W9-BXG-579

Kenrick-Glennon
Seminary Library

Charles L. Souvay Memorial

CYCLOPÆDIA

OF

BIBLICAL,

THEOLOGICAL, AND ECCLESIASTICAL

LITERATURE.

PREPARED BY

THE REV. JOHN M'CLINTOCK, D.D.,

AND

JAMES STRONG, S.T.D.

VOL. VI.—ME–NEV.

220. 3
M158C
1969
v. 6

BAKER BOOK HOUSE
Grand Rapids, Michigan

57373

Reprinted 1969 by
Baker Book House Company

Library of Congress Catalog Card Number: 68-56007

Entered according to Act of Congress, in the year 1876, by

HARPER & BROTHERS,

In the Office of the Librarian of Congress, at Washington.

Printed in the United States of America

LIST OF WOOD-CUTS IN VOL. VI.

CYCLOPÆDIA

OF

BIBLICAL, THEOLOGICAL, AND ECCLESIASTICAL LITERATURE.

ME.

Mead, Matthew, an English divine, was born in Buckinghamshire in 1629. Of his early history we know but little. He first came prominently into public notice during the Cromwellian movement. Mead identified himself with the cause of the Independents, and was appointed by the Protector to the living of Shadwell in 1658. Four years later he was ejected for nonconformity, and removed to Holland, in common with many other ministers of that age. He became acquainted with the duke of Orange, and was greatly favored by him and the States. Afterwards he returned to England, and gathered about him one of the largest congregations in London. He settled at Stepney as pastor of a dissenting congregation in 1674, and the community betokened their love and esteem for him by presenting him with building material for a new chapel. He died in 1699. Matthew Mead, whom his friend and associate, Howe (*Funeral Sermon* for Mead), describes as "that very reverend and most laborious servant of Christ," was as indefatigable in Christian work as he was amiable in spirit, and, in consequence of his mild temperament and the moderation of his opinions, formed the strongest personal link between the Presbyterians and Independents of England in the second half of the 17th century. Among his publications are, *The Almost Christian,* or seven sermons on Acts xxvi, 28 (Lond. 1666, 8vo) :— *The Almost Christian Discovered* (1684, 4to; Glasgow, 1755, 12mo; with Essay by Dr. Young of Perth, Lond. 1825; 1849, 12mo) :—*Life and Death of Nathaniel Mather* (1689, 8vo) :—*Vision of the Wheels:* sermon on Ezek. x, 13 (1689, 4to). See Calamy, *Nonconformists;* Skeats, *Hist. of the Free Churches of England,* p. 167; Allibone, *Dict. of Brit. and Amer. Auth.* ii, 1257.

Mead, Richard, a distinguished English physician, who was born at Stepney in 1673, and after studying at the most eminent medical schools on the Continent, returned and settled in England, and became one of the most celebrated practitioners of his time, wrote a treatise on the diseases mentioned in Scripture, entitled *Medicina Sacra, seu de morbis insignioribus qui in Biblis memorantur* (Lond. 1749, 8vo; republished at Amsterdam, 1749, 8vo). A translation of this work was made by Dr. T. Stark, and was published with a memoir of the author (Lond. 1755, 8vo). Dr. Mead died in 1754. See Allibone, *Dict. Brit. and Amer. Biog.* s. v.

Mead, Stith, an early Methodist Episcopal minister, was born in Bedford County, Va., Sept. 25, 1767; was converted in 1789, and feeling called of God to preach the Gospel, entered the itinerancy in 1793; was located in 1816; readmitted superannuate in 1827, and died in 1835. Mr. Mead was eminently useful as a preacher, and particularly conspicuous in the great revivals of his time, yet remembered in the Southern States. See *Minutes of Conferences,* ii, 347.

Mead, Zechariah, a clergyman of the Protestant Episcopal Church, was born at Greenwich, Conn., some time in the first half of our century (perhaps 1802), and was educated at Yale College (class of 1825). He was

ordained priest at Norfolk, Va., May 22, 1831; became rector of Grace Church, Boston, Mass.; from 1837–1840 was editor of the *Southern Churchman,* published at Richmond, Va.; and died Nov. 27, 1840. See *General Catal. of the Divinity School of Yale College,* p. 7.

Meade, WILLIAM, D.D., a noted prelate of the Protestant Episcopal Church, was born at Millwood, Clarke County, Nov. 11, 1789, his father being Col. Richard K. Meade, aide-de-camp to Gen. Washington, and was connected both by birth and marriage with some of the oldest and best families in Virginia. His great-grandfather was an Irish Romanist, who came to this country, married a Quakeress in Flushing, L. I., and removed to Virginia. His grandmother was a descendant of Richard Kidder, bishop of Bath and Wells. William was educated at Princeton College, N. J. (class of 1808); was ordained deacon by bishop Madison, Feb. 24, 1811, in Williamsburg, Va.; and priest by bishop Claggett, in St. Paul's Church, Alexandria. He commenced his ministry in his own native parish, Frederick (now Clarke) County, as assistant to the Rev. Alexander Balmaine; in the fall of 1811 he took charge of Christ Church, Alexandria, where he remained two years, when he returned to Millwood, and, on the death of Mr. Balmaine, became rector of that Church. In 1826 he was a candidate as assistant bishop in Pennsylvania, but failed by one vote of nomination by the clergy; and in the following year the Rev. H. U. Onderdonk, D.D., was elected. In 1828 he was elected assistant bishop to bishop Moore, and was consecrated Aug. 19, 1829, in St. James's Church, Philadelphia, by bishops White, Hobart, Griswold, Moore, Croes, Brownell, and H. U. Onderdonk. On the death of bishop Moore, Nov. 11, 1841, he became bishop of the diocese of Virginia. In this capacity he labored unceasingly, up to the hour of his death, March 14, 1862, for the good of evangelical Christianity. He advanced the interests of his Master's cause not only in the pulpit, but in many and various ways he labored for the good of humanity. Several educational and missionary societies owe their origin to him, and the Theological School of Virginia, lately at Alexandria, was largely indebted to him for its existence (though the plan of a theological seminary in Virginia was not original with him). He gave to this school of the prophets his personal care and labors, nearly to the close of his life. During the exciting days of 1861 bishop Meade made many fervent though futile efforts to save Virginia from the troubles of the impending civil war. He steadfastly opposed secession to the very last. Taken altogether, but few men in the nation have enjoyed the confidence of the people to a greater degree than did this honest ecclesiastic, who sought in more ways than one to serve his day and generation as a truly Christian man. For years before his death bishop Meade was the recognised head of the evangelical branch of the Protestant Episcopal Church in the United States. On bishop Meade's ecclesiastical position, the *Church Review* (July, 1862) thus comments: "The gross worldliness, and even the open immorality of many of the early clergy of Virginia; the moral-essay style of preaching which characterized many of the missionaries; the French infidelity introduced during the Revolution, and the absence of that bitter opposition to Church principles which was, and even now is waged in the Northern States, led the bishop to regard as not only mainly, but only important, the development of the subjective in religion. His 'extraordinary will,' as the *Episcopal Recorder* calls it, and his Calvinistic doctrines, led him to separate evangelical truth from apostolic order, and to make him, we doubt not an honest, but a most determined opponent to any earnest presentation of the positive institutions of Christianity." Bishop Meade was buried from St. Paul's Church, Richmond, March 17. His principal published works are, *Family Prayer* (1834):—*Lectures on the Pastoral Office*, and *Lectures to Students* (1849): —*Old Churches and Families in Virginia* (Philad. 1856, 2 vols. 8vo):—*The Bible and the Classics* (1861, 12mo). Besides these, he also published *Memorials of [his] Two Beloved Wives*, which the *Church Review* informs us was suppressed. His controversial writings are numerous. See *Life*, by bishop Johns (Baltimore, 1868). (J. H. W.)

Meadow, a term used in the A. V. as the translation of two Heb. words, neither of which seems to have this meaning, although terms otherwise rendered doubtless have. See ABEL.

1. Gen. xli, 2 and 18. Here the word in the original is הָאָחוּ (with the definite article), *ha-Achû'*. It appears to be an Egyptian term, literally transferred into the Hebrew text, as it is also into that of the Alexandrian translators, who give it as τῷ Ἄχει. (This is the reading of Codex A. Codex B, if we may accept the edition of Mai, has ἔλος; so also the rendering of Aquila and Symmachus, and of Josephus [*Ant.* ii, 5, 5]. Another version, quoted in the fragments of the Hexapla, attempts to reconcile sound and sense by ὄχϑη. The Veneto-Greek has λειμών.) The same form is retained by the Coptic version. Its use in Job viii, 11 (A. V. "flag")—where it occurs as a parallel to *gômê* (A. V. "rush"), a word used in Exod. ii, 3 for the "bulrushes" of which Moses's ark was composed—seems to show that it is not a "meadow," but some kind of reed or waterplant. This the Sept. supports, both by rendering in the latter passage βούτομον, and also by introducing Ἄχι as the equivalent of the word rendered "paperreeds" in Isa. xix, 7. Jerome, in his commentary on the passage, also confirms this meaning. He states that he was informed by learned Egyptians that the word *achi* denoted in their tongue any green thing that grew in a marsh—*omne quod in palude virens nascitur*. But, as during high inundations of the Nile—such inundations as are the cause of fruitful years—the whole of the land on either side is a marsh, and as the cultivation extends up to the very lip of the river, is it not possible that *Achu* may denote the herbage of the growing crops? The fact that the cows of Pharaoh's vision were feeding there would seem to be as strong a figure as could be presented to an Egyptian of the extreme fruitfulness of the season: so luxuriant was the growth on either side of the stream, that the very cows fed among it unmolested. The lean kine, on the other hand, merely stand on the dry brink. See NILE. No one appears yet to have attempted to discover on the spot what the signification of the term is. See REED.

2. Judg. xx, 33 only: "the meadows of Gibeah." Here the word is מַעֲרֵה, *Maareh'*, which occurs nowhere else with the same vowels attached to it. The sense is thus doubly uncertain. "Meadows" around Gibeah can certainly never have existed: the nearest approach to that sense would be to take *maareh* as meaning an open plain. This is the dictum of Gesenius (*Thesaur.* p. 1069), on the authority of the Targum. It is also adopted by De Wette ("Die Pläne von G."). But, if an open plain, where could the ambush have concealed itself? See PLAIN.

The Sept., according to the Alex. MS. (the Vatican Codex transfers the word literally—Μαρααγαβέ), read a different Hebrew word—מַעֲרָב—"from the west of Gibeah." Tremellius, taking the root of the word in a figurative sense, reads "after Gibeah had been left open," i. e. by the quitting of its inhabitants—*post denudationem Gibhæ*. This is adopted by Bertheau (*Kurzgef. Handb.* ad loc.). But the most plausible interpretation is that of the Peshito-Syriac, which by a slight difference in the vowel-points makes the word מְעָרָה, "the cave;" a suggestion quite in keeping with tne locality, which is very suitable for caves, and also with the requirements of the ambush. The only thing that can be said against this is that the liers-in-wait were "set round about" Gibeah, as if not in one spot, but several. See GIBEAH.

Me'ah (Heb. *Meäh'*, מֵאָה, a *hundred*, as often; Sept. ἑκατόν, Μιά; Vulg. *centum, Emath*), a tower in Jerusalem, situated on the eastern wall (Neh. iii, 1; xii, 39), probably at the north-eastern angle of the Temple enclosure (Strong's *Harmony and Expos. of the Gospels*, Append. ii, p. 19; but it is not likely that the outer wall was different from that of the Temple, as supposed by Dr. Barclay, *City of the Great King*, p. 152). See JERUSALEM.

Meal (קֶמַח, *ke'mach*, in pause קָמַח, prob. *fat*, i. e. *marrow*; hence the *fatness* of wheat or barley, i. e. its ground substance, Gen. xviii, 6; Numb. v, 15; 1 Kings iv, 22; xvii, 12, 14, 16; 2 Kings iv, 41; 1 Chron. xii, 40; Isa. xlvii, 2; Hos. viii, 7; "*flour*," as elsewhere rendered, 1 Sam. i, 24; xxviii, 24; 2 Sam. xvii, 28; Gr. ἄλευρον, Matt. xiii, 33; Luke xiii, 21; also סֹלֶת, *so'leth, stripped* of its bran, the finest portion of the ground grain, Gen. xviii, 6 [where it stands after the preceding term, in apposition]; elsewhere "flour" or "fine flour," Sept. σεμίδαλις), the ground produce of any species of grain. See GRITS. This is usually prepared in the East by females in hand-mills. See FLOUR.

Meals. See DINE; REPAST; SUP; and the article following.

Meal-time (אָכַל עֵת, *eth o'kel*, the *season of eating*, Ruth ii, 14). That the Hebrews took their principal meal (*cœna, supper*) in the latter part of the afternoon or towards evening, follows as well from the circumstance that banquets and convivial entertainments generally (perhaps always) occurred near the close of the day (sometimes being continued far into the night, Josephus, *Life*, 44), as from the custom still prevalent in the East (Wellsted, *Trav.* i, 113; the Persians sup about six or seven o'clock), a usage to which the Essenes were an exception (Josephus, *War*, ii, 8, 5). See FEAST. The agricultural and laboring portion of the community, however, probably took their principal meal at noon (1 Kings xx, 16). See DINE. In the forenoon a slight repast was partaken (*breakfast*, ἄριστον, comp. Luke xiv, 12; John xxi, 22). Among the later Jews, it was usual for the deeply religious not to taste anything before the hour of morning prayer (comp. Acts ii, 15; see Lightfoot, *Hor. Heb.* ad loc.; the passage in *Berach.* fol. xxvii, 2, quoted by Kuinöl, refers to the blessing before eating, see *Gemar. Bab.* vi, 1, 1); on the Sabbath, the synagogue worship led to the rule of not eating before the sixth hour, or noon. Before each meal, persons were accustomed, especially in later times, carefully to wash (Matt. xv, 2; Luke xi, 38; Mark vi, 2; sec the younger Buxtorf's *Dissert. philol. theol.* p. 397 sq.), like the ancient Greeks (*Iliad*, x, 577; *Odyss.* i, 136 sq.; iv, 216 sq.; Aristoph. *Vesp.* 1216) and the modern Orientals (Niebuhr, *Beschr.* p. 54; Shaw, *Trav.* p. 202), and also to "say grace" (בְּרָכָה, the *blessing*, εὐλογία, εὐχαριστία; Matt. xiv, 19; xv, 36; xxvi, 26; Luke ix, 16; John vi, 11; comp. Tim. iv, 3; see the Gemara, *Berach.* p. 278; and the rabbinical tract, *Berachoth*, p. 6–18; also Kuinöl, *De precum ante et post cibum ap. Jud. et Chris-*

tian. antiquitate, Lips. 1764). While eating, the Hebrews originally *sat* (Gen. xxvii, 19; Hengstenberg, *Mos.* p. 36, incorrectly infers their recumbency at table from Gen. xviii, 4; comp. Judg. xix, 6; 1 Sam. xx, 5, 24; 1 Kings xiii, 20), like the Greeks in the heroic period (*Iliad*, x, 578; *Odyss.* i, 144; xv, 134; Athen. viii, 363; xi, 459), and the Romans anciently (Serv. *ad Æn.* vii, 176; Varro, *Ling. Lat.* l, p. 236 Bip.; see Becker, *Charikl.* i, 425), and in this posture are the early Egyptians represented on the monuments (Wilkinson, ii, 201). In later times the practice of reclining (ἀνακεῖσθαι, κατακεῖσθαι, κατακλίνεσθαι, see the Mishna, *Berach.* vi, 6) on cushions or divans (מִטּוֹת; κλῖναι, Xen. *Cyrop.* viii, 8, 16; κατακλίματα, Josephus, *Ant.* xv, 9, 3; comp. A. Baccius, *De conviv. antiq.* ii, 1 sq., in Gronov. *Thesaur.* ix), at first only in special entertainments (Amos vi, 4; comp. ii, 8; Matt. ix, 10; xxvi, 7; Mark vi, 22; xiv, 3; Luke v, 29; vii, 37; xiv, 10; John xii, 2; xiii, 23, etc.), but eventually in common life (Luke xvii, 7), without any particular invitation to that effect (Terent. *Heautont.* i, 1, 72; Plaut. *Trucul.* ii, 14, 16; Martial, iii, 50, 3; comp. Plat. *Conviv.* p. 213), and universally (see H. Mercurialis, *Diss. de accubitu triclinio*, in his *Ars gymnast.* p. 75 sq.). See ACCUBATION. Every such divan or dinner-bed accommodated (according to Roman fashion) three persons (*triclinium* [Plin. xxxvii, 6], a prevalent form of luxury [Plin. xxxiii, 52; Josephus, *Ant.* xv, 9, 3; Philo, ii, 478], introduced from the Babylonians, who used a carpet or tapestry over it [Plin. viii, 74], whence the terms descriptive of *spreading* it [*sternere*, Cic. *Mur.* 36; Macrob. *Sat.* ii, 9; στρωννύειν, Xen. *Cyrop.* viii, 3, 6; which explains the ἀνάγαιον ἐστρωμένον of Mark xiv, 15; see generally Ciacon. *De triclinio*, Amst. 1699]), sometimes as many as five, who leaned upon the left arm, the feet being stretched out behind. Each one on the right touched with the back of his head the breast of his left neighbor, whence the phrase "to lie in one's bosom" (ἀνακεῖσθαι ἐν τῷ κόλπῳ, John xiii, 23; xxi, 20), as being the place of the spouse (among the Jews, however, wives ate sitting, which the Romans generally held to be the most becoming attitude, Isidor. *Orig.* xx, 11; comp. Sueton. *Claud.* 32; Val. Max. ii, 1, 2; the "sitting at the feet" in Luke x, 39, was not an act of participation in the meal), a friend, or a favorite (Plin. *Ep.* iv, 22; see Kype, *Observ.* i, 402; comp. Talm. Babyl. *Berach.* vii, 2, 5); the place of honor being in the middle of the three (Talm. Hieros. *Taanith*, lxviii, 1; comp. Potter, *Archæol.* ii, 661). The tables (comp. 1 Sam. xx, 29; 2 Sam. ix, 7, 11; 1 Kings x, 5; Ezek. xxxix, 20; Luke xxii, 21; Acts xvi, 34, etc.) were probably, as still in the East (Mariti, *Trav.* p. 283; Shaw, *Trav.* p. 202; Mayr, *Schicksale*, i, 51; Robinson, *Researches*, ii, 726), low (among modern Orientals consisting of a round skin [*sufra*] or reed-mat, Rüppel, *Abyssin.* ii, 85, spread on the floor in the middle of the room, Arvieux, *Voyage*, iii, 237; Pococke, *East*, i, 292; Harmar, *Observ.* ii, 453, or on a stool, and furnished with rings on the edge, so that after the meal it may be folded together, and hung up like a bag, the food being laid on mats, or upon cloths covering it, comp. Niebuhr, *Trav.* i, 372; Paulus, *Samml.* iii, 101), as appears likewise from the pattern of the table of show-bread. See TABLE. Meat and vegetables, the first cut into small pieces (the loins and shoulders affording what were regarded as choice morsels, Ezek. xxiv, 4), were set on the table in large platters, out of which each guest took his share with his fingers upon the flat pieces of bread, and ate without either knife or fork (comp. Zorn, in the *Miscell. Duisburg.* ii, 437 sq.; Mariti, *Trav.* p. 284); or was sometimes helped by the host (1 Sam. i, 4; comp. John xiii, 26; Xen. *Cyrop.* i, 3, 7). The pieces of bread were dipped into the sauce (Matt. xxvi, 23; Aristoph. *Eq.* 1176), and the vegetables were conveyed from the dish by means of the hand or fingers to the mouth (comp. Prov. xix, 24; xxvi, 15; Ruth ii, 14 is not in point), a custom which still prevails in the East even at the royal table (Tavernier, *Trav.* i,

282; Arvieux, *Voyage*, iii, 238; Pococke, ii, 63; Niebuhr, *Besch.* p. 53; Shaw, *Trav.* p. 203; Burckhardt, *Wahaby*, p. 51; Rosenmüller, *Morgenl.* iv, 138; Robinson, ii, 726; iii, 201). Whether they drank wine during the meal (like the Romans) or after it (like the Egyptians, Herod. ii, 278, and Persians, Herod. v, 18, and as is still the practice of most Arabians and Persians, Chardin, iv, 44, 52; Arvieux, iii, 277; Burckhardt, *Sprachen*, p. 137; comp. Josephus, *Ant.* xv, 1, 2), is not positively stated, although the Talmud (Babylon. *Berach.* p. 251) seems to imply that the Jews did both, the draught following the meal, however, being the principal one (*Berach.* viii, 4, 7; comp. Robinson, ii, 726). See EATING. (See generally M. Geier, in the *Biblioth. Lubec.* v, 1 sq.) See ENTERTAINMENT.

Meal-tub Plot is the name of a plot concocted on the part of Romanists, but intended to be fathered on a number of eminent persons engaged in the interests of the Protestants during the reign of Charles II, in the year 1679. A conspiracy on the part of the Jesuits to dethrone or make away with Charles, and place the duke of York (who was in favor of the papal rule) on the throne, having come to light, the papists, exasperated, determined to set on foot a sham plot, and brand the Presbyterians as the originators. The dastardly attempt was timely discovered, and heaped infamy upon the already spotted character of the Jesuits. For a full account, see Neale, *Hist. of the Puritans*, ii, 290; Stoughton, *Eccl. Hist. of Engl.* (*Ch. of the Restoration*), ii, 21 sq.

Meä'ni (Μεανί v. r. Μανί and Μααví), a less correct form (1 Esdr. v, 31) for the MEHUNIM (q. v.) of the Heb. text (Ezra ii, 50).

Means OF GRACE, a convenient but unscientific and unscriptural phrase for those exercises or agencies which become the channel or occasion of spiritual influences to the Christian. The doctrine concerning the means of grace is based on that of grace itself. It has only received its adequate form through the Reformation, which, in opposition to the Roman Church, who considers that grace is imparted by the visible Church, particularly by the priest, asserts as the only regular means of grace the Word of God and the sacraments instituted by Christ. In popular language, however, the term "means of grace" is extended so as to include those duties which we perform for the purpose of improving our minds, affecting our hearts, and of obtaining spiritual blessings; such as hearing the Gospel, reading the Scriptures, self-examination, meditation, prayer, praise, Christian conversation, etc. The means are to be used without any reference to merit, solely with a dependence on the divine Being; nor can we ever expect happiness in ourselves, nor be good exemplars to others, while we live in the neglect of them. It is in vain to argue that the divine willingness to bestow grace supersedes the necessity of them, since God has as certainly appointed the means as the end. Besides, he himself generally works by them, and the more means he thinks proper to use, the more he displays his glorious perfections. Jesus Christ, when on earth, used means; he prayed, he exhorted, and did good, by going from place to place. Indeed, the systems of nature, providence, and grace are all carried on by means. The Scriptures abound with exhortations to them (Matt. v; Rom. xii), and none but enthusiasts or immoral characters ever refuse to use them. In the following article we use the term in its more restricted sense, as related to the sacramental controversy between Roman Catholics and Protestants, condensing the statements in Herzog's *Real-Encyklop.* v, 200 sq.

The starting-point of the Protestant doctrine on this subject is contained in the fifth article of the *Confession of Augsburg.* Grace itself is presupposed, such as exists in the form of justification by faith. The hearing of the Word and the partaking of the sacraments are methods of arriving at this faith: "Nam per verbum et sacramenta, tamquam per instrumenta donatur Spiritus

Sanctus, qui fidem afficit, ubi et quando visum est Deo in iis, qui audiunt Evangelium," etc. To this statement is joined the declaration, "Damnant Anabaptistas et alios, qui sentiunt, Spiritum Sanctum contingere sine verbo externo hominibus per ipsorum præparationes ad opera." The *Heidelberg Catechism* enounces the same doctrine, and at the same time states still more emphatically the connection between the sacraments and the Word of God in quest. 65: "Whence comes saving grace? It is the effect of the Holy Spirit in our heart by means of the preaching of the holy Gospel, and confirmed by the use of the holy sacraments." (The most important passages of symbols on this point are: *Apoleg.* iv, 153; *Artic. Smalc.* pars ii, 2, 8; *Catechism. maj.* Præceptum iii, p. 426; *Symbol. apost.* p. 502; *Formul. conc.* Epitome: "De lib. arbitr." Negativa vi; *Solid. decl.* p. 655, 669, 828; *Conf. Helv.* ii, c. 1; *Conf. Gall.* art. 25, 35; *Conf. Belg.* art. 24.) The means of grace are called *instrumenta gratiæ, media, adminicula gratiæ.* In the Lutheran Church the union between the Word and the sacraments is made much closer than in the Reformed. The *Helvetic Confession* treats of the Word of God in the first chapter, and of the sacraments in the nineteenth. The reason of this separation is that the Bible, as the Word of God, is the foundation of the whole system. Yet their connection and union are not lost sight of: "Prædicationi verbi sui adjunxit Deus mox ab initio in ecclesia sua sacramenta, vel signa sacramentalia." The idea of the unity of the means of grace is not considered by the evangelical Church as only a formal, human, or theological connection between the Word of God, baptism, and the Lord's Supper, but as the consequence of a divine act, the institution of the Church and of the ecclesiastical office. The means of grace are not mere possessions of the Church, but its foundation itself. The Church is called into existence by the Word of God, while by baptism and communion it is manifested as a religious community (see *Conf. Aug.* art. vii). Schleiermacher himself recognised in them the essential and unchangeable foundations of the Church (ii, § 127). Thus he contradicts himself when further on, treating of the connection between baptism and the Lord's Supper, he refuses to consider it as an actual dogmatic point (p. 416). The unity of the means of grace may be briefly said to consist in their constituting the Church as the organ of transmission of grace. The inner ground of their unity is grace itself, of which they are the channels; the outer aspect is the *ministerium*, the office appointed by Christ, which has to administer both forms of the means of grace.

This brings us to the significance and necessity of these means of grace, or to the views of the Protestant Church as opposed to the Roman Catholic Church on these points. The first point of difference lies in the conception of the ecclesiastical office. Both, indeed, consider it as a divine institution, but the Protestants look upon it as a *ministerium*, which can be considered as a continuous Christian working of the Church in the Word and sacraments, while the Roman Catholics retain the idea of a *sacerdotium* forming the real fundamental means of grace, and creating itself the distinct means of grace after the manner of the apostles (see Dieringer, *Lehrbuch d. Kath. Dogmatik*, p. 512), "The substitution of the Son of man by the apostleship." If its sacerdotal character is susceptible of being defended by Scripture and tradition, it yet is certain that it is only through tradition that it obtained this superior importance, as capable of creating the other means of grace. The practical results of this superior importance became manifest in the prohibition to read the Bible, the refusal of the chalice in communion, etc., thus diminishing the other means of grace, while they were increased on the other hand by the promulgation of the commandments of the Church, and the institution of additional sacraments; and also modified in the doctrine of the sacrificial character of the Eucharist, etc. Thus the Protestant doctrine of the means of grace dif-

fers at once from the Roman Catholic, by its conception of a *ministerium* in the place of a *sacerdotium*. They next differ in the relative position they assign to the means of grace. Protestants maintain that this grace is first communicated through the Word of God, and confirmed by the sacraments; Roman Catholics, on the contrary, consider the sacraments as the chief means of grace, and the Word of God as accessory. Then, as regards the Word of God, Protestants consider it as consisting essentially in Scripture, together with explanations, while by it Roman Catholics understand only the *prædicatio verbi*. The latter also increase the number of sacraments, and recognise other means of grace. On these points, see WORD OF GOD and SACRAMENTS. Another distinction is the difference in which the means of grace themselves are apprehended in their connection with grace and forgiveness. According to the *Concil. Trident.*, sess. 7, the sacraments work *ex opere operato*, a doctrine which the *Conf. Aug.* art. xiii, rejects. We must, of course, refer to Roman Catholic theologians to find the sense which that Church attaches to the *opus operatum* (Bellarmine, *De sacr.* ii, 1). According to them, infant baptism is efficient in itself to regenerate them, without any resistance being for a moment to be thought of. The opposition of adults to baptism, confession, and the mass could only consist in an obstacle (*ponere obicem*), a deceitful hiding of a mortal sin, and the persistence in it, for absolution presupposes a full and candid confession. But a passive faith as saving faith, in the Protestant sense, is not required to give efficiency to the sacraments. We might then suppose that the Word would here, as a means of grace, be placed before the sacrament, and produce conversion, which would insure the effect of the sacrament. But we must remember that, for the most part, Roman Catholics are such from being born of Roman Catholic parents. Of converts themselves nothing further is demanded than that they should have enough *fides implicita* in the word announced to them to submit to the authority of the Church. History teaches us how even the word itself may become the *opus operatum.*

In opposition to the Roman Catholic Church, Protestants generally draw a distinction between grace and the means of grace, although they recognise their relation. We must, however, distinguish between such as reject altogether the necessity and ordinance of the means of grace, and those who recognise as such the Word of God but not the sacraments. Among the former we find in the time of the Reformation the Anabaptists, in later times the Quakers. They maintain that the Holy Spirit, without the aid of the Word, illuminates each man immediately by an inner light at a certain time, and that by it only is man able to understand the Word of God (see Barclay, *Apol.*). Still it would be unjust to say that they altogether reject the notion of means of grace, for the Quakers are especially distinguished for diligent searching of the Scriptures. But they deny the existence of divinely-ordained, special means of grace of the Church. The Socinians and Mennonites, on the other hand, consider, in a certain sense, the Word of God as an objective means of grace; the former considering the sacraments purely as symbols of the Christian faith (*cerimoniæ*), while the Mennonites consider them also as objective signs of the action of grace (Riz, *Conf.* art. 30). Here also we miss the objective character of the means of grace, but we find it again among the Arminians. Necessarily as the sphere of action of the sacraments is restricted as means of grace, that of grace itself, as immediately active, becomes enlarged; this we see exemplified in the doctrine of restoration of the Anabaptists, in the Quaker doctrine of the action of the revealing Spirit ("Deus spiritus revelatione se ipsum semper filiis hominum patefecit," Barclay, *Apol.* thes. ii), and in the Socinian notion of an extraordinary and special action of the divine Spirit aside from its general action through the Gospel (Osterodt, *Unterricht. K.* p. 34). The Protestant Church, in its doctrine of *gratia præveniens*, recognises, with some restriction, the truth of these views, but still maintains the necessity of the sacraments. According to Scripture, the sphere of the *gratia præveniens* extends beyond that of the theocratic revelation. The Spirit dwells where it chooses, the Logos shines in all human souls, and the *gratia præveniens* is active in all receptive hearts. Yet the prepared soul only arrives to an *experimental* knowledge of salvation within the sphere of revelation, and to a *certainty* of it by the ordained means of grace. On this point of the necessity of the means of grace, the difference, such as it is, which exists between the Lutheran and the Reformed Church on that doctrine, cannot but appear. The possibility of the spiritual enlightenment of individual members of the Church, *sine externo ministerio*, is clearly recognised by the *Conf. Helv.* ii, cap. i. Still the article considers it as divinely ordained that it is imparted by the *usitata ratio instituendi homines*. It insists still more strongly on the necessity of the *prædicatio dei verbi*, to which, of course, is joined the *interna Spiritus illuminatio*. But this necessity is defined as a *necessitas præcepti, non absoluta*, i. e. God, in the work of redemption, is not confined to these means, as is proved by the prophets and by revelation, but, in consideration of the weakness of our nature, has appointed these means (see Schweizer, *Glaubenslehre d. ev. ref. Kirche*, ii, 561). Luther, on the contrary, refers even the inspiration of the prophets to the *verbum vocale* (*Art. Smal.* p. 333). Another difference consists in the close connection existing in the Lutheran Church between the sacrament and the Word, while in the Reformed theology the Word takes the prominent position as the *causa instrumentalis fidei* (see Ebrard, *Christliche Dogmatik*, p. 578). The Lutheran Church teaches an organic joint action of grace and the means of grace, without, however, making them identical. The Reformed Lutherans understand only an economic joint action, which, however, does not exclude irregularities or rather exceptions. As regards the Word of God, the Lutheran theologians strongly uphold its *efficacia*, and Calovius and Quenstedt speak of a *unio mystica gratiæ sive virtutis divinæ cum verbo* (see Hahn, *Lehrbuch*, p. 549). At this point orthodoxy approaches the idea of the *opus operatum* (see Lange, *Dogmatik*, p. 1119). According to Reformed theology, the connection of the Spirit with the Word is conditioned by the number of the elect among the number of hearers, while the *Heidelberg Catechism* holds that the Spirit awakens faith in our heart through the preaching of the holy Gospel. According to Nitzsch, the point of union of the two confessions on this doctrine lies in the conception of the *pignus*. We further notice that the Reformed Church does not insist as strongly on the necessity of baptism as the Lutheran. The *Confessio Scotica* (p. 127) emphatically rejects the Roman Catholic doctrine of the damnation of children dying without baptism; so does also Calvin, in his *Instit.* iv, 16, 26. As regards the connection between baptism and regeneration, the twenty-seventh article of the *Conf. Anglic.* takes a middle course, saying that baptism is a *signum regenerationis per quod recte baptismum suscipientes ecclesiis inseruntur.* By this is meant that the ecclesiastic, social regeneration is accomplished, the individual, social regeneration made thereby perceptible to the senses, and sacramentally promised. See REGENERATION.

With regard to the action and the necessity of the means of grace, the differences of the different confessions come again into play. While the evangelical churches teach that the sacraments are agents of sanctification for those who receive them with faith, strengthening and increasing that faith, the Roman Catholic holds that they are the agents of faith, requiring none to be worthily participated in beyond faith in the authority of the Church, and that mortal sin alone can render them ineffectual, and the Baptists and Socinians look upon the participation in the sacraments only as outward acts, professions of the Christian faith.

In dogmatics, the means of grace represent the eternal presence of Christ in the spiritual Church, and through her in the world. In his institutions, Christ, by the Holy Spirit, identifies himself with them, and in his eternal presence draws the world to his salvation. The Word and the sacraments are inseparably connected with each other: the Word receives its fulfilment and seal in the sacrament, while the sacrament receives light and spiritual life from the creative power of the Word. The Word, without the seal of the sacrament, is only a scholastic knowledge; the sacrament, without the vivifying influence of the Word, is a piece of priestly magic. But though the means of grace, in their connection with the Holy Spirit, set at work the saving power of the life of Christ, as a participation in his salvation, still they must be preceded by faith, since Christ required faith when personally present on earth. Yet he no more requires a perfect faith than he compels to believe. Those who ask shall receive. See SACRAMENT.

See Fletcher, *Works;* Wesley, *Works;* Hagenbach, *Hist. of Doctrines;* Winer, *Symbol.* p. 113; Kurtz, *Ch. Hist.* vol. i; Niedner, *Philos.* p. 441.

Mea′rah (Heb. *Meärah′*, מְעָרָה, a *cave*, as often; Sept. ἀπὸ Γάζης, apparently reading מֵעַזָּה *from Gaza;* Vulg. *Maara*), a place mentioned in Josh. xiii, 4 as situated in the northern edge of Palestine: "From the south, all the land of the Canaanites, and Mearah that is beside the Sidonians, unto Aphek." Some find it in the town *Marathos* (Strabo, xvi, 753; Pliny, v, 17; Ptolemy, v, 15, 16). Most interpreters, following the Chaldee and Syriac (see the *Critici Biblici*, s. v.), are of the opinion that the term should rather be rendered as an appellative—*the cave* (Keil's *Comment.* ad loc.); but if a mere cave were intended, and not a place called Mearah, the name would surely have been preceded by the definite article, and would have stood as הַמְּעָרָה, "the cave." Besides, the scope of the passage shows that some place—either a city or district—must be meant. "Reland (*Palæst.* p. 895) suggests that Mearah may be the same with Meroth, a village named by Josephus (*Ant.* iii, 3, 1) as forming the limit of Galilee on the west (see also *Ant.* ii, 20, 6), and which again may possibly have been connected with the waters of Merom. A village called *el-Mughar* is found in the mountains of Naphtali, some ten miles west of the northern extremity of the Sea of Galilee (Robinson, iii, 79, 30; Van de Velde's *Map*), which may possibly represent an ancient Mearah." "About half-way between Tyre and Sidon, close to the shore, are the ruins of an ancient town; and in the neighboring cliffs are large numbers of caves and grottos hewn in the rock, and formerly used as tombs. Dr. Robinson suggested that this may be 'Mearah of the Sidonians' (ii, 474). The ruins are now called *'Adlân*, but perhaps take that name from the village on the mountain-side." Ritter (*Erdk.* xvii, 10; also xvi, 8, 9), on the other hand, identifies Mearah, under the name *Mughara*, with the remarkable cavern (Rosenmüller, *Alterth.* II, i, 39 sq., 66) which the Crusaders fortified, and which is described by William of Tyre (*Histor. Hieros.* xix, 2, 11) as "a certain fortress of ours in the Sidonian territory, namely, an impregnable grotto, commonly called the *Cave of Tyre* (*Cavea de Tyron*)." It was afterwards the last retreat of the emir Fakhr ed-Din. The place is now also known as *Shukif Tairûn* (Abulfeda, *Table*). Schultz is the first traveller who mentions it in modern days. It is situated in the high cliff east of Sidon, between Jezim and Michmurhy (Van de Velde, *Memoir*, s. v.). See CAVE.

Mears, THOMAS, M.A., an English divine of note, flourished near the opening of the present century. He was at one time rector of St. Lawrence and vicar of St. Michael's, in Southampton, and chaplain to the corporation of that town. He died about 1810. Mr. Mears was a prolific writer, and a pulpit orator of no mean ability. He contributed many articles to the *Orthodox Churchman's Magazine*, and published several of his sermons, among which the following deserve special mention: *England expects every Man to do his Duty* (1805, 8vo):—*Religious Example* (1807, 8vo):—*On the Lord's Supper* (1807, 8vo).

Measure is the rendering in the Auth. Vers. of a number of Hebrew and Greek terms, some of which are descriptive of dimension or extent generally, while others denote a specific length or capacity. Again, there are other words in the original denoting a particular quantity or space, which are still differently rendered in the Auth. Vers. It is our purpose in the present article to present merely a general view of the various renderings, leaving the determination of the modern equivalents to the special head of METROLOGY (q. v.). The following are the words rendered "measure" in the A.V.:

1. *Those that are of indefinite Import.*—(1) חֹק, *chôk* (Isa. v, 14; a *statute*, as elsewhere usually rendered); (2) מַד, *mad* (Job xi, 9; Jer. xiii, 25; reduplicated plur. Job xxxviii, 5; elsewhere a *garment*, as usually rendered); (3) properly מִדָּה, *middah'*, the usual word thus rendered (Exod. xxvi, 2, 8; Josh. iii, 4; 1 Kings vi, 25; vii, 9, 11, 37; 2 Chron. iii, 3; Job xxviii, 25; Psa. xxxix, 4 [5]; Jer. xxxi, 39; Ezek. xl, 3, 5, 10, 21, 22, 24, 28, 29, 32, 33, 35; xli, 17; xlii, 15, 16, 17, 18, 19; xliii, 13; xlv, 3; xlvi, 22; xlviii, 16, 30, 33; Zech. ii, 1 [5]; elsewhere "piece," etc.); (4) מְשׂוּרָה, *mesurah'* (Lev. xix, 35; 1 Chron. xxiii, 39; Ezek. iv, 11, 16); (5) מִשְׁפָּט, *mishpat'* (Jer. xxx, ii; xlvi, 28; *judgment*, as elsewhere usually rendered); (6) מִתְכֹּנֶת, *mithko'neth* (Ezek. xlv, 11; "tale," Exod. v, 8; "composition," Exod. xxx, 32, 37; "state," 2 Chron. xxiv, 13); (7) תֹּכֶן *to'ken* (Ezek. xlv, 11; "tale," Exod. v, 18); (8) μέτρον, the usual and proper Greek word (Matt. vii, 2; xxiii, 32; Mark iv, 24; Luke vi, 38; John iii, 34; Rom. xii, 3; 2 Cor. x, 13; Eph. iv, 7, 13, 16; Rev. xxi, 17).

2. *Such as represent a definite Value.*—(1) אֵיפָה, *ey-phah'* (Deut. xxv, 14, 15; Prov. xx, 10; Mic. vi, 10; elsewhere "*ephah*" [q. v.]); (2) אַמָּה, *ammah'* (Jer. li, 13; "post," Isa. vi, 4; elsewhere "*cubit*" [q. v.]); (3) כֹּר, *kor* (1 Kings iv, 22 [v, 2]; v, 11 [25]; 2 Chron. ii, 10 [9]; xxvii, 5; Chald. plur. Ezra vii, 22; elsewhere "*cor*" [q. v.]), Gr. κόρος (Luke xvi, 7); (4) סְאָה, *seäh'* (Gen. xviii, 6; 1 Sam. xxv, 18; 1 Kings xviii, 32; 2 Kings vii, 1, 16, 18; a *seah* [q. v.]), the Gr. σάτον (Matt. xiii, 33; Luke xiii, 21), and the reduplicated form סַאסְּאָה, *sasseäh'* (Isa. xxvii, 8; used indeterminately); (5) שָׁלִישׁ, *shalish'* (Isa. xl, 12; "great measure," Psa. lxxx, 5; lit. a *third*, i. e. prob. of the ephah, but used indefinitely; (6) βάτος (Luke xvi, 6; the Hebrew *bath* [q. v.]); (7) χοῖνιξ (Rev. vi, 6; the Greek *chœnix* [q. v.]).

Meat.—I. It does not appear that the word "meat" is used in any one instance in the Authorized Version of either the O. or N. Testament in the sense which it now almost exclusively bears of animal food. The latter is denoted uniformly by "flesh."

1. The only possible exceptions to this assertion in the O. T. are: (*a*) Gen. xxvii, 4, etc., "savory meat;" Gen. xlv, 23, "corn and bread and meat." Here the Hebrew word, מַטְעַמִּים, *matammim'*, which in this form appears in this chapter only, is derived from a root which has exactly the force of our word "taste," and is employed in reference to the manna. In the passages in question the word "dainties" would be perhaps more appropriate. (*b*) In Genesis the original word is one of almost equal rarity, מָזוֹן, *mazon'*; and if the Lexicons did not show that this had only the general force of *food* in all the other Oriental tongues, that would be established in regard to Hebrew by its other occurrences, viz. 2 Chron. xi, 23, where it is rendered "victual;" and Dan. ix., 12, 21, where the meat spoken of is that to be furnished by a tree.

2. The only real and inconvenient ambiguity caused by the change which has taken place in the meaning of the word is in the case of the "meat-offering," the second of the three great divisions into which the sacrifices of the Law were divided—the burnt-offering, the meat-offering, and the peace-offering (Lev. ii, 1, etc.)—and which consisted solely of flour, or corn, and oil, sacrifices of flesh being confined to the other two. The word thus translated is מִנְחָה, *minchah'*, elsewhere rendered "present" and "oblation," and derived from a root which has the force of "sending" or "offering" to a person. It is very desirable that some English term should be proposed which would avoid this ambiguity. "Food-offering" is hardly admissible, though it is perhaps preferable to "unbloody or bloodless sacrifice." See MEAT-OFFERING.

3. There are several other words, which, though entirely distinct in the original, are all translated in the A. V. by "meat;" but none of them present any special interest except טֶרֶף, *te'reph*. This word, from a root signifying "to tear," would be perhaps more accurately rendered "prey" or "booty." Its use in Psa. cxi, 5, especially when taken in connection with the word rendered "good understanding" in ver. 10, which should rather be, as in the margin, "good success," throws a new and unexpected light over the familiar phrases of that beautiful Psalm. It seems to show how inextinguishable was the warlike, predatory spirit in the mind of the writer, good Israelite and devout worshipper of Jehovah as he was. Late as he lived in the history of his nation, he cannot forget the "power" of Jehovah's "works" by which his forefathers acquired the "heritage of the heathen;" and to him, as to his ancestors when conquering the country, it is still a firm article of belief that those who fear Jehovah shall obtain most of the spoil of his enemies—those who obey his commandments shall have the best success in the field.

4. In the N. T. the variety of the Greek words thus rendered is equally great; but dismissing such terms as ἀνακεῖσθαι or ἀναπίπτειν, which are rendered by "sit at meat"—φαγεῖν, for which we occasionally find "meat" —τράπεζα (Acts xvi, 34), the same—εἰδωλόθυτα, "meat offered to idols"—κλάσματα, generally "fragments," but twice "broken meat"—dismissing these, we have left τροφή and βρῶμα (with its kindred words, βρῶσις, etc.), both words bearing the widest possible signification, and meaning everything that can be eaten or can nourish the frame. The former is most used in the Gospels and Acts. The latter is found in John and in the Epistles of Paul. It is the word employed in the famous sentences, "for meat destroy not the work of God," "if meat make my brother to offend," etc. See ALISGEMA.

II. Meat, however, in the proper modern sense (בָּשָׂר, *basar', flesh*, as it is rendered in the Auth. Vers.), i. e. of clean beasts (Lev. xi,), namely, lambs (Isa. liii, 7; Amos vi, 4), calves (1 Sam. xxviii, 24; Gen. xviii, 7; Amos vi, 4; Luke xv, 23; comp. Russell, *Aleppo*, i, 145), oxen (Isa. xxii, 13; Prov. xv, 17; 1 Kings iv, 23; Matt. xxii, 4), kids (1 Sam. xvi, 20; Judg. vi, 19), also venison (1 Kings iv, 23), and poultry (1 Kings iv, 23; see Gesenius, *Thes. Heb.* p. 715; Michaelis, *Mos. Recht.* iv, 198), was a favorite dish among the Hebrews, either roasted entire, or cooked with choice vegetables and eaten with bread (2 Sam. vi, 19; 1 Kings xvii, 6); yet only royal personages partook of it daily (1 Kings iv, 23; Neh. v, 18), the less wealthy merely on festive occasions (Luke xv, 23; comp. Niebuhr, *Besch.* p. 52), especially at the great sacrificial festivals; and we find that the modern Arabs, namely, the Bedouin, as a general rule, but seldom eat flesh (Shaw, *Trav.* p. 169; comp. Burckhardt, *Trav.* ii, 1003; Wellsted, i, 248; those of the peninsula of Sinai live mostly on sour milk, dried dates, and unleavened bread, Rüppel, p. 203; but among the ancient Egyptians flesh was very commonly eaten, Exod. xvi, 3; comp. Rosellini, *Monum. civ.* i, 151). The shoulder was the most esteemed piece of the animal (1 Sam. ix,

24; comp. Harmar, i, 311). Flesh which contained the blood was forbidden (Lev. iii, 17; vii, 26; xvii, 10; Deut. xii, 16, 27), because the life was regarded as residing in the blood (Gen. ix, 4; comp. Oedmann, vi, 89 sq.). See BLOOD. The pieces of flesh were taken by each guest from the common dish with his fingers. See EAT; MEAL-TIME. The Jews were very careful to avoid the flesh of heathen victims (Aboda Sara, ii, 3). See CLEAN; OFFERING.

III. As above noted, in the English version the word "meat" means food in general; or when confined to one species of food, it always signifies meal, flour, or grain, but never flesh, which is now the usual acceptation of the word. See FLESH. A "meat-offering" in the Scriptures is always a vegetable, and never an animal offering; and it might now be rendered a bread-offering, or a meal-offering, instead of a meat-offering. It does not appear that the ancient Hebrews were very nice about the dressing of their food. We find among them roast meat, boiled meat, and ragouts. See COOK. Their manner of living would be much like that of the ancient Egyptians, among whom they had long resided. Wilkinson says, "No tray was used on the Egyptian table, nor was it covered by any linen; like that of the Greeks, it was probably wiped with a sponge or napkin after the dishes were removed, and polished by the servants when the company had retired. The dishes consisted of fish; meat, boiled, roasted, and dressed in various ways; game, poultry, and a profusion of vegetables and fruit, particularly figs and grapes during the season; and a soup or pottage of lentils. Of figs and grapes they were particularly fond. Fresh dates during the season, and in a dried state at other periods of the year, were also brought to table." See FOOD. Among the Hebrews meats that were offered were boiled in a pot (1 Sam. ii, 14, 15). They were forbidden to seethe a kid in the milk of its dam (Exod. xxiii, 19; xxxiv, 26). They might not kill a cow and its calf on the same day; nor a sheep or goat and its young one at the same time. They might not cut off a part of a living animal to eat it, either raw or dressed. If any lawful beast or bird should die of itself or be strangled, and the blood not drain away, they were not allowed to taste of it. He that by inadvertence should eat of any animal that died of itself, or that was killed by any beast, was to be unclean till the evening, and was not purified till he had washed his clothes. They ate of nothing dressed by any other than a Hebrew, nor did they ever dress their victuals with the kitchen implements of any but one of their own nation.

The prohibition of eating blood, or animals that are strangled, has been always rigidly observed by the Jews. In the council of the apostles held at Jerusalem, it was declared that converts from paganism should not be subject to the legal ceremonies, but that they should refrain from idolatry, from fornication, from eating blood, and from such animals as were strangled, and their blood thereby retained in their bodies; which decree was observed for many ages by the Church (Acts xv, 20–29).

In reference to "meats offered to idols," it may be observed that at the first settling of the Church there were many disputes concerning the use of meats offered to idols (1 Cor. viii, 7, 10). Some newly-converted Christians, convinced that an idol was nothing, and that the distinction of clean and unclean creatures was abolished by our Saviour, ate indifferently of whatever was served up to them, even among pagans, without inquiring whether the meats had been offered to idols. They took the same liberty in buying meat sold in the market, not regarding whether it were pure or impure, according to the Jews; or whether it had been offered to idols or not. But other Christians, weaker or less instructed, were offended at this liberty, and thought that eating of meat which had been offered to idols was a kind of partaking in that wicked and sacrilegious offering. This diversity of opinion produced some scan-

dal, for which Paul thought that it behoved him to provide a remedy (Rom. xiv, 20, 21; Tit. i, 15). He determined, therefore, that all things were clean to such as were clean, and that an idol was nothing at all; that a man might safely eat of whatever was sold in the shambles, and need not scrupulously inquire whence it came; and that if an unbeliever should invite a believer to eat with him, the believer might eat of whatever was set before him (1 Cor. x, 25, etc.). But at the same time he enjoins that the laws of charity and prudence should be observed; that believers should be cautious of scandalizing or offending weak minds; for though all things might be lawful, yet all things were not always expedient. See SACRIFICE.

Meat-offering (מִנְחָה, minchah'; sometimes more fully קָרְבַּן מִנְחָה, to mark its sacrificial character; Sept. fully δῶρον θυσία, but generally simply δῶρον or θυσία, sometimes προσφορά; Vulg. oblatio sacrificii, or simply sacrificium). The word minchah (from the obsolete root מָנַח, "to distribute" or "to give") signifies originally a gift of any kind, and appears to be used generally of a gift from an inferior to a superior, whether God or man (Lat. fertum). Thus in Gen. xxxii, 13 it is used of the present from Jacob to Esau, in Gen. xliii, 11 of the present sent to Joseph in Egypt, in 2 Sam. viii, 2, 6 of the tribute from Moab and Syria to David, etc.; and in Gen. iv, 3, 4, 5 it is applied to the sacrifices to God offered by Cain and Abel, although Abel's was a whole burnt-offering. Afterwards this general sense became attached to the word corban (קָרְבָּן), and the word minchah restricted to an "unbloody offering," as opposed to זֶבַח, a "bloody" sacrifice. It is constantly spoken of in connection with the drink-offering (נֶסֶךְ, Sept. σπονδή, Vulg. libamen), which generally accompanied it, and which had the same meaning. See DRINK-OFFERING. The law or ceremonial of the meat-offering is described in Lev. ii and vi, 14–23. It was to be composed of fine flour, seasoned with salt, and mixed with oil and frankincense, but without leaven; and it was generally accompanied by a drink-offering of wine. A portion of it, including all the frankincense, was to be burnt on the altar as "a memorial;" the rest belonged to the priest; but the meat-offerings offered by the priests themselves were to be wholly burnt.

Its meaning (which is analogous to that of the offering of the tithes, the first-fruits, and the showbread) appears to be exactly expressed in the words of David (1 Chron. xxix, 10–14), "All that is in the heaven and in the earth is thine . . . All things come of thee, and of thine own have we given thee." It recognised the sovereignty of the Lord, and his bounty in giving us all earthly blessings, by dedicating to him the best of his gifts: the flour, as the main support of life; oil, as the symbol of richness; and wine, as the symbol of vigor and refreshment (see Psa. civ, 15). All these were unleavened and seasoned with salt, in order to show their purity, and hallowed by the frankincense for God's special service. This recognition, implied in all cases, is expressed clearly in the form of offering the first-fruits prescribed in Deut. xxvi, 5–11.

It will be seen that this meaning involves neither of the main ideas of sacrifice—the atonement for sin and the self-dedication to God. It takes them for granted, and is based on them. Accordingly, the meat-offering, properly so called, seems always to have been a subsidiary offering, needing to be introduced by the sin-offering, which represented the one idea, and forming an appendage to the burnt-offering which represented the other. Thus, in the case of public sacrifices, a "meat-offering" was enjoined as a part of (1) the daily morning and evening sacrifice (Exod. xxix, 40, 41); (2) the Sabbath-offering (Numb. xxviii, 9, 10); (3) the offering at the new moon (Numb. xxviii, 11–14): (4) the offerings at the great festivals (Numb. xxviii, 20, 28; xxix, 3, 4, 14, 15, etc.); (5) the offerings on the great day of atonement

(Numb. xxix, 9, 10). The same was the case with private sacrifices, as at (1) *the consecration of priests* (Exod. xxix, 1, 2; Lev. vi, 20; viii, 2) *and of Levites* (Numb. viii, 8); (2) *the cleansing of the leper* (Lev. xiv, 20); (3) *he termination of the Nazaritish vow* (Numb. vi, 15).

The unbloody offerings offered alone did not properly belong to the regular meat-offering. They were usually substitutes for other offerings. Thus, for example, in Lev. v, 11, a tenth of an ephah of flour is allowed to be substituted by a poor man for the lamb or kid of a trespass-offering: in Numb. v, 15 the same offering is ordained as the "offering of jealousy" for a suspected wife. The unusual character of the offering is marked in both cases by the absence of the oil, frankincense, and wine. We find also at certain times libations of water poured out before God; as by Samuel's command at Mizpeh during the fast (1 Sam. vii, 6), and by David at Bethlehem (2 Sam. xxiii, 16), and a libation of oil poured by Jacob on the pillar at Bethel (Gen. xxxv, 14). But these have clearly especial meanings, and are not to be included in the ordinary drink-offerings. The same observation will apply to the remarkable libation of water customary at the Feast of Tabernacles, but not mentioned in Scripture. See TABERNACLES, FEAST OF.

From the above statements it appears that the "meat-offering" (or, rather, food-offering) was in general such eatable but bloodless articles (of vegetable growth) as were to be presented to Jehovah as devout gifts (comp. the early instance, Gen. iv, 3 sq.), and in a special sense only gifts of meal, raw or baked, which were brought to the altar of burnt-offerings, Exod. xl, 29; comp. xxx, 9), and either wholly or partially burnt to the honor of Jehovah (commonly with incense) by the hand of the priest. The portion of such "meat-offering" that was to be consumed is called אַזְכָּרָה, in contradistinction from that part which fell to the priest (Lev. ii, 2, 9, 16; Numb. vi, 26; comp. Lev. xxiv, 7, where the incense of the showbread is so called, which was also consumed). This word certainly has not the signification of *odoramentum* (Saadias), or in general *offering* (as Michaelis thinks), but is a verbal noun from הִזְכִּיר (*to cause to remember*), and the Sept. translates μνημόσυνον accordingly (see Gesen. *Thesaur.* p. 417). The Mishnic tract *Menachoth* (v, 2; comp. Otho, *Lex. Rabb.* p. 649) treats of the "meat-offering" in the above broad sense as an important part of the sacred ritual. The Bible itself specifies, of the *not* burned "meat-offerings," only the Pentecostal bread expressly by the name of a *minchah* (Lev. xxiii, 18; comp. ver. 17), while the Passover sheaf and the showbread belong by their own nature to the same category. The proper "meat-offerings," as above particularized, were either independent gifts (Talm. הבאות בפני עצמן), or simply additions to other principal offerings (הבאות עם הזבח). For example, no burnt-offering could be presented without a meat or drink offering (see Lev. vii, 8 sq.); and drink-offerings were associated likewise with thank-offerings (Lev. vii, 12 sq.), and in a certain case with a sin-offering (Lev. xiv, 10, 20). This appears to have been on the principle that men do not eat flesh without bread and wine; a signification which also lay at the bottom of the Greek οὐλαί (coarse ground barley grains) and the Roman *mola salsa*, with which the victim was strewn. Bahr (*Symbol.* i, 216), however, regards the supplementary unbloody offering as a sort of compensation for the life taken from the sacrifice. Such additional meat-offerings, at all events, appear regularly in connection with the principal offerings, whether (*a*) free-will (Numb. xvi, 4 sq.; comp. Judg. vi, 19) or (*b*) enjoined. The latter, again, were sometimes offered *publicly* in the name of the whole people (מנחת צבור), as those in connection with the daily morning and evening oblation (Exod. xxix, 40; xxviii, 6; Numb. iv, 16), or with the sabbatical (Numb. xxviii, 9) and feast offerings (Numb. xxviii,

11 sq.; Lev. xxiii); at other times they were *private* (מנחת יחיד), as that of the purification of the leper (Lev. xiv, 20 sq.), the Nazarite who had fulfilled his vow (Numb. vi, 16, 17), and the consecration of Levites (Numb. viii, 8 sq.), and perhaps of priests (Exod. xxix, 2, Lev. viii, 2). In these cases the essential part of the meat-offering was fine wheat flour (סֹלֶת; Josephus, ἄλευρον καθαρώματον, *Ant.* iii, 9, 4), mixed with olive-oil (these were both to be the best procurable in Palestine; see the Mishna, *Menach.* viii, 1), and it was all consumed upon the altar. The proportions were: for a lamb, $\frac{1}{10}$ ephah of flour and $\frac{1}{4}$ hin of oil; for a ram, $\frac{2}{10}$ ephah of flour and $\frac{1}{3}$ hin of oil; finally, for a bullock, $\frac{3}{10}$ ephah of flour and $\frac{1}{2}$ hin of oil (Numb. xv, 4 sq.; xxviii, 5, 9, 12 sq., 28 sq.; xxix, 3 sq., 8 sq., 13 sq.; Lev. xiv, 21). For the lamb offered with the Passover sheaf, $\frac{3}{10}$ ephah of fine flour was prescribed (Lev. xxiii, 13). In the case of the Nazarite still different regulations are made (Numb. vi, 16 sq.). See NAZARITE. From the fact that in connection with (free-will) burnt-offerings a handful of the meal only as a meat-offering was to be sprinkled upon the altar to be consumed with the incense, while the remainder fell to the priest's lot (Lev. vii, 14 sq.), we see that priestly festivities were associated with the thank-offerings.

It likewise appears from the foregoing account that the independent "meat-offerings" were sometimes free-will (Lev. ii), and sometimes obligatory. To the latter belonged the cases specified above: (*a*) that of a poor man, who had made himself liable in the manner stated in Lev. v, 1 sq. (comp. ver. 11); and (*b*) the "jealousy-offering" of a wife charged with adultery (Numb. v, 15, 26); to which is to be added (*c*) the consecration-offering of a priest (high-priest) on entering upon his office (Lev. vi, 20 [13] sq.). The Talmud (see *Menach.* iv, 5; xi, 3) applies this law exclusively to the oblation of the high-priest, and makes the meat-offering to be a *daily* one (מנחה תמיד), with which Josephus agrees (*Ant.* iii, 10, 7). In both the first cases the meat-offering consisted of $\frac{1}{10}$ ephah of meal (without oil or incense), of which, as above noted, only a handful was burned, and the rest, as usual, went to the priest; whereas in the third case, the whole meat-offering was to be consumed (if so we may understand the somewhat dark passage of Lev. vi, 22). The meal in cases (*a*) and (*c*) was to be of wheat, but in the case (*b*) of barley. The free-will offering might be brought in either of three conditions, namely, as raw flour, upon which oil was poured and incense laid (strewed) (Lev. ii, 1 sq.); or as roasted and pounded (firstling) grains, likewise with oil and incense (Lev. ii, 14 sq.); or, lastly, as baked dough. The dough, moreover, might be baked either in the oven, and in that case the oil must be spread under the loaves, or sprinkled upon them (Lev. ii, 14); or in a pan (מחבת), when the dough must be mixed with the oil, and in the presentation the loaves were broken in pieces and oil poured on them (Lev. ii, 5 sq.); or, finally, in the מרחשת, i. e., according to the Jews, a deep stew-pan, so that the loaves swam in oil (Lev. ii, 7). See CAKE. The priest always burned of these free-will offerings a handful of meal with oil (or a batch), with all the incense, on the altar (Lev. ii, 2); the remainder fell sometimes to him, sometimes to the other priests (Lev. vii, 9 sq.), and must be consumed in the sanctuary (Lev. ii, 3; x, 10, 12 sq.; comp. Josephus, *Ant.* iii, 9, 4). Leaven or honey must not be mixed with the meat-offering (Lev. ii, 11; a rule which, with one exception [Lev. vii, 13], applied to all such offerings; see Exod. xxix, 2; Lev. vii, 12; viii, 26; x, 12; Mishna, *Menach.* v, 1), but they must be salted (Lev. ii, 13). Even in eating the meat-offering the priests were not allowed to use ferment (see Lev. vi, 16 [9]; x, 12). See generally Reland, *Antiq. Sacr.* iii, 7; Iken, *Antiq. Hebr.* i, 14; Carpzov, *Appar.* p. 708 (brief); Bauer, *Gottesd. Verd.* i, 187 sq. (incomplete and inexact). See

Vollborth, *De sacrificio farreo Hebræorum* (Gottingen, 1780). See OFFERING.

Mebane, WILLIAM N., a Presbyterian minister, was born in Guilford County, N. C., March 10, 1809. His preparatory education was received in Greensborough, N. C., under the Rev. Drs. Pressly and Carothers. He graduated at the University of North Carolina in 1833, and at Princeton Theological Seminary in 1837; in 1838 and 1839 labored as a missionary in the bounds of the states of Louisiana and Texas; in 1840 was ordained and installed pastor of Spring Garden Church, N. C.; in 1852 took charge of Madison Church. He died in May, 1859. Mr. Mebane possessed fine conversational powers, together with a striking independence of thought; as a pastor he was very successful, as he was gifted with the happy faculty of introducing the subject of personal religion. See *Presb. Hist. Almanac,* 1861, p. 97.

Mebun'nai (Heb. *Mebunnay',* מְבֻנַּי, constructive, if genuine; Sept. ἐκ τῶν υἱῶν [apparently pointing מִבְּנֵי], but v. r. Σαβουχαί; Vulg. *Mebounai*), a person named as one of David's body-guard (2 Sam. xxiii, 27), but elsewhere more correctly SIBBECHAI (2 Sam. xxi, 18; 1 Chron. xx, 4) or SIBBECAI (1 Chron. xi, 29; xxvii, 11). See DAVID.

Mecaskey, JOHN W., A.M., a minister of the Methodist Episcopal Church, born in 1821, was the son of pious parents, and inherited an honored name, a fine physical form, a vigorous intellect, and an amiable disposition. On the death of his devoted mother in his twelfth year, he was placed by his remaining parent in the academy of the Rev. Mr. Andrews, of Doylestown, Pa., and there completed his academical course. His inclinations were for the legal profession, and he consequently fitted himself for admission to the bar, with fair promises of a bright future. Suddenly brought to acknowledge his need of religion, he gave himself to Christianity, and, believing himself to be called to preach the Gospel, at once prepared for the great work. After rendering good service in the Sunday-school, and as a class-leader and exhorter, he was licensed to preach; and being further proved by one year's travel on the Newtown Circuit, he was recommended to the Philadelphia Conference, by which he was received in 1844, and sent to Radnor Circuit. His subsequent fields of labor were Grove Circuit, Mauch Chunk, Stroudsburg, Bustleton, St. John's, the Tract Agency, and West Philadelphia. After this he was stationed in Columbia, Reading, Norristown, and Pottsville. In 1862 he was again brought to Philadelphia, and stationed in Asbury, West Philadelphia, and here he worked for the Master's cause until death, Oct. 16, 1863. "He was instant in season and out of season, an able minister of the New Testament, and a faithful steward of the mysteries of God. Purity, dignity, and earnestness, culminating in deep, constant devotion to God and his work, marked and illuminated his whole course." See *Minutes of Conferences,* 1864, p. 26.

Mecca (*Om Al-Kora,* Mother of Cities), the birthplace of Mohammed, and therefore the central and most sacredly guarded and honored city of Arabia, is one of its oldest towns, the capital of the province of Hejaz. It is situated in 21° 30′ N. lat., and 40° 8′ E. long., 245 miles south of Medina (q. v.), and about 65 miles east of Jiddah, the well-known port on the Red Sea, in a narrow, barren valley, surrounded by bare hills and sandy plains, and watered by the brook Wady Al-Tarafeyn. The city is about 1500 paces long, and about 650 broad, and is divided into the Upper and Lower City, with twenty-five chief quarters. The streets are broad and rather regular, but unpaved; excessively dusty in summer, and muddy in the rainy season. The houses, three or four stories high, are built of brick or stone, ornamented with paintings, and their windows open on the streets. The rooms are much more handsomely furnished, and altogether in a better state than is usual in the East, the inhabitants of Mecca making their living

chiefly by letting them to the pilgrims who flock hither to visit the Beit Allah (House of God), or chief mosque, containing the Kaaba (q. v.). This mosque, capable of holding about 35,000 persons, is surrounded by nineteen gates surmounted by seven minarets, and contains several rows of pillars, about twenty feet high, and about eighteen inches in diameter, of marble, granite, porphyry, and common sandstone, which at certain distances are surmounted by small domes. A great number of people are attached to the mosque in some kind of ecclesiastical capacity, as katibs, muftis, mueddins, etc. Pilgrimages have very much decreased of late years, and in consequence the inhabitants of this city, at one time containing 100,000, now scarcely counts 40,000 regular residents. The age of the city of Mecca is not exactly known. We find that it was in quite a flourishing condition in the days of Ptolemy, under the name of *Macoraba.* Mohammed, who had been obliged to quit it quite precipitately in A.D. 622, returned to it in 627, forcing his entrance as conqueror. At first it belonged to the tribe of the Kosaites, later to the Koreish (q. v.). Within the course of the present century (1803) Mecca was taken by the Wahabies (q. v.), but given up again to the pacha of Egypt, Mehemet Ali (1833), whose son Ibrahim was made sheik El-Haram —"of the Sacred Place." At present, however, Mecca is directly dependent on the sultan of Turkey. A certain balm, the "Balm of Mecca," is made from a plant called *Besem,* which grows in abundance in the neighborhood of the city. Another chief article of manufacture, and a great source of income to the residents of Mecca, are the *chaplets* for pious pilgrims. See Chambers, *Cyclop.* s. v.; *Der Christliche Apologete,* 1872, Nov. 12.

Mechanic. The Hebrews appear to have learned in Egypt the elements at least of all the forms of handicraft practiced in that highly-civilized country, and later their neighbors the Phœnicians, famous in early times for their progress in the industrial arts, doubtless exerted a further influence upon them; nevertheless, down at least to the close of the period of the judges, the skill of the Hebrews in manufactures was quite inconsiderable (1 Sam. xiii, 20). Many of the handicrafts were practiced by the proprietor of the house (landowner) himself (comp. Homer, *Odyss.* v, 243), chiefly the coarser kinds of work (i. e. in wood), while other sorts fell to the female head of the family, such as baking (2 Sam. xiii, 8), weaving and embroidering (Exod. xxxv, 28; Prov. xxxi, 24), and the making up of garments, including those of the men (Prov. xxxi, 21; 1 Sam. ii, 19; Acts ix, 39). See WOMAN, and comp. the Mishna, *Kethuboth,* v, 5. But all the varied forms of manufacture, which, being generally executed by dint of actual manipulation, required a good degree of personal dexterity, were carried on among the Hebrews by the owners themselves, who were not slaves. So in the Homeric poems several kinds of mechanic arts appear (*Iliad,* iv, 110, 485; xviii, 601; *Odyss.* iii, 425, 432; see Wachsmuth, *Hellen. Alterth.* II, i, 47 sq.).

Accordingly we find mention of the *gold* and *silver* smith (צוֹרֵף or מְצָרֵף, Judg. xvii, 4; Isa. xl, 19; Jer. x, 14, etc.), who especially fabricated idols, or plated and ornamented them; the apothecary (רֹקֵחַ or רַקָּח, Exod. xxx, 35; comp. μυρεψός, Ecclus. xxxviii, 7); the *artificer* (חָרָשׁ, Exod. xxxv, 35; Deut. xxvii, 15; 1 Sam. xiii, 19), a term inclusive of blacksmiths (חָרָשׁ בַּרְזֶל, Isa. xliv, 12; 2 Kings xxiv, 14; 1 Sam. xiii, 19; Talm. נַפָּחִין, Mishna, *Chel.* xiv, 3) and braziers (ח' נְחֹשֶׁת, 1 Kings vii, 14; comp. χαλκεύς, 2 Tim. iv, 14), as well as carpenters (ח' עֵץ, 2 Sam, v, 11; Isa. xliv, 13; comp. τέκτων, Matt. x iii, 55; Mark vi, 3; also cabinet-makers, Mishna, *Baba Kamma,* ix, 3) and masons (חָרָשֵׁי קִיר, 1 Chron. xiv, 1); the *stone-squarers* (חֹצְבֵי אֶבֶן, 2 Kings xii, 12), which was distinct from the last named,

VI.—1*

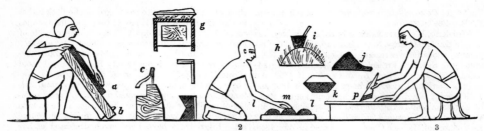

Veneering and the Use of Glue. (Wilkinson.)

a, a piece of dark wood applied to one of ordinary quality, *b*. *c*, adze, fixed into a block of wood of the same color as *b*. *e*, a ruler; and *f*, a square, similar to those used by our carpenters. *g*, a box. Fig. 2 is grinding something. *i*, glue-pot on the fire. *j*, a piece of glue. Fig. 3, applying glue with a brush, *p*.

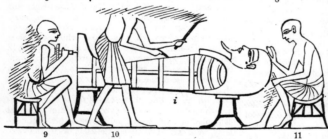

Bandaging Mummies and making the Cases. (Wilkinson.)

Fig. 1, sawing wood. 2, cutting the leg of a chair, indicating the trade of the carpenter. 3, a man fallen asleep. *c c*, wood ready for cutting. *d*, onions and other provisions, which occur again at *g*, with vases, *f f*. 4 and 7, binding mummies. 6, brings the bandages. 9, using the drill. 8, 10, and 11, painting and polishing the case.

high rank in the fine styles of work, especially those in which labor passes over into an art, appears from the fact that a single individual often carried on several trades at once (Exod. xxxi, 3 sq.; 2 Chron. ii, 14); while David and Solomon are recorded as having imported for their structures Phœnician (Sidonian) artificers (1 Kings v, 6; 1 Chron. xiv, 1; 2 Chron. ii, 7, 14, etc.). See PHŒNICIA.

After the exile handicrafts and arts in general stood in greater esteem among the Jews, so that experts were found among them, and their productions acquired considerable reputation (see Rosenmüller, *Morgenland*, vi, 42). It passed for a sign of a bad bringing up when a father failed to teach his son a trade (Mishna, *Kiddush.* iv. 14; Lightfoot, p. 616; comp. *Pirke Aboth*, ii, 2; Wagenseil, *Sota*, p. 597; Otho, *Lex. Rabb.* p. 491). In the Apocrypha of the Old Test. there are mentioned the κεραμεύς, as a moulder of figures of clay (Wisd. xv, 8), the χρυσουργός, ἀργυρο-

but whether the *plasterers* (תָּפֵל טָחַי, Ezek. xiii, 11) were a separate trade from the masons is not clear; the *potter* (יֹצֵר, Isa. xxix, 16, etc.; κεραμεύς, Matt. xxvii, 7, 10; comp. Gesenius, *Monum. Phœn.* p. 161); the *locksmith* (מַסְגֵּר, Jer. xxix, 2); the *fuller* (כֹּבֵס or מְכַבֵּס, 2 Kings xviii, 17; γναφεύς, Mark ix, 3; comp. Gesen. *ut sup.* p. 181); the *weaver* (אֹרֵג) early (Exod. xxviii, 32) formed a separate branch of industry (especially in fabrics of byssus, 1 Chron. iv, 21), and in large cities the *baker* (אֹפֶה, Hos. vii, 4; Jer. xxxvii, 21; see Josephus, *Ant.* xv, 9, 2; but Luke xi, 2, does not prove the absence of such a trade); later also the *barber* (גַּלָּב, Ezek. v, 1) is named (סְפָר, according to the Targum of Jonath. at Lev. xiii, 45; Mishna, *Shabb.* i, 2). See each in its place. Nevertheless, that the Hebrews took no very

χόος, and χαλκοπλάστης among metal-workers (Wisd. xv, 19), chiefly as tributary to idol image-makers; in the New Test. the tanner (βυρσεύς, Acts ix, 43; x, 6, 32; Talm. מורסירן or צבדנין, *Chel.* xv, 1), the tent-maker (σκηνοποιός, Acts xviii, 3); in Josephus occur the cheese-makers (τυροποιοί, *War*, v, 4, 1), the barbers (κουρεῖς, *Ant.* xvi, 5; *War*, i, 27, 5), who were of service to princes; in the Talmud, among others, the tailor (חירט, *Shabb.* i, 3), the shoemaker (רצען, *Pesach.* iv, 6), the plasterer (סריד, *Chel.* xxix, 3), the glazier (גזז, *Chel.* viii, 9), the goldsmith (זהר, *Chel.* xxix, 6), the dyer (צבע, comp. Thilo, *Apocr.* p. 111). Some of these occupations were of so low repute that those who followed them could not attain the office of high-priest (*Kiddush.* lxxxii, 1); viz. those of the weaver, the barber, the fuller, the apothecary, the blood-letter, the bath-keeper, the tanner, which avocations, especially the barber's and the tanner's, were very odious (*Kiddush.* iv, 14; *Megilla*, iii, 2; comp. Otho, *Lex. Rabb.* p. 155; Wetstein, *Nov. Test.* ii, 516). The workshops or place of business of the artisans appear (in the larger cities) to have been in certain streets or squares (*bazaars*, Tournefort, *Trav.* ii, 322), where they were collected (Jer. xxxix, 21); as in the Talmud, for instance, there is mention (Surenhusius, *Mischna*, v, 169, 225) of a *meat-market* (אטלם or ארטלין), and in Josephus (*War*, v, 4, 1) of a *cheese-maker's* valley (the Tyropœon), as likewise of forges and dealers in wool and garments (*War*, v, 8, 1). On occasions of public mourning such places were closed (Philo, ii, 525). See generally, Iken, *Antiq. Hebr.* ii, 578 sq.; Bellermann, *Handb.* i, 221 sq. See HANDICRAFT.

Mecherah. See MECHERATHITE.

Mech'erathite (Heb. *Mekerathi'*, מְכֵרָתִי, gentile from מְכֵרָה, *Mekerah'*, a *sword*, as in Gen. xlix, 5; Sept. Μεχουραθί v. r. Μεχωραθρί, Vulg. *Mecherathites*), an epithet applied to Hepher, one of David's famous warriors, probably as being a native of MECHERAH, a place otherwise unknown (1 Chron. xi, 36); but from the parallel passage (2 Sam. xxiii, 34) it would appear to be a corruption for MAACHATHITE. See UR.

Mechitar (or **Melkhitar**), DA PETRO, the founder of the Order of Mechitarists (q. v.), was born at Sebaste, a town of Armenia Minor, Feb. 7, 1676. His father's name was Peter Manukean (i. e. son of Manug), but he exchanged his family name (Manug) for that of Mechitar, or "Consoler," on entering into ecclesiastical orders. His early education had been intrusted to monastics; they, no doubt, influenced him to devote himself to the service of the Church. At the age of fifteen he became an inmate of the Convent of the Holy Cross, near Sebaste; and a few years after, being made secretary of the archbishop Michael, who took him to Erzerum, he became acquainted with a fellow-countryman who had travelled in Europe, and who lent him an Armenian work by Galanus, an Italian missionary, *On the Reconciliation of the Armenian Church with that of Rome* (published at Rome in 1650). Though Mechitar still continued professedly a member of the Armenian priesthood, he appears from this time to have become in secret a proselyte to the Church of Rome; but the exact date of his passing over seems to have been unknown to all his biographers. He was anxious to make himself acquainted with the civilization of the West, it is urged by some; others believe that Mechitar had fallen into the hands of Romish priests, and was induced, as early as 1693, to accept the Romish interpretation of the sacred writings, and, consequently, of the doctrines and faith of the hierarchy, and that he determined on a visit to Rome to enjoy an interview with the holy father and the great dignitaries of the Latin Church. There is some reason also for the belief that Mechitar was at once, after his entry into the Latin Church, made a member of the Society of Jesus, and that he secretly worked for the good of the order. On his way to Rome he was attacked by severe illness in the island of Cyprus, and compelled to return, begging his way as he went. In 1696 he re-entered the convent, determined to become a worker for higher religious and literary culture among his countrymen, and to further this undertaking effectually he sought to gather about him young men desiring to work as missionaries. In 1699 he was made D.D., and shortly after he removed to the Byzantine capital. In 1700, when he was a preacher at Constantinople, some dissensions between the partisans of two rival patriarchs divided the Armenian community into two hostile parties. Mechitar at first advised reconciliation, and afterwards, to their surprise, preached submission to the Church of Rome, and this roused such a storm against him that he was obliged to claim the protection of the French ambassador, which was readily afforded.

Thenceforth Mechitar appeared openly as a Roman Catholic. To escape from the animosity of his countrymen he still found it necessary to remove in disguise to Smyrna, and finally he settled at Modon, in the Morea, under the protection of the Venetian government, to whom it then belonged. As early as Sept. 8, 1701, he had founded at Constantinople a new religious community, in which ten other persons joined with him; at Modon, on Sept. 8, 1703, he took possession of an estate given him by the Venetians, to build a convent of the new order, which was called after his own name. The war between the Turks and the Venetians drove Mechitar in 1715 to Venice, where he remained until after the conquest of the Morea by the Mussulman. His petition for a place instead of Modon found a willing ear at the Venetian Senate in 1717, and he was presented with the little island of San Lazaro, near the Lido, and there Mechitar built the convent which still attracts the attention of every visitor to Venice. It was opened on the day of the Virgin Mary's birth, Sept. 8. Thenceforth Mechitar labored assiduously for the good of the Church of Rome and the elevation of his countrymen. He is acknowledged even by his opponents of the Armenian Church to have revived the high literary attainments of his country in former days. He not only contributed to this by his own efforts as a voluminous writer, but in a still more important degree by establishing printing-presses. He died April 27, 1749. His own productions are, besides many hymns, which are still sung in the Armenian churches, because they were written before his apostasy, a translation of Thomas à Kempis's *Imitation of Christ*, and of Thomas Aquinas's *Theology*, and many philological works of value. The fullest account of Mechitar, of his work, and of his followers, in English, is to be found in *Brief Account of the Mechitaristican Society*, by Alexander Gorde (Venice, 1835). See MECHITARISTS.

Mechitarists, a congregation of Armenian Christians, who reside on the island of San Lazaro at Venice, but who have also obtained a footing in France and Austria. They derive their name from MECHITAR DA PETRO (q. v.), who in the year 1701 founded this religious society for the purpose of diffusing a knowledge of the old Armenian language and literature. The Mechitarists, like their founder and instructor, acknowledge the supremacy of the Roman pontiff, and seek to spread the faith and practices of the Church of Rome in the East. The rules of the Mechitarists are modelled after those of the Benedictines, but every member must be of the Armenian nation, and promise an active devotion to the cultivation of the Armenian language and literature. The result, as we have said above, has been the formation not only of a convent but of an academy; and, in fact, the best schools for the study of Armenian are in the houses of the order. A division was provoked in 1773, and some of the Mechitarists settled at Trieste, and there founded an institution like that at San Lazaro. In 1810 these seceders removed to Vienna, the Austrian capital, and there they still remain, busy mainly in the publication of Armenian classical productions and instructing young Armenians. A third society has recently been founded at Paris, and efforts are making for the establishment of a fourth at Constantinople. Several hundred volumes have already been published by the Mechitarists. Of these the theological portion has a Roman Catholic circulation only, but the others have been welcomed by the Armenians generally. They publish a periodical like the English *Penny Magazine*. See Bozé, *De Convent de St. Lazare à Venise, ou Histoire succincte de l'Ordre des Méchitaristes Arméniens* (Paris, 1837).

Mechthildis, ST., a younger sister of St. Gertrude (q. v.), of the ancient and renowned family of Hackeborn, was born at Eisleben in the early part of the 13th century. She early manifested a decided taste for religious exercises, and at the age of seven, having gone one day with her mother to visit the Convent of Rodersdorf, occupied by Benedictine nuns, she was so much delighted with it that she insisted on remaining in it. She was allowed to become a novice, and fulfilled all the duties imposed upon her in that position with great zeal, showing herself particularly serviceable in taking care of the poor and the afflicted. At the end of her noviciate she took the veil, and remained in the convent until 1258, when, together with the other nuns, she removed to that of Helpede, where she died shortly after. Inclining from youth to mysticism, she, like her sister Gertrude, claimed to have had visions, but she steadfastly declined writing them down; this was, however, done against her will by one of her friends, under the title *Revelationes selectæ S. Mathildis*, together with a short biographical notice. These mystic pieces are not only full of elevated thoughts and aspirations, but give evidence of a thorough acquaintance with Scripture. The best edition is that published, together with a German translation, in the *Bibliotheca mystica et ascetica* (Cologne, 1854, pt. x).

Another Mechthildis, also honored as a saint in the Roman Catholic Church, flourished near the middle of the 12th century. She was a descendant of the counts of Andechs. In early youth she commenced to manifest signs of piety, and when she attained the requisite age she became a nun in the Convent of Diessen, in Bavaria. Here she acquired such reputation for piety and zeal that she was elected abbess in 1153. Some years afterwards she was obliged, at the command of the bishop, to go as abbess to the Convent of Edelstetten, which she was to renovate. She labored there with her usual zeal, and proved very successful, yet she always regretted leaving her former convent, and during her last illness was removed to it. She died May 31, 1160. She is commemorated April 10. See Herzog, *Real-Encyklop.* ix, 223; Wetzer u. Welte, *Kirchen-Lex.* xii, 788.

Mecklenburg, a North German territory, now part of the German empire, consists of two grand-duchies, the larger one called Mecklenburg-Schwerin, and the smaller one called Mecklenburg-Strelitz.

(1.) *Mecklenburg-Schwerin*, bounded on the north by the Baltic, on the east by Pomerania, on the south by Brandenburg, and on the west by Lauenburg, covers an area of about 5126 square miles, and has a population of 560,618 (in 1867), of which 556,290 are Lutherans (200 Reformed), 1195 communicants of the Church of Rome, and 3064 adherents to the Jewish faith. The Mecklenburgers are for the most part of Slavonic origin, but amalgamation with their Saxon neighbors has largely Germanized the original race. The predominating form of religion is the Lutheran, the religion of the reigning prince. The grand-duke, whose powers are limited by a mixed feudal and constitutional form of government, has the title of royal highness, and is styled prince of the Wends, and of Schwerin and Ratzeburg, count of Schwerin, and lord of Rostock, Stargard, etc. The state Church divides the territory into 331 rectories, with 475 churches, which are controlled by six superintendents and thirty-seven præpositors. Much has been done of late years in extending the educational organization of Mecklenburg, although the lower classes do not yet enjoy as many advantages as in some other districts of Germany. Besides the university at Rostock (q. v.), there are five gymnasia, and numerous burgher, parochial, and other schools. The principal towns are the capital Schwerin, Ludwigslust, Rostock, Güstrow, and Wismar.

(2.) *Mecklenburg-Strelitz*, the other grand-duchy, is composed of two distinct portions of territory, viz. Stargard (by far the larger division, lying to the east of Mecklenburg-Schwerin) and the principality of Ratzeburg (between Mecklenburg-Schwerin and Lauenburg), and comprises an area of rather more than 1000 square miles, with a population of 98,770 (in 1867), of which 97,937 are Lutherans (1000 Reformed), 169 Roman Catholics, and 466 Jews. Like the other Mecklenburg duchy, the country is in the hands of the Lutherans. It is

divided into sixty-two rectories, and is governed by seven diocesan superintendents (propste).

The two Mecklenburg duchies have provincial estates in common, which meet once a year, alternately at Malchin and Sternberg. This united chamber consists of noble landowners and the representatives of fortyseven provincial boroughs, each of which has, however, its separate municipal government.

History.—The Mecklenburg territory, anciently occupied by Germanic and afterwards by Slavonic tribes, was in the 12th century conquered by Henry the Lion, duke of Saxony, who, after thoroughly devastating the country, and compelling the small number of inhabitants remaining after the war to adopt Christianity, restored the greater part of the territory to Burewin, the heir of the slain Slavonic prince, Niklot, and gave him his daughter in marriage. The country at that period received its present designation from its principal settlement, Mikilinborg, now a village between Wismar and Bruël. Christianity was, however, known to the inhabitants of this country long before the inroads of Henry the Lion. Missionaries of the Cross are said to have been there in the days of Charlemagne; but true Christian principles and faithful adherents to the Christian cause were not made there until the first half of the 10th century. After Henry I had vanquished the natives in the battle at Leuzen (931), bishop Adalward, of Verden, in that very year baptized one of their rulers, and by the close of that century many converts had been gathered. But Christianity was still unpopular, and its confessors suffered much persecution, especially near the middle of the 11th century (comp. Jaffé, *Lothar*, p. 147, 232; *Conrad III*, p. 16). Not until the successful incursions of Henry the Lion can Christianity be really said to have found a hold in Mecklenburg territory, and hence he is generally looked upon not only as the author of the consolidation of the territory as Mecklenburg, but also as the founder of Christianity within its bounds. Shortly after the middle of the 12th century convents were built, and several monastic establishments founded. We find one Vicelin († 1154), bishop of Lubeck, and his successor Gerold, especially active as missionaries. But Christianity did not attain to a really prosperous condition during the Middle Ages in this part of the Teutonic domains, although it was elevated into a duchy in 1349 by the emperor Charles. The Protestant doctrines were first introduced here in 1550 by duke Johann Albrecht, and his grandsons, Wolf-Friedrich and Johann Albrecht, who founded the lines of Mecklenburg-Schwerin and Mecklenburg-Güstrow. They were, however, deprived of the ducal title in 1627, in consequence of their adhesion to the Protestant cause, and the imperial general Wallenstein was proclaimed duke of all Mecklenburg. In 1632 Gustavus Adolphus of Sweden restored his kinsmen, the deposed dukes, to their domains. Kötzer, alias Schlüter (q. v.), who was poisoned in 1532, was particularly prominent in the cause of the Reformers. The fruit of his labors was seen in 1534 in the decree against the reading of the mass, and in the final official adoption of the Protestant cause in 1550. The secular affairs of Mecklenburg continued to undergo changes. After various subdivisions of the ducal line into the branches of Schwerin, Strelitz, and others, and the successive extinction of several of these collateral houses, the Imperial Commission, which met at Hamburg in 1701, brought about the settlement of a family compact, by which it was arranged that Schwerin and Güstrow should form one duchy, and Strelitz, with Ratzeburg and Stargard, Mirow and Nemerow, another independent sovereignty. After this, very few events of importance occurred till the accession in Schwerin, in 1785, of Friedrich Franz, who obtained the title of grandduke in 1815, and died in 1837, after a long reign, which he had made highly conducive to the internal welfare and external reputation of his hereditary dominions. The reign of Friedrich Franz II, who succeeded his father, Paul Friedrich, in 1842, was disturbed by a contest between the nobles and the burgher and equestrian landowners, the former arrogating to themselves the exclusive right of electing members into the equestrian order, nominating to benefices, and monopolizing other prerogatives of the ancient feudal nobility. The revolutionary excitement of 1848 gave a fresh stimulus to the popular ferment, and the disturbances could only be quelled by the intervention of Prussian troops. In 1866 the duchies were incorporated in the North German Confederation, and since the establishment of the new German empire they form part of the latter. Religious toleration and freedom of speech, which were comparatively unknown in the duchies of Mecklenburg, have since 1866 gained quite a footing there, and promise much aid in the extinction of a very lukewarm profession of Christianity, and the establishment of vital Christianity in its stead. See Adam. Bremens. *Hist. Eccles.* in Pertz, *Mon. Script.* vol. iii; Ernst Boll, *Geschichte Mecklenburg's mit besonderer Berücksichtigung der Culturgesch.* (Neubrandenburg, 1855-56); Herzog, *Real-Encyklopädie,* s. v.; *Deutsch-Amerik. Conv. Lexikon,* s. v.   (J. H. W.)

Med'aba ($M\eta\delta\alpha\beta\acute{a}$, 2 Macc. ix, 36). See MEDEBA.

Me'dad (Heb. *Meydad'*, מֵידָד, *low;* Sept. $M\omega\delta\acute{a}\delta$), a person mentioned in connection with Eldad, as two of the seventy elders who were nominated to assist Moses in the government of the people, but who remained in the camp, probably as modestly deeming themselves unfit for the office, when the others presented themselves at the tabernacle. The divine Spirit, however, rested on them even there, "and they prophesied in the camp" (Numb. xi, 24-29). The Targum of Jonathan alleges that these two men were brothers of Moses and Aaron by the mother's side, being sons of Jochebed and Elizaphan. B.C. 1657. See ELDAD.

Me'dan (Heb. *Medan'*, מְדָן, *contention,* as in Prov. vi, 14, 19; Sept. $M\alpha\delta\acute{a}\nu$ v. r. in Chron. $M\alpha\delta\iota\acute{a}\mu$; Vulg. *Madan*), the third son of Abraham by Keturah (Gen. xxv. 2). B.C. post 2024. He and his brother Midian are believed to have peopled the country of Midian, east of the Dead Sea. "It has been supposed, from the similarity of the name, that the tribe descended from Medan was more closely allied to *Midian* than by mere blood-relation, and that it was the same as, or a portion of the latter. There is, however, no ground for this theory beyond its plausibility. The traditional city Medyen of the Arab geographers (the classical Modiana), situate in Arabia on the eastern shore of the Gulf of Eyleh, must be held to have been Midianitish, not Medanitish (but Bunsen, *Bibelwerk,* suggests the latter identification). It has been elsewhere remarked [see KETURAH] that many of the Keturahite tribes seem to have merged in early times into the Ishmaelite tribes. The mention of 'Ishmaelite' as a convertible term with 'Midianite,' in Gen. xxxvii, 28, 36, is remarkable; but the Midianite of the A.V. in ver. 28 is Medanite in the Hebrew (by the Sept. rendered $M\alpha\delta\iota\eta\nu\alpha\tilde{\iota}o\iota$, and in the Vulg. *Ismaelitæ* and *Madianitæ*); and we may have here a trace of the subject of this article, though Midianite appears on the whole to be more likely the correct reading in the passages referred to." See MIDIAN.

Medard, ST., bishop of Noyon, in France, was born about 456, in the village of Sallency, near Noyon. Through his father, Nectardus, he belonged to a noble Frank family; his mother, Protagia, a Gallo-Roman, also claimed high connections. He was educated in the school of his native city, and early manifested that zeal and charity for which he afterwards became distinguished. He entered the Church under the guidance of the bishop of Vermand, and on the death of the latter, in 530, was appointed his successor. In consequence, however, of the frequent invasions which desolated that district, he exchanged this see for Noyon, a strongly-fortified town. When St. Eleutherus, bishop of Tournay, died, in 532, Medard was invited to join this see to that of Noyon;

he refused at first, but was finally induced to accept by king Clotaire himself, and the two dioceses continued to be administered by the same bishop until 1146, when they were again divided. St. Medard was one of the most influential and most universally-respected bishops of his time. King Clotaire came to visit him shortly before his death, which occurred about 545, and afterwards caused his remains to be buried in the royal estate of Crouy, near Soissons. The renowned cathedral of St. Medard is erected over his grave. He is commemorated on June 8. He is highly praised by Gregory of Tours (lib. iv, c. 19), who, like his biographers Venantius, Fortunatus, and Radbodus, attributes to him a great number of miracles. The best biography of St. Medard is contained in the *Acta Sanctorum* for July 8. See Perz, *Monum. Hist. Germ.* vol. i and ii; Gregorius Turon. *Hist. Franc.* lib. iv, c. 19; same, *De Gloria Confess.* c. 95; Radbodus, *Vita S. Medardi, Noviom. episc. apud Surium,* 8 *Junii; Gallia Christ.* vol. ix, col. 979.   (J. N. P.)

Medatha. See HAMMEDATHA.

Mede (Heb. *Maday'*, מָדַי, a word of Indian origin, meaning, according to Gesenius, *Thes. Heb.* p. 768, the *middle* country, from its position, as in Polybius, v, 44; Auth. Vers. "Medes," "Media," "Madai," Gen. x, 2; 2 Kings xvii, 6; xviii, 11; 1 Chron. i, 5; Esth. i, 3, 14, 18, 19; x, 2; Isa. xiii, 17; xxi, 2; Jer. xxv, 25; li, 11, 28; Dan. viii, 20; ix, 1; also *Madi'*, מָדִי, "Mede," Dan. xi, 1; Chald. *Maday'*, מָדַי, "Mede," "Medes," Ezra vi, 2; Dan. v, 28; vi, 8, 12, 15; and *Madaah'*, מָדָאָה, "Median," or *Madaa'*, מָדָא, Dan. v, 31; Gr. $M\tilde{\eta}\delta o\varsigma$), the ethnographic title of a *Median,* or inhabitant of Media; the same of that of MADAI [q. v.]. The Hebrew form, "which occurs in Gen. x, 2, among the list of the sons of Japheth, has been commonly regarded as a personal appellation; and most commentators call Madai the third son of Japhet, and the progenitor of the Medes. But it is extremely doubtful whether, in the mind of the writer of Gen. x, the term *Madai* was regarded as representing a person. That the genealogies in the chapter are to some extent ethnic is universally allowed, and may be seen even in our Authorized Version (verse 16-18). As Gomer, Magog, Javan, Tubal, and Meshech, which are conjoined in Gen. x, 2 with Madai, are elsewhere in Scripture always ethnic and not personal appellatives (Ezek. xxvii, 13; xxxviii, 6; xxxix, 6; Dan. viii, 21; Joel iii, 6; Psa. cxx, 5; Isa. lxvi, 19, etc.), so it is probable that they stand for nations rather than persons here. In that case no one would regard Madai as a person; and we must remember that it is the exact word used elsewhere throughout Scripture for the well-known nation of the Medes. Probably, therefore, all that the writer intends to assert in Gen. x, 2 is that the Medes, as well as the Gomerites, Greeks, Tibareni, Moschi, etc., descended from Japhet. Modern science has found that, both in physical type and in language, the Medes belong to that family of the human race which embraces the Cymry and the Greco-Romans" (see Prichard's *Phys. Hist. of Mankind,* iv, 6-50; chap. x, § 2-4; and comp. the article on MEDIA). For "Darius the Mede," see DARIUS.

Mede, JOSEPH, B.D., a learned English divine, was descended from a respectable family at Berden, in Essex, and was born in 1586. When but a boy ten years old he lost his father, but his education was provided for by friends. He became a commoner of Christ Church, Cambridge, in 1602, where he took the degree of master of arts in 1610, having made such progress in all kinds of learning that he was universally esteemed an accomplished scholar. He was appointed Greek lecturer on Sir Walter Mildmay's foundation, and particularly employed himself in studying the history of the Chaldæans and Egyptians. He appears to have had many offers of preferment, but unhesitatingly declined them all in favor of this position, which afforded him leisure for favorite studies. He died in 1638. "Mr.

Mede," says his biographer, "was an acute logician, an accurate philosopher, a skilful mathematician, an excellent anatomist, a great philologist, a master of many languages, and a good proficient in history and chronology." His principal production, worthy the labors of a lifetime, he sent forth in 1627, under the title *Clavis Apocalyptica* (Cambridge, 1627, 4to) ; to which he added in 1632, *In Sancti Joannis Apocalypsin Commentarius, ad amussim Clavis Apocalypticæ.* An English translation of this celebrated work was published in London in 1650, entitled *The Key of Revelation searched and demonstrated out of the natural and proper Characters of the Visions, etc. ; to which is added a Conjecture concerning Gog and Magog.* This work has been honored with high commendation from the learned Dr. Hurd, in his *Introduction to the Study of the Prophecies* (ii, 122, etc.), where Mede is spoken of as "a sublime genius, without vanity, interest, or spleen, but with a single, unmixed love of truth, dedicating his great talents to the study of the prophetic Scriptures, and unfolding the mysterious prophecies of the Revelation." A collection of the whole of Mede's writings was published in 1672, in 2 vols. folio, by Dr. Worthington, who added to them a life of the author. He was a pious and profoundly learned man ; and in every part of his works the talents of a sound and learned divine are eminently conspicuous. He was distinguished for his meekness, modesty, and prudence, and for unbounded liberality towards the needy. A very full account of Mede is given in Allibone's *Dict. Brit. and Amer. Authors,* s. v. See also *English Cyclop.* s. v.; *Gen. Biog. Dict.* s. v.; Darling, *Cyclop. Bibliog.* i, 2028 ; Horne, *Bibl. Bibl.* 1839, p. 331 ; Orme, *Biblioth. Biblia,* s. v.; Hunt, *Hist. of Religious Thought in England,* i, 167.

Med'eba (Heb. *Meydeba'*, מֵידְבָא, *water of quiet ;* Sept. $M\eta\delta\alpha\beta\dot{\alpha}$ in Chron., $M\alpha\iota\delta\alpha\beta\dot{\alpha}$ in Josh., $M\omega\dot{\alpha}\beta$ in Numb., and $M\omega\alpha\beta\tilde{\iota}\tau\iota\varsigma$ v. r. $M\eta\delta\alpha\beta\dot{\alpha}$, $M\eta\delta\alpha\mu\dot{\alpha}$, $M\iota\delta\alpha\beta\dot{\alpha}$ in Isa.; Vulg. *Medaba ;* Joseph. $M\eta\delta\dot{\alpha}\beta\alpha$ and $M\epsilon\delta\dot{\alpha}\beta\eta$), a town east of the Jordan, in a plain of the same name in the southern border of the tribe of Reuben (Josh. xiii, 9, 16), before which was fought the great battle where Joab defeated the Ammonites and their allies (1 Chron. xix, 7 ; comp. with 2 Sam. x, 8, 14, etc.). In the time of Ahaz, Medeba was a sanctuary of Moab (Isa. xv, 2) ; but in the denunciation of Jeremiah (xlviii), often parallel with that of Isaiah, it is not mentioned. It originally belonged to the Moabites (Numb. xxi, 30), from whom it was conquered by Sihon the Amoritish king (Josephus, *Ant.* xiii, 1, 2, and 4) ; but upon the captivity of the tribes beyond the Jordan, the Moabites again took possession of it (Isa. xv, 2), and retained it after the return from exile (1 Macc. ix, 36). See JAMBRI. It was the scene of the capture and possibly the death of John Maccabæus, and also of the revenge subsequently taken by Jonathan and Simon (Josephus, *Ant.* xiii, 1, 4 ; the name is omitted in Maccabees on the second occasion, see ver. 38). About B.C. 110 it was taken, after a long siege, by John Hyrcanus (*Ant.* xiii, 9, 1 ; *War,* i, 2, 4), and then appears to have remained in the possession of the Jews for at least thirty years, till the time of Alexander Jannæus (xiii, 15, 4) ; and it is mentioned as one of the twelve cities by the promise of which Aretas, the king of Arabia, was induced to assist Hyrcanus II to recover Jerusalem from his brother, Aristobulus (*Ant.* xiv, 1, 4). Ptolemy calls it *Medaua* ($M\dot{\eta}\delta\alpha\nu\alpha$), in Arabia Petræa, in long. 68° 30', lat. 30° 45' (v, 17, 6). Stephen of Byzantium (p. 566) assigns it to Nabatene. The *Onomasticon* places it near Heshbon ; and it was once the seat of one of the thirty-five bishoprics of Arabia (Reland, *Palæstina,* p. 217, 223, 226). The place, although in ruins, still retains the name *Madeba,* and is situated upon a round hill seven miles south of Heshbon. The ruins are about a mile and a half in circuit, but not a single edifice remains perfect, although the remains of the walls of private houses are traceable, and an immense tank (Irby and Mangles, p. 471) is visible

(Seetzen, in Zach's *Monat. Corresp.* xviii, 431 ; Burckhardt, *Trav. in Syria,* p. 365 sq.). The foundations of an ancient temple observed by these travellers on the west of the town are perhaps those of the Christian church which it once contained ($\dot{\eta}$ $\pi\dot{o}\lambda\iota\varsigma$ $M\eta\delta\dot{\alpha}\beta\omega\nu$, Le Quien, *Oriens Christianus,* 769–772). A large tank, columns, and other marks of former structures are still to be seen ; the remains of a Roman road exist near the town, which seems formerly to have connected it with Heshbon. "Taken as a Hebrew word, Me-deba means 'waters of quiet ;' but, except the above tank, what waters can there ever have been on that high plain ? The Arabic name, though similar in sound, has a different signification."

The *plain* (מִישׁוֹר) from Medeba to Dibon, given in Josh. xiii, 9 as the southern portion of the territory of the Amorites, is the modern *Belka,* a fertile tract thus described by Raumer (*Palästina,* p. 70) : "Southwards from Rabbath Ammon as far as the Arnon the country is mostly table-land, in sóme places for a considerable distance without a tree, but covered with the ruins of cities that have been destroyed. Towards the east it stretches away into the desert of Arabia, and on the west it slopes away to the Jordan." The part of this plateau here referred to is elsewhere (Numb. xxi, 20) called, after its former inhabitants, "the field of Moab," or (Numb. xxiii, 14) "the field of the watchmen" (comp. Hengstenberg, *Bileam,* p. 241, 243). See MISHOR.

Medhurst, WALTER HENRY, D.D., an English missionary and Chinese scholar, was born in London in 1796. He first entered the missionary field of labor in 1816, when he was sent to China by the London Missionary Society to ascertain if the country was open to the Gospel, and, if so, to furnish this people with a correct version of the Scriptures in Chinese. After having labored successfully in India, on the island of Malacca, and other Asiatic countries, he was again sent to China in 1835, with the Rev. Edwin Stevens ; but he did not commence active missionary work in that country until 1845, when he was joined by Lockhart, and settled at Shanghai. He had charge of the printing establishment which was owned by this society, and had up to this time been operated at Batavia ; he now removed it to Shanghai, and began the publication of sermons and tracts. In spite of the opposition of the numerous Romanists, the mission grew so rapidly that in the year 1847 34,000 copies of different works were printed, and 500 tracts were weekly distributed. This same year delegates from several stations convened in Shanghai for the revision of the New Testament in Chinese. Medhurst was engaged in this important labor until 1850, when he withdrew, and gave his whole time to the revision of the Old Testament. He died Jan. 24, 1857, a few days after his return to England, closing a life of valuable service spent in the interests of Christian missions. Medhurst founded several orphan asylums, and did much good among the Asiatics in various ways. His works of special interest are, *China, its State and Prospects, with especial Reference to the Diffusion of the Gospel* (Lond. 1838, 8vo) :—*Dissertation on the Theology of the Chinese* (8vo) :—*The Chinese Version of the Scriptures* (1851, 8vo) :—also a *Chinese Dictionary* (1838, 4to), and a *Japanese and English Vocabulary.* See Vapereau, *Dictionnaire des Contemporains,* s. v.; Allibone, *Dict. of Brit. and Amer. Authors,* vol. ii, s. v.

Me'dia (מָדַי). The same Hebrew word is used in the O. T. as the name of a son of Japhet, of the nation which he founded, and of their country. Hence we find it rendered in four different ways in our A.V. In most cases these renderings are arbitrary, and tend to confuse rather than explain—(1.) *Madai,* the proper rendering (Gen. x, 2 ; $M\alpha\delta o\dot{\iota}$; Alex. $M\alpha\delta\alpha\dot{\iota}$; *Madai ;* 1 Chron. i, 5, $M\alpha\delta\alpha\dot{\iota}\mu$) ; (2.) *Medes* ($M\dot{\eta}\delta o\iota$, 2 Kings xvii, 6 ; xviii, 11 ; Esther i, 19 ; Isa. xiii, 17 ; Jer. xxv, 25 ; Dan. ix, 1 ; v, 28 ; $M\dot{\eta}\delta\epsilon\iota\alpha$, Ezra vi, 22 ; *Medoi*) ; (3.) *Media* ($M\dot{\eta}\delta o\iota$, *Medoi,* Esther i, 3 ; x, 2 ; Isa. xxi, 2 ; Dan. viii, 20) ;

(4.) *Mede*, only in Dan. xi, 1. In the following account we chiefly refer of course to ancient territorial distributions and descriptions.

I. *Geography.*—The general situation of the country is abundantly clear, though its limits may not be capable of being precisely determined. Media lay northwest of Persia Proper, south and south-west of the Caspian, east of Armenia and Assyria, west and north-west of the great salt desert of Iran. Its greatest length was from north to south, and in this direction it extended from the 32d to the 40th parallel, a distance of 550 miles. In width it reached from about long. 45° to 53°; but its average breadth was not more than from 250 to 300 miles. Its area may be reckoned at about 150,000 square miles, or three fourths of that of modern France. The natural boundary of Media on the north was the river Aras; on the west Zagros, and the mountain-chain which connects Zagros with Ararat; on the south Media was probably separated from Persia by the desert which now forms the boundary between Farsistan and Irak Ajemi; on the east its natural limit was the desert and the Caspian Gates. West of the gates it was bounded, not (as is commonly said) by the Caspian Sea, but by the mountain range south of that sea, which is the natural boundary between the high and the low country. It thus comprised the modern provinces of Irak Ajemi, Persian Kurdistan, part of Luristan, Azerbijan, perhaps Talish and Ghilan, but not Mazanderan or Asterabad.

The division of Media commonly recognised by the Greeks and Romans was that into Media Magna and Media Atropatene (Strabo, xi, 13, § 1; comp. Polyb. v, 44; Pliny, *H. N.* vi, 13; Ptolem. vi, 2, etc.). 1. *Media Atropatene*, so named from the satrap Atropates, who became independent monarch of the province on the destruction of the Persian empire by Alexander (Arrian, *Exped. Alex.* iii, 8; vi, 29; Diod. Sic. xviii, 3), corresponded nearly to the modern Azerbijan, being the tract situated between the Caspian and the mountains which run north from Zagros, and consisting mainly of the rich and fertile basin of Lake Urumiyeh, with the valleys of the Aras and the Sefid Rud. This is chiefly a high tract, varied between mountains and plains, and lying mostly three or four thousand feet above the sea level. The basin of Lake Urumiyeh (the Spanta of Strabo) has a still greater elevation, the surface of the lake itself, into which all the rivers run, being as much as 4200 feet above the ocean. The country is fairly fertile, well-watered in most places, and favorable to agriculture; its climate is temperate, though occasionally severe in winter; it produces rice, corn of all kinds, wine, silk, white wax, and all manner of delicious fruits. Tabriz, its modern capital, forms the summer residence of the Persian kings, and is a beautiful place, situated in a forest of orchards. The ancient Atropatene may have included also the countries of Ghilan and Talish, together with the plain of Moghan, at the mouth of the combined Kur and Aras rivers. These tracts are low and flat; that of Moghan is sandy and sterile; Talish is more productive; while Ghilan (like Mazanderan) is rich and fertile in the highest degree. The climate of Ghilan, however, is unhealthy, and at times pestilential; the streams perpetually overflow their banks; and the waters which escape stagnate in marshes, whose exhalations spread disease and death among the inhabitants. 2. *Media Magna* lay south and east of Atropatene. Its northern boundary was the range of Elburz from the Caspian Gates to the Rudbar pass, through which the Sefid Rud reaches the low country of Ghilan. It then adjoined upon Atropatene, from which it may be regarded as separated by a line running about south-west by west from the bridge of Menjil to Zagros. Here it touched Assyria, from which it was probably divided by the last line of hills towards the west, before the mountains sink down upon the plain. On the south it was bounded by Susiana and Persia Proper, the former of which it met in the modern Luristan, probably about lat. 33° 30', while it struck the latter on the eastern side

of the Zangros range, in lat. 32° or 32° 30'. Towards the east it was closed in by the great salt desert, which Herodotus reckons to Sagartia, and later writers to Parthia and Carmania. Media Magna thus contained a great part of Kurdistan and Luristan, with all Ardelan and Irak Ajemi. The character of this tract is very varied. Towards the west, in Ardelan, Kurdistan, and Luristan, it is highly mountainous, but at the same time well-watered and richly wooded, fertile and lovely; on the north, along the flank of Elburz, it is less charming, but still pleasant and tolerably productive; while towards the east and south-east it is bare, arid, rocky, and sandy, supporting with difficulty a spare and wretched population. The present productions of Zagros are cotton, tobacco, hemp, Indian corn, rice, wheat, wine, and fruits of every variety; every valley is a garden; and besides valleys, extensive plains are often found, furnishing the most excellent pasturage. Here were nurtured the valuable breed of horses called Nisæan, which the Persians cultivated with such especial care, and from which the horses of the monarch were always chosen. The pasture grounds of Khawah and Alishtar, between Behistun and Khorram-abad, probably represent the "Nisæan plain" of the ancients, which seems to have taken its name from a town Nisæa (Nisaya), mentioned in the cuneiform inscriptions.

Although the division of Media into these two provinces can only be distinctly proved to have existed from the time of Alexander the Great, yet there is reason to believe that it was more ancient, dating from the settlement of the Medes in the country, which did not take place all at once, but was first in the more northern and afterwards in the southern country. It is indicative of the division, that there were two Ecbatanas—one, the northern, at Takht-i-Suleiman; the other, the southern, at Hamadan, on the flanks of Mount Orontes (Elwand) —respectively the capitals of the two districts. See ECBATANA.

Next to the two Ecbatanas, the chief town in Media was undoubtedly Rhages—the Raga of the inscriptions. Hither the rebel Phraortes fled on his defeat by Darius Hystaspis, and hither, too, came Darius Codomannus after the battle of Arbela, on his way to the eastern provinces (Arrian, *Exped. Alex.* iii, 20). The only other place of much note was Bagistana, the modern Behistun, which guarded the chief pass connecting Media with the Mesopotamian plain.

No doubt both parts of Media were further subdivided into provinces, but no trustworthy account of these minor divisions has come down to us. The tract about Rhages was certainly called Rhagiana, and the mountain tract adjoining Persia seems to have been known as Parætacene, or the country of the Parætacæ. Ptolemy gives as Median districts Elymais, Choromithrene, Sigrina, Daritis, and Syromedia; but these names are little known to other writers, and suspicions attach to some of them. On the whole, it would seem that we do not possess materials for a minute account of the ancient geography of the country, which is very imperfectly described by Strabo, and almost omitted by Pliny.

In Great Media lay the metropolis of the country, the Ecbatana of that district (Pliny, *Hist. Nat.* vi, 17), as well as the province of Rhagiana and the city Rhagæ, with the above Nisæan plain, celebrated in the time of the Persian empire for its horses and horse-races (Herod. iii, 106; Arrian, vii, 13; Heeren, *Ideen*, i, l. 305). This plain was near the city Nisæa, around which were fine pasture lands producing excellent clover (*Herba Medica*). The horses were entirely white, and of extraordinary height and beauty, as well as speed. They constituted a part of the luxury of the great, and a tribute in kind was paid from them to the monarch, who, like all Eastern sovereigns, used to delight in equestrian display. Some idea of the opulence of the country may be had when it is known that, independently of imposts rendered in money, Media paid a yearly tribute of not less than 3000 horses, 4000 mules, and nearly 100,000 sheep. The breeds, once celebrated through the world, appear to exist no more; but Ker Porter saw the shah ride on festival occasions a splendid horse of pure white. Cattle abounded, as did the richest fruits, as pines, citrons, oranges, all of peculiar excellence, growing as in their native land. Here also was found the silphium (probably assafœtida), which formed a considerable article in the commerce of the ancients, and was accounted worth its weight in gold.

II. *History.*—1. *Its Early Stages.*—In Gen. x, 2 we are told that Madai was the third son of Japhet (comp. 1 Chron. i, 5). The names in that invaluable ethnological summary were not merely those of individuals but of the nations which descended from them; for the historian says, "By these were the isles of the Gentiles divided in their lands, every one after his tongue, after their families, in their nations" (ver. 5). For a period of fifteen centuries the Medes are not again mentioned in Scripture. Then Isaiah, in pronouncing the prophetic doom of Babylon, says, "I will stir up the Medes against them" (xiii, 17). This prophecy was uttered about B.C. 720. There is no direct evidence connecting Madai, the son of Japhet, and the nation he founded, with the Medes (*Madai*) of whom Isaiah speaks; but the names are identical in Hebrew; and the genealogical tables of Genesis appear to have been intended to show the origin of those nations which afterwards bore an important part in the history of God's people.

Berosus, the Babylonian priest and historian, states that at a very remote period (B.C. cir. 2000) the Medes ruled in Babylon (Eusebius, *Chron.* i, 4). Though we may not be able to rely upon either his dates or his facts, yet we may infer from his words and references that the Medes were one of the great primeval races which established themselves in Central Asia. Herodotus gives a very graphic and circumstantial account of the early history of the Medes, and the establishment of the empire: "The Medes were called anciently by all people *Arians*; but when Medêa, the Colchian, came to them from Athens, they changed their name. Such is the account which they themselves give" (vii, 62). This is opposed to what appears to be the opinion of the sacred writers; but there can be no doubt that during the time of ascendency of Greek arms, literature, and art, Eastern nations were all anxious to claim some sort of connection with Greece, and this may account for Herodotus's story (comp. Rawlinson's *Herod.* iv, 61, 1st ed.).

The Medes appear, however, to have been a branch of the Arian family, who probably had their primitive seat on the east bank of the Indus, and thence sent their colonies eastward into India, and westward to Media, Persia, Greece, etc. (Müller, *Science of Language*). There are independent grounds for thinking that an Arian element existed in the population of the Mesopotamian valley, side by side with the Cushite and Shemitic elements, at a very early date. It is therefore not at all impossible that the Medes may have been the predominant race there for a time, as Berosus states, and may afterwards have been overpowered and driven to the mountains, whence they may have spread themselves eastward, northward, and westward, so as to occupy a vast number of localities from the banks of the Indus to those of the middle Danube. The term Arians, which was by the universal consent of their neighbors applied to the Medes in the time of Herodotus (Herod. vii, 62), connects them with the early Vedic settlers in Western Hindustan; the *Mati*-eni of Mount Zagros, the Sauro-*Matæ* of the steppe-country between the Caspian and the Euxine, and the *Mætæ* or *Mæotæ* of the Sea of Azov, mark their progress towards the north; while the *Mædi* or *Medi* of Thrace seem to indicate their spread westward into Europe, which was directly attested by the native traditions of the Sigynnæ (Herod. v, 9). It has been supposed by some that there was a Scythic tribe of Madai who conquered and held Babylonia long previous to the irruption of the Arian family,

and that it is to them Berosus alludes. There are no good grounds for this belief; and it is worthy of note as tending to disprove the theory that the name "Mede" does not appear upon the Assyrian monuments before the year B.C. 880 (Rawlinson's *Commentary on Assyrian Inscriptions*). To that date is assigned the inscription on the famous black obelisk, discovered by Layard at Nimrûd, which contains a record of the victories of Temen-bar, the Assyrian monarch. In the twenty-fourth year of his reign he invaded the territory of the Medes (Vaux, *Nineveh and Persepolis*, p. 263, where a translation of the inscription is given). At that time the Medes were independent, occupying an extensive country with many cities, and divided, like the Persians, into a number of tribes having each a chief. This remarkable monument thus fixes the date of the first conquest of the Medes by the Assyrians; but it does not determine the date of the settlement of the former in Media. Sir H. Rawlinson thinks that the way in which the nations are grouped in that inscription seems to indicate that the Medes when attacked were in the act of migrating (*Commentary*). This, however, is very uncertain.

The invasion of Temen-bar was probably more like an Arab raid than a military conquest. His successors on the Assyrian throne were almost incessantly engaged in hostilities with the Medes (Rawlinson's *Herodot.* i, 404); and Sargon appears to have been the first who attempted to occupy the country with regular garrisons. He built cities in Media, and reduced the people to tribute (Rawlinson's *Herod.* l. c.; and *Comment.*). Sargon was that king of Assyria "who took Samaria, and carried Israel captive," and placed some of them "*in the cities of the Medes*" (2 Kings xvii, 6; comp. xviii, 17; Isa. xx, 1). The truth of Scripture history is here strongly confirmed by monuments recently disentombed from the ruins of Sargon's palace at Khorsabad. On its walls are inscribed the records of his conquests, in which both Media and Judæa are mentioned—the former as on the eastern, and the latter on the western limits of his vast empire (Rawlinson's *Comment.* p. 61; Rawlinson's *Herodot.* i, 405). See SARGON.

Media was not yet a kingdom. It was occupied by a number of petty chiefs, each ruling his own tribe. From these chiefs the Assyrian monarchs exacted tribute. The tribes increased in numbers, influence, and power. They held a country naturally strong. The Assyrian yoke was galling to their free spirits, and probably this first induced them to unite their forces, elect a common leader, and assert their independence. The exact date of this revolution cannot now be fixed, but the fact of it is certain. Herodotus's account of it is as follows: "The Assyrians had held the empire of Upper Asia for a space of 520 years, when the Medes set the example of revolt. They took arms for the recovery of their freedom, and fought a battle with the Assyrians, in which they behaved with such gallantry as to shake off the yoke of servitude" (i, 95). He then tells how the empire was formed by a certain Deioces, who, in consequence of his wisdom and justice, was elected monarch by the six tribes composing the nation (i, 96-101). Deioces built the great city of Ecbatana; and, after a prosperous reign of fifty-three years, left the throne to his son Phraortes. Phraortes conquered Persia, vastly enlarged the Median empire, and reigned twenty-two years. He was succeeded by his son Cyaxares. During his reign, while engaged in a war against Nineveh, Media was overrun by a horde of Scythians, who held a great part of Western Asia for twenty-eight years. The Scythian leaders were at length treacherously murdered by Cyaxares, and the Median monarchy re-established. He ruled forty years, and then left the kingdom to his son Astyages, whose daughter Mandane was married to a Persian noble, and became the mother of the great Cyrus. According to this narrative, the Median monarchy was established about B.C. 708 (Rawlinson's *Herodot.* i, 407). There is good reason to believe, however, that the early

According to Herodotus.	Years of Reign.	According to Diodorus.	Reign.	Eusebius.	Reign.	Syncellus.	Reign.
		1. Arbaces.......	28	1. Arbaces ...	28	1. Arbaces..............	28
		2. Mandauces....	60	2. Sosarmus..	30	2. Mandauces.........	20
		3. Sosarmus	30	3. Medidus...	40	3. Sosarmus	30
		4. Articas.......	50	4. Cardiccas..	13	4. Articas	30
		5. Arbacines....	22				
		6. Artæus........	40				
1. Deioces	53	7. Artynes.......	22	5. Deioces....	54	5. Diœces.............	54
2. Phraortes.......	22	8. Antibarnes....	40	6. Phraortes..	24	6. Aphraartes.........	51
3. Cyaxares........	40	9. Astibares, or		7. Cyaxares...	32	7 Cyaxares	32
4. Astyages........	35	10. Astyages......		8. Astyas.....	38	8. Astyages, or Darius...	28
Total..........	150	Total........	282	Total.....	259	Total.............	283

Herodotus.	B.C.	Presumed Original Authority.	B.C.	Rawlinson's Chronology.	B.C.
Revolt of the Medes.......		Revolt of the Medes.............		Medes at war with Assyria.........	
Deioces (53 years)..........	708	Deioces (22 years)............	708	Media conquered by Assyria......	710
Phraortes (22 yrs.) conquers Persia, and	655	Phaortes (53 yrs.) conquers Persia, and		Media generally subject to Assyria, but often in revolt..............	
Cyaxares (40 years).........	633	Cyaxares (40 years)	633	Cyaxares begins his conquests......	633 (?)
Attacks Nineveh	632	28 { Attacks Nineveh	632		
Drives out the Scyths	604	yrs. { Drives out the Scyths	604	Wars with Scyths................	
Takes Nineveh	603	Takes Nineveh ...	603	Takes Nineveh	625
Attacks Halyattes........	602			Wars with Lydia	
Makes peace..............	596			Aids Nebuchadnezzar	597
Astyages (35 years).........	593	Astyages (35 years)........	593	Astyages, or Aspadas.............	593
Conquered by Cyrus.....	558	Conquered by Cyrus.......	558	Conquered by Cyrus.............	558

portion of the narrative is apocryphal, and that Cyaxares was the real founder of the Median empire. He is so represented by most ancient historians (Diodorus Sic. ii, 32; Æschylus, *Persæ*, 761; see Grote's *History of Greece*, vol. iii). The Assyrian monumental annals are almost complete down to the reign of the son of Esarhaddon (B.C. 640), and they contain no mention of any Median irruptions; on the contrary, they represent the Median chiefs as giving tribute to Esarhaddon (Rawlinson's *Herodot*. i, 405, 408).

Ctesias, as quoted by Diodorus Siculus (ii, 32), assigns to the Median monarchy a still older date than Herodotus. He gives a list of eight kings who ruled before Astyages, for an aggregate period of 282 years, which would fix the establishment of the monarchy about B.C. 875. The names of the kings are different from those of Herodotus; and it is vain to attempt to reconcile the narratives (see, however, Hales's *Analysis of Chronology*, iii, 84; Heeren, *Manual of Ancient Hist.*). Rawlinson has clearly shown that Ctesias's narrative is fabulous (*Herodot*. i, 406).

2. *The Median Empire.*—(1.) *Its Establishment.*—From the foregoing notices we may conclude that the Medes migrated from beyond the Indus to the country on the southern shores of the Caspian Sea not later than the 9th century B.C.; that they settled there as a number of distinct tribes (probably *six*, as Herodotus states, *l. c.*), and so remained during a period of three or four centuries; that some Scythian tribes either occupied the country with them or invaded it at a later date; and that (about B.C. 633) Cyaxares rose suddenly to power, united the Medes under his sway, drove out the Scythians, and established the monarchy. Before this time the Medes are only once mentioned in Scripture, and then, as has been seen, their country was subject to Assyria (2 Kings xvii, 6).

A few years after the establishment of his empire Cyaxares made a league with the Babylonian monarch, and invaded Assyria. Nineveh was captured and destroyed, B.C. 625. The incidents of the siege and capture, as related by Diodorus Siculus (ii, 27, 28), contain a remarkable fulfilment of the prophecies uttered by Nahum (i, 8; ii, 5, 6; iii, 13, 14) nearly a century previously; and recent excavations by Layard illustrate both (*Nineveh and Babylon*, p. 71, 103, etc.). See NINEVEH. The Assyrian monarchy was then overthrown (Rawlinson, *Ancient Monarchies*, ii, 521).

Abydenus (probably following Berosus) informs us that in his Assyrian war Cyaxares was assisted by the Babylonians under Nabopolassar, between whom and Cyaxares an intimate alliance was formed, cemented by a union of their children; and that a result of their success was the establishment of Nabopolassar as independent king on the throne of Babylon, an event which we know to belong to the above-mentioned year. It was undoubtedly after this that Cyaxares endeavored to conquer Lydia. His conquest of Assyria had made him master of the whole country lying between Mount Zagros and the river Halys, to which he now hoped to add the tract between the Halys and the Ægæan Sea. It is surprising that he failed, more especially as he seems to have been accompanied by the forces of the Babylonians, who were perhaps commanded by Nebuchadnezzar on the occasion. See NEBUCHADNEZZAR. After a war which lasted six years he desisted from his attempt, and concluded the treaty with the Lydian monarch of which we have already spoken. The three great Oriental monarchies — Media, Lydia, and Babylon — were now united by mutual engagements and intermarriages, and continued at peace with one another during the remainder of the reign of Cyaxares, and during that of Astyages, his son and successor.

(2.) *Extent of the Empire.*—The conquest of Assyria produced a great change in the Median empire, and on the whole of Western Asia. Babylon then regained its independence, and formed a close alliance with Media. The Israelites, who had been led captive by the Assyrians, were placed under new rulers. Cyaxares led his victorious armies into Syria and Asia Minor (Herod. i, 103). When Pharaoh-necho marched to the banks of the Euphrates against Babylon, the Babylonians were aided by the Medes (Joseph. *Ant*. x, 5, 1). It was in attempting to oppose this expedition of the Egyptian monarch that king Josiah was slain at Megiddo (Jer. xlvi, 2; 2 Chron. xxxv, 20; 2 Kings xxiii, 29). We also learn that Nebuchadnezzar was aided by the Medes in the conquest of the Jews and capture of Jerusalem (Eusebius, *Pr. Evang.*; comp. 2 Kings xxiv, 1; 2 Chron. xxxvi, 5). Media was now the most powerful monarchy in Western Asia.

The limits of the Median empire cannot be definitely fixed, but it is not difficult to give a general idea of its size and position. From north to south its extent was in no place great, since it was certainly confined between the Persian Gulf and the Euphrates on the one side, and the Black and Caspian seas on the other. From east to west it had, however, a wide expansion, since it reached from the Halys at least as far as the Caspian Gates, and possibly farther. It comprised Persia, Media Magna, Northern Media, Matiene or Media Mattiana, Assyria, Armenia, Cappadocia, the tract between Armenia and the Caucasus, the low tract along the south-west and south of the Caspian, and possibly some portion of Hyrcania, Parthia, and Sagartia. It was separated from Babylonia either by the Tigris, or more probably by a line running about half-way between that river and the

Euphrates, and thus did not include Syria, Phœnicia, or Judæa, which fell to Babylon on the destruction of the Assyrian empire. Its greatest length may be reckoned at 1500 miles from north-west to south-east, and its average breadth at 400 or 450 miles. Its area would thus be about 600,000 square miles, or somewhat greater than that of modern Persia.

(3.) *Its Character.*—With regard to the nature of the government established by the Medes over the conquered nations, we possess but little trustworthy evidence. Herodotus in one place compares, somewhat vaguely, the Median with the Persian system (i, 134), and Ctesias appears to have asserted the positive introduction of the satrapial organization into the empire at its first foundation by his Arbaces (Diod. Sic. ii, 28); but, on the whole, it is perhaps most probable that the Assyrian organization was continued by the Medes, the subject nations retaining their native monarchs, and merely acknowledging subjection by the payment of an annual tribute. This seems certainly to have been the case in Persia, where Cyrus and his father Cambyses were monarchs, holding their crown of the Median king before the revolt of the former; and there is no reason to suppose that the remainder of the empire was organized in a different manner. The satrapial organization was apparently a Persian invention, begun by Cyrus, continued by Cambyses, his son, but first adopted as the regular governmental system by Darius Hystaspis.

(4.) *Its Duration.*—Of all the ancient Oriental monarchies the Median was the shortest in duration. It commenced, as we have seen, after the middle of the 7th century B.C., and it terminated B.C. 558. The period of three quarters of a century, which Herodotus assigns to the reigns of Cyaxares and Astyages, may be taken as fairly indicating its probable length, though we cannot feel sure that the years are correctly apportioned between the monarchs. Its rise was rapid, and appears to have been chiefly owing to the genius of one man—Cyaxares. The power of Media was short-lived. With Cyaxares it rose, and with him it passed away. At his death he left his throne to Astyages, of whom little is known except the stories told by Herodotus (i, 110–129) and Nicolaus of Damascus (*Frag. Hist. Gr.* iii, 404-6), who probably borrowed from Ctesias; and on these little reliance can be placed. They are founded on fact, and we may infer from them that during the reign of Astyages a war broke out between the Medes and Persians, in which the latter were victorious, and Cyrus, the Persian king, who was himself closely related to Astyages, united the two nations under one sceptre (B.C. 558). The life of Astyages was spared, and even the title of king continued with him.

This is as far as the authorities we have followed carry us. But Xenophon, in his *Cyropædia*, gives us a very different account of the relationship of Cyrus to the Median king, at the time of the capture of Babylon by their allied arms. See DARIUS THE MEDE.

(5.) *Coalescence with the Persian Empire.*—It is universally allowed that the Median king who succeeded Cyaxares was his son Astyages; but of the character of this king and the events and duration of his reign there exists an absolute contradiction. In so far as Scripture is concerned, the accounts are chiefly of importance from their relation to Cyrus and Darius, the only personages mentioned in Scripture as connected with this period of Median history. But having already been considered under the two names in question, it becomes unnecessary to relate the circumstances afresh here. From chronological considerations we have leaned to the authority of Xenophon in those previous articles, but it is impossible to arrive at certainty. We simply state that whichever account be preferred of the birth and relations of Cyrus, the notices in Daniel oblige us to hold that at the time of the capture of Babylon there was a superior in rank, though not in power, to Cyrus; and this can only have been either Astyages or Cyaxares II. If it were the latter, the description

given us by Xenophon of his vain, capricious, and fickle disposition perfectly accords with the idea suggested respecting him by the narrative in Dan. vi.

Whether we suppose Cyrus himself to have been king of Persia at the period of the conquest of Babylon, or Cambyses his father to have still reigned there, the Darius of Daniel would properly be head only of the Median kingdom; and it was not until Cyrus came to the throne that the great empire was united under one head. Cyrus was consequently the first king of the Medo-Persian dominions, without any discredit to Daniel's statement that Darius, the head of the older kingdom of Media, and the uncle and father-in-law, according to Xenophon, of Cyrus, received during his brief reign the rank that gratified his excessive vanity. In regard to the position and character of Cyrus, this is not the place for any detailed account. He was the real founder of the vast empire which ruled Asia and threatened Europe until the time of Alexander. He is the hero whom the poets and historians of Persia delighted to celebrate, and whose real character doubtless was of the grand and heroic cast. The praises of Xenophon had been anticipated in that sublime address in which Jehovah, nearly 200 years before, calls upon Cyrus his shepherd to advance on his career of conquest (Isa. xlv, 1-6). The statement of Xenophon that the Medes voluntarily submitted to Cyrus (*Cyrop.* i, 1) seems much more agreeable to the scriptural accounts of things after the conquest of Babylon, and to the manner in which foreign nations regarded the newly-risen empire, than is the narrative of Herodotus, who relates that Media was conquered by Cyrus, and held in subjection by force (Herodotus, i, 125, 130). The accession of Darius the Mede (Dan. v, 31) seems inconsistent with this latter view. Throughout his reign we always find the Medes mentioned first in rank, which they would scarcely be if they were a conquered people (Dan. v, 28; vi, 8, 12, 15). At a subsequent period, when the Persian line of kings had succeeded to the throne, while we find the Medes ever ranked side by side with the Persians, we find, as was natural, that the language of the court placed Persia, the country of the reigning king, first in rank (Esth. i, 3, 18, 19, etc.). We have, however, in the conclusion of this book an indication that while the language of the court gave the preference to Persia, the state chronicles still ran under their ancient title, "the chronicles of the kings of Media and Persia"—pointing plainly to the original superiority of rank of Media over Persia, quite inconsistent with the idea of a conquered race (Esth. x, 2). With this view of Scripture the notions entertained by foreign nations of the new empire agree. So far from looking on the Medes as a conquered dependency of Persia, both the Greeks of Europe and the barbarians of Asia look on the Median as the preponderant element, quite obscuring the more recent power of Persia. The queen of the Massagetæ addresses Cyrus as the "sovereign of the Medes," ignoring the Persian nation (Herodotus, i, 206). Thucydides, who ranks in the foremost place of Grecian history, invariably styles the barbarous power that had nearly conquered Greece Median, and never calls it Persian (bk. i). All this points to the original superiority of the Median kingdom—a superiority which still belonged to it in foreign eyes, but which could not well have attached to it if Media had been violently subdued to the rule of Persia. Scripture, which in its early silence as to the very existence of Persia was true to the political obscurity of this latter power, is also the first to recognise the superiority to which it rose under Cyrus. Before the allied armies had marched through the empty bed of the Euphrates into the heart of Babylon, prophecy described the rising empire as a ram with two horns, one of which was higher than the other, and the higher came up last (Dan. viii, 3). Scripture history, penetrating the veil of tradition, and looking through the thin disguise which the assumption of Median dress and manners by the Persians had cast over reality, was the first to recognise that Persia, not Media, had become the ruler of Asia. It is Persia that is spoken of throughout the book of Ezra, the Jewish scribe being better acquainted with the facts of history than Thucydides was. Nor are the subsequent revolts of the Medes against Persian rule any argument that at the first rise of the empire they were not one of two great nations united together on friendly and equal terms. So long as Cyrus and Cambyses his son, descended from the Median as from the Persian dynasty, sat on the throne, Media made no attempt at revolt. Nor did they do so under the foreign the pseudo Smerdis, who was supposed to be the son of Cyrus. It was not until the discovery of the imposture practiced by Smerdis, and the elevation of a purely Persian family in the person of Darius Hystaspis to the throne, that Media sought for a separate existence. Her ancient line of kings no longer ruled over the mountains of Media, and hence probably she sought to return to that independence which had been her pride during the centuries when Assyria vainly sought to rule over Median land.

According to some writers (as Herodotus and Xenophon) there was a close relationship between Cyrus and the last Median monarch, who was therefore naturally treated with more than common tenderness. The fact of the relationship is, however, denied by Ctesias; and whether it existed or no, at any rate the peculiar position of the Medes under Persia was not really owing to this accident. The two nations were closely akin; they had the same Arian or Iranic origin, the same early traditions, the same language (Strabo, xv, 2, 8), nearly the same religion, and ultimately the same manners and customs, dress, and general mode of life. It is not surprising therefore that they were drawn together, and that, though never actually coalescing, they still formed to some extent a single privileged people. Medes were advanced to stations of high honor and importance under Cyrus and his successors, an advantage shared by no other conquered people. The Median capital was at first the chief royal residence, and always remained one of the places at which the court spent a portion of the year; while among the provinces Media claimed and enjoyed a precedency, which appears equally in the Greek writers and in the native records. Still it would seem that the nation, so lately sovereign, was not altogether content with its secondary position. On the first convenient opportunity Media rebelled, elevating to the throne a certain Phraortes (*Frawartish*), who called himself Xathrites, and claimed to be a descendant from Cyaxares. Darius Hystaspis, in whose reign this rebellion took place, had great difficulty in suppressing it. After vainly endeavoring to put it down by his generals, he was compelled to take the field himself. He defeated Phraortes in a pitched battle, pursued and captured him near Rhages, mutilated him, kept him for a time "chained at his door," and finally crucified him at Ecbatana, executing at the same time his chief followers (see the *Behistun Inscription*, in Rawlinson's *Herodotus*, ii, 601, 602). The Medes thereupon submitted, and quietly bore the yoke for another century, when they made a second attempt to free themselves, which was suppressed by Darius Nothus (Xenophon, *Hell.* i, 2, 19). Thenceforth they patiently acquiesced in their subordinate position, and followed through its various shifts and changes the fortune of Persia.

Media, with the rest of the Persian empire, fell under the sway of Alexander the Great. At his death the northern province was erected by the satrap Atropates into an independent state, and called Atropatene. The southern province, Media Magna, was attached with Babylon to the kingdom of the Seleucidæ. The whole country eventually passed over to the Parthian monarchy (Strabo, xvi, 745). It is now included in the dominions of the shah of Persia.

III. *Antiquities.*—1. *Internal Divisions.*—According to Herodotus the Median nation was divided into six tribes (ἔθνη), called the Busæ, the Paretaceni, the Struchates,

the Arizanti, the Budii, and the Magi. It is doubtful, however, in what sense these are to be considered as ethnic divisions. The Paretaceni appear to represent a geographical district, while the Magi were certainly a priest-caste; of the rest we know little or nothing. The Arizanti, whose name would signify "of noble descent," or "of Arian descent," must (one would think) have been the leading tribe, corresponding to the Pasargadæ in Persia; but it is remarkable that they have only the *fourth* place in the list of Herodotus. The Budii are fairly identified with the eastern *Phut*—the *Putiya* of the Persian inscriptions—whom Scripture joins with Persia in two places (Ezek. xxvii, 10; xxxviii, 5). Of the Busæ and the Struchates nothing is known beyond the statement of Herodotus. We may perhaps assume, from the order of Herodotus's list, that the Busæ, Paretaceni, Struchates, and Arizanti were true Medes, of genuine Arian descent, while the Budii and Magi were foreigners admitted into the nation.

2. *Character, Manners, and Customs.*—The ancient Medes were a warlike people, particularly celebrated, as Herodotus (vii, 61) and Strabo (xi, 525) inform us, for their skill in archery. Xenophon says their bows were three ells long. This illustrates the language of Isaiah describing the attack of the Medes on Babylon: "Their *bows* also shall dash the young men to pieces" (xiii, 18). Their cavalry was also excellent, their horses being fleet and strong, and their men skilful riders. It is doubtless in reference to this fact that Jeremiah, speaking of the overthrow of Babylon, says, "They (the enemies) shall hold the bow and the lance . . . *and they shall ride upon horses*" (l, 42). Strabo states that the province of Atropatene alone was able to bring into the field an army of 10,000 horse (xi, 523). Xenophon affirms that the Medes did not fight for plunder. Military glory was their great ambition, and they would never permit gold or silver to turn them aside from their object. How striking do the words of Isaiah thus appear! "Behold I will stir up the Medes against them, which shall not regard silver, and as for gold, they shall not delight in it" (xiii, 18). The wealth of Babylon could not save it, for the Medes could not be bought off (Rosenmüller, *Bib. Geog.* i, 176). The conquests of the Medes, and their intercourse with other nations, produced a marked change upon their character. They became fond of dress and display; those settled in cities engaged in commerce, and lost their hardy habits and bravery. The splendor of the Median robes became proverbial, and their princes and nobles ruled the fashion in the East. They were imitated by the Persian court (Herodot. vi, 112; Xenoph. *Cyrop.* i, 3, 2; Strabo, xi, p. 525). It was this dress, that is, of the highest class, which seems to have gained a sort of classical authority, and to have been at a later period worn at the Persian court, probably in part from its antiquity. This dress the Persian monarchs used to present to those whom they wished to honor, and no others were permitted to wear it. It consisted of a long white loose robe or gown, flowing down to the feet, and enclosing the entire body, specimens of which, as now used in those countries, may be seen in plates given in Perkin's *Residence in Persia* (N. Y. 1843). The nature and the celebrity of this dress combine with the natural richness of the country to assure us

Median Dress (from the Monuments of Persepolis).

that the ancient Medians had made no mean progress in the arts; indeed, the colors of the Persian textures are known to have been accounted second only to those of India. If these regal dresses were of silk, then was there an early commerce between Media and India; if not, weaving, as well as dyeing, must have been practiced and carried to a high degree of perfection in the former country (Ammian. Marcell. xxiv, 6, p. 353, ed. Bip.; Athen. xii, p. 512, 514 sq.; Heeren, *Ideen*, i, 205, 307; Herod. vi, 112; Dan. iii, 21). The Medes thus gave way to luxury and its consequent vices, and they soon became an easy prey to their more warlike neighbors. The northern mountaineers retained their primitive habits, and consequently their independence, for a much longer period.

3. *Religion.*—The ancient religion of the Medes must undoubtedly have been that simple creed which is placed before us in the earlier portions of the Zendavesta. Its peculiar characteristic was Dualism, the belief in the existence of two opposite principles of good and evil, nearly if not quite on a par with one another. Ormazd and Ahriman were both self-caused and self-existent, both indestructible, both potent to work their will—their warfare had been from all eternity, and would continue to all eternity, though on the whole the struggle was to the disadvantage of the Prince of Darkness. Ormazd was the God of the Arians, the object of their worship and trust; Ahriman was their enemy, an object of fear and abhorrence, but not of any religious rite. Besides Ormazd, the Arians worshipped the sun and moon, under the names of Mithra and Homa; and they believed in the existence of numerous spirits or genii, some good, some bad, the subjects and ministers respectively of the two powers of Good and Evil. Their cult was simple, consisting in processions, religious chants and hymns, and a few plain offerings, expressions of devotion and thankfulness. Such was the worship and such the belief which the whole Arian race brought with them from the remote east when they migrated westward. Their migration brought them into contact with the fire-worshippers of Armenia and Mount Zagros, among whom Magism had been established from a remote antiquity. The result was either a combination of the two religions, or in some cases an actual conversion of the conquerors to the faith and worship of the conquered. So far as can be gathered from the scanty materials in our possession, the latter was the case with the Medes. While in Persia the true Arian creed maintained itself, at least to the time of Darius Hystaspis, in tolerable purity, in the neighboring kingdom of Media it was early swallowed up in Magism, which was probably established by Cyaxares or his successor as the religion of the state. The essence of Magism was the worship of the elements, fire, water, air, and earth, with a special preference of fire to the remainder. Temples were not allowed, but fire-altars were maintained on various sacred sites, generally mountain-tops, where sacrifices were continually offered, and the flame was never suffered to go out. A hierarchy naturally followed, to perform these constant rites, and the magi became recognised as a sacred caste entitled to the veneration of the faithful. They claimed in many cases a power of divining the future, and practiced largely those occult arts which are still called by their name in most of the languages of modern Europe. The fear of polluting the elements gave rise to a number of curious superstitions among the professors of the Magian religion (Herod. i, 138); among the rest to the strange practice of neither burying nor burning their dead, but exposing them to be devoured by beasts or birds of prey (Herod. i, 140; Strabo, xv, 3, § 20). This custom is still observed by their representatives, the modern Parsees. See Rhode, *Heil. Sage der Baktr. Meder und Perser*, p. 820; *Abbildungen aus der Mythol. der Alten Welt; Pers. Med.* plate 10, 11.

4. The *language* of the ancient Medes was not connected with the Shemitic, but with the Indian, and divided itself into two chief branches, the Zend, spoken in North Media, and the Pehlvi, spoken in Lower Media and Parthia, which last was the dominant tongue among the Parthians (Adelung, *Mithridates*, i, 256 sq.; Eichhorn, *Gesch. der Lit.* v, 1, 294 sq.).

5. *References to the Medes in Scripture.*—The references to the Medes in the canonical Scriptures are not very numerous, but they are striking. We first hear of certain "cities of the Medes," in which the captive Israelites were placed by "the king of Assyria" on the destruction of Samaria, B.C. 721 (2 Kings xvii, 6; xviii, 11). This implies the subjection of Media to Assyria at the time of Shalmaneser, or of Sargon, his successor, and accords (as we have shown) very closely with the account given by the latter of certain military colonies which he planted in the Median country. Soon afterwards Isaiah prophesies the part which the Medes should take in the destruction of Babylon (Isa. xiii, 17; xxi, 2), and this is again still more distinctly declared by Jeremiah (li, 11 and 28), who sufficiently indicates the independence of Media in his day (xxv, 25). Daniel relates, as a historian, the fact of the Medo-Persic conquest (v, 28, 31), giving an account of the reign of Darius the Mede, who appears to have been made viceroy by Cyrus (vi, 1–28). In Ezra we have a mention of Achmetha (Ecbatana), "the *palace* in the province of the Medes," where the decree of Cyrus was found (vi, 2–5)—a notice which accords with the known facts that the Median capital was the seat of government under Cyrus, but a royal residence only and not the seat of government under Darius Hystaspis. Finally, in Esther, the high rank of Media under the Persian kings is marked by the frequent combination of the two names in phrases of honor.

In the apocryphal Scriptures the Medes occupy a more prominent place. The chief scene of one whole book (Tobit) is Media, and in another (Judith) a very striking portion of the narrative belongs to the same country. But the historical character of both these books is with reason doubted, and from neither can we derive any authentic or satisfactory information concerning the people. From the story of Tobias little could be gathered, even if we accepted it as true, while the history of Arphaxad (which seems to be merely a distorted account of the struggle between the rebel Phraortes and Darius Hystaspis) adds nothing to our knowledge of that contest. The mention of Rhages in both narratives as a Median town and region of importance is geographically correct, and it is historically true that Phraortes suffered his overthrow in the Rhagian district. But beyond these facts the narratives in question contain little that even illustrates the true history of the Median nation.

IV. *Literature.*—The ancient authorities for the history and geography of Media and the Medes are Herodotus, especially when read with the learned and valuable notes of Rawlinson; Strabo, Xenophon, Ptolemy, Diodorus Siculus, Arrian, and Josephus. The monuments and inscriptions discovered, and in part deciphered, within the last few years, add vastly to our stores of information. The various works and articles of Sir H. Rawlinson referred to in the body of this article serve to set forth and illustrate their contents. Among modern writers the student may consult Bochart, Cellarius, Ritter; Grote's *History of Greece*, iii, 301–312; Prof. Rawlinson's *Ancient Monarchies;* Bosanquet's *Chronology of the Medes*, read before the Royal Asiatic Society, June 5, 1858; Brandis, *Rerum Assyriarum tempora emendata*, p. 1–14; and Hupfeld's *Exercitationum Herodotearum Specimina duo*, p. 56 sq. For the present state of the country, see Sir K. Porter's *Travels;* Kinnier's *Persian Empire;* Layard's *Nineveh and Babylon;* Chesney's *Euphrates Expedition;* Sir H. Rawlinson's articles in the *Journal of R. G. S.* vols. ix and x; and the valuable dissertations in Rawlinson's *Herodotus*, vol. i.

Me'dian (Chald. *Madaya'*, מָדָיָא, marg. מָדָאָה;

Sept. ὁ Μῆδος, Vulg. *Medus*), a patrial epithet of Darius, "the son of Ahasuerus, of the seed of the Medes" (Dan. ix, 1), or "the Mede" (xi, 1), as described in Dan. v, 31. See MEDE.

Mediation, in the Christian sense, is the intervention of Jesus Christ between God and sinners. It implies a condition of alienation and hostility on the part of man towards God, and a corresponding state of disfavor and condemnation in the divine mind with respect to man. Such a mutual relation of dissatisfaction lies at the basis of the whole remedial scheme of salvation, originating in the fall (q. v.), and provided for in the atonement (q. v.). It is presumed in every form of religion and worship, whether heathen, Jewish, or any other; and has its natural exponents in sacrifice (q. v.), the priesthood (q. v.), and ritual (q. v.). In addition to the considerations adduced under the head Mediator (q. v.), there remain certain fundamental aspects of this question which we propose here briefly to discuss. See EXPIATION.

1. *Man's Enmity towards God.*—This is a fact too apparent to require detailed proof. Its historical origin is given in the Bible in the account of Eden, its record is engraven in the whole course of human conduct, and its conclusive attestation is found in the deepest consciousness of man's nature. The sense of guilt and condemnation, to which it inevitably and legitimately gives rise in the human conscience, is a testimony so universal, so profound, and so overwhelming as to call for little if any external corroboration.

2. *God's Displeasure towards Man.*—This is a doctrine which of necessity results from the preceding one. If God be holy, as the Scriptures represent him, and as the purest forms of faith depict him, he cannot but regard all sin with the utmost abhorrence, and he cannot be supposed to entertain amicable emotions towards those who commit and delight in sin. This feeling in the divine mind, however, must not be regarded as one of vindictiveness or personal hatred. A pure and unselfish being, raised above the petty jealousies and hazards of earth, cannot be conceived as entertaining sentiments of *malice*. Such a view of the divine nature is inconsistent with the emphatic statements of Scripture (such as that "God is love," etc.), with the interest he still takes in fallen humanity ("God so *loved* the world that he gave his only-begotten Son," etc.), and even with the benevolent provision which he makes in nature for the continuation and comfort of the race. In like manner Christians are forbidden to indulge any malevolence towards their own personal enemies, much more towards their fellow-creatures at large. That view of the Almighty which represents or imagines him as taking any delight in human suffering is characteristic of heathenism, not of Bible truth. See LOVE.

Nevertheless the purest ethics, as well as the soundest theology, demands a place in the divine mind for that sense of indignation with moral evil, and that call for its punishment, which are instinctive in the human breast. In this light are to be interpreted the many and pointed declarations of the Bible respecting God's anger against sin, and his inexorable determination to inflict vengeance upon its perpetrators. Justice, no less than mercy, is one of the indispensable attributes of a holy deity. The ultimate grounds of this doctrine are not to be sought so much in any considerations of administrative policy or governmental consistency—mere views of expediency and safety—as in the essential contradiction of the divine nature itself to all that is inconsistent with its own character.

3. These premises being settled as the actual relations between the parties, the grand problem arises, How can this mutual disagreement be removed? That the change, if any, must take place in man, is obvious, not only because God is immutable, but because he certainly has not been at fault. The offender alone must make the amends. The Being offended against may indeed propose advances towards reconciliation, as it belongs

to him to lay down the terms of satisfaction, but these cannot involve any concession nor imply any retraction. The standard of righteousness must not be lowered, nor wrong exculpated. The case presents a difficulty in two aspects, neither of which can be overlooked in any scheme proposing its settlement. They relate respectively to the *past* and the *future*. Two questions therefore arise: 1. How can the sinful acts already committed be properly forgiven? 2. How can their recurrence be most effectively prevented in time to come? These two subordinate problems must be wrought out together, as the omission to solve the latter would render the solution of the former nugatory. The mediation of Jesus Christ exactly meets all the conditions of both these problems. It is spontaneous on the part of God, voluntary on the part of the Mediator, and does not infringe on the freedom of man. It cancels the past debt, takes away the sense of present guilt, and removes the disposition to transgress thereafter. It releases, reconciles, and renews at once. Pardon, peace, purity are its harmonious results. Justification, regeneration, sanctification are its immunities. The first frees from the judicial sentence, the second restores to the heavenly family, and the third fits for life here and forever. All this is due to the *vicarious* principle of the atonement. It remains to show more particularly how the substitution of Christ as a victim for man in undergoing the penalty accomplishes these ends successfully and satisfactorily. The transfer of the punishment due to human crimes, as effected in the life and death of our Saviour, is not a mere forensic device, nor simply a diplomatic artifice; it is no stratagem invented to elude justice, nor a pretence set up to screen impunity. If, with regard to its individual objects, it was unconditional and absolute, as Universalism generally on the one hand represents it by extension, and strict Predestinarianism on the other by limitation, it would justly be liable to this charge. But inasmuch as it secures the permanent reformation of the culprit in the very process of amnesty, it is not purely penal, but also prophylactic; it changes the relations of the sinner by converting him into a saint.

(1.) The chief, if not the only difficulty in our conceptions of the method of Christian redemption, relates to the justice of substituting an innocent for a guilty person in the expiation of crime. This is, to be sure, an abstract question, but it is a fundamental one. Its determination, however, rests with the Being to be placated, and with the individual submitting to become the victim, rather than with ourselves, the beneficiaries of the arrangement, or with any other intelligences who may be merely spectators. As the compact, in pursuance of which this mediation is effected, was confined to the bosom of the Godhead, we might fairly be excused from attempting its vindication; especially as the Father and the Son, regarded as the contracting parties, are so identified in nature and action that any moral discrepancy or personal disagreement, such as this question implies, is necessarily excluded. Indeed, if they two freely consent, as the plan presupposes, it is hard to see who can have a right to raise a doubt or utter complaint on the subject. Still, to obviate all cavil, it may not be amiss to pursue this point as far as we may without presumption or arrogance.

Instances of a similar but far less extensive vicarious suffering have occurred in human history, and are often pointed to as rare but striking illustrations of this principle. These were applauded at the time of their occurrence, and have been commended ever since by the common voice of mankind, without incurring the imputation of unfairness or compromise. If we look into the design of judicial exactions, so far as human legislation and administration enable us to discern it, we find it to be fourfold: 1, the appeasement of the wrath of the injured party; 2, the moral cure of the offending party; 3, the allaying of the sense of wrong in the convictions of the community; and, 4, the deterring of others from similar crimes. Most laws for earthly retribution have chiefly in view the pecuniary reparation of the wrong, and the protection of society against its recurrence; and in these respects Christ's atonement is as parallel as possible. In cases of capital punishment, with which the present is most analogous, the first two ends of penal infliction are necessarily excluded, by the death of the murdered and the execution of the murderer; so that there remain only the moral influence and the preventive effect upon others as the essential objects to be attained. See PUNISHMENT. But, in the case in hand, these external and disinterested observers can consist only of the angels and inhabitants of other worlds, inasmuch as our own race is wholly included in the culprit himself. Of the moral constitution or even existence of the latter of these two classes of presumed spectators we have absolutely no knowledge, nor any reason to suppose that they could become informed of the transaction. Of the former we know but little more, and that little leads us to the belief that they have already passed their probation, and are therefore incapable of being influenced by example, while the interest which they take in the scene is that of intense satisfaction at its progress and consummation. All objectors are thus removed, and the substitution is ratified by common consent.

We have assumed that man's demurral to this procedure is silenced by the fact of his being himself the convict. Yet a prisoner may be imagined to have a right to protest against another's taking his place as accused or condemned. This, however, he can only be allowed in court to do when he confesses his crime, and demands to bear its penalty in person. Both these privileges, if such they can be called, are reserved to him by the scheme under consideration. Nay, he is required to make confession before he can avail himself of the benefits of Christ's mediation, and that with a sincerity and fulness which admit of no retraction; and he is at last compelled to undergo the penalty himself unless he voluntarily and actively apply for the exemption offered him. These provisions are the saving clauses of the bill of amnesty, and by virtue of them the vicarious redemption receives its final approval.

(2.) Nevertheless the sinner realizes a partial effect of the atonement unconditionally, in the respite from punishment till the close of his earthly career. But for this the whole race had been cut off in embryo at the first transgression. Hence there is an opportunity for the exercise of the remedial or curative as well as preventive influence of that penal retribution, which is temporarily suspended and may be wholly averted from himself. The only problem here arising is, How can impunity be allowed without encouraging vice? or rather, to state it more radically, How can the criminal go scot-free and yet be reformed? It has of late years only been discovered in families, schools, armies, and diplomacy that pardon is often the best discipline; but God knew long ago the true philosophy of the prevention of crime. The spectacle of another suffering the penalty due to ourselves has been found to be the most effectual softener of the rebel heart, and the condition of genuine contrition is the best safeguard against the abuse of clemency. In this light the scheme of Christian mediation is most abundantly sanctioned by actual experiment, and the Cross becomes the glory of the redeemed. See REDEMPTION.

(3.) It is not to be imagined, however, that in this vicarious atonement Jesus Christ actually experienced the aggregate amount of suffering due for the sins of every human being. In the first place, this was unnecessary. The object to be attained was not a given amount of penal infliction, whether to placate the Almighty, to reform the offender, or to vindicate the statutes infracted. This is obvious from the foregoing discussion. Had these ends rigidly required an exact balance-sheet of debit and credit on this basis, no substitution or vicarious satisfaction had been admissible at all. The strict terms of the law are, "The soul that sinneth,

it shall die." The mediation under consideration was an equivalent, such as met the moral design of the penalty. Nor is it correct to argue that as man incurred infinite guilt by sinning against infinite holiness, so Christ offered an infinite satisfaction by reason of his divine and perfect nature. Neither part of this proposition is tenable. No finite creature is capable of infinite guilt, not even the sum total of all humanity, for it is limited both in its numbers and nature, and so is likewise the sum of its sins. Christ therefore did not need to make an infinite atonement, but only an adequate or commensurate one. His expiation was sufficient, not because it was made by his divine nature—for that was by hypothesis incapable and incompetent—but because it contained such a degree of merit, in view of its completeness and the exalted character of the offerer, that the divine Being could consistently accept it in lieu of the actual obedience of the race represented, and thus remit the penalty due them. In the next place, an absolute equality or identity of retribution was impossible in the remedial scheme. The supposition that Jesus endured—whether during his whole lifetime, or in the brief agonies of the garden and the cross—the sum total of the torments that will be and that would have been experienced by the eternally damned, is simply preposterous. Not only had he no opportunity for this, but he was not capable of it, either physically or spiritually. His bodily pain was such, indeed, as to take his life, but other men have known as great, if not greater. His mental anguish, especially the hiding of his Father's face, was so intense as to literally break his heart; but it cannot have been the same, either in character, extent, or continuance, as the everlasting pangs of conscious guilt. All that was practicable, in him as a substitute for man, was to undergo an ordeal as similar in kind and degree as his pure human nature would admit. In this sense he drank the bitter cup of atonement to its very dregs, but it was not the identical draught intended for mankind. Finally, such an absolute vicariousness would have been useless, and that in two most vital respects: it would so fully have exhausted the penalty for all possible or foreseen human transgression as to render the personal punishment of any offender thereafter impossible, because unjust; and it would have been no gain or saving of suffering on the whole, but a mere shifting of a specific load from the shoulders of one being to those of another. No larger average of happiness could have resulted, nor any greater glory redounded to God. Such an atonement would have defeated instead of furthering the main design of its merciful Projector. It would have been fatal to all the advantages seen above to be secured by Christ's mediation. See VICARIOUS SUFFERING.

Mediator, a person who intervenes between two parties at variance, in order to reconcile them. The term does not occur in the Old Test., but the idea is contained in that remarkable passage (Job ix, 33) which is rendered in the Auth. Vers. "Neither is there any daysman betwixt us, that might lay his hand upon us both." The Hebrew words are, לֹא יֵשׁ־בֵּינֵינוּ מוֹכִיחַ יָשֵׁת יָדוֹ עַל־שְׁנֵינוּ; literally, "There is not between us a reprover—he shall place his hand upon us both." This the Sept. translates, or rather paraphrases, εἴθε ἦν ὁ μεσίτης ἡμῶν, καὶ ἐλέγχων, καὶ διακούων ἀναμέσον ἀμφοτέρων. See DAYSMAN. In the New Test. it is the invariable rendering of μεσίτης, a word which is rather rare in classical Greek—Polybius and Lucian being, it would appear, nearly the only classical authors who employ it (see Robinson, N.-T. Lex. s. v.). Its meaning, however, is not difficult to determine. This seems evidently to be, qui medio inter duo stat—he who takes a middle position between two parties, and principally with the view of removing their differences. Thus Suidas paraphrases the word by μεσέγγυος, and also by ἐγγυητής, μέσος δύο μερῶν. In the Sept. the word appears to occur only once, namely, in the above passage of Job.

1. It is used, in an accommodated sense, by many of the ancient fathers, to denote *one who intervenes between two dispensations.* Hence it is applied by them to John the Baptist, because he came, as it were, between the Mosaic and Christian dispensations. Thus Greg. Nazianzen (*Orat.* xxxix, p. 633) calls him ὁ παλαιᾶς καὶ νέας μεσίτης. Theophylact, commenting on Matt. iii, gives him the same denomination.

2. Again, it signifies, in its more proper sense, an *internuncius,* or ambassador, one who stands as the channel of communication between two contracting parties. Thus most commentators think that the apostle Paul, in Gal. iii, 19, calls Moses *mediator,* because he conveyed the expression of God's will to the people, and reported to God their wants, wishes, and determinations. In reference to this passage of Scripture, Basil (*De Spiritu Sancto,* cap. xiv), says, "Mosen figuram representâsse quando inter Deum et populum intermedius extiterit." Many ancient and modern divines, however, are of opinion that Christ himself, and not Moses, is here meant by the apostle, and this view would seem to be confirmed by comparing Deut. xxxiii, 2 with Acts vii, 38–52. Christ it was who, surrounded by angelic spirits, communicated with Moses on Mount Sinai. On this point, the words of the learned and pious Chrysostom, on Gal. iii, are very express: "Here," says he, "Paul calls Christ Mediator, declaring thereby that he existed before the law, and that by him the law was revealed." This application of the passage will be the more evident if we consider the scope of the apostle's argument, which evidently is to point out the dignity of the law. How could he present a clearer demonstration of this than by showing that it was the second person of the everblessed Trinity who stood forth on the mount to communicate between God the Father and his creature man! Moreover, to contradistinguish Christ's mediation from that of Moses, the former is emphatically styled μεσίτης κρείττονος διαθήκης (Heb. viii, 6). This, however, implies that Moses was the mediator of the former covenant, and Eadie, in his *Commentary on Galatians* (ad loc.), shows at length that this is the meaning of the passage, in opposition to all other views. Moses is likewise often styled סרסור, or mediator, in the rabbinical writings (see Schöttgen and Wetstein, ad loc.). But be this as it may, far more emphatically and officially

3. CHRIST is called Mediator (1 Tim. ii, 5; Heb. viii, 6; ix, 15; xii, 24) by virtue of the reconciliation he has effected between a justly-offended God and his rebellious creature man (see Grotius, *De Satisfactione Christi,* cap. viii). In this sense of the term Moses was, on many occasions, an eminent type of Christ. The latter, however, was not *Mediator* merely by reason of his coming between God and his creatures, as certain heretics would affirm (see Cyril. Alex. *Dial. I de Sancta Trinitate,* p. 410), but because he appeased his wrath, and made reconciliation for iniquity. "Christ is the Mediator," observes Theophylact, commenting on Gal. iii, "of two, i. e. of God and man. He exercises this office between both by making peace, and putting a stop to that spiritual war which man wages against God. To accomplish this he assumed our nature, joining in a marvellous manner the human, by reason of sin unfriendly, to the divine nature." "Hence," he adds, "he made reconciliation." Œcumenius expresses similar sentiments on the same passage of Scripture. Again, Cyril, in his work before quoted, remarks: "He is esteemed Mediator because the divine and human nature being disjointed by sin, he has shown them united in his own person; and in this manner he reunites us to God the Father." If, in addition to the above general remarks, confirmed by many of the most ancient and orthodox fathers of the Church, we consider the *three great offices* which holy Scripture assigns to Christ as Saviour of the world, viz. those of *prophet, priest,* and *king,* a further and more ample illustration will be afforded of his Mediatorship.

(1.) One of the first and most palpable predictions which we have of the prophetic character of Christ is that of Moses (Deut. xviii, 15): "The Lord thy God will raise up unto thee a prophet from the midst of thee, of thy brethren, like unto me; unto him ye shall hearken." That this refers to Christ we are assured by the inspired apostle Peter (Acts iii. 22). Again, in Isaiah lxi, 1, 3, Christ's consecration to the prophetic office, together with its sacred and gracious functions, is emphatically set forth (see Luke iv, 16–21, where Christ applies this passage to himself). In order, then, to sustain this part of his mediatorial office, and thus work out the redemption of the world, we may see the necessity there was that Messiah should be both *God* and man. It belongs to a prophet to expound the law, declare the will of God, and foretell things to come: all this was done, and that in a singular and eminent manner, by Christ, our prophet (Matt. v, 21, etc.; John i, 8). All light comes from this prophet. The apostle shows that all ministers are but stars which shine by a borrowed light (2 Cor. iii, 6, 7). All the prophets of the Old, and all the prophets and teachers of the New Testament, lighted their tapers at this torch (Luke xxi, 15). It was Christ who preached by Noah (1 Pet. iii, 19), taught the Israelites in the wilderness (Acts vii, 37), and still teaches by his ministers (Eph. iv, 11, 12). On this subject bishop Butler (*Analogy,* part ii, ch. v) says: "He was, by way of eminence, *the prophet,* 'the prophet that should come into the world' (John vi, 14) to declare the divine will. He published anew the law of nature, which men had corrupted, and the very knowledge of which, to some degree, was lost among them. He taught mankind, taught us authoritatively, to live soberly, righteously, and godly in this present world, in expectation of the future judgment of God. He confirmed the truth of this moral system of nature, and gave us additional evidence of it, the evidence of testimony. He distinctly revealed the manner in which God would be worshipped, the efficacy of repentance, and the rewards and punishments of a future life. Thus he was a prophet in a sense in which no other ever was." Hence the force of the term ὁ λόγος, by which John designates Christ. See PROPHET.

But, on the other hand, had the second person of the Trinity come to us in all the majesty of his divine nature, we could not have approached him as our instructor. The Israelites, terrified at the exhibitions of Deity, cried out that the Lord might not so treat with them again; it was then that he, in gracious condescension to their feelings, promised to communicate with them in future through a prophet like unto Moses. The son of God, in assuming the form of an humble man, became accessible to *all.* This condescension, moreover, enabled him to sympathize with his clients in all their trials (Heb. ii, 17, 18; iv, 14, 15). Thus we perceive the connection of Christ's prophetic office—he being both God and man—with the salvation of man. On this subject Chrysostom (*Homil.* cxxxiv, tom. v, p. 860) remarks: "A mediator, unless he has a union and communion with the parties for whom he mediates, possesses not the essential qualities of a mediator. When Christ, therefore, became mediator between God and man (1 Tim. ii, etc.), it was indispensable that he should be both God and man." Macarius, also (*Homil.* vi, 97), on this question more pointedly observes: "The Lord came and took his body from the virgin; for if he had appeared among us in his naked divinity, who could bear the sight? But he spoke as man to us men."

Again, the Redeemer was not only to propound, explain, and enforce God's law, but it was needful that he should give a practical proof of obedience to it in his own person (comp. Rom. v, 19). Now, if he had not been *man,* he could not have been subject to the law; hence it is said, Gal. iv, 4, "When the fulness of the time was come, God sent forth his son, made of a woman, made under the law;" and if he had not been God, he could not, by keeping the law, have *merited* forgiveness for us, for he had done but what was required of him. It was the fact of his being *very God and very man* which constituted the *merit* of Christ's obedience.

(2.) Moreover, in working out the mighty scheme of redemption the mediator must assume the office of *priest*. To this office he was solemnly appointed by God (Psa. cx, 4; Heb. v, 10), being qualified for it by his incarnation (Heb. x, 6, 7), and he accomplished all the ends thereof by his sacrificial death (Heb. ix, 11, 12); as in sustaining his *prophetic* character, *so in this,* his Deity and humanity will be seen. According to the exhibition of type and declaration of prophecy, the mediator must die, and thus rescue us sinners from death by destroying him who had the power of death. "But we see Jesus," says the apostle (Heb. ii, 9), "who was made a little lower than the angels for the suffering of death, crowned with glory and honor, that he by the grace of God should taste death for every man. Forasmuch, then, as the children are partakers of flesh and blood, he also himself likewise took part of the same, that through death he might destroy him who had the power of death, that is, the devil." On the other hand, had he not been *God* he could not have raised himself from the dead. "I lay down my life (saith he, John x, 17, 18), and take it up again." He had not had a life to lay down if he had not been man, for the Godhead could not die; and if he had not been God, he could not have acquired *merit* by laying it down: it must be his own, and not in the power of another, else his voluntarily surrendering himself unto death—as he did on the charge that he, being only man, made himself equal with God—was an act of *suicide*, and consequently an act of blasphemy against God! It was, then, the mysterious union of both natures in the one person of Christ which constituted the *essential glory* of his vicarious obedience and death.

Nor are the two natures of Christ more apparent in his *death* than they are in the *intercession* which he ever liveth to make in behalf of all who come unto God by him (Heb. vii, 25). The author of the Epistle to the Hebrews teaches us (chaps. vii, ix) that the high-priest under the Levitical dispensation typified Christ in his intercessory character: as the high-priest entered *alone* within the holiest place of the tabernacle once a year with the blood of the sacrifice in his hands, and the names of the twelve tribes upon his heart, so Christ, having offered up himself as a lamb without spot unto God, has gone into glory bearing on his *heart* the names of his redeemed. We may then ask with the apostle (Rom. viii, 33), "Who shall lay anything to the charge of God's elect? It is God that justifieth, who is he that condemneth? It is Christ that died, yea rather, that is risen again, who is even at the right hand of God, who also maketh *intercession* for us." In this part of his mediatorial work God's *incommunicable* attributes of *omniscience, omnipresence,* and *omnipotence* are seen. He must therefore have been God, and on the ground of his being able from personal experience to sympathize with the suffering members of his mystical body, he must have been man; being perfect God and perfect man, he is then a perfect *intercessor*.

(3.) We come, lastly, to notice Christ's mediatorial character *as king.* The limits of this article will not admit of our even alluding to the varied and multiplied passages of Scripture which delineate Christ as "Head over all things to the Church" (see Psa. ii, 6; lxx; Isa. xxxii, 1; Dan. ix, 25; Col. i, 17, 18, etc.). Suffice it here to say that Christ could not, without the concurrence of his *divine* nature, gather and govern the Church, protect and defend it against all assailants open and secret, and impart to it his Holy Spirit, to enlighten and renew the minds and hearts of men and subdue Satan—all these are acts of his kingly office.

Such, then, is the work of Christ's mediatorship—salvation revealed by him as prophet, procured by him as priest, and applied by him as king—the work of the whole person wherein both natures are engaged. Hence it is that some of the ancients speaking of it, designate it $\theta\epsilon\alpha\nu\delta\rho\iota\kappa\eta$ $\epsilon\nu\epsilon\rho\gamma\epsilon\iota\alpha$, "a divine-human operation" (see Dionys. Areopag. *Epist. IV ad Caiam Damascenum,* iii, 19).

Thus Jesus Christ is the mediator between an offended God and sinful man (1 Tim. ii, 5). Both Jews and Gentiles have a notion of a mediator: the Jews call the Messiah אמצעא, the Mediator, or Middle One. The Persians call their god Mithras $\mu\epsilon\sigma\iota\tau\eta\varsigma$, a mediator; and the dæmons, with the heathens, seem to be, according to them, mediators between the superior gods and men. Indeed, the whole religion of paganism was a system of mediation and intercession. The idea, therefore, of salvation by a mediator is not so novel or restricted as some imagine; and the Scriptures of truth inform us that it is only by this way human beings can arrive to eternal felicity (Acts iv, 12; John xiv, 6). Man, in his state of innocence, was in friendship with God; but, by sinning against him, he exposed himself to his just displeasure; his powers became enfeebled, and his heart filled with enmity against him (Rom. viii, 6); he was driven out of his paradisaical Eden, and was totally incapable of returning to God, and making satisfaction to his justice. Jesus Christ, therefore, was the appointed mediator to bring about reconciliation (Gen. iii, 12; Col. i, 21); and in the fulness of time he came into this world, obeyed the law, satisfied justice, and brought his people into a state of grace and favor; yea, into a more exalted state of friendship with God than was lost by the fall (Eph. ii, 18).

We have seen above some of the reasons why in order to accomplish this work it was necessary that the Mediator should be God and man in one person. We may specify the following in addition. (*a*) It was necessary that he should be man: 1. That he might be related to those to whom he was to be a mediator and redeemer (Phil. ii, 8; Heb. ii, 11–17). 2. That sin might be atoned for, and satisfaction made in the same nature which had sinned (Rom. v, 17–21; viii, 3). 3. It was meet that the mediator should be man, that he might be capable of suffering death; for, as God, he could not die, and without shedding of blood there was no remission (Heb. ii, 10, 15; viii, 3–6; ix, 15–28; 1 Pet. iii, 18). 4. It was necessary that he should be a holy and righteous man, free from all sin, that he might offer himself without spot to God (Heb. vii, 26; ix, 14; i, 19; 1 Pet. ii, 22. (*b*) But it was not enough that the mediator should be truly man, and an innocent person; he must be more than a man; it was requisite that he should be really God. 1. No mere man could have entered into a covenant with God to mediate between him and sinful men (Rom. ix, 5; Heb. i, 8; 1 Tim. iii, 16; Tit. ii, 13). 2. He must be God, to give virtue and value to his obedience and sufferings (John xx, 28; Acts xx, 28; 2 Pet. ii, 1; Phil. ii, 5–11). 3. The Mediator being thus God and man, we are encouraged to hope in him. In the person of Jesus Christ the object of trust is brought nearer to ourselves. If he were God and not man, we should approach him with fear and dread; and if he were man and not God, we should be guilty of idolatry to worship and trust in him at all (Jer. xvii, 5). The plan of salvation by such a Mediator is therefore the most suitable to human beings; for here "Mercy and truth are met together, righteousness and peace have kissed each other" (Psa. lxxxv, 10).

The properties of Christ as Mediator are these: 1. He is the only Mediator (1 Tim. ii, 4). Praying, therefore, to saints and angels is an error of the Church of Rome, and has no countenance from Scripture. 2. Christ is a Mediator of men only, not of angels; good angels need not any; and as for evil angels, none is provided nor admitted. 3. He is the Mediator both for Jews and Gentiles (Eph. ii, 18; 1 John ii, 2). 4. He is the Mediator both for Old and New Testament saints. 5. He is a suitable, constant, willing, and prevalent Mediator; his mediation always succeeds, and is infallible.

For a more ample view of this important subject, see

Flavel, *Panstratia of Shamier*, vol. iii (Geneva, folio), vii, 1, in which the views of the Romish Church are ably controverted. See also Brinsley (John), *Christ's Mediation* (Lond. 1657, 8vo); Gill's *Body of Divinity*, i, 336; Witsii *Œcon. Fœd.* lib. ii, c. 4; Fuller's *Gospel its own Witness*, ch. iv, p. 2; Hurrion's *Christ Crucified*, p. 103, etc.; Owen, *On the Person of Christ*; Goodwin's *Works*, b. iii; M'Laughlan, *Christ's Mediatorship* (Edinb. 1853); Kitto, *Bibl. Cyclop.* s. v.; Buck, *Theol. Dict.* s. v.; *Amer. Presb. Rev.* 1863, p. 419. See ATONEMENT.

Medicamentum, or MEDICĪNA CORPORIS ET MENTIS, a name occasionally found in the writings of the Church fathers as a synonyme of our term "*the Lord's Supper.*" Ignatius and others not unusually speak of "the medicine of immortality," "medicine or preservative of the soul." See Riddle, *Christian Antiquities*, p. 551.

Medici, THE HOUSE OF, one of the most noted families of Italy's nobility, figures so largely in the ecclesiastical history of mediæval times and the days of the Renaissance that we cannot pass it without a somewhat detailed account of its different members.

1. The early history of the family of the Medici is obscure, although some authors have traced their genealogy from the age of Charlemagne. But it must be remembered that these genealogies were made after the elevation of this family to supreme power in the republic of Florence—a position which they attained only by degrees, after the accumulation of wealth sufficient to control the affairs of the Italian nation. It appears, however, from authentic monuments, that many individuals of this family had signalized themselves on various important occasions even in early times. Giovanni de' Medici, in the year 1251, with a body of only one hundred Florentines, forced his way through the Milanese army, then besieging the fortress of Scarperia, and entered the place with the loss of twenty lives. Francesco de' Medici was at the head of the magistracy of Florence in 1348, at the time when the black plague, which had desolated so large a portion of the world, extended its ravages to that city. Salvestro de' Medici acquired great reputation by his temperate but firm resistance to the nobles, who, in order to secure their power, accused those who opposed them of being attached to the party of the Ghibelines, then in great odium at Florence. The persons so accused were said to be *ammoniti* (admonished), and by that act were excluded from all offices of government. In the year 1379, Salvestro, being chosen chief magistrate, exerted his power to reform this abuse, which was not, however, effected without a violent commotion, several of the nobility losing their lives in the attempt. It is from this time that we date the rise of the Medici to prominence in political, and finally also in ecclesiastical affairs.

2. The founder, however, of that almost regal greatness which the Medici enjoyed for more than two centuries was not Salvestro, who first received great public distinctions, but Giovanni de' Medici. His immense wealth, honorably acquired by commercial dealings, which had already rendered the name of *Medici* celebrated in Europe, was expended with liberality and magnificence. Of a mild temper and averse to cabals, Giovanni de' Medici did not attempt to set up a party, but contented himself with the place in the public councils to which even his enemies declared him entitled in virtue of his eminence, his acquirements, and the purity of his character. He died in 1429, leaving to his sons, Cosmo and Lorenzo, a heritage of wealth and honors hitherto unparalleled in the republic.

Cosmo (born 1389, died 1464), on whom was gratefully bestowed the honored title of "Father of his country," really began the glorious epoch of the Medici. Cosmo's life, except during a short period, when the Albizzi and other rivals re-established a successful opposition against the policy and credit of the Medici, was one uninterrupted course of prosperity; at once a mu-

nificent patron and a successful cultivator of art and literature, he did more than any other sovereign in Europe to revive the study of the ancient classics, and to foster a taste for mental culture. He assembled around him learned men of every nation, and gave liberal support to numerous Greek scholars, whom the subjection of Constantinople by the Turks had driven into exile; and by his foundation of an academy for the study of the philosophy of Plato, and of a library of Greek, Latin, and Oriental MSS., he inaugurated a new æra in modern learning and art. In the lifetime of his father, Cosmo had engaged not only in the extensive business by which the family had acquired its wealth, but also in the affairs of state. Such was his authority and reputation that in the year 1414, when Balthasar Cossa, who had been elected pope, and had assumed the name of John XXIII, was summoned to attend the Council of Constance, he chose to be accompanied by Cosmo de' Medici, among other men of eminence, whose characters might countenance his cause. By this council, which continued nearly four years, Balthasar was deprived of his pontifical dignity, and Otto Colonna, who took the name of Martin V, was elected pope. Cosmo did not desert in adversity the man to whom he had attached himself in prosperity. At the expense of a large sum of money, he redeemed him from the hands of the duke of Bavaria, who had seized upon his person; and afterwards gave him a hospitable shelter at Florence during the remainder of his life. The successful pontiff, instead of resenting the kindness shown to his rival, soon afterwards paid a public visit to Florence, where, on the formal submission of Balthasar, and at the request of the Medici, he created the ex-pope a cardinal, with the privilege of taking the first place in the sacred college. The new-made cardinal died in 1419, and it was rumored that the Medici at his death possessed themselves of immense wealth which he had acquired during his pontificate. This rumor was afterwards encouraged by those who well knew its falsehood. The true source of the wealth of the Medici was their superior talents and application to business, and the property of the cardinal was scarcely sufficient to discharge his debts and legacies. During the retirement of his latter days, his happiest hours were devoted to the study of letters and philosophy, and the conversation of learned men. He also endowed numerous religious houses, and built a hospital at Jerusalem for the relief of distressed pilgrims.

3. Cosmo's grandson, Lorenzo, afterwards surnamed the "Magnificent" (born Jan. 1, 1448, died April 8, 1492), was introduced to a knowledge of public affairs, on account of the infirmities of his father, immediately upon the decease of Cosmo. Though only a youth, he was at once pushed forward to take upon himself the work supposed to belong to a much maturer mind. To afford him a clearer insight into political affairs than he could secure at home, he was sent to visit the principal courts in Italy. Upon the accession of Sixtus IV to the papal throne, he went, with other citizens of Florence, to congratulate the new pope, and was invested with the office of treasurer of the holy see; and while at Rome embraced the opportunity to add to the remains of ancient art which his family had collected. One of the first events after he undertook the administration of affairs was a revolt of the inhabitants of Volterra, on account of a dispute with the Florentine republic. By the recommendation of Lorenzo, force was used, and the result was the sack of Volterra. Like his grandfather, he encouraged literature and the arts, employed learned men to collect choice books and antiquities for him from every part of the known world, established printing-presses in his dominions as soon as the art was invented, but, above all, he deserves special commendation for his re-establishment of the Academy of Pisa, to which city he removed in order to complete the undertaking: he selected the most eminent professors, and contributed a large sum from his private fortune, in addition to that granted by the state of Florence. In another respect also Lorenzo

resembled his grandfather Cosmo. He was, or affected to be, an admirer of Plato, took an active part in the establishment of an academy for the cultivation of the Platonic philosophy, and instituted an annual festival in honor of Plato.

While Lorenzo was dividing his time between the administration of the state and the promotion of literature, the Pazzi, a numerous and distinguished family in Florence, of all the opponents of the Medici the most inveterate, formed a conspiracy to assassinate Lorenzo and his brother; experience having taught them the impossibility of overthrowing the reign of the Medici in any other way. Giuliano was killed, but Lorenzo escaped. "A horrible transaction this, which has been justly quoted as an incontrovertible proof of the practical atheism of the times in which it took place—one in which a pope, a cardinal, an archbishop, and several other ecclesiastics, associated themselves with a band of ruffians to destroy two men who were an honor to their age and country; and purposed to perpetrate their crime at a season of hospitality, in the sanctuary of a Christian Church, and at the very moment of the elevation of the host, when the congregation bowed down before it, and the assassins were presumed to be in the immediate presence of their God. The plan was concocted at Rome, with the participation of pope Sixtus IV. On the 26th of April, 1478, in the church of the Reparata, during the mass, while the host was elevated and the multitude were kneeling, the murderous blow was struck, the very mass-bell itself sounding the signal to the other conspirators to possess themselves of the palace and government." The failure of this dastardly scheme only made the Medici the more invincible. The people, who had always been attached to them, exasperated by this open and daring attempt to rob them of those whom they conceived to be their best friends, now took the execution of the law in their own hands, and put to death or apprehended the assassins. Salviati, archbishop of Pisa, was hung through the windows of the palace, and was not allowed to divest himself even of his robes; and Jacopo de' Pazzi, with one of his nephews, shared the same fate. The name and arms of the Pazzi family were suppressed, its members were banished, and Lorenzo rose still higher in the regard of his fellow-citizens. The troubles of the Medici, however, did not stop here. For them yet remained the punishment at the disposal of the papal party, and the latter, maddened by the failure of their plot, determined now to avail themselves of the advantages which Rome could afford as "ecclesiastical thunderer." Sixtus IV promptly excommunicated Lorenzo and the magistrates of Florence, laid an interdict upon the whole territory, and, forming a league with the king of Naples, prepared to invade the Florentine dominions. Lorenzo appealed to all the surrounding potentates, and, zealously supported by his fellow-citizens, commenced hostilities, and carried on two campaigns. At the close of 1479, Lorenzo took the bold resolution of paying a visit to the king of Naples, and, without obtaining any previous promise of security, trusted himself to the mercy of his enemy. The result of this confidence was a treaty of mutual defence and friendship between the king of Naples and Florence, and this finally forced Sixtus to consent to a treaty of peace. In 1484 Sixtus IV died, and his successor on the papal throne, Innocent VIII, manifesting a determination to re-establish friendly relations with the different Italian princes [see INNOCENT VIII], the contest of the Medici with the Church seemed to have come to a happy close. There was, however, still one dark cloud on the firmament of the heavens, and it threatened sooner or later to bring trouble and discomfiture to the Medici—we refer to Savonarola, the great Italian reformer, who was in the very strength of his manhood at this time. The Italian monk had long opposed the licentious habits of the court and the nobility. He was opposed, moreover, to the display of regal splendor, and boldly preached in favor of democracy and re-

publican institutions. Lorenzo sought in more than one way to conciliate the sturdy reformer, but all efforts proved futile. Not even the cardinalate could tempt him [see SAVONAROLA], and Lorenzo was forced to admit himself, "Besides this man, I have never seen a true monk." Gradually Savonarola gave system to his republican ideas, and, gathering about him a host of followers, these opponents of the ruling administration came to be known by the name of *Piagnoni* (q. v.) or "weepers," so called because of their determination to stem the progress of the voluptuous refinement of the day by ascetic severity of morals. Lorenzo himself saw clearly the inherent insufficiency of art and philosophy alone for the security of a state; but while he sighed for a purely religious influence, he feared the dangerous tendency of the *Piagnoni* towards a popular and democratic form of government, and he had failed to extinguish or abate this opposition when suddenly cut down by disease and death, April 8, 1492.

Lorenzo is credited with even greater love and devotion to the development of literary life and the study of the fine arts than any of his predecessors. His own productions are sonnets, canzoni, and other lyric pieces; some longer works in stanzas, some comic satires, carnival songs, and various sacred poems. Many of the lighter kind were popular in their day. Although the ancestors of Lorenzo laid the foundation of the immense collection of manuscripts contained in the Laurentian library, Lorenzo has the credit of adding most largely to the stock. For the purpose of enriching his collection of books and antiquities, he employed learned men in different parts of Italy, and especially his intimate friend Politian, who made several journeys in order to discover and purchase the valuable remains of antiquity. Two journeys were undertaken at the request of Lorenzo into the East by John Lascaris, and the result was the acquisition of a great number of manuscripts. On his return from his second expedition, Lascaris brought two hundred manuscripts, many of which he had procured from a monastery at Mount Athos; but this treasure did not arrive till after the death of Lorenzo, who in his last moments expressed to Politian and Pico of Mirandola his regret that he could not live to complete the collection which he was forming. On the discovery of the art of printing, Lorenzo quickly saw and appreciated its importance. At his suggestion, several Italian scholars devoted their attention to collating the manuscripts of the ancient authors, for the purpose of having them accurately printed. On the capture of Constantinople by the Turks, many learned Greeks took refuge in Italy; and an academy was established at Florence for the purpose of cultivating the Greek language, partly under the direction of native Greeks, and partly under native Italians. The services of these learned men were procured by Lorenzo, and were amply rewarded by his bounty. "Hence," as Roscoe observes (in his *Life of Lorenzo de' Medici*, 1795, 2 vols. 4to; Bohn's edit. Lond. 1851, 12mo), "succeeding scholars have been profuse of their acknowledgments to their great patron, who first formed that establishment, from which (to use their own scholastic figure), as from the Trojan horse, so many illustrious champions have sprung, and by means of which the knowledge of the Greek tongue was extended, not only through Italy, but through France, Spain, Germany, and England, from all which countries numerous pupils attended at Florence, who diffused the learning they had there acquired throughout the rest of Europe." Lorenzo also augmented his father's collection of the remains of ancient art. He appropriated his gardens in Florence to the purpose of an academy for the study of the antique, which he furnished with statues, busts, and other works of art, the best of their kind that he could procure. The higher class of his fellow-citizens were incited to these pursuits by the example of Lorenzo, and the lower class by his liberality. To the latter he not only allowed competent stipends while they attended to their studies, but gave considerable premiums as rewards of their proficiency. To this institution, more than to any other circumstance, Roscoe ascribes the sudden and astonishing advance which, towards the close of the 15th century, was evidently made in the arts, and which, commencing at Florence, extended itself to the rest of Europe.

4. Lorenzo's successor in the government of Florence was his eldest son Pietro; but of far greater interest to the ecclesiastical student is the history of his younger son Giovanni, and that of his nephew Giulio. The former of the two last named, Giovanni, was honored, by the prudent manipulations of Lorenzo, with the cardinal's hat when only a boy of thirteen years, at the hands of Innocent VIII, and, on the death of Julius II, brought credit upon the name of Medici by his accession to the papal throne. See LEO X. Of Giulio's history we have the following from Roscoe. Shortly after the attempt at assassination, he says, "Lorenzo received a visit from Antonio da San Gallo, who informed him that the untimely death of Giuliano had prevented his disclosing to Lorenzo a circumstance with which it was now become necessary that he should be acquainted: this was the birth of a son, whom a lady of the family of Gorini had borne to Giuliano about twelve months before his death, and whom Antonio had held over the baptismal font, where he received the name of Giulio. Lorenzo immediately repaired to the place of the infant's residence, and, taking him under his protection, delivered him to Antonio, with whom he remained until he had arrived at the seventh year of his age. This concealed offspring of illicit love, to whom the kindness of Lorenzo supplied the untimely loss of a father, was destined to act an important part in the affairs of Europe. The final extinction of the liberties of Florence, the alliance of the family of Medici with the royal house of France, the expulsion of Henry VIII of England from the bosom of the Roman Church, and the consequent establishment of the doctrines of the Reformers in Great Britain, are principally to be referred to this illegitimate son of Giuliano de' Medici, who through various vicissitudes of fortune at length obtained the supreme direction of the Roman see, and, under the name of Clement VII, guided the bark of St. Peter through a succession of the severest storms which it has ever experienced."

Pietro possessed neither capacity nor prudence, and in the troubles which the ambition of her princes and the profligacy of her popes brought upon Italy, by plunging her into civil and foreign war, he showed himself treacherous and vacillating alike to friends and foes. Lodovico Sforza, surnamed the "Moor," relying on the friendship which, from the middle of the 15th century, had prevailed between the Sforza family of Milan and the Medici, applied to him for assistance in establishing his claim to the duchy of Milan; but, seeing that no reliance could be placed on Pietro, he threw himself into the arms of Charles VIII of France. The result was the invasion of Italy by a French army of 32,000 men. Pietro, in hopes of conciliating the powerful invader, hastened to meet the troops on their entrance into the dominions of Florence, and surrendered to Charles the fortresses of Leghorn and Pisa, which constituted the keys of the republic. The magistrates and people, incensed at his perfidy, drove him from the city, and formally deposed the family of the Medici from all participation of power in 1494.

The attempts of Giovanni, then a cardinal, to uphold the Median authority, and his success in the reestablishment of his house in 1512, we have narrated in our article on Leo X. Pietro was slain in 1503, while fighting in the French ranks.

It was during the invasions of the French in Italy, in the days of Pietro, that Florence was robbed of one of her greatest treasures—the invaluable library which had been collected by the care of his father and grandfather. "The French troops, which had entered the city without opposition, led the way to this act of barbarism, in which they were joined by the Florentines themselves,

who openly carried off or purloined whatever they could discover that was rare or valuable. Besides the numerous manuscripts, the plunderers carried off the inestimable specimens of the arts which the palace of the Medici contained, and which had long made it the admiration of strangers and the chief ornament of the city. Exquisite pieces of ancient sculpture, vases, cameos, and gems of various kinds, were lost amid the indiscriminate plunder, and the rich accumulations of half a century were destroyed or dispersed in a single day." During the interregnum, the labors of the Piagnoni were suddenly checked by the martyrdom of their beloved leader, Savonarola, in 1498; and, when the Medici came again to rule over Florence, this disposition of some of their strongest opponents threw a weight of power into the hands of the Medici which rendered all attempts to maintain even a show of independence futile on the part of the Florentines. The faintest indication of republican spirit was at once crushed by the combined aid of pope and emperor.

5. The accession of Clement VII only strengthened the Medici in Florence, and, though the legitimate male line of Cosmo was extinct (with the exception of the pope), Clement VII gave, in 1529, to Alessandro, natural son of the last prince Lorenzo II, the rank of duke of Florence; and on his death, by assassination, without direct heirs, in 1537, raised Cosmo I, the descendant of a collateral branch, to the ducal chair.

Cosmo, known as the Great, possessed the astuteness of character, the love of elegance, and taste for literature, but not the frank and generous spirit that had distinguished his great ancestors; and while he founded the academies of painting and of fine arts, made collections of paintings and statuary, published magnificent editions of his own works and those of others, and encouraged trade, for the protection of which he instituted the ecclesiastical order of St. Stephen, he was implacable in his enmity, and scrupled not utterly to extirpate the race of the Strozzi, the hereditary foes of his house. His acquisition of Sienna gained for him the title of grand-duke of Tuscany from Pius V; and he died in 1574, leaving enormous wealth and regal power to his descendants, who, throughout the next half century, maintained the literary and artistic fame of their family. In the 17th century the race rapidly degenerated, and, after several of its representatives had suffered themselves to be made the mere tools of Spanish and Austrian ambition, the main line of the Medici family became extinct in 1737. The genealogy of the Medici to the present time is given in a splendid work but little known, entitled *Famiglie celebri Italiane*, by Litta. The Medici and their descendants are comprised in *Fascicolo XVII* (in seven parts, Milan, 1827–30, folio). See also *Modern Universal History*, vol. xxxvi; Noble, *Memoirs of the House of Medici*, illustrated with genealogical tables; Tenhove, *Memoirs of the House of Medici*, translated from the French by Sir R. Clayton (Bath, 1797, 2 vols. 4to); Roscoe, *Life of Lorenzo de' Medici*, and his *Life and Pontificate of Leo X* (Liverp. 1805, 4 vols. 4to); Guicciardini, *Storia d'Italia*; Botta, *Storia d'Italia*; Sismondi, *Hist. des Republiques Italiennes*; Leo, *Gesch. v. Italien*; Trollope, *Hist. of Florence* (Lond. 1865, 4 vols. 8vo); Hallam, *Middle Ages* (Smith's ed., Harpers, 1872), p. 229 sq.; *National Quart. Rev.* Dec. 1863, art. iii; *Foreign Quart. Rev.* v, 475; and the excellent article in the *English Cyclopædia*, s. v.

Medicine (תְּרוּפָה, *teruphah'*, a medical powder, Ezek. xlvii, 12; Sept. ὑγίεια, comp. θεραπεία of Rev. xxii, 2; Vulg. *medicina*; also the plur. רְפֻאוֹת, *rephuoth'*, *medicaments*, or remedies for wounds, Jer. xxx, 13; xlvi, 11; "healed," Ezek. xxx, 21; but גֵּהָה, *gehah'*, in Prov. xvii, 12, is properly the *removal* of the bandages from a sore, hence its *healing;* therefore render, "a joyful heart perfects a *cure*"). In the following article we endeavor as far as possible to treat the subject from the modern scientific point of view. See HEAL.

I. *Sources of Medical Science among the Hebrews.*—1. *Natural.*—Next to care for food, clothing, and shelter, the curing of hurts takes precedence even among savage nations. At a later period comes the treatment of sickness, and recognition of states of disease, and these mark a nascent civilization. Internal diseases, and all for which an obvious cause cannot be assigned, are in the most early period viewed as the visitation of God, or as the act of some malignant power, human—as the evil eye—or else superhuman, and to be dealt with by sorcery, or some other occult supposed agency. The Indian notion is that all diseases are the work of an evil spirit (Sprengel, *Gesch. der Arzeneikunde*, ii, 48). But among a civilized race the pre-eminence of the medical art is confessed in proportion to the increased value set on human life, and the vastly greater amount of comfort and enjoyment of which civilized man is capable.

2. *Egyptian.*—It would be strange if their close connection historically with Egypt had not imbued the Israelites with a strong appreciation of the value of this art, and with some considerable degree of medical culture. From the most ancient testimonies, sacred and secular, Egypt, from whatever cause, though perhaps from necessity, was foremost among the nations in this most human of studies purely physical. Again, as the active intelligence of Greece flowed in upon her, and mingled with the immense store of pathological records which must have accumulated under the system described by Herodotus, Egypt, especially Alexandria, became the medical repertory and museum of the world. Thither all that was best worth preserving amid earlier civilizations, whether her own or foreign, had been attracted, and medicine and surgery flourished amid political decadence and artistic decline. The attempt has been made by a French writer (Renouard, *Histoire de Médicine depuis son Origine*, etc.) to arrange in periods the growth of the medical art as follows: 1st. The Primitive or Instinctive Period, lasting from the earliest recorded treatment to the fall of Troy. 2dly. The Sacred or Mystic Period, lasting till the dispersion of the Pythagorean Society, B.C. 500. 3dly. The Philosophical Period, closing with the foundation of the Alexandrian Library, B.C. 320. 4thly. The Anatomical Period, which continued till the death of Galen, A.D. 200. But these artificial lines do not strictly exhibit the truth of the matter. Egypt was the earliest home of medical and other skill for the region of the Mediterranean basin, and every Egyptian mummy of the more expensive and elaborate sort involved a process of anatomy. This gave opportunities of inspecting a vast number of bodies, varying in every possible condition. Such opportunities were sure to be turned to account (Pliny, *N. H.* xix, 5) by the more diligent among the faculty, for "the physicians" embalmed (Gen. l, 2). The intestines had a separate receptacle assigned them, or were restored to the body through the ventral incision (Wilkinson, v, 468); and every such process which we can trace in the mummies discovered shows the most minute accuracy of manipulation. Notwithstanding these laborious efforts, we have no trace of any philosophical or rational system of Egyptian origin, and medicine in Egypt was a mere art or profession. Of science the Asclepiadæ of Greece were the true originators. Hippocrates, who wrote a book on "Ancient Medicine," and who seems to have had many opportunities of access to foreign sources, gives no prominence to Egypt. It was no doubt owing to the repressive influences of her fixed institutions that this country did not attain to a vast and speedy proficiency in medical science, when *post mortem* examination was so general a rule instead of being a rare exception. Still it is impossible to believe that considerable advances in physiology could have failed to be made there from time to time, and similarly, though we cannot so well determine how far, in Assyria. Recent researches at Kouyunjik have given proof, it is said, of the use of the microscope in minute devices, and yielded up even specimens of magnifying lenses. A cone engraved with a table of cubes, so small as to be unintelligible without a lens, was brought home by Sir H. Rawlinson, and is now in the British Museum. As to whether the invention was brought to bear on medical science, proof is wanting. Probably such science had not yet been pushed to the point at which the microscope becomes useful. Only those who have quick, keen eyes for the nature-world feel the want of such spectacles. The best guarantee for the advance of medical science is, after all, the interest which every human being has in it, and this is most strongly felt in large gregarious masses of population. Compared with the wild countries around them, at any rate, Egypt must have seemed incalculably advanced. Hence the awe with which Homer's Greeks speak of her wealth, resources, and medical skill (*Il.* ix, 381; *Od.* iv, 229. See also Herod. ii, 84, and i, 77). The simple heroes had reverence for the healing skill which extended only to wounds. There is hardly any recognition of disease in Homer. There is sudden death, pestilence, and weary old age, but hardly any fixed morbid condition, save in a simile (*Od.* v, 395). See, however, a letter *De rebus ex Homero medicis*, D. G. Wolf (Wittenberg, 1791). So likewise even the visit of Abraham, though prior to this period, found Egypt no doubt in advance of other countries. Representations of early Egyptian surgery apparently occur on some of the monuments of Beni-Hassan. Flint knives used for embalming have been recovered; the "Ethiopic stone" of Herodotus (ii, 86; comp. Ezek. iv, 25) was probably either black flint or agate [see KNIFE], and those who have assisted at the opening of a mummy have noticed that the teeth exhibit a dentistry not inferior in execution to the work of the best modern experts. This confirms the statement of Herodotus that every part of the body was studied by a distinct practitioner. Pliny (vii, 57) asserts that the Egyptians claimed the invention of the healing art, and (xxvi, 1) thinks them subject to many diseases. Their "many medicines" are mentioned (Jer. xlvi, 11). Many valuable drugs may be derived from the plants mentioned by Wilkinson (iv, 621), and the senna of the adjacent interior of Africa still excels all other. Athothmes II, king of the country, is said to have written on the subject of anatomy. Hermes (who may perhaps be the same as Athothmes, intellect personified, only disguised as a deity instead of a legendary king), was said to have written six books on medicine, in which an entire chapter was devoted to diseases of the eye (Rawlinson's *Herod.* note to ii, 84), and the first half of which related to anatomy. The various recipes known to have been beneficial were recorded, with their peculiar cases, in the memoirs of physic, inscribed among the laws, and deposited in the principal temples of the place (Wilkinson, iii, 396, 397). The reputation of its practitioners in historical times was such that both Cyrus and Darius sent to Egypt for physicians or surgeons (Herod. iii, 1, 129-132); and by one of the same country, no doubt, Cambyses's wound was tended, though not, perhaps, with much zeal for his recovery.

Of midwifery we have a distinct notice (Exod. i, 15), and of women as its practitioners, which fact may also be verified from the sculptures (Rawlinson's note on Herod. ii, 84). The sex of the practitioners is clear from the Heb. grammatical forms. The names of two, Shiphrah and Puah, are recorded. The treatment of new-born Hebrew infants is mentioned (Ezek. xvi, 4) as consisting in washing, salting, and swaddling—this last was not used in Egypt (Wilkinson). The physicians had salaries from the public treasury, and treated always according to established precedents, or deviated from these at their peril, in case of a fatal termination; if, however, the patient died under accredited treatment, no blame was attached. They treated gratis patients when travelling or on military service. Most diseases were by them ascribed to indigestion and excessive eating (Diod. Sicul. i, 82), and when their science failed them magic was called in. On recovery it was also

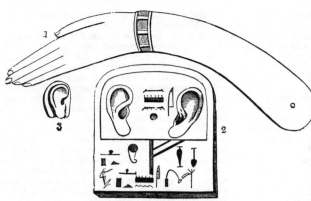

Ancient Egyptian Exvotos, for Cures.
1. Ivory hand, in Mr. Salt's collection.
2. Stone tablet, dedicated to Amun-re, for the recovery of a complaint in the ear; found at Thebes.
3. An ear, of terra cotta, from Thebes, in Sir Gardiner Wilkinson's possession.

customary to suspend in a temple an exvoto, which was commonly a model of the part affected; and such offerings doubtless, as in the Coan Temple of Æsculapius, became valuable aids to the pathological student. The Egyptians who lived in the corn-growing region are said by Herodotus (ii, 77) to have been specially attentive to health. The practice of circumcision is traceable on monuments certainly anterior to the age of Joseph. Its antiquity is involved in obscurity, especially as all we know of the Egyptians makes it unlikely that they would have borrowed such a practice, so late as the period of Abraham, from any mere sojourner among them. Its beneficial effects in the temperature of Egypt and Syria have often been noticed, especially as a preservative of cleanliness, etc. The scrupulous attention paid to the dead was favorable to the health of the living. Such powerful drugs as asphaltum, natron, resin, pure bitumen, and various aromatic gums, suppressed or counteracted all noxious effluvia from the corpse; even the saw-dust of the floor, on which the body had been cleansed, was collected in small linen bags, which, to the number of twenty or thirty, were deposited in vases near the tomb (Wilkinson, v, 468, 469). For the extent to which these practices were imitated among the Jews, see EMBALMING. At any rate, the uncleanness imputed to contact with a corpse was a powerful preservative against the inoculation of the living frame with morbid humors. But, to pursue to later times this merely general question, it appears (Pliny, N. H. xix, 5) that the Ptolemies themselves practiced dissection, and that, at a period when Jewish intercourse with Egypt was complete and reciprocal, there existed in Alexandria a great zeal for anatomical study. The only influence of importance which would tend to check the Jews from sharing this was the ceremonial law, the special reverence of Jewish feeling towards human remains, and the abhorrence of "uncleanness." Yet those Jews—and there were, at all times since the Captivity, not a few, perhaps—who tended to foreign laxity, and affected Greek philosophy and culture, would assuredly, as we shall have further occasion to notice that they in fact did, enlarge their anatomical knowledge from sources which repelled their stricter brethren, and the result would be apparent in the general elevated standard of that profession, even as practiced in Jerusalem. The diffusion of Christianity in the 3d and 4th centuries exercised a similar but more universal restraint on the dissecting-room, until anatomy as a pursuit became extinct, and, the notion of profaneness quelling everywhere such researches, surgical science became stagnant to a degree to which it had never previously sunk within the memory of human records.

3. *Grecian.*—In comparing the growth of medicine in the rest of the ancient world, the high rank of its practitioners—princes and heroes—settles at once the question as to the esteem in which it was held in the Homeric and pre-Homeric period. To descend to the historical, the story of Democedes at the court of Darius illustrates the practice of Greek surgery before the period of Hippocrates—anticipating, in its gentler waiting upon nature, as compared (Herod. iii, 130) with that of the Persians and Egyptians, the methods and maxims of that father of physic, who wrote against the theories and speculations of the so-called Philosophical school, and was a true empiricist before that sect was formularized. The Dogmatic school was founded after his time by his disciples, who departed from his eminently practical and inductive method. It recognized hidden causes of health and sickness arising from certain supposed principles or elements, out of which bodies were composed, and by virtue of which all their parts and members were attempered together and became sympathetic. Hippocrates has some curious remarks on the sympathy of men with climate, seasons, etc. He himself rejected supernatural accounts of disease, and especially dæmoniacal possession. He refers, but with no mystical sense, to numbers as furnishing a rule for cases. It is remarkable that he extols the discernment of Orientals above Westerns, and of Asiatics above Europeans, in medical diagnosis. The Empirical school, which arose in the 3d century B.C., under the guidance of Acron of Agrigentum, Serapion of Alexandria, and Philinus of Cos, waited for the symptoms of every case, disregarding the rules of practice based on dogmatic principles. Among its votaries was a Zachalias (perhaps Zacharias, and possibly a Jew) of Babylon, who (Pliny, N. H. xxxvii, 10; comp. xxxvi, 10) dedicated a book on medicine to Mithridates the Great; its views were also supported by Herodotus of Tarsus, a place which, next to Alexandria, became distinguished for its schools of philosophy and medicine; as also by a Jew named Theudas, or Theudas, of Laodicea (see Wunderbar, *Biblisch-Talmudische Medicin,* i, 25), but a student of Alexandria, and the last, or nearly so, of the empiricists whom its schools produced. The remarks of Theudas on the right method of observing, and the value of experience, and his book on medicine, now lost, in which he arranged his subject under the heads of *indicatoria, curatoria,* and *salubris,* earned him high reputation as a champion of empiricism against the reproaches of the dogmatists, though they were subsequently impugned by Galen and Theodosius of Tripoli. His period was that from Titus to Hadrian. "The empiricists held that observation and the application of known remedies in one case to others presumed to be similar constitute the whole art of cultivating medicine. Though their views were narrow, and their information scanty when compared with some of the chiefs of the other sects, and although they rejected as useless and unattainable all knowledge of the causes and recondite nature of diseases, it is undeniable that, besides personal experience, they freely availed themselves of historical detail, and of a strict analogy founded upon observation and the resemblance of phenomena" (Dr. Adams, *Paul. Ægin.* ed. Sydenham Soc.).

This school, however, was opposed by another, known as the Methodic, which had arisen under the leading of Themison, also of Laodicea, about the period of Pompey the Great. Asclepiades paved the way for the "method" in question, finding a theoretic basis in the corpuscular or atomic theory of physics which he borrowed from Heraclides of Pontus. He had passed some early years in Alexandria, and thence came to Rome shortly before Cicero's time ("Quo nos medico amicoque usi sumus," Cicero, *de Orat.* i, 14). He was a transitional link between the Dogmatic and Empiric schools and this later, or Methodic (Sprengel, *ut sup.* pt. v, 16), that sought to rescue medicine from the bewildering mass of particulars into which empiricism had plunged it. He reduced diseases to two classes, chronic and acute, and endeavored likewise to simplify remedies. In the meanwhile, the most judicious of medical theorists since Hippocrates, Celsus, of the Augustan period, had reviewed medicine in the light which all these schools afforded, and, not professing any distinct teaching, but borrowing from all, may be viewed as eclectic. He translated Hippocrates largely *verbatim,* quoting in a less degree Asclepiades and others. Antonius Musa, whose " cold-water cure," after its successful trial on Augustus himself, became generally popular, seems to have had little of scientific basis, but by the usual method, or the usual accidents, became merely the fashionable practitioner of his day in Rome. Attalia, near Tarsus, furnished also, shortly after the period of Celsus, Athenæus, the leader of the last of the schools of medicine which divided the ancient world, under the name of the "Pneumatic," holding the tenet "of an etherial principle ($\pi\nu\epsilon\tilde{\nu}\mu\alpha$) residing in the microcosm, by means of which the mind performed the functions of the body." This is also traceable in Hippocrates, and was an established opinion of the Stoics. It was exemplified in the innate heat, $\theta\epsilon\rho\mu\dot{\eta}\ \check{\epsilon}\mu\phi\nu\tau\sigma\varsigma$ (Aret. *de Caus. et Sign. Morb.Chron.* ii, 13), and the *calidum innatum* of modern physiologists, especially in the 17th century (Dr. Adams, *Pref. Aretæus,* ed. Sydenh. Soc.).

4. *Effect of these Systems.*—It is clear that all these schools may easily have contributed to form the medical opinions current at the period of the N.T.; that the two earlier among them may have influenced rabbinical teaching on that subject at a much earlier period; and that, especially at the time of Alexander's visit to Jerusalem, the Jewish people, whom he favored and protected, had an opportunity of largely gathering from the medical lore of the West. It was necessary, therefore, to pass in brief review the growth of the latter, and especially to note the points at which it intersects the medical progress of the Jews. Greek Asiatic medicine culminated in Galen, who was, however, still but a commentator on his Western predecessors, and who stands literally without rival, successor, or disciple of note, till the period when Greek learning was reawakened by the Arabian intellect. The Arabs, however, continued to build wholly upon Hippocrates and Galen, save in so far as their advance in chemical science improved their pharmacopœia: this may be seen on reference to the works of Rhazes, A.D. 930, and Haly Abbas, A.D. 980. The first mention of small-pox is ascribed to Rhazes, who, however, quotes several earlier writers on the subject. Mohammed himself is said to have been versed in medicine, and to have compiled some aphorisms upon it; and a herbalist literature was always extensively followed in the East from the days of Solomon downwards (Freind's *History of Medicine,* ii, 5, 27). Galen himself belongs to the period of the Antonines, but he appears to have been acquainted with the writings of Moses, and to have travelled in quest of medical experience over Egypt, Syria, and Palestine, as well as Greece, and a large part of the West, and, in particular, to have visited the banks of the Jordan in quest of opobalsamum, and the coasts of the Dead Sea to obtain samples of bitumen. He also mentions Palestine as producing a watery wine, suitable for the drink of febrile patients.

II. *Historical Notices.*—Having thus described the external influences which, if any, were probably most potent in forming the medical practice of the Hebrews, we may trace next its internal growth. The cabalistic legends mix up the names of Shem and Heber in their fables about healing, and ascribe to those patriarchs a knowledge of simples and rare roots, with, of course, magic spells and occult powers, such as have clouded the history of medicine from the earliest times down to the 17th century.

1. *In the Old Testament.*—So to Abraham is ascribed a talisman, the touch of which healed all disease. We know that such simple surgical skill as the operation for circumcision implies was Abraham's; but severer operations than this are constantly required in the flock and herd, and those who watch carefully the habits of animals can hardly fail to amass some guiding principles applicable to man and beast alike. Beyond this, there was probably nothing but such ordinary obstetrical craft as has always been traditional among the women of rude tribes, that could be classed as medical lore in the family of the patriarch, until his sojourn brought him among the more cultivated Philistines and Egyptians. The only notices which Scripture affords in connection with the subject are the cases of difficult midwifery in the successive households of Isaac, Jacob, and Judah (Gen. xxv, 26; xxxv, 17; xxxviii, 27), and so, later, in that of Phinehas (1 Sam. iv, 19). Doubts have been raised as to the possibility of twins being born, one holding the other's heel; but there does not seem to be any such limit to the operations of nature as an objection on that score would imply. After all, it was perhaps only just such a relative position of the limbs of the infants at the mere moment of birth as would suggest the "holding by the heel." The midwives, it seems, in case of twins, were called upon to distinguish the first-born, to whom important privileges appertained. The tying on of a thread or ribbon was an easy way of preventing mistake, and the assistant in the case of Tamar seized the earliest possible moment for doing it. "When the hand or foot of a living child protrudes, it is to be pushed up . . . and the head made to present" (*Paul. Ægin.* ed Sydenh. Soc. i, 648, Hippocr. quoted by Dr. Adams). This probably the midwife did, at the same time marking him as first-born in virtue of being thus "presented" first. The precise meaning of the doubtful expression in Gen. xxxviii, 27 and marg. is discussed by Wunderbar, *ut sup.* p. 50, in reference both to the children and to the mother. Of Rachel a Jewish commentator says, "Multis etiam ex itinere difficultatibus prægressis, viribusque post diu protractos dolores exhaustis, atonia uteri, forsan quidem hæmorrhagia in pariendo mortua est" (*ibid.*). The traditional value ascribed to the mandrake, in regard to generative functions, relates to the same branch of natural medicine; but throughout this period there occurs no trace of any attempt to study, digest, and systematize the subject.

But, as Israel grew and multiplied in Egypt, they doubtless derived a large mental cultivation from their position until cruel policy turned it into bondage; even then Moses was rescued from the lot of his brethren, and became learned in all the wisdom of the Egyptians, including, of course, medicine and cognate sciences (Clem. Alex. i, p. 413), and those attainments, perhaps, became suggestive of future laws. Some practical skill in metallurgy is evident from Exod. xxxii, 20. But, if we admit Egyptian learning as an ingredient, we should also notice how far exalted above it is the standard of the whole Jewish legislative fabric, in its exemption from the blemishes of sorcery and juggling pretences. The priest, who had to pronounce on the cure, used no means to advance it, and the whole regulations prescribed exclude the notion of trafficking in popular superstition. We have no occult practices reserved in the hands of the sacred caste. It is God alone who doeth great things, working by the wand of Moses, or the brazen serpent; but the very mention of such instruments is such as to expel all pretence of mysterious virtues in the things themselves. Hence various allusions to God's "healing mercy," and the title "Jehovah that healeth" (Exod. xv, 26; Jer. xvii, 14; xxx, 17; Psa. ciii, 3; cxlvii, 3; Isa. xxx, 26). Nor was the practice of physic a privilege of the Jewish priesthood. Any one might practice it, and this publicity must have kept it pure. Nay, there was no scriptural bar to its practice by resident aliens. We read of "physicians," "healing," etc., in Exod. xxi, 19; 2 Kings viii, 29; 2 Chron. xvi, 12; Jer. viii, 22. At the same time the greater leisure of the Levites and their other advantages would make them the students of the nation, as a rule, in all science, and their constant residence in cities would give them the opportunity, if carried out in fact, of a far wider field of observation.

The reign of peace in Solomon's days must have opened, especially with renewed Egyptian intercourse, new facilities for the study. He himself seems to have included in his favorite natural history some knowledge of the medicinal uses of the creatures. His works show him conversant with the notion of remedial treatment (Prov. iii, 8; vi, 15; xii, 18; xvii, 22; xx, 30; xxix, 1; Eccles. iii, 3); and one passage (Eccles. xii, 3, 4) indicates considerable knowledge of anatomy. His repute in magic is the universal theme of Eastern story. It has even been thought he had recourse to the shrine of Æsculapius at Sidon, and enriched his resources by its records or relics; but there is some doubt whether this temple was of such high antiquity. Solomon, however, we cannot doubt, would have turned to the account, not only of wealth but of knowledge, his peaceful reign, wide dominion, and wider renown, and would have sought to traffic in learning, as well as in wheat and gold. To him the Talmudists ascribe a "volume of cures" (ספר רפואות), of which they make frequent mention (Fabricius, Cod. Pseudep. V. T. p. 1043). Josephus (Ant. viii, 2) mentions his knowledge of medicine, and the use of spells by him to expel dæmons who cause sicknesses, "which is continued among us," he adds, "to this time." The dealings of various prophets with quasi-medical agency cannot be regarded as other than the mere accidental form which their miraculous gifts took (1 Kings xiii, 6; xiv, 12; xvii, 17; 2 Kings i, 4; xx, 7; Isa. xxxviii, 21). Jewish tradition has invested Elisha, it would seem, with a function more largely medicinal than that of the other servants of God; but the scriptural evidence on the point is scanty, save that he appears to have known at once the proper means to apply to heal the waters, and temper the noxious pottage (2 Kings ii, 21; iv, 39-41). His healing the Shunammite's son has been discussed as a case of suspended animation, and of animal magnetism applied to resuscitate it; but the narrative clearly implies that the death was real. As regards the leprosy, had the Jordan commonly possessed the healing power which Naaman's faith and obedience found in it, would there have been "many lepers in Israel in the days of Eliseus the prophet," or in any other days? Further, if our Lord's words (Luke iv, 27) are to be taken literally, Elisha's reputation could not have been founded on any succession of lepers healed. The washing was a part of the enjoined lustration of the leper after his cure was complete; Naaman was to act as though clean, like the "ten men that were lepers," bidden to "go and show themselves to the priest" —in either case it was "as thou hast believed, so be it done unto thee." The sickness of Benhadad is certainly so described as to imply treachery on the part of Hazael (2 Kings viii, 15). Yet the observation of Bruce, upon a "cold-water cure" practiced among the people near the Red Sea, has suggested a view somewhat different. The bed-clothes are soaked with cold water, and kept thoroughly wet, and the patient drinks cold water freely. But the crisis, it seems, occurs on the third day, and not till the fifth is it there usual to apply this treatment. If the chamberlain, through carelessness, ignorance, or treachery, precipitated the application, a fatal issue may have suddenly resulted. The "brazen serpent," once the means of healing, and worshipped idolatrously in Hezekiah's reign, is supposed to have acquired those honors under its Æsculapian aspect. This notion is not inconsistent with the Scripture narrative, though not therein traceable. It is supposed that something in the "volume of cures," current under the authority of Solo-

mon, may have conduced to the establishment of these rites, and drawn away the popular homage, especially in prayers during sickness, or thanksgivings after recovery, from Jehovah. The statement that king Asa (2 Chron. xvi, 12) "sought not to Jehovah but to the physicians," may seem to countenance the notion that a rivalry of actual worship, based on some medical fancies, had been set up, and would so far support the Talmudical tradition.

The captivity of Babylon brought the Jews into contact with a new sphere of thought. Their chief men rose to the highest honors, and an improved mental culture among a large section of the captives was no doubt the result which they imported on their return. Wunderbar regards the Babylonian captivity as parallel in its effects to the Egyptian bondage, and seems to think that the people would return debased from its influence. On the contrary, those whom subjection had made ignoble and unpatriotic would remain. If any returned, it was a pledge that they were not so impaired; and, if not impaired, they would certainly be improved by the discipline they had undergone. He also thinks that sorcery had the largest share in any Babylonian or Persian system of medicine. This is assuming too much: there were magicians in Egypt, but physicians also (see above) of high cultivation. Human nature has so great an interest in human life that only in the savage, rudimentary societies is its economy left thus involved in phantasms. The earliest steps of civilization include something of medicine. Of course superstitions are found copiously involved in such medical tenets, but this is not equivalent to abandoning the study to a class of professed magicians. Thus in the Ueberreste der altbabylonischen Literatur, p. 123, by D. Chwolson, St. Petersb. 1859 (the value of which is not, however, yet ascertained), a writer on poisons claims to have a magic antidote, but declines stating what it is, as it is not his business to mention such things, and he only does so in cases where the charm is in connection with medical treatment and resembles it; the magicians, adds the same writer on another occasion, use a particular means of cure, but he declines to impart it, having a repugnance to witchcraft. So (p. 125-6) we find traces of charms introduced into Babylonian treatises on medical science, but apologetically, and as if against sounder knowledge. Similarly, the opinion of fatalism is not without its influence on medicine; but it is chiefly resorted to where, as often happens in pestilence, all known aid seems useless. We know, however, too little of the precise state of medicine in Babylon, Susa, and the "cities of the Medes," to determine the direction in which the impulse so derived would have led the exiles; but the confluence of streams of thought from opposite sources, which impregnate each other, would surely produce a tendency to sift established practice and accepted axioms, to set up a new standard by which to try the current rules of art, and to determine new lines of inquiry for any eager spirits disposed to search for truth. Thus the visit of Democedes to the court of Darius, though it seems to be an isolated fact, points to a general opening of Oriental manners to Greek influence, which was not too late to leave its traces in some perhaps of the contemporaries of Ezra. That great reformer, with the leaders of national thought gathered about him, could not fail to recognise medicine among the salutary measures which distinguished his epoch. Whatever advantages the Levites had possessed in earlier days were now speedily lost even as regards the study of the divine law, and much more therefore as regards that of medicine; into which competitors would crowd in proportion to its broader and more obvious human interest, and effectually demolish any narrowing barriers of established privilege, if such previously existed.

2. In the Interval between the Old and the New Testament.—It may be observed that the priests in their ministrations, who performed at all seasons of the year barefoot on stone pavement, and without perhaps any vari-

ation of dress to meet that of temperature, were peculiarly liable to sickness (Kall, *De Morbis Sacerdotum*, Hafn. 1745). Hence the permanent appointment of a Temple physician has been supposed by some, and a certain Ben-Ahijah is mentioned by Wunderbar as occurring in the Talmud in that capacity. But it rather appears as if such an officer's appointment were precarious, and varied with the demands of the ministrants.

The book of Ecclesiasticus shows the increased regard given to the distinct study of medicine by the repeated mention of physicians, etc., which it contains, and which, as probably belonging to the period of the Ptolemies, it might be expected to show. The wisdom of prevention is recognised in Ecclus. xviii, 19; perhaps also in x, 10. Rank and honor are said to be the portion of the physician, and his office to be from the Lord (xxxviii, 1, 3, 12). The repeated allusions to sickness in vii, 35; xxx, 17; xxxi, 22; xxxvii, 30; xxxviii, 9, coupled with the former recognition of merit, have caused some to suppose that this author was himself a physician. If he was so, the power of mind and wide range of observation shown in his work would give a favorable impression of the standard of practitioners; if he was not, the great general popularity of the study and practice may be inferred from its thus becoming a common topic of general advice offered by a non-professional writer. In Wisd. xvi, 12, plaister is spoken of; anointing, as a means of healing, in Tob. vi, 8.

3. *In the New Testament.*—Luke, "the beloved physician," who practiced at Antioch while the body was his care, could hardly have failed to be conversant with all the leading opinions current down to his own time. Situated between the great schools of Alexandria and Cilicia, within easy sea-transit of both, as well as of the Western homes of science, Antioch enjoyed a more central position than any great city of the ancient world, and in it accordingly all the streams of contemporary medical learning may have probably found a point of confluence. The medicine of the New Test. is not solely, nor even chiefly, Jewish medicine; and even if it were, it is clear that the more mankind became mixed by intercourse, the more medical opinion and practice must have ceased to be exclusive. The great number of Jews resident in Rome and Greece about the Christian æra, and the successive decrees by which their banishment from the former was proclaimed, must have imported, even into Palestine, whatever from the West was best worth knowing; and we may be as sure that its medicine and surgery expanded under these influences as that, in the writings of the Talmudists, such obligations would be unacknowledged. But, beyond this, the growth of large mercantile communities, such as existed in Rome, Alexandria, Antioch, and Ephesus, of itself involves a peculiar sanitary condition from the mass of human elements gathered to a focus under new or abnormal circumstances. Nor are the words in which an eloquent modern writer describes the course of this action less applicable to the case of an ancient than to that of a modern metropolis. "Diseases once indigenous to a section of humanity, are slowly but surely creeping up to commercial centres, whence they will be rapidly propagated. One form of Asiatic leprosy is approaching the Levant from Arabia. The history of every disease which is communicated from man to man establishes this melancholy truth, that ultimately such maladies overleap all obstacles of climate, and demonstrate a solidarity in evil as well as in good among the brotherhood of nations" (Dr. Ferguson, *Pref. Essay to Gooch on Diseases of Women*, New Sydenham Society, London, 1859, p. xlvi). In proportion as this "melancholy truth" is perceived would an intercommunication of medical science prevail also.

4. *In Contemporary Heathen Writers.*—The medicine and surgery referred to in the New Test., then, was probably not inferior to that commonly in demand among educated Asiatic Greeks, and must have been, as regards its basis, Greek medicine, and not Jewish. Hence a

standard Gentile medical writer, if any is to be found of that period, would best represent the profession to which the evangelist belonged. Without absolute certainty as to date, we seem to have such a writer in Aretæus, commonly called "the Cappadocian," who wrote certainly after Nero's reign began, and probably flourished shortly before and after the decade in which Paul reached Rome and Jerusalem fell. If he were of Luke's age, it is striking that he should also be perhaps the only ancient medical authority in favor of dæmoniacal possession as a possible account of epilepsy. If his country be rightly indicated by his surname, we know that it gave him the means of intercourse with both the Jews and the Christians of the apostolic period (Acts ii, 9; 1 Pet. i, 1). It is very likely that Tarsus, the nearest place of academic repute to that region, was the scene of, at any rate, the earlier studies of Aretæus, nor would any chronological difficulty prevent his having been a pupil in medicine there when Paul and also, perhaps, Barnabas were, as is probable, pursuing their early studies in other subjects at the same spot. Aretæus, then, assuming the date above indicated, may be taken as expounding the medical practice of the Asiatic Greeks in the latter half of the first century. There is, however, much of strongly-marked individuality in his work, more especially in the minute verbal portraiture of disease. That of pulmonary consumption in particular, is traced with the careful description of an eye-witness, and represents with a curious exactness the curved nails, shrunken fingers, slender, sharpened nostrils, hollow, glazy eye, cadaverous look and hue, the waste of muscle and startling prominence of bones, the scapula standing off like the wing of a bird; as also the habit of body marking predisposition to the malady, the thin, veneer-like frames, the limbs like pinions, the prominent throat and shallow chest, with a remark that moist and cold climates are the haunts of it (Aret. περὶ φθίσεως). His work exhibits strong traits here and there of the Pneumatic school, as in his statement regarding lethargy, that it is frigidity implanted by nature; concerning elephantiasis even more emphatically, that it is a refrigeration of the innate heat, "or, rather, a congelation—as it were one great winter of the system." The same views betray themselves in his statement regarding the blood, that it is the warming principle of all the parts; that diabetes is a sort of dropsy, both exhibiting the watery principle; and that the effect of white hellebore is as that of fire: "so that whatever fire does by burning, hellebore effects still more by penetrating inwardly." The last remark shows that he gave some scope to his imagination, which indeed we might illustrate from some of his pathological descriptions; e. g. that of elephantiasis, where the resemblance of the beast to the afflicted human being is wrought to a fanciful parallel. Allowing for such overstrained touches here and there, we may say that he generally avoids extravagant crotchets, and rests chiefly on wide observation, and on the common-sense which sobers theory and rationalizes facts. He hardly ever quotes an authority; and though much of what he states was taught before, it is dealt with as the common property of science, or as become *sui juris* through being proved by his own experience. The freedom with which he follows or rejects earlier opinions has occasioned him to be classed by some among the Eclectic school. His work is divided into—I, the causes and signs of (1) acute and (2) chronic diseases; and, II, the curative treatment of (1) acute and (2) chronic diseases. His boldness of treatment is exemplified in his selection of the vein to be opened in a wide range of parts—the arm, ankle, tongue, nose, etc. He first has a distinct mention of leeches, which Themison is said to have introduced; and in this respect his surgical resources appear to be in advance of Celsus. He was familiar with the operation for the stone in the bladder, and prescribes, as Celsus also does, the use of the catheter, where its insertion is not prevented by inflammation, then the incision into the neck of the bladder, nearly as in modern lithotomy. His views of the internal economy were a strange mixture of truth and error, and the disuse of anatomy was no doubt the reason why this was the weak point of his teaching. He held that the work of producing the blood pertained to the liver, "which is the root of the veins;" that the bile was distributed from the gall-bladder to the intestines; and, if this vesica became gorged, the bile was thrown back into the veins, and by them diffused over the system. He regarded the nerves as the source of sensation and motion; and had some notion of them as branching in pairs from the spine. Thus he has a curious statement as regards paralysis, that in the case of any sensational point *below* the head, e. g. from the membrane of the spinal marrow being affected injuriously, the parts on the right side will be paralyzed if the nerve towards the right side be hurt, and similarly, conversely, of the left side; but that if the head itself be so affected, the inverse law of consequence holds concerning the parts related, since each nerve passes over to the other side from that of its origin, decussating each other in the form of the letter X. The doctrine of the Pneuma, or ethereal principle existing in the microcosm by which the mind performs all the functions of the body, holds a more prominent position in the works of Aretæus than in those of any of the other authorities (Dr. Adams's *Preface to Aret.* p. x, xi). He was aware that the nervous function of sensation was distinct from the motive power; that either might cease and the other continue. His pharmacopœia is copious and reasonable, and the limits of the usefulness of this or that drug are laid down judiciously. He makes large use of wine, and prescribing the kind and the number of *cyathi* to be taken; and some words of his on stomach disorders ($\pi\epsilon\rho i \ \kappa\alpha\rho\delta\iota\alpha\lambda\gamma i\eta\varsigma$) forcibly recall those of Paul to Timothy (1 Tim. v, 23), and one might almost suppose them to have been suggested by the intenser spirituality of his Jewish or Christian patients. "Such disorders," he says, "are common to those who toil in teaching, whose yearning is after divine instruction, who despise delicate and varied diet, whose nourishment is fasting, and whose drink is water." As a purge of melancholy, he prescribes "a little wine, and some other more liberal sustenance." In his essay on *causus*, or "brain" fever, he describes the powers acquired by the soul before dissolution in the following remarkable words: "Every sense is pure, the intellect acute, the gnostic powers prophetic; for they prognosticate to themselves in the first place their own departure from life; then they foretell what will afterwards take place to those present, who fancy sometimes that they are delirious: but these persons wonder at the result of what has been said. Others also talk to certain of the dead, perchance they alone perceiving them to be present, in virtue of their acute and pure sense, or perchance from their soul seeing beforehand, and announcing the men with whom they are about to associate. For formerly they were immersed in humors, as if in mud and darkness; but when the disease has drained these off, and taken away the mist from their eyes, they perceive those things which are in the air, and, through the soul being unencumbered, become true prophets." To those who wish further to pursue the study of medicine at this æra, the edition of Aretæus by the Sydenham Society, and in a less degree that by Boerhaave (Lugd. Bat. 1735), to which the references have here been made, may be recommended.

As the general science of medicine and surgery of this period may be represented by Aretæus, so we have nearly a representation of its *Materia Medica* by Dioscorides. He too was of the same general region—a Cilician Greek—and his first lessons were probably learnt at Tarsus. His period is tinged by the same uncertainty as that of Aretæus; but he has usually been assigned to the end of the first or beginning of the second century (see Smith, *Dict. of Class. Biog.* s. v.). He was the first author of high mark who devoted his attention

to *Materia Medica*. Indeed, this branch of ancient science remained as he left it till the times of the Arabians; and these, though they enlarged the supply of drugs and pharmacy, yet copy and repeat Dioscorides, as, indeed, Galen himself often does, on all common subject-matter. Above 90 minerals, 700 plants, and 168 animal substances are said to be described in the researches of Dioscorides, displaying an industry and skill which has remained the marvel of all subsequent commentators. Pliny, copious, rare, and curious as he is, yet, for want of scientific medical knowledge, is little esteemed in this particular branch, save when he follows Dioscorides. The third volume of *Paulus Ægin.* (ed. Sydenham Soc.) contains a catalogue of medicines simple and compound, and the large proportion in which the authority of Dioscorides has contributed to form it will be manifest at the most cursory inspection. To abridge such a subject is impossible, and to transcribe it in the most meagre form would be far beyond the limits of this article.

III. *Pathology in the Bible.*—Before proceeding to the examination of diseases in detail, it may be well to observe that the question of identity between any ancient malady known by description and any modern one known by experience is often doubtful. Some diseases, just as some plants and some animals, will exist almost anywhere; others can only be produced within narrow limits depending on the conditions of climate, habit, etc.—and were only equal observation applied to the two, the *habitat* of a disease might be mapped as accurately as that of a plant. It is also possible that some diseases once extremely prevalent may run their course and die out, or occur only casually; just as it seems certain that, since the Middle Ages, some maladies have been introduced into Europe which were previously unknown. See *Biblioth. Script. Med.* (Geneva, 1731), s. v.; Hippocrates, Celsus, Galen; Leclerc's *History of Medicine* (Paris, 1723; transl. London, 179( ); Freind's *History of Medicine.*

1. *General Maladies.*—Eruptive diseases of the acute kind are more prevalent in the East than in colder climes. They also run their course more rapidly; e. g. common itch, which in Scotland remains for a longer time vesicular, becomes, in Syria, pustular as early sometimes as the third day. The origin of it is now supposed to be an acarus, but the parasite perishes when removed from the skin. Disease of various kinds is commonly regarded as a divine infliction, or denounced as a penalty for transgression; "the evil diseases of Egypt" (perhaps in reference to some of the ten plagues) are especially so characterized (Gen. xx, 18; Exod. xv, 26; Lev. xxvi, 16; Deut. vii, 15; xxviii, 60; 1 Cor. xi, 30); so the emerods [see HÆMORRHOIDS] of the Philistines (1 Sam. v, 6); the severe dysentery (2 Chron. xxi, 15, 19) of Jehoram, which was also epidemic [see BLOOD, ISSUE OF; and FEVER], the peculiar symptom of which may perhaps have been *prolapsus ani* (Dr. Mason Good, i, 311–13, mentions a case of the entire colon exposed); or, perhaps, what is known as *diarrhœa tubularis*, formed by the coagulation of fibrine into a membrane discharged from the inner coat of the intestines, which takes the mould of the bowel, and is thus expelled; so the sudden deaths of Er, Onan (Gen. xxxviii, 7, 10), the Egyptian first-born (Exod. xi, 4, 5), Nabal, Bathsheba's son, and Jeroboam's (1 Sam. xxv, 38; 2 Sam. xii, 15; 1 Kings xiv, 1, 5), are ascribed to the action of Jehovah immediately, or through a prophet. Pestilence (Hab. iii, 5) attends his path (comp. 2 Sam. xxiv, 15), and is innoxious to those whom he shelters (Psa. xci, 3–10). It is by Jeremiah, Ezekiel, and Amos associated (as historically in 2 Sam. xxiv, 13) with "the sword" and "famine" (Jer. xiv, 12; xv, 2; xxi, 7, 9; xxiv, 10; xxvii, 8, 13; xxviii, 8; xxix, 17, 18; xxxii, 24, 36; xxxiv, 17; xxxviii, 2; xlii, 17, 22; xliv, 13; Ezek. v, 12, 17; vi, 11, 12; vii, 15; xii, 16; xiv, 21; xxxiii, 27; Amos iv, 6, 10). The sicknesses of the widow's son of Zarephath, of Ahaziah, Benhadad, the leprosy of Uzziah, the boil

of Hezekiah, are also noticed as diseases sent by Jehovah, or in which he interposed (1 Kings xvii, 17, 20; 2 Kings i, 3; xx, 1). In 2 Sam. iii, 29, disease is invoked as a curse, and in Solomon's prayer (1 Kings viii, 37; comp. 2 Chron. xx, 9) anticipated as a chastisement. Job and his friends agree in ascribing his disease to divine infliction; but the latter urge his sins as the cause. So, conversely, the healing character of God is invoked or promised (Psa. vi, 2; xli, 3; ciii, 3; Jer. xxx. 17). Satanic agency appears also as procuring disease (Job ii, 7; Luke xiii, 11, 16). Diseases are also mentioned as ordinary calamities; e. g. the sickness of old age, headache (perhaps by sunstroke), as that of the Shunammite's son, that of Elisha, and that of Benhadad, and that of Joram (Gen. xlviii, 1; 1 Sam. xxx. 13; 2 Kings iv, 20; viii, 7, 29; xiii, 14; 2 Chron. xxii, 6).

2. Among *special* diseases mentioned in the Old Test. are, ophthalmia (Gen. xxix, 17, מְבַלּוֹת עֵנַיִם), which is perhaps more common in Syria and Egypt than anywhere else in the world, especially in the fig season, the juice of the newly-ripe fruit having the power of giving it. It may occasion partial or total blindness (2 Kings vi, 18). The eye-salve (κολλύριον, Rev. iii, 18; Hor. *Sat.* i) was a remedy common to Orientals, Greeks, and Romans (see Hippocr. κολλούριον; Celsus, vi, 8, *De oculorum morbis*, [2] *De diversis collyriis*). Other diseases are—barrenness of women, which mandrakes were supposed to have the power of correcting (Gen. xx, 18; comp. xii, 17; xxx, 1, 2, 14-16); "consumption," and several, the names of which are derived from various words, signifying to burn or to be hot (Lev. xxvi, 16; Deut. xxviii, 22) [see FEVER]; compare the kinds of fever distinguished by Hippocrates as καῦσος and πῦρ. The "burning boil," or "of a boil" (Lev. xiii, 23, צָרֶבֶת הַשְּׁחִין, Sept. οὐλή τοῦ ἕλκους), is again merely marked by the notion of an effect resembling that of fire, like the Greek φλεγμονή, or our "carbuncle;" it may possibly find an equivalent in the Damascus boil of the present time. The "botch (שְׁחִין) of Egypt" (Deut. xxviii, 27) is so vague a term as to yield a most uncertain sense; the plague, as known by its attendant *bubo*, has been suggested by Scheuchzer. It is possible that the *Elephantiasis Græcorum* may be intended by שְׁחִין, understood in the widest sense of a continued ulceration until the whole body, or the portion affected, may be regarded as one שְׁחִין. Of this disease some further notice will be taken below; at present it is observable that the same word is used to express the "boil" of Hezekiah. This was certainly a single locally-confined eruption, and was probably a carbuncle, one of which may well be fatal, though a single "boil" in our sense of the word seldom is so. Dr. Mead supposes it to have been a fever terminating in an abscess. The diseases rendered "scab" and "scurvy" in Lev. xxi, 20; xxii, 22; Deut. xxviii, 27, may be almost any skin-disease, such as those known under the names of lepra, psoriaris, pityriasis, icthyosis, favus, or common itch. Some of these may be said to approach the type of leprosy as laid down in Scripture, although they do not appear to have involved ceremonial defilement, but only a blemish disqualifying for the priestly office. The quality of being incurable is added as a special curse, for these diseases are not generally so, or at any rate are common in milder forms. The "running of the reins" (Lev. xv, 2, 3; xxii, 4, marg.) may perhaps mean *gonorrhœa*, or more probably *blennorrhœa* (mucous discharge). If we compare Numb. xxv, 1, xxxi, 7, with Josh. xxii, 17, there is ground for thinking that some disease of this class, derived from polluting sexual intercourse, remained among the people. The existence of *gonorrhœa* in early times —save in the mild form—has been much disputed. Michel Lévy (*Traité d'Hygiène*, p. 7) considers the affirmative as established by the above passage, and says of syphilis, "Que pour notre part, nous n'avons jamais pu considérer comme une nouveauté du xvᵉ siecle." He

certainly gives some strong historical evidence against the view that it was introduced into France by Spanish troops under Gonzalvo de Cordova on their return from the New World, and so into the rest of Europe, where it was known as the *morbus Gallicus*. He adds, "La syphilis est perdue confusément dans la pathologie ancienne par la diversité de ses symptômes et de ses altérations; leur interprétation collective, et leur redaction en une seule unité morbide, a fait croire à l'introduction d'une maladie nouvelle." See also Freind's *History of Med.*, Dr. Mead, Michaelis, Reinhart (*Bibelkrankheiten*), Schmidt (*Biblisch. Med.*), and others. Wunderbar (*Bib.-Talm. Med.* iii, 20, commenting on Lev. xv, and comparing Mishna, *Zabim*, ii, 2, and Maimonides, ad loc.) thinks that *gonorrhœa benigna* was in the mind of the latter writers. Dr. Adams, the editor of *Paul. Ægin.* (Sydenh. Soc. ii, 14), considers syphilis a modified form of elephantiasis. For all ancient notices of the cognate diseases, see that work, i, 593 sq. The "issue" of xv, 19, may be the *menorrhagia*, the duration of which in the East is sometimes, when not checked by remedies, for an indefinite period (Matt. ix, 20), or uterine hemorrhage from other causes.

In Deut. xxviii, 35 is mentioned a disease attacking the "knees and legs," consisting in a "sore botch which cannot be healed," but extended, in the sequel of the verse, from the "sole of the foot to the top of the head." The latter part of the quotation would certainly accord with *Elephantiasis Græcorum;* but this, if the whole verse be a mere continuation of one described malady, would be in contradiction to the fact that this disease commences in the face, not in the lower members. On the other hand, a disease which affects the knees and legs, or more commonly one of them only—its principal feature being intumescence, distorting and altering all the proportions—is by a mere accident of language known as *Elephantiasis Arabum, Bucnemia Tropica* (Rayer, iii, 820–841), or "Barbadoes leg," from being well known in that island. Supposing, however, that the affection of the knees and legs is something distinct, and that the latter part of the description applies to the *Elephantiasis Græcorum*, the incurable and all-pervading character of the malady are well expressed by it. This disease is what now passes under the name of "leprosy" (Michaelis, iii, 259)—the lepers, e. g. of the huts near the Zion gate of modern Jerusalem are elephantiacs. It has been asserted that there are two kinds, one painful, the other painless; but, as regards Syria and the East, this is contradicted. There the parts affected are quite benumbed and lose sensation. It is classed as a tubercular disease, not confined to the skin, but pervading the tissues and destroying the bones. It is not confined to any age or either sex. It first appears in general, but not always, about the face, as an indurated nodule (hence it is improperly called tubercular), which gradually enlarges, inflames, and ulcerates. Sometimes it commences in the neck or arms. The ulcers will heal spontaneously, but only after a long period, and after destroying a great deal of the neighboring parts. If a joint be attacked, the ulceration will go on till its destruction is complete, the joints of finger, toe, etc., dropping off one by one. Frightful dreams and fetid breath are symptoms mentioned by some pathologists. More nodules will develop themselves, and, if the face be the chief seat of the disease, it assumes a leonine aspect (hence called also *Leontiasis*), loathsome and hideous; the skin becomes thick, rugose, and livid; the eyes are fierce and staring, and the hair generally falls off from all the parts affected. When the throat is attacked the voice shares the affection, and sinks to a hoarse, husky whisper. These two symptoms are eminently characteristic. The patient will become bed-ridden, and, though a mass of bodily corruption, seems happy and contented with his sad condition, until, sinking exhausted under the ravages of the disease, he is generally carried off, at least in Syria, by diarrhœa. It is hereditary, and may be inoculated, but does not propagate itself by the closest

contact; e. g. two women in the aforesaid leper-huts remained uncontaminated though their husbands were both affected, and yet the children born to them were, like the fathers, elephantisiac, and became so in early life. On the children of diseased parents a watch for the appearance of the malady is kept; but no one is afraid of infection, and the neighbors mix freely with them, though, like the lepers of the Old Test., they live "in a several house." Many have attributed to these wretched creatures a *libido inexplebilis* (see *Proceedings of Med. and Chirurg. Soc. of London*, Jan. 1860, iii, 164, from which some of the above remarks are taken). This is denied by Dr. Robert Sim (from a close study of the disease in Jerusalem), save in so far as idleness and inactivity, with animal wants supplied, may conduce to it. It became first prevalent in Europe during the crusades, and by their means was diffused, and the ambiguity of designating it leprosy then originated, and has been generally since retained. Pliny (*Nat. Hist.* xxvi, 5) asserts that it was unknown in Italy till the time of Pompey the Great, when it was imported from Egypt, but soon became extinct (*Paul. Ægin.* ed. Sydenh. Soc. ii, 6). It is, however, broadly distinguished from the λέπρα, λεύκη, etc. of the Greeks by name and symptoms, no less than by Roman medical and even popular writers; comp. Lucretius, whose mention of it is the earliest—
"Est elephas morbus, qui propter flumina Nili,
Gignitur Ægypto in mediâ, neque præterea usquam."
It is nearly extinct in Europe, save in Spain and Norway. A case was seen lately in the Crimea, but may have been produced elsewhere. It prevails in Turkey and the Greek Archipelago. One case, however, indigenous in England, is recorded among the medical facsimiles at Guy's Hospital. In Granada it was generally fatal after eight or ten years, whatever the treatment. This favors the correspondence of this disease with one one of those evil diseases of Egypt, possibly its "botch," threatened in Deut. xxviii, 27, 35. This "botch," however, seems more probably to mean the foul ulcer mentioned by Aretæus (*De Sign. et Caus. Morb. Acut.* i, 9), and called by him ἄφθα or ἐσχάρη. He ascribes its frequency in Egypt to the mixed vegetable diet there followed, and to the use of the turbid water of the Nile, but adds that it is common in Cœle-Syria. The Talmud speaks of the elephantiasis (*Baba Kama*, 80 *b*) as being "moist without and dry within" (Wunderbar, *Biblisch-Talmudische Med.* 3tes Heft, 10, 11). Advanced cases are said to have a cancerous aspect, and some even class it as a form of cancer, a disease dependent on faults of nutrition.

It has been asserted that this, which is perhaps the most dreadful disease of the East, was Job's malady. Origen, *Hexapla* on Job ii, 7, mentions that one of the Greek versions gives it, *loc. cit.*, as the affliction which befel him. Wunderbar (*ut sup.* p. 10) supposes it to have been the Tyrian leprosy, resting chiefly on the itching implied, as he supposes, by Job ii, 7, 8. Schmidt (*Biblischer Med.* iv, 4) thinks the "sore boil" may indicate some graver disease, or complication of diseases. But there is no need to go beyond the statement of Scripture, which speaks not only of this "boil," but of "skin loathsome and broken," "covered with worms and clods of dust;" the second symptom is the result of the first, and the "worms" are probably the larvæ of some fly, known so to infest and make its *nidus* in any wound or sore exposed to the air, and to increase rapidly in size. The "clods of dust" would of course follow from his "sitting in ashes." The "breath strange to his wife," if it be not a figurative expression for her estrangement from him, may imply a fetor, which in such a state of body hardly requires explanation. The expression my "bowels boiled" (xxx, 27) may refer to the burning sensation in the stomach and bowels, caused by acrid bile, which is common in ague. Aretæus (*De Cur. Morb. Acut.* ii, 3) has a similar expression, θερμασίη τῶν σπλάγχνων οἷον ἀπὸ πυρός, as attending syncope. The "scaring dreams" and "terrifying visions" are perhaps a mere

symptom of the state of mind bewildered by unaccountable afflictions. The intense emaciation was (xxxiii, 21) perhaps the mere result of protracted sickness.

The disease of king Antiochus (2 Macc. ix, 5–10, etc.) is that of a boil breeding worms (*ulcus verminosum*). So Sulla, Pherecydes, and Alcman, the poet, are mentioned (Plut. *Vita Sullæ*) as similar cases. The examples of both the Herods (Josephus, *Ant.* xvii, 6, 5; *War*, i, 33, 5) may also be adduced, as that of Pheretime (Herod. iv, 205). There is some doubt whether this disease be not allied to phthiriasis, in which lice are bred, and cause ulcers. This condition may originate either in a sore, or in a morbid habit of body brought on by uncleanliness, suppressed perspiration, or neglect; but the vermination, if it did not commence in a sore, would produce one. Dr. Mason Good (iv, 504–6), speaking of μάλις, μαλιασμύς=cutaneous vermination, mentions a case in the Westminster Infirmary, and an opinion that universal phthiriasis was no unfrequent disease among the ancients; he also states (p. 500) that in gangrenous ulcers, especially in warm climates, innumerable grubs or maggots will appear almost every morning. The camel, and other creatures, are known to be the habitat of similar parasites. There are also cases of vermination without any wound or faulty outward state, such as the *Vena Medinensis*, known in Africa as the "Guineaworm," of which Galen had heard only, breeding under the skin, and needing to be drawn out carefully by a needle, lest it break, when great soreness and suppuration succeed (Freind, *Hist. of Med.* i, 49; De Mandelslo's *Travels*, p. 4; and *Paul. Ægin.* t. iv, ed. Sydenh. Soc.). Rayer (iii, 808–819) gives a list of parasites, most of them in the skin. This "Guinea-worm," it appears, is also found in Arabia Petræa, on the coasts of the Caspian and Persian Gulf, on the Ganges, in Upper Egypt and Abyssinia (ib. 814). Dr. Mead refers Herod's disease to ἐντοζῶα, or intestinal worms. Shapter, without due foundation, objects that the word in that case should have been not σκώληξ, but εὐλή (*Medica Sacra*, p. 188).

In Deut. xxviii, 65 it is possible that a palpitation of the heart is intended to be spoken of (comp. Gen. xlv, 26). In Mark ix, 17 (comp. Luke ix, 38) we have an apparent case of epilepsy, shown especially in the foaming, falling, wallowing, and similar violent symptoms mentioned; this might easily be a form of dæmoniacal manifestation. The case of extreme hunger recorded in 1 Sam. xiv was merely the result of exhaustive fatigue; but it is remarkable that the bulimia of which Xenophon speaks (*Anab.* iv, 5, 7), was remedied by an application in which "honey" (comp. 1 Sam. xiv, 27) was the chief ingredient.

Besides the common injuries of wounding, bruising, striking out eye, tooth, etc., we have in Exod. xxi, 22 the case of miscarriage produced by a blow, push, etc., damaging the fœtus.

The plague of "boils and blains" is *not* said to have been fatal to man, as the murrain preceding was to cattle; this alone would seem to contradict the notion of Shapter (*Medica Sacra*, p. 113), that the disorder in question was small-pox, which, wherever it has appeared, until mitigated by vaccination, has been fatal to a great part, perhaps a majority of those seized. The small-pox also generally takes some days to pronounce and mature, which seems opposed to the Mosaic account. The expression of Exod. ix, 10, a "boil" flourishing, or ebullient with blains, may perhaps be a disease analogous to phlegmonous erysipelas, or even common erysipelas, which is often accompanied by vesications such as the word "blains" might fitly describe. This is Dr. Robert Sim's opinion. On comparing, however, the means used to produce the disorder (Exod. ix, 8), an analogy is perceptible to what is called "bricklayer's itch," and therefore to leprosy. A disease involving a white spot breaking forth from a boil related to leprosy, and clean or unclean according to symptoms specified, occurs under the general *locus* of leprosy (Lev. xiii, 18–23).

The "withered hand" of Jeroboam (1 Kings xiii, 4–6),

and of the man (Matt. xii, 10–13; comp. Luke vi, 10), is such an effect as is known to follow from the obliteration of the main artery of any member, or from paralysis of the principal nerve, either through disease or through injury. A case with a symptom exactly parallel to that of Jeroboam is mentioned in the life of Gabriel, an Arab physician. It was that of a woman whose hand had become rigid in the act of swinging, and remained in the extended posture. The most remarkable feature in the case, as related, is the remedy, which consisted in alarm acting on the nerves, inducing a sudden and spontaneous effort to use the limb—an effort which, like that of the dumb son of Crœsus (Herod. i, 85), was paradoxically successful. The case of the widow's son restored by Elisha (2 Kings iv, 19), was probably one of sunstroke. The disease of Asa "in his feet" (Schmidt, *Biblischer Med.* iii, 5, 2), which attacked him in his old age (1 Kings xv, 23; 2 Chron. xvi, 12), and became exceeding great, may have been either *œdema*, dropsy, or *podagra*, gout. The former is common in aged persons, in whom, owing to the difficulty of the return upwards of the sluggish blood, its watery part stays in the feet. The latter, though rare in the East at present, is mentioned by the Talmudists (*Sotah*, 10 *a*, and *Sanhedrin*, 48 *b*), and there is no reason why it may not have been known in Asa's time. It occurs in Hippocr. *Aphor.* vi, *Prognost.* 15; Celsus, iv, 24; Aretæus, *Morb. Chron.* ii, 12, and other ancient writers.

In 1 Macc. vi, 8, occurs a mention of "sickness of grief;" in Ecclus. xxxvii, 30, of sickness caused by excess, which require only a passing mention. The disease of Nebuchadnezzar has been viewed by Jahn as a mental and purely subjective malady. It is not easy to see how this satisfies the plain, emphatic statement of Dan. iv, 33, which seems to include, it is true, mental derangement, but to assert a degraded bodily state to some extent, and a corresponding change of habits. The "eagles' feathers" and "birds' claws" are probably used only in illustration, not necessarily as describing a new type to which the hair, etc., approximated. (Comp. the simile of Psa. ciii, 5, and that of 2 Kings v, 14.) We may regard it as Mead (*Med. Sacr.* vol. vii), following Burton's *Anatomy of Melancholy*, does, as a species of the melancholy known as *Lycanthropia* (Paulus Ægin. iii, 16; Avicenna, iii, 1, 5, 22). Persons so affected wander like wolves in sepulchres by night, and imitate the howling of a wolf or a dog. Further, there are well-attested accounts of wild or half-wild human creatures, of either sex, who have lived as beasts, losing human consciousness, and acquiring a superhuman ferocity, activity, and swiftness. Either the lycanthropic patients or these latter may furnish a partial analogy to Nebuchadnezzar in regard to the various points of modified outward appearance and habits ascribed to him. Nor would it seem impossible that a sustained lycanthropia might produce this latter condition.

Here should be noticed the mental malady of Saul. His melancholy seems to have had its origin in his sin; it was therefore grounded in his moral nature, but extended its effects, as commonly, to the intellectual. The "evil spirit from God," whatever it mean, was no part of the medical features of his case, and may therefore be excluded from the present notice. Music, which soothed him for a while, has entered largely into the milder modern treatment of lunacy.

The palsy meets us in the New Test. only, and in features too familiar to need special remark. The words "grievously tormented" (Matt. viii, 6) have been commented on by Baier (*De Paral.* p. 32), to the effect that examples of acutely painful paralysis are not wanting in modern pathology, e. g. when paralysis is complicated with neuralgia. But if this statement be viewed with doubt, we might understand the Greek expression (βασανιζόμενος) as used of paralysis agitans, or even of chorea (St. Vitus's dance), in both of which the patient, being never still for a moment save when asleep, might well be so described. The woman's case who was "bowed

together" by "a spirit of infirmity" may probably have been paralytic (Luke xiii, 11). If the dorsal muscles were affected, those of the chest and abdomen, from want of resistance, would undergo contraction, and thus cause the patient to suffer as described.

Gangrene (γάγγραινα, Celsus, vii, 33, *de gangrœnâ*), or mortification in its various forms, is a totally different disorder from the "canker" of the A. V. in 2 Tim. ii, 17. Both gangrene and cancer were common in all the countries familiar to the scriptural writers, and neither differs from the modern disease of the same name (Dr. M. Good, ii, 669, etc., and 579, etc.).

In Isa. xxvi, 18; Psa. vii, 14, there seems an allusion to false conception, in which, though attended by pains of quasi-labor and other ordinary symptoms, the womb has been found unimpregnated, and no delivery has followed. The medical term (Dr. M. Good, iv, 188) ἐμπνευμάτωσις, *mòla ventosa*, suggests the scriptural language, "We have, as it were, brought forth wind;" the whole passage is figurative for disappointment after great effort.

Poison, as a means of destroying life, hardly occurs in the Bible, save as applied to arrows (Job vi, 4). In Zech. xii, 2, the marg. gives "poison" as an alternative rendering, which does not seem preferable, intoxication being probably meant. In the annals of the Herods poisons occur as the resource of stealthy murder.

The bite or sting of venomous beasts can hardly be treated as a disease, but in connection with the "fiery (i. e. venomous) serpents" of Numb. xxi, 6, and the deliverance from death of those bitten, it deserves a notice. Even the Talmud acknowledges that the healing power lay not in the brazen serpent itself, but "as soon as they feared the Most High, and uplifted their hearts to their heavenly Father, they were healed, and in default of this were brought to naught." Thus the brazen figure was symbolized only; or, according to the lovers of purely natural explanation, was the stage-trick to cover a false miracle. It was customary to consecrate the image of the affliction, either in its cause or in its effect, as in the golden emerods, golden mice, of 1 Sam. vi, 4, 8, and in the ex-votos common in Egypt even before the exodus; and these may be compared with the setting up of the brazen serpent. Thus we have in it only an instance of the current custom, fanciful or superstitious, being sublimed to a higher purpose. The bite of a white she-mule, perhaps in the rutting season, is, according to the Talmudists, fatal; and they also mention that of a mad dog, with certain symptoms by which to discern his state (Wunderbar, *ut sup.* p. 21). The scorpion and centipede are natives of the Levant (Rev. ix, 5, 10), and, with a large variety of serpents, swarm there. To these, according to Lichtenstein, should be added a venomous solpuga, or large spider, similar to the Calabrian tarantula; but the passage in Pliny adduced (*H. N.* xxix, 29) gives no satisfactory ground for the theory based upon it, that its bite was the cause of the emerods. It is, however, remarkable that Pliny mentions with some fulness a *mus araneus*—not a spider resembling a mouse, but a mouse resembling a spider—the shrewmouse, and called *araneus*, Isidore says from this resemblance, or from its eating spiders. Its bite was venomous, caused mortification of the part, and a spreading ulcer attended with inward griping pains, and when crushed on the wound it was its own best antidote. See DISEASE.

The disease of old age has acquired a place in Biblical nosology chiefly owing to the elegant allegory into which "The Preacher" throws the succeeding tokens of the ravage of time on man (Eccles. xii). The symptoms enumerated have each their significance for the physician; for, though his art can do little to arrest them, they yet mark an altered condition calling for a treatment of its own. "The Preacher" divides the sum of human existence into that period which involves every mode of growth, and that which involves every mode of decline. The first reaches from the point of birth or even of generation, onwards to the attainment of the "grand climacteric," and the second from that epoch backwards through a corresponding period of decline till the point of dissolution is reached. These are respectively called the ימי הצליה and the ימי העמידה of the rabbins (Wunderbar, 2tes Heft). This latter course is marked in metaphor by the darkening of the great lights of nature, and the ensuing season of life is compared to the broken weather of the wet season, setting in when summer is gone, when after every shower fresh clouds are in the sky, as contrasted with the showers of other seasons, which pass away into clearness. Such he means are the ailments and troubles of declining age, as compared with those of advancing life. The "keepers of the house" are perhaps the ribs which support the frame, or the arms and shoulders which enwrap and protect it. Their "trembling," especially that of the arms, etc., is a sure sign of vigor past. The "strong men" are its supporters, the lower limbs "bowing themselves" under the weight they once so lightly bore. The "grinding" hardly needs to be explained of the teeth, now become "few." The "lookers from the windows" are the pupils of the eyes, now "darkened," as Isaac's were, and Eli's; and Moses, though spared the dimness, was yet in that very exemption a marvel (Gen. xxvii; comp. xlviii, 10; 1 Sam. iv, 15; Deut. xxxiv, 7). The "doors shut" represent the dulness of those other senses which are the portals of knowledge; thus the taste and smell, as in the case of Barzillai, became impaired, and the ears stopped against sound. The "rising up at the voice of a bird" portrays the light, soon-fleeting, easily-broken slumber of the aged man; or rather "to the voice of the bird," i. e. the high key, the

—— "big, manly voice
Now turn'd again to childish treble."

The "daughters of music brought low" suggest the cracked voice of age, or, as illustrated again by Barzillai, the failure in the discernment and the utterance of musical notes. The fears of old age are next noticed: "They shall be afraid of *that which is high;*" an obscure expression, perhaps, for what are popularly called "nervous" terrors, exaggerating and magnifying every object of alarm, and "making," as the saying is, "mountains of mole-hills." Or, even more simply, these words may be understood as meaning that old men have neither vigor nor breath for going up hills, mountains, or anything else that is "high;" nay, for them the plain, even the road has its terrors — they walk timidly and cautiously even along that. "Fear in the way" is at first less obvious; but we observe that nothing unnerves and agitates an old person more than the prospect of a long journey. Thus regarded, it becomes a fine and subtile touch in the description of decrepitude. All readiness to haste is arrested, and a numb despondency succeeds. The "flourishing" of the "almond-tree" is still more obscure; but we observe this tree in Palestine blossoming when others show no sign of vegetation, and when it is dead winter all around—no ill type, perhaps, of the old man who has survived his own contemporaries and many of his juniors. Youthful zest dies out, and their strength, of which "the grasshopper" is probably a figure, is relaxed. The "silver cord" has been thought to be that of nervous sensation, or motion, or even the spinal marrow itself. Possibly some incapacity of retention may be signified by the "golden bowl broken;" the "pitcher broken at the well" suggests the vital supply stopping at the usual source—derangement perhaps of the digestion or of the respiration; the "wheel shivered at the cistern" has been imagined to convey, through the image of the water-lifting process familiar in irrigation, the notion of the blood, pumped, as it were, through the vessels, and fertilizing the whole system; for "the blood is the life."

IV. *Hebrew Therapeutics.*—This careful register of the tokens of decline might lead us to expect great care for the preservation of health and strength; and this indeed is found to mark the Mosaic system, in the regulations concerning diet, the "divers washings," and the pollution imputed to a corpse—nay, even in circumcision itself. These served not only the ceremonial purpose of imparting self-consciousness to the Hebrew, and keeping him distinct from alien admixture, but had a sanitary aspect of rare wisdom, when we regard the country, the climate, and the age. The laws of diet had the effect of tempering, by a just admixture of the organic substances of the animal and vegetable kingdoms, the regimen of Hebrew families, and thus providing for the vigor of future ages, as well as checking the stimulus which the predominant use of animal food gives to the passions. To these effects may be ascribed the immunity often enjoyed by the Hebrew race amid epidemics devastating the countries of their sojourn. The best and often the sole possible exercise of medicine is to prevent disease. Moses could not legislate for cure, but his rules did for the great mass of the people what no therapeutics, however consummate, could do—they gave the best security for the public health by provisions incorporated in the public economy. Whether we regard the laws which secluded the leper as designed to prevent infection or repress the dread of it, their wisdom is nearly equal, for of all terrors the imaginary are the most terrible. The laws restricting marriage have in general a similar tendency, degeneracy being the penalty of a departure from those which forbid commixture of near kin. Michel Lévy remarks on the salubrious tendency of the law of marital separation (Lev. xv) imposed (Lévy, *Traité de Hygiène*, p. 8). The precept also concerning purity on the necessary occasions in a desert encampment (Deut. xxiii, 12–14), enjoining the return of the elements of productiveness to the soil, would probably become the basis of the municipal regulations having for their object a similar purity in towns. The consequences of its neglect in such encampments is shown by an example quoted by Michel Lévy, as mentioned by M. de Lamartine (*ib.* 8, 9). Length of life was regarded as a mark of divine favor, and the divine legislator had pointed out the means of ordinarily insuring a fuller measure of it to the people at large than could, according to physical laws, otherwise be hoped for. Perhaps the extraordinary means taken to prolong vitality may be referred to this source (1 Kings i, 2), and there is no reason why the case of David should be deemed a singular one. We may also compare the apparent influence of vital warmth enhanced to a miraculous degree, but having, perhaps, a physical law as its basis, in the cases of Elijah, Elisha, and the sons of the widow of Zarephath, and the Shunammite. Wunderbar has collected several examples of such influence similarly exerted, which, however, he seems to exaggerate to an absurd pitch. Yet it would seem not against analogy to suppose that, as pernicious exhalations, miasmata, etc., may pass from the sick and affect the healthy, so there should be a reciprocal action in favor of health. The climate of Palestine afforded a great range of temperature within a narrow compass—e. g. a long seacoast, a long, deep valley (that of the Jordan), a broad, flat plain (Esdraelon), a large portion of table-land (Judah and Ephraim), and the higher elevations of Carmel, Tabor, the lesser and greater Hermon, etc. Thus it partakes of nearly all supportable climates. In October its rainy season begins with moist westerly winds. In November the trees are bare. In December snow and ice are often found, but never lie long, and only during the north wind's prevalence. The cold disappears at the end of February, and the "latter rain" sets in, lasting through March to the middle of April, when thunder-storms are common, torrents swell, and the heat rises in the low grounds. At the end of April the hot season begins, but preserves moderation till June, thence till September becomes extreme; and during all this period rain seldom occurs, but often heavy dews prevail. In September it commences to be cool, first at night, and sometimes the rain begins to fall at the end of it. The migration with the season from an inland to a sea-coast position, from low to high ground, etc., was a point of social development never systematically reached during the scriptural history of Palestine. But men inhabiting the same regions for centuries could hardly fail to notice the connection between the air and moisture of a place and human health, and those favored by circumstances would certainly turn their knowledge to account. The Talmudists speak of the north wind as preservative of life, and the south and east winds as exhaustive, but the south as the most insupportable of all, coming hot and dry from the deserts, producing abortion, tainting the babe yet unborn, and corroding the pearls in the sea. Further, they dissuade from performing circumcision or venesection during its prevalence (Jebamoth, 72 a, ap. Wunderbar, 2tes Heft, vol. ii, A). It is stated that "the marriage-bed placed between north and south will be blessed with male issue" (Berachoth, 15, ib.), which may, Wunderbar thinks, be interpreted of the temperature when moderate, and in neither extreme (which these winds respectively represent), as most favoring fecundity. If the fact be so, it is more probably related to the phenomena of magnetism, in connection with which the same theory has been lately revived. A number of precepts are given by the same authorities in reference to health; e. g. eating slowly, not contracting a sedentary habit, regularity in natural operations, cheerfulness of temperament, due sleep (especially early morning sleep is recommended), but not somnolence by day (Wunderbar, ut sup.). We may mention likewise in this connection that possession of an abundance of salt tended to banish much disease (Psa. lx, 2; 2 Sam. viii, 13; 1 Chron. xviii, 12). Salt-pits (Zeph. ii, 9) are still dug by the Arabs on the shore of the Dead Sea. For the use of salt to a new-born infant, Ezek. xvi, 4; comp. Galen, De Sanit. lib. i, cap. 7.

The rite of circumcision, besides its special surgical operation, deserves some notice in connection with the general question of the health, longevity, and fecundity of the race with whose history it is identified. Besides being a mark of the covenant and a symbol of purity, it was perhaps also a protest against the phallus-worship, which has a remote antiquity in the corruption of mankind, and of which we have some trace in the Egyptian myth of Osiris. It has been asserted also (Wunderbar, 3tes Heft, p. 25) that it distinctly contributed to increase the fruitfulness of the race, and to check inordinate desires in the individual. Its beneficial effects in such a climate as that of Egypt and Syria, as tending to promote cleanliness, to prevent or reduce irritation, and thereby to stop the way against various disorders, have been the subject of comment to various writers on hygiene. In particular a troublesome and sometimes fatal kind of boil (phymosis and paraphymosis) is mentioned as occurring commonly in those regions, but only to the uncircumcised. It is stated by Josephus (Cont. Ap. ii, 13) that Apion, against whom he wrote, having at first derided circumcision, was circumcised of necessity by reason of such a boil, of which, after suffering great pain, he died. Philo also appears to speak of the same benefit when he speaks of the "anthrax" infesting those who retain the foreskin. Medical authorities have also stated that the capacity of imbibing syphilitic virus is less, and that this has been proved experimentally by comparing Jewish with other, e. g. Christian populations (Wunderbar, 3tes Heft, p. 27). The operation itself consisted of originally a mere incision, to which a further stripping off the skin from the part, and a custom of sucking the blood from the wound, was in a later period added, owing to the attempts of Jews of the Maccabæan period, and later (1 Macc. i, 15; Josephus, Ant. xii, 5, 1: comp. 1 Cor. vii, 8), to cultivate heathen practices. The reduction of the remaining portion of the præputium after the more simple operation, so as to cover what it had exposed, known as epispasmus, accomplished by the elasticity of the skin itself, was what this anti-Judaic practice sought to effect, and what the

later, more complicated and severe, operation frustrated. To these were subjoined the use of the warm-bath, before and after the operation, pounded cummin as a styptic, and a mixture of wine and oil to heal the wound. It is remarkable that the tightly-swathed rollers, which formed the first covering of the new-born child (Luke ii, 7), are still retained among modern Jews at the circumcision of a child, effectually preventing any movement of the body or limbs (Wunderbar, p. 29). See CIRCUMCISION.

No surgical operation beyond this finds a place in holy Scripture, unless, indeed, that adverted to under the article EUNUCH. The Talmudists speak of two operations to assist birth, one known as קריצת הדופן (gastrotomia), and intended to assist parturition, not necessarily fatal to the mother; the other known as קריצת הבמן (hysterotomia, sectio cæsarea), which was seldom practiced save in the case of death in the crisis of labor, or, if attempted on the living, was either fatal, or at least destructive of the powers of maternity. An operation is also mentioned by the same authorities having for its object the extraction piecemeal of an otherwise inextricable fœtus (ibid. p. 53, etc.).

Wunderbar enumerates from the Mishna and Talmud fifty-six surgical instruments or pieces of apparatus; of these, however, the following only are at all alluded to in Scripture. A cutting instrument, called צור, supposed to be a "sharp stone" (Exod. iv, 25). Such was probably the "Æthiopian stone" mentioned by Herodotus (ii, 86), and Pliny speaks of what he calls Testa samia, as a similar implement. Zipporah seems to have caught up the first instrument which came to hand in her apprehension for the life of her husband. The "knife" (מאכלת) of Josh. v, 2 was probably a more refined instrument for the same purpose. An "awl" (מרצע) is mentioned (Exod. xxi, 6) as used to bore through the ear of the bondman who refused release, and is supposed to have been a surgical instrument. A seat of delivery, called in Scripture אבנים, Exod. i, 16, by the Talmudists משבר (comp. 2 Kings xix, 3), "the stools;" but some have doubted whether the word used by Moses does not mean rather the uterus itself, as that which moulds and shapes the infant. Delivery upon a seat or stool is, however, a common practice in France at this day, and also in Palestine. The "roller to bind" of Ezek. xxx, 21 was for a broken limb, as still used. Similar bands, wound with the most precise accuracy, involve the mummies. A scraper (חרס), for which the "potsherd" of Job was a substitute (Job ii, 8).

Exod. xxx, 23–5 is a prescription in form. It may be worth while also to enumerate the leading substances which, according to Wunderbar, composed the pharmacopœia of the Talmudists—a much more limited one— which will afford some insight into the distance which separates them from the leaders of Greek medicine. Besides such ordinary appliances as water, wine (Luke x, 34), beer, vinegar, honey, and milk, various oils are found; as opobalsamum ("balm of Gilead"), the oil of olive, myrrh, rose, palma christi, walnut, sesamum, colocynth, and fish; figs (2 Kings xx, 7), dates, apples (Cant. ii, 5), pomegranates, pistachio-nuts, and almonds (a produce of Syria, but not of Egypt, Gen. xliii, 11); wheat, barley, and various other grains; garlic, leeks, onions, and some other common herbs; mustard, pepper, coriander seed, ginger, preparations of beet, fish, etc., steeped in wine or vinegar, whey, eggs, salt, wax, and suet (in plasters), gall of fish (Tob. vi, 8; xi, 11), ashes, cowdung, etc.; fasting-saliva, urine, bat's blood, and the following rarer herbs, etc.; ammeisision, menta gentilis, saffron, mandragora, Lawsonia spinosa (Arab. alhenna), juniper, broom, poppy, acacia, pine, lavender or rosemary, cloverroot, jujub, hyssop, fern, sampsuchum, milk-thistle, laurel, Eruca muralis, absynth, jasmine, narcissus, madder, curled mint, fennel, endive, oil of cotton, myrtle, myrrh, aloes, sweet cane (acorus calamus), cinnamon, canella *alba,* cassia, *ladanum, galbanum,* frankincense, *storax,* nard, gum of various trees, musk, *blatta byzantina;* and these minerals—bitumen, natrum, borax, alum, clay, aëtites, quicksilver, litharge, yellow arsenic. The following preparations were also well known: *Theriacas,* an antidote prepared from serpents; various medicinal drinks, e. g. from the fruit-bearing rosemary; decoction of wine with vegetables; mixture of wine, honey, and pepper; of oil, wine, and water; of asparagus and other roots steeped in wine; emetics, purging draughts, soporifics, potions to produce abortion or fruitfulness; and various salves, some used cosmetically, e. g. to remove hair; some for wounds and other injuries. The forms of medicaments were cataplasm, electuary, liniment, plaster (Isa. i, 6; Jer. viii, 22; xlvi, 11; li, 8; Josephus, *War,* i, 33, 5), powder, infusion, decoction, essence, syrup, mixture.

An occasional trace occurs of some chemical knowledge, e. g. the calcination of the gold by Moses; the effect of "vinegar upon nitre" (Exod. xxxii, 20; Prov. xxv, 20; comp. Jer. ii, 22). The mention of "the apothecary" (Exod. xxx, 35; Eccl. x, 1), and of the merchant in "powders" (Cant. iii, 6), shows that a distinct and important branch of trade was set up in these wares, in which, as at a modern druggist's, articles of luxury, etc., are combined with the remedies of sickness (see further, Wunderbar, 1stes Heft, p. 73, ad fin.).

Among the most favorite of external remedies has always been the bath. As a preventive of numerous disorders its virtues were known to the Egyptians, and the scrupulous Levitical bathings prescribed by Moses would merely enjoin the continuance of a practice familiar to the Jews, from the example especially of the priests in that country. Besides the significance of moral purity which it carried, the use of the bath checked the tendency to become unclean by violent perspirations from within and effluvia from without; it kept the porous system in play, and stopped the outset of much disease. In order to make the sanction of health more solemn, most Oriental nations have enforced purificatory rites by religious mandates—and so the Jews. A treatise collecting all the dicta of ancient medicine on the use of the bath has been current ever since the revival of learning, under the title *De Balneis.* According to it, Hippocrates and Galen prescribe the bath medicinally in peripneumonia rather than in burning fever, as tending to allay the pain of the sides, chest, and back, promoting various secretions, removing lassitude, and suppling joints. A hot bath is recommended for those suffering from *lichen (De Baln.* p. 464). Those, on the contrary, who have looseness of the bowels, who are languid, loathe their food, are troubled with nausea or bile, should not use it, as neither should the epileptic. After exhausting journeys in the sun, the bath is commended as the restorative of moisture to the frame (p. 456-458). The four objects which ancient authorities chiefly proposed to attain by bathing are—1, to warm and distil the elements of the body throughout the whole frame, to equalize whatever is abnormal, to rarefy the skin, and promote evacuations through it; 2, to reduce a dry to a moister habit; 3 (the cold bath), to cool the frame and brace it; 4 (the warm bath), a sudorific to expel cold. Exercise before bathing is recommended, and in the season from April till November inclusive it is the most conducive to health; if it be kept up in the other months, it should then be but once a week, and that fasting. Of natural waters some are nitrous, some saline, some aluminous, some sulphureous, some bituminous, some copperish, some ferruginous, and some compounded of these. Of all the natural waters the power is, on the whole, desiccant and calefacient, and they are peculiarly fitted for those of a humid and cold habit. Pliny (*H. N.* xxxi) gives the fullest extant account of the thermal springs of the ancients (*Paul. Ægin.* ed. Sydenh. Soc. i. 71). Avicenna gives precepts for salt and other mineral baths; the former he recommends in case of scurvy and itching, as rarefying the

skin, and afterwards condensing it. Waters medicated with alum, natron, sulphur, naphtha, iron, litharge, vitriol, and vinegar, are also specified by him. Friction and unction are prescribed, and a caution given against staying too long in the water (*ibid.* p. 338-340; comp. Aëtius, *De Baln.* iv, 484). A sick bather should lie quiet, and allow others to rub and anoint him, and use no strigil (the common instrument for scraping the skin), but a sponge (p. 456). Maimonides, chiefly following Galen, recommends the bath, especially for phthisis in the aged, as being a case of dryness with cold habit, and to a hectic-fever patient as being a case of dryness with hot habit; also in cases of ephemeral and tertian fevers, under certain restrictions, and in putrid fevers, with the caution not to incur shivering. Bathing is dangerous to those who feel pain in the liver after eating. He adds cautions regarding the kind of water, but these relate chiefly to water for drinking (*De Baln.* p. 438, 439). The bath of oil was formed, according to Galen and Aëtius, by adding the fifth part of heated oil to a waterbath. Josephus speaks (*War,* i, 33, 5) as though oil had, in Herod's case, been used pure. There were special occasions on which the bath was ceremonially enjoined—after a leprous eruption healed, after the conjugal act, or an involuntary emission, or any gonorrhœal discharge, after menstruation, childbed, or touching a corpse; so for the priests before and during their times of office such a duty was prescribed. The Pharisees and Essenes aimed at scrupulous strictness of all such rules (Matt. xv, 2; Mark vii, 5; Luke xi, 38). River-bathing was common, but houses soon began to include a bath-room (Lev. xv, 13; 2 Kings v, 10; 2 Sam. xi, 2; Susanna 15). Vapor-baths, as among the Romans, were latterly included in these, as well as hot and cold bath apparatus, and the use of perfumes and oils after quitting it was everywhere diffused (Wunderbar, 2tes Heft, vol. ii, *B*). The vapor was sometimes sought to be inhaled, though this was reputed mischievous to the teeth. It was deemed healthiest after a warm to take also a cold bath (*Paul. Ægin.* ed. Sydenh. Soc. i, 68). The Talmud has it—"Whoso takes a warm bath, and does not also drink thereupon some warm water, is like a stove hot only from without, but not heated also from within. Whoso bathes, and does not withal anoint, is like the liquor outside a vat. Whoso having had a warm bath does not also immediately pour cold water over him, is like an iron made to glow in the fire, but not thereafter hardened in the water." This succession of cold water to hot vapor is commonly practiced in Russian and Polish baths, and is said to contribute much to robust health (Wunderbar, *ibid.*). See BATHE.

V. *Literature.*—Besides the usual authorities on Hebrew antiquities, Talmudical and modern, Wunderbar (1stes Heft, p. 57-69) has compiled a collection of writers on the special subject of scriptural, etc., medicine, including its psychological and botanical aspects, as also its political relations; a distinct section of thirteen monographs treats of the leprosy; and every various disease mentioned in Scripture appears elaborated in one or more such short treatises. Those out of the whole number which appear most generally in esteem, to judge from references made to them, are the following, which include a few from other sources: Rosenmüller's *Natural History of the Bible* (in the *Biblical Cabinet,* vol. xxvii); De Wette, *Hebräisch-jüdische Archäologie,* § 271 *b;* Calmet (Augustin), *La Médecine et les Médecins des anc. Hebreux* (in his *Comm. litérale,* Paris, 1724, vol. v); idem, *Dissertation sur la Sueur du Sang* (Luke xxii, 43, 44); Pruner, *Krankheiten des Orients;* Sprengel (Kurt), *De medic. Ebræorum* (Halle, 1789, 8vo); idem, *Beiträge zur Geschichte der Medicin* (Halle, 1794, 8vo); idem, *Versuch einer pragm. Geschichte der Arzeneikunde* (Halle, 1792, 1803, 1821; the last edition by Dr. Rosenbaum, Leipsic, 1846, 8vo, vol. i, § 37-45); idem, *Histor. Rei Herbar.* (lib. i, cap. i, *Flora Biblica*); Bartholini (Thom.), *De morbis biblicis, miscellanea medica* (in Ugolini, xxx, 1521); idem, *Paralytici novi Testamenti* (in Ugolini, xxx, 1459);

Schmidt (Joh. Jac.), *Biblischer Medicus* (Züllichau, 1743, 8vo, p. 761); Kall, *De morbis sacerdot. V. T.* (Hafn. 1745, 4to); Reinhard (Chr. Tob. Ephr.), *Bibelkrankheit., welche im alten Testam. vorkommen* (i and ii, 1767, 8vo, p. 384; v, 1768, 8vo, p. 244); Shapter (Thomas), *Medica sacra, or Short Expositions of the more important Diseases mentioned in the Sacred Writings* (London, 1834); Wunderbar (R. J.), *Biblisch-Talmudische Medicin* (in 4 parts, Riga, 1850–1853, 8vo; new series, 1857); Celsius (Ol.), *Hierobotanicon, s. de plantis sacræ scripturæ dissertationes breves* (2 parts, Upsal, 1745, 1747, 8vo; Amstelod. 1748); Bochart (Samuel), *Hierozoicon, s. bipartitum opus de animalibus sacræ scripturæ* (London, 1665, fol.; Frankfort, 1675, fol.; edited by, and with the notes of Ern. F. G. Rosenmüller, Lips. 1793, 3 vols. 4to); Spencer, *De legibus Hebræorum ritualibus* (Tübingen, 1732, fol.); Reinhard (Mich. H.), *De cibis Hebræorum prohibitis; Diss. I. respon. Seb. Müller* (Viteb. 1697, 4to); *Diss. II respon. Chr. Liske* (ibid. 1697, 4to); Eschenbach (Chr. Ehrenfr.), *Progr. de lepra Judæorum* (Rostock, 1774, 4to; in his *Scripta medic. bibl.* p. 17–41); Schilling (G. G.), *De lepra commentationes*, rec. J. D. Hahn (Lugd. Bat. 1788, 8vo); Chamseru (R.), *Recherches sur le véritable caractère de la lèpre des Hébreux* (in *Mém. de la Soc. médic. d'émulation de Paris*, 1810, iii, 335); *Rélation Chirurgicale de l'Armée de l'Orient* (Paris, 1804); Wedel (Geo. W.), *De lepra in sacris* (Jena, 1715, 4to; in his *Exercitat. med. philolog.* Cent. II, dec. 4, p. 93–107); idem, *De morb. Hiskiæ* (Jena, 1692, 4to; in his *Exercitat. med. philolog.* Cent. I, dec. 7); idem, *De morbo Jorami exercitat.* I, II (Jena, 1717, 4to; in his *Exercitat. med. philolog.* Cent. II, dec. 5); idem, *De Saulo energumeno* (Jena, 1685; in his *Exercitat. med. philolog.* Cent. I, dec. 2); idem, *De morbis senum Solomonæis* (Jena, 1686, 4to; in his *Exercitat. med. philolog.* Cent. I, dec. 3); Lichtenstein, *Versuch*, etc. (in Eichhorn's *Allgem. Bibliothek*, vi, 407–467); Mead (Dr. R.), *Medica Sacra* (London, 4to); Gudius (G. F.), *Exercitatio philologica de Hebraica obstetricum origine* (in Ugolini, xxx, 1061); Kall, *De obstetricibus matrum Hebræarum in Ægypto* (Hamburg, 1746, 4to); Israels (Dr. A. H.), *Tentamen historico-medicum, exhibens collectanea Gynæcologica, quæ ex Talmude Babylonico depromsit* (Gröningen, 1845, 8vo); Börner (F.), *Dissert. de statu Medicinæ ap. Vett. Hebr.* (1735); Norberg, *De Medicina Arabum* (in *Opusc. Acad.* ii, 404); Aschkenazei (Mos.), *De ortu et progressu Medicinæ inter Hebræos* (Hamburg, 17. , 8vo); Ginsburger (B. W.), *De Medica ex Talmudis illustrata* (Götting. 1743, 4to); Goldmann, *De rebus medices Vet. Test.* (Bresl. 1846, 4to); Leutenschläger (J. H.), *De medicis veterum Hebr.* (Schleiz. 1786, 8vo); Lindlinger (J. S.), *De Hebr. vett. medica de Dæmoniacis* (Wittenb. 1774, 2 vols. 8vo); Reineccius (Chr.), *Dictum Talmudicum de optimo medico, Gehenne digno* (Weissenb. 1724, fol.). See PHYSICIAN.

MEDICINE, HEATHEN. See SUPERSTITION.

Mediety (or **Portion**) is the name given to the division of a rectory church into several parsonages or vicarages.

Medigo, Elia ben-Mose, ABBA DEL, a noted Jewish savan of the 15th century, celebrated for his attainments as a philosopher, flourished at Padua, Italy, as teacher of metaphysics. He died in 1493. For his works, see Fürst, *Bibl. Jud.* ii, 338.

Medigo, Joseph Salomo del, another Jewish writer of note, and of the same family as the preceding, was born at Candia in 1591. He was highly educated, and though busily engaged in the practice of medicine as one of the most eminent of his profession, he nevertheless devoted much time and attention to the study of Jewish philosophical productions and the writings of Jewish mystics. He published dissertations on different philosophical subjects and on the Cabala, and biographies of several eminent Hebrew literati. He died at Prague in 1655. See Fürst, *Bibl. Judaica*, ii, 338 sq.

Medina (Arab. *city*), or, more fully, MEDINAT AL-NABI (City of the Prophet), also called *Tabah, Tibah*,

etc. (the Good, Sweet, etc.), and mentioned by Ptolemy as *Jathrippa:* the holiest city of Mohammedan countries, next to Mecca, and the second capital of Hejaz in Western Arabia, is situated about 270 miles north of Mecca, and 140 north by east of the port of Jembo, on the Red Sea, and contains about 16,000 inhabitants (Burton). Medina is about half the size of Mecca. The streets, between fifty and sixty in number, are deep and narrow, paved only in a few places. The houses are flat-roofed and double-storied, and are built of a basaltic scoria, burned brick, and palm-wood. Very few public buildings of any importance are to be noticed besides the great mosque Al-Haram (the Sacred), supposed to be erected on the spot where Mohammed died, and to enclose his tomb. It is of smaller dimensions than that of Mecca, being a parallelogram, 420 feet long and 340 feet broad, with a spacious central area, called El-Sahn, which is surrounded by a peristyle, with numerous rows of pillars. The Mausoleum, or Hujrah, itself is an irregular square, 50–55 feet in extent, situated in the southeast corner of the building, and separated from the walls of the mosque by a passage about 26 feet broad. A large gilt crescent above the "Green Dome," springing from a series of globes, surmounts the Hujrah, a glimpse into which is only attainable through a little opening, called the Prophet's Window; but nothing more is visible to the profane eye than costly carpets or hangings, with three inscriptions in large gold letters, stating that behind them lie the bodies of the Prophet of Allah and the two caliphs — which curtains, changed whenever worn out, or when a new sultan ascends the throne, are supposed to cover a square edifice of black marble, in the midst of which stands Mohammed's tomb. Its exact place is indicated by a long pearly rosary (Kaukab al-Durri) — still seen — suspended to the curtain. The Prophet's body is supposed to lie (undecayed) stretched at full length on the right side, with the right palm supporting the right cheek, the face directed towards Mecca. Close behind him is placed, in the same position, Abubekr, and behind him Omar. The fact, however, is that when the mosque, which had been struck by lightning, was rebuilt in 892, three deep graves were found in the interior, filled only with rubbish. Many other reasons, besides, make it more than problematic whether the particular spot at Medina really contains the Prophet's remains. That his coffin, said to be covered with a marble slab, and cased with silver (no European has ever seen it), rests suspended in the air, is a stupid story, invented by Christians, and long exploded. Of the fabulous treasures which this sanctuary once contained, little now remains. As in Mecca, a great number of ecclesiastical officials are attached in some capacity or other to the Great Mosque, as ulemas, mudarisin, imaums, khatibs, etc.; and not only they, but the townspeople themselves live to a great extent only on the pilgrims' alms. There are few other noteworthy spots to be mentioned in Medina, save the minor mosques of Abubekr, Ali, Omar, Balal, etc.

Mediolānum. See MILAN.

Mediocres, or SECOND GRADE, an epithet of that class of monks, from the age of twenty-four to forty, who were exempted from being taper-bearers, from the reading of the epistle, gospel, martyrology, collation in chapter, parva cantaria, and chanting the offices. See Walcott, *Sacred Archæology*, s. v.

Mediterranean SEA, a later name (Solin. xxii, 18; see Forbiger, *Handb. de alt. Geogr.* ii, 13 sq.) for the usual Roman title (*Mare Internum*) of that immense body of water between Europe, Asia, and Africa, styled by the Hebrews "the Great Sea" (הַיָּם הַגָּדוֹל, Numb. xxxiv, 6 sq.; Josh. i, 4; Ezek. xlvii, 10, etc.; likewise in the Talmud, ימא רבא; so ἡ μεγάλη θάλασσα, Hecat. *Fragm.* p. 349), or "the hinder (i. e. Western) sea" (הַיָּם הָאַחֲרוֹן, Deut. xii, 24; in distinction from "the forward [i. e. Eastern] sea," i. e. the Dead Sea, Zech. xiv, 8, etc.), "sea of the Philistines" (יָם הַפְּלִשְׁתִּים, Exod. xxiii, 31), and also simply "the Sea" (Josh. xix, 36; as likewise in the Greek, ἡ θάλασσα, 1 Macc. xiv, 34; xv, 11; Acts x, 6, 32), and bounding Palestine on the west. It has, from Tyre to Ptolemais, a high and rocky shore, which farther south becomes low and sandy (Strabo, xvi, 758 sq.; comp. Josephus, $Ant.$ xv, 9, 6; $War,$ i, 21, 5; see Scholz, $Reise,$ p. 136); it makes at Mount Carmel a great bay (that of Accho or Ptolemais), but elsewhere it affords very few good harbors (chiefly those of Cæsarea, Joppa, and Gaza). Its surface lies higher than that of the Dead Sea. The ebb and flow of the tide in the Mediterranean is irregular, and noticeable only in particular localities, and unimportant on the coast of Palestine (see Michaelis, $Einleit. ins A. T.$ i, 74, anm.). The current of the sea is regularly from south to north, and is doubly strong at the time of the Nile freshet, so as to carry the deposit of mud and sand against the southern (Philistian) shore, which accordingly is continually pushing farther and farther into the sea (see Ritter, $Erdk.$ ii, 460, 462). Under the water there are found at the coast from Gaza to Jaffa large coral reefs (Volney, $Voyage,$ ii, 246); and the sea abounds in fish. Commerce finds on it a great sphere; but the Phœnicians and Egyptians had nearly a monopoly of this, as the Mosaic legislation was unfavorable even to coast trading. Particular portions of this vast body of water were designated by special names, but of these only the Adriatic (ὁ Ἀδρίας) is distinctively named in the Bible (Acts xxvii, 27). See ADRIA. Vague mention, however, is made likewise of the Ægæan Sea, the modern Archipelago (Acts xvii, 14, 18), the sound between Cilicia and Cyprus (Acts xxvii, 5), and the Syrtis of the Lybian Sea (Acts xxvii, 17). See generally Bachiene, $Paläst.$ I, i, 87 sq.; Hamesveld, $Bibl. Geogr.$ i. 440 sq.— Winer, ii, 70. See SEA. The whole of the coast, from the Nile to Mount Carmel, was anciently called the Plain of the Mediterranean Sea. The tract between Gaza and Joppa was simply called the Plain; in this stood the five principal cities of the Philistine satrapies —Ascalon, Gath, Gaza, Ekron or Accaron, and Azotus or Ashdod. The countries bordering on the Mediterranean were unquestionably the cradle of civilization, and they have in all ages been the scene of mighty changes and events, the investigation of which belongs to the general historian; all, however, that has relation to scriptural subjects will be found stated under the heads CYRENE, EGYPT, GREECE, SYRIA, etc., and therefore to enter into the detail here would be superfluous, as would any lengthened notice of the sea itself, the Hebrews having never been a maritime people. See Smith, $Dict. of Class. Geogr.$ s. v. Internum Mare; M'Culloch, $Dict. of Geogr.$ s. v. See PALESTINE.

Medler, NICHOLAS, one of the three principal disciples of Luther, was born at Hof, in Saxony, in 1502. He studied at Erfurt and Wittenberg, where he held conferences on the Old Test. and mathematics. He afterwards opened a school at Eger, but came into conflict with the authorities of that city for teaching the doctrines of Luther to his pupils. He then took a situation as teacher in his native city, and was appointed pastor there in 1530, but preached such violent sermons that he was obliged to leave in 1531. Retiring to Wittenberg, he remained there six years as deacon. Luther often allowed him to supply his place in the pulpit, as he highly esteemed Medler for his great talents as well as zeal. He was made chaplain of the wife of Joachim I, who had fled to Wittenberg. In 1535 he was, together with Jerome Weller, made D.D., and in 1536 superintendent at Naumburg. Here he engaged in numerous controversies, but was much beloved and respected both by the people and by the authorities. Maurice of Saxony succeeded in attracting him to the University of Leipsic. In 1541, as he went by order of the elector to hold the first evangelical worship in the

cathedral of Naumburg, he found that the canon regulars had closed the doors: Medler caused one of them to be broken open and another he burned down. In the same year he got into a controversy with Sebastian Schwebinger, who was surnamed the Greek, on account of his philosophical acquirements and his devotion to the cause of the canons. He also quarrelled with his colleague Amsdorf, and with the senate of Naumburg, particularly with Mohr, to whom he addressed the reproach, "Quod numquam palam et expresse taxarit vel errores papisticæ doctrinæ et cultus impios, vel manifesta scandala in vita illius gregis." The faculty of Wittenberg approved the accusation, and deposed Mohr, but Medler himself was also obliged to resign. Medler now went to Spandau, near Berlin, where the Reformed doctrines were becoming established, and in 1546 finally became superintendent of Brunswick, after having three times declined the appointment, notwithstanding the advice of Melancthon and Luther. In Brunswick he succeeded, after great efforts, in establishing a school, where afterwards Melancthon, Urbanus Regius, Justus Jonas, and Flacius taught for a while after the downfall of Wittenberg in 1547. In 1551 he left Brunswick on account of his health, and went to Leipsic, where he was made superintendent of Bernburg, but on his first preaching he was struck with apoplexy, and died shortly after at Wittenberg. He was full of controversial zeal for the doctrines of Luther. His works are enumerated by Streitperger, v, 4, and by Schamelius, $Numburgum literatum,$ p. 19, 37. A sermon of his against the Interim of Leipsic (q. v.) was often reprinted; also in Schamelius, $Numburgum literatum.$ See M. A. Streitperger, $De vita D. N. Medl.$ (in $Actus promotionis—per Ambrosium Reudenium,$ fol. O sq., Jena, 1591); Hummel, $Neue Bibliothek,$ iii, 536 sq.; Rethmeyer, $Kirchengesch. v. Braunschweig,$ iii, 173, 194; Danz, $Epistolæ P. Melanch. ad N. Medl.;$ Döllinger, $Reformationsgesch.$ ii, 74 sq.; Herzog, $Real-Encyklopädie,$ ix, 234. (J. N. P.)

Meë'da (Μεϊδά v. r. Δεϊδά), a Græcized form (1 Esdr. v, 32) of the MEHIDA (q. v.) of the Heb. lists (Ezra ii, 52; Neh. vii, 54).

Meekness (עֲנָוָה, πραότης), a calm, serene temper of mind, not easily ruffled or provoked to resentment (James iii, 7, 8). Where the great principles of Christianity have disciplined the soul, where the holy grace of meekness reigns, it subdues the impetuous disposition, and causes it, trusting in God, both to submit and to forgive. It teaches us to govern our own anger whenever we are at any time provoked, and patiently to bear the anger of others, that it may not be a provocation to us. The former is its office, especially in superiors; the latter in inferiors, and both in equals (James iii, 13). The excellency of such a spirit appears, if we consider that it enables us to gain a victory over corrupt nature (Prov. xvi, 32); that it is a beauty and an ornament to human beings (1 Pet. iii, 4); that it is obedience to God's word, and conformity to the best patterns (Eph. v, 1, 2; Phil. iv, 8). It is productive of the highest peace to the professor (Luke xxi, 19; Matt. xi, 28, 29). It fits us for any duty, instruction, relation, condition, or persecution (Phil. iv, 11, 12). To obtain this spirit, consider that it is a divine injunction (Zeph. ii, 3; Col. iii, 12; 1 Tim. vi, 11). Observe the many examples of it: Jesus Christ (Matt. xi, 28), Abraham (Gen. xiii, xvi, 5, 6), Moses (Numb. xii, 3), David (Zech. xii, 8; 2 Sam. xvi, 10, 12; Psa. cxxxi, 2), Paul (1 Cor. ix, 19). Note how lovely a spirit it is in itself, and how it secures us from a variety of evils; that peculiar promises are made to such (Matt. v, 5; Isa. lxvi, 2); that such give evidence of their being under the influence of divine grace, and shall enjoy the divine blessing (Isa. lvii, 15). See Henry, $On Meekness;$ Dunlop, $Sermons,$ ii, 434; Evans, $Sermons on the Christian Temper,$ ser. 29; Tillotson, $Sermon on$ 1 $Pet. ii,$ 21, and $on Matt. v,$ 44; Logan, $Sermons,$ vol. i, ser. 10; Jortin, $Sermons,$ vol. iii, ser. 11.

Meene, HEINRICH, a German theologian, was born at Bremen April 11, 1710, and was educated at the universities of Helmstädt and Leipsic. In 1734 he entered the ministry as pastor at Volkersheim, near Hildesheim, and in 1737 removed to Quedlinburg, where, in addition to his pastoral labors in town, he served as court preacher. He was honored at this time with the title of "Consistorial-Rath." In 1758 he accepted a call to Jever, and there he flourished until his death, May 20, 1782. Besides many contributions to different periodicals, to Sinceri's *Sammlung Hamburgischer Kanzelraden*, and to Cramer's *Sammlungen zur Kirchengesch. u. theol. Gelehrsamk.*, etc., Meene published a large number of books in the department of religious literature. His works of special interest are, *Die treffliche Fürsprache des heiligen Geistes für die Gläubigen* (Helmstädt, 1745, 8vo; 2d edition much enlarged, 1754, 8vo):—*Unpartheiische Prüfung der Abhandlung: Schrift und Vernunftmäszige Ueberlegung der beiderseitigen Gründe für und wider die ganz unendliche Unglückseligkeit der Verbrecher Gottes und deren endliche selige Wiederbringung, angestellt, und zur Rechtfertigung der Gedanken des hochwürdigen Herrn Abts Mosheim von dem Ende der Höllenstrafen* (Helmstädt, 1747-1748, 3 vols, 8vo; also published under the title, *Die gute Sache der Lehre von der unendlichen Dauer der Höllenstrafen*. See Döring, *Gelehrte Theol. Deutschlands*, ii, 458 sq.

Meerza. See MIRZA.

Meeting. The Society of Friends, vulgarly called Quakers, have adopted the use of this word to designate their official gatherings for various purposes.

(1.) *Meeting for Sufferings.*—Its origin and purpose are thus given: "The yearly meeting of London, in the year 1675, appointed a meeting to be held in that city, for the purpose of advising and assisting in cases of suffering for conscience sake, which hath continued with great use to the society to this day. It is composed of Friends, under the name of correspondents, chosen by the several quarterly meetings, and residing in or near the city. The same meetings also appoint members of their own in the country as correspondents, who are to join their brethren in London on emergency. The names of all these correspondents, previously to their being recorded, are submitted to the approbation of the yearly meeting. Such men as are approved ministers and appointed elders are also members of this meeting, which is called the 'Meeting for Sufferings,' a name which arose from its original purpose, and has not yet become entirely obsolete. The yearly meeting has intrusted the Meeting for Sufferings with the care of printing and distributing books, and with the management of its stock; and, considered as a standing committee of the yearly meeting, it hath a general care of whatever may arise, during the intervals of that meeting, affecting the society, and requiring immediate attention, particularly of those circumstances which may occasion an application to government." See FRIENDS.

(2.) *Monthly Meeting*, a gathering of Friends of several particular congregations, situated within a convenient distance of one another. The business of the monthly meeting is to provide for the subsistence of the poor, and for the education of their offspring; to judge of the sincerity and fitness of persons appearing to be convinced of the religious principles of the society, and desiring to be admitted into membership; to excite due attention to the discharge of religious and moral duty; and to deal with disorderly members. Monthly meetings also grant to such of their members as remove into the limits of other monthly meetings certificates of their membership and conduct. It is likewise the duty of this body to appoint overseers for the proper observance of the rules of discipline, and for the disposal of difficulties among members by private admonition, agreeably to the Gospel rule (Matt. xviii, 15-17), so as to prevent, if possible, their being laid before the monthly meeting. When a case, however, is introduced to the monthly meeting, it is usual for a small committee to be appointed to visit the offender, in order to endeavor to convince him of his error, and induce him to forsake and condemn it. Time is allowed to judge of the effect of this labor of love, and if needful the visit is repeated. If these endeavors prove successful, the person is by minute declared to have made satisfaction for the offence; if not, he is disowned by the society. In disputes between individuals, it has long been the decided judgment of the society that its members should not sue each other at law. It therefore enjoins all to end their differences by speedy and impartial arbitration, agreeably to rules laid down. If any refuse to adopt this mode, or, having adopted it, to submit to the award, it is the direction of the yearly meeting that such be disowned. To monthly meetings also belongs the allowing of marriages; for the society has always scrupled to acknowledge the exclusive authority of the priests in the solemnization of marriage. A record of marriages is kept by the monthly meeting, as also of the births and burials of its members. A certificate of the date, of the name of the infant, and of its parents, is the subject of one of these last-mentioned records; and an order for the interment, countersigned by the gravemaker, of the other.

(3.) *Quarterly Meeting*, among the Society of Friends, is an assembly composed of several monthly meetings. At the quarterly meeting are produced written answers from the monthly meetings to certain queries respecting the conduct of their members, and the meetings' care over them. The accounts thus received are digested into one, which is sent, also in the form of answers to queries, by representatives to the yearly meeting. Appeals from the judgment of monthly meetings are brought to the quarterly meetings, whose business also is to assist in any difficult case, or where remissness appears in the care of the monthly meetings over the individuals who compose them. See QUARTERLY MEETING.

(4.) *Yearly Meeting*, an annual meeting of the Society of Friends. "The yearly meeting has the general superintendence of the society in the country in which it is established; and therefore, as the accounts which it receives discover the state of inferior meetings, as particular exigencies require, or as the meeting is impressed with a sense of duty, it gives forth its advice, makes such regulations as appear to be requisite, or excites to the observance of those already made, and sometimes appoints committees to visit those quarterly meetings which appear to be in need of immediate advice." At the yearly meeting another meeting (a sort of subcommittee) is appointed, bearing the name of the *morning meeting*, for the purpose of revising the denominational manuscripts previous to publication; and also the granting, in the intervals of the yearly meeting, of certificates of approbation to such ministers as are concerned to travel in the work of the ministry in foreign parts, in addition to those granted by their monthly and quarterly meetings. When a visit of this kind does not extend beyond Great Britain, a certificate from the monthly meeting of which the minister is a member is sufficient. If to Ireland, the concurrence of the quarterly meeting is also required. Regulations of similar tendency obtain in other yearly meetings. The "stock" of the yearly meeting consists of occasional voluntary contributions, which is expended in printing-books, salary of a clerk for keeping records, the passage of ministers who visit their brethren beyond sea, and some small incidental charges; but not, as has been falsely supposed, the reimbursement of those who suffer distraint for tithes and other demands with which they scruple to comply. Appeals from the quarterly meetings are heard at the yearly meetings. There are ten yearly meetings—namely, one in London, to which representatives from Ireland are received; one in Dublin; one in New England; one in New York; one in Pennsylvania: one in Maryland; one in Virginia; one in the Carolinas:

one in Ohio; and one in Indiana. Reports of each of these may be found in the *Annual Monitor*.

MEETING, QUARTERLY. Among the Methodists, the quarterly meeting is a general meeting of the stewards, leaders, and other officers, for the purpose of transacting the general business of the "circuit" or "district;" in the Methodist Episcopal Church presided over by the "presiding elder," or the minister in charge. Its special object is, besides the celebration of the *Love-feast* (q. v.), to examine the spiritual and financial conditions of the Church. See *Discipline*, chap. ii, sect. i, 3. See CONFERENCE, QUARTERLY.

Meeting-house, a place appropriated for the purpose of public Christian worship. In England the churches of Dissenters are so called by the Anglican communicants, and in the United States the Quakers thus name their places of public worship. See CHURCH; CHAPEL.

Meganck, FRANÇOIS DOMINIQUE, a noted Dutch theologian and valiant defender of the cause of the Jansenists, was born at Menin about 1683; studied at the University of Louvain, and then devoted himself wholly to the polemical field of theology. At first he wielded his pen only, but after a time he entered the pulpit also, determined to combat the Romanism of the Ultramontanes. He was a member at the council, in 1763, at Utrecht. He died at Leyden, Oct. 12, 1775. His principal works are, *Réfutation abrégée du Traité du Schisme* (1718, 12mo; Paris, 1791, 8vo):—*Défense des contrats de vente rachetables des deux côtés* (1730, 4to):—*Primauté de Saint Pierre et de ses Successeurs* (1763 and 1772, 12mo). In the last-named work he questions the pope's supremacy over a council.

Megander (also known under the name of *Grosmann*), CASPAR, was born at Zürich in 1495. He was educated at the University of Basle, where he secured the degree of M.A. in 1518, and soon after was appointed chaplain of the hospital at Zürich. Here he early espoused the doctrines of Zwingle, and with him, in 1525, publicly demanded the suppression of the mass and the evangelical celebration of the Lord's Supper. After the Berne disputation, in 1528, he was called as professor of theology to Berne, where he soon obtained the first position among the leading personalities, and zealously labored in this place for the advance of Zwinglian doctrines. In 1532, at Zofingen, he took part in the deliberations of the Anabaptists; and again, as deputy of the council, at the disputes at Lausanne in 1536, and of the synod at the same place in 1537. He also compiled the Berne Catechism in 1536. His Zwinglianism involved him in many serious disputes with Bucer in the latter's attempts at union. As one of the originators of the Helvetic Confession of 1536, he successfully defended the Wittenberg Formula of Concord at the convent at Berne, Oct. 19, 1536, and in consequence Bucer was dismissed. In 1537, however, Bucer's justification of his conduct was finally accepted, and Megander was charged to modify his Catechism in conformity with the Formula of Concord. Megander no longer opposed the alteration, the revised Catechism was at once prepared by Bucer, and was accepted by the Council of Berne in 1537. Megander, however, refusing to be governed by these alterations, was deposed from office, and returning to Zürich was there reappointed archdeacon at the cathedral, and in this position he arduously labored to oppose the efforts of Bucer. Megander died in 1545. Of his works, the *Anmerkungen* to Genesis and Exodus, Hebrews and Epistles of John, deserve special mention. See Hundeshagen, *Conflicte des Zwingl., Luterth., und Calv. in Berne* (Berne, 1842).

Megapolensis, Joannes, a minister of the (Dutch) Reformed Church, was the second clergyman sent out by the Classis of Amsterdam to this country, under the patronage of the Dutch West India Company and the patroon Van Rensselaer (in 1642). He was also *the first missionary to the Indians*, preceding the cele-

brated "apostle to the Indians," John Eliot, some three years. His original family name was VAN MEKELENBURG, which, after the pedantic fashion of the age, was Hellenized into Megapolensis. Leaving his two congregations in Holland, he engaged with the patroon to serve for six years, his outfit and expenses of removal to be paid, and at a salary of eleven hundred guilders per year ($440). In addition to the usual duties of a missionary pastor at an outpost of civilization, like Rensselaerwyck, he soon interested himself in the Indians who came thither to trade, and learned what he called "their heavy language" so as to speak and preach fluently in it. The early records of the First Reformed Church in Albany contain many names of Indians converted, baptized, and received into the communion of the Church under his labors. Thus completely were the home and foreign missionary work and spirit combined in this apostolic man. In 1644 he wrote a tract (which was published in 1651 in Holland) on *the Mohawk Indians in New Netherlands* (now translated in the New York Historical Society's Collections, vol. ii, series i, p. 158). While our subject was residing in Albany, the celebrated Jesuit missionary, father Isaac Jogues, was captured on the St. Lawrence by the Mohawks, and subjected to horrible cruelties by the savages. The Dutch at Fort Orange tried to ransom him. At length, escaping from his captors, he remained in close concealment for six weeks. During this time Megapolensis was his constant friend, and rendered him every kindness that was in his power. The Jesuit father was at length ransomed by the Dutch, and sent to Manhattan, whence he returned to Europe. But in 1646 he came back again to Canada, and revisited the Mohawks, who put him to a cruel death. Another Jesuit, father Simon le Moyne, who discovered the salt springs at Onondaga in 1654, also became intimate with the dominie of Fort Orange, and wrote "three polemical essays" to convert his "Dutch clerical friend to the Romish doctrine." But the stanch minister wrote a vigorous and elaborate reply, which, however, was lost in the wreck of the ship by which he sent it to Canada. At the close of his stipulated term of service Megapolensis proposed to return to Holland, but governor Stuyvesant persuaded him to remain in New Amsterdam (now New York) as pastor of the Dutch Church. Here, for twenty years, he labored as senior pastor, being assisted from 1664 to 1668 by his son Samuel. He died in 1670, in the sixty-seventh year of his age, retaining his pastoral relation to the last. "He was a man of thorough scholarship, energetic character, and devoted piety, and he is entitled to a high, if not pre-eminent position in the roll of early Protestant missionaries among the North American savages. For nearly a quarter of a century he exercised a marked influence in the affairs of New Netherlands. He saw the infancy of the Dutch province, watched its growth, and witnessed its surrender to overpowering English force. His name must ever be associated with the early history of New York, towards the illustration of which his correspondence with the Classis of Amsterdam, now in the possession of the General Synod of the Reformed Protestant Dutch Church, and his sketch of the Mohawk Indians, form original and very valuable contributions." See J. Romeyn Brodhead, in the *N. Y. Hist. Society's Coll.* vol. iii; Rev. E. P. Rogers, D.D., *Historical Discourse;* Sprague, *Annals*, vol. ix. (W. J. R. T.)

Megapolensis, Samuel, son of the above, was born in 1634, and was educated at Harvard College, Cambridge, Mass., where he spent three years; afterwards went to the University of Utrecht, Holland, and there he graduated in 1659, having pursued a full theological course. He next went to Leyden University, and, after a complete course in that most celebrated medical school of Europe, obtained the degree of doctor of medicine. Returning to America, he was associate pastor of the Church of New Amsterdam with his venerable father for over four years—1663–68. In 1664 he was appointed one of the Dutch commissioners who prepared the terms of surrender to the English government. "Probably it was through his influence that the rights of the Reformed Church were so carefully guarded." In 1668 he returned to Holland, and settled at Wernigerode, where he ministered seven years, 1670 to 1677. Afterwards, "being well skilled in both the English and Dutch languages," he served the English or Scotch churches of Flushing (1677–85) and Dordrecht (1685–1700), when he was declared *emeritus*, or honorably laid aside from his work, after a ministry of thirty-seven years. The date of his death is not known. See Rev. Dr. DeWitt, in Sprague's *Annals*, vol. ix; Corwin's *Manual of the Ref. Church*, s. v. (W. J. R. T.)

Megara, School of, one of the schools founded by disciples of Socrates, but so modified in position from their teacher as to deserve the name of a peculiar society. Its principal supporter was Euclid of Megara, who was born about 440 B.C., and was himself a pupil of Parmenides, one of the most prominent leaders in the *Eleatic School* (q. v.). After the death of Socrates, his disciples, fleeing for safety from Athens, found a pleasant home in the house of Euclid, and there, guided by him, finally established principles which gave them the name of *Megarists.* They taught that ethics stands in the service of dialectics. The essence of good is unity—unity so entire as to embrace immobility, identity, and permanence. Hence the sensible world has no part in existence. Being and good are thus the same thing, viz. unity; good therefore alone exists, and evil is but the absence of existence. It does not follow, however, that there is but a single being and a single sort of good, for unity may be found contained in various things. Euclid expressly taught that, in spite of their unity, being and good clothe themselves in different forms, present themselves under different points of view, and receive different names, as wisdom, God, intelligence, and the like. Euclid also anticipated Aristotle in distinguishing the act from the power, and resolved, according to his ideas of being, the relation between the two. Other supporters of this school were Eubulicles, Alexinos, Diodorus, Chronos, Philo, and Stilpo. See Dyck, *De Megaricorum doctrina* (Bonn, 1827); Ritter, *Ueber die Philosophie der Megarischen Schule;* Ueberweg, *History of Philosophy,* vol. i.

Megerlin, DAVID FRIEDRICH, a noted German Orientalist and mystic, was born at Stuttgard near the opening of the 18th century. After holding for some time a professorship at the gymnasium at Montbelliard, he preached at Laubach, whence, in 1769, he removed to Frankfort-on-the-Main to continue in the pastorate. He died in August, 1769. Megerlin took a lively interest in the welfare of the Jews, and labored earnestly for their conversion. In 1756 he gained great notoriety by his public intercession in behalf of rabbi Eibeschütz, who had published a cabalistic work containing many points to which his brethren had taken decided exception, particularly the favorable allusions to Sabbathai Zewi (q. v.). The Jews were greatly provoked with Eibeschütz because they had found him a believer in the messiahship of the pretender Sabbathai, but Megerlin insisted that Eibeschütz had been misinterpreted, and that the rabbi was a believer in Jesus Christ. He made these views public in his *Geheime Zeugnisse für die Wahrheit der christlichen Religion* (Leipsic, 1756, 4to); and in *Neue Erweckung der Zerstreuten Judenschaft* (1756), and *Christlicher Zuruf an die Rabbinen* (1757). His other valuable works are, *De scriptis et collegiis orientalibus; item Observationes critico-theologicæ* (Tübing. 1729, 4to):—*Hexas orientalium collegiorum philologicorum* (1729, 4to):—*De Bibliis Latinis Moguntiæ primo impressis* 1450–1462 (1750, 4to); and a translation of the Koran into German. See Meusel, *Gelehrten-Lexikon*, s. v.; Grätz, *Gesch. der Juden*, x, 416.

Megethius. See MARCION.

Megid'do (Heb. *Megiddo'*, מְגִדּוֹ, according to Ge-

senius, perh. *place of troops*, according to Fürst, *rich in ornaments*, i. e. *noble, fruitful;* Sept. Μαγεδδώ, but Μαγεδώ in Judg. i, 27, Μαγδώ in 1 Kings ix, 15, and Μαγεδών v. r. Μαγεδδών and Μαγεδδώ in 2 Chron. xxxv, 22; Vulg. *Mageddo*), once in the prolonged form MEGIDDON (Zech. xii, 11, Heb. *Megiddon'*, מְגִדּוֹן, Sept. renders ἐκκοπτόμενος, Vulg. *Mageddon*), a town belonging to Manasseh (Judg. i, 27), although at first within the boundaries of Issachar (Josh. xvii, 11), and commanding one of those passes from the north into the hill-country which were of such critical importance on various occasions in the history of Judah (Judith iv, 7). It had originally been one of the royal cities of the Canaanites (Josh. xii, 21). This tribal arrangement was made partly to supplement the mountain-territory of Manasseh, and partly to give those strongly-fortified places to a tribe who, from their courage and their alliance with Ephraim, might be able to drive out the old inhabitants. The task, however, proved too great even for the warlike Manassites; but when the power of Israel was fully established, the Canaanites were reduced to slavery (Josh. xvii, 13–18; Judg. i, 27, 28). Indeed, we do not read of Megiddo being firmly in the occupation of the Israelites till the time of Solomon. That monarch placed one of his twelve commissariat officers, named Baana, over "Taanach and Megiddo," with the neighborhood of Beth-shean and Jezreel (1 Kings iv, 12). In this reign it appears that some costly works were constructed at Megiddo (ix, 15). These were probably fortifications, suggested by its important military position. Nearly all the notices of the place are connected with military transactions. Of these there were three notable ones, the sacred records of which, and perhaps some profane or monumental reminiscences, remain. See ESDRAELON.

(1.) The first was the victory of Barak. The song of Deborah brings the place vividly before us, as the scene of the great conflict. Jabin, king of Hazor, successor of the prince who had organized the northern confederation against Joshua, was now the oppressor of Israel, and Sisera was his general. The army of Jabin, with its 900 chariots of iron, was led down into the great plain, and drawn up at Megiddo, in a position to afford the best ground for the terrible war-chariots. With much difficulty Deborah the prophetess induced Barak to collect the warriors of the northern tribes. They assembled on Tabor. Deborah gave the signal, and the Israelites marched down to attack the enemy, full of hope and enthusiasm. At this moment a hail-storm from the east burst over the plain, and drove full in the faces of the advancing Canaanites (Josephus, *Ant.* v, 4). "The stars in their courses fought against Sisera." His army was thrown into confusion. The waters of the Kishon rose rapidly, the low plain became a morass; chariots, horses, soldiers, all together were engulfed (Judg. iv and v). Those who have visited Megiddo and traversed its plain in the spring, after a heavy fall of rain, have found the Kishon greatly swollen, its banks quagmires, and all the ordinary roads impassable. See KISHON.

(2.) To this place Ahaziah fled when his unfortunate visit to Joram had brought him into collision with Jehu, and here he died (2 Kings iv, 27), within the confines of what is elsewhere called Samaria (2 Chron. xxii, 9). As there are some difficulties in the history, we give the texts at length:

Short (2 Kings ix, 27).	*Full* (2 Chron. xxii, 7–9).
"And when Ahaziah the king of Judah saw this, he fled by the way of the garden-house. And Jehu followed after him, and said, Smite him also in the chariot. And they did so at the going up to Gur, which is by Ibleam. And he fled to Megiddo, and died there. And his servants carried him in a chariot to Jerusalem, and buried him in his	"And the destruction of Ahaziah was of God by coming to Joram: for when he was come, he went out with Jehoram against Jehu the son of Nimshi, whom the Lord had anointed to cut off the house of Ahab. And it came to pass that when Jehu was executing judgment upon the house of Ahab, and found the princes of Judah, and the

sepulchre with his fathers in the city of David."

sons of the brethren of Ahaziah, that ministered to Ahaziah, he slew them. And he sought Ahaziah: and they caught him (for he was hid in Samaria), and they brought him to Jehu: and when they had slain him, they buried him: Because, said they, he is the son of Jehoshaphat, who sought the Lord with all his heart. So the house of Ahaziah had no power to keep still the kingdom."

With reference to the above two accounts of the death of Ahaziah, which have been thought irreconcilable (Ewald, iii, 529; Parker's De Wette, p. 270; Thenius, etc.), it may be here remarked that the order of the events is sufficiently intelligible if we take the account in Chronicles, where the kingdom of Judah is the main subject, as explanatory of the brief notice in Kings, where it is only incidentally mentioned in the history of Israel. The order is clearly as follows: Ahaziah was with Jehoram at Jezreel when Jehu attacked and killed him. Ahaziah escaped and fled by the Beth-gan road to Samaria, where the partisans of the house of Ahab were strongest, and where his own brethren were, and there concealed himself. But when the sons of Ahab were all put to death in Samaria, and the house of Ahab had hopelessly lost the kingdom, he determined to make his submission to Jehu, and sent his brethren to salute the children of Jehu (2 Kings x, 13), in token of his acknowledgment of him as king of Israel (not, as Thenius and others, to salute the children of Jehoram, and of Jezebel, the queen-mother). Jehu, instead of accepting this submission, had them all put to death, and hastened on to Samaria to take Ahaziah also, who he had probably learned from some of the attendants, or as he already knew, was at Samaria. Ahaziah again took to flight northwards, towards Megiddo, perhaps in hope of reaching the dominions of the king of the Sidonians, his kinsman, or more probably to reach the coast where the direct road from Tyre to Egypt would bring him to Judah. See CÆSAREA. He was hotly pursued by Jehu and his followers, and overtaken near Ibleam, and mortally wounded, but managed to get as far as Megiddo, where it would seem Jehu followed in pursuit of him, and where he was brought to him as his prisoner. There he died of his wounds. In consideration of his descent from Jehoshaphat, "who sought Jehovah with all his heart," Jehu, who was at this time very forward in displaying his zeal for Jehovah, handed over the corpse to his followers, with permission to carry it to Jerusalem, which they did, and buried him in the city of David. The whole difficulty arises from the account in Kings being abridged, and so bringing together two incidents which were not consecutive in the original account. But if 2 Kings ix, 27 had been even divided into two verses, the first ending at "garden-house," and the next beginning "and Jehu followed after him," the difficulty would almost disappear. Jehu's pursuit of Ahaziah would only be interrupted by a day or two, and there would be nothing the least unusual in the omission to notice this interval of time in the concise abridged narrative. We should then understand that the word *also* in the *original* narrative referred, not to Jehoram, but to the brethren of Ahaziah, who had just before been smitten, and the death of Ahaziah would fall under 2 Kings x, 17. If Beth-gan (A. V. "garden-house") be the same as En-gannim, now Jenin, it lay directly on the road from Jezreel to Samaria, and is also the place at which the road to Megiddo and the coast, where Cæsarea afterwards stood, turns off from the road between Jezreel and Samaria. In this case the mention of Beth-gan in Kings as the direction of Ahaziah's flight is a confirmation of the statement in Chronicles that he concealed himself in Samaria. This is also substantially Keil's explanation (p. 288, 289). Movers proposes an alteration of the text (p. 92, note), but not very successfully

(וַיְבִיאֻהוּ אֶל־יֵחוּ) instead of וַיָּבֹא הוּא לִיהוּדָה). See JEHU.

(3.) But the chief historical interest of Megiddo is concentrated in Josiah's death. On this occasion Megiddo saw a very different sight from the first, and heard, instead of a song of triumph, a funeral wail from the vanquished host of Israel (Zech. xii, 11). Pharaoh-Necho was on his march against the king of Assyria. He passed up the plains of Philistia and Sharon, and king Josiah foolishly attempted to stop him while defiling through the glens of Carmel into the plain of Megiddo. He was defeated, and as he fled the Egyptian archers shot him in his chariot. He was taken to Jerusalem, but appears to have died on the road (2 Kings xxiii, 29). The story is told in the Chronicles in more detail (2 Chron. xxxv, 22–24). There the fatal action is said to have taken place "in the valley of Megiddo" (Sept. ἐν τῷ πεδίῳ Μαγεδδών). This calamity made a deep and permanent impression on the Jews. It is recounted again in 1 Esd. i, 25–31, where in the A.V. "the plain of Magiddo" represents the same Greek words. The lamentations for this good king became "an ordinance in Israel" (2 Chron. xxxv, 25). "In all Jewry" they mourned for him, and the lamentation was made perpetual "in all the nation of Israel" (1 Esd. i, 32). "Their grief was no land-flood of present passion, but a constant channel of continued sorrow, streaming from an annual fountain" (Fuller's *Pisgah Sight of Palestine*, p. 165). Thus, in the language of the prophets (Zech. xii, 11), "the mourning of Hadadrimmon in the valley (Sept. πεδίῳ) of Megiddon" becomes a poetical expression for the deepest and most despairing grief; as in the Apocalypse (Rev. xvi, 16) ARMAGEDDON, in continuance of the same imagery, is presented as the scene of terrible and final conflict. For the Septuagint version of this passage of Zechariah, we may refer to Jerome's note on the passage. "Adadremmon, pro quo LXX transtulerunt Ροῶνος, urbs est juxta Jesrælem, quæ hoc olim vocabulo nuncapata est, et hodie vocatur Maximianopolis in Campo Mageddon." *Ar-Mageddon* may be for עָר מְגִדֹּה, that is, "the city of Megiddo;" or if we regard the aspirated ἁρ as equivalent to the Hebrew הַר, then the meaning will be "mountain of Megiddo," which would likewise be appropriate (Alford, ad loc.). That the prophet's imagery is drawn from the occasion of Josiah's death there can be no doubt. In Stanley's *S. and P.* (p. 347) this calamitous event is made very vivid to us by an allusion to the "Egyptian archers, in their long array, so well known from their sculptured monuments." For the mistake in the account of Pharaoh-Necho's campaign in Herodotus, who has evidently put Migdol by mistake for Megiddo (ii, 159), it is enough to refer to Bähr's *excursus* on the passage (see below). The Egyptian king may have landed his troops at Acre; but it is far more likely that he marched northwards along the coast-plain, and then turned round Carmel into the plain of Esdraelon, taking the left bank of the Kishon, and that there the Jewish king came upon him by the gorge of Megiddo.

Eusebius and Jerome (*Onomast.*) do not attempt to mark the situation of the place, and it appears that the name Megiddo was in their time already lost. They often mention a town called *Legio* (Λεγεών), which must in their day have been an important and well-known place, as they assume it as a central point from which to mark the position of several other places in this quarter (e. g. fifteen miles west of Nazareth, and three or four from Taanach). This has been identified (Reland, *Palæst.* p. 873; comp. Benjamin of Tudela, ii, 433) with the village now called *Lejjun*, which is situated upon the western border of the great plain of Esdraelon, where it begins to rise gently towards the low range of wooded hills that connect Carmel with the mountains of Samaria (*Onomast.* s. v. Gabathon). This place was visited by Maundrell, who speaks of it as an old village near a brook, with a khan then in good repair (*Journey*, March

22). This khan was for the accommodation of the caravan on the route between Egypt and Damascus, which passes here. Having already identified the present village of Taannuk with the ancient Taanach, the vicinity of this to Lejjun induced Dr. Robinson (*Bibl. Researches*, iii, 177–180; also new ed. iii, 116–118) to conceive that the latter might be the ancient Megiddo, seeing that Taanach and Megiddo are constantly named together in Scripture (1 Kings iv, 12; 1 Chron. vii, 29); and to this a writer in a German review (Grosse, in the *Stud. u. Krit.* 1845, i, 252 sq.) adds the further consideration that the name of Legio was latterly applied to the plain or low valley along the Kishon, as that of Megiddo had been in more ancient times (עֵמֶק מְגִדּוֹ, 2 Chron. xxxv, 22; בְּקַעַת מְגִדּוֹן, Zech. xii, 11; τὸ πεδίον Μαγεδδώ, 3 Esdr. i, 27). See ESDRAELON. Herodotus (ii, 159) appears to allude to the overthrow of Josiah at this place (2 Kings ix, 23, 29), but instead of Megiddo he names the town *Magdolum* (Μάγδολον), the MIGDOL of Egypt (see Harenberg, *Bibl. Brem.* vi, 281; Rosenmüller, *Alterth.* II, ii. 99). Rosellini (*Monum. stor.* ii, p. 133) thinks that Herodotus may still refer to the Palestinian locality, and he imagines that he finds traces of the name on the monuments (*Makto*, i. e. Magdo, *ib.* iv, p. 158), but Ewald (*Isr. Gesch.* iii, 406) finds the Magdolum of Herodotus in *el-Mejdel* (the MIGDAL of Josh. xix, 38), between the Kishon and Acco (comp. Hitzig, *Philist.* i, 96). Megiddo or Lejjun is probably the place mentioned by Shaw as the *Ras el-Kishon*, or the head of the Kishon, under the south-east brow of Carmel (*Trav.* p. 274). It was visited and described by Mr. Wolcott in 1842, who found it to be an hour and forty minutes distant from Taanach. The Nahr Lejjun is a stream five or six feet wide, running into the Kishon, and feeding three or four mills. A little distance up it is situated the Khan el-Lejjun, and on a small eminence on the opposite side the remains of the ancient Legio. Among the rubbish are the foundations of two or three buildings, with limestone columns mostly worn away⊹ and another with eight or ten polished columns still remaining, and others of limestone among them. The finest structure appears to have been in the south-west corner of the ruins, by the side of the brook. Among its foundations are two marble columns with Corinthian capitals, and several of granite. A gateway with a pointed arch is still standing. A small bridge is thrown over the stream, and leads to the khan, which is of Saracenic structure (*Bibliotheca Sacra*, 1843, p. 77). Van de Velde visited the spot in 1852, approaching it through the hills from the south-west. He describes the view of the plain as seen from the highest point between it and the sea, and the huge *tells* which mark the positions of the "key-fortresses" of the hills and the plain, Taanûk and el-Lejjûn, the latter being the most considerable, and having another called Tell Metzellim, half an hour to the north-west (*Syr. and Pal.* i, 350–356). About a month later in the same year Dr. Robinson was there, and convinced himself of the correctness of his former opinion. He, too, describes the view over the plain, northwards to the wooded hills of Galilee, eastwards to Jezreel, and southwards to Taanach, Tell Metzellim being also mentioned as on a projecting portion of the hills which are continuous with Carmel, the Kishon being just below (*Bib. Res.* ii, 116–119). Both writers mention a copious stream flowing down this gorge (March and April), and turning some mills before joining the Kishon. Here are probably the "waters of Megiddo" (מֵי מְגִדּוֹ) of Judg. v, 19, though it should be added that by professor Stanley (*S. and P.* p. 339) they are supposed rather to be "the pools in the bed of the Kishon" itself, which has its springs in Tabor (ver. 21; see Hollman, *Commentar. in carm. Deboræ*, Lips.1818, p. 42 sq.), and not (as in Michaelis, *Suppl.* p. 339; Hamesveld, iii, 138) the Sea of *Cendevia* (Pliny, v, 17; xxxvi, 65), at the foot of Carmel. The same author regards the "plain (or valley) of Megiddo" as denoting not the

whole of the Esdraelon level, but that broadest part of it which is immediately opposite the place we are describing (p. 335, 336). The supposition of Raumer (*Palästina*, p. 402), that Legio represented the ancient *Maximianopolis* (which is given by Jerome as the later name for *Hadadrimmon*), based upon the presumption that the remains of a Roman road said to be still visible to the south of Lejjun are those of the thoroughfare between Cæsarea and Jezreel, is without good foundation (see *Bibliotheca Sacra*, 1844, p. 220). Yet Van de Velde (*Memoir*, p. 333) holds this view to be correct. He thinks he has found the true Hadadrimmon in a place called *Rummaneh*, " at the foot of the Megiddo hills, in a notch or valley about an hour and a half south of Tell Metzellim," and would place the old fortified Megiddo on this tell itself, suggesting further that its name, "the Tell of the Governor," may possibly retain a reminiscence of Solomon's officer, Baana the son of Ahilud. Porter believes this tell was the site of the stronghold of Megiddo itself (*Family Treasury*, Dec. 1864).

Megid'don (Zech. xii, 1). See MEGIDDO.

Megillah. See TALMUD.

Megillôth (מְגִלּוֹת, *rolls*, from גָּלַל). The Hebrew MSS. were on rolls of parchment, usually written on one side, though sometimes also on both (Ezek. ii, 10). Afterwards the term מגלה was used of a *book* consisting of several leaves fastened together (Jer. xxxvi, 23, 24); once it occurs in Scripture as designating the Pentateuch (Psa. xl, 8 [7]). In later Jewish usage the term Megilloth was applied to the five books, viz. Song of Songs, Ruth, Lamentations, Ecclesiastes, and Esther, which were read on certain festivals in the synagogue. See HAPHTHARAH. The title of Megillah was used κατ᾽ ἐξοχήν of the book of Esther [see ESTHER, BOOK OF]; and from this it is supposed it was transferred to the others. To the reading of this at the Feast of Purim special importance was attached by the Jews (Talmud, Tr. *Megillah*, ed. Surenhus. ii, 387). See ROLL.

Megma, THE, a Mohammedan name for an assembly or council specially convened to judge of the merits or demerits of their highest functionary. The members of the Megma are the *imams*, or "doctors of the law." See IMAM.

Mehadu is the name of a Hindû deity of inferior rank, supposed to have been created before the world, and which they hold will be used when the end of the world shall come as an instrument to destroy all created things. See Broughton, *Biblioth. Hist. Sac.* ii, 78.

Mehemet Ali, one of the most noted of Egypt's sovereigns, who filled the viceroyalty from 1804 to 1848, deserves a place here for his philanthropic acts towards the Christians, and his beneficence towards all men, without distinction of creed. He was born in 1769, and died at Cairo Aug. 3, 1849. Mehemet Ali was particularly noted for his successful wars against the Mamelukes, and for his reduction of Syria, which he conquered in 1830. "As a ruler," says a contemporary, "Mehemet Ali displayed talents of a very high order, and few princes have founded more beneficent institutions or shown a more just and liberal spirit. He established schools and colleges, created an army and navy, and introduced the manufactures of Europe. He protected his Christian subjects, and aided by his liberality the researches of Champollion, Lepsius, and other eminent savants." See F. Mengin, *Histoire de l'Égypte sous le Gouvernement de Mohammed Ali* (1839); A. de Vaulabelle, *Histoire de l'Égypte;* Creasy, *Hist. of the Ottoman Turks*, ii, 392.

Mehet'abeël (Neh. vi, 10). See MEHETABEL.

Mehet'abel (Heb. *Meheytabel'*, מְחֵיטַבְאֵל, whose *benefactor* is *God;* or, according to Gesenius, a Chald. form for מֵיטִיב אֵל, *blessed* by *God;* Vulg. *Metabeel*), the name of a man and of a woman.

1. (Sept. Μετεβεήλ, Μεταβεήλ.) The daughter of

Matred, and wife of Hadad, the last named of the original kings of Edom, whose native or regal city was Pai or Pau (Gen. xxxvi, 39; 1 Chron. i, 50). B.C. prob. cir. 1619.

2 (Sept. Μηταβειήλ v. r. Μεταβειήλ, Auth. Vers. "Mehetabeel.") The father of Delaiah, and grandfather of the Semaiah who connived with Sanballat in his attempts to decoy Nehemiah into signs of fear (Neh. vi, 10). B.C. considerably ante 446.

Mehi'da (Heb. *Mechida'*, מְחִידָא, prob. *joining;* Sept. in Ezra Μειδά v. r. Μαουδά, in Neh. Μειιδά v. r. Μιδά; Vulg. *Mahida*), a name given in Ezra ii, 52; Neh. vii, 54, apparently as that of a person whose descendants (or possibly a place whose inhabitants) were among the Nethinim of the "children" (i. e. probably residents) of Bazlith, after the exile. B.C. ante 536.

Me'hir (Heb. *Mechir'*, מְחִיר, *price,* as often; Sept. Μαχείρ v. r. Μαχίρ), the son of Chelub and father (? founder) of Eshton, of the tribe of Judah (1 Chron. iv, 11), but of what particular family does not clearly appear. B.C. perhaps cir. 1618.

Meholah. See ABEL-MEHOLAH.

Meho'lathite (Heb. *Mecholathi'*, מְחֹלָתִי, Gentile adj. from *Meholah;* Sept. Μαουλαθίτης, Μοουλαθί), a native doubtless of ABEL-MEHOLAH (1 Sam. xviii,19; 2 Sam. xxi, 8).

Mehu'jaël (Heb. *Mechuyaël'*, מְחוּיָאֵל, *smitten by God;* v. r. in the same verse *Mechiyaël'*, מְחִיָּאֵל; Sept. has Μαλελεήλ v. r. Μαϊήλ; Vulg. *Maniael*), the son of Irad and father of Methusael, third antediluvian patriarch in descent from Cain (Gen. iv, 18). B.C. cir. 3840.

Mehu'man (Heb. *Mehuman'*, מְהוּמָן, either from the Syr. *faithful,* or from some unknown Persian word; Sept. Ἀμάν, Vulg, *Mehuman*), the first named of the seven eunuchs whom Xerxes commanded to bring in Vashti to the royal presence (Esth. i, 10). B.C. 483.

Mehu'nim (Heb. *Meünim,'* מְעוּנִים, *habitations,* as in 1 Chron. iv, 41, etc.; Sept. in Ezra, Μοουνείμ v. r. Μοουνίμ, Auth.Vers. "Meunim;" in Neh. Μεεινώμ v. r. Μείνών; Vulg. constantly *Munim*), apparently a person whose "children" returned among the Nethinim from Babylon (Ezra ii, 50; Neh. vii, 52); but rather, perhaps, to be regarded as indicating the inhabitants of some town in Palestine where they settled after the exile, and in that case probably identical with the inhabitants of MAON (or possibly the "Mehunims" [below] of 2 Chron. xxvi, 7). See MAONITE.

MEHUNIMS, THE (הַמְּעוּנִים, i. e. *the Me'ûnim;* Sept. οἱ Μειναῖοι v. r. οἱ Μιναῖοι; Vulg. *Ammonitæ*), a people against whom king Uzziah waged a successful war (2 Chron. xxvi, 7). Although so different in its English dress, yet the name is in the original merely the plural of MAON (מָעוֹן), a nation named among those who in the earlier days of their settlement in Palestine harassed and oppressed Israel. Maon, or the Maonites, probably inhabited the country at the back of the great range of Seir, the modern esh-Sherah, which forms the eastern side of the Wady el-Arabah, where at the present day there is still a town of the same name (Burckhardt, *Syria,* Aug. 24). This is quite in accordance with the terms of 2 Chron. xxvi, 7, where the Mehunim are mentioned with "the Arabians of Gur-baal," or, as the Sept. renders it, Petra. Another notice of the Mehunims in the reign of Hezekiah (B.C. cir. 726–697) is found in 1 Chron. iv, 41. Here they are spoken of as a pastoral people, either themselves Hamites, or in alliance with Hamites, quiet and peaceable, dwelling in tents. They had been settled from "of old," i. e. aboriginally, at the east end of the valley of Gedor or Gerar, in the wilderness south of Palestine. A connection with Mount Seir is hinted at, though obscurely (ver. 42). Here, however, the Auth.Vers.—probably following the translations of Luther and Junius, which in their turn

follow the Targum—treats the word as an ordinary noun, and renders it "habitations;" a reading now relinquished by scholars, who understand the word to refer to the people in question (Gesenius, *Thesaur.* p. 1002 *a,* and *Notes on Burckhardt,* p. 1069; Bertheau, *Chronik*). A third notice of the Mehunim, corroborative of those already mentioned, is found in the narrative of 2 Chron. xx. There is every reason to believe that in ver. 1 "the Ammonites" should be read as "the Maonites," who in that case are the "men of Mount Seir" mentioned later in the narrative (ver. 10, 22).

In all these passages, including the last, the Sept. renders the name by οἱ Μειναῖοι—the Minæans—a nation of Arabia renowned for their traffic in spices, who are named by Strabo, Ptolemy, and other ancient geographers, and whose seat is now ascertained to have been the south-west portion of the great Arabian peninsula, the western half of the modern Hadramaut (Smith, *Dict. of Geography,* s. v. Minæi). Bochart has pointed out (*Phaleg,* vol. ii, cap. xxii), with reason, that distance alone renders it impossible that these Minæans can be the Meunim of the Bible, and also that the people of the Arabian peninsula are Shemites, while the Meunim appear to have been descended from Ham (1 Chron. iv, 41). But, with his usual turn for etymological speculation, he endeavors nevertheless to establish an identity between the two, on the ground that *Carn al-Manasil,* a place two days' journey south of Mecca, one of the towns of the Minæans, signifies the "horn of habitations," and might therefore be equivalent to the Hebrew *Meonim.* Josephus (*Ant.* ix, 10,3) calls them "the Arabs who adjoined Egypt," and speaks of a city built by Uzziah on the Red Sea to overawe them. Ewald (*Geschichte,* i, 323, note) suggests that the southern Minæans were a colony from the Maonites of Mount Seir, who in their turn he appears to consider a remnant of the Amorites (see the text of the same page). That the Minæans were familiar to the translators of the Sept. is evident from the fact that they not only introduce the name on the occasions already mentioned, but that they further use it as equivalent to NAAMATHITE. Zophar the Naamathite, one of the three friends of Job, is by them presented as "Sophar the Minæan," and "Sophar king of the Minæans." In this connection it is not unworthy of notice that as there was a town called Maon in the mountain-district of Judah, so there was one called Naamah in the lowland of the same tribe. El-Minyây, which is or was the first station south of Gaza, is probably identical with Minoïs, a place mentioned with distinction in the Christian records of Palestine in the 5th and 6th centuries (Reland, *Palæst.* p. 899; Le Quien, *Oriens Christ.* iii, 669), and both may retain a trace of the Minæans. BAAL-MEON, a town on the east of Jordan, near Heshbon, still called *Ma'in,* probably also retains a trace of the presence of the Maonites or Mehunim north of their proper locality.

The latest appearance of the name MEHUNIMS in the Bible is in the lists of those who returned from the captivity with Zerubbabel. Among the non-Israelites from whom the Nethinim—following the precedent of what seems to have been the foundation of the order—were made up, we find their name (Ezra ii, 50, A. V. "Mehunim;" Neh. vii, 52, A.V. "Meunim"). Here they are mentioned with the Nephishim, or descendants of Naphish, an Ishmaelitish people whose seat appears to have been on the east of Palestine (1 Chron. v, 19), and therefore certainly not far distant from Ma'an, the chief city of the Maonites.

Meichelbeck, CHARLES, a German monastic and scholar, was born May 29, 1669, at Oberndorf, in Algau. He was admitted in 1687 to the Order of the Benedictines of Buren, in Bavaria. From 1697 he taught Latin, and subsequently theology, in the different convents of his order. After having prepared a history of the abbey of Buren—*Chronico Benedicto-Buranum* (Buren, 1752, fol.)—he was commissioned in 1722, by the chief bishop of Freisingen, to write one of that city—*Historia*

Frisingensis, ab anno 724 (Augsburg, 1724–29, 2 vols. fol.); the numerous diplomas contained in this work render it very valuable as a history of Germanic institutions. Called later to Vienna to write the annals of the house of Austria, he declined the task on account of the bad state of his health. He died at Freisingen April 2, 1734. P. Haidenfeld prepared a life of Meichelbeck, but it was never published. See Hirsching, *Hist. liter. Handbuch ;* Zapf, *Literarische Reisen*, vol. i; Meusel, *Gelehrten-Lexikon*, s. v.

Meier, Ernst Heinrich, a German Orientalist, was born at Rusbendt, in Schaumburg-Lippe, May 17, 1813. He studied at the University of Tübingen, and was appointed professor there in 1848. He died March 2, 1866. Of his writings, the following deserve especial mention: *Uebersetzung und Erklärung des Proph. Joel* (Tübing. 1840) :—*Hebräisches Wurzelwörterbuch* (Manh. 1845) :—*Ueber die Bildung und Bedeutung des Plural in den sem. und germanischen Sprachen* (ibid. 1846) :—*Die ursprüngliche Form des Dekalogs* (1846) :—*Commentar zu Jesaia*, vol. i (Pforzh. 1850) :—*Die Form der hebr. Poesie* (Tübing. 1853) :—*Geschichte der poetischen Nationalliteratur der Hebräer* (ibid. 1856). This last-named work was an attempt to transform the introduction of the Old Test. into a history of the literature of the Hebrews.

Meier, Friedrich Karl, a German theologian, was born Aug. 11, 1808. He became privat-docent in 1832, and professor of theology at Jena in 1835. In 1836 he removed to Giessen to labor in the same capacity, and there he died, Feb. 13, 1841. His principal writings are, *Geschichte der Transubstantionslehre* (Heidelb. 1832) :—*Commentar zum Briefe an die Ephesier* (Berlin, 1834) :—*Girolamo Savonarola* (ibid. 1836) :—*Lehrbuch der Dogmengeschichte* (Giess. 1840).

Meier, Georg Friedrich, a German philosopher, was born in 1718 at Ammendorf; was a student, and in 1746 was appointed professor of philosophy, at Halle. He died there in 1777. His writings are, *Anfangsgründe der schönen Wissenschaften* (Halle, 1748, 3 vols.; 2d edit. ibid. 1754) :—*Betrachtungen über den ersten Grundsatz aller schöner Künste und Wissenschaften* (ibid. 1757) :—*Metaphysik* (ibid. 1756, 4 vols.) :—*Philosophische Sittenlehre* (ibid. 1756–61, 5 vols.) :—*Recht der Natur* (ibid. 1767) :—*Versuch eines neuen Lehrgebäudes von den Seelen der Thiere* (ibid. 1756) :—*Versuch einer allgemeinen Auslegungskunst* (ibid. 1756) :—*Untersuchung verschiedener Materien aus der Philosophie* (ibid. 1768–71, 4 vols.). See his biography by S. G. Lange (ibid. 1778).

Meier, Gerhard, a German theologian, was born at Hamburg Aug. 26, 1664. He received his first instruction in the schools of his native city; studied theology at the university at Leipsic and at Wittenberg. In 1684 he received his degree, and in 1687 was appointed adjunct to the faculty of philosophy. In 1692 he received his degree of licentiate of theology. His dissertation at this time was *De mysteriis pentecostalibus in Paradiso revelatis.* In December of the same year he was called to the gymnasium of his native city as professor of logic and metaphysics. He was next appointed pastor of St. Benedict's Church, and later was made superintendent and a Church councillor. In 1698 he went to Wittenberg to receive the degree of doctor of divinity. In 1700 he accepted a call to Bremen as councillor of the consistory, and superintendent and pastor of the cathedral. In 1715 the position of general superintendent and professor of theology at Greifswalde was offered him, but he declined it. He died Feb. 25, 1723. Meier was esteemed for his sound theological research, which he displayed in several dissertations, mostly of a dogmatic character. A complete list of his works is given by Döring, *Gelehrte Theol. Deutschlands*, ii, 462.

Meier, Johann Christian Wilhelm, a German theologian, was born at Engter July 5, 1731. He received his first instruction in languages and sciences at home, and afterwards at the gymnasium at Osnabrück.

He studied theology in Jena and Göttingen. In 1753 he returned home, a candidate of theology, and was soon assigned a place as assistant to an aged pastor at Westen, near Nienburg. In this position he secured for himself the respect of his superior, and added to his literary fame by contributions to a theological periodical. In 1756 he formed the acquaintance of major Von Busch at Nienburg, who appointed him field chaplain to his regiment. In this capacity he accompanied the regiment to Canterbury, England. During his stay there he collected material for a history of the Methodists. After having travelled much for this purpose, he returned to Nienburg with his regiment in February, 1757. The history, we are sorry to say, was never published. Some of his dissertations, but particularly one, crowned with a prize, *Schrift und Vernunftmäszige Abhandlung von dem versöhnen der Zeitpunkte im Leben Jesu*, published in 1756, recommended him to the favor of the count of Schaumburg-Lippe. With the title of a councillor of consistory, he became presiding superintendent of Bückeburg and supreme pastor at Stadthagen. At Rinteln he obtained the degree of a doctor of divinity by the defence of his dissertation *De effectibus concionum Methodisticarum haud Miraculosis nec mirabilibus* (Rintelii, 1758, 4to). He died in 1775. Meier was esteemed a theologian of great learning and sincere piety, and was untiring in his endeavors to elevate the moral qualities of the heart. (J. H. W.)

Meigs, BENJAMIN CLARK, D.D., a missionary of the American board in Ceylon, was born at Bethlehem, Conn., Aug. 9, 1789; was educated at Yale College (class of 1809), and while a student there he was hopefully converted, and united with the college Church in 1809. His religious exercises were very deep and marked. He taught for a time in an academy at Bedford, New York, and then spent two and a half years at the Andover Theological Seminary. During his course there he attended, in connection with Samuel J. Mills and others, those select meetings of inquiry and prayer in reference to the subject of missions to the heathen which were commenced with the formation of the American board. Mr. Meigs, determined to devote himself to a missionary's life, was ordained at Newburyport, Mass., June 21, 1815, and sailed from that place October 23 following, to found the Ceylon mission at Jaffna. In connection with this mission he labored more than forty years, sharing in its toils and trials, its fears and hopes. In 1840, after an absence of twenty-five years, he returned to his native land, and sailed again from Boston Oct. 17, 1841, to continue his missionary labors. In 1858 the failure of his health compelled him to return again to America, and relinquish the work to which his life had been devoted. He died from a disease contracted by his long residence in India, at New York City, May 12, 1862. See *Missionary Herald*, July, 1862. •

Meïlah. See TALMUD.

Meindaerts, PETER JOHN, a Dutch theologian of note, was born Nov. 7, 1684, at Groningen. After having concluded his studies at Malines and Louvain, he became attached to the cause of Peter Codde, a Jansenistic prelate, who had just been dismissed by the pope from the vicarship of the United Provinces. Meindaerts was therefore obliged to go to Ireland to receive his sacerdotal ordination (1716). On his return he was made pastor of Leuwarden. In 1739 he was elected archbishop of Utrecht, in the place of Theodore van der Croon, and occupied the see until his death. Like his predecessors, Meindaerts was often obliged to defend the rights of his see against the encroachments of the court of Rome. Censured by Clement XII, he appealed from him to the first council, and executed the project, a long time meditated, of filling the vacant sees of his metropolis. It was thus that he revived the extinct bishoprics of Harlem and Deventer, by giving them, one to Jerome de Bock (1742), the other to Jean Byeveld (1758). These acts of authority drew upon him new censures from

Benedict XIV and Clement XIII. In 1763 Meindaerts held a council at Utrecht, in which were seated his suffragans, his clergy, and many French Jansenists. This act further provoked the most animated controversies. He died at Groningen Oct. 31, 1767, after having presided many times at Utrecht over a religious assembly, to which he gave the name of Provincial Synod. His principal writings are, *Recueil de témoignages en faveur de l'église d'Utrecht* (Utrecht, 1763, 4to; reprinted in 2 vols. 12mo):—the *Actes* of the Council of Utrecht, in Latin, translated into French, 4to:—*Lettre à Clément XIII* (Utrecht, 1768, 12mo). See Chalmot, *Biograph. Woordenbock*, s. v.; Hoefer, *Nouv. Biog. Générale*, s. v.

Meineke, JOHANN HEINRICH FRIEDRICH, a German theologian, was born at Quedlinburg Jan. 11, 1745, and was educated at the University of Helmstädt, which he entered, when in his nineteenth year, as a student of divinity; later he studied at Halle. He returned to Quedlinburg in 1767, and was two years after appointed to a position in the high-school of that city. He gave himself up to the study of literature and philosophy, especially Kant's system, which he studied diligently for several years. Though much engaged in his profession as a teacher, he yet wished, as he advanced in years, to leave the pedagogical sphere, and he very readily accepted an appointment as minister at St. Blasius' Church at Quedlinburg. In the beginning of 1825 he was taken ill, and died July 25, 1825. Meineke united a perfect knowledge of theology, philosophy, and ancient languages, with a talent for the practical application of his knowledge. Though liberal in sentiment, he yet displayed the most decided abilities of a polemic who gave no quarter. He knew only one cause, that of his God and of his Church, and to serve it faithfully was his only endeavor. His best polemical production, entitled *Finsterlinge unserer Zeit*, he published under the nom de plume of Aloysius Frey (in 1822). For the use of ministers, he published in 1811 *Repertorium für alle Kanzelbedürfnisse der Prediger an Sonn- und Festtagsfrühpredigten oder in der Woche* (Quedlinburg, 1811, 8vo), vol. i; the second volume was never published, but an appendix to this he published in 1817:—*Tägliches Handbuch für Prediger und Predigamts-Candidaten zur leichtern Auffindung der Materialien zu ihren Kanzelvorträgen* (ibid. 1817, 8vo). But perhaps the most valuable production of his life was *Die Bibel ihrem Gesammtinhalte nach summarisch erklärt zurichtiger Beurtheilung und zweckmässigem Gebrauche derselben für Lehrer in Bürger und Landschulen* (Quedlinburg, 1819, 2 vols. 8vo). See Döring, *Gelehrte Theol. Deutschlands*, s. v.

Meiners, CHRISTOPH, a celebrated German philosopher, was born at Otterndorf, Hanover, in 1747. About his early life but little is known. He studied at the University of Göttingen, and became a professor at his alma mater in 1772. He died in 1810. He wrote, *Revision der Philosophie* (Göttingen, 1772):—*Versuch einer Religionsgeschichte der ältesten Völker besonders Aegyptens* (ibid. 1775):—*Historia doctrinæ de vero Deo* (Lemgo, 1780, 2 vols.):—*Geschichte des Ursprungs der Wissenschaften in Griechenland und Rom* (ibid. 1781, 2 vols.): —*Geschichte des Verfalls der Sitten und Staatsverfassung der Römer* (Leips. 1782):—*Geschichte des Verfalls der Sitten, Wissenschaften und Sprache der Römer* (Wien, 1791):—*Geschichte aller Religionen* (Hanover, 1806, 2 vols.):—*Geschichte der Ethik* (ibid. 1800, 2 vols.):—*Untersuchungen über die Denk- und Willenskräfte* (Götting. 1806):—*Geschichte der Entstehung und Entwickelung der hohen Schulen* (ibid. 1802, 4 vols.):—*Geschichte des weiblichen Geschlechts* (Hanov. 1798, 4 vols.):—*Lebensbeschreibungen von Männern aus der Zeit der Wiederherstellung der Wissenschaften* (Zürich, 1796):—*Historische Vergleichung der Sitten des Mittelalters mit denen unseres Jahrhunderts* (Hanov. 1793, 3 vols.). Besides these, his own works, he edited, in connection with T. G. Feder, *Philosophische Bibliothek* (Götting. 1788-91, 4 vols.); in connection with Spittler, *Göttingisches historisches Magazin* (Hanov. 1787-90); *Neueres Magazin* (ibid. 1791-92, 3 vols.). Meiners's literary works evince great activity, and at the same time a great variety in his themes; the most of his writings, however, are devoted to show the difference between past and present morals.

Meinhold, JOHANN WILHELM, a German theologian, was born Feb. 27, 1797, at Netzelkow, on the isle of Usedom, and was educated at Greifswalde. In 1820 he was appointed rector of the school at Usedom, and soon after minister at Koserow, near the Baltic; in 1826 at Krummin, and in 1844 at Rehwinkel, near Stargard. He resigned this position in 1850, and joined the Roman Catholic confession. He died in 1851 at Charlottenburg. He published *Athanasia oder die Verklärung Friedrich Wilhelm III* (1844):—*Die babylonische Sprachen und Ideenverwirrung der modernen Presse* (Leips. 1848). His works were collected and published at Leipsic (1846-52), entitled *Gesammelte Schriften.*

Meinrad, ST., a German Roman Catholic ascetic, was born towards the close of the 8th century. He was educated at the abbey of Reichenau. He secluded himself in a desert near the Etzel Mountains, and afterwards near the spot where now stands the Benedictine convent of Einsiedeln, which was built in 934 by the canon Benedictus of Strasburg. Meinrad was murdered Feb. 21, 863.

Meintel, CONRAD STEPHEN, a German theologian, was born at Schwabach, Bavaria, in the early part of the 18th century. In his very youth he made such rapid progress in old and modern languages that he had finished in his twelfth year the reading of the Bible in the original. He studied theology at the university at Altdorf in 1745; continued in 1746 at Jena; went in 1747 home to Peternaurach, where his father was then installed as a minister of the Gospel. In 1751 he returned to Altdorf. He gained great notoriety in 1751 by means of his dissertation *De locis quibusdam Jobi, in quibus celeberr. Schultens majorem lucem desideravit.* In the latter part of 1751 he went home to assist his father, and stayed there till 1754, when he went to Erlangen, and then gained great distinction by his defence of the dissertation *Observationes philologico-philosophicæ in Ecclesiastis septem priores versus.* He was given the privilege of holding public lectures. He had hopes of a professorship, but love for his home made him return to it again, and he became an assistant of his father. He finally accepted a call from St. Petersburg, Russia, and died, as minister of the Protestant congregations at Wassili-Ostrow, Aug. 13, 1764. A short time before his death the doctorate in divinity was given to him by the University of Königsberg. Besides several literary essays, he published the following: *Notæ selectissimorum commentatorum Judaicorum in Psalmos Davidi ex collectione Hebraica celeberr.* H. J. v. Bashuysen, Latine redditæ (Suabaci, 1744, 8vo):—*Cento quattro historie scelte della Biblia raccolte dal fee Sgr. Giov. Hubner ed hora tradotte de original Tedesco in Italiano* (ibid. 1745, 4to).

Meir, *Rabbi* (surnamed "*illuminator,*" i. e. the enlightener, from the estimate which his contemporaries had formed of his merit), lived about 120. He was a native of Asia Minor. Legend traces his origin to the emperor Nero. He was a disciple of the famous rabbi Akiba (q. v.), and was very intimate with Elisa ben-Abua, who, after his apostasy and subserviency to the Romans, was called *Acher*, i. e. the other one. Meir's talents early procured him ordination from his teacher Akiba. As an instructor, he was remarkable for a thorough and effective investigation of his subject. The rabbins used to say, in their Oriental manner, that he dealt with difficulties of the law as a giant would uproot the mountains, and shatter them against each other. So replete was he with knowledge, and so successful in the communication of it, that "were a man even to touch the staff of rabbi Meir, he would become wise." His wife was Beruria, the talented and accomplished daughter of Chananja ben-Teradion, who was burned, wrapped in the roll which he had been discovered studying, during the persecution under Hadrian. Meir supported himself by making copies of the Scriptures. This occupation required not only considerable learning, but especially scrupulous exactness, a quality for which Meir was not particularly distinguished. His teacher, the conscientious Ishmael, anxiously set these things before him, representing the danger which must result from any neglect on his part. But Meir, who felt no peculiar scruples, and was vain of his excellent memory, which on one occasion had enabled him to copy the whole book of Esther, set these prudent counsels aside. It was the practice of Jewish copyists to use an ink which, in case of any mistake, could easily be obliterated. On the other hand, Meir, confident of his accuracy, used an indelible ink prepared from sulphate of copper (Chalcanthon). Referring to this, he replied to Ishmael's admonitions in his usual off-hand manner, "Oh, I have a remedy at hand against all mistakes: I use sulphate of copper." As has already been said, his talents had procured him ordination from Akiba. The youthful appearance of the rabbi excited the jealousy of some, whom he reminded that, as it was not the vessel but its contents which were precious, it might happen that, while a new vessel contained old, an old-looking vessel might only enclose new wine. Meir was very fond of illustrating his doctrine by apologue and parable, and is reported to have invented no less than three hundred fables about foxes (Sanh. 38, b; Sota, 49, a). The only lasting merit of rabbi Meir was his continuation of the labors of Akiba in the arrangement of the Halacha. This he carried a stage further, by dividing, according to their contents, the traditions which had hitherto been only strung together according to their number. In this respect Jehuda Hakkodesh, the compiler of the Mishna, was much indebted to his tuition.

The domestic history of Meir is in many respects touching. "It has already been stated that our rabbi was married to Beruria, so famed for her talents and rabbinical lore as, in the opinion of contemporaries, to occupy a high place among the sages of the time. Her sister had, after the martyrdom of their parents, been carried to Rome for the purpose of public prostitution. But there Providence had watched over her honor. When the persecutions ceased, Beruria found no rest till Meir went to Rome to rescue his sister-in-law from infamy. Before entering on the dangerous undertaking, he resolved to try whether her principles had remained unshaken. Disguising himself as a Roman, he approached her, and, having satisfactorily ascertained her steadfastness, he bribed the attendants and procured her escape, though in the attempt he himself escaped capture only by disguise and feigning to eat forbidden meat. . . . Beruria, throughout all these trials, proved herself not only an attached, but a devoted wife. She had shared his trials when, during the persecutions, Meir had fled from Palestine. On his return she cheered and encouraged him, and by her conduct softened the domestic afflictions with which he was visited. For example, while on a certain Sabbath the rabbi was engaged in the college, his two sons were suddenly taken ill and died. To spare her husband some hours of grief, and especially not to commute the festivities of the Sabbath into a season of mourning, the mother carefully repressed her own feelings and concealed the sad tidings. The Sabbath had been spent as usual, and its holy exercises and stillness were ended with the evening, when Beruria asked her husband whether it were not duty readily and cheerfully to restore to its owner any property, however pleasant, which had been intrusted for safe-keeping. When the astonished rabbi answered the strange inquiry in the affirmative, his weeping wife took him by the hand, and led him to the bed on which the lifeless remains of their two children were stretched, reminding him that he whose two children these rightfully were had taken back what for a time he had intrusted to their keeping." Unfortunately Beruria after-

wards compromised her character and committed suicide. Her death appears to have unsettled Meir's tranquillity. He left Palestine and resided some time in Babylonia, whence he returned to his colleagues with another and less learned bride.

Meir, besides cultivating intercourse with the most noted theologians of his own time, was also on friendly and even intimate terms with heathen sages, especially with Naumenius the philosopher, of Apamea, in Syria. The principles of this philosopher were essentially those of Neo-Platonism, in the peculiar modification of that philosophy which the influx of Eastern elements had brought about. The most noted, if not the most sophistical, among Meir's numerous pupils, was Symmachus, of Samaritan origin, known as a translator of the Bible into Greek. He had attended Meir's prelections, and thoroughly imbibed his method. It is said that this dialectician on one occasion undertook by forty-nine arguments to prove that the touch of a certain dead reptile could not defile a person. It was opprobriously said of Symmachus by his contemporaries that his ancestors could not have heard the law on Mount Sinai. Symmachus afterwards joined the Christian sect of the Ebionites. His translation of the Bible is stated to have been more free from errors and more faithful than that of Aquila. According to Grätz, this Symmachus is not the translator of the Bible.

Meir had frequently changed his residence. When the Sanhedrim was restituted under Simeon (q. v.), he returned to the Holy Land, and was elected vicar of the rabbinical see; but his continual disagreements with the Nasi induced him at last to leave Palestine for Asia Minor, where he died, bequeathing to his countrymen the following proud and characteristic message: "Tell the children of the Holy Land that their Messiah has died in a strange country." According to his expressed wish, the tabernacle of his unquiet spirit found its last resting-place by the sea-shore, where his grave was washed by the waves, and looked out upon the wide, storm-tossed ocean. See Etheridge, Intr. to Hebr. Literature, p. 79 sq.; Grätz, Gesch. d. Juden, iv, 188-196, 468-470; Edersheim, Hist. of the Jewish Nation (Edinburgh, 1857), p. 251-259. (B. P.)

Meir, Abulafia, EL-LEWI BEN-TODROS, a Jewish savant of note, was born about 1180, and was a native of Burgos. He taught the law at Toledo, where he died in 1244. He wrote various cabalistical works, such as the לִפְנֵי וְלִפְנִים, a part of which was published in Hebrew and Latin by Rittangel in the סֵפֶר יְצִירָה (Amst. 1662). He wrote also a letter against Maimonides's אִגְּרוֹת, a treatise on the Masorah, entitled "The Fence of the Law," מָסֹרֶת סְיָג לַתּוֹרָה, and some novellas on parts of the Mishna. See Fürst, Bibl. Jud. i, 16; Etheridge, Introd. to Hebr. Literature, p. 276, 277; Grätz, Gesch. d. Juden, vii, 33 sq.; Jost, Gesch. d. Judenthums, iii, 8, 9; Lindo, History of the Jews of Spain and Portugal, p. 81; Finn, Sephardim, or the History of the Jews in Spain and Portugal, p. 193 (Lond. 1841). (B. P.)

Meir ben-Baruch (also called by the Jews Maharam, from the initial letters= מורנו הרב מאיר מהר״ם, our teacher the rabbi Meir), one of the most distinguished Jewish literati during the Middle Ages, was born in 1230. He was the first official chief rabbi in the German empire, to which dignity he was nominated by the emperor Rudolph I of Hapsburg. He had his seat and college at Rottenburg-an-der-Tauber, whence he is also called Meir of Rottenburg or Meier Rottenburg. The unsettled condition of the Jews in the German empire, especially the oppressions and persecutions which threatened them every year, obliged Meir to leave the country. In the spring of 1286 he prepared to go to Syria. There, it was said, a Messiah had appeared to deliver the unhappy people. When about to enter the vessel which would convey him and his co-religionists who had followed him from Italy to the East, he was recognised by a former co-religionist, named Knippe, who was in the suite of the bishop of Basle. Rabbi Meir was imprisoned by the emperor, not so much for punishment as for the purpose of extorting from him or his co-religionists a sum of money. Meir died in 1293 in prison at Worms, where his tombstone was discovered a few years since in the "Gottesacker," or cemetery. The Ashkenazim, or German Jews, venerate him as a saint. Meir wrote *Theological Decisions*, or *Questions and Answers* (שאלות ותשובות), which have been published at Cremona, 1557; Prague, 1603. He also wrote *Commentaries on the Masorah* (באורי מסרת), which are still in MS. in the public libraries. He also wrote some liturgical pieces, which are still in use among the Jews; among other pieces, the famous lamentation שאלי שרופה באש, in commemoration of the burning of the law at Paris in 1242. See Etheridge, *Introd. to Heb. Literature*, p. 288; Grätz, *Gesch. d. Juden*, vii, 107, 170–172, 188–191, 445, 456–60 (new edit. Leipsic, 1873); Jost, *Geschichte des Judenthums u. s. Sekten*, iii, 32, 58; Fürst, *Biblioth. Jud.* iii, 176, 177; Zunz, *Geschichte und Literatur*, p. 40, 92, 128 (Berlin, 1845); *Literaturgeschichte der Synagogales Poesie*, p. 357–62, 623 (Berlin, 1865). (B. P.)

Meir ibn-Gabbai, a Jewish writer, was born in 1481 in Spain. When eleven years old he was obliged to leave his country on account of the edict of Ferdinand and Isabella, which banished all Jews from the land. Little is known of his personal history after this time. He wrote several cabalistical works: דֶּרֶךְ אֱמוּנָה, i. e. *the way of truth*, ten sections on the ten Sephiroth (Padua, 1563; Berlin, 1850, by N. A. Goldberg):—עֲבֹדַת הַקֹּדֶשׁ, also מַרְאוֹת אֱלֹהִים, in four sections: a, *on the unity of God*; b, *on the mysteries of the adoration of God*; c, *on the end of the higher and lower creatures*; d, *on the mysteries of the law* (Mantua, 1545, folio; Venice, 1567; Krakau, 1578); and a work on *prayer*, entitled תּוֹלַעַת יַעֲקֹב (Kstpl. 1560; Zolkiew, 1799). See Fürst, *Biblioth. Jud.* i, 311, 312; Jost, *Geschichte des Judenthums*, iii, 138; Grätz, *Geschichte d. Juden*, ix, 239 (Berl. 1866). (B. P.)

Meir Joseph BEN-JOSHUA, surnamed *Ha-Sephardi*, i. e. the Spaniard, a Jewish savant of note, flourished in the early part of the 16th century. He was born in 1496 at Avignon, whither his father had retired on leaving Spain. He is the author of a most valuable historic work, entitled דִּבְרֵי הַיָּמִים, *Chronicles of the Kings of France and the Ottoman Sovereigns*, in two parts; the first from the creation till 1520, and the second of transactions from that time till 1553 (Venice, 1554; Amsterd. 1733). The value of the work consists in the fact that it throws aside much of the fable and wild imagination which render almost worthless all other rabbinical histories. Though contemporary with those events, the chronicler must be regarded as an impartial historian. A part of this work has been translated into Latin by L. Ferrand (Paris, 1670). To English readers this work is made accessible by C. H. Bialloblotzky's translation, *The Chronicles of R. Joseph ben-Joshua Meir, the Sephardi* (Lond. 1836–38). See Fürst, *Biblioth. Jud.* ii, 115; Etheridge, *Introd. to Heb. Literat.* p. 453; Lindo, *Hist. of the Jews of Spain and Portugal*, p. 451; Jost, *Geschichte des Judenthums*, iii, 124; Milman, *History of the Jews*, iii, 461 (New York, 1870); Da Costa, *Israel and the Gentiles*, p. 397 sq. (New York, 1855). (B. P.)

Meir Rofe, OF HEBRON. Like his father Chija Rofe, he was a physician. Little is known of his life, except that he was one of the adherents of Sabbathai Zewi (q. v.), or Aga Mohammed Effendi, the Messiah, who during the 17th century excited the whole of Europe and Asia. (B. P.)

Meïri (מֵאִירִי, or לְבֵית מֵאִיר), MENACHEM BEN-SALOMO, also called *Don Vidal Salomo*, also *Menachem ben-Salomo*, a Jewish savant, was born at Perpignan, in France, in 1249. He was a man of great learning, and, like Maimonides, he tried to harmonize philosophy with the Talmud. He wrote in a lucid style, and in this respect made an exception to that bombastic method which was prevalent in his times. In his explanations of the holy Scriptures he kept aloof from the philosophical and mystical interpretation, and, though he acknowledged that some passages contain a higher hidden sense, he nevertheless adhered to the literal interpretation of the Word. He died between 1317 and 1320. Besides a commentary on the book of Proverbs, he wrote commentaries on the Talmudical tract *Megilla* (עַל בֵּית הַבְּחִירָה מְגִלָּה; new edition Königsberg, 1860, 4to); on *Joma*, printed with Is. Nuñes-Vaez's שׁיּח יִצְחָק (Livorno, 1760); on *Jebamoth, Sabbath, Nedarim, Nazir, Sota* (Livorno and Salonica, 1794 and 1795). But his greatest commentary is on the tract *Aboth* (בֵּית אָבוֹת or פֵּרוּשׁ לְאָבוֹת, with an introduction to the Talmud, etc. This latter work has been edited by M. Stern (Vienna, 1854), with biographical and bibliographical matter. See Grätz, *Gesch. d. Juden*, vii, 240–42 (Leipsic, 1873); Jost, *Gesch. des Judenthums u. s. Sekten*, iii, 57; Fürst, *Biblioth. Jud.* ii, 345, 346; Zunz, *Zur Gesch. u. Literatur*, p. 476–481 (Berl. 1845). (B. P.)

Meisel, MARCO or MORDECHAI, a great Jewish philanthropist, was born in 1528 and died in 1601. Little is known of his life, except that he was one of the wealthiest men at that time in Germany, and that he used his means for philanthropic purposes. He built homes, hospitals, synagogues, colleges, and did all in his power to elevate the condition of his brethren, especially at Prague. The German emperor, Rudolph I, honored him by the appointment of councillor. See Grätz, *Gesch. d. Juden*, ix, 497–99 (Leipsic, 1866); Jost, *Gesch. d. Judenthums*, iii, 281. (B. P.)

Meisels, BÄR, a celebrated rabbi, was born in 1797, and died on the 15th of February, 1871, at Warsaw, where for many years he had ably filled the eminent distinction of a leader in Israel. A decided republican in politics, he was long the eyesore of the Russian government, but the very eye-apple of the Poles. Of his life we hardly know anything, because the papers were prohibited by the police from giving any biographical notices of the deceased, or any description of the demonstration at his funeral. That Meisels's death was felt as a loss to the community at large, we may gather from the fact that forty thousand people, representing all creeds, nationalities, and races, attended his funeral. In him the Poles lost one of their stanchest patriots, a man who was never afraid to utter his political sentiments. In 1861 he suffered imprisonment for six months on account of his political activity. (B. P.)

Meisner, BALTHAZAR, one of the most eminent German Protestant theologians of the early part of the 17th century, was born in 1587. He studied at Wittenberg, Giessen, Strasburg, and Tübingen, and in 1613 became professor at Wittenberg. In connection with B. Mentzer (q. v.) of Giessen, and J. Gerhard of Jena, he perceived the requirements of the Church, and did his utmost to satisfy them. This we see in a remarkable sketch of his on the subject, published anonymously at Frankfort in 1679, under the title *B. Meisneri pia desideria paulo ante beatum obitum ab ipso manifestata*. The principal passages of it were also published in Tholuck's *Wittenberger Theologen*, p. 96. He had made himself known in the literary world when but twenty-four years of age by his *Philosophia sobria* (Giessen, 1611), which passed through several editions. This work involved him in a controversy with Cornelius Martin of Helmstädt, the champion of the Aristotelian school (see Henke, *Calixtus*, i, 258). His merits as a theologian have lately been fully recognised by Kaltenborn, in his *Vorläufer d. Grotius auf dem Gebiete des "Jus naturæ gentium"* (1848), p. 220. Meisner died Dec. 29, 1626. See Herzog, *Real-Encyklop.* ix, 251. (J. N. P.)

Meisnic Interim is the former name for the first formula of the LEIPSIC INTERIM (q. v.).

Meister, Christoph Andreas, a German theologian, was born at Ahornberg Aug. 23, 1671. He was the son of a minister, who gave him his first education. Afterwards he attended school at Mönchberg, Hof, and Bayreuth, where he excelled in the study of the ancient languages. He went to Wittenberg to study theology, and, thanks to several influential men, he became in 1693 minister at Langensteinach, but resigned in 1701, when he was appointed minister at the court of Limburg-Speckfeld, and located at Mark Eimersheim. In 1704 he became chief minister and inspector at Sommerhausen, and in 1709 minister at the court of Hohenlohe; also superintendent and counsellor of the consistory at Weikersheim, where he died Oct. 31, 1728. Meister bore the reputation of one thoroughly acquainted with the theology of his time. He was above all things tolerant towards those who differed from him in their religious opinions. Several of his sermons were published. A list of them is given by Döring, *Gelehrte Theol. Deutschlands*, s. v.

Meister, Christoph Georg Ludwig, a German theologian, was born at Halle Aug. 12, 1738, where he began his education at Franke's orphan school; in riper years he was a student at the university of his native town. In 1763 he was appointed second minister at Ballenstedt. In 1784 he was called to Duisburg, on the Rhine, where he filled, besides the office of a minister, a professorship of theology. In the autumn of 1784 he was called to Bremen, and was there installed as third minister of the Liebfrauen Kirche, at the same time serving also as professor of theology at the highschool; he became in 1789 second minister of the same church, and in 1795 first minister. He died Jan. 26, 1811, holding in his hands the manuscript of a sermon which he was to deliver the day after. Meister was highly esteemed by his contemporaries as the author of several ascetic works. He published also *J. L. von Mosheim's Erklärung wichtiger Stellen der heiligen Schrift, aus dessen Werken gezogen und mit practischen Zusätzen für die häusliche Andacht begleitet* (Leipsic and Wesel, 1777, 8vo); and *Kleine theologische Schriften* (Brem. 1790, 8vo).

Me-jar'kon (Heb. *Mey-Hay-yarkon'*, מֵי הַיַּרְקוֹן, *waters of yellowness*, or *clear water*; Sept. Θάλασσα Ἰαρακών, Vulg. *Mejarcon*), a town in the tribe of Dan, mentioned between Gath-rimmon and Rakkon (Josh. xix, 46); probably so called from a spring in its vicinity. Schwarz (*Palest.* p. 141) regards the name as equivalent to *river of disease* (lit. *of paleness*), and states that there is a "*Wady Udshi* which descends from the mountains of Lod" (probably referring to the ravine in the south rear of Ludd), a nearly synonymous epithet, according to him, on the strength of which he is disposed to identify the locality. "It is difficult not to suspect that the name following that of Me-hajjarkon, har-Rakon (A. V. Rakkon), is a mere corrupt repetition thereof, as the two bear a very close similarity to each other, and occur nowhere else".

Mekhitar Kosh, surnamed *the Beardless*, a learned Armenian ecclesiastic, who was born about 1140, founded a monastery in the valley of Dandsoud, in Eastern Armenia, in 1191, and became its first abbot. He died in 1213. Mekhitar Kosh left several works, but they still continue in MS. form, and are of minor value. See Hoefer, *Nouv. Biog. Générale*, xxxiv, 786.

Meko'nah (Heb. *Mekonah'*, מְכֹנָה, a *base*, as in 1 Kings vii, 27, etc.; Sept. in most editions omits, but v. r. Μαχνά and Μαβνή, Vulg. *Mochona*), a town in the southern part of the tribe of Judah, and inhabited after the exile (Neh. xi, 28). From its being coupled (in that passage) with Ziklag, we should infer that it was situated far to the south, while the mention of the "daughter towns" (בְּנוֹת, A.V. "villages") dependent on it, seem to show that it was a place of some magnitude. Re-

land (*Palæst.* p. 892) thinks it may be identical with *Mechanum*, a village located by Jerome between Eleutheropolis and Jerusalem, eight miles from the former (*Onomast.* s. v. Bethmacha). It seems strange that Jerome should speak of a village south of Jerusalem when describing Beth-maachah, which lay at the northern extremity of Palestine (2 Sam. xx, 14). The only unappropriated site at about the required distance is *Jerash*, not far north-east of Beit Nettif (Robinson, *Researches*, ii, 342, note).

Mekshirim. See TALMUD.

Mel (or **Mell**), CONRAD, a German theologian, was born Aug. 14, 1666, at Gudensberg (Hesse). He was the son of a Protestant minister, studied theology at the Dutch University of Groningen, then returned to Germany, and performed pastoral duties at Mittau, Memel, and Königsberg. In 1705 he was called to take charge of the Gymnasium of Hersfeld as director, and later received due recognition for his services from his prince, the landgrave, in the position of superintendent of the churches of Hesse. He died at Cassel, May 3, 1733. Mel had made sacred antiquity a special study, and, if his works were written too hastily, it must be attributed to the necessity of providing for the support of a large family. Mel belonged to the Royal Societies of London and Berlin. Of his works we notice *Die Posaune der Ewigkeit*—sermons (Königsb. 1697, 4to; 7th edit. Cassel, 1755, 4to); there is a kind of sequel, under the title *Der Herold der Ewigkeit* (Berlin, 1729, 4to):—*Legatio orientalis Sinensium, Samaritanorum, Chaldæorum, et Hebræorum, cum interpretationibus* (Königsberg, 1760, fol): —*Omina bruta* (1704, 8vo); inserted in D'Haubert's *Bibl. magica :—Der würdige Gast an des Herrn Tafel*—sermons (Königsberg, 1704, 4to, eight editions):—*Antiquarius sacer, seu de usu antiquitatum Judaicarum, Græcarum, et Romanarum in explicandis obscurioribus Scripturæ dictis* (Schleusingen, 1707, 8vo; the edition of Frankfort, 1719, 4to, is augmented by the addition of four small works):—*Pantometrum nauticum* (Hersfeld, 1707, fol.). He invented a machine by which he pretended to measure longitude at sea with great exactness, and offered models to several academies; those of London and Berlin presented several objections, to which he replied in the *Pharus illustrans* (ibid. 1709, fol.):—*Der Tabernackel oder gründiche Beschreibung der Stiftshütte, sammt allen ihren Theilen und heiligen Gerähten* (Frankfort, 1709, 1711, 4to; Cassel, 1720, 4to):—*Missionarius evangelicus* (Hersfeld, 1711, 8vo):—*Zion's Lehre und Wunder*—sermons (Frankfort, 1713, 4to, eight editions):—*Das Leben der Patriarchen* (Frankfort, 1715, 1716, 2 vols. 4to):—*Die Lust der Heiligen* (Cassel, 1715, 8vo; 15th edit. ibid. 1779);—*Salomon's Tempel* (Frankfort, 1724, 4to; Cassel, 1726, 4to). The manuscripts of Mel are preserved in the library of Cassel, among which is a *Histoire littéraire de la Hesse*. See *Acta Histor. Eccles.* i, 105; J. H. Lederhose, *Ehrengedächtniss Conrad Mel* (Cassel, 1733, 4to); Streides, *Grundl. zu einer Hess. Gelehrten Geschichte*, viii, 391. (J. H. W.)

Melach. See SALT.

Melah. See TEL-MELAH.

Melancholy, in so far as it is a mental disease, and must more or less affect the religious state of the believer, demands our consideration. It is generally held that melancholy is the exaggeration of the natural and legitimate feelings of grief, despondency, and apprehension, which become morbid where the emotion is without a cause, or is disproportioned to the actual cause, or is so intense as to disturb and destroy the exercise of the other mental powers. This dejection and suffering is found associated with exalted sensations, or delusions as to the personal or physical condition of the individual, which originate in habitually cherishing certain impressions, in fixing the attention upon certain vital processes, which may be unhealthy, or become so by the very concentration of thought bestowed upon them. The patient lives in fear of death, in the conviction that he is differently or more exquisitely constructed than those around; that he labors under some foul or fatal disease; that he is destitute of strength or comeliness. This has been regarded as hypochondriacal melancholy —the *maladie Anglaise*, and affects the opening of life. Similar feelings are called forth in reference to the social position. There arises a dread of poverty and want. The victim is haunted by imaginary debts, obligations, peculations. He feels incapable of extricating himself. The poor, as well as the rich, entertain such doubt and dread. They starve in order to husband their resources. This affection prevails at maturity—at the period of greatest activity and usefulness. Towards the decline of life—although encountered at every age—morbid depression assumes the form of religious anxiety, despair, remorse. Moral statistics show that among the inhabitants of Northern Europe the number of cases of melancholy exceeds those of mania; and it has been supposed that the rudiments of the malady may be detected in the original character, the temperament and habits of the race, as well as in the climate, domestic condition, and diet, by which these are modified. Defective blood nutrition, or anæmia, appears to be the physical state with which the great majority of cases of melancholy are connected, and to which all modes of treatment are directed. Powerful and permanent and depressing moral emotions act as effectively in arresting healthy digestion and alimentation as the use of injudicious food, or the use of proper nourishment under circumstances such as the respiration of impure air, or indulgence in intemperate or degraded tendencies, which render assimilation impossible. The aspect of the melancholiac corroborates the view of inanition and exhaustion. The surface is pale, dry, cold, attenuated, even insensible; the muscles are rigid; the frame is bent; the eyes sunk, and fixed or flickering; the lips parched and colorless. There is a sense of exhaustion or pain, or impending dissolution. It has been remarked that in proportion to the intensity of the internal agony is there an obtuseness or anæsthesia to wounds or external injuries. Such an immunity causes in lunatics an indifference to the most grievous forms of suffering, and has given rise to the supposition, on the part of those scientists who cannot see any virtue in religion, that Christian martyrs displayed at the stake a fortitude inspired rather by a lunatic condition than by heroic faithfulness to their convictions.—Chambers, *Cyclop.* s. v.

To remove the oppressiveness of melancholy the following remedies may be applied: 1, early rising; 2, plain, nourishing food; 3, strict temperance; 4, exercise in the open air. Or, if it arises particularly from the mind: 1, associate with the cheerful; 2, study the Scriptures; 3, consider the amiable character of God, and the all-sufficient atonement of his Son; 4, avoid all sin; 5, be much in prayer, so as to enjoy the promised presence of the Holy Spirit, the infallible Comforter; 6, be constantly engaged in such employments as combine the sense of duty and the feelings of benevolence. See Burton, Baxter, and Rogers, *On Melancholy;* Cecil, *Remains;* Fuller, *Works;* Haslam, *Observations on Madness and Melancholy;* Esquirol, *Maladies Mentales,* i, 398; Crichton, *Inquiry into the Nature and Origin of Mental Derangement.* See also MIND; MONOMANIA.

Melancthon, PHILIP, the most noted associate of Luther in the German Reformation.

Life.—Philip was born at Bretten, then in the Lower Palatinate, but now in the grand-duchy of Baden, Feb. 16, 1497. His father, George *Schwartzerd,* was a skilful armorer, and an earnest, pious man, whose personal worth and success in his art had gained for him the patronage and esteem of many of the princes of Germany. His mother, Barbara Reuter, was a frugal, industrious, and energetic woman, the daughter of the burgomaster of the village, and the supposed authoress of several household rhymes still popular in Germany. His education was begun, under the superintendence of his grandfather Reuter, at his native place. Among

his earliest teachers was John Unger, to whose thoroughness Melancthon, in later years, paid the tribute, "He made me a grammarian." Already, under Unger, his quickness of comprehension, the facility with which he memorized, the readiness with which he clearly explained what he knew, his deep interest in his studies, and his eagerness to converse upon them, marked the young pupil as a boy of rare promise. Upon the death of his grandfather, he was removed in 1508 to Pforzheim, in Baden, where he attended a Latin school, and made his home with a female relative (according to some authorities, his grandmother), who was a sister of the renowned Reuchlin. Here he became a favorite of this great classical scholar, who presented him with books, and in recognition of his extraordinary attainments, according to a custom of the times, translated his German name *Schwartzerd* into the Greek *Melanchthon* ($\mu\acute{\epsilon}\lambda\alpha\varsigma$, black; $\chi\vartheta\acute{\omega}\nu$, earth)—a name retained throughout his life, although he usually spelled it Melanthon; at present many writers have come to adopt the spelling Melancthon, and, as this is the orthography of this Cyclopædia, we have conformed to it. In October, 1509, he entered the University of Heidelberg, where, notwithstanding his extreme youth, he soon gained great distinction as a linguist, being known among his fellow-students as "the Grecian." When only a few months over fourteen he received the degree of bachelor of arts, became private tutor to the sons of count Lowenstein, and composed the Greek Grammar which was published several years afterwards. The severity of the climate occasioning repeated attacks of fever, and the refusal of the faculty, on account of his youth, to admit him to the master's degree, induced him in 1512 to remove to Tübingen. Here he devoted himself to a wide range of study, embracing Greek and Latin literature, philosophy, history, rhetoric, logic, mathematics, medicine, jurisprudence, and theology. In theology he attended the lectures of Lempan, and read William Occam. In medicine, he studied Galen with such diligence that he could repeat the most of that author from memory. In 1514 he received his master's degree, and began to lecture on Virgil and Terence. The next year found him aiding Reuchlin in the controversy with the monks. About the same time (1515) Erasmus expressed his unqualified admiration of the young master's attainments. "What promising hopes does Philip Melancthon give us, who, yet a youth, yes, almost a boy, deserves equal esteem for his knowledge of both languages. What sagacity in argument, what purity of expression, what a rare and comprehensive knowledge, what extensive reading, what delicacy and elegance of mind does he not display!" Three years later he wrote: "Christ designs this youth to excel us all: he will totally eclipse Erasmus." In 1516 he lectured on rhetoric, and expounded Livy and Cicero; and before leaving Tübingen had published his Greek Grammar.

Of the spiritual struggles of Melancthon during this period we know nothing. His great modesty prevented him from giving publicity to the details of his inner history. Whatever was the mode in which God was preparing this chosen vessel for his service we cannot discern, as in the case of Luther, any crisis, marked on the one side by the anguish of felt guilt and agonizing efforts to satisfy God's law, and on the other by rest in the merits of Christ and joy in the assurance of personal salvation. From his earliest youth God's Spirit seems to have sanctified his mind through the principles of the divine Word, which he had made the object of the most conscientious study; so that when he was called to the assistance of Luther, by his personal experience of the grace of God, he had already apprehended the great doctrine of justification by faith, which he was summoned to expound and defend. Called in 1518, upon the recommendation of Reuchlin, to the Greek professorship at Wittenberg, he declined, on his way thither, invitations from both Ingolstadt and Leipsic. At his arrival, his boyish appearance, and his timid and retiring manners, caused a feeling of disappointment; but when, four days later (Aug. 29), he delivered his inaugural lecture, "*On reforming the Studies of Youth*," he won the enthusiastic applause of all his hearers. Luther, especially, was delighted. Two days afterwards he wrote: "We quickly forgot all our thoughts about his person and stature, and rejoiced and wondered at his treatment of his theme. . . . I really desire no other teacher of Greek so long as he lives." And again, Sept. 2, "Philip has his lecture-room crowded with students. He has especially infused an enthusiasm for the study of Greek into the students of theology of all classes." This favorable opinion was only strengthened by further intimacy, which revealed the extensive erudition of Melancthon, and called forth eulogiums still more ardent. "A wonderful man, in whom everything is almost supernatural, yet my most cherished and intimate friend" (Luther to Reuchlin, Dec. 14, 1518). Although repeatedly called elsewhere, even to France and England, he remained at Wittenberg until the close of his life, exerting, by his varied attainments, marvellous industry, and simple piety, an influence second only to that of the great Reformer. Married in 1520 to Catharine Krapp, daughter of the burgomaster of Wittenberg, whom his friend Camerarius describes as a pious and devoted wife and mother, Melancthon enjoyed in his domestic life much happiness, but during his later years suffered great trouble and anxiety. Of his two sons, one died in infancy; Philip died in 1603, a pious but not a gifted man, at one time secretary of the Consistory. Of his two daughters, Anna married the learned but erratic and unprincipled George Sabinus, provost of the University of Königsberg, and died in 1547; while Magdalena became the wife of Dr. Caspar Reucer, afterwards professor at Wittenberg, and survived her father.

Melancthon's last years were embittered not only by domestic griefs, but also by the distracted condition of the Church. He longed to be delivered, as he said, from the "*rabies theologica.*" A violent cold, contracted in travelling, April, 1560, terminated in a fever, which eventually proved fatal. Although in much feebleness, he continued to lecture until a week before his death, which occurred April 19. Almost his last words were, "Nothing but heaven." Two days afterwards his body was laid by the side of that of Luther, where, on the anniversary of his death, in 1860, the corner-stone of a monument to his memory was laid with appropriate ceremonies. It has since been reared, in 1869.

Melancthon as a Teacher. — His reputation as a teacher gave him the title of *Præceptor Germaniæ*, and attracted to Wittenberg crowds of students not only from all parts of Germany, but also from England, France, Poland, Hungary, Denmark, and even Italy and Greece. He frequently lectured to an audience of 2000. His lectures covered Old and New Testament exegesis, dogmatic theology, the explanation of the principal Latin and Greek classics, ethics, logic, physics, and occasionally metaphysics. In addition, he received private pupils at his house, and exercised over them a truly paternal oversight. By his work in the organization of many of the schools of Germany, and more especially by his valuable text-books, he continued for many years after his death to exert a more powerful influence than any living teacher, and became, as Hallam (*Hist. of Lit.* i, 145) remarks, "far above all others, the founder of general learning throughout Europe." His *Latin Grammar*, prepared originally for his private pupils, was almost universally adopted in Europe, running through fifty-one editions, and continuing until 1734 to be the text-book even in the Roman Catholic schools of Saxony. His *Greek Grammar* also enjoyed great popularity. Of his *Terence*, 73 editions had been published within 106 years of its first publication. He also published either scholia upon or expositions or paraphrases of the *De Officiis, Lælius, De Oratore, Orator, Topicæ, Epistles,* and 19 *Orations* of Cicero, Porcius Latro, Sallust, the *Germania* of Tacitus, Pliny, Quintilian,

l. xii, six orations of Demosthenes, one of Æschines, Lycurgus, Stobæus, Ælian, Lucian, Thucydides, Xenophon, Plutarch, Lysis, Ptolemæus, selections from Homer and Sophocles, 18 tragedies of Euripides, Aristophanes, Menander, 19th Idyl of Theocritus, Tyrtæus, Solon, Theognis, Calimachus, Pindar, Empedocles, Virgil, Ovid, the *Miles* of Plautus, and the *Theognis* of Seneca, in addition to composing 391 Latin and Greek odes. His style (*genus dicendi Philippicum*), which is said, in purity of diction and correctness of classical taste, to excel even that of Erasmus, for a time was regarded in the schools as a model, even to the exclusion of Cicero and Quintilian.

In philosophy, although, in his first edition of his *Loci Communes*, he sympathizes with Luther's antagonism to Aristotle, yet he soon learned to distinguish between the use and the abuse of that author, and, while condemning Aristotle as perverted by Romish scholasticism, he effectually employed him in his true meaning as an important aid to the student of theology for the detection of sophistry and the attainment of a clear method of thought. He declared that he had never understood the use of philosophy until he had apprehended the pure doctrine of the Gospel. Among his philosophical works were an *Epitome of Moral Philosophy; Elements of Ethics; Explanation of Aristotle's Ethics; Commentary on Aristotle's Politics; Elements of Rhetoric; Logical Questions;* and dissertations on various ethical subjects, such as oaths, contracts, etc. For many years instruction in these works was the regular course in ethics in most of the schools of Protestant Germany. A writer before quoted pronounces them "more clear, elegant, and better arranged than those of Aristotle himself or his commentators" (Hallam's *Literature,* ii, 50). He was the author, also, of an elementary text-book of physics, and a sketch of universal history, from the creation to the Reformation (*Chronicon Carionis*). His miscellaneous orations, lectures, and essays fill over two volumes of the *Corpus Reformatorum.*

Melancthon as a Theologian and Reformer.—But it is with Melancthon as a theologian that we have chiefly to do. He never entered the ministry, and therefore performed his work in the Church entirely in the capacity of a layman. Immediately upon going to Wittenberg he identified himself with the Reformation, which had begun the preceding year. During his first fall and winter there he delivered lectures on Titus, following them by a course on the Psalms, Matthew, and Romans. His published exegetical lectures embrace, in addition, Genesis, Proverbs, Ecclesiastes, Isaiah, Jeremiah, Lamentations, Daniel, Haggai, Zechariah, Malachi, John, Corinthians, Colossians, and Timothy. His lectures on Romans and Corinthians were published by Luther without the author's knowledge. Extemporaneous explanations of the Gospels, during a later period of his life, delivered on Sundays at his residence, were committed to writing by some of his hearers, and, after revision by Pezel, were published under the title of *Postils.*

He accompanied Luther to the Leipsic Disputation (1519), at which he remained a mere spectator, but afterwards published a letter to Œcolampadius, in which he gave a succinct account of the discussion. Though written in the best spirit, it provoked a very bitter reply from Dr. Eck, in which, while acknowledging Melancthon's pre-eminence as a grammarian, he expressed the utmost contempt for his theological attainments, and advised him thereafter to confine his attention to classical pursuits, and not to attempt to enter a higher sphere. The reply of Melancthon is brief and modest, but the indignation of Luther manifested itself in a severer answer, in which he pronounced Melancthon better versed in Scripture than all the Ecks together. During the same year Melancthon received the degree of B.D.

Early in 1521, under the assumed name of Didymus Faventinus, he published an apology for the Reformation, in reply to Emser (Rhadinus). About Easter of the same year he laid the foundation of Protestant systematic theology by the publication of his *Loci Communes seu Hypotyposes Theologicæ.* It originated from a very brief summary of doctrine, prepared for his private use, which was afterwards delivered to his pupils, as an introduction to his lectures on Romans, and published by them without his consent or revision. The *Loci Communes* were intended to take the place of this meagre, and, to its author, very unsatisfactory sketch. They are marked by the clearness of method and purity of style for which Melancthon was distinguished. Luther declared that the little book could not be refuted, and that it was worthy not only of immortality, but even of canonical authority. Chemnitz affirms that Luther often remarked in private conversation that there was more solid doctrine contained in it than in any other volume since the days of the apostles. The same author quotes the Romish theologian, Alphonso de Zamara, as declaring: "It explains its doctrinal statements in such appropriate and accurate terms, and, by a methodical treatment, renders them so clear and strong, that it is injuring the papal power more than all other writings of the Lutherans." Erasmus termed it "a wondrous army, ranged in order of battle against the Pharisaic tyranny of false teachers;" and Calvin, "So beautiful is the proof that it affords, that the most perfect simplicity is the noblest method of handling the Christian doctrine." The couplet of Selnecker was often repeated:

"Non melior liber est ullus post biblia Christi,
Quam qui doctrinæ, corpusque, locique vocatur."

During the author's life it passed through over sixty editions, but was subjected to constant changes. The only exception of any moment taken within the Lutheran Church to the first edition is against its statement of the doctrine of the freedom of the will, to which Hutter and others have objected that it inclines towards fatalism. Seckendorf, on the contrary, claims that on this point it was misunderstood. In 1535 the objectionable sentence, "All things happen necessarily," was omitted. After 1543 the work was greatly enlarged, and so far changed on that subject as to seem far more in harmony with the teaching of Erasmus than that of Luther. It was repeatedly translated into the German. The translation of Justus Jonas was revised by Luther, who suggested that, while the articles on justification and the holy supper were well treated, they were not sufficiently full. A French translation appeared, with the commendation of Calvin, in 1546, and one into Italian (1534 or 1535) found eager readers even at Rome. There were also Dutch and Wendic versions. Portions of it have been translated into English—"On the Divine Essence," by Dr. J. A. Seiss, in the *Evangelical Review*, xii, 1–46; "On the Nature of Sin." *Theological Essays from the Princeton Review*, p. 218-228. It was attacked by the papist, Richard Smyth, of England, and defended by Paulus ab Eitren, a Hamburg theologian, who prepared an edition with additional notes, and citations from the fathers. The renowned *Loci Theologici* of Chemnitz is a commentary upon it. Similar commentaries were written by Prætorius, Pezel, Strigel, and Fabricius, while Spangenberg, Sohn, Mayer, and Hemmingius have prepared abridgments. For many years it continued to be a text-book in the Lutheran schools, until supplanted by Hutter's Compend.

During Luther's absence at the Wartburg, the care of the Reformation rested mainly upon Melancthon. With great ability he defended Luther against the theologians of Paris, but found himself unable to withstand the storm of fanaticism which arose among some of his former friends. He was even for a time greatly in doubt as to whether the pretensions of Carlstadt and the Zwickau prophets might not be true, and received from Luther a reproof because he dealt with them with so much mildness. Without any reserve, he insisted on

his own inability to meet the crisis, and urged the return of Luther as the only solution of the difficulty.

After Luther's return, he was diligently occupied in revising the translation of the Bible—a work in which his philological attainments were at several periods of invaluable service to the Church. In 1522 Luther wrote to Spalatine, asking that Melancthon might be relieved of teaching the classics, in order to devote his entire time to theology, but the latter objected, and preferred even to cease his theological instructions. In 1526, however, he was formally appointed professor of theology. During the two succeeding years he was the principal member of the commission to visit the churches and church-schools of Thuringia. The *Articles of Visitation*, prepared in connection with this commission, to give the ministers some directions concerning their preaching and teaching, are sometimes regarded as the earliest confession of the Lutheran Church. The importance which they attach to the preaching of the law, in order to guard against the abuse of the doctrine of justification by faith, excited the opposition of Agricola and others, and led to a conference at Torgau (q. v.), November, 1527, in which the position of Melancthon was approved. In February, 1529, he accompanied his prince to the Diet of Spires, and assisted in the preparation of the Protest, presented April 19th, from which the friends of the Reformation obtained the name Protestants. A few months later, October 1-3, he participated, together with Luther, Brentius, and others, in the Colloquy at Marburg (q. v.) with Zwingle and his adherents. In 1530 he accompanied the evangelical princes to the Diet of Augsburg, and there, on the basis of the seventeen articles prepared by Luther at Schwabach, elaborated the *Augsburg Confession*, which was presented to the emperor June 25. During its preparation the work was repeatedly revised by Luther, then at Coburg, in almost daily correspondence with Melancthon. "Melancthon, then, was by pre-eminence the composer of the Confession, not as a private individual, but as chief of a body of advisers, without whose concurrence nothing was fixed; Luther, by pre-eminence, as the divinely-called representative of the Church, its author." For a thorough examination of the relation which Melancthon sustained to the Augsburg Confession, the reader is referred to Krauth's *Conservative Reformation*, p. 201-267. The hypothesis of the rationalist Rückert, that Melancthon intended by it to effect a compromise with Rome, and that, for this purpose, a conspiracy was formed to keep Luther in ignorance of the plan, is there completely overthrown. Melancthon's excessive love of peace, and his desire to bring together into an organic union all the Protestant churches, caused him in after years to forget that the Augsburg Confession was the work of the Church, and not his own; for he felt himself at liberty to publish numerous revised editions, in which he made frequent changes. These changes, originating the distinction between the *Variata* and *Invariata*, almost caused a rupture with Luther, and ultimately resulted in controversies which imperilled the life of the Lutheran churches. Notwithstanding these changes, it cannot be proved that his personal convictions were at any succeeding period actually different from the teaching of the unaltered Confession. He repeatedly declared, until the close of his life, that his faith was unchanged. His object in the alterations was simply to generalize those statements which were so specific in their declaration of the Lutheran faith as to prevent the endorsement of the adherents of Calvin and others. He was constantly seeking for a generic form of agreement in which the specific differences might be lost sight of. He remained at Augsburg until late in September, employed in fruitless negotiations with the Romish theologians. The confutation of the Augsburg Confession, presented August 3, led him in reply to prepare the Apology—a masterpiece which the Lutheran Church has prized so highly as to number it among her symbols.

His Catechism (*Catechesis Puerilis*) appeared in 1532. In 1535 and 1536 he was actively engaged in negotiations with Bucer to secure a union of the Protestant churches on the doctrine of the Lord's Supper. As the result of these efforts, the Wittenberg Concord was signed May 28, 1536. In February, 1537, he was a member of the convention at Smalcald, and signed the *Articles*, with the proviso that he would acknowledge the supreme authority of the pope, *jure humano*, if the latter would permit the preaching of the pure Gospel. In the negotiations with the papists at Worms (1540), and at Ratisbon (1541), he was the principal theologian of the Protestants. At the latter conference his compromising spirit acceded to articles clothed in such ambiguous language as to admit the interpretation either of an affirmation or a denial of the doctrine of justification by faith; but the object of the conference failed, because of an irreconcilable difference concerning the externals of religion, in which Melancthon displayed more than his ordinary firmness. In 1542 and 1543 he was employed by the archbishop and elector of Cologne to superintend the introduction of the Reformation into his territories. The book of instruction prepared in connection with this work excited the indignation of Luther against Melancthon, until the latter assured him that Bucer was alone responsible for the article on the Lord's Supper. Early in 1545, at the request of the elector, he prepared a pamphlet on *The Reformation of Wittenberg*, which was sent to the Council of Trent as a summary of the doctrines of the Lutheran Reformers. After the death of Luther, in 1546, he was the acknowledged head of the Reformation, but unfortunately became again involved in negotiations with the papists. to whom he made the most remarkable concessions. His connection with the Leipsic Interim (1548) was the most unfortunate act of his life. Under the form of an apparent compromise, he yielded to the papists many of the most essential points of difference between them and the Protestants. "He was willing to tolerate both a popedom and a hierarchy, stripped, however, of divine rights, and deprived of all power in matters of faith. The relation of faith to works, and the doctrine of the sacraments, might, in his estimation, be veiled in a judicious obscurity of phrase." In every part of the evangelical Church the *Interim* was most violently resisted, and his connection with it strongly condemned. In addition to private rebukes from Calvin and Brentius, Agricola, Flacius, and others publicly attacked him. In 1550 he published his *Explanation of the Nicene Creed*, and in the succeeding year the *Confessio Saxonica*, in which he had gained courage to entirely repudiate the concessions of the *Interim*. In 1552 he was engaged in a controversy with Osiander, who had confounded justification with sanctification; in 1553 he published brief treatises against Schwenckfeldt and Stancar, and in 1554 his *Examen Ordinandorum*, a brief outline of doctrinal, ethical, and polemical theology, for the use of candidates for the ministry. His efforts during his last years to unite the followers of Calvin with those of Luther, and his attendance at another religious conference at Worms (1557) with the papists, were equally unsuccessful.

Melancthon was undoubtedly the great theologian of the Lutheran Reformation. Yet the very gifts which were of such great service in reducing the purified doctrine to a connected system, and organizing the outward form of the Church, constantly tempted him to seek for external union, even at the expense of principles essential to all true inner harmony. This tendency, fostered by his classical tastes and natural amiability and timidity, rendered him very unsafe as a leader, although so strong when under the guidance of a firmer will, as that of Luther. It is to this that Calvin referred when he heard of Melancthon's death: "O, Philip Melancthon! for it is upon thee whom I call, upon thee, who now livest with Christ in God, and art waiting for us, until we shall attain that blessed rest. A hundred times, worn out with fatigue and overwhelmed with care, thou hast laid thy head upon my breast and said, Would God I might die here. And a thousand times since then I have earnestly desired that it had been granted us to be together. Certainly thou wouldst have been more valiant to face danger, and stronger to despise hatred, and bolder to disregard false accusations."

Literature.—The first edition of his collected works was published at Basle, 1541; the second, edited by his son-in-law, Peucer, Wittenberg, 1562–64 (4 vols. fol.). The most valuable is that of the *Corpus Reformatorum*, edited by Bretschneider and Bindseil (1834–60, 28 vols. fol.). A complete catalogue of Melancthon's writings, and of their different editions, etc., was published by H. E. Bindseil, entitled *Bibliotheca Melancthoniana* (Halle, 1868, 8vo, 28 pp.). The tercentenary of Melancthon's decease has called forth a large number of addresses and essays to celebrate his memory. Besides the admirable orations of Dorner, Kahnis, and Rothe, are W. Thilo, *Melancthon in the Service of the Holy Scriptures;* F. A. Nitzelnadel, *Philip Melancthon, the Teacher of Germany;* W. Beyschlag, *Phil. Mel., a Sketch in Church History;* F. W. Genthe, *Oration at Eisleben;* H. Keil, *Laudatio Phil. Melancthonis;* H. K. Sack, a *Sermon at Magdeburg;* C. Schlottmann, *De Phil. Mel. reipublicæ literariæ Reformator;* J. Classen, *Melancthon's Relations to Frankfort-on-the-Main.* Other works have been published upon some of the pupils and friends of Melancthon; e. g. J. Classen, on Jacob Micyllus, rector at Frankfort, and professor in Heidelberg, 1526 to 1558; E. W. Löhn, on Dr. Caspar Creutziger (Cruciger), a pupil of both Melancthon and Luther, Reb. Tagmann, on Petrus Vincentius of Breslau. The earliest life of Melancthon was written by his friend Camerarius. The *Annales Vitæ*, in vol. xxviii, Corp. Ref., afford the richest biographical material. Biographies have been written by Camerarius (1566), Strobel (1777), Niemeyer (1817), Köthe (1829), Facius (1832), Ulenberg (1836), Heyd (1839), Galle (1840), Matthes (1841), Ledderhose (1847), Wohlfahrt (1860), C. Schmidt (1861), Meurer, Plank (1866), and others. Those accessible to English readers are the valuable but brief sketch by Dr. F. A. Cox, and an excellent translation of Ledderhose by Dr. G. F. Krotel (Phila. 1855). See also Krauth's *Conservative Reformation*, p. 220 sq.; Seckendorf's *Historia Lutheranismi;* Ranke, *Hist. Ref.* p. 132; Cunningham, *Reformers;* D'Aubigné, *Hist. Ref.* i, 97,325; Nisard, *Études sur la Renaissance;* Hardwick, *Hist. Ref.* p. 30 sq.; Burnet, *Hist. Ref.;* Gieseler, *Church Hist.* vol. iv, ch. i; Mosheim, *Eccles. Hist.* vol. iii; Hagenbach, *Kirchengesch.* vol. iii; Fisher, *Hist. Ref.* p. 97 sq.; Dorner, *Gesch. der protestant. Theologie*, p. 108, 320, 329; *Bibliotheca Sacra*, 1846, p. 301; 1864, p. 448; *Jahrbuch deutscher Theol.* vol. x, pt. i, p. 185; 1870, iii, 503; iv, 615; *Mercersburg Rev.* 1850, p. 325, Kitto, *Journ. Sac. Lit.* 1854, p. 185; *Meth. Qu. Rev.* 1855, p. 163; 1860, p. 676; *Studien u. Kritiken*, 1859, vol. ii; *Brit. and For. Ev. Rev.* 1861, Jan.; 1868, Oct.; *Am. Theol. Rev.* 1861, April; 1860, p. 529; *Amer. Presbyt. Rev.* 1861, p. 261; *Zeitschr. f. wissensch. Theol.* 1871, vol. ii, art. viii. (H. E. J.)

Melangists (or **Convulsionists**) is the name of a degenerate sect of Jansenists (q. v.). It originated in 1727, upon the decease of François de Paris. He had been noted for his piety and asceticism, and, now that he had left his earthly abode, multitudes flocked to his grave, and there, in various ways, testified their superstitious regard and veneration. Marvellous cures were claimed to be wrought there, and miracles were said to be performed. Strong religious emotions were manifested, and some were seized with convulsions. Some were endowed with the spirit of prophecy, and predicted the overthrow of Church and State. Many of the fanatics themselves claimed that their miraculous doings were divinely inspired, while others ascribed them to evil influences. Those who considered these curious works inspired by evil influences were called "Discernents," while the believers received the name of *Melanigists*, because they supposed themselves partly actively, partly passively inspired. The superstition and fanaticism which prevailed at François's grave soon after his death were not wholly confined to the common people, but were shared by a considerable number of men of rank and learning. These religious excesses, however, tended to create a general prejudice against Jansenism, and really ruined the cause—at least in France; or, as Voltaire aptly remarks, "The grave of St. François of Paris became the grave of Jansenism."

Melania, St., called THE YOUNGER, a Roman lady of a noble family, who was born about A.D. 388, became a convert to Christianity and founded a convent in Palestine, and subsequently a monastery near Mount Calvary. She was the daughter of a Roman consul, and one of the many noble ladies of the Eternal City who joined the cause of the Christians. She died in 439, and her death is commemorated by the Church of Rome Dec. 31. See Macé, *Hist. de Sainte-Mélanie* (Paris, 1729, 12mo).

Melati′ah (Heb. *Melatyah′*, מְלַטְיָה, *deliverance of Jehovah;* Sept. Μαλτίας, but most copies omit), a Gibeonite who repaired part of the walls of Jerusalem on the northern side, after the return from Babylon (Neh. iii, 7). B.C. 446.

Mel′chi (Μελχί, for Heb. מַלְכִּי, *my king*), the name of two of Christ's maternal ancestors. See GENEALOGY OF JESUS CHRIST.

1. The son of Addi and father (maternal grandfather) of Neri or Neriah (Luke iii, 28); probably identical with the MAASEIAH of 2 Chron. xxxiv, 8).

2. The son of Janna and father of Levi, fourth in ascent from the Virgin Mary (Luke iii, 24). B.C. much ante 22.

Melchi′ah (Heb. *Malkiyah*, מַלְכִּיָה, *Jehovah's king;* Sept. Μελχίας), a priest, the father of Pashur (Jer. xxi, 1); elsewhere called MALCHIAH (Jer. xxxviii, 1; Neh. xi, 12) and MALCHIJAH (1 Chron. ix, 12).

Melchi′as (Μελχίας), the Greek form (in the Apocrypha) of the Heb. MALCHIAH; namely, (*a*) 1 Esdr. ix, 26; (*b*) 1 Esdr. ix, 32; (*c*) 1 Esdr. ix, 44.

Mel′chiël (Μελχιήλ)), a person whose son Charmis was one of the three governors of Bethulia (Judith vi, 15). The Vulgate has a different reading, making Charmis the same as Gothoniel; and the Peshito gives the name *Manshajel*.

Melchior, the name attributed in Romish legends to one of the wise men who visited the infant Saviour. See MAGI.

Melchior, ALBRECHT WILHELM, a German theologian, was born at Herborn March 12, 1685. His father, who died in 1690, was superintendent and professor of theology. Albrecht commenced his academic course at Duisburg, but continued his studies at the university at Franecker. He paid special attention to Oriental languages and literature. He finished his studies at Utrecht, and returned to Duisburg. He was in 1709 installed as minister at Mühlheim, and made professor of theology at Hanau in 1718. Upon taking this position he delivered an essay, *De religione et veræ religionis criteriis*. In 1723 he was called to a professorship of theology and Church history at Franecker, where he died, Aug. 11, 1738. Melchior made quite a name for himself in theological literature. He published several dogmatic and exegetical dissertations to prove the authenticity of the miracles of Christ. A list of all his productions, of minor value at present, is given by Döring, *Gelehrte Theol. Deutschl.* s. v.

Melchis′edec (Heb. v–vii). See MELCHIZEDEK.

Melchi-shu′a (1 Sam. xiv, 49; xxxi, 2). See MALCHISHUA.

Melchites or MELEKITES (from מֶלֶךְ, *a king*), i. e. *Royalists*, is the name given to those Syriac, Egyptian,

and other Christians of the Levant, who acknowledge the authority of the pope and the doctrines of the Church of Rome. Excepting some few points of little or no importance, which relate only to ceremonies and ecclesiastical discipline, the Melchites are in every respect professed Greeks; but they are governed by a particular patriarch, who assumes the title of Patriarch of Antioch. Their origin is referred to the labors of the Jesuits in the 17th century, and the name of *Melchites* was given to them because they agreed with the Greeks who submitted to the Council of Chalcedon, and was designed by their enemies to brand them with the reproach of having done so merely in conformity to the religion of the emperor. They celebrate mass in the Arabic language, use unleavened bread in the Eucharist, and their priests (not their bishops) are allowed to marry. They have also some monastic establishments, whose inmates follow the rule of St. Basil, the common rule of all the Greek monks. See Farrar, *Eccles. Dict.;* Eadie, *Eccles. Cyclop.;* Neale, *Hist. East. Church*, ch. ii, 7; Neander, *Church Hist.* iii, 176.

Melchiz′edek (Heb. *Malki′-Tse′dek*, מַלְכִּי־צֶדֶק, *king* of *righteousness*, i. e. righteous king, comp. Heb. vii, 2; Sept. and N. T. Μελχισεδέκ, and so Anglicized in the N. T. "Melchisedec;" Josephus, Μελχισεδέκης, *Ant.* i, 10, 2), the "priest of the most high God," and king of Salem, who went forth to meet Abraham on his return from the pursuit of Chedorlaomer and his allies, who had carried Lot away captive. The interview is described as having occurred in the "valley of Shaveh (or the level valley), which is the king's valley." He brought refreshment, described in the general terms of "bread and wine," for the fatigued warriors, and bestowed his blessing upon their leader, who, in return, gave to the royal priest a tenth of all the spoil which had been acquired in his expedition (Gen. xiv, 18, 20). B.C. cir. 2080. See ABRAHAM. In one of the Messianic Psalms (cx, 4) it is foretold that the Messiah should be "a priest after the order of Melchizedek;" which the author of the Epistle to the Hebrews (vi, 20) cites as showing that Melchizedek was a type of Christ, and the Jews themselves, certainly, on the authority of this passage of the Psalms, regarded Melchizedek as a type of the regal-priesthood, higher than that of Aaron, to which the Messiah should belong. The bread and wine which were set forth on the table of show-bread, was also supposed to be represented by the bread and wine which the king of Salem brought forth to Abraham (Schöttgen, *Hor. Heb.* ii, 615). In the following discussions respecting his person, office, and locality, we substantially adhere to the traditionary view of this character.

There is something surprising and mysterious in the first appearance of Melchizedek, and in the subsequent references to him. Bearing a title which Jews in after-ages would recognise as designating their own sovereign, bringing gifts which recall to Christians the Lord's Supper, this Canaanite crosses for a moment the path of Abraham, and is unhesitatingly recognised as a person of higher spiritual rank than the friend of God. Disappearing as suddenly as he came in, he is lost to the sacred writings for a thousand years, and then a few emphatic words for another moment bring him into sight as a type of the coming Lord of David. Once more, after another thousand years, the Hebrew Christians are taught to see in him a proof that it was the consistent purpose of God to abolish the Levitical priesthood. His person, his office, his relation to Christ, and the seat of his sovereignty, have given rise to innumerable discussions, which even now can scarcely be considered as settled. Hence the faith of early ages ventured to invest his person with superstitious awe. A mysterious supremacy came also to be assigned to him ("the great high-priest," Philo, *Opp.* ii, 34) by reason of his having received tithes from the Hebrew patriarch; and on this point the Epistle to the Hebrews (vii, 1–10) expatiates strongly. But the Jews, in admitting this official or personal superiority of Melchizedek to Abraham, sought to account for it by alleging that the royal priest was no other than Shem, the most pious of Noah's sons, who, according to the shorter chronology, might have lived to the time of Abraham (Bochart, *Phaleg*, ii, 1), and who, as a survivor of the deluge, is supposed to have been authorized by the superior dignity of old age to bless even the father of the faithful, and entitled, as the paramount lord of Canaan (Gen. ix, 26), to convey (xiv, 19) his right to Abraham. Jerome, in his *Ep.* lxxiii, *ad Evangelum* (in *Opp.* i, 438), which is entirely devoted to a consideration of the person and dwelling-place of Melchizedek, states that this was the prevailing opinion of the Jews in his time; and it is ascribed to the Samaritans by Epiphanius (*Hær.* lv, 6, p. 472). It was afterwards embraced by Luther and Melancthon, by H. Broughton, Selden, Lightfoot (*Chor. Marco præm.* ch. x, 1, § 2), Jackson (*On the Creed*, bk. ix, § 2), and by many others. Equally old, perhaps, but less widely diffused, is the supposition, not unknown to Augustine (*Quæst. in Gen.* lxxii, in *Opp.* iii, 396), and ascribed by Jerome (*l. c.*) to Origen and Didymus, that Melchizedek was an angel. The fathers of the 4th and 5th centuries record with reprobation the tenet of the Melchizedekians that he was a Power, Virtue, or Influence of God (August. *De Hæresibus*, § 34, in *Opp.* viii, 11; Theodoret, *Hæret. fab.* ii, 6, p. 332; Epiphan. *Hær.* lv, 1, p. 468; comp. Cyril Alexand. *Glaph. in Gen.* ii, 57) superior to Christ (Chrysost. *Hom. in Melchiz.* in *Opp.* vi, p. 269), and the not less daring conjecture of Hieracas and his followers that Melchizedek was the Holy Ghost (Epiphan. *Hær.* lxvii, 3, p. 711, and lv, 5, p. 472). Epiphanius also mentions (lv, 7, p. 474) some members of the Church as holding the erroneous opinion that Melchizedek was the Son of God appearing in human form, an opinion which Ambrose (*De Abrah.* i, § 3, in *Opp.* i, 288) seems willing to receive, and which has been adopted by many modern critics. Similar to this was a Jewish opinion that he was the Messiah (ap. Deyling, *Obs. Sacr.* ii, 73; Schöttgen, *l. c.*; comp. the book Sohar, ap. Wolf, *Curæ Phil.* in Heb. vii, 1). Modern writers have added to these conjectures that he may have been Ham (Jurieu), or a descendant of Japhet (Owen), or of Shem (ap. Deyling, *l. c.*), or Job (Kohlreis), or Mizraim, or Canaan, or even Enoch (Deyling, *Observat. Sacr.* ii, 71 sq.; Clayton, *Chronology of the Heb. Bible*, p. 100). Other guesses may be found in Deyling (*l. c.*) and in Pfeiffer (*De personâ Melch.* in *Opp.* p. 51). All these opinions are unauthorized additions to Holy Scripture—many of them seem to be irreconcilable with it. The conjecture, however, which holds Melchizedek to have been Shem (see Jerome, ad *Isa.* xli), and which we find in Rashi on Gen. as well as in the Jerusalem Targum, and also that of Jonathan (ad loc. Gen.), but not in that of Onkelos, requires an explanation how his name came to be changed, how he is found reigning in a country inhabited by the descendants of Ham, how he came forth to congratulate Abraham on the defeat of one of his own descendants, as was Chedorlaomer, and how he could be said to have been without recorded parentage (Heb. vii, 3), since the pedigree of Shem must have been notorious. In that case, also, the difference of the priesthoods of Melchizedek and Levi would not be so distinct as to bear the argument which the Epistle to the Hebrews founds upon it. Rejecting on such grounds this opinion, others, as we have seen, in their anxiety to vindicate the dignity of Abraham from marks of spiritual submission to any mortal man, have held that Melchizedek was no other than the Son of God himself. But in this case it would hardly have been said that he was made "*like*" unto the Son of God" (Heb. vii, 3), or that Christ was constituted " a priest" after the order of Melchizedek (Heb. vi, 20), or, in other words, was a type of himself. The best founded opinion seems to be that of Carpzov (*Apparat. Antiq. Sacr. Cod.* chap. iv, p. 52) and most judicious moderns, who, after Josephus (*War*, vi, 10), allege that he was a principal person among the

Canaanites and posterity of Noah, and eminent for holiness and justice, and therefore discharged the priestly as well as regal functions among the people; and we may conclude that his twofold capacity of king and priest (characters very commonly united in the remote ages; see N. Schwebel, *De causis conjunctæ olim c. regno sacerdotii dignitatis*, Onold. 1769; J. G. Müller, *De regibus ap. antiq. populos sacerdotibus*, Jen. 1746) afforded Abraham an opportunity of testifying his thankfulness to God, in the manner usual in those times, by offering a tenth of all the spoil. This combination of characters happens for the first time in Scripture to be exhibited in his person, which, with the abrupt manner in which he is introduced, and the nature of the intercourse between him and Abraham, render him in various respects an appropriate and obvious type of the Messiah in his united regal and priestly character. The way in which he is mentioned in Genesis would lead to the immediate inference that Melchizedek was of one blood with the children of Ham, among whom he lived, chief (like the king of Sodom) of a settled Canaanitish tribe. This was the opinion of most of the early fathers (ap. Jerome, *l. c.*), of Theodoret (*in Gen.* lxiv, p. 77), and Epiphanius (*Hær.* lxvii, p. 716), and is now generally received (see Grotius *in Hebr.*; Patrick's *Commentary in Gen.*; Bleek, *Hebräer*, ii, 303; Ebrard, *Hebräer*; Fairbairn, *Typology*, ii, 313, ed. 1854). As Balaam was a prophet, so Melchizedek was a priest among the corrupted heathen (Philo, *Abrah.* xxxix; Euseb. *Præp. Evang.* i, 9), not self-appointed (as Chrysostom suggests, *Hom. in Gen.* xxxv, § 5; comp. Heb. v, 4), but constituted by a special gift from God, and recognised as such by him.

Melchizedek combined the offices of priest and king, as was not uncommon in patriarchal times. Nothing is said to distinguish his kingship from that of the contemporary kings of Canaan; but the emphatic words in which he is described, by a title never given even to Abraham, as a "priest of the most high God," as blessing Abraham and receiving tithes from him, seem to imply that his priesthood was something more (see Hengstenberg, *Christol.* Psa. cx) than an ordinary patriarchal priesthood, such as Abraham himself and other heads of families (Job i, 5) exercised. Although it has been observed (Pearson, *On the Creed*, p. 122, ed. 1843) that we read of no other sacerdotal act performed by Melchizedek, but only that of blessing [and receiving tithes, Pfeiffer], yet it may be assumed that he was accustomed to discharge all the ordinary duties of those who are "ordained to offer gifts and sacrifices" (Heb. viii, 3); and we might concede (with Philo, Grotius, *l. c.*, and others) that his regal hospitality to Abraham was possibly preceded by an unrecorded sacerdotal act of oblation to God, without implying that his hospitality was in itself, as recorded in Genesis, a sacrifice.

The " order of Melchizedek," in Psa. cx, 4, is explained by Gesenius and Rosenmüller to mean "manner"=likeness in official dignity=a king and priest. The relation between Melchizedek and Christ as type and antitype is made in the Epistle to the Hebrews to consist in the following particulars: 1. Melchizedek was the priest of the most high God by an immediate divine constitution; so Christ was a priest after his order, and not after that of Aaron. 2. Melchizedek derived his priestly office from no predecessor, and delivered it down to no successor; in this respect Christ also stands alone: "Our Lord sprang from the tribe of Judah, of which tribe Moses spake nothing concerning priesthood." 3. Melchizedek was superior to Abraham, consequently his priesthood was superior to that of Levi and his descendants. So Christ's priesthood was superior to the Aaronic. 4. Melchizedek was *the priest appointed* to exercise his office in behalf of all the worshippers of the true God; so Christ is the universal priest, the only one appointed to make intercession for our guilty race. 5. Melchizedek's priesthood was limited to no definite time; this circumstance is noticed just as it would have been had his priesthood had neither beginning nor end: "Christ is a priest forever" (Psa. cx, 4). 6. Each sustained the high honors of king and priest; and the significant appellations are applied to both—"Righteous King and King of Peace" (Isa. xxxii, 1; viii, 6, 7). In the Messianic prediction (Psa. cx, 4), "Thou art a priest forever after the order of Melchizedek," the phrase "*forever*" is not to be understood in the absolute sense, either of Melchizedek's priesthood or of Christ's. Melchizedek's priesthood terminated with his life; so Christ's priestly and kingly office as Mediator will both cease when the work of redemption is fully accomplished (1 Cor. xv, 24-28). But in neither case is there any statute which limits the specified accession to office and of egress from it. To these points of agreement, noted by the apostle, human ingenuity has added others which, however, stand in need of the evidence of either an inspired writer or an eye-witness before they can be received as facts and applied to establish any doctrine. Thus J. Johnson (*Unbloody Sacrifice*, i, 123, ed. 1847) asserts on very slender evidence that the fathers who refer to Gen xiv, 18, understood that Melchizedek offered the bread and wine to God; and hence he infers that one great part of our Saviour's Melchizedekian priesthood consisted in offering bread and wine. Bellarmine asks in what other respects is Christ a priest after the order of Melchizedek. Waterland, who does not lose sight of the deep significancy of Melchizedek's action, has replied to Johnson in his *Appendix* to "the Christian Sacrifice explained" (ch. iii, § 2, *Works*, v, 165, ed. 1843). Bellarmine's question is sufficiently answered by Whitaker, *Disputation on Scripture* (Quest. ii, ch. x, p. 168, ed. 1849). The sense of the fathers, who sometimes expressed themselves in rhetorical language, is cleared from misinterpretation by bishop Jewel, *Reply to Harding*, art. xvii (*Works*, ii, 731, ed. 1847). In Jackson, *On the Creed* (bk. ix, § 2, ch. vi–xi, p. 955 sq.), there is a lengthy but valuable account of the priesthood of Melchizedek; and the views of two different theological schools are ably stated by Aquinas (*Summa*, iii, 22, § 6) and Turretin (*Theologia*, ii, 443–453).

Another fruitful source of discussion has been found in the site of Salem and Shaveh, which certainly lay in Abraham's road from Hobah to the plain of Mamre, and which are assumed to be near to each other. The various theories may be briefly enumerated as follows: (1) Salem is supposed to have occupied in Abraham's time the ground on which afterwards Jebus and then Jerusalem stood; and Shaveh to be the valley east of Jerusalem through which the Kidron flows. This opinion, abandoned by Reland (*Pal.* p. 833), but adopted by Winer, is supported by the facts that Jerusalem is called Salem in Psa. lxxvi, 2, and that Josephus (*Ant.* i, 10, 2) and the Targums distinctly assert their identity; that the king's dale (2 Sam. xviii, 18), identified in Gen. xiv, 17, with Shaveh, is placed by Josephus (*Ant.* vii, 10, 3), and by mediæval and modern tradition (see Ewald, *Gesch.* iii, 239), in the immediate neighborhood of Jerusalem; that the name of a later king of Jerusalem, Adonizedek (Josh. x, 1), sounds like that of a legitimate successor of Melchizedek; and that Jewish writers (*ap.* Schöttgen, *Hor. Heb.* in Heb. vii, 2) claim Zedek = righteousness, as a name of Jerusalem. (2) Jerome (*Opp.* i, 446) denies that Salem is Jerusalem, and asserts that it is identical with a town near Scythopolis or Bethshan, which in his time retained the name of Salem, and in which some extensive ruins were shown as the remains of Melchizedek's palace. He supports this view by quoting Gen. xxx, 18, where, however, the translation is questionable; compare the mention of Salem in Judith iv, 4, and in John iii, 23. (3) Stanley, (*S. and P.* p. 237) is of opinion that there is every probability that Mount Gerizim is the place where Melchizedek, the priest of the Most High, met Abraham. Eupolemus (ap. Eusebius, *Præp. Evang.* ix, 17), in a confused version of this story, names Argerizim, the mount of the Most High, as the place in which Abraham was hospita-

bly entertained. (4) Ewald, *Gesch.* iii, 239) denies positively that it is Jerusalem, and says that it must be north of Jerusalem on the other side of Jordan (i, 410): an opinion which Rödiger (Gesen. *Thesaurus*, p. 1422 *b*) condemns. There, too, Stanley thinks that the king's dale was situate, near the spot where Absalom fell. See KING'S DALE.

Some Jewish writers have held the opinion that Melchizedek was the writer and Abraham the subject of Psa. cx. See Deyling, *Obs. Sacr.* iii, 137. It may suffice to mention that there is a fabulous life of Melchizedek printed among the spurious works of Athanasius, iv, 189.

Reference may be made to the following works in addition to those already mentioned: two tracts on Melchizedek by M. J. H. von Elswick, in the *Thesaurus Novus Theolog.-philologicus;* L. Borgisius, *Historia Critica Melchisedeci* (Bern. 1706); Quandt, *De sacerdotio Melch.* (Regiom. 1737); Gaillard, *Melchisedecus Christus* (Leyd. 1686); M. C. Hoffman, *De Melchisedeco* (1669); H. Broughton, *Treatise on Melchizedek* (1591); Kirchmaier, *De Melchisedecho* (Rotterd. 1696); Lange, *idem* (Hal. 1713, 1714); Danhauer, *idem* (Strasb. 1684); Pietsch, *idem* (Halle, 1713); Reinhart, *idem* (Wittenb. 1751); Wähner, *idem* (Gött. 1745); Henderson, *Melchisedek* (Lond. 1839); and other monographs cited in Darling, *Cyclop. Bibliogr.* col. 183, 1607. See also J. A. Fabricius, *Cod. Pseudepig. V. T.;* P. Molinæus, *Vates*, etc. (1640), iv, 11; J. H. Heidegger, *Hist. Sacr. Patriarcharum* (1671), ii, 288; Hottinger, *Ennead. Disput.;* P. Cunæus, *De Republ. Heb.* iii, 3, apud *Crit. Sacr.* vol. v; Ursini, *Analect. Sacr.* i, 349; Krahmer, in Illgen's *Zeitschr.* vii, 4, p. 87; Auberlein, in the *Stud. u. Krit.* iii, 1857, 453 sq.; *Presb. Quar. Rev.* Oct. 1861.

Melchizedekians, a sect which arose in the Christian Church about the beginning of the 3d century, and was composed mainly of Jewish converts. They affirmed that Melchizedek was not a man, but a heavenly power superior to Jesus Christ; for Melchizedek, they said, was the intercessor and mediator of the angels; and Jesus Christ was only so for man, and his priesthood only a copy of that of Melchizedek. Similar views were revived among the *Hieracites*. See Theodoret, *Hæres. Sat.* ii, 5, 6.

Meldenius, RUPERTUS, a German Protestant theologian of the 17th century, is known especially by his work entitled *Parænesis votiva pro pace ecclesiæ ad Theologos Augustanæ Confessionis s.* 1, *et a.* Very little is known of his life, and it was even at one time supposed that the name was fictitious. Yet the existence of Meldenius appears now well established. He was a warm supporter of the *Formula Concordiæ*, and did not contemplate a union of the two churches, but at the same time he wished the spirit of scholastic controversy which then ruled the churches to give way to real, practical piety and peace. In the first part of his work he denounces the state of the Lutheran Church, and in the second he presents the remedy for it. He accused theologians of not distinguishing sufficiently between essentials and non-essentials, and maintains that, while they should always be ready to defend their opinions, they ought not to be ceaselessly engaged in controversies. He claims that in order to labor efficiently for the edification of his flock the minister must himself lead a holy life, and nothing, in his opinion, can be worse than Pharisaical hypocrisy, which is the origin of φιλοδοξία, φιλαργυρία, and φιλονειχία. He ends his description of these besetting sins of the Church with the exclamation, *Serva nos Domine, alioqui(n) perimus.* In the second part he contrasts with these faults the opposite virtues of humility, moderation, and peacefulness which the Christian should possess. Want of Christian love he considers as the true cause of the state of affairs; there is enough of science, but a great lack of love. He cannot understand a minister whose sins have been pardoned by God not hiding under the shield of love the faults of his colleague. "Omnium vero norma," says Rupertus, "sit caritas cum prudentia quadam pia et humilitate non ficta conjuncta." He does not wish all controversies to cease, but to be conducted in a more moderate, charitable spirit. He then compares the actual state of religion with its state in the early ages, and concludes by saying, "Si nos servaremus in necessariis unitatem, in non necessariis libertatem, in utrisque caritatem, optimo certe loco essent res nostræ." As essentials, Rupertus considers those principles which refer directly to the articles of faith or principal points in the Catechism, or such as can be clearly established from Scripture, such as were held by the early Church, proved such by the acts of synods or symbolic works, and, finally, those which all orthodox theologians agree upon as such. On the other hand, he holds as non-essential such points as are not clearly demonstrated by Scripture, do not form an article of the Catechism, were not held by the ancient Church, or considered necessary by the greater number of orthodox theologians. Rupertus openly declares that he does not hold the views of those who consider purity of doctrine as essential. The work is published by J. G. Pfeiffer in his *Miscellanea Theologica* (Leips. 1736); also by Lücke, *Ueber das Alter, den Verfasser*, etc., *des Kirchlichen Friedenspruches: In necessariis unitas, in non necessariis libertas, in utrisque caritas* (Götting. 1850). See Herzog, *Real-Encyklopädie*, ix, 304.

Mel'eä (Μελεᾶς, of uncertain signification), a person named as the son of Menan and father of Eliakim, among the maternal ancestry of Jesus, in the private line of David (Luke iii, 31), but the name itself is of doubtful authenticity (see *Meth. Quar. Rev.* 1852, p. 597).

Me'lech (Heb. *Me'lek*, מֶלֶךְ, *king;* Sept. Μελάχ and Μαλάχ v. r. Μαλώχ and Μαλώθ), the second named of the four sons of Micah, the grandson of Saul's son Jonathan (1 Chron. viii, 35; ix, 41). B.C. post 1037. See also HAMMELECH; EBED-MELECH; NATHAN-MELECH; REGEM-MELECH.

Meletians, ASIATIC. The Arians in 331 had deposed Eustathius, bishop of Antioch, a learned and zealous Nicene; but a party who adhered to the Nicene symbol, and who called themselves Eustathians, continued to exist at Antioch. After appointing several successors to Eustathius, the Arians, in 360, transferred Meletius from the bishopric of Sebaste to that of Antioch. Although the Arians found they had made a mistake, and soon deposed him as an enemy of Arianism, yet only a part of the Nicenes at Antioch would acknowledge him as bishop, since the Eustathians regarded an Arian ordination as invalid. In this way two parties were formed among the Nicenes at Antioch—a strict party, the Eustathians; and a moderate party, the Meletians. This schism, after Athanasius had tried in vain to remove it, Lucifer made worse by ordaining as bishop over the Eustathians the presbyter Paulinus, in opposition to the wishes of Eusebius of Vercelli, who had been sent with him to Antioch, by the Alexandrian Synod, as his co-deputy. The entire Nicene portion of Christendom now became divided, in reference to this matter, into two parties; the Occidentals and Egyptians recognising Paulinus as the true bishop of Antioch, and the majority of the Orientals, whose Nicene proclivities had been somewhat weakened by semi-Arian influences, recognising Meletius. See EUSTATHIANS. See also MELETIUS OF ANTIOCH.

Meletios, M., an Eastern prelate, was born in the latter part of the 16th century, in Janina, in Epirus, and flourished first as metropolitan at Lepanto and Arta, and in the same position, after 1703, at Athens. He died at Constantinople in 1714. He wrote *Kirchengeschichte, aus dem Altgriechischen in's Neugriechische übertragen* (Wein. 1780, 3 vols., with Notes by J. Vendoti).

Meletius OF ANTIOCH, an eminent Greek ecclesiastic, was born in the beginning of the 4th century at Melitene, in Armenia Minor. His first important appointment was that of bishop of Sebaste (A.D. 357), to which office he succeeded Eustathius, who had been deposed. See EUSTATHIANS. The wilful conduct of the people soon caused Meletius to resign, and he retired to Berœa, in Syria. At this time the Arian controversy caused so much excitement that sectarian zeal was fast displacing true piety. Meletius, however, by confining himself to the essential doctrines of the Gospel and ignoring polemical subjects, succeeded in winning the esteem of all except the extremists of both factions, and by universal assent was raised to the bishopric of Antioch (A.D. 360). His new position gave such importance to his opinions that he could no longer remain indifferent to the disputes which were marring the concord of the Christian world. At the request of the emperor Constantius he gave an exposition of Prov. viii, 22, in which he expressed himself as being in sympathy with the orthodox party. At this avowal the Arians became greatly excited, and succeeded in influencing the emperor to banish him to his native Melitene. Euzoius was installed in his place, and the orthodox party separated from the communion of the Arians. Previous to this the most zealous portion of the orthodox had withdrawn on account of the deposition of Eustathius, but the two seceding parties remained separate—the Eustathians adhering at this time to presbyter Paulinus, the intended successor of Eustathius, who had died in the mean while, and the other orthodox gathering around Meletius. On the accession of Julian as emperor (362), Meletius was recalled, and for two years endeavored to reconcile and unite the two factions of the orthodox party; but the Eustathians refused to recognise him, and elected Paulinus as their bishop, who was duly ordained by Lucifer of Cagliari. On the accession of Valens, Meletius was again banished, but by an edict of Gratian (378) was recalled, and shortly after reinstated. The unrelenting prejudice of Paulinus frustrated all attempts at reconciliation, though Meletius proposed to him a just plan of union. Meletius died at an advanced age while attending the Council of Constantinople in A.D. 381. His funeral oration, pronounced by Gregorius Nyssenus, is still extant. The schism in the Church lasted until 413 or 415, when bishop Alexander succeeded in reconciling the old orthodox party with the successor of Meletius. See Schaff, *Ch. Hist.* i, 372 and 394; Gieseler, *Eccles. Hist.* i, 201 sq.; Smith, *Dict. of Gr. and Rom. Biog.* vol. ii, s. v.; Walch, *Ketzerhistorie*, vol. iv. See MELETIANS. (H. W. T.)

Meletius OF LYCOPOLIS flourished in the Egyptian district of Thebais in the beginning of the 4th century. He was a prelate in the Church, and the founder of the *Meletian* sect, or, as they termed themselves, the *Church of the Martyrs*. During the bitter persecutions which the Christians suffered under the reign of Diocletian, he and his superior, Peter, archbishop of Alexandria, were thrown into prison. Many Christians had abjured their religious belief for the sake of freedom from persecution, and some of these, regretting their faithlessness, repaired to the two imprisoned bishops, desiring to receive absolution, and to become reconciled with the Church. Peter was in favor of granting the request of these *lapsi*, provided they would do penance; but Meletius, denouncing them as traitors, refused to have any intercourse with them, until at least all persecution had ceased. A majority of the Christians then in confinement approved of his course. This gave rise to a schism, which gained some prominence after the release of Meletius, who became the leader of the rebels, and from whom they received their name. After regaining his freedom he ordained some twenty-nine bishops, and even encroached upon the diocese of Peter with ordinations and excommunications. He was finally checked by the Council of Nice, who censured him, but allowed him to retain his title. The council also agreed to confirm his appointments, provided they would receive a new ordination from the proper authorities. The sect to which he gave rise, sometimes called *Egyptian Meletians*, lasted for nearly a century and a half, when its members made common cause with the Arians. See Schaff, *Ch. Hist.* i, 451; Gieseler, *Eccles. Hist.* i, 166; Stanley, *Hist. of the East. Ch.* p. 256; Mosheim, *Eccles. Hist.* i, 75; Hase, *Ch. Hist.* p. 690. (H. W. T.)

Mel'icu (Heb. marg. *Meliku'*, מְלִיכוּ, text *Meloki'*, מְלֹוכִי; Sept. Μαλούχ v. r. Ἀμαλούχ, Vulg. *Milicho*; Neh. xii, 14). See MALLUCH.

Melissus OF SAMOS, a Greek philosopher, was born at Samos, and flourished in the 5th century (about 444) before Christ. It is said that he was not less distinguished as a citizen than as a philosopher, and that he commanded the fleet of his country during its insurrection against Athens. Melissus seems to have been the disciple of Parmenides; he studied at least the writings of the philosophers of the Eleatic school, and adopted their doctrines in a modified form; or, as one has it, "he took up the letter rather than the spirit of their system." He made his opinions known in a work written in Ionic prose, probably entitled *Of Being and of Nature*. He treated not of the infinite variety of things produced or engendered, but of eternal nature considered abstractly, apart from all concrete things, and, like Parmenides, called it *being*. Simplicius has preserved some fragments of this treatise, and the author (Aristotle or Theophrastus) of the book on Melissus, Xenophanes, and Gorgias, has made its doctrines well known. Melissus taught the same system of *idealism* as did the leaders of the Eleatic school, Xenophanes and Parmenides, but he is characterized by greater boldness in his way of stating it, and in some respects by profounder views. What really existed, he maintained, could neither be produced nor perish; it exists without having either commencement or end; infinite (differing in this respect from Parmenides), and consequently one; invariable, not composed of parts, and indivisible: which doctrine implies a denial of the existence of bodies, and of the dimensions of space. All that our senses present to us (that is to say, the greater part of things which exist) is nothing more than an *appearance* relative to our senses (τὸ ἐν ἡμῖν), and is altogether beyond the limits of real knowledge. He thus made the first though weak attempt, which was afterwards carried out by Zeno with far more acuteness and sagacity, to prove that the foundations of all knowledge derived from experience are in themselves contradictory, and that the reality of the actual world is inconceivable. As for the relation between real existence and the Deity, we are ignorant of the sentiments of Melissus on this head; for what is reported by Diogenes Laertius (ix, 24) can be considered as relating only to the *popular* notions. Some important fragments of Melissus have been collected by Brandis in the first part of the *Commentationum Eleaticarum*, pars prima, p. 185 sq., and by M. Mullach in his excellent edition of the treatise *Aristotelis de Melisso, Xenophane, et Gorgia, Disputationes, cum Eleaticorum philosophorum fragmentis* (Berlin, 1846). The same editor inserts them in the *Fragmenta Philosophorum Græcorum* of the Didot collection (1860, 8vo). See Diogenes Laertius, ix, 24; Plutarch, *Pericles*, p. 26, 27; Simplicius, *In Arist. Phys. de Cœlo*; Ritter, *Gesch. der Philosophie*, vol. i; Tenneman's *Manual of Philosophy*, p. 68, 69; Smith, *Dict. of Class. Biog.* s. v.; Hoefer, *Nouv. Biog. Générale*, s. v.

Mel'ita (Μελίτη; probably of Phœnician etymology, and signifying *refuge*, otherwise *clay*; but according to Hammeker, *Miscell. Phœnic.* p. 46, so named from its abundance of *ash*-trees), an island in the Mediterranean, on which the ship which was conveying the apostle Paul as a prisoner to Rome was wrecked, and which was the scene of the interesting circumstances recorded in Acts xxvii, 28 (see J. Ab. Ciantari *Diss. apol. de Paulo in Melitam naufragio ejecto*, Ven. 1738).

I. *Identification of the Locality.*—Melita was the ancient name of *Malta* (see J. F. Wandalin, *Diss. de Melita Pauli*, Havn. 1707), and also of a small island in

the Adriatic, now called *Meleda* (Μελιτίνη νῆσος, Ptol. ii, 17, 39; comp. Pliny, iii, 30; Apollon. Rhod. iv, 572), and each of these has found warm advocates for its identification with the Melita of Scripture (see Ciantar's edition of Abela's *Malta Illustrata*, i, 608), the former being the traditionary and long-established opinion (see Ign. Giorgi, *Paulus in mari quod nunc Venetus sinus dicitur, naufragus*, Ven. 1730; Jac. de Rhoer, *De Pauli ad insul. Melit. naufragio*, Traj. ad R. 1743; comp. *Bibl. Ital.* xi, 127; *Nov. Miscell. Lips.* iv, 308; Paulus, *Samml.* iv, 356), liable only to the objection that the part of the Mediterranean in which it is situated was not properly "the Sea of Adria" (Dr. Falconer's *Dissertation on St. Paul's Voyage*, 1817), which has been shown (see Wetstein's *Comment.* ad loc.) to be without force (see J. Smith, *Voyage and Shipwreck of St. Paul*, Lond. 1848; also Conybeare and Howson's *Life of St. Paul*, ii, 353). As, however, the controversy on this subject has been somewhat voluminous, we will discuss it in detail, referring to other articles for confirmation of the opinions and conclusions here expressed.

1. *Arguments in Favor of Malta.*—(1.) We take St. Paul's ship in the condition in which we find her about a day after leaving Fair Havens, i. e. when she was under the lee of Clauda (Acts xxvii, 16), laid to on the starboard tack, and strengthened with "undergirders" [see SHIP], the boat being just taken on board, and the gale blowing hard from the east-north-east. See EUROCLYDON. (2.) Assuming (what every practiced sailor would allow) that the ship's direction of drift would be about west by north, and her rate of drift about a mile and a half an hour, we come at once to the conclusion, by measuring the distance on the chart, that she would be brought to the coast of Malta on the thirteenth day (see ver. 27). (3.) A ship drifting in this direction to the place traditionally known as St. Paul's Bay, would come to that spot on the coast without touching any other part of the island previously. The coast, in fact, trends from this bay to the south-east. This may be seen on consulting any map or chart of Malta. (4.) On Koura Point, which is the south-easterly extremity of the bay, there must infallibly have been breakers, with the wind blowing from the north-east. Now the alarm was certainly caused by breakers, for it took place in the night (ver. 27), and it does not appear that the passengers were at first aware of the danger which became sensible to the quick ear of the "sailors." (5.) Yet the vessel did not strike; and this corresponds with the position of the point, which would be some little distance on the port side, or to the left of the vessel. (6.) Off this point of the coast the soundings are twenty fathoms (ver. 28), and a little farther, *in the direction of the supposed drift*, they are fifteen fathoms (ver. 28). (7.) Though the danger was imminent, we shall find from examining the chart that there would still be time to anchor (ver. 29) before striking on the rocks ahead. (8.) With bad holding-ground there would have been great risk of the ship dragging her anchors. But the bottom of St. Paul's Bay is remarkably tenacious. In Purdy's *Sailing Directions* (p. 180) it is said of it that "while the cables hold there is no danger, as the anchors will never start." (9.) The other geological characteristics of the place are in harmony with the narrative, which describes the creek as having in one place a sandy or muddy beach (κόλπον ἔχοντα αἰγιαλόν, ver. 39), and which states that the bow of the ship was held fast in the shore, while the stern was exposed to the action of the waves (ver. 41). For particulars we must refer to the work (mentioned below) of Mr. Smith, an accomplished geologist. (10.) Another point of local detail is of considerable interest—viz. that, as the ship took the ground, the place was observed to be διθάλασσος, i. e. a connection was noticed between two apparently separate pieces of water. We shall see, on looking at the chart, that this would be the case. The small island of Salmonetta would at first appear to be a part of Malta itself; but the passage would open on the right

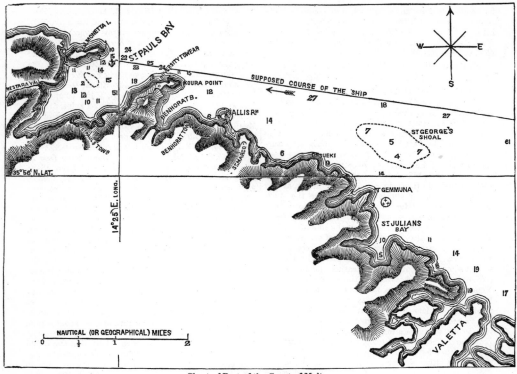

Chart of Part of the Coast of Malta.

as the vessel passed to the place of shipwreck. (11.) Malta is in the track of ships between Alexandria and Puteoli; and this corresponds with the fact that the "Castor and Pollux," an Alexandrian vessel which ultimately conveyed St. Paul to Italy, had wintered in the island (Acts xxviii, 11). (12.) Finally, the course pursued in this conclusion of the voyage, first to Syracuse and then to Rhegium, contributes a last link to the chain of arguments by which we prove that Melita is *Malta*.

2. *Objections to Malta*.—The case is established to demonstration. Still it may be worth while to notice one or two objections. It is said, in reference to xxvii, 27, that the wreck took place in the Adriatic or Gulf of Venice. It is urged that a well-known island like Malta could not have been unrecognised (xxvii, 39), nor its inhabitants called "barbarous" (xxviii, 2). And as regards the occurrence recorded in xxviii, 3, stress is laid on the facts that Malta has no poisonous serpents, and hardly any wood. To these objections we reply at once that ADRIA, in the language of the period, denotes not the Gulf of Venice, but the open sea between Crete and Sicily; that it is no wonder if the sailors did not recognise a strange part of the coast on which they were thrown in stormy weather, and that they did recognise the place when they did leave the ship (xxviii, 1); that the kindness recorded of the natives (xxviii, 2, 10), shows that they were not "barbarians" in the sense of being savages, and that the word denotes simply that they did not speak Greek; and, lastly, that the population of Malta has increased in an extraordinary manner in recent times, that probably there was abundant wood there formerly, and that with the destruction of the wood many indigenous animals would disappear.

3. *Objections to Meleda*.—In adducing positive arguments and answering objections, we have indirectly proved that Melita in the Gulf of Venice was not the scene of the shipwreck. But we may add that this island could not have been reached without a miracle under the circumstances of weather described in the narrative; that it is not in the track between Alexandria and Puteoli; that it would not be natural to proceed from it to Rome by means of a voyage embracing Syracuse; and that the soundings on its shore do not agree with what is recorded in the Acts.

4. *History of the Controversy*.—An amusing passage in Coleridge's *Table Talk* (p. 185) is worth noticing as the last echo of what is now an extinct controversy. The question has been set at rest forever by Mr. Smith, of Jordan Hill, in his *Voyage and Shipwreck of St. Paul*, the first published work in which it was thoroughly investigated from a sailor's point of view. It had, however, been previously treated in the same manner, and with the same results, by admiral Penrose, and copious notes from his MSS. are given in *The Life and Epistles of St. Paul*. In that work (2d ed. p. 426, *note*) are given the names of some of those who carried on the controversy in the last century. The ringleader on the Adriatic side of the question, not unnaturally, was padre Georgi, a Benedictine monk connected with the Venetian or Austrian *Meleda*, and his *Paulus Naufragus* is extremely curious. He was, however, not the first to suggest this untenable view. We find it, at a much earlier period, in a Byzantine writer, Const. Porphyrog. *De Adm. Imp.* (c. 36, vol. iii, p. 164, of the Bonn ed.).

II. *Description and History of the Locality*.—(In this portion we chiefly use the statements found in Kitto's *Cyclopædia*, s. v.).—1. *The immediate Scene*.—The name of St. Paul's Bay has been given to the place where the shipwreck is supposed to have taken place. This, the sacred historian says, was at "a certain creek with a shore," i. e. a seemingly practicable shore, on which they purposed, if possible, to strand the vessel, as their only apparent chance to escape being broken on the rocks. In attempting this the ship seems to have struck and gone to pieces on the rocky headland at the entrance of the creek. This agrees very well with St. Paul's Bay, more so than with any other creek of the island. This bay is a deep inlet on the north side of the island, being the last indentation of the coast but one from the west-

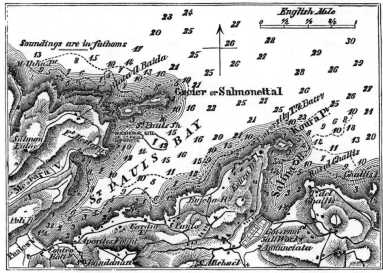

Map of "St. Paul's Bay," on the Island of Malta.

sociated with piracy. The Christianity, however, introduced by Paul was never extinct. Melita, from its position in the Mediterranean, and from the excellence of its harbors, has always been important both in commerce and war.

The island was first colonized by the Phœnicians (hence the term "barbarian," that is, neither Greek nor Roman, used in the sacred narrative, Acts xxviii, 2), from whom it was taken by the Greek colonists in Sicily, about B.C. 736; but the Carthaginians began to dispute its possession about

ern extremity of the island. It is about two miles deep, by one mile broad. The harbor which it forms is very unsafe at some distance from the shore, although there is good anchorage in the middle for light vessels. The most dangerous part is the western headland at the entrance of the bay, particularly as there is close to it a small island (Salamone), and a still smaller islet (Salmonetta), the currents and shoals around which are particularly dangerous in stormy weather. It is usually supposed that the vessel struck at this point. From this place the ancient capital of Malta (now Citta Vecchia, Old City) is distinctly seen at the distance of about five miles; and on looking towards the bay from the top of the church on the summit of the hill whereon the city stands, it is evident that the people of the town might easily from this spot have perceived in the morning that a wreck had taken place; and this is a circumstance which throws a fresh light on some of the circumstances of the deeply interesting transactions which ensued. See SHIPWRECK.

2. *The Island in General.*—The island of Malta lies in the Mediterranean, about sixty miles south from Cape Passaro, in Sicily. It is about seventeen miles in length, and nine or ten in breadth. Near it, on the west, is a smaller island, called Gozo, the ancient Gaulos. Malta has no mountains or high hills, and makes no figure from the sea. It is naturally a barren rock, but has been made in parts abundantly fertile by the industry and toil of man. It was famous for its honey and fruits, for its cotton-fabrics, for excellent building-stone, and for a well-known breed of dogs. A few years before St. Paul's visit, corsairs from his native province of Cilicia made Melita a frequent resort; and through subsequent periods of its history, Vandal and Arabian, it was often as-

B.C. 528, and eventually became entire masters of it. The Phœnician language, in a corrupted form, continued to be spoken there in St. Paul's day (Gesenius, *Versuch üb. malt. Sprache*, Leips. 1810). From the Carthaginians it passed to the Romans in the Second Punic War, B.C. 242, who treated the inhabitants well, making Melita a municipium, and allowing the people to be governed by their own laws. The government was administered by a proprætor, who depended upon the prætor of Sicily; and this office appears to have been held by Publius when Paul was on the island (Acts xxviii, 7). Its chief officer (under the governor of Sicily) appears from inscriptions

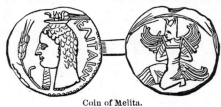

Coin of Melita.

to have had the special title of πρῶτος Μελιταίων, or *Primus Melitensium*, and this is the very phrase which Luke uses (xxviii, 7). Mr. Smith could not find these

"St. Paul's Bay," Malta.
(This view is taken from a point at the back of the bay, near the castle. The island shown as shutting in the bay is Salmonetta.)

inscriptions. There seems, however, no reason whatever to doubt their authenticity (see Bochart, *Opera*, i, 502; Abela, *Descr. Melitœ*, p. 146, appended to the last volume of the *Antiquities* of Grævius; and Böckh, *Corp. Insc.* iii, 5754). On the division of the Roman empire, Melita belonged to the western portion; but having, in A.D. 553, been recovered from the Vandals by Belisarius, it was afterwards attached to the empire of the East. About the end of the 9th century the island was taken from the Greeks by the Arabs, who made it a dependency upon Sicily, which was also in their possession. The Arabs have left the impress of their aspect, language, and many of their customs upon the present inhabitants, whose dialect is to this day perfectly intelligible to the Arabians and to the Moors of Africa. Malta was taken from the Arabs by the Normans in A.D. 1090, and afterwards underwent other changes till A.D. 1530, when Charles V, who had annexed it to his empire, transferred it to the Knights of St. John of Jerusalem, whom the Turks had recently dispossessed of Rhodes. Under the knights it became a flourishing state, and was the scene of their greatest glory and most signal exploits (see Porter, *Malta and its Knights*, Lond. 1872). The institution having become unsuited to modern times, the Order of St. John of Jerusalem, commonly called Knights of Malta, gradually fell into decay, and the island was surrendered to the French under Bonaparte when on his way to Egypt in 1798. From them it was retaken by the English with the concurrence and assistance of the natives; and it was to have been restored to the Knights of Malta by the stipulations of the treaty of Amiens; but as no sufficient security for the independence of the order (composed mostly of Frenchmen) could be obtained, the English retained it in their hands; and this necessary infraction of the treaty was the ostensible ground of the war which only ended with the battle of Waterloo. The island is still in the hands of the English, who have lately remodelled the government to meet the wishes of the numerous inhabitants. It has recently become the actual seat of an Anglican bishopric, which, however, takes its title from Gibraltar out of deference to the existing Catholic bishopric of Malta. See, in addition to the works above cited, P. Carlo, *Origine della Fede in Malta* (Milan, 1759); Carstens, *De apothesi Pauli in Melita* (Lubec, 1754); L. de Boisgelin, *Malte ancienne et moderne* (Par. 1809); Bartlett's *Overland Route* (Lond. 1851), p. 3–118; Smith's *Dict. of Class. Geogr.* s. v. Melita; M'Culloch's *Gazetteer*, s. v. Malta; also the observations and travels cited by Engelmann, *Bibl. Geog.* (see Index, s. v. Malta); and the monographs cited by Volbeding, *Index Program.* p. 84. See PAUL.

Melito OF SARDIS, bishop of the place after which he is named, and a writer of considerable eminence, flourished in the 2d century. So little is known of his personal history that it cannot be determined at what date he was elevated to the episcopacy, though he probably held the bishopric when the controversy arose at Laodicea respecting the observance of Easter, which caused him to write a book on the subject. This took place under Marcus Aurelius, to whom Melito presented an *Apology for Christianity*, according to Eusebius, in his *Chronicon*, in A.D. 169–170. In this apology (which, recently re-discovered in a Syriac translation and placed in the British Museum, was lately [1866] rendered into English by the celebrated Cureton) Christianity is described as a philosophy that had indeed originated among the barbarians, but had attained to a flourishing condition under the Roman empire, to the benefit of which it greatly redounded. According to a fragment preserved by Eusebius, he beseeches the emperor "to examine the accusations which were brought against the Christians, and to stop the persecution by revoking the edict which he had published against them. He represents to him that the Roman empire was so far from being injured or weakened by Christianity that its foundation was more firmly established and its bounds considerably enlarged since that religion

had taken footing in it. He puts him in mind that the Christian religion had been persecuted by none but the worst emperors, such as Nero and Domitian; that Hadrian and Antoninus had granted privileges in its favor, and that he hoped from his clemency and goodness that they should obtain the same protection of their lives and property from him." According to the testimony of Tertullian (in a work now lost, but which Jerome cites), Melito was regarded as a prophet by many of his contemporaries. The Church of Rome commemorates him as a saint April 1. From a passage in Origen, quoted by Theodoret (*Quæst. in Genesim*, c. 20), Melito appears to have believed that God possessed a bodily form, and to have written in support of that doctrine. This assertion of Origen is supported by the testimony of Grenadius of Massilia (*Lib. Dogm. Eccles.* c. 4); and Tillemont, though unwilling to allow this, admits that the early Church may possibly have been withheld from honoring his memory by an appointed office on account of this imputation, or else on account of the ascription to him of the book *De Transitu Beatœ Virginis*. The surnames of *Asianus* and of *Sardensis* given him by Jerome designate rather his see than his birthplace. Polycrates of Ephesus, a somewhat later writer, in a letter to Victor, bishop of Rome, calls him *Eunuchus;* yet this is not to be taken in the literal sense, but rather indicates only that he remained faithful to his vow of chastity. As to the particulars of the death of Melito, scarcely anything is known. Polycrates, in a letter addressed to pope Victor (A.D. 196), says, "What shall I say of Melito, whose actions were all guided by the operations of the Holy Spirit? who was interred at Sardis, where he waits the resurrection and the judgment." From this it may be inferred that he had died some time previous to the date of this letter at Sardis, the place of his interment. Melito was especially skilled in the literature of the Old Testament, and was one of the most prolific authors of his time. Eusebius furnishes the following list of Melito's works: Περὶ τοῦ πάσχα δύο; Περὶ πολιτείας καὶ προφητῶν; Περὶ κυριακῆς; Περὶ φύσεως ἀνθρώπου; Περὶ πλάσεως; Περὶ ὑπακοῆς πίστεως αἰσθητηρίων; Περὶ ψυχῆς καὶ σώματος; Περὶ λουτροῦ; Περὶ ἀληθείας; Περ. κτίσεως καὶ γενέσεως Χριστοῦ; Περὶ προφητείας; Περὶ φιλοξενίας; Ἡ κλείς; Περὶ τοῦ διαβόλου καὶ τῆς ἀποκαλύψεως Ἰωάννου; Περὶ ἐνσωμάτου Θεοῦ; Πρὸς Ἀντωνῖνον βιβλίδιον; Ἐκλογαί; Περὶ σαρκώσεως Χριστοῦ, against Marcion; Λόγος εἰς τὸ πάθος. Although these works are lost, the testimony of the fathers remains to inform us how highly they were esteemed. Eusebius gives some important fragments of Melito's works; some others are found in the works of different ecclesiastical writers. The best collection of these fragments is found in Routh, *Reliquiœ Sacrœ* (Oxford, 1814, 8vo), i, 109. Dom Pitra published several fragments in the *Spicilegium Solesmense*. Fragments of his works, found preserved in a Syriac translation, are now stored in the library of the British Museum. Cureton has translated some; others have been published in Kitto's *Journal of Sacred Literature*, vol. xv. A satire against monks was published in France under the title *Apocalypse de Méliton*. See Eusebius, *Hist. Eccles.* vol. iv; Jerome, *De Vir illust.;* *Chronon Paschale;* Cave, *Hist. Litteraria*, ad ann. 170; Tillemont, *Mém. pour servir à l'hist. ecclés.* ii. 407 sq., 663 sq.; Ceillier, *Auteurs Sacrés*, ii, 78 sq.; Lardner, *Credibility*, pt. ii, c. 15; Le Clerc, *Hist. Eccles. duorum prim. sœculor.;* Ittig, *De Hœresiarch.* sec. ii, c. xi; Woog, *Dissertationes de Melitone* (Leips. 1744–51, 4to); Semler, *Hist. Eccles. selecta capita sœculi*, vol. ii, c. 5; Dupin, *Nouvelle Bibliothèque des auteurs ecclés.* vol. i; Galland, *Bibl. Patrum*, vol. ii, Proleg.; Pressensé, *Histoire des trois premiers siecles*, ii, 2, p. 166; Smith, *Dict. of Gr. and Rom. Biog. and Mythol.* ii, 1023; Herzog, *Real-Encyklopädie*, ix, 313; Neale, *Hist. of the East. Ch.* Introd. i, 38; Donaldson, *Ch. Literature;* Schaff, *Ch. Hist.* i, 166, et al.; *Journal Sacred Lit.* vols. xv, xvi, and xvii; Piper, in *Studien und Kritiken*, 1838; Steitz, *ibid.* 1856 and 1857; Welte, *Tübinger theol. Quartalschrift*, 1862, p. 302 sq.

Melitonians, so called from MELITO OF SARDIS (q. v.), a sect who maintained that not the soul, but the body of man, was made after God's image.

Melius, JOHN PETER, a Hungarian theologian, was born at Horki in 1536. After having embraced Calvinism, he became in 1558 professor in the school of Debrezin, and later superintendent. He died in 1572. Melius contributed largely towards propagating the Reformed religion among the nobles of Transylvania. He is mainly known, however, by his translations of the New Testament and many parts of the Old into Hungarian. See Gerdes, *Scrinium Antiquarium*, vol. vii; Selig, *Historie der Augsburgischen Confession*, vol. ii.

Melkart. See HERCULES.

Mellen, John (1), a Unitarian divine, was born at Hopkinton, Mass., in 1722. He graduated at Harvard College in 1741, was pastor of the Church in Lancaster, Mass., and subsequently at Hanover, and died in 1807. Mr. Mellen was the author of *Eight Occasional Sermons*, 1735–95, and *Fifteen Discourses on Doctrinal Subjects*, 1765. See Allibone, *Dict. of Brit. and Amer. Authors*, vol. ii, s. v.

Mellen, John (2), a Unitarian divine, was born in 1752. He graduated at Harvard College in 1770, was minister of Barnstable, Mass., and died in 1828. Mr. Mellen published eight separate *Sermons* and *Discourses* (1791, '93, '95, '97, '99), and also two *Dudleian Lectures* (1795, '99).

Mellin, GEORG SAMUEL ALBRECHT, a German theologian, was born at Halle in 1775. After finishing his education he was appointed minister and counsellor of the consistory at Magdeburg, where he died in 1825. He wrote, *Marginalien und Register zu Kant's Kritik des Erkenntnissvermögens* (Züllichau, 1794, 2 vols. 8vo):— *Encyklopädisches Wörterbuch der kritischen Philosophie* (ibid. 1797–1804, 6 vols. 8vo):—*Marginalien und Register zu Kant's metaphysischen Anfangsgründen der Rechtslehre* (ibid. 1800):—*Wörterbuch der Philosophie* (Magdeburg, 1805–7, 2 vols. 8vo).

Mellitus, a noted prelate of the Church in the Anglo-Saxon period, flourished in the 7th century. He was sent in A.D. 601, by pope Gregory the Great, as missionary to the assistance of Augustine, who was then laboring in England. Mellitus, with other zealous missionaries, proved a valuable help in the promotion of Christianity on the Anglican shores. He brought from Rome all the paraphernalia necessary for the performance of Church services; also a manuscript copy of the Bible in two volumes, two copies of the Psalms, as they were sung in the churches, two copies of the Gospels, Lives of the Apostles and Martyrs, and a Commentary on the Gospels and Epistles. These were the first books ever known among the Saxons. Sebert, king of Essex, permitted Mellitus to preach the Gospel to his subjects, made him first bishop of the Saxons in London, and favored him with a life-long friendship. At his death Sebert was succeeded by three pagan sons, who did not continue their father's protection. It is related that after the decease of Sebert, Mellitus encountered much opposition, and was finally required to leave the country; and consequently he, with others of the persecuted, crossed over to France. Subsequently Edbald, who succeeded Ethelbert in Kent, embracing Christianity and relenting towards the exiles, Mellitus was recalled, and afterwards labored zealously in the cause of Christianity, which from that time became firmly established in Kent. Mellitus appears to have been endowed with much prudence as well as piety: not making fierce inroads upon paganism, but watching for and seizing the favorable moment for speaking and doing, he effected much for Christianity. He was afterwards made archbishop of Canterbury, and died about the year 625. See Maclear, *Hist. of Missions*, p. 105 sq.; Churton, *Hist. of the Early Engl. Ch.*; Inett, *Hist. of the Engl. Ch.* (see Index).

Mello, GUILLAUME DE, an ascetic French author, a native of Nantes, flourished in the latter half of the 17th century. He was canon of the collegiate church of Notre Dame of Nantes. He wrote *Les Élévations de l'âme à Dieu par les degrés de Créatures*, taken from the Latin of cardinal Bellarmine (Nantes, 1666, 4to):—*Le Devoir des Pasteurs*, translated from the Latin of Barthélemi des Martyr (Paris, 1672, 12mo):—*Les divines Opérations de Jésus* (Paris, 1673, 12mo):—*Le Prédicateur évangelique* (Paris, 1685, 7 vols. 12mo). These works are anonymous. It is believed that Mello is also the author of a *Vie des Saints* (Paris, 1688, 4 vols. 8vo).

Melody (זִמְרָה, *zimrah'*, a *song* or music, of the voice, Isa. li, 3 ["psalm," Psa. lxxxi, 2; xcviii, 5], or of an instrument, Amos v, 23; metaphorically, a *song of the land*, i. e. its "best fruits," Gen. xliii, 11; נָגַן, *nagan'*, to *strike*, i. e. sound a musical chord, Isa. xxiii, 13, elsewhere "play"=ψάλλω, Eph. v, 19, elsewhere "sing") is strictly a musical science, the pleasing variation between notes of a different pitch in the same part or strain, in distinction from *harmony*, which is the accord of sounds between the different parts; but in general terms it is synonymous with *music* or sweetness of sound. See MUSIC.

Melon (only in the plur. אֲבַטִּחִים, *abattichim'*, from בָּטַח, according to Gesenius by transposition for טָבַח, to *cook*, but perh. rather a foreign word; Sept. likewise πέπονες, Vulg. *pepones*) occurs only in Numb. xi, 5, where the murmuring Israelites say, "We remember the fish which we did eat freely in Egypt, the cucumbers and the *melons*," etc. The correctness of this translation is evident from the kindred word *butikh* used for the melon generically by the Arabs (Abdul. p. 52, 54; Rhaz. *De var.* p. 56; Abulf. *Ann.* ii, 65), whence the Spanish *budiecas*, and French *pastêques*. The Mishna, however (*Jemmoth*, viii, 6; *Maaser*, i, 4), distinguishes this term from watermelons (דְלוּעִים); but it uses the singular (*Chilaim*, i, 8; *Edujoth*, iii, 3) undoubtedly in the sense of muskmelon, a signification which all the versions (Onkelos, Syr., Arab., and Samar.) have affixed to it. A similar distinction prevails among the Arabs, who call the watermelon *butikh-hindi*, or Indian melon. The muskmelon is called in Persian *khurpúzeh*, and in Hindî *khurbúja*. It is probably a native of the Persian region, whence it has been carried south into India, and north into Europe, the Indian being a slight corruption of the Persian name. As the Arabian authors append *fufash* as the Greek name of *butikh*, it is more than probable that this is intended for πέπων, especially if we compare the description in Avicenna with that in Dioscorides. By Galen it was called *Melopepo*, from *melo* and *pepo*, the former from being roundish in form, like the apple. The melon is supposed to have been the σίκυος of Theophrastus, and the σίκυος πέπων of Hippocrates. It was known to the Romans, and cultivated by Columella, with the assistance of some precaution at cold times of the year. It is said to have been introduced into England about the year 1520, and was called muskmelon to distinguish it from the pumpkin, which was then usually called melon. All travellers in Eastern countries have borne testimony to the refreshment and delight they have experienced from the fruit of the melon (Hasselquist, *Trav.* p. 528; Bellon, *Observ.* ii, 75; Joliffe, *Trav.* p. 231; Tournefort, iii, 311; Chardin, iii, 330; Sonnini, ii, 216, 328). Alpînus speaks of their very general use, under the title *Batech*, by the Egyptians (*Rerum Ægypt. Hist.* i, 17). He also describes in the same chapter the kind of melon called *Abdellavi*, which, according to De Sacy, is oblong, tapering at both ends, but thick in the middle (*De Plantis Ægypti*, tab. xli); but Forskål applies this name also to the *Chate* (which is separately described by Alpinus, and a figure given by him at tab. xl), and says it is the commonest of all fruits in Egypt, and is cultivated in all their fields,

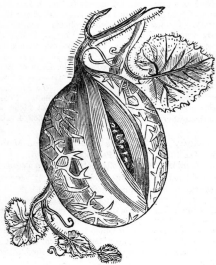

Cucumus Chate, Egyptian Melon.

and that many prepare from it a very grateful drink (*Flora Ægyptiaco-Arabica*, p. 168). The *Chate* is a villous plant with trailing stems, leaves roundish, bluntly angled, and toothed; the fruit pillose, elliptic, and tapering at both ends (Alpin. *l. c.* p. 54). Hasselquist calls this the "Egyptian melon" and "queen of cucumbers," and says that it grows only in the fertile soil round Cairo; that the fruit is a little watery, and the flesh almost of the same substance as that of the melon, sweet and cool. "This the grandees and Europeans in Egypt eat as the most pleasant fruit they find, and that from which they have the least to apprehend. It is the most excellent fruit of this tribe of any yet known" (Hasselquist, *Travels*, p. 258). These plants, though known to the Greeks, are not natives of Europe, but of Eastern countries, whence they must have been introduced into Greece. They probably may be traced to Syria or Egypt, whence other cultivated plants, as well as civilization, have travelled westwards. In Egypt they formed a portion of the food of the people at the very early period when the Israelites were led by Moses from its rich cultivation into the midst of the desert. The melon, the watermelon, and several others of the Cucurbitaceæ, are mentioned by Wilkinson (*Thebes*, p. 212; *Ancient Egyptians*, iv, 62) as still cultivated there, and are described as being sown in the middle of December, and cut, the melons in ninety and the cucumbers in sixty days.

It is not necessary to exclude from the generic term *abattich* in the above passage the watermelon (*Cucurbita citrullus*), which is clearly distinguished by Alpinus as cultivated in Egypt, and called by names similar to the above. Serapion, according to Sprengel (*Comment. in*

Oriental Watermelon.

Dioscor. ii, 162) restricts the Arabic *Batikh* to the watermelon. It is mentioned by Forskål, and its properties described by Hasselquist. Though resembling the other kinds very considerably in its properties, it is very different from them in its deeply-cut leaves. The plant is hairy, with trailing cirrhiferous stems. Hasselquist says that it is cultivated on the banks of the Nile, in the rich clayey earth which subsides during the inundation, and serves the "Egyptians for meat, drink, and physic. It is eaten in abundance, during the season, even by the richer sort of the people; but the common people, on whom Providence hath bestowed nothing but poverty and patience, scarcely eat anything but these, and account this the best time of the year, as they are obliged to put up with worse at other seasons of the year" (*Travels*, p. 256).

The common melon (*Cucumis melo*) is cultivated in the same places and ripens at the same time with the watermelon, but the fruit in Egypt is not so delicious (see Sonnini's *Travels*, ii, 328); the poor in Egypt do not eat this melon. "A traveller in the East," says Kitto (note on Numb. xi, 5), "who recollects the intense gratitude which a gift of a slice of melon inspired while journeying over the hot and dry plains, will readily comprehend the regret with which the Hebrews in the Arabian Desert looked back upon the melons of Egypt."

For further details, see Ol. Celsius, *De Melonibus Ægyptiis* (Lugd. B. 1726), and *Hierobot.* i, 356 sq.; Salmasii *Homon. hyles iatricæ*, c. 35; Rosenmüller, *Morgenl.* ii, 241 sq.; Thomson, *Land and Book*, ii, 261; Tristram, *Nat. Hist. of the Bible*, p. 468.

Melugin, THOMAS MADDIN, a minister of the Methodist Episcopal Church, South, was born near Covington, Ky., Sept. 17, 1838; in 1853 he was converted, and joined the above Church; was licensed to preach in August, 1861, and in November following was admitted into the Memphis Conference on trial, and sent to La Grange Circuit; in 1862 to Randolph Circuit; in 1863 to Huntingdon Circuit, where his health failed, and he was compelled to leave the work. In 1864 he received a supernumerary relation, in which he was assigned to Randolph Circuit, and in 1865 to Covington Station, where he remained until his death, April 2, 1866. Mr. Melugin was ever devoted to his work, and in his last illness exemplified the power of the Christian's faith. See *Minutes of the M. E. Church, South*, 1866.

Melville, Andrew, one of Scotland's celebrated characters, the most eminent worker in the "Kirk" next to John Knox himself, and denominated by Anglican churchmen "the father of Scottish Presbytery" (Stephen, i, 258; compare, however, Hetherington, p. 78, col. 1), was born Aug. 1, 1545. He was the youngest of the nine sons of Richard Melville of Baldovy, a small estate on the banks of the South Esk, near Montrose. He had the misfortune to lose both his parents when only about two years old, his father falling at the battle of Pinkie in 1547, and his mother dying in the course of the same year; and the education of young Andrew devolved upon his eldest brother, who was minister of the neighboring parish of Maritoun after the establishment of the Reformation in 1560. Even as a child Andrew distinguished himself by the quickness of his capacity, and, though a delicate boy, it was determined that he should have all the advantages the schools of his day could afford him. At the age of fourteen he was removed from the grammar-school of Montrose, where he had been for some time, to St. Mary's College, in the University of St. Andrew's. Here he studied for four years most devotedly, and, upon the completion of the curriculum, bore away the reputation of being "the best philosopher, poet, and Grecian of any young master in the land." We are told that John Douglas, who was at that time rector of St. Andrew's, showed Andrew Melville much marked attention, and that the old rector was so much pleased with his shrewdness and accuracy of observation, that, on parting with him, Douglas exclaimed.

"My silly fatherless and motherless boy, it's ill to wit what God may make of thee yet.". Anxious to continue his studies under the guidance of master minds, he determined to go abroad, and take his place at the feet of the learned of other lands. First among the high-schools of that day figured Paris, and thither he now directed his steps. He was only a boy of nineteen, but he had the purposes of a man, and without the loss of a moment, he made haste to reach Paris, and recommenced his studies at the French capital. After a two-years' stay he proceeded to Poitiers, to devote some time to the study of civil law, not, however, for the purpose of preparing for the legal profession, but only as a source of discipline "connected with a complete course of education."

Melville had gone to Poitiers, as he imagined, a perfect stranger, but his reputation as a scholar had reached the place long before he made his actual début, and he was greeted with the offer of a professorship at the high-school which he had intended to enter as a student. For three years he labored at the College of St. Marceon with most marked success, at the same time, however, adhering steadfast to the chief intention of his visit thither, viz. the study of civil law. In 1567 the renewed political disturbances obliged him to quit France. He retired to Geneva, and by the exertions of Beza the chair of humanity, which happened to be then vacant, in the academy of that place, was secured for him. Andrew Melville was now more in his element, both politically and religiously, and Geneva was a scene to which his mind often recurred in after-life. It was there he made that progress in Oriental learning for which he became so distinguished. There also he enjoyed the society of some of the best and most learned men of the age; but above all it was there the hallowed flame of civil and religious liberty began to glow in his breast, with a fervor which continued unabated ever after. In the spring of 1574, at the urgent request of his friends at home, he resigned his position here, and decided to return to his native country, from which he had now been absent altogether about ten years. On this occasion Beza addressed a letter to the General Assembly, in which, among other expressions of a like kind, he declared that Melville was "equally distinguished for his piety and his erudition, and that the Church of Geneva could not give a stronger proof of affection to her sister Church of Scotland than by suffering herself to be bereaved of him that his native country might be enriched with his gifts."

On Melville's arrival in Edinburgh, in July, 1574, he was invited by the regent Morton to enter his family as a domestic tutor; but this invitation was declined by Melville, who was averse to a residence at court, and preferred an academic life. He was early gratified in this wish, for, having taught for a short time as private tutor in the house of a near relative, he was urged by archbishop Boyd and other leading men for the principalship of Glasgow College, and was promptly appointed by the General Assembly. In this new position his learning, energy, and talents were eminently serviceable, not only to the university over which he presided, but to the whole kingdom and to literature in general. He introduced improvements of great importance in teaching and discipline, and infused an uncommon ardor into his pupils. It was not, however, as a mere scholar or academician that Melville now distinguished himself. The constitution of his office, as a professor of divinity, entitled him to a seat in the ecclesiastical judicatories, and he took a prominent part in the ecclesiastical disputes of the time, and was active in the Church courts and in the conferences held with the Parliament and privy council on the then much agitated subject of Church government. During Melville's absence from Scotland, an incongruous species of Church government—nominally Episcopalian, but which neither satisfied Episcopalians nor Presbyterians—had been introduced. He, however, was not a believer in prelacy. He

insisted that prelacy is not founded upon scriptural authority, and that it is foreign to the institutions and practices of apostolical times. His stay in Geneva, moreover, had afforded him a very favorable opportunity to judge of the workings of the Presbyterian parity, and, in consequence, he was determined to exert himself for the establishment of like institutions in his own country. Hetherington will have it that the Episcopalians are in "the habit of ascribing the decided Presbyterian form of Church government in Scotland to the personal influence of Andrew Melville, who, they say, had brought from Geneva the opinions of Calvin and Beza, and succeeded in infusing them into the Scottish ministers, who had previously been favorable to a modified prelacy." But no less an authority than Dr. Cook, himself a Presbyterian, holds that until Melville's arrival from Geneva "a modified and excellent form of episcopacy" was prevailing in the Church of Scotland, and that it was the indifference of the earl of Morton, who was now acting regent, that resulted perniciously to the country, and paved the way for the agitation of "new plans of ecclesiastical polity" (i, 237, 238). He certainly was not given the name of Episcopomastrix, or the "scourge of bishops," by any Episcopalian, and there seems every reason for the opinion that Melville was really the first Scotchman to press the interests of Presbyterianism. There is one thing certain, however, that even though Melville did not come determined to oust prelacy from Scottish churches, he yet steered clear of the regent's proposals, which, if Melville had acceded to them, "might have enabled that crafty statesman [Morton] to rivet securely the fetters with which he was striving to bind the Church, instead of being mightily instrumental in wrenching them asunder" (Hetherington, p. 78, col. 2). Melville's intrepidity was often very remarkable. On one occasion, when threatened by Morton in a menacing way, which few who were acquainted with the regent's temper could bear without apprehension, Melville replied, "Tush, man! threaten your courtiers so. It is the same to me whether I rot in the air or in the ground; and I have lived out of your country as well as in it. Let God be praised; you can neither hang nor exile his truth!"

In March, 1575, Melville had an opportunity to publicly press his reforming schemes. He was at this time a member of the General Assembly, and his name was included in a committee appointed to confer with the government on the subject of the polity of the Church, and to prepare a scheme of ecclesiastical administration to be submitted to a general assembly. In 1578 his labors were finally crowned with success. He presided this year over the assembly, and had the pleasure to take the vote approving the second book of Discipline, from that period the standard of Presbyterian Church government. Another matter to which the attention of the General Assembly was at this time directed was the reformation and improvement of the universities. Here Melville also took a leading part. The high state of learning and discipline to which the University of Glasgow had been raised by him, and the comparatively low grade of education in the other colleges, had become an object of public notoriety, and it was necessary that measures be taken for reforming and remodelling them. A new theological school was agreed upon for St. Andrew's, and it was resolved to translate Melville thither. At the end of the year 1580 he was installed principal of St. Mary's College, in the University of St. Andrew's, and in this new position he distinguished himself by his usual zeal and ability. Besides giving lectures on theology, he taught the Hebrew, Chaldee, Syriac, and rabbinical languages, and his prelections were attended not only by young students in unusual numbers, but also by several masters of the other colleges. But his scholastic labors, however arduous and multifarious, could not prevent him from continuing an active worker for the interests of the Church, even in the pulpit. Immediately after his removal to St. Andrew's, Melville began to perform divine service, and he also took a share of the other ministerial duties of the parish. His gratuitous labors were highly gratifying to the people in general, but the freedom and fidelity with which he reproved vice exposed him to the resentment of several leading individuals, and the most atrocious calumnies against Melville were conveyed to the king, whose mind was predisposed to receive any insinuations to his disadvantage. A bad matter was made worse in 1582, when Melville was sent to the General Assembly, and was by that body honored with the office of moderator. In this prominent place he had many opportunities to advocate the interests of his pet plans on ecclesiastical government. But even here matters did not rest. He was invited to preach before the assembly, and in his sermon he boldly inveighed against the tyrannous measures of the court, and against those who had brought into the country the "bludie gullie" of absolute power. This fearless charge, which the assembly had applauded, and had seconded by a written remonstrance, intrusted to Melville for presentation at court, led to a citation before the privy council for high-treason, and, though the crime was not proved, he was sentenced to imprisonment for contempt of court, as he had refused to appear, maintaining that whatever a preacher might say in the pulpit, even if it should be called treason, he was not bound to answer for it in a civil court until he had been first tried in an ecclesiastical court. Apprehensive that his life was really in danger, he set out for London, and did not return to the North till the faction of Arran was dismissed in the year following. After being reinstated in his office at St. Andrew's, Melville and his nephew took an active part in the proceedings of the Synod of Fife (q. v.), which terminated in the excommunication of archbishop Adamson, for having dictated and defended the laws subversive of ecclesiastical discipline. When Adamson was relaxed from censure, and restored to his see, Melville was charged to retire to the north of the Tay, and was not permitted to return to his post till the college had reluctantly consented to gratify one of the king's menial servants by renewing a lease, to the great diminution of the rental. Not long afterwards, the king, accompanied by Du Bartas, the poet, on a visit to St. Andrew's, had an opportunity of hearing from Melville a most spirited and learned, though extemporaneous, refutation of an elaborate lecture by Adamson in favor of his views of royal prerogative, and, upon the decease of Adamson in 1592, Melville had the pleasure of seeing the passage of an act of Parliament ratifying the government of the Church by general assemblies, provincial synods, presbyteries, and kirk sessions, and explaining away or rescinding the most offensive of the acts of the year 1584 — the *black acts*, as they were usually called. This important action is considered to this day as the legal foundation of the Presbyterian government, and it was regarded by Melville as an ample reward for his laborious efforts. The king, however, was not sincerely in favor of these measures, and secretly displayed a strong desire to make the "Kirk" a mere tool of political power, or to restore episcopacy. Melville strenuously resisted every such attempt, whether made in an open or clandestine form.

In 1596 a very favorable opportunity seemed to present itself for the court to effect its purposes. A tumult had taken place at Edinburgh on December 16, and this opportunity was seized by the court as a handle for the purpose of effecting a change in the constitution of the Church. Melville, and the Synod of Fife, and many leading clergymen, protested. To reach the king's ears, Melville was selected as chairman of a deputation to the king. Upon this occasion Melville displayed the same intrepidity of character that he had exhibited on meeting Morton while in the regency. King James seemed to be displeased with the Protestants, and reminded Melville that he was *his* vassal. "Sirrah," retorted Melville, "ye are *God's* silly vassal; there are two kings and two kingdoms in Scotland:

there is king James, the head of the commonwealth; and there is Christ Jesus, the king of the Church, whose subject James the Sixth is, and of whose kingdom he is not a king, nor a lord, nor a head, but a member." It is not to be wondered at that such plain speaking met the displeasure of the man who had a peculiar liking for stratagems, or who was accustomed to look upon the works of darkness as the essence of "kingcraft." A general assembly was summoned by the king to meet at Perth; and as it was composed chiefly of ministers from the north, who were studiously infected with prejudices against their southern brethren, the adherents of Melville were left in the minority. But the next assembly at Dundee, as we shall see presently, was not quite so tractable, and it became quite clear to king James that in this way he would not succeed in annihilating, nor even lessening, Melville's ascendency. An opportunity, however, was not long wanting for such a nefarious attempt. A royal visitation of the university was determined upon, and king James went to St. Andrew's in person, where, after searching in vain for matter of accusation against Melville, it was ordained that all professors of theology or philosophy, not being actual pastors, should thenceforth be precluded from sitting in sessions, presbyteries, synods, or assemblies, and from teaching in congregations. When the assembly met at Dundee in 1588, Melville made his appearance, notwithstanding the restrictions under which he had just been placed; but, when his name was called, king James objected, and declared that he would not permit any business to be done until Melville had withdrawn. Melville defended himself, and boldly told the king that the objection was invalid; to prevent difficulty, however, he finally withdrew under protest. Preparation was now made for restoring the order of bishops, and the first approach to this measure was to induce the commissioners of the General Assembly to solicit that the ministers and elders of the Church might be represented in Parliament. A statute was accordingly passed, declaring prelacy to be the third estate, and asserting the right of such ministers as should be advanced to the episcopal dignity to the same legislative privileges which had been enjoyed by the former prelates. The next conference, held at Falkland, Melville attended, and there, in presence of his majesty, maintained his sentiments with his accustomed fearlessness and vehemence, and the king judged it prudent to refer all the matters which were still intended to be adjusted to an assembly which met at Montrose in March, 1600. Melville appeared as a commissioner from his presbytery, and though, by the king's objections, he was not suffered to take his seat, his counsels and his unconquerable zeal served to animate and confirm the resolution of his brethren; and the assembly was with great difficulty prevailed upon to adopt the scheme of the court, under certain modifications. In 1601 Melville, nothing daunted by the fierce opposition of his royal master, attended the assembly at Burnt Island. Melville's conduct was grossly misrepresented, and James, incensed by the perseverance of his subject, immediately set out for St. Andrew's, and there, without even the sanction of his privy council, issued a *lettre de cachet*, charging Melville to confine himself within the walls of the college; the royal mandamus decreeing, at the same time, "if he fail and do in the contrary, that he shall be incontinent thereafter, denounced rebel, and put to the law, and all his movable goods escheat to his highness's use for his contemption." The king's conduct towards the Church from this time forward we have already treated in detail in the article JAMES I (q. v.).

James's accession to the English throne brought to Melville a permit enlarging his circle of activity to within six miles of the college, and three congratulatory poems, which he had written for the occasion, seemed even to have established peace between the two combatants. In 1606, however, the war broke out anew, and this time it ended only with the removal of the sturdy reformer. In 1604 and in 1605, Melville had sorely provoked the king by his activity against the royal measures. In 1606 Melville was selected to represent his presbytery at Parliament, and protest against the act of restoring episcopacy and reviving chapters. This action was unfavorably commented upon before the king, and the latter determined to punish Melville. One fine day Melville quite unexpectedly received a letter from his majesty desiring him to repair to London before September 15, that his majesty might consult him and others of his learned brethren on ecclesiastical matters. Melville and others went accordingly, and had various interviews with the king, who at times condescended even to be jocular with them; but they soon learned that they were interdicted from leaving the place without special permission from his majesty, and that James was only waiting for a favorable opportunity to vent his wrath upon Melville. The occasion was not long wanting. Melville having written a short Latin epigram, in which he expressed his feelings of contempt and indignation at some rites of the English Church on the festival of St. Michael, was immediately summoned before the privy council, found guilty of "scandalum magnatum," and, after a confinement of nearly twelve months, first in the house of the dean of St. Paul's, and afterwards in that of the bishop of Winchester, was committed to the Tower, and was there kept a prisoner for more than four years, in violation of every principle of justice. The first year of his imprisonment was particularly severe. He was deprived of all opportunity to give expression to his thoughts either by writing or oral communication. Through the influence of Sir James Sempill, he was removed, at the end of ten months, to a more healthy and spacious apartment, and was allowed the use of pen, ink, and paper. When the rigor of his confinement was relaxed, he was consulted both by Arminius and his antagonist Lubbertus on their theological disputes. He continued to refresh his mind by occasionally writing a poem, and in two or three letters to his nephew, James Melville, whom he loved as a son, he reviewed Dr. Downham's sermon on Episcopacy. In 1610 he printed a specimen of poetical translations of the Psalms into Latin verse, and he never wrote a letter to his nephew without transmitting copies of some of his verses. In 1611 he was released, on the solicitation of the duke of Bouillon, who wanted his services as a professor in the university at Sedan, in France. Melville, now in his sixtysixth year, would fain have gone home to Scotland to lay his bones there, but the king would on no account hear of such a thing, and he was forced to spend his old age in exile. Melville died about 1622, but neither the date of his death nor the events of his last years are ascertained.

Melville appears to have been low in stature and slender in his person, but possessed of great physical energy. His voice was strong, his gesture vehement, and he had much force and fluency of language, with great ardor of mind and constancy of purpose. His natural talents were of a superior order, and he was a scholar and divine of no common attainments. "As a preacher of God's word, he was talented in a very high degree—zealous, untiring, instant in season and out of season, and eminently successful—and as a saint of God, he was a living epistle of the power of religion on the heart. Sound in faith, pure in morals, he recommended the Gospel in his life and conversation—he fought the good fight; and, as a shock cometh in at its season, so he bade adieu to this mortal life, ripe for everlasting glory. If John Knox rid Scotland of the errors and superstitions of popery, Andrew Melville contributed materially, by his fortitude, example, and counsel, to resist, even to the death, the propagation of a form of worship uncongenial to the Scottish character" (Howie, p. 278). Dr. McCrie concludes his two interesting volumes of Melville's *Life* (1819) with the declaration, "Next to the Reformer, I know no individual from whom Scotland

has received such important services, or to whom she continues to owe so deep a debt of national respect and gratitude, as Andrew Melville." See, besides McCrie's biography, Hetherington, *Hist. of the Church of Scotland* (N. Y. 1856, 8vo), p. 78 sq.; Cook, *Reformation in Scotland*, chap. xxvii; Stephen, *Hist. of the Church of Scotland* (Lond. 1845, 4 vols. 8vo), i, 258 sq.; Russel, *Hist. of the Church of Scotland* (Lond. 1834, 2 vols. 18mo), i, chap. ix; ii, chap. x sq.; Howie, *Scots Worthies*, p. 239 sq.; Chambers and Thomson, *Biog. Dict. of Eminent Scotsmen* (1855), iv, 1 sq.; *Blackwood's Magazine*, Sept. 1824. (J. H. W.)

Melville, Henry, B.D., an eminent English divine and pulpit orator, was born at Pendennis Castle, Cornwall, Sept. 14, 1800; was educated at St. Peter's College, Cambridge, graduated B.A. in 1821, and soon after became a fellow and tutor; later he determined to take holy orders, and was appointed minister of Camden Chapel, Camberwell, London; in 1843 he was made principal of East India College, Haileybury; in 1846 he accepted the appointment as chaplain to the Tower of London, and incumbent of the church within its precincts; about 1848 he was elected to the Golden Lectureship of St. Margaret's, Lothbury; in 1853 he became chaplain to the queen, and in 1856 canon of St. Paul's; in 1863 rector of Barnes and rural dean. He died in London Feb. 9, 1871. A number of Mr. Melville's *Lectures* and *Sermons* were published, many of them without his consent (1845, 1846, 1850, 1851, 1853); they have also been several times republished in this country. Also *Voices of the Year: Readings for the Sundays and Holidays through the Year* (1856, 2 vols.) :—*Golden Counsels: Persuasions to a Christian Life* (1857); and other works. "No other clergyman of the English Church during the present century has had the reputation for eloquence and rhetorical finish in his discourses which Mr. Melville retained to the last. His sermons were very carefully and elaborately written, and delivered with great earnestness and fervor. If there was fault anywhere, it was in the superabundance of his imagery, and his more than Oriental wealth of style."—*New Amer. An. Cyclop.* 1871, p. 495; Allibone's *Dict. of Brit. and Amer. Authors*, ii, 1262; *English Encyclop.* vol. ii, s. v.

Melville, James, an eminent Scotch scholar and divine, was born in 1556. He was professor of Hebrew and Oriental languages in the University of St. Andrew's in 1580, minister of Anstrutherwerter in 1596, and subsequently of Kilrenny. He died in 1614. Mr. Melville was a zealous advocate of Presbyterian discipline. He was the author of *Ad Jacobum I Ecclesiæ Scotianæ Libellus supplex* (1645), and his *Autobiography and Diary* (1556-1610). See Dr. M'Crie's *Life of Andrew Melville; Blackwood's Magazine*, xvi, 256.

Mel'zar (Heb. *meltsar'*, מֶלְצַר, prob. from the Pers. *master of wine*, i. e. chief butler; so Bohlen, *Symbol.* p. 22; others, *treasurer*), the title rather than the name of an officer in the Babylonian court (as in the margin, "steward," but Sept. Ἀμερσάρ, on account of the Heb. art., Vulg. *Malasar*), being that of the person who had charge of the diet of the Hebrew youths in training for promotion as magi (Dan. i, 11, 16; comp. Lengerke, Stuart, *Comment.* ad loc.). "The *melzar* was subordinate to the 'master of the eunuchs;' his office was to superintend the nurture and education of the young; he thus combined the duties of the Greek παιδαγωγός and τροφεύς, and more nearly resembles our 'tutor' than any other officer. As to the origin of the term, there is some doubt; it is generally regarded as of Persian origin, the words *mal çara* giving the sense of 'head cup-bearer;' Fürst (*Lex.* s. v.) suggests its connection with the Hebrew *nazar*, 'to guard.'"

Member (in the plur. רְצָרִים, *yetsirim'*, *forms*, Job xvii, 7; μέλη, *parts*, i. e. limbs) properly denotes a part of the natural body (1 Cor. xii, 12-25); figuratively, sensual affection, like a body consisting of many members (Rom. vii, 23); also true believers, members of

Christ's mystical body, as forming one society or body, of which Christ is the head (Eph. iv, 25).

Memento Mori—*remember death.* It was God himself who first gave this admonition to fallen Adam (Gen. iii, 19). Such admonitions we find in the Old and New Testament, and that very frequently, no doubt with intent to remind us constantly of the final day, of the end of life. Philip, king of Macedon, it is said, ordered his attendant to remind him of his death every morning by saying, " King, thou art a mortal being; live in the thought of death." Human beings are but too apt to forget the " Memento mori" when called to high places of honor. An exception, however, was a certain general who, when holding his triumphal processions, had a servant advance to him and cry out repeatedly, " Do not forget that you are a mortal man." We should be mindful that every one of us is but a *mortal* being. Even to this day the sinister thought of this is impressed upon the pope at his coronation, when the master of the ceremony advances toward the holy father with a silver staff, on which is fastened a tuft of oakum; this is lighted by a candle borne by a clerical, who bends his knee, and, holding up the burning oakum, exclaims, " Holy father, be reminded that all earthly existence will be extinguished like this tuft of oakum." Another occasion the Romanists furnish in their liturgy, so especially solemn on Ash Wednesday, where the sentence occurs, " Memento homo, quia pulvis es, et in pulverem reverteris." There are two ecclesiastical orders, the *Carthusians* and *Trappists*, whose members, on meeting a person, utter aloud the words "Memento mori." The Trappists always keep in their gardens an open grave, surely a good warning and constant reminder of the uncertainty of earthly existence. See DEATH.

Memling, HANS or JAN, a celebrated Flemish painter, was born at Constanz in 1439, according to Dr. Boisserée, but other authorities, among whom may be cited Mrs. Heaton, assert positively that his birthplace was Bruges, and that he was born in 1430. There was for a long time a fierce controversy as to this painter's name, some writers insisting that it should be written *Hemling* or *Hemmelinck*, and that he was of German origin; there is, however, very little reason for doubting that Memling was the real name of the painter whose works adorn the Chapel of St. John at Bruges. There is but little known of his life; he appears to have lived some years in Spain, and is supposed to have visited Italy and Germany—certainly Cologne; he is also said to have served Charles the Bold of Burgundy, both as painter and as warrior. He was admitted, wounded and destitute, into the Hospital of St. John at Bruges, a religious institution, in which none but inhabitants of Bruges were entered (which fact is also given to prove that he was born in Bruges), and, upon recovering, painted, from gratitude at his kind treatment, the beautiful picture of *Sibyl Zambeth.* There are a number of works of art in this hospital by Memling, prominent among which is the history, in minute figures, of *St. Ursula,* the virgin saint of Cologne, and her companions, exquisitely painted in oil in many compartments, upon a relic case of Gothic design, known as La Châsse de Ste. Ursule. Memling painted also during his stay at this hospital the *Adoration of the Magi,* the large altar-piece of the *Marriage of St. Catharine,* the *Madonna and Child,* and a *Descent from the Cross.* Nine pictures by Memling are in the Munich Gallery, among which the greatest are, *Israelites collecting Manna, St. Christopher carrying the infant Christ, Abraham and Melchizedek,* the *Seizure of Christ in the Garden,* a *Sancta Veronica* or *Face of Christ,* the *Joys and Sorrows of the Virgin,* and the *Journey of the three Kings of the East.* Rathgeber enumerates over one hundred works which are attributed to Memling, but few of them, however, can be authenticated. He also decorated missals and other books of Church service, one of which is in the Library of St. Mark at Venice. Memling proba-

bly died in the year 1499, as an authentic document preserved in the records of the town of Bruges, dated in 1499, speaks of him as "the late Meestre Hans." See Mrs. Heaton, *Masterpieces of Flemish Art* (Lond. 1869, 4to); Kugler's *Hand-book of Painting,* transl. by Waagen (Lond. 1860, 2 vols. 12mo); Mrs. Jameson, *Legends of the Madonna,* p. 19, 89, 105, 202, 304.

Memmi, SIMON, an eminent Siennese painter, was born in 1285. Vasari says he was a pupil of Giotto; Lanzi, however, claims him as a scholar of the Siennese maestro Mino. He was a close imitator of the style of Giotto, whom he accompanied to Rome. After his master's death he painted a *Virgin* in the portico of St. Peter, also two figures of *St. Paul* and *St. Peter* upon the wall between the arches of the portico on the outer side. He then returned to Sienna, where he was appointed by the Signoria to paint one of the halls of their palace in fresco, the subject being a *Virgin,* with many figures around her. He painted three other pictures in the same palace, one of which, an *Annunciation,* was afterwards removed to the gallery of the Uffizi. The other represented the Virgin holding the Child in her arms, and was destroyed by the earthquake of 1798. He was invited to Florence by the general of the Augustines, where he painted a very remarkable *Crucifixion.* Vasari says, "In this painting the thieves on the cross are seen expiring, the soul of the repentant thief being joyfully borne to heaven by angels, while that of the impenitent departs, accompanied by devils, and roughly dragged by these dæmons to the torments of hell" (*Lives of the Painters,* i, 184). He also painted three of the walls of the chapter-house of Santa Maria Novella. On the first wall, over the entrance, is the *Life of San Domenico;* on that which is nearest the church he represented the *Brethren of the Dominican Order contending against the Heretics;* on the third, which is where the altar stands, was depicted the *Crucifixion of Christ.* Many other works are attributed to him jointly with his brother Lippo Memmi, who also practiced the art of painting with great success. About 1342 the two brothers returned to Sienna, where Simon commenced a work of vast extent, being a *Coronation of the Virgin,* with an extraordinary number of figures. He died before its completion at Avignon, in July, 1344. See Vasari, *Lives of the Painters,* transl. by Foster (Lond. 1850, 5 vols. 8vo), i, 181; Lanzi's *History of Painting,* transl. by Roscoe (Lond. 1847, 3 vols. 8vo), i, 278; Mrs. Jameson, *Legends of the Madonna* (Lond. 1857, 8vo), p. 172, 273.

Mem'mius, QUINTUS (Κόϊντος Μέμμιος), one of the Roman ambassadors sent to the Jews by Lysias (2 Macc. xi, 34) about B.C. 163–2. See MANLIUS.

Memorial is the name (1) of a prayer of oblation; the prayer in the order of the communion beginning " O Lord and heavenly Father," which follows the communion of the faithful. (2) The tomb of a martyr, or a church dedicated to his memory. (3) The commemoration of a concurrent lesser festival by the use of its collect. (4) Exequies, an office for the dead said by the priest in the 14th century in England.

Memory, that faculty of the mind which enables us to recall past impressions, whether of external facts or internal consciousness. It applies to sensations, perceptions, creations of the fancy, matters acquired by learning, in short, to anything, actual or imaginary, which has previously occupied the mind. It is the great mental storehouse of knowledge. The clearness of the impression so recalled depends, other things being equal, upon the strength and vividness of the original impression, and this largely depends upon the degree of *attention* given to the object of it at the time. Other conditions are, chiefly, length of interval since the first impression, frequency of its reiteration, variety of intervening and confusing impressions, etc. There are two accessory ideas usually included in the definition of memory.

namely, the power of *retaining* as well as recalling previous impressions, and an accompanying consciousness that the impressions recalled relate to the past. But both these are logically involved in the definition above given; for the power of retention is only indicated and measured by the facility or ability of recalling, and the past character of the thing remembered is implied in its being *re*-called rather than conceived, perceived, or originated. Memory is thus a definite act, which serves as the exponent or index of the faculty by virtue of which it is performed; and the power itself is estimated and characterized according to the ease, rapidity and completeness of the function. Memory can hardly be said to be voluntary, yet the will may assist it indirectly. The recurrence of the past impression depends upon what is called the *association of ideas*, i. e. the connection in which the impression was first made; and this furnishes the link for retrieving it. This association differs greatly in different minds, and, indeed, with almost every occasion. By attentively fixing the mind upon something connected with the matter sought to be recalled, the train of thought may often be recovered; yet, when it does at last recur, it is spontaneous. Hence memory has been distinguished into simple *remembrance*, or passive memory without effort, and *recollection*, or active memory accompanied by a mental endeavor. Memory of a particular point may be clear or faint. Memory in general may be either weak or strong. In some individuals these last characteristics are constitutional. The memory, however, may be greatly improved by habit. Artificial helps are called *mnemonics*. Memory may also be weak in one respect, and strong in another. Hence the distinction of *verbal* memory, etc. Names and numbers are proverbially difficult to remember. Yet some remarkable instances of these species of memory are on record. Singular instances also of disordered memory, either excessively acute or defective in some peculiar respects, have been observed. It is held by many that nothing is absolutely lost by the memory; and some are of the opinion that this faculty will furnish the conscience with the whole catalogue of past sins at the final judgment. See MIND.

Mem'phis ($M\acute{\epsilon}\mu\phi\iota\varsigma$, Herod. ii, 99, 114, 136, 154; Polyb. v, 61; Diod. i, 50 sq.), a very ancient city, the capital of Lower Egypt, standing at the apex of the Delta, ruins of which are still found not far from its successor and modern representative, *Cairo.* In the following account of it, we shall of course mainly have in view the Scripture relations and notices of this important ancient site, but at the same time we shall introduce whatever illustration seems pertinent from profane and monumental sources. See EGYPT.

I. *The Name.*—Memphis occurs once in the A. V., in Hosea ix, 6, where the Hebrew has *Môph* (מֹף, Sept. $M\acute{\epsilon}\mu\phi\iota\varsigma$, Vulg. *Memphis*). Elsewhere the Hebrew name appears as *Noph* (נֹף), under which form it is mentioned by Isaiah (xix, 13), Jeremiah (ii, 16; xlvi, 14, 19), and Ezekiel (xxx, 13, 16). These two *Hebrew* forms are contractions of the ancient Egyptian MEN-NUFR or MEN-NEFRU, whence the Coptic *Menfi, Memfi, Membe* (Memphitic forms), and *Memfe* (Sahidic), the Greek name, and the Arabic *Menf.* The Hebrew forms were probably in use among the Shemites in Lower Egypt, and perhaps among the Egyptians, in the vulgar dialect.

The ancient Egyptian *common* name (as above) signifies either "the good abode," or "the abode of the good one." Plutarch, whose Egyptian information in the treatise *De Iside de Osiride* is generally valuable, indicates that the latter or a similar explanation was current among the Egyptian priests. He tells us that some interpreted the name the "haven of good ones," others, "the sepulchre of Osiris" ($\kappa a\grave{\iota}\ \tau\grave{\eta}\nu\ \mu\grave{\epsilon}\nu\ \pi\acute{o}\lambda\iota\nu\ o\acute{\iota}\ \mu\grave{\epsilon}\nu\ \acute{o}\rho\mu o\nu\ \grave{a}\gamma a\vartheta\tilde{\omega}\nu\ \grave{\epsilon}\rho\mu\eta\nu\epsilon\acute{\nu}o\nu\sigma\iota\nu,\ o\acute{\iota}\ \delta'\ [\grave{\iota}\delta\iota]\omega\varsigma\ \tau\acute{a}\phi o\nu$ $'O\sigma\acute{\iota}\rho\iota\delta\iota\varsigma$, c. 20). "To come to port" is, in hieroglyphics, ΜΕΝΑ or ΜΑΝ, and in Coptic the long vowel is not only preserved but sometimes repeated. There is, how-ever, no expressed vowel in the name of Memphis, which we take therefore to commence with the word MEN, "abode," like the name of a town or village MEN-HEB, "the abode, or mansion, of assembly," cited by Brugsch (*Geographische Inschriften*, i, 191, No. 851, tab. xxxvii). "The good abode" is the more probable rendering, for there is no preposition, which, however, might possibly be omitted in an archaic form. The special determinative of a pyramid follows the name of Memphis, because it was the pyramid-city, pyramids having perhaps been already raised there as early as the reign of Venephes, the fourth king of the first dynasty (Manetho, ap. Cory, *Anc. Frag.* p. 96, 97; comp. Brugsch, *Geogr. Inschr.* i, 240).

The *sacred* name of Memphis was HA-PTAH, PA-PTAH, or HA-PTAH-KA, or HA-KA-PTAH, "the abode of Ptah," or "of the being of Ptah" (Brugsch, i, 235, 236, Nos. 1102, 1103, 1104, 1105, tab. xlii).

II. *Geographical Position.*—Memphis was well chosen as the capital city of all Egypt. It stood just above the ancient point of the Delta, where the Pelusiac, Sebennytic, and Canopic branches separated. It was within the valley of Upper Egypt, yet it was close to the plain of Lower Egypt. If farther north it could not have been in a position naturally strong; if anywhere but at the division of the two regions of Egypt, it could not have been the seat of a sovereign who wished to unite and command the two. Where the valley of Upper Egypt is about to open into the plain it is about five miles broad. On the east, this valley is bounded almost to the river's brink by the light yellow limestone mountains which slope abruptly to the narrow slip of fertile land. On the west, a broad surface of cultivation extends to the low edge of the Great Desert, upon which rise, like landmarks, the long series of Memphite pyramids. The valley is perfectly flat, except where a village stands on the mound of some ancient town, and unvaried but by the long groves of date-palms which extend along the river, and the smaller groups of the villages. The Nile occupies the midst with its great volume of water, and to the west, not far beneath the Libyan range, is the great canal called the Bahr Yûsuf, or "Sea of Joseph." The scene is beautiful from the contrast of its colors, the delicate tints of the bare desert-mountains or hills bright with the light of an Egyptian sun, and the tender green of the fields, for a great part of the year, except when the Nile spreads its inundating waters from desert to desert, or when the harvest is yellow with such plenteous ears as Pharaoh saw in his dream. The beauty is enhanced by the recollection that here stood that capital of Egypt which was in times very remote a guardian of ancient civilization; that here, as those pyramids—which triflers in all ages have mocked at—were raised to attest, the doctrine of a future state was firmly believed and handed down till revelation gave it its true significance; and that here many of the great events of sacred history may have taken place, certainly many of its chief personages may have wondered at remains which in the days of Abraham were the work of an older and stronger generation.

But for the pyramids it would now be difficult to ascertain the precise site of Memphis, and the pyramids, extending for twenty miles, do not minutely assist us. No lofty mounds, as at Bubastis and Saïs, mark the place of the great city; no splendid temples, as at Thebes, enable us to recall its magnificence. The valley between the Libyan Desert and the Nile is flat and unmarked by standing columns, or even, as at neighboring Heliopolis, by a solitary obelisk. Happily a fallen colossal statue and some trifling remains near by, half buried in the mud, and annually drowned by the inundation, show us where stood the chief temple of Memphis, and doubtless the most ancient part of the city, near the modern village of Mît-Rahîneh (fully *Minyet Rahineh;* comp. Robinson, *Researches*, i, 40, 41). This central position is in the valley very near the present west bank of the river, and three miles from the

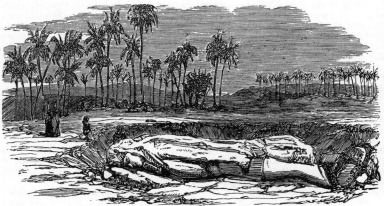

Present View of the Site of Memphis, with a fallen colossal Statue of Rameses II.

The climate of Memphis may be inferred from that of the modern Cairo — about ten miles to the north —which is the most equable that Egypt affords. The city is said to have had a circumference of about nineteen miles (Diod. Sic. i, 50), and the houses or inhabited quarters, as was usual in the great cities of antiquity, were interspersed with numerous gardens and public areas.

edge of the Great Desert. The distance above Cairo is about nine miles, and that above the ancient head of the Delta about sixteen. The ancient city was no doubt of great extent, but it is impossible, now that its remains have been destroyed and their traces swallowed up by the alluvial deposit of the Nile, to determine its limits, or to decide whether the different quarters mentioned in the hieroglyphic inscriptions were portions of one connected city; or, again, whether the Memphis known to classical writers was smaller than the old capital, a central part of it, from which the later additions had, in a time of decay, been gradually separated. In the inscriptions we find three quarters distinguished: The "White Wall," mentioned by the classical writers ($\lambda \varepsilon \nu \kappa \delta \nu$ $\tau \varepsilon \tilde{\iota} \chi o \varsigma$), has the same name in hieroglyphics, SEBT-HET (Brugsch, ut sup. i, 120, 234, 235; 1 tab. xv, Nos. 1091–1094; tab. xlii). That Memphis is meant in the name of the nome appears not only from the circumstance that Memphis was the capital of the Memphitic Nome, but also from the occurrence of HA-PTAH-KA or HA-KA-PTAH, as the equivalent of SEBT-HET in the name of the nome (Brugsch, $ibid.$ i, tab. xv; i, 1; ii, 1, etc., and $Nomen$ aus dem $neuen$ $Reiche$, p. 1). The White Wall is put in the nome-name for Memphis itself, probably as the oldest part of the city. Herodotus mentions the White Wall as the citadel of Memphis, for he relates that it held a garrison of 120,000 Persians (iii, 91), and he also speaks of it by the name of the Citadel simply ($\tau \delta$ $\tau \varepsilon \tilde{\iota} \chi o \varsigma$, p. 13, 14). Thucydides speaks of the White Wall as the third, and, as we may infer, the strongest part of Memphis, but he does not give the names of the other two parts (i, 104). The Scholiast remarks that Memphis had three walls, and that whereas the others were of brick, the third, or White Wall, was of stone (ad loc.). No doubt the commentator had in his mind Greek towns surrounded by more than a single wall, and did not know that Egyptian towns were rarely if ever walled. But his idea of the origin of the name white, as applied to the citadel of Memphis, is very probably correct. The Egyptian forts known to us are of crude brick; therefore a stone fort, very possible in a city like Memphis, famous for its great works in masonry, would receive a name denoting its peculiarity. It is noticeable that the monuments mention two other quarters, "The two regions of life" (Brugsch, $ibid.$ i, 236, 237, Nos. 1107 sq., tab. xlii, xliii), and AMHI or PER-AMHI ($ibid.$ p. 237, No. 1114 a, tab. xliii).

III. $History.$—1. The foundation of the city is assigned to Menes, the first king of Egypt, head of the first dynasty (Herod. ii, 99). The situation, as already observed, is admirable for a capital of the whole country, and it was probably chosen with that object. It would at once command the Delta and hold the key of Upper Egypt, controlling the commerce of the Nile, defended upon the west by the Libyan mountains and desert, and on the east by the river and its artificial embankments.

The building of Memphis is associated by tradition with a stupendous work of art, which has permanently changed the course of the Nile and the face of the Delta. Before the time of Menes the river, emerging from the upper valley into the neck of the Delta, bent its course westward towards the hills of the Libyan Desert, or at least discharged a portion of its waters through an arm in that direction. Here the generous flood, whose yearly inundation gives life and fertility to Egypt, was largely absorbed in the sands of the desert or wasted in stagnant morasses. It is even conjectured that up to the time of Menes the whole Delta was an uninhabitable marsh. The rivers of Damascus, the Barada and 'Awaj, now lose themselves in the same way in the marshy lakes of the great desert plain south-east of that city. Herodotus informs us, upon the authority of the Egyptian priests of his time, that Menes, "by banking up the river at the bend which it forms about a hundred furlongs south of Memphis, laid the ancient channel dry, while he dug a new course for the stream half-way between the two lines of hills. To this day," he continues, "the elbow which the Nile forms at the point where it is forced aside into the new channel is guarded with the greatest care by the Persians, and strengthened every year; for if the river were to burst out at this place, and pour over the mound, there would be danger of Memphis being completely overwhelmed by the flood. Mên, the first king, having thus, by turning the river, made the tract where it used to run dry land, proceeded in the first place to build the city now called Memphis, which lies in the narrow part of Egypt; after which he further excavated a lake outside of the town, to the north and west, communicating with the river, which was itself the eastern boundary" (Herod. ii, 99). From this description it appears that—like Amsterdam diked in from the Zuyder Zee, or St. Petersburg defended by the mole at Cronstadt from the Gulf of Finland, or more nearly like New Orleans protected by its levee from the freshets of the Mississippi, and drained by Lake Pontchartrain—Memphis was created upon a marsh reclaimed by the dike of Menes and drained by his artificial lake. The dike of Menes began twelve miles south of Memphis, and deflected the main channel of the river about two miles to the eastward. Upon the rise of the Nile, a canal still conducted a portion of its waters westward through the old channel, thus irrigating the plain beyond the city in that direction, while an inundation was guarded against on that side by a large artificial lake or reservoir at Abusir. The skill in engineering which these works required, and which their remains still indicate, argues a high degree of material civilization, at least in the mechanic arts, in the earliest known period of Egyptian history. The manufactures of glass at Memphis were famed for the superior quality of their workmanship, with which Rome continued to be supplied long after Egypt became a province of the empire.

The environs of Memphis presented cultivated groves of the acacia-tree, of whose wood were made the planks and masts of boats, the handles of offensive weapons of war, and various articles of furniture (Wilkinson, iii, 92, 168).

Sir Gardner Wilkinson observes, " The dike of Menes was probably near the modern Kafr el-Eiyát, fourteen miles south of Mît-Rahîneh, where the Nile takes a considerable bend, and from this point it would (if the previous direction of its course continued) run immediately below the Libyan mountains, and over the site of Memphis. Calculating from the outside of Memphis, this bend agrees exactly with the hundred stadia, or nearly eleven and a half English miles—Mît-Rahîneh being about the centre of the old city. No traces of these dikes (sic) are now seen" (Rawlinson's Herod. ii, 163, note 6). That the dike has been allowed to fall into neglect, and ultimately to disappear, may be accounted for by the gradual obliteration of the old bed, and the cessation of any necessity to keep the inundation from the site of Memphis, which, on the contrary, as the city contracted, became cultivable soil and required to be annually fertilized. But are we to suppose that Menes executed the great engineering works attributed to him? It is remarkable that the higher we advance towards the beginnings of Egyptian history, the more vast are the works of manual labor. The Lake Mœris, probably excavated under the 6th dynasty, cast into the shade all later works of its or any other kind executed in Egypt. The chief pyramids, which, if reaching down to this time, can scarcely reach later, increase in importance as we go higher, the greatest being those of El-Gîzeh, sepulchres of the earlier kings of the 4th dynasty. This state of things implies the existence of a large serf population gradually decreasing towards later times, and shows that Menes might well have diverted the course of the Nile. The digging of a new course seems doubtful, and it may be conjectured that the branch which became the main stream was already existent.

The mythological system of the time of Menes is ascribed by Bunsen to "the amalgamation of the religion of Upper and Lower Egypt;" religion having "already united the two provinces before the power of the race of This in the Thebaid extended itself to Memphis, and before the giant work of Menes converted the Delta from a desert, checkered over with lakes and morasses, into a blooming garden." The political union of the two divisions of the country was effected by the builder of Memphis. "Menes founded the Empire of Egypt by raising the people who inhabited the valley of the Nile from a little provincial station to that of a historical nation" (Egypt's Place, i, 441 ; ii, 409).

2. It would appear from the fragments of Manetho's history that Memphis continued the seat of government of kings of all Egypt as late as the reign of Venephes, the third successor of Menes. Athothis, the son and successor of Menes, built the palace there, and the king first mentioned built the pyramids near Cochome (Cory's Anc. Frag. 2d ed. p. 94–97); pyramids are scarcely seen but at Memphis, and Cochome is probably the name of part of the Memphitic necropolis, as will be noticed later. The 3d dynasty was of Memphitic kings, the 2d and part of the 1st having probably lost the undivided rule of Egypt. The 4th dynasty, which succeeded about B.C. 2440, was the most powerful Memphitic line, and under its earlier kings the pyramids of El-Ghîzeh were built. It is probable that other Egyptian lines were tributary to this, which not only commanded all the resources of Egypt to the quarries of Syene on the southern border, but also worked the copper mines of the Sinaitic Peninsula. The 5th dynasty appears to have been contemporary with the 4th and 6th, the latter being a Memphitic house which continued the succession. At the close of the latter Memphis fell, according to the opinion of some, into the hands of the Shepherd kings, foreign strangers who, more or less, held Egypt for 500 years. At the beginning of the 18th dynasty we once

more find hieroglyphic notices of Memphis after a silence of some centuries. During that dynasty and its two successors, while the Egyptian empire lasted, Memphis was its second city, though, as the sovereigns were Thebans, Thebes was the capital.

3. After the decline of the empire, we hear little of Memphis until the Persian period, when the provincial dynasties gave it a preference over Thebes as the chief city of Egypt. Herodotus informs us that Cambyses, enraged at the opposition he encountered at Memphis, committed many outrages upon the city. He killed the sacred Apis, and caused his priests to be scourged. "He opened the ancient sepulchres, and examined the bodies that were buried in them. He likewise went into the temple of Hephæstus (Ptah), and made great sport of the image. . . . He went also into the temple of the Cabîri, which it is unlawful for any one to enter except the priests, and, not only made sport of the images, but even burned them" (Herod. iii, 37). Memphis never recovered from the blow inflicted by Cambyses. With the Greek rule, indeed, its political importance somewhat rose, and while Thebes had dwindled to a thinly-populated collection of small towns, Memphis became the native capital, where the sovereigns were crowned by the Egyptian priests ; but Alexandria gradually destroyed its power, and the policy of the Romans hastened a natural decay.

4. At length, after the Arab conquest, the establishment of a succession of rival capitals, on the opposite bank of the Nile—El-Fustát, El-Askar, El-Katá-ë, and El-Kahireh, the later Cairo—drew away the remains of its population, and at last left nothing to mark the site of the ancient capital but ruins, which were long the quarries for any who wished for costly marbles, massive columns, or mere blocks of stone for the numerous mosques of the Moslem seats of government. The Arabian physician, Abd-el-Latif, who visited Memphis in the 13th century, describes its ruins as then marvellous beyond description (see De Sacy's translation, cited by Brugsch, Histoire d'Egypte, p. 18). Abulfeda, in the 14th century, speaks of the remains of Memphis as immense; for the most part in a state of decay, though some sculptures of variegated stone still retained a remarkable freshness of color (Descriptio Ægypti, ed. Michaelis, 1776). At length, so complete was the ruin of Memphis that for a long time its very site was lost. Pococke could find no trace of it. Recent explorations, especially those of Messrs. Mariette and Linant, have brought to light many of its antiquities, which have been dispersed in the museums of Europe and America. Some specimens of sculpture from Memphis adorn the Egyptian hall of the British Museum; other monuments of this great city are in the Abbott Museum in New York. The dikes and canals of Menes still form the basis of the system of irrigation for Lower Egypt; the insignificant village of Mît-Rahîneh occupies nearly the centre of the ancient capital.

IV. Edifices, Ruins, and Monuments.—Of the buildings of Memphis, none remain above ground; the tombs of the neighboring necropolis alone attest its importance. It is, however, necessary to speak of those temples which ancient writers mention, and especially of such of these as are known by remaining fragments.

1. Herodotus states, on the authority of the priests, that Menes "built the temple of Hephæstus, which stands within the city, a vast edifice, well worthy of mention" (ii, 99). The divinity whom Herodotus thus identifies with Hephæstus was Ptah, "the creative power, the maker of all material things" (Wilkinson, in Rawlinson's Herod. ii, 289; Bunsen, Egypt's Place, i, 367, 384). Ptah was worshipped in all Egypt, but under different representations in different nomes; ordinarily "as a god holding before him with both hands the Nilometer, or emblem of stability, combined with the sign of life" (Bunsen, i, 382). But at Memphis his worship was so prominent that the primitive sanctuary of his temple was built by Menes: successive monarchs

greatly enlarged and beautified the structure by the addition of courts, porches, and colossal ornaments. Herodotus and Diodorus describe several of these additions and restorations, but nowhere give a complete description of the temple, with measurements of its various dimensions (Herod. ii, 99, 101; 108–110, 121, 136, 153, 176; Diod. Sic. i, 45, 51, 62, 67). According to these authorities, Mœris built the northern gateway; Sesostris erected in front of the temple colossal statues (varying from thirty to fifty feet in height) of himself, his wife, and his four sons; Rhampsinitus built the western gateway, and erected before it the colossal statues of Summer and Winter; Asychis built the eastern gateway, which "in size and beauty far surpassed the other three;" Psammetichus built the southern gateway; and Amosis presented to this temple "a recumbent colossus seventy-five feet long, and two upright statues, each twenty feet high." The period between Menes and Amosis, according to Brugsch, was 3731 years; according to Wilkinson only about 2100 years; but upon either calculation the temple, as it appeared to Strabo, was the growth of many centuries. Strabo (xvii, 807) describes this temple as "built in a very sumptuous manner, both as regards the size of the Naos and in other respects." The Dromos, or grand avenue leading to the temple of Ptah, was used for the celebration of bull-fights, a sport pictured in the tombs. But these fights were probably between animals alone—no captive or gladiator being compelled to enter the arena. The bulls having been trained for the occasion, were brought face to face and goaded on by their masters, the prize being awarded to the owner of the victor. But though the bull was thus used for the sport of the people, he was the sacred animal of Memphis.

This chief temple was near the site of the modern village of Mît-Rahîneh. The only important vestige of this great temple, probably second only, if second, to that of Amen-ra at Thebes, now called the temple of El-Karnak, is a broken colossal statue of limestone representing Rameses II, which once stood, probably with a fellow that has been destroyed, before one of the propyla of the temple. (See cut, p. 72.) This statue, complete from the head to below the knees, is the finest Egyptian colossus known. It belongs to the British government, which has never yet spared the necessary funds for transporting it to England.

2. Near this temple was one of Apis, or Hapi, the celebrated sacred bull, worshipped with extraordinary honors at Memphis, from which the Israelites possibly took the idea of the golden calf. Apis was believed to be an incarnation of Osiris. The sacred bull was selected by certain outward symbols of the indwelling divinity; his color being black, with the exception of white spots of a peculiar shape upon his forehead and right side. The temple of Apis was one of the most noted structures of Memphis. It stood opposite the southern portico of the temple of Ptah; and Psammetichus, who built that gateway, also erected in front of the sanctuary of Apis a magnificent colonnade, supported by colossal statues or Osiride pillars, such as may still be seen at the temple of Medinet Abu at Thebes (Herod. ii, 153). Through this colonnade the Apis was led with great pomp upon state occasions. Two stables adjoined the sacred vestibule (Strabo, xvii, 807).

The Serapeum, or temple of Serapis, or Osirhapi, that is, Osiris-Apis, the ideal correspondent to the animal, lay in the desert to the westward, between the modern villages of Abû-Sîr and Sakkarah, though to the west of both. Strabo describes it as very much exposed to sand-drifts, and in his time partly buried by masses of sand heaped up by the wind (xvii, 807). The sacred cubit and other symbols used in measuring the rise of the Nile, were deposited in the temple of Serapis. Near this temple was the burial-place of the bulls Apis, a vast excavation, in which they were sepulchred in sarcophagi of stone in the most costly manner. Diodorus (i, 85) describes the magnificence with which a deceased Apis was interred and his successor installed at Memphis. The place appropriated to the burial of the sacred bulls was a gallery some 2000 feet in length by twenty in height and width, hewn in the rock without the city. This gallery was divided into numerous recesses upon each side; and the embalmed bodies of the sacred bulls, each in its own sarcophagus of granite, were deposited in these "sepulchral stalls." A few years since this burial-place of the sacred bulls was discovered by M. Mariette, and a large number of the sarcophagi have already been opened. These catacombs of mummied bulls were approached from Memphis by a paved road, having colossal lions on either side.

3. At Memphis was the reputed burial-place of Isis (Diod. Sic. i, 22); it had also a temple to that "myriad-named" divinity, which Herodotus (ii, 176) describes as "a vast structure, well worthy of notice," but inferior to that consecrated to her in Busiris, a chief city of her worship (ii, 59).

Herodotus describes "a beautiful and richly-ornamented enclosure," situated upon the south side of the temple of Ptah, which was sacred to Proteus, a native Memphitic king. Within this enclosure there was a temple to "the foreign Venus" (Astarte?), concerning which the historian narrates a myth connected with the Grecian Helen. In this enclosure was "the Tyrian camp" (ii, 112). A temple of Ra or Phre, the Sun, and a temple of the Cabiri, complete the enumeration of the sacred buildings of Memphis.

4. The necropolis of Memphis has escaped the destruction that has obliterated almost all traces of the city, partly from its being beyond the convenient reach of the inhabitants of the Moslem capitals, partly from the unrivalled massive solidity of its chief edifices. This necropolis, consisting of pyramids, was on a scale of grandeur corresponding with the city itself. The "city of the pyramids" is a title of Memphis in the hieroglyphics upon the monuments. The great field or plain of the pyramids lies wholly upon the western bank of the Nile, and extends from Abû-Roësh, a little to the northwest of Cairo, to Meydûm, about forty miles to the south, and thence in a south-westerly direction about twenty-five miles farther, to the pyramids of Howara and of Biahmû in the Fayum. Lepsius regards the "pyramid fields of Memphis" as a most important testimony to the civilization of Egypt (Letters, Bohn, p. 25; also Chronologie der Aegypter, vol. i). These royal pyramids, with the subterranean halls of Apis, and numerous tombs of public officers erected on the plain or excavated in the adjacent hills, gave to Memphis the pre-eminence which it enjoyed as "the haven of the blessed."

The pyramids that belong to Memphis extend along the low edge of the Libyan range, and form four groups—those of El-Ghîzeh, Abû-Sîr, Sakkarah, and Dahshûr—all so named from a neighboring town or village. The principal pyramids of El-Ghîzeh—those called the First or Great, Second, and Third—are respectively the tombs of Khufu or Shufu, the Cheops of Herodotus and Suphis I of Manetho, of the 4th dynasty; of Khafra or Shafra, Cephren (Herod.), of the 5th? and of Menkaura, Mycerinus or Mencheres of the 4th. The Great Pyramid has a base measuring 733 feet square, and a perpendicular height of 456 feet, having lost about twenty-five feet of its original height, which must have been at least 480 feet (Mr. Lane, in Mrs. Poole's Englishwoman in Egypt, ii, 121, 125). It is of solid stone, except a low core of rock, and a very small space allowed for chambers and passages leading to them. The Second Pyramid is not far inferior to this in size. Next in order come the two stone pyramids of Dahshûr. The rest are much smaller. In the Dahshûr group are two built of crude brick, the only examples in the Memphitic necropolis. The whole number that can now be traced is upwards of thirty, but Lepsius supposes that anciently there were about sixty, including those south of Dahshûr, the last of which are as far as the Faiyum, about sixty miles above the site of Memphis by the course of the river. The principal pyramids in the Memphitic necropolis are twenty in number, the pyramid of Abû-Roësh, the three chief pyramids of El-Ghîzeh, the three of Abû-Sîr, the nine of Sakkarah, and the four of Dahshûr. The "pyramids" built by Venephes near Cochome may have been in the groups of Abû-Sîr, for the part of the necropolis where the Serapeum lay was called in Egyptian KEM-KA or KA-KEM, also KEM or KEMI, as Brugsch has shown, remarking on its probable identity with Cochome (ut sup. i, 240, Nos. 1121, 1122, 1123, tab. xliii).

The pyramids were tombs of kings, and possibly of members of royal families. Around them were the tombs of subjects, of which the oldest were probably in general contemporaneous with the king who raised each pyramid. The private tombs were either built upon the rock or excavated, wherever it presented a suitable face in which a grotto could be cut, and in either case the mummies were deposited in chambers at the foot of deep pits. Sometimes these pits were not guarded by the upper structure or grotto, though probably they were then originally protected by crude brick walls. A curious inquiry is suggested by the circumstance that the Egyptians localized in the neighborhood of Memphis those terrestrial scenes which they supposed to symbolize the geography of the hidden world, and that in these the Greeks found the first ideas of their own poetical form of the more precise belief of the older race, of the Acherusian Lake, the Ferry, Charon, and the "Meads of Asphodel," but this captivating subject cannot be here pursued (see Brugsch, i, 240, 241, 242). See PYRAMIDS.

V. *Biblical Notices.*—The references to Memphis in the Bible are wholly of the period of the kings. Many have thought that the land of Goshen lay not very far from this city, and that the Pharaohs who protected the Israelites, as well as their oppressors, ruled at Memphis. The indications of Scripture seem, however, to point to the valley through which ran the canal of the Red Sea, the Wâdi-t-Tumeylât of the present inhabitants of Egypt, as the old land of Goshen, and to Zoan, or Tanis, as the capital of the oppressors, if not also of the Pharaohs who protected the Israelites. A careful examination of the narrative of the events that preceded the Exodus seems indeed to put any city not in the easternmost portion of the Delta wholly out of the question. See GOSHEN.

It was in the time of the decline of the Israelitish kingdom, and during the subsequent existence of that of Judah, that Memphis became important to the Hebrews. The Ethiopians of the 25th dynasty, or their Egyptian vassals of the 23d and 24th, probably, and the Saites of the 26th, certainly, made Memphis the political capital of Egypt. Hosea mentions Memphis only with Egypt, as the great city, predicting of the Israelitish fugitives, "Mizraim shall gather them up, Noph shall bury them" (ix, 6). Memphis, the city of the vast necropolis, where Osiris and Anubis, gods of the dead, threatened to overshadow the worship of the local divinity, Ptah, could not be more accurately characterized. No other city but Abydos was so much occupied with burial, and Abydos was far inferior in the extent of its necropolis. With the same force that personifies Memphis as the burier of the unhappy fugitives, the prophet Nahum describes Thebes as walled and fortified by the sea (iii, 8), as the Nile had been called in ancient and modern times, for Thebes alone of the cities of Egypt lay on both sides of the river. See NO-AMMON. Isaiah, in the wonderful Burden of Egypt, which has been more marked and literally fulfilled than perhaps any other like portion of Scripture, couples the princes of Zoan (Tanis) with the princes of Noph as evil advisers of Pharaoh and Egypt (xix, 13). Egypt was then weakly governed by the last Tanitic king of the 23d dynasty, as ally or vassal of Tirhakah; and Memphis, as already remarked, was the political capital. In Jeremiah, Noph is spoken of with "Tahapanes," the frontier stronghold

Daphnæ, as an enemy of Israel (ii, 16). It is difficult to explain the importance here given to "Tahapanes." Was it to warn the Israelites that the first city of Egypt which they should afterwards enter in their forbidden flight was a city of enemies? In his prophecy of the overthrow of Pharaoh-Necho's army, the same prophet warns Migdol, Noph, and "Tahpanhes" of the approach of the invader (xlvi, 14), as if warning the capital and the frontier towns. When Migdol and "Tahpanhes" had fallen, or whatever other strongholds guarded the eastern border, the Delta could not be defended. When Memphis was taken, not only the capital was in the hands of the enemy, but the frontier fort commanding the entrance of the valley of Upper Egypt had fallen. Later he says that "Noph shall be waste and desolate, without an inhabitant" (ver. 19). And so it is, while many other cities of that day yet flourish—as Hermopolis Parva and Sebennytus in the Delta, and Lycopolis, Latopolis, and Syene, in Upper Egypt; or still exist as villages, like Chemmis (Panopolis), Tentyra, and Hermonthis, in the latter division—it is doubtful if any village on the site of Memphis, once the most populous city of Egypt, even preserves its name. Latest in time, Ezekiel prophesies the coming distress and final overthrow of Memphis. Egypt is to be filled with slain; the rivers are to be dried and the lands made waste; idols and false gods are to cease out of Noph; there is to be "no more a prince of the land of Egypt." So much is general, and refers to an invasion by Nebuchadnezzar. Noph, as by Hosea, is coupled with Egypt —the capital with the state. Then more particularly Pathros, Zoan, and No are to suffer; Sin and No again; and with more vivid distinctness the distresses of Sin, No, Noph, Aven, Pi-beseth, and "Tehaphnehes" are foretold, as if the prophet witnessed the advance of fire and sword, each city taken, its garrison and fighting citizens, "the young men," slain, and its fair buildings given over to the flames, as the invader marched upon Daphnæ, Pelusium, Tanis, Bubastis, and Heliopolis, until Memphis fell before him, and beyond Memphis Thebes alone offered resistance, and met with the like overthrow (xxx, 1–19). Perhaps these vivid images represent, by the force of repetition and their climax-like arrangement, but one series of calamities: perhaps they represent three invasions—that of Nebuchadnezzar, of which we may expect history one day to tell us; that of Cambyses; and last, and most ruinous of all, that of Ochus. The minuteness with which the first and more particular prediction as to Memphis has been fulfilled is very noticeable. The images and idols of Noph have disappeared; when the site of almost every other ancient town of Egypt is marked by colossi and statues, but one, and that fallen, with some insignificant neighbors, is found where once stood its greatest city.

VI. *Literature.*—The chief authorities on the subject of this article are Lepsius, *Denkmäler aus Aegypten und Aethiopien*; Brugsch, *Geographische Inschriften*; Col. Howard Vyse, *Pyramids of Gizeh*, fol. plates, and 8vo text and plates; Sir J. G. Wilkinson, *Modern Egypt and Thebes*, and *Hand-book to Egypt*; and Mrs. Poole, *Englishwoman in Egypt*, where the topography and description of the necropolis and the pyramids are by Mr. Lane. See further, Fourmont, *Descript. des Plaines d'Heliop. et de Memphis* (Par. 1755); Niebuhr, *Trav.* i, 101; Du Bois Aymé, in the *Descript. de l'Égypte*, viii, 63; Prokesch, *Erinner.* ii, 38 sq.; also Gesenius, *Thes. Heb.* p. 812; Smith's *Dict. of Class. Geogr.* s. v. See NOPH.

Memu′can (Heb. *Memukan′*, מְמוּכָן, of unknown but prob. Persian origin; Sept. Μονχαῖος, Vulg. *Mamuchan*), the last named of the seven satraps or royal counsellors at the court of Xerxes, and the one at whose suggestion Vashti was divorced (Esth. i, 14, 16, 21). B.C. 483. "They were 'wise men who knew the times' (skilled in the planets, according to Aben-Ezra), and appear to have formed a council of state; Josephus says that one of their offices was that of interpreting the laws

(*Ant.* xi, 6, 1). This may also be inferred from the manner in which the royal question is put to them when assembled in council; '*According to law* what is to be done with'the queen Vashti?' Memucan was either the president of the council on this occasion, or gave his opinion first in consequence of his acknowledged wisdom, or from the respect allowed to his advanced age. Whatever may have been the cause of this priority, his sentence for Vashti's disgrace was approved by the king and princes, and at once put into execution. The Targum of Esther identifies him with 'Haman, the grandson of Agag.' The reading of the *Kethib*, or written text, in ver. 16, is מומכן."

Men, THE, are a class of persons who occupy a somewhat conspicuous place in the religious communities of Northern Scotland, chiefly in those parts of it where the Gaelic language prevails, as in Ross, Sutherland, and the upland districts of Inverness and Argyle. Large and undivided parishes, a scanty supply of the means of grace, patronage, and other causes peculiar to such localities, seem to have developed this abnormal class of self-appointed instructors and spiritual overseers, who sustain in the Church of Scotland a relation very similar to that of our lay-preachers. They are designated "Men" by way of eminence, and as a title of respect, in recognition of their superior natural abilities, and their attainments in religious knowledge and personal piety. There is no formal manner in which they pass into the rank or order of *Men*, further than the general estimation in which they are held by the people among whom they live, on account of their known superior gifts and religious experience. If they are considered to excel their neighbors in the exercises of prayer and exhortation, for which they have abundant opportunities at the *lyke-wakes*, which are still common in the far Highlands, and at the meetings for prayer and Christian fellowship, and if they continue to frequent such meetings, and take part in these religious services, so as to meet with general approbation, they thus gradually gain a repute for godliness, and naturally glide into the order of "The Men."

There are oftentimes three or four "Men" in a parish; and as, on communion occasions, Friday is specially set apart for prayer and mutual exhortation, these lay-workers have then a public opportunity of exercising their gifts by engaging in prayer, and speaking on questions bearing on religious experience. This, in many parts of the Highlands, is considered as the great day of the communion season, and is popularly called the "Men's day;" and, as there may be present twenty or thirty of these "Men" assembled from the surrounding parishes, the whole service of the day is, so to speak, left in their hands—only the minister of the parish usually presides, and sums up the opinions expressed on the subject under consideration. Many of the "Men" assume on these occasions a peculiar garb in the form of a large blue cloak; and in moving about from one community to another, they are treated with great respect, kindness, and hospitality. The influence which was thus acquired by the "Men" over the people was very powerful, and no wonder that some of them grievously abused it. Yet there can be no doubt that, in many parishes in the Highlands, where the ministers have been careless and remiss in the performance of their duties, these lay-workers have often been useful in keeping spiritual religion alive. It is not to be wondered that the heads of some of them were turned, and that the honor in which they were held begat spiritual pride in them. But these are always said to have been the exception. Since the period of the disruption, when the Highlands have been furnished with a more adequate supply of Gospel ordinances, and spiritual feudalism has been broken, it has been observed that the influence of the "Men," for the most part connected now with the Free Church, has been gradually on the wane. See Auld, *Min. and Men of the Far North* (1868), p. 142–262. (J. H. W.)

Men of Understanding, a religious sect which seems to have been a branch of the *Brethren and Sisters of the Free Spirit*, has already been considered under the heading HOMINES INTELLIGENTIÆ.

Menachoth. See TALMUD.

Menæa (or Μεναῖον), a part of the liturgy of the Eastern Church, containing all the changeable parts of the services used for the festival days of the Christian year. It is usually arranged in twelve volumes, one for every month, but the whole is sometimes compressed into three volumes. The *Menæa* of the Eastern Church nearly answers to the *Breviary* of the Western Church, omitting, however, some portions of the services which the latter contains, and inserting others which are not in it. See Zacharius, *Bibliotheca Rit.;* Neale, *Eastern Church*, p. 829. See BREVIARY.

Ménage, MATTHIEU, a French theologian, was born about 1388, in Maine, near Angers. He studied at the University of Paris, and there received the degree of M.A. in 1408, and was called to the chair of philosophy after 1413. The success he obtained caused him to be elected vice-chancellor in 1416, and rector of the university in 1417. He afterwards established himself at Angers, where he taught theology. In the year 1432 he was sent by the Church of Angers, with Guy of Versailles, to the Council of Basle, and by the council to pope Eugene IV at Florence. He did not return to Basle until 1437. In 1441 he received the functions of a theologian. He died Nov. 16, 1446. His biography has been written by Gilles Ménage. See Hoefer, *Nouv. Biog. Générale*, s. v.

Men'ahem (Heb. *Menachem'*, מְנַחֵם, *comforting* [comp. *Manaen*, Acts xiii, 1]; Sept. Μαναήμ, Vulg. *Manahem;* Josephus, Μανάημος, *Ant.* ix, 11, 1), the seventeenth separate king of Israel, who began to reign B.C. 769, and reigned ten years. He was the son of Gadi, and appears to have been one of the generals of king Zachariah. When he heard the news of the murder of that prince, and the usurpation of Shallum, he was at Tirzah, but immediately marched to Samaria, where Shallum had shut himself up, and slew him in that city. He then usurped the throne in his turn, and forthwith reduced Tiphsah, which refused to acknowledge his rule. He adhered to the sin of Jeroboam, like the other kings of Israel. His general character is described by Josephus as rude and exceedingly cruel (*Ant.* ix, 11, 1). The contemporary prophets, Hosea and Amos, have left a melancholy picture of the ungodliness, demoralization, and feebleness of Israel; and Ewald adds to their testimony some doubtful references to Isaiah and Zechariah. (For the encounter with the Assyrians, see below.) Menahem died in B.C. 759, leaving the throne to his son Pekahiah (2 Kings xv, 14–22). There are some peculiar circumstances in the narrative of his reign, in the discussion of which we follow the most recent elucidations. See ISRAEL, KINGDOM OF.

(1.) Ewald (*Gesch. Isr.* iii, 598), following the Sept., would translate the latter part of 2 Kings xv, 10, "And Kobolam (or Keblaam) smote him, and slew him, and reigned in his stead." Ewald considers the fact of such a king's existence a help to the interpretation of Zech. xi, 8; and he accounts for the silence of Scripture as to his end by saying that he may have thrown himself across the Jordan, and disappeared among the subjects of king Uzziah. It does not appear, however, how such a translation can be made to agree with the subsequent mention (ver. 13) of Shallum, and with the express ascription of Shallum's death (ver. 14) to Menahem. Thenius excuses the translation of the Sept. by supposing that their MSS. may have been in a defective state, but ridicules the theory of Ewald. See KINGS.

(2.) In the brief history of Menahem, his ferocious treatment of Tiphsah occupies a conspicuous place. The time of the occurrence and the site of the town have been doubted. Keil says that it can be no other place than the remote Thapsacus on the Euphrates, the northeast boundary (1 Kings iv, 24) of Solomon's dominions; and certainly no other place bearing the name is mentioned in the Bible. Others suppose that it may have been some town which Menahem took in his way as he went from Tirzah to win a crown in Samaria (Ewald); or that it is a transcriber's error for Tappuah (Josh. xvii, 8), and that Menahem laid it waste when he returned from Samaria to Tirzah (Thenius). No sufficient reason appears for having recourse to such conjectures where the plain text presents no insuperable difficulty. The act, whether perpetrated at the beginning of Menahem's reign or somewhat later, was doubtless intended to strike terror into the hearts of reluctant subjects throughout the whole extent of dominion which he claimed. A precedent for such cruelty might be found in the border wars between Syria and Israel (2 Kings viii, 12). It is a striking sign of the increasing degradation of the land, that a king of Israel practiced upon his subjects a brutality from the mere suggestion of which the unscrupulous Syrian usurper recoiled with indignation. See TIPHSAH.

(3.) But the most remarkable event in Menahem's reign is the first appearance of a hostile force of Assyrians on the north-east frontier of Israel. King Pul, however, withdrew, having been converted from an enemy into an ally by a timely gift of 1000 talents of silver, which Menahem exacted by an assessment of fifty shekels a head on 60,000 Israelites. This was probably the only choice left to him, as he had not that resource in the treasures of the Temple of which the kings of Judah availed themselves in similar emergencies. It seems, perhaps, too much to infer from 1 Chron. v, 26 that Pul also took away Israelitish captives. The name of Pul (Sept. Phaloch or Phalos) appears, according to Rawlinson (Bampton Lectures for 1859, Lect. iv, p. 133), in an Assyrian inscription of a Ninevite king, as Phallukha, who took tribute from Beth Kumri (= the house of Omri = Samaria), as well as from Tyre, Sidon, Damascus, Idumæa, and Philistia; the king of Damascus is set down as giving 2300 talents of silver, besides gold and copper, but neither the name of Menahem, nor the amount of his tribute, is stated in the inscription. Rawlinson also says that in another inscription the name of Menahem is given, probably by mistake of the stonecutter, as a tributary of Tiglath-pileser. See NINEVEH.

Menahem (BEN-ZERACH) OF ESTELLA, a Jewish savant, was born in 1306 at Estella, whither his father had fled after the expulsion of the Jews from France. In 1328, six years after his marriage to the daughter of Benjamin Abiz, the rabbi of Estella, the Navarrese massacre occurred, in which his father, mother, and four younger brothers were murdered, while he himself, severely wounded, was left for dead. A soldier riding by, late in the night, heard him groan, and lifted the unfortunate Jew upon his horse, bound up his wounds, clothed him, and secured a physician's care for him. Thus preserved, Menahem repaired to Toledo, and studied the Talmud for two years. Thence he went to Alcala, where he joined R. Joshua Abalesh in his studies. Upon the death of the latter in 1350, Menahem succeeded as ruler of the college, and held this place till 1368. Having lost all his property during the civil war, Don Samuel Abarbanel, of Seville, liberally supplied him during the remainder of his life, which he spent at Toledo, where he died in 1374. To this benefactor he dedicated his book on Jewish rites and ceremonies, in 327 chapters, entitled *Provision for the Way*, צֵדָה לַדֶּרֶךְ וּזְנֵי לְאָרְחָא (Ferrara, 1554). Comp. Grätz, *Gesch. d. Juden* (Leipsic, 1873), vii, 312; Jost, *Gesch. d. Judenthums u. s. Sekten*, iii, 86; Zunz, *Zur Gesch. u. Literatur* (Berlin, 1845), p. 415; Dessauer, *Gesch. d. Israeliten* (Breslau, 1870), p. 323 sq.; Fürst, *Bibl. Judaica*, ii, 353; Lindo, *History of the Jews of Spain and Portugal* (London, 1848), p. 157 sq.; Finn, *Sephardim, or the History of the Jews in Spain and Portugal* (London, 1841), p. 307;

Etheridge, *Introd. to Hebr. Literature*, p. 265; Manasseh ben-Israel, *The Conciliator*, transl. by E. H. Lindo (London, 1842), p. xxx; Zunz, *Literaturgeschichte der synagogalen Poesie* (Berlin, 1865), p. 506. (B. P.)

Menahem OF MERSEBURG, a rabbi of great distinction among Jewish scholars of the 14th century, and one of the representatives of truly German synagogal teachers, flourished about 1360. He lived in very troublesome times, and because the literary remains of this period were scanty, it was called the דּוֹר יָתוֹם, "the destitute generation." To the prominent literati of that period, who left some monuments of their learning, belongs Menahem of Merseburg, who wrote *annotations on Rabbinical decisions*, entitled מְפוּקִים, reprinted in Jak. Weit's שו"ת, "questions and answers" (Vened. 1549; Hanau, 1610). Comp. Grätz, *Geschichte der Juden*, viii, 149; Jost, *Geschichte des Judenthums u. s. Sekten*, iii, 116; Zunz, *Zur Geschichte u. Literatur* (Berlin, 1845), p. 193; Fürst, *Bibl. Judaica*, ii, 352.

Me'nan, or rather MAINAN (Μαϊναν [with much variety of readings], of uncertain signification), a person named as the son of Mattatha and father of Melea, among the private descendants of David and ancestors of Christ (Luke iii, 31); but of doubtful authenticity (*Meth. Quart. Rev.* 1852, p. 597). See GENEALOGY OF JESUS CHRIST.

Menandrians, one of the most ancient branches of the Gnostics, received their name from their leader, Menander. He was a Samaritan by birth, and is said to have received instruction from Simon Magus. This supposition is not well founded, however, and has arisen, no doubt, from the similarity which existed, to some extent, between his teachings and those of Simon, as well as from the erroneous idea that all the Gnostic sects sprung from the Simonians. Menander aspired to the honor of being a Messiah, and, according to the testimonies of Irenæus, Justin, and Tertullian, he pretended to be one of the æons sent from the pleroma, or celestial regions, to succor the souls that lay groaning under bodily oppression and servitude, and to maintain them against the violence and stratagems of the dæmons that hold the reins of empire in this sublunary world. One of the conditions of salvation was baptism in his name, according to a peculiar form instituted by him. He claimed also the power to make his followers immortal. His daring pretensions and fanatical teachings should cause him to be ranked as a lunatic rather than the founder of a heretical sect. The influence of the Menandrians continued through several minor sects until some time in the 6th century. They were often confounded, by those not well informed on the subject, with the orthodox followers of Christ. See Eusebius, *Hist. Eccles.* iii, 26,; iv, 22; Irenæus, *Adv. hæres.* i, 21; Justin M., *Apolog.* i, 26; Schaff, *Ch. Hist.* i, 235; Gieseler, *Eccles. Hist.* i, 56; Mosheim, *Commentary on Eccles. Hist.*; Wetzer und Welte, *Kirchen-Lexikon*, vol. vi, s. v.; Walch, *Hist. der Ketzereien*, i, 185 sq., 276, 284; Schröckh, *Kirchen-Gesch.* ii, 244. See also GNOSTICS; MAGUS, SIMON.

Ménard, Claude, a French theologian, was born at Angers in 1580. He began his career as a barrister, and was made a lieutenant-general of the provostship. Becoming depressed in mind by the loss of his wife, he forsook his calling, and intended to retire from the world. His friends prevented his entering a cloister, but his embraced the ecclesiastical profession, and showed his interest in monastic institutions by contributing to the erection of several convents. He applied himself to researches in the antiquities of his province with so much success that his compatriot Ménage calls him "Le père de l'histoire d'Anjou." He died Jan. 20, 1652. He is noted for the following works: *Les deux premiers livres de St. Augustin contre Julien* (Paris, 1617, folio and 8vo):—*S. Hieronymi endiculus de Hæresibus Judæorum* (ibid. 1617, 4to). Ménard published this history from a manuscript which he had found at Lasal. He added different Latin treatises of the same age, and notes, in which he showed much judgment and erudition. Ménard's edition served as a basis for that of Ducange, in which the notes and observations of the former are upheld :—*Itinerarium B. Antonini martyris, cum annotationibus* (Angers, 1640, 4to) :—*Recherches et avis sur le corps de St. Jacques le Majeur* (Angers, 1610). In this work he maintains, against general opinion, that the relics of this apostle are kept in St. Maurille's Church at Angers. To Ménard is also attributed *L'histoire de l'ordre du Croissant,* a MS. in the library at Paris. See *Biographie Universelle,* s. v.

Ménard, François, a Dutch writer of note, was born at Stellewroof, in Friesland, in 1570. He established himself at Poitiers, where he was at first professor of humanity, and later professor of jurisprudence. He obtained a pension from Louis XIII. The time of his death is not known. His important works are, *Regicidium detestatum, quæsitum, præcœutum* (Poitiers, 1610), written on the occasion of the death of Henry IV :— *Disputationes de juribus episcoporum* (Poitiers, 1612, 8vo), which displays a deep knowledge of civil and canonical law; and *Des notes sur la vie de Ste.-Radegerel et sur la règle de Saint-Césaire* (edited by Charles Pidoux, Poitiers, 1621).

Ménard, Jean, a French ecclesiastic and writer, was born at Nantes Sept. 23, 1650. He studied law at Paris, and met with great success at Nimes as a pleader. But, influenced by conscientious scruples, he entered the Seminary of Saint-Magloire in 1675 as a student of theology, and, after receiving orders at Paris, returned to his native place to devote himself to the furtherance of true Christianity. Believing that an ascetic life of the very strictest sort is required of all devout Christians, he determined to give himself entirely to works of charity and kindred offices. He refused the canonship to Sainte-Chapelle, and also the bishopric of Saint-Pol de Léon, preferring the humble position of warden of the seminary at Nimes, where he labored with great satisfaction for more than thirty years. He died at Nimes April 15, 1717. Ménard is the author of a *Catéchisme* (Nimes, 1695, 8vo), which has been approved by many prelates. His memory for some time was the object of a kind of worship, and his tomb, it is said, was a place of miracles and wonderful cures.

Ménard, Léon, a French antiquary, was born Sept. 12, 1706, at Tarasçon. After having studied successfully at the college of the Jesuits at Lyons, he took his degree in law at Toulouse, and succeeded his father in the position of counsellor to the inferior court of Nimes. After 1744 he resided almost continually at Paris, whither he had been sent in the interest of his clients. Largely devoted to the study of history and antiquity, he made himself known by his *History of the Bishops of Nimes,* the success of which opened to him in 1749 the doors of the Academy of Inscriptions. He also became a member of the academies of Lyons and of Marseilles. In 1762 he went to Avignon, and, at the express invitation of the magistrates, he spent two years in collecting the materials necessary for a history of that city; but, his health failing, he was obliged to desist from this work. He died Oct. 1, 1767, at Paris. Ménard wrote, *Histoire des Évêques de Nimes* (La Haye [Lyons], 1737, 2 vols. 12mo) ; revised in the *Histoire* of that city :—*Histoire civile, ecclésiastique, et littéraire de la Ville de Nimes, avec des Notes et les Preuves* (Paris, 1750–58, 7 vols. 4to). The only fault of this learned work is its excessive prolixity. An abridgment of it has appeared, continuing as far as 1790 (Nimes, 1831–33, 3 vols. 8vo) :—*Réfutation du Sentiment de Voltaire qui traite d'Ouvrage supposé le "Testament du Cardinal Richelieu"* (anonymous, 1750, 12mo). Foncemagne joined Ménard in sustaining the authenticity of a writing that Voltaire persisted in declaring apocry-

phal :—*Pièces fugitives pour servir a l'Histoire de France, avec des Notes historiques et géographiques* (Paris, 1759, 3 vols. 4to). This valued collection, published in cooperation with the marquis D'Aubois, contains a number of researches respecting persons, places, dates, etc., from 1546 to 1653 :—*Vie de Fléchier,* at the head of an edition of the works of that prelate, but of which only the first volume appeared (1760, 4to). Ménard is also the author of several dissertations, which have been printed in the *Mémoires de l'Académie des Inscriptions.* See Le Beau, *Éloge de Ménard,* in the *Mém. de l'Acad. des Inscript.* vol. xxxvi; *Nécrologe des Hommes illustres de la France* (1770).

Ménard, Nicolas Hugues, a French theologian, was born at Paris in 1585. Having finished his studies at the college of the cardinal Le Moine, Hugues Ménard joined the Benedictines in the Monastery of St. Denis, Feb. 3, 1608. He at first devoted himself to preaching, and was very successful in the principal pulpits of Paris. Finding the discipline not sufficiently severe in the Abbey of St. Denis, he repaired to Verdun, to enter the reformed Monastery of St. Vanne. Later he taught rhetoric at Cluni, and finally went to St. Germain-des-Prés, where he terminated his laborious career, Jan. 20, 1644. He wrote, *Martyrologium SS. ord. S. Benedicti* (Paris, 1629, 8vo), a work that is still read —*Concordia Regularum, auctore S. Benedicto, Anian abbate,* with notes and learned observations (Paris, 1628, 4to) :—*D. Gregorii papæ, cognomento* Magni, *Liber Sacramentorum* (Par. 1642, 4to) :—*De unico Dyonisio, Areopagitica Athenarum et Parisiorum episcopo* (Paris, 1643, 8vo), against the canon of Launoy :—*S. Barnabæ, apostoli, Epistola catholica* (Paris, 1645, 4to), an epistle taken by H. Ménard from a MS. of Corbie, and published after his death by D'Achery. See Nicéron, *Mémoires,* vol. xxii; Ellies Dupin, *Bibl. des Aut. ecclés. du dix-septième siècle : Hist. litt. de la Cong. de Saint-Maur.* p. 18 sq.

Ménart, QUENTIN, a French prelate, was born at Flavigny, diocese of Autun, about the beginning of the 15th century. He was successively treasurer to the chapel of Dijon, provost of St. Omer, counsellor to the duke Philippe de Bourgogne, and his ambassador to the kings of France, England, and Germany. The letters of pope Eugenius IV, who afterwards promoted him to the metropolitan see of Besançon, bear the date of Sept. 18, 1439. He made his entrance into that city Aug. 1, 1440. There was at that time no kingdom or republic whose administration was more difficult than that of the Church of Besançon. The archbishop pretended, by virtue of ancient titles, to be temporal lord of the city; but the citizens contested these assumed rights, and reserved to themselves unqualified freedom, which they did not hesitate to defend at all times even at the point of the sword, so that between the archbishop and his people there was continual war. Quentin Ménart had just taken possession of his see as his procurator had arrested a citizen whom he accused of heresy, and caused to be condemned by the ecclesiastical judge. The citizens declared that this crime of heresy was only a pretext, and came to the archbishop's palace bringing a complaint which greatly resembled a menace. The latter was obliged to yield, blamed the conduct of his procurator, and restored liberty to the condemned heretic. Very soon other tumults arose. On the heights of Brégille the archbishop possessed a castle, which overlooked and irritated the city of Besançon. A pretext offering itself, the citizens repaired to Brégille, and entirely demolished not only the castle, but the adjacent houses also. Ménart complained in his turn, but they scarcely listened to him. He then retired to his castle of Gy, with all his court, and hurled against the city a sentence of interdiction. The citizens of Besançon, however, were not superstitious enough to fear this punishment, and submitted without a murmur to the suffering inflicted by the resentment of the archbishop, and refused to yield in order to obtain a repeal of the interdict. Ménart proceeded to Rome, and invoked the authority of the pope; the pope delegated the affair to a cardinal, who even aggravated the sentence pronounced upon the rebels. But the people carried the cause before the tribunal of the emperor, and the latter sent many of his counsellors successively to Besançon—Didier of Montreal, Hartung of Cappel—who in their turn declared Quentin Ménart accused and guilty of rebellion. At last, in April, 1450, this great lawsuit was terminated, Ménart coming forth victor. The castle of Brégille was reconstructed at the expense of the citizens. Then the archbishop of Besançon returned to his city and to his palace, where he died, Dec. 18, 1462. See Dunod, *Hist. de l'Église de Besançon*, vol. i; L'Abbé Richard, *Hist. des Dioc. de Besançon et de Saint-Claude.*

Menasseh ben-Israel. See MANASSEH BEN-ISRAEL.

Menasseh Vital. See VITAL.

Mencius (or **Meng**), one of the two great Chinese sages (the other being Confucius), is supposed by Legge (whose statements we condense) to have been born about the year B.C. 371, one hundred years after the death of Confucius, and to have been contemporary with Plato, Aristotle, Zeno, Epicurus, and Demosthenes. His name, like that of his great exemplar, was Latinized by the Jesuits from *Meng-tse*, as that of the earlier sage was from Koong-foo-tse, to conform to which the later worthy should have been called *Meng-foo-tse*, or *Menfucius*. The Chinese language is monosyllabic, and the original one hundred family names of the empire are all monosyllables. In transferring the names Koong and Meng into Latin or English, foreigners have fallen into the ludicrous mistake of confounding name and title, and making a single polysyllabic surname out of the two—as if the Chinese were to make Popjohn out of pope John, or Lordbut out of lord Bute!

Men often owe their greatness to their mothers. The mother of Meng is celebrated throughout China as a model of feminine wisdom in family training. The first home of her widowhood was near a cemetery, and her little boy, with the instinctive imitativeness peculiar to children, began to practice funeral ceremonies, and to perform Liliputian burial-rites. "This will never do," said Madam Meng, "my son will grow up an undertaker," and she promptly removed to a house in the market-place. Here the boy imitated the cries, disputes, and chafferings of the buyers and sellers. "This will not answer," said the watchful mother, "he will make only a pedler or an auctioneer," and again she removed and took up her abode in the vicinity of a school. The youth forthwith took to chanting lessons in concert with the loud chorus peculiar to the Chinese school-room. "This will do," said the prudent dame, "my son will become a scholar," and she was not disappointed in her forecasting. Nevertheless he was, like all boys, indifferent and careless, and we are told that, to quicken his zeal and give him a striking lesson, his mother one day surprised and alarmed him by suddenly cutting asunder the web she was weaving. Upon his inquiring why she did it, she replied that thus, by his idleness, he was cutting asunder the web of opportunity, and destroying his prospects for life, just as she had destroyed the product of the loom. The boy was affected, and gave greater diligence to his studies. These are all the glimpses we have of philosopher Meng, until we meet him in public life at forty years of age. He must have spent his early years in diligent study of the classics, but how, or under what masters, we are not informed. In his writings he says, "Although I could not be a disciple of Confucius myself, I have endeavored to cultivate my character and knowledge by means of others who were." Like his master Confucius, Mencius doubtless assumed the office of a teacher—not a teacher or professor in our Western sense, but a peripatetic advocate of morals, po-

litical philosophy, and good government—one to whom youthful and perplexed inquirers resorted for counsel and encouragement. In the times of Confucius and Mencius, China was not a consolidated empire as at present, but consisted of a number of states or provinces under independent chieftains or kings. To the court of one of these Mencius resorted at about the age of forty years, and at the court of one or another of these petty rulers he lingered for nearly a quarter of a century —the period which his published works cover—when he retired to obscurity, and spent the remaining twenty years of his life with his disciples in social converse, or the preparation of the seven books that constitute his writings. It was a long time before his reputation became national; but the time came at last, when a native writer says, "Since the time when Han, duke of Literature, delivered his eulogium—'Confucius handed the scheme of doctrine to Mencius, on whose death the line of transmission was interrupted'—all the scholars of the empire have associated Confucius and Mencius together." Meng lived to an advanced age, dying B.C. 288. The influence of his doctrines and opinions in China is second only to that of Confucius. "Confucius," says a native writer, "spoke only of benevolence; Mencius speaks of benevolence and righteousness." "Confucius spoke only of the will or mind; Mencius enlarged on the nourishment of the passion-nature."

The pet doctrine of Mencius was the intrinsic goodness of human nature, although he admitted that by far the greater part of mankind had, through unfavorable circumstances or influences, become perverted. He says, "The way in which a man loses his natural goodness is like the way in which trees are deprived by the woodman of their branches and foliage; and, if they still send forth some buds or sprouts, then come the cattle and goats and browse upon them. As in the tree all appearance of life and beauty is destroyed, so in man, after a long exposure to evil influences, all traces of native goodness seem to be obliterated." But he maintains that "there is an original power of goodness in the race," and that "all men may, if they will, become like Yao and Shun, two of the early sages and kings, who were pre-eminent for their virtue." Mencius attributed the decline in morals to the neglect of the precepts of Confucius. He was determined, therefore, to correct the evils which had sprung up, and, by securing the attention of the people to the study of morals, to restore the virtues of the primitive ages. One well versed in Chinese scholarship says, "The great object of Mencius is to rectify men's hearts. 'If a man once rectify his heart,' says he, 'little else will remain for him to do.' In another place he says, 'The great or superior man is he who does not lose his child's heart,'" an expression which vividly recalls those beautiful lines of the great German poet—

"Wohl dem der frei von Schuld und Fehle
    Bewahrt die kindlich reine Seele" (Schiller).

It is evident, however, that, owing to his sanguine and ardent nature, or to some other cause, Mencius did not very fully realize the exceeding difficulty of "rectifying one's heart." He did not like disputing, yet, when forced to it, showed himself master of the art. His reasonings are often marked by an enjoyable ingenuity and subtlety. "We have more sympathy with him than with Confucius. He comes closer to us; he is not so awful, but he is more admirable." The people he considered the most important element of a nation, the sovereign of the least consequence. The ground of the relation between sovereign and people is the will of God. He asserts the doctrine, *Vox populi, vox Dei.* "Heaven sees as the people see, Heaven hears as the people hear." The highest compliment to the Chinese sage Meng is paid him by Dr. Legge, who finds his views of human nature identical with those of the great author of the "Analogy," bishop Butler, whom Wardlaw, in his Christian Ethics, compares to the Greek Zeno. It would please us to quote largely from the Seven Books, as the best means of showing the real character and teachings of this teaching "celestial." His writings abound in gems of illustration. Opening them at random, we everywhere light upon striking sayings: "To dig a well, and stop without reaching the spring, is to throw away the well." "People cannot live without fire or water, yet, if you knock at a man's door and ask for water or fire, there is no man who will not give them, such is the abundance of these things: a sage king will cause pulse and grain to be as abundant as fire and water." "To the truly great man belong by nature benevolence, righteousness, prosperity, and knowledge." "Good government is feared by the people, good instructions are loved by them: good government gets their wealth, good instructions their hearts." "Honor and virtue delight in righteousness." "Death in the discharge of duty may be ascribed to the will of Heaven." "Life springs from sorrow and calamity, death from ease and pleasure." "The value of benevolence depends on its being brought to maturity." "I like life and I like righteousness: if I cannot keep the two together, I will let the life go and choose righteousness." "The tendency of man's nature to good is like the tendency of water to flow downwards." "As you do violence to wood in order to make it into cups and bowls, so you must do violence to humanity to fashion it to benevolence and righteousness." "No man can bend himself and at the same time make others straight."

Legge finds fault with Confucius and Mencius because their views were so human—both said so little of God and heaven. To these influential teachers he attributes the gross materialism of the Chinese literati to-day. We have no apology to offer for their atheism. Mencius is an object of reverence, but he does not indirectly contribute, like Confucius, to idolatry, in the sanctification of tables, altars, sacrifices, and victims to himself. Mencius is only human, Confucius is divine. The distinguished Orientalist Rémusat, in drawing a comparison between Confucius and Mencius, says the former "is always grave, and even austere; he exalts men of virtue, of whom he presents an ideal portrait; he speaks of bad men only with a cool indignation. Mencius, with the same love of virtue, seems to feel for vice rather contempt than abhorrence. He assails it with the force of argument; he does not disdain even to employ against it the weapons of ridicule." Mencius combined a certain modesty with a just and manly appreciation of himself. He seemed greatly surprised when one of his disciples was disposed to rank him as a sage; yet he said on another occasion, "When sages shall rise up again, they will not change my words." He believed that he was appointed by Heaven to uphold or restore the doctrines of the ancient sages, such as Yao, Shun, and Confucius. Han-Yu, a celebrated Chinese critic, says, "If we wish to study the doctrines of the sages, we must begin with Mencius. . . . It is owing to his words that learners nowadays still know how to revere Confucius, to honor benevolence and righteousness, to esteem the true sovereign, and to despise the mere pretender." See, besides the notice prefixed to the Chinese-English edition of Legge's *Chinese Classics* (Hong-Kong, 1861), vol. ii, Panthier's translation of Mencius's writings (Paris, 1851), and his *Chine*, p. 187 sq.; Loomis, *Confucius and the Chinese Classics* (San Francisco, 1867, 12mo), bk. iv; Rosny, in Hoefer's *Nouv. Biog. Générale*, s. v.; and the excellent article in Thomas's *Dict. of Biog. and Mythol.* s. v. (E. W.)

Mencke, Johann, son of the following, was born at Leipsic in 1674, and was admitted master of arts in that university in 1694. He spent some time there in the study of divinity, and then travelled in Holland and England. The reputation of his father secured him ready admission to literary circles, but, to the great disappointment of his father, he turned away from theology, and gave himself to the pursuit of studies in history and jurisprudence. He died April 1, 1732.

Mencke, Otto, a learned German divine, was born at Oldenburg, in Westphalia, in 1644. When a youth of seventeen, he left the parental roof to seek further educational advantages than his native place could afford him at the large harbor of Bremen, and there he pursued the study of philosophy; he next removed to the University of Leipsic, where he was admitted master of arts in 1664. Thereafter he continued his studies at the universities of Jena, Wittemberg, Groningen, Franeker, Utrecht, Leyden, and Kiel. Returning to Leipsic, he applied himself for some time to divinity and civil law. In 1668 he was chosen professor of morality in that university, and in 1671 took the degree of licentiate in divinity. He discharged the duties of his professorship with great reputation till his death, which happened in 1707. He was five times rector of the University of Leipsic, and seven times dean of the faculty of philosophy. He published several works of his own, and edited many valuable productions of others. They are all, however, of a secular character. See *Gen. Biog. Dict.* s. v.; *Biographie Universelle*, s. v.

Mendæans (or **Mendians**), also known as CHRISTIANS OF ST. JOHN, are an Eastern religious sect of Christians, who appear to retain some New-Testament principles, tainted, however, very much with Jewish doctrines and customs, and even with many heathen practices and phases of religious opinion. See HEMERO-BAPTISTÆ. They style themselves *Mendei Yochanan*, i. e. *Disciples of John.*

Names.—The name מַנְדָּיָא, *Mandâyê*, derived from *Manda de-Chayê*, מַנְדָּא דְהַיָּא, the λόγος τῆς ζωῆς, or *word of life*, is equivalent to οἱ λογικοί, in opposition to those holding different views, who are designated by them as ἄλογοι. But it is only among themselves they use that appellation; in public they call themselves *Sobba* (from the Arabic *tsabbah*), and allow themselves to be considered by the Mohammedans as the followers of the *Sabæans* mentioned in the Koran. This erroneous opinion, it is said, took its rise from their habit of turning to the polar star when praying. The name of *Christians of St. John* was never assumed by them, and originated with travellers. Their most learned and distinguished men are called by them *Nasôrâyê*, נְצוֹרָיֵא.

Sacred Books.—Most of their standard works, which might have given us authentic views of their principles, were destroyed by the Turks, and their religious works now extant are only, 1, the סִדְרָא רַבָּא, *Sidra Rabba*, "the great book;" also called גְּנְזָא, *Gensa*, "the treasure." This is their principal work, and contains their doctrines, only in unconnected fragments, evidently the production of a number of different persons. It is divided into two parts, the first forming about two thirds of the whole, is written for the living, and is called יְמִינָא, "*the right;*" the other, smaller, for the dead, is called סְמָלָא, "*the left,*" and contains an account of the death of Adam, as also the prayers to be used by the priests on the occasion of deaths and funerals. Norberg has given some information on that work under the title "*Liber Adami,*" which is quite improper, and which he probably took from Abraham Ecchellensis; his version also is full of errors arising from erroneous interpretation of the text, which he gives also incorrectly, so that this work can only be used with great caution. 2. סִדְרָא נְשַׁמְתָא, "the book of souls;" it contains the prayers of the priests, and constitutes the liturgy, which every priest is to know by heart. 3. קוֹלַסְתָא. This contains the marriage ritual. 4. בָּאוָתָא דְרַחֲמֵא, in which are found the prayers for each day. 5. אָ אֲנְדְנֵי דְדִרְבְשָׁא, prayers to be recited before the cross, both at home and in the church, but exclusively by the priests. 6. דְרַשָׁא דְיַחֲנָא, a history of John the Baptist. 7. אָסְפַר מַלְוָשִׁיא, a treatise on astrology. Aside from these they have formulas for all kinds of sorcery, and amulets for sickness and other misfortunes which evil spirits may bring; these charms are to be worn on the breast. Those used against incurable diseases are called קְמָחַיָא, those against curable disorders פְּשֵׁרַיָא. According to Ignatius a Jesu, they also possess another work, entitled "Divan," of which he gives an account; yet the characteristics he furnishes of it seem to apply equally to the Sidra Rabba, and it is thought that the latter may be the work he refers to.

Belief.—Their religion, which is a singular mixture of the most opposite systems of antiquity, is very obscure and confused, the more as, in the course of time, it underwent different and often contradictory modifications, which we find in their religious works. Another very perplexing feature of the system for those who study it is that the same deities or angels are sometimes designated by entirely different names, until it becomes almost impossible to establish their identity.

In a single abstract from the Sidra Rabba (i, 130-236) we find no less than three conflicting accounts of the creation. They agree in placing at the beginning of all things פִּירָא רַבָּא, Pira Rabba, "the great fruit," the בְּגוֹ פִּירָא רַבָּא, Bego Pira Rabba, "in the great fruit." This recalls the Orphean myth of a world's egg, containing the germ of all that exists. Norberg, in his preface, remark 3, not being able to understand פירא, transformed it into פְרחָא, which, in his Onomasticon, he explains "volucris, sc. Phœnix," and translates the preceding words "(fuit) Ferho per Ferho," which, in the Onom., he explains by "Summum Numen per se exstitit." At the same time with the great fruit was the מָאנָא רַבָּא דֶאֶקָרָא, "Mana the Lord of Glory," and the אָיַר זִיוָא רַבָּא, "the Ether of great brilliancy," which latter is the world, in which the Mana Rabba reigns, and which contains the יַרְדְנָא רַבָּא, "the great Jordan" (they call all rivers Jordans), which proceeds from him. Mana Rabba finally called forth "the life," חִיָא (sc. קַדְמָיָא, "the first"). This accomplished the act of creation, and the Mana Rabba at once went into the most absolute retirement, where he dwells invisible to all but the purest emanations, and the most pious among the Mendæans, who, after their death, are permitted, but only once, to contemplate the Almighty. As the revealed, active, and governing deity—but not similar to the semigods of the Gnostics—stands the Chayê Kadmâyê, "the first life," which is therefore entitled to the first worship and adoration. Hence also it is it, and not the Mana Rabba, who is first invoked in all prayers, and with whose name every book begins. It is designated under a variety of names, even sometimes by those applied to the Mana Rabba, with whom it is occasionally confounded. Like him, it dwells in the pure, brilliant ether, which is considered as a world in itself, in which all that exists is pervaded by the waters of the fire of life, and is inhabited by numberless Uthrê, עוּתְרַיָא, "angels," who dwell there in eternal blessedness. From the Chayê Kadmâyê emanated first the Chayê Thinyânê, חִיָא תִנְיָנָיָא, "the second life," often called also וּשְׁמִין, and then the מַנְדָא דְחַיָא, Mandâ de-Chayê. This is sometimes (ii, 208) called דַכְיָא, the "pure," yet is described as susceptible of impure thoughts: thus it attempted to usurp the place of the first life, and was on that account exiled from the pure ether into the world of light, being separated from it by the הַפִיקְרָא מָיָא (the Cabalists call them אפיקר מים). It is similar to Cain, while its younger brother, Mandâ de-Chayê, represents Abel. He is called the father, master, and king of the Uthrê, lord of the worlds, the beloved son, the good shepherd, the high-priest, the word of life, the λόγος, the teacher and redeemer of mankind, who descended into hell and chained the devil:

he is, in short, the Christ of the Mendæans; and as the followers of our Saviour, so are they named after the founder of their faith. He dwells with the father, who is supposed to be sometimes Chayê Kadmâyê, sometimes Mana Rabba, and is, like the "first life," called אָדָם קַדְמָיָא (comp. in the Cabala, אָדָם קַדְמוֹן). He revealed himself, however, to humanity in his three sons, who are also called his brothers, שִׁיתִיל, הִיבִיל, and אֲנוּש (Abel, Seth, and Enoch). In another place it is said that Hebil alone is his son, Shethil his grandson, and Anush his great-grandson. Hebil, the most important among them, is almost equally venerated with the Mandâ de-Chayê, receives the same names, and is often confounded with him. He is generally named הִיבִיל זִרְוָא. Among the Uthrê, "angels," who emanated from Chayê Thinyânê, the first and most eminent is חַיָא תְלִיתָיָא, "the third life;" often also called אָבָתוּר, Abâthur. This is not the "buffalo," as erroneously asserted by Gesenius (in Ersch und Gruber, Encyklop. s. v. Zabier), but only has that name because of his being called κατ' ἐξοχήν, "the father of the Uthrê," אָבָא דְעוּתְרַיָא. He is also called "the old, the hidden, the watcher." He sits at the limit of the world of light, where, at the door which leads to the middle and lower regions, and in a scale which he always holds in his hand, he weighs the deeds of the departed as they appear before him to gain admittance. Under him there was in the beginning an immense void, and at the bottom of it the troubled, black waters, מַיָא סְיָאוַיָא. As he looked down and saw his image reflected in it, arose פְּתָאהִיל, who is also called Gabriel, and retains in part the nature of the dark waters from which he proceeded. He received from his father the mission to build the earth and to create man. This he is represented sometimes as having performed alone; at others, with the aid of the dæmons. When he had created Adam and Eve, he found himself unable to give them an upright posture, or to breathe the spirit into them. Hebil, Shethil, and Anush then interfered, and obtained from Chayê Kadmâyê (or took from Pethahil at his instigation) the spirit of Mana, and infused it into man, that he might not worship Pethahil as his creator. The latter was on that account exiled from the world of light by his father, and consigned to a place below, where he is to remain until the day of judgment. He will then be raised up by Hebil-Siva, be baptized, made king of the Uthrê, and will be generally worshipped. The nether world consists of four entrances into hell, or limbo, each of which is governed by a king and queen. Then only comes the real kingdom of darkness, divided into three parts, governed by three old, single kings—Shedum, the grandson of darkness; Gio, the great; and Krun, or Karkum, "the great mountain of flesh," who, as the oldest and greatest among them, the first-born king of darkness, inhabits the lowest region. In the entrances to hell there is yet dirty, slimy water; in the real hell there is none, and Krun's kingdom consists only of dust and vacancy. In hell and its entrance there is no longer any brilliancy in fire, but only a consuming power. Hebil-Siva (or Mandâ de-Chayê), sustained by the power of Mana Rabba, descended into it, unravelled the mysteries of the lower regions, took all power from their kings, and closed the door of the different worlds. By subterfuge he brought out Rucha, daughter of Kin, the queen of darkness, and prevented her return to the nether world. She then bore the worst of all devils, אוּר, the fire, i. e. the destroyer, whom Hebil-Siva, when in his zeal he sought to storm the worlds of light, threw into the black waters, bound, and surrounded with iron and seven golden walls. While Pethahil was occupied in the creation of the world and of man, Rucha bore first seven, then twelve, and again five sons to the fire. These twenty-four sons were by Pethahil transplanted into the heavens; the first seven are the seven planets, one for each of the seven heavens; the sun, as the greatest, stands in the central or fourth heaven; the twelve became the signs of the zodiac; the fate of the remaining five is unknown. They are intended to be serviceable to man, but only seek to injure him, and are the source of all evil and wrong upon earth. The seven planets have their stations, מַטָּרְתָא, where they return always, after accomplishing their course in the heavens. They, like the earth, and another world situated in its neighborhood, to the north, rest on anvils which Hebil-Siva placed on the belly of the "fire." The Mendæans consider the heavens as built of the clearest, purest water, but so solid that even diamond will not cut it. On this water the planets and other stars are sailing; they are of themselves dark, being evil dæmons, but are illuminated by brilliant lights carried by the angels. The clearness of the sky enables us to see through the seven heavens as far as the polar star, around which, as the central sun, all the other stars are revolving. It stands at the dome of heaven, before the door of the Abâthur, and is therefore the place to which the Mendæans direct their prayers. They consider the earth as a circle, inclining somewhat to the south. It is surrounded on three sides by the sea; on the north, on the contrary, is a great mountain of turquoise, whose reflection causes the sky to appear blue. Immediately on the other side of that mountain is another world, in which Pharaoh, a king and high-priest of the Mendæans, and the Egyptians, who did not perish in the Red Sea, but were saved, lead a happy life. Both worlds are surrounded by the outer sea, יַמָּא רַבָּא דְסוּף (which Norberg erroneously translates "the Red Sea"), and immediately behind this are the stations of the seven planets. Man consists of three parts: the body, פַּגְרָא; the animal soul, רוּחָא; and the heavenly soul, the spirit, נִשְׁמְתָא, or $\sigma\tilde{\omega}\mu\alpha$, $\psi\nu\chi\acute{\eta}$, $\nu o\tilde{\nu}\varsigma$. It is $Rucha$, $\psi\nu\chi\acute{\eta}$, who leads him into evil; one virtue only is assigned to her—she plays the part of Juno Lucina at confinements.

Although the Mendæans were originally Christians, they have entirely estranged themselves from the true principles of Christianity. When in the Syriac N. T. they found the Holy Spirit called $Rucha$ $de\text{-}Kodsha$, as for them $Rucha$, as $\psi\nu\chi\acute{\eta}$, was the mother of the devil, they identified them, considered the Messiah as her son, and therefore looked upon him as a sorcerer, and, as Mercury, placed him among the planets. They consider the earth as altogether 480,000 years old, during which it has been alternately under the influence of the various planets for an equal length of time; the human race has been three times destroyed by the sword, fire, and water, only one couple remaining alive after each time. At the time of Noah the world was 466,000 years old; 6000 years after him, when the sun (whom they call also קָדוֹשׁ, אֲדוֹנָי, אֲרִל אִרִל) came to reign over the world, and Jerusalem (called אוּרְשְׁלֵם) was built at its command, her first prophet, Abraham, אַבְרָהִם, appeared; her second was Moses, מִישָׁא, after whom came Shlimun bar-Davith, to whom the dæmons yielded obedience. As the third false prophet, they name רִשׁוֹ מְשִׁיחָא, whom they consider as an impostor, taught by the Rucha de-Kodsha, calling himself God and the son of God, but was unmasked as an impostor by Anush (perhaps so called in view of the בַּר אֲנָשָׁא of the Syriac N. T.), and was put to death by the Jews. Anush himself was baptized by John the Baptist, the only true prophet, and he performed the miracles and resurrections attributed by Christians to Christ. The last of the false prophets was Mohammed, whom they call Achmat, and there will be none after him. After 4000 or 5000 years mankind will again be destroyed: this time by a terrific storm. But the world will be again repeopled by a man and a woman from the upper world, and their descendants shall dwell on the earth for 50,000 years in piety and innocence. Then will the fire, also called leviathan, destroy the earth and the other medium worlds, as well as the nether worlds; their spirits will be annihilated, and the universe become a realm of light.

Priesthood. — There are different degrees in their priesthood. The lower class is called $Sheganda$, שְׁגַנְדָּא, and forms a sort of medium between the clergy, properly so called, and the laity. The members of it are actually but assistants, $\delta\iota\acute{\alpha}\kappa o\nu o\iota$, of the priests, and can be received into it while yet mere boys. They are consecrated to that office by the imposition of hands, and the recital of a short formula at baptism. Many remain always in this subordinate position; if they desire to go higher, which they are not permitted to do before they are fifteen years of age, they must study diligently the religious books and customs of their people, undergo a strict trial for sixty days, and pass seven days and nights awake and in prayer with a priest; if admitted, they then become $Tarmides$, תַּרְמִידָא (probably for תַּלְמִידָא, "scholars"), to which office they are consecrated by seven priests. This is the true priestly order, which qualifies them for every ecclesiastical office. Those who distinguish themselves by their science and conduct can become גַּנְזִבְרָא, which probably is equivalent to גִּזְבָּר, גִּזְבָּר, Ezra i, 8; vii, 21, or "thesaurarius," he who possesses the great treasure in himself. It corresponds to the office of high-priest or bishop, and requires only a short probation and the consecration by another of that rank. His functions are only to consecrate others, and to preside at marriages, which can, however, be legally administered by the tarmides, without his participation. A priest who officiates at the marriage of a woman not a maiden, a widow, or a woman divorced from her husband, loses the right to perform afterwards any religious ceremony except such marriages; he is then called פּוֹרִיסָק, "one cut off." Finally, the highest ecclesiastical dignity, similar to that of patriarch or pope, is that of the רִישׁ עַמָּא, "chief of the people," who is also considered as their civil chief. Their princes—when they had princes—were to be at the same time their high-priests, as they assert was the case with Pharaoh. At present they have none. Women are also allowed by them to become members of the clergy; they must be virgins to enter into the order of shegandi, but when they enter the order of tarmides they must at once marry a priest of that order or of a higher. They can in this manner arrive to the degree of $R\hat{e}sh$ $Amma$, if their husband is invested with that title, for in no case can the woman have a higher title than her husband. The official dress of the priests is pure white, is very simple, and consists of white linen underclothing, and a shirt of the same material tied with a white belt. From both shoulders hangs a white stole, about the width of the hand, extending down to the feet. They wear a white cloth on their head, twisted like a turban, the end of which, about a yard in length, hangs down on the left side in front. On the right forearm they wear, during divine worship only, the תָּגָא, "crown," which consists of a piece of white linen, two finger-lengths in breadth, sewed on three sides, and which, when not in use, is put under the turban. On the little finger of the right hand the tarmides wear a gilt and the superior priests a golden seal-ring, bearing the inscription שׁוּם יַוַר זִיוָא, "the name of the $Javar\text{-}Siva$," and carry an olive-branch in the left hand. They must always be barefooted in exercising their functions.

Houses of Worship.—The churches, which are only intended for the use of the priests and their assistants, the laymen remaining in the entry, are so small that only two persons can stand in them at the same time. They are built from west to east, and are distinguished by gable-roofs. They have no altar and no ornaments, only a few boards in the corners to put things on when needed, but they must be provided with flowing water for baptism.

Religious Worship, Practices, and Observances.—Their year is the solar year of 365 days, divided into twelve months of thirty days each; the remaining five days do not belong to any month. Their months are generally named after the signs of the zodiac; they have also retained for them the Jewish appellation, with a few alterations. They observe the Sabbath, and have besides four ecclesiastical festivals: 1, on New-year's-day, at the beginning of the "Waterman;" 2, on the 18th day of "Taurus;" 3, between the Virgin and the Balance; 4, on the first day of the Capricorn. Their greatest festival is the Pantesha, the five days of baptism: it is the third in the above list. On this occasion all Mendæans are baptized again; the most pious among them are baptized every Sunday. The Lord's Supper is always connected by them with baptism; for it they use paste, prepared in the church by the priest, instead of bread, and water in the place of wine. It is only on the occasion of marriage, which is always preceded by baptism, that the laymen commune with wine, prepared also in the church by the priest. The priests, on the contrary, always commune with wine.

Number.—In the 17th century the Mendæans still counted some 20,000 families; they have since considerably decreased in number. They are located, some on the Euphrates and Tigris, south of Bagdad, or between the two rivers; some in various cities of Kurdistan, where they carry on the trades of jewellers, blacksmiths, shipbuilders, carpenters, or joiners. The statement of Germanus Conti, that there are persons of the same creed in Lebanon, appears to have originated in a mistake between them and the Nosairians. The Mendæans do not outwardly distinguish themselves from the Mohammedans among whom they reside. They should, however, according to their law, dress entirely in white; but, as the Mohammedans claim the exclusive use of that color, the Mendæans wear mostly brown, or brown and white garments. They must avoid dark colors, as belonging to the kingdom of darkness, yet this rule cannot always be observed. Polygamy is not only permitted, but advised, as their "great book" repeatedly recommends them to diligently increase the race. It is a very general practice with them, although, according to the statement of the priests, they do not usually have more than two wives. See Herzog, *Real-Encyklop.* ix, 318 sq.; also Farrar, *Eccles. Dict.* s. v.; *Deutsche Zeitschrift f. christl. Wissenschaft u. christl. Leben*, 1854, No. 23; 1856, No. 42, 43, 46, 49; Burckhardt, *Les Nazorées ou Mandai-Jahja appelés ordinairement Zabiens et Chrétiens de St. Jean Baptiste* (Strasb. 1840); Chwolsohn, *Die Szabier* (Petersb. 1856); Petermann, *Reisen im Orient*, (1861), vol. ii.

Mendelssohn, Bartholdy-Felix, the first musical composer of eminence who, since Bach and Händel bequeathed to the world their sacred harmonies, devoted his best efforts and great talents chiefly to sacred music. Felix was the grandson of Moses Mendelssohn, the philosopher; his father was the eminent Jewish banker, Abraham Mendelssohn - Bartholdy, who embraced the Christian religion and became a member of the Lutheran Church. Felix was born Feb. 3, 1809, at Hamburg. As a boy he displayed a wonderful talent for music, which attracted the attention of the poet Goethe, who warmly interested himself in Felix, and greatly encouraged him to develop that talent with which the Creator had so largely endowed him. Upon the removal of his parents to Berlin in 1812, his instruction in music was intrusted to Zelter and Berger, both masters in the art: the former a profound musical theorist, and the latter a renowned pianist and teacher. It is not to be wondered at that, under the care and guidance of such masters, the progress of Felix in his musical studies more than fulfilled their expectations. At the age of nine we find him giving his first concert in Berlin, delighting the audience by his graceful performance on the piano. He

now commenced to write musical compositions of every form. At the early age of sixteen, he composed his first opera, the music of which is not only charming, but full of dramatic element. This composition shows what Mendelssohn might have accomplished in operatic music had he not left this field for a higher and nobler one —that of sacred music. Another proof of his dramatic power is in his music to Shakespeare's *Midsummer Night's Dream*, which is regarded as one of his best efforts in dramatic music. In 1821 he composed his second opera, and finished one half of a third one, besides writing six symphonies, one quartette for the piano and stringed instruments, a cantata, six fugues, and a number of etudes, sonatas, and songs. At the age of twenty Mendelssohn visited England for the first time, and was there deeply influenced for the whole course of his afterlife. He arrived in London in 1829, and, being known by reputation to the most eminent musicians, was most cordially received. At the first concert with the Philharmonic Society, his overture to *Midsummer Night's Dream* was most enthusiastically received by those who had not even heard his name. In the same year Mendelssohn visited Scotland, and was warmly welcomed by literary and musical societies fully able to appreciate his genius. He made an extended tour through the Highlands, being deeply impressed with the wild and romantic beauty of the old Caledonian music, which some years after gave rise to his celebrated Scotch symphony in A minor. His music to the Isles of Fingal also owes its origin to the impression made upon his mind by the wild and stormy shores of the Hebrides. In the following year he visited Italy, and two years afterwards Paris. Later he revisited London, and from that time to the end of his life was a frequent sojourner there. He began to be even more appreciated in England than in his native country, and it became to him, as it were, the land of his adoption. Benedict, in his life of Mendelssohn, says: "The mean cabals which were always at work against him in Berlin increased his dislike to that city, so much so as to induce him to leave it, as he then thought, forever." At Leipsic he accepted the conductorship of the celebrated Gewandhaus concerts, and remained there until 1844, when, induced by the invitation of the king of Prussia, he returned to Berlin.

His entrance upon his glorious career as a composer of sacred music may be ascribed to the committee of the Birmingham Festival, which called forth the oratorio of St. Paul for its festival of 1837. The impression which this composition made at Birmingham is described by those present as truly grand. In 1840 Mendelssohn composed his *Hymn of Praise*, written expressly for the Birmingham Festival, and performed under his direction. It is a work called a symphony cantata, of marvellous beauty. His third and last oratorio was also written for Birmingham, and, although he commenced it in 1837, it was only finished in time for the festival of 1846, and during these nine years he bestowed upon it his greatest care and attention. The first performance of it took place Aug. 26, 1846, he being the conductor. The enthusiasm was unbounded, and it was universally pronounced his masterpiece, and the greatest oratorio since Händel brought out his *Messiah*.

Although king Frederick William IV bestowed the greatest honors upon Mendelssohn, and offered him every inducement to stay in Berlin, yet he preferred Leipsic, and it was mostly there and in England that he devoted his time to further everything noble and true in art. Mendelssohn was also a diligent scholar in philology, history, and other sciences. His *Letters from Italy and Switzerland* (translated from the German by lady Wallace, London, 1862) bear evidence of his superior attainments, and may be regarded as a fine literary production. In the selection of a text for his oratorios he was very exact, and to the careful student of sacred music it must be apparent that in Mendelssohn's compositions, founded upon a scriptural text, not only love of music as an art, but also a genuine spirit of piety is revealed. No one could give more true and deeply-felt expression than he did in his music to such passages as these: "As the hart pants for cooling streams," "I waited for the Lord," "He, watching over Israel," "It is enough," etc. By the student and lover of sacred music Mendelssohn must ever be regarded as a shining light. If not endowed with the genius of a Bach, Händel, Mozart, or Beethoven, the great talent, exquisite taste, and depth of feeling which he displayed in all his compositions will ever secure him a place among the first of masters. Riehl, in his *Musikalische Karakterköpfe* (i, 106), says, "Many thousands have, by the influence of Mendelssohn's music, been led to the study of the works of Bach and Händel, and enabled to form a more correct idea of their true and lasting value." Again, Riehl says (p. 101), "He made the severe forms of sacred music more elegant and more charming by uniting the formal part of it with a subjective wealth of feeling." In his private life he was a man of most charming disposition, making all who came in contact with him his ardent friends and admirers. Towards his fellow-artists he was perfectly free from envy, always encouraging those in whom he discovered talent. Death plucked him when in his best years, at Leipsic, Nov. 4, 1847. It is impossible to speak here in detail of Mendelssohn's works. They are very numerous, and embrace every branch of his art, but it was in sacred music that his highest powers were displayed; and *St. Paul* and *Elijah* will descend to posterity along with the *Messiah* and *Israel in Egypt*. See Benedict, *Leben u. Werke des F. Mendelssohn-Bartholdy* (1850); Lampadius, *Leben d. Felix Mendelssohn-Bartholdy* (Leips. 1848; in English, N. Y. 1865); Fétis, *Biographie Universelle des Musiciens*; V. Magnien, *Étude biographique sur Mendelssohn-Bartholdy* (1850); Hiller, *Mendelssohn-Bartholdy* (Cologne and Lond. 1874); *Fraser's Magazine*, April, 1848; *British Quarterly Review*, October, 1862.

Mendelssohn, Moses (also called RAMBAN [רמבמ״ן], from the initials of ר׳ משה בן מנחם מנדל, R. Moses ben-Menachem Mendel, and MOSES DESSAU), whom Mirabeau describes as "un homme jeté par la nature au sien d'une horde avilie, né sans espèce de fortune, avec un tempérament faible et même infirme, un caractère timide, une douceur peut-être excessive, enchaîné toute sa vie dans une profession presque méchanique, s'est élevé rang des plus grands écrivains que ce siècle a vu naître en Allemagne" (*Sur Moses Mendelssohn*, London, 1787), was born at Dessau, Germany, Sept. 6, 1729. His father was a copier (סופר) of Biblical writings upon parchment. Moses gave early tokens of an intelligent and scrutinizing mind. Fortunately for his nascent talents, the rabbi of the congregation, David Herschel Fränkel, perceiving the eagerness of the boy for learning, undertook to instruct him in all those branches which then constituted a Jewish education—the Bible in the original Hebrew, with its chief commentaries, and rabbinical literature. At an early age Mendelssohn also became acquainted with Maimonides's (q. v.) famous work, the *More Nebuchim*, or "Guide of the Perplexed," the intense study of which made a new æra in his life, and that in two ways—it laid the foundation of his mental culture, and also of his bodily disease and suffering. (Mendelssohn was hump-backed, and extremely small and feeble in person.) The German language the rabbins of Mendelssohn's early days proscribed as Gentile learning, and hence his studies had been entirely confined to the Hebrew; but as he branched out in his studies he also acquired the German tongue. When hardly fourteen years of age he was obliged to relinquish learning for the choice of a profession. He went to Berlin in search of employment, and there gained his scanty subsistence by following the occupation of copyist and corrector for the press, carefully making use of every leisure moment to learn the ancient languages, and to gain in-

struction in general literature and philosophy. Chance favored him with the acquaintance of a Polish Jew who possessed a profound knowledge of mathematics. The Pole became his instructor in Euclid, which he studied from a copy of the work in Hebrew, this being the only language understood by his teacher. Besides Locke's *Essay on the Human Understanding*, he studied the writings of Wolf, Leibnitz, and Spinoza, which exercised the greatest influence upon his mental development. Thus passed seven of the most laborious years of his life; it was the period of apprenticeship served to science. Gradually this most reserved but most persevering and highly-cultivated youth became known in wider circles. His fortune now began to turn. A rich co-religionist of Berlin, Isaac Bernhard, a silk manufacturer, engaged him as tutor for his children. Henceforth he was in easy if not affluent circumstances. His connection with the house of Bernhard continued throughout life, first as tutor in the family, afterwards as book-keeper in the manufactory, and eventually as manager if not as partner in the concern. In the intervals of business he published, in concert with his friend, Tobias Bock, some essays on natural philosophy in Hebrew, for the use of young men studying the Talmud. This publication, which appeared in the קהלת מוסר, i. e. "The Hebrew Preacher," gave some offence to the rabbins, and he escaped persecution only by his strict observance of the Oral Law, to which he undeviatingly submitted all the rest of his life, although his internal convictions were little in accordance with its practices. About this time (1754) he became acquainted with Lessing (q. v.) and Nicolai (q. v.). With the former he formed an intimate friendship, always regarded by Mendelssohn as among the most fortunate circumstances of his life; for in "Lessing, than whom no man was ever more free from the prejudices of creed and nation, Mendelssohn found a hearty sympathy and an effective fellow-laborer in his projects for bettering the condition of the German Jews, an object which then and at all times lay nearest his heart. Indeed, the known friendship of so eminent a man for one of that tribe, in defiance of all the prejudices of his age, was scarcely less important to the Jews in general than it was to Mendelssohn in particular." For two hours every day regularly they met and discussed together literary and philosophical subjects, a circumstance which led Mendelssohn to write his *Philosophische Gespräche*, the very first effort by which he became distinguished beyond the pale of Judaism. The MS. of these dialogues Mendelssohn left with Lessing for examination; but how great was the former's surprise when one day Lessing returned his dialogues in print, published without the author's knowledge. He next sent forth *Pope, ein Metaphysiker* (together with Lessing [1755]), and several other essays, and finally his *Briefe über die Empfindungen* (1764). In the same year he also wrote *Abhandlungen über die Evidenz der metaphysischen Wissenschaften* as a prize essay for the Berlin Academy, which was crowned by that learned body, who besides unanimously resolved to elect him a member of their number. Frederick the Great, however, generally prejudiced against the Jews, struck the name off the list, and the Jew had to content himself with the consciousness that he enjoyed less than his contemporaries believed him entitled to. Mendelssohn afterwards, at the instigation of Nicolai and Lessing, collected all his philosophical lucubrations, and published them in 1761 under the title of *Philosophische Schriften*, of which in a short time three editions were published (3d ed. 1777, 2 vols. 8vo). At thirty-one Mendelssohn married a lady from Hamburg, by whom he had several children, among them a son, whose birth gave rise to one of his most celebrated works, the *Morgenstunden*, which treats on the existence of God, in refutation of Pantheism and Spinozism—the result of many years' inquiry on that subject. Mendelssohn had formerly defined the universe as a creation out of the divine substance, a view involving the main principle of Spinozism, and directly opposed to the notions of deity and creation prevalent in his day. He now attempted, by concessions and modifications, to get rid of the ethical objections usually brought against kindred theories. The work is a fragment; only the first volume appeared (in 1785), the death of the author arresting its progress. The most popular work, however, was his *Phädon, oder über die Unsterblichkeit der Seele*, a colloquy on the doctrine of immortality. The characters are taken from Plato's dialogue of the same name, and the descriptive parts are mere translations of the original. The Jewish philosopher, however, has made Socrates produce new arguments in place of those attributed to him by his disciple Plato, thinking these substitutions better adapted to modern readers. The following is his principal, and, indeed, his only peculiar argument, the rest of the dialogue being employed in its defence, and in expressions of reliance on the goodness of the Deity. For every change three things are required: first, a state of the changeable thing prior to its change; secondly, the state that follows the change; and, thirdly, a middle state, as change does not take place at once, but by degrees. Between being and not-being there is no middle state. Now the soul being simple, and not, as a compound body, capable of resolution into parts, must, if it perish, be absolutely annihilated; and in its change from death to life, it must pass at once from being to not-being, without, of course, going through any middle state—a change which, according to the three requisitions of change, is impossible. Thus by "reductio ad absurdum" the immortality of the soul was proved. Kant, in his *Kritik der reinen Vernunft* (2d ed.; it is not in the 1st ed.; see the complete edition of Kant's works by M. Rosenkranz [Leipsic]), has shown the futility of Mendelssohn's argument, while he admits his acuteness in perceiving that mere incapability of resolution into parts was of itself not sufficient to preserve the immortality of the soul, as had been supposed by many philosophers of the time. Mendelssohn, by assuming that change must be gradual and not sudden, thought that he had established his point, as the soul, being simple, could not admit of gradual resolution. Kant, however, shows that we may conceive a gradual annihilation even without resolution into parts—or, to use his own expression, a diminution of the "intensive magnitude." Thus a deep red color may grow fainter and fainter till at last all the redness is gone, and this without any diminution of the surface colored. Another fallacy in Mendelssohn's argument is that his definition of change applies only to a transition from one state of being to another, and therefore does not include a transition from being to not-being. For if not-being be considered a state of being, there is no occasion for an argument at all, as the continuance of being is assumed in the definition of change, nor would anything be gained by supposing the soul in such a paradoxical state as nonentity with still a sort of being attached to it. This work not only immortalized its author's name, but conferred upon him for the strength of his reasoning the name of "the Jewish Socrates," and "the Jewish Plato" for the amenity of his diction. In less than two years after its first appearance (1767) it went through three large editions, and was translated into Hebrew, and into almost every modern language; English editions were published in 1789 and 1838. Mendelssohn's fame was at its height both among Christians and Jews, and he was lauded both as a philosopher and literary character. Zealous Christians were wondering that so enlightened and exemplary a man should retain the faith of his fathers, and regarded it as a sacred duty to bring him over to the Church. Foremost among them was John Caspar Lavater (q. v.), who sought to drag him into theological controversy, though with no unkind intentions. In order to bring about this result, he dedicated to Mendelssohn his translation of Bonnet's *Inquiry into*

the *Evidences of Christianity*, with the request that he would refute it in case he should find the argument untenable; and that, if it should seem to him conclusive, he would "do what policy, love of truth, and probity demanded—what Socrates doubtless would have done, had he read the work and found it unanswerable;" thus offering him the alternative either to incur the odium of his own people by formally abjuring the faith of his fathers, or to draw upon himself the wrath of the Christian clergy by a public assault on their religion. This was in the year 1769. The position in which Mendelssohn was thus placed was not only most delicate, but also not without peril. He clung to the ancestral religion not only with the tenacity of early habits, but also with the fulness of conviction which profound study of the subject had given him. How was it possible to reply to the arguments brought forward in favor of Christianity without giving offence to the dominant churches, and becoming liable to the severe penalties enacted by the laws against the assailants of the established creeds? Mendelssohn, however, did reply. He wrote a courteous but decided letter to the pastor of Zurich, in which he not only speaks of his "veneration for the moral character of the founder of Christianity," but also defines very fully his position as a liberal-minded and enlightened Jew. This letter not only satisfied all parties, but also drew from Lavater a public apology and retraction of his peremptory challenge. The agitation caused by this transaction aggravated Mendelssohn's constitutional complaints, threatening his life, and for a long time incapacitating him for intellectual labor. After his recovery he published a Hebrew commentary on Ecclesiastes (Berl. 1769; ibid. 1788), translated into German by Rabe (Anspach, 1771), and into English by Preston (Lond. 1845). The author complains that "nearly all the commentators who have preceded me have almost entirely failed in doing justice to their task of interpretation. . . . I have not found in one of them an interpretation adequate to the correct explanation of the connection of the verses of the book, but, according to their method, nearly every verse is spoken separately and unconnectedly; and this would not be right in a private and insignificant author, much less in a wise king." As to the design of the book, Mendelssohn thinks "that Solomon wrote it to propound the doctrine of the immortality of the soul, and the necessity of leading a cheerful and contented life, and interspersed these cardinal points with lessons of minor importance, such as worship, politics, domestic economy, etc." Soon after this appeared a German translation of the Pentateuch, made by himself, with a grammatical and exegetical commentary in Hebrew, contributed by several Jewish literati, viz. Sal. Dubno (q. v.), Aaron Jaroslaw, N. H. Wessely (q. v.), and H. Homberg. This important work, which is entitled סֵפֶר נְתִיבוֹת הַשָּׁלוֹם, i. e. *The Book of the Paths of Peace* (Berlin, 1780–83), is preceded by an elaborate and most valuable introduction, written in Hebrew, called אוֹר לִנְתִיבָה, *A Light to the Path*, in which Mendelssohn discusses various topics connected with Biblical exegesis and literature. The introduction, which was published separately before the completion of the commentary (Dec. 1782), now accompanies the translation and commentary, and is given in German in his *Collected Works* (Leips. 1845), vii, 18 sq.; and in English in the *Hebrew Review*, edited by Breslau (Lond. 1860). The work soon found its way into the principal synagogues and schools in Germany, and, thus encouraged, he produced afterwards a version of the Psalms and the Song of Solomon, which are considered classical. "It was in this especially," says Da Costa, "that the philosopher kept up the striking resemblance to Maimonides, his celebrated predecessor and model. Both, under the outward forms of Rabbinical Judaism, desired to give an entirely new direction to the religion of the Jews—to reform it, to develop it." Nothing, indeed, could have more powerfully affected the Orientalism of his countrymen than these efforts of Mendelssohn for Biblical criticism from a modern Platonic stand-point. The new medium of vision brought new insight; critical inquiry took the place of fanaticism; the divergences of Shemitic and European thought proved not so irreconcilable after all. Cabalism and other kindred superstitions quietly dropped out of sight; the old dialectical barbarism was extirpated; the Jews who read his Scriptures in the translation attained purity of idiom, and with it the power of appreciating the writings of the great minds of Germany, to whom they had remained strangers. Ere long the best minds of the race became thoroughly associated with the intellectual movement of Germany, content to abandon mystical ambitions and theocratic pretensions, and to find their Canaan in Europe. Mendelssohn's next work declared more clearly (though always with a degree of vagueness) his own ideas on religion than any other work hitherto published. It was written in answer to the treatise of his friend the councillor Dohm (*Ueber die bürgerliche Verbesserung der Juden*). The statesman in his work "had started from the principle that every amendment must proceed from liberty and equality of rights in society bestowed upon the Jew; from an entire reform in the systems of instruction and education; from free admission to the practice of all arts and sciences, and even a participation in some posts and offices of state; the authority of the synagogue over its members to be maintained, in cases of religious difference, by the power of casting them out of its bosom for a time or entirely." On this last point Mendelssohn took exception. He would not allow the synagogue or any other religious society to impose any restriction whatever on the rights of thinking and teaching. In the preface to his German translation of Manasseh ben-Israel's (q. v.) *Salvation of Israel*, he plainly declared his conviction "that every society had certainly the right to exclude its members when they ceased to conform to the principle of the society; but that this rule could not in any way apply to a religious society, whether church or synagogue, because true religion exerts no authority over ideas and opinions, but, being all heart and spirit, only desires to use the power of conviction; and Jews especially should take from Christians, among whom they live, an example of charity, and not of hatred or intolerance, and begin by loving and bearing with each other, that they might themselves be loved and tolerated by others." The influence produced by the writings of Mendelssohn was to destroy all respect for the Talmud and the rabbinical writers among the Jews, who approved his opinions. This is the more remarkable, inasmuch as Mendelssohn professed all the while to be himself an admirer of those works; and this obvious inconsistency called forth a publication entitled *Ein Brief an Mendelssohn*, in which this contradiction was clearly pointed out, and the assertion made that he was in reality a Christian, without having the courage to avow his true sentiments. To this attack he replied by his *Jerusalem, oder über religiöse Macht und Judenthum* (Berlin, 1783), in which he contended that "the state, which has the right to compel actions, cannot justly attempt to constrain its citizens to unanimity in thought and sentiment; it should, however, seek by wise provisions to produce those sentiments from which good actions spring. Religious differences should not prejudice civil equality; the true ideal is not unity, but freedom of belief." He says, "All religion is solely a matter of the heart, and should not be under any control, either of the State, Church, or Synagogue;" while at the same time he insists that "the law of Moses was not a law of faith, but merely of statutes and prohibitions." "Whatever may have caused the inward struggles of the philosopher of Berlin," says Da Costa, "it is certain that, without wishing or suspecting it, Mendelssohn—as, six centuries earlier, Maimonides—stirred up among his co-religionists a feeling of void." Soon, however, Mendelssohn

was doomed to experience another trial of his sensibility in an attack on his deceased friend Lessing by Jacobi (q. v.), who published *Briefe an Mendelssohn über die Lehre des Spinoza*, in which he charged Lessing with being an "implicit Spinozist" — a charge then much severer than at present, when many German philosophers are avowed admirers of Spinoza. Mendelssohn endeavored to refute the charge in a work entitled *Moses Mendelssohn an die Freunde Lessing's* (1786), in which he stated that "if Lessing was able absolutely and without all further limitation to declare for the system of any man, he was at that time no more in harmony with himself, or he was in a strange humor to make a paradoxical assertion which, in a serious hour, he himself rejected." The answer was considered triumphant, and drew from Kant the remark, "It is Mendelssohn's fault that Jacobi thinks himself a philosopher." In a hurried preparation of this latter work Mendelssohn overtasked his physical powers, and the exhaustion thus produced led to his premature death, which took place Jan. 4, 1786. Ramler wrote this epitaph on Mendelssohn: "True to the religion of his forefathers, wise as Socrates, teaching immortality, and becoming immortal like Socrates." Besides many Hebrew and German essays which we have not room to mention, Mendelssohn contributed freely to the *Bibliothek der schönen Wissenschaften*, edited by Lessing (q. v.). His complete works were collected and edited by his grandson, G. B. Mendelssohn (Leips. 1843–5, 7 vols.). The influence which he exercised over the Jewish nation is incalculable. He roused the Jews of Germany, if not of the world, from the mental apathy with which in his day they regarded all that had not a distinct reference to religion. On the other hand, he acted in the most beneficial manner on his Christian contemporaries by exterminating the brutal prejudices which they entertained against Jews, and through his most distinguished Christian friends brought about the abrogation of the disgraceful laws with respect to them. See JEWS. He effected a reformation in Judaism, and founded that new school of Hebrew literature and Biblical exegesis which has now produced so many and such distinguished Jewish literati not only in Germany, but throughout Europe. No wonder that the Jews express their gratitude to him and reverence for him in the saying, "From Moses (the law-giver) to Moses (Maimonides) and Moses (Mendelssohn), no one hath arisen like Moses" (ממשה למשה ועד משה לא הם כמשה). See Kayserling, *M. Mendelssohn, seine Leben u. s. Werke* (Leips. 1862); Samuels, *Memoirs of Moses Mendelssohn*, etc. (2d ed. Lond. 1827); Hedge, *Prose Writers of Germany*, p. 99 sq.; Adler, *Versöhnung von Gott, Religion, und Menschenthum durch M. Mendelssohn* (Berlin, 1871); Axenfeld, *Moses Mendelssohn im Verhältniss zum Christenthum* (Erlangen, 1865); Grätz, *Gesch. d. Juden*, xi, 1 sq.; Ueberweg, *History of Philosophy*, ii, 118, 523, 528 (Engl. transl. by Morris, New York, 1874); Milman, *Hist. of the Jews*, iii, 408 sq.; McCaul, *Sketches of Judaism and the Jews*, p. 43 sq.; Da Costa, *Israel and the Gentiles*, p. 544 sq.; Schmucker, *Hist. of the Modern Jews* (Philadelphia, 1867), p. 239 sq.; Kalkar, *Israel u. d. Kirche* (Hamburg, 1869), p. 117 sq.; *Jewish Intelligence* (Lond. 1866), p. 31 sq.; Etheridge, *Introduction to Hebrew Literature*, p. 475 sq.; *Miscellany of Hebrew Literature* (Lond 1872), p. 22 sq.; Dessauer, *Gesch. d. Israeliten* (Breslau, 1870), p. 497 sq.; Stern, *Gesch. d. Judenthums* (ibid. 1870), p. 54 sq.; Cassel, *Zeitfaden für Jüd. Gesch. u. Literatur* (Berlin, 1872), p. 108 sq.; Fürst, *Bibl. Jud.* ii, 359–367; De Rossi, *Dizionario storico degli autori Ebrei* (German transl. by Hamberger), p. 224 sq.; id., *Bibliotheca Judaica antichristiana*, p. 69; Jost, *Gesch. d. Israeliten*, ix, 66; id., *Gesch. d. Juden. u. s. Sekten*, iii, 293 sq.; Zedner, *Auswahl historischer Stücke* (Berl. 1840), p. 204 sq.; Farrar, *Crit. History of Free Thought*; Hurst's Hagenbach, *Church Hist. 18th and 19th Century*; *Christian Remembrancer*, Oct. 1866, p. 267. (B. P.)

Mendez, Alphonso, a noted missionary of the Roman Catholic Church, flourished in Abyssinia in the early part of the 17th century. He was a Portuguese by birth, but we know little of his personal history disconnected from his labors in the East. He belonged to the Society of Jesus, and was created patriarch of the Abyssinians in 1626, by the emperor Suscenius, or Socinios, who, quite contrary to general practices, not only himself paid allegiance to the Roman pontiff, but also obliged his subjects to abandon the religious rites and tenets of their ancestors, and to embrace the doctrine and worship of the Romish Church. Mendez, as patriarch, by his intemperate zeal, imprudence, and arrogance, ruined the cause in which he had embarked, and occasioned the total subversion of the Roman pontiff's authority and jurisdiction, which seemed to have been established upon solid foundations. "He began his ministry," says Mosheim (*Eccles. Hist.*, Harper's edit., ii, 193), "with the most inconsiderate acts of violence and despotism. Following the spirit of the Spanish Inquisition, he employed formidable threatenings and cruel tortures to convert the Abyssinians; the greatest part of whom, together with their priests and ministers, held the religion of their ancestors in the highest veneration, and were willing to part with their lives and fortunes rather than forsake it. He also ordered those to be rebaptized who, in compliance with the orders of the emperor, had embraced the faith of Rome, as if their former religion had been nothing more than a system of paganism. Nor did the insolent patriarch rest satisfied with these arbitrary and despotic proceedings in the Church; he excited tumults and factions in the state, and, with an unparalleled spirit of rebellion and arrogance, encroached upon the prerogatives of the throne, and attempted to give law to the emperor himself. Hence arose civil commotions, conspiracies, and seditions, which excited in a little time the indignation of the emperor, and the hatred of the people against the Jesuits, and produced at length, in 1631, a public declaration from the throne, by which the Abyssinian monarch annulled the orders he had formerly given in favor of popery, and left his subjects at liberty either to persevere in the doctrine of their ancestors or to embrace the faith of Rome. This rational declaration was mild and indulgent toward the Jesuits, considering the treatment which their insolence and presumption had so justly deserved; but in the following reign much severer measures were employed against them. Basilides, or Facilidas, the son of Segued, who succeeded his father in 1632, thought it expedient to free his dominions from these troublesome and despotic guests, and accordingly, in 1634, he banished from his territories the patriarch Mendez, with all the Jesuits and Europeans who belonged to his retinue, and treated the Roman Catholic missionaries with excessive severity. From this period the very name of Rome, its religion, and its pontiff, were objects of the highest aversion among the Abyssinians." Le Grand, himself a Roman Catholic, makes the following remark upon the conduct of the patriarch Mendez: "It is to be wished that the patriarch had never intermeddled in such a variety of affairs" (by which mitigated expression the author means his ambitious attempts to govern in the cabinet as well as in the Church), "or carried his authority to such a height as to behave in Ethiopia as if he had been in a country where the Inquisition was established; for by this conduct he set all the people against him, and excited in them such an aversion to the Roman Catholics in general, and to the Jesuits in particular, as nothing has hitherto been able to diminish, and which subsists in full force to this day" (in the fourth dissertation subjoined to vol. ii of Lobo's *Voyage d'Abyssinie*, which the reader will do well to consult, especially p. 116, 130, 144). See also Ludolfi *Histor. Æthiopica*, lib. iii, cap. xii; Geddes, *Ch. Hist. of Ethiopia*, p. 233; La Croze, *Hist. du Christianisme d'Éthiopie*, p. 79; Lockman, *Travels of the Jesuits*, i, 308 sq. (J. H. W.)

Mendez, Gonzalez Juan, a Roman Catholic prelate of note, flourished in the latter half of the 16th century. He was an Augustinian friar of the province of Castile, when he was chosen by the king of Spain to become ambassador to the emperor of China in 1584. In 1593 he was made bishop of Lipari, in Italy; in 1607, bishop of Chiapi, in New Spain; and in 1608, bishop of Propajan, in the West Indies. He died in 1617. He wrote *A History of China* in Spanish, which has been translated into several languages.

Mendez, Gonzalez Pedro, a noted Roman Catholic prelate in the Church of Spain, called the "grand cardinal," was born at Guadalajara in 1428, of an ancient and noble family. He made rapid progress in his studies, especially in the languages, in civil and canon law, and in belles-lettres. His uncle, Gautier Alvarez, archbishop of Toledo, gave him an archdeaconry in his church, and sent him to the court of John II, king of Castile. His merit and quality soon made him friends, and he acquired the bishopric of Calahorra. Henry IV, who succeeded John, trusted him with the most important affairs of state, and with the bishopric of Siguenca, and finally procured a cardinal's hat for him, from Sixtus IV, in 1473. When Henry died, in the year following, he named cardinal Mendez for his executor, and dignified him at the same time with the title of the Cardinal of Spain. He did great service afterwards to Ferdinand and Isabella, in the war against the king of Portugal, and in the conquest of the kingdom of Granada from the Moors. He was then made archbishop of Seville and Toledo successively; and, after governing some years in his several provinces with great wisdom and moderation, he died Jan. 11, 1495. He founded the magnificent college of Santa Cruz at Valladolid, and a hospital at Toledo. See Salazar de Mendoza, *Chronica del gran Cardinal de España* (1625).

Mendicants, Order of, also known as *Begging Friars*, is the name of several religious organizations within the boundaries of the Roman Catholic Church, intended to depend for support on the voluntary contributions of the laity. This sort of society began in the 13th century, and the members of it, by the tenor of their institution, were to remain entirely destitute of all fixed revenues and possessions. Innocent III was the first of the popes who perceived the necessity of instituting such an order; and though his far-seeing eye took in the possible dangers of fierce and ascetic enthusiasm, he nevertheless felt constrained to give those monastic societies making a profession of poverty the most distinguishing marks of his protection and favor. The peculiar state and circumstances of the time seem to have rendered such an establishment very essential for the preservation of the Church. The monastic orders then existing wallowed in opulence, and were by the corrupting influence of their ample possessions lulled into a luxurious indolence. They lost sight of all their religious obligations, trampled upon the authority of their superiors, suffered heresy to triumph unrestrained, and the sectaries to form various assemblies; in short, they were incapable of promoting the true interests of the Church, and abandoned themselves, without either shame or remorse, to all sorts of crimes. On the other hand, the "heretics" of the Church, the sects which had left its communion, followed certain austere rules of life and conduct, which formed a strong contrast between them and the religious orders, and contributed to render the licentiousness of the latter still more offensive and shocking to the people. These sects maintained that voluntary poverty was the leading and essential quality in a servant of Christ; obliged their doctors to imitate the simplicity of the apostles; reproached the Church with its overgrown opulence, and the vices and corruptions of the clergy, that flowed thence as from their natural source; and, by their commendation of poverty and contempt of riches, acquired a high degree of respect, and gained a prodigious ascendency over the minds of the multitude. In consequence, the great desire of the Church was the formation of a society composed of a set of men who—by the austerity of their manners, their contempt of riches, and the external gravity and sanctity of their conduct and maxims—might resemble those doctors that had gained such reputation for the heretical sects, and who might rise so far above the allurements of worldly profit and pleasure as not to be seduced by the promises or threats of kings and princes from the performance of the duties which they owed to the Church, or from persevering in their subordination to the Roman pontiffs.

The favors which the Mendicants received at the hands of Innocent III were extended to them likewise by his successors in the pontifical chair, as experience had demonstrated their public and extensive usefulness. But when it became generally known that they had such a peculiar place in the esteem and protection of the rulers of the Church, their number grew to such an enormous and unwieldy multitude, and swarmed so prodigiously in all the European provinces, that they became a burden, not only to the people, but to the Church itself. The great inconvenience that arose from the excessive multiplication of the Mendicant orders was first attempted to be remedied by Gregory X in a general council which he assembled at Lyons in 1272; for here all the religious orders that had sprung up after the council held at Rome in 1215, under the pontificate of Innocent III, were suppressed; and the extravagant multitude of Mendicants, as Gregory called them, were reduced to a smaller number, and confined to four societies or denominations, viz. the *Dominicans*, the *Franciscans*, the *Carmelites*, and the *Augustines*, or Hermits of St. Augustine (see each). As the pontiffs allowed these four Mendicant orders the liberty of travelling wherever they thought proper, of conversing with persons of every rank, of instructing the youth and multitude wherever they went, and as these monks exhibited in their outward appearance and manner of life more striking marks of gravity and holiness than were observable in the other monastic societies, they arose all at once to the very summit of fame, and were regarded with the utmost esteem and veneration through all the countries of Europe. The enthusiastic attachment to these sanctimonious beggars went so far that, as we learn from the most authentic records, several cities were divided or cantoned out into four parts, with a view to these four orders: the first part being assigned to the Dominicans, the second to the Franciscans, the third to the Carmelites, and the fourth to the Augustines. The people were unwilling to receive the sacraments from any other hands than those of the Mendicants, to whose churches they crowded to perform their devotions while living, and were extremely desirous to deposit there their remains after death. Nor did the influence and credit of the Mendicants end here, for we find in the history of this and the succeeding ages that they were employed not only in spiritual matters, but also in temporal and political affairs of the greatest consequence—in composing the differences of princes, concluding treaties of peace, concerting alliances, presiding in cabinet councils, governing courts, levying taxes, and other occupations, not only remote from, but absolutely inconsistent with the monastic character and profession. However, the power of the Dominicans and Franciscans greatly surpassed that of the other two orders, insomuch that these two orders were, before the Reformation, what the Jesuits have been since that period—the very soul of the hierarchy, the engines of the state, the secret spring of all the motions of the one and the other, and the authors and directors of every great and important event, both in the religious and political world.

By very quick progression, the pride and confidence of the Mendicants arrived at such a pitch that they had the presumption to declare themslves publicly possessed of a divine impulse and commission to illustrate and maintain the religion of Jesus. They treated with the utmost insolence and contempt the priesthood; they affirmed without a blush that the true method of salvation was revealed to them alone; proclaimed with ostentation the superior efficacy and virtue of their indulgences; and vaunted beyond measure their interest at the court of heaven, and their familiar connections with the Supreme Being, the Virgin Mary, and the saints in glory. By these impious wiles they so deluded and captivated the ignorant and blinded the multitude that they would not intrust any others but the Mendicants with the care of their souls. They retained their credit and influence to such a degree nearly to the close of the 14th century that great numbers of both sexes—some in health, others in a state of infirmity, others at the point of death—earnestly desired to be admitted into the Mendicant order, which they looked upon as a sure and infallible method of rendering Heaven propitious. Many made it an essential part of their last wills that their bodies, after death, should be wrapped in old, ragged Dominican or Franciscan habits, and interred among the Mendicants; for such was the barbarous superstition and wretched ignorance of this age, that people universally believed they should readily obtain mercy from Christ at the day of judgment if they appeared before his tribunal associated with the Mendicant friars. About this time, however, the Mendicants fell under a universal odium; but, being resolutely protected against all opposition, whether open or secret, by the popes, who regarded them as their best friends and most effectual supports, they suffered little or nothing from their numerous adversaries.

In the 15th century, besides their arrogance, which was excessive, a quarrelsome and litigious spirit prevailed among the Mendicants, and drew upon them justly the displeasure and indignation of many. By affording refuge at the time to the Beguins (q. v.) in their order, they became offensive to the bishops, and were involved in difficulties and perplexities of various kinds. They lost their credit in the 16th century by their rustic impudence, their ridiculous superstitions, their ignorance, cruelty, and brutish manners. They displayed the most barbarous aversion to the arts and sciences, and expressed a like abhorrence of certain eminent and learned men, who had endeavored to open the paths of science to the pursuits of the studious youth, and had recommended the culture of the mind, and attacked the barbarism of the age in their writings and discourses. The general character of the society, together with other circumstances, concurred to render a reformation desirable, and had the effect of bringing it about. Among the number of Mendicants are also ranked the Capuchins, Recollets, Minims, and others, who are branches or derivations from the former. Buchanan says that the Mendicants of Scotland, under an appearance of beggary, lived a very luxurious life; whence one wittily called them, not *Mendicant*, but *Manducant* friars. See Jean le Rond d'Alembert, *Hist. des Moines mendiants* (Paris, 1768, 12mo; German by J. Scheubner, Nuremb. 1769); J. Gurlitt, *Gesch. d. Bettelmönchsorden im 13 Jahrh.* (*Theol. Studien u. Kritiken*, i, 109 sq.); Gieseler, *Eccles. Hist.* ii, 287 sq.; iii, 46 et al.; Mosheim, *Eccles. Hist.* vol. ii (see Index); Neander, *Ch. Hist.* vol. v (see Index); Milman, *Hist. of Latin Christianity*, vii, 321 et al.; Hardwick, *Ch. Hist.* (Middle Ages) p. 252 sq., 320 sq. et al.; Mrs. Jameson, *Legends of the Monastic Orders*, p. 227 sq.; Lea, *Sacerdotal Celibacy*, p. 377; *Chr. Review*, vol. xx, Jan. (J.H.W.)

Mendoza. See MENDEZ.

Mends, HERBERT, an English Protestant divine, born at Brinkworth, in Wiltshire, about the middle of the 18th century, was the son of Christopher Mends, also a clergyman. He early decided to devote himself to the ministry, and was accordingly placed at a grammar-school at Plymouth, where he obtained the rudiments of a classical education; and was after that instructed by the Rev. Samuel Buncombe, a minister of the Independent Church at Ottery St. Mary, Devon, where he continued three years. In 1777, having completed his academical studies, he removed to Sherborne, in Dorset, and was ordained pastor of the Church. In 1782, his father's infirmities increasing, he was invited to assist him at Plymouth; here he was very successful, his Church augmenting greatly, not only in the number of hearers, but in the membership. He was steadfast and consistent in his attachment to evangelical truth in the midst of various and conflicting errors, which at that period pervaded the West of England, and which led him to express his sentiments with unusual energy in his confession of faith delivered at his ordination. If in his later years he insisted more earnestly on the obligations of true Christians to maintain good works, it did not arise from any diminished sense of the value of other religious duties; but local circumstances induced him to inveigh against certain errors which seemed to him dangerous to practical religion. Another great cause of his success was the animation and warmth of his address, which not only attracted a large congregation, but kept them still united at a period when a minister's waning energies frequently impair his usefulness. In 1785 Mr. Mends became the first and most active promoter of the Association of Independent Ministers of Churches in the West of England, by which society valuable aid was contributed to the extension and success of the Gospel. He died about the opening of this century. Mends did not write much for publication. In 1785 he published an *Elegy on the Death of William Shephard, Esq.*; in 1789, *A Sermon on the Injustice and Cruelty of the Slave-trade*; in 1790, *A Sermon on the Education of the Children of the Poor*; in 1797, *A Defence of Infant Baptism*; and, in 1801, *A Sermon preached in London before the Missionary Society.*

Me′ne, a word Anglicized in the Auth. Vers. of the Chaldee sentence MENE, MENE, TEKEL, UPHARSIN (מְנֵא מְנֵא תְּקֵל וּפַרְסִין, mene′, mene′, tekel′, u-pharsin′, *numbered, numbered, weighed, and dividing*, as each term is immediately interpreted, the last being given in its sing. and pass. form פְּרֵס, peres′, *divided*; Sept. [i. e. Theodotion] in both passages μανή, θεκέλ, φάρες; Vulg. *mane, thecel, phares*), an inscription supernaturally written "upon the plaster of the wall" in Belshazzar's palace at Babylon (Dan. v, 5–25); which "the astrologers, the Chaldæans, and the soothsayers" could neither read nor interpret, but which Daniel first read and then interpreted. Yet the words, as they are found in Daniel, are pure Chaldee, and, if they appeared in the Chaldee character, could have been read, at least, by any person present on the occasion who understood the alphabet of his own language. To account for their inability to decipher this inscription, it has been supposed that it consisted of those Chaldee words written in another character. Dr. Hales thinks that it may have been written in the primitive Hebrew character, from which the Samaritan was formed, and that, in order to show on this occasion that the writer of the inscription was the offended God of Israel, whose authority was at that moment peculiarly despised (ver. 2, 3, 4), he adopted his own sacred character, in which he had originally written the decalogue, in which Moses could transcribe it into the law, and whose autograph copy was found in Josiah's days, and was most probably brought to Babylon in the care of Daniel, who could therefore understand the character without inspiration, but which would be unknown to "the wise men of Babylon" (*New Analysis of Chronology* [Lond. 1811], i, 505). This theory has the recommendation that it involves as little as possible of miraculous agency. Josephus makes Daniel discourse to Belshazzar as if the inscription had been in Greek. "He (Daniel) explained the writing thus: MANH. 'This,' said he, '*in the Greek language*, may mean *a number*; thus God hath numbered so long a time for thy life and for thy government, and that there remains a short time for thee.' ΘEKEΛ. This signifies *weight*; hence he says, 'God having weighed in a

balance the time of thy kingdom, finds it already going down.' ΦAPEΣ. This also, according to *the Greek language*, denotes *a fragment*; hence 'he will break in pieces thy kingdom, and divide it among the Medes and Persians'" (*Ant.* x, 11, 3). It has been supposed by some that "the wise men" were not so much at fault to read the inscription as to explain its meaning, which, it is said, they might sufficiently understand to see its boding import to the monarch, and be unwilling to consider further—like the disciples in regard to the predictions of our Lord's death (Luke ix, 45), where it is said, "This saying was hid from them, they perceived it not; and they feared to ask him of that saying." Certainly it is said throughout our narrative that "the wise men could not read the writing, nor make known the interpretation of it," phrases which would seem to mean one and the same thing; since, if they mean different things, the order of ideas would be that they could not interpret nor even read it, and Wintle accordingly translates, "could not read so as to interpret it" (*Improved Version of Daniel*, Lond. 1807). At all events, the meaning of the inscription by itself would be extremely enigmatical and obscure. To determine the application, and to give the full sense, of an isolated device which amounted to no more than "he or it is numbered, he or it is numbered, he or it is weighed, they are divided" (and there is even a riddle or paranomasia on the last word פְרֵס; comp. Susannah, ver. 54, 55, and 58, 59, Greek, and Jer. i, 11, 12, Hebrew; which may either mean "they divide," or "the Persians," with little difference of pronunciation in the sing. [פְּרֵס and פָּרַס] and none in the plur. [פַּרְסִין]), must surely have required a supernatural endowment on the part of Daniel—a conclusion which is confirmed by the exact coincidence of the event with the prediction, which he propounded with so much fortitude (ver. 30, 31).

Menedēmus, a Greek philosopher and teacher, flourished in the 3d century B.C.

Life.—He was born in Eretria of a noble family, the Theopropidæ. Being poor, he labored as a tent-maker and builder for a livelihood. According to Diogenes Laertius, he was sent on some military service to Megara, where he profited by the occasion to hear Plato. He then relinquished the army, and devoted himself to philosophy. But it is not probable that he was old enough to have heard Plato before the death of the latter. If the length of his life as Diogenes gives it is correct, it would not have been possible; for at the period of Plato's death he would have been only four years of age. According to the story in Athenæus (iv, p. 168), he and his friend Asclepiades labored for a maintenance as millers, passing the night in toil in order to gain time for philosophy during the day. They subsequently became pupils of Stilpo at Megara, whence they proceeded to Elis, to profit by the instructions of some disciples of Phædo. Menedemus, on his return to Eretria, established a school of philosophy, which was called the Eretrian. He did not devote himself entirely to philosophy, but was an active participant in the politics of his native city, becoming the most influential man in the state, although in his earlier days he was regarded with dislike. He was sent on various missions to Ptolemæus (probably Ptolemæus Ceraunus), to Lysimachus, and to Demetrius, and obtained for his native city a repeal of a portion of the tax paid to Demetrius. During some portion of his life he visited Cyprus, and greatly enraged the tyrant Nicocreon by his freely-expressed opinions. The story of his being in Egypt, and sharing in the making of the Septuagint version, which is found in Aristeas, is doubtless unworthy of credence. He enjoyed the favor of Antigonus Gonatus, and persuaded the Eretrians to present to him a public congratulation after his victory over the Gauls. This induced the suspicion of an intention on his part of betraying Eretria into the power of Antigonus. According to one account, these surmises led him to depart secretly from

Eretria, and take refuge in the sanctuary of Amphiaraus at Oropus. Some golden vessels, the property of the temple, being lost while he was there, the Bœotians compelled him to leave, when he fled to the court of Antigonus, where he soon died of grief, probably in the year B.C. 277, at the age of seventy-four. Another account says that he went to Antigonus to solicit his interference in behalf of the freedom of his native city.

As a Philosopher and Teacher.—As a teacher, Menedemus, in his intercourse with his disciples, was characterized by the absence of formality and restraint, although noted for the severity with which he rebuked all dissoluteness and intemperance, so that the fear of his censure seems to have acted as a check. He lived with his friend Asclepiades, between whom and himself there existed a close friendship. In the latter part of his life he seems to have lived in affluence. Of the philosophy of Menedemus little is known, excepting that it closely resembled that of the Megarian school, and that of Phædo of Elis. Indeed, he may be said to have continued Philo's philosophy. Its leading feature was the dogma of the oneness of the Good, which he carefully distinguished from the Useful. All distinctions between virtues he regarded as merely nominal. The Good and the True he looked upon as identical. In dialectics he rejected all merely negative propositions, maintaining that truth could be predicated only of those which were affirmative, and of these he admitted such alone as were identical propositions. He was a vehement and keen disputant, but none of his philosophical controversies or doctrines were committed to writing. Epicrates, in a passage quoted by Athenæus (ii, p. 59), classes Menedemus with Plato and Speusippus; but it appears from Diogenes Laertius that his opinion of Plato and Xenocrates was not very high. Stilpo he greatly admired. See Diogenes Laertius, ii, 125-144; Plutarch, *De Adul. et Amic. Disc.* p. 55; Strabo, lx, p. 393; Ritter, *Geschichte der Philosophie*, bk. vii, c. 5.

Menela'üs (Μενέλαος, a common Greek name), a usurping high-priest who obtained the office from Antiochus Epiphanes (B.C. cir. 172) by a large bribe (2 Macc. iv, 23-25), and drove out Jason, who had obtained it not long before by similar means. When he neglected to pay the sum which he had promised, he was summoned to the king's presence, and by plundering the Temple gained the means of silencing the accusations which were brought against him. By a similar sacrilege he secured himself against the consequences of an insurrection which his tyranny had excited, and also procured the death of Onias (ver. 27-34). He was afterwards hard pressed by Jason, who, taking occasion from his unpopularity, attempted unsuccessfully to recover the high-priesthood (2 Macc. v, 5-10). For a time he then disappears from the history (yet comp. ver. 23), but at last he met with a violent death at the hands of Antiochus Eupator (B.C. cir. 163), which seemed in a peculiar manner a providential punishment of his sacrilege (xiii, 3, 4).

According to Josephus (*Ant.* xii, 5, 1) he was a younger brother of Jason and Onias, and, like Jason, changed his proper name, *Onias*, for a Greek name. In 2 Macc., on the other hand, he is called a brother of Simon the Benjamite (2 Macc. iv, 23), whose treason led to the first attempt to plunder the Temple. If this account be correct, the profanation of the sacred office was the more marked by the fact that it was transferred from the family of Aaron.

Menès was the name of the first king of the first Egyptian dynasty. He marks a great chronological epoch, being placed by different chronologers as early as B.C. 3643, 3892, or even 5702. Stricter Egyptologists make his accession B.C. 2717. This name, which signifies *the conductor*, has been found on inscriptions, but no contemporary monuments of him are known. Menes is the most usual form of his name, but it is also written

Menas, Menis, Meinis, Men, Min, and *Mein*. It is singularly in accordance with the Indian *Menu*, the Greek *Minos*, the Teutonic *Mannus*, and similar appellations of a primeval king; although the oldest Egyptian language seems to have had nothing akin with the Aryan family, to which the others belong. Herodotus says that he built Memphis on the original bed of the Nile, which he turned from its former course, and erected therein a beautiful temple to Hephæstus or Pthah II (comp. Diod. i, 50, ed. Wess. ad loc.). Diodorus informs us that he introduced into Egypt the worship of the gods, the practice of sacrifices, and many luxuries. For this last innovation he was subsequently held in great dishonor, as Plutarch mentions a pillar at Thebes, in Egypt, on which was inscribed an imprecation against Menes as an introducer of luxury. There is a legend preserved by Diodorus which narrates—in defiance of chronology, unless *Mendes* is to be substituted for *Menas*—his being saved from death in Lake Mœris by a crocodile, in gratitude for which he inaugurated the worship of that animal, and built a city in the neighborhood of the lake called the City of Crocodiles, and a pyramid to serve as his own tomb. During his reign there was a revolt of the Libyans. That he made foreign conquests we learn from an extract from Manetho, preserved by Eusebius. By Marsham and others he is considered as identical with the *Mizraim* of Scripture. According to some accounts he was killed by a hippopotamus. See Lepsius, *Königsbuch*, Quellentaf, p. 5; Böckh, *Manetho*, p. 386; Poole, *Hor. Ægypt.* p. 219; Herodotus, ii, 4, 99; Diodorus, i, 43, 45, 89 (ed. Wess. ad loc.); Plutarch, *De Is. et Osir.* p. 8; Perizon, *Orig. Ægypt.* c. 5; Shuckford's *Connection*, bk. iv; Bunsen, *Ægyptens Stelle in der Weltgeschichte*, ii, 38-45. See EGYPT; MEMPHIS.

Meneses, ALEIXIO DE, a Portuguese prelate and statesman, was born Jan. 25, 1559. His father had directed the education of king Sebastian. Brought up in the palace, he entered, contrary to his parent's wishes, the convent of the Augustines at Lisbon, Feb. 24, 1574, and finished his studies at Coimbra. He was appointed archbishop of Goa by Philip II, and took possession of his see in September, 1595. He convened a provincial synod, in which useful reforms were established; he organized many missions, and evangelized, among others, the savage inhabitants of the island of Socotra. He devoted himself also to the Christians of Abyssinia, and, above all, to those schismatic Nestorians known under the name of "Christians of St. Thomas," who have taken refuge for centuries in the mountains of Malabar. That in which the bishop of Cochin, the Jesuits, the Dominicans, and even the disciples of St. Francis were unsuccessful, he was enabled to accomplish, and after many centuries of division the Roman Church received into its bosom the greater part of this branch of the Christian family. Pope Clement testified to Meneses his satisfaction by a brief April 1, 1599. Meneses was subsequently appointed to the government of the Indies, and performed the duties of viceroy from May 3, 1606, to May 28, 1609. He showed himself stern and severe towards some of the Mohammedan princes, but tranquillity at least was preserved in the Indies during his administration. He died May 3, 1617. His memorable journey in the mountains is published under this title: *Jornadado Arcebispo de Goa D. Aleixo de Menezes quandofoi a serras do Malavar, em que morão os antiguos Christaõs de S.-Tomé por Fr. Antonio de Gouvea* (Coimbra, 1606, fol.). There is added generally to this curious narration: *Sinodo diocesano de igreja e bispado de antiguos Christaõs de S.-Tomé das serras de Malavar celebrado por D. Fr. Aleixo de Menezes* (ibid. 1606; translated into Spanish in 1608 by Francis Muños . He also wrote *Histoire Orientale des grands progrès de l'Église catholique en la réduction des anciens Chrétiens dits de St. Thomas, avec la messe des anciens Chrétiens en l'évêché d'Angamale* (Bruxelles, 1609, 8vo; the translator, J. B. de Glen, has unfortunately left many blanks in his version). See Barbosa Machado, *Bibliotheca Lusitana*; Ternaux-Compans, *Biblioth. Asiatique et Africaine*; Veyssière la Croze, *Hist. du Christianisme des Indes*; Pedro Barreto de Regende, *Tratado dos Vizos-Reis da India*, in MS. in the Biblioth. imp. de Paris.

Menes'theus (Μενεσθεύς v. r. Μενέσθεσις, Vulg. *Mnestheus*), the father of Apollonius (q. v.), the ambassador of Antiochus Epiphanes to Ptolemy Philometor (2 Macc. iv, 21).

Meng. See MENCIUS.

Mengs, ANTON RAFAEL, a distinguished artist of the 18th century, was born at Aussig, in Bohemia, in 1728. His father, also a painter, adopted a very cruel course of treatment to his son, forcing him, at the age of six years, to draw the entire day without other nourishment than a crust of bread and a bottle of water, and chastising him severely if the task given was unfinished in the allotted time. In 1741, at the age of thirteen, he was taken to Rome, where he was employed in copying the works of Raphael in miniature for Augustus III, elector of Saxony and king of Poland. In 1744 he returned to Dresden, and was appointed court-painter by Augustus, with permission to return to Rome to continue his studies. He there painted several original pictures, among which was a lovely *Virgin and Child*, in which the Virgin was painted from a beautiful peasant-girl, of whom he became so enamoured that he turned Roman Catholic for her sake and married her. Soon after this he again returned to Dresden, where he remained three years, when the tyranny of his father became so oppressive that he received permission from his royal patron to visit Rome again, in order to execute his commission for an altar-piece for the royal chapel. Shortly after his arrival he was deprived of his pension, the king's finances having suffered by the Seven-Years' War; and thus suddenly thrown upon his own resources, Mengs painted at low prices for the support of his family. In 1754 he received an appointment as director of the new academy at Rome, and in 1757 was employed by the Celestines to paint the ceilings of the Church of St. Eusebio. In 1761 the king of Spain invited Mengs to his court at Madrid, and granted him a liberal pension. Here he executed, among other works, a *Descent from the Cross* and the *Council of the Gods*. The air of Spain proved detrimental to his health, and he returned to Rome, and was there engaged, immediately upon his arrival, by Clement XIV, to paint in the Vatican a picture of *Janus dictating to History*, and one of the *Holy Family*. One of his finest productions is the *Nativity*, painted for the royal collection of the king of Spain. He died in 1779. See Giobals, *Éloge historique de Mengs* (1781); Bianconi, *Elogio storico di R. Mengs* (1780); Spooner, *Biographical History of the Fine Arts* (N. Y. 1865, 2 vols. 8vo), vol. ii; Chev. Don Joseph Nicholas d'Azara, *The Works of Anthony Raphael Mengs* (Lond. 1796, 2 vols. 12mo); Kugler's *Hand-book of Painting* (transl. by Waagen, Lond. 1860, 2 vols. 12mo), ii, 519, 521.

Meni (Heb. *Meni'*, מְנִי, from מָנָה, to *distribute*; Sept. τύχη, Vulg. *ea*, i. e. *fortuna*, just mentioned [see GAD]; Auth. Vers. "that number," marg. "Meni"), apparently an idol which the captive Israelites worshipped by libations (lectisternia), after the custom of the Babylonians (Isa. lxvi, 11), and probably symbolical of destiny (a sense indicated by the first clause of the next verse), like the Arabic *manan, fate* (from the same root), and the Greek μοῖρα. Pococke (*Specim. hist. Arab.* p. 92) has pointed out the resemblance to *Manát*, an idol of the ancient Arabs (Koran, Sur. liii, 19. 20), "What think ye of Allat, and Al-Uzzah, and *Manah*, that other third goddess?" Manah was the object of worship of "the tribes of Hudheyl and Kuzá'ah, who dwelt between Mekkeh and El-Medîneh, and, as some say, of the tribes of Ows, El-Khazraj, and Thakîk also. This idol was a large stone, demolished by one Saad in the

eighth year of the flight, a year so fatal to the idols of Arabia" (Lane's *Sel. from the Kur-ân*, pref. p. 30, 31). But Al-Zamakhshari, the commentator on the Koran, derives *Manah* from a root signifying "to flow," because of the blood which flowed at the sacrifices to this idol, or, as Mill explains it, because the ancient idea of the moon was that it was a star full of moisture, with which it filled the sublunary regions.

"That the word is a proper name, and also the proper name of an object of idolatrous worship cultivated by the Jews in Babylon, is a supposition which there seems no reason to question, as it is in accordance with the context, and has every probability to recommend it. But the identification of Meni with any known heathen god is still uncertain. The versions are at variance. In the Sept. the word is rendered 'fortune' or 'luck.' The old Latin version of the clause is 'impletis *dæmoni* potionem;' while Symmachus (as quoted by Jerome) must have had a different reading, מִמֶּי, *minni*, 'without me,' which Jerome interprets as signifying that the act of worship implied in the drink-offering was not performed for God, but for the dæmon ('ut doceat non sibi fieri sed dæmoni'). The Targum of Jonathan is very vague—'and mingle cups for their idols;' and the Syriac translators either omit the word altogether, or had a different reading, perhaps לָמוֹ, *lâmô*, 'for them.' Some variation of the same kind apparently gave rise to the *super eam* of the Vulgate, referring to the 'table' mentioned in the first clause of the verse. From the old versions we come to the commentators, and their judgments are equally conflicting. Jerome (*Comm. in Es.* lxv, 11) illustrates the passage by reference to an ancient idolatrous custom which prevailed in Egypt, and especially at Alexandria, on the last day of the last month of the year, of placing a table covered with dishes of various kinds, and a cup mixed with mead, in acknowledgment of the fertility of the past year, or as an omen of that which was to come (comp. Virgil, *Æn.* ii, 763). But he gives no clue to the identification of Meni, and his explanation is evidently suggested by the renderings of the Sept. and the old Latin version; the former, as he quotes them, translating *Gad* by 'fortune,' and *Meni* by 'dæmon,' in which they are followed by the latter. In the later mythology of Egypt, as we learn from Macrobius (*Saturn.* i, 19), Δαίμων and Τύχη were two of the four deities who presided over birth, and represented respectively the Sun and Moon. A passage quoted by Selden (*De Dis Syris*, i, c. 1) from a MS. of Vettius Valens of Antioch, an ancient astrologer, goes also to prove that in the astrological language of his day the sun and moon were indicated by δαίμων and τύχη, as being the arbiters of human destiny. This circumstance, coupled with the similarity between Meni and Μήν or Μήνη, the ancient name for the moon, has induced the majority of commentators to conclude that Meni is the Moon god or goddess, the *Deus Lunus*, or *Dea Luna* of the Romans; masculine as regards the earth which she illumines (*terræ maritus*), feminine with respect to the sun (*solis uxor*), from whom she receives her light. This twofold character of the moon is thought by David Mill to be indicated in the two names Gad and Meni, the former feminine, the latter masculine (*Diss.* v, § 23); but as both are masculine in Hebrew, his speculation falls to the ground. Le Moyne, on the other hand, regarded both words as denoting the sun, and his double worship among the Egyptians: *Gad* is then the goat of Mendes, and *Meni* =Mnevis worshipped at Heliopolis. The opinion of Huetius that the *Meni* of Isaiah and the Μήν of Strabo (xii, c. 31) both denoted the sun, was refuted by Vitringa and others. Among those who have interpreted the word literally 'number' may be reckoned Jarchi and Abarbanel, who understand by it the 'number' of the priests that formed the company of revellers at the feast, and later Hoheisel (*Obs. ad. diffic. Jes. loca*, p. 349) followed in the same track. Kimchi, in his note on Isa.

lxv, 11, says of Meni, 'It is a star, and some interpret it of the stars which are *numbered*, and they are the seven stars of motion,' i. e. the planets. Buxtorf (*Lex. Hebr.*) applies it to the 'number' of the stars which were worshipped as gods; Schindler (*Lex. Pentagl.*) to the 'number and multitude' of the idols, while according to others it refers to 'Mercury, the god of numbers;' all which are mere conjectures, *quot homines, tot sententiæ*, and take their origin from the play upon the word Meni, which is found in the verse next following that in which it occurs ('therefore will I *number* [וּמָנִיתִי, *û-mânithi*] you to the sword'), and which is supposed to point to its derivation from the verb מָנָה, *mânâh*, to number. But the origin of the name of Noah, as given in Gen. v, 29, shows that such plays upon words are not to be depended upon as the bases of etymology. On the supposition, however, that in this case the etymology of Meni is really indicated, its meaning is still uncertain. Those who understand by it the moon, derive an argument for their theory from the fact that anciently years were *numbered* by the courses of the moon."

The fact of Meni being a Babylonian god renders it probable that some planet was worshipped under this name: but there is much diversity of opinion as to the particular planet to which the designation of *destiny* would be most applicable (see Lakemacher, *Observ. philol.* iv, 18 sq.; David Mill's diss. on the subject in his *Dissert. selectæ*, p. 81–132). Münter considers it to be *Venus* (see Gesenius, *Comment.* ad loc.), as the lesser star of good fortune (the *Nanæa* of the Persians [2 Macc. i, 13] or *Anætis* [Strabo, xv, 733] of the Armenians [xi, 532; xii, 559]); Ewald takes it to be *Saturn*, the chief dispenser of evil influences; and Movers (*Phönic.* i, 650) has returned to the old opinion that Meni is the *moon*, which was also supposed to be an arbitress of fortune: the best arguments for which last view are collected by Vitringa (ad loc.). It also deserves notice that there are some, among whom is Hitzig, who consider Gad and Meni to be names for one and the same god, and who chiefly differ as to whether the sun or the moon is the god intended. It would seem on the whole that, in the passage under consideration, the prophet reproaches the idolatrous Jews with setting up a table to Fortune, and with making libations to Fate; and Jerome (ad loc.) observes that it was the custom as late as his time, in all cities, especially in Egypt, to set tables before the gods, and furnish them with various luxurious articles of food, and with goblets containing a mixture of new wine, on the last day of the month and of the year, and that the people drew omens from them in respect to the fruitfulness of the year; but in honor of what god these things were done he does not state. Numerous examples of this practice occur on the monuments cf Egypt (Wilkinson, *Anc. Eg.* i, 265). See GAD.

Menifee, QUINN M., a minister of the Methodist Episcopal Church, South, son of Hon. William Menifee, was a native of Texas. He first studied law, and took his place at the bar with a good prospect of success in that profession. At the call of duty, however, he relinquished the practice of jurisprudence, and entered the Methodist itinerancy in 1857. During the war he served, for nearly two years, as a private soldier in the army of Virginia, losing a leg at the battle of Sharpsburg. After the restoration of peace he entered upon ministerial work in Texas, and there labored faithfully till his death in 1867. "Quinn Menifee was a young man of noble and generous impulses, a high-toned gentleman, and a pure-minded Christian. . . . Notwithstanding the loss of one of his limbs, his friends predicted for him a useful and successful career in the ministry. But his sun of life went down ere it had reached its meridian." See Thrall, *Hist. of Meth. in Texas*, p. 164.

Menippus, one of the most noted Cynic philosophers, was born at Gadara, in Cœle-Syria, in the first century B.C. He was originally a slave, but afterwards became one of the pupils of Diogenes. He satirized the philosophers of his time in such severe terms that the most bitter satires were afterwards denominated Menippean. Lucian pronounces him "the greatest snarler and snapper among the old dogs" (the Cynics), and in his "Dialogues of the Dead" makes Diogenes describe him as an old bald-headed man, in a tattered cloak, incessantly ridiculing the pedantry of his brother philosophers. He was the author of thirteen treatises, which contained, we are told, nothing serious, but were filled with cutting sarcasms. These works are all lost, but we have fragments of Varro's *Saturæ Menippeæ*, written in imitation of Menippus. According to Diogenes (vi, 101), these works were entitled as follows: Νεκυία, Διαϑῆκαι, Ἐπιστολαί, etc. He amassed great wealth as a usurer, but, having been cheated out of all of it, was so mortified that he strangled himself.

Menius (or **Menig**), JUSTUS, an eminent German theologian of the Reformation period, noted for his part in the spread of the Protestant doctrines, was born at Fulda Dec. 13, 1499. He studied for the Church, and intended to become a monastic in order to serve the cause of Rome the more faithfully, but, while living as deacon at Meilberg, he was made acquainted with the doctrines of Luther, and he became so interested in the reformatory movement that he decided to go to the very stronghold of the heretics and judge for himself. He accordingly set out for Wittenberg to hear Luther preach, and while there was made a convert to the new cause, and at once identified himself with the Protestants. In 1546 he was made ecclesiastical superintendent of Gotha, and afterwards he became pastor of St. Thomas's Church at Leipsic, which situation he retained until his death, Aug. 11, 1588. Menius was a devoted friend of Luther, whom he accompanied to the Colloquy of Marburg (q. v.), and in 1532 he signed the articles of Smalcald (q. v.). Together with George Spalatin, Cruciger, Myconius, and John Webern, he drew up the first ecclesiastical ritual used in Saxony. Among his works, we notice *Commentaria in lib. Samuelis et Acta Apostolorum* (Wittenb. 1532, 8vo):—*Sepultura Lutheri* (1538, 4to):—*Vom Geist d. Wiedertäuffer* (Wittenb. 1544, 4to):—*Von d. Nothwehr* (Wittenb. 1547, 8vo):—*Historica Descriptio de Bello Gothico* (1568, 8vo). See Motschmann, *Erfordia Literata;* Albrecht, *Sächsische Kirchengesch.* i, 306; Tentzel, *Suppl. Reliqua Hist. Gothanæ*, p. 787; Schmidt, *Justus Menius, der Reformator Thüringens* (1867, 2 vols. 8vo); *Jahrb. deutsch. Theol.* 1870, No. iv; Herzog, *Real-Encyklopädie*, ix, 325 sq.

Menken, GOTTFRIED, D.D., an eminent German Protestant divine, was born at Bremen May 29, 1768. His early education was somewhat imperfect, from want of means, but in 1788 he entered the University of Jena, bringing with him only his Bible, a lexicon, and the works of Jacob Böhme. The rationalistic tendency which prevailed in the German universities at that time was thoroughly repugnant to his nature, and he determined to give himself to a close and quiet study of his Bible, and of those languages which could assist him in that object, leaving entirely aside the divers purely theological systems. He wrote at the time a number of essays and expositions, which, however, not being satisfied with them, he afterwards destroyed at Wetzlar, with the exception of some valuable pieces forming one volume of about 150 pages. In 1790 he went to the University of Duisburg, where he found the same general tendency prevailing as at Jena. He met, however, with some kindred spirits, such as Achelis († judge at Duisburg in 1857) and Schlechtendal, earnest evangelical men, with whom he formed a friendship which lasted all his life. About 1791 he became an inmate in the family of the rector, Fr. A. Hasenkamp, whose example and precepts appear to have exerted a lasting influence over him. In 1794 he became assistant preacher at Frankfort-on-the-Main; in 1796, pastor of the Protestant Church at Wetzlar; removed in the same capacity to Bremen in 1802, and died there June 1, 1831. He was a great admirer of Bengel, and opposed not only Wolf and Baumgarten's views, but also those of such men as Lavater, Pfenninger, Häfeli, Stolz, Ewald, and Yung Stilling, whom he accused of conceding too much to the philosophical notions of the times. Among his numerous works we notice *Beitrag z. Dämonologie, oder Widerlegung d. exegetischen Aufsätze d. H. Prof. Grimm* (Frankf. and Leips. 1793) :—*Ueber Glück u. Sieg d. Gottlosen* (Frankf. and Leips. 1795)—both of which were published anonymously :—*Christliche Homilien* (Nurenb. 1798) :—*Neue Sammlung* (1802) :—*Homilien ü. d. Propheten Elias* (1804) :—*Predigten* (1825). After his death there appeared *Letzte Sammlung christlicher Predigten* (Cologne, 1847) :—*Anleitung z. eigenen Unterricht in d. Wahrheiten d. Heiligen Schrift* (Frankf. 1805; 2d edit. 1825) :—*Leitfaden z. Unterricht f. Confirmanden* (1817 ; 3d edit. 1826). See Osiander (J. E.), in the *Tübinger Zeitschrift*, 1832, vol. ii ; also, separately, *Menken als Schriftsteller* (Bremen, 1832) ; Herzog, *Real-Encyklopädie*, ix, 328 sq. (J. N. P.)

Mennander, CARL FREDRIK, a learned Swedish prelate, was born July 19, 1712, at Stockholm. After having been bishop of Abo, in Finland, he was called to teach physics at the University of Upsala. Towards the close of his life he was made archbishop of that city. He was a member of the Academy of Sciences at Upsala, in which city he died, May 22, 1786. He wrote *De Usu Logices in historia* (Abo, 1748) :—*De Ophiolatria Gentilium* (ibid. 1752, 4to) :—*De Synodis Aboensibus* (ibid. 1773, 4to) ; and many papers on archæology inserted in the collection of the society of Upsala.

Mennas, a patriarch of the Eastern Church, flourished in the first half of the 6th century. He was for a time superintendent of the great hospital "Holy Samson," at Constantinople. In 536 he became patriarch of that city by the choice of the emperor Justinian and the clergy, to supersede the Monophysite Antimus I, who had left his episcopal seat at Trapezunt, and had usurped the patriarchal dignity. Mennas was the first among Oriental patriarchs who was consecrated as bishop by a Roman pope (March 13, 563) (see Labbe, *Concil.* col. 47 sq.; also Baronius, *Annal.* ad ann. 536, n. 27 ; Pagi, *Critica*, ad ann. 536, n. 6). Mennas attended quietly to his duties at the Church of Constantinople till the war of the "Three Chapters" broke out and involved him [see CHAPTERS, THREE], and finally brought about his deposition from Rome, because of his adhesion to the side of the emperor against the Roman pontiff. In this trying hour Mennas displayed a most amiable disposition, and acted the part of a truly honorable man. He bowed submissively to the severe decision of the pope, and even used his influence to persuade the other bishops of the Eastern Church, who had suffered like him the displeasure of the papal vicegerent, to bear patiently with the holy father and to approve his decisions, and to revoke their previous approval of the imperial decrees (Hardouin, iii, 10 ; Labbe, v, 338). Mennas soon after died, August, 552. He had presided over the Church of Constantinople for sixteen years and six months. He is commemorated in the Latin Martyrologium Aug. 25, and in the Greek Menologium Aug. 24. A pretty full account of the life of Mennas is furnished both in the Latin and Greek *Martyrologies* under the dates of commemoration. See also Wetzer und Welte, *Kirchen-Lexikon*, vii, 57.

Menno, SIMON, one of the "shining lights" of the 16th century, a Reformer whose apostolic spirit and labors have thus far failed to receive the recognition they deserve, probably because of the relation he sustained to that peculiar sect of Christians called after him, *Mennonites* (q. v.).

Life.—The early history of Menno is somewhat obscured ; it has not yet been definitely determined when he was born. The year generally fixed upon is 1498 ;

his friends of the Netherlands believe it to have occurred in 1496, but Göbel, the noted German Church historian, holds that Menno saw the light of day in 1505 (*Gesch. d. christl. Lebens in d. Rhein. Westph. evangel. Kirche*, i, 191). His native place was the little village of Witmarsum, in Friesland. He was reared and educated under the influence of the Church, and finally decided to devote his life to her service. In 1524 he took orders as priest, and was located at the village of Pingium. His religious condition at this time was anything but desirable. "He was," we are told, "in utter darkness of mind and worldliness of spirit, yet not without some tenderness of conscience and apparent piety." In 1530 he was induced to examine the New Testament with diligence, in consequence of doubts concerning transubstantiation. He now became through grace gradually enlightened, his preaching changed, and he was called by some an evangelical preacher, though he says of himself, "At that time the world loved me, and I the world." His preaching found favor among the people, and he gained daily in popularity. In 1531 finally came the turning-point which resulted in his departure from the mother Church. In this year he witnessed the martyrdom of Sieke Snyder, at Leeuwarden, for Anabaptism. This severity towards one who had dared to differ for conscience sake rather enlisted his sympathy, roused him to a similar inquiry concerning the sacrament of *Baptism*, and resulted in his embracing the views of the persecuted Baptists, though he for several years struggled to suppress his secret convictions, on account of the odium and suffering which the avowal must incur. "By the gracious favor of God," he observes, "I have acquired my knowledge, as well of baptism as of the Lord's Supper, through the enlightening of the Holy Spirit, attendant on my much reading and contemplating the Scriptures, and not through the efforts and means of seducing sects, as I am accused."

Mosheim has taken advantage of this hesitating course on the part of Menno after his conversion to the cause of the Anabaptists, and has accused our subject of duplicity, as guilty of having held "clandestine intercourse with the Anabaptists" until he found it convenient "to throw off the mask." This, however, is unjust and cruel. Menno was never truly an Anabaptist. He never sympathized with the excesses committed at Münster and elsewhere (for he actually published a severe censure against the erroneous opinions and vile practices of John of Leyden in 1535), and his views of baptism were so peculiar that to this day the *Mennonites* stand alone in their mode of observing this sacrament. The only thing he held in common with the Anabaptists was opposition to infant baptism. Menno, however, associated quite freely with the Anabaptists, and exerted a most salutary influence over them, making many friends among that sect. In 1537 he was actually invited by a number of Anabaptists of Groningen to assume among them the rank and functions of a public teacher ; and as he looked upon the persons who made this proposal as exempt from the fanatical frenzy of their brethren at Münster, he yielded to their entreaties. His conversion from Romanism he himself alludes to in the following strain : "I besought my God with sighing and tears that to me, a troubled sinner, he would grant the gift of his grace ; that he would endue me with wisdom, spirit, frankness, and manly fortitude, so that I might preach his worthy name and holy word unadulterated, and proclaim his truth to his praise. At length the great and gracious Lord, perhaps after the course of nine months, extended to me his fatherly spirit, help, and mighty hand, so that I freely abandoned at once my character, honor, and fame, which I had among men, as also my antichristian abominations, mass, infant baptism, loose and careless life, and all, and put myself willingly in all trouble and poverty under the pressing cross of Christ my Lord. In my weakness I feared God ; I sought pious people, and of these I found some, though few, in good zeal and doctrine. I disputed with the perverted, and some I gained through God's help and power, and led them by his word to the Lord Christ; but the stiff-necked and obdurate I commended to the Lord. Thus has the gracious Lord drawn me, through the free favor of his great grace. He first stirred in my heart; he has given me a new mind; he has humbled me in his fear; he has led me from the way of death, and, through mere mercy, has called me upon the narrow path of life into the company of the saints. To him be praise forever. Amen." According to Van Oosterzee (in Herzog's *Real-Encyklopädie*, ix, 339 sq.), Menno was led to separation from Rome by the cruel treatment of the Anabaptists in 1535. Many of the sufferers at this time had been hearers of the word of God as dispensed by Menno, and had been made disciples of the new sect by his declarations against infant baptism and the opinion of a "real presence" in the Eucharist. Indeed, his own brother had suffered a martyr's death on this occasion, and this may have contributed in no small measure to the decided step which Menno took shortly after.

With Menno's appointment to the ministry of a class of "Anabaptists" at Groningen opens the most eventful period of his life's work. His withdrawal from the Church of Rome relieved him of the vow of celibacy, and he made haste to select a companion for life, by whom he had several children. All these things would make it appear that Menno settled quietly at Groningen, and there enjoyed life's ease. But this is not the record of Simon Menno. Anxious to spread the Reformed doctrines, and more especially his own peculiar views of the Bible's teachings, he travelled constantly far and near. He visited not only all Friesland, but traversed Holland and Germany, determined to make new converts, and to organize and unite the scattered members of the Anabaptists into his own fold. Although oftentimes exposed to persecution, he nevertheless continued steadfast in the work. When he found it impossible to remain any longer in Friesland he removed to Wismar; finally he settled at Oldeslohe, in Holstein, where he was granted not only protection, but even encouragement, and was allowed to establish a printing-press for the diffusion of his religious opinions. There he died, January 13, 1561, in the satisfaction of having gathered a large and flourishing sect, which continues to this day. See MENNONITES.

Menno as a Protestant.—Mosheim (*Eccles. Hist.* 16th century) thus speaks of Menno's labors after his establishment at Groningen as a Protestant minister: "East and West Friesland, with the province of Groningen, were first visited by this zealous apostle of the Anabaptists; whence he directed his course into Holland, Guelderland, Brabant, and Westphalia; continued it through the German provinces that lie on the coast of the Baltic Sea, and penetrated so far as Livonia. In all these places his ministerial labors were attended with remarkable success, and added to his sect a prodigious number of followers. Hence he is deservedly considered as the common chief of almost all the Anabaptists, and the parent of the sect that still subsists under that denomination." As Mosheim persists in mentioning Menno in connection with the Anabaptists, and as the public is prejudiced against all who were known under that name, we think it but just to insert here Menno's own account of his labors: "Through our feeble service, teaching, and simple writing, with the careful deportment, labor, and help of our faithful brethren, the great and mighty God has made so known and public, in many cities and lands, the word of true repentance, the word of his grace and power, together with the wholesome use of his holy sacraments, and has given such growth to his churches, and endued them with such invincible strength, that not only many proud, stout hearts have become humble, the impure chaste, the drunken temperate, the covetous liberal, the cruel kind, the godless godly, but also, for the testimony which

they bear, they faithfully give up their property to confiscation, and their bodies to torture and to death; as has occurred again and again to the present hour. These can be no fruits nor marks of false doctrine (with that God does not co-operate); nor under such oppression and misery could anything have stood so long were it not the power and word of the Almighty. See, this is our calling, doctrine, and fruit of our service, for which we are so horribly calumniated, and persecuted with so much enmity. Whether all the prophets, apostles, and true servants of God did not through their service also produce the like fruits, we would gladly let all the pious judge. He who bought me with the blood of his love, and called me to his service, unworthy as I am, searches me, and knows that I seek neither gold and goods, nor luxury, nor ease on earth, but only my Lord's glory, my salvation, and the souls of many immortals. Wherefore I have had, now the eighteenth year, to endure so excessive anxiety, oppression, trouble, sorrow, and persecution, with my poor, feeble wife and little offspring, that I have stood in jeopardy of my life and in many a fear. Yes, while the priests lie on soft beds and cushions, we must hide ourselves commonly in secret corners. While they at all nuptials and christenings, and other times, make themselves merry in public with fifes, drums, and various kinds of music, we must look out for every dog, lest he be one employed to catch us. Instead of being greeted by all as doctors and masters, we must be called Anabaptists, clandestine holders-forth, deceivers, and heretics. In short, while for their services they are rewarded in princely style, with great emoluments and good days, our reward and portion must be fire, sword, and death. What now I, and my true coadjutors in this very difficult, hazardous service, have sought, or could have sought, all the well-disposed may easily estimate from the work itself and its fruit. I will then humbly entreat the faithful and candid reader once more, for Jesus's sake, to receive in love this my forced acknowledgment of my enlightening, and make of it a suitable application. I have presented it out of great necessity, that the pious reader may know how it has happened, since I am on all sides calumniated and falsely accused, as if I were ordained and called to this service by a seditious and misleading sect. Let him that fears God read and judge."

In the article ANABAPTISTS we have already alluded to the general mistake of supposing that all Anabaptists were engaged in the Münster excesses, and that usually persons fail to make a distinction between the sober Christians and the worst fanatics of the party. In our sketch of the life and labors of *David Joris* (q. v.), we had occasion to point out the earnestness which characterized his followers of the "Anabaptists;" but it is in this place that we would enlist our reader's attention to the injustice of suffering a whole sect to be despised and forsaken because of the faults of a few who may have secured membership in order to make their religious garb a stepping-stone to abused power. The two large Protestant bodies of Lutheran and Reformed have always been characterized by jealousy towards any new sects, and have quickly charged their weaker rivals with all the infirmities which flesh is heir to, if any one member of the new comers was open to criticism. Even in our very day the Methodists and Baptists suffer more or less persecution from the communicants of the State churches in Germany; how much more likely in those days of the 16th century, when first the iron hold of the papacy, which had cramped the Church for ages, was suddenly relaxing. From all the sources now at our command, we gather the fact that Menno was a gentle, earnest, modest man, of a spiritual nature, with no trace about him of wild fanaticism; ready to encourage all that was noble, pure, and good in his fellow-men, constantly reproving those of his followers who appeared guilty of misdemeanors of any sort. Flourishing in the Reformation period, he was frequently involved in controversies; thus in 1543 he was visited by the celebrated

John à Lasko, who was determined to draw Menno into the party of the Reformed or Lutherans. For three or four days the two eminent divines held public disputations upon Christ's humanity, infant baptism, etc., etc., but so gentle was Menno in his manner that at the close of the controversy the two combatants parted in peace, promising good-will towards each other. In 1550 he published a special tract to defend the doctrine of the Trinity against the Unitarians, who were coming to his country from Italy and Switzerland; in 1552, *A thorough Confession on Disputed Points,* for the use of other religious bodies than his own.

Result of Menno's Labors.—The whole system of theology as taught by Simon Menno presents few, if any, new developments. In his controversies with John à Lasko and Micronius, he confessed a peculiar Christology. He did not believe in a Son *sundered* and *divided* into two persons (*"zerstückelt oder zertheilt"*) of a human and divine nature. He confessed one and the same Son and Only-begotten, who in his very flesh is the God-Logos, who in his flesh came down from heaven, and in very flesh became man. He believed that Christ, in this way, was born *in* Mary, but not *of* Mary; that he became flesh, and was made man, without taking upon him Mary's flesh and blood. Anxious to ascribe to our Lord the highest purity possible, he seems to have indulged in speculations which rendered the reality of Christ's human nature somewhat doubtful. He probably borrowed this vague notion from the Münster Anabaptists. As a writer of systematic theology, Simon Menno was inferior to most of his contemporaries, and his main work, *Das Fundamentbuch* (1539), shows his want of adaptedness to a systematic treatment of religious doctrines. Following the example of the apostles, he taught his followers, as the occasion required, in a simple, childlike way, and never allowed himself to be drawn into abstruse, or even abstract questions, when preaching to them. A complete and systematic statement of his doctrines was never given by Simon Menno, and the great influence which he and his followers exercised on the internal and external history of the Reformation was due to the *principle* they represented.

Like the other Protestant Reformers, Menno accepted the *formal* and *material* principles of the Reformation; but, besides these, he aimed at a *moral, practical* end. It was his earnest desire to restore the kingdom of God, or the Christian Church, to that purity which is taught in the New Testament, and which he believed had existed in the Apostolic Church. To bring back this golden age of Christianity, and to organize a congregation μὴ ἔχουσαν σπῖλον, ἢ ῥυτίδα, ἤ τι τῶν τοιούτων (Ephes. v, 27), was the constant aim of all his efforts. This accounts for the singular asceticism of the sect, and explains why the Mennonites did not, like other evangelical bodies, concern themselves about abstract religious speculations, but about moral laws and duties. For the same reasons they also separated themselves from the unbelieving world, and tried to purify the Church by administering the ordinance of baptism only to those who had made a personal profession of faith in Christ. The validity of infant baptism was rejected, while only adults "who do actually profess repentance towards God and obedience to our Lord Jesus Christ" were considered proper subjects of this ordinance. We quote here article seven of a Mennonite Confession of Faith: "We confess of baptism that all repenting believers, who by faith, regeneration, and renewal of heart by the Holy Spirit, have been united with God, and whose names are written down in heaven, are to be baptized in the name of the Father, and the Son, and the Holy Ghost, to show forth in a solemn and beautiful emblem their faith in the crucified, buried, and risen Redeemer, with its effect to live up to whatsoever things Christ taught his followers." The necessity of the power of excommunication in the Church was earnestly asserted by Menno, "for without the right usage of excommunication the spiritual kingdom of God on earth cannot exist intact in purity and piety. A Church without the proper apostolical ban or excommunication is like a city without walls or gates, like a field or garden without a fence, or like a house without walls or doors. For without it the Church would stand open to all seducers and evil-doers, to idolators and wilfully persistent sinners." He insisted upon excommunication to such an extent that members of his congregation at Wismar who had listened to the sermons of Lutheran clergymen were excommunicated as if they had committed public crimes, or indulged in gross passions.

The works of Simon Menno, of which the last were printed in his own printing establishment, were published collectively in 1600, under the title *Sommaria of Byllwergadering van sommige schriftelyke Bekentenissen des geloofs, mitsgaders eenige waarachtige Verant woordingen, gedaan door Menno Simons.* It was, however, a very imperfect compilation; much better was that of 1646, 4to; but the best appeared in 1681, in sm. fol., at Amsterdam, entitled *Opera omnia theologica, of al de Godgeleerde werken van Menno Simonis,* etc.

Besides the histories on his followers, quoted in the article MENNONITES, see *Biographie des Protest. celèbres* (Paris), ii, 59–70; Cramer, *Het leven an de verrigtingen von Menno Simons* (Amst. 1837), perhaps the most important work to be consulted; Harder, *Leben Menno Simons* (Königsb. 1846); Roosen, *Menno Simons den evangelischen Mennonitengemeinden geschildert* (Leipsic, 1848). (J. H. W.)

Mennonites is the name of a Christian sect which sprung up in Holland and Germany about the time of the Reformation, though it cannot be said to have actually originated in the great revolution of the 16th century. The Baptists claim the Mennonites as their forerunners, and regard them to be the direct descendants of the Waldenses (q.v.); but this origin of the Mennonites is disputed by most Pædobaptist writers, who recognise them simply as the followers of one Simon Menno (q.v.), who gathered the more moderate of the *Anabaptists* (q.v.), gave them a new code of discipline, and became to them the interpreter of the law and the Gospel. Because of the excesses committed by the more fanatic and unruly of the German Anabaptists in the reformatory period, the Baptists and Mennonites take exception to this classification. M. Herman Schyn, a Mennonite minister, who has published their history and apology, seeks to maintain that they are not Anabaptists, either by principle or by origin. Besides the necessity of adult baptism, the Mennonites in the 16th century held, in common with the Anabaptists, the belief in Christ's personal reign during the millennium—the unlawfulness of oaths and wars, even in resistance to injury—the impropriety of engaging in lawsuits—and the exclusion of the civil magistrate from the Church. But with the wild notions, which were indulged in by many, of setting up Christ's kingdom on earth by violence and bloodshed, they had no sympathy. Every immoral practice, also, they as a sect discountenanced; and they deserve to be held up as a Christian body characterized by consistency and moderation. In the days of their founder they were certainly among the most pious Christians the Church ever saw, and the worthiest citizens the State ever had. "It must be at once conceded," says Hardwick (*Church Hist. during the Ref.* p. 280), "that the principles of the sect are free from nearly all the dark fanaticism which stains the records of the older party."

Mennonites, the Anabaptists of the Netherlands first called themselves in 1536, the year in which the hitherto scattered community celebrated its union. Menno, seeing clearly that "in union lies strength," had obtained a regular state of Church order, separate from all Dutch and German Protestants, and thus secured an ecclesiastical establishment. He laid down rules for the guidance of the congregations, and furnished them with a sort of "confession of faith." His doctrines were free from the anti-social and licentious tenets and the pretensions to inspiration which are ascribed to the Anabaptists; but he agreed with them in condemning the baptism of infants (Matt. xxviii, 19), in expecting a personal reign of Christ on earth for a thousand years at the millennium, in excluding magistrates from the Christian Church (Schyn, i, 214), and in maintaining that all war was unlawful (Matt. xxvi, 52), that the taking of oaths was prohibited by Christ (Matt. v, 37), and that human science is useless and pernicious to a Christian. But these tenets were so explained and modified by Menno as to differ very little from the doctrines generally held by the Reformed churches, securing a high degree of credit to the religious system of this famous teacher, and thus contributing to the rapid progress of his followers both in numbers and in influence. He insisted upon the strictest attention to moral duties, and exercised a most severe discipline upon offenders, and in a very short time succeeded in excluding from this fellowship those fanatics that had so dishonored the name of Anabaptists, and gradually built up a large and flourishing sect.

The severe discipline which Menno exercised over his followers had, however, ultimately the effect of producing divisions within his flock. Oftentimes the propriety or impropriety of excommunicating from the fellowship of the Church those who had incurred its censures was questioned. Menno insisted upon the expulsion of all guilty of misdemeanor, even if the erring ones showed signs of repentance. Some in the flock took exception to this severity, and insisted upon it that an excommunicated might at least be readmitted if signs of repentance were clearly manifest. This division of opinion resulted finally in the division of the sect into two parties, named respectively "*die Feinen,*" the Fine, and "*die Groben,*" the Coarse. They were also called "Flemings" or "Flandrians" and "Waterlanders," from the districts in which they resided. The former was the more rigid of the two; but ere long it was also divided into Flandrians and Frieslanders. This separation arose out of a question as to what should constitute a sufficient cause for excommunication. One party regarded those only who were open contemners of the divine law to be deserving the highest censure of the Church, while the other party considered offences of the most trivial kind a reason for the instant rejection of the offender. Menno himself officially sided with the Flemings, and he was forced to pronounce the expulsion of the milder party, although his sympathies were supposed to be with them.

Other particular sentiments that divided the Mennonites are the following: The Flemingians maintain, with various degrees of rigor, the opinions of their founder Menno as to the human nature of Christ, alleging that it was produced in the womb of the Virgin by the creating power of the Holy Ghost, and hence object to the terms *person* and *trinity* as not consistent with the simplicity of the Scriptures; they hold to the obligation that binds us to wash the feet of strangers, in consequence of our Saviour's command; the necessity of excommunicating and avoiding, as one would do the plague, not only avowed sinners, but also all those who depart, even in some slight instances pertaining to dress, etc., from the simplicity of their ancestors; the contempt due to human learning, and to other matters of less moment. Another separation took place at Amsterdam in 1664, and had a much wider influence, extending also to the other Dutch churches; it was between the Mennonites who held to the opinions of the *Remonstrants* (q. v.) and the old orthodox party. The leader of the Remonstrants, or Socinians, was Dr. Galenus Abrahams (see Benthem, *Holländ. Kirche- u. Schulenstaat,* i, 832; Jehring, p. 30), hence called *Gallenists* (q. v.), and, from the house where they assembled (*bij het Lam*), Lamists; the opponents were called Apostoolians, from their leader, Dr. Samuel Apostool; and Zonists, from their house in *de Zon* (sun). By the *Algemeene Doopsgezinde Societeit,* founded in 1811, the two

churches came again into closer fellowship (see *Jahrboekje voor de Doopsgez. Gemeenten,* 1838 and 1839, p. 118; comp. p. 99).

But, though divided, all Mennonites are agreed in regard to the fundamental doctrine of baptism, which is administered by pouring, and only to adults. "The opinions," says Mosheim (*Eccles. Hist.* iv, 142 sq.), "that are held in common by the Mennonites, seem to be all derived from this fundamental principle, that the kingdom which Christ established upon earth is a visible Church, or community, into which the holy and just alone are to be admitted, and which is consequently exempt from all those institutions and rules of discipline that have been invented by human wisdom for the correction and reformation of the wicked. This fanatical principle was avowed by the ancient Mennonites, but it is now almost wholly renounced. Yet from this ancient doctrine many of the religious opinions that distinguish the Mennonites from all other Christian communities seem to be derived. In consequence of this doctrine, they admit none to the sacrament of baptism except persons that are come to the full use of their reason; they neither admit civil rulers into their communion, nor allow any of their members to perform the functions of magistracy; they pretend to deny the lawfulness of repelling force by force, and consider war, in all its shapes, as unchristian and unjust; they entertain the utmost aversion to the execution of justice, and more especially to capital punishments; and they also refuse to confirm their testimony by an oath."

The first settlement of the Mennonites in the United Provinces was granted them by William, prince of Orange, towards the close of the 16th century. During the War of Liberation they had played no unimportant part. Although their obligation not to carry arms prevented them from entering the army, they nevertheless greatly aided the cause by liberal contributions of money, etc. It was not, however, before the 17th century that their liberty and tranquillity were fixed upon solid foundations, when, by a Confession of Faith published in the year 1626, they cleared themselves from the imputations of those pernicious and detestable errors that had been laid to their charge. In order to appease their intestine discords, a considerable part of the Anabaptists of Flanders, Germany, and Friesland concluded their debates in a conference held at Amsterdam in the year 1630, and entered into the bonds of fraternal communion, each reserving to themselves a liberty of retaining certain opinions. This association, simply nominal, however, was renewed and confirmed by new resolutions in the year 1649, in consequence of which the rigorous laws of Menno and his successors were in various respects mitigated and corrected. Their association at that time was very much like that of the Congregationalists in the United States. Indeed, in cultus they had much in common with this religious body. Each congregation chooses its own pastor, whom they call *exhorter,* and upon him they lean in his strength or weakness. These preachers frequently were not paid by their congregations, but depended upon business or trade enterprises for their daily bread. When no preacher could be secured, the deacon would minister unto the male portion, and the deaconess unto the female portion of the congregation.

In the 17th and 18th centuries the persecution of the Mennonites in Germany and Switzerland drove many to Holland, and the "parent" body was thus largely increased. It was estimated about the middle of the 18th century at some 160,000. Since that time the Dutch Mennonites have again considerably decreased in number. An important event in their history was the provision of the theological training of their ministry by the establishment of a seminary in 1735. There are no buildings connected with this college, but the students receive theological instruction in a room, containing the library, over the Mennonite chapel. The lectures are delivered in Latin; and each student before his entrance must be acquainted with Latin and Greek. They attend at a literary institution for instruction in Hebrew, ecclesiastical history, physics, natural and moral philosophy, etc. They have private lodgings in different parts of the city. The college was established nearly a century ago, and was at first supported by the Amsterdam Mennonites alone; but lately other churches send in their contributions. Some of the students receive support from the public fund; they are all intended for the Christian ministry. Thus provided with an educated ministry, they were placed on a more equal footing with the other Protestant bodies of the country. The names Oosterbaan, Stinstra, and Hesselink are mentioned with pride as theologians of Holland, and not simply as Mennonite ministers, by every Dutchman. In 1795 they were granted equality with the other Protestants, and soon after they began gradually to drop peculiar characteristics, so as to form substantially only one national body. In 1811 all Mennonites united in the formation of a society for the support and encouragement of theological education. In 1835 the tercentennial date of Menno's withdrawal from the Papal Church was unitedly observed by all his followers. A missionary society, sustaining three laborers in Java, is supported by all Mennonites, and so is the *Teyler Theological Society* at Haarlem. According to the Mennonite "Year-Book" of 1850 (the last published by the denomination), they had then in Holland 127 congregations and 140 ministers, not counting the retired preachers and those engaged as professors.

The Mennonites in Germany, etc.—In Germany the Mennonites were rather numerous in the 17th century. In Moravia alone they counted some 70,000. They were expelled from that country by Ferdinand II in 1622, and, after a short stay in Hungary and Transylvania, finally found a resting-place in Russian territory (see below). The Mennonites were very largely represented in Eastern Prussia. They were particularly numerous at Dantzic, Marienburg, and Elbing. Their Dutch neatness and Dutch industry soon made these desolate and swampy regions to flourish like a garden. But almost incessant persecution largely reduced their number by emigration. In 1730 and in 1732 they were threatened with expatriation on account of their refusal to serve in the army; but the storm passed by, and king Frederick II gave them additional privileges—not, however, until the order had been weakened by emigration. Gradually they increased again until 1789, when they were forbidden to purchase landed property. But, notwithstanding all difficulties, the Mennonites have remained, in part at least, on Prussian soil, particularly the valley of the Vistula, called "the Garden Spot of Prussia." Their number in all Germany is estimated at about 50,000.

The Mennonites in Russia.—Russia gladly availed herself of Prussia's intolerance, and did much to secure these valuable citizens for her own territory. Catharine II in 1786 had invited the Mennonites to Russia, along with other German colonists, and in 1789 228 families arrived in Russia, and between 1793 and 1796 there was an immigration of 118 more families. These all settled on and near the island of Khortitz, on the Lower Dnieper, below Tekaterinoslav. The conditions on which they came to Russia were: Protection from all attacks, freedom of worship, a gift of lands to the amount of 190 acres for each family, exemption from all taxes and imposts for ten years, money for their journey, and money and wood with which to establish themselves, freedom of trade and manufactures, the administration of oaths in their own way, and exemption forever from military service. These privileges were confirmed by the emperor Paul, and extended to all Mennonites who should come thereafter. In spite, therefore, of the repeal and mitigation of the severe laws against them in Prussia, there was a continued and large immigration of Mennonites into Russia up to the year 1817. These colonists settled near their brethren in the government of Tau-

rid, in the region between the rivers Molotchna, Dnieper, and Tokmak, not far from the town of Berdiansk. From that time the Mennonites have gone on increasing and prospering, until they now number about 40,000 souls. They have always been protected and favored by the government, so that they have almost entirely governed themselves, and have preserved their German character and institutions intact. This they in great part owe to the character and efforts of Johann Cornies, who, up to his death in 1848, exercised a very powerful influence over them, though he held no office and no rank. Titles and orders were on several occasions offered to him by the imperial government, which highly appreciated his services, but they were always refused. His advice was several times asked by the minister of domains, and the governor-general of New Russia rarely took an important measure without first consulting Cornies. These Mennonites not only had their own schools and churches, and retained in their integrity the language, habits, and usages of their ancestors, but had a sort of self-government, each group of villages being under a governor appointed by themselves from their own ranks, who acted as the organ of communication between them and the general government. In 1861, the present czar (Alexander II) granted new lands and renewed all the old concessions to a colony of Mennonites who settled on the Volga. These lands, however, as also those ceded by Catharine, were not given in fee simple. The receivers were allowed to leave them to their children and to sell them to each other, but could not dispose of them to any other than a Mennonite without special permission of the government.

In our own day the attitude of the Russian government towards the Mennonites has decidedly changed, and a harsh and unfriendly spirit been manifested in regard to them. The sharp-sighted among them foresaw an invasion of their liberties from the tone of the Russian newspapers and the attitude of Russian officials. On June 4, 1871, the expected blow came. An edict, addressed to all the colonists in the empire—German Lutherans and Roman Catholics, as well as Mennonites, Bulgarians, and others, to all of whom, as to the Mennonites, grants of lands and special privileges had been given—set the limit of ten years as the terminal period of exemption from military service, with the proviso that, as to furnishing recruits, the laws ruling colonists should remain in force only till the publication of a general law on military duty. Such a law might be promulgated at any day, and the Mennonites, with others, be obliged to furnish recruits, in spite of their religious convictions against bearing arms. By the general law of Russia emigration is not permitted; but, for the benefit of the aggrieved colonists, ten years were given them in which to take themselves out of Russia, if unwilling to come under the full intent of Russian law. After that time no emigration is to be permitted. Meanwhile some of the Mennonites had been busy making inquiries to guide them in the selection of new homes. Cornelius Jonsen, a leading Mennonite, acting as German consul at Berdiansk, had written letters to members of the sect in this country and Canada, asking information as to the advantage of America for settlement by their people. Very full and encouraging replies were received from John Funk, at Elkhart, Indiana, and from others in Canada, Pennsylvania, and the West. Jonsen had these letters printed, and distributed them, together with little pamphlets, telling of the attractions of America. So enthusiastic did the people become over the hope of freer and happier homes in the New World, that in a short time $20,000 was raised to aid a deputation to America, to visit its finest sections, and to return to Russia with a report of the result of their spying out of the land. The delegates sent were twelve in number, and left Russia for this country at various times from February to May, 1873, and the result is manifest in the large arrival of this people, who have purchased lands on the Western prairies, and in some of our Southern states. The probability is that all the Mennonites of Russia will settle in the United States.

Those Mennonites who, after their emigration to Russia, settled in the Crimea, and there lived on land bought by themselves, and not included in the grants of either Catharine or Alexander, are likewise emigrating to this country. An advance guard of some thirty families, who were able to sell their estates at once, quitted the Russian territory and arrived here Aug. 15 (1873). They are essentially German, still speaking the language of the land they were obliged to leave nearly a century ago, and are from the villages of Friedenstein ("Stone of Peace") and Bruderfeld ("Brother's Field"), in the Crimea, in the neighborhood of the Black Sea. They marry only within their own Church. A correspondent of the *New York Tribune* writes from St. Petersburg, under date of April 19 (1873), concerning this people: "That the Mennonites are thrifty, industrious, and economical, their prosperity is sufficient proof. They are, besides this, very clean, neat, and orderly (a lady could go into every peasant's stable), and quiet, contented, honest, moral, and deeply religious. There is no drunkenness or gambling among them. Crime is exceedingly rare. The latest statistics I can find are dated 1841, and those show that for 37 years there were only 88 crimes in the Mennonite colonies on the Molotchna, including about 12,000 people. Of these crimes, 41 sprang from the sexual relation, and 9 were thefts; all the rest were minor offences, such as disobedience to the authorities. Besides all this, the Mennonites are educated. Every child knows how to read and write; in every village there is a school. The Bible and other religious books are, of course, to be found in every house. The Mennonites were visited by Haxthausen in 1843. and by Petzholdt in 1855, and both travellers bear testimony to the worth and the prosperity of the colonists. Petzholdt says: 'It is my firm conviction that Russia possesses no more useful or more industrious citizens than the Mennonites.' Up to this time the Mennonites have always been loyal subjects to Russia. They have never been remiss in their taxes; and during the Crimean War sent large voluntary gifts of grain and provender to the besieged army. It is only because the privileges granted to them are infringed, and they will be compelled to enter the army against their conscience, that they now wish to emigrate from Russia."

The Mennonites in the United States. —These newcomers are not by any means the first Mennonites in the United States. They came as early as 1683. Holding much in common with the Friends, the Mennonites received an invitation from William Penn to settle in the new province of Pennsylvania. Many accepted the kind offer of the Quaker leader, and in little more than half a century the sect had migrated to the number of about 500 families. In 1708 a school and meeting-house were erected by them in Germantown, Pa. In the following year another colony was established in what is now known as Lancaster County, Pa. Other emigrations followed in 1711, 1717, 1727, and 1733 successively. In 1735 there were nearly if not quite 500 families settled in Lancaster County. Afterwards their families settled also in various parts of Maryland, Ohio, Indiana, New York, and Canada; and they are now found in nearly every part of the Union and of Canada, though they are most numerously presented in Pennsylvania, Ohio, Maryland, and Virginia. It is difficult to arrive at their whole number, as they keep no accessible records for that purpose, believing public displays of this nature to be only one of the vanities of denominations, and of no good service, as the Great Head of the Church well sees and knows how many are his. They probably number, however, as nearly as can be ascertained, about 350 ministers and €6,000 members. They have a publishing-house at Elkhart, Indiana. Their bishops, ministers, and deacons meet semi-annually in district conferences for the purpose of learning the state of the Church, and deliberating upon sug-

gested methods for advancing her spiritual prosperity. Their religious views are similar to those held by their brethren in Europe. They have, however, distinguishing peculiarities. Their office-bearers—bishops, ministers, and deacons—are all of them chosen by lot. Their pastors give their services gratuitously. Their views and character as a body meeting with much misrepresentation, and exciting considerable prejudice against them, they translated and published at Philadelphia, in 1727, their Confession of Faith. For details, see *American Christian Record*, p. 145 sq.

Besides the *Old* Mennonites, there are in America : 1. *The Reformed* or *Strict Mennonites*, who in 1811 branched off from the parent American body. They follow strictly the injunctions of Simon Menno in regard to foot-washing, non-resistance of evil, abstinence from oaths, and separation from all excommunicated persons. This sect numbers not more than 4000, and is confined chiefly to Pennsylvania, where it first originated. Their doctrines are too rigid for general acceptance, and they progress but slowly. They are a worthy, honest, and exemplary people. 2. *The New Mennonites*, numbering about 10,000, organized in 1847 by J. H. Oberholtzer and ten other ministers of the Old Mennonites in Eastern Pennsylvania. They introduced various reforms, and spread rapidly, not only in Pennsylvania, but in other states, and were the first Mennonites to found a theological seminary, located at Wadsworth, Ohio. In 1872 they had three teachers and twenty-two pupils. They also have a publishing-house at Milford Square, Pa. 3. *The Evangelical Mennonites*, organized from the preceding body in 1856, who hold stated meetings for prayer as a Christian necessity. They number only about 300. 4. *The Omish Mennonites*, numbering about 22,500, followers of Jacob Amman, of Alsace, and very much like the Reformed. They discard the use of buttons on their clothes, substituting the hook, and hence are frequently called *Hookers.*

The Mennonites all over the world count probably 800,000. Their oldest authoritative "Confession of Faith" dates from 1580, entitled *De Waterlandsche Belydenis;* in 1591 was published the *Concept von Köln;* in 1617, *De Friesche Belydenis;* and later (1766), the most complete and generally accepted Confession was prepared by John Ries, preacher of the Waterlanders in Alcmar, and by Lubbert Gerard, in Latin (comp. Schyn, ii, 78, 279 ; i, 172).

For information respecting the Mennonites, see Ottus, *Annales Anabaptistici* (Basle, 1672, 4to) ; *Gründliche Historie von den Begebenheiten, Streitigkeiten, und Trennungen, so unter den Taufgesinnten bis 1615 vorgegangen* (from the Dutch of Van Gent), by Jehring (Jena, 1720) ; Schyn, *Hist. Christianorum, qui in Belgio fœderato Mennonitæ appellantur* (Amstelod. 1725); id., *Historiæ Mennonitarum plenior Deductio* (Amsterd. 1729), which is a defence of the sect, and in which the author protests against their being confounded with the Anabaptists ; Van Huyzen, *Epitome doctr. Mennonitarum ;* Botsace, *Wiederbelebung der Wiedertäufferischen Lehre ;* Crichton, *Gesch. der Mennoniten ;* Starck, *Gesch. d. Taufe u. Taufgesinnten ;* V. Reiswitz u. Wadzeck, *Glaubensbekenntniss der Mennoniten u. Nachricht von ihren Colonieen nebst Lebensbeschreib. Menno Simonis* (Berl. 1824); Reiswitz, *Beiträge zur Kenntniss der Mennoniten* (Breslau, 1829) ; Blaupot Ten Cate, *Geschiedenis der Doopsgezinden in Friesland, Holland, Zeeland, etc.* (Amsterd. 1837–50) ; Cornelius, *Gesch. d. Münstersch. Aufruhrs* (Leips. 1855) ; Wigandus, *In Dogmatibus Anabaptistarum ;* Hase, *Neue Propheten ;* De Bussière, *Les Anabaptistes* (Paris, 1853) ; Rues, *Gegenwärtiger Zustand der Mennoniten ;* Mosheim, *Eccles. Hist.* cent. xvi, § iii, pt. ii, c. 3 ; and cent. xvii, § ii, pt. ii, c. 5 (it is to be wished that Mosheim had written the history of this sect in a spirit of greater candor) ; Gieseler, *Eccles. Hist.* iv, 371 sq.; Möhler, *Symbolics,* p. 355 sq.; Hagenbach, *Hist. of Doctrines,* vol. ii (see Index) ; and Van Oosterzee, in Herzog, *Real-Encyklop.* vol. ix, s. v.

Menochius, GIOVANNI STEFFANO, a learned Italian, the son of Jacques Menochius, a celebrated lawyer, was born at Pavia in 1576. At the age of seventeen he entered the Order of the Jesuits. He taught theology in different colleges of his order, was principal of those of Modena and Rome, then became inspector for the province of Milan, next for that of Venice, and was finally appointed assistant to the superior-general. He died at Rome Feb. 4, 1655. Of his works we mention *Hieropoliticon, sive institutiones politicæ e Scripturis depromptæ* (Lyons, 1625, 8vo) :—*Institutiones œconomicæ e Scripturis depromptæ* (Lyons, 1627, 8vo) :— *Brevis Expositio sensus litteralis totius Scripturæ* (Cologne, 1630, 2 vols. fol. : this estimable work was reprinted several times ; the best edition is that published at Paris [1719, 2 vols. fol.], by P. Tournemine — reproduced at Avignon [1768, 4 vols. 4to] ; it contains an appendix to the commentaries on the Bible, and to different Jesuitical authors. See Simon, *Histoire critique des principaux Commentateurs du Nouv. Test.* p. 651) : — *Storie tessute di varie eruditione sacra, morale e profana* (Rome, 1646-54, 6 vols. 4to) ; the first published under the fictitious name of J. Corona : — *De Republica Hebræorum* (Paris, 1648 and 1652, fol.) : — *De Œconomia Christiana* (Venice, 1656, 4to) : — *Storia Miscellanea Sacra* (Venice, 1658, 4to). See also Alegambe and Sottwell, *Scriptores Societatis Jesu ;* Dupin, *Bibl. des Auteurs Ecclés.* vol. xviii.

Menologium (μηνηλόγιον, from μήνη and λόγος), a name given by the Greek Christians to such of their Church books as contained, besides the *Menæa* (q. v.), or special prayers and hymns for each festival and saint's day, short biographical notices and descriptions of the death of the saints and martyrs. The Menologia were generally divided into monthly parts ; sometimes into two semi-annual volumes. There are yet a number of them extant in MS., and extracts of them for the use of the Greek Church were repeatedly printed in the 17th century. It nearly corresponds to the *Martyrology* of the Roman Church. The Greeks give the names of the saints, together with short biographical notices of them, taken from the μηναῖα, and also the Gospel lessons for the day. Allatius, in *De libris Græcorum,* p. 83-86, gives an account of their origin and contents. Several of them are very ancient, and known to us by the accounts of Assemani, Genebrardus, and Ant. Contius. The most important are : *Menol. ex versione Cardinalis Sirleti in Canisii lectt. antiquarum* (tome v) :—*Menol. ex Menæis Græcorum erutum et in linguam vern. versum a Maximo Margunio ed. Anton. Pinello* (Venet. 1529) : — *Menol. Græcorum jussu Basilii Imperatoris Græce olim editum — nunc primum Gr. et Lat. prodit studio et opera Annibalis Tit. S. Clementis* (Urbini, 1727). Still more remarkable than this edition of the so-called *Menologium Basilianum* is the Μηνολόγιον τῶν εὐαγγέλων ἑορταστιχῶν sive *Calendarium Ecclesiæ Constantinopolitanæ primitus ex Bibliotheca Romana Albanorum in lucem editum,* etc., *cura Steph. Anton. Morcelli* (Rome, 1788, 2 vols.). The text in this edition, revised with great care, was, according to the opinion of the author, written during the reign of Constantinus Copronymus. See Augusti, *Denkwürdigkeiten,* vi, 208 ; xii, 300 ; Suicer and Du Fresne, *Lexicon,* s. v. ; Siegel, *Christl. Alterthümer* (see Index) ; Neale, *Introd. Hist. East. Church.*

Menot, MICHEL, a French preacher, was born about 1440. He belonged to the Order of the Gray Friars, among whom he taught theology for several years. His sermons were of a peculiar make-up—half in barbarous Latin, half in burlesque French, and filled with coarse jests and trivialities ; he nevertheless gained great reputation, rather for his oddity than any display of ability, and his enthusiastic hearers surnamed him " the golden trigend." Menot died at Paris in 1518. The

printer Claude Chevalier collected a certain number of Menot's sermons, which appeared under the title *Sermones quadragesimales olim Turonis declamati* (Paris, 1519 and 1525, 8vo), very rarely seen at present. See Nicéron, *Mémoires,* etc., vol. xxiv ; *Dict. Hist.* (ed. of 1822), s. v. ; Le Bas, *Dict. Encycl. de la France,* s. v.

Ménoux, JOSEPH DE, a French Jesuit, was born October 14, 1695, at Besançon. He belonged to an ecclesiastical family, and, destined for the Church, he entered the Society of Jesus at an early age, studied the classics at different colleges, and applied himself with success to preaching. He obtained the confidence of king Stanislas, who appointed him preacher and superior of the seminary of missions for Lorraine. He is represented as a man of mind, intriguing and serviceable, a useful friend and a dangerous enemy. Voltaire says that he persuaded pope Benedict XIV, the author of some large treatises in folio on the canonization of the saints, that he should translate them into French. He sent several pages of it to him, and obtained a good benefice for his seminary, of which the Benedictines were robbed. Voltaire, who in his secret correspondence calls Ménoux a false brother, was assured of the protection of the learned Jesuit in all circumstances ; but the alliance established between them was not sincere on either side. Ménoux was one of the first members of the Academy of Nancy, and was associated with those of the Arcades of Rome. He wrote : *Notions Philosophiques des vérités fondamentales de la Religion, ouvrage didactique d'un ordre nouveau* (7th edition, revised and corrected ; Nancy, 1758, 8vo. This work appeared at first under the title of *Défi général à l'incredulité.* " There are few," says Fréron, " so methodical, so clear, so precise, so consistent") :—*Heures du Chrétien, à l'usage des Missions* (Nancy, 1741, 12mo) :—*Discours prononcé en 1753 à la séance publique de la Société Littéraire de Nanci* (ibid. 1753, 4to ; translated into Italian by order of pope Benedict XIV) :—*Coup d'œil sus l'arrêt du Parlement de Paris concernant l'institut des Jésuites* (Avignon, 1761, in two parts, 8vo). Ménoux is regarded as the author of this writing, signed by P. Griffet, and he furnished to Cerutti the materials for *L'Apologie générale de l'institut des Jésuites.* He was a co-laborer in the moral and religious works of Stanislas. See Fréron, *Année littéraire,* 1753, 1758 ; Durival, *Descript. de la Lorraine,* i, 236 ; J. J. Rousseau, *Confessions,* bk. viii.

Mensa, Mensal (*table*), a name anciently given to a church erected over a martyr's grave. See MARTYR. Such edifices received this appellation from the distinctive altar or communion table. Thus Augustine speaks of a church called *mensa Cypriani*—Cyprian, as he explains, not having eaten there, but having there been offered up. Prior to the Reformation in Scotland, when the revenue of a popish bishopric arose from the annexation of parish churches, those allotted to the bishop himself were called *mensal* churches, as furnishing his table ; the other churches being called *common,* as bishop and chapter had an interest in them. *Mensa* is used by some writers in the same sense as *Martyrium* (q. v.). See Eadie, *Eccles. Cyclop.* s. v. ; Riddle, *Christian Antiquities* (Index) ; Walcott, *Sacred Archæol.* s. v.

Mensa Capitulāris and **Mensa Episcopālis** are the technical terms severally given to the *table support* of chapter members and the incumbents of the episcopal office. So long as communistic life prevailed in churches endowed by monastic institutions, the expense for the table was provided for by the common property of the chapter. But in the 10th and 11th centuries, when canonical life was done away with, and the canons supported their own private establishments, the endowment was reduced by deducting therefrom the amount necessary to defray the expense of the table, and this sum was apportioned, and consequently the term (1) *mensa capitularis* for that share of the table endowment which was to defray the table expenses of the chapter members, and (2) *mensa episcopalis* for the episcopal share. The chapter's portion was again subdivided according to the number of members belonging to a chapter, and the proportion of allowance for each particular person was determined by rank. The administration of the capitular property was usually intrusted to the provost, and that of the episcopal table estate to an official appointed by the bishop himself (vice-dominus) (Carol. M., capit I ao. 802, c. 13; Lothar I, capit ao. 824, c. 8). If any of the capitulary estates were to be sold, a permit of the bishop and all capitularies must be secured (c. 1, 2, 3, 8, x, *De his quæ fuint a prælat.* iii, 10; sext. c. 2, *De reb. eccl. non alien.* iii, 9). If any of the episcopal estates were to be sold, a permit of the pope had to be asked for (c. 8, x, *De reb. eccl. non alien.*). In cases where the episcopal chair is endowed with such goods, this regulation remains yet in force. See Wetzer und Welte, *Kirchen-Lexikon,* s. v.

Mensa Dei (*the Lord's table*), a term which has immediate reference to the Lord's Supper. The opposition between the expressions, "table of the Lord" and "table of dæmons" (see 1 Cor. xi), at once marks it out as a table set apart for sacred purposes. See ALTAR; TABLE.

Menses Papāles is the technical term for one form of papal investiture claimed by the incumbent of St. Peter's chair, in case the vacancy occurs within certain stated months. The present rules of the Roman chancel on this point are: "Cupiens Sanctissimus Dominus Noster pauperibus clericis et aliis benemeritis personis providere omnia beneficia ecclesiastica cum cura et sine cura, sæcularia et quorumvis ordinum regularia qualitercumque qualificata, et ubicumque existentia in singulis Januarii, Februarii, Aprilis, Maii, Julii, Augusti, Octobris, et Novembris mensibus, usque ad suæ voluntatis beneplacitum extra Romanam curiam, alias, quam per resignationem quocumque modo vacatura, ad collationem, provisionem, præsentationem, electionem, et quamvis aliam dispositionem quorumcunque collatorum et collatricium sæcularium et quorumvis ordinum regularium (non autem S. R. E. cardinalium, aut aliorum sub concordatis inter sedem apostolicam et quoscunque alios initis, et per eos qui illa acceptare et observare debuerant acceptatis, quæ lædere non intendit, comprehensorum) quomodolibet pertinentia dispositioni suæ generaliter reservavit," etc. It is to be remarked that the term *alternativa mensium* is sometimes used to designate the papal months, although they do not really have the same meaning. In the case of patriarchs, archbishops, or bishops, residing in their dioceses, the papal months are reduced from eight to six, the pope retaining only the uneven months (January, March, May, July, September, November).

The papal months originated in the 12th century. The reason was a desire of the popes to secure benefices to worthy but destitute members of the clergy. At first this was done by recommendations (*preces*); when this did not succeed, a real command was issued (*mandatum de providendo*). Gratian's decretal of 1151 contains no such mandate, as they originated shortly afterwards. One example of them, of the times of Innocent II, is given by Peter, abbot of Cluny, in his *Epistol.* lib. ii, ep. 33–35 (quoted in Gonzales Tellez, cap. 37, x, *De rescriptis,* i, 3, No. 4); another from Adrian IV (1154–1159), epist. 13 (Würdtwein, *Subsidia diplomatica* [Heidelb. 1774], tom. iv, p. ix); Mansi, *Collectio Conciliorum,* xxi, 805. If these mandates were not obeyed, it was then the practice to issue successively *literæ monitoriæ, præceptoriæ,* and *executoriæ.* The *mandata de providendo* came afterwards to be issued not only for actually vacant benefices, but also in advance (c. 19, x, *De rescriptis,* i, 3 : "Si qua [præbenda] tunc in eorum vacaret ecclesia vel proxima vacaturam"). The Council of Lateran of 1179, however, forbade to present to or even to promise benefices before they were vacant (c. 2, x, *De concess. præb. non vacatis,* iii, 8), and this defence

was renewed by Innocent III, Honorius III, and Boniface VIII; the practice was, however, justified on the ground that the promise did not specify any particular benefice. The churches often resisted these papal encroachments (see Richter, *Lehrbuch d. Kirchenrechts,* § 148; Thomassin, *Vetus ac nova ecclesiæ disciplina,* pt. ii, lib. i, cap. xliii, xliv), but their protestations were disregarded until, in the Council of Costnitz (1418), pope Martin V declared: "Ultra reservationes juris duæ partes sint in dispositione Papæ, et tertia pars remaneat in dispositione Ordinariorum; ita, quod duo prima cedant Papæ et tertium Ordinario, ita, quod per quamcumque aliam reservationem aut prærogativas non minuatur" (Van der Hardt, *Concilium Constantiense,* i, 1022 sq.). In France this was understood, in 1425, to give the pope eight months, the bishops four. By the Concordat of Vienna, in 1448, the pope was to have the disposal of vacant benefices during the six uneven months, and the bishops during the six others. The text of the concordat further states: "De cæteris dignitatibus et beneficiis quibuscunque, sæcularibus et regularibus vacaturis, ultra reservationes jam dictas, majoribus dignitatibus post pontificales in cathedralibus et principalibus in collegiatis exceptis, de quibus jure ordinario provideatur per illos inferiores, ad quos alias pertinet; idem sanctissimus dominus . . . non impediet, quo minus de illis, cum vacabunt de mensibus Februarii . . . libere disponatur per illos, ad quos collatio, provisio, præsentatio, electio aut alia quævis dispositio pertinebit . . . ." This seems evidently to signify that the other dignities are excepted from the *alternativa mensium;* but from the first this was understood to take the appointment to such dignities out of the *alternativa* to confer it on the pope. That the first was the true interpretation is apparent from its being the view taken by Martin V in the Council of Costnitz, whose tenor was more favorable even than that of the Concordat of Vienna to the papal cause. The later interpretation, however, was asserted by Pius II.

Vacancies occurring in consequence of a simple resignation, or of an exchange of benefices, are excepted from the *alternativa mensium* (Schlör, *De reservatione beneficiorum et dignitatum ex qualitate vacationis per resignationem* [Francf. ad M. 1777, 4to]), as also benefices under lay patronage (Ferraris, *Bibliotheca Canonica,* s. v. Beneficium, art. xi, note 18–20); most curacies, and other subordinate offices, are also excepted (Hedderich, *Diss. de parochiis in Germania,* etc. [Bonn, 1780, 4to], vol. i; Koch, *Sanctio pragmatica Germanorum illustrata* [Argentorati, 1789, 4to], p. 228, note 64).

Some dioceses, however, managed to elude the papal months entirely, by means of special papal edicts rendered for the purpose of securing other advantages (see Probst, *Turnarii ecclesiarum Germaniæ,* in Ullheimer, *Ad concordata nationis Germ. integra documentorum,* fasc. iv [Frankf. and Leips. 1777], p. 360, 376; Gudenus. *Codex diplomat.* tom. iv, No. cccxxiv, p. 717; Le Bret, *Magazin z. Gebrauche d. Staaten- u. Kirchengesch.* pt. viii, p. 4, etc.).

This law is still in force, but has in later times undergone various modifications. In Bavaria, the Concordat of 1817, art. x, states: "Regia Majestas ad canonicatus in sex mensibus apostolicis sive papalibus nominabit." For Prussia, the bull *De salute animarum,* of 1821, regulates that "Futuro autem tempore . . . canonicatus in mensibus Januarii, Martii, Maii, Julii, Semtembris, ac Novembris . . . vacantes conferentur, quemadmodum hactenus in capitulo Wratislaviensi hactenus factum est" (see Laspeyre, *Gesch. u. heutige Verfassung d. Kath. K. Preussens* [Halle, 1840], i, 339, 369, 370). In several other countries the law has fallen into disuse, and the appointments are made by the dioceses. See Herzog, *Real-Encyklop.* ix, 359.

Men-stealer (ἀνδραποδιστής), one who kidnaps or decoys a free person into slavery, an act condemned by the apostle among the highest crimes (1 Tim. i, 10). The seizing or stealing of a free-born Israelite, either to treat him as a slave or sell him as a slave to others, was by the law of Moses punished with death (Exod. xxi, 16; Deut. xxiv, 7), which the Jewish writers inform us was inflicted by strangling (see Wetstein, ad loc.). The practice was likewise forbidden among the Greeks (see Smith's *Dict. of Class. Ant.* s. v. Andrapodismou Graphe), and was condemned by law among the Romans (see Adams's *Roman Antiq.* p. 24). See SLAVE.

Mensurius, bishop of Carthage, of whose personal history but little is known, figured very prominently during the Diocletian persecutions. He seems to have been identified with the liberal or Arian party, and to have entertained heretical opinions, to which he gave publicity in books published under the title of " Sacred Scriptures." He opposed the enthusiastic veneration of the confessors who were kept in prison At the synod held at Ceuta, A.D. 305, he was arraigned for these acts, but, as most of the African bishops were accused of the same crime, the matter was passed over. Later a new charge was brought against Mensurius, and he had to defend himself at Rome in 311. It seems that he there cleared himself, but on his return home he died. Under his successor in the bishopric the Donatist quarrels opened. See DONATISTS.

Mental Reservation is a term for withholding or failing to disclose something that affects a statement, promise, oath, etc., and which, if disclosed, would materially vary its import. As this is a false and deceitful way of acting, it can not be approved by true morality. The Jesuits, indeed, allowed and taught their pupils to delude people by all kinds of mental reservations and deceitful intentions. With many of them the end sanctified the means, and so they taught that even deceit by false promises and perjuries is allowable, if only good things were attained thereby in the end. They defended this manner of action by the shallow pretext that mentally something very different has been promised or sworn to from what the spoken words declared. See CASUISTRY; MORAL PHILOSOPHY.

Mentone, BERNARD DE. See BERNARD.

Mentzer, Balthasar (1), a German Lutheran divine, greatly noted for his decided opposition to the Reformed Church theologians, was born in Allendorf, Hesse, February 27, 1565. He studied at the University of Marburg, where he excelled by the display of unusual talents and knowledge. After preaching for several years at Kirtorf, he was appointed in 1596 professor of theology at his alma mater. While in this position he was involved in many controversies because of his prince's tendency towards the doctrines of the Reformed Church. Mentzer was especially radical in his opposition to their views on the doctrine of *Ubiquity,* on *Iconoclasm,* the *Lord's Supper,* and the *Decalogue,* and in 1605 was actually forced to quit Marburg, and, together with his colleagues, Winckelmann and Leuchter, removed to Giessen, to take a position in the new university founded by landgrave Lewis, and there became one of the most renowned teachers. He died Jan. 6, 1627, at Marburg, to which place the university had been removed in the mean time.

Mentzer was a pure Lutheran; his Christian faith was a truly orthodox belief in the Christological dogma as furnished in the idiomatic and ubiquistic doctrine. He published many works, most of which bore a polemic character. His Latin works were afterwards collected and published by his son : *Opera theologica Latina* (Frankf. 1669, 2 vols. 8vo). His apologetic works against Romanism and the Reformed Church contain the *Exegesis Confessionis Augustanæ* (Giessen, 1603). Similar to this is his *Repetitio Chemnitiana.* Challenged by the work of the Romanist John Pistorius (*Wegweiser für alle verführte Christen*), he wrote *Anti-Pistorius sui disputatio de præcipuis quibusdam controversis capitibus* (Marburg, 1600):—*Evangelischer Wegweiser* (Marburg, 1603); and many others. He engaged in a controversy with John Crocius, professor at Marburg, against

whom he sent forth *Abstersio calumniarum J. Crocii, Apologetica, Anticrocia, Collatio Augustanæ Confessionis cum doctrina Calvini, Bezæ et sociorum* (1610). He had also a controversy with John Sadeel, of Paris and Geneva, Matthias Martinius, at Herborn, Paul Stein, at Cassel, Schönfeld, and Pareus : *Elencheus errorum J. Sadeelis in libello de veritate humanæ naturæ Christi* (Giessen, 1615):—*Elencheus errorum J. Sadeelis in libello de sacramentali manducatione* (Giessen, 1612):—*Anti-Martinius sive modesta et solida responsio,* etc. (Giessen, 1612); and many others. These polemics concerning the human nature of Christ, the sacramental use of the Lord's Supper, and the idiomatic use of *impanation,* give an idea of the logic of the Reformed criticism and the tenacity of the Lutheran defence. The humanity of Christ, the "Word was made flesh, and dwelt among us," are the principal points of Mentzer's theological grounds. He condemns his opponent's view as Arianistic: "Non igitur existimo, unquam exstitisse inter Christianos, qui Christo homini vel naturæ ejus humanæ minus gloriæ et auctoritatis et potentiæ tribuendum censuerint, quam Martinium hunc Freienhagensem" (*Anti-Martinius,* p. 167). In a communication to Martinius, Mentzer's assertion, "Ipsa divina præsentia juxta sacras literas est actio," provoked another controversy with his colleagues at Giessen, professors Winckelmann and Gisenius. This controversy was settled by the landgrave's personal interference only, who in 1607 imposed silence and peace on all parties. Mentzer's principal work is *Necessaria et justa defensio contra injustas criminationes L. Osiandri, M. Nicolai, Th. Tummii, in qua multi de persona et officio Christi erroris deteguntur et refutantur* (1624). This was answered in 1625 in Thummi's *Acta.* In 1618 Mentzer was called to Wolfenbüttel to give his opinion on Calixtus's *Epitome theologiæ.* He never went thither, but sent a criticism to his son-in-law, superintendent Wiedeburg, acknowledging the eminent talents of the author, but judging his epitome from his own narrow and exclusive stand-point. See Witten, *Mem. Theol.* i, 223 sq.; Strieder, *Hessische Gelehrtengeschichte,* vol. viii ; Walch, *Relig. Streitigkeiten innerhalb der Luth.-Kirche;* also, *Streitigkeiten ausserhall der Luther.-Kirche,* iii, 505 ; Henke, *Georg. Calixtus,* i, 123, 282, 307, 321 ; ii, 23 ; *Memor. Theol.* i, 223 sq. ; Gasz, *Gesch. der protest. Theol.* i, 277, 278 ; Walch, *Biblioth. theologica,* ii, 654 ; Dorner, *Doctrine of the Person of Christ,* ii, 243 et al. (J. H. W.)

Mentzer, Balthasar (2), son of the preceding, was born May 14, 1614, at Giessen, and was educated at the University of Marburg, which he entered in 1628, but completed his education at Strasburg and Jena. In 1640 he became professor at Marburg, in 1648 at Rinteln. He returned four years after and got a position at the University cf Giessen, and died July 28, 1679. His most important works are, *Compendium Theol. Christ.* (Rinteln, 1649):—*Quæstt. Theol. ad Aug. Conf.* (Darmst. 1668; often republished; at last at Rinteln, 1753):— *De termino vitæ* (1647), and *Abgenöthigte fernere Erklärung der Frage vom Ziel des menschlichen Lebens* (Rinteln, 1649):—*Kurzes Bedenken über Wahrenberg's Gespräch von der Polygamie* (Darmst. 1671); etc.

Menu. See MANU.

Menúchah (Heb. *Menuchah'*, מְנוּחָה, *rest,* as often) appears in the marg. of the A. V. at Judg. xx, 43 (Sept. [Vat.] ἀπὸ Νουά, Vulg. and A. V. "with ease," as if מִמְּנוּחָה), and Jer. li, 59 (Sept. δώρων, Vulg. *prophetiæ,* A. V. "quiet"). The Sept. likewise, in the remarkable list of additional towns in Judah (Josh. xv, 59), seems to make mention of it (Μανοχώ). Fürst (*Heb. Lex.* s. v.) thinks it the place in Benjamin called *Manochath* (1 Chron. viii, 6) or *Hatsi-ham-Menuchoth* (1 Chron. ii, 54). But all this is doubtful, and the word is rather an appellative. See MENUCHITE.

Menúchite or **Menúchoth** is given in the margin of the A. V. at 1 Chron. ii, 52, 54, in place of "Manahethite" of the textual rendering, as an alternative rendering of the Heb. *Menuchoth'* (מְנָחוֹת, ver. 52) or *Menachti'* (מְנַחְתִּי, ver. 54), which, as far as can be gathered from the obscure and confused passage, seems to be assigned as a general name of certain descendants of Judah, classified according to some locality settled or inhabited by them. Some (as apparently the A. V.) have referred this presumed place to the Manahath (q. v.) of 1 Chron. viii, 6; but this was either in Benjamin or Moab, certainly not in Judah. Others have found it in the Menuchah (q. v.) supposed to be referred to in Judg. xx, 43; but of the existence of this latter there is very great doubt. The ancient versions are able to make nothing intelligible out of the passage. Thus much is clear, that the *Hatsi-ham-Menuchoth* of ver. 52 corresponds as one half either of a lineage or of a district to the other half which appears in ver. 54 as *Hatsi-ham-Menachti*; but the relation between the noun Menuchoth and the adjective Menachthite we cannot discover. The latter of these two moieties is predicated of the son of Salma, the former of the son of Shobal. As of Shobal, however, *sons* are announced, we must recognise in Haroeh the name of another son; moreover, in chap. iv, 2, Reaiah appears as a son of Shobal, and this name so closely resembles Haroeh that we may suppose them identical. Haroeh and Reaiah are thus associated as the two sons of Shobah, and the ו connective ("and") may have originally stood between them in the text. Haroeh, indeed, may be resolved into the article and a participle (הָרֹאֶה = *the seer*), and thus be reduced to a mere appellation or attribute, but this would not help the narrative. Hatsi-ham-Menuchoth, on the other hand, is a less natural form for a patrial name than Hatsi-ham-Menachti, and this would seem to designate an original or ancestor by the name of Manachath (מְנַחַת), a form which actually occurs elsewhere as the name of a man. See MANAHATH. Now as Shobal is repeatedly stated to be the "father" (founder) of Kirjath-jearim, his sons of course, in part at least, settled there. We may therefore clear up ver. 52 by interpreting it as meaning that Shobal had two sons, Reaiah and Manahath, and that part of the descendants of the latter settled at Kirjath-jearim, becoming the heads of the families named in ver. 53. The other portion of the Manahathites appear to have colonized at Zorah, in the adjoining territory of Dan; and are hence, for some reason not clear, classed in ver. 54 with the descendants of Shobal's brother Salma as "Zorites," that city being perhaps chiefly occupied by the latter. Yet it is a singular circumstance that in chap. iv, 1, 2, Reaiah's posterity are said to have peopled this city, if, indeed, that be the just interpretation of "Zorathites." See ZORAH.

Menyměni (Μενυμένοι, *the initiated*) was the name given, especially in the 4th and 5th centuries, to full members of the Church of Christ. It originated in the supposed analogy between baptism and the rites of initiation into the sacred mysteries of the heathen. The phrase ἴσασιν οἱ μεμυημένοι, "the initiated know," occurs about fifty times in the works of Augustine and Chrysostom. In like manner μῶσται, μυσταγώγηγτοι, μυσταγωγοί, and other terms borrowed from the heathen mysteries, are applied to the Christian rites. All these expressions, which came into general use in the 4th century, mark the prevalence of that system of secret instruction or doctrine which we noticed in the article ARCANI DISCIPLINA. See Riddle, *Christian Antiquities*, p. 195.

Meön. See BAAL-MEON; BETH-BAAL-MEON; BETH-MEON.

Meön'enim (Heb. *Meönenim'*) occurs in the Auth. Vers. (Judg. ix, 37) in the proper name Elon-Meonenim (אֵלוֹן מְעוֹנְנִים), "the plain;" or, as it should be rendered, *the oak of Meonenim* (Sept. Ἠλων Μαωνενίμ v. r. δρύος ἀποβλεπόντων, marg. "regarders of times"). Me-

onenim (variously rendered in the Auth. Vers. "soothsayers," "regarders of times," etc.) means *sorcerers*, and is derived either from עוֹנָה, "time" (Exod. xxi, 10), from עַיִן, "the eye," or else, which is more probable, from עָנָן, "a cloud;" it means, therefore, those dealers in forbidden arts who observe times, or practice fascination, or take auguries from the signs of the sky. See DIVINATION. Whatever was its original meaning, Meonenim was afterwards used in a perfectly general sense (Deut. xviii, 10, 14; 2 Kings xxi, 6; Micah v, 12) for wizards. In this article, therefore, we are only concerned with "the oak of the sorcerers," a celebrated tree near Shechem, mentioned in Judg. ix, 37, where Gaal, son of Ebed, the Shechemite conspirator, standing "in the entering of the gate," saw the soldiers of Abimelech first on the hilltops, and then in two companies, of which one approached by the "oak of the sorcerers," which is evidently pointed out as a conspicuous land-mark. It would be the better suited for this purpose because oaks are rare in Palestine, except in the hills. For other trees used as land-marks, see Gen. xxxv, 8; 1 Sam. xxii, 6; x, 3; xiv, 2, etc. Now it happens that in Scripture no less than *four* other celebrated trees in the immediate neighborhood of Shechem are prominently mentioned in connection with important events, and it is interesting to inquire whether all or any of these can be identified with "the sorcerer's oak." See OAK.

1. In Gen. xii, 6 we are told that Abraham "passed through the land unto the place of Sichem, unto the oak of Moreh" (Sept. τὴν δρῦν τὴν ὑψηλήν), where the use of the singular points to *one* tree of note, although at Shechem there was a grove of oaks (Deut. xi, 30). It was, therefore, in all probability conspicuous for size and beauty, and the vision which Abraham there commemorated by building an altar would add to it a sacred and venerable association. See ABRAHAM.

2. In Gen. xxxv, 4 we read that Jacob, on his way to Bethel, took from his family all the strange gods which were in their hand, and all their ear-rings which were in their ears, and hid them under the oak which was by Shechem (הָאֵלָה אֲשֶׁר עִם־שְׁכֶם). The use of the article in this verse is not, indeed, absolutely decisive, but would lead naturally to the supposition that this tree was the one already so famous in the religious history of the Israelitish family. That אֵלָה is used (Sept. τερέβινθος) and not אַלּוֹן, is a consideration of no importance, for it seems certain that the two words are synonymous (see Gesenius, *Thesaur.* p. 50, 51), or at any rate are used interchangeably. See TEREBINTH.

3. In Josh. xxiv, 26, Joshua, after addressing the assembled tribes at Shechem, "took a great stone and set it up there under an oak (*the* oak, הָאֵלָה) that was by the sanctuary of the Lord." The use of the definite article again renders it probable that this is the same tree as that which had been connected with the memories of Abraham's vision, and Jacob's rejection of idolatrous possessions; and the probability is strengthened into certainty by the fact that Joshua's injunction in ver. 14 ("put away the gods which your fathers served on the other side of the flood") is almost identical with that which Jacob had addressed to his family on that very spot (Gen. xxxv, 2) some 300 years before. Kalisch, indeed, objects that a "sanctuary of the Lord" would never have been erected at the place of idols (*Genesis*, p. 586); but, to say nothing of the fact that *several* of the Jewish high-places seem to have been also connected with the worship of the Canaanites, a place where idols had been buried, and so rejected and scorned, would surely be most fitted for the sanctuary, especially if it had been hallowed by a previous protest made by the great forefather of the race against the idolatry which there surrounded him (Gen. xii, 7).

4. In Judg. ix, 6, we read that "all the men of Shechem . . . made Abimelech king, by the oak (A. V.

plain) of the pillar that was in Shechem" (עִם־אַלּוֹן מֻצָּב אֲשֶׁר בִּשְׁכֶם. The word מֻצָּב, *mutstsab'*, is very obscure, and Jerome's version, "quercus quæ stabat in Sichem," seems to show that it may once have *followed* אֲשֶׁר. The Sept. renders it πρὸς τῇ βαλάνῳ (τῇ εὑρετῇ τῆς στάσεως τῆς ἐν Σικίμοις, where στάσις means "a military station," a rendering approved by Gesenius (*Thesaur.* p. 904), who compares Isa. xxix, 3. Our A.V. refers it to the sacred stone set up by Joshua, and this seems a very probable rendering, from the constant use of the word *matstsebáh* for similar erections (Gen. xxviii, 18; Exod. xxiv, 4; 2 Kings iii, 2; Micah v, 13, etc.). It seems further possible that during the confusions which prevailed in the country after Joshua's death, the stone which he had erected beneath it, and which he invested, even though only in metaphor, with qualities so like those which the Canaanites attributed to the stones they worshipped — during these confused times this famous block may have become sacred among the Canaanites, one of their "matstsebahs" [see IDOL], and thus the tree have acquired the name of "the oak of Mutstsab" from the fetish below it. The argument that this tree cannot be identical with Jacob's, because *that* is spoken of as *near* (עַם), and *this* as in (ב) Shechem, is quite unconvincing, both because the use of the prepositions by Hebrew writers is by no means minutely accurate, in this way corresponding to their general ἀγεωγραφία, and because Shechem may mean the *district round the city*, as well as the city itself. (For a decisive case in point, see Josh. v, 13, where the Vulgate rightly renders בִּירִיחוֹ by "*in agris urbis* Jericho.") We believe, therefore, that all these trees are one and the same, which thus becomes connected with four most memorable events in the lives of Abraham, Jacob, Joshua, and Abimelech.

Was this tree also the "oak of the sorcerers?" There might at first seem to be a positive reason *against* the identification, because (1.) The name "sorcerers," or "enchanters," would not be particularly suitable to the tree, which Kalisch also thinks might with more propriety have been called the "oak of idols," or of "witchcraft," than the oak of enchanters (*Genesis*, p. 586); and (2.) Because Gaal evidently points to the Elon-Meonenim at a distance from the city, whereas Jacob's tree was in it. Of this second argument we have already disposed; and besides, Gaal's expression may merely mean that one company was on the *road which led by* "the sorcerer's oak." As regards the first argument, the Elon-Meonenim may have been the same as Jacob's tree, and yet *not* have received its name from the idols and amulets which Jacob buried there. The close connection of ear-rings with talismans and magic arts is well known, and in the Chaldee the word used for ear-ring is קדישא, so that it does seem reasonable to suppose that there is a connection between the name and the event. But if not, *may not the name have originated in some use made of the tree by the priests and necromancers of the neighboring shrine of Baal-Berith?* (Judg. viii, 33; ix, 36). If it be asked how it was that a tree so sacred as this could have received *an opprobrious name*, it must be borne in mind that this name only occurs on the lips of Gaal, who in all probability was an aboriginal Canaanite of the old royal family (ix, 28; comp. Gen. xxxiv, 2, 6), and who would therefore be likely to call the tree by a name derived from its associations with idolatrous rather than with Jewish worship. See GAAL.

Meön'othai (Heb. *Meönothay'*, מְעוֹנֹתַי, my habitations; Sept. Μαναθί v. r. Μαωναθεί), the father (? founder) of Ophrah, and apparently the brother of Hathath, the son of Othniel (1 Chron. iv, 14). B.C. post 1612.

Meph'aath [some *Mepha'ath*] (Heb. *Meypha'ath*, מֵיפַעַת, prob. *splendor*; once defectively written מֵפַעַת Josh. xiii, 18, and once [Kethib] מוֹפַעַת, Jer. xlviii, 21;

Sept. Μηφάαθ in Josh., Φαάθ v. r. Μαεφλά in Chron., and Μαφάς v. r. Μωφάθ in Jer.), a Levitical (Merarite) city (Josh. xxi, 37; 1 Chron, vi, 79) of the tribe of Reuben (Josh. xiii, 18), doubtless originally (like Heshbon, of which it formed a dependency) in the hands of the Amorites (Numb. xxi, 26), but afterwards belonging to Moab (Jer. xlviii, 21); probably situated near Kedemoth and Jahazah, in connection with which it is always mentioned. Eusebius (*Onomast.*) calls it *Mephath* (Μηφάθ), and states that it was still occupied by a Roman garrison as a defence against the Arabs of the neighboring desert. As the name implies a conspicuous position, the site may possibly correspond with that of the modern village with ruins on an eminence marked as *Um el-Weled* on Van de Velde's *Map*, east of Medeba. "The extended, and possibly later, form of the name which occurs in Chronicles and Jeremiah, as if *Mey Phaath*, 'waters of Phaath,' may be, as in other cases, an attempt to fix an intelligible meaning on an archaic or foreign word;" although the fuller form appears to be radical (so both Gesenius and Fürst, from יָפַע, *to glitter, be eminent*).

Mephib'osheth (Heb. *Mephibo'sheth*, מְפִיבֹשֶׁת [twice defectively מְפִבֹשֶׁת, 2 Sam, xix, 24; xxi, 8], *exterminator of* the *shame*, i. e. idols or Baal, see Simonis *Lex. V. T.* p. 160; Ewald, *Isr. Gesch.* ii, 383; Sept. Μεφιβόσεθ v. r. Μεμφιβοσθέ, Vulg. *Miphiboseth*, Josephus Μεμφιβοσθος), the name of two of king Saul's descendants. "Bosheth appears to have been a favorite appellation in Saul's family, for it forms a part of the names of no fewer than three members of it—Ish-bosheth and the two Mephi-bosheths. But in the genealogies preserved in 1 Chronicles these names are given in the different forms of Esh-baal and Merib-baal. The variation is identical with that of Jerub-baal and Jerub-besheth, and is in accordance with passages in Jeremiah (xi, 13) and Hosea (ix, 10), where Baal and Bosheth appear to be convertible or, at least, related terms, the latter being used as a contemptuous or derisive synonyme of the former. One inference from this would be that the persons in question were originally named Baal; that this appears in the two fragments of the family records preserved in Chronicles; but that in Samuel the hateful heathen name has been uniformly erased, and the nickname of Bosheth substituted for it. It is some support to this to find that Saul had an ancestor named Baal, who appears in the lists of Chronicles only (1 Chron. viii, 30; ix, 36). But such a change in the record supposes an amount of editing and interpolation which would hardly have been accomplished without leaving more obvious traces, in reasons given for the change, etc. How different it is, for example, from the case of Jerub-besheth, where the alteration is mentioned and commented on. Still the facts are as above stated, whatever explanation may be given of them." See ISHBOSHETH.

1. Saul's son by his concubine Rizpah, the daughter of Aiah (2 Sam. xxi, 8). He and his brother Armoni were among the seven victims who were surrendered by David to the Gibeonites, and by them crucified in sacrifice to Jehovah, to avert a famine from which the country was suffering. There is no doubt about this being the real meaning of the word יָקַע, translated here and in Numb. xxv, 4 "hanged up" (see Michaelis's *Supplement*, No. 1046; also Gesenius, *Thesaur.* p. 620; and Fürst, *Handwb.* p. 539 b). Aquila has ἀναπήγνυμι, understanding them to have been not crucified but impaled. The Vulgate reads *crucifixerunt* (ver. 9), and *qui affixi fuerant* (ver. 13). The Hebrew term is entirely distinct from תָּלָה, also rendered "to hang" in the A.V., which is its real signification. It is this latter word which is employed in the story of the five kings of Makkedah; in the account of the indignities practiced on Saul's body, 2 Sam. xxi, 12; on Baanah and Rechab by David, 2 Sam. iv, 12; and elsewhere.

The seven corpses, protected by the tender care of the mother of Mephibosheth from the attacks of bird and beast, were exposed on their crosses to the fierce sun of at least five of the midsummer months, on the sacred eminence of Gibeah. This period results from the statement that they hung from barley harvest (April) till the commencement of the rains (October); but it is also worthy of notice that the Sept. has employed the word ἐξηλιάζειν, "to expose to the sun." It is also remarkable that on the only other occasion on which this Hebrew term is used—Numb. xxv, 4—an express command was given that the victims should be crucified "in front of the sun." At the end of that time the attention of David was called to the circumstance, and also possibly to the fact that the sacrifice had failed in its purpose. A different method was tried: the bones of Saul and Jonathan were disinterred from their resting-place at the foot of the great tree at Jabesh-Gilead, the blanched and withered remains of Mephibosheth, his brother, and his five relatives, were taken down from the crosses, and father, son, and grandsons found at last a resting-place together in the ancestral cave of Kish at Zelah. When this had been done, "God was entreated for the land," and the famine ceased. B.C. 1053-1019. See RIZPAH.

2. The son of Jonathan and grandson of king Saul (2 Sam. iv, 4; in which sense "the son of Saul" is to be taken in 2 Sam. xix, 24; see Gesenius, Thesaur. p. 216); called also by the equivalent name of MERIBBAAL (1 Chron. ix, 40). The following account of his history and character is sufficiently detailed to set forth the important relations which he held to the adventures and reign of his father's successor.

1. His life seems to have been, from beginning to end, one of trial and discomfort. The name of his mother is unknown. There is reason to think that she died shortly after his birth, and that he was an only child. At any rate, we know for certain that when his father and grandfather were slain on Gilboa he was an infant of but five years old. B.C. 1053. He was then living under the charge of his nurse, probably at Gibeah, the regular residence of Saul. The tidings that the army was destroyed, the king and his sons slain, and that the Philistines, spreading from hill to hill of the country, were sweeping all before them, reached the royal household. The nurse, perhaps apprehending that the enemy were seeking to exterminate the whole royal family, fled, carrying the child on her shoulder. This is the statement of Josephus (ἀπὸ τῶν ὤμων, Ant. vii, 5, 5); but it is hardly necessary, for in the East children are always carried on the shoulder (see Lane's Mod. Egyptians, ch. i, p. 52, and the art. CHILD). But in her panic and hurry she stumbled, and Mephibosheth was precipitated to the ground with such force as to deprive him for life of the use of both feet (2 Sam. iv, 4). These early misfortunes threw a shade over his whole life, and his personal deformity—as is often the case where it has been the result of accident—seems to have exercised a depressing and depreciatory influence on his character. He can never forget that he is a poor lame slave (2 Sam. xix, 26), and unable to walk; a dead dog (ix, 8); that all the house of his father were dead (xix, 28); that the king is an angel of God (ib. 27), and he his abject dependent (ix, 6, 8). He receives the slanders of Ziba and the harshness of David alike with a submissive equanimity which is quite touching, and which effectually wins our sympathy.

2. After the accident which thus embittered his whole existence, Mephibosheth was carried with the rest of his family beyond the Jordan to the mountains of Gilead, where he found a refuge in the house of Machir ben-Ammiel, a powerful Gadite or Manassite sheik at Lo-debar, not far from Mahanaim, which during the reign of his uncle Ishbosheth was the head-quarters of his family. By Machir he was brought up (Josephus, Ant. vii, 5, 5); there he married, and there he was living at a later period, when David, having completed the

subjugation of the adversaries of Israel on every side, had leisure to turn his attention to claims of other and less pressing descriptions. The solemn oath which he had sworn to the father of Mephibosheth at their critical interview by the stone Ezel, that he "would not cut off his kindness from the house of Jonathan forever: no, not when Jehovah had cut off the enemies of David each one from the face of the earth" (1 Sam. xx, 15); and again, that "Jehovah should be between Jonathan's seed and his seed forever" (ver. 42), was naturally the first thing that occurred to him, and he eagerly inquired who was left of the house of Saul, that he might show kindness to him for Jonathan's sake (2 Sam. ix, 1). So completely had the family of the late king vanished from the western side of Jordan that the only person to be met with in any way related to them was one Ziba, formerly a slave of the royal house, but now a freed man, with a family of fifteen sons, who, by arts which, from the glimpse we subsequently have of his character, are not difficult to understand, must have acquired considerable substance, since he was possessed of an establishment of twenty slaves of his own. From this man David learned of the existence of Mephibosheth. Royal messengers were sent to the house of Machir at Lo-debar, in the mountains of Gilead, and by them the prince and his infant son Michah (comp. 1 Chron. ix, 40) were brought to Jerusalem. The interview with David was marked by extreme kindness on the part of the king, and on that of Mephibosheth by the fear and humility which have been pointed out as characteristic of him. He leaves the royal presence with all the property of his grandfather restored to him, and with the whole family and establishment of Ziba as his slaves, to cultivate the land and harvest the produce. He himself is to be a daily guest at David's table. From this time forward he resided at Jerusalem (2 Sam. ix). B.C. cir. 1037. See Kitto's Daily Bible Illust. ad loc.

3. An interval of about fourteen years now passes, and the crisis of David's life arrives. See DAVID. Of Mephibosheth's behavior on this occasion we possess two accounts—his own (2 Sam. xix, 24-30), and that of Ziba (xvi, 1-4). They are naturally at variance with each other. (1.) Ziba meets the king on his flight at the most opportune moment, just as David has undergone the most trying part of that trying day's journey, has taken the last look at the city so peculiarly his own, and completed the hot and toilsome ascent of the Mount of Olives. He is on foot, and is in want of relief and refreshment. The relief and refreshment are there. There stand a couple of strong he-asses ready saddled for the king or his household to make the descent upon; and there are bread, grapes, melons, and a skin of wine; and there—the donor of these welcome gifts—is Ziba, with respect in his look and sympathy on his tongue. Of course the whole, though offered as Ziba's, is the property of Mephibosheth: the asses are his, one of them his own riding animal (חֲמוֹר, both in xvii, 2, and xix, 26); the fruits are from his gardens and orchards. But why is not their owner here in person? Where is the "son of Saul?" He, says Ziba, is in Jerusalem, waiting to receive from the nation the throne of his grandfather, that throne from which he has so long been unjustly excluded. Such an aspiration would be very natural, but it must have been speedily dissipated by the thought that he at least would be likely to gain little by Absalom's rebellion. Still it must be confessed that Ziba's tale at first sight is a most plausible one, and that the answer of David is no more than was to be expected. So the presumed ingratitude of Mephibosheth is requited with the ruin he deserves, while the loyalty and thoughtful courtesy of Ziba are rewarded by the possessions of his master, thus reinstating him in the position which he seems to have occupied on Mephibosheth's arrival in Judah. (2.) Mephibosheth's story—which, however, he had not the opportunity of telling

until several days later, when he met David returning to his kingdom at the western bank of the Jordan—was very different from Ziba's. He had been desirous to fly with his patron and benefactor, and had ordered Ziba to make ready his ass that he might join the cortége. But Ziba had deceived him, had left him, and not returned with the asses. In his helpless condition he had no alternative, when once the opportunity of accompanying David was lost, but to remain where he was. The swift pursuit which had been made after Ahimaaz and Jonathan (2 Sam. xvii) had shown what risks even a strong and able man must run who would try to follow the king. But all that he could do under the circumstances he had done. He had gone into the deepest mourning possible (the same as in xii, 20) for his lost friend. From the very day that David left he had allowed his beard to grow ragged, his crippled feet were unwashed (Jerome, however, *pedibus infectis*—alluding to false wooden feet which he was accustomed to wear, *Quæst. Heb.* ad loc.) and untended, his linen remained unchanged. That David did not disbelieve this story is shown by his revoking the judgment he had previously given. That he did not entirely reverse his decision, but allowed Ziba to retain possession of half the lands of Mephibosheth, is probably due partly to weariness at the whole transaction, but mainly to the conciliatory frame of mind in which he was at that moment. "Shall, then, any man be put to death this day?" is the key note of the whole proceeding. David could not but have been sensible that he had acted hastily, and was doubtless touched by the devotedness of his friend's son, as well as angry at the imposition of Ziba; but, as he was not wholly convinced of Mephibosheth's innocence, and as there was at the time no opportunity to examine fully into the matter, perhaps also actuated by the pride of an already expressed judgment or by reluctance to offend Ziba, who had adhered to him when so many old friends forsook him, he answered abruptly, "Why speakest thou any more of thy matters? I have said, Thou and Ziba divide the land." The answer of Mephibosheth was worthy of the son of the generous Jonathan, and, couched as it is in Oriental phrase, shows that he had met a better reception than he had expected : "Yea, let him take all; forasmuch as my lord the king is come again in peace unto his own house" (2 Sam. xix, 24-30). B.C. cir. 1023.

4. We hear no more of Mephibosheth, except that David was careful that he should not be included in the savage vengeance which the Gibeonites were suffered to execute upon the house of Saul for the great wrong they had sustained during his reign (2 Sam. xxi, 7). B.C. cir. 1019. Through his son Micah the family of Saul was continued to a late generation (1 Chron. ix, 40 sq.).

On the transaction between David and Mephibosheth, see J. G. Elsner, *Ueb. die gerechte Unschuld u. Redlichkeit Mephiboseths* (Frankf. u. Leipz. 1760); Niemeyer, *Charakt.* iv, 434 sq.; Kitto's *Daily Bible Illust.* ad loc.; Blunt, *Undesigned Coincidences,* ad loc.; Hall, *Contemplations,* ad loc.; H. Lindsay, *Lectures,* ii, 102; Doddridge, *Sermons,* i, 177; Ewald, *Hist. of Israel* (Engl. transl. iii, 191). See ZIBA.

Me′rab (Heb. *Merab′,* מֵרָב, *increase;* Sept. Μερόβ and Μερώβ; Josephus Μερόβη, *Ant.* vi, 6, 5), the eldest of the two daughters of king Saul (doubtless by his wife Ahinoam), and possibly the eldest child (1 Sam. xiv, 49). She first appears (B.C. cir. 1062) after the victory over Goliath and the Philistines, when David had become an inmate in Saul's house (1 Sam. xviii, 2), and immediately after the commencement of his friendship with Jonathan. In accordance with the promise which he made before the engagement with Goliath (xvii, 25), Saul betrothed Merab to David (xviii, 17), but it is evidently implied that one object of thus rewarding his valor was to incite him to further feats, which might at last lead to his death by the Philistines. David's hesi-

VI.—4*

tation looks as if he did not much value the honor, although his language in ver. 18 may be only an Oriental form of self-depreciation (comp. 1 Sam. xviii, 23; xxv, 42; 2 Sam. ix, 8); at any rate before the marriage Merab's younger sister Michal had displayed her attachment for David, and Merab was then married to Adriel the Meholathite, who seems to have been one of the wealthy sheiks of the eastern part of Palestine, with whom the house of Saul always maintained an alliance. To Adriel she bore five sons, who formed five of the seven members of the house of Saul who were given up to the Gibeonites by David, and by them impaled as a propitiation to Jehovah on the sacred hill of Gibeah (2 Sam. xxi, 8). See RIZPAH.

The Authorized Version of this passage is an accommodation, rendering יָלְדָה, "she brought up," although it has "she bare" for the same Hebrew word in the previous part of the verse. The Hebrew text has "the five sons of Michal, daughter of Saul, which she bare to Adriel," and this is followed in the Sept. and Vulgate. The Targum explains the discrepancy thus : "The five sons of Merab (which Michal, Saul's daughter, brought up) which she bare," etc. The Peshito substitutes Merab (in the present state of the text "Nodob") for Michal. J. H. Michaelis, in his Hebrew Bible (2 Sam. xxi, 10), suggests that there were two daughters of Saul named Michal, as there were two Elishamas and two Eliphalets among David's sons. Probably the most feasible solution of the difficulty is that "Michal" is the mistake of a transcriber for "Merab;" but, if so, it is manifest from the agreement of the versions and of Josephus (*Ant.* vii, 4, 30) with the present text, that the error is one of very ancient date. See MICHAL.

Meraï′ah (Heb. *Merayah′,* מְרָיָה, *resistance;* Sept. 'Αμαρία v. r. Μαρέα; Vulg. *Maraja*), a chief priest, the "son" of Seraiah, contemporary with the high-priest Joiakim (Neh. xii, 12). B.C. post 536.

Merai′oth (Heb. *Merayoth′,* מְרָיוֹת, *rebellions;* Sept. Μεραιώθ, Μεραώθ, and Μαριώθ v. r. Μαριήλ), the name of one or more leading priests.

1. The son of Zerahiah and father of Amariah, a high-priest of the line of Eleazar (1 Chron. vi, 6, 7, 52; Ezra vii, 3). B.C. considerably ante 1062. It was thought by Lightfoot that he was the immediate predecessor of Eli in the office of high-priest, and that at his death the high-priesthood changed from the line of Eleazar to the line of Ithamar (*Temple Service,* iv, § 1). In 1 Chron. ix, 11; Neh. xi, 11, his name appears to have become transposed between those of Zadok and Ahitub, instead of its proper place after the latter, as may be seen from 1 Chron. vi, 6-12. See HIGH-PRIEST.

2. A chief priest whose son Helkai was contemporary with the high-priest Joiakim (Neh. xii, 15); doubtless identical with the MEREMOTH of ver. 3.

Me′ran (Μερράν, Vulg. *Merrha*), a place mentioned along with Theman as famous for its merchants and its wise men (Bar. iii, 23). The association with the Hagarenes leads us to seek for Meran in Arabia. It may be *Mohrah* in Desert Arabia, or *Marane,* of which Pliny speaks (*N. H.* vi, 28, 32). Strabo (xvi, 4, p. 776) and Diodor. Sic. (iii, 43) also mention the Μαραΐται. The conjecture of Grotius that it is the *Mearah* mentioned in Josh. xiii, 4, and that of Hävernick (*De libro Baruch,* p. 5) that it is the Syrian town *Maarah,* are mere guesses (comp. Fritzsche, *Exeget. Hdb. z. Apok.* ad loc.).—Kitto. The suggestion of Hitzig (*Psalmen,* ii 119) that Meran is merely a corruption of "Medan" or "Midian," owing to the ready mistake by a translator of ד for ר, is more plausible, although there is little evidence of a Hebrew original for this portion of Baruch. Junius and Tremellius give *Medanœi,* and their conjecture is supported by the appearance of the Midianites as nomade merchants in Gen. xxxvii. Both Medan and Midian are enumerated among the sons of Keturah in Gen. xxv, 2, and are closely connected with the Dedanim, whose "travelling companies," or caravans, are frequently alluded to (Isa. xxi, 13; Ezek. xxvii, 15).

Mera'ri (Heb. *Merari'*, מְרָרִי, *sad;* Sept. Μεραρί), the youngest son of Levi, probably born in Canaan (Gen. xlvi, 11; Exod. vi, 16; Numb. iii, 17; 1 Chron. vi, 1). B.C. 1874. Of Merari's personal history, beyond the fact of his birth before the descent of Jacob into Egypt, and of his being one of the seventy who accompanied Jacob thither, we know nothing whatever (Gen. xlvi, 8, 11). He became the head of the third great division (מִשְׁפָּחָה) of the Levites, whose designation in Hebrew is the same as that of their progenitor, only with the article prefixed, viz. הַמְּרָרִי, i. e. the Merarites (Exod. vi, 19), who during the march through the desert had charge of the materials of the Tabernacle (Numb. iii, 36; iv, 30 sq.), for the transportation of which they were provided with four carts, each drawn by a yoke of oxen (Numb. vii, 8). In Palestine they were assigned twelve trans-Jordanic cities for a residence (Josh. xxi, 7, 34 sq.). See MERARITE.

Merari (Μεραρί v. r. Μεραρεί) was likewise the name of the father of Judith (Judith viii, 1; xvi, 7).

Mera'rite (Heb. same as *Merari*, Sept. Μεραρί, Auth. Vers. "Merarites"), the patronymic title of the descendants of MERARI (Numb. xxvi, 57). Their prominence among the Levitical families justifies a somewhat copious treatment of the subject.

At the time of the exodus, and the numbering in the wilderness, the Merarites consisted of two families, the Mahlites and the Mushites, Mahli and Mushi being either the two sons or the son and grandson of Merari (1 Chron. vi, 19, 47). Their chief at that time was Zuriel, and the whole number of the family, from a month old and upwards, was 6200; those from thirty years old to fifty were 3200. Their charge was the boards, bars, pillars, sockets, pins, and cords of the Tabernacle and the court, and all the tools connected with setting them up. In the encampment their place was to the north of the Tabernacle, and both they and the Gershonites were "under the hand" of Ithamar, the son of Aaron. Owing to the heavy nature of the materials which they

GENEALOGICAL TABLE OF THE MERARITES.

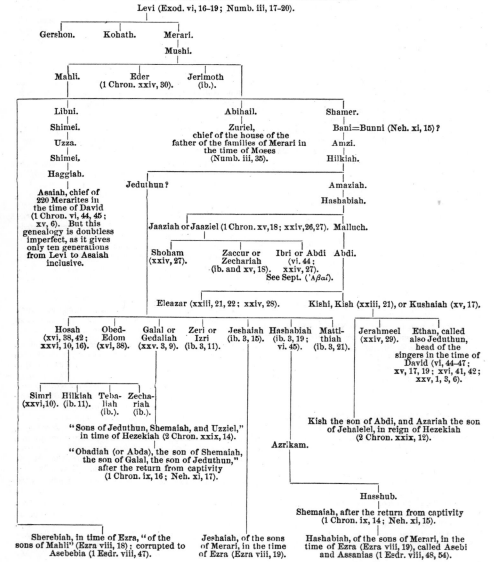

had to carry, four wagons and eight oxen were assigned to them; and in the march both they and the Gershonites followed immediately after the standard of Judah, and before that of Reuben, that they might set up the Tabernacle against the arrival of the Kohathites (Numb. iii, 20, 33–37; iv, 29–33, 42–45; vii, 8; x, 17, 21). In the division of the land by Joshua, the Merarites had twelve cities assigned to them, out of Reuben, Gad, and Zebulon, of which one was Ramoth-Gilead, a city of refuge, and in later times a frequent subject of war between Israel and Syria (Josh. xxi, 7, 34–40; 1 Chron. vi, 63, 79–81). In the time of David Asaiah was their chief, and assisted with 220 of his family in bringing up the ark (1 Chron. xv, 6). Afterwards we find the Merarites still sharing with the two other Levitical families the various functions of their caste (1 Chron. xxiii, 6, 21–23). Thus a third part of the singers and musicians were Merarites, and Ethan or Jeduthun was their chief in the time of David. See JEDUTHUN. A third part of the door-keepers were Merarites (1 Chron. xxiii, 5, 6; xxvi, 10, 19), unless, indeed, we are to understand from ver. 10 that the door-keepers were all either Kohathites or Merarites, to the exclusion of the Gershonites, which does not seem probable. In the days of Hezekiah the Merarites were still flourishing, and Kish, the son of Abdi, and Azariah, the son of Jehalelel, took their part with their brethren of the two other Levitical families in promoting the reformation, and purifying the house of the Lord (2 Chron. xxix, 12, 15). After the return from captivity Shemaiah represents the sons of Merari, in 1 Chron. ix, 14; Neh. xi, 15, and is said, with other chiefs of the Levites, to have "had the oversight of the outward business of the house of God." There were also at that time sons of Jeduthun under Obadiah or Abda, the son of Shemaiah (1 Chron. ix, 16; Neh. xi, 17). A little later again, in the time of Ezra, when he was in great want of Levites to accompany him on his journey from Babylon to Jerusalem, "a man of good understanding of the sons of Mahli" was found, whose name, if the text here and at ver. 24 is correct, is not given. "Jeshaiah, also, of the sons of Merari," with twenty of his sons and brethren, came with him at the same time (Ezra viii, 18, 19). But it seems pretty certain that Sherebiah, in ver. 18, is the name of the Mahlite, and that both he and Hashabiah, as well as Jeshaiah, in ver. 19, were Levites of the family of Merari, and not, as the actual text of ver. 24 indicates, priests. The copulative ו has probably fallen out before their names in ver. 24, as appears from ver. 30 (see also 1 Chron. ix, 14; Neh. xii, 24). See LEVITE.

The above table gives the principal descents, as far as it is possible to ascertain them. But the true position of Jaaziah, Mahli, and Jeduthun is doubtful. Here too, as elsewhere, it is difficult to decide when a given name indicates an individual, and when the family called after him, or the head of that family. It is sometimes no less difficult to decide whether any name which occurs repeatedly designates the same person, or others of the family who bore the same name, as e. g. in the case of Mahli, Hilkiah, Shimri, Kishi or Kish, and others. As regards the confusion between Ethan and Jeduthun, it may perhaps be that Jeduthun was the patronymic title of the house of which Ethan was the head in the time of David. Jeduthun might have been the brother of one of Ethan's direct ancestors before Hashabiah, in which case Hashabiah, in 1 Chron. xxv, 3, 19, might be the same as Hashabiah in vi, 45. Hosah and Obededom seem to have been other descendants or clansmen of Jeduthun, who lived in the time of David; and, if we may argue from the name of Hosah's sons, Simri and Hilkiah, that they were descendants of Shamer and Hilkiah, in the line of Ethan, the inference would be that Jeduthun was a son either of Hilkiah or Amaziah, since he lived after Hilkiah, but before Hashabiah. The great advantage of this supposition is, that while it leaves to Ethan the patronymic designation Jeduthun, it draws a

wide distinction between the term "sons of Jeduthun" and "sons of Ethan," and explains how in David's time there could be sons of those who are called sons of Jeduthun above thirty years of age (since they filled offices, 1 Chron. xxvi, 10), at the same time that Jeduthun was said to be the chief of the singers. In like manner it is possible that Jaaziah may have been a brother of Malluch or of Abdi, and that if Abdi or Ibri had other descendants besides the lines of Kish and Eleazar, they may have been reckoned under the headship of Jaaziah. The families of Merari which were so reckoned were, according to 1 Chron. xxiv, 27, Shoham, Zaccur (apparently the same as Zechariah in 1 Chron. xv, 18, where we probably ought to read "Zaccur, son of Jaaziah," and xxvi, 11), and Ibri, where the Sept. has Ὠβδί, Ἀβαί, and Ἀβδί. See each name in its place.

Meratha'im (Heb. *Meratha'yim*, מְרָתַיִם, *double rebellion;* Sept. πικρῶς,Vulg. *dominantes*), a name given to Babylon (Jer. l, 21), symbolical of its intensely perverse character (see Henderson, *Comment.* ad loc.). The expression "the land of two dominations" seems especially to allude "to the double captivity which Chaldæa had inflicted on the nation of Israel (Jer. l, 21). This is the opinion of Gesenius, Fürst, Michaelis (*Bibel für Ungelehrten*), etc., and in this sense the word is taken by the versions generally, excepting that of Junius and Tremellius, which the A. V.—as in other instances—has followed here."

Merati, GAETANO MARIA, an Italian theologian, was born at Venice Dec. 23, 1668. He was educated in the regular order of the Theatians, afterwards taught philosophy and theology in the college belonging to his order, and in 1705 accompanied the Venetian ambassador to London. He went to Rome in 1716 as procurator-general of his order. Pope Benedict XIV honored him with his friendship. He died at Rome Sept. 8, 1744. Some of Merati's works are, *La vita soavemente regolata delle donne* (Venice, 1708, 12mo) :—*La Verità della Religione Cristiana e Cattolica di.nostrata ne' suoi fondamenti* (1721, 2 vols. 4to) :—*Novæ Observationes et Additiones ad Gavanti Commentaria in rubricas Missalis et Breviarii Romani* (Augsburg, 1740, 2 vols. 4to) :—six *Lettres dans les Epistolæ claror. Venetorum* (1746, 2 vols.), addressed to Mogliobecchi. He was also the editor of *Thesaurus sacrorum Rituum de Gavanti* (Rome, 1736–38, 4 vols. 4to), a work to which he made valuable contributions.

Merault, ATHANASE RÉNÉE, a noted French educator, was born at Paris in 1744, and was educated at the College of Jeuilly. Although possessing a very large fortune, he entered the Oratory in order to devote himself to the instruction of the young. After his twenty-fifth year he was director of the house of education. Compelled to leave Paris by the Revolution, he retired to Orleans, where his parents resided. Imprisoned in 1793, and set free again after the 9th of Thermidor, he remained in the city, and became in 1805 grand vicar of the bishopric of Bernier, which placed him at the head of the great seminary. The Church of Orleans is indebted to the abbot Merault for several religious and charitable institutions, to the foundation of which he devoted a large portion of his money. He died at Orleans June 13, 1835. His works are, *Les Apologistes Involontaires ou la Religion éternelle prouvée et défendue par les objections mêmes des incrédules* (Paris, 1806, anonymous, and 1820, 12mo) :—*Les Apologistes, ou la Religion Chrétienne prouvée par ses ennemis comme par ses amis* (Orleans, 1821, 8vo and 12mo); a continuation of the preceding work : — *Conspiration de l'impiété contre l'humanité* (Paris, 1822, 8vo) : — *Rapport sur l'histoire des Hébreux rapprochée des temps contemporains* (Orleans, 1825, 12mo) : — *Enseignements de la Religion* (Orleans, 1827, 5 vols. 12mo) : — *Recueil des Mandements sur l'instruction des peuples* (Paris, 1830, 12mo).

Merbes, BON DE, a French theologian, was born

in 1616 at Montdidier. He entered the congregation of the Oratory, and rose to much distinction. The doctorate of theology was conferred upon him. He died Aug. 2, 1684. His Latin works are excellent. Especial notice is due to his *Summa Christiana seu Orthodoxa morum disciplina ex Sacris Litteris, sanctorum patrum monumentis, conciliorum oraculis, summorum denique pontificum decretis fideliter excerpta,* etc. See Du Pin, *Bibliothèque du dix-septième siècle,* iv, 271.

Mercati, GIOVANNI BAPTISTA, a painter of the 17th century, was a native of S. Sepolcro, Tuscany. He achieved a high reputation at home, and his fame extended as far as Rome. Two of his historical frescos, representing *Our Lady,* are in S. Chiara; and at S. Lorenzo there is a picture of the titular, with other saints. In the Guides to Venice and Rome several of his works are mentioned; and in that of Leghorn, the only picture in the cathedral esteemed worthy of notice is that of the *Five Saints,* painted by Mercati with great care. See Lanzi's *History of Painting,* transl. by Roscoe (London, 1847, 3 vols. 8vo), i, 255.

Mercator, MARIUS. See MARIUS.

Mercein, T. F. RANDOLPH, a minister of the Methodist Episcopal Church, was born in New York City Nov. 27, 1825. He was converted in early youth, and joined the Presbyterian Church, to which his parents belonged. His educational advantages were very superior, as he was intended for the ministry. In his second year at college his health failed, and he was obliged to desist from all study. While at home he fell in with books that gave him a distaste for Calvinistic theology. He promptly joined the Methodists, was licensed to preach, and exercised his power as a Christian pastor for eleven years. He died at Sheffield, Mass., Sept. 15, 1856. "Of a high order of intellect, carefully educated, deeply serious and thoughtful, with a profound sense of ministerial responsibility, bold and faithful in the discharge of duty, gentle, amiable, and genial, he was eminently fitted to adorn both public and private life. His deep, ardent piety pervaded and beautified his whole being. He was emphatically a pure, humble, heavenly-minded man. His rare gifts made him an attractive speaker, a fine writer, a successful author, an accomplished debater, a choice friend. He was *loved* even more than he was admired" (Smith, *Sacred Memories of the N. Y. and N. Y. East Conf.* p. 75 sq.). His published works are, *Natural Goodness:—The Wise Master-Builder: — Childhood and the Church;* and numerous essays, etc., in the periodicals of the Church. All these evince great genius and earnest study, deeply imbued with the spirit of Christian love.—*Minutes of Conferences,* vi, 321; Dr. Dewey's *Lecture* (p. 298), of the "Pitt's Street Chapel Lectures" (Boston, Jewett & Co., 1858).

Mercer, JESSE, D.D., a Baptist minister, was born in Halifax County, N. C., Dec. 16, 1769. His early education was limited, yet he began to preach when only eighteen years of age; was ordained Nov. 7, 1789, and soon became pastor of a Church at Hutton's Fork (now Sardis), in Wilkes County. In 1793 he accepted a call to Indian Creek (or Bethany), in Oglethorpe County, whence he removed in 1796 to Salem, where he became preceptor in the academy, and also succeeded his father in the charge of the Phillips Mill, Powelton, and Bethesda churches for some time, and finally removed to the fork of the Little River, in Green County. In 1826 he attended the General Convention in Philadelphia, and at the end of the next year accepted a call from the Church at Washington, Wilkes County, where he continued until 1833, when he became editor of the *Christian Index,* a religious periodical. He was made D.D. by Brown University in 1835. He was for many years identified with the Georgia Association, acting as clerk of that body from 1795 till 1816, and afterwards as moderator till 1839; he was also connected with the Baptist Convention of the State of Georgia from its beginning in 1822, being its moderator until 1841, when his impaired health obliged him to resign. He became also one of the trustees of the college at Washington, and president of the mission board of the Georgia Association from 1830 to 1841. He died Sept. 6, 1841. Dr. Mercer published a large number of *Addresses, Circular Letters, Essays,* etc. See Mallory, *Memoir of the Rev. Jesse Mercer, D.D.;* Sprague, *Annals,* vi, 283.

Merchant (this and kindred terms, as *merchandise,* etc., are properly expressed by some form of the Heb. סָחַר, *sachar',* to *travel* about; Gr. ἔμπορος, a *passenger* to and fro; sometimes also by רָכַל, *rakal',* to *go* about; and occasionally by the title CANAANITE). Trade is of very great antiquity in the East (Niebuhr, *Trav.* iii, 4 sq.), and was sometimes carried on by sea (Prov. xxxi, 14; Psa. cvii, 23), but more commonly on land by means of a company associated for a mercantile journey (Gen. xxxvii, 25; Job vi, 18). See CARAVAN. The itinerant character and temporary location which appear in all the ancient notices of Oriental merchants, whether individuals or an association of several persons, is still a marked trait of the same class in the East (Hackett's *Illustrat. of Script.* p. 63). In the patriarchal times such parties of Ishmaelites passed through Canaan on their way to Egypt (Gen. xxxvii, 25, 28), and bartered with the nomades for various products of their herds in exchange for implements, apparel, and similar articles, and sometimes purchased slaves (Gen. xxxvii, 28; xxxix, 1). After the Hebrews became settled in Palestine, they were drawn into those forms of commercial relations that early existed, but rather passively than actively, since the Mosaic law little favored this profession (Michaelis, *Mos. Recht,* i, 238 sq.; Josephus's denial of all mercantile pursuits by his nation, *Apion,* i, 12, is probably too strong an expression), although the geographical position of their country would seem to be in general advantageous for it; but the circumscribed extent of their territory, the prevailing direction of the population to agriculture, which left few poor, their almost total want of those natural and artificial products most in demand for general traffic, and the preoccupation of the trade between Asia and Africa by two mercantile nations (the Phœnicians and Arabians), mostly precluded them from an independent commerce, for which, indeed, they were further incapacitated by the continuance of their sea-coast for the most part in the hands of the Canaanites and Philistines, who had, moreover, secured to themselves the great commercial route to Damascus, through the prominence of several cities in the northern part of Palestine (Bertheau, *Isr. Gesch.* p. 287). Yet the north-western Israelites appear quite early to have occupied a post in the Phœnician marts (Gen. xlix, 13; Deut. xxxiii, 18; Judg. v, 17). Solomon not only (as a royal monopoly) imported horses from Egypt, and traded them away in Syria by governmental salesmen (1 Kings x, 26; 2 Chron. i, 16, 17), but formed a commercial treaty with the king of Tyre for maritime enterprise (1 Kings ix, 26), and launched from the Edomitish ports of Ezion-geber and Elath, which David had acquired on the Red Sea, a fleet that sailed under the pilotage of Tyrian seamen into the Indian Ocean, and, after a three years' voyage, brought back gold, silver, ivory, sandal-wood, ebony, apes, peacocks, and other products of Chin-India (1 Kings x, 11; xxii, 22, 50; 2 Chron. ix, 10, 21). See OPHIR. After the death of Solomon this marine commerce shared the neglect of all the royal affairs, and the trade never revived, with the single exception of Jehoshaphat's undertaking (1 Kings xxii, 49), until these harbors passed entirely out of the control of the Israelites. See EDOMITE. What position the Jews held in the Phœnician traffic, or what profit the transit of Phœnician merchandise brought them, is only to be gleaned indirectly from the historical records (Bertheau, *Isr. Gesch.* p. 354); but that both these were not inconsiderable is clear from Ezek. xxvi;

2; xxvii, 17. The kingdom of Israel was probably more favored in this latter particular than that of Judah, as the principal thoroughfares of trade passed through its bounds. Commercial relations subsisted between Tyre and Judæa after the exile (Neh. xiii, 16), and even in New-Testament times (Acts xii, 20). From the Phœnicians the Hebrews imported, besides timber for edifices (1 Kings v; 1 Chron. xiv, 1), and sea-fish (Neh. xiii, 16), a great many foreign necessaries, and even luxuries (such as variegated stuffs, unguents, and peltries, purple garments, etc.), which for the most part came from Arabia, Babylonia, and India (comp. Ezek. xxvii), and sold in exchange wheat (comp. Acts xii, 20), oil (1 Kings v, 11), honey, dates, balsam (Hos. xii, 2; see Ezek. xxvii, 17), and also a fine species of fancy fabric, which the diligent hands of the women had prepared (Prov. xxxi, 24). Respecting the balance of trade we have no certain means of judging, and it is the more difficult to ascertain how this was adjusted, inasmuch as Palestine must have derived its supply of the metals likewise from foreigners. Yet we nowhere find any indication that the national wealth had sensibly diminished; on the contrary, the Israelites were able to endure an almost unbroken series of hostile attacks, often resulting in pillage, and always very exhaustive of money (1 Kings xiv, 26; xv, 18; 2 Kings xii, 18; xiv, 14; xvi, 18, etc.), while certain periods (Isa. ii, 7), and even individual tribes (Hos. xii, 9), were distinguished for opulence and luxury; perhaps the revenue was derived through the surrounding districts of Edom, Moab, and Phœnicia (see T. C. Tychsen, *De commerciis et navigationibus Hebræor. ante exil. Bab.*, in the *Comment. Gott.* vol. xvi; *Class. Hist.* p. 150 sq.; Hartmann, *Ueb. Pentat.* p. 751 sq.). After the exile the Hebrew commerce had a wider range, especially as many Jews had become scattered in foreign countries where they experienced many favors, so that the nation took a greater relish in this avocation and in its safe emoluments. Prince Simon invited commercial intercourse by the improvement of the harbor of Joppa; the Palestinian Jews, however, being still restrained by the discouragement of their law and their early mercantile prejudices, appear not to have risen to any great degree of activity in trade; and Herod's improved port at Cæsarea (Josephus, *Ant.* xv, 9, 6) was mostly occupied by foreigners, while under the Roman

Shop of an Eastern Clothes-dealer.

dominion traffic was encumbered by tolls and imposts, many commodities being even included in the list of government monopolies. Still Jewish love of gain prevailed wherever a favorable opportunity offered (Josephus, *Life*, p. 13), and laid claim to trading privileges (Josephus, *War*, ii, 21, 2). Internal, especially retail trade (enactments relative to which are contained in Lev. xix, 36; Deut. xxv, 13 sq.; comp. Hos. xii, 8), was particularly promoted by the high festivals, to which every adult Israelite resorted in pursuance of the national religion. In the cities open spaces at the gates were designated for the exposure of wares, and even Tyrian merchants frequented the market at Jerusalem (Neh. xiii, 16; see Hartman, ad loc.; comp. Zeph. i, 10; Zech. xiv, 2; and see Movers, *Phönic.* i, 50); a mart for sacrificial victims and sacred shekels being established in the outer court of the Temple itself (John ii, 14 sq.; Matt. xxi, 12). The Mishna contains notices of the early practice of beating down in price (*Nedar.* iii, 1), and of shop-keepers (*Maaseroth*, ii, 3). For the commerce of the Phœnicians, Egyptians (Isa. xlv, 14), Babylonians (Nah. iii, 16), and Arabians, see those articles respectively. See COMMERCE. In modern Oriental cities the retail trade is chiefly carried on in small shops, usually gathered together in a particular quarter or street, like the stalls in an Occidental market. See BAZAAR.

Merchants' Lecture, a lecture originally set up at Pinner's Hall in 1672 by the Presbyterians and Independents to defend the doctrines of the Reformation against popery and Socinianism. Some misunderstanding occurring, the Presbyterians removed to Salter's Hall. See LECTURE.

Mercier, Barthélemi, a learned French ecclesiastic and bibliographer, was born at Lyons April 4, 1734. At the age of fifteen he became a novice among the regular prebendaries of the collegiate church of Saint-Geneviève, in Paris, and after one year of probation he was allowed to take the vow. Immediately thereafter he was sent to the Abbey of Chatrices, in Champagne, and there studied rhetoric and philosophy. In 1754 he was made assistant to the learned Perigré, librarian of Saint-Geneviève, and in 1760 was appointed his successor. Four years later Mercier was invested with the abbotship of Saint-Léger, which was then vacant, at Soissons. In 1772, in consequence of some trouble which he had with his associates, he resigned his functions as an abbot. Being thus liberated from official duties, he travelled through Holland and the Netherlands, where he was in hopes of collecting the materials necessary for the compilation of certain works on which he was engaged. Although he had yet published only the *Supplement* to the history of printing by Marchand, he was warmly greeted wherever he went. In 1792 he was appointed a member of the so-called Monument Commission. In this capacity he exerted himself to rescue from destruction all private and public collections of art and literature. He also drew up for the use of librarians minute instructions touching the books intrusted to their custody, and a method for classifying them. Towards the latter part of his life, François de Neufchâteau, a clergyman and a fosterer of letters, granted him a pension of 2400 francs, the first annual instalment of which was paid to him in 1798. This assistance enabled Mercier to decline the generous offer of La Serna Santander, who had proposed to relinquish in favor of Mercier his own office of librarian at Brussels. He died in 1799. His writings are characterized by an evidence of profound erudition, together with system and perspicuity in all his researches. He published a large number of works, among which we may cite, *Lettres sur la Bibliographie instructive de M. Debure* (Paris, 1763, 8vo):—*Lettre sur le véritable auteur du Testament politique du Cardinal de Richelieu* (Paris, 1765, 8vo; all of which were extracted from the *Mémoires de Tréveux*):—*Consultation sur la question de savoir si les religieux de*

Saint-Geneviève sont ou ne sont pas Chanoines Réguliers (new ed. Paris, 1772, 4to):—*Opinion sur de prétendues prophéties qu'on applique aux événements presents* (Paris, 1791):—*Dissertations sur l'auteur de l'Imitation de Jésus-Christ*, par l'abbé Ghesquière (1775, 12mo). See *Notice sur la vie et les écrits de Mercier de Saint-Léger*, by Chardon de la Rochette.

Mercier, Christopher, a French ascetic author, was born at Dôle near the opening of the 17th century. He entered the Order of the Carmelites, and changed his worldly name to *Albert de Saint-Jacques.* He died in 1680. His most celebrated works are, *Vie de la Mère Thérèse de Jésus, fondatrice des Carmelites de la Franche Course* (Lyons, 1673, 4to) ; and *La Lumière aux vivants par l'expériences des morts* (Lyons, 1675, 8vo).

Mercier (or Le Mercier), Jean, in Latin *Mercerus*, a distinguished Huguenot, was born in Uzès, France, near the beginning of the 16th century. Destined for the bar, he studied law in Avignon, and also in Toulouse. But the dead languages having a powerful attraction for him, he devoted much of his time to the study of Greek, and ere long confined himself entirely to the pursuit of Hebrew and other Shemitic tongues. After having been the most noted pupil of Vatable, he became his successor, in 1546, to the chair of professor of Hebrew in the Royal College of France. Casaubon believed that Mercier was the most learned Hebraist of his day. When the second religious war broke out, Mercier was constrained to quit Paris. After the treaty of peace at Saint-Germain, he returned to France, but while passing through his native city he was carried away by the pestilence. He died a Protestant in 1562. Mercier published almost the whole of Jonathan's *Targum* on the Prophecies. He also wrote in Latin valuable commentaries on all the books of the Old Testament, and on the Gospel according to Matthew. His commentaries furnished matter to the *Synopsis Criticorum* of Utrecht (1634). He is also the author of *Tractatulus de accentibus Jobi, Proverbiorum, et Psalmorum, auctore R. Juda, filio Betham Hispano,* a translation from Hebrew (Paris, 1556, 4to):—*Liber de accentibus Scripturæ, auctore R. Juda, filio Balaam* (Paris, 1565, 4to):—*In Decalogum commentarius Rabbini Abraham, cognomento Ben-Ezra, interpr. J. Mercero* (Lyons, 1568, 4to) : — *Notæ in Thesaurum Linguæ Sanctæ Pagnini* (Lyons, 1575–95, fol.) — *Observationes ad Horæpollinis hieroglyphica* (Strasburg, 1595, 4to). He also published a *Commentary on the Canticles* and *Lectures on Genesis.* See Haag, *La France Protestante.*

Mercurianus, *Father,* a noted Romanist of the Order of the Jesuits, was a Belgian by birth. We know but little of his personal history, except that he stood very high in the estimation of pope Gregory XIII, who caused his advancement to the generalship of the order. He died Aug. 1, 1580. Nicolini, *Hist. of the Jesuits* (p. 150), tells us that "he was a simple and weak old man. Mercurianus," he continues, "exercised very little influence on the destinies of the order, and was the first general whose authority was held in little account."

Mercu'rius (the Roman name of the god *Mercury*, the *Hermes* of the Greeks, Ἑρμῆς, Acts xiv, 12 ; comp. Rom. xvi, 14 ; the name is of uncertain etymology), properly a Greek deity, whom the Romans identified with their god of commerce and bargains. In the Greek mythology Hermes was the son of Zeus and Maia, the daughter of Atlas, and is constantly represented as the companion of his father in his wanderings upon earth. On one of these occasions they were travelling in Phrygia, and were refused hospitality by all save Baucis and Philemon, the two aged peasants of whom Ovid tells the charming episode in his *Metam.* viii, 620–724, which appears to have formed part of the folk-lore of Asia Minor. See LYCAONIA. Mercury was the herald of the gods (Homer, *Od.* v, 28 ; *Hym. in*

Herm. 3), and of Zeus (*Od.* i, 38, 84 ; *Il.* xxiv, 333, 461), the eloquent orator (*Od.* i, 86 ; Horace, *Od.* i, 10, 1), inventor of letters, music, and the arts. He was equally characterized by adroitness of action and readiness of speech, being the representative of intelligence and craft among men (see Pauly's *Real-Encyklop.* iv, 1842). He was usually represented as a slender, beardless youth, but in an older Pelasgic figure he was bearded. The fact that he was the customary attendant of Jupiter when he appeared on earth (Ovid, *Fast.* v, 495; comp. *Metam.* ii, 731 sq.), explains why the inhabitants of Lystra (Acts xiv, 12), as soon as they were disposed to believe that the gods had visited them in the likeness of men, discovered Hermes in Paul, as the chief speaker, and as the attendant of Jupiter (see Kuinöl, *Comment.* ad loc.). It seems unnecessary to be curious whether the representations of Mercury in ancient statues accord with the supposed personal appearance of Paul (see Walch, *Diss. ad Acta Ap.* iii, 183 sq.), and especially in the matter of the *beard* of the latter, for all known representations of the god differ in much more important particulars from the probable costume of Paul (e. g. in the absence of any garment at all, or in the use of the short chlamys merely ; in the caduceus, the petasus, etc. (see Müller, *Ancient Art,* § 379–381.) It is more reasonable to suppose that those who expected to see the gods mixing in the affairs of this lower world, in human form, would not look for much more than the outward semblance of ordinary men.

Hermes (Mercury).

Mercurius. See HERMES TRISMEGISTUS.

Mercy (properly חֶסֶד, *che'sed,* kindness ; ἔλεος, *pity*), a virtue which inspires us with compassion for others, and inclines us to assist them in their necessities. That works of mercy may be acceptable to God, as Christ has promised (Matt. v, 7), it is not enough that they proceed from a natural sentiment of humanity, but they must be performed for the sake of God, and from truly pious motives. In Scripture mercy and truth are commonly joined together, to show the goodness that precedes and the faithfulness that accompanies the promises ; or, a goodness, a clemency, a mercy that is constant and faithful, and that does not deceive. Mercy is also taken for favors and benefits received from God or man ; for probity, justice, goodness. Merciful men—in Hebrew, *chasdim*—are men of piety and goodness. Mercy is often taken for giving of alms, Prov. xiv, 34; xvi, 6; Zach. vii, 9. See CHARITY.

Mercy, as derived from *misericordia,* may import that sympathetic sense of the suffering of another by which the heart is affected. It is one of the noblest traits of character. The object of mercy is misery : so God pities human misery, and forbears to chastise severely ; so man pities the misery of a fellow-man, and assists to diminish it ; so public officers occasionally moderate the strictness of national laws from pity to the culprit. But only those can hope for mercy who express penitence and solicit mercy; the impenitent, the stubborn, the obdurate, rather brave the avenging hand of justice than beseech the relieving hand of mercy. See PARDON.

Mercy is an essential attribute of Jehovah, for the knowledge of which we are indebted wholly to revelation. By the propitiatory sacrifice of our Divine Redeemer a way is opened for the exercise of mercy and grace towards the human family perfectly honorable to the attributes and government of God. He appears a just God and a Saviour: "He is just, and yet he justifieth him that believeth in Jesus." Thus the plan of salvation by Jesus Christ provides for the exercise of infinite mercy, consistently with the most rigid demands of truth and righteousness; so that, under this gracious dispensation, "mercy and truth" are said to "have met together," and "righteousness and peace have kissed each other" (Gen. xix, 19; Exod. xx, 6; xxxiv, 6, 7; Psa. lxxxv, 10; lxxxvi, 15, 16; ciii, 17; Luke xviii, 13; Rom. ix, 15–18; Heb. iv, 16; viii, 12). The expression "I will have mercy, and not sacrifice" (Hos. vi. 6; Matt. ix, 13), signifies, as the connection indicates, that God is pleased with the exercise of mercy rather than with the offering of sacrifices, though sin has made the latter necessary (1 Sam. xv, 22; Mic. vi, 6–8). See ATONEMENT.

Mercy is also a Christian grace, and no duty is more strongly urged by the Scriptures than the exercise of it towards all men, and especially towards such as have trespassed against us (Matt. v, 7; xviii, 33–35).

Mercy, Sisters of. See SISTERS OF MERCY.

Mercy, WILHELM, a German Roman Catholic theologian, was born Feb. 9, 1753, at Ueberlingen, near the Bodensee, and was educated at Oberschwangar. In 1787 he was called to the court of duke Charles of Würtemberg, and in 1798 became minister at Gruol, principality of Hohenzollern-Sigmaringen. His advanced age obliged him to resign his position in 1819, and he died July 1, 1825. Mercy was an extremely well-educated man. He published in 1801 an essay on the necessity of reform within the Roman Catholic Church, which caused considerable sensation. He aimed at an entire reform of the Church constitution and the clergy. Besides several articles in the *Jahresschriften für Theologie und Kirchenrecht der Katholiken* (Ulm, 1806–10), he published several other valuable but minor productions in theological literature. See Döring, *Gelehrte Theol. Deutschlands*, s. v.

Mercy-seat (כַּפֹּרֶת, *kappo'reth*, a *covering*, i. e. lid of a vessel, spoken only of the top of the sacred ark; Sept. and New Test. ἱλαστήριον, Vulg, *propitiatorium*), the cover of the box or ark containing the tables of the Sinaitic law, and overspread by the cherubim, between which appeared the shekinah, or visible radiant symbol of the divine presence; it is properly represented as a plank of acacia overlaid with gold, for it was not probably a solid plate or sheet of the purest gold (Exod. xxv, 17 sq.; xxx, 6; xxxi, 7, etc.). Hence the holy of holies is sometimes called the "house of the mercy-seat" (1 Chron. xxviii, 11, Heb.). Josephus simply calls it a lid (ἐπίθεμα, *Ant.* iii, 6, 5); but the versions have all regarded the term as indicative of *propitiation* (as if from the Piel of כָּפַר), and the same view appears to be taken by the New-Testament writers, who compare it with the throne of grace in heaven, access to which has been opened by the blood of Christ (Heb. ix, 5; Rom. iii, 24). See ARK. Comp. 1 Chron. xxviii, 11, where the holy of holies is called the בֵּית הַכַּפֹּרֶת, "house of the mercy-seat." "It was that whereon the blood of the yearly atonement was sprinkled by the high-priest; and in this relation it is doubtful whether the sense of the word in the Heb. is based on the material fact of its 'covering' the ark, or from this

notion of its reference to the 'covering' (i. e. atonement) of sin. See ATONEMENT. But in any case the notion of a 'seat,' as conveyed by the name in English, seems superfluous and likely to mislead. Jehovah is indeed spoken of as 'dwelling' and even as 'sitting' (Psa. lxxx, 1; xcix, 1) between the cherubim, but undoubtedly his seat in this conception would not be on the same level as that on which they stood (Exod. xxv, 18), and an enthronement in the glory above it must be supposed. The idea with which it is connected is not merely that of 'mercy,' but of formal atonement made for the breach of the covenant (Lev. xvi, 14), which the ark contained in its material vehicle—the two tables of stone. The communications made to Moses are represented as made 'from the mercy-seat that was upon the ark of the testimony' (Numb. vii, 89; comp. Exod. xxv, 22; xxx, 6); a sublime illustration of the moral relation and responsibility into which the people were by covenant regarded as brought before God" (Smith). It is not without significance that the mercy-seat was *above* the ark and below the symbols of the divine presence and attributes, as if to foreshadow the supersedence of the law of ordinances contained in the ark by the free grace of the Gospel. See Pratenius, *De Judæa arca* (Upsal. 1727); Werner, *De Propitiatoria* (Giessen, 1695). See SHEKINAH.

Me'red (Heb. *id.*, מֶרֶד, *rebellion*, as in Josh. xxii, 22; Sept. Μωράδ and Μωρήδ, Vulg. *Mered*), a person named as the second son of Ezra (or Ezer), of the tribe of Judah (1 Chron. iv, 17). See EZRAH. Great confusion prevails in the account of his lineage and family, and indeed in the whole chapter in question. Ver. 17, after mentioning the four sons of Ezra, immediately adds, "and she bore Miriam," etc.; where the Sept., by an evident gloss, attributes these children to Jethro, the first named of Ezra's sons; the Vulg. has *genuit*, referring them to Ezra as additional sons, in defiance of the text וַתַּהַר, which is undoubtedly feminine; while Luther renders this word as a proper name, *Thahar*, equally at variance with the text, which joins the following word by the accus. particle אֶת, a construction that does not here allow the resolution by the rendering *with*. In ver. 18 we find several sons attributed to "his wife Jehudijah," and the statement added, "And these are the sons of Bithiah, the daughter of Pharaoh, which Mered took:" the Sept., Vulg., and Luth. follow the Heb., which yields no intelligible connection. Ver. 19: "And the sons of his wife Hodiah, the sister of Naham, the father of Keilah the Garmite, and Eshtemoa the Maachathite;" where, however, the Heb. text would be more naturally rendered "the sons of the wife of Hodijah," בְּנֵי אֵשֶׁת הוֹדִיָּה, the form אֵשֶׁת being rarely absolute (see Nordheimer's *Heb. Gramm.* § 604); the Sept. renders: "And the sons of the wife of his Jewish sister [υἱοὶ γυναικὸς τῆς Ἰουδαίας ἀδελφῆς] were Nachem, and Dana the father of Keeila, and Someion the father of Joriam. And the sons of Naem, the father of Keeila, were Garmi and Jesthemoe, Machatha" [various readings, "of the Idumæan sister" (or "of Odia the sister") of Nachain, the father of Keeila, were Garmi (others "Hotarmi" or "Hogarmi") and Eshthaimon, Nochathi]; the Vulg. and Luther are like the Heb., except the ambiguous renderings, "Et filii uxoris Odajae," "Die Kinder des Weibes Hodija." The Syr. and Arab. omit ver. 17 and 18 (Davidson's *Revis. of the Heb. Text*, ad loc.). The corruption of the text is evident. We suggest a conjectural restoration by transposing the latter part of ver. 18 to the middle of ver. 17, and the whole of ver. 19 to the end of ver. 17; these simple changes will supply the manifest incongruities as follows: "And the sons of Ezra [or Ezer] were Jether, and Mered, and Epher, and Jalon. And these are the sons of Bithiah (the daughter of Pharaoh), whom Mered [first] married; she bore Miriam, and Shammai, and Ishbah (founder of Eshtemoa): and the sons of his [second] wife Hodijah (the sister of Naham, father [founder] of Keilah the Garmite [? strong city] and of Eshtemoa the Maachathite) — this Jewish wife bore Jered (founder of Gedor), and Heber (founder of Socho), and Jekuthiel (founder of Zanoah)." This essentially agrees with Bertheau's rectification of the passage (*Erklär.* ad loc.), adopted by Keil (*Comment.* ad loc.).

"It has been supposed that Pharaoh is here the name of an Israelite, but there are strong reasons for the common and contrary opinion. The name Bithiah, 'daughter,' that is, 'servant of the Lord,' is appropriate to a convert. It may be observed that the Moslems of the present day very frequently give the name Abdallah, 'servant of God,' to those who adopt their religion. That another wife was called the Jewess, is in favor of Bithiah's Egyptian origin. The name Miriam, if, as we believe, Egyptian, is especially suitable to the child of an Egyptian." See BITHIAH. Pharaoh, whose daughter Mered espoused, was therefore undoubtedly some one of the Egyptian kings, and hence Mered himself would appear to have been a person of note among the Israelites. As his children by his other wife (who was also highly related), were recognised as chief men or rebuilders of Canaanitish cities, and hence must have lived soon after the conquest and settlement of Palestine by the Hebrews, Mered himself will be placed in the period of the exode, and he may be supposed to have married the daughter of the predecessor of that Pharaoh by whom the Israelites were detained in so cruel bondage; perhaps his Egyptian wife refused to accompany him to the promised land, and the later children may have been the fruit of a subsequent marriage during the wanderings in the desert with a Hebrewess Hodijah. B.C. cir. 1658.

Mered's wife Bithiah "is enumerated by the rabbins among the nine who entered Paradise (Hottinger, *Smegma Orientale*, p. 515), and in the Targum of R. Joseph on Chronicles she is said to have been a proselyte. In the same Targum we find it stated that Caleb, the son of Jephunneh, was called Mered because he withstood or rebelled against (מָרַד) the counsel of the spies, a tradition also recorded by Jarchi. But another and very curious tradition is preserved in the *Quæstiones in libr. Paral.*, attributed to Jerome. According to this Ezra was Amram; his sons Jether and Mered were Aaron and Moses; Epher was Eldad, and Jalon Medad. The tradition goes on to say that Moses, after receiving the law in the desert, enjoined his father to put away his mother because she was his aunt, being the daughter of Levi: that Amram did so, married again, and begat Eldad and Medad. Bithiah, the daughter of Pharaoh, is said, on the same authority, to have been 'taken' by Moses, because she forsook idols, and was converted to the worship of the true God. The origin of all this seems to have been the occurrence of the name 'Miriam' in 1 Chron. iv, 17, which was referred to Miriam the sister of Moses. Rabbi D. Kimchi would put the first clause of ver. 18 in a parenthesis. He makes Bithiah the daughter of Pharaoh the first wife of Mered, and mother of Miriam, Shammai, and Ishbah; Jehudijah, or 'the Jewess,' being his second wife."

Meredith, C. G., a Methodist Episcopal minister, was born in Baltimore County, Md., May 5, 1820; was converted at eleven, joined the Ohio Conference in 1846, travelled with usefulness eight years, and died at Lebanon Station, Ohio, July 16, 1854. Mr. Meredith was amiable and serious from childhood, was full of good works, and by his own efforts acquired not only a fine general English education, but read Greek and Latin fluently. He was a sound theologian, and a dignified, instructive, and useful minister of the Gospel. See *Minutes of Conferences*, v, 467.

Meredith, Thomas, a Baptist minister, was born at Warwick, Bucks County, Pa. After graduating (Jan. 4, 1816) in the University of Philadelphia, he began the study of theology, was licensed Dec. 30, 1816, and two

years after he was ordained at Edenton. In 1819 he was settled as pastor of the Baptist Church at Newbern. In 1822 he accepted a call of the Baptist Church of Savannah, and finally settled in 1825 as pastor of the Church at Edenton, N. C., where he remained for nine years. He commenced the publication of the *Baptist Interpreter*, the first Baptist paper printed in North Carolina. In 1835 he returned to the Church of Newbern, where he published the *Biblical Recorder*. In 1840 he removed to Raleigh, where he continued to issue the paper, though his health was too feeble to allow him to take a pastoral charge. He died Nov. 13, 1850. He published a pamphlet entitled *Christianity and Slavery* in 1847, which had previously appeared in the *Biblical Recorder*.

Mer'emoth (Heb. *Meremoth'*, מְרֵמוֹת, *exaltations*), the name of two men at the close of the captivity.

1. (Sept. Μεραμώς, Μαρεμώς, Μαρμώς, ἀπὸ 'Ραμώς v. r. Μαριμώς, etc.; Vulg. *Merimuth*). A priest, son of Urijah, and grandson (descendant) of Koz, who returned from Babylon with Zerubbabel (Neh. xii, 3), B.C. 536, and to whom were afterwards consigned the bullion and sacred vessels forwarded by Ezra (Ezra viii, 33). B.C. 459. "After the statement in Ezra ii, 62, respecting the exclusion of the family of Koz from the priesthood, it is puzzling to find one of this family recognised as a priest; but probably the exclusion did not extend to the whole family, some being able to establish their pedigree" (Kitto). He repaired two sections of the walls of Jerusalem (Neh. iii, 4, 21), B.C. 446, and lived to join in the sacred covenant of fidelity to Jehovah (Neh. x, 5). B.C. cir. 410. In Neh. xii, 15 he is mentioned by the name of MERAIOTH, as the father of Helkai.

2. (Sept. Μαριμώς, Vulg. *Marimuth*.) An Israelite of the "sons" (? inhabitants) of Bani, who divorced his Gentile wife after the exile (Ezra x, 36). B.C. 459.

Mererius, a French prelate, flourished in the latter half of the 6th century as bishop of Angoulême. He was originally count of Angoulême. At that period of history the civil government differed so little from the ecclesiastical that, without any change of habits or alteration of moral life, the appellation of count was not unfrequently exchanged for that of bishop, in order to transmit to a son, or perhaps a nephew, the title thus relinquished. In this way the prerogatives of both titles were retained in the same family. But it was considered an abuse of authority to have any one person invested with the combined privileges and distinctions of a count and of a bishop. The count Mererius was canonically settled in the see of Angoulême by St. Germain, bishop of Paris, and St. Euphrone, archbishop of Tours, with the consent of king Charibert. Nantin, the nephew of Mererius, inherited the immunities and possessions attached to the title of count. This occurred about 570. After seven years of episcopacy Mererius was poisoned by Frontonius, who seized the bishop's mitre, and was apparently recognised without opposition as the bishop of Angoulême. It is worthy of notice that in those troublesome times it was not uncommon through such crimes to reach the highest offices. The authors of *L'Histoire Littéraire* and the *Gallia Christiana* have fancied the identity of Mererius, bishop of Angoulême, with one Maracharius, who, according to Fortunatus, attended the dedication of the church at Nantes in 568; but father Lecointe would rather believe that this Maracharius Romacharius was the bishop of Coutances. Yet neither the bishop of Coutances nor the bishop of Angoulême was a fellow-provincial of the bishop of Nantes. It is much more likely that the Maracharius mentioned by Fortunatus is the same with Maclianus, bishop of Vannes, who died probably in 577. It is said that some writings by Mererius were deposited in the library of Cluni, but they seem to have been lost.

Me'res (Heb. *id.*, מֶרֶס, from the Sanscrit *meresh*, *worthy*, according to Benfey, p. 200; Sept. Μέρες, but most copies omit; Vulg. *Mares*), one of the seven satraps or viziers of Xerxes (Esth. i, 14). B.C. 483.

Méri, FRANÇOIS, a French Benedictine monk, was born at Vierzon in 1675. He died Oct. 18, 1723, in the Abbey of Saint-Martin de Maçai, province of Berry. Méri published a work entitled *Discussion critique et théologique des Remarques de M. sur le dictionnaire de Moréri*, under the nom de plume *M. Thomas* (1720). He has sometimes been mistaken for Dom Philippe Billouet, his contemporary, who never published any work.

Meriadec, ST., a French prelate, whose name in Latin is *Mereadocus*, was born in Vannes about AD. 605. He was a lineal descendant of the ancient kings of Armorica, and was brought up at the court of Joël III, king of Brittany. He was ordained a priest by Hingueten, the bishop of Vannes, and afterwards retired into the waste and sterile country of Stival, near Pontivy. At the death of Hingueten, the clergy and the laity alike with one acclaim appointed Meriadec his legitimate successor. St. Meriadec is mentioned in the *Vita Sanctorum* by Bollandus (ii, 36). It is not known when he was canonized, but his name is still much venerated in Brittany, where many churches and chapels have been consecrated under the inspiration of his memory. He died in Vannes in the year 666.

Merian, HANS BERNHARD, a noted philosopher, was born in 1723 at Lichstall, in the canton of Basle, where his father was a minister. After finishing an academical course of philosophical and philological studies, he became private tutor of a young Dutch nobleman. At the recommendation of M. de Maupertuis, Frederick the Great called him to Berlin. Here he became a member of the Academy of Sciences, and soon distinguished himself so much that in 1771 he was nominated director of the philosophical department, and in 1797 (after Formey's death) secretary of the academy. Of his numerous philosophical works, some of which show superior merits, we mention the following: *Diss. de autochiria* (Basle, 1740) : — *Discours sur la métaphysique* (Basle, 1766) : — *Système du monde* (Bouillon, 1770) : — *Examen de l'histoire naturelle de la religion par Mr. Hume, ou l'on refute les erreurs*, etc. (Amsterdam, 1779). Numerous philosophical essays of his are printed in the "Mém. de l'Acad. des Sciences à Berlin," e. g. *Mém. sur l'apper-*

ception de sa propre existence ; Mém. sur l'apperception considérée relativement aux idées, ou sur l'existence des idées dans l'âme (vol. v) ; *Refléxions philos. sur la ressemblance* (vol. xii) ; *Examen d'une question concernant la liberté* (vol. ix) ; *Parallèle de deux principes de psychologie* (vol. xiii) ; *Sur le sens moral* (vol. xiv) ; *Sur le désir* (vol. xvi) ; *Sur la crainte de la mort ; Sur le mépris de la mort ; Sur le suicide* (vol. xix) ; *Sur le durée et sur l'intensité du plaisir et de la peine* (vol. xii). For further details, see Fred. Ancillon, *Éloge historique de J. B. Merian*, etc. (Berlin, 1810).

Mer'ibah (Heb. *Meribah'*, מְרִיבָה, *quarrel*, or "strife," as in Gen. xiii, 8 ; Numb. xxvii, 14), the designation of two places, each marked by a spring.

1. (Sept. λοιδόρησις ; Vulg. joins with the preceding name in one, *tentatio*, Exod. xvii, 7 ; but in Psa. lxxxi, 8, λοιδορία, *contradictio*.) The latter of the two names given by Moses to the fountain in the desert of Sin, on the western gulf of the Red Sea, which issued from the rock which he smote by the divine command, the other equivalent name being MASSAH ; and the reason is assigned, "because of the *chiding* of the children of Israel, and because they did there *tempt* the Lord" (Exod. xvii, 1–7). This spot is only named once again by this title (Psa. lxxxi, 8). The general locality is designated by the name REPHIDIM (ver. 1, 8). See EXODE. The monks of Sinai still pretend to show the identical rock from which Moses brought forth the water (Olin's *Travels*, i, 416). Stephens describes it as an isolated stone, about twelve feet high, with several artificial gashes from which water trickles (*Trav.* i, 285). Burckhardt, also, who was one of the first travellers that critically examined the locality, thinks it bears indubitable marks of art, yet one of the later travellers, D. Roberts, holds that the orifice has been naturally formed by the oozing of water for a long period (*Holy Land, Egypt*, etc., vol. iii, pl. iii). The rock rests isolated where it has fallen from the face of the mountain. It is of red granite, fifteen feet long, and ten feet wide. Down the front of the block, in an oblique direction, runs a seam, twelve or fourteen inches wide, of apparently a softer material ; the rock also has ten or twelve deep horizontal crevices, at nearly equal distances from each other. There are also other apertures upon its surface from which the

"The Rock of Moses."

water is said to have issued—in all about twenty in number, and lying nearly in a straight line around the three sides of the stone, and for the most part ten or twelve inches long, two or three inches broad, and from one to two inches deep; but a few are as deep as four inches. The rock is highly revered both by the Christians and Bedouins. It lies in the valley called Wady el-Lejah, in the very highest region of the Sinai group, running up narrow and choked with fallen rocks between the two peaks that claim to be the Mount of Moses, and contains the deserted convent of El-Abein (Kitto, *Pict. Bible*, ad loc.).

2. (Sept. ἀντιλογία, in Numb. xx, 13; xxvii, 14; Deut. xxxii, 51; λοιδορία in Numb. xx, 24; Vulg. *contradictio;* but in Psa. xcv, 8, πειρασμός, *tentatio*, Auth. Vers. "provocation;" and in Ezek. xlvii, 19, Μαριμώθ; xlviii, 28, Βαριμώθ—in which last two passages, as well as in Psa. cvi, 32, the Auth. Vers. has "strife.") Another fountain produced in the same manner, and under similar circumstances, in the desert of Zin (Wady Arabah), near Kadesh; to which the name was given with a similar reference to the previous misconduct of the Israelites (Numb. xx, 13, 24; Deut. xxxiii, 8). In the last text, which is the only one where the two places are mentioned together, the former is called Massah only, to prevent the confusion of the two Meribahs, "Whom thou didst prove at Massah, and with whom thou didst strive at the waters of Meribah." Indeed, this latter Meribah is almost always indicated by the addition of "waters," as if further to distinguish it from the other (Numb. xx, 13, 24; Deut. xxxiii, 8; Psa. lxxxi. 8; cvi, 32; Ezek. xlvii, 19; xlviii, 28), a title that is but once applied to the other Meribah (Psa. lxxxi, 8); and the locality we are now considering is still more distinctly called "waters of Meribah in Kadesh" (Numb. xxvii, 14), and even Meribah of Kadesh (A. V. "Meribah-Kadesh," Deut. xxxii, 51). Only once is this place called simply Meribah (Psa. xcv, 8). It is strange that, with all this carefulness of distinction in Scripture, the two places should rarely have been properly discriminated. Indeed many commentators have regarded the one as a mere duplicate of the other, owing to a mixture of earlier and later legend. The above monkish tradition has contributed to confound the two localities. But, besides the differences already noted, there was this very important one, that in smiting the rock at the second place Moses himself exhibited impatience with the multitude (Numb. xx, 10–12); whereas he showed no signs of passion on the former occasion. See MOSES. The distance of place from the former Meribah, the distance of time, and the difference of the people in a new generation, are circumstances which, when the positive conditions of the two wells were so equal, explain why Moses might give the same name to two places. See KADESH.

Merib′-Baäl (Heb. *Merib′-Ba′al*, מְרִיב בַּעַל, *contender with Baal*, 1 Chron. viii, 34; Sept. Μεριβαάλ v. r. Μεφριβαάλ, Vulg. *Meribaal;* also in the contracted form *Meri′-Ba′al*, מְרִי בַעַל, 1 Chron. ix, 40; Sept. Μεριβαάλ v. r. Μεχριβαάλ, Vulg. *Meribaal*), the son of Jonathan, elsewhere called MEPHIBOSHETH (2 Sam. iv, 4, etc.), apparently from an unwillingness to pronounce the idolatrous name of Baal. See ISHBOSHETH.

Merici, ANGELA, foundress of the Order of Ursulines, was born at Desenzano, on the lake of Guarda, in 1511. Her family name was *De Brescia*. She was brought up by her uncle, and at an early age entered the Order of St. Francis. She made a pilgrimage to the Holy Land, and after her return established at Brescia, in 1537, a new order of nuns, of which she was appointed superior. Angela Merici died March 21, 1540. Her order was so successful that at the end of a century after its organization it counted in France alone over three hundred and fifty convents. See Helyot, *Hist. des ordres monastiques*, iv, 150; D'Emillianne, *Hist. des ordres monastiques*, p. 247–249; Moréri, *Dict. hist.* s. v.; Hoefer, *Nouv. Biog. Générale*, ii, 638. See URSULINES.

Meridian is the technical term for the siesta or noon-day sleep in a convent, allowed to be taken during one hour after hall-time.

Merino, JOHN ANTON DIAZ, a Roman Catholic prelate, was born in 1771. In his twelfth year he had made such extraordinary progress in his studies that he was ready to enter the University of Alcala. Later he lectured as professor of theology at several universities in Spain and Cuba, then joined the Dominicans, and was shortly after promoted general of this order. On account of his great wisdom and sagacity, he was often consulted by the bishops in cases of an intricate character. In 1832 he was ordained, and in his position led a most exemplary and simple life, and greatly devoted himself to the sufferings of the poor. His firm and vivid faith was a bulwark against the evils of his time, and, for refusing to support irreligious edicts of his government, he was finally expelled from his see and had to leave Spain. He spent his last years in France in exile, and died at Marseilles in 1844. He published *Coleccion Ecclesiastica* and *Biblioteca de la Religion*, the first work containing all the acts of the Spanish bishops in defence of the system of the Church pursued during the constitutional epoch, and the latter comprising the translation of the works of Lamennais, Maistre, etc.

Merit signifies *desert*, or that which is earned; originally the word was applied to soldiers and other military persons, who, by their labors in the field, and by the various hardships they underwent during the course of a campaign, as also by other services they might occasionally render to the commonwealth, were said, *merere stipendia*, to merit, or earn their pay; which they might properly be said to do, because they yielded in real service an equivalent to the state for the stipend they received, which was therefore due to them in justice. Here, then, we come at the true meaning of the word *merit;* from which it is very clearly to be seen that, in a theological sense, there can be no such thing as merit in our best obedience. One man may merit of another, but all mankind together cannot merit from the hand of God. This evidently appears, if we consider the imperfections of all our services, and the express declaration of the divine Word (Ephes. ii, 8, 9; Rom. xi, 5, 6; Tit. iii, 5; Rom. x, 1, 4). The scholastic distinction between *merit of congruity* and *merit of condignity* is thus stated by Hobbes (*Of Man*, pt. i, ch. iv): "God Almighty having promised Paradise to those that can walk through this world according to the limits and precepts prescribed by him, they say he that shall so walk shall *merit* Paradise *ex congruo*. But because no man can demand a right to it by his own righteousness, or any other power in himself, but by the free grace of God only, they say no man can *merit* Paradise *ex condigno*." See MERITUM. See South's *Sermons, The Doctrine of Merit stated*, vol. iii, ser. 1; Toplady's *Works*, iii, 471; Hervey's *Eleven Letters to Wesley;* Robinson's *Claude*, ii, 218. See also WORKS.

MERITS OF CHRIST, a term used to denote the influence or moral consideration resulting from the obedience of Christ—all that he wrought and all that he suffered for the salvation of mankind. See ATONEMENT ; IMPUTATION ; RIGHTEOUSNESS OF CHRIST.

MERITS OF SAINTS. See SUPEREROGATION.

Meritum DE CONDIGNO, or DE CONGRUO (*desert of worth* or *fitness*). This distinction in the idea of the merit of good works, as it was first interpreted by Thomas Aquinas, may be looked upon as a compromise between the strict Augustinian doctrine to which he himself was attached, and the Pelagian tendencies of the Church in general, particularly on the subject of good works. He therefore considers meritorious works under two aspects: 1. According to the substance of the work itself, in so far as proceeding from beings endowed with free will, it is an effect of their free volition. 2. As proceeding in a measure from the grace of the Holy Spirit. Under the last aspect, being, in fact, an effect of the divine grace in man, it is meritorium vitæ æternæ *ex condigno.* While considered as a result of free will, the immense disproportion between the creature and the supernatural communicated grace prevents there being any *condignitas,* any absolute desert, but only a *congruitas,* propter quandam æqualitatem proportionis. For it appears suitable that " ut homini operanti secundum *suam* virtutem Deus recompenset secundum excellentiam *suæ* virtutis." From this Thomas Aquinas concludes : 1. That no one but Christ can gain by *meritum condigni* any *primam gratiam* for another. 2. That, on the contrary, it is possible to all as regards *meritum congrui,* since " secundum amicitiæ proportionem Deus implet hominis voluntatem in salvatione alterius." The conclusion, which opens wide the door to the practice of supererogatory works, is consequently this, that "fides aliorum *valet alii* ad salutem *merito congrui,* non condigni." Duns Scotus goes even further in this Pelagian direction, and asserts that man can, de congruo, prepare *(disponere)* himself for the reception of the grace offered him. By Protestants this distinction is of course rejected, as well as the whole doctrine of good works. The *Apol. Conf.* (ii, 63) declares that this scholastic distinction is but a screen for Pelagianism : "Nam si Deus necessario dat gratiam pro merito congrui, jam non est meritum congrui, sed condigni;" elsewhere (iii, 127) it opposes to it the following arguments: 1. That this doctrine tends to diminish the mediatorial character of Christ, qui perpetuo est mediator, non tantum in principio justificationis. 2. That it continually awakens doubts in the conscience, for hypocrites could always rely on their good works to merit justification, while conscientious believers would be in doubt as to all their works, and always seeking for more. "Hoc est enim de congruo mereri, dubitare et sine fide operari, donec desperatio incidit." See Münscher, *Lehrbuch d. Dogmengesch.* ii. 1, 145, 146, 176; Neander, *Gesch. d. christl. Religion u. Kirche,* ii, 294, 610; Herzog, *Real-Encyklop.* ix, 365.

Merlat, ELIE, a French theologian, was born at Saintes in March, 1634, and was educated at Saumur and Montauban; he afterwards visited Switzerland, Holland, and England, and in 1658 secured a position as minister at the church of All Saints. In 1678 he presided over the provincial synod at Jonzac. His reply to *Renversement de la Morale d'Arnauld* brought upon him the displeasure of the government in 1679; he was sent to prison, and in 1680 the Parliament of Guienne banished him from the country. Merlat escaped to Lausanne, where he was appointed professor of theology. He died there Nov. 18, 1705. His most celebrated works are, *Réponse générale au livre de M. Arnauld: Le Renversement de la Morale de Jésus Christ* (Saumur, 1672, 12mo):—*Le moyen de discerner les esprits;* this sermon was directed towards the visionaries, and created great disturbance :—*Le vrai et le faux Piétisme* (Lausanne, 1700, 12mo).

Merle d'Aubigné, JEAN HENRI, D.D., one of the illustrious characters of the Church of the 19th century, the popular historian of the most prominent event of modern times—the great Reformation of the 16th century—was born at the village of Eaux Vives, on Lake Leman, in the canton of Geneva, Switzerland, Aug. 16, 1794. He was the descendant of celebrated French Protestants. His first French ancestor to leave the native soil was his great-grandfather, John Lewis Merle, who quitted his home at Nismes after the revocation of the Edict of Nantes (1685), and found a refuge in the home of Switzerland's greatest character—John Calvin. In 1743 Francis, son of John Lewis, married Elizabeth D'Aubigné, daughter of the celebrated French Protestant nobleman, and direct descendant of the noted chevalier, Theodore Agrippa d'Aubigné, the grandfather of Madame de MAINTENON (q.v.). According to French usage, the family name of Elizabeth's illustrious ancestry was

appended to the family name of her own offspring. One of these was her son, Aimé Robert (born in 1755, murdered in 1799), the father of this subject, and of two other sons who now figure in American mercantile life —one of them has been for many years a resident of Brooklyn, L. I.; the other a resident of New Orleans.

Jean Henri was educated in the Academy, or, as it is more commonly called, the University of Geneva. Determined to enter the ministry, he inaugurated his theological course at his alma mater. While engaged in his studies, under the leadership of a faculty decidedly rationalistic in tendency, he fell in with the Haldanes, and was led to dedicate himself to Christ as a faithful and devoted servant. In his own account of his conversion, Dr. d'Aubigné states that his professor of divinity disbelieved the doctrine of the Trinity, and that, instead of the Bible, "St. Seneca and St. Plato were the two saints whose writings he held up for admiration." The pupil followed the master throughout. He was chairman of a meeting of students who protested most vehemently, in a public document, against "the odious aggression" of a pamphlet entitled "Considerations upon the Divinity of Jesus Christ," by Henri Empeytaz, which was addressed to them, and had produced a great excitement. "But soon," he continues, "I met Robert Haldane, and heard him read from an English Bible a chapter from Romans about the natural corruption of man— a doctrine of which I had never before heard. In fact, I was quite astonished to hear of man being corrupt by nature. I remember saying to Mr. Haldane, 'Now I see that doctrine in the Bible.' 'Yes,' he replied; 'but do you see it in your heart?' That was but a simple question, yet it came home to my conscience. It was the Sword of the Spirit; and from that time I saw that my heart was corrupted, and knew from the Word of God that I can be saved by grace alone. So that, if Geneva gave something to Scotland at the time of the Reformation—if she communicated light to John Knox— Geneva has received something from Scotland in return in the blessed exertions of Robert Haldane." See HALDANE; MALAN.

Upon the completion of his theological course at Geneva, Merle d'Aubigné went abroad and studied at the universities of Leipsic and Berlin. In the last-named place he attended the lectures of the "father of modern Church history," Neander. On his way to Berlin he had passed through Eisenach, and visited the castle of Wartburg, made famous by Luther's sojourn. It was in this spot that he first conceived the purpose of writing the "History of the Reformation." His stay at Berlin, and association with the immortal Neander, only confirmed the purpose, and he rested not until the work was in the possession of the world. In 1817 he was ordained to preach, and became the pastor of an interesting French Protestant Church at Hamburg. There he labored diligently for his people and his God for some five years, when he was invited to Brussels, by the late king himself, as pastor of a newly-formed French congregation. He rapidly rose in favor and distinction, and enjoyed the position of president of the Consistory of the French and German Protestant churches of the Belgian capital. In 1830, the revolution delivering the country from Protestant rule and Dutch authority, all persons friendly to the king of Holland were regarded as enemies of the Belgians, and Merle d'Aubigné, fearing for his life, determined to return to his native country. The pious "Switzers" were actively canvassing at this time for the establishment of an independent theological school —a training place for the ministry of the orthodox churches. His arrival gave a new impetus to the project, and resulted in the formation of the "Evangelical Society" in 1831, and the founding of the long-desired seminary. Merle was appointed professor of Church history, and intrusted with the management of the school, a position which he continued to hold for the remainder of his life, adorning it by his piety, learning, and eloquence, and sanctified by the divine blessing upon his ever-memorable labors. His associates in the school were Gaussen, celebrated as the author of a work on "Inspiration," Pilet, and La Harpe. Though possessed of an ample fortune, Dr. Merle d'Aubigné lived a life of laborious activity. At seventy-eight he was still vigorous, and went to bed on Sunday night, October 20, after partaking of the sacrament, and subsequent devotions, with no sense of pain or illness. Like Dr. Chalmers, whom in some points he may be said to have resembled, he was found to have died quietly in his room at night, and to have been some hours dead before his family knew their loss. His death occurred on Oct. 21, 1872, at Geneva. Upon his country's loss, the *Christian Intelligencer* (Oct. 24, 1872) thus comments in a beautifully-written obituary of our subject: "Not since the impressive death-scene of John Calvin, which took place 308 years ago, has Geneva been called to mourn over the loss of a more illustrious citizen and minister of the Lord Jesus Christ. The Free Church, of which he was founder, pastor, professor—which differs from the Established Church in having no connection with the State government—partakes largely of the nature of Calvinistic Methodism. But the man himself was broader and greater than any sect. His beautiful tribute to the memory of Calvin is his own most appropriate epitaph : 'He was not a Genevan ; he was not a Swiss ; he was of the City of God.'" Henry Baylies, in a short report of "An Evening with D'Aubigné" (*Zion's Herald*, Nov. 14, 1872), has furnished a description of Merle's appearance of late years: "D'Aubigné stood, I should say, full six feet, rather more than less ; was large, but not corpulent. His face was long, not full, and smooth, I think. His iron-gray locks were combed back, exposing a high forehead ; his eyebrows were heavy and black. His features and expression were somewhat severe, and marked, as if he had inherited the spirit and fought the battles of the old Scotch Covenanters. He conversed in English with tolerable readiness. His health was then feeble, but he was hopeful of improvement."

Merle d'Aubigné as an Author.—The duties incumbent upon a professor of theology are so varied, especially at Geneva, where the influences, as in most large European cities, are decidedly rationalistic, that the manner in which D'Aubigné discharged his duty towards his pupils was of itself sufficient to entitle him to the very highest regards on the part of all followers of Jesus the Christ. The task, however, which D'Aubigné had set for himself at Eisenach, the writing of *a history of the great Reformation*, was the one that mainly occupied him ; and while a most devoted pastor and a truly laborious professor, he yet found time for the completion of a work that has immortalized the name of its author. His *Histoire de la Réformation au Seizième Siècle* (Paris, 1835–53, 5 vols. 8vo) gained for him literally a world-wide reputation. His warm, devotional manner made him singularly popular as a preacher and speaker, and threw a charm over his hearers. His vigorous Protestantism, and his belief in the special providential mission of the evangelical forms of Protestant Christianity, made his history almost a manifesto of Protestantism. His style is brilliant, and generally clear, and, as was said of him by one of the most eminent of the English reviewers, "He wrote for time, and his writings will endure for eternity." The sale of this work was immense. More than 200,000 copies were sold in France alone ; while the English translation has circulated in more than 300,000 copies in Great Britain and the United States. In Germany also the work proved an immense success. But while the fascinations of its style, as well as the transcendent interest and importance of its matter, captivated the people, there are many scholars who have taken exception to his "one-sidedness," and have declared it uncritical and unscholarly. One of the latest writers on the subject, Prof. Fisher, of Yale, actually ignores D'Aubigné as an authority, and refuses to place him by the side of such men as Gieseler and Ranke. This we think

a great injustice to D'Aubigné. We do not ourselves believe that he has done anything more than *popularize* the great Protestant story ; but to ignore him who may be said to have been virtually the first to write the history of the Reformation is a shortcoming to be regretted. See Preface to Fisher, *The Reformation* (N. Y. 1873, 8vo) ; and compare Baird, *D'Aubigné and his Writings, with a Sketch of the Life of the Author* (N.Y. 1846, 12mo), p. xx. Says the writer in the *Christian Intelligencer*, whom we have already had occasion to quote : "It is impossible to estimate the far-reaching influence of this work in reproducing the characters, scenes, and struggles of the Reformation times, and in its strong hold upon the popular mind. We are well aware of the critical ordeal which it has passed through among the scholars of Europe, and that its scientific value is not rated so high as that of histories written for learned men. But as a book for the people it has no rival, either in its immense circulation, or in its acknowledged power in behalf of the great principles of the Protestant Reformation. The work is, moreover, the bright and best reflection of its gifted author's genius, learning, and grace. Brilliant in style, picturesque in description, sententious, full of striking thoughts and powerful word-painting, it also glows with his profound love for the dear old faith, and with burning zeal against the corruptions and iniquities of the great apostasy of Rome. In no other book in our language do Luther and Erasmus, Melancthon, Farel, Calvin, Tetzel, and Dr. Eck, the great emperor and the greater elector, Leo X, and other characters, so live and move, and act in all their personal traits and historical deeds." In 1862 he supplemented his great work by the publication of *The History of the Reformation in Europe in the Time of Calvin*, the fourth volume of which was published in 1868. The other works of M. d'Aubigné, although less widely celebrated, are in their way scarcely inferior to his greatly-renowned production. They are: *Le Luthéranisme et la Réforme* (Paris, 1844) :—*Le Protecteur, ou la Republique d'Angleterre aux Jours de Cromwell* (ibid. 1848, 8vo) : rendered into English, and largely circulated under the title, "The Protector, or the English Republic in the Days of Cromwell," a thoughtful and admirably written review of the rule of the Puritan dictator. It is based upon Carlyle's famous monogram on the Protector, and was expressly designed as an exhibit of that "Protestantism which in Cromwell's mind was far above his own person:"—*Germany, England, and Scotland, or Recollections of a Swiss Minister* (London, 1848, 8vo), a work that showed great powers of observation and clearness of expression:—*Three Centuries of Struggling in Scotland, or Two Kings and Two Kingdoms* (Paris, 1850, 18mo) : a brief—if we may so style it—in which are presented the main features of the Scottish Reformation :—*L'Ancien et le Ministre* (1856) :—and *Character of the Reformer and the Reformation of Geneva* (1862, 8vo). M. Merle d'Aubigné has also contributed largely to periodical publications, the most noted of his papers being a series on the *Archives of Christianity*. See, besides the writers already quoted, *La France Protestante, ou vies des Protestants Français* (1853) ; Charles de Remusat, *Mélanges de Littérature et Philosophie ;* Vapereau, *Dict. des Contemporains*, s.v.; Hoefer, *Nouv. Biog. Générale*, s. v.; *Brit. and For. Evang. Rev.* 1843, 101 sq.; *New-Englander*, iv, 344; *Harper's Magazine*, 1872, Nov. (J. H. W.)

Merle, Matthieu, a noted Huguenot soldier, was born at Uzès, Languedoc, in 1548. He was not, as De Thou represents, the son of a wool-carder, nor did he follow in his youth the trade of wool-carding. He belonged to a noble but poor family of Lower Languedoc, did not receive any school education, and never learned either to read or to write. Having a decided liking for war and the profession of arms, Merle, at the age of twenty, enlisted in a guard commanded by D'Acier, who subsequently became the duke of Uzès. As a member of that guard, Merle went through the campaign of 1569 in Poitou. After the pacification in 1570, he entered the service of François de Peyre, a gentleman of the horse, who intrusted him with the supervision of his castle in Génaudau. Shortly after the massacre of St. Bartholomew, hostilities having been kindled afresh, Merle inflicted the bloodiest retaliation upon the Romanists, and by his deeds of valor and prowess became so redoubtable that the mere mention of his name was sufficient to cause far and near the direst consternation among his enemies. He died about 1590. Goudin, in his *Mémoires*, published a brief sketch of Merle, and his career as a soldier. See De Thou, *Historia sui temporis*; M. Imberais, *Hist. des guerres religieuses en Auvergne*; Hoefer, *Nouv. Biog. Générale*, s. v.

Merlin, Charles, a French critic, was born at Amiens in 1678. He joined the Society of Jesus; at first was a teacher of belles-lettres, and subsequently instructed in theology with much success. He was also one of the editors of the *Mémoires de Trévoux*. Merlin died in Paris about 1747. He is the author of *Réfutation des critiques de M. Bayle sur St. Augustin* (Paris, 1732, 4to). He had also undertaken to examine or refute Bayle's criticisms on religious matters, but this work was never given to the public. Nearly all the articles which Merlin contributed to the *Mémoires de Trévoux* were intended to controvert Bayle's religious opinions. Other works of his are, *Véritable clef des ouvrages de St. Augustin* (Paris, 1732, 4to):—*Examen exact et détaillé du fait d'Honorius* (1738, 12mo):—*Traité historique et dogmatique sur les paroles ou les formes des Sacrements de l'Église* (Paris, 1745, 12mo; reprinted in 1840 by Migne).

Merlin, Jacques (1), a French theologian, was born in Saint-Victurnin, Limousin, about the latter part of the 15th century. After having received his diploma as a doctor of theology at Navarre (1499), he became lecturer on divinity to the chapter of Saint-Etienne de Limoges. Subsequently he was ordained curate of Montmartre, near Paris. In 1525 he was appointed chief penitentiary of the cathedral of Notre-Dame, of which he had previously been resident canon. In 1527, king Francis I caused his arrest and incarceration for preaching against certain courtiers who were suspected of sympathy with the reform movement. He was cast into the dungeon of the Louvre. At the entreaties of the prebendaries of Paris he was liberated, after having suffered incarceration for two years, but even then was confined in his residence at Nantes. He was allowed, however, to return to Paris in 1530, when he was installed grand-vicar to the bishop of Paris, and also curate and archpriest of La Madeleine. In the introduction to the edition of Origen's works, which he published in 1511, he wrote an *Apologie d'Origène*. This apology, wherein, for the first time, the errors imputed to Origen are justified, caused Merlin's condemnation by the Paris Faculty of Theology, and by the impetuous syndic Noël Beda. He likewise published a *Collection de tous les Conciles*, the first ever issued from the press (Paris, 1524, fol.; Cologne, 1530, 8vo; and Paris, 1535, 8vo). He also edited the works of *Richard de Saint-Victor* (Paris, 1518):—*Pierre de Blois* (Paris, 1519):—*Durand de Saint-Pourçain* (1515); and six *Homélies en Français, sur ces paroles de l'Évangile: Missus est angelus Gabriel* (Paris, 1538, 8vo). Merlin died in Paris Sept. 26, 1541, and was buried in the crypt of Notre-Dame. See Dupin, *Aut. eccl. du seizième siècle*, iv, 545; Salmon, *Traité de l'Étude des Conciles*, p. 197, 474.

Merlin, Jacques (2), a Protestant clergyman, the son of Pierre Merlin, was born at Alençon Feb. 5, 1566. He studied at Geneva, and at Oxford, England. In 1589 he was appointed incumbent of La Rochelle, where he continued to labor until the end of his life. In 1601 he was a delegate from his province to the political assembly at Sainte-Foi. He was chosen vice-president of the national synod held at La Rochelle in 1607, and

president of the synod convened two years later in Saint-Maxent. He wrote *Diaire ou Journal du ministre Merlin* (Geneva, 1855, 8vo, 65 pp.), published by M. Crottet from a MS. deposited in the library at La Rochelle. In this same library there is another MS. by Jacques Merlin, which contains a chronological record of the events noted by him in La Rochelle. He died about 1620. See Haag, *La France Protest.*; Arcère, *Hist. de La Rochelle.*

Merlin, Jean-Raymond (surnamed *Monroy*), a Protestant theologian, was born at Romans, France, about 1510. He was a professor of Hebrew at Lausanne, probably from 1537 to 1558, when he resigned his position in order the better to protest against the removal from office of two of his colleagues, Pierre Viret and Jacob Valier, by act of the Bernese government. He afterwards retired to Geneva, where he was pastor for three years. Called to Paris in 1561, at the instance of Coligny, he was intrusted with a mission to La Rochelle, and attended the Conference at Poissy, where he took, however, only a secondary part. Jeanne d'Albret then invited him to visit the Béarn, and engaged him to propagate the doctrines of the Reformation. He returned to Geneva about the middle of 1564. Shortly thereafter he came in conflict with the civil authorities, and, because of his decided opposition to civil interference in ecclesiastical affairs, was removed. Merlin then went into the Dauphiné, from which the massacre of St. Bartholomew drove him away. He sought refuge in Geneva. He died about 1578. Merlin wrote a French translation entitled *Commentaires d'Œcolampade sur Job et Daniel* (Geneva, 1561, 8vo). He also published *Catéchisme extrait de celui de Genève, pour examiner ceux qu'on veut recevoir à la Cène, avec la translation en langue Béarnoise* (Limoges, s. d. 8vo):—*Les dix Commandements de la loi de Dieu, translatés d'Hébreu en Français, et exposés avec six autres translations* (Geneva, 1561, 8vo). See Marchand, *Dict. Historique*; Haag, *La France Protestante.*

Merlin, Pierre, a French Protestant theologian, the son of Jean-Raymond, was born about 1535. After having been a disciple of Theodore de Beza, according to De Thou, he became religious adviser to the prince de Condé. D'Aubigné, however, maintains that he was a minister of the Gospel under admiral de Châtillon. The latter version is the likelier of the two. Certain it is that he was with admiral de Châtillon during the St. Bartholomew massacre. Through a fortunate circumstance he escaped the slaughter and fled to Geneva, where he formed the acquaintance of J. J. Scaliger. In process of time, however, he returned to France, and then became the pastor in ordinary of a nobleman named Laval, residing at Vitré. He was highly esteemed by his co-religionists, and presided at the general synods held respectively at Sainte-Foi, in 1578, and at Vitré, in 1583. As a delegate from the churches in Brittany, he also attended the Synod of Saumur in 1596. Pierre de L'Estoile relates that the impetuous Covenanter, Jean Boucher, in a sermon preached in July, 1591, represented that Merlin was really the father of Henry of Navarre (Henry IV). From this singular fabrication likewise sprang the other story that he had clandestinely married Jeanne d'Albret, the queen of Navarre, and that the celebrated D'Aubigné was the issue from that union. Prosper Marchand, in his *Dictionnaire*, took great pains to refute all these allegations made by the Covenanters, or opposers of Henry IV. Merlin died about 1603. He wrote: *Vingt Sermons sur le livre d'Esther* (La Rochelle, 1591, 8vo; Geneva, 1594, 8vo):—*Job Commentariis illustratus* (Geneva, 1599, 18mo):—*Sainctes Prières recueillies de plusieur passages de l'Ancien et du Nouveau Testament* (Geneva, 1609, 8vo):—*Discours théologiques de la tranquillité et vrai repos de l'âme* (Geneva, 8vo). See Haag, *La France Protestante.*—Hoefer, *Nouv. Biog. Générale*, s. v.

Mero. See MEROTH.

Mer'odach (Heb. *Merodak'*, מְרֹדַךְ, apparently a syncopated form of מְרֹאדַךְ; Sept. Μαιρωδάχ v. r. Μεωδάχ and Μαωδάχ; Vulg. *Merodach*) occurs in Jer. l, 2, in such connection with idols as to leave no doubt that it is the name of a Babylonian god. In conformity with the general character of Babylonian idolatry, Merodach is supposed to be the name of a planet; and, as one of the Tsabian and Arabic names for Mars is *Mirrich*, "arrow" (the latter of which Gesenius thinks may be for *Mirdich*, which is very nearly the same as Merodach), there is some presumption that it may be Mars, but in other respects he more closely resembles Jupiter. As for etymologies of the word, Hitzig has suggested (*Comment.* on Isa. xxxix, 1) that it is the Persian *mardak*, the diminutive of *mard*, "man," used as a term of endearment; but more probably it is from the Persian and Indo-Germanic *mord*, or *mort* (which means death, and is so far in harmony with the conception of Mars, as the lesser star of evil omen), and the affix *och*, which is found in many Assyrian names, as Nisroch, etc. (Gesenius, *Thes. Heb.* p. 818). The bloody rites with which Mars was worshipped by the ancient Arabs are described in Norberg's *Onomast. Codicis Nasar.* p. 107. Of the worship of this idol by the Assyrians and Babylonians, besides the passages in Isa. xxxix, 1; Jer. l, 2, we have testimony in the proper names of the kings of Assyria and Babylonia, which are often compounded with this name, as Evil-Merodach, and Merodach-Baladan, who is also called Berodach-Baladan (see Gesenius, *Comment. zu Jesa.* i, 281). In the above passage of Jeremiah, "Bel and Merodach are coupled together, and threatened with destruction in the fall of Babylon. It has commonly been concluded from this passage that Bel and Merodach were separate gods; but from the Assyrian and Babylonian inscriptions it appears that this was not exactly the case. Merodach was really identical with the famous Babylonian Bel or Belus, the word being probably at first a mere epithet of the god, which by degrees superseded his proper appellation. Still a certain distinction appears to have been maintained between the names. The golden image in the great temple at Babylon seems to have been worshipped distinctly as Bel rather than Merodach, while other idols of the god may have represented him as Merodach rather than Bel. It is not known what the word Merodach means, or what the special aspect of the god was, when worshipped under that title. In a general way Bel-Merodach may be said to correspond to the Greek Jupiter. He is 'the old man of the gods,' 'the judge,' and has the gates of heaven under his especial charge. Nebuchadnezzar calls him 'the great lord, the senior of the gods, the most ancient,' and Neriglissar 'the first-born of the gods, the layer-up of treasures.' In the earlier period of Babylonian history he seems to share with several other deities (as Nebo, Nergal, Bel-Nimrod, Anu, etc.) the worship of the people, but in the later times he is regarded as the source of all power and blessings, and thus concentrates in his own person the greater part of that homage and respect which had previously been divided among the various gods of the Pantheon." See Rawlinson, *Herodotus*, i, 267 sq.; *Ancient Monarchies*, i, 169.

Mer'odach-bal'adan (Heb. *Merodak'-Baladan'*, מְרֹאדַךְ בַּלְאֲדָן, *Mars* [or *Jupiter*] is his *lord* [see MERODACH]; Bohlen less well compares the Persian *mardak balaudaun, honored man;* Sept. Μαρωδὰχ Βαλαδάν v. r. Μαιωδὰχ Ἀλαδάν, Vulg. *Merodach Baladan*), a king of Babylonia, the son of Baladan, and contemporary of Hezekiah (B.C. 711), with whom he cherished friendly relations (Isa. xxxix, 1; 2 Kings xx, 12; 2 Chron. xxxii, 31; in two of which passages the name is written BERODACH-BALADAN, by an interchange of letters). He is unquestionably the *Mardokempad* (Μαδοκέμπαδος) of Ptolemy's *Canon* (comp. Ewald, *Isr.*

Gesch. iii, 344), who reigned at Babylon for twelve years, B.C. 721–709. Josephus (*Ant.* x, 2, 2) calls him simply *Baladas* (Βαλάδας), apparently identifying his name with that of his father. He is usually identified (Gesenius, *Comment.* on Isa. ad loc.) with the Merodach-Baladan mentioned by Berosus (in Eusebius, *Chron. Armen.* i, 42, ed. Aucher) as a viceroy of the king of Assyria, who rebelled and seized the kingdom of Babylon for himself (see Knobel, *Comment.* on Isa. p. 282); but this person is probably one who fell in a part of the two years' interregnum some years later (B.C. 702–699), since he is said to have been slain by Elibus (the Belibus of Ptolemy's *Canon*) after a reign of only six months (see Hitzig, *Comment.* on Isa. p. 450). Merodach-Baladan is mentioned in the Assyrian inscriptions at Khorsabad, deciphered by Dr. Hincks and Col. Rawlinson, according to which he was conquered by Sennacherib in the first year of the latter's reign. Merodach-Baladan is there called king of Kar-Duniyas, a city and country frequently mentioned in the Assyrian inscriptions, and comprising the southernmost part of Mesopotamia, near the confluence of the Tigris and Euphrates, together with the districts watered by these two rivers, to the borders of Susiana. This king, with the help of his Susianian allies, had recently recovered Babylon, from which Sargon, Sennacherib's father, had expelled him in the twelfth year of his reign. The battle seems to have been fought considerably to the north of that city. The result was that Sennacherib totally defeated Merodach-Baladan, who fled to save his life, leaving behind him all his military equipments. In the cuneiform annals of the fourth year of Sennacherib's reign, Merodach-Baladan is further mentioned as having escaped to an island, where himself and all his family were finally captured by Sennacherib (Layard's *Nineveh and Babylon*, p. 140, 145). The dates of these notices would seem to identify the Merodach-Baladan of the monuments with the temporary usurper of the same name alluded to by Berosus, rather than with the one of Scripture; possibly future investigations may show that they were all three identical, as also the Mardokempadus of the *Canon*, since the records of the inscriptions appear to speak of an occupancy of Babylon by him at two distinct periods, the first during the reign of Sargon (being probably that referred to in the Scriptures and the *Canon*), and the second for a shorter space and after a considerable interval, in the first of Sennacherib (being that alluded to by Berosus). A different but analogous solution of the above difficulty is to suppose two kings of the same name at the two periods in question. See HEZEKIAH.

"Putting all our notices together, it becomes apparent that Merodach-Baladan was the head of the popular party, which resisted the Assyrian monarchs, and strove to maintain the independence of the country. It is uncertain whether he was self-raised or was the son of a former king. In the second book of Kings he is styled 'the son of Baladan;' but the inscriptions call him 'the son of *Yagin*;' whence it is to be presumed that Baladan was a more remote ancestor. Yagin, the real father of Merodach-Baladan, is possibly represented in Ptolemy's *Canon* by the name Jugæus—which in some copies replaces the name Elulæus, as the appellation of the immediate predecessor of Merodach-Baladan. At any rate, from the time of Sargon, Merodach-Baladan and his family were the champions of Babylonian independence, and fought with spirit the losing battle of their country. The king of whom we are here treating sustained two contests with the power of Assyria, was twice defeated, and twice compelled to fly his country. His sons, supported by the king of Elam, or Susiana, continued the struggle, and are found among the adversaries of Esar-Haddon, Sennacherib's son and successor. His grandsons contended against Asshur-bani-pal, the son of Esar-Haddon. It is not till the fourth generation that the family seems to become extinct, and the Babylonians, having no champion to maintain their cause, contentedly acquiesce in the yoke of the stranger. The increasing power of Assyria was at this period causing alarm to her neighbors, and the circumstances of the time were such as would tend to draw Judæa and Babylonia together, and to give rise to negotiations between them. The astronomical marvel, whatever it was, which accompanied the recovery of Hezekiah, would doubtless have attracted the attention of the Babylonians; but it was probably rather the pretext than the motive for the formal embassy which the Chaldæan king despatched to Jerusalem on the occasion. The real object of the mission was most likely to effect a league between Babylon, Judæa, and Egypt (Isa. xx, 5, 6), in order to check the growing power of the Assyrians. Hezekiah's exhibition of 'all his precious things' (2 Kings xx, 13) would thus have been, not a mere display, but a mode of satisfying the Babylonian ambassadors of his ability to support the expenses of a war. The league, however, though designed, does not seem to have taken effect. Sargon, acquainted probably with the intentions of his adversaries, anticipated them. He sent expeditions both into Syria and Babylonia—seized the stronghold of Ashdod in the one, and completely defeated Merodach-Baladan in the other. That monarch sought safety in flight, and lived for eight years in exile. At last he found an opportunity to return. In B.C. 703 or 702 Babylonia was plunged in anarchy—the Assyrian yoke was thrown off, and various native leaders struggled for the mastery. Under these circumstances the exiled monarch seems to have returned, and recovered his throne. His adversary, Sargon, was dead or dying, and a new and untried prince was about to rule over the Assyrians. He might hope that the reins of government would be held by a weaker hand, and that he might stand his ground against the son, though he had been forced to yield to the father. In this hope, however, he was disappointed. Sennacherib had scarcely established himself on the throne when he proceeded to engage his people in wars, and it seems that his very first step was to invade the kingdom of Babylon. Merodach-Baladan had obtained a body of troops from his ally, the king of Susiana; but Sennacherib defeated the combined army in a pitched battle; after which he ravaged the entire country, destroying 79 walled cities and 820 towns and villages, and carrying vast numbers of the people into captivity. Merodach-Baladan fled to 'the islands at the mouth of the Euphrates' (Fox Talbot's Assyrian Texts, p. 1)—tracts probably now joined to the continent—and succeeded in eluding the search which the Assyrians made for him. If we may believe Polyhistor, however, this escape availed him little. That writer relates (ap. Euseb. Chron. Can. i, 5) that he was soon after put to death by Elibus, or Belibus, the viceroy whom Sennacherib appointed to represent him at Babylon. At any rate, he lost his recovered crown after wearing it for about six months, and spent the remainder of his days in exile and obscurity." See BABYLONIA.

Meroë. See SEBA.

Me′rom (Heb. *Merom′*, מֵרוֹם, *height;* Sept. Μερώμ), a lake (מֵרוֹם, "waters") among the hills (hence the name, Burckhardt, *Trav.* ii, 553) of northern Palestine, whose shores were the scene of the great victory of the Hebrews over the northern Canaanites (Josh. xi, 5–7); doubtless the same with that through which the Jordan flows three miles from its source, called by Josephus *Samechonitis* (Σαμοχωνῖτις or Σεμεχωνῖτις, *Ant.* v, 5, 1; *War*, iii, 10, 7; iv, 1, 1). In his account of the battle (*Ant.* v, 1, 18), the confederate kings encamp "near Beroth, a city of upper Galilee, not far from Kedes;" nor is there any mention of water. In the *Onomasticon* of Eusebius the name is given as "Merran" (Μερράν), and it is stated to be "a village twelve miles distant from Sebaste (Samaria), and near Dothaim." Abulfeda (*Tab. Syr.* p. 155) calls it the *Sea of Banias*, but its usual modern name is *Bakrat el-Hûleh* (Burck-

hardt, *Trav.* i, 87). It was visited by Lieut. Lynch (*Expedition*, p. 471), and is most fully described by Thomson (in the *Bibliotheca Sacra*, 1846, p. 185; see also 1843, p. 12, and map; 1854, p. 56; Robinson's *Res.* new ed. p. 395; comp. Reland, *Palæst.* p. 261 sq.; Hamelsveld, i, 482 sq.; Schwarz, *Palest.* p. 47). As regards the modern name of Hûleh, by which the native inhabitants of the district commonly designate the lake, there are some grounds for tracing it also to a very ancient source. Josephus (*Ant.* xv, 10, 3) speaks of Herod as having obtained from Cæsar the territory of a troublesome prince named Zenodorus—a territory that lay between Trachon and Galilee, and which "contained Ulatha (Οὐλάθαι) and Paneas." The country so described is the very region in which Lake Merom is situated; and Οὐλάθα has every appearance of being the Greek form of Hûleh. It is also conjectured that this *Ulatha* of Josephus and *Hûleh* of modern times may derive their common origin from a period so remote as that of *Hul*, the son of Aram, mentioned in the book of Genesis (x, 23), a personage whom Josephus calls Ὄυλος (*Ant.* i, 6, 4). Hence, not improbably, the name (see Ritter, *Palest. und Syr.* ii, 234; Stanley, *Sin. and Pal.* p. 283). The word, both in Hebrew and Arabic, seems to have the force of *depression*—the low land (see Michaelis, *Suppl.* Nos. 687, 720); and Michaelis most ingeniously suggests that it is the root of the name Κοιλησυρία, although in its present form it may have been sufficiently modified to transform it into an intelligible Greek word (*Spicilegium*, ii, 137, 138). The name *Samechonitis* may perhaps be derived from the Arabic root *samak*, "to be high," and would thus be identical in meaning with the Hebrew Merom (Gesenius, *Thesaur.* p. 1276; Reland, *Palæst.* p. 262). Perhaps the phrase מֵי מְרוֹם might be rendered "the upper waters;" that is, the upper lake or collection of waters formed by the river Jordan (see Reland, p. 262). Several other explanations of the Greek name as found in Josephus have been given: 1. It is derived from the Chaldee סָמַק, "red," because of the ruddy color of its water. 2. From סְבָךְ, "a thorn," because its shores abound with thorn-bushes (Lightfoot, *Opp*, ii, 172). 3. From the Arabic *samk*, "a fish" (Reland, p. 262). These explanations appear to be all too fanciful (Stanley, *Sin. and Pal.* p. 383, note). Josephus mentions a city called *Meroth* (Μηρώθ or Μηρώ, *Life*, p. 37; *War*, ii, 20, 6), which Ritter connects with the Heb. name of the lake (*Pal. und Syr.* ii, 235).

This interesting lake—Merom, Samechonitis, or Hûleh—lies embedded in the midst of one of the finest scenes in Palestine. The Ard el-Hûleh, the centre of which the lake occupies, is a nearly level plain of sixteen miles in length, from north to south; and its breadth, from east to west, is from seven to eight miles. On the west it is walled in by the steep and lofty range of the hills of Kedesh-Naphtali; on the east it is bounded by the lower and more gradually ascending slopes of Bashan; on the north it is shut in by a line of hills hummocky and irregular in shape, and of no great height, and stretching across from the mountains of Naphtali to the roots of Mount Hermon, which towers up, at the north-eastern angle of the plain, to a height of 10,000 feet. At its southern extremity the plain is similarly traversed by elevated and broken ground, through which, by deep and narrow clefts, the Jordan, after passing through Lake Hûleh, makes its rapid descent to the Sea of Galilee, the level of which is from 600 to 700 feet lower than that of the waters of Merom (Van de Velde, *Memoir*, p. 181). This noble landscape, when seen, for the first time and suddenly, from the lofty brow of the mountains of Naphtali, can never fail to excite the liveliest admiration : the intense greenness, so unusual in Palestine, of the abundantly-watered plain—the bright blue lake reflecting from its bosom the yet brighter and bluer sky—the singularly-picturesque ranges of the surrounding hills; and, rising far above them all, the Jebel esh-Sheikh, the monarch of the mountains, the mighty Hermon, dark and shaggy to its shoulders with the forests that clothe its sides, and with its double summit covered with perpetual snow. The lake itself in form is not far from a triangle, the base being at the north and the apex at the south; and, though no exact measurement of it seems ever to have been made, it is about four and a half miles in length by about three miles in breadth. According to Josephus (*War*, iv, 1, 1) it is sixty stadia long and thirty wide, and full of fish (Burckhardt, *Trav.* ii, 554). Robinson states (*Researches*, iii, 339 sq.) that its size varies somewhat according to the season, being when he saw it (in summer) about two miles long, but in the northern part bounded by an extensive marsh, which explains the length sometimes assigned of eight or ten miles (Seetzen, in Zach's *Monatl. Corresp.* xviii, 344). It is surrounded on all sides, and especially on the south, west, and north, by broad morasses, and by such impervious brakes of tall sedges, reeds, and canes, as to be all but unapproachable. It is the receptacle for the drainage of the highlands on each side, but more especially for the waters of the Merj Ayûn, an elevated plateau which lies above it among the roots of the great northern mountains of Palestine. On the north-western side of the lake the morasses extend almost to the very base of the Kedesh-Naphtali hills. The Hasbâny river, which falls almost due south from its source in the great Wady et-Teim, is joined at the north-east corner of the Ard el-Hûleh by the streams from Banias and Tell el-Kady, and the united stream then flows on through the morass, rather nearer its eastern than its western side, until it enters the lake close to the eastern end of its upper side. From the apex of the triangle at the lower end the Jordan flows out. In addition to the Hasbâny, and the innumerable smaller watercourses which filter into it the waters of the swamp above, the lake is fed by independent springs on the slope of its enclosing mountains. Of these the most considerable is the Ain el-Mellâhah, near the upper end of its western side, which sends down a stream of forty or fifty feet in width. Though this name signifies "the fountain of salt," neither is the water brackish, nor is there any saline incrustation in its neigborhood, to account for such a designation. This spring gives to the lake one of its names. William of Tyre calls it *Lacus Meleha* (*Hist.* xviii, 13); and the name now frequently given to it by the neighboring Arabs is *Bahret el-Mellâhah*. The water of the lake is clear and sweet; it is covered in parts by a broad-leaved plant, and abounds in water-fowl. The only inhabitants of the plain are a few tribes of Arabs who dwell in tents. There is not a single village or house in any part of it. Its soil is singularly fertile, and where cultivated, as it is partially to the south and east of the lake, yields luxuriant crops. Its rich, swampy pastures are covered with large herds of buffaloes. This cultivated district is called the Ard el-Khait, perhaps "the undulating land" (otherwise "the land of wheat," from its fertility), el-Khait being also the name which the Arabs sometimes call the lake (Thomson, in the *Bibl. Sacra*, iii, 199; Robinson, *Bib. Res.* iii, App. p. 135, 136). In fact the name Hûleh appears to belong rather to the district, and only to the lake as occupying a portion of it. It is not restricted to this spot, but is applied to another very fertile district in northern Syria lying below Hamah. A town of the same name is also found south of and close to the Kasimiyeh river, a few miles from the castle of Hunin. See PALESTINE.

Meron. See SHIMRON-MERON.

Méron, PHILIPPE VAN, a Dutch visionary and doctor of theology, was born at Goude in 1435. He was a member of the Brethren of the Conference, and distinguished himself by his eloquence. He was sent as a missionary to Sweden, and died in 1506. His works are of a mystical character. The most important of them is *Historie van den Heiligen Patriach Joseph, bruydegom*

der Mœgh Maria, ende opvoeder Ons Heeren Jhesu Christi (Goude, 1496, 8vo). In this work Méron narrates a revelation which he claims to have had in Sweden, when he ascertained by divine intuition that Joseph "became the foster-father of Jesus Christ on the 19th of January." In consequence of this revelation he exhorted all good Christians to fast on that day, and to keep the festival of St. Joseph. But this alleged revelation did not in any way alter the custom of the Church to honor the memory of Joseph on the 19th of March. See Walvis, *Beschr. v. Goude*, ii, 144; Prosper Marchand, *Dictionnaire*, p. 106.

Meronoth. See MERONOTHITE.

Meron'othite (Heb. *Meronothi'*, מֵרֹנֹתִי, gentile from מֵרֹנוֹת, *Meronoth'*, signif. uncertain, a place elsewhere unknown; Sept. ἐκ Μεραϑών or Μαραϑών, Μηρωνωϑύτης, Vulg. *Meronothites*), an epithet applied to Jehdeiah, the herdsman of the royal asses in the time of David and Solomon (1 Chron. xxvii, 30), and also to Jadon, one of those who repaired the walls of Jerusalem (Neh. iii, 7); apparently as being natives of some town called MERONOTH, of the position or existence of which no other notice is extant, but from the latter passage it may be conjectured to have lain not far from Gibeon and Mizpah, and appears to have been inhabited after the captivity.

Merorim. See BITTER (HERBS).

Meroth (Μηρώϑ) or **Mero** (Μηρώ), a fortified town of Galilee (Josephus, *War*, ii, 20, 6; *Life*, p. 37), probably the *Meiron* (מירון) of the Talmud (Reland, *Palœst.* p. 817); now the village of *Meirôn*, about 1¾ hours west-north-west of Safed; famous for Jewish pilgrimages to the tombs of their ancient rabbis (Wilson, *Lands of the Bible*, ii, 311; Carmoly, *Itin.* p. 133, 260; Robinson, *Researches*, iii, 334; *Later Res.* p. 73, 74; Schwarz, *Palest.* p. 70 note, 186; Van de Velde, *Memoir*, p. 334). See AMERYTHA; MEROM; MEROZ.

Me'roz (Heb. *Meroz'*, מֵרוֹז, perh., as suggested by Gesenius, for מֵאָרוֹז, from the Arabic, *refuge*; but Fürst disapproves of this etymology; Sept. Μηρώζ, Vulg. *terra Meroz*), a place in the northern part of Palestine, the inhabitants of which were severely reprehended (Judg. v, 23) for not having taken the field with Barak against Sisera (comp. Judg. xxi, 8–10; 1 Sam. xi, 7). It would seem as if they had had an opportunity of rendering some particular and important service to the public cause which they neglected (see Dr. Robinson's note in the *Bib. Repos.* 1831, p. 606). The tradition of its site was lost as early as the time of Procopius of Gaza, who had attempted in vain to recover it (Reland, *Palœst.* p. 896). Possibly the city was utterly destroyed in consequence of the curse. In the Jewish traditions preserved in the Commentary on the Song of Deborah attributed to Jerome, Meroz, which may be interpreted as *secret*, is made to signify the evil angels who led on the Canaanites, and are cursed by Michael, the angel of Jehovah, the leader of the Israelites. Eusebius and Jerome (*Onomast.* s. v. Merrus) fix it twelve Roman miles from Sebaste, on the road to Dothaim; but this position would place it south of the field of battle, and therefore scarcely agrees with the history. Schwarz (*Palest.* p. 36) says it is mentioned in the Talmud under the name of *Marchesheth* or *Maresheth*, and locates it (*ib.* p. 168) at the village of *Murussus*, two or three miles north or north-west of Bethshan, on the line of hills separating the basin of Tayibeh from the valley of Jezreel (Robinson's *Researches*, new ed. iii, 339). The town must have commanded the Pass, and if any of Sisera's people attempted, as the Midianites did when routed by Gideon, to escape in that direction, its inhabitants might no doubt have prevented their doing so, and have slaughtered them. Fürst (*Lex.* s. v.) suggests that it was a locality in a district of Galilee partly inhabited by Gentiles (1 Kings ix, 11), not far from Kedesh-Naphtali, and consequently in the neighborhood of the Lake Merom, perhaps the locality (reading מְרוֹם, *high place*) which gave name to the lake itself. Wilson (*Lands of the Bible*, ii, 89) identifies it with the *Kefr-Mesr*, on the southern slope of Mount Tabor, and this Van de Velde approves (*Memoir*, p. 334). Thomson thinks it may be the present *Meiron*, a famous Jewish cemetery six miles west of Safed; this would be between Barak's residence and Tabor (Judg. iv, 12), and therefore render the inhabitants liable to a summons to arms by the Hebrew general (*Land and Book*, i, 424). This last place is possibly the *Meroth*, strongly fortified by Josephus (*Life*, p. 37; *War*, ii, 20, 6; iii, 3, 1).

Merriam, Edwin Elisha, a Presbyterian minister, was born in Mason, Hillsborough County, N. H., in 1837. He graduated with honor at Amherst College, Mass., in 1858, and at Union Theological Seminary, N.Y., in 1863; was ordained and installed pastor of the Church in Salem, Wayne County, Pa., in 1864, where he died Feb. 17, 1865. Mr. Merriam possessed superior qualifications for usefulness as a minister, and was much beloved as a pastor. See *Presb. Hist. Almanac*, 1866, p. 218.

Merriam, W. W., an American missionary to Turkey, of whose personal history we know but little, deserves a place here for his activity and zeal in behalf of the cause of missions, a devotion which cost him his life in June, 1862, when he was assassinated near Philippopolis, Turkey, on his return from a missionary meeting at Constantinople. Merriam was appointed by the American Board.

Merrick, James, an English divine, noted for his theological and, especially, for his poetical productions, called by Lowth "one of the best of men and most eminent of scholars," was born Jan. 8, 1720, and was educated at Trinity College, Oxford. He became a "probation fellow" at his alma mater in 1744, took holy orders shortly after, and became noted for his philanthropic labors. Owing to infirm health he never undertook the task of supplying the pulpit. He died Jan. 5, 1769. When yet a mere boy at school at Reading, Merrick published a poetical production that deserves to be placed among the classical writings of the English. His chief works are, *A Dissertation on Proverbs*, ch. ix (Lond. 1744, 8vo): —*Prayers for a Time of Earthquakes and Violent Floods*, written in 1756, soon after the earthquake at Lisbon:—*Annotations, Critical and Grammatical, on the Gospel of St. John* (Reading, 1764, 8vo; 2d pt. 1767, 8vo):—*Annotations on the Psalms* (ibid. 1767, 8vo; 1768, 4to), of which only part were his own; archbishop Secker, bishop Lowth, and Kennicott were contributors: —*An Encouragement to a Good Life*, particularly addressed to soldiers quartered at Reading, among whom he labored much for the good of the Christian cause. Indeed, he appears to have paid great attention to this class of men, who at that time especially required it. He also wrote *Poems on Sacred Subjects*, and made an excellent *Translation of the Psalms into English Verse*. This, beyond all doubt the best poetical translation in English, was unfortunately not adapted for parochial choirs, inasmuch as it was divided into stanzas for music. This work is not perhaps as generally known as its merits would justify. He published several other minor religious treatises. See Orme, *Bibliotheca Biblica*, p. 313; Allibone, *Dict. Brit. and Amer. Authors*, s. v.; *English Cyclop.* s. v.; Holland, *Psalmists of Great Britain*, ii, 210 sq.

Merrick, James Lyman, a Presbyterian minister, was born at Monson, Mass., Dec. 11, 1813. He graduated at Amherst College in 1830, and in 1833 at the theological seminary at Columbia, S. C.; was ordained as a missionary to the Persians in 1834; in August of the same year he sailed for Constantinople, and in October, 1835, arrived at Tabriz, Persia. He labored, travelled, and explored among the Mohammedans about two years, then joined the Nestorian Mission at Oroomiah, and in 1845 returned to America, and in 1849 was installed pastor of the Congregational Church at Am-

herst, Mass. He died June 18, 1866. Mr. Merrick had a strong mind, and was a good scholar, a faithful pastor, and an earnest missionary. He was thoroughly acquainted with the Persian, and well read in the Arabic, Hebrew, Turkish, Greek, Latin, and French tongues. He was altogether absorbed in the interests of the Persian language and literature, and bequeathed his property to the literary institutions which had afforded him his early advantages, for the founding of four Persian scholarships. He was the author of *The Pilgrim's Harp*, a volume of poems (1847):—*The Life and Religion of Mohammed*, translated from the Persian (1850):—*Keith's Evidences of Prophecy*, translated into Persian (1846). He also left in MS., *A Full Work on Astronomy*, selected, compiled, and translated into Persian, *A Friendly Treatise on the Christian Religion*, and *A Treatise on the Orthography and Grammar of the English Language*. See *Presb. Hist. Almanac*, 1867, p. 181, 182; *N. Amer. Rev.* lxxi, 273; Brownson's *Quar. Rev.* 2d ser., iv, 408. (J. L. S.)

Merriken, Joseph, a Methodist Episcopal minister, was born at Annapolis, Md., Nov. 25, 1811; entered the Baltimore Conference in 1831; in 1835–8 was stationed in Baltimore; in 1838–9, in Lewiston, Pa.; in 1840–1, in Hagerstown, Md.; in 1842–3, in Annapolis; in 1844–5, in Baltimore; and in 1847 in Alexandria, where he died, in February (?), 1848. He was a man of great energy and labor, and one of the best preachers of his time, not in great talents, but in sound judgment, clear and earnest study, and great faith. He was especially noted for excellence and faithfulness as a pastor. See *Minutes of Conferences*, iv, 197.

Merrill, Daniel, an American Baptist minister, noted for his opposition to open communion and Pædobaptists, flourished as pastor at Sedgwick, Me., where he died in 1833, about sixty-five years of age. His works are, *Seven Sermons on Baptism* (10th ed. 1812):—*Eight Letters on Open Communion* (1805):—*Letters occasioned by Worcester's Discourses:—Balaam Disappointed;* and several sermons preached on important public occasions.

Merrill, David, a Presbyterian minister, was born at Peacham, Vt., in 1798, and was educated at Dartmouth College (class of 1821). He was called to preach at Urbanna, Ohio, in 1827; thence to the Church at Peacham in 1841, where he died in 1850. Mr. Merrill published *Three Occasional Sermons*, and contributed to several periodicals. A volume of his sermons, with a sketch of his life, was published by Thomas Scott Pearson (Windsor, Vt., 1855, 8vo). See Allibone, *Dict. of Brit. and Amer. Authors*, s. v.

Merrill, Franklin, a Presbyterian minister, was born in 1819. He was educated at Princeton College, studied divinity at the Princeton Theological Seminary, and was ordained pastor of the Presbyterian Church at Hempstead, Long Island, N. Y., in 1848. In 1853 he accepted a call to the Presbyterian Church of Stillwater, N. Y., and in 1858 to the Reformed Dutch Church of Schuylerville, N. Y., where he died, March 31, 1861. Mr. Merrill was an earnest and instructive preacher, and possessed the high art of impressing the message of God with peculiar directness and pungency. See *Presb. Hist. Almanac*, 1862, p. 206.

Merrill, Joseph A., a noted Methodist Episcopal minister, was born at Newbury, Mass., Nov. 22, 1785; was converted in 1804; entered the New England Conference in 1807; was stationed in Boston in 1813–14; in 1815–18 was presiding elder on Vermont District; in 1819 was agent of the Wesleyan Academy at New Market, and the first missionary of the first missionary society of the Methodist Episcopal Church, which was formed by the Lynn Common Church, and his field was New Hampshire. In 1826–27 he was stationed in Boston; 1830–33 was presiding elder on Providence District; 1834–38 was on Springfield District; 1843–47, in Salem, Boston, and Cambridge; and died at Wilbraham, Mass., July 22, 1849. "Mr. Merrill was an able and useful minister, and greatly devoted to the interests of the Church. He was one of the original trustees of the Wesleyan University, and remarkably successful as an agent for the academy, of which he secured the removal to Wilbraham. He was one of the earliest and most devoted friends of the anti-slavery cause, and his name is honorably identified with the rise and progress of that important movement." His administrative and practical talents were of the highest order, and his firm integrity made him trusted and respected by all. See *Minutes of Conferences*, iv, 536; Steven's *Memorials of Methodism*, ii, ch. xxxii. (G. L. T.)

Merrill, Thomas Abbott, D.D., a Congregational minister, was born January 18, 1780, in Andover, Mass.; graduated at Dartmouth College in 1801; was chosen tutor in 1803; and in 1804 tutor in Middlebury College, which office he held a year, and was then ordained pastor in Middlebury, Dec. 19, 1805. He labored on this charge until Oct. 19, 1842. He died April 25, 1855. He was one of the formers of the Vermont Domestic Missionary Society in 1818, and secretary of the same until 1821; and he was president of the Peace Convention in 1853. In 1842 he was chosen treasurer of Middlebury College. He published two of his sermons (1806; 1833). See Sprague, *Annals*, ii, 481.

Merritt, TIMOTHY, an early and eminent Methodist Episcopal minister, was born at Barkhamstead, Conn., October, 1775. He was converted about 1792, and entered the New England Conference in 1796. From 1803 to 1817 he located; was stationed in Boston in 1817–18; in 1822 was at Providence; in 1825–26 preached at Boston; in 1831 at Malden, and also "devoted much time to the editorship of *Zion's Herald;*" from 1832 to 1836 was assistant editor of the *Christian Advocate and Journal*, New York. He died at Lynn, Mass., 1845. Mr. Merritt was an able and powerful writer, an eloquent preacher, an accomplished debater, and in all respects one of the foremost ministers of his time. He was a well-read man, and worthy of a place among the scholars of his Church. His ministry was made especially useful by the enjoyment and earnest preaching of the doctrine of Christian perfection. His influence was wide and blessed, and his memory is precious. Mr. Merritt published *Convert's Guide and Preacher's Assistant:—Christian Manual:—Discussion against Universal Salvation:—On the Validity and Sufficiency of Infant Baptism:*—and (together with Dr. Wilbur Fisk) *Lectures and Discussions on Universal Salvation*. See *Minutes of Conferences*, iii, 616; Steven's *Memorials of Methodism*, i, ch. xxiii; ii, ch. xxvii; Sherman's *New Engl. Divines*, p. 312. (G. L. T.)

Merriwether, JOHN T., a minister of the Methodist Episcopal Church South; joined the Memphis (Tenn.) Conference in 1854, and was appointed to Dyersburg Circuit; in 1855 to Dresden Station; in 1856 to Trenton Station; in 1857 to Holly Springs Station; in 1858 to Asbury Chapel, Memphis; in 1859 and 1860 to Aberdeen Station; in 1861 was made presiding elder of Aberdeen District; in 1865 was appointed to Denmark Circuit; and in 1866 took a supernumerary relation. He died in Denmark, Tenn., April 10, 1867. "He possessed a strong and highly-cultured mind, a soul imbued with the spirit of Christ, and an intelligent yet burning zeal in his high calling." See *Minutes of the M. E. Church South*, 1867.

Mersennus (Fr. MERSENNE), MARIN, a very learned French ecclesiastic and philosopher, was born in 1588 at Oyse, in the present department of Maine. He received his education at the College of La Flèche, where he was a fellow-student of Des Cartes, and with him he formed an intimacy, which a similarity of pursuits ripened into a friendship dissolved only by death. He also studied at the University of Paris, and subsequently at the Sorbonne. In 1612 he took the vows at the Minimes, in the neighborhood of Paris. In the year following entering the priesthood, he deemed it incum-

bent on him to study the Hebrew language, and addressed himself to the accomplishment of this task. In 1615 he filled the chair of philosophy at Nevers, and there taught till the year 1619, when he was chosen superior of the convent, and, on completing the term of his office, he travelled in Germany, Italy, and the Netherlands. He finally settled in Paris, where his gentle temper and polite and engaging manners procured him a number of distinguished friends. Of these the chief was the founder of the Cartesian philosophy, who entertained the highest opinion of his abilities, and consulted him upon all occasions. It has been stated —though the story seems highly improbable—that Des Cartes, by the advice of Mersenne, at once changed his intention of founding his system on the principle of a vacuum, and adopted that of a plenum. The discovery of the cycloid has been ascribed to him and also to Des Cartes, but it now seems pretty clear that to neither are we indebted for the first notice of this curve. Mersenne died at Paris in 1648. Père Mersenne was undoubtedly a man of great learning and unwearied research, and deserved the esteem in which he was held by the philosophers and literati of his age; but, except his *Harmonie Universelle*, his works are now unread and almost unknown. If by some he was overrated, by others he has been undervalued; and when Voltaire mentioned him as "Le minime et très minime Père Mersenne," he indulged his wit at the expense of one with whose writings, it is to be suspected, he was very little acquainted. His eulogist, however, in the *Dictionnaire Historique*, admits that Mersennus very ingeniously converted the thoughts of others to his own use; and the abbé Le Vayer calls him "Le bon Larron"—a skilful pilferer. Nevertheless, the work above named, *L'Harmonie Universelle, contenant la Théorie et la Pratique de la Musique* (1637, 2 vols. fol.), has proved of the utmost value to all later writers on the subject. The work was, in 1648, translated into Latin and enlarged by the author; but both the original and translation have now become as rare as they are curious. Another, but earlier production of his, *La Verité des Sciences contre les Sceptiques* (Paris, 1625), discusses at considerable length the nature of mathematical evidence, and concludes by maintaining that mental philosophy, jurisprudence, and all the arts and sciences, should be taught and illustrated through the aid of mathematics (liv. i, ch. viii, x, xiii, xiv). "The mind itself," he held, "is the real and effective source of all its powers and perceptions of abstract truth" (p. 193). See Hilarion de Coste, *Vie du R. P. Marin de Mersenne;* Nicéron, *Hommes illustres*, vol. xxxiii; Blakey, *Hist. of the Philosophy of Mind*, ii, 423 sq. (J. H. W.)

Merton, WALTER, an English prelate noted for his philanthropy, flourished in the 13th century. He was surnamed from the place of his birth, a village in Surrey. His education he received at a neighboring convent, and was there influenced to enter the ecclesiastic life. After filling various important offices in the Church, he was in 1258 advanced to the post of chancellor of England; but he held this position only a very short time. In 1264 he founded a college at Oxford, which still bears his name. In 1274 he was advanced to the see of Rochester. He died before the expiration of 1277.

Merû or **Merus** (Gr. Μηρός), a word of doubtful etymology, is in Hindû mythology the name of a mythical mountain. It is said to be situated in the centre of the seven continents, and its height is supposed to be 84,000 *yojanas*, of which 16,000 are below the surface of the earth. (A yojana is usually reckoned at 16,000 yards, or about nine of our miles; but, according to some authorities, it is only five miles.) The sacred river Ganges (Ganga), we are told, falls from heaven on its summit, and flows to the surrounding worlds in four streams, of which the southernmost is the Ganges of India. Brahma, attended by *rishis* (sages) and celestial minstrels, is supposed to visit them, and also Siva and his consort Pârvatî. See Wilson, *Sanscrit Dictionary*, s. v.; Moor, *Hindû Pantheon*, s. v.; Coleman, *Hindû Mythology*, p. 253.

Me'ruth ('Εμμερούϑ, Vulg. *Emerus*), put (1 Esdr. v, 24) for IMMER (Ezra ii, 37).

Merwin, SAMUEL, an early and eminent Methodist Episcopal minister, was born at Durham, Conn., Sept. 13, 1777; was converted while young; entered the New York Conference in 1800; in 1803 was stationed at Montreal, Canada; in 1804 at New York; in 1806 at Boston; in 1807-8 at Newport, R. I.; in 1812-13 at Albany; in 1814 at Brooklyn; from 1815 to 1818 was presiding elder on New York District; in 1819 preached in New York; in 1820 in Albany; from 1821 to 1823 was on the New Haven District; in 1824-5 at Baltimore; in 1826-7 at Philadelphia; in 1828-9 at Troy; in 1830-31 at New York; from 1832 to 1835 on the New York District; in 1836 at New York; in 1837-8 at Rhinebeck, N. Y., where he died, Jan. 13, 1839. Mr. Merwin was a man of great influence and usefulness in his whole public career. His ministerial and administrative talents were of the highest order. He possessed a mind of great richness and power, a vivid imagination, a commanding voice and person, and fervent piety; these, combined with the gift of utterance, made him one of the most eloquent men of his time; and the important stations which he filled in the New England, New York, Philadelphia, and Baltimore Conferences, testify to the opinion of his brethren respecting his abilities. In the presiding eldership his masterly judgment and influence over men made him conspicuous as a peace-maker and an organizer. Many souls were converted through his labors, and his memory in the church is blessed. See *Minutes of Conferences*, ii, 669; Sprague, *Annals of American Pulpit*, vol. vii. (G. L. T.)

Merz, PHILIPP PAUL, a German theologian, was born at Augsburg near the close of the seventeenth century. After having been received as a candidate for orders in the evangelical ministry in 1724, he suddenly turned to Romanism; was subsequently ordained a priest, and became the curate of Schwabsoyen, and sometime afterwards retired into his native city. He died in 1754. He wrote *Thesaurus Biblicus* (Augsburg, 1733-38, 1751, 1791, 2 vols. 4to; Venice, 1758, 4to). This work is very useful to preachers. At the end of each important word it contains a reference to such passages of Scripture as bear upon it. Merz also published *Quotlibet Catecheticum* (Augsburg, 1752, 5 vols. 4to), which is a complete and methodical abstract of the best catechisms then extant. See Zapf, *Augsburgische Bibliothek*, p. 11; Veith, *Bibliotheca Augustana*; Meusel, *Gelehrten-Lexikon*, s. v.

Mesa, CHRISTOBAL DE, a Spanish poet, was born at Zafra (Estramadura) in 1550. The little that is known of him is gathered from his own poetical compositions, and particularly his two epistles to the count de Lemos, together with that addressed to the count de Castro. From these productions it appears that in his youth Mesa was the pupil of Sanchez, the most eminent of Spanish philologists, and that he had also deeply studied both Fernand de Herrera and Louis de Soto. In after-life he spent some years in Italy, where he became intimately acquainted with the poet Tasso. He died, poor and obscure, about 1620. One of his poems is founded upon the tradition that the corpse of St. James, after his martyrdom in Jerusalem, was miraculously translated to Spain and deposited at Compostella, where from that day to this James has been honored as the patron saint of the realm. See JAMES. Another of his poems treats of Pelagius and the struggles of the Christians against the Moors up to the battle of Covadonga. His third poetical work relates the battle of Tolosa, which destroyed the power of the Mohammedans, and secured the emancipation of the Peninsula. He also wrote *El Patron de España* (Madrid, 1611, 12mo). See Ticknor,

History of Spanish Literature, ii, 462; Hoefer, *Nouv. Biog. Générale*, s. v.

Me'sech (Psa. cxx, 5). See MESHECH.

Mesengui, FRANÇOIS PHILLIPPE, a French ecclesiastic, celebrated for his connection with Jansenism, was born at Beauvais, in August, 1677. His parents being poor, friends defrayed the expenses of his education in the College of Beauvais and at the Seminary of Trente-Trois in Paris. After having been invested with the first minor orders, he became a professor of humanities in his native city. On his return to Paris in 1707, through the influence of his friends he was appointed superintendent of the department of rhetoric in the college at Beauvais. Coffin, who succeeded Rollin as the director of that institution, selected the abbé Mesengui for his coadjutor, and upon him devolved the duty of teaching the catechism to the students. The opposition, however, which he manifested to the papal bull known as *Unigenitus* constrained him in 1728 to resign his official functions. He subsequently became a member of the clergy at Saint-Etienne-du-Mont. Suspected of harboring the doctrines of Jansenism, he was in consequence prohibited from all ecclesiastical avocations, and confined to privacy and obscurity. He took up his residence in Paris, and devoted himself to the composition of various works designed for the propagation of the Jansenistic doctrines, which he finally adopted. He died in February, 1763, at Saint-Germain-en-Laye. Mesengui published: *Idée de la vie et de l'esprit de N. Choart de Buzauval, évêque de Beauvais, avec un abrégé de la vie de M. Hermant* (Paris, 1717, 12mo):— *Abrégé de l'histoire et de la morale de l'Ancien Testament* (Paris, 1728, 12mo):—*Le Nouveau Testament, trad. en Français, avec des notes littérales* (Paris, 1729, 12mo; 1752, 3 vols. 12mo):— *Vie des Saints pour tous les jours de l'année* (Paris, 1730, 6 vols. 12mo):—*Abrégé de l'histoire de l'Ancien Testament, avec des éclaircissements et des réflexions* (Paris, 1735-53, 10 vols. 12mo): —*Abrégé de l'histoire de l'Ancien et du Nouveau Testament* (Paris, 1737-38, 3 vols. 12mo):—*Épitres et Évangiles, avec des réflexions* (Paris, 1737; Lyons, 1810, 12mo): —*Exposition de la doctrine Chrétienne, ou instructions sur les principales vérités de la religion* (Utrecht [Paris], 1744, 6 vols. 12mo; new edition, revised and enlarged, Paris, 1754-58, 4 vols. 12mo). Some writers state that the duke of Orleans endeavored to prevail upon Mesengui to expunge from his works such passages as reflected upon the religious controversies of his day; but Mesengui evidently turned a deaf ear to the duke's entreaties. A new edition of the last work, issued in Italy, was placed in the *Index Expurgatorius* by an apostolic brief from pope Clement XIII in 1761. In a posthumous *Mémoire*, addressed to the cardinal Passionei, Mesengui attempted to justify his religious views. Among his other works may be mentioned, *La Constitution Unigenitus, avec des Remarques* (Paris, 1746, 12mo):—*Entretien de Théophile et d'Eugène sur la religion* (ibid. 1760, 12mo). Mesengui took part with Vigier and Coffin in the liturgical writings which M. de Vintimille, archbishop of Paris, disseminated in his diocese. See Lequeux, *Mémoire abrégé sur la vie et les ouvrages de l'abbé Mesengui* (Paris, 1763, 8vo).

Me'sha, the name of a place and of three men, differently written in the Heb.

1. (Heb. *Mesha'*, מֵשָׁא, probably of Arabic origin; Sept. Μασσή, Vulg. *Messa*.) A place mentioned in describing the boundaries of that part of Arabia inhabited by the descendants of Joktan (Gen. x, 30), where it is stated that "their dwelling was from Mesha even unto Sephar, (and beyond even unto) a mount of the east." In this passage it has been assumed by many that "the mountain of the east" (הַר הַקֶּדֶם) is not put by apposition in conjunction with Sephar, but is some third locality to which the boundary extends, as

Saadias interprets; and, if so, it is doubtless none other than the chain running across the middle of Arabia from the region of Mecca and Medina as far as the Persian Gulf, now called Nesjd, the highlands (see Jomard, *Notice sur le pays de l'Arabie centrale*, Paris, 1823). Sephar would then be the modern Sephr, the chief city of the district Shehr in the province of Hadramant. See SEPHAR. Bochart (*Phaleg*, ii, 20) thinks that Mesha, from which the boundary extends, is the *Musa* or *Muza* (Μοῦσα, Ptol. vi, 8; Μοῦζα, Arrian, *Peripl.*; *Muza*, Pliny, vi, 23) spoken of as a maritime city on the western coast of Arabia, not far from Mocha, where *Muzaa* (Niebuhr, *Arabien*, p. 223; Janaen, *Hist. Jemanæ*, p. 286), or rather *Mausij* (Niebuhr, p. 224, 225; Mannert, *Geogr.* vi, 1, p. 63), now stands. It was a town of note in classical times, but has since fallen into decay, if the modern *Musa* be the same place. The latter is situated in about 13° 40′ N. lat., 43° 20′ E. long., and is near a mountain called the *Three Sisters*, or Jebel Musa, in the Admiralty Chart of the Red Sea, drawn from the surveys of captain Pullen, R.N. But as neither of these Arabic names can well be compared with that of Mesha, it may be better (with J. D. Michaelis, *Spicileg.* ii, p. 214; *Suppl.* No. 1561) to understand *Mesene* or *Meisan*, situated among the mouths of the Tigris (in the Shat el-Arab) on the Persian Gulf—a place described by Philostogius (iii, 7; comp. Dion Cass. lxviii, 28; Asseman. *Bibl. Orient.* iii, 2, p. 430, 603; Abulfeda in *Tab. Iracæ* ap. Michael. in *Spicil.* l. c.; D'Anville, *l'Euphrate et le Tigre*, p. 135), the name perhaps signifying the *river island*, from its being enclosed by the branches of the Tigris, as often alluded to by the Greek geographers (see Steph. Byz. s. v. Orathra and Messene; Pliny, v, 27,31; Cellar. *Notit.* ii, p. 749; D'Anville, p. 130, 131). The sacred writer would thus in his description begin with the eastern limits of the Joktanidæ, and end with the western and northern, Sephar being sought between them. "But it is very doubtful whether the island, which has been formed by the deposits of the river, was in existence in the days of Moses; and it is still more doubtful whether such a spot could at that early period have attained to any political or geographical notoriety. Besides, it is not likely that an accurate writer would describe a purely Arabian territory as commencing on the east side of the Tigris. The theory of Mr. Forster is much more probable than either of the preceding. He identifies Mesha with a mountain-range called *Zames* by Ptolemy (vi, 7), which commences near the Persian Gulf, and runs in a south-western direction nearly across the peninsula. It is an undoubted fact that the various Joktanitic tribes, or Beni-Kahtân, as they are called by Arab writers, are still found, and have been from the earliest period, in the wide region extending from Mount Zames to the Indian Ocean and Red Sea; and that this range separates them from the Ishmaelitish Arabs (Forster, *Geography of Arabia*, i, 95 sq.). Forster further conjectures that the name Zames is radically identical with Mesha, the syllables being inverted, as is very common in Arabic words—thus Mesza = Mesha. The Zames range is now called by the general name of the 'Nejd Mountains,' and the country extending thence to the Indian Ocean on the east, and the Red Sea on the south, embraces the most fertile part of Arabia—the classic Arabia Felix, now called Yemen (Ritter, *Erdkunde*, xii, 708 sq.). The mountains of Nejd are famous for their pastures and for their horses, which are considered the best in Arabia (Ritter, p. 918–1035; Fresnel, *Lettres sur la Géog. de l'Arabie*, in *Journ. Asiat.* vol. v." "The position of the early Joktanitic colonists is clearly made out from the traces they have left in the ethnology, language, and monuments of Southern Arabia; and, without putting too precise a limitation upon the possible situation of Mesha and Sephar, we may suppose that these places must have fallen within the south-western quarter of the peninsula; including the modern Yemen on the west, and the districts of 'Oman, Mahreh, Shihr, etc., as far as

Hadramaut, on the east. These general boundaries are strengthened by the identification of Sephar with the port of Zafâri, or Dhafâri; though the site of Sephar may possibly be hereafter connected with the old Himyeritic metropolis in the Yemen, but this would not materially alter the question. In Sephar we believe we have the eastern limit of the early settlers, whether its site be the sea-port or the inland city; and the correctness of this supposition appears from the Biblical record, in which the migration is apparently from west to east, from the probable course taken by the immigrants, and from the greater importance of the known western settlements of the Joktanites, or those of Yemen."

2. (Heb. *Meysha'*, מֵישָׁע, *deliverance;* Sept. Μαρισάς v. r. Μαρισά, Vulg. *Mesa*.) The eldest son of Caleb or Chelubai (brother of Jerahmeel and son of Hezron), and the father (founder) of Ziph, of the tribe of Judah (1 Chron. ii, 42). B.C. cir. 1618.

3. (Heb. *Meysha'*, מֵישָׁא, *retreat;* Sept. Μωσά v. r. Μισά, Vulg. *Mosa*.) One of the sons of Shaharaim of the tribe of Benjamin, by the latter of his two wives, Baara or Hodesh (1 Chron. viii, 9). B.C. cir. 1612. See SHAHARAIM.

4. (Heb. *Meysha'*, מֵישַׁע, *deliverance;* Sept. Μισά v. r. Μωσά, Vulg. *Mesa*.) A king of Moab, who possessed an immense number of flocks and herds (2 Kings iii, 4). Probably the allegiance of Moab, with that of the tribes east of the Jordan, was transferred to the northern kingdom of Israel upon the division of the monarchy, for there is no account of any subjugation of the country subsequent to the war of extermination with which it was visited by David, when Benaiah displayed his prowess (2 Sam. xxiii, 20), and "the Moabites became David's servants, bearers of gifts" (2 Sam. viii, 2). When Ahab had fallen in battle at Ramoth Gilead, Mesha seized the opportunity afforded by the confusion consequent upon this disaster, and the feeble reign of Ahaziah, to shake off the yoke of Israel, and free himself from the burdensome tribute of a "hundred thousand lambs and a hundred thousand rams with their wool." These numbers may seem exaggerated if understood as the amount of yearly tribute. It is therefore more probable that the greedy and implacable Ahab had at some one time levied this enormous impost upon the Moabites; and it is likely that it was the apprehension of a recurrence of such ruinous exactions which incited the revolt (2 Kings i, 1; iii, 5). The country east of the Jordan was rich in pasture for cattle (Numb. xxii, 1), the chief wealth of the Moabites consisted in their large flocks of sheep, and the king of this pastoral people is described as *nokéd* (נוֹקֵד), "a sheepmaster," or owner of herds. About the signification of this word *noked* there is not much doubt, but its origin is obscure. It occurs but once besides in Amos i, 1, where the prophet Amos is described as "among the *herdmen* (נוֹקְדִים, *nokedim*) of Tekoah." On this Kimchi remarks that a herdsman was called *noked*, because most cattle have black or white spots (comp. נָקֹד, *nakód*, Gen. xxx, 32, A. V. "speckled"), or, as Buxtorf explains it, because sheep are generally marked with certain signs so as to be known. But it is highly improbable that any such etymology should be correct, and Fürst's conjecture that it is derived from an obsolete root, signifying to keep or feed cattle, is more likely to be true (*Concord.* s. v.). See HERD.

When, upon the death of Ahaziah, his brother Jehoram succeeded to the throne of Israel, one of his first acts was to secure the assistance of Jehoshaphat, his father's ally, in reducing the Moabites to their former condition of tributaries. The united armies of the two kings marched by a circuitous route round the Dead Sea, and were joined by the forces of the king of Edom. See JEHORAM. The disordered soldiers of Moab, eager only for spoil, were surprised by the warriors of Israel and their allies, and became an easy prey. In the panic which ensued they were slaughtered without mercy, their country was made a desert, and the king took refuge in his last stronghold and defended himself with the energy of despair. With 700 fighting men he made a vigorous attempt to cut his way through the beleaguering army, and, when beaten back, he with- drew to the wall of his city, and there, in sight of the allied host, offered his first-born son, his successor in the kingdom, as a burnt-offering to Chemosh, the ruthless fire-god of Moab. There appears to be no reason for supposing that the son of the king of Edom was the victim on this occasion, whether, as R. Joseph Kimchi supposed, he was already in the power of the king of

The Moabitic Stone.

(The numbers in the margin designate the lines corresponding to the verses below. The dots over some of the characters show that the decipherment is doubtful. The small letters, a b, c e, indicate the two large fragments rescued from the Arabs, who had broken the stone after impressions had been taken from it by the discoverer. The whole stone was about three feet seven inches long, by one foot eleven inches wide.)

Moab, and was the cause of the Edomites joining the armies of Israel and Judah; or whether, as R. Moses Kimchi suggested, he was taken prisoner in the sally of the Moabites, and sacrificed out of revenge for its failure. These conjectures appear to have arisen from an attempt to find in this incident the event to which allusion is made in Amos ii, 1, where the Moabite is charged with burning the bones of the king of Edom into lime. It is more natural, and renders the narrative more vivid and consistent, to suppose that the king of Moab, finding his last resource fail him, endeavored to avert the wrath and obtain the aid of his god by the most costly sacrifice in his power. On beholding this fearful sight, the besiegers withdrew in horror, lest some portion of the monstrous crime might attach to their own souls (comp. Josephus, *Ant.* ix, 3, 2; Ewald, *Isr. Gesch.* iii, 226 sq.). By this withdrawal they, however, afforded the king the relief he desired, and this was, no doubt, attributed by him to the efficacy of his offering, and to the satisfaction of his god therewith. The invaders, however, ravaged the country as they withdrew. and returned with much spoil to their own land (2 Kings iii, 25–27). B.C. cir. 891. See MOAB-ITE.

The exploits of "Mesha, son [i. e. votary] of Chemosh, king of Moab," are recorded in the Phœnician inscription lately discovered by M. Ganneau on a block of black basalt at Dibon in Moab (see *Quarterly Statement*, No. 5, of "The Palestine Exploration Fund," Lond. 1870); which, according to the decipherment given by him in the *Revue Archéologique* (Jan. and June, 1870), is as below (see the *Wesleyan Magazine*, April, 1870). Prof. Neubauer has published the text in modern Hebrew characters in Grätz's *Monatschrift*, and Prof. J. Derenbourg a translation in the *Revue Israélite* (April 8, 1870), substantially as below. See also the *Church Gazette*, N. Y. 1871, No. 6. Several other commentaries have been published upon it, especially by Dr. Deutsch of the British Museum. See also Nöldeke, *Inschrift des Mesa* (Kiel, 1870); Schlottman, *Siegessäule Mesa's* (Halle, 1870); De Costa, *The Moabite Stone* (N. Y. 1871). The fullest exhibit, together with the literature of the subject, is that of Dr. Ginsburg (2d ed. Lond. 1871).

1. I, Mesha, son of Chemosh, . . . King of Moab, [son]
2. of Yabni . . . My father reigned over Moab (thirty years), and I reigned
3. after him; I made this altar for Chemosh at Karhah on account
4. of the assistance he gave me in all battles, and because he made me successful against my enemies the men
5. of the King of Israel, who oppressed Moab a long time, for Chemosh was angry against
6. his land. His son succeeded him, and he also said, I will oppress Moab. In my days he (Chemosh) said, [I will go]
7. and appear (be favorable) to Moab and his temple; then Israel wasted continually. Omri took [the plain of]
8. Mahdeba and dwelt in it . . . built forty . . . [and dwelt]
9. Chemosh there in my days. I built Baal-Meon and made (sacrifices) there . . . and I [built]
10. Kiryathan. The men of Gad [dwelt] in [this] land from early times, and there built the King
11. of Israel [Yaazer]; I besieged the city, took it, and killed all [who dwelt]
12. in the city, to the gratification of Chemosh and Moab; I made captive there . . .
13. [and brought] it to Chemosh at Keriyoth. I remained here with the chiefs and [the soldiers until]
14. the next day. Then Chemosh bade me go and take Nebo from Israel. [I arose and]
15. went in the night and fought against it from the break of day till noon; I
16. took it, killed all, seven thousand . . . [to please Astor].
17. . . . for Chemosh devoted to Astor. . . . I took from there all
18. the vessels of Jehovah, and [offered] them to Chemosh. And the King of Israel built
19. Yahaz, and dwelt there, when I made war upon him. Chemosh drove him out from thence; I
20. took from Moab two hundred men, all chiefs, transferred them to Yahaz, and began
21. to make war against Dibon. I built Kirhah, Hamath-ha-Yearim, and Hamath.
22. H . . .; I constructed their gates and their towers; I

23. built the palace, and I made aqueducts (?) in the interior
24. of the town. There were no cisterns in the interior of the town of Kirhah, and I said to all the people, Make
25. every one a cistern in his house. And I made a ditch round Kirhah with [the men]
26. of Israel. I built (Aro)ër, and I made the passage over the Arnon.
27. I built Beth-Bamoth, which had been overthrown, and Bezer, which had been destroyed.
28. I fortified Dibon to hold it in subjection, and I constructed
29. fortresses in the towns which I added to [my] land. I built
30. . . . Beth-Diblathan, Beth-Baal-Meon, and transported thither [Moabites]
31. [in order to take possession of] the land. At Horonan dwelt [the children of Reuben] . . .
32. Chemosh told me, Go, fight against Horonan [I fought against it and took it],
33. [and there dwelt] Chemosh in my days . . .
34. . . .

Me'shach (Heb. or Chald. *Meyshak'*, מֵישַׁךְ, of foreign etymology; Sept. Μισάκ v. r. Μισάχ, Vulg. *Misach*), the title given by the Babylonian court to MICHAEL (q. v.), one of the Hebrew youths in training for the rank of magi (Dan. i, 7; ii, 49; iii, 12–30). "Gesenius resolves the name into the Persic *miz-shah*, 'the guest of the shah' (*Thesaur.* s. v.); Hitzig (*Exeget. Hdb.* ad loc.) and Fürst (*Heb.-Lex.* s. v.) refer it to the Sanscrit *Méshah*, 'a ram,' and regard it as a name of the sun-god. The changing of the names of persons taken into a family as servants or slaves was common in ancient times among both the Orientals and the Greeks (Jahn, *Archäol.* pt. i, vol. ii, p. 280: Theodoret on Dan. i, 7: Chrysostom, *Opp.* v, 286; Hävernick, *Comm. üb. Dan.* p. 30)" (Kitto). "That Meshach was the name of some god of the Chaldæans is extremely probable, from the fact that Daniel, who had the name of Belteshazzar, was so called after the god of Nebuchadnezzar (Dan. iv, 8), and that Abednego was named after Nego, or Nebo, the Chaldæan name for the planet Mercury." See DANIEL.

Me'shech (Heb. *Me'shek*, מֶשֶׁךְ, a *drawing* out, as in Psa. cxxvi, 6; or *possession*, as in Job xxviii, 18; Sept. Μοσόχ, Vulg. *Mosoch;* a pronunciation which the Samaritan codex also exhibits, מֹשֹׁוּךְ; but in Ezek. xxxviii, 2, 3; xxxix, 1, Sept. v. r. Μοσόκ and Μεσόχ; in Ezek. xxvii, 13, τὰ παρατείνοντα; in Psa. cxx, 5, Sept. ἐμακρύνϑη, Vulg. *prolongatus est*, Auth. Vers. "Mesech"), the sixth son of Japheth, B.C. cir. 2500 (Gen. x, 2), and founder of a tribe mentioned among his descendants (1 Chron. i, 5), and later (Ezek. xxvii, 13) as engaged in traffic with Tyre, in connection with Gog (Ezek. xxxviii, 2, 3; xxxix, 1). In nearly every instance they are coupled with Tubal or the Tibareni as neighbors (Gen. x, 2; Ezek. xxvii, 13; xxxii, 26; xxxviii, 2, 3; xxxix, 1: so also Herodotus, iii, 94; vii, 78; comp. Hengstenberg, *Moses*, p. 206; Wilkinson, i, 378 sq.); and from one passage at least (Ezek. xxxii, 26) they appear to have lived near Assyria and Elymais. They are without doubt the same with the *Moschi* (Bochart, *Phaleg*, iii, 12), a barbarous people of Asia, inhabiting what were known as the Moschian Mountains (Ptol. v, 6, 1; 13, 5), between the Black and Caspian seas (Strabo, xi, 344, 378, 498 sq.; Pliny, vi, 11), in the later Iberia (comp. Josephus, *Ant.* i, 6, 1), who are named by ancient authors as forming a single department of the Persian empire under a separate jurisdiction with the Tibarenians (Herod. iii, 94; vii, 78). In confirmation of the trade alluded to in Ezek. xxvii, 13, Reineggs remarks (*Beschreib. des Caucas.* i, 6; ii, 61) that the Moschian Mountains contain rich copper-mines, and this region has always been noted for the export of slaves, especially females, whose beauty usually commands a ready market for the Turkish harems (see Rosenmüller, *Alterth.* I, i. 248 sq.). In Psa. cxx, 5, the name occurs in connection with Kedar as a synonyme for foreigners or barbarians (Michaelis, *Suppl.* p. 1569), like the modern phrase "Turks and Hottentots."—Winer, ii, 86. The same name, but in a plural form, appears, according to some, in Isa. lxvi, 19 (מֹשְׁכֵי קֶשֶׁת, Sept. Μοσόχ, Vulg. *tendentes sagittam*, Auth. Vers. "that draw the bow"), but it there is rather an appellation of the archers (comp. Jer. xlvi, 9); also, but with still less probability, in Jer. v, 8 (מַשְׁכִּים, Sept. Θηλυμανεῖς, Vulg. *emissarii*, Auth. Vers. "fed"). "The Colchian tribes, the Chalybes more especially, were skilled in working metals, and hence arose the trade in the 'vessels of brass' with Tyre; nor is it at all improbable that slaves were largely exported thence as now from the neighboring district of Georgia. Although the Moschi were a comparatively unimportant race in classical times, they had previously been one of the most powerful nations of Western Asia. The Assyrian monarchs were engaged in frequent wars with them, and it is not improbable that they had occupied the whole of the district afterwards named Cappadocia. In the Assyrian inscriptions the name appears under the form of *Muskai*: a somewhat similar name, *Mashoash*, appears in an Egyptian inscription which commemorates the achievements of the third Rameses (Wilkinson, *Anc. Eg.* i, 398, Abridg.). The subsequent history of Meshech is unknown; Knobel's attempt to connect them with the Ligurians (*Völkertaf.* p. 119, etc.) is devoid of all solid ground." "The names of the Moschians and Tybarenians are also joined frequently on the Assyrian inscriptions (Rawlinson's *Herodotus*, i, 651; comp. Pliny, vi, 4). The primitive seat of the Moschi appears to have been among the Caucasus Mountains, on the south-eastern shores of the Black Sea, immediately north of Armenia (Strabo, xi, p. 498 sq.); and, according to Strabo, a part of the great chain or group of mountains took their name (xi, p. 521). The Moschi were, however, a wild and warlike race, and extended their depredations and conquests far beyond the confines of their native hills. Cappadocia appears to have been, at least in part, occupied by them (Josephus, *Ant.* i, 6, 1), and probably from them its capital city took its name *Mazaka* (Strabo, xii, p. 538; Rawlinson's *Herodotus*, iv, 222). In the time of the Hebrew prophets their power was felt even in Syria and Egypt in conjunction with their Scythic allies, Gog and Magog, under whose command they had apparently placed themselves. It is interesting to observe how Ezekiel's description of their equipments—'bucklers, small shields (מָגֵן), and swords' (Ezek. xxxviii, 1-5)—corresponds with that of Herodotus (vii, 78). During the ascendency of the Babylonians and Persians in Western Asia the Moschi were subdued; but it seems probable that a large number of them crossed the Caucasus range and spread over the northern steppes, mingling with the Scythians. There they became known as *Muskovs*, and gave that name to the Russian nation, and its ancient capital, by which they are still universally known throughout the East (Rawlinson's *Herod.* iv, 222)." See ETHNOLOGY.

Meshed-Ali and **Meshed-Hossein** is the name of a Mohammedan cemetery situated near the ruins of Babylon, which is one of the most celebrated places of pilgrimage of the Shiites. Many thousands of corpses are brought thither during the year for interment from all parts of the East.

Meshelemi'ah (Heb. *Meshélemyah'*, מְשֶׁלֶמְיָה, *friendship of Jehovah*, 1 Chron. ix, 21; Sept. Μοσολλάμ v. r. Μοσολλαμί, Vulg. *Mosollamia*; also, in the prolonged form, *Meshelemya'hu*, מְשֶׁלֶמְיָהוּ, 1 Chron. xxvi, 1; Μοσολλάμ v. r. Μοσελλεμία; ver. 2, Μασελλαμία v. r. Μοσελλαμία; ver. 9, Μεσολλεμία v. r. Μοσελλεμία; Vulg. *Mesellemia*), a Levite of the Korhite branch, who, with his seven sons and ten other relatives, was appointed by David warden of the east gate of the Temple; called SHELEMIAH in 1 Chron. xxvi, 14; and apparently also SHALLUM in 1 Chron. ix, 19. B.C. 1014. "As we learn from ver. 9 that he had eighteen strong men of his sons and brethren under him, we may conclude that all his sons except Zechariah the first-born

(ver. 14) served with him, and therefore Elioenai likewise. There were six Levites daily on guard at the east gate, whose turn would therefore come every third day."

Meshez'abeël (Heb. *Mesheyzabel'*, מְשֵׁיזַבְאֵל, whose *deliverer* is *God*; Sept. Μαζαβήλ, Μεσωζεβηλ, and Βασηζά v. r. Μασεζειηλ; Vulg. *Mesezebel* and *Mesizebel*), one of the chief Israelites that subscribed the sacred covenant after the captivity, B.C. cir. 410 (Neh. x, 21); apparently the same with the father of Pethahiah the Zerahite of Judah, which latter had previously (B.C. cir. 440) assisted in the administration of civil affairs (Neh. xi, 24); and perhaps the same with the father of Berechiah and grandfather of Meshullam, which last had (B.C. 446) assisted in repairing the walls of Jerusalem (Neh. iii, 4).

Meshi. See SILK.

Meshil'lemith (1 Chron. ix, 12). See MESHILLEMOTH.

Meshil'lemoth (Heb. *Meshillemoth'*, מְשִׁלֵּמוֹת, *requitals*; Vulg. *Mosollamoth*), the name of two men.

1. (Sept. Μοσολλαμώθ v. r. Μοσολαμώθ.) The father of the chief Ephraimite Berechiah, which latter was one of those who opposed the reduction of their captive brethren of Judah to slavery (2 Chron. xxviii, 12). B.C. ante 738.

2. (Sept. Μεσαριμίθ.) A priest, son of Immer and father of Ahasai (Neh. xi, 13); doubtless the same with the priest MESHILLEMITH (Heb. *Meshillemith'*, מְשִׁלֵּמִית, *retribution*; Sept. Μοσολλαμώθ v. r. Μασελμώθ, Vulg. *Mosollamith*), the son of Immer and father of Meshullam (1 Chron. ix, 12). B.C. long ante 440.

Mesho'bab (Heb. *Meshobab'*, מְשׁוֹבָב, *returned*; Sept. Μεσωβάβ), one of the chief Simeonites, whose enlarged family induced him to migrate to Gedor in the time of Hezekiah (1 Chron. iv, 34). B.C. cir. 711.

Meshul'lam (Heb. *Meshullam'*, מְשֻׁלָּם, *befriended*; Sept. usually Μοσολλάμ), the name of several persons in the later periods of Jewish history.

1. One of the chief Gadites resident in Bashan in the time of Jotham's viceroyship (1 Chron. v, 13). B.C. 781.

2. The father of Azaliah and grandfather of Shaphan, which last was the scribe sent by Josiah to direct the contributions for repairing the Temple (2 Kings xxii, 3). B.C. considerably ante 623.

3. A priest, son of Zadok and father of Hilkiah (1 Chron. ix, 11; Neh. xi, 11). Probably the same as SHALLUM (q. v.), the high-priest (1 Chron. vi, 13; Ezra vii, 1).

4. A Levite of the family of Kohath, one of the overseers of the Temple repairs undertaken by Josiah (2 Chron. xxxiv, 12). B.C. 623.

5. One of the chief Benjamites of the family of Elpaal resident at Jerusalem (1 Chron. viii, 17). B.C. ante 589. He is perhaps the Benjamite (son of Hodaviah, and grandson of Hasenuah) whose son (or descendant) Sallu resided at Jerusalem after the captivity (1 Chron. ix, 7); but this person seems elsewhere to be called the son of Joed (Neh. xi, 7).

6. The eldest of the children of Zerubbabel (1 Chron. iii, 19). B.C. cir. 536.

7. A chief priest, son of Ezra, contemporary with Joiakim (Neh. xii, 13). B.C. post 536.

8. A chief priest, son of Ginnethon, contemporary with Joiakim (Neh. xii, 16). B.C. post 536.

9. One of the leading Israelites sent for by Ezra to accompany his party to Jerusalem (Ezra viii, 16). B.C. 459. He appears to be the same with one of those who assisted in the investigation concerning the foreign marriages of those who had returned (Ezra x, 15). He was perhaps the same with one of the Temple wardens, as afterwards arranged (Neh. xii, 25). B.C. cir. 440. This last is also called MESHELEMIAH (1 Chron. xxvi, 1), SHELEMIAH (1 Chron. xxvi, 14), and SHALLUM (Neh. vii, 45).

10. An Israelite, of the "sons" (or residents) of Bani, who divorced his Gentile wife after the exile (Ezra x, 29). B.C. 459.

11. A priest, son of Meshillemith and father of Jahzerah (1 Chron. ix, 12; comp. Neh. xi, 13). B.C. long ante 440.

12. The son of Berechiah and grandson of Meshezabeel; he repaired two portions of the walls of Jerusalem after the captivity (Neh. iii, 4, 30). B.C. 446. It was his daughter that Tobiah's son Johanan married (Neh. vi, 18).

13. The son of Besodeiah, who, in connection with Jehoiada, repaired the "old gate" of Jerusalem after the exile (Neh. iii, 6). B.C. 446.

14. One of the Jewish leaders who made the tour of the walls of Jerusalem on their completion after the captivity (Neh. xii, 33). B.C. 446.

15. A chief Benjamite (son of Shephathiah), who dwelt at Jerusalem after the captivity (1 Chron. ix, 8). B.C. cir. 440.

16. One of the principal Israelites who supported Ezra on the left while expounding the law to the people (Neh. viii, 4). B.C. cir. 410. He may have been identical with No. 9, 12, 13, 14, or 15. He is probably the same with one of those who subscribed the sacred covenant on the same occasion (Neh. x, 20).

17. One of the priests who joined in Nehemiah's solemn bond of allegiance to Jehovah (Neh. x, 7). B.C. cir. 410. He is perhaps the same with either No. 6 or No. 7.

Meshul'lemeth (Heb. *Meshulle'meth*, מְשֻׁלֶּמֶת, *friend*; Sept. Μεσολλάμ, Vulg. *Messalemeth*), the daughter of Haruz of Jotbah; she was the mother of king Amon, and consequently the wife of Manasseh, whom she appears to have survived (2 Kings xxi, 19). Her character may be inferred from the idolatry of her son as well as of her husband. B.C. 664–642.

Mesitys (μεσίτης, i. e. *mediator*) was the name given to a presbyter while engaged in discharging the functions of the Eucharist. This was considered by the ancient Church as the highest point of a presbyter's dignity and office. The appellation was very properly censured by Augustine as derogating from the dignity and office of the true and only Mediator of the Christian covenant (*Contr. Parmen.* lib. ii, c. 8; comp. *De Civ. Dei*, lib. ix, c. 15). This word also denoted the middle rank occupied by the presbyter between the bishop and deacon. See Riddle, *Christian Antiquities* (see Index).

Mesmer, FRANZ (according to others, FRIEDRICH ANTON), the founder of the doctrine of animal magnetism, or, as it is more generally termed, mesmerism, was born at a village near the Bodensee May 23, 1733. He studied mathematics and natural science at the Jesuit school in Dillingen, and, later, medicine at the University of Vienna, and there took the degree of doctor of medicine in 1766. About 1772 he commenced, assisted by father Hell, to investigate the curative powers of the magnet, and was led to adopt the opinion that there exists a power similar to magnetism, which exercises an extraordinary influence on the human body. This he called *animal magnetism*, and published an account of his discovery, and of its medicinal value, in 1775: *Précis historique et faits relatifs au magnétisme animal;* and in 1776, in his thesis, *On the Influence of the Planets on the Human Body.* Honors were conferred upon him in Germany. In 1778 he went to Paris, where he attracted much attention. His system obtained the support of members of the medical profession, as well as of others; but he refused two offers, one of 30,000 livres, and the other of 340,000 livres, to reveal his secret; and this, combined with other circumstances, gave rise to suspicion, and induced the French government to appoint a commission, composed of physicians and naturalists, among them Bailly, our own Franklin, and Lavoisier, whose report was unfavorable to him. He now fell into disrepute, and after a visit to

England, retired to Meersburg, near his native place, where he spent the rest of his life in complete obscurity. He died March 5, 1815. See MESMERISM.

Mesmerism. Under this heading we propose to consider the various phenomena which have at different times been presented for public consideration under the names of *Mesmerism, Animal Magnetism, Magnetic Somnambulism, Clairvoyance,* etc., etc. The nature of this *Cyclopædia* of course limits us in the consideration of this subject from a theological stand-point.

Animal magnetism is a supposed influence or emanation by means of which one person can act upon another, producing wonderful effects upon his body, and controlling his actions and thoughts. It was fancied to have some analogy to the magnetism of the loadstone, and hence its name. The term has been used to group together a multitude of manifestations deemed to be of a wonderful kind, which have given rise to an amount of delusion and credulity hardly exemplified on any other subject. Electro-biology, odylism, table-turning, spirit-rapping, table-talking, spiritism, have been classed as only modifications of the same phenomena. For the sake of securing a thorough review of the various phenomena which mesmerism, so called, or better, animal magnetism, has been conceived to produce in those who were brought under its influence, we divide the subject into two classes: cases which are effected while the person operated upon remains awake, and those which take place while the patient is in a state of sleep, or in a state resembling it. These two classes of phenomena, moreover, belong to different periods of the history of mesmerism. To those of the first class chiefly the early practitioners of this mysterious art confined their pretensions, and it was only at a later period that the magnetizers laid claim to the power of producing those wonderful manifestations included under the second class.

Mesmerism Proper.—Anthony Mesmer, whose personal history we have detailed above, is supposed to be the first in modern times who claimed to have discovered the process of healing physical derangements by the application of animal magnetism, as already defined. Many were the cures pretended to be wrought by Mesmer and his disciples, until he was suddenly checked in his auspicious career by the unfavorable report of the committee which the French government appointed in 1785. "This pretended agent," said they, "is not magnetism; for on examining the grand reservoir of the fluid by a needle and electrometer, neither magnetism nor electricity could be detected. We tried it upon ourselves and others without effect. On blindfolding those who professed great susceptibility of its influence, all its ordinary effects were produced when nothing was done, but they imagined they were magnetized; while none of its effects were produced when they were really magnetized, but imagined nothing was done. So also when brought under a magnetized tree; nothing happened if they thought they were at a distance from it, while they immediately went into violent convulsions when they thought they were near the tree, though really not so. The effects, therefore," say the commissioners, "are purely imaginary; and although they have wrought some cures, they are not without evil results, for the convulsions sometimes spread among the feeble of mind and body, and especially among women. And, finally, there are parts of the operations which may readily be turned to vicious purposes, and in fact immoral practices have already actually grown out of them."

Mesmerism Modified.—But even long before the supposed discovery of Mesmer had been subjected to the test of scientific investigation, mesmerism had entered on a new phase, and assumed a form differing widely in many respects from that which it obtained from the hands of its author. We allude to what is scientifically termed *Magnetic Somnambulism*, and which was first brought before the public for consideration by one of

Mesmer's pupils, the marquis de Puysegur. In the hands of Mesmer animal magnetism was simply a curative agent; in the hands of Puysegur, however, we find it not only to be a curative means, but to confer the power of detecting the morbid condition of parts, both in the person operated on and in others, and the instinctive knowledge of the remedies required to effect a cure. With this important advance, the mesmeric system was after this time advocated by Mesmer himself, and hence the mistake on the part of some that Mesmer was acquainted with the phenomena of somnambulism and had discoursed upon them from the very first during his stay in Paris. But whether De Puysegur or Mesmer be the discoverer of magnetic somnambulism, certain it is that if this discovery had not been made, animal magnetism would have found its resting-place in the grave of Mesmer. Remodelled by this valuable addition, new life was infused into the expiring system; "a life so vigorous, indeed, that it has been sufficient to keep it alive till the present time."

The art of inducing the magnetic state, as practiced by its discoverer, Mesmer, involved the use of apparatus—the *baquet*, or magnetic tub, iron rods, etc.; but the means which De Puysegur first used, and which became the more common, are *passes* made by the hands of the magnetizer from the head of the "subject" or patient downward, or simply making him fix his eyes on the operator. "Ordinarily," we are told, "the magnetizer and the patient are seated opposite to each other; the former, with each hand, lays hold of the opposite hand of the latter, with the balls of the thumbs resting against each other. Thus they sit for five or ten minutes, or until the influence begins to be felt. The magnetizer then withdraws his hands, and makes slow passes with open hands and outspread fingers over the patient from the head to the foot, turning the hands away while moving them upward, and while making the downward passes keeping the points of the fingers within an inch or two of the patient's clothing. After making a dozen or two of such passes, the magnetizer resumes his former position. During the whole of this process he keeps his attention on the patient, and exercises his will in silent commands that he shall become somnambulic. The patient should be still, quiet, and resigned. Some persons can be mesmerized within a few minutes; others can not be affected by trials of an hour daily for weeks; but after the experiment has once succeeded, it can be more easily repeated. The patient becomes more susceptible, and the magnetizer more powerful, by every successful trial. The patient who could not, at first, be thrown into the mesmeric sleep in less than an hour of constant contact with the operator, may at last be magnetized in a few minutes or seconds, without contact, by the mere outstretched hand, glance, or even will of the mesmerist." According to the mesmeric theory, the nervous energy of the operator has overpowered that of the subject, as a powerful magnet does a weak one, and the two are in *rapport*, as it is termed. In some cases the mesmeric trance assumes the form of *clairvoyance.*

The various stages of the magnetic influence mesmerizers distinguish as six different classes. "The first stage is that of waking magnetization. The patient feels a singular influence pervading his body, frequently a pricking, somewhat like that felt in a limb asleep. Sometimes there is an increase of temperature and sweat. The second stage is that of drowsiness. The pulse becomes fuller, the breathing slower; there is a feeling as though warmth were radiating from the stomach; there is a heavy pressure on the eyelids, which close against the will of the patient, and he is unable to open them; but still he retains his normal consciousness and sensation. The third stage is that of coma, or senseless sleep, wherein he is insensible to the loudest noises, and all the nerves of sensation are as if benumbed. The fourth stage is that of magnetic somnambulism. The patient awakes from the third stage into a new sphere of exist-

VI.—5

ence, and as another person. He has consciousness and sensation, but they differ greatly from those of his normal condition. He hears only the voice of his magnetizer, or of some person in contact with him. The magnetizer can make his muscles rigid in almost any position, and has the power of governing his physical motions. His own senses of touch, taste, and smell appear to be dormant, but he perceives all the impressions produced on those senses in the magnetizer's frame. The fifth stage is that of clairvoyance. This is a heightened condition of the fourth stage. The patient has means of perception unknown to man in his normal state, and so singular that the assertion of their possession, measured by the general experience of the race, appears to be an impudent falsehood or imposture. The somnambulist can see with his eyes closed and bandaged; he can then even see what waking men in his place can not see with their eyes open. He can read the contents of letters unopened; he can see through clothing, wood and metal boxes, and walls of brick or stone; he can tell what is going on in the room above him or in the room below. Sometimes the sense of sight, or a faculty capable of perceiving things which the normal man perceives only by means of the organ of vision, seems to reside in the forehead, in the back-head, in the fingers, or in the knuckles of the hand. Thus the clairvoyant will sometimes move about holding his fist in front of him for the purpose of seeing where he is going. How this means of perception can exist apart from the organs of vision, why it exists in one part of the body more than another, and why one should have it in the hand, another in the forehead, and a third in the back-head, are questions very proper to be asked, but to which there is no satisfactory answer. . . . The clairvoyant not only sees things outside of his body, but even in it. His whole physical frame is transparent to him; he looks through and sees all the functions of life as though they were going on in a glass case. He can see through the bodies of others placed in magnetic connection with him in the same way. Frequently he will describe, with the accuracy of high anatomical, physiological, and pathological knowledge, the operations of healthy and diseased organs; and will even prescribe remedies for disease." While in this state the functions of the body are liable to be much affected—the pulsations of the heart and the respirations are quickened or retarded, and the secretions altered, and that chiefly at the will of the operator. At his direction the limbs are made rigid, or become endowed with unnatural strength; one liquid tastes as any other, and is hot or cold, sweet or bitter, as the subject is told; in short, *every thought, sensation, and movement of the subject obeys the behest of the mesmerizer*, if we may take the word of mesmerists for the subject's experience. The sixth and last stage, finally, the mesmerists claim to be that of "perfect clairvoyance," and a far more exalted position than the fifth. "The perfect clairvoyant," we are told, "sees what is going on at a distance of hundreds of miles, reads the thoughts of all persons about him, reads the past, and can truly foretell the future. His soul dwells in light and delight; he often regrets that he cannot continue in that state forever; he shudders at the necessity of being brought down into the dull, tiresome, base world of normal life." Between these different stages of the mesmeric condition, as here described, no precise line can be drawn. The transition from one stage to the other is gradual, and generally imperceptible at the time. Thus many of the characteristics of the clairvoyant stage belong also to the somnambulic stage, in which they are, indeed, most frequently observed.

These are the phenomena alleged by mesmerists. To say that they are not true statements, or to decide which only are true, if any there be that are false, does not lie within our domain as encyclopædists, but it may be well enough to state here that physiologists, physicians, and savans are pretty well agreed that the notion of a force of any kind whatever proceeding in such cases from a person, or from a magnetizing apparatus, is a *delusion.* The effects, whatever they are, must have their cause somewhere else. Where it is to be looked for was already indicated in the earliest days of mesmerism by the committee appointed by the French government, who closed their report by saying, "*the effects actually produced were produced purely by the imagination.*" This part of the science of human nature — the reflex action of the mental upon the physical—had not then, however, been sufficiently studied, and is not now widely enough known to render the conclusion of the reporters a satisfactory explanation of the phenomena; and the fallacies of mesmerism, though subjected to many similar exposures (Dr. Falkoner, of Bath, e. g., annihilated the patent metallic tractors of Perkin by making wooden ones exactly like them, which produced exactly the same effects), have constantly revived in some shape or other. One chief cause of the inveteracy of the delusion is that the opponents of mesmerism do not distinguish between denying the theory of the mesmerists and the facts which that theory pretends to explain, and have been too ready to ascribe the whole to delusion and fraud. It thus happens that the most sceptical often become all of a sudden the most credulous. Finding that things do actually happen which they cannot explain, and had been accustomed to denounce as impostures, they rush to the other extreme, and embrace not only the facts but the theory, and call this, too, believing the evidence of their senses. Now the reality of the greater part of the manifestations appealed to by the mesmerist must be admitted, though we deny his explanation of them; and even where their reality must be denied, it does not follow that the mesmerist is not sincere in believing them; there is only greater room than in any other case for suspecting that he has deceived himself.

The first to give a really scientific direction to the investigation of appearances of this class was Mr. Braid, a surgeon in Manchester, who detaches them altogether from the semblance of power exerted by one individual over another, or by metallic disks or magnets, and traces the whole to the brain of the subject, acted on by *suggestion,* a principle long known to psychologists, though never yet made so prominent as it ought to be. The subject has been ably handled in a paper in the *Quarterly Review* for September, 1853 (said to be by Dr. Carpenter). The reviewer traces the operation of this principle through the most ordinary actions, which no one thinks wonderful, up to the most miraculous of the so-called "spiritual" manifestations. Ideas become associated in our minds by habit or otherwise, and one being awakened brings on another, thus forming a train of thought; this is *internal* suggestion. But impressions from without originate and modify those trains, constituting *external* suggestion. While awake and in a normal condition, the *will* interferes with and directs these trains of thought, selecting some ideas to be dwelt upon, and comparing them with others and with present impressions. A comparative inactivity of this selecting and comparing faculty, leaving the flow of ideas to its spontaneous activity, produces the state of mind called *reverie* or *abstraction.* In dreaming and somnambulism, the will and judgment seem completely suspended; and under internal suggestions the mind becomes a mere automaton, while external suggestions, if they act at all, act as upon a machine. These are well-known facts of the human constitution, and independent of mesmerism, though their bearing upon it is obvious. Another fact of like bearing is the effect of concentrated attention on any object of thought in intensifying the impression received. This may proceed so far, in morbid states of the nervous system, that an idea or revived sensation assumes the vividness of a present impression, and overpowers the evidence of the senses. Ideas thus become *dominant,* overriding the impressions of the outer world, and carrying themselves out into action independently

of the will, and even *without the consciousness* of the individual. These dominant ideas play a greater part in human actions and beliefs than most are aware of. "Expectant attention" acts powerfully on the bodily organs, and often makes the individual see and hear what he expects to see and hear, and, without his consciousness, moves his muscles to bring it about. These, too, are recognised facts in the sciences of physiology and psychology. See Carpenter's *Human Physiology* and Dr. Holland's *Chapters on Mental Physiology.*

In the *Illustrations of Modern Mesmerism, from Personal Observation,* published by Dr. (the late Sir John) Forbes in 1845, we have in small compass a complete exposure of the pretended clairvoyant powers of some of the most notorious persons of this class. In the preface he states that he only professes, by a simple narrative of facts, to illustrate the actual pretensions and performances of the mesmerists of the present day, and to show on what sandy foundations the popular belief in their marvels rests. He expresses the modest hope that what is contained in this little book may teach a useful lesson to those numerous unscientific persons who are accustomed to attend mesmeric exhibitions, public or private, from motives of rational curiosity, or with the commendable object of investigating what seem to be important truths. He believes that such persons must now feel convinced that no reliance whatever is to be placed on the results presented at such exhibitions as evincing the truth and powers of mesmerism. He found that it was impossible for the ordinary visitor at these exhibitions to discriminate the true from the false, and that the coarsest juggling might pass with the trusting spectator, seated at a distance from the scene of action, for mysterious and awful truths. Mesmerism or clairvoyance may be true or false, and he professes to be ready to believe them on obtaining sufficient proof of their reality. If, however, we find the most eminent, and apparently the most trustworthy of the clairvoyants, not only uniformly unsuccessful when the necessary precautions are taken to test their powers, but actually detected, and confessing with shame that they have been guilty of the grossest imposture and deceit— where are we to look for the means of establishing the truths of this mysterious science? If we were to believe a fiftieth part of the pretensions put forth in the works and lectures of professional mesmerists, it would be the easiest matter in the world to carry off the prizes offered to any one who could read writing contained in an envelope so secured that it could not be read in the ordinary way. If it is an easy matter to see what is going on in the arctic regions, it cannot surely be difficult to see what is contained in a deal-box. In July, 1839, M. Bourdin, a member of the French academy of science and medicine, as one of a commission of that celebrated body, appointed to inquire into the merits of clairvoyance, made the following offer to the mesmerists: " Bring us a person magnetized or not magnetized, asleep or awake; let that person read with the eyes open, through an opaque substance, such as tissue of cotton, linen, or silk, placed at six inches from the face, or read even through a simple sheet of paper, and that person shall have 3000 francs." *No candidate appeared.* (*Bull. de l'Acad.* iii, 1123.) If such a power as seeing in any other way than by the organ of vision really existed, as was vaunted to be possessed by so many persons both before the prize was offered and since, surely some one of the clairvoyants would have come forward and established a just claim to the prize, but, as none appeared, we may conclude with safety that both then and now no such marvellous power exists or is developed in the human constitution.

So signal and repeated were the failures of the magnetists to establish the truth of their doctrines in France, that the whole subject seems to have fallen into merited contempt and oblivion. In more recent times the exciting phenomena of spirit-rapping have superseded those of somnambulism, and spiritual media have of late too much occupied the public attention to leave any room for those who can boast no higher powers than those of which magnetic clairvoyants claim the possession.

Our limits do not permit us to pursue the subject at greater length. See SPIRITISM. We must content ourselves with stating briefly the following general conclusions advanced by the *Encyclopædia Britannica:* 1. That it has not been proved that there is any magnetic influence, or nervous fluid, which passes from the operator to the person operated on, and produces in him the various phenomena of magnetic somnambulism. 2. That it has been proved that all the phenomena recorded, which have received sufficient scientific scrutiny to convince men of their truth and reality, can be accounted for on ordinary principles, without the aid of mesmerism. 3. That the lower phenomena—such as sleep, diminished or exalted sensibility, loss of voluntary motion, muscular rigidity, and the like, can be produced by persons acting on themselves by means of fixed staring at objects, which are incapable of giving out any nervous or magnetic influence. 4. That the evidence which can be obtained of the reality of the existence of magnetic somnambulism, in any case, is inconclusive; that it is possible that the person supposed to be in such a state may really be awake, and simply feigning sleep; and that in many cases there is the most conclusive evidence that the persons pretending to be so affected are impostors, while in other cases, in which no intention to deceive may have existed, the patients have acted under a peculiar state of mind, to which only the weak and nervous are liable. 5. That though numerous cases of surgical operations are recorded in which the patients are reported not to have felt pain, it is probable that some at least may have really experienced painful sensations without giving any outward expression of their sensations; that we have no evidence or means of knowing, except from their own testimony, that they did not really feel pain, but that it is very probable that in some cases, from a peculiar state of the mind acting upon the nervous system, the patients were really rendered unconscious of pain. 6. That it does not appear from experiment that immunity from pain in operations can be induced, in any but exceptional cases, in Europeans; though it appears, from the experience of Dr. Esdaile, that it can be produced with comparative facility in the natives of India. 7. That the higher phenomena of clairvoyance, pre-vision, intro-vision, and retro-vision, do not rest on adequate and satisfactory evidence. That it has never been proved in a single instance, when the necessary precautions have been taken, that a person could read or see objects through opaque substances; and that the alleged instances of the possession of such a power, when put to the test, have proved uniformly unsuccessful, and have amounted to nothing more than attempts at vague guessing. That it has been proved in some cases that the persons pretending to know events which happened at a distance were fully acquainted with the events through ordinary channels of information. That the description of events pretended to have been discovered by means of clairvoyance has not been in accordance with the truth, unless it has been possible for the patient to employ the usual means of discovering them; and that in most instances there are observed the most manifest attempts, on the part of their friends, to assist clairvoyants by suggestions and leading questions. That the attempts to describe what is going on in the interior of their own bodies, to diagnose diseases in themselves or others, and to prescribe remedies for the cure of the diseases which they pretend to discover, have been complete failures, and mere repetitions of such notions of anatomy, of disease, and of treatment, as they may have acquired by casual reading, conversation, or more careful study. 8. That there is no recorded instance, worthy of credit, of transference of the senses — that is, of persons being able to read, taste, smell, or hear, by the fingers, stomach, or any other part

of the body, other than the organs by which these functions are naturally performed—and that pretended instances of the possession of such powers have been proved to be cases of fraud and wilful imposition. 9. That phreno-mesmerism does not prove the truth of phrenology, or throw any light upon the doctrine that the faculties of the mind have a local seat in special parts of the brain, which can be tied up and let loose—mesmerized or de-mesmerized—at pleasure; and that the experiments designed to prove the excitement of the so-called phrenological organs by magnetic operations have all resulted in manifest failures or impositions when properly tested. 10. That the phenomena described by different authors, under the various designations of animal magnetism, magnetic somnambulism, hypnotism, odyle, and electro-biology, are identical in their nature, and can be explained, in so far as they possess any truth or scientific value, upon recognised physiological principles. That the whole subject has been systematically obscured by its cultivators with a cloud of mystery, which has given rise to difficulties, and placed impediments in the way of rational and scientific investigation. That the real phenomena which not unfrequently occur in the weak and nervous subjects of magnetic operations are in themselves very remarkable, but that they are not different from phenomena which occur spontaneously; and that they are to be explained by the reciprocal influence exerted by the mind and the nervous system upon each other, and by the unnatural influence thus induced of the nervous upon the muscular systems. See Thouret, *Recherches et Doutes sur le Magnétisme animal* (1784); Eschmayer, *Versuch über die scheinbare Magik des Magnetismus* (Stuttg. and Tüb. 1816, 8vo); *Théorie du Mesmérisme* (Paris, 1818, 8vo); Jozwik, *Sur le Magnétisme animal* (1832); Townshend, *Facts in Mesmerism* (Lond. 1853); id. *Mesmerism Proved True* (Lond. 1857); Sandys, *Mesmerism and its Opponents; Amer. Bib. Repository,* 2d Ser. i, 362; *Brit. Qu. Rev.* ii, 402; *Christ. Examiner,* i, 496; li, 395; *For. Qu. Rev.* v, 96; xii, 413; *North Brit. Rev.* xiii, 1; xv, 69; *Lond. Qu. Rev.* lxi, 151; 1871, Oct. art. i; *Blackw. Mag.* lvii, 219; lxx, 70 sq.; *New-Engl.* iv, 443; *Bib. Sacra.* i, 333.

Mesobaiah. See MESOBAITE.

Meso'baïte (Heb. *Metsobayah'*, מִצֹּבָיָה, *garrison of Jehovah,* being apparently the name of the place itself, used for a gentile, the preceding noun being regarded as in the construct; Sept. Μεσωβία v. r. Μεινα-βεία, Vulg. *Masobia*), a designation of Jasiel, the last named of David's body-guard (1 Chron. xi, 47), probably meaning *of Mesobaiah,* as being his place of residence; but, no other clue being given to its locality there is no room even to conjecture its position. Possibly it is rather the name of a person from whom he was descended; but the form and construction are equally difficult as a patronymic. Perhaps we should point הַמְצֹבָיָה, and thus refer to ZOBAH as the place of his nationality. Kennicott's conclusion (*Dissertation,* p. 233, 234) is that originally the word was "the Metsobaites" (הַמְצֹבָיִם), and applied to the three names preceding it.

Mesopota'mia (Μεσοποταμία, Acts ii, 9; vii, 2; so called as lying *between the rivers;* see Tzchucke, *Mela,* iii, 335 sq.; the ARAM, אֲרָם, of the Hebrews, usually rendered "Aram," or "Syria," in the Auth. Vers.), the Greek and Roman name for the entire region lying between the rivers Euphrates and Tigris, and bounded on the north by Mt. Taurus, and by Mt. Masius on the north-east (Ptol. v, 18; Pliny, v, 13; vi, 9; Philostr. Apol. i, 20). It never formed a distinct state, and the Greek name, which does not appear to extend back beyond the time of Alexander (comp. Arrian, *Alex.* vii, 7; Tacit. *Annal.* vi, 37), applies rather to its natural than political geography, but was generally employed by the Romans, who (under the emperors) joined it with

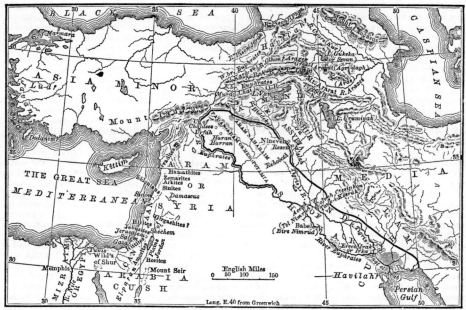

Map of Mesopotamia.

Syria (Mela, i, 11, 1; Pliny, vi, 13); and hence it appears in Acts ii, 9. In the Old-Test. geography it is designated as a part of Aramæa, under the names PADAN-ARAM (פַּדַּן אֲרָם, the plain of Aram, Gen. xxv, 20; xxi, 18; xxxiii, 18; comp. the field of Aram, שְׂדֵה אֲרָם, Hos. xii, 12; and so campi Mesopotamiæ, Curt. iii, 2, 3; iv, 9, 6) and ARAM-NAHARAIM (אֲרַם נַהֲרַיִם, Aram of the two rivers, Gen. xxiv, 10; Deut. xxiii, 5), for which the Sept. has Mesopotamia, or Mesopotamia of Syria; the Syriac renders house of the rivers (Peshito at Acts ii, 9; vii, 2; see Assemani, Biblioth. Orient. i, 462), and the Arabs call it the island (i. e. peninsula; see Abulfeda, Tab. Mesopot. ed. Paulus; and Tuch, Abulfed. descriptionis Mesopot. spec. [Hal. 1830]). In this early-inhabited land, the northern portion of which was an uncommonly fertile plateau, rich in fat cattle (Strabo, xvi, 747), and not destitute of forests (Dio Cass. lxviii, 26; lxxv, 9), dwelt the nomade ancestors of the Hebrews (Gen. xi; comp. Acts vii, 2). From hence Isaac obtained his wife Rebecca (Gen. xxiv, 10, 19; xxv, 20); here Jacob served as a herdsman for Rachel (Gen. xxviii sq.), and here most of his sons were born (Gen. xxxv, 26; xlvi, 15). The principal cities, situated not only on the two main rivers, but also along their tributaries, the Chaboras (Habor) and Mygdonius, were Nisibis, Edessa, Canæ (Haran), and Circesium (Carchemesh); in the interior were only villages (Philostr. Apoll. i, 20). The inhabitants were of Syrian origin (Strabo, xvi, 737), and spoke a dialect of the Aramæan (Strabo, ii, 84; comp. Gen. xxxi, 47). Southern Mesopotamia, on the contrary, is a flat, uncultivated, and poorly-irrigated steppe, a resort of lions (Ammin. Marc. xviii, 7), ostriches, and (formerly) wild asses, and roamed over by predatory hordes of Arabs (see Strabo, xvi, 747, 748; comp. Xenoph. Anab. i, 5, 1). Only on the banks of the two principal rivers is it susceptible of much tillage. Yet through this barren tract from the earliest ages passed the great caravan route for commerce from the shore of the Euphrates to Seleucia and Babylon (Strabo, xvi, 748), as it still does to Bagdad. See generally Cellar. Notit. ii, 602 sq.; Olivier, Voyaye, iv, ch. xiv, p. 372 sq.; Ainsworth, Researches; Heeren, Ideen, I, i, 183 sq.; Ritter, Erdk. xi, pl. 36 [1844]; Forbiger, Handb. ii, 625 sq.; Southgate's Tour; Buckingham's Travels; Layard's Nineveh and Bab. eh. xi–xv.

Of the history of this whole country we have but little information till the time of the Persian rule. "According to the Assyrian inscriptions, Mesopotamia was inhabited in the early times of the empire (B.C. 1200–1100) by a vast number of petty tribes, each under its own prince, and all quite independent of one another. The Assyrian monarchs contended with these chiefs at great advantage, and by the time of Jehu (B.C. 880) had fully established their dominion over them. The tribes were all called 'tribes of the Naïri,' a term which some compare with the Naharaim of the Jews, and translate 'tribes of the stream-lands.' But this identification is very uncertain. It appears, however, in close accordance with Scripture, first, that Mesopotamia was independent of Assyria till after the time of David; secondly, that the Mesopotamians were warlike, and used chariots in battle; and, thirdly, that not long after the time of David they lost their independence, their country being absorbed by Assyria, of which it was thenceforth commonly reckoned a part." The Mesopotamian king Chushan-Rishathaim, who for eight years (B.C. 1575–1567) held the (trans-Jordanic) tribes of Israel in subjection (Judg. iii, 8, 10), was probably only the petty chieftain of one of the principalities nearest the Euphrates. In the time of David (B.C. 1040) the kings of Syria-Zoba appear to have had dominion over the Mesopotamian clans (2 Sam. x, 16). See ZOBAH. In the beginning of the 8th century B.C., Shalmaneser of Assyria had brought the different states of Mesopotamia under his sway (2 Kings xix, 13); and in after-times the Mesopotamians shared the conquest of the other Asiatic nations under the successive empires of the Babylonians, Persians, and Macedonians. After Alexander's death, this country fell under the Syrian rule of the Seleucidæ (comp. Josephus, Ant. xii, 3, 4); and after the fall of this dynasty it became the arena for the Parthian, Armenian, and finally the Roman arms. In New-Test. times many Jews had settled in Mesopotamia (Josephus, Ant. xii, 3, 4; comp. Acts ii, 9). The Romans under Lucullus and Pompey began to disturb Mesopotamia; and, somewhat later, Crassus was there defeated and slain. Trajan wrested the whole province, with several adjacent territories, from the Parthians; and although Hadrian had to relinquish these conquests, Lucius Verus and Severus again subdued Mesopotamia, and it remained a Roman province until the end of the 4th century. On the death of Julian, Jovian found himself obliged to abandon the greater part of the country to the Persians, the Romans only retaining so much of Western Mesopotamia as was enclosed by the Chaboras and Euphrates, and on the north by the Mons Masius (see Smith's *Dict. of Class. Geog.* s. v.). When the Sassanian dynasty in Persia was overthrown by the Arabs, towards the middle of the 7th century, Mesopotamia came under the dominion of the caliphs. Since the year 1516 it has formed an integral part of the Ottoman empire. See SYRIA.

Mesorion ($\mu\epsilon\sigma\dot{\omega}\rho\iota o\nu$) is the technical term for an intermediate office in the Greek Church after *Proton, Triton, Ekton, Ennaton;* but omitted after *Luchnikon* and *Hesperinon, Apodeipnon, Mesonuktion* (matins), and *Orthron* (lauds). See CANONICAL HOURS.

Mespelbrunn, JOHANN ECHTER VON, an eminent German theologian, of princely birth, was born at Mespelbrunn, near Mayence, March 18, 1545. In 1555, when but ten years old, he obtained a canonicate in Würzburg, and in 1559 one in Mayence. He studied at Mayence, Cologne, Louvain, Douay, Paris, and Pavia; became prebendary of Würzburg in 1569, and soon after dean of the cathedral, and finally prince bishop of Würzburg, Dec. 1, 1573. He was ambitious of honors and consideration, but aimed at the same time at the moral and religious improvement of his diocese. The emperor Rudolph II often employed him, particularly in 1578-79, to quell the disturbances in the Spanish Netherlands, and as envoy on affairs of state; in this capacity Echter was one of the prime motors of the Ligue. Yet in a difficulty he had with the abbot of Fulda concerning that abbey, both the pope and, in 1602, the emperor decided against him. In order to check the progress of the evangelical doctrines of the Reformation in Würzburg, he occupied himself zealously with the interior affairs of his diocese, and endeavored to reform its Church. In 1576 he took part in the Diet of Regensburg, and in 1582 in that of Augsburg. He improved the system of education, organized several public schools, and in 1582 founded the University of Würzburg. The chairs of philosophy and theology he filled with Jesuits, and founded three colleges, which were afterwards united into one under the name of Seminary of St. Kilian. On the other hand he deposed and exiled all the evangelical ministers and preachers, and even the civil officers of his diocese who favored the principles of the Reformation, whenever an occasion presented. He sought to retain the people in their allegiance to the Roman Catholic Church by means of preaching and visiting tours, while he tried to reform the immorality of the clergy, and to restore them to a better standing. With this view he wrote his *Constitutiones pro cultu divino, statuta ruralia pro Clero* (1584; in German, 1589); several *Antiphonien u. Psalterien* (1602), and a *Missal.* He also founded the Julius Hospital at Würzburg. He died Sept. 13, 1617. See J. N. Buchinger, *J. Echter v. Mespelbrunn* (Würzb. 1843). (J. H. W.)

Mesplède, LOUIS, a French canonist, was born at Cahors about 1601. He became a Dominican monk, was made a prior, and then a provincial of Languedoc; but in the latter capacity he had to contend with many difficulties, and failed in his efforts to bring about a general reform of the order to which he belonged. He died at Cahors in 1663. The following works of his, written in tolerably good Latin, deserve our notice: *Quærela apologetica provinciæ Occitaniæ Ordinis Prædicatorum* (Cahors, 1624, 4to) :—*Catalaunia Galliæ vindicata, adversus Hispaniarum scriptorum imposturas* (Paris, 1643, 8vo) : — *Notitia antiqui status Ordinis Prædicatorum* (Paris, 1643, 8vo; reprinted in Cahors, 1644, with appendices, under the title *Commonitorium de Ordinis Prædicatorum Renovatione*). See Echard et Quétif, *Script. Ord. Prædicat;* Bayle, *Dict. Crit.* s. v.; Hoefer, *Nouv. Biog. Générale,* s. v.

Mësrop, also called *Mashtoz,* the noted translator of the Armenian version of the Bible, was born in the latter half of the 4th century in a small village of the province Taron. He was at first secretary of the Armenian patriarch Nerses the Great, and afterwards became his minister of ecclesiastical affairs. After filling this position seven years, he went into a convent, but, failing to find any satisfaction there, he went into a desert, where he gathered about him a number of young men as scholars. Under the government of the patriarch Isaak (Sa'ak) the Great (A.D. 390-440) Mësrop was commissioned to preach as missionary, for which position he was especially fitted by his thorough knowledge of foreign languages. He now found need of an Armenian version of the Scriptures, the version of the clergy being in the Syriac, a language but little understood by the populace. After having spent several years in the arduous task, and that with but little show of success, he resolved to throw himself upon the mercy of his Lord and God, and seek at his hands the wisdom and knowledge required for the successful accomplishment of his undertaking. Nor did he wait long for answer to his prayer. While sojourning at Samosata, we are told, he was led to see the different types engraved in a rock, and that he could remember every single letter so plainly that he was able to describe them to the distinguished calligraph Rufanus, who finally composed the desired alphabet. He immediately commenced the gigantic work of translating the Bible from the Greek into the Armenian, a version which was introduced afterwards into that part of Armenia governed by his king Vramshapuh. By request of other sovereigns, he made also translations for the Georgian and Albanian countries. A change in the government obliged him to quit Persian territory, and he sought a new home in Grecian Armenia, where he continued his activity under the special protection of the emperor Theodosius of Constantinople and the patriarch Atticus. In spite of the severe crusades against the members of the new religion, he continued to inspire his scholars and friends with confidence in their final success, and defeated several times the various attempts to introduce idolatry in the practices of a pure Catholic religion. One of his later great works was the translation of the liturgical books of the Greeks into the modern Armenian language. After the death of his old companion Isaak I, Mësrop was elected patriarch of Armenia, but he died the next year, February 19, 441. A critical edition of Mësrop's translation of the Bible appeared in Venice in 1805, in four volumes. As an energetic and scientific man, Mësrop ranks among the most important combatants of the Christian religion in the early centuries, when the communication of the new religion met especially with great obstacles in the East for want of written languages. Mësrop furthered literature among his countrymen not only by his own literary productions, but by founding "a whole school of remarkable thinkers and writers, that created what is called 'the golden period' for the enlightenment of ancient Armenia" (Malan). See Naumann, *Versuch einer Gesch. d. Armenischen Lit.* (Leips. 1836, 8vo); *Quadro della storia letteraria di Armenia estesa da Mons Placido Tukias Somal.* etc. (Ven. 1829), p. 14 sq.; *Quadro delle opere di vari autori anticamente tradotte in Armeno* (Ven. 1825), p. 7-9; Goriund, *Life of St. Mësrop;* Malan, *Life and Times of Gregory the Illuminator,* etc. (Lond. 1868, 8vo), p. 28 sq. See ARMENIAN VERSION. (J. H. W.)

Mess (מַשְׂאֵת, *maseth'*, a *lifting up,* as of the hands, Psa. cxli, 2; or of *flame,* Judg. xx, 38, 40; so of a *sign,* Jer. vi, 1; hence an *oracle* or "burden," Lam. ii, 14), properly a *gift* ("oblation," "reward," etc., Esth. ii, 18; Jer. xl, 5; Amos v, 11); also *tribute* ("oblation," "collection," 2 Chron. xxiv, 6, 9; Ezek. xx, 40); specially a portion of food to a guest (Gen. xliii, 34; 2 Sam. xi, 8). See EATING.

Mess Johns, in the Church of England, is, according to Broughton (*Bibliotheca Hist. Sac.* s. v.), a name given last century to a certain class of chaplains kept by the nobility and families of higher rank, who were generally expected to rise from table after the second course, and were in little better esteem than menials. In Scotland, Eadie (*Eccles. Cyclop.* s. v.) informs us, the name of *Mass* or *Mess John* was given to Presbyterian ministers, not from any connection with the mass, or because they succeeded mass-priests, but probably because they were called *Mr.* or *Messrs.*, the title "*reverend*" not being applied to them.

Message (prop. for מַלְאָכוּת, Hag. i, 13; ἀγγελία, 1 John iii, 11; elsewhere דָּבָר, a *word*; ἐπαγγελία, a *promise*; πρεσβεία, an *embassy*). See MESSENGER.

Messalians (from Chald. מְצַלִּין), or EUCHITES (from εὔχομαι, *to pray*) is the name borne by two heretical sects of Christian mendicants. (1.) An ancient sect, composed of roaming mendicant monks, flourished in Mesopotamia and Syria towards the end of the 4th century (dating from 360) as a distinct body, although their doctrine and discipline subsisted in Syria, Egypt, and other countries before the birth of Christ. They were a sort of mystics, who believed that two souls exist in man, the one good, the other evil. They were anxious to expel the evil soul, and hasten the return of the good Spirit of God, by contemplation and prayer, believing that only prayer could save them, and therefore taught the duty of every Christian to make life a period of unintermitted prayer. They despised all physical labor, moral law, and the sacraments, and embraced many opinions nearly resembling the Manichæan doctrine, derived from Oriental philosophy. When their heretic principles became fully known towards the end of the 4th century, the persecution of both the ecclesiastical and civil authority fell upon them; yet they perpetuated themselves to the 7th century, and reappeared in the Bogomiles and Messalians (2) of the Middle Ages.

(2.) Another sect of this name arose in the 12th century, in which there appears a revival or extension of the opinions held by those of the same name in the 4th century. They are charged with holding heterodox views respecting the Trinity. They rejected marriage, abstained from animal food, treated with contempt the sacraments of baptism and the Lord's Supper, and the various ordinances of external worship, placing the essence of religion in prayer, and maintaining the efficacy of perpetual supplications to the Supreme Being for expelling the evil genius which dwells in the breast of every mortal. The term *Euchite*, or *Messalian*, became an invidious appellation for persons of piety in the Eastern churches, just as the terms Albigenses, Waldenses, and Bogomiles were used subsequently to designate all enemies of the Roman pontiff. See Neander, *Ch. Hist.* iii, 589; Haweis, *Ch. Hist.* ii, 222; Mosheim, *Ch. Hist.* bk. iii, ch. xii; pt. ii, ch. v; Schaff, *Ch. Hist.* ii, 199 sq. (J. H. W.)

Messemakers, ENGELBERT (Latin, *Cultrificus*), a Belgian theologian, was born at Nimègue about the opening of the 15th century. He joined the Dominican friars, became a doctor of theology, probably at Cologne, and in 1465 undertook to establish a convent in Zwolle, of which he was appointed the first friar. He died about 1492. Among other works, he wrote *Epistola declaratoria privilegiorum F. F. Mendicantium contra curatos parochales et Epistola de simonia vitanda in receptione noviciorum* (Nimègue, 1479, 4to; Cologne, 1497, 8vo; Paris, 1507, 8vo; Delft, 1508, 16mo):— *Carmen de Pane:— Manuale Confessorum metricum* (Cologne, 1497, 4to). See De Jonghe, *Desolata Batavia Dominicana*, p. 186–87; Hartzheim, *Prodromus Hist. univers. Coloniensis*, vol. ii.

Messenger (properly מַלְאָךְ, *malak'* [see MALACHI], ἄγγελος, both words often rendered *angel* [q. v.];

in a more general sense צִיר, ἀπόστολος, Prov. xxv, 13; Isa. lvii, 9 [see APOSTLE]; in a special sense for forms of בָּשַׂר, *to convey good news* [see GOSPEL]; also vaguely for נָגַד, to *tell*; צִוָּה, to *command*). It is a practice in the East to employ messengers who run on foot to convey despatches (Job i, 14), and these men sometimes go a hundred and fifty miles in less than twenty-four hours. See FOOTMAN. Such messengers were sent by Joab to acquaint David with the fate of his son Absalom. Ahimaaz went with such speed that he outran Cushi, and was the first to appear before the king, who sat at the gate of Mahanaim, anxiously awaiting tidings from the battle (2 Kings ix, 18). The common pace of travelling in the East is very slow. Camels go little more than two miles an hour; but dromedaries are often used for the purpose of conveying messages in haste, especially to a distance, as they are said to outrun the swiftest horses. To this practice Job alludes when he says, "My days are swifter than a post" (ix, 25). Instead of passing away with a slowness of motion like that of a caravan, my days of prosperity have disappeared with a swiftness like that of a messenger carrying despatches.

Messer, Asa, D.D., LL.D., a noted American educator and Baptist minister, was born in Methuen, Mass., in 1769. He studied at Brown University, where he graduated in 1790. The next year he became a tutor in that institution; a professor of languages in 1796. of mathematics and natural philosophy in 1799, and president in 1802, which latter position he held until 1826. Having been licensed in 1792, and ordained in 1801, he preached occasionally, both while professor and president, for congregations of different denominations. After retiring from the presidency, he was elected to several civil offices of trust by the citizens of Providence. He died Oct. 11. 1836. Dr. Messer published a number of discourses and orations. See Sprague, *Annals of the Amer. Pulpit*, vi, 326.

Messer, Leon, also called MESTRE LEON, LEONE HEBREO, was the oldest son of the famous statesman, philosopher, theologian, and commentator, Don Isaac b.-Jehudah Abrabanel (q.v.), whose full name was *Don Jehuda Leon b.-Isaak Abravanel*. He is better known as *Leo Hebræus*. Leon Messer was born at Lisbon near the close of the 15th century. When the Jews were expelled from Spain in 1492, he accompanied his father in all his peregrinations, and finally settled at Genoa, where he practiced medicine with great repute, for which cause he was also called "Medico Hebreo." He was a profound philosopher, and an excellent poet. His *Philography*, or *Dialoghi di Amore* (Rome, 1535; Venice, 1607), contains disquisitions on the doctrines of Neo-Platonism, the symbols of mythology, the Hebrew Kabala, and the Arabian philosophy. It exists in French, Spanish, and Latin translations, all made in the 16th century. He also wrote some poems in honor of his father, an elegy on his death, and a poem of 130 stanzas descriptive of the vicissitudes of his life, and containing exhortations to his son. He was also a good mathematician, and an amateur in music. The date of his death is not known. Comp. Fürst, *Biblioth. Jud.* ii, 230 sq.; Lindo, *History of the Jews of Spain and Portugal*, p. 268 sq.; Finn, *Sephardim*, p. 418; Etheridge, *Introd. to Hebr. Lit.* p. 449 sq.; Da Costa, *Israel and the Gentiles*, p. 377; Ueberweg, *History of Philosophy* (transl. by C. Morris, N. Y. 1872), p. 428; Munk, *Esquisse historique de la philosophie chez les Juifs* (Germ. transl. by B. Beer, Leipsic, 1852), p. 37, 84 sq.; Zunz, *Literaturgesch. d. Synagog. Poesie*, p. 524; *Geschichte und Literatur*, p. 250, 316; Ticknor, *Hist. of Spanish Literature* (Am. ed.), iii, 189, 190, note; Jost, *Geschichte d. Jud. u. s. Sekten*, iii, 117; Grätz, *Gesch. d. Jud.* vol. viii; but especially Delitzsch's lucid treatise in the *L. B. d. Orients*, 1840, c. 81 sq., *Leo der Hebräer: Characteristik seines Zeitalters, seiner Richtung und seiner Werke.* (B. P.)

Messi'ah, the special title of the Saviour promised to the world through the Jewish race. We have space for the discussion of a few points only of this extensive theme, and we here treat especially those points not particularly discussed under other heads. See REDEEMER.

I. *Official Import of the Name.*—The Hebrew word מָשִׁיחַ, *Mashi'ach,* is in every instance of its use (thirty-nine times) rendered in the Sept. by the suitable term Χριστός, which becomes so illustrious in the N. T. as the official designation of the Holy Saviour. It is a verbal noun (see Simonis *Arcanum Form. Hebr. Ling.* p. 92 sq.), derived from מָשַׁח, and has much the same meaning as the participle מָשׁוּחַ (2 Sam. iii, 39, and occasionally in the Pentateuch), i. e. *Anointed.* The prevalent and all but universal (Isa. xxi, 5 and Jer. xxii, 14 being perhaps the sole exceptions) sense of the root מָשַׁח points to the consecration of objects to sacred purposes by means of anointing-oil. Inanimate objects (such as the tabernacle, altar, laver, etc.) are included under the use of the verb; but the noun מָשִׁיחַ is applied only to animate objects. There is, however, some doubt as to 2 Sam. i, 21—כָּמָגֵן שָׁאוּל בְּלִי מָשִׁיחַ בַּשָּׁמֶן —where, according to some (Maurer, Gesenius, Fürst; see also Corn. à Lapide, ad loc.), the phrase, "not anointed with oil," is applied to *the shield* (comp. Isa. xxi, 5). The majority of commentators refer it to *Saul,* "as if he had not been anointed with oil." So the A. V., which seems to follow the Vulgate: This version, however (*quasi non esset unctus oleo*), is really as inexplicit as the original, admitting the application of "*anointed*" to either the king or his shield. This double sense is avoided by the Septuagint (Θυρεὺς Σαοὺλ οὐχ ἐχρίσϑη ἐν ἐλαίῳ), which assigns the anointing, as an epithet, to the shield. The Targum of Jonathan refers the מָשִׁיחַ to Saul, but drops the negative. To us the unvarying use of the word, as a *human* epithet, in all the other (thirty-eight) passages, two of them occurring in the very context of the disputed place (2 Sam. i, 14, 16), settles the point in favor of our A. V., as if the king had fallen on the fatal field of Gilboa like one of the common soldiers, "not as one who had been anointed with oil." See ANOINTING.

The official persons ("the Christs of the O.T.:" Perowne, *Coherence of O. and N. T.*) who were consecrated with oil were *priests* (Exod. xxviii, 41; Levit. iv, 3, 5, 16; Numb. xxxv, 35), *kings* (1 Sam. ix, 16; xvi, 3; 2 Sam. xii, 7; 1 Kings i, 34), and *prophets* (1 Kings xix, 16). The great Antitype, the Christ of the N. T., embraced and exhausted in himself these several offices, which, in fact, were shadows of his threefold functions as the Prophet, Priest, and King of his people. It is the pre-eminence which this combination of anointed offices gave him that seems to be pointed at in Psa. xlv, 8, where the great Messiah is anointed "*above his fellows;*" above the Christs of old, whether of only one function, as the priest Aaron, or the prophet Elisha, or the king Saul; or of two functions, as Melchizedek the priest and king, or Moses the priest and prophet, or David the king and prophet. In our Saviour Christ is uniquely found the triple comprehension, the recapitulation in himself of the three offices (see Eusebius, *Hist. Eccles.* i, 3, vol. i, p. 24, by Burton [Oxon. 1848]). But not only were the ancient offices typical, the material of consecration had also its antitype in the Holy Ghost (Cyril of Jerusalem, *Catech. Illum.* x, 99; *Catech.* Νεοφ. p. 202, 203; Basil, *contra Eunom.* v; Chrysostom on Psa. xlv; Theodoret, *Epit. divin. Decret.* xi, p. 279; Theophylact on Matt. i; Œcumenius on Rom. i, etc.). The prophecy of Isa. lxi, 1 ("The Spirit of the Lord Jehovah is upon me, because Jehovah hath anointed me") was expressly claimed by Jesus for fulfilment in the synagogue at Nazareth (Luke iv, 16–21) on his return to Galilee "*in the power of the Spirit*" (ver. 14), which

he had plenarily received at his recent baptism (ver. 1), and by which he was subsequently led into the wilderness (ver. 1). This anointing of our Lord to his Messianic functions is referred to in a general sense in such passages as Isa. xi, 2 and Acts x, 38. But from the more specific statement of Peter (Acts ii, 36), it would appear that it was not before his resurrection and consequent ascension that Christ was fully inducted into his Messianic dignities. "He was anointed to his prophetical office at his baptism; but thereby rather initiated to be, than actually made Christ and Lord. Unto these two offices of everlasting Priest and everlasting King he was not actually anointed, or fully consecrated, until his resurrection from the dead" (dean Jackson, *Works,* vii, 368). As often as the evangelists style him *Christ* before his resurrection from the dead, it is by way of *anticipation (ibid.* p. 296). On this point, indeed, the grammatical note of Gersdorf (*Sprachchar.* i, 39, 272), as quoted by Winer (*Gram. des N. T. sprachid.* iii, 18, p. 107; Clark, p. 130), is interesting: "The four evangelists almost always write ὁ Χριστός [the expected Messiah, like ὁ ἐρχόμενος], while Paul and Peter employ Χριστός, as the appellation had become more of a proper name. In the epistles of Paul and Peter, however, the word has the article when a governing noun precedes" (for extremely elaborate tables, containing every combination of the sacred names of Christ in the N. T., the reader is referred to the last edition of bishop Middleton's *Doctrine of the Greek Article,* by H. J. Rose, B.D., App. ii, p. 486–496). Twice only in the N. T. does the Hebrew form of it (Messias) occur, in John i, 41 and iv, 25; and twice only in the O.T. have our translators retained the same form (Messiah), in Dan. ix, 25 and 26. In these passages, both in the Greek of the evangelist [Μεσσίας, or (as Griesbach preferred to read) Μεσίας, more closely like the original] and in the Hebrew of the prophet [מָשִׁיחַ], there is an absence of the article—the word having, in fact, grown out of its appellative state, which so often occurs in the earlier books, into a proper name; thus resembling the course of the Χριστός of the Christian Scriptures. See CHRIST.

II. *The gradual Growth of the Messianic Revelation.* —1. *First or Patriarchal Period.*—(1.) In the primeval promise (Gen. iii, 15) lies the germ of a universal blessing. The tempter came to the woman in the guise of a serpent, and the curse thus pronounced has a reference both to the serpent which was the instrument, and to the tempter that employed it; to the natural terror and enmity of man against the serpent, and to the conflict between mankind redeemed by Christ its Head, and Satan that deceived mankind. Many interpreters would understand by the seed of the woman the Messiah only; but it is easier to think with Calvin that mankind, after they are gathered into one army by Jesus the Christ, the Head of the Church, are to achieve a victory over evil. The Messianic character of this prophecy has been much questioned by those who see in the history of the fall nothing but a fable: to those who accept it as true, this passage is the primitive germ of the Gospel. "The seed of the woman," the vagueness and obscurity of which phrase was so suited to the period of the protevangelium, is cleared in the light of the N. T. (see Gal. iv, 4, where the γενόμενον ἐκ γυναικός explains the original זַרְעָהּ). The deliverance intimated was no doubt understood by our first parents to be universal, like the injury sustained, and it is no absurdity to suppose that the promise was cherished afterwards by thoughtful Gentiles as well as believing Jews; but to the latter it was subsequently shaped into increasing precision by supplementary revelations, while to the former it never lost its formal vagueness and obscurity. The O. T. gives us occasional gleams of the glorious primeval light as it struggled with the gross traditions of the heathen. The nearer to Israel the clearer the light; as in the cases of the Abimelechs (Gen. xx, 6; xxvi,

28), and Melchizedek (Gen. xiv, 18), and Job (xix, 25), and Balaam (Numb. xxiv, 17), and the magi (Matt. ii), and the Samaritan woman (John iv, 25; and see, on the Christology of the Samaritans, Westcott's *Introduction*, p. 148, 149). But even at a distance from Israel the light still flickered to the last, as "the unconscious prophecies of heathendom" show, as archbishop Trench happily designates—though in a somewhat different sense—the yearnings of the Gentiles after a deliverer (*Hulsean Lectures* for 1846; see also bishop Horsley's *Dissert. on the Messianic Prophecies dispersed among the Heathen*, in *Sermons*, ed. 1829, ii, 263–318; and comp. Virgil's well-known eclogue *Pollio*, and the expectations mentioned by Suetonius, *Vit. Vespasian.* iv, 8, and Tacitus, *Hist.* v, 9, 13, and the Sibylline oracles, discussed by Horsley [*ut sup.*], with a strong leaning to their authenticity). See below, § iv, 1 (3). But although the promise was absolutely indefinite to the first father of man (on which see bishop Horsley, *Sermon* xvi, p. 234, 235, comp. with Faber's *Prophetical Dissert.* vii, 4 and 5), additional light was given, after the deluge, to the second father of the human race.

(2.) To Noah was vouchsafed a special reservation of blessing for one of his sons in preference to the other two, and—as if words failed him—he exclaimed, "Blessed be Jehovah, the God of Shem!" (Gen. ix, 26). Not that at any time God meant to *confine* a monopoly of blessing to the individual selected as the special depositary thereof. In the present instance Japheth, in the next verse, is associated with his brother for at least some secondary advantage : " God shall enlarge Japheth, and he shall dwell in the tents of Shem." Instead of blessing Shem, as he had cursed Canaan, he carries up the blessing to the great fountain of the blessings that were to follow Shem.

(3.) The principle of limitation goes on. One of Shem's descendants has three sons. Only one of these is selected as the peculiar treasurer of the divine favor. But not for himself alone was Abraham chosen. As in Shem's instance, so here again Abraham was to be the centre of blessing to even a larger scope. More than once was he assured of this : "In thy seed ["in thee," xii, 3] shall all the nations of the earth be blessed" (Gen. xxii, 18). The Messianic purport of this repeated promise cannot be doubted after Christ's own statement (John viii, 56) and Paul's comment (Gal. iii, 16). The promise is still indefinite, but it tends to the undoing of the curse of Adam by a blessing to all the earth through the seed of Abraham, as death had come on the whole earth through Adam. When our Lord says " Your father Abraham rejoiced to see my day, and he saw it and was glad" (John viii, 56), we are to understand that this promise of a real blessing and restoration to come hereafter was understood in a spiritual sense, as a leading back to God, as a coming nearer to him, from whom the promise came; and he desired with hope and rejoicing ("gestivit cum desiderio," Bengel) to behold the day of it.

(4.) In Abraham's son—the father of twin sons— we meet with another limitation; Jacob not only secures the traditional blessing to himself, but is inspired to concentrate it at his death on Judah, to the exclusion of the eleven other members of his family. " Judah, thou art he whom thy brothers praise. . . . The sceptre shall not depart from Judah, nor a lawgiver from between his feet, until *Shiloh* come" (Gen. xlix, 8, 10; see Perowne's *Essay*, p. 26, 188; Delitzsch, ad loc.; bishop Pearson, *Creed*, art. ii; Hengstenberg, *Christol.* i, 59, 60; Davison, *On Prophecy*, p. 106; Döllinger, *Gentile and Jew in the Courts of the Temple of Christ*, translated by Darnell, ii, 392. Onkelos and Raschi, it may be worth while to add, make *Shiloh* here to refer to the Messiah, as do D. Kimchi and Abendana). To us the Messianic interpretation of the passage seems to be called for by the principle of periodical limitation, which amounts to a law in the Christological Scriptures. We accept the conclusion, therefore, that the שִׁילֹה of this verse is the

שַׂר־שָׁלוֹם, "Prince of Peace," of Isa. ix, 5 [6]; and the זֶה שָׁלוֹם, "This man is peace," of Micah v, 4; and the דְּבֶר שָׁלוֹם, "the peace-speaker," of Zech. ix, 10; and the Εἰρήνη ἡμῶν, "our peace," of Paul, Eph. ii, 14—in a word, our Messiah, Jesus Christ. This, then, is the first case in which the promises distinctly centre in one person; and he is to be the man of peace; he is to wield and retain the government, and the nations shall look up to him and obey him. See SHILOH.

2. *Mosaic Period.* — (1.) The next passage usually quoted is the prophecy of Balaam (Numb. xxiv, 17-19). The *star* points indeed to the glory, as the sceptre denotes the power, of a king. Onkelos and Jonathan (pseudo) see here the Messiah. But it is doubtful whether the prophecy is not fulfilled in David (2 Sam. viii, 2, 14); and though David is himself a type of Christ, the direct Messianic application of this place is by no means certain.

(2.) The prophecy of Moses (Deut. xviii, 18), "I will raise them up a prophet from among their brethren, like unto thee, and will put my words in his mouth; and he shall speak unto them all that I shall command him," claims attention. Does this refer to the Messiah? The reference to Moses in John v, 45–47—"He wrote of me" —seems to point to this passage; for it is a cold and forced interpretation to refer it to the whole types and symbols of the Mosaic law. On the other hand, many critics would fain find here the divine institution of the whole prophetic order, which, if not here, does not occur at all. Hengstenberg thinks that it does promise that an order of prophets should be sent, but that the singular is used with direct reference to the greatest of the prophets, Christ himself, without whom the words would not have been fulfilled. "The spirit of Christ spoke in the prophets, and Christ is in a sense the only prophet" (1 Pet. i, 11). Jews in earlier times might have been excused for referring the words to this or that present prophet; but the Jews whom the Lord rebukes (John v) were inexcusable; for, having the words before them, and the works of Christ as well, they should have known that no prophet had so fulfilled the words as he had.

(3.) The passages in the Pentateuch which relate to " the Angel of the Lord" have been thought by many to bear reference to the Messiah.

3. *Period of David.*—Here another advance is found in prophetic limitation. Jacob had only specified *the tribe*, now the particular *family* is indicated from which Messiah was to spring. From the great promise made to David (2 Sam. vii, 11–16), and so frequently referred to afterwards (1 Kings xi, 34, 38; Psa. lxxxix, 30–37; Isa. lv, 3; Acts xiii, 34), and described by *the sweet psalmist of Israel* himself as "an everlasting covenant ordered in all things, and sure" (2 Sam. xxiii, 5), arose that concentrated expectation of the Messiah expressed by the popular phrase *Son of David*, of which we hear so much in the N. T. (comp. Matt. ix, 27; xii, 23; xxi, 9; xxii, 42; Mark x, 47, 48; xi, 10; Luke i, 32; xviii, 38, 39; John vii, 42; Rom. i, 3; Rev. xxii, 16; with Jer. xxiii, 5).

In the promises of a kingdom to David and his house " forever" (2 Sam. vii, 13), there is more than could be fulfilled save by the eternal kingdom in which that of David merged; and David's last words dwell on this promise of an everlasting throne (2 Sam. xxiii). Passages in the Psalms are numerous which are applied to the Messiah in the N. T.: such are Psa. ii, xvi, xxii, xl, cx. Other psalms quoted in the N. T. appear to refer to the actual history of another king; but only those who deny the existence of types and prophecy will consider this as an evidence against an ulterior allusion to Messiah; such psalms are xlv, lxviii, lxix, lxxii. The advance in clearness in this period is great. The name of Anointed, i. e. King, comes in, and the Messiah is to come of the lineage of David. He is described in his exaltation, with his great kingdom that shall be spiritual rather than temporal (Psa. ii, xxi, xl, cx). In other places he is seen in suffering and humiliation (Psa. xxii, xvi, xl).

Having now confined the Messiah's descent to the family of the illustrious king who was "the man after God's own heart," prophecy will await God's own express identification of the *individual* (see it given in Matt. iii, 17; xvii, 5; Mark i, 11; ix, 7; Luke iii, 22; ix, 35; and referred to in 2 Pet. i, 17). But it will not idly wait. It has other particulars to announce, to give point and precision to a nation's hopes.

4. *Period of Prophetism.*—After the time of David the predictions of the Messiah ceased for a time, until those prophets arose whose works we possess in the canon of Scripture. They nowhere give us an exact and complete account of the nature of the Messiah; but different aspects of the truth are produced by the various needs of the people, and so they are led to speak of him now as a Conqueror, or a Judge, or a Redeemer from sin; it is from the study of the whole of them that we gain a clear and complete image of his person and kingdom. This third period lasts from the reign of Uzziah to the Babylonian captivity. The Messiah is a King and Ruler of David's house, who shall come to reform and restore the Jewish nation and purify the Church, as in Isa. xi, xl–lxvi. The blessings of the restoration, however, will not be confined to Jews; the heathen are made to share them fully (Isa. ii, lxvi). Whatever theories have been attempted about Isa. liii, there can be no doubt that the most natural is the received interpretation that it refers to the suffering Redeemer; and so in the N. T. it is always considered to do. The passage of Mic. v, 2 (comp. Matt. ii, 6) left no doubt in the mind of the Sanhedrim as to the birthplace of the Messiah. The lineage of David is again alluded to in Zech. xii, 10–14. The time of the second Temple is fixed by Hagg. ii, 9 for Messiah's coming; and the coming of the Forerunner and of the Anointed is clearly revealed in Mal. iii, 1; iv, 5, 6.

All the more important events of the coming Redeemer's life and death, and subsequent kingdom and exaltation, were foretold. Bethlehem was to be his birthplace (Mic. v, 2; comp. with Matt. ii, 1–6); Galilee his country (Isa. ix, 1, 2; comp. with Matt. iv, 14–16); a virgin his mother (Isa. vii, 14; comp. with Matt. i, 23); he was to preach glad tidings to the meek and to bind up the broken-hearted (Isa. lxi, 1; comp. with Luke iv, 17–21); though her king, he was to come to the daughter of Zion, just and having salvation, lowly and riding upon an ass, and upon a colt, the foal of an ass (Zech. ix, 9; comp. with John xii, 14, 15); he was to be despised and rejected of men; was to be led like a lamb to the slaughter (Isa. liii, 3, 7; comp. with Psa. xxii, 6; John i, 11; xviii, 40; Mark xiv, 61 and xv, 5); his garments were to be parted, and lots cast upon his vesture (Psa. xxii, 18; comp. with John xix, 23, 24); his hands and feet were to be pierced (Psa. xxii, 16; comp. with Luke xxiii, 33, and John xx, 25); he was to have vinegar given to him to drink (Psa. lxix, 21; comp. with Matt. xxvii, 34, 38); he was to pour out his soul unto death; was to be numbered with the transgressors; and his grave, though intended to be with wicked men (see this translation in Mason and Bernard's *Hebr. Gram.* ii, 305), was in reality destined to be with a rich man (Isa. liii, 9; comp. with Matt. xxvii, 57, 58); his soul was not to be left in hell, nor his flesh to see corruption (Psa. xvi, 10; comp. with Acts ii, 31, and xiii, 34–36); he was to sit on the right hand of Jehovah till his foes were made his footstool (Psa. cx, 1; comp. with 1 Pet. iii, 22; Heb. i, 3; Mark xvi, 19, and 1 Cor. xv, 25); his kingdom was to spread until ultimately "the kingdom and dominion, and the greatness of the kingdom under the whole heaven, should be given to the saints of the Most High" (Dan. vii, 27; see Perowne, *Coherence*, p. 29, 30). Slight as is this sketch of the prophetic announcements with which God was pleased to sustain human hope amid human misery, "as a light that shineth in a dark place" (2 Pet. i, 19),

"shining more and more unto the perfect day" (Prov. iv, 18), it is yet enough to suggest to us how great must have been the longing for their Deliverer which such persistent and progressive promises were likely to excite in the hearts of faithful men and women.

The expectation of a golden age that should return upon the earth was, as we have seen, common in heathen nations (Hesiod, *Works and Days*, p. 109; Ovid, *Met.* i, 89; Virgil, *Ecl.* iv; and passages in Eusebius, *Præp. Ev.* i, 7; xii, 13). It was doubtless inspired by some light that had reached them from the Jewish revelation. This hope the Jews also shared, but with them it was associated with the coming of a particular person, the Messiah. It has been asserted that in him the Jews looked for an earthly king, and that the existence of the hope of a Messiah may thus be accounted for on natural grounds and without a divine revelation. But the prophecies refute this: they hold out not a King only, but a Prophet and a Priest, whose business it should be to set the people free from sin, and to teach them the ways of God, as in Psa. xxii, xl, cx; Isa. ii, xi, liii. In these and other places, too, the power of the coming One reaches beyond the Jews and embraces all the Gentiles, which is contrary to the exclusive notions of Judaism. A fair consideration of all the passages will convince us that the growth of the Messianic idea in the prophecies is owing to revelation from God. The witness of the N. T. to the O.-T. prophecies can bear no other meaning; it is summed up in the above-cited words of Peter (2 Pet. i, 19–21; comp. the elaborate essay on this text in Knapp's *Opuscula*, vol. i). Our Lord affirms that there are prophecies of the Messiah in the O. T., and that they are fulfilled in him (Matt. xxvi, 54; Mark ix, 12; Luke xviii, 31–33; xxii, 37; xxiv, 27; John v, 39, 46). The apostles preach the same truth in Acts ii, 16, 25; viii, 28–35; x, 43; xiii, 23, 32; xxvi, 22, 23; 1 Pet. i, 11, and in many passages of Paul. Even if internal evidence did not prove that the prophecies were much more than vague longings after better times, the N. T. proclaims everywhere that although the Gospel was the sun, and O.-T. prophecy the dim light of a candle, yet both were light, and both assisted those who heeded them to see aright; and that the prophets interpreted, not the private longings of their own hearts, but the will of God, in speaking as they did (see Knapp's Essay for this explanation) of the coming kingdom.

5. The period after the close of the canon of the O. T. is known to us in a great measure from allusions in the N. T. to the expectation of the Jews. From such passages as Psa. ii, 2, 6, 8; Jer. xxiii, 5, 6; Zech. ix, 9, the Pharisees, and those of the Jews who expected the Messiah at all, looked for a temporal prince only. The apostles themselves were infected with this opinion till after the resurrection (Matt. xx, 20, 21; Luke xxiv, 21; Acts i, 6). Gleams of a purer faith appear (Luke ii, 30; xxiii, 42; John iv, 25). On the other hand, there was a sceptical school which had discarded the expectation altogether. No mention of the Messiah appears in the Book of Wisdom, nor in the writings of Philo; and Josephus avoids the doctrine. Intercourse with heathens had made some Jews ashamed of their fathers' faith.

It is quite consistent with the prospects which, as we have seen, the prophecies were calculated to raise, that we are informed by Luke of the existence of what seems to have been a considerable number of persons "that looked for redemption in Israel" (ii, 38). The demeanor of these believers was exhibited in a close and conscientious adherence to the law of Moses, which was, in its statutes and ordinances, at once the rule of pious life and the schoolmaster to guide men to their Messiah (Gal. iii, 24). As examples of these "just and devout" persons, the evangelist presents us with a few short but beautiful sketches in his first and second chapters. Besides the blessed Mary and faithful Joseph, there are Zacharias and Elisabeth, Simeon and Anna—pictures of holiness to be met with among men and women, married and unmarried, whose piety was strongly toned with this eminent feature, which is expressly attributed to one of them, "waiting for the consolation of Israel" (comp. Luke i, 6 with ii, 25, and 37, 38). Such hopes, stimulated by a profound and far-sighted faith, were exhibited at the birth and infancy of the Messiah Jesus by these expectant *Jews;* and they were not alone. *Gentiles* displayed a not less marvellous faith, when "the wise men from the East" did homage to the babe of Bethlehem, undeterred by the disguise of humiliation with which the Messiah's glory was to the human eye obscured (Matt. ii, 2, 11). But at his death, no less than at his birth, under a still darker veil of ignominy, similar acknowledgments of faith in his Messiahship were exhibited. Mark mentions it as one of the points in the character of Joseph of Arimathæa that he "waited for the kingdom of God;" and it would seem that this faith urged him to that holy "boldness" of using his influence with Pilate to rescue the body of Jesus, and commit it to an honorable tomb, as if he realized the truth of Isaiah's great prophecy, and saw in the Crucified no less than the Messiah himself (Mark xv, 43). To a like faith must be imputed the remarkable confession of the repentant thief upon the cross (Luke xxiii, 42)— a faith which brought even the Gentile centurion who superintended the execution of Jesus to the conviction that the expiring sufferer was not only innocent (Luke xxiii, 47), but even "the Son of God" (Matt. xxvii, 54, and Mark xv, 39). This conjunction of Gentile faith with that of Hebrews is most interesting, and, indeed, consistent with the progress of the promise. We have seen above how, in the earliest stages of the revelation, Gentile interests were not overlooked. Abraham, who saw the Messiah's day (John viii, 56), was repeatedly assured of the share which all nations were destined to have in the blessings of his death (Gen. xii, 3; xxii, 18; Acts iii, 25). Nor was the breadth of the promise afterwards narrowed. Moses called "the nations" to rejoice with the chosen people (Deut. xxxii, 43). Isaiah proclaimed the Messiah expressly as "the light of the Gentiles" (xlii, 6; xlix, 6); Haggai foretold his coming as "the desire of all nations" (ii, 7); and when he came at last, holy Simeon inaugurated his life on earth under the title of "a light to lighten the Gentiles" (Luke ii, 32). When his Gospel was beginning to run its free course, the two missionaries for the heathen quoted this great prophetic note as the warrant of their ministry: "I have set thee to be a light of the Gentiles, that thou shouldest be for salvation unto the ends of the earth" (Acts xiii, 47). Plain, however, as was the general scope of the Messianic prophecies, there were features in it which the Jewish nation failed to perceive. Framing their ideal not so much from their Scriptures as from their desires, and impatient of a hated heathen yoke, they longed for an avenging Messiah who should inflict upon their oppressors retaliation for many wrongs. This wish colored all their national hopes; and it should be borne in mind by the student of the Gospels, on which it throws much light. Not only was the more religious class, such as Christ's own apostles and pupils, affected by this thought of an external kingdom, even so late as his last journey to Jerusalem (Mark x, 37); but the undiscriminating crowds, who would have forcibly made him king (John vi, 15)—so strongly did his miracles attest his Messianic mission even in their view (ver. 14) —and who afterwards followed him to the capital and shouted hosannas to his praise, most abruptly withdrew their popular favor from him and joined in his destruction, because he gave them no signs of an earthly empire or of political emancipation. Christ's kingdom was "not of this world" — a proposition which, although containing the very essence of Christianity, offended the Jewish people when Jesus presented himself as their veritable Messiah, and led to their rejection of him. Moreover, his lowly condition, sufferings, and death, have been a stumbling-block in the way of their recognition of him ever since. See SAVIOUR.

III. *Jewish Views respecting the Messiah.*—"Even in

the first prediction of the woman's seed bruising the serpent's head, there is the idea of a painful struggle and of a victory, which leaves the mark of suffering upon the Conqueror" (Smith's *Messianic Prophecies of Isaiah* [1862], p. 164). This thought has tinged the sentiments of all orthodox believers since, although it has often been obscured by the brilliant fancy of ambition. See SON OF MAN.

1. *Early Jewish Opinions.*—The portrait of an afflicted and suffering Messiah is too minutely sketched by the Psalmist (Psa. xxii, xlii, xliii, lxix), by Isaiah (ch. liii), by Zechariah (ch. xi–xiii), and Daniel (ix, 24– 27), to be ignored even by reluctant Jews; and strange is the embarrassment observable in Talmudic Judaism to obviate the advantage which accrues to Christianity from its tenure of this unpalatable doctrine. Long ago did Trypho, Justin Martyr's Jew, own the force of the prophetic Scriptures, which delineated Messiah as "a man of sorrows" (Justin. *Dial.* 89). In later times, after the Talmud of Babylon (7th century) became influential, the doctrine of two Messiahs was held among the Jews. For several centuries it was their current belief that Messiah *Ben-David* was referred to in all the prophecies which spoke of glory and triumph, while on Messiah *Ben-Joseph* of Ephraim fell all the predicted woes and sufferings. By this expedient they both gratified their traditional idea which exonerated their chief Messiah, of David's illustrious race, from all humiliation, and likewise saved their nominal deference to the inspired prophets who had written of the sorrows of Messiah. (For a popular sketch of this opinion of two Messiahs, the reader is referred to Smith's sermons *On the Messianic Prophecies of Isaiah,* p. 177–181; see also Buxtorf's *Lexicon Talmud.* s. v. משיח, p. 1126, 1127, and s. v. אַרְמִילוֹס; Eisenmenger's *Entdecktes Judenthum,* ii, 720–750; Otho's *Lexicon Rabbin.;* Schöttgen, *Horæ Heb. et Rabbin.* ii, 1–778.) All the references to a *suffering* Messiah made by great writers, such as Rashi, Ibn-Esra, and D. Kimchi, are to "Messiah *Ben-Joseph;*" while of the more than seventy quotations cited by Buxtorf from the Targums, including Onkelos, not one refers to the Messiah *as suffering.* This early Targumistic literature (as distinguished from the latter Rabbinical) dwells on the glories, triumphs, and power of a conquering Messiah. However absurd this distortion was, it was yet felt to be too great a homage to the plain interpretation of the prophetic Scriptures as given by Christian writers, who showed to the votaries of the Talmud that their earlier authors had applied to the Son of David the very passages which they were for referring to the Son of Joseph. From the tenth and eleventh centuries, therefore, other interpretations have been sought for. Maimonides omits the whole story of Messiah *Ben-Joseph* in his account of the Messiah; see Pococke, *Append. on Malachi. The Messiah has been withdrawn altogether from the reach of all predicted sufferings.* Such passages as Isa. liii, have been and still are applied to some persecuted servant of God, Jeremiah especially, or to the aggregate Jewish nation. This anti-Messianic exegesis is prevalent among the Neologians of Germany and France, and their "free-handling" disciples of the English school (see Dr. Rowland Williams, *Essays and Reviews,* p. 71–75 [edit. 2]). Thus Jewish sentiment has either reverted to that low standard of mere worldly expectation which recognises no humiliation in Messiah, but only a career of unmixed triumph and glory, or else has collapsed in a disappointment and despair which forbid all speculation of a Messiah whatever (Eisenmenger, *Entdecktes Judenth.* i, 677). Jewish despair does not often resolve itself into Christian hope. Here and there affecting instances of the genuine change occur, such as the two mentioned by bishop Thirlwall (*Reply to Dr. W.'s earnestly respectful letter,* p. 78); in the second of which—that of Isaac da Costa—conversion arose from his thoughtful reflections on the present dispersion of the Jewish race

for its sins. His acceptance of Jesus as the Messiah solved all enigmas to him, and enabled him to estimate the importance of such prophetic promises as are yet unfulfilled to Israel. But the normal state of Jewish Messianic opinion is that sickness of heart which comes from deferred hopes. This despair produces an abasement of faith and a lowering of religious tone, or else finds occasional relief in looking out after pretended Messiahs. Upwards of thirty cases of these have deluded the nation in its scattered state since the destruction of Jerusalem. See MESSIAHS, FALSE. The havoc of life and reputation caused by these attempts has tended more than any thing else to the discouragement of Messianic hopes among the modern Jews. Foremost in the unhappy catalogue of these fanatics stands the formidable rebellion under Bar-Cocheba, in the 2d century. Rabbi Akiba, "the second Moses," the great light of the day in Jewry, declared before the Sanhedrim that Bar-Cocheba was the Messiah. Rabbi Jochanan alone made opposition, and said, "Grass, O Akiba, will grow out of thy jaws, and yet the Son of David not have come." We know not what was the fate of Bar-Cocheba (or Bar-Coseba, "the son of lying," as his disappointed dupes at length called him), but the gray-headed Akiba was taken by the Romans and executed. More are said to have perished in this attempt than in the previous war of Titus. Embarrassing as all these failures are to the Jews, they only add one more to the many proofs of the Messiahship of Jesus of Nazareth, who expressly foretold these delusions of "false Christs" (Matt. xxiv, 24; Mark xiii, 22), as one class of retributions which should avenge on Israel the guilt of his own rejection. Not only, however, from the lowliness and suffering of the Christian Messiah, but in a still greater degree from his exalted character, there arises a difficulty of faith to the Jewish objection. The divinity of nature which Jesus claimed is perhaps the greatest doctrinal obstacle to his reception among the Jews. See Gfrörer, *Gesch. d. Urchristenthums* (Stuttg. 1838); Solani, *Croyances Messianiques* (Strasb. 1864). See SON OF GOD.

2. *Modern Jewish Views.*—The hope of a Messiah—the bounteous benefactor and inaugurator of a glorious reign on earth, firmly establishing forever and ever the greatness of Abraham's descendants—had prevailed even among the children of Israel, but it required the days of trial and tribulation, such as came in the days of the exile, to create a yearning for the appearance of the King, the Conqueror, the God of Israel. Within the domains of a foreign ruler, and subject to his rule, the Messiah became an ever-present being to the thoughts and to the visions of the Jews; and yet when at last the Son of man came to his own, his own knew him not. But though they rejected him of whom Moses and the prophets wrote, the faith in a Restorer of Israel for many centuries continued to knit together the nation in their dispersed condition. Of late only a change has come over them, and the Jewish camp may be truly said to have divided into three distinct branches: (1) the extreme right, (2) the extreme left, and (3) the centre.

(1) The Jews belonging to the first class are those who remain either (*a*) orthodox in their adherence to the liberal interpretation of the Bible and tradition, or (*b*) who, though accepting both Bible and tradition, favor a liberal construction of the traditional usages. This class of Jews continue to look for a personal reign of Messiah, and their restoration to the land of their forefathers. Their number is daily decreasing, however, and the time promises to be soon when they shall be counted among the things that were.

(2) To the second class belong those Jews generally denominated *Reformed.* They would sweep away Talmudism and the ceremonial law, claiming a complete emancipation from religious thraldom as their indefeasible right. They question the propriety of interpreting the prophets as predicting a personal Messiah, and deny the possibility of a restoration of Israel as a nation of political entity. In 1840 they for the first time gave

public expression to their belief in a meeting at Frankfort, when they declared that "a Messiah who is to lead back to Palestine is neither expected nor desired by the associated, and they acknowledge that alone to be their country to which they belong by birth or civil relation." In 1869 a meeting of the educated Jews of Germany was held in the city of Leipsic, at which eighty-four different Jewish congregations were represented. Twenty-four of the attendants were rabbis of high repute; the lay members men who had secured the highest places in the gift of the nation, among them the late Dr. Fürst, then professor at the University of Leipsic, the learned Lazarus, of the University of Berlin, etc. In 1840 the gathering had been composed of a handful of rationalistic Jews; in 1869 the meeting at Leipsic was attended by Israel's ablest and most devoted adherents. Yet these men *rejected* the belief in Israel's restoration, and passed the following resolution: "Those portions of our prayers which refer to the re-establishment of the annual sacrifices at the Messianic period, or to the return of the Jews to Jerusalem, must be modified." How widespread the opinion represented at this meeting may be best judged if such a conservative journal as the *London Jewish Chronicle* is led to comment that "Although every Jew is bound to believe in a Messiah, the question whether that expression indicates a person or a time, and whether he or it has arrived or not, is, according to the Talmud, an open question."

(3) The main portion of modern Judaism consists of the moderate party, embracing those Jews who seek to develop a higher spirituality from the old form of Judaism. With them the ceremonial law is valuable only as a hedge to keep the people apart from other forms of religion till the times are fulfilled. Like Kimchi, Abrabanel, and other Jewish commentators, they apply the oracle in Isa. xi, 1–10 to the age of the Messiah, whose advent they place at the very time when the final gathering of the Jewish people is to be accomplished. "The one," says the Rev. Prof. Marks (*Jewish Messenger*, January, 1872), "is to be immediately consequent upon the other; or, rather, they are prophesied as synchronous events." Denying the accuracy of Christian interpretation, which refers the 11th chapter to the first, and the 12th chapter to the coming of Christ in the final day, they insist that the Hebrew Scriptures teach only *one* Messianic appearance, and that chapter 11 warrants no distinction in point of time between "the clearly-defined occurrences which are to mark Messiah's advent;" "and," continues Prof. Marks, "so far from representing the complete regeneration of the moral world as the result of many centuries after the promised Messiah shall have appeared, the prophet of the text mentions the *universal peace and harmony that shall prevail, as well as the ingathering of the dispersed of Judah and of Israel*, as the especial events which are to characterize the inauguration of the Messianic age. *The promised regenerator of mankind is to be known by the accomplishment of these his appointed tasks;* and no one, according to the Jewish view of prophetic Scripture, is entitled to the name of 'the Messiah' who does not vindicate his claim to that high office by means of the fulfilment of the conditions which the word of inspiration has assigned to his coming."

As is well known, the Jews looked for a Messiah in the days of our Saviour. For centuries after the whole nation was incessantly on the watch: their prosperity seemed the harbinger of his coming; their darkest calamities, they believed, gathered them only to display, with the force of stronger contrast, the mercy of their God and the glory of their Redeemer. Calculation upon calculation failed, until at last, their courage threatening desertion, the rabbinical interdict was sent forth to repress the dangerous curiosity which, often baffled, would still penetrate the secrets of futurity. "Cursed is he who calculates the time of the Messiah's coming" was the daily message to the faithful of the synagogue; and at last it was declared that "No indication is given with regard to the particular epoch at which the prophecy of the 11th chapter (of Isaiah) is to be accomplished," but that the inspired messenger of God has furnished means of determining by the evidence of our senses the *distinctive signs* by which the advent of the Messiah is to be marked, viz. (1) the arrival of the *golden age* (ver. 7, 8, 9); (2) the rallying of the nations, unsought and uninvited, around the Messianic banner (ver. 10); and (3) the *second* ingathering of the whole of the Jewish people, including the tribes of Judah and Benjamin, as well as those which composed the kingdom of Samaria, and are popularly spoken of as "the lost tribes" (ver. 11 and 12. Compare on this point Lindo, *The Conciliator of R. Manasseh ben-Israel* [Lond. 1842, 2 vols. 8vo], ii, 143). "As Jews, we," they say, "maintain that the promised Messiah has not yet appeared, and that the world has never witnessed such a moral picture as the prophets predict of the Messianic age." And yet they are obliged themselves to confess that "*Various opinions prevail* [among them] *with respect to what is to be precisely understood by the coming of the Messiah.* Some hold that it implies the birth of a particular personage; others, that it describes the conjunction of certain events which are to act with extraordinary moral power on the world at large. But what it does especially behoove us to bear in mind is, first, that the prophets identify the Messianic advent with an *age* when brute force shall have come to an end, when warfare and strife shall have disappeared from the earth, and when love shall have become the sole governing principle of humanity; and, secondly, that this important work of the regeneration of mankind is to be brought about by the instrumentality of the Jewish people, *if not by some remarkable individual born of that race.*"

Jesus the Christ they refuse to recognise as that "remarkable individual," "because," as one of their number has declared, "we do not find *in the present comparatively imperfect stage of human progress the realization of that blessed condition of mankind which the prophet Isaiah associates with the æra when Messiah is to appear. And as our Hebrew Scriptures speak of one Messianic advent only, and not of two advents* (even those in the synagogue who speak of a Messiah from the house of Joseph concurrently with one from the house of David make their advent synchronous); *and as the inspired Book does not preach Messiah's kingdom as a matter of faith, but distinctly identifies it with matters of fact which are to be made evident to the senses, we cling to the plain inference to be drawn from the text of the Bible, and we deny that Messiah has yet appeared, and upon the following grounds:* First. Because of the three distinctive facts which the inspired seer of Judah inseparably connects with the advent of the Messiah, viz. the cessation of war and the uninterrupted reign of peace, the prevalence of a perfect concord of opinion on all matters bearing upon the worship of the one and only God, and the ingathering of the remnant of Judah and of the dispersed ten tribes of Israel—not one has, up to the present time, been accomplished. Second. We dissent from the proposition that Jesus of Nazareth is the Messiah announced by the prophets, because the Church which he founded, and which his successors developed, has offered, during a succession of centuries, a most singular contrast to what is described by the Hebrew Scriptures as the immediate consequence of Messiah's advent, and of his glorious kingdom. The prophet Isaiah declares that when the Messiah appears, peace, love, and union will be permanently established; and every candid man must admit that the world has not yet realized the accomplishment of this prophecy. Again, in the days of Messiah, all men, as Scripture saith, 'are to serve God with one accord;' and yet it is very certain that since the appearance of him whom our Christian brethren believe to be Messiah, mankind has been split into more hostile divisions on the grounds of religious belief, and more antagonistic sects have sprung

up, than in any historic age before Christianity was preached." For the articles of confession, see the article JUDAISM, iv, 1057, col. 1 (9 and 12), 1058, and especially those portions in *Conservative* and *Reformed* JUDAISM; also RESTORATION OF THE JEWS.

IV. *Proof of the Messiahship of Jesus.*—This discussion resolves itself into two questions. See JESUS CHRIST.

1. The promised Messiah *has already come.* To prove this assertion, we shall confine our remarks to *three* prophecies. (1.) The first is the passage above commented on, occurring in Gen. xlix, 8, 10, where Jacob is giving his sons his parting benediction, etc. When he comes to Judah, he says: "The sceptre shall not depart from Judah, nor a lawgiver from between his feet, until Shiloh come; and unto him shall the obedience of the people be." It is evident that by Judah is here meant, not the *person,* but the *tribe;* for Judah died in Egypt, without any pre-eminence. By *sceptre* and *lawgiver* are obviously intended the legislative and ruling power, which did, in the course of time, commence in David, and which for centuries afterwards was continued in his descendants. Whatever variety the form of government—whether monarchical or aristocratical—might have assumed, the *law* and polity *were still the same.* This prediction all the ancient Jews referred to the Messiah. Ben-Uzziel renders it, "Until the time when the king Messiah shall come." The Targum of Onkelos speaks to the same effect, and that of Jerusalem paraphrases it thus: "Kings shall not cease from the house of Judah, nor doctors that teach the law from his children, until that the king Messiah do come, whose the kingdom is; and all nations of the earth shall be subject unto him." Now that the sceptre has departed from Judah, and, consequently, that the Messiah has come, we argue from the acknowledgments of some most learned Jews themselves. Kimchi thus comments on Hosea: "These are the days of our captivity, wherein we have neither king nor prince in Israel; but we are in the power of the Gentiles, and under their kings and princes." Again, Abarbanel, commenting on Isa. liii, says that it is a great part of their misery in their captivity that they have neither kingdom nor rule, nor a sceptre of judgment! The *precise* time when all authority departed from Judah is disputed. Some date its departure from the time when Herod, an Idumæan, set aside the Maccabees and Sanhedrim. Thereupon the Jews are said to have shaved their heads, put on sackcloth, and cried, "Woe to us, because the sceptre is departed from Judah, and a lawgiver from beneath his feet!" Others think that it was when Vespasian and Titus destroyed Jerusalem and the Temple that the Jews lost the last vestige of authority. If, therefore, the sceptre *has* departed from Judah—and who can question it who looks at the broken-up, scattered, and lost state of that tribe for ages?—the conclusion is clearly irresistible that the Messiah *must have long since come!* To avoid the force of this conclusion the Jews now say that the שֵׁבֶט, *she'bet,* which we render *sceptre,* may be translated *rod,* and metaphorically signifies, in the above passage, *affliction.* That the word cannot bear this meaning *here* is evident, because, for a long while after the prophecy was uttered, especially in the reigns of David and Solomon, the tribe of Judah was in a most prosperous state. See SCEPTRE.

(2.) The next proof that the Messiah has long since come we adduce from Dan. ix, 25, 26, 27. It is evident that the true Messiah is here spoken of. He is twice designated by the very name. If we consider what the work is which he is here said to accomplish, we shall have a full confirmation of this. Who but he could finish and take away transgression, make reconciliation for iniquity, bring in everlasting righteousness, seal up the vision and prophecy, confirm the covenants with many, and cause to cease the sacrifice and oblation? Indeed, there is a saying extant in the Talmud, as the tradition of former times, "In Daniel is delivered to us the end of the Messiah," i. e. the term wherein he ought to come, as it is explained by Jarchi. Grotius (*De Veritat.* v) speaks of a Jew, R. Berachia, who lived fifty years before our Lord, and who declared that the time fixed by Daniel could not go beyond fifty years! If then it be the *true* Messiah who is described in the above prophecy, it remains for us to see how the time predicted for his coming has long since transpired. This is expressly said to be seventy weeks from the going forth of the commandment to restore and build Jerusalem. That by seventy weeks are to be understood seventy sevens of years, a day being put for a year, and a week for seven years, making up 490 years, is allowed by Kimchi, Jarchi, rabbi Saadias, and other learned Jews, as well as by many Christian commentators. It is clear that these seventy weeks cannot consist of weeks of days, for all put together make but one year, four months, and odd days—a space of time too short to crowd so many various events into as are here specified; nor can any such time be assigned between the two captivities, wherein like events did happen (see Prideaux, *Connect.* lib. v, pt. 1). This period of time then *must have long since* elapsed, whether we date its commencement from the first decree of Cyrus (Ezra i, 1, 2), the second of Darius Hystaspes (vi, 15), or that of Artaxerxes (viii, 1). See Grotius, *De Veritat.* v; Josephus, *War*, vii, 12, 13. See SEVENTY WEEKS.

(3.) We can only barely allude to one remarkable prediction more, which fixes the time of the Messiah's advent, viz. Hag. ii, 7–9: "I will shake all nations, and the desire of all nations shall come: and I will fill this house with glory, saith the Lord of Hosts. The silver is mine, and the gold is mine, saith the Lord of Hosts. The glory of this latter house shall be greater than of the former, saith the Lord of Hosts." The glory here spoken of *must* be in reference to the Messiah, or on some other account. It could not have been said that the second Temple exceeded in glory the former one; for in many particulars, according to the acknowledgment of the Jews themselves, it was far inferior, both as a building (Ezra iii, 3, 12) and in respect of the symbols and tokens of God's special favor being wanting (see Kimchi and R. Salomon on Hag. i, 8). The promised glory, therefore, must refer to the coming and presence of him who was promised to the world before there was any nation of the Jews; and who is aptly called the "*Desire of all nations.*" This view is amply confirmed by the prophet Malachi (iii, 1). Since, then, the very Temple into which the Saviour was to enter has for ages been destroyed, *He must*, if the integrity of this prophecy be preserved, *have come*. Nor is the force of this passage for our present purpose greatly diminished if we take the interpretation of many, that חֶמְדָּה, "desire," here, being fem., cannot directly refer to the Messiah personally; for in any case the prophecy refers to some glorification, at the time future, of the then existing Temple; and as that Temple has now utterly passed away, its fulfilment cannot be looked for under any Messiah yet to come. See DESIRE.

That there was, at the time of our Lord's birth, a great expectation of the Messiah, both among Jews and Gentiles, may be seen from three celebrated historians, as well as from the sacred Scriptures. Tacitus (*Hist.* c. 13) says: "Pluribus persuasio inerat, antiquis sacerdotum literaris contineri, eo ipso tempore fore ut valesceret *Oriens*, profectique Judæa rerum potirentur." Again, Suetonius (in *Vespas.* 4) says: "Percrebruerat Oriente toto vetus et constans opinio, esse in fatis ut eo tempore Judæi profecti rerum potirentur." Josephus, not being able to find any calculation by which to protract the general expectation of the Messiah, applies it in the following words to Vespasian (*War*, vii, 31): "That which chiefly excited the Jews to war was an ambiguous prophecy, which was also found in the sacred books, that at that time some one within their country should

arise who would obtain the empire of the whole world." We are, moreover, informed again by Suetonius (*Octav.* 94), that, upon the conception of Augustus, it was generally thought that *Nature* was then in labor to bring forth a king who would rule the Romans. Some suppose that the words of Virgil (*Eclog.* iv) point at our Saviour, but they were intended by him to apply to the son of Pollio. We may just add that as there was a general expectation of the Messiah at this time, so there were many impostors who drew after them many followers (Josephus, *Ant.* xx, 2, 6; *War*, lvii, 31). See also a full account of the false Christs who appeared by John à Lent, *Schediasm.* c. 2; Maimonides, *Ep. ad Judæos Marsilienses;* Christ prophesies of such persons (Matt. xxiv, 24, 29).

2. The limits of this article will admit of our only touching upon the proofs that Jesus of Nazareth, and none other, is the very Messiah that was to come. (1.) What was predicted of the Messiah was fulfilled in Jesus. Was the Messiah to be of the seed of the woman (Gen. iii, 15), and this woman a virgin? (Isa. vii, 14). So we are told (Gal. iv, 4; Matt. i, 18, and 22, 23) that Jesus was made of a woman, and born of a virgin. Was it predicted that he (Messiah) should be of the tribe of Judah, of the family of Jesse, and of the house of David? (Mic. v, 2; Gen. xlix, 10; Isa. xi, 10; Jer. xxiii, 5). This was fulfilled in Jesus (Luke i, 27, 69; Matt. i, 1). See GENEALOGY OF CHRIST. (2.) If the Messiah was to be a prophet like unto Moses, so was Jesus also (Isa. xviii; John vi, 14). If the Messiah was to appear in the second Temple, so did Jesus (Hag. ii, 7, 9; John xviii, 20). (3.) The Messiah was to work miracles (Isa. xxxv, 5, 6; comp. Matt. xi, 4, 5). See MIRACLE. (4.) If the Messiah was to suffer and die (Isa. liii), we find that Jesus died in the same manner, at the very time, and under the identical circumstances, which were predicted of him. The very man who betrayed him, the price for which he was sold, the indignities he was to receive in his last moments, the parting of his garments, and his last words, etc., were all foretold of the Messiah, and accomplished in Jesus! (5.) Was the Messiah to rise from the dead? So did Jesus. How stupendous and adorable is the providence of God, who, through so many apparent contingencies, brought such things to pass! See Kidder, *Demonstration of the Messiah* (Lond. 1726, fol.); Olearius, *Jesus d. wahre Messias* (Leips. 1714, 1737); M'Caul, *Messiahship of Jesus* (Warburton Lect. 1852); Black, *Messiahs and anti-Messiahs* (Lond. 1853); Browne, *Messiah as foretold and expected* (Lond. 1862); Higginson, *Hebrew Messianic Hope and Christian Reality* (Lond. 1871). Comp. also Malcolm's *Theological Index*, s. v.; Volbeding's *Index Programmatum*, p. 38 sq.; Hase's *Leben Jesu*, p. 86; and Danz, *Wörterbuch*, p. 855 sq. See CHRISTOLOGY.

MESSIAHS, FALSE. Jesus warned his disciples that false Christs should arise (Matt. xxiv, 24), and the event has verified the prediction. No less than twenty-four such impostors have been enumerated as having appeared in different places and at different times; and even this does not exhaust the list. One by the name of *Simeon* was the first of any note who made a noise in the world. Being dissatisfied with the state of things under Hadrian, he set himself up as the head of the Jewish nation, and proclaimed himself their long-expected Messiah. He was one of those banditti that infested Judæa, and committed all kinds of violence against the Romans; and had become so powerful that he was chosen king of the Jews, and by them acknowledged their Messiah. However, to facilitate the success of this bold enterprise, he assumed the name of Bar-Cocheba (q. v.), alluding to the star foretold by Balaam; for he pretended to be the star sent by heaven to restore his nation to its ancient liberty and glory. This epithet was changed by his enemies into that of Bar-Cozeba, i. e. *son of a lie.* He chose a forerunner, raised an army, was anointed king, coined money inscribed with his own name, and proclaimed himself Messiah and prince of the Jewish nation. Hadrian raised an army, and sent it against him: he retired into a town called Bither, where he was besieged. Bar-Cocheba seems to have been killed in the siege, the city was taken, and a dreadful havoc succeeded. The Jews themselves allow that during this short war against the Romans in defence of this false Messiah they lost five or six hundred thousand souls. This was in the first half of the 2d century. In the reign of Theodosius the Younger, A.D. 434, another impostor arose, called *Moses Cretensis*. He pretended to be a second Moses, sent to deliver the Jews who dwelt in Crete, and promised to divide the sea and give them a safe passage through it. Their delusion proved so strong and universal that they neglected their lands, houses, and other concerns, and took only so much with them as they could conveniently carry. On the day appointed, this false Moses, having led them to the top of a rock, men, women, and children threw themselves headlong down into the sea, without the least hesitation or reluctance, till so great a number of them were drowned as to open the eyes of the rest, and make them sensible of the cheat. They then began to look for their pretended leader, but he had disappeared, and escaped out of their hands.

In the reign of Justin, about A.D. 520, another impostor appeared, who called himself the son of Moses. His name was *Dunaan*. He entered into a city of Arabia Felix, and there he greatly oppressed the Christians; but he was taken prisoner and put to death by Elesban, an Ethiopian general. The Jews and Samaritans rebelled against the emperor Justinian, A.D. 529, and set up one *Julian* for their king, and accounted him the Messiah. The emperor sent an army against them, killed great numbers of them, took their pretended Messiah prisoner, and immediately put him to death. In the time of Leo the Isaurian, about A.D. 721, arose another false Messiah in Spain: his name was *Serenus*. He drew great numbers after him, to their no small loss and disappointment; but all his pretensions came to nothing.

The 12th century was particularly fruitful in producing Messiahs. About 1137 there appeared one in France, who was put to death, and numbers of those who followed him. In A.D. 1138 the Persians were disturbed with a Jew who called himself the Messiah. He collected a vast army; but he, too, was put to death, and his followers were treated with great inhumanity. A false Messiah stirred up the Jews at Cordova, in Spain, A.D. 1157. The wiser and better part looked upon him as a madman, but the great body of the Jewish nation believed in him. On this occasion nearly all the Jews in Spain were destroyed. Another false Messiah who arose in the kingdom of Fez, A.D. 1167, under the name of *David Alrui* (Alroy), brought great troubles and persecutions upon the Jews that were scattered throughout that country. Disraeli has taken this historical event as the plot of his *Alroy*. In the same year an Arabian professed to be the Messiah, and pretended to work miracles. When search was made for him, his followers fled, and he was brought before the Arabian king. Being questioned by him, he replied that he was a prophet sent from God. The king then asked him what sign he could show to confirm his mission. "Cut off my head," said he, "and I will return to life again." The king took him at his word, promising to believe him if his prediction was accomplished. The poor wretch, however, never came to life again, and the cheat was sufficiently discovered. Those who had been deluded by him were grievously punished, and the nation was condemned to a very heavy fine. Not long after this, a Jew who dwelt beyond the Euphrates called himself the Messiah, and drew vast multitudes of people about him. He gave this for a sign of it, that he had been leprous, and had been cured in the course of one night. He, like the rest, perished, and brought great persecution on his countrymen. A magician and false Christ arose in Persia, A.D. 1174, who seduced many of the common peo-

ple, and brought the Jews into great tribulation (see Maimonides, *Epistol. ad Judæos in Massilia agentes*). Another of these impostors, a great cabalist, arose, A.D. 1176, in Moravia, who was called *David Almasser*. He pretended he could make himself invisible; but he was soon taken and put to death, and a heavy fine laid upon the Jews. A famous cheat and rebel exerted himself in Persia, A.D. 1199, called *David el-David*. He was a man of learning, a great magician, and pretended to be the Messiah. He raised an army against the king, but was taken and imprisoned; and, having made his escape, was afterwards retaken and beheaded. Vast numbers of the Jews were butchered for taking part with this impostor.

In the 13th and 14th centuries the Messiah imposition had come to a comparative stand-still. It is true the most learned of the rabbis, the celebrated Saadia, Abraham Ibn-Chija, Nachman, and Gersoni, had taken upon themselves to calculate the time of the actual coming of the veritable deliverer, and had fixed upon 1358 as the Messiah year; but no one came forward and sought to impose himself upon the waiting multitude. Towards the close of the 15th century, however, the opportunity was renewed by the terrible fate of the Jews, especially in the Iberian peninsula, where for so many years they had enjoyed a haven of rest. On the Continent the Jews had suffered from the very start of the Crusading movement, but in the Iberian peninsula they had found a pleasant home and a quiet retreat, frequently even positions of power and of honor. Gradually, however, their position was undermined. First the Church of Rome trained men as polemics against the Jews. Later it was determined to make converts of them at any price, and if they could not be secured peacefully, to subject them to bloody persecution. This policy was inaugurated at Seville in 1391–92, and soon spread over the peninsula. Escape was difficult, and, if made, hardly augured a brighter future in other lands; and thus reasoning, they remained, and some 200,000 Jews were made to accept baptism at the point of the sword. This event forms the saddest turning-point in Jewish history. Persecution upon persecution followed. The Jew, finding no alternative, was forced to play the part of the hypocrite, and, while pressing the cross to his lips, vowed in his heart more faithful devotion to the cause of Israel. The gloomiest day came with the date of America's discovery. The year that shed new light upon Europe shrouded the Jew in darkness, and forms at the same time the grandest and the most melancholy hour of modern history. But though at first many had been made converts in the hours of oppression, they gradually came to believe in the vital truths of Christianity; and though the examples before them were not promotive of a true Christian life, the fact that no deliverer had come to Israel in the most trying hour made them not only faint but wavering, and there seemed danger that, if not soon inspired with new hope, the last day had come for the Jewish race. There remained, it is true, a small remnant that had continued thus far in open defiance to all demands of the government, and valiantly contended for liberty of conscience. But even these successive trials had broken their courage, and had robbed them of the prospect of a more auspicious future. Not only the uneducated, but even the learned and the devoted, were yielding up the long cherished Messianic hope, as a sweet dream, an idle fancy, which lacked all chance of reality. The Jewish race, they declared, was born to suffer forever, and the day would never come for deliverance from oppression; never should they see a day of freedom and independence. This hopeless and hapless condition of his countrymen determined the learned Jewish rabbi Abrabanel (q. v.) to employ his pen in defence of the O.-T. Scriptures, and of Jewish interpretation. Aware that if this spirit of discontent and unbelief were suffered to grow it would result in the ultimate defunction of the Jewish ranks, he essayed to combat it by inspiring them anew with the prospects of an early delivery from oppression, and the dawn of a happy change. Though hoary with age, he wrote with trembling hands book after book to explain the principal Messianic passages of the O. T., especially those of Daniel, and argued that Israel could safely depend upon a glorious future, and that the day of the Messiah was near at hand. He even went so far as to determine the date, and fixed upon 1503 as the year of their delivery. As a leader in Israel, Abrabanel's word commanded attention, and the wretched people were encouraged to take new hope.

At such a moment there was room for imposition, and it came immediately with the very opening of the 16th century. Enthusiasts declared that the time had arrived for removal to the Holy Land, to anticipate the change so near at hand. One German rabbi, Ascher Lämmlein (or Lämmlin), a resident within the Austrian dominions, actually gave himself out as the forerunner of the approaching Messiah, and, as pseudo-John, about A.D. 1502, called the people to repentance, and urged an immediate removal to the East. He pulled down his own house, presaging that by another year he and his brethren who would follow him should live in peace under the reign of the "King of the Jews." Lämmlein lived near Venice, but his admonitions travelled all through Germany, Italy, Spain, and France. Everywhere his cause made converts; even Christians are said to have believed in his mission (see Grätz, Gesch. d. Juden, ix, 243). But the prophet died suddenly, and all hopes lay prostrate in the dust. The agony of the people, so basely deceived, lacks description. A few flocked to the cross of Christ, and in this their most trying hour declared that Jesus was the Christ; but the greater number, with that stubbornness characteristic of the Shemitic race, yet refused to look for help from the *great* Physician.

The Messiah-hope still lingered, however faintly, in the heart of the Jew, particularly in the Iberian peninsula, where he now suffered most; and it was not long before a new impostor arose to abuse the confidence of his much dejected brethren. This time the pretender played his part more acutely, and it was some time before his deception was discovered. During the eventful reign of Charles V a person suddenly turned up at the court of the king of Portugal, who, calling himself *David Reubeni*, declared that he had come from India as ambassador of his brother, the king of the Jews, to propose an alliance for the recovery of the Holy Land from the Mussulman. He had so carefully prepared himself for his rôle that he appeared natural, and his story apparently bore truth upon its face. He readily found friends both among Jews and Gentiles, and he was favorably received wherever he went. To persuade the Iberian government of the verity of his mission, he had brought papers confirming his claims; and he kept at such a respectful distance from the Jews that they became doubly anxious to approach him. Those who had been forcibly converted to Christianity fairly worshipped the ground he had stood upon; and great was the joy among the Jews of Italy when David found favor in the eyes of Clement VII (1523-34), and gained distinctions at the papal court. In the midst of his successes he was joined by one *Solomon Molcho* (q. v.), a Portuguese New-Christian, who openly apostatized to Judaism, and set up as the prophet of the movement. He submitted to circumcision, and in many other ways sought to prove his sincerity. At first he travelled with David, but, anxious to visit the Holy Land, he parted with the prince and set out for the East. On his return he visited Clement VII, and found even greater favor with the pope than David. Indeed, Molcho enjoyed Clement's protection thereafter, and, though an apostate, he was suffered to pour out his apocalyptic rhapsodies without restraint. But he finally came to a woful end. He had met David again, and together they had gone to Ratisbon, the seat of Charles V, to convert the emperor. Charles was hardhearted, and both David and Solomon were thrown into prison; the former escaping, we hardly know how, the

latter expiating his daring at the stake. This put an end to the Messiah promises of the 16th century.

In the 17th century the first false Christ arose in the East Indies, A.D. 1615, and was largely followed by the Portuguese Jews who are scattered over that country. Another in the Low Countries declared himself to be the Messiah of the family of David, and of the line of Nathan, A.D. 1624. He promised to destroy Rome, and to overthrow the kingdom of Antichrist and the Turkish empire.

The year 1666 was a year of great expectation, and some wonderful thing was looked for by many. This was a fit time for an impostor to set up, and accordingly lying reports were carried about. It was said that great multitudes marched from unknown parts to the remote deserts of Arabia, and they were supposed to be the ten tribes of Israel, who had been dispersed for many ages; that a ship had arrived in the north part of Scotland with sails and cordage of silk; that the mariners spoke nothing but Hebrew; that on the sails was this motto, "The Twelve Tribes of Israel." The auspicious moment was embraced to advantage by one *Sabbathai Zebi* (q. v.), the greatest of all Jewish pretenders, who made a great noise, and gained a great number of proselytes. He was born at Aleppo, and imposed on the Jews for a considerable time with great success as "King of the kings of the earth;" but when the Turkish government, under whose protection he lived, questioned his wholesome influence on the people, he forsook the Jews and turned Mohammedan for the sake of saving his life, which he believed in danger—a presentiment that proved but too true, for he was finally beheaded. Sabbathai Zebi's influence is still incalculable; he demands so much notice at our hands that we refer our readers to the special article under his name. Suffice it to say here that this man formed a considerable sect, which—notwithstanding that the conduct of its founder might, one would suppose, have disabused the most blind and fanatic enthusiasm—long existed, and still continues to exist.

Another false Christ that made any considerable number of converts was one rabbi *Mordecai*, a Jew of Germany: he appeared A.D. 1682. It was not long before he was found out to be an impostor, and was obliged to flee from Italy to Poland to save his life: what became of him afterwards does not seem to be recorded. About the middle of the 18th century an extraordinary adventurer, named Frank, by birth a Polish Jew, and by profession, in his younger days, a distiller of brandy, suddenly came to the front, and revived the expiring Sabbathaic party by the propagation of a new creed, which leaned towards Christianity, while it was really neither that nor Judaism. This lofty eclectic rejected the Talmud, but insisted on a hidden sense in the Scriptures. He admitted the trinity and the incarnation of the Deity, but preserved an artful ambiguity as to the person in whom the Deity was incarnate. He was himself a believer in Sabbathai Zebi, and yet he dared not to speak out against Christ; consequently he preferred to leave the question unsettled, until his connection with the Christian world seemed to demand a more decided confession, when he openly embraced Christianity as a member of the Roman Catholic Church. In his last years he flourished as "baron" Frank, and his followers dared even to presume that he was of royal lineage, and closely related to the reigning house of Russia. The extent of his influence may be fairly estimated by our readers when we tell them that 800 persons attended his funeral. A cross was set up over his tomb. For some time a daughter whom he had left guided his followers; but these gradually dispersed, and, deprived of pecuniary aid, the family of Frank gave to the world a work written by him many years before his decease, counselling the Jews to embrace the Christian religion. See FRANK, JACOB. Frank evidently preferred to continue the work of Sabbathai Zebi rather than declare himself a Messiah. He frequently declared that his mission was to unite together all religions, sects, and confessions. Among the paradoxical opinions he is said to have advanced was the idea that the Lord Jesus Christ is still upon earth, and that he would soon again send forth twelve apostles to publish the Gospel. All that now remains of the Frankists is contained within the Roman Catholic Church of Poland; they are therefore virtually Christians, though distinguishing themselves by marked remains of Judaism. Some consider that they still retain in secret a belief in the religion of the synagogue. They are found in Poland, especially at Warsaw, dispersed among all, even the highest, classes of society, chiefly in the profession of law and medicine. They are said to have taken a considerable share in the war of insurrection against Russia in the year 1830; it has even been said that the chief of the Frankists was a member of the Diet of Poland, and afterwards obliged to take refuge as an exile in France. But little is known of them at present, as they mix so largely with the Christians as such.

In our own day the Messiah question is again enlivened by the appearance of new claimants. One of these lately made his début in the far East, at Sana, in the kingdom of Yemen, and created much excitement, which has scarcely subsided yet. The well-known Œastern traveller, baron De Maltzahn, furnishes the following account of this modern Messiah of the Orient: The pretender, of a fascinating exterior, remarkably brilliant eyes, and a melodious voice, after studying the mysteries of the great cabalistical work, the Zohar, withdrew from intercourse with his fellow-men, and eventually retired into a desert, where he submitted to bodily mortifications and self-denial. He soon became distinguished as a worker of miracles, and as such attracted the attention of the superstitious Bedouins. These, seeking to obtain his good graces, brought various descriptions of food, and were pleased that he condescended to accept their offerings. The increase of their flocks and of their household, and even their success in the attack upon hostile troops, were attributed to the power peculiar to this worker of marvels. His reputation spread far and wide among the Arabian population, and many incredible stories were circulated about this "wise man." It was said of him that his face had the splendor of the sun; that the name, "Son of David," was engraved upon his hand; that he possessed the valuable power of discovering treasures; that he was invulnerable, etc. His Jewish compatriots, not pleased with the connection between their favorite scholar and the members of a strange religion, were about to bring him back to his own people, when a sudden calamity gave the position of this man a new turn. An epidemic broke out among the flocks of the Bedouins, who in consequence of this calamity were in a short time reduced to extreme want. These changes in the fortune of the Arabs were assigned to the secret influence of the mysterious man. It was then remembered that he was a Jew, and he all at once became the object of bitter hatred. The recluse had meanwhile quitted his solitude and returned to his native place. Here he was declared, chiefly by the Arabs, to be a Messiah, and he became a dreaded and unapproachable power even in the eyes of his fiercest enemies. His Jewish countrymen were in expectation that he would crush the Arabs and lead his own brethren to the Holy Land. His heated imagination accepted the messianic part which the delusion of the people had conferred upon him; and he beheld in the opinion of the multitude an evidence of his high mission. He received everywhere munificent presents, lived in a princely style, was reverenced by his own people, and dreaded by the Moslems, until some daring Arabs finally waylaid and killed him, and thus proved that he was vulnerable. But superstition is more invulnerable than false Messiahs. *Ari Shocher* (such was his name) is not considered as dead by his followers. He appeared after the murder, they say, under another form, in the neighborhood of Sana,

and proclaimed that, at a later time, he would assume again his former shape. The government has taken steps to seize him, but he has since disappeared, and his present whereabouts are unknown.

Very recently "a new Messiah," writes the *Fremdenblatt* (August, 1872), "has made his appearance, and he has been graciously pleased to address his first official communication to the Jewish congregation of Berlin. The royal 'whom it may concern' bore a seal which had on it the crown of Israel, the shield of David, and the following words as motto: '*Lo bechail velo bekoach ki im beruchi, amar Adonai Zebaoth*—not with power, nor with force, but with my Spirit, says the Lord Zebaoth.' The congregation is commanded to cause to be proclaimed in the synagogue the commemoration day of the destruction of Jerusalem, that thenceforth that day shall be celebrated no longer as a day of mourning, but as a day of joy and jubilation, because he, '*Jekuthiel*, king of Israel,' has come, and is about to assume the throne of his empire as the veritable Messiah. Should they refuse to carry out his behest, he will pour out the vial of his anger on the unbelievers, and the infidels will fall under the ban of excommunication, on his entering Berlin. The communication is accompanied by a memorial containing the rules of government which 'Jekuthiel, the king of Israel,' prescribes for the government of his people, and a copy of the diplomatic notes which his royal majesty has caused to be transmitted to the Porte and the other great powers for a peaceable cession of Palestine and Syria." Although a year has passed since he issued his *address*, nothing has been heard of his entry into the new capital of the German empire.

See Buxtorf, *Lex. Chald. Talm. et Rabbin.* (Basle, 1640, fol.), coll. 1267 sq.; id. *Synagoga Judaica*, ch. i; Hulsius, *Theol. Jud.* (Bredæ, 1653, 4to); Pocock, *Theol. Works*, i, 159 sq.; Johannes à Lent, *Hist. of False Messiahs* (in Ugolini's *Thesaurus*, entitled *De Pseudo-Messiis*); Eisenmenger, *Entdecktes Judenthum* (Königsb. 1711, 2 vols. 4to), ii, 647 sq., a book to be read very guardedly; Jortin, *Remarks on Eccl. Hist.* iii, 330; Birch, *De Messia* (Havn. 1789); Harris, *Sermons on the Messiah*; Simpson, *Key to the Prophecies*, sec. 9; Maclaurin, *On the Prophecies relating to the Messiah*; Fuller, *Jesus the true Messiah*; Stehelin, *Traditions of the Jews* (Lond. 1751–52, fol.); De Rossi, *Della vana aspettazione degli Ebrei del loro Re Messia* (Parma, 1773, 4to); Bertholdt, *Christologia Jud. Jesu apostolorumque Ætate* (Erlangen, 1811)—convenient but superficial; Lange, *Life of Christ* (see Index); Liddon, *Divinity of Christ*, p. 69, 77, 91; Alger, *Hist. Fut. Life*, p. 169, 219, 353; Sadler, *Emanuel*, p. 97 sq.; Milman, *Hist. of the Jews*, ii, 432 sq.; iii, 366; Allen, *Mod. Judaism*, p. 253 sq.; Young, *Christology of the Targums* (Edinb. 1853); Jost, *Gesch. der Israeliten*, vol. viii; Grätz, *Gesch. der Juden* (see Index in vol. vi, vii, viii, and x); Michel Nicolas, *Des doctrines rel. des Juifs pendant les deux siècles antérieurs à l'ère Chrétienne* (Paris, 1860, 8vo), p. 266 sq.; Langen, *Judenth. zur Zeit Christi* (Freib. 1866), p. 391 sq.; Grau, *Semiten und Indogermanen* (2d ed. Stuttg. 1867, sm. 8vo), Introd. and chap. v; Rule, *Karaites* (Lond. 1870, 12mo), p. 132 sq.; *Journ. Sac. Lit.* 1873, Jan. art. viii; *Jahrb. deutsch. Theol.* 1867, ii, 340 sq.; *Christian Examiner*, 1869, p. 96; *Engl. Rev.* viii, 182; *Christian Monthly*, 1844, Nov. p. 581; *National Rev.* April, 1863, p. 466 sq.; 1864, p. 554 sq.; *Old and New*, 1870, April, p. 545; *New-Englander*, v, 360 sq.; x, 102 sq.; *Biblioth. Sac.* xi, 609 sq.; Hamburger, *Real-Encyklop. f. Bibel u. Talmud*, art. Messias. (J. H. W.)

Messi'as (Μεσσίας), the Græcized form (John i, 41; iv, 25) of the Heb. title MESSIAH (q. v.), translated *Christ*.

Messina, ANTONELLA DA, an Italian painter, was born at Messina some time between 1414 and 1426; studied in the Netherlands in the school of Johann van Eyck, where he learned the secret of the preparation and use of oil-colors, and spread the knowledge of it afterwards among the Venetians. Authors differ widely as to this artist, and very little is known of his life. His principal works are the head of *St. Sebastian* and a *Madonna and Child*, in the Berlin Museum. A *Christ bound to a Pillar* is in the Manfrini Gallery at Venice, and a *Dead Christ*, with three weeping angels, in the Imperial Gallery of Vienna. A *Crucifixion*, with the Virgin and St. John, is in the Antwerp Museum; and in the Academy of Venice is a *Weeping Nun*. Two altarpieces by him are recorded, which were painted for the two churches of the Dominante, besides several Madonnas and sacred subjects for individuals. He died about 1490. See Vasari, *Lives of the Painters*, transl. by Foster (London, 1850, 5 vols. 8vo), ii, 55; Spooner, *Biographical History of the Fine Arts* (N. Y. 1865, 2 vols. 8vo), vol. ii, s. v.

Mestrezat, Jean, a distinguished French Protestant theologian, was born at Geneva in 1592. He studied theology at Saumur, and was in 1615 appointed pastor at Charenton, near Paris, which position he held until his death, May 2, 1657. He took part in the national synod held at Charenton in 1623, and presided over that of 1631. Among the important events of his life, we must mention three public conferences he held, the first with P. Véron, a Jesuit, the great polemic of his order; the second with P. Regourd, in the presence of Anne of Austria; and the third with abbot De Retz (afterwards cardinal), who relates the most striking features of it in his *Mémoires*. Mestrezat was distinguished for his inflexible firmness of purpose. It is said that he once defended the cause of Protestantism in the presence of the cardinal De Richelieu with so much vivacity that that prelate could not help remarking, "Here is the most daring minister in France." Like his colleague Daillé (q. v.), he inclined towards the views of the theologians of Saumur concerning hypothetical universalism. His most important works are: *De la Communion de Jésus Christ au sacrement de l'Eucharistie, contre les Cardinaux Bellarmin et Du Perron* (Sedan, 1624, 8vo):—*Traité de l'Ecriture Sainte, contre le Jésuite Regourd et le Cardinal Du Perron* (Gen. 1642, 8vo):—*Traité de l'Église* (Gen. 1649, 4to):—*Sermons sur la venue et la naissance de Jésus Christ au monde* (Gen. 1649, 8vo):—*Sermons sur les chapitres XII et XIII de l'Épitre aux Hébreux* (Gen. 1655, 8vo):—*Vingt sermons sur divers textes* (Sedan, 1625, 12mo; Gen. 1658, 8vo). See *Mémoires du Cardinal de Retz* (Petitot's collection), xliv, 130; Bayle, *Dict. Hist.*; Senebier, *Hist. Litt. de Genève*; Haag, *La France Protest.* vii, 400; André, *Essai sur les œuvres de J. Mestrezat* (Strasb. 1847); Hoefer, *Nouv. Biog. Générale*, xxxv, 184; Herzog, *Real-Encykl.* ix, 443; A. Vinet, *Hist. de la Prédication*, p. 143. (J. N. P.)

Mestrezat, Philippe, a Reformed theologian, son of Jean, was born at Geneva. In 1641 he was a professor of philosophy in his native city; in 1644 the pastor of a church; and in 1649 a professor of theology. He acquired the reputation of being an original thinker and a good preacher. He died at Geneva in 1690. He published many dissertations, among which may be mentioned: *De Unione Personarum in Christo* (Gen. 1682, 4to):—*De Communicatione idiomatum toti Christo facta* (ibid. 1675, 4to):—*De Tolerantia fratrum dissidentium in præter-fundamentalibus* (1663, 4to):—*Quæstionum philosophico-theologicarum de libero arbitrio Decas* (1655, 4to). See Senebier, *Hist. Littér. de Genève*; Hoefer, *Nouv. Biog. Générale*, s. v.

Metabolism (from μεταβάλλω, to *change*) is a term coined by the German theologian Rückert to describe the doctrinal views of the Christian fathers Ignatius, Justin, and Irenæus on the Lord's Supper. They stand midway between strict transubstantiation and the merely symbolical view, and hold fast to an objective union of the sensible with the supersensible. See LORD'S SUPPER; ZWINGLE.

Metagnostics is a synonyme of *metaphysics* (q. v.) (from μετά, *beyond*, and γνῶσις, *knowledge*), because it

transcends common knowledge. This name, of course, might be given to the whole system of philosophy.

Metal, a term that nowhere occurs in the Auth.Ver., although the various metals and operations with them are frequently referred to. The allusions indeed are of such a character as to show that the art of metallurgy was well advanced in those ancient times.

The mountains of Palestine contained metals, nor were the Hebrews ignorant of the fact (Deut. viii, 9); but they do not appear to have understood the art of mining, unless indeed the numerous allusions apparently to mining operations in Job xxviii are an evidence that these were carried on in the period of the monarchy. See MINE. They therefore obtained from others the superior as well as the inferior metals, and worked them up. They received also metal utensils ready made, or metal in plates (Jer. x, 9), from neighboring and distant countries of Asia and Europe. The Hebrews, in common with other ancient nations, were acquainted with nearly all the metals known to modern metallurgy, whether as the products of their own soil or the results of intercourse with foreigners. The trade in these metals was chiefly in the hands of the Phœnicians (Ezek. xxvii, 7), who obtained them from their colonies, principally those in Spain (Jer. x, 9; Ezek. xxvii, 12). Some also came from Arabia (Ezek. xxvii, 19), and some apparently from the country of the Caucasus (Ezek. xxvii, 13).

I. One of the earliest geographical definitions is the one describing the country of Havilah as the land which abounded in *gold*, and the gold of which was good (Gen. ii, 11, 12). The first artist in metals was a Cainite, Tubal-cain, the son of Lamech, the forger or sharpener of every instrument of *copper* (A. V. "brass") and *iron* (Gen. iv, 22). "Abraham was very rich in cattle, in *silver*, and in *gold*" (Gen. xiii, 2); silver, as will be shown hereafter, being the medium of commerce, while gold existed in the shape of ornaments during the patriarchal ages. The vast quantity of silver and gold used in the Temple in the time of Solomon, and otherwise possessed by the Jews during the flourishing time of the nation, is very remarkable, under whatever interpretation we regard such texts as 1 Chron. xxii, 14; xxix, 4, etc. In like manner, we find among other ancient Asiatic nations, and also among the Romans, extraordinary wealth in gold and silver vessels and ornaments of jewelry. As all the accounts, received from sources so various, cannot be founded on exaggeration, we may rest assured that the precious metals were in those ancient times obtained abundantly from mines—gold from Africa, India, and perhaps even then from Northern Asia; and silver principally from Spain. *Tin* is first mentioned among the spoils of the Midianites which were taken when Balaam was slain (Numb. xxxi, 22), and *lead* is used to heighten the imagery of Moses's triumphal song (Exod. xv, 10).

Whether the ancient Hebrews were acquainted with *steel*, properly so called, is uncertain; the words so rendered in the A. V. (2 Sam. xxii, 35; Job xx, 24; Psa. xviii, 34; Jer. xv, 12) are in all other passages translated *brass*, and would be more correctly *copper*. The "northern iron" of Jer. xv, 12 is believed by commentators to be iron hardened and tempered by some peculiar process, so as more nearly to correspond to what we call steel (q. v.); and the "flaming torches" of Nah. ii, 3 are probably the flashing steel scythes of the war-chariots which should come against Nineveh.

Besides the simple metals, it is supposed that the Hebrews used the mixture of copper and tin known as *bronze*, and probably in all cases in which copper is mentioned as in any way manufactured, bronze is to be understood as the metal indicated. But with regard to the *chashmal* (A. V. "amber") of Ezek. i, 4, 27; viii, 2, rendered by the Sept. ἤλεκτρον, and the Vulg. *electrum*, by which our translators were misled, there is considerable difficulty. Whatever be the meaning of *chashmal*, for which no satisfactory etymology has been proposed, there can be but little doubt that by $\dot{\eta}\lambda\epsilon\kappa\tau\rho\sigma\nu$ the Sept. translators intended, not the fossil resin known by that name to the Greeks and to us as "amber," but the metal so called, which consisted of a mixture of four parts of gold with one of silver, described by Pliny (xxxiii, 23) as more brilliant than silver by lamp-light. There is the same difficulty attending the $\chi\alpha\lambda\kappa\sigma\lambda i$-$\beta\alpha\nu\sigma\nu$ (Rev. i, 15; ii, 18; A.V. "fine brass"), which has hitherto successfully resisted all the efforts of commentators, but which is explained by Suidas as a kind of electron more precious than gold. That it was a mixed metal of great brilliancy is extremely probable, but it has hitherto been impossible to identify it. Whether it was the same as that precious compound known among the ancients as Corinthian brass is uncertain, but it is likely that in later times the Jews possessed splendid vessels of the costly compound known by that name. Indeed, this is distinctly affirmed by Josephus (Life, p. 13). See BRASS.

In addition to the metals actually mentioned in the Bible, it has been supposed that mercury is alluded to in Numb. xxxi, 23 as "the water of separation," being "looked upon as the mother by which all the metals were fructified, purified, and brought forth," and on this account kept secret, and only mysteriously hinted at (Napier, Metal. of the Bible, Introd. p. 6). Mr. Napier adds, "There is not the slightest foundation for this supposition."

With the exception of iron, gold is the most widely diffused of all metals. Almost every country in the world has in its turn yielded a certain supply; and as it is found most frequently in alluvial soil, among the débris of rocks washed down by the torrents, it was known at a very early period, and was procured with little difficulty. The existence of gold and the prevalence of gold ornaments in early times are no proof of a high state of civilization, but rather the reverse. Gold was undoubtedly used before the art of working iron or copper was discovered. We have no indications of gold streams or mines in Palestine. The Hebrews obtained their principal supply from the south of Arabia, and the commerce of the Persian Gulf. The ships of Hiram, king of Tyre, brought it for Solomon (1 Kings ix, 11; x, 11), and at a later period, when the Hebrew monarch had equipped a fleet and manned it with Tyrian sailors, the chief of their freight was the gold of Ophir (1 Kings ix, 27, 28). It was brought thence in the ships of Tarshish (1 Kings xxii, 48), the Indiamen of the ancient world; and Parvaim (2 Chron. iii, 6), Raamah (Ezek. xxvii, 22), Sheba (1 Kings x, 2, 10; Psa. lxxii, 15; Isa. lx, 6; Ezek. xxvii, 22), and Uphaz (Jer. x, 9), were other sources of gold for the markets of Palestine and Tyre. It was probably brought in the form of ingots (Josh. vii, 21; A.V. "wedge," lit. "tongue"), and was rapidly converted into articles of ornament and use. Ear-rings, or rather nose-rings, were made of it—those given to Rebecca were half a shekel ($\frac{1}{4}$ oz.) in weight (Gen. xxiv, 22)—bracelets (Gen. xxiv, 22), chains (Gen. xli, 42), signets (Exod. xxxv, 22), bullæ, or spherical ornaments suspended from the neck (Exod. xxxv, 22), and chains for the legs (Numb. xxxi, 50; comp. Isa. iii, 18; Pliny, xxxiii, 12). It was used in embroidery (Exod. xxxix, 3; 2 Sam. i, 24; Pliny, viii, 74); the decorations and furniture of the Tabernacle were enriched with the gold of the ornaments which the Hebrews willingly offered (Exod. xxxv-xl); the same precious metal was lavished upon the Temple (1 Kings vi, vii); Solomon's throne was overlaid with gold (1 Kings x, 18), his drinking-cups and the vessels of the house of the forest of Lebanon were of pure gold (1 Kings x, 21), and the neighboring princes brought him as presents vessels of gold and silver (1 Kings x, 25). So plentiful indeed was the supply of the precious metals during his reign that silver was esteemed of little worth (1 Kings x, 21, 27). Gold and silver were devoted to the fashioning of idolatrous images (Exod. xx, 23; xxxii, 4; Deut. xxix, 17; 1 Kings xii, 28). The crown on the head of Malcham (A.V. "their king"),

the idol of the Ammonites at Rabbah, weighed a talent of gold, that is, 125 lbs. troy, a weight so great that it could not have been worn by David among the ordinary insignia of royalty (2 Sam. xii, 30). The great abundance of gold in early times is indicated by its entering into the composition of every article of ornament and almost all of domestic use. Among the spoils of the Midianites taken by the Israelites, in their bloodless victory when Balaam was slain, were ear-rings and jewels to the amount of 16,750 shekels in gold (Numb. xxxi, 48–54), equal in value to more than $150,000. 1700 shekels of gold (worth more than $15,000) in nose jewels (A.V. "ear-rings") alone were taken by Gideon's army from the slaughtered Midianites (Judg. viii, 26). These numbers, though large, are not incredibly great, when we consider that the country of the Midianites was at that time rich in gold streams, which have since been exhausted, and that, like the Malays of the present day and the Peruvians of the time of Pizarro, they carried most of their wealth about them. But the amount of treasure accumulated by David from spoils taken in war is so enormous that we are tempted to conclude the numbers exaggerated. From the gold shields of Hadadezer's army of Syrians and other sources he had collected, according to the chronicler (1 Chron. xxii, 14), 100,000 talents of gold, and 1,000,000 talents of silver; to these must be added his own contribution of 3000 talents of gold and 7000 of silver (1 Chron. xxix, 2–4), and the additional offerings of the people, the total value of which, estimating the weight of a talent to be 125 lbs. troy, gold at 73s. per oz., and silver at 4s. 4$\frac{1}{2}$d. per oz., is reckoned by Mr. Napier to be £939,929,687. Some idea of the largeness of this sum may be formed by considering that in 1855 the total amount of gold in use in the world was calculated to be about $4,100,000,000. Undoubtedly the quantity of the precious metals possessed by the Israelites might be greater in consequence of their commercial intercourse with the Phœnicians, who were masters of the sea; but in the time of David they were a nation struggling for political existence, surrounded by powerful enemies, and without the leisure necessary for developing their commercial capabilities. The numbers given by Josephus (Ant. vii, 14, 2) are only one tenth of those in the text, but the sum, even when thus reduced, is still enormous. But though gold was thus common, silver appears to have been the ordinary medium of commerce. The first commercial transaction of which we possess the details was the purchase of Ephron's field by Abraham for 400 shekels of silver (Gen. xxiii, 16); slaves were bought with silver (Gen. xvii, 12); silver was the money paid by Abimelech as a compensation to Abraham (Gen. xx, 16); Joseph was sold to the Ishmaelite merchants for twenty pieces of silver (Gen. xxxvii, 28); and generally in the Old Testament, "money" in the A.V. is literally silver. The first payment in gold is mentioned in 1 Chron. xxi, 25, where David buys the threshing-floor of Ornan, or Araunah, the Jebusite, for "six hundred shekels of gold by weight." But in the parallel narrative of the transaction in 2 Sam. xxiv, 24, the price paid for the threshing-floor and the oxen is fifty shekels of silver. An attempt has been made by Keil to reconcile these two passages, by supposing that in the former the purchase referred to was that of the entire hill on which the threshing-floor stood, and in the latter that of the threshing-floor itself. But the close resemblance between the two narratives renders it difficult to accept this explanation, and to imagine that two different circumstances are described. That there is a discrepancy between the numbers in 2 Sam. xxiv, 9 and 1 Chron. xxi, 5 is admitted, and it seems impossible to avoid the conclusion that the present case is but another instance of the same kind. With this one exception there is no case in the O.T. in which gold is alluded to as a medium of commerce; the Hebrew coinage may have been partly gold, but we have no proof of it. See GOLD.

Silver was brought into Palestine in the form of

plates from Tarshish, with gold and ivory (1 Kings x, 22; 2 Chron. ix, 21; Jer. x, 9). The accumulation of wealth in the reign of Solomon was so great that silver was but little esteemed : " the king made silver to be in Jerusalem as stones" (1 Kings x, 21, 27). With the treasures which were brought out of Egypt, not only the ornaments, but the ordinary metal-work of the Tabernacle was made. Silver was employed for the sockets of the boards (Exod. xxvi, 19; xxxvi, 24), and for the hooks of the pillars and their fillets (Exod. xxxviii, 10). The capitals of the pillars were overlaid with it (Exod. xxxviii, 17); the chargers and bowls offered by the princes at the dedication of the Tabernacle (Numb. vii, 13, etc.), the trumpets for marshalling the host (Numb. x, 2), and some of the candlesticks and tables for the Temple, were of silver (1 Chron. xxviii, 15, 16). It was used for the setting of gold ornaments (Prov. xxv, 11) and other decorations (Cant. i, 11), and for the pillars of Solomon's gorgeous chariot or palanquin (Cant. iii, 10). See SILVER.

From a comparison of the different amounts of gold and silver collected by David, it appears that the proportion of the former to the latter was 1 to 9 nearly. Three hundred talents of silver and thirty talents of gold were demanded of Hezekiah by Sennacherib (2 Kings xviii, 14); but later, when Pharaoh-nechoh took Jehoahaz prisoner, he imposed upon the land a tribute of 100 talents of silver, and only one talent of gold (2 Kings xxiii, 33). The difference in the proportion of gold to silver in these two cases is very remarkable, and does not appear to have been explained. See MONEY.

Brass, or more properly copper, was a native product of Palestine, "a land whose stones are iron, and out of whose hills thou mayest dig copper" (Deut. viii, 9; Job xxviii, 2). It was so plentiful in the days of Solomon that the quantity employed in the Temple could not be estimated, it was so great (1 Kings vii, 47). Much of the copper which David had prepared for this work was taken from the Syrians after the defeat of Hadadezer (2 Sam. viii, 8), and more was presented by Toi, king of Hamath. The market of Tyre was supplied with vessels of the same metal by the merchants of Javan, Tubal, and Meshech (Ezek. xxvii, 13). There is strong reason to believe that brass, a mixture of copper and zinc, was unknown to the ancients. To the latter metal no allusion is found. But tin was well known, and from the difficulty which attends the toughening of pure copper so as to render it fit for hammering, it is probable that the mode of deoxidizing copper by the admixture of small quantities of tin had been early discovered. "We are inclined to think," says Mr. Napier, "that Moses used no copper vessels for domestic purposes, but bronze, the use of which is less objectionable. Bronze, not being so subject to tarnish, takes on a finer polish, and being much more easily melted and cast, it probably was more extensively used than copper alone. These practical considerations, and the fact that almost all the antique castings and other articles in metal which are preserved from these ancient times are composed of bronze, prove in our opinion that where the word 'brass' occurs in Scripture, except where it refers to an ore, such as Job xxviii, 2 and Deut. viii, 9, it should be translated bronze" (Metals of the Bible, p. 66). Arms (2 Sam. xxi, 16; Job xx, 24; Psa. xviii, 34) and armor (1 Sam. xvii, 5, 6, 38) were made of this metal, which was capable of being so wrought as to admit of a keen and hard edge. The Egyptians employed it in cutting the hardest granite. The Mexicans, before the discovery of iron, "found a substitute in an alloy of tin and copper; and with tools made of this bronze they could cut not only metals, but, with the aid of silicious dust, the hardest substances, as basalt, porphyry, amethysts, and emeralds" (Prescott, Conq. of Mexico, ch. v). The great skill attained by the Egyptians in working metals at a very early period throws light upon the remarkable facility with which the Israelites, during their wanderings in the desert, elaborated the works of art connected with the structure

of the Tabernacle, for which great acquaintance with metals was requisite. In the troublous times which followed their entrance into Palestine this knowledge seems to have been lost, for when the Temple was built the metal-workers employed were Phœnicians. See COPPER.

Iron, like copper, was found in the hills of Palestine. The "iron mountain" in the trans-Jordanic region is described by Josephus (War, iv, 8, 2), and was remarkable for producing a particular kind of palm (Mishna, Succa, ed. Dachs, p. 182). Iron mines are still worked by the inhabitants of Kefr Hûneh in the S. of the valley Zaharâni; smelting-works are found at Shemuster, three hours W. of Baalbek, and others in the oak-woods at Masbek (Ritter, Erdkunde, xvii, 73, 201); but the method employed is the simplest possible, like that of the old Samothracians, and the iron so obtained is chiefly used for horse-shoes. See IRON.

Tin and lead were both known at a very early period, though there is no distinct trace of them in Palestine. The former was among the spoils of the Midianites (Numb. xxxi, 22), who might have obtained it in their intercourse with the Phœnician merchants (comp. Gen. xxxvii, 25, 36), who themselves procured it from Tarshish (Ezek. xxvii, 12) and the tin countries of the West. The allusions to it in the Old Testament principally point to its admixture with the ores of the precious metals (Isa. i, 25; Ezek. xxii, 18, 20). It must have occurred in the composition of bronze : the Assyrian bowls and dishes in the British Museum are found to contain one part of tin to ten of copper. "The tin was probably obtained from Phœnicia, and consequently that used in the bronzes in the British Museum may actually have been exported, nearly three thousand years ago, from the British Isles" (Layard, Nin. and Bab. p. 191). See LEAD; TIN.

Antimony (2 Kings ix, 30; Jer. iv, 30; A.V. "painting"), in the form of powder, was used by the Hebrew women, like the kohl of the Arabs, for coloring their eyelids and eyebrows. See PAINT.

III. As above stated, the invention of the metallurgic arts is in Scripture ascribed to Tubal-cain (Gen. iv, 22). In later times the manufacture of useful utensils and implements in metals seems to have been carried on to a considerable extent among the Israelites, if we may judge from the frequent allusions to them by the poets and prophets. But it does not appear that, in the finer and more elaborate branches of this great art, they made much, if any, progress during the flourishing times of their commonwealth; and it will be remembered that Solomon was obliged to obtain assistance from the Phœnicians in executing the metal work of the Temple (1 Kings vii, 13). Among the ancient Egyptians the operations of metallurgy were carried to great perfection, as the delineations extant upon the monuments still testify (see Wilkinson, ii, 133 sq.). The Assyrians likewise had made great proficiency in the same art (see Layard's Nineveh, ii, 315 sq.; Nin. and Bab. p. 191 sq.).

The Hebrew workers in iron, and especially such as made arms, were frequently carried away by the different conquerors of the Israelites (1 Sam. xiii, 19; 2 Kings xxiv, 14, 15; Jer. xxiv, 1; xxix, 2); which is one circumstance among others to show the high estimation in which this branch of handicraft was anciently held.

The following are the metallic manufactures named in the Old Testament : Of iron, axes (Deut. xix, 5-2; 2 Kings vi, 5); saws (2 Sam. xii, 31); stone-cutters' tools (Deut. xxvii, 5); sauce-pans (Ezek. iv, 3); bolts, chains, knives, etc., but especially weapons of war (1 Sam. xvii, 7; 1 Macc. vi, 33). Bedsteads even were sometimes made of iron (Deut. iii, 11); "chariots of iron," i. e. war-chariots, are noticed frequently. Of copper we find vessels of all kinds (Lev. vi, 28; Numb. xvi, 39; 2 Chron. iv, 16; Ezek. viii, 27); and also weapons of war, principally helmets, cuirasses, shields, spears (1 Sam. xvii, 5; vi, 38; 2 Sam. xxi, 16); also chains (Judg. xvi, 21); and even mirrors (Exod. xxxviii, 8). Gold and *silver* furnished articles of ornament, also vessels, such as cups, goblets, etc. The holy vessels of the Temple were mostly of gold (Ezra v, 14). Idolaters had idols and other sacred objects of silver (Exod. xx, 20; Isa. ii, 20; Acts xvii, 29; xix, 24). *Lead* is mentioned as being used for weights, and for plumb-lines in measuring (Amos vii, 7; Zech. v, 8). Some of the tools of workers in metal are also mentioned: פַּעַם, *pa'am*, the *anvil* (Isa. xli, 7); מַקָּבָה, *makkabah'*, the *hammer* for carpenters (Isa. xliv, 12); פַּטִּישׁ, *pattish'*, the *stone-hammer* (Isa. xli, 7); מַל קְחִים, *mal kachim'*, the *pincers*; מַפֻּחַ, *mappu'ach*, the *bellows* (Jer. vi, 29); מַצְרֵף, *matzreph'*, the *crucible* (Prov. xvii, 3); כּוּר, *kûr*, the *melting-furnace* (Ezek. xxii, 18). See each of these articles in alphabetical order.

There are also allusions to various operations connected with the preparation of metals. (1.) The smelting of metal was not only for the purpose of rendering it fluid, but in order to separate and purify the richer metal when mixed with baser minerals, as silver from lead, etc. (Isa. i, 25; comp. Pliny, *Hist. Nat.* xxxvii, 47; Ezek. xxii, 18–20). The dross separated by this process is called סִגִים, *sigim'*, although this word also applies to metal not yet purified from its dross. For the actual or chemical separation other materials were mixed in the smelting, such as alkaline salts, בּוֹר, *bôr* (Isa. i, 25), and lead (Jer. vi, 29; comp. Pliny, *Hist. Nat.* xxxiii, 31). (2.) The casting of images (Exod. xxv, 12; xxvi, 37; Isa. xl, 19), which are always of gold, silver, or copper. The casting of iron is not mentioned, and was perhaps unknown to the ancients (Hausmann, in *Commentatt. Soc. Gœtt.* iv, 53 sq.; Müller, *Archäol.* p. 371). (3.) The hammering of metal, and making it into broad sheets (Numb. xvi, 38; Isa. xliv, 12; Jer. x). (4.) Soldering and welding parts of metal together (Isa. xli, 7). (5.) Smoothing and polishing metals (1 Kings vii, 45). (6.) Overlaying with plates of gold, and silver, and copper (Exod. xxv, 11–24; 1 Kings vi, 20; 2 Chron. iii, 5; comp. Isa. xl, 19). The execution of these different metallurgic operations appears to have formed three distinct branches of handicraft before the exile; for we read of the blacksmith, by the name of the "worker in iron" (חֹרֵשׁ בַּרְזֶל, Isa. xliv, 12); the brass-founder (1 Kings vii, 14); and the gold and silver smith (Judg. xvii, 4; Mal. iii, 2). See MECHANIC.

See generally, Bellermann, *Handb.* i, 221 sq.; De Wette, *Archäol.* p. 130 sq.; Faber, *Archäol.* i, 394 sq.; Link, *Urwelt*, i, 435 sq.; Winer, *Realw.* s. v. Metalle. See further under MINE.

Metallurgy. See METAL; MINE.

Metamorphoses (Gr. μεταμόρφωσις, *change of form*) denoted, in the mythology of the ancients, those transformations of human beings into beasts, stones, trees, and even into fire, water, etc., in fables of which that mythology abounded. The origin and significance of such fables it is often impossible to determine. Some of them probably originated in observation of the wonderful transformations of nature; some in a misapprehension of the metaphors employed by the older poets; and some perhaps in mere superstition and love of the marvellous. The wild imagination of the Orientals filled their mythologies with metamorphoses in the greatest number; and the classic mythology approaches to them in this respect. The mediæval days of Europe, especially of Germany, gave forth the fairy tales and other forms of folk-lore, wonderfully rich in metamorphoses. See MYTHOLOGY.

Metaphor (Gr. μεταφόρα, a *transference*), a figure of speech by means of which one thing is put for another which it only resembles. It differs from other comparisons, e. g. *simile*, etc., in consisting of a *single word.* Thus the Psalmist speaks of God's law as being "a light to his feet and a lamp to his path." The metaphor is therefore a kind of comparison, in which the

speaker or writer, casting aside the circumlocution of the ordinary similitude, seeks to attain his end at once by boldly identifying his illustration with the thing illustrated. It is thus of necessity, when well conceived and expressed, graphic and striking in the highest degree, and has been a favorite figure with poets and orators, and the makers of proverbs, in all ages. Even in ordinary language the meanings of words are in great part metaphors; as when we speak of an *acute* intellect or a *bold* promontory.

Metaphrastes, SIMEON, a Byzantine writer of the Middle Ages, acquired great reputation by his compilation of the lives of many saints and martyrs. Very little is known of his individual history. It appears, however, to be proved that he lived at Constantinople, and there filled an official position. The name Metaphrastes was given him on account of the manner in which he commented and *paraphrased* (ἐμετέφρασε) the materials for his biographical work. The greatest variety of opinion prevails as to the time when he lived: Blondell, Vossius, Ceillier, Baronius, Simler, Volaterra, Allatius, Cave, Oudin, Fabricius, all give different dates, varying from the 9th to the 14th century. It even appears uncertain whether there may not have existed two men of that name at different times. The more ancient date is that of Leo Allatius, who in his work *De Simeonum Scriptis* (Par. 1664, p. 49 sq.) enters into deep researches concerning Metaphrastes, the result of which is adopted by Cave (*Histor. Litter.* [Lond. 1688], p. 573) and Fabricius (*Bibl. Gr.* vi, 509; in ed. Harl. x, 180 sq.). His conclusions were opposed by Oudin in his *Dissertatio de œtate et scriptis Sim. Met.* (*Comment.* ii, 1300 sq.). From various passages in works undoubtedly written by Metaphrastes, it appears to be pretty well established that he lived during the reign of the emperor Leo VI (Philosophus), and was sent as ambassador to the Arabs of Crete in 902, and in 904 to those who had conquered Thessalonica, whom he persuaded not to destroy that city, as they originally intended. It seems also well established that he was still alive in the time of the emperor Constantine VII (Porphyrogenitus). His principal works are: *Vitæ Sanctorum*, undertaken, it is said, at the suggestion of the emperor Constantine. This assertion, however, has often been contradicted. The work is not original; Metaphrastes only arranged and paraphrased, in very good style for the times, various biographies which existed previously in the libraries of churches and convents. He omitted many details which he considered useless or unproved, and substituted others which he looked upon as more important or authentic. He has been accused of having by these modifications destroyed the simplicity of the ancient biographies. His own work has undergone many alterations and additions, as well as curtailment, so that, according to Fabricius, out of 539 biographies generally ascribed to him, only 122 are undoubtedly genuine. Cave, on the other hand, maintains that the greater part of the 417 manuscript biographies extant in the various libraries of Europe are the work of Metaphrastes. Agapius, a monk, gave an extract of them under the title *Liber dictus Paraclitus, seu illustrium sanctorum vitæ desumptæ ex Simeone Metaphraste* (Venice, 1541, 4to). The most important among these biographies were published, in Greek and Latin, in the Bollandists' *Acta Sanctorum*:—*Annales*, commencing with the emperor Leo the Armenian (813–820), and ending with Romanus, the son of Constantine Porphyrogenitus (959–963). It is evident that Metaphrastes, who was already an ambassador in 902, could not have been tho historian of events which occurred sixty years later. Some critics consequently consider the later part of the *Annales* to have been written by another Metaphrastes, while Baronius thinks that the whole work was composed by a writer living in the 12th century. These *Annales*, which are of great historical value, were published with a Latin translation by Combéfis in his *Hist. Byzantinæ Scriptores post Theophanem*, of which the edition by Immanuel Bekker (Bonn, 1838, 8vo) is a carefully-revised reprint :—*Epistolæ IX*, published in Greek and Latin by Leo Allatius, *Diatriba de Simeonibus; Carmina pia duo politica*, in Allatius; and in Lectius, *Poëtæ Græci veteres* (Geneva, 1614, fol.):—*Sermo in Diem Sabbati sancti*, in Latin only, by Combéfis, *Biblioth. Concionator.* vol. iii :—Εἰς τὸν ϑρῆνον τῆς ὑπεραγίας ϑεοτόκου, etc., in Greek and Latin by Allatius; several hymns, or *canons*, still in use in the Greek Church :—Ἠϑικοὶ λόγοι, an extract from the works of St. Basil, and published in Greek and Latin by Morel (Paris, 1556, 8vo). See Fabricius, *Biblioth. Græca*, vii, 683 ; x, 180 ; Cave, *Histoire Litt.*; Hankius, *Scriptores Byzant.* ch. xxiv ; Oudin, *Dissert. de Ætate et Scriptis Simeonis Metaphrastis*, in his *Comment. de script. eccles.*; Baronius, *Annales* ad ann. 859.—Herzog, *Real-Encykl.* ix, 446 ; Hoefer, *Nouv. Biog. Gén.* xxxv, 188 ; Smith, *Dict. of Gr. and Rom. Biog. and Mythol.* ii, 1055. (J. N. P.)

Metaphysics, in its strictest sense, is applied, as a term, to that department of *philosophy* which has for its object the investigation of existences out of ourselves—"that knowledge of causes and principles which we should carry with us into every department of inquiry." Inasmuch as mind cannot properly know what is not in contact with itself, the question, "What is the nature of our knowledge of the external world?" has been asked by philosophers, and answered in various ways; and this is the great question of metaphysics, if the term is applied in a strictly historical sense. Among modern writers of note in the field of philosophy, Prof. Ferrier, in his *Institutes of Metaphysics* (Edinb. and Lond. 1854, 12mo), accordingly occupies himself solely with the questions connected with knowledge, or the nature of our perception of an external world; his explanatory title is, *The Theory of Knowing and Being.* On the other hand, the lately-deceased Scotch philosopher Mansel, in his article *Metaphysics* (*Cyclopædia Britannica*, 8th ed. vol. xiv, s. v.), divided the subject into two parts—"*Psychology*, or the science of the facts of consciousness [which expresses the science of mind generally] as such; and *Ontology*, or the science of the same facts considered in their relation to realities existing without the mind"—that is, the problem of perception or metaphysics in the narrower sense. "Metaphysics," says the writer of the article on that subject in the *Edinburgh Cyclopædia*, "have been called the *First philosophy*, or the Science of Sciences, as their object is to explain the principles and causes of all things existing, and to supply the defects of inferior sciences, which do not demonstrate, or sufficiently explain, their principles." Here we have a still further departure from our first and somewhat circumscribed sphere to the vast expanse of the department itself known as *philosophy.* Of the above two branches of philosophy or metaphysics, *psychology* (q. v.) investigates the faculties and operations of the human mind, while *ontology* (q. v.) seeks to develop the nature and laws of real existence. The former deals with the phenomena of consciousness, the constitution of the mind, the laws of thought; the latter with the essential characteristics of being *per se*, the constitution of the universe, the laws of things. The former is descriptive, and the latter scientific metaphysics. "Metaphysics," says Sir William Hamilton (*Lect.* vii, p. 85), "in whatever latitude the term be taken, is a science, or complement of sciences, exclusively occupied with mind. Now the philosophy of mind—psychology or metaphysics, in the widest signification of the terms—is threefold, for the object it immediately proposes for consideration may be either, 1, *Phenomena* in general ; or, 2, *Laws;* or, 3, *Inferences* and *Results.* . . . The whole of philosophy is the answer to these three questions : 1. What are the facts or phenomena to be observed ? 2. What are the laws which regulate these facts, or under which these phenomena appear? 3. What are the real results, not immediately manifested, which these facts or phenomena warrant us in drawing?"

The great authority which Aristotle enjoyed in the Middle Ages, and the little actual knowledge respecting the laws of existence, induced his followers to form from his philosophical fragments a system, which served as a canon for the philosophy of the time. The oldest commentators of Aristotle had directed their endeavors to this point; but metaphysics, as an independent science, was developed by the schoolmen of the Middle Ages (Thomas Aquinas, Duns Scotus, William Occam, and others). In the 17th century, however, the metaphysics of the schoolmen was undermined by the introduction of a critical spirit of investigation. Lord Bacon, More, Hobbes, appeared in England; Th. Campanella, in Italy; Des Cartes, in France, as adversaries of the Aristotelian school-philosophy. For details, see PHILOSOPHY.

As regards the origin of the name, the most recent discussions appear, on the whole, to confirm the commonly-received opinion, according to which the term *Metaphysics*, though originally employed to designate a treatise of Aristotle, was probably unknown to that philosopher himself. It is true that the oldest and best of the extant commentators on Aristotle refers the inscription of the treatise to the Stagyrite (Alexander, in *Arist. Meth.* p. 127, ed. Bonitz); but in the extant writings of Aristotle himself, though the work and its subject are frequently referred to under the titles of the *First Philosophy*, or *Theology*, or *Wisdom* (Asclepius, apud Brandis *Scholia*, p. 519, b. 19; Bonitz, in *Arist. Metaph.* p. 5), no authority is found for the latter and more popular appellation. On the whole, the weight of evidence appears to be in favor of the supposition which attributes the inscription τὰ μετὰ τὰ φυσικά to Andronicus Rhodius, the first editor of Aristotle's collected works. The title, as given to the writings on the first philosophy, probably indicates only their place in the collection, as coming *after the physical treatises* of the author (comp. Bonitz *ad Arist. Metaph.* p. 3, 5). In this respect the term *Metaphysics* has been aptly compared to that of *Postils;* both names signifying nothing. more than the fact of something else having preceded. Shakespeare used *metaphysical* as synonymous with *supernatural.*

> "Fate and *metaphysical* aid doth seem
> To have thee crowned."—*Macbeth*, Act i, Scene 3.

Clemens Alexandrinus (*Strom.* i) considered *metaphysical* as equivalent to *supernatural;* and is supported by the Greek commentator Philoponus. But if μετά be interpreted, as it may, to mean *along with*, then *metaphysics*, or metaphysical philosophy, will be that philosophy which we should take *along with* us into physics, and into every other philosophy—that knowledge of causes and principles which we should carry with us into every department of inquiry. Aristotle called it the governing philosophy, which gives laws to all, but receives laws from none (*Metaphys.* lib. i, cap. 2). Lord Bacon (*Advancement of Learning*, bk. ii) has limited its sphere, when he says, "The one part (of philosophy), which is *physics*, inquireth and handleth the *material* and *efficient* causes; and the other, which is *metaphysics*, handleth the *formal* and *final* cause." But all causes are considered by Aristotle in his writings which have been entitled *Metaphysics.* "Aristotle," says Schwegler (*Hist. of Philos.* p. 112), "held that every science must have for investigation a determined province and separate form of being, but that none of these sciences reaches the conception of being itself. Hence there is needed a science which should investigate that which the other sciences take up hypothetically, or through experience. This is done by the first philosophy, which has to do with being as such, while the other sciences relate only to determined and concrete being. The *metaphysics*, which is this science of being and its primitive grounds, is the *first philosophy*, since it is presupposed by every other discipline. Thus, says Aristotle, if there were only a physical substance, then would physics be the first and the only philosophy; but if there be an immaterial and unmoved essence which is the ground of all being, then must there be also an antecedent, and, because it is antecedent, a universal philosophy. The first ground of all being is God, whence Aristotle occasionally gives to the first philosophy the name of theology." "The aim of metaphysics," says D'Alembert (*Mélanges*, iv, 143), "is to examine the generation of our ideas, and to show that they come from *sensations*." This is the ideology of Condillac and De Trace. "Metaphysics," says Stewart (*Dissert.* pt. ii, p. 475), "was a word formerly appropriated to the ontology and pneumatology of the schools, but now understood as equally applicable to all those inquiries which have for their object to trace the various branches of human knowledge to their first principles in the constitution of the human mind;" and in the Preface to the same *Dissertation* he says that by metaphysics he understands the "inductive philosophy of the human mind." For literature, see PHILOSOPHY. (J. H. W.)

Metastasio, PIETRO BONAVENTURA, an eminent Italian poet, deserves our notice as the author of several sacred dramas, oratorios, etc. He was born at Rome in 1698, and was originally named TRAPASSI. He manifested at an early age extraordinary talents for improvisation on any subject. Having attracted the notice of the celebrated jurist Gravina, he was adopted by him, and his name was changed to Metastasio (a "changing"), in allusion to his adoption. His benefactor died in 1718, leaving his property to Metastasio, who now devoted himself principally to literary pursuits and the publication of his different poetical productions. In 1729 he was invited to Vienna to become poet laureate, and flourished at the Austrian capital until his death in 1782. The genius of Metastasio is eulogized by Voltaire and La Harpe, the former of whom compares some of his scenes to the most sublime of the Greek poets. Rousseau, in his *Nouvelle Héloïse*, pronounces him "the only poet of the heart, the only genius who can move by the charm of poetic and musical harmony;" and Schlegel observes that his purity of diction, grace, and delicacy have rendered him, in the eyes of his countrymen, a classic author—the Racine of Italy. Of Metastasio's seven sacred dramas, or oratorios, *La Passione, La Morte d'Abel*, and *Isacco*, are best known; but all of them, Calsabigi justly observes, are as perfect as this kind of composition will allow. See Burney, *Memoirs of Metastasio* (1796, 3 vols.); Torcia, *Elogio del Abbate P. Metastasio* (1782); Hiller, *Ueber P. Metastasio und seine Werke* (1786); Altanesi, *Vita di P. Metastasio* (1787); *Lives of the Italian Poets*, by the Rev. Henry Stebbing (London, 1831). (J. H. W.)

Metcalfe, WILLIAM, M.D., a prominent minister of the Bible-Christian Church, was born in the parish of Orton, Westmoreland, England, March 11, 1788. He became a disciple of the Rev. Dr. Cowherd, a noted minister of the Swedenborgian Church, who in 1809 organized the Bible-Christian Church. Metcalfe in 1811 was ordained as a minister of this Church by Dr. Cowherd, and in 1817, with a small company of his fellow-believers, immigrated to Philadelphia, where he continued his ministerial labors till the day of his death in 1862. According to his biographer, the specific work of Mr. Metcalfe's life was "that of sowing the seeds and cultivating the principles of temperance and vegetarianism, and permanently establishing the Bible-Christian Church in this country." The Bible-Christian Church in England founded its doctrinal basis mainly upon the writings of Swedenborg. It propounded views upon two subjects, however, which have never been generally received in the *New Jerusalem Church*, as the Swedenborgians prefer to call themselves. It inculcated the duty of total abstinence from all intoxicating drinks as a beverage, and from the use of animal food. These two requirements were made conditions of Church membership, more particularly by Mr. Metcalfe. He was one

of the original members of the American "Vegetarian Society," and was one of its most earnest supporters. On the death of Dr. William A. Alcott, the first president of the society, in 1859, Dr. Metcalfe was elected his successor. He rendered efficient service also in the cause of temperance, and may be termed one of the pioneers of the movement in this country. "As a preacher," we are told by his biographer, "he was not what is called an orator, but his delivery was easy, plain, distinct, and impressive. His action was moderate and graceful. He was never boisterous, never sensational, and seldom allowed his imagination to display its powers in the pulpit. His sermons were suggestive and instructive, always including some teaching on practical, every-day duties. He sought all fields for the illustration of Bible truths, especially availing himself of the lights of modern science and of ancient history in the elucidation of his subject." Seventeen of his *Discourses* were lately published by his son Joseph, under the title *Out of the Clouds into the Light* (Phila. 1872, 12mo). See *New Jerusalem Messenger*, Oct. 23, 1872; *Memoir of the Rev. William Metcalfe, M.D.*, by his son Joseph (Phila. 1866, 12mo).

Metel (Lat. *Metellus*), HUGUES, a French canon, was born at Toul, in Lorraine, about 1080. He was the offspring of wealthy parents. While yet a child he lost his father, and was indebted to the solicitude of his mother for a liberal education. He studied theology at Laon under the celebrated teacher Anselm, and embraced Christianity at Toul about 1118, when he was entered a member of the regular canons in the abbey of Saint-Léon. He remained in that institution until his death, which occurred near 1157. Fifty-five noted epistles bear his authorship. The first of them is addressed to St. Bernard, whom Hugues Metel calls a "*clarissima lampas*," while to himself he attributes the humbler qualifications of *quondam nugigerulus, nunc crucis Christi bajulus*. See Calmet, *Histoire de la Lorraine*, i, cxxi; Fortin d'Urban, *Histoire et Œuvrages de Hugues Metel* (Paris, 1839, 8vo).

Metempsychōsis. See TRANSMIGRATION.

Mete′rus (Μετήρους v. r. Βαιτηρούς, Vulg. omits), given (1 Esdr. v, 17) among those whose "sons" returned from the captivity with Zerubbabel; but the Heb. lists (Ezra ii; Neh. vii) have no corresponding name.

Mete-yard (מִדָּה, *middah'*, Lev. xix, 35; *measure* simply, as elsewhere rendered).

Meth, EZECHIEL, a noted leader of a mystic sect who at the beginning of the 17th century created great excitement in Thuringia. Meth was practicing medicine in the city of Langensalza, Thuringia, when his uncle, a merchant in the same town, who had become an enthusiastic mystic, presented him with his peculiar conceptions of Christian fellowship and responsibility. Meth was readily won in favor of the heretical doctrines, and became one of the leaders of a sect which soon became numerous. He afterwards moved to Leipsic, where he died in 1640. Stiefel and Meth found their first followers among their own relatives and friends at Langensalza and Erfurt. They also gained access to the house of count Hans Ludwig de Gleichen, whose wife, the countess Juliana, became so ensnared in their mystic doctrines that she was finally excluded from the Lord's table. But matters did not rest here. She imagined she was a second Virgin Mary, and was to give birth to the new Messiah. She therefore separated herself from the count, and to the day of her death (July 28, 1633) remained steadfast in her hopes that she would bring forth the Messiah. The authorities tried in various ways to bring these enthusiasts to their senses, but kindness as well as punishment proved in vain, until at last Stiefel died—Stiefel who had been considered immortal by Meth and all his followers. A change took place in Stiefel's mind, and he is said to have died a truly converted Christian.

The doctrines of Stiefel and Meth were for the most

part identical with the mysticism of the Anabaptists and of Schwenkfeld, as specified and condemned in the Formula of Concord. Only Christ, the living Word, is recognised, while the revealed Word, i. e. the Bible, is despised, the ministry, with all its officers, rejected, and the sacraments—baptism and communion—are declared works of witchcraft. They further taught that as the law of God has been fulfilled by Christ, the true Church can neither sin nor err; that no resurrection can take place, nor eternal life be hoped for, as all true Christians are already dead to the world, and feel the promised joys of eternity in their lives, to the fullest extent possible. See Arnold, *Kirchen u. Ketzer Historie* (see Index). See STIEFEL.

Metheg. See METHEG-AMMAH.

Me′theg-am′mah (Heb. *me′theg ha-ammah′*, מֶתֶג הָאַמָּה, *bridle* [as in 2 Kings xix, 28, etc.] *of the mother* [i. e. mother-city = אֵם, in 2 Sam. xx, 19]; Sept. ἡ ἀρωρισμένη, Vulg. *frenum tributi*), a figurative term for a chief city, occurring in the statement (2 Sam. viii, 1), " David took the bit of the metropolis (Auth. Vers. 'Metheg-Ammah') out of the hand of the Philistines," i. e. he subdued their capital or strongest town, meaning GATH, as is expressly affirmed in the parallel passage (1 Chron. xviii, 1). Other interpretations may be seen in Glassii *Philol. Sacr.* ed. Dathe, p. 783. Gesenius (*Thes. Heb.* p. 113) compares the Arabic proverb, " I give thee not my bridle," i. e. I do not submit to thee (see Schultens *ad Job*, xx, 11; and Hariri *Cons.* iv; *Hist. Tamerl.* p. 243; *Vit. Tim.* i, 50). On the other hand, Ewald (*Gesch.* iii, 190) less naturally takes Ammah as meaning the " forearm," and treats the words as a metaphor to express the perfect manner in which David had smitten and humbled his foes, had torn the bridle from their arm, and thus broken forever the dominion with which they curbed Israel, as a rider manages his horse by the rein held fast on his arm. He objects to the other interpretation that Gath had its own king still in the days of Solomon; but it may be replied that the king in Solomon's time may have been, and probably was, tributary to Israel, as the kings "on this side the Euphrates" (1 Kings iv, 24) were. It is an obvious objection to Ewald's interpretation, that to control his horse a rider must hold the bridle, not on his arm, but fast in his hand.

Methen. See MITHNITE.

Methoar. See REMMON-METHOAR.

Methodism, as a distinctive form of Church life and polity, dates from the revival of religion in England under the labors of the brothers Wesley and of Whitefield. See these names respectively.

I. *Origin.*—In November, 1729, the Wesleys, Whitefield, and their associates—about a dozen young men, students at Oxford University—formed themselves into a society for purposes of mutual moral improvement. They had a sincere desire to please God; and, by diligence, self-denial, and active benevolence, they sought to know and do his will. By instructing the children of the neglected poor, by visiting the sick and the inmates of prisons and almshouses, by a strict observance of the fasts ordained by the Church, and by scrupulous exactness in their attendance upon public worship, they became objects of general notice. Many grave men thought them righteous overmuch, and attempted to dissuade them from an excess of piety; while profane-wits treated them with sarcasm and contempt. Nothing could save from ridicule men who in that age and in such a place professed to make religion the great business of life. Hence by their fellow-students they were called in turn, *Sacramentarians, Bible-bigots, Bible-moths, The Godly Club.* One, a student of Christ-Church College, with greater reverence than his fellows, and more learning, observed, in reference to their *methodical* manner of life, that a new sect of METHODISTS had sprung up, alluding to the ancient school of physicians known by that name. The appellation obtained currency, and, al-

though the word is still sometimes used reproachfully as expressive of enthusiasm, or undue religious strictness, it has become the acknowledged name of one of the largest and most rapidly increasing evangelical Christian denominations (comp. Tyerman, *The Oxford Methodists*, N. Y., Harpers, 1873, 8vo).

From this time Methodism may be said to have started. In 1739 the first Methodist "meeting-house" in England was built at Kingswood. "Wesley's idea at this time, and for many years afterwards," says Skeats (*Hist. of the Free Churches of England*, p. 363), "was merely to revive the state of religion in the Church; but he knew enough of the condition of society in England, and of human nature, to be aware that unless those who had been brought under the awakening influence of the Gospel met together, and assisted each other in keeping alive the fire which had been lit in their hearts, it must, in many instances, seriously diminish, if not altogether die out." Originally, therefore, it was no part of the design of Wesley and his associates to found a new religious sect. *He* considered them all members of the Church of England—zealous for her welfare, and loyal to her legitimate authorities. For a full discussion of this point, see the article WESLEY. They were all tenacious of her order, and great sticklers for what they deemed decency and decorum. One of them tells us, "I should have thought the saving of souls almost a sin if it had not been done in a church;" and such was the sentiment of John Wesley, when, to his horror, he first heard that his bosom friend, Whitefield, had attempted to preach the Gospel in the open air. This was in the year 1739, on Saturday, the 17th of February. The discourse was addressed to the colliers at Kingswood, near the city of Bristol. "I thought," said Whitefield, "that it might be doing the service of my Creator, who had a mountain for his pulpit, and the heavens for a sounding-board; and who, when his Gospel was rejected by the Jews, sent his servants into the highways and hedges." In a little while John Wesley was induced to follow his example. Being providentially at Bristol, and a great assembly (estimated at 3000) having come together at a place called Race Green, "I submitted," he says, "to be more vile, and proclaimed in the highways the glad tidings of salvation." This was Wesley's first attempt in England. He had previously preached in the open air while in this country as a missionary to the Indians in Georgia, but he had no intention of resuming the practice in England, till he was stimulated by the example and urgent advice of his friend. His brother Charles was even more opposed to this departure from Church usages, and this apparent breach of ecclesiastical order. He had confined himself to the usual labors of the ministry in such pulpits as were opened to him, preaching the Gospel with earnestness and simplicity, more especially in London, where he also devoted much of his time to the felons in Newgate, not a few of whom were brought through his instrumentality to repentance and faith in Christ. Being strenuously urged by Whitefield, he at length consented to make one effort. "I prayed," he says, "and went forth in the name of Jesus Christ. I found near a thousand helpless sinners waiting for the Word in Moorfields. I invited them in my Master's words, as well as name, 'Come unto me, all ye that labor and are heavy laden, and I will give you rest.' The Lord was with me, even me, the meanest of his messengers, according to his promise. . . . My load was gone, and all my doubts and scruples. God shone on my path, and I knew this was his will concerning me." Thenceforth, in various parts of the kingdom, they continued to preach the Gospel in the open air as opportunity was afforded. Immense crowds thronged everywhere to hear the Word, and multitudes were converted from the error of their way. As a consequence of this violation of ecclesiastical order, and more especially because of the earnest and energetic style of the preachers, most of the pulpits of the Established Church were soon closed against them. Many dignitaries of the Church were above measure enraged at this *new way*, and zealous in opposing it. "Some clergymen," says Wesley, "objected to this 'new doctrine,' salvation by faith; and, because of my unfashionable doctrine, I was excluded from one and another church, and at length shut out of all." In many places, too, Wesley and his associates were treated as disturbers of the peace, and subjected to annoyance and persecution. They were reviled, mobbed, imprisoned. They bore everything with patience. "Not daring to be silent," says Wesley, "it remained only to preach in the open air; which I did at first not out of choice, but necessity. I have since seen abundant reason to adore the wise providence of God herein, making a way for myriads of people who never troubled any church, nor were likely so to do, to hear that Word which they soon found to be the power of God unto salvation."

The result of these labors was not only the conversion of many souls, but the formation of religious societies. The young converts, neglected, and in many instances treated contemptuously by the established clergy, were as sheep having no shepherd. They naturally longed for the fellowship of kindred spirits. At their own request, they were united together for mutual comfort and edification. Wesley gives the following account of the origin of what was then called simply "the United Society." The rules which were drawn up for them are to the present day recognised, with two or three very slight alterations, as the *General Rules* of all branches of the great Methodist family in England, in the United States, and elsewhere:

"1. In the latter end of the year 1739 eight or ten persons came to me in London, who appeared to be deeply convinced of sin, and earnestly groaning for redemption. They desired (as did two or three more the next day) that I would spend some time with them in prayer, and advise them how to flee from the wrath to come, which they saw continually hanging over their heads. That we might have more time for this great work, I appointed a day when they might all come together; which, from thenceforward, they did every week, viz. on Thursday in the evening. To these, and as many more as desired, to join with them (for their number increased daily), I gave those advices from time to time which I judged most needful for them; and we always concluded our meetings with prayer suitable to their several necessities.

"2. This was the rise of the United Society, first in London, and then in other places. Such a society is no other than 'a company of men having the form and seeking the power of godliness; united in order to pray together, to receive the word of exhortation, and to watch over one another in love, that they may help each other to work out their salvation.'

"3. That it may the more easily be discerned whether they are indeed working out their own salvation, each society is divided into smaller companies, called classes, according to their respective places of abode. There are about twelve persons in every class; one of whom is styled the Leader. It is his business,

"(1.) To see each person in his class once a week, at least, in order

"To inquire how their souls prosper;

"To advise, reprove, comfort, or exhort, as occasion may require;

"To receive what they are willing to give towards the support of the Gospel;

"(2.) To meet the ministers and the stewards of the society once a week, in order

"To inform the minister of any that are sick, or of any that walk disorderly, and will not be reproved;

"To pay to the stewards what they have received of their several classes in the week preceding; and

"To show their account of what each person has contributed.

"4. There is one only condition previously required of those who desire admission into these societies; viz. 'a desire to flee from the wrath to come, and be saved from their sins.' But wherever this is really fixed in the soul, it will be shown by its fruits. It is therefore expected of all who continue therein that they should continue to evidence their desire of salvation,

"First, by doing no harm, by avoiding evil in every kind; especially that which is most generally practiced. Such as

"The taking the name of God in vain;

"The profaning the day of the Lord, either by doing ordinary work thereon, or by buying or selling;

"Drunkenness; buying or selling spirituous liquors; or drinking them, unless in cases of extreme necessity;

"Fighting, quarrelling, brawling; brother going to law with brother; returning evil for evil, or railing for railing; the using many words in buying or selling;

"The buying or selling uncustomed goods;

"The giving or taking things on usury, viz. unlawful interest;

"Uncharitable or unprofitable conversation; particularly speaking evil of magistrates or of ministers;

"Doing to others as we would not they should do unto us;

"Doing what we know is not for the glory of God; as,

"The putting on of gold and costly apparel;

"The taking such diversions as cannot be used in the name of the Lord Jesus;

"The singing those songs or reading those books which do not tend to the knowledge or love of God;

"Softness, and needless self-indulgence;

"Laying up treasure upon earth;

"Borrowing without a probability of paying; or taking up goods without a probability of paying for them.

"5. It is expected of all who continue in these societies, that they should continue to evidence their desire of salvation,

"Secondly, by doing good, by being in every kind merciful after their power, as they have opportunity; doing good of every possible sort, and as far as is possible to all men:

"To their bodies, of the ability that God giveth, by giving food to the hungry, by clothing the naked, by helping or visiting them that are sick or in prison;

"To their souls, by instructing, reproving, or exhorting all we have any intercourse with; trampling under foot that enthusiastic doctrine of devils, that 'we are not to do good, unless our hearts be free to it.'

"By doing good, especially to them that are of the household of faith, or groaning so to be; employing them preferably to others, buying one of another, helping each other in business; and so much the more, because the world will love its own, and them only

"By all possible diligence and frugality, that the Gospel be not blamed.

"By running with patience the race that is set before them, denying themselves, and taking up their cross daily; submitting to bear the reproach of Christ; to be as the filth and offscouring of the world; and looking that men should say all manner of evil of them falsely, for the Lord's sake.

"6. It is expected of all who desire to continue in these societies that they should continue to evidence their desire of salvation,

"Thirdly, by attending upon all the ordinances of God: such are

"The public worship of God;

"The ministry of the word, either read or expounded;

"The supper of the Lord;

"Family and private prayer;

"Searching the Scriptures; and

"Fasting or abstinence.

"7. These are the general rules of our societies: all which we are taught of God to observe, even in his written Word—the only rule, and the sufficient rule, both of our faith and practice. And all these we know his Spirit writes on every truly awakened heart. If there be any among us who observe them not, who habitually break any of them, let it be made known unto them who watch over that soul, as they that must give an account. We will admonish him of the error of his ways: we will bear with him for a season. But then, if he repent not, he hath no more place among us. We have delivered our own souls."

The "societies" thus formed increased so rapidly that very soon there arose a necessity for additional ministerial service. As the leaders in this wonderful revival of religion had been led providentially into the practice of field-preaching, and into the formation of religious societies, so they were induced in the same manner to accept the assistance of preachers who had not been educated for the ministry, nor ordained to that service. This was at that time regarded by many as the most heinous of their offences. The Wesleys themselves at first hesitated at what seemed so monstrous an innovation; and the elder brother, when he first heard that a layman had taken a text and preached a sermon, hastened to London to put a stop to the irregularity. The man, Thomas Maxfield by name, had been left in charge of the little flock during the absence of the ordained ministers, had prayed with them, read to them passages of Scripture, attempted an exposition of a verse or two, and found himself preaching almost before he was aware of it. Happily for the interests of the new sect, and happily, too, for the cause of Christ, Wesley was met by his mother before he had time to censure the young preacher, or publicly to denounce this innovation. Mrs.

Wesley, the widow of a stanch minister of the Establish-ed Church, had been educated in its doctrines, and she revered its prelatical assumptions. But she had heard the young man preach several times. On the arrival of her son, seeing that his countenance was expressive of dissatisfaction, she inquired the cause. "Thomas Maxfield," said he, abruptly, "has turned preacher, I find." She looked attentively at him, and replied, "John, you know what my sentiments have been. You cannot suspect me of readily favoring anything of this kind; but take care what you do with respect to that young man, for he is as surely called of God to preach as you are." Her advice was followed, and the result justified her opinion. Wesley recognised the validity of the young man's call; and thereafter it became a set-tled conviction with him, as it is with his followers to this day, that a warrant to preach the Gospel does not of necessity come only through one channel. In process of time, as instances of this kind increased, it became necessary to devise some criterion by which to test those who professed to believe themselves called of God to preach. This was a subject to which John Wesley early turned his attention; and the question, with his answer, continues to the present day to be incorporated among the rules recognised by all Wesleyan Methodists. We say *Wesleyan* Methodists because, previous to the preach-ing of Maxfield, Whitefield had separated himself from his associates, and thenceforward became known as the leader of the Calvinistic division of Methodism. The question and answer were in the following words:

"*Quest.* How shall we try those who profess to be moved by the Holy Ghost to preach?

"*Ans.* 1. Let the following questions be asked, namely: Do they know God as a pardoning God? Have they the love of God abiding in them? Do they desire nothing but God? And are they holy in all manner of conversation?

"2. Have they the gifts (as well as the grace) for the work? Have they (in some tolerable degree) a clear, sound understanding, a right judgment in the things of God, a just conception of salvation by faith? And has God given them any degree of utterance? Do they speak justly, readily, clearly?

"3. Have they fruit? Are any truly convinced of sin, and converted to God by their preaching?

"As long as these three marks concur in any one, we believe he is called of God to preach. These we receive as sufficient proof that he is moved by the Holy Ghost."

From the time of Maxfield's admission as a preacher, many others of similar piety and gifts offered their ser-vices and were accepted. As the work went on, and additions were made to the "societies" in all parts of the kingdom, the demand for preachers increased. Wesley had always thought that preachers would be supplied from the pulpits of the Established Church, but, disap-pointed in this, he came to favor the admission of those who, although not episcopally ordained, were wholly devoted to the work of preaching the Gospel, and gladly recognised them as ministers of Christ. The employ-ment of this class of auxiliaries constantly increasing, finally led to a meeting, held annually thereafter, and known as "the Conference" (q. v.). The first of these assemblies was held in 1744, and from this year Meth-odism began to assume the appearance of an organized system. It was in 1744 that the brothers John and Charles Wesley, with two or three other regularly-or-dained clergymen, met with such of the "preachers" as could conveniently attend, to clothe Methodism with the conventional forms of established ecclesiastical gov-ernment. Of course neither John nor Charles could brook the idea of becoming Dissenters, and Methodism was organized as an independent Church body only af-ter the death of John Wesley. See WESLEYANS. To all intents and purposes the Church was organized at this first Conference in 1744, and yet by this very body one of the questions asked was, "Are we Dissenters?" and its answer an emphatic "*No.*" "Although we call sinners to repentance in all places of God's dominion, and although we frequently use extemporary prayer, and unite together in a religious society, yet we are not Dis-senters in the only sense which our law acknowledges,

viz. those who renounce the service of the Church. We do not, we dare not, separate from it. We are not se-ceders, nor do we bear any resemblance to them. We set out upon quite opposite principles. The seceders laid the very foundation of their work in judging and condemning others. We laid the foundation of our work in judging and condemning ourselves. They be-gin everywhere with showing their hearers how fallen the Church and its ministers are; we begin everywhere with showing our hearers how fallen they are them-selves" (Coke, *Life of Wesley*, p. 287). "Monday, June 25, and the five following days," says the leader of this little band, "we spent in conference with our preachers, seriously considering by what means we might the most effectually save our own souls and them that heard us, and the result of our consultations we set down to be the rule of our future practice." Already had the larger portion of England been divided into "circuits," to each of which several preachers were sent for one or two years. A part of the work of each annual assembly was to arrange these appointments and changes. At the early Conferences various theological questions were dis-cussed with reference to the agreement of all the par-ties in a common standard; and when this was settled, and the doctrinal discussions were discontinued, new regulations of another kind were from year to year adopted, as the state of the societies, and the enlarging opportunities of doing good, seemed to require. The first indication of a desire to see a separate establish-ment was given by John Wesley in 1784, when he or-dained Coke (q. v.) bishop of the Methodist Church in this country. See METHODIST EPISCOPAL CHURCH. On neither side of the ocean had adherents of Wesley hitherto organized as a Church. They were simply up to this time non-ecclesiastical religious societies, en-tirely voluntary on the part of the members, and all governed by a common discipline, of which their found-er was the sole dictator and the chief executor. Yet even this step to provide for the Methodists in Amer-ica a separate ecclesiastical organization does not clear-ly reveal whether Wesley changed his mind as to his former relation and that of his adherents within the Anglican rule to the Church of England. Says Dr. Curry, of the *Christian Advocate* (N. Y., May 25, 1871), "No fact respecting the history of John Wesley is more clearly manifest than that he was always a strenuous supporter of the authority of the Established Church of England. He jealously regarded the exclusive ec-clesiastical authority of that Church in all that he did as an evangelist, and seemed always determined that while he lived and ruled—and it was always under-stood that he would rule as long as he lived—nothing should be tolerated in his societies at all repugnant to the sole and exclusive ecclesiastical authority of the Established Church. This rule was applied to his so-cieties in America before the Revolution just as strictly as to those in England. But the political separation of America from Great Britain, as it also ended the au-thority of the English Church in this country, made it lawful, according to his theory of the case, for the Meth-odist societies in America to become regularly organized churches."

II. The *theological doctrines* of Wesleyan Methodism are, with perhaps two or three modifications, the same as those which, by common consent, are at present deemed evangelical. The articles of religion drawn up by Wes-ley for his immediate followers, and substantially adopted by all Methodist bodies since, are but slightly modified from those of the Established Church of England. They were originally prepared for the churches in the States. See ARTICLES, TWENTY-FIVE. The sermons of John Wesley, and his notes on the New Testament, are rec-ognised by his followers in Great Britain and America as the standard of Methodism, and as the basis of their theological creed. The unity of the Godhead, and the coequal divinity of the Father, the Son, and the Holy Ghost; the death, resurrection, ascension, and intercession of Jesus Christ; salvation by faith; the sufficiency and divine inspiration of the Holy Scriptures; a final day of judgment, and the eternity of future rewards and punishments, are doctrines held in common with other evangelical branches of the Church of Christ. Maintaining man's total depravity through the fall of Adam, and his utter inability, unless aided by divine grace, to take one step towards his recovery, Methodists hold that this grace is free, extending itself equally, by virtue of the atonement, to all the children of men. Hence they deny the doctrine of special election, with its counterpart, reprobation, as taught in Calvinistic formularies, and maintain, in opposition to those who hold to a limited atonement, that Jesus Christ, "by his oblation of himself once offered, made a full, perfect, and sufficient sacrifice, oblation, and satisfaction for the sins of the whole world." They recognise two sacraments as ordained by Christ— Baptism and the Lord's Supper. Infant children and believing adults have a right to the former; and penitent seekers of salvation, as well as professing Christians, are invited to partake of the latter, both being regarded not only as "badges or tokens of Christian men's profession, but as certain signs of grace and God's good will towards us, by the which he doth work invisibly in us, and doth not only quicken, but also strengthen and confirm our faith in him." As to the *mode* of baptism, so that the ceremony be performed by an authorized minister in the name of the Father, the Son, and the Holy Ghost, it is optional whether the water be applied by sprinkling or pouring, or by the immersion of the candidate; and although kneeling is the usual mode of receiving the elements at the Lord's table, those who prefer may partake of them in a standing or sitting posture. They deny the doctrine usually styled the "perseverance of the saints," believing that a true child of God may fall from grace and finally perish; but they hold the doctrine of assurance, in the sense that it is the privilege of the justified sinner now to know his sins forgiven. The Holy Spirit, they teach, bears witness of the fact of present pardon and acceptance; but this is deemed to be the privilege of believers, not the indispensable evidence of regeneration. "It does not follow," says Wesley, "that all who do not *know* their sins forgiven are children of the devil." Methodism teaches also that it is the privilege of believers in this life to reach that maturity of grace, and that conformity to the divine nature, which cleanses the heart from sin, and fills it with love to God and man—the being filled, as Paul phrases it, with all the fulness of God. This they call Christian perfection, a state which they declare to be attainable through faith in Christ. Wesley says on this subject, and none of his authorized followers have gone beyond him, "Christian perfection implies the being so crucified with Christ as to be able to testify, 'I live not, but Christ liveth in me.' It does not imply an exemption from ignorance or mistake, infirmities or temptations. I believe," he adds, "there is no such perfection in this life as excludes these involuntary transgressions, which I apprehend to be naturally consequent on the ignorance and mistakes inseparable from mortality. Therefore 'sinless perfection' is a phrase I never use, lest I should seem to contradict myself. I believe a person filled with the love of God is still liable to these involuntary transgressions. Such transgressions you may call sins, if you please: I do not, for the reasons above mentioned." This doctrine Wesley calls "the grand depositum which God has given to the people called Methodists;" and he gives it as his opinion that God raised them up chiefly to preach, and exemplify, and propagate it. See WESLEYANISM.

III. As to *the government and usages of Methodism*, they are similar, but not entirely uniform, in all its branches and divisions. In the parent body, the Wesleyan Methodists of England, the ecclesiastical government is entirely in the hands of the ministry. "The Conference," originally instituted, as we have seen, by Wesley, has the power of making rules and regulations for the government of the body. This power is, however, restricted within certain limits prescribed in what is known as "the deed of declaration," executed by John Wesley a little while before his death, and enrolled in the archives of the high court of chancery in 1794. By the provisions of this deed, the Conference consists of one hundred ministers, who were originally named therein, and to whom and to their successors was committed the duty of filling vacancies as they occur. The Conference, by the deed of declaration, is to meet annually, and to continue in session not less than five days nor more than three weeks. Other ministers attend and take part in the discussions, but the legal body consists of the "hundred" only. Their first business, after filling vacancies, is the election from their own number of a president, who holds his office for one year, but is eligible to a reelection after an interval of eight years. Any member of the "legal hundred" absenting himself without leave from two successive Conferences, and not appearing on the first day of the third, forfeits his seat. The Conference admits preachers on trial; receives them into full membership by ordination; examines and scrutinizes the character of every minister in the connection, and has power to try those against whom any charge is brought, and to censure, suspend, or excommunicate, if necessary. By the Conference the proceedings of subordinate bodies are finally reviewed, and the state and prospects of the Church at large are considered, and regulations enacted for its increasing efficiency. The most important of these subordinate judicatories is "the district meeting," which is composed of ministers and laymen "residing within a district of country embracing from ten to twenty or more circuits"—a circuit being the prescribed field of labor for two, three, or, in some cases, four ministers. The district meeting has authority: 1. To examine candidates for the ministry; and without their recommendation no candidate can come before the Annual Conference. 2. To try and suspend ministers who are found immoral, erroneous in doctrine, unfaithful to their ordination vows, or deficient in ability for the work they have undertaken. 3. To decide preliminary questions concerning the building of chapels. 4. To review the demands from the less wealthy churches, which draw upon the public funds of the connection for aid in supporting their ministers. 5. To elect a representative, who is thus made a member of a committee appointed to sit previously to the meeting of "the Conference," in order to prepare a draft of the stations of all the ministers for the ensuing year; regard being had to the wishes of the people in the allocation of individual pastors. The judgment of this "stationing committee" is conclusive until Conference, to which an appeal is allowed in all cases, either from ministers or people. But the appointments are made for one year only, and no preacher can be appointed to the same charge more than three years successively. In the District Conference laymen take part, equally with ministers, in all that affects the general welfare of the body; and the lay influence predominates still more in "the quarterly meeting," which is held, as its name indicates, every three months on every circuit. All *local preachers*, a numerous and influential body of men, who preach on Sundays, and follow some secular employments for a livelihood; *stewards*, whose duty it is to attend more especially to the temporalities of the society; *class-leaders*, of whom mention is made above in the general rules, are members of the quarterly meeting, at which candidates for the sacred office are first proposed, and, if rejected by their fellow-members, they have no appeal to another tribunal. A similar balance of power is maintained in the "leaders' meeting," which is held monthly, in regard to various affairs of the particular society to which it belongs. Many of these meetings are attended by one minister only, or, at the most, by two or three, while the lay members are very numerous. No leader, or other society officer, is appointed but with the concurrence of a leaders' meeting; no steward without that of the quarterly meeting. Among the usages peculiar to Methodism we have already noticed "the class-meeting," at which, although chiefly designed for spiritual instruction and improvement, it is expected that weekly contributions shall be made for the support of the ministry; and in which it is necessary for all who desire to become Methodists to undergo a period of probation of three among the Methodists of England, and of six months among those of the Methodist Episcopal Church (in the Church South there is no probationism), and attendance upon which thereafter is a term of membership. There is also in England what is known as the band-meeting, which differs from the class-meeting in that it is a voluntary association, and does not allow males and females to meet together, nor the married to belong to the same "band" with the single. The love-feast is a meeting held at the discretion of the preacher, quarterly or oftener; and the watchnight is a meeting for prayer, preaching, and mutual exhortation, held at first frequently, but now only on the last night of the year, and continuing until after midnight. John Wesley is claimed to have been the originator of religious tracts for gratuitous distribution, and of cheap volumes for the dissemination of the principles of Christianity. His followers have continued the system of publishing, and from "the Book-room" in London still emanate religious publications, tracts, and periodicals, the profits arising from the sale of which are applied to connectional purposes. For further details, see WESLEYANS.

The duties of a Methodist minister were thus defined by Mr. Wesley, and they have since remained substantially in all branches of the denomination (see Discipline, etc., § 138 sq.): "Q. What is the office of a Christian minister? A. To watch over souls, as he that must give an account. To feed and guide the flock. Q. How shall he be fully qualified for his great work? A. By walking closely with God, and having his work greatly at heart; by understanding and loving every branch of our discipline, and by carefully and constantly observing the twelve rules of a helper, viz.: 1. Be diligent; never be unemployed; never be triflingly employed; never WHILE away time, nor spend more time at any place than is strictly necessary. 2. Be serious; let your motto be, Holiness to the Lord; avoid all lightness, jesting, and foolish talking. 3. Converse sparingly and cautiously with women, particularly with young women. 4. Take no step towards marriage without solemn prayer to God, and consulting with your brethren. 5. Believe evil of no one; unless fully proved, take heed how you credit it: put the best construction you can on everything—you know the judge is always supposed to be on the prisoner's side. 6. Speak evil of no one, else your word especially would eat as doth a canker; keep your thoughts within your own breast till you come to the person concerned. 7. Tell every one what you think wrong in him, lovingly and plainly, and as soon as may be, else it will fester in your own heart; make all haste to cast the fire out of your bosom. 8. Do not affect the gentleman; a preacher of the Gospel is the servant of all. 9. Be ashamed of nothing but sin; no, not of cleaning your own shoes when necessary. 10. Be punctual; do everything exactly at the time; and do not mend our rules, but keep them, and that for conscience' sake. 11. You have nothing to do but to save souls, and therefore spend and be spent in this work; and go always, not only to those who want you, but to those who want you most. 12. Act in all things, not according to your own will, but as a son in the Gospel, and in union with your brethren. As such, it is your part to employ your time as our rules direct; partly in preaching and visiting from house to house; partly in reading, meditation, and prayer. Above all, if you labor with us in our Lord's vineyard, it is needful that you should do that part of the work which the Conference shall advise, at those times and places which they shall judge most for his glory. Observe: It is not

your business to preach so many times, and to take care merely of this and that society, but to save as many souls as you can; to bring as many sinners as you possibly can to repentance; and with all your power to build them up in that holiness without which they cannot see the Lord; and, remember, a Methodist preacher is to mind every point, great and small, in the Methodist discipline; therefore you will need all the grace and all the sense you have, and to have all your wits about you." See ITINERANCY.

The latest writer on Methodism (the Rev. L. Tyerman, Life and Times of John Wesley) who dares to hold that it is "the greatest fact in the history of the Church of Christ," thus comments upon the present condition of the parent body of Methodism, the Wesleyan Methodist Church (q. v.): "The 'Methodist,' or parent 'Conference,' employs in Great Britain and Ireland 1782 regular ministers. Besides these, there were, in 1864, in England only, 11,804 lay preachers, preaching 8754 sermons every Sabbath-day. In the same year, the number of preaching-places in England only was 6718, and the number of sermons preached weekly, by ministers and lay preachers combined, was 13,852. To these must be added the lay preachers, preaching-places, etc., in Wales, Scotland, Ireland, Shetland, and the Channel Islands. The number of Church members in Great Britain and Ireland is 365,285, with 21,223 on trial; and, calculating that the hearers are three times as numerous as the Church members, there are considerably more than a million persons in the United Kingdom who are attendants upon the religious services of the parent Conference of 'the people called Methodists.' Some idea of their chapel and school property may be formed from the fact that, during the last seven years, there has been expended, in Great Britain only, in new erections and in reducing debts on existing buildings, £1,672,541; and towards that amount of expenditure there has been actually raised and paid (exclusive of all connectional collections, loans, and drafts) the sum of £1,284,498. During the ten years from 1859 to 1868, inclusive, there was raised for the support of the foreign missions of the connection £1,408,235; and if to this there be added the amount of the Jubilee Fund, we find more than a million and a half sterling contributed during the decade for the sustenance and extension of the Methodist work in foreign lands. The missions now referred to are carried on in Ireland, France, Switzerland, Germany, Italy, Gibraltar, India, Ceylon, China, South and West Africa, the West Indies, Canada, Eastern British America, Australia, and Polynesia. In these distant places the committee having the management of the missions employ 3798 paid agents, including 994 who are regularly ordained, and are wholly engaged in the work of the Christian ministry. Besides these, there are about 20,000 agents of the society (as lay preachers, etc.) who are rendering important service gratuitously, while the number of Church members is 154,187, and the number of attendants upon the religious services more than half a million. Space prevents a reference to the other institutions and funds of British Methodism, except to add that, besides 174,721 children in the mission schools, the parent connection has in Great Britain 698 day-schools, efficiently conducted by 1532 certificated, assistant, and pupil teachers, and containing 119,070 scholars; also 5328 Sunday-schools, containing 601,801 scholars, taught by 103,441 persons who render their services gratuitously; and that the total number of publications printed and issued by the English Book Committee only, during the year ending June, 1866, was four millions one hundred and twenty-two thousand eight hundred, of which nearly two millions were periodicals, and more than a quarter of a million were hymn-books."

IV. Subdivisions.—The different branches of the great Methodistic body are as follows:

1. The WESLEYAN METHODISTS, or main and original body of the Methodists in Great Britain, often spoken of above. See WESLEYANS.

2. The CALVINISTIC METHODISTS date from a dispute between Whitefield and the Wesleys on doctrinal points. The former, with his associates, under the special patronage of the countess of Huntingdon, and greatly aided by her liberal contributions, organized societies and built chapels in various parts of England, Scotland, and Wales. For their particular doctrinal tenets, see CALVINISM. After the death of Whitefield they were divided into three separate sects. (1.) The first was known as *Lady Huntingdon's Connection*, which observed strictly the liturgical forms of the English Established Church, with a settled pastorate instead of an itinerant ministry. They have not increased with much rapidity since her death, having at the present time less than a hundred ministers, and between sixty and seventy chapels. They have maintained from the beginning a theological school for the education of ministers, now known as Cheshunt College, in Hertfordshire, England. See HUNTINGDON. Although the name "connection" continues to be used, the Congregational polity is practically adopted; and, of late years, several of the congregations have become, in name as well as virtually, Congregational Churches. The number of chapels, mentioned in the census of 1851, as belonging to this connection, was 109, containing accommodations for 38,727 persons, and the attendance on the census Saturday was 19,151. (2.) The second of these divisions was called the *Tabernacle Connection*, or *Whitefield Methodists*. They had no connectional bond after the death of their founder, and each separate society regarding itself as independent, they are now lost as a distinctive sect, and found only among the churches known as Congregationalist or Independent. (3.) The *Welsh Calvinistic Methodists*, the third of these branches, was organized in 1743. They have continued to increase and prosper until the present day, being confined, however, mostly to the principality of Wales, where they at present number about 60,000 communicants. In the United States there are about 4000 members of this denomination, with four annual Conferences, one in each of the states of New York, Pennsylvania, Ohio, and Wisconsin. The members are mostly Welsh, or of Welsh descent, and their religious services are generally celebrated in the Welsh language.

3. The WESLEYAN METHODIST NEW CONNECTION was the result of the first secession from the parent body after the death of Wesley. It originated in 1797, under the leadership of Alexander Kilham, after whom they are sometimes called *Kilhamites* (q. v.). He had been a preacher among the Wesleyans, and was expelled from the Conference in 1796. His offence was a publication in which he criticised severely the then present order of things, and submitted proposals for what he deemed reform. In accordance with his sentiments a secession Church was organized, and the New Connection sprang into existence with about 5000 members. Their Conference is constituted upon the representative system, laymen having an equal voice with the clergy in the government of the Church, while in doctrine and general usage they differ not at all from the old connection. Their history has not been marked by any great success. They have a few chapels in Ireland, and in Canada there are from 8000 to 10,000 members. Of late years they have decreased in the number of membership. In 1890 the body contained about 35,000 members.

4. THE BAND-ROOM METHODISTS originated in Manchester in 1806. The name is derived from the *Band Room* in North Street, Manchester, where a class of overzealous revivalists used to gather, and, contrary to the rules of the *Connection*, admitted parties not members. They were also guilty of acting independently of leaders' meetings, and when remonstrated with, withdrew and formed an independent body. The Band-Room Methodists still exist; but are now called *The United Free Gospel Churches*. They differ from the "parent" body in having no paid ministers. They have, however, annual conferences.

5. The PRIMITIVE METHODISTS are, next to the Wesleyans, the largest Methodist body in England. They date from the year 1810. A few regular Wesleyan preachers introduced, on their circuits, the American practice of holding camp-meetings. These were disapproved by the Conference, and denounced as "highly improper." Other questions entered into the controversy, and the result was the formation of the new sect. Their discipline and theology are strictly Wesleyan, but they go beyond any other denomination in committing the duty of Church government to the laity. Their Conference is composed of one third preachers and two thirds laymen. From the stir they make in their religious services, they have been called *Ranters*. They allow women to preach. They have several missions in foreign lands, and in England and Wales, according to the last official report of 1890, the connection had 193,658 members. In the United States, also, they have secured a footing; they here count a membership of 5639. See PRIMITIVE METHODISTS.

6. The BRYANITES, or BIBLE CHRISTIANS, are a sect of Methodists very similar to the preceding. They date from 1815. Their leader was a Wesleyan local preacher of considerable talent, by the name of O'Bryan (q. v.). Among them, as among the Primitive Methodists, females are regularly licensed to preach in public. They principally exist in Cornwall and the West of England, but also have mission stations in the Channel Islands, the United States, Canada, Prince Edward's Island, and Australia. They had, according to their report of 1873, 26,427 full and accredited Church members.

7. The PRIMITIVE METHODISTS OF IRELAND. This body of Primitive Methodists is of later origin than that of England, and is entirely independent of the other organization of like name. The *Primitive Methodists of Ireland* date from 1816. The English Conference in 1795 granted to the members the privilege of receiving from their own ministers, under certain guards and restrictions, the sacraments. The Irish Conference thereupon, in the following year, came to the conclusion that among them "it was not expedient;" but in 1816, after the subject had been freely discussed by the people, and numerous petitions asking that it might be administered were brought before the Conference, the request was granted by a majority of sixty-two against twenty-six. The minority, with the Rev. Adam Averell, one of their most influential ministers, at their head, separated, and took with them about ten thousand members, full one third of the whole. (It is worthy of remark that the secession in 1797 [see 3] was the result of the *non*-compliance of the English Conference with the wishes of the people to have the sacrament from their own ministers.) The only difference between the Irish Primitive Methodists and the Wesleyans remains to this day the liberty of members in the former body to partake of the sacraments in the *churches*. The preachers are regarded simply as laymen, because of the failure of this secession among them. The *real* lay members, however, have also a voice in the government of the *societies*. In 1861 the Irish Primitive Methodists numbered 14,247 members. See PRIMITIVE METHODISTS.

8. The UNITED METHODIST FREE CHURCH is a union, recently formed, of three different divisions of seceders from Wesleyan Methodism.

(*a*) The PROTESTANT METHODISTS, who organized into a distinct body in 1828, then counting 28 local preachers, 56 leaders, and upwards of 1000 members, seceders from the Leeds societies, because of the opposition to the introduction of an organ.

(*b*) The WESLEYAN METHODIST ASSOCIATION, which was organized in 1835, under the leadership of Samuel Warren, one of the opponents (in 1834) to the proposed establishment of a theological institution, to be presided over by Dr. Jabez Bunting. The Leeds seceders joined the Associationists in 1828; both amalgamated with the *Free Methodists* in 1857. See UNITED METHODIST FREE CHURCH.

(c) The REFORMERS, who were organized into a body in 1849. At the Manchester Conference held in that year, six members, suspected of private intrigue with members of the Wesleyan Methodist Association (see b), were placed at the bar, without having received any regular notice of the charges to be preferred against them, as required by the standing laws and usages of the connection, and without a trial, without any evidence that they had violated any law, human or divine, three of them were reprimanded and three were expelled. The act excited the astonishment of the nation, convulsed the connection, and led to the loss of one hundred thousand members. Many of them, after a while, for want of ministers and suitable places of worship, returned to the old body, but others formed themselves into a distinctive body styled the Reformed Methodists. These amalgamated bodies differ from the "parent" body only in Church government and usages. One of their professed objects is the reformation of the body from which they are separated. Their annual assembly admits lay representatives, circuits with less than 500 members sending one; less than 1000, two; and more than 1000, three delegates. Each circuit governs itself by its local courts, without any interference as to the management of its internal affairs. At their Annual Assembly, held at Bristol, England, in August, 1890, they reported 85.461 members.

9. The WESLEYAN REFORM UNION is a body composed of those of the seceders of 1849 (see 7 [c]) who refused to amalgamate with the United Methodist Free Church. In 1868 it numbered nearly a thousand Church members.

The above comprise all the Methodist branches now existing in Great Britain and Ireland. Some others have occasionally sprung up, such as the Tent Methodists, the Independent Methodists, etc., but they are now either extinct or incorporated with other churches.

10. In the United States, the main body of Wesley's followers are incorporated in the METHODIST EPISCOPAL CHURCH, which was formally organized in 1784. Previous to that time local preachers from England, prominent among whom were Philip Embury and an officer in the British army by the name of Webb, had preached in New York and other places, and organized societies on the English model. In 1769 the first regular itinerant Methodist preachers, Boardman and Pilmoor, were sent over by Mr. Wesley. The former took his station in New York, the latter in Philadelphia—occasionally changing with each other, and often making short excursions into the country. They were very successful in their labors; and, by their instrumentality, not only were multitudes converted, but quite a number of lay preachers were received and employed. At the English Wesleyan Conference of 1771, Francis Asbury and Richard Wright volunteered to come to America as missionaries. They landed in Philadelphia in the month of October of that year, and were received by the societies with great cordiality. In the year 1773 two additional missionaries, Rankin and Shadford, were sent over, and the first American "Conference" was held at Philadelphia in July of that year. The number of members in the society was stated to be 1160; and resolutions were adopted recommending continued conformity to the discipline and doctrines of the English Methodists. From that time, all through the stormy season of the Revolutionary War, success seems to have attended their efforts, so that, at the Conference of 1784, there were reported to be about 15,000 members in the connection. In this year Wesley, for the first time, performed the solemn rite of ordination by setting apart two men as elders for the flock in America, and by consecrating to the episcopal office Dr. Thomas Coke, at that time a presbyter in the Church of England. The doctor and his two associates immediately thereafter sailed for America, and were present at the Conference in Baltimore, at which the Methodist Episcopal Church was organized. The first act of that Conference was the ratification with entire unanimity of Coke's ordination, and the election of one of their own number, Francis Asbury, to the same office. The Conference also received Wesley's abridgment of the Articles of the Church of England, which continue to be their standard of doctrine to the present day, and also an abridgment of the Book of Common Prayer, prepared by the same hand, and sent over with the recommendation that it should be used in the Methodist chapels. This was done in some of the large cities for a season, but soon fell into disuse, with the exception of the sacramental services and the forms of ordinations, which are still retained and used. The bishops are elected by a General Conference, which meets every four years, and is composed of delegates from the several Annual Conferences in the ratio of one delegate for a certain number of members, which has been changed from time to time according to the increase of the general body. The ratio fixed by the General Conference of 1872 as a basis of future representation is one delegate for every forty-five members of an Annual Conference. At the same Conference lay members, in the ratio of two for every Annual Conference, were also admitted. The bishops, like the preachers, are itinerant; and it is specially enacted that if one of them ceases from travelling without the consent of the General Conference, he shall not thereafter exercise the episcopal office. His powers are similar to those of the president of the English Conference, with the additional duty of fixing the appointments of the preachers, deciding all questions of law in an Annual Conference, and ordaining bishops, elders, and deacons. The limit of three years, beyond which the preachers of the British Wesleyan Connection may not continue in the same place, is now also the rule of the Methodist Episcopal Church in the United States; and to this is added the regulation that they may not be returned to the same place more than three years in six. Presiding elders in this branch of the Church occupy a position very similar to that of the chairmen of districts in England, except that they have no separate pastoral charge. They are appointed by the bishops, and may remain four years on the same district. They form a kind of advisory committee in assisting the bishops to fix the appointments of the preachers. The "Book Concern," situated in New York, with a branch at Cincinnati, and depositories in various other cities, has a capital of more than a million of dollars, and is one of the largest publishing houses in the world. Under the patronage and control of the Church are weekly papers published in New York, Syracuse (N.Y.), Pittsburgh (Pa.), Cincinnati (O.), Chicago (Ill.), St. Louis (Mo.), San Francisco (Cal.), Portland (Oregon), and Atlanta (Ga.). They publish also several illustrated papers for Sunday-schools, one of a similar kind for the Tract Society, a monthly Sunday-school journal, a monthly magazine in English, another in German, and a quarterly review. See METHODIST EPISCOPAL CHURCH.

11. The METHODIST EPISCOPAL CHURCH, SOUTH, projected at Louisville, Ky., in 1845, was formally organized by delegates from Conferences within the slave-holding states in May, 1846. In doctrine, discipline, and general usages, it is the same as the preceding. The same is true of its forms of worship and usages. But while the Church North made open declaration against the institution of slavery, the Church South ignored the subject. Now that the institution is abolished in the United States, the two bodies can hardly be said to differ. The Methodist Episcopal Church, South, has a flourishing publishing house (at Nashville, Tenn.), and issues several periodicals. See METHODIST EPISCOPAL CHURCH, SOUTH.

12. The METHODIST PROTESTANT CHURCH was organized in the city of Baltimore, Md., in the year 1830, by a convention composed of an equal number of clerical and lay delegates from various states of the Union. The convention continued in session three weeks, and adopted a "Constitution" for the new association. Its

fundamental doctrines, and most of its usages, are the same as those of the Episcopal Methodists, the body from which it seceded. Following the example of the British Wesleyans, the episcopal office is denied, and a president called to rule over each Annual Conference, elected by the ballot of that body. The laity is admitted to an equal participation with the clergy in all Church legislation and government. The General Conference, which meets every four years, consists of an equal number of ministers and laymen, who are elected by the Annual Conferences. The slavery question divided the Methodist Protestant Church into two bodies —the *Methodist Protestant Church of the North-western States* and the *Methodist Protestants of the Southern States.* The head-quarters of the former were established at Springfield, Ohio; those of the latter at Baltimore, Md. Their members were found only in certain parts of the United States. Their greatest strength is in Virginia, Maryland, and in some portions of Ohio and Pennsylvania. Of late years, a union of all non-episcopal Methodists having been proposed, the Protestant Methodists North changed their official name to *The Methodist Church.* The Wesleyan Methodist Church was one of the churches expected to be merged into this newly-constituted body, but hitherto all efforts at union have failed, and there seems to be no immediate prospect of their amalgamation. *The Methodist Church* numbers about 75,000 members; altogether the Methodist Protestants count about 148,000. The head-quarters of the Church South remain at Baltimore, Md.; those of *The Methodist Church* have been removed from Springfield, Ohio, to Pittsburgh, Pa. See METHODIST PROTESTANT CHURCH; METHODISTS, THE.

13. The WESLEYAN METHODIST CHURCH was formed by a convention of clerical and lay delegates which met in the city of Utica, N.Y., in 1843. The principal part of the delegates in attendance were ministers or members of the Methodist Episcopal Church, and the main reason for the establishment of the new body was their hostility to slavery. At their organization as a Church they adopted a Discipline and plan of Church government, and divided the connection into six Annual Conferences, having about 600 ministers and preachers (mostly local), and a reported membership of about 20.000. Their Articles of Faith are the same as those of the Methodist Episcopal Church, and their General Rules are similar, with the exception that they are more stringent on the subject of slavery. They discard episcopacy and presiding elders, but, like the English Wesleyans, they have chairmen of districts, and elect the presidents of their Annual Conferences at each successive session. Ministers are appointed to their respective fields of labor by a stationing committee, the decisions of said committee being subject to approval by the Conference. Societies and churches are permitted to negotiate beforehand with any minister for his services; but such engagements, if made, must receive the sanction of the Conference. Both General and Annual Conferences are composed of ministers and lay delegates, the local preachers also having a representation.

14. The AFRICAN METHODIST EPISCOPAL CHURCH was formed by a party of colored members, under the leadership of Richard Allen, hence sometimes called *Allenites,* who seceded from their white brethren at Philadelphia in 1816. They adopted, in the main, the doctrines and usages of the body from which they seceded. Mr. Allen was elected to the office of bishop, and ordained by four elders of their Church, assisted by a colored presbyter of the Protestant Episcopal denomination. They are found in various parts of the states of Pennsylvania, New York, New Jersey, Delaware, and Maryland. There are also some in the Western States, and a few in Upper Canada, their congregations being largest and most influential in the city of Philadelphia. The *Methodist Almanac* of 1891 assigns them 7 bishops, 3000 preachers, and 400,000 members.

15. The AFRICAN METHODIST EPISCOPAL (Zion)

CHURCH was formed by another secession of colored members in the city of New York in 1819. They elect annually one of their elders as general superintendent, but do not ordain or set him apart to that office by the imposition of hands. The *Methodist Almanac* of 1891 credits them with 7 bishops, 3000 preachers, and 412,513 members.

16. The UNITED BRETHREN IN CHRIST is the designation of a body of Christians, sometimes called *German Methodists.* They must not be confounded with the Moravians, or Unitas Fratrum, who are sometimes called the United Brethren. "The United Brethren in Christ," although mostly consisting of Germans and their immediate descendants, are of American origin, and date as a distinct sect from the year 1800, when their first Annual Conference was held. From that time they have continued to increase in Pennsylvania, Maryland, Virginia, Ohio, Indiana, and other portions of the United States. They have four bishops, nine Annual Conferences, and a General Conference, which meets every fourth year. In doctrines and Church government they are, with few unimportant variations, the same as the Methodist Episcopalians.

17. The EVANGELICAL ASSOCIATION are in doctrine and Church government nearly allied to the Episcopal Methodists. They date from the year 1800, and are sometimes called *Albrights,* after one of the founders of the sect. They elect bishops from the body of the elders, and have several Annual Conferences, and a General Conference, the supreme law-making authority, which meets quadrennially. The members are mostly Germans or of German descent, and are numerous only in Pennsylvania, Ohio, and Illinois. The *Methodist Almanac* of 1891 reports 1 bishop, 1187 preachers, 428 local preachers, and 145,903 members.

18. The FREE METHODIST CHURCH was organized by former members of the Methodist Episcopal Church, Aug. 23, 1860. The main occasion for the establishment of this body was the expulsion of two ministers from the Genesee Conference. The Free Methodists rigidly enforce the rule for *simplicity of dress;* the privilege of free seats in all houses of worship; congregational singing, without the aid of choir or musical instrument; extemporaneous preaching. In doctrine they are one with other Methodist bodies, but adhere strictly to Wesley's views on *sanctification,* and teach *everlasting torment.* They have abandoned the episcopacy, but have one *superintendent,* who is elected every four years at the meeting of their General Conference. They report, in 1890, 513 preachers and 19,998 members. See METHODISTS, FREE.

19. The COLORED METHODIST EPISCOPAL CHURCH IN AMERICA was organized by order of the General Conference of the Methodist Episcopal Church, South, December 16, 1870. The new Church consists of the colored preachers and members heretofore belonging to the Methodist Episcopal Church, South. Two bishops were elected—Rev. William H. Miles, of Kentucky, and Rev. R. H. Vanderhorst, of Georgia. The *Christian Index,* edited by Rev. Samuel Watson, at Memphis, Tenn., was adopted as the organ of the new Church, and Rev. L. J. Scurlock was elected assistant editor and book agent. The structure of the new Church, counting about 17,000 members, conforms in all essential particulars to that of the Methodist Episcopal Church, South, viz. in doctrine, discipline, and economy, but is entirely independent of that organization, though in sympathy with and fostered by it. White people are not admitted to membership.

There are a few other minor subdivisions of the Methodist family, e. g. the Independent (or Congregational) Methodist Church, the names and statistics of which are given in the tabular summary below. In connection with one or other of the larger bodies, Methodists are found not only in England and North America, but they have "Conferences" in France, Germany, Africa, and Australia. They have missionary stations (for more particulars concerning which. see section VI).

20. *Defunct Methodist Bodies.* — Of these, the most important are:

(*a*) The REFORMED METHODIST CHURCH. This body, which is now merged into the *Wesleyan Methodist Church* (see 13), originated in a secession from the Methodist Episcopal Church in 1814. The seceders considered themselves restricted under the episcopal form of government, and, with a view to obtain redress of their grievances, petitioned the General Conference. Their representations met with no favorable reception, and in consequence they withdrew from the membership of the Methodist Episcopal Church. Their formal separation from that body took place Jan. 16, 1814. In the leading doctrines of Christianity they agreed with the Church which they left; but as to the government of the Church, they conducted their affairs on the Congregational principle. They held peculiar views regarding the efficacy of faith. They believed that all blessings given in answer to prayer are in consequence of faith; and in cases of sickness and distress, faith exercised is the restoring principle. They also taught moral perfection in the present state. They admitted to membership all who simply exhibited clear evidence that their sins were forgiven, and that their hearts were renewed. They held that subscription to any record of Christian principles is altogether unnecessary. In 1818 they spread in Upper Canada, and there made great progress. For some time after the organization of the Wesleyan Methodist Church they united with that body in publishing a magazine—a circumstance which ultimately led to a union between the two bodies.

(*b*) The METHODIST SOCIETY, a body which originated in a secession from the Methodist Episcopal Church in New York in 1820, in consequence of what was deemed an undue interference on the part of the ruling preacher with the temporalities of the Church. In Church doctrine the new body adhered to the rules of the "parent" society, but in the government of the Church there was a considerable difference. 1. No bishop was allowed, but a president of each Annual Conference was chosen yearly by ballot from the members thereof. 2. All ordained ministers, whether travelling or not, were allowed a seat in the Annual Conference. "The property of the societies to be vested in trustees of their own choice, and the minister to have no oversight of the temporal affairs of the Church." After the

organization of the *Methodist Protestant Church* (see 12), the Methodist Society was merged in the former.

21. *Methodists in Canada and other British Dominions in America.*—A little more than sixty years ago Methodism was for the first time represented in those parts by William Losee, whom the sainted Asbury had appointed as a worker of the Gospel, "to range at large." The work has prospered there as elsewhere, and there are now five large bodies, presided over by no less than 900 itinerant ministers. Four of these large bodies, viz. the *Wesleyans, Primitives, New Connectionists,* and *Bible Christians,* are either an offspring of like associations in the United Kingdom, or in intimate relations at present.* But the fifth of them is an independent organization, like the great Methodist body of the United States, from which it sprang, and after which it is named the *Methodist Episcopal Church of Canada,* dating its origin as a separate body in 1828. The Canada Wesleyans, though adhering to the polity of the English Wesleyans, are now agitating the adoption of lay-representation, in order to effect a union of all the Methodist bodies in Canada; their aggregate membership amounts at present to a little over 100,000, their preachers to over 600 in all the different bodies. See METHODIST EPISCOPAL CHURCH IN CANADA; WESLEYAN METHODISTS; PRIMITIVE METHODISTS; NEW-CONNECTION METHODISTS; etc.

V. *Aggregate.*—Not reckoning the Band-Room Methodists, nor the countess of Huntingdon's Connection, and making a moderate *estimate* of the Sunday-school scholars belonging to the Welsh Calvinistic Methodists and to the Primitive Methodists in Ireland, we arrive at the results given in the table below. Reckoning two additional hearers for each Church member and Sunday-school scholar, we make a total of more than twelve millions of persons receiving Methodist instruction, and from week to week meeting together in Methodist buildings for the purpose of worshipping Almighty God. The statement is startling, but the statistics given entitle it to the fullest consideration.

But rightly to estimate the results of Methodism during the last hundred and thirty years, there are other facts to be remembered.

"Who will deny, for instance, that Methodism has

* The *Canada Wesleyan Church* was not only founded by, but for many years belonged to the *Methodist Episcopal Church* of the United States.

GREAT BRITAIN AND IRELAND.
The number of members is for the United Kingdom; of chapels and scholars, Great Britain only.

Denomination.	Ministers.	Lay Preachers.	Members.	On Probation.	Chapels.	Number of Sunday-school Scholars.
Wesleyan Methodists	2,209	15,841	446,288	34,575	7,310	928,506
Methodist New Connection	189	1,915	29,492	4,969	449	87,247
Primitive Methodists	1,038	16,299	194,347	....	4,436	430,641
Bible Christians	179	1,479	25,112	832	584	38,738
United Methodist Free Churches	340	3,066	67,235	6,868	1,242	193,173
Independent Methodists	....	323	5,866	395	110	19,291

AMERICA.

Denomination.	Date of Organization.	Number of Ministers.	Number of Church Members.	Number of Sunday-school Scholars.
Methodist Episcopal Church (in 1891)	1784	13,279	2,226,463	2,222,728
United Brethren	1800	1,455	195,709	....
Evangelical Association (Albrights)	1800	1,187	145,705	....
African Methodist Episcopal	1816	3,000	400,000	....
African Methodist Episcopal (Zion)	1819	3,000	412,713	....
Canadian Wesleyans				
Eastern British American Wesleyan Methodists	1828	1,748	253,863	226,050
Methodist Episcopal Church of Canada				
Methodist Protestants	1830	1,441	147,604	....
American Wesleyans (Connection)	1843	about 300	18,000	....
Methodist Episcopal Church, South (in 1890) †	1844	4,862	1,161,666	694,533
Free Methodists	1860	513	19,998	....
Primitive Methodists	....	63	5,502	....
Four minor sects	....	542	30,500	....
Totals	....	31,390	5,017,723	3,143,311

† This does not include the colored membership now separately organized as the *Colored Methodist Episcopal Church, South.*

exercised a potent and beneficial influence upon other churches: Episcopal, Presbyterian, Independent, and Baptist churches have all been largely indebted to Methodism, either directly or indirectly, for many of the best ministers and agents they have ever had. It is a remarkable fact that, during Wesley's life-time, of the 690 men who acted under him as itinerant preachers, 249 relinquished the itinerant ministry. These 249 *retirers* included not a few of the most intelligent, energetic, pious, and useful preachers that Wesley had. Some left him on the ground of health; others began business, because as itinerant preachers they were unable to support their wives and families; but a large proportion became ordained ministers in other churches. In some instances, the labors of these men, and their brother Methodists, led to marvellous results. To give but one example: David Taylor, originally a servant of lady Huntingdon, was one of Wesley's first preachers, but afterwards left the work. Taylor, however, was the means of converting Samuel Deacon, an agricultural laborer; and the two combined were the instruments, in the hands of God, in raising up a number of churches in Yorkshire and the midland counties, which, in 1770, were organized into the New Connection of General Baptists; and that connection seventy years afterwards, in 1840, comprised 113 churches, having 11,358 members, a foreign missionary society, and two theological academies" (*Methodist Magazine* [1856], p. 335).

Sunday-schools are now an important appendage of every church, and have been a benefit to millions of immortal souls; but it deserves to be mentioned that Hannah Ball, a young Methodist lady, had a Methodist Sunday-school at High Wycombe fourteen years before Robert Raikes began his at Gloucester; and that Sophia Cooke, another Methodist, who afterwards became the wife of Samuel Bradburn, was the first who suggested to Raikes the Sunday-school idea, and actually marched with him, at the head of his troop of ragged urchins, the first Sunday they were taken to the parish church.

The first British Bible Society that existed, "The Naval and Military," was projected by George Cussons, and organized by a small number of his Methodist companions. The London Missionary Society originated in an appeal from Melville Horne, who for some years was one of Wesley's itinerant preachers, and then became the successor of Fletcher as vicar of Madeley. The Church Missionary Society was started by John Venn, the son of Henry Venn, the Methodist clergyman. The first Tract Society was formed by John Wesley and Thomas Coke in 1782, seventeen years before the organization of the present great Religious Tract Society in Paternoster Row—a society, by the way, which was instituted chiefly by Rowland Hill, and two or three other Calvinistic Methodists. It is believed that the first Dispensary that the world ever had was founded by Wesley himself in connection with the old Foundery, in Moorfields. The Strangers' Friend Society, paying every year from forty to fifty thousand visits to the sick poor of London, and relieving them as far as possible, is an institution to which Methodism gave birth in 1785.

Building churches is one of the great features of the age. Unfortunately, England has had no religious worship census since 1851; but even then, according to the tables of Horace Mann, Methodism had, in England and Wales only, 11,835 places of worship, with 2,231,017 sittings. In America, according to the census of 1860, Methodism nine years ago provided church accommodation for 6,259,799, which was two and a quarter millions more than was provided by any other Church whatever.

The public press is one of the most powerful institutions of the day. England has four Methodist newspapers; Ireland, one; France, one; Germany, one; India, one; China, one; Australia, two; Canada and British America, five; and the United States about fifty.

VI. *Outgrowth in Missionary Labors.* 1. *In English, or chiefly so.*—Methodism was from its very inception a missionary movement, domestic and foreign. It initiated, so to speak, both the spirit and plan of modern English mission work. Protestant England had manifested but a faint interest in this species of Christian labor until the birth of Methodism, and the spirit of life may be said to have been breathed into English missionary societies by Methodism. Nor need this astonish us. The Church of England recognised as its field the territory held by the Anglican throne; cold and almost lifeless at home, the residents in the colonies and other dependencies received but little religious care. Methodism, the outgrowth of a reawakened zeal for holy living, sought its fields not only in England and Ireland, but manifested early a strong desire for the spread of the Gospel into all parts. To this end Dr. Thomas Coke, in 1786, issued "An Address to the Pious and Benevolent, proposing an Annual Subscription for the Support of Missionaries in the Highlands and adjacent Islands of Scotland, the Isles of Jersey, Guernsey, and Newfoundland, the West Indies, and the Provinces of Nova Scotia and Quebec;" and in the year following the Wesleyan missions bore the distinctive title of "Missions established by the Methodist Society." Even before this organization had been effected, missionary labors were put forth in behalf of the residents of the West Indies. In 1791 Methodism reached out its hand after France, and its great schemes to Christianize Africa were brought to trial as early as 1811. In Asia labor was commenced in 1814; in Australasia in 1815; in Polynesia in 1822; until, from the first call of Wesley for American evangelists, in the Conference of 1769, down to our day, we see the grand enterprise reaching to the shores of Sweden, to Germany, France, and the Upper Alps; to Gibraltar and Malta; to the banks of the Gambia, to Sierra Leone, and to the Gold Coast; to the Cape of Good Hope; to Ceylon, to India, and to China; to the colonists and aboriginal tribes of Australia; to New Zealand, and the Friendly and Fiji Islands; to the islands of the western as well as of the southern hemisphere; and from the Gulf of St. Lawrence to Puget's Sound (comp. Alder, *Wesleyan Missions* [Lond. 1842], p. 4). From 1803 to the present time Wesleyan Methodism has contributed more than twenty millions of dollars for foreign evangelization. In England the Wesleyan Society to-day enrolls more communicants in its mission churches than all other British missionary societies combined. The historian of religion during the last and present centuries would find it difficult to point to a more magnificent monument of Christianity.

Methodist missions may, however, be said to have had their origin long before the founding of a society for the specific purpose of spreading its doctrines in foreign parts. "From its very beginning," says Stevens (*Hist. of Methodism*, iii, 312), "Methodism was characterized by a zealous spirit of propagandism. It was essentially missionary. Its introduction into the West Indies by Gilbert in 1760, and into Nova Scotia by Coughlan in 1765; the appointment of Pilmoor and Boardman to America in 1769, and its commencement at New York at least three years before this date; the formation successively of its Irish, Welsh, and English domestic missions, and the organization of a missionary 'institution' at least two years before the first of what are called modern missionary societies, attest its character as an energetic system of evangelization." But these wide developments of missionary energy, grand as some of them are in their historical importance, were but initiatory to that denominational missionary system which arose from Coke's project of an Asiatic mission (in 1786), to be headed by himself in person, requiring his life as a sacrifice, and thus constituting him, above the mere fact of being first bishop of American Methodism, and the first Protestant bishop of the New World, as the representative character of Methodist missions.

American Methodism has been aptly termed by Dr. Abel Stevens (*Centenary of Amer. Meth.* p. 187) "a missionary scheme," for it was clearly "the great home mission enterprise of the North American continent." The independent establishment of the colonies as a republic in 1776 largely altered the relation to England, and the missionary body gradually ripened into a Church organization, from which, in turn, went out enterprises. The year 1819 is memorable in the history of American Methodism as the epoch of the formal organization of its missionary work. But these early labors were confined to the "home" fields, and aimed mainly at the conversion of the aborigines and slaves. It was some thirteen years later, during the session of the General Conference of 1832, that foreign missions were decided upon, and American Methodism commissioned its Gospel harbingers to carry the truth as it is in Jesus to the dark nations of South Africa, the Romish adherents of Mexico, and of South America. We give below some of the details of this great work in particular fields. Besides its very extensive domestic work, the Methodist Episcopal Church has now missions in China, Corea, India, Africa, Bulgaria, Germany, Switzerland, Denmark, Norway, Sweden, and South America. Its missions, foreign and domestic, in the year 1889 numbered 1239 circuits and stations, 3325 paid laborers (preachers and assistants), and 261,987 communicants. The funds contributed to its treasury, from the beginning down to 1865, amounted to about $6,000,000. About 350 of the missionaries were in 1866 reported to preach in the German and Scandinavian languages, and more than 30,000 of the communicants of German and Scandinavian origin.

"American, like British Methodism," says Stevens (*Centenary of Amer. Meth.* p. 199), "has become thoroughly imbued with the apostolic idea of foreign and universal evangelization. With both bodies it is no longer an incidental or secondary attribute, but is inwrought into their organic ecclesiastical systems. It has deepened and widened till it has become the great characteristic of modern Methodism, raising it from a revival of vital Protestantism, chiefly among the Anglo-Saxon race, to a world-wide system of Christianization, which has reacted on all the great interests of its Anglo-Saxon field, has energized and ennobled most of its other characteristics, and would seem to pledge to it a universal and perpetual sway in the earth. Taken in connection with the London and Church Missionary societies, the British and Foreign Bible Society, the London Tract Society, to all of which Methodism gave the originating impulse, and the Sunday-school institution, which it was the first to adopt as an agency of the Church, it is not too much to say that it has been transforming the character of English Protestantism and the moral prospects of the world. Its missionary development has preserved its primitive energy. According to the usual history of religious bodies, if not indeed by a law of the human mind, its early heroic character would have passed away by its domestic success and the cessation of the novelty and trials of its early circumstances; but by throwing itself out upon all the world, and especially upon the worst citadels of paganism, it has perpetuated its original militant spirit, and opened for itself a heroic career, which need end only with the universal triumph of Christianity. English Methodism was considered, at the death of its founder, a marvellous fact in British history; but to-day (1866) the Wesleyan missions alone comprise more than twice the number of the regular preachers enrolled in the English Minutes in the year of Wesley's death, and nearly twice as many communicants as the Minutes then reported from all parts of the world which had been reached by Methodism. The latest (1865) reported number of missionary communicants in the Methodist Episcopal Church equals nearly one half the whole membership of the Church in 1819, the year in which the Missionary Society was founded, and is nearly double the membership with which the

denomination closed the last century, after more than thirty years of labors and struggles."

2. *Methodism among the French.* — In the year 1790 Methodism was introduced among the French by English Wesleyan preachers, and in 1791 Dr. Coke ordained in a small village of Normandy the first French Methodist preacher. The work was successful, and a society of 100 members had been gathered when the storm of the Revolution prevented further progress, and in 1817 the work had to be begun anew. In 1819 Methodism was introduced into the south of France by Charles Cook, whose labors were eminently successful among the Protestants, who were then in such a state of ignorance and religious indifference that, out of some 400 ministers, not ten could be found who knew and preached the Gospel. Revivals ensued, classes were formed, societies were organized, preachers were raised, and in 1844 there was in France a Church of nearly 1500 members, with 24 travelling preachers. During the progress of the work the other churches had profited, however, by the reviving influence, and Methodism, being regarded as a "foreign importation," began gradually to lose in membership, so that by 1852 there were only 900 actual adherents to the Methodist Church, notwithstanding that the work of evangelization had progressed as usual. These circumstances prompted the Wesleyans to counsel the independent establishment of French Methodism in a distinct French Church, dependent upon the "parent body" for an annual stipend only. The first French Conference was held at Nismes in 1852. From that moment the tide turned again in favor of Methodism; and, notwithstanding the organization of other churches, some of which, it must be owned, have grown more rapidly, the Conference of 1890 reported 1518 members, 184 chapels and preaching-rooms, 53 Sunday-schools, 2539 Sunday-scholars, 101 local preachers, and 36 ministers, and some 9000 regular hearers at the public services. The official title of the Methodist body in France is *The Evangelical Methodist Church of France and Switzerland.* The French Methodists sustain a publishing-house at Paris, and issue a weekly paper, entitled *L'Evangelist.* The "Methodist Episcopal Church" sustains one missionary in the suburbs of Paris, but he is a member of the Swiss Mission Conference, and his labors are intended to benefit only the German residents of the French metropolis.

3. *Methodism among the Germans.* — The Germans were first brought into direct contact with the Methodists in the United States of America. The United Brethren, who have always been in close communion with the Methodists, may really be said to have paved the way for the success of the work among the Germans. The labors of the Rev. William Otterbein, the founder of the United Brethren Church, and a warm personal friend of bishop Asbury, were thoroughly Methodistic, and the United Brethren Church was for many years considered by the Methodists a co-ordinate branch of their own Church, having a special mission to labor and spread the doctrines of Methodism among the Germans. Turning their attention to the young generation and its wants, the United Brethren came to drop the tongue of the Fatherland, and thus alienated themselves from the field which Methodism anxiously sought to supply. A helper offered in the hour of need in the person of Jacob Albright, who, having been converted, and feeling himself called of God to preach the Gospel among the Germans of Pennsylvania, prayed for the sympathies of the Methodist Episcopal Church for his project. Failing to secure the aid asked for, he finally struck out for himself, organized the converts God had given him into a Church, which he called the Evangelical Association, a work that has since been owned of God to the salvation of thousands upon thousands of Germans throughout the land. The Evangelical brethren have always claimed to be Methodists, are known as such among the Germans, and were in former years very much in the habit of styling themselves "The Evangelical Associa-

tion, commonly called Albrights, or Albright Methodists." With but slight modification, they have adopted the Methodist Discipline and Methodist usages. In the matter of doctrine they are Methodistic throughout, laying peculiar emphasis upon those experimental doctrines of Christianity—repentance, faith, regeneration and adoption, growth in grace, and the duty and privilege of entire sanctification. Wesley, Watson, and Clarke are their standard authorities. They lay claim to the fathers of Methodism, thus priding themselves in a common origin with Methodists. At a very early date of their history, when they numbered but a few hundred members, they proposed organic union with the Methodist Episcopal Church upon the sole condition of being permitted to use the German language in the public worship of their congregations, and of laboring exclusively among the Germans. Strange as it may now seem, the offer was rejected, under the erroneous impression which then prevailed that the German language would necessarily die out in a generation or so. Of course emigration had not then attained its present gigantic dimensions, nor were there any indications of results in this direction such as we witness in our day. Efforts looking to organic union between the Methodist Episcopal Church and the Evangelical Association have since been renewed.

In 1836 the conversion and call to the ministry of William Nast, a highly-educated German, a graduate of Tübingen University, moved the leading men in the Methodist Church to establish a domestic mission among the Germans, and it was intrusted to the newly-made convert. He travelled extensively through Ohio and Pennsylvania, and was eminently successful in impressing his countrymen with the need of a "higher" life. The progress of forming a congregation, however, was very slow. Thus after a whole year's labor at Cincinnati, among its thousands of Germans, subjected to the grossest insults, and in constant danger of bodily harm, preaching in the streets and market-places, distributing tracts and talking about Jesus and his salvation in the beer saloons and the tenement houses, he went up to Conference and reported the reception of *three* members, all told. But the final result was, after all, great and glorious. The influence of Nast's example gradually spread among the Germans, and converts came in numbers. From the little congregation, in the old Burke chapel on Vine Street, in Cincinnati, Methodism has made its inroads among the Germans of the United States with such a force that this branch of the Church now presents the results given in the tables below.

The German Methodists now possess two colleges—one in Berea, Ohio, and one in Warrenton, Mo.; one Normal School in Galena, Ill.; and a "Mission House" at New York. They have also two orphan asylums—

one in Berea, Ohio, with sixty-five orphans, and one in Warrenton, Mo., with thirty-five orphans; the running expenses of these orphan asylums amount to nearly $14,000 per year, which sum is contributed by German Methodists. The value of the property of these institutions is over $250,000, besides an endowment fund of $57,000 of the German Wallace College at Berea, Ohio. The circulation of their official organ, the *Christliche Apologete*, is 1915, and of the *Sonntag- und Schul-Glocke* (their Sunday-school paper) 26,000. Very recently a religious German monthly family magazine has been started, and it promises to be a success. The Germans of the Methodist Episcopal Church, South, issue an official organ weekly, and a Sunday-school paper.

German Methodists returning to their native country impressed the German mind with the value of experimental religion, and in 1849 a mission was established in Germany by the Methodist Episcopal Church. Its first superintendent and most efficient worker was the Rev. L. S. Jacoby, D.D., himself a German. But long before any effort had been made to establish missions in that country Methodism was already known there. Wesley had spent in 1738 nearly three months in Germany and Holland, and again in 1783 and 1786 shorter periods in the latter country, where he became acquainted with some of the most godly and learned men in those two centres of Protestant Christianity and enlightenment. The friendship of the Moravians contributed to make his name and doings still more widely known there. Nor was the German press silent while such a revival was going on in England. Dr. Burckhardt, a godly minister, of the Savoy Chapel, in the Strand, and an admirer of the Wesleys, published in Nuremberg a *Complete History of the Methodists in England*, which reached a second edition in 1795. Wesley's sermons were translated into German by Lutheran ministers, several of whom visited England and became greatly interested in Methodism. Since then Methodist literature has multiplied in Germany, until it would make up quite a formidable list both for and against the Methodists.

The first Methodists who established themselves on German soil were the converts of a German named Albrecht, or Albright, who, having embraced the Methodist doctrines in America, was pressed in spirit to engage actively in caring for the religious wants of his fellow-countrymen in the United States. The work which he first organized, about the beginning of the century, has grown into vast proportions, under the name of the "Evangelical Association," noticed above. After having extended to thousands of the Germans of America, the Albrecht Methodists, as they are called abroad, began to extend their efforts towards the Germans in Europe. They held their sixtieth Conference in 1872 at Strasburg, where they commenced a work several years

STATISTICS OF THE GERMAN METHODIST EPISCOPAL CHURCH IN THE U. S. FOR 1890.*

Conferences.	Ministers.	Local Preachers.	Members and Probationers.	Sunday-schools.	Officers and Teachers.	Scholars.	Churches.	Probable Value.	Parsonages.	Probable Value.	Missionary Collections.
Central German	141	98	14,484	172	2,369	13,092	182	$750,200	79	$144,700	$8,358 56
Chicago German	83	4	7,921	192	1,033	13,723	118	372,600	64	78,400	4,312 25
East German	47	32	5,122	65	1,101	7,264	58	572,678	37	113,300	7,489 00
North German	68	41	4,870	105	1,199	4,729	86	235,383	41	56,798	2,280 33
Northwest German	56	43	4,129	107	589	3,884	56	111,050	32	38,350	2,221 60
St. Louis German	135	105	10,609	151	1,748	9,457	154	442,950	87	100,950	5,773 31
South German	33	29	1,830	41	312	1,671	38	70,220	25	22,850	1,465 75
West German	84	76	5,449	115	1,188	5,177	96	248,050	55	60,725	3,838 65
California German	20	17	829	17	178	1,063	16	92,350	9	13,400	956 00
North Pacific German	15	3	452	17	102	442	11	35,500	5	8,300	519 00
Total	687	445	55,695	982	9,819	60,502	815	$2,930,981	434	$637,773	$37,214 45

* The Methodist Episcopal Church, South, supports a mission for the Germans within its boundaries. This field of labor was entered by the Methodist Episcopal Church, South, immediately upon its organization in 1846. Superintendents are set apart by the conferences laboring in Texas, Louisiana, Maryland, and Virginia. Very recently a German congregation has been started in Memphis, Tennessee. The Rev. E. N. Blogg, superintendent of the German mission in the Baltimore and Virginia conferences, reports in 1873 a gradual and healthful growth. "The work," he says, " extends now to Norfolk, Petersburg, Richmond, Baltimore, and Hookstown, with four missionaries in the field besides myself, who are zealously engaged in the duties of aggressive missionary labor.....

since. They have in all Germany 10,231 Church members, 286 Sunday-schools with 11,322 scholars, and 64 itinerant preachers. They have two periodicals, and have lately extended their field to Switzerland.

This work was strengthened by the establishment of a mission from the Wesleyans of England. A German layman of the name of Muller had been converted in London, and had become an exhorter and class-leader. Upon his return to Würtemberg, his native place, after an absence of fourteen years, he could not conceal from his family the change which had been wrought in his heart, and he soon began to hold meetings from village to village. A revival took place, and the persons converted organized themselves in classes. Muller, finding himself in a work that demanded all his ability, gave up his secular business and devoted himself to the evangelization of his fellow-countrymen. This work, begun in 1831, has resulted in the founding of a number of small churches, which comprise (in 1873) a membership of 7026, and 6778 Sunday-school scholars, with 101 travelling and local ministers; and has extended from Würtemburg into the duchy of Baden and to the borders of Austria.

But the grandest and most enterprising of the branches of German Methodism is unquestionably that of the American Methodist Episcopal Church, which, as we have seen above, took its rise from the work among the German emigrants in the United States. In 1852 this missionary field was constituted into an Annual Conference, and it now covers all the German-speaking people in Germany, Switzerland, and France, divided into seven districts: Bremen, Berlin, Frankfort, Ludwigshaven, Carlsruhe, Zurich, and Basle, which comprise more than sixty circuits or stations, with (in 1872) 73 travelling ministers, 386 places of worship, 229 Sunday-schools

with 10,071 scholars, 6230 Church members, and 1369 probationers. This mission is thoroughly organized. It has a book publishing-house, which issues, besides a variety of treatises or books, every fortnight the *Evangelist* and *Kinder-Freund;* every month the *Missionar-Sammler* and *Monatlicher Bote;* and every quarter the*Wächter-Stimmen.* It has also a theological college, which has had as its professors Dr. Warren, of Boston University, and Dr. Hurst, of Drew Theological Seminary. Its present instructors are Dr. Sulzberger and L. Nippert. It had had an existence of fourteen years, when, by the timely and princely gift of John T. Martin, of Brooklyn, N. Y., the present commodious and substantial building, four stories high, standing on a lot one hundred by five hundred feet, was erected, free of debt, at Frankfort-on-the-Main. The property is estimated at about $30,000. The following branches are taught: Greek, Latin, English, German, Hebrew, geography, arithmetic, music, homiletics, dogmatics, discipline of the Methodist Episcopal Church, history of Methodism, Church history, profane history, literature, archæology, exegesis. There are at present twenty-seven young men in this school preparing for the ministry. Sixty or seventy ministers have already gone forth in the course of twelve years. About fifty-four labor in Germany, and others have come to America and are laboring here.

4. *Methodism among the Scandinavians.*—The Methodist Episcopal Church has also done immense service to the cause of personal religion by its missionary efforts among the Scandinavians, with whom the Church was brought face to face in this country. As early as 1845 these labors were commenced, under the auspices of the Home Missionary Society. The work has grown until it presents this imposing array:

STATISTICS OF THE SCANDINAVAIAN MISSIONS OF THE M. E. CHURCH IN THE U. S. FOR 1890.

Conferences.	Ministers.	Local Preachers.	Members and Probationers.	Sunday-schools.	Officers and Teachers.	Scholars.	Churches.	Probable Value.	Parsonages.	Probable Value.	Missionary Collections.
N. W. Norwegian and Danish	73	4	508	12	69	279	13	$78,400	8	$6,700	$382 00
Norwegian and Danish.......	55	67	4,408	76	566	3,176	70½	165,650	30	33,550	3,011 05
Total Norwegian and Danish	128	71	4,916	88	635	3,455	83⅜	244,050	38	40,250	3,393 05
Northwest Swedish..........	81	110	8,811	105	965	6,331	112	364,777	53	68,890	5,484 10
Total..................	209	181	13,727	193	1,600	9,786	195⅜	$608,827	91	$109,140	$8,877 15

STATISTICAL REPORT OF THE METHODIST EPISCOPAL CHURCH MISSIONS IN SWEDEN FOR 1890.

	Missionaries.	Missions.	Ordained Native Preachers.	Unordained Native Preachers.	Native Teachers.	Other Helpers.	Members.	Probationers.	Aver. Attend. on Sunday Worship.	Children Baptized.	Churches and Chapels.	Estimated Value.	Sunday-schools.	Scholars.	Missionary Collection.	Other Benevolent Societies.	For Self-support.	For Church Buildings, &c.	For Other Local Purposes.	Volumes Printed.
This year	7	82	73	96	96	448	13,333	2,664	28,260	353	95	Kronas 839,644	216	16,139	Kronas 14,946	Kronas 13,677	Kronas 49,202	Kronas 51,253	Kronas 81,461	402,900
Last year	..	80	70	26	84	496	12,959	3,051	33,050	390	87	722,659	208	15,547	14,063	16,163	51,507	31,593	76,099	381.900
Increase..........	..	2	3	70	12	....	381	....	....	....	8	116,985	8	592	883	.....	.....	19,660	5,362	21,000
Decrease..........	..	..	..	..	..	48	....	387	4,790	37	..	.....	....	.....	.....	2,486	2,305	.....	.....	.. ...

STATISTICAL REPORT OF THE METHODIST EPISCOPAL CHURCH MISSIONS IN NORWAY FOR 1890.

	Ordained Preachers.	Unordained Native Preachers.	Local Preachers.	Members.	Probationers.	Aver. Attend. on Sunday Worship.	Children Baptized.	Sunday-schools.	Scholars.	Churches and Chapels.	Estimated Value.	Halls Rented.	Debt on Property.	Collected for Church Buildings, &c.	Collected for Missions.	For Self-support.	For Other Local Purposes.	Volumes Printed.
This year..............	31	12	34	4,418	714	8,072	225	59	5,014	37	Crowns 542,275	12	Crowns 149,274	Crowns 21,288	Crowns 4,723	Crowns 10,560	Crowns 42,305	247,661
Last year..............	29	11	35	4,159	601	6,360	210	59	5,039	36	529,000	7	164,406	6,867	4,388	11,675	44,068	308,310
Increase..............	2	1	..	259	113	1,712	15	..	.....	1	13,275	5	.....	14,421	335	.....	1,703	.....
Decrease..............	..	..	1	.....	....	.....	..	..	25	..	.....	..	15,032	.....	....	1,115	.....	60,649

The annual statistics covering my operations in the Baltimore Conference are as follows: Local preachers, 2; members, 32; infants baptized, 12; Sunday-schools, 2; superintendents, 3; teachers, 16; scholars, 178; volumes in library, 210." The Missionary Report for 1873 furnishes no other statistics of the German work, but the secretary prefaces the reports from the superintendents (under date of June 1) with the remark that "a very important question will be agitated at the next General Conference [May, 1874]—that of erecting the Germans into a separate Conference." A German paper for the members in this field is published by the Methodist Episcopal Church, South, under the editorial guidance of the Rev. J. A. B. Ahrens, at New Orleans, Louisiana.

For the last three years a monthly, called *Missionaren*, devoted to religion, has been published. A hymn-book has also been prepared for the members of this branch of the Methodist Episcopal Church.

The success of this work at home gave rise to the establishment of a mission to the Scandinavians in 1854. It now extends over Denmark, Sweden, and Norway. Its importance may be judged by the last annual report. In Denmark there are now 301 members, 6 class-leaders, 3 exhorters, 2 local preachers, 20 regular appointments, and 4 missionaries, under the superintendence of the Rev. Karl Schon, at Copenhagen, where the mission possesses a very elegant church. In the other two countries the reports are as given in the two preceding tables.

5. *Methodism in Australia.*—Methodism at the beginning of this century found its adherents in Australia. The first class was organized March 6, 1812. The first missionary to this colony was Samuel Leigh, who landed in 1815. At first the labors of the preacher were confined to the whites, particularly the convicts who had been transported hither from the mother country. Gradually the work was extended to the natives also. In 1853 Methodism had progressed so well that the formation of an independent Conference was counselled by the home Church, and in January, 1855, the first session of the Wesleyan Conference was held at Melbourne, and was presided over by the Rev. W. B. Boyce, at that time general superintendent of Methodist missions in Australia, now secretary of the Wesleyan Missionary Society, London. At that time there were some 60 preachers and 11,000 members. Now this bough of the vigorous tree planted by John Wesley divides itself into three branches. The first extends over Australia Proper and Van Diemen's Land, the Methodist districts in which adapt themselves to the colonial divisions of New South Wales, Victoria, South Australia, Western Australia, and Tasmania. These are the home districts of Methodism in that region, the work in them being missionary only as regards a few surviving relics of the feeble aborigines, or the swarms of immigrant Chinese. The second branch of Australian Methodism divides itself over New Zealand into the two districts of Auckland and Wellington, and the work is of a mixed character, embracing the British settlers and the Maori. The third branch is purely missionary, and extends over the Friendly and the Fiji Islands. "These," said the Rev. G. T. Perks, at the anniversary of the Wesleyan Missionary Society, May 5, 1873, "have been among the most successful of modern missions." See FIJI ISLANDS. "The statistics of these missions speak for themselves: 23 European missionaries labor in connection with 63 native missionaries, and 906 native catechists, and 1796 local preachers; the number of Church members is 33,149. There are above 133,000 attendants at public worship in 802 chapels and in 357 other preaching-places. The work of education has not been neglected; 1568 day-schools, taught by 148 head teachers, and by 2469 subordinate masters, return 53,804 day-scholars, and about the same number attend the Sunday-schools, in which there are 3551 teachers." At the fifteenth session of the Conference in 1868, held at Sydney, the reports from all parts of the work were very encouraging. There were then 241 preachers and 57 native helpers. The collective totals of the Australian connection were, in 1868, 30,590 members, with 8953 persons "on trial." Australian Methodism has three flourishing high-schools—Newington College, at New South Wales; Wesley College, at Victoria; and Horton College, in Tasmania. Of late a theological school has been projected.

6. *Methodism in the West Indies.* — In no other missionary field has Methodism met with greater success than among this portion of the globe's inhabitants. The West Indies was, moreover, the first foreign field sought by the Wesleyans, and its history is closely linked to that of the founder, John Wesley, and his own associates. One of the natives, Nathaniel Gilbert, from Antigua,

came under the influence of the Methodists while on a visit to England, and in 1760 returned to his native land to preach their doctrines to his countrymen. As they were bound by the heavy chains of slavery, he determined to bestow upon them the liberty of the Gospel. When he died two hundred had embraced the cause of Methodism. Their next leader was John Baxter, an Englishman, who had been licensed as "local preacher," and who had gone to the West Indies as a ship-carpenter. He preached for eight years, and did much good among the blacks. When the missionaries finally arrived, he was able to turn over two thousand adherents as the result of *preparatory* labors. In 1786 the home society set aside one man for the spread of missions in the West Indies. He was to accompany Dr. Coke to America, and then be transferred to his new field. On the way the company suffered shipwreck, and by mere accident all landed at Antigua, and, when Coke witnessed the glorious work begun, he left the three missionaries by his side—Warrener, Clarke, and Hammet—in the country, and sailed alone to the United States. In 1792, when Coke visited the West Indies, and held a Conference at Antigua, the missionaries reported 20 stations, with 12 preachers and 6500 members. In 1873 the progress of Methodism in these parts was thus commented upon by the Rev. G. T. Perks, at the annual meeting of the Wesleyan Missionary Society (May 5): "The West Indian missions occupy a peculiar position in relation to other missions. The colonies of Jamaica, the Windward and Leeward Islands, the Bahamas, British Guiana, Honduras, and Hayti are mainly inhabited by the descendants of the Africans emancipated in 1834. The European population is comparatively small. No missions have had greater difficulties to contend against. Earthquakes, hurricanes, the pestilence, and occasional fires have from time to time destroyed life and property; the changes in the commercial policy of the British government operated for a while most injuriously in reducing the value of the staples of these colonies, and in some localities fearful droughts reduced the population to poverty and starvation. Our Maya mission to Honduras has been disturbed by Indian raids on the colony; and our societies in Ruatan, an island belonging to the republic of Honduras, have suffered from a political revolution, which is no strange event in the Spanish republics of America. Yet, in spite of these untoward circumstances, the West Indian colonies are gradually improving—agriculturally, commercially, and socially. The great want is an educated native ministry. The time since the emancipation has been but a short period in the history of a nation, and our moral and educational agencies have not been equal to the task of thoroughly changing the character and habits of the people within the lifetime of a generation. Yet over many of our churches we have great reason to rejoice; and, from what has been effected in their case, to look hopefully in reference to the future. In these missions we have 97 missionaries, 44,728 members, and 28,038 scholars."

7. *Methodism in India.* — Next in importance is the missionary work in India. The Wesleyans have labored there for years, but their expenditure on the field, both in men and money, is far inferior to that of the Methodist Episcopal Church, which has, especially within a very recent period, met with unprecedented success. But all Methodists have an equal interest in the success of this missionary field, to which the sainted Coke gave his life. See COKE. Work was commenced in 1813 at Ceylon. By 1819 the impression made warranted the establishing of schools in the principal cities along the western coast. In the mean time missionary labors had been commenced (1817) on the continent itself, with head-quarters at Bombay. At the time of the centennial of Methodism (1839) the mission in India counted 21 stations, 43 missionaries and helpers, and 1200 members. At present (1873) the field covering the Tamil and Singhalese districts, Calcutta, Mysore, and Madras.

contains 2976 members, with 13,987 children in the schools, guided by 75 missionaries. These statistics do not give, however, an adequate impression of the nature and character of the work itself. In India and Ceylon the missionaries preach in the streets and bazars, as well as in the chapels; they make frequent missionary tours in their respective districts, to preach and converse, and circulate books in the villages. Much time is necessarily occupied in the training of native agents, and in the charge of the higher classes in the schools, as well as in the general superintendence of the educational department of this work.

The Methodist Episcopal Church sent its missionaries to these parts in 1856. The pioneer operations were confined to efforts for the education of the natives. By 1864 the work had progressed sufficiently to warrant the organization of an Annual Conference, divided into three districts. That field has since been covered by three distinct conferences and the mission of Malaysia.

liam Taylor, at Bombay, have added Western India to the missionary field of the Methodist Episcopal Church. No statistics have been published authoritatively, but accounts have appeared in the newspapers of the remarkable revival at Bombay, Poonah, and vicinity. Six itinerants are describing the Bombay circuit, and they do not consider their work as designed for the English and Eurasian populations alone, but for people in India— European, Eurasian, Mahratta, Hindû, nominally Christian, Pagan, or Mohammedan.

8. *Methodism among the Chinese and Japanese.*—In 1847 the Methodist Episcopal Church opened operations in China, and the field has returned more than it at first promised. The gradual success of the work of this body has been given in the article on *China* (q. v.). The "parent" body—the Wesleyans—were introduced into this field by the voluntary labors of George Piercy, a preacher, in 1851. Two years later the Missionary Society of his Church came to his aid by sending two assistants. The Methodist Episcopal Church, South, has

MISSIONS OF THE METHODIST EPISCOPAL CHURCH IN INDIA IN 1890.

CONFERENCES.	SOCIETY AGENTS.					CHURCH.							EDUCATIONAL.								MISSION PROPERTY.			
	Amer-ican.		Native Assist's.										Theological Schools.											
	Male.	Female.	Ordained.	Local Preachers.	Exhorters.	Members.	Probationers.	Total Membership.	Conversions during the Year.	Children Baptized.	Adherents.	Sunday-school Scholars.	Total Baptisms.	Students.	High Schools.	Students.	Other Day-Schools.	Scholars.	Total Scholars.	Churches and Chapels.	Parsonages.	Estimated Value of all Property.	Debt on Real Estate.
North India	53	21	67	245	724	5,958	7,463	13,421	2,402	2,501	12,603	30,823	6,105	3	76	11	1,706	655	15,951	17,733	64	105	1,149,465	109,795
South India	39	7	2	10	76	616	263	879	202	95	1,067	7,719	185			3	365	70	2,557	2,922	21	13	341,685	55,585
Bengal	36	10	6	50	57	965	1,275	2,240	1,057	296	3,526	3,881	981			2	281	74	2,412	2,693	18	11	495,398	44,650
Total	128	38	75	305	857	7,539	9,001	16,540	3,661	2,892	17,196	42,423	7,271	3	76	16	2,352	799	20,920	23,348	103	129	1,986,548	209,960

(Rupees. for Estimated Value and Debt columns)

"Four male and five female missionaries left for India in October last; these are included in the above totals. There are 541 members, 526 probationers, 735 non-communicant adherents (regular attendants on worship), with 1178 Sabbath-scholars, and the 86 native helpers, making a Christian community of 3066 souls under the charge of the India Conference in Oude and Rohilcund, all won for Christ since the Great Rebellion closed. In the 34 Sunday-schools there are 107 officers and teachers, 1177 scholars, and 1088 volumes in the libraries; conversions during last year, 56. In the 45 vernacular day-schools for boys there are 1437 pupils; in the 25 Anglo-vernacular boys' schools, 1968 scholars; in the 46 vernacular day-schools for girls, 915 pupils; in the Anglo-vernacular schools, 142 girls: being a total of 116 schools, 234 teachers, and 4462 scholars, including 138 orphan boys and 142 orphan girls—the entire expense of which, including the two orphanages, was $29,423 for the past year, the whole of which was contributed by friends in India and the Ladies' Missionary Society of the Methodist Episcopal Church, with the American patrons of the orphan children."

Medical instruction is afforded by some of the missionaries, and the natives have by this means been largely interested in Christian work and life. A Biblical institute for the training of native helpers is supported under the name of the "India Conference Theological Seminary." The school was commenced April 15, 1872. The number of young men in attendance has been sixteen, of whom thirteen have received scholarships. Three local preachers attended during the "hot-season term." The following is the course of study pursued this first year, viz.: Old-Testament Exegesis; Church Catechism, Nos. 1, 2, and 3; Sacred Geography; Ecclesiastical History; Compend of Theology (Ileni-Ilahi ka usul); Hand-book of the Bible (Miftah ul-Kitab); Homiletics; the Persian and Arabic languages. The Rev. D. W. Thomas, one of the missionaries in India, has given to this institution $20,000, and is now in the United States to increase the endowment, in order to make the school self-supporting.

Very recently the successful labors of the Rev. Wil-

also an interest in this field. The Wesleyans support at present in the Canton and Wuchang districts 11 missionaries, with 178 members, and 386 children in the schools. Work has recently been commenced by them at Kwang-chi, with prospects of success. They also support medical institutions. The great coolie traffic moved the establishment of a Chinese mission in Australia, and it is prospering. The mission of the Methodist Episcopal Church in 1890 reported its condition in China to be as follows: Missionaries in the field, 40; assistant missionaries, 29; missionaries of the Women's Foreign Missionary Society (a body lately formed as auxiliary to the regular Missionary Society of the Methodist Episcopal Church), 6; native preachers ordained, 79; adults baptized the past year, 558; children baptized the past year, 663; total baptisms during the year, 1221; members in full connection, 3987; probationers, 2385; baptized children, 6379; total members, probationers, and baptized children, 4387; increase, 78; Sunday-school scholars, 4387. A Biblical institute for the training of native helpers is supported. A Christian native teacher is employed, and each American missionary devotes part of one day every week to giving instruction in some special part in the course of study. There is a press connected with the mission, and last year one million and a half of pages of tracts were printed and distributed. The property of the mission is valued at $252,620. The mission has also two boarding-schools, one for boys and another for girls; a day-school, with 75 scholars; and a foundling asylum, with 30 inmates. The Woman's Foreign Missionary Society has greatly aided the work in these parts within the past two years by the employment of deaconesses.

The influx of Chinese on our Pacific coast aroused the interest of the Methodist Episcopal Church, and in 1867 a home mission was inaugurated for their conversion. The present status of this field of labor is as follows: Missionaries, 2; members, 115; 1 church, value $20,000; 1 parsonage, value $1000; missionary collections, $40; missions, 1; money, $3500. The Methodist Episcopal Church, South, has also very recently commenced operations there.

Near the close of last year a Methodist mission was established at *Japan* under the auspices of the Methodist Episcopal Church. Dr. Maclay, formerly superintendent of the mission in China, has supervision, and he hopes to make this new effort a glorious success. Already a native of influence and rank in the empire has espoused this cause, and is now preaching.

9. *Methodism in Africa.*—Dr. Coke was early drawn towards this field of missionary labor. But all efforts proved unsuccessful until 1811, when a Methodist mission was established at Sierra Leone, commencing its labor with a membership of 110, and three local preachers, who had fostered the work for some time. Gradually the mission extended to the Gambia districts. In these parts of Western Africa the natives are in process of training, under the Christianizing influences of the Wesleyans, to benefit them by the civilization which too often has been made a means of degradation to their race. The majority of the ministers in Africa are natives, educated and trained for their work. Twenty-one missionaries labor in this field, which has 8974 Church members. "In the Cape Colony, the Orange Free State, Trans-Vaal Republic, and Natal, the native and European populations are so mingled that it is impossible to separate the returns of the colonial work from those of the missions in Kaffirland and in the Bechuana country. The early history of the mission is identified with the names of Barnabas and William Shaw, the latter, the honored father of the Kaffir mission, is no longer among us, but his work survives. These missions have been, since their beginning, tried by native wars, and by the unsettlement of the population occasioned by emigration, and by the discovery of the diamond fields; but the work is rapidly advancing. A large number of the Kaffir population have been brought under Christian influence; thousands of scholars have been trained to read the Word of God in their own tongue, and many able native ministers have been raised up. The difficulty now is to meet the enlarged educational wants and requirements of the native people. In these missions 85 ministers labor; the number of Church members is 13,748, and the scholars reported are 13,821" (Perks, in his address already quoted).

The Methodist Episcopal Church established a mission in Liberia in 1832. By 1836 the formation of an Annual Conference became necessary, and at present a bishop presides over this field. We have the following summary of statistics for 1890: Members, 2954; deaths, 67; probationers, 224; local preachers, 58; baptisms—adults, 121; children, 85; churches, 36, of the probable value of $31,430; parsonages, 1, of the probable value of $150; Sabbath-schools, 41; officers and teachers, 405; scholars, 2614; day-schools, 15; scholars in day-schools, 450; volumes in libraries, 1127; collections for the support of the Gospel, $1282. See LIBERIA.

The Conference, at its last session, expressed its deep sense of the need of a more thorough training of men for the holy ministry, and took incipient steps towards the establishment of a Biblical institute. Measures have also been taken for the establishment of a mission in the Kong mountains, north and east of Liberia and Sierra Leone, where dwell the Mandingoes, perhaps the most cultivated tribe on the western coast of Africa. See MANDINGO. Ten thousand dollars have been appropriated for this work.

10. *Methodism in Italy, Spain, and Portugal.*—For some time the Wesleyans have supported missionaries in each of these countries. Late events have given a new impetus to the work, and it promises to yield fruit in abundance. Besides two English ministers, seventeen Italians are preaching Methodist doctrines. At Rome the Wesleyans are now in possession of suitable buildings for preaching and educational purposes, and at Naples the new chapel and schools are advancing towards completion, while their educational establishment at Padua is in efficient operation.

The Methodist Episcopal Church in 1871 decided to establish a mission in that country, and placed the Rev. Dr. Vernon in charge. Bologna has been selected as head-quarters.

In Spain, Methodism supported for years a mission at Gibraltar, the only spot available until the new order of things developed. At present there are stations at Barcelona and Port Mahon (in the island of Minorca), and in Portugal at Oporto.

11. *Methodism in South America and Mexico.*—In 1836 missionary work was commenced in South America, but the success of the mission has not yet been fairly established. There are connected with this work 18 ordained preachers and 6 assistants, with 985 members. The Sunday-schools number 2113 teachers and scholars, and the day-school 1379 scholars. About half of these are charity scholars.

In November, 1872, the Methodist Episcopal Church organized a mission for Mexico, under the superintendence of the Rev. William Butler, D.D., formerly superintendent of her work in India. The enterprise is too recent to enable us to say much about it.

12. In *Bulgaria* the Methodist Episcopal Church established a mission in 1857. Connected with it are two ordained preachers, one at Constantinople and the other at Tultcha. These missionaries are engaged in preaching the Gospel, scattering religious reading, and translating the New Testament into the Bulgarian tongue. The appropriation is $19,320.

13. *Recapitulation.*—The number of Methodists outside of England and America, according to the best information we can obtain, was in 1866 as follows:

Australia	42,194
West Indies	41,592
Ireland	29,060
Africa	19,403
British Provinces	15,297
Germany and Switzerland	7,620
France	1,884
Ceylon	1,661
Norway	1,200
India	1,000
China	336
South America	193
Turkey	75
Total	161,515

The whole number of Methodists in the world would therefore figure at the present time about as follows:

United States and Canada	2,591,875
Great Britain and Ireland	931,450
All others	276,675
Total	4,000,000

VII. *Literature.*—The sources for the history and doctrine of the Methodists are as follows: *Works of John Wesley* (first complete edition, Bristol, 1771–74, 32 small volumes, full of typographical errors; 2d ed. 1809–13, 16 vols. 8vo, with a register, also containing errors; a critical edition was prepared by Thomas Jackson and published, London, 1831, 14 vols. 8vo; N.Y. 1831, 7 vols. 8vo); *Memoirs of the late John Wesley, with a Review of his Life and Writings, and a History of Methodism from its Commencement in* 1729 *to the present Time,* by John Hampson, A.B. (Sunderland, 1791, 3 vols. 12mo; translated into German, with remarks and additions by Niemeyer, Halle, 1793, 2 vols.); Burkhardt, *Complete History of the Methodists in England* (Nürnb. 1795, 2 vols.); *Life of the Rev. John Wesley, A.M., including an Account of the great Revival of Religion in Europe and America, of which he was the first and chief Instrument,* by Dr. Coke and Mr. Moore (Lond. 1792, 8vo); *Life of John Wesley, collected from his private Papers and printed Works, and written at the Request of his Executors; to which is prefixed some Account of his Ancestors and Relations; with the Life of Charles Wesley, collected from his private Journal, and never before published—the whole forming a History of Methodism, in which the Principles and Economy of Methodism are unfolded* (chiefly from a London edition published by John Whitehead, M.D., Dublin, 1805, 2 vols. 8vo). For the sources of these biographies, see Curry, *Remarks,* in the addition to his revision of Southey's edition, i, 405, 406; *Sermons by Charles Wesley, with a Memoir of the Author* (Lond. 1816); *Journals of Charles Wesley, to which are appended Selections from his Correspondence and Poetry, with an Introduction and Notes* by the Rev. T. Jackson (Lond. 2 vols. 8vo); Thomas Jackson, *Memoirs of Charles Wesley, comprising Notices of his Poetry, of the Rise and Progress of Methodism, and of contemporary Events and Characters* (Lond. 8vo); William Myles, *Chronological History of the People called Methodists, of the Connection of the late Rev. John Wesley, from their Rise in the Year 1729 to their last Conference in the Year 1802* (Lond. 1803, 12mo); *Life of Wesley, and Rise and Progress of Methodism,* by Robert Southey, Esq., LL.D., with Notes by the late Samuel Taylor Coleridge, Esq.; and Remarks on the Life and Character of John Wesley, by the late Alexander Knox, Esq., edited by the Rev. Charles C. Southey, M.A. (2d American edition, with Notes, etc., by the Rev. Daniel Curry, D.D., 2 vols. 12mo, N.Y. 1847); Richard Watson, *Observations on Southey's Life of Wesley* (Lond. 1820); R. Watson, *Life of the Rev. John Wesley* (Lond. 1831); A. Clarke, *Memoirs of the Wesley Family* (Lond. and N.Y.); Wm. C. Larrabee, *Wesley and his Coadjutors* (N.Y. 2 vols. 16mo); E. Janes, *Wesley his own Historian* (N.Y. 1872, 12mo); the Rev. L. Tyerman, *Life and Times of John Wesley, Founder of the Methodists* (Lond. and N.Y. 1872, 3 vols. 8vo); and by the same author, *The Oxford Methodists* (Lond. and N.Y. 1873, 8vo); *Complete Works of John Fletcher* (Lond. 1815, 10 vols. 8vo; N.Y. 1831, 4 vols. 8vo); Joseph Benson, *Life of the Rev. John William de la Flechère* (Fletcher), compiled from the Narrative of the Rev. Mr. Wesley, the biographical Notes of the Rev. Mr. Gilpin, from his own Letters, and other authentic Documents (Lond. 1817, 8vo; in German, with a Preface by A. Tholuck, Berlin, 1833); Samuel Drew, *Life of the Rev. Thomas Coke, LL.D., including in Detail his various Travels and extraordinary Missionary Exertions in England, Ireland, America, and the West Indies, with an Account of his Death* (Lond. 1817, 8vo; N.Y. 1847, 12mo); *Extracts of the Journals of the Rev. Dr. Coke's Five Visits to America* (Lond. 1793, 12mo); Stevenson, *City Road Chapel, London* (Lond. 1863, 12mo); *Annual Minutes of the Methodist Conference, from the First held in London by the late Rev. John Wesley, in the Year 1744* (several vols.); *Arminian Magazine,* from 1778, now styled *Wesleyan Methodist Magazine* (Lond.); *London Quarterly Review,* since 1853; the great ecclesiastical weeklies—*Watchman, Wesleyan Times,* etc. See also Gillie, *Life of the Rev. George Whitefield* (Lond. 1813); Philip, *Life of Whitefield; Life and Times of the Countess of Huntingdon* (Lond. 2 vols.); Mudge, *Lady Huntingdon Portrayed* (N.Y. 1857); *Lives of Early Methodist Preachers,* edited by the Rev. Thomas Jackson (Lond. 1839, 2 vols. 12mo); and numerous biographies from the time of the origin of Methodism.

Sources for the history of the Methodist Episcopal Church especially: *Journals of the Rev. Francis Asbury, Bishop of the Methodist Episcopal Church* (new ed., N.Y. 1854, 3 vols. 12mo); *Minutes of the Annual Conferences of the Methodist Episcopal Church* (N.Y. 29 vols. 8vo); *Journals of the General Conference of the Methodist Episcopal Church* (N.Y. 12 vols. 8vo); *Methodist Quarterly Review* (N.Y. 54 vols.); A. Stevens, *Memorials of the Introduction of Methodism into the Eastern States* (N.Y. 2 vols.); J.B. Finley, *Sketches of Western Methodism* (N.Y. 12mo); and similar researches by Peck, Raybold, and others; Wakely, *Lost Chapters recovered from the Early History of American Methodism;* id. *Heroes of Methodism* (N.Y. 12mo); Coles, *Heroines of Methodism* (N.Y. 12mo); Stevens, *Women of Methodism* (N.Y. 12mo); Rev. W. Reddy, *Inside Views of Methodism* (N.Y. 18mo); W.P. Strickland, *History of Missions of the Methodist Episcopal Church* (N.Y. 12mo); Bishop Thomson, *Our Oriental Missions* (N.Y. 2 vols. 16mo); W.C. Smith, *Pillars in the Temple, or Lives of Deceased Laymen of the Methodist Episcopal Church*

(N.Y. 16mo); Deems, *Annals of Southern Methodism;* Miller, *Experience of German Meth. Preachers* (Cincinnati, 1859); Strickland, *Life of Bishop Asbury;* id. *Pioneers of the West* (N.Y. 12mo); Stevens, *Life and Times of Nathan Bangs* (N.Y. 1863); id. *Sketches and Incidents* (N.Y. 18mo); Larrabee, *Asbury and his Coadjutors; Life and Letters of Bishop Hamline* (N.Y. 12mo); Sandford, *Wesley's Missionaries to America;* G. Peck, *Episcopacy and Slavery.*

Collective histories of Methodism: the best universal history of Methodism which the Methodist Episcopal Church has ever produced is Dr. Abel Stevens's *History of the Religious Movement of the Eighteenth Century called Methodism, considered in its different denominational Forms, and in its Relation to British and American Protestantism* (N.Y. and Lond. 1858–61, 3 vols. 8vo and 12mo). The best history which was ever written in England is by Dr. George Smith: *History of Methodism*—vol. i, *Wesley and his Times;* vol. ii, *The Middle Age of Methodism;* vol. iii, *Modern Methodism* (Lond. 1857–62, 3 vols. 8vo). Earlier works: Jackson, *Centenary of Wesleyan Methodism* (Lond. 1839); Jonathan Crowther, *Portraiture of Methodism, or the History of the Wesleyan Methodists, showing their Rise, Progress, and present State; Biographical Sketches of some of their most eminent Ministers; the Doctrines the Methodists believe and teach fully and explicitly stated; with the whole Plan of their Discipline, including their original Rules and subsequent Regulations. Also a Defence of Methodism* (Lond. 1815, 8vo). Concerning the history of the Methodist Episcopal Church especially: Nathan Bangs, *Hist. of the Meth. Episc. Church from the Year 1766 to 1840* (N.Y. 1839–41, 4 vols. 12mo); A. Stevens, *Hist. of the Meth. Episc. Church* (N.Y. 1865–67, 4 vols. 8vo and 12mo); Lee, *Hist. of the Methodists;* Strickland, *Hist. of the Missions of the M.E. Church* (1st ed. Cincinnati, 1849); Goss, *Statistical Hist. of Methodism* (N.Y. 1866, 18mo); R. Emory, *Hist. of the Discipline of the M.E. Church,* revised and brought down to 1856 by W.P. Strickland (1st ed. N.Y. 1843); Charles Elliott, *Hist. of the great Secession from the M.E. Church in the Year 1845, eventuating in the Organization of the new Church, entitled the M.E. Church South* (Cincinnati, 1855, 8vo); *Hist. of the M.E. Church in the South-west from 1844 to 1864,* by the Rev. Charles Elliott, D.D., LL.D., edited and revised by the Rev. Leroy Vernon, D.D. (St. Louis, Mo., 1872, 12mo). On Canada: G.F. Playter, *Hist. of Methodism in Canada* (Toronto, 1862, 12mo); Gorrie, *Lives of Eminent Methodist Ministers;* etc.

Books on Methodism. (*a*.) Polemical books. Innumerable anti-Methodistic works have been published since the days of Wesley. A list of 277 such books, which, however, are now almost forgotten, is given in alphabetic order by H.D. Decanver: *Catalogue of Works in Refutation of Methodism, from its Origin in 1729 to the present Time* (Phila. 1846). (*b*.) Philosophical (pragmatical) studies: Isaac Taylor, *Wesley and Methodism* (Lond. 1851)—Introduction; 1, *Founders of Methodism;* 2, *Substance of Methodism;* 3, *Form of Methodism;* 4, *Methodism of the Future.* Mr. Taylor, a copious Calvinistic writer of the Anglican Church, was once a Dissenter; B.F. Tefft, *Methodism Successful, and the Internal Causes of its Success* (N.Y. 1859). (*c*.) More or less apologetic are, James Porter, *Compendium of Methodism, embracing the History and present Condition of its various Branches in all Countries, with a Defence of its Doctrinal, Governmental, and Prudential Peculiarities* (N.Y. 1851; 16th ed. 1860, 12mo); George Smith, *The Polity of Wesleyan Methodism exhibited and defended* (Lond. 1852, 12mo); P.D. Gorrie, *Episcopal Methodism as it was and is* (Auburn, N.Y. 1852, 12mo); Bishop Emory, *Defence of our Fathers* (N.Y. 8vo); T.E. Bond, *Economy of Methodism* (N.Y. 8vo); J. Dixon, *Methodism in its Economy* (Lond. and N.Y. 18mo); N. Bangs, *Responsibilities of the M.E. Church* (N.Y. 18mo); A. Stevens, *Church Polity* (N.Y. 12mo); Morris, *Church Polity* (N.Y. 12mo); L.S. Jacoby, *Handbuch des Methodismus,* embracing its history, doctrine, government, and peculiar ceremonies (Bremen, 1853, 12mo); Thomas Jackson, *Wesleyan Methodism a Revival of Apostolical Christianity*, a centenary sermon (Lond. and N. Y. 1839); Dixon, *Methodism in its Origin, Economy, and present Position* (Lond. and N. Y. 1843, 18mo); Wise, *Popular Objections to Methodism Considered and Answered* (Boston, 1856, 12mo); Rigg, *Essay on the Principles of Methodism* (Lond.); Shrewsbury, *Methodism Scriptural* (Lond.); Thomas Bond, *The Economy of Methodism Illustrated and Defended* (N. Y. 8vo); Jackson, *Letter to Dr. Pusey, being a Vindication of the Tenets and Character of the Wesleyan Methodists against his Misrepresentations and Censures* (Lond. and N. Y.); F. Hodgson, *Ecclesiastical Polity of Methodism Defended* (Lond. and N. Y.); Henkle, *Primary Platform of Methodism* (Louisville, Ky., 1851); F. J. Jobson, *America and American Methodism* (N. Y. 1857, 12mo); Strickland, *Genius and Mission of Methodism* (N. Y. 1851); Turner, *Constitution of Methodism* (Lond. 12mo); W. J. Sassnett, *Progress, considered with particular Reference to the M. E. Church, South* (Nashville, 1855, 12mo); N. Bangs, *Present State, Prospects, and Responsibilities of the M. E. Church* (N. Y. 1850); John Bakewell, *Admonitory Counsels to a Methodist*, etc. (N. Y. 18mo); Bishop Baker, *Guide in the Administration of the Discipline of the M. E. Church* (N. Y. 16mo); Hawley, *Manual of Methodism* (N. Y. 12mo).

Among the earlier apologetical works of Methodism, Fletcher's *Checks to Antinomianism*, covering the first two volumes of his whole works (see below), ranks deservedly as the ablest and most learned defence of Arminianism; and, indeed, it proved quite a polemic against Calvinism. The same writer furnished one of the best polemics against Socinianism, provoked by Priestley. The ablest treatise on systematic theology, from a Methodistic stand-point, was furnished by Dr. Richard Watson in his *Theological Institutes*, a work which to this day remains the text-book of Methodist students in divinity. An elaborate *Analysis* was prepared for it by the late senior editor of this Cyclopædia, the Rev. Dr. John M'Clintock. Editions innumerable have been published of the *Institutes*, with the *Analysis*, both in this country and in England (1st edition Lond. 1822–1828, in 6 parts; N. Y. 2 vols. 8vo; Nashville, Tenn., 1 vol. 8vo). There is also a compilation of Methodist doctrines, entitled *Wesleyana: a System of Wesleyan Theology* (N. Y. 12mo). See also *Meth. Qu. Rev.* 1853, Jan. p. 136 sq.; *North. Amer. Rev.* 1865, April, p. 593 sq.; *Wesleyan Meth. Magazine*, 1866, Feb.; *Good Words*, 1866, Jan.; *Lond. Qu. Rev.* Oct. 1872; D. D. Whedon, in the *Bibliotheca Sacra*, April, 1862; J. T. Peck, in the *Meth. Qu. Rev.* April, 1870; J. Porter, in the *Meth. Qu. Rev.* 1871; D. A. Whedon, in the *Meth. Qu. Rev.* Jan. 1868, and April, 1870; D. D. Whedon, in the *Meth. Qu. Rev.* 1866, p. 124, 276, 312, 443; 1872, April and Oct. art. iii; 1873, Jan. p. 138 sq.; *Lond. Rev.* Oct. 1854, art. v; *North Brit. Rev.* 1852, Feb.; *Ch. Examiner*, vol. iv; *North Brit. Rev.* xxxii, 269; Newell Culver, *Methodism Forty Years Ago and Now* (N. Y. 1873, 18mo); Malcom, *Theological Index*, s. v.; and the excellent *Catalogue of the Boston Library* (2d or consolidated edition, July, 1873). Dr. Abel Stevens, in his *Hist. of Methodism*, reckons that at least 1500 titles would be required to make up a fair bibliography of Methodism. The Rev. William F. Warren, D.D., in his *Systematische Theologie einheitlich behandelt* (Bremen, 1865, 8vo), besides giving the position of Methodism in systematic theology somewhat in detail, has furnished a very elaborate compilation of Methodist literature, which is quite complete up to the time of the publication of his book; it covers p. 168–186. In England, Dr. Osborn prepared a treatise on the literature of the Wesleyans (Lond. 1868, 8vo). Very recently a work was commenced by the Rev. Dr. Sulzberger, of Frankfort-on-the-Main, which is intended to be a full treatment of Methodist doctrinal theology for the use, especially, of German students. Vol. i appeared in 1873.

Methodist Episcopal Church, THE, is the official title of the largest body of Methodists in the United States, with branches in different parts of the world.

I. *Organization.*—This title was assumed by the American Methodists as a distinct body at what is historically known as the "Christmas Conference," which commenced its session on Friday, Dec. 24, 1784, and was continued through Christmas week, and until the second day of the new year. Previous to this period the American Methodists had constituted *societies*, like those in Great Britain, in connection with and under the jurisdiction of the Rev. John Wesley, whom they all alike reverenced and obeyed as their spiritual father and head. The first Methodist service in America is believed to have been held in the year 1766, in the city of New York, by Philip Embury, an Irish immigrant and local preacher, a carpenter by trade, who was moved thereto by the stirring appeals of Barbara Heck, an Irishwoman, whose name is illustrious in the annals of the denomination. Thomas Webb, a captain in the British army, who was then staying in America, Robert Strawbridge, and Robert Williams, all local preachers, were, with Embury, the prosecutors of the work thus begun, until, in the autumn of 1769, Richard Boardman and Joseph Pilmoor arrived at Philadelphia as missionaries sent out by Mr. Wesley. Seven others afterwards came; but the entire service of all Wesley's missionaries in the colonies was less than twenty-eight years, leaving out of the account Francis Asbury, who alone of them remained in the country during the Revolutionary War, and who became the apostle and bishop of the Church. Though several of them were not fortunate in their associations with their American brethren, two soon becoming Presbyterians, a third, by his active Toryism, causing grave scandal and even persecution, and none, except Asbury, staying long, they, as a whole, by their labors, zeal, and adherence to the well-proved Wesleyan discipline, were instrumental in settling the cause upon a firm basis, and raising up scores of native preachers to carry on the work.

The first Conference, held in 1773, presided over by Rankin as superintendent, consisted of ten members, all Europeans, with an aggregate in the societies of 1160. In May, 1784, eleven years later, notwithstanding all the adverse influences of the war, they numbered 14,988 members, several hundred local preachers and exhorters, 84 itinerant preachers, with more than sixty chapels, and probably not less than 200,000 attendants upon their worship. By the system of itinerancy, which had been rigidly enforced during this period, Methodism had been prevented from localizing itself, and had established organized societies in every state of the Union outside of New England, become the dominant, popular, religious power in Maryland and Delaware, and at several points planted its standard beyond the Alleghanies. Though thus widely spread, nearly nine tenths of its membership were south of Mason and Dixon's line, and of these a large proportion were in the Middle States, where the Anglican, or the English Established Church, once so flourishing, had become nearly extinct.

Most of the Methodists of 1784 were without the sacraments; for the English clergy upon whom they had generally depended had, with few exceptions, either left the country or forsaken their parishes. Thousands had been received into the societies without baptism; their children were growing up without that sacred rite; and preachers were ministering in their pulpits who had never even partaken of the Lord's Supper. The growing necessity for some provision for the administration of the sacraments had led to so serious thought and discussion in successive Conferences that the regular session of 1779, deeming the exigency sufficient to warrant a departure from ecclesiastical usage, constituted four of their number a presbytery, who with solemn forms proceeded to ordain one another, and afterwards others of their brethren. At the end of a year the sacramental party yielded to the minority for peace' sake; the administration of the sacraments was suspended; and it was agreed to seek the counsel of Wesley, and abide by his judgment. He advised them to "continue on the old plan until further direction." Wesley found for his American societies no way of relief until subsequent to the conclusion of the war. Then, after long and mature thought, and consultation with his friends, among whom was Fletcher, the saintly vicar of Madeley, he resolved to use the power which he believed himself as a presbyter to possess, and ordain a ministry that should meet the demands of the thousands who sought aid from him as their spiritual founder. He proposed to the Rev. Thomas Coke, LL.D., to receive ordination at his hands as their superintendent, to which Coke, whose sympathies were profoundly stirred in their behalf, consented, when study and reflection had convinced him of Wesley's power to ordain to the Episcopal office. It was also arranged that two of the English preachers should be ordained to accompany him as elders. Accordingly, on the first day of September, 1784, at Bristol, using the convenient and solemn forms of the Church of England, and, assisted by Dr. Coke and the Rev. Thomas Creighton, a presbyter of the English Church, Wesley ordained Richard Whatcoat and Thomas Vasey to the office of deacon. On the next day he ordained them elders, and, assisted by Creighton and Whatcoat, he also ordained Coke superintendent, or bishop, as this officer was afterwards called. He then sent them upon their mission, with instructions to organize the societies into a distinct Church, and to ordain Asbury joint superintendent with Coke. To facilitate their work, he furnished them with a "Sunday Service," or liturgy, a collection of psalms and hymns, and also "The Articles of Religion." Upon their arrival in America, a special conference or convention of the itinerant preachers was summoned, and on the 24th of December sixty of them assembled in the Lovely Lane Chapel, in the city of Baltimore. Dr. Coke took the chair, and presented the following letter from Wesley, written eight days after the ordinations, and tersely stating the grounds of what he had done and advised:

"*To Dr. Coke, Mr. Asbury, and our Brethren in North America:*

"By a very uncommon train of providences, many of the provinces of North America are totally disjoined from their mother country, and erected into independent states. The English government has no authority over them, either civil or ecclesiastical, any more than over the states of Holland. A civil authority is exercised over them, partly by the Congress and partly by the provincial assemblies; but no one either exercises or claims any ecclesiastical authority at all. In this peculiar situation, some thousands of the inhabitants of these states desire my advice; and, in compliance with their desire, I have drawn up a little sketch.

"Lord King's Account of the Primitive Church convinced me, many years ago, that bishops and presbyters are the same order, and consequently have the same right to ordain. For many years I have been importuned, from time to time, to exercise this right, by ordaining part of our travelling preachers. But I have still refused, not only for peace' sake, but because I was determined as little as possible to violate the established order of the National Church, to which I belonged.

"But the case is widely different between England and North America. Here there are bishops who have a legal jurisdiction. In America there are none, neither any parish ministers; so that for some hundred miles together there is none either to baptize or to administer the Lord's Supper. Here, therefore, my scruples are at an end, and I conceive myself at full liberty, as I violate no order and invade no man's right, by appointing and sending laborers into the harvest.

"I have accordingly appointed Dr. Coke and Mr. Francis Asbury to be joint superintendents over our brethren in North America, as also Richard Whatcoat and Thomas Vasey to act as elders among them, by baptizing and ministering the Lord's Supper. And I have prepared a liturgy, little differing from that of the Church of England (I think, the best constituted national Church in the world), which I advise all the travelling preachers to use on the Lord's day in all the congregations, reading the litany only on Wednesdays and Fridays, and praying extempore on all other days. I also advise the elders to administer the Supper of the Lord on every Lord's day.

"If any one will point out a more rational and script-

ural way of feeding and guiding those poor sheep in the wilderness, I will gladly embrace it. At present I cannot see any better method than that I have taken.

"It has indeed been proposed to desire the English bishops to ordain part of our preachers for America; but to this I object: (1.) I desired the bishop of London to ordain only one; but could not prevail. (2.) If they consented, we know the slowness of their proceedings; but the matter admits of no delay. (3.) If they would ordain them now, they would likewise expect to govern them; and how grievously would this entangle us! (4.) As our American brethren are now totally disentangled both from the state and from the English hierarchy, we dare not entangle them again, either with the one or the other. They are now at full liberty simply to follow the Scriptures and the Primitive Church. And we judge it best that they should stand fast in that liberty wherewith God has so strangely made them free."

After the reading and consideration of this document, it was, without a single dissenting voice, regularly and formally "agreed to form a Methodist Episcopal Church, in which the liturgy (as presented by the Rev. John Wesley) should be read, and the sacraments be administered by a superintendent, elders, and deacons, who shall be ordained by a presbytery, using the Episcopal form, as prescribed in the Rev. Mr. Wesley's Prayer-book;" or, in the language of the Minutes of the Conference, "following the counsel of Mr. John Wesley, who recommended the Episcopal mode of government, we thought it best to become an Episcopal Church, making the Episcopal office elective, and the elected superintendent, or bishop, amenable to the body of ministers and preachers." Asbury refused the high office to which Wesley had appointed him unless it were ratified by the Conference, and, in accordance with the act of organization, both he and Coke were formally and unanimously elected superintendents. On the second day of the session, Asbury was ordained deacon, elder on the third, and superintendent on the fourth, Coke being assisted by Whatcoat and Vasey in the services, and also in the last by Otterbein, a personal friend of Asbury, and a minister in the German Reformed Church. The "Sunday Service" and "Articles" prepared by Wesley were adopted; the Rules and Discipline were revised and adapted to the new order of things; the establishment of a college was resolved upon; twelve preachers were ordained elders, and one deacon, and the work of the Conference was done.

Different views have been taken of these transactions, though not among Methodists. On the one hand it is held that Wesley did not ordain Coke as bishop, but to an undefined superintendency; that he found fault with Asbury for assuming to be a bishop; that he did not intend the separation of his societies from the Church of England, or an authority by his ordinations to administer the sacraments. The view taken by Methodist writers may be stated as follows: 1. Wesley's letter, above quoted, shows his understanding of the condition of those in whose behalf he acted. Their one great demand was some provision for the sacraments, and this he proposed to answer, not only for the time being, but in perpetuity forever. The Church of England had ceased to exist in the United States, so that he violated no law or regulation of that Church in what he might do for America. He provided for no separation, for there was nothing left to separate from. By the terms of the letter, Whatcoat and Vasey, whom he ordained, were to administer the sacraments, as they proceeded to do immediately after their arrival. He intended the step taken to obviate forever all necessity for any connection of American Methodism with the English hierarchy. The liturgy which he prepared, with the forms used in the English Church for ordinations to the three distinct offices of the ministry, indicates his intent that the three offices should be perpetuated in the Methodist Episcopal Church. To him the name was not important, but the function was. He therefore said "superintendent" and "elder," instead of bishop and presbyter—more modest titles, perhaps, but the same in import; and any newly-elected superintendent was to be presented to the superintendent "to be ordained." 2. For forty years Mr.

Wesley had believed that bishops and presbyters constituted but one order, with the same right to ordain. He knew that for two centuries the succession of bishops in the Church of Alexandria was preserved through ordination by presbyters alone. "I firmly believe," he said, "I am a scriptural $\dot{\epsilon}\pi\acute{\iota}\sigma\kappa\sigma\pi\sigma\varsigma$, as much as any man in England or in Europe; for the uninterrupted succession I know to be a fable which no man ever did or can prove;" but he also held that "neither Christ nor his apostles prescribe any particular form of Church government." He was a true bishop of the flock which God had given to his care. He had hitherto refused "to exercise this right" of ordaining, because he would not come into needless conflict with the order of the English Church to which he belonged. But after the Revolution, his ordaining for America would violate no law of the Church; and when the necessity was clearly apparent, his hesitation ceased. "There does not appear," he said, " any other way of supplying them with ministers." Having formed his purpose, in February, 1784, he invited Dr. Coke to his study in City Road, laid the case before him, and proposed to ordain and send him to America. Coke was startled at first, doubting Wesley's right to ordain him, though why, if the ordination were not to the office of bishop, the next higher to that which he already held, is inexplicable. He finally assented, and wrote, "The power of ordaining others should be received by me from you, by the imposition of your hands." 3. History records no other plan as proposed than that of an Episcopal organization. This is what was laid before the few preachers called for counsel immediately after Coke's arrival in America. The title assumed by the Church is "Episcopal." The Minutes of the organization say that this was done, "following the counsels of Mr. John Wesley, who recommended the Episcopal mode of Church government, making the Episcopal office elective, and the elected superintendent, or bishop, amenable to the body of ministers and preachers;" and he had no reproof for the statement or the title, though the document was printed under his eye. The Minutes of 1789 say of him: "Preferring the Episcopal mode of Church government, he set apart Thomas Coke for the Episcopal office, and having delivered to him letters of Episcopal orders, directed him to set apart Francis Asbury for the same Episcopal office, in consequence of which the said Francis Asbury was solemnly set apart for the said Episcopal office," which statements Wesley never disputed, and none of these things did he condemn. If Coke and the Methodists of that day misunderstood or exceeded his intentions and acts, that he took no pains to correct their error is the strangest and most unaccountable thing of all. 4. The language of Charles Wesley is to the point. He certainly knew what was done, and the intention in doing it. He says that his brother "assumed the Episcopal character, ordained elders, consecrated a bishop, and sent him to ordain our lay preachers in America." He wrote bitterly to his brother John of Coke's "Methodist Episcopal Church in Baltimore," of the readiness of the London preachers to receive orders from him, of Coke's ambition and rashness. Coke distinctly said, after his return to England, that "he had done nothing but under the direction of Mr. Wesley;" and Wesley replied to Charles that Coke "has done nothing rashly." Silence in such circumstances becomes assent. 5. Wesley, then, intended an Episcopal Church. But an Episcopal Church must have an Episcopacy, and therefore an $\dot{\epsilon}\pi\iota\sigma\kappa\sigma\pi\sigma\varsigma$, bishop, or superintendent, names alike in signification. He preferred the latter, as did Coke, who spoke in his sermon at Asbury's ordination of "our bishops, or superintendents, as we rather call them." When it began to be applied as a personal title to the incumbents of the office, Wesley wrote, "How can you, how dare you, suffer yourself to be called bishop?" though he well knew that an Episcopal Church must have its bishop. To the title, not to the thing, he did object, and most strongly, for as it met him in England, its

pomp and pretentiousness were far removed from that character of simplicity which he had so laboriously stamped upon Methodism. "I study to be little," he truly said in the same letter; but when he added, "You study to be great," he took counsel of his fears, and showed how little he knew the real character of Asbury, to whom he was writing. The truth is, he made a bishop, and called him superintendent. American Methodists early saw fit to sometimes use the other word. 6. "The eldership is by scriptural precedent, and by the natural course of things, as embodying the mass of the mature ministry, the main body and trunk of the ministerial strength and power. As such it is naturally and crudely the undeveloped one order. Just as, naturally, and by sacred precedent and expediency, it reserves the diaconate order as its preparatory pupilage, so it flowers up into the Episcopacy as its concentrated representative order. Fundamentally, there may thus be one order; subsidiarily, a second order; and derivatively, yet superior in function, a third order. The ordership and organic permanence is constituted in all three cases, according to sacred precedent, by ordination. The highest of the three orders is especially, as it happens, perpetuated by a series of ordaining hands, passing from predecessor to successor, bishop authenticating bishop, as elder does not authenticate elder, or deacon, deacon. Hence, though, as derivative, it is in origin less an order, and an inferior order, yet, as constituted, it becomes more distinctively an order than either of the other two. The New Testament furnishes, indeed, no decisive precedent of an ordained and permanently fixed superpresbyterial order; but it does furnish classes and instances of men exercising superpresbyterial authority, so that pure and perfect parity of office is not divinely enjoined. Such classes and cases are the apostles, perhaps the evangelists, St. James of Jerusalem, and Timothy and Titus. . . . Wesley held that the episcopate and eldership were so one order that the power constituting an Episcopal order inhered in the eldership; but he did not believe that there lay in the eldership a right to exercise that power without a true providential and divine call. Hence, in his Episcopal diploma given to Coke, he announces, 'I, John Wesley, think myself providentially CALLED at this time to set apart,' etc." (D. D. Whedon, Meth. Quar. Rev. Oct. 1871, p. 676.)

II. Doctrines.—1. The "Articles of Religion" prepared by Wesley for the new Church, twenty-four in number, are an abridgment of the Thirty-nine Articles of the Church of England. Fifteen of the latter are entirely omitted, and several others considerably amended. While all traces of Calvinism, as well as of Romish leanings, are carefully eliminated, there is no insertion of Wesley's Arminianism, or of his doctrines of the "Witness of the Spirit" and "Christian Perfection." Several important protests against Pelagian, Romish, and other errors, are retained, as are also, in substance, those articles which are in accordance with the sentiments of the universal Church. On the Trinity, the person and work of Christ, the Holy Spirit, the Scripture canon, original sin, free will, justification by faith, vicarious atonement, and good works, they speak clearly and in the most orthodox language. The design was to provide a broad and liberal platform upon which the great body of Christians who hold the essentials of Christianity might stand together in love and charity. With a few verbal changes, and the insertion of one new article (the twenty-third), they stand as they were adopted in 1784; and from the year 1832 it has been placed beyond the power of the Church to "revoke, alter, or change" them. See ARTICLES, TWENTY-FIVE, of the Methodist Episcopal Church.

2. The theology of the Church is thoroughly Arminian, as it has been from the beginning. In this it agrees with universal Wesleyan Methodism. It has been stoutly and bitterly accused of Pelagianism by those who formed their estimate of Arminianism from the writings of men who received a part only of that

system, and incorporated with it other and objectionable principles, rather than from a familiarity with the views of Arminius himself. The articles on "Original Sin" and "Free Will" should forever have saved it from that reproach. Wesley's doctrinal sermons, Notes on the New Testament, and other writings, have been its standards of Arminian orthodoxy, while the rigid examination to which all candidates for the ministry are subjected is its chief security that only what is deemed correct and sound in doctrine shall be preached in its pulpits.

3. Wesley's doctrine of the "Witness of the Spirit," known to many by the term "Assurance," holds an important place in the system of the Church. He defines it as "an inward impression on the soul, whereby the Spirit of God immediately and directly witnesses to my spirit that I am a child of God; that Jesus Christ hath loved me, and given himself for me; that all my sins are blotted out, and I, even I, am reconciled to God;" and to effect this persuasion, he supposes that the Holy Spirit "works upon the soul by his immediate influence, and by a strong though inexplicable operation." The possession of this assurance is taught to be the privilege of all believers, and penitents are diligently instructed not to rest until it is received; while it is a constant theme in the pulpit and the social meeting. Such is the emphasis practically placed upon it.

4. Sanctification, or "Christian Perfection," as Wesley preferred to style it, is a doctrine of all Methodism, and is firmly held by the Church. It teaches no state attainable in this life like that of the angels, or of Adam in Paradise, or in which there is an exemption from mistakes, ignorance, infirmities, or temptations; and, positively, that all saints may by faith be so filled with the love of God that all the powers of the soul shall be recovered from the abnormal, perverted, sinful condition, and, together with the outward conduct, be controlled in entire harmony with love. See METHODISM.

III. *Government.* — 1. The *General Conference*, the highest of the five judicatories of the Church, assembles on the first day of May in every fourth year, and is the only legislative body of the denomination. As in the Christmas Conference, it was for many years, constructively at least, an assembly of the whole ministry; but their increasing number, the impossibility of a general attendance from the constantly-extending field, and the felt necessity of settling the doctrinal and ecclesiastical systems upon a basis less easily changed, led to the arrangement, in 1808, that thenceforth it should be composed of ministerial delegates from the several Annual Conferences, acting under certain clearly-defined restrictions. These restrictive rules, or articles, as they are termed, have been modified from time to time, though the most important change was effected in 1872, providing for the introduction of laymen into the body, with equal powers with the clergy. The General Conference now (1873) consists of one minister for every forty-five members of each Annual Conference, chosen by the clergy, and two laymen, chosen by lay electors from the several Quarterly Conferences within the same territory. The regulations defining its functions are as follows: "The General Conference shall have full powers to make rules and regulations for our Church, under the following limitations and restrictions, namely:

"I. The General Conference shall not alter, revoke, or change our Articles of Religion, nor establish any new standards or rules of doctrine contrary to our present existing and established standards of doctrine.

"II. They shall not allow of more than one ministerial representative for every fourteen members of the Annual Conference, nor allow of a less number than one for every forty-five, nor more than two lay delegates for any Annual Conference; *provided*, nevertheless, that when there shall be in any Annual Conference a fraction of two thirds the number which shall be fixed for the ratio of representation, such Annual Conference shall be entitled to an additional delegate for such fraction; and *provided*, also, that no Conference shall be denied the privilege of one delegate.

"III. They shall not change or alter any part or rule of our government, so as to do away Episcopacy, or destroy the plan of our itinerant general superintendency; but may appoint a missionary bishop or superintendent for any of our foreign missions, limiting his jurisdiction to the same respectively.

"IV. They shall not revoke or change the General Rules of the united societies.

"V. They shall not do away the privileges of our ministers or preachers of trial by a committee, and of an appeal; neither shall they do away the privileges of our members of trial before the society, or by a committee, and of an appeal.

"VI. They shall not appropriate the produce of the Book Concern, nor of the Charter Fund, to any purpose other than for the benefit of the travelling, supernumerary, superannuated, and worn-out preachers, their wives, widows, and children.

Provided, nevertheless, that upon the concurrent recommendation of three fourths of all the members of the several Annual Conferences who shall be present and vote on such recommendation, then a majority of two thirds of the General Conference succeeding shall suffice to alter any of the above restrictions excepting. the first article; and also, whenever such alteration or alterations shall have been first recommended by two thirds of the General Conference, so soon as three fourths of the members of all the Annual Conferences shall have concurred as aforesaid, such alteration or alterations shall take effect."

These *Restrictive Rules*, together with the *Articles of Religion* and the *General Rules* [see METHODISM], are commonly held to be the Constitution of the Church. They make the General Conference supreme in authority, with entire supervision over all the interests and work of the denomination, and the bond of the whole connectional system. It elects the bishops and other general officers; the bishops, who are its presiding officers, but not members of the body, are subject to its direction, and answerable to it for their moral as well as official conduct.

2. The *Judicial Conference* is instituted for the trial of bishops who may be accused of wrong-doing, and of appeals of convicted members of an Annual Conference. The Annual Conferences severally elect annually seven "Triers of Appeals." In case of an appeal, the triers from three Conferences contiguous to that whose decision is appealed from, constitute the Judicial Conference, whose action is final, except that all decisions of questions of law are reviewed by the General Conference. For the trial of an accused bishop, the triers from five neighboring Conferences are necessary.

3. The *Annual Conference* is composed wholly of travelling preachers. It selects the place of its sessions, the bishops appointing the time, and presiding. It possesses no legislative power: its functions are purely administrative. It holds the power of discipline over its own members, inquiring annually into the Christian character and ministerial efficiency of each by name. It gathers the ecclesiastical statistics of its several societies, though its jurisdiction is over the ministers, rather than over the churches. The proceedings and action of this body, as recorded in its journal, are reviewed by the General Conference, to which it is subject.

4. The *District Conference* embraces the churches of a presiding elder's district, and is composed of the pastors, local preachers, exhorters, and one steward and Sunday-school superintendent from each pastoral charge. It licenses local preachers, recommends them to the Annual Conference for orders or for admission on trial, and holds jurisdiction over them; it is also charged with a general supervision of the temporal and spiritual affairs of the district. Specifically, it inquires into the work of Sunday-schools, forms plans for the occupation of new fields within its territory, and promotes attention to the charities of the Church.

5. The *Quarterly Conference* is limited to a single pastoral charge, over which it exercises entire supervision, subject to the provisions of the Discipline. Its members are the pastor, local preachers, exhorters, stewards, and class-leaders, together with the trustees and Sunday-school superintendent, if members of the Church. Besides the functions of the District Conference, which devolve upon it where no District Conference is held, it inquires carefully into the condition and work of every department of the local society.

6. The *Leaders' and Stewards' Meeting*, presided over by the pastor, and consisting of all the class-leaders and stewards of his charge, is usually held monthly, for the purpose of inquiring after the sick, needy, and any that, by neglect of the means of grace or by incorrect life, may need the admonitions of good discipline. The meeting recommends probationers for reception into the Church, as also candidates for license to exhort or preach. See LEADERS' MEETINGS.

7. The legislation of 1784 gave new force to the essential features which Rankin and Asbury, who had been trained in the school and under the eye of Wesley, had stamped upon the American societies. Evangelization and supervision, the former to extend the work, the latter to secure and build up what had been won, were fundamental in the methods then adopted, as they were in the measures of Wesley. The bishops were chief evangelists, almost plenary in power, yet sharing with the humblest in fare and labor, inspecting the local societies and classes, meeting leaders and trustees, and holding themselves responsible for even the details of the work throughout the denomination. The preacher in charge of a circuit was the bishop's "assistant," and the other preachers of the circuit were the assistant's "helpers," and under his direction. In still closer contact with the membership was the class-leader, appointed by the assistant, and in his subordinate sphere of pastorship aiding him by watching over the little band while he might be in other parts of the circuit. This "military regimen," as the historian of the Church has styled it, very remote from a democracy, which, indeed, it never pretended to be, gave surprising vigor to all the movements of the system. In all the modifications which have been from time to time effected, and the numerous limitations of power which the ministry have imposed upon themselves, these features of evangelization and supervision have been steadily maintained. The bishop presides in the Conferences; forms the districts according to his judgment; appoints the preachers to their fields, allowing none to remain more than three years in succession in the same charge, except the presiding elders, who may remain four years, and a few others specially designated; ordains; travels through the connection at large, and oversees, in accordance with the prescribed regulations of the General Conference, to which he is subject, the spiritual and temporal business of the Church. The bishops are not diocesan, but have a joint jurisdiction over the whole Church, constituting an "itinerant general superintendency." The arrangement and division of their work is annually made by themselves, giving to each his portion (though their respective residences are assigned by the General Conference), and for its faithful and orderly performance they are responsible to the General Conference. See EPISCOPACY; ITINERANCY.

8. Ordinations of preachers were at first designed simply to supply the sacraments to the societies, and soon an elder came for this purpose to be placed in charge of a district containing several circuits. Thus originated the office of presiding elder, a sub-episcopate, with duties of oversight and administration indispensable in the system of the Church. Their constant travel through their districts, their presidency in the Quarterly Conferences, and familiarity with both churches and pastors, enabled the presiding elders to give the bishop the information and counsel necessary for the best adjustment of the appointments. In this work usage has made them his advisers, or, in more popular phrase, his "cabinet," though without authority of law. The wisdom of the Church has judged it best that the sole responsibility of the appointments shall be with the Episcopacy.

9. Admission into an Annual Conference is preceded by a two years' probation in the itinerant work, and a rigid examination in a prescribed course of study; and all preachers thus admitted as members are ordained deacons, and in two years more, on the completion of the required studies, they are ordained elders. It devolves upon the former to "administer baptism, solemnize matrimony, assist the elder in administering the Lord's Supper, and to do all the duties of a travelling preacher;" and upon the latter, in addition to these, to "administer the Lord's Supper" and to "conduct divine worship." But an elder, deacon, or preacher may be in charge of a circuit or station, with no difference in function except in the matter of the sacraments. He is the chief executive officer of the local society, charged to "take care" of its interests in accordance with the provisions of the Discipline, and is responsible to the Annual Conference both for the proper discharge of his duties and for his moral conduct. While he is the pastor of the flock, sub-pastors, denominated class-leaders, are charged with the oversight of small bodies of the membership, whom they are to meet weekly "for social and religious worship, for instruction, encouragement, and admonition." The local preachers, without a share in the government of the Church, except in the District and Quarterly Conferences, constitute a lay ministry, a corps of self-supporting evangelists, numerically larger than the travelling preachers, which has been of great efficiency. See LAY MINISTRY. All churches and parsonages are the property of the local society, held by trustees chosen in accordance with the law of the state or territory wherever a specific mode is required, and otherwise by the Quarterly Conference.

10. Admission to membership in the Church is preceded by a probation of at least six months, during which period the candidate has opportunity for acquiring that familiarity with the Church, its doctrines, rules, and usages, which enables him to intelligently assume the obligations of a member therein. The one preliminary condition for reception on trial is "a desire to flee from the wrath to come, and to be saved from their sins," which is expected to show itself by such fruits as are specified in the General Rules. Genuine spiritual life is more carefully sought than rigid dogmatic orthodoxy, the only test of the latter sort being "the doctrines of holy Scripture, as set forth in the Articles of Religion," which, as shown above, embrace little more than the fundamentals of Christian doctrine as accepted by evangelical churches. The probationer, having been previously baptized, and also recommended by the Leaders' and Stewards' Meeting, or by his leader if there is no such meeting, may be received into the Church upon giving assurance in presence of the Church of his doctrinal belief as just expressed, his purpose to observe and keep the rules of the Church, and to contribute of his worldly goods, according to his ability, for the support of its institutions. Nevertheless, persons coming from other orthodox churches are received at once into full fellowship without the usual probation.

IV. *History and Progress.*—Under this head we propose to give a rapid sketch of the work performed by the Methodist Episcopal Church and its gradual growth, noting, as we pass, its relations to public questions, its changes of internal economy, and the principal controversies that have grown up from time to time, with their effects.

1. *Pioneer Work.*—"Methodism presented itself to the new nation," says Stevens, "an Episcopal Church, with all the necessary functions and functionaries of such a body; the only one, of Protestant denomination, now in the nation, for the colonial fragments of the English Establishment had not yet been reorganized." Led by Coke and Asbury, the little band of itinerants went forth to their self-sacrificing toils with a new sense of consolidation and certainty, and feeling in their souls, as they said, that they were "raised up to reform the continent, and to spread scriptural holiness over these lands." Under the new system, the eucharist was immediately administered to thousands of disciples who had never partaken of it, and large numbers of both adults and children were baptized, scores of the latter receiving the rite at a single meeting. The work ex-

tended in every direction. The post of hardship and severity was the post of honor. Going in the true spirit of evangelists, with the conviction that they had "nothing to do but to save souls," they not only held and strengthened the fields already won, but pressed on to the regions beyond, continually forming new circuits, and proclaiming their message wherever men would hear—in churches, in barns and log-cabins, in the forest and highway. They crossed the mountains, and kept pace with the constantly-advancing frontier; they penetrated Canada, and established themselves in New England and Nova Scotia. Gown, and band, and prayer-book were too cumbersome for their use, and were soon laid aside. The system was providentially adapted to self-propagation. "Its class and prayer meetings trained most, if not all, the laity to practical missionary labor, and three or four of them, meeting in any distant part of the earth by the emigrations of these times, were prepared immediately to become the nucleus of a Church. The lay or local ministry, borne on by the tide of population, were almost everywhere found, prior to the arrival of regular preachers, ready to sustain religious services—the pioneers of the Church in every new field." Such was their success that in sixteen years, at the end of the century, their 15,000 members had become 64,894, and the 84 itinerants had increased to 287, not counting the scores who had fallen out of their ranks from pure physical inability to endure the terrible severity of the system, but were still working nobly in their local sphere. Bishop Coke's stay in the country at his first visit was but five months, a fair type of his subsequent visits. After 1787 his Episcopal work was limited to ordinations, presiding in Conference when present, itinerating through the country, and preaching, the stationing of the preachers being left with bishop Asbury.

Coke threw himself with zeal into the work of raising funds for the college at Abingdon, Md., whose cornerstone Asbury laid three days after his first departure for Europe. In 1789 he stood with Asbury in the presence of Washington, presenting to him, in behalf of the Church, a congratulatory address upon his inauguration as president, approving the recently-adopted Federal Constitution, and professing allegiance to the government. The Methodist Episcopal Church was the first ecclesiastical body to recognise the Constitution of the United States, and, in its article afterwards adopted, it declared its faith that they are a "sovereign and independent nation," rather than a confederacy of sovereign states. Coke's indefatigable labors in travelling and preaching in behalf of the cause of education, and for the emancipation of slaves, show him worthy of his high position. Yet Asbury was the chief apostle of the Church, giving it his entire energies, becoming an example to his brethren in labors and sacrifices, and carefully attending to even the most minute and local details, meeting classes, trustees, and often visiting pastorally from house to house. He instituted in 1786, in Virginia, the first Sunday-school in America, and four years later the Conference ordered Sunday-schools to be established for the instruction of poor children, white and black, in "learning and piety," being the first American Church to recognise this institution. Official attention was given as early as 1788 to the publication of books, a "book steward" being appointed; and a borrowed capital of six hundred dollars became the foundation of the future "Book Concern." Additional legislation from time to time, as necessity demanded, gave greater efficiency and solidity to the body, but innovations upon well-tried methods found no favor.

2. *Early Secessions.*—As early as 1792, James O'Kelly introduced into the Conference a resolution permitting a preacher who might feel aggrieved by the appointment assigned him, to "appeal to the Conference and state his objections," and requiring the bishop, if his objections were found valid, to appoint him to another circuit. The proposition was lost by a large majority;

but the defeat cost the Church the secession of the mover with a few other preachers and a large number of members, who ultimately styled themselves "the Christian Church."

Attempts were made in 1800 to make the presiding eldership elective in the Annual Conferences, to introduce the English method of making the appointments by requiring them to be read in open session, "to hear what the Conference may have to say on each station," and to aid the bishop in making the appointments by a committee of preachers chosen by the Conference for the purpose; but they signally failed, though some of them were revived in subsequent years.

3. *Early Emancipation Movements.*—The most vexing question of those early, as well as of later times, was that of *slavery.* The Methodist preachers of those days were thoroughly hostile to the institution. At the organization of the Church they pronounced it "contrary to the golden law of God and the unalienable rights of mankind, as well as every principle of the Revolution;" and their enactments required all members holding slaves to set them free, wherever it could be legally done, and forbade all future admission of slaveholders into the Church or to the Lord's Supper, while all who might buy or sell slaves were "immediately to be expelled, unless they buy them on purpose to free them."* Could they have looked forward a century, and seen that either the Gospel or the sword must solve the problem of slavery, these men who believed themselves divinely sent to "reform the continent," would surely, with their clear convictions on the subject, not have failed to discern that it was a part of their mission to destroy the great crime of the nation, and they would doubtless have maintained the high ground they had so firmly taken. But they compromised with the evil because of the great embarrassments attending the execution of their rules, which in six months were suspended, never again to be enforced. Yet the Church was always anti-slavery. Its preachers, holding "the power of the keys," effected the liberation of thousands of slaves kept by those who sought admission into its fold. The Discipline never ceased to pronounce a condemnation upon the system; and, from 1804, it perpetually asked, "What shall be done for the extirpation of the evil of slavery?" while successive General Conferences sought by legislation, addresses to the Church, and measures for memorials to the state Legislatures, to remove and abolish it.

4. *Completed Organization.*—The absences of Dr. Coke in Europe rendering an additional bishop necessary, Richard Whatcoat was elected to that office in 1800, as was William M'Kendree in 1808, the first native American elevated to the episcopate.

The latter year is the epoch of the plan of a *delegated General Conference*, adopted to "preserve, strengthen, and perpetuate the union of the connection," and to render "the doctrine, form of government, and General Rules, sacred and inviolable." The "Council" devised by the bishops, composed of themselves and the presiding elders, had proved abortive after two trials, and the General Conference, as then constituted, practically placed the doctrinal and administrative systems of the denomination in the power of the more centrally located ministers. The new plan was conservative of every fundamental principle of the Church, and at the same

* The General Rule on Slavery *certainly* existed in May, 1787, and was *probably* written by Wesley, brought over by Coke, and adopted by the Christmas Conference. Elliott so holds without the "probably." Neither Articles nor Rules were printed in the Discipline till 1789, nor the Articles till 1790. In 1789 was issued the "fifth edition" of the "Discipline," "considered and approved" in 1784. That of 1792 was "*revised* and approved." But the edition of 1789 has the Rule on Slavery with Wesley's rules, and is dated "May 27, 1787." In 1785 Asbury and Dickens changed "the order and arrangement" of the Discipline. April 25, 1786, Asbury read it in manuscript arranged in "sections;" but it was not published till May, 1787, when it had received the sanction of Coke, who had been absent from June, 1785, to March, 1787.

time gave to the remotest Conference equal power with the most central, in proportion to its number of ministers. The first session, held in 1812, was composed of 90 members, representing 688 preachers, and a membership of 195,357; the sixteenth, held in 1872, was composed of 421 members, 292 clerical and 129 lay, representing, according to the Minutes of 1871, 9699 travelling preachers, 11,382 local preachers, and 1,421,323 members and probationers. Taking a fresh departure with the adoption of this measure, the Church pressed forwards in its practical work with added zeal.

5. *Denominational Institutions.* — The Book Concern, already (in 1804) removed from Philadelphia to New York, multiplied its publications, and scattered a vigorous Methodist literature through the circuits by the agency of the preachers. They were too busy to make books, but they could sell them, and thus educate a people trained in the truth as they received it. In 1818 the *Methodist Magazine* was started—the beginning of the periodical literature of the denomination. It is now known as the *Methodist Quarterly Review*, one of the ablest of the quarterlies, with the largest circulation of all. The first weekly, *The Christian Advocate,* was issued in 1826, though *Zion's Herald*, under the auspices of New England Methodists, preceded it nearly four years, and in its second half-century it is full of beauty and power. A second publishing-house was established in 1820 in Cincinnati; and depositories are located in several of the principal cities of the country. The increase of the business led in 1833 to a removal from Crosby Street, in New York, where it had been carried on for nine years, to Mulberry Street. The whole establishment was swept away by fire early in 1836, at a loss of at least a quarter of a million. New and better buildings soon rose on the same spot, which, with their subsequent additions, have been used as a manufactory of the house since the date of the removal of the principal office to its present location (805 Broadway), procured for it and the Missionary Society at the cost of about a million dollars. Its entire capital in 1873 was $1,052,448. There is also a " Western Methodist Book Concern," with a capital of $467,419.

To the relief of worn-out and needy preachers, and the widows and orphans of preachers, the denomination has always been attentive. At first, in 1784, the preachers themselves instituted a " Preachers' Fund," each paying out of his poverty a specified sum annually into its treasury. It was afterwards merged in the "Chartered Fund," instituted in 1796 for the same purposes. This fund has never been a favorite charity; it amounts to only about $40,000, and its dividends to the Conferences have, of course, always been small. Many of the Annual Conferences hold trust funds, whose proceeds are devoted to the same end. Surplus profits of the Book Concern were for many years employed for their relief, but the chief reliance is on the annual contributions of the congregations, amounting now yearly to $150,000.

The missionary work of the Church took an organized form in 1819, when its Missionary Society was instituted. Methodism was itself a missionary system, "the great home-mission enterprise of the North American continent, and its domestic work, demanded all its resources of men and money." The Conference of 1784 ordered an annual collection in every principal congregation to provide a fund for " carrying on the whole work of God," chiefly for the expenses of preachers sent to new or feeble fields. Missionaries were early sent among the slaves and Indians, and the constant extension of the Church, whether in the older states or on the ever-advancing frontier, has been a missionary movement. The society, organized primarily to aid the home-mission work, grouped with it the foreign field; and now, besides more than 2000 missionaries in the English-speaking Conferences, 161 in the German Conferences, and 90 among the Indians and other peoples of foreign birth in the United States, supported in whole or in part by the society, its foreign missionaries, in-

cluding native preachers and teachers, number 679, and are scattered in Africa, South America, China, India, Japan, Germany, Switzerland, Denmark, Norway, Sweden, Bulgaria, Italy, and Mexico. Its receipts in 1872 amounted to $661,056 60. It is supplemented by the Woman's Foreign Missionary Society, and by other organizations of a *quasi* missionary character, equally with it under the control of the General Conference, its Sunday-school Union, its Tract, Freedman's Aid, and Church Extension societies.

The educational movements of the Church began with the Church itself. John Dickens, afterwards the first book agent, suggested to Asbury the plan of an academic institution as early as 1780, and at their first meeting the latter submitted it to Coke, who heartily approved it. It was laid before the Christmas Conference, which agreed upon measures to establish a college. Five thousand dollars—a large sum for those days—were raised for it before the building was begun; its foundations were laid at Abingdon, Md., in the following June, and in the last month of 1787 it was solemnly dedicated under the name of Cokesbury College. The curriculum embraced " English, Latin, Greek, logic, rhetoric, history, geography, natural philosophy, and astronomy, and, when the finances will admit of it, Hebrew, French, and German." More than seventy students were at one time within its halls. Unfortunately it was burned down in 1795: "a sacrifice of £10,000 in about ten years," says Asbury. A new edifice was soon provided in Baltimore, and the college reopened with fair prospects, but in a year it also was lost by fire. Another college was projected in Georgia in 1789, and several academies were opened before the close of the century. The disastrous fate of Cokesbury led Asbury to think the Lord had "not called Methodists to build colleges," a saying of his that has been most sadly perverted. He would have had the same thing, but would have called it a " school," and not a " college," and he would place one in every Conference. He actually framed a scheme to bring " two thousand children under the best plan of education ever known in this country." In 1818 a second attempt was made to establish a college in Baltimore, but without success. The educational plans of the early Methodists were simply broader than their financial ability. At no time has the slander been just that they were enemies to education. In 1817 an academy was opened in Newmarket, N. H., since removed to Wilbraham, Mass.; and in 1819 another in New York City. In 1820 the General Conference took up the subject, and recommended that each Annual Conference establish as soon as practicable a literary institution under its own control. This action was followed by new efforts. Several Conference seminaries were soon opened, and, to meet the increasing demand for higher education, within twelve years no less than five colleges were put in successful operation. Theological schools are of a later date, and assumed at first the modest title of " Biblical Institute." The first, projected in 1839, after various fortunes, was located at Concord, N. H., in 1847; in 1867 it removed to Boston, and in 1871 became the school of theology in the Boston University. The Garrett Biblical Institute, at Evanston, Ill., founded in 1855, received an endowment of $300,000 and its name from a liberal Methodist lady of Chicago. The Drew Theological Seminary was originated in the Centenary movement at Madison, N. J., through the munificence of the gentleman whose name it bears. There is also a mission institute at Frankfort-on-the-Main, in Germany, named *Martin Institute,* after the gentleman whose munificence mainly endowed the school; and there are similar schools in India, and at two or three points in the Southern States. By the close of the centennial year of American Methodism, " the Methodist Episcopal Church alone reported no less than 25 colleges (including theological schools), having 158 instructors, 5345 students, about $4,000,000 in endowments and other property, and 105,531 volumes in their libraries. It reports also 77 academies, with 556 instructors, and 17,761 students, 10,462 of whom are females, making an aggregate of 102 institutions, with 714 instructors, and 23,106 students. The Southern division of the denomination [the Methodist Episcopal Church, South] reported before the Rebellion 12 colleges and 77 academies, with 8000 students, making an aggregate for the two bodies of 191 institutions and 31,106 students" (Stevens's *Hist. of Am. Meth.* p. 540). In the thank-offerings of the Centenary, education was made a prominent object of the contributions of the people.

6. *Later Divisions.*—Various causes have operated to prevent the continued unity of the denomination whose origin and progress are here traced, but it should be noted that no division has ever occurred on doctrinal grounds. The separation of O'Kelly and his friends, as already stated, took place in 1792, because the Conference refused to restrict the power of the bishops in the appointments of ministers to their fields of labor. In 1816 the colored members of Philadelphia and its vicinity withdrew and organized the "African Methodist Episcopal Church;" and in 1820 a secession in New York City originated the African Methodist Episcopal Zion Church. They are large and useful bodies.

Embarrassments arose in Canada after the War of 1812, through jealousies of the Conference, because of its connection with a foreign ecclesiastical body, which finally became so severe that in 1828 the General Conference was formally requested to set off the Canada Conference as a distinct Church. The General Conference, after full deliberation, held that it had no power to divide the Church, as it was constituted to preserve, not to destroy, its unity. Deeming the case to be one of necessity, it consented to the voluntary withdrawal of the Canada brethren; allowed the bishops, if requested, to ordain the bishop whom the separating Conference might elect; and proposed to the Annual Conferences such a change in the Restrictive Rules as would permit a *pro rata* division with them of the common property in the Book Concern. The requisite vote not being obtained, the property was not divided; but a satisfactory arrangement was effected through heavy discounts in sales of books, giving what was on all hands considered a full equivalent. The Canada Conference separated itself from the Church; but between the two sections the most friendly relations have ever subsisted.

The circumstances which led in 1830 to another secession, and the formation of the "Methodist Protestant Church," were of a more serious sort. The subject of lay representation in the General Conference, though from an early day deemed by a few to be important, began about 1820 to agitate the Church. The measures of the "Reformers," as the friends of the movement styled themselves, were unfortunate, leading not only to a most acrimonious controversy, but to such disorders as rendered necessary ecclesiastical trials and expulsions. Out of the controversy arose Emory's masterly production, "The Defence of Our Fathers." The subject came before the General Conference by petitions and memorials, and received the fullest attention. The report refusing the radical change asked for, written by Dr. Thomas E. Bond, a local preacher, and not a member of the body, and presented by Dr. Emory, was unanimously adopted. "The great body of our ministers, both travelling and local, as well as of our members—perhaps not much, if any, short of one hundred to one—oppose their wishes," says the report; and Bangs thought that "nine tenths of our people were decidedly opposed to the innovation." The result was a new denomination, starting with 83 preachers and 5000 members, and a long and bitter controversy that finally died of exhaustion.

The subject of slavery, which for many years agitated the whole country, and finally plunged it into a civil war, could not fail, in the progress of events, to involve in its complications a Church which constantly put slavery under its ban, but did not make absolute non-slaveholding a test of membership. Two important secessions resulted—one in the North, the other in the South. One of the General Rules—the moral code of the Church from the beginning—forbade "the buying or selling of men, women, or children, with an intention to enslave them." The legislation of the Church was steadily adverse to the institution, though always embarrassed by the obstacles which the civil laws placed in the way of a legal emancipation. The prohibition, however, of buying or selling slaves with any other intent than their freedom, remained unchanged. Moreover, from the year 1800, the Discipline provided that "when any travelling preacher becomes an owner of a slave or slaves by any means, he shall forfeit his ministerial character in the Methodist Episcopal Church unless he execute, if it be practicable, a legal emancipation of such slaves, conformably to the laws of the state in which he lives;" from 1816, that "no slaveholder shall be eligible to any official station in our Church hereafter, where the laws of the state in which he lives will admit of emancipation, and permit the liberated slave to enjoy freedom;" and from 1824 it contained provisions for the religious instruction of slaves, and concerning colored local preachers. These regulations were in force at the commencement of the "abolition movement," and continued unchanged until 1860, when the formula in the Discipline declares that "the buying, selling, or holding of human beings, to be used as chattels, is contrary to the laws of God and nature, and inconsistent with the golden rule;" and both preachers and people are admonished to "keep themselves pure from this great evil, and to seek its extirpation by all lawful and Christian means." The discussions in Great Britain from the year 1823, that resulted in emancipation in all the British colonies in 1834, drew attention to the system of slavery as it existed in the United States, which was not greatly unlike that of the West Indies. Philanthropic men became aroused by numerous well-authenticated facts of the wicked and inhuman treatment of slaves. They were led to examine the system of chattel slavery and its practical workings, and found them so adverse to the right to himself of every person of full age and sane mind, except for the commission of crime, that they pronounced slaveholding to be a crime in God's sight, and immediate, unconditional emancipation a duty. Leading ministers, chiefly in New England at first, espoused these views, and advocated them in the pulpit, at camp-meetings, in conventions, through the press, and by all those means that could act upon the public mind. In the controversies that followed, in which some of the most able pens of the denomination were engaged, the question was examined in all its aspects. The subject was introduced into Quarterly and Annual Conferences, and ultimately became involved with questions of Conference rights, Episcopal prerogatives, and the rights of the laity. The General Conference of 1836 passed a vote of censure upon two of its members who had attended and spoken at an anti-slavery meeting in Cincinnati, where the session was held, (a resolution which in 1868, so greatly had opinion changed with events, it rescinded and pronounced void), and exhorted the "members and friends" of the Church "to abstain from all abolition movements and associations, and to refrain from patronizing any of their publications." But Methodism had not overlooked the welfare of the slave. At the culmination of these troubles, a hundred thousand colored persons, mostly slaves, were enrolled as members of the Church, amounting to one tenth of the whole. But many apologies for quietness and tolerance of the legal relation of master were nullified by a resolution of the Georgia Conference, "that slavery, as it exists in the United States, is not a moral evil." At length, the General Conference of 1840 having found it "inexpedient to express any opinion, or to adopt any measures additional to those already in the Discipline," many began to abandon all hope of seeing the Church purged of slavery, and to regard withdrawal as necessary to free themselves from the guilt of connection with it. Others, who had been prominent in the anti-slavery ranks, and had advocated such modifications in the law of the Church as would prevent the holding of slaves as chattels, maintained that the Discipline was against slavery, and that secession was not an anti-slavery measure. They preferred to fight the battle within the Church. But Orange Scott, Jotham Horton, Luther Lee, and others, felt impelled by their consciences to withdraw. At a convention held at Utica, N. Y., in 1843, they organized the "Wesleyan Methodist Connection." This was but the beginning of a struggle in which churches were rent in twain through most of the Northern States. The organization thus formed numbered at one period a considerable number of preachers and members; but time and events have produced such changes that many of its first leaders and warmest friends have returned to the old Church in the belief that the denomination has accomplished its mission.

But a severer convulsion was preparing in the South. The discriminations of the Discipline against slaveholding had come to be distasteful to a generation that held views on slavery widely different from those of the fathers, though six Conferences, lying wholly or partly in slave states, the Baltimore being one, rigidly enforced the old rule requiring ministers to emancipate the slaves of whom they might become owners by inheritance, marriage, or any other means, wherever the civil law allowed it, and never permitted slaveholders in their ranks. It was also the ancient and settled policy and constant usage to place no slaveholder in the Episcopacy; and in 1832 James O. Andrew was put in nomination for that high office by Southern delegates, because, though of the South, he was free from all personal connection with slavery, and was elected. This was upon the principle that a bishop, in a system of general superintendency which gave him equal jurisdiction in Massachusetts and South Carolina, must be free from whatever would prevent the exercise of his functions with acceptance in any part of the Church. A slaveholding bishop could never have presided in the Northern Conferences, and the election of one would be an infraction of the law forbidding the General Conference to "destroy the plan of our itinerant general superintendency." The increasing restiveness under this exclusion from the highest office of the Church led to an attempt by Southern delegates, in 1836, to elect to it a slaveholder, and, upon its failure, to great agitation and threats of secession, if what was termed "this proscriptive system" should not be abandoned. The renewal of the effort in 1844 was fully determined upon, and the purpose of resistance on the part of the Northern Conferences was equally firm, when the marriage of bishop Andrew, in January of that year, with a lady who was the owner of slaves, suddenly gave the friends of the movement precisely what they wanted, but could not have obtained by the suffrages of the General Conference—a slaveholding bishop. That trouble was ahead was evident, and the Southern ministry became at once a unit in sustaining him. It could not be expected that the Church would quietly submit to the revolutionizing of its ancient policy by a marriage; and nothing could have more astounded the Northern delegates to the General Conference of 1844 than the intelligence, which met them upon their arrival in New York, the place of the session, that slaveholding was already intrenched in the Episcopacy. Early in the session an appeal of the Rev. Francis A. Harding from the action of the Baltimore Conference was presented. That gentleman having become by marriage the owner of five slaves, the Conference, in pursuance of its old purpose to "not tolerate slavery in any of its members," required him to legally emancipate them within the year, and, upon his refusal, suspended him from the ministry. The General Conference, after a full hearing of the case, it being clear that emancipation could be legally effected in

Maryland, affirmed the decision of the Baltimore Conference by a vote of 117 to 56. That body, though few were "abolitionists," certainly was in no mood to yield further to the encroachments of slavery; and it was equally evident that should bishop Andrew be touched, secession would ensue. His voluntary resignation could have saved both the South and the Church; and this step he promptly resolved to take, but he was overruled by the Southern delegates. They preferred disruption to a non-slaveholding Episcopacy. The committee on the Episcopacy was instructed to ascertain and report the facts in relation to the bishop's alleged connection with slavery, when it was found that, besides the legal ownership of several others, he had married a lady owning slaves, and had secured them to her by a deed of trust, thus putting their freedom out of his power. A resolution, with a preamble reciting the facts, was promptly offered by Mr. Griffith, a delegate from Baltimore, affectionately requesting him to resign his office; but the final action, after ten days' debate, was the adoption of the following substitute by a vote of 111 yeas and 69 nays:

"*Whereas*, The Discipline of our church forbids the doing anything calculated to destroy our itinerant general superintendency; and whereas bishop Andrew has become connected with slavery by marriage and otherwise, and this act having drawn after it circumstances which, in the estimation of the General Conference, will greatly embarrass the exercise of his office as an itinerant general superintendent, if not in some places entirely prevent it; therefore,

"*Resolved*, That it is the sense of this General Conference that he desist from the exercise of his office so long as this impediment remains."

Evidently this was the mildest action possible without the abandonment of the established principles and usage of the Church. It left him still a bishop, free to choose his own course, and with unquestioned right to the full exercise of his powers the hour the "impediment" should be removed; and private individuals vainly opened the way for his relief by offering to bind themselves to purchase all his slaves and their connections, and set them free. The Southern delegates took no steps from first to last towards an amicable settlement of the difficulty; and acquiescence in the doctrine of a non-slaveholding bishop or separation from the Church were the only alternatives left. All their measures were in the latter direction. First, Dr. Capers proposed a plan of two independent General Conferences, with a joint interest in the Book Concern and the Missionary Society. This, being in reality a division of the Church, was held impossible. Then, as a second step, the following declaration was presented, signed by fifty-one delegates from the thirteen slaveholding Conferences, and one from Illinois:

"The delegates of the Conferences in the slaveholding states take leave to *declare* to the General Conference of the Methodist Episcopal Church, that the continued agitation on the subject of slavery and abolition in a portion of the Church; the frequent action on that subject in the General Conference; and especially the extra-judicial proceedings against bishop Andrew, which resulted, on Saturday last, in the virtual suspension of him from his office as superintendent, must produce a state of things in the South which renders a continuance of the jurisdiction of this General Conference over these Conferences inconsistent with the success of the ministry in the slaveholding states."

This paper was at once referred to a committee of nine, who were afterwards instructed (according to the Journal), in case they could not frame an "amicable adjustment of the difficulties now existing in the Church on the subject of slavery, to devise, if possible, a constitutional plan for a mutual and friendly division of the Church." But Mr. Hamline (afterwards bishop), one of the committee, refused to go out with such instructions. "Being urged to go, he said, 'I will not go out with instructions to devise a plan to divide the Church.' 'Then will brother Hamline go if the instructions be so changed as simply to read, if the South should separate, to make provision in such a contingency to meet the emergency with Christian kindness and the strictest equity?' Mr. Hamline said, 'I will go out with such instructions'" (Hamline's *Life and Letters*, p. 165). The instructions were modified accordingly. On the next day a protest against the action of the majority was read, affirming in stronger terms the position of the Declaration, which was followed some days later by a Reply. Whether, after this formal notice of the coming separation, it would not have been the wiser to allow events to take their course, is an open question. The protesting delegates, about to renounce the jurisdiction of the General Conference, could claim nothing, as of right, at its hands; and it was certainly an act of the highest magnanimity on the part of the two-thirds' majority to prescribe for itself beforehand a law of most liberal treatment of the withdrawing Conferences, and to provide for the conditional division with them of the property of the Church. Yet this was done in the report of the committee on the Declaration. (See the paper quoted in full under METHODIST EPISCOPAL CHURCH, SOUTH.) This document was adopted with great unanimity. An analysis of it shows that (1) it is based upon one fundamental condition, namely, a necessity to be found by the slaveholding Conferences for a distinct ecclesiastical connection, produced by the action of the General Conference. (2) It assumes that such distinct organization, if formed at all, will come into being by the action of those Conferences, and upon their own responsibility. (3) It does not arrange a division of the Church. For this the General Conference had no power, as was agreed in the Committee; and that it did not and could not divide the Church was as freely asserted by Southern as by Northern delegates, both during and after the debate. The term "division" does occur, but solely with reference to property. (4) It is not a "plan of separation," as it afterwards came to be styled, for it does not authorize, direct, or sanction any step of the withdrawing party; but is purely an enactment of the rules to be observed by the Methodist Episcopal Church in case a "not improbable contingency" becomes, by the sole action of the South, an accomplished fact. (5) To avoid the strife and bitterness that so generally attend a disruption, it enacts that, in case a new Church is formed, the Methodist Episcopal Church shall exercise no jurisdiction beyond certain limits, if the Church South shall act upon the same friendly principle. The Church simply lays down for itself the rule of non-interference. (6) Nine of the twelve resolutions relate entirely to property, which, even if a Southern Church should be formed, can have no force whatever without the three-fourths' concurrent vote of the Annual Conferences for the proposed change of the Restrictive Rule. All this was well understood at the time.

By this eminently Christian enactment the General Conference made provision for peace and quiet in view of the threatened withdrawal of a large and powerful portion of the Church. History must, however, record that the Southern delegates, at a meeting held on the day following the adjournment, and without waiting for the "necessity" to develop itself, and to be found by the Conferences, called a convention of delegates from the slaveholding Conferences, with a defined ratio of representation, to assemble at Louisville, Ky., on May 1, 1845, invited bishop Andrew to attend and preside in their Conferences, and also issued an address to the ministers and members in the South, stating what they term "the facts and reasons connected with the proposed separation of the Southern Conferences into a distinct organization." This precipitated and virtually decided the question of separation. In the controversies that followed this summary proceeding, the whole Church was stirred. The various questions involved were discussed in public meetings, in Quarterly and Annual Conferences, in Church periodicals and pamphlets. Bishop Soulé, the senior bishop of the Church, in September called bishop Andrew into the field, to attend with himself the Conferences, in contravention

of the expressed judgment of the General Conference. The slaveholding Conferences appointed delegates to the proposed convention, although several of them had not found the "necessity" for a separate organization. The recommendation to change the sixth Restrictive Rule failed by 269 votes to receive the concurrence of the Annual Conferences. The Louisville Convention met May 1, 1845; bishops Soulé and Andrew were in attendance, and upon invitation presided over its deliberations. On May 17 the new Church was organized by the adoption of the following resolution, whose language may seem singular to the curious reader who remembers that what is styled the "provisional plan of separation" gave no direction, authority, or consent for the assembling or action of the convention, and that the provisions referred to relate solely to the action of the Church separated from, and not at all to the action of the parties separating:

"Be it resolved, by the delegates of the several Annual Conferences of the Methodist Episcopal Church in the slaveholding states, in general convention assembled, That it is right, expedient, and necessary to erect the Annual Conferences represented in this convention into a distinct ecclesiastical connection, separate from the jurisdiction of the General Conference of the Methodist Episcopal Church, as at present constituted; and accordingly we, the delegates of said Annual Conferences, acting under the provisional plan of separation adopted by the General Conference of 1844, do solemnly *declare* the jurisdiction hitherto exercised over said Annual Conferences by the General Conference of the Methodist Episcopal Church *entirely dissolved;* and that said Annual Conferences shall be, and they hereby are, *constituted* a separate ecclesiastical connection, under the provisional plan of separation aforesaid, and based upon the Discipline of the Methodist Episcopal Church, comprehending the doctrines and entire moral, ecclesiastical, and canonical rules and regulations of said Discipline, except only in so far as verbal alterations may be necessary to a distinct organization, and to be known by the style and title of 'THE METHODIST EPISCOPAL CHURCH, SOUTH.'"

By this secession the Methodist Episcopal Church lost 1345 travelling and 3166 local preachers, and 495,288 members. Bishop Andrew at once gave in his adhesion to the new Church, and bishop Soulé followed him at its first General Conference in May, 1846.

Troubles soon occurred upon the border line of the two churches. The Southern General Conference took summary possession of the newspapers within its territory, and of the Charleston Book Depository, with their books, notes, presses, etc., all of which belonged to the Book Concern. The understanding in relation to boundaries was not kept. Though the rule had not been changed, a *pro rata* division of the Book Concern was demanded on pain of a suit at law. In this state of affairs, the General Conference of 1848 was met by the Rev. Dr. Lovick Pierce, as delegate from the Church South, bearing the "Christian salutations" of that body, and proposing fraternal relations between the two churches; but the existing difficulties were so evidently incompatible with the proposed fraternity, that it could not "at present" be entered into, though all personal courtesies, with an invitation to a seat within the bar, were tendered to Dr. Pierce. As the report on the Declaration was an enactment of the General Conference, it was, like any other enactment, repealable at its pleasure; and in the exercise of its wisdom it said, "Having found, upon clear and incontestable evidence, that the three fundamental conditions of said proposed plan have severally failed, and the failure of either of them separately being sufficient to render it null and void, and having found the practical working of said plan incompatible with certain great constitutional principles elsewhere asserted, we have found and declared the whole and every part of said provisional plan to be null and void." But in its desire to amicably adjust the claims made by the Church South upon the funds of the Book Concern, it authorized the book agents to offer to submit them to disinterested arbiters, provided eminent counsel learned in the law should advise them that it could be legally done: otherwise, and in case a suit at law should be commenced, to propose an arbitration under authority of the court; and in case they could not offer arbitration, and no suit should be commenced, it was recommended to the Annual Conferences to "so far suspend the sixth Restrictive Article of the Discipline as to authorize the book agents at New York and Cincinnati to submit said claim to arbitration." This was going to the utmost limit of its power. The question of the suspension of the sixth article was midway in its progress through the Annual Conferences when it was arrested by the commencement of suits in the civil courts. The case in New York came to a hearing before judge Nelson, but before the issuing of the final decree the matter was amicably adjusted through the friendly offices of judge M'Lean. The Cincinnati case resulted in favor of the defendants in the Circuit Court; but on a hearing of the appeal by the Supreme Court, to which it was carried by the Southern commissioners, the decision of the court below was reversed, on the alleged ground that the General Conference had full power to divide the Church, and that that body did, in the adoption of the report on the Declaration, actually divide the Church, when the division of the property follows, as a matter of course. The Church at once obeyed the decision; but no intelligent minister or member of the denomination has ever accepted the exposition given by the Supreme Court, through the lips of judge Nelson, of the law of the Church, the facts of its history, or the action of the General Conference of 1844. The relations between the two churches have not as yet become cordial. The bishops of the Methodist Episcopal Church in 1869 made some advances towards a reunion, which were ungraciously received; but the General Conference of 1872 ordered the appointment of a delegation of two ministers and one layman to convey its greetings to the General Conference of the Church South at its next ensuing session.

Aside from these troubles, and others growing out of the increasing intensity of the conflict between freedom and slavery, the work of the Church was vigorously and successfully pressed. It stood arrayed with its full moral power on the side of the Union in the war provoked by slavery, and more than a hundred thousand of its members gave themselves to the armies of their country. Before the close of the war it entered upon preparations for the celebration of the centenary of Methodism in America, by all the churches and people, "with devout thanksgiving, by special religious services and liberal thank-offerings," setting apart the month of October, 1866, for that purpose. The Church had attained by the end of the century, notwithstanding its losses by the several secessions, more than a million of members, and it was hoped that "not less than two millions of dollars" would be contributed to render its agencies more efficient in the future. Appropriate services were held throughout the Church, and at the close of the joyful month the aggregate contributions amounted to $8,709,498 39.

7. An important organic change in the economy of the Church was effected in 1872 by the introduction of laymen into the General Conference. In 1860 that body expressed its approval of the measure "when it shall be ascertained that the Church desires it," and also provided for the submission of the question to the votes of both the ministry and members. The result showed a large majority against the proposed change. Nevertheless, while the General Conference felt precluded by this expression of the popular will from adopting it, it reaffirmed in 1864 its approval of it upon the same condition as before. At its next session it took up the subject anew, recommending a definite plan to the consideration of the Church, ordering the submission afresh of the question of lay delegation to the vote of the laity, and proposing to the Annual Conferences the requisite alterations in the second Restrictive Rule. A large majority of the former, and more than the necessary three-fourths vote in the latter, having been obtained in favor of the change, the General Conference, with the assent of 283 out of its 292 members, concurred in the same.

The lay delegates, who had been provisionally elected in anticipation of this action, were at once admitted to their seats. It is provided that "the ministerial and lay delegates shall sit and deliberate together as one body, but they shall vote separately whenever such separate vote shall be demanded by one third of either order; and in such cases the concurrent vote of both orders shall be necessary to complete an action."

8. The Bishops are assigned to certain residences, and some of them are limited to particular foreign fields. The following are their names, with the year of their ordination, and other facts:

Thomas Coke..............1784.—Died at sea, May 3, 1814, aged 66.
Francis Asbury...........1784.—Died in Virginia, March 31, 1816, aged 70.
Richard Whatcoat........1800.—Died in Delaware, July 5, 1806, aged 71.
William M'Kendree.......1808.—Died in Tennessee, March 5, 1835, aged 77.
Enoch George.............1816.—Died in Virginia, August 23, 1828, aged 60.
Robert R. Roberts........1816.—Died in Indiana, March 28, 1843, aged 64.
Joshua Soule ....1824.—Ent. M. E. Church, South, 1845; died March 6, 1867, aged 85.
Elijah Hedding ....1824.—Died in Poughkeepsie, April 9, 1852, aged 72.
James O. Andrew.........1832.—Bishop M. E. Church, South, 1845; died March 2, 1871, aged 77.
John Emory...............1832.—Died in Maryland, Dec. 16, 1835, aged 46.
Beverly Waugh............1836.—Died in Maryland, Feb. 9, 1858, aged 69.
Thomas A. Morris.........1836.—Died in Ohio, Sept. 2, 1874, aged 80.
Leonidas L. Hamline.....1844.—Resigned, 1852; died in Iowa, March 22, 1865, aged 67.
Edmund S. Janes.........1844.—Died in N. Y. City, Sept. 18, 1876, aged 69.
Levi Scott................1852.—Died in Odessa, Del., July 13, 1882, aged 80.
Matthew Simpson ....1852.—Died in Philadelphia, June 18, 1884, aged 73.
Osmon C. Baker..........1852.—Died in Concord, N. H., Dec. 20, 1871, aged 58.
Edward R. Ames..........1852.—Died in Baltimore, April 25, 1879, aged 73.
Francis Burns............1858.—Miss. Bp. to Liberia; died in Baltimore, April 18, 1863.
Davis W. Clark...........1864.—Died in Cincinnati, May 23, 1871, aged 59.
Edward Thomson.........1864.—Died in Wheeling, W. Va., March 22, 1870, aged 59.
Calvin Kingsley ....1864.—Died in Beirût, Syria, April 6, 1870, aged 57.
John W. Roberts..........1866.—Died in Liberia, Jan. 30, 1876, aged 54.
Thomas Bowman.........1872.—Residence, St. Louis.
William L. Harris........1872.—Died in N. Y. City, Sept. 2, 1887, aged 69.
Randolph S. Foster.......1872.—Residence, Roxbury, Mass.
Isaac W. Wiley...........1872.—Died in Foochow, China, Nov. 22, 1884, aged 59.
Stephen M. Merrill.......1872.—Residence, Chicago, Ill.
Edward G. Andrews......1872.—Residence, New York City.
Gilbert Haven............1872.—Died in Malden, Mass., Jan. 3, 1880, aged 59.
Jesse T. Peck.............1872.—Died in Syracuse, N. Y., May 17, 1883, aged 72.
Henry W. Warren........1880.—Residence, Denver, Col.
Cyrus D. Foss............1880.—Residence, Philadelphia, Pa.
John F. Hurst............1880.—Residence, Washington, D. C.
Erastus O. Haven........1880.—Died in Salem, Ore., Aug. 2, 1881, aged 61.
William X. Ninde ....1884.—Residence, Topeka, Kan.
John M. Walden ....1884.—Residence, Cincinnati, O.
Willard F. Mallalieu.....1884.—Residence, New Orleans, La.
Charles H. Fowler.......1884.—Residence, San Francisco, Cal.
William Taylor...........1884.—Miss. Bishop to Africa.
John H. Vincent..........1888.—Residence, Buffalo, N. Y.
James N. Fitzgerald......1888.—Residence, Minneapolis, Minn.
Isaac W. Joyce...........1888.—Residence, Chattanooga, Tenn.
John P. Newman.........1888.—Residence, Omaha, Neb.
Daniel A. Goodsell.......1888.—Residence, Fort Worth, Tex.
James M. Thoburn.......1888.—Miss. Bp. to India and Malaysia.

V. *Statistics.*—There are in the denomination 76 Annual Conferences, whose statistics show in 1872 10,242 travelling preachers, 11,964 local preachers, 1,458,441 members and probationers, 17,471 Sunday-schools, with 1,278,559 scholars and 193,691 officers and teachers, and 14,008 churches and 4484 parsonages, valued together at $8,575,877. The baptisms for the year were 53,459 children and 61,311 adults. The benevolent contributions for the year were, for the Missionary Society, $671,000 21; Woman's Foreign Missionary Society, $18,755 34; Church Extension Society, $94,572 63; Tract Society, $21,585 67; Sunday-school Union, $22,674 15; American Bible Society, $42,528 35; Freedman's Aid Society, $12,048 97; Education, $6,660 42; and for necessitous ministers, $150,140 62—making an aggregate of $1,039,966 36. See METHODISM. (D. A.W.)

Methodist Episcopal Church in Canada.
The first Canadian Methodist Society, as nearly as can be ascertained, was formed in the township of Augusta, in Upper Canada (now Ontario), in 1778. Its first members were some of the parties who had constituted the first Methodist Society in New York. See METHODIST EPISCOPAL CHURCH. Prominent names

were those of Paul and Barbara Heck, their three sons, John, Jacob, and Samuel; John and Catharine Lawrence—Mrs. Lawrence had been the widow of Philip Embury; and Samuel Embury, a son of Philip Embury. Besides these, it was joined by such others of the scattered settlers of Augusta as wished to unite with them in Christian fellowship. Samuel Embury was the class-leader. About two years after the organization of this society, viz. in 1780, Mr. Tuffey, a Methodist local preacher from England, then connected with a regiment stationed at Quebec, preached to his comrades and to the towns-people; but it does not appear that he attempted to form any regular class.

Methodism was introduced into the country about Niagara and westward by the Rev. George Neal, who was born in Pennsylvania Feb. 28, 1751. He was converted under the ministry of the Rev. Hope Hull. Mr. Neal became a local preacher, and went into Canada in 1786. He settled in the Niagara District, taught school during the week, and preached to the people on the Sabbath, and frequently on week-day evenings. Following the illustrious examples of Nelson, in England, Williams, in Ireland, and Embury, in New York, Neal collected together those who had been converted through his instrumentality, and formed a society in the township of Stamford in 1790, appointing Christian Warner the class-leader, an office which he continued to fill until his death, March 21, 1833. This class, collected without the intervention of any travelling preacher, as was also the above class in Augusta, embraced among its members a number who afterwards distinguished themselves as pillars in the Church of God (*Hist. of the M. E. Church in Canada*, p. 34). The ministrations of Mr. Neal were approved by his brethren in the United States and Canada, and he was therefore ordained deacon by bishop Asbury July 23, 1810, at the Annual Conference held that year at Lyons, in the State of New York.

The Rev. William Losee was the first itinerant Methodist preacher on Canadian soil. In 1789 or the beginning of 1790 he was visiting some of his friends and relatives near Kingston, Upper Canada. Being zealous in the Master's work, he improved his visit by preaching whenever opportunity offered. The people heard him gladly, and, having been edified by his labors, they sent a petition to the New York Conference, of which he was a member, requesting that body to send Losee among them, and he was appointed. The first class was organized Feb. 20, 1791; the second March 2 of the same year—the very day on which John Wesley died. From this year the Methodist societies and congregations were regularly supplied with missionaries from the Church in the United States. The ministers in what was then a wilderness endured great privations, and encountered formidable dangers; but they were indefatigable in their labors, through zeal for God and for the salvation of the people.

Early Methodism in Canada, as well as in Europe and the United States, had to contend with great opposition. Its most formidable foes were those who were determined upon the aggrandizement and dominancy of what they called the Established Church, although no such thing as a Church establishment had been constituted in those provinces by legal enactment. These would-be adherents of the Church of England were violent in their hostility to Methodism, as were also the members of some other Protestant churches, to say nothing about the Roman Catholics. An instance of the intolerant spirit manifested towards the early Methodist preachers is presented by the following facts. In 1788 Mr. James M'Carty, an adherent of Mr. Whitefield, went from the United States and settled in Earnestown, near the shore of the Bay of Quinté. Feeling it to be his duty to preach the Gospel to his neighbors, he collected them together in their little log-cabins, and dispensed to them the Word of Life. He was interfered with by parties from Kingston, who, clothed with a little brief author-

ity, caused him to be dragged from the place of worship, from his peaceful and happy home, and from the bosom of his family. They cast him into prison, and, after giving him some sort of a trial, sentenced him to banishment from the country. He was taken away from Kingston by his persecutors, and his family saw his face no more. He is supposed to have been murdered. Mr. Neal was likewise ordered to leave the country; but the hand of God interposed, and finally he was allowed to remain, and to continue his Christian labors. The spirit of intolerance continued for many years, though, as time advanced, it manifested itself in somewhat less violent forms. Lawsuits were entered against some of the early preachers for celebrating marriage between the members of their own congregations, and they were ordered into exile on this account. But none of these things moved the devoted men who were sent by bishop Asbury and the New York and Genesee conferences. Steady to their purpose, namely, the advancement of the cause of Christ, their watchword was "Onward!" At the commencement of this century, about ten years after Mr. Losee first entered Canada, the work stood as follows: 1 district, 4 circuits, 7 preachers, and 936 members.

During the next decade the increase in Church membership was still more encouraging. The privations of the preachers were nearly the same, and their labors, if possible, still more arduous, because they had to extend their work yet further into the forest. They had to ford dangerous streams, plod through deep swamps, and often camp out during the night in the dreary woods, with their saddle-bags for a pillow, the canopy of heaven and the foliage of the trees for covering, the faithful horse standing sentinel near his master, suffering with him from cold and hunger. Many a long and dismal night was thus spent by these self-sacrificing men, sometimes aroused from their brief repose by the screeching of owls, the howling of wolves, or the war-whoop of the savage. But the great desire of their hearts was realized — the success of the Gospel cause. In 1810 there were 2 districts, 15 circuits, 19 preachers, and 2795 members. The Upper Canada district was placed under the direction of the Genesee Annual Conference in 1810, and the Lower Canada district in 1811.

Great success attended the preaching of the Word, and the connection continued to prosper until the occurrence of the unhappy War of 1812. Several of the preachers appointed to Canadian circuits were prevented from entering upon their charges because the Canadian government had issued a proclamation ordering all Americans to leave the country before the 3d of July. A few of the preachers already resident determined to risk the danger of remaining; others were British-born subjects, and these, with the assistance of local preachers, supplied the work. During the unhappy conflict, the societies sustained great loss, as will appear from the statistics of the Church at the Genesee Conference of 1815, which was held shortly after peace was declared. The Canada work was reported at that Conference as follows: 2 districts, 9 circuits, 14 preachers, and 1765 members—a decrease since 1810 of 1030 members. The war-cloud having passed over, and the sunshine of peace once more shedding its benign rays upon both countries, the Genesee Conference resumed its care of the Canadian Church. But, though the two nations continued at peace, the Methodist societies were doomed to be agitated and divided by men sent out by the English Methodists as missionaries. The bitterness and heartburnings which were produced by the rivalry that ensued retarded to some extent the advancement of the cause in certain localities; but in the greater part of their field the American Methodists steadily increased in numbers, influence, and spirituality.

The year 1817 was distinguished for the most remarkable revival influence that had yet been witnessed in Canada. The Genesee Annual Conference that year was held in Elizabethtown, Upper Canada, commencing

June 21, bishop George presiding. An Annual Conference was a new thing in Canada, and therefore great crowds of people attended the ministry of the Word, especially on the Sabbath. The number of preachers present was large, and all were anxious to build up the walls of Zion. Religious services commenced at eight o'clock on Sabbath morning, and the Lord manifested himself with power. Many were seeking redemption before the hour had arrived at which the bishop was to preach, so that when he entered the house the congregation was aglow with the fire of divine love. Hundreds were present. The bishop preached one of his most able and impressive sermons, and the discourse had a powerful effect upon his hearers. The services continued all day with but little intermission, and it was not until late in the evening that the people dispersed. It is believed that more than one hundred souls were brought to Christ at this Conference. But the work of reformation did not end there. The preachers went from the Conference refreshed and strengthened, preaching with great effect Christ, the power of God, and the wisdom of God. On all the circuits the Word prevailed mightily, sinners were converted, and believers quickened. For more than three years there were constant additions to the Church throughout the Canadian work; and in some instances the revival influence extended to the border circuits in the United States. In 1820 the Genesee Conference was again held in Canada. The church in which it assembled was at the west end of "Lundy's Lane," near the spot where six years previously the British and American soldiers had met in deadly conflict. How great the change now. Americans and Canadians, actuated by the love of Christ, united harmoniously in council and effort to build up the walls of Zion, and rejoiced together in the triumphs of the Gospel of peace. There were about one hundred preachers present at the Conference. Bishop George presided, still exerting the same holy influence upon preachers and people as in 1817. Thirty preachers were ordained at this Conference. Some of this number were local preachers residing in Canada. The state of the work in 1820 was 2 districts, 17 circuits, 28 preachers, 47 local preachers, 65 exhorters, and 5557 members.

In the same year a settlement was effected between the General Conference and the English Conference, by which it was agreed that the Methodist Episcopal Church should withdraw its ministers from Lower Canada, and give up that province, with all its Church property therein, to the management of the English Conference; and that the English Conference should in like manner withdraw its missionaries from Upper Canada, and give up that province, with all its Church property therein, to the Methodist Episcopal Church (comp. *History of the Methodist Episcopal Church in Canada*, p. 127–154). The rival interest having been withdrawn from Upper Canada—with the exception of Kingston, where the English Conference continued to keep one of its missionaries—the societies of the Methodist Episcopal Church, once more in the enjoyment of peace, soon recovered from the effects of the recent agitations, and were greatly prospered in spiritual things. So rapidly had the work extended, that in 1824 the General Conference held in Baltimore consented to the establishment of an Annual Conference for Canada.

The Canada Conference was organized at Hallowell, Upper Canada, August 25, 1824. Bishops George and Hedding were present, and presided in turn. The preachers numbered, including the two bishops and those on trial, thirty-three persons. This was a small number compared with the numbers who met at Elizabethtown in 1817, or at Lundy's Lane in 1820. For four years longer the bishops went into Canada and presided at the sessions of the Canada Conference, appointing the preachers to the several charges, both preachers and societies cheerfully accepting such appointments. The work continued to extend and prosper, and Methodism was fast becoming a power in the land. But the good

it was accomplishing among the people, instead of removing the prejudices of its opponents, only tended to infuse fear of its great and growing influence among the advocates of a State Church. Among the Methodists, also, there were some who advocated the independent establishment of the Canadian Methodist Episcopal Church, on the ground that it would secure to the Canadian Methodists greater civil and religious liberty. Prominent among these was the Rev. H. Ryan, who had been agitating for a separation of the societies in Canada from the parent Church in the United States since 1820. The scheme was presented to the people on national and patriotic grounds, and the General Conference was memorialized on the subject, and at its session held at Pittsburgh, May, 1828, the request was granted. Accordingly, the Canadian Methodists were on October 2, 1828, organized into the Methodist Episcopal Church of Canada. In 1828 there were 3 districts, 48 travelling preachers, 7 superannuated preachers, and 32 circuits, with a membership of 9678. The increase for the year was 1033.

From 1828 until 1832 the infant Church in Canada had unprecedented success, considering the opposition it met with from the Rev. H. Ryan and his followers, who separated themselves from the connection in 1829, and organized another body. The provisional government was quite as hostile to the Methodist Episcopal Church in Canada after 1828 as it had been before its separation from the parent body. Parliament vindicated the rights of the preachers and Church, but the executive was not only confederated with the Church and State party in the country to cripple the energies of the original Methodists of the province, but was intriguing with the English Wesleyan Missionary Committee to induce that body—in violation of the settlement of 1820—to send their agents again into the country to form rival societies, large sums of money from the public revenue being promised if these missionaries would come. The scheme of the executive was successful, and Dr. Alder was sent out by the Missionary Committee to commence operations in Upper Canada in 1832. It was to avoid a collision with these agents of the English Conference, and also in evident anticipation of large financial supplies, that the great majority of the preachers consented to revolutionize the newly-organized Methodist Episcopal Church in Canada, and to become a mere dependency of the English Conference.

This unconstitutional movement was resisted by some of the preachers, and by hundreds of the members. Despite remonstrance, however, the Canada Conference consummated its union with the English body, taking with it most of the Church property, nearly all the preachers, and the principal part of the membership. Some of the former, and hundreds of the latter, disapproving of the proceedings of the Conference, yet submitted from hopelessness of successful resistance. A respectable minority protested against the action of the Conference, maintaining that the discipline of the Church did not vest in the Conference the powers assumed by it in that action, and that therefore the action was null and void. They also maintained that if the General Conference had possessed the powers it claimed, its action was nevertheless null and void, because persons were allowed to take part in its proceedings who, according to the discipline of the Church, were not members of the General Conference. The protestants further claimed that, having joined an Episcopal Church, they could not without their own consent be made members of a non-Episcopal Church; neither could they, without fault of their own, be deprived of their membership in the Church they had joined; that they therefore were still members of the Methodist Episcopal Church in Canada, and that said Church remained in its constitution and government intact—the action of the Conference amounting to nothing more than the withdrawal of the Conference and those who followed it from the Church.

Those preachers, travelling and local, who continued to adhere to the Methodist Episcopal Church, therefore exerted themselves to collect together the scattered remnants remaining faithful to the old Church. The winter of 1833–34 was spent in this particular work—no easy task, because of the extent of country which had to be traversed; but the few preachers who adhered to the original Church organization were indefatigable in their efforts to rebuild the broken-down walls of their beloved Zion. The Conference assembled at Yonge Street in June, 1834, when it was ascertained that only fourteen preachers could be calculated upon who were prepared to take work the ensuing year; with a membership of 1100—a decrease during eight months of 13,899. These statistics, however, did not represent the true status of the Church, for many more of the people returned to the old fold as soon as they found that there was sufficient vitality left in it to reconstruct and carry on the work of God in the land. Ten years after the disruption of 1833, viz. in 1843, there were seventy effective ministers and preachers supplying circuits and stations in Upper Canada, besides superannuated and supernumerary preachers, and a goodly staff of local preachers, who were doing efficient service in the Master's vineyard. The membership had increased to 8880, and there had been a corresponding increase of Church property. It will be remembered that at the union in 1833 the Church had lost almost all its connectional property, and this made the subsequent increase the more marked.

In January, 1845, the *Canada Christian Advocate*, a weekly paper, was established to supply the place in Church literature formerly occupied by the *Christian Guardian*. This medium of communication drew the societies and preachers more closely together, and enabled all better to understand the true position of the Church, and the work accomplished through its agency. It is still the weekly official paper.

The connection has now a book-room and publishing-house, located in the thriving and beautiful city of Hamilton, at the head of Lake Ontario. The class of publications and papers sent out from it very greatly benefits the Church, and assists in advancing the cause of Christ through the country generally.

There are two colleges under the direction and control of the Methodist Episcopal Church in Canada, viz. Albert College, vested with university powers, and Alexandra College, for the education of young ladies. These educational establishments are located in Belleville, in a healthy situation, surrounded by pleasing scenery, and in full view of the pure and placid waters of the Bay of Quinté, about fifty miles west from Kingston. Under the able management of the president, Rev. A. Carman, M.A., these institutions are prospering, and are exerting an influence for good in the country.

The Methodist Episcopal Church in Canada is composed of three Annual Conferences, with a delegated General Conference which meets every fourth year, and has the same legislative powers as the parent body in the United States. The present position of the Church, therefore, is: One General Conference, three Annual Conferences—Niagara, Ontario, and Bay of Quinté—ten extensive districts, 145 circuits and stations, 228 travelling preachers, 225 local preachers, 21,818 members, with Church property amounting to $2,149,776. Great attention is given to the Sabbath-school work. As nearly as can be estimated, from reports at hand, there are not far from 30,000 children in the Sunday-schools.

The polity of the Methodist Episcopal Church in Canada is like that of the Methodist Episcopal Church in the United States: the bishop taking the general oversight of the connection, presiding at the Conferences, and proceeding in almost every respect in a similar manner to that of the bishops of the parent body. The late incumbent of the bishopric, the Rev. J. Richardson, D.D., Yorkville, Ontario, died in 1874. See Webster, *Hist. M. Epis. Ch., Canada*; *Meth. Qu. Rev.* 1863, Jan. p. 169 sq.; 1863, Apr. p. 204; 1868, Apr. p. 264; 1871, Jan. p. 173. (T. W.)

Methodist Episcopal Church, South. — I. *Early History.*—In the year 1766 Philip Embury and Captain Thomas Webb, Methodist local preachers, began to preach in New York, and in the same year Robert Strawbridge, also a local preacher, in Maryland. In 1769 Richard Boardman and Joseph Pilmoor were sent over to America as missionaries by the Rev. John Wesley; and they were followed in 1771 by Francis Asbury and Richard Wright. In 1772 Asbury was made general assistant, that is, superintendent, under Wesley, of the Methodist societies in America. They were all connected with the Colonial Church of England, until that Church was disbanded after the Revolution. As they had no ordained ministers, and the English bishops would not ordain any for them, though importuned to do so by Wesley, he undertook to ordain some for them himself, and to organize his societies into a regular Episcopal Church, to take the place, so far as the Methodists were concerned, of the old Colonial Church. The Methodist Episcopal Church in America, as it was styled, was organized in 1784. The Rev. John Wesley, M.A., consecrated the Rev. Thomas Coke, LL.D., who was, like himself, a presbyter of the Church of England, to the office of superintendent, or bishop, of the new organization—other clergymen of the Church of England assisting in the consecration. Richard Whatcoat and Thomas Vasey were at the same time ordained elders, or presbyters, for the American Church. Conferences of the preachers had been held annually from the year 1773; but now a special Conference was convened in Baltimore, and bishop Coke consecrated Francis Asbury as bishop, and several elders and deacons were ordained at the same time. The Conference gave its suffrage to all these appointments. Wesley and his associates proceeded upon the true principle that the Episcopacy is derived from the Presbytery of the Church, so far as it differs from the latter—in this respect reverting to the ancient regimen which recognised the bishop as *primus inter pares*. Certain functions of government are ordinarily restricted to the Episcopacy to prevent schism and confusion, but with no idea of a *jus divinum*—as if bishops were, by God's ordinance, a third order in the ministry, and that there can be no Church without one of them. Thus the American Methodists became truly Episcopal, without any tincture of either Romish, Oriental, or Anglican prelacy—that, indeed, being precluded by the repudiation of the dogma of uninterrupted apostolical succession. The Church being thus organized with a Liturgy and Confession of Faith, judiciously abridged by Mr. Wesley from the Prayer-book and Thirty-nine Articles of the Church of England, and a Discipline essentially the same as that of the parent Wesleyan body in England, went forward with astonishing success, extending all over the territory of the United States and Canada. As the exigencies required, new bishops were consecrated, and various modifications took place in the discipline of the Church. In 1792 it was ordered that all the travelling preachers in full connection should attend the General Conference; in 1800 this was restricted to all who had travelled four years; in 1804 this was explained to mean "from the time they were received on trial by an Annual Conference." But as their number multiplied, a delegated General Conference was organized to meet quadrennially—the first meeting being in 1812. The ratio of representation was one delegate to every five travelling preachers in full connection. This ratio has been repeatedly altered, in view of the constant increase of the Annual Conferences. The General Conference was bound by the following restrictive rules: "The General Conference shall have full powers to make rules and regulations for our Church, under the following limitations and restrictions, namely: 1. The General Conference shall not revoke, alter, or change our articles of religion, nor establish any new standards or rules of doctrine contrary to our present existing and established standards of doctrine. 2. They shall not allow of more than one representative for every five members of the Annual Conference, nor allow of a less number than one for every seven. 3. They shall not change or alter any part or rule of our government, so as to do away Episcopacy, or destroy the plan of our general superintendency. 4. They shall not revoke or change the General Rules of the United Societies. 5. They shall not do away the privileges of our ministers or preachers of trial by a committee, and of an appeal; neither shall they do away the privileges of our members of trial before the society, or by a committee, and of an appeal. 6. They shall not appropriate the produce of the Book Concern, nor of the Chartered Fund, to any purpose other than for the benefit of the travelling, supernumerary, superannuated, and worn-out preachers, their wives, widows, and children. Provided, nevertheless, that upon the joint recommendation of all the Annual Conferences, then a majority of two thirds of the General Conference succeeding shall suffice to alter any of the above restrictions." In 1832 the proviso was changed thus: "Provided, nevertheless, that upon the concurrent recommendation of three fourths of all the members of the several Annual Conferences who shall be present and vote on such recommendation, then a majority of two thirds of the General Conference succeeding shall suffice to alter any of the above restrictions excepting the first article; and also, whenever such alteration or alterations shall have been first recommended by two thirds of the General Conference, so soon as three fourths of the members of all the Annual Conferences shall have concurred as aforesaid, such alteration or alterations shall take effect."

II. *The Slavery Question.*—From the beginning the American Methodists legislated on the subject of negro slavery—at first (1780) advising the members holding slaves to emancipate them; then (1783) warning local preachers that it may be necessary to suspend them if they did not in one year emancipate their slaves, if they held them "contrary to the laws which authorize their freedom in any of the United States;" then (1784) ordering that those who bought negroes to hold them as slaves, being previously warned, should be expelled; and forbidding them to sell them on any consideration; and suspending the local preachers in Maryland, Delaware, Pennsylvania, and New Jersey who refused to emancipate them, but "trying those in Virginia another year." All this was before the Church was organized. At the time of the organization of the Church, the following rules were adopted:

"*Quest.* 41. Are there any directions to be given concerning the negroes? *Ans.* Let every preacher, as often as possible, meet them in class; and let the assistant always appoint a proper white person as their leader. Let the assistants also make a regular return to the Conference of the number of negroes in society in their respective circuits.

"*Quest.* 42. What methods can we take to extirpate slavery? *Ans.* We are deeply conscious of the impropriety of making new terms of communion for a religious society already established, excepting on the most pressing occasion; and such we esteem the practice of holding our fellow-creatures in slavery. We view it as contrary to the golden law of God, on which hang all the law and the prophets, and the inalienable rights of mankind, as well as every principle of the Revolution, to hold in the deepest debasement, in a more abject slavery than is perhaps to be found in any part of the world except America, so many souls that are all capable of the image of God. We therefore think it our most bounden duty to take immediately some effectual method to extirpate this abomination from among us; and for that purpose we add the following to the rules of our society, viz.: 1. Every member of our society who has slaves in his possession shall, within twelve months after notice given to him by the assistant (which notice the assistants are required immediately, and without any delay, to give in their respective circuits), legally execute and record an instrument whereby he emancipates and sets free every slave in his possession who is between the ages of forty and forty-five immediately, or at furthest when they arrive at the age of forty-five; and every slave who is between the ages of twenty-five and forty immediately, or at furthest at the expiration of five years from the date of the said instrument; and every slave who is between the ages of twenty and twenty-five immediately, or at furthest when they arrive at the age of thirty; and every slave under

the age of twenty, as soon as they arrive at the age of twenty-five, at furthest; and every infant born in slavery after the above-mentioned rules are complied with, immediately on its birth. 2. Every assistant shall keep a journal, in which he shall regularly minute down the names and ages of all the slaves belonging to all the masters in his respective circuit, and also the date of every instrument executed and recorded for the manumission of the slaves, with the name of the court, book, and folio in which the said instruments respectively shall have been recorded; which journal shall be handed down in each circuit to the succeeding assistants. 3. In consideration that these rules form a new term of communion, every person concerned, who will not comply with them, shall have liberty quietly to withdraw himself from our society within the twelve months succeeding the notice given as aforesaid: otherwise the assistant shall exclude him in the society. 4. No person so voluntarily withdrawn, or so excluded, shall ever partake of the Supper of the Lord with the Methodists till he complies with the above requisitions. 5. No person holding slaves shall, in future, be admitted into society or to the Lord's Supper till he previously complies with these rules concerning slavery. N.B.—These rules are to affect the members of our society no further than as they are consistent with the laws of the states in which they reside. And respecting our brethren in Virginia that are concerned, and after due consideration of their peculiar circumstances, we allow them two years from the notice given to consider the expedience of compliance or non-compliance with these rules.

"*Quest.* 43. What shall be done with those who buy or sell slaves, or give them away? *Ans.* They are immediately to be expelled, unless they buy them on purpose to free them."

In 1785 these rules were suspended, as it was thought they "would do harm," though still the destruction of slavery was to be sought "by all wise and prudent means." In 1796 the following section was inserted in the Discipline:

"*Quest.* What regulations shall be made for the extirpation of the crying evil of African slavery? *Ans.* 1. We declare that we are more than ever convinced of the great evil of the African slavery which still exists in these United States, and do most earnestly recommend to the Yearly Conferences, quarterly meetings, and to those who have the oversight of districts and circuits, to be exceedingly cautious what persons they admit to official stations in our Church; and in the case of future admission to official stations, to require such security of those who hold slaves for the emancipation of them, immediately or gradually, as the laws of the states respectively, and the circumstances of the case will admit; and we do fully authorize all the Yearly Conferences to make whatever regulations they judge proper, in the present case, respecting the admission of persons to official stations in our Church. 2. No slaveholder shall be received into society till the preacher who has the oversight of the circuit has spoken to him freely and faithfully on the subject of slavery. 3. Every member of the society who sells a slave shall immediately, after full proof, be excluded the society. And if any member of our society purchase a slave, the ensuing quarterly meeting shall determine on the number of years in which the slave so purchased would work out the price of his purchase. And the person so purchasing shall, immediately after such determination, execute a legal instrument for the manumission of such slave at the expiration of the term determined by the quarterly meeting. And in default of his executing such instrument of manumission, or on his refusal to submit his case to the judgment of the quarterly meeting, such member shall be excluded the society. *Provided also,* that in the case of a female slave it shall be inserted in the aforesaid instrument of manumission that all her children who shall be born during the years of her servitude shall be free at the following times, namely: every female child at the age of twenty-one, and every male child at the age of twenty-five. *Nevertheless,* if the member of our society executing the said instrument of manumission judge it proper, he may fix the times of manumission of the children of the female slaves before mentioned at an earlier age than that which is prescribed above. 4. The preachers and other members of our society are requested to consider the subject of negro slavery with deep attention till the ensuing General Conference; and that they impart to the General Conference, through the medium of the Yearly Conferences, or otherwise, any important thoughts upon the subject, that the Conference may have full light, in order to take further steps towards the eradicating this enormous evil from that part of the Church of God to which we are united."

In 1800 the following new paragraphs were inserted:

"5. When any travelling preacher becomes an owner of a slave or slaves by any means, he shall forfeit his ministerial character in our Church, unless he execute, if it be practicable, a legal emancipation of such slaves, conformably to the laws of the state in which he lives. 6. The Annual Conferences are directed to draw up addresses for the gradual emancipation of the slaves to the legislatures of those states in which no general laws have been passed for that purpose. These addresses shall urge, in the most respectful but pointed manner, the necessity of a law for the gradual emancipation of the slaves; proper committees shall be appointed by the Annual Conferences, out of the most respectable of our friends, for the conducting of the business; and the presiding elders, elders, deacons, and travelling preachers, shall secure as many proper signatures as possible to the addresses, and give all the assistance in their power in every respect to aid the committees, and to further this blessed undertaking. Let this be continued from year to year till the desired end be accomplished."

In 1804 the following alterations were made: the question reads, "What shall be done for the extirpation of the evil of slavery?" In paragraph 1 (1796), instead of "more than ever convinced," it reads, "as much as ever convinced;" and instead of "the African slavery which still exists in these United States," it reads simply "slavery." In paragraph 4 (3 of 1796), respecting the selling of a slave, before the words "shall immediately," the following clause is inserted: "Except at the request of the slave, in cases of mercy and humanity, agreeably to the judgment of a committee of the male members of the society, appointed by the preacher who has the charge of the circuit." This new proviso was inserted: "*Provided also*, that if a member of our society shall buy a slave with a certificate of future emancipation, the terms of emancipation shall, notwithstanding, be subject to the decision of the Quarterly-meeting Conference." All after "*nevertheless*" was stricken out, and the following substituted: "The members of our societies in the states of North Carolina, South Carolina, Georgia, and Tennessee shall be exempted from the operation of the above rules." The paragraphs about considering the subject of slavery and petitioning legislatures were cancelled, and this was added: "6. Let the preachers, from time to time, as occasion serves, admonish and exhort all slaves to render due respect and obedience to the commands and interests of their respective masters." In 1808 it was ordered that "no slaveholder shall be eligible to the office of an elder, where the laws will admit of emancipation, and permit the liberated slave to enjoy freedom;" but all that related to slaveholding among private members, and paragraph 5 of 1804, were cancelled, and the following substituted: "3. The General Conference authorizes each Annual Conference to form their own regulations relative to buying and selling slaves." In 1812 this was altered thus: "3. Whereas the laws of some of the states do not admit of emancipating of slaves without a special act of the legislature, the General Conference authorizes each Annual Conference to form their own regulations relative to buying and selling slaves." In 1816 paragraph 1 of 1796 was altered thus: "1. We declare that we are as much as ever convinced of the great evil of slavery; therefore no slaveholder shall be eligible to any official station in our Church hereafter, where the laws of the state in which he lives will admit of emancipation, and permit the liberated slave to enjoy freedom." In 1820 the paragraph leaving it to the Annual Conferences "to form their own regulations about buying and selling slaves" was cancelled. In 1824 the following paragraphs were added: "4. All our preachers shall prudently enforce upon our members the necessity of teaching their slaves to read the Word of God; and to allow them time to attend upon the public worship of God on our regular days of divine service. 5. Our colored preachers and official members shall have all the privileges which are usual to others in the District and Quarterly Conferences, where the usages of the country do not forbid it. And the presiding elder may hold for them a separate District Conference, where the number of colored local preachers will justify it. 6. The Annual Conferences may employ colored preachers to travel and preach where their services are judged necessary; provided that no one shall be so employed without having been recommended according to the Form of Discipline."

The General Rules drawn up by Mr. Wesley for the Methodist societies in England were not placed in the Discipline at the time of the organization of the Methodist Episcopal Church in America in 1784. They were inserted, with some alterations, by bishops Coke and Asbury in 1789. The bishops took the liberty of interpolating the rule forbidding "the buying or selling the bodies and souls of men with an intention to enslave them."* In 1792 it was altered thus: "The buying or selling of men, women, or children, with an intention to enslave them." In 1808 thus: "The buying and selling of men, women, and children, with an intention to enslave them." In view of the time and manner of its introduction, and its peculiar phraseology, this rule was considered to refer to the African slave-trade, and not to the transfer of those already in slavery from one person to another; hence it met with but little opposition in the South, which denounced that odious traffic. The later General Conferences, down to that of 1840, were conservative on this subject, and this latter affirmed the right of local preachers in Maryland and Virginia who held slaves to ordination, from which they had been debarred by the Baltimore Conference. As the Southern States did not allow the emancipation of slaves without expatriation, both ministers and members held them without violation of the Discipline. As slavery was a civil and social institution, it was impossible for the Church to exist in the South without this permission. In this respect the Methodist Episcopal Church only imitated the Apostolic and Primitive Church, which allowed of slavery among both the membership and ministry, and made laws for the regulation of the same. Mr. Wesley pursued the same course in the West Indies, licensing Mr. Gilbert, a slaveholder, to preach, and baptizing his slaves. The British Conference did so too, charging its ministers in the West Indies to have nothing to do with the institution of slavery, as that was a matter belonging to the legislature, but to preach the Gospel alike to master and slave. Thus, after a tortuous legislation on the vexed question, which scarcely knows a parallel in Church history, the Methodist Episcopal Church in America appears to have been settling down upon a satisfactory and permanent basis.

III. *The Separation.*—But when the General Conference met in 1844, in New York, the Rev. Francis A. Harding, of the Baltimore Conference, appealed to it from the decision of that Conference, which had suspended him from the ministry for not manumitting slaves belonging to his wife. The General Conference confirmed the decision of the Baltimore Conference, despite the laws of Maryland and of the Discipline. It was ascertained, too, that one of the bishops, James Osgood Andrew, residing in Georgia, had become connected with slavery. Neither he nor Mr. Harding had either bought or sold a slave. Bishop Andrew was *legally* in possession of a slave, bequeathed him by a lady, and whom he would liberate at any time, but she would not receive her freedom; also a boy, left by his former wife to his daughter without will; him, too, he would willingly manumit if he could do so by the laws of Georgia; also slaves legally his by his second marriage, whom he could not own, but secured them by deed to his wife, to whom they belonged—the law not allowing their emancipation. But after a lengthened, excited, and very able discussion of the question on both sides, the General Conference adopted the following preamble and resolution: "Whereas, the Discipline of the Church forbids the doing anything calculated to destroy our itinerant and general superintendency; and whereas, bishop Andrew has become connected with slavery, by marriage and otherwise, and this act having drawn after it circumstances which, in the estimation of the General Conference, will greatly embarrass the exercise of his office as an itinerant general superintendent, if not, in some places, entirely prevent it; therefore, *Resolved*, That it is the sense of this General Conference that he

* [See, however, foot-note on p. 173 of the art. METHOD- IST EPISCOPAL CHURCH.—ED.]

desist from the exercise of this office so long as this impediment remains." The vote stood 111 for and 69 against—all in the affirmative, except one (and he a Northerner), being from Northern Conferences, the Baltimore Conference being equally divided: several from the Northern Conferences, however, voted in the negative. The bishops had requested the General Conference to suspend action in the premises, suggesting that arrangements might be made to retain bishop Andrew in office, as his services would be "welcome and cordial" in the South. Resolutions declaring the action in the case of bishop Andrew, to be advisory only, and not to be considered in the light of a judicial mandate, and postponing its final disposition, according to the suggestion of the bishops, were laid on the table by a vote of 75 to 68 —the South, of course, voting in the negative. Resolutions proposing two General Conferences were referred to a committee, which could not agree on a report. The Southern delegates then presented the following "Declaration:" "The delegates of the Conferences in the slaveholding states take leave to *declare* to the General Conference of the Methodist Episcopal Church that the continued agitation on the subject of slavery and abolition in a portion of the Church, the frequent action on that subject in the General Conference, and especially the extra-judicial proceedings against bishop Andrew, which resulted on Saturday last in the virtual suspension of him from his office as superintendent, must produce a state of things in the South which renders a continuance of the jurisdiction of the General Conference over these Conferences inconsistent with the success of the ministry in the slaveholding states." This declaration was referred to a committee of nine, composed of Northern and Southern delegates, with instructions to devise a constitutional plan for a mutual and friendly division of the Church, provided the difficulties could not be otherwise adjusted. The minority, through Dr. Bascom, presented an elaborate protest against the action of the majority in the case of bishop Andrew, characterizing it as extra-judicial and unconstitutional—the Episcopacy being a co-ordinate branch of the government of the Church, a bishop cannot be subjected by a delegated Conference to any official disability without formal presentation of a charge of the violation of law, and conviction on trial, and no law concerning slavery had been violated by bishop Andrew; the action therefore in his case was unconstitutional, and would establish a dangerous precedent, subversive of the union and stability of the Methodist Episcopal Church. This protest was allowed to go on the Journal, and a reply was made to it on the part of the majority. Resolutions were adopted allowing bishop Andrew's name to remain in the Minutes, Hymn-book, and Discipline as formerly; allowing him and his family a support; and leaving to him to decide what work he would do, if any, in view of the action of the Conference—the third resolution being adopted by a vote of 103 to 67. The committee of nine made their report on a plan of separation, which, after discussion and amendment, and earnest advocacy by Drs. Olin, Hamline, Bangs, Elliott, and other Northern delegates, was adopted by a nearly unanimous vote. The leaders of the North considered that the Conference was shut up to this course, as they affirmed that, under the circumstances, bishop Andrew could not preside in some of the Northern Conferences, and they believed that if he were suspended, and the Southern Church submitted to it, Methodism could not prosper in the South. Hundreds of thousands of negroes were supplied with the Gospel by the Southern Church, and access to them, especially on the plantations, would be debarred if the measure in question were submitted to by the South. Division, therefore, was inevitable. It was accomplished in the spirit of candor and charity— and the rather as the Connection was getting too large, as Dr. Elliott said, for one General-Conference jurisdiction. The following is the *Plan of Separation:*

"The select committee of nine to consider and report on the declaration of the delegates from the Conferences of the slaveholding states, beg leave to submit the following report:

"*Whereas*, a declaration has been presented to this General Conference with the signatures of *fifty-one* delegates of the body, from thirteen Annual Conferences in the slaveholding states, representing that, for various reasons enumerated, the objects and purposes of the Christian ministry and Church organization cannot be successfully accomplished by them under the jurisdiction of this General Conference as now constituted; and whereas, in the event of a separation, a contingency to which the declaration asks attention as not improbable, we esteem it the duty of this General Conference to meet the emergency with Christian kindness and the strictest equity, therefore, *Resolved*, by the delegates of the several Annual Conferences in General Conference assembled,

"1. That should the Annual Conferences in the slaveholding states find it necessary to unite in a distinct ecclesiastical connection, the following rule shall be observed with regard to the northern boundary of such connection: All the societies, stations, and Conferences adhering to the Church in the South, by a vote of a majority of the members of said societies, stations, and Conferences, shall remain under the unmolested pastoral care of the Southern Church; and the ministers of the Methodist Episcopal Church shall in no wise attempt to organize churches or societies within the limits of the Church South, nor shall they attempt to exercise any pastoral oversight therein; it being understood that the ministry of the South reciprocally observe the same rule in relation to stations, societies, and Conferences adhering by a vote of a majority to the Methodist Episcopal Church; provided, also, that this rule shall apply only to societies, stations, and Conferences bordering on the line of division, and not to interior charges, which shall in all cases be left to the care of that Church within whose territory they are situated.

"2. That ministers, local and travelling, of every grade and office in the Methodist Episcopal Church, may, as they prefer, remain in that Church, or, without blame, attach themselves to the Church South.

"3. *Resolved*, by the delegates of all the Annual Conferences in General Conference assembled, That we recommend to all the Annual Conferences at their first approaching sessions to authorize a change of the sixth Restrictive Article, so that the first clause shall read thus: 'They shall not appropriate the produce of the Book Concern, nor of the Chartered Fund, to any other purpose other than for the benefit of the travelling, supernumerary, superannuated, and worn-out preachers, their wives, widows, and children, and to such other purposes as may be determined upon by the votes of two thirds of the members of the General Conference.'

"4. That whenever the Annual Conferences, by a vote of three fourths of all their members voting on the third resolution, shall have concurred in the recommendation to alter the sixth Restrictive Article, the agents at New York and Cincinnati shall, and they are hereby authorized and directed to deliver over to any authorized agent or appointee of the Church South, (should one be organized), all notes and book accounts against the ministers, Church members, or citizens within its boundaries, with authority to collect the same for the sole use of the Southern Church; and that said agents also convey to the aforesaid agent or appointee of the South all the real estate, and assign to him all the property, including presses, stock, and all right and interest connected with the printing establishments at Charleston, Richmond, and Nashville, which now belong to the Methodist Episcopal Church.

"5. That when the Annual Conferences shall have approved the aforesaid change in the sixth Restrictive Article, there shall be transferred to the above agents of the Southern Church so much of the capital and produce of the Methodist Book Concern as will, with the notes, book accounts, presses, etc., mentioned in the last resolution, bear the same proportion to the whole property of said Concern that the travelling preachers in the Southern Church shall bear to all the travelling ministers of the Methodist Episcopal Church, the division to be made on the basis of the number of travelling preachers in the forthcoming Minutes.

"6. That the above transfer shall be in the form of annual payments of $25,000 per annum, and specifically in stock of the Book Concern, and in Southern notes and accounts due the establishment, and accruing after the first transfer mentioned above; and until the payments are made the Southern Church shall share in all the net profits of the Book Concern in the proportion that the amount due them, or in arrears, bears to all the property of the Concern.

"7. That Nathan Bangs, George Peck, and James B. Finley be, and they are hereby appointed commissioners to act in concert with the same number of commissioners appointed by the Southern organization (should one be formed), to estimate the amount which will fall due to the South by the preceding rule, and to have full powers to carry into effect the whole arrangements proposed with regard to the division of property, should the separation take place. And if by any means a vacancy occur in this

Board of Commissioners, the Book Committee at New York shall fill said vacancy.

"8. That whenever any agents of the Southern Church are clothed with legal authority or corporate power to act in the premises, the agents at New York are hereby authorized and directed to act in concert with said Southern agents, so as to give the provisions of these resolutions a legally binding force.

"9. That all the property of the Methodist Episcopal Church in meeting-houses, parsonages, colleges, schools, Conference funds, cemeteries, and of every kind within the limits of the Southern organization, shall be forever free from any claim set up on the part of the Methodist Episcopal Church, so far as this resolution can be of force in the premises.

"10. That the Church so formed in the South shall have a common right to use all the copyrights in possession of the Book Concerns at New York and Cincinnati at the time of the settlement by the commissioners.

"11. That the book agents at New York be directed to make such compensation to the Conferences South for their dividend from the Chartered Fund as the commissioners above provided for shall agree upon.

"12. That the bishops be respectfully requested to lay that part of this report requiring the action of the Annual Conferences before them as soon as possible, beginning with the New York Conference."

The Southern delegates sent out an address to their constituents, showing what they had done, and counselling moderation and forbearance. They called for a convention of the Annual Conferences—in the ratio of one to eleven of their members—to meet in Louisville, Ky., May 1, 1845. Meanwhile the Church in the South, in Quarterly and Annual Conferences, took action in the premises, and declared in favor of the plan of separation with a very near approach to unanimity. The convention met in Louisville at the appointed time, bishops Soulé, Andrew, and Morris being present. The bishops were invited to preside, and the two former did so. The convention, acting under the plan of separation, declared the Southern Conferences there represented a distinct connection, under the style of "The Methodist Episcopal Church, South," and made provision for the holding of its first General Conference in Petersburg, Va., May, 1846. Bishops Soulé and Andrew were requested to become regular and constitutional bishops of the Methodist Episcopal Church, South; the latter complied with the request, but the former, in view of outstanding engagements, postponed doing so till the session of the General Conference. The action of the convention was nearly unanimous, and it gave great satisfaction throughout the South. Bishop Soulé gave in his formal adherence at the General Conference in Petersburg; two other bishops were consecrated, viz. William Capers, D.D., and Robert Paine, D.D.; the Discipline was revised; missions, etc., were projected; Henry B. Bascom, Alexander L. P. Green, and Charles B. Parsons were appointed commissioners, and John Early agent and appointee, according to the provisions of the plan of separation; editors, etc., were chosen, and all the operations of the Church went on as though no separation had taken place. Lovick Pierce, D.D., was commissioned to attend the session of the Northern General Conference in 1848, to tender to that body the Christian regards and fraternal salutations of the General Conference of the Methodist Episcopal Church, South; but he was not received in his official capacity. A change had come over the Northern Church, and the General Conference repudiated the plan of separation. The Church-property question had to be settled by the Supreme Court of the United States, which decided in favor of the South. The property was divided according to the provisions of the plan. A publishing-house was established in Nashville; a quarterly review, weekly papers, Sunday-school papers, books, tracts, etc., were published; and all things progressed prosperously till the war interfered with the operations of the Church, and sadly crippled its institutions. Much of its property was appropriated by others during the military occupancy of the South; but most of it has been restored, and it is hoped all the rest will soon be. Tentative movements have been made by some in the Northern Church for reunion; but as that is deemed inexpe-

dient and impracticable, the Northern General Conference of 1872 empowered the bishops to send a deputation to the General Conference of the Methodist Episcopal Church, South, in 1874, to see if fraternal intercourse cannot be established between the two connections. It is hoped that this will take place on a basis honorable to both parties. The fraternal messenger sent to the Northern Conference in 1848, assured that body that the Methodist Episcopal Church, South, was always ready for fraternization on the basis of the plan of separation.

III. *Present Condition.*—The Church has been rapidly recovering from the sad effects of the war. At the time of the separation, in 1844, there were about 450,000 communicants in the Southern Church. In 1860 there were 757,205, of whom 207,766 were colored members. These figures were greatly reduced during the war. In 1890 the number of communicants was 1,161,666, of whom only 520 were colored. There were 4862 travelling and 6269 local preachers—all embraced in the foregoing figures. Most of the colored members had joined other colored bodies of Methodists. Many of them are connected with the Colored Methodist Episcopal Church in America, which was organized in 1870 by the sanction of the General Conference of the Methodist Episcopal Church, South, with a distinct connection in fraternal relation with this Church, the bishops of the latter consecrating as bishops two colored ministers chosen by a colored General Conference. One of them died in 1872; but the Connection is prosperous, having a number of Annual Conferences, and at a special General Conference, held in Augusta, Ga., in 1873, three other bishops were elected. Their Discipline, *mutatis mutandis,* is the same as that of the Methodist Episcopal Church, South. The bishops of the Southern Church have been : Soulé, Andrew, Bascom, Capers, Pierce, Early, Kavanagh, Wightman, Doggett, Marvin, and McTyeire; and they now are Keener, Wilson, Granberry, Hargood, Duncan, Galloway, Hendrix, Key, Haygood, and Fitzgerald. There are 46 Annual Conferences, composed of travelling ministers and lay delegates—four of the latter (one of whom may be a local preacher) from every district. The General Conference is constituted of an equal number of ministers and laymen. District Conferences are held in all the districts once a year, for the purpose of review, etc., but without legislative or judicial power. Quarterly Conferences are held in all the pastoral charges, at which exhorters and local preachers are licensed, and preachers are recommended to the Annual Conference for ordination or admission into the travelling ministry. Church Conferences are ordered once a month, to review all the spiritual and temporal affairs of the pastoral charges. Sunday-schools, love-feasts, class-meetings, and prayer-meetings enter into the economy of the Church. The General Conference ordered a revised edition of the Liturgy, as abridged by Mr. Wesley for the Methodist Episcopal Church in America, to be published for those congregations that might desire to use it; but few, if any, do so. The Ritual is still in use for all occasional services, and it has been carefully revised and improved, as also has been the psalmody of the Church. The Sunday-school cause has received a great impulse, and many valuable publications are issued to meet its demands. Universities, colleges, and academies, for both sexes, have been multiplying all over the Connection. Many original works, which are held in high estimation, such as histories, biographies, sermons, commentaries, and other works on theology, have been issued from the publishing-house of the Church; and the great staple works of the Wesleyan press have been carefully revised and re-printed. The publishing-house was in part destroyed by fire in February, 1872, but a magnificent edifice, approaching completion, is to take its place. The missionary work of the Church was well-nigh broken up by the war; but it is recuperating —except the missions to the colored people, which were considered the crowning glory of the Southern Methodist Church. The missions to China and Brazil have received a great impetus and promise well; so do the Indian missions. A mission has been established in Mexico under favorable auspices. But the destitute portions of the South—destroyed by the war—require a vast amount of missionary work, and in rendering this the Church is restricted, for want of sufficient men and means, from extending its work in the foreign field.— *Disciplines, General Minutes, Journals* of the General Conferences of the Methodist Episcopal Churches North and South; Emory's *History of the Discipline; Methodist Church Property Case;* Redford's *History of the Organization of the Methodist Episcopal Church, South.* See METHODISM. (T. O. S.)

Methodist Protestant Church is the name assumed by a body of Christians who seceded from the Methodist Episcopal Church in 1830. The primary causes for this step were opposition to the episcopate, and the decided refusal of the Methodist Episcopal ministry to vest any authority in the laity. From the very outset efforts were made by a minority in the Methodist Episcopal Church to secure the representation of the laity in the conferences. See KILHAMITES; LAY REPRESENTATION. In 1824 a so-called Union Society was founded at Baltimore, Md., for the purpose of agitating the question of a change of the Church government, and a periodical was established called *The Mutual Rights of the Ministers and Members of the Methodist Episcopal Church.* In the spring of 1826 the Baltimore Union Society initiated a movement to inquire into the expediency of making a united petition for a general representation to the General Conference of 1828. The convention was held in November, 1827, and the petition was presented, but received an unfavorable reply. The Union Society, persisting in its efforts, a number of individuals were expelled in Tennessee, North Carolina, and Baltimore. This provoked many friends of the radicals, and caused the secession of considerable numbers. A convention which met at Baltimore, Md., Nov. 12, 1828, drew up provisional articles of association; and on Nov. 2, 1830, another convention, composed of an equal number of clerical and lay delegates from various states of the Union, assembled at the same place, and, after a session protracted for three weeks, adopted a Constitution and a Book of Discipline, and formed a new society, under the name of *Methodist Protestant Church.* The Rev. Francis Waters, D.D., of Baltimore, was president of this convention.

The Methodist Protestant Church holds the same doctrinal views as the parent body, and differs from it only in a few points of ecclesiastical government. Following the example of the British Wesleyans, the Episcopal office is abolished, and a president called to rule over each Annual Conference, elected by the ballot of that body. The laity is admitted to an equal participation with the clergy in all Church legislation and government. The General Conference, which at first met every seventh, but now congregates every fourth year, is composed of an equal number of ministers and laymen, who are elected by the Annual Conferences at the ratio of one delegate of each order from every one thousand communicants. The General Conference has authority, under certain restrictions, to make such rules for the government of the Church as may be necessary to carry into effect the laws of Christ; to fix the compensation and duties of travelling ministers and preachers, etc.; to devise means for raising money, and to regulate the boundaries of Annual Conference districts. The Annual Conference, which consists of all the ordained itinerant ministers of the district, has power to elect to orders, station ministers, preachers, and missionaries; make rules for defraying the expenses of their support, and fix the boundaries of circuits and stations. It elects its own president yearly. The Quarterly Conference is composed of the trustees, ministers, preachers, exhorters, leaders, and stewards in the circuit of which it is the immediate official meeting. It examines

the official character of its members, licenses preachers, recommends candidates for ordination to the Annual Conference, etc. There are classes, leaders, and stewards, as in the Methodist Episcopal Church.

The slavery question divided the Methodist Protestant Church into two bodies—*the Methodist Protestant Church of the North-western States,* and *the Methodist Protestants of the Southern States.* The head-quarters of the former were established at Springfield, Ohio; those of the latter at Baltimore, Md. The members of the Methodist Protestant Church were at that time scattered mainly over the Border States and certain parts of the West; their principal strength has since developed in Virginia, Maryland, and in some portions of Ohio and Pennsylvania. Of late years a union of all non-Episcopal Methodists having been proposed, the Protestant Methodists North changed their official name to *the Methodist Church.* Their head-quarters were lately removed from Springfield, Ohio, to Pittsburgh, Pa. Each body has a board of foreign and domestic missions and a Book Concern—the Protestant Church South at Baltimore, Md.; the Methodists at Pittsburgh, Pa. At the beginning the Methodist Protestant Church counted 83 ministers and about 5000 members; and at the seventh General Conference in 1858 there were 2000 stationed ministers, 1200 churches, 90,000 members, and $1,590,000 worth of property. In their present divided form they figure, according to the *New York Observer Year-book* of 1873, as follows: (1) The Methodist Church counts 28 conferences, 766 preachers, and about 75,000 members, with a Church property of $1,609,425; and (2) the Methodist Protestant Church, within 25 conferences, employs 423 preachers, and has about 70,000 members.

The Methodist Protestants have three colleges: the Western Maryland, at Westminster, Carroll County, Md.; Yadkin College, North Carolina; and one in West Virginia. The *Methodist Protestant,* a weekly paper, of which the Rev. L. W. Bates, D.D., is the editor, published at their Book Concern, is the official organ. The eleventh General Conference of this body is to be held at Lynchburg, Virginia, on the first Friday of May, 1874.

The Methodist Church issues a weekly newspaper, the *Methodist Recorder,* edited by Alexander Clark, and published by the Book Concern at Pittsburgh, Pa. Also a semi-monthly Sunday-school journal, edited by the same. A new Hymn-book, entitled *The Voice of Praise,* has just been compiled and published, which compares favorably with that of any other denomination. Among the recent literary productions of the Church are the following works: *Pulpit Echoes,* by John Scott, D.D.; *Non-Episcopal Methodism,* by T. H. Colhouer, A.M.; *Wonders of the East,* by J. J. Smith, D.D.; *The Impending Conflict,* by J. J. Smith, D.D.; *Recollections of Itinerant Life,* by George Brown, D.D.; *The Lady Preacher,* by the same; *The Gospel in the Trees,* by Alexander Clark, A.M.; *Work-day Christianity,* by the same; etc. Adrian College, Adrian, Mich., is under their control, and is in a most promising condition. Its president is George B. McElroy, D.D. It admits both males and females. The Missionary Board—William Collier, D.D., president, and C. H. Williams, corresponding secretary—is devising large plans for the West, and initiating foreign work. The Board of Ministerial Education—J. B. Walker, corresponding secretary—is doing a good work for young men preparing for the ministry. There is a fair prospect that at an early day an organic reunion with the Methodist Protestant Church will be effected. The initiatory steps have already been taken, and will probably lead to a united Methodist Church of non-episcopal order. The General Conference of the Methodist Church will meet at Pittsburgh, Pa., May 17, 1874. See the *Discipline of the Methodist Church,* and *Discipline of the Methodist Protestant Church;* also Stevens, *Hist. of Methodism,* iii, 463; Bangs, *Hist. Meth. Ch.* iii, 432 sq.; Sprague, *Annals Amer. Pulpit,* vol. vii, Introd. p. 18. See METHODISM.

Methodists, Camp, is a term of reproach which in the days of early Methodism was fastened upon those Methodists in the Western States of North America who, with a view to promote revivals of religion, adopted camp-meetings, at which religious services were conducted. Now that camp-meetings have become popular, in this country the term is no longer employed.

Methodists, Dialectic, or Romish, as they have also been called, flourished near the middle of the 17th century. They were priests of the Church of Rome, who attempted, by ingenious sophistry, to refute the arguments employed against them by the Protestant (Huguenot) party. Mosheim (*Eccles. Hist.* vol. iii) arranges these "Methodists" under two classes. According to his classification, the one party in their controversies urged their opponents to adduce direct proof of their doctrines by an appeal to the statements of the Holy Scripture. The other party refused to encounter the Protestants by arguing with them on the various disputed points, but sought to overcome them by adducing certain great principles involving the whole subject. Thus they insisted that the Church which was chargeable with changing or modifying its doctrines could not have the Holy Spirit for its guide.

In England the term *Methodist* is frequently applied to a person who becomes religious, without reference to any particular sect or party, and especially to ministers of the Church of England who are evangelical and zealous in their preaching.

Methodists, Free (properly "THE FREE METHODIST CHURCH"). This body, the youngest of the Methodist family, an offshoot of the Methodist Episcopal Church, dates its existence from Aug. 23, 1860, when it was organized at a convention held at Pekin, Niagara Co., N. Y., composed of laymen and ministers who were then or had been of the Methodist Episcopal Church.

I. *Origin, etc.*—The causes for the establishment of this independent body were manifold. Most prominent, however, were a desire for primitive Methodist *simplicity*, and more faithful adherence to the doctrines and usages of Wesley and his associates. Its organizers were ministers expelled from the "parent" body because of their course in opposing what they called innovations or departures from the rules of the Discipline. It was and is claimed by those engaged in the Free Methodist movement that the Methodist Church has declined in spirituality since their early history, and that in the rapid progress made by the Church in adding numbers, acquiring property, etc., sufficient care has not been taken to guard its purity, and preserve its primitive power and spiritual efficiency—the *toleration* of many worldly practices, and a departure from correct doctrine on several important points. In proof of this it is asserted that widely divergent and contradictory teachings are heard from the pulpit on the doctrine of entire sanctification without official rebuke, some preachers claiming sanctification as a work done concomitantly with justification, others regarding it as a result to be reached by a gradual process of spiritual growth, and yet others preaching it as a second distinct attainment to be received instantaneously by faith. The Free Methodists also hold that hearty and thorough repentance, evinced by honest confession, and complete abandonment of all sin, is practically not enough insisted on, and that many are accepted as converts who are not even scripturally awakened; that a merely intellectual belief, born of human reason, is allowed to take the place of the supernatural faith taught by Paul and Wesley; that the direct witness of the Spirit is not now enjoyed by multitudes of professed Methodists; that power over all sin is not experienced; that entire sanctification is even professedly a rare attainment; that the execution of discipline is so neglected as to become difficult; and in many societies impossible; that Methodists generally have abandoned plainness of dress, and are as fashionably attired as the world itself; that they are allowed and countenanced

in the transaction of unscriptural business enterprises, and transact lawful business on worldly principles; and especially that secret and oath-bound fellowship with societies composed in large part of unsaved men is tolerated and encouraged; and that the relaxing of the rule requiring attendance at class is especially fatal to spirituality. It is also further asserted that other evidences of the spiritual decline of the Church are exhibited by the partial and frequent abandonment of the free-seat system in its houses of worship; and in the substitution of choir singing and instrumental performances for congregational praise; by the reading instead of preaching of sermons; by the building of extravagantly costly churches, and resorting to improper modes of Church support, such as Church fairs, picnics, donation parties, etc.

The movement for the organization of this independent body had its commencement within the bounds of the Genesee Conference (N. Y.) of the Methodist Episcopal Church. A number of ministers of that body had written and spoken against these alleged departures from the primitive faith of Methodism. By the year 1855 a state of feeling had been engendered which resulted in acrimonious disputes, accusations, Church trials, etc., and finally, in the year 1858, in the expulsion of the Rev. B. T. Roberts and the Rev. Joseph M'Creery on a charge of contumacy. Mr. Roberts had been tried the previous year by his Conference for alleged "immoral and unchristian conduct." (Said conduct consisted in publishing an article in the *Northern Independent* entitled "New-school Methodism," in which the writer set forth views such as have been recited above, and which he offered to retract and confess as publicly as they had been promulgated if proved untrue or incorrect.) His article was assumed to be slanderous, however, and he was found guilty, and was sentenced to be rebuked by the bishop. The contumacy charged against him in the following year consisted in publishing and circulating a second edition of *New-school Methodism*, and a pamphlet signed by George W. Estes, which gave a short account of the trial of the year preceding. On this charge (which was disproved as to the *publishing*), and on the testimony of one witness (whose veracity was impeached) as to the circulation, Mr. Roberts, in connection with one or two colleagues, was expelled from the Genesee Conference and the Methodist Episcopal Church. This proceeding was regarded as a measure of high-handed persecution by many ministers and laymen of the Church, and during the ensuing year one hundred and ninety-five prominent laymen met in convention at Albion, Orleans County, N. Y., and passed resolutions expressing their entire and unabated confidence in the expelled preachers, and recommending them to continue to labor for the salvation of souls. This sympathy of the laymen was shared by many of the ministers of the Conference, and this was so publicly expressed that at the ensuing Conference four of them were expelled on charges of "contumacy," while two others were located for the same cause. A large number of the lay members were also excluded from the Church. The ensuing General Conference, held at Buffalo in 1860, was respectfully petitioned by fifteen hundred members of the Methodist Episcopal Church within the bounds of the Conference from which these expulsions had taken place to investigate the judicial action of said Conference in relation to these matters. A committee was appointed for this purpose; but was finally discharged. B. T. Roberts had appealed from both of the decisions of the Conference in his case. The first only was entertained, and on that, "The verdict of reproof," the appeal committee stood equally divided. The other appeal was not entertained. Thus these ministers and members were shut out of the Church. As they believed that the causes which had led to their expulsion existed more or less in all the other churches bearing the Methodist name, they felt compelled to organize a new denomination, that would, in their judgment, more fully carry out the purposes and designs of Methodism.*

II. *Organization, Doctrines, etc.*—In the formation of the new Church, while everything calculated to sustain and cherish the original spirit of Methodism has been carefully retained, care has been taken to incorporate into its modes of government everything shown by the progress of Methodism for a century past to be necessary. The Episcopacy is abandoned, and general superintendency substituted; the incumbents of the office are elected every four years. Quadrennial, Annual, and Quarterly Conferences are retained as in the parent body, while the last addition to the machinery of the Methodist Episcopal government, viz. the District Conference, adopted in 1872, has been in use among the Free Methodists from their beginning. In all the before-named Church courts a number of laymen, equal to the ministry, are admitted, and their right to speak and vote is fully guaranteed. The official board is retained, and there is provision for annual meetings of all members of the societies for the appointment of delegates to the Annual Conferences, and stewards. Class-meetings are held, and attendance is a condition of membership in the Church. The preachers in charge nominate and the classes elect the class-leaders. The office of presiding elder is retained, but the name of the officer is *district chairman.*

The articles of faith adopted are the same as those of the Methodist Episcopal Church, with two additions, designed to secure uniformity of belief, and guard against the introduction of errors on the important points to which they relate. The first is on entire sanctification, and the first part is in the words of John Wesley, viz.: "Justified persons, while they do not outwardly commit sin, are nevertheless conscious of sin still remaining in the heart. They feel a natural tendency to evil, a proneness to depart from God, and cleave to the things of earth. Those that are sanctified wholly are saved from all inward sin—from evil thoughts and evil tempers. No wrong temper, none contrary to love remains in the soul. All their thoughts, words, and actions are governed by pure love. Entire sanctification takes place subsequently to justification, and is the work of God wrought instantaneously upon the consecrated, believing soul. After a soul is cleansed from all sin, it is then fully prepared to grow in grace" (*Discipline*, "Articles of Religion," ch. i, § 1, p. 23). This doctrine is regarded as of so much importance that no person is admitted to the full membership of the Church who does not endorse it, and pledge himself definitely to seek diligently the experience thereof. No minister would be tolerated in the body who could be truthfully regarded as out of accordance in views or teaching therewith.

The second new article of faith is on *future reward and punishment*, and reads as follows: "God has appointed a day in which he will judge the world in righteousness by Jesus Christ, according to the Gospel. The righteous shall have in heaven an inheritance in-

corruptible, undefiled, and that fadeth not away. The wicked shall go away into everlasting punishment, where their worm dieth not, and their fire is not quenched" (*Discipline*, "Articles of Religion," ch. i, § 1, p. 23).

A noteworthy difference of polity exists between this and all other Methodist bodies in respect to admitting members on probation. None are received simply on expressing "a desire to flee from the wrath to come," but all are required to give evidence of such a desire by confessing a "saving faith in Christ." In other words, none are added to the Church, even on probation, unless it is believed that they "are saved." Free Methodists claim that much of the defection alleged to have taken place in the Methodist Episcopal and other churches is due to the fact that multitudes have joined the Church as seekers of salvation, but have gone no further spiritually.

It is also definitely required of all who join the Free Methodist Church that they shall lay aside all superfluous ornaments in dress, "laying aside gold, pearls, and costly array" (*Discipline*, ch. i, § 3, ¶ 4). That they shall keep free from connection with all societies requiring an oath, affirmation, or promise of secrecy as a condition of membership therein (*ibid.* ¶ 5). Also that they shall refrain from the use of all intoxicating liquors, and from the use of tobacco, except as medicine (*ibid.* p. 31, ¶ 4).

III. *Present Condition, etc.*—The progress of the denomination is rapid, considering the bold stand it makes against many customs and usages quite popular even in the churches, and the nature of the requirements made of those who become members. During the first years of its history it had to encounter some of the difficulties which beset early Methodism in the form of wild fanaticism and a spirit of insubordination to proper church regulations, and it suffered considerably from the doings and sayings of some who were never members of the Church, but who, taking advantage of the circumstances under which it was formed, and acting somewhat in connection with its movements, promulgated ideas and encouraged practices contrary to pure Gospel; but the young denomination has had power to shake off these parasites, and free itself from these incumbrances, and bids fair to march on its way successfully in the mission of spreading scriptural holiness as understood by Wesley and his immediate coadjutors. The religious services of the Free Methodists are generally characterized by the warmth and fervor so noticeable among early Methodists. Congregational singing is universal.

The Free Methodist Church is at present composed of seven Annual Conferences, embracing portions of nearly every Northern state in the Union. The following is an abstract of statistics taken from the reports of the Conferences for the year ending September, 1890; Members, 208,861; travelling preachers, 700; local preachers, 159; Sabbath-schools, 155; scholars, 4894; teachers, 973; value of Church property, $263,550.

Two educational institutions have been started under the auspices of the Church, one at North Chili, Monroe County, N. Y., the other at Spring Arbor, Michigan. These are conducted with strict reference to the principles and usages of the people by whom they are sustained, and bid fair to become successful.

The publication of a monthly magazine was commenced by the Rev. B. T. Roberts in the year 1860, entitled *The Earnest Christian*, devoted to the advocacy of Bible holiness. It has been from the first well sustained, and, though it is an exponent of the principles taught by Free Methodists, is still conducted as an independent enterprise, and regarded as an unsectarian publication. It has a large circulation outside the Church, which supplies its chief patronage. A weekly paper, entitled *The Free Methodist*, and edited by the Rev. Levi Wood, was started in the interests of the denomination Nov. 2, 1867. This also is a private enterprise, though depending on the patronage of the body for support. It is now published at Chicago, Ill., and its

---

* In adherence to our rule respecting denominational articles, we have permitted our contributor to state his case in his own way. Justice to all parties concerned, however, requires us to add that several of the above statements relative to the origin of the Church in question are made from a partisan point of view, and consequently fail to give a fair representation of the grounds of controversy. This is true, at least, in the following particulars: (1) The original difficulty grew out of a spirit of censoriousness and insubordination exhibited by the parties in question. (2) The expulsion of the ministers from the Annual Conference was in accordance with the regular forms of ecclesiastical discipline; and the private members were dropped, in accordance with an episcopal decision, after they had really abandoned their former communion. (3) The appeal to the General Conference was dismissed, as being unsustained by adequate reasons. In all these proceedings, the Church from which they were excluded acted in the sovereign right of self-defence, and its legitimate authorities were the ultimate judges of the necessity and propriety of the course pursued. Those who had incurred the penalty had therefore no just cause to complain of the action taken, however severe it might seem to them.—ED.

present editor is the Rev. L. Bailey. It has a very large circulation.

At present the labors of the Free Methodist Church are confined to the poor and comparatively uneducated classes of the community, and its ministers are mostly drawn from them. It can scarcely claim much denominational literature. The Rev. E. Bowen, D.D., wrote a history, entitled *The Origin of the Free Methodist Church*, which is rather a plain, straightforward statement of historical facts than an attempted literary monument. The Rev. B. T. Roberts, who has from its organization been general superintendent of the body, having been thrice re-elected to that position, graduated at Middletown, Conn., and is a writer of considerable power. His editorials, tracts, and essays display argumentative ability, and the faculty of uttering truths concisely.

Methodists, The. See METHODISM.

Methodius, ST. (surnamed also *Eubulus* and *Eubulius*), a noted theologian of the Eastern Church of the 3d century, one of the "fathers" and "martyrs" of the Church, flourished first as bishop of Olympus and Patara, in Lycia (hence also oftentimes surnamed *Patarensis*), and later presided over the see of Tyre, in Palestine. He is supposed to have died early in the 4th century. According to Suidas, he suffered a martyr's death at Chalcis ('Ανατολῆς) during the reign of Decius (249–251) and Valerian. This seems improbable, however, since Valerian reigned after and not contemporary with Decius, and since the chronology of the reign of these emperors is far from accurate. It seems pretty well established now that Methodius was a contemporary of Porphyry; and if he died in a persecution, it was probably, as Cave supposes, in that of A.D. 303, or, as Fabricius thinks, in that of A.D. 311. The last-named date is quite generally accepted as the year of Methodius's decease. Epiphanius says that "he was a very learned man, and a strenuous assertor of the truth." Jerome has ranked him in his catalogue of Church writers, but Eusebius has not mentioned him; which silence is attributed by some, though merely upon conjecture, to Methodius's having written very sharply against Origen, who was favored by Eusebius. His principal works are, Περὶ 'Αναστάσεως, *De Resurrectione*, against Origen, divided into two or three parts; fragments of it are to be found in Epiphanius (*Panarium*), in Photius (*Bibliotheca*), and in the works of Damascenus:—Περὶ τῶν γενετῶν, *De Creatis*, in Photius:—Περὶ Αὐτεξουσίου καὶ πόθεν τὰ κακά, *De Libero Arbitrio*. Leo Allatius gave the full text, together with a Latin version, but the work, as contained in Combéfis's edition of Methodius, is not complete:—Περὶ τῆς ἀγγελομιμήτου παρθενείας καὶ ἀγνείας, *De Angelica Virginitate et Castitate*, written in the form of a dialogue: it is a curious work, partaking at once of the character of Plato's *Banquet* and of the *Song of Solomon*, thoroughly Christian in its doctrines, but very free in its language. Photius claims that it was interpolated, and contains traces of Arianism; these, however, have disappeared from the MSS. at present extant, from which the work was first published by Leo Allatius, under the title *S. Methodii, episcopi et martyris, Convivium decem Virginum Leo Allatius hactenus non editum primus Grœce vulgavit, Latine verit; notas et diatriben de Methodiorum scriptis adjecit* (Rome, 1656, 8vo). About the same time Possinus prepared another edition, which was published at Paris under the title *S. Methodii Convivium Virginum Grœce et Latine nunc primum editum* (1657, 8vo). It is also to be found in Combéfis, *Auctuar. Bibl. Patr.* (Paris, 1672):—*Oratio de Simeone et Anna, seu In Festum Occursus et Purificationis B. Mariœ*, published by Petrus Plantinus (Antwerp, 1598); this has by some been considered as the work of a later Methodius, but this opinion is contradicted by Allatius:—Λόγος περὶ Μαρτύρων, *Sermo de Martyribus:*—Εἰς τὰ Βαΐα, *In Ramos Palmarum:* Photius gives extracts of this oration, but some doubt Methodius being its author:—*Libri Adversus Porphyrium*, fragments of which are given by Damas-

cenus:—*De Pythonissa contra Origenem*, lost:—*Commentarii in Cantica Canticorum*, of which only fragments remain:—Ξένων, lost; etc. Another work, *De Revelatione*, sometimes attributed to him, is more likely from a later Methodius. The *De Libero Arbitrio, De Resurrectione, De Angelica Virginitate et Castitate*, two homilies, and the extracts contained in Photius, were published by Combéfis in Greek and Latin, with notes (Paris, 1644, fol.), together with the works of Amphilochus and Andreas Cretensis. Galland has collected the preserved works supposed to be the production of Methodius, as well as all fragments, and published them in his *Biblioth. Patr.* vol. iii. See Photius, *Cod.* p. 234–237; Mai, *Script. vet. nov. coll.* vii, 1; Cave, *Histor. Litt.;* Henschen, in the Bollandists, *Acta Sanctorum*, vol. iv; Nath. Lardner, *Credibility of the Gospel History*, vol. v; Oudin, *Comment. de Scriptoribus eccles.* vol. i; Andrea Sixt, *Dissert. de Methodio* (Altorf, 1787, 4to); Fabricius, *Bibl. Grœca* (edit. of Harless), vii, 746 et al.; Donaldson, *Hist. Ch. Lit.;* Milman, *Hist. Lat. Christianity* (see Index); Schaff, *Ch. Hist.* i, 356 sq., 511; Neander, *Christ. Dogmas*, i, 121, 256; *Meth. Qu. Rev.* 1871, January, p. 164.

Methodius OF BOHEMIA, a native of Thessalonica, who flourished during the 9th century, became distinguished by his missionary zeal, his learning, and his skill as a painter. He first entered a convent at Constantinople, and afterwards spent some time in Rome, where he acquired that remarkable skill as an artist which leads Le Beau (*Hist. du Bas Empire*, xiv, 362) to speak of him as the most eminent painter of his time —a high compliment, indeed, when we note that among his contemporaries were Modalulph, in France, Tutilo, in Germany, and Lazarus, in Constantinople, all of whom are considered artists of great ability. After his return to Constantinople, he received an invitation from Bogoris, king of Bulgaria, to visit his court, and instruct him and his subjects in the principles of Christianity. This king's heart had been softened towards the Christian religion by the influence of his sister, who had shortly before returned from Constantinople, whither, thirty-eight years before, she had been conveyed as a captive, and where she had been brought up and educated a Christian. A severe pestilence oppressed Bulgaria, and led Bogoris formally to implore the aid of his sister's God. The plague was stayed, and the king acknowledged the might and goodness of the Christian's God in hearing and answering his prayer; but still he shrank from deserting entirely the faith of his fathers, lest his subjects should revolt against him in defence of paganism. At this critical moment he bethought himself of the strange expedient of using the skilful pencil of Methodius, knowing that his people could be more readily affected by images of terror than by eloquent words of persuasion. By his advice Methodius painted the last judgment, and so vividly represented the tortures of the damned that the heart of the king himself was struck with terror, and he sought to escape this terrible destiny by numbering himself among the sons of the Church. He was accordingly baptized in 863 or 864; and, though much opposition was shown, paganism was rapidly compelled to yield to the Christian religion as introduced by Methodius. After working with such success in Bulgaria, Methodius was sent into Greek Moravia, where, in conjunction with his brother Cyril (q. v.), he accomplished a great work, his holy zeal meeting with grand results. Christianity had already found its way to some parts of the tribe by its connection with the Frankish empire under Charlemagne, but the nation, as a whole, was still devoted to paganism. Its ruler, Radislav or Rastices, had formed an alliance with the Greek empire for political purposes. This afforded an opportunity for the sending forth of these two missionary brothers. Methodius rendered valuable assistance to his brother Cyril in his task of inventing an alphabet for the Sclavonic language, and in the work of translating the Bible, as well as several liturgical works, into the language of the people.

A schism breaking out between the Latin and the Greek churches, the Moravian prince was induced, by political changes, to enter into a closer relation with the German empire and the Western Church. Methodius and Cyril, in this emergency, proved themselves to be men who valued Christianity more highly than sect. They repaired to Rome, where they easily entered into an understanding with pope Adrian I, so that party strife caused no delay in the good work. Cyril remained in Rome as a monk, while Methodius, after acknowledging submission to the Romish Church, and giving a satisfactory confession of faith, was consecrated archbishop of the Moravian Church. It was while Methodius was laboring in Moravia that duke Borzivoy, of Bohemia, visited the court of Swatopluk (871), and becoming acquainted with the Christian religion, acknowledged his belief in it by causing himself, his wife, and his attendants to be baptized. On his return to Bohemia, Methodius accompanied him, and for a short time labored successfully, converting many, and causing several convents and churches to be erected. From this new field he returned to Moravia, where he remained until the wars with which the country was then distracted obliged him to transfer the field of his labors to the adjacent provinces connected with the German empire. The clergy of Salzburg, envious of his success, and prejudiced against the Eastern Church, complained to pope John VIII that Methodius was attached to the customs of the Greek Church, and that he made use of the Sclavonic language in public worship, and accused him of infringing on the see of the archbishop of Salzburg. The pope, though little inclined to listen to accusations which German bishops might make against any prelate ordained at Rome, could not altogether allay his suspicions as to the relations between Methodius and the Eastern Church, especially at a time when there were constant bickerings between the Latin and the Greek churches. Methodius hastened to Rome in obedience to the call of the pope (879), and an interview took place, which resulted in a complete refutation of the charges made against him. The pope even defended the use of the Sclavonic instead of the Latin language, in a letter written to the Moravian prince, in which he says: "The alphabet invented by a certain philosopher, Constantine (Cyril), to the end that God's praise may duly sound forth in it, we rightly commend; and we order that in this language the messages and works of our Lord Christ be declared; for we are exhorted by Holy Scripture to praise the Lord, not in three languages alone, but in all tongues and nations (Psa. cxvii, and Philip. ii). And the apostles, full of the Holy Ghost, proclaimed in all languages the great works of God. And the apostle Paul exhorts us (1 Cor. xiv) that, speaking in tongues, we should edify the Church. It stands not at all in contradiction with the faith to celebrate the mass in this language, to read the Gospel or lessons from the Scriptures properly translated into it, or to rehearse any of the Church hymns in the same, for the God who is the author of the three principal languages created the others also for his own glory. Only it is necessary, in order to greater solemnity, that in all the Moravian churches the Gospel should, in the first place, be publicly read in Latin, and then repeated in the Sclavonic language, so as to be understood by the people" (Neander, iii, 318). The pope also formed the Moravians into a separate diocese, independent of the German Church, and confirmed Methodius as their archbishop, making him directly responsible to himself instead of to the German prelate. This led to new disputes, in which the German clergy succeeded in influencing the Moravian prince against Methodius. One of his subordinate bishops, named Wichin, also attached himself to the German party. His difficulties and controversies became so numerous that he reported the matter in detail to the pope, and requested permission to appear before him in person. John VIII granted this request, and, though expressing a desire to hear

both sides of the controversy, assured him of his kindly feelings towards him, and exhorted him not to allow the work to suffer, but to prosecute it faithfully. In 881 Methodius went to Rome, after which time his name disappears from the records of history. It cannot be determined whether he died soon after, or whether the hostile party in Moravia prevented his return. He was canonized by the Church. The Greeks and Sclavonians celebrate him on May 11, although in the Martyrologium the day is March 9. See F. X. Richter, *Cyrill und Method der Slaven Apostel* (1825); Ginzel, *Gesch. der Slaven Apostel* (1857); Baxmann, *Politik der Päpste* (Elberf. 1869), vol. ii; Neander, *Ch. Hist.* iii, 318 sq.; Hardwick, *Ch. Hist. Middle Ages*, p. 111 sq.; Maclear *Hist. of Missions in Middle Ages*, p. 284 sq. (H. W. T.)

Methodius OF CONSTANTINOPLE, a patriarch in the Eastern Church who flourished about 1240, is probably the author of *De Revelatione*, which some attribute to Methodius Eubulus. The Greek text, with a Latin version, is contained in the first volume of the *Græcia Orthodoxa*, as well as in some of the *Biblioth. Patrum.* He also wrote *Ænigmata*, in iambic tristichs, extant in MS. See Fabricius, *Bibl. Græc.* vii, 275; Cave, p. 662 (ed. Geneva).

Methodology ($\mu\acute{\epsilon}\vartheta o\delta o\varsigma$ and $\lambda\acute{o}\gamma o\varsigma$) is the scientific plan of investigating any department of knowledge. In the science of theology, it is the practical application of encyclopedia. The one leads to the other. A clear insight into the nature and connections of any science will lead to a right mode of treating it; and as the complete knowledge of a science is essential to a good method, so, on the other hand, a good method is the best test and verification of knowledge. The aims of methodology are to furnish a plan of theological study, showing the order in which the topics should be taken up, and indicating the best methods of study, and necessary books and helps of all kinds. Some writers hold that methodology should be treated and studied entirely apart from encyclopedia. In a strictly scientific sense, this view is correct; but, for practical purposes, these two branches are generally blended into one connected whole. The whole treatment taken together is therefore called by the double name of theological encyclopedia and methodology. Of these, encyclopedia is the objective side, the outline of the science itself; methodology is the subjective side, having reference to the work of the student of the science.

The science of theological encyclopedia and methodology is a comparatively recent study. The history of the science has been so fully treated in the article on ENCYCLOPEDIA (q. v.), and the methods of the chief writers on the subject so amply set forth, that we simply refer to it. Since the publication of that article, however, an important work, *Lectures by the late John McClintock, D.D., LL.D., on Theological Encyclopedia and Methodology* (N. Y. 1873, 12mo), has appeared, which contains so many new thoughts that we here insert Dr. McClintock's division of the subject. He divides theological science into the following four departments:

1. *Exegetical* Theology, which is concerned with the records of revelation.
2. *Historical* Theology, which is concerned with the development of revelation in the life and thought of the Church. This definition gives a twofold division of Historical Theology:
   a. The Life of the Church; that is, *Church History.*
   b. The Thought of the Church; that is, *Doctrinal History.*
3. *Systematic* Theology, which is concerned with the matter of revelation—with the scientific treatment of its contents; making a fourfold subdivision:
   a. Apologetics, or the defence of Christianity from attacks from without.
   b. Dogmatics, or the scientific statement of doctrines as admitted by the Church.
   c. Ethics, or a scientific statement of duty in which man stands to God.
   d. Polemics, or the vindication of doctrine from heretical attacks from within the Church.
4. *Practical Theology*, which is concerned with the preservation of revelation and its propagation in and through

the Church, as the outward and visible form of the kingdom of Christ among men. Here we have two general divisions:

    a. The Functions of the Church; and
    b. The Organization and Government of the Church.

This treatment, which has largely prevailed since the 16th century, rests upon the theory that Christianity is a system founded upon divine revelation, and that theology is really the product of the application of the human intellect to the contents of revelation.

See Crooks and Hurst, *Theol. Encycl. and Methodology* (N. Y. 1884) ; also *Jahrb. Deutsch. Theol.* Oct. 1871.

Methu- (מַת‍), construct-state of מַת, an adult *man*, used like the old English *folk*), a frequent prefix in Heb. proper names, as those here following; so likewise in the old Punic names *Metuastartus*, *Methymnatus*, etc. (Gesenius, *Monum. Phœn.* p. 399, 411).

Methu'saël (Heb. *Methushaël'*, מְתוּשָׁאֵל, *man that* is from *God;* Sept. Μαθουσάλα, Vulg. *Mathusael*), the son of Mehujael and father of Lamech, of the family of Cain (Gen. iv, 18). B.C. cir. 3770. The resemblance of the name to the following, on which (with the coincidence of the name Lamech in the next generation in both lines) some theories have been formed, is apparent rather than real.

Methu'selah (Heb. *Methushe'lach*, מְתוּשֶׁלַח, *man of* the *dart;* Sept. and N. T. Μαθουσάλα ; Josephus, Μαθουσάλας, *Ant.* i, 3, 3 and 4 ; Vulg. *Mathusala* and *Mathusale;* Auth. Vers. "Mathusala," in Luke iii, 37), the son of Enoch, and eighth of the Sethite antediluvian patriarchs (Gen. v, 21, 22, 25, 26, 27 ; 1 Chron. i, 3). He was born (according to the Heb. text) B.C. 3484. When he had attained the age of 187 years, his son Lamech was born, after which he lived 782 years, and died (B.C. 2516) only a few months before the flood, at the extreme age of 969; which, being the greatest term attained by any on record, has caused his name to become a proverb of long life. See LONGEVITY.

Metochīta, Georgius (Γεώργιος ὁ Μετοχίτης), a Greek theologian, flourished in the latter half of the 13th century. He was the archdeacon of the Church at Constantinople, the intimate friend and zealous partisan of the emperor Andronicus, and favored a union of the Greek Church with the Latin. Under the reign of Andronicus the Younger he was ostracized on account of his religious opinions, and died in exile. He was the relative, perhaps the father, of Theodorus Metochita, with whom he has often been confounded. He wrote several works of great importance for their bearing on the history of his times; but his literary style, although energetic, is rude and well-nigh barbarous. His *Refutation* ('Αντίρρησις) *of the three Chapters of Planude*, and his *Reply to Manuel Nepos of Crete*, were published by Leo Allatius, in the *Græcia Orthodoxa*, vol. ii. The same publisher has given to the public a fragment of Metochita's *Discourse on the Union of the Churches*, together with a portion of the fourth book of his treatise *On the Procession of the Holy Ghost*, bound in one volume with *Diatriba contra Hottingerum*. See Fabricius, *Bibliotheca Græca*, x, 412 ; Cave, *Hist. Litt.* s. v.

Metochīta, Theodorus (Θεύδωρος ὁ Μετοχίτης), a Greek theologian, flourished in the days of the emperor Andronicus the Elder, who appointed him the chief *logothete*, or chancellor, of the Church at Constantinople, and intrusted him with several missions. Amid all his official duties, Metochita found time to compose sundry works which reflect honor upon his learning. He was banished from the country shortly after the usurpation of power by Andronicus the Younger, in 1328. The emperor was not slow to recall him; but Metochita being disgusted with the complexion which matters had assumed, retired into a convent, where he died about 1332. His principal works are *Commentaries* (Παράφρασις) on several treatises by Aristotle : *Physica, De Anima, De Cœlo, De Ortu et Interitu, De Memoria et Reminiscentia, De Somno et Vigilia.* These commenta-

ries were published in Latin by Gent. Hervet (Basle, 1550, 4to; Ravenna, 1614, 4to) ; but the original Greek text of the *Commentaries* has remained inedited. He also wrote two books on ecclesiastical history, and several works of a secular character, which were never printed. See Fabricius, *Bibl. Græca*, x, 412 sq. ; C. F. de Bodenbourg, *De Th. Metochitæ Scriptis Notheias vulgo insimulatis*, in the *Miscellan. Lipsiensia*, vol. xii.

Metonymy (μετωνυμία, "*denominatio nominis pro nomine posita*," Quintillian, 8, 6, 23), a technical term in rhetoric designating a "trope, in which a word is used to express a thing differing from its original meaning in kind" (E. D. Haven, *Rhetoric*, p. 78). Metonymies are a little bolder than synecdoches (q. v.), and, as Aristotle observes, may be employed either to elevate or to degrade the subject, according to the design of the author. The substance may be named for the quality, the cause for the effect, the precedent for the consequent, or the reverse, e. g. "*Addison* was smooth, but *Prescott* smoother." Here *Addison* means *the writings of Addison; smooth* means *pleasing to the ear.* Both words are metonymic. "Always respect *old age*"—a metonymy for *aged people.* Thus, "*gray hairs*" may stand for "*old age*," the name of Virgil for that of his writings, the "*head*" for the "*intellect*," and the "*olive-branch*" for "*peace.*" Metonymies may be classified as follows:

(1.) *The sign for the thing signified*, signum pro signato. *Sword* for war; Θρόνος for power (Luke i, 32; Heb. i, 8); ἀνατολή, δυσμή, for east and west (Matt. ii, 3 ; Luke xiii, 29; Psa. xlvi, 6) ; *red tape*, for the difficulties in obtaining the completion of a work that must pass the inspection of several officers; a *pen* for literature—"The pen is mightier than the sword."

(2.) *The container for the thing contained*, continens pro contento. "The *country* is jealous of the *city.*" "The *army* yielded, but the *navy* resisted ;" ὁ κόσμος, world, for the human beings contained in the world (Matt. xviii, 7 ; John i, 10; iii, 16, 17); ὁ οἶκος, the house, for domestics (John iv, 53 ; Acts x, 2, 11, 14, 16).

(3.) *A cause may be put for an effect, and an effect for a cause.* "The *savage* desolation of war." The *cause* of the desolation is a savage spirit; here it is transferred to the effect. In an opposite transference, we may speak of *pale death, joyful* health, a *proud* testimony. This is sometimes called a *transferred epithet.*

(4.) *A man may be named for his works.* Thus we speak of "Shakespeare," meaning his writings. "Blackstone," meaning his works on law. So the "Prophets" are referred to (Mark i, 2; Luke xvi, 29; xxiv, 44; Acts viii, 28), meaning their writings. This is akin to personification (q. v.).

Metre (Gr. μέτρον) is, in its most extensive signification, the *measure* by which any thing is determined with exactness and due proportion. In its classical sense the word is used for the subdivision of a verse. The Greeks measured some species of verses (the dactylic, choriambic, antispastic, Ionic, etc.) by considering each foot as a metre; in others (the iambic, trochaic, and anapæstic, each dipodia, or two feet, formed a metre. Thus the dactylic hexameter (the heroic verse) contained six dactyls or spondees ; the iambic, anapæstic, and trochaic trimeter, six of those feet respectively. A line is said to be acatalectic when the last syllable of the last foot is wanting ; brachicatalectic, when two syllables are cut off in the same way ; hypercatalectic, when there is one superfluous syllable.

In religious poetry, as adapted to music, metre denotes the regular consecution in a stanza of lines containing a certain number of syllables of a given kind of verse. The usual number of lines is four, and these may be alike or different in length. For example, in what is called *Long Metre*, each line consists of four iambic measures ; in *Common Metre*, the lines contain alternately four and three iambi, or their prosodiac equivalents; and in *Short Metre* every line has three iambi, except the third, which has four. All other kinds are called "*particular metres*," as 6 lines of 8 syllables each, 4 lines of 7, 6 lines of 7, 4 lines of 10, 4 of 6 and 2 of 8, 8 of 8 and 7 alternately, etc.

Metrētès. See FIRKIN.

Metrical Psalms and Hymns. Several of the Psalms were translated into English metre, during the latter part of the reign of Henry VIII, by Sir Thomas Wyatt, and printed in 1549. This version, however, is supposed to be lost. It has been thought that a reference to some metrical psalms existed in the 7th section of the 1st Act of Uniformity in the reign of Edward VI, 1549, authorizing the use of the Prayer-book, where it was enacted "that it shall be lawful for all men, as well in churches, chapels, oratories, or other places, to use openly any psalm or prayer taken out of the Bible at any due time; not letting or omitting thereby the service, or any part thereof, mentioned in the said book." But this was several years antecedent to the appearance of any regular version. The metrical Psalms, called the "Old Version," originated with Sternhold, who was groom of the robes to Henry VIII and Edward VI, and was continued by others until 1641, when the revisers of the Prayer-book declared that "singing of hymns in metre is no part of the liturgy," and therefore they refused to consider them, as not in their commission. See Proctor, *On Common Prayer* (see Index); Cardwell, *Conferences*, s. v.; Bates, *Christ. Antiq.* s. v.; Staunton, *Eccles. Dict.* s. v. See PSALMS, VERSIONS OF.

Metrodōrus, a leading Epicurean philosopher, was, according to the best authorities, a native of Lampsacus, although some claim that he was an Athenian. He flourished in the second half of the 3d century B.C. From his earliest connection with this school of philosophy until his death, he lived in daily and intimate intercourse with Epicurus, absenting himself only six months during the whole period. He is regarded as the founder of that baser and more sensual form of Epicurean philosophy which many, who sought for "pleasure as the chief good," substituted for the intellectual enjoyment adopted by Epicurus as his ideal good. According to Cicero, he made perfect happiness to consist in having a well-constituted body, and knowing that it would always remain so. One of his sayings, as quoted by Athenæus, was that "the belly is the foundation of all philosophy." He claimed that all pertaining to a happy life should be tested and measured by this organ. Metrodorus became the favorite disciple of Epicurus, and may justly be ranked second only to him in importance. He died in 277 B.C., at the age of fifty-three, seven years before the death of his master, who had intended to make him his successor. He left two children, a son and daughter, whom Epicurus protected while he was living, and for whom he generously provided in his will. Metrodorus left to the world some of his thoughts in the tangible form of thirteen volumes, as enumerated by Diogenes. All these have disappeared, except some fragments found among the Herculanean Papyri; the most important of which is a portion of his treatise Περὶ Αἰσθησίαν, contained in the sixth volume of the Neapolitan collection. For many years the Epicureans kept the 20th of each month as a festal day in honor of their master and of Metrodorus, whose name will ever be linked with that of Epicurus. Another philosopher of like name flourished in *Chios*, in Greece, about 400 B.C. He was the author of a *Treatise on Nature*, which was very celebrated. See Bayle, *Hist. and Crit. Dict.* s. v.; Fabricius, *Biblioth. Græca*, iii, 606; Pliny, *Hist. Nat.* xxxv, 40; Plutarch, *Paulus Æmilius*, 32. (H. W. T.)

Metrology, the science of determining the relative value of measures, whether these belong to pecuniary standards or to fixed quantities of capacity or extent. Indeed, these three are intimately connected, for coins can only be accurately determined by weight, and the bulk of solids or liquids is ultimately ascertained by linear measurements in cubic dimensions, or by a given weight of a certain substance of uniform density. Specific gravity, therefore, lies at the basis of all quantitative admeasurements. In the present article we are, of course, strictly concerned only with the Biblical, especially Hebrew, weights and measures; but as the value of these has come down to us chiefly in Greek equivalents, it becomes necessary to take the latter also into consideration. "The Roman measures came from Greece, the Grecian from Phœnicia, the Phœnician from Babylon. Accordingly each system will throw light on the other, and all may be made to contribute something to the elucidation of the Hebrew weights and measures. This method of viewing the subject, and the satisfactory lessons which have been hence deduced, are to be ascribed to Böckh (*Metrologischen Untersuchungen*, Berlin, 1838), who, availing himself of the results ascertained by English, French, and German scholars, and of the peculiar facilities afforded by a residence in the midst of the profound and varied erudition of the Prussian capital, has succeeded, by the application of his unwearied industry and superior endowments, in shewing that the system of weights and measures of Babylon, Egypt, Palestine, Phœnicia, Greece, Sicily, and Italy, formed one great whole, with the most intimate relationships and connections." To these researches must be added later investigations and comparisons by different antiquarians as to the value of particular specimens of coins and measures still extant, which sometimes considerably modify the conclusions of Böckh.

I. *Coins and Weights.*—1. *Names of the principal Hebrew Standards.*—The following are the regular gradations, beginning with the highest:

(1.) The *talent*, כִּכָּר, *kikkár*, strictly a *circle*, hence any round object; and thus a circular piece of money. It was of two kinds, the talent of gold (1 Kings ix, 14) and the talent of silver (2 Kings v, 22). See TALENT.

(2.) The *manéh*, מָנֶה, the Greek *mina*, or μνᾶ, strictly a *portion*, i. e. a subdivision of the "talent."

(3.) The *shékel*, שֶׁקֶל, Græcized σίκλος, properly a *weight*, the usual unit of estimation, applied to coins and weights. It likewise was of two kinds, the sacred (Lev. v, 15) and the royal (2 Sam. xiv, 26).

(4.) The *béka*, בֶּקַע, strictly a *cleft* or fraction (Gen. xxiv, 22).

(5.) The *geráh*, גֵּרָה, properly a *kernel* or bean, like our "grain," and the Greek ὄβολος.

2. *Values of these as compared with each other.*—The relation of the talent to the shekel is determined by the statement in Exod. xxx, 13, that every Israelite above twenty years of age had to pay the poll-tax of half a shekel as a contribution to the sanctuary. Exod. xxxviii, 26 tells us that this tax had to be paid by 603,550 men. The sum amounted to 100 talents and 1775 shekels (Exod. xxxviii, 25), which are, therefore, equal to 603,550 half shekels, or 301,775 full shekels. This gives for the value of the talent in shekels, $\frac{301,775-1775}{100} = 3000$. The relation of the maneh to the shekel, and consequently to the talent, is not so clear. In Ezek. xlv, 13, it seems to have consisted of 60 shekels $(20+25+15)$; but a comparison of 1 Kings x, 17 with 2 Chron. ix, 16 would make it to consist of 100 shekels (3 manehs = 300 shekels). Some explain these discrepancies by supposing that the sacred shekel was double the commercial, or that the talent and maneh of gold were respectively double those of silver. In this uncertainty it is generally agreed to reckon 60 manehs to the talent, and 50 shekels to a maneh. The beka was a half-shekel (Exod. xxxviii, 26); and the gerah was $\frac{1}{20}$ the shekel (Exod. xxx, 13; Lev. xxvii, 25; Numb. iii, 47; Ezek. xlv, 20).

3. *Values of the Hebrew Weights as determined by a Comparison with the Greek and Roman.*—Josephus states (*Ant.* iii, 6, 7) that the Hebrew talent of gold contained 100 minæ (μνᾶς), but whether by this latter he means

the Greek or the Hebrew weight corresponding to that term, is not clear. Again he states ($Ant.$ xiv, 7, 1) that the gold mina ($\mu\nu\tilde{a}$) was equal to two and a half Roman pounds ($\lambda\acute{\iota}\tau\rho\alpha\varsigma$). On the presumption that the same kind of mina is spoken of in both passages, the talent would be equivalent to 250 pounds. On the other hand, Epiphanius ($De\ Pond.\ et\ Mens.\ Heb.$) estimates the Hebrew talent at 125 Roman pounds. This difference, being just one half, leads to the suspicion that it is connected with the above variation in the value of the talent, maneh, and shekel; and this, in connection with the nearer correspondence to the Greek measures of similar name, renders the lower estimate the more probable. Taking the Roman pound (presumed to be equivalent to the Greek $\lambda\acute{\iota}\tau\rho\alpha$) at 5204 grains (Smith, $Dict.\ of$ $Class.\ Antiq.$ s. v. $Libra$), we have the Hebrew talent equal to 650,500 grains, or 112.79 pounds troy, or 92.9 pounds avoirdupois. Once more, Josephus says the gold shekel was equal to a daric ($Ant.$ iii, 8, 10), a Persian coin in Greek circulation, specimens of which have come down to us weighing an average of 128.5 grains (Smith, $ibid.$ s. v. Daricus). This would yield a talent of 385,500 grains; which is much less, yet confirms the above conclusion sufficiently for an approximate equivalent, as it evidently was meant to be, especially as the darics extant have of course lost considerable weight by time. Moreover, foreign coin usually passes for less than its true value.

4. $Absolute\ Determination\ of\ the\ Value\ of\ the\ Hebrew$ $Weights.$—This has been attempted by means of the coins that have actually come down to our time. The heavier specimens of silver of the Maccabæan mintage that have been found give an average weight to the shekel of 220 grains. See SHEKEL. This affords a talent of 660,000 grains, very nearly agreeing with the above result. The copper coins of the same period that have survived are on the average much heavier, being about double the weight, showing a variation in the standard for that metal similar to that noticed above in the case of gold. Böckh, by averaging the shekels of every kind of metal, arrives at a mean weight of 274 grains; but this is too high for the preceding estimates. See MONEY.

"In the New Testament (Matt. xvii, 24) the Temple-tax is a $didrachm$; from other sources we know that this 'tribute' was half a shekel; and in verse 27 the $stater$ is payment of this tax for two persons. Now the stater—a very common silver Attic coin, the $tetradrachm$ —weighed 328.8 Parisian grains: thus considerably surpassing the sacred shekel. Are we, then, to hold the stater of the New Testament for an Attic tetradrachm? There is reason in the passage of Matthew and in early writers for regarding the two as the same. The Attic tetradrachm sank from its original weight of 328.8 to 308 and 304. This approximation must have gone on increasing, for under the empire a $drachm$ was equal to a Roman $denarius$, which in the time of Tiberius weighed 69.8 Parisian grains. Four denarii were equal to 279 Parisian grains; so that, if the denarius is regarded as an Attic drachm, the sacred shekel may be correctly termed a tetradrachm. With this Josephus agrees ($Ant.$ iii, 8, 2), who says that the shekel ($\sigma\acute{\iota}\kappa\lambda o\varsigma$), a Hebrew coin, contains four Attic drachms." See DRACHMA.

II. $Measures\ of\ Dimension\ or\ Extent.$—These are chiefly taken from some natural standard, such as the various portions of forearm and hand, or the distance of travel, etc.; so, among other nations, the $foot$, $fathom$, etc. In the descriptive portion of this and the following section we shall endeavor to bring these disputed questions to something like a practical conclusion.

1. $Measures\ of\ Length.$—(1.) The principal of these were as follows: (a) The אֶצְבַּע, $etsbá$, or finger-breadth, mentioned only in Jer. lii, 21. (b) The טֶפַח, $téphach$, or hand-breadth (Exod. xxv, 25; 1 Kings vii, 26; 2 Chron. iv, 5), applied metaphorically to a short period

of time in Psa. xxxix, 5. (c) The זֶרֶת, $zéreth$, or span, the distance between the extremities of the thumb and the little finger in the extended hand (Exod. xxviii, 16; 1 Sam. xvii, 4; Ezek. xliii, 13), applied generally to describe any small measure in Isa. xl, 12. (d) The אַמָּה, $ammâh$, or cubit, the distance from the elbow to the extremity of the middle finger. This occurs very frequently in the Bible in relation to buildings, such as the Ark (Gen. vi, 15), the Tabernacle (Exod. xxvi, xxvii), and the Temple (1 Kings vi, 2; Ezek, xl, xli), as well as in relation to man's stature (1 Sam. xvii, 4; Matt. vi, 27), and other objects (Esth. v, 14; Zech. v, 2). (e) The גֹּמֶד, $gómed$, lit. a rod, applied to Eglon's dirk (Judg. iii, 16). Its length is uncertain, but it probably fell below the cubit, with which it is identified in the A. V. (f) The קָנֶה, $kanéh$, or reed (comp. our word "cane"), for measuring buildings on a large scale (Ezek. xl, 5–8; xli, 8; xlii, 16–19).

(2.) Little information is furnished by the Bible itself as to the relative or absolute lengths described under the above terms. With the exception of the notice that the reed equals six cubits (Ezek. xl, 5), we have no intimation that the measures were combined in anything like a scale. We should, indeed, infer the reverse from the circumstance that Jeremiah speaks of "four fingers," where, according to the scale, he would have said "a hand-breadth;" that in the description of Goliath's height (1 Sam. xvii, 4), the expression "six cubits and a span" is used instead of "six cubits and a half;" and that Ezekiel mentions "span" and "half a cubit" in close juxtaposition (xliii, 13, 17), as though they bore no relation to each other either in the ordinary or the long cubit. That the denominations held a certain ratio to each other, arising out of the proportions of the members in the body, could hardly escape notice; but it does not follow that they were ever worked up into an artificial scale. But by comparing together Exod. xxv, 10 with Josephus ($Ant.$ iii, 6, 5), we find the span equal to half a cubit; for the length which Moses terms two cubits and a half, Josephus designates five spans. The relation of tephach (hand-breadth) and etsba (finger) to ammâh (cubit) appears from their several names and their import in other systems. The hand-breadth is four fingers; the span contains three times the breadth of the hand, or twelve fingers. This is the view which the rabbins uniformly take. We find a similar system among the Greeks, who reckoned in the cubit twenty-four fingers, six hand-breadths, and two spans. The same was the case with the Egyptians.

The most important conclusion usually drawn from the Biblical notices is to the effect that the cubit, which may be regarded as the standard measure, was of varying length, and that, in order to secure accuracy, it was necessary to define the kind of cubit intended, the result being that the other denominations, if combined in a scale, would vary in like ratio. Thus in Deut. iii, 11, the cubit is specified to be "after the cubit of a man;" in 2 Chron. iii, 3, "after the first," or, rather, "after the older (רִאשׁוֹנָה) measure;" and in Ezek. xli, 8, "a great cubit," or, literally, "a cubit to the joint," which is further defined in xl, 5 to be "a cubit and a hand-breadth." These expressions involve one of the most knotty points of Hebrew archæology, viz. the number and the respective lengths of the scriptural cubits. A cubit "after the cubit of a man" implies the existence of another cubit, which was either longer or shorter than it, and from analogy it may be taken for granted that this second cubit would be the longer of the two. But what is meant by the "$ammâh$ of a man?" Is it the $cubitus$ in the anatomical sense of the term—in other words, the bone of the forearm between the elbow and the wrist? or is it the full cubit in the ordinary sense of the term, from the elbow to the extremity of the middle finger? What, again, are we to understand by Ezekiel's expression, "cubit to the joint?" The term אַצִּיל, $atstsil$, is explained by Gesenius (*Thesaur.* p. 144) of the *knuckles*, and not of the "armholes," as in the A.V. of Jer. xxxviii, 12, where our translators have omitted all reference to the word *yadêka*, which follows it. A "cubit to the knuckles" would imply the space from the elbow to the knuckles, and as this cubit exceeds by a hand-breadth the ordinary cubit, we should infer that it was contradistinguished from the cubit that reached only to the wrist. The meaning of the word is, however, contested : Hitzig gives it the sense of a *connecting wall* (*Comm. on Jer.*). Sturmius (*Sciagr.* p. 94) understands it of the *edge* of the walls, and others in the sense of a *wing* of a building (Rosenmüller, *Schol. in Jer.*). Michaelis, on the other hand, understands it of the knuckles (*Supplem.* p. 119), and so does Saalschütz (*Archäol.* ii, 165). The expressions now discussed, taken together, certainly favor the idea that the cubit of the Bible did not come up to the full length of the cubit of other countries. (See below.) A further question remains to be discussed, viz. whether more than two cubits were in vogue among the Hebrews. It is generally conceded that the "former" or "older" measure of 2 Chron. iii, 3 was the Mosaic or legal cubit, and that the modern measure, the existence of which is implied in that designation, was somewhat larger. Further, the cubit "after the cubit of a man" of Deut. iii, 11 is held to be a *common* measure, in contradistinction to the Mosaic one, and to have fallen below this latter in point of length. In this case we should have three cubits—the common, the Mosaic or old measure, and the new measure. We turn to Ezekiel and find a distinction of another character, viz. a long and a short cubit. Now it has been urged by many writers, and we think with good reason, that Ezekiel would not be likely to adopt any other than the old orthodox Mosaic standard for the measurements of his ideal temple. If so, his *long* cubit would be identified with the *old* measure, and his short cubit with the one "after the cubit of a man," and the *new* measure of 2 Chron. iii, 3 would represent a still longer cubit than Ezekiel's long one. Other explanations of the prophet's language have, however, been offered : it has been sometimes assumed that, while living in Chaldæa, he and his countrymen had adopted the long Babylonian cubit (Jahn, *Archæol.* § 113) ; but in this case his short cubit could not have belonged to the same country, inasmuch as the difference between these two amounted to only three fingers (Herod. i, 178). Again, it has been explained that his short cubit was the ordinary Chaldæan measure, and the long one the Mosaic measure (Rosenmüller, *in Ezek.* xl, 5) : but this is unlikely, on account of the respective lengths of the Babylonian and the Mosaic cubits, to which we shall hereafter refer. Independently of these objections, we think that the passages previously discussed (Deut. iii, 11 ; 5 Chron. iii, 3) imply the existence of three cubits.

It remains to be inquired whether from the Bible itself we can extract any information as to the length of the Mosaic or legal cubit. The notices of the height of the altar and of the height of the lavers in the Temple are of importance in this respect. In the former case three cubits is specified (Exod. xxvii, 1), with a direct prohibition against the use of steps (Exod. xx, 26) ; in the latter, the height of the base on which the laver was placed was three cubits (1 Kings vii, 27). If we adopt the ordinary length of the cubit (say 20 inches), the height of the altar and the base would be 5 feet. But it would be extremely inconvenient, if not impossible, to minister at an altar or to use a laver placed at such a height. In order to meet this difficulty without any alteration of the length of the cubit, it must be assumed that an inclined plane led up to it, as was the case with the loftier altar of the Temple (Mishna, *Middoth*, iii, § 1, 3). But such a contrivance is contrary to the spirit of the text; and, even if suited to the altar, would be wholly needless for the lavers. Hence Saalschütz infers that the cubit did not exceed a Prussian foot, which is less than an English foot (*Archäol.* ii,

167). The other instances adduced by him are not so much to the point. The molten sea was not designed for the purpose of bathing (though this impression is conveyed by 2 Chron. iv, 6, as given in the A. V.), and therefore no conclusion can be drawn from the depth of the water in it. The height of Og, as inferred from the length of his bedstead (9 cubits, Deut. iii, 11), and the height of Goliath (6 cubits and a span, 1 Sam. xvii, 4), are not inconsistent with the idea of a cubit about 18 inches long, if credit can be given to other recorded instances of extraordinary stature (Pliny, vii, 2, 16 ; Herod. i, 68 ; Josephus, *Ant.* xviii, 4, 5). At the same time the rendering of the Sept. in 1 Sam. xvii, 4, which is followed by Josephus (*Ant.* vi, 9, 1), and which reduces the number of cubits to four, suggests either an error in the Hebrew text, or a considerable increase in the length of the cubit in later times.

(3.) We now turn to collateral sources of information, which we will follow out, as far as possible, in chronological order. The earliest and most trustworthy testimony as to the length of the cubit is supplied by the existing specimens of old Egyptian measures. Several of these have been discovered in tombs, carrying us back at all events to B.C. 1700, while the Nilometer at Elephantinè exhibits the length of the cubit in the time of the Roman emperors. No great difference is exhibited in these measures, the longest being estimated at about 21 inches, and the shortest at about $20\frac{1}{3}$, or exactly 20.4729 inches (Wilkinson, *Anc. Eg.* ii, 258). They are divided into 28 digits, and in this respect contrast with the Mosaic cubit, which, according to rabbinical authorities, was divided into 24 digits. There is some difficulty in reconciling this discrepancy with the almost certain fact of the derivation of the cubit from Egypt. It has generally been surmised that the Egyptian cubit was of more than one length, and that the sepulchral measures exhibit the shorter as well as the longer by special marks. Wilkinson denies the existence of more than one cubit (*Anc. Eg.* ii, 257–259), apparently on the ground that the total lengths of the measures do not materially vary. It may be conceded that the measures are intended to represent the same length, the variation being simply the result of mechanical inaccuracy ; but this does not decide the question of the double cubit, which rather turns on the peculiarities of notation observable on these measures. For a full discussion of this point we must refer the reader to Thenius's essay in the *Theologische Studien und Kritiken* for 1846, p. 297–342. Our limits will permit only a brief statement of the facts of the case, and of the views expressed in reference to them. The most perfect of the Egyptian cubit measures are those preserved in the Turin and Louvre museums. These are unequally divided into two parts, the one on the right hand containing 15, and the other 13 digits. In the former part the digits are subdivided into aliquot parts from $\frac{1}{2}$ to $\frac{1}{16}$, reckoning from right to left. In the latter part the digits are marked on the lower edge in the Turin, and on the upper edge in the Louvre measure. In the Turin measure the three left-hand digits exceed the others in size, and have marks over them indicating either fingers or the numerals 1, 2, 3. The four left-hand digits are also marked off from the rest by a double stroke, and are further distinguished by hieroglyphic marks supposed to indicate that they are digits of the old measure. There are also special marks between the 6th and 7th, and between the 10th and 11th digits of the left-hand portion. In the Louvre cubit two digits are marked off on the lower edge by lines running in a slightly transverse direction, thus producing a greater length than is given on the upper side. It has been found that each of the three above specified digits in the Turin measure = $\frac{1}{24}$ of the whole length, less these three digits; or, to put it in another form, the four left-hand digits = $\frac{1}{6}$ of the 25 right-hand digits : also that each of the two digits in the Louvre measure = $\frac{1}{24}$ of the whole length, less these two digits; and further, that twice the left half of either measure =

the whole length of the Louvre measure, less the two digits. Most writers on the subject agree in the conclusion that the measures contain a combination of two, if not three, kinds of cubit. Great difference of opinion, however, is manifested as to particulars. Thenius makes the difference between the royal and old cubits to be no more than two digits, the average length of the latter being 484.289 millimètres, or 19.066 inches, as compared with 523.524 millimètres, or 20.611 inches, and 523 millimètres, or 20.591 inches, the lengths of the Turin and Louvre measures respectively. He accounts for the additional two digits as originating in the practice of placing the two fingers crosswise at the end of the arm and hand used in measuring, so as to mark the spot up to which the cloth or other article has been measured. He further finds, in the notation of the Turin measure, indications of a third or ordinary cubit 23 digits in length. Another explanation is that the old cubit consisted of 24 or 25 new digits, and that its length was 462 millimètres, or 18.189 inches; and, again, others put the old cubit at 24 new digits, as marked on the measures. The relative proportions of the two would be, on these two hypotheses, as 28 : 26, as 28 : 25, and as 28 : 24. (See below.)

The use of more than one cubit appears to have also prevailed in Babylon, for Herodotus states that the "royal" exceeded the "moderate" cubit ($\pi\tilde{\eta}\chi\upsilon\varsigma\ \mu\acute{\epsilon}\tau\rho\iota\upsilon\varsigma$) by three digits (i, 178). The appellation "royal," if borrowed from the Babylonians, would itself imply the existence of another; but it is by no means certain that this other was the "moderate" cubit mentioned in the text. The majority of critics think that Herodotus is there speaking of the ordinary Greek cubit (Böckh, p. 214), though the opposite view is affirmed by Grote in his notice of Böckh's work (Class. Mus. i, 28). Even if the Greek cubit be understood, a further difficulty arises out of the uncertainty whether Herodotus is speaking of digits as they stood on the Greek or on the Babylonian measure. In the one case the proportions of the two would be as 8 : 7, in the other case as 9 : 8. Böckh adopts the Babylonian digits (without good reason, we think), and estimates the Babylonian royal cubit at 234.2743 Paris lines, or 20.806 inches (p. 219). A greater length would be assigned to it according to the data furnished by M. Oppert, as stated in Rawlinson's Herod. i, 315; for if the cubit and foot stood in the ratio of 5 : 3, and if the latter contained 15 digits, and had a length of 315 millimètres, then the length of the ordinary cubit would be 525 millimètres, and of the royal cubit, assuming, with Mr. Grote, that the cubits in each case were Babylonian, 588 millimètres, or 23.149 inches.

Reverting to the Hebrew measures, we should be disposed to identify the new measure implied in 2 Chron. iii, 3, with the full Egyptian cubit; the "old" measure and Ezekiel's cubit with the lesser one, either of 26 or 24 digits; and the "cubit of a man" with the third one of which Thenius speaks. Böckh, however, identifies the Mosaic measure with the full Egyptian cubit, and accounts for the difference in the number of digits on the hypothesis that the Hebrews substituted a division into 24 for that into 28 digits, the size of the digits being of course increased (p. 266, 267). With regard to the Babylonian measure, it seems highly improbable that either the ordinary or the royal cubit could be identified with Ezekiel's short cubit (as Rosenmüller thinks), seeing that its length on either of the computations above offered exceeded that of the Egyptian cubit.

In the Mishna the Mosaic cubit is defined to be one of six palms (Celim, 17, § 10). It is termed the moderate cubit (א׳ הבינונית), and is distinguished from a lesser cubit of five palms on the one side (Celim, ib.), and on the other side from a larger one, consisting, according to Bartenora (in Cel. 17, § 9), of six palms and a digit. The palm consisted, according to Maimonides (ibid.), of four digits; and the digit, according to Arias

Montanus (Ant. p. 113), of four barleycorns. This gives 144 barleycorns as the length of the cubit, which accords with the number assigned to the cubitus justus et mediocris of the Arabians (Böckh, p. 246). The length of the Mosaic cubit, as computed by Thenius (after several trials with the specified number of barleycorns of middling size, placed side by side), is 214.512 Paris lines, or 19.0515 inches (Stud. u. Krit. p. 110). It seems hardly possible to arrive at any very exact conclusion by this mode of calculation. Eisenschmid estimated 144 barleycorns as equal to 238.35 Paris lines (Böckh, p. 269), perhaps from having used larger grains than the average. The writer of the article on "Weights and Measures" in the Penny Cyclopædia (xviii, 198) gives, as the result of his own experience, that 38 average grains make up 5 inches, in which case 144 = 18.947 inches; while the length of the Arabian cubit referred to is computed at 213.058 Paris lines (Böckh, p. 247). The Talmudists state that the Mosaic cubit was used for the edifice of the Tabernacle and Temple, and the lesser cubit for the vessels thereof. This was probably a fiction; for the authorities were not agreed among themselves as to the extent to which the lesser cubit was used, some of them restricting it to the golden altar, and parts of the brazen altar (Mishna, Cel. 17, § 10). But this distinction, fictitious as it may have been, shows that the cubits were not regarded in the light of sacred and profane, as stated in works on Hebrew archæology. Another distinction, adopted by the rabbinists in reference to the palm, would tend to show that they did not rigidly adhere to any definite length of cubit; for they recognised two kinds of palms, one wherein the fingers lay loosely open, which they denominated a smiling palm; the other wherein the fingers were closely compressed, and styled the grieving palm (Carpzov, Appar. p. 674, 676).

(4.) Prof. T. O. Paine, the acute and accurate author of Solomon's Temple, etc. (Bost. 1861), presents some original and ingenious views on the subject, which appear to us to solve most of the above difficulties. He maintains that there was but one cubit in use among the Hebrews, and that essentially the same with the Egyptian cubit. The "hand-breadth" he regards as an addition (a b) to the rod itself (b c), for convenience of holding, as in the annexed figure. This,

Cubit-rule, according to Paine.

he thinks, likewise explains the peculiar phraseology in Ezekiel xliii, 13: אַמָּה אַמָּה וָטֹפַח. A cubit [i. e. the rule] is a cubit and a hand-breadth long (p. 72). So also by means of the following figure he shows that only six cubits were counted on the reed (b c), while the hand-breadth (a b) was a handle to hold the reed by. Thus Ezek. xl, 5, "And in the man's hand a measuring-reed six cubits by the [regular] cubit, and a hand-breadth" [additional];" again, Ezek. xli, 8, "A full reed of six great cubits," הַקָּנֶה שֵׁשׁ אַמּוֹת אַצִּילָה, literally, as the Masoretic accents require, the reed, six cubits to the joint, i. e., as Mr. Paine shrewdly interprets the joint of the reed, one of its knots or sections, as in the subjoined cut (ibid.). All this suggests the surmise that the three larger and separate digits over the cubits described above as extant were actually no part of the measure itself, but only the finger-marks or *handle* by means of which it was grasped in use. If these be deducted, the cubit will be reduced to the usual or traditionary reckoning, which is about 18 inches.

We take the liberty of adding some interesting researches from a private communication by the same writer, in which he believes that he has discovered *the cubit locked up in the sockets* of the Tabernacle walls. Having determined that these were each $\frac{1}{2}$ cubit square and $\frac{1}{8}$ cubit thick, he makes the following curious calculation: The 96 silver sockets of the planks (Exod. xxvi, 15-25) would make 4 cubit cubes, i. e., if piled together, a solid mass 2 cubits in each dimension; or, in other terms, 24 sockets made a solid cubit. As each socket weighed a talent (Exod. xxxviii, 27), we have the formula,

$$1 \text{ cubit (in inches)} = \sqrt[3]{\frac{24 \text{ talents in silver}}{\text{weight of 1 cub. inch of silver}}}$$

As the talent contained 3000 shekels, and as silver weighs 2651 grains per inch, we have, by substitution,

$$1 \text{ cubit} = \sqrt[3]{\frac{72,000 \text{ shekels silver}}{2651 \text{ grains}}};$$

or, assuming the ancient shekel to have weighed (as above) 220 grains,

$$1 \text{ cubit (in inches)} = \sqrt[3]{\frac{15,840,000}{2651}} = \sqrt[3]{5975} = 18.14 \text{ inches.}$$

This strikingly agrees with the result attained above. Prof. Paine remarks that the *cores* for the tenons in the sockets may safely be neglected, as the dross would fully counterbalance them. The alloy, if at all used in manufacturing, would not materially raise the value of the cubit in this calculation.

(5.) Land and area were measured either by the cubit (Numb. xxxv, 4, 5; Ezek. xl, 27) or by the reed (Ezek. xlii, 20; xliii, 17; xlv, 2; xlviii, 20; Rev. xxi, 16). There is no indication in the Bible of the use of a square measure by the Jews. Whenever they wished to define the size of a plot, they specified its length and breadth, even if it were a perfect square, as in Ezek. xlviii, 16. The difficulty of defining an area by these means is experienced in the interpretation of Numb. xxxv, 4, 5, where the suburbs of the Levitical cities are described as reaching outward from the wall of the city 1000 cubits round about, and at the same time 2000 cubits on each side from without the city. We can hardly understand these two measurements otherwise than as applying, the one to the width, the other to the external boundary of the suburb, the measurements being taken respectively perpendicular and parallel to the city walls. But in this case it is necessary to understand the words rendered "from without the city," in ver. 5, as meaning *to the exclusion of* the city, so that the length of the city wall should be added in each case to the 2000 cubits. The result would be that the size of the areas would vary, and that where the city walls were unequal in length, the sides of the suburb would be also unequal. For instance, if the city wall were 500 cubits long, then the side of the suburb would be 2500 cubits; if the city wall were 1000 cubits, then the side of the suburb would be 3000 cubits. Assuming the existence of two towns, 500 and 1000 cubits square, the area of the suburb would in the former case = 6,000,000 square cubits, and would be 24 times the size of the town; while in the latter case the suburb would be 8,000,000 square cubits, and only 8 times the size of the town. This explanation is not wholly satisfactory, on account of the disproportion of the suburbs as compared with the towns; nevertheless any other explanation only exaggerates this disproportion. Keil, in his comment on Josh. xiv, 4, assumes that the city wall was in all cases to be regarded as 1000 cubits long, which, with the 1000 cubits outside the wall, and measured in the same direction as the wall, would make up the 2000 cubits, and would give to the side of the suburb in every case a length of 3000 cubits. The objection to this view is that there is no evidence

as to a uniform length of the city walls, and that the suburb might have been more conveniently described as 3000 cubits on each side. All ambiguity would have been avoided if the size of the suburb had been decided either by absolute or relative acreage; in other words, if it were to consist in all cases of a certain fixed acreage outside the walls, or if it were made to vary in a certain ratio to the size of the town. As the text stands, neither of these methods can be deduced from it. See LEVITICAL CITY.

2. The measures of distance noticed in the Old Testament are the three following: (*a*) The צַ֫עַד, *tsá'ad*, or pace (2 Sam. vi, 13), answering generally to our yard. (*b*) The כִּבְרַת הָאָֽרֶץ, *kibráth ha-árets*, rendered in the A. V. "a little way" or "a little piece of ground" (Gen. xxxv, 16; xlviii, 7; 2 Kings v, 19). The expression appears to indicate some definite distance, but we are unable to state with precision what that distance was. The Sept. retains the Hebrew word in the form Χαβραθά, as if it were the name of a place, adding in Gen. xlviii, 7 the words κατὰ τὸν ἱππόδρομον, which is thus a second translation of the expression. If a certain distance was intended by this translation, it would be either the ordinary length of a race-course, or such a distance as a horse could travel without being overfatigued—in other words, a stage. But it probably means a locality, either a race-course itself, as in 3 Macc. iv, 11, or the space outside the town walls where the race-course was usually to be found. The Sept. gives it again in Gen. xlviii, 7 as the equivalent for Ephrath. The Syriac and Persian versions render *kibrath* by *parasang*, a well-known Persian measure, generally estimated at 30 stades (Herod. ii, 6; v, 53), or from 3$\frac{1}{2}$ to 4 English miles, but sometimes at a larger amount, even up to 60 stades (Strab. xi, 518). The only conclusion to be drawn from the Bible is that the *kibrath* did not exceed and probably equalled the distance between Bethlehem and Rachel's burial-place, which is traditionally identified with a spot 1$\frac{1}{2}$ miles north of the town. (*c*) The דֶּ֫רֶךְ יוֹם, *dérek yôm*, or מַהֲלַךְ יוֹם, *mahalák yóm*, a day's journey, which was the most usual method of calculating distances in travelling (Gen. xxx, 36; xxxi, 23; Exod. iii, 18; v, 3; Numb. x, 33; xi, 31; xxxiii, 8; Deut. i, 2; 1 Kings xix, 4; 2 Kings iii, 9; Jonah iii, 3; 1 Macc. v, 24, 28; vii, 45; Tobit vi, 1), though but one instance of it occurs in the New Testament (Luke ii, 44). The distance indicated by it was naturally fluctuating, according to the circumstance of the traveller or the country through which he passed. Herodotus variously estimates it at 200 and 150 stades (iv, 101; v, 53); Marinus (*ap. Ptol.* i, 11) at 150 and 172 stades; Pausanias (x, 33, § 2) at 150 stades; Strabo (i, 35) at from 250 to 300 stades; and Vegetius (*De Re Mil.* i, 11) at from 20 to 24 miles for the Roman army. The ordinary day's journey among the Jews was thirty miles; but when they travelled in companies, only ten miles. Neapolis formed the first stage out of Jerusalem, according to the former, and Beeroth according to the latter computation (Lightfoot, *Exerc. in Luc.* ii, 44). It is impossible to assign any distinct length to the day's journey: Jahn's estimate of 33 miles, 172 yards, and 4 feet, is based upon the false assumption that it bore some fixed ratio to the other measures of length.

In the Apocrypha and New Testament we meet with the following additional measures: (*d*) The Sabbath-day's journey, σαββάτου ὁδός, a general statement for a very limited distance, such as would naturally be regarded as the immediate vicinity of any locality. (*e*) The στάδιον, *stadium*, or "furlong," a Greek measure introduced into Asia subsequently to Alexander's conquest, and hence first mentioned in the Apocrypha (2 Macc. xi, 5; xii, 9, 17, 29), and subsequently in the New Testament (Luke xxiv, 13; John vi, 19; xi, 18; Rev. xiv, 20; xxi, 16). Both the name and the length of the stade were borrowed from the foot-race course at Olympia. It equalled 600 Greek feet (Herod. ii, 149), or 125 Roman paces (Plin. ii, 23), or $606\frac{3}{4}$ feet of our measure. It thus falls below the furlong by $53\frac{1}{4}$ feet. The distances between Jerusalem and the places Bethany, Jamnia, and Scythopolis, are given with tolerable exactness at 15 stades (John xi, 18), 240 stades (2 Macc. xii, 9), and 600 stades (2 Macc. xii, 29). In 2 Macc. xi, 5 there is an evident error, either of the author or of the text, in respect to the position of Bethsura, which is given as only 5 stades from Jerusalem. The Talmudists describe the stade under the term *rês*, and regarded it as equal to 625 feet and 125 paces (Carpzov, *Appar.* p. 679). (*f*) The mile, μίλιον, a Roman measure, equalling 1000 Roman paces, 8 stades, and 1618 English yards. See each in its place.

III. *Measures of Capacity.*—1. Those for *liquids* were: (*a*) The לֹג, *log* (Lev. xiv, 10, etc.), originally signifying a "basin." (*b*) The הִין, *hin*, a name of Egyptian origin, frequently noticed in the Bible (Exod. xxix, 40; xxx, 24; Numb. xv, 4, 7, 9; Ezek. iv, 11; etc.). (*c*) בַּת, βάτος, the *bath*, the name meaning "measured," the largest of the liquid measures (1 Kings vii, 26, 38; 2 Chron. ii, 10; Ezra vii, 22; Isa. v, 10; Luke xvi, 16).

With regard to the relative values of these measures we learn nothing from the Bible, but we gather from Josephus (*Ant.* iii, 8, 3) that the bath contained 6 hins (for the bath equalled 72 *xestæ* or 12 *choës*, and the hin 2 *choës*), and from the rabbinists that the hin contained 12 logs (Carpzov, *Appar.* p. 685).

2. The dry *measure* contained the following denominations: (*a*) The קַב, *cab*, mentioned only in 2 Kings vi, 25, the name meaning literally *hollow* or *concave.* (*b*) The עֹמֶר, *ómer*, mentioned only in Exod. xvi, 16–36. The same measure is elsewhere termed עִשָּׂרוֹן, *issarón*, as being the tenth part of an ephah (compare Exod. xvi, 36), whence in the A. V. "tenth deal" (Lev. xiv, 10; xxiii, 13; Numb. xv, 4, etc.). The word omer implies a *heap*, and secondarily a *sheaf*. (*c*) The סְאָה, *sêâh*, or "measure," this being the etymological meaning of the term, and appropriately applied to it, inasmuch as it was the ordinary measure for household purposes (Gen. xviii, 6; 1 Sam. xxv, 18; 2 Kings vii, 1, 16). The Greek equivalent, σάτον, occurs in Matt. xiii, 33; Luke xiii, 21. The seah was otherwise termed שָׁלִישׁ, *shalish*, as being the third part of an ephah (Isa. xl, 12; Psa. lxxx, 5). (*d*) The אֵיפָה, *epháh*, a word of Egyptian origin, and of frequent recurrence in the Bible (Exod. xvi, 36; Lev. v, 11; vi, 20; Numb. v, 15; xxviii, 5; Judg. vi, 19; Ruth ii, 17; 1 Sam. i, 24; xvii, 17; Ezek. xlv, 11, 13, 14; xlvi, 5, 7, 11, 14). (*e*) The לֶתֶךְ, *léthek*, ἡμίκορος, or "half-homer," literally meaning what is *poured out:* it occurs only in Hos. iii, 2. (*f*) The הֹמֶר, *hómer*, meaning *heap* (Lev. xxvii, 16; Numb. xi, 32; Isa. v, 10; Ezek. xlv, 13). It is elsewhere termed *cor*, כֹּר, from the circular vessel in which it was measured (1 Kings iv, 22; v, 11; 2 Chron. ii, 10; xxvii, 5; Ezra vii, 22; Ezek. xlv, 14). The Greek equivalent, κόρος, occurs in Luke xvi, 7.

The relative proportions of the dry measures are to a certain extent expressed in the names *issarón*, meaning a tenth, and *shalish*, a third. In addition, we have the Biblical statement that the omer is the tenth part of the ephah (Exod. xvi, 36), and that the ephah was the tenth part of a homer, and corresponded to the bath in liquid measure (Ezek. xlv, 11). The rabbinists supplement this by stating that the ephah contained three seahs, and the seah six cabs (Carpzov, p. 683).

The scale is constructed, it will be observed, on a combination of decimal and duodecimal ratios, the former prevailing in respect to the omer, ephah, and homer, the latter in respect to the cab, seah, and ephah. In the liquid measure the duodecimal ratio alone appears, and hence there is a fair presumption that this was the original, as it was undoubtedly the most general principle on which the scales of antiquity were framed (Böckh, p. 38). Whether the decimal division was introduced from some other system, or whether it was the result of local usage, there is no evidence to show.

3. The absolute values of the liquid and dry measures form the subject of a single inquiry, inasmuch as the two scales have a measure of equal value, viz. the bath and the ephah (Ezek. xlv, 11): if either of these can be fixed, the conversion of the other denominations into their respective values readily follows. Unfortunately, the data for determining the value of the bath or ephah are both scanty and conflicting. Attempts have been made to deduce the value of the bath from a comparison of the dimensions and the contents of the molten sea as given in 1 Kings vii, 23–26. If these particulars had been given with greater accuracy and fulness, they would have furnished a sound basis for a calculation; but, as the matter now stands, uncertainty attends the statement. The diameter is given as 10 cubits, and the circumference as 30 cubits, the diameter being stated to be "from one brim to the other." Assuming that the vessel was circular, the proportions of the diameter and circumference are not sufficiently exact for mathematical purposes, nor are we able to decide whether the diameter was measured from the internal or the external edge of the vessel. The difference, however, in either respect, is not sufficiently great to affect the result materially. The shape of the vessel has been variously conceived to be circular and polygonal, cylindrical and hemispherical, with perpendicular and with bulging sides. The contents are given as 2000 baths in 1 Kings vii, 26, and 3000 baths in 2 Chron. iv, 5, the latter being probably a corrupt text. The conclusions drawn have been widely different, as might be expected. If it be assumed that the form of the vessel was cylindrical (as the description *prima facie* seems to imply), that its clear diameter was 10 cubits of the value (often estimated) of 19.0515 English inches each, and that its full contents were 2000 baths, then the value of the bath would be 4.8965 gallons; for the contents of the vessel would equal 2,715,638 cubic inches, or 9793 gallons. If, however, the statement of Josephus (*Ant.* viii, 3, 5), as to the hemispherical form of the vessel, be adopted, then the estimate would be reduced. Saigey, as quoted by Böckh (p. 261), on this hypothesis calculates the value of the bath at 18.086 French litres, or 3.9807 English gallons. If, further, we adopt Saalschütz's view as to the length of the cubit, which he puts at 15 Dresden inches at the highest, the value of the bath will be further reduced, according to his calculation, to $10\frac{1}{4}$ Prussian quarts, or 2.6057 English gallons; while at his lower estimate of the cubit at 12 inches, its value would be little more than one half of this amount (*Archäol.* ii, 171). On the other hand, if the vessel bulged, and if the diameter and circumference were measured at the neck or narrowest part of it, space might be found for 2000 or even 3000 baths of greater value than any of the above estimates. It is therefore hopeless to arrive at any satisfactory conclusion from this source. Nevertheless, we think the calculations are not without their use, as furnishing a certain amount of presumptive evidence. For, setting aside the theory that the vessel bulged considerably, for which the text furnishes no evidence whatever, all the other computations agree in one point, viz. that the bath fell far below the value placed on it by Josephus, and by modern writers on Hebrew archæology generally, according to whom the bath measures between 8 and 9 English gallons. See BRAZEN SEA.

We turn to the statements of Josephus and other early writers. The former states that the bath equals 72 *xestæ* (*Ant.* viii, 2, 9); that the hin equals 2 Attic *choës* (*ibid.* iii, 8, 3; 9, 4); that the seah equals $1\frac{1}{2}$ Italian *modii* (*ibid.* ix, 4, 5); that the cor equals 10 Attic *medimni* (*ibid.* xv, 9, 2); and that the issaron or omer equals 7 Attic *cotylæ* (*ibid.* iii, 6, 6). It may further be implied from *Ant.* ix, 4, 4, as compared with 2 Kings vi, 25, that he regarded the cab as equal to 4 *xestæ*.

Now, in order to reduce these statements to consistency, it must be assumed that in *Ant.* xv, 9, 2, he has confused the *medimnus* with the *metrètes*, and in *Ant.* iii, 6, 6, the *cotylè* with the *xestès*. Such errors throw doubt on his other statements, and tend to the conclusion that Josephus was not really familiar with the Greek measures. This impression is supported by his apparent ignorance of the term *metrètes*, which he should have used not only in the passage above noticed, but also in viii, 2, 9, where he would naturally have substituted it for 72 *xestæ*, assuming that these were Attic *xestæ*. Nevertheless, his testimony must be taken as decisively in favor of the essential identity of the Hebrew bath with the Attic *metrètes*. Jerome (*in Matt.* xiii, 33) affirms that the seah equals $1\frac{1}{2}$ *modii*, and (*in Ezek.* xlv, 11) that the cor equals 30 *modii*: statements that are glaringly inconsistent, inasmuch as there were 30 seahs in the cor. The statements of Epiphanius, in his treatise *De Mensuris*, are equally remarkable for inconsistency. He states (ii, 177) that the cor equals 30 *modii*. On this assumption the bath would equal 51 *sextarii*, but he gives only 50 (p. 178); the seah would equal 1 *modius*, but he gives $1\frac{1}{4}$ *modii* (p. 178), or, according to his estimate of 17 *sextarii* to the *modius*, $21\frac{1}{4}$ *sextarii*; though elsewhere he assigns 56 *sextarii* as its value (p. 182); the omer would be $5\frac{1}{10}$ *sextarii*, but he gives $7\frac{1}{2}$ (p. 182), implying 45 *modii* to the cor; and, lastly, the ephah is identified with the Egyptian *artabè* (p. 182), which was either $4\frac{1}{2}$ or $3\frac{1}{3}$ *modii*, according as it was in the old or the new measure, though, according to his estimate of the cor, it would only equal 3 *modii*. Little reliance can be placed on statements so loosely made, and the question arises whether the identification of the bath with the *metrètes* did not arise out of the circumstance that the two measures held the same relative position in the scales, each being subdivided into 72 parts; and, again, whether the assignment of 30 *modii* to the cor did not arise out of there being 30 seahs in it. The discrepancies can only be explained on the assumption that a wide margin was allowed for a long measure, amounting to an increase of fifty per cent. This appears to have been the case from the definition of the seah or σάτον given by Hesychius (μόδιος γέμων, ἥγουν ἐν ἥμισυ μόδιον Ἰταλικόν), and again by Suidas (μόδιον ὑπερπεπληρωμένον, ὡς εἶναι μόδιον ἕνα καὶ ἥμισυν). Assuming, however, that Josephus was right in identifying the bath with the *metrètes*, its value would be, according to Böckh's estimate of the latter (p. 261, 278), 1993.95 Paris cubic inches, or 8.7053 English gallons; but, according to the estimate of Bertheau (*Gesch.* p. 73), 1985.77 Paris cubic inches, or 8.6696 English gallons.

The rabbinists furnish data of a different kind for calculating the value of the Hebrew measures. They estimated the log to be equal to six hen eggs, the cubic contents of which were ascertained by measuring the amount of water they displaced (Maimonides, *in Cel.* 17, § 10). On this basis, Thenius estimated the log at 14.088 Paris cubic inches, or .06147 English gallon, and the bath at 1014.39 Paris cubic inches, or 4.4286 gallons (*St. u. Kr.* p. 101, 121). Again, the log of water is said to have weighed 108 Egyptian drachmæ, each equalling 61 barleycorns (Maimonides, *in Peah*, 3, § 6, ed. Guisius). Thenius finds that 6588 barleycorns fill about the same space as 6 hen eggs (*St. u. Kr.* p. 112). Again, a log is said to fill a vessel 4 digits long, 4 broad, and $2\frac{7}{10}$ high (Maimonides, *in Præf. Menachoth*). This vessel would contain 21.6 cubic inches, or .07754 gallon. The conclusion arrived at from these data would agree tolerably well with the first estimate formed on the notices of the molten sea.

In the New Testament we have notices of the following foreign measures: (*a*) The *metrètes*, μετρητής (John ii, 6; A.V. "firkin"), for liquids. (*b*) The *chænix*, χοῖνιξ (Rev. vi, 6; A.V. "measure"), for dry things. (*c*) The *xestes*, ξέστης, applied, however, not to the particular measure so named by the Greeks, but to any

small vessel, such as a cup (Mark vii, 4, 8; A.V. "pot"). (*d*) The *modius*, similarly applied to describe any vessel of moderate dimensions (Matt. v, 15; Mark iv, 21; Luke xi, 33; A.V. "bushel"); though properly meaning a Roman measure, amounting to about a peck.

The value of the Attic *metrètes* has already been stated to be 8.6696 gallons, and consequently the amount of liquid in six stone jars, containing on the average $2\frac{1}{2}$ *metrètæ* each, would exceed 110 gallons (John ii, 6). Very possibly, however, the Greek term represents the Hebrew *bath*, and if the bath be taken at the lower estimate assigned to it, the amount would be reduced to about 60 gallons. Even this amount far exceeds the requirements for the purposes of legal purification, the tendency of Pharisaical refinement being to reduce the amount of water to a minimum, so that a quarter of a log would suffice for a person (Mishna, *Yad.* 1, § 1). The question is one simply of archæological interest as illustrating the customs of the Jews, and does not affect the character of the miracle with which it is connected. The *chænix* was $\frac{1}{48}$ of an Attic *medimnus*, and contained nearly a quart. It represented the usual amount of corn for a day's food, and hence a *chænix* for a penny, or denarius, which usually purchased a bushel (Çicero, *Verr.* iii, 81), indicated a great scarcity (Rev. vi, 6).

With regard to the use of fair measures, various precepts are expressed in the Mosaic law and other parts of the Bible (Lev. xix, 35, 36; Deut. xxv, 14, 15; Prov. xx, 10; Ezek. xlv, 10), and in all probability standard measures were kept in the Temple, as was usual in the other civilized countries of antiquity (Böckh, p. 12).

IV. The following are the various Biblical weights and measures of all kinds, in the alphabetical order of the original terms, with their correct and conventional renderings, and the nearest modern representative:

Heb. or Gr.	Name.	A.V.	Equivalent.
Adarkón	*Daric*	"dram"	*quarter-eagle.*
Argúrion	*Silverling*	"piece of silver," etc.	*half-crown.*
Assárion	*Assarius*	"farthing"	*penny.*
Ammáh	*Cubit*	"cubit"	*half-yard.*
Bath	*Bath.*	"bath"	*quarter-barrel.*
Bátos	*Bath.*	"measure"	*quarter-barrel.*
Béka	*Beka.*	"bekah," etc.	*quarter-ounce.*
Chœnix.	*Chœnix.*	"measure"	*quart.*
Darkemón	*Daric.*	"dram"	*quarter-eagle.*
Denárion	*Denarius*	"penny"	*shilling.*
Dérek, etc.	*Travel.*	"journey"	*[general].*
Didráchmon	*Didrachm.*	"tribute"	*quarter-dollar.*
Dráchmè	*Drachma.*	"piece of silver"	*shilling.*
Epháh	*Ephah.*	"ephah"	*half-bushel.*
Etsbá	*Finger*	"finger"	*finger-length.*
Geráh	*Gerah*	"gerah"	*half-penny-w't.*
Gómed	*Span*	"cubit"	*quarter-yard.*
Hin.	*Hin*	"hin"	*gallon.*
Hómer.	*Homer*	"homer"	*double-barrel.*
Issarón	*Tenth.*	"tenth deal"	*half-peck.*
Kab	*Kab.*	"cab"	*quart.*
Kanéh	*Reed.*	"reed"	*half-rod.*
Késheth, etc.	*Bow*	"bow," etc.	*bow-shot.*
Kesitáh	*Kesita.*	"piece of money"	*ingot.*
Kibráth, etc.	*Space.*	"way," etc.	*short distance.*
Kikkár	*Talent.*	"talent"	*hundred-w'ght.*
Kodrántes	*Quadrans.*	"farthing"	*farthing.*
Kómets	*Handful*	"handful"	*handful.*
Kor	*Kor*	"cor"	*hogshead.*
Kóros	*Kor*	"measure"	*hogshead.*
Lépton	*Scale*	"mite"	*mill.*
Léthek	*Lethek.*	"measure"	*half-hogshead.*
Lithos, etc.	*Stone.*	"stone's-throw"	*stone-throw.*
Lítra	*Pound.*	"pound"	*pound.*
Log.	*Log*	"log"	*half-pint.*
Manéh	*Maneh.*	"maneh"	*double-pound.*
Metrétes	*Metretes.*	"firkin"	*firkin.*
Milion	*Mile*	"mile"	*mile.*
Mna	*Mina*	"pound"	*triple-half-eagle.*
Módios	*Modius*	"bushel"	*peck.*
Omer	*Omer*	"omer"	*half-peck.*
Orguia	*Fathom.*	"fathom"	*fathom.*
Péchus	*Ell*	"cubit"	*half-yard.*
Réba	*Fourth.*	"fourth"	*half-quarter-ounce.*
Sáton	*Seah*	"measure"	*peck.*
Seáh.	*Seah,*	"seah"	*peck.*
Shalish	*Third.*	"third"	*peck.*

Heb. or Gr.	Name.	A. V.	Equivalent.
Shékel.......	Shekel.......	"shekel"...	{ half-ounce. / half-dollar.
Stadios or } / Stadion }	..Stade.........	"furlong"....	furlong.
Stater	Stater	"piece of money"....	half-crown.
Talantion	Talent........	"talent"....	thousand dollars.
Téphach......	Hand-breadth.	"hand-breadth"	..hand-breadth.
Tsáade	Pace..........	"pace"........	pace.
Xéstès.......	Sextarius.....	"measure"...	pint.
Zéreth........	Span..........	"span".......	span.

V. The following tables exhibit at one view the approximate results of the foregoing investigations:

I. HEBREW WEIGHTS.

Troy Weight.					Grains.	Lbs.	Oz.
Gerah..................................					11		$\frac{1}{40}$
10	Beka.......................				110		$\frac{1}{4}$
20	2	Shekel			220		$\frac{1}{2}$
1000	100	50	Maneh........		11,000	1	11
60,000	6000	3000	60	Kikkar.	660,000	114	7

II. SCRIPTURE MONEYS.

Name.	Nation.	Metal.	Prop.Valuation.			Current Worth.		
			$	cts.	mills.	$	cts.	mills.
Lepton	Greek	Copper						1.9
Quadrans	Roman	"			3.8			3.8
Assarius	"	"		1	5.4		1	5.4
Denarius	"	Silver		15	4.7		15	4.7
Drachma	Greek	"		17	5.9		15	4.7
Didrachm	"	"		35	1.9		30	9.4
Stater	"	Gold		70	3.7		61	8.9
Shekel	Jewish	Silver		60				
Mina	Greek	"		17 59	3.2		15 47	3.8
Talent	"	Gold	1058	59		928	43	

III. HEBREW MEASURES OF LENGTH.

					Inches.
Finger...					0.75
4	Palm....				3.02
12	3	Span....			9.07
24	6	2	Cubit....		18.14
144	36	12	6	Reed........	108.84

IV. HEBREW LIQUID MEASURES.

	JOSEPHUS.			RABBINS.		
	gals.	qts.	pts.	gals.	qts.	pts.
Log...................			0.99			0.56
12	Hin..........					
		1	1.85	3	0	0.72
72	6	Bath..........		8 2	3.2	5 0 0.32
720	60	10	Cor......	89		50 1 1.2

V. HEBREW DRY MEASURES.

	JOSEPHUS.	RABBINS.
	bsh.pks.qts.pts.	bsh.pks.qts.pts.
Cab....	2	1 0.24
1$\frac{4}{5}$	Omer	2
	3 1.1	
6	3$\frac{1}{3}$	Seah..........	1 3 1.7	6 1.44
18	10	3	Ephah........	1 0 2 3.2	2 4 0.32
180	100	30	10	Homer	11 0 4	6 1 1 1.2

VI. *Literature.*—J. D. Michaelis, *Supplem. ad Lex. Hebr.* p. 1521; Hussey, *Essay on the Ancient Weights, Money,* etc. (Oxford, 1836); F. P. Bayer, *De Nummis Hebræo-Samaritanis* (Valentiæ Edetanorum, 1781: written in reply to *Die Unächtheit der Jüd. Münzen,* Bützow, 1779); Hupfeld, *Betrachtung dunkler Stellung der A. T. Textgeschichte,* in the *Studien und Kritiken,* 1830, ii, 247–301; Thenius, *ibid.* 1846, i, 78 sq.; G. Seyffarth, *Beiträge zur Kenntniss der Literatur, Kunst, Mythol. und Geschichte des alten Aegypten;* Cumberland, *Essay on Weights and Measures;* Arbuthnot, *Tables of Ancient Coins,* etc.; Böckh's *Metrologische Untersuchungen;* Mommsen's *Geschichte des Römischen Münzwesens;* Don V. Vazquez Queipo's *Essai sur les Systèmes Métriques et Monétaires des Anciens Peuples;* Müller, *Ueb. d. heil. Maase der Hebräer und Hellenen* (Freib. 1859); Hezfeld, *Metrologische Voruntersuchungen* (Leips. 1863–5); Tuckermann, *Das jüdische Maas-System* (Breslau, 1867).

Metrophǎnès (Μητροφάνης), a Greek theologian, bishop of Smyrna, flourished in the 9th century. He is particularly known for his opposition to Photius. He was already bishop of Smyrna when his friend, the patriarch Ignatius, was replaced by Photius, and, although he at first recognised the new patriarch, he subsequently opposed him so fiercely as to be himself deposed and cast into prison. When Ignatius was restored by emperor Basil I, Metrophanes regained his see, and in the Council of Constantinople (869) showed himself one of the most ardent of Photius's adversaries. After the death of Ignatius, in 879, Photius became again patriarch, and Metrophanes was again deposed. He nevertheless continued to speak and to write against Photius, and was excommunicated in 880. We have no details concerning his life after that date. He wrote a letter to Manuel concerning the dispute with Photius from 858 to 870, which is preserved both in Greek and Latin in Labbe, *Concilia,* vol. viii, and in Raderus, *Acta Concilii* (Ingolstadt, 1604, 4to). See Fabricius, *Biblioth. Græca,* xi, 700; Baronius, *Annal.* ad ann. 870; Hankius, *Scriptores Byzantini,* xvii, 1; xviii, 66; Hoefer, *Nouv. Biog. Générale,* xxxv, 220. (J. N. P.)

Metrophǎnès, CRITOPULUS, a Greek theologian of the 17th century, was born in Berœa, was educated at the convent school at Athos. Afterwards he served in an intimate relation to the celebrated patriarch, Cyril Lucar, who in 1616 sent him to England to be instructed in the doctrine and discipline of the Church of England, and to continue his education at the University of Oxford, even then a very celebrated educational institution. Lucar, in a letter to George Abbott, archbishop of Canterbury, at this time complained bitterly of the progress made by the Jesuits in the Eastern Church, and of the inability of his clergy to successfully resist them for want of sufficient instruction (see that letter in P. Colomesii *Clarorum ver. epist.* [Lond. 1687], Ep. 46; also in his *Opp.* ed. Fabric. [Hamb. 1709], p. 557). Metrophanes, on his arrival in England, was well received by archbishop Abbott and king James. In 1620 or 1621 Metrophanes went to Germany, where he visited the Protestant universities of Wittenberg, Tübingen, Altdorf, Strasburg, and Helmstadt. In the latter place he made the acquaintance of Conring, Calixtus, and Conrad Hornejus, at whose suggestion he wrote, in 1625, a confession of the tenets of the orthodox Greek Church, with an exposition of its principal customs. This was subsequently published, together with a Latin translation, by John Hornejus, son of Conrad, and an introduction by Conring (see Conringii *Opp.* vi, p. 391), at Helmstadt, in 1661. Among his other productions in Germany we find, *De vocibus quibusdam liturgicis epist.* ed. J. J. Crudelius (Jüterb. 1737):—*Oratio Græca panegyrica et dogmatica in nativitatem domini Latine versa,* per M. G. Queccium (Alt. 1626):—*Responsio ad quæstionem de dicto apostolico "Spiritu ambulate," Gr. et Lat.* ed. a M. Rindero, *Emendationes et animadversiones in Joh. Meursii Gloss. Græco-barbarum* ed. *Franzius* (Stendal, 1787):—*De pronunciatione literæ* Θ, ed. Schwenterus (Norimb. 1625); and letters to be found in G. Richteri *Epistolis,* p. 729, and in J. Chr. Wolfii *Conspectu supell. epist.* p. 26, 66, 129. He next went for some time to Venice as a teacher of Greek, and finally returned to Constantinople, in what year is uncertain. He subsequently became patriarch of Alexandria. The most important of all his works is the above-mentioned confession (Ὁμολογία τῆς ἀνατολικῆς ἐκκλησίας τῆς καθολικῆς καὶ ἀποστολικῆς, κ.τ.λ.). It is a rather full, clear exposition of the doctrines and customs of the Greek Church, more in the form of a theological analysis than of a strictly symbolic work. He shows in it great opposition to the Romish Church, but at the same time avoids all Protestant polemics. The charge that Metrophanes was *Lutheran* in tendency is unjust, and is ignored by all able theologians. According to Metrophanes, the Greek doctrines can be divided into two parts, forming a "simple" and an "economical" system of theology (*Conf.* p. 13, ed. Weissenb.). The first treats of God and of the Trinity, leading naturally to the exposition of the Greek doctrine concerning the Holy Ghost (*Confess.* p. 15 sq.). If we compare the doctrine of the author on the point with the tradition of the Greek fathers, we find the doctrine much more complete, and somewhat similar to that of the Latin Church. Each of the three divine persons stands in a definite relation to the two others, and at the same time constitute one form of the Deity. The first person stands as the father of the second and the sender ($\pi\rho o\beta o\lambda\epsilon\dot{v}\varsigma$), but embraces them both in himself as $vo\tilde{v}\varsigma$. The second person, or son, possesses a $\lambda\dot{o}\gamma o\varsigma$, the third the $\pi\rho\dot{v}\beta\lambda\eta\mu\alpha$ of the first, as $\pi\nu\epsilon\tilde{v}\mu\alpha$, an identity with both. See Weissenborn, *Præfatio* to his *Appendix litt. Symbol. Eccles. Orientalis* (Jena, 1850); Ditelmaier, *De Metrophane Critopule* (Altenb. 1769); Neale, *Florent. Council*, p. 168.

Metropolitan ($M\eta\tau\rho o\pi o\lambda\dot{\iota}\tau\eta\varsigma$) is the name of an ecclesiastical dignitary—an episcopal officer—who, by virtue of his residence in the capital of a country or province, exercises not only the authority of a presiding officer in his own diocese, but exerts, in some sense, jurisdiction over the other bishops of the same country or province; and in this respect differs from the *archbishop* (q. v.), who simply enjoys some additional privileges of honors and respect not common to the plain bishop (comp. Schaff, *Ch. Hist.* i, 270).

The office originated in the Roman countries, when the chief city of a province was called $\mu\eta\tau\rho\dot{o}\pi o\lambda\iota\varsigma$. The date of its origin cannot be exactly fixed, but "the third century," says Coleman (*Manual of Prelacy and Ritualism*, p. 235), "may be regarded as the period in which it was chiefly consolidated and established." Romanists hold that it can be traced, at least in germ, to the days of the apostles, and that mention is made of the office in the letters of Paul to Timothy and to Titus (comp. Pierre de Marca, *Concord.* lib. vi, Giorgi, *De Antiquo Ital. Metropol.*). Several of the Church fathers also mention the fact that the metropolitan office existed in apostolic days (e. g. Chrysostom, 15 *Hom. in V. Tim.*, and Eusebius, *Hist. Eccles.* iii, c. 4); but it is clear that "the *name* of metropolitan does not occur until the 4th century" (Coleman, *Anc. Christianity Exemplified*, p. 143). The title was first publicly adopted by the Church at the Council of Nicæa, A.D. 325, and there seems good ground for the belief that, like all other episcopal offices, the metropolitan government "was not the production of a day, but the result of a gradual modification of the diocesan government, by a further concentration of episcopal power, and the extension of its influence over a wider range of territory" (Coleman, *Prel. and Rit.* p. 242; comp. Schaff, *Ch. Hist.* ii, 270).

The following may be considered as the rights and privileges of the office. The metropolitan had precedence of all other bishops of his province, a decisive voice in their election, and the power of confirming and ordaining them. He summoned provincial councils, presided in them, and drew up the decrees. He had the oversight of the provincial bishops, and the ecclesiastical superintendence of the whole province. He had the privilege of determining all causes of special importance in provincial council, but in concurrence with the other bishops of the province. In extreme cases, appeal was made to him, when he had the power of controlling a provincial bishop, without the assistance of other bishops. He could give and receive letters of communion, and publish and carry into effect laws enacted either by emperors or by councils relating to the Church. The bishops of a province elected and ordained their metropolitan, without the concurrence of the metropolitan of any other province.

The ninth canon of the Council of Antioch (341) thus defines the office of the metropolitan: "The bishops of each eparchy (province) should know that upon the bishop of the metropolis (the municipal capital) also de-

volves a care for the whole eparchy, because in the metropolis all, who have business, gather together from all quarters. Hence it has been found good that he should also have a precedence in honor, and that the other bishops should do nothing without him—according to the old and still binding canon of our fathers—except that which pertains to the supervision and jurisdiction of their parishes (i. e. dioceses in the modern terminology), and the provinces belonging to them; as in fact they ordain presbyters and deacons, and decide all judicial matters. Otherwise they ought to do nothing without the bishop of the metropolis, and he nothing without the consent of the other bishops." In the nineteenth canon, this council forbade a bishop being ordained without the presence of the metropolitan, and the presence or concurrence of the majority of the bishops of the province. The writers of the Latin Church use promiscuously the words archbishop and metropolitan, making either name denote a bishop, who, by virtue of his see, presides over or governs several other bishops. Thus in the newly-constituted hierarchy of the Roman Catholic Church in England the archbishop of Westminster has the rank of *metropolitan*. In the Roman Catholic Church of Ireland, the archbishops of Armagh, Dublin, Cashel, and Tuam, all possess the same rank. In the Church of England, also, the real meaning of the term metropolitan seems to have been lost sight of, and the archbishops of Canterbury and York, in England, and in Ireland those of Armagh and Dublin, are called metropolitans. The Greeks, however, use the name only to denote him whose see is really a civil metropolis. See Farrar, *Eccles. Dict.* s. v.; Hook, *Church Dict.* s. v.; Walcott, *Sacred Archæology*, s. v.; Siegel, *Handbuch d. christl.-kirchl. Alterthümer*, iii, 264 sq.; Planck, *Gesch. d. christl.-kirchl. Gesellschaftsverfassung*, i, 572 sq.; Ziegler, *Versuch d. kirchl. Verfassungsformen*, p. 61 sq.

Metropoliticum is the name of the archiepiscopal ordinariate and consistory, a sort of ecclesiastical supreme court, or second court of appeals, in the Church of Rome, installed by the metropolitans or archbishops. Occasionally it has the special power conferred which constitutes it also a third court of appeals, but, as a rule, this court hears all appeals in matters of discipline and matrimonial difficulties. As the duties of the archbishop are both to attend to the management of his own diocese and the dioceses of his subaltern bishops, the metropolitan council is divided into two boards or senates, one of which constitutes the court in cases of discipline and matrimonial differences of the archdiocese, the other hearing appeals from the ordinaries and consistories of the assistant bishops. But it is against the nature of archiepiscopal jurisdiction that the metropoliticum can also take the appeals against the sentence of the archiepiscopal vicary and ordinary and decide upon those. An appeal ab eadem ad eundem is not admissible, for it cannot be thought of that the general vicary or the archiepiscopal ordinary represents the archbishop as common bishop in propria diœcesi, the metropoliticum representing him as such, inasmuch as the archbishop is in his own archdiocese as ordinarius. The archbishop certainly cannot fill the offices of two dignitaries; the cognition or decision of appeals from sentences of archiepiscopal general vicaries and metropolitan courts should therefore be sent to other, hence to the metropolitan court of another archbishopric. Appeals from the decisions of the metropolitan courts in second instance are usually presented to the pope himself, securing acquittal at Rome by the Curia Romana, unless his holiness may please to order a judices in partibus, i. e. confer upon the metropoliticum the power of acting as a court of appeal of the third instance. See Wetzer und Welte, *Kirchen-Lexikon*, s. v.

Mets, LAURENT DE, a Flemish prelate, was born at Grammont about 1520. He studied theology at Louvain, became a curate at Deinse, almoner and canon of

Saint-Gudula's church at Brussels, and shortly after the opening of the year 1562 he was appointed vicar to cardinal de Granvelle, archbishop of Malines, and installed ecclesiastical judge, or official, for the district of Brussels. In 1569, the University of Louvain constituted him the conservator of its privileges and vested rights, which were then hotly contested. Laurent de Mets did not long discharge the intricate functions of this last office, for in November, 1569, he was preferred to the bishopric of Bois-le-Duc. Mets founded a seminary, and published a Ritual for the use of his clergy. In November, 1577, he was constrained to yield to the insurrection of the Calvinists. At first he took refuge in Cologne, and then in Namur, where, in 1578, Gregory XIII invested him with the episcopal see rendered vacant by the death of Anthony Havet. He died at Namur, 1580. He is the author of *Statuta Synodi Diœcesanæ Buscoducensis anno Domini* MDLXXI (Bois-le-Duc, 1571, 8vo):—*Manuale Pastorum diœcesis Sylvœducensis*, (ibid. 1572, 4to). See Paquot, *Mémoires pour servir à l'histoire littéraire des Pays-Bas*, xii, 319–27; Valère André, *Bibliotheca Belgica*; Guillaume Gazet, *Histoire ecclésiastique des Pays-Bas.*; Foppens, *Bibliotheca Belgica*, p. 810.

Metsiah. See TALMUD.

Mettray, Reformatory of. This noted institution for the reformation of juvenile delinquents is the parent of all institutions of this character, and deserves our notice therefor. The object of the Reformatory of Mettray and other like institutions, which have, especially of late, been fast multiplying, is the mild punishment and ultimate restoration to society of juvenile delinquents. The founder of the reformatory—whose labors, like those of the prison reformers of our day, deserve to be cherished forever—was M. Demetz, a French lawyer, a member of the Parisian bar, who, struck with the evils and hardships attending the committal to prison of young persons, and considering the training and habits of scarcely responsible criminals, condemned to languish hopelessly for a time, incapable of producing results other than their emerging worse than when they entered, resolved, in conjunction with the vicomte Bretignères de Courteilles, to found a school which should have for its object the reformation of this class of offenders. In 1839, accordingly, the Reformatory, or, as it is called, the Colony of Mettray, was set on foot, about five miles from the city of Tours, in France. From that day to this, M. Demetz has, by his assiduous labors and self-devotedness, rendered to France and Europe one of the greatest benefits that could be conferred on society, proving that, by agricultural and other labors of industry, and well-considered rules of organization and discipline, the neglected and criminal may be trained to take their place honestly and honorably in society; the relapses into crime being in the institution of Mettray only 3.81 per cent. See PRISON REFORM. (J. H. W.)

Metus, an aged and venerable Christian of Alexandria, who, in the persecution of that city A.D. 249, for refusing to blaspheme his Saviour, was first beaten with clubs, then pierced with sharp reeds, and finally stoned to death. Quinta and Apollonia, two Christian females, and many others whose names are not preserved, were fellow-sufferers. Fox, *Book of Martyrs*, p. 26.

Metz, an important fortified city of the province of Lorraine, lately conquered by the Prussians in their contest with France, and situated on the Moselle, at its confluence with the Seille, holds an important position in Church history.

This place, known to the Romans by the name of *Divodorum*, was the chief town of a people called the *Mediomatrici*, whose name it took at a later date. In the 5th century the corrupted form *Mettis* first came into use, whence the modern *Metz*. It was destroyed by the Huns in 452. At the death of Clovis it became the capital of Austrasia, and later the capital of Lor-

raine. In 985 it became a free imperial town. It was finally secured to France by the peace of Westphalia in 1648, and was held by the French until ceded to the Germans in 1870. It has a population of over 50,000, somewhat diminished of late by the excursions of families unwilling to live under Prussian rule. Its streets are wide and clean, and it contains numerous spacious squares. The cathedral, a Gothic edifice, begun in 1014, and finished in 1546, is remarkable for its boldness, lightness, and elegance, and has a beautiful spire of open work, 373 feet in height. The church of Notre-Dame-de-la-Ronde is a noteworthy structure. Its choir was built in 1130. Metz contains also many other noble edifices and institutions, religious, civil, and military. Its industry is active, the chief employments being lace-making, tanning, embroidering, and the manufacture of brushes, clothing for the army, flannels, pins, and canes; there are also brass and copper foundries.

Metz figures quite prominently in the history of religious persecutions during the 16th and 17th centuries. The Huguenot war, especially, affected the peace of the Protestants of this place. The revocation of the Edict of Nantes was put in force at this place only five days after its publication. More than 4000 people left the place. (Comp. *La persécution de l'église de Metz*, d'écrite par le sieur Olry [2d ed], by O. Cuvier [Paris, 1860]).

METZ, COUNCIL OF (*Concilium Metense*). Church councils were held at Metz as early as A.D. 590. At this time Ægidius, archbishop of Rheims, was deposed and banished for high-treason against king Childebert. Of far greater importance, however, was a council held here in A.D. 835, which revoked the excommunication of Louis le Débonnaire, who had been unjustly treated by Ebbo, archbishop of Rheims. Another council, in the year following, supplemented the action of 835 by crowning Louis, Ebbo himself receding from his former position. See LOUIS LE DÉBONNAIRE. See also Landon, *Manual of Councils*, s. v.

Metz, Christian. See INSPIRED.

Metz, Joseph von, a German Roman Catholic theologian, was born at Ebenhofen, Bavaria, March 9, 1758. He was educated by Meinrad Meichelbeck, prior of the monastery at Reichenau, continued his education at the monastery at Benedictheuren, and graduated in 1779 at Augsburg. Afterwards he studied at the seminary at Pfaffenhausen; was ordained at Augsburg in 1785; became in the same year tutor of the children of the count of Stauffenberg, with whom he went to Strasburg, Mentz, and Würzburg; was then installed as minister at Freighalden, and a few years after as chaplain at Eberstall. In 1801 he was nominated clerical counsellor by Carl Theodor of Dalberg, bishop at Constance. In 1802 he got a position as minister to Riszdissen, and in 1804 as deacon at Laupheim; in 1809 poor health forced him to resign both positions, but in 1810, being restored to health, he became clerical counsellor of the government of the bishopric of Constance; in 1812 general counsellor of the vicarage at Elwangen; resigned in 1817, and died January 4, 1819. His manifold duties as pastor prevented the composition of extended literary works. Besides several essays in journals, he published *Katechismus, oder Leitfaden zum Christ-katholischen Religionsunterricht* (Const. 1812, 8vo). See Döring, *Gelehrte Theol. Deutschlands des 18ten u. 19ten Jahrhunderts*, ii, s. v.

Meucci, VINCENZIO, a Florentine artist, born in 1694, was chiefly employed in works of perspective, which he executed at various places in Tuscany, and in the cupola of the royal chapel in S. Lorenzo. Several works of Meucci are dispersed through various churches in Florence, and in a chapel of the Wunziata, where he painted a lovely *Madonna*, which is allowed to be one of his best works. He died in 1776. See Lanzi's *History of Painting*, transl. by Roscoe (London, 1847, 3 vols. 8vo), i, 253.

Meuillon, RAYMOND DE, a French preacher and

theologian, was born about 1235 in Dauphiny. After having declared to adhere to the rules of St. Dominic at the Convent of Sisteran, he was elected in 1264 general preacher of that order, and some time afterwards he was nominated definitor. In 1278 he was commissioned to go to England to suppress the too liberal discourses of some Dominicans, accused of irreverence to the memory of St. Thomas. After having accomplished the mission assigned to him, Raymond gave an account of his journey to the assembled chapels in Paris in May, 1279. The delinquents were condemned, and the priors authorized to punish vigorously whosoever should attempt new excesses. As a reward for his zeal, Raymond was nominated definitor for a second time. Some years after he was introduced to the secular Church in the capacity of a bishop. In 1289 Raymond was promoted archbishop of Embrun. He died June 29, 1294. Raymond de Meuillon's writings may be divided into two distinct categories, viz. his statutes and his dogmatical books. L'Histoire Littéraire analyzes them both. His dogmatical books have been translated into Greek. The only copy of this version, once kept in the Monastery of St. Germain-des-Prés at Paris, is now in the imperial library of St. Petersburg, with a great number of other manuscripts of his. See Le Catalogue des MSS. Bibl. impér. by M. Edouard de Muralt, and the valuable article of M. V. Le Clerc in L'Histoire Littéraire.

Meü'nim (Neh. vii, 52). See MEHUNIM.

Meur, VINCENT, a noted French divine, the inspirer of French foreign missions, was born at Tonguedec, in the diocese of Frézuier, France, in 1628. When yet a young man, he obtained the post of almoner to the court of Louis XIV. Tiring, however, of the idleness which frequently intervened in the discharge of his duties, he induced several other ecclesiastics, his friends and colleagues, to unite with him in founding an institution to prepare zealous apostles and effective preachers of the Word, and by this movement originated the French Board of Foreign Missions. In its incipiency, twelve persons assembled for consultation and deliberation in a small house in the Rue de la Harpe. Meur presided at this meeting. The Jesuits, comprehending the advantages which their society would derive from cooperative work with such auxiliaries, in 1652 affiliated with them. Meur, the moving spirit of these Roman Catholic missionaries, advised that work be inaugurated in South-eastern Asia, and, to obtain the approval of pope Alexander VII, in 1657 repaired to Rome. The pontiff warmly approved the project. Meur himself, however, instead of accompanying his associates, returned to Paris, and there engaged in theological discussions. He attacked Jansenius and his followers; in 1664 was appointed superior of the Seminary for Foreign Missions; assumed the priorate of St. André, in Brittany; and went on some religious missions to Dijon, Auxerre, and other cities of Burgundy, where he had friends. He had just returned from Brittany, to receive property bequeathed to him by his father and his brother, when he died, at Vieux-Chateaux-en-Brie, in 1668. See Richard et Giraud, Biblioth. Sacrée; Hoefer, Nouv. Biog. Générale, s. v.

Meuschen, JOHANN GERHARD, a learned German Protestant theologian, was born at Osnabrück, in Westphalia, May 4, 1680, a son of the minister Johann Conrad Meuschen at the St. Catharinenkirche. He commenced his education at the gymnasium of his native town; in 1699 entered the University of Jena, where, in 1702, he secured the title of master of arts. In 1703, being about to take a position as professor at Copenhagen, but detained accidentally at Kiel, he was appointed professor extraordinary of philosophy at the university of that place. He returned to Osnabrück in 1704, whither he was called by the St. Catharinenkirche as assistant to his father. In 1708 he was called to the Hague as pastor of the Lutheran congregation of that place, and

here he labored until 1716, when he went to Hanau as chief court and city minister, with the character of counsellor of the consistory; in 1720 he was appointed clerical superintendent of the district of Hanau-Lichtenberg. In 1723, after having refused several important offers made to him, he removed to Coburg as ecclesiastical counsellor, superintendent-general, and professor of theology, and died there December 15, 1743. Meuschen was a decided opponent of the papists, and especially of the Jesuits; and had to suffer considerably from their animosity towards him. One of his pamphlets against the machinations of Jesuitism, Nugæ venales Rullenses, was even publicly destroyed by fire under the hands of the executioner. The larger part of his works are of an ascetic tendency. The most important of his productions are: Postilla mythica, and Die neu eröffnete Bahn des wahren Christenthums:—Madonna et santa casa di Loretto, oder historische Beschreibung der lieben Frauen und des heiligen Hauses zu Loretto (Jena, 1702, 8vo):—Diss. academica de Cynisis philosophis (Kilon. 1703, 4to):— Diss. de præjudicio auctoritatis (ibid. 1704, 4to):—Diss. de antiquo et moderno ritu salutandi sternutantes (ibid. 1704, 4to):—Diss. de fabis Pythagoricis mysticis (ibid. 1704, 4to):—Anweisung zur Verleugnung der Welt und seiner selbst (Osnabrück, 1706, 12mo):—Das hohe Geheimniss der Geburt Christi in der Seele (Amsterdam, 1709, 8vo):—Die in der ersten Kirche gebräuchliche apostolische Consecration des heil. Abendmahls, aus den Patribus und Kirchengeschichten erwiesen. Meuschen was a very superior student in the ancient and Oriental languages, and his contributions to exegetical theology are perhaps among the most valuable productions of his age and country. His best works in the field of Biblical literature are: Diatribe de Nasi principe et directore Synedrii Magni Hebræorum (Coburg, 1724, 4to):—Novum Testamentum e Talmude illustratum (Leip. 1736, 4to):—Bibliotheca medici sacri, seu recensio scriptorum qui Scripturam Sacram ex medicina et philosophia naturali illustrarunt (The Hague, 1712, 8vo). He also edited Eygas's Chronicon Universale, under the title Herm. Eygantis Ord. minor. flores temporum s. chronicon universale ab anno Christi ad A.D. 1340 et adhinc ad a. 1513 continuatum a M. Eysenhart; editum præmisse glossario Latinitatis ferreæ J. G. Meuschenii (Lugd. Batav. 1743, 4to). See Programma funebre in Meuschenium (in the Acta Historico Ecclesiastica [Leipsic, vol. vii]); Strieder, Hessische gelehrten geschichte, vol. ix; Götten, Gelehrtes Europa, vols. ii and iii. (J. H. W.)

Meusel (or **Mösel**), WOLFGANG (Latin Musculus), a German Protestant theologian and Hebraist, was born at Dieuze, Lorraine (lately in France, but now in Germany), in 1497. At the age of fifteen, through the good offices of the prior, he was entered as a novice in the monastery of the Benedictines near Lixheim. After a course of arduous studies he was ordained a priest, and then devoted himself to preaching. In 1518 the writings of Luther strongly inclined Meusel to embrace the doctrines of the Reformation. Though elected prior of the cloister with which he was connected, he declined that office in order to maintain his independence. About this time he began so openly to preach the dogmas of Protestantism that he became generally known as the "Lutheran monk." Soon afterwards he quitted the monastery and went to Strasburg, where, in 1527, he married a relative of his former superior in the priory. A series of misfortunes and vicissitudes involved Meusel in obscurity until 1529, when he was appointed vicar at the cathedral at Strasburg. It was then that he diligently applied himself to the pursuit of Hebrew under the tuition of Bucer and Capito. In 1531 the Augsburg Senate invited him to come and labor for the spiritual good of the city. His principles of liberality and toleration so pleased the Senate that they intrusted him with some important missions. In 1536 he was sent to the assembly at Wittemburg, where he executed the formulary of a union designed to bind together the churches of Germany, North and South, in the matter of the Eucharist. In 1540 the Augsburg Senate delegated him to the councils held at Worms by the Protestants and the Catholics, and afterwards to the conferences which took place at Ratisbon. In the following year he drew up the heads of the controversy between Melancthon and Eck. In 1544 he established at Donauwörth the principles of the Reformation, and distinguished himself as a preacher. In 1549 he was installed professor of theology at Bern. He died in that city about 1563. Meusel wrote, *Anti-Cochlæus primus, adversus J. Cochlei de sacerdotio ac sacrificio novæ legis libellum* (Augsburg, 1644, 4to) : — *Commentarii in D. Joannis Evangelium* (Basle, 1545, fol.) :—*Commentarii in Matthæum* (ibid. 1548, fol.) :—*Dialogi IV de Quæstiont: Liceat homini Christiano evangelicæ doctrinæ guaro papisticis superstionibus ac falsis cultibus externa societate communicare?* (1549, 8vo) :—*Commentarii in Psalmos* (ibid. 1553, fol.) :—*In Decalogum Explanatio* (ibid. 1553) :—*Commentarii in Genesin* (ibid. 1554, fol.) :— *Commentarii in Epistolam ad Romanos* (ibid. 1555, fol.) :—*Commentarii in Esaiam prophetam* (ibid. 1567, fol.) :—*Commentari in Epistolas ad Corinthios, ad Galatos, ad Ephesios* (ibid. 1559, fol.) :—*Loci communes Theologiæ sacræ* (ibid. 1560, fol.):—*Commentarii in Epistolas ad Philippenses, Colossenses, Thessalonicenses et in primam ad Timotheum* (ibid. 1565, fol.). See *Synopsis festalium concionum, auctore Wolf. Musculo Dusano. Ejusdem vita, obitus, erudita carmina. Item clariss. virorum in ipsius obitu epicedia* (Basle, 1595, 12mo). See Haag, *Le France Protest.*; Melch. Adam, *Vitæ Theologorum;* Bayle, *Hist. Dictionary,* s. v.; Hoefer, *Nouv. Biog. Générale,* s. v.

Mexico, a federal republic of North America, and by far the most powerful representative of the Spanish American states.

I. *General.*—Mexico is situated between latitude 15° and 32° north, and longitude 97° and 117° west. The area is estimated by Behm and Wagner (*Bevölkerung der Erde,* Gotha, 1872) at 776,280 square miles; by other authorities somewhat differently. The population amounted in 1868, according to the calculations of the Mexican statistician, Cubas y Garcia, to 9,173,052. The country was, in 1518, conquered by Cortes for Spain, and from that time to 1821 constituted the vice-kingdom of New Spain. Up to 1843, when Texas separated from Mexico and declared itself independent, the area of Mexico was more than double what it is at present, embracing an area of about 1,500,000 square miles, but soon after the loss of Texas, the entire country north of the Rio Grande had, in consequence of the war of 1846 to 1848, to be ceded to the United States. In 1821 Mexico declared independence from Spain, and constituted itself a republic. The attempt of the Creole, Iturbide, to convert the country into an empire (1822), ended after about one year with his expulsion; and from that time Mexico, though continually torn by civil wars, remained a republic, with the single exception of the interval from 1864 to 1867 when Maximilian I was emperor of Mexico. The Mexican population embraces about 1,140,000 whites (40,000 Europeans, 300,000 Creoles, 800,000 Chapetones, or persons of mixed descent, who claim to be white), 1,500,000 to 2,000,000 Mestizoes of mixed descent, and about 16,000 negroes; all the others are Indians. Nearly all of these last are Christianized (*fideles*), only about 100,000 are still unbaptized (*Indios bravos*), and inhabit in small tribes the northern regions of the republic. All races have equal rights before the law; slavery was abolished on Sept. 16, 1829, under president Guerrero. The general language of the country is Spanish; of the Indian dialects, about twenty have maintained themselves to the present day; those most extensively spoken are the Aztec, or Mexican, and the Otonutian. The population in 1883 was 10,447,974.

II. *History of the Roman Catholic Church.*—The conquest of the country was soon followed by its Christianization. The first missionaries (after 1522) belonged to the Franciscan order, and one of the first Franciscan

monks, Peter of Ghent, reported that the missionaries of his order had, during the first six years of their labors, converted 200,000 Indians; and according to a report of the first bishop of Mexico, Zumaraga, in 1531, the number of the converts had risen to 1,000,000. Even the missionaries, however, complain that the conversion in many cases was little more than nominal, and many hid their idols under the cross in order to be able to worship them with impunity. The Franciscans were, in 1526, followed by the Dominicans, who gave to the country most of its bishops, by the Mercedarians (Order of Mercy), and (after 1553) by the Augustinians. When the Jesuits arrived in the country in 1572, the Christianization of the districts settled by the colonists was nearly complete; but the Jesuits established a number of prosperous missions in the territories of Northern Mexico, which at that time did not belong to the Spanish dominions. About the year 1600 Mexico abounded in magnificent churches, convents, and charitable institutions. The cruel treatment of the Indians by many Spaniards often called forth the remonstrances of monks and bishops, who prevailed upon king Charles V of Spain to interfere in behalf of the Indians, and upon pope Paul III to declare authoritatively that the Indians were rational beings, and must be treated as such. At the same time the bishops took good care of their own interests, and the Church of Mexico was one of the wealthiest on the globe. In 1767 the Jesuits were expelled from the country, and about the same time the influence of the liberal and rationalistic tendencies which prevailed in South-western Europe invaded Mexico, and gradually undermined both the Spanish rule and the influence of the Catholic Church. Among the leaders of the war of independence were many liberals. After the establishment of the federative republic, the Church generally sided with the Centralists, or Escosesos (so called after the Scotch rite of Freemasonry), and thereby provoked the bitter hostility of the Federalists, or Yorkinos (so called after the York rite of the Freemasons), who confiscated very large amounts of Church property whenever they were in power. In consequence of the refusal of the Spanish government to relinquish its historical rights in Mexican Church affairs, nearly all the episcopal sees became gradually vacant, until a convention with Rome for the reorganization of the Mexican Church was concluded and proclaimed, in 1831, as a law of the state. In 1851, under the presidency of Arista, a papal nuncio, Clementi, was appointed for Mexico, but the Chamber of Deputies did not recognise him, and even a portion of the clergy received him with distrust. In an allocution of Dec. 15, 1856, the pope complained that in the previous year (1855) the ecclesiastical jurisdiction had been abolished, the property of the diocese of Puebla confiscated, and the bishop of that city exiled; that in 1856 the Church had been stripped of all her possessions, the bishop of Guadalajara exiled, the sale of the Church property ordered, and the monks prevailed upon to leave their convents; that liberty of worship, speech, and the press had been introduced, many priests fined, a number of convents destroyed, and others suppressed; and that in general the government of president Santa Anna had shown a bitter hostility to the Church. President Commonfort (elected in 1856) was regarded as a still worse enemy of the Church than Santa Anna. A good understanding between Church and State was for a short time re-established under president Zuloaga (1858); but after his speedy overthrow (1859) the conflict began anew. A papal allocution of Sept. 30, 1861, deplored the new persecution of the Church in Mexico, when under the administration of president Juarez the possessions of the Church had been declared as national property, churches plundered, bishops expelled, clergymen, monks, and nuns exposed to many annoyances, and so forth. When Maximilian I was proclaimed emperor, the entire Church party supported him. Maximilian, before going to Mexico, implored at Rome the papal blessing, conferred many favors upon the Church, and received a new papal nuncio in Mexico; but the negotiations for a new concordat failed from reasons that have not yet been fully cleared up. After the re-establishment of the republican government under Juarez, the Church again complained of the liberal policy pursued by the government, and these complaints continued when Juarez was succeeded (1872) by president Lerdo de Tejada. The new president, as well as the majority of the Mexican Congress, adhered to the principles of religious toleration. In May, 1873, the Mexican Congress adopted a new law for the regulation of the affairs of the Roman Catholic Church, and the relation between Church and State, which contained the following provisions: Art. 1. Church and State are independent of each other. Congress can issue no laws which establish or prohibit any religion. Art. 2. Marriage is a civil contract, which is under the exclusive jurisdiction of the state authorities, and regulated by law. Art. 3. Religious societies can possess no real estate. Art. 4. All inhabitants of the republic are declared free from religious vows. The first article of this law was adopted unanimously, the remainder by overwhelming majorities, the minority in no case consisting of more than seventeen votes.

III. *Constitution and Statistics of the Roman Catholic Church.*—Soon after the conquest of the country by the Spaniards, the first bishopric was established in Mexico. About 1600 the vice-kingdom was divided into 7 dioceses: Mexico, Chiapa, Michoacan, Oajaca, Puebla, Guadalajara, and Yucatan, forming the ecclesiastical province of Mexico. Subsequently the number of dioceses rose to 11, and the number of parishes, in 1856, amounted to 1235. In 1863 pope Pius IX raised the dioceses of Michoacan and Guadalajara to archbishoprics, and erected 7 new dioceses. Accordingly the country is at present divided into 3 ecclesiastical provinces: *Mexico*, with the dioceses of Puebla, Chiapa, Oajaca, Yucatan, Vera Cruz, Chilapa, and Tulancingo; *Michoacan*, with the dioceses of San Luis Potosi, Queretaro, Leon, and Zamora; and *Guadalajara*, with the dioceses of Durango, Linares, Sonora, and Zacatecas. All the old dioceses have chapters. According to the decrees of the third Provincial Council of Mexico, each cathedral shall have 5 dignitaries (dean, archdeacon, cantor, theologus, thesaurarius), 10 canons, 6 prebendates, 6 half-prebendates, and 6 clerks, "with a good income." The new dioceses have as yet no chapter. Besides the regular parishes, there are many missionary stations, part of which were supported by six collegios de propaganda fide. Most of the latter were, however, suppressed by a decree of president Santa Anna, and parishes erected in their place. Under the Spanish rule the bishops were appointed by the king. After the establishment of the republic, the president of Mexico claimed the same right, and appointed bishops for every see that became vacant. But the popes refused to recognise the rights claimed by the presidents, and to confirm the appointments. Thus in 1829 all the dioceses, with the exception of one, had become vacant. In 1830 the canon Valdez, as envoy of the Mexican republic, succeeded in concluding a convention with the pope, which regulated the election of Mexican bishops by providing that the chapter were to propose to the government three candidates, among whom the latter would designate one as the future bishop, who thereupon would receive the canonical institution from the pope. The emperor Maximilian again claimed all the rights and privileges which the Spanish kings had possessed in Mexico, inclusive of the right of appointing the bishops. These, as well as other controverted points, were to be settled by a concordat, for the conclusion of which he was negotiating with the pope; but before an agreement had been arrived at, Maximilian lost his throne and life. The Mexican bishops formerly enjoyed all the rights conferred upon the bishops by the canon law as it prevailed in Spain; but the presidents of the Mexican republic refused to recognise many of these rights, and pope Pius IX, in an allocution of Dec. 15, 1856, complained that

president Commonfort had abolished the ecclesiastical jurisdiction altogether. The emperor Maximilian also failed to meet the expectations of Rome in this respect; for a note of the cardinal secretary of state to the Mexican ambassador in Rome, dated March 9, 1864, reclaimed from the imperial government "the full freedom of the bishops in the exercise of their pastoral office." The income of the bishops during the Spanish rule amounted to from 25,000 ducats to 100,000 ducats annually. The republic confiscated the entire property of the Church, and promised to give to the bishops a fixed income from the public revenue; but the bishops protested against this, and declared that they preferred to be supported by the voluntary gifts of the faithful. The number of priests is variously estimated at from 6000 to 10,000; they are partly educated in diocesan seminaries, partly in convents. Nearly all of them are of Indian descent; the native Spanish priests were in 1828 expelled from the country, in common with all the other Spaniards. The parish priests derived their income formerly from the very high fees which had to be paid for the ecclesiastical function. These fees were abolished by a decree of Santa Anna (Aug. 17, 1833), and again by Maximilian (Dec. 27, 1864), and it was provided that they should receive salaries from the state; but the bishops refused to accept this arrangement. Monks and nuns were very numerous in Mexico during the Spanish rule. In 1810 the Franciscans had 6 provinces, the Dominicans 3, the Augustinians 2, the Carmelites and Mercedarians 1 each. There were in all 1931 monks in 149 monasteries. The female orders in the same year had 57 convents with 1962 nuns. The property of the monasteries amounted to about 10,000,000 pesos, exclusive of the large amount of alms. The female orders had, in 1845, 50 convents, with real estate yielding a net annual income of 500,000 piastres; and had besides a capital of 4,500,000 piastres. The republic abolished the obligatory character of the monastic vows, and suppressed several convents; yet the number of convents did not begin to show any marked decrease until about 1860, when the Franciscans had 30 houses, the Dominicans 25, the Augustinians 10, the Carmelites 10, the Jesuits 1, the Oratorians 3, the Benedictines 1, the Brothers of Charity 2. The female orders were all suppressed by a decree issued in 1863, except the Sisters of Charity. The public educational institutions are under the exclusive control of the state authorities. They embrace one university in the city of Mexico, founded in 1551, 2 lyceums in Potosi and Guanajuato, and colleges in most of the large cities. Elementary instruction has severely suffered from the constant civil wars; but, according to recent accounts (*Annual American Cyclopædia*, 1872), "in most of the states each municipality has primary schools for both sexes, the teachers being paid out of municipal funds. The Lancasterian Society of the city of Mexico furnishes examined teachers for the elementary branches of those schools, and by its untiring efforts for the advancement of the cause of education generally, is establishing a firm basis for the future welfare of the country." There is, however, also a large number of schools established by the Church, and under her exclusive control, and their number has of late considerably increased. Besides the religious societies found in all Catholic countries, Mexico has some peculiar confradias and hermandados, the members of which engage to pay monthly contributions for defraying the extraordinary pomp at the festivals of the patron saints of the churches. Some of these confraternities are very wealthy. One of these secular brotherhoods is called the "Brotherhood of the Coachmen of our Lord." It was founded in 1758, and the members engage to act as coachmen for the priests who carry the Eucharist to sick persons. The confiscation of the immense Church property was begun by the Spanish government soon after the expulsion of the Jesuits. During the War of Independence, the government of Mexico drew largely upon the possessions of the Church in order to get the money needed for carrying on the war. The value of the tithe, which in 1810 yielded about 2,000,000 pesos, had decreased in 1826 to about one half, and decreased still more when the Mexican Congress in 1833 abolished the co-operation of the secular arm in the collection of the tithe, leaving the payment of it wholly to the individual piety of the citizens. President Commonfort, in 1855, confiscated all the property of the Church of Puebla. Under president Juarez, in 1859, the entire possessions of the clergy were declared to be a national domain, and their sale ordered. The income from this property was estimated at about 20,000,000 pesos. The regency which was appointed after the French invasion did not dare to stop the progress of the sale, and was therefore excommunicated by the bishops. After the establishment of the empire, the clerical party demanded the restoration of all the property that had belonged to the Church, and which was estimated at one third of the entire real estate of the republic. As a considerable portion of the sold property had already changed hands, the emperor found it impossible to concede the demand, and by decree of Dec. 27, 1864, ordered the secularization of the Church property to be proceeded with. Commissioners were subsequently sent to Rome, to come, if possible, to an understanding with the pope; but they were unsuccessful. Four provincial synods were held by the Mexican bishops—the first three in 1555, 1565, 1585; the fourth by archbishop Lorenzana (1766-1771).

IV. *Protestant Missions.*—The history of the Protestant missions in Mexico began in 1860, when the government proclaimed religious freedom. Until then, Protestant Christianity in any form had been prohibited. But previously to that year Miss Rankin had (in 1852) opened at Brownsville, in Texas, just opposite the Mexican town of Matamoras, a school for the children of the large Mexican population. She sent a considerable number of Spanish Bibles, which were supplied by the American Bible Society, into Mexico, and in 1854 established a Protestant seminary for Mexican girls likewise at Brownsville. In 1856 the American Foreign and Christian Union took charge of the Mexican mission. After all obstructions to the establishment of Protestant worship had been removed in 1860, the Rev. Mr. Thompson, of the Methodist Episcopal Church, South, went (in November, 1860) as agent of the American Bible Society into Mexico as far as Monterey. He was cordially received, the authorities giving him leave to plant Protestant missions and to circulate the Bible; but when the outbreak of the civil war in the United States interrupted the communication with New York, he had to suspend his labors, and to return to Texas. When the communication with New York had been re-established by the opening of a port on the Mexican side of the Rio Grande, the Rev. Mr. Hickey, a colportor of the American Bible Society, who, being a Union man, had to flee the South, went to Matamoras, and accepted in 1863 an agency of the Bible Society for Mexico. He subsequently went to Monterey, collected a congregation, and after a little time administered baptism to a dozen Mexicans. When his duties compelled him to leave Monterey, he selected a suitable man from the converts to continue religious services. In 1865 Miss Rankin went to Monterey, where she erected a missionhouse, suited for chapel, school, and residence of the missionary. The building was completed in 1868, and several of the converts were sent out as colportors and Bible-readers. Two of these men went to the state of Zacatecas, in company with two of the Bible Society's agents. Their labors resulted in the conversion of thirty persons, among whom were two highly educated men, who took up the work after the departure of the colportors, and carried it forward with great success. An evangelical paper, the *Antorcha Evangelical*, was published, which proved a very efficient aid to Protestant preaching. In 1871 the number of converts amounted to more than one hundred. In 1872 the mission of

Zacatecas was transferred by the American and Foreign Christian Union to the Board of the Presbyterian Church, which in the same year also stationed missionaries at San Luis Potosi and in the city of Mexico. In 1873, there were in all from ten to fifteen little congregations connected with the missions of the Presbyterian boards. Two schools, one for each sex, had been formed in the capital, and two also at Cos, a small town of 4000 inhabitants in the state of Zacatecas. The mission at Monterey, at the beginning of 1873, numbered six regularly organized churches, the number of members in these ranging from twelve to sixty. As the American and foreign Christian Union in 1873 suspended operations in foreign lands, Miss Rankin offered the Monterey mission to the American Board of Commissioners of Foreign Missions, which, in September, 1872, had sent from California the first missionaries into Mexico. During the decline and ruin of the empire of Maximilian, the foreign committee of the Board of Missions of the Protestant Episcopal Church of the United States sent out an agent to collect information in regard to the prospects of an effort for the establishment of a congregation under the jurisdiction of the Protestant Episcopal Church. It was found that there was a widespread preparation for a reformation of the National Church, and that a large number of priests sympathized with the movement. Though the government of Maximilian strongly favored the Roman Catholic Church, the foundation of a Reformed Catholic Church, called "the Church of Jesus," was laid. After the re-establishment of the republic, the movement soon assumed large dimensions. The government sold to the Reformers some of the most beautiful churches in the capital. During the greater portion of this time the Rev. Dr. Riley, a clergyman of the Protestant Episcopal Church, who had been born and educated in one of the Spanish republics of South America, had been the constant adviser and friend of the Reformers. He had brought with him from New York to Mexico a printing-press, and used it for the dissemination of the principles of the Reformed Church. He had prepared a Liturgy in Spanish, conformed in all essential respects to that of the Protestant Episcopal Church. He had purchased one church in the capital and one half of another, and presented them to a board of trustees, to be held in trust for the benefit of the movement. As the foreign committee of the Protestant Episcopal Church was restricted by its constitution to the support of missions of its own Church, and on that account could not comprise an independent Church like that of the Church of Jesus, the American Church Missionary Society in 1873 took the movement under its charge. The Methodist Episcopal Church established a mission in Mexico in 1872. In November of that year the Rev. Dr. William Butler was appointed superintendent of the mission. He accepted, and arrived in the city of Mexico in February, 1873. He reported the statistics of the work of the Church at the close of its first quarter as follows: four Mexican congregations—two in the city of Mexico, 75 persons; one in Pachuca, capital of the state of Hidalgo, 45 persons; one in Rio del Monte, five miles beyond, 10 persons; total, 130 souls; two English congregations—in the city of Mexico, 60 attendants, and Pachuca, 45; being an aggregate of 235 persons in six congregations; 12 scholars in day-schools, and 42, with 9 teachers and officers, in two Sunday-schools. The mission had two class-meetings, about 14 Mexicans and 16 English and Americans attending. A missionary property has been purchased in Puebla. The Methodist Episcopal Church, South, also resolved in 1872 to take up Mexico as a missionary field. Bishop Keener proceeded to Mexico and purchased a chapel for the mission, and in 1873 the first missionary was stationed there. The progress of these Protestant missionary labors produced a great excitement among the strict adherents of the Roman Catholic Church. In a number of places mobs insulted the Protestants, as well as the members of the Reformed Church of Jesus. At Chapulhuac three persons were killed and several wounded. The Methodist and Presbyterian missionaries in the city of Mexico, with the representatives of the British Bible Society, solicited through the United States minister, the Hon. Thomas H. Nelson, an interview with the president of Mexico, in order to seek from him an assurance of his disposition to protect Prot-.estants in Mexico in the enjoyment of their religious rights under the constitution. The interview took place on April 25, 1873, when president Lerdo de Tejada assured the missionaries that the opinion of all the enlightened classes of society favored religious toleration, and that he, the president, would answer for the conduct of all the authorities depending directly upon the federal government.

See Lorenzana, *Concilio (Mexic.) primero y segundo* (Mexico, 1769); Lorenzana, *Histor. de Nueva España escrito por su esclarecido conquistador H. Cortez, aumentada con otros documentos y notas* (Mexico, 1770); Prescott, *Hist. of the Conquest of Mexico; Baluffi, L'America un tempo Spagnuola, riguardata sotto l'aspetto religioso dall' epoca del suo discuoprimento sino al* 1843 (Ancona, 1844); Brasseur du Bourbourg, *Hist. des nations civilisées du Mexique* (Paris, 1858–50, 4 tom.); Mühlenpfordt, *Schilderung der Republic Mexico* (Hanover, 1844); Richthofen (Prussian ambassador in Mexico), *Die äussern u. innern polit. Zustände der Republic Mexico* (Berlin, 1859); Neher, *Kirchl. Statistik*, iii, 337, sq.; Kalkar, *Gesch. der röm-kathol. Mission* (Germ. transl. [Erlangen, 1867]). (A. J. S.)

Meyer, Hermanus, D.D., a noted Dutch Reformed minister, was born in Bremen, Lower Saxony, July 27, 1733. He was educated at the Latin school and gymnasium of that Saxon city, and subsequently at the theological academy in Groningen, where in 1758 he became a candidate for the ministry. Having received a call to the Dutch Church of Kingston, New York, he was ordained March 31, 1763, and sailed from London for New York, where he arrived in October of that year, and immediately assumed the duties of his pastoral charge. He found the Church sadly divided on the old quarrel of the Coetus and Conferentie parties as to ordination in this country or in Holland. He sympathized with the former, which was the liberal side, in favor of a ministry trained in America; but his efforts to keep the peace were vain. His pungent, practical preaching also made him many foes among the formal and worldly people. Thus, after preaching on regeneration, one of his Church officers said to him, "Flesh and blood cannot endure such preaching." "Flesh and blood cannot inherit the kingdom of God," was his quick reply. The ecclesiastical difficulties alluded to above culminated in his suspension from the active duties of the ministry by an exparte and illegal body of Conferentie ministers in 1766. For nearly seven years afterwards, although this discipline was declared illegal, he remained in Kingston, preaching to his adherents in private houses. In 1772 he removed to New Jersey, as pastor of the united churches of Pimpton and Totowa (now Paterson). Brighter days had dawned. He was a member of the convention of 1771, which reunited the long-sundered churches. The General Synod elected him to two professorships in their theological institution—Hebrew (1784) and lector in divinity (1786), both of which he held during life; and in 1789 he was made a doctor of divinity by Queen's College. He died Oct. 27, 1791, lamented as "one of the pillars of the Church." Dr. Meyer was a truly learned divine. In Latin, Greek, and Hebrew he was a critical scholar, and had made considerable attainment in the Syriac. He had long meditated a new translation of the Old Testament, but the ecclesiastical troubles of his life prevented its completion. He left "the beginning of that work in a full translation of the Psalms of David, in Latin interlineations between the text, with copious commentaries and emendations in the finest German writing upon a broad margin." His person was small, his features fine and

benevolent, his voice and manner in the pulpit good, and his delivery very animated. In theological sentiment he was thoroughly evangelical. His faithful preaching made him pre-eminent among the godly ministers of his day. Amiable and kind-hearted, punctual and exact, faithful as a pastor, and humble in his private and official walk, his severe trials chastened and exalted his sterling piety, and his last days were crowned with honor. His death was pre-eminently peaceful and happy. See *Magazine of Ref. Dutch Church*, ii, 300; Sprague, *Annals*, vol. ix; Corwin's *Manual of Ref. Church*, s. v. (W. J. R. T.)

Meyer, Johann Friederich von, an eminent German theologian and jurist, was born at Frankfort-on-the-Main, Sept. 12, 1772. In 1789 he entered the University of Göttingen, where he applied himself with great zeal to jurisprudence, not however neglecting his favorite study, Greek. In 1790 he published his *Commentatio de diis ac deabus Græcorum et Romanorum δαδούχοις cum vi tabulis æreis*, which attracted great attention. In 1793 he went to Leipsic, where he turned his attention mainly to the study of philosophy. After holding various official positions, which he successively lost in consequence of the French invasion, he was, in 1807, appointed counsellor to the municipal court of Frankfort; became member of the senate in 1816; judge in 1821, and finally, in 1837, president of the criminal court and of the court of appeals. At the same time he was a member of the diet, and thrice, in 1825, 1839, and 1843, filled the office of burgomaster. He died Jan. 27, 1849. In the early part of his life Meyer inclined to rationalism—this still appears in his poem of *Tobias*, in seven cantos, published in 1800; but he was subsequently converted, and thenceforth became very active as a theologian. In 1806 and 1807 he translated Cicero's works on the nature of the gods, divination, and fate; in 1813, Xenophon's *Cyropædia* (2d ed. 1823). In 1812 he published his *Bibeldeutungen*, in which he found full play for his acquirements in philology, jurisprudence, etc. He next turned his attention to a new translation of the Bible, as he wished to correct the philological errors contained in Luther's translation. It assumed the form of a revision of Luther's translation, with annotations, and was published in 1819 (2d ed. without the notes, 1823; latest ed. Frankf. 1855). The value of this work was recognised by the University of Erlangen, and he was honored with the doctorate in divinity, and in 1816 was made president of the Bible Society of Frankfort. On emerging from rationalism, Meyer took a leaning towards mysticism, in the better sense of the word. This is apparent in such works as his *Blätter für höhere Wahrheit* (Frankf. 1820–32); *Wahrnehmungen einer Seherin* (Frankf. 1827). Aside from the above-named works, he wrote, *Der Rosenkreuzer, die Fama u. d. Confession* (Frankf. 1828):—*Kritische Kränze* (Berl. 1830):—*Das Buch Jezira, hebräisch u. deutsch* (Leips. 1830):—*Inbegriff d. christlichen Glaubenslehre* (Kempt. 1832):—*Hesperiden*, (Kempt. 1836):—*Prosodisches Hülfsbuch* (1836):—*Zur Aegyptol.* (1840). See Döring, *Gelehrte Theol. Deutschl.* s. v. (J. H. W.)

Meyer, Johann Hermann, a German Protestant theologian, was born at Hamburg October 6, 1737, and was educated at the University of Helmstädt. He was appointed minister at Hamburg in 1766, in 1778 at Rendsburg. He was elected deacon in 1771 by the parishioners of the Nicolai Kirche at Kiel, and made, in 1778, archdeacon, and in 1786 pastor of that church. He died August 26, 1795. Meyer was very much beloved for his strict sense of honesty, morality, friendship, and love. He was very devoted to his vocation as minister, and found but little time for the publication of books. The following dissertations are the most important works he gave to the public: *Hamburgische Abschiedsrede- und Rendsburgische Antrittspredigt.* (Hamburg, 1768, 4to); *Gedenkverse mit dem Inhalt Predigten vom J.* 1774 (Kiel, 1774, 8vo); *Der Verlust der Gnade:*

in einer Wahlpredigt (Hamburg, 1775, 8vo); *Das Andenken voriger Zeiten* (Kiel, 1776, 8vo).

Meyer, John, a noted Dutch theologian and Hebraist, was born about the middle of the 17th century. He flourished as professor of theology at the University of Haderwyk, and died in 1725. His works are of great value to the exegete. Those most worthy of notice are his *Uxor Christiana, sive de conjugio inter duos, deque incestu et divortiis, dissertationes tres* (Amst. 1688, 4to); *Tractatus de temporibus et fasti diebus Hebræorum* (Amst. 1724); and his edition of *Seder Olam*, a Hebrew chronicle of great esteem among the Jews, usually attributed to rabbi Jose ben-Chilpeta.

Meyer, John H., son of Dr. Herman Meyer (q.v.), another distinguished minister of the Reformed Church, was born at Pequinet, N. J., Oct. 19, 1774; graduated at Columbia College in 1795; studied theology under Dr. Livingston, and was licensed to preach in 1798; settled as pastor of the Dutch churches at New Paltz and New Hurley, N. Y., from 1799 to 1803, and at Schenectady from 1803 to 1806. He was an accomplished scholar, and preached with great elegance and ease in the Dutch and English languages. He was remarkable for unction and popularity as a preacher.

Meyerbeer, GIACOMO, a very noted German composer of music, was born in Berlin Sept. 5, 1794, and was of Jewish descent. At the age of nine years he was regarded as a masterly pianist in a city full of cultivated musicians, and at ten he commenced his career as a composer, producing many songs and pieces for the piano-forte, which excited the wonder and admiration of his friends by their spirit and originality. At fifteen he was placed under the tuition of abbé Vogler, who had established a celebrated school of composition in the city of Darmstadt. Here, under the abbé's instruction, young Meyerbeer composed a quantity of classic and elaborate sacred music in the severest scholastic style of his master, all of which, however, is lost to the world, as the composer, when his ideas became more matured, did not care to preserve it. One of these compositions, however, brought him into notoriety: it was an oratorio bearing the title *God and Nature*, and was performed in the presence of the grand-duke of Darmstadt, gaining for its author the distinction of being appointed composer to the court. When Meyerbeer was eighteen, his first dramatic piece, *Jephthah's Daughter*, was performed at Munich. Though intended for the stage, it was more of an oratorio than an opera; but on account of its severe style, and the evident inattention to the minor attractions of melody, it was not received in a flattering manner by the Bavarian public. After a series of professional disappointments, his first success was achieved at Padua in 1818, in the performance of *Romilda e Costanza*, which, together with *Semiramide*, produced at Turin in 1819, and *Emma di Resburgo*, at Venice in 1820, firmly established the composer's reputation. In 1831 he gave to the public *Robert the Devil*. His subsequent works are operatic. He died May 2, 1864. See L. de Loménie, *M. Meyerbeer, par un Homme de Rien* (1849); De Bury, *Meyerbeer et son temps* (1865); Mentel, *Meyerbeer, s. Leben u. Werke* (1868).

Meyere, LIÉVIN DE, a Belgian Jesuit, was born at Gand in 1655. In 1700 he became a member of the Society of Jesus. He subsequently taught philology, philosophy, and theology, and was made rector of a college at Louvain. He bitterly opposed the tenets of the Jansenists. His numerous writings, nearly all poetical, are replete with animadversions against them. Meyere died at Louvain in 1730. The following work, said to have been written by Théod. Eleutherius, was edited by Meyere: *Historia Controversiarum de divinæ gratiæ auxiliis sub pontif. Sixto V, Clemente VIII, et Paulo V,* lib. vi (Antwerp, 1705, fol.). See Moréri, *Grand Dict. Hist.* s.v.; Goethals, *Lectures relatives à l'hist. des sciences et des lettres en Belgique*, vol. i.

Meyfart (or Mayfart), JOHANN MATTHÆUS, a Lutheran theologian of considerable note, son of a Protestant divine, was born at Jena in 1590. He received an excellent philological and philosophical education at Gotha, and afterwards entered the University of Wittenberg, where he devoted himself to the study of logic, physics, ethics, and the classics. In 1611, having secured the degree of A.M., he began the study of theology. In 1616 Meyfart was called to a professorship at the newly-founded University of Coburg. He published his first theological essays in 1617. In 1624 he was created doctor of theology by the University of Jena. In the same year he began the preparation of a large dogmatic work entitled *De theologia, de philosophiæ sobrio usu, de S. S., et de symbolis*; but he never completed this work. In 1627, however, he went before the public with quite large and valuable works: *Anti-Becanus sive manualis controversiarum theol., a Becano collecti, confutatio* (Leipsic, 1627, 2 vols.); *Nodus Gordius Sophistarum solutus, i. e. de ratione solvendi argumenta sophistica*, etc., libri iv (Coburg, 1627, 8vo). Meyfart is one of the most remarkable characters of the 17th century, and can justly be called the forerunner of Spener (q.v.). With an intense longing for the highest ideals, which undoubtedly had been fostered by his classical studies, he united a true, living faith in Christ, and desired to leave this earth to be with his Saviour. At the same time he was quick to perceive the many errors and the moral decay of the Church, and, with an earnestness seldom surpassed, he raised his voice against the manifold sins and imperfections of the Church of his day and country. In 1626 he issued his *Tuba novissima*, i. e. of the four last things, viz. death, judgment, eternal life, and condemnation. These were originally four sermons preached by him at Coburg; but they created such an impression that he had not only to publish them in book form, but was also urged to publish more sermons and admonitions on these and similar subjects. Thus he published six more volumes on *The Heavenly Jerusalem, Eternal Damnation*, and the *Final Judgment*. Some of these books passed through five and more editions. Henke, in just appreciation of his merits, calls Meyfart "a German Dante, full of poetry and knowledge." During his later life Meyfart published several books and essays which were written in the spirit of the Reformation. One of his essays contains an earnest address to the clergy how to live and how to pray; another is directed against the vice of nepotism and simony; and in another, *De concilianda pace inter ecclesias per Germaniam evangelicas*, he enumerates seventeen characteristic reasons why theologians are so ill adapted to peace, e. g. *insufficientia morum et eruditionis, metus odii et invidiæ, intuitus humanæ auctoritatis*, etc. After the capture of Erfurt by Gustavus Adolphus, Meyfart was called as professor of theology to the newly-reorganized Lutheran University of Erfurt, and in 1635 he was elected rector of the university, and senior of the theological department. He died Jan. 26, 1642.

Mez'ahab (Heb. *Mey-Zahab'*, מֵי זָהָב, *water of gold*, i. e. of a golden lustre; Sept. Μαιζοώβ, but omits in Chron.; Vulg. *Mezaab*), the father of Matred and maternal grandfather of Mehetabel, which last was wife of Hadar, or Hadad, the last mentioned of the early Edomitish kings (Gen. xxxvi, 39; 1 Chron. i, 50), B.C. considerably ante 1619. "His name has given rise to much speculation. Jarchi renders it, 'What is gold?' and explains it, 'He was a rich man, and gold was not valued in his eyes at all.' Abarbanel says he was 'rich and great, so that on this account he was called Mezahab, for the gold was in his house as water.' 'Haggaon' (writes Aben-Ezra) 'said he was a refiner of gold, but others said that it pointed to those who made gold from brass.' The Jerusalem Targum of course could not resist the temptation of punning upon the name, and combined the explanations given by Jarchi and Haggaon. The latter part of Gen. xxxvi, 39 is thus rendered: 'The name of his wife is Mehetabel, daughter of Matred, the daughter of a refiner of gold, who was wearied with labor (מַטְרְדָא, matredâ) all the days of his life; after he had eaten and was filled, he turned and said, What is gold? and what is silver?' A somewhat similar paraphrase is given in the Targum of the Pseudo-Jonathan, except that it is there referred to Matred, and not to Mezahab. The Arabic version translates the name ' water of gold,' which must have been from the Hebrew, while in the Targum of Onkelos it is rendered ' refiner of gold,' as in the Quæstiones Hebraicæ in Paralip., attributed to Jerome, and the traditions given above; which seems to indicate that originally there was something in the Hebrew text. now wanting, which gave rise to this rendering, and of which the present reading, מֵי, mey, is an abbreviation."

Mezuzáh (מְזוּזָה) or **Mezuzôth** (מְזוּזוֹת), the sing. and plur. forms of a "door-post," the place on which the Mosaic law is interpreted by the Jews as enjoining the Israelites to write passages of Scripture (Deut. vi, 9; xi, 20). In the following account we especially treat of the Rabbinical regulations.

1. *Signification of the Word, and Design of the Injunction.*—The word מזוזה (from זוז, to push about, to move) denotes either that which is most prominent, hence *the post of a door*, or that on which the door moves, or on which the hinges turn—hence a *door-post*. This is the sense in which it occurs in the Hebrew Scriptures. From the fact, however, that on it were written passages of the law, the term *Mezuzah* came afterwards synedochically to denote the writing itself, or the passages of Scripture affixed to the door-post, and this is the sense in which the word is used in the Chaldee paraphrases, and in the Jewish writings generally. As books were exceedingly rare and expensive in ancient times, and could only be possessed by very few, the practice obtained among the nations of antiquity, and still prevails in the East, of writing, engraving, or painting such sacred mottoes or sage maxims over the doors of dwellings as the parents were especially anxious to record or to impart to their children. Thus the ancient Egyptians had brief hieroglyphical legends over their doorways (Wilkinson, *Manners and Customs of Ancient Egypt*, ii, 102; Wathen, p. 101); the Greeks and Romans had inscriptions over their doors (Virgil, *Georg.* iii, 26 sq.). Other nations had their laws written upon their gates (Huetius, *Demonstratio Evangelica*, p. 58); and the Moslems to the present day, "never set up a gate, cover a fountain, build a bridge, or erect a house, without writing on it choice sentences from the Koran, or from their best poets" (Thomson, *The Land and the Book*, p. 98). Now Moses in this instance, as in many other cases, availed himself of a prevalent custom, in order to keep the divine precepts ever before the eyes of the people, and to enable them to instruct their children in the law of God. Hence Maimonides beautifully remarks: "The commandment about *the Mezuzah* is binding on every one. For whenever an Israelite comes into the house, or goes out, he, seeing on it the name of the Holy One, blessed be he, will thereby be reminded of his love; and when he awakens from his sleep, and from his thoughts about the vanities of time, he will thereby be led to remember that there is nothing which endures forever and throughout all eternity except the knowledge of the everlasting Rock, and he will reflect and walk in the paths of righteousness" (*Jad Ha-Chezaka, Hilchoth Tephillin*, vi, 13).

2. *The Manner in which this Injunction has been and still is observed.*—That the Jews of old literally observed this injunction is not only evident from the above-mentioned prevailing custom of antiquity, but also from Josephus, who distinctly says that the Jews "inscribe the greatest blessings of God upon their doors" (*Ant.* iv, 8, 13); from the Chaldee paraphrase of Onkelos, who translates Deut. vi, 9; xi, 20, "And thou shalt write them upon scrolls, and affix them on the door-posts of thy

houses and thy gates;" from the Jerusalem Targum, Jonathan ben-Uziel, Jerusalem Talmud (*Pesach*, i, 1), Babylonian Talmud (*Erubin*, 96 b; *Aboda Sara*, 11 a), etc. These authorities, moreover, show that the Hebrews, at least after the Babylonian captivity, and at the time of Christ, wrote the passages containing this injunction on a piece of parchment, and affixed it to the door-posts; and that this *Mezuzah*, as it is called, is substantially the same as the Jews now have it, which is made in the following manner: On the inside of a piece of square parchment, prepared by a Jew especially for this purpose, are written Deut. vi, 4–9, and xi, 13–21, while on the outside are written the divine name שדי, *the Almighty*, on the place where the first passage ends, and the words כוזו במוכסז כוזו, *Kuzu Bemuksaz Kuzu*, to the left at the bottom. Thus written, the schedule is then rolled up in such a manner that the divine name שדי is outside, and is put into a reed, or hollow cylinder made of lead, brass, or silver, varying in costliness according to the circumstances of the people. In this tube there is a little hole, just large enough to show the divine name, which is protected by a piece of glass, forming, as

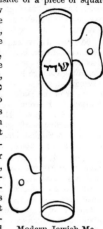

Modern Jewish Mezuzah.

it were, a little window, through which שדי is seen. Such a *Mezuzah* must be affixed to the right-hand doorpost of every door in the house by a nail at each end. The fixing of it is accompanied by the following prayer: "Behold I prepare my hands to perform the commandment which my Creator has given me about the *Mezuzah*. In the name of the one, holy, most blessed God and his Shechinah, who is concealed, mysterious, and incorporated in the name of all Israel. Blessed art thou, O Lord our God, king of the universe, who hast sanctified us by thy commandments, and hast enjoined us to affix *the Mezuzah*." Like the Greeks and Romans, who attached amulets to the jambs of the doors, and ascribed to them magic power, the Jews from a very early period believed that *the Mezuzah* guarded the house against the entrance of diseases and evil spirits, as may be seen from the remarks in the Talmud (*Jerusalem Pesach*, i, 1; and *Babylonian Aboda Sara*, 11 a; *Menachoth*, 33 b), and the Chaldee paraphrase of the Song of Solomon (viii, 3), which is, "I have affixed *the Mezuzah* to the right side of my door, in the third part thereof, towards the inside, so that the evil spirits may have no power to hurt me." Hence the divine name שדי is made to denote *the Guardian of the dwellings of Israel*, the ש standing for שומר, the ד for דירת, and the י for ישראל, according to the exegetical rule called נוטריקון (=*notaricum*, from *notarius*, a short-hand writer, one who writes with abbreviations), which regards every letter of a word as an initial or abbreviation of a word; while the words כוזו במוכסז כוזו, supposed to be the name of the guardian angel, or of God himself, are made to stand for יהוה יהוה אלהינו, *Jehovah our God is Jehovah*, by another exegetical rule, which exchanges each letter of a word with its immediate predecessor in the alphabet; e. g. the כ in כוזו is exchanged for י, the ו for ה, the ז for ו, and the ו for ה, thus yielding יהוה. Every pious Jew, as often as he passes *the Mezuzah*, in leaving the house or in entering it, touches the divine name with the finger of his right hand, puts it to his mouth, and kisses it, saying in Hebrew, "The Lord shall preserve thy going out and thy coming in, from this time forth, and for evermore" (Psa. cxxi, 8); and when leaving on a business expedition, he says, after touching it, בשמך כוזו במוכסז כוזו אלך ואצצלריח, "in thy name, *Kuzu Bemuksaz Kuzu* (=God), I go out and shall prosper."

III. *Literature.*—Maimonides, *Jad Ha-Chezaka Hilchoth Tephillin U-Mezuzah Ve-Sepher Torah*, v, vi; *Jork Dea*, § 285-295; the Jewish ritual entitled *Derek Ha-Chajim*, containing a summary of all the laws connected with the Jewish observances (Vienna, 1859), p. 31 sq.; Buxtorf, *Synag. Jud.* p. 482-487; Leo Modena, *Rites and Customs*, pt. i, ch. ii, § 3; Allen's *Modern Judaism*, p. 327-329. See DOOR-POST.

Mezzofanti, JOSEPH CASPAR, a Roman Catholic prelate, celebrated as the greatest linguist the world has ever seen, was born at Bologna Sept. 17, 1774. His father, Francis Mezzofanti, was a carpenter; and he himself, being destined for the same humble career, was placed at one of the free schools of the Oratory in his native city. Father Respighi, a priest of that congregation, observed the remarkable talents of the boy, and saved him for literature. He was removed to a higher school—one of the so-called "*Scuole Pie*" of Bologna —and eventually to the archiepiscopal seminary, where, after completing the usual course of letters, philosophy, divinity, and canon law in the university, he was admitted to priest's orders in September, 1797. Of the details of his progress in the study of languages during these early years no accurate record is preserved; but it is known that, like most eminent linguists, he was gifted, even in childhood, with a very wonderful memory, and that, partly under the various professors in the university, partly by the aid of foreign residents in the city, partly by his own unassisted studies, he had acquired, before the completion of his university career, the Latin, Greek, Hebrew, Arabic, Spanish, French, German, and Swedish languages. In 1797, at the early age of twenty-two, he was appointed professor of Arabic in the university; but on the annexation of Bologna, as one of the papal legations, to the newly-established Cisalpine republic, he, refusing to take the oaths of the new constitution, was set aside from the professorship. After the conclusion of the concordat between Pius VII and the first consul, the ancient constitution of the university was restored. In 1803 Mezzofanti was named to the higher professorship of Oriental languages, and in the same year became assistant librarian of the public library of the city. In 1808 the professorship was discontinued, and Mezzofanti was reduced to great distress. He made a scanty living by private tuition; but, nothing daunted, steadily followed in private what had become his engrossing pursuit—the study of languages. A letter of his, dated in 1804, to the celebrated Orientalist, John Bernard de Rossi, whose personal acquaintance he subsequently formed during a short visit to Modena in 1805, enclosed a composition in twelve languages, which he submitted to the judgment of his correspondent; and by 1812 Mezzofanti's reputation as a linguist was thoroughly established. The well-known Pietro Giordani, in several of his letters to his friends, calls him "the divine Mezzofanti," and declares that his skill in living and dead languages entitles him to be regarded as "a man of all ages and all nations." The war of which Northern Italy was so long the theatre afforded Mezzofanti many opportunities of extending his stock of languages. In the hospital of Bologna, to which he was attached as volunteer chaplain, were to be met —among the invalids of the Austrian, Russian, and French armies—Germans, Hungarians, Bohemians, Wallachians, Servians, Russians, Poles, and Croats. Partly in the desire to offer these sufferers the consolations of religion, partly from his love of the study itself, Mezzofanti labored assiduously to turn these and all similar opportunities to account; and several instances are recorded in which, without the assistance of a grammar or dictionary, he contrived to establish a mode of communication with a stranger who was utterly ignorant of every language except his own, and eventually to master that language sufficiently for all the purposes of conversation. He has left an account of his mode of study during these years, which is not a little curious and interesting. "The hotel-keepers," he says, "were in the habit of notifying me of the arrival of all strangers at Bologna; and I never hesitated, when anything was to be learned thereby, to call upon them, to interrogate them, to make notes of their communications, and to take lessons in the pronunciation of their several languages. There were a few learned Jesuits too, and several Spaniards, Portuguese, and Mexicans residing in Bologna, from whom I received valuable assistance, both in their own and in the learned languages. I made it a rule to learn every strange grammar, and to apply myself to every new dictionary that came within my reach. I was constantly filling my head with new words. Whenever a stranger, whether of high or low degree, passed through Bologna, I tried to turn the visit to account, either for the purpose of perfecting my pronunciation, or of learning the familiar words and turns of expression. Nor did all this cost me so much trouble; for, in addition to an excellent memory, God had gifted me with remarkable flexibility of the organs of speech." In the year 1812 Mezzofanti was appointed assistant librarian of the university; in 1814 he was reinstated in his professorship; and in 1815 he became chief librarian. From this period, especially after the restoration of peace, his reputation rapidly extended. Every visitor of Bologna related fresh marvels regarding his prodigious attainments. Tourists from every nation, whether of Europe or of the East, united in representing him as perfect, each one in his own language. Lord Byron, about 1820, pronounced him "a walking polyglot, a monster of languages, and a Briareus of parts of speech." M. Molbech, a Danish traveller of the year 1820, reports the number of his languages at "more than thirty," and testifies to his speaking Danish "with almost entire correctness." French, German, Spanish, Polish, Russian, Greek, and Turkish travellers concur in the same report, not only with regard to their own, but also to many other languages. During all these years—except a short visit to Pisa, Leghorn, Florence, and Rome—he had resided altogether at Bologna, though invited, with many flattering offers, to transfer his residence to Paris, to Vienna, to Florence, and to Rome. At length, having gone to Rome as a member of the deputation sent by the Bolognese to offer their submission to pope Gregory XVI, after the revolution in 1831, he was induced by the pontiff to settle permanently in Rome, and to accept a prebend in the Church of St. Mary Major, which was soon after exchanged for a canonry in St. Peter's, and, on the promotion of the celebrated Angelo Mai, then keeper of the Vatican Library, to the secretaryship of the Propaganda, Mezzofanti was appointed to succeed him in the important charge of the Vatican. He held this office till 1838, in which year, conjointly with Mai, he was elevated to the cardinalate. His residence in a great centre of languages, such as Rome, and especially the facilities of intercourse with the various races represented in the College of the Propaganda, gave a new impulse to Mezzofanti's linguistic studies. The reports of his visitors at Rome are still more marvellous than those of the Bolognese period. An eminent German scholar, Herr Görres, who had much intercourse with him in the year 1841, writes thus: "He is familiar with all the European languages; and by this I mean not only the ancient classical tongues and the modern ones of the first class—such as the Greek and Latin, or the Italian, French, German, Spanish, Portuguese, and English—his knowledge extends also to the languages of the second class, viz., the Dutch, Danish, and Swedish; to the whole Sclavonic family —Russian, Polish, Bohemian, or Czechish; to the Servian, the Hungarian, the Turkish; and even those of the third and fourth classes—the Irish, the Welsh, the

Wallachian, the Albanian, the Bulgarian, and the Illyrian. The Romani of the Alps and the Lettish are not unknown to him; nay, he has made himself acquainted with Lappish. He is master of the languages which fall within the Indo-Germanic family—the Sanscrit and Persian, the Kurdish, the Georgian, the Armenian; he is familiar with all the members of the Shemitic family —the Hebrew, the Arabic, the Syriac, the Samaritan, the Chaldee, the Sabaic—nay, even with the Chinese, which he not only reads, but speaks. Among the Hamitic languages, he knows Coptic, Ethiopic, Abyssinian, Amharic, and Angolese." What is especially notable in this marvellous gift possessed by Mezzofanti is that his knowledge of each among this vast variety of languages was almost as perfect as though his attention had been devoted to such language exclusively. The reports of all the great students of language concur in describing him as speaking even their own tongues always with the precision and, in most cases, with the fluency of a native. His pronunciation, his idiom, his vocabulary, were alike unexceptionable. Even the familiar words of every-day life, and the delicate turns of conversational language, were at his command; and in each language he was master of the leading dialects, and of the provincial peculiarities of idiom, of pronunciation, or of expression. In French, he was equally at home in the pure Parisian of the Faubourg St. Germain or in the Provençal of Toulouse. He could accommodate himself in German to the rude jargon of the Black Forest or to the classic vocabulary of Hanover; and he often amused his English visitors with specimens of the provincialisms of Yorkshire, Lancashire, or Somersetshire. With the literature of those various countries, too, he was well acquainted. He loved to talk with his visitors of the great authors in their respective languages; and his remarks are described as invariably sound and judicious, and exhibiting careful and various reading, often extending to departments with which it would never be supposed that a foreigner could be familiar. A Dutch traveller, for instance, Dr. Wap, was surprised to find him acquainted with his own national poets, Vondel and Cato; a Dane, with the philological works of Rask; a Swede, with the poetry of Ochsentsjerna. To a Sicilian he would repeat whole pages of the poetry of Meli; and an English gentleman was astounded to hear him discuss and criticise Hudibras, of all English writers the least attractive, as well as the least intelligible to a foreigner. He was in the habit, too, of amusing himself by metrical compositions in the various languages which he cultivated, and often wrote for his visitors a couplet or two in their native language, as a little memento of their interview. Dr. Wap, the Dutch traveller just referred to, speaks in high praise of some extempore lines in Dutch by which Mezzofanti replied to a sonnet which Dr. Wap had addressed to him; and the well-known Orientalist, Dr. Tholuck, having asked Mezzofanti for some memorial of his visit, received from him a Persian couplet, after the manner of Hafiz, which he composed (although not without some delay) during Dr. Tholuck's visit. After his removal to Rome, although he had already passed his fiftieth year, he added largely to his stock of languages. His most notable acquisition during this period was Chinese, which he acquired (partly at the Chinese college in Naples, partly among the Chinese students of the Propaganda) in such perfection as to be able not only to write and converse freely in it, but even to preach to the young Chinese ecclesiastics. During the same period he acquired the Abyssinian, the Californian, some of the North American Indian languages, and even the "impossible" Basque. It was in Rome, and especially in the Propaganda, that he displayed in its greatest perfection his singular power of instantaneously passing in conversation from one language to another, without the slightest mixture or confusion, whether of words or of pronunciation.

Mezzofanti, by virtue of his position as cardinal, was member of many ecclesiastical congregations in Rome, but he never held any office of state. He died on the 15th of March, 1849, and was buried in the Church of St. Onofrio, beside the grave of Torquato Tasso. His personal character was gentle, humble, modest, humane, and he was a sincere and devout man.

It is difficult to determine with accuracy the number of languages known by Mezzofanti, and still more so to ascertain how many of these he spoke, and with what degree of fluency in each. During his lifetime, as we have seen, report varied considerably at different times; nor was he himself believed to have made any very precise statement on the subject. To a Russian traveller, who visited him before the year 1846, and who begged of him a list of all the languages and dialects in which he was able to express himself, he sent a paper in his own hand containing the name of God in fifty-six languages. The author of a memoir which appeared soon after the cardinal's death in a Roman journal, the *Civilta Catolica* (now known to be by father Bresciani, a Roman Jesuit), states that in the year 1846 Mezzofanti himself informed him that he was able to express himself in seventy-eight languages. Marvellous as these statements may appear, they seem fully borne out by inquiries (with a view to the preparation of a biography) which have been made since the death of the cardinal. Reports have been received from a vast number of individuals, natives of different countries, whose collective testimony, founded on their own personal knowledge of Mezzofanti, places beyond all question the fact of his having spoken fluently considerably more than fifty different languages. There are others among the languages ascribed to him, regarding which it is difficult to institute any direct inquiry; but, judging from analogy, and relying on the well-known modesty and truthfulness of Mezzofanti, we need not hesitate to accept his own statement as reported by F. Bresciani; the more so as among his papers now in the possession of his family is a list, drawn up from memoranda contained therein, of no less than a hundred and twenty languages with which he possessed some acquaintance, unaccompanied, however, by any note specifying those among the number which he spoke, or the degree of his knowledge of each. His English biographer, Russell, comes to the following results, which are, in brief (for details see that work): 1. Languages frequently tested, and spoken by the cardinal with rare excellence—thirty. 2. Stated to have been spoken fluently, but hardly sufficiently tested—nine. 3. Spoken rarely and less perfectly—eleven. 4. Spoken imperfectly; a few sentences and conversational form—eight. 5. Studied from books, but not known to have been spoken—fourteen. 6. Dialects spoken, or their peculiarities understood—thirty-nine dialects of ten languages, many of which might justly be described as different languages. This list adds up one hundred and eleven, exceeding by all comparison everything related in history. Jonadab Almanor and Sir William Jones are not claimed to have gone beyond twenty-eight; while Mithridates and Pico of Mirandola have been made famous by twenty-two.

In general learning Mezzofanti's attainments were highly respectable. He was a well-informed theologian and canonist, and an impressive though not eloquent preacher. M. Libri, the historian of mathematical science in Italy, found him well acquainted with algebra, and reports an interesting conversation which he had with him on the Bija Gannita (the algebra of the Hindûs), as well as on the general subject of Indian history and antiquities. Other writers describe him as entering freely into the history as well as the literature of their several countries. But as an author he is almost unknown. He occasionally read papers at various literary and scientific societies in Bologna and Rome; but his only known publication is a short memoir of his friend and brother professor, father Emanuel da Ponte, which was printed at Bologna in 1820; and he leaves no monument for posterity beyond the tradition that he was incomparably the greatest linguist the world has ever seen. See G. Stolz, *Biographia del Cardinal Giuseppe Mezzofanti*, in the *Journal de Rome* of Feb. 5, 1850; A. Manavit, *Esquisse historique sur le Cardinal Mezzofanti* (Paris, 1854, 8vo); Russell, *Life of the Cardinal Mezzofanti*, etc. (Lond. 1857, 8vo); *L'Ami de la Religion* (1849); *Revue Catholique de Louvain*, Sept. 1853; *Engl. Cyclop.* s. v.; *Bibliotheca Sacra*, 1849, p. 407; *English Review*, Jan. 1855; *Princeton Review*, 1858, p. 645 sq.; *Catholic World*, March, 1870, p. 857.

Miako, one of the largest cities of Japan, was, until the recent abolishment of the ecclesiastical emperor, the seat of the *mikado*, or spiritual prince. The city, containing nearly one million of inhabitants, is situated in the south-west of the island of Nipon, in the midst of an extensive plain, and about thirty miles from Osaca. Miako is also noted as the great stronghold of *Sintuism* (q. v.)—the ancient religion of Japan—of temple-worship, priests, monks, ceremonies, and ritualism. Some of the temples are of great size and splendor. Don Rodrigo de Vivero, the Spanish governor of Manilla, who visited Miako in 1608, was told that it then contained 5000 temples. He describes one in which was an immense bronze image of Buddha, the construction of which was begun by the tycoon in 1602. He says, "I ordered one of my people to measure the thumb of the right hand; but, although he was a person of the ordinary size, he could not quite encircle it with both arms. But the size of the statue is not its only merit: the feet, hands, mouth, eyes, forehead, and other features are as perfect and as expressive as the most accomplished painter could make a portrait. When I first visited this temple it was unfinished; more than 10,000 men were daily employed upon it. The devil could not suggest to the emperor a surer expedient to get rid of his immense wealth." This colossus was injured by an earthquake in 1662, after which it was melted down, and a substitute prepared of wood gilded. Kämpfer, who was at Miako in 1691, describes the temple which contained this image as enclosed by a high wall of freestone, some of the blocks of which were twelve feet square. "A stone staircase of eight steps led up to the gateway, on either side of which stood a gigantic image twenty-four feet high, with the face of a lion, but otherwise well proportioned, black, and almost naked, and placed on a pedestal six feet high. Within the gateway were sixteen stone pillars on each side for lamps, and on the inside of the enclosing wall was a spacious gallery covered with a roof supported by two rows of pillars eighteen feet high and twelve feet distant from each other. Opposite the gateway, in the middle of the court, stood the temple, much the loftiest structure which Kämpfer had seen in Japan, with a double roof supported by ninety-four immense wooden pillars, nine feet in diameter. The floor of the temple was paved with square flags of marble. There was nothing inside but the great image of Buddha sitting on a *terete*, or lotus flower, supported by another flower of which the leaves were turned upwards, the two being raised about twelve feet from the floor. The idol was gilded all over, had long ears, curled hair, and a crown on the head which appeared through the window over the first roof of the temple. The shoulders were so broad as to reach from one pillar to another, a distance of thirty feet. In front of this temple is an edifice containing a bell, which is described in the Japanese guide-books as seventeen feet two and a half inches high, and weighing 1,700,000 Japanese catties, equal to 2,066,000 English pounds, a weight five times greater than that of the famous bell at Moscow. Kämpfer, however, who had seen the great bell at Moscow, describes this Japanese bell as inferior in size to that, and as being rough, ill cast, and ill shaped. It was sounded by striking it on the outside with a large wooden mallet. Another temple, dedicated to Quanwon, was very long in proportion to its breadth. In the centre was a gigantic image of Quanwon, with thirty-six arms. Sixteen black images

larger than life stood round it, and on each side two rows of gilt idols, with twenty arms each. On either side of the temple, running from end to end, were ten platforms rising like steps one behind the other, on each of which stood fifty images of Quanwon as large as life —1000 in all, each on its separate pedestal, so arranged as to stand in rows of five, one behind the other, and all visible at the same time, each with its twenty hands. On the heads and hands of all these are placed smaller idols, to the number of forty or more. The whole number of images is stated by the Japanese to be 33,000" (*New American Cyclopædia*, vol. xi, s. v.). Miako is also the head-quarters of literature, science, and art. The imperial palace, on the northern side of the city, is, together with its ward, a town of itself. See JAPAN; MIKADO.

Mi'amin (Heb. *Miyamin'*, מִיָּמִן, a contracted form of the name *Miniamin*), the name of three persons after the exile.

1. (Sept. Μεϊαμείν v. r. Μεϊαμίν, Vulg. *Maiman*, Auth. Vers. "Mijamin.") The head of the sixth division of the sacerdotal order as distributed by David (1 Chron. xxiv, 9). B.C. 1014.

2. (Sept. Μεαμείν v. r. Μιαμίν, Vulg. *Miamim*.) One of the chief priests who returned from Babylon with Zerubbabel (Neh. xii, 5). B.C. 536. He must have attained a great age if identical with the priest who subscribed the religious covenant with Nehemiah (Neh. x, 7, where the name is Anglicized "Mijamin"). B.C. cir. 410. He is probably the same person called MINIAMIN in Neh. xii, 17, but his son's name appears there to have accidentally escaped from the text. See MOADIAH.

3. (Sept. Μεαμίν v. r. Μεαμίμ, Vulg. *Miamin*.) One of the Israelites, a "son" (i. e. inhabitant) of Parosh, who divorced his Gentile wife after the captivity (Ezra x, 25). B.C. 459.

Miautsé, the hill-tribes of China, are generally supposed to be the *aborigines* of that country. From the dawn of Chinese history, we find the people of the plains contending against those of the high lands, and to the present day the hardy mountaineers have maintained their independence. The Miautsé consist of forty-one tribes, occupying large portions of Kwang-se, Kwei-chow, Yun-nan, Sze-chuen, and adjacent provinces. Some of them own Chinese sway; other tribes are absolutely independent. They are smaller in size and stature, and have shorter necks, and their features are somewhat more angular, than the Chinese. Their dialects are various, and wholly different from the Chinese; their affinity is most likely with the *Laos* and other tribes between Burmah, Siam, and China. Dr. Macgowan, a well-known ethnologist, describes them as skilful in manufacturing. He holds to an identity of the Miautsé of Western China and the hill-tribes of Burmah. See KARENS. The degree of civilization they have attained to is much below that of the Chinese. Both sexes wear their hair braided in a tuft on the top of the head, but never shaven and twisted as the Chinese; they dress in loose garments of cotton and linen; ear-rings are in universal use among them. They live in huts constructed upon the branches of trees, and in mud hovels. Their agriculture is rude, and their garments are usually obtained by barter from other people. Their religious observances are of the same peculiar nature as those of the other Asiatic tribes uninfluenced by Christian civilization. Their marriage and funeral usages are particularly striking. In one tribe it is the custom for the father of the new-born child, as soon as the mother has become strong enough to leave her couch, to get into bed himself, and there receive the congratulations of his acquaintances as he exhibits his offspring. See *Chinese Repository*, i, 29; xiv, 105 sq.; Williams, *The Middle Kingdom*, i, 37, 147 sq.

Mib'har (Heb. *Mibchar'*, מִבְחָר, *choice*, as in Isa. xxii, 7, etc.; Sept. Μαβάρ v. r. Μεβααλ), a Hagarene ("son of Haggeri"), one of David's famous warriors (1 Chron. xi, 38); apparently the same called in the parallel passage (2 Sam. xxiii, 36) BANI the Gadite. B.C. 1046. See DAVID. "It is easy to see, if the latter be the true reading, how בְּנֵי הַגָּדִי, *Bani hag-gadi*, could be corrupted into בֶּן־הַגְּרִי, *ben-hag-geri*; and הגדי is actually the reading of three of Kennicott's MSS. in 1 Chron., as well as of the Syriac and Arabic versions, and the Targum of R. Joseph. But that 'Mibhar' is a corruption of מִצְבָה (or מצבא, acc. to some MSS.), *mitstsôbâh*, 'of Zobah,' as Kennicott (*Dissert.* p. 215) and Cappellus (*Crit. Sacr.* i, c. 5) conclude, is not so clear, though not absolutely impossible. It would seem from the Sept. of 2 Sam., where instead of Zobah we find πολυδυνάμεως, that both readings originally co-existed, and were read by the Sept. מִבְחַר הַצָּבָא, *mibchar hats-tsâbâ*, 'choice of the host.' If this were the case, the verse in 1 Chron. would stand thus: 'Igal the brother of Nathan, flower of the host; Bani the Gadite.'"

Mib′sam (Heb. *Mibsam′*, מִבְשָׂם, *fragrance*), the name of two men.

1. (Sept. Μασσάμ v. r. in Chron. Μαβσάν.) The fourth named of the twelve sons of Ishmael, and head of an Arabian tribe bearing his name (Gen. xxv, 13; 1 Chron. i, 29). B.C. post 2061. "The signification of his name has led some to propose an identification of the tribe sprung from him with some one of the Abrahamic tribes settled in Arabia aromatifera, and a connection with the *balsam* of Arabia is suggested (Bunsen, *Bibelwerk*; Kalisch, *Genesis*, p. 483). The situation of Mekkeh is well adapted for his settlements, surrounded as it is by traces of other Ishmaelitish tribes; nevertheless the identification seems fanciful and farfetched." See ARABIA.

2. Sept. Μαβασαν v. r. Μαβασάμ.) The son of Shallum and father of Michma, apparently the grandson of Shaul, a son of Simeon (1 Chron. iv, 25). B.C. ante 1658.

Mib′zar (Heb. *Mibtsar′*, מִבְצָר, *fortress*, as often; Sept. in Chron. Μαβσάρ v. r. Βαβσάρ, in Gen. Μαζάρ). The ninth named of the petty Edomitish chieftains descended from Esau contemporary with the Horite kings (Gen. xxxvi, 42; 1 Chron. i, 53). B.C. long post 1905. "These phylarchs are said to be enumerated 'according to their settlements in the land of their possession;' and Knobel (*Genesis*), understanding Mibzar as the name of a place, has attempted to identify it with the rocky fastness of Petra. 'the strong city' (עִיר מִבְצָר, *'ir mibstar*, Psa. cviii, 11; comp. Psa. lx, 11). 'the cliff,' the chasms of which were the chief stronghold of the Edomites (Jer. xlix, 16; Obad. 3)." See EDOM.

Mi′cah (Heb. *Mikah′*, מִיכָה [in Judg. xvii, 1, 4, the prolonged form *Mika′yehu*, מִיכָיְהוּ, is used], a contracted form of the name *Micaiah*; Sept. Μιχά, but Μιχαία in 2 Chron. [xviii, 14, where the name is for that of "Micaiah," and is so rendered in the Auth. Vers.] xxxiv, 20; and Μιχαίας in Jer. xxvi, 18; Mic. i, 1), the name of several men. See also MICAIAH; MICHAH; MICHAIAH.

1. An Ephraimite, apparently contemporary with the elders who outlived Joshua. B.C. cir. 1590–1580. He secretly appropriated 1100 shekels of silver which his mother had saved; but being alarmed at her imprecations on the author of her loss, he confessed the matter to her, and restored the money. She then forgave him, and returned him the silver, to be applied to the use for which it had been accumulated. Two hundred shekels of the amount were given to the founder, as the cost or material of two teraphim, the one molten and the other graven; and the rest of the money served to cover the other expenses of the semi-idolatrous establishment formed in the house of Micah, of which a wandering Levite, named Jonathan, became the priest, at a yearly stipend (Judg. xvii). Subsequently the Danite army, on their journey to settle northward in Laish, took away both the establishment and the priest, which they afterwards maintained in their new settlement (Judg. xvii). See DAN; JONATHAN.

The establishments of this kind, of which there are other instances—as that of Gideon at Ophrah—were, although most mistakenly, formed in honor of Jehovah, whom they thus sought to serve by means of a local worship, in imitation of that at Shiloh (see Kitto's *Daily Bible Illustra.* ad loc.). This was in direct contravention of the law, which allowed but one place of sacrifice and ceremonial service; and was something of the same kind, although different in extent and degree, as the service of the golden calves, which Jeroboam set up, and his successors maintained, in Dan and Bethel. The previous existence of Micah's establishment in the former city no doubt pointed it out to Jeroboam as a suitable place for one of his golden calves.—Kitto. See JEROBOAM. The preservation of the story here would seem to be owing to Micah's accidental connection with the colony of Danites who left the original seat of their tribe to conquer and found a new Dan at Laish—a most happy accident, for it has been the means of furnishing us with a picture of the "interior" of a private Israelitish family of the rural districts, which in many respects stands quite alone in the sacred records, and has probably no parallel in any literature of equal age. But apart from this the narrative has several points of special interest to students of Biblical history in the information which it affords as to the condition of the nation, of the members of which Micah was probably an average specimen.

(1.) We see how completely some of the most solemn and characteristic enactments of the law had become a dead letter. Micah was evidently a devout believer in Jehovah. While the Danites in their communications use the general term *Elohim*, "God" ("ask counsel of God," Judg. xviii, 5; "God hath given it into your hands," ver. 10), with Micah and his household the case is quite different. His one anxiety is to enjoy the favor of Jehovah (xvii, 13); the formula of blessing used by his mother and his priest invokes the same awful name (xvii, 2; xviii, 6); and yet so completely ignorant is he of the law of Jehovah that the mode which he adopts of honoring him is to make a molten and a graven image, teraphim or images of domestic gods, and to set up an unauthorized priesthood, first in his own family (xvii, 5), and then in the person of a Levite not of the priestly line (ver. 12)—thus disobeying in the most flagrant manner the second of the Ten Commandments, and the provisions for the priesthood—laws both of which lay in a peculiar manner at the root of the religious existence of the nation. Gideon (viii, 27) had established an ephod; but here was a whole chapel of idols, "a house of gods" (xvii, 5), and all dedicated to Jehovah.

(2.) The story also throws a light on the condition of the Levites. They were indeed "divided in Jacob and scattered in Israel" in a more literal sense than that prediction is usually taken to contain. Here we have a Levite belonging to Bethlehem-judah, a town not allotted to the Levites, and with which they had, as far as we know, no connection; next wandering forth, with the world before him, to take up his abode wherever he could find a residence; then undertaking, without hesitation, and for a mere pittance, the charge of Micah's idol-chapel; and, lastly, carrying off the property of his master and benefactor, and becoming the first priest to another system of false worship, one, too, in which Jehovah had no part, and which ultimately bore an important share in the disruption of the two kingdoms. It does not seem at all clear that the words "molten image" and "graven image" accurately express the original words *Pesel* and *Massekah*. See IDOL. As the Hebrew text now stands, the "graven image" only was carried off to Laish, and the "molten" one remained behind with Micah (xviii,.20, 30; comp. 18). True the Sept. adds the molten image in ver. 20, but in ver. 30 it agrees with the Hebrew text.

(3.) But the transaction becomes still more remarkable when we consider that this was no obscure or ordinary Levite. He belonged to the chief family in the tribe; nay, we may say to the chief family of the nation, for, though not himself a priest, he was closely allied to the priestly house, and was the grandson of no less a person than the great Moses himself. For the "Manasseh" in xviii, 30 is nothing less than an alteration of "Moses," to shield that venerable name from the discredit which such a descendant would cast upon it. See MANASSEH, 3. In this fact we possibly have the explanation of the much-debated passage, xviii, 3: "They knew the voice of the young man the Levite." The grandson of the Lawgiver was not unlikely to be personally known to the Danites; when they heard his voice (whether in casual speech or in loud devotion we are not told) they recognised it, and their inquiries as to who brought him hither, what he did there, and what he had there, were in this case the eager questions of old acquaintances long separated.

(4.) The narrative gives us a most vivid idea of the terrible anarchy in which the country was placed when "there was no king in Israel, and every man did what was right in his own eyes," and shows how urgently necessary a central authority had become. A body of six hundred men completely armed, besides the train of their families and cattle, traverses the length and breadth of the land, not on any mission for the ruler or the nation, as on later occasions (2 Sam. ii, 12, etc.; xx, 7, 14), but simply for their private ends. Entirely disregarding the rights of private property, they burst in wherever they please along their route, and, plundering the valuables and carrying off persons, reply to all remonstrances by taunts and threats. The Turkish rule, to which the same district has now the misfortune to be subjected, can hardly be worse.

At the same time it is startling to our Western minds —accustomed to associate the blessings of order with religion—to observe how religious were these lawless freebooters: "Do ye know that in these houses there is an ephod, and teraphim, and a graven image, and a molten image? Now therefore consider what ye have to do" (xviii, 14). "Hold thy peace and go with us, and be to us a father and a priest" (ver. 19).

(5.) As to the date of these interesting events, the narrative gives us no direct information beyond the fact that it was before the beginning of the monarchy; but we may at least infer that it was also before the time of Samson, because in this narrative (xvii, 12) we meet with the origin of the name of Mahaneh-dan, a place which already bore that name in Samson's childhood (xiii, 25, where it is translated in the Auth. Vers. "the camp of Dan"). That the Danites had opponents to their establishment in their proper territory before the Philistines entered the field is evident from Judg. i, 34. Josephus entirely omits the story of Micah, but he places the narrative of the Levite and his concubine, and the destruction of Gibeah (chaps. xix, xx, xxi)—a document generally recognised as part of the same (see Bertheau, Kommentar, p. 192) with the story of Micah, and that document by a different hand from the previous portions of the book—at the very beginning of his account of the period of the judges, before Deborah or even Ehud (Ant. v, 2, 8-12). This is supported by the mention of Phinehas, the grandson of Aaron, in Judg. xx, 28. An argument against the date being before the time of Deborah is drawn by Bertheau (p. 197) from the fact that at that time the north of Palestine was in the possession of the Canaanites—"Jabin, king of Canaan, who reigned in Hazor," in the immediate neighborhood of Laish. The records of the southern Dan are too scanty to permit our fixing the date from the statement that the Danites had not yet entered on their allotment—

that is to say, the allotment specified in Josh. xix, 40-48. But that statement strengthens the conclusion arrived at from other passages, that these lists in Joshua contain the towns allotted, but not therefore necessarily possessed by the various tribes. "Divide the land first, in confidence, and then possess it afterwards," seems to be the principle implied in such passages as Josh. xiii, 7 (comp. 1); xix, 49, 51 (Sept. "So they went to take possession of the land").

The date of the insertion of the record may perhaps be more nearly arrived at. That, on the one hand, it was after the beginning of the monarchy is evident from the references to the ante-monarchical times (xviii, 1; xix, 1; xxi, 25); and, on the other hand, we may perhaps infer from the name of Bethlehem being given as "Bethlehem-judah," that it was before the fame of David had conferred on it a notoriety which would render any such affix unnecessary. The reference to the establishment of the house of God in Shiloh (xviii, 31) seems also to point to the early part of Saul's reign, before the incursions of the Philistines had made it necessary to remove the tabernacle and ephod to Nob, in the vicinity of Gibeah, Saul's head-quarters. Some, like Le Clerc, argue for a later date, from the phrase, "until the day of the captivity of the land," in xviii, 30, as if it necessarily referred to the Assyrian invasion. The reading is doubtful. Studer and Hitzig take the 30th verse as a later interpolation; Kimchi, Hävernick, Hengstenberg, and Bleek refer the phrase to the captivity of the ark in the time of Eli, but on no good ground, unless the reading הָאָרֶץ be changed, as some prefer, into הָאָרוֹן. Stähelin and Ewald, regarding the verse as a later addition, place the composition about the period of Asa or Jehoshaphat; Stähelin insisting, too, that the diction does not belong to the purer period of the language. Verse 30, indeed, does not quite agree with 31, which seems to limit the duration of the Danite idolatry to the period of the station of the ark at Shiloh; and the phrase, "until the day of the captivity," as Keil remarks (Commentary, ad loc.), may refer to some unknown invasion on the part of the neighboring Syrians. Besides, it can scarcely be supposed that this idolatrous cultus, so directly and openly opposed to the spirit and letter of the Mosaic law, would have been allowed to stand in the zealous days of Samuel and David. See Stanley's Lectures on the Jewish Church, p. 296, 297. See JUDGES, BOOK OF.

2. The son of Mephibosheth, or Meribbaal (son of Jonathan and grandson of king Saul), and the father of several sons (1 Chron. viii, 34, 35; ix, 40, 41). B.C. post 1037. In 2 Sam. ix, 12, he is called MICHA.

3. The first in rank of the priests of the Kohathite family of Uzziel, under the sacerdotal arrangement by David (1 Chron. xxiii, 20). B.C. 1014. He had a son named Shamir, and a brother Isshiah (1 Chron. xxiv, 24, 25; Auth. Vers. "Michah").

4. The son of Shimei and father of Reaia, of the descendants of Reuben (1 Chron. v, 5). B.C. ante 782.

5. A prophet, apparently of the kingdom of Judah, and contemporary with Isaiah (Mic. i, 1). B.C. cir. 750. He is styled "the Morasthite," as being a native of Moresheth of Gath (i, 14, 15), so called to distinguish it from another town of the same name in the tribe of Judah (Josh. xv, 44; 2 Chron. xiv, 9, 10). Micah is thus likewise distinguished from a former prophet of the same name, called also Micaiah, mentioned in 1 Kings xxii, 8. The above place of Micah's birth "Jerome and Eusebius call Morasthi, and identify with a small village called Eleutheropolis, to the east, where formerly the prophet's tomb was shown, but which in the days of Jerome had been succeeded by a church (Epit. Paulæ, c. 6). As little is known of the circumstances of Micah's life as of many of the other prophets. Pseudo-Epiphanius (Opp. ii, 245) makes him, contrary to all probability, of the tribe of Ephraim; and besides confounding him with Micaiah the son of Imlah, who lived more than a century before, he betrays additional ignorance in describing Ahab as king of Judah. For rebuking this monarch's son and successor Jehoram for his impieties, Micah, according to the same authority, was thrown from a precipice, and buried at Morathi in his own country, hard by the cemetery of Enakim (Ἐνακείμ, a place which apparently exists only in the Sept. of Mic. i, 10), where his sepulchre was still to be seen. The *Chronicon Paschale* (p. 148 c) tells the same tale. Another ecclesiastical tradition relates that the remains of Habakkuk and Micah were revealed in a vision to Zebennus, bishop of Eleutheropolis, in the reign of Theodosius the Great, near a place called Berathsatia, which is apparently a corruption of Morasthi (Sozomen, *H. E.* vii, 29; Nicephorus, *H. E.* xii, 48). The prophet's tomb was called by the inhabitants *Nephsameemana*, which Sozomen renders μνῆμα πιστόν."

MICAH, Book of, the sixth of the minor prophets in the usual arrangement, but the third in the Sept. (after Hosea and Amos). In the following account of it we treat in special detail those points that have created controversies in modern times.

1. *The Name.*—This, which the prophet bears in common with the other persons above and below, is found with considerable variation in the Heb. and A. V. The full form is מִיכָיָהוּ, *Mikâyá'hû*, "who is like Jehovah," which is found in 2 Chron. xiii, 2; xvii, 7. This is abbreviated to מִיכָיְהוּ, *Mikâ'yĕhû*, in Judg. xvii, 1, 4; still further to מִכָיְהוּ, *Mikâ'yĕhû* (Jer. xxxvi, 11), מִיכָיָה, *Mikâyâh'* (1 Kings xxii, 13); and finally to מִיכָה, *Mikâh'*, or מִיכָא, *Mikâ'* (2 Sam. ix, 12).

II. *Date.*—The period during which Micah exercised the prophetical office is stated, in the superscription to his prophecies, to have extended over the reigns of Jotham, Ahaz, and Hezekiah, kings of Judah, giving thus a maximum limit of 59 years (B.C. 756–697), from the accession of Jotham to the death of Hezekiah, and a minimum limit of 16 years (B.C. 742–726), from the death of Jotham to the accession of Hezekiah. In either case he would be contemporary with Hosea and Amos during part of their ministry in Israel, and with Isaiah in Judah. According to rabbinical tradition, he transmitted to the prophets Joel, Nahum, and Habakkuk, and to Seraiah the priest the mysteries of the Kabbala, which he had received from Isaiah (R. David Ganz, *Tsemach David*), and by Syncellus (*Chronogr.* p. 199 c) he is enumerated in the reign of Jotham as contemporary with Hosea, Joel, Isaiah, and Oded. The date of the book itself may be fixed at about B.C. 725. His prediction with impunity of the desolation of Jerusalem (iii, 12) is expressly alluded to in Jeremiah (xxvi, 18, where the text has מִיכָיָה, Micaiah), as having been uttered during the reign of Hezekiah. The allusions to idolatry (vii, 13) and to Babylon (iv, 10) have induced Berthold (*Einleitung*, § 411) to refer the prophecy of Micah to the time of the captivity; but De Wette truly observes that this supposition is unnecessary, as idolatry existed under Hezekiah (2 Kings xxiii), and Babylon equally belonged to the kingdom of Assyria. Hartmann's attempt to regard the passage respecting Babylon as an interpolation (see *Micha neu übersetzt*), De Wette regards as even still more venturesome; nor had this writer the slightest authority for supposing that some only of the prophecies are Micah's, and that the work was compiled during the exile. The time assigned to the prophecies by the only direct evidence which we possess agrees so well with their contents that it may fairly be accepted as correct.

Why any discrepancy should be perceived between the statement in Jeremiah, that "Micah the Morasthite prophesied in the days of Hezekiah king of Judah," and the title of his book, which tells us that the word of the Lord came to him "in the days of Jotham, Ahaz, and Hezekiah," it is difficult to imagine. The former does not limit the period of Micah's prophecy, and at most

applies only to the passage to which direct allusion is made. A confusion appears to have existed in the minds of those who see in the prophecy in its present form a connected whole, between the actual delivery of the several portions of it, and their collection and transcription into one book. In the case of Jeremiah, we know that he dictated to Baruch the prophecies which he had delivered in the interval between the 13th year of Josiah and the 4th of Jehoiakim, and that when thus committed to writing they were read before the people on the fast day (Jer. xxxvi, 2, 4, 6). There is reason to believe that a similar process took place with the prophecies of Amos. It is, therefore, conceivable, to say the least, that certain portions of Micah's prophecy may have been uttered in the reigns of Jotham and Ahaz, and for the probability of this there is strong internal evidence, while they were collected as a whole in the reign of Hezekiah and committed to writing. Caspari (*Micha*, p. 78) suggests that the book thus written may have been read in the presence of the king and the whole people on some great fast or festival day, and that this circumstance may have been in the minds of the elders of the land in the time of Jehoiakim, when they appealed to the impunity which Micah enjoyed under Hezekiah. Knobel (*Prophetismus*, ii, § 20) imagines that the prophecies which remain belong to the time of Hezekiah, and that those delivered under Jotham and Ahaz have perished. It is evident from Mic. i, 6 that the section of the prophecy in which that verse occurs must have been delivered before the destruction of Samaria by Shalmaneser, which took place in the 6th year of Hezekiah (cir. B.C. 722), and connecting the "high-places" mentioned in i, 5 with those which existed in Judah in the reigns of Ahaz (2 Kings xvi, 4; 2 Chron. xxviii, 4, 25) and Jotham (2 Kings xv, 35), we may be justified in assigning chap. i to the time of one of these monarchs, probably the latter; although, if chap. ii be considered as part of the section to which chap. i belongs, the utter corruption and demoralization of the people there depicted agree better with what history tells us of the times of Ahaz. Caspari maintains that of the two parallel passages, Mic. iv, 1–5, Isa. ii, 2–5, the former is the original, and the latter belongs to the times of Uzziah and Jotham, and this view is maintained by Hengstenberg (*Christology*, i, 480), and accepted by Pusey (*Minor Prophets*, p. 289). But the evidence on the point is not at all conclusive. Mic. iv, 1–4 may possibly, as Ewald and others have suggested, be a portion of an older prophecy current at the time, which was adopted by both Micah and Isaiah (Isa. ii, 2–4). The denunciation of the horses and chariots of Judah (v, 10) is appropriate to the state of the country under Jotham, after the long and prosperous reign of Uzziah, by whom the military strength of the people had been greatly developed (2 Chron. xxvi, 11–15; xxvii, 4–6). Compare Isa. ii, 7, which belongs to the same period. Again, the forms in which idolatry manifested itself in the reign of Ahaz correspond with those which are threatened with destruction in Mic. v, 12–14; and the allusions in vi, 16 to the "statutes of Omri," and the "works of the house of Ahab," seem directly pointed at the king, of whom it is expressly said that "he walked in the way of the kings of Israel" (2 Kings xvi, 3). It is impossible in dealing with internal evidence to assert positively that the inferences deduced from it are correct; but in the present instance they at least establish a probability that, in placing the period of Micah's prophetical activity between the times of Jotham and Hezekiah, the superscription is correct. In the first years of Hezekiah's reign the idolatry which prevailed in the time of Ahaz was not eradicated, and in assigning the date of Micah's prophecy to this period there is no anachronism in the allusions to idolatrous practices. Maurer contends that chap. i was written not long before the taking of Samaria; but the third and following chapters he places in the interval between the destruction of Samaria and the time that Jerusalem was menaced by the army of Sennacherib in the 14th year of Hezekiah. The passages, however, which he quotes in support of his conclusion (iii, 12; iv, 9, etc.; v, 5, etc.; vi, 9, etc.; vii, 4, 12, etc.) do not appear to be more suitable to that period than to the first years of Hezekiah, while the context, in many cases, requires a still earlier date. In the arrangement adopted by Wells (pref. to Micah, § iv–vi), chap. i was delivered in the contemporary reigns of Jotham king of Judah and of Pekah king of Israel; ii, 1–iv, 8 in those of Ahaz, Pekah, and Hosea; iii, 12 being assigned to the last year of Ahaz, and the remainder of the book to the reign of Hezekiah.

It is remarkable that the prophecies commence with the last words recorded of the prophet's namesake, Micaiah the son of Imlah, "Hearken, O people, every one of you" (1 Kings xxii, 28). From this, Bleek (*Einleitung*, p. 539) concludes that the author of the history, like the ecclesiastical historians, confounded Micah the Morasthite with Micaiah; while Hengstenberg (*Christology*, i, 409, Eng. tr.) infers that the coincidence was intentional on the part of the later prophet, and that "by this very circumstance he gives intimation of what may be expected from him, and shows that his activity is to be considered as a continuation of that of his predecessor, who was so jealous for God, and that he had more in common with him than the mere name." Either conclusion rests on the extremely slight foundation of the occurrence of a formula which was at once the most simple and most natural commencement of a prophetic discourse.

III. *Contents.*—But, at whatever time the several prophecies were first delivered, they appear in their present form as an organic whole, marked by a certain regularity of development. Three sections, omitting the superscription, are introduced by the same phrase, שִׁמְעוּ, "Hear ye," and represent three natural divisions of the prophecy—i–ii, iii–v, vi–vii—each commencing with rebukes and threatenings, and closing with a promise. 1. The first section opens with a magnificent description of the coming of Jehovah to judgment for the sins and idolatries of Israel and Judah (i, 2–4), and the sentence pronounced upon Samaria (ver. 5–9) by the Judge himself. The prophet, whose sympathies are strong with Judah, and especially with the lowlands which gave him birth, sees the danger that threatens his country, and traces in imagination the devastating march of the Assyrian conquerors from Samaria onward to Jerusalem and the south (i, 8–16). The impending punishment suggests its cause, and the prophet denounces a woe upon the people generally for the corruption and violence which were rife among them, and upon the false prophets who led them astray by pandering to their appetites and luxury (ii, 1–11). The sentence of captivity is passed upon them (ver. 10), but is followed instantly by a promise of restoration and triumphant return (ii, 12, 13). 2. The second section is addressed especially to the princes and heads of the people; their avarice and rapacity are rebuked in strong terms; and as they have been deaf to the cry of the suppliants for justice, they too "shall cry unto Jehovah, but he will not hear them" (iii, 1–4). The false prophets who had deceived others should themselves be deceived; "the sun shall go down over the prophets, and the day shall be dark over them" (iii, 6). For this perversion of justice and right, and the covetousness of the heads of the people who judged for reward, of the priests who taught for hire, and of the prophets who divined for money, Zion should "be ploughed as a field," and the mountain of the temple become like the uncultivated woodland heights (iii, 9–12). But the threatening is again succeeded by a promise of restoration, and in the glories of the Messianic kingdom the prophet loses sight of the desolation which should befall his country. Instead of the temple mountain covered with the wild growth of the forest, he sees the mountain of

the house of Jehovah established on the top of the mountains, and nations flowing like rivers unto it. The reign of peace is inaugurated by the recall from captivity, and Jehovah sits as king in Zion, having destroyed the nations who had rejoiced in her overthrow. The predictions at the close of this section form the climax of the book, and Ewald arranges them in four strophes, consisting of seven or eight verses each (iv, 1–8; iv, 9–v, 2; v, 3–9; v, 10–15), with the exception of the last, which is shorter, and in which the prophet reverts to the point whence he started: all objects of politic and idolatrous confidence must be removed before the grand consummation. 3. In the last section (vi, vii) Jehovah, by a bold poetical figure, is represented as holding a controversy with his people, pleading with them in justification of his conduct towards them and the reasonableness of his requirements. The dialogue form in which chap. vi is cast renders the picture very dramatic and striking. In vi, 3–5 Jehovah speaks; the inquiry of the people follows in ver. 6, indicating their entire ignorance of what was required of them; their inquiry is met by the almost impatient rejoinder, "Will Jehovah be pleased with thousands of rams, with myriads of torrents of oil?" The still greater sacrifice suggested by the people, "Shall I give my first-born for my transgressions?" calls forth the definition of their true duty, "to do justly, and to love mercy, and to walk humbly with their God." How far they had fallen short of this requirement is shown in what follows (ver. 9–12), and judgment is pronounced upon them (ver. 13–16). The prophet acknowledges and bewails the justice of the sentence (vii, 1–6), the people in repentance patiently look to God, confident that their prayer will be heard (ver. 7–10), and are reassured by the promise of deliverance announced as following their punishment (ver. 11–13) by the prophet, who in his turn presents his petition to Jehovah for the restoration of his people (ver. 14, 15). The whole concludes with a triumphal song of joy at the great deliverance, like that from Egypt, which Jehovah will achieve, and a full acknowledgment of his mercy and faithfulness to his promises (ver. 16–20). The last verse is reproduced in the song of Zacharias (Luke i, 72, 73).

The predictions uttered by Micah relate to the invasions of Shalmaneser (i, 6–8; 2 Kings xvii, 4, 6) and Sennacherib (i, 9–16; 2 Kings xviii, 13), the destruction of Jerusalem (iii, 12; vii, 13), the captivity in Babylon (iv, 10), the return (iv, 1–8; vii, 11), the establishment of a theocratic kingdom in Jerusalem (iv, 8), and the Ruler who should spring from Bethlehem (v, 2). The destruction of Assyria and Babylon is supposed to be referred to in v, 5, 6; vii, 8, 10. According to many, iv, 13 refers to the heroic deeds of the Maccabees, and their victories over the Syrians or Syro-Macedonians, called Assyrians in Micah v, as well as in Zechariah x, 11.

There is no prophecy in Micah so interesting to the Christian as that in which the native place of the Messiah is announced (v, 2), which is cited by the evangelist (Matt. ii, 6) with slight verbal variations, but substantially the same import (see Kuinöl, *Comment.* ad loc. Mat.). In Micah emphasis is laid on the actual smallness of Bethlehem to enjoy such an honor; in Matthew the prominent idea is the honor itself, and its ideal grandeur—the converse side of the statement. Pocock cuts the knot by adopting rabbi Tanchum's odd opinion that the term צָעִיר means both little and great, the prophet selecting the one sense and the evangelist the other. It is evident that the Jews in the time of Jesus interpreted this passage of the birthplace of the Messiah (Matt. ii, 5; John vii, 41, 42). The Targum gives the reference formally to the Messiah. The later rabbinical writers, however, such as Kimchi, Aben-Ezra, Abrabanel, etc., have maintained that it had only an indirect reference to the birthplace of the Messiah, who was to be a descendant of David, a Bethlehemite, but not of necessity himself born in Bethlehem. Others, however, as David Ganz (*B. Zemach David*), expressly mention Bethlehem as the birthplace of the Messiah. The interpretation which considered this prophecy as intimating only that the Messiah was to be a descendant of David, was that current among the Jews in the time of Theodoret, Chrysostom, Theophylact, and Euthymius Zigabenus, from whom we learn that it was maintained to have been fulfilled in Zerubbabel, the leader of the Jews on their return from Babylon, of which, and not of Bethlehem, he was a native. (See Sozomen, vii, 729; Carpzov, *Introd.* iii, 374 sq.; Jerome, *Ep. ad Eustach.* i, 704.) This interpretation was held among Christians by the celebrated Theodore of Mopsuestia (as we learn from his condemnation by the council at Rome under pope Vigilius), and afterwards by Grotius (*Comment.*), who, however, regarded Zerubbabel as a type of Christ, and considered Christ's birthplace at Bethlehem as an outward representation of his descent from the family of David. Many of the moderns have been attached to this interpretation of the prophecy, referring it to the general idea of the Messiah rather than to Zerubbabel, while some among them have, after the example of some Jews, ventured to assert that the account of the birth of Christ at Bethlehem was not to be depended on. Some have asserted, after Jerome (*Comm. in Mic.*), that the citation in Matt. ii, 6 is that of the Sanhedrim only, not of the evangelist (Hengstenberg's *Christology*). Jahn (*Append. Hermeneut.*) observes that it is evident that the Jews in the time of Christ expected the Messiah's birth to take place at Bethlehem; and although he admits that the prophecy may be understood tropically in the sense applied to it by Grotius, he contends that the context will not admit of its applicability either to Hezekiah or any other monarch than the Messiah; nor is it possible to apply the prophecy fully and literally to any but him who was not only of the house and lineage of David, but was actually born at Bethlehem, according to the direct testimony of both Matthew's and Luke's gospels. The plain meaning is that the Messiah, as David's son, should be born in David's town (Hofmann, *Weiss. u. Erf.* p. 249). Tertullian also presses the argument that the Messiah has come, for Bethlehem was deserted—"Neminem de genere Israel in civitate Bethlehem remansisse" (*Adv. Judæos*, vol. xiii; *Opera*, ii, 734, ed. Oehler). To give the vague sense of Davidic extraction, and yet to deny that the words point out the place of birth, was thus a necessary but feeble Jewish subterfuge. Rénan admits the usual interpretation of the prophecy, though he affirms that Jesus was really not of the family of David, and was born at Nazareth (*Vie de Jésus*, chap. ii). (See generally, Eichhorn, *Einleit.* iv, 369 sq.; Bertheau, *Einl.* iv, 1633 sq.; Knobel, *Prophet.* iii, 199 sq.) See MESSIAH.

IV. The *genuineness* of the book has not been called in question. Only Ewald, in his *Jahrb.* xi, 29, is disposed to maintain that the two concluding chapters are the work of a different author. His objections, however, have no force against the universal opinion. The language of Micah is quoted in Matt. ii, 5, 6, and his prophecies are alluded to in Matt. x, 35, 36; Mark xiii, 12; Luke xii, 53; John vii, 42.

V. The *style* of Micah is rich, full, and musical—as nervous, vehement, and bold, in many sections, as Hosea, and as abrupt, too, in transitions from menace to mercy. He presents, at the same time, no little resemblance to Isaiah in grandeur of thought, in richness and variety of imagery, and in roundness and cadence of parallelism. The similarity of their subjects may account for many resemblances in language with the latter prophet, which were almost unavoidable (comp. Mic. i, 2 with Isa. i, 2; Mic. ii, 2 with Isa. v, 8; Mic. ii, 6, 11 with Isa. xxx, 10; Mic. ii, 12 with Isa. x, 20–22; Mic. vi, 6–8 with Isa. i, 11–17). The diction of Micah is vigorous and forcible, sometimes obscure from the abruptness of its transitions, but varied and rich in figures derived from the pastoral (i, 8; ii, 12; v, 4, 5, 7, 8; vii,

14) and rural life of the lowland country (i, 6; iii, 12; iv, 3, 12, 13; vi, 15), whose vines, and olives, and fig-trees were celebrated (1 Chron. xxvii, 27, 28), and supply the prophet with so many striking allusions (i, 6; iv, 3, 4; vi, 15; vii, 1, 4) as to suggest that, like Amos, he may have been either a herdsman or a vine-dresser, who had heard the howling of the jackals (i, 8; A.Vers. "dragons") as he watched his flocks or his vines by night, and had seen the lions slaughtering the sheep (v, 8). The sudden changes are frequently hidden from the English reader, because our version interprets as well as translates; the simple connective ‫ו‬ being often rendered by some logical term, as "therefore" (i, 6), "then" (iii, 7), "but" (iv, 1), "notwithstanding" (vii, 13), etc. Concise and pointed questions are put suddenly; persons are changed rapidly; the people are spoken of, and then in a moment spoken to; the nation is addressed now as a unit, and now edged appeals are directed to individuals. The language is quite pure and classical—intercourse with northern countries had not yet debased it. An under-tone of deep earnestness pervades the book; everywhere are discerned the workings of an intensely honorable and patriotic soul. Micah is successful in the use of the dialogue, and his prophecies are penetrated by the purest spirit of morality and piety (see especially vi, 6–8; and vii, 1–10).

One peculiarity which Micah has in common with Isaiah is the frequent use of paronomasia; in i, 10–15 there is a succession of instances of this figure in the plays upon words suggested by the various places enumerated (comp. also ii, 4), which it is impossible to transfer to English, though Ewald has attempted to render them into German (*Propheten des A. B.* i, 329, 330). In these verses there is also vivid grouping, as place after place is challenged along the line of the conqueror's march. Each turn is seen to carry its doom in its very name. That doom is told in many ways—either to them or of them; either in the prophet's name or as a divine burden; either as an event about to come or as a judgment which will certainly overtake them. Perhaps in vii, 18 there is an allusion to the meaning of the prophet's own name. The divine name which appears with greatest frequency is, as is usual with the prophets, Jehovah; but we also meet with Adonai and Adonai Jehovah (i, 2), also "the Lord of the whole earth" (iv, 13), and "Jehovah of hosts" (iv, 4). Elohim is used distinctively of the divine as opposed to the human in iii, 7. Allusions to the past history of the people are found in many places. There are also several expressions which are found in the Mosaic writings, though it might be rash to say that Micah takes them directly from the Pentateuch. Nor would we endorse all the instances in which, as Caspari affirms, later prophets, as Jeremiah and Ezekiel, Habakkuk and Zephaniah, have adopted the language of Micah (*Micha*, p. 449, etc.). The poetic vigor of the opening scene, and of the dramatic dialogue sustained throughout the last two chapters, has already been noticed.

VI. *Commentaries.* — The following are the especial exegetical helps on the whole book alone, to a few of the most important of which we prefix an asterisk: Ephrem Syrus, *Explanatio* (in *Opp.* v, 272): Theophylact, *Commentarius* (in *Opp.* vol. iv); Luther, *Commentarius* (ed. Theodore, Vitemb. 1542, 8vo; also in his *Works*, both Germ. and Lat.); Brentz, *Commentaria* (in *Opp.* vol. iv): Gerlach, *Commentarius* (Aug. Vind. 1524, 8vo); Biblaander, *Commentarius* (Tigur. 1534, 8vo); Phrygio, *Commentarius* (Argent. 1538, 8vo); Gilby, *Commentary* (Lond. 1551, 1591, 8vo); Chytræus, *Explicatio* [includ. Neh.] (Vitemb. 1565, 8vo); Draconis, *Explicatio* [includ. Joel and Zech.] (Vitemb. 1565, 8vo); Graxar, *Commentarius* (Salmant. 1570, 8vo); Selnecker, *Anmerckungen* (Leips. 1578, 4to); Bang, *Fontium trias* [includ. Jonah and Ruth] (Hafn. 1631, 8vo); Graver, *Expositio* (Jen. 1619, 1664, 4to); *Pocock, *Commentary* (Oxf. 1677, fol.; also in *Works*); Van Toll, *Vitleyginge* (Utrecht, 1709,

4to); Schnurrer, *Animadversiones* (Tübing. 1783, 4to); Bauer, *Animadversiones* [on chap. i, ii] (Altorf, 1790, 4to); Grosschopff, *Uebersetzung* (Jena, 1798, 8vo); *Justi, *Erläuterung* (Leips. 1799, 8vo); *Hartmann, *Erläuterung* (Lemgo, 1800, 8vo); Wolf, מִנְחָה טְהוֹרָה (Dessau, 1805, 8vo); Gliemann, *Illustratio* (Hall. 1842, 4to); *Caspari, *Micha der Morasthiter* (Marb. 1852, 8vo); Roorda, *Commentarius* (Leyd. 1869, 8vo). See PROPHETS, MINOR.

6. The father of Abdon (2 Chron. xxxiv, 20); elsewhere called MICHAIAH, the father of Achbor (2 Kings xxii, 12).

7. A Levite of the descendants of Asaph (1 Chron. ix, 15); elsewhere properly called MICHA (Neh. xi, 17, 22).

Micai'ah, the prevailing form of the name of several persons (one a Levite, 2 Chron. xiii, 2), written with considerable diversity in the original and in the ancient translations, as well as the Auth. Vers. (properly, for Heb. *Mikayah'*, מִיכָיָה, *who is like Jehovah?* 2 Kings xxii, 12; Sept. Μιχαίας, Vulg. *Micha,* Auth. Vers. "Michaiah," Neh. xii, 35, Μιχαία, *Michaja,* "Michaiah;" Neh. xii, 41, Μιχαίας, *Michœa,* "Michaiah;" Jer. xxvi, 18, Μιχαίας, *Michœas,* "Micah;" paragogically, Heb. *Mikah'yehu,* מִיכָיְהוּ; Judg. xvii, 1, 4, Μιχά, *Michas,* "Micah;" 1 Kings xxii, 8, 9, 13, 14, 15, 24, 25, 26, 28, Μιχαίας, *Michœas,* "Micaiah;" 2 Chron. xviii, 7, 8, 12, 13, 23, 24, 25, 27, Μιχαίας, *Michœas,* "Micaiah;" Jer. xxxvi, 11, 13, Μιχαίας, *Michœas,* "Michaiah;" fully, Heb. *Mikaya'hu,* מִיכָיָהוּ; 2 Chron. xiii, 2, Μααχά, *Michaja,* "Michaiah;" 2 Chron. xvii, 7, Μιχαίας, *Michœas,* "Michaiah;" contracted, Heb. *Mikah'*, מִיכָה; Judg. xvii, 5, 8, 9, 10, 12, 13, and xviii, 2, 3, 4, 13, 15, 18, 22, 23, 26, 27, 31, Μιχά, *Michas,* "Micah;" 1 Chron. v, 5, and viii, 34, 35, and ix, 40, 41, and xxiii, 20, Μιχά, *Michas,* "Micah;" 1 Chron. xxiv, 24, 25, Μιχά, *Micha,* "Michah;" 2 Chron. xviii, 14, Μιχαίας, *Michœas,* "Micaiah;" 2 Chron. xxxiv, 20, Μιχαία, *Micha,* "Micah;" Jer. xxvi, 18, Μιχαίας v. r. Μιχέας and Μηχαίας, *Michœas,* "Micah;" Micah i, 1, Μιχαίας, *Michœas,* "Micah;" by Chaldaism, *Mika',* מִיכָא; 2 Sam. ix, 12, and Neh. x, 11, and xi, 17, Μιχά, *Micha,* "Micha;" 1 Chron. ix, 15, Μιχά, *Micha,* "Micah;" Neh. xi, 22, Μιχά, *Michas,* "Micha"). The only person invariably thus called was the son of Imla, and a prophet of Samaria (1 Kings xxii, 1–35; 2 Chron. xviii). B.C. 895. The following abstract of the narrative concerning him is sufficiently copious on certain disputed points. Three years after the great battle with Benhadad, king of Syria, in which the extraordinary number of 100,000 Syrian soldiers is said to have been slain, without reckoning the 27,000 who, it is asserted, were killed by the falling of the wall at Aphek, Ahab proposed to Jehoshaphat, king of Judah, that they should jointly go up to battle against Ramoth-Gilead : which Benhadad was, apparently, bound by treaty to restore to Ahab. Jehoshaphat, whose son Jehoram had married Athaliah, Ahab's daughter, assented in cordial words to the proposal; but suggested that they should first "inquire at the word of Jehovah." Accordingly, Ahab assembled 400 prophets, while, in an open space at the gate of the city of Samaria, he and Jehoshaphat sat in royal robes to meet and consult them. "That these were, however, no true prophets of Jehovah, is evident from their being afterwards emphatically designated Ahab's prophets, in contradistinction to the Lord's (ver. 22, 23). It is evident also from the suspicion created in the mind of Jehoshaphat respecting their character by their manner and appearance; for, after they had all spoken, and as having yet to learn the real purpose of heaven, Jehoshaphat asked whether there was not yet a prophet of Jehovah. In consequence of this request Micaiah was mentioned by Ahab, but with the notification that he hated him, 'for he doth not prophesy good concerning me, but evil' (ver. 8); which, in the circumstances, cannot be regarded otherwise than as a further proof of the essential difference between the actual position of this man and the others who assumed

the name of prophets of the Lord." The prophets unanimously gave a favorable response; and among them, Zedekiah, the son of Chenaanah, made horns of iron as a symbol, and announced, from Jehovah, that with those horns Ahab would push the Syrians till he consumed them. For some reason which is unexplained, and can now only be conjectured, Jehoshaphat was dissatisfied with the answer, and asked if there was no other prophet of Jehovah at Samaria? Ahab replied that there was yet one, Micaiah, the son of Imla; but, in words which obviously call to mind a passage in the *Iliad* (i, 106), he added, "I hate him, for he does not prophesy good concerning me, but evil." Micaiah was, nevertheless, sent for; and after an attempt had in vain been made to tamper with him, he first expressed an ironical concurrence with the 400 prophets, and then openly foretold the defeat of Ahab's army and the death of Ahab himself. In opposition to the other prophets, he said that he had seen Jehovah sitting on his throne, and all the host of heaven standing by him, on his right hand and on his left: that Jehovah said, Who shall persuade Ahab to go up and fall at Ramoth-Gilead; that a spirit (the Heb. has the art. *the spirit,* as if some special emissary of evil) came forth and said that he would do so; and on being asked, Wherewith? he answered, that he would go forth and be a lying spirit in the mouth of all the prophets. Irritated by the account of this vision, Zedekiah struck Micaiah on the cheek, and Ahab ordered Micaiah to be taken to prison, and fed on bread and water, till his return to Samaria. Ahab then went up with his army to Ramoth-Gilead; and in the battle which ensued, Benhadad, who could not have failed to become acquainted with Micaiah's prophecy, uttered so publicly, which had even led to an act of public personal violence on the part of Zedekiah, gave special orders to direct the attack against Ahab, individually. Ahab, on the other hand, requested Jehoshaphat to wear his royal robes, which we know that the king of Judah had brought with him to Samaria (1 Kings xxii, 10); and then he put himself into disguise for the battle; hoping thus, probably, to baffle the designs of Benhadad and the prediction of Micaiah; but he was, nevertheless, struck and mortally wounded in the combat by a random arrow. We hear nothing further of the prophet. Josephus dwells emphatically on the death of Ahab, as showing the utility of prophecy, and the impossibility of escaping destiny, even when it is revealed beforehand (*Ant.* viii, 15, 6). He says that it steals on human souls, flattering them with cheerful hopes, till it leads them round to the point whence it will gain the mastery over them. This was a theme familiar to the Greeks in many tragic tales, and Josephus uses words in unison with their ideas. (See Euripides, *Hippolyt.* 1256, and compare Herodot. vii, 17; viii, 77; i, 91). From his interest in the story, Josephus relates several details not contained in the Bible, some of which are probable, while others are very unlikely; but for none of which does he give any authority. Thus, he says, Micaiah was already in prison when sent for to prophesy before Ahab and Jehoshaphat, and that it was Micaiah who had predicted death by a lion to the son of a prophet, under the circumstances mentioned in 1 Kings xx, 35, 36; and had rebuked Ahab after his brilliant victory over the Syrians for not putting Benhadad to death. There is no doubt that these facts would be not only consistent with the narrative in the Bible, but would throw additional light upon it; for the rebuke of Ahab in his hour of triumph, on account of his forbearance, was calculated to excite in him the intensest feeling of displeasure and mortification; and it would at once explain Ahab's hatred of Micaiah, if Micaiah was the prophet by whom the rebuke was given. Nor is it unlikely that Ahab, in his resentment, might have caused Micaiah to be thrown into prison, just as the princes of Judah, about 300 years later, maltreated Jeremiah in the same way (Jer. xxxvii, 15). But some other statements of Josephus cannot so readily be regarded as probable. Thus he relates that, when Ahab disguised himself, he gave his own royal robes to be worn by Jehoshaphat in the battle of Ramoth-Gilead, an act which would have been so unreasonable and cowardly in Ahab, and would have shown such singular complaisance in Jehoshaphat, that, although supported by the translation in the Septuagint, it cannot be received as true. The fact that some of the Syrian captains mistook Jehoshaphat for Ahab is fully explained by Jehoshaphat's being the only person in the army of Israel who wore royal robes. Again, Josephus informs us that Zedekiah alleged, as a reason for disregarding Micaiah's prediction, that it was directly at variance with the prophecy of Elijah, that dogs should lick the blood of Ahab, where dogs had licked the blood of Naboth, in the city of Samaria: inasmuch as Ramoth-Gilead, where, according to Micaiah, Ahab was to meet his doom, was distant from Samaria a journey of three days. It is unlikely, however, that Zedekiah would have founded an argument on Elijah's insulting prophecy, even to the meekest of kings who might have been the subject of it; but that, in order to prove himself in the right as against Micaiah, he should have ventured on such an allusion to a person of Ahab's character, is absolutely incredible. See AHAB.

It only remains to add, that the history of Micaiah offers several points of interest, among which the two following may be specified: 1. Micaiah's vision presents what may be regarded as transitional ideas of one origin of evil actions. In Exodus, Jehovah himself is represented as directly hardening Pharaoh's heart (vii, 3, 13; xiv, 4, 17; x, 20, 27). In the Book of Job, the name of Satan is mentioned; but he is admitted without rebuke, among the sons of God, into the presence of Jehovah (Job i, 6–12). After the captivity, the idea of Satan, as an independent principle of evil, in direct opposition to goodness, becomes fully established (1 Chron. xxi, 1; and compare Wisd. ii, 24). See SATAN. Now the ideas presented in the vision of Micaiah are different from each of these three, and occupy a place of their own. They do not go so far as the Book of Job— much less so far as the ideas current after the captivity; but they go farther than Exodus. See Ewald, *Poet. Bücher*, iii, 65. 2. The history of Micaiah is an exemplification in practice of contradictory predictions being made by different prophets. Other striking instances occur in the time of Jeremiah (xiv, 13, 14; xxviii, 15, 16; xxiii, 16, 25, 26). The only rule bearing on the judgment to be formed under such circumstances seems to have been a negative one, which would be mainly useful after the event. It is laid down in Deut. xviii, 21, 22, where the question is asked, how the children of Israel *were to know* the word which Jehovah had not spoken? The solution is, that "if *the thing follow not, nor come to pass, that* is the thing which Jehovah has not spoken." See PROPHET.

Mice. See MOUSE.

Mi′cha (for the Heb., etc., see MICAIAH), the name of three men.

1. A son of Mephibosheth (2 Sam. ix, 12); elsewhere (1 Chron. viii, 34, 35) called MICAH (q. v.).

2. The son of Zabdi and father of Mattaniah, a Levite of the family of Asaph (Neh. xi, 17, 22); probably the same that joined in the sacred covenant after the captivity (Neh. x, 11). B.C. cir. 410. In 1 Chron. ix, 15 his name is incorrectly Anglicized "Micah." He must not be confounded with the Michaiah of Neh. xii, 35.

3. "A Simeonite, father of Ozias, one of the three governors of the city of Bethulia in the time of Judith (Judith vi, 15). His name is remarkable as being connected with one of the few specific allusions to the ten tribes after the captivity."

Michæ′as (Vulg. *id.*), an erroneous form (2 Esdr. i, 39) of the name of the prophet MICAH.

Mi′chaël (Heb. *Mikaël′*, מִיכָאֵל, *who is like God?*

Sept. and N. T. Μιχαήλ), the name of an archangel and of several men.

1. The title given in the angelology of the Jews adopted during the exile, to one of the chief angels, who, in Dan. x, 13–21; xii, 1, is described as having special charge of the Israelites as a nation, and in Jude 9 as disputing with Satan about the body of Moses, in which dispute, instead of bringing against the archenemy any railing accusation, he only said, "The Lord rebuke thee, O Satan!" Again, in Rev. xii, 7–9, Michael and his angels are represented as warring with Satan and his angels in the upper regions, from which the latter are cast down upon the earth. "This representation served not only to give that vividness to man's faith in God's supernatural agents, which was so much needed at a time of captivity, during the abeyance of his local manifestations and regular agencies, but also to mark the finite and ministerial nature of the angels, lest they should be worshipped in themselves. Accordingly, as Gabriel represents the ministration of the angels towards man, so Michael is the type and leader of their strife, in God's name and his strength, against the power of Satan. In the O. T. therefore he is the guardian of the Jewish people in their antagonism to godless power and heathenism. In the N. T. (see Rev. xii, 7) he fights in heaven against the dragon— 'that old serpent called the Devil and Satan, which deceiveth *the whole world:*' and so takes part in that struggle which is the work of the Church on earth. The nature and method of his war against Satan are not explained, because the knowledge would be unnecessary and perhaps impossible to us: the fact itself is revealed rarely, and with that mysterious vagueness which hangs over all angelic ministrations, but yet with plainness and certainty." On the authority of the first of these texts the Jews have named Michael not only one of the "seven" archangels, but the chief of them (comp. the Targum on Cant. viii, 9); and on the authority of all three the Christian Church has been disposed to concur in this impression (see J. D. Häberlin, *Selecta de Mich. ejusque apparitionibus, gestis et cultu*, Helmst. 1758). The Jews regard the archangels as being such, not simply as a class by themselves, but as respectively the chiefs of the several classes into which they suppose the angels to be divided; and of these classes Michael is the head of the first, and therefore chief of all the archangels (*Sepher Othioth*, fol. 16). "The rabbinical traditions constantly oppose him to Sammael, the accuser and enemy of Israel, as disputing for the *soul* of Moses; as bringing the ram the substitute for Isaac, which Sammael sought to keep back, etc.: they give him the title of the 'great high-priest in heaven,' as well as that of the 'great prince and conqueror;' and finally lay it down that 'wherever Michael is said to have appeared, there the glory of the Shechinah is intended.' It is clear that the sounder among them, in making such use of the name, intended to personify the divine power, and typify the Messiah (see Schöttgen, *Hor. Hebr.* i, 1079, 1119; ii, 8, 15, ed. Dresd. 1742)." Hengstenberg maintains at length (both in his *Christology* and his *Commentary on the Apocalypse*) that Michael is no other than the Lord Jesus Christ himself; but this is hardly in accordance with the mention of the other archangel, Gabriel, nor with the other theophanies of the O. T., in which the Logos appears only as the Angel [of] Jehovah, or the Angel of the Covenant. The passages in Daniel and Revelations must be taken as symbolical, and in that view offer little difficulty. In the former, one of the guardian angels of the Jews (probably Gabriel, Dan. ix, 21) exhibits himself as a protector, and as struggling with the prince of Persia for the liberation of the Jewish exiles. In the discharge of this duty, Michael, the chief guardian of the same people, comes to help him. The first angel promises to return (from his visit to Daniel) to renew the contest, and indicates his success by declaring that "the prince of Greece will come," i. e. to overthrow the

Gnostic Gem of Michael. (The lower figure shows the size of the gem.)

days, and on the last day, when they came opposite to the tomb of Hadrian, Gregory beheld the archangel Michael hovering over the city; and he alighted on the top of the mausoleum and sheathed his sword, which was dripping with blood. Then the plague was stayed, and the tomb of Hadrian has been called the Castle of Sant' Angelo from that day, and a chapel was there consecrated, the name of which was Ecclesia Sancti Angeli usque ad Cœlos. Michael is also said to have appeared to command the building of two churches (see Mrs. Clement, *Legendary and Mytholog. Art*, p. 229). The first was on the eastern coast of Italy, and was called the church of Monte Galgano, which became a resort for numerous pilgrims. Again, in the reign of Childebert II, Michael appeared to Aubert, bishop of Avranches, and commanded that a church should be built on the summit of a rock in the Gulf of Avranches, in Normandy; and Mont-Saint-Michel became one of the most celebrated places of pilgrimage, as it is one of the most picturesque in scenery. From this time Michael was greatly venerated in the Church of Rome, especially in France. He was selected as patron saint of the country and of the order which Louis instituted in his honor.

Representations of the Archangel as a Saint.—"Michael is always represented as young and beautiful.

Persian empire. Here also Michael, in particular, is designated as the prince of the Jews. So in Zech. i, 8, 14, the guardian angel of the Jews exhibits his solicitude for them and his care over them. The same thing is again exhibited in Zech. iii, 1, 2, where the angel of the Lord rebukes Satan on account of his malignant intentions towards the high-priest Joshua. So again in Rev. xii, 7, 9, Michael and his angels are represented as waging war with Satan and his angels. This passage stands connected with ver. 5 of the context, which represents the Man-Child (Jesus) as caught up to the throne of God. The war waged would seem to have arisen from the efforts of Satan to annoy the ascending Saviour. Such appears to be the symbolic representation (see Stuart's *Comment.* ad loc.). The allusion in Jude 9 is more difficult to understand, unless, with Vitringa, Lardner, Macknight, and others, we regard it also as symbolical; in which case the dispute referred to is that indicated in Zech. iii, 1; and "the body of Moses" as a symbolical phrase for the Mosaical law and institutions [see JUDE], in accordance with the usual mode of speaking among Christians, who called the Church "the body of Christ" (Col. i, 18, 24; Rom. xii, 5). A comparison of Jude 9 with Zech. i, 8-14 gives much force and probability to this conjecture (see F. U. Wolter, *De Michaëli cum diabolo litigante* [Rinteln, 1727-9]). According to others, "the body of Moses" here means his proper and literal body, which the Lord secretly buried (Deut. xxxiv, 5, 6), and which Satan wished to present to the Jews as an object of idolatry (comp. 2 Kings xviii, 4). "The allusion seems to be to a Jewish legend attached to Deut. xxxiv, 6. The Targum of Jonathan attributes the burial of Moses to the hands of the angels of God, and particularly of the archangel Michael, as the guardian of Israel. Later traditions (see Œcumen. *in Jud.* cap. 1) set forth how Satan disputed the burial, claiming for himself the dead body because of the blood of the Egyptian (Exod. ii, 13) which was on Moses's hands" (see Quistorp, *Num Michaëlis de corpore Mosis disceptatio fabula sit?* [Gryph. 1770]).

Michael as a Saint in the Church of Rome.—This archangel is canonized in the Roman calendar, and his festival, called Michaelmas (q. v.), is celebrated on the 29th of September. The legends preserved by Roman Catholics relate that Michael appeared to the Virgin Mary to announce to her the time of her death, and that he received her soul and bore it to Jesus. And again, that during the 6th century, when a fearful pestilence was raging in Rome, St. Gregory advised that a procession should be made, which should pass through the streets singing the service which since then has been called the Great Litanies. This was done for three

St. Michael.

As patron of the Church Militant, he is 'the winged saint,' with no attribute save the shield and lance. As conqueror of Satan, he stands in armor, with his foot upon the Evil One, who is half human or like a dragon in shape. The angel is about to chain him, or to transfix him with the lance. But the treatment of this subject is varied in many ways, all, however, easily recognised. As lord of souls, St. Michael is unarmed; he holds a balance, and in each scale a little naked figure representing the souls; the *beato* usually joins the hands as in thankfulness, while the rejected one expresses horror in look and attitude. Frequently a dæmon is seizing the falling scale with a Plutonic hook, or with his talons. In these pictures the saint is rarely without wings. When introduced in pictures of the Madonna and Child he presents the balance to Christ, who seems to welcome the happy soul. Whether with or without the balance, he is always the lord of souls in pictures of the death, assumption, or glorification of the Virgin Mary, for tradition teaches that he received her spirit, and cared for it until it was reunited to her body and ascended to her Son. The old English coin called an angel was so named because it bore the image of this archangel."

On the subject generally, see Surenhusius, *Bibl. Katall.* p. 701; Fabricius, *Pseudepigr.* i, 839 sq.; Wetstein, i, 649; ii, 735; Hartmann, *Verbind.* p. 83; Eisenmenger, *Judenth.* i, 806 sq.; Thilo, *Apocryph.* i, 691; Trigland, *Dissert. theol.* p. 198 sq.; Laurmann, *Collectan. in ep. Jud.* p. 71 sq.; Seeland, in the *Brem. u. Verdensch. Biblioth.* iii, 89 sq.; Braun, *De Michaële* (Altorf, 1726); Hurenius, *De Michaële* (Vitemb. 1593). See ANGEL; MOSES.

2. The father of Sethur, which latter was the Asherite commissioner to explore the land of Canaan (Numb. xiii, 13). B.C. ante 1657.

3. One of the four sons of Izrahiah, the great-grandson of Issachar (1 Chron. vii, 3). B.C. prob. post 1618. Possibly the same with No. 8.

4. One of the "sons" of Beriah, a son of Elpaal, of the tribe of Benjamin (1 Chron. viii, 16). B.C. post 1612.

5. A chief Gadite resident in Bashan (1 Chron. v, 13), B.C. apparently post 1093. He was perhaps identical with the son of Jehishai and father of Gilead, some of the posterity of whose descendant Abihail are mentioned as dwelling in the same region (1 Chron. v, 14). B.C. long ante 782.

6. One of the Manassite chiliarchs who joined David when he returned to Ziklag (1 Chron. xii, 20). B.C. 1053.

7. The son of Baaseiah and father of Shimea, among the ancestors of the Levite Asaph (1 Chron. vi, 40). B.C. considerably ante 1014.

8. The "father" of Omri, which latter was the phylarch of the tribe of Issachar under David and Solomon (1 Chron. xxvii, 18). B.C. ante 1014.

9. One of the sons of king Jehoshaphat, whom he portioned before the settlement of the succession upon Jehoram, but whom the latter, nevertheless, out of jealousy, caused to be slain upon his own accession (2 Chron. xxi, 2). B.C. 887.

10. A "son" (prob. descendant) of Shephatiah, whose son Zebadiah returned with eighty males from Babylon (Ezra viii, 8). B.C. ante 459.

Michael, St., and all Angels, Feast of. This festival of the Latin and Greek churches, commemorating the ministry of the holy angels to the heirs of salvation, originated in some provincial festivals which were introduced between the 3d and 5th centuries, and which were then combined into one common celebration on the 29th of September by pope Felix III in 480 (Mansi, xiv, 73). Its observance was not enjoined upon the Greek Church before the 12th century (Guericke, *Kirchen-Gesch.* p. 194 sq.). The Collect is taken from the Missal: "Deus, qui miro ordine angelorum ministeria hominumque dispensas; concede propitius ut a quibus tibi ministrantibus in cœlo semper assistitur, ab his in terra vita nostra muniatur. Per dominum" (*Missal Sar.* "In festo sancti Michaelis Archangeli," fol. ccvi). See Procter, *Hist. Book of Common Prayer*, p. 301.

Michael Alexandrīnus, a noted patriarch of Alexandria, flourished near the middle of the 9th century. He was very active in behalf of a union of the Eastern and Western churches, and wrote, about A.D. 869, *De Unitate Ecclesiæ* (printed in Labbe's *Concil.* vol. viii, and in Hardouin, *Concil.* vol. v). See Cave, *Hist. Lit.* ad an. 869; Fabricius, *Bibl. Græca*, xi, 188.

Michael Anchiălus, another distinguished Eastern ecclesiastic, patriarch of Constantinople from 1167 to 1185, was a decided opponent to the attempt at union of the Eastern and Western churches. He was also noted as an eminent disciple of Aristotelian philosophy. His extant works are five synodal decrees, published in Greek and Latin in the *Jus Gr. Rom.* (iii, 227), and a dialogue with the emperor Manuel Comnenus concerning the claims of the Roman pontiff. Of the latter work only some extracts have been published by Leo Allatius.

Michael Angelo BUONAR(R)OT(T)I, an Italian artist, who, in an age when Christian art had reached its zenith, stood unrivalled as a painter, sculptor, poet, and architect, was born March 6, 1474, at the Castle of Caprese, in Tuscany. He was of noble origin, having descended on his mother's side from the ancient family of Canossa, in Tuscany, while the Buonarotti had long been associated with places of trust in the Florentine republic. Michael Angelo was very early afforded the advantages of association with first-class artists, and this gave rise to the saying that "he sucked in sculpture with his milk." About 1488 he was admitted as a student into the seminary which was established by Lorenzo the Magnificent for the study of ancient art in connection with the collections of statuary in the Medicean Gardens, and there he attracted the notice of Lorenzo by his artistic skill, and was invited by that generous Florentine prince to take up his residence at the palace of the Medici. As an inmate of the palace, he enjoyed the society of eminent literary men, one of whom, Angelo Poliziano (Politian), became his intimate friend. Among his earliest works was a marble bass-relief, the subject of which was *The Battle of Hercules with the Centaurs.* This work, which was approved by his own mature judgment, is preserved in Florence. Lorenzo's death in 1492, and the temporary reverses which befell the Medici family in consequence of the incapacity of Lorenzo's successor, Pietro, led Michael Angelo to quit Florence for Bologna. There, however, he remained only about a year, and gladly enough turned his face towards Florence again. Michael now found a patron in the person of Pietro Soderini, the gonfaloniere (chief ruler) of Florence. About 1497 he produced an admirable marble group called a "Pietà," representing "The Virgin weeping over the Dead Body of her Son." "In none of his works," says Ernest Breton, "has he displayed more perfect knowledge of design and anatomy, or more profound truth of expression" (*Nouv. Biog. Générale*, s. v.). This *Mater Dolorosa* now adorns a chapel in the Church of St. Peter at Rome. After this he executed a gigantic marble statue of the psalmist David, which stands in front of the Palazzo Vecchio, in Florence. He received 400 ducats for this work, on which he spent about eighteen months, and which he finished in 1504. Next in order of time, and, according to some of his contemporaries, first in merit, ranks his great cartoon for the ducal palace at Florence, which, together with the pendant executed by Leonardo da Vinci, has long since perished. This work, which represented a scene in the wars with Pisa, when a number of young Florentines, while bathing in the Arno, are surprised by an attack of the Pisans, showed so marvellous a knowledge of the anatomical development of the human figure, and such extraordinary facility in the powers of execution, that it became a study for artists of every land, creating actually a new era in art. "Such was the excellence of this work," says Vasari, "that some thought it absolute perfection." Another production which belongs to this period, and which is of special interest to the student of Christian art, is an oil-painting of the *Holy Family* (about 1504). Shortly after his accession to the pontificate, Julius II called Michael Angelo to Rome, and commissioned him to make the pope's monument, which was to be erected within St. Peter's. Although this work was never completed on the colossal scale on which it had been designed, and was ultimately erected in the Church of St. Pietro ad Vincol, it is a magnificent composition, and is memorable for having given occasion to the reconstruction of St. Peter's on its present sublime plan, in order the better to adapt it to the colossal dimensions of the proposed monument. In 1506 Michael Angelo, incensed by the indifference of the pontiff towards him, quitted Rome; but after a short time the repeated and urgent entreaties of Julius led him to return, and at the pope's request he now painted with his own hand the ceiling of the Sistine Chapel, and, although unwillingly, he began in 1508, and completed within less than two years his colossal task, which proved one of the most marvellous of his works. The subjects of these cartoons are taken from the book of Genesis, but between these and the representations of the persons of the Saviour's genealogy are colossal figures of prophets and sibyls.

Julius II died in 1513, and was succeeded by Leo X, who, together with successive popes, is censured for illiberal conduct towards Michael Angelo. Leo ordered him to build the façade of the Church of San Lorenzo, at Florence, and compelled him, against his will, to spend several years in procuring marble for that purpose. "It is a mortifying reflection," says Duppa, "that the talents of this great man should have been buried and his time consumed, during the whole reign of Leo X, in little else than in raising stone out of a quarry and making a road to convey it to the sea" (*Life of M. Angelo*). Under the patronage of Clement VII (1523), Michael Angelo devoted himself to the library and sacristy of San Lorenzo, at Florence, and in 1528 or 1529 he spent his time at Florence in the erection of fortifications to resist the attempts of the expelled Medici to recover possession. He also fought in the defence of that city against the papal troops. On the surrender of Florence he returned to Rome, and after the accession of pope Paul III, in 1534, was permitted to resume the monument of Julius II, which he completed on a smaller scale than he had first designed. It consists of seven statues, one of which represents Moses, and was placed in the Church of San Pietro ad Vincolo. This statue of Moses is called one of his masterpieces. Another great production of this period is his great picture of *the Last Judgment*, painted for the altar of the Sistine Chapel. This colossal fresco, nearly 70 feet in height, which was completed in 1541, after some eight years of close confinement, was regarded by contemporary critics as having surpassed all his other works for the unparalleled powers of invention and the consummate knowledge of the human figure which it displayed. On a comparison with Raphael it loses, however, much of its value, for, as has been truly said, "one will seek in vain for that celestial light and divine inspiration which appears in the Transfiguration." After its completion, Michael Angelo devoted himself to the perfecting of St. Peter's, which by the touch of his genius was converted from a mere Saracenic hall into the most superb model of a Christian church. He refused all remuneration for this labor, which he regarded as a service to the glory of God. He never married; and upon his death in 1563, at Rome, his remains were removed to Florence, and laid within the Church of Santa Croce. His piety, benevolence, and liberality made him generally beloved; and in the history of art no name shines with a more unsullied lustre than that of Michael Angelo. "He was the bright luminary," says Sir Joshua Reynolds, "from whom painting has borrowed a new lustre, under whose hands it assumed a new appearance and became another and superior art, and from whom all his contemporaries and successors have derived whatever they have possessed of the dignified and majestic" (*Discourses on Painting*, vol. ii). Always a student, always dissatisfied with what he had done, many of his works were left unfinished; but his fragments have educated eminent men. In disposition he was proud and passionate, but highminded; not greedy of gold, but princely in his generosity. His mind was full of great conceptions, for which he was ready to sacrifice and forego physical comforts. Of his merits as an artist, it is enough to say that Ra-

phael thanked God that he was born in the time of Michael Angelo Buonarotti. Comparing him with Raphael, Quatremère de Quincy marks Michael Angelo as "the greatest of draughtsmen." "In painting," says Duppa, "the great work on which Michael Angelo's fame depends, and, taking it for all in all, the greatest work of his whole life, is the ceiling of the Sistine Chapel. ... His sibyls and prophets exhibit with variety and energy the colossal powers of his mind. ... In his great works, his superior abilities are shown in the sublimity of his conceptions, and the power and facility with which they are executed." See Condivi, *Vita di Michael Angelo Buonarotti* (Rome, 1553; new ed. Pisa, 1823); Vignali, *Vita di Michael Angelo* (1753); Richard Duppa, *Life of Michael Angelo* (London, 1806); Hauchecorne, *Vie de Michel-Ange*; Quatremère de Quincy, *Vie de Michel-Ange* (1835); J. S. Harford, *Life of Michael Angelo* (1856–7, 2 vols. 8vo); Hermann Grimm, *Michael Angelo's Leben*, and English version of the same (London, 1865, 2 vols.); Vasari, *Lives of Painters and Sculptors*; Lanzi, *Storia della Pittura*; Winckelmann, *Neues Maler-Lexikon*, s. v.; Nagler, *Künstler-Lexikon*, s. v.; Marie Henri Bayle, *Histoire de la Peinture en Italie*; Pater, *Studies in the History of the Renaissance* (Lond. and N. Y., Macmillan & Co., 1873, 8vo), ch. v, contains an interesting essay on the poetry of *Michael Angelo*.

Michael Apostolius, an eminent Greek scholar, who contributed largely to the revival of learning in Italy, flourished in the 15th century. He was an intimate friend of Gemistus Pletho, and an adherent of the Platonic philosophy, two circumstances which, together with his own merits, caused him to be well received by cardinal Bessarion in Italy, where he settled about 1440. Later in life Michael retired to Candia, where he got a livelihood by teaching children and copying manuscripts. There he died, some time after 1457, for in that year he wrote a panegyric on the emperor Frederick III. His principal works are, a defence of Plato against Theodore Gaza, extant in MS. in the Vienna library:—*Menexenus*, a dialogue on the Holy Trinity, investigating whether the Mohammedans and Jews are right in believing a Mono-Deus; or the Christians, in believing a Deus Trin-unus; extant in MS., ibid.:—*Oratio consultoria ad Socerum sibi irascendum cum ad secundas transiret nuptias*, extant in the Bodleian:—*Appellatio ad Constantinum Palæologum ultitum Imperatorum:—Oratio ad Ioannem Argyropulum:—Epistolæ XLV*; these letters are extremely important for the history of the writer's time, as Lambecius asserts, who perused all or most of them, and it is to be regretted that none of them are printed. The first is addressed to Gemistus, the others to Manuel Chrysolaras, Chalcocondylas, Argyropulus, Bessarion, and other celebrated men of the time. They are extant in MS. in the Bodleian; some of them are also to be found in the Vatican and at Munich:—*Oratio Panegyrica ad Fredericum III*, written about or perhaps in 1457; it was published in Greek and Latin by Freherus in the second vol. of his *Rerum German. Script.:—Oratio Funebris in Laudem Bessarionis*, does credit to the heart of Michael, for it seems that the cardinal had not behaved very generously towards the poor scholar. Still it is very questionable whether our Michael is the author of it; Bessarion died in 1472, and as Michael, previously to leaving Constantinople, in or before 1440, had enjoyed, during many years, the friendship of Gemistus, whose name became conspicuous in the very beginning of the 15th century, and who was a very old man in 1441, he must have attained a very great age if he survived Bessarion:—*Disceptatio adversus eos qui Occidentales Orientalibus superiores esse contendebant*, extant in MS. in the Bodleian:—*De Figuris Grammaticis*, which Leo Allatius esteemed so highly that he intended to publish it, but was unfortunately prevented:—*An Etymological Dictionary*; doubtful whether still extant; a work of great importance:—'Ιωνία, *Violets*, a pleasing title given to a collection of sentences of celebrated persons. Arsenius, of Malvasia, made an extract of it ($Ἀποφθέγματα$ [Rome, 8vo]), which he dedicated to pope Leo X, who reigned from 1513 to 1522:—$Συναγωγὴ Παροιμιῶν$, containing 2027 Greek proverbs, a very remarkable little work, which soon attracted the notice of the lovers of Greek literature; it was dedicated by the author to Casparus Uxama, or Osmi, a Spanish prelate, whom Michael met at Rome. Editions: the Greek text by Hervagius (Basle, 1558, 8vo); the text, with a Latin version and valuable notes, by P. Pantinus and A. Scholl, (Leyd. 1619, 4to); also cum Clavi Homerica, by George Perkins. See Cave, *Hist. Lit.* ad an. 1440; Fabricius, *Bibl. Græc.* xi, 189; Smith, *Dict. Greek and Rom. Biog. and Mythol.* s. v.

Michael Balsämon, a noted Eastern ecclesiastic, flourished in the latter half of the 15th century. He is supposed to have been a native of Constantinople, where he always lived. He was one of the Greek deputies sent in 1438 to the Council of Florence, discovered the secret intrigues of the Latins, and prognosticated the ultimate fate of the union of the two churches, to which he subscribed reluctantly. He wrote and addressed to the emperor Joannes Palæologus *Anaphora Cleri Constantinopolitani,* of which Leo Allatius gives a few fragments in his work *De Consensu utriusque Ecclesiæ.* See Cave, *Hist. Lit.* ad an. 1440; Fabricius, *Bibl. Græca,* x, 373, note.

Michael Bradacius, the first Moravian bishop, flourished originally as a Hussite priest at Zamberg, in the eastern part of Bohemia, about the middle of the 15th century. In 1467, when the Moravian Brethren (q. v.) separated from the National Church, and instituted a ministry of their own, Michael, who had in the mean time joined the Moravian Brethren, was sent, together with two other priests, to a Waldensian colony on the frontiers of Bohemia and Austria, in order to secure the episcopacy. These Waldenses were on friendly terms with the Calixtines, and openly fraternized with them at the mass. John Rokyzan, the Calixtine leader, who had ambitious projects with regard to the archiepiscopal chair at Prague, which had long been vacant, hoped to win the support of the Waldenses. Hence, when their ministry had become extinct, he induced bishop Philibert, who had come to Prague as a delegate of the Council of Basle, to ordain two members of the Waldensian colony, Frederick Nemez and John Wlach, as priests, on the 14th of September, 1433. In the summer of the following year (1434)—when the Taborites had been defeated by the Calixtines; when the utmost confusion prevailed throughout Bohemia in Church and State; when an open feud was raging between the council and the pope; when, however, the former did everything in its power to conciliate the Bohemians—these two Waldensian priests were consecrated bishops at Basle by bishops of the Roman Catholic Church. This act was meant as an example and encouragement for the Bohemians, that they might be the more ready to accept the compactata of the council. Nemez and Wlach consecrated other bishops, of whom two were living in 1467, the name of the senior being Stephen. He and his associate consecrated Michael Bradacius and his two companions, who thus became the first bishops of the Bohemian Brethren. A Church council was organized, of which Michael Bradacius was constituted the president. After a time he resigned the presidency in favor of Matthias of Kunwalde (q. v.), but remained in the council. He died at Reichenau in 1501. Zezschwitz, in his article *Lukas v. Prag,* in Herzog's *Real-Encykl.* vol. xx, calls in question the authenticity of the above narrative, but fails to make good his doubts. He is misled by preconceived notions against the Moravian episcopacy, as his article plainly shows. The transfer of the Waldensian episcopate to the Brethren is established by a number of documents, whose dates range from 1476 to 1600, in the "Lissa Folios," at Herrnhut (see MORAVIAN BRETHREN, THE ANCIENT); by the of-

ficial report (1478) of Wenzel Koranda, the administrator of the Utraquist Consistory at Prague (Palacky's *Geschichte v. Böhmen,* i, 191, 192); and by the earliest histories of Blahoslaw, Lasitius, Regenvolscius, and Comenius; while the origin of the Waldensian episcopacy is set forth in the official answers with which the Brethren met the attacks of the learned Jesuit, Wenzel Sturm, in the reign of Maximilian II. These answers were written by the assistant bishop Jaffet, and are preserved in the archives at Herrnhut. The validity of the episcopate of the Brethren was not doubted either by the Roman Catholic or by the National Church, and the fact that they had secretly secured it from the Waldenses brought about a severe persecution immediately after the truth became known (1468). Compare Benham's *Origin and Episcopate of the Boh. Breth.* (Lond. 1867); Schweinitz's *Moravian Episcopate* (Bethlehem, 1865); Palacky's *Geschichte v. Böhmen,* vii, 492; Gindely's *Geschichte d. B. B.* i, 37; Czerwenka's *Persekutionsbüchlein* (Gütersloh, 1869), c. xx, n. 31; Cröger's *Gesch. d. Alten Brüderkirche* (Gnadan, 1865), vol. i. (E. de S.)

Michael Cerularius, a noted Eastern ecclesiastic, flourished as patriarch of Constantinople near the middle of the 11th century. He gained great notoriety mainly by his violent attacks upon the Latin Church. He caused so much scandal that pope Leo IX sent cardinals Humbert and Frederick, with Peter, archbishop of Amalfi, to Constantinople in order to persuade Cerularius to a more moderate conduct. Their efforts were not only unsuccessful, but they were treated with such abuse that Humbert excommunicated the virulent patriarch. Cerularius in his turn excommunicated the three legates, and he caused the name of pope Leo IX to be erased from the diptychs. In 1057 he prevailed upon the emperor Michael Stratioticus to yield to his successful rival, Isaac Comnenus, whose interest he took care of for some time. Differences, however, soon broke out between them; and when he was once quarrelling with Isaac about the respective authority of the Church and the State, he impudently cried out, "I have given you the crown, and I know how to take it from you again." Banishment was his due reward, and Isaac was about to remove him from his see when death removed him from the earth (1058). Cerularius wrote: *Decisio Synodica de Nuptiis in Septimo Gradu:—De Matrimonio prohibito* (the former printed, Greek and Latin, in the third book, and fragments of the latter in the fourth book of Leunclavius, *Jus Græco-Roman.*):—*Epistolæ II ad Petrum Antiochenum* (Greek and Latin, in the second vol. of Cotelerius, *Eccles. Græc. Monument.*):—*De Sacerdotis Uxore Adulterio polluta* (in Cotelerius, *Patres Apostol.*):—$Σημείωμα$, s. *Edictum Synodale adversus Latinos de Pittacia, seu De Excommunicatione a Latinis Legatis in ipsum ab ipso in Legatos vibrata, anno* 1054, *die septimo Junii factum* (Græce et Latine, in Leo Allatius, *De Libr. Eccles. Græcis*):—*Homilia* (ed. Græce et Latine, by Montfaucon, under the title *Epistola Synodi Niceanæ ad Sanctam Alexandriæ Ecclesiam* [Paris, 1715, fol.]). There are, farther, extant in MS. fragments of several letters, as *Contra Rebelles Abbates, Contra Armenios, De Homicidio facto in Ecclesia, De Episcoporum Judiciis,* etc. See Cave, *Hist Lit.* ad an. 1043; Fabricius, *Bibl. Græc.* xi, 195, 196.

Michael Glycas, a noted ecclesiastical historian of the Greek Church of the 12th century (some place him as late as the 15th), was a native of Sicily, and flourished about A.D. 1120. His most important production, the *Annales Quadripartiti,* is a work not only historical, but also philosophical and theological. Part I describes the creation of the world in six days; Part II extends from the creation to the birth of Christ; Part III to Constantine the Great; and Part IV to the death of Alexius Comnenus, A.D. 1118. It was published in Gr. and Lat., with notes, by Labbe (Paris, 1660, fol.). Glycas also wrote *Disputationculæ II,* and likewise many epistles, of which fragments are preserved.

Michael Monăchus, a theologian of the Church of the East, flourished as presbyter at Constantinople probably towards the close of the 9th century. He is noted as the author of *Encomium Ignatii Patriarchæ* (who died in 877), edited, Greek and Latin, in a very mutilated form, by Raderus in his *Acta Concilii* (Ingolstadt, 1604, 4to), also in the eighth vol. of the *Concilia:* —*Encomium in Angelicorum Ordinum Ductores, Michælem et Gabrielem:*—*Encomium in gloriosum Christi Apostolum Philippum:*—Perhaps *Vita et Miracula S'ti Nicolai:*—*Vita Theodori Studitæ,* of which Baronius gives some fragments in his *Annales* ad an. 795 and 826. The complete text, with a Latin translation, was published by Jacobus de la Baune, in the fifth vol. of *Opera Sirmondi* (Paris, 1696, fol.). The life of Theodore Studita, as well as one or two of the other productions, was perhaps written by another Michael Monachus, a contemporary and survivor of Studita, who died as early as 826. The author of this life was a very incompetent writer. Cave, *Hist. Lit.* ad an. 876; Fabricius, *Biblioth. Grœc.* ix, 505.

Michael Psellus, Jr., a noted Greek philosopher and teacher, flourished at Constantinople from 1020 to 1105, as teacher of theology and philosophy. He is noted as the writer of Διδασκαλία παντοδαπή in Fabricius, *Biblioth. Grœca* (vol. x):—Περὶ δυνάμεων τῆς ψυχῆς, edited by Tarin (Par. 1618 sq.):—a Paraphrase of Aristotle's Περὶ ἑρμενείας (Ven. 1503):—Synopsis of Aristotle's *Organon,* edited by Ehlinger (Augsb. 1597): —Commentary on Aristotle's *Natural Philosophy,* in Lat. by Camotius (Ven. 1554):—Περὶ τῶν πέντε φωνῶν of Porphyrius (Basle, 1542):—Περὶ ἐνεργείας δαιμόνων, edited by Gaulinenus (Paris, 1615). See Leo Allatius, *De Psellis eorumque scriptis* (Rome, 1634); Ueberweg, *Hist. Philos.* i, 404; Enfield, *Hist. Philos.* p. 474.

Michael Scotus, a learned author of the 13th century, was born at Durham, England; or, as some assert, at Balweary, Scotland. He attended lectures at Oxford, and afterwards at Paris, and devoted himself to the study of mathematics and Oriental languages. Emperor Frederick II, who reigned at that time in Germany, was the most prominent protector of art and sciences, and Michael went to his court, studying medicine and chemistry. After a stay of several years in Germany, he returned to England, where he became a great favorite of king Edward II. He died in 1291, at a very advanced age. Michael Scotus was celebrated on account of his knowledge in secret arts and magic (comp. Dante, *Inferno*, xx, 115–118). It is said that his books on magic were buried with him. He was also actively engaged in the translation of Aristotle, which was made by command of emperor Frederick II, and was afterwards printed at Venice in 1496: *Aristotelis opera Latine versa, partim e Grœco, partim e Arabico, per viros lectos et in utriusque linguæ prolatione peritos, jussu imperatoris Fridirici II.* He probably translated the natural philosophy of Aristotle from the Arabic version of Avicenna. Michael is the author of *De secretis naturæ, sive de procreatione hominis et physiognomia,* and of the *Quæstio curiosa de natura solis et lunæ,*" i. e. of gold and silver. He has also been considered the author of *Mensa philosophica seu enchiridion, in quo de quæstionibus mensalibus et variis ac jucundis hominum congressibus agitur,* which has been printed several times. This latter work, however, has been attributed, by some at least, to Theobald Anguilbertus, a learned Irishman, who lived about the year 1500 as doctor of medicine and philosophy at Paris. See Tennemann, *Manual Hist. Philos.* p. 223; Wetzer u. Welte, *Kirchen-Lexikon,* s. v.

Michael VIII, surnamed PALÆOLŎGUS (ὁ Παλαιολόγος), emperor of Nicæa, and afterwards of Constantinople, from A.D. 1260 to 1282, the restorer of the Greek empire, and the laborer for the "unity of the Church," was born of noble parentage in 1234. At an early age he rose to eminence, which he owed more to his uncommon talents than to his illustrious birth. He was in great favor with the emperor Theodore (II) Lascaris. This sovereign died in August, 1259, leaving a son, John III, who was only nine years old, and over whom he had placed the patriarch Arsenius, and the magnus domesticus Muzalon, as guardians. Michael, the friend of the soldiers, was determined to secure for himself the place of Muzalon, who was despatched by the imperial guard, and Michael Palæologus, whom Theodore shortly before his decease had appointed magnus dux, was chosen as guardian instead, and soon afterwards received or gave himself the title and power of despot. Next he made himself master of the imperial treasury, bribed or gained the Varangian guard and the clergy, and secured his proclamation as emperor at Magnesia. Michael and the boy John were crowned together at Nicæa, on the 1st of January, 1260. While the event was hailed with satisfaction at home, it failed to secure friends abroad. The Latins, especially, were dissatisfied; assumed a haughty tone towards Michael, and demanded the cession of those parts of Thrace and Macedonia which belonged to Nicæa, as a condition of acknowledging him as emperor. But Michael treated the Latin ambassadors with ridicule, and, in answer, took prompt measures for driving the Latins out of Constantinople; and, before the end of the year 1260, Baldwin II was shut up within his capital. Michael, however, was not strong enough to reduce the city, and was obliged to convert the siege into a blockade; until one day, one Curtrizacus, the commander of a body of volunteer auxiliaries, was informed of the existence of a subterranean passage leading from a place outside the walls into the cellar of a house within them, and which seemed not to be generally known. Upon the strength of this information, a plan was formed for the surprise of the garrison by means of the passage, and, after concerting measures with the commander-in-chief, he ventured with fifty men through the passage into the city. His plan succeeded completely. No sooner was he within than he took possession of the nearest gate, disarmed the post, opened it, and the main body of the Greeks rushed in. The stratagem was executed in the dead of night. The inhabitants, roused from their slumber, soon learned the cause of the noise, and kept quiet within their houses, or joined their daring countrymen. The Latins, dispersed in various quarters, were seized with a panic, and fled in all directions, while the emperor Baldwin had scarcely time to leave his palace and escape on board of a Venetian galley, which carried him immediately to Italy. On the morning of the 25th of July, 1261, Constantinople was in the undisputed possession of the Greeks, after it had borne the yoke of the Latins during fifty-seven years, three months, and thirteen days.

Michael, informed of the success of his arms, lost no time in repairing to Constantinople; and on the 14th of August held his triumphal entrance, saluted by the people with demonstrations of the sincerest joy. Constantinople, however, was no more what it had been. During the reign of the Latins plunder, rapine, and devastation had spoiled it of its former splendor; trade had deserted its harbor, and thousands of opulent families had abandoned the palaces or mansions of their forefathers in order to avoid contact with the hated foreigners. To restore, repeople, and readorn Constantinople was now Michael's principal task; and, in order to accomplish his purpose the better, he confirmed the extensive privileges which the Venetian, the Genoese, and the Pisan merchants had received from the Latin emperors. Although the Nicæan emperors considered themselves the legitimate successors of Constantine the Great, the possession of Constantinople was an event of such magnitude as to suggest to Michael the idea of a new coronation, which was accordingly solemnized in the cathedral of St. Sophia. But Michael was crowned alone, without John—an evil omen for the friends of the young emperor, whose fears were but too soon realized, for on

Christmas-day of the same year, 1261, John was deprived of sight and sent into exile to a distant fortress. This hateful crime caused a general indignation among the people, and might have proved the ruin of Michael had he been a man of a less energetic turn of mind. The patriarch Arsenius, coguardian to John, was irreconcilable; he fearlessly pronounced excommunication upon the imperial criminal, and years of trouble and commotion elapsed before Michael was readmitted into the communion of the faithful by the second successor of Arsenius, the patriarch Joseph.

The loss of Constantinople pope Urban IV regarded as robbing him of the hope of effecting a union between the Latin and the Greek churches, and he therefore urged the European princes to undertake a crusade against the Greek schismatics; but Michael avoided the danger by promising the pope to do his utmost in order to effect himself a mediation between the belligerents, and, as both the parties were tired of bloodshed, peace was soon restored (1263). In 1265 Arsenius was deposed, because he would not revoke the excommunication he had pronounced against the emperor; whereupon the prelate's adherents, the Arsenites, caused a schism which lasted till 1312. See ARSENIUS. In this skilful manner he also avoided troubles which threatened him in 1269, when Charles, king of Sicily, took up arms on pretence of restoring the fugitive Baldwin to the throne, and forthwith marching upon Constantinople, placed the capital in jeopardy. Michael, afraid that these hostilities were only the forerunners of a general crusade of all the Latin princes against him, made prompt proposals for a union of the Greek Church with that of Rome. The learned Veccus, accompanied by several of the most distinguished among the Greek clergy, were sent to the council which was called to assemble at Lyons in 1274; and there the union was effected by the Greeks giving way in the much disputed doctrine of the procession of the Holy Ghost, and submitting to the supremacy of the pope. See LYONS, II. The union, however, was desired only by a minority of the Greeks, and the orthodox majority accordingly did their utmost to prevent the measure from being carried out. Michael, in his turn, supported his policy with force. The patriarch Joseph was deposed, and Veccus appointed in his stead; cruel punishment was inflicted upon all those who opposed the union; and Greece was shaken by a religious commotion which forms a remarkable event in the ecclesiastical history of the East. As space forbids us to dwell here longer upon these important transactions, we can only remark that the union was never effectually carried out, and was entirely abandoned upon the death of Michael. See FILIOQUE; GREEK CHURCH.

The manifest duplicity and the cruelty with which the emperor behaved finally made him odious to his own subjects and contemptible to his Latin friends, and the latter part of his reign was an uninterrupted series of domestic troubles and foreign wars. His dearly-bought friendship with the Latin, and especially the Italian powers, was brought to a very speedy end. Upon the decease of the ex-emperor Baldwin, his son Philip assumed the imperial title, and formed an alliance between pope Martin IV, Charles of Anjou, king of Sicily, and the Venetians, with a view of reconquering Constantinople and dividing the Greek empire. But the invaders failed, and Michael, not satisfied with the glory of his arms and the material benefit he derived from his victory, resolved to take terrible revenge: he paid twenty thousand ounces of gold towards equipping a Catalan fleet, with which king Peter of Aragon was to attack Sicily; and the "Sicilian Vespers," in which eight thousand Frenchmen were massacred, and in consequence of which Sicily was wrested from Charles of Anjou and united with Aragon, were in some degree the work of Michael's fury. In the autumn of 1282 he fell ill, and died Dec. 11, 1282, leaving the renown of a successful but treacherous tyrant. See Niceph. Gregor. lib. iv-v;

Acropol. c. 76, etc.; Phranz. lib. i; Pachymeres, *Historia Rerum a Michaele Palæologa gestarum* (1666); Neale, *Hist. of the East. Ch.* ii, 311 sq.; Hase, *Ch. Hist.* p. 269, 354 sq.; Schröckh, *Kirchengeschichte,* xxviii, 315 sq.; Gieseler, *Eccles. Hist.* iii, 232, 413; Ffoulkes, *Divisions in Christendom,* vol. i; Neander, *Ch. Hist.* viii, 264; Hardwick, *Ch. Hist. of the Middle Ages,* p. 279-282; Hefele, *Conciliengeschichte,* vol. iv; Smith, *Dict. of Greek and Roman Biogr.* s. v.

Michaelensi, JEAN, a Swiss theologian of the 12th century, the date of whose birth and death are unknown, figured as a bishop of Lausanne in 1166. We know so little of his life that we cannot say whether this same Michaelensi was the one that assisted at the Council of Troyes in 1128, and who was commissioned to draw up a body of rules for the Temple order. These rules have often been reprinted, but appeared for the first time in the *Chronique de Citeaux,* by Aubert Lemire. They have also been attributed to Saint Bernard, but without foundation. See, for the scanty information accessible, Fleury, *Hist. Ecclés.* liv. 67, n. 55; Mabillon, *Op. S. Bernarde,* i, 571; *Hist. Littér. de la France,* xi, 66; Ruchat, *Abrégé de l'Histoire Ecclés. du pays de Vaud.* p. 75.

Michaelis is the name of a German family distinguished in the Protestant theological world. The following are the most eminent members of this family:

1. CHRISTIAN BENEDIKT was born at Elrich, in Hohnstein, Jan. 26, 1680. He was educated at Halle, and in 1713 was made a professor extraordinary of philosophy, and in 1731 ordinary professor of theology at his alma mater. In 1738 he was transferred to the departments of Greek and Oriental literature. He died Feb. 22, 1764. He was not a very prolific writer, but his few productions display unusual talent and ripe scholarship. He was a thorough master of the Biblical languages, particularly the Hebrew. His principal works are, 1. *On Hebrew Grammar and Philology: Dissertatio, qua solœcismus casuum ab Ebraismo S. Codicis depellitur* (Halle, 1729):—*Dissert. qua solœcismus generis a Syntaxi S. Codicis Ebraici depellitur* (Halle, 1739):—a treatise against the etymological hypothesis, defended by Hermann Hardt and others, that Hebrew and the cognate tongues were derived from Greek (Halle, 1726): —a treatise on the Hebrew points, in which he took the side of Capellus (Halle, 1739):—a dissertation on *Scripture Paronomasia* (Halle, 1737):—a disputation on *Hebrew Ellipses* (Halle, 1724). 2. *On Biblical Exegesis: De Herba Borith* (Halle, 1728):—*De Idumœa et ejus Antiq. Historia* (Halle, 1733):—*Philologemata Medica* (in which he discusses certain points of the *ars medica* of the Bible):—*Observationes philologicæ de nominibus propriis Ebræis,* a work which was a worthy predecessor of Simon's *Onomasticon V. T.*:—*Dissertatio philologica de antiquitatibus œconomiæ patriarchalis* (reprinted in Ugolino, *Thesaur.* xxiv, 323). In the year 1749 he published *Tractatus criticus de variis lectionibus N. T. caute colligendis et dijudicandis,* an elaborate treatise on the various readings of the Greek Testament, exhibiting proofs of an accurate critical judgment. It gives some account of the MSS. known in his day, both Greek and Latin; of the ancient versions, and of the patristic quotations. We must not omit to mention his co-operation with his uncle, *Johann Heinrich Michaelis* (q. v.), in the valuable commentary on the *Hagiographa.* Our author contributed the annotations on the Proverbs, Lamentations, and Daniel. He was also associated with J. H. Michaelis in a commentary on the first two of the greater prophets. Simultaneously with the work of the latter on Isaiah, noticed above, appeared C. B. Michaelis's treatise, *De Jeremia et de Vaticinio ejus* (Halle, 1712). In the year 1736 he published a short work, *De vaticinio Amosi prophetæ.* See Kitto, *Cyclop. Bibl. Lit.* s. v.; Herzog, *Real-Encyklopädie,* s. v.

2. JOHANN DAVID, one of the ablest of Germany's theologians, and son of the preceding, was born at Halle

Feb. 27, 1717. After receiving instruction for some time from private tutors, Michaelis spent four years in the Orphan School at Halle, where his attention was particularly directed to languages and philosophy. In 1733 he began to attend the lectures at the university, and it was here that he obtained from the chancellor Ludwig's lectures on German history the foundation of that knowledge of general law and of the constitution of society which was afterwards displayed in his *Mosaisches Recht*. (See below.) In 1740 he visited England, where he made the acquaintance of several eminent scholars both in London and in Oxford. During part of his residence in England he preached in the German chapel at St. James's Palace. On his return to Germany, he devoted himself to the study of history, Oriental languages, and Biblical criticism. Upon the death of the chancellor Ludwig, Michaelis was commissioned to arrange and catalogue his immense library. The catalogue was published in 1745, and is considered a model for such works. Michaelis published his first book in 1739. It was a *Dissertatio de Punctuorum Hebr. Antiquitate*, and was quite ultra-orthodox, written in the Buxtorfian manner. But later he appears to have joined the school of Schultens, if we may judge by the Hebrew Grammar he published in 1745. The pietistic air of Halle finally led him to accept the proffered position at Göttingen, and he removed to that place in 1746, and there he spent the rest of his life, although he was invited by Frederick the Great in 1763 to return to Prussia. To the University of Göttingen Michaelis rendered the most important services as professor of theology and Oriental literature from 1745 to 1791; as secretary and director of the Royal Society of Sciences, from 1751 to 1770, when he left it on account of some differences with the members; as editor of the journal entitled *Gelehrte Anzeigen*, from 1753 to 1770; and as librarian and director of the philological seminary, which would have been abandoned after the death of Gesner in 1761 if Michaelis had not consented to direct it gratuitously.

In order to throw new light upon Biblical science, Michaelis planned the expedition to Arabia and India which was conducted by Carsten Niebuhr. The first project of this enterprise was submitted in the year 1756 to baron Von Bernstorff, then minister of Frederick V, king of Denmark. The course of the travellers was directed mainly by Michaelis, who drew up a series of questions for their guidance. These questions discuss the most interesting points of Biblical science—sacred geography, Oriental habits and customs, natural productions mentioned in the Bible, and diseases which still affect men in the East as they did of old. "The perspicuity, and precision, and learning with which our author proposes the questions, and the information in answer to them obtained by Niebuhr and Forskål (as embodied in the *Voyage en Arabie* and *Description de l'Arabie* of the former, and in the *Descriptiones Animalium*, etc., of the latter), strikingly illustrate the sagacity of Michaelis; and the literary results of the expedition, though short of the exaggerated expectations of the time, have, in the shape of five quarto volumes, been permanently beneficial to Biblical science. In 1775 Michaelis was made a knight of the Polar Star by the king of Sweden; in 1786 he was appointed an Aulic counsellor of Hanover, and in 1789 he was elected a Fellow of the Royal Society of London. He was also a member of the Academy of Inscriptions, Paris. He died Aug. 22, 1791.

The works of Michaelis are very numerous; the following are some of the most important. In Oriental literature, grammars of Hebrew, Chaldee, Syriac, and Arabic, and treatises on various subjects connected with these languages: *Orientalische und Exegetische Bibliothek* (a valuable periodical commenced by Michaelis in 1771, and of which he conducted 24 vols.) :—*Supplementa in Lexica Hebraica* (6 pts. in 2 vols. 4to—useful, not more for the language illustrated, than for the information afforded on Biblical geography, archæology, and

natural history. In philosophy: an essay *On the Influence of Opinions on Language, and of Language on Opinions*, which obtained a prize from the Prussian Academy of Sciences in 1759; a treatise on *moral philosophy*, and other works. In history, geography, and chronology: *Spicilegium Geographiæ Hebræorum exteræ post Bochartum* (Götting. 1769, 1780); other treatises on geography and chronology; several separate dissertations on the laws and antiquities of the Jews, the substance of most of which is embodied in his *Mosaisches Recht*, in 6 vols. 1770-75; a second edition of the first 5 vols. of this work was published in the years 1775-80. This work, which is considered the masterpiece of Michaelis, was translated into English by Dr. Alexander Smith, under the title of *Commentaries on the Laws of Moses* (1814, 4 vols. 8vo). "The great object of Michaelis in this work is to investigate and illustrate the philosophy of the Mosaic laws, to show their wonderful adaptation in every respect to the very peculiar circumstances in which the people to whom they were given had been placed by Providence; and, while he takes every opportunity of establishing the claims of Moses to the character of an ambassador from heaven, to inculcate upon human legislators the important lesson of studying those particulars respecting the nature and political situation, the ideas and prejudices, the manners and customs of their countrymen, by attention to which alone they can ever hope to make them virtuous, prosperous, and happy" (Dr. Smith's Preface, p. xvii). In Biblical criticism, Michaelis's *Introduction to the New Testament* is well known in England by the translation of the late bishop Marsh; he also published part of an *Introduction to the Old Testament; a Translation of the Bible, with Notes, for the Unlearned;* a monograph on the three chief Messianic psalms (viz. x, xl, cx), in which he ably defended their prophetic character (comp. cardinal Wiseman, *Lectures*, p. 378); a commentary on the *Book of Maccabees* (1778); on *Ecclesiastes* (1762). He also wrote an able vindication of the sacred narrative on *the Burial and Resurrection of Christ according to the Four Evangelists* (Halle, 1783; English transl. 1827); and published learned notes on an edition of bishop Lowth's *Sacra Poesis Hebræorum* (reprinted in the Oxford edition, with further annotations by E. F. C. Rosenmüller, 1821).

Johann David Michaelis has been in many respects more influential as a Biblical writer than any other of the numerous savants whom Germany has produced within the last 150 years. He exhibited an indomitable energy in the prosecution of his studies, and, hurried forward by an inquiring spirit, he could not fail to produce valuable writings. Unfortunately, however, he was inconsistent as a writer. Anxious to adhere to the established system of Lutheranism, he displayed outwardly great respect for the Christian religion, while he was really too light-minded, as he himself acknowledges, to adopt their tone of pious feeling. It is true, however, that his early pietistic training nevertheless sustained in him a certain conviction of the truth of Christianity. He endeavored constantly, by new and singularly ingenious theories, to remove objections to Christianity; and, much to the surprise of his younger contemporaries, whose rationalistic views were ripening apace, he held to the last many parts of the older system, which they had either modified or thrown aside. The melancholy consequences, however, of this merely natural persuasion are abundantly manifest. Destitute of that conviction which alone can give a comprehensive insight into the real character of revelation, and the harmonious relation of its several parts, he had no guide to enable him to perceive what might be safely admitted without detriment to the system itself; he consequently, according to the usual custom of persons taking only a partial view of subjects, frequently opposed the objection, instead of the principle on which the objection was founded; endeavored to remove it by theories in conformity with mere human systems, and strengthened it equally by his concessions and by his own inadequate and arbitrary defences. Possessed of no settled principles, every minute difficulty presented itself with intrinsic force and perplexity to his mind; his belief was a reed ready to be shaken by every fresh breeze; all that he had previously gained seemed again staked on the issue of each petty skirmish; and, in the very descriptive comparison of Lessing, he was like the timid soldier who loses his life before an outpost, without once seeing the country of which he would gain possession. The theological opinions of this celebrated man are never to be trusted; and, indeed, the serious student cannot but be disgusted with the levity which too frequently appears in his writings, and the gross obscenity which frequently defiles them. After all drawbacks, however, the discriminating and careful student will seldom consult Michaelis without benefiting by his erudition and clearness of illustration; and often will he find objections on Scripture refuted with much force and felicitous originality. Dr. Tholuck describes Michaelis as one of the chief pioneers of neology, though not because he indulged in bold neological assumptions, but because he was devoid of religious life, retaining only the external form of orthodoxy, but abandoning its essence and spirit (comp. Tholuck, *Vermischte Schriften*, ii, 130). See *Lebensbeschreibung von ihm selbst abgefasst* (Leipsic and Rinteln, 1793); C. G. Heyne, *Elogium J. D. Michaelis* (1791); Kitto, *Cyclop. Bibl. Lit.* s. v.; *English Cyclop.* s. v.; Döring, *Gelehrte Theol. Deutschlands*, vol. ii, s. v.; Hagenbach, *Ch. Hist. of the 18th and 19th Centuries*, i, 157 sq.; Kahnis, *Hist. of German Protestantism*, p. 120.

3. JOHANN FRIEDRICH, another writer of this family, a pupil of Danzius, is the author of a philological dissertation on the derivation and meaning of the sacred name אֱלֹהִים (reprinted in Ugolino, *Thesaur.* xxiv, 105–138). With this treatise it is worth while to compare J. D. Michaelis's remarks, *Supplement. ad Lex. Hebraic.* p. 85–87; and Gesenius, *Thesaur.* p. 95–99.

4. JOHANN GEORG, who flourished as divinity professor at Halle, was born at Zerbst May 22, 1690; was educated at the University of Franeker; in 1715 entered the ministry; in 1717 accepted a position in the gymnasium at Frankfort-on-the-Oder; and in 1730 was promoted to a professorship in the university then at that place. In 1735 he was called to Halle, and died there July 16, 1758. He is the author of several learned works; one, on the famous Catechetical School of Alexandria, was first published in 1739; another work is entitled *De progressu et incremento doctrinæ salutaris inde a protevangelio usque ad Noachum* (1752); he is, however, better known for his *Observationes Sacræ*, a volume of great and varied erudition, comprising certain disputations which he had held at the University of Frankfort. This volume was published at Utrecht in 1738; we add the titles of such as claim mention in this work: *De incisura propter mortuos:—De Elisæo, a propro puerorum Bethlehensium justo Dei judicio vindicato:—De cane, symbolo prophetæ:—De Spiritu Sancto, sub externo linguarum ignearum symbolo Apostolis communicato:—De crustulis quotidianis pontificis maximi:—De Sacerdote, ex ministerio suffitus non divite*. In Ugolino, *Thesaur.* xi. 727–748, there occurs a valuable dissertation, *De Thuribulo Adyti*, in which our author fully considers the high-priest's sacrificial duties on the great day of atonement, and takes occasion to illustrate, in an interesting manner, the priesthood of Christ in some of its features as indicated in the Epistle to the Hebrews (ix, 7–15). See Döring, *Gelehrte Theol. Deutschlands*, ii, 516 sq.; Kitto, *Cyclop. Bibl. Lit.* s. v. (J. H.W.)

5. JOHANN HEINRICH, upon the whole, the most accurately learned of all the accomplished members of his family, was born at Klettenberg, in Hohnstein, July 26, 1668. He studied Oriental literature for some years at Frankfort-on-the-Oder, where he had the celebrated Ludolf for his instructor in Ethiopic. He next

studied for a time at Leipsic, and then removed to Halle, the head-quarters of Spener's influence, and became librarian to the university, later professor of the Oriental languages, and eventually of divinity. Halle was at that time the most renowned of the German universities; its professors were eminent men, and its schools crowded with eager students, and J. Heinrich Michaelis was the soul of the place. In connection with A. H. Franke, he instituted the *Collegium Orientale Theologicum*, a seminary for instruction in the Biblical languages. Fifty years before Kennicott's publication, J. H. Michaelis, after some thirty years' conscientious labor, led the way in Old-Testament textual criticism by issuing from the press a carefully-edited Hebrew Bible (Halle, 1720, 2 vols. 4to). Kennicott, who was impetuous in judgment, spoke slightingly of this work, as if the author, from favor of the Masoretic text, had improperly used his manuscripts (see Kennicott's *Annual Account of Hebrew Collections*, p. 146). He afterwards modified his opinion in the following statement, which we extract, as giving a good description of Michaelis's labors: "This edition was the first which contained any various readings collected from Hebrew MSS. by a Christian editor. The text is taken from Jablonski's edition, with some few emendations. . . . There were collated for this Bible most of the best printed editions, and also five Hebrew MSS. belonging to the library at Erfurt; two of which contain the verses in Joshua excluded by the Masora. The propriety of selecting various readings from Hebrew MSS. and ancient versions is set forth in the preface" (*Hist. of Hebr. Text. Dissert.* ii, 487, Teller's ed. p. 465). Three quarto volumes of exegesis, in the shape of a commentary on the *Hagiographa*, entitled *Annotationes Philologico-Exegeticæ in Hagiographis* (Halle, 1720), accompanied the critical text. This is a work of still acknowledged value. J. H. Michaelis was the general editor of the whole work; but he received assistance from his nephew, and from Rambach in portions of it. The annotations on the Psalms, Job, Canticles, Ezra, and the Chronicles were contributed by him (on the critical merit of our author, see Wiseman, *Connection between Science*, etc. 2d ed. p. 349). Other works of his, worthy of mention here, are, a dissertation, *De Paradiso:*—a tract, *De peculiaribus Hebræorum loquendi modis* (Halle, 1702):—*De Iesaia propheta ejusque vaticinio* (Halle, 1710):—and on the N. T., *De textu N. T. Græco* (Halle, 1707:—*Introductio in Jacobi epistolam* (Halle, 1722, 4to). Johann Heinrich Michaelis died in 1738. See Döring, *Gelehrte Theol. Deutschlands*, vol. ii, s. v.; Herzog, *Real-Encyklopädie*, ix, 522 sq.

Michaelis, Sebastien, a French Dominican, was born in 1543, at Saint-Zacharie, Provence. He introduced reforms into many houses of his order, for which, with the consent of the court of Rome, he raised a particular congregation. Michaelis was the first vicar-general of this body, and, after having refused in 1579 the bishopric of Fréjus, became prior of the new convent of the Friar Preachers at Paris in 1613. He may be regarded as the restorer of the Order of St. Dominic in France, a work with which in our days Lacordaire's name has figured prominently. Besides some religious works, he wrote *L'Histoire véritable de ce qui s'est passé sous l'exorcisme de trois filles possédées au pays de Flandre, avec un Traité des Sorciers et des Magiciens* (Paris, 1623, 2 vols. 8vo); and edited Le Fevre, *Calendrier historique et chronologique de l'Église de Paris*. See Hoefer, *Nouv. Biog. Générale*, s. v.

Michaelius, JONAS, a Reformed (Dutch) minister, the *first* minister of the Reformed Church in America, was born in 1577; was educated at Leyden University; settled in Holland in 1612–16, in St. Salvador in 1624–25, in Guinea in 1626–27, and then migrated to this country, and arrived at Manhattan (now New York) in 1628. He organized a consistory, administered the sacraments, and performed all the functions of a minister of the Gospel. In 1633 he was succeeded by the Rev. Everardus Bogardus, who was accompanied by Adam Roelandsen, the first schoolmaster. After a few years of service he returned to Holland, and "the Classis of Amsterdam wished to send him back to New York in 1637, but he did not return. At his first communion here he had fifty communicants. He paints a sad picture of the low condition of the natives, and proposes to let the parents go and try to educate the children. His letter breathes a spirit of deep piety, and of submission to the divine will in all his bereavements." His wife died in 1628, only seven weeks after their arrival in this country, leaving him with three small children. This letter, and other particulars respecting this pioneer of the Dutch churches in this country, are found in *Colonial Hist. of New York*, ii, 759-770. See also Corwin's *Manual Ref. Church*, p. 164. (W. J. R. T.)

Michaelmas, a day which, according to the Church of Rome, was set apart to express her thankfulness to God for the many benefits she had received by the ministry of holy angels; and called Michaelmas because St. Michael is alluded to in Scripture as an angel of great power and dignity, and as presiding and watching over the Church of God with particular vigilance and application, and as triumphant over the devil. It originated in some provincial festivities which were introduced between the 3d and 9th centuries, and which were then combined into one common celebration on the 29th of September, the day on which St. Michael's Church on Mount Garganus was dedicated, as mentioned in the Saxon Chronicle in 1011, and in Ethelred's laws in 1014. There is a tradition that this feast was instituted by Alexander, bishop of Alexandria. It was generally observed in the 8th century; in the 12th century by the Council of Mayence, and indeed by the whole Greek Church, in accordance with an injunction of the emperor Manuel Comnenus. The apparition of St. Michael, "the prince seraphim, leader of the angelic hosts, prefect of Paradise, and conductor of souls to the place of repose," to whom cemetery chapels and churches on hills were in consequence dedicated, was observed on the 8th of May. In the 10th century there was a curious superstition that on every Monday morning St. Michael held high mass in the churches.

The Greek and other Eastern churches, the Church of England, as well as several other evangelical churches, continue to observe the Feast of St. Michael, according to Wheatly, in order "that the people may know what benefits Christians receive by the ministry of angels" (*On the Common Prayer*, p. 190).

The Romish Church, besides observing St. Michaelmas, also celebrates three appearances of St. Michael, which have happened (we are told) in these later years. The first is the appearance of this archangel at Colossus, in Phrygia; but at what time the Romanists do not know themselves. They observe Sept. 6 as the day. The second is that of Mount Garganus, in the kingdom of Naples, about the end of the 5th century. May 8 is set apart as the day to commemorate the event. The third is his reputed appearance to Aubert, bishop of Avranches, upon a rock called the *Tomb*, where now stands the abbey of St. Michael. This was about 706. October 16 is observed in memory of this event. See Broughton, *Biblioth. Hist. Sacra*, ii, 93; Procter, *On the Book of Common Prayer*, p. 301; Wheatly, *On the Common Prayer*, p. 253; Butler, *Lives of Fathers, Martyrs, and Saints*, ii, 94; iii, 177; Michaelis, *Denkwürdigkeiten a. d. christl. Archäol.* iii, 28 sq.

Mi'chah (Heb. as in MICAIAH), a son of Uzziel and a Kohathite priest (1 Chron. xxiv, 24, 25); elsewhere (1 Chron. xxiii, 20) more correctly Anglicized MICAH (q.v.).

Michaï'ah (for the Heb., etc., see MICAIAH), the name of several men and one woman.

1. The queen-mother of king Abijah (2 Chron. xiii, 2); elsewhere (2 Chron. xi, 20) called MAACHAH (q. v.).

2. One of the national chieftains to whom Jehosha-

phat gave orders to instruct the people of the various cities of Judah in the sacred law (2 Chron. xvii, 7). B.C. 910.

3. The father of Achbor, which latter was one of the courtiers (perhaps a Levite) sent by Josiah to inquire of the prophetess Huldah concerning the newly-discovered copy of the Pentateuch (2 Kings xxii, 12). B.C. ante 623. In the parallel passage (2 Chron. xxxiv, 20) he is called MICAH, and his father's name is written Abdon.

4. The son of Gemariah and grandson of Shaphan: after having heard Baruch read the terrible predictions of Jeremiah in his father's hall, he went, apparently with good intentions, to report to the king's officers what he had heard (Jer. xxxvi, 11-13). B.C. 605. "Michaiah was the third in descent of a princely family, whose names are recorded in connection with important religious transactions. His grandfather Shaphan was the scribe, or secretary, of king Josiah, to whom Hilkiah the high-priest first delivered the book of the law which he said he had found in the House of Jehovah—Shaphan first perusing the book himself, and then reading it aloud to the youthful king (2 Kings xxii, 10). It was from his father Gemariah's chamber in the Temple that Baruch read the prophecies of Jeremiah in the ears of all the people. Moreover, Gemariah was one of the three who made intercession to king Zedekiah, although in vain, that he would not burn the roll containing Jeremiah's prophecies." See JEREMIAH.

5. The son of Zaccur and father of Mattaniah, Levites ("priests' sons") of the line of Asaph (Neh. xii, 35). B.C. considerably ante 446.

6. One of the priests who celebrated with trumpets the completion of the walls of Jerusalem after the exile (Neh. xii, 41). B.C. 446.

Mi'chal (Heb. *Mikal'*, מִיכַל, *rivulet*, as in 2 Sam. xvii, 20; Sept. Μεχόλ v. r. Μελχόλ; Josephus, Μιχάλα, *Ant.* vi, 11, 4), the younger of king Saul's two daughters (1 Sam. xiv, 49), doubtless by his wife Ahinoam (1 Sam. xiv, 50). In the following statement of the Biblical history, we chiefly dwell upon those points that relate to his successor. See DAVID.

The king had proposed to bestow on David his eldest daughter Merab; but before the marriage could be arranged an unexpected turn was given to the matter by the behavior of Michal, who fell violently in love with the young hero. The marriage with her elder sister was at once put aside. Saul eagerly caught at the opportunity which the change offered him of exposing his rival to the risk of death. The price fixed on Michal's hand was no less than the slaughter of a hundred Philistines. For these the usual "dowry" by which, according to the custom of the East, from the time of Jacob down to the present day, the father is paid for his daughter, was relinquished. David by a brilliant feat doubled the tale of victims, and Michal became his wife (1 Sam. xviii, 20-28). What her age was we do not know—her husband cannot have been more than twenty. B.C. cir. 1063.

It was not long before the strength of her affection was put to the proof. They seem to have been living at Gibeah, then the head-quarters of the king and the army. After one of Saul's attacks of frenzy, in which David had barely escaped being transfixed by the king's great spear, Michal learned that the house was watched by the myrmidons of Saul, and that it was intended on the next morning to attack her husband as he left his door (1 Sam. xix, 11). That the intention was real was evident from the behavior of the king's soldiers, who paraded round and round the town, and "returning" to the house "in the evening," with loud cries, more like the yells of the savage dogs of the East than the utterances of human beings, "belched out" curses and lies against the young warrior who had so lately shamed them all (Psa. lix, 3, 6, 7, 12). Michal seems to have known too well the vacillating and ferocious disposition of her father when in these dæmoniacal moods. The attack was ordered for the morning; but before the morning arrives the king will probably have changed his mind and hastened his stroke. So, like a true soldier's wife, she meets stratagem by stratagem. She first provided for David's safety by lowering him out of the window; to gain time for him to reach the residence of Samuel, she next dressed up the bed as if still occupied by him; one of her teraphim, or household gods, was laid in the bed, its head enveloped, like that of a sleeper, in the usual net (so Ewald, *Gesch.* iii, 101, renders כְּבִיר, rather perhaps a *quilt* or mattress, A.V. "pillow" [q. v.]) of goat's hair for protection from gnats, the rest of the figure covered with the wide *béged* or plaid. It happened as she had feared; Saul could not delay his vengeance till David appeared out of doors, but sent his people into the house. The reply of Michal is that her husband is ill and cannot be disturbed. At last Saul will be baulked no longer: his messengers force their way into the inmost apartment, and there discover the deception which has been played off upon them with such success. Saul's rage may be imagined: his fury was such that Michal was obliged to fabricate a story of David's having attempted to kill her (1 Sam. xix, 12–17). B.C. cir. 1062.

This was the last time she saw her husband for many years; and when the rupture between Saul and David had become open and incurable, Michal was married to another man, Phalti, or Phaltiel, of Gallim (1 Sam. xxv, 44; 2 Sam. iii, 15), a village apparently not far from Gibeah. Her father probably did not believe her story concerning David's escape; but he had taken advantage of it by cancelling her former marriage. David, however, as the divorce had been without his consent, felt that the law (Deut. xxiv, 4) against a husband taking back a divorced wife could not apply in this case; he therefore formally reclaimed her of Ish-bosheth, who employed no less a personage than Abner to take her from Phaltiel, and conduct her with all honor to David. It was under cover of this mission that Abner sounded the elders of Israel respecting their acceptance of David for king, and conferred with David himself on the same subject at Hebron (2 Sam. iii, 12–21). As this demand was not made by David until Abner had contrived to intimate his design, it has been supposed by some that it was managed between them solely to afford Abner an ostensible errand in going to Hebron; but it is more pleasant to suppose that, although the matter happened to be so timed as to give a color to this suspicion, the demand really arose from David's revived affection for his first wife and earliest love. After the death of her father and brothers at Gilboa, Michal and her new husband appear to have betaken themselves, with the rest of the family of Saul, to the eastern side of the Jordan. If the old Jewish tradition inserted by the Targum in 2 Sam. xxi may be followed, she was occupied in bringing up the sons of her sister Merab and Adriel of Meholah. At any rate, it is on the road leading up from the Jordan valley to the Mount of Olives that we first encounter her with her husband—Michal under the joint escort of David's messengers and Abner's twenty men, *en route* to David at Hebron, the submissive Phaltiel behind, bewailing the wife thus torn from him. It was at least fourteen years since David and she had parted at Gibeah, since she had watched him disappear down the cord into the darkness, and had perilled her own life for his against the rage of her insane father. That David's love for his absent wife had undergone no change in the interval seems certain from the eagerness with which he reclaims her as soon as the opportunity is afforded him. Important as it was to him to make an alliance with Ishbosheth and the great tribe of Benjamin, and much as he respected Abner, he will not listen for a moment to any overtures till his wife is restored. Every circumstance is fresh in his memory. "I will not see thy face except thou first bring Saul's daughter

. . . my wife Michal whom I espoused to me for a hundred foreskins of the Philistines" (2 Sam. iii, 13, 14). The meeting took place at Hebron. B.C. cir. 1047. How Michal comported herself in the altered circumstances of David's household, how she received or was received by Abigail and Ahinoam we are not told; but it is plain from the subsequent occurrences that something had happened to alter the relations of herself and David. They were no longer what they had been to each other. The alienation was probably mutual. On her side must have been the recollection of the long contests which had taken place in the interval between her father and David; the strong anti-Saulite and anti-Benjamite feeling prevalent in the camp at Hebron, where every word she heard must have contained some distasteful allusion, and where at every turn she must have encountered men like Abiathar the priest or Ismaiah the Gibeonite (1 Chron. xii, 4; comp. 2 Sam. xxi, 2), who had lost the whole or the greater part of their relatives in some sudden burst of her father's fury. Add to this the connection between her husband and the Philistines who had killed her father and brothers; and, more than all perhaps, the inevitable difference between the boy-husband of her recollections and the matured and occupied warrior who now received her. The whole must have come upon her as a strong contrast to the affectionate husband whose tears had followed her along the road over Olivet, and to the home over which we cannot doubt she ruled supreme. On the side of David it is natural to put her advanced years, in a climate where women are old at thirty, and probably a petulant and jealous temper inherited from her father, one outburst of which certainly produced the rupture between them which closes our knowledge of Michal.

It was the day of David's greatest triumph, when he brought the Ark of Jehovah from its temporary resting-place to its home in the newly-acquired city. It was a triumph in every respect peculiarly his own. The procession consisted of priests, Levites, the captains of the host, the elders of the nation; and conspicuous in front, "in the midst of the damsels playing on the timbrels" (comp. Psa. lxviii, 25), was the king dancing and leaping. Michal watched this procession approach from the window of her apartments in the royal harem; the motions of her husband, clothed only in a thin linen ephod (1 Chron. xv, 27), shocked her as undignified and indecent—"she despised him in her heart." B.C. cir. 1043. It would have been well if her contempt had rested there; but it was not in her nature to conceal it, and when, after the exertions of the long day were over —the last burnt-offering and the last peace-offering offered, the last portion distributed to the crowd of worshippers—the king entered his house to bless his family, he was received by his wife, not with the congratulations which he had a right to expect, and which would have been so grateful to him, but with a bitter taunt, which showed how incapable she was of appreciating either her husband's temper or the service in which he had been engaged. David's retort was a tremendous one, conveyed in words which once spoken could never be recalled. It gathered up all the differences between them which made sympathy no longer possible, and we do not need the assurance of the sacred writer, that "Michal had no child unto the day of her death," to feel quite certain that all intercourse between her and David must have ceased from that date. Josephus (*Ant.* vii, 4, 3) intimates that she returned to Phaltiel, but of this there is no mention in the records of the Bible; and it would be difficult to reconcile such a thing with the known ideas of the Jews as to women who had once shared the king's bed. See ABISHAG; ADONIJAH. The fanciful Jewish tradition, preserved in the Targum on Ruth iii, 3, states that Phaltiel had from the first acted in accordance with the idea alluded to in the text. He is placed in the same rank with Joseph, and is commemorated as "Phaltiel, son of Laish, the pious (חֲסִידָא,

Assidæan, the word used for the Puritans of the New-Testament times), who placed a sword between himself and Michal, Saul's daughter, lest he should go in unto her." It was thus, perhaps, as Abarbanel remarks, ordered by Providence that the race of Saul and David should not be mixed, and that no one deriving any apparent right from Saul should succeed to the throne.

Her name appears but once again (2 Sam. xxi, 8), as the bringer-up, or more accurately the mother, of five of the grandchildren of Saul who were sacrificed to Jehovah by the Gibeonites on the hill of Gibeah. But it is probably more correct to substitute Merab for Michal in this place (see Hitzig, *Begr. der Krit.* p. 145 sq.; Flieschmann, *De filiis Michal*, Altorf, 1716). See ADRIEL.

Michel, Augustin, a German Roman Catholic theologian, was born in 1661, at Unterstorff, Bavaria, and was educated at the University of Dillingen. He studied both theology and law, and secured the doctorate in divinity and also in law. After finishing his studies, he returned as teacher to the convent-school of his native place, where he had prepared for the university. He was afterwards appointed ecclesiastical counsellor by the prince elector of Cologne, the prince bishop of Freising, and the prince abbot of Kempten. He died in 1751. Some of his most important works, besides many dissertations and contributions to periodicals, are, *Expositiones in Psalmos, in Cantica, Cenciones dominicales*, etc. (never published):—*Theologia canonico-moralis* (1707, fol.):—*De juro et justitia, juridice et theologice tractata contra L. B. de Schmid* (Romæ, 1699, 8vo):—*Discussio theologica de contritione et attritione* (ibid. 1710, 4to):—*Confutatio infamis libri cui Litalis Expostulatio contra damnationem Quesnellii*, etc. (Landeshuti, 1719, 4to).

Michel, François, a French visionary, was born at Salon, in Provence, in 1661. To this name is attached the memory of an extraordinary adventure, which, towards the close of the summer of 1699, created a great sensation in France. Michel practiced at Salon the trade of a farrier. When thirty-eight years of age, the father of a family, and well known in his vicinity, he claimed to have the following vision: "One evening, in the field, returning home, he saw at the foot of a tree, and surrounded by a great light, a beautiful fair woman, clothed in white, with a mantle arranged in court-fashion, who, calling Michel by his name, told him that she was the late queen, Marie Thérèse, who had been married to the king. After having confided to him some things of great importance, she ordered him, under pain of death, to go and reveal them to the king, adding that if at first he could not obtain an audience with the king, he should demand to see a minister of state, but that he should reserve certain secrets for the king alone. This apparition was renewed three times. Yielding finally to these injunctions, the farrier repaired to Aix, to the intendant of Provence, who, surprised at the good sense and firmness of this man, gave him letters to the ministers, and paid his way. This marvellous story spread in all directions. Michel had scarcely arrived at Marseilles, when he sought M. de Brissac, major of the body-guard, and, without permitting himself to be disheartened, insisted on having access to the king. Louis XIV, informed of the singular obstinacy of Michel, finally consented to receive the farrier, and had with him two interviews; but to this day the conversation between the king and his subject remains a mystery. To his friends the king pronounced Michel a man of great good sense. Michel returned to his province, furnished with a sum of money, and provided for during the remainder of his life." This singular case was much commented upon. While some admitted the reality of a providential mission, others saw in it only a tissue of bold trickery, of which Michel, in his simplicity, was the first dupe. We are told to place all this story to the account of a Madame Arnoul, a romantic and intriguing woman, widow of the intendant of ma-

rine at Marseilles, and who preserved a secret and intimate friendship for a long time with Madame de Maintenon. Michel, fatigued with the curiosity of which he was the object, retired to Lançon, a village near Aix, where he died, December 10, 1726. Saint-Simon, *Mémoires*, xi, 16 sq. (edit. Cheruel); Proyart, *Vie du Dauphin père de Louis XVI*. See Hoefer, *Nouv. Biog. Générale*, s. v.

Michel, Georg Adam, a German theologian, was born Sept. 23, 1708, at Walpheim; was educated at the school of his native place, and studied theology at the University of Jena. Afterwards he assisted his father in his ecclesiastical functions for seven years, was then appointed inspector of the orphan asylum at Oettingen, with the title Counsellor of the Consistory; and died March 21, 1780. Michel combined with a great knowledge in theology a thorough acquaintance with history. He contributed largely to the *Oettingische Bibliothek* (Oettingen, 1758, 8vo), and to the *Oettingische politische kirchliche und gelehrten Geschichte* (ibid. 1772-79, 3 vols. 8vo).

Michel, Jean, a French ecclesiastic, was born at Beauvais about the close of the 14th century. He was at first counsellor to Louis II, king of Sicily; then canon of Rouin, of Aix, and of Angiers. He was appointed bishop of Angiers by the state, February 28, 1439; archdeacon Guillaume d'Estouteville, of the same diocese, however, obtained edicts from the pope for the bishopric. Fortified with these bulls, he presented himself to the chapter, and demanded the deposition of Michel; but, instead, the supplicant himself was removed. Guillaume persisted notwithstanding, and seated himself as bishop of Angiers in the Council of Florence, while Jean Michel was seated with the same title in the Council of Basle. Stormy dissensions ensued, which the pope Eugenius endeavored to terminate by appointing Guillaume successively bishop of Digne and cardinal. But a man of so great an origin, and so powerful in his alliances, was not to be satisfied with these transactions. His intrigues continued to involve the bishopric in constant agitation. The plebeian Jean Michel had, however, resolute partisans. Few prelates have left in the Church of Angiers such honorable memories. The kings of France have several times demanded, though in vain, his canonization by the Church of Rome. Michel died Sept. 11, 1447. See *Gallia Christiana*, vol. xiv, col. 580; Hoefer, *Nouv. Biog. Générale*, s. v.

Michele, PARRASIC, a Venetian painter, flourished about 1590. He was a pupil of Paul Veronese. He executed several works for the churches, especially a *Pieta*, in a chapel of the church of San Giuseppe, into which he introduced a portrait of himself. See Spooner, *Biog. Hist. of the Fine Arts* (N. Y. 1865, 2 vols. 8vo).

Michelians. See HAHN, MICHEL; KORNTHAL, SOCIETY OF.

Michelini, GIO. BATTISTA, a painter of religious subjects, who flourished about 1650, was a native of Foligno. He was a pupil of Guido Reni, and wrought in the churches of the Romagna. Lanzi says there are several of his works at Gubbio, and mentions particularly a *Dead Christ*. But little is known of him. See Lanzi's *Hist. of Painting*, transl. by Roscoe (Lond. 1847, 3 vols. 8vo), i, 460; Spooner, *Biog. Hist. of the Fine Arts* (N. Y. 1865, 2 vols. 8vo).

Michelozzi (or **Michelozzo**), a celebrated Florentine sculptor and architect, was born in 1396. He was a pupil of Donatello, and the greater part of the sepulchral monument erected for pope Giovanni Coscia, in the church of San Giovanni at Florence, by Donatello, is in reality the work of Michelozzi. In the same church is a beautiful statue of *Faith*, which was executed by Michelozzi as a companion to the two statues of *Hope* and *Charity* by his master. Over the sacristy and the rooms of the superintendents, which are opposite to San Giovanni, Michelozzi executed a full relief of

San Giovanni, which was afterwards removed, and is now in the Florentine Gallery, in the corridor of bronzes. As an architect, Michelozzi had deservedly a high reputation. He built, among many other fine buildings, the library of the monastery of San Giorgio Maggiore, a house of the Black Monks of Santa Giustina. In 1437 he commenced the construction of the convent of San Marco, which was finished, at a cost of 36,000 ducats, in 1452. Michelozzi also constructed for Cosmo de' Medici the noviciate of Santa Croce, which, for beauty of form and decoration, will compare favorably with any work of this master. The convent of the Barefooted Monks of St. Francis, the church and convent of the monks of San Girolamo, and many other works of purely secular character, are by this distinguished man. He died in 1470, and was buried in his own tomb, in the church of San Marco, in Florence. See Vasari, *Lives of the Painters,* transl. by Mrs. Foster (Lond. 1850, 5 vols. 8vo), i, 494; Quatremère de Quincy, *Vies des Architectes illustres.*

Michl, ANTON, a German Roman Catholic theologian, was born in 1753 at Ebersberg, Bavaria; was educated at Freysing, and ordained in 1776. He afterwards studied law and ecclesiastical history, and was in 1799 appointed professor of ecclesiastical law and history at Landshut. He was a faithful adherent of the government party, at that time, as in our own day, decidedly anti-Romanistic in feeling and tendency, and Michl thereby made many friends even among the Protestants, who looked upon him as a friend of liberty and of light. He died at Landshut in 1813. Besides several dissertations, he published *Kirchenrecht für Katholiken und Protestanten, mit Hinsicht auf den Code Napoleon und die bayerischen Landesgesetze* (Munchen, 1809); and *Kirchengeschichte* (ibid. 1807–11, 2 vols. 8vo). See Cl. A. Baaders, *Lexikon verstorbener bayer. Schriftsteller* (Augsburg and Leipsic, 1824); Wetzer u. Welte, *Kirchen-Lexikon,* s. v.

Mich'mas (Heb. *Mikmas',* מִכְמָס, something *hidden;* Ezra ii, 27, Sept. Μαχμάς v. r. Χαμμάς; Neh. vii, 31, Μαχεμάς), or MICHMASH (Heb. *Mikmash',* מִכְמָשׁ, id. Neh. xi, 31, Sept. Μαχαμάς, in pause מִכְמָשׁ, 1 Sam. xiii, 2, 5, 11, 16, 23; xiv, 5, 31; Isa. x, 28; Sept. Μαχμάς, and so in 1 Macc. ix, 13; Josephus, Μαχμά [*Ant.* xiii, 1, 6]), a town of Benjamin (Ezra ii, 27; Neh. xi, 31; comp. vii, 31), east of Bethel or Beth-aven (1 Sam. xiii, 5), and south from Migron, on the road to Jerusalem (Isa. x, 28). "If the name be, as some scholars assert (Fürst, *Handwb.* p. 600*b*, 732*b*), compounded from that of Chemosh, the Moabitish deity, it is not improbably a relic of some incursion or invasion of the Moabites, just as Chephar-haammonai, in this very neighborhood, is of the Ammonites. But though in the heart of Benjamin, it is not named in the list of the towns of that tribe (comp. Josh. xvii)." The words of 1 Sam. xiii, 2; xiv, 4; and Isa. x, 29, show that at Michmas was a pass where the progress of a military body might be impeded or opposed, since it was held by the Philistines while Saul and the Israelites were at Gibeah; it was also on the line of march of an invading army from the north, and the Assyrians are represented as depositing their baggage there on their way to Jerusalem, just before reaching Gibeah (Isa. x, 28). It was perhaps for this reason that Jonathan Maccabæus fixed his abode at Michmas (1 Macc. ix, 73); and it is from the chivalrous exploit of another hero of the same name, the son of Saul, that the place is chiefly celebrated (1 Sam. xiii, xiv, 4–16). "Saul was occupying the range of heights above mentioned, one end of his line resting on Bethel, the other at Michmas (1 Sam. xiii, 2). In Geba, close to him, but separated by the wide and intricate valley, the Philistines had a garrison with a chief officer. The taking of the garrison or the killing of the officer by Saul's son Jonathan was the first move. The next was for the Philistines to swarm up from their sea-side plain in such numbers that no alternative was left for Saul but to re-

tire down the wady to Gilgal, near Jericho, that from that ancient sanctuary he might collect and reassure the Israelites. Michmas was then occupied by the Philistines, and was their furthest post to the east. But it was destined to witness their sudden overthrow. While he was in Geba, and his father in Michmas, Jonathan must have crossed the intervening valley too often not to know it thoroughly; and the intricate paths which render it impossible for a stranger to find his way through the mounds and hummocks that crowd the bottom of the ravine—with these he was so familiar—the passages here, the sharp rocks there—as to be able to traverse them even in the dark. It was just as the day dawned (Joseph. *Ant.* vi, 6, 2) that the watchers in the garrison at Michmas descried the two Hebrews clambering up the steeps beneath. We learn from the details furnished by Josephus, who must have had an opportunity of examining the spot when he passed it with Titus on their way to the siege of Jerusalem (see *War,* v, 2, 1), that the part of Michmas in which the Philistines had established themselves consisted of three summits, surrounded by a line of rocks like a natural entrenchment, and ending in a long and sharp precipice, believed to be impregnable. Finding himself observed from above, and taking the invitation as an omen in his favor, Jonathan turned from the course which he was at first pursuing, and crept up in the direction of the point reputed impregnable. It was there, according to Josephus, that he and his armor-bearer made their entrance to the camp (Josephus, *Ant.* vi, 6, 2)" (Smith). See GIBEAH; JONATHAN. It was inhabited, after the return from Babylon (Neh. xi, 31), by 122 returned colonists (Ezra ii, 27; Neh. vii, 31). Eusebius describes Michmas as a large village nine Roman miles from Jerusalem, on the road to Ramah (*Onomast.* s. v. Μαχμά). Travellers have usually identified it with *Bir* or *el-Bireh* (see Maundrell, March 25; and the details in Quaresmius, *Elucidato,* ii, 786, 787); but Dr. Robinson (*Researches,* ii, 117) recognises it in a place still bearing the name of *Mukhmas,* at a distance and position which correspond well with these intimations. It is small, and almost desolate, but bears marks of having once been a place of strength and importance. There are many foundations of hewn stones, and some columns lie among them. The steep and precipitous *Wady es-Suweinit,* a valley into which the two ravines on the low ridge between which the village is situated run, is probably the "passage of Michmash" mentioned in Scripture (1 Sam. xiii, 23; Isa. x, 29). "In it," says Dr. Robinson, "just at the left of where we crossed, are two hills of a conical, or rather spherical form, having steep rocky sides, with small wadys running up between each so as almost to isolate them. One of them is on the side towards Jeba (Gibeah), and the other towards Mukhmas. These would seem to be the two rocks mentioned in connection with Jonathan's adventure (1 Sam. xiv, 4, 5). See BOZEZ; SENEH. They are not, indeed, so sharp as the language of Scripture would seem to imply; but they are the only rocks of the kind in this vicinity. The northern one is connected towards the west with an eminence still more distinctly isolated" (*Bib. Researches,* ii, 116; comp. new ed. iii, 289; see Thenius, in the *Sachs. exeget. Stud.* ii, 147 sq.). "Immediately facing Mukhmas, on the opposite side of the ravine, is the modern representative of Geba; and behind this again are Ramah and Gibeah—all memorable names in the long struggle which has immortalized Michmas. Bethel is about four miles to the north of Michmas, and the interval is filled up by the heights of Burka, Deir Diwan, Tell el-Hajar, etc., which appear to have constituted the Mount Bethel of the narrative (xiii, 2)." In the Talmud (*Menachoth,* viii, 1; comp. Schwarz, *Palest.* p. 131) the soil of Michmas is celebrated for its fertility (Reland, *Palæst.* p. 897). "There is a good deal of cultivation in and among groves of old olives in the broad, shallow wady which slopes down to the north and east of the village; but Mukhmas itself is a very poor place, and the country close to it has truly a most forbidding aspect. Huge gray rocks raise up their bald crowns, completely hiding every patch of soil, and the gray huts of the village, and the gray ruins that encompass them, can hardly be distinguished from the rocks themselves. There are considerable remains of massive foundations, columns, cisterns, etc., testifying to former prosperity greater than that of either Anathoth or Geba" (Porter, *Handbk.* p. 215, 216).

Mich'mash (1 Sam. xiii, 2–23; xiv, 5, 31; Neh. xi, 31; Isa. x, 28). See MICHMAS.

Mich'methah (Heb. *Mikmethath'*, מִכְמְתָת, perh. *hiding-place;* Sept. Μαχϑώϑ, Vulg. *Machmethath*), a town on the northern border of Ephraim (and the southern of Manasseh), situated eastward of Shechem and southward from Asher, in the direction of Tappuah (Josh. xvii, 7), also not very far west of Jordan, but beyond Taanath-Shiloh (Josh. xvi, 6; where part of the verse appears to have become transposed from its proper location at the beginning of ver. 8; see Keil's *Comment.* ad loc.). These notices appear to fix it not far from Wady Bidan, north-east of Salem. See TRIBE. This position corresponds to the location assigned to the associated places by Eusebius (Schwarz, *Palest.* p. 147); and M. de Saulcy found a little village in this vicinity, called *el-Makhna*, which he thinks may be a vestige of the Biblical locality (*Narrative*, i, 93); but Dr. Robinson, who passed through this region during his last visit, speaks only of "several villages" visible in this vicinity (*Researches*, new ed. iii, 298), and applies the name el-Makhna to a large fertile valley south of Nablûs (*ibid.* p. 132, etc.); which, however, according to Van de Velde's *Map*, runs into Wady Bidan.

Mich'ri (Heb. *Mikri'*, מִכְרִי, *salable;* Sept. Μοχορέ v. r. Μαχίρ), the father of Uzzi and grandfather of Elah, which last was one of the principal Benjamites resident in Jerusalem after the exile (1 Chron. ix, 8). B.C. considerably ante 440.

Mich'tam (Heb. *miktam'*, מִכְתָּם, prob. for מִכְתָב, *written;* Sept. στηλογραφία, Vulg. *tituli inscriptio*), a term found in the titles of several psalms (xvi, lvi, lvii, lviii, xl), and signifying a *writing*, i. e. a *poem* or song (see Gesenius, *Thesaur.* p. 724), like מִכְתָב (*miktab'*, "writing," in Isa. xxxviii, 9). Others (as Luther, after Aben-Ezra, Kimchi, and others) unaptly translate it *golden*, i. e. precious, distinguished, as if from כֶּתֶם, gold. Still others (as Hezel, Ewald) refer to an Arabic root meaning to *conceal*, as if written from retirement, or in a plaintive strain; and some (after the rabbins) make it a compound of מָךְ וְתָם, i. q. *humble and perfect*, referring to David. See PSALMS.

Micislaus, duke of Poland in the 10th century, is noted in ecclesiastical history as the promulgator of Christianity among the Poles, A.D. 965. His own conversion was brought about by his wife, Dambrowka, daughter of a Bohemian prince. John XIII was at that time the Roman pontiff, and he despatched Ægidius, bishop of Tusculum, to the aid of the duke and his wife. See POLAND.

Micqueau, JEAN-LOUIS, a French Protestant theologian, was born at Rheims about 1530. He took part in the Reformation; established a school at Orleans in 1557, and taught the humanities in the college of the same city. Allied by friendship with Gentien Hervet, a canon of Rheims and native of Orleans, the difference in their religions brought on a polemical correspondence. He died near the close of the 16th century. Micqueau wrote, *Lycampæi castri obsidio et excidium* (1554): — *De constituenda apud Aurelios juventutis disciplina Oratio* (1558) :—*Aureliæ urbis memorabilis ab Anglis obsidio, anno 1428, et Joannæ Virginis Lotharingæ res gestæ* (1560) :—*Résponse au discours de Gentien Hervet, sus ce que les pilleurs, voleurs et branleurs de l'églises disent qu'ils ne veulent qu'aux prières* (1564) :—*Deuxième*

Résponse de Jean-Louis Micqueau, maistre d'école à Orleans, aux folies reveries, exécrables blasphèmes, erreurs et mensonges de G. Hervet (1564). See *Revue historique et littéraire de la Champagne*, No. 11, 15 (November, 1854), p. 74; Hoefer, *Nouv. Biog. Générale*, s. v.

Micrælius, JOHANN, a German Lutheran professor, was born at Cösslin, in Pomerania, Sept. 1, 1597. He began his studies at the college of his own town, and in 1614 removed to Stettin, where he studied theology under professor Aamer. In 1616 he maintained a dispute, "*De Deo uno et trino*," which secured him much reputation. A year after he disputed at the University of Königsberg, "*De veritate transcendentali*." He received in 1621 the degree of master of philosophy at the University of Greifswald, after having maintained a thesis, "*De meteoris*." He finished his studies at Leipsic. He was made professor of rhetoric in the royal college at Stettin in 1624, rector of the Senate School in 1627, and rector of the royal college and professor of theology in 1649. He had a famous dispute with John Bergius, first preacher at the court of the elector of Brandenburg, upon the differences between the Lutherans and Calvinists. On a visit to Sweden, in 1653, he had the honor to pay his respects to queen Christina, who received him with very marked attention. She defrayed the charges of his doctor's degree. He died Dec. 3, 1658. Micrælius wrote, *Lexicon Philologicum:— Lexicon Philosophicum:—Syntagma Historiæ Mundi:— Syntagma Historiæ Ecclesiasticæ:—Ethnophronius contra Gentiles de Principiis Religionis Christianæ:*—he afterwards added a continuation, *Contra Judæas Depravationes:—Tabellæ Historicæ, ad Millen. et Rerumpublic. Tempora dijudicanda Necessariæ:—Tractatus de copia Rerum et Verborum, cum Praxi continua Præceptorum Rhetor.:—Archæologia, Arithmetica, usus Globorum et Tabular. Geographicar.:—Orthodoxia Lutherana contra Bergium;* and numerous theses, disputations, orations, etc. See *Allgemeines Historisches Lexikon* (Leips. 1731, 5 vols. fol.), iii, 560 sq.; Witte, *Memor. theol.* p. 282 sq.; Bayle, *Hist. Dict.* s. v. (J. H.W.)

Micronesia (from Greek μικρός, *small*, and νῆσος, *island*, signifying a region of small islands or islets) is a term of recent application, and is applied to a portion of the Central Archipelago, Pacific Ocean, including the Kingsmill group. Micronesia proper extends from the westernmost island of the Sandwich group to near Japan and the Philippines, and reaches south of the equator, including the Ladrone Islands, the Carolinas, and the Pellew Islands. The Kingsmill group lies on both sides of the equator, and consists of fifteen principal islands, all coral, and densely covered with cocoa-nut groves.

Customs. — The population of these islands amounts to about 50,000 souls. They are governed by independent chiefs or kings, and mostly lead a life of indolence. They are divided into three classes—chiefs, landholders, and slaves. They live in small communities, regarding the eldest of their number as a kind of patriarch. Polygamy is common. They are hospitable, and ready to share the last morsel with the needy. In each town is a "stranger's house," where travellers find a temporary home. The cocoa-nut, which everywhere abounds, supplies the few wants of the natives with little labor. Their chief employment is the manufacture of cocoa-nut oil. Almost everything which the natives eat, drink, wear, live in, or use in any way, is obtained from the cocoa-nut tree.

Religion. — There exists hardly any well-developed form of worship or religion. They have no idols and no priests. A loose system of spirit worship, or, better said, of veneration for the spirits of the dead, used to prevail among these people, but is gradually dying out. When a Micronesian dies, the body is placed upon mats, in the centre of the house, and rubbed with cocoa-nut oil till the flesh is gone; then the bones are placed in a loft or thrown into the sea. A stone is placed near the house as a resting-place for the spirit, and offerings are made to it twice a year. There are but few traditions, and the people cannot be said to be very superstitious.

Missions.—Prosperous missions have been established in these groups by agents of the American Board of Foreign Missions; several of the workers have been selected from among their converts in Honolulu. As the result of the mission to Micronesia, during the nineteen years since its commencement, it would appear that a wonderful change has been produced in the social and moral condition of the once wild and savage inhabitants. A number of the natives have been converted to Christianity, and, according to the last report, 668 converts are united in Church fellowship. See *The Missionary World* (N.Y. 1873, 12mo), p. 457 and 1123; Grundemann, *Miss. Atlas*, s. v.; Newcomb, *Cyclop. of Missions*, p. 539 sq. See SANDWICH ISLANDS.

Micronius, MARTIN, a very distinguished Dutch divine, was born about 1523 at Ghent, of a noble Dutch family. We know little of Micronius's early years. He was at first a physician, and is said to be the author of several medical books and essays. In 1550, when the Protestant Church was bitterly persecuted by the Spaniards, Micronius, with many others of his countrymen, fled to England, and there proved himself a very efficient helpmate to John à Lasko (q. v.) in the establishment and organization of the foreign Protestant congregation in London. He translated John à Lasko's system of Church order and liturgical formulars into Dutch, and introduced them into the congregation of Dutch refugees in London. The death of the king wrought an entire change in the prospects of the exiles, and on the accession of queen Mary they prepared to leave for other parts. Micronius accompanied them to Denmark and East Friesland, and finally became pastor at Norden. He died towards the close of the 16th century. In his disputations and writings Micronius opposed Simon Menno (q. v.) and David George; and when Westphal (q. v.), a Lutheran divine, had called his fellow-pilgrims "martyrs of the devil," on account of Lasko's views of the sacraments, Micronius sought to convince, or at least silence him, but failed. In Norden he edited his larger and smaller Catechism, 1592: *De cleyne catechismus of kinderbere der Duitschen Ghemeynte van London, etc., weeke nu hier ende daer verstrogt is. Ghemaect door Martin Micron. Ghedruckt bey Gellium Itematium anno* 1555. These catechisms were consulted in the composition of the Heidelberg Catechism (q. v.). Micronius also wrote an apology of the foreign Protestant congregation, defending them against the accusation of high-treason, which had furnished a pretext for their expulsion from England. See Köcher, *Katech. Gesch. der reform. Kirche;* Bartel's *Johannes à Lasko.*

Mid-day (צָהֳרַיִם, *double light,* 1 Kings xviii, 29, i. e. noon, as elsewhere rendered; מַחֲצִית הַיּוֹם, *half of the day,* Neh. viii, 3; ἡμέρα μέση, *middle day,* Acts xxvi, 13). See DAY.

Mid'din (Heb. *Middin',* מִדִּין, *distance;* Sept. Μαδδίν v. r. Μαδών), a town in the desert of Judah, mentioned between Beth-arabah and Secacah (Josh. xv, 61); and probably situated not far from the Dead Sea, about opposite its middle, or possibly at the ruins near a well marked on Van de Velde's *Map* as *Khan Mardeh,* near the north end of the Dead Sea. "By Van de Velde (*Memoir,* p. 256, and *Map*) mention is made of a valley on the south-western side of the Dead Sea, below Masada, called *Um el-Bedun,* which may contain a trace of the ancient name."

Middle Ages. The barbarism of this period may be said to have begun about A.D. 510, when the barbarians had made an irruption into the West very prejudicial to the interests of literature. Learning was preserved in the bishops' schools and monasteries: the works of ancient authors were kept in the libraries of the monasteries, but the libraries of monks and church-men were composed chiefly of ecclesiastical and ascetic works. Greek literature was generally neglected, Latin but poorly cultivated; rhetoric was turned into bombast, the liberal arts comprised within a few rules, and the study of philosophy abandoned and decried. This barbarism almost *extinguished the light* (hence the name "*Dark* Ages") and life of Christianity, as the influence of the Church in the course of its previous corruption had already suppressed ancient literature. See Riddle's *Eccl. Chron.;* Eden, *Theol. Dict.;* Farrar, *Eccles. Dict.*

Middle Wall (μεσότοιχον), spoken of the *chel* or sacred fence ("partition") between the Court of the Gentiles and the interior sanctum of the Temple (Eph. ii, 14). See TEMPLE.

Middlekauff, SOLOMON, a German Reformed minister, was born near Hagerstown, Md., in 1818; was educated at Marshall College, Mercersburg, Pa. (class of 1839); studied theology in the theological seminary of the German Reformed Church located in the same place; was ordained in 1842, and became pastor of the Lincolnton charge in North Carolina. He died at the mineral springs, Catawba County, N. C., May 21, 1845. His ministry was brief but blessed. Energetic, mild, and peaceful in spirit, well educated and zealous, his influence was widely felt, and his memory is faithfully cherished.

Middleton, Conyers, a celebrated divine and scholar of the Church of England, was born Dec. 27, 1683, at Richmond, in Yorkshire. His father, the Rev. William Middleton, rector of Hinderwell, gave him a liberal education. At the age of seventeen he was sent to Trinity College, Cambridge, of which college he was two years afterwards chosen a scholar. He took his degree of B.A. in 1702, and was shortly after ordained deacon. In 1706 he was elected a fellow of Trinity College, and in 1708 joined with other fellows of his college in a petition to the bishop of Ely, as the visitor of the college, against Bentley (q. v.), the master. Middleton, who was then a young man, did not take a prominent part in this proceeding; but the feelings of hostility to the master originated by these disputes sank deep into his mind, and made him subsequently the most determined and dangerous of Bentley's enemies. Soon after this petition, he withdrew himself from Bentley's jurisdiction by marrying a lady of ample fortune. He subsequently resided for a short time in the Isle of Ely, on a small living in the gift of his wife, but the unhealthiness of the situation induced him to return to Cambridge at the end of a year. In October, 1717, when George I visited the University of Cambridge, Middleton, with several others, was created doctor of divinity by mandate; but Bentley, who was regius professor of divinity, refused to confer the degree unless a fee of four guineas was given to him in addition to the so-called "broad-piece," which had by ancient custom been allowed as a present on this occasion. This demand was resisted by Middleton, who, however, at last consented to pay it under protest. An appeal to court proved unfavorable to Bentley, but still he kept the money. Middleton thereupon sued Bentley for it in the vice-chancellor's court; and Bentley, refusing to pay the money or to acknowledge the jurisdiction of the court, was deprived of his degrees. Bentley petitioned the king for relief from that sentence, and, as he was a firm supporter of the Whig ministry then in power, it was feared that a commission might be issued by the crown to inquire into the state of the university. Middleton, to justify himself and his friends, published *A full and impartial Account of all the late Proceedings in the University of Cambridge against Dr. Bentley;* which, says Dr. Monk, "was the first published specimen of a style which, for elegance, purity, and ease, yields to none in the whole compass of the English language. The acrimonious and resentful feeling which prompted every line, is in some measure disguised by the pleasing language, the harmony of the periods, and the vein of scholarship which enliven the whole tract" (Monk, *Life of Bentley*, p. 388). A few months afterwards Middleton published *A Second Part of the full and impartial Account of all the late Proceedings*, and also *A true Account of the present State of Trinity College, in Cambridge, under the oppressive Government of their Master, R. Bentley, late D.D.* These books seem to have been written in order to destroy the suspicion which many then had, viz. that the proceedings of the university against Dr. Bentley did not flow so much from any real demerit in the man, as from a certain spirit of opposition to the court, the great promoter of whose interest he was thought to be. Middleton, in one of his pamphlets, had very imprudently declared "that the fellows of Trinity College had not been able to find any proper court in England which would receive their complaints;" and Bentley, perceiving that his adversary had been guilty of an expression which might be considered as a libel upon the administration of justice in the whole kingdom, brought an action against him, in which the jury returned a verdict of guilty. The court, however, was unwilling to pronounce sentence, and the matter was eventually settled by Middleton's begging pardon of Bentley, and consenting to pay all the expenses of the action.

But Middleton had not done with Bentley yet. The latter, in 1720, published proposals for a new edition of the Greek Testament, with a specimen of the intended work. The former, in 1721, published *Remarks, Paragraph by Paragraph, upon the Proposals lately published by R. Bentley for a new Edition of the Greek Testament.* Although Middleton professed, in the commencement of the pamphlet, that "his remarks were not drawn from him by personal spleen or envy to the author of the *Proposals*, but by a serious conviction that he had neither talents nor materials proper for the work he had undertaken, and that religion was much more likely to receive detriment than service from it," the whole tenor and style of the pamphlet showed that it was the result of the most virulent personal animosity. He followed up his attack on Bentley by *Some further Remarks;* and it must be conceded that these two books against Bentley are written with great acuteness and learning, and, though Bentley affected to despise them, they destroyed the credit of his *Proposals* so effectually that his intended publication of the New Testament came to nothing.

Upon the great enlargement of the public library at Cambridge, a new office of principal librarian was established, to which Middleton was elected, notwithstanding a violent opposition. He afterwards travelled through France and Italy, and spent some months in Rome in 1724. After his return, Middleton published his celebrated *Letter from Rome* (1729), in which he attempted to show that "the religion of the present Romans was derived from that of their heathen ancestors;" and that, in particular, the rites, ceremonies, dress of the priests, etc., in the Roman Catholic Church, were taken from the pagan religion. This work was received with great favor by the learned, and went through four editions in the author's lifetime. The free manner, however, in which he attacked the miracles of the Roman Catholic Church gave offence to many Anglican divines, and they charged Middleton with entertaining as little respect for the miracles of the apostles as for those of the Roman Catholic saints.

Hitherto Dr. Middleton stood well with mankind; for notwithstanding the offence he had given to some bigots by certain passages in the above-mentioned pamphlet, yet the reasonable part of Christians were well pleased with his writings, believing that he had done great service to Protestantism by his exposé of the absurdities of popery. He was, in fact, a general favorite with the public, when, by the publication of a new work, *Christianity as old as Creation* (1731), he not only gave great offence to the clergy, but also ruined all his hopes for preferment. This letter, which was first published anonymously, was soon known to be writ-

ten by Middleton. Pearce (q. v.), bishop of Rochester, replied to it, treating the author as an infidel; and so strong was the feeling against Middleton that he was in danger of losing his degree and office of librarian. Promising, however, to publish a satisfactory vindication of his course, the authorities withheld their intended degradation, and in 1732 Middleton gave to the world *Some Remarks on Dr. Pearce's second Reply;* wherein the author's sentiments, as to all the principal points in dispute, are fully, clearly, and satisfactorily explained. In this manifesto, Middleton strongly asserted his belief in Christianity, and disavowed any intention to cast doubt upon its evidences; and thereby saved himself from degradation, but not from strong suspicion of hypocrisy—a charge which has ever since attached to his name.

Middleton regarded Christianity in scarcely any other light than as a republication of the law of nature, and endeavored to reduce, as far as possible, everything supernatural in the Bible to mere natural phenomena. He expressly maintained that there were contradictions in the four evangelists which could not be reconciled (*Reflections on the Variations found in the Four Evangelists*); he accused Matthew "of wilfully suppressing or negligently omitting three successive descents from father to son in the first chapter of his Gospel" (see vol. ii, 24); he asserted that the apostles were sometimes mistaken in their applications of prophecies relating to Christ (ii, 59); he considered "the story of the fall of man as a fable or allegory" (ii, 131), and, with respect to the prophecy given at the fall, he did not hesitate to declare (iii, 183) "that men who inquire into things will meet with many absurdities which reason must wink at, and many incredibilities which faith must digest, before they can admit the authority of this prophecy upon the evidence of this historical narration." Such being the opinions of Middleton, it cannot excite surprise, notwithstanding his assertions to the contrary, that he should have been looked upon as a disbeliever in the fundamental doctrines of Christianity.

While these discussions were going on, Middleton was appointed to the professorship of natural history, which appointment he resigned in 1734. In the following year he published *A Dissertation concerning the Origin of Printing in England*, showing that it was first introduced and practiced by an Englishman, William Caxton, at Westminster, and not, as commonly supposed, by a foreign printer at Oxford. In 1741 he published by subscription his most celebrated work, *The History of the Life of M. Tullius Cicero* (Lond. 2 vols. 4to). There were three thousand subscribers to this work, and the profits arising from its sale were so considerable as to enable Middleton to purchase a small estate at Hildersham, six miles from Cambridge, where he chiefly resided during the remainder of his life. Two years afterwards Middleton published a translation of Cicero's letters to Brutus, and of Brutus's to Cicero, with the Latin text, and a prefatory dissertation, in which he defended the authenticity of the Epistles. In 1745 he published *Germana quædam Antiquitatis eruditæ Monumenta*, etc., in which he gave an account of the various specimens of ancient art which he had collected during his residence at Rome. Two years afterwards he published his *Treatise on the Roman Senate*, in which he maintained that all vacancies in the senate were filled up by the people. But the work which has a peculiar interest for us he published shortly after, under the title *An Introductory Discourse to a larger Work, designed hereafter to be published, concerning the Miraculous Powers which are supposed to have subsisted in the Christian Church from the earliest Ages, through several successive Centuries; by which it is shown that we have no sufficient Reason to believe, upon the Authority of the primitive Fathers, that any such Powers were continued to the Church after the Days of the Apostles* (1748). The *Introductory Discourse* to the work, and the *Free Inquiry* itself, elicited numerous controversial tracts. Middleton was attacked by Stebbing and Chapman, the former of whom endeavored chiefly to show that Middleton's scheme was inseparably connected with the fall of Christianity, while the latter labored to support the authority of the fathers. These attacks Middleton repelled by *Some Remarks on Two Pamphlets (by Drs. Stebbing and Chapman) published against the Introduction.* "The discourse," remarks Mr. Orme (*Bibl. Bib.* s. v.), referring to the whole controversy, "is worthy of attention, for, though the combatants on both sides carried matters too far, considerable information may be collected from them—on the character and testimony of the fathers, the nature of miracles, and on other points closely connected with the Christian revelation." The controversy began to grow very hot. Besides Stebbing and Chapman, Parker, Brook, Johnson, Dodwell, Church, and others attacked him, while he was defended by Yates, Jenkins, Toll, etc. A full list of the principal publications on the subject are enumerated by Kippis in a note to the 6th part of Doddridge's *Course of Lectures* (see also Orme's *Bibl. Bib.*; Strong's *Cat. of Engl. Theol.* 1830, No. 9441 sq.; Lord Brougham, *Men of Letters of the Times of George III*, p. 384). It was declared by Middleton's opponents that the tendency of his inquiry was to destroy the evidence of miraculous interpositions; but Middleton explicitly disavowed such intentions, and should have the benefit of the doubt. This much, however, must be admitted, that he seems never to have been so much pleased as when, by broaching some startling point of disputation, he succeeded in horrifying the minds of his orthodox brethren. Accordingly, before the theological world had recovered from the surprise and indignation into which they had been thrown by the *Free Inquiry*, its fearless author put forth upon the world an attack upon bishop Sherlock, entitled *An Examination of the Lord Bishop of London's Discourses concerning the Use and Intent of Prophecy; with some cursory Animadversions on his late Appendix, or additional Dissertation, containing a further Inquiry into the Mosaic Account of the Fall* (1750). In this work he attempted to refute Sherlock's (q. v.) theory of a chain of prophecy running through the different portions of the Old Testament. He was refuted by Dr. Rutherforth, divinity professor at Cambridge; but Middleton, whose end seems to have been answered, which was to abuse the bishop a little, pursued the argument no further. The obstinate controversialist died with the armor on his back and the lance in his hands. He was meditating a general answer to all the objections made against the *Free Inquiry;* but, being seized with illness, and imagining he might not be able to go through it, he singled out Church and Dodwell, as the two most considerable of his adversaries, and employed himself in preparing a particular answer to them. This, however, he did not live to finish, but died July 28, 1750, at Hildersham, in Cambridgeshire. A little before his death, he thought it prudent to accept a small living from Sir John Frederick. A few months after his death was published his *Vindication of the Free Inquiry into the Miraculous Powers, etc., from the Objections of Dr. Dodwell and Dr. Church.* The piece is unfinished, but very able as far as it goes. In 1752 all the before-mentioned works, except *The Life of Cicero*, were collected and printed in four volumes, 4to, under the title of *Miscellaneous Works;* among which were inserted the following pieces, never before published, viz., *A Preface to an intended Answer to all the Objections made against the Free Inquiry;—Some cursory Reflections on the Dispute, or Dissension, which happened at Antioch, between the Apostles Peter and Paul; —Reflections on the Variations, or Inconsistencies, which are found among the Four Evangelists in their different Accounts of the same Facts;—An Essay on the Gift of Tongues, tending to explain the proper Notion and Nature of it, as it is described and delivered to us in the sacred Scriptures, and as it appears also to have been understood by the learned both of ancient and modern times;— Some short Remarks on a Story told by the Ancients concerning St. John the Evangelist and Cerinthus the Here-*

tic; and on the Use which is made of it by the Moderns, to enforce the Duty of shunning Heretics;—An Essay on the allegorical and literal Interpretation of the Creation and Fall of Man;—De Latinarum literarum pronunciatione dissertatio;—Some Letters of Dr. Middleton to his Friends. A second edition of these *Miscellaneous Works* was published in five volumes, 8vo, in 1755. "Dr. Middleton," says Parr, in his preface *Bellendenus*, "was a man of no common attainments; his learning was elegant and profound, his judgment was acute and polished, his taste was fine and correct; his style was so pure and harmonious, so vigorously flowing without being inflated, that, Addison alone excepted, he seems to me without a rival." See Leckey, *Hist. of Rationalism* (see Index in vol. ii); Jortin, *Eccles. Remarks*, i, 298; Disraeli, *Miscell. of Literature, Quarrels of Authors*, p. 313; Nichols, *Lit. Anec.* p. 414 sq.; Knox, *Essays*, ii, 56; *N. Amer. Review*, xxxv, 440; Chancellor Kent, *Course of Engl. Reading;* Macaulay, *Crit. and Hist. Essays*, ii, 132; Orme, *Bibl. Bib.* s.v.; *Biogr. Brit.* s.v.; Chalmers's *Biogr. Dict.* s. v.; *General Biogr. Dict.* s. v.; *English Cyclop.* s. v.; Hook, *Eccles. Biogr.* s. v.; Darling, *Cyclop. Bibl.* i, 2057; Allibone, *Dict. of Brit. and Amer. Authors*, ii, 1273 sq.; *Blackwood's Magazine*, xiv, 257; xv, 461; xxviii, 440 sq.; xxxii, 607; Bickersteth, *Christ. Student*, p. 298.

Middleton, Erasmus, a noted English divine, was born about 1740. He received his education at St. Edmund's Hall, Oxford, but was expelled from that university, together with five other youths, on account of his sympathy with the Methodists. This circumstance gave rise to MacGowan's satire of *The Shaver*. Middleton then entered King's College, Cambridge, and, after his graduation, became pastor of an Episcopal congregation at Dalkeith, Scotland, and curate successively to Romaine and Cadogan, and at St. Margaret's, Westminster. He was presented to the rectory of Turvey, Bedfordshire, in 1764, and was thus a predecessor of Leigh Richmond (q. v.). He died April 25, 1805. Dr. Middleton was a man of warm piety, and of a Catholic spirit. He is the well-known author of *Biographia Evangelica, or an historical Account of the Lives and Deaths of the most eminent evangelical Authors or Preachers, both British and Foreign, in the several Denominations of Protestants* (1779, 4 vols. 8vo). This great biographical work is a collection of invaluable materials, and must immortalize his memory, while doing immense good. Of his other works we mention: *Archbishop Leighton's whole Works, with Life* (1805, 4 vols.):—*Versions and Imitations of the Psalms of David* (1806):—*Luther's Commentary on the Epistle to the Galatians, with his Life* (1807). See Allibone, *Dict. of Brit. and Amer. Authors*, ii, 1275; Cooper, *Biog. Dict. of Eminent Persons*, p. 865.

Middleton, Thomas Fanshawe, D.D., the first English bishop of Calcutta, largely identified with the Anglican Church missionary work in India, only son of the Rev. T. Middleton, rector of Kedleston, Derbyshire, was born at that village Jan. 26, 1769. His early training he received under his father. In 1779 he was admitted into Christ's Hospital, London, and thence proceeded to Pembroke Hall, Cambridge, where he took his degree of B.A., with honors, in January, 1792. Shortly after he received ordination, and entered upon the curacy of Gainsborough, in Lincolnshire. Here he edited a periodical work entitled the *Country Spectator*, which continued to appear for about seven months, Middleton sustaining the paper mainly by his own compositions. This connection brought him to the notice of Dr. John Pretyman, archdeacon of Lincoln, who in 1794 appointed him tutor to his two sons. Middleton in consequence removed first to Lincoln, and afterwards to Norwich, where he became curate of St. Peter's Mancroft in 1799, having previously (in 1795) been presented by Dr. Pretyman to the rectory of Tansor, in Northamptonshire. In 1802 he was presented with the rectory of Bytham, in Lincolnshire. About this time he wrote his chief work, *The Doctrine of the Greek Article applied to the Criticism and Illustration of the New Testament*, which he published in 1808, with a dedication to Dr. Pretyman. The object of this work is, first, to establish the rules which govern the use of the article, and then to apply these rules to the interpretation of various passages in the New Testament, many of which are of such a nature that they furnish arguments for or against the divinity of Christ, according to the different views which are taken of the force of the article. Owing to this circumstance, the doctrine of the Greek article has become the subject of warm discussion among theologians; and some Unitarian divines have strongly opposed the views of Middleton. His chief rules have, however, been received as sound by the great majority of Biblical critics. (A second and improved edition was published by Prof. Scholefield in 1828; and a third by the Rev. Hugh James Rose in 1833. An abstract of the work is prefixed to Valpy's edition of the Greek Testament.) In the same year in which he published this work he took his degree of D.D. at Cambridge, and removed to his living at Tansor, where he discharged his duties in such a manner as to gain the affection and esteem of his people. In 1809 he was appointed by bishop Pretyman to a stall in the cathedral of Lincoln, and in 1812 to the archdeaconry of Huntingdon. In 1811 he resigned his two livings for the vicarage of St. Pancras, Middlesex, and the rectory of Rottenham, in Hertfordshire. He fixed his residence at St. Pancras, and made the acquaintance of several dignitaries of the Church and other distinguished individuals. He was in sympathy with the object of the Society for Promoting Christian Knowledge, and was earnest and untiring in advancing its interests, as well as those of other societies in connection with the Church. The knowledge thus acquired of their plans, resources, and activities greatly aided him in his subsequent career in India, and the discernment and good judgment which he brought to their meetings contributed materially to their efficiency. About this time the Anglican Church established a bishopric in India, constituting Calcutta as the episcopal residence. For this distinguished position Dr. Middleton was selected; and he was accordingly consecrated the first colonial bishop ever set apart by the Anglican Church by the archbishop of Canterbury, May 8, 1814. A short time prior to his departure for Calcutta, bishop Middleton was made a fellow of the Royal Society. He arrived in Calcutta Nov. 28, 1814— a little more than a year from the time of the death of Henry Martyn, that valued worker in this field. During the voyage Middleton had diligently employed himself in increasing his qualifications for his office, especially by the study of Hebrew and Persian. As bishop of Calcutta he made every effort to promote the interests of Christianity, and to aid the cause of education. He made three visitations of his immense diocese, in two of which he directed his particular attention to the state of the Syrian Christians in the neighborhood of Cochin, on the coast of Malabar. By his efforts the Bishop's College at Calcutta was established for the education of clergymen and missionaries for the British possessions in Asia; and he laid the first stone of its buildings Dec. 15, 1820. He instituted a consistory court at Calcutta, and would have done the same at Madras but for the opinion of the advocate-general of Madras that he regarded such a measure as illegal. These extended labors and extraordinary exertions, embarrassed by daily annoyances from the civil authorities in their application of regulations applicable only to the home clergy, could not result otherwise than in depressing him and diminishing his vigor, especially in India's unhealthy climate, and greatly hastened the end of his days. He died July 8, 1822, absolutely worn out by toil and fatigue. His successor in the work was the sainted Reginald Heber (q. v.). Bishop Middleton was large and dignified in form, animated in manner, and generous and kind in disposition. As a preacher he was very impressive, his

voice clear and pleasing, his style simple and manly, generally argumentative, and strongly imbued with the doctrines of the Church of England. In accordance with his last desires, bishop Middleton's papers were destroyed, and we have, therefore, none of his greater works excepting the one he had published in his earlier years on "the Greek Article," the periodical publication mentioned above, and some sermons, charges, and tracts, which have been collected into a volume, to which a memoir of bishop Middleton is prefixed, by H. K. Bonney, D.D., archdeacon of Bedford (London, 1824). See Charles Webb Le Bas, *Life of the Right Rev. Thomas Fanshawe Middleton* (London, 1831, 2 vols. 8vo); Miss Yonge, *Pioneers and Founders*, ch. vii; *Monthly Review*, 1810 (May); Kaye, *Christianity in India*. (J. H. W.)

Middoth. See TALMUD.

Midgard's Serpent, or the *World-Serpent (Jörmungand)*, is, in the mythology of the Norsemen, the great serpent which surrounds the world. As the offspring of Loki (q. v.), the principle of evil, the other gods feared the new-born, and determined to get early possession of it and Fenrir, another of Loki's offspring, and, when secured, Midgard's Serpent was cast into the ocean, where it grew till it encircled the world, biting its own tail. At the end of the world, the world-serpent will fight among the enemies of the gods and be slain by Thor, who, however, will die immediately afterwards from the effect of its venom. The myth of the world-serpent is supposed to signify the deep or main ocean, which, excited by Loki (subterranean fire or earthquake), is thrown upon the land, thus proving scarcely less fatal to the works of man than the direct action of volcanic fire, represented under the form of Fenrir. For further particulars, see Thorpe's *Northern Mythology*, i, 80 sq., 161 sq.; Mallet's *Northern Antiquities*, vol. ii, Fables xvi, xxv, xxvi, xxvii; Keyser's *Religion of the Northmen*; Petersen's *Nordisk Mythologi*.

Mid'ian (Heb. *Midyan'*, מִדְיָן, strife, as in Prov. xviii, 18; xix, 13; Sept. Μαδιάμ v. r. Μαδιάν; N. T. Μαδιάμ, Acts vii, 29, where the Auth. Vers. has "Madian;" the Heb. often stands collectively for the "Midianites" also, as it is frequently rendered in all the versions), the fourth son of Abraham by Keturah, and the progenitor of the Midianites (Gen. xxv, 2; 1 Chron. i, 32). B.C. post 2024. His five sons are enumerated in Gen. xxv, 4; 1 Chron. i, 33. Of his personal history nothing further is known. See MIDIANITE.

Mid'ianite (Heb. *Midyani'*, מִדְיָנִי, Numb. x, 29, used collectively, and so rendered "Midianites," which is the usual translation for *Midian* itself; Sept. Μαδιανίτης; but the plur. מִדְיָנִים also occurs, Gen. xxxvii, 28, and the fem. מִדְיָנִית, Numb. xxv, 15; see also MADIAN), a tribe of people descended from Abraham's son Midian (q. v.), a branch of the Arabians dwelling principally in the desert north of the peninsula of Arabia. Southwards they extended along the eastern shore of the Gulf of Aileh; and northwards they stretched along the eastern frontier of Palestine; while the oases in the peninsula of Sinai seem to have afforded them pasture-grounds, and caused it to be included in the "land of Midian." The notion that there were two peoples called Midian, founded on the supposed shortness of the interval for any considerable multiplication from Abraham to Moses, and on the mention of Moses's Cushite wife, seems to be untenable. Even conceding the former objection, which is unnecessary, one tribe has often become merged into another and older one, and only the name of the latter retained. See Burton, *Gold Mines of Midian and Ruined Midianitish Cities* (Lond. 1878, 8vo).

I. *History.*—Midian, though not the oldest, was the most celebrated son of Keturah. What Judah became among the tribes of Israel, Midian became among the tribes of Arabia. It is true we find the other branches of the Keturites spoken of a few times in sacred history, and mentioned in such a way as to prove that as tribes they never lost their individuality; yet the Midianites were the dominant people, and Midian is the great name which always comes out prominently before the historian. Not only so, but the Midianites appear to have been for a lengthened period the virtual rulers of Arabia, combining into a grand confederacy, and then guiding or controlling, as circumstances required, all the Arabian branches of the Hebrew race. This fact comes out incidentally in many parts of Scripture; and we require to keep it carefully in view in order to understand the sacred narrative.

1. Midian had five sons, who, doubtless, in accordance with Arab custom, became heads of distinct tribes (Gen. xxv, 4; comp. Numb. xxxi, 8). We are told that while "Abraham gave all that he had to Isaac," that is, made him his heir—head of his house and patrimony—"to the sons of the concubines Abraham gave gifts, and sent them away from Isaac his son while he yet lived, eastward, to the land in the east" (ver. 5, 6). This is the first indication of the country occupied by the Midianites and other descendants of Keturah. The expression is not very definite. Abraham's principal place of residence was Southern Palestine—Mamre and Beersheba. The "country of the east" appears to have included the whole region on the east side of the Arabah or great valley which reaches from the fountains of the Jordan to the Ælanitic Gulf. All Arabia, in fact, and even Mesopotamia were included in the "country of the East" (Gen. xxix, 1; Numb. xxiii, 7, etc.). See BENE-KEDEM. Another incidental notice in Gen. xxxvi, 35 points more clearly to the exact territory of Midian. Hadad, one of the early kings of Edom, is said to have "smitten Midian in the field of Moab." We may conclude from this that the Midianites were at that time settled on the eastern borders of Moab and Edom. They were, like all Arabians, a nomad or semi-nomad people; having some settlements around fountains and in fertile valleys, but forced to wander in their tents from place to place to secure sufficient pasture for their flocks. The Midianites were an enterprising people. They were not satisfied with the dull routine of pastoral and agricultural life. From the first they appear to have engaged in commercial pursuits. Some districts of Arabia, Eastern Palestine, and Lebanon, yielded valuable spices and perfumes which were in great demand in Egypt, not merely for the luxuries of the living, but for the embalming of the dead. In this profitable trade the Midianites engaged. It was to one of their caravans passing through Palestine from Gilead to Egypt that Joseph was sold by his brethren (Gen. xxxvii, 25 sq.). Slaves at that time found as ready a market in Egypt as they do now. It will be observed that the traders are called by the historian both *Ishmaelites* and *Midianites*, the two names being used as synonymous. The reason probably is that these were the dominant tribes in Arabia, and carried on the trade jointly; hence they were known among strangers by both names. It would seem, however, that the merchants in this caravan were true Midianites, though they may have been accompanied by Ishmaelites (ver. 28, 36; but comp. 25, 27). In ver. 36 the Hebrew is הַמְּדָנִים, the *Medanites*, which is the regular plural of *Medan* (מדן), the third son of Keturah (Gen. xxv, 2); while in ver. 28 the word is מִדְיָנִים, the regular plural of מִדְיָן. There can be little doubt that the Midianites are referred to in both passages, as represented in the Septuagint, Vulgate, Targums, and other ancient versions. See MEDAN. By a similar latitude of expression, the Midianites sometimes appear to be reckoned among the Ishmaelites (Judg. vii, 12; viii, 22, 24); elsewhere they are distinguished from them (Gen. xxv, 2, 4, 12, 16). This probably arose from their being nomadic in their habits, so that bands of them often moved from place to place. But the difficulty may be avoided by supposing that the terms "Midianite" and "Ishmaelite" are used as a synonyme of travelling mer-

chant, such as they became in later times. See ISHMAELITE.

2. The next notice of Midian is in connection with the eventful history of Moses—"Moses fled from the face of Pharaoh, and dwelt in the land of *Midian*" (Exod. ii, 15). Reuel or Jethro, the priest of Midian, became his master and father-in-law. Moses kept his flock. The subsequent incidents of this strange narrative show clearly the region then inhabited by Jethro, and called "the land of Midian." It was the peninsula of Sinai, and it was while watching his flock there on the side of Horeb that Moses saw the glory of the Lord in the burning bush, and received the commission to return to Egypt for the deliverance of Israel (Exod. iii, 1 sq.). It would appear, from a comparison of the several incidental notices of Jethro given in the Pentateuch, that the peninsula of Sinai was not his settled place of abode. When Israel was encamped at Horeb, Jethro brought thither Moses's wife and his two sons; and, after a brief stay, we are told that "he went his way into his own land" (Exod. xviii, 1-3, 27; comp. Numb. x, 29, 30). The Midianites were nomads roaming over a very wide region, but, like most Arab tribes, having one permanent nucleus. This nucleus was specially their home: it was the "land of their kindred;" yet they also claimed the whole region in which they pastured their flocks as their own. The nucleus of the Midianites was somewhere on the eastern border of Edom, but their pasture-grounds probably extended as far as Gilead and Bashan on the north, while on the south they embraced an extensive territory along both shores of the Ælanitic Gulf. Hence Horeb was said to be in the land of Midian (Exod. ii, 15 with iii, 1), while the chief seat of Jethro's tribe was on the east of Edom. The Midianites were thus accustomed to lead their flocks and herds over the whole of that region which the Israelites afterwards traversed—the choice pastures, the fountains, and the wells in the desert were all known to them. This fact throws light on Moses's urgent request to his father-in-law—"Leave us not, I pray thee: forasmuch as thou knowest how we are to encamp in the wilderness, and thou mayest be to us instead of eyes" (Numb. x, 31). It should, however, be remembered that the name of Midian (and hence the "land of Midian") was perhaps often applied, as that of the most powerful of the northern Arab tribes, to the northern Arabs generally, i. e. those of Abrahamic descent (comp. Gen. xxxvii, 28, but see respecting this passage above; and Judg. viii, 24); just as BENE-KEDEM embraced all those peoples, and, with a wider signification, other Eastern tribes. If this reading of the name be correct, "Midian" would correspond very nearly with our modern word "Arab;" limiting, however, the modern word to the Arabs of the northern and Egyptian deserts: all the Ishmaelitish tribes of those deserts would thus be Midianites, as we call them Arabs, the desert being their "land." At least it cannot be doubted that the descendants of Hagar and Keturah intermarried; and thus the Midianites are apparently called Ishmaelites in Judg. viii, 24, being connected, both by blood and national customs, with the father of the Arabs. The wandering habits of nomadic tribes must also preclude our arguing from the fact of Moses's leading his father's flock to Horeb, that Sinai was necessarily more than a station of Midian: those tribes annually traverse a great extent of country in search of pasturage, and have their established summer and winter pastures. The Midianites were mostly (not always) dwellers in tents, not towns; and Sinai has not sufficient pasture to support more than a small, or a moving people. But it must be remembered that perhaps (or we may say *probably*) the peninsula of Sinai has considerably changed in its physical character since the time of Moses; even the adjacent isthmus has been thought, since that period, to have risen many feet, so that "the tongue of the Egyptian Sea" has "dried up;" and this supposition would much diminish the difficulty of accounting for the means of subsistence found by the

Israelites in their wanderings in the wilderness, when not miraculously supplied. Apart from this consideration, we know that the Egyptians afterwards worked mines at Sarábet el-Khádim, and a small mining population may have found sufficient sustenance, at least in some seasons of the year, in the few watered valleys, and wherever ground could be reclaimed: rock-inscriptions (though of later date) testify to the number of at least passers-by; and the remains of villages of a mining population have recently been discovered. Whatever may have been the position of Midian in the Sinaitic peninsula, if we may believe the Arabian historians and geographers, backed as their testimony is by the Greek geographers (see below), the city of Midian was situate on the opposite or Arabian shore of the Arabian Gulf; and thence northwards, and spreading east and west, we have the true country of the wandering Midianites. See SINAI.

3. The next occurrence of the name of this people in the sacred history marks their northern settlements on the border of the Promised Land, "on this side Jordan [by] Jericho," in the plains of Moab (Numb. xxii, 1-4). The Midianites were a wise and a wily people. So long as the Israelites only traversed their outlying pasture-grounds on the west of the Arabah, they were content to cultivate their friendship; but when, in the latter part of their journey, having passed round the southern end of Edom, they entered the proper territory of Midian, the Midianites tried every plan and used every effort to work their destruction. They consulted with their neighbors, the chiefs of Moab, and resolved to bring the prophet Balaam to curse the powerful strangers (Numb. xxii, 4-7). Balaam came, and the Lord turned the intended curse into a blessing. The prophet, however, adopted a more effectual mode of injuring the Israelites than by the agency of enchantments. He persuaded the women of Midian and Moab to work upon the passions of the Israelites, and entice them to the licentious festivals of their idols, and thus bring upon them the curse of heaven (xxxi, 16). This infamous scheme proved only too successful (ch. xxv), and, had it not been checked by the almost complete annihilation of the Midianites, it would have brought destruction upon the whole host of Israel (xxv, 17; xxxi, 2). The vengeance then executed upon Midian was terrible. Their cities and castles were burned; the entire males that fell into the hands of the conquerors were put to death, including the five kings of Midian—Evi, Rekem, Zur, Hur, and Reba, together with Balaam—and with them all the married females; and the young women and children were reduced to slavery. It has been affirmed that these acts of vengeance are so cruel, so barbarous in their character, that they could never have been prompted by a God of love, and that, therefore, the narrative cannot be considered as of divine authority. Those who bring such an accusation against the Scriptures must surely overlook the leading circumstances of the case—they must forget that the God of love is also the God of justice. The whole Midianitish nation, male and female, had deliberately combined and conspired, by wile and stratagem, to wean the Israelites from their allegiance to the God of heaven, and not only so, but wantonly to allure them to the commission of the most foul and degrading crimes. Was it inconsistent with justice for the moral Governor of the universe to punish such guilt? Could any punishment less sweeping have freed the earth from crime so deep-rooted and so dangerous? The influence of the Midianites on the Israelites was clearly most evil, and directly tended to lead them from the injunctions of Moses. Much of the dangerous character of their influence may probably be ascribed to the common descent from Abraham. While the Canaanitish tribes were abhorred, Midian might claim consanguinity, and more readily seduce Israel from its allegiance.

The details of this war given by Moses afford us some little insight into the nature of the country of Midian,

and the occupations of the people. The Midianites were not pure nomads; they had cities and goodly castles (xxxi, 10). Their principal wealth consisted, however, in flocks and herds, for the Israelites captured 675,000 sheep, 72,000 beeves, and 61,000 asses. It is singular that camels are not mentioned; but it is probable that, as the Israelites were all footmen, the camels escaped to the desert. Recent investigations have shown that the whole desert east of Edom and Moab is thickly studded with the ruins of ancient cities and castles (Wallin, in Journal of R. G. S. xxiv, 115 sq.; Porter, Damascus, ii, 188; Wetstein, Reisebericht über Hauran, etc.; Graham, in Journal of R. G. S. for 1859). These were doubtless the habitations of the Midianites. The whole region around their cities, extending from the mountains of Haurân to the Ælanitic Gulf, though now dreary and desolate, is not barren. In spring and early summer it is covered with vegetation, and it has many rich valleys, a few patches of which are still here and there cultivated by the Arab tribes. Everywhere there are evidences of partial cultivation in former days, and there are also traces of a comparatively dense population (see Porter, Hand-book, p. 501, 508, 523, etc.).

Some time previous to the exodus it appears that the Midianites had allied themselves closely to the Moabites. Sihon, king of the Amorites, made war upon Moab and Ammon, conquered a large part of their territory, and retained possession of it (Judg. xi, 13-23). At the same time he made Midian, the ally of Moab, tributary; and hence the five princes of Midian are called by Joshua vassals (נְסִיכֵם; Keil on Josh. xiii, 21) or "dukes" of Sihon. The defeat of Sihon by the Israelites secured the freedom of the Midianites; and then they, fearing lest they should in like manner be subdued by Moses, conspired to destroy Israel, and thus brought destruction upon themselves. The government of Midian was doubtless similar to that of all the nations of Arabia—patriarchal. The nation was divided into a number of tribes, each of which was independent, and led by its own sheik or chief. In time of common danger or of war, the sheiks of the various tribes formed a council, but always acknowledged the presidency of the head of one leading family, who was (and still is) styled the "prince" (emir) of the nation. Five of the sheiks of Midian are mentioned in Judges as subjects of Sihon. In Numb. xxxi, 8 they are called "kings" (מלכים); while in xxii, 4 Moab is said to have consulted with the "elders" (זקנים) of Midian. The great Arab tribes have two classes of chiefs: one class is composed of the rulers of the leading divisions of the tribe, the other of the rulers of subdivisions. The former are hereditary, the latter are simply influential or warlike men who, by their talents, have gathered around them a number of families. It would seem to be the former class—the hereditary rulers of Midian—who are called "kings;" while the others, the influential leaders or senators of the tribe, are termed "elders." In the transaction with Balaam, the elders of Midian went with those of Moab, "with the rewards of divination in their hand" (xxii, 7); but in the remarkable words of Balaam the Midianites are not mentioned. This might be explained by the supposition that Midian was a wandering tribe, whose pasture-lands reached wherever, in the Arabian desert and frontier of Palestine, pasture was to be found, and who would not feel, in the same degree as Moab, Amalek, or the other more settled and agricultural inhabitants of the land allotted to the tribes of Israel, the arrival of the latter. But the spoil taken in the war that soon followed, and more especially the mention of the dwellings of Midian, render this suggestion very doubtful, and point rather to a considerable pastoral settlement of Midian in the trans-Jordanic country. Such settlements of Arabs have, however, been very common. In this case the Midianites were evidently tributary to the Amorites, being "dukes of Sihon, dwelling in the country" (יֹשְׁבֵי הָאָרֶץ): this inferior position explains their omission from Balaam's prophecy. The rank of the Midianitish woman Cozbi, that of a daughter of Zur, who was "head over a people, of a chief house in Midian," throws a strange light over the obscure page of that people's history. The vices of the Canaanites, idolatry and licentiousness, had infected the descendants of Abraham, doubtless connected by successive intermarriages with those tribes; and the prostitution of this chief's daughter, caught as it was from the customs of the Canaanites, is evidence of the ethnological type of the latter tribes. Some African nations have a similar custom: they offer their unmarried daughters to show hospitality to their guests.

4. There is no further mention of the Midianites in history for two hundred and fifty years. During that period the nation had completely recovered its ancient influence and power, probably by the arrival of fresh colonists from the desert tracts over which their tribes wandered; and they again turned their arms against their old enemies, the Israelites. For seven years they oppressed them so grievously that the people were forced to flee from the open country, and to seek an asylum in mountain fastnesses, in caves, and in fortified cities (Judg. vi, 1, 2). Midian was now at the head of a great confederacy, comprising the Amalekites and the leading tribes of Arabia, called by the sacred historian *Beni Kedem* ("children of the East," ver. 3). In early spring the confederates assembled their vast flocks and herds, descended through the defiles of Gilead, crossed the Jordan, and overran the rich plains of Central Palestine, plundering and destroying all before them — "sheep, oxen, asses," property, the young corn, and the luxuriant pastures: "For they came up with their cattle, and their tents, and they came as grasshoppers for multitude; for both they and their camels were without number; and they entered into the land to destroy it" (ver. 5). In their distress the Israelites cried unto the Lord, and he sent a deliverer in the person of Gideon (ver. 8–13). The invaders were concentrated on Esdraelon—their flocks covering the whole of that splendid plain, and their encampment lying along the base of "the hill of Moreh," now called Little Hermon (ver. 33; vii, 1, 12). Gideon assembled his band of warriors at the well of Harod, or fountain of Jezreel, situated at the foot of Gilboa, and famed in after-days as the scene of Saul's defeat and death (vii, 1). See HAROD. The romantic incidents in this memorable campaign have been treated of elsewhere [see GIDEON], but the Midianitish side of the story is pregnant with interest. The scene over that fertile plain, dotted with the enemies of Israel, "the Midianites, and the Amalekites, and all the Bene-Kedem, [who] lay along (נֹפְלִים, *fell*, i. e. *pitched* their tents) in the valley like locusts for multitude, and their camels were without number, as the sand by the sea-side for multitude" (vii, 12), has been picturesquely painted by Prof. Stanley (*Sinai and Palestine*, p. 333).

The descent of Gideon and his servant into the camp, and the conversation of the Midianitish watch, forms a vivid picture of Arab life. It does more: it proves that as Gideon, or Phurah, his servant, or both, understood the language of Midian, the Shemitic languages differed much less in the 14th century B.C. than they did in after-times [see ARABIA]; and we besides obtain a remarkable proof of the consanguinity of the Midianites, and learn that, though the name was probably applied to all or most of the northern Abrahamic Arabs, it was not applied to the Canaanites, who certainly did not then speak a Shemitic language that Gideon could understand. The stratagem of Gideon receives an illustration from modern Oriental life. Until lately the police in Cairo were accustomed to go their rounds with a lighted torch thrust into a pitcher, and the pitcher was suddenly withdrawn when light was required (Lane's *Mod. Eg.* 5th edit. p. 120)—a custom affording an exact parallel to the ancient expedient adopted by Gideon.

The consequent panic of the great multitude in the valley, if it have no parallels in modern European history, is consistent with Oriental character. Of all peoples, the nations of the East are most liable to sudden and violent emotions; and a panic in one of their heterogeneous, undisciplined, and excitable hosts has always proved disastrous. In the case of Gideon, however, the result of his attack was directed by God, the divine hand being especially shown in the small number of Israel, 300 men, against 135,000 of the enemy. At the sight of the 300 torches, suddenly blazing round about the camp in the beginning of the middle-watch (which the Midianites had newly set), with the confused din of the trumpets, "for the three companies blew the trumpets, and brake the pitchers, and held the lamps in their left hands, and the trumpets in their right hands to blow [withal], and they cried, [The sword] of the Lord and of Gideon" (vii, 20), "all the host ran, and cried, and fled" (ver. 21). The panic-stricken multitude knew not enemy from friend, for "the Lord set every man's sword against his fellow even throughout all the host" (ver. 22). The rout was complete, the first places made for being Beth-shittah ("the house of the acacia") in Zererath, and the "border" (שָׂפָה, *lip*) of Abel-meholah, "the meadow of the dance," both being probably down the Jordan valley, unto Tabbath, shaping their flight to the ford of Beth-barah, where probably they had crossed the river as invaders. The flight of so great a host, encumbered with slow-moving camels, baggage, and cattle, was calamitous. All the men of Israel, out of Naphtali, and Asher, and Manasseh, joined in the pursuit; and Gideon roused the men of Mount Ephraim to "take before" the Midianites "the waters unto Beth-barah and Jordan" (ver. 23, 24). Thus cut off, two princes, Oreb and Zeeb (the "raven," or, more correctly "crow," and the "wolf"), fell into the hands of Ephraim, and Oreb they slew at the rock Oreb, and Zeeb they slew at the wine-press of Zeeb (vii, 25; comp. Isa. x, 26, where the "slaughter of Midian at the rock Oreb" is referred to). It is added, in the same verse, that they pursued Midian, and brought the heads of the princes to Gideon "on the other side Jordan." This anticipates the account of his crossing Jordan (viii, 4), but such transpositions are frequent, and the Hebrew may be read "On this side Jordan." But though we have seen that many joined in a desultory pursuit of the rabble of the Midianites, only the 300 men who had blown the trumpets in the valley of Jezreel crossed Jordan with Gideon, "faint yet pursuing" (viii, 4). With this force it remained for the liberator to attack the enemy on his own ground, for Midian had dwelt on the other side Jordan since the days of Moses. Fifteen thousand men, under the "kings" of Midian, Zebah and Zalmunna, were at Karkor, the sole remains of 135,000, "for there fell a hundred and twenty thousand men that drew sword" (viii, 10). The assurance of God's help encouraged the weary three hundred, and they ascended from the plain (or *ghór*) to the higher country by a ravine or torrent-bed in the hills, "by the way of them that dwelt in tents [that is, the pastoral or wandering people as distinguished from towns-people], on the east of Nobah and Jogbehah, and smote the host, for the host was secure" (viii, 11)—secure in that wild country, on their own ground, and away from the frequent haunts of man. A sharp pursuit seems to have followed this fresh victory, ending in the capture of the kings and the final discomfiture of the Midianites. The overthrow of Midian in its encampment, when it was "secure," by the exhausted companies of Gideon (they were "faint," and had been refused bread both at Succoth and at Penuel, viii, 5–9), set the seal to God's manifest hand in the deliverance of his people from the oppression of Midian. Zebah and Zalmunna were slain, and with them the name itself of Midian almost disappears from sacred history. That people never afterwards took up arms against Israel, though they may have been allied with the nameless hordes who, under the common designation of "the people of the East," Bene-Kedem, harassed the eastern border of Palestine.

To this victory there are subsequent allusions in the sacred writings (Psa. lxxxiii, 10, 12; Isa. ix, 4; x, 6); but the Midianites do not again appear in sacred or profane history. The name, indeed, occurs after the exile in Judith ii, 16, but it seems to be there confounded with the Arabians. Josephus, however, asserts ($Ant.$ iv, 7, 1) that Petra, the capital of Arabia (i. e. Idumæa), was called by the natives Areceme, from the Midianitish king Rekem slain by Moses (Numb. xxxi, 8). Eusebius and Jerome also mention a city $Madian$, so named after the son of Abraham by Keturah, situated beyond Arabia (Idumæa) to the south, by the Red Sea, from which the district was called; and another city of the same name near the Arnon and Areopolis, the ruins of which only existed in their days ($Onomast.$ s. v.; comp. Jerome, $Comment.$ ad $Jes.$ lx, and $Ezech.$ xxv). These were doubtless traditionary recollections of the different branches of the Midianitish stock, showing their prevalence throughout Idumæa and the Sinaitic peninsula as a migratory tribe.

II. $Geographical$ $Identification.$—From all the above notices, we may gather with considerable certainty that there were at least two main branches of the Midianites. It seems to have been that portion of the tribe dwelling about the eastern arm of the Red Sea, among whom Moses found refuge when he fled from Egypt, and whose priest or sheik was Jethro, who became the father-in-law of the future lawgiver (Exod. iii, 1; Numb. x, 29). See KENITE. These in like manner are usually reckoned along with the Ethiopians of Cushite origin. It is certain that some Cushite tribes did settle in and on the outskirts of Arabia, which was therefore called Cush, in common with other districts occupied by Cushite tribes; and, under this view, is observable that the wife of Moses is called a Cushite (Numb. xii, 1), and that, in Hab. iii, 7, the Midianites are named with the Cushites; for these are undoubtedly the Midianites who trembled for fear when they heard that the Israelites had passed through the Red Sea. We do not again meet with these Midianites in the Jewish history, but they appear to have remained for a long time settled in the same quarter, where indeed is the seat of the only Midianites known to Oriental authors. The Arabian geographers of the middle age (Edrisi, $Clim.$ iii, 5, p. 3; Ibn el-Wardi, and Abulfeda, $Arab.$ $descr.$ p. 77; comp. Seetzen, xx, 311) speak of the ruins of an ancient town called $Madian$, on the eastern side of the Red Sea, where was still to be seen the well at which Moses watered the flocks of Shoaib or Jethro. This was doubtless the same as $Modiana$, a town in the same district, mentioned by Ptolemy ($Geog.$ v, 19); and Niebuhr conjectures that the site is now occupied by Moilah, a small town or village on the Red Sea, on the Haj road from Egypt ($Descript.$ $Arab.$ p. 377); but, as Rosenmüller remarks ($Bibl.$ $Geog.$ iii, 224), this place is too far south to be identified with the Midian of Jethro. The Madian of Abulfeda is doubtless that mentioned by Josephus ($Ant.$ xii, 11, 1) as $Madiene$ (Μαδνηνή), situated at the Red Sea, properly identified by Reland ($Palæst.$ p. 98, 100) with the modern $Midyan$, situated about half-way down the eastern coast of the Ælanitic Gulf (Forster's $Geogr.$ of $Arabia$, ii, 116, and Index, s. v.). To the same effect are the notices of the city Madian in Eusebius and Jerome above.

Another branch of the Midianites occupied the country east and south-east of the Moabites, who were seated on the east of the Dead Sea; or rather, perhaps, we should say that, as they appear to have been a semi-nomad tribe, they pastured their flocks in the unsettled country beyond the Moabites, with whom, as a kindred, although more settled tribe, they seem to have been on the most friendly terms, and on whose borders were situated those "cities and goodly castles which they possessed" (Numb. xxxi, 10). It is to these Mid-

ianites that we must refer the brief statements of a collision with Hadad, one of the early Edomitish kings (Gen. xxxvi, 35). These Midianites, like the other tribes and nations who had a common origin with them, were highly hostile to the Israelites.

Midian is named authentically only in the Bible. It has no history elsewhere. The names of places and tribes occasionally throw a feeble light on its past dwellings; but the stories of Arabian writers, borrowed, in the case of the northern Arabs, too frequently from late and untrustworthy Jewish writers, cannot be seriously treated. For trustworthy facts we must rest on the Biblical narrative. The city of "Medyen [say the Arabs] is the city of the people of Shu'eib, and is opposite Tabûk, on the shore of Bahr el-Kulzum [the Red Sea]: between these is six days' journey. It [Medyen] is larger than Tabûk; and in it is the well from which Moses watered the flock of Shu'eib" ($Marásid$, s. v.). El-Makrîzî (in his $Khitat$) enters into considerable detail respecting this city and people. The substance of his account, which is full of incredible fables, is as follows: Medyen are the people of Shu'eib, and are the offspring of Medyán [Midian], son of Abraham, and their mother was Kantûrà, the daughter of Yuktán [Joktan] the Canaanite: she bare him eight children, from whom descended peoples. He here quotes the passage above cited from the $Marásid$ almost verbatim, and adds that the Arabs dispute whether the name be foreign or Arabic, and whether Medyen spoke Arabic, so called. Some say that they had a number of kings, who were respectively named Abjad, Hawez, Huttî, Kelemen, Saafas, and Karashet. This absurd enumeration forms a sentence common in Arabic grammars, which gives the order of the Hebrew and ancient Arabic alphabets, and the numerical order of the letters. It is only curious as possibly containing some vague reference to the $language$ of Midian, and it is therefore inserted here. These kings are said to have ruled at Mekkeh, Western Nejd, the Yemen, Medyen, and Egypt, etc., contemporaneously. That Midian penetrated into the Yemen is, it must be observed, extremely improbable, notwithstanding the hints of Arab authors to the contrary: Yákût, in the $Moajam$ (cited in the $Journal$ of the $Deutsch.$ $Morgenl.$ $Gesellschaft$), saying that a southern Arabian dialect is of Midian; and El-Mes'ûdî ($ap.$ Schultens, p. 158) inserting a Midianitish king among the rulers of the Yemen; the latter being, however, more possible than the former, as an accidental and individual, not a national occurrence. The story of Shu'eib is found in the Kurán. He was sent as a prophet to warn the people of Midian, and being rejected by them, they were destroyed by a storm from heaven (Sale's $Kurán$, vii and xi). He is generally supposed to be the same as Jethro, the father-in-law of Moses; but some, as Sale informs us, deny this; and one of these says that "he was first called Buyûn, and afterwards Shu'eib; that he was a comely person, but spare and lean, and of few words." The whole Arab story of Medyen and Shu'eib, even if it contain any truth, is encumbered by a mass of late rabbinical myths. El-Makrîzî tells us that in the land of Midian were many cities, of which the people had disappeared, and the cities themselves had fallen to ruin; that when he wrote (in the year 825 of the Hegira) forty cities remained, the names of some being known, and of others lost. Of the former, he says there were, between the Hijáz and Palestine and Egypt, sixteen cities; and ten of these in the direction of Palestine. They were El-Khalasah, El-Sanîtah, El-Medereh, El-Minyeh, El-Aawaj, El-Khuweyrak, El-Bîrein, El-Má-eyn, El-Seba, and El-Mu'allak. The most important of these cities were El-Khalasah and El-Sanîtah; the stones of many of them had been removed to El-Ghazzah (Gaza) to build with them. This list, however, must be taken with caution.

III. $Condition$ and $Customs.$—Much of this has already been incidentally mentioned. The whole account of the doings of the Midianites with Israel—and it is only thus that they find a place in the sacred writings —plainly marks them as characteristically Arab. We have already stated our opinion that they had intermarried with Ishmael's descendants, and become nationally one people, so that they are apparently called Ishmaelites; and that, conversely, it is most probable their power and numbers, with such intermarriages, had caused the name of Midian to be applied to the northern Abrahamic Arabs generally. They are described as true Arabs—now Bedawin, or "people of the desert;" anon pastoral or settled Arabs—the "flock" of Jethro; the cattle and flocks of Midian, in the later days of Moses; their camels without number, as the sand of the sea-side for multitude when they oppressed Israel in the days of the Judges—all agree with such a description. Like Arabs, who are predominantly a nomadic people, they seem to have partially settled in the land of Moab, under the rule of Sihon the Amorite, and to have adapted themselves readily to the "cities" (עָרִים) and forts (A. V. "goodly castles," טִירֹת), which they did not build, but occupied, retaining even then their flocks and herds (Numb. xxxi, 9, 10), but not their camels, which are not common among settled Arabs, because they are not required, and are never, in that state, healthy. Israel seems to have devastated that settlement, and when next Midian appears in history it is as a desert horde, pouring into Palestine with innumerable camels; and, when routed and broken by Gideon, fleeing "by the way of them that dwelt in tents" to the east of Jordan. The character of Midian we think is thus unmistakably marked. The only glimpse of their habits is found in the vigorous picture of the camp in the valley of Jezreel, when the men talked together in the camp, and one told how he had dreamed that "a cake of barley-bread tumbled into the host of Midian, and came into a tent, and smote it that it fell, and overturned it, that the tent lay along" (Judg. vii, 13).

The spoil taken in both the war of Moses and that of Gideon is remarkable. On the former occasion, the spoil of 675,000 sheep, 72,000 beeves, and 61,000 asses, seems to confirm the other indications of the then pastoral character of the Midianites; the omission of any mention of camels has already been explained. But the gold, silver, brass, iron, tin, and lead (Numb. xxxi, 22), the jewels of gold, chains, and bracelets, rings, earrings, and tablets" (ver. 50)—the offering to the Lord being 16,750 shekels (ver. 52)—taken by Moses, is especially noteworthy; and it is confirmed by the booty taken by Gideon; for when he slew Zebah and Zalmunna he "took away the ornaments that [were] on their camels' necks" (Judg. viii, 21), and (ver. 24-26) he asked of every man the ear-rings of his prey, "for they had golden ear-rings, because they [were] Ishmaelites." "And the weight of the golden ear-rings that he requested was a thousand and seven hundred [shekels] of gold; besides ornaments and collars, and purple raiment that [was] on the kings of Midian, and besides the chains that [were] about their camels' necks." (The rendering of the A. V. is sufficiently accurate for our purpose here, and any examination into the form or character of these ornaments, tempting though it is, belongs more properly to other articles.) We have here a wealthy Arab nation, living by plunder, delighting in finery (especially their women, for we may here read "nose-ring"), and, where forays were impossible, carrying on the traffic southwards into Arabia, the land of gold—if not naturally, by trade—and across to Chaldæa, or into the rich plains of Egypt. See ARABIA.

Midlent Sunday (or **Mothering Sunday**), imperfectly explained in the *Antiquitates Vulgares*, is founded on the Roman Hilaria (q. v.), or feast in honor of Cybele, the mother of the gods, who, the legend tells us, was converted by Christianity into the mother Church, whence, in the second step, the *Antiquitates Vulgares* deduces the origin of Midlent. See Brough-

ton, *Bibl. Historico-Sacra*, i, 194; Fosbrook, *British Monachism*, p. 61.

Midnight (לַיְל, *night*, νύξ, in connection with חֲצִי, חֲצוֹת, or תּוֹךְ, μέσος, *middle*; μεσονύκτιον simply. See NIGHT.

Midrash (Heb. מִדְרָשׁ) is a word applied to the oldest Jewish exposition of the Scriptures—a peculiar, somewhat wild mode of interpretation, which appeals more to the feelings than to the reason.

I. *Title and its Signification, etc.*—The term מדרש, which is strangely rendered in the text of the A. V. by *story* (2 Chron. xiii, 22; xxiv, 27), is derived from the root דרש, *to search into, to examine, to investigate, to explain*, and primarily denotes *the study, the exposition of Holy Scripture*, in the abstract and general sense. Thus it is said, "Not the study of it (תמדרש), but the doing of the law is the chief thing" (*Aboth*, i, 17). The study or exposition of Holy Writ (מדרש) was effected in earlier times through public discourses, delivered on Sabbaths, festivals, and days of assembly, by the priests, Levites, elders of Israel, and prophets. During the period of the second Temple, when the canonical books and the written discourses of the older prophets became unintelligible to the mass of the people, who spoke Hebraized Aramaic, these public expositions became more formal, and were delivered on a large scale by the lawyers, or Scribes (סופרים), as they are called in the N. T., the directors of schools (רבנן), graduated rabbins (רבות, only with suff. רבותינו), or learned men in general and members of societies (חברים).

II. *Design and Classification.*—The design of the Midrash or exposition varied according to circumstances. Sometimes the lecturer (דורש, דרשן) confined himself to giving a running paraphrase (מתורגמן) into the vulgar Aramaic, or the other dialects of the country, of the lessons from the Law and Prophets which were read in Hebrew (see HAPHTARAH), thus gradually giving rise to the Chaldee, Syriac, and Greek versions, so that these Targumim may be regarded as being the result, or forming part of the Midrash. The chief design of the Midrash, however, was to propound the Scriptures either *logically* or *homiletically*. Hence obtained that twofold mode of expression called *the legal* or *Halachic exegesis*, and the *homiletic* or *Hagadic exegesis*, and their respective literatures.

1. *The Legal or Halachic Exegesis.*—The object of this branch of exposition is to ascertain, by analogy, combination, or otherwise, the meaning of the law respecting exceptional cases about which there is no direct enactment in the Mosaic code, as it was the only rule of practice in the political and religious government of the Jews under all vicissitudes of the commonwealth, and as the motto of the expositors and administrators of it was "Turn it (i. e. the inspired code) over and over again, for everything is in it, and will be discovered therein" (*Aboth*, v, 22). The laws thus obtained, either by deduction from the text or introduction into it, are called *Halachoth* (הלכות, sing. הלכה, from הלך, *to go*), *the rule by which to go, the binding precept, the authoritative law*, being equivalent to the Hebrew word משפטים (comp. Chaldee Paraphrase on Exod. xxi, 9), and this mode of exposition, which is chiefly confined to the Pentateuch as the legal part of the O. T., is termed *Halachic exegesis*. These Halachoth (הלכות), some of which are coeval with the enactments in the Pentateuch itself (Deut. xvii, 11), while some are the labors of the Great Synagogue or the Sopherim=Scribes—beginning with Ezra, and terminating with Simon the Just—were for centuries transmitted orally, and hence are also called *Shematha* (שמעתא), i. e. that which was heard, or that which was received by members of the chain of tradition. Those prohibitory

laws or fences (גדר, סיג, later גזרה) which the Sopherim were obliged to make on their own account in consequence of the new wants of the times, without being indicated in the Pentateuch, and which are called Sopheric precepts (דברי סופרים), and in the N. T. Tradition of the Elders (παράδοσις τῶν πρεσβυτέρων, Matt. xv, 2; Mark vii, 3), are distinguished from the traditional laws which are deduced from the Bible. The latter are designated Deductions from the Law (עקר דאורייתא), and are of equal authority with the Biblical precepts. The few learned men who during the period of the Sopherim (B.C. 450–300) wrote down some of these laws, or indicated them by certain signs (סמנים) or hints (רמזים) in their scrolls of the Pentateuch, only did so to assist their memory, and the documents are called Secret Scrolls (מגלות סתרים). These marginal glosses in the MSS. of the Law became the basis of the Masorah (q.v.). Gradually, however, these Halachoth were fully written down, and are embodied in the following works.

(1.) It was not till the period of the Tanaim (an honorable appellation given to those doctors who transmitted the oral law), B.C. 220–A.D. 220, that the fixing, collecting, and final redaction of the Halachah—this mass of juridico-political and religious practice, or doctrine of human and divine law (humani et divini juris)—took place. The first attempt at a compilation and rubrification of it was made by Hillel I (B.C. 75–A.D. 8), who classified and arranged the diverse laws under six sedarim (סדרים) or orders. In this he was followed by 'Akiba (A.D. 20–120), and Simon III b.-Gamaliel II, who was the president of the Sanhedrim A.D. 140–163, and whose son R. Jehudah I the Holy, called Rabbi κατ' ἐξοχήν (died A.D. cir. 193), completed the final redaction of the code called Mishna (q. v.).

(2.) The Mishna, however, like the Pentateuch, soon became the subject of discussion or study, as many of its expositions and enactments are not only couched in obscure language, but are derived from antagonistic sources. Hence, like the divine code of the law, which it both supplements and expounds, the Mishna itself was expounded during the period of the Amoraim, or expositors; an appellation given to the public expositors of the oral law (הלכות), recorded by the Tanaim, A.D. 220–540, both in Jerusalem and Babylon. The result of these expositions is the two Talmuds, or more properly Gemaras, viz. the Jerusalem and the Babylon. See TALMUD.

(3.) Prior in point of age to the compilation of the Mishna is the commentary on Exodus, called Mechilta, which is composed of nine Tractates (מסיכתות), subdivided into sections (פרשיות), and treating on select sections of Exodus in the following order: The first tract treats on Exod. xii, 1–xiii, 6, in eighteen sections; the second is on xiii, 7–xiv, 31, in six sections; the third is on xv, 1–21, in ten sections; the fourth is on xv, 22–xvii, 7, in seven sections; the fifth is on xvii, 8–xviii, 27, in four sections; the sixth is on xix, 1–xx, 22, in eleven sections; the seventh is on xxi, 1–xxii, 22, in eight sections; the eighth is on xxii, 23–xxiii, 19, in two sections; and the ninth tract is on chap. xxix, 12–17; xxxv, 1–3, in two sections. The first compilation of the Mechilta was most probably made under the influence of R. Ishmael b.-Elisa, A.D. cir. 90 [see ISHMAEL B.-ELISA], which accounts for the many maxims contained in it, and not to be found elsewhere. It was re-edited afterwards, and greatly altered (comp. Geiger, Urschrift, p. 434 sq.). It was printed at Constantinople in 1515; then again at Venice in 1545; then, with a commentary and revised text by M. Frankfurter (Amst.), in 1712; but the best edition is that by Landau (Vilna), in 1844. A Latin translation of it by Ugolino is given in his Thesaurus Antiquitatum Sacrum, vol. xiv (Venice, 1752).

(4.) Commentary on Leviticus, called Siphra, Sifra

(ספרא), the Book; also Siphra D'be Rab (ספרא דבי רב), Siphra of the school of Rab, because Rab=Abba Areka, the first of the Amoraim, and founder of the celebrated school at Sora, of which he was president twenty-eight years (A.D. 219–247), is its author; and by some it is denominated Boraitha shel Torath Cohanim (ברייתא של תורת כהנים), because the book of Leviticus which it expounds is called by the Jews the Code of the Priests (תורת כהנים, Jebamoth, 72 b; Rashi, on Levit. ix, 23). The Siphra is divided into treatises (דיבורים), which are subdivided into sections (פרשות), and these again into chapters (פרקים). The first edition of it appeared, together with the Mechilta and Siphri, at Constantinople in 1515; then at Venice in 1545; and, with a very extensive commentary by Ibn Chajim, at Venice in 1609–11; with the commentary Ha-Tora Veha-Mitzva, by M. L. Malbim, at Bucharest in 1860. The best edition, however, is that by Schlossberg, with the commentary of Abraham b.-David, and the Massoreth Ha-Talmud of Weiss (Vienna, 1862). A Latin translation of it by Ugolino is given in his Thesaurus Antiquitatum Sacrum (Venice, 1752), vol. xiv.

(5.) Commentary on Numbers and Deuteronomy, called Siphre or Siphri (ספרי), the Books, also Siphre D'be Rab (ספרי דבי רב), because Rab, the author of the preceding work, is also the author of this commentary, and Vishallechu (וישלחו), because it begins with Numb. v, 2, where this word occurs. The commentary on Numbers is divided into one hundred and sixty-one chapters, and that on Deuteronomy into three hundred and fifty-seven. The Siphre first appeared with the Mechilta and Siphra at Constantinople in 1515; at Venice in 1545. The best edition of it is in two volumes, with the extensive commentary by Lichtstein (vol. i, Dyrhenfort, 1810; vol. ii, Radvill, 1819). A Latin translation of it by Ugolino is given in his Thesaurus Antiquitatum Sacrum (Venice, 1753), vol. xv.

2. The Homiletic or Hagadic Exegesis.—The design of this branch of the Midrash or exposition is to edify the people of Israel in their most holy faith, to encourage them to obedience, to commend to them the paths of virtue and morality, to stimulate them to all good works, and to comfort them in tribulation by setting before them the marvellous dealings of Providence with the children of man, the illustrious examples of the holy patriarchs, and the signal punishment of evil-doers from by-gone history—investing each character, and every event, with the halo or contumely, the poetry or the legend, which the fertile genius of the Hebrew nation and the creative power of tradition had called into existence in the course of time. This branch of exposition extends over the whole Hebrew Scriptures, while the Halachic interpretation, as we have seen, is chiefly confined to the Pentateuch, which is the civil and legal portion of the Bible. It is also called Hagadah (הגדה; Chaldee אגדה, from נגד, to say), said, reported, on dit, without its having any binding authority, in contradistinction to the Halachah, which is authoritative law. When it is stated that this department of Biblical exegesis is interspersed with homiletics, the beautiful maxims and ethical sayings of illustrious men, attractive mystical expositions about angels and dæmons, paradise and hell, Messiah and the Prince of Darkness; poetical allegories, symbolical interpretations of all the feasts and fasts, charming parables, witty epithalamiums, touching funeral orations, amazing legends, biographical and characteristic sketches of Biblical persons and national heroes; popular narratives, and historical notices of men, women, and events of by-gone days; philosophical disquisitions, satirical assaults on the heathen and their rites, able defences of Judaism, etc., etc., it will be readily understood why the Jewish nation gradually transferred to this storehouse of Biblical and national lore the name Midrash = the exposition, κατ'

ἐξοχήν. This branch of public and popular exposition, in which the public at large naturally felt far more interest than in the dry disquisitions about legal enactments, being thus called by them *The Midrash*, the collection of works which contain this sacred and national lore obtained the name *Midrashim* (מדרשים), *Commentaries*, in the sense of Cæsar's *Commentaries*. Hence the term *Midrashic* or *Hagadic* exegesis, so commonly used in Jewish writings, by which is meant an interpretation effected in the spirit of those national and traditional views. The following are the principal *Midrashim*, or commentaries, in the more restricted sense of the word, which contain the ancient Hagadic expositions. (It must here be remarked that as this branch of the Midrash embraces the whole cycle of ethics, metaphysics, history, theosophy, etc., as well as Biblical exposition, it has been divided into—1, *General Hagadah* or *Hagadah Midrash*, in its wider sense, treating almost exclusively on morals, history, etc.; and, 2, into *Special Hagadah* or *Hagadah Midrash*, in its narrower, and *Midrash* in its narrowed sense, occupying itself almost entirely with Biblical exposition, and making the elements of the general Hagada subservient to its purpose. It would be foreign to the design of this article were we to discuss anything more than the Midrash in its narrowest sense.)

(1.) *Midrash Rabboth* (מדרש רבות), or simply *Rabboth* (רבות), which is ascribed to Oshaja b.-Nachmani (fl. A.D. 278), and derives its name from the fact that this collection begins with a *Hagadah* of Oshaja *Rabba*, contains ten Midrashim, which bears the respective names of—1. *Bereshith Rabba* (בראשית רבא), abbreviated from *Bereshith d'Rabbi Oshaja Rabba* (בראשית דבי אושעיא רבא), on Genesis, divided into a hundred sections (פרשות). 2. *Shemoth Rabbah* (שמות רבה), on Exodus, in fifty-two sections. 3. *Va-jikra Rabbah* (ויקרא רבה), on Leviticus, in thirty-seven sections. 4. *Ba-midbar Rabbah* (במדבר רבה), on Numbers, in twenty-three sections. 5. *Debarim Rabbah* (דברים רבה), on Deuteronomy, in eleven sections. 6. *Shir Ha-Shirim Rabbah* (שיר השירים רבה), also called *Agadath Chasith* (אגדת חזית), because the text begins with the word *Chasith*, on the Song of Songs. 7. *Midrash Ruth Rabbah* (מדרש רות רבה), on Ruth. 8. *Midrash Eichah Rabbathi* (איכה רבתי), on Lamentations. 9. *Midrash Coheleth* (מדרש קהלת), on Ecclesiastes. 10. *Midrash Megillath Esther* מדרש מגילת אסתר), also called *Hagadath Megillah* (הגדת מגלה), on Esther. This *entire* collection, which was first published at Venice in 1545, has been reprinted many times since (best edition by Schrentzel, with the different commentaries, Stettin, 1863, 2 vols.). Excerpts of the Midrash on Ruth, Esther, and Lamentations have been published in Latin by Schnell (Altdorf, 1650). The age of the compilation of the separate Midrashim constituting this collection is critically and elaborately discussed by Zunz, *Die Gottesdienstlichen Vorträge der Juden*, p. 174-184, 263 sq.

(2.) *Pesikta* (פסיקתא), compiled by Cahana or Kahana ben-Tachlifa, who was born about A.D. 330, and died in 411. This Midrash, which comprises a complete cycle of lectures on the Pericopes of the feasts and fasts [see HAPHTARAH], and which was lost for several centuries, has been restored by an anonymous writer about the year A.D. 846, and edited under the name *Pesikta Rabbathi* (פסיקתא רבתי), intermixing it, however, with portions from the *Midrash Jelammedenu*. In this new form the *Pesikta* was first published by Isaac ben-Chajim Ha-Cohen (Prague, 1655). An excellent edition, entitled פסקתא רבתי עם הגדות ופרוש, with divisions into paragraphs, an emended text, extensive references,

and a critical commentary and indices by Seeb (Wolf) ben-Israel Isser, was published in Breslau in 1831. The nature and date of this Midrash are discussed in a most masterly manner by Zunz, *Die Gottesdienstlichen Vorträge*, p. 185-226, 239-251; Rapaport, *Erech Millin*, p. 171.

(3.) *Midrash Tanchuma* (מדרש תנחומא), i. e. the Midrash compiled by Tanchuma ben-Abba (flourished cir. A.D. 440), also called *Midrash Jelammedenu* (מדרש ילמדנו), from the fact that eighty-two sections begin with the formula ילמדנו, *it will teach us*. This Midrash extends over the whole Pentateuch, and consists of 140 sections. It contains extracts from the Mechilta, Siphre, Va-Ikra Rabba, Pesikta, and Boraitha de Rabbi Eliezer, and was first published after a redaction of the first Geonim period, when a great deal of it was lost, altered, and interpolated by Joseph ben-Shoshan (Constantinople, 1520; also Venice, 1545; Mantua, 1563; Salonica, 1578; with corrections after two MSS. and additions, Verona, 1595; and at different other places); the best edition is that with the twofold commentary by Chan. Sandel ben-Joseph (Vilna, 1833). For a thorough analysis of this Midrash we must refer to Zunz, *Die Gottesdienstlichen Vorträge*, p. 226-238.

(4.) *Pirke Rabbi Eliezer* (פרקי רבי אליעזר), also called *Boraitha* or *Agada de Rabbi Eliezer* (אגדא או ברייתא דרבי אליעזר), because Eliezer ben-Hyrcanus (flourished cir. A.D. 70) is its reputed author. This Midrash, which discusses the principal events recorded in the Pentateuch, consists of fifty-four sections, treating respectively on the following important subjects: the life of R. Eliezer (secs. i and ii); the creation (iii-vi); new moon (vii); intercalary year (viii); the fifth day's creation (ix); the flight of Jonah, and his abode in the fish (x); the sixth day's creation (xi); Adam, paradise, and the creation of the plants (xii); the fall (xiii); the curse (xiv); paradise and hell (xv); Isaac and Rebecca (xvi); the offices to be performed to bridal pairs and mourners (xvii); the creation (xviii); the ten things created on the eve of the sixth creation day (xix); the expulsion from paradise (xx); Adam, Eve, Cain, and Abel (xxi); the degeneracy of Cain's descendants and the flood (xxii); the ark and its occupants (xxiii); the descendants of Noah, the tower of Babel (xxiv); Sodom, Lot, and his wife (xxv); the ten temptations of Abraham (xxvi); his rescuing Lot (xxvii); God's covenant with Abraham (xxviii); his circumcision (xxix); the sending away of Hagar and Ishmael, the condition of the Jews in the days of Messiah (xxx); Abraham about to sacrifice Isaac (xxxi); Isaac bestowing the blessing on Jacob (xxxii); the resurrection (xxxiii); future state (xxxiv); Jacob's dream (xxxv); his sojourn with Laban (xxxvi); his wrestling with the angel (xxxvii); the selling of Joseph (xxxviii); Jacob's sojourn in Egypt (xxxix); God's manifestation in the bush (xl); the giving of the law (xli); the exodus (xlii); the power of repentance (xliii); the conflict of Moses with Amalek (xliv); the golden calf (xlv); the tables of stone and the atonement (xlvi); the exploit of Phineas (xlvii); the birth of Moses and the redemption from Egypt (xlviii); Samuel, Saul, Agag, Haman, Mordecai, Titus, Nebuchadnezzar, Ahasuerus, Vashti, and Esther (xlix, l); the new creation (li); the seven wonders of the world (lii); the punishment of calumny, Absalom and David (liii); and the leprosy of Miriam (liv). This Midrash, which is chiefly written in pure and easy Hebrew, was first published at Constantinople in 1514, and has since been reprinted numerous times; but the best edition is with the critical commentary called *the Great Edifice* (בית הגדול), emended text and references to Talmud and Midrashim by Broda (Vilna, 1838; a more convenient edition of it, Lemberg, 1858). A Latin translation by Vorst was published under the title *Capitula R. Eliezeris continentia imprimis succinctam historiæ sacræ recensionem, etc., cum vett. Rabb. Commentariis* (Leyden, 1644). The composition and age of this Midrash are discussed by Zunz, *Die Gottesdienstlichen Vorträge*, p. 271-278.

(5.) Midrash on Samuel, called (מדרש שמואל [רבתא]) *Midrash Shemuel [Rabbatha]*, divided into thirty-two sections (פרשות), twenty-four of which are devoted to 1 Sam. and eight to 2 Sam. It is chiefly made up of excerpts from older works, and the compiler is supposed to have lived about the beginning of the 11th century. Rashi is the first who quotes this Midrash (*Comment. on Chron.* x, 13). It was first published at Constantinople in 1517, and has since been frequently reprinted with the Midrash described below. The best editions of it are the one with the twofold commentary Ez Joseph and Anaph Joseph, references to the parallel passages in the Talmud and Midrashim, etc., by Schrentzel (Stettin, 1860); and the other published together with the Midrash on Proverbs and the commentary of Isaac Cohen (Lemberg, 1861).

(6.) Midrash on the Psalms, called (מדרש תלים [רבתא]) *Midrash Tillim [Rabbatha], Hagadath Tillim* (הגדת תלים), or *Shochar Tob* (שחר טוב), after the words with which it commences. With the exceptions of seven psalms—viz. xlii, xcvi, xcvii, xcviii, cxv, cxxiii, and cxxxi—this Midrash extends over the whole Psalter. As it contains extracts from the Babylonian Talmud, the Pesikta, Boraitha of R. Eliezer, Tanchuma, and Pesikta Rabbathi, it must have been compiled about the end of the 10th century, most probably in Italy. It was first published at Constantinople in 1512. The portion on Psa. cxix, which extends to the first verses of the letter ק, is called *Midrash Alpha Betha* (מדרש אלפא ביתא), from the fact that this is an alphabetic psalm; it has been published separately (Salonica, 1515). The Midrash on the Psalms has frequently been published together with the Midrash on Samuel, under the title *Midrash Shochar Tob* (שוחר טוב), which properly belongs only to that on the Psalms.

(7.) Midrash on Proverbs, called (מדרש משלי [רבתא]) *Midrash Mishle [Rabbatha]*, consists of a compilation of those maxims and expositions from former works which are best calculated to illustrate and explain the import of the book of Proverbs. The compiler, who lived about the middle of the 11th century, omits all the references to the original sources, discards the form of lectures, and assumes that of a commentary. The first edition of this Midrash appeared at Constantinople in 1512-17, with the commentary Sera Abraham (Vilna, 1834), and the commentary of Isaac Cohen (Stettin, 1861).

(8.) *Midrash Jalkut* (מדרש ילקוט), or *Jalkut Shimoni* (ילקוט שמעוני), i. e. *the collection* or *compilation of Simeon*, who flourished in the 11th century. This Midrash, which extends over the whole Hebrew Scriptures, is described in the article CARA in this *Cyclopædia*.

III. *Method and Plan of the Midrash.*—In discussing its method and plan, it must be borne in mind that the Midrash first developed itself in public lectures and homilies; that the ancient fragments of these discourses became afterwards literary commodities, serving frequently as the groundwork of literary productions; and that the Midrashic writers or compilers mixed up other matters and pieces of their own composition with the remnants of expository lectures. The ancient relics, however, are easily discernible by their dialect, diction, etc., and by the authority to whom they are ascribed. That there was a method in them has been shown by the erudite and indefatigable Jellinek, than whom there is no greater authority on the subject. He points out the following plan as gathered from the ancient fragments:

1. The lecturer first set forth the theme of his discourse in a passage of Scripture enunciating the particular truth which he wished to unfold, and then illustrated it by a parable, and enforced it by a saying which was popular in the mouth of the people. This rule is given in the Midrash itself (comp. יש להן וכולהון, מקרא, ויש להם משל, ויש להם מליצה, *Midrash on the Song of Solomon*, 1 a).

2. The attention of the audience was roused and the discourse was enlivened by the lecturer using a foreign word instead of a well-known expression, or by employing a Greek, Latin, Aramaic, or Persian term in addition to the Hebrew (comp. *Aruch*, s. v. אדודקר). This accounts for the striking fact that so many foreign words occur in the Midrash to express things for which the Hebrew has expressions, and that both Hebrew and foreign words, *expressing the same idea*, stand side by side (comp. מחדר לחדר ומקיטון לקיטון, *Midrash Rabbah on Genesis*, c. vii; בת טובים ובת גינוסרין, *Midrash on the Song of Solomon*, 1 a).

3. The lecturer increased the beauty of his discourse by trying to discover analogies between numbers and persons related to each other—e. g. between David and Solomon. Comp. *Midrash on the Song of Songs*, ibid.

4. The lecture was also rendered more attractive by being interspersed with plays upon words, which were not intended to explain or corroborate a statement, but were simply meant to create a pleasant feeling in the audience. Hence, to judge of the frequent plays upon words by the rules of hermeneutics is to misunderstand the æsthetics of the Hagadah.

5. It was considered as ornamenting the discourse, and pleasing to the audience, when single words were reduced to their numerical value in order to put a certain point of the lecture in a clearer light. Thus, e. g., the lecturer speaking of Eliezer, Abraham's faithful servant, and being desirous to show that he alone was worth a host of servants, remarked that Eliezer (אליעזר, $1+30+10+70+7+200=318$) is exactly as much as the three hundred and eighteen young men mentioned in Gen. xiv, 14. Comp. *Midrash Rabboth on Genesis*, ch. xlii. When it is remembered that the Hebrew letters were commonly used as numbers, it will be easily understood how the audience would be rejoiced to see a word converted so dexterously into figures.

6. To relieve the discourse of its monotony, the lecturer resolved a long word into several little words, or formed new words by taking away a letter or two from the preceding and following words in the same sentence. "If the Midrash is read with the guidance of these æsthetical canons," continues Dr. Jellinek, "we shall find in it less arbitrariness and more order. We shall, moreover, understand its method and plan, and often be put in a position to distinguish the original discourse from the literary element of a later date, as well as from interpolations. For the confirmation of our æsthetical canons, let the reader compare and analyze chapters ii, iii, and v of *Midrash Rabboth* on Genesis" (*Ben Chananja*, iv, 383 sq.).

IV. *Halachic and Hagadic Rules of Interpretation.*— The preceding exposition of the method and plan of the Midrash has prepared us to enter upon the Halachic and Hagadic rules of interpretation which were collected and systematized by Elieser ben-Jose the Galilæan (יוסי הגלילי), one of the principal interpreters of the Pentateuch in the 2d century of the Christian æra. According to this celebrated doctor, whose sayings are so frequently recorded in the Talmud and the Siphri, there are thirty-two rules (שלשים ושתים מדות) whereby the Bible is to be interpreted, which are as follows:

1. *By the superfluous use of the three particles* את, גם, *and* אך, *the Scriptures indicate in a threefold manner that something more is included in the text than the apparent declaration would seem to imply.* Thus, e. g., when it is said, Gen. xxi, 1, "And the Lord visited (את שרה) Sarah;" the superfluous את, which sometimes

denotes *with*, is used to indicate that *with* Sarah the Lord also visited other barren women. The second, גם, is used superfluously in the passage "take also your herds, and *also* (גם) your flocks" (Exod. xii, 32), to indicate that Pharaoh also gave the Israelites sheep and oxen, in order to corroborate the declaration made in Exod. x, 25; while the superfluous את, 2 Kings ii, 14, "He also (את) had smitten the waters," indicates that more wonders were shown to Elisha at the Jordan than to Elijah, as it is declared in 2 Kings ii, 9. This rule is called רבוי, *inclusion*, more being meant than said.

2. *By the superfluous use of the three particles* אך, רק, *and* מן, *the Scriptures point out something which is to be excluded.* Thus, e. g., אך in Gen. vii, 23, "And Noah only (אך) remained," shows that even Noah was near death, thus indicating exclusion. The superfluous רק in "Only (רק) the fear of God is not in this place" (Gen. xx, 11), shows that the inhabitants were not altogether godless; while מן in Exod. xviii, 13, "And the people stood by Moses from (מן) the morning unto the evening," indicates that it did not last all day, but only six hours (*Sabbath*, 10 a). This rule is called מיעוט, *diminution, exclusion.*

3. *If words denoting inclusion follow each other, several things are included.* Thus in 1 Sam. xvii, 36, "Thy servant slew also (גם את) the lion, also (גם) the bear," three superfluous expressions follow each other, to show that he slew three other animals besides the two expressly mentioned in the text. This rule is called רבוי אחר רבוי, *inclusion after inclusion.*

4. *If words denoting exclusion follow each other, several things are excluded.* Thus in Numb. xii, 2, "Hath the Lord indeed only spoken to Moses? hath he not also spoken to us?" the superfluous expressions רק and אך which follow each other denote that the Lord spoke to Aaron and Miriam before he spoke to Moses, thus not only without the lawgiver *being present* to it, but *before* God spoke to him, and not only did he speak to Aaron, but also to Miriam, so that there is here a twofold exclusion. If two or more inclusive words follow each other, and do not admit of being explained as indicative of inclusion, they denote *exclusion.* Thus, e. g., if the first word include the whole, while the second only includes a part, the first inclusion is modified and diminished by the second. If, on the contrary, two or more exclusive words follow each other, and do not admit of being explained as indicative of exclusion, they denote *inclusion.* Thus, e. g., if the first exclude four, while the second only excludes two, two only remain included, so that the second exclusive expression serves to include or increase. This rule is called מיעוט אחר מיעוט, *exclusion after exclusion*, and the two exceptions are respectively denominated אין רבוי אחר רבוי אלא למעט, *inclusion after inclusion effecting diminution*, and אין מיעוט אחר מיעוט אלא לרבות, *exclusion after exclusion effecting increase* (comp. *Pessachim*, 23 a; *Joma*, 43 a; *Megilla*, 23 b; *Kiddushin*, 21 b; *Baba Kama*, 45 b; *Sanhedrin*, 15 a; with *Menachoth*, 34 a).

5. *Expressed inference from the minor to the major*, called קל וחומר מפורש. An example of this rule is to be found in Jer. xii, 5, "If thou hast run with the footmen, and they have wearied thee, [inference] then how canst thou contend with horses?"

6. *Implied inference from the minor to the major*, called קל וחומר סתום. This is found in Psa. xv, 4: "He sweareth to his own hurt, and changeth not," hence how much less if he swear to his advantage (comp. *Maccoth*, 24 a).

7. *Inference from analogy or parallels*, called גזרה שוה. Thus it is said of Samuel, that "there shall no razor come upon his head" (1 Sam. i, 11), and the same language is used with respect to Samson—"No razor shall come on his head" (Judg. xiii, 5); whereupon is based the deduction from analogy, that just as Samson was a Nazarite, so also Samuel (*Nasir*, 66 a).

8. *Building of the father* (בנין אב) is the property of any subject which is made the starting-point, and to constitute a rule (אב, *a father*) for all similar subjects. Thus, e. g., in Exod. iii, 4, it is stated, "God called unto him out of the midst of the bush, and said, Moses, Moses;" hence it concludes that whenever God spoke to Moses, he addressed him in the same manner. See HILLEL and ISMAEL BEN-ELISA.

9. *Brachylogy* (דרך קצרה). The Scriptures sometimes express themselves briefly, and words must be supplied. Thus, e. g. ותכל דוד, where it ought to be ותכל נפש דוד, *and David's soul was consumed*, נפש being omitted; again, 1 Chron. xvii, 5, where ואהיה ואהיה מתהלך מאוהל אל אוהל וממשכן ought to be מאוהל אל אוהל וממשכן למשכן, "And I went from tent to tent, and from tabernacle to tabernacle," the words מתהלך and למשכן being omitted.

10. *Repetition* (דבר שהוא שנוי). The Scriptures repeat a thing in order to indicate thereby something special. Thus it is said in Jer. vii, 4, "Trust ye not in lying words, saying, The temple of the Lord, the temple of the Lord, the temple of the Lord;" the last phrase is repeated three times, to indicate that though his people Israel celebrate feasts in the temple three times in the year, the Lord will not regard it because they do not amend their ways.

11. *The separation and order of the verses* (סדור שנחלק) are designed to convey some explanation. Thus verses 18 and 19 of 2 Chron. xxx ought to be differently placed (comp. *Rashi*, ad loc.).

12. *A subject often explains itself while it imparts information on other subjects* (דבר שבא ללמד ונמצא למד). Thus, "Its cry, it shall arise like that of a serpent" (Jer. xlvi, 22), indicates that the serpent must have raised a tremendous cry after the curse which the Lord pronounced against it, since we are nowhere else told that there was any occasion on which it cried; and that Egypt raises an equally loud cry—thus serving to give information upon another subject, and at the same time explaining itself (comp. *Sota*, 9 b).

13. *A general statement is made first, and is followed by a single remark, which is simply to particularize the general.* This rule is called כלל שאחריו מעשה ואינו אלא פרטו של ראשון, and is illustrated by Gen. i, 27, where the creation of man is recorded in general terms—"Male and female created he them;" while ii, 7, which describes the creation of Adam, and ii, 21, which speaks of the creation of Eve, are simply the particulars of i, 27, and not another record or contradiction.

14. *A great and incomprehensible thing is represented by something small to render it intelligible.* This rule is called דבר גדול שנתלה בקטן להשביע האוזן כדרך שהיא שומעת, and is illustrated by Deut. xxxii, 2—"My doctrine shall drop as the rain;" where the great doctrines of revelation are compared with the less significant rain, in order to make them comprehensible to man; and by Amos iii, 8—"When the lion roareth, who doth not fear? the Lord speaketh," etc.; where the lion is compared with the Deity, to give man an intelligible idea of the power of God.

15. *When two Scriptures seem to contradict each other, a third Scripture will reconcile them* (שני כתובים המכחישרם את זה את זה עד שיבא הכתוב השלישי ויכריע ביניהים). Thus it is said in 2 Sam. xxiv, 9,

"There were in Israel eight hundred thousand valiant men," in contradiction to 1 Chron. xxi, 5, where "a thousand thousand and a hundred thousand men that drew sword"—three hundred thousand more are said to have been among all Israel. The apparent contradiction is reconciled by xxvii, 1, where it is said, "The children of Israel after their number; to wit, the chief fathers and captains of thousands and hundreds, and their officers who served the king in all matters of the courses, who came in and went out, was, month by month, through all the months of the year, twenty-four thousand in each course." From this it is evident that the number of these servants for twelve months amounted to two hundred and eighty-eight thousand, and as the chief fathers of Israel consisted of twelve thousand, we obtain the three hundred thousand who were noted in the registers of the king, and therefore are not mentioned in 2 Sam. xxiv, 9. Thus the two apparently contradictory Scriptures are reconciled by a third Scripture. It deserves to be noticed that this ancient interpretation is now generally followed, and that it is espoused by Dr. Davidson, *Sacred Hermeneutics* (Edinb. 1843), p. 546, etc.

16. *An expression used for the first time is explained by the passage in which it occurs* (דבר מיוחד במקומו). Thus, e. g., Hannah is the first who in her prayer addresses God as "Lord of Hosts;" whence it is concluded that the superfluous expression *hosts* indicates that she must have argued to this effect—"Lord of the universe, thou hast erected two worlds (צבאות); if I belong to the nether world I ought to be fruitful, and if to the upper I ought to live forever." Hence the expression is designed for this passage (*Berachoth*, 31 b).

17. *A circumstance is not fully described in the passage in which it first occurs, but is explained elsewhere* (דבר שאינו מתפרש במקומו ומתפרש במקום אחר). Thus it is stated in Gen. ii, 8, where the garden of Eden is first mentioned, that there were in it all manner of fruit; but it is not to be gathered from this passage that there was anything else in the garden; while from Ezek. xxviii, 13, where this passage is further explained, it is evident that there were also precious stones in Paradise.

18. *A thing is named in part, but comprises the whole* (דבר שנאמר במקצת והוא נוהג בכל). Thus in Exod. xxii, 30 it is forbidden to eat flesh "torn of beasts in the field;" and in Lev. xxii, 8, it is said, "That which is torn he shall not eat," here also forbidding that which is torn in the city. The use of the expression *field* in the first passage is owing to the fact that beasts are far more frequently torn in it than in the city; and the Scriptures mention the common and not the uncommon occurrences. Hence in the expression *field* everything is comprised—city, country, forest, mountain, valley, etc.

19. *The respective predicates of two subjects in the same passages may refer to both alike* (דבר שנאמר בזה וה״ה לחבירו). Thus, "Light is sown for the righteous, and gladness for the upright in heart" (Psa. xcvii, 11), does not imply that the former is without gladness and the latter without light, but what is predicated of one also belongs to the other (comp. *Taanith*, 15 a).

20. *The predicate of a subject may not refer to it at all, but to the one next to it* (דבר שנאמר בזה ואינו ענין לו והוא ענין לחבירו). Thus the remark, "This to Judah" (Deut. xxxiii, 7), does not refer to Judah, since it is said further on, "And he said, Hear, Lord, the voice of Judah," but to Simeon, whom Moses hereby blesses after Reuben.

21. *When a subject is compared with two things, it is to receive the best attributes of both* (דבר שהוקש לשתי מדות ואתה נותן לו כח היפה שבשתיהן). Thus, "The righteous shall flourish like the palm-tree; he shall grow up like a cedar in Lebanon" (Psa. xcii, 12)—

the comparison is with the best qualities of both (comp. *Taanith*, 25 a).

22. *The first clause explains by its parallelism the second, to which it refers* (דבר שחורו מוכיח עליו). Thus, "A gift in secret pacifieth anger," in the first hemistich signifying the anger of God, shows that "and a reward in the bosom strong wrath" (Prov. xxi, 14), in the second hemistich, refers to the strong wrath of God (comp. *Baba Bathra*, 9 b).

23. *The second clause in parallelism explains the first hemistich, to which it refers* (דבר שהוא מוכיח חבירו). Thus, "The voice of the Lord shaketh the wilderness; the Lord shaketh the wilderness of Kadesh" (Psa. xxix, 8). Here Kadesh, though comprised in the expression wilderness of the first clause, is used in the second clause to heighten the strength of the first hemistich, by showing that the wilderness must have been shaken exceedingly, since Kadesh, the great wilderness, was shaken (comp. Deut. i, 16).

24. *A subject included in a general description is excepted from it to convey a special lesson* (דבר שהיה בכלל ויצא מן הכלל ללמד על עצמו יצא). Thus, "Joshua, the son of Nun, sent out of Shittim two men to spy secretly, saying, Go, view the land, and Jericho" (Josh. ii, 1). Here Jericho is superfluous, since it is comprised in the general term *land*, but it is especially mentioned to indicate that Jericho by itself was equal in power and strength to the whole country. Hence that which is excepted teaches something special about itself.

25. *A subject included in a general description is excepted from it to teach something special about another subject* (דבר שהיה בכלל ויצא מן הכלל ללמד על חבירו). Thus the command, "Ye shall take no redemption-price for the life of a murderer who is guilty of death" (Numb. xxxv, 31), is entirely superfluous, since it is included in the declaration already made—"As he hath done, so shall it be done to him" (Lev. xxiv, 19). It is, however, mentioned especially to be a guide for other punishments, since it is concluded from it that it is only for murderers that no redemption-price is to be taken, but that satisfaction may be taken in case of one knocking out his neighbor's tooth or eye (comp. *Kethuboth*, 37 b, 38 a).

26. *Parable* (משל). Thus, "The trees went forth on a time to anoint a king over them, and they said unto the olive-tree, Reign thou over us" (Judg. ix, 8), where it is the Israelites and not the trees who said to Othniel, son of Kenaz, Deborah and Gideon reign over us. So also the remark, "And they shall spread the cloth before the elders of the city" (Deut. xxii, 17), is parabolic, meaning that they should make their testimony as clear as the cloth (comp. *Kethuboth*, 46 a).

27. *The preceding often explains what follows* (מנין שדורשין ממעל בהגדה). Thus, "And the Lord said unto Jehu, Because thou hast done well, executing that which is right in mine eyes . . . thy children of the fourth generation shall sit on the throne of Israel" (2 Kings x, 30), is to be explained by what precedes. Because Jehu destroyed four generations of the house of Ahab—viz. Omri, Ahab, Joram, and his sons, as is stated (comp. ver. 13)—therefore shall four generations of his house remain on the throne.

28. *Antithetic sentences often explain each other by their parallelism* (מנין שדורשין מנגד בהגדה). Thus in Isa. xxx, 16, "But ye said, No; for we will flee upon horses; therefore shall ye flee, and ride upon rapid runners; therefore shall your pursuers run;" the words wherewith they have sinned are put in parallelism with the words of punishment, couched in the same language and in similar expressions.

29. *Explanations are obtained by reducing the letters of a word to their numerical value* (מנין שדורשים גמטריא בהגדה), *and substituting for it another word*

or phrase of the same value, or by transposing the letters (חלוף אותיות). For an instance of the first we must refer to the reduction of אליעזר to 318, given in the preceding section. The second part of this rule is illustrated by examples which show that several modes of transposing the letters were resorted to. Thus ששך, *Sheshach*, is explained by בבל, *Babel* (Jer. xxv, 26; li, 41), and לב קמי by כשדים (*ibid.* li, 1), by taking the letters of the alphabet in their inverse order; א, the first letter, is expressed by ת, the last letter of the alphabet; ב, the second letter, by ש, the last but one; ג by ר; ד by ק; ה by צ, and so on. This principle of commutation is called *Atbash* (א״ת ב״ש), from the first two specimen pairs of letters which indicate the interchange. Or the commutation is effected by bending the alphabet exactly in the middle, and putting one half over the other, and the interchange is א for ל, ב for מ, ג for נ. This mode is termed *Albam* (א״ל ב״ם), from the first two specimen pairs of letters which indicate the interchange (comp. *Nedarim*, 32 a; *Sanhedrin*, 22 a).

30. *An explanation is to be obtained by either dividing a word into several words, or into syllables, and transposing these syllables, or into letters, and taking each letter as an initial or abbreviation of a word.* This rule is termed מנין שדורשין נוטריקון בהגדה, and is illustrated by the word אברהם being divided into אב המון גוים, *the father of many nations;* by כרמל being divided into מל and כר, and the latter transposed into רך, viz. *soft* and *grindable;* and by every letter of נמרצת (1 Kings ii, 8) being taken as standing for a word, viz.: נ=נואף, *adulterer;* מ=מואבי, *Moabite;* ר=רוצח, *murderer;* צ=צורר, *apostate;* and ת= תועבה, *abhorred* (comp. *Sabbath*, 105 a).

31. *Words and sentences are sometimes transposed* (מוקדם שהוא מאוחר בעניין). Thus 1 Sam. iii, 3, "And ere the lamp of God went out, and Samuel was lying in the temple of the Lord," the words בהיכל יהוה *in the temple of the Lord,* which are placed later in the sentence, evidently belong to רכבה, *went out,* since no one was allowed to sit down in the Temple except the kings of the house of David, much less to lie down. So also in Psa. xxxiv, where ver. 18 must be taken up to ver. 16 (comp. *Kiddushin*, 78 b; *Baba Kama*, 106).

32. *Whole sentences are sometimes transposed* (מוקדם מאוחר שהוא בפרשות). Thus, e. g. the record, "And he said unto him, Take me a heifer of three years old," etc. (Gen. xv, 9, etc.), ought properly to precede ch. xiv, inasmuch as it is anterior in point of time. This reversed order is owing to the fact that the Scriptures for some reason put certain events which occurred earlier in time after later occurrences (comp. *Berachoth*, 7 b, with *Pessachim*, 6 b).

Besides these thirty-two rules, the following laws of interpretations must be mentioned:

i. *Deduction from Juxtaposition.* — When two laws immediately follow each other, it is inferred that they are similar in consequences. Thus it is said in Exod. xxii, 18, 19, "Thou shalt not suffer a witch to live. Whosoever lieth with a beast shall surely be put to death;" whence it is inferred that these two enactments are placed close to each other to indicate the manner of death a witch is to suffer, which the Scriptures nowhere define. Now, as he who cohabits with an animal is, according to *the Halachah* based upon Lev. xx, to be stoned to death, hence it is concluded that a witch is to die in the same manner.

ii. All repetitions of words, as well as the construction of the finite verb with the infinite, e. g. השב תשיב, העבט תעביטנו, have a peculiar signification,

and must be explained. Some, however, maintain that the Bible, being written in human language, employs these repetitions (דיברה תורה כלשון בני אדם) in accordance with the *usus loquendi* (*Mishna Baba Mezia*, ii, 9; xii, 3; *Gemara*, ibid. 31; *Jerusalem Nedarim*, i, 1; *Kethuboth*, 77 b; *Berachoth*, 31 b).

iii. *Letters are to be taken from one word and joined to another, or formed into new words.* Thus, e. g. ונתתם את נחלתו לשארו, "Then ye shall give his inheritance unto his kinsman" (Numb. xxvii, 11), is explained by ונתתם את נחלת שאר לו, "And ye shall give the inheritance of his wife to him," i. e. the husband, by taking away the ו from נחלתו and the ל from לשארו, thus obtaining the word לו; and it is deduced therefrom that a man inherits the property of his (שאר) wife (comp. *Baba Bathra*, iii, 6; *Menachoth*, 74 a). This rule is called גורעין ומוסיפין ודורשין.

iv. *A word is to be explained both with the preceding and following words.* Thus, ושרי אשת אברם לא ילדה לו ולה שפחה מצרית ושמה הגר, "And Sarai, Abraham's wife, bare him no children; and she had a handmaid, an Egyptian, whose name was Hagar" (Gen. xvi, 1), is explained, "And Sarai, Abraham's wife, bare no children to him and to herself" (לו ולה); and then again, *to him* (i. e. Abraham) *and to her* (i. e. Sarai) *there was a handmaid* (לו ולה שפחה). This rule is called מקרא נדרש לפניו ולאחריו, and is not admitted by some (comp. *Sabbath*, 32 b; *Menachoth*, 19 a).

v. *The letters of a word are sometimes transposed.* Thus עמלנו, "our labor" (Deut. xxv, 7), is made to mean *our children*, עלמנו, by transposing the מ and the ל.

vi. *Letters resembling each other in sound or appearance, or belonging to the same organ of speech, are interchanged.* Thus תורה צוה לנו משה מורשה קהלת יעקב, "Moses commanded us the law, an inheritance of the congregation of Jacob" (Deut. xxxiii, 4), is explained, "The law which Moses has given us, is the BETROTHED or WIFE (מְאֹרָשָׂה) of the congregation of Jacob," by changing the ו in מורשה for א, and ש for שׂ.

The alteration produced by rules v and vi, and which are in the Talmudic and post-Talmudic period generally introduced by the remark אל תקרי כך אלא כך, *Read not so and so, but so and so,* must not be taken for emendations of the text of *various readings,* but are simply another mode of obtaining an additional meaning of the text. It was argued that as the literal and limited sense of the Bible, read in the stereotyped order, could not yield sufficiently the divine and inexhaustible mind couched in those letters, every transposition, commutation, etc., ought to be resorted to in order to obtain as much as possible of the infinite idea; especially as every such effort yielded that sense and meaning thoroughly in harmony with what might justly be expected from Holy Scripture. It was therefore regarded as probable that the Bible designed to indicate it in addition to what the regular order and reading of the words conveyed. It must also be remembered that some of these rules, especially those which involved an alteration of the text and a departure from the literal meaning, were not used in *Halachic exegesis,* and that *the Hagadic exegesis* employs many more than those we have specified. In fact, anything and everything is resorted to which can make the text speak comfort and consolation in every time of need, or connect the legends about Scriptural characters with the Biblical record. The puerility and extravagance of many of the rules are obvious, while others are of acknowledged value. See CABALA.

V. *Importance of the Halachic and Hagadic Exegesis.* —When it is borne in mind that the annotators and punctuators of the Hebrew text, and the translators of the ancient versions, were Jews impregnated with the theological opinions of the nation, and prosecuted their Biblical labors in harmony with these opinions, and the above-named exegetical rules, the importance of the Halachic and Hagadic exegesis to the criticism of the Hebrew text, and to a right understanding of the Greek, Chaldee, Syriac, and other versions, as well as of the quotations of the O. T. in the N. T., can hardly be overrated. If it be true—and few will question the fact— that every successive English version, either preceding or following the Reformation, reflects the peculiar notions about theology, Church government, and politics of each period and of every dominant party; and that even the most literal translation of modern days is, in a certain sense, a commentary of the translator; we ought to regard it as natural that the Jews, without intending to deceive, or wilfully to alter the text, should by the process of the *Midrash* introduce or indicate, in their Biblical labors, the various opinions to which shifting circumstances gave rise. Let a few specimens from the Hebrew text, and the ancient versions, suffice to illustrate the Midrashic process, and its paramount importance to Biblical criticism.

1. *The Hebrew Text and the Masorah.*—The influence of the Halachic and Hagadic exegesis on the formation of the Hebrew text and the Masorah is far greater than has hitherto been imagined, though the limits of this article only admit of a few examples. Thus, e. g., the question put by Isaiah to Hezekiah, "The shadow has gone forward (הָלַךְ) ten degrees; shall it go back ten degrees?" (2 Kings xx, 9) as the Hebrew text has it, is not only grammatically incorrect, inasmuch as the repetition of the *ten degrees* a second time requires the article, but is at variance with the king's reply given in ver. 10, from which it is evident that the prophet asked him whether the shadow should *go forwards* OR *backwards* ten degrees, that Hezekiah chose the latter because it was more difficult and wonderful, and that the original reading was הֲיֵלֵךְ, instead of הָלַךְ; and, indeed, this reading is still preserved by the Chaldee, the Syriac, the Vulgate, etc.; is followed by Luther and the Zurich version, whence it found its way into Coverdale, the Bishop's Bible, and has finally got into the A. V. The mystery about the origin of the present textual reading is solved when we bear in mind the Hagadic explanation of the parallel passage in Isa. xxxviii, 8. Now, tradition based upon this passage tells us that the shadow or the sun had gone ten degrees forwards at the death of Ahaz, and the day was thus shortened to two hours (אותו היום שמת בו אחז שתי שעות היה), *Sanhedrin,* 96 a), in order that his burial might be hasty and without royal honors, and that now these ten degrees went backwards. Hence the present reading, which was effected by the trifling alteration of הילך into הלך, i. e. "the shadow," the prophet is made to say to the king, "Has once gone forward ten degrees" (i. e. at the death of Ahaz); "shall it now go backward ten degrees?" Thus the Midrashic exposition of Isa. xxxviii, 8, it may be supposed, gave rise to the textual reading of 2 Kings xx, 9. For the influence of the Halachic and Hagadic exegesis on the Masorah and the various readings, we must refer to Krochmal, *More Neboche Ha-Jeman* (Lemberg, 1851), p. 169 sq. See KERI AND KETHIB; NETHINIM.

2. *The Greek Versions.*—That the Septuagint is pervaded by the Halachic and Hagadic exegesis may almost be seen on every page of this version. A few examples must suffice. Thus, e. g., the Septuagint rendering of חיה by ζωογονοῦντων, in Lev. xi, 47, is only to be explained when it is borne in mind that, according to the Halachah, the prohibition respecting טרפה (Exod.

xxii, 30, etc.) does not simply refer to animals torn by wild beasts, but to every animal which is sickly and maimed, though belonging to the clean animals allowed to be eaten in Lev. xi; and that one of the sure tests whether an animal is healthy, and hence eatable, is when it *bears young ones;* barrenness is an infallible sign of its sickly condition (comp. *Chulin,* 24 with 58; Salomon ben-Adereth, *Respons.* xcviii; *Torath Cohanim,* 124)—hence the Septuagint rendering, "Between those which bear young ones and [for this reason] may be eaten, and those which bear young ones and may not be eaten," because they belong to the animals proscribed. Again, the rendering of Josh. xiii, 22, ואת בלעם . . . בחרב . . . הרגו, by καὶ τὸν Βαλαὰμ . . . ἀπέκτειναν . . . ἐν ῥοπῇ, which has caused such perplexity to commentators and given rise to diverse emendations (e. g. προνομῇ, Oxf.; ἐν ῥομφαίᾳ ἐν τροπῇ, Ald. and Complut.), is at once explicable when reference is made to the Hagadah, which is quoted in Jonathan ben-Uzziel's Chaldee Paraphrase of Numb. xxxi, 6, and is as follows: "Balaam flew into the air by his magic arts, and Phinehas threw him down;" so that ἐν ῥοπῇ means *in the fall* (comp. also Rashi on Numb. xxxi, 6).

Symmachus, too, cannot be understood in many of his translations without reference to the Halachic and Hagadic exegesis. Thus the apparently strange rendering of לא תבשל גדי בחלב אמו by οὐ σκευάσεις ἔριφον διὰ γάλακτος μητρὸς αὐτοῦ (Exod. xxiii, 19) becomes intelligible when it is remembered that the Halachah not only prohibits the cooking, but the mixing and eating of animal meat and milk in any form (comp. *Mechilta,* ad loc.; *Cholin,* 115). Hence the rendering of תבשל by σκευάσεις. The rendering of ויראל משה by ὥρκισε δὲ Μωϋσήν (Exod. i, 21), which has been thought very extraordinary and inexplicable, becomes perfectly plain when the Hagadah on this passage is consulted, which tells us that Jethro demanded of Moses to swear that he would devote to idolatry his first-begotten son by Zipporah, and that Moses consented to it; and remarks further, *Then said Jethro, Swear, and Moses swore to him, as it is written,* ויראל משה. Now אלה denotes *to swear,* as in 1 Sam. xiv, 24, and 2 Kings v, 23 (comp. *Mechilta,* sec. Jethro, beginning quoted in *Jalkut,* ad loc.; *Nedarim,* 65 a).

These few specimens must suffice, for, greatly important as the subject is, the limits of this article prevent us from giving illustrations of the influence which the Halachic and Hagadic exegesis exercised upon the other Greek versions, as well as upon the Chaldee paraphrases, the Syriac version, the Vulgate, the Arabic, and the expositions of the early fathers.

VI. *Literature.* — Zunz, *Die gottesdienstlichen Vorträge der Juden* (Berlin, 1832), p. 35 sq.; Hirschfeld, *Halachische Exegese* (Berlin, 1840); by the same author, *Die hagadische Exegese* (Berlin, 1847); Sachs, *Die religiöse Poesie der Juden in Spanien* (Berlin, 1845), p. 141 sq.; Rapaport, *Erech Millin* (Prague, 1852), art. Agada, p. 6 sq.; Frankel, *Vorstudien zur der Septuaginta* (Leipsic, 1841), p. 179 sq.; by the same author, *Ueber den Einfluss der palästinischen Exegese auf die alexandrinische Hermeneutik* (Leipsic, 1851); and *Programm zur Eröffnung des jüdisch-theologischen Seminars zu Breslau* (Breslau, 1854); Luzzatto, *Oheb. Ger.* (Vienna, 1831); Pinner, *Vorstudien zum Talmud* (Berlin, 1831); Geiger, *Urschrift und Uebersetzung der Bibel* (Breslau, 1857); Steinschneider, *Jewish Literature* (London, 1857), p. 5 sq.; Deutsch, in *Lond. Quarterly Review,* April, 1867 sq., art. on Talmud; Ginsburg, *Historical and Critical Commentary on Ecclesiastes* (London, 1861), p. 30 sq., 455 sq.; and the literature there referred to.

Midwife (מְיַלֶּדֶת, part. in Piel of יָלַד, "to bring forth;" Sept. μαῖα, Vulg. *obstetrix;* Gen. xxxv, 17; xxxviii, 28). It must be remarked that חָיוֹת, Exod. i,

19, "lively," is also in rabbinical Hebrew "midwives," an explanation which appears to have been had in view by the Vulg., which interprets *chayoth* by "ipsæ obstetricandi habent scientiam." It is also rendered "living creatures," implying that the Hebrew women were, like animals, quick in parturition. Gesenius renders "vividæ, robustæ" (*Thes.* p. 468). In any case the general sense of the passage Exod. i, 19 is the same, viz. that the Hebrew women stood in little or no need of the midwives' assistance. Parturition in the East is usually easy. See WOMAN. The office of a midwife is thus, in many Eastern countries, in little use, but is performed, when necessary, by relatives (Chardin, *Voy.* vii, 23; Harmer, *Obs.* iv, 425). See CHILD. It may be for this reason that the number of persons employed for this purpose among the Hebrews was so small, as the passage Exod. i, 19 seems to show; unless, as Knobel and others suggest, the two named were the principal persons of their class. In the description of the transaction mentioned in Exod. i, one expression, "Upon the stools," receives remarkable illustration from ancient as well as modern usage. On the walls of the palace of Luxor, in Upper Egypt, there is a grand painting, which is faithfully copied in Lepsius's *Denkmäler*, representing the birth of the eldest son of Thothmes IV, and very possibly the "first-born" of the Pharaoh who was drowned in the Red Sea. Queen Mautmes is represented as receiving a message through the god Thoth, that she is to give birth to a child. The mother is placed *upon a stool*, while two midwives chafe her hands, and the babe is held up by a third (Sharpe's *History of Egypt*, i, 65). Gesenius doubts the existence of any custom such as the direct meaning of the passage implies. and suggests a wooden or stone trough for washing the new-born child. But the modern Egyptian practice, as described by Mr. Lane, exactly answers to that indicated in the book of Exodus. "Two or three days before the expected time of delivery, the *Layeh* (midwife) conveys to the house the *kursi elwiládeh*, a chair of a peculiar form, upon which the patient is to be seated during the birth" (Lane, *Mod. Egypt.* iii, 142). See STOOL. The moral question arising from the conduct of the midwives does not fall within the scope of the present article. The reader, however, may refer to St. Augustine, *Contr. mendacium*, xv, 32, and *Quæst. in Hept.* ii, 1; also Corn. à Lap. *Com. on Ex.* i. When it is said, "God dealt well with the midwives, and built them houses," we are probably to understand that their families were blessed either in point of numbers or of substance. Other explanations of inferior value have been offered by Kimchi, Calvin, and others (Calmet, *Com. on Ex.* i; Patrick; Corn. à Lap.; Knobel; Schleusner, *L.V.T.* οἰκία; Gesenius, *Thesaur.* p. 193; *Crit. Sacr.*). It is worth while to notice only to refute on its own ground the Jewish tradition which identified Siphrah and Puah with Jochebed and Miriam, and interpreted the "houses" built for them as the so-called royal and sacerdotal families of Caleb and Moses (Josephus, *Ant.* iii, 2, 4; Corn. à Lap. and *Crit. Sacr.* l. c.; Schöttgen, *Hor. Hebr.* ii, 450; *De Mess.* c. iv). See BIRTH.

Mieg, Johann Casimir, a German theologian and philologist, was born at Heidelberg Oct. 6, 1712. His father was a professor of theology and minister at the Heiligengeistkirche of that place. He entered the university of his native place when fourteen years of age; continued his studies at Zürich, Basle, and Berne; returned to Heidelberg in 1732, and finished his education at Marburg and Halle. He was appointed a professor of philosophy at Herborn in 1733, and in 1743 professor of divinity and philology at Lingen. This position he resigned in 1757, and returned to Herborn as professor of theology and preacher. He died Sept. 28, 1764. Some of his most celebrated works are, *Diss.* חדבות עבדים, *hoc est Constitutiones servorum tam in genere, quam in Hebræorum specie* (Herbornæ Nassoviarum, 1734, 4to):—חלכית עבדי עבר, *hoc est: Constitutio*

res servi Hebræi e Scriptura et Rabbinorum monumentis collectæ nec non cum ceterarum gentium consuetudinibus huic inde collatæ (ibid. 1735, 8vo) :—*Commentatio theologico-practica, de virtute in præcordiis objecto* εὐαρεσίας *divinæ ad Psa. li* (Lemgoviæ, 1749, 8vo).

Mieg, Ludwig Christian, a German Reformed theologian, was born Aug. 20, 1668, at Heidelberg, and received his education at his native place and at Basle, where he defended his dissertation "De regulis communicationis motus." In 1689, during the French war, when Heidelberg was destroyed, he was vicar of the French congregation at Manheim. Later he made a voyage through the Netherlands, and returned in 1691 to Heidelberg, and was appointed professor of Greek, and minister of the Reformed congregation at Rinteln. In 1694 he was made professor of ecclesiastical history at Marburg, and in 1697 professor of theology. He returned in 1706 to Heidelberg as ecclesiastical counsellor, professor of divinity, and first minister of the church of the Holy Ghost; resigned his place in 1730, and died Jan. 19, 1740. His most noted works are, *Diss. de regulis communicationis motus* (Basle, 1685, 4to): —*Theses historico-practicæ ex historia et vita Abrahami desumtæ* (Marburg, 1696, 4to) :—*Diss. historica, qua A. Pagii sententia de occasione Apologiarum a veteris ecclesiæ doctoribus conscriptarum examinatur* (ibid. 1696, 4to):—*Diss. theologica de terrore Dei* (ibid. 1699, 4to): —*Disquisitio theologica de perspicuitate et universalitate institutionis naturalis, ad Psa. xix*, 4, 5 (ibid. 1699, 4to): —*Diss. theologico-philologica I et II de cura pauperum apud Hebræos* (ibid. 1700, 4to) :—*Theses theologicæ de traditionibus* (ibid. 1700, 4to) :—*Diss. de propheta promisso, Deut. xviii*, 15, *contra D. Hugueminum* (ibid. 1704, 4to) :—*Oratio de providentia divina circa nascentem Univers. Heidelberg. cum elencho Professor. Heidelberg.* (ibid. 1770, 4to). See Döring, *Gelehrte Theol. Deutschlands*, s. v.

Miel, JAN, a distinguished Flemish painter, was born in a small village near Antwerp in 1599. Lanzi says he was a pupil of Vandyck. He resided some time at Rome, where he studied under Andrea Sacchi, to whom he gave such proofs of genius that he was employed to assist him in his works at the Palazzo Barberini. Miel, whose disposition led him to the grotesque, introduced something ludicrous into the work, which was deemed unworthy the dignity of the subject, and he was dismissed. He then visited Lombardy to study the works of Correggio, and also passed some time in Parma and Bologna. On his return to Rome he was employed by pope Alexander VII to paint a picture of *Moses striking the Rock* for the gallery of Monte Cavallo. He also painted a *Baptism of St. Cyrillio* for the church of S. Martino de' Monti, and the *Annunciation*, and some frescos of the life of St. Lamberti, in S. Maria dell' Anima. Subsequently he was invited to Turin by Charles Emanuel, duke of Savoy, who appointed him court painter, and in whose service he was retained the residue of his life. After his engagement by the duke he painted no more religious works. He was elected a member of the Academy of St. Luke in 1648, and thereafter devoted himself almost entirely to hunting scenes and battle pieces. He died at Turin in 1664. Many of Miel's best works are in the Imperial Gallery at Vienna. See Lanzi, *History of Painting*, transl. by Roscoe (Lond. 1847, 3 vols. 8vo), iii, 307; Spooner, *Biog. Hist. of the Fine Arts* (N. Y. 1865, 2 vols. 8vo).

Mielk, JOHANN BERTRAM, a German theologian, was born at Kiel March 24, 1736, where he was also educated. In 1758 the dignity of master of arts was conferred upon him as a reward for the defence of his dissertation "*De divisione in infinitum.*" In 1768 he was appointed deacon at Neustadt, in Holstein; in 1771, second minister at the Fleckenkirche at Preetz, and in 1784 chief minister at Oldenslohe, where he died June 14, 1801. He was very much renowned as editor of *Beiträge zur Beförderung der häuslichen Andacht in*

Predigten (1777–83). He deserves also much credit for his translation of Millot's *Universal History.*

Mieris, FRANS, Jr., a Dutch artist and writer of note, deserves a place here as the author of a work on *History and Ecclesiastical Antiquities of the Seven United Provinces* (1726). He was born at Leyden in 1689, and died in 1763.

Mies, JACOB VON. See JACOB.

Migdal-Edar ("tower of the flock"), a place on the route of Jacob (Gen. xxxv, 21), probably about two miles south of Jerusalem, near the Bethlehem road, where the cluster of ruins called *Kirbet Um–Moghdala* is now situated (Tobler, *Dritte Wanderung*, p. 81). See EDAR.

Mig´dal-el (Heb. *Migdal´-El*, מִגְדַּל־אֵל, *tower of God*; Sept. Μαγδαλιήλ v. r. Μαγδαλιηωράμ or Μεγαλααρίμ), a fortified city of the tribe of Naphtali (Josh. xix, 38), "named between Iron and Horem, possibly deriving its name from some ancient tower—the 'tower of El, or God.' By Eusebius (*Onomasticon*, Μαγδιήλ) it is spoken of as a large village lying between Dora (Tantura) and Ptolemais (Akka), at nine miles from the former, that is, just about *Athlit*, the ancient 'Castellum peregrinorum.' No doubt the Castellum was anciently a *migdol* or tower; but it is impossible to locate a town of Naphtali below Carmel, and at least twenty-five miles from the boundaries of the tribe. It may, however, have been the *Magdôlum* named by Herodotus (ii, 159) as the site of Pharaoh Necho's victory over Josiah (see Rawlinson's *Herod.* ii, 246, note). But this was not the only Migdol along this coast. If the modern Hurah is Horem and Yarûn Iron, there is a possibility in finding Migdal-el in *Mujeidel*, at no great distance from them, namely, on the left bank of the Wady Kerkerah, eight miles due east of the Ras en-Nakurah, six miles west of Hurah and eight of Yarûn (see Van de Velde's *Map*, 1858)." The enumeration of the towns in the above passage of Joshua, however, favors the connection of this name with the preceding as one, i. e. Migdal-el-Horem, as in the Sept. In any case the present Migdal is probably the MAGDALA (q. v.) of the New Test. (Matt. xv, 39), which lay within the limits of Naphtali (q. v.).

Mig´dal-gad (Heb. *Migdal´-Gad*, מִגְדַּל־גָּד, *tower of fortune*; Sept. Μαγδαλγάδ), a town in the plain of Judah, mentioned between Hadashah and Dilean (Josh. xv, 37); probably the *el-Mejdel* a short distance northeast of Ascalon (Schwarz, *Palest.* p. 103 ; Van de Velde, *Memoir*, p. 334). It is a prosperous village, encircled by luxuriant orchards and olive groves, and fields unsurpassed in fertility. Among the houses are many traces of antiquity—large hewn stones and broken columns. Some three miles south-east of Mejdel is the village of Jenin, which may perhaps be the Zenan noted by Joshua in the group with Migdal-gad ; and ten miles distant in the same direction are the ruins of Lachish and Eglon (Porter, *Hand-book*, p. 261, 272).

Migdal-Sannah, a large village located by Jerome (*Onomast.* s. v. Senna, "Magdal-senna, quod interpretatur Turris Senna ;" but perhaps he has merely misread Eusebius, μεγάλη Σεννά) at seven (Euseb. eight) Roman miles north of Jericho, on the border of Judæa. Dr. Robinson (*Bib. Res.* iii, 295) inclines to identify it with the *Mejdel* in the central mountains of Palestine, near the edge of the Ghor, at the upper end of the Wady Fasail, and not far from Daumeh, the ancient Edumia (Van de Velde, *Syr. and Pal.* ii, 307).

Mig´dol (Heb. *Migdol´*, מִגְדֹּל, a *tower*; Sept. Μάγδωλον or Μαγδωλόν), a town in Lower Egypt (Jer. xliv, 1 ; xlvi, 14), the northern limit of the country (opposite Syene, Ezek. xxix, 10 ; xxx, 6). It is apparently the *Magdolum* of the *Antonine Itinerary* (p. 171), situated twelve Roman miles from Pelusium ; and, as it is doubtless also the place mentioned (Exod. xiv, 2 ; Numb. xxxiii, 7) in the description of the passage of the Red Sea by the Israelites (see Gesenius, *Thesaur.* p. 268; Ewald, *Isr. Gesch.* ii, 55), a difficulty has been experienced from the statements of those texts that this occurred "between Migdol and the sea," and "before Migdol," arising from the much greater distance of this locality from Pelusium, which the explanation of Hengstenberg (*Mos. u. Aeg.* p. 58 sq.), that these expressions simply refer to the general region within which the Israelites were hemmed, scarcely meets. It is therefore better to regard the distance given in the *Itinerary* as somewhat vague, so that Migdol may have been situated sufficiently near to be said to be opposite the scene of the miracle. See EXODE. The name has been traced in the Coptic *Meshtol*, which signifies *many* hills (Champollion, *L'Égypte sous les Pharaons*, ii, 79), and has been referred (see Niebuhr, *Descr. Arabiæ*, p. 409) to the *Meshtul* of Arabian geographers, in the province of Sharkje, in Lower Egypt, on the island Myecphor (Rosenmüller, *Alterth.* iii, 260); but it is better (with Forster, *Ep. ad Michael.* p. 29) to consider it as alluding to a mountainous situation (suitable for a watch-tower on the frontier), and we may then (with Tischendorf, *De Israel. per mare rubrum transitu*, p. 25 sq.; Kutscheit, *Lepsius u. der Sinai*, p. 6 sq.; and other earlier travellers) identify it with Jebel *Ataka* (see Olin's *Travels in the East*, i, 350). The only objection to this identification that remains, worthy of consideration, is that, according to some travellers, a gentle slope, some two or three miles wide, intervenes between this range of hills and the sea-shore, containing many camel-paths, and offering an easy escape for the Israelites hemmed in by the Egyptians that came down upon them through Wady Tuwarik (Aiton's *Lands of the Messiah*, p. 120) ; but it is doubtful whether so extensive a shore existed here anciently (see *ib.* p. 106), and even if this margin were not at that time covered by the waves, it may easily have been preoccupied by a detachment of the Egyptian troops sent round by way of the isthmus to cut off the retreat of the Israelites. Herodotus (ii, 159) doubtless alludes to this place under the name of *Magdolum*, which he describes as a frontier town towards Palestine, where Josiah was slain by Necho; evidently confounding it with Megiddo. See RED SEA, PASSAGE OF.

Miget, ST., a prelate of the French Church, was born about the beginning of the 7th century. His life was written in the 10th century by an anonymous hagiographer, and published by the Bollandists, June 6. Another chronicler of the same century, Adson, in his *Legende de Saint Waldebert, abbé de Luxueil*, says that St. Miget presided at the obsequies of this abbot, who was his dearest friend. St. Miget is spoken of as a reformer within the Church. It appears that he introduced great changes in the liturgy of his diocese, and instituted first in the church of Besançon five archdeacons, to whom he gave important privileges. He died about the year 670. His name is found in the *Martyrologe Gallican* of the date of Aug. 7.—Dunod de Charnage, *Hist. de l'Église de Besançon;* J.-Jacques Chifflet, *Vesuntio*, pt. ii; *Vie des Saints de Franche Comté*, by the professors of the college of St. Francis Xavier, i, 236. See Hoefer, *Nouv. Biog. Générale*, s. v.

Miglionico. ANDREA, a Neapolitan painter, was a pupil of Luca Giordano. According to Dominici, he acquired considerable reputation, and executed many works for the churches at Naples, among which the *Descent of the Holy Ghost*, in the church of S. S. Nunziata, is highly commended. He died about 1710.—Lanzi's *History of Painting*, transl. by Roscoe (Lond. 1847, 3 vols. 8vo), ii, 59; Spooner, *Biog. Hist. of the Fine Arts* (N. Y. 1865, 2 vols. 8vo).

Mignard, Pierre (1) (called *the Roman*), an eminent French painter, was born at Troyes in 1610. After receiving some instruction at home, his father placed him in the school of Jean Boucher at Bruges; subsequently under Vouet. In 1636 he went to Rome, to study after Raphael and Michael Angelo ; there he remained twenty-two years, painting a number of fine Madonnas, and the portraits of popes Urban VIII and Alexander VII. One of the finest frescos in France, the cupola of the Val de Grace, was executed by Mignard. He also adorned the great hall at St. Cloud with mythological subjects. He died in 1695, after having received many distinctions and honors.—Lanzi's *History of Painting* (Lond. 1847, 3 vols. 8vo), i, 476.

Mignard, Pierre (2), a French architect, and nephew of the preceding, was born at Avignon in 1640. After a series of extensive journeys throughout France and Italy, during which he devoted himself to the study of architecture, he settled in Paris. He built the Abbey de Montmajour, near Arles, which gained him great reputation; and he was intrusted with many important works. Among these may be mentioned the façade of the church of St. Nicholas and the Porte St. Martin. Subsequently the Abbey de Montmajour was destroyed by fire, but was rebuilt precisely according to the designs of Mignard. He was one of the six architects who, in 1671, founded the French Academy of Architecture, of which he was appointed professor. He died in 1725. See Spooner, *Biog. Hist. of the Fine Arts* (N. Y. 1865, 2 vols. 8vo), ii, 564.

Mig'ron (Heb. *Migron'*, מִגְרוֹן, *precipice;* Sept. in 1 Sam. Μαγδών, in Isa. Μαγεδδώ v. r. Μαγγεδώ, apparently reading ד for ר; Vulg. *Magron*), a town of Benjamin, which, from the historical indications, must have been between Ai and Michmas, on the route of the invading Assyrian army southward (Isa. x, 28). From Michmas a narrow valley extends northward out of and at right angles with that which has been identified as the passage of Michmas (q. v.). The town of Migron seems to have been upon and to have commanded the pass through this valley, somewhere between the modern Deir Diwan and Mukhmus (Robinson's *Researches*, ii, 149). Saul was stationed at the further side of Gibeah (? Geba), "under a pomegranate-tree which is by Migron" (1 Sam. xiv, 2), when Jonathan performed his great exploit at Michmas; and this is to be explained (see Rosenmüller, *Alterth.* II, ii, 170 sq.; Bachiene, II, ii, 145) on the supposition that Migron was on the border (perhaps extending considerably north-west of Michmas) of the district to which Gibeah gave its name. Migron, therefore, was in all probability situated on, or close to, the ravine now called Wady Suweinit. It was a commanding position (Josephus, *Ant.* vi, 6, 2, where it is said to be "a high hill"), for Saul was able to see from it the commotion which followed the attack of Jonathan on the Philistine camp. The ravine is not quite half a mile in breadth from brow to brow. According to Schwarz (*Palest.* p. 130), there are extant some ruins about half a mile south of the site of Bethel, which the Arabs still call Burj (fort) *Magrun;* but no map exhibits here more than a ruined church, and the position is too far north. Keil thinks the Migron of 1 Samuel was a different place from that of Isaiah (*Comment. on Sam.* ad loc.), but this is an unnecessary supposition. The only locality that seems to combine the scriptural requirements is the eminence just north-west of Mukhmus, which separates Wady Suweinit from its branch running up directly north to Deir Diwan; and some ancient town appears to be indicated by the sepulchres in the latter valley.

Mihill, NORRIS, a minister of the Methodist Episcopal Church, was born in Sheffield, C. W., about 1823. He was converted at eighteen, while resident at Wilmington, N. Y.; but continued in his trade until 1861, when he was placed in charge of West Peru Circuit, which he served with marked ability for two years. At the end of this time he joined the Troy Conference on trial, and was sent to Beekmantown, where he was serving for the third year with great efficiency at the time of his death, Oct. 3, 1868. Mihill was earnestly devoted to the interests of his Master, and was beloved by his

associates and parishioners. See *Minutes of Conferences,* 1869, p. 117.

Mih-Teih, or Mé-Teih, an eminent Chinese philosopher, who flourished about 400 B.C., says Dr. Legge, "was an original thinker, and exercised a bolder judgment on things than Confucius or any of his followers. He taught that all the evils in society arise from the want of mutual universal love. For example, a prince loves only his own state, and does not love the neighboring state. Therefore he makes war against it." "If princes," he asked, "regarded other states as their own, who would begin a war? If every one regarded his neighbor's person as his own, who would be found to rob? If universal love prevailed, all enmities, usurpations, and miseries would disappear. Princes, loving one another, would have no battle-fields; the chiefs of families, loving one another, would attempt no usurpation; men, loving one another, would commit no robberies." See Dr. Legge, *Chinese Classics*, vol. ii, ch. iii; Thomas, *Dict. of Biog. and Mythol.* s. v.

Mij'amin (*a*, 1 Chron. xxiv, 9; *b*, Neh. x, 7). See MIAMIN.

Mikkelsen, HANS, a noted Danish Biblical student, author of the first Danish version of the New Testament, was originally mayor of Malmoe, in Scaiaa, and subsequently secretary to Christian II of Denmark. When the king was, in 1523, obliged to flee from his dominions and take refuge in Holland, Mikkelsen accompanied him, and it was while there that, at the suggestion of his sovereign, he set himself to the work of translating the New Testament. Driven by the bigoted jealousy of the papal party in the Netherlands from his place beside the king, he retired to Harderwick, in Guelderland, where he died about the year 1532. His translation, which was published in 1524 (small 4to), professes to be made from the Latin, but this applies only to the four Gospels, in translating which he seems to have followed the version of Erasmus; for the other books he has closely followed the German version of Luther. See Henderson, *Dissertation on Hans Mikkelsen's Translation* (Copenhagen, 1813); W. L. Alexander, in Kitto, *Cyclop. Bibl. Lit.* s. v.

Mik'loth (Heb. *Mikloth'*, מִקְלוֹת, prob. i. q. מַקְלוֹת, *staves*, as in Gen. xxx, 37, etc.; Sept. Μακαλώθ, Μακελώθ, and Μακελλώθ), the name of two men.

1. The principal officer of the second contingent of troops under Dodo, during the reign of David and Solomon (1 Chron. xxvii, 4). B.C. 1014.

2. A descendant of Benjamin resident at Jerusalem, and father of Shimeah or Shimean, of the family of king Saul, but in what degree of relationship is not clear (1 Chron. viii, 32; ix, 37, 38). B.C. perhaps cir. 536.

Miknei'ah (Heb. *Mikneya'hu*, מִקְנֵיָהוּ, *possession of Jehovah;* Sept. Μακενία or Μακενίας), a Levitical door-keeper of the Temple and harper in the time of David (1 Chron. xv, 18, 21). B.C. 1014.

Mikron. See MICRONIUS.

Mikvaoth. See TALMUD.

Mil'alai (Heb. *Milalay'*, מִלֲלַי, *eloquent;* Sept. omits; Vulg. *Malalai*), one of the Levitical musicians who made the circuit of the newly-completed walls of Jerusalem after the exile (Neh. xii, 36). B.C. 446.

Milan, one of the large cities of Italy, capital of Lombardy, situated on the River Olona, contains a population of 295,543. It is a very ancient city, and is noted in ecclesiastical history as the seat of several important Church councils. Milan (Lat. *Mediolanum*) was originally a town or village of the Insubrian Gauls. It was conquered by the Romans 222 B.C., received the Latin franchise about 89 B.C., and the full Roman franchise 49 B.C. Under the Romans it became a conspicuous centre of wealth and civic influence; its inhabitants were noted for their refined manners and literary tastes.

and the public buildings for their beauty and elegance. In the beginning of the 4th century it was selected as the residence of the imperial court by Maximian. Milan was sacked by the Huns (under Attila) in 452; by the Goths (under the brother of Vitiges) in 539; and passed to the Longobards and Franks previous to its subjection by the German Empire. After 961, it was long governed by dukes in the name of the emperors. The feuds of the Guelphs and Ghibellines distracted Milan, like all the other Italian cities. Supreme power became eventually vested in the Ghibelline Visconti, by whom the ascendency of Milan was extended over the whole of Lombardy. From 1545 to 1714, Milan submitted to the successive predominance of France and Austria. Under Bonaparte, it was declared the capital of the Cisalpine republic, of the Italian republic, and, finally, of the kingdom of Italy. In 1815, Milan was restored to Austria, and continued the capital of the Austro-Italian kingdom until the annexation of Lombardy to Piedmont, in 1859, by the peace of Villafranca.

MILAN, ARCHBISHOPRIC OF. We have no trustworthy information as to its early history. There is a vague tradition that Barnabas (q. v.), the colaborer of the apostle Paul, established the Christian Church at Milan, and was the first bishop. This account lacks support, and scarcely deserves notice. But though of no historical value, the legend is significant in regard to the position which the archbishopric of Milan held in the controversies between the Oriental and Occidental churches. It has been aptly remarked by Reuchlin that, "just as Barnabas was the connecting link between Paul and the other apostles, so the Church of Milan attempted to reconcile the Greek and Roman opinions." The first bishop of Milan, of whom we have any historical knowledge, is Auxentius (q. v.), A.D. 355-374. He was the leader of the Arians in the Western churches. When the orthodox bishops, at a provincial synod held at Rome in 369, condemned Arianism, they did not dare to pronounce the anathema against Auxentius, because they knew him to be protected by the emperor Valentinian I. Although they were at last prevailed upon by Athanasius to pronounce against Auxentius in their synodal epistle to the Illyrians, Auxentius maintained himself in his see until his death. But the divisions thus created in the Church by the Arian heresy (q. v.) rendered the election of a successor to Auxentius no easy matter. The contest was carried on between Catholics and Arians with such violence that Ambrose, who was the consular prefect of Liguria and Æmilia, was obliged to proceed himself to the church to exhort the people to order. At the close of his speech the whole assembly, Catholics and Arians, with one voice demanded him for their bishop, and he was constrained to accept the proffered honor. Ambrose devoted himself to his work with great zeal, and soon acquired great influence both with the people and the emperor Valentinian. He opposed the Arians from the very beginning of his episcopacy, and in 382 presided at an episcopal synod at Aquileia, at which the Arian bishops Palladius and Secundianus were deposed. Ambrose died at Milan, April 4, 397. All succeeding archbishops and bishops were in like manner elected by the people, the Church of Milan not being subject to the Roman bishop until the days of Gregory the Great (q. v.). After the overthrow of the Gothic kingdom, the archbishops of Milan, owing to the religious differences and the feeling of enmity which existed between the people and their conquerors, the Lombards (q. v.), resided at Geneva. But when, in 653, Aribert, the son of duke Garduald, was chosen king of the Lombards, matters changed. "Rex Heribertus," says Döllinger, "pius et catholicus, Arianorum abolevit hæresem et Christianam fidem fecit crescere." The Lombards now became enthusiastic churchmen, and the archbishop returned to Milan. But although the archbishop of Milan was henceforth considered the first bishop of the kingdom, crowning the kings with the so-called *iron crown*, and obtaining increasing power, he

nevertheless remained subject to the king, and the inferior clergy to the subordinate judges — in short, the Church was subject to the State. After the downfall of the Longobard kingdom, the archbishops of Milan at first lost much of their power; but during the fights and quarrels of the 9th, 10th, and 11th centuries, they not only regained their former influence, but became even more independent than ever before. Owing to the then prevailing German policy, large feudal estates were bestowed upon the bishops of Milan, and, during the reign of the Ottos (q. v.), the archbishops of Milan were considered the most influential allies of the German emperors.

Eriberto di Argago, who filled the archiepiscopal chair of Milan from 1019 to 1045, was one of the most powerful princes, and though unsuccessful in the revolt which he organized in 1034 against emperor Conrad the Salic, his influence was scarcely diminished after his return from the expulsion to which his rebellion had subjected him. At the time of his death, Milan was passing through one of its accustomed civil dissensions, and the election of Eriberto's successor caused great excitement. Erlembaldo, the popular chief (dominus populi), called the citizens together to nominate candidates, and induced them to select four. These four were sent to the emperor Henry III (q. v.), for him to make the appointment; but the faction of the nobles despatched a rival in the person of Guido di Valate, who had recommended himself to the emperor by his zealous services, and who was given the coveted dignity, to the great disgust of the popular nominees. Their expostulations were unavailing with the emperor, and both parties returned— Guido to assume an office harassed by the opposition of the people on whom he had been forced, and the disappointed candidates to brood over the wrongs they had experienced. We shall presently see how thoroughly these men avenged themselves on Guido, with whom the independence of the Milanese archbishopric came to an end.

It is historically evident, then, that Milan was at one time completely independent of the papacy. Rome was not even thought of in creating the archbishop, whose spiritual and temporal power were granted by the imperial investiture. But when, soon after, the German popes had rescued the pontificate from the contempt into which it had fallen, its domination over Milan became a necessary step in its progress to universal supremacy.

Marriage, at that time, was a universal privilege of the Milanese clergy. Pope Leo IX (q. v.) and his successors attacked the Milanese on this account, and, in a council held at Rheims by Leo IX in 1049, many laws were enacted against clerical matrimony. Archbishop Guido defended the position of the Milanese clergy, not only by Scripture texts, but also by a decision which he affirmed was rendered by St. Ambrose, to whom the question of the permissibility of sacerdotal marriage had been referred by the pope and bishops. The popes by their emissaries excited great tumults in Milan, inflaming the popular passion against, what they called, the irregularities of the clergy. Guido in vain endeavored to repress the agitation thus produced, and argued in favor of the married clergy. Armed resistance was offered to the papal faction, the result of which was incessant fights and increasing bloodshed. Nicholas II (q. v.), who then occupied the papal chair, sent Hildebrand and Anselm on a mission to Milan, with instructions to allay the passions which led to such deplorable civil strifes. The milder Anselm might perhaps have succeeded in this errand of reconciliation, but the unbending Hildebrand refused to listen to aught but unconditional subjection to Rome. The quarrel, therefore, waxed fiercer and deadlier (see Arnulf, *Gest. Archiep. Mediolan.* lib. iii, c. 9; Landulf, *Sen.* lib. iii, c. 9).

In 1059 another papal legation was sent, with full authority to force the recalcitrant archbishop and clergy to submission. An assembly was held, where the legates asserted the papal pre-eminence by taking the place of honor, to the general indignation of the Milanese, who did not relish the degradation of their archbishop before the representatives of a foreign prelate. The authority of Rome, which at first was stoutly denied by the archbishop, was finally acknowledged, the archbishop and the clergy signing a paper in which they expressed their contrition in the most humiliating terms (see Damiani, *Opusc.* xlii, c. i).

The pride of the Milanese, however, was deeply wounded by such a subjection to Rome, unknown for many generations, and ill endured by men who gloried in the ancient dignity of the Ambrosian Church. When, therefore, in 1061, after Nicholas's death, their townsman, Anselm, was elevated from the episcopate of Lucca to that of the holy see, under the name of Alexander II, the Milanese Church attempted to regain its former independence. A council of German and Lombard bishops convened at Basle, and unanimously elected as pontiff Cadalus, bishop of Parma, under the title of Honorius II. By the assistance of the German emperors, the Lombard bishops, with Guido, the archbishop of Milan, at their head, assembled a considerable army in 1062, with which they conducted their new pope to Rome, while the popular party in Milan and Northern Italy assumed a formidable aspect in its alliance to the Lombard bishops. At this juncture Alexander II was rescued from probable defeat by the occurrence of a most unexpected event—the German bishops, under the influence of Hanno, archbishop of Cologne, sided with Alexander, and in 1064 the Synod of Mantua pronounced the deposition of Honorius. The archbishop of Milan, being unable to support the pretensions of the rival pope without German aid, of which there was no prospect, yielded, and was excommunicated by the pope in 1066. Guido, however, disregarding this excommunication, resolved to officiate in the solemn services of Pentecost (June 4, 1066), and, braving all opposition, appeared at the altar. Excited to fury at this unexpected contumacy, the papal party attacked him in the church; his followers rallied in his defence, but, after a stubborn fight, were forced to leave him in the hands of his enemies, by whom he was nearly beaten to death. Some few months later archbishop Guido succeeded in reorganizing his party, and the war was for several years carried on with varying fortune. At last, in 1069, Hildebrand proposed that both the Milanese clergy and laity should take an oath that in future their archbishops should apply to the pope, and not to the emperor, for confirmation. Guido sought to anticipate this movement, and, old and wearied with the endless strife and contention, resigned his archbishopric to the subdeacon Gotefrido, who had long been his principal adviser. The latter procured his confirmation from Henry IV (q. v.), but the Milanese, defrauded of their electoral privileges, refused to acknowledge him. The papal party, taking advantage of this popular feeling, excited a tumult, and Gotefrido was glad to escape at night from the rebellious city.

Meanwhile Azzo, the papal aspirant, fared no better than his rival. The people rushed in to his inaugural banquet, unearthed him from the corner where he had hidden himself, dragged him by the heels in the street, and, placing him in a pulpit, forced him to swear that he would make no further pretensions to the see, and Azzo quitted the city, content to have saved his life.

The city remained thus without an archbishop, and in 1074 Hildebrand, who in April, 1073, had succeeded to Alexander, launched an interdict against Milan. The Milanese were disposed to disregard the interdict, and applied to Henry IV, requesting the appointment of another archbishop. To this the emperor responded by nominating Tedaldo, who was duly consecrated. Tedaldo was the leader of the disaffected bishops, who at the Synod of Pavia, in 1076, excommunicated pope Gregory himself; and though, after the interview at Canossa in 1077, the Milanese, disgusted with Henry's voluntary humiliation before that papal power which they had

learned to despise, abandoned the imperial party for a time, yet Tedaldo kept his seat until his death in 1085, notwithstanding the repeated excommunications launched against him by Gregory (see Arnulf, lib. iv; v, c. 2, 5, 9; Landulf, *Sen.* lib. iii, c. 29; iv, 2; Muratori, *Annales*, ann. 1085). With his death the independence of the Milan archbishopric ceased.

At present the clergy of Milan seem to be inclined to follow the lead of the Old Catholic party. Their programme, which contains the following reforms: election of the priests by the parish, the use of the vernacular at all Church-services, reform of Mariolatry and adoration of saints, marriage of the priests, etc., shows a healthy reaction against papal abuses. E. Serra Gropelli may be pointed out as the leader of the Milanese reform party.

See Hefele, *Conciliengeschichte*, iv, 297 sq.; Riddle, *Hist. of the Papacy*, ii, 119 sq.; Dupin, *Eccles. Hist.* ix, chap. viii; Mosheim, *Church Hist.* iii, xi, pt. ii; Lea, *Hist. of Sacerdotal Celibacy*, chap. xiii; Schröckh, *Kirchengesch.* xxii, 523 sq.; Böhringer, *Kirche Christi*, i, 90; iii, 92 sq.; Milman, *Hist. of Lat. Christianity*, iii, 240 sq.; Reichel, *Roman See in the Middle Ages*, p. 189, 191 sq.; Wetzer und Welte, *Kirchen-Lexikon*, v, 318 sq.; Herzog, *Real-Encyklop.* xx, 72 sq.

MILAN, COUNCIL OF. There is no historical proof extant to warrant the assertion that any Church councils or synods were held at Milan before 355 A.D. We have no reliable information concerning the synod which is said to have been held at Milan in 344 (see Hardouin, *Acta Conciliorum et Epistolæ decretales ac Constitutiones*, etc. [Paris, 1715], i, 627 sq.), and very little is known of the synod of 346 (or 347). In that year a council of Western bishops was summoned at Milan, when the so-called *Long Creed* (μακρόστιχος, to be found in Socrates, *Hist. Eccl.* ii, 18), which had been drawn up by the Arian Council of Antioch (A.D. 345), was rejected. The council also required the deputies who brought it to sign a condemnation of Arianism. Of course they left the council in wrath (see J. Dominic, *Mansi Sacrorum conciliorum nova et amplissima collectio*, etc. [Florent. 1759], ii, 1370). After the death of Constance (A.D. 350), and the victory over Magnentius (A.D. 353), Constantius endeavored to establish Arianism by force in the West. In the synods of Arles (A.D. 354) and of Milan (A.D. 358), he compelled the assembled bishops to sign the condemnation of Athanasius, though most of them were, it is thought, orthodox. Constantius was now sole master of the Roman world, and by bribes, by threats, and by force, the condemnation of Athanasius was extorted from the assembled bishops. Even Liberius (q. v.), the successor of Julius I, rejected Athanasius, from fear of Constantius, but soon afterwards threw off his timidity, and refused to subscribe to his condemnation (see Mansi, iii, 233 sq.; Hefele, i, 631).

The next council was held A.D. 390, St. Ambrose presiding. It is commonly supposed that in this council the sentence of the Gallic bishops against Ithacius Ursacius (who had caused the death of the Priscillianists by their fiery zeal against their errors) was confirmed by the bishops of Italy. Baronius (as well as the collection of councils) states that this same council condemned Jovinian, the author of a new heresy, which decried the merit of virginity. St. Jerome reduces his doctrine to the four following heads: 1. That virgins, widows, and married women, being baptized, have the same degree of merit, if there be no difference between them in other respects. 2. That they who have been regenerated in baptism cannot be overcome by the devil. 3. That there is no difference in point of merit, between those who abstain from meat and those who partake of it with thanksgiving. 4. That all those who have kept their baptismal state shall have the same glory in heaven. From these principles other errors were deduced, viz. that there is no difference of degree in sin; that fasting is not requisite; that there will be no distinction of merits in heaven. The fathers of the council condemned the opinions of Jovinian and his followers, and they were driven out of the city. See Mansi, *l. c.* 690; Gieseler, i, 333; Hefele, ii, 48.

Another council was held at Milan in 451, convoked by Eusebius, bishop of Milan, at the request of St. Leo the Great. All the suffragans of Milan were present, in all twenty bishops, among whom were Crispinus of Pavia, Maximus of Turin, Abundius of Como, Optatianus of Brescia. The letter of the pope to Eusebius was read; the legates then made a report of what was passing in the East, and especially of the miseries existing from the acts of the Latrocinium at Ephesus; afterwards the celebrated letter of St. Leo to Flavianus was read, and the council unanimously declared that it contained the true doctrine of the Catholic Church upon the subject of the *Incarnation* (q. v.), and that it was built upon the teachings of the prophets, evangelists, and apostles. At the same time they decreed that all who should oppose this doctrine should be anathematized. Finally, a synodal letter was addressed to the pope filled with expressions of esteem and respect (Mansi, ii, 78 sq.; Hefele, *Conciliengeschichte*, ii, 374 sq.). In A.D. 679 pope Agatho summoned a council at Milan to condemn anew the heresy of *Monothelism* (q. v.) (Mansi, xi, 174; Hefele, iii, 228). The provincial synods of A.D. 842, 860, 880, and 1009 have no bearing upon the general history of the Church, but those interested in these are referred to Mansi, xiv, 790; xv, 590; xvii, 535, and xix, 310; Hefele, iv, 99, 217, 770. September 12, 1287, a synod was held by Otto, the archbishop, assisted by eight of his suffragans, and the deputies of all the chapters of the province. Ten canons were published, in which they ordered the observation of the papal constitutions, and the laws of the emperor Frederick II against heretics. Abbots and abbesses, monks and nuns, were ordered to observe the rule of St. Benedict or that of St. Augustine, and monks were forbidden to enter nunneries. The power of building churches and oratories was declared to be solely in the hands of the bishop (Mansi, xxiv, 868 sq.; Hefele, vi, 225; Muratori, *Rev. Ital.* vol. iv). From 1565 to 1582 six provincial councils were held at Milan. For information concerning their enactments, see *Concil,* xv, 242, 337, 365 sq., 408, 556, 706; Jo. Harduini *Acta,* x, 633, 1140; Christ. Wilhelm-Franz Walch, *Entwurf einer vollständigen Historie der Kirchenversammlungen* (Leipsic, 1759).

Milanese Liturgy. The Liturgy of Milan, commonly attributed to Ambrose, is substantially the same as that of Rome until the time of Gregory the Great, and appears to have been derived from the same origin. "In the time of Gregory, the Church of Milan did not adopt the chief alteration made by him. From that time, if not previously, the Liturgy of Milan began to be considered a peculiar rite; and as the Romans gave their sacramentaries the names of Gelasius and Gregory, so the Milanese gave theirs the name of Ambrose; who, in fact, may have composed some parts of it. After the time of Gregory, the Milan Liturgy doubtless received several additions. The earliest ecclesiastical writer who has been cited as speaking of the Ambrosian rite is Walofred Strabo, who died A.D. 849" (Riddle, *Christian Antiquities,* p. 417). See LITURGY.

Milani, Aureliano, nephew of the following, was born at Bologna, Italy, in 1675. He painted in the style of Caracci, and, next to Carlo Cignani, no one did more to maintain the dignity and credit of the Bolognese school. Lanzi says he was not so excellent in his coloring. His principal works in Bologna are the *Resurrection,* in the church of La Puritá; the *Stoning of St. Stephen,* in St. Mascarella; and *St. Jerome,* in Sta. Maria della Vita. He afterwards went to Rome, where his finest work is the *Beheading of St. John the Baptist,* in the church of the Bergamaschi. He died in 1749. See Lanzi, *History of Painting,* transl. by Roscoe (London, 1847, 3 vols. 8vo), iii, 152.

Milani, Giulio Cesare, a Bolognese painter,

who was born in 1621, executed many works for the churches in Bologna and the adjacent cities. His finest productions are the *Marriage of the Virgin,* in the church of St. Giuseppe; *St. Antonio di Padova,* in St. Maria del Costello; and a *Holy Family,* at the Lervi. According to Lanzi, "he was the most eminent of Torre's disciples, and was rather admired in the churches of Bologna, and extolled in many adjacent states." He died in 1678. See Lanzi, *History of Painting,* transl. by Roscoe (Lond. 1847, 3 vols. 8vo), iii, 107; Spooner, *Biog. History of the Fine Arts* (N. Y. 1865, 2 vols. 8vo).

Milbourne, LUKE, an English divine, was born at Wroxhall, Warwickshire. He was educated at Pembroke Hall, Cambridge, after which he became rector of St. Ethelburga, London, and lecturer of Shoreditch in 1704. He died April 13, 1720. He published thirty-one single sermons between 1692 and 1720; several theological treatises, poems, etc.; and the following work, by which he is best known: *Notes on Dryden's Virgil* (Lond. 1698). Among Milbourne's theological works, we regard as the most important his *Legacy to the Church of England* (new ed. 1726, 2 vols. 8vo), in which he vindicates her orders from the objections of Papists and Dissenters. This work, it is stated, was undertaken by the special command of archbishop Sancroft and Dr. Lloyd, bishop of Norwich. See Cooper, *Biograph. Dict.* p. 806; Ellis, *Hist. of Shoreditch;* Malone's *Dryden,* i, 214; iv, 633, 645; Johnson, *Lives of the Poets,* ed. Cunningham, i, 371 sq.; Allibone, *Dict. of Authors,* ii, 1277.

Mil'cah (Heb. *Milkah',* מִלְכָּה, *advice;* Sept. Μελχά), the name of two women.

1. The daughter of Haran, and sister of Lot and Iscah (or Sarah); she married Nahor (Gen. xii, 29), by whom she had eight sons (Gen. xx, 20, 23), one of whom was Bethuel, the father of Rebekah (Gen. xxiv, 15, 24, 47). She was thus Abraham's sister-in-law, and the grandmother of Isaac's wife. B.C. cir. 2047.

2. The fourth named of the five daughters of Zelophehad, of the tribe of Manasseh (Numb. xxvi, 33), who became heiresses for the want of brothers (Numb. xxvii, 1), and, having married members of the same tribe (Numb. xxxvi, 11), were assigned portions in Gilead (Josh. xvii, 3). B.C. 1619–1612.

Mil'com (Heb. *Milkom',* מִלְכֹּם, *their king,* 1 Kings xi, 5; Sept. Μελχώμ and Μελχόμ, Vulg. *Moloch;* 2 Kings xxiii, 13, Μολόχ, *Melchom;* also MALCHAM, Heb. *Malkam',* מַלְכָּם, *id.,* Jer. xlix, 1, 3, Sept. Μελχόλ, Vulg. *Melchom,* "their king;" but this last is the proper rendering in Amos i, 15; Zeph. i, 5, in which latter passage the Auth. Vers. has "Malcham"), the principal deity of the Ammonites (Jer. xlix, 1, 3), for whose worship Solomon erected altars on the Mount of Olives, hence called the Hill of Offence (2 Kings xxiii, 13). Milcom is usually regarded as the same as *Molech* or *Moloch,* although the latter was worshipped in a different place and manner, namely, by the offering of children in the flames of the valley of Hinnom (see Keil, *Comment.* ad loc. Kings; Movers, *Phön.* p. 324 sq.; Ewald, *Isr. Gesch.* iii, 100). See MOLOCH.

Mildew (יֵרָקוֹן, *yerakon', greenness,* i. e. pallor, as the "paleness" by affright, Jer. xxx, 6) is properly a species of fungus or parasitic plant generated by moisture, and corrosive of the surface to which it adheres. In Scripture it is applied to grain, and refers to the pale green or yellowish color indicative of fading or withering of plants (Deut. xxviii, 22; 1 Kings viii, 37; 2 Chron. vi, 28; Amos iv, 9; Hag. ii, 17; in all which passages it is connected with "blasting"). The Arabic applies the word *yerakon* to human beings as well as to corn, and thus describes the disease called in Europe yellow jaundice. Forskål was informed in Arabia by a Jew that it was the general opinion there that it is a mild breeze, dangerous to the corn, by which the ears are turned yellow. See LEPROSY.

Mile (μίλιον, the Greek form of the Latin *milliari-*

um, from *mille,* a *thousand,* Matt. v, 41), a Roman measure of 1000 geometrical paces (*passus*) of five feet each, and therefore equal to 5000 Roman feet (see Smith's *Dict. of Greek and Roman Antiq.* s. v. Milliare). Taking the Roman foot at 11.6496 English inches, the Roman mile would be 1618 English yards, or 142 yards less than the English statute mile (see *Penny Cyclopædia,* s. v.). By another calculation, in which the foot is taken at 11.62 inches, the mile would be little more than 1614 yards. The number of Roman miles in a degree of a large circle of the earth is little more than 75 (see Ukert, *Geogr. d. Griech.* I, ii, 75). The most common Latin term for the mile is *mille passuum,* or only the initials M. P.; sometimes the word *passuum* is omitted. The Roman mile contained eight Greek stadia (Pliny, ii, 21). Hence it is usual with the earlier writers on Biblical geography to translate the Greek "stade" into the English "furlong" in stating the measurements of Eusebius and Jerome, who, like the early itineraries, always reckon by Roman miles. See FURLONG. The Talmudists also employed this measure (which they call מיל, Otho, *Lex. Rabb.* p. 421), but estimate it at 7½ stadia (*Baba Mezia,* xxxiii, 1), as also the Roman historians frequently reckon it, without geographical or mathematical accuracy (Forbiger, *Handbuch d. alt. Geogr.* i, 555). Mile-stones were set up along the roads constructed by the Romans in Palestine (Reland, *Palæst.* p. 401 sq.), and to this day they may be seen, here and there, in that country (Robinson, *Bib. Res.* ii, 161, note; ii, 306). The mile of the Jews is said to have been of two kinds, long or short, dependent on the length of the pace, which varied in different parts, the long pace being double the length of the short one (Carpzov, *Apparat.* p. 679). See METROLOGY.

Miles, HENRY G., a Presbyterian minister, was born in Amsterdam, N. Y., about the year 1811. He was educated in Hudson, Ohio, studied theology in the Union Theological Seminary, New York; was licensed by the New York Third Presbytery, and ordained by the Rochester Presbytery in 1851. He received and accepted a call to the Church at Dover, Ohio, and subsequently preached at Hublinsbury, Pa., and Parma Centre and Woodhull, N. Y., where he died, July 21, 1860. Mr. Miles had to struggle with many difficulties, but in all his duties he was conscientious and zealous. As a preacher he was clear and practical. See *Presb. Hist. Almanac,* 1862, p. 189. (J. L. S.)

Mile'tum (2 Tim. iv, 20). See MILETUS.

Mile'tus (Μίλητος, from the name of a fabled son of Apollo, who is said to have founded the city, Apollod. iii, 1, 2), a city and seaport of Ionia, in Asia Minor, about thirty-six miles south of Ephesus (Cramer's *Asia Minor,* ii, 385 sq.). The apostle Paul touched at this port on his voyage from Greece to Syria, and delivered to the elders of Ephesus, who had come to meet him there, a remarkable and affecting address (Acts xx, 15-38). "In the context we have the geographical relations of the latter city brought out distinctly, as if it were Luke's purpose to state them. In the first place, it lay on the coast to the south of Ephesus. Next, it was a day's sail from Trogyllium (ver. 15). Moreover, to those who are sailing from the north, it is in the direct line for Cos. We should also notice that it was near enough to Ephesus by land communication for the message to be sent and the presbyters to come within a very narrow space of time. All these details correspond with the geographical facts of the case. As to the last point, Ephesus was by land only about twenty or thirty

miles distant from Miletus. There is a further and more minute topographical coincidence, which may be seen in the phrase, 'They accompanied him to the ship,' implying as it does that the vessel lay at some distance from the town. The site of Miletus has now receded ten miles from the coast, and even in the apostle's time it must have lost its strictly maritime position (Hackett, *Comm. on the Acts,* 2d ed. p. 344; comp. Acts xxi, 5). In each case we have a low, flat shore, as a marked and definite feature of the scene." Miletus was a place of considerable note, and the ancient capital of Ionia and Caria (Herod. i, 142; Pliny, v, 31). It was the birthplace of several men of renown—Thales, Timotheus, Anaximander, Anaximenes, Democritus (Pomp. Mela, i, 17; Diog. Laertius, *Vit. Philosoph.* p. 15, 88, 89, 650). Ptolemy (*Geogr.* v, 2, 9) places Miletus in Caria by the sea, and it is stated to have had four havens, one of which was capable of holding a fleet. (See J. E. Rambach, *De Mileto ejusque coloniis* [Hal. 1790]; Soldan,

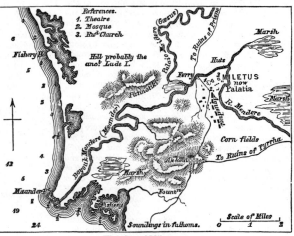

References.
1. Theatre
2. Mosque
3. Ru^d Church

Vicinity of Miletus.

Rer. Miles. Comment. [Darmst. 1829]; Schroeder, *Comment. de rebus Miles.* [Strals. 1827].) "In early times it was the most flourishing city of the Ionian Greeks. The ships which sailed from it were celebrated for their distant voyages. Miletus suffered in the progress of the Lydian kingdom and became tributary to Crœsus. In the natural order of events, it was absorbed in the Persian empire; and, revolting, it was stormed and sacked. After a brief period of spirited independence, it received a blow from which it never recovered, in the siege conducted by Alexander when on his Eastern campaign. But still it held, even through the Roman period, the rank of a second-rate trading town, and Strabo mentions its four harbors. At this time it was politically in the province of Asia, though Caria was the old ethnological name of the district in which it was situated. Its preeminence on this coast had now long been yielded up to Ephesus. These changes can be vividly traced by comparing the whole series of coins of the two places. In the case of Miletus, those of the autonomous period are

Coin of Miletus.

numerous and beautiful, those of the imperial period very scanty. Still Miletus was for some time an episcopal city of Western Asia. Its final decay was doubtless promoted by the silting up of the Mæander." It was noted for a famous temple of Apollo, the oracle of which is known to have been consulted so late as the 4th century (Apollodorus, *De Orig. Deor.* iii, 130). There was, however, a Christian church in the place; and in the 5th, 7th, and 8th centuries we read of bishops of Miletus, who were present at several councils (Magdeburg, *Hist. Eccles.* ii, 192; iv, 86; v, 3; vii, 254; viii, 4). The city fell to decay after its conquest by the Saracens, and is now in ruins, not far from the spot where the Mæander falls into the sea. (See Büsching, *Erdbeschr.* XI, i, 100; Tzschucke, *ad Mel.* III, i, 481.) The exact site, however, is somewhat a matter of uncertainty (Rosenmüller, *Bibl. Geogr.* I, ii, 187), owing to the altered character of the coast in modern times; but it appears to be in part covered by the remains now called *Palatia*, i. e. the palace (Leake, *Asia Minor*, p. 240). It lies in a triangular plot of ground, bounded by two branches of the river Mendere—the ancient Mæander. These unite a little to the north of the ruins, and the stream thus formed disembogues through marshy ground into the sea about two miles distant. The harbor is filled up by the alluvial soil brought down by the river, which has already created a delta of no insignificant dimensions. The ruins of the ancient Miletus are even at

Ruins of Miletus.

the present time striking and picturesque, especially those of the theatre, one of the largest in Asia Minor. Seen from the south-west, it makes still a splendid object; to the south is a mosque, and farther still, in the same direction, a line of ruined arches, once forming an aqueduct. The fragments of a church remain, in which the current tradition of the place asserts that St. John preached the Gospel; but it is unquestionably of a date far later than that of the evangelist. In the plain, between the theatre and the aqueduct, are a few pillars, indicating the site of a temple, probably dedicated to Diana. See Texier, *Asie Mineure*, p. 316 sq.

Some take the Miletus where Paul left Trophimus sick (2 Tim. iv, 20; Auth. Vers. "Miletum") to have been in Crete, and therefore different from the above; but there seems to be no need for this conclusion. "This passage presents a very serious difficulty to the theory that there was only one Roman imprisonment. When Paul visited the place on the occasion just described, Trophimus was indeed with him (Acts xx, 4); but he certainly did not 'leave him sick at Miletus,' for at the conclusion of the voyage we find him with the apostle at Jerusalem (Acts xxi, 29). Nor is it possible that he could have been so left on the voyage from Cæsarea to Rome, for in the first place there is no reason to believe that Trophimus was with the apostle then at all; and in the second place the ship was never to the north of Cnidus (Acts xxvii, 7). But on the hypothesis that Paul was liberated from Rome and revisited the neighborhood of Ephesus, all becomes easy, and consistent with the other notices of his movements in the pastoral epistles. (See Conybeare and Howson, *Life and Epistles of St. Paul*, ch. xxvii; Birks, *Horæ Apostolicæ*.)" See further in Schmidt, *Res Milesianæ* (Gött. 1855); Smith,

Dict. of Gr. and Rom. Geogr. s. v.; Conybeare and Howson, *St. Paul*, ii, 214 sq.; Tschihatscheff, *L'Asie Mineure* (Par. 1853), i, 252 sq.; Rawlinson, *Herod.* i, 218 sq.

Milēum, a city of Numidia, in the northern part of Africa, is celebrated in Church history as a place where, at the beginning of the 5th century, two synods were held. The first of them, which is of little importance, convened Aug. 27, 402. Aurelius of Carthage presided. The canons of Hippo and Carthage were confirmed, and five canons of discipline published, which are contained in the African Code (comp. *Codex Canon. Eccl. Afric.* p. 85–90). It was decided that the younger bishops should give place to those of older standing, excepting the primates of Numidia and Mauritania, who always took precedence of all other primates of whatever standing (*Conc.* ii, 1323). The second synod, which was held towards the autumn of A.D. 416, is known as the *Concilium Milevitanum.* This was a provincial council of Numidia, and was attended by sixty-one bishops of the province. It was chiefly owing to Augustine's (q. v.) influence, and to the happy issue of the synod at Diospolis (q. v.), that the African bishops assembled in a synodical meeting. Having learned the proceedings of the Council of Carthage of the same year, they wrote a synodalletter to pope Innocent I (q. v.), in which, after enlarging upon the enormity of the Pelagian heresy, which denied the necessity of *prayer in adults* and of baptism for children, and, after showing how worthy it was of the notice and censure of the Church, they entreated him, since the salvation of Pelagius (q. v.) and Cœlestius (q. v.) could not be secured, that he would at least provide for that of others by condemning their heresies. They did not ask the excommunication of Pelagius and Cœlestius, as has sometimes been stated, but that they should be commanded to renounce their heresies, and that only the heresies themselves should be condemned. "Hoc gestum," they concluded, "Domino frater, sanctæ caritati tuæ intimandum ducimus, ut statutis nostræ mediocritatis etiam apostolicæ sedis adhibeatur auctoritas." Among the names attached to this letter are those of Silvanus, primate of the province of Numidia, Alypius, St. Augustine, Severus of Mileum, Fortunatus of Citha, and Possidius. Another and more confidential letter was addressed to Innocent by five North African bishops, of whom Augustine was one (see Mansi, iv, 321 sq.). Pelagius also sent him a letter and a confession of faith, which, however, were not received in due time. Innocent understood both the controversy and the interests of the Roman see. In his reply, which is to be found in *August. Epist.* p. 182, he commended the Africans for having addressed themselves to the Church of St. Peter, before which it was seemly that all the affairs of Christendom should be brought. He praised the zeal and pastoral care of the African bishops, briefly established the true doctrine of grace, and condemned Pelagius and Cœlestius, with their followers, declaring them to be separated from the Catholic Church. "Non solum enim," he says, "qui faciunt sed etiam qui consentiunt facientibus, digni sunt morto; quia non multum interesse arbitror inter committentis animum et consentientis favorem." He refrained, however, from giving judgment respecting the Synod of Diospolis. He also replied to the letters which Augustine and the four bishops—Aurelius, Alypius,

Evodius, and Possidius—had addressed to him. These letters of Innocent were written in a council held at Rome upon the subject in January, 417, and are to be found in Mansi (iii, 1071 sq.). See Schulstraten, *Antiq. Eccles. Afric. Diss.* vol. iii; Norris, *Hist. Pelag.* i, 10; Hefele, *Conciliengeschichte*, ii, 100; Gieseler, *Eccles. Hist.* i, 330 sq.; Schaff, *Church Hist.* iii, 797; Milman, *Hist. of Christianity*, p. 389, 414 sq.

Milicz VON KREMSIER (*Kromesize*), JOHN, was one of the most eminent precursors of the Bohemian Reformation. Of his early years little is known. The fact that in his mature years he first engaged in the study of the German language, would indicate that his education must have been acquired elsewhere than in a German university; possibly in Italy or at Paris, or in his own country, Moravia. Commencing his public career as a priest about the year 1350, he soon attracted the notice of the emperor Charles IV, who was also king of Bohemia, and became his secretary. At the same time, as canon of the cathedral at Prague, and archdeacon, he occupied a conspicuous ecclesiastical position. Resigning, however, all his prospects of promotion, notwithstanding the entreaties of the bishop, he chose a lot of poverty and hardship, that he might more fully imitate the example of Christ. For six months he preached to the people at Bishop-teinitz; but fearing lest his position there was too tempting, in a worldly point of view, he returned to Prague, first officiating in the church of St. Nicholas, in the Kleine Seito, and afterwards in that of St. Ægidius, in the old city. At first his hearers were few. Perhaps his Moravian dialect was not attractive. His reproof of sin, and his earnest words, however, soon attracted notice. Multitudes thronged to hear him. He preached daily, and often three, and sometimes five sermons. To be more extensively useful, he applied himself to the study of German, that he might address himself to the Germans of Prague. The evils and corruptions of the times doubtless led him to select his themes of discourse largely from the Apocalypse, and the prophets of the Old Testament, and ere long the coming of Antichrist became the burden of his pulpit discourses. He fixed the date of his coming at A.D. 1365-67, nor did he fear to expose the iniquities which, to his view, seemed to herald it. Priests, bishops, and magistrates, and even the emperor himself, were not spared. It is to the credit of his reputation for sincerity that, notwithstanding the hostility which he provoked in some quarters, he was sustained and befriended by the highest powers in Church and State.

In 1367, on the report that the pope was about to return from Avignon to Rome, Milicz resolved to visit and confer with him. The pope's arrival was delayed; and Milicz, obedient to what he regarded as the voice of the Spirit within him, nailed upon the doors of St. Peter's the sentence which had so long occupied his thoughts—"The Antichrist has come." He zealously warned the people and the clergy to withdraw themselves from iniquity. The inquisitor, encouraged by reports of Milicz's course in Bohemia, ordered his arrest and imprisonment. From his prison he was summoned to preach to an assembly of the clergy, but his full release did not take place till the pope's arrival in Rome in 1368. In free conference with the pope and some of the cardinals who befriended him, he moderated, if he did not modify his views. On his return to Prague, where he succeeded Conrad Waldhauser in the Tein Church, his enthusiastic zeal assumed a new phase. He devoted himself earnestly to the reform of the vicious and abandoned. Scores of prostitutes were recalled to repentance and virtue. The quarters they had occupied, heretofore the scandal of the city, were transformed. A chapel to St. Mary Magdalene was erected there, and buildings were provided for the residence and support of the hundreds, if not thousands, that were recovered to the paths of virtue. Milicz's course made him many enemies. Of the clergy, some were jealous of him, and others hated him for his rebukes. Charges were drawn up against him, and forwarded to the pope at Avignon. It is quite significant that these articles, twelve in number, are almost silent as to any doctrinal errors. The pope, however, was prejudiced against Milicz, and summoned him to his court, to answer in person. Milicz, promptly responded to the summons. He met a kindly reception, and succeeded in vindicating his innocence. But his career was drawing to a close. He was taken sick at Avignon, and died June 29, 1374. At Prague his decease gave occasion for public and general lamentation.

Of the Christian character and devotion of Milicz, Matthias of Janow speaks in terms that might seem extravagant if the actual results of Milicz's labors did not go so far to justify them. Notwithstanding the envy which was felt towards him by some of the clergy, and the hostility which he provoked by his sharp rebuke of prevailing iniquity, he does not seem to have laid himself open to the charge of departing seriously from the accepted doctrines and usages of the Church. Indeed, his zeal took more of a practical than a speculative direction, and in this respect only can he be considered as a precursor who prepared the way for Huss.

Of Milicz's writings, some are still extant in manuscript, and some have been preserved by his friend and admirer, Matthias von Janow (q. v.). His Latin works were, *Libellus de Antichristo; Gratia Dei*, or sermons on the occasion of Church festivals throughout the year; and *Sermones Quadrigesimales*. Of his Bohemian works, consisting of sermons and postils, one only has been printed, and, though it found a place in the Prohibitory Index, not a copy of it is now known to exist.

A somewhat detailed account of Milicz is given by Neander in his *History of the Church* (vol. v). To the other sources of information—besides Balbinus (*Miscell.* i, lib. iv, 34) and the writings of Matthias of Janow—to which Neander had access, must be added P. Jordan's *Die Vorläufer des Hussitenthums in Böhmen*, which presents a concise sketch of Conrad of Waldhausen, Milicz, and Matthias of Janow. This sketch, really drawn up by F. Palacky, the historian of Bohemia, was published at first in Germany, with the name of P. Jordan affixed, since at the time it was doubtful whether the laws of the press in Austria would permit its publication in any of its states. It was republished, however, in 1868, under the name of its real author, F. Palacky; and doubtless furnishes the most trustworthy account extant of the subject of this article. See also Gillett, *Life of Huss* (see Index in vol. ii); Hardwick, *Ch. Hist.* p. 397, 399; Gieseler, *Eccles. Hist.* iii, 184 sq.; Riddle, *Hist. of the Papacy*, ii, 363; Czerwonka, *Gesch. der evangel. Kirche in Böhmen* (Bibf. 1869), vol. i. (E. H. G.)

Militant, Church, a term applied to the *whole congregation* of faithful men on earth (in distinction from the Church *triumphant* in heaven), as engaged "to fight manfully" under Christ's banner against sin, the world, and the devil; and to continue his faithful *soldiers* (milites) and servants unto their life's end.

Military Orders is a term applied to three celebrated fraternities which sprang up in the period of the *Crusades* (q. v.). They were religious associations which arose from a mixture of the religious enthusiasm and the chivalrous love of arms which almost equally formed the characteristics of mediæval society. The first origin of such associations may be traced to the necessities of the Christian residents of the Holy Land, in which the monks, whose first duty had been to serve the pilgrims in the hospital at Jerusalem, were compelled, by the necessity of self-defence, to assume the character of soldiers as well as of monks. These were termed *Knights of St. John*. See HOSPITALLERS. The second, the order of the *Templars* (q. v.), and the third, the *Teutonic Knights*, were the outgrowth of the days of the Crusades. See KNIGHTHOOD. These military orders professed to unite religious vows with the duties and discipline of a warrior. The chief objects they claimed to have in view were to defend and support Christianity, by force of arms, against the Mohammedans; to keep the public roads of Palestine from being infested with robbers; and to assist the poor, and minister to the sick, among those who were prompted by the spirit of the times to visit, as pilgrims, the various places reputed to be scenes of our Lord's earthly career.

The inferior orders of Alcantara and Calatrava, in Spain, having for their immediate object the defence of their country against the Moors, as well as those of Avis, in Portugal, claimed to have been instituted for like reasons as those above mentioned. They followed the Cistercian rule, and all three differed from the Templars and the Knights of St. John in being permitted by their institute to marry once. The same privilege was enjoyed in the Savoyard order of Knights of St. Maurice and the Flemish order of St. Hubert. On the contrary, the Teutonic Knights, who had their origin in the Crusades [see TEUTONIC KNIGHTS], were bound by an absolute vow of chastity.

With the varying conditions of society, these religious associations have at various times been abolished or fallen into disuse; but most of them still subsist in the form of orders of knighthood, and, in some of them, attempts have recently been made to revive, with certain modifications, the monastic character which they originally possessed. See Lea, *Hist. of Sacerdotal Celibacy*, ch. xxii; Giustinani, *Ordini Militari*, s. v.

Militz. See MILICZ.

Milk is designated by two Hebrew words of distinct signification.

1. חָלָב (*chalab'*, *fat*, i. e. rich; Gr. γάλα) denotes new or *sweet* milk. This, in its fresh state, appears to have been used very largely among the Hebrews, as is customary among people who have many cattle, and yet make but sparing use of their flesh for food (see Job xxi, 24; Judg. iv, 19). It is not a mere adjunct in cookery, or restricted to the use of the young, although it is naturally the characteristic food of childhood, both from its simple and nutritive qualities (1 Pet. ii, 2), and particularly as contrasted with meat (1 Cor. iii, 2; Heb. v, 12); but beyond this it is regarded as substantial food adapted alike to all ages and classes. Hence it is enumerated among "the principal things for the whole use of a man's life" (Ecclus. xxxix, 26). It frequently occurs in connection with honey, as a delicacy (Exod. iii, 8; xiii, 5; Josh. v, 6; Jer. xi, 5; comp. Dio Chrys. xxxv, p. 434; Strabo, xv, p. 715). In reading of milk in Scripture, the milk of cows naturally presents itself to the mind of the European reader; but in Western Asia, and especially among the pastoral and semi-pastoral people, not only cows, but goats, sheep, and camels are made to give their milk for the sustenance of man. That this was also the case among the Hebrews may be clearly inferred even from the slight intimations which the Scriptures afford. Thus we read of "butter of kine, and milk of sheep" (Deut. xxxii, 14); and in Prov. xxvii, 27, the emphatic intimation, "Thou shalt have goats' milk for food," seems to imply that this was considered the best for use in the simple state (comp. Pliny, xxviii, 33; see Russell's *Aleppo*, ii, 12; Sonnini, *Trav.* i, 329 sq.; Bochart, *Hieroz.* i, 717 sq.). "Thirty milch camels" were among the cattle which Jacob presented to his brother Esau (Gen. xxxii, 15), implying the use of camels' milk.

The most striking scriptural allusion to milk is that which forbids a kid to be seethed in its mother's milk, and its importance is attested by its being thrice repeated (Exod. xxiii, 19; xxxiv, 26; Deut. xiv, 21). The following are the most remarkable views respecting it: (1.) That it prohibits the eating of the foetus of the goat as a delicacy: but there is not the least evidence that the Jews were ever attached to this disgusting

luxury. (2.) That it prevents the kid being killed till it is eight days old, when, it is said, it might subsist without the milk of its mother. (3.) This ground is admitted by those who deduce a further reason from the fact that a kid was not, until the eighth day, fit for sacrifice. But there appears no good reason why a kid should be described as "in its mother's milk," in those days, more than in any other days of the period during which it is suckled. (4.) Others, therefore, maintain that the eating of a sucking kid is altogether and absolutely prohibited. But a goat suckles its kid for three months, and it is not likely that the Jews were so long forbidden the use of it for food. No food is forbidden but as unclean, and a kid ceased to be unclean on the eighth day, when it was fit for sacrifice; and what was fit for sacrifice could not be unfit for food. (5.) That the prohibition was meant to prevent the dam and kid from being slain at the same time. But this is forbidden with reference to the goat and other animals in express terms, and there seems to be no reason why it should be repeated in this remarkable form with reference to the goat only. (6.) Others understand it literally, as a precept designed to encourage humane feelings. But, as Michaelis asks, how came the Israelites to hit upon the strange whim of boiling a kid in milk, and just in the milk of its own mother? (7.) Still, understanding the text literally, it is possible that this was not a common act of cookery, but an idolatrous or magical rite. Maimonides, in his *More Nebochim*, urges this opinion, and adduces the fact that in two of the above passages the practice is spoken of in immediate connection with the three great annual feasts (Exod. xxiii, 17, 19; xxxiv, 23, 26), although he admits that he "had not yet been able to find it in the Zabian books." This opinion is confirmed by an extract which Cudworth (*Discourses concerning the True Notion of the Lord's Supper*, p. 30) gives from an ancient Karaïte commentary on the Pentateuch; it has been supported by Spencer (*De Legibus Hebr.* ii, 9, § 2), and has been advocated by Le Clerc, Dathe, and other able writers; it is also corroborated by the addition in the Samaritan copy, and in some degree by the Targum. (8.) Michaelis, however, advances a quite new opinion of his own. He takes it for granted that בָּשַׁל, rendered "seethe," may signify to roast as well as to boil, which is hardly disputable; that the kid's mother is not here limited to the real mother, but applies to any goat that has kidded; that חָלָב here denotes not *milk*, but *butter*; and that the precept is not restricted to kids, but extends not only to lambs (which is generally granted), but to all other not forbidden animals. Having erected these props, Michaelis builds upon them the conjecture that the motive of the precept was to endear to the Israelites the land of Canaan, which abounded in *oil*, and to make them forget their Egyptian *butter*. Moses, therefore, to prevent their having any longing desire to return to that country, enjoins them to use oil in cooking their victuals, as well as in seasoning their sacrifices (*Mosaisches Recht*, pt. iv, p. 210). This is ingenious, but it is open to objection. The postulates cannot readily be granted, and, if granted, the conclusion deduced from them is scarcely just, seeing that, as Geddes remarks, "there was no need nor temptation for the Israelites to return to Egypt on account of its butter, when they possessed a country that flowed with milk and honey" (*Critical Remarks*, p. 257). See KID.

In its figurative use, milk occurs sometimes simply as the sign of abundance (Gen. xlix, 12; Ezek. xxv, 4; Joel iii, 18, etc.); but more frequently in combination with honey—"milk and honey" being a phrase which occurs about twenty times in Scripture. Thus a rich and fertile soil is described as a "land flowing with milk and honey;" which, although usually said of Palestine, is also applied to other fruitful countries, as Egypt (Numb. xvi, 13). This figure is by no means peculiar to the Hebrews, but is frequently met with in classical writers. A beautiful example occurs in Euripides (*Bacch.* 142). Hence its use to denote the food of children. Milk is also constantly employed as a symbol of the elementary parts or rudiments of doctrine (1 Cor. iii, 2; Heb. v, 12, 13); and, from its purity and simplicity, it is also made to symbolize the unadulterated Word of God (1 Pet. ii, 2; comp. Isa. lv, 1).

The term rendered "milk out" in Isa. lxvi, 11, is צִיץ, *matsats'*, which occurs only in that passage, and apparently signifies to *suck* or draw out something sweet with relish, as milk from the breast; it is put as a symbol of abundant satisfaction.

2. הֶמְאָה, *chemah'*, from חָמָה, to *coagulate*), is always translated "butter" in the Authorized Version. It seems to mean both butter and curdled milk, but most generally the latter; and the context will, in most cases, suggest the distinction, which has been neglected by our translators. It was this curdled milk, highly esteemed as a refreshment in the East (where it is called *lebben*, see Russell's *Aleppo*, i, 150; Burckhardt, *Trav.* ii, 697, 727; Robinson, ii, 405; iii, 574), that Abraham set before the angels (Gen. xviii, 8); and it was the same that Jael gave to Sisera, instead of the water which he asked (Judg. v, 25), as Josephus particularly notes (γάλα διαφϑορὸς ἤδη, *Ant.* v, 5, 4); it was produced from one of the goat-skin bottles which are still used for the purpose by the Bedouins (Judg. iv, 19; comp. Burckhardt's *Notes*, i, 45). As it would keep for a considerable time, it was particularly adapted to the use of travellers (2 Sam. xvii, 29). In this state milk acquires a slightly inebriating power, if kept long enough. Isa. vii, 22 is the only text in which the word is coupled with "honey," and there it is a sign of scarcity, not of plenty, as when honey is coupled with fresh milk. It means that there being no fruit or grain, the remnant would have to live on milk and honey; and, perhaps, that milk itself would be so scarce that it would be needful to use it with economy, and hence to curdle it, as fresh milk cannot be preserved for chary use. Although, however, this word properly denotes curdled milk, it seems also to be sometimes used for milk in general (Deut. xxxii, 14; Job xx, 15; Isa. vii, 15). See BUTTER; CHEESE.

Lebben is still extensively used in the East: at certain seasons of the year the poor almost live upon it, while the upper classes eat it with salad or meat (Russell, i, 118). It is still offered in hospitality to every passing stranger (Robinson, *Bib. Res.* i, 571; ii, 70, 211)—so freely, indeed, that in some parts of Arabia it would be regarded as a scandal if money were received in return (Burckhardt's *Arabia*, i, 120; ii, 106). The method now pursued in its preparation is to boil the milk over a slow fire, adding to it a small piece of old *lebben* or some other acid in order to make it coagulate (Russell, *Aleppo*, i, 118, 370; Burckhardt, *Arabia*, i, 60). See FOOD.

MILK AND HONEY *used at Baptism.* — The practice of tasting milk and honey at baptism appears to have been founded upon the promises made to the Israelites (Exod. iii, 8, 17; xxxiii, 3). They were probably regarded as appropriate emblems at the administration of that sacrament by which we are introduced into that new land "flowing with milk and honey," the spiritual kingdom of God under the Gospel. The tasting of milk may be supposed to refer especially to the words of St. Peter, "As new-born babes, desire the sincere milk of the word, that ye may grow thereby" (1 Pet. ii, 2); a passage which was applied to baptism. As milk denoted the spiritual nourishment afforded by God's Word, so honey denoted its pleasantness or agreeableness to the mind and heart of a renewed person (Psa. xix, 11; cxix, 103; Rev. x, 9, 10). And the use of honey at baptism may have served to remind believers of the superiority of the Christian dispensation over the Jewish, since under the latter there was a law against the use of honey at sacrifices, on account of its liability to corrupt. See

HONEY. The emblems of milk and honey were in use as early as the third and fourth centuries. Salmasius and some others suppose that they were given to the communicant instead of the Eucharist. This, however, is a mistake, for the Eucharist was administered at the same time (Salmasius, ap. *Suicer. Thesaur.* pt. ii, p. 236). Tertullian says it was a sign of new birth, and that the communicants became as children adopted into God's family—"Inde suscepti lacti et mellis concordiam prægustamus" (Tertull. *De cor. Mil.* c. 3). St. Jerome says this was done in allusion to those passages of the apostle, "I have fed you with milk, and not with strong meat;" and to St. Peter's saying above; for milk denotes the innocency of children (*Comment. in Es.* LV, i). Clemens Alexandrinus also takes notice of this custom, saying, "As soon as we are born, we are nourished with milk, which is the nutriment of the Lord; and when we are born again, we are honored with the hope of rest by the promise of Jerusalem which is above, where it is said to rain milk and honey: for by these material things we are assured of that sacred food" (Clem. Alexandr. i, 6, 103). We learn further, from the third Council of Carthage, that the milk and honey had a peculiar consecration distinct from that of the Eucharist (*Cod. Eccles. Afric.* can. 37, ap. Justellun)—"Nothing else should be offered in the sacraments of the body and blood of the Lord but what the Lord commanded, that is, bread and wine mingled with water. But the first-fruits, and honey and milk, which are offered on one most solemn day for the mystery of infants, though they be offered at the altar, shall have their own peculiar benediction, that they may be distinguished from the sacrament of the body and blood of the Lord." Here we see that milk and honey were only to be offered on one solemn day, that is, on the great Sabbath, or Saturday before Easter, which was the most solemn time of baptism; and only for the mystery of infants, that is, persons newly baptized, who were commonly called infants, in a mystical sense, from their new birth, in the African Church. In the time of the Council of Trullo the offering of milk and honey at the altar was forbidden (comp. *Conc. Trull.* can. 57). See Riddle, *Christian Antiquities*, p. 520; Ayer, *Treasury of Bible Knowledge*, p. 591; Coleman, *Ancient Christianity*, p. 402; Bingham, *Antiquities of the Latin Church*, i, 500 sq.; ii, 755 sq.; Eadie, *Eccles. Dict.*; Augusti, *Christl. Archæology*, ii, 446 sq.

Mill (רֵחַיִם, *recha'yim*, the *two millstones*, from רָחַה, to *bruise*, Exod. xi, 5; "mills," Numb. x, 8; "millstones," Isa. xlvii, 2; Jer. xxv, 10; "nether" millstone, Deut. xxiv, 6; μύλων, Matt. xxiv, 21. Each millstone was called פֶּלַח, *pe'lach*, a *slice* or piece, as of fruit, in Cant. iv, 3; 1 Sam. xxx, 12; always "piece" of a millstone, Judg. ix, 53; 2 Sam. xi, 21; Job xli, 24; Gr. μύλος, Matt. xviii, 6; Luke xvii, 2; Rev. xviii, 21, 22). The mill (properly טְחָנָה, *tachanah'*, a "grinding," Eccl. xii, 4; טְחוֹן, *techon'*, "to grind," Lam. v, 13; Gr. μύλη) for grinding grain had not wholly superseded the mortar in pounding it in the time of Moses (Numb. xi, 8). See MORTAR. But fine meal—that is, meal ground or pounded fine—is mentioned so early as the time of Abraham (Gen. xviii, 6): hence mills and mortars must have been previously known. See GRITS. The mill common among the Hebrews differed little from that which is in use to this day throughout Western Asia and Northern Africa. It consisted of two circular stones, two feet in diameter and half a foot thick. The lower is called the "nether millstone" (Job xli, 16 [24]), and the upper the "rider" (Judg. ix, 53; 2 Sam. xi, 21). The former was usually fixed to the floor, and had a slight elevation in the centre, or, in other words, was slightly convex in the upper surface. The upper stone had a concavity in its under surface fitting to, or receiving, the convexity of the lower stone. There was a hole in the top, through which the grain was introduced by handfuls at a time. The upper stone had an upright stick fixed in it as a handle, by which it was made to turn upon the lower stone, and by this action the grain was ground, and came out at the edges. As there were neither public mills nor bakers, except the king's (Gen. xl, 2; Hos. vii, 4–8), each family possessed a mill; and, as it was in daily use, it was made an infringement of the law for a person to take another's mill or millstone in pledge (Deut. xxiv, 6). See MILLSTONE. On the second day, in warm climates, bread becomes dry and insipid; hence the necessity of baking every day, and hence also the daily grinding at the mills early in the morning. See BREAD. It is worked by women, sometimes singly and sometimes two together, who are usually seated on the bare ground (Isa. xlvii, 1, 2) "facing each other; both have hold of the handle by which the upper is turned round on the 'nether' millstone. The one whose right hand is disengaged throws in the grain as occasion requires through the hole in the upper stone. It is not correct to say that one pushes it half round, and then the other seizes the handle.

Modern Egyptian Mill.

Oriental Hand-mill.

This would be slow work, and would give a spasmodic motion to the stone. Both retain their hold, and pull *to*, or push *from*, as men do with the whip or cross-cut saw. The proverb of our Saviour (Matt. xxiv, 41) is true to life, for *women* only grind. I cannot recall an instance in which men were at the mill" (Thomson, *Land and Book*, ii, 295). The labor is very hard, and the task of grinding is in consequence performed only by the lowest servants (Exod. xi, 5; comp. Plaut. *Merc.* ii, 3) and captives (Judg. xvi, 21; Job xxxi, 10; Isa. xlvii, 1, 2; Lam. v, 13; comp. Homer, *Od.* vii, 103; Suetonius, *Tib.* c. 51). Grinding is reckoned in the Mishna (*Shabbath*, vii, 2) among the chief household duties, to be performed by the wife unless she brought with her one servant (*Cethuboth*, v, 5); in which case she was relieved from grinding, baking, and washing, but was still obliged to suckle her child, make her husband's bed, and work in wool. Among the Fellahs of the Hauran, one of the chief articles of furniture described by Burckhardt (*Syria*, p. 292) is the "*hand-mill*, which is used in summer when there is no water in the wadies to drive the mills." The operation occasions considerable noise, and its simultaneous performance in a great number of houses or tents forms one of the sounds as indicative of an active population in the East as the sound of

wheel-carriages in the West. Hence the sound of the mill is the indication of peaceful household life, and the absence of it is a sign of desolation and abandonment: "When the sound of the mill is low" (Eccl. xii, 4). No more affecting picture of utter desolation could be imagined than that conveyed in the threat denounced against Judah by the mouth of the prophet Jeremiah (xxv, 10): "I will take from them the voice of mirth, and the voice of gladness, the voice of the bridegroom and the voice of the bride, *the sound of the millstones*, and the light of the candle" (comp. Rev. xviii, 22). The song of the women grinding is supposed by some to be alluded to in the above passage of Ecclesiastes, and it was evidently so understood by the Sept.; but Dr. Robinson says (i, 485), "We heard no song as an accompaniment to the work," and Dr. Hackett (*Bibl. Illust.* p. 49) describes it rather as shrieking than singing. It is alluded to in Homer (*Od.* xx, 105–119); and Athenæus (xiv, p. 619 *a*) refers to a peculiar chant which was sung by women winnowing corn, and mentioned by Aristophanes in the *Thesmophoriazusæ*.

The hand-mills of the ancient Egyptians appear to have been of the same character as those of their descendants, and like them were worked by women (Wilkinson, *Anc. Eg.* ii, 118, etc.). "They had also a large mill on a very similar principle, but the stones were of far greater power and dimensions; and this could only have been turned by cattle or asses, like those of the ancient Romans and of the modern Cairenes." It was the millstone of a mill of this kind, driven by an ass, which is alluded to in Matt. xviii, 6 (μύλος ὀνικός), to distinguish it, says Lightfoot (*Hor. Hebr.* ad loc.), from those small mills which were used to grind spices for the wound of circumcision, or for the delights of the Sabbath, and to which both Kimchi and Jarchi find a reference in Jer. xxv, 10. Of a married man with slen-

Roman Hand-mills.

der means it is said in the Talmud (*Kiddushin*, p. 29 *b*), "With a millstone on his neck he studies the law," and the expression is still proverbial (Tendlau, *Sprichwörter*, p. 181). The ordinary mill of the Romans, however, was essentially like the conical hand-mill of the East, as specimens preserved among the ruins of bake-houses in Pompeii show (see Smith's *Dict. of Gr. and Rom. Antiq.* s. v. Mola).

It was the movable upper millstone of the hand-mill with which the woman of Thebez broke Abimelech's skull (Judg. ix, 53). It is now generally made, according to Dr. Thomson, of a porous lava brought from the Hauran, both stones being of the same material; but, says the same traveller, "I have seen the *nether* made of a compact sandstone, and quite thick, while the *upper* was of this lava, probably because from its lightness it is the more easily driven round with the hand" (*Land and Book*, ii, 296). The porous lava to which he refers is probably the same as the black tufa mentioned by Burckhardt (*Syria*, p. 57), the blocks of which are brought from the Lejah, and are fashioned into millstones by the inhabitants of Ezra, a village in the Hauran. "They vary in price according to their size, from fifteen to sixty piastres, and are preferred to all others on account of the hardness of the stone."

One passage (Lam. v, 13) is deserving of notice, which Hoheisel (*De Molis Manual. Vet.* in Ugolini, vol. xxix) explains in a manner which gives it a point that is lost in our Auth. Vers. It may be rendered, "The choice (men) bore the mill (טְחוֹן, *techôn*), and the youths stumbled beneath the wood;" the wood being the woodwork or shaft of the mill, which the captives were compelled to carry. There are, moreover, allusions to other apparatus connected with the operation of grinding—the sieve, or bolter (נָפָה, *naphah'*, Isa. xxx, 28; or כְּבָרָה, *kěbarah'*, Amos ix, 9), and the hopper, though the latter is only found in the Mishna (*Zabim*, iv, 3), and was a late invention. We also find in the Mishna (*Demai*, iii, 4) that mention is made of a miller (טוֹחֵן, *tochên*), indicating that grinding grain was recognised as a distinct occupation. Wind-mills and water-mills are of more recent date.

Mill, David, D.D., a noted German Orientalist, was born at Königsberg, Prussia, April 13, 1692. Called to Holland, he accepted a professorship in the University of Utrecht. He died May 22, 1755. His ablest work is, *Dissertationes Selectæ Varia S. Litt. et Antiquitatis Orientalis Capita exponentes et illustrantes, curis secundis* (Lugd. Bat. 1743).

Mill, James, an eminent British metaphysician and political economist, was born of humble parentage in the neighborhood of Montrose, Scotland, April 6, 1773. After having received a thorough education in the house of Sir John Stuart, M.P., he was sent to the University of Edinburgh, where he was educated for the Church. He entered into holy orders in 1798, but, instead of devoting himself to his sacred calling, he went to London in 1800; became editor of the *Literary Journal*, and wrote for various periodicals, including the *Eclectic* and the *Edinburgh Review*. In 1806 he commenced a *History of British India*, which he completed and published in 1818. The impression produced by this masterly history on the Indian authorities was such that in 1819 Mill was appointed assistant-examiner of Indian correspondence. He continued in this office till 1832, when he was appointed head of the examiner's office, where he had the control of all the departments of Indian administration. Shortly after his appointment to the India House, he contributed the articles on *Government, Education, Jurisprudence, Law of Nations, Liberty of the Press, Colonies*, and *Prison Discipline* to the *Encyclopædia Britannica*. These essays were reprinted in a separate form and became widely known. The powers of analysis, of clear statement, and thorough application of principles exhibited in these articles had probably never before

been brought to bear on this class of subjects. In 1821–1822 he published his *Elements of Political Economy*, a work prepared primarily with a view to the education of his eldest son, John Stuart Mill (q. v.).

In 1829 Mr. Mill came before the public with his *Analysis of the Phenomena of the Human Mind*, a work on which he bestowed more of the labor of thought than on any other of his productions, and on a subject of special interest to the theologian and the philosopher. In this work Mill has attempted to resolve all the powers of the human mind into a very small number of simple elements. From an examination of a number of the more complicated cases of consciousness, he arrives at the conclusion that they all resolve themselves into three simple elements—sensations, ideas, and the train of ideas. He thus explains what he means by the terms *sensations* and *ideas*: "We have two classes of feeling: one, that which exists when the object of sense is present; another, that which exists after the object of sense has ceased to be present. The one class of feelings I call sensations, the other class of feelings I call ideas" (i, 41). He begins with the simpler phenomena, and thence proceeds to the exposition of the more complex ones. "The feelings," he says, "which we have through the external senses are the most simple, at least the most familiar, of the mental phenomena. Hence the propriety of commencing with this class of our feelings" (*Analysis*, i, 1). Accordingly he begins with sensation, under which head he ranges the feelings which we have by the five senses—smell, taste, hearing, touch, and sight; the muscular sensations, and the sensations in the alimentary canal. He next treats of ideas, or, as he calls them, the images of sensation. He then comments on ideas put together or associated in trains, and of the order of their association and the causes of that order. He then treats of consciousness and conception, which philosophers, he says, have erroneously created into what they called powers of the mind; whereas, he says, consciousness is merely a name applied to sensations, and to ideas whether simple or complex—to all the feelings of our sentient nature: and conception a name applied only to ideas, and to ideas only in a state of combination. "Imagination," he says, "is the name of a train of ideas. I am said to have an imagination when I have a train of ideas. There is a great diversity of trains. Not only has the same individual an endless variety of trains, but a different character belongs to the whole series of trains which pass through the minds of different individuals or classes of individuals. The different pursuits in which the several classes of men are engaged render particular trains of ideas more common to them than other trains. One man is a merchant, and trains respecting the goods in which he buys and those in which he sells are habitual in his mind. Another man is a lawyer, and ideas of clients and fees, and judges and witnesses, and legal instruments and points of contestation, and the practice of his court, are habitually passing in his mind. Ideas of another kind occupy the mind of the physician; of another kind still the mind of the warrior. The statesman is occupied with a train different from that of any of the classes that have been mentioned, and one statesman with a very different train from another, according as his mind is running upon expedients which may serve the purpose of the day, or arrangement which may secure the happiness of the population from generation to generation. A peculiar character belongs to the train which habitually occupies the mind of the mathematician. The mind of the metaphysician is also occupied by a train distinguished from that of other classes. And there is one man yet to be mentioned, the poet, the peculiarity of whose trains has been a subject of particular observation. To such a degree, indeed, have the trains of the poet been singled out for distinction, that the word imagination, in a more restricted sense, is appropriated to them. We do not call the trains of the lawyer, or the trains of the merchant, imagination. We do not speak of them as imagining, when they are revolving each the ideas which belong to his peculiar occupation; it is only to the poet that the epithet of imagination is applied. His train, or trains analogous to his, are those which receive the name of imagination" (i, 179).

In some parts of his philosophy Mill has, we think, been led into error, by carrying his notion of association, as an explanation of these phenomena, too far. Thus, in the chapter on classification, after very ably showing how long men had been led away by mere jargon from the real nature and object of classification, he says: "Man first becomes acquainted with individuals. He first names individuals. But individuals are innumerable, and he cannot have innumerable names. He must make one name serve for many individuals." Then, after alluding to the case of "synchronous sensations so concreted by constant conjunction as to appear, though numerous, only one, of which the ideas of sensible objects—a rose, a plough, a house, a ship—are examples," he thus proceeds: "It is easy to see wherein the present case agrees with and wherein it differs from those familiar cases. The word man, we shall say, is first applied to an individual; it is first associated with the idea of that individual, and acquires the power of calling up the idea of him; it is next applied to another individual, and acquires the power of calling up the idea of him; so of another, and another, till it has become associated with an indefinite number, and has acquired the power of calling up an indefinite number of those ideas indifferently. What happens? It does call up an indefinite number of the ideas of individuals as often as it occurs; and calling them up in close connection, it forms them into a species of complex idea" (i, 204). From this simple basis he builds up with remarkable dexterity a comprehensive system, all the errors or defects of which lie at the very threshold. His conclusions are inevitable, if his premises, his representation of the facts of consciousness, be accepted. Sensation, ideation, association, and naming are the elementary processes in his analysis, by which he accounts for all the complex phenomena of the mind—for abstraction, memory, judgment, ratiocination, belief, and the power of motives. He devotes the latter half of the second volume of his *Analysis* to the phenomena in which the sensations and ideas are to be considered as not merely existing, but also as exciting to action. He treats of pleasurable and painful sensations, and of the causes of the pleasurable and painful sensations; then of ideas of the pleasurable and painful sensations, and of the causes of them. He treats of wealth, power, and dignity, and their contraries; of our fellow-creatures, and of the objects called sublime and beautiful, and their contraries, contemplated as causes of our pleasures and pains. Chapter xxii is devoted to the subject of motives, and chapter xxiv to that of the will; chapter xxv (the last) to intention. Mr. Mill's exposition of all these phenomena is mainly grounded on the law of association, by which he means simply the fact that the order of occurrence among our ideas is the order of occurrence among our former sensations, of which those ideas are the copies.

The last publication of Mill was a fragment containing a severe criticism on James Macintosh's dissertation on the progress of ethical philosophy. Mill, who had always exercised a particular championship for the doctrines of Thomas Hobbes (q. v.), was not at all pleased with the unceremonious manner in which his favorite was handled by Sir James. If Hobbes and Mill are right, then many great names are liable to the charge of error. Mill took a leading part in the founding of University College, London, and gave a powerful intellectual stimulus to a number of young men, some of whom (including his own son, and Grote, the Greek historian) have risen to eminence. He died at Kensington June 23, 1836. See *Engl. Cyclop.* s. v.; *Amer. Cyclop.* xi, 501 sq.; Chambers, *Cyclop.* s. v.; Lewis, *Biog. Hist. of Philosophers*, ii, 507; *Westminst. Rev.* xiii, 265; *Blackwood's Magazine*, xlvi, 671; Allibone, *Dict. of Brit. and Amer. Authors*, ii, 1279 sq.

Mill, John, D.D., a very learned English divine and Biblical critic, was born at Shapp, Westmoreland, in 1645. In 1661 he became a servitor in Queen's College, Oxford, where he secured the master of arts in 1669. He was afterwards elected a fellow, and became eminent as a tutor. Having entered into orders, he was greatly admired for his pulpit eloquence. In 1676 he became chaplain to the bishop of Oxford. In 1680 he received from his college the living of Bletchingdon, in Oxfordshire, and in the year following received the degree of D.D., and became chaplain in ordinary to Charles II. In 1685 he was elected principal of St. Edmund's Hall, Oxford, and in 1704 was appointed prebendary of Canterbury. He died in 1708. He is famous for having devoted the labor of thirty years to the preparation of a new edition of the Greek Testament, finishing it only fourteen days before his death. It appeared under the title of Ἡ Καινὴ Διαθήκη, *Novum Testamentum Græcum, cum Lectionibus Variantibus MSS. Exemplarium, Versionum, Editionum, SS. Patrum et Scriptorum Ecclesiasticorum, et in easdem notis; Studio et labore Joannis Millii, S. T. P. Oxonii, e Theatre Sheldoniano* (1707, fol.). The various readings are reckoned at about 30,000, the text being that of Robert Stephens's edition of 1550. The collection of such a mass of various readings, instead of supplying arms for infidelity, as some seem to have feared, has served to place the uncorrupted integrity of the Scriptures in a stronger light than ever. Dr. Whitby (q. v.) attacked the work in his *Examen variantum lectionum Joh. Millii* (1710), but Dr. Bentley (q. v.), under the signature of Phileleutheros Lipsiensis, ably vindicated the labors of Mill; and Michaelis, Marsh, Harewood, and critical scholars generally, attest the great value of his edition. It has been aptly remarked that "the infancy of criticism ends with the edition of Gregory, and the age of manhood commences with that of Mill." Mill's edition ranks next to that of Wetstein in importance and utility, its prolegomena being beyond price. See Marsh, *Divinity Lectures*, vii, 9, 10, 13; Wood, *Athen. Oxon.*; Jones, *Christ. Biography*, s. v.; *Brit. and For. Rev.* 1871, Feb. art. viii; *Lond. Qu. Rev.* July, 1871; *Blackwood's Mag.* xxviii, 443; Chambers, *Cyclop.* s. v.; Allibone, *Dict. of Brit. and Amer. Authors*, ii, 1279 sq.; Horne, *Bibl. Bib.* (1839), p. 16; Orme, *Bibl. Bib.* s. v. See CRITICISM.

Mill, John Stuart, the British philosopher whose writings have done much to shape the thinking of this generation, was the son of James Mill (q. v.), and was born in London May 20, 1806. His intellectual training was conducted by his learned father, who, holding that all men are born with equal faculties, and that character is the result solely of association and circumstance, preferred, it would seem, the sole control of the boy in order to test upon him the theories he had espoused and preached. At an age when children are usually weaned, John Stuart began the study of Greek, followed shortly after by arithmetic, with Latin at eight, and logic in his twelfth year, and before he had completed his fourteenth year, as he tells us himself, he had gone over the whole range of ancient literature and philosophy, as well as the most noted of modern historians, civil and ecclesiastical, besides having himself composed volumes of history. Such an education, conducted by a person of his father's ability, could not fail of remarkable results. By it he also gained lasting habits of application, and a wonderful power of sustained and accurate thinking; and by the constant use of his pen he early became master of a style whose point and lucidity are unrivalled among logical and metaphysical writers. But with these advantages there came also a most serious drawback. The training intentionally left one side of his nature untouched. It ignored all culture of the imagination, the emotions, or the sympathies. Of the tender associations, the sweet charities that cluster about the thought of home, this young philosopher knew nothing. He cannot bring himself to say that he loved his father, and of his mother he makes no mention whatever. Nor was the solitude of his early life broken by the cheerful intercourse of school. Indeed, he was carefully kept apart from all his contemporaries lest he should be corrupted by their prejudices or their example, insomuch that he was not himself aware that his own education and acquirements were not those of any other boy of his age. As this education, especially with respect to religion, has an important bearing on the life and work of this so justly celebrated man, we quote here at length from his *Autobiography* :

"I was brought up from the first without any religious belief, in the ordinary acceptation of the term. My father, educated in the creed of Scotch Presbyterianism, had by his own studies and reflections been early led to reject not only the belief in revelation, but also the foundations of what is commonly called Natural Religion. . . . Finding no halting-place in deism, he remained in a state of perplexity until, doubtless after many struggles, he yielded to the conviction that *concerning the origin of things nothing whatever can be known.* This is the only correct statement of his opinion, for dogmatic atheism he looked upon as absurd; as most of those whom the world has considered atheists have always done. These particulars are important, because they show that my father's rejection of all that is called religious belief was not, as many might suppose, primarily a matter of logic and evidence: the grounds of it were moral still more than intellectual. He found it impossible to believe that a world so full of evil was the work of an Author combining infinite power with perfect wisdom and righteousness. . . . His aversion to religion, in the sense usually attached to the term, was of the same kind with that of Lucretius: he regarded it with the feelings due not to a mere mental delusion, but to a great moral evil. He looked upon it as the greatest enemy of morality: first, by setting up fictitious excellences—belief in creeds, devotional feelings, and ceremonies, not connected with the good of the human race—and causing them to be accepted as substitutes for genuine virtues; but, above all, by radically vitiating the standard of morals, making it consist in doing the will of a being on whom it lavishes all the phrases of adulation, but whom in sober truth it depicts as eminently hateful. I have a hundred times heard him say that all ages and nations have represented their gods as wicked in a constantly increasing progression; that mankind have gone on adding trait after trait till they reached the most perfect conception of wickedness which the human mind can devise, and have called this God, and prostrated themselves before it. This *ne plus ultra* of wickedness he considered to be embodied in what is commonly presented to mankind as the creed of Christianity. Think (he used to say) of a being who would make a hell—who would create the human race with the infallible foreknowledge, and therefore with the intention, that the great majority of them were to be consigned to horrible and everlasting torment!"

It does not seem to have occurred to James Mill to inquire whether what was presented as the creed of Christianity by the Kirk and its divines really was the only lesson to be learned from the religion of the Gospel and the idea of God. But, holding this entirely negative belief, essentially and directly, as was well said by Browne before the Christian Evidence Society, because he did not admit the freedom of the will, he based the education of his son upon it. Hence we are not astonished when a little after the passage quoted above we find John Stuart Mill writing:

"It would have been wholly inconsistent with my father's ideas of duty to allow me to acquire impressions contrary to his convictions and feelings respecting religion; and he impressed upon me from the first that the manner in which the world came into existence was a subject on which nothing was known; that the question, 'Who made me?' cannot be answered, because we have no experience or authentic information from which to answer it; and that any answer only throws the difficulty a step further back, since the question immediately presents itself, 'Who made God?'"

That is to say, because he could not solve the problem of the origin of evil, he took refuge in a cheerless nescience, and denied the possibility of knowing anything relative to the origin or the destiny of mankind, denied the authority of conscience, and substituted the principle of utility for any intuitive standard of right and wrong. In his own life this dismal philosophy had already borne its bitter fruit, and his son writes that

"He deemed very few pleasures worth the price paid for them; he thought human life a poor thing after the

freshness of youth and of unsatisfied curiosity had gone by. He would sometimes say that if life were made what it might be by good government and good education, it would be worth having; but he never spoke with any enthusiasm even of that possibility. He used to say he had never known a happy old man, except those who were able to live over again in the pleasures of the young."

At first young Mill accepted without hesitation the leading ideas of his father, and of the circle of his father's friends, among whom were chief the philosopher Bentham (q. v.) and the political economist Ricardo. They had many projects on foot for the improvement of mankind, and the youthful and inexperienced Mill entered into their plans with the zeal becoming his age and wisdom; indeed, he believed he had a call "to be a reformer of mankind," and felt as if all his earthly happiness hung upon this design. His studies were directed to this end, and he began when only sixteen to employ his pen in the work. The enthusiasm lasted until his twentieth year. He was in the midst of eager discussion, he had already made himself a reputation in the new *Westminster Review*, and was hard at work upon his edition of *Judicial Evidence*, when he stopped to ask himself this question, "Suppose that all your objects in life were realized, that all the changes in institutions and opinions which you are looking forward to could be completely effected at this very instant, would this be a great joy and happiness to you?" He got the inevitable answer, "No." In an hour the light faded out of all his visions. His labor had lost its motive and its charm. He had nothing, he thought, to live for; and he sank into a dull and dreary melancholy. He had heretofore made happiness the end of existence, and the test of all right action; but he now found it impossible, in his own experience, to realize that end or apply that test, because he was forced to confess that no action, however apparently successful, was competent to bring him happiness. His philosophy of life had broken down under him. It was evidently necessary to reconstruct it; and as the six months' melancholy wore away he elaborated his new theory. He still considered happiness the end of life, but "thought this end only to be attained by not making it the direct end. Ask yourself whether you are happy, and you cease to be so. The only chance is to treat, not happiness, but some end external to it, as the purpose of life." These utilitarian doctrines became the life of his theory of morals, and the principles in his expansion of the Benthamite formulas. They are, it must be confessed, "the least earthy forms of this earthy philosophy," and yet how very far from the Christian doctrine of duty and of right is any such theory of morals as this! Still, had he but followed the free and uncontrollable bent of his philosophical growth from this point in his life, or had he fallen into hands other than those which subsequently enchained him, we think that he might have arrived at far higher and more sound results in moral and metaphysical science than he ever attained to. For it may be here remarked that one of the distinctive peculiarities of Mill was what, for want of a simpler term, must be called his *receptivity*. Seldom has so powerful a thinker been so subject to the unconscious influence of others; but in him sympathy was more powerful than individuality—he had more of the feminine principle that receives than the masculine power which imparts an impression. Hence through life, whenever his sympathies and affections were excited, his opinions followed.

In 1820 John was first suffered to pass beyond the narrow limit of his father's study, and he was sent for a year to France, where he studied some of the sciences and the higher mathematics. On his return he continued his philosophical studies, and in the winter of 1822–23 had the pleasure of starting a "Utilitarian Society," where he enjoyed discussions upon some of the heaviest metaphysical topics that occupied the British mind, and he himself tells us that he always dated from them his own "real inauguration as an original and independent thinker." He also obtained valuable instructions from the "Co-operative Society," composed of the disciples of Owen, the Communist, with whom Mill and a few other political economists, sworn enemies of Communism, had discussions in order to "settle" the question whether the Owenites had any right to exist. The result was the formation of a "Speculative Society," composed of a body of young men who became almost as famous as Mill—Macaulay, Thirlwall, Wilberforce, and the Bulwers, among others, were of that circle. In May, 1823, his father procured for him employment in the East India Company, which he himself was serving, and John was thus afforded the necessary competency for the continuation of his literary labors, besides enjoying that training in accurate and perspicuous writing for which he afterwards became noted. There can be no doubt that his work in the India House was of great value to him. It considerably enlarged his knowledge of social and political subjects, and in a more direct and *human* way than by the study of books. He was led to study mind in the concrete. His despatches had to pass the scrutiny of the directors; then they were to be read and acted on by men living on the other side of the world—both of which facts led him to choose not only the strongest arguments, but the strongest way of putting them. Mr. W. T. Thornton, his colleague, thus describes the vast amount of his work in that relation:

"In 1828 he was promoted to be assistant examiner, and in 1856 he succeeded to the post of chief examiner, after which his duty consisted rather in supervising what his assistants had written than in writing himself; but for the three-and-twenty years preceding he had had immediate charge of the political department, and had written almost every 'political' despatch of any importance that conveyed the instructions of the merchant princes of Leadenhall Street to their pro-consuls in Asia. Of the quality of these documents it is sufficient to say that they were John Mill's; but in respect to their quantity, it may be worth mentioning that a descriptive catalogue of them completely fills a small quarto volume of between 300 and 400 pages, in their author's handwriting, which now lies before me; also that the share of the Court of Directors in the correspondence between themselves and the Indian government used to average annually about ten huge vellum-bound volumes, foolscap size, and five or six inches thick, and that of these volumes, two a year, for more than twenty years running, were exclusively of Mill's composition: this, too, at times when he was engaged upon such voluntary work in addition as his *Logic* and *Political Economy*" (*Memorial*, p. 31).

Mill remained with the East India Company until its extinction in 1858. In 1865 he was elected to Parliament, and acted with the advanced liberals, but lost his seat in 1868. In 1867 he was chosen rector of St. Andrew's University, Edinburgh. In 1869 his wife, whom he adored, died, and in order to be ever near her grave he removed to Avignon, France, and there spent the remainder of his life. He died May 9, 1873.

While yet a youth we have seen Mill a writer of various essays. They were of such a bold and thoughtful character as to secure him even then a prominent place in the *Edinburgh* and *Westminster Reviews*, and from 1834 to 1840 he was editor in chief of the latter. In 1827 he was intrusted with the editorship of Bentham's *Rationale of Judicial Evidence*. But his great production he brought out when he was thirty-eight years old, and at once secured by the *System of Logic, Ratiocinative and Inductive* (Lond. 1843, 2 vols. 8vo; republished, N. Y., Harpers, 1864, from the 8th ed.), a world-wide reputation. It is a perfect exhibit of his philosophy, notwithstanding his claim that he seeks simply to discover and expound the proper method of investigating truth, without pledging himself to any system of speculative philosophy. "There are so many points of a speculative nature touched upon, all in the spirit of the *Analysis*, that he must necessarily be regarded as a partisan of the modern Lockian school of metaphysics" (Morell, p. 252). Mill has developed in his *Logic* the deductive principle and its application to logic as a sci-

ence, and thus has lent special value to his work. The last hundred pages are taken up with what the author calls "the logic of the moral sciences." Here, as he tells us, he makes "an attempt to contribute towards the solution of a question which the decay of old opinions, and the agitation which disturbs European society to its inmost depths, render as important in the present day to the practical interests of human life as it must at all times be to the completeness of our speculative knowledge, viz. whether moral and social phenomena are really exceptions to the general certainty and uniformity of the course of nature, and how far the methods by which so many of the laws of the physical world have been numbered among truths irrevocably acquired and universally assented to can be made instrumental to the formation of a similar body of received doctrine in moral and political science." The *Logic*, together with an *Examination of Sir William Hamilton's Philosophy* (1865), and his editorial corrections and comments on his father's *Analysis of the Human Mind*, constitute John Stuart Mill's philosophical works. From these it is apparent that, as Dr. Porter says (in Ueberweg's *Hist. of Philos.* ii, 427–429),

"The physiological foundation on which he builds is the system of James Mill, modified by that of Dr. Thomas Brown. He carefully insists, however, that he neither accepts nor inculcates any system of metaphysics. But the system of metaphysics which he usually applies is substantially that of Hobbes, Hume, and Comte. He does not rigidly adhere, however, either to the psychology or to the philosophy which characterizes or controls his conclusions. He differs from his father in holding the act of belief to be something more than an inseparable association of one object with another (compare James Mill's *Analysis*, 2d edition, chap. xi, note); that causation is a term which it is indispensable we should use in our analysis of the conceptions of matter and mind; and that certain axioms are the necessary foundations of mathematical and physical sciences, but are themselves the products of induction (comp. *Logic*, passim). After a long and laborious analysis, he reaches the conclusion that matter must be defined as 'a permanent possibility of sensation,' and that 'mind is resolved into a series of feelings, with a background of possibilities of feeling.' He concedes that in adhering to this definition 'we are reduced to the alternative of believing that the mind, or *ego*, is something different from any series of feelings or possibilities of them, or else of accepting the paradox that something which, *ex hypothesi*, is but a series of feelings can be aware of itself as a series.' In respect to the belief, in the real existence of the external world, he concedes that it cannot be proved philosophically, and can only be justified by the consideration that 'the world of possible sensations, succeeding one another according to laws, is as much in other beings as it is in me; it has therefore an existence outside me; it is an external world' (comp. *Exam. of Sir W. Hamilton's Philosophy*, ch. xi, xii, xiii)."

Mill's posthumous publications—*Three Essays on Religion; Nature; The Utility of Religion* (Lond. and N. Y. 1874, 8vo)—teach more clearly, however, than the preceding works that he believed very positively in matter and very hesitatingly in spirit; very strongly in man and very feebly in God; very earnestly in human government and social organization, and not at all in divine providence. Indeed, "the perfectibility of man through an enlightened self-interest—by means of popular government and universal education, especially in the elements of political economy and the Malthusian doctrines of population—was the chief article of his philosophical creed" (Dr. Porter, in *Internat. Rev.* N. Y. 1874, May–June, pt. vi). For further particulars, we refer our readers to Allibone, *Dict. of Brit. and Amer. Authors*, ii, 1280; see also *Edinb. Rev.* July, 1866, art. iv; Jan. 1874, art. iv; Jan. 1875, art. i; *Brit. Qu. Rev.* July, 1868, art. i; Jan. 1874, art. ix; *New-Englander*, Oct. 1874, art. i; *Westminster Rev.* Jan. 1875, art. i; *Christian Qu.* April, 1874, art. i; Masson, *Recent Brit. Philos.* (N. Y. 1866, 12mo), especially p. 245–335; Porter, *Human Intellect* (see Index); *John Stuart Mill, his Life and Works* (1873), twelve sketches by J. R. Fox Bourne, W. T. Thornton, Herbert Spencer, and others (reprinted in *Popular Science Monthly*, July, 1873, art. xii; and the *Autobiography* (Lond. and N. Y. 1873, 8vo).

Mill, William Hodge, D.D., an eminent English divine, was born at Cambridge in 1791. He was educated at Trinity College, Cambridge, and was ordained deacon in 1817, and priest in 1820. Immediately after his ordination he was appointed principal of Bishop's College, Calcutta, which position he held till 1838, when he was obliged to return to England in consequence of impaired health. In the year following he was appointed domestic and examining chaplain to archbishop Howley, and in 1840 was elected Christian advocate in the University of Cambridge. In 1843 he was presented to the living of Brasted, Kent, and in 1848 was chosen regius professor of Hebrew at Cambridge, and canon of Ely. His profound learning in mathematics, languages, and other branches of intellectual research, gained him a deservedly high reputation at home and abroad. His great work, *Christii Sangita, or the Sacred History of Jesus,* in Sanskrit, rendered him famous as a thorough Oriental philologist. He died Dec. 25, 1853. Dr. Mill was a prolific author, and of his numerous works we mention only the most important: *Observations on the attempted Application of Pantheistic Principles to the Theory and Historic Criticism of the Gospel* (Camb. 1840–44; 5 div. 8vo; 2d ed. 1855, 8vo) :—*Prelectio theologica* (1843):—*On the Temptation of Christ* (1844) :—*On the Nature of Christianity* (1848) :—*Lectures on the Catechism,* ed. by the Rev. B. Webb (1856). See Cooper, *Biog. Dict.* p. 866; Allibone, *Dict. of Brit. and Amer. Authors,* ii. 1281.

Milledoler, PHILIP, D.D., a noted American divine, was born at Rhinebeck, N. Y., Sept. 22, 1775. His parents were Swiss Germans, who emigrated to America from the canton of Berne about the middle of the last century. Philip was converted in very early youth; was educated at Columbia College; and at nineteen years of age was licensed to preach the Gospel, and became pastor of the German Reformed Church in Nassau Street, New York, succeeding the Rev. Dr. Gross, his pastor and theological professor. He preached there in both German and English from 1795 to 1800. His reputation for unction and eloquence drew large audiences; he became generally known, and in 1800 was called to the Third Presbyterian Church in Philadelphia. He accepted the offer, and, removing to the city of brotherly love, labored there for five years with great success, large additions being made to the communion of the Church. In 1805 he accepted a unanimous call as first pastor of the Rutgers Street Presbyterian Church, New York, and remained there until 1813, when he transferred his relation to the Reformed Church, and became one of the pastors of the Collegiate Church of that city. In 1825 he was elected professor of didactic and polemic theology by the General Synod of the Reformed Church, to succeed the venerable Dr. John H. Livingston. At the same time he was appointed president of Rutgers College, and professor of moral philosophy. These offices he accepted and held until 1841, when he resigned, and retired to private life at New Brunswick. He died, full of years, labors, and honors, Sept. 22, 1852. His wife died the next day, and both were buried in the same grave, with a common funeral service. Dr. Milledoler's professional career was marked by diligent and faithful services, by great dignity of character and kind demeanor towards his students, and by a saintly piety which shone through all his life. His gentleness of heart perhaps diminished his ability as a disciplinarian, and unfitted him to cope successfully with the difficulties of his double office. His forte was in the pulpit. His whole ministry in New York was remarkable for the constant divine blessing that followed his labors. In prayer he seemed almost like a man inspired. His use of scriptural language at the throne of grace was most wonderful, and it was woven together with a skill and power that were only to be accounted for by the influence of the Holy Spirit upon his suppliant soul. This fervor and unction in prayer characterized him till the very close of life. His preaching partook of much

of the same elevated and tender spirit. His sermons were clear, earnest, solemn, and impressive. His sentences were short, often highly rhetorical in structure, and always pregnant with Gospel truth. As a pastor, and in the sick-room, he was not surpassed. But in nothing did he so soar heavenward, and seem so full of divine power, as in public prayer. A number of powerful revivals of religion occurred under his ministry. Dr. Milledoler declined several pressing offers of high positions in the Church. In 1823, with Dr. Gardner Spring, he visited, as commissioner of the General Assembly, the missions among the Tuscarora, Seneca, and Cattaraugus Indians. In the great benevolent movements of his time he was an earnest actor. He was moderator of the Presbyterian General Assembly in 1808, and president of the General Synod of the Reformed Church in 1823, and was one of the members of the convention that formed the American Bible Society in 1816. He helped to organize and was the first president of the Society for Evangelizing the Jews, and an active original member and corresponding secretary of the United Foreign Missionary Society formed in 1817. He published a number of sermons, public addresses, and other pamphlets. In his old age Dr. Milledoler was most venerable in appearance, elegant in manners, and saint-like in spirit. His snow-white hair, and almost ruddy complexion, and scrupulous neatness in dress, his unfailing courtesy and radiant goodness, stamped him not merely as a Christian gentleman of the old school, but as one who lived for two worlds, blessing this one and waiting for the glory of the next. See Sprague, *Annals of the Amer. Pulpit,* vol. ix; Corwin's *Manual of the Ref. Church,* s. v. (W. J. R. T.)

Millenarians (or Chiliasts), a name given to those who believe that the saints will reign on earth with Christ a thousand years. See MILLENNIUM.

Millenary Petition is the name of the paper which was presented to king James VI of Scotland (James I of England), as he passed through England on his way to London, by the Puritans. It contained a petition signed by nearly a thousand ministers, and hence the name *Millenarian.* It prayed for such changes or alterations in ceremonial as the Puritans had generally contended for. An answer to it was published by the University of Oxford, and the divines of Cambridge thanked their Oxonian brethren. The conference at Hampton Court, however, was the result of the famous petition. See Fisher, *Hist. of the Reformation,* p. 434; Neale, *Hist. of the Puritans* (Harper's edition), *i* 228; Fuller, *Church History,* book x, p. 21. See PURITANS.

Millennium. This term signifies a period of a thousand years, and in its religious use is applied to the prophetic æra mentioned in Rev. xx, 1–7. The Millenarians or Chiliasts, in ancient and modern times, are characterized by their tenet respecting the second advent of Jesus, which they believe will be accompanied by the resurrection of the martyrs and saints, who will reign with him on earth, in a state of blessedness and rest, for a thousand years, when the resurrection of the wicked will occur, together with the final judgment and its eternal awards. They have differed somewhat among themselves concerning the character of this millennial kingdom, some viewing it as more and some as less spiritual in its nature, employments, and joys. They have also differed in other minor particulars; but in the main opinion relative to the advent, the first resurrection, and the temporal reign of Christ, the various classes of Millenarians are agreed. This doctrine is generally attributed to a Jewish origin. Josephus (*Ant.* xviii, i, 3) says of the Pharisees that they hold to the confinement of the souls of the wicked in an everlasting prison, but that the righteous "have power to revive and live again." In a second passage (*War,* ii, 8, 14) he describes the Pharisaic doctrine in a similar manner, for it is not probable that, in this last place, he intends to ascribe to the Pharisees a doctrine of transmigration. In the Book of Daniel (xii, 2) it is declared that both the righteous and wicked will be raised from the grave, although it is not certain whether the sacred writer at the moment has in mind the whole human race or only Israel. The New Testament teaches us that both the righteous and the wicked will be raised from the dead (John v, 28, 29; Acts xxiv, 15; Rev. xx, 11–15). The passages on this topic in the writings of Paul pertain chiefly to the consequences of redemption, and hence relate to the resurrection of believers. The idea of a resurrection of the saints, and of their participation in a temporal, millennial reign of Christ, was early adopted, especially by Jewish Christians. In the Epistle of Barnabas (cir. 100) we find the rest of the seventh day (Gen. ii, 2, 3) symbolically interpreted, with the aid of Psa. xc, 4, and made to prefigure a rest of Christ and his saints, to continue for a thousand years (ch. xv). The millennial theory was embraced in a sensuous form by Cerinthus (Eusebius, *Hist. Eccl.* iii, 28; vii, 25). It is found in apocryphal books by Jews and Jewish Christians in the first age of the Gospel—in the Book of Enoch, in the Testament of the Twelve Patriarchs, and in the Sibylline Books. It penetrated into the Gentile branch of the Church, and spread extensively. Papias, who is supposed to have been a contemporary of John the Apostle, is mentioned by Irenæus and Eusebius as an adherent of this doctrine. The colossal grapes which Papias supposed that the millennial days would provide suggest the idea which he entertained of this happy period. It is true that the Chiliastic doctrine wears a Judaic stamp, and arose, in some degree, from Judaic influences; but, as Dorner has observed, there is one marked distinction between the millenarian views of Christians and all Jewish theories of the Messianic kingdom. Christian millenarians unanimously considered the earthly kingdom as limited in its duration, and as introductory to a spiritual and eternal state of being. The triumph of the Gospel through the agency of a present Redeemer was to be attended with the renovation of the earth, and to be succeeded by the everlasting, heavenly blessedness of the righteous, the proper sequel of the last judgment. Tracing down the history of the doctrine, we find that Justin Martyr (cir. 150) received it. In the dialogue with Trypho (c. 80), he says that he himself and "many others" hold that Jerusalem will be built again as a residence for Christ, with the patriarchs and saints. He says that there are "many of a pure and devout Christian mind who are not of the same opinion;" but he adds, "I, and all other Christians whose belief is in every respect correct, know that there will be both a resurrection of the flesh and a thousand years in Jerusalem, which will then be rebuilt, adorned, and enlarged, as the prophets Ezekiel, Isaiah, and others declare." Justin quotes in support of his opinion Isa. lxv, 17 sq.; Gen. ii, 2, in connection with Psa. xc, 3; Rev. xx, 4–6, and other passages. Irenæus is likewise a millenarian. He speaks (*Adv. Hær.* V, xxxiii, 2) of "the times of the kingdom," when the "righteous shall bear rule upon their rising from the dead; when also the creation, having been renovated and set free, shall fructify with an abundance of all kinds of food, from the dew of heaven and from the fertility of the earth." Here follows the citation from Papias in regard to the colossal fruit of the vine. Tertullian advocated the same doctrine. Notwithstanding the extensive spreading of the millenarian tenet, it would be a rash inference to assume that it was universal, or accepted as the creed of the Church. On this point Neander has good observations (*Ch. Hist.*, Torrey's transl., i, 651). The first decided opponent of whom we have a knowledge was Caius, the Roman presbyter, about the year 200. The crass form in which Chiliasm entered into the heresy of Montanism contributed materially to the strengthening of the antagonism to millenarian views. The Alexandrian school opposed them with energy, particularly Origen, with whose peculiar opinions it was inconsistent. Nepos, an

Egyptian bishop, about the middle of the 3d century, wrote, in defence of the doctrine, a work entitled *A Confutation of the Allegorists*, by which name were designated such as explained allegorically the passages on which the opinion of a millennium rested. This work, which acquired much reputation, was refuted with equal zeal and candor by Dionysius of Alexandria. It was still common, however, in the time of Jerome, who himself was one of its opponents. But gradually the tenet which had so widely prevailed became obnoxious and proscribed. One great reason of this remarkable change of sentiment is to be found in the altered condition and prospects of the Church. Christians at first yearned for the reappearance of the Lord. Moreover, it was impossible for them to raise their faith and hopes so high as to expect the conquest of the Roman empire by the moral power of the cross, independently of the personal and supernatural interposition of Christ. But as the Gospel made progress, the possibility and probability of a peaceful victory of the Christian cause over all its adversaries, by the might of truth and of the Spirit, gained a lodgment in the convictions of good men. It is believed that Origen (b. 180, d. 254) is the first of the ancient ecclesiastical writers to affirm the practicableness of such a triumph of the Gospel through its own inherent efficacy. The Judaic and Judaizing associations of the millenarian opinion were not without a strong influence in rendering it suspected and unpopular. Augustine's treatment of the subject marks an epoch. He says (*De Civitate Dei*, xx, 7) that he had once held to a millenarian Sabbath; nor does he consider the doctrine objectionable, provided the joys of the righteous are figured as spiritual. But, proceeding to discuss the subject, he advocates the proposition that the earthly kingdom of Christ is the Church, which was even then in the millennial æra, and on the road to a glorious ascendency over all its enemies. It would seem that this modified interpretation of prophecy, sustained as it was by the authority of the principal Latin father, gave color to the mediæval speculations on this subject. As the year of our Lord 1000 approached, it was a natural corollary that the judgment and the end of the world would then occur. Hence there was a widespread excitement throughout Western Europe, from the apprehension that the "dies iræ" was at hand. There were not wanting in the Middle Ages "apocalyptic parties" —enthusiasts, whether individuals or in bands—who looked for the miraculous advent of Jesus as the indispensable means of purifying and extending the Church.

At the Reformation, the traditional method of interpreting the Book of Revelation was abandoned. The papacy was extensively regarded as Antichrist, and Luther and other leading Reformers frequently supposed themselves authorized by the signs of the times to expect the speedy coming of the Lord. A fanatical form of millenarianism was espoused by the Anabaptists of Germany, who took possession of the city of Münster, and set up the reign of the saints.

The millenarian doctrine, in its essential characteristics, has had adherents among some of the sober-minded theologians of the Lutheran Church in later times. Of these, one of the most distinguished is John Albert Bengel, the author of the *Gnomon*, who defended his opinion in his commentary on the Apocalypse, published in 1740. He was followed by other divines of repute; and the doctrine has not been without prominent supporters among the Lutherans down to the present time. One of the latest of their number who has discussed this question is the Rev. A. Koch (*Das tausendjährige Reich*, Basle, 1872). This writer endeavors, in particular, to refute the arguments adduced against the doctrine of a millennium by the German commentators Hengstenberg, Keil, and Kliefoth.

In all the other various orthodox Protestant bodies there are many who believe in the personal advent of Christ for the purpose of establishing a millennial kingdom. Now, as in former ages, the literal restoration of the Jews to Palestine, and their conversion to Christianity, is frequently a part of this creed. The coming of Christ in visible glory is to be signalized, it is held, by this among other wonderful events. The Chiliastic tenet forms one of the distinguishing features of the "Catholic Apostolic Church," or the religious denomination commonly known as Irvingites. (See the art. CATHOLIC APOSTOLIC CHURCH, and IRVING, EDWARD, in this Cyclopædia.) Christ is to come and gather his elect together; the Jews are to be brought back to their ancient land; the Gospel is to be extended by their instrumentality, and by the new agencies connected with the personal presence of the Lord, over the earth. Then is to follow the judgment and the end of the world. Such are the main points of the millenarian view, as cherished by the followers of Mr. Irving.

In the course of the history of the Church many sects have arisen by whom the speedy coming of Christ to set up a visible empire has been proclaimed. One of these is the class designated as "Millerites" (q. v.), the disciples of William Miller (q. v.). He was born in Pittsfield, Mass., in 1781, and died in 1849. With slender resources of learning, he began, about the year 1833, to preach on the subject of the second advent, which he declared, on the ground of his interpretation of the prophecies, to be near at hand. The Millerites at length went so far as to fix a certain day in the year 1843 when the Lord was to appear in the clouds of heaven. Some gave up their ordinary occupations, and prepared robes in which to ascend and meet Christ. Subsequently the members of this sect—if sect it is to be called—ceased to define the precise time of the miraculous advent, but continued to wait for it as near. See ADVENTISTS. The Millerites, in common with many other Chiliasts, have supposed themselves to be furnished by the prophecies with the means of calculating with mathematical accuracy the time of the Saviour's glorious advent.

When we leave the history of the doctrine, and look at the exegetical arguments of the several parties, it becomes plain that they are guided by diverse principles of interpretation. With respect to certain passages, millenarians adopt a second sense, or a figurative, tropical interpretation. This is the character of their view of the sabbatical rest, as predicted in Gen. ii, 2, 3, and Psa. xc, 4. On the contrary, to the passages in Isaiah and other prophets which describe Jerusalem as the centre and resort of worshippers of all nations, promise Canaan as an everlasting possession to the Jews, and depict their splendid restoration to power and plenty, they give a literal interpretation. The same course is pursued by them with regard to Rev. xx, and with regard to all that is said of the first and the second resurrection. They attach often a literal sense to the declaration of Jesus (Matt. xxvi, 29; Mark xiv, 25) in which he speaks of drinking new wine in his Father's kingdom. They consider their general view to be favored by Luke xiv, 14 ("the resurrection of the just"); Luke xx, 35 ("they which shall be accounted worthy to obtain that world and the resurrection of the dead"); by John vi, 39, 44 (which speaks of the resurrection of believers, without any mention of others). The promise of Christ that the disciples at "the regeneration"—or the restitution of all things, and the deliverance of all things from corruption—shall sit on thrones, judging the tribes of Israel (Matt. xix, 28), is confidently referred to as proving the millenarian hypothesis. So the statements of John and Paul with respect to Antichrist, and the sins and perils to immediately precede the advent—corroborated, as they suppose, by the Saviour's own predictions in Matt. xxiv and xxv, and the parallel passages—are brought forward in defence of their position.

The opponents of the millenarians rely principally upon the passages in which the resurrection of the good and evil is spoken of as if it were simultaneous, or without any considerable interval of time interposed. They appeal also to the passages in the Gospels and Epistles in which the general judgment is connected immedi-

ately with the second advent. Their conception of the prospects and destiny of the kingdom of Christ are derived from passages like the parables of the leaven, of the mustard-seed, and of the husbandman. That it was expedient for Christ to go away from his disciples in order that his visible presence might give way to his invisible presence and influence everywhere, and to the dispensation of the Spirit, is considered an argument against the general philosophy on which the millenarian tenet rests. It is thought to be more consonant with the genius of Christianity, as contrasted with the Jewish economy, to look for a triumph of the Gospel in the earth by moral forces and by the agency of the Holy Spirit within the souls of men, than to expect the stupendous miracle of Christ's reappearance as a Ruler on this globe, for the spiritual subjugation of unbelievers and enemies. Hence those who reject Chiliasm give a figurative rendering to the prophetic passages in the Apocalypse which are the most plausible argument for that theory. The tendency of the millenarian theory to chill the hopes, and thus repress the missionary activity of Christians, by exhibiting the world as in a process of deterioration, and by representing the efforts of Christians to convert mankind as fruitless, until the coming of Christ, constitutes not the least serious objection to such opinions.

There is in England at the present time an energetic propaganda of millenarian notions, called the "Prophecy Investigation Society," which consists of fifty members, some of them prominent Churchmen, and which has published a series of volumes on prophetic subjects, adding largely to apocalyptic literature. There are also numerous journals published in England to support these views. The most important is the *Quarterly Journal of Prophecy*, edited by Dr. Bonar, of the Free Church of Scotland, which has been established fourteen years, and has a large circulation. The *Rainbow* is a monthly periodical; the *Christian Observer*, the monthly journal of the evangelicals, often displays millenarian tendencies. There are, besides, numerous weeklies of small circulation, the chief being the *Revivalist*, originally established to promote revivals in personal religion, but now devoted to the spread of millenarian views. Nor is the interest in this subject confined to Dissenters in England or Scotland; a certain class of minds in the Established Church seem to be just as strongly contaminated. For many successive years, during Lent, courses of lectures have been delivered in St. George's Church, Bloomsbury, on the subject of the second advent, by clergymen of the Church of England. The course for the year 1849 was printed, under the title of *The Priest upon his Throne*, being lectures by twelve clergymen of the Church of England, with a Preface by the Rev. James Haldane Stewart, M.A., rector of Limpsfield (Lond. 1849). This is, next to Dr. Brown's *Second Coming of our Lord*, the ablest book against the millenarian doctrine. One of the latest productions in English is *The End of all Things, or the Coming of Christ*, by an anonymous author, a clergyman of the Church of England. It is an argument against millenarianism, and is interesting for its sketch of the rise of the doctrine with the well-meaning but weak-minded Papias, and its progress through all the sects and shades of belief, until "more than half of the evangelical clergy of the Church of England are at this moment millenarians."

Among the most important writings on the millennium are Corrodi, *Krit. Gesch. d. Chiliasmus* (Frankfort, 1871); Dorner, *Gesch. d. Person Christi*, vol. i; Herzog, *Real-Encyklop.* art. Chiliasmus. See also the exegetical criticism in Rothe's *Dogmatik*, pt. ii, sec. ii. Most of the recent treatises on doctrinal theology—for example, that of Gass, *Dogmengeschichte*, ii, 477 sq.; and the able work by Dr. Hodge—contain discussions of this subject. Among the special writers on the subject may be consulted, on the millenarian side, Mede, Abbadie, Beverley, Burnet, Hartley, Price, Frere, Irving, Birks, Bickersteth, Brooks, the duke of Manchester Begg,

Burgh, Greswell, Gilfillan, Bonar, Elliot, Homes, Burchell, Wood, Tyso, Molyneux, etc.; and on the other side, bishop Hall, R. Baxter, Gipps, Dr. David Brown, Waldegrave, Fairbairn, Urwick, Bush, and many others. Floerke (evangelical pastor in Lübz), *Die Lehre vom tausendjährigen Reiche. Ein theologischer Versuch.* (Marburg, 1859, 8vo) ; Volck, *Der Chiliasmus seiner neuesten Bekämpfung gegenüber, eine historisch-exegetische Studie* (Dorpat, 1869, 8vo); Carson, *The Personal Reign of Christ during the Millennium proved to be impossible* (1873, 12mo); *Second Adventism in the Light of Jewish History*, by the Rev. T. M. Hopkins, edited by Joseph R. Boyd, D.D. (N.Y. 1873, 12mo). The following periodicals may be consulted to advantage : *Church of England Rev.* 1854, Oct. p. 443; *Lond. Rev.* No. x, art. ix; *Meth. Qu. Rev.* 1845, Jan. art. v and vii; 1850, July, p. 485; 1851, April, p. 325; 1868, Oct. p. 615; Kitto, *Journal of Sacred Literature*, 1854, July, p. 505; Oct. p. 19 sq.; 1856, Jan. p. 467; *Amer. Presb. Rev.* 1861, April, p. 403; 1864, April, p. 177 sq.; July, p. 411; 1865, April, p. 195; *Princet. Rev.* 1867, Jan. p. 160; *Evangel. Qu. Rev.* 1861, Jan. art. ii; 1868, July, p. 337; *Theological Medium* (Cumberland Presb. Church), 1873, April, art. ix; *Bibliotheca Sacra*, 1873, Jan. art. iv; *Qu. Rev. Evang. Luth. Church*, 1873, Jan. art. ii. (G. P. F.)

Miller, Armistead, a Presbyterian missionary of African parentage, was born in North Carolina about 1830 as a slave, but was liberated and went to Africa when a boy; was educated in the Alexander High School, Liberia, and afterwards returned to America, and received a theological training in the Ashmun Institute, Oxford, Pa. In 1859 he was licensed and ordained by New Castle Presbytery, and soon afterwards went to Africa, and became pastor of Mount Coffee Church, Liberia, where he died, Jan. 15, 1865.—Wilson, *Presb. Hist. Almanac*, 1866, p. 131.

Miller, Charles W., a minister of the Methodist Episcopal Church, South, was born in Wayne County, Ind., in 1820. He entered the ministry in 1840, and continued faithful in the prosecution and studies of the work. When failing health obliged him to seek the climate of the Rocky Mountains, he went to Colorado as a laborer for the Church of which he was a member, and acceptedly applied himself to his task. He died in Colorado City, Colorado, April 8, 1872, universally deplored, and long to be remembered for his great activity. Three thousand persons are said to have been converted under his preaching. See F. H. Sutherland, in the *Central Christian Advocate* (M. E. Ch., South), May 1, 1872.

Miller, David, a minister of the Methodist Episcopal Church, was born at New Hartford, Conn., Nov. 24, 1792. He entered the ministry in 1816 as a member of the New York Conference. For several years he was chaplain at the State Prison at Wethersfield. In 1855 he was appointed presiding elder of the Hartford District. He died at Bristol, Conn., Dec. 26, 1855. David Miller was a man of good judgment and a practical mind, which aided him in his own affairs and also in giving counsel to others. As a preacher, he was plain and earnest, relying upon the truth which he endeavored always to proclaim in the spirit of one determined not to know anything among men save Jesus Christ and him crucified.

Miller, George, D.D., an Irish divine, distinguished for his eminence in theology, history, and literature, was born at Dublin Oct. 22, 1764. He was educated at Trinity College in his native city, and, after receiving holy orders, soon rose to prominence. In 1801 he was appointed vicar-general of Armagh, and lecturer of modern history at his alma mater. His lectures attracted universal attention, and were published in 1816, under the title of *Lectures on the Philosophy of Modern History from the Fall of the Roman Empire to the French Revolution* (Dublin, 1816, 8 vols.; 1852, 4 vols. 8vo). This work of Dr. Miller "possesses unity of subject, har-

mony of proportion, and connection of parts; thereby constituting one of the best of modern histories in English, and affording a systematic view of the progress of civilization" (*For. Qu. Rev.*). "Dr. Miller assumes, as the basis of his system, that all the events of this world have an intrinsic connection, which gives them the coherence and the unity of a moral drama. A single event or period, taken by itself, is a grain of dust in this mighty balance" (*Edinb. Rev.* 1, 287 sq.). "Dr. Miller," says a prominent critic in the *Dublin University Magazine* (xiii, 572), "advances and establishes his great principle, that God reigneth in the affairs of men, and that the end of the divine government is man's improvement." In the winter of 1817 Dr. Miller was induced to apply for the head-mastership of the Royal School of Armagh, which was immediately conferred upon him. In conjunction with many able champions of Protestantism, he made a noble stand against the fatal policy of English statesmen, by which Roman Catholics were admitted to political power. While Dr. Miller, in 1793, had hailed with pleasure the commencement of political concessions to the Romish Church, and had even lent a helping hand to these reforms, he now, with deeper philosophy and wider statesmanship, opposed the growing political power of the Romanists. His *Letter to Mr. Plunkett on the Policy of the Roman Catholic Question* (Lond. 1826) is a fair index to his opinions. In the same year he showed himself the champion of the true faith by attacking the modern Arian opinions in his *Observations on the Doctrines of Christianity and on the Athanasian Creed;* and when the Pusey (q. v.) discussions were at their height, he published *A Letter to Dr. Pusey in reference to his Letter to the Lord Bishop of Oxford* (1840, 8vo). *A Second Letter to Dr. Pusey* was published in the winter of 1841, and it suffices to say that Dr. Miller was thereafter considered one of the most formidable opponents of Puseyism. In his position as head-master of the Royal School of Armagh he showed himself uncompromising in his defence of Scriptural education in Ireland. Dr. Miller, being firmly persuaded that "most of our relations to our fellow-men, for which education is to prepare us, grow out of our relations to God," advocated Scriptural education as the only true system. Christian influence must pervade the whole educational institution, he asserted, and all our knowledge must be derived from the holy Scriptures. His *Case of the Church Education Society of Ireland argued in Reply to Dr. Elrington* (Lond. 1847), and his *Supplement to the Case of the Church Education Society* (Dublin, 1847), are most important statements of what true education ought to accomplish. Blessed with a mind peculiarly cheerful, contented and happy in his disposition, devout in his religion, truly philosophic in his learning, Dr. Miller was beloved and esteemed by all who came into official or private connection with him. He died Oct. 6, 1848. See *Memoir of Dr. Miller* in Bohn's edition of Miller's *History*, iv, 5 sq.; *Dublin University Mag.* xvii, 674 sq.; *Edinburgh Review*, i, 287 sq.; Allibone, *Dict. of Brit. and Amer. Authors*, ii, 1282.

Miller, George Benjamin, D.D., an eminent divine of the Lutheran Church, was born of Moravian parentage at Emmons, Lehigh County, Pa., June 10, 1795. His father, the Rev. George G. Miller, connected with the classical and theological school at Nazareth, and descended from a long line of Moravian clergymen, furnished him with special facilities for intellectual and moral culture. He entered Nazareth Hall as a pupil when only eight years of age, and there he continued his studies for eight years. He then left for Philadelphia, and commenced his career as a teacher in a private school. Subsequently he turned his attention to mercantile pursuits, but he soon discovered that the work was not adapted to his natural tastes and inclinations. In less than a year he resumed his former employment, and became associated with the Rev. Dr. Hazelius as an instructor in an academy at New Germantown, N. J.

and at the same time continued his theological studies, which had been commenced at Nazareth. In the autumn of 1818 he entered upon the work of the ministry at Canajoharie, N. Y., having been previously licensed to preach by the New York Ministerium, then under the presidency of the Rev. Dr. Quitman. In connection with his pastoral labors he established a classical school, and gave regular instruction. In this position he faithfully labored till 1827, when he accepted a professorship in Hartwick Seminary, N. Y., and again became the colleague of Dr. Hazelius, whom he succeeded as principal of the institution in 1830. With the exception of five years spent in the work of teaching and preaching elsewhere, he continued connected with this seminary, either as principal or professor of theology, until his death, devoting all his energies to the preparation of young men for college or of candidates for the holy ministry. His name will always be as closely identified with the history of the institution as that of its benevolent founder. He died with the harness on, April 5, 1869. Dr. Miller was married to Delia B. Snyder in 1816, and in 1866 commemorated his "golden wedding" with a large number of relatives and friends, who had gathered from different parts of the country to present their congratulations and good wishes, the whole family, twenty-three in number, on the evening preceding the wedding festivities, uniting in the celebration of the Lord's Supper, and the reverend patriarch, surrounded by three generations, administering the sacred ordinance. Dr. Miller was a man of quick, acute, and discriminating intellect. He was distinguished for his accurate and ripe scholarship. As a man of learning, he had few superiors in the country. He had a perfect command of his own vernacular, and spoke and wrote German and French with wonderful facility. He was familiar with the exact sciences, his acquaintance with history was very extensive, and his knowledge of the ancient classics critical and complete. He was also a profound Hebraist, and thoroughly versed in the Scriptures, so that he never found it necessary to use a concordance, but could turn with almost unfailing intuition to the required passage of the sacred page. Dr. Miller was noted as a man of original thought and independent research. As a writer, he was universally commended as clear, accurate, and instructive. The productions of his pen show his power of analysis, of generalization, and great condensation in the method of statement. His extensive erudition and enlarged experience were only surpassed by the loveliness of his Christian character; and his earnest, simple-hearted, active piety made a deep impression upon all who came within the range of his influence. His elevated type of Christian excellence, his high culture, his unpretending, modest character, his life unsullied by a single stain, attracted towards him by the strongest sympathies all men. He was a bright and shining light in the Church, and his name will ever be cherished with the most affectionate interest. All his acquisitions were made subordinate to that which most deeply interested his active mind —the study of divine truth. All his treasures were laid at the Master's feet, and devoted entirely to his service. When, in 1836, he received the distinction of D.D. from Union College, he meekly submitted, remarking to a friend that the letters would serve as a good Scriptural motto, *Deo Duce*. The Lutheran Church owes to him as much as to any other laborer in this country. The only works published by Dr. Miller are a volume of *Sermons on some of the Fundamental Principles of the Gospel*, and a text-book on German Grammar, which never reached an extensive circulation. For a more detailed account, see *Evangel. Qu. Rev.* 1870, Jan. p. 25 sq.; *Memorial Volume of Hartwick Seminary*. (M. L. S.)

Miller, George W., a minister of the Methodist Episcopal Church, was born near Westminster, Md., in 1826. He was converted at sixteen; entered the ministry of the United Brethren Church in his twenty-fifth year, and travelled for seven consecutive years. He then joined the ministry of the Methodist Episcopal Church, in which he labored until his death, at Pioneer, Ohio, Aug. 10, 1872. He was an earnest and successful minister, a faithful and beloved pastor.

Miller, Hugh, one of the most noted characters among the English-speaking nations of our century, the champion of the Free Church of Scotland, and the defender of revelation from "scientists," falsely so called, was born of very humble parentage at Cromarty, in Scotland, Oct. 10, 1805. He received his first education at the parish school, where he was distinguished for his fondness for poetry and poetical composition. At that early age he was an extensive reader, and placed under contribution the libraries of the parish. In this way he laid the foundation of an extended knowledge of literature, which availed him in after-life. But the most important part of his education consisted in the natural-history instruction he received from an uncle who had acquired a taste for the observation of natural phenomena. His poverty proved an obstacle to a collegiate education, and he was obliged to learn a trade in order to secure a livelihood. He determined fortunately, as his later history proved, to become a stone-mason. This occupation unexpectedly fostered the taste he had acquired for the study of natural history; and while hewing blocks of stone in the quarry, he was diligently studying the traces they exhibited of their past history. It was in this way that he prepared himself to become the historian of the old red sandstone, among the rocks of which he principally worked. "It was the necessity which made me a quarrier that taught me to be a geologist," he himself wrote in after-life. He labored as a quarryman and stone-mason for about fifteen years, constantly improving himself in his leisure hours by reading and study. The publication of a volume of poems which he wrote during that time attracted the attention of some persons, who, by procuring him a situation in a bank of his native village, enabled him to devote more time to his studies. He now commenced contributing to several newspapers. The Church of Scotland was at that time a prey to internal dissensions, which ultimately led to a division. The Independents, who wished to throw off the yoke of the higher clergy, received great support from the people; Miller rendered them great service when the contest came to a close by the decision of the House of Lords in the Auchterarder case, in 1839, by his pamphlet, entitled *A Letter from One of the Scottish People to the Right Honorable Lord Brougham and Vaux on the Opinions expressed by his Lordship in the Auchterarder Case*. This remarkable letter drew towards him the attention of the evangelical party, and he was selected as the most competent person to conduct the newly-started *Witness* newspaper. the principal metropolitan organ of the Free Church. This paper owed its success to his able contributions—political, ecclesiastical, and geological. His articles on geology he contributed to the first congress of the British Association, held at Glasgow in 1840. They were highly praised by Charles Lyell, Murchison, Buckland, and Agassiz, and the name of Miller was by them associated with the wonderful fossil, the Pterichthys Milleri, which he had discovered in the red sandstone, and which had previously been thought to contain scarcely any fossils. Miller published these articles in book form, under the title *The Old Red Sandstone, or New Walks in an Old Field* (Edinburgh, 1841, 8vo; often reprinted, both in England and America). In 1847 appeared his *First Impressions of England and its People* (3d ed. 1853, 8vo), the result of a tour made during the previous year. Some parts of this book, especially the account of the pilgrimages to Stratford-on-Avon, and the Leasowes, and Olney, and other places, memorable for their literary associations, are among the very finest pieces of descriptive English. A magic style characterized all his works, whether those of a more popular kind or his scientific treatises, such as the *Footprints of the Creator* (1849), a work suggested by the *Vestiges of Crea-*

tion, and subversive of the fallacies of that superficial and plausible book. "There was nothing in Miller's works," says the *Edinburgh Review* for July, 1858, "which so much surprised the reader as their mere literary merit. Where could this Cromarty mason have acquired his style?" Not one of the authors of our day has approached Hugh Miller as a master of English composition, for the equal of which we must go back to the times of Addison, Hume, and Goldsmith. During the later part of his life he suffered severely from disease of the brain, and he finally shot himself while in a fit of somnambulism, Dec. 24, 1856. His death caused a most painful excitement. Few men have occupied a higher position in the estimation of his countrymen. He was a noble example of what self-education can do for a man; and, whether regarded as the fearless and independent writer, or the man of literature and science, his character must claim the respect and admiration of posterity. The personal appearance of Mr. Miller, or "Old Red," as he was familiarly named by his scientific friends, is thus described by one who had the good fortune to see him: "A head of great massiveness, magnified by an abundant profusion of sub-Celtic hair, was set on a body of muscular compactness, but which in later years felt the undermining influence of a life of unusual physical and mental toil. Generally wrapped in a bulky plaid, and with a garb ready for any work, he had the appearance of a shepherd from the Rossshire hills rather than an author and a man of science. In conversation or in lecturing the man of original genius and cultivated mind at once shone out, and his abundant information and philosophical acuteness were only less remarkable than his amiable disposition, his generous spirit, and his consistent, humble piety" (*Literary Gazette*). His other works are, *The Geology of the Bass* (1848, 8vo):—*On certain Peculiarities of Structure in some ancient Ganoids* (fishes) (1850):—*On the Fossil Flora of Scotland* (1855):—*My School and Schoolmasters*, a very interesting autobiography, in which he relates his early history, and his struggles in pursuit of science (1855):—*The Testimony of the Rocks* (Lond. 1858), in which he discusses the Biblical bearings of geology, published after his death. "Hugh Miller," says the writer in the *Edinburgh Review* whom we have already had occasion to quote, "must undoubtedly be regarded as one of the most remarkable men whom Scotland has produced. . . . The interest of his narrative, the purity of his style, his inexhaustible faculty of happy and ingenious illustration, his high imaginative power, and that light of genius which it is so difficult to define yet so impossible to mistake, all promise to secure for the author of the *Old Red Sandstone* the lasting admiration of his countrymen." The different scientific works of Hugh Miller mark an important epoch in the progress of the study of geology. He was one of the first to popularize the subject. "Besides adding much to our knowledge, and placing things previously known in a clear and pleasing light, Mr. Miller's performance will be very acceptable also to geologists both of the old and young school" (*Lond. Athen.* 1842, p. 523). "But what is in a great degree peculiar to our author is the successful combination of Christian doctrines with pure scientific truth" (Agassiz, Introd. to Amer. ed. of *Footprints of the Creator*). See *Labor and Triumph: the Life and Times of Hugh Miller*, by Thomas N. Brown, D.D. (Glasgow and N.Y. 1858, 12mo); *Lond. Gentleman's Magazine*, 1857, pt. i, p. 244 sq.; *Lond. Athen.* 1856, p. 1609; *Edinb. Rev.* July, 1858, art. Hugh Miller (reprinted in the *Living Age*, Aug. 21, 1858); *North Brit. Rev.* Aug. 1854; Allibone, *Dict. of Brit. and Amer. Authors*, s. v.; *Men of the Time*, s. v.; *Engl. Cyclop.* s. v.; Hoefer, *Nouv. Biog. Générale*, xxxv, 524; *New-Englander*, viii, 237; *North Amer. Rev.* lxxiii, 448; *Eclectic Rev.* 4th series, xxvii, 685; xv, 690; *Brit. Qu. Rev.* 1871, July, p. 40; *Meth. Qu. Rev.* 1859, Oct. p. 513; *Westminster Rev.* 1871, April, p. 269.

Miller, Jacob (1), D.D., was born Dec. 11, 1788,

at Goshenhoppen, Pa., and was reared under religious influences in accordance with the views and practices of the Lutheran Church. He was engaged in the prosecution of his literary and theological studies for five years, under the direction of the Rev. Dr. Geissenhainen, and completed them under the instruction of Drs. Helmuth and Schmidt, who at that time had charge of a private seminary in Philadelphia for the education of candidates for the ministry. His first field of labor was the Goshenhoppen District, among the people in whose midst he had lived all his life. Here he labored twenty-one years, "not only with acceptance," says the record, "but with profit." In 1829 he removed to Reading, Pa., where he continued to labor till his death, just twenty-one years. He died May 16, 1850. Dr. Miller was a man of marked ability. His natural endowments were of a superior order, and they had been brought under the influence of careful culture. He wielded an immense influence. In whatever position he was placed his power was felt. In 1838 he was honored with the doctorate of divinity by the University of Pennsylvania, but he never recognised or used the degree. (M. L. S.)

Miller, Jacob (2), a minister of the Methodist Episcopal Church, a native of Germany, came to this country when but seventeen years of age (1832); was converted while a resident of Quincy, Ill., and connected with the German Lutheran Church. Himself the product of a revival, he labored earnestly for the renewing of God's love in the hearts of his lukewarm Lutheran brethren, but the minister of the Church with which he was connected opposed him, and Miller was finally obliged to leave that body. With thirty others, like-minded, he joined the Methodist Episcopal Church. In 1848 he was admitted into the Illinois Conference, and labored with great success until, by reason of failing health, he was obliged to ask for a superannuated relation. In 1860 he was again placed on the active list, and sent to Alton, Ill., where he labored successfully. In 1866 he was sent to Petersburg Circuit, Ill.; thence to Bushnell, where he died, March 7, 1871. See *Minutes of Annual Conferences*, 1871, p. 188.

Miller, James, a Presbyterian minister, was born near New Milns, Ayrshire, Scotland, Feb. 4, 1803. He was educated at Glasgow College, Scotland; studied divinity in the theological seminary at Glasgow, and was licensed by Kilmarnock Presbytery of the United Secession Church. Soon after he came to the United States; was ordained in 1841 by the Associate Reformed Presbyterian Church of Ohio as pastor over the Church in Perrysburg and Scotch Ridge, Wood Co., Ohio; subsequently removed to Iowa, preaching as opportunity offered, and died Jan. 26, 1867. Mr. Miller was a successful and useful minister, and did much to advance the cause of truth. See Wilson, *Presb. Hist. Almanac*, 1868, p. 274.

Miller, Johann Peter, a German Protestant theologian, was born at Leipheim April 26, 1725; was educated at the university at Helmstädt; in 1747 went to Göttingen, and in 1750 became rector of the Latin school at Helmstädt. In 1756 he accepted a similar position at the Lutheran Gymnasium at Halle, but returned in 1766 to Göttingen, as professor of theology, and there died, May 29, 1789. Miller wrote and published a continuation of Mosheim's *Sittenlehre*. His productions of value are, *Das Reich der Natur und Sitten* (Halle, 1757–1762):—*Diss. in locum ad Roman. S.* 28 (Helmstädt, 1747):—*Diss. locus antologicus de Eodem et Diverso* (Götting. 1748, 4to):—*Diss. de notabili et maximo versionis Italæ ad verba Christi Matt. xx*, 28 additamento (ibid. 1749, 4to):—*J. L. Mosheimii Commentationes et orationes varii generis* (Hamburg, 1751, 8vo):—*Vollständiger Auszug aus allen neuen Theilen der Mosheimischen Sittenlehre der heiligen Schrift* (Halle, 1765, 8vo; 2d auflage, ibid. 1777, 8vo):—*Die Hoffnung besserer Zeiten für Schulen* (ibid. 1765, 4to):—*Progr. quo probatur, cum theopneustea Apostolorum nec omniscientiam quasi* *aliquam, nec anamartesiam fuisse conjunctam* (Götting. 1789, 4to).

Miller, John E., a minister of the Reformed (Dutch) Church, was born at Albany in 1792; graduated at Union College in 1812; was licensed in 1817; served the Church as missionary in the South and West in 1817 and 1818; was pastor at Chester, N. J., Presbyterian Church from 1818 to 1823; and then of the Reformed Church, Tompkinsville, Staten Island, until he died, in 1847, in the midst of a powerful revival of religion in his Church. Miller was also chaplain in the Marine Hospital and at the Seaman's Retreat. In this place he exhibited the highest degree of moral courage and religious faith and zeal in times of appalling pestilence, and among sufferers of all kinds. Contagious diseases had no fears for him. He was a simple-hearted, bold, tender, and faithful preacher of the Gospel; a guileless, outspoken, honest soul; a hater of strife; and a brave, calm, earnest, uncompromising lover and defender of the faith once delivered to the saints. His memoir is to be found in a goodly volume, called *An Old Disciple and his Descendants*, by Rev. F. M. Kip, D.D., which contains brief biographies of his patriarchal father (Christian Miller, Esq., of Albany) and several of his family, who were noted for unusual gifts of mind, character, and piety. Among these was a grandson, Isaac Livingston Kip Miller, a youth of unusually brilliant and powerful intellect, and of great promise, who died in 1846, while studying for the ministry. He was the elder brother of Dr. W. A. Miller (q. v.). (W. J. R. T.)

Miller, John Peter, a talented but eccentric American minister, was born in the Palatinate, Germany, about the year 1715; was thoroughly educated in his native land; came to this country in 1730; was licensed and ordained by the Philadelphia Synod of the Presbyterian Church; and in 1731 became pastor of the German Reformed Church in Tulpehocken, Berks County, Pa., where he labored successfully for about four years. In 1735 he fell in with an enthusiast by the name of Beissel, by whom he was immersed, and so became identified with the Seventh-day Baptists. Flying from the society of the world, he entered upon a solitary or monastic life at the base of a mountain, near a "limpid spring." He afterwards, urged by the force of his trials, entered the cloister of the Seventh-day Baptists at Ephrata, Pa. "Here, under the name of Jabez, he lived a quiet life as a Protestant monk, using a board for his bed at night, and devoting himself by day to what he imagined to be the service of God in severe self-castigation." See Harbaugh, *Fathers of the Ref. Church*, i, 301-311. (D. Y. H.)

Miller, John Wesley, a minister of the Methodist Episcopal Church, South, was born at Charleston, South Carolina, Oct. 27, 1829. He enjoyed a collegiate education, and entered the ministry in 1850; was, as licentiate, deacon, and elder, on circuits, stations, missions, and in the Southern army as chaplain of hospitals, always a faithful, devoted servant of Christ. He died in the village of Darlington, South Carolina, June 29, 1866. See *Minutes of the M. E. Church, South*, 1866.

Miller, Louis Pilketon, a minister of the Methodist Episcopal Church, was born in Union County, Pa., Jan. 8, 1809. He joined the Church in his sixteenth year. He was soon after impressed by a strong conviction that it was his duty to preach the Gospel to others. He worked in his father's fields by moonlight, that he might procure religious books to qualify himself for this station in life. In 1828 he entered the academy at Milton, Pa., and in 1830 he was admitted into the Ohio Conference. He was successively stationed at Athens, Norwich, Georgetown, Madisonville, South Charleston, Wilmington, Franklin, White Oak, Madisonville, Amelia, Williamsburg, Lockland, West White Oak, Amelia, Milford, New Carlisle, Raysville, Batavia, Madisonville, Miami, Jamestown, and Moscow. In 1864 he entered the army as chaplain, and served until peace was re-

stored. He died in 1872. Mr. Miller was a man of great humility and piety, and his ministry was a glorious success.

Miller, Nathan W., a minister of the Methodist Episcopal Church, was born at Washington, Me., Dec. 24, 1831; was converted and united with the Church in June, 1842. In 1853 he was licensed as a local preacher, and in 1859 was employed by the presiding elder of the Rockland District to preach at Benton and vicinity, where he labored successfully. He entered the itinerancy in 1862 as a member of the East Maine Conference, and was appointed to North Searsport; in 1864 and 1865, to Bear Hill, Charleston, and Garland; in 1866, to Garland; in 1867, to Abbott and Greenville; in 1868, to Danforth, Weston, and Topsfield. In 1869 he was granted a superannuated relation; and in June following he moved to Benton, where he could be near his family friends. Here he assisted in the public service as long as his strength would permit. He died Feb. 22, 1870. "Brother Miller, as a Christian minister, had clear perceptions; a high sense of honor, combined with a deep sense of obligation; as a citizen, he was kind and obliging; as a friend, true, trusty, and confiding; as a companion and father, affectionate, kind, and faithful." See *Minutes of Annual Conferences*, 1870.

Miller, Samuel (1), D.D., LL.D., an eminent Presbyterian divine, whose name is cherished as that of one who materially assisted in laying the foundations of the Presbyterian Church in this country, was born Oct. 31, 1769, at Dover, Delaware. He received his early literary training under the direction of his father, the Rev. John Miller, a native of Boston, who early settled as a Presbyterian pastor in Delaware. Samuel was educated at the University of Pennsylvania (class of 1789), and graduated with the highest honor in his class; commenced the study of theology under his father, and finished his theological course under the Rev. Dr. Nesbit, at Dickinson College, Carlisle, Pa.; in 1791 was licensed to preach, and in 1793 was installed as colleague pastor with Drs. McKnight and Rodgers over the First Presbyterian Church in New York City, and, after the dissolution, was pastor of the Wall Street Church until 1813. He was instrumental in the establishment of Princeton Seminary, and subsequently was appointed to the chair of ecclesiastical history and Church government, which he held for more than thirty-six years. He died Jan. 7, 1850. Dr. Miller was an extensive author, and published, *Sermon on Psa. ii*, 11 (Feb. 1799):—*A Pastoral Discourse* (1800):—*A Brief Retrospect of the 18th Century* (1803, 2 vols. 8vo):—*Letters on the Constitution and Order of the Christian Ministry* (1807, 12mo):—*Discourse designed to Commemorate the Discovery of New York* (1809):—*Memoir of Rev. John Rogers, D.D.* (1813, 8vo):—*Letters on Unitarianism* (1821, 8vo):—*On the Eternal Sonship of Christ* (1823):—*Lectures at the Seminary* (1827):—*Letters on Clerical Manners and Habits* (1827, 12mo):—*Lectures at the Seminary* (1830):—*Essay on the Utility and Importance of Creeds and Confessions:—On the Office of Ruling Elder* (1831, 12mo):—*On Baptism:—Letters on the Observance of the Monthly Concert in Prayer:—Memoir of the Rev. Charles Nesbit, D.D.* (1840):—*The Primitive and Apostolical Order of the Church of Christ vindicated* (1840, 12mo):—*Letters from a Father to his Son in College* (1843):—*Thoughts on Public Prayer* (1848):—*On Christian Education of Children*. Dr. Miller also contributed a *Life of Jonathan Edwards* to Sparks's "American Biography." Dr. Miller possessed admirable natural qualities that constituted the foundation of his eminently attractive character. His countenance, full of generosity and manliness, was indicative of great purity and nobility of character; his manners were uncommonly dignified and polished; his conversation brilliant and attractive. He was pre-eminently a man of system and method. His intellect was naturally clear, comprehensive, and symmetrical. As a minister, he was singularly adapted to profit theological students—

his preaching clear, direct, and full of evangelical truth. As a professor, he was eminently qualified; his lectures were luminous exhibitions of his subject, full of well-digested thought, and arranged with graceful naturalness. As an author, he was at home in almost every field, whether literary or theological. His taste was beyond criticism, insomuch that, in reading his works, one rarely meets with an expression that admits of being essentially improved. His style is marked by an elegant simplicity—generally easy and flowing, but occasionally rising to the more artificial, condensed, and elevated strain. See *Life of Samuel Miller, D.D., LL.D.*, by Samuel Miller (1869); *The Biblical Rep. and Princeton Rev.* Jan. 1870, p. 33; *Amer. Presb. Rev.* July, 1869, p. 619; *Presb. Hist. Almanac*, 1863, p. 52; *N. Amer. Rev.* xxviii, 505–531; *Sketches of the Lit. of the United States; London Athen.* 1835, p. 716; Dr. J. W. Francis's *Old New York* (2d. ed. 1858), p. 57; *Life of Archibald Alexander, D.D.*, by his son, p. 380.

Miller, Samuel (2), a minister of the German Reformed Church, was born in Union County, Pa., March 23, 1815. He was licensed in 1842, and ordained the following year. He first labored in Dauphin, and then in Butler County, Pa. In 1852 he removed to Chambersburg, Pa., where he stood in connection with the publication office of the Reformed Church as associate editor of the *Messenger* and *Kirchenzeitung.* After laboring in this capacity about six years, he returned to the pastoral work, residing for several years in Lebanon, and afterwards in Pottsville, Pa. His health failing, he removed to Philadelphia, where he died, Oct. 11, 1873. Mr. Miller was a man of decided talent, genial spirit, and indomitable energy, patience, and perseverance. He is the author of a work of some merit, entitled *Mercersburg and Modern Theology compared*, and of quite a number of articles in the *Mercersburg Review.* See *Ref. Church Messenger*, Nov. 5, 1873. (D. Y. H.)

Miller, Samuel J., an American divine of some note, figured first as missionary to Africa, and later as agent of the Colonization Society. He died in 1818. He was the editor of the celebrated *Report of the Presbyterian Church: The Commonwealth of Pennsylvania vs. Ashbel Green and Others* (Phila. 8vo; new ed. 1855, 8vo, p. 596).

Miller, Thomas, one of the pioneer preachers of American Methodism, largely identified with the spread of Methodist doctrine in Maryland, was born about the year 1770, of Irish parentage, and was reared in the Presbyterian Church. About 1800 he joined the Methodist Episcopal Church, and soon became an official member; in 1808 he was licensed to exhort and preach. His itinerant life commenced in 1809, under the elder Dr. Chandler, and continued till 1848, nearly forty years. In his early ministry he was healthy and strong, and never spared his strength; in fact, his health and strength served him well through all his ministerial course. He was stationed for twelve years at different times in Philadelphia, and held other important charges. His early education was limited, but constant reading and close application, added to great natural abilities, made him an able minister of the New Testament. He was known by the title of "Old Father Miller" far and wide, and he was loved and honored by all who knew him, both in and out of the Church. He was a good friend to the young, and took great interest in the Sabbath-school. He took many a young man by the hand, and helped him into the ministry. He died in 1848.

Miller, Tobias Ham, a Universalist minister and journalist, was born about 1802. In early life he was settled in Maine as an orthodox clergyman, but later he became a firm Universalist. He was the original "Uncle Toby" of the Boston *Carpet Bag;* was on the *Chronicle* (Portsmouth) eighteen years, and the *Portsmouth Journal* twenty years. He died in Portsmouth, New Hampshire, March 30, 1870.

Miller, William, the founder of the *Millerites*

(q. v.), was born at Pittsfield, Mass., in 1781. He enjoyed but slender educational advantages. During the war of 1812 he served as a volunteer with the rank of captain. About 1833, while a resident of Low Hampton, N. Y., he began his career as an apostle of the new doctrine, which taught that the world was coming to an end in 1843. The main argument on which his belief rested was that relative to the termination of the 2300 days in Dan. viii, 14, which he regarded as years. Then considering the seventy weeks in Dan. ix, 24, as the key to the date of the 2300 days of the preceding chapter, and dating the periods B.C. 457, when Artaxerxes, king of Persia, sent up Ezra from his captivity, to restore the Jewish polity at Jerusalem (Ezra vii), and ending the seventy weeks, as commentators generally do, in A.D. 33, with the crucifixion of Christ, he found the remainder of the 2300 days, which was 1810, would end in 1843. For ten years he held forth to this purport, and succeeded in gathering a large number of followers, which is said to have reached fifty thousand, who awaited, with credulous expectation, the appointed day. The result, however, turning out contrary to the teaching of their apostle, the Adventists, as they are sometimes termed, gradually forsook Miller. He died at Low Hampton, Washington County, N. Y., Dec. 20, 1849. His followers esteemed him as a man of more than ordinary mental power, as a cool, sagacious, and honest reasoner, a humble and devoted Christian, a kind and affectionate friend, and a man of great moral and social worth. See MILLERITES.

Miller, William A., D.D., a minister of the Reformed (Dutch) Church, was born at Albany, N. Y., in 1824; graduated at Union College in 1842, and at the theological seminary of the Reformed Church at New Brunswick in 1845. He was a grandson of the "Old Disciple," and nephew of Rev. John E. Miller, whom we notice above, and inherited the robust intellect, strong character, and religious peculiarities of his remarkable family. After a brief settlement as pastor of the Reformed Church of Glenham, N. Y. (1846–49), he became professor of languages, and subsequently principal of the Albany Academy, a celebrated classical and mathematical school (1849–56). From 1856 to 1859 he was the useful pastor of the Reformed Church of Rhinebeck, when his health failed from pulmonary disease, of which he died in 1863. Dr. Miller was a highly-gifted man, a thoroughly accurate and critical scholar, an enthusiastic and competent instructor, a logical, practical, and profitable preacher, and a man who always devoted himself completely to his professional duties. He dealt much in careful expository preaching, for which his turn of mind, classical culture, and love of the truth admirably fitted him. Had his life been spared, he would doubtless have risen to higher positions in the Church which he so greatly adorned by his scholarship and services. He was "chosen in the furnace of affliction," and his graces were beautifully developed by the protracted trials of bereavement, disease, and suffering, and especially by being obliged to desist from all labor for Christ, just when he felt most anxious and best qualified for it. His Christian experiences during his last years and in death were delightful and impressive exhibitions of the triumphs of grace. (W. J. R. T.)

Millerites, or Adventists, as they are sometimes called, are those millenarians [see MILLENNIUM] who adhere to the doctrines as expounded by William Miller (q. v.). When in 1833 he first began to proclaim millennial doctrines, the earnestness of his manner, his evident familiarity with the Scriptures and with history, and the bold confidence with which he proclaimed his views, made so deep and wide an impression that he everywhere left in his wake large numbers examining the evidences for themselves. Among his most ardent followers was Joshua V. Himes, a minister of the Christian connection, who, having become a believer, commenced, in 1840, without subscribers or funds, the publication of a semi-monthly journal entitled *Signs of the Times and Exposition of Prophecy*; and, meeting with success, two years later issued a weekly, under the title of the *Advent Herald*, which largely aided in disseminating the doctrines of the Adventists, who now comprise many thousands, in the United States, British America, and Great Britain. This journal (still published in Boston, Mass.), together with the labors of Mr. Miller, who gave his time, his energies, and his property to the extension of his views, and the efforts of numerous proselytes that everywhere rose up, soon established great numbers in a belief in the general correctness of Mr. Miller's interpretation of the prophecies, and the personal appearing of the Lord was eagerly looked for by some 50,000 followers. Though disappointed at the time set, and frequently from time to time since, there are still many adherents to Miller's views. Their aggregate number is quite respectable, and their efforts for the dissemination of their convictions generous and unfaltering. While as a body they make little or no pretension to influence, as individuals they are necessarily close Bible students; are liberal, according to their means, to the poor and for the support of the Gospel; and noticeable in the main for the modesty and uprightness of their walk, and their careful conformity to virtue and to law. As a body they accept the great leading doctrines of the evangelical Church, and are distinguished only for their peculiar belief in the personal coming of Christ, and his bodily reign with his saints on the earth. They have no creed nor form of discipline other than the Word of God, which they regard as a sufficient rule of faith and duty. They hold conferences, composed of lay and clergy, as often as it is deemed necessary for the discussion of such subjects and measures as the interests of the cause may demand; but these are purely voluntary and advisory, and claim to exercise no authority over the conscience of any.

In round numbers, the Millerites are supposed to comprise in this country from fifteen to twenty thousand, scattered over all the states of the Union, in which estimate those in the different churches, who are numerous, are not included.

General Doctrines of Belief.—1. They cannot see, if, according to Isa. vii, 14, Christ was foretold to be born of a virgin, and it came to pass (Matt. i, 18–25); if, as foretold (Micah v, 2), Christ was literally born in Bethlehem (Matt. ii, 1); if, as foretold (Dan. ix, 26), Messiah came at the expiration of seven weeks and sixty-two weeks (Mark i, 15), and if after the sixty-two weeks Messiah was literally cut off; if, as foretold (Isa. liii, 8, 9), he was cut off out of the land of the living for the transgression of his people, and made his grave with the wicked and with the rich in his death; if (Psa. xvi, 10) Christ's soul was not left in hell, nor did his flesh see corruption; if (Psa. cx, 1) Christ did sit on the right hand of God, and is to sit there till his enemies be made his footstool — if all these predictions have literally come to pass, and they think they have, then they cannot see ground for doubting that the same rule will be observed in the fulfilment of all other predictions relating to Christ.

2. Prophecy (Gen. xxii, 18) foretells Christ as the seed of Abraham, in whom all the families of the earth shall be blessed. It also promises to the seed of Abraham all the land of Canaan, for an everlasting possession, in connection with Abraham himself (Gen. xvii, 8); hence the land is called Emannel's land (Isn. viii, 8). But, when Christ was on earth, he had not where to lay his head. Therefore he must return personally to inherit it.

3. Christ is the predicted Son of David, who is to sit forever on David's throne; he is the Son of David according to the flesh (Psa. cxxxii, 11). But, while on earth, he never sat on David's throne. He went to Jerusalem, as foretold, on an ass's colt; claimed his rights, and was proclaimed king by the children, but rejected by the rulers (Matt. xxi). Hence he must return to enjoy his kingdom and reign over the house of Jacob forever (Luke i, 32, 33).

4. Christ has the promise of the uttermost parts of the earth for his possession (Psa. ii, 8), but he never yet had it. Therefore he must come back to earth to possess it.

5. Prophecy (Dan. vii, 13, 14) points out the coming of Christ to receive his kingdom and dominion over all nations, to be in the "clouds of heaven." But he has never yet come thus. He must, therefore, fulfil the prediction in futurity, at his second advent. He cannot have universal dominion till he does.

6. Christ rose from the dead in the identical body in which he was crucified and buried, and was so identified

(John xx, 24–31). Those who thus identified his person, of flesh and bones, saw him go from earth up into heaven, and a cloud received him out of their sight. They were told by divine messengers that this same Jesus, whom they saw go into heaven, "shall so come back again in like manner" (Acts i, 2–11).

7. That the second advent will be pre-millennial. First, because the millennial reign is placed after the first resurrection (Rev. xx, 1–6), which cannot be till the second advent of Christ. [Those who have part in the first resurrection are saints, and will live forever. The second death has no power on them. But they that are Christ's are to be raised at his coming; and that is the order of the resurrection to follow Christ's resurrection (1 Cor. xv, 23). Christ's coming, and the resurrection of the just, must therefore precede the millennial reign.] Second, because the millennial period follows the casting the beast and the false prophet into the lake of fire, and the shutting up of the devil in the bottomless pit (Rev. xix, 20, and xx, 1–3). Third, because thus, before the millennium, all the great anti-Christian powers are to be put down. The man of sin, however, the son of perdition, is only to be destroyed by the brightness of Christ's coming (2 Thess. ii, 8). The coming of Christ, for his destruction, must therefore be pre-millennial.

8. That there will be two resurrections, a thousand years apart, viz. the "first resurrection," "the resurrection of life," "the resurrection of the just;" and the "resurrection of the rest of the dead," the "resurrection of damnation," the "resurrection of the unjust."

9. That the general view that the millennium will be a thousand years of peace, and be introduced by the conversion of the world to Christ, and consist in his universal spiritual reign; and the millenarian view that though Christ will come and reign personally on earth during the millennium, yet that that period will be one of probation, in which the heathen who had never heard of Christ, and the Jews who have been cut off during the Christian dispensation, will have the Gospel preached to them and be converted, are both unscriptural and not to be received, because both the general and specific teachings of the Bible are against it. Thus the dream of Nebuchadnezzar (Dan. ii) foretells four universal empires which are to fill up the period from then till the everlasting kingdom of God comes and destroys them, and fills the whole earth. But there can be no everlasting kingdom without immortality, which cannot be till the resurrection at the second advent of Christ. The seventh chapter of Daniel presents, in vision, the same four empires, with the divisions and successions of the fourth empire, which only end (ver. 13, 14) when the Son of Man comes in the clouds of heaven to receive his everlasting dominion, which is also universal. Till the judgment, the little blasphemous horn wears out the saints, and prevails against them. So, also, in the twenty-fourth of Matthew, the course of events from the time of Christ to his second coming and the end of the world is given. There were to be wars, famines, pestilences, persecutions of the saints, false prophets, false Christs, abominations, great tribulations, mournings by all the tribes of the earth, the preaching of his Gospel to all the world for a witness to all nations, and *then* the end should come, and they see the Son of Man coming in the clouds of heaven with power and great glory. There is no peace in the prediction till he comes. Therefore he will come personally to judge the world and reign, and not spiritually to convert and save the world. The tares and wheat, too (the righteous and wicked), are to grow together till the end of the world or age, and then they are to be cast off and punished, and the other glorified in the kingdom of God (Matt. xiii, 24–43). For these and many other reasons, they cannot believe in the conversion of the world before the second advent of the Saviour.

10. That the thousand years will be one of judgment rather than probation. For they read in the second Psalm that when the heathen are given to Christ for his inheritance, and the uttermost parts of the earth for his possession, that he is to break or rule them (Rev. xii, 5, and ii, 27) with a rod of iron, and dash them in pieces like a potter's vessel, which they consider to be anything else besides conversion. They also read in Psa. cxlix that all the saints will "bind their kings with chains, and their nobles with fetters of iron, and execute upon them the judgments written." From Isa. lx and Zech. xiv they likewise learn that the worship and service of the heathen will be compulsory service.

11. That final and eternal retribution will be awarded to all nations when the Son of Man comes in his glory (Matt. xxv and Luke xiii).

12. That the promises made to Israel of a yet future and final gathering to the land of Canaan will be literally accomplished, and Israel forever dwell there in peace. But that this cannot be fulfilled before the resurrection of the just, when the believing remnant of Israel, of every generation, including Abraham, Isaac, and Jacob, will be raised from the dead, and restored to their own land. This Ezek. xxxvii declares will be the way the whole house of Israel will be restored: "I will open your graves, and bring you up out of your graves, and bring you into your own land." The resurrection, according to Paul, is "the

hope of Israel." But if the resurrected and glorified Israel are to have the land and dwell there forever, the Jews in flesh and blood, as a nation, cannot have it forever. All the promises, however, of a future return, promise an everlasting possession of the land. But mortal Jews cannot possess it forever—glorified and immortal ones can. Therefore they are the heirs of promise.

13. That the coming of the Lord is at the door for the following reasons, viz.: First, the four great empires are to be succeeded by the kingdom of God; and it is very manifest that the last—the Roman government—has passed its predicted divisions, and must soon end. Second, the waning of the Ottoman or Mohammedan power is another index pointing to the speedy coming of the kingdom of Christ. Third, the universal movements and agitations, the famines, pestilences, and earthquakes, the wars and rumors of wars, together with the signs in the sun, moon, and stars, etc., are conclusive evidence of his speedy approach. Fourth, the Gospel, which was to be preached in all the world, for a witness to all nations, is now completing its work.

14. That the advent doctrine, embracing, as it does, the resurrection of the body, the personal and visible appearance and reign of Christ on earth, the restitution of the heavens and earth to their paradisical state, as the eternal inheritance of the saints, etc., is the only view which will explain and harmonize the Word of God.

The intelligent reader will perceive, however, that most of the above arguments are merely precarious inferences from passages of Scripture whose meaning is greatly disputed. See MILLENNIUM. (J. H. W.)

Milles, JEREMIAH, D.D., a celebrated English divine and antiquary, was born in 1714, and received his preparatory education at Eton. He studied at Corpus Christi College, Oxford, and took the degree of M.A. in 1735, and that of D.D. in 1747. His uncle, Dr. Thomas Milles, bishop of Waterford and Lismore, collated him to a prebend in the cathedral of Waterford, and presented him to a living near that city. In 1762 Dr. Milles was nominated to the deanery of Exeter, and in 1767 he was chosen president of the Society of Antiquaries. He died Feb. 13, 1784. In the "Archæologia" are several communications by him, particularly one entitled *Observations on the Wardrobe Account of the Year* 1483, wherein are contained the deliveries made for the coronation of king Richard III; and another (*Archæol.* iv, 331 sq.) in which he denies the genuineness of the Apamæan medal. In connection with E. Pococke (q. v.), he edited *Inscriptiones Antiquæ* (1752). He also published some of his sermons. Dr. Milles is, however, best known in the literary world by his edition in defence of the antiquity of the "Poems of Rowlay." See Chambers, *Cyclopædia,* s. v.; Allibone, *Dict. of Brit. and Amer. Authors,* ii, 1288.

Millet (הֹחַן, *do'chan,* so called from the dark-green or *smoky* color of the leaf; Sept. κέγχρος, Vulg. *milium*) occurs in Scripture only in Ezek. iv, 9, where the prophet

is directed to take unto him wheat, and barley, and beans, and lentiles, and *millet,* and fitches, and to put them into one vessel, and to make bread thereof for himself. All the grains enumerated in this verse continue to form the chief articles of diet in the East at the present day, as they appear to have done in ancient times. The Hebrew word *dochan* is identical with the Arabic *dukhun,* which is applied in the present day by the Arabs to a small grain cultivated from the middle of Europe to the most southern part of India. This is the common millet, *Panicum miliaceum* of botanists, which is sometimes cultivated in England on account of the seeds being used for feeding birds and poultry. But the grain is usually imported from the Mediterranean. In India it is cultivated in the cold weather, that is, in the same season with wheat and barley, and is an article of diet with the inhabitants. The culms are erect, from two to four feet high, the whole plant being very hairy; leaves large, with long sheaths, which involve most part of the culm; panicle oblong, much branched, bending down with the weight of the grain; glumes cuspidate; corol three-valved, adventitious valve emarginate; seed oval and smooth, colored longitudinally with five streaks. The name, *miliaceum,* is said to have been applied to this plant from its producing such a quantity of grain, as if one stalk bore a thousand seeds. Tournefort says (*Voyage,* ii, 95) that in the isle of Samos the inhabitants, in preparing their bread, knead together one half wheat and the other half barley and millet mixed together. It is also an article of diet both in Persia and India. Forskål applies the name *dukhun* to another corn-grass, which he first found in a garden at Rosetta, cultivated on account of its seed being given as food to birds. Afterwards he found it commonly cultivated in Arabia. It grows to a great size, being about five cubits in height, with seeds of the size of rice. To it he has given the name of *Holcus dochna,* but the plant is as yet unknown to botanists. The Biblical "millet" is confounded by many writers with the broom-corn varieties, which belong to the genus Sorghum, a species of which is the modern Egyptian *durra.* It is possible that the Heb. *dochan* includes the common species, *Sor-*

Panicum Miliaceum.

Sorghum Vulgare.

ghum vulgare. There is, however, little doubt that the true *dukhun* of Arab authors is the above-described *Panicum miliaceum.* This is so universally cultivated in the East as one of their smaller corn-grasses that it is most likely to be the kind chiefly alluded to in the passage of Ezekiel. Two cultivated species of *Panicum* are named as occurring in Palestine, viz. *P. miliaceum* and *P. italicum* (Strand's *Flor. Palœst.* Nos. 35, 37). The genera *Sorghum* and *Panicum* belong to the natural order *Gramineæ,* perhaps the most important order in the vegetable kingdom. See Celsii *Hierobot.* i, 453 sq.; Oedmann, *Verm. Samml.* v, 92 sq.; Niebuhr, *Arabia,* p. 295; *Trav.* i, 158; Forskal, *Flora Ægypt.* p. 174; Wellsted, *Trav.* i, 295; Gesenius, *Thes. Heb.* p. 333; *Penny Cyclopædia,* s. v. Panicum.

Millet, SIMON-GERMAIN, a French Benedictine, was born at Venisy, near Sens, in 1575. He died near Paris, June 28, 1647. But little is known of his life's history. The following are his works: *Les Dialogues de Saint-Grégoire* (translated into French; Paris, 1624, 1644, 8vo):—*Le Trésor sacré, ou inventaire des saintes reliques etau tres précieux joyaux de l'église et du trésor de Saint-Denys* (Paris, 1638, 12mo):—*Vindicata Ecclesiæ Gallicanæ de suo Areopagita Dionysio Gloria* (Paris, 1638, 8vo):—*Ad Dissertationem nuper evulgatam de Duobus Dionysiis Responsio,* against the canon of Launoy (Paris, 1642, 8vo).—*Hist. Litter. de la Congregation de Saint-Maur,* p. 28. See Hoefer, *Nouv. Biog. Gén.* s. v.

Milletière. See LAMILETIÈRE.

Milligan, JAMES, D.D., a Presbyterian divine, was born in Dalmellington, Ayrshire, Scotland, Aug. 7, 1785. At the age of fourteen he united with the Established Church of Scotland. His early education was obtained while out upon the moor watching the sheep, reciting two or three times a week to a teacher in a neighboring village. In 1801, dissatisfied with the government of Scotland, he emigrated to America, and came to Westmoreland County, Pa. After engaging in mercantile life for some months, he entered Jefferson College, Pa. His funds becoming exhausted, he was obliged to leave, and went to Greensburg, Pa.; instituted an academy, taught eighteen months, realized a sum sufficient to complete his collegiate course, and graduated with honors. He next accepted a call as teacher of languages in the Philadelphia University. While there he pursued his theological studies in the Reformed Presbyterian Seminary. He was licensed by the Northern Presbytery in 1811, and in 1812 was ordained pastor of Coldenham Congregation, Orange County, N. Y.; in 1818 he accepted a call to the Scotch Covenanter Congregation at Ryegate, Caledonia County, Vt.; thence he went to New Alexandria, Pa., in 1839; and in 1848 to Eden, Ill., where he continued to preach until 1855. He died about the year 1861. Dr. Milligan was a warm friend of the Scotch Covenanters. He was instrumental in inaugurating the first temperance reform movement in the State of Vermont; and was first also to introduce the scriptural office of deacon in the American Reformed Presbyterian Church. His publications are, *A Narrative of the Secession Controversy in Vermont:—Sermon on Free Agency:—Sermon on the Prospects of a True Christian in a Sinful World:—A Defence of Infant Baptism.* See Wilson, *Presb. Hist. Almanac,* 1863, p. 188.

Millington, WILLIAM, D.D., an eminent Anglican divine of the Reformatory period, and one of the most learned men of his day, was a native of Pocklington, Yorkshire. He was ordained priest March 8, 1420. He took his doctor's degree at Cambridge, and is said to have been a member of Clare Hall, in that university; but however that may be, certain it is that in 1443 he was appointed the provost of King's College. This important position, however, he voluntarily resigned in 1446, on a point of conscience. The oft-repeated statement that he was deprived of the provostship for unduly favoring natives of Yorkshire is without foundation.

It is said that on leaving King's he retired to Clare Hall. He died in May, 1466, and was buried in St. Edward's Church, Cambridge. An interesting memoir of Dr. Millington, by George Williams, B.D., was communicated to the Cambridge Antiquarian Society in 1858.

Million (רְבָבָה, *rebabah',* Gen. xxiv, 60), *ten thousand,* as elsewhere rendered.

Mil'lo (Heb. always with the art. *ham-millo',* הַמִּלּוֹא, *the fulness;* Sept. [Alex.] in 1 Kings ix only ἡ Μελίο; Vulg. *Mello*), properly a mound or rampart, as being filled in with stones and earth; hence a fortress or castle; applied to two structures or fortifications:

(*a*) According to Gesenius (*Thes. Heb.* p. 789), a part of the citadel of Jerusalem, probably the rampart or intrenchment; or, as Winer thinks (*Wörterb.* s. v.), the tower afterwards called Hippicus (2 Sam. v, 9; 1 Kings ix, 15, 24; xi, 27; 1 Chron. xi, 8; 2 Chron. xxxii, 5). In the last of these texts, where David is said to have restored or fortified the Millo "of" (not "in") the city of David, the Sept. has τὸ ἀνάλημμα τῆς πόλεως, "the *fortification* of the city of David;" in the other passages it has simply ἄκρα, the *mound* or tower. The Targum merely Chaldaizes the Heb. term (מְלֵיתָא, *vallum*). "Both name and thing seem to have been already in existence when the city was taken from the Jebusites by David. His first occupation, after getting possession, was to build 'round about, from the Millo and to the house' (A. V. 'inward,' 2 Sam. v, 9); or, as the parallel passage has it, 'he built the city round about, and from the Millo round about' (1 Chron. xi, 8). Its repair or restoration was one of the great works for which Solomon raised his 'levy' (1 Kings ix, 15, 24; xi, 27); and it formed a prominent part of the fortifications by which Hezekiah prepared for the approach of the Assyrians (2 Chron. xxxii, 5)." The same place is probably meant by the "house of Millo," where Joash was killed (2 Kings xii, 21). Others are of the opinion that Millo was the name of a valley in Jerusalem, which separated ancient Jebus from the city of David, but which was afterwards filled up by David and Solomon (Barclay, *City of the Great King,* p. 113). Schwarz (*Palest.* p. 241) holds that it was on the eastern declivity towards the spring of Siloam (reading Shiloah for Silla). The most natural impression from the notices is that it was some region or space adjacent to Mount Zion, perhaps that portion of the Tyropœon enclosed by the first wall, the bridge, and the Temple. (See Lightfoot, *Works,* ii, 189; Hamelsveld, *Bibl. Geogr.* ii, 46 sq.; Ewald, *Isr. Gesch.* iii, 70; Strong's *Harm. and Expos. of the Gospels,* Append. ii, p. 24; Schulz, *Jerusalem,* p. 80.) See JERUSALEM.

(*b*) The fortress or citadel of Shechem, all the occupants or garrison of which joined in proclaiming Abimelech their king (Judg. ix, 6, 20). See BETH-MILLO; SILLA.

Mills, Abraham, LL.D., a prominent American author, was born in Dutchess County, N. Y., in 1796. After having received a thorough academic education, he opened a classical school in New York City. He had not been long engaged in this school when he was appointed professor of mathematics and philosophy in the Baptist Literary and Theological Institute, then established in New York. Three years after, when the institute was transferred to Hamilton, N. Y., Mills severed his connection, and flourished as a highly-esteemed teacher and lecturer on rhetoric and belles-lettres. He died July 8, 1867. Mills issued text-books on the topics on which he gave instruction. The honorary degree of LL.D. was conferred on him by Madison University. He deserves a place here on account of his *Compendium of the History of the Ancient Hebrews* (1856). See Drake, *Dict. of Amer. Biogr.* s. v.; Appleton's *Annual Cyclop.* 1867, p. 511.

Mills, Henry, D.D., a Presbyterian divine, was born at Morristown, N. J., March 12, 1786; pursued his preparatory studies in his native town; graduated at Princeton College in 1802; for a considerable time taught in the academy at Morristown, and also at Elizabethtown, N. J.; was tutor for two years at Princeton College; studied theology with the Rev. Dr. James Richards; was licensed by the Presbytery of New Jersey, and in 1816 was ordained pastor of the Presbyterian Church in Woodbridge, N. J. In 1821 he was called to the professorship of Biblical criticism in the theological seminary at Auburn, N. Y., where he continued to perform his duties with eminent ability until 1854, when he resigned, and was made professor emeritus. He died June 10, 1867. Dr. Mills was a man of marked characteristics—impressive in personal appearance, instructive in conversation, sharp in intellect. As a preacher, his style was simple, chaste, and direct. As a scholar, he was most eminent—thoroughly versed in Hebrew and master of the German language. He published in 1845 *Horæ Germanicæ, a Version of German Hymns.* See Wilson, *Presb. Hist. Almanac,* 1868, p. 218.

Mills, Nathaniel B., an early and eminent minister of the Methodist Episcopal Church. He was born in Newcastle County, Del., Feb. 23, 1766; was converted in 1783; entered the Baltimore Conference in 1787; in 1790 was stationed at Hartford, Conn.; in 1804 at Baltimore; filled various important circuits, etc., until 1835, when he became superannuated. He died in Carroll County, Md., Feb. 20, 1845. He preached with great zeal and success for nearly sixty years.—*Minutes of Conferences,* iii, 594; Stevens, *Memorials of Methodism.*

Mills, Samuel, a minister of the Methodist Episcopal Church, was born in Northampton County, N. C., in 1780; was converted in 1800; entered the itinerancy in 1804; was stationed at Columbia in 1806, at Charleston in 1809, at Milledgeville in 1810, and at Camden in 1811, where he died, June 8, 1811. He was a plain, earnest preacher, possessed of good abilities, and "a witness of sanctification, which he frequently pressed on his hearers." See *Minutes of Conferences,* i, 206.

Mills, Samuel John (1), a Congregational minister, was born May 16, 1743, in Kent, Conn. He graduated at Yale College in 1764, and was ordained June 29, 1769, in Torringford, Conn., where he resided until his death, May 11, 1833. He published a few occasional sermons, and two sermons on the religious sentiments of Christ, in a volume entitled *Sermons Collected* (1797). See Sprague, *Annals of the American Pulpit,* i, 672.

Mills, Samuel John (2), popularly called the "Father of Foreign Mission Work in Christian America," an efficient minister of the Congregational Church, was the son of the minister of Torrington, Conn., and was born April 21, 1783. He was educated at Williams College (class of 1809). He next entered the theological seminary, having decided to preach the Gospel, and while at school in Andover his mind was deeply impressed with the importance of foreign missions, and he endeavored to awaken a similar feeling in the hearts of his fellow-students. He united with Judson, Newell, Nott, and Hall in a resolution to undertake a foreign mission. In 1812 and 1813 he and J. F. Schermerhorn made a missionary tour in the Western States. He was ordained, with other missionaries, at Newburyport, June 21, 1815. He ascertained in March, 1815, that not a Bible could be found for sale or to be given away in New Orleans; he thereupon distributed many Bibles in French and English, and visited the sick soldiers. Finding that seventy or eighty thousand families at the South and West were destitute of a Bible, he suggested at the close of his report the formation of a national society like the British. His efforts contributed to the establishment of the *American Bible Society,* May 8, 1816. The plan of the *United Foreign Mission Society,* which, however, accomplished but little, originated with him while residing with Dr. Griffin at Newark, N. J., as did also the African school, which existed a few years

at Parsippany, near Newark. He attended the first meeting of the Colonization Society, Jan. 1, 1817, which was established by his and Dr. Finley's exertions, and Mills was at that time appointed, together with Dr. Burgess, to visit England, and explore the coast of Africa for the society. He sailed in November, 1817, and in a wonderful manner escaped shipwreck on the coast of France. He sailed from England for Africa Feb. 2, 1818, and arrived on the coast March 12. After a laborious inspection of more than two months, he embarked on his return in the brig Success, May 22, 1818. A severe cold, which he took early in June, was succeeded by a fever, and he died at sea, June 16, 1818. He was buried in the depths of the ocean. See Spring, *Memoirs of John Samuel Mills* (N. Y. 1820, 8vo); Sprague, *Annals Amer. Pulpit,* ii, 566; *Cyclop. Missions,* p. 263 sq.; Anderson, *Hist. Missions of A. B. For. M. in India* (1874).

Mills, Thornton A., D.D., a Presbyterian divine, was born in Paris, Ky., September, 1810. He early enjoyed excellent educational advantages; graduated at Miami University, Oxford, Ohio, in 1830; studied theology for a short time in Lane Theological Seminary, and afterwards privately, and was licensed in 1833. He labored for some time in Frankfort, Ky., and in 1836 was installed pastor of the Third Presbyterian Church, Cincinnati. In 1848 he purchased *The Watchman of the Valley,* and continued to edit that paper, first under the name of *Central Watchman,* and later of *Central Christian Herald,* until January, 1853, when it was bought by the synods of Ohio, Indiana, Cincinnati, and Wabash. During 1853 he was secretary and general agent for the Church Erection Committee; in 1854 accepted a call to the Second Church, in Indianapolis; in 1856 was chosen as general secretary of the Permanent Committee of the General Assembly on Education for the Ministry, to which work he devoted the remainder of his life. He died June 21, 1867. Dr. Mills was a man of firm grasp of mind, clear and positive views of truth, and indomitable energy and perseverance. See Wilson, *Presb. Hist. Almanac,* 1868, p. 220; *Meth. Qu. Rev.* Jan. 1872, p. 27. (J. L. S.)

Mills, William, an early minister of the Methodist Church, was born in Monmouth County, N. J., Aug. 26, 1747; entered the United States army in 1776; suffered various vicissitudes during the war until he was carried a prisoner to Europe, whence he returned after the war; was converted through Methodist instrumentality in 1792; entered the itinerancy at Philadelphia in 1799, and died at Long Branch, N. J., Dec. 5, 1813. He was a most amiable and excellent man, and a very successful preacher. Several extensive revivals resulted from his labors. See *Minutes of Conferences,* i, 239.

Mills, William Robert, a minister of the Methodist Episcopal Church, was born in Alexandria, Va., July 5, 1816. He enjoyed the advantages of a liberal academical training, and was for some time a student at William and Mary College. At an early age he was converted, and shortly after became fully persuaded of a divine call to the ministry; was licensed to preach, and was admitted into the Baltimore Conference in the spring of 1840. He labored successively on Berwick Circuit; in 1841 on Huntington Circuit; 1842, Northumberland; 1843, Lycoming; 1844, Lock Haven; 1845–46, Penn's Valley; 1847, Northumberland; 1848–49, Warrior's Mark; 1850–51, Huntingdon; 1852–53, Lewistown Circuit; 1854–55, Newport; 1856, Mercersburg; 1857–58, Liberty, Md.; 1859–60, East Baltimore Station; 1861–62, North Baltimore Station; 1863–65, Altoona; 1866–67, Lewisburg; 1868, Carlisle; 1869, York. In the last-named place he died, Dec. 18, 1869. Mills was a faithful pastor and an eloquent preacher. His sermons evinced deep research, were argumentative, and logically arranged, and enlivened with illustrative incidents. See *Minutes of Conferences,* 1870, p. 54.

Millstone (רֶכֶב, *re'keb,* usually a *chariot,* hence the "upper millstone" or *rider,* Deut. xxiv. 6; more fully

כֶּלַח רֶכֶב, Judg. ix, 53; 2 Sam. xi, 21; in Job xli, 24 there is no Hebrew word corresponding; in Isa. xlvii, 2; Jer. xxv, 10, רֵחַיִם; elsewhere rendered "mill;" Gr. μύλος). See MILL.

Milman, Henry Hart, D.D., one of the leaders of the Broad Church party in the Anglican communion of our day, an ecclesiastic of distinction also, both as a historian and a poet, was the youngest son of Sir Francis Milman, physician to George III, and was born in London Feb. 10, 1791. He was educated at Eton, and afterwards at Brasenose College, Oxford, where he took the degrees of B.A. and M.A., and of which he was elected a fellow. He wrote several poems, and secured much distinction by his efforts. In 1817 he took holy orders, and was appointed vicar of St. Mary's, Reading. In 1820 Mr. Milman published *The Fall of Jerusalem*, a dramatic poem, founded on Josephus's narrative of the siege of the sacred city. This, in some respects his most beautiful poetical production, established his reputation. In 1821 he was elected professor of poetry in the University of Oxford. He now published three other dramatic poems: *The Martyr of Antioch, Belshazzar*, and *Anne Boleyn.* In 1827 he published his sermons, delivered as the Bampton Lecture, and entitled *The Character and Conduct of the Apostles considered as the Evidence of Christianity* (8vo), and in 1829, without his name, *The History of the Jews* (Lond. and N. Y. 3 vols. 18mo). This work was written in so liberal a spirit that orthodox ecclesiastics could hardly fail to be offended. Its weak point was a want of adequate learning, especially in the department of Biblical criticism. A new edition, greatly improved, and more critical, yet still far from being very accurate, or built on solid foundations, prefaced by an interesting introduction, was published in 1863 (Lond. and N. Y. 3 vols. 12mo). In this new form the work has had a large circulation both among Jews and Gentiles. It is to this day the only worthy record of the "chosen people of God" in the English tongue. In 1840 he came again before the public as a historian; this time with a *History of Christianity from the Birth of Christ to the Abolition of Paganism in the Roman Empire* (Lond. 3 vols. 8vo; N. Y., Harpers, 1 vol. 8vo). In this work he professes to view Christianity as a historian, in its moral, social, and political influences, referring to its doctrines no further than is necessary for explaining the general effect of the system. It is a far better effort than his previous work, and marks the advance of an accomplished and liberal-minded student. His scholarly attainments received the acknowledgment of the Church by various appointments. In 1849, after having been honored successively with the rectory of St. Margaret's, Westminster, and the canonship of Westminster, he was promoted to the deanery of St. Paul's. This position he held until his death, Sept. 24, 1868.

The works already mentioned will secure for dean Milman an honorable place in the literary history of England, but they are by no means his ablest productions. His greatest work, and one of the most valuable productions in the English language, is his *History of Latin Christianity, including that of the Popes to the Pontificate of Nicholas V* (Lond. and N. Y. 1854, 8 vols. 8vo); a continuation of the author's *History of Christianity*, and yet in itself a complete work. To give it that completeness, dean Milman has gone over the history of Christianity in Rome during the first four centuries. It brings the history down to the close of the pontificate of Nicholas V, that is, to 1455. It is a work of great learning, liberality, and chastened eloquence; it displays a broad grasp of human nature in its religious workings; something of the philosopher, and still more of the poet, is seen in the strong and vivid spirit of sympathy with which he deals with men of the most different opinions. The work has secured for its author a position in the first rank of English historians. "No such work," says the *Qu. Rev.* of London, "has appeared in English ecclesi-

astical literature—none which combines such breadth of view with such depth of research, such high literary and artistic eminence with such patient and elaborate investigation." Perhaps we should add the estimate of one of our own historical writers, than whom no greater or more competent critic could be heard; we refer to William H. Prescott (*Philip II*, ii, 500, n. 69), who says of it: "One of the most remarkable works of the present age, in which the author reviews, with curious erudition and in a profoundly philosophical spirit, the various changes that have taken place in the Roman hierarchy; and, while he fully exposes the manifold errors and corruptions of the system, he shows throughout that enlightened charity which is the most precious of Christian graces, as, unhappily, the rarest." Dean Milman also earned the gratitude of the Christian world by an edition of Gibbon's *Decline and Fall of the Roman Empire*, which presented the great historian with more ample illustration than he had before received, and set at rest many exceptions taken by Gibbon against Christianity. The notes were further elucidated and verified by Dr. W. Smith, and Gibbon's works are now sought for only in this amended form. Other works of Milman are a *Life of Keats*, and *Hebrew Prophecy*, a sermon, published in 1865. He also edited an illustrated review of Horace, with a Life of the poet; translations from the Agamemnon of Æschylus, Bacchanals of Euripides, etc. He was a frequent contributor to the [London] *Quarterly Review*. A collected edition of his "Poetical Works," including *Fazio*, a tragedy, which has frequently been on the stage, was published in 1840, and, besides the works above mentioned and his smaller poems, contains the *Nala and Damayanti*, translated from the Sanscrit. Since his death *Annals of St. Paul's Cathedral* (1868), and *Savonarola, Erasmus, and other Essays* (1870), have been published.

Dean Milman was also an important contributor to English hymnology. Some of his productions are familiar to every English-speaking Christian; in the Anglican Church he is a particular favorite, and as the author of "When our heads are bowed with woe," "Bound upon the accursed tree," "Ride on, ride on in majesty," and the more subjective composition, "Brother, thou art gone before us" (from the *Martyr of Antioch*), has established a household name, and has secured popular love. As he occupied for years the pulpit of one of the largest and most influential of English churches, we append the following portrayal of dean Milman from the *Saturday Rev.* (Oct. 1868): "He was no speaker; he had not the very least of platform tricks; with a superb scorn, he disdained the arts which win fame at public meetings; and in a certain sense he was not a good preacher. He was too refined, too much habituated to limitations, too sensitive, and too careful, to be able to fling out those broad statements which must be hazarded by the popular preacher. But in a certain sort of preaching he was first-rate. His eulogium on the duke of Wellington—we doubt whether it is published—struck us, as we were fortunate enough to hear it, as equal to the best of the French models of pulpit eloquence." See Vapereau, *Dict. des Contemporains*, s. v.; Allibone, *Dict. of Brit. and Amer. Authors*, s. v.; *English Cyclop.* s. v.; *Men of the Times*, s. v.; Hagenbach, *Hist. Doctrines*, ii, 423 sq.; Schaff, *Christ in Song*, p. 206–209; Lecky, *Hist. of European Morals from Augustus to Charlemagne* (Preface) (1869); *Edinb. Rev.* Jan. 1858; Jan. 1864; and Jan. 1869; *Lond. Qu. Rev.* April, 1816; July, 1818; May, 1820; and April, 1869; *Blackwood's Mag.* March and July, 1822; Dec. 1868; *North Brit. Rev.* Nov. 1854; March, 1869: *Fraser's Mag.* Oct. 1854; *Christian Remembrancer*, 1854, Oct. p. 266; Kitto, *Journ. of Sac. Lit.* 1854, Oct.; *Westminst. Rev.* 1870, Oct. p. 219; *Princeton Rev.* 1842, p. 238; *Pen Pictures of popular English Preachers* (Lond. 1852), p. 175–178.

Milne, COLIN, a Scottish divine, noted for his attainments in natural science, was born at Aberdeen, Scotland, about 1744. He was educated at Marischal

College under the supervision of his uncle, Dr. Campbell, who was both principal and divinity professor at the college. After completing his studies there, Milne entered the University of Edinburgh. He joined the Church of England, and by the aid of the duke of Northumberland obtained the rectory of North Chapel, in Sussex. His pulpit eloquence soon made him widely known, and he received the appointment of preacher to the London Hospital, and also the lectureship of Deptford, a position which he held for many years. He died in 1815. His sermon preached at the anniversary meeting of the Royal Humane Society was published in 1779 (8vo). A volume of his sermons was published in 1780 (8vo). His other publications were in a line foreign to our work.

Milner, Isaac (1), D.D., an Anglican divine of note, eminent for his piety as well as for his great attainments in divinity and the sciences, was born of humble parentage near Leeds, Yorkshire, in 1751. As a boy of six he entered the grammar school of his native place, but the straitened circumstances of his family obliged the removal of Isaac, and he was transferred from the schoolroom to the factory. Though apprenticed to a weaver, he continued to devote his leisure hours to study, and gradually acquired sound learning. His brother, the noted Joseph Milner (q. v.), who had enjoyed many educational advantages, was in 1767 appointed head-master of the grammar school at Hull. By him Isaac was relieved of his obligation at the factory, and afforded opportunity to continue his studies in the position of assistant to Joseph. In 1770 Isaac was admitted a student at Queen's College, Cambridge, and there received his degree in 1774, and was appointed tutor. He received among his pupils Mr. Pitt and Mr. Wilberforce, with whom he travelled abroad, and became the honored instrument in the conversion of the latter. See WILBERFORCE. In 1775 Isaac Milner was elected fellow of Queen's College. In 1783, returning to the university, he was chosen professor of natural philosophy, and master of his college in 1788, when he proceeded doctor in divinity. In 1791 he was appointed to the deanery of Carlisle. He was elected vice-chancellor of the university in 1792, and six years afterwards became Lucasian professor of mathematics. He died at the house of Wilberforce, at Kensington Gore, April 1, 1820. Dean Milner wrote, besides several papers in the *Philosophical Transactions*, and the continuation of his brother's *Church History*, the following works: *Animadversions on Dr. Haweis's Impartial History of the Church of Christ* (1800, 8vo):—*Strictures on some of the Publications of the Rev. Herbert Marsh, intended as a Reply to some of his Objections against the Bible Society* (1813, 8vo):— *Essays on Human Liberty; Sermons* (2 vols. 8vo); besides works of a mathematical kind. "Dean Milner was possessed of very extensive and accurate learning, which he always had at his command. He had great talents for conversation, and a dignified simplicity of manner. His religious and political principles agreed pretty closely with his brother's." See *Meth. Qu. Rev.* 1840 (July), p. 407; Jones, *Christ. Biog.* s. v.; *English Cyclop.* s. v.; Allibone, *Dict. of Brit. and Amer. Authors,* s. v.; Mary Milne, *Life of Isaac Milner* (1842).

Milner, Isaac (2), a minister of the Methodist Episcopal Church, South, was born in Yorkshire, England, April 2, 1818. His parents were of the old English Wesleyan stock, and young Milner was educated with great piety and care. In his seventeenth year he was converted, and, believing himself called of God to preach the Gospel, he hesitatingly prepared to enter the ministry. While human reasoning held him back, divine love impelled him forward. He began his elementary studies alone and after the midnight hour, and in this way gained his education. Being of a studious habit, he soon acquired a storehouse of knowledge, and was numbered among the promising youths of the ministry.

Seized with a desire to visit America, he came to New Orleans in 1848. Many and severe trials awaited him in his new home. He was taken sick of typhoid fever, and for three months he lay hovering between life and death. After his recovery he was for a time a member of the Memphis Conference. He afterwards joined the Tennessee Conference, and remained a member of it till his death, which occurred near Columbia, Tenn., June 16, 1872. Isaac Milner was one of the most popular Methodist preachers. He knew no failure; if he ever did, his audience knew nothing about it. In every department he proved himself to be a man of great ability and usefulness. His mind was naturally vigorous and receptive; his memory tenacious; his well-balanced mind, like a rich, productive field, yielded a wealth of thought, independent of the production of other men. His fancy was vigorous, his figures original and bold— always pleasing, often overwhelming. Milner served his Church in various ways, but in every department he proved himself not only a workman that needeth not to be ashamed, but a workman of great ability, usefulness, and popularity. See *Minutes of the Annual Conferences of the M. E. Church, South,* 1872, p. 715 sq.

Milner, John (1), an English nonjuring divine of note, was born near Halifax in 1627 or 1628. He was educated at Christ's College, Cambridge, and after his graduation took orders. He was, however, obliged to live retired till the Restoration, when he obtained the curacy of Beeston, and in 1673 was appointed vicar of Leeds. In 1681 he was chosen prebendary of Ripon; but, on refusing the oaths at the Revolution, he quitted his preferments and went to St. John's College, Cambridge, where he died, Feb. 16, 1702. Dr. Milner was a prolific writer, and published several controversial theological tracts and critical dissertations upon various portions of the Scriptures. Of his numerous works we mention the following: *Church History of Palestine from the Birth of Christ to Diocletian* (1688, 4to):— *Conjectanea in Isaiam* ix, 1, 2:—*De Nethinim sive Nethinæis:—Defence of Archbishop Usher against Drs. Cary and Vossius:—Account of Mr. Locke's Religion:—Animadversions on Le Clerc's Reflections upon our Saviour and his Apostles.* See Watson, *Halifax;* Thoresby, *Vicaria Leodensis,* p. 114 sq.; Wilford, *Memorials;* Cooper, *Biog. Dict.* p. 869; Allibone, *Dict. of Brit. and Amer. Authors,* ii, 1293.

Milner, John (2), D.D., more properly named MILLER, an eminent Romish theologian and antiquary, was born in London, Oct. 14, 1752. He was educated at the schools of Sedgley Park and Edgbaston, and then went to study theology at Douai. Having taken orders, he was in 1779 attached to Winchester Chapel. Although a zealous Roman Catholic, he refused to join in the efforts made by his Church in England in 1788 and in 1791 to obtain from Parliament the repeal of the ancient laws against Roman Catholics. In after-times he was engaged in numerous controversies, both with Protestant theologians and with members of the Roman Catholic committee, who accused him of too great vivacity in his discussions. He declared against the right of the king of vetoing the appointment of bishops, and, together with the Irish Roman Catholic clergy, obstinately refused to yield the point to the solicitations of his own party. In 1814 he even took a journey to Rome, to consult with the pope on this point. The esteem in which he was held in the midst of these difficulties is evinced by the appointment he received in 1803 as apostolic vicar of the midland district, under the title of bishop of Castabala *in partibus.* Dr. Milner settled at Wolverhampton, where he died, April 19, 1826. He was quite distinguished as an archæologist, belonged to the Antiquarian Society, and contributed many learned papers to the *Archæologia.* He wrote *The History, Civil and Ecclesiastical, and Survey of the Antiquities of Winchester* (1798, 2 vols. 4to; 2d ed., corrected and enlarged, 1809, 2 vols. 4to):—*The End of Religious Controversy,* addressed to Dr. Burgess, Bishop of St. David's, in answer to his Protestant Catechism (1818; 2d ed., revised, 1819, 8vo; transl. into French under the title Excellence de la Religion Catholique, Paris, 1823, 2 vols. 8vo):—A Vindication of the End of Religious Controversy from the Exceptions of Bishop Burgess and the Rev. R. Grier (Lond. 1822, 8vo):—Letters to a Prebendary, being an Answer to Reflections on Popery by the Rev. John Sturges, LL.D. (Winchester, 1800, 4to):—A short Description of the Hospital of St. Cross, near Winchester (21st ed. Winchester; no date):—An Historical and Critical Inquiry into the Existence and Character of St. George, Patron of England (1795, 8vo):—A Treatise on the Ecclesiastical History of England during the Middle Ages (1811, royal 8vo):—Letter to the Author of a Book called A candid and impartial Sketch of the Government of Pope Clement XIV (Lond. 1785, 8vo):—Divine Right of the Episcopacy (1791, 8vo):— The Case of Conscience solved, or the Catholic Claims proved to be compatible with the Coronation Oath (1802, 8vo):—Inquiry into certain Opinions concerning the Catholic Inhabitants and the Antiquities of Ireland (1808, 8vo). Of all the advocates of the papal Church, no one has displayed more learning and acuteness than Milner, though not unmixed with partisan gall and misrepresentation. See Lond. Qu. Rev. 1810 (May), 1811 (Oct.); Rose, New Biog. Dict. s. v.; Darling, Cyclop. Bibliog. ii, 2771; Hoefer, Nouv. Biog. Générale, xxxv, 554; Allibone, Dict. of Brit. and Amer. Authors, s. v.; Dr. Husenbeth, Life of Dr. Milner (Dublin, 1862, 8vo).

Milner, Joseph, an eminent Anglican divine and ecclesiastical historian, the elder brother of Isaac, was born near Leeds, Yorkshire, Jan. 2, 1744. He was sent to the grammar school at Leeds, where, by his industry and talents, among which a memory of most extraordinary power was conspicuous, he gained the warm regard of his master. Milner's father had always been in very narrow circumstances; his death only made the task greater; but, by the assistance of some gentlemen in Leeds, whose children Milner had lately engaged in teaching, and by the offer of the office of chapel-clerk at Catharine Hall, Cambridge, he was enabled to enter that hall at the age of eighteen. In the year 1766 he took his degree of B.A., and gained the chancellor's second gold medal for classical knowledge. He was made assistant in the school, and afterwards the curate of the Rev. Mr. Atkinson, of Thorp Arch, near Tadcaster. While in this place he undertook the completion of an epic poem, entitled Davideis, which he had commenced at Cambridge. It was submitted to Dr. (afterwards bishop) Hurd, who highly complimented the author on the talent it displayed, but advised him to defer its publication. On entering into deacon's orders, Milner was elected head-master of the grammar school, and afternoon lecturer of the principal church of Hull. In this position he succeeded beyond the most ardent expectations of his dearest friends, especially in the capacity of an instructor, and the school increased under his care. About the year 1770 Joseph Milner embraced the sentiments of the evangelical party in the Church of England. This change in his religious views brought upon him neglect, and in some cases open opposition from many among the upper classes who had once been his admirers and friends; but his church was soon crowded with others, chiefly from the lower orders of the people, in whose sentiments and manners his preaching produced a striking change; and at length he not only recovered the esteem of his fellow-townsmen, but lived to see his own religious sentiments become so popular in the town that many of the pulpits of the churches were filled by his friends and pupils, and he himself was chosen vicar of Hull by the mayor and corporation. Mr. Milner had been appointed vicar of North Ferriby, near Hull; subsequently he had been appointed to the vicarship of the Holy Trinity, Cambridge. His election as vicar of Hull occurred only a few weeks before his death, which took place on the 15th

of November, 1797. A monument, executed by Bacon, was erected to his memory in the high church of Hull by several of his friends and former pupils. The excellences of Mr. Milner's personal character were of the highest order. He was deeply pious, upright in all his conduct, singularly open and sincere, and kind, cheerful, and amusing in social life. In his political principles he was strongly attached to the established order of things in Church and State.

His principal works are Gibbon's Account of Christianity considered (1781, 8vo), in which he not only exposes the sophistry of that infidel theologian, but gives the true character of the religion which he had attempted to undermine:—Some Passages in the Life of Wm. Howard (1785, 8vo):—Essays on the Influence of the Holy Spirit (1789, 12mo):—Practical Sermons (1801, 2 vols. 8vo; 2d edit. revised, corrected, and enlarged by Rev. Isaac Milner, D.D., dean of Carlisle, 1801–23, 3 vols. 8vo):—The Way of Salvation, or the Christian Doctrine of Justification explained (Lond. 1814, 24mo); and, lastly, a History of the Church of Christ—a work by which Dr. Joseph Milner is principally known. He lived to complete only four volumes; but the task was taken up by his brother Isaac, who completed it by the addition of another volume, in which he was largely aided by the MS. left at his command. The work extends from the rise of Christianity to the Reformation. The first edition appeared in 5 vols. 8vo, 1794 to 1812, and a second edition in 1810. The latest edition was published at London in 1847, 8vo. It was also translated into French (1836–8, 3 vols. 12mo) and German (1804). As it omits nearly all discussion of ecclesiastical controversies, as well as of rites, ceremonies, and forms of Church government—in fact, whatever did not agree with the writer's own opinions—Milner's work cannot be well termed a Church history, but its value as a contribution to ecclesiastical history is very considerable; only it should be read with much caution, and constant reference to Dr. Maitland's Strictures on Milner's Church History, and his Notes on Milner's History, etc. Dr. Milner's historical work certainly surpasses most other Church histories previously produced in the use made of the writings of the fathers, though the reverence which the author professes for those venerable men has led him to trust them too much. Most modern critics speak only in derogatory terms of this work, and an English writer of recent times thus comments upon it: "The principles on which the History of the Church of Christ is written are of the narrowest kind; the scholarship is poor, the literary merit still poorer, and the critical insight poorest of all. It deserves mention only for the estimation in which it was formerly held." The author of the Natural History of Enthusiasm, in commenting upon the characteristic defects of Mosheim and Milner as historians of Christianity, observes that "Mosheim gives us the mere husk of history, and Milner nothing but some separated particles of pure farina." A collection of Dr. Joseph Milner's works was published by his brother Isaac (Lond. 1810, 8 vols. 8vo). See Isaac Milner, Life of Joseph Milner, prefixed to his "Sermons;" Perry, Ecclesiastical History (see Index in vol. iv); Bibliotheca Sacra, Jan. 1850, p. 65; North Brit. Rev. Nov. 1858, p. 186; Bickersteth, Christian Student, p. 320; English Cyclop. s. v.; Darling, Cyclop. Bibliog. ii, 2771; Hook, Eccles. Biog. s. v.; Allibone, Dict. of Brit. and Amer. Authors, s. v.

Milnor, James, D.D., a distinguished divine of the Protestant Episcopal Church, was born at Philadelphia June 20, 1773. He studied for a while at the University of Pennsylvania, but about 1789 turned his attention to jurisprudence. His first settlement as a legal practitioner was at Norristown, but about 1797 he returned to Philadelphia, where he married. Until then he had lived, as he had been educated, a Quaker; but, as he had not been trained to any great strictness in the customs of the Friends, and as his wife belonged to an Episcopal family, it cost him little sacrifice to change his denomination. In consequence of his marriage, he had, moreover, been in due form "read out of meeting." In 1805 Mr. Milnor was elected a member of the select council of Philadelphia for two years. In 1807 he was elected for three years to the same body; and in 1808 was raised to the presidency of the council for one year. In 1810 he was elected to the Congress of the United States, as a member of the House of Representatives, from the city and county of Philadelphia: his term there closed March 4, 1813. He was for a long time a man of the world, though in the better sense of that expression; but about the year 1800 he began to turn his attention to religion. At first he inclined to Universalism, but finally, in 1812, became a communicant in the Episcopal Church. Soon after the expiration of his term in Congress he removed to Norristown, where, while preparing himself to enter the ministry, he acted as lay-reader in St. John's Church by permission of bishop White. He was ordained deacon in St. James's Church, Philadelphia, Aug. 14, 1814, and was admitted to the order of Presbyters in the same place Aug. 27, 1815. On October 21 following he was unanimously elected by the vestry a minister of the United Churches in Philadelphia. He finally received a call from St. George's Church, in New York, which he accepted after much hesitation, and was installed by bishop Hobart Sept. 30, 1816. He was made D.D. by the University of Pennsylvania in 1819. In 1830 he was sent to the British and Foreign Bible Society as a delegate of the American Bible Society, and of various other religious and benevolent institutions. On his return he resumed his charge at St. George's, and continued there until his death, April 8, 1844. Dr. Milnor was distinguished for his dignity and wisdom, and especially for his benevolence and piety. He ardently labored for the advancement of the kingdom of Christ, and his life is full of incident and instruction, "alike attractive to the ardent youth, the man of business, the humble Christian, and the mature theologian." Dr. Milnor published an *Oration on Masonry* (Phila. 1811):—a *Thanksgiving Sermon* (New York, 1817):—*A Sermon on the Death of his Excellency De Witt Clinton* (New York, 1828):—*Two Sermons* in the *National Preacher* (1836):—*A Charitable Judgment of the Opinions and Conduct of Others* (New York, 1845). See the Rev. John S. Stone, D.D., *Memoir of the Rev. James Milnor, D.D.* (New York, 1848, 12mo); *Prot. Epis. Qu. Rev. and Ch. Register*, April, 1855, p. 311; *N. Y. Ch. Rev.* ii, 31; *New-Englander*, vii, 122 sq.; *Princeton Rev.* xxi, 236; Sprague, *Annals of the Amer. Pulpit*, v, 562; *Meth. Qu. Rev.* July, 1849, p. 407; Drake, *Dict. of Amer. Biog.* s. v.

Milo OF RHEIMS, a noted character in the ecclesiastical history of the 8th century, flourished as archbishop of Rheims and Trèves. In his early life he was decidedly irreligious; dedicated himself to a soldier's profession, and gained much notoriety as one of Charles Martel's warriors. When the Carlovingian was involved in a quarrel with St. Rigobert, the archbishop of Rheims, he ended the dispute by deposing Rigobert, and bestowed the primatical see upon Milo, who soon after succeeded in obtaining possession also of the equally important archiepiscopate of Trèves. He is described as being a clerk in tonsure, but in every other respect an irreligious laic; yet when pope Boniface interfered and sought his removal, the holy father, with all the aid of his royal patrons, was unable to oust Milo from his inappropriate dignities; and in 752, ten years after the beginning of his reforms, we find pope Zachary, in response to an appeal for advice, counselling to leave Milo to the divine vengeance (*Epist.* 142). Nothing more is known of Milo's personal history. See Lea, *Hist. of Sacerdotal Celibacy*, p. 132.

Milon (1), a French monastic, was born about the beginning of the 9th century. In his youth he submitted to the monastic rules of the abbey of Saint Amand. Some critics have reckoned him among the abbots of that house, but this is an erroneous opinion. Milon was superintendent of the schools attached to Saint Amand, when Charles the Bald confided to him the education of his two sons, Pepin and Drogon. He died June 20, 872. A great number of the poems of Milon have been preserved. His *Vie de Saint Amand*, in heroic verse, is preserved in the collection of Bollandus of February 5th. It is to be regretted that we cannot find in this collection a supplement in prose to the *Vie de Saint Amand* by the monk Baudemond. Henschenius pretends, it is true, that this supplement is not the work of Milon; but the manuscripts, the epitaph of Milon, and the authority of Mabillon condemn the assertion of Henschenius. This supplement can be found in Surius of February 6th. Mabillon and Bollandus have, besides, published two sermons of Milon on Saint Amand, which are also found in the works of Philip, abbot of Bonne-Espérance. To the writings already mentioned we may add a *Homélie sur Saint Principe*, edited by Surius; a little poem, *Sur le Printemps et l'Hiver*, published by Casimir Oudin, in his *Supplementum de Scriptoribus ecclesiasticis a Bellarmino omissis*; an epitaph on the princes Drogon and Pepin, in the collection of Bollandus, June 16th, ascribed to Milon by Mabillon; two pieces in hexameter verse, *Sur la Croix*, which are still unedited; also a poem, *Sur la Sobriété*, published by Martène, *Anecd.* i, 44. See Trithemius, *De Script. eccles.* c. 283; Mabillon, *Annal.* i, 427; *Hist. Litt. de la France*, v, 409; Hoefer, *Nouv. Biog. Générale*, s. v.

Milon (2), a French prelate, was born about the beginning of the 11th century. He joined the Benedictine order in the monastery of Saint-Aubin, at Angers. Milon was sent to Rome by his abbot to pope Urban II, and was by him presented with the cardinal's hat, and made bishop of Palestrine. He was finally ordered to return to France, and preach against simony. Milon assisted in 1095 at the Council of Clermont. After the death of Urban II, Milon was appointed by Pascal II papal legate. Milon died about the year 1112. Marbode wrote a eulogy upon him, which Mabillon has published in the fifth volume of his *Annales*. Martène has published, in his *Voyage Littéraire*, ii, 244, some verses of a certain Milon which are believed to be written by the chief bishop of Palestrine. See *Hist. Litt. de la France*, x, 20; Hoefer, *Nouv. Biog. Générale*, s. v.

Milon (3), a French prelate, was born in the latter part of the 11th century. In his youth he lived in strict seclusion, but later embraced the rules of the canons of Prémontré; in 1121 was made abbot of the monastery of Dompmartin; and finally, in 1131, was elected and confirmed bishop of Térouanne. The first act of his episcopate appears to have been the consecration of Simon, abbot of Saint-Bertin. Milon was a strict disciplinarian. In 1148 he assisted in the Council of Rheims, at the trial of Gilbert de la Porrée. In 1150 he was engaged in a debate with Thierry, count of Flanders. In 1157, delegated by the sovereign pontiff, he adjusted a dispute which arose between the bishop of Amiens and the abbot of Corbie. Baronius has praised the religious character and wisdom of Milon; others have greatly extolled his humility. Claude la Saussaye has given him a place in his martyrology; and Luc, abbot of Saint-Corneille, has dedicated to him his *Commentaires sur le Cantique des Cantiques*. Thus Milon, who lived in an age fruitful in illustrious prelates, was one of the glories of his province. No one has to this day made a rigorous distinction between his authentic writings and the more numerous works which appear to have been improperly attributed to him. He died July 16, 1158. See *Gallia Christ.* x, col. 1347, 1546; *Hist. Litt. de la France*, xiii, 286; Hoefer, *Nouv. Biog. Générale*, s. v.

Milon (4), a French prelate, was born in England, of French descent, about the latter part of the 11th century. Milon, bishop of Térouanne, having died in 1158, Milon was appointed his successor, having formerly been archdeacon of that church. A letter written to pope

Alexander III, in favor of Thomas à Becket, has been attributed to him. A friend of John of Salisbury, bishop of Chartres, has addressed two of his epistles to him. He died at Térouanne, Sept. 14, 1169. See *Gallia Christ.* x, col. 1548; *Hist. Litt. de la France*, xiii, 287; Hoefer, *Nouv. Biog. Générale*, s. v.

Milon (5), a French ecclesiastic, was born about the beginning of the 12th century. He was sent by Innocent III to preach a crusade against the Albigenses. Subsequently he led the crusaders, marched under the walls of Béziers, and besieged and burned that place, after having slaughtered the inhabitants. Milon is mentioned for the last time as being present at the council held at Avignon, Sept. 6, 1209. In the collection of the letters of Innocent III published by Baluze are two letters from his legate. They also attribute to this fanatic a prayer to the Virgin, which has been inserted by P. Benoit in his *Histoire des Albigeois*, i, 279. See *Hist. Litt. de la France*, xvii, 26; Hoefer, *Nouv. Biog. Générale*, s. v.

Milon, JOHANN NICOLAUS, a German theologian, was born at Hamburg Nov. 2, 1738; was educated at the Johanneum, and later at the gymnasium of his native city. In 1760 he entered the University of Göttingen, where he studied ancient languages and Church history. He returned in 1764 to Hamburg, and was appointed in 1765 professor of philosophy at Kiel; in 1769 he was appointed minister at Lüneburg, and in 1770 at Wandsbeck, where he died, June 10, 1795. Some of his important works are, *Diss. de scribarum erroribus in textu Hebraico V. T. impresso* (Kilouii, 1764, 4to):—*Observationes criticæ in aliquot Veteris Fœderis loca* (ibid. 1765, 4to):—*Kritische Anmerkungen über einige Stellen des Alten Testaments* (Kiel, 1768, 8vo):—*Etwas über* 1 *Mos. xlix,* 10 *und Matt. v,* 31, 32 (Hamburg, 1788, 8vo).

Miltiädes, an early ecclesiastical writer, noted for his able defence of the orthodox Church against the Montanists, is supposed to have flourished towards the close of the 2d century. Eusebius and Jerome mention his writings, but there is now no trace of these supposed valuable productions. He is said to have lived under Marcus Aurelius (161–180), and under his son and successor Commodus (180–192). Miltiades was an able polemic, and waged war successfully, not only against the Montanists, but also combated Judaism and heathenism in its various phases. See Eusebius, *Hist. Eccles.* v, 17.

Miltiädes, also called *Melchiades* or *Melciades,* a bishop of Rome, was born about the middle of the 3d century. He early occupied as a priest a very conspicuous place by his arduous efforts to protect the rights and interests of the Roman Church against the many wrongs enacted by pope Maxentius, and was, besides, prominent in the protection of Christians during the persecutions. He succeeded Eusebius on the pontifical throne in 310, and, in 313, was ordered by the emperor Constantine the Great, who was opposed to the Donatists, to bring the Donatist difficulties to a close. In council with twenty Gallican and Italian bishops, he reinstated Cæcilian as bishop of Carthage. For his zeal and exertion in trying to bring back the Donatists into the union of the Church he was slandered, but Augustine (*Epist.* 162) speaks of him as "vir optimus, filius Christianæ pacis et pater Christianæ plebis." The Manichæans also, who worked secretly at Rome, found in him a watchful guardian against their doctrines. He was the first pope to live in a royal palace, which was presented to him by the emperor Constantine the Great, with other rich endowments. Miltiades issued two well-known edicts: the one interdicting fasting on Sundays and Thursdays, because the heathens celebrated these days "quasi sacrum jejunium;" and he also enacted, "Ut oblationes consecratæ per ecclesias ex consecratu episcopi dirigerentur, quod declaratur fermentum." The true meaning of the latter edict has often been a matter of dispute. Miltiades died in 314: it is erroneously reported of him that he died a martyr. St. Bernard, who described the life

of this pope, makes no mention of the manner of his death. His remains were interred in the Calixtine Chapel, but by pope Paul I they were removed "in capite" to the Church of St. Sylvester. See Bower, *Hist. of the Popes* (see Index in vol. vii); D'Artaud, *Life and Times of the Roman Pontiffs* (N. Y. 1865, 2 vols. roy. 8vo), i, 67; Herzog, *Real-Encyklop.* ix, 300; Wetzer u. Welte, *Kirchen-Lexikon*, vol. vi, s. v.

Miltitz, KARL VON, a Roman ecclesiastic, celebrated as the papal chamberlain and legate to the Reformers, was the son of a Saxon nobleman, and was born about 1490. He flourished first as canon at Mayence, Trêves, and Missonia. In 1515 he removed to Rome and became papal notary. In 1518, when cardinal Cajetan had so signally failed in bringing "little brother Martin" to submission, Leo X became aware of the greatness of the schism likely to occur in the German Church. The strife against the Latin system had assumed gigantic proportions. Around Luther were now gathered the great, and the strong, and the learned of the Teutonic race. Frederick, the electoral prince of Saxony, was Luther's staunch friend and protector, and Leo X, knowing the influence and power of this prince, felt loth to incur his ill-will by harsh measures against Luther. Miltitz was therefore despatched to the electoral court with a valuable present—the consecrated golden rose. This was to give the electoral prince assurance of the good intentions of pope Leo towards Saxony, and of his special friendship for Frederick; at the same time he was instructed to conciliate Luther, and, if possible, to make an end of the whole Lutheran controversy. In December, 1518, Miltitz arrived in Saxony, but, being careful to find out first how matters stood, he did not take the consecrated rose with him on his first call. This was a mistake on Miltitz's part, for, when the rose afterwards arrived, the prince acted very coolly, and, instead of accepting the present in person, commissioned three of his noblemen to receive the pope's gift, and Luther aptly remarked that "its odor had been lost on the long journey" (see *Luther's Briefe*, edited by De Wette, i, 108, 109). Miltitz's special instructions were to *conciliate* Luther, and we must acknowledge that he acted with much policy and skill. He carefully abstained from visiting cardinal Cajetan, who, by his imperious and arrogant treatment of Luther, had lost all influence with the electoral prince. When among friends, or even while staying in public houses, he did not hesitate to denounce the indulgence traffic, and assured his hearers that the shameful trade was carried on without the pope's consent. It was therefore perfectly natural that the electoral prince and Luther should have put confidence in Miltitz, and that his mission of conciliation seemed in a fair way to succeed (comp. however, Fisher, *Ref.* p. 97, note 2). On Jan. 3, 1519, Miltitz had a conference with Luther at Altenburg. The papal legate received the Reformer kindly, embraced and kissed him, and then addressed him as follows: "Dear brother Martin, how much I have been mistaken! I always imagined you an old doctor, sitting behind the stove, and full of whims and chimerical notions. But now I see that you are in the very height of manly strength. Not with five thousand armed men would I dare to take you to Rome. All my investigations have shown me that, wherever one person is for the pope, three are against him and for you." He then in the kindest manner remonstrated against Luther's violence, showing him how much harm the Church had to suffer in consequence. He failed, however, to procure any recantation, and succeeded simply in obtaining from Luther an expression of submissiveness. Silence was imposed on him, as well as on his opponents, and it was agreed to transfer the whole matter to the judgment of the archbishop of Trêves. In consequence of this agreement, Luther wrote to the pope a letter full of courtesy and humility, and went even so far as to declare publicly "that separation from a Church for which St. Paul and St. Peter, and one hundred thousand martyrs, had shed their blood, was not permissible, and that on no account must we resist her teachings and commands" (see Walch, xv, 812). This attitude of the great Reformer has often been stigmatized by the Romanists as an act of hypocrisy and simulation (see Wetzer u. Welte, *Kirchen-Lex.* vii, 148; Pallavicini, *Gesch. d. Conc. v. Trient*); but Luther's design, it must be borne in mind, was not to array himself against the Church, but to vindicate her against what he believed to be an abuse of her sacred name. Luther's movements were so completely churchly that even archbishop Manning (*Unity of the Church*, p. 328 sq.) is obliged to acknowledge it. At this critical moment (February, 1519) Dr. Eck, one of Luther's most prominent opponents, who in 1518 had challenged Carlstadt to a public disputation, published an outline of his *Theses*, which clearly proved to Luther that the main object of his attack was not Carlstadt, but himself. Luther considered this a breach of the agreement which he had concluded with Miltitz, and, as his adversaries did not hold themselves bound thereby, he, of course, felt relieved from his promise, and he so declared to the elector Frederick on the 13th of March. Luther's position at these disputations widened the breach with Rome [see LUTHER]; and the reformatory writings, *To the Christian Nobles of the German Nation, of the Bettering of the Christian State* (August, 1520), and *Of the Babylonish Captivity of the Church* (October, 1520), tended to fix the fact that reconciliation with the Church of Rome was no longer possible. Yet Miltitz would not despair of it. October 12, 1520, he had another conference with Luther at Lichtenberg, and then and there Luther expressed himself willing once more to test the question. It was too late, however, for in September, 1520, Eck had appeared in Germany with the papal bull, condemning as heresies forty-one propositions extracted from Luther's writings, and summoning him, on pain of excommunication, to retract his errors within sixty days. This ended Miltitz's mission as far as Luther was concerned. But as Miltitz's instructions extended not only against Luther, but also against Tetzel, whose behavior in the traffic in indulgences had been marked with peculiar impudence and indecency, he now repaired to Leipsic (December, 1519), sent for Tetzel, and subjected him to a most searching examination, which is given in a letter written by Miltitz to Pfeffinger (see Löscher, *Reformationsacten*, iii, 20 [Leipsic, 1729]): "I know enough of Tetzel's scandalous and lying life and actions. I convicted him of his crimes by well-attested testimony. I showed him the receipts of Fugger's commissioners, which proved beyond doubt that he received one hundred and thirty florins per month for his trouble, besides all expenses paid; a carriage with three horses, and ten florins per month extra for his servant. Thus did Tetzel, who, moreover, has two illegitimate children in the employ of the Church. No one can estimate how much he may have stolen. I shall report all these things to Rome, and expect a papal judgment." Tetzel, in consequence of his fear and anxiety, was taken dangerously sick, and died soon after. All efforts of reconciliation having failed, Miltitz returned to Rome, but, after a short stay, he returned to Germany, and died there in 1529—some say while on his homeward journey. See Seidemann, *Carl v. Miltitz* (Dresden, 1844, 8vo); id. *Die Leipziger Disputation im Jahre* 1519 (Dresden, 1843, 8vo); *Luther's Briefe* (edited by De Wette), i, 108, 109, and 115; Ranke, *Hist. of the Reformation*, i, 386 sq.; Hagenbach, *Kirchengesch.* iii, 83 sq.; Krauth, *Conservat. Reformation; Fisher, Hist. of the Reformation*, p. 97; Waddington, *Hist. of the Reformation*, vol. i, ch. iii; Gieseler, *Eccles. Hist.* vol. iv; Herzog, *Real-Encyklopädie*, viii, 326, 577; iii, 629; xv, 579.

Milton, JOHN, among the brightest glories of the rich and varied literature of England, one of the four master-singers of the English Helicon, has taken rank with Homer and Virgil and Dante. Dryden's eulogy was well-merited, though too epigrammatic. In splen-

dor of conception and in majesty of language, he is without a peer. Gray recognises in him no inferiority to Shakespeare. John Wilson, a graceful poet himself, and an appreciative critic, concludes that England has produced but one perfect poem, and that that poem is Milton's *Paradise Lost*. Poetry, however, was not the exclusive occupation of Milton's life. He was also a laborious and prolific writer of prose, and was long engaged in religious polemics and political controversy. His wreath of immortality was woven of poetic flowers; but his distinction in his own day was more largely due to his writings as a publicist and theological disputant. Milton is even more remarkable in the phases and circumstances of his life than in the brilliancy of his genius. His mature years coincided with that turbulent period when civil dudgeon first grew high, and passed into the turmoil and strife which constitute at once the shame and the glory of English history. The evening glories of the Elizabethan age lingered along the horizon at the commencement of his career; the serener but fainter radiance of the æra of queen Anne was prognosticated before his death. In the wide interval, one name of eminent renown in literature stretches its single and unbroken line of light across the darkened heavens. That name is the name of John Milton. His birth was amid the glories that had ennobled the reign of the maiden queen; he gathered strength for the stern and shifting duties of life throughout the reign of James; he illustrated the early rule of Charles I by strains that seemed echoes from the fairy land behind; he dignified the times of civil warfare and theological contention by prose compositions which occasionally united the grand cathedral harmonies of Hooker with the yet unanticipated magnificence of Burke. In poverty and depression, and blindness and age, he sought consolation from his music on that sacred harp, whose melting and piercing melodies no hand could ever awaken but his own. In character, and in the vicissitudes of his career, he was the true representative of the struggle which fills the seventeenth century. He bridges over the vast abyss between Shakespeare and Dryden, and marks the changing phases of the revolution in Church and State. Hence the consideration of his works can scarcely be severed from the notice of his life, which divides itself into four sharply-defined and well-contrasted periods.

I. *Period* 1608-1629.—Infancy, and education till he attains his majority, from the fifth year of James I to the fifth year of Charles I.

II. *Period* 1629-1639.—Completion of education at the university, in retirement and by foreign travel. From his majority to his return from the Continent.

III. *Period* 1639-1660.—Participation in the turmoil of the times. Active and public life.

IV. *Period* 1660-1674.—Milton's age, and blindness and seclusion. Production of his great poems.

Milton's Life and Works. I. *Period* 1608-1629.—John Milton, the illustrious son of obscure but reputable parents, was born at the sign of "the Spread Eagle," in Bread Street, in the parish of All-hallows, London, on the 9th of December, 1608. His father, of the same name, was a scrivener, who had been disinherited by his Roman Catholic parents for adopting the Protestant faith. His exertions in pursuit of a livelihood had secured comfort, if not wealth, and had not repressed his tastes for literature and art. Thus may be explained the conjunction of Puritan principles, of romantic fancies, of chivalrous sentiments, of literary and artistic sensibilities, so strangely, and not always congruously, exhibited in the poetry of his son.

That son received the tenderest care and the most sedulous instruction from his hopeful and appreciative sire. He was of frail constitution, and was, in consequence, educated at first at home. From his instructor—the eminent scholar and zealous Puritan, Thomas Young— he imbibed his taste for poetry, as he gratefully acknowledged. At the age of thirteen he was sent to St. Paul's

School, London, and after two years was transferred to Christ Church, Cambridge, where he remained, with some interruptions, over eight years. He carried with him to college great proficiency in the classic tongues, and had added to them an acquaintance with Hebrew, French, and Italian, and some skill in music and fencing. These liberal pursuits he continued to prosecute at the university with unusual diligence and with admirable results. Indications of his progress are supplied by his Latin and English poems, by notices in his polemical writings, and by his college exercises, which Mr. Masson has reclaimed from oblivion. From these sources we learn that he was exceedingly handsome, though of slight frame and moderate stature, and was skilled in all manly exercises. He is said to have been called "the lady of his college," not less for the purity of his character than for his delicate beauty.

Along with his extensive acquirements, Milton bore with him to Cambridge the germs of all his future tastes, the beginnings of all his future accomplishments. In his boyhood he had been "smit with the love of sacred song." Aubrey states that he was a poet at ten years of age. The love of the Muse grew strong with his growth. His devotion to his native tongue was early displayed. He soon aspired to the production of a poem which "future ages would not willingly let die." He was already consecrating himself to his high vocation, and disciplining his young genius with patient diligence. In this calm and industrious tenor of life, Milton ripened to his majority.

II. *Period* 1629-1639.—On the 8th of December, 1629, Milton was twenty-one years of age. On the Christmas-day ensuing he produced that magnificent choral song, *The Ode on the Nativity.* Admirable and exquisite as it is in itself, it is amazing as the composition of a young man who had just assumed the *toga virilis,* and was in the midst of his college career. Its remarkable merit may be best appreciated by comparing it with the nearly contemporaneous poems of George Herbert, Ben Jonson, and Vaughan on the same subject. The ode is equally remarkable for its startling indication at so early a period of the characteristics of his grandest works. The lyric movement of thought and expression, the intricate melody and skill of the metre, the strength and propriety of the epithets, the concentration and point of the language, the harmonies of sound, the dexterous accumulation of suggested names, the solemnity and reverential awe of the whole utterance, are anticipations of his final glories. Grand as is this choral hymn, Milton felt that his powers of song were not sufficiently matured to sustain the yet vague splendor of his conceptions. The *Ode on the Passion*—the companion-piece to the *Ode on the Nativity*—was never completed. "This subject the author finding to be above the years he had when he wrote it, and nothing satisfied with what was begun, left it unfinished." These two odes are the first outlines of the *Paradise Lost* and *Paradise Regained.* The self-censure, patience, diligence, and humility of Milton are as notable as his lordly tone and conscious power. Three years later, just before leaving Cambridge, he laments that "my late spring no bud nor blossom shew'th;" but adds,

"It shall be still in strictest measure even
    To that same lot, however mean or high
To which Time leads me, and the will of Heaven."

Milton was designed for the Church, and had been trained in all secular and theological learning for that holy office. The depression of the Puritans under the stern domination of Laud closed the prospect to the young candidate. He waited long and patiently, in doubt and hope; but in 1632 withdrew from Cambridge, having taken both his degrees. He left the university with credit and honor, and retired to the grateful seclusion of his father's villa at Horton—not far from Eton and Windsor. Here he remained for five years, spending the sunny summer-time of his life in multifarious study. He plunged into the mysteries of Hebrew lore,

familiarized himself with the best lessons of history, and carefully perused the whole series of the Greek and Latin authors, from Homer to Ducas and Phranza.

It was during the earlier half of his residence at Horton that Milton produced his *L'Allegro* and *Il Penseroso,* and his two masques, the *Arcades* and *Comus.* These poems were not composed for the noisy public, but as relaxations from study, which embodied the shifting lights and shadows of his life at Horton. They are photographs of the scenery that surrounded his retreat, lighted up by the bright glow of his changing moods. They reveal also the character and ingredients of the ambrosia on which his mind had feasted from boyhood, and betray the flowers from which the honey was distilled. The subjects, the contrasts, the metre, and many of the thoughts, phrases, and rhymes, are imitated from the poetical "Abstract of Melancholy" prefixed by Burton to his quaint *Anatomy of Melancholy.* Other obligations are due to the exquisite "Song on Melancholy" in Beaumont and Fletcher's *Nice Valor.* The same royal seizure, which ennobles what it appropriates, and which is declared by Longinus to be no theft, signalizes all of Milton's compositions. It is his manner. It is his genius. He claims the spoils of learning as his own. He made the triumphs of others the stepping-stones of his fame. To the year 1634 we probably owe the *Arcades ;* to it we certainly owe the more splendid *Comus.* Both were written under circumstances which are curiously illustrative of the social, political, and theological condition of the times, and of the great controversy in respect to dramatic performances. The *Arcades* is a much slenderer performance than the *Comus,* but possesses the same general characteristics: purity, grace, fancy, melody, learning, and gorgeous expression. The *Comus* is an almost perfect gem. It is as distinctly unique in its charms as Shakespeare's *Midsummer Night's Dream.* Its authorship was not avowed. It was published by Henry Lawes, in 1637, to escape the constant importunities for copies of the manuscript. In this year the plague raged with great violence, and many notable deaths occurred. On the 3d of April Milton's mother died; on the 6th of August Ben Jonson expired; on the 10th Edward King, of Christ Church, was lost at sea on his way to Ireland.

The death of Mrs. Milton broke up the family retreat at Horton, and Milton made preparations for foreign travel. He was meditating a great poem—an epic on the Round Table, or on the story of the Trojan Brutus. "Do you ask what I am meditating?" says he, in a letter to Deodati. "By the help of Heaven, an immortality of fame! But what am I doing? I am letting my wings grow, and preparing to fly; but my Pegasus has not yet feathers enough to soar aloft in the fields of air."

One more poem—the last song of his young and fresh life—preceded his going abroad. The admirers of "Rare Ben" honored his memory by a volume of *epicedia,* or funeral eulogies, entitled *Jonson Virbius.* The scholars of Cambridge proposed a similar tribute to the ghost of Edward King. To this collection Milton contributed that finest of elegies, the *Lycidas.* It is the echo of the pastoral music of the ancient Greeks, and recalls the plaintive strains of Bion, while adopting the metrical forms of the Italian *canzoni.*

Not long after this Milton set out on his Continental tour. Northern Europe was closed against him by the Thirty-Years' War, which was ravaging the whole of Germany. France was writhing beneath the tyranny of Richelieu, who was consolidating the monarchy at home, and strangling the supremacy of the House of Austria abroad. Milton crossed over to Paris, where he formed the acquaintance of Grotius; proceeded to Lyons, and, descending the Rhone, reached Marseilles. Thence he followed the *littorale* to Nice. From Nice he went to Genoa, and to Florence, in which city, the centre of Italian culture, he was welcomed with the highest distinction, and was elected a member of the

Florentine academies. While at Florence he visited "the starry Galileo," now seventy-five years of age, at his pleasant villa of Arcetri, in the neighborhood. Continuing his journey, he reached Rome, spending two months there "in viewing the antiquities," and listening to Leonora Baroni—the Jenny Lind of those days—who seems to have touched his heart, and to whom he addressed three Latin epigrams. He next proceeded to Naples, where he was hospitably entertained by Manso, marquis di Villa, the friend of Tasso. Everywhere he was received with honor, admiration, and the interchange of complimentary verses.

Milton had proposed to extend his travels to Sicily and Greece, but was not permitted to anticipate lord Byron in a poetic pilgrimage to the land of Helicon and Parnassus, and of the Vale of Tempe. He was recalled from Naples by the political agitations at home, and the dull murmurs of approaching civil war. On his homeward journey he was met by intelligence of the death of his friend, Charles Deodati, whereupon he wrote the *Epitaphium Damonii*—the Latin counterpart of the *Lycidas*. From this it is evident that he was still revolving an epic on the *Brut d'Angleterre* or the *Morte d'Arthur*. But he deserted the fountains of Hippocrene, and for twenty-one years devoted himself to polemics, politics, and prose.

III. *Period* 1649–1660.—*Milton as a Polemic, Theologian, Politician, and Prose-writer.*—On his return to England, Milton undertook the education of his two nephews, John and Edward Phillips. He was induced to receive other boys also, and accordingly took a large house in Aldersgate Street, and opened a school. Out of his academical employments sprung his *Tractate on Education*, his *Accidence commenced Grammar*, and his posthumous work *On Christian Doctrine*, which lay unknown till 1825. (It was edited by the present incumbent of the episcopal chair of Winchester [bishop Sumner]; a translation has also been published.) The first expounded his views on education, which resembled those of Roger Ascham and of John Lyly. The second was a practical exemplification of his method for the use of his school. The third was an expansion and systematization of the religious instructions given by him to his pupils. It has a much higher significance. It presents Milton's peculiar and utterly heterodox theology—which is thoroughly Arian, and in a great measure materialistic. It was the theological preparation for the *Paradise Lost* and *Paradise Regained*, and is their best commentary. Indeed, it is impossible to understand the esoteric meaning of those great poems, to estimate their spirit, or to appreciate many of their details, without the continuous illustration afforded by this long-lost treatise in prose. "His active imagination and impetuous spirit," it has been well said, "mingle too strongly with his theology, and in several particulars corrupt it; but though, like Locke, he sometimes mistakes the sense of Scripture, no man had a higher opinion of its supreme authority, or held more firmly its most vital truths. His name cannot be classed with modern Unitarians."

In 1641 Milton reappeared as a writer before the public with his first prose work, *Of Reformation in England*, "to prove that the Church of England still stood in need of reformation." He continued the subject in four other works, replying to bishop Hall and archbishop Usher in a short essay, *Of Prelatical Episcopacy*, and in a more elaborate response, entitled *The Reason of Church Government urged against Prelaty*. It is in this latter work that Milton commences the remarkable series of autobiographical sketches whence so much of our information in regard to his tastes, studies, habits, sentiments, principles, and occupations is gathered. Bishop Hall and archbishop Usher had aroused other assailants. Chief among such attacks in that pamphleteering day was a pamphlet designated *Smectymnuus*, from the initials of its five authors—Stephen Marshal, Edmund Calamy, Thomas Young, Matthew Newcomen, and William Spurston. To this attack bishop Hall replied in a

Defence of the Remonstrance. Milton, who had assailed the original Remonstrance, and was the grateful pupil of Thomas Young, now brought out *Animadversions on the Remonstrants' Defence.* A rejoinder from bishop Hall's son followed, to which Milton responded in 1642 by his celebrated *Apology for Smectymnuus.* These productions thus all hang together. Their object and interdependence are pointed out in the author's *Second Defence for the People of England.*

In 1643, during the brief superiority of the Cavaliers, Milton, now in his thirty-fifth year, hastily married Mary Powell, a gay, thoughtless, pretty girl of seventeen—"the daughter of Richard Powell, Esq., of Forrest Hill, near Shotover, Oxfordshire, an active royalist." The match was a singular and ill-assorted union. It was unhappy. It could scarcely have been otherwise. The fair malignant, in her young beauty, could not endure the gloomy yoke of her sedate Puritan husband. After the honeymoon was over, she visited her father, and remained all summer, heedless of the entreaties, remonstrances, and commands of her grim lord. He turned to his books, and to the examination of nice points of theological ethics. He studied the nature and obligations of marriage, and soon arrived at the foregone conclusion to divorce his recalcitrant bride. The result of his eager inquiries was *The Doctrine and Discipline of Divorce, restored to the Good of both Sexes*—published anonymously in 1644. Another fruit of his studies and experiences was his undisguised contempt for women. Before concluding his inquiries, he proceeded to the practice of his theory by paying his addresses to another fascinating young lady. Mrs. Milton, after a year's absence, sought a reconciliation, entreated forgiveness on her knees, was pardoned, and returned to her repellent home. She died in 1653, leaving three daughters, the only children of the poet, who grew up without culture or companionship. The husband, who took back the wife, did not put away his scandalous doctrine, which was earnestly denounced. He enforced it in three other works: *The Judgment of Martin Bucer concerning Divorce; Tetrachordon*, a consideration of his four chief texts of Scripture on the subject; and *Colasterion*, a bitter castigation of an illiterate and anonymous opponent. The *Colasterion* is Milton's solitary attempt at humor—and very questionable humor it is, except as ill-humor. In the same year with *The Doctrine of Divorce* appeared the *Tractate on Education*, addressed to "Master Samuel Hartlib," and the noble *Areopagitica, or Speech for the Liberty of unlicensed Printing.* The *Areopagitica* is the finest of Milton's prose compositions in subject, treatment, spirit, and expression. It is the earliest of the grand English arguments for the liberty of the press. Written with the forms of Greek oratory, and in imitation of the orations of Isocrates, its stiff, stately, and sonorous periods roll on with involved Hellenistic phrase, but are distinguished by fervor of feeling, breadth and truth of conception, and radiant utterance. Leckey (*Rationalism in Europe*, ii, 80) says, "The *Paradise Lost* is, indeed, scarcely a more glorious monument of the genius of Milton than the *Areopagitica*."

Milton's prose style is not in general either good or attractive. It is not merely intricate and cumbrous, but it is prolix, vagabond, and wearisome. Its high reputation has been derived from the *Areopagitica*, and from rare bursts of rhetorical brilliancy in other writings. Only a small part of the prose works merits the eulogies bestowed upon the glorious "purple patches;" and even these are more worthy of admiration than of unrestricted praise.

On March 15, 1649—six weeks after the execution of Charles I—Milton was appointed secretary for foreign tongues to the Council of State. He had probably gained the favor of the Republican authorities by his *Tenure of Kings* and *Observations on the Articles of Peace* in Ireland. He held the position till a short time before the Restoration; but the salary was reduced by nearly one half after 1655; and after 1652, when he became blind, the duties were discharged, first, by Philip Meadowes, and afterwards by Andrew Marvell. The appointment called him away from his preparations for his Arthurian epic, which was published towards the close of his life as a *Historie of Britanie.*

His first task under his political taskmasters was *Eikonoclastes*, in answer to the *Icon Basilike*—the political testament ascribed to Charles I, and bequeathed by him on the scaffold to his people. Milton's reply is bold, defiant; breathing all the exhilarating airs of sanguine freedom, but coarse, vituperative, passionate, and ungenerous. It was a suitable prelude for the Latin "Apologies for the People of England" (*Defensio pro Populo Anglicano, Prima et Secunda*), composed in 1651 and 1654 as a refutation of the celebrated scholar Salmasius. In his various "Letters of State"—extending from Aug. 10, 1649, to May 15, 1659—including the "Manifesto of the Lord Protector" in 1655, there are many lofty sentiments and sounding periods; but it would be scarcely fair to transfer to the secretary the praise for sagacious or audacious policy, which may belong exclusively to the Republican councillors, or to the great Republican sovereign. Cromwell was not a man to borrow his policy from a subordinate, and from a subordinate awed into unscrupulous homage by his resolute character.

In the composition of the *Defence for the People of England* Milton's sight gave way. As early as 1644 it had been seriously impaired by much study, frequent vigils, and constant writing. He became totally blind in 1652. He was warned by his physicians to abstain from literary labor. He refused to spare his eyes by the renunciation of what he conceived to be a high patriotic duty. He studied and wrote for his party and country till "the drop serene" totally darkened his vision. The assertion of his lofty resolve is imbedded in his *Second Defence for the People of England*, and a touching account of the advancing stages of his blindness is given in a letter to a Greek friend, which is much less known than his pathetic allusions to his great privation in the *Paradise Lost*, the *Samson Agonistes*, and two of his sonnets.

Shut out from the light of day, cut off from the direct pursuit of his official duties, denied personal communion with his books, the companions of his solitary hours, Milton's thoughts were turned inwards, employed on poetic visions, and fed with the treasures of his vast memory. During the long years of darkness and enforced leisure, he gradually conceived and moulded and commenced his *Paradise Lost.* When Cromwell died, confusion and anarchy returned, and the hope or fear of the restoration of the Stuart line occupied the public expectation. The blind seer then resumed his political labors, endeavored to preserve or to improve the recent order in the Church, and to uphold the late scheme of government, in several small publications. His ideas of religious and civil freedom tolerated only views consonant in spirit with his own; and would have sought to perpetuate English freedom and republicanism by rendering the remnant of the Long Parliament a close, permanent, and self-renewing oligarchy. His urgent clamors awoke no echo. His voice was too faint, too wild, too foreign to the necessities of the country and the time, and to the wisdom of sober statesmanship, to meet with any acceptance. Fairfax and Monk insured Charles II's return to his ancestral throne. Milton's political life was ended. All his hopes, all his dreams, all his cherished plans, were turned to dust and ashes. Poor, forlorn, outlawed, helpless, but not wholly dejected, he entered on the last period of his life in difficulty and danger and distress.

IV. *Period 1660–1674.*—The closing years of Milton's life offer little biographical detail. He was blind, in want, helpless; shunning the world, and shunned by it. Vane and other leaders of the lately dominant faction perished on the scaffold; others were outlawed or exiled. Milton was threatened with the like fate in con-

sequence of his prompt and virulent denunciation of his slaughtered monarch. He was spared, tradition says, through the intercession of Sir William Davenant. He was compelled to remain in hiding. His second wife, née Woodcock, had died in 1659, within a year of her marriage. He took a third in 1665, Elizabeth Marshal, daughter of Sir Edward Marshal, of Cheshire. She must have been a young bride, as she survived her husband more than fifty years. Of his second and third wives, of his daughters in their young womanhood, of his domestic life, of his intercourse with his still remaining friends, scarcely anything is heard at this period. Andrew Marvell and a few other intimates still consoled his loneliness and obscurity with their fervent attachment. Dryden, in the flush of his young and garish reputation, did reverence to him; but the desolate poet disappears from public gaze, and communes with his thoughts, his memories, and his God. "Forgetting the world, and of the world forgot," he worked out his immortal fame. Content with "audience fit, though few," he created those wondrous poems, which were the sublimated essence of his life and learning and labors—his own undying glory, and the pride of the English tongue.

When Milton retired from the plague in London, in 1665, to the house which Elwood, the Quaker, had presented to him, at Chalfont, in Buckinghamshire, he ex-

Milton's Cottage at Chalfont.

hibited to his friends the MS. of *Paradise Lost.* It may have been unfinished. It was sold, April 27, 1667, to Samuel Simmons, of London, for £5 down, and £5 on each of three future contingencies. Only two payments were made, whence it is inferred that less than 2800 copies were disposed of in the seven years preceding his death. This poem was the crowning labor of the poet's life. It had engaged his thoughts as early as 1654, and had occupied his solitary meditations during the ensuing years. It had been completed amid the boisterous license, and obscene dissonance, and reckless debauchery of the Restoration. He had poured into it all the wealth of learning and reflection and observation, and experience gathered in a studious, thoughtful, and full life—crystallizing into radiant gems the rich materials he employed. Like his own Pandemonium,

"Out of the earth a fabric huge
Rose like an exhalation, with the sound
Of dulcet symphonies, and voices sweet."

From his college days he had contemplated the production of a great poem. In penury and wretchedness and scorn he achieved his ideal, after the lapse of a whole stormy generation. The currents of his life changed the course of his fancies. He renounced the charms of old romance to sing the songs of heaven, and "tell of things invisible to mortal sight."

Milton selected for his subject the fall of man—a subject of universal interest—of special interest to all believers in the redemption—of more peculiar interest to the religious enthusiasts and reformers of the 17th century; and pre-eminently attractive to Milton from his peculiar idiosyncrasies. It was no new theme. In whole or in part it had been treated by Avitus in the 5th century; by Cædmon in the 6th; by Proba Falconia in the 10th; by Fra Giacomo, of Verona, in the 12th; by the mediæval writers of miracle plays between the 11th and 16th; by Andreini in the 17th, and by other writers. To most of these predecessors Milton was indebted, without sacrificing his own essential originality, which stamps every page with the seal of his own majesty. He hesitated long before settling the form of the poem. His genius was distinctly lyrical, but the *Ode on the Nativity* had exhausted the compass of the lyric strain, and demonstrated its insufficiency. He tried a dramatic cast, and commenced the play with Satan's invocation to the sun in the fourth book. His own temperament, the personages, the scene, the action, the incidents, were all unsuited to the drama. He finally adopted the epic mould, without creating a true epic, for the lyric spirit and strong predominance of his own personality still remain. If Satan is his hero, Satan is a glorified though fallen image of Milton himself. The poem is singular, alone, unapproached, a work *sui generis*. As Wordsworth said of the poet's soul, the poem

"Was like a star, and dwelt apart,
It had a voice whose sound was like the sea,
Pure as the naked heavens, majestic, free."

There is neither need nor room here for any criticism of this noble masterpiece. It is nearly perfect in subject, plan, impersonations, sentiments, moral aim, language, decoration, episodes, and rhythm. It is unequalled in grandeur, sublimity, verisimilitude of invention, and pathos. The blemishes indicated by Addison and other censors are less failures of the poet than weaknesses of the theologian, as may be seen from his treatise *De Doctrina Christiana*. Even the blank verse, which was adopted by him on an erroneous theory, and would have failed utterly in feebler hands, becomes with him "the Dorian mood of flutes and soft recorders." All the lavish rhetoric of praise of Macaulay, in the sparkling essay which his matured judgment disapproved throughout, may be bestowed on the *Paradise Lost*.

Four years after the completion of this signal work, Milton brought forth his *Paradise Regained* and *Samson Agonistes*. The former was preferred by the poet to its greater predecessor, was its natural counterpart, and probably was designed in its opening lines. The author's partiality for this smaller work doubtless rested on theological caprices; but, as a work of art, it has striking excellences of its own. It is more quiet, more smooth, more uniform, and more symmetrical. Its radiance has a gentler glow than the fierce splendor of the more imposing poem. Its habitual depreciation may be due to the same cause which secured the parental preference—the mistake in determining the supreme moment of the Saviour's life, as the subject of the tale. The temptation was more significant to Milton than the crucifixion. By the temptation Christ's divinity was earned; it was scarcely attested by the crucifixion, according to his views. The *Samson Agonistes* is Greek in form and expression; Hebrew in conception and spirit; English and personal in aim. It is a martyr's death-song—the agonizing wail of Milton's crushed, mangled, writhing, but triumphant soul; expostulating, like Job, with the Almighty and the Omniscient, who

"Now hath cast me off as never known.
And to those cruel enemies,
Whom I by his appointment had provoked,
Left me, with the irreparable loss
Of sight, reserved alive to be repeated
The subject of their cruelty and scorn.
Nor am I in the list of them that hope;
Hopeless are all my evils, all remediless:
This one prayer yet remains, might I be heard,
No long petition: speedy death,
The close of all my miseries, and the balm."

The death invoked came soon. He sank rapidly under attacks of gout, which became both more frequent and more violent; yet in his paroxysms "he would be very cheerful, and sing." He expired placidly in his own house on Sunday, Nov. 8, 1674, and the seer of things celestial was buried near his father, who had so sanguinely cherished his young genius.

It would be presumptuous to close this concise notice of John Milton with any summary estimate of ours upon his character and genius. He may be admired by all—he can be judged only by his peers. "It may be doubted," says Walter S. Landor, "whether the Creator ever created one altogether so great as Milton—taking into one view at once his manly virtues, his superhuman genius, his zeal for truth, for true piety, true freedom, his eloquence in displaying it, his contempt of personal power, his glory and exultation in his country's." "Milton," says Macaulay, "did not strictly belong to any of the classes which we have described. He was not a Puritan. He was not a Freethinker. He was not a Cavalier. In his character the noblest qualities of every party were combined in harmonious union. . . . We are not much in the habit of idolizing either the living or the dead; but there are a few characters which have stood the closest scrutiny and the severest tests, which have been tried in the furnace and have proved pure, which have been declared sterling by the general consent of mankind, and which are visibly stamped with the image and superscription of the Most High. These great men we trust we know how to prize; and of these was Milton. . . . His thoughts are powerful not only to delight, but to elevate and purify. Nor do we envy the man who can study either the life or the writings of the great poet and patriot without aspiring to emulate, not indeed the sublime works with which his genius has enriched our literature, but the zeal with which he labored for the public good, the fortitude with which he endured every private calamity, the lofty disdain with which he looked down on temptation and dangers, the deadly hatred which he bore to bigots and tyrants, and the faith which he so sternly kept with his country and with his fame" (*Essay on Milton*).

Literature.—Miltonic bibliography is so extensive that it would be ridiculous to enumerate even the most important works. A general reference to Allibone, *Dict. of Brit. and Amer. Authors*, will answer a better purpose than any copious list presented here. It may then suffice to mention a few authorities of special interest for the assistance they afford for the appreciation of the poet and his labors. Masson, *Life and Times of Milton, narrated in connection with the Political, Ecclesiastical, and Literary History of his Time* (Lond. 3 vols. 8vo; 1859 sq.; still unfinished); Keightley, *Account of the Life, Opinions, and Writings of John Milton* (Lond. 1855, 8vo); Brydges, *The Poetical Works of John Milton* (Lond. 1835, 6 vols. 12mo); St. John, *The Prose Works of John Milton* (Lond. 5 vols. 12mo); Prendergast, *A complete Concordance to the Poetical Works of John Milton* (Madras, 1857–59); Hamilton, *Original Papers illustrative of the Life of John Milton* (Camden Society); Dunster, *Considerations on Milton's Early Reading, and on the Prima Stamnia of the Paradise Lost* (Lond. 1800); Coleridge, *Lectures on Shakespeare and Milton* (Lond. 1857); Channing, *Remarks on the Character and Genius of Milton;* De Quincey, *Milton,* in *Theological Essay;* Skeats, *Hist. of the Free Churches of England,* p. 61; Perry, *Ch. Hist.* vol. ii; Tulloch, *Puritan Leaders,* ch. v; Hunter, *Religious Thought in England* (see Index, vol. iii); Hallam, *Hist. of Lit.* (Harper's edition), ii, 375 sq.; Hume, *Hist. of England,* ch. lxii; Kitto, *Journal of Sac. Lit.* i, 236 sq.; vol. xxiii; *Christian Examiner,* ii, 423 sq.; iii, 29 sq.; vol. lvii; *Retrospective Rev.* 1825, vol. xiv; Emerson, in the *North Amer. Rev.* lxxxii, 388 sq.; *Biblioth. Sac.* 1859, p. 857; 1860, p. 1; *Meth. Qu. Rev.* 1859, p. 495 sq.; *North British Rev.* May, 1859; *Edinb. Rev.* April, 1860; *Lond. Qu. Rev.* April, 1872; Prescott, *Biog.*

and Crit. Miscellanies; Bayne, *Contemporary Rev.* Aug. 1873; *Brit. Qu. Rev.* Jan. 1871, p. 115; July, 1872, p. 127 sq.; July, 1871, p. 111 sq.; *Presb. Qu. Rev.* April, 1872, art. x; *Catholic World*, Feb. 1, 1873. Those who desire to know how the English Homer is regarded by a nation whose taste and habits of thought differ most widely from the Anglo-Saxon race, may consult the article "Milton" in the *Biographie Universelle*, from the pen of the justly-celebrated French critic Villemain. He admits that Milton's picture of our first parents in Eden surpasses, in graceful and touching simplicity, anything to be found in the creations of any other poet, ancient or modern, and that the human imagination has produced nothing more grand or more sublime than some portions of *Paradise Lost*. Compare also the lately issued work on the *History of English Literature* by Taine (Lond. and N. Y. 1872, 2 vols. 8vo); Geoffroy, *Études sur les Pamphlets Politiques et Religieux de Milton* (Paris, 1848), and *Revue Chrétienne*, 1869, p. 19 sq. A revised edition of Milton's *poetical works* has been prepared under the editorship of Prof. David Masson, the able biographer of Milton, and a multifarious worker, which when published will no doubt be the standard edition of the poetical writings of John Milton. (G. F. H.)

Mîmânsâ (from the Sanscrit *mân*, to investigate; hence, literally, *investigation*) is the collective name of two of the six divisions of orthodox Hindû philosophy. See HINDÛISM. These two divisions are respectively distinguished as *Pûrva-mîmânsâ* and *Uttara-mîmânsâ*, the latter being more commonly called *Vedânta* (q. v.), while the former is briefly styled *Mîmânsâ*. Native writers rank the Mîmânsâ with the five other philosophical systems; but the term philosophy—as understood in a European sense—can scarcely be applied to it, as it is neither concerned with the nature of the absolute or of the human mind, nor with the various categories of existence in general—topics which are dealt with more or less by the other five philosophies. The object of the Mîmânsâ is in reality simply to lay down a correct interpretation of such Vedic passages as refer to the Brahminic ritual, to solve doubts wherever they may exist on matters concerning sacrificial acts, and to reconcile discrepancies—according to the Mîmânsâ always apparent only—of Vedic texts.

The foundation of this system is therefore preceded by a codification of the three principal Vedas [the fourth Veda, the "Atharvan," never attained in India the high consideration paid to the others, and is not universally accepted as a Veda (q. v.)]—the Rik, Black-Yajus, and Sâman—and by the existence of schools and theories which, by their different interpretations of the Vedic rites, had begun to endanger, or, in reality, had endangered a correct, or at least authoritative understanding of the Vedic texts. It is the method, however, adopted by the Mîmânsâ which imparted to it a higher character than that of a mere commentary, and allowed it to be looked upon as a philosophy; for, in the first place, the topics explained do not follow the order in which they occur in the Vedic writings, especially in the Brâhminic portion of the Vedas (q. v.); they are arranged according to certain categories, such as authoritativeness, indirect precept, concurrent efficacy, co-ordinate effect, etc.; and, secondly, each topic or case is discussed according to a regular scheme, which comprises the proposition of the subject-matter, the doubt or question arising upon it, the *prima facie* or wrong argument applied to it, the correct argument in refutation of the latter, and the conclusion devolving from it. Some subjects treated of in the Mîmânsâ, incidentally, as it were, and merely for the sake of argument, belong likewise rather to the sphere of philosophic thought than to that of commentatorial criticism —such, for instance, as the association of articulate sound with sense, the similarity of words in different languages, the inspiration or eternity of the Veda, the invisible or spiritual operation of pious acts, etc.

The reputed founder of this system is Jaimini—of unknown date—who taught it in twelve books, each subdivided into four chapters, except the third, sixth, and tenth books, which contain eight chapters each; the chapters, again, are divided into sections, generally comprising several Sûtras or aphorisms, but sometimes only one. The extant commentary on this obscure work is the *Bhâshya* of Sabara-swâmin, which was critically annotated by the great Mîmânsâ authority, Kumârila-swâmin. Out of these works, which, in their turn, quote several others, apparently lost, has arisen a great number of other writings, explaining and elucidating their predecessors. The best compendium, among these modern works, is the *Jaiminiya-nyâya-mâlâ-vistura*, by the celebrated Mâdhavâchârva (q. v.). See Mullens, *The Religious Aspects of Hindû Philosophy* (Lond. 1860); the Rev. K. M. Banerjew, *Dialogues on the Hindû Philosophy* (Lond. 1861); Chunder Dutt, *Essay on the Vedanta* (Calcutta, 1854); Duncker, *Gesch. des Alterthums*, i, 205; Clarke, *Ten Great Religions*, p. 116 sq.

Mina (in Greek μνᾶ, A. V. "pound"), a weight and coin which, according to the Attic standard, was equivalent to 100 *drachmæ* (Plutarch, *Solon*, xvi; Pliny, xxi, 109) or Roman *denarii*, i. e. (estimating the average value at the time of Christ) about $16. It is the sum named in the parable of Luke xix, 13 sq., where the amount of 100 *minæ* is therefore some $1600. On the other hand, the *mina* mentioned in 1 Macc. xiv, 24 (comp. xv, 18) is a weight, and (as being originally equivalent to the Heb. *shekel*) it may be reckoned at 8220 Paris grains (Böckh, *Metrol. Untersuch.* p. 124); and the sum of 1000 *minæ* of gold would then amount to about $16,910. See MONEY.

Different from this is the Heb. *maneh* (מָנֶה), originally likewise a weight, but used of the precious metals, and hence ultimately determining the value of coin. The word has perhaps an etymological connection with the Greek *mina*. See METROLOGY.

Minæans (i. e. *deniers, heretics*) is the name of a Jewish sect mentioned in the writings of the Church fathers. This is only another name for the *Nazaræans* (q. v.). Comp. Keim, *Leben Jesu*, p. 608.

Minard, Abel, a prominent layman of the Methodist Episcopal Church, noted for his great philanthropic labors, was born in Massachusetts September 25, 1814. His father died soon after his birth, and he lost his mother when he was about eight years old, so that as a mere youth he was left alone in the world. His early life was an earnest struggle for success; he was subjected to all the disadvantages which attend those who are compelled to work their own way from poverty to fortune. He learned the trade of a tanner; but his energy of character soon sought a broader field of action in business operations, which proved successful, and rapidly secured him wealth and influence. In 1846 he went to California; in 1856 removed to Lockport, N. Y.; and in 1866 settled at Morristown, N. J., where he died, Jan. 31, 1871. In early life Mr. Minard was a member of the Free-will Baptist Church, but in the prime of his days he neglected his Church privileges. In the spring of 1870 he united with the Methodist Episcopal Church at Morristown, in whose communion he spent his last days. In early life he promised his God that if he would bless him he would give away the tenth part of his income, and he dealt out largely to the poor and to the Church; in later years, fearing that he had not kept the vow fully, he failed not to make compensation for his neglect by numerous private and public benefactions. The churches both of Morristown and Lockport were remembered in his will. He also left a sum, the interest of which is annually applied for the education of four young men in Drew Theological Seminary at Madison, N. J. But the crowning work of his life was the establishment of the "Minard Home," in Morristown (valued at $50,000), for the education of the female orphans of missionaries and home ministers of the Methodist Episcopal Church. See *New York Christian Advocate*, June 15, 1870; Prof. Buttz, in the *Ladies' Repository*, 1872.   (J. H. W.)

Minard, Louis Guillaume, a French ecclesiastical writer, was born at Paris January 31, 1725. Educated at the College of France by the care of Rivard, with whom he was a favorite pupil, he joined the "Brothers of the Christian Doctrine," and was appointed while still young to some of the superior offices of his congregation. He entered the secular clergy and obtained the benefice of Bercy, near Paris. His tolerance and easy profession of religion brought upon him many admonitions from his superiors; finally, Christophe de Beaumont, archbishop of Paris, suspended him from his sacred functions—having been offended by a book that Minard had written, entitled *Panégyrique de Saint Charles Borromée*. Minard continued to dwell among his ex-parishioners, devoting all his time to study and to charity. In 1778 he refused the generalship offered him by the lay brethren. In 1795 he became a member of the Presbytery of Paris. He died, poor and infirm, at Paris, April 22, 1798. Besides the *Panégyrique de Saint Charles Borromée*, condemned by the Sorbonne and his provisor the archbishop of Paris, Minard wrote *Avis aux fidèles sur le schisme dont l'Église de France est menacée* (Paris, 1795, 8vo). In this tract, written to establish peace with the Jansenists, he says that all parties should unite to establish harmony in the Church, and that the resistance of a part of the clergy to the laws is as injurious to the divine service as to the state. It was replied to by Bernard Lambert la Plaigne, a Dominican Jansenist, who, aided by Maultrot, wrote four *Lettres aux ministres de la ci-devant église constitutionelle* (1795–1796). Minard afterwards replied to these by a *Supplément* to the *Avis aux Fidèles*. See *Nouvelles ecclésiastiques* (Utrecht, 1798); *Dict. historique*, s. v.

Minaret (or **Minar**) is the name of a tall turret used in Saracenic architecture. The minaret, as it is called by the Turks, contains a staircase, and is divided into several stories, with balconies from which the priests summon the Mohammedans to prayer —bells not being permitted in their religion [see MOHAMMEDANISM]—and is terminated with a spire or ornamental finial. The minarets are among the most beautiful features of Mohammedan architecture, and are an invariable accompaniment of the mosques (q. v.). In India, *minars*, or pillars of victory, are frequently erected in connection with mosques; some of these are lofty and splendid monuments, that of Kûtub, at Old Delhi, being 48 feet 4 inches in diameter at the base, and about 250 feet high. They are often built on a plan of a star-like form, and are divided into stories by projecting balconies, like the minarets.

Mincháh (מִנְחָה), properly a *gift* (as often rendered) or present (Gen. xxxii, 14; xix, 21; xliii, 11 sq.), especially to nobles and kings (Judg. iii, 15; 1 Sam. xi, 23; 2 Chron. xvii, 5, 11; Psa. xlv, 13; Isa. xxxix, 1; 1 Kings x, 25); hence *tribute* from a subject nation (2 Sam. viii, 2, 6; 1 Kings v, 1 [iv, 21]; 2 Kings xvii, 4; Psa. lxxii, 10); but specifically an offering to God, i. e. *sacrifice* (Isa. i, 13; 1 Chron. xvi, 29), particularly a bloodless one, "meat-offering," consisting of flour, meal, or cakes, with oil and frankincense, burned upon the altar by itself, or in connection with a bloody offering (Lev. ii, 1 sq.; vii, 9, etc.). See OFFERING.

In Jewish liturgy the word *Minchah* is the technical term for the afternoon service of prayer. See LITURGY (I).

Mincing (טָפַף, *taphaph'*, Isa. iii, 16) occurs in the prophet's description of the behavior of the "daughters of Jerusalem." The Hebrew word, as well as the Arabic *taf*, refers to the taking small and quick steps, the affected pace of a coquettish woman. The passage might be rendered, "They walk and trip along." Although the Hebrew word has perhaps a slightly different sense, yet the gait of the females seems to have been very much like the modern practice of swaying the body in walking. See WOMAN.

Mind, the exercise or expression of the spiritual part of man's nature. It is obviously divisible into the

Minaret.

three elementary functions, thought, emotion, and volition; but scientific writers greatly differ as to the subordinate or detailed faculties, as they are called. Reid thus classifies the mental powers: Perception, memory, conception, abstraction, judgment, reasoning. Stewart thus: Perception, attention, conception, abstraction, association, imagination, reason. Others propose a deeper analysis of the intellectual faculties, and find three properties which appear fundamental and distinct, no one in any degree implying the other, while the whole taken together are sufficient to explain all intellectual operations: namely, discrimination, retentiveness, and association of ideas. Sir W. Hamilton, departing from common classifications, sums the intellections into six:

(1.) The presentative faculty, or the power of recognising the various aspects of the world and of the mind. (2.) The conservative faculty or memory, meaning the power of storing up. (3.) The reproductive faculty, or the means of recalling sleeping impressions or concepts. (4.) The representative faculty, or imagination. (5.) The elaborative faculty, or the power of comparison, by which classification, generalization, and reasoning are performed. (6.) The regulative faculty, or the cognition of the *a priori* or instinctive notions of the intellect, as space, time, causation, necessary truths, etc. Noah Porter divides his "Human Intellect" into four parts: (a.) He treats of natural consciousness, philosophical consciousness; sense perception, its conditions and process; of the growth and products of sense perception. (b.) He treats of representation and representative knowledge; by which he means memory, imagining power, etc. (c.) He treats of thinking and thought knowledge; by which he means the formation and nature of the concept, judgment, reasoning, etc. (d.) He treats of intuition and intuitive knowledge, in which he discourses on mathematical relations, causation, design, substance, attribute; the finite and conditioned; the infinite and absolute. Berkeley and his school teach a pure idealism, which asserts that everything we can take cognizance of is mind or self; that we cannot transcend our mental sphere; whatever we know is our own mind. Others, again, as Locke, resolve all into empiricism, and look on mind as simply the result of material organization. These two views contain the extreme angles to which speculation has run. The former is idealism or spiritualism, the latter materialism or empiricism.

The pre-Socratic school of philosophers was materialistic, of which Anaximenes, Pythagoras, Heraclitus, were patrons. Between these and Plato, Socrates was a transitional link. The post-Platonic philosophers were spiritualistic in the main, notwithstanding French materialism and German rationalism. See MATERIALISM. Dr. McCosh, in his *Intuitions of the Mind,* makes a triplet of parts. In part first (which is on the "Nature of the Intuitive Convictions of the Mind") he shows that there are no innate mental images; no innate or general notions; no *a priori* forms imposed by the mind on objects; no intuitions immediately before consciousness as law principles. But there are intuitive principles operating in the mind; these are native convictions of the mind, which are of the nature of perceptions or intuitions. Intuitive convictions rise up when contemplations of objects are presented to the mind. The intuitions of the mind are primarily directed to individual objects. The individual intuitive convictions can be generalized into maxims, and these are entitled to be represented as philosophic principles. In part second he shows that the mind begins its intelligent acts with knowledge; that the simple cognitive powers are sense, perception, and self-consciousness. It is through the bodily organism that the intelligence of man attains its knowledge of all material objects beyond. The qualities of matter—extension, divisibility, size, density or rarity, figure, incompressibility, mobility, and substance—are known by *intuition;* and it is by cognition we know self as having being, and as not depending for existence on our observation; as being in itself an abiding existence; as exercising potency in spirit and material being—"Cogito, ergo sum." The primitive cognitions recognise being, substance, mode, quality, personality, number, motion, power. The primitive beliefs recognise space, time, and the infinite. The mind intuitively observes the relations of identity, of whole to part, of space, time, quantity, property, cause, and effect. The motive and moral convictions—as appetencies, will, conscience—are involved in the exercise of conscience. In part third he shows that the sources of knowledge are sense, perception, self-consciousness, and faith exercise. But there are limits to our knowledge, ideas, and beliefs. We cannot know any substance other than those re-

vealed by sense, consciousness, or faith. We can never know any qualities or relations among objects except in so far as we have special faculties of knowledge. The material for ideas must be brought from the knowledge sources. These sources are limited, and our belief is limited. Professor Bain, in his book, shows that human knowledge falls under two departments—the object department, marked by extension; the subject department, marked by the absence of extension. Subject experience has three functions—feeling, will, thought. The brain is the organ of the mind. The nervous systems are only extensions or ramifications of the brain, and through these the mind transmits its influence. In this nervous system, which acts as a channel for the transmission of messages from the mind, are two sets of nerves—the in-carrying, the out-carrying. The intellectual functions are commonly expressed by memory, reason, imagination. The primary attributes of intellect are difference, agreement, retentiveness, or continuity. J. S. Mill propounds a psychological theory of the belief in a material world—postulates, expectation, association, laws, substance, matter. The external world is a permanent possibility of sensation. Then follows the distinction of primary and secondary qualities; application to the permanence of mind, etc.

The true theory is both scriptural and scientific, methodic and encyclopedic; and though it may not explain all ideation amply, yet it shows that the nature and functions of mind can only be seen in connection with all the other parts of the human system, just as the nature and functions of a fountain are only seen when considered in connection with the other parts of the cosmos. We can only understand the nature and office of ducts, glands, veins, or arteries when we view them in their mutual relations, and in their relations with all the other parts of the physical system. We can only understand civil polity, social statics, natural phenomena, when taken in their reciprocal relations; and so we can only understand mind when viewed in connection with everything else it touches. Views taken from any other premise must be partial and imperfect. We hold that mind has seven great forces or modes. The so-called scientific writers acknowledge this, at least substantially. These are consciousness, conception, abstraction, association, memory, imagination, reason. Now if science shows us that there are seven great corresponding qualities or forces in the body, and if Scripture (which reveals what science cannot) shows us that there are seven great corresponding powers in the soul which lie back of and control all powers of body and of mind, why not conclude that this trinal septenary of forces interlace and overlap each other, so as to constitute a human personality? We do not claim for this theory a scientific status, but is it not worthy of a speculative niche? Our observation shows us that this universe progresses by a duplex method, unfolding and infolding, or evolving and involving. Scripture shows that this unfolding comes *from* a sevenfold force; science shows that it comes *through* a sevenfold faculty. The following curious coincidences may not be out of place here, as illustrating a somewhat abstruse problem of this subject. The Revelation by John reveals ἑπτὰ πνεύματα, or "the seven spirits," as the constituent powers of Deity. The question arises, What are these seven spirits? (Isa. xi, 2; Psa. cxi, 10; Prov. i, 7; Job xxviii, 28). It is held by many influential writers that the spirits mentioned in these references are to be taken in connection with Zechariah's sevenfold lamp (Zech. iv, 1). Delitzsch, in his work on *Psychology,* endeavors to find these elements in the Hebraistic distinctions of "the spirit of fear," i. e. of divine veneration (יִרְאָה), "the spirit of knowledge" (דַּעַת), "the spirit of power" (גְּבוּרָה), etc.; but these are highly mystical and even fanciful. Whatever, however, may be thought of such abstractions, as to what Scripture says, or is imagined to say, about the sevenfold *doxa* or soul life, science does seem to discover, or at least point out, a sevenfold means of mind representation in the body. She recognises seven forms of life: the embryonic, the breathing, the blood, the heart, the sensation, containing the five senses, the externalization of the $\nu o\tilde{\upsilon}\varsigma$ by the tongue, and the outpressure of the entire mental phases and spirit feelings through the entire bodily habitus. In the trichotomy of nature the soul is first, the mind second, the body third. The mind is therefore moulded by the soul, and the body by the mind. As the soul lies at the base of the being, all its ramifications are tinged with the hues of the soul. The mind, nevertheless, is moulded by whatever it plays upon. Thus mind is a middleman standing between the world of morals and of matter (yet interlacing both), communicating the will of the spirit to the external sphere. It is not a monarch, but a marshal; yet it is august in its capacity; in its elasticity, eternal. See PSYCHOLOGY.

For further discussion of the mind, see the works mentioned above; also the early Greek writers, as Diogenes, Anaxagoras, Heraclitus, Empedocles, Democritus, and the Socratic school, as Plato, Aristotle, etc. The modern schoolmen who treat of the subject are chiefly the following: Gassendi (1592–1655), Des Cartes (1596–1650), Geulinx (1625–1699), Spinoza (1632–1677), Malebranche (1688–1715), Hume (1711–1776), Reid (1710–1796), Brown (1778–1820), Condillac (1715–1780), Collard (1763–1845), Leibnitz (1646–1716), Kant (1724–1804), Schleiermacher (1768–1834). Many of these were rather metaphysicians than mental philosophers; yet their theories and discussions involve the nature and functions of the human mind, especially in its intellectual aspects; and they therefore may be said to have laid the foundations for mental science in its present development. The principal works more expressly relating to the intellectual faculties are Stewart, *Treatise* and *Essay on the Mind*; Brown, *Philosophy of the Human Mind*; Abercrombie, *Intellectual Powers*; Watts, *On the Mind*; Cudworth, *Intellectual System*; Reid, *Essays on the active Powers of the Human Mind*; Mill (James), *Analysis of the Phenomena of the Human Mind*; McCosh, *Intuitions of the Mind*; Wilson (W. D.), *Lectures on the Psychology of Thought and Action*; Bain, *Mind and Body: the Theories of their Relation*; Carpenter, *Principles of Mental Physiology*; Maudsley, *Body and Mind: their Connection and mutual Influence*. The works on *Mental Science* treat likewise of the emotional elements of the mind. See PHILOSOPHY. Most of the works named include the third or causative faculty of the mind, i. e. the will; but the importance of this, in its theological bearings, requires a separate treatment. See WILL. See also *Christian Monthly Spectator*, viii, 141, 184; *Lit. and Theol. Rev.* i, 74, 169, 614; ii, 261, 576; *North Amer. Rev.* xix, 1; xxiv, 56; *Monthly Rev.* cxviii, 441; *Brit. Qu. Rev.* Dec. 1871, p. 308; *Contemporary Rev.* April and Oct. 1872; *Meth. Qu. Rev.* iv, 243; April, 1870, p. 221; *Popular Science Monthly*, July, 1873, art. x; Dec. art. iv and vi; *The Academy*, Nov. 1, 1873, p. 445. See MONOMANIA.

Mine. The word does not occur in the Bible, but that mining operations were familiar to the Hebrew people from an early age is evident from many Scriptural allusions. See METAL. A remarkable description of the processes of ore mining occurs in the book of Job (xxviii, 1–11):

Why, [there] exists for silver a vein;
And a place for gold, [which] they may filter:
   Iron from clod can be taken,
   And stone will pour forth copper.
An end has [one] put to the [subterranean] darkness,
And to every recess [is] *he* prying [after]
The stone of gloom and death-shade.
   He has pierced a shaft [down] away from [any] sojourner,
   [Where] the [miners] forgotten of foot-[hold]
   Have hung [far] from man, [and] swung.
Earth—from it shall issue [means to procure] bread,
Though under it [its bosom] has been overturned as [by] fire:

A sapphire-place [are] its stones,
   And gold-clods [are] his [that explores it].
A beaten [path thither]—bird of prey has not known it,
Nor hawk's eye scanned it;
   Sons of rampancy [fierce beasts] have not trodden it,
   Roarer [lion] has not wended over it.
On the flint he has stretched forth his hand;
He has overturned from [the] root mountains:
   In the cliffs channels has he cleft,
   And every precious [thing] has his eye seen.
     From trickling [the adjacent] rivers has he stopped,
     While [the] concealed [thing] he shall bring forth [to] light.

The following comments on this passage (which may be a later addition of the time of Solomon), as well as the remarks on metallurgy in general, are indicative of its pertinence to the subject. See JOB, BOOK OF.

It may be fairly inferred from the description that a distinction is made between gold obtained in the manner indicated, and that which is found in the natural state in the alluvial soil, among the débris washed down by the torrents. This appears to be implied in the expression "the gold they refine," which presupposes a process by which the pure gold is extracted from the ore, and separated from the silver or copper with which it may have been mixed. What is said of gold may be equally applied to silver, for in almost every allusion to the process of refining the two metals are associated. In the passage of Job which has been quoted, so far as can be made out from the obscurities with which it is beset, the natural order of mining operations is observed in the description. The whole point is obviously contained in the contrast, "Surely there is a source for the silver, and a place for the gold which men refine; but where shall wisdom be found, and where is the place of understanding?" No labor is too great for extorting from the earth its treasures. The shaft is sunk, and the adventurous miner, far from the haunts of men, hangs in mid-air (v, 4): the bowels of the earth—which in the course of nature grows but corn—are overthrown as though wasted by fire. The path which the miner pursues in his underground course is unseen by the keen eye of the falcon, nor have the boldest beasts of prey traversed it, but man wins his way through every obstacle, hews out tunnels in the rock, stops the water from flooding his mine, and brings to light the precious metals as the reward of his adventure. No description could be more complete. The poet might have had before him the copper mines of the Sinaitic peninsula. In the Wady Maghârah, "the valley of the Cave," are still traces of the Egyptian colony of miners who settled there for the purpose of extracting copper from the freestone rocks, and left their hieroglyphic inscriptions upon the face of the cliff. That these inscriptions are of great antiquity there can be little doubt, though Lepsius may not be justified in placing them at a date B.C. 4000 (*Letters from Egypt*, p. 346, Eng. tr.). In the Maghârah tablets, Mr. Drew (*Scripture Lands*, p. 50, note) "saw the cartouche of Suphis, the builder of the Great Pyramid, and on the stones at Sarâbit el-Khâdim there are those of kings of the eighteenth and nineteenth dynasties." But the most interesting description of this mining colony is to be found in a letter to the *Athenæum* (June 4, 1859, No. 1649, p. 747), signed M. Δ., and dated from "Sarâbit el-Khâdim, in the desert of Sinai, May, 1859." The writer discovered on the mountain exactly opposite the caves of Maghârah traces of an ancient fortress, intended, as he conjectures, for the protection of the miners. The hill on which it stands is about 1000 feet high, nearly insulated, and formed of a series of precipitous terraces, one above the other, like the steps of the Pyramids. The uppermost of these was entirely surrounded by a strong wall, within which were found remains of 140 houses, each about ten feet square. There were, besides, the remains of ancient hammers of green porphyry, and reservoirs "so disposed that when one was full the surplus ran into the others, and so in succession, so that they must have had water enough to last for years. The ancient furnaces are still to be seen, and on the coast of the Red Sea are found the piers and wharves whence the miners shipped their metal in the harbor of Abu Zenî-meh. Five miles from Sarâbit el-Khâdim the same traveller found the ruins of a much greater number of houses, indicating the existence of a large mining population, and, besides, five immense reservoirs formed by damming up various wadys. Other mines appear to have been discovered by Dr. Wilson in the granite mountains east of the Wady Mokatteb. In the Wady Nasb the German traveller Rüppell, who was commissioned by Mohammed Ali, the viceroy of Egypt, to examine the state of the mines there, met with remains of several large smelting-furnaces, surrounded by heaps of slag. The ancient inhabitants had sunk shafts in several directions, leaving here and there columns to prevent the whole from falling in. In one of the mines he saw huge masses of stone rich in copper (Ritter, *Erdkunde*, xiii, 786). The copper mines of Phæno, in Idumæa, according to Jerome, were between Zoar and Petra: in the persecution of Diocletian the Christians were condemned to work them.

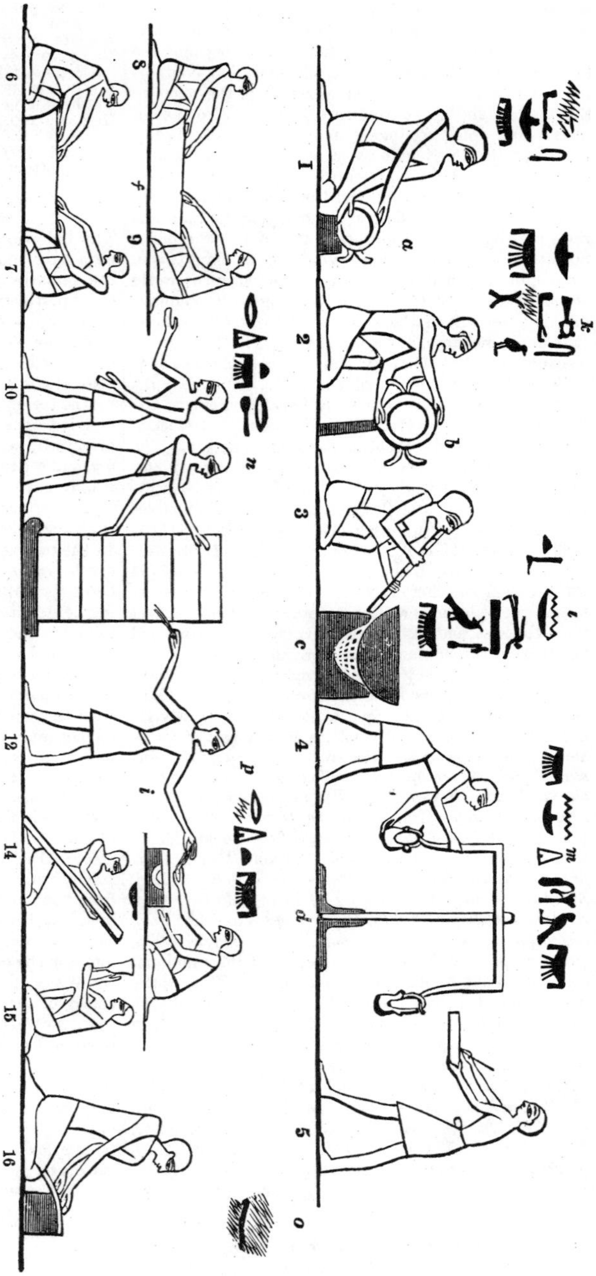

The gold mines of Egypt in the Bishárî desert, the principal station of which was Eshuranib, about three days' journey beyond Wady Allaga, have been discovered within the last few years by M. Linant and Mr. Bonomi, the latter of whom supplied Sir G. Wilkinson with a description of them, which he quotes (*Anc. Eg.* iii, 229, 230). Ruins of the miners' huts still remain as at Sarâbit el-Khâdim. "In those nearest the mines lived the workmen who were employed to break the quartz into small fragments, the size of a bean, from whose hands the pounded stone passed to the persons who ground it in hand-mills, similar to those now used for corn in the valley of the Nile, made of granitic stone; one of which is to be found in almost every house at these mines, either entire or broken. The quartz, thus reduced to powder, was washed on inclined tables, furnished with two cisterns, all

Figs. 1, 2. Making jewelry. 3. Blowing the fire for melting the gold. 4. Weighing the gold. 5. Clerk or scribe. 6, 7, 8, 9. Washing gold. 10. Superintendent. The remaining part relates to the preparation of the metal before it is worked.

Egyptian Goldsmiths.

built of fragments of stone collected there; and near these inclined planes are generally found little white mounds, the residuum of the operation." According to the account given by Diodorus Siculus (iii, 12–14), the mines were worked by gangs of convicts and captives in fetters, who were kept day and night to their task by the soldiers set to guard them. The work was superintended by an engineer, who selected the stone and pointed it out to the miners. The harder rock was split by the application of fire, but the softer was broken up with picks and chisels. The miners were quite naked, their bodies being painted according to the color of the rock they were working, and in order to see in the dark passages of the mine they carried lamps upon their heads. The stone as it fell

was carried off by boys; it was then pounded in stone mortars with iron pestles by those who were over thirty years of age, till it was reduced to the size of a lentil. The women and old men afterwards ground it in mills to a fine powder. The final process of separating the gold from the pounded stone was intrusted to the engineers who superintended the work. They spread this powder upon a broad slightly-inclined table, and rubbed it gently with the hand, pouring water upon it from time to time so as to carry away all the earthy matter, leaving the heavier particles upon the board. This was repeated several times; at first with the hand, and afterwards with fine sponges gently pressed upon the earthy substance, till nothing but the gold was left. It was then collected by other workmen, and placed in earthen crucibles, with a mixture of lead and salt in certain proportions, together with a little tin and some barley bran. The crucibles were covered and carefully closed with clay, and in this condition baked in a furnace for five days and nights without intermission. Three methods have been employed for refining gold and silver: 1, by exposing the fused metal to a current of air; 2, by keeping the alloy in a state of fusion and throwing nitre upon it; and, 3, by mixing the alloy with lead, exposing the whole to fusion upon a vessel of bone-ashes or earth, and blowing upon it with bellows or other blast; the last appears most nearly to coincide with the description of Diodorus. To this process, known as the cupelling process [see LEAD], there seems to be a reference in Psa. xii, 6; Jer. vi, 28-30; Ezek. xxii, 18-22, and from it Mr. Napier (*Metals of the Bible*, p. 24) deduces a striking illustration of Mal. iii, 2, 3, "He shall sit as a refiner and purifier of silver," etc. "When the alloy is melted . . . upon a cupel, and the air blown upon it, the surface of the melted metals has a deep orange-red color, with a kind of flickering wave constantly passing over the surface. . . . As the process proceeds, the heat is increased . . . and in a little time the color of the fused metal becomes lighter. . . . At this stage the refiner watches the operation, either standing or sitting, with the greatest earnestness, until all the orange color and shading disappears, and the metal has the appearance of a highly-polished mirror, reflecting every object around it; even the refiner, as he looks upon the mass of metal, may see himself as in a looking-glass, and thus he can form a very correct judgment respecting the purity of the metal. If he is satisfied, the fire is withdrawn, and the metal removed from the furnace; but if not considered pure, more lead is added and the process repeated."

Silver mines are mentioned by Diodorus (i, 33), with those of gold, iron, and copper, in the island of Meroë, at the mouth of the Nile. But the chief supply of silver in the ancient world appears to have been brought from Spain. The mines of that country were celebrated (1 Macc. viii, 3). Mount Orospeda, from which the Guadalquivir, the ancient Baltes, takes its rise, was formerly called "the silver mountain," from the silver mines which were in it (Strabo, iii, p. 148). Tartessus, according to Strabo, was an ancient name of the river, which gave its name to the town that was built between its two mouths. But the largest silver mines in Spain were in the neighborhood of Carthago Nova, from which, in the time of Polybius, the Roman government received 25,000 drachmæ daily. These, when Strabo wrote, had fallen into private hands, though most of the gold mines were public property (iii, p. 148). Near Castulo there were lead mines containing silver, but in quantities so small as not to repay the cost of working. The process of separating the silver from the lead is abridged by Strabo from Polybius. The lumps of ore were first pounded, and then sifted through sieves into water. The sediment was again pounded, and again filtered, and after this process had been repeated five times the water was drawn off, the remainder of the ore melted, the lead poured away, and the silver left pure. If Tartessus be the Tarshish of Scripture, the metal workers of Spain in those days must have possessed the art of hammering silver into sheets, for we find in Jer. x, 9, "silver spread into plates is brought from Tarshish, and gold from Uphaz."

We have no means of knowing whether the gold of Ophir was obtained from mines or from the washing of gold streams. Pliny (vi, 32), from Juba, describes the *littus Hammæum* on the Persian Gulf as a place where gold mines existed, and in the same chapter alludes to the gold mines of the Sabæans. But in all probability the greater part of the gold which came into the hands of the Phœnicians and Hebrews was obtained from streams; its great abundance seems to indicate this. At a very early period Jericho was a centre of commerce with the East, and in the narrative of its capture we meet with gold in the form of ingots (Josh. vii, 21, A. V.

"wedge," lit. "tongue"), in which it was probably cast for the convenience of traffic. That which Achan took weighed twenty-five ounces.

As gold is seldom if ever found entirely free from silver, the quantity of the latter varying from two per cent. to thirty per cent., it has been supposed that the ancient metallurgists were acquainted with some means of parting them, an operation performed in modern times by boiling the metal in nitric or sulphuric acid. To some process of this kind it has been imagined that reference is made in Prov. xvii, 3, "The *fining-pot* is for silver, and the *furnace* for gold;" and again in xxvii, 21. "If, for example," says Mr. Napier, "the term *fining-pot* could refer to the vessel or pot in which the silver is dissolved from the gold in parting, as it may be called with propriety, then these passages have a meaning in our modern practice" (*Metals of the Bible*, p. 28); but he admits that this is at best but plausible, and considers that "the constant reference to certain qualities and kinds of gold in Scripture is a kind of presumptive proof that they were not in the habit of perfectly purifying or separating the gold from the silver."

A strong proof of the acquaintance possessed by the ancient Hebrews with the manipulation of metals is found by some in the destruction of the golden calf in the desert by Moses: "And he took the calf which they had made, and burnt it in fire, and ground it to powder, and strewed it upon the water, and made the children of Israel drink" (Exod. xxxii, 20). As the highly malleable character of gold would render an operation like that which is described in the text almost impossible, an explanation has been sought in the supposition that we have here an indication that Moses was a proficient in the process known in modern times as calcination. The object of calcination being to oxidize the metal subjected to the process, and gold not being affected by this treatment, the explanation cannot be admitted. M. Goguet (quoted in Wilkinson's *Anc. Eg.* iii, 221) confidently asserts that the problem has been solved by the discovery of an experienced chemist that "in the place of tartaric acid, which we employ, the Hebrew legislator used natron, which is common in the East." The gold so reduced and made into a draught is further said to have a most detestable taste. Goguet's solution appears to have been adopted without examination by more modern writers, but Mr. Napier ventured to question its correctness, and endeavored to trace it to its source. The only clew which he found was in a discovery by Stahll, a chemist of the 17th century, "that if one part gold, three parts potash, and three parts sulphur are heated together, a compound is formed which is partly soluble in water. If," he adds, "this be the discovery referred to, which I think very probable, it certainly has been made the most of by Bible critics" (*Met. of the Bible*, p. 49). The whole difficulty appears to have arisen from a desire to find too much in the text. The main object of the destruction of the calf was to prove its worthlessness and to throw contempt upon idolatry, and all this might have been done without any refined chemical process like that referred to. The calf was first heated in the fire to destroy its shape, then beaten and broken up by hammering or filing into small pieces, which were thrown into the water, of which the people were made to drink as a symbolical act. "Moses threw the atoms into the water as an emblem of the perfect annihilation of the calf, and he gave the Israelites that water to drink, not only to impress upon them the abomination and despicable character of the image which they had made, but as a symbol of purification, to remove the object of the transgression by those very persons who had committed it" (Kalisch, *Comm. on Exod. xxxii*, 20). See CALF, GOLDEN.

How far the ancient Hebrews were acquainted with the processes at present in use for extracting copper from the ore, it is impossible to assert, as there are no references in Scripture to anything of the kind, except in the passage of Job already quoted. Copper smelting, however, is in some cases attended with comparatively small difficulties, which the ancients had evidently the skill to overcome. Ore composed of copper and oxygen, mixed with coal and burned to a bright red heat, leaves the copper in the metallic state, and the same result will follow if the process be applied to the carbonates and sulphurets of copper. Some means of toughening the metal, so as to render it fit for manufacture, must have been known to the Hebrews as to other ancient nations. The Egyptians evidently possessed the art of working bronze in great perfection at a very early time, and much of the knowledge of metals which the Israelites had must have been acquired during their residence among them.

Of tin there appears to have been no trace in Palestine. That the Phœnicians obtained their supplies from the mines of Spain and Cornwall there can be no doubt, and it is suggested that even the Egyptians may have procured it from the same source, either directly or through the medium of the former. It was found among the possessions of the Midianites, to whom it might have come in the course of traffic; but in other instances in which allusion is made to it, tin occurs in conjunction with other metals in the form of an alloy. The lead mines of Gebel er-Rossass, near the coast of the Red Sea, about half-way between Berenice and Kossayr (Wilkinson, *Handb. for Egypt*, p. 403), may have supplied the Hebrews with that metal, of which there were no mines in their own country, or it may have been obtained from the rocks in the neighborhood of Sinai. The hills of Palestine are rich in iron, and the mines are still worked there, though in a very simple, rude manner, like that of the ancient Samothracians: of the method employed by the Egyptians and Hebrews, we have no certain information. It may have been similar to that in use throughout the whole of India from very early times, which is thus described by Dr. Ure (*Dict. of Arts*, etc., art. Steel): "The furnace or bloomery in which the ore is smelted is from four to five feet high; it is somewhat pear-shaped, being about five feet wide at bottom and one foot at top. It is built entirely of clay.... There is an opening in front about a foot or more in height, which is built up with clay at the commencement, and broken down at the end of each smelting operation. The bellows are usually made of a goat's skin.... The bamboo nozzles of the bellows are inserted into tubes of clay, which pass into the furnace. ... The furnace is filled with charcoal, and a lighted coal being introduced before the nozzles, the mass in the interior is soon kindled. As soon as this is accomplished, a small portion of the ore, previously moistened with water to prevent it from running through the charcoal, but without any flux whatever, is laid on the top of the coals, and covered with charcoal to fill up the furnace. In this manner ore and fuel are supplied, and the bellows are urged for three or four hours. When the process is stopped, and the temporary wall in front is broken down, the bloom is removed with a pair of tongs from the bottom of the furnace."

It has seemed necessary to give this account of a very ancient method of iron smelting, because, from the difficulties which attend it, and the intense heat which is required to separate the metal from the ore, it has been asserted that the allusions to iron and iron manufacture in the Old Testament are anachronisms. But if it were possible among the ancient Indians in a very primitive state of civilization, it might have been known to the Hebrews, who may have acquired their knowledge by working as slaves in the iron furnaces of Egypt (comp. Deut. iv, 20). The question of the early use of iron among the Egyptians is fully disposed of in the following remarks of Sir Gardner Wilkinson (*Ancient Egyptians*, ii, 154–156): "In the infancy of the arts and sciences, the difficulty of working iron might long withhold the secret of its superiority over copper and bronze; but it cannot reasonably be supposed that a nation so advanced, and so eminently skilled in the art of working metals as the Egyptians and Sidonians, should have remained ignorant of its use, even if we had no evidence of its having been known to the Greeks and other people; and the constant employment of bronze arms and implements is not a sufficient argument against their knowledge of iron, since we find the Greeks and Romans made the same things of bronze long after the period when iron was universally known. ... To conclude, from the want of iron instruments, or arms, bearing the names of early monarchs of a Pharaonic age, that bronze was alone used, is neither just nor satisfactory; since the decomposition of iron, especially when buried for ages in the nitrous soil of Egypt, is so speedy as to preclude the possibility of its preservation. Until we know in what manner the Egyptians employed bronze tools for cutting stone, the discovery of them affords no additional light, nor even argument; since the Greeks and Romans continued to make bronze instruments of various kinds long after iron was known to them; and Herodotus mentions the iron tools used by the builders of the Pyramids. Iron and copper mines are found in the Egyptian desert, which were worked in old times; and the monuments of Thebes, and even the tombs about Memphis, dating more than 4000 years ago, represent butchers sharpening their knives on a round bar of metal attached to their apron, which from its blue color can only be steel; and the distinction between the bronze and iron weapons in the tomb of Rameses III, one painted red, the other blue, leaves no doubt of *both* having been used (as in Rome) at the same periods. In Ethiopia iron was much more abundant than in Egypt, and Herodotus states that copper was a rare metal there; though we may doubt his assertion of prisoners in that country having been bound with fetters of gold. The speedy decomposition of iron would be sufficient to prevent our finding implements of that metal of an early period, and the greater opportunities of obtaining copper ore, added to the facility of working it, might be a reason for preferring the latter whenever it answered the purpose instead of iron." See METAL.

Mineralogy. This science, like all others of modern date, was in a very imperfect state among the Hebrews. Hence the sacred writers speak of minerals without any scientific classification, and according to their merely external characteristics. This occasions the utmost difficulty in identifying any but the commonest mineral substances. In precious stones, particularly, this vagueness of name and description precludes the possibility of any certainty as to the actual mineral intended, or, rather, leads to the presumption that in most instances no one substance is denoted, but that the name is generic, including all stones of the same general appearance, color, hardness, etc. See GEM. The following is a list of the mineral productions mentioned in the Bible, with their probable modern representatives. For details, see each word in its place.

Achlamáh	Amethyst	"amethyst."
Alabastron	Alabaster	"alabaster."
Amethustos	Amethyst	"amethyst."
Argúros	Silver	"silver."
Bahát	Marble	"red marble."
Baréketh } *Barkáth* }	Emerald?	"carbuncle."
Barzél	Iron	"iron."
Bedíl	Alloy?	"tin."
Bedólach	Bdellium	"bdellium."
Berullos	Beryl	"beryl."
Bétser	Ore	"gold."
Bor } *Boríth* }	Alkali	"soap," etc.
Chalkídon	Chalcedony	"chalcedony."
Chalkolibánon	Electrum	"fine brass."
Chalkos	Copper	"brass."
Challamísh	Flint	"flint," etc.
Chashmál	Burnished Copper	"amber."
Chemár	Bitumen	"slime."
Chol	Sand	"sand."
Chrusoléthos	Chrysolite	"chrysolite."
Chrusoprásos	Chrysoprase	"chrysoprase."
Chrusos	Gold	"gold."
Dar	Pearl-stone	"white marble."

Ekdôch............	Carbuncle.........	" carbuncle."
Gabish............	Crystal............	" pearl."
Gir..............	Lime..............	" chalk."
Gophríth..........	Sulphur............	" brimstone."
Hals............	Salt...............	" salt."
Huakinthos.........	Hyacinth..........	" jacinth."
Huálos...........	Glass.............	" glass."
Jaspis............	Jasper	" jasper."
Kadkód...........	Ruby..............	" agate."
Kérach...........	Crystal............	" crystal."
Késeph...........	Silver.............	" silver."
Kéthem,.........	Virgin Gold........	" gold."
Krustallos..........	Crystal............	" crystal."
Léshem...........	Opal ?.............	" ligure."
Margarítès.........	Pearl..............	" pearl."
Marmáros..........	Marble.............	" marble."
Mélach	Salt...............	" salt."
Nechásh ⎱ *Nechósheth* ⎰	.......Copper........	" brass."
Néther............	Nitre..............	" nitre."
Nóphek...........	Emerald ?..........	" emerald."
O'dem............	Garnet............	" sardius."
Ophéreth..........	Lead...............	" lead."
Paldáh...........	Steel..............	" torch."
Paz	Refined Gold........	" fine gold."
Pitdáh...........	Topaz ?............	" topaz."
Puk..............	Antimony..........	" paint."
Sappheiros ⎱ *Sappîr* ⎰	....Sapphire........	" sapphire."
Sardínos ⎱ *Sardios* ⎰	........Carnelian	⎱ " sardine." ⎰ " sardius."
Sardónux.........	Sardonyx..........	" sardonyx."
Sháish	Alabaster..........	" marble."
Shamír............	Diamond..........	" diamond," etc.
Shashér	Red Ochre	" vermilion."
Shebó.............	Agate ?...........	" agate."
Shesh............	White Marble.......	" marble."
Shóham	Onyx ?............	" onyx."
Sidêros............	Iron...............	" iron."
Sig..............	Scoriæ, etc........	" dross."
Smaragdos	Emerald..........	" emerald."
Sochéreth..........	Spotted Marble.....	" black marble."
Tarshísh	Topaz ?............	" beryl."
Theíon	Brimstone..........	" brimstone."
Topazion...........	Topaz.............	" topaz."
Tsar	Nodule............	" flint."
Yahalôn...........	Onyx ?............	" diamond."
Yashephéh	Jasper	" jasper."
Zaháb......... ...	Gold..............	" gold."
Zekukíth	Glass..............	" crystal."

See Rosenmüller, *Biblical Mineralogy and Botany* (Edinb. 1846, 12mo); Moore, *Ancient Mineralogy* (N. Y. 1834, 12mo).

Minerva, the name of a Roman goddess, identified by the later Grecizing Romans with the Greek *Athene*, whom she greatly resembled, though, like all the old Latin divinities, there was nothing anthropomorphic in what was told concerning her. Her name is thought to spring from an old Etruscan word preserved in the roots of *mens* (the mind) and *monēre* (to warn or advise); and the ancient Latin scholar and critic, Varro (ap. August. *De Civ. Dei*, vii, 28), regarded her as the impersonation of divine thought—the plan of the material universe, of which Jupiter was the creator, and Juno the representative. Hence all that goes on among men, all that constitutes the development of human destiny (which is but the expression of the divine idea or intention), is under her care. She is the patroness of wisdom, arts, and sciences, the personification, so to speak, of the thinking, inventive faculty—and was invoked alike by poets, painters, teachers, physicians, and all kinds of craftsmen (Ovid, *Fast.* iii, 809, etc.; August. *l. c.* vii, 16). She also guides heroes in war; and, in fact, every wise idea, every bold act, and every useful design, owes something to the high inspiration of this virgin goddess (Livy, xlv, 33; Virgil, *Æn.* ii, 615). Popular tradition accounted for her origin as follows: "She was the offspring of the brain of Jupiter, from which she issued in full armor." She was always represented as a virgin. In war she was contradistinguished from Mars (the god of brute force) as the patroness of scientific warfare, and hence, according to the ancient poets, was always superior to him. The favorite plant of Minerva was the olive, and the animals consecrated to her were the owl and the serpent. As she was a maiden goddess, her sacrifices consisted of calves which had not borne the yoke or felt the sting (Fulgentius, p. 651). She had many temples and festivals dedicated to her. Her oldest temple in

Minerva.

Rome was that on the Capitol. Her most popular festival was held in March, and lasted five days, from the 19th to the 23d inclusive. Minerva was popularly believed to be the inventor of musical instruments, especially wind instruments, the use of which was very important in religious worship, and which were accordingly subjected to an annual purification, which took place during the festival just alluded to (Ovid, *Fast.* iii, 849).

ATHENE, or PALLAS ATHENE, the Greek goddess corresponding, as we have said, to the Roman Minerva, was one of the few truly grand *ethical* divinities of Greek mythology. Different accounts are given of her origin and parentage, probably from the jumbling together of local legends; but the best known, and, in ancient times, the most orthodox version of the myth represented her as the daughter of Zeus and Metis. Zeus, we are told, when he had attained supreme power after his victory over the Titans, chose for his first wife Metis (Wisdom); but being advised by both Uranus and Gæa (Heaven and Earth), he swallowed her, when she was pregnant with Athene. When the time came that Athene should have been born, Zeus felt great pains in his head, and caused Hephæstus (Vulcan) to split it up with an axe, when the goddess sprang forth—fully armed, according to the later stories. Throwing aside the thick veil of anthropomorphism which conceals the significance of the myth, we may see in this account of Athene's parentage an effort to set forth a divine symbol of the combination of power and wisdom. Her father was the greatest, her mother the wisest of the gods. She is literally born of both, and so their qualities harmoniously blend in her. It is possible that the constant representation of her as a strictly maiden goddess, who had a *real*, and not a merely *prudish* antipathy to marriage, was meant to indicate that qualities like hers could not be mated, and that, because she was perfect, she was doomed to virginity.

Athene is not represented, however, by the Greeks as a cold, unfeeling divinity; on the contrary, tradition will have it that she warmly and actively interested herself in the affairs of both gods and men. She sat at the right hand of Zeus, assisting by her councils. She was regarded as the patroness of poetry and oratory; agriculture also she was supposed to protect and cherish; and as a warlike divinity she was regarded as the protectress in battle of those heroes who were distinguished as well for their wisdom as their valor. Pope, in his *Temple of Fame*, alludes to her twofold character as the patroness of arts and arms, where he says:

"There Cæsar, graced with both Minervas, shone."

In the Trojan war she fought for the Greeks—who, in point of fact, were in the right. The poets feigned that Neptune and Minerva disputed for the possession of Attica, which the gods promised to him or her who should produce the most useful gift to mankind. Neptune, striking the earth with his trident, produced a war-horse, and Minerva produced the olive (the symbol of peace), by which she gained the victory. She was sometimes called Pallas, Parthenos (i. e. "virgin"), Tritonia or Tritogeneia, and other names.

Her worship was universal in Greece, and representations of her in statues, busts, coins, reliefs, and vase paintings were and are numerous. She is always dressed, generally in a Spartan tunic with a cloak over it, and wears a helmet, beautifully adorned with figures of different animals, the ægis, the round argolic shield, a lance, etc. Her countenance is beautiful, earnest, and thoughtful, and the whole figure majestic. There was a celebrated statue of Minerva, called "Palladium," which was said to have fallen from the sky, and on which the safety of Troy depended (Milman, *Hist. of Christianity*, see Index). See G. Hermann, *Dissertatio de Græca Minerva* (1837); Hartung, *Die Religion der Römer*, ii, 78 sq.; Guigniaut, *Religions de l'Antiquité*; Smith, *Dictionary of Greek and Roman Biography and Mythology*, s. v.; Vollmer, *Mythol. Wörterbuch*, s. v.; *Biographie Universelle* (Partie mythologique); Chambers, *Encyclop.* s. v.

Mingarelli, Fernando, an eminent Italian theologian, was born at Bologna in 1724. He flourished as professor of theology at the University of Malta for several years. Impaired health finally obliged his return to France. He died at Faenza Dec. 21, 1777. He was a member of the Academy of the Arcadians. Mingarelli wrote several works; the most important are, *Vetera monumenta ad classem Ravennatem nuper eruta* (Faenza, 1756, 4to; notes of Mauro Fattorini and of Bianchi): — *Veterum testimonia de Didymo Alexandrino cæco, ex quibus tres libri de trinitate nuper detecti eidem asseruntur* (Rome, 1764, 4to).

Mingarelli, Giovanni Lodovico, an eminent Italian bibliographer, the elder brother of the preceding, was born at Bologna Feb. 27, 1722. He held successively the principal offices of the congregation of the regular canons of San Salvatore. Afterwards he was a professor of Greek literature at the College della Sapienza, at Rome. Mingarelli employed his hours of leisure in visiting the principal libraries of the great papal city, and published some important works which he thus discovered. He died at Rome March 6, 1793. We owe to him, as editor, the *Annotationes literales in Psalmos* of father Marini (Bologna, 1748–50); he added new explanations of the Psalms, which are included in the Roman liturgy, and a life of the author, the exactitude of which is praised by Tiraboschi: — *Veterum Patrum Latinorum opuscula numquam antehac edita* (Bologna, 1751): — *Sopra un' opera inedita d'un antico teologo lettera* (Venice, 1763, 12mo; and in the *Nuova Raccolta Calogerana*, tom. xi). This is a treatise on the Trinity, which Mingarelli regards as the product of the 11th century, and he ascribes its authorship to Didymus of Alexandria. There is an analysis of his dissertation in the *Journal de Bouillon*, Jan. 1766: — *Ægyptiorum codicum reliquiæ*

Venetiis in Bibliothecâ Nanianâ asservatæ (ibid. 1785, 2 pts. 4to). These catalogues are greatly valued by scholars. He left a number of works in MS. form; they are now kept at Bologna. See Cavalieri, *Vita di Mingarelli* (Novara, 1817, 8vo); Tipaldo, *Biographia degli Ital. illustr.* v, 59.

Mingled People (עֶרֶב, *e'reb*, a *mixture*), spoken of a "mixed" multitude, such as accompanied the Israelites from Egypt (Exod. xii, 38), and joined them after their return from Babylon (Neh. xiii, 3); but specifically (with the def. article) of the promiscuous mass of foreign auxiliaries, e. g. of Solomon (1 Kings x, 15), of Egypt (Ezek. xxx, 5; Jer. xxv, 20, 24), of Chaldæa (Jer. l, 37). "The phrase (הָעֶרֶב, *hâ-ereb*), like that of 'the mixed multitude,' which the Hebrew closely resembles, is applied in Jer. xxv, 20, and Ezek. xxx, 5, to denote the miscellaneous foreign population of Egypt and its frontier-tribes, including every one, says Jerome, who was not a native Egyptian, but was resident there. The Targum of Jonathan understands it in this passage, as well as in Jer. l, 37, of the foreign mercenaries, though in Jer. xxv, 24, where the word again occurs, it is rendered 'Arabs.' It is difficult to attach to it any precise meaning, or to identify with the mingled people any race of which we have knowledge. 'The kings of the mingled people that dwell in the desert,' are the same apparently as the tributary kings (A. V. 'kings of Arabia') who brought presents to Solomon (1 Kings x, 15); the Hebrew in the two cases is identical. These have been explained (as in the Targum on 1 Kings x, 15) as foreign mercenary chiefs who were in the pay of Solomon, but Thenius understands by them the sheiks of the border tribes of Bedouins, living in Arabia Deserta, who were closely connected with the Israelites. The 'mingled people' in the midst of Babylon (Jer. l, 37) were probably the foreign soldiers or mercenary troops, who lived among the native population, as the Targum takes it. Kimchi compares Exod. xii, 38, and explains *hâ-ereb* of the foreign population of Babylon generally, 'foreigners who were in Babylon from several lands,' or it may, he says, be intended to denote the merchants, *ereb* being thus connected with the עֹרְבֵי מַעֲרָבֵךְ of Ezek. xxvii, 27, rendered in the A. V. 'the occupiers of thy merchandise.' His first interpretation is based upon what appears to be the primary signification of the root עָרַב, *'ârab*, to *mingle*, while another meaning, 'to pledge, guarantee,' suggested the rendering of the Targum 'mercenaries,' which Jarchi adopts in his explanation of 'the kings of *hâ-ereb*,' in 1 Kings x, 15, as the kings who were pledged to Solomon and dependent upon him. The equivalent which he gives is apparently intended to represent the French *garantie*. The rendering of the A. V. is supported by the Sept. σύμμικτος in Jeremiah, and ἐπίμικτος in Ezekiel." See MIXED MULTITUDE.

Mingrelia, an Asiatic province of Russia, situated between the Black and Caspian seas, in the country formerly called Colchis. It covers a territory of 2600 square miles, inhabited by nearly 250,000 people. The country is mountainous, but is largely cultivated. Tobacco, rice, and millet are raised, and a great deal of silk, honey, and wine are produced. Mingrelia became subject to Russia in 1803, but was until 1867 governed by its own prince, called Dadian, who resided in the small town of Zoobdidee. The inhabitants of Mingrelia are generally inferior in appearance to the mountaineers of the Caucasus. We are told by travellers that they are an ignorant, superstitious, and corrupt people.

Religious Condition.—The Mingrelians are ostensibly members of the Greek Church, but their religion consists rather in outward practices and observances than in inward purity and heart devotion. Many of their practices are open to severe censure. They observe four Lents, comprehending (1) the forty-eight days before Easter; (2) the forty days before Christmas; (3) the month preceding St. Peter's day; and (4) a Lent devoted to the Virgin Mary, and observed for a fortnight. Their chief saint is St. George, who is also the special patron of the Georgians, the Muscovites, and the Greeks. Their worship of images is of such a description that even Romanists declare it deserving the reproach of idolatry. They offer them stags' horns, tusks of boars, pheasants' wings, and weapons, with a view of insuring a happy success to their wars and hunting expeditions. It is even said that, like the Jews, they offer bloody sacrifices, immolate victims, and, like our Western savages, feast on them in general assembly; that they kill animals at the ombs of their parents, and pour wine and oil over the graves, as the pagans did. They abstain from meat on Mondays, out of regard for the moon, and Friday is observed as a holiday. They are exceedingly thievish: theft is not regarded as a crime, but rather a proof of skill that disgraces no one; he who is caught in the act has nothing to fear beyond a trifling fine.

Introduction of Christianity.—Some ecclesiastical historians insist that the king, the queen, and the nobility of Colchis were converted to the Christian faith by a female slave, under the reign of Constantine (Socrates, lib. i, c. 20; Sozomen, lib. ii, c. 7). Others assert that the Mingrelians were instructed in the Christian doctrines by one Cyrillus, whom the Sclavonians in their own tongue call *Chiusi,* and who is said to have lived about A.D. 806. Perhaps religion was extinguished altogether in these regions during the time that elapsed between the fifth and the ninth centuries. The Mingrelians show, on the sea-shore, near the Corax River, a large church, in which, according to their statement, St. Andrew preached; but this is to be taken "cum grano salis." In former times the Mingrelians acknowledged the spiritual supremacy of the patriarch of Antioch; but this supremacy has been transferred to the patriarchal see of Constantinople. Nevertheless they have two primates of their own nation, whom they call *catholicos:* one for Georgia, the other for Mingrelia. There were formerly twelve bishoprics. There are only six left at the present time, the other six having been changed into abbeys. The primate or chief bishop of Mingrelia, who resides at Constantinople, makes his appearance in Mingrelia only once in his life, and then only for the purpose of consecrating the holy oil, or chrism, which the Greeks call *myron.*

The statements of some travellers respecting the treasures of the primate and the bishops of the Mingrelians, the splendor of their garments, the extortions they commit, and the enormous sums of money they exact for mass, confession, ordination, etc., are rather at variance with the statements relating to the general poverty of the nation; there is likely to be exaggeration on both sides. What is said of the ignorance and corruption of the clergy in general may be more readily believed. The bishops, who are very loose in their morals, are regarded as acceptable if they abstain from meat, strictly observe Lent, and say mass in conformity with the Greek rite. Priests are allowed to marry, not only before their ordination, but also afterwards, and even to take a second wife, with dispensation.

The observances at baptism are very peculiar. As soon as a child is born, the priest anoints his forehead, drawing a cross on it with the chrism. The baptism is deferred until the child is two years of age, when he is christened by immersion in warm water; again unctions are made on almost every part of his body; holy bread is given him to eat, and wine to drink. The priests do not stick to the traditional form of baptism, and have been known to use wine for the christening of great people's offspring.

There are in Mingrelia monks of the order of St. Basil, who are called *berres.* They are dressed like Greek monks, and do not differ from them in their manner of living. A very condemnable abuse is that parents are allowed to engage their children to this state, in their tenderest years, when they are themselves in-

capable of choice. There are also nuns of the same order; they wear a black veil, and observe the same fastings and abstinence as the monks; but they do not submit to claustration, and make no vows, being thus at liberty to leave the monastic state when so inclined. The cathedral churches are adorned with painted images (no rilievi), covered, it is said, with gold and gems; but the parochial churches are sadly neglected. It is asserted that the Mingrelians are in possession of quite a number of precious relics, brought to them by the Greek fugitives, after the downfall of Constantinople; among others they claim to have a piece of the true cross, eight inches long; but the statements of the Greeks and the Romanists, in the matter of relics, are somewhat subject to caution. The Theatins of Italy in 1627 established a mission in Mingrelia, and so have the Capuchins in Georgia, and the Dominicans in Circassia; but the small success which attended these endeavors caused the missions to be suffered to fall into decay, and finally to be abandoned. See Dr. J. Zampi, *Relation de Mingrélie;* Cerry, *État présent de l'Église Romaine;* Chardin, *Voyage de Perse;* and especially Bergier, *Dictionnaire de Théologie,* iv, 347 sq.

Min'iamin (Heb. *Minyamin',* מִנְיָמִין, *from* the *right* hand, or perhaps corrupted from *Benjamin*), the name of two men. See also MIAMIN.

1. (Sept. Βενιαμείν v. r. Βενιαμίν, Vulg. *Benjamin.*) One of the Levites (or priests) who had charge of the distribution of the sacred offerings among the families of the sacerdotal order under Hezekiah (2 Chron. xxxi, 15). B.C. 726.

2. (Sept. Μιαμίν, Vulg. *Miamin.*) One of the priests that returned with Zerubbabel from Babylon (Neh. xii, 17), and celebrated with trumpets the completion of the walls of Jerusalem (Neh. xii, 41); probably the same elsewhere called MIAMIN (Neh. xii, 5) or MIJAMIN (Neh. x, 7).

Miniātis, ELIAS, an Eastern theologian and teacher, was born at Liguri, Cephalonia, in 1669, and was educated at Venice. He filled offices as public instructor, and became afterwards clergyman at Constantinople, Corfu, and the Peloponnesus, and was finally bishop of Calaoryta. He died in 1714. His works are: Πέτρα σκανδάλου (Leipsic, 1718), a treatise on the schism between the Greek and Latin churches: a Latin and German version of it was published at Leipsic in 1843, and at Vienna in 1888:— Διδαχαὶ εἰς τὴν ἁγίαν καὶ μεγάλην Τεσσαρακοστὴν καὶ εἰς ἄλλας ἐπιστήμους ἑορτάς (Venice, 1727, and often).

Miniato (or **Minias**), ST., an Armenian prince, who belonged to the Roman army, and served under Decius. When that emperor was encamped outside the city of Florence, according to the Florentine legend, this saint was denounced as a Christian, and condemned to be thrown to the beasts of the amphitheatre. A panther was first set upon him, but the saint was delivered from him in answer to his prayers. He was then hanged, put in boiling oil, and stoned, without being destroyed, for an angel descended to comfort him, and clothed him in a garment of light. Finally he was beheaded. It is said that this severe measure was executed in A.D. 254. Miniato is represented dressed as a prince, with scarlet robe and a crown. His attributes are the palm, the lily, and javelins.

Miniature is a picture illustrating the text of a MS.; so called because filling up the outline sketched in vermilion (*minimum*).

Minims (*ordo fratrum minimorum S. Francisci de Paula*), a religious order in the Church of Rome, founded by St. Francis de Paula, of Calabria, in the year 1453. The new order was called at first *Hermits of St. Francis* (*Eremitæ Minimorum Fratrum S. Francisci de Paula*). Pope Sixtus IV, in 1474, confirmed the statutes of the order, thus uniting them in conventual order, and named

Francis superior-general. He enjoined on his disciples a total abstinence from flesh, wine, and fish; besides which they were always to go barefoot, and not permitted to quit their habit and girdle night or day. Their habit is a coarse, black woollen stuff, with a woollen girdle of the same color, tied in five knots. The order increased rapidly; it gained many disciples, especially in France, where Francis was in high favor with Louis XI, Charles VIII, and Louis XII. Many houses of the order were established throughout the kingdom, and the friars themselves were called *les bons hommes* (*Boni homines*). In Spain they also gained influence, Ferdinand the Catholic building their first monastery for them at Malaga. A new name, "the Fathers of Victory," was bestowed upon them, because Ferdinand believed that only by their prayerful intercession Malaga had been captured from the Moors. In 1497 the emperor Maximilian called them to Germany, and founded three monasteries for the order.

For a long time the order had no special rules and regulations, the example of the superior-general serving as a pattern. In 1493 Franciscus finished his threefold rules, and they were confirmed by pope Alexander VI. Humility and repentance, poverty, fasting, praying, and silence form the principal features of these ascetic rules, and Franciscus called his brethren " *Minimos Fratres.*" This name was given them because they should be "the least among the brethren," and Christ's words (Matt. xxv, 40), "Quamdiu fecistis uni de his fratribus meis minimis, mihi fecistis," should have a peculiar reference to them. The austerity of the rules is particularly great in the selection of food. The brethren are debarred not only the use of meat, but also of eggs, butter, milk, and cheese. In 1493 Franciscus also instituted a female order of *Minims*, and subjected it to the guidance of the older order.

The order is at present divided into thirty-one provinces, of which twelve are in Italy, eleven in France and Flanders, seven in Spain, and one in Germany. In the beginning of the last century the order had about 450 convents. At present their number has greatly decreased. The Minims have passed even into the Indies, where there are some convents which do not compose provinces, but depend immediately on the general. Their principal house is at Rome. The superior of each male body is called *corrector;* that of each female body, *correctrix;* the superior of the order is called *generalis corrector.* There are now but few houses for female Minims. The tertiaries of the order are secular persons; but while they are not obliged to retire from society, they are required to observe the abstinence from meat, etc. They have also correctors and correctrices, and are subject to the order of the general corrector. Their distinguishing mark is a girdle with only two knots. See Bonanni, *Verz. der geistlichen Ordensleute,* ii, 58 sq.; Wetzer und Welte, *Kirchen-Lexikon,* v,i, 152; Herzog, *Real-Encyklopädie,* ix, 538.   (J. H. W.)

Minister, one who acts as the less (from *minus* or *minor*) or inferior agent, in obedience or subservience to another, or who serves, officiates, etc., as distinguished from the master, *magister* (from *magis*), or superior. It is used in the A. V. to describe various officials of a religious and civil character. The words so translated in the Scriptures are the following:

1. מְשָׁרֵת, *meshareth'*, which is applied, (1) to an attendant upon a person in high rank, as to Joshua in relation to Moses (Exod. xxiv, 13, Sept. παρεστηκὼς αὐτῷ; Aquila and Symm. ὁ λειτουργὸς αὐτοῦ; comp. Exod. xxxiii, 11, Sept. Θεράπων Ἰησοῦς; Numb. xi, 28; Josh. i, 1, Sept. ὑπουργὸς Μωυσῆ; Alex. λειτουργός), and to the attendant on the prophet Elisha (2 Kings iv, 43; vi, 15, Sept. λειτουργός; comp. 2 Kings iii, 11; 1 Kings xix, 21); (2) to the *attachés* of a royal court (1 Kings x, 5 [Sept. λειτουρός], where, it may be observed, they are distinguished from the "servants" or officials of higher rank [עֶבֶד, a more general term, Sept. παῖς], an-

swering to our *ministers*, by the different titles of the chambers assigned to their use, the "sitting" of the servants meaning rather their *abode*, and the "attendance" of the ministers the ante-room in which they were stationed); persons of high rank held this post in the Jewish kingdom (2 Chron. xxii, 8); and it may be in this sense, as the attendants of the King of kings, that the term is applied to the angels in Psa. ciii, 21 (λειτουργοί); comp. Psa. civ, 4 (Heb. i, 7; and see Stuart's *Comment.* ad loc.); (3) to the priests and Levites, who are thus described by the prophets and later historians (Jer. xxxiii, 21; Ezek. xliv, 11; Joel i, 9, 13; Ezra viii, 17; Neh. x, 36), though the verb, whence *mesháreth* is derived, is not uncommonly used in reference to their services in the earlier books (Exod. xxviii, 43; Numb. iii, 31; Deut. xviii, 5, etc.). Persons thus designated sometimes succeeded to the office of their principal, as did Joshua and Elisha. Hence the term is used of the Jews in their capacity as a sacred nation, "Men shall call you the ministers of our God" (Isa. lxi, 6).

2. פְּלַח, *pelach'* (Chald.), Ezra vii, 24, "minister" of religion, λειτουργός (comp. פְּלַח, ver. 19), though he uses the word מְשָׁרְתִם in the same sense, ch. viii, 17. In the N. T. we have three terms, each with its distinctive meaning.

3. Λειτουρός, a term derived from λεῖτον ἔργον, "public work," and the *leitourgia* was the name of certain personal services which the citizens of Athens and some other states had to perform gratuitously for the public good. From the sacerdotal use of the word in the N.T., it obtained the special sense of a "public divine service," which is perpetuated in our word "liturgy." The verb λειτουργεῖν is used in this sense in Acts xiii, 2. It answers most nearly to the Hebrew *mesháreth*, and is usually employed in the Sept. as its equivalent. It betokens a subordinate public administrator, whether civil or sacerdotal, and is applied in the former sense to the magistrates in their relation to the divine authority (Rom. xiii, 6), and in the latter sense to our Lord in relation to the Father (Heb. viii, 2), and to St. Paul in relation to Jesus Christ (Rom. xv, 16), where it occurs among other expressions of a sacerdotal character, "ministering" (ἱερουργοῦντα), "offering up" (προσφορά, etc.). In all these instances the original and special meaning of the word, as used by the Athenians, namely, with respect to those who administered the public offices (λειτουργίαι) at their own expense (Böckh, *Staatshaush. der Athener*, i, 480; ii, 62; Potter's *Gr. Ant.* i, 85), is preserved, though this comes, perhaps, yet more distinctly forward in the cognate terms λειτουργία and λειτουργεῖν, applied to the sacerdotal office of the Jewish priest (Luke i, 23; Heb. ix, 21; x, 11), to the still higher priesthood of Christ (Heb. viii, 6), and in a secondary sense to the Christian priest who offers up to God the faith of his converts (Phil. ii, 17, λειτουργία τῆς πίστεως), and to any act of public self-devotion on the part of a Christian disciple (Rom. xv, 27; 2 Cor. ix, 12; Phil. ii, 30).

4. The second Greek term, ὑπηρέτης, differs from the two others in that it contains the idea of actual and personal attendance upon a superior. Thus it is used of the attendant in the synagogue, the חַזָּן, *chazán*, of the Talmudists (Luke iv, 20), whose duty it was to open and close the building, to produce and replace the books employed in the service, and generally to wait on the officiating priest or teacher (Carpzov, *Apparat.* p. 314). It is similarly applied to Mark, who, as the attendant on Barnabas and Saul (Acts xiii, 5), was probably charged with the administration of baptism and other assistant duties (De Wette, ad loc.); and again to the subordinates of the high-priests (John vii, 32, 45; xviii, 3, etc.), or of a jailor (Matt. v, 25 = πράκτωρ in Luke xii, 58; Acts v, 22). Josephus calls Moses τὸν ὑπηρέτην Θεοῦ (*Ant.* iii, 1, 4). Kings are so called in Wisd. vi, 4. The idea of *personal attendance* comes prominently forward in Luke i, 2; Acts xxvi, 16, in both of which places it

is alleged as a ground of trustworthy testimony ("ipsi *viderunt*, et, quod plus est, *ministrarunt*," Bengel). Lastly, it is used interchangeably with διάκονος in 1 Cor. iv, 1, comp. with iii, 5, but in this instance the term is designed to convey the notion of subordination and humility. In all these cases the etymological sense of the word (ὑπὸ ἐρέτης) comes out. It primarily signifies an *under-rower* on board a galley, of the class who used the longest oars, and consequently performed the severest duty, as distinguished from the Θρανίτης, the rower upon the upper bench of the three, and from the ναῦται, sailors, or the ἐπιβάται, marines (Dem. 1209, 11, 14; comp. also 1208, 20; 1214, 23; 1216, 13; Pol. i, 25, 3): hence in general a hand, agent, minister, attendant, etc. The term that most adequately represents it in our language is "attendant."

5. The third Greek term, διάκονος, is the one usually employed in relation to the ministry of the Gospel: its application is twofold, in a general sense to indicate ministers of any order, whether superior or inferior, and in a special sense to indicate an order of inferior ministers. In the former sense we have the cognate term διακονία applied in Acts vi, 1, 4, both to the ministration of tables and to the higher ministration of the Word, and the term διάκονος itself applied, without defining the office, to Paul and Apollos (1 Cor. iii, 5), to Tychicus (Eph. vi, 21; Col. iv, 7), to Epaphras (Col. i, 7), to Timothy (1 Thess. iii, 2), and even to Christ himself (Rom. xv, 8; Gal. ii, 17). In the latter sense it is applied in the passages where the διάκονος is contra-distinguished from the bishop, as in Phil. i, 1; 1 Tim. iii, 8–13. The word is likewise applied to false teachers (2 Cor. xi, 15), and even to heathen magistrates (Rom. xiii, 4), in the sense of a minister, assistant, or servant in general, as in Matt. xx, 26. The term διάκονοι denotes among the Greeks a higher class of servants than the ὁοῦλοι (Athen. x, 192; see Buttm. *Lex.* i, 220; comp. Matt. xxii, 13, and Sept. for משרת, Esth. i, 10; ii, 2; vi, 3). It is worthy of observation that the word is thus of very rare occurrence in the Sept., and then only in a general sense: its special sense, as known to us in its derivative "deacon" (q. v.), seems to be of purely Christian growth. See MINISTRY.

MINISTER is a Latin word applied in that portion of the Christian Church known as the Western to designate that officer who is styled *deacon* in Greek. The word was applied generally to the Anglican clergy about the time of the great rebellion, since which time it has come into general use, and is now applied to any preacher of the Gospel. Even the Jews have adopted the use of this word, and *rabbi* is scarcely ever heard in English-speaking congregations of that people. Ministers are also called divines, and may be distinguished into *polemic*, or those who possess controversial talents; *casuistic*, or those who resolve cases of conscience; *experimental*, those who address themselves to the feelings, cases, and circumstances of their hearers; and, lastly, *practical*, those who insist upon the performance of all those duties which the Word of God enjoins. An able minister will have something of all these united in him, though he may not excel in all; and it becomes every one who is a candidate for the ministry to get a clear idea of each, that he may not be deficient in the discharge of that work which is the most important that can be sustained by mortal beings. Many volumes have been written on this subject, but we must be content in this place to offer only a few remarks relative to it.

1. In the first place, then, it must be observed that ministers of the Gospel ought to be *sound as to their principles*. They must be men whose hearts are renovated by divine grace, and whose sentiments are derived from the sacred oracles of divine truth. A minister without principles will never do any good; and he who professes to believe in a system should see to it that it accords

with the Word of God. His mind should clearly perceive the beauty, harmony, and utility of the doctrines, while his heart should be deeply impressed with a sense of their value and importance.

2. *They should be mild and affable as to their dispositions and deportment.* A haughty, imperious spirit is a disgrace to the ministerial character, and generally brings contempt. They should learn to bear injuries with patience, and be ready to do good to every one; be courteous to all without cringing to any; be affable without levity, and humble without pusillanimity; conciliating the affections without violating the truth; connecting a suavity of manners with a dignity of character; obliging without flattery; and throwing off all reserve without running into the opposite extreme of volubility and trifling.

3. *They should be superior as to their knowledge and talents.* Though many have been useful without what is called learning, yet none have been so without some portion of knowledge and wisdom. Nor has God Almighty ever sanctified ignorance, or consecrated it to his service; since it is the effect of the fall, and the consequence of our departure from the fountain of intelligence. Ministers therefore, especially, should endeavor to break these shackles, get their minds enlarged, and stored with all useful knowledge. The Bible should be well studied, and that, especially, in the original languages. The scheme of salvation by Jesus Christ should be well understood, with all the various topics connected with it. And in the present day a knowledge of history, natural philosophy, logic, mathematics, and rhetoric is peculiarly requisite. A clear judgment, also, with a retentive memory, inventive faculty, and a facility of communication, should be obtained.

4. *They should be diligent as to their studies.* Their time, especially, should be improved, and not lost by too much sleep, formal visits, indolence, reading useless books, studying useless subjects. Every day should have its work, and every subject its due attention. Some advise a chapter in the Hebrew Bible, and another in the Greek Testament, to be read every day. A well-chosen system of divinity should be accurately studied. The best definitions should be obtained, and a constant regard paid to all those studies which savor of religion, and have some tendency to public work.

5. *Ministers should be extensive as to their benevolence and candor.* A contracted, bigoted spirit ill becomes those who preach a Gospel which breathes the purest benevolence to mankind. This spirit has done more harm among all parties than many imagine, and is, in our opinion, one of the most powerful engines the devil makes use of to oppose the best interests of mankind; and it is really shocking to observe how sects and parties have all, in their turns, anathematized each other. Now, while ministers ought to contend earnestly for the faith once delivered to the saints, they must remember that men always think differently from each other; that prejudice of education has great influence; that difference of opinion as to subordinate things is not of such importance as to be a ground of dislike. Let the ministers of Christ, then, pity the weak, forgive the ignorant, bear with the sincere though mistaken zealot, and love all who love the Lord Jesus Christ.

6. *Ministers should be zealous and faithful in their public work.* The sick must be visited, children must be catechised, the ordinances administered, and the Word of God preached. These things must be taken up, not as a matter of duty only, but of pleasure, and executed with faithfulness; and, as they are of the utmost importance, ministers should attend to them with all that sincerity, earnestness, and zeal which that importance demands. An idle, frigid, indifferent minister is a pest to society, a disgrace to his profession, an injury to the Church, and offensive to God himself.

7. *Lastly, ministers should be consistent as to their conduct.* No brightness of talent, no superiority of intellect, no extent of knowledge, will ever be a substitute

for this. They should not only possess a luminous mind, but set a good example. This will procure dignity to themselves, give energy to what they say, and prove a blessing to the circle in which they move. In fine, they should be men of prudence and prayer, light and love, zeal and knowledge, courage and humility, humanity and religion.

See Dr. Smith, *Lecture on the Sacred Office;* Gerard, *Pastoral Care;* Macgill, *Address to Young Clergymen;* Massillon, *Charges;* Baxter, *Reformed Pastor;* Herbert, *Country Parson;* Burnet, *Pastoral Care;* Dr. Edwards, *Preacher;* Mason, *Student and Pastor;* Brown, *Address to Students;* Mather, *Student and Preacher;* Ostervald, *Lectures on the Sacred Ministry;* Robinson, *Claude;* Doddridge, *Lectures on Preaching;* Miller, *Letters on Clerical Manners;* Burder, *Hints;* Ware, *Lecture on the Connection of Pulpit Eloquence and the Pastoral Care; Christ. Examiner;* Plumer, *Pastoral Theology;* Tyng, *Office and Duty of a Christian Pastor;* Bridge, *Christian Ministry;* Kidder, *The Christian Pastorate;* Townsend, *Tongue and Sword; Presb. Qu. and Princet. Rev.* 1854, p. 386, 708; 1859, p. 15, 366; Jan. 1873, art. vi and vii; *Universalist Qu.* Oct. 1872, art. vii; Kitto, *Journal,* April, 1853, p. 192; *Meth. Quar. Review,* July, 1851, p. 430. See MINISTRY.

Minister of the Altar was a title applied in the Church of Rome, since the close of the 12th century, to the provider of pure bread, wine, and water for the mass. The *ministrant,* as he is called by the clergy, also responds to the prayers and benedictions. Originally a clerk, deacon, or subdeacon was delegated for this position, but now the duty is assigned to boys, except on unusually solemn and festive occasions.

Ministerial Call, a term used to denote that right or authority which a person receives to preach the Gospel. This call is considered as twofold: *divine* and *ecclesiastical.* The following things seem essential to a divine call: 1. A holy, blameless life; 2. An ardent and constant inclination and zeal to do good; 3. Abilities suited to the work: such as knowledge, aptness to teach, courage, etc.; 4. An opportunity afforded in Providence to be useful. The Methodists hold that no man should seek to enter the ministerial ranks who does not feel especially called to preach the Gospel. They are quite decided on this point. An *ecclesiastical* call consists in the election which is made of any person to be a pastor. But here those governed by an episcopacy differ from the Presbyterians, Baptists, Congregationalists, etc.; the former believing that the choice and call of a minister rest with the superior clergy, or those who have the gift of an ecclesiastical benefice; the latter teaching that it should rest on the suffrage of the people to whom he is to minister. See EPISCOPACY; ORDINATION.

Ministerial Education. It is rather an inference than a demonstrable historical fact that in the Levitical cities of the Jews schools were maintained for the instruction of priests and Levites in the knowledge and ceremonies of the law. See EDUCATION. It is certain, however, that under Samuel "schools of the prophets" were established for the purpose of training men for the high function of moral and spiritual teaching. Not less than five such schools are named in sacred history; one at Naioth, one at Bethel, one at Jericho, one at Gilgal, and another at Mount Ephraim. The number of the sons of the prophets was often large. Obadiah hid one hundred of them in a cave to save them from the malice of Jezebel, and at the translation of Elijah fifty of the sons of the prophets were present to witness the wonderful scene.

At a subsequent period of Jewish history a species of schools came into vogue, known as the "assemblies of the wise." The Talmud mentions some twelve of these institutions, of which those at Tiberias and Jerusalem were the most celebrated. Nevertheless they were not exclusively for the education of the priests, but also of elders and teachers. When Jesus the Christ ap-

peared among men, no inconsiderable portion of his ministry was employed in the instruction and training of his disciples in a kind of peripatetic school, of which he was the great Teacher, as he went about doing good and explaining the things of the kingdom of God. From the Acts and the Epistles it is evident that the apostles imitated their divine Lord in giving personal attention to the instruction of younger disciples designed to succeed them in the holy vocation. As the great Head of the Church had commanded his disciples to "go teach all nations," so Paul, in handing down his apostolical responsibility to the future Church, exhorts Timothy and his successors in this language: "The things that thou hast heard of me among many witnesses, the same commit thou to faithful men, who shall be able to teach others also" (2 Tim. ii, 2).

In harmony with such examples and precepts, it is recorded, in the early history of the Church, that the apostle John spent his advanced years at Ephesus in qualifying youth for the Christian ministry, that Mark founded a ministerial school at Alexandria, and Polycarp another at Smyrna. Subsequently, similar schools were established at Cæsarea, in Palestine; at Antioch, Laodicea, Nicomedia, Athens, Edessa, Nisibis in Mesopotamia, Seleucia, Rome, and Carthage. Less distinguished than these were many episcopal schools connected with the prominent dioceses of the ancient Church. In some of the better periods and phases of monasticism conventual schools were established, in which young ecclesiastics were qualified as missionaries and teachers for the tribes and nations to which they were sent forth. Prominent among these were the schools at Iona, at Bangor, in Wales, and Armagh, in Ireland. During the mediæval period the Waldenses, although few in number and obscure in their seclusion, required all their candidates for the ministry to be diligent students, prescribing to them a course of study, and testing them by specific examinations.

The schools of Charlemagne, and the various universities founded in sequence of the Crusades, appear to have contemplated primarily, though not exclusively, the instruction of ecclesiastics. The University of Prague and that of Strasburg are celebrated for their aid to religion and the diffusion of piety in the Church. Nor must Paris be omitted. All these institutions exerted their influence for the purifying of Christian doctrine, not only at home, but abroad. We need but mention the names of John Huss and Jerome of Prague; and here let us not forget John Wickliffe, who labored so faithfully at Oxford, and instilled English students with those principles that gave life to the Reformation. D'Aubigné says: "The first rays of the sun from on high gilded with their fires at once the Gothic colleges at Oxford and the antique schools at Cambridge." During the Reformatory period, the Continental universities became the main agencies for the spread of the new doctrines. Wittenberg, then but recently founded, became the nursery, the citadel, of the Protestants. The lecture-rooms of the Reformers were their principal pulpits; and, as has been declared by Melancthon in his *Life of Luther,* the great cause owes its success to the universities. The University of Heidelberg heard with joy the lectures of the exile Reuchlin. Wittenberg was the starting-point of the great Reformer himself, and from all Europe students flocked thither to sit at the feet of the immortal Melancthon. All the leaders of the new cause, in short, were university men—most of them professors, who diffused their opinions through attentive listeners. Calvin, first at Strasburg, and later, aided by Beza, at Geneva, exerted an influence chiefly through the famous schools with which he was connected. Fleury says, in his *Life of Calvin:* "He was indebted to the academy (at Geneva), which soon became greatly frequented, for the rapid diffusion of his doctrines in Germany, Holland, and France." In passing, we may remind our readers also of those university laborers, the ardent servants for the Christian cause, Erasmus of

Paris, Œcolampadius of Strasburg, Peter Martyr and Martin Bucer of Oxford and Cambridge, and Arminius of Leyden.

From those days to the present all complete universities had had faculties of theology of greater or less extent. Their character and influence we shall consider in an article on *Theological Education* (q. v.). We confine ourselves for the present to a review of the educational advantages offered by the various religious organizations independent of the state; and as even such are in Europe subject to more or less state aid, we shall consider here only those of religious bodies in the United States of America, but mainly in so far as they have in view the instruction of ministers.

In the colonial days of this country's history the ministers were, with few exceptions, men who had been trained for the work in Europe, and in a majority of cases were skilled laborers in the vineyard before they left the old country. It has been estimated that there was in the New England colonies, twenty years after the landing of the Pilgrims, a graduate of college for every 240 inhabitants. A few of these graduates were employed in the civil administration of the colonies, but most of them were in the ministry. As the population increased, it became necessary to supply the ministry from the rising generation. For this purpose, and this mainly, the university at Cambridge was founded in 1636, and as its motto was chosen "Christo et ecclesiæ" (*To Christ and the Church*). Amid much sacrifice and denial this school was started, and for years, yea, decades, as new churches were planted, or as the early ministers passed away by death, the ministerial office was supplied, in great measure, from among the graduates of the infant college. More than half of its graduates, during the first century of its existence, entered into the labors of the ministry. Cotton Mather, in his *Magnolia*, furnishes a list of the New England churches in 1696, from which it appears that of the 129 pulpits supplied by 116 pastors, 107 of the preachers were graduates of Harvard College. In the charters of several of the oldest colleges it is declared that *virtue and religion* are the principal objects for the founding of these higher institutions of learning. "The Virginians have souls to be saved" was the plea presented by the pioneers in 1693, when the college was asked for Virginia; "and though the chancellor cursed their souls, saying, 'Let them raise tobacco,' William and Mary granted both a charter and money to the college which still bears their name." In a few generations all the leading churches, as they grew and found a need for training-schools to supply the ministry, founded colleges, until at present full four hundred chartered *Christian colleges* have grown into life as the outward material expression of the Christian zeal within American bosoms. What is peculiarly strange about American colleges is that all of them have felt more or less constrained to consecrate their work to religion. "Secular and state colleges, so called, many of them, surpass those under denominational control in their vigorous appeals to the religious feelings of the people." Placing some eminent worker of the Christian Church in the presidency, they install the Word of God in the daily college prayers. They require all the students to attend church each Sabbath. They have daily prayer-meetings among the students. These students generally attend Sabbath-schools. The Greek Testament is read in the college lessons. The evidences of Christianity are taught in the classes. Free tuition and other inducements are offered to attract candidates for the ministry to these institutions. Revival measures are introduced. All the means of grace known to the evangelical churches are used as regularly, as frequently, as earnestly in the colleges as they are in any of the congregations. Of late years, the Church, working unitedly under the auspices of the "Evangelical Alliance," has appointed a day of prayer to be observed once annually—now on the last Thursday in January—and many have

been the conversions and fruits for the ministry. It is asserted by those who have carefully searched the records of our colleges that nearly one third of their graduates enter the ministry. Of Amherst College, e. g., it is told that "nearly half of its 'alumni,' since the beginning of its career, have become ministers of the Gospel." "Even West Point Military Academy, where they talk of war, and drill to the time of martial music every day, the cross of Jesus has won many a trophy. In one of the awakening seasons there the college chaplain was busy circulating tracts. A cadet to whom he gave a tract called soon afterwards to see him, exclaiming, 'I am a lost sinner; what must I do to be saved?' The chaplain led him gently to Jesus. The cadet was afterwards bishop Polk." Such is the religious influence upon the higher literary institutions in the United States of America.

Theological Seminaries.—Ministerial education, properly so called, was afforded to but few of the earlier preachers of this country. In the colleges no special advantages were known, except what the instructors could grant by special arrangement. Principally the custom prevailed in some churches of associating ministerial candidates as students with experienced pastors, from whom they might receive instruction in theology and pastoral duty, and to whom in turn they might render some assistance. In other churches, in which the pressure for ministerial aid was great, young and inexperienced men were associated in actual service with senior ministers, by whom they were expected to be taught. While such modes of instruction and training were the best practicable at an initial period of Church development, and, indeed, not without some intrinsic advantages, yet the increase of general education, and the necessity for more thorough study on the part of ministers, were thought to demand the establishment of a class of institutions specially devoted to ministerial preparation and the cultivation of sacred learning.

The history of this class of institutions in the United States is limited to the present century, with the single exception of a Roman Catholic seminary in Baltimore, founded in 1791. The first theological seminary of the Congregationalists, that of Andover, was founded in 1807. The dates at which the other principal denominations followed these examples are as follows: The Presbyterians at Princeton in 1812; the Protestant Episcopalians at New York in 1817; the Baptists at Hamilton, N. Y., in 1820; the Methodists at Newbury, Vt., in 1843—consolidated with Concord, N. H., in 1847.

The extent to which institutions for ministerial education have since been multiplied is indicated by the following summary, given in the report of the United States commissioner of education for 1886-7.

Denomination.	Number of Institutions.	Number of Instructors.	Number of Students.
Roman Catholic......	20	140	646
Presbyterian..........	14	81	739
Baptist..............	18	101	1011
Protestant Episcopal..	12	68	286
Methodist Episcopal..	13	101	655
Congregational.......	11	65	378
Lutheran	14	59	1013
Reformed.............	6	21	95
Christian	6	19	229
Minor sects..........	25	36	987
Total	139	691	6039

Of the influence of this class of institutions as a whole, it may be said that it is greatly conducive to the advancement of sacred learning. By the accumulation of libraries, by the classification of studies, by the devotion of able men to special departments, more thorough instruction is provided, and students are enabled to secure, within limited periods, a more thorough acquaintance with the various branches of theological science than would be possible by any form of isolated or individual effort. (D. P. K.)

Educational Aid Societies.—In this connection a word must be said about the many educational societies founded by the various religious bodies to aid young men financially during their preparations for the sacred office of the ministry. The amount of work accomplished by these agencies may be estimated by reference to the following items: The American Education Society (including the parent society at Boston and its Presbyterian branches), since its formation in the year 1815, has raised and expended in the work of ministerial education not far from $2,000,000. It has afforded aid to over 5000 young men in their course of education for the ministry. The amount raised by this society for one year was $38,914, and the number of young men assisted for the same year was 432. The American Board of Commissioners for Foreign Missions since its formation has sent out into the great foreign mission field not far from 500 ordained ministers. Of these over one half have been beneficiaries of the American Education Society. About one third of the Congregational ministers of New England at the present time were aided in their education by this society, while more than one third of that large body of men who have labored so efficiently in connection with the Home Missionary Society were raised up in the same way. The Board of Education of the Presbyterian Church (Old School) has since its formation furnished aid to about 2200 young men. How many of these men have been employed in foreign and home missionary service we have no means at hand for determining. The amount raised by this board from year to year for the purposes of ministerial education is not far from $50,000, and the number of young men now assisted yearly is but little less than 400. There is also an Education Society in connection with the Baptist churches, which has rendered efficient aid in the same great work. In the Methodist Episcopal Church this agency has assumed such vast importance that special provision was made for a "Board of Education" during the American Centennial of Methodism, and there is now (1874) a fund of $100,000, the interest of which is annually expended to aid candidates for the Methodist ministry There are also educational societies for the same purpose in connection with most of the Annual Conferences. Even the non-evangelical churches support such agencies. See Knight, *Utility of Theol. Seminaries;* Kentish, *Importance of Min. Education;* Clarke (Adam), *Letter to a Preacher;* Mason, *Student and Pastor;* Raike, *Remarks on Clerical Education; New-Englander,* i, 126; *Eclectic Rev.* (new series), i, 99; *Princeton Rev.* v, 55; xv, 587; *Christian Examiner,* xi, 84; *Amer. Bible Repository,* ix, 474; xi, 187; 2d series, viii, 444; x, 462; *Evangel.* (Luth.) *Qu. Rev.* 1868, July; *Meth. Qu. Rev.* July, 1845, art. ii; Jan. 1872, p. 94; *Theol. Medium* (*Cumberland Presbyt. Rev.*), Jan. 1873, art. i.

Ministerium is a term applied to an ecclesiastical body within the pale of the Lutheran Church. It is composed only of ordained ministers, and transacts business pertaining only to the interests of the ministry, such as the *examination, licensure,* and *ordination of candidates* for the ministry. "This is the specific and chief business of the ministerium. It also, when necessary, examines and decides charges of heresy against any of its own members, and may, by appeal, act in the cause of a layman charged with heresy—but only by appeal 'from the decision of a Church Council.'" It will thus be seen that the business transacted by the ministerium is of a special and definite character; and to preclude any attempt to go beyond this, it is expressly provided that "all business not specifically intrusted to the ministerium . . . shall belong to the synod." Of late efforts have been made, especially in this country, to abolish the ministerium, and to transfer its power to the synod, in order that the lay members of the Church may have a voice in the management of the affairs now within the jurisdiction of the ministerium; and this demand has been made upon the ground that the Lutheran Church has suffered more from heresy and immorality in her ministry than other churches, because the minis-

ter is amenable only to his clerical brethren. See an able discussion on this subject in the *Quarterly Review of the Evangelical Luth. Church,* January, 1873, art. v.

Ministration ($\delta\iota\alpha\kappa o\nu\iota\alpha$, $\lambda\epsilon\iota\tau o\nu\rho\gamma\iota\alpha$, both usually rendered "ministry"), the period during which an office is administered (Luke i, 23). The law of Moses is called the "ministration of death" and "condemnation." It convinces men of sin, the penalty for which is eternal death; and to this they are already condemned. The Gospel is the "ministration of the Spirit" that "giveth life;" it proceeds from the Holy Ghost; is confirmed and applied by him; and by means of it he conveys life, and all spiritual graces and benefits, to the souls of men (2 Cor. iii, 7, 8). The term is also used for the distribution of alms (Acts vi, 1; 2 Cor. ix, 13).

Ministry (עֲבוֹדָה, *work;* שָׁרֵת, *attendance;* $\lambda\epsilon\iota\tau o\nu\rho\gamma\iota\alpha$, *waiting upon;* $\delta\iota\alpha\kappa o\nu\iota\alpha$, *service*). Besides the ordinary applications of this term to the common affairs of life, it is specially used in the Scriptures, chiefly those of the New Testament, to denote a devotion to the interests of God's cause, and, in a technical sense, the work of advancing the Redeemer's kingdom. It is in this sense, namely, of the *Christian Ministry,* that we propose here to treat of some features of this office, leaving to special titles other parts, such as the literary qualification for it [see MINISTERIAL EDUCATION], and a more general view of its relations to the article PASTORAL THEOLOGY. The essential functions of evangelical ministry are the following:

I. *Preaching.*—The duty of disseminating the Gospel is not confined to the ministry. A comparison of all the narratives relative to the event in the New Testament renders it clear that the great commission in Matt. xxviii, 19, 20 was not delivered to the eleven apostles merely, but to the general body of the disciples then assembled (1 Cor. xv, 6). It is the great character of evangelization. In like manner it appears that, although the twelve apostles were originally sent out on a preaching tour of Galilee (Matt. x), subsequently seventy others were despatched on a similar mission (Luke x). So on the day of Pentecost the whole mass of believers at Jerusalem seem to have been inspired with preaching powers, and they actually exercised them (Acts ii, 4). Nor was this an occasional though extraordinary instance; on the contrary, a similar practice is implied in all the later exhibitions of the then universal gift of the Holy Spirit (Acts x, 44–47; xix, 6, 7; 1 Cor. xii, xiv). Indeed, the technical distinction between clergy and laity in this particular is almost ignored in the New Testament, and we find members of the Church, whether official or private, male or female, freely exercising their liberty in proclaiming Jesus everywhere (Acts vi, 8; viii, 1, 4–8; ix, 20; xviii, 24–28; xxi, 9). This is in accordance with the universal impulse of the newly-converted soul to communicate the glad tidings of his own salvation to others, without waiting for any formal license or authorization. Such evangelization is the very essence of preaching, by whatever name it may be called, or by whatever conventionalities it may be surrounded. We may add that whoever loses this spirit of his early zeal, has lost, be his success or attainments in other respects what they may, the great divine seal of his call to preach. See LAY PREACHING.

The call, as above defined, to preach the Gospel to the best of our ability and opportunity, is one that every Christian should recognise and obey. It is, however, a duty entirely distinct from, although in some cases closely related to, the general question of our vocation in life. It is precisely at this point that the thought of the ministry has probably occurred, sooner or later, to every considerate young man of the Church. If earnest and devoted, he is apt to infer the farther duty of giving himself exclusively as an avocation to the work of preaching. The idea having once been vividly presented to his imagination, is likely, in proportion to his conscientiousness, to fasten more and more deeply upon his convictions, while at the same time his judgment of his fitness, his inclinations, and his circumstances may be totally adverse to the course. Hence he is in a two-fold danger of error; on the one hand he may mistake for a distinctive divine call his own general promptings to do anything, however uncongenial, for the sake of his Master; or, on the other, he may yield to a self-depre-cating modesty and the force of obstacles, and neglect a real call. Under this balancing of arguments, per-haps the safest guides are two—one internal, the other external. In the first place, let him carefully examine his own heart, and see what motive secretly prompts him in this direction. If it be the love of applause, a desire for distinction, a vanity for public prominence, or a wish to gain a ready mode of subsistence, of course he must conclude himself to be unworthy and unfit for the holy office. If, again, he is chiefly drawn to the work under a mere sense of condemnation if he refuse, we ap-prehend he has not reached the highest intimation of an incentive to duty in this path. He, like every other believer, of course, must quiet his conscience by being *willing* to do any duty, even this, if clearly made known; but it does not follow that he is called upon to do any and every disagreeable thing, simply because it would be a cross to him. A better and more decisive, as well as consistent test, is to ask himself, "Do I seek this place, or consent to assume it, because I look upon it as the most exalted and useful one I could occupy? Is it one in which I feel that I can most effectually glorify God and serve my generation?" If he still have doubt in answering the question, then let him turn to the other outward test. Let him *try it*, and experiment will soon satisfy him whether his call is genuine or not. This experience will especially determine four points; namely, 1. His natural qualification or disqualification, in point of physical, mental, and spiritual adaptation; 2. His probable measure of success, as evinced by the fruit of his efforts; 3. His greatest lack, and consequent-ly the points where, by study and care, he should more fully prepare himself in the future; 4. The providential indications, by way of opening, means, etc., for his far-ther progress. The Church, meanwhile, through his friends, fellow-members, and the pastor, will thus have an opportunity of judging on all these points, and then advice will not only be welcomed by him, but must in the end be conclusive.

Our result, therefore, under this head is, that while preaching the Gospel in some form, and as a specific work, is the general duty of all believers, it is the sole or exclusive duty of those only who, by undoubted in-ternal and external marks, are divinely called to the office, and sanctioned in it by the Church at large. This last is the ultimate or determinative sign.

II. *Ordination.*—The second great and peculiar func-tion of the Christian ministry is the administration of the holy sacraments—namely, Baptism and the Lord's Supper. Other clerical offices—such as officiating at marriages, funerals, chaplaincy, expounding the Script-ures, dispensing ritual duties, etc.—are entirely subor-dinate and immaterial to these. The sacraments like-wise may, no doubt, lawfully be administered by a lay unordained person, or even by a woman, in case of emergency or private celebration; but, for the sake of propriety and system, they should be a matter of Church order, and this is the meaning of the term "ordination." This, therefore, is a purely *ecclesiastical* distinction, which affects the ordained individual only as to certain churchly relations or functions appertaining to himself individually. For this reason it is performed but once, and as a ceremony. Whether it be executed by the bishop, a presbyter, or neighboring pastor, is entirely conventional. The true "apostolical succession" is maintained wherever the line is in accordance with the established Church usage in the case.

It will be observed that preaching and "orders" do not necessarily concur in the same person. Hence some

churches have ordained elders who are not clergymen. Hence, likewise, there are ordained local preachers and unordained travelling preachers. The election to cleri-cal orders rests, in the Episcopal churches, with the bish-op; in the Presbyterian churches, with the Presbyterial Synod; in Methodist churches, with the Annual Con-ference; among Congregationalists, Baptists, etc., with the congregation itself.

III. *The Pastorate.*—This is the last and crowning office of the Christian ministry. It does not necessarily involve the two preceding, for in all churches there are occasionally pastors who are not ordained men. In the Methodist Church there are at least sub-pastors, namely, class-leaders, who have no other clerical functions; and many of the Roman Catholic priests do not preach at all. On the other hand, there are numerous "evangelists" who, as local preachers, have no pastoral relations, nor any ordained status. The pastorate, moreover, differs from the preaching element of the ministry in its *local* and *transferable* character. The commission to preach is world-wide, long as mind and body last; but the pas-toral jurisdiction is necessarily limited to a particular community and on stipulated terms. The appointment under it always implies a mutual understanding and consent between the pastor and his people; and it is a piece of clerical imposition when the latter are permit-ted to have no voice in its formation and dissolution; as it is an act of prelatical tyranny when the former is not consulted, or allowed to express his wishes and judg-ment.

We have said that the pastorate is the highest func-tion of the ministry. It is so, because it combines in their most complete, regular, and effective form all the elements of the ministerial relation. A man who has the hearts of his people, and can sway them from the pulpit, as well as touch them in the tender and intimate connections of his pastoral ministrations; who intro-duces their babes to Christ, and dispenses to them the symbols of the body and blood of their Lord, wields a power which kings might envy, and holds a place with which Gabriel's cannot vie. He is God's ambassador to a dying community, and his angel in the Church.

IV. To the foregoing ministerial functions many are disposed to add a fourth, namely, *administration.* This, so far as it applies to the execution of discipline in any particular Church, is merely a part of the pastorate; and even here it is very doubtful whether the pastor have legitimately any power beyond that of presiding in meetings, and guiding in a general way the affairs of the Church. His personal influence, of course, is very great; and if the people have confidence in his judgment, his advice will be freely sought and cheerfully followed. But the assumption of any dictatorial rights will quickly be resented and resisted as a "lording over God's heri-tage" equally unwarranted by Scripture or ecclesiastical law.

The extension of the clerical administration to the general Church, in distinction from the laity, is a prelat-ical usurpation characteristic only, and everywhere, of High-Churchism. It is the essence of popery, and is not the less offensive if advocated or practiced by a bishop in any Protestant Church. Even the Episcopal churches, strictly so called, do not hold this theory; the Methodist Church has lately discarded it, and the Pres-byterians admit the lay elders to a full participation in the highest legislative assemblies.

Referring once more to our Lord's constitutional be-hest (Matt. xxviii, 19, 20), we find four duties enjoined upon his disciples: 1. Preaching—that is, evangelization. 2. Discipling—that is, enrolling as followers of Jesus. 3. Baptism—that is, initiation by a public ordinance. 4. Instruction—that is, inculcation of Christian doctrine in detail. Not one of these is the essential or peculiar, much less exclusive prerogative of the ministry; al-though the minister, as such, naturally takes the lead in them, devoting himself professionally to them, espe-cially in the more public and formal relations. Of all the really characteristic functions of the ministry, we have found—to recapitulate—that the true basis of authorization arises in the Church itself, as the final earthly judge of qualification and fidelity; and that she expresses her decision with respect to it through the preacher's own immediate brethren; while she signs his credentials to the second through the ecclesiastical organism which he thereby enters; and she issues her mandate respecting the third through the local community which thus invites his care.

See, besides the works quoted under MINISTER, Schaff, Hist. Apostol. Ch. p. 495 sq.; Bearcroft, Thirteen Discourses on the Ministry; Boardman, On the Christian Ministry; Collings, Vindication of a Gospel Ministry; Crosthwaite, On the Christian Ministry; Edmonson, On the Christian Ministry; Fancourt, Nature and Expediency of a Ministry; Taylor, Institution and Necessity of the Ministry; Turner, The Christian Ministry Considered; Vinet, Theory of the Evangel. Ministry; Wallace, Guide to the Christian Ministry; Wayland (Francis), Letters on the Christian Ministry; Amer. Bible Repository, ix, 64; Christian Exam. v, 101; xv, 334; Christian Monthly Spectator, iii, 401; viii, 441; ix, 487; Christian Observer, xiv, 13; xix, 433; xx, 533, 544; xxii, 329, 546; xxviii, 137, 416; Christian Qu. Spect. iv, 207; vi, 542; vii, 353; viii, 411; Christian Rev. i, 15; iii, 254, 576; xi, 256; xiii, 501; xv, 400; Edinb. Rev. xix, 360; North Amer. Rev. xlix, 206; Kitto, Journ. of Sac. Lit. vol. xxix; Cumberl. Presb. Qu. Oct. 1871. See also Poole, Index to Periodical Lit. s. v.; Malcom, Theol. Index, s. v.

Min'ni (Heb. Minni', מִנִּי, etymology unknown; Sept. παρ' ἐμοῦ, Vulg. Menni) occurs only in Jer. li, 27 (and so in the Targ. at Psa. xlv, 9, but wrongly), as the name of an Armenian province, joined with Ararat; i.e., as Bochart well observes (Phaleg, i, 3, p. 19, 20), probably the Minyas (Μινύας) of Nicholas of Damascus in Josephus (Ant. i, 3, 6), a tract of Armenia overhung by the mountain Baris, on which are the traces of the ark. St. Martin (Mémoires sur l'Arménie, i, 249) rightly compares the region of the Manavassœi, in the middle of Armenia, so called from Manavas, the son of Haigus, who is said to have been the founder of Armenia (Moses Choren. i, 11). Less likely is the supposition (Bochart, ut sup.) that the Greek name Armenia itself sprung from הַר־מִנִּי, "mountain of Minni," since it is rather derived from Aram (see St. Martin, ut sup. p. 259). "The name may be connected with the Minnai of the Assyrian inscriptions, whom Rawlinson (Herod. i, 464) places about lake Urumiyeh, and with the Minuas who appears in the list of Armenian kings in the inscription at Wan (Layard's Nin. and Bab. p. 401). At the time when Jeremiah prophesied, Armenia had been subdued by the Median kings (Rawlinson, Herod. i, 103, 177)." See ARMENIA.

Minnis, WILLIAM, D.D., a Presbyterian divine, was born, of Scotch-Irish parents, in Blount County, Tenn., Dec. 28, 1799. He was educated at Maryville College, Tenn.; studied divinity in the South-western Theological Seminary at Maryville; was licensed in 1825, and ordained in 1826 as pastor of Westminster Church, Tenn. In 1838 he received and accepted a call to the charge of Salem and New Market, Tenn.; became a member of the United Synod at its organization in 1857, and died May 5, 1863. Dr. Minnis was a man of extraordinary energy, thorough in the investigation of every subject, clear in the illustration of the deepest thought, and truly in earnest in the conversion of souls. See Wilson, Presb. Hist. Almanac, 1867, p. 446.

Min'nith (Heb. Minnith', מִנִּת, distribution; Sept. in Judg. Μενίθ v. r. Ἀρνών, Vulg. Mennith; in Ezek. μύρα, balsamum), a town in the country of the Ammonites, to which Jephthah pursued them (Judg. xi, 33), celebrated for the excellence of its wheat, which was exported to the markets of Tyre (Ezek. xxvii, 17). It

still existed in the age of Eusebius, four Roman miles from Heshbon, on the road to Philadelphia (Onomast. s. v. Μαανίθ, Jerome Mannith). Schwarz (Palest. p. 280) thinks it the same with the present Minja, five miles east of Hesban. "'From Aroer to the approach to Minnith' (עַד בּוֹאֲךָ מ) seems to have been a district containing twenty cities. Minnith was in the neighborhood of Abel-Ceramim, the 'meadow of vineyards.' In this vicinity were possibly situated the vineyards in which Balaam encountered the angel on his road from Mesopotamia to Moab (Numb. xxii, 24). An episcopal city of 'Palestina secunda,' named Mennith, is quoted by Reland (Palœst. p. 211), but with some question as to its being located in this direction (p. 209). A site bearing the name Menjah is marked in Van de Velde's Map, perhaps on the authority of Buckingham, at seven Roman miles east of Heshbon, on a road to Ammân, though not on the frequented track."

Mino, MAESTRO, a distinguished sculptor, flourished during the 15th century. The exact dates of his birth and death are unknown. He is sometimes called MINO DEL REGNO. The statues of San Pietro and San Paolo, which are in the sacristy of St. Peter's, at Rome, but which until 1847 stood at the foot of the steps of St. Peter's, are his work; also the Tomb of Pope Paul II, in the Basilica of St. Peter's. See Vasari, Lives of the Painters, transl. by Mrs. Foster (Lond. 1850, 5 vols. 8vo), ii, 85.

Minor Canon is the name frequently applied to a petty canon, petty prebendary, or sub-canon:

(1.) A vicar in priest's orders in the old foundations; a representative and auxiliary who celebrated at the high altar in the absence of a canon. Generally there were four, occasionally as many as eight. In most cases they were the vicars of the four dignitaries. In the Romish Church of England the word designated in some instances the prebendaries who were in minor orders, and at York a major canon was one who had kept the greater residence. At St. Paul's they form a college, instituted in 1395, over and above the thirty vicars. The latter sung the matin and lady mass, but the minor canons chanted the mass of requiem for their founder, as well as the apostles' and high or chapter masses, being required in addition to attend all the hours. All were priests under a superior, called a warden. Their almoner looked after the choristers. The two cardinals, who had a doubled stipend, were parish priests of the close. They furnished the librarian, subdean, succentor, and divinity lecturer, and the perpetual gospeller and epistoler. In 1378 they wore surplices, dark almuces of calaba, lined with minever, with a black cope and hood, trimmed with silk or linen.

(2.) A subordinate or stipendiary priest, appointed by the dean and chapter in the new foundations; and by the original constitution the number equalled that of the canons, and the stipend half that of the latter. They had a share in the quotidian. In the time of Charles I their numbers were reduced. They had no estates of their own, and lived in a common hall, along with the schoolmasters, lay singers, and choristers. Minor canons are removable by the dean and chapter, and are now choral substitutes of the canons residentiary, officiating in turn, under their authority, jointly with the dean. See Walcott, Sacred Archæology, s. v.; Staunton, Eccles. Dict. s. v. See also CANON, ECCLESIASTICAL.

Minor, Launcelot Byrd, a missionary of the Protestant Episcopal Church, was born at Topping Castle, Carolina County, Va., Sept. 9, 1813. In 1833 he entered the theological seminary of Virginia. Missionaries being required for West Africa, he determined to give himself to the work. He was ordained in 1836, and sailed from Baltimore for Cape Palmas May 8, 1837. Immediately after arrival in his field of labor, he assumed the charge of a school at Mount Vaughan, Cape Palmas. In April, 1839, he visited the Gold Coast, of which he gave a graphic account to the Board of Missions. In the same year he returned to the United States on a visit, and while here he married. Shortly after he returned to Africa, to take charge of a small chapel at Mount Vaughan. In 1841 he took part in an exploring expedition, having for its object the establishment of a station in the district of Taboo, and in 1843 he removed his family to that locality; but just as he was ready to commence his labors there he died. He possessed neither brilliant talents nor a strong intellect, but his devotion to his work made him so earnest and zealous that everything gave way before him. The natives were attracted by the amiableness of his character, and his influence over them was most potent and blessed. See H. W. Pierson, *American Missionary Memorial*, p. 449.

Minor, Melchior Gottlieb, a German theologian, was born at Zilzendorf, in the Silesian county of Brieg, Dec. 28, 1693; received his preparatory education at the orphan school at Halle, where he distinguished himself by great proficiency in the ancient languages; in 1709 he entered the gymnasium at Zittau, and in 1712 the university. He studied theology and philosophy at Wittenberg; soon afterwards he went to Halle, to study modern languages, civil and ecclesiastical law, and mathematics. Upon the completion of his course in 1715, he returned to his native city, where he got a position as tutor; in 1720 he was appointed minister at Teppliwode, in the principality of Münsterberg; and in 1722 minister at Landshut. Some time after he was appointed counsellor of the Prussian consistory, and inspector of churches and schools of the district of Schweidnitz. He died Sept. 24, 1748. Some of his most important works are, *Das Leben im Leiden, eine Leichenpredigt über Psa. xlii*, 2, 3 (Landshut, 1723, fol.) :—*Das nöthige Wissen eines Christen* (Janer, 1723, 12mo): —*Kurze Nachricht von den Altären der Juden, Heiden und Christen, mit einer Beschreibung des in der Gnadenkirche von Landshut erbauten Altars* (Landshut, 1725, 4to):—*Hauptsumme der christlichen Lehre* (ibid. 1726, 12mo):—*Geistliche Reden und Abhandlungen* (Leipsic and Breslau, 2 vols. 1752, 8vo):—*Heilige Betrachtungen über die Evangelien* (ibid. 1756, 8vo):—*Heilige Betrachtungen über die Leidensgeschichte Jesu* (ibid. 1757, large 8vo). See Döring, *Gelehrte Theol. Deutschlands*, s. v.

Minorca (Span. *Menorca*), one of the Balearic Isles, some twenty-five miles distant from Majorca, the largest of the group, is 31 miles long and 13 miles wide, covering in all a territory of about 300 square miles, and counting 37,280 inhabitants, subject to the Spanish government. The coast of Minorca, broken into numerous bays and inlets, is fringed with islets and shoals, and its surface, less mountainous than that of Majorca, is undulating, rising to its highest point in Mount Toro, 4793 feet above the sea-level. Its chief productions are marble, slate, plaster, the common cereals and legumes, oranges, silk, lemons, oil, wine, olives, and aromatic herbs. The chief towns are Port Mahon, the capital, and Ciudadela, the former capital, with a population of about 4000. There are many remains of Celtic civilization on the island. The people of Minorca (*Menorquines*) are very indolent, the women very stylish and polite. The religious history of the *Menorquines* is so intimately connected with that of their rulers that we must refer to the article SPAIN.

Minoress is another name under which the followers of St. Clare are distinguished. See CLARE, ST.

Minorites, a name of the Franciscan order, derived from the later denomination adopted by their founder, *Fratres Minores*. See FRANCISCANS.

Minos, a Cretan hero and lawgiver, figures in Greek mythology and legends. There are many writers who speak of two characters of that name, but Homer and Hesiod know of only one Minos, the king of Cnossus, and son and friend of the god Jupiter himself. We are told that Minos secured the throne by promising sacrifices to the gods, and that when he had acquired the power he was cruel and tyrannical; and that after he had subjected the Athenians he treated them mercilessly, and required their boys and virgins as sacrifices to the Minotaur (q. v.). Although these legends and fables are of but little interest, Minos deserves a place here as a benefactor of the race; and, if his existence be not mythical, he must be ranked among the wise men of the earth. To him the celebrated *Laws of Minos*, which served as a model for the legislation of Lycurgus, are ascribed. He is said to have dealt out justice, and to have so pleased the gods that he became a judge of the souls which entered the infernal regions. Minos has by some writers on antiquity been identified with Manu (or Menu), the great Hindû lawgiver.

Minotaur (i. e. the *Bull of Minos*) is one of the most repulsive conceptions of Grecian mythology. He is represented as the son of Pasiphaë and a bull, for which she had conceived a passion. It was half man, half bull—a man with a bull's head. Minos, the husband of Pasiphaë, shut him up in the Cnossian Labyrinth, and there fed him with youths and maidens, whom Athens was obliged to supply as an annual tribute, till Theseus, with the help of Ariadne, slew the monster. See MINOS. The Minotaur is, with some probability, regarded as a symbol of the Phœnician sun-god.

Minshall, ROBERT, a minister of the Methodist Episcopal Church, was born in Pennsylvania in 1788; entered the Baltimore Conference in 1813; and died in Mercersburg, Pa., July 15, 1828. He was a man of fine talents and great piety and zeal. He was especially useful as a promoter of Sunday-schools and tract societies, and was also an excellent and faithful minister of the Word. See *Minutes of Conferences*, ii, 37.

Minster signified originally, as in the writings of Cassian, St. Athanasius, and Jerome, the cell of a solitary; but the word was extended by Eusebius to embrace the church or the abode of a religious community. (1.) A church of regular canons. (2.) A church formerly served by monks (in Germany the term *Münster* is still employed, and *Marmoutier* in France—*majus monasterium*, or great minster). (3.) A cathedral. (4.) Many large churches, held by secular canons, were dignified by the title of minster. (5.) Paris churches, in 960, were called minsters, and several retain the name. These were the original outposts of the Church, isolated stations of priests living under rule and in community, which in time became parishes.

Minster Ham is the term applied to a sanctuary-house, in which persons were afforded refuge for three days. If it were burdened with the king's purveyance, they might remain for a longer period.

Minstrel (מְנַגֵּן, *menaggen'*, one *striking* the harp, 2 Kings iii, 15; αὐλητής, Matt. ix, 33, a *flute-player*, "piper," Rev. xviii, 22). Music was often employed by the Hebrews for sacred purposes, and in the case of Elisha it appears to have conduced to inspiration (2 Kings iii, 15). See MUSIC. It was a usual accompaniment of funerals likewise (Matt. ix, 33; comp. Josephus, *War*, iii, 9, 5), as it is still in the East (see Hackett's *Illustra. of Script.* p. 113). See BURIAL.

The English word *minstrel* represents the French word *ménestral*, which is itself a diminutive of *ministre*, and is applied to the class of persons who *administered* to the amusement of their patrons by their skill in music and poetry. Chaucer uses the word *minister* in the sense of minstrel in his *Dreame* (Richardson, s. v., and Du Cange, *Gloss.*). The class of minstrels had in mediæval times a social position almost akin to the bards and scalds whose *Sagas* they sung and whose inspiration they imitated at humble distance. Musical sound has been an accompaniment of religious worship in all countries. The expert player on the musical instrument has been associated with the possessor of yet higher faculties (see Wilkinson's *Ancient Egyptians*, chap. ii, and representations of harpers in the tomb of Rameses III, Thebes; Müller's *Hist. of Greek Literature*, chap. xii). The "pleasant voice and lovely song," and the art of "playing well on an instrument," were associated with the functions of prophecy (Ezek. xxxiii, 31-33). Various passages of Holy Scripture show that the skilful performance of sacred music formed a large portion of the education of the sons of the prophets; 1 Sam. x, 5, "Thou shalt meet a company (חֶבֶל, Sept. χορός) of prophets coming down from the high place, with a psaltery, a tabret, a pipe, and a harp *before them* [see PROPHET], and they shall prophesy." It is not certain whether the prophets were here distinct from the players on instruments, but most probably they were the same individuals as those of whom we read elsewhere, that they "should prophesy with harps, with psalteries, and with cymbals" (1 Chron. xxv, 1); that they resembled "the sons of Asaph, of Heman, and of Jeduthun, who should prophesy with a harp, according to the order of the king, to give thanks and to praise the Lord" (see also ver. 6, 7). In this passage the performance of sacred song and choral music in the temple received the exalted designation of prophecy. Sacred music, "a joyful noise unto the Lord," and "thanksgiving to the Lord upon an instrument of ten strings, and upon the psaltery" (Psa. lxvi, 1; lxxxvii, 7; xcii, 1-3; c, 1), were characteristics of close communion with God. The effect produced upon the auditors is described (1 Sam. x, 6) as being in that instance very remarkable—Saul is assured that when he hears the prophetic minstrelsy, "the Spirit of the Lord will come upon him, and he shall prophesy with them, and be turned into another man." See ver. 11, and comp. 1 Sam. xix, 20-24, the account of the prophets being instructed by Samuel, and the effect of the holy song under the influence of the Spirit of God upon Saul's messengers, and afterwards upon Saul himself. Saul is thus seen to be peculiarly accessible to the highest influences of music, and hence the advice tendered to him by his servants (1 Sam. xvi, 16), "Seek out a man who is a cunning *player* on a harp, and it shall come to pass that when the evil spirit from God is upon thee, that he shall play with his hand and thou shalt be well." The participial form מְנַגֵּן (from נָגַן, in Piel, which is used of striking the strings of a musical instrument) is here translated "a player," and in 2 Kings iii, 15, "minstrel." The effect produced on Saul was remarkable. See SAUL. The custom of applying such a remedy to mental disturbance may be traced in other writings. Thus Quintil. (*Instit. Orat.* lib. ix, chap. 4) says, "Pythagoreis moris fuit, cum somnum peterent ad lyram prius lenire mentes, ut si quid fuisset turbidiorum cogitationum componerent" (comp. Plutarch, *De Musica*, and Aristotle, *Pol.* lib. viii, chap. 5; Apollonius Dyscolos, *De Miris*, quoted by Grotius, ad loc., Ἰᾶται ἡ κατάλαυσις τῆς διανοίας ἐκστάσεις. See also *King Lear*, act. ii, sc. v, where music is used to bring back the wandering mind of Lear). Josephus (*Ant.* vi, 8, 2), in his account of the transaction, associates the singing of hymns by David with the harp-playing, and shows that though the tragedy of Saul's life was lightened for a while by the skilful minstrelsy of David, the raving madness soon triumphed over the tranquillizing influence (comp. 1 Sam. xviii, 10; xix, 10). Weemse (*Christ. Synagogue*, chap. vi, § 3, par. 6, p. 143) supposes that the music appropriate to such occasions was "that which the Greeks called ἁρμονίαν, which was the greatest and the saddest, and settled the affections."

In many references of Holy Scripture the minstrel and the prophet appear to be identical, and their functions the same; but in 2 Kings iii, 15 their respective functions are clearly distinguished. The prophet Elisha needed the influence of "the *minstrel*" to soothe the irritation occasioned by the aggravating alliance of Israel with Judah. Not until this was effected would the prophetic influence guide him to a sound vaticination of the duty and destiny of the allied forces. The minstrelsy was produced, according to Procopius, by a Levite, who sung the Psalms of David in the hearing of the prophet; if so, he was thus the means of producing that condition of mind by which the prophet was lifted above the perceptions of his senses, and the circumstances which surrounded him, into a higher region of thought, where he might by divine grace penetrate the secret purposes of God. Jarchi says that "on account of anger the Shechinah had departed from him;" Ephraem Syrus, that the object of the music was to attract a crowd to hear the prophecy; J. H. Michaelis, that the prophet's mind, disturbed by the impiety of the Israelites, might be soothed and prepared for divine things by a spiritual song. According to Keil (*Comm. on Kings*, i, 359, Eng. tr.), "Elisha calls for a minstrel, in order to gather in his thoughts by the soft tones of music from the impression of the outer world, and, by repressing the life of self and of the world, to be transferred into the state of internal vision, by which his spirit would be prepared to receive the divine revelation." This in effect is the view taken by Josephus (*Ant.* ix, 3, 1), and the same is expressed by Maimonides in a passage which embodies the opinion of the Jews of the Middle Ages. "All the prophets were not able to prophesy at any time that they wished; but they prepared their minds, and sat joyful and glad of heart, and abstracted; for prophecy dwelleth not in the midst of melancholy, nor in the midst of apathy, but in the midst of joy. Therefore the sons of the prophets had before them a psaltery, and a tabret, and a pipe, and a harp, and [thus] sought after prophecy" (or prophetic inspiration) (*Yad hachazakah*, vii, 5, Bernard's *Creed and Ethics of the Jews*, p. 16; see also note to p. 114). Kimchi quotes a tradition to the effect that, after the ascension of his master Elijah, the spirit of prophecy had not dwelt upon Elisha because he was mourning, and the spirit of holiness does not dwell but in the midst of joy. The references given above to the power and dignity of song may sufficiently explain the occurrence. The spiritual ecstasy was often bestowed without any means, but many instances are given of subordinate physical agencies being instrumental in its production (Ezek. ii, 2; iii, 24; Isa. vi, 1; Acts x, 9, 10; Rev. i, 9, 10).

The word *minstrel* is used of the αὐλήτας who, in Matt. ix, 23, are represented as mourning and making a noise on the death of Jairus's daughter. The custom of hiring mourners at the death of friends is seen on Etruscan amphoræ, tombs, and bass-reliefs (see Dennis's *Etruria*, i, 295; ii, 344, 354, where music was considered appropriate; and Wilkinson, *Ancient Egyptians*, ii, 366-373). Skill in lamentation (Amos v, 16; Jer. ix, 17) was not necessarily skill in playing on the pipe or flute, but probably included that accomplishment (Eccles. xii, 5; 2 Chron. xxxv, 25). See MOURNING.

Minstrels' Gallery, in a church, forms a sort of orchestra for the accommodation of vocal and instrumental performers. It is quite common in Continental churches, but is very rarely met with in England. There is a gallery of this sort over the altar-screen at Chichester cathedral, and another, much more remarkable, near the middle of the north side of the choir of Exeter cathedral. It is supported upon thirteen pillars, between every two of which, in a niched recess, there is a sculptured representation of an angel playing upon a musical instrument. Among these we observe the cittern, bagpipe, harp, violin, pipe, tambourine, etc. The roof of Outwell Church, Norfolk, and the minstrels' column at Beverley, also exhibit a great variety of musical instruments anciently used in our churches, independent of the organ and the regalls, which was a small portable organ, having one row of pipes giving the treble notes, the same number of keys, and a small pair of bellows moved with the left hand.

Mint (ἡδύοσμον, *sweet-scented*) occurs (Matt. xxiii,

23; Luke xi, 42) among the smaller garden herbs which the Pharisees punctiliously tithed. See ANISE; DILL. It was much esteemed as a warming condiment by the ancients (Pliny, xix, 47; xx, 53; xxi, 18; Dioscor. iii, 41; Martial, x, 48, 8 sq.; the Romans calling it *mentha*, and the Greeks μίνθη) as well as the Jews (Mishna, *Okzim.* i, 2; *Ohol.* viii, 1; also the Talmudical tracts *Shem ve-Jobel*, vii, 2; *Sheb.* vii, 1; the rabbins call it מִרְתָּא; it was even strewed, for the sake of its odor, upon the floors of houses and synagogues, Buxtorf, *Lex. Rab.* p. 1228), and as it still is in Eastern countries (Raffenau Delîle, *Flora Aegypt.* in the *Descr. de l'Égypte*, xix). "Some commentators have supposed that such herbs as mint, anise (dill), and cumin, were not tithable by law, and that the Pharisees solely from an overstrained zeal paid tithes for them; but as dill was subject to tithe (*Masseroth*, iv, 5), it is most probable that the other herbs mentioned with it were also tithed, and this is fully corroborated by our Lord's own words: 'These ought ye to have done.' The Pharisees, therefore, are not censured for paying tithes of things untithable by law, but for paying more regard to a scrupulous exactness in these minor duties than to important moral obligations."

"It is difficult to determine the exact species or variety of mint employed by the ancients. There are numerous species very nearly allied to one another. They usually grow in moist situations, and are herbaceous, perennial. of powerful odor, especially when bruised, and have small reddish-colored flowers, arranged in spikes or whorls. The taste of these plants is bitter, warm, and pungent, but leaving a sensation of coolness on the tongue; in their properties they are so similar to each other, that, either in medicine or as a condiment, one species may safely be substituted for another. The species most common in Syria is *Mentha sylvestris*, found

Mentha Sylvestris.

by Russell at Aleppo, and mentioned by him as one of the herbs cultivated in the gardens there. It also occurs in Greece, Taurus, Caucasus, the Altai Range, and as far as Cashmere. *M. arvensis* is also a widely-diffused species, being found in Greece, in parts of Caucasus, in the Altai Range, and in Cashmere." (See Celsii *Hierob.* i, 543 sq.) Lady Calcott (*Script. Herb.* p. 280) makes the following ingenious remark: "I know not whether mint were originally one of the bitter herbs with which the Israelites eat the Paschal lamb, but our use of it with roast lamb, particularly about Easter time, inclines me to suppose it was." The same writer also observes that the modern Jews eat horseradish and chervil with lamb. The wood-cut represents the horse mint (*M. sylvestris*), which is common in Syria, ana, according to Russell (*Nat. Hist. of Aleppo*, p. 39), found in the gardens at Aleppo: *M. sativa* is generally supposed

to be only a variety of *M. arvensis*, another species of mint; perhaps all these were known to the ancients. The mints belong to the large natural order *Labiatæ*.

Mintert, PETER, a Dutch theologian, flourished for many years at Heerle, in Holland, about the beginning of the 18th century. He was noted for his great learning as a Biblical scholar and theologian. His principal work was the *Lexicon Græco-Latinum in Novum Testamentum Jesu Christi; cum Præfatione J. G. Pritii* (Francof. 1728, 4to). There was no better lexicon than this of Mintert previous to the publication of Schleusner's *Novum Lexicon*. It is valuable for its numerous references to the Hebrew Scriptures and the Septuagint; and is helpful as a concordance as well as a lexicon to the student of the N.-T. Scriptures in the original version.

Minturn, ROBERT BROWNE, an American philanthropist, who was born in New York City Nov. 16, 1805, and with a good preparatory education entered business and became a successful merchant, deserves a place here as one of the founders of the celebrated *St. Luke's Hospital*, one of the noblest of New York charities. Minturn also labored for the poor and the sick in many other ways, and his name deserves to be remembered in Christian society. He was one of the first commissioners of emigration, and an originator of the association for improving the condition of the poor. He died Jan. 9, 1866.

Minuccio (or **Minucci**), a learned Roman Catholic prelate, was born at Serravalle, Italy, in 1551. After having been prevost at Oettingen, Germany, he became counsellor to the duke of Bavaria. He was next secretary successively to popes Innocent IX and Clement VIII. The latter appointed him in 1596 archbishop of Zara, in Dalmatia. He was appointed by the republic of Venice to negotiate a peace with the Uscoques (adventurers), fugitives from Dalmatia, who availed themselves of the difficulties existing between Austria and Venice to rob and ransack the inhabitants of the borders of both countries. Minuccio died in Munich in 1604. He wrote in Italian the history of these filibusters up to 1602; it was published at Venice (1676, 4to) under the title of *Storia degli Uscocchi*, with a continuation as far as 1616 by Paoli Sarpi. He also wrote *Vita sanctæ Augustæ de Serravalle*, in the Bollandists (of March 27), and in the *Supplément de Surius*. See Ughelli, *Italia Sacra*, vol. v; Hoefer, *Nouv. Biog. Générale*, s. v.

Minucius FELIX, MARCUS, one of the most celebrated apologists of the early Latin Church, flourished in the 3d century. But little is known of his early history beyond the fact that he was a native of Africa, but removed to Rome, and there successfully exercised the profession of advocate until his conversion to Christianity. Lactantius (*Inst. Div.* l. i, c. q, l. v, vi) and Jerome are loud in his praise, and assure us that Minucius was much admired for his eloquence. He is ever to be remembered by the Christian Church as one of her ablest defenders in a work of his entitled *Octavius*, which is a dialogue between a Christian called Octavius and a heathen called Cæcilius, concerning the merits of the two religions which were then striving for supremacy. In this dialogue, Octavius repels the absurd imputations of the heathens against the early Christians, whom they accused of all sorts of impurities and crimes in their religious meetings. Through fear of persecution, these meetings took place mostly at night and in concealed places, which circumstances exposed them to the obloquy of vulgar ignorance. At the same time Octavius retorts upon his co-disputant by exposing the notoriously licentious practices of the heathens. The style of this work is argumentative and sufficiently pure; the language is animated, and the mode of treating the subject attractive, being mixed up with mythological learning and much information concerning the customs and opinions of that interesting period. "It is," says Neander, "a felicitous and dramatic representation seized from life, replete with good-sense, and pervaded by a lively Christian feeling." As an apology of Christianity, the work of Minucius Felix is a companion to those of Clemens Alexandrinus, Athenagoras, Theophilus of Antioch, Justin, Tertullian, and other early advocates of the Christian faith in its times of trial and depression, and forms a link between them and those of Arnobius, Lactantius, Eusebius, Ambrose, and the other fathers of the 4th century. *Octavius* was at one time attributed to Arnobius, and was inserted as the eighth book of his disputations *Adversus Gentes;* but Balduin published a *Dissertation on Minucius* (Kiel, 1685), which unquestionably places the authorship where it belongs —with Minucius. *Octavius* is now extant only in one MS. copy, which had remained unnoticed in the Vatican library until the pontificate of Leo X, who gave it to Francis I of France. It has gone through many editions, among which those by James Gronevius (Leyden, 1709), by Davis (Cambridge, 1712), and by Orelli (Turic. 1836), deserve notice. The latter is accompanied by numerous notes by Dr. Davis and others, and a dissertation, or commentary, by Baldwin. It has been translated into French by the abbé De Gourcy, into German by Kusswurm (Turic. 1836) and Lübkert (Leips. 1836), and into English, also, in Reeve's *Apologies of Justin Martyr,* etc., vol. ii. The latest and best edition of the original is by Carl Halm (Vienna, 1867).

Another work, entitled *De Fato,* against astrologers, is mentioned by Jerome as being ascribed to Minucius, although Jerome expresses doubts concerning its authorship. This work is not known to be extant now. See Schaff, *Ch. Hist.* vol. i; Hagenbach, *Hist. of Doctrines,* i, 63 sq.; Du Pin, *Biblioth. des aut. Eccles.* i, 117 sq.; Schröckh, *Kirchengesch.* iii, 420 sq.; *Jahrb. deutsch. Theol.* 1867, Oct.; Meier, *De Minucio Felice* (Zurich, 1824, 8vo). (J. H. W.)

Minution is a term applied by monastics of the Middle Ages to phlebotomy, which was much in fashion in those times. In some abbeys a bleeding-house, called *Flebotomaria,* was sustained. For details on the practices of the monastics in minution, see Fosbrooke, *British Monachism* (Lond. 1817, 4to), p. 321.

Minzocchi, FRANCESCO, a renowned painter of the Bolognese school, sometimes called *Il vecchio di San Bernardo,* was born in Florence in 1513. In his youth he studied the works of Palmigiani in his native city, and from him he acquired a weak style, as evinced in his picture of the *Crucifixion* at the Padri Osservanti. Afterwards he changed his manner, assuming a more correct and beautiful style; and his subsequent productions are marked by a beauty and grace rivalling nature herself. Among his most careful works may be mentioned two lateral pictures at the cathedral of Loretto, in a chapel of S. Francisco di Paola. They represent the *Sacrifice of Melchizedek* and the *Miracle of the Manna,* in which the prophets and principal characters are given with great dignity and nobleness. Scanneli extols a specimen of his works in fresco on the ceiling of S. Maria della Grata in Forli, representing the *Deity* surrounded by a number of angels: figures full of spirit, majestic, varied, and painted with a power and skill in foreshortening which entitles him to greater celebrity than he enjoys. He left, also, a number of productions in the cathedral at S. Domenico. He was so much admired that upon the demolition of the chapels his least celebrated frescos were carefully cut out and preserved. He died in 1574. See Lanzi's *History of Painting,* trans. by Roscoe (London, 1847, 3 vols. 8vo), iii, 56.

Miph'kad (Heb. *Miphkad'*, מִפְקָד, *review* or census of the people, as in 2 Sam. xxiv, 9, etc.; or *mandate,* as in 2 Chron. xxxi, 13; Sept. Μαφεκάδ, Vulg. *judicialis*), the name of a gate of Jerusalem, situated opposite the residence of the Nethinim and the bazaars, between the Horse-gate and the angle of the old wall near the Sheep-gate (Neh. iii, 31); probably identical with the Prison-gate (Neh. xii, 39), under the middle of the

bridge spanning the Tyropœon (see Strong's *Harm. and Expos. of the Gosp.* Append. ii, p. 15). Barclay (*City of the Great King,* p. 156) identifies it with the High-gate of Benjamin (Jer. xx, 2), and locates it at the west end of the bridge; but that gate was probably situated elsewhere. "The name may refer to some memorable census of the people, as, for instance, that of David (2 Sam. xxiv, 9, and 1 Chron. xxi, 5, in each of which the word used for 'number' is *miphkad*), or to the superintendents of some portion of the worship (*Pekidim,* see 2 Chron. xxxi, 13)." See JERUSALEM.

Mirabaud, JEAN BAPTISTE, a French philosopher of some celebrity, was born in Paris in 1675, and died in 1760. He was at home in the literature of Italy and of Spain, and made many valuable translations; among others, he rendered Tasso's *Jerusalem Delivered* and the *Orlando Furioso.* He also wrote several philosophical treatises, which in 1726 secured him admission to the French Academy. His most important works are, *Le Monde, son origine, son antiquité;* and *Sentimens des Philosophes sur la nature de l'âme.* Mirabaud was for a long time regarded as the author of the *Système de la Nature,* now known to have been written by baron D'Holbach. See D'Alembert, *Histoire des Membres de l'Academie Française;* Hoefer, *Nouv. Biog. Générale,* s. v.; Ueberweg, *Hist. of Philosophy,* vol. ii.

Miracle Plays. See MYSTERIES.

Miracles. In every age there are certain great movements of human thought, which more or less influence the convictions of men in the mass, and carry them on to conclusions which, but a few years before, would have seemed altogether improbable. Sometimes it is very difficult to account for these movements. There has often been no master-mind leading the way: whatever works have been written have rather been the result of the wave of thought passing over that small portion of the world which thinks than the cause of the wave. As far as cause can be traced, the new movement is a reaction, a recoil of the mind, from that which has gone before, whether in the way of dissatisfaction at the sloth and inactivity of the previous age, and at its being ignobly content to have no high aspiration, no high sense of the nobleness of man's mission, or a rebound from overstrained dogmatism and principles urged on to an extent which made them practically a burden and wearisomeness too great for men to endure.

The latter is perhaps the more common origin of new developments of thought, and is a power larger and more constantly at work than men are apt to imagine. But the explanation of the movements of the mind in our own time is rather to be sought in the meanness of the last century. Upon the whole, it was not a time of high purposes, though the War of Independence on the one side of the Atlantic, and the resistance to the despotism of Napoleon on the other, show that it was not wanting in great practical results. But as the present century advanced, the old lethargy which had enwrapped the minds of the English-speaking race gave way. Some men became intensely active in working for practical reforms; others set new modes of thought in motion, and everywhere there was an eager desire for thoroughness, and for probing the principles of things to the very bottom. The old argument of "continuance"—that a thing should still exist because it had existed—gave way to an intense realism, which would let nothing exist unless it could prove its right to existence. Utilitarianism became the order of the day, and that poetry which often gilds a sleepy age, and makes it dwell at peace in a dreamland of repose, vanished before the energy of men keenly alive to the necessities and imperfections of the present.

It is this intense realism that has made men restless and ill at ease at having to believe in miracles. A miracle stands on entirely different grounds from the whole present order of things, and is out of harmony with the main current of our thoughts. There have been ages when men lived for the future, when the present was neglected, and things unseen were the realities which engrossed their thoughts. When we read the accounts of the trials for witchcraft in New England a century or two ago, we find not the accusers only, but the accused full of ideas of the preternatural. What they saw had but slight influence upon them; what they imagined had alone power over their minds. We, on the contrary, live in the present. The turn of our minds is to verify everything. We call for proof, and whatever cannot be proved we reject. It is not merely miracles which we treat thus, but most of what the last century regarded as historical realities. The intense historical activity of the present day, which has rewritten for us the annals of Greece and Rome, of the Church and of England, of the great æras of Spain and the Netherlands, besides special studies of great value, has its origin in that same spirit for searching and proving which leads so many to reject miracles.

It is altogether unfair to lay the rejection of miracles to the charge of physical science. The leaders of science are as thoroughly realistic as our historians and men of letters, but not more so. They are themselves phenomena of an age which perpetually asks What is? They inquire into the conformation of the earth and its constituents; into the motions of the heavenly bodies, and the laws which govern them, with the same eagerness to find out present facts, and the explanation of them, as animates the historian and the practical reformer. Old beliefs in our day can no more stand their ground than old laws and old customs, unless they can prove their right to stand by an appeal to present usefulness. It is of no use to appeal to anything else. In the present state of men's minds, if a thing does not fit in to the present, it seems to have no right to exist at all.

But if the progress of physical science has little to do with the dislike to miracles and the supernatural, the rapid increase of material wealth, and the advance made in everything which tends to present comfort and enjoyment, have much to do with it. We are living in an age when the present is full of enjoyment. By our large ascendency over the powers of nature, the earth yields us its treasures with a bountifulness never known before. Our homes are replete with comforts and luxuries little dreamed of by those who went before; and the secret forces of nature are pressed into our service, and do our bidding. Side by side with this subjection of nature there has grown up a greatness of material enterprise unknown before. Vast projects are undertaken and persevered in, before which the greatest merchant princes of antiquity would have quailed. There is a grandeur of conception, a nobleness of purpose, an unflinching courage in many of the commercial undertakings of the present day, which, though gain may be their final object, yet give them a dignity and a poetry that make them for the time enough to conceal the deep cravings which are man's peculiar endowment, and which mark him out as a being destined for no common purposes.

Yet this present greatness of material things dwarfs many of man's higher gifts. Its influence begins early. Even in education it makes men aim chiefly at utilitarian objects, and at too early results. Parents do not care for anything which does not lead directly and at once to profit and pay. Whatever develops man's thinking powers, and aims simply at making him better and nobler in himself, is thrust aside. It would take too much time; defer too long the quick harvest of gains; might make men even indifferent to worldly prosperity, and unwilling to sacrifice everything to material wealth. Or, at all events, it lies out of the circle of men's every-day thoughts. Life is an eager race, with boundless prizes for all who press onwards and upwards. In so active a contest, with every energy on the stretch, and every exertion richly rewarded, it is no wonder if the present is enough; and in its enjoy-

ment men thrust from them indignantly everything that would interfere with and render them less fit for the keen struggle after earthly success.

It is this spirit which makes it so difficult for men to believe in miracles. The purpose of miracles, and their whole use and intention hold so entirely distinct a place from that which is now the main purpose of the mass of men, that they will hear no evidence for them, nor stop calmly to consider whether they may not after all hold a necessary place in the order of things, and be as indispensable for man's perfectness as is this present activity. What too many do is to put aside the consideration of them entirely. They have a sort of notion that miracles contradict the laws of nature, and are therefore impossible. Without perhaps denying the historical accuracy of the Gospels in the main, they yet suppose that they were written by credulous men in a credulous age, and that if cool observers had been present, they could have explained on natural grounds all that took place. Probably they do not think much about the supernatural at all. They have plenty to occupy them; have no spare time; find their lives full of interest; they rise early to their labor and late take rest; and so are content with a general feeling that, whatever may be the explanation of man being what he is, and of the world being what it is, time will reveal it, and that no obligation lies upon a busy man to inquire into abstruse questions, with no present profit. When business is over and old age has come, then it will be his duty to make his peace with God. And he will do so in the ordinary way, as other men do. Religion is a thing relegated to the background for the present; in due time he will attend to it as a practical matter, in the same way in which he will attend to the making of his will.

This thorough realism of the 19th century, intensified by the vast facilities of combined action and mutual intercourse, which make us live constantly in one another's company, would banish all care and thought of the future from our minds, if it were not that the belief in the existence of a God and of a future life is an undying conviction of our nature. It is a necessary part of ourselves to look forward. No present gains or successes can content us. We turn always to the future, and that with an eagerness which would make life unendurable if we were forced to believe that life were all. The doctrine of annihilation may be professed, but can never really be believed; for it violates the deepest instincts of our hearts. And thus compelled by the very constitution of our natures to believe that there is a God, and that we exist after death, religion itself becomes a very real thing, and supplies a real need. The existence of a God and the immortality of man are not doctrines which need proving. They are intuitions, innate ideas, which may and do gain form and shape from advancing knowledge, but which grew out of the soul itself. Over the savage they have little influence, but civilized and thinking man can never be complete and entire unless these deep instincts of his inner being have their needs fully met and satisfied. In a man who stands perfect and complete, the necessities of the future must be as fully and entirely recognised and supplied as the requirements of the present. He must have a religion.

Now religion is either natural or revealed. Not that these two are opposed. The revealed religion which we Christians profess contains and gives new authority to all the truths of natural religion, while extending itself far beyond them. Natural religion is a dim feeling and groping after God as manifested in his works, and a distinguishing of right from wrong, as far as the indications of a righteous government existing now, and the laws of our own nature, and the marvellous gift of conscience, enable us to do so. In revealed religion we have fuller knowledge: knowledge of God's attributes, not merely as far as we can trace them in his works, but still more as they are manifested in his dealings with man, as made known to us in revelation itself; knowledge of man, both as regards his present state and his future hopes; more exact knowledge, too, of right and wrong, the appeal now lying not to the varying codes of human morality, nor even to the inner conscience, which, as a faculty capable of education and development, is no rigid rule, but one which bends to every state of things, and adapts itself to every stage and degree of human progress and decay. Under a revealed religion the appeal is to an unchanging law of God. Morality has at last a settled basis, and man a fixed standard by which to judge his actions.

Now it seems almost supererogatory to show that natural religion does not suffice for man's wants. We know of no one who has definitely asserted that it does. Even Kant, though he appears to think that Christianity might now be dispensed with, yet distinctly holds that natural religion, without the teaching of Christianity, would not even now have been enlightened enough, or pure enough, or certain enough, to guide man's life.* But the whole state of the heathen world before Christ came, and now wherever Christianity is unknown, is proof sufficient of the utter powerlessness of natural religion. The Greek world, with its marvellous taste in art and appreciation of the beautiful, was yet intensely wicked. The state of things at Rome under the empire was so foul that modern pens would blush to describe it. What natural religion is where civilization does not exist, the condition now of savage tribes proves clearly enough. We will touch therefore only upon one point, that of progress. Apart from Christianity, there are at most in the world the very faintest indications of progress; usually none at all. In no form of natural religion, in no heathen religion, was there anything to lead man onward, or to make him better. At best, as under Mohammedanism, or the religion of Confucius, there was stagnation. And when, as in the case of so many of the older civilizations of the world, decay set in, there was no recuperative force. Man sank steadily and hopelessly. In the Old Testament alone do we find the thought of progress. A nation is there formed for a high and unique purpose; and to shape it for its end it is placed in a special and immediate relation to God, and is taught by messengers sent directly by him. Under this special dispensation, its one business was to grow fit for the work prepared for it; its one motto, progress. In the New Testament, progress is the central thought everywhere present; but no longer now for one nation—it is progress for all mankind. It is a new kingdom that is proclaimed, and all who enter it are required to put away old things, and become new. It belongs to men who have left their previous condition far behind, and who, forgetting what is past, "reach forth unto those things which are before." And special stress is laid everywhere upon the duty of bringing all men into this new kingdom, and of Christians being the purifying salt which is to preserve the whole world.

The means by which Christianity thus renovates mankind, and becomes the moving force of all modern and real progress, is partly that it alone proposes to us principles so perfect that at the utmost our approach to their realization is a very distant one. The complete abnegation of self, the treatment of others with that justice, liberality, and love with which we would wish ourselves to be treated, and a holiness as absolute and entire as that of God himself—such principles, while practically aiding us in our upward course, yet set us a standard which, as a matter of fact, is unattainable. How often this is misunderstood! Men contrast our Christianity with what is set before us in the Gospels, and, either in mockery or in grief at the disparity, assert that our state is practically a mere heathenism. But while there is ample room for lamentation that we

Christians are content to remain so very much below the standard set us, yet, so far as there is progress towards it—so far as it can be truly said that this generation is in a higher stage than the last was, and is training the youth to attain in the next to a still nearer approximation to Christian perfectness, so far Christianity is doing its work; not merely its work on individuals—these constantly, even where the general state of things is bad and low, it raises to a high degree of virtue and holiness—but its work on the mass. If nationally we are making no progress, then our Christianity is not having its proper work, and, in an age which judges by results, is not proving its right still to exist. But even at the worst no Christian nation is hopeless: heathen nations sank without hope. Christian nations have again and again risen from the lowest degradation.

But Christianity tends to progress not merely by the high ideal it sets before us, but by its power over men's sympathies. This power resides mainly in the human nature of Christ, but only when viewed in its relation to his Godhead. As the great proof of the Father's love to man, it does arrest our feelings, dwell upon our imagination, and inspire our conduct with motives such as no other supposed manifestation of the Deity to man has ever produced. Christ incarnate in the flesh is not merely the realization of the high standard of Christianity, and the model for our imitation, but acts also as a motive power, by which men are aroused and encouraged to the attempt to put into practice the principles of the religion which Christ taught.

If there be a God—and the man who denies it contradicts the intuitions of his own nature—it is religion, and revealed religion only, that gives us adequate knowledge of his nature and attributes. If there be a future—and the very instincts of our nature testify that there is—again it is revealed religion only that tells us what the future life is, and how we may attain to it. Yet necessary parts as both these beliefs are of our nature, men may bring themselves to deny them. For a time they can put away from them both the future and a God. But if there be a present—and this is just the one thing in which the 19th century does thoroughly believe—even then, granting only this, if this present is to have any progress, and is to move onwards to anything better; if there is to be in it anything of healthful and vigorous life, this, too, is bound up with the one religion, which has satisfactory proof to give that it is revealed; proof that it did come really from God; and proof that it is the one motive power of human progress. If the light of nature hitherto has been insufficient to secure virtue or raise men towards it, that light will not suffice now, even though it has been fed and strengthened by centuries of Christian teaching. In asserting this, Kant asserted too much. Neither Christians nor Christian communities have as yet risen to anything like a high general standard of morality, to say nothing about holiness; remove the high ideal and the strong motives supplied by the religion of Christ, and there would result, first stagnation, and then decay. An "enlightened self-love" never yet successfully resisted any carnal or earthly passion. Christianity has effected much; the contrast between heathen and Christian communities is immense: but it has not raised men yet to its own standard, nor even to a reasonably fair standard of moral excellence.

Now, grant but the possibility of there being a God; grant but the possibility of there being a future, as there must necessarily be a connection between man's future and his present, and as our idea of God forbids our excluding any existent thing from connection with him, then at least a revelation would be useful, and as God must be good, there is no antecedent improbability in his bestowing upon man what would be of use and benefit to him. You must get rid of God—must resolve him into a sort of nebulous all-pervading ether, with no attributes or personal force or knowledge (the Pantheists do this beautifully, and call God *cosmic force*)—you

---

* "We may well concede that if the Gospel had not previously taught the universal moral laws, reason would not yet have attained so perfect an insight into them."—Letter of Kant to Jacobi, in Jacobi's *Werke*, iii, 523.

must get rid of a future life, and account yourselves simple phenomena, like the monkey, and ascidian jelly-bags, from which you are supposed to be descended, with no connection with the past, no reason for your present existence, mere shooting-stars in the realms of space, coming from nowhere, and going nowhither, and so only, by the extirpation of these two ideas from your nature, can you make a revelation improbable. Even then your position is open to grave doubt. We can understand the law of evolution; and if the law be proved, though as yet it is unproved, it would involve me in no religious difficulties, provided that evolution really worked towards a solid end. Accustomed everywhere else in nature to see things fitted to their place, and all things so ordered that there is a use for everything, I could understand the meanest thing in creation rising upwards in the scale through multitudinous forms and infinite periods of time, if finally there were some purpose for all this rising. The plan is vast and marvellous. It can be justified only by some useful end. And such an end there would be if, after vast ages of development, the tiny atom ended in becoming a reasonable and responsible creature, with some purpose for all this vast preparation, because capable of still rising upwards, and of "becoming partaker of the divine nature." But if the law of evolution stops at man without a future, then its product is not worthy of it, and so purposeless a law, ending in so mean a result—for what is there meaner than man without Christ?—falls to the ground as too grand in its design for so bare and worthless a result.

Yet even this is but part of the argument; the evidences in favor of Christianity have a collective force, and it is upon them as a whole that one fain rests secure. But we may well contend that if Christianity is necessary for our present well-being; if the advance of society; if the removal of the bad, the vile, and the sorrowful in our existing arrangements; if the maintenance and strengthening of the noble, the earnest, the generous, and the pure, is bound up with Christianity, as being the only sure basis and motive towards progress, then; at all events, religion can show cause enough for existence to make it the duty of men to examine the evidence which it offers in its proof. Nineteenth-century men may decline to listen to arguments which concern only things so remote as God and the future. Have they not built railways, laid the Atlantic telegraph, found out the constituent elements of the sun through the spectrum, and gained fortunes by gambling on the stock exchange? What can men want more? Well, they want something to bind society together: even the worst want something to control in others those passions to which they give free play in themselves. No man wants society to grow worse, however much he may do himself to corrupt it. But the one salt of society, the one thing that does purify and hold it together, is religion.

Now antecedently there is no reason why God might not have made natural religion much more mighty and availing. As it is, nothing is more powerless in itself, though useful as an ally to revelation. Religion or no religion means revelation or no revelation. Reject revelation, and the only reason for not rejecting natural religion is that it is not worth the trouble. If religion, then, is a necessity of our present state, this means that revelation is a necessity. We are quite aware that even revealed religion does not explain all the difficulties of our present state. There is very much of doubt suggested by our philosophy to which Christianity gives only this answer, Believe and wait. It is, in fact, rigidly careful in refusing to give any and every explanation of things present except a practical one: in the most marked way it is silent as to the cause of our being what we are, and as to the nature of the world to come. It tells us that we do not now see the realities themselves, but only reflections of them in a mirror, and even that only in a riddling way (1 Cor. xiii, 12). Hereafter it promises that we shall see the things themselves,

and understand the true nature and exposition of the enigmas of life. Meanwhile it gives us every practical help and necessary guidance for the present. Judged thus by practical results and by its working powers, it is a thing indispensable. Without it man is imperfect, and society has nothing to arrest its dissolution, or arouse it to a struggle after amendment. Reformation is essentially a Christian idea. That a state should throw off its ignoble past and start on a new quest after excellence and right is possible only where there is a religion strong enough to move men, and noble enough to offer them a high ideal. Reform movements have therefore been confined to Christian states; and for the individual, his one road to perfection has been a moving forwards towards God.

Upon this, then, we base our argument for miracles. The universal instincts of men prove the necessity of the existence of religion. Without it the promptings of our hearts, compelling us to believe in a God and to hope for a future, would be empty and meaningless; and this no human instincts are. There is no instinct whatsoever which has not in external nature that which exactly corresponds to it, and is its proper field of exercise. And, in the next place, natural religion, though in entire agreement with revealed, is, as we have shown, insufficient for the purposes for which religion is required. And, finally, there is the phenomenon that the revealed religion which we profess does act as a motive to progress. Christian nations—in morals, in freedom, in literature, in science, in the arts, and in all that adorns or beautifies society and human life—hold undoubtedly the foremost place, and are still moving forward. And in proportion as a Christian nation holds its faith purely and firmly, so surely does it advance onwards. It is content with nothing to which it has attained, but sees before it the ideal of a higher perfection (Phil. iii, 13, 14).

Now a revealed religion can be proved only by that which involves the supernatural. What our Lord says to the Jews, that "they would not have sinned in rejecting him but for his works" (John xxv, 24), commends itself at once to our reason. No proof can rise higher than the order of things to which it belongs. And thus all that can be proved by the elaborate examination of all created things, and the diligent inquiry into their conformation and uses and instincts, and the purposes for which each organ or faculty was given them; yea, even the search into man's own mind, and all the psychologic problems which suggest so very much to us as to the purposes of our existence—all this can rise no higher than natural religion. They are at best but guesses and vague conjectures, and a feeling and groping after truth. Nothing of this sort could prove to us a revealed religion. For how are we to know that it is revealed? In order to its being revealed, God must be the giver of it. And how are we to know that it is he who speaks? Its strength, its value, its authority, all depend upon its being the voice of God. No subjective authority can prove this. The nature of the truths revealed, their adaptability to our wants, their usefulness, their probability—nothing of this would prove that they had not been thought out by some highly-gifted man. We must have direct evidence—something pledging God himself—before we can accept a religion as revealed.

We shall see this more clearly if we reflect upon the nature of the obedience which we are required to render to a revealed religion. Its authority is summary, and knows no appeal. It is God who speaks, and there is no higher tribunal than his throne. Take, for instance, the Ten Commandments. Essentially they are a republication of the laws of natural religion, excepting perhaps the fourth commandment. But upon how different a footing do they stand! The duty of not killing is in natural religion counteracted by the law of self-preservation, and in heathen communities has been generally very powerless, and human life but little valued.

Even in fairly-civilized communities murder was not a crime to be punished by the state, but to be avenged by the relatives of the murdered man. This even was the state of things among the Jews when the Ten Commandments were promulgated, and Moses, by special enactments, modified and softened the customs which he found prevalent, and which did not distinguish between wilful murder and accidental homicide. Natural religion, therefore, gave no special sanctity to human life, but regarded only the injury done to the family of the sufferer. The divine commandment has gone home straight to the conscience. It has made the shedding of blood a sin, and not merely an injury. Accordingly, Christian states have recognised the divine nature of the law by punishing murder as a public offence, instead of leaving it to be dealt with as a private wrong.

A revealed religion therefore claims absolute power over the conscience as being the direct will of God. No question of utility or public or private expediency may stand in its way. It must be obeyed, and disobedience is sin. But plainly we ought not to yield such absolute obedience to anything that we do not know to be the law of God. Man stands too high in the scale of existence for this to be right. Were it only that he is endowed with a conscience, and thereby made responsible for his actions, it is impossible for him to give up the control over his own actions to any being of less authority than that One to whom he is responsible. But a revelation claims to be the express will of that very Being, and therefore a sufficient justification of our actions before his tribunal. Surely, before we trust ourselves to it, we may fairly claim adequate proof that it is his will. The issues are too serious for less than this to suffice.

But, besides this, when we look at Christianity, the nature of its doctrines brings the necessity of supernatural proof before us with intense force. It teaches us that God took our nature upon him, and in our nature died in our stead; and, as we have pointed out before, the strength of Christianity, and that which makes it a religion of progress, is this union of the divine and human natures in Christ. He is not merely the "man of sorrows," the ideal of suffering humanity—and a religion that glorifies a sinless sufferer may do much to alleviate sorrow and sweeten the bitter cup of woe—but he is much more than this. It is only when that sinless sufferer is worshipped as our Lord and our God that we reach the mainspring which has given Christianity its power to regenerate the world.

But how could such a doctrine be believed on any less evidence than that which directly pledged the divine authority on its behalf? The unique and perfect character of the Jesus of the evangelists; the pure and spotless nature of the morality he taught; the influence for good which Christian doctrines have exercised; the position attained by Christian nations, and the contrast between the ideals of heathenism and of Christianity —all this and more is valuable as subsidiary evidence. Some of it is absolutely necessary to sustain our belief. Even miracles would not convince us of the truth of a revelation which taught us a morality contrary to our consciences. For nothing could make us believe that the voice of God in nature could be opposed to his voice in revelation. It is a very axiom that, however it reaches us, the voice of God must be ever the same. But these subsidiary proofs are but by-works. They are not the citadel, and can never form the main defence. A doctrine such as that of God becoming man must have evidence cognate to and in pari materie with the doctrine itself. Thus, by a plain and self-evident necessity, revelation offers us supernatural proof of its reality. This supernatural proof is twofold, prophecy and miracle.

Now these two not merely support one another, but are essentially connected. They are not independent, but correlative proofs. It was the office of the prophet gradually to prepare the way for the manifestation of the Immanuel upon earth. In order to do so effectually he often came armed with supernatural authority. But a vast majority of the prophets had no other business than to impress on the consciences of the people truths already divinely vouched for and implicitly accepted; and such no more needed miracles than the preachers of Christianity do at the present day. But among the prophets were here and there men of higher powers, whose office was to advance onwards towards the ultimate goal of the preparatory dispensation. Such men offered prediction and miracle as the seals which ratified their mission. In general men could be prepared to receive so great a miracle as that set forth in the opening verses of John's Gospel only by a previous dispensation which had brought the supernatural very near to man. If the Old Testament had offered no miracles, and had not taught the constant presence of God in the disposal of all human things, the doctrines of the New Testament would have been an impossibility.

But we shall understand their connection better when we have a clearer idea of the true scriptural doctrine of miracles. The current idea of a miracle is that it is a violation of the laws of nature, and as the laws of nature are the laws of God, a miracle would thus signify the violation by God of his own laws. This is not the teaching of the Bible itself, but an idea that has grown out of the Latin word which has supplanted the more thoughtful terms used in the Hebrew and in the Greek Scriptures. A "miracle," miraculum, is something wonderful—marvellous. Now no doubt all God's works are wonderful; but when the word is applied to his doings in the Bible, it is his works in nature that are generally so described. In the Hebrew, especially in poetry, God is often described as doing "wonders," that is, miracles. But the term is not merely applicable to works such as those wrought by him for his people in Egypt and the wilderness (Exod. xv, 11; Psa. lxxviii, 12), but to a thunder-storm (Psa. lxxvii, 14), and to his ordinary dealings with men in providence (Psa. ix, 1; xxvi, 7; xl, 5), and in the government of the world. But this term wonder is not the word in the Hebrew properly applicable to what we mean by miracles, and in the New Testament our Lord's works are never called "miracles" ($\vartheta a \dot\upsilon \mu a \tau a$) at all. The people are often said to have "wondered" (Matt. ix, 33; xv, 31) at Christ's acts, but those acts themselves were not intended simply to produce wonder; they had a specific purpose, indicated by the term properly applicable to them, and that term is sign.

This is the sole Hebrew term for what we mean by miracle; but there are other words applied to our Lord's doings in the New Testament which we will previously consider. And, first, there is a term which approaches very nearly to our word miracle, namely, $\tau \dot\epsilon \rho a \varsigma$, portent, defined by Liddell and Scott, in their Greek Lexicon, as a "sign, wonder, marvel, used of any appearance or event in which men believed that they could see the finger of God." But, with that marvellous accuracy which distinguishes the language of the Greek Testament, our Lord's works are never called $\tau \dot\epsilon \rho a \tau a$ in the Gospels. The word is used of the false Christs and false prophets, who by great signs and portents shall almost deceive the very elect (Matt. xxiv, 24; Mark xiii, 22). The populace, however, expected a prophet to display these portents (John iv, 48), and Joel had predicted that such signs of God's presence would accompany the coming of the great and notable day of Jehovah (Acts ii, 19).

In the Acts of the Apostles our Lord is said to have been approved of God by portents as well as by powers and signs, the words literally being "Jesus of Nazareth, a man displayed of God unto you by powers, and portents, and signs;" but the portents refer to such things as the star which appeared to the magi, and the darkness and earthquake at the crucifixion. Exactly parallel to this place are the words in Heb. ii, 4, where God is said to have borne witness to the truth of the apostles' testimony "by signs and portents, and manifold powers, and diversified gifts of the Holy Ghost," the description being evidently intended to include every manifestation of God's presence with the first preachers of the Gospel, ordinary and extraordinary, in providence and in grace, and not merely the one fact that from time to time they wrought miracles.

But the term *portents* is freely applied to the miracles wrought by the apostles, being used of them no less than eight times in the Acts, and also in Rom. xv, 19, and 2 Cor. xii, 12. In every case it is used in connection with the word *signs*, the Greek in Acts vi, 8; xv, 12, being exactly the same as that in Acts ii, 43; iv, 30; v, 12; xiv, 3, though differently rendered. The two words, however, express very different sides of the apostles' working, the term *sign*, as we shall see hereafter, having reference to the long-previous preparation for the Messiah's advent, while *portents* were indications of the presence with them of the finger of God.

In the Synoptic Gospels, the most common term for our Lord's miracles is $\delta \upsilon \nu \acute{\alpha} \mu \epsilon \iota \varsigma$, *powers*. Full of meaning as is the word, it nevertheless is not one easy to adapt to the idiom of our language, and thus in the Gospels it is usually translated "mighty works" (Matt. xi, 20, 21, 23, etc.), but *miracles* in Acts ii, 22; viii, 13; xix, 11; 1 Cor. xii, 10, 28, etc. Really it signifies the very opposite of miracles. A $\delta \acute{\upsilon} \nu \alpha \mu \iota \varsigma$ is a faculty, or capacity for doing anything. We all have our faculties— some physical, some mental and moral—and these are all strictly natural endowments. We have also spiritual faculties, and these also primarily are natural endowments of our inner being, though heightened and intensified in believers by the operation of the Holy Ghost. Yet even this is, by the ordinary operation of the Spirit, in accordance with spiritual laws, and not in violation of them. The teaching therefore of this word $\delta \upsilon \nu \acute{\alpha} \mu \epsilon \iota \varsigma$, *powers* or *faculties*, is that our Lord's works were perfectly natural and ordinary to him. They were his capacities, just as sight and speech are ours. Now in a brute animal articulate speech would be a miracle, because it does not lie within the range of its capacities, and therefore would be a violation of the law of its nature; it does lie within the compass of our faculties, and so in us is no miracle. Similarly, the healing of the sick, the giving sight to the blind, the raising of the dead—things entirely beyond the range of our powers, yet lay entirely within the compass of our Lord's capacities, and were in accordance with the laws of his nature. It was no more a "miracle" in him to turn water into wine than it is with God, who works this change every year. Nor does John call it so, though his word is rendered miracle in our version (John ii, 11).

His language, as becomes the most thoughtful and philosophic of the Gospels, is deeply significant. He does not use the term $\delta \acute{\upsilon} \nu \alpha \mu \iota \varsigma$, *faculty*, at all, but has two words, one especially his own, namely, $\check{\epsilon} \rho \gamma o \nu$, a *work* (yet used once by Matthew, xi, 2, who has so much in common with John); the other, the one proper term for miracle throughout the whole Bible, $\sigma \eta \mu \epsilon \tilde{\iota} o \nu$, a *sign*.

Our Lord's miracles are called $\check{\epsilon} \rho \gamma \alpha$, *works*, by John some fifteen or more times, besides places where they are spoken of as "the works of God" (ix, 3; v, 20, 36). Now this term stands in a very close relation to the preceding word, $\delta \acute{\upsilon} \nu \alpha \mu \iota \varsigma$, a *faculty*. A faculty, when exerted, produces an $\check{\epsilon} \rho \gamma o \nu$, or work. Whatever powers or capacities we have, whenever we use them, bring forth a corresponding result. We have capacities of thought, of speech, of action, common to the species, though varying in the individual; and what is not at all remarkable in one man may be very much so in another, simply because it is beyond his usual range. But outside the species it may be not only remarkable but miraculous, because it lies altogether beyond the range of the capacities with which the agent is endowed. And so, on the contrary, what would be miraculous in one class of agents is simply natural in another class, because it is in accordance with their powers.

Now had our Lord been merely man, any and every work beyond the compass of man's powers would have been a miracle. It would have transcended the limits of his nature; but whether it would necessarily have violated the laws of that nature is a question of some difficulty. Supposing that man is an imperfect being, but capable of progress, the limits of his powers may be indefinitely enlarged. Those who hold the theory of evolution concede this, and therefore concede that there is nothing miraculous in a remarkable individual being prematurely endowed with capacities which finally and in due time will be the heritage of the whole species. It is the doctrine of the Bible that the spiritual man has a great future before him, and the prophets of old, and the apostles and early Christians, endowed with their great charismata, or gifts, may be but an anticipation of what the spiritual man may finally become. Still, among the "works" of our Lord and his apostles, there is one which seems distinctly divine, namely, the raising of the dead. Gifts of healing, of exciting dormant powers, such as speech in the dumb, of reading the thoughts of others' hearts, may be so heightened in man as he develops under the operations of the Spirit that much may cease to be astonishing which now is highly so. But the raising of the dead travels into another sphere; nor can we imagine any human progress evolving such a power as this. We cannot imagine man possessed of any latent capacity which may in time be so developed as naturally to produce such a result. So, too, the multiplying of food seems to involve powers reserved to the Creator alone.

But the Gospel of John does not regard our Lord as a man prematurely endowed with gifts which finally will become the heritage of the whole species; it is penetrated everywhere with the conviction that a higher nature was united in him to his human nature. It shows itself not merely in formal statements like the opening words of the Gospel, but in the language usual with him everywhere. And so here. Our Lord's miracles to him are simply and absolutely $\check{\epsilon} \rho \gamma \alpha$, *works* only. But, as we have seen before, they are also divine works, "works of God." Still in Christ, according to John's view, they were perfectly natural. They were the necessary and direct result of that divine nature which in him was indissolubly united with his human nature. The last thing which the apostle would have thought about them was that they were miraculous, *wonderful*. That God should give his only-begotten Son to save the world was wonderful. That such a being should ordinarily do works entirely beyond the limits of man's powers did not seem to John wonderful, and hence the simple but deeply significant term by which he characterizes them.

Yet such works were not wrought without a purpose; nor did such a being come without having a definite object to justify his manifestation. If wisdom has to be justified of all her children, of all that she produces, there must be some end or purpose effected by each of them, and especially in one like Christ, confessedly the very highest manifestation of human nature, and, as we Christians believe, reaching high above its bounds. Now John points this out in calling our Lord's works $\sigma \eta \mu \epsilon \tilde{\iota} \alpha$, *signs*. It is devoutly to be hoped that in the revised translation of the New Testament this term will be restored to its place, instead of being mistranslated *miracle*, as in our present version. Really, in employing it, John was only following in the steps of the older Scriptures, and the unity of thought in the Bible is destroyed when the same word is translated differently in one book from its rendering in another. However wonderful may be God's works, they are not wrought simply to fill men with astonishment, and least of all are those so wrought which lie outside the ordinary course of God's natural laws.

The word $\sigma \eta \mu \epsilon \tilde{\iota} o \nu$, *sign*, tells us in the plainest language that these works were tokens calling the attention of men to what was then happening; and especially is it used in the Old Testament of some mark or signal confirming a promise or covenant. Such a sign (or mark) God gave to Cain in proof that his life was safe (Gen. iv, 15). Such a sign (or token) was the rainbow to Noah, certifying him and mankind throughout all time that the world should not be again destroyed by water (Gen. ix, 13). And here learn we incidentally that God's signs need not be miraculous. The laws of refraction probably were the same before as after the flood, and the fact of the rainbow being produced by the operation of natural laws does not make it a less fit symbol of a covenant between God and man relative to a great natural convulsion. So, again, circumcision was a sign (or token) of the covenant between God and the family of Abraham (Gen. xvii, 11). It was to recall the minds of the Israelites to the thought not merely that they stood in a covenant relation to God, but that that covenant implied personal purity and holiness. In the same way the Sabbath was a sign (Exod. xxxi, 13; Ezek. xx, 12) of a peculiar relation between the Jew and his God.

But there are places where it distinctively means what we call a miracle. Thus Ahaz is told to ask a sign, and a choice is given him either of some meteor in the heavens, or of some appearance in the nether world: "Make it deep unto Hades, or high in the vault of heaven above" (Isa. vii, 11). And when the unbelieving king will ask no sign, the prophet gives him that of the Immanuel, the virgin's son. So the sign unto Hezekiah of his recovery was the supernatural retrogression of the shadow upon the sundial of Ahaz, however significant it might also be of the hand of time having gone back as regards Hezekiah's own life (Isa. xxxviii, 7). Elsewhere the divine foreknowledge is the sign (Exod. iii, 12; Isa. xxxvii, 30), and generally signs of God's more immediate presence with his people would either be prophecy (Psa. lxxiv, 9) or miracle (ib. cv, 27; Jer. xxxii, 20; Dan. iv, 2).

Very much more might be learned by a fuller consideration of the manner in which the word *sign* is used in the Old Testament, but what is said above is enough to explain the reason why John so constantly used the term to express our Lord's miracles. The water changed into wine at Cana he calls "the beginning of signs" (ii, 11), and the healing of the centurion's son is "the second sign" (iv, 54), as being the first and second indications of Christ's wielding those powers which belong to God as the Creator and Author of nature, and which therefore pledged the God of nature, as the sole possessor of these powers, to the truth of any one's teaching who came armed with them (iii, 2, where again the Greek is *signs*). So he tells us that the people assembled at Jerusalem for the Passover believed Jesus "when they saw the *signs* which he did" (ib. ii, 23). It was, in fact, the very thing they had asked (Matt. xii, 38; xvi, 1; John ii, 18; vi, 30), and candid minds confessed that they were a sufficient ground for belief (ib. vi, 14; vii, 31; ix, 16; xii, 18); in fact, they were wrought for that purpose (ib. xx, 30, 31), though men might and did refuse to accept them as proof conclusive of the Saviour's mission (xi, 47; xii, 37), and vulgar minds saw in them nothing more than reason for astonishment (vi, 2, 26). To them they were simply *miracles*—wonders.

A sign is more and means more than a miracle, for it does not stand alone, but is a token and indication of something else. Thus John's word shows that our Lord's *works* had a definite purpose. They were not wrought at random, but were intended for a special object. What this was is easy to tell. The Old Testament had always represented the Jews as holding a peculiar position towards the Godhead. They were a chosen people endowed with high privileges and blessings, but so endowed because they were also intended for a unique purpose. They were the depositaries of revelation, and in due time their *Torah*, their revealed law, was to go forth out of Zion (Isa. ii, 3) to lighten the whole Gentile world (ib. xlii, 6). This promise of

a revelation extending to the whole world was further connected with the coming of a special descendant of Abraham (Gen. xxii, 18; Deut. xviii, 15), and prophecy had gradually so filled up the outline that a complete sketch had been given of the person, the offices, the work, and the preaching of the great Son of David, to whose line the promise had subsequently been confined (Isa. xi, 1; Jer. xxiii, 5; Hos. iii, 8; Mic. v, 2, etc.).

But how were people to know when he had come? The prophets had indeed given some indications of the time, especially Daniel (ix, 24–27), and so clear were their words that all the world was expecting the arrival of some mighty being, in whom *magnus ab integro sæclorum nascitur ordo*, and an entire transformation of the world should take place. But how, among many claimants, was he to be known? He might come, perhaps, as a conqueror, and by force of arms compel men to submit to his authority. But no! Prophecy had described him as the Prince of Peace; nor was his kingdom to be of this world, but a spiritual empire. Now, if we reflect for a little, we shall see that there is no obligation incumbent upon men to accept, or even examine, the claims of any and every one professing to be the bearer of a revelation from God. Before this duty arises, there must at least be something to call our attention to his claims. Mere self-assertion imposes no obligation upon others, unless it have something substantial to back it up. Life is a practical thing, with very onerous duties, and few, like the Athenians of old, have the taste or the leisure to listen to and examine everything new. The herald of a divine dispensation must have proof to offer that he does come from God, and such proof as pledges the divine attributes to the truth of his teaching. This is the reason why the Old-Testament dispensation was one of *signs*. On special occasions justifying the divine interference, and in the persons of its great teachers, the prophets, supernatural proof was given in two ways of God's presence with his messengers in a manner superior to and beyond his ordinary and providential presence in the affairs of life. The divine *omniscience* was pledged to the truth of their words by the prediction of future events; and his *omnipotence* by their working things beyond the ordinary range of nature. The two Old-Testament proofs of a revelation were prophecy and miracle. We can think of no others, and nothing less would suffice.

As we have said, the whole of the Old Testament looked forward to the manifestation of a divine person, in whom revelation would become, in the first place, perfect; in the second, universal; and, thirdly, final. As being a final revelation, prophecy, which was the distinctive element of the preparatory dispensation, holds in it no longer an essential place, though it is present in the New Testament in a subordinate degree. But miracle must, in the bearer of such a revelation, rise to its highest level; first because of the superiority of his office to that of the prophets. For he was himself the end of prophecy, the person for whose coming prophecy had prepared, and in whom all God's purposes of love towards mankind were to be fulfilled. The office of Christ as the bearer to mankind of God's final and complete message involves too much for us lightly to ascribe it to him. And no merely natural proof would suffice. We could not possibly believe what we believe of him had he wrought no miracles. We could not believe that he was the appointed Saviour, to whom "all honor was given in heaven and earth" (Matt. xxviii, 18), for man's redemption, if he had given no proof during the period of his manifestation on earth of being invested with extraordinary powers. But we go further than this. Perhaps no one would deny that the sole sufficient proof of such a religion as Christianity must be supernatural. We assert that no revealed religion whatsoever can be content with a less decided proof. The sole basis upon which a revelation can rest is the possession by the bearer of it of prophetic and miraculous powers.

For a revealed religion claims authority over us. If it be God's voice speaking to us, we have no choice but to obey. Our reason might not approve; our hearts and wills might detest what we were told; yet if we knew that it was God's voice, we must sadly and reluctantly submit to it. But it would be wrong in the highest degree to yield up ourselves to anything requiring such complete obedience unless we had satisfactory proof that God really was its author. And no subjective proof could be satisfactory. The purity of the doctrines of Christianity, their agreement with the truths of natural religion, their ennobling effects upon our characters, and the way in which they enlighten the conscience—all this and more shows that there is no impossibility in Christianity being a divine revelation: the perfectness of our Lord's character, the thoroughness with which Christ's atonement answers to the deepest needs of the soul, the way in which Christianity rises above all religions of man's devising—all this and more makes it probable that it is God's gift. But at most these considerations only prepare the mind to listen without prejudice to the direct and external proofs that Christianity is a revelation from God. The final proof must pledge God himself to its truth. But what are the divine attributes which would bear the most decisive witness? Surely those which most entirely transcend all human counterfeits — omniscience and omnipotence. Now these are pledged to Christianity by prophecy and miracle.

The first had performed its office when Christ came. All men were musing in their hearts upon the expected coming of some Great One. His miracles, his *works*, the products of his *powers*, were the *signs* that prophecy was in course of fulfilment. The two must not be separated. Our Lord expressly declares that but for his *works* the Jews would have been right in rejecting him (John xv, 24). His claims were too high for any less proof to have sufficed. But the nature of his works did put men under a moral obligation to inquire into his claims; and then he sent them to the Scriptures (John v, 39). The miracles were thus not the final proof of Christ's mission. Had they been such, we might have expected that they would still be from time to time vouchsafed, as occasion required, even to the end of the world. The agreement of Christ's life and death and teaching with what had been foretold of the Messiah is the leading proof of his mission, and, having this, we need miracles no more. Christ's works called men's attention to this proof, and made it a duty to examine it. They also exalt his person, and give him the authority of a messenger accredited from heaven; but the Old Testament remains for all ages the proper proof of the truth of the New. Miracles were *signs* for the times; prophecy is for all time, and as Christianity no longer requires anything especially to call men's attention to its claims, prophecy is proof enough that it is a message from God.

The more clearly to set this before our readers, we repeat that prediction was the distinctive sign of God's presence under the Old-Testament dispensation, and miracles subordinate. Revelation was then a growing light, and was ever advancing onward; and thus the prophets were ever preparing for the future. It was only on special occasions that miracle was needed. But when revelation became perfect and final in the person of One who, according to the terms of prophecy, transcended the bounds of human nature, it was necessary that miracle should rise in him to its highest level, both because of the dignity of his person, as one invested with all power, human and divine, and also as the proper proof at the time of his being the Son, the last and greatest therefore whom the Father could send; and, finally, to call the attention of men to his claims, and compel them to examine them. For this reason they were called *signs*. But as soon as the dispensation thus given could force its claims on men's atten-

tion by other means, and its divine founder had withdrawn, miracles necessarily ceased, as being inconsistent with man's probation. Look over the list of Scripture names for miracles, and ask what one would be appropriate now? Of what would they now be *signs?* Of what person would they be the proper *faculties?* For whom now would they be suitable *works?* The whole scriptural theory of miracles is contravened by the supposition of miracles being continued after Christianity had once been established. What history teaches us, namely, that they were rapidly withdrawn, is alone consistent with what we gather from Scripture concerning them.

They were an essential part of the proof at the time, and have an essential use now. For we could not believe what is taught us of Christ if he had not been accredited by miracles. But the proper evidence for the truth of Christianity now is that of prophecy, not as existing any longer in living force, but as manifested in the agreement of the long list of books forming the Old Testament with one another; and still more in the fulfilment of the Old Testament in the New. It is a proof in everybody's hands, and open to every one to examine. The proof of miracles requires, of course, large historical evidence, and not every one possesses bishop Stillingfleet's *Origines Causæ*, or even Paley; but every Christian has his Bible, and in it will find the proper proof now of its truth.

Agreeably with this, dean Lyall, in his *Propædia Prophetica*, has well remarked that the apostles "scarcely allude to Christ's miracles at all, and never in the way of proof" (p. 4). Miracles, he shows, now hold a disproportionate place in the argument from that assigned to them in the New Testament; and, in fact, it is very remarkable that Peter but twice refers in his speeches to Christ's miracles, and never but once to those wrought by himself. Paul, in his thirteen epistles, only thrice appeals to his own miraculous powers, and never mentions Christ's miracles, or even directly alludes to them. The key of this we have in the names applied to them by the apostles, and especially by John. They were the natural works of one such as was Christ, but also signs that in him the long preparation of the Old-Testament dispensation had reached its final purpose, and that the new and lasting dispensation had begun.

In their proper place and degree, however, they were and still remain essential to the proof of a divine revelation. We could not accept a revelation, or give it the authority over our conscience due to the direct voice of God, unless we had indubitable proof that it was God's voice. The supernatural can only be proved by the supernatural. If, then, a revelation was necessary as well for the present progress of mankind as for their future perfectness, miracle was also necessary, and the believer in revelation cannot possibly discard it from its place among the evidences.

Necessarily, therefore, from first to last, the Bible is a book of miracle. Miracle is present not as an accident, separable from the main thread, but is itself the very essence of the narrative. The facts of the Old Testament were the basis of the faith of the Jew. They were so as being *miracles*, and because, as such, they involved certain dogmatic propositions concerning the divine Being and his relations to themselves. So as regards ourselves. When we repeat the Apostles' Creed, we acknowledge our belief first in the existence of a God—an instinct, as we have shown, of our nature—but upon this follow certain historical facts recorded in the New Testament, which are either directly miraculous, or become dogmatic because of being based upon miracle. Without miracle Christianity is absolutely nothing. All that distinguishes it from simple Theism is miraculous.

Miracles in the present day are at a discount. Our men of science have so well studied the laws of the material universe, and shown us so clearly the existence there of a calm, unbroken, unvarying order, that our minds, enamored of so grand a truth, are impatient of any truth or theory rising above these material laws. Thus the controversy whether Christianity is true or not really turns upon miracle. The close and exact examination of all the facts of holy Scripture which has marked our days has served only to confirm men's belief in the authenticity of the sacred writings. Our increased knowledge, especially that obtained from the cuneiform inscriptions corroborative of the Old-Testament history, and from similar unquestionable authorities contemporaneous with the New-Testament records, has well-nigh swept away every so-called historical difficulty; while subjective criticism has not merely failed in substantiating any case against the several books of the Bible, but has done very much to place them upon a surer basis. At no time was the external evidence in favor of Christianity, or the argument drawn from prophecy, so clear and so little liable to objection as at the present day. And this is no slight matter. A host of eager and competent critics have examined with unfavorable intentions the whole line of our defences, and the result of their operations has been to show how thoroughly tenable it is in every part.

Thus the whole attack is now thrown upon miracle. Miracle is roundly asserted to be contrary to the whole course of nature, and to be a violation of that grand law of invariable order which we find everywhere else throughout the universe. In this way a sort of induction is drawn against miracle. Wherever we can examine into the causes of phenomena, we always find them the products of forces acting according to unchanging laws. Whole regions of phenomena, which were once supposed to be under the sway of chance, have now been reduced to order, and the causes of them made manifest. Men of science have entered one field after another, and have added it to their domains, by showing what laws govern it, and how those laws work. With some show of reason therefore they affirm that law prevails everywhere, and that where at present it cannot be shown to prevail, we may yet be sure of its presence, and convinced that the patient investigations of science will in due time demonstrate its sway. And therefore miracle, as being a violation of these universal laws, is not merely, they say, contrary to that experience of men of which Mr. Hume spoke, and upon which he founded an argument repeatedly shown to be untenable, but of an induction drawn from a vast field of observation and scientific inquiry. In miracle, and miracle alone, science finds something which contradicts its experience. The examination of this most important objection will complete our inquiry.

The proposition contained in this objection, when we consider it, seems a most true conclusion as regards the material universe. All material things apparently are governed by general laws, and it is probable that scientific men are quite right in endeavoring to show that even in creation all things were produced by law. For our own part, we cannot imagine a perfect Being like the Deity working except by law, and therefore we read all theories about evolution and selection, and the formation of the solar system by slow degrees out of a vast nebula, and the like, with no prejudice regarding them, however intended, simply as attempted answers to the question, In what way—by what secondary processes—did God create and shape the world? If, after reading the arguments, we conclude by thinking them often ingenious rather than true, and put the book down with the Scotch verdict, "Not proven," we do not therefore think that science is on the wrong track, nor doubt that all these inquiries do in the main give us juster views of God's method of working. But miracle seems to us to belong to another field of thought, and to be outside the domains of science. For we venture to ask, Is the material universe everything? Is there nothing but matter? nothing but dull, inert particles, acted upon by material forces—attraction, repulsion,

affinity, and the like. What is force? What is law? If there be a God—a perfect, omnipotent, omnipresent Being—then law has to us a meaning. It is his will, working permanently and unchangeably because he is a perfect and omnipotent worker. We can understand force. It is his presence, acting upon and controlling all things, but always in the same way, because he changes not. To believe in universal order without a universal will to order all things, to believe in universal laws without a universal lawgiver, is to us an absurdity. *Ex nihilo nihil fit.* In a world where every effect has a cause, who and what is the cause of all? Who but God? And who sustains the world now but he who first made it?

But it is not the office of science to inquire into the being and attributes and nature of this First Great Cause. Science is solely occupied with the *secondary processes*. When it has reached the law, it has done its work. It is not the business of science to examine into the law as such, but only into the mode of its operations. Whose is the law, what power sustains it, how it came into being—all this lies outside the domain of science. Thus science never rises above material things; and by remembering this — by remembering that, after all, the field of science (of course we mean physical science) is limited—we see that an induction made in its proper field does not justify any conclusions in fields outside its limits.

Let us take the case of man. Science, looking at him in his physical aspect, tells us that he consists of several pounds of salts and earths, combined with a larger number of gallons of water. It tells us by what chemical affinities these commonplace materials are held together, how they operate upon one another, by what processes the waste is renewed, and by what a mass of curious mechanical contrivances man's body, considered as a machine, performs its operations. If we ask how it comes to think, science tells us much about the brain; how like it is to a galvanic trough, and by what an elaborate, threefold apparatus of nerves it sends its commands to every part of the body. But when we ask how it is that the brain does consciously what the voltaic battery does unconsciously; how it is that these earths and salts, when combined into a man, know that they are a man, we get only the unmeaning answer that it is the result of organization. But give science all the bottles in a chemist's shop, and it cannot organize a sentient being out of them. In fact, it owns itself that life is a mystery. It can tell how life works, but not what life is. Life is as much beyond the reach of science as is God. It knows the laws of life, but no more.

Man therefore, when considered only physically, contains more than science can master. But is life the only mystery in man? Why does man think? Why does he speculate upon his own actions? Why muse upon the purpose of all things here below? Of all beings upon this earth, man alone is self-conscious. He alone knows that he exists; he alone feels that he exists for a purpose, and can and does consciously interfere with other things in order to shape them to his own ends. He alone has not the mere rudiments, but the full gift of a conscience, which is always interfering with him, and giving him endless annoyance, because it will pass judgment upon his actions, and condemn much that he does.

Now it is in connection with this higher world that miracle has its proper place. It distinctly has reference to man as a being in whom there is more than mere material forces at work. Prove that there is nothing more in man than salts and earths and water, and there would be no place for miracle. Now physical science stops at proving this. The most skilful analyst could get nothing more out of man than salts, earths, and water; but then, confessedly, he labors under this disadvantage, that he cannot begin his analysis until life, and with it the sentient soul, has withdrawn from the machine. All he can examine is the residuum only.

We want some science therefore which can examine man while he is alive, and report upon him. For physical science is not the sole science. There are other sciences, and each is authoritative only upon its own domain. The psychologist, who examines into the workings of man's inner nature, is quite as worthy of a hearing as the physicist, who examines into the materials out of which he is composed. *Ne sutor ultra crepidam*—a homely but wise motto, which a rising and progressive study, such as is physical science, in the hours of its first triumphs, is in danger of neglecting. After all, a man of only one science tries to see with only one eye, and to walk with only one leg. Before we can form a true estimate of the question that so deeply concerns us—What is man's place and work and purpose in the world?—we must include a far wider induction than that offered by physical science.

If, as the instincts of our nature teach us, there be a God; if man be more than a very highly-organized machine; if within him there be an immortal soul, and before him a future life, then miracle is essential to his well-being. It is the sole possible proof of conscious relation between man and God. Man could not be sure that God had spoken to him, had revealed to him any knowledge requisite for his use, had entered into covenant relation with him, without miracles. We know nothing in physical science to disprove this relation. Suppose that we find a stage elaborately constructed and adorned. No theory, however true, of the manner in which this stage was constructed, no examination of the mechanical laws by which it is still kept in being, will justify us in concluding that it was not intended for some further purpose. Nor, because the boards are all safely nailed in their place, does it follow that actors may not enter upon it, higher in nature than the boards, and capable of spontaneous motion. Nor, because we have never seen the builder, does it follow that he did not erect the stage on purpose that these actors might play upon it their parts. Geology, chemistry, astronomy, so far from proving that the world had no purpose, and that the actors upon it have no freedom and no responsibility, rather suggest the contrary. They teach us what a vast amount of skill, patience, wisdom, and goodness has been expended in forming the stage. *Quorsum hæc?* What was the object of all this? What the end? Oh! but some physicists answer, We reject teleology. That is, we reject something which lies beyond our province, and on which we have no authority to speak. They tell us all about the stage, and then, instead of saying frankly, We have done our part, *Plaudite* (and richly they deserve our applause), they tell us, Be satisfied with the stage. It is very pretty, very nicely constructed, but utterly unmeaning. An elaborate universe without a purpose, is a poor, mean thing, unworthy to exist. It would be a disgrace to a man to erect a noble structure without a purpose: there are many buildings in England called So-and-So's Folly, because erected without a sufficient purpose. Let us beware of ascribing such child's play to that Power which called the universe into being.

No. The more we consider man, and the more we learn about him, and about the world which he inhabits, the more sure we are that he is no fortuitous concurrence of atoms, but the chief and culminating point, in whom, and in whom alone, all the skill and wisdom and long patience displayed in the formation of the world find their purpose and their justification. The wonders of physical science all lead up to this. There are some among its teachers who would persuade us that the universe is a mere curiosity shop, fitted to raise our wonder, but never reasonable, because nowhere the product of mind, or controlled by mind. But the very harmony which they find in nature, and the calm reign of law, proves that mind does pervade all nature. Without mind there can be no harmony; without a universal mind no universal law. But grant that mind may exist as well as matter, and you grant the possibility of this world having a purpose—a purpose which, as we have shown, can be realized only in man. But to realize this purpose men's finite mind may need converse with the universal, the infinite mind, and, if so, miracle is justified by this necessity.

Thus, then, miracle is not contrary to nature, but rises simply above the sphere of mere material forces. And it is untrue and unphilosophic to regard it as an interference by God with his universal laws, much less a violation of them. Man daily interferes with the material laws and forces of nature, but we never violate them. The stone thrown into the air interferes with the law of gravitation, but does not violate it. And if God be an intelligent and moral worker like man, only in a superior and perfect degree, he, too, must be capable of bending the powers of nature to instantaneous obedience to his will, or he could not do what man can do. His own laws he could not violate, because they are his laws; but his interference with them would necessarily be what we call a miracle, something which the ordinary operations of nature could not produce; something which transcends nature, and goes utterly beyond it. If a sheep possessed the power of reasoning upon its own actions and those of man, the latter would seem to it absolutely miraculous, because they so entirely exceed its own powers. Yet to man they would be no miracles, but the ordinary exercise of his powers. And so what we call miracles are not miracles to the Deity, and therefore the evangelists call them in Christ simply δυνάμεις, ' is ..unies; and John calls them ἔργα, *works*, only, the natural products of his faculties; yet not wrought without a purpose. They were also σημεῖα, *signs*, tokens indicating that something was done, which man was thereby required to examine and observe; and living as the Jews did under a preparatory dispensation, they were signs that the fulness of time had come, and the final dispensation being ushered in.

In conclusion. Without miracles there can be only natural religion; revealed religion is impossible. Revelation is itself a miracle; and its very object is to tell us things which we could not otherwise know. Such things cannot be verified as we verify the facts of science. No man hath or can see God. No man can tell us by experience what is the state of the soul after death, for from that bourne no traveller returns. Yet some knowledge of the relations of the soul with God may be absolutely necessary for our moral and spiritual well-being. Now the utter failure of natural religion convinces us that it is necessary. And therefore we feel no difficulty in the belief that God, in creating the world such as it is, and placing man upon it such as he is, and under such circumstances as those in which we find ourselves, did from the first purpose this reasonable interference with the material laws of his own framing, by which he grants man the only sufficient proof that he is willing to enter into covenant relations with him. If the physicist reply that such action on God's part is inconceivable, we answer that he also must conceive of some such action. Students of physical science deal in long numbers, but these numbers are as nothing compared with the eternity past. Work back with the geologist, and you come at last to a first beginning of matter. Looked at by the light of mental science, the eternal existence of matter is impossible. To the metaphysician, matter is but a phenomenon of mind. Confining ourselves, then, to our universe, what a momentous change was that in God when he passed from the passive state of not willing it to the active state of willing the existence of our system! Grant that by his fiat he only called into existence an atom, out of which by evolution all things here below have sprung, what a stupendous act it was, and how entirely it placed the Deity in relations, and to speak with all reverence, under obligations from which he was free before! For the Creator is under the obligations of justice and love to his creatures. He made us, and not we ourselves. But he neither was nor is under any moral obligations to his material laws. They abide in power and might because he abideth continually. And miracle simply means that he, the Creator, has from time to time, under the operation of a higher law, given us the necessary proof that he does love us, and that certain messengers, chosen from among men, had authority to teach us truths which concerned our peace; and that, finally, by "powers and portents and signs, he has manifested and displayed Jesus of Nazareth in the midst of us" as "a leader and Saviour, to give repentance unto his people and the remission of sins."

Miracles, then, were no after-thought, no remedial process to set right what had gone wrong before. They form an essential and necessary part and condition of the intercourse between the universal mind of God and the finite mind of man, and that intercourse was necessary for man's good. Why man is just what he is, and why the state of things in which he finds himself is what it is, we cannot tell. We can only reason from facts as we find them. But man being such as he is, we assert that the world would be a failure without miracles; for either man would exist without a purpose, or, having been placed here for some purpose, he would not know with sufficient certainty or clearness what that purpose was, and therefore would neither have the means of effecting it, nor even any obligation laid upon him of trying to accomplish what his Maker had willed in his creation. (R. P. S.)

For the relations of miracles to prayer, see PRAYER.

We have thus far considered simply the positive evidences on which the belief in miracles properly rests, and it remains to notice the objections that have from time to time been urged against it, and the different views as to the character and office of miracles.

The Christians even of apostolic days were in the habit of appealing to the miracles and prophecies in support of the truth of their religion, and hence it became important to define exactly the idea of a miracle; and in consequence of a desire for such preciseness division arose among the interpreters of Scripture, provoking heresy in the Church, while from without attacks were constantly made against the credibility of the Gospel history, the divine authenticity of the prophetic announcements, and the wonderful works claimed to have been wrought under the old dispensation. Dean Trench, in his *Notes on Miracles*, has furnished an excellent and interesting account of the various assaults made on the argument for miracles, and to it we must refer for detailed information. Suffice it to say here that the controversy respecting the possibility of miracles is as old as philosophic literature. Indeed, from the writings of Jewish savans, it would appear that the controversy respecting the possibility of miracles commenced even in the days of the O.-T. dispensation, and that near the appointed time for the coming of the Saviour the world was greatly animated by a controversy on the subject. There is a very clear view of it, as it stood in the pagan world, given by Cicero in his books *De Divinatione*. In the works of Josephus there are occasionally suggestions of naturalistic explanations of O.-T. miracles; but these seem rather thrown out for the purpose of gratifying sceptical pagan readers than as expressions of his own belief. The other chief authorities for Jewish opinion are Maimonides's *Moreh Nebochim*, lib. ii, c. 35, and the *Pirke Aboth*, in Surenhusius's *Mishna*, iv, 469, and Abrabanel, *Miphaloth Elohim*, p. 93.

Dean Trench, in his classification of the objectors, places the Jewish first, then follows with the heathen (Celsus, etc.), and puts as third in the list the pantheistic objectors led by Spinoza. He evidently regards Cardan (*De Contradictione Medicorum*, 2, tract. 2), and those other Italian atheists who referred the Christian miracles to the influence of the stars, as unworthy of notice. If these be omitted, as Trench has done, the controversy in the modern Christian world regarding miracles may be said to date back to the 17th century,

and to have been ushered in by Spinoza's *Tractatus Theologici Politici*, "which contained the germ of almost all the infidel theories that have since appeared." Rationalists since the days of Spinoza have opposed the reality and credibility of miracles, while the adherents of the modern (formal) supernaturalism rested belief in revelation especially on that branch of evidence. One of these objections, urged by Spinoza, and repeated in various forms by subsequent writers, is thus stated by dean Mansel: "The laws of nature are the decrees of God, and follow necessarily from the perfection of the divine nature; they must therefore be eternal and immutable, and must extend to all possible events. Therefore, to admit an exception to these laws is to suppose that God's order is broken, and that the divine work is but an imperfect expression of the divine will. This objection is perfectly intelligible in the mouth of a pantheist, with whom *God* and *nature* are convertible terms, and a divine supernatural act is a self-contradiction; but it is untenable in any system which admits a personal God distinct from nature, and only partially manifested in it. In such a system nature is not infinite, as Spinoza makes it, but finite. There is a distinction between the actual and the possible; between the visible world as a limited system, with limited laws, and the whole mind of God, embracing all possible systems as well as the present. From this point of view, nature, as actually existing, *does* express a portion, and a portion only, of the divine purpose; the miracle expresses another portion belonging to a different and more comprehensive system. But in addition to this consideration, even the actual world furnishes us with an answer to the objection. God's order, we have too much reason to know, actually is broken. His will is not carried out. Unless we make God the author of evil, we must admit that sin is a violation of his will, a breach made in his natural order, however impossible it may be to give an account of its origin. The pantheist evades the difficulty by denying that evil has any real existence; but to the theist, who admits its existence, it is conclusive evidence that, as a fact, however little we may understand how it can be, the world, as it exists, is not a perfect expression of God's law and will. The miracle, as thus viewed, belongs to a spiritual system appointed to remedy the disorders of the natural system; and against the self-complacent theory which tells us that disorders in the natural system are impossible, we have the witness of a melancholy experience which tells us that they are actually there. Thus viewed, the miracle is in one sense natural, in another supernatural. It is natural as forming a part of the higher or spiritual system; it is supernatural as not forming a part of the lower or material system. The same considerations may serve to obviate another form of the same objection—a form in which it is likewise suggested by Spinoza, though developed by other writers in a form more adapted to the language of theism. We are told that it is more worthy of God to arrange a plan which shall provide by its original laws for all possible contingencies than one which requires a special interposition to meet a special emergency. We know so little about the process of creating and governing a world, that it is difficult for us to judge what method of doing so is most worthy of God; but this whole objection proceeds on the gratuitous assumption that the plan of the world, as it exists in the counsels of God, must be identical with the plan of the world as it is contemplated by man in relation to physical laws. Doubtless the miracle, like any other event, was foreseen by God from the beginning, and formed part of his eternal purpose; but it does not therefore follow that it is included within that very limited portion of his purpose which is apprehended by man as a system of physical laws. To Omnipotence no one event is more difficult than another; to Omniscience no one event is more wonderful than another. The distinction between miracles and ordinary events, as has already been observed, is a distinction, not in relation to God, but in relation to man. Moreover, even from the human point of view, the miracle is not wrought for a physical, but for a moral purpose; it is not an interposition to adjust the machinery of the material world, but one to promote the spiritual welfare of mankind. The very conception of a *revealed*, as distinguished from a *natural* religion, implies a manifestation of God different in kind from that which is exhibited by the ordinary course of nature; and the question of the probability of a miraculous interposition is simply that of the probability of a revelation being given at all." A list of the principal replies to the pantheistic objectors may be seen in Fabricius, *Delectus Argumentorum*, etc., c. 43, p. 697 (Hamburg, 1725). A full account of the controversy in England with the deists during the last century will be found in Leland's *View of the Deistical Writers* (reprinted at London, 1836). The debate was renewed about the middle of that century by the publication of Hume's celebrated essay, which teaches that "a miracle is a violation of the laws of nature; and as a firm and unalterable experience has established these laws, the proof against a miracle, from the very nature of the fact, is as entire as any argument from experience can possibly be imagined." According to the position taken in the preceding remarks by the dean of Canterbury, it cannot with any accuracy be said that a miracle is "a violation of the laws of nature." It is the effect of a supernatural cause, acting along with and in addition to the natural causes constituting the system of the world. It is produced, therefore, by a different combination of causes from that which is at work in the production of natural phenomena. The laws of nature are only general expressions of that uniform arrangement according to which the same causes invariably produce the same effect. They would be violated by the production, at different times, of different effects from the same cause; but they are not violated when different effects are produced from different causes. The experience which testifies to their uniformity tells us only what effects may be expected to follow from a repetition of the same cause; it cannot tell us what effects will follow from the introduction of a different cause. This, which is in substance the answer given to Hume by Brown, appears the most satisfactory among the various arguments by which the sceptical philosopher's position has been assailed. It is questioned by some of the critics of Hume (notably Sir William Hamilton; comp. Hamilton's Reid, p. 129, 444, 457, 489), whether his sceptical arguments are offered in a spirit of hostility to the processes of common-sense and the truths of religion, and not rather in a spirit of hostility to philosophy itself, by representing the results of its analysis as equally probable in favor of and against two opposite directions of thought. The form of dialogue which is adopted by Hume in this discussion favors somewhat this construction; but it cannot be reconciled with the impression left upon the unbiased mind that Hume had no confidence in speculation of any kind when applied to supersensual or spiritual beings and relations (comp. Ueberweg, *Hist. Philos*. ii, 379). The ablest replies to Hume's arguments were sent forth by Principal Campbell in his *Dissertation on Miracles*; Hey, *Norrisian Lectures*, i, 127 sq.; Elrington, *Donellan Lectures* (Dublin, 1796); Dr. Thomas Brown, *On Cause and Effect*; Paley, *Evidences of Christianity* (Introduction); Archbp. Whately, *Logic* (Appendix); and *Historic Doubts respecting Napoleon Bonaparte*; Dean Ryall, *Propædia Prophetica* (reprinted, 1854); Bp. Douglas, *Criterion, or Miracles Examined*, etc. (Lond. 1754); Farrar, *Critical Hist. of Free Thought*, p. 150 sq. See HUME. Within the last few years the controversy has been reopened by the late professor Baden Powell in the *Unity of Worlds*, and some remarks on the study of evidences published in the now-celebrated volume of *Essays and Reviews*. See Goodwin, in *Am. Theol. Rev*. July, 1861; *Christian Remembrancer*, July, 1861.

From England the controversy shifted again to the Continent, and finds its ablest representatives against the supernaturalists now not only in the camp of the atheistic and pantheistic, but also among theologians, and dean Trench therefore adopts as his next or fifth class those who regard miracles, as such, only subjectively, placing as its standard-bearer the celebrated Schleiermacher, who advanced a doctrine as incompatible with any belief in a real miracle as was that taught by Hume. "A miracle," says Schleiermacher, "has a positive relation, by which it extends to all that is future, and a negative relation, which in a certain sense affects all that is past. In so far as that does not follow which would have followed, according to the natural connection of the aggregate of finite causes, in so far an effect is hindered, not by the influence of other natural counteracting causes belonging to the same series, but notwithstanding the concurrence of all effective causes to the production of the effect. Everything, therefore, which from all past time contributed to this effect is in a certain measure annihilated; and instead of the interpolation of a single supernatural agent into the course of nature, the whole conception of nature is destroyed. On the positive side, something takes place which is conceived as incapable of following from the aggregate of finite causes. But, inasmuch as this event itself now becomes an actual link in the chain of nature, every future event must be other than it would have been had this one miracle not taken place." On this and other grounds, Schleiermacher is led to maintain that there is no real distinction between the natural and the supernatural; the miracles being only miraculous relatively to us, through our imperfect knowledge of the hidden causes in nature, by means of which they were wrought. "This objection," says dean Mansel, "proceeds on an assumption which is not merely unwarranted, but actually contradicted by experience. It assumes that the system of material nature is a rigid, not an elastic system; that it is one which obstinately resists the introduction of new forces, not one which is capable of adapting itself to them. We know by experience that the voluntary actions of men can be interposed among the phenomena of matter, and exercise an influence over them, so that certain results may be produced or not, according to the will of a man, without affecting the stability of the universe, or the coherence of its parts as a system. What the will of man can effect to a small extent, the will of God can surely effect to a greater extent; and this is a sufficient answer to the objection which declares the miracle to be *impossible*; though we may not be able to say with certainty whether it is actually brought to pass in this or in some other way. There may be many means, unknown to us, by which such an event may be produced; but if it can be produced in any way it is not impossible."

The rationalists, thus encouraged by the mediating theologians, endeavored to explain the miraculous as something natural, while the natural philosophers asserted that nature transfigured by spirit (the blending of the two in one) is the only true miracle. But thus the reality of the miracle (in the scriptural sense) was destroyed, and it was regarded simply as the symbolical expression of a speculative idea. See Schelling, *Methode*, p. 181, 203; and comp. Bockshammer and Rosenkranz, cited in Strauss, *Dogmatik*, p. 244 sq. [Bockshammer (*Freiheit der Willens*, transl. by Kaufman, Andov. 1840) says that what is willed in the spirit of truth and purity with a mighty will, is willed in the Spirit of God, and it is only a postulate of reason that nature cannot withstand such a will. Hence Christ is the great miracle-worker. Rosenkranz (*Encykl. d. Theol.* p. 160) defines miracle as nature determined by spirit; spirit is the basis of nature, and hence nature cannot limit it. This power was fully concentrated in Christ.] The *natural* interpretation of miracles rather served the purposes of rationalism, while the adherents of modern speculative philosophy gave the preference to the hypothesis that the miracles related in Scripture are myths, because it is more agreeable to the negative tendency of that school—that the antecedent improbability of a miracle taking place must always outweigh that of the testimony in its favor being false; and thus that the occurrence of a miracle, if not impossible, is at least incapable of satisfactory proof. Such is in the main the argument of Hume, but it came more recently to be revived and assumed as an axiomatic principle by the so-called naturalistic, or, better, rationalistic Paulus, and by the *historico-critical school*, represented mainly by Woolston, Strauss, and Renan. "The fallacy of this objection," says dean Mansel, "consists in the circumstance that it estimates the opposed probabilities solely on empirical grounds; i. e. on the more or less frequent occurrence of miraculous events as compared with false testimony. If it is ever possible that an event of comparatively rare occurrence may, in a given case and under certain circumstances, be more credible than one of more ordinary occurrence, the entire argument falls to the ground in reference to such cases. And such a case is actually presented by the Christian miracles. The redemption of the world is an event unique in the world's history: it is therefore natural to expect that the circumstances accompanying it should be unique also. The importance of that redemption furnishes a 'distinct particular reason' for miracles, if the divine purpose can be furthered by them. Under these circumstances the antecedent probability is for the miracles, not against them, and cannot be outweighed by empirical inductions drawn from totally different data, relating to the physical, not to the religious condition of the world. It must, however, be always remembered that abstract and general considerations like the above, though necessary to meet the unbelieving objections which are unhappily rife on this subject, do not constitute the grounds of our belief in the miracles of Scripture, especially those of Christ. The abstract argument is the stronghold of scepticism, and to deal with it at all it is necessary to meet it on its own ground. On the other hand, the strength of the Christian argument rests mainly on the special contents of the Gospel narrative, particularly as regards the character of the Saviour portrayed in it, and the distinctive nature of his miracles as connected with his character, and on the subsequent history of the Christian Church. It is far easier to talk in general terms about the laws of nature, and the impossibility of their violation, than to go through the actual contents of the Gospels in detail, and show how it is possible that such a narrative could have been written, and how the events described in it could have influenced, as they have, the subsequent history of the world, on any other supposition than that of its being a true narrative of real events. Accordingly we find that, while the several attacks on the Gospel miracles in particular, with whatever ability they may have been conducted, and whatever temporary popularity they may have obtained, seem universally destined to a speedy extinction beyond the possibility of revival, the general *a priori* objection still retains its hold on men's minds, and is revived from time to time, after repeated refutations, as often as the changing aspects of scientific progress appear to offer the opportunity of a plausible disguise of an old sophism in new drapery. The minute criticisms of Woolston and Paulus on the details of the Gospel history are utterly dead and buried out of sight; and those of Strauss show plain indications of being doomed to the same fate, though supported for a while by a spurious alliance with a popular philosophy. And the failure which is manifest in such writers, even while they confine themselves to the merely negative task of criticising the Gospel narrative, becomes still more conspicuous when they proceed to account for the origin of Christianity by positive theories of their own. The naturalistic theory of Paulus breaks down under the sheer weight of its own accumulation of cumbrous and awkward explanations; while the

mythical hypothesis of Strauss is found guilty of the logical absurdity of deducing the premise from the conclusion: it assumes that men invented an imaginary life of Jesus because they believed him to be the Messiah, when the very supposition that the life is imaginary leaves the belief in the Messiahship unexplained and inexplicable. On the other hand, the *a priori* reasonings of Spinoza and Hume exhibit a vitality which is certainly not due to their logical conclusiveness, but which has enabled them in various disguises to perplex the intellects and unsettle the faith of a different generation from that for which they were first written. Hence it is that a writer who is required, by the exigencies of his own day, to consider the question of miracles from an apologetic point of view, finds himself compelled to dwell mainly on the abstract argument concerning miracles in general, rather than on the distinctive features which characterize the Christian miracles in particular. The latter are the more pleasant and the more useful theme, when the object is the edification of the believer; the former is indispensable when it is requisite to controvert the positions of the unbeliever. There is, however, one phase of the sceptical argument which may be met by considerations of the special rather than of the general kind. It has been objected that no testimony can prove a miracle as such. 'Testimony,' we are told, 'can apply only to apparent, sensible facts; testimony can only prove an extraordinary and perhaps inexplicable occurrence or phenomenon; that it is due to supernatural causes is entirely dependent on the previous belief and assumptions of the parties.' Whatever may be the value of this objection as applied to a hypothetical case, in which the objector may select such occurrences and such testimonies as suit his purpose, it is singularly inapplicable to the works actually recorded as having been done by Christ and his apostles. It may, with certain exceptions, be applicable to a case in which the assertion of a supernatural cause rests solely on the testimony of the *spectator* of the fact; but it is not applicable to those in which the cause is declared by the *performer*. Let us accept, if we please, merely as a narrative of 'apparent sensible facts,' the history of the cure of the blind and dumb dæmoniac, or of the lame man at the Beautiful Gate; but we cannot place the same restriction upon the words of our Lord and of St. Peter, which expressly assign the supernatural cause— 'If I cast out devils by the Spirit of God, then the kingdom of God is come unto you.' 'By the name of Jesus Christ of Nazareth doth this man stand here before you whole.' We have here, at least, a testimony reaching to the supernatural; and if that testimony be admitted in these cases, the same cause becomes the most reasonable and probable that can be assigned to the other wonderful works performed by the same persons. For if it be admitted that our Lord exercised a supernatural power at all, there is, to use the words of bishop Butler, 'no more presumption worth mentioning against his having exerted this miraculous power in a certain degree greater, than in a certain degree less; in one or two more instances, than in one or two fewer.' This brings us to the consideration on which the most important part of this controversy must ultimately rest; namely, that the true evidence on behalf of the Christian miracles is to be estimated, not by the force of testimony in general, as compared with antecedent improbability, but by the force of the peculiar testimony by which the Christian miracles are supported, as compared with the antecedent probability or improbability that a religion of such a character should have been first introduced into the world of superhuman agency. The miracles of Christ, and, as the chief of them all, that great crowning miracle of his resurrection, are supported by all the testimony which they derived from his own positive declarations concerning them, taken in conjunction with the record of his life, and the subsequent history of the Christian religion.

The alternative lies between accepting that testimony, as it is given, or regarding the Gospels as a fiction, and the Christian faith as founded on imposture. In adopting this argument, we do not, as is sometimes said, reason in a circle, employing the character of Christ as a testimony in favor of the miracles, and the miracles again as a testimony in favor of the character of Christ. For the character of Christ is contemplated in two distinct aspects: first, as regards his human perfectness; and, secondly, as regards his superhuman mission and powers. The first bears witness to the miracles, the miracles bear witness to the second. When our Lord represents himself as a human example to be imitated by his human followers, he lays stress on those facts of his life which indicate his human goodness: 'Take my yoke upon you, and learn of me; for I am meek and lowly of heart.' When, on the other hand, he represents himself as divinely commissioned for a special purpose, he appeals to the superhuman evidence of his miracles as authenticating that mission: 'The works which the Father hath given me to finish, the same works that I do, bear witness of me that the Father hath sent me.' It is true that the evidence of the miracles, as addressed to us, has a different aspect, and rests on different grounds, from that which belonged to them at the time when they were first performed. But this change has not diminished their force as evidences, though it has somewhat changed its direction. If we have not the advantage of seeing and hearing and questioning those who were eye-witnesses of the miracles, the deficiency is fully supplied by the additional testimony that has accrued to us, in the history of Christianity, from their day to ours. If we have stricter conceptions of physical law, and of the uniformity of nature, we have also higher evidence of the existence of a purpose worthy of the exercise of God's sovereign power over nature. If the progress of science has made many things easy of performance at the present day which would have seemed miraculous to the men of the 1st century, it has also shown more clearly how inimitable and unapproachable are the miracles of Christ, in the maturity of science no less than in its infancy. And when it is objected that 'if miracles were, in the estimation of a former age, among the chief supports of a former Christianity, they are at present among the main difficulties and hinderances to its acceptance,' we may fairly ask, What is this Christianity which might be more easily believed if it had no miracles? Is it meant that the Gospel narrative, in general, would be more easy to believe were the miracles taken out of it? The miracles are so interwoven with the narrative that the whole texture would be destroyed by their removal. Or is it meant that the great central fact in the apostolic preaching—the resurrection of Christ—would be more natural and credible if he who thus marvellously rose from the dead had in his lifetime exhibited no signs of a power superior to that of his fellow-men? Or is it meant that the great distinctive doctrines of Christianity—such as those of the Trinity and the Incarnation—might be more readily accepted were there no miracles in the Scripture which contains them? We can scarcely imagine it to be seriously maintained that it would be easier to believe that the second person of the divine Trinity came on earth in the form of man, were it also asserted that while on earth he gave no signs of a power beyond that of ordinary men. In short, it is difficult to understand on what ground it can be maintained that the miracles are a hinderance to the belief in Christianity, except on a ground which asserts also that there is no distinctive Christianity in which to believe. It may with more truth be said that the miraculous element, which forms so large a portion of Christianity, has its peculiar worth and service at the present day as a protest and safeguard against two forms of unchristian thought to which an intellectual and cultivated age is liable—pantheism, the danger of a deeply speculative

philosophy; and materialism, the danger of a too exclusive devotion to physical science. Both these, in different ways, tend to deify nature and the laws of nature, and to obscure the belief in a personal God distinct from and above nature; against both these, so long as the Christian religion lasts, the miracles of Christ are a perpetual witness; and in so witnessing they perform a service to religion different in kind, but not less important than that which they performed at the beginning. The miracles of the O. T. may be included in the above argument, if we regard, as Scripture requires us to regard, the earlier dispensation as an anticipation of and preparation for the coming of Christ. Many of the events in the history of Israel as a people are typical of corresponding events in the life of the Saviour; and the earlier miraculous history is a supernatural system preparing the way for the later consummation of God's supernatural providence in the redemption of the world by Christ. Not only the occasional miracles of the O.-T. history, but, as bishop Atterbury remarks, some of the established institutions under the law—the gift of prophecy, the Shechinah, the Urim and Thummim, the sabbatical year—are of a supernatural character, and thus manifest themselves as parts of a supernatural system, ordained for and leading to the completion of the supernatural in Christ."

A question has also been raised whether it is not possible that miracles may be wrought by evil spirits in support of a false doctrine. This question affects Christian evidences simply, and in this line the only question that can practically be raised is whether the Scripture miracles—supposing them not to be pure fabrications—are real miracles wrought by divine power, or normal events occurring in the course of nature, or produced by human means. Indeed, the possibility of real miracles other than divine is a question rather of curiosity than of practical value. An able discussion of this subject will be found in Farmer's *Dissertation*, though the author has weakened his argument by attempting too much. So far as he undertakes to show that there is no sufficient evidence that miracles actually have been wrought by evil spirits in behalf of a false religion, his reasoning is logical and satisfactory, and his treatment of the supposed miracles of the Egyptian magicians is in this respect highly successful. But when he proceeds from the historical to the theological argument, and maintains that it is inconsistent with God's perfections that such miracles ever should be wrought, he appears to assume more than is warranted either by reason or by Scripture, and to deduce a consequence which is not required by the former, and appears difficult to reconcile with the latter. That there may be such a thing as "the working of Satan, with all power and signs and lying wonders," and that such working will actually be manifested before the last day in support of Antichrist, is the natural interpretation of the language of Scripture. That such a manifestation has as yet taken place is, to say the least, a conclusion not established by existing evidence.

Another question has been raised as to the means of distinguishing between true and false miracles, meaning by the latter term phenomena pretended to be miraculous, but in fact either natural events or human impostures or fabrications. Various rules for distinguishing between these have been given by several authors, the best known being the four rules laid down in Leslie's *Short and Easy Method with the Deists*, and the three given in bishop Douglas's *Criterion*, and to some extent the six given by bishop Stillingfleet in *Origines Sacra*, bk. ii, chap. x, and the very acute observations in a similar kind of work, J. H. Newman's *Life of Apollonius Tyanæus*, published in the *Encyclopædia Metropolitana*. Yet the practical value of these rules, though considerable as compared with the inquiry previously noticed, is available rather for particular and temporary phases of controversy than for general and perpetual edification. A more permanent principle in relation to this question is suggested by Leslie in his remarks on the pretended miracles of Apollonius, where he shows that the assumed miracles, even if admitted, have no important connection with our belief or practice. "But now," he says, "to sum up all, let us suppose to the utmost that all this said romance were true, what would it amount to? Only that Apollonius did such things. What then? What if he were so virtuous a person that God should have given him the power to work several miracles? This would noways hurt the argument that is here brought against the deists, because Apollonius set up no new religion, nor did he pretend that he was sent with any revelation from heaven to introduce any new sort of worship of God; so that it is of no consequence to the world whether these were true or pretended miracles; whether Apollonius were an honest man or a magician; or whether there ever were such a man or not. For he left no law or gospel behind him to be received upon the credit of those miracles which he is said to have wrought." "To this," says dean Mansel, "it may be added that there is an enormous *a priori* improbability against miracles performed without any professed object, as compared with those which belong to a system that has exercised a good and permanent influence in the world. This improbability can only be overcome by a still more enormous mass of evidence in their favor; and until some actual case can be pointed out in which such evidence exists, the unimportance of a reported series of miracles is a valid reason for withholding belief in them. The Scripture miracles, in this respect, stand alone and apart from all others as regards the evidence of their reality, combined with their significance, if real."

Among the most important works on Scripture miracles, and not incidentally mentioned in the article on Christian Evidences, are: Fleetwood, *Essay upon Miracles* (1701); Locke, *Discourse of Miracles* (1701–2); Pearce, *The Miracles of Jesus Vindicated* [in reply to Woolston] (1729); Smallbrook, *Vindication of our Saviour's Miracles* [in reply to Woolston] (1729, 2 vols. 8vo); Lardner, *Vindication of Three of our blessed Saviour's Miracles* [in reply to Woolston] (1729); Sherlock, *The Trial of the Witnesses* (1729); Stevenson, *Conference upon the Miracles of our Saviour* (1730, 8vo); Sykes, *Credibility of Miracles*, etc. (1749, 8vo); Douglas, *The Criterion* (1754); Claparede, *Miracles of the Gospel* [in answer to Rousseau] (Lond. 1758, 8vo); Campbell, *Dissertation on Miracles* (1763); Farmer, *Dissertation on Miracles* (1771); Bishop Douglas, *Criterion of Miracles* (1774, 8vo); De Haen, *De Miraculis* (Francf. 1776, 8vo); Scherer, *Ausf. Erklärung der Weissagungen d. N. T.* (Lpz. 1803, 8vo); *The Hulsean Prize Essay* for 1814; Collyer, *Miracles* (1812); Penrose, *Evidence of the Scripture Miracles* (1826); Le Bas, *Considerations on Miracles* (1828); Newman, *Life of Apollonius Tyanæus*, in *Encycl. Metrop.* [written before his defection to Rome]; Tholuck, *Glaubenswürdigkeit d. evangel. Gesch.* (Hamb. 1837); Müller, *Disputatio de Miraculorum Jesu Christi Natura et Necessitate* (1839–1841); Nitzsch, in *Studien und Kritiken* of 1843; Wardlaw, *On Miracles* (1852; New York, 1853); Rothe, in *Studien und Kritiken* of 1858; Trench, *Miracles of our Lord* (6th ed. 1858); Koestlin, *De Miraculorum, quæ Christus et primi ejus discipuli fecerunt, natura et ratione* (1860); Evans, *Christian Miracles* (Lond. 1861); McCosh, *The Supernatural in Relation to the Natural* (1862); Mozley, *Lectures on Miracles* (Bampton for 1865; Lond. 1865, 8vo); Fisher, *Supernat. Origin of Christianity* (1865); Duke of Argyle, *Reign of Law* (1866); Litton, *Miracles* (Lond. 1867); Uhlhorn, *Modern Rep. of the Life of Jesus* (Bost. 1868); Fowler, *Mozby and Tyndale on Miracles* (Lond. 1868); Archbishop of York, *Limits of Philos. Inquiry* (Edinb. 1868); Mountford, *Miracles, Past and Present* (Boston, 1870, 12mo); Bender, *Wunderbegriff d. N. T.* (Frankfort a. M. 1873); Upham, *Star of our Lord* (N. Y. 1873, 8vo); Belcher, *Our Lord's Miracles of Healing Considered* (London, 1873); Fowle, *Religion and Science* (1873,

8vo); Christlieb, *Mod. Doubts* (1874), ch. v; Bushnell, *Nature and the Supernatural* (new ed. 1874); Cudworth, *Intellectual System* (see Index in vol. iii); Watson, *Theol. Instit.* i, 73 sq., 146 sq., 234; Hodge, *Systematic Theol.* vol. i, ch. xii; Hagenbach, *Hist. Doctr.* i, 314 sq., 414 sq.; ii, 467 sq.; Haag, *Histoire des Dogmes Chrétiens*, pt. i, ch. iv, et al.; J. Pye Smith, *First Lines of Christian Theol.* p. 62 sq., 582 sq., et al.; Pascal, *Pensées*, pt. ii, art. 19, § 9; Lyall, *Prop. Proph.* p. 441; Kitto, *Cyclop. Bibl. Lit.* s. v.; Smith, *Bibl. Dict.* s. v.; *Christian Magazine*, 1797; *Christian Instructor*, xvii, 145; *Christian Rev.* July, 1856; *Theol. Rev.* vol. iv; *For. Qu.* vol. xxii; *Bibl. Sacra*, vols. ii and vii; *North Brit. Rev.* Feb. 1846, art. viii; April, 1862, art. iv; *North Amer. Rev.* July, 1860; *Journ. of Sac. Lit.* April, Oct. 1854; Jan. 1856; *South. Presb. Rev.* 1856; *South. Qu. Rev.* July, 1857; *Princet. Rev.* April, 1856; *Amer. Theol. Rev.* July, 1861; *Christian Remembrancer*, July, 1861; (Lond.) *Qu. Rev.* Oct. 1862, p. 242; *Amer. Presb. Rev.* April, 1863, art. i; Jan. 1865; *Brit. and For. Rev.* x, 11, 55; *Bulletin Théologique*, Sept. 1863, p. 137; *Theol. Eclectic*, vol. v, No. 3; *Westm. Rev.* Jan. 1818, p. 106; *Meth. Rev.* April, 1853, p. 181; 1870, p. 299; 1872 (Jan.), p. 154; *Brit. and For. Ev. Rev.* 1863 (Jan.), p. 29–55; *Blackwood's Magazine*, June, 1867; *Bibl. Sacra*, April, 1863, art. iii; 1867, p. 189; *Jahrb. deutscher Theol.* 1869, p. 572; *Contemp. Rev.* May, 1869, p. 89 sq.; Nov. 1872, art. v; *Christian Qu.* Oct. 1873, art. iii; *Brit. Qu. Rev.* July, 1873, art. vi; *Bapt. Qu. Rev.* 1870; Jan. 1874, art. i; *Qu. Rev. of Luth. Ch.* July, 1874, art. v.

MIRACLES, ECCLESIASTICAL. The Port Royalists taught that "there would never have been any false miracles if there had been none true." Many Protestants, taking hold of this wise adage, set down as incontrovertible the assertion that the so-called "miracles" wrought in the Church since the patristic period *are not of God*, because they are not prophesied as were those of the Israelitish and apostolic days (see Exod. iii, 12; Mark xvi, 17, 18), and that, as Dr. Hodge has it, "while there is nothing in the N. T. inconsistent with the occurrence of miracles in the post-apostolic age of the Church . . . when the apostles had finished their work, the necessity of miracles, so far as the great end they were intended to accomplish was concerned, ceased" (*Syst. Theol.* iii, 452).

This position of Protestant writers seems to gain strength from a close examination of the practices of the early patristic period, for it is an uncontested statement that during the first hundred years after the death of the apostles we hear little or nothing of the working of miracles by the early Christians. Says bishop Douglas, "If we except the testimonies of Papias and Irenæus, who speak of raising the dead . . . I can find no instances of miracles mentioned by the fathers before the 4th century" (*Criterion*, p. 228–232); and if we come down to the fathers of the 4th century, we find that they freely speak of the age of miracles as past; that such interpositions, being no longer necessary, were no longer to be expected. Whatever may appear to the contrary in the more oratorical and panegyrical writings of the fathers, whenever they address themselves theologically to the question of miracles, they admit clearly and unreservedly the truth that this kind of evidence has ceased in the Christian Church. The miracles of divine power (according to St. Augustine) are now to be sought in the works of nature, in the wonders of its ever-recurring changes, and in the regular course of the divine providence. After enumerating the miracles of Christ, he asks, "Cur (inquis) ista modo non fiunt? Quia non moverent nisi mira essent; at si solita essentia mira non essent" (*De Utilitate Credendi*), which he only so far qualifies in his retractions as not absolutely to deny the possibility of a modern miracle. In another place he speaks of "miracles not being permitted to last to our times," or to survive the propagation of Christianity over the world (*De vera Religione*, c. 25, § 47). St. Chrysostom bears the same testimony to the cessation of miracles in his beautiful sermons on the Resurrection and on the Feast of Pentecost (*Ser.* xxxiii and xxxvi), where he solves the same question—"Why are no signs and miracles intrusted to us now?"—by claiming those higher miracles of grace and inward change which enable us to use the prayer of faith, and to exclaim, "Our Father, which art in heaven!" Chrysostom says himself: "Ne itaque ex eo, quod nunc signa non fiunt, argumentum ducas tunc etiam non fuisse. Etenim tunc utiliter fiebant, et nunc utiliter non fiunt" (*In Epistolam i, ad Corinth.* Homil. vi, 2; comp. Augustine, *De Civitate Dei,* xxii, viii, 1). Yet these fathers also supply us with accounts of deeds wrought by Christian believers, which the Roman Catholic Church has pleased to stamp as miraculous, but which these early writers of the Church mark out clearly as *natural* results. If indeed they pleased to call them miracles, they yet betray that even in their own view there' was a vast difference between the scriptural and ecclesiastical miracles, and that they did not count them as of the same category. St. Augustine, referring to the wonderful deeds wrought by the faithful of the Church in his day, concedes also that they were not wrought with the same lustre as in the apostolic days, nor with the same significance and authority for the whole Christian world (comp. Fr. Nitzsch, jun., *Augustinus' Lehre vom Wunder* [Berlin, 1865], p. 32 sq.). Bishop Douglas says that these miraculous workings were confined to "the cures of diseases, particularly the cures of dæmoniacs, by exorcising them; which last indeed seems to be their favorite standing miracle;" and Prof. Newman, one of the richest prizes gained by the Romanists from the Church of England in this generation, is candid enough to admit the contrast between the scriptural and what he calls ecclesiastical miracles. He says, "The miracles of Scripture are, as a whole, grave, simple, and majestic: those of ecclesiastical history often partake of what may not unfitly be called a romantic character, and of that wildness and inequality which enters into the notion of romance." "It is obvious," he says elsewhere, "to apply what has been said to the case of the miracles of the Church, as compared with those in Scripture. Scripture is to us a garden of Eden, and its creations are beautiful as well as 'very good;' but when we pass from the apostolic to the following ages, it is as if we left the choicest valleys of the earth, the quietest and most harmonious scenery, and the most cultivated soil, for the luxuriant wilderness of Africa or Asia, the natural home or kingdom of brute nature uninfluenced by man" (*Two Essays on Scripture Miracles and on Ecclesiastical,* 2d ed. Lond. 1870, p. 116, 150). Dr. Hodge, in commenting upon Romish miracles, quotes these words of Prof. Newman, and says of them, "A more felicitous illustration can hardly be imagined. The contrast between the Gospels and the legends of the saints is that between the divine and the human, and even the animal; between Christ (with reverence be it spoken) and St. Anthony" (iii, 455).

The Roman Catholic Church, notwithstanding the want of any trustworthy patristic testimony, asserts that the power of performing all manner of miraculous works remains with the Church since the days of its first founding, henceforth and forever. "Roman Catholics," says Butler, "relying with entire confidence on the promises of Christ [quoting Acts ii, 3 sq.; John xiv, 12; Mark xvi, 17, 18], believe that the power of working miracles was given by Christ to his Church, and that it never has been, and never will be withdrawn from her" (*Book of the Rom. Cath. Ch.* Letter iii, p. 37 sq.; see also p. 46 sq.). Another, even greater celebrity, the learned Bellarmine, goes so far as to prove from this continuity of the miraculous power in the Church of Rome that the Protestant Church, lacking this, is manifestly not of God. He argues that miracles are necessary to evince any new faith or extraordinary mission; that miracles are efficacious and sufficient. By the for-

mer, he then tells us, may be deduced that the Church is not to be found among Protestants; by the latter, that it is most assuredly among Catholics: "Undecima nota est gloria miraculorum; sunt autem duo fundamenta præmittenda. Unum quod miracula sint necessaria ad novam fidem vel extraordinariam missionem persuadendam. Alterum, quod sint efficacia et sufficientia; nam ex priore deducemus non esse apud adversarios veram ecclesiam, ex posteriore deducemus eam esse apud nos. Quod igitur miracula sint necessaria, probatur primo Scripturæ testimonio, Exod. iv, cum Moses mitteretur a Deo ad populum, ac diceret: 'Non credent mihi, neque audient vocem meam.' Non respondet Deus, 'Debent credere, velint nolint,' sed dedit illi potestatem faciendi miracula, et ait: 'Ut credant, quod apparuerit tibi Dominus,' etc. Et in Novo Testamento, Matt. x, 'Euntes, prædicate, dicentes: Appropinquovit regnum cœlorum; infirmos curate, mortuos suscitate, leprosos mundate, dæmones ejicite.' Joan. xv, 'Si opera non fecissem in eis quæ nemo alius fecit, peccatum non haberent'" (*Opera,* vol. ii; *De Notis Ecclesiæ,* lib. iv, cap. xiv, col. 206 D [Col. 1619]). Even the liberal-minded Dr. Milner, who displayed learning in almost every department of science; who possessed experience, intelligence, and taste; who wrote well and reasoned acutely; teaches, in a letter devoted to the subject of miracles, that "if the Roman Catholic Church were not the only true Church, God would not have given any attestation in its favor. . . . Having demonstrated the distinction," by which he means the exclusive holiness of the Roman Catholic Church, he professes himself "prepared to show that God has borne testimony to that holiness by the many and incontestable (?) miracles he has wrought in her favor, *from the age of the apostles down to the present time*" (Lett. xxvi, p. 163 sq., et al.).

The reasoning of Dr. Milner brings us to reconsider the statement made in the early part of this article that "no miraculous events mark the history of the Church after the days of the apostles, if we may depend on the authority of the patristic writers." Romanists frequently refer us to what St. Ignatius, who flourished in the 1st century after Christ, relates about the wild beasts which were let loose upon the martyrs being frequently restrained by a divine power from hurting them, and also to the miracle which deterred the apostate Julian (this, however, brings us to the 4th century) from rebuilding the Temple of Jerusalem. As to the first of these miraculous workings, a single observation must suffice. The words of Ignatius are: "Ne sicut in aliis, territæ sint et non eos tetigerunt;" implying that the fierce animals did not behave as in ordinary cases, but that, being terrified at the sight of the surrounding spectators, they refused to fight. Ignatius himself considered the occurrence purely accidental and natural; otherwise he would have given the glory to God, and have besought him to repress their fury. As to the second miracle, it must of necessity have occurred, or the prophecy which related to it could not be fulfilled (Dan. ix, 27). Says Elliott: "In its exact completion I perfectly agree with Dr. Milner, and for the very reason assigned by Gibbon himself, that if it were not verified, 'the imperial sophist would have converted the success of his undertaking into a specious' (he should have said solid) 'argument against the faith of prophecy and the truth of revelation' (*Decline and Fall,* iv, 104). But I am not equally disposed to admit that there were other as extraordinary miracles, besides the one mentioned, since the apostolic age; or, if there were, that they were performed for the purpose alleged by him" (*Delin. of Romanism,* p. 527). Dr. Neander, bishop Kaye, Dr. Schaff, and others, hold to the *gradual cessation theory.* That is to say, they teach that "there is an antecedent probability that the power of working miracles was not suddenly and abruptly, but gradually withdrawn, as the necessity of such outward and extraordinary attestation of the divine origin of Christianity diminished and gave way to the natural operation of truth and moral suasion." They also hold that "it is impossible to fix the precise termination, either at the death of the apostles, or their immediate disciples, or the conversion of the Roman empire, or the extinction of the Arian heresy, or any subsequent æra, and to sift carefully in each particular case the truth from legendary fiction." "Most of the statements of the apologists," says Dr. Schaff, "are couched in general terms, and refer to extraordinary cures from dæmoniacal possession (which probably includes, in the language of that age, cases of madness, deep melancholy, and epilepsy) and other diseases, by the invocation of the name of Jesus. Justin Martyr speaks of such cures as a frequent occurrence in Rome and all over the world, and Origen appeals to his own personal observation, but speaks in another place of the growing scarcity of miracles, so as to suggest the gradual cessation theory. Tertullian attributes many, if not most, of the conversions of his day to supernatural dreams and visions, as does also Origen, although with more caution. But in such psychological phenomena it is exceedingly difficult to draw the line of demarcation between natural and supernatural causes, and between providential interpositions and miracles proper. The strongest passage on this subject is found in Irenæus (Adv. hær. ii, 31, § 2, and ii, 32, § 4), who, in contending against the heretics, mentions, besides prophecies and miraculous cures of dæmoniacs, even the raising of the dead among contemporary events taking place in the Catholic Church; but he specifies no particular case or name; and it should be mentioned also that his youth still bordered almost on the Johannean age" (Ch. History, i, 206, 207). In another place, referring to the testimony of Ambrose and Augustine for belief in a continuation of miracles, Dr. Schaff, while himself advocating the gradual cessation theory, and also the possibility of miraculous power dwelling in the Church of to-day, teaches, nevertheless, that even the best of patristic testimonies may be impeached if they appear on the witness stand in behalf of miraculous deeds wrought in the Church in post-apostolic days: "We should not be bribed or blinded by the character and authority of such witnesses, since experience sufficiently proves that even the best and most enlightened men cannot wholly divest themselves of superstition and of the prejudices of their age. Recall, e. g., Luther and the apparitions of the devil, the Magnalia of Cotton Mather, the old Puritans and their trials for witchcraft, as well as the modern superstitions of spiritual rappings and table-turnings, by which many eminent and intelligent persons have been carried away" (iii, 461).

But, differ as we may regarding the cessation or non-cessation of miraculous power in the Church of Christ, there is, nevertheless, one point on which Protestants unite in opposing the pretensions of Rome; some betraying an undue dogmatic bias, but all agreeing that it is remarkable that the genuine writings of the ante-Nicene Church are more free from miraculous and superstitious elements than the annals of the Middle Ages, and especially of monasticism. Indeed, it would appear that the Nicene age is the first marked as one of miracles, and that miracles rapidly increased in number from henceforth until they became matters of every-day occurrence. Dr. Isaac Taylor adds: "No such miracles as those of the 4th century were pretended in the preceding æra, when they might seem to be more needed. If, then, these miracles were genuine, they must be regarded as opening a new dispensation" (Anc. Christianity, ii, 357). This new dispensation, no doubt, they heralded, for it is manifest that the miracles of the Nicene age and post-Nicene age "were always intended to propagate the belief of certain rites and doctrines and practices which had crept into the Church; to advance the reputation of some particular chapel or image or religious order, or to countenance opinions, either such as were contested among themselves, or such as the whole Church did not teach" (Bishop Douglas, Criterion, p. 40).

Says Dr. Taylor: "Whereas the alleged supernatural occurrences related, or appealed to by the earlier Christian writers, are nearly all of an ambiguous kind, and such as may, with little difficulty, be understood without either the assumption of miraculous interposition, or the imputation of deliberate fraud, it is altogether otherwise with the miracles of the Church of the 4th, 5th, and 6th centuries. From the period of the Nicene Council and onward miracles of the most astounding kind were alleged to be wrought from day to day, and openly, and in all quarters of the Christian world. These wonders were solemnly appealed to and seriously narrated by the leading persons of the Church, Eastern and Western; and in many instances these very persons—the great men now set up in opposition to the leaders of the Reformation—were themselves the wonder-workers, and have themselves transmitted the accounts of them. But then these alleged miracles were, almost in every instance, wrought expressly in support of those very practices and opinions which stand forward as the points of contrast distinguishing Romanism from Protestantism. We refer especially to the ascetic life—the supernatural properties of the eucharistic elements—the invocation of the saints, or direct praying to them, and the efficacy of their relics; and the reverence or worship due to certain visible and palpable religious symbols" (ii, 235).

Dr. Hodge, commenting upon these Romish miracles, says, "they admit of being classified on different principles. As to their nature, some are grave and important; others are trifling, childish, and even babyish; others are indecorous; and others are irreverent, and even blasphemous. . . . Another principle on which they may be classified is the design for which they were wrought or adduced. Some are brought forth as proofs of the sanctity of particular persons or places or things; some to sustain particular doctrines, such as purgatory, transubstantiation, the worshipping of the saints and of the Virgin Mary, etc., some for the identification of relics. It is no injustice to the authorities of the Church of Rome to say that whatever good ends these miracles may in any case be intended to serve, they have in the aggregate been made subservient to the accumulation of money and to the increase of power. . . . The truth of Christianity depends on the historical truth of the account of the miracles recorded in the N. T. The truth of Romanism depends on the truth of the miracles to which it appeals. What would become of Protestantism if it depended on the dæmonology of Luther, or the witch-stories of our English forefathers? The Romish Church, in assuming the responsibility for the ecclesiastical miracles, has taken upon itself a burden which would crush the shoulders of Atlas" (iii, 456; comp. Princet. Rev. April, 1856, art. v, especially p. 272). And Dr. Schaff, who, as we have already seen, inclines to the belief that miracles may have been wrought in post-apostolic days, and may continue to be wrought to-day and hereafter, yet ventures to say that "the following weighty considerations rise against the miracles of the Nicene and post-Nicene age; not warranting, indeed, the rejection of all, yet making us at least very cautious and doubtful of receiving them in particular: 1. These miracles have a much lower moral tone than those of the Bible, while in some cases they far exceed them in outward pomp, and make a stronger appeal to our faculty of belief. Many of the monkish miracles are not so much supernatural and above reason as they are unnatural and against reason, attributing even to wild beasts of the desert, panthers and hyenas, with which the misanthropic hermits lived on confidential terms, moral feelings and states, repentance and conversion, of which no trace appears in the N. T. 2. They serve not to confirm the Christian faith in general, but for the most part to support the ascetic life, the magical virtue of the sacrament, the veneration of saints and relics, and other superstitious practices, which are evidently of later origin, and are more or less offensive to the healthy evangelical mind. 3. The further they are removed from the apostolic age, the more numerous they are, and in the 4th century alone there are more miracles than in all the three preceding centuries together, while the reason for them, as against the power of the heathen world, was less. 4. The Church fathers, with all the worthiness of their character in other respects, confessedly lacked a highly-cultivated sense of truth, and allowed a certain justification of falsehood *ad majorem Dei gloriam*, or *fraus pia*, under the misnomer of policy or accommodation (so especially Jerome, *Epist. ad Pammachium*); with the single exception of Augustine, who, in advance of his age, rightly condemned falsehood in every form. 5. Several Church fathers, like Augustine, Martin of Tours, and Gregory I, themselves concede that in their time extensive frauds with the relics of saints were already practiced; and this is confirmed by the fact that there were not rarely numerous copies of the same relict, all of which claimed to be genuine. 6. The Nicene miracles met with doubt and contradiction even among contemporaries, and Sulpitius Severus makes the important admission that the miracles of St. Martin were better known and more firmly believed in foreign countries than in his own (*Dialog.* i, 18). 7. Church fathers, like Chrysostom and Augustine, contradict themselves in a measure in sometimes paying homage to the prevailing faith in miracles, especially in their discourses on the festivals of the martyrs, and in soberer moments, and in the calm exposition of the Scriptures, maintaining that miracles, at least in the Biblical sense, had long since ceased (comp. Robertson, *Hist. of the Christian Church to Gregory the Great* [Lond. 1854], p. 334). We must, moreover, remember that the rejection of the Nicene miracles by no means justifies the inference of intentional deception in every case, nor destroys the claim of the great Church teachers to our respect. On the contrary, between the proper miracle and fraud there lie many intermediate steps of self-deception, clairvoyance, magnetic phenomena and cures, and unusual states of the human soul, which is full of deep mysteries, and stands nearer the invisible spirit-world than the every-day mind of the multitude suspects. Constantine's vision of the cross, for example, may be traced to a prophetic dream; and the frustration of the building of the Jewish Temple under Julian, to a special providence, or a historical judgment of God. The mytho-poetic faculty, too, which freely and unconsciously produces miracles among children, may have been at work among credulous monks in the dreary deserts, and magnified an ordinary event into a miracle. In judging of this obscure portion of the history of the Church we must, in general, guard ourselves as well against shallow naturalism and scepticism as against superstitious mysticism, remembering that

'There are more things in heaven and earth
Than are dreamt of in our philosophy'"

(*Ch. Hist.* iii, 463–465).

If we institute a direct and careful comparison between the Biblical and the ecclesiastical miracles, we find, besides matter of fact, as to the certainty of the thing and the reasons of credibility, there is a great difference in the force and efficacy of the former and a confirmation of that for which it is produced, while it is not so in the case of the latter. "Those Biblical miracles," says Butler, "were generally very beneficial to human nature, doing mighty offices of kindness towards those who were the subjects of them, such as healing the sick, raising the dead, restoring the deaf, the lame, and the blind, etc.; all which bore an excellent proportion to the great design of redeeming and saving mankind. And if at any time there were any mixture of severity in the very act, such as striking some dead by a word spoken, or putting others in the immediate possession of the devil by excommunication; yet was even this done either in kindness to posterity, by fixing, in the first institution of

things, one or two standing pillars of salt, that might be for example and admonition to after-ages, against some practices that might otherwise in time destroy Christianity; as, in the first instance, of Ananias and Sapphira, against the sin of hypocrisy; or else to some good purposes for the persons themselves, as in the last instance of excommunication; so in the case of the incestuous person, it was adjudged by Paul, 'to deliver such a one unto Satan for the destruction of the flesh, that the spirit may be saved in the day of the Lord Jesus' (1 Cor. v, 5). None of these miracles were such useless, ludicrous actions as the Romish authors have filled their histories with; such as that of St. Berinus, who, 'being under full sail for France, and half his voyage over, finding he had forgot something, walks out upon the sea, and returns back dryshod;' such as St. Mochua, by his prayer and staff hindering the poor lambs from sucking their dams, when they were running towards them with full appetites; such, again, as St. Francis bespeaking the ass in the kind compellation of brother, 'to stand quiet till he had done preaching, and not disturb the solemnity;' and such as St. Fiutanus keeping the calf from the cow, that they should neither of them move towards one another; such, in a word, as St. Frimianus and St. Ruadanus, sporting their miracles with each other, as if they had the power given them for no other end but mere trial of skill, or some pretty diversion of bystanders" (*Notes*, p. 252–258). The *Breviary* (q. v.) teems with descriptions of all manner of miraculous manifestations, but we have not room to enumerate others here, and must refer the reader to it and to Elliott (*Delineation of Romanism*, p. 527–543). On the most important so-called miracles claimed by the Church of Rome in modern days, see the articles ST. FRANCIS; HOLY COAT OF TRÈVES; ST. JANUARIUS; LOURDES; XAVIER, etc. See also SUPERSTITION; VISIONS.

It appears, moreover, from the writings of many distinguished Roman Catholic authors that the post-Nicene miracles are not generally accepted. Thus Peter, abbot of Cluny, as far back as the 13th century, says: "You know how much those Church sonnets grieve me" (lib. v, *Epist.* xxix). He mentions one of Benedict which he declares contained no less than twenty-four lies. Ludovicus Vives, speaking of the *Legenda Aurea*, observes: "How unworthy both of God and man is the story of their saints, which, I do not know why, was called the Golden Legend, it having been written by one who had an iron mouth and a leaden heart" (lib. ii, *De Currupt. Artib.*, in fine). And Espencius declares: "No stable is fuller of dung than their legends are of fables" (*in* 2 *Tim. iv, Digress.* 21). These authorities might be multiplied to a great extent. We must content ourselves with a few of the leading minds since the reformatory ideas took root in the Church of Rome. First among these we must place the learned French chancellor Gerson, of Paris University, who, when, in the Council of Constance, the canonization of St. Bridget (q. v.) was proposed, thus spoke out: "It cannot be said how much this curiosity for knowing future and hidden things, and for seeing miracles and performing them, hath deluded most persons, and constantly turned them away from true religion. Hence all those superstitions among the people which destroy the Christian religion, while, like the Jews, they only seek a sign, exhibiting to images the worship due to God, and attaching their faith to men yet uncanonized, and to apocryphal writings, more than to the Scriptures themselves."

In the 15th century the appearance of a rival to the Franciscan visionary in the person of St. Catharine of Sienna as the champion of the more powerful Dominicans, provoked the following utterance from cardinal Cajetan, utterly nullifying the former declarations of the Church in her favor: "It is alleged," he writes, "that St. Bridget had a revelation that the Blessed Virgin was preserved from original sin. But the probability of this opinion is very slender, for it is opposed to very many saints, and none of those alleged were themselves canonized. To St. Bridget, moreover, we may oppose St. Catharine of Sienna, who said that the contrary doctrine had been revealed to her, as the archbishop of Florence relates in the first part of his *Summa*. And St. Catharine would seem to deserve greater credit, because she was canonized like the other saints, while St. Bridget was canonized in the period of the schism, during the obedience of Boniface IX, in which there was no certain and undoubted pope." Further on he adds the fatal words: "New revelations against so many saints and ancient doctors must seem to the wise to bring in an angel of Satan transformed into an angel of light, to bring in fancies, and even figments. These, truly, with the so-called miracles which are cited in this cause, are rather for old women than for the holy synod, whence I do not deem them worthy of mention." "There is need of great caution," writes this great divine, "first on account of the miracle itself, inasmuch as Satan transforms himself into an angel of light, and can work many signs and wonders, such as we might deem that none but God could work—as works of healing, power over the elements, and the like. Hence it is said that Antichrist will perform so many miracles in the sight of men that, if it were possible, he would deceive the very elect themselves. Secondly, there is need of caution on the ground of illusions, as happens in the case of prophesyings. Thirdly, it may be urged that signs (according to 1 Cor. xiv, and St. Gregory, *Hom.* x) are given to the unbelieving, and not to believers; while to the Church as faithful, and not unfaithful, are given the prophetical and apostolical revelations. Hence the way of signs . . . unless not merely a wonder, but a true and indisputable miracle, is wrought before the Roman Church in the most evident manner, ought not to determine any doubtful doctrine; and the reason is, because we have from God an ordinary way for the determination of matters of faith; insomuch that if an angel from heaven were to say anything contrary to this ordinary way he ought not to be believed (Gal. i, 8). Add to this that the miracles received by the Church in the canonization of saints, which are most authentic of all, are not, inasmuch as they rest on human testimony, absolutely certain (for it is written, 'Every man is a liar'); although they may be certain after a human manner. But the certainty of the Christian faith ought not to be certain after a human manner, but ought to have altogether an infallible evidence such as no human being, but only God, can produce. Hence the apostle Peter, after giving his own testimony to the heavenly voice heard by him in the transfiguration of our Lord, as a human evidence, subjoins: 'And we have a more sure word of prophecy,' adding that 'Prophecy came not by the will of man.' Wherefore certainty in the judicial determination of the things of faith must be obtained by divine and not by human testimony" (*De Conceptione B. V. M.* cap. i).

We can even go to the chair of St. Peter and learn from some of its incumbents a like disposition to ignore, or even to reject the miraculous manifestations in the Church. Thus pope Gregory XI, having been persuaded by the prophecies of St. Catharine of Sienna to return to Rome from Avignon, "when on his death-bed, and having in his hands the sacred body of Christ, protested before all that they ought to beware of human beings, whether male or female, speaking under pretence of religion the visions of their own brain. For by these (he said) he was led away; and, setting aside the reasonable advice of his own people, had drawn himself and the Church to the verge of an imminent schism, unless her merciful Spouse, Jesus, should save her," which the dreadful result too clearly proved (Gerson, *De Exam. Doctrinarum,* pt. ii, consid. iii). Nor need pope Benedict XIV be forgotten. His utterances are clearly laid down in his great work on the *Canonization of the Saints* (lib. iv, ch. xxxi, § 21–25).

If from these celebrated Romish authorities we come down to our own day, we find bishop Milner, who is himself an advocate of the doctrine, yet admitting "that a vast number of incredible and false miracles, as well as other fables, have been forged by some and believed by other Catholics in every age of the Church, including that of the apostles. I agree . . . in rejecting the *Legenda Aurea* of Jacobus de Voragine, the *Speculum* of Vincentius Belluacensis, the *Saints' Lives* of the patrician Metaphrastes, and scores of similar legends, stuffed as they are with relations of miracles of every description" (*End of Controversy,* Lett. xxvii, p. 175, 176).

It is, however, by no means to be inferred from what we have said that these miraculous exhibitions are confined to the Church of Rome. The Protestants have now and then prophets and visionaries who claim supernatural power. But while the Protestant Church has always discarded the authors, or at least, under the most favorable circumstances, has refused to accord to such exhibitions any divine origin, the Church of Rome clearly teaches that these things are so to be. Hence, occasionally, sects departing from the Church of Rome have tried to establish their authority by miraculous signs and works. Thus some of the persecuted *Jansenists* availed themselves of the utility of modern miracles for the purpose of propagating a new doctrine or deciding a controverted one, and had recourse to the same weapons of defence against their implacable adversaries. François de Paris, the son of an advocate of the Parliament of Paris, became in this sense the apostle of the Jansenist doctrine, and the prophet against the famous bull Unigenitus. His holiness and mortification of life, and the reaction of public opinion after the cruel persecutions of the Jesuits, greatly favored the success of his claim to work miracles, which, according to his biographers, was proved both in his life and at his tomb after death, in a degree that few canonized saints have attained to. The learned reviewer of his life, in the *Acta Eruditorum* of Leipsic, merely concludes from his history that the city of Paris was filled at the time with the followers of Jansenius, and that they were compelled to appeal thus to the popular superstition in order to lessen the persecutions of the Jesuits, and in a manner to attack them with their own weapons. These miracles chiefly involved powers of healing and restoration of outward faculties, and bore (if true) a much closer resemblance to the healing gifts which inaugurated Christianity than to the senseless and aimless wonders of mediæval miracle-working. But the contagion which was thus spread over the Church, and throughout almost every age, was by no means confined to the Roman Church, its orders or disorders.

Though the churches of the Reformation, in their bold appeal "to the law and to the testimony," had treated the visions and miracles upon which the inner power of Rome had been built with as little ceremony as they treated the forged decretals on which her external power had been carried up in the darkness of the Middle Ages, it was not long before the old love of the marvellous, and the inextinguishable longing after the forbidden fruit of visions and revelations which had been so abundantly enjoyed but a little before, extended into the churches of the Reformation. But the occasion of their appearance was different altogether from that which had evoked it in the Roman Church, though by a singular coincidence the scene of the Protestant and of the Romish revelations was the same. The province of Dauphiny, which gave a birthplace to the peasant visionaries of La Salette, was also, in an earlier day, the native country of Isabel Vincent, whose miraculous preachings in her sleep and ecstatic visions enlisted the faith of the good and learned M. Jurieu, and produced from him an energetic and not ineloquent appeal in behalf of modern miracles. The very title of his treatise in its English dress is almost as sensational as a novel of Miss Braddon: *The Reflections of the reverend and learned M. Jurieu upon the strange and miraculous Ecstasies of Isabel Vincent, the Shepherdess, of*

Saon, in Dauphiné, who ever since February last hath sung Psalms, prayed, preached, and prophesied about the present Times in her Trances; as also upon the wonderful and portentous Trumpetings and singing of Psalms that were heard by thousands in the air in many Parts of France in the Year 1686. Not nursed into life in the bosom of Rome, and nourished as the visions of Lourdes and La Salette by a priesthood too deeply interested in the success of the imposition, the Protestant wonders sprang into a vigorous and sturdy existence out of the terrible hot-bed of cruelty and persecution which the revocation of the Edict of Nantes had produced in every province of France, and which, in the more imaginative region of the south, bore strange and exotic fruits. The visions of the poor shepherdess and her preachings were little more, in fact, than the broken and wild recollections of the Protestant services then so cruelly prohibited—prophecies of future trials or deliverances being intermingled with her sermons in the same manner as they had doubtless been by the exiled and often martyred pastors of that period of bitter persecution, whose judgment, "though of a long time," was read in the dreadful anarchy of the first Revolution, and seems hardly fully ended in our own day.

The crushing out of a rational faith was followed by the rise of the school of Voltaire and Diderot, and it well might shame the advocates of the Church of Rome in every age to find that the proscribed infidel was the first to bring to justice, or, rather, to public reprobation, the judges who, at the instigation of the Jesuits, so horribly tortured and murdered the poor silk-mercer of Toulouse, Calas, whose only crime, like that of the victims of Thorn in a somewhat earlier day, was his firm and consistent Protestantism. The wonderful sounds in the air—which were testified by so many thousands, and described in a public letter by M. de Besse, a pastor who had contrived to escape from his prison to Lausanne—might perhaps be referred, without charge of scepticism, to the effects of this dreadful persecution upon the minds and the nerves of its wretched and homeless victims, of whom it might well be said, in the words of Paul, "They were slain with the sword; they wandered about in sheep-skins and goat-skins; being destitute, afflicted, tormented, they wandered in deserts, and in mountains, and in dens, and in caves of the earth." Indeed, some even imagined, as M. de Besse tells us, that the wonderful sounds which were heard by so many were but the singing of the poor exiles met together in woods or in caves; but the variety of places in which he himself heard these mysterious harmonies soon convinced him that so simple a solution of them was erroneous. In vain the ear-witnesses of these phenomena were taken to prison for declaring them, and forbidden to say anything about them again. The witnesses multiplied more and more. Sometimes the sounds were like those of a trumpet, and had a warlike character; at other times they are described as combining the most ravishing strains of harmony; sometimes they were heard by day, sometimes, again, at night, "but in the night in a more clear and distinct manner than in the day" (Jurieu, *Reflections*, p. 36). "The trumpet always sounds as if an army were going to charge, and the harmony is like the composition of many voices, and of an infinite number of musical instruments." "I do believe," adds the good pastor, who found it more easy to interpret the sign than to account for it, "that the trumpet is a sign of a cruel war that will be made in a little time, and that the harmony comes from the mouth of angels, who, to put our enemies to the last confusion, thunder out the praises of God at a time when these wretched men forbid it to reformed Christians." The outbreak of the French Revolution, and the overthrow of the Church just a century after, would seem to verify, though at a later date, the interpretation of the poor exile, whose fellow-witness was a "Sieur Calas," probably one of the family of the martyr of a later day; while the testimony to the authenticity of his letter is given by an exiled minister, bearing the equally suggestive name of Murat.

Passing over to Germany, we find that the contagion of new revelations and prophecies had spread itself in the eastern part of the empire at an earlier period in the 17th century. Temporarily with the mystical and hieroglyphical system of Jacob Böhme, there sprang up in Silesia and Saxony the cognate revelations of Kotter, Drabitz, and Christina Poniatovia, all having a political rather than strictly religious character, and foretelling the final triumph of Protestantism in the empire, and the regeneration of Christianity, by the overthrow of the Roman power. Kotter, fortunately for his head, escaped into Lusatia, where some noblemen of influence became his adherents. Drabitz, not so fortunate, lost his head at Presburg, by order of the emperor, to whom his visions had a somewhat treasonable aspect; while Poniatovia, more fortunate than either, closed her revelations by marrying the tutor of the son of the king of Bohemia, and the threefold revelations, though introduced with much pomp and circumstance, and with a vast number of curious illustrations of the dreams and visions in which they were disclosed, by the famous Amos Comenius, fell still-born on the world, and have now a place on the shelves of the curious, on the ground of their rarity and of the grotesque ingenuity of their pictorial representations. (Two editions of these revelations, both in 4to, appeared under the editorship of Comenius. The former is called *Lux in Tenebris*, the latter *Lux è Tenebris.* A copy of one of these was burned with Drabitz after he was beheaded at Presburg. Both editions are very rare.) In Western Germany they were almost unknown, and it is memorable that almost all the prophets and mystics of Central Europe belonged to that mixed Teutonic and Sclavonic race which peoples the eastern frontier lands of the empire. But, though Germany contributed so little to the visionary lore of Europe at this period in a direct manner, it had produced a system of mystical divinity which laid the foundations of many future visions and ecstasies. The wild theology or theosophy, or whatever else it might be called, of Jacob Böhme, was a fruitful soil for the growth of new revelations and prophecies, and might well prepare the mind it obscured for the most startling apparitions of the beings of another world. The writings of this celebrated enthusiast, forbidden and suppressed in his own country, found vent in Holland and England. The mysticism of Jane Leade (q. v.) and her followers, the *Philadelphians* (q. v), the Quietism of Molina (q. v.), are subjects for consideration in the article MYSTICISM. But it may not be amiss, in this place, to call attention to the singular contrast between the Roman Catholic miracles, visions, and revelations, and those of the Protestant world. While the former are always invoked in order to found some new and undiscovered system of worship or object of superstition, the latter have a very practical end, and stand in close connection with holiness of life, which modern Roman revelations tend so little to promote. Even Jane Leade's revelations had a really Christian moral, which cannot in any sense be affirmed of the wonders of Lourdes or La Salette, and of the miracles with which, as Dr. Newman affirmed, the Roman Church is hung about on every side. "The Anglo-Saxon nature," says a writer in the *British Quarterly Review* (July, 1873, p. 97), "does not often indulge in visions, but when it does they seem to partake of that practical character which belongs to the race. No doubt some good may have arisen even from Mrs. Leade and her *Philadelphian Society* in its various branches in that age of spiritual deadness in which her lot was cast. Possibly even now we may be deriving some advantage from the example and the labors of this aged enthusiast, even as the decayed vegetation of an earlier year may have contributed to the fruitfulness of our own. The Philadelphian Society seems but a short time to have survived its foundress, though the ramifications of it were so extended, and its temporary success so remarkable. But *notwithstanding the success of visionaries and pretenders to miraculous powers, both in mediæval and modern times, it cannot be denied that the current of feeling in the general body of the Church has run strongly and steadily against their pretensions*, and that even those which had been attributed to a divine influence in the beginning, have often been referred to a diabolical inspiration in the end. Nor was this the only peril to which miracle-mongers and visionaries were exposed. So long as they fell in with the ruling power, and flattered the prejudices or the tastes of the day, all was well with them. St. Bridget, whose bitter denunciations against the crimes of the court of Rome made her the popular saint of those who looked for their reformation during the great schism, or who began that difficult work at Constance, would have been handed over to Satan in the day when the 'Curia' was again restored in all its old deformity, and only pledged to a reform which it never attempted to carry out. Nicholas Bulwersdorf, whose revelations against Rome were uttered, unhappily for himself, in the Council of Basle, and were mixed up with the old heresy of the Millenarians, expiated for them at the stake; while the poor monk whose revelations and prophecies are mentioned by the Dominican, Nyder, was found to have derived his inspiration, or, rather, his diabolic possession, from having swallowed the devil through greedily devouring a most tempting cauliflower in the garden of the monastery without saying grace—'avide comedit, ac dæmonem ignoranter deglutivit.' Another monk, who had a revelation which led him to found a new order, of which he assumed the government, incurred bodily as well as spiritual destruction—'incineratus est rector cum regula.' The presumption of diabolic influence was, however, not less decisive in Protestant England than in Rome itself, and the grotesque history of the *Surey Demoniack, or Satan's strange and dreadful Actions in and about the Person of Richard Dugdale*, in 1697, exhibits the popular superstition in the fullest degree. This poor creature, who seems to have been an epileptic patient, fortunately escaped the Roman ordeal, for we read that he was 'dispossessed by God's blessing on the fastings and prayers of divers ministers and people.' It had been well if the spiritual authorities of Lourdes and La Salette, instead of 'believing every spirit,' had 'dispossessed' the poor visionary peasants of their fond conceit, instead of instituting pilgrimages for the canonization of so foolish a story." Well might they have fallen back from the visions and miracles of a darker age upon that great and last revelation of God to man, those Scriptures of eternal truth, that "pure and living precept of God's Word, which, without more additions, nay, with the forbidding of them, hath within itself the promise of eternal life, the end of all our wearisome labors and all our sustaining hopes" (Milton, *On Prelatical Episcopacy*). The question of ecclesiastical miracles was slightly touched by Spencer in his notes on *Origen against Celsus*, and more fully by Le Moine; but did not attract general attention till Middleton published his famous *Free Inquiry* (1748). Several replies were written by Dodwell (junior), Chapman, Church, etc., which do not seem to have attracted much permanent attention. Some good remarks on the general subject occur in Jortin's *Remarks on Ecclesiastical History*, and in Warburton's *Julian*. This controversy has also of late years been reopened by Dr. Newman, in an essay on *miracles*, originally prefixed to a translation of Fleury's *Ecclesiastical History*, and since republished in a separate form.

See, besides, Elliott; Cramp, *Text-book of Popery;* Hodge, *Divinity;* Forsyth, *Italy*, ii, 154 sq.; *Rome in the 19th Century*, i, 40, 86; ii, 356; iii, 193 sq.; Lady Morgan, *Italy*, ii, 306; iii, 189; Graham, *Three Months' Residence*, etc., p. 241; Middleton, *Letter from Rome;* Southey, *Vindiciæ Ecclesiæ Anglicanæ*, p. 125 sq.; Blanco White, *Poor's Man's Preservation against*

Popery, p. 90; Brownlee, *Letters in the Roman Catholic Controversy;* Brand, *Popul. Antiq.;* Hone, *Anc. Mysteries.*

Miraculous Conception, a term used to denote the supernatural formation of the human nature of Jesus Christ, i. e. that it was brought forth not in the ordinary method of generation, but out of the substance of the Virgin Mary, by the immediate operation of the Holy Ghost. The evidence upon which this article of the Christian faith rests is found in Matt. i, 18–23, and in the more particular narration which Luke has given in the first chapter of his Gospel. If we admit this evidence of the fact, we can discern the emphatic meaning of the appellation given to our Saviour when he is called "the seed of the woman" (Gen. iii, 15); we can perceive the meaning of a phrase which Luke has introduced into the genealogy of Jesus (Luke iii, 23), "being (as was supposed) the son of Joseph," and of which, otherwise, it is not possible to give a good account; and we can discover a peculiar significance in an expression of the apostle Paul (Gal. iv, 4), "God sent forth his Son, made of a woman." The conception of Jesus is the point from which we date the union between his divine and human nature; and, this conception being miraculous, the existence of the Person in whom they are united was not physically derived from Adam. But, as Dr. Horsley says in his sermon on the Incarnation, the union with the uncreated Word is the very principle of personality and individual existence in the Son of Mary. According to this view of the matter, the miraculous conception gives a completeness and consistency to the revelation concerning Jesus Christ. Not only is he the Son of God, but, as the Son of man, he is exalted above his brethren, while he is made like them. He is preserved from the contamination adhering to the race whose nature he assumed; and when the only-begotten Son, who is in the bosom of the Father, was made flesh, the intercourse which, as man, he had with God, is distinguished, not in degree only, but in kind, from that which any prophet ever enjoyed; and it is infinitely more intimate, because it did not consist in communications occasionally made to him, but arose from the manner in which his human nature had its existence. See INCARNATION; JESUS CHRIST.

Miradoro, LUIGI, a noted Italian painter of the school of Cremona, was born at Genoa about the commencement of the 17th century. He is commonly designated *Il Genovesino*, from his native city, from whence, after being initiated into the rudiments of his art, he appears to have gone to Cremona, where he began to study the works of Panfilo Nuvolone. Afterwards he painted in the manner of the Caracci—bold, large, correct in coloring, and productive of fine effect. While he appears to be little known in his native city, he nevertheless enjoyed a high reputation in Cremona and in parts of Lombardy. His *S. Gio. Damasceno*, in the church of S. Clemente, at Cremona, is highly commended. The Merchants' College at Piacenza possesses likewise a beautiful *Pietà* from his hand, representing the *Dead Christ in the Lap of the Virgin*. He appears to have been remarkably successful in the treatment of all subjects, but especially so in compositions of a terrific or tragic nature. The exact time of his death is unknown: but one of his works in S. Imerio bears the date 1651; therefore his demise must have been subsequent to this date. See Lanzi's *Hist. of Painting* (transl. by Roscoe, Lond. 1847, 3 vols. 8vo), ii, 451; Spooner, *Biog. Hist. of the Fine Arts* (N. Y. 1865, 2 vols. 8vo), ii, 568.

Miræus, ALBERT (*Aubert le Mire*), a Roman Catholic theologian of Belgium, was born at Brussels in 1573, and was educated for the Church at the high-schools of Douai and Louvain. Shortly after taking orders he was appointed canon at Antwerp; in 1598 he became also private secretary to his uncle, bishop John Miræus; afterwards he became court preacher and librarian to the archduke Albert of Austria; and in 1624 dean of the cathedral at Antwerp, where he died in 1640. Most of his life was consecrated to the good of his Church and country. Miræus was also a multifarious writer. Many of his works are on ecclesiastical history. We will mention here *Bibliotheca Ecclesiastica* (Antwerp, 1639–1649, 2 vols. fol.; a new edition of this work was published at Hamburg in 1718 by Joh. Alb. Fabricius, who says in the preface, "Vir et hoc et tot aliis monumentis in lucem editis non minus de veteri memoria quam de posteritate omni insigniter promeritus") :— *De statu religionis Christianæ per totum orbum* (Helmst. 1671) : —*Notitia episcopatum orbis Christiani* (Antwerp, 1613) :— *Chronicon Cisterciense* (Cologne, 1614 : — *Geographia Ecclesiastica:* — *Codex regularum et constitutionum clericalium :—Origines cœnobiorum Benedictinorum, Carthusianorum,* etc. : — *Opera historica et diplomatica, Elogia illustrium Belgii scriptorum, Chronicon rerum Belgicarum, Chronicon rerum toto orbe gestarum,* etc. All his works were collected and published at Brussels in 1733, in 4 vols. fol.

Mirage, the French name of an optical illusion common in the East, and directly referred to by Isaiah (שָׁרָב, *sharab'*, "parched ground," xxxv, 7; "heat," xlix, 10), and perhaps indirectly by Jeremiah (xv, 18, "waters that fail;" literally, *that cannot be trusted*). It is still known by the name of *seráb*, the Arabic equivalent of the above Heb. term. This phenomenon is as simple in its origin as it is astonishing in its effects. Under it are classed the appearance of distant objects as double, or as if suspended in the air, erect or inverted, etc. The cause of mirage is a diminution of the density of the air near the surface of the earth, produced by the transmission of heat from the earth, or in some other way; the denser stratum being thus placed *above,* instead of, as is usually the case, *below* the rarer. Now rays of light from a distant object, situated in the denser medium (i. e. a little above the earth's level), coming in

a direction nearly parallel to the earth's surface, meet the rarer medium at a very obtuse angle, and, instead of passing into it, are reflected back to the dense medium, the common surface of the two media acting as a mirror. Suppose, then, a spectator to be situated on an eminence, and looking at an object situated like himself in the denser stratum of air, he will see the object by means of directly transmitted rays; but, besides this, rays from the object will be reflected from the upper surface of the rarer stratum of air beneath to his eye.

Mirage, fig. 1.

(See fig. 1.) The image produced by the reflected rays will appear inverted, and below the real object, just as an image reflected in water appears when observed from a distance. If the object is a cloud or portion of sky, it will appear by the reflected rays as lying on the surface of the earth, and bearing a strong resemblance to a sheet of water. (See fig. 2.) This form of mirage, which is

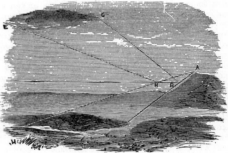

Mirage, fig. 2.

most common in sandy, desert countries, is an illusive appearance of pools and lakes of water, in places where water is most needed and least likely to occur. This

Mirage, fig. 3.

phenomenon offers so perfect a delusion in all its circumstances that the most forewarned and experienced travellers are deceived by it, as are even the natives of the deserts, when not sufficiently acquainted with the locality in which it appears to be aware that no water actually exists. No one can imagine, without actual experience, the delight and eager expectation, followed by the most intense and bitter disappointment, which the appearance of the *serâb* often occasions to travelling parties, particularly when the supply of water which they are obliged to carry with them upon their camels is nearly or quite exhausted. (See fig. 3.)

> " Still the same burning sun ! no cloud in heaven !
> The hot air quivers, and the sultry mist
> Floats o'er the desert, with a show
> Of distant waters mocking their distress."—SOUTHEY.

Major Skinner, in his *Journey Overland to India*, describes the appearance of the *serâb* in that desert, between Palestine and the Euphrates, which probably supplied the images employed by Isaiah : "About noon the most perfect deception that can be conceived exhilarated our spirits and promised an early resting-place. We had observed a slight mirage before, but this day it surpassed all I had ever fancied. Although aware that these appearances have often led people astray, I could not bring myself to believe that this was unreal. The Arabs were doubtful, and said that, as we had found water yesterday, it was not improbable that we should find some to-day. The seeming lake was broken in several parts by little islands of sand, that gave strength to the delusion. The dromedaries of the sheiks at length reached its borders, and appeared to us to have commenced to ford, as they advanced and became more surrounded by the vapor. I thought they had got into deep water, and moved with greater caution. In passing over the sand banks their figures were reflected in the water. So convinced was Mr. Calmun of its reality that he dismounted and walked towards the deepest part of it, which was on the right hand. He followed the deceitful lake for a long time, and to our sight was strolling on its bank, his shadow stretching to a great length beyond. There was not a breath of wind; it was a sultry day, and such a one as would have added dreadfully to the disappointment if we had been at any time without water." See PARCHED GROUND.

Miramion, MARIE BONNEAU, *Lady*, a very estimable French female philanthropist of the 17th century, was born at Paris Nov. 2, 1629. She was the daughter of Jacques Bonneau, lord of Rubelles, and of Maria d'Issy, both very wealthy. She married (March, 1645) Jean Jacques de Beauharnais, lord of Miramion, who died the same year. Many desirable parties solicited her hand, but she preferred to consecrate herself to God and to the care of the poor and sick, and took religious vows Feb. 2, 1649, when only twenty years of age. Every hour of her life was devoted to some charitable or pious act. In 1660 she collected twenty-eight poor monks driven from Picardy by the war, and nourished and cared for them for six months. Her zeal and liberality prompted her to found at Paris the House of Refuge and that of Sainte-Pelagie; she drew up the rules for these two houses, destined to serve as asylums for wives and repentant women. She contributed largely for the establishment of the Seminary of Foreign Missions. Civil war had increased the misery of the people of Paris; Madame de Miramion sold her necklaces, estimated at 24,000 pounds, and her plate, and distributed the proceeds in alms. In 1661 she established a society of twelve girls to teach country children how to dress wounds and succor the sick. This little community was called the " Sainte-Famille ;" Madame de Miramion subsequently united it to the daughters of "Sainte-Geneviève." She bought for them a large house on the wharf of the Tournelle, sufficiently endowed the establishment, and consented to become superior. She gave more than 70,000 pounds to her parish of Saint-Nicolas de Chardonnet, the seminary of which she endowed with

a sum of 35,000 francs. The hospital for foundlings was also greatly indebted to her. She died March 24, 1696. See Abbé de Choisy, *Vie de Madame de Miramion* (Paris, 1706, 4to, and 1707, 8vo) ; Saint-Simon, *Mémoires*; Richard and Giraud, *Bibliothèque Sacrée*; Hoefer, *Nouv. Biog. Générale*, s. v. See GENEVIÈVE, ST., DAUGHTERS OF.

Mirandula, Giovanni Francesca della, a noted theological and philosophical writer of the 16th century, was born about 1469. He cultivated learning and the sciences, after the example of his uncle. (See below the article MIRANDULA, GIOVANNI PICO DELLA.) Upon the death of his father, in 1499, he succeeded, as eldest son, to his estates, and thus became involved in great trouble, which finally cut short not only his literary labors but also his life. His brothers Lewis and Frederick combined against him, and, by the assistance of the emperor Maximilian I and Hercules I, duke of Ferrara, succeeded in driving him from his principality in 1502, and he was forced to seek refuge abroad, until at length pope Julius II, invading and becoming master of Mirandula, re-established him in 1511. After the pope's defeat at Ravenna (April 11, 1512), Giovanni Francisca became a refugee a second time, and so continued for two years. After the French were driven out of Italy he was restored to his possessions. He died in October, 1533, when Galeoti Picus, his nephew, i. e. the son of his brother Lewis, entered his castle by night with forty armed men, and assassinated him and his eldest son Albert. He seems to have been a more voluminous writer than his uncle. His earlier works were inserted in the Strasburg edition of his uncle's, in 1504, and continued in those of Basle, 1573 and 1601. Among these are : (1.) *De studio divinæ et humanæ philosophiæ libri duo :* in this he compares profane philosophy with a knowledge of Holy Scripture, and shows how preferable the latter is to the former. (2.) *De imaginatione liber.* (3.) *De imitatione ad Petrum Bembum epistolæ duæ, et ejus responsum.* (4.) *De rerum prænotione libri ix :* in this book of the Prescience of things, he treats of the divine prescience, and of that knowledge which some pretend to have of things future, by compacts with evil spirits, by astrology, chiromancy, geomancy, and the like means, which he confutes at large. (5.) *Examen vanitatis doctrinæ gentium et veritatis disciplinæ Christianæ*, etc., wherein he opposes the errors of philosophers, Aristotle particularly. (6.) *Epistolarum libri quatuor.* (7.) *De reformandis moribus oratio ad Leonem X.* These are the most important of his writings to be found in the editions above mentioned of his uncle's works; but there are other works, which have never been collected together, but have always continued separate, as they were first published: such are—*Vita Hieronymi Savonarolæ :—De veris calamitatum temporum nostrorum causis liber :—De animæ immortalitate :—Dialogus cui nomen Strix, sive de ludificatione dæmonum :—Hymni heroici tres ad Trinitatem, Christum, et Virginem :—De Venere et Cupidine expellendis carmen heroicum :— Liber de Providentia Dei contra philosophastros :—De auro tum æstimando, tum conficiendo, tum utendo libri tres*, etc. "There is not," says Du Pin, "so much wit, sprightliness, subtlety, and elegance in the works of Francis Pico as in those of his uncle ; no, nor yet so much learning: but there is more evenness and solidity." See the books referred to in the article following.

Mirandula, Giovanni Pico della, an Italian philosopher and theologian, one of the writers of the days of the Renaissance, noted for his attempt to reconcile Christianity with the ideas of paganism, was one of the greatest lights of the 15th century. He was born Feb. 24, 1463. Even as a youth, the prince of Mirandula was noted for his precociousness, and remarkable for his memory and intelligence. He challenged disputations on abstruse subjects with the learned of his day, as if one of their number. In 1477 he entered the University of Bologna, to study canonical law, besides which he devoted himself especially to the study of philosophy and theology. After this he visited the other universities of note on the Continent, and everywhere attracted attention by his learning and the facility with which he acquired knowledge. Besides a mastery of Greek and Latin, he could claim acquaintance with the Hebrew, Chaldee, and Arabic. He was also well acquainted with the various philosophical systems of antiquity, and with those of the scholastics and of Raymond Lully. But vain of his knowledge, he came to consider himself qualified to solve the problem of reconciling philosophy and theology, and even to conciliate the philosophical systems of Plato and Aristotle. This would have required a critical knowledge more profound than was to be found in the 15th century, as well as an originality of mind which Mirandula did not possess. He has, indeed, in his writings, rendered great service to theology, in pointing out the aid it may derive from the knowledge of Oriental languages, but we vainly seek in them a single new metaphysical idea.

After many wanderings, "wanderings of the intellect as well as physical journey," says Parr, "Pico came to rest at Florence." But his stay at the different universities had made him only the more sanguine of carrying out the plan formed of reconciling the philosophers with each other, and all alike with the Church. To Rome, the centre of the Church, he therefore now directed his steps, satisfied that there he should first disclose to the world his great project, and there he should promptly receive the honors of the clergy. Mirandula arrived at Rome in 1487. Innocent VIII was then reigning. Like some knight-errant, the young man of only twenty-three summers now, published, to the astonishment of the learned world, nine hundred propositions on subjects of dialectics, morals, natural philosophy, mathematics, theology, natural magic, and cabalism, taken not only from Greek and Latin, but also from Hebrew and Arabic writers, and declared himself ready to defend these propositions openly against any one. For that object, he invited all the savans of Europe to come to argue against him at Rome, offering to defray the expenses of such as would have to travel a great distance. These famous theses, De omni re scibili, as Mirandula called them (et de quibusdam aliis, adds Voltaire, thus making the best criticism on Mirandula's pretensions), were posted all over Rome, and awakened great curiosity as well as jealousy. Parties envious of Mirandula's reputation succeeded in awakening the doubts of the papal court as to the orthodoxy of some of the propositions, and Mirandula not only struggled in vain for over a year at Rome simply to obtain leave to publish his theses, but even the reading of the book containing them was forbidden by the pope. Disgusted with this treatment, Mirandula finally quitted Rome for Florence. Made restless by the opposition he had encountered, he remained here but a short time, went to France, and did not return to Italy till several years later. Shortly after Alexander VI had ascended the papal throne (1492) the case of Mirandula was reconsidered, and, June 18, 1493, Pico was finally absolved from all heresy by a brief of the pontifical court. Mirandula by this time had, however, given up all profane sciences, to devote himself exclusively to theology. The remainder of his life was spent in attempts to refute Judaism, Mohammedanism, and judicial astrology. He died at Florence, Nov. 17, 1494, the day when Charles VIII, who had received him at Paris, entered the city. He was interred in the cemetery of St. Mark, in the habit of a Jacobin, having taken a resolution, just before his death, to enter into that order; and upon his tomb was inscribed this epitaph:

"Joannes jacet hic Mirandula: cætera norunt
Et Tagus, et Ganges; forsan et Antipodes."

The greater part of his immense fortune he gave over in his last days to his friend, the mystical poet Benivieni, to be spent by him in works of charity, chiefly in

the sweet charity of providing marriage-dowries for the peasant girls of Florence.

Short as his life was, Mirandula composed a great number of works, which have often been printed separately and together. They have been printed together at Bologna (1496), at Venice (1498), at Strasburg (1504), and at Basle (1557, 1573, 1601)—all in folio. The principal works in the collection are, Heptaplus, id est de Dei creatoris opere sex dierum libri septem (Strasburg, 1574, fol.; translated into French by Nicolas le Fèvre de la Boderi, under the title L'Heptaple, où en sept façons et autant de livres est exposée l'histoire des sept jours de la création du monde [Florence, about 1480; Paris, 1578, fol.]). "Pico de la Mirandula," says Matter, "convinced that the books of Moses, interpreted with the aid of the Cabala and of Neo-Platonism, would appear as the source of all speculative science, wrote an exposition of Genesis according to the seven meanings given to it by some of the exegetes of that period. But this work, rather short for such a subject and such a purpose, is really but a weak imitation, even in regard to its title, of the works of some of the fathers. Here is a specimen of his manner of interpretation. The words 'God created the heavens and the earth,' are made by him to signify that God created the soul and the body, which can very well be considered as represented by heavens and earth. The waters under the heavens are our sensitive faculties, and their being gathered together in one place indicates the gathering of our senses in a common sensorium. This allegorical manner, borrowed from Origen, or rather from Philo, is probably anterior even to the latter; and it is evident that this could not afford the means of reconciling philosophy and theology. Generally speaking, Mirandula, whose genius was so precocious, so brilliant, and so comprehensive, wrote too young and too fast, and with too much confidence in secondhand learning, while his imagination was too vivid not to prevent his giving full satisfaction to the claims of reason. All his works bear the marks of that general kind of knowledge one possesses in leaving the schools, but nowhere do they evince that depth and originality which are the fruits of meditation and of patient research. He was a prodigy of memory, of elocution, of dialectics; he was neither a writer nor a thinker." The reader may do well to compare with this estimate of Mirandula, Pater's enthusiastic tribute to the author of the "Heptaplus:"—Conclusiones philosophicæ, cabalisticæ et theologicæ (Rome, 1486, fol.); these are the famous theses which made such a sensation at the time, but are now looked upon only as curiosities:—Apologia J. Pici Mirandulani, Concordiæ comitis (1489, fol., very scarce); it is Mirandula's defence against the charge of heresy; the writer corrects some singular instances of ignorance on the part of his accusers: one of them, for instance, took Cabala for the name of a man, and asserted that it was a scoundrel who had written against Christ:—Disputationes adversus astrologiam divinatricem libri xii (Bologna, 1495, fol.):—Aureæ ad familiares epistolæ (Paris, 1499, 4to; Venice, 1529, 8vo; reprinted by Cellarius, 1682, 8vo):—Elegia deprecatoria ad Deum (Paris, 1620, 4to):—De Ente et Uno opus, in quo plurimi loci in Moise, in Platone et Aristotele explicantur; De hominis dignitate (Basle, 1580, 8vo):—Commento del signor Giovanni Pico sopra una canzone de amore, composta da Girolamo Benivieni, cittadino Fiorentino, secundo la mente ed opinione dei Platonici (Florence, 1519, 8vo; Venice, 1522, 8vo), a commentary in the manner of Plato's Banquet, and very readable. "With an ambitious array of every sort of learning, and a profusion of imagery borrowed indifferently from the astrologers, the Cabala, Homer, Scripture, and Dionysius the Areopagite, he attempts to define the stages by which the soul passes from the earthly to the unseen beatitudes." It has been well said that the Renaissance of the 15th century was in many things great rather by what it designed than by what it achieved. The same may be appropriately applied to Mirandula's efforts.

"He had sought knowledge, and passed from system to system, and hazarded much; but less for the sake of positive knowledge than because he believed there was a spirit of order and beauty in knowledge, which would come down and unite what man's ignorance had divided, and renew what time had made dim. And so while his actual work has passed away, yet his own qualities are still active, and he himself remains, as one alive in the grave, 'cæsiis et vigilibus oculis,' as his biographer describes him, and with that sanguine clear skin, 'decenti rubore interspersa,' as with the light of morning upon it; and he has a true place in that group of great Italians who fill the end of the 15th century with their names" (Pater). See Paul Jove, *Elogia*; Sir Thos. More, *Pico, Earl of Mirandula, and a great Lord of Italy* (from the Italian of Francis della Mirandula); Nicéron, *Mémoires*, vol. xxxiv; Tiraboschi, *Storia della litteratura Italiana*, vi, 323; Ginguené, *Hist. littéraire d'Italie*, vol. iii; Matter, *Dict. des sciences philosophiques*; Meiners, *Lebensbeschreibungen berühmter Männer*, etc., vol. ii; Hoefer, *Nouv. Biog. Générale*, xl, 43; Sigwart, *Ulrich Zwingle, der Charakter seiner Theologie, mit besonderer Rücksicht auf Picus von Mirandula* (Stuttg. 1855), p. 14 sq.; Dreydorft (Georg), *Das System des John Picus Graf von Mirandula* (Marburg, 1858); Pater. *Studies in the History of the Renaissance* (Lond. and N. Y. Macmillan, 1873, 12mo), chap. ii.

Mirepoix, GUI DE LEWIS, *Seigneur de*, one of the great soldiers of the French who battled for the Church in the days of the Crusades, flourished in the early part of the 13th century. He was a friend of Simon de Montfort, marshal of France, conducted the warfare against the Albigenses, and was rewarded for his blind adherence to the papal cause with the title of "Marshal of the Faith." He died in 1230.

Mir'iam (Heb. *Miryam'*, מִרְיָם, *rebellion*; Sept. Μαριάμ, but in 1 Chron. iv, 17 Μαών v. r. Μαρών; Josephus Μαριάμμη, *Ant.* iv, 4, 6), the name of a woman and of a man. The name reappears in the N. T., Μαριάμ being the form always employed for the nominative case of the name of the *Virgin Mary*, though it is declined Μαρίας, Μαρίᾳ; while Μαρία is employed in all cases for the three other Marys. At the time of the Christian æra it seems to have been common. Among others who bore it was Herod's celebrated wife and victim, *Mariamne*. See also MARY.

1. The sister of Moses and Aaron, and supposed (so Josephus, *Ant.* ii, 9, 4) to be the same that watched her infant brother when exposed on the Nile; in which case she was probably ten or twelve years old at the time (Exod. ii, 4 sq.). B.C. 1738. She was the daughter of Amram and Jochebed, of the tribe of Levi (Numb. xxvi, 59; comp. Mic. vi, 4). When the Israelites left Egypt, Miriam naturally became the leading woman among them. "The sister of Aaron" is her Biblical distinction (Exod. xv, 20). In Numb. xii, 1 she is placed before Aaron; and "Miriam the Prophetess" is her acknowledged title (Exod. xv, 20). The prophetic power showed itself in her under the same form as that which it assumed in the days of Samuel and David—poetry, accompanied with music and processions. The only instance of this prophetic gift is when, after the passage of the Red Sea, she took a cymbal in her hand, and went forth, like the Hebrew maidens in later times after a victory (Judg. v, 1; xi, 34; 1 Sam. xviii, 6; Psa. lxviii, 11, 25), followed by the whole female population of Israel, also beating their cymbals and striking their guitars (מְחֹלֹת, otherwise "dances"). It does not appear how far they joined in the whole of the song (Exod. i, 15–19); but the opening words are repeated again by Miriam herself at the close, in the form of a command to the Hebrew women. "She answered them, saying, Sing ye to Jehovah, for he hath triumphed gloriously: the horse and his rider hath he thrown into the sea." B.C. 1658. The arrival of Moses's Cushite wife in the camp seems to have created in her an un-

seemly dread of losing her influence and position, and led her into complaints of and dangerous reflections upon Moses, in which Aaron joined (see Kitto's *Daily Bible Illustr.* ad loc.). See ZIPPORAH. Their question, "Hath Jehovah spoken by Moses? Hath he not spoken also by us?" (Numb. xii, 1, 2), implies that the prophetic gift was exercised by them; while the answer implies that it was communicated in a less direct form than to Moses. "If there be a prophet among you, I Jehovah will make myself known unto him in a vision, and will speak unto him in a dream. My servant Moses is not so. . . . With him will I speak mouth to mouth, even apparently, and not in dark speeches" (Numb. xii, 6–8). A stern rebuke was administered in front of the sacred tent to both Aaron and Miriam. But the punishment fell on Miriam, as the chief offender. The hateful Egyptian leprosy, of which for a moment the sign had been seen on the hand of her younger brother, broke out over the whole person of the proud prophetess. How grand was her position, and how heavy the blow, is implied in the cry of anguish which goes up from both the brothers—"Alas, my lord! . . . Let her not be as one dead, of whom the flesh is half consumed when he cometh out of his mother's womb. . . . Heal her now, O God! I beseech thee." And it is not less evident in the silent grief of the nation: "The people journeyed not till Miriam was brought in again" (Numb. xii, 10–15). The same feeling is reflected, though in a strange and distorted form, in the ancient tradition of the drying up and reflowing of the marvellous well of the Wanderings. See BEER. This stroke, and its removal, which took place at Hazeroth, form the last public event of Miriam's life. She died towards the close of the wanderings at Kadesh, and was buried there (Numb. xx, 1). B.C. 1619. Her tomb was shown near Petra in the days of Jerome (*Onomast.* s. v. Cades Barnea). According to the Jewish tradition (Josephus, *Ant.* iv, 4, 6), her death took place on the new moon of the month Xanthicus (i. e. about the end of February), which seems to imply that the anniversary was still observed in the time of Josephus. The burial, he adds, took place with great pomp on a mountain called Zin, i. e. the wilderness of Zin); and the mourning—which lasted, as in the case of her brothers, for thirty days—was closed by the institution of the purification through the sacrifice of the heifer (Numb. xix, 1–10), which in the Pentateuch immediately precedes the story of her death. According to Josephus (*Ant.* iii, 2, 4; 6, 1), she was married to the famous Hur, and, through him, was grandmother of the architect Bezaleel. In the Koran (ch. iii) she is confounded with the Virgin Mary; and hence the Holy Family is called the Family of Amram, or Imram (see also D'Herbelot, *Bibl. Orient.* s. v. Zakaria). In other Arabic traditions her name is given as *Kolthum* (see Weil's *Bibl. Legends*, p. 101).

2. The first named of the sons of Mered (the son of Ezra, of the family of Caleb) by Bithiah, the daughter of Pharaoh (1 Chron. iv, 17). B.C. prob. cir. 1658. See MERED.

Mirkhond, MOHAMMED EBN-EMIR KHOWAND SHAH, a noted Eastern historian, a native of Persia, was born in 1434, and died in 1498. He is the author of a work containing legends concerning Persian kings and sages, extracts of which were first published by Davity (*États, empires, royaumes du monde*). He also wrote a history of the Samanites, published in German by Wilken (*Geschichte der Samaniden*), at Göttingen, in 1808, and in French by Defremeny (Paris, 1845).

Mir'ma (Heb. *Mirmah'*, מִרְמָה, *deceit*, as often; Sept. Μαρμά), the last named of the sons of Shaharaim by Hodesh, and a chieftain of the tribe of Benjamin (1 Chron. viii, 10). B.C. post 1612.

Miron, CHARLES, a French prelate, was born in 1569. At eighteen, holding already the abbotship of Cormeri and Airvaux, he was appointed by the king bishop of Angers. Of the different parties which then divided

France, Miron espoused the cause of Henry IV. He was also one of the preachers who pronounced a funeral eulogy upon the king when assassinated by the hand of Ravaillac. Miron, upon removing from Angers to Paris, continued to hold his relation to the Church at Angers, and thereby provoked a grave dispute between the bishop and his chapter. The chapter, insisting upon the pope's appointment, declared themselves free from Miron's episcopal jurisdiction, to which the bishop took decided exception, and the disputes called forth by this affair finally led Miron to vacate his bishopric. He transmitted his insignia to Guillaume Fouquet de la Varenne, and became, by exchange, abbot of Saint-Lomer de Blois. This transaction took place in 1615. But in 1621, Guillaume Fouquet having died, Miron reclaimed his bishopric, obtained it a second time, and entered Angers April 23, 1622. Very soon the discussions between the bishop and the chapter were resumed, and only terminated by the papal appointment of Miron to the archbishopric of Lyons, Dec. 2, 1626. This nomination was denounced by Salon as detrimental to the liberties of the Gallican Church. He died, however, before much could come of the opposition, Aug. 6, 1628. See *Gallia Christiana*, iv, col. 192; xiv, col. 584, 585; Hoefer, *Nouv. Biog. Générale*, xxxv, 668.

Mirror. Although this word does not occur in the Auth. Vers., except in the Apocrypha (Wisd. vii, 26), it is the proper representative of at least two Heb. and one Gr. term, for which our translators employ the less correct rendering "LOOKING-GLASS" (מַרְאָה, *marah'*, a *vision*, as often, Exod. xxxviii, 8; Sept. κάτοπτρον, Vulg. *speculum;* רְאִי, *reï'*, a *spectacle*, Job xxxvii, 18, Sept. ὅρασις, Vulg. *æs;* גִּלָּיוֹן, *gilyon'*, a *tablet* of wood, stone, or metal on which to inscribe anything, so called as being made *bare*, Isa. viii, 1; in Isa. iii, 23 the plural refers, according to the Chald., Abarbanel, Jarchi, and others, with the Vulg. *specula*, and the Auth. Vers. "glasses," to mirrors or polished plates of metal, see Gesenius, *Comment.* ad loc., but Kimchi and others understand, with the Sept., διαφανῆ Λακονικά, transparent garments, such as show the body, comp. Schröder, *De Vest. mul. Heb.* p. 311, 312). In the first of the foregoing passages the mirrors in the possession of the women of the Israelites, when they quitted Egypt, are described as being of *brass ;* for "the laver of brass, and the foot of it," were made from them. In the second, the firmament is compared to "a molten mirror." In fact, the mirrors used in ancient times were almost universally of metal (the passage in the Mishna, *Chelim*, xxx, 2, does not allude to glass mirrors); and as those of the Hebrew women in the wilderness were brought out of Egypt, they were doubtless of the same kind as those which have been found in the tombs of that country, and many of which now exist in our museums and col-

lections of Egyptian antiquities. These are of mixed metals, chiefly copper, most carefully wrought and highly polished; and so admirably did the skill of the Egyptians succeed in the composition of metals that this substitute for our modern looking-glass was susceptible of a lustre, which has even been partially revived at the present day in some of those discovered at Thebes, though buried in the earth for so many centuries. The mirror itself was nearly round, and was inserted in a handle of wood, stone, or metal, the form of which varied according to the taste of the owner (see Wilkinson's *Ancient Egyptians*, iii, 384–386). In the N. T. mirrors are mentioned (ἔσοπτρα, James i, 23; comp. 1 Cor. xiii, 12; see Harenberg, in *Hasæi et Iken. nov. thesaur.* ii, 829 sq.). They are alluded to in the Rabbinical writings (אספקלריא, i. e. *specularia*, Targ. Jon. *in Exod.* xix, 17; Deut. xxxiii, 19; Mishna, *Chelim*, xvii, 15; *Edujoth*, ii, 7; see Lightfoot, *Hor. Heb.* p. 379). See generally, Th. Carpzov, *De speculis Hebræor.* (Rostock, 1752); Jahn, I, ii, 155 sq.; Hartmann, *Hebr.* ii, 240 sq.; iii, 245 sq. It appears likewise from other positive statements that mirrors anciently were of metal, namely, of copper (χαλκεῖον, Xenoph. *Symp.* vii, 4) or tin, also of an alloy of both these metals, answering to brass, and sometimes even of silver (Pliny, xxxiii, 45; xxxiv, 48; comp. Rosell. *Monum.* II, ii, 528 sq.; Becker, *Gallus*, III, iii). Occasionally they were of great size (Senec. *Nat. Quæst.* i, 16, 17, p. 185, Bip.; Quintil. *Inst.* ii, 3, 68). Finally, mirrors of polished stone are mentioned (Pliny, xxxvi, 45; comp. Sueton. *Domit.* xiv). "Pliny mentions that anciently the best were made at Brundusium. Praxiteles, in the time of Pompey the Great, is said to have been the first who made them of silver, though these were afterwards so common as, in the time of Pliny, to be used by the ladies' maids. Silver mirrors are alluded to in Plautus (*Mostell.* i, 4, ver. 101) and Philostratus (*Icon.* i, 6); and one of steel is said to have been found. They were even made of gold (Eur. *Hec.* 925; Senec. *Nat. Quæst.* i, 17). According to Beckmann (*Hist. of Inv.* ii, 64, Bohn's transl.), a mirror which was discovered near Naples was tested, and found to be made of a mixture of copper and regulus of antimony, with a little lead. Beckmann's editor (Mr. Francis) gives in a note the result of an analysis of an Etruscan mirror, which he examined and found to consist of 67.12 copper, 24.93 tin, and 8.13 lead, or nearly eight parts of copper to three of tin and one of lead; but neither in this, nor in one analyzed by Klaproth, was there any trace of antimony, which Beckmann asserts was unknown to the ancients. Modern experiments have shown that the mixture of copper and tin produces the best metal for specula (*Phil. Trans.* lxvii, 296). Beckmann is of the opinion that it was not till the 13th century that glass, covered at the back with tin or lead, was used for this purpose, the doubtful allusion in Pliny (xxxvi, 66) to the mirrors made in the glass-houses of Sidon having reference to experiments which were unsuccessful. Other allusions to bronze mirrors will be found in a fragment of Æschylus preserved in Stobæus (*Serm.* xviii, p. 164, ed. Gesner, 1608) and in Callimachus (*Hym. in Lav. Pall.* 21). Convex mirrors of polished steel are mentioned as common in the East in a manuscript note of Chardin's upon Ecclus. xii, 11, quoted by Harmer (*Observ.* vol. iv, c. 11, obs. 55). The metal of which the mirrors were composed being liable to rust and tarnish, required to be constantly kept bright (Wisd. vii, 26; Ecclus. xii, 11). This was done by means of pounded pumice-stone, rubbed on with a sponge, which was generally suspended from the mirror. The Persians used emery-powder for the same purpose, according to Chardin (quoted by Hartmann, *Die Hebr. am Putztische*, ii, 245). The obscure image produced by a tarnished or imperfect mirror appears to be alluded to in 1 Cor. xiii, 12. On the other hand, a polished mirror is among the Arabs the emblem of a pure reputation. 'More spotless than the mirror of a foreign woman' is with

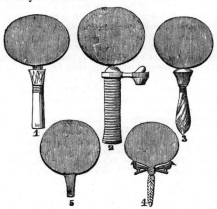

Ancient Mirrors of Bronze. (From the British Museum: 1 to 4, Egyptian; 5, Assyrian.)

them a proverbial expression, which Meïdani explains of a woman who has married out of her country, and polishes her mirror incessantly, that no part of her face may escape her observation (De Sacy, *Chrest. Arab.* iii, 236). Mirrors are mentioned by Chrysostom among the extravagances of fashion for which he rebuked the ladies of his time, and Seneca long before was loud in his denunciation of similar follies (*Nat. Quæst.* i, 17). They were used by the Roman women in the worship of Juno (Senec. *Ep.* 95; Apuleius, *Metam.* xi, c. 9, p. 770). In the Egyptian temples, says Cyril of Alexandria (*De ador. in Spir.* ix; *Opera,* i, 314, ed. Paris, 1638), it was the custom for the women to worship in linen garments, holding a mirror in their left hands and a sistrum in their right; and the Israelites, having fallen into the idolatries of the country, had brought with them the mirrors which they used in their worship." This is a practice to which one of the above Scripture passages (Exod. xxxviii, 8) appears to allude (see Gesenius, *Comment. on Isa.* i, 215; on the contrary, B. F. Quistorp, *Die speculis labri œnei,* Gryph. 1773).

Mirth, the expression of joy, gayety, merriment, is thus distinguished from its synonym, cheerfulness: *Mirth* is considered as an act, *cheerfulness* a habit of the mind. *Mirth* is short and transient; *cheerfulness* fixed and permanent. Those are often raised into the greatest transports of mirth who are subject to the greatest depressions of melancholy: on the contrary, cheerfulness, though it does not give such an exquisite gladness, prevents us from falling into any depths of sorrow. Mirth is like a flash of lightning, that breaks through a gloom of clouds, and glitters for a moment; cheerfulness keeps up a kind of daylight in the mind, and fills it with a steady and perpetual serenity.

Mirth is sinful, 1. When men rejoice in that which is evil. 2. When unreasonable. 3. When tending to commit sin. 4. When a hinderance to duty. 5. When it is blasphemous and profane.

Mis'aël ($M\iota\sigma\alpha\dot{\eta}\lambda$), the Greek form (*a,* 1 Esdr. ix, 44; comp. Neh. viii, 4; *b,* Song of the Three Child. 66; comp. Dan. i, 6 sq.) of the Heb. name MISHAEL (q. v.).

Misanthropist (from the Greek $\mu\iota\sigma\epsilon\tilde{\iota}\nu$, *to hate,* and $\dot{\alpha}\nu\vartheta\rho\omega\pi o\varsigma$, *man*), a hater of mankind; one that abandons society from a principle of discontent. The consideration of the depravity of human nature is certainly enough to raise emotions of sorrow in the breast of every man of the least sensibility; yet it is our duty to bear with the follies of mankind; to exercise a degree of candor consistent with truth; to lessen, if possible, by our exertions, the sum of moral and natural evil; and by connecting ourselves with society, to add at least something to the general interests of mankind. The misanthropist, therefore, is an ungenerous and dishonorable character. Disgusted with life, he seeks a retreat from it; like a coward, he flees from the scene of action, while he increases his own misery by his natural discontent, and leaves others to do what they can for themselves.

The following is his character more at large: "He is a man," says Saurin (*Sermons*), "who avoids society only to free himself from the trouble of being useful to it. He is a man who considers his neighbors only on the side of their defects, not knowing the art of combining their virtues with their vices, and of rendering the imperfections of other people tolerable by reflecting on his own. He is a man more employed in finding out and inflicting punishments on the guilty than in devising means to reform them. He is a man who talks of nothing but banishing and executing, and who, because he thinks his talents are not sufficiently valued and employed by his fellow-citizens, or, rather, because they know his foibles, and do not choose to be subject to his caprice, talks of quitting cities, towns, and societies, and of living in dens or deserts."

Misciroli, TOMMASO, a painter of the Bolognese school, was born at Faenza in 1636. He gained consid-

erable reputation, and executed several works for the churches. His principal picture is the *Martyrdom of St. Cecilia,* an altar-piece in the church of St. Cecilia at Faenza, which is finished with great care. Lanzi says that in some of his works Misciroli equals the best Viennese painters, but accuses him of plagiarism in many instances, notably in the picture above alluded to, in which he introduced an executioner stirring up the flames, a feature copied almost entirely from Lionello's grand picture of the martyrdom of St. Domenico in the church of that name at Bologna. Misciroli died in 1699. See Lanzi's *Hist. of Painting,* transl. by Roscoe (Lond. 1847, 3 vols. 8vo), iii, 131; Spooner, *Biog. Hist. of the Fine Arts* (Phila. 1865, 2 vols. 8vo), ii, 569.

Miser (Lat. *unhappy*), a term formerly used in reference to a person in wretchedness or calamity; but it now denotes a parsimonious person, or one who is covetous to extremity; who denies himself even the comforts of life to accumulate wealth. "Avarice," says Saurin, "may be considered in two different points of light. It may be considered in those men, or rather those public bloodsuckers, or, as the officers of the Roman emperor Vespasian were called, those *sponges* of society, who, infatuated with this passion, seek after riches as the supreme good, determine to acquire it by any methods, and consider the ways that lead to wealth, legal or illegal, as the only road for them to travel. Avarice, however, must be considered in a second point of light. It not only consists in committing bold crimes, but in entertaining mean ideas and practicing low methods, incompatible with such magnanimity as our condition ought to inspire. It consists not only in omitting to serve God, but in trying to associate the service of God with that of mammon. How many forms doth avarice take to disguise itself from the man who is guilty of it, and who will be drenched in the guilt of it till the day he dies! Sometimes it is *prudence,* which requires him to provide not only for his present wants, but for such as he may have in future. Sometimes it is *charity,* which requires him not to give society examples of prodigality and parade. Sometimes it is *parental love,* obliging him to save something for his children. Sometimes it is *circumspection,* which requires him not to supply people who make ill use of what they get. Sometimes it is *necessity,* which obliges him to repel artifice by artifice. Sometimes it is *conscience,* which convinces him, *good man,* that he hath already exceeded in compassion and alms-giving, and done too much. Sometimes it is *equity,* for justice requires that every one should enjoy the fruit of his own labors and those of his ancestors. Such, alas! are the awful pretexts and subterfuges of the miser" (*Sermons,* vol. v, ser. 12). See AVARICE; COVETOUSNESS.

Miserēre (Lat. *have compassion*), the name of a liturgic prayer, set to music, and used in Roman Catholic worship. It is a sort of paraphrase on the 51st or 57th Psalm, and is used on penitential occasions, and particularly in Passion-week. It is therefore not only set to a regular Gregorian melody (see Keller, *Die acht Psalmentöne,* etc., Aix-la-Chap. 1856, p. 18), but has also become a theme for compositions to the most eminent masters, such as Palestrina, Orlando di Lasso, Allegri, Scarlatti, Leonardo Leo, Thomas Bai, Zingarelli, Pergolese, Jomelli, Fioravanti, Fétis, Vogler, Stadler, etc. The most renowned among these compositions is that by Gregorio Allegri (a descendant of Correggio, born at Rome in 1590, † 1640), in which two choirs, one of four, the other of five parts, sing alternately until the finale, where all join in *pianissimo,* the measure also becoming gradually slower. This piece, from the time it was composed, has always been sung on Wednesday and Friday of Passion-week in the Sistine Chapel at Rome. One writer says: "Never by mortal ear was heard a strain of such powerful, such heart-moving pathos. The accordant tones of a hundred human voices, and one which seemed more than human, ascended together to heaven for mercy to mankind—for pardon to a guilty and sinning world. It had nothing in it of this earth—nothing that breathed the ordinary feelings of our nature. Its effects upon the minds of those who heard it were almost too powerful to be borne, and never can be forgotten. One gentleman fainted and was carried out; and many of the ladies near me were in agitation even more distressing, which they vainly struggled to suppress. It was the music of Allegri; but the composition, however fine, is nothing without the voices which perform it here." Another writer says: "At the conclusion of this portion of the service, and when the darkness is complete by the concealment of the last light, commences the *Miserere.* This is the 51st Psalm. And as it is breathed by the choir—the most perfect and practiced choir in the world —as it is heard in all the stillness and solemnity of the scene, wrapped in darkness, and leaving nothing to distract the eye where all looks dim and shadowy, it has a strange and wonderful effect. It is designed to express, as far as music can express, the deep and mental agonies of the dying Saviour; and certainly there never yet was heard, except among the shepherds of Bethlehem on the night of the nativity, such sounds, so unearthly, and unlike the music of the world. It is plaintive, intensely melancholy, and has a powerful effect under the peculiar circumstances of the scene." It was formerly the exclusive property of the Sistine Chapel, the partition being jealously kept there; Mozart succeeded, however, in writing it down after hearing it twice. It has since been repeatedly published. While the Miserere is sung, the pope kneels at the altar, the cardinals at their desks, and as it proceeds the lights at the altar are extinguished one by one, which is explained by Gavanti, *Thes.* ii, 99: "Ad unumquemque psalmum (there are other psalms sung before the Miserere) exstinguitur una candela, una post aliam, quia apostoli paulatim defecerunt a Christo." In fact, the whole use of this psalm in Passion-week is intended *ad designandum apostolorum timorem.* The word *miserere* has in modern days come to be applied to any sacred composition of a penitential character. See Herzog, *Real-Encyklopädie*, ix, 547; Eadie, *Eccles. Cyclop.* s. v.; Siegel, *Christliche Alterthümer* (see Index in vol. iv).

Misérèrès. Elbowed stalls, often found in cathedral, collegiate, and minster churches, with seats that may be turned up, so as to give an opportunity of kneeling in those parts of the service in which the language of *supplication* ("miserere") occurs. They were allowed in the Roman Catholic Church as a relief to the infirm during the long services that were required to be performed by the ecclesiastics in a standing posture. They are always more or less ornamented with carvings of leaves, small figures, animals, etc., which are generally very boldly cut. Examples are to be found in almost all English churches which retain any of the ancient stalls; the oldest is in Henry the Seventh's Chapel at Westminster, where there is one in the style of the 13th century.

Miserere in Henry the Seventh's Chapel, Westminster.

Misericord is a term used to denote various offices and articles. (1) Subsellia—Spanish *subsilia*—the folding seat of a stall. See MISERERES. (2) A compassionate mitigation of full penance. (3) According to Lyndwood, a custom in certain monasteries of relieving

a number of monks, in alternate weeks, from attendance in choir and claustral duties. (4) A hall for eating flesh-meat in a monastery. Some convents, as Canterbury and Westminster, had country hospitals for convalescents. (5) The word also implied stated indulgences and allowances, according to circumstances, of food, drink, wine or beer, or clothing or bedding, beyond the rule. And, finally, some writers, misled by the glossarist of Matthew Paris, have called a misericord *a guzzle of wine*, an imperfect definition taken from the refreshment of that liquor granted during the above period. See Walcott, *Sacred Archæology*, s. v.; Fosbrooke, *British Monachism*, ch. xlviii.

Misericordia Domĭni is the name of the second Sunday from Easter, so called from the opening lines of the mass read on that day in the Romish churches. In the Greek Church the day is frequently called St. Thomas's Sunday.

Mis′gab (Heb. *Misgab′*, מִשְׂגָּב, *height*, as often; Sept. Ἀμάϑ τὸ κραταίωμα v. r. Μασιγάϑ, and τὸ ὀχύρωμα Μωάβ, Vulg. *fortis*), a town in Moab, situated on the desolating track of the invading Babylonians (Jer. xlviii, 1), probably so called from being located on an eminence. De Saulcy (*Narrative*, i, 391) suggests a connection with the present Wady *el-Mujeb*, the ancient Arnon; but this is merely fanciful. The place is doubtless to be sought near the associated localities of Kiriathaim and Heshbon; perhaps it is only an appellative (as it usually has the article) for the older locality BAMOTH (q. v.). Others think it may be the MIZPEH of Moab (1 Sam. xxiii, 3), or a general name for the highlands of Moab, as in Isa. xxv, 12 (without the art. A. V. "high fort"). See MOAB.

Mish′aël (Heb. *Mishaël′*, מִישָׁאֵל, *who* is *like God?* Sept. Μισαήλ), the name of three men.

1. The eldest of the three sons of Uzziel (the son of Kohath and grandson of Levi), and consequently the cousin of Aaron (Exod. vi, 22). He, with his brother Elzaphan, at the command of Moses, carried out the bodies of Nadab and Abihu to burial (Lev. x, 4). B.C. 1657. They may thus have been two of those whose defilement by a dead body prevented their keeping the passover at Sinai on the regular day (Numb. ix, 6; see Blunt, *Coincidences*, ad loc.).

2. The second named of the three Hebrew youths (Dan. i, 6) trained along with Daniel at the Babylonian court (Dan. i, 11), and promoted to the rank of magi (Dan. i, 19). Having assisted Daniel in solving the dream of Nebuchadnezzar (Dan. ii, 17), they were advanced to civil dignities (Dan. iii, 12); but were afterwards cast into the blazing furnace for refusing to worship the royal idol; and, being miraculously delivered from it, they were still more highly honored by the king (Dan. iii, 13–30). His Chaldæan name was MESHACH (Dan. i, 7). B.C. cir. 580.

3. One of those (apparently chief Israelites) who supported Ezra on the left hand while reading the law to the people after the captivity (Neh. viii, 4). B.C. 410.

Mi′shal (Heb. *Mishal′*, מִשְׁאָל, prob. *entreaty;* Sept. Μισαλά), a city of the tribe of Asher (Josh. xix, 26, where it is Anglicized "Misheal"), assigned to the Levites of the family of Gershom (Josh. xxi, 30); elsewhere called MASHAL (1 Chron. vi, 74). It is doubtless the *Masan* referred to by Eusebius (*Onomast.* s. v. Μασάν) as situated on the Mediterranean, near Carmel, a position with which the text (Josh. xix, 26) agrees (see Keil, *Comment.* ad loc.). It is probably the modern ruined village *Misalli*, near the shore about three miles north of Athlit (Van de Velde, *Memoir*, p. 335).

Mi′sham (Heb. *Misham′*, מִשְׁעָם, according to Gesenius, *their cleansing* or *their beholding;* according to Fürst, *madness;* Sept. Μισαάλ, Vulg. *Misaam*), one of the sons of Elpaal, of the tribe of Benjamin, mentioned as the rebuilders of Ono, Lod, and their suburbs (1 Chron. viii, 12). B.C. post 1612.

Mish'eäl (Josh. xix, 26). See MISHAL.

Mish'ma (Heb. *Mishma'*, מִשְׁמָע, *hearing*, as in Isa. xi, 3; Sept. Μασμά), the name of two men.

1. The fifth of the twelve sons of Ishmael, and heads of Arabian tribes (Gen. xxv, 14; 1 Chron. i, 30). B.C. considerably post 2061. The people called by Ptolemy *Mæsæmanes* (vi, 7, 21, Μαισαιμανείς), who were located to the north-east of Medina, were probably descended from him. Arabic writers mention the *Beni-Mismah* (Freytag, *Hamas*, II, i, 220), but nothing is known of them (Knobel, *Genes.* ad loc.). See ARABIA.

2. The son of Mibsan, of the tribe of Simeon, and father of Hamuel (1 Chron. iv, 25, 26). B.C. considerably ante 1053.

Mishman'nah (Heb. *Mishmannah'*, מִשְׁמַנָּה, *fatness*; Sept. Μασμάν v. r. Μασμανά), the fourth of the Gadite braves who repaired to David in the wilderness of Adullam (1 Chron. xii, 10). B.C. cir. 1061.

Mishna (Heb. מִשְׁנָה, *Mishnáh*), the code of Jewish laws arranged about the year A.D. 200 or 220, at Tiberias, in Palestine, by R. Jehudah, surnamed Hakkadosh (q. v.). The title is by some understood as importing "second," like מִשְׁנֶה in Gen. xliii, 23, the rabbinical code being second or next to the Pentateuch; it is so interpreted in the rabbinical lexicon *Schulchan Aruch*, but we think it is more likely derived from שָׁנָה, *to study*, also *to teach*, which perhaps at first meant only "to repeat." In the Talmud (q.v.), quotations from the Mishna are introduced by the Aramaic word תְּנַן, *Tenan*, i. e. *we have studied*; and the book itself is called מַתְנִיתִין, *Mathnithin*; while the rabbins who lived before the publication of the Mishna are spoken of as תַּנָּאִין, *learners*, or perhaps *teachers*; and their sayings, not found in that collection, are quoted תְּנָיָא, "it was learned or taught." The version "learners" for Tannain is not unnatural, as the Heb. official name for Rabbins is תַּלְמִידֵי חֲכָמִים, *disciples of the wise*. The sons of R. Jehudah are named among the Tannain, and they most probably assisted in the completion of the work of the Mishna.

The sayings recorded in the Mishna reach back to the times of Simon the Just, a contemporary of Alexander the Great; and it expounds also some religious and political usages introduced by Ezra; but the bulk of the book is made up of the decisions or opinions of the rival schools of Hillel and Shammai, who arose at the beginning of the 1st century of the Christian æra, and of the subsequent teachers, who followed generally the rulings of Hillel's school, and among whom Hillel's descendants were prominent. In a few instances a case (מַעֲשֶׂה) is stated to have arisen, and the decision of the Sanhedrin (q. v.) upon it, or of some prominent rabbi, is given; very often the names of the teachers who taught any particular point are mentioned, even where no disagreement is spoken of; but much oftener in cases of disagreement. Still oftener, however, the text of the law appears without any one to propound it: these parts of the Mishna are ascribed to R. Meir, who flourished about A.D. 145, and it is therefore probable that R. Meir made an older collection, of which the Mishna as now found is only an enlargement.

The authority for the laws of the Mishna is best explained in the first section of the first chapter of its treatise, אָבוֹת (Aboth, fathers): "Moses received the law from Sinai, and handed it over to Joshua, and Joshua to the elders, and the elders to the prophets, and the prophets to the men of the Great Synod" (the companions and followers of Ezra down to about B.C. 300). The meaning hereof is, that Moses received not only the written law from God, but also certain rules for its construction and application; and that even in the most corrupt times

of Israel's history there were always some pure and holy men, who kept up the study of this tradition, and handed it over unbroken to their successors. Moreover, it was inferred from Deut. xvii, 9 that the supreme judges for the time being might make authoritative decisions on facts as they arose; and that these decisions must serve as precedents for the future, unless reversed by a court of "greater wisdom and greater number." The words "priests and Levites" in that verse were construed by the Pharisees merely to indicate the place at which the supreme judges must hold their sessions. The rules of construction of the Pentateuch are stated as thirteen, among which the foremost are קַל וָחֹמֶר, *Kal ve-chomer*, *a minori ad majus*, and גְּזֵרָה שָׁוָה, *Gezerah shavah*, "like decision." The latter, however, rests generally on the arbitrary comparison of the same word in two wholly disconnected passages, and is not allowed unless tradition itself sanction it. Besides these rules of construction, certain ceremonies in their full form were also believed to have thus been handed down, while the letter of the law only hinted at the manner of performing them. Thus Exod. xiii, 9, 16; Deut. vi, 10; xi, 18, command the tying of those respective passages to the hand and between the eyes of the Israelite; but tradition supplied the manner of doing it, that is, the construction of the phylacteries. The second section of the above-quoted chapter proceeds: "They (the men of the great synod) said three things: . . . make a *fence to the law*." That is, put around the law a wall of restrictions and injunctions, which the Israelite will have to break through before he feels tempted to break the law itself. This was, in fact, done to a great extent by the teachers whose sayings are recorded in the Mishna. Many of their so-called גְּזֵרוֹת (decisions)—a name given to the extra-Mosaic laws—refer to a stricter observance of the Sabbath, and these are comprehended under the name of שַׁבּוּת, which decisions Selden renders *Sabbathismus*; forbidding, for instance, the handling on the Sabbath of anything that has been unlawfully made on that day; the causing a Gentile (unless in case of necessity) to work on the Sabbath for the Israelite; to play musical instruments on that day, etc. Others refer to Levitical cleanness; among these are numberless rules about the washing of hands, of cups, etc., at the ordinary meals, in imitation of the rules which the Aaronitic priesthood had to observe at their sacrificial meals. It was principally by these observances that the followers of the rabbins, whom Christian writers generally denote as the Pharisaic sect, but who called themselves חֲבֵרִים (companions), distinguished themselves not only from the Sadducees (q. v.), but also from the indifferent mass, who are known in the Mishna as עַם הָאָרֶץ (people of the land), and are often spoken of with a great deal of bitterness.

The writers of the Mishna never seek to make their readers believe that a rabbinical ordinance, which is intended only as a part of the fence around the law, is of divine origin; but where doubt can arise about the meaning, they expressly show what is intended for a construction of the law, and what is their own addition, often by the words פָּטוּר (free; that is, not liable to stripes for a wilful offence, or to a sin-offering for offence through ignorance or forgetfulness); yet אָסוּר (forbidden). In the very first section of the first chapter of the Mishna—where the question arises how late at night the passages Deut. vi, 5–10; xi, 13–21, may be read in fulfilment of the command to speak of them "when thou liest down," we find: "The learned (חֲכָמִים —as opposed to any one rabbi by name) say until midnight; and rabbi Gamaliel said until the morning dawn; in fact, when his sons came home from a feast, and told him We have not read the Shemâ (Hear, O Israel), he told them, As the morning has not dawned, you should read it; not this only, but wherever the wise have said until midnight, the command reaches to dawn, etc.; and why have they said till midnight? in order to keep man from transgression."

The style of the Mishna is, with very few exceptions, dry and crowded, with not a word to spare; and the book is written for men who already know the great principles of which they only seek the details. Historical or legendary notices are rare; and the few dogmatic passages—for instance, the chapter about a future life—run in the same style as if they were given for the guidance of an ordinary court of justice; the chapter, Who has no share in the world to come? follows naturally upon the chapters, Who are to be hanged? Who are to be stoned? A few instances will be given below.

The language of the Mishna is in the main not Aramaic, but Hebrew; stripped, however, of all that is idiomatic about Hebrew, such as the use of the conversive vav, and filled with many Aramaic forms, such as the masculine plurals in רִין for the truly Hebrew רִים. That the people of Palestine generally spoke pure Aramaic as early as the days of Christ, and even long before, is well enough known from other sources; but the Mishna attests it by quoting terse sayings in that language, e. g. כְּפוּם צַעֲרָא אַגְרָא—"like the toil. is the reward." A very large number of Greek words are also found: thus אסטניס (ἀσθενής) is always put for "sickly;" לסטים (λῃσταί) for "robbers." Latin words also occur, but not so frequently, and generally in a somewhat corrupt form, while the Greek words are rendered about as exactly as the Hebrew alphabet will allow. (Comp. Bondi, אוֹר אֶכְתֵּר, Beleuchtung der in Talmud. v. Babylon u. Jerusalem, in d. Targumim u. Midraschim vorkommenden fremden, besonders lateinischen Wörter [Dessau, 1812, 8vo]; Hartmann, Supplementa [Rost. 1813, 4to]; especially his Thesaurus linguæ Hebraicæ e Mishna augendæ [3 pts. 1825–26, 4to]).

We proceed to give an analysis of the Mishna, keeping strictly to it, and leaving out of view anything that may be taught by the Tannain, but which is regarded as בָּרַיְתָא, Baraytha, i. e. "outside," although known to be sayings of these teachers, because they are not collected in the Mishna, and simply occur either in quotations in the Talmud or elsewhere.

The Mishna is divided into six parts (סְדָרִים, Sedarim, arrangements), which contain 62 treatises (מַסָּבוֹת, Massakoth), and 514 chapters (פְּרָקִים, Perakim). The latter, again, are divided into numbered sections, each of which is called a Mishna. The great parts and the treatises are named after their contents, the chapters after their opening words. (The figures set after each treatise show its number of chapters.)

i. The first part—זְרָעִים, Zerâ'im, seeds—contains eleven treatises. The first of these—בְּרָכוֹת, Berakoth, benedictions (9)—treats of the reading of the Shemâ (see above), daily prayers, and grace before and after meals, the purgations to be made as a preparation for prayer, and like subjects. The ten other treatises refer to the laws of the field and of its produce: פֵּאָה, Peah, corner (8), treats of the field corners, gleanings, etc., to be left to the poor; דְּמַאי, Demai, doubtful (7), of corn or fruits coming from the indifferent, who might have failed to tithe it; כִּלְאָיִם, Kilayim, mixtures (9), of the prohibited mingling of fruit and grain crops on the same field or vineyard, and incidentally of the forbidden mixture of wool and flax in garments (Lev. xix, 19); שְׁבִיעִית, Shebi'ith, seventh (10), of the Sabbatic year; תְּרוּמוֹת, Terumoth, tributes (11), of the tributes from the crop, which were due to the Aaronitic priests, including the tithe of tithe due them from the Levites; מַעַשְׂרוֹת, Ma'aseroth, tithes (5), of the tithes due to the Levites; מַעֲשֵׂר שֵׁנִי, Ma'aser Sheni, second tithe (5), of the tithe which was

eaten or otherwise spent in the joy of the yearly feasts, but which in the third year was given to the poor; חַלָּה, Challah, dough (4), refers to the tribute from the baking-trough, which was given to the priests; עָרְלָה, 'Orlah, literally foreskin (3), of the forbidden fruits of the trees in Palestine during the first three years of their growth (Lev. xix, 23); בִּכּוּרִים, Bikkurim, first-fruits (4), treats in its first three chapters of the first-fruits which were to be brought to the tabernacle and given to the priests (Deut. xxvi, 5), while the fourth chapter is only added to it to bring it to the close of one of the six great parts, and is called Ἀνδρόγυνος, androgynos, spelled in Hebrew אנדרוגינוס, the man-woman, and contains a few laws as to persons of doubtful sex.

ii. The next great division, מוֹעֵד, Mô'ed, season, contains twelve treatises. The first, שַׁבָּת, Sabbath (24), treats of the duties of that day; remarkable for the enumeration of thirty-nine different kinds of work, by each of which, separately, the guilt of Sabbath-breaking may be incurred. Of each kind a type is given, to which many other actions may be compared as falling within the same reason. A very great proportion of the treatise is taken up with the laws of mere "Sabbathismus" (see above). The next treatise, עֵרוּבִין, 'Erubin, mingling (10), deals with those ceremonies by which the Sabbath boundary was extended, "mingling" a whole town into one fictitious yard, so that carrying within it should not be unlawful; or how the Sabbath boundary of a town, within which one might walk on the Sabbath-day, can be extended. Then comes פְּסָחִים, Pesachim (10), which relates to the Passover, and all things connected with its celebration; שְׁקָלִים, Shekalim, shekel-pieces (8), about various tributes, going to the Temple, and various rites in it, at different seasons of the year; יוֹמָא, Yoma, the day (8), on the service of the day of Atonement; סוּכָּה, Sukkah, hut (5), about the hut and festival bunch of the Feast of Tabernacles, and the rules about reading the Psalms of Praise (cxiii–cxviii) on that and other feasts; בֵּיצָה, Bêtsah, egg (5), so called from its first word. An egg laid on a feast-day, the school of Shammai says, may be eaten; the school of Hillel says, may not be eaten (i. e. on the same day)—this being one of the very few cases in which the latter school is stricter than the other. It is not pretended that "guilt" under the law is incurred by eating fresh-laid eggs on holidays. The treatise deals mostly with what may or may not be done on the great holidays in the preparation of food, actions which on the Sabbath would be clearly unlawful. Next, ראֹשׁ הַשָּׁנָה, Rosh Hash-shanah, New-year (4), gives the laws of the feast which goes by that name among the later Jews, but which in the Bible (Lev. xxiii, 24) is called the first of the seventh month; it also teaches how to fix the days of new moon. The treatise תַּעֲנִית, Ta'anith, fast (4), refers principally to the prayers for rain, and to the fasts, private and public, that were kept in years of drouth; מְגִלָּה, Megillah, the scroll (4), refers to the feast of Purim, the reading of (the scroll of) the Book of Esther, then of the reading of the Pentateuch and Prophet lessons, and denounces as heretical certain variations in the liturgy and certain spiritual modes of construing passages of the law; for instance, "He who takes the law of incest figuratively should be silenced;" that is, he who extends it to the disgracing his father or mother. This passage is evidently directed against the early Christians, and their modes of teaching. The treatise מוֹעֵד קָטָן, Mô'éd Katan, small holiday (3), treats mainly of the mourning rites, these being forbidden on all feasts, even on the half-holidays between the first and last day of Passover and of the Feast of Huts; while the last treatise, חֲגִיגָה, Chagigah, feasting (3), speaks of the voluntary sacrifice—other than the Paschal lamb—offered by the individual Jews on the great feasts.

iii. The third part of the Mishna is called נָשִׁים, Nashim, women, and embraces seven treatises. The first of these, יְבָמוֹת, Yebamoth, Levirate (16), discusses the law found in Deut. xxv, 5–9. Its first section may give a good idea of the manner of the Mishna: "Fifteen women free their rival wives and their rival's rivals from the 'shoe-pulling' (Deut. xxv, 9) and brother's marriage to the world's end: his daughter (the dead brother's wife being the daughter of a surviving brother), son's daughter or daughter's daughter; his wife's daughter, wife's son's daughter, or wife's daughter's daughter; his mother-in-law, mother-in-law's mother, father-in-law's mother; his sister on the mother's side, mother's sister or wife's sister, and the wife of his brother by the mother's side, and the wife of his brother, who was not alive at the same time with him, and his daughter-in-law; all these free their rival wives," etc. (that they are free themselves is taken for granted). The treatise כְּתוּבוֹת, Kethuboth (13), discusses the prescribed marriage contracts and marital rights in general, and shows a much higher regard for the rights of wives and daughters than most, if not all, ancient codes of law; נְדָרִים, Nedarim (11), treats of vows, and contains some of that harsh casuistry which meets with rebuke in the New Testament; נָזִיר, Nazir, the crowned (9), of the special vow of the Nazarite (Numb. vi, 2); סוֹטָה, Sotah, the erring woman (9), of the ordeal for wives suspected of faithlessness (Numb. ch. v). The last chapter of this treatise relates the gradual decay and downfall of national and religious life in Israel from the times of the early Maccabees; it foretells the signs of the approaching Messiah, and winds up with setting forth the qualities that lead upwards to eternal life. The next treatise, גִּטִּין, Gittin, divorce-bills (9), is set apart to the law of divorce; and קִדּוּשִׁין, Kiddushin, betrothals (4), the last of this great division, to the laws of the marriage ceremony. But a great part of it is taken up with counsels as to the trade or profession in which an Israelite should bring up his son; and many occupations are named which unmarried men should not follow, on account of the great facilities they offer for unchaste practices.

iv. The fourth grand division is styled נְזִיקִין, Nezikin, injuries, and most of the ten treatises contained in it deal with the principles and the practice of civil and criminal law. The first three treatises, each of ten chapters, are called by Aramaic names — בָּבָא קַמָּא, Baba Kamma, the first gate, i. e. court; בָּבָא מְצִיעָא, Baba Metsi'a, the middle gate; בָּבָא בַתְרָא, Baba Bathra, last gate—and discuss the laws between man and man in matters of property, that are deducible from the Pentateuch, or had been suggested by experience. In the "first gate" the law of bailment is taught, without being involved in the obscurities of the degrees of negligence which the Roman lawyers have thrown around it; the only principle recognised is, What was the intent of the bailor when he made the loan, or pledge, or deposit of his goods? against what dangers did he intend to secure them? what risks did he intend to take? The text in Exod. xxii, 6–14 shows that even a depositary without hire is liable for theft, though not for forcible robbery; for that the goods should not be stolen was the very object of the deposit. The same general doctrine prevailed in the English law, till lord Holt, chief justice during the reign of queen Anne, disturbed it by views imported from Roman jurisprudence. The measure of damages for assault and bodily injuries is also given, and the "eye for eye" of the sacred text is construed as meaning only damages in money for the lasting injury; while an additional allowance must be made for loss of time, cost of cure (Exod. xxi, 19), pain and disgrace—this

last element of damages being derived from the "cutting off the hand" in Deut. xxv, 21, which is taken figuratively only. The fourth treatise is named סַנְהֶדְרִין, Sanhedrin (i. e. Συνέδρια), courts of justice (11). The first two chapters set forth the constitution of the Jewish commonwealth, rather as the Pharisaic party would have wished to see it, than as it ever was, with all the great powers, political and judicial, in the hands of the supreme court of seventy-one learned judges; and both the high-priest and king as figure-heads. Of the latter it is said, "The king does not judge, and none judges him; does not testify, and none testifies concerning him." The practice in criminal cases is minutely set forth; while cases of bailments or trespasses, arising under the peculiar Mosaic law, were to be tried by three judges, and ordinary commercial cases even by a single judge; criminal charges must be tried before courts composed of twenty-three members. The forms were analogous to those of England and America—that is, based on the idea of accusation and defence, not of inquiry and confession. No person once acquitted could be retried, but all facilities were given, to the last moment, to establish the innocence of the convicted, either on points of law or fact. The modes of capital execution are also given—stoning and burning in such a way as to cause instant death. Among the chapters which begin, "The following are stoned," "The following are hung," we find also one which begins thus, "The following have no share in the world to come: he who says, The resurrection is not found in the law, or the law is not from heaven, and the Epicurean (materialist)." The next treatise, מַכּוֹת, Makkoth, stripes (3), treats of the punishment of false witnesses, and of crimes punishable by stripes; then comes שְׁבוּעוֹת, Shebu'oth, oaths (8), about the decisive oath in civil causes; there was no other oath, as witnesses always testified without oath under sanction of the commandment not to bear false witness. The admission and forms of testimony are then discussed in עֵדְיוֹת, 'Edayoth, testimonies (8). Then comes עֲבוֹדָה זָרָה, 'Abôdah Zarah, idolatry (5), showing what manner of intercourse with idolaters and what things connected with idolatry are forbidden to the Israelite; for instance, the use of wine handled by a Gentile; for he might have made an idolatrous libation of it. The next treatise, אָבוֹת, Aboth, fathers (5), contains the collected wisdom of the "fathers," which name here, but nowhere else, is bestowed upon the sages of the Mishna. The whole of it, with a good English translation, can be found in the common (orthodox) Jewish prayer-book [see LITURGY], where a sixth chapter of somewhat later origin is added. The treatise opens, as above stated, by bringing the tradition down from Moses to the Great Synod; it then carries it from (1) Simon the Just, one of its last survivors, to (2) Antigonus of Socho, who taught to despise reward, and is said to have given rise to the Sadducæan heresy; (3) Jose of Zeredah and Jose of Jerusalem; (4) Joshua, son of Perahiah, whom later legends, by an anachronism, describe as the teacher of Jesus, and Nittai the Arbelite; (5) Jehudah, son of Tabbai, and Simeon ben-Shetah, the reformer of the criminal and civil law, and defender of religion and liberty against the tyranny of king Jannæus; (6) Shemaiah and Abtalyon, said to be of convert descent; (7) Hillel and Shammai, the founders of the great rival schools; (8) Johanan, or John, the son of Zaccai; (9) Gamaliel, known as the teacher of Paul, and seemingly a son or grandson of Hillel; (10) Simeon, his son; (11) Gamaliel, the son of Simeon; (12) Jehudah Hakkadosh, the compiler of the Mishna. The "couples" in this chain are generally thought to consist of the president and vice-president of the Sanhedrin for the time being, called respectively נָשִׂיא (prince) and אָב בֵּית דִּין (father of the court). The treatise contains the favorite moral and dogmatic sayings of these and other rabbins. Many of them are merely practical rules of life; some address themselves to judges; but more of them exhort to the study of the law, and still more to good works. The future world is much referred to; and one rabbi Jacob (ch. iv, § 21) says, in the spirit of the early Christians. "This world is the anteroom to the coming world; prepare in the anteroom, that thou mayest enter the banqueting-hall" (triclinium). But the study of the law and good works (מִצְוֹת, Mitzvoth, commandments), and not faith, is recommended as the road to future happiness. Elsewhere unbelief is denounced as forfeiting the world to come; but it seems that in the present treatise this tenet was not insisted on. A very remarkable point is the endeavor (ch. v, § 9) to reconcile the philosophic view of unchangeable laws of nature with the Biblical account of miracles: "Ten things were created in the twilight of the eve of Sabbath (of creation week)—that is, the mouth of the earth (which swallowed Korah), the mouth of the well (in the wilderness), the mouth of Balaam's ass, the rainbow, the manna, the rod (of Moses), the diamond worm (said to have cut the stones for the Temple), the alphabet, the writing (on the tables), and the tables." The last treatise of this part is הוֹרָיוֹת, Horayoth (3), concerning forms of trial.

v. The fifth grand division, קָדָשִׁים, Kodashim, with its eleven treatises, relates mostly to sacrifices, and was obsolete when the Mishna was composed. The very full treatment given to this subject shows how strong were the hopes of a speedy restoration. We have here זְבָחִים, Zebachim, slaughtered offerings (14); מְנָחוֹת, Menachoth, offerings made of flour (13), whose subject is indicated by their title, though somewhat more is comprised in them. But the next treatise, חוֹלִין, Cholin, unsanctified things (12), treats of the food allowed or disallowed to the Jew; especially of the mode of slaughtering beasts and fowls, and of the marks of disease, which render the eating of their flesh unlawful. We have then בְּכוֹרוֹת, Bekoroth, (sacrifices of) first-born animals (9); עֲרָכִין, 'Erakin, estimates (9), i. e. for redeeming consecrated men or beasts in money, according to the standard laid down in Leviticus (ch. v and xxvii); תְּמוּרָה, Temurah, exchange (7), referring to the exchange of tithe beasts; כְּרִיתוֹת, Kerithoth, excisions (6), which teaches what sins are threatened with the punishment, "That soul shall be cut off from its people." This treatise is put in this connection because most of the sacrifices dealt with in this division are penances for sin. It is followed by מְעִילָה, Me'ilah, (the sacrifice for) embezzlement (6), see Lev. v, 15; and תָּמִיד, Tamid, daily sacrifice (7), whose titles express their main subjects. The latter closes with the list of the psalms that were sung by the Levites in the Temple on the seven days of the week: Sunday, Psa. xxiv; Monday, Psa. xlviii; Tuesday, Psa. lxxxii; Wednesday, Psa. xciv; Thursday, Psa. lxxxi; Friday, Psa. xciii; on the Sabbath, of course, Psa. xcii. The next treatise, מִדּוֹת, Middoth, measures (5), gives an exact description of the Herodian temple, and of all its appointments. The division closes with the rather mystical treatise, קִנִּים, Kinnim, nests (3), which discusses the law on birds' nests (Deut. xxii, 6).

vi. The last grand division, טָהֳרוֹת, Tohoroth, cleanness, is the largest of all, though it was also in most of its parts useless when the Mishna was written: as the right to enter the Temple or to eat of sanctified food (respectively to be eaten as sanctified food) are the main tests of technical cleanness. We find here twelve treatises: כֵּלִים, Kelim, vessels (30); אֹהָלוֹת, Ohaloth, tents (18), the latter of which treats of the communication to a house and to its contents of uncleanness by the presence of a dead body in it. This remained of interest to the Aaronitish priests, who must not defile themselves with a dead body other than of their next blood

relations; which law is supposed to remain in force notwithstanding the disuse of sacrifices. Then comes נְגָעִים, Nega'im, plagues (14), about leprosy; פָּרָה, Parah, the cow (12), the ashes of which were used to purge the defilement by the touch of the dead (Numb. xix, 2); טָהֳרוֹת, Tohoroth, here in the sense of purification (10); מִקְוָאוֹת, Mikvaoth, bathing-cisterns (10), which retain an interest beyond the Holy Land, and beyond the times of the Temple, in connection with the next treatise; נִדָּה, Niddah, the separated, i. e. the menstruating woman (10). Then we have מַכְשִׁירִין, Makshirin, what renders fit (to receive uncleanness) (6); זָבִים, Zabim, spermatorrhœa (5); טְבוּל יוֹם, Tibbul Yom, dipping of the (same) day (4), the ablution of vessels in cisterns, which, as a shadow of Levitical cleanness, was kept up in post-templic times; יָדַיִם, Yadayim, hands (4), which refers to the washing of hands, an avowedly rabbinic institution. The last treatise of the whole collection is עוּקְצִין, 'Ukatsin, fruitstems (3), with some unimportant laws about Levitical cleanness; among others, those that relate to fruitstems. At the end is placed a reflection on the blessing of peace, so that the book may close with the favorite verse (Psa. xxix, 11), "The Lord give strength to his people; the Lord bless his people with peace."

The principal commentaries on the Mishna are, of course, the Talmuds—Jerusalem and Babylonian: the former covers the whole work, while the latter omits much of the obsolete parts. But the Mishna, or by the more appropriate phrase מִשְׁנָיוֹת, in the plural (setting aside the singular form for the single section), is found published, without either Talmud, in six volumes, each of which contains one of the great divisions. It is generally accompanied by two running commentaries, both of which take most of their matter from the Talmud; the first of these, by R. Obadiah, of Bartenora, is explanatory; the other, called the Tosephoth (i. e. additions), of R. Yom Tob, of Prague, raises and solves difficulties and seeming contradictions, and was written towards the beginning of the Thirty-Years' War. Maimonides wrote a much more valuable commentary on the Mishna in 1168; but being written in Arabic, and but partially rendered into the rabbinical Hebrew, it is seldom used or seen. The Hebrew abridgment, entitled מִשְׁנֵה תּוֹרָה, or סֵפֶר הַיָּ"ד, i. e. the book of fourteen (books), and divided into four parts, was published at Soncino (1490, 2 vols. fol.): republished at Venice (1524, 3 vols. fol.) and at Amsterdam (1701, 4 vols. fol.). Selections from it were made in English by Bernard, entitled The Main Principles of the Creed and Ethics of the Jews, exhibited in Selections from the Yad Hachazakah of Maimonides, with a literal English Translation, copious Illustrations from the Talmud, etc. (Camb. 1832, 8vo); and an entire version into English made by several writers, under the editorship of E. Soloweyezik, was begun at London (1863, 8vo). Various commentaries in the rabbinical language, of no great merit, written during the 17th and 18th centuries, are printed in the ordinary editions of the Mishna, which are quite cheap. To the Persian Jews the Mishna is the only standard, as the Talmuds are almost unknown among them. (L. N. D.)

Editions of the Mishna.—The principal editions of the Mishna are by (1) Menasse ben-Israel, with short glosses (Amsterd. 1631); (2) Jose ben-Israel (ibid. 1646); (3) Israel ben-Elijah Götz, with Cabalistic Book Jetsira (Venice, 1704, 8vo); (4) with the commentary of Maimonides (Naples, 1492, fol.); (5) do., Mishnaioth in Perush Rambam (Venice, 1606, fol.); (6) and by far the best and favorite edition, by Prof. Surenhusius of Amsterdam, which is furnished not only with the commentaries, but also with a Latin translation. It is entitled, Mischna, sive totius Hebræorum Juris, Rituum, Antiquitatum, et Legum oralium Systema, cum clarissimorum Rabbinorum Maimonidis et Bartenoræ Commentariis in-

tegris, quibus accedunt variorum Auctorum Notæ et Versionis in eos quos ediderunt Codices (Amst. 1668-1703, 6 vols. fol.). The several treatises of the Mishna have also been translated into Latin by different authors, the principal of whom are:

Order.	Treatise.	Translator.	Publication.
I.	Berakoth	Edzard	Hamb. 1713, 4to.
	Peah	Gnisius	Oxf. 1690, 4to.
	Demai	"	"
	Kilaim	"	"
	Shebiith	"	"
	Terumoth	"	"
	Maaseroth	"	"
	Maaser Sheni	Surenhusius.	
	Challah	"	
	Orlah	Ludwig	Leipsic, 1695.
	Bikkurim	"	" 1696.
II.	Sabbath	Schmid & Wotton	" 1670.
	Erubin	" "	
	Pesachim	Surenhusius.	
	Shekalim	Otho	Geneva, 1675.
	Yoma	Sheringham	London, 1648.
	Sukkah	Dachs	Cologne, 1726.
	Betsah	Surenhusius.	
	Rosh-hashanah	Houting	Amsterd. 1695.
	Taanith	Lundy	Cologne, 1694.
	Megillah	Surenhusius.	
	Moed Katan	"	
	Chagigah	Ludwig	Leipsic, 1796.
III.	Yebamoth	Surenhusius.	
	Kethuboth	Faust	Basle, 1699.
	Nedarim	Ulmann	Leipsic, 1663.
	Nazir	"	
	Sotah	Wagenseil	Altorf, 1663.
	Gittin	Surenhusius.	
	Kiddushin	"	
IV.	Baba Kama	L'Empereur	1637.
	Baba Metsia	Surenhusius.	
	Baba Bathra	"	
	Sanhedrin	Cocceius	Amsterd. 1629.
	Makkoth	"	
	Shebuoth	Ulmann	1663.
	Edaoth	Surenhusius.	
	Aboda Zara	Peringer	Altorf, 1680.
	Aboth	Surenhusius.	
	Horioth	Ludwig	Leipsic, 1696.
V.	Zebachim	Ulmann	1663.
	Menachoth	Surenhusius.	
	Cholin	"	
	Bekoroth	"	
	Erakin	"	
	Temurah	"	
	Kerithoth	Ulmann	1663.
	Meïla	Surenhusius.	
	Tamid	Peringer	Altorf, 1680.
	Middoth	L'Empereur	1630.
	Kinnim	Surenhusius.	

VI. Kelim, Ohaloth, Negaim, Parab, Tohorôth, Mikvaoth, Niddah, Makshirin, Zabim, Tibbul Yom, Yadaim, and Ukazin—all by Surenhusius.

The entire Mishna has been translated into Spanish by Abraham ben-Reuben (Venice, 1606, fol.); into German by Rabe: *Die ganze Mischna* (Ausbach, 1760-63, 6 vols. 4to); and by Dr. Jost (Berlin, 1832-33, 6 vols. 4to). Into English have been rendered the treatises *Sabbath* and *Erubin* by Dr. Wotton (Lond. 1718); the treatise *Aboth*, in the *Jewish Prayer-book*, by Young (Edinb.); the treatises *Berakoth, Kilaim, Sabbath, Erubin, Pesachim, Yoma, Sukkah, Yom Tob, Rosh-hashanah, Taanith, Megilla, Moed Katan, Yebamoth, Kethuboth, Gittin, Kiddushin, Cholin,* and *Yadaim,* wholly or in part by De Sola and Raphall (Lond. 1843, 8vo; 2d ed. 1845).

From all this it appears that the Christian Church has been largely identified with a study of the *Mishna,* and that the charge, so frequently reiterated, that Christian theologians are unacquainted with Jewish traditional lore is unjust. Indeed it is very apparent that even the Church fathers were more or less familiar with the Mishna, which they termed δευτερώσεις. Jerome first mentions it (*Epist. ad Algas,* qu. 10): "I cannot declare how vast are the traditions of the Pharisees, or how anile their myths, called by them δευτερώσεις (Mishnaioth); neither would their bulky nature permit the attempt." Epiphanius also says, but with a dislocation of text (*Hær.* xv, Jud.; also *Hær.* xiii, 26): "The Jews have had four streams of those traditions that they term δευτερώσεις—the first bears the name of Moses the prophet; the next they attribute to a teacher named Akiba; the third is fathered on a certain Andon, or Annon, whom they also call Judas [Hannasi]; and the

sons of Apamonæus [Asamonæi] were the authors of the fourth." So, too, Augustine, writing shortly before the date of the Jerusalem Talmud, says: "Besides the Scriptures of the law and the prophets, the Jews have certain traditions belonging to them, not written, but retained in memory, and handed down from one to another. named δευτερώσεις" (c. *Adv. Leg. et Ptoph.* ii, 1); and again, "Deliramento Judæorum ad eas traditionis quas δευτερώσεις vocant pertinentia." In the Middle Ages the gross ignorance of the clergy left this important field unstudied. With the Reformation, the Mishna became again an open book to the Christian clergy; and in modern days many of their number, especially in Germany, Holland, and England, have carefully covered this department of Biblical knowledge. Perhaps exception will be taken to this term by some, but let it be remembered that the Mishna, "as the original text of the Talmud, and as a faithful picture of Jewish theology and ecclesiology in the apostolic and post-apostolic ages, should be known to every Christian student —at least in its general outlines—and a nearer acquaintance with its contents is indispensably required for successful investigation of the Hebrew element in primitive Christianity, as found in the New Testament, and in the New Testament alone" (Rule, *Karaites,* p. 57-58). As to the estimate of this compiled tradition by the orthodox Hebrew, let us refer to a Jewish historian, who, in his eulogy of the Mishna, pronounced it "a work, the possession of which by the Hebrew nation compensates them for the loss of their ancestral country; a book which constitutes a kind of homestead for the Jewish mind, an intellectual and moral fatherland of a people who, in their long discipline of suffering, are exiles and aliens in all the nations of the earth."

The dogmatic and moral teachings of the Tannain are well sketched by Jost in his *Geschichte des Judenthums u. seiner Sekten,* vol. ii. The sketches in Milman's *History of the Jews,* ii, 461 sq., are instructive on some points, though they do not always distinguish between the teaching of the Tannain and of later rabbins. See also Chiarini, *Le Talmude;* Geiger, *Das Judenthum;* Grätz, *Gesch. d. Juden,* vol. iv (transl. N.Y. 1874); Rule, *Karaites,* ch. vi; Etheridge, *Introd. to Hebr. Lit.* p. 114 sq.; the excellent articles on the *Talmud* by Dr. Deutsch in the *Quarterly Review,* Oct. 1867, reprinted in the *Eclectic Review,* 1867; *Christian Remembrancer,* 1868, Oct.; *Amer. Biblical Repository,* 2d series, ii, 261 sq.; Kitto, *Journal of Sacred Lit.* vi, 42 sq.; *Edinburgh Rev.* 1873, July, art. ii; Fürst, *Bibliotheca Judaica,* ii, 40 sq.

Mishneh. See HULDAH.

Mishór, THE (הַמִּישׁוֹר; Sept. Μισώρ, also πεδίνη; Vulg. *planities* and *campestria;* A.V. "the plain"). This word is applied in Scripture to any *plain* or level tract of land, as in 1 Kings xx, 23, and 2 Chron. xxvi, 10; but in a number of passages it is used with the article as the proper name of the plateau of Moab; and when thus employed it is generally Græcized in the Sept. (Deut. iii, 10; Josh. xiii, 9, 16, 17, 21; Jer. xlviii, 8, 21). Stanley brings out the meaning of this word: "The smooth downs (of Moab) received a special name (Mishor), expressive of their contrast with the rough and rocky soil of the west" (*Sin. and Pal.* p. 317); and probably, it might be added, in contrast with the wooded heights and picturesque vales of Gilead. The word comes from the root יָשַׁר, to be *level* or *just,* and is sometimes employed in a moral sense (Psa. xlv, 6; cxliii, 10). Stanley supposes that the whole of the upland downs east of the Jordan are called Mishor, and that this fact fixes the true site of the battle of Aphek (1 Kings xx, 23 sq.). It seems doubtful, however, whether the word Mishor, in the description of that battle, will bear the meaning thus assigned to it. It appears to be simply put in opposition to *harim,* "hills." "Their gods are gods of the *hills,* therefore they were stronger than we, but let us fight against them *in the plain"* (*mishor*). In 2 Chron xxvi, 10, *mishor* also means "a plain" west of the Jordan. As a proper name, or a special appellative, it was given only to the great plateau of Moab, even as distinguished from that of Bashan (Deut. iii, 10). This plateau commences at the summit of that range of hills, or rather lofty banks, which bounds the Jordan valley, and extends in a smooth, gently undulating surface far out into the desert of Arabia. Medeba was one of its chief cities, and hence it is twice called "the Mishor of Medeba" (Josh. xiii, 9, 16). It formed the special subject of the awful curse pronounced by Jeremiah—"Judgment is come upon *the land of the Mishor*" (xlviii, 21). It was chiefly celebrated for its pastures; but it also contained a number of large and strong cities, the ruins of which still dot its surface (Porter, *Damascus*, ii, 183). See MOAB; TOPOGRAPHICAL TERMS.

Mishpat. See EN-MISHPAT.

Mishra. See MISHRAITE.

Mish'raïte (Heb. *Mishraï'*, מִשְׁרָעִי, gentile, used collectively, from some noun *Mishra'*, מִשְׁרָע, perhaps *slippery*; Sept. Ἡμασαραείν v. r. Ἡμασαραΐμ, Vulg. *Maserei*, Auth. Vers. "Mishraites"), an inhabitant of a place called MISHRA, alluded to only in 1 Chron. ii, 53, as founded by the descendants of Caleb, and associated with the Ithrites and others, who were in some way connected with Kirjath-jearim; probably therefore a village in the vicinity of this last town.

Misology (from μισεῖν, to hate, and λόγος, *reason*) is a term employed to designate the hatred of reason—the most unreasonable kind of hatred that can possibly be thought of. But as *reason* is the point of demarcation between man and brute, the misologist generally claims to be opposed only to the false application of the reasoning powers. See REASON.

Misotheia (μισέω, to hate, and Θεός, *God*) is hatred of God and everything divine—hatred of truth, wisdom, virtue, and reason. In classic Greek we only find μισόθεος, hating the gods, godless (Æsch. *Ag.* 1090). Sometimes the word is changed to Θεομίσης, a person hating the gods, and to Θεομίσητος, a person hated by the gods. The *misotheist* is akin to the *misologist.* See MISOLOGY.

Mispe'reth (Heb. *id.* מִסְפֶּרֶת, *enumerating*; Sept. Μαασφαράθ v. r. Μασφαράθ), one who returned from Babylon with Zerubbabel (Neh. vii, 7); elsewhere called MIZPAR (Ezra ii, 2).

Misrachi, Elia, BEN-ABRAHAM (called also *Elia Parnas*), a noted rabbi, flourished at Constantinople towards the close of the 15th century. Misrachi was versed not only in rabbinic lore, but also in astronomy and mathematics. He maintained a lively controversy with his contemporary, Mose Kapsoli, a teacher and judge in the old Romanesque congregation of Jews at Constantinople about 1500, on the question whether the children of Karaites ought to be admitted into the rabbinical schools. Kapsoli denounced the practice as illegal. Misrachi argued not only that it was lawful, but highly expedient, as a means of bringing them to conform to rabbinism. Misrachi labored much in the cause of Jewish education. He died about 1525. Besides his *Chidushim* (חִדּוּשִׁים), a collection of novellas on the *Sepher Mizvoth Gadol* of Moses de Coucy, and a super-commentary on Rashi's Pentateuch (ס׳ הַמִּזְרָחִי, or ס׳) אֵלֶּה מִזְרָחִי עַל הַתּוֹרָה); he wrote also a treatise on arithmetic, מְלֶאכֶת הַמִּסְפָּר; also ס׳ הַמִּסְפָּר, which was translated into Latin by O. Schreckfuchs and S. Münster (Basle, 1546). See Fürst, *Bibl. Jud.* ii, 381; id. *Gesch. d. Karäerthums*, ii, 304; De Rossi, *Dizionario* (Germ. transl. by Humberger), p. 201; Etheridge, *Introd. to Hebr. Literat.* p. 461 sq.; Cassel, *Leitfaden für jüd. Gesch. u. Literat.* (Berlin, 1872), p. 91; Grätz, *Gesch. d. Juden*, viii, 292, 297; Jost, *Gesch. d. Juden. u. s. Sekten*, iii, 127; Lindo's *Conciliator of R. Manasseh ben-Israel* (Lond. 1842), p. xxviii. (B. P.)

Mis'rephoth-ma'im (Heb. *Misrephoth'-Ma'yim*, מִשְׂרְפוֹת מַיִם, *burnings of water;* according to Kimchi, with allusion to warm baths; but, as Gesenius thinks, from lime-kilns or smelting-furnaces situated near the water; Sept. Μασρεφώθ Μαΐν, Vulg. *aquæ Maserephoth*), a place between Zidon and the valley of Mizpeh, whither Joshua pursued the allied Canaanites after the defeat of Jabin (Josh. xi, 8); from which passage, as well as from the only other where the place is mentioned (Josh. xiii, 6), it appears to have been a valley (containing springs or a running stream; see Unger, *De thermis Sidonis*, Lips. 1803), situated in the mountainous region, near the northern border of Canaan, opposite Mount Lebanon; probably therefore in the middle portion of the valley of the Leontes—a position that may have given occasion for the name (i. q. glass-houses by the water side, see Keil, *Comment.* ad loc.) by furnishing facilities for the manufacture of glass (a substance said to have been first invented in this region) from the sand washed down by the stream. Dr. Thomson (*Land and Book*, i, 469) still adheres to a location given by him and Schulz (*Bibliotheca Sacra*, 1855, p. 826) at a collection of springs called *Ain-Mesherfi*, with ruins adjacent on the shore near Ras en-Nakura, at the foot of Jebel Mushakka, on the northern border of the plain of Akka (Van de Velde, *Memoir*, p. 335); but the locality is entirely too far south of Sidon.

Misrepresentation, the act of wilfully representing a thing otherwise than it is. We ought to be careful not to misrepresent the actions of others; and we should, with equal solicitude, avoid any misrepresentations of their words. Verbal misrepresentations may be productive of the greatest injury, and are indicative of radical malevolence. Words, in themselves, and taken in their insulated state, are capable of diverse meanings; and he who reports any impressions without noticing what went before, or what followed after, may easily pervert the most harmless into the most criminal expressions; or cause the foulest inferences to be drawn from the most innocent discourse. What confusion and inquietude in society, what suspensions of confidence, what interruptions of good neighborhood, what bitterness and animosity, are occasioned by verbal misrepresentations! How often has the fondest love been thus blighted, and the warmest friendship turned cold! The perverse construction, the imperfect repetition, or the mutilated statement of what others have said, is one of the common expedients which the artful and treacherous know so well how to employ to serve their own sinister ends, to promote their own interested views, and to produce endless feuds, inextinguishable jealousies, and irreconcilable animosities. As the words of men may thus be misrepresented to serve the most mischievous purposes, it earnestly behooves us, on all occasions, when we repeat the discourse of others, to adhere as closely as possible to the words, and never wilfully to deviate from the sense. We ought to beware of stating that to have been designed as a positive declaration which was intended only as a casual supposition; we are not to represent that as a literal affirmation which was meant only as an incidental illustration, or as a figurative ornament; for it is possible in this way to render an exact copy of the words, and yet a malicious perversion of the sense. But when we report what others have said, and particularly when the interest of the individual is in the least degree concerned in the fidelity of the representation, we are not only to repeat the expressions that were used, but the sense in which they were at the time designed to bear, and which was evident either from the context of the discourse or from the manner of the speaker. See TRUTH.

By subtle queries, invidious remarks, and treacherous insinuations, the slanderer infuses doubt into the mind of one respecting the integrity or the conduct of another; and thus he often effects his purpose with more safety than he could by a more open and direct attack.

Thus he gradually but surely undermines the reputation of his neighbor, or supplants those who seem to stand in the way of his own advancement. As secret is more dangerous than open hostility, so the characters of men are often more irreparably injured by calumnious suggestions than by unreserved and unqualified calumnies. Sometimes slander is covered under the garb of praise, but then the praise is never bestowed except where it is likely to prove injurious to the person, by the aversion which it occasions, or the jealousy which it inflames. We all have many faults, but the slanderer aggravates them by his description. Regardless of adherence to truth, he distorts and magnifies whatever he relates. Where the habit of falsehood, as in the base calumniator, is joined with a malevolent disposition, venial defects are magnified into criminal atrocities; and a trivial speck, almost too small to be noticed, is spoken of as an incurable ulceration. The malevolence of the slanderer is never willing to balance the vices with the virtues, the defects with the perfections of the human character; but he censures and condemns without moderation or indulgence. Men cannot insure the effect which they intend, the issue of their actions, or the success of their exertions. We may deserve, but we cannot command success. Good endeavors and honest efforts are in our power, but the ultimate event is in the hands of God. But when things go wrong, when good endeavors are frustrated, and pernicious effects issue from good principles or meritorious attempts, which could neither have been prevented nor foreseen, then how apt are men to impute the unexpected effect to deliberate contrivance, and to slander the intention which they ought to praise! Thus, those who are ever ready to calumniate what merits praise, impute the good which follows any particular action to chance, and the evil to design. See Fellowes, *Body of Theology*, ii, 324–329. See SLANDER.

Misri-Effendi, a Turkish poet and religious enthusiast, is noted for his attempt at a revolution, under a religious garb, during the reign of Achmet III (1703–1739). Misri was born in Egypt about 1660. Of his personal history but little is known previous to 1693. At this time he was flourishing at Broussa as mollah, an office both of an ecclesiastical and civil character, corresponding somewhat to our "justice of the peace." See MOLLAH. Dissatisfied with the manner in which the war against Austria was conducted, and believing himself inspired for leadership, he gathered about him three thousand fanatics, and with these crossed the Bosphorus, landed at Adrianople, and stormed the great mosque, in which the sultan, with his court, was at the time attending the noon-service. Misri was defeated in his attempt, and he was arrested with his ringleaders and carried back to Broussa. No other punishment was inflicted, because Misri had gained popular favor by his religious enthusiasm. The occurrence of a large fire and a violent earthquake two days after Misri's removal disturbed the popular mind, and it was generally held that Misri had been truthful in his declarations, and he was hereafter regarded as endowed with supernatural visions. The sultan even requested Misri to return; but he refused, declaring his mission finished, as he had accomplished the task of rousing the authorities to more vigorous action towards the Austrians. Hereafter Misri gave himself up to religious studies, and wrote poetry on sacred subjects. The most important of his productions celebrates the *incarnation of Christ*, wherein it is said, "I am always with Jesus, and united with him." These verses, because Misri's production, received the certificate of orthodoxy, but it was ordered also that they be prefaced by these warning words: "Whosoever writes verses like these of Misri shall be committed to the flames; Misri alone shall be spared, for we cannot condemn one who is possessed with enthusiasm." There is little left of the poetical compositions of Misri, and that little is not printed. The patriarch Callinicos, who was in friendly relations with

some eminent Protestant members of the German universities, was Misri's intimate friend. Misri died at Broussa in 1710.

Missabib. See MAGOR-MISSABIB.

Missa Catechumenōrum is the name of that portion of the liturgies of the early Church at which catechumens were permitted to be present. It consisted of the Prefatory Prayer, the Hymn, the Little Entrance, the Trisagion, the Epistle and Gospel, and the Prayers after the Gospel. Before the Great Entrance, or procession of the elements to the altar, all the catechumens were obliged to leave the church, with such words of dismissal as those used in the Liturgy of St. Chrysostom: "As many as are catechumens depart; catechumens depart; as many as are catechumens depart; let none of the catechumens remain." The catechumens being still unbaptized, it was not considered fitting that they should witness the actual celebration of the holy Eucharist, though they were permitted to take part in the earlier prayers of the liturgy, and to hear the reading of holy Scripture. See Bona, *Rer. Liturg.* i, 16; Bingham, *Origines Ecclesiasticæ*, p. 10, 114, 567, 677 et sq.; Riddle, *Christian Antiquities*, p. 192 sq.; Coleman, *Ancient Christianity Exemplified*, p. 110, 180, 185, 415. See CATECHUMENS.

Missa Fidelium, a term for the latter part of the liturgy, as distinguished from that portion at which only catechumens were allowed to be present. See MISSA CATECHUMENORUM.

Missa Præsanctificatōrum is the term applied to a eucharistic office, observed by the advocates of the doctrine of transubstantiation, and in which the great oblation is made and communion administered with elements consecrated at a previous celebration.

The 49th canon of Laodicea (q. v.), which dates from the 4th century, states that bread ought not to be offered during Lent, save on the Sabbath-day and Lord's-day. The 52d canon of the council in Trullo, or Quinisext (A.D. 692), renewed this canon, and ordered the use of the rite of the presanctified every day in Lent except on Saturday, the Lord's-day, and the Feast of the Annunciation. The Greek Church has accepted these regulations, and closely followed them, excepting that the Liturgy of Basil is said on Maundy-Thursday and on Easter eve, instead of the presanctified mass (Neale, *Hist. East. Ch.* pt. i, chap. vii, p. 713). For the rite itself we refer to Goar, *Euchologium;* Neale, *Hist. East. Ch.;* and Renaudot, *Liturg. Or. Collectio* (ed. 1847), i, 76. We have room here only for its essentials, and in presenting these depend chiefly upon Neale, who says that, technically speaking, the office of the presanctified is merely an addition to the usual vespers.

In the prothesis of the Sunday preceding, when reservation is to be made, the priest, having as usual cut and stabbed the first loaf, cuts also the other loaves, saying for each, "In remembrance," etc., as in the usual office. Then he pours forth wine and water in the holy chalice. When he is about to sign the loaves, he speaks in the singular, "Make this bread," because Christ is one. He elevates all the loaves together, and breaks the first loaf of the oblations, and puts the portion in the holy cup, and pours in the warm water as usual. Then taking the holy spoon in his right hand, he dips it in the holy blood; and in the left hand he takes each loaf by turns, and holding the holy spoon that has been dipped in the holy blood, he moves it crosswise on the part where the cross has been made on the crumb, and puts it away in the artophorion. So with the other loaves of reservation. In the rite itself, after the prayers and responses of the three antiphons, while the troparia are sung, the priest goes to the holy prothesis, and taking the presanctified bread from the artophorion, puts it with great reverence on the holy disk, putting also wine and water, after the accustomed manner, into the holy chalice, and saying, not the prayer of prothesis, but only, *Through the prayers of our holy Fa-*

ther, Lord, God, Jesus Christ, have mercy upon us. For the sacrifice is presanctified and accomplished. After the Cathisma, etc., the little entrance takes place without the Gospel; then the prayers of the catechumens, and the prayers of the faithful, in the second of which is, "Behold at the present time his spotless body and quickening blood entering in, and about to be proposed on this mystic table, invisibly attended by the multitude of the heavenly host." Then is sung the hymn, "Now the heavenly powers invisible minister with us, for behold the King of Glory is borne in. Behold the mystic sacrifice, having been perfected, is attended by angels: with faith and love let us draw near, that we may become partakers of life eternal." After this the great entrance is made, but instead of the prayer of the cherubic hymn, the fifty-first Psalm is said. After the entrance, the deacon says, "Let us accomplish our evening supplication unto the Lord. For the proposed and presanctified gifts, let," etc. In the following prayer occur the words, "Look down on us who are standing by this holy altar as by thy cherubic throne, on which thine only-begotten Son and our God is resting in the proposed and fearful mysteries." After further prayers, the priest, the divine gifts being covered, stretches out his hand and touches the quickening blood with reverence and great fear; and when the deacon says, "Let us attend," the priest exclaims, "Holy things presanctified for holy persons." Then, having unveiled them, he finishes the participation of the divine gifts. The communion being finished, and the holy things that remain being taken away from the holy table, the concluding prayers are made.

In the controversy regarding this rite between cardinal Humbert and Nicetas Pectoratus, the only matter of real liturgical interest appears to be Humbert's objection that a double oblation is made of the same thing —first in the liturgy, in which it is consecrated, next in that in which it is received. Neale denies the existence of the second oblation. "The mere fact of the great entrance," he writes, "without any formal oblation, and simply considered, does not involve of necessity a sacrifice."

Leo Allatius, in his tract on this rite (at the end of his work, *De Eccl. Occ. et Or. Perpetua Consensione*), names several variations. One is on the point just mentioned: "Alii sustollebant Præsanctificata. Alii non exaltabant, sed tantum modo tangebant" (1595). Another important variation is, "Constantinopolitanus præsanctificatum panem sanguine non tingit; cæteri tingunt" (1593). Again, as to the times when the rite is used, "Alii, prima et secunda primæ jejuniorum hebdomadis feriis, Præsanctificata non celebrant; alii celebrant" (1594).

In the Roman Church the omission of consecration is limited to Good Friday and Easter eve. The Missal rubric for "Feria v in Cœna Domini" is, "Hodie sacerdos consecrat duas hostias, quarum unam sumit, alteram reservat pro die sequenti, in quo non conficitur sacramentum; reservat etiam aliquas particulas consecratas, si opus fuerit, pro infirmis; sanguinem vero totum sumit; et ante ablutionem digitorum ponit hostiam reservatam in alio calice, quem diaconus palla et patena cooperit, et desuper velum expandit, et in medio altaris collocat."

On Good Friday the reserved host is brought in procession to the altar, after the adoration of the cross, while the hymn is sung, "Vexilla Regis prodeunt." "Cum venerit sacerdos ad altare, posito super illud calice, genuflexus sursum incensat et accedens deponit hostiam ex calice super patenam quam diaconus tenet; et accipiens patenam de manu diaconi, hostiam sacram ponit super corporale, nihil dicens. . . . Interim diaconus imponit vinum in calicem et subdiaconus aquam, quam sacerdos non benedicit, nec dicit super eam orationem consuetam; sed accipiens calicem a diacono ponit super altare nihil dicens; et diaconus illum cooperit palla." After censing the oblations and the altar, the

priest, turning to the people, says as usual, "Orati fratres ut meum ac vestrum sacrificium acceptabile fiat.' "Tunc celebrans . . . supponit patenam sacramento, quod in dextera accipiens elevat ut videri possit a populo; et statim supra calicem dividit in tres partes, quarum ultimam mittit in calicem more solito, nihil dicens. Pax Domini non dicitur nec Agnus Dei, neque pacis osculum datur." The priest's prayer before reception follows. "Et sumit Corpus reverenter." "Deinde omissis omnibus quæ dici solent ante sumptionem sanguinis, immediate particulam hostiæ cum vino reverenter sumit de calice." "Quod ore sumpsimus," etc. "Non dicitur Corpus tuum Domine, nec Post Communio, nec Placeat Tibi, nec datur Benedictio; sed facta reverentia coram altare sacerdos cum ministris discedit; et dicuntur Vesperæ sine cantu; et denudatur altare."

The principle upon which these regulations regarding Lent are founded is that the Eucharist is a feast, and the consecration service is proper only for festivals. The Sabbath as well as the Sunday was a stated feast in the early Church, and the Western Church received the Laodicæan canon; but in later times in the Roman obedience Saturday has been held a fast. Yet Socrates (*E. H.* v, 21) tells us that at Rome they fasted three weeks before Easter, excepting Saturdays and Sundays. See Bingham, *Origines Ecclesiasticæ*, bk. xv, ch. iv, § 12.

For a statement of the position in which the Church of England stands on these questions, see Blunt, *Annotated Book of Common Prayer* (in the notes for Good Friday.)

Missa Sicca, or *dry service*, as it is sometimes called, consists in the recital of the ordinary of the mass without the canon, there being neither consecration nor communion. The rite is described and commented upon by Durandus, *Rationale*, IV, i, 23; Durantus, *De Ritibus*, II, iv; Bona, *Rerum Liturg.* I, xv, 6; Martene, *De Ant. Eccl. Ritibus*, I, iii, 1; Bingham, *Antiq.* XV, iv, 5; Neale, *Eastern Church*, I, vii, 4. "As the canons forbid priests to celebrate the liturgy more than once in the day, except in cases of urgent necessity; and as some covetous and wicked priests were desirous of celebrating more frequently, with the object of receiving oblations from the people; they availed themselves of the *missa sicca*, and thus deceived the people, who intended to offer their prayers and alms at a real commemoration of the sacrifice of Christ" (Palmer). The earliest mention of this abuse is its condemnation in the Capitulars of Charlemagne (Neale), that is, in A.D. 805: the leading example is its practice by St. Louis, who died A.D. 1270. Durantus says that the book *Liber Sacerdotalis*, in which this rite is described, was approved by Leo X; and he finds the Missa Sicca in the passage of Socrates, *Hist.* v, 22, where Leo Allatius finds the rite of the presanctified. The more learned Roman theologians of the 16th century condemned this abuse, and Bona states its general suppression. Neale, however, says that it was common in Belgium as late as A.D. 1780. The rite was never in use in the East, except in Egypt.

Neale has charged the Church of England with deliberately retaining the Missa Sicca, but Blunt (*Dict. of Hist. and Doctrinal Theol.* s. v.) holds that "this charge is without foundation. There is an essential difference between the use of the eucharistic hymns, without which the rite could hardly be called a Missa, and the use of the prayer for the Church militant only, made real, as far as can be, by the offering of alms. The English custom is not an approval of abstaining from communion, such as certainly was more or less implied in the Missa Sicca, but a practical illustration of the words of the priest's exhortation, 'I for my part shall be ready,' and a protest against the remissness of the people." See Palmer, *Origines Liturgicæ*, ii, 164, 165. (J. H. W.)

Missal (Lat. *Missale plenarium*, or simply *Plenarium*) is the name given to an office-book of the Roman Catholic Church, containing the liturgy, i. e. all of the litturgy required for the celebration of the *Mass* (q. v.) or Missa, viz. the fixed *Ordinary* (q.v.), and *Canon* (q.v.), with the changeable *Introits, Collects, Epistles, Gospels,* etc. In the early Western Church it was called *sacramentarium,* but it then contained only parts of what is now comprehended in the *Missal.* Some copies, as required in every parish by the bishops, contained the Gospels, the sacramentary, prayers, prefaces, benedictions, and the canon, the lectionary, a book of epistles, and the antiphon, or, in a word, all that was to be sung by the priest at the altar, and by the ministers in the ambon. These books were called *Plenars* (q. v.), i. e. complete or full; but usually their contents were distributed into separate volumes—the Gradual, Collectar, Benedictional, Hymnar, etc. The complete Missal was requisite when priests, from the 9th century, began to say low masses, and especially for country clergy; as laymen, by the Capitulars of 789, were forbidden to sing the lessons and alleluia, and the priests were required to sing the Sanctus with the people before the canon was commenced. The earliest Frank, Gothic, or Gallican missals, of the 6th century, contained only the portion of the liturgy recited by a bishop or priest—that is, the canon, prayers, and prefaces. At a later date, those of small churches comprised the Introit, Gradual, Alleluia, Tract, Offertory, Sanctus, and Communion, where, although there were a deacon and subdeacon, the smallness of the choir required the celebrant and his two assistants to chant together.

The Missal was probably compiled near the close of the 5th century, was amplified by Gelasius I, and corrected by pope Gregory I. But, although the Missal was contained in the Gregorian rite, it appeared in such varied forms in different churches, and frequently with so many improper additions, that the wish for an emendation became general, and, having been expressed at the Council of Basle, and in 1536 at a synod at Cologne, it was successfully urged at the Council of Trent. During the early part of the council no agreement could be effected. In the eighteenth session a commission was appointed, which, however, could not bring to an end the work intrusted to it; whereupon the council, in the twenty-fifth session, resolved upon recommending to the pope the reform of the Breviary, Missal, and Rituals. As the question was not to create a new liturgy, but to purify the existing one, to restore it to its original simplicity, etc., the work was recommended to be done in Rome. It was commenced under Pius IV, and completed under Pius V. The only members of the commission whose names are known are cardinal Bernardino Scossi and Tomaso Golduelli, bishop of Asaph. Perhaps a great share in the execution of the work may be ascribed to cardinal Sirlet and to the learned Giulio Poggi. The new Missal appeared in 1570; it was followed by two revisions under Clement VIII (bull of July 7, 1604) and Urban VIII (bull of Sept. 2, 1634). It is composed of an introduction, three parts, and an appendix. The introduction gives the calendar, the general rubrics, a summary of the rite, and instructions about possible deficiencies. The three parts are: 1. "Proprium missarum de tempore," with the formularies for the successive solemnities of the year. It treats of all the Sundays, from the first Sunday of Advent to the last after Pentecost. The whole ecclesiastical year pivots around the three capital feast-days: Christmas, Easter, and Pentecost—Easter being the centre. Between the Saturday before Easter and Easter Sunday the Ordo Missal is inserted. 2. "Proprium missarum de sanctis" contains the formularies for the celebration of the mass on particular feasts of saints, etc. This part of the Missal is arranged after the months and days of the civil year. 3. "Commune sanctorum" is a kind of complement of the preceding for such saint-days as have no particular mass-formular in proprium. The division is founded on the character of the saint, and on the order of rank as given by the litany of All Saints. There are mass-formularies for the vigil of an apostle-day, for the days of the martyrs,

within and without the Easter period, for the days of the confessors, the virgins, and of those who did not die in the virginal state. The *Appendix* is very comprehensive: it gives the annual mass, different votival masses, and the masses for the deceased, several benedictions, and, lastly, the masses for such feasts or commemorations as are celebrated in certain places with papal approbation, and called therefore " Missæ ex indulto apostolico."

In the Anglican Church, previous to the Reformation, the missals used varied very greatly; and even after the compilation of the Roman Missal, the English missals known as "Sarum Use," "Hereford Use," "Lincoln Use," "Bangor Use," etc., continued to be general. Near the end of the 16th century, however, the Jesuits succeeded in forcing the Roman Missal into the Romish churches of England. The old missals, before the invention of the art of printing, were generally written in the most sumptuous manner, ornamented with beautiful initials, and most splendidly bound. A kind of large Gothic letters (monachal writing), for the writing of the missals, came into use in the 13th century. After the invention of the art of printing, patterns were cut after these letters, and used for the printing of missals; hence the name of missal letters given to a certain kind of large types. The missal of the Oriental rites differs from that of the Roman Church, each having, for the most part, its own proper form. See Rosarius, *Observationes;* Pisart, *Expositio Rubicarum missalis;* Mohrenius, *Expos. Missæ atque Rubicarum;* Huebner, *Historia Missæ;* Lewis, *Bible, Missal, and Breviary;* Maskell, *Dissert.* ch. iv, p. xlix sq., lxix sq.; Zaccaria, *Bibliotheca Ritualis,* i, 39 sq.; Palmer, *Origines Liturgicæ,* i, 111, 308; Walcott, *Sacred Archæology,* s. v.

Missi Dominici is the name of a class of extraordinary commissaries sent by the Carlovingian dynasties to different parts of their dominions for various purposes of civil and ecclesiastical government. The importance of these officers was vastly increased by Charles the Great, who employed them as an efficacious means of restraining the dangerous power of the dukes; but the importance thus given to these dignitaries having proved under Pepin to be dangerous to royal authority, Charles strove to weaken them, and destroy their power altogether, by transferring their supervisory functions over the jurisdictions of the counts, the administration of the bishops, etc., to the *missi dominici.* The whole empire was accordingly divided into districts (missatica, legationes), coinciding generally with the province of a metropolitan. The missi received special instructions regarding the different points of their mission. So great was the importance the emperor attached to the careful execution of his designs, that to the written instructions always given to his travelling representatives, he frequently added oral explanation and discussion. Thus the missi became the organ by which the central authority managed the administration of the whole empire; and there was, in fact, no part of the affairs of government entirely removed from their competence. Their principal duties were as follows: (1) To see that the laws, both of the State and the Church, were observed. (2) To superintend jurisdiction. In whatever cause or suit there was no decision given by the court, the decision was expected from the missi; they also received complaints against the courts. To that effect they held sessions four times every year in different places. They appointed *meliores et veteriores,* whose duty it was to denounce the crimes, transgressions, etc., that had transpired. (3) To superintend the execution of the laws regarding the army, and to exact the fine of sixty solidi (heribannum) from the defaulters. (4) To generally supervise the possessions of the State and of the Church, and to make registers and descriptions thereof. To carry out these measures the missi held a kind of diet (placita provincia), and at these sessions the superior clergy, the counts, and some other officers, were obliged to appear, under penalty of the heribann. Those who persisted in their refusal were denounced to the king.

The missi were expected to give detailed accounts of their mission at court. In difficult matters, of which they declined to take the responsibility, the decision was left to the king. Every one to whom justice had been denied by the court and the missi had always resort to the king. In order to give the missi sufficient authority, they were allowed the right of imposing the fine of-the heribann; and the disobedient were threatened even with death. Compensations were allowed them for the expenses of their travels. See Franc. de Roye, *De Missis dominicis, eorum officio et potestate;* Neuhauss, *De Miss. domin. ad disciplin. publ.* (Leipsic, 1744, 8vo). (J. H. W.)

Mission is the word used by Roman Catholics, Anglicans, and American Ritualists in a sense somewhat synonymous to the word *Revival* (q. v.). Among Roman Catholics the *Mission* is a series of special services, conducted generally by propagandists, who do not themselves preside over a parish; they are mostly members of a monastic order. The word "Mission" in this sense is of recent use. In the Church of England and the Protestant Episcopal Church the word designates "a series of services in which prayer, praise, preaching, and personal exhortation are the main features, and is intended to call souls to repentance and faith, and deepen the spiritual life in the faithful." The "mission" is conducted in a particular parish, or in a number of parishes at once, directed by the rector, or by some priest experienced in such matters, whom he obtains to aid him. "Its themes are heaven, hell, the judgment, sin, the atonement for sin, God's justice, and God's mercy." "The purpose is the proclamation of the old foundations of faith and repentance to souls steeped in worldliness and forgetful of their destiny, whether they be the souls of the baptized or the unbaptized." The usual period of the year for the "mission" is the season of *Lent* (q. v.). In England it has been the practice for years. A correspondent of the New York *Church Journal* (March 12, 1874), after describing the interest awakened by the mission services in the English metropolis (in 1874), says that the bishops, persuaded by the good results of the propriety of the missions, "have declined to lay down special rules, and trust to the loyalty of the clergy to conduct the mission in accordance with the rules of the Church," and then adds that "the clergy are now too busy with the real work of the mission to discuss the proper pronunciation of 'Amen,' the length of surplices, and the color of stoles." In the United States it has as yet found favor with few of the Protestant Episcopal churches. A serious obstacle is the *Liturgy.* In the mission the largest spontaneity and freedom are allowed. Prayers are extemporaneous. The preaching is pungent and personal. The singing is participated in by the whole congregation, and familiar hymns and tunes are selected. The tendency is towards a general introduction of the "mission" into all Protestant Episcopal churches. *The Church Journal and Gospel Messenger* of Dec. 25, 1873, made a special plea in its behalf, and the Rev. B. P. Morgan has published a book to enlist his Church in revival work. See RETREAT. (J. H. W.)

Mission, Inner. See INNER MISSIONS.

Mission-Priests is the name by which those priests of Rome are designated who have been educated for mission work at home or abroad. There are certain monastic institutions that greatly aid in this work. Indeed, several monastic orders aim particularly at missionary work, e. g. the *Congregation of the Oratory,* the *Congregation of St. Vincent of Paula,* or *Lazarists* (q. v.), the *Congregation of the Sacred Sacraments,* the *Congregation of Jesus and Mary* [see EUDISTS], etc.

Mission-Schools. These are of two kinds.

(1.) The schools aiming to supply the particular want of the missionary before he enters the field, fitting him in his theological studies, and in the knowledge of languages, etc., for the work in view. This class of schools have been but recently organized among the English-speaking people. In Germany they have existed for some time. Usually, however, the course of study is inferior to the university course in theology. English and American schools for missionaries seek to afford the best advantages possible. Several American religious bodies have schools for the training of native missionaries in the country where they are to labor. Thus, for example, the Methodist Episcopal Church has such an institution at Frankfort-on-the-Main. The Church of England has a number of them, particularly in India and Africa. In the United States there are facilities for missionary training provided at Yale College, Boston University, and Syracuse University. The different theological seminaries have lectures on *Missions* and on *Comparative Religion* to aid those preparing for the ministry with a possibility of missionary service.

(2.) Institutions aiming to aid the missionary in propagating Christianity, or seeking to prepare the way by educating the minds of the people, in order that they may be more capable of understanding and appreciating the facts and evidences, the doctrines and duties of Scripture. Another reason for such an education is that it procures means and opens ways of access to the people, and opportunities of preaching to them. "Ignorant of God and his law, as well as of their own, and the moral character of the world; content with mental inactivity, and indifferent to moral elevation; untaught in the principles of science, and fast bound in errors venerated for their antiquity; vicious in their habits, and absorbed in sensual indulgences; accustomed to the profane rites of religions glittering yet grovelling, and degrading yet commanding and terrible—the heathen nations are unprepared to listen to the annunciation of glory to God in the highest, and to appreciate the Gospel as proclaiming deliverance from the dominion of sin and death. . . . The stupidity of the Hottentot, the sensuality of the Hindû, the prejudice of the Mohammedan, the ancestral pride of the 'son of heaven,' and the sottishness of the South Sea Islander, alike interpose a wall high as heaven between the Christian missionary and the child of ignorance" (Dr. Storrs, *Sermon before the A. B. C. F. M. in* 1850). In such circumstances schools become very important as a means of communication with different classes of people, with children and parents, with men and women. Mission-schools, therefore, are a wise and most effective agency in prosecuting the missionary work. They communicate true science, and thus undermine the errors of heathenism; they inspire and foster a love for knowledge, and thus help to overcome the deep debasement of the heathen mind and heart. They conciliate the favorable regards of the heathen, convincing them that the missionary seeks to benefit them, and thus furnish an opportunity for the systematic instruction of youth and children in the principles of Christianity. These mission-schools have been of different grades, according to the circumstances and requirements of the case. *Boys' schools* have usually been found most practicable, especially at the commencement of a mission, and most effective for accomplishing the objects in view. The heathen readily appreciate the value of education for their boys, and both the pupils and their parents are usually found as hearers at preaching services. *Girls' schools* were of necessity a later supply, for these find the strongest prejudices of the heathen to contend with. Woman is of an inferior condition; she is secluded, and no foreigner surely is to have access to her; hence girls' schools are usually established after other schools have succeeded in winning confidence and making the natives understand the true objects of the mission. Indeed, in heathen communities, whenever an attempt was made to establish female schools at the outset of the mission, great prejudice and misapprehension have been the consequence, often seriously embarrassing the progress of all mission work. There is hardly a field occupied for missionary labor but within its territory schools are located and in successful operation. As a rule, female teachers are employed; generally the wives of the missionaries or their lady friends. Of course all missionary workers are Christians, holding a connection with some religious body. The most successful schools are now found in India (see Butler, *Land of the Veda*). In China and Japan there are several in successful operation. In Constantinople, the American Roberts College may be looked upon as a valuable auxiliary of Christian mission work. In Beirut also there is an American college greatly aiding the Protestant cause. In Africa, where the people to be converted are in a very abject state of mind, missionaries have largely availed themselves of educational aids. Many of the most successful mission-workers advocate the building up of schools as a very essential step to progress in converting the heathen world, and to this end missionary societies are founding schools in their respective fields. In the heathen world evidently the secular school supplies the same want that is afforded us in the religious school, better known as the *Sunday-School*. See *American Bible Repository*, xii, 87; *Christian Rev.* v, 580.

Missions. True Christianity is essentially missionary in character. The Gospel having been designed for all nations, and its field being the world, it was from the first associated with means for its own extension. In a highly important sense, the Lord Jesus may be considered the first missionary. He was sent by the Eternal Father to set up his own kingdom upon the earth. The patriarchs, and all faithful priests and prophets among the Jews, were agents preparatory to the introduction of that kingdom. Having called disciples and established a Church, the risen Saviour, before his ascension, commissioned his chosen apostles, in the presence of the great body of the disciples, the then existing Church. To them, as the leaders and representatives of the actual and the prospective Church, he addressed the great missionary command, "Go ye into all the world, and preach the Gospel to every creature."

Christ's mission had been to the Jews. He said, "I am not sent but to the lost sheep of the house of Israel." The apostles were sent to the Jews and Gentiles. "The Acts of the Apostles" is the first official missionary report—the first volume of missionary history; unless, indeed, it rank second, as it is subsequent to the Gospel history of him "who went about doing good." So vast has been the expansion of the missionary enterprise since the outpouring of the Holy Spirit on the day of Pentecost, and so voluminous have become its records, that this article is of necessity limited to a very brief sketch of the subject as a whole. Nevertheless, the design of the article is to give, in the briefest practicable space, a just and duly proportioned view of the principal missionary agencies of successive periods, and some indication of their results, together with references to the sources of more detailed information.

There are two leading modes of studying the subject of missions. The first regards primarily the agencies employed, following them to their different fields of action. The second contemplates in succession the several fields, where necessarily it gives attention to the different agencies employed upon them. Each mode has some peculiar advantages, as well as defects or difficulties, and both are essential to a full comprehension of the subject. They will consequently be followed in the order named. As a natural guide to study and help to memory, the order of time will be followed in the survey of missionary agencies.

I. *Apostolic Missions.*—It is safe to affirm that no just or adequate comprehension of the New-Testament history can be gained by any one who does not read or study it from a missionary point of view. But when, in the light of their great commission, the apostles are regarded as Christian missionaries going forth to evangelize the nations, not only the narrative of their *Acts* or doings, but their epistles to the churches which they planted and trained, become instructive, both as to their

modes of proceeding, their difficulties, and their successes.

Paul, as the apostle to the Gentiles, stands forth in deserved prominence as a model missionary. Although originally a relentless persecutor of the Christians, he experienced a thorough spiritual conversion, and thus became "a new man in Christ Jesus." Having been called of God to be an apostle or missionary of Jesus Christ, he "conferred not with flesh and blood," he "counted not his life dear unto him," but went forth preaching the everlasting Gospel wherever he could find hearers, encountering perils of robbers, perils by his own countrymen, perils by the heathen, perils in the city, perils in the wilderness, and perils among false brethren (2 Cor. xi, 26); nevertheless winning souls to Christ, rescuing communities from paganism, founding churches, training ministers, and at length finishing his course with joy, having won both the martyr's crown and the crown of eternal life. Until the consummation of all things, the study of Paul's missionary character, travels, and labors, will be a standard and profitable topic for all who desire to comprehend the true principles, agencies, and measures of Christian propagandism. In the subsequent history of the Church it will be found that all departures from the spirit of his example have been aberrations from the line of true success; whereas efforts put forth from similar motives and in a like spirit have been invariably attended by the divine blessing and the salvation of men.

But although prominent as the founder of the infant Church in the principal cities of the Roman empire, and although, for some wise but not easily comprehended reason, his successive missionary journeys chiefly occupy the sacred narrative, yet Paul was only one of the noble band of apostolic missionaries. Peter was the acknowledged leader of the opening mission of the infant Church to Jerusalem, and afterwards of missionary efforts in behalf of Jews throughout the world. Not only was he the chief actor in the scenes of the Pentecost, but he laid the foundation for missions to the Gentiles by baptizing the centurion Cornelius and other Gentiles at Cæsarea. According to Origen and Eusebius, he preached to the Jews scattered in Pontus, Galatia, Cappadocia, Asia, and Bithynia. Many scholars have become satisfied that his mission extended to Babylon, on the Euphrates, while the general voice of antiquity ascribes to him a martyr's death at Rome. Whatever may have been true as to his actual presence at those extreme points of the East and the West, his general epistles sufficiently demonstrate his personal acquaintance, as well as ministerial authority, in vast regions intermediate.

Next to that of Peter we recognise the prominence of the apostle John, who, after protracted labors among the Jews in Palestine, took up his abode at Ephesus, from which centre he exercised supervision of the churches of Asia Minor till the period of his exile to Patmos, whence he yet speaks to the churches.

As to the other apostles, neither Scripture nor history gives definite information, but early and uncontradicted tradition assigns them severally to important and widespread mission fields. According to the general voice of antiquity, James the Just remained at Jerusalem. Andrew preached in Scythia, Thrace, Macedonia, Thessaly, and Achaia; Philip in Upper Asia, Scythia, and Phrygia, where he suffered martyrdom. Bartholomew penetrated India. Thomas visited Media and Persia, and possibly the coast of Coromandel and the island of Ceylon. Matthew went to Ethiopia, Parthia, and Abyssinia; Simon Zelotes to Egypt, Cyrene, Lybia, and Mauritania; and Jude to Galilee, Samaria, Idumæa, and Mesopotamia. Whatever of literal truth is embodied in the traditions quoted, they at least show that the grand missionary idea was associated with the history of the several apostles from the earliest period; and, taken in connection with known results, they leave no doubt that the lives of those chosen men were spent in zealous and self-sacrificing efforts for the spread of the Gospel. Nor was this true only of the apostles, but also of the Christian believers of that period generally, who, when even scattered by persecution, "went everywhere preaching the word" (Acts viii, 4). On no other hypothesis than that of universal missionary activity on the part of both ministers and members of the Church of the apostles and their immediate successors, attended also by the divine blessing, is it possible to account for the extensive spread of early Christianity. During the last sixty years of the 1st century the new religion became diffused, to a greater or less extent, throughout the numerous countries embraced in the Roman empire, inclusive of Egypt, Northern Africa, Spain, Gaul, and Britain. As a direct result of the apostolic missions, the Christian Church is supposed to have contained in the year 100 half a million of living members, those of the first and second generations having mostly gone forward to join the Church triumphant.

The churches of the present and the future will find the most important lessons as to their responsibilities and duties in the history of apostolic missions. It may also be said that modern missions, and the comparatively recent development of the missionary spirit, have thrown much light upon the instrumentalities by which Christianity was first established in the earth, and by which it was designed to become universal. From both classes of events it appears that consecrated men and consecrated means are the active agencies to be employed for the establishment of Christ's kingdom upon the earth; and that these combined, under the guidance and blessing of the Head of the Church, may be expected to triumph over the most frigid indifference and the most violent opposition.

In the penury, the obscurity, and the lack of facilities of the early Church, the work of promoting the salvation of men, and of extending the truth, was one of individual and personal exertion, supplemented, of course, by the influence of the Holy Spirit. At first there were no churches for public assembly, no books for auxiliary influence, no organizations for the support of missionaries, home or foreign. Nevertheless, regenerated men went everywhere preaching the word. They founded churches wherever the word was received by believers, and the members of the churches were taught to sustain those who labored among them in the Lord, and also to let the riches of their liberality abound, even out of their deep poverty, for the furtherance of the Gospel. They were also taught the duty of constant prayer, not only for one another, but especially that the word of God might have free course and be glorified, and that God would open to his servants a door of utterance to speak the mystery of Christ (2 Thess. iii, 1; Col. iv, 3). Thus the whole Apostolic Church was an agency for self-extension, and for the propagation of the truth. Though public preaching was practiced to the greatest extent practicable, yet the inference is inevitable that the extension of Christian truth was accomplished largely by means of personal influence in conversation, example, and private persuasion. In this way all could be "helpers of the truth." And by public and private means, united and in constant action, Christianity was diffused, notwithstanding the apparently insuperable obstacles that confronted it on every hand. There is good reason to believe that had the true character of the Apostolic Church been preserved, and its singleness of missionary aim and action been maintained, the development of Christianity in the world would have been constant, if not rapid, and that long ere this the remotest nations would have been evangelized.

II. *Ancient Missions.*—Under this head, allusion will be made to the aggressive movements of the Church between the apostolic and mediæval periods. That the 2d and 3d centuries witnessed great missionary activity on the part of Christians in the countries to which access could be secured, is proved not only by the multi-

plication of their numbers and influence, but by the bloody persecutions that were waged against them under successive Roman emperors. Owing to various causes there have come down to us but few details of the precise work that was done, or of the modes in which it was done. It is, however, but reasonable to suppose that apostolic measures and usages were, during the earlier parts of this period, quite in the ascendant. Eusebius says that "the followers of the apostles imitated their example in distributing their worldly goods among necessitous believers, and, quitting their own country, went forth into distant lands to propagate the Gospel." It was at the beginning of the 2d century that the younger Pliny, governor of Bithynia, after official investigation, made to the emperor Trajan his celebrated report concerning the customs and prevalence of the Christians. Said he, "Many persons, of all ages, of every rank, and of both sexes, likewise are accused, and will be accused [of Christianity]. Nor has the contagion of this superstition pervaded cities only, but the villages and open country." The allegations of this persecutor of Christians, in respect to the numbers accused of Christianity, are corroborated by various statements of Christians themselves. Justin Martyr, writing about one hundred and six years after the ascension, says, "There is not a nation, either of Greek or barbarian, or of any other name, even of those who wander in tribes and live in tents, among whom prayers and thanksgivings are not offered to the Father and Creator of the universe in the name of the crucified Jesus." Tertullian, in his Apology, written fifty years later, says, "Though of yesterday, we have filled every sphere of life: cities, castles, islands, towns; the exchange, the very camps, the plebeian populace, the seats of judges, the imperial palace, and the forum." When it is remembered that these results had been attained in the face of persecution, and in spite of tortures and martyrdom, no other comment is needed upon the missionary diligence and devotedness of those who were the agents of such wide-spread and effective evangelization. In harmony with measures of this character was the translation of the Scriptures into several important languages, as the Latin, the Syriac, the Ethiopian, and the Egyptian. In the absence of statistics, which were then impossible, all attempts to estimate numbers must be chiefly based upon probabilities. Yet some have estimated that the number of Christians at the end of the 2d century was not less than two millions, and increased during the 3d century to perhaps twice that number.

The opening of the 4th century, A.D. 313, witnessed the issue of Constantine's edict of toleration, an event which shows about as conclusively as figures could the continuous growth of Christian influence and numbers. That edict was proclaimed in immediate sequence of the *Æra Martyrium,* the Diocletian persecution—the tenth in the series of those fierce attacks upon the non-offending and non-resisting followers of Christ, which successively proved that "the blood of the martyrs was the seed of the Church." As the edict referred to suppressed official persecution in all parts of the empire, it may be regarded as in itself an unmingled blessing, a recognition of an indefeasible right of humanity, and all that Christianity needed on the part of the world for further advancement and complete success. When the way of the Lord had been thus prepared, through so much toil and suffering, it was to be expected that thenceforward the cause of Christian truth would be advanced with accumulated moral and spiritual power. It is, however, a sad, but, in the history of missions, a usually overlooked fact, that the very period at which so much had been gained, and from which so much was to be hoped in the legitimate extension of Christianity, witnessed the development of agencies and influences that antagonized the peculiar aims of the Gospel and marred its missionary character, sowing throughout the extended field of its influence the seeds of premature and almost fatal decay. The circumstance of these influences being more or less antagonistic to each other did not relieve their evil effect, but rather increased their power, as multiplied diseases sooner reduce the vital energies of the human system. Had there been no previous departures from the true spirit of the Gospel, and had the Christians of the 4th century been content to rely on spiritual agencies for the promotion of Christianity, the advantages which followed the professed conversion of Constantine might in all probability have tended to extend and consolidate a pure type of Christianity. But, unhappily, insidious influences had already been initiated, which, in the sunshine of apparent prosperity, grew with the rankness and rapidity of noxious weeds. Of these influences, allusion can only be made summarily to doctrinal errors, monasticism, and worldly conformity. It was not merely that Docetism, Ebionism, Gnosticism, Montanism, Arianism, and other heresies induced bitter and protracted controversies, thus dividing the Church with partisan strife, but they absorbed the thought and energies of thousands of professed Christian ministers, who ought to have been exclusively engaged in preaching the Gospel. So when, in the 2d century, the doctrine of a Christian priesthood began to be developed with an attempted imitation of the Jewish, the evil was not merely the diversion of ministerial talent from the one work of preaching and teaching in the name of Christ to a burdensome routine of ritual ceremonies, but a direct step towards conformity with certain pagan theories and practices which in later periods were put forward as elements of Christianity itself.

As it has often been asserted, and indeed extensively believed, that the world owes something to monasticism in consideration of certain missionary labors conducted by members of monastic orders, it seems proper to set forth the true bearing of that subject, from which it will appear that monasticism was, in fact, one of the earliest and greatest hindrances to the missionary development of the Church, and that whatever good was subsequently done by missionaries who were monks was done by force of Christian impulse or character, in direct contravention of the spirit and intent of monasticism. It is unnecessary to dwell upon the historic fact that monasticism existed in the far East as a heathen practice anterior to the Christian æra. The first strictly ascetic sect in the Church was that of the Montanists, which arose in Phrygia about A.D. 150, from Montanus, who had been previously a priest of the heathen deity Cybele. During the 2d and 3d centuries a growing disposition manifested itself in the Church to exaggerate the virtue of fasting, and to attach special merit to celibacy, specially among the clergy. Vows of celibacy began to be taken by persons of both sexes, in the idea that such a life was more holy than that of wedlock. About the year A.D. 250 the Decian persecution raged with extreme severity in Upper Egypt, causing many to flee for their lives to deserts and secluded places. Already the minds of many Christians in Egypt had been predisposed to asceticism by the writings of Clement, Origen, and Dionysius of Alexandria. Under a combination of these and similar influences, many persons who ought to have been contending earnestly for "the faith once delivered to the saints" withdrew themselves from society, and wasted their lives in idleness, and in useless struggles with the phantoms of their own excited imaginations. The true spirit of Christianity would have given them courage to face danger, and doubtless have enabled them in many cases to win even their persecutors to the faith. But the impulse of cowardice, whether moral or physical, is contagious; hence multitudes of well-meaning but weak persons abandoned scenes of Christian conflict, and betook themselves to desert solitudes and caves of the mountains. At first they lived as hermits, and sought by means of labor to provide for themselves, and to devote a surplus of their earnings to charitable objects. By degrees the austerities of some won for them notoriety, and caused them to become objects of charity, and even of superstitious reverence,

among the ignorant. Thus such men as Anthony of Egypt, Paul of Thebes, Hilarion of Palestine, and others, became severally the centres of great communities of men, who might at their homes or in mission fields have been very useful, but who now wasted their lives in idleness and self-mortifications, to the disgrace of the Christianity which they professed. Pachomius, originally a soldier, but afterwards an anchoret, developed a certain organizing power by gathering his imitators out of their individual huts into a *cœnobium*, or community residence, thus founding the first Christian monastery. It was at Tabenna, an island of the Nile. Pachomius also founded cloisters for nuns; and the members of his community, during his lifetime, reached the large number of 3000. By the middle of the 5th century this order of monks alone, and there were various others, had attained the great number of 50,000. From this brief statement as an index let the mind of the reader survey the vast expansion of the monastic idea and of monastic ambition as orders of monks became multiplied and powerful, spreading themselves throughout Europe and the East during the long period of fifteen centuries. See BENEDICTINES; CARMELITES; CARTHUSIANS; DOMINICANS; JESUITS; MONASTICISM; MONKS; etc. Considering the hundreds of thousands, and even millions, of persons whose lives were by this unscriptural and unnatural system withdrawn from spheres of Christian usefulness in society and in mission fields to profitless and often degrading austerities, to say nothing of worse excesses that sometimes followed in its train, it is easy to perceive that monasticism acted as a gigantic and wide-spread antagonism to the evangelization of the world. It may be assumed that the persons embraced within its influence meant well, and as a rule lived up to the theories of which they were the victims. But how different might have been the position and influence of the Christian Church had the lives and sacrifices of all those persons been applied in accordance with the Saviour's precept, "Go teach all nations."

While, therefore, monasticism was decimating the Church by the profitless seclusion of thousands of its best members, worldly conformity, on the other hand, came into the Church like a flood, with the elevation of many of the clergy to imperial favor. Thus the ancient Church, instead of remaining a unit in its zeal and efforts for the conversion of the world, became embarrassed by two opposite and equally injurious systems of error and practice, both alike fatal to its missionary faithfulness and progress. To this day the Greek Church remains under the incubus of the monastic system fastened upon it at that early period, while the Latin Church soon after became so closely identified with secular power that, although it resumed propagandism, it practiced it with motives and measures often highly exceptionable, and thus contaminated and enfeebled the Christianity it disseminated. "In regard to missions, the inaction of the Eastern churches is well known. As a general rule, they have remained content with the maintenance of their own customs." "The preaching of Ulphilas to the Goths, of the Nestorian missions in Asia, of Russia in Siberia and the Aleutian Islands, are but striking exceptions. The conversion of the Russian nation was effected, not by the preaching of the Byzantine clergy, but by the marriage of a Byzantine princess. In the midst of the Mohammedan East the Greek populations remain like islands in the barren sea, and the Bedouin tribes have wandered for twelve centuries round the Greek convent of Mount Sinai, probably without one instance of conversion to the creed of men whom they yet acknowledge with almost religious veneration as beings from a higher world" (Stanley, *Eastern Ch.*).

In taking a historical view, however brief, of the Christian missions of successive ages, it seems desirable to exercise charity in the largest degree consistent with truth. And, in fact, great allowance must be made for the ignorance and difficulties of ancient and mediæval times. Nevertheless, in the light of the Saviour's rule, "by their fruits shall ye know them," it is necessary to concede that much in ecclesiastical history that has passed for Christianity is scarcely less than a caricature of the reality. So of missionary propagandism and the conversion of nations, it must be confessed that many familiar and comprehensive phrases, such as the "conversion of the Roman empire," "the conversion of the Northern nations," "the conversion of Germany," "of Poland," "of Norway," etc., can only signify nominal conversion, and such outward changes as might take place wholly apart from the influence of that true faith which "works by love and purifies the heart." While, therefore, facts may be mentioned as they are represented to us in history, a careful judgment will discriminate as to their true moral or evangelical significance. Nor must the important consideration be overlooked that God, who can make the wrath of man praise him, and overrule the most untoward events to the accomplishment of his own glory, could, and doubtless did, overrule much that was imperfect, and even censurable, in the mode of promoting a nominal Christianity for the ultimate furtherance of the truth.

III. *Period and Elements of Transition.*—There is no positive line of demarcation between the ancient and the mediæval churches. Indeed writers never cease to differ in regard to the limits assigned to each. In point of fact, the former gradually and almost insensibly blended into the latter; but, in a missionary point of view, we are forced to consider the ancient Church as coming to a close when her purity and her aggressiveness began simultaneously to decline. During the first three centuries Christianity maintained a complete antagonism to false religions and pagan worship in all its forms. Conversions to Christianity were individual, not national; the new faith made its way upward from the humbler strata of society to the higher, from the Catacombs to the palace, till at length the number of converts became too great and too influential to be ignored either by emperors or by senates. In the 4th century we have the example of the emperor Constantine, as yet unbaptized, taking an active part in preaching and in the councils of the Church; and subsequently the leading missionary efforts were specially addressed to kings and princes, to whose determination their subjects were expected to conform.

One of the saddest aspects of the closing period of the ancient Church appeared in the growing tendency on the part of the clergy to accept nominal instead of real conversions, outward conformity instead of actual faith. Many bishops encouraged this tendency, wishing to make what they called conversion as easy as possible. Hence they baptized even those who lived in open sin, and who plainly indicated their purpose to continue in it. Perhaps they imagined that such persons, when once introduced to the Church, would be more easily and certainly reformed, although, for the most part, they merely told them what they would have to believe in order to be Christians, without insisting on the obligations of a holy life, lest the candidates should decline baptism. "These corrupt modes of procedure originated partly in the erroneous notions of worth attached to a barely outward baptism and outward Church fellowship, and partly in the false notions of what constituted faith, and of the relation of the doctrines of faith and of morals in Christianity to each other" (Neander, *Church Hist.* ii, 100). Against such views and measures there were not wanting remonstrances on the part of such men as Chrysostom and Augustine. The former, reprobating bishops animated by a false zeal for increasing the numbers of nominal Christians, says: "Our Lord utters it as a precept, 'Give not that which is holy unto the dogs, neither cast ye your pearls before swine.' But, through foolish vanity and ambition, we have subverted this command too by admitting those corrupt, unbelieving men, who are full of evil, before they have given us any satisfactory evidence of a change of mind, to partake of the sacraments. It is on this account many of those

who were thus baptized have fallen away and occasioned much scandal." Augustine complained: "How many seek Jesus only that he may benefit them in earthly matters! One man has a lawsuit, so he seeks the intercession of the clergy; another is oppressed by his superior, so he takes refuge in the Church; and still another that he may secure the wife of his choice. The Church is full of such persons. Seldom is Jesus sought for Jesus's sake." Nor were worldly motives the only agencies which led to spurious and hypocritical conversions. Many were awakened by outward impressions: some supposed they had seen miraculous effects produced by the sign of the cross; others were affected by dreams, and did little more than exchange one superstition for another. Against these insidious and contagious errors Augustine uttered faithful exhortations and warnings in his tract *De Catechizandis Rudibus* and other writings, but the current of things, and the swelling tide of barbarian invasion, greatly antagonized his influence. Some were doubtless led from poor beginnings to better results, becoming in the end true Christians, although they entered the Church from unworthy motives; but far earlier, and more extensively than is generally supposed, the true spiritual character of the ancient Church, as a whole, had lamentably declined, and with it all genuine zeal for the spiritual conversion of men.

IV. *Mediæval Missions.*—It is not to be denied that the mediæval period was one of revolution, and therefore unfavorable to the propagation of true religion; but it is by no means conceded, as is argued by some Protestant writers, including Milman, Guizot, and others of high reputation, that a defective development of Christianity was therefore inevitable, or that the semi-monastic and secular measures employed to civilize and Christianize the barbarians of Europe were "adapted as a transitionary stage for the childhood of those races." On the other hand, it is claimed, in the light of Scripture and experience, both among ancient and modern heathen, that the grand desideratum for those times, as for all others, was the unadulterated Gospel of Christ and his apostles, which not only would have availed tenfold more than did all worldly and semi-secular expedients, but would have remained as a pure, instead of a corrupting, leaven to work in after ages. It is pleasing to observe that in some of the earlier missions, of which brief sketches will now be submitted, there was no inconsiderable mixture of just and appropriate evangelical agencies, such as the translation and circulation of the Scriptures, and self-denying examples of missionary life. Instead of attempting, as has often been done, to sum up by centuries what was done, or said to have been done, to extend Christianity, it is thought better to present from historic sources a few sample missionary events and characters from successive periods of mediæval Church history, illustrating the actual introduction of the Church into different countries and among various races.

1. *The Mission of Ulphilas to the Goths.*—"When we proceed to inquire in what way a knowledge of Christianity was diffused among the nations which thus established themselves on the ruins of the Roman empire, we find, at least at the outset, that ecclesiastical history can give us but scanty information. 'We know as little in detail, remarks Schlegel, 'of the circumstances under which Christianity became so universally spread in a short space of time among all the Gothic nations as of the establishment, step by step, of their great kingdom on the Black Sea.' The rapid and universal diffusion, indeed, of the new faith is a proof of their capacity for civilization, and of the national connection of the whole race; but where shall we find the details of their conversion? We have not a record, not even a legend, of the way in which the Visigoths in France, the Ostrogoths in Pannonia, the Suevians in Spain, the Gepidæ, the Vandals, the followers of Odoacer, and the fiery Lombards, were converted to the Christian faith. We may trace this, in part, to the terrible desolation which

at this period reigned everywhere, while nation warred against nation, and tribe against tribe; we may trace it, still more, to the fact that every one of the tribes above mentioned was converted to the Arian form of Christianity, a sufficient reason in the eyes of Catholic historians for ignoring altogether the efforts of heretics to spread the knowledge of the faith. And till the close of the 6th, and the opening of the 7th century, we must be content with the slenderest details, if we wish to know anything of the early diffusion of Christianity on the European continent.

"The record, however, of one early missionary has forced its way into the Catholic histories.' In the reigns of Valerian and Gallienus, the Goths, descending from the north and east, began, from their new settlements on the Danube, to threaten the safety of the southern provinces of the empire. Establishing themselves in the Ukraine and on the shores of the Bosphorus, they spread terror throughout Pontus, Bithynia, and Cappadocia. In one of these inroads they carried off from the latter country a multitude of captives, some belonging to the clergy, and located them in their settlements along the northern bank of the Danube. Here the captives did not forget their Christian duties towards their heathen masters, nor did the latter scorn to receive from them the gentle doctrines of Christianity. The work, indeed, went on in silence, but from time to time we have proofs that the seed had not been sown in vain. Among the 318 bishops at the Council of Nice, the light complexion of the Gothic bishop Theophilus must have attracted notice, as contrasted 'with the dark hair and tawny hue of almost all the rest.' But Theophilus was the predecessor and teacher of a still greater missionary. Among the involuntary slaves carried off in the reign of Gallienus were the parents or ancestors of Ulphilas, who has won for himself the title of 'Apostle of the Goths.' Born, probably, in the year 318, he was, at a comparatively early age, sent on a mission to Constantinople, and there Constantine caused him to be consecrated bishop by his own chaplain, Eusebius of Nicomedia. From this time he devoted himself heart and soul to the conversion of his countrymen, and the Goths were the first of the barbarians among whom we see Christianity advancing general civilization, as well as teaching a purer faith.

" But his lot was cast in troublous times: the threatened irruption of a barbarous horde, and the animosity of the heathen Goths, induced him to cross the Danube, where the emperor Constantine assigned to his flock a district of country, and here he continued to labor with success. The influence he had already gained, and the natural sense of gratitude for the benefits he had bestowed upon the tribes by procuring for them a more peaceful settlement, rendered his efforts comparatively easy. Rejoicing in the woodlands and pastures of their new home, where they could to advantage tend their numerous flocks and herds, and purchase corn and wine of the richer provinces around them, they listened obediently to the voice of their bishop, whom they likened to a second Moses. And the conduct of Ulphilas justified their confidence. With singular wisdom he did not confine his efforts to the oral instruction of his people; he sought to restore to them the art of writing, which probably had been lost during their migration from the east to the north of Germany. Composing an alphabet of twenty-five letters, some of which he was fain to invent, in order to give expression to sounds unknown to Greek and Latin pronunciation, he translated the Scriptures into the native language of his flock, omitting only the four books of Kings, a precaution he adopted from a fear that their contents might tend to rouse the martial ardor and fierce spirit of a people who, in this matter, to use the quaint language of the historian, 'required the bit rather than the spur.'

"After a while he was constrained to act the part of mediator between the Visigothic nation and the Roman emperor Valens. In the year A.D. 374 the barbarous horde of the Huns burst upon the kingdom of the Ostrogoths, and, having subdued it, turned their eyes to the lands and possessions of the Visigoths. Unable to defend the line of the Dniester, the latter fell back upon the Pruth, hoping for safety amid the inaccessible defiles of the Carpathian mountains. But, sensible that even here they were not secure, a considerable party began to long for an asylum within the Roman dominions, and it was agreed that ambassadors, with Ulphilas among their number, should repair to the court of Valens, and endeavor to obtain a new settlement.

"Valens was an Arian and a controversialist. At this very time he was enforcing at Antioch, 'by other weapons than those of reason and eloquence,' a belief in the Arian theology; and when the poor bishop presented himself, and requested aid in the dire necessity of his people, the emperor is reported to have persecuted him with discussions on the hypostatic union, and to have pressed upon him the necessity of repudiating the Confession of Nice, and adopting that of Rimini. Ulphilas was in a great strait, but, being a simple-minded man, and considering the question one of words, and involving only metaphysical subtleties, not worthy of consideration in comparison with the sufferings of his people, he assented to the emperor's proposal, and promised that the Gothic nation should adopt the Arian Confession. The emperor, on his part, consented to give up certain lands in Mœsia, but annexed to this concession two harsh and rigorous conditions: that before they crossed the Danube the Goths should give up their arms, and suffer their children to be taken from them as hostages for their own fidelity, with the prospect of being educated in the different provinces of Asia.

"On these hard terms instructions were issued to the military governors of the Thracian diocese, bidding them make preparations for the reception of the new settlers. But it was found no easy matter to transport across a river more than a mile in breadth, and swelled by incessant rains, upwards of a million of both sexes and of all ages. For days and nights they passed and repassed in boats and canoes, and before they landed not a few had been carried away and drowned by the violence of the current. But, besides the disciples of Ulphilas, thousands of Goths crossed the river who still continued faithful to their own heathen priests and priestesses. Disguising, it is even said, their priests in the garb of Christian bishops and fictitious ascetics, they deceived the credulous Romans; and only when on the Roman side of the river did they throw off the mask, and make it clear that Valens was not easily to have his wish gratified, and see them converted to Arianism. One of the hereditary chiefs, Fritigern, a disciple of Ulphilas, adopted the creed of the empire, the other, Athanaric, headed the numerous party which still continued devoted to the altars and rites of Woden. The latter faction, placing their chief god on a lofty wagon, dragged it through the Gothic camp; all who refused to bow down, they burned, with their wives and children; nor did they spare the rude church they had erected, or the confused crowd of women and children who had fled to it for protection. But while the great bulk of the Gothic nation were involved in constant wars with the Roman armies, and, under the two great divisions of Ostrogoths and Visigoths, were gradually spreading themselves over Gaul, Italy, and Spain, Ulphilas continued, till the year 388, to superintend the temporal and spiritual necessities of the peaceful and populous colony of shepherds and herdsmen which, as in another Goshen, he had formed on the slopes of Mount Hæmus, and to whom he had presented the Gothic Bible in their own tongue.

"The zeal he had displayed found an imitator in the great Chrysostom. What was the measure of his success we have no means of judging, but it is certain that he founded in Constantinople an institution in which Goths might be trained and qualified to preach the Gospel to their fellow-countrymen. Even during the three years of his banishment to the remote and wretched little town of Cucusus, among the ridges of Mount Taurus, amid the want of provisions, frequent sickness without the possibility of obtaining medicines, and the ravages of Isaurian robbers, his active mind, invigorated by misfortunes, found relief not only in corresponding with churches in all quarters, but in directing missionary operations in Phœnicia, Persia, and among the Goths. In several extant epistles we find him advising the despatch of missionaries, one to this point, another to that, consoling some under persecution, animating all by the example of the great apostle Paul, and the hope of an eternal reward. And in answer to his appeals, his friends at a distance supplied him with funds so ample that he was enabled to support missions and redeem captives, and even had to beg of them that their abundant liberality might be directed into other channels. How far his exertions prevailed to win over any portion of the Gothic nation to the Catholic communion we have no means of judging. Certain it is that from the Western Goths the Arian form of Christianity extended to the Eastern Goths, to the Gepidæ, the Alans, the Vandals, and the Suevi; and it has been justly remarked that we ought not to forget 'that when Augustine, in his great work on the "city of God," celebrates the charity and clemency of Alaric during the sack of Rome, these Christian graces were entirely due to the teaching of Oriental missionaries'" (Maclear's *Missions in the Middle Ages*, p. 37–43).

2. *The Conversion of Clovis and the Franks.*—In the year 481 Clovis succeeded to the chieftaincy of the Salian Franks. In 493 he married Clotilda, the daughter of the king of Burgundy, who professed Christianity, and sought to persuade her husband to embrace it also; but her efforts for a time were without success. "At length, on the battle-field of Tolbiac, his incredulity came to an end. The fierce and dreadful Alemanni, fresh from their native forests, had burst upon the kingdom of his Ripuarian allies; Clovis, with his Franks, had rushed to the rescue, and the two fiercest nations of Germany were to decide between them the supremacy of Gaul. The battle was long and bloody; the Franks, after an obstinate struggle, wavered, and seemed on the point of flying, and in vain Clovis implored the aid of his own deities. At length he bethought him of the vaunted omnipotence of Clotilda's God, and he vowed that if victorious he would abjure his pagan creed and be baptized as a Christian. Thereupon the tide of battle turned; the last king of the Allemanni fell, and his troops fled in disorder, purchasing safety by submission to the Frankish chief. On his return Clovis recounted to his queen the story of the fight, the success of his prayer, and the vow he had made. Overwhelmed with joy, she sent without delay for Remigius, the venerable bishop of Rheims, and on his arrival the victorious chief listened attentively to his arguments. Still he hesitated, and said he would consult his warriors. These rough soldiers evinced no unwillingness; with, perhaps, the same indifference that he himself had permitted the baptism of his children, they declared themselves nothing loth to accept the creed of their chief. Clovis therefore yielded, and the baptism was fixed to take place at the approaching festival of Christmas. The greatest pains were taken to lend as much solemnity as possible to the scene. The church was hung with embroidered tapestry and white curtains, and blazed with a thousand lights, while odors of incense, 'like airs of paradise,' in the words of the excited chronicler, 'filled the place.' The new Constantine, as he entered, was struck with awe. 'Is this the heaven thou didst promise me?' said he to the bishop. 'Not heaven itself, but the beginning of the way thither,' replied the bishop. The service proceeded. As he knelt before the font to wash away the leprosy of his heathenism, 'Sicambrian,' said Remigius, 'gently bow thy neck, burn that thou didst adore, adore that which thou didst burn.' Thus, together with three thousand

of his followers, Clovis espoused Clotilda's creed, and became the single sovereign of the West who adhered to the Confession of Nicæa. Everywhere else Arianism was triumphant. The Ostrogoth Theodoric in Italy, the successors of Euric in Visigothic France, the king of Burgundy, the Suevian princes in Spain, the Vandal in Africa—all were Arians.

"The conversion of Clovis, like that of Constantine, is open to much discussion. It certainly had no effect upon his moral character. The same 'untutored savage' he was, the same he remained. But the services he rendered to Catholicism were great, and they were appreciated. 'God daily prostrated his enemies before him, because he walked before him with an upright heart, and did what was pleasing in his eyes.' In these words Gregory of Tours expresses the feelings of the Gallic clergy, who rallied round Clovis to a man, and excused all faults in one who could wield the sword so strenuously in behalf of the orthodox faith. His subsequent career was a succession of triumphs: Gundebald, the Burgundian king, felt the vengeance of Clotilda's lord on the bloody field of Dijon on the Ousche, and the cities on the Saone and the Rhone were added to the Frankish kingdom. A few more years and the Visigothic kingdom in the south felt the same iron hand. The orthodox prelates did not disguise the fact that this was a religious war, and that the supremacy of the Arian or the Catholic Creed in Western Europe was now to be decided. Clovis himself entered fully into the spirit of the crusade: on approaching Tours, he made death the penalty of injuring the territory of the holy St. Martin; in the church of the saint he publicly performed his devotions, and listened to the voices of the priests as they chanted the 18th Psalm: '*Thou hast girded me, O Lord, with strength unto the battle; thou hast subdued unto me those which rose up against me. Thou hast also given me the necks of mine enemies, that I might destroy them that hate me.*' Whether he understood the words or not, they seemed prophetic of the subsequent career of the new champion of Catholicism. The orthodox historians exhaust the treasury of legends to adorn his progress. A 'hind of wonderful magnitude' guided him through the swollen waters of the River Vienne; a pillar of fire blazed forth from the cathedral as he drew nigh Poitiers, to assure him of success. At last the bloody plains of Vouglé witnessed the utter defeat of the Arian Goths, and Alaric, their king, was mingled with the crowd of fugitives. Bordeaux, Auvergne, Rovergne, Toulouse, Angoulême, successively fell into the hands of the Frankish king, and then before the shrine of St. Martin the 'eldest son of the Church' was invested with the titles of Roman Patricius and Consul, conferred by the Greek emperor Anastasius.

"We have thus sketched the rise of the Frankish monarchy because it has an important connection with the history of Christian missions. Orthodoxy advanced side by side with the Frankish domination. The rude warriors of Clovis, once beyond the local boundaries of their ancestral faith, found themselves in the presence of a Church which was the only stable institution in the country, and bowed before a creed which, while it offered infinitely more to the soul and intellect than their own superstitions, presented everything that could excite the fancy or captivate the sense. Willingly, therefore, did they follow the example of their king; and for one that embraced the faith from genuine, a thousand adopted it from lower motives. And while they had their reward, the Frankish bishops had theirs too, in constant gifts of land for the foundation of churches and monasteries, and in a speedy admission to wealth and power.

"But the Frankish Church was not destined to evangelize the rude nations of Europe. The internal dissensions and constant wars of the successors of Clovis were not favorable to the development of Christian civilization at home or its propagation abroad. Avitus of Vienne, Cæsarius of Arles, and Faustus of Riez, proved what might be done by energy and self-devotion. But the rapid accession of wealth more and more tempted the Frankish bishops and abbots to live as mere laymen, and so the clergy degenerated, and the light of the Frankish Church grew dim. Not only were the masses of heathendom lying outside her territory neglected, but within it she saw her own members tainted with the old leaven of heathenism, and relapsing, in some instances, into the old idolatries. A new influence, therefore, was required, if the light of the Frankish Church was to be rekindled, and the German tribes evangelized. And this new influence was at hand. But to trace its origin, we must leave the scenes of the labors of Ulphilas and Severinus for two sister isles high up in the Northern Sea, almost forgotten amid the desolating contest which was breaking up the Roman world. We must glance first at the origin of the Celtic Church in Ireland and the Scottish highlands, whose humble oratories of timber and rude domes of rough stone might, indeed, contrast unfavorably with the prouder structures of the West, but whose missionary zeal burned with a far steadier flame. We must then turn to the shores of Kent, where the story of Clovis and Clotilda was to be re-enacted, and a Teutonic Church was destined to arise, and send forth, in its turn, missionary heroes among their kindred on the Continent" (Maclear's *Missions in the Middle Ages*, p. 54–58).

3. *Patrick and the Irish Missionaries.*—"The Gospel was planted in Ireland by a single missionary, self-moved—or, rather, divinely moved—and self-supported. His historic name was Patrick, and the Roman Catholics (claiming him, without reason, as their own) call him St. Patrick. He was born about the year 410, and most probably in some part of Scotland. His parents were Christians, and instructed him in the Gospel. Patrick's first visit to the field of his future mission was in his youth, as a captive of pirates, who carried him away, with many others, as a prisoner. Patrick was sold to a chieftain, who placed him in charge of his cattle. His own statement is that his heart was turned to the Lord during the hardships of his captivity. 'I prayed many times a day,' he says. 'The fear of God and love to him were increasingly kindled in me. Faith grew in me, so that in one day I offered a hundred prayers, and at night almost as many; and when I passed the night in the woods or on the mountains, I rose up to pray in the snow, ice, and rain before daybreak. Yet I felt no pain. There was no sluggishness in me, such as I now find in myself, for then the spirit glowed within me.' This is extracted from what is called the 'Confession' of Patrick, written in his old age.

"Some years later he was again taken by the pirates, but soon regained his liberty, and returned home. His parents urged him to remain with them, but he felt an irresistible call to carry the Gospel to those among whom he had passed his youth as a bondman. 'Many opposed my going,' he says in his 'Confession,' 'and said behind my back, "Why does this man rush into danger among the heathen, who do not know the Lord?" It was not badly intended on their part, but they could not comprehend the matter on account of my uncouth disposition. Many gifts were offered me with tears if I would remain. But, according to God's guidance, I did not yield to them; not by my own power—it was God who conquered in me, and I withstood them all; so that I went to the people of Ireland to publish the Gospel to them, and suffered many insults from unbelievers, and many persecutions, even unto bonds, resigning my liberty for the good of others. And if I am found worthy, I am ready to give up my life with joy for his sake.' In such a spirit did this apostle to Ireland commence his mission, about the year 440; not far from the time when Britain was finally evacuated by the Romans. . . .

"Patrick being acquainted with the language and customs of the Irish people, as a consequence of his early captivity, gathered them about him in large assemblies at the beat of a kettle-drum, and told the story of Christ so as to move their hearts. Having taught them to read, he encouraged the importation of useful books from England and France. He established cloisters after the fashion of the times, which were really missionary schools for educating the people in the knowledge of the Gospel, and for training a native ministry and missionaries; and he claims to have baptized many thousands of people. . . .

"'The people may not have adopted the outward profession of Christianity, which was all that, perhaps, in the first instance they adopted, from any clear or intellectual appreciation of its superiority to their former religion; but to obtain from the people even an outward profession of Christianity was an important step to ultimate success. It secured toleration, at least, for Christian institutions. It enabled Patrick to plant in every tribe his churches, schools, and monasteries. He was permitted, without opposition, to establish among the half-pagan inhabitants of the country societies of holy men, whose devotion, usefulness, and piety soon produced an effect upon the most barbarous and savage hearts. This was the secret of the rapid success attributed to Patrick's preaching in Ireland. The chieftains were at first the real converts. The baptism of the chieftain was immediately followed by the adhesion of the clan. The clansmen pressed eagerly around the missionary who had baptized the chief, anxious to receive that mysterious initiation into the new faith to which their chieftain and father had submitted. The requirements preparatory to baptism do not seem to have been very rigorous; and it is, therefore, not improbable that in Tirawley, and other remote districts, where the spirit of clanship was strong, Patrick, as he himself tells us he did, may have baptized some thousands of men.' . . .

"When this zealous missionary died, about the year 493, his disciples, who seem all to have been natives of Ireland—a native ministry—continued his work in the same spirit. The monasteries became at length so numerous and famous that Ireland was called *Insula Sanctorum*, the 'Island of Saints.' It gives a wrong idea of these institutions to call them monasteries, or to call their inmates monks. 'They were schools of learning and abodes of piety, uniting the instruction of the college, the labors of the workshop, the charities of the hospital, and the worship of the Church. They originated partly in a mistaken view of the Christian life, and partly out of the necessity of the case, which drove Christians to live together for mutual protection. The missionary spirit, and consequent religious activity, prevailing in the Irish monasteries, preserved them for a long time from the asceticism and mysticism incidental to the monastic life, and made them a source of blessing to the world.' The celibacy of the clergy was not enjoined in those times. Married men were connected with the cloisters, living, however, in single houses. The Scriptures were read, and ancient books were collected and studied. The missions which went forth from these institutions, as also those from England and Wales, are frequently called 'Culdee' missions. See CULDEES and IONA.

"The names of Columba and Columbanus are familiar to the readers of ecclesiastical history. Both were Irish missionaries, and both were from the institution at Bangor, in Ireland. Columba's mission was to the Picts of Scotland, and was entered upon at the age of forty-two, in the year 563. This was thirteen hundred years ago, and about seventy years after the time of Patrick. He was accompanied by twelve associates, and was the founder of the celebrated monastery on Iona, an island situated on the north of Scotland, now reckoned one of the Hebrides. This school, which had an enduring fame, became one of the chief lights of that age. Continuing thirty-five years under Columba's management, it attained a high reputation for Biblical studies and other sciences; and missionaries went from it to the northern and southern Picts of Scotland, and into England, along the eastern coast to the Thames, and to the European continent. Columbanus entered on his mission to the partially Christianized, but more especially to the pagan portions of Europe, in the year 589. That he was an evangelical missionary may be confidently inferred from the tenor of his life, and from the records of his Christian experience. He thus writes: 'O Lord, give me, I beseech thee, in the name of Jesus Christ, thy Son, my God, that love which can never cease, that will kindle my lamp but not extinguish it, that it may burn in me and enlighten others. Do thou, O Christ, our dearest Saviour, thyself kindle our lamps, that they may evermore shine in thy temple; that they may receive unquenchable light from thee that will enlighten our darkness and lessen the darkness of the world. My Jesus, I pray thee, give thy light to my lamp, that in its light the most holy place may be revealed to me in which thou dwellest as the eternal Priest, that I may always behold thee, desire thee, look upon thee in love, and long after thee.' Columbanus went first to France, taking with him twelve young men, as Columba had done, to be his co-laborers—men who had been trained under his special guidance. Here, as a consequence of continual wars, political disturbances, and the remissness of worldly-minded ecclesiastics, the greatest confusion and irregularity prevailed, and there was great degeneracy in the monastic orders. Columbanus preferred casting his lot among the pagans of Burgundy, and chose for his settlement the ruins of an ancient castle in the midst of an immense wilderness, at the foot of the Vosges Mountains. There they often suffered hunger, until the wilderness had been in some measure subdued and the earth brought under cultivation. The mission then became self-supporting, but we are not informed by what means the previous expenses were defrayed. Preaching was a part of their duty, though there is less said of this than of their efforts to impart the benefits of a Christian education to the children of the higher classes. The surrounding poor were taught gratuitously. All the pupils joined in tilling the fields, and such was their success in education that the Frankish nobles were forward to place their sons under their care. It was the most famous school in Burgundy, and there was not room in the abbey for all who pressed to gain admittance; so that it became necessary to erect other buildings, and to bring a large number of teachers over from Ireland to meet the demand. Here the eminent missionary pursued his labors for a score of years. As he represents himself to have buried as many as seventeen of his associates during twelve years, the number of his co-laborers must have been large. The discipline which Columbanus imposed on the monastic life was severe, but perhaps scarcely more so than was required by the rude spirit of the age; and he took pains to avoid the error, so prevalent in the Romish Church, of making the essence of piety consist in externals. The drift of his teaching was that everything depended on the state of the heart. Both by precept and example he sought to combine the contemplative with the useful. At the same time he adhered, with a free and independent spirit, to the peculiar religious usages of his native land. As these differed in some important respects from what were then prevalent among the degenerate Frankish clergy, he had many enemies among them, who sought to drive him from the country. This they at length effected, with the aid of the wicked mother of the reigning prince. Columbanus was ordered to return to Ireland, and to take his countrymen with him. This he did not do, but repaired first to Germany, and then to Switzerland. He spent a year near the eastern extremity of the Lake Constance, laboring among the Suevi, a heathen people in that neighborhood. This territory coming at length under the dominion of his enemies, he crossed the Alps, in the year 612, into Lombardy, and founded a monastery near Pavia; and there this apostle to Franks, Swabians, Bavarians, and other nations of Germany, passed the remain-

der of his days, and breathed out his life Nov. 21, 615, aged seventy-two years. Gallus, a favorite pupil and follower of Columbanus, remained behind in consequence of illness, and became the apostle of Switzerland. He also was an Irishman, and was characterized, as was his master, by love for the sacred volume. In what was then a wilderness he founded a monastery, 'which led to the clearing up of the forest, and the conversion of the land into cultivable soil, and it afterwards became celebrated under his name, St. Gall.' Here he labored for the Swiss and Swabian population till his death, in the year 640. This monastery was pre-eminent for the number and beauty of the manuscripts prepared by its monks; many of which, and, among others, some fragments of a translation of the Scriptures into the Allemanni language, about the year 700, are said to be preserved in the libraries of Germany.

"Neander is of the opinion that the number of missionaries who passed over from Ireland to the continent of Europe must have been great, though of very few is there any exact information. Wherever they went, cloisters were founded, and the wilderness soon gave place to cultivated fields. According to Ebrard, there were more than forty cloisters in the vicinity of the Loire and Rhone, which were governed according to the rules of Columbanus, and to which emigrants came from Ireland as late as the close of the 7th century. He also affirms that Germany was almost wholly heathen when that missionary entered it. But before the year 720 the Gospel had been proclaimed by himself and his countrymen from the mountains of Switzerland down to the islands in the delta of the Rhine, and eastward from that river to the River Inn, and the Bohemian forest, and the borders of Saxony, and still farther on the seacoast; and all the really German tribes within those borders were in subjection to the Christian faith as it had been taught by the Irish missionaries. Ebrard's earnest testimony to the evangelical nature of the Irish missions should not be overlooked. He declares that they read the Scriptures in the original text, translated them wherever they went, expounded them to the congregations, recommended the regular and diligent perusal of them, and held them to be the living Word of Christ. The Scriptures were their only rule of faith. They preached the inherited depravity of man, the atoning death of Christ, justification without the merit of works, regeneration as the life in him who died for us, and the sacraments as signs and seals of grace in Christ. They held to no transubstantiation, no purgatory, no prayers to saints, and their worship was in the native language. But, though they used neither pictures nor images, they seem to have been attached to the use of the simple cross; and Gallus, the distinguished champion of Columbanus, is said, when marking out a place on which to erect a monastery, to have done it by means of a cross, from which he had suspended a capsule of relics. Complete exemption from superstition was perhaps among the impossibilities of that age" (Anderson's *Foreign Missions*, p. 69–82).

4. Similar in interest, though varied in detail, are the stories of Augustine's mission to England, A.D. 596; that of Boniface to Germany, A.D. 715; and that of Anksgar to Scandinavia, A.D. 826; together with that of many of their associates and successors. Nor were the missions among the Sclavonic races during the 9th and 10th centuries without many incidents of great interest. See Maclear's *Missions in the Middles Ages*; Milman's *Latin Christianity*; Merivale's *Conversion of the Northern Nations*; Guizot's *History of Civilization*: etc.; S. F. Smith, *Mediæval Missions*.

5. A period has now been reached when it is necessary to take note of another important element in the history and character of missions, viz., papal influence. Gregory the Great, A.D. 568–604, was the first of the bishops of Rome who exerted any decided official influence on the propagation of Christianity by means of missions. "His project of sending missionaries to Eng-

land, formed before his attaining the pontifical dignity, was among the first to be carried into execution. In the year 596 he despatched Augustine, with forty assistant monks, to effect the conversion of the Anglo-Saxons. *Conversion*, in the dialect of Rome, signified nothing more than proselytism; and it was sanguinely hoped that by influencing the chiefs to renounce idolatry their subjects would soon be converted in a mass. . . . The success of Augustine and his brethren was even beyond their expectation. Landing on the Isle of Thanet, they applied to Ethelbert, the king of Kent, for permission to preach in his kingdom. Ethelbert had married a Christian princess, and was therefore not unfavorably disposed towards his uninvited guests. Yet so ignorant was he of the nature of their errand that he insisted that their first interview with him should take place in the open air, lest he should fall a victim to their magical arts. Augustine's eloquence, however, soon inspired the king with confidence, and Ethelbert then granted to the missionaries an old, ruinous church at Canterbury, dedicated to St. Martin, and which had existed from the time of the Romans, as their first station for preaching the Gospel. Ere long the king yielded to the arguments of Augustine or the persuasions of his wife, and his baptism was followed by that of many of his subjects, no fewer than ten thousand being thus nominally received into the Church on a single occasion. . . . Gregory was overjoyed at the success of his mission, and needed no solicitations to send a re-enforcement of preachers, all of whom were monks. He next divided the whole island into two archbishoprics, appointing Augustine to be archbishop of London, and constituting York the metropolitan city of the north when Christianity should have penetrated so far. As London had not yet, however, embraced the new religion, and was not within the domains of Ethelbert, Augustine made Canterbury his abode and see. In the true spirit of Roman arrogance, Augustine assumed to himself the right of governing all the churches in Britain, whether planted by the recent laborers or existing from earlier times. But the ancient British churches were indignant at such an encroachment on their independence and liberties. 'We are all prepared,' said Deynoch, abbot of Bangor, on one occasion, 'to hearken to the Church of God, to the pope of Rome, and to every pious Christian, so as to manifest to all, according to their several stations, perfect charity, and to uphold and aid them both by word and deed. What other duty we can owe to him whom you call *pope*, or father of fathers, we do not know; but this we are ready to exercise towards him and every other Christian.' This independence by no means pleased Augustine; and he was heard to say to his Anglo-Saxon followers, 'Well, then, since they will not own the Anglo-Saxons as brethren, or allow *us* to make known to them the way of life, they must regard them as enemies, and *look for revenge*.' The horrible spirit which dictated such a speech is too apparent to need comment, and shows how little of real Christianity the Roman missionaries mingled with their zeal for the papal see. In the contests which the new Church thus waged with the old, the influence of Augustine and his followers with the Saxon kings generally enabled them to triumph; and although the British churches long persevered in maintaining their freedom, they gradually became absorbed in the Anglican hierarchy; and, long before the Norman invasion, those who ventured to dissent from the Roman forms of worship were only to be found in the extreme parts of the island.

"During the pontificate of Gregory, the Spanish Church also became subject to the primacy of Rome. Before this period the Goths, who had established their power in Spain, were of the Arian party; but on their king, Reckared, professing his belief in the doctrine of the Trinity, the bishops in a body requested the pope to undertake the supervision of their affairs—a request with which Gregory was only too happy to comply.

He attempted, moreover, to obtain the subjection of the French clergy, but in this he could only partly succeed. Nevertheless, he formed alliances with the French princes, nobles, and bishops; and, considering their Church as subject to his inspection, did not hesitate to interfere on many occasions both with advice and with admonition.

"It was, perhaps, the zeal of Gregory for multiplying nominal converts to Christianity that led him to introduce alterations in the forms of worship, which were so exaggerated by succeeding pontiffs as to change the solemn service of God into a ridiculous show. Observing the influence which the harmonies of music and the beauties of painting and sculpture exerted upon the minds of the Lombards and other half-civilized tribes, he resolved to employ the arts as handmaids to religion" (*Lives of the Popes*, p. 78-81).

For more than one hundred years following, although the papacy was constantly making advances towards temporal sovereignty, no one of the popes possessed the character of Gregory. In 715 Gregory II came to the papal chair. It was he that sent Corbinian as missionary to France and Boniface to Germany. Gregory III, about 741, sent the first ambassador of Rome to France. From the middle of the 8th century the popedom laid claim to a temporal sovereignty, and from A.D. 800, when pope Leo III crowned Charlemagne as emperor of the West, that monarch assumed the protectorate of Christendom, and stood ready to the extent of his power to promote the interests of the Roman see, which he chiefly did by means of conquest. From that time, more than before, missions were made an agency for the propagandism not merely of a ceremonial Christianity, but of the power of the popes. Monasticism, already widely extended, became an auxiliary of great power, that could be wielded for any special object contemplated by the Roman see. The popes wielded the prerogative of establishing and controlling the various orders of monks, and, by granting them exemption from the local supervision of bishops, were able always to hold them in the most direct subservience to their own ambitions. From the middle of the 9th century onward there was a vast increase of monasteries in various parts of Europe. The Benedictine order was in the ascendency, but, notwithstanding repeated reforms of its rule and practice, many of the monks were dissolute, and, as the clergy of various countries were chiefly taken from the monasteries, anarchy, simony, and concubinage largely prevailed. This was the *sæculum obscurum*, the darkest of the dark ages; and, in the general stagnation which prevailed, there was but little activity in any form of missionary effort. Europe was considered Christian, and there were no elements at work to improve the type of Christianity it had received, while, on the contrary, many germs of evil that had been sowed as tares were springing up to choke whatever of wheat was left to grow.

6. *The Crusades.*—About this period rumors of violence and insult to Christian pilgrims in the East began to excite attention, and the certainty that Christians were greatly oppressed by the Moslems at Jerusalem and throughout Palestine became the pretext for the crusades. The idea of rescuing by force the Holy Sepulchre from the pollution of the infidels was first developed as a duty of the Church under pope Sylvester II, A.D. 999-1003. It took form and action in eight successive crusades or wars of the cross, extending through two centuries and a half. These so-called holy wars scarcely differed in principle from the wars of Clovis, Charlemagne, and others, by which the Church had been extended among the nations and tribes of Northern Europe; and also of Cortez and Pizarro, made after the discovery of the New World, to Christianize (?) the nations of Mexico and Central and South America. The peculiarity of the crusades consisted in the remoteness of the land they aimed to conquer, the resistance offered by the Moslem races, and the defeats which overwhelmed in one form or another the armies of eight succes-

sive crusades, until, by the loss of millions of men and treasure, all Europe was exhausted.

The only proper view to take of these wars is to regard them as grand but mistaken missionary expeditions. As such they were sanctioned by the popes, preached by the monks, sustained by the people, and enterprised by the warriors, who went forth prepared to sacrifice treasure and life, but confident of winning heaven as a result. Mark the history and language of pope Innocent III, A.D. 1198–1216: "The event of the crusades might have crushed a less lofty and religious mind than that of Innocent to despair. Armies after armies had left their bones to crumble on the plains of Asia Minor or of Galilee; great sovereigns had perished or returned discomfited from the Holy Land. The great German crusade had ended in disgraceful failure. All was dissension, jealousy, hostility. The king of Antioch was at war with the Christian king of Armenia. The two great orders, the only powerful defenders of the land, the Hospitallers and the Templars, were in implacable feud. The Christians of Palestine were in morals, in character, in habits, the most licentious, most treacherous, most ferocious of mankind. But the darker the aspect of affairs the more firmly seemed Innocent to be persuaded that the crusade was the cause of God. In every new disaster, in every discomfiture and loss, the popes had still found unfailing refuge in ascribing them to the sins of the Christians, and their sins were dark enough to justify the strongest language of Innocent. It needed but more perfect faith, more holiness, and one believer would put to flight twelve millions; the miracles of God against Pharaoh and against the Philistines would be renewed in their behalf. For the first two or three years of Innocent's pontificate, address after address, rising one above another in impassioned eloquence, enforced the duty of contributing to the holy war. This was to be the principal, if not the exclusive theme of the preaching of the clergy. In letters to the bishop of Syracuse, to all the bishops of Apulia, Calabria, and Tuscany, he urges them to visit every city, town, and castle; he exhorts not only the nobles, but the citizens, to take up arms for Jesus Christ. Those who cannot assist in person are to assist in other ways, by furnishing ships, provisions, and money. Somewhat later came a more energetic epistle to all archbishops, bishops, abbots, priors, and princes and barons of France, England, Hungary, and Sicily. The vicar of Christ himself would claim no exemption from the universal call; he would, as became him, set the example, and in person and in estate devote himself to the sacred cause. He had therefore himself invested with the cross two cardinals of the Church, who were to precede the army of the Lord, and to be maintained, not by any mendicant support, but at the expense of the holy see. After the pope's example, before the next March, every archbishop, bishop, and prelate was to furnish a certain number of soldiers, according to his means, or a certain rate in money for the support of the crusading army. Whoever refused was to be treated as a violator of God's commandments, threatened with condign punishment, even with suspension. To all who embarked in the war Innocent promised, on their sincere repentance, the remission of all their sins, and eternal life in the great day of retribution. Those who were unable to proceed in person might obtain the same remission in proportion to the bounty of their offerings and the devotion of their hearts. The estates of all who took up the cross were placed under the protection of St. Peter" (Milman, *Lat. Christianity*, v, 75 sq.). Had such language been used, such influence exerted, and such sacrifices made in harmony with the Saviour's plan of evangelizing the world, who can tell what happy and far-reaching results might not have been attained as the issue? But bad efforts in a good cause, no less than well-meant efforts in a bad cause, can only be expected to result disastrously. Hence true Christianity, instead of being promoted, was perverted and antagonized, till the hope

of its very existence had well-nigh fled the earth. Nevertheless, some fragments of the true leaven still remained, sometimes in the Church, and sometimes in small and obscure sects like the Waldenses. A specimen of the higher and better aspirations cherished by individuals is illustrated in the history of Raymond Lull (see LULLY), but the difficulties in their way were insuperable. It need not be denied that the terrible evils of the crusades were in a subsequent period in many respects overruled for the good of humanity. But as it does not enter into the scope of providential action to atone for the crimes of men or the errors of Christians, the world and the Church are destined to suffer perpetual loss as a result of the milito-missionary fanaticisms of the mediæval Church. What was needed to bring in the light of truth and civilization into the dreary centuries under consideration was the simple, earnest Gospel, accompanied by the pure Word of God, and illustrated by the lives of its teachers. But a long period was destined to elapse before that most desirable consummation was to be realized. Indeed, it was only by slow degrees, and through long and painful struggles, that the Church again recovered the apostolic idea of missions.

7. Roman Catholic missions assumed a new and, in some respects, an improved phase during the 13th and 14th centuries, chiefly through the mendicant and preaching orders of Dominic and Francis d'Assisi. By them a vigorous effort was made to revive the Catholic faith in all the countries of Europe, and even to extend it by peaceful foreign missions among pagans and Mohammedans in various parts of Asia and Africa. "In one important respect the founders of these new orders absolutely agreed—in their entire identification with the lowest of mankind. At first amicable, afterwards emulous, eventually hostile, they, or rather their orders, rivalled each other in sinking below poverty into beg-. gary. They were to live upon alms; the coarsest imaginable dress, the hardest fare, the narrowest cell, was to keep them down to the level of the humblest. Both the new orders differed in the same manner, and greatly to the advantage of the hierarchical faith, from the old monkish institutions. Their primary object was not the salvation of the individual monk, but the salvation of others through him. Though, therefore, their rules within their monasteries were strictly and severely monastic, bound by the common vows of chastity, poverty, and obedience, seclusion was no part of their discipline. Their business was abroad rather than at home; their dwelling was not like that of the old Benedictines, or others, in uncultivated swamps and forests of the North, on the dreary Apennines, or the exhausted soil of Italy, in order to subdue their bodies, and occupy their dangerously unoccupied time, merely as a secondary consequence, to compel the desert into fertile land. Their work was among their fellow-men, in the village, in the town, in the city, in the market, even in the camp. Monastic Christianity would no longer flee the world; it would subjugate it, or win it by gentle violence" (Milman, *Lat. Christianity*, v, 238). But, being monastic still, this form of Christianity lacked the vital elements of evangelical power, and soon ran into fearful excesses. Dominic himself personally took part in the bloody crusade against the Albigenses, which ere long was followed by the establishment of the Spanish Inquisition, with Dominican friars as its generals and chief inquisitors. See INQUISITION. The pretext in both cases was the conversion of heretics, for which confiscation, torture, and murder were as relentlessly applied to praying and Bible-reading Christians as to Jews and Moors. Thus the world had still to wait long centuries before the apostolic idea of Christian missions returned to the Church.

V. *Modern Missions.*—1. *Roman Catholic.*—Prior to the close of the 15th century, the zeal of the Church of Rome had been roused to a fervid state of excitement by the reported successes of the missionaries of the mendicant orders who had followed in the train of Portuguese discoveries along the coast of Africa and beyond the Cape of Good Hope to India. At that period the New World was discovered, and the grandeur of the fields that as a consequence were opened to conquest and adventure inflamed anew the zeal of propagandism. The idea of planting the cross upon the islands and continents of America was deemed sufficient to justify if not to hallow any violence necessary to subjugate the native idolators. Missionaries sailed in every fleet, and every new discovery was claimed by the Church in the name of some Christian sovereign. About the same period the order of the Jesuits was founded, which by its rapid increase and decisive influence soon rivalled all preceding orders, sending forth its missionaries to India, China, and Japan. See JESUITS. Thus a new and exciting impulse was given to agencies which succeeded in planting Latin Christianity throughout regions of vastly greater extent than it had ever before occupied.

No unprejudiced mind can become acquainted with the vast extent of the missionary operations undertaken and maintained by the missionaries of the Church of Rome during the 16th, 17th, 18th, and 19th centuries without according to the actors in them the meed of high admiration for their devotion and self-sacrifice, however he may lament the defects and errors of the system in connection with which they acted, and the low grade of Christian life they promoted.

"In the East, missions were founded in Hindustan, the East India Islands, Japan, China, Tonquin, Abyssinia; in America, the half-civilized natives of Peru and Mexico were converted, and their descendants now form the mass of the people, and the Church of Rome has enrolled two of Indian blood among her canonized saints. The nomadic tribes from Labrador to Cape Horn were visited; many were completely gained, in other parts reductions were formed, and such as could be persuaded to enter were instructed alike in the truths of Christianity and the usages of civilized life. Close on these discoveries came the religious feuds of the 16th century, and the defection of nearly every prince in Northern Europe from the Roman see. State churches were formed in many of the German states, the Scandinavian kingdoms, Holland, England, and Scotland, based on the doctrines of Luther and Calvin. This led to a new species of mission: colleges were established in Catholic countries for the education of their fellow-believers in the northern countries, and the training of such as wished to enter the priesthood; and from these seminaries missionaries proceeded to their native country to minister to their brethren, and to gain back such as seemed to repent the late change. Many suffered the penalty of death; but this, as usually happens, only raised up others to fill their places. From this period the Catholic missions were either home missions for instructing the ignorant and neglected in Catholic countries, or those in which the exercise of religion is permitted (comp. Nitzsch, *Praktische Theologie*, vol. iii, pt. i); missions in Protestant countries to supply clergy for the Catholic portion; missions among schismatics to reunite them to Rome; missions to pagan nations. These missions became at last so important a part of the Church government that Gregory XV (1621-23) instituted the Congregation de Propaganda Fide [see PROPAGANDA], which gave a new impulse to the zeal and fervor of missionaries, and all interested in the missionary cause. This congregation or department consisted of thirteen cardinals, two priests, a religious, and a secretary; and to it exclusively was committed the direction of missions and Church matters in mission countries. Considerable sums were bestowed by public and private munificence on this department, and under Urban VIII a college, usually styled the Urban College, or the Propaganda, was erected and richly endowed. Here candidates for the priesthood and the missions are received from all quarters of the globe, and a printing-

press issues devotional works in a great number of languages. Besides this college, there soon rose the Armenian College at Venice, the Germanic, English, Irish, and Scotch colleges at Rome, the English colleges at Rheims and Douay, the Irish and Scotch at Paris, the Irish colleges at Louvain and Valladolid, and some others, all intended to train the missionaries for their own countries; and at a later date the Chinese college at Naples was founded in the same view, and of late years a missionary college has arisen at Drumcondra. Convents and religious houses of various orders were also founded on the Continent for natives of the British Isles, and from these also missionaries annually set out for the missions in the English dominions. Most of these latter have, however, since disappeared, swept away by the French Revolution, or transferred to England or the United States" (Newcomb, *Cyclopædia of Missions*, p. 299 sq.). See *English Review*, xvi, 421 sq. We also extract from Newcomb a detailed account of the results of these missionary operations; for still later particulars we refer the reader to the articles on the several countries in this Cyclopædia.

"I. *Missionary Societies.*—There are, properly speaking, no missionary societies in the Catholic Church similar to those among Protestants. Three societies, of quite recent origin—the *Society for the Propagation of the Faith*, centring at Lyons; the *Leopoldine Society*, at Vienna; and the *Society of the Holy Childhood*, in France—raise funds by a small weekly contribution, which the directors distribute to various missions, as they think proper, but over the missionaries and stations they exercise no control. The various missions are conducted entirely independent of this aid, relying, in default of it, on other resources. The last-named society is made up of children, and has a special object, the raising of money to save and baptize children exposed to death by their unnatural parents in China and Annam. Besides the aid thus given, some missions have funds established before the present century, and formerly French, Spanish, and Portuguese missionaries received a regular stipend from the government. The great mass of the missions at present are individual efforts, supported by the zeal and sacrifices of the bishops and clergy employed on them.

"II. *Receipts.*—The amount raised in 1852 by the Society for the Propagation of the Faith was $950,000; by the Society of the Holy Childhood, $117,000; total, $1,067,000.

"III. *Missionary Stations.*—*A*. EUROPE.—1. Among the Protestant states of Europe, the only countries where the Catholic Church is still a mere mission are Denmark, Norway, and Sweden. Here the number of Catholics is very small, and no details are published, as many severe civil penalties are still enforced against members; and especially converts of the Roman Church. The whole number does not probably exceed 150,000.

"2. *Turkey.*—The United Armenians have an archbishop at Constantinople; the Latins, several bishops and vicars apostolic; the distinct missions are those of the Franciscans in Moldavia, Jesuits in Herzegovine, and Lazarists at Constantinople and Salonica—the latter aided in their labors by the Sisters of Charity. The whole number of Latin Christians is estimated at 613,000, and is constantly on the increase.

"3. *Greece.*—In this kingdom there are constant accessions to the Latin and United Greek churches, especially at Athens, Piræus, Patras, Nauplia, Navarino, and Heraclia. There are in this kingdom and the Ionian republic flourishing missions of the Capuchins and Jesuits.

"*B*. ASIA.—1. *Turkey in Asia.*—The Franciscans have had missions in the Holy Land since the crusades, which, more or less active at times, are now pushed with energy. The Jesuits have since their origin had missions among the Eastern Christians, won many back to Rome, established schools, and raised the standard of clerical instruction. At Antioch there are Maronite, United Greek, and Syrian patriarchs, and elsewhere an Armenian and a Chaldæan patriarch, all in communion with Rome; and the number of Christians who acknowledge the supremacy of Pius IX is about a million.

"2. *Persia.*—In this country there is a mission directed by the Lazarists and protected by France, as well as a United Armenian Church well established and tolerated.

"3. *India.*—The Hindû mission dates back to the conquest of Goa by the Portuguese in 1510, and was at first conducted by the Franciscans, Dominicans, and zealous secular priests. Its progress was, however, slow, till the arrival of Francis Xavier in 1542. By his labors, and those of other fathers of the Society of Jesus, numbers were converted on the Fishery Coast, the islands of Manar and Ceylon, and Travancore, while the former missionaries renewed their efforts in other parts, and gained to Rome all the Chaldaic Christians who had fallen into Nestorianism. The Jesuit mission is, however, the most celebrated, and, after Xavier, owed its chief progress to

Robert de Nobili, nephew to pope Marcellus II, who originated the plan of having missionaries for each caste, adopting the life of each. He himself became a Brahminsamassi. The blessed John de Brito converted the Maravas; Aquaviva, at Delhi, won Akbar to the Christian religion; and Goes traversed Thibet and Tartary to Pekin. These missions were affected by the overthrow of the Portuguese and French power in India, by the persecution of the Danes, by the disputes as to the Malabar rites, by the suppression of the Jesuits, and by the troubles of the French Revolution. A large number of converts had, however, been made, and their descendants remained faithful. During the Dutch rule in Ceylon, Catholicity was maintained there by the labors of the Portuguese Oratorians. All Hindustan is now divided into vicariates apostolic for European and native Christians, the most extensive Hindû missions being those of Madura, conducted by the Jesuits; of Mysore, conducted by the priests of the Foreign Missions; and of Ceylon, by the priests of the Oratory—all of which are rapidly gaining the ground lost in darker days. Hindustan contains 15 vicariates, 16 bishops, a large number of priests, including 500 native clergymen, and nearly 4,000,000 of Latin and Chaldee Christians. Ceylon contains 2 vicariates, 3 bishops, and 150,000 Catholics.

"4. *Farther India.*—The Tonquin mission was founded by the Jesuit Alexander Rhodes, who labored in that field from about 1624 to 1648, and gathered a Church of 60,000 Christians. Driven at last from the country, he originated at Paris the Seminary of the Foreign Missions, founded in 1633, and induced the Holy See to appoint bishops to Tonquin. Since then the priests of the Foreign Missions have had the chief direction of the mission in Annam and the neighboring province of Su-Tchuen, in China. The Jesuits also continued their mission, and by the labors of both many native clergy were formed. The Cochin China mission was founded about the same time by F. Rossi, and passed also to the Foreign Missions. Both churches have undergone terrible persecutions, even of late years, under the emperor Minh-Menh, but have steadily increased. Tonquin contains 6 vicariates apostolic, governed by 12 bishops. One of these vicariates in 1847 contained 10 European and 91 native priests, 200 catechists, and about 200,000 Christians. Another, 2 bishops, 3 European and 43 native priests, 60 catechists, and 70,000 Christians. Cochin China contains 3 vicariates apostolic, all directed by clergy of the Seminary of the Foreign Missions and native priests.

"*Siam, Laos, and Cambodia.*—These missions are also directed by the priests of the Foreign Missions and native clergymen. They have been subjected to repeated persecutions, but are now at peace. Ava, Pegu, and Malacca are vicariates, with 2 bishops and about 10,000 Catholics.

"5. *China.*—The Chinese mission was attempted in the 13th century by John de Montecorvino, who founded a metropolitan see at Pekin, which subsided for over a century. Xavier attempted to restore it in 1552, but died near Canton. After several other attempts, the Jesuits Ruggieri and Pazio founded a mission, which, under the great Matthew Ricci (1584–1610), obtained a permanent footing in the empire. The early Jesuits adopted the dress of literati, and thus secured the esteem of the emperors, and would probably have gained them to Christ but for the Tartar invasion. After that change persecutions began, and as differences arose between the Jesuits on the one side, and the Dominicans in Fokien and the priests of Foreign Missions in Suchuen on the other, as to the use of certain ceremonies, these dissensions formed a pretext for very severe edicts. For many years the blood of the Chinese Christians and their missionaries flowed in torrents. At present the Church enjoys peace, although the insurgents are decidedly hostile to the Chinese Catholics, and treat them with great severity. Among the celebrated Chinese missionaries may be named Ricci, Schall, and Verbiest, mathematicians; Marin, an American, who attempted a mission in 1556; Lopez, a native Chinese priest and bishop; Denis de la Cruz, another Chinese, who died at Carthagena, in South America; Navarrette, Amiot, Sanz, Perboyre, a recent martyr. The suppression of the Jesuits and the French Revolution seriously affected these missions by cutting off a supply of learned and adventurous missionaries. Since the restoration of peace in Europe, and especially since the establishment of the Society for the Propagation of the Faith, the mission has recovered much of its former extent. At the present time China contains 21 sees or vicariates, 23 bishops, 628 European and 335 native priests, many convents and houses of religious women, and a population of 541,720 Catholics. The great mass of the old Jesuit missions are directed by the French Lazarists; the missions in Suchuen, Yunnan, Quaychoo, and Leatong, by the priests of the Foreign Missions; those in Chansi, Chensi, and Honquang, by Italian Franciscans; those in Fokien by Spanish Dominicans; and those in Chantong and Kiangnan by French Jesuits, who have recently returned.

"6. *Corea.*—Christianity was introduced here from China about 1632, and has since grown amid persecution of the severest kind. The history of the Corean Church is written in blood. Her first neophyte was a martyr; her first Chinese apostle, a martyr; her first native priest, a martyr; her first European missionaries, all martyrs. The number of Catholics is about 13,650, directed by a bishop, 18 European priests, if still alive, and some native clergy. This mission is intrusted to the Seminary of the Foreign Missions.

"7. *Mongol Tartary.*—This is a Lazarist mission, directed by a bishop, 3 European and 10 native priests, a college seminary, 8 schools, and 5000 Christians.

"8. *Mantchûria.* — A mission under the priests of the Foreign Missions, with a bishop and some European clergymen.

"9. *Thibet.*—Missions were attempted here in the 13th and 14th centuries by Hyacinth of Poland, and Oderic of Fruili; in the 17th century by the Jesuits and Capuchins; but in the interval Buddhism had grown up and expelled all but the traces of Christianity. The mission was restored in 1846 by the Lazarists Huc and Gabet. Others have followed, and a bishop has lately been appointed.

"*East India Islands.*—Missions exist on some of these of ancient date, but the data are not very full or recent.

"10. *Japan.*—Christianity was introduced into this empire in 1549 by Francis Xavier, who had converted a Japanese at Goa. During a stay of two years he visited several kingdoms, and founded missions, which he confided to zealous priests of his order. The faith spread rapidly. In 1562 the prince of Omura, and soon after the kings of Bungo and Arima, embraced Christianity, and sent a splendid embassy to pope Gregory XIII. Soon after Taycosoma, a powerful general, usurped the throne, and in 1586 issued a law against Christianity, which his predecessor, Nabunanga, had greatly favored. The number of Christians increased with the persecution, and in 1638 they rose in arms in Arima, but were crushed by Dutch aid. Since then the faith has been almost entirely extinguished. The number of Christians put to death has been estimated at nearly two millions, and the annals of the Jesuits, Franciscans, and Dominicans are filled with narratives of the deaths of members of their orders in Japan. Besides Xavier, the greatest missionaries were Valignani, father John Baptist, a Spanish Franciscan, Philip of Jesus, a Mexican Franciscan, both crucified at Nagasaki, father Charles Spinola, etc. The last Catholic priest who entered Japan was M. Sedotti, who in 1709 found means to land, but he was never again heard of. Within a few years great efforts have been made to reach the forsaken Christians still said to exist in Japan; and a bishop appointed to the mission has already founded stations on the Lew-Chew Islands.

"*C.* AFRICA.—1. *Congo.* —The earliest missions were those of Congo, begun by the Dominicans, Franciscans, and Jesuits. From 1500 to about 1560 the success was great; the king and many of his people were converted, native priests ordained, and one raised to the episcopacy. Catholicity flourished there for many years, but insensibly declined for want of priests. The Carmelites established missions in Guinea, the Jesuits in Angola and Loango; and on these chiefly the Catholics of Congo depended as late as 1622. In 1642 the Capuchins undertook the mission, headed by Fray Francisco de Pampeluna, once a military officer of high rank. This body and their successors continued the mission till about 1700, when Cistercians took their place. About the middle of the last century the priests of the Foreign Missions established stations in Loango, and converted many. These missions still exist in several parts:

"2. *Barbary.* — Missions have from the earliest times been conducted there by Franciscans, Dominicans, Trinitarians, and Mercedarians; still later by the Jesuits and Lazarists. The number of Christians is, however, very small, and the clergy do not number a score.

"3. *Egypt.*—The Latin mission there is due chiefly to the Jesuits, of whom father Sicard was the leader. Many Copts were recalled to the Latin Church, and are now directed by Lazarist missionaries, aided by brothers of the Christian School.

"4. *Abyssinia.*—The Portuguese, about 1530, attempted to convert the schismatics of Abyssinia, and revive morality and learning, but the efforts and the zeal of the Jesuits failed; the missionaries were excluded, after a long persecution. In 1839 the mission was revived by the Lazarists, and a bishop appointed, while the Galla country was allotted to the Capuchins in 1846.

"5. *Madagascar.*—The first missions among the Malagasies was begun by the Lazarists in 1648, and continued till 1674, when Louis XIV forbade French vessels to stop at the island. The mission was revived in 1837 by Mr. Dalmond, who founded the station of Nossibe in 1840. Since 1845 this mission has been confided to the Jesuits, who have made rapid progress.

"6. *Other Parts.*—Missions have been founded at different spots on the eastern and western coast, which have been discontinued, or are not yet firmly established. That of Guinea is the most thriving. A bishop was at first selected for it from among the Catholic clergy in the United States; but on the failure of his health the mission was transferred to the Society of the Sacred Hearts of Jesus and Mary, who still administer it.

"*D.* OCEANICA.—The first Catholic mission in Oceanica was that of Messrs. Bachelot, Armand, and Short, of the

'Congregation of the Sacred Hearts of Jesus and Mary,' at the Sandwich Islands. They began it in 1826, and continued it till their expulsion by the government in 1832. In the following year vicars apostolic were appointed, and missions begun at Gambier, Tahiti, and, for a second time, at the Sandwich Islands. These missions are chiefly directed by priests of the Society of Picpry and the Marists. Other stations were begun in New Zealand, at Futuna, in the Marquesas, Nukahwa, and elsewhere. These missions extended so rapidly that several new vicariates were formed; and, in spite of martyrdom, disease, and shipwreck, they are still advancing. Oceanica now contains 8 bishops, 10 vicariates, and 300 missionaries.

"*E. America.*—1. *Spanish Missions.*—Missions were established in all Spanish America, and great numbers were converted, especially in Mexico and Peru, where their descendants are still the majority, mingled with the Spanish race. Even in Cuba the Spanish blood is much mixed with Indian blood. The missions among the wild tribes were of a different character. The most celebrated are those of the Jesuits in Paraguay and California, the missions among the Moxos and Abipones in Chili and New Grenada. Few of these are now properly missions, and they are matter for a history rather than a gazetteer.

"2. *Portuguese Missions.*—The missions of Brazil were chiefly conducted by Portuguese Jesuits, who converted several tribes, although their numbers were diminished by the cruelty of the savages on land and pirates at sea. Several of these missions still subsist, but details are not easily accessible as to their numbers and extent.

"3. *United States and Canada.*—The early Catholic missions in New Mexico, Florida, and California were Spanish. The natives of New Mexico were converted, and, being now Christians, are not considered a mission. In Florida, while a Spanish province, the Indians were converted by Franciscans, and formed villages on the Apalachicola and around the city of St. Augustine. The English drove these Indians from their villages, and their descendants, now called Seminoles, or wanderers, have lost all traces of Christianity. The Upper California missions were conducted by Franciscans, and till a recent period were in a very flourishing state, but are now destroyed. The Canada missions were begun by French Jesuits, in Nova Scotia and Maine, about 1612. The Recollects followed, succeeded again by the Jesuits. This mission converted the Abenaquis of Maine, now forming two villages in the state of Maine and two in Canada; the Hurons of Upper Canada, a part of whom are Catholics, are still at Lorette, near Quebec; a part of the Iroquois, or Five Nations, who form the three Catholic villages at Caughnawaga, St. Regis, and the Lake of the Two Mountains; the Algonquins, who form a mission village with the last-named band of Iroquois; the Micmacs of Nova Scotia, now attended by the secular clergy; the Montagnais, at Chicoutimi and Red River, under a bishop and missionaries; the Ottawas of Lake Superior, who, with the Ojibwas and Menomonees, are now under the care of Canadian clergy on the north, and on the south of bishop Baraga, a philologist, whose talents have been acknowledged by the government; the Illinois and Miamis, whose descendants are now on Indian Territory and in Louisiana; the Arkansas, whose descendants, under the name of Kappas, are also there. The Catholics of Maryland began missions among the neighboring tribes, but tribe and mission have long since disappeared. Since the Revolution and the establishment of a Catholic hierarchy in the United States, attention has been gradually turned to the Indian missions; 2 vicariates are devoted to them alone. That of Upper Michigan contains 1 bishop, 5 priests, 6 schools, and a large number of Catholic Ottawas and Ojibwas; that of Indian territory has a bishop, 8 clergymen, 4 schools, 5300 Catholics of the Pottawatomies, Osages, Miamis, Illinois, Kansas, and Kappas. Besides these, there are in the diocese of Milwaukee a Menomonee and an Ojibwa mission; in that of St. Paul's, Minnesota, a Sioux, a Winnebago, and 3 Ojibwa missions; and in Oregon there are missions among the Waskos, Cayusus, Pointed Hearts, and Flatheads—the Indian Catholics of the territory numbering 3400. Besides these, a few hundred converted Indians are to be found in California.

"This is an outline of the widely-extended and much-diversified Catholic missions. As to their history, the work of Henrion, *Histoire Générale des Missions Catholiques;* Wittmann, *Die Herrlichkeiten der Kirche in ihren Missionen* (Augsburg, 1841); Marshall, *Missions,* Roman Catholic and Protestant (Lond. 1865); and the annals of the Society for the Propagation of the Faith, will give a general idea; but the sources are the accounts of the various religious bodies engaged on the several missions, voluminous works which would alone form a library." See also Wetzer u. Welte, *Kirchen-Lexikon,* vii, 157 sq.; (Regensburg) *Real-Encyklopädie,* vol. ix, s. v.

2. *The Greek Church.*—Movements have recently occurred in Russia, the principal stronghold and promoter of the Greek Church, indicating some slight development of the modern missionary spirit.

A Russian Bible Society has been organized at St. Petersburg, with the sanction of the emperor Alexander.

A former society, which had 279 auxiliaries, and had circulated 861,000 copies of the Scriptures, was suppressed by the emperor Nicholas.

The Russian government has also organized the establishment of a missionary society for the spread of the orthodox religion among the heathen Mussulmen and Buddhists within its territory. The operations of the society have primary reference to the conversion of the pagan tribes of the Altai and Trans-Balkan country, the Caucasus being assigned to another society of the same kind. The following is an account of the inauguration of the missionary society first referred to: "In 1870 the Greek Church of Russia organized an institution called 'The Orthodox Society on behalf of Missions,' the object of which was the conversion of the non-Christians of all parts of the Russian empire except the Caucasian and Trans-Caucasian provinces already provided for, and both the spiritual edification and social advancement of the converts thus made. The society was inaugurated at Moscow under the presidency of Innocent, metropolitan of that city, and therefore known as 'the Apostle of Kamtchatka.' Liturgy and *Te Deum* were performed, and a sermon preached in the cathedral before a crowded congregation, among whom were present the governor-general of the province and others of the highest officials, although the solemnity had no official character. The society is placed under the patronage of the Russian empress, and the ultimate control of the holy synod. The president is the metropolitan of Moscow, and the society's affairs are administered by a council at that place. Committees are also to be formed in every city under the local bishop. The society is annually to observe the day of Sts. Cyril and Methodius, May 11 (O. S.). Any person subscribing at least three roubles may be a member of the society. Its council possesses, besides the president, two vice-presidents, chosen for two years, one by the president from his coadjutor bishops, and one by the members of the society from the laity. Of the twelve members of the council, four are biennially nominated by the president, and the rest by the members of the society at a general meeting."

3. *Protestant Missions.*—(1.) *Beginnings and Gradual Development.*—The 16th century covered the period of the great Reformation, in which, by severance from the Church of Rome, an effort was made to escape from the accumulated errors and abuses of more than ten centuries, and to establish Christianity on a Scriptural basis. See Reformation. On the part of the Reformers, it was for a long time a struggle for existence, and the first and everywhere present necessity was the establishment of churches as the nuclei of future action. Unhappily a lack of unity, combined with the inherited spirit of intolerance, for a time led to strifes among themselves, which greatly retarded the development of the Protestant churches, and postponed the day of their active efforts for the conversion of the world. Nevertheless the Church of Geneva, as early as 1556, inaugurated foreign missions by sending a company of fourteen missionaries to Rio de Janeiro, in hope of being able to introduce the Reformed religion into Brazil; but the mission was defeated by a combination of treachery with religious and political opposition (see Kidder, *Sketches of Brazil,* vol. i, ch. i). In 1559 a missionary was sent into Lapland by the celebrated Gustavus Vasa, king of Sweden. Early in the 17th century the Dutch, having obtained possession of Ceylon, attempted to convert the natives to the Christian faith. About the same time, many of the Nonconformists who had settled in New England began to attempt the conversion of the aborigines. Mayhew in 1643, and the laborious Eliot in 1646, devoted themselves to this apostolic service. In 1649, during the protectorate of Cromwell, there was incorporated by act of Parliament the "Society for the Propagation of the Gospel in New England." In 1660 the society was dissolved; but, on urgent application, it was soon restored, and the celebrated Robert Boyle was appointed its first

governor. The zeal of this distinguished individual for the diffusion of the Gospel in India and America, and among the native Welsh and Irish; his munificent donations for the translations of the sacred Scriptures into Malay and Arabic, Welsh and Irish, and of Eliot's Bible into the Massachusetts Indian language, as well as for the distribution of *Grotius de Veritate Christianæ Religionis;* and, lastly, his legacy of £5400 for the propagation of Christianity among the heathens, entitle him to distinct attention. Besides these incipient efforts to diffuse the Gospel, glowing sentiments on the subject are to be found scattered through the sermons and epistolary correspondence of the age, which show that many a Christian heart was laboring and swelling with the desire of greater things than these. Still the century closed with witnessing little more than individual and unsustained endeavors. The "Society for Promoting Christian Knowledge," which will be noticed hereafter, whose objects, to a certain extent, embrace the labors of missionaries, was organized in England in 1698; but it was not till the early part of the 18th century that what has been denominated the age of missionary association fairly began to dawn. It opened very faintly and slowly, but nevertheless it has since been growing brighter and brighter to the present day.

(2.) *Present Extent.*—To convey some faint idea of what has subsequently been accomplished, and put in the way of accomplishment, it is deemed proper now to submit a brief sketch of the principal missionary organizations and agencies of the Protestant world. In this exhibit a grouping is adopted which is designed to show primarily the countries in which the several societies originated and have been sustained; secondly, the date of their origin, and a summary view of their character and early history; and, thirdly, the fields of their operation, the amount of their income, and the present condition of their enterprises. For further particulars, consult the articles on each country and society in this Cyclopædia.

The principal Protestant missionary societies may be classified as—I. *Continental;* II. *British;* III. *American.*

"I. *Continental Missionary Societies.—Danish College and Missions.*—As early as the year 1714 the Danish College of Missions was opened in Copenhagen by Frederick IV, king of Denmark, for the training of missionaries. Danish missions to the heathen had been commenced even before this period, agents having been obtained from the University of Halle, in Saxony. On July 9, 1706, two missionaries arrived from Denmark on the Coromandel coast, in India, and settled at Tranquebar. They immediately commenced the study of Tamil, the language spoken in that part of the country. Although they had gone to a part of the Danish empire, and were patronized by royalty, the missionaries encountered great opposition from the prejudices of the natives, and even from the Danish government, who on several occasions arrested and imprisoned the missionaries for months together. Privation, as well as persecution, was the lot of the mission-staff at an early period of their labors. The first remittance sent from Europe, which at that time was greatly needed, was lost at sea, but friends were raised up in a manner unexpected, and loans of money were offered them till they could obtain supplies from the society at home. When their borrowed stock was nearly exhausted, remittances reached them, along with three more missionaries, in 1709. This was but the beginning of better times, for shortly afterwards the London Society for Promoting Christian Knowledge became a liberal patron of their mission, giving them not only an edition of the Portuguese New Testament for circulation among the people, but also a printing-press, with a stock of types and paper, and a Silesian printer. When opposition to the mission subsided, and the cause expanded somewhat, a type-foundery and paper-mill were established, and the work of translation and printing was prosecuted with vigor. In 1715 the Tamil New Testament was completed, and eleven years afterwards the Old Testament made its appearance. Several of the elder missionaries were called away by death, but zealous young men were sent out from Europe from time to time, and a native pastorate was raised up as the fruit of missionary labor, which rendered good service to the cause. In 1758 a mission was opened at Calcutta by one of this society's missionaries, but at the expense of the Society for Promoting Christian Knowledge. In 1762 the celebrated missionary Schwartz, who had already been in the Indian field for twelve years, commenced his labor in Trichinopoly, in connection with which he fulfilled a long, honorable, and successful period of labor, and finished his course with joy in 1798. In the year 1835 the principal Danish missions in India, which had been so largely sustained by the Christian Knowledge Society, were transferred to the Society for the Propagation of the Gospel in Foreign Parts.

"*Mission to Greenland.*—In 1721 the Danish mission to Greenland was commenced by the Rev. Hans Egede, a zealous Christian pastor of Vogen, in Norway. For thirteen years this good man had prayed and planned for a mission to that dreary region. Having at length obtained the consent and patronage of the king of Denmark to the undertaking, the missionary convened a few friends together, opened a subscription list, and in the face of formidable difficulties pushed forward the work, till a ship was purchased to convey him and a small party of settlers to Greenland. During the voyage, which lasted eight weeks, they suffered much from storms, floating mountains of ice, and a leak in the vessel, which they were obliged to stop with their clothes. On landing at their destination, their first work was to build a house of turf and stone, in which the natives, who appeared friendly, assisted them as best they could, intimating by signs, however, that if they intended to live in it they would be frozen to death. While engaged in these exercises, and in striving to acquire the strange language of the Greenlanders, Mr. Egede encountered innumerable difficulties. His greatest trial was the dissatisfaction of the colonists, several of whom resolved to return home, as they were very uncomfortable, and found the natives unwilling to trade. He was supported by the courage and resolution of his heroic wife, however, and by the arrival of two ships with provisions in the summer of 1722, when their stores were nearly exhausted. The missionary found it extremely difficult to induce the people to attend to receive such instruction as he was able to give, and it was only by offering a fish-hook for every letter of the alphabet they learned that he succeeded in getting a few children to come to school. The following year another missionary came to the assistance of Mr. Egede; and the mission was carried on with praiseworthy perseverance, but with little success for a long time. On the accession of Christian VI to the throne of Denmark, government aid was withdrawn from the mission; but the senior missionary, having the option to remain in the country, nobly stood to his post, and continued his labors amid untold privations, troubles, and sufferings, not the least of which arose from the introduction of small-pox into the settlement, which swept off about 2000 of the natives. In 1734 the mission was re-enforced by the appointment of three new agents, one of whom was the son of the pioneer missionary, Mr. Egede. The following year, his beloved wife having been called away by death, Mr. Egede returned to Denmark, but still exerted himself on behalf of the mission. Through his influence the colony and the mission were re-enforced, his son published a Greenland lexicon, the Scriptures were translated into the native language of the people, and 4000 persons were reported as having been brought under religious instruction, although it is admitted that very few of them could be regarded as converts to the faith of the Gospel. The Danish mission to Greenland was ultimately transferred to the 'United Brethren.' Here should be mentioned the mission to *Lapland* (q. v.).

"*United Brethren's Missions* [see MORAVIANS].—The missionary spirit of the Moravian Church manifested itself at an early period after the establishment of the settlement at Herrnhut. When falsely accused, and declared an exile from Germany, count Zinzendorf gave a reply which indicated the spirit by which he was actuated, and the genius of the people with whom he had cast in his lot. He said: 'Now we must collect a congregation of pilgrims, and train laborers to go forth into all the world, and preach Christ and his salvation to every creature.' He was led to this by a visit made to the Danish capital in 1731. When the new colony only numbered about 600 persons, all of whom were poor exiles, and when just beginning to build a church for their own accommodation in what had lately been a wilderness, they resolved to labor for the conversion of the heathen world. Within ten years from that date, 1732, they sent missionaries to St. Thomas and St. Croix, in the West Indies; to the Indians in North and South America; to Lapland, Tartary, Algiers, Western Africa, the Cape of Good Hope, and Ceylon. About the year 1831 an association was formed in London, which raised about £5000 per annum in aid of Moravian missions, and this proved a great help to the cause. Subsequently the United Brethren sent out agents to other West India islands, including Jamaica, Tobago, Antigua, Barbadoes, and St. Christopher's; to South America, Labrador, Greenland, Egypt, Persia, and India. The first missions of the Moravian Brethren were not very successful, but their agents persevered amid numerous difficulties, privations, and sufferings, to which they had been well trained by the painful experience of their previous history, and the ultimate result has been very gratifying.

"*Statistics of Moravian Missions.*—A recent publication says: 'The Moravian mission statistics for 1889 show 127 stations; 286 missionary agents; 1663 native assistants and overseers; 84,201 communicants; 18,280 non-communicants under regular instruction. £16,803 are raised from home sources, and £50,000 is the full amount received annually from all sources. A "Leper Home" at Jerusalem is under their care. In the year 1887 five Christian workers were ministering to about 25 sufferers from that terrible disease. Alaska is the scene of their latest missionary enterprise. It was commenced in 1885 and is directed to the Eskimo of the North-west. Since 1818 the number of members in the entire field has increased from 30,000 to 84,000.

"*Netherlands Missionary Society.*—This institution was formed at Rotterdam in 1796, mainly through the influence of Dr. Vanderkemp. Before the eccentric doctor embarked for his distant sphere of labor in South Africa, to which he had been appointed by the London Missionary Society, he visited Rotterdam to take leave of his friends, and while there he found leisure to publish a Dutch version of an earnest address which had emanated from the London Society, the result of which was the organization of the Netherlands Missionary Society. For some time the financial aid offered to the enterprise was very slender, and no immediate steps were taken towards commencing operations. This interval was wisely employed by the directors in endeavoring to leaven the Dutch mind with the true missionary spirit. When the funds were available, and they contemplated entering upon foreign fields of labor, they were deterred from doing so from the loss of most of the Dutch colonies, which had fallen into the hands of France during the war. The directors therefore made an arrangement with the London Missionary Society to supply men and means for carrying on the work in Africa and India under their anspices and management. In this way they trained and sent out several excellent missionaries to the Cape of Good Hope and the East, where their knowledge of the Dutch language was at once available for carrying on the work. In 1814 Holland rose again to independence, and recovered its colonies, when the Netherlands Society took immediate advantage of the favorable change in national affairs, and sent out five young missionaries from their seminary on their own account, to enter favorable openings which presented themselves in the Eastern Archipelago among the Malays. Other agents followed from year to year, and that part of the world was largely and well occupied by the society. In 1820 two missionaries were sent out to India, and a few years afterwards they were followed by Dr. Gutzlaff, who, finding a number of Chinese at Riosew, his appointed station, was ultimately induced to extend his labors to the 'Celestial Empire.' A mission was also established at Surinam, in Dutch Guiana, and the Netherlands Society was able to report 17 stations and 19 missionaries under their direction, with a goodly number of native converts to the faith of the Gospel united in Church fellowship.

"*Other Dutch Missions.*—It must not be supposed that the organization of the Netherlands Missionary Society is all that Holland has done for the conversion of the heathen. Long anterior to that event, even as early as 1612, the famous Anthony Walwens planted a seminary at Leyden for the preparation of foreign missionaries, the Dutch East India Company countenancing and approving of the institution. When Ceylon came under the power of Holland, in 1636, a number of missionaries were sent out to propagate the Reformed religion among the idolatrous natives. A very superficial mode of making converts seems to have been adopted, however, for when they were reported as amounting to 400,000 in number, there were only 100 communicants. The sad disproportion reveals a system of action which was not only reprehensible in itself, but greatly prejudicial to all subsequent missionary labor, as has been proved by painful experience. Dutch missionaries were also sent out at an early period to Southern Africa, Java, Formosa, Amboyna, and other places.

"*Basle Missionary Society.*—In the year 1815 a seminary was established for the training of missionaries at Basle, in Switzerland. It owed its origin to the gratitude of a few pious people who recognised the providence of God in a violent storm which occurred at a particular juncture, and which proved the means of preserving their town from ruin when the armies of Russia and Hungary were hurling shells into it. The form which the gratitude of these people assumed was a desire to educate pious teachers to send to the heathen, to make them acquainted with the good news of salvation. The school was at first very small, with few scholars, and a slender income of about £50 per annum. In the course of a few years a missionary college was built, and liberal support came from Germany and France, as well as from various parts of Switzerland, so that the income rose to £5000. This result flowed from the formation of auxiliary or branch societies in those countries. The institution was now conducted with vigor, and furnished the English Church Missionary Society with some of its most devoted laborers. In forty years after its commencement it had sent forth nearly 400 missionaries to foreign lands, and 80 were still under training. It was no part of the original plan of this institution to engage in the support and management of foreign missions, but merely to prepare agents for the work. In 1821, however, a society was formed for this object, and from year to year missionaries were sent to North America, Western Africa, India, and China. A society was also organized for the special purpose of disseminating the Gospel among the Jews. The missionaries of the Basle Society are not all ministers. They send out pious mechanics and agriculturists to teach the natives the arts of civilized life, at the same time that they instruct them in the principles of Christianity by the preaching of the Gospel and the establishment of schools. The *Basle Missionary Society* is generally conceded to have first awakened an interest in missions among the Germans. See Ostertag, *Entstehungsgesch. der Missionsgesellschaft zu Basel* (1865).

"*Paris Evangelical Missionary Society.*—The origin of this institution is somewhat curious and interesting. In the year 1822 a meeting was convened at the house of an American merchant, S. V. S. Wilder, Esq., then residing in Paris, to take into consideration the best means of propagating the Gospel in heathen lands. There were present the presidents of the Lutheran and Reformed consistories, as well as many of the ministers of these churches, and others of different persuasions then in the French metropolis. The result was the formation of this society, which, in its commencement, contemplated two objects: the one to employ the press as a means to enlighten the public mind on the nature and character of Protestant missions, and the other to educate young men, who had been duly recommended, in a knowledge of the languages of the East. The Rev. Jonas King was then in Paris, and received an invitation to go to the Holy Land with the Rev. Mr. Fisk, the new society charging itself with his support for a certain period. Subsequently the society devoted all its efforts to South Africa, where its agents have labored for many years with great advantage to several scattered tribes of natives. In 1829 three missionaries were sent by the society to the Cape of Good Hope, one of whom settled among the French refugees at Wellington, near Cape Town, and the other two proceeded to the Bechuana country, and commenced a station at Motito. Re-enforcements arrived from time to time, which enabled the missionaries to extend their labors to various parts of a country that stood in great need of the light of the Gospel. That part of the interior known as Basutoland was occupied by the French missionaries. New stations were formed, schools were established, and chapels built at Bethulia, Morjia, Beersheba, Thaba, Bassion, Mekuatling, Friedor, Bethesda, Berea, and Carmel. At several of these places a goodly number of natives were brought to a saving knowledge of the truth, and united in Church fellowship, although the notorious chief Moshesh still adhered to his heathenism, notwithstanding his superior intelligence. The French mission in South Africa has repeatedly suffered from devastating wars among the natives and settlers, but the greatest blow to its prosperity was the war which raged in France in 1870–71, through which the supplies of the missionaries were in a great measure cut off. Providence, however, raised up friends in the time of need, and the work still goes on.

"*Rhenish Missionary Society.*—The institution now known as the Rhenish Missionary Society was organized in 1828 by the amalgamation of three other associations, which had previously maintained a separate existence in Elberfeld, Barmen, and Cologne. The society was afterwards further strengthened by the incorporation of several other small associations in the Rhenish provinces and Westphalia. In 1829 three missionaries were sent out to South Africa. These were followed in after-years by several others, and stations were ultimately established at Stellenbosch, Worcester, Tulbagh, Saron, Schietfontein, Ebenezer, Kamaggas, and other places within the boundaries of the Cape Colony; and at Bethany, Berseba, Rehoboth, Rood-Volk, Wesley Vale, and Barmen in Namaqualand, and Damaraland. Some of these stations were originally commenced by Wesleyan missionaries who had for many years labored on the south-western coast of Africa. But in 1851 an arrangement was made by which they were given over to the Rhenish Society, as was also the station at Nisbett Bath a few years afterwards, the Wesleyans finding it necessary to concentrate their labors in other localities. In 1834 the Berlin Missionary Society sent two agents to Borneo, and others followed at intervals, who were employed in educational labors. In 1846 the work was extended to China, where several baptisms were soon reported as having taken place. Indeed, undue importance appears to have been attached to baptism by the missionaries of this institution, for when this society had been in existence about twenty-two years, nearly 5000 baptisms were reported, when comparatively few of the number could be regarded as communicants, or Church members. Perhaps this and some other peculiarities may be accounted for by the Lutheran type of theology which the agents generally seem to have espoused.

"*Berlin Missionary Society.*—This society was formally organized in 1824, but it arose out of efforts which had been previously made for missionary objects. As early as the year 1800 an institution was formed in the Prussian capital by members of the Lutheran Church to educate pious youths for foreign mission service. During the following twenty-five years forty students were so educated. In 1834 the Berlin Missionary Society sent out four missionaries to South Africa. These were followed by others during successive years, and arrangements were made for carrying on the work on an extensive scale. One of the first stations occupied by this society was at Beaufort, and thence the missionaries went among the Korannas and Kaffirs. Subsequently the work was extended to Zoar, Bethel, Emmaus, Bethany, Priel, New Germany, and other stations, some of which are situated within the boundaries of the Cape Colony, others in the Orange Free State, the Trans-Vaal Republic, Kaffraria, and in the distant regions of Natal. The last report gives forty-seven stations in South Africa, with sixty-four laborers and 9772 communicants. China was entered in 1883 and now has three stations, ten workers, and 446 communicants. The number of scholars for both missions was 3542 ; native contributions were £4338.

"*Swedish Missionary Society.*—The Swedes made vigorous though unsuccessful efforts to propagate the Gospel in heathen lands as early as the year 1559. The sphere of their operations was Lapland, and their work was conducted under royal auspices. Gustavus Vasa headed the missionary movement of his country for the enlightenment of the Laplandese, and succeeding monarchs threw the weight of their influence into the Christian enterprise. In 1775 the New Testament, translated into Laplandese, was published. The mission was far from prosperous, however, and, after years of hoping against hope, it was abandoned. Nor is this to be wondered at, if one half of what has been recorded in reference to the drinking and other immoral habits of both priests and people is true. After an interval of nearly three centuries, Lapland again engrossed the attention of the Swedes. In 1835 the Swedish Missionary Society was formed, and sent forth a pious young man, named Carl Ludovic Tellstroem, the fruit of the Wesleyan Mission in Stockholm, as a catechist to Lapland. He had many difficulties to encounter from the migratory and dissipated habits of the people; but by following them to their markets and fairs with his Bible, to instruct them in the truths of the Gospel, there is reason to hope that his labors were productive of some good results. Schools were afterwards established for the training of the rising generation, and the children were taught, fed, and clothed at the expense of the society, and at the end of two years were sent home with tracts and books to interest and instruct their parents, families, and friends. It also has a mission in Lapland.

"*Evangelical Lutheran Mission.*—This society was instituted in 1836, with its head-quarters at Dresden. The seat of direction was in 1848 removed to Leipsic. Its efforts have been chiefly turned to Southern India, to the occupation of those fields of labor which had been previously cultivated by the Danish missionaries. From a report published some time ago, it appears that they had in their employ 24 missionaries, with 12 native candidates, in 22 different stations, counting 14,014 Church members and 3653 scholars under their pastoral care. They have also labored as a society in New South Wales, but the results did not long warrant the continuance of this work.

"*North German Missionary Society.*—This institution was organized in the year 1836, with its seat first at Hamburg and afterwards at Bremen. The scene of its earliest labors was India, one station being in the Telogoo country, and the other in the Neilgherries. A serious diminution in the financial receipts led to the transference of the mission for some years to the United States Evangelical Lutheran Church. When the finances revived, however, the responsibilities connected with carrying on the work were again assumed by the Bremen Union, and the field of effort has recently called forth a large amount of sympathy in North Germany. 10 missionaries, 409 communicants, and 321 scholars are now reported.

"*Norwegian Missionary Society.*—This society was formed in 1842, and soon afterwards sent out missionaries to labor among the warlike Zulus in South-eastern Africa. The aim of the institution is to supply agents who are able and willing to instruct the people in the arts of civilized life, as well as in religious knowledge. With this object an estate was purchased in Natal, and an industrial institution established, which has already been productive of much good, reporting 20,660 adherents.

"*Swedish (Lund) Mission.*—In 1846 this society was established at Lund, and three years afterwards it sent out 2 missionaries to China, who were killed by pirates. Other agents were at length sent out, who were spared to take their share in attempting to evangelize the Chinese, with a hopeful prospect of success.

"*Berlin Missionary Union for China.*—This society was established in the month of June, 1850, during a visit of Dr. Gutzlaff to Berlin. Dr. F. W. Krummacher was appointed president, and Prof. Lachs secretary. The object of the society is to send out European laborers, and to aid training institutions. In a field so wide as the vast Chinese empire there is ample room for all, and from the last published accounts it is pleasing to learn that the missionaries of this small but useful association were actively employed in diffusing abroad the light of the Gospel.

"Of minor account is the *Evangelical Mission Society*, founded in 1858 by Gützlaff, until then a member of the *Berlin Missionary Society*. No stress is laid upon the education of the missionary, but the mission field as a life-

home is insisted upon. This society labors in New South Wales, among the Papuas, and in the South Sea Islands and East India.

The *Hermannsburg Mission*, with head-quarters at Hanover, founded by pastor Harms, labors in East Africa, India, Australia, and New Zealand. 13,424 native Christians are connected with them.

"*Miscellaneous Jewish Societies.*—On the continent of Europe there are sundry associations which have for their object the evangelization of the lost sheep of the house of Israel, but their labors are so local and diversified that they cannot well be described separately. The Jewish Society at Berlin was formed in 1822, the Bremenlehe Society in 1839, the Rhenish Westphalia Union in 1843, the Hamburg-Altona in 1844, the Hesse-Cassel in 1845, and the Hesse-Darmstadt in 1845. These are but a few of the many organizations which exist in connection with Christian churches of various denominations for the special benefit of the Jews, and the interest in the spiritual welfare of Abraham's seed is deepening and widening every year.

"II. *British Missionary Societies.—Society for the Propagation of the Gospel in Foreign Parts.*—This is the oldest Protestant missionary society in England, and its origin may be traced to a very remote period. About the year 1644, while the civil wars still continued in that country, a petition was presented to Parliament by a clergyman of the Church of England, supported by many English and Scotch divines, urging the duty of attempting to convert the natives of North America to Christianity. This, no doubt, led to the ordinance passed on July 27, 1648, by the Independents of the Commonwealth, by which a corporation was established, entitled 'The President and Society for the Propagation of the Gospel in New England.' The preamble recites that 'the Commons of England assembled in Parliament, having received intelligence that the heathens in New England are beginning to call upon the name of the Lord, feel bound to assist in the work.' They ordered the act to be read in all the churches of the land, and collections to be made in aid of the object. This was the first missionary association formed in England, and may be considered as the parent of the present 'venerable' Society for the Propagation of the Gospel in Foreign Parts. The colonial settlements first attracted public attention to the spiritual wants of their European and heathen populations. The colonists of New England from the commencement displayed great zeal for the conversion of the Indians. The labors of Eliot, Mather, and others will never be forgotten by the Christian Church. After the Restoration in Great Britain, Baxter and Boyle distinguished themselves by their practical sympathy with the work in which these excellent men were engaged. Meanwhile the Church of England became interested in supplying the new colonies with Episcopalian ministers. In 1675 it was found 'that there were scarcely four members of the Church of England in all the vast tracts of North America.' In view of this lamentable state of things, royalty was moved to liberality. Charles II was induced by Compton, bishop of London, to allow £20 for passage money for ministers and schoolmasters willing to go out to supply the deficiency, and the sum of £1200 was also granted to supply American parishes with Bibles and other religious books. The Society for the Propagation of the Gospel in Foreign Parts was organized June 16, 1701, when it received a charter from William III. The main objects for which it was instituted are stated to be twofold. It was designed 'to provide for the ministrations of the Church of England in the British colonies, and to propagate the Gospel among the native inhabitants of those countries.'

"The income of the Society for the Propagation of the Gospel in Foreign Parts is derived from various sources, embracing Parliamentary grants, collections in churches, schoolrooms, and public halls, in which anniversary sermons are preached and missionary meetings held, and subscriptions and legacies from individuals. In this way the institution is liberally supported, and a large amount of agency is brought to bear upon the people where mission stations have been formed.

"During the long period of its existence the venerable Society for the Propagation of the Gospel in Foreign Parts has gradually extended its labors to various parts of the world, and has been instrumental of much good, especially to British colonists at an early period of their struggles, long before modern missionary societies had commenced their operations. This useful institution now occupies important stations in the British provinces of North America, the Dominion of Canada, British Columbia, the West Indies, Southern Africa, Australia, New Zealand, India, and China. To all these places Anglican bishops and clergymen have gone forth, carrying with them their own views of Church order and discipline; and in connection with every important colony a diocese has been formed, and parishes have been organized after the style of the mother country. The main object of the institution is to supply the services and the ordinances of the Church of England to the tens of thousands of British emigrants who have been annually leaving the shores of their native country from generation to generation, to better their condition in foreign lands. And with much zeal and earnestness have the agents of this society followed their countrymen in all their wanderings, ministering to their spiritual necessities, and bringing home to their recollections the tender associations of the 'old country,' where they were favored in times of yore to listen with pleasure to the sound of the 'church-going bell.' Nor have the dark, benighted heathen population within the boundaries and in the neighborhood of the respective colonies been neglected by this time-honored institution. Many poor wandering Indians in the north-western wilds of America, as well as idolatrous Hindûs in the East, and warlike Kaffirs in Southern Africa, to say nothing of the aborigines of other lands, have been favored with the means of grace and religious instruction through its instrumentality, especially of late years, since attention was more particularly directed to this department of the work.

" *The Society for the Promotion of Christian Knowledge.*—Although not strictly missionary in its primary object, this was at a very early period an auxiliary to Christian missions, and is at this day a most powerful help to the Church of England in her desolate places abroad, as well as at home. It was founded in 1698, mainly by a private clergyman, Dr. Thomas Bray, who, subsequently acting as commissioner in Maryland, and seeing the great necessity for some further effort at home for the advancement of religion in the colonies, happily succeeded in rousing public attention to the matter. Having afterwards been the chief instrument in the formation of the Gospel Propagation Society, Dr. Bray may be fairly considered the founder of both these institutions, and in them of many other noble societies which followed them, by imitation or natural consequence. As early as the year 1709 the Society for the Promotion of Christian Knowledge established a connection with the Danish mission to the Hindûs at Tranquebar, and rendered considerable aid towards the support of the work. The Tanjore mission originated in 1726, and the one at Trichinopoly in 1762, which, with the celebrated Schwarts as its missionary, was taken up five years afterwards by the Christian Knowledge Society, and prosecuted with vigor and success. When other institutions of the Church of England were afterwards organized for the express purpose of propagating the Gospel in foreign lands, the Christian Knowledge Society thenceforth confined its attention to the circulation of religious works—Bibles, Prayer-books, tracts, etc.—at a cheap rate in Great Britain and its several dependencies. There are branch societies in various parts of the country, and persons are constituted members by subscribing annually a sum not less than one guinea.

" *The Church Missionary Society* was instituted in London April 12, 1799. The original design of the society was to act more especially in Africa and the East. That fact was embodied in its first designation, but afterwards dropped. Though the sphere contemplated by the first board of directors was neither small nor unimportant, this society has planted missions over still more widely-extended regions. At first, and for a long time after its commencement, this society was simply supported and governed by the members of the Episcopal Church, and was not in any way subject to ecclesiastical authority. At length the appointment of English bishops to foreign countries rendered a change in the administration of the Church Missionary Society absolutely necessary; and it was decided that in future the institution should be conducted in strict conformity with the ecclesiastical principles of the Establishment. Hence all the missionaries who now go out in its service are placed under the government and direction of the bishops nearest to their respective stations. The funds of the Church Missionary Society are supplied in the usual way by personal contributions, legacies, collections after sermons, and at public meetings; and hitherto the institution has been supported in a very liberal manner.

"The principal spheres of labor entered upon and efficiently worked by the agents of the Church Missionary Society have been in Western Africa, Continental India, and Ceylon, British North America, and the West Indies. In all these countries, but especially in the one first named, the missionaries, catechists, and teachers of this institution have toiled with commendable zeal and diligence, and have been favored to see the fruit of their labor on a large scale. In 1882 Egypt and Arabia were entered. The *Missionary Year-Book*, for 1890, gives the statistics of the society as follows: 294 stations, 282 ordained, 43 lay, and 40 female foreign workers; 266 ordained, 2940 lay, 690 female native workers; 185,538 adherents, 47,531 communicants, 1928 schools, 77,451 scholars. The total income of the society amounted to £221,330 19s. 11d. In 1830 there were only 318 communicants; in 1870 only 21,705. Only 30 missionaries were employed in 1830, and 203 in 1870. In 1830 there was not a single native ordained clergyman employed by the society; in 1870 there were only 109. Up to March 1, 1862, there had gone forth on foreign service, in connection with the Church Missionary Society, 562 men of various countries and races, of whom 121 were Germans.

" *The Colonial Church and School Society* may be regarded as supplementary to the Church Missionary Society. It has rendered valuable assistance to the missionaries employed in the far north-western wilds of British America, formerly included in the Hudson's Bay territo-

ries, to clergymen and teachers laboring among the scattered settlers of Australia, and to mission stations and schools in several of the British colonies.

" *The London Society for Promoting Christianity among the Jews* was founded in the year 1808, although it was not fully organized until the following year. The constitution originally contemplated two objects: 'To relieve the temporal distress of the Jews, and to promote their spiritual welfare.' Public worship, and the education of the children under the care of the society, within the United Kingdom, are conducted in strict conformity to the principles and formularies of the Church of England, with which it has always been identified both in its management and principal support. The first sphere of its action was among the Jews in London. In 1811 a printing-press was established to give employment to poor Jewish converts. Two years later a chapel and schools were opened for the benefit of seventy-nine proselytes and their families. In 1818 the first foreign missionary was sent forth to labor in Poland, where a seminary was soon afterwards established for the training of Jewish converts as missionaries. The society also published a Hebrew edition of the Scriptures for the Jews generally, and prepared a Judæo-Polish version for Poland, and a Syriac version for the Cabalistic Jews. In 1840 the Jewish college for the complete training of missionary agents was established. It has proved an important auxiliary to Jewish missions, not only in connection with the London society, but also to kindred institutions which were afterwards called into existence. The London Society has above 30 mission stations for the benefit of the Jews in Europe, Asia, and Africa; more than 100 missionaries, of whom upwards of 60 are converted Israelites; about 20 schools, with an aggregate of Hebrew children during the last thirty years of upwards of 10,000. This society has seen 50 of its converts ordained as clergymen of Christian congregations at home, and it has distributed above 212,000 copies of the Hebrew Scriptures.

" *Scottish Society for Propagating Christian Knowledge.*—This institution was established in Edinburgh in the year 1709, being the first missionary association organized by the Presbyterians of North Britain. Its original design was the extension of religion in the British empire, and especially in the Highlands and Islands of Scotland. The pagan world subsequently arrested the attention of the directors, and called forth their sympathies and efforts. About twenty years after its formation this society entered into correspondence, with a view to forming stations among the American Indians in the vicinity of New England. Three agents were appointed to labor among the aborigines of these settlements; but, from some untoward circumstances which occurred, they appear to have been wanting in adaptation for their work, and were withdrawn. In 1741 a mission was established among the Delaware Indians, which met with great success. A number of native converts were received into the Church by baptism, and the heart of the missionary was cheered by manifest tokens of the divine presence and blessing. A good work was also carried on for some time among the Indians of Long Island by the agency of this society; but an attempt to evangelize the natives settled on the banks of the Susquehanna was not so successful.

" *The Scottish Missionary Society* was instituted in the month of February, 1796, under the designation of the Edinburgh Missionary Society. The first mission of this society to Sierra Leone was not a success. Nothing daunted by the comparative failure of the mission to Western Africa, in 1802 the Scottish Missionary Society sent out two missionaries to Tartary. This mission also failed in consequence of the oppressive and restrictive measures of government. The agents of this society were more successful, however, in Asiatic Russia, where they commenced their labors in 1805. In 1822 missionaries were also sent to India, when Bombay and Puna were occupied as principal stations. In 1835 this branch of the work was transferred to the General Assembly of the Church of Scotland, which had recently commenced operations in India. In 1824 a mission was organized for Jamaica, which was productive of much good. This produced a mission to Old Calabar, Western Africa, which has been prosecuted with vigor and success. In 1847 the stations of this society in Jamaica were transferred to the United Presbyterian Church, by which they are now carried on with efficiency and success.

" *The Glasgow Missionary Society* was organized in February, 1796. It sent missionaries to Western and Southern Africa, but without very marked success. In 1844 the missions of the Glasgow Society were transferred to the Free Church of Scotland.

" *The Church of Scotland's Foreign Mission Scheme.*—The formation of several missionary societies of a general nature towards the close of the last century appears to have excited the zeal, if not the jealousy, of the Church of Scotland, and overtures were presented to the General Assembly from different synods, praying that attention might be paid to the claims of the heathen world. For some time these were disregarded; but in 1824 the subject was brought forward again, and a committee was appointed to prepare a programme for the organization of what was justly designated as 'a pious and benevolent object.' At the next Assembly, in 1825, the committee reported in favor of British India as a field of labor, and advised the establishment of a great central seminary, with auxiliary district schools for the instruction of Hindû children and young persons of both sexes. In 1829 the Rev. Alexander Duff sailed for Calcutta as the head of the educational institution. The ship was wrecked off the Cape of Good Hope, but without loss of life. After some delay and many dangers, Mr. and Mrs. Duff arrived at Calcutta on May 27, 1830, having lost a valuable library, and 'being more dead than alive.' The seminary was opened in the month of August, and met with remarkable success. Within a few days of the opening 200 pupils were in attendance. Both the elementary and collegiate sections of the institution prospered. The English language was chosen as the medium of instruction in the highest classes, but as soon as qualified teachers and suitable school-books could be obtained, due attention was paid to the vernacular. In 1835 three missionaries—the Rev. James Mitchell, John Wilson, and Robert Nisbet—were transferred by their own desire from the Scottish Missionary Society to the General Assembly's Mission; and in 1843 still further changes were made by the disruption of the General Assembly, which issued in the formation of the Free Church of Scotland, to which all the missionaries in India adhered, with the buildings, furniture, and property of the respective stations. After laboring in connection with the Indian Mission for nearly thirty-five years, Dr. Duff finally returned to his native land in 1863, having meanwhile made but a brief visit to England and the United States in 1854 and 1855.

"The Free Church of Scotland's Foreign Mission.—This Church, after its organization in 1843, made arrangements for carrying on the missionary work both at home and abroad. The educational establishment at Calcutta, under the able superintendence of Dr. Duff, and the mission stations at Bombay, Puna, Nagpore, Madras, and other places in India, as well as those in Southern Africa, the colonies of Canada, Nova Scotia, New Brunswick, the West Indies, Madeira, the Mediterranean, Australia, and Natal, were prosecuted with vigor and success under the new administration.

"The Free Church of Scotland also assumed the responsibility of supporting and carrying on a mission to the Jews which had been organized a short time before the disruption. The history of this branch of the work, so far as Hungary and Austria are concerned, is of more than ordinary interest. Pesth was the scene of a remarkable awakening among the scattered seed of Abraham. Hundreds of Jews, many of them persons of distinction, became simultaneously interested inquirers into the truth of Christianity. The revolution in Hungary caused the suspension of the mission for a time, and the despotism of Austria well-nigh extinguished it. Of late years there have been considerable changes in the scene of its operations, and Frankfort, Amsterdam, Breslau, Pesth, Galatz, and other places are mentioned in the society's report as places where its agents are now laboring for the conversion of the Jews to the faith of the Gospel.

"United Presbyterian Synod's Foreign Mission.—In the year 1835 the United Secession Church planted a mission in the West Indies by the agency of the Revs. William Paterson and James Niven. In the course of a few years several stations were opened in Jamaica, Trinidad, and the Grand Caymanas. The progress of the mission to these parts is indicated by the following scenes of labor, and the dates when the work was commenced at each place respectively: Jamaica—Stirling, 1835; New Broughton, 1835; Friendship, 1837; Goshen, 1837; Mount Olivet, 1839; Montego Bay, 1848; Kingston, 1848. Trinidad—Port of Spain, 1839; Arauca, 1842. The Great Caymanas—Georgetown, 1846. In 1846 a mission was commenced at Old Calabar, in Western Africa, intended to be worked chiefly by converted negroes from Jamaica. The synod also sent several missionaries to Canada, who have since succeeded in forming self-sustaining congregations, and even in organizing large and influential presbyteries. The first work of the United Presbyterian Church, formed in May, 1847, was to accept of the transference of the stations and agents of the Scottish Missionary Society in Jamaica, and of the Glasgow African Missionary Society in Kaffraria, which it has since conducted with vigor and success. It has also a Jewish mission to Algiers, Aleppo, and other places.

"English Presbyterian Synod's Foreign Mission.—This Church entered upon foreign missionary operations in 1844. The principal scene of its labors is China, and although the work has not as yet been conducted on a large scale, it is hoped that lasting good will be the result. The funds of the society were considerably augmented a few years ago by the handsome bequest of the late Mr. Sandeman, to whose benevolence and general Christian character a graceful tribute is paid in the annual report for 1859. Promising mission stations have been formed at Amoy and Swatow, where a few converted natives have been united in Church fellowship, and an additional missionary has recently been ordained and sent forth to strengthen the hands of the brethren who have been some time in the field.

"Reformed Presbyterian Church Mission.—Foreign mis-

VI.—12*

sionary operations were commenced by this body in 1842. The principal scene of its labor has been the South Sea Islands, especially New Zealand and the New Hebrides. The Rev. John Inglis labored for many years in the island of Aneiteum with considerable success. By the blessing of God on his unwearied efforts a goodly number of converted natives were gathered into the fold of Christ, some of whom became efficient Church officers and teachers of others, while the rising generation were carefully trained in a knowledge of God's holy Word to an extent which is not often witnessed even on mission stations. At one time, out of a population of 1900 in a certain district, 1700 were able to read the Bible—a proportion of readers perhaps scarcely surpassed in any country.

"Irish Presbyterian Church's Mission.—The General Assembly of the Presbyterian Church in Ireland commenced its missionary operations in 1840. Their first field was India. Considerable attention has also been paid to the British colonies by this body, missionaries having been sent out at different times to North America, Australia, Tasmania, and New Zealand. The Assembly has also Jewish missions at Hamburg, Bonn, and in Syria.

"Scottish Society for the Conversion of Israel.—This society was instituted in the year 1845, not in connection with any particular branch of the Christian Church, but on a broad and catholic basis, the directors being chosen from different denominations. It was originally designed to afford temporal relief to the migrating Jews who visited Glasgow. Subsequently it extended its operations to the seed of Abraham in foreign lands, and sought their spiritual benefit as well as temporal welfare. Stations were formed and agents employed at Hamburg, Algiers, and Alexandria; but in 1857, when the United Presbyterian Church originated a mission to the Jews, these foreign stations were transferred to that body, from which most of the funds had been derived, and the Scottish Society again confined its labors to home, as before.

"Edinburgh Medical Missionary Society.—In the year 1841 several of the leading medical practitioners in the Scotch metropolis, in the course of their reading, having come to the conclusion that medical skill might be greatly helpful to Christian missions, formed themselves into an association for this object. Their first efforts were directed to China, where the want of medical knowledge was sorely felt. The constitution of the society does not restrict its operations to the Celestial empire, but leaves it at liberty to afford its aid to the missionary enterprise in any part of the world. The intention of its patrons is to give gratuitous medical aid to the suffering poor, and at the same time to embrace every opportunity of imparting religious instruction to the dark, benighted heathens who are the objects of its benevolence.

"London Missionary Society.—Towards the close of the year 1794 a spirited paper appeared in the Evangelical Magazine advocating the formation of a mission to the heathen on the broadest possible basis. This led to the organization of the London Missionary Society. The Rev. David Bogue, D.D., of Gosport, the author of the paper alluded to, may therefore be regarded as the father and founder of this noble institution; and his name will ever be held in grateful remembrance by the friends of missions. Two months after the appearance of Dr. Bogue's practical paper, a conference was held to take steps for giving effect to the laudable proposal. That conference was attended by representatives from several evangelical bodies, in accordance with the proposed catholicity of the spirit of action. The result of that conference was a carefully-prepared address to the ministers and members of the various churches, and the appointment of a committee to diffuse information, and to learn the sentiments of the Christian public upon the subject. A conference upon a larger scale was held in September, 1795—twelve months after the publication of Dr. Bogue's paper. The conference lasted three days, and comprised a large and influential body of Christians. The Rev. Dr. Haweis preached an eloquent and impressive sermon on the occasion, taking for his subject the great commission (Mark xv, 16); and the Rev. J. Burder and the Rev. Rowland Hill also took part in the preliminary work which issued in the formation of the institution. Thus, amid many prayers, much fraternal love, and the promise of large support both in counsel and contributions, the London Missionary Society was launched.

"The first question which pressed upon the attention of the directors of the London Missionary Society after its formation was the selection of the most suitable fields of labor. Wishing to commence their operations in a part of the world where no efforts had as yet been made by any other society for the evangelization of the natives, and encouraged by the reports which had been brought to England from the South Seas by an exploring expedition which had discovered many new islands, they decided, in the first place, to send missionaries to Polynesia. The field once chosen, and that choice published, it was found that neither agents nor money were wanting for the enterprise. The enthusiasm which prevailed was broad and deep, and the readiness with which service was offered and funds furnished cheered the hearts of the directors, and was regarded by them as a clear indication of the divine favor. In the early part of 1796 the missionary ship *Duff* was purchased, and freighted with a suitable cargo; and twenty-nine agents who had volunteered their services embarked for their distant sphere of labor. These were not all missionaries, properly so called, only four of them being ordained ministers, and the rest mechanics or artisans of different kinds, intended to take a part in the good work. Everything appeared providential hitherto, and, to crown all, Mr. James Wilson, a retired captain of excellent spirit and great professional skill, proffered his services to navigate the ship with its precious cargo to Polynesia. After some detention at Portsmouth, the *Duff* went to sea on Sept. 23, followed by the earnest prayers of thousands; and by the good providence of God reached her destination in safety, notwithstanding a severe storm which she encountered off the Cape of Good Hope.

"The missionary ship *Duff* arrived at Tahiti on March 6, 1797, and anchored safely in Matavia Bay, at a distance of about three quarters of a mile from the shore. In the afternoon the captain and a member of the mission landed, and were met on the beach by Paitia, the aged chief of the district, who welcomed them to the country, and offered them a large native house for their accommodation. It was arranged that to the four ordained ministers and fourteen of the unmarried brethren should be confided the establishment and prosecution of the mission at Tahiti; that ten should endeavor to effect a settlement at Tonga, one of the Friendly Islands; and that two should proceed to the Marquesas. The agents were distributed according to this arrangement, and commenced their labors, no doubt, with the best intentions. It would be an exercise of painful interest, if our space permitted us, to give the sequel of this enterprise in all its particulars. It may suffice to say that in this large band of missionary agents, selected in such haste, there were several men who proved altogether deficient in mental power, moral courage, and other necessary qualifications for the work. Consequently, some proved unfaithful and abandoned the enterprise altogether; others were discouraged, and the few who were stout-hearted and courageous labored under many difficulties. In some of the islands the mission totally failed, several of the agents being murdered, and the rest having to flee for their lives. In after-years the London Missionary Society learned to select its missionaries with greater care, and seminaries for their proper training were speedily established. After numerous reverses, disappointments, and long delay, the missionaries of the London Society ultimately prosecuted their labors in various islands of Polynesia, with results of a most remarkable character, in connection with which the name of John Williams, the martyr of Erromanga, and those of other worthies, will be handed down to posterity as entitled to affectionate remembrance.

"In 1798, about three years after its commencement, the London Missionary Society sent forth four missionaries to Southern Africa: Dr. Vanderkemp and Mr. Edmonds to labor in that part of the Cape Colony which bordered upon Kaffraria, and Messrs. Kitchener and Edwards were stationed north of the colony among the Bushmen. In the following year Dr. Vanderkemp and his colleague penetrated into Kaffirland, and offered the Gospel to the warlike natives, but with little success at that time. They afterwards labored among the Hottentots living within the colonial boundary, several of whom were successfully instructed in the things of God, and brought to a saving knowledge of the truth. In 1806 the missionaries crossed the Orange River, and commenced their labors among the wild Namaquas. Here the celebrated Robert Moffatt began his honorable and eventful career, and was favored to rejoice over the notorious Hottentot chief Africaner. Mr. Moffatt afterwards established a prosperous mission at Kuruman, among the Bechuanas, many of whom he saw gathered into the fold of Christ, and into whose language he translated the Holy Scriptures. After a long, laborious, and honorable missionary career, extending over half a century, Mr. Moffatt finally returned to England in 1870, a remarkable instance of God's preserving goodness and of entire devotion to the mission cause. To the north of Bechuanaland, in the region of the Zambeze, Dr. Livingstone performed his wonderful missionary travels, and there also the ill-fated mission of the London Society to the Makololo was attempted.

"British India was the next field of labor on which the London Missionary Society entered. In 1804 the Rev. Messrs. Ringeltaube, Cran, and Des Granges were sent out with the view of establishing a mission on the coast of Coromandel. On their arrival, Messrs. Cran and Des Granges proceeded to Vizagapatam, which lies about 500 miles south-west of Calcutta, and which was then unoccupied by any other society's missionaries. There they met with a cordial reception, and soon succeeded in establishing schools, and in translating portions of the Scriptures into the Telinga language. In 1808 the mission was greatly strengthened by the conversion of a celebrated Brahmin, named Ananderayer, an interesting account of which was given in the *Evangelical Magazine*. In 1809 Mr. Cran died, and his colleague, Mr. Des Granges, only survived him about twelve months. Thus was the station left desolate for a time; but other zealous missiona-

ries were sent out, and the cause again prospered. The good work was afterwards extended to Madras, Belgaum, Bellary, Bangalore, Mysore, Salem, Combaconum, Coimatoor, Travancore, Chinsarah, Berhampore, Benares, Surat, and other parts of India. At all these places schools were established, congregations gathered, the Gospel faithfully preached, and many souls won for Christ through the agency of this excellent institution.

"At an early period of its history, the London Missionary Society was led to turn its attention to the West Indies. In 1807 a Dutch planter in British Guiana made an earnest appeal to the directors for a missionary, accompanied by a liberal offer of pecuniary assistance. This led to the appointment of the Rev. John Wray as the first agent of the society in Demerara. As the work extended, additional missionaries were sent out, and stations were ultimately established in George Town, Berbice, and various parts of the colony, much to the advantage of the poor negroes, who made rapid progress in religious knowledge. The mission was progressing delightfully, when it received a severe check by the general rising of the slaves. But after the emancipation in 1834, the London Missionary Society realized the benefit of the change in common with other kindred institutions, and their numerous stations in Demerara, Berbice, and Jamaica have been favored with a pleasing measure of prosperity under the more favorable circumstances of entire and unrestricted freedom.

"To the London Missionary Society must be awarded the honor of organizing the first Protestant mission from England to China. In the year 1807 the Rev. Robert Morrison was sent out, chiefly for the purpose of securing, if possible, a good translation of the Scriptures into the difficult language of the Chinese empire. In this he succeeded beyond the expectations of the most sanguine friends of the enterprise. He proved admirably adapted for the peculiar and untried sphere upon which he entered. After laboring at his translation for some years, Dr. Morrison was joined by other missionaries, and the work of preaching and teaching was commenced in good earnest. The progress of the mission was slow at first, and it was not till the year 1814 that the first convert was baptized. Afterwards, however, a considerable number of Chinese were brought to a saving knowledge of the truth, and gathered into the fold of Christ, through the united labors of the missionaries of this society.

"But the most interesting mission of the London Society was the one which was undertaken to the island of Madagascar in 1818 by the appointment of the Rev. Messrs. Jones and Bevan as the first missionaries. Returning for their families, whom they had left at the Mauritius until they should learn the state of the country, these excellent brethren proceeded to Tamatave in the course of the following year, and commenced their work. Within seven weeks of their arrival five of this little band sickened and died, and Mr. Jones was left alone. He nobly resolved to persevere in his solitary work as he best could, and having returned from the Mauritius, whither he was obliged to retire for a season for the recovery of his health, he was joined by other missionaries from England, and their united labors proved very successful. During the first fifteen years of this mission the entire Bible was translated into the Malagasy language, and printed at the mission press in the capital, and the missionaries frequently preached to a congregation of 1000 persons with the most blessed results. Then came a dark and gloomy night of persecution, during the bloody reign of a cruel pagan queen. The missionaries were driven from the island, hundreds of the converted natives suffered martyrdom rather than deny Christ, and the once promising mission was laid desolate. This state of things had continued for more than a quarter of a century, when, in the order of divine providence, by the death of the queen in 1867, the way was opened once more for the preaching of the Gospel in Madagascar. The mission was now recommenced, and it was found that the native Christians had generally proved faithful, numerous accessions also having been made to their number. Several memorial churches were built to commemorate the death of the martyrs, and the work was extended to various parts of the island, with the prospect of still greater good in time to come.

"The report of the London Missionary Society for 1888 stated : 'In China there are connected with the society 39 missionaries; in India, 97; in Madagascar, 32; in South Africa, 25; in the West Indies, and in the South Sea district, 141. The total income of the society amounted to £124,860 1*s.* 9*d.*, the expenditure to £128,254 5*d.* Three magazines are published by the society—the *Chronicle*, the *Juvenile Monthly*, and *Quarterly News of Woman's Work*. Up to 1888 the society had sent out 887 missionaries.

"*British Society for the Propagation of the Gospel among the Jews.*—This institution was established in London in the year 1842, and draws its chief support from the various Dissenting communities in England. Its object is identical with the Episcopal Society for Propagating Christianity among the Jews; but, being organized on a more catholic and general basis, it affords an appropriate sphere of evangelical labor in this department of missionary work for Nonconformists of every name. This society does not aim so much to baptize and found churches as to preach the Gospel and circulate the Scriptures and religious tracts among the seed of Abraham in various countries. Its first sphere of operations was among the Jews in the cities and seaport towns of Great Britain. It afterwards extended its labors to the Continent, and opened stations at Frankfort, Paris, Lyons, Würtemberg, and Breslau, and also at Gibraltar and Tunis, the place last named having been found an excellent centre from which to work in Northern Africa, as well as a position of great influence from its being in the direct highway to the Holy Land. This society has also its mission college for the Jews, in which it trains many of its own agents. The twenty-four missionaries employed by this institution are all converted Jews, with the exception of two or three, more than one half of whom were trained at the mission college. Nor are the religious interests of the rising generation neglected. From the beginning attention has been paid to Sabbath and week-day schools for Jewish children; and a few years ago an orphan asylum was established, in which a considerable number of destitute Hebrew boys and girls are fed, clothed, and instructed; and when they grow up they are put to useful trades and occupations, that they may earn their own livelihood.

"*Congregational Home Missions.*—The report presented to the last anniversary of this association stated that the society consists of 475 home mission pastors, who occupy central positions composed of four, five, or six villages, where, with the help of 121 voluntary lay preachers, the Gospel is preached in 786 mission chapels and rooms, the attendance in which had exceeded 102,000 persons. There is in connection with this organization a department of lay and colportor evangelists, 100 of whom are now at work, who had visited 80,000 families during the year, distributed 250,000 tracts, sold 3000 copies of the Bible, and 120,000 periodicals. One thousand members had been added to the churches by means of this agency during the year.

"*Baptist Missionary Society.*—Like most other great and good things, the Baptist Missionary Society had a small and humble beginning. Its early history is inseparably connected with that of William Carey, who may be fairly regarded as its father and founder, as well as its first missionary to the heathen world. Although of humble parentage and low condition in life, Mr. Carey was a man of great mental energy and unwearied perseverance. While plying his lowly avocations, first as a shoemaker and afterwards as a humble pastor and village schoolmaster, he conceived the grand idea of attempting to propagate the Gospel among heathen nations; and, to make himself better acquainted with the wants of the world, and to prepare himself for future action, he constructed maps of various countries, read numerous books, and studied two or three different languages. At length, in 1784, the Nottingham Baptist Association, to which he belonged, resolved upon holding monthly concerts for prayer. Mr. Carey's one topic at these meetings was the degraded state of heathen lands; but few entirely sympathized with him in his views. Seven years later, when he had removed to Leicester, he introduced his favorite theme, and pressed it upon the attention of his ministerial brethren when assembled together. He respectfully submitted for their consideration, 'Whether it was not practicable, and their bounden duty, to attempt somewhat towards spreading the Gospel in the heathen world.' At the next meeting of the association, in the month of May, 1792, Mr. Carey preached his ever-memorable sermon from Isa. liv, 2, 3, and dwelt with great power on his two leading divisions —'Expect great things from God, and attempt great things for God.' The impression produced by this discourse was so deep and general that the association resolved upon instituting a mission to the heathen at their next meeting in autumn. On Oct. 2 the society was formed, and although the collection on the occasion only amounted to £13 2s. 6d., ample funds speedily flowed in from various quarters.

"After the formation of the Baptist Missionary Society, the next great question was in reference to the specific field in which operations should commence. Mr. Carey had thought long and anxiously about the South Sea Islands, and held himself in readiness to proceed thither if he could be promised support even for one year. Just at that time he met with a Mr. Thomas, from India, who was busily engaged in collecting funds for the establishment of a Christian mission in Bengal. In consequence of the representations made by this well-meaning but somewhat eccentric stranger, it was arranged that Mr. Carey should accompany him to the East, and that they should unite their efforts to establish a Baptist mission among the Hindûs. After encountering numerous and complicated difficulties, financial, domestic, and political, they at length embarked for India in the *Princess Maria*, a Danish East Indiaman, on June 13, 1793. They landed in safety at Balasore on Nov. 10; but finding the way closed by the restrictions of the East India Company against their openly pursuing their sacred vocation as Christian missionaries, and being uncertain as to what amount of support, if any, they would receive for themselves and their families from England, they went up the country, and took situations which were offered to them in connection

with establishments for the cultivation and manufacture of indigo. At the same time they studied the language of the natives, held religious meetings with the people, and labored in every way to bring them to a saving knowledge of the truth. Mr. Carey, moreover, from the beginning gave great attention to the translation of the Scriptures into the Bengalee and other languages of the East, and the extent to which he succeeded was perfectly marvellous. As the prospects of success improved, additional missionaries were sent out from England; the head-quarters of the mission were removed to the Danish settlement of Serampore; printing-presses were set up, and the work of translating and preaching the Gospel was carried on in a manner which has scarcely ever been equalled in any other part of the mission field. Mr. Carey became one of the most learned men in India, and for several years held the high office of professor of languages in the Calcutta College, in addition to his missionary duties. After a long and honorable career, during which he saw the Baptist mission in India greatly extended, and the whole or parts of the sacred Scriptures translated into about forty different languages of the East, Dr. Carey died in peace at Serampore, at the advanced age of seventy-three, on Monday, June 9, 1834, leaving a noble example of disinterested zeal and entire devotedness to the service of Christ among the heathen.

"The attention of the Baptist Missionary Society was directed at an early period to the West Indies, and in 1814 the first station was commenced at Falmouth, in Jamaica. The first regular missionary appointed to this interesting sphere of labor was the Rev. John Rowe, but the ground had been partially prepared by Mr. Moses Baker, a man of color from America. The favorable reports sent home by the first missionary to Jamaica induced the society to send out two more laborers in the course of the following year. The number of agents was increased still further afterwards, till, in the course of fifteen years, fourteen pastors were employed, and the Church members numbered upwards of 10,000. Prosperous stations were established not only at Falmouth, but also in Kingston, Montego Bay, and in most of the other chief towns on the island. All went on well till the year 1831, when there occurred one of those insurrections of the Negro slaves which have repeatedly been so disastrous in their results to the missionary enterprise. As usual, the planters strove to involve the missionaries in the consequences of their own folly. In their fury the colonists destroyed nearly all the chapels of the Baptist Missionary Society throughout the island, with a view to secure the expulsion of their agents; but in this they were disappointed. The value of the property thus wantonly destroyed was estimated at £20,000. The local government gave no redress; but the Imperial Parliament made handsome grants to compensate for the loss, and the British public came forward most liberally to help to restore the waste places of Zion. When the storm had passed over, the work again revived and prospered, not only in Jamaica, but also in the Bahama Islands, Trinidad, Honduras, St. Domingo, and other parts of the West Indies.

"In the year 1848 the Baptist Missionary Society extended its labors to Western Africa, and stations were established in the island of Fernando Po, and also on the banks of the Camaroons, in the Bight of Benin. The Rev. A. Saker was the first missionary to this part of the coast, and he was spared to labor for many years, and to see the fruit of his labor, while many others fell a sacrifice to the climate soon after their arrival. At length the Baptist missionaries were expelled from Fernando Po by the Spanish government on their taking possession of the island and on the termination of their agreement with the English. On the mainland, however, where unrestricted religious liberty was allowed by the native chiefs, the good work took deep root, and a goodly number of hopeful converts were gathered into the fold of Christ. When China was thrown open to European missionaries, the Baptist Missionary Society responded to the call for Gospel preachers, and sent out two or three agents, who succeeded in making a good beginning, notwithstanding numerous difficulties which had to be encountered. Nor has this institution been unmindful of the claims of Europe. It has recently appointed missionaries to Norway and Italy; and in Rome itself its agents are taking their share in the glorious work of shedding the light of divine truth on the darkness of popish error and superstition.

"According to the last annual report, the number of European missionaries employed in various parts of the world by the Baptist Missionary Society (not including the Jamaica Baptist Union) is 118, in addition to 306 native pastors and preachers, who have been raised up in distant lands as the fruit of missionary labor. These occupy 446 stations, and minister in 320 chapels of various kinds, and they have under their pastoral care 7822 European and 12,776 native Church members. The number of scholars attending the mission schools is 3777. In connection with the Jamaica Baptist Union there are 59 pastors, 144 churches, 32,342 Church members.

"*General Baptist Missionary Society.*—The General Baptists, so called from their general or Arminian views of redemption, formed a missionary society in 1816. The origin of this association is, under God, traceable mainly to the able advocacy of the Rev. J. G. Pike. Regarding the field as wide enough for all the agents that could be sent into it, this society also first turned its attention to India. In the month of May, 1821, two missionaries, the Rev. Messrs. Bampton and Peggs, sailed for Cuttach, the principal town in Orissa, the seat of the notorious idol Juggernaut. The first of these devoted servants of Christ soon finished his course; but other agents followed at intervals, and opened new stations in adjoining districts. They were driven, however, by the force of external circumstances, to make frequent changes in their locations and plans of action. Their chief work consisted in combating the prejudices and practices of idolatry, and their stations were generally found in the neighborhood of the head-quarters of the venerated idols. The missionaries succeeded in establishing schools for both sexes, and an asylum for orphan or destitute children. Many a precious life they instrumentally preserved, which had been devoted to the blood-stained altar. As elsewhere, the great enemy to Christianity in Orissa was caste, change of creed being attended by enormous sacrifices—not only separation from kindred, but the loss of the wonted means of support. Despite all obstacles, and they were many and serious, the Gospel was ultimately embraced by considerable numbers, although the missionaries had to wait six years for their first convert. To counteract in some measure the evils which followed upon the loss of caste, the missionaries set themselves to the formation of villages, where the converts might be mutually helpful to each other. A carefully executed translation of the Bible into the Orissa language, and the preparation of a dictionary and grammar, were the work of Mr. Sutton, one of the society's missionaries, who exerted himself nobly in this department of Christian labor. In 1845 this society established a mission at Ningpo, in China, which, although feeble in its commencement, encourages the hope of its friends and patrons as to a fair measure of success in time to come.

"*Wesleyan Methodist Missionary Society.*—The name of Dr. Coke must ever be associated with the early history of Methodist missions. He was raised up and called by the providence of God to this department of Christian labor just at the time when his services were specially required. Mr. Wesley was fully engaged in guiding that great religious movement which took place in the United Kingdom in the latter part of the 18th century, when the foreign work was commenced, and could ill afford to have his attention called off to distant fields of labor. It was at this critical period that Dr. Coke appeared on the stage of action. Wearied with the restrictions and petty annoyances which he met with in the discharge of his duties as a parish clergyman, and with a heart fired with true missionary zeal, after his remarkable conversion to God, he joined the Methodist connection, and at Mr. Wesley's request took the general superintendency of the home and foreign missions—an office which he filled with credit to himself and advantage to the cause during the remainder of his long, active, and useful life. In the prosecution of his arduous duties, Dr. Coke crossed the Atlantic eighteen times, established a number of new missions, and went about from door to door himself to collect the means for their support in the most praiseworthy manner, long before the Missionary Society was regularly organized.

"Methodism had only been planted in the United States of America a few years when, in 1780, the work was extended to Canada; in 1783, to Nova Scotia; in 1791, to New Brunswick, and about the same time to Prince Edward's Island and Newfoundland. A few years afterwards Wesleyan missions were established in the Hudson's Bay Territory and British Columbia; while at the same time the Methodist Episcopal Church was spreading itself over every state in the Union, and planting mission stations in California and Oregon, and in other distant parts of the great continent. Dr. Coke was on his voyage to Nova Scotia with three missionaries—Messrs. Warrener, Hammett, and Clarke—when the vessel in which they sailed was driven by a storm to the West Indies. Observing, as they believed, the hand of God in this event, the missionaries at once began to labor in those interesting islands, where their services were much required; and their numbers being soon increased, on the return of the zealous doctor to Europe, the foundation of a great and glorious work was laid, which continued to grow and expand from year to year, with great advantage to all classes of people. Dr. Coke had crossed the Atlantic eighteen times in superintending and carrying on the missions in America and the West Indies, and was advanced in years when, in 1813, he conceived the grand idea of Methodist missions to India. Bent upon his noble purpose, he pushed onwards through every difficulty, and on the last day of the year he sailed for the far-distant East, accompanied by six devoted young missionaries appointed to this service by the Wesleyan Conference. On the morning of May 3, 1814, Dr. Coke was found dead in his cabin, having, it is supposed, expired in the night in a fit of apoplexy. The Rev. Messrs. Harvard, Clough, Squance, Ault, Erskine, and Lynch keenly felt the sudden removal of their leader and head; but, having committed his remains to their watery grave in the Indian Ocean, they proceeded

to India in the true missionary spirit, and by the blessing of God succeeded in laying the foundation of the present prosperous Wesleyan mission in Ceylon and continental India.

"The burden of superintending and collecting for the support of the early Methodist missions devolved almost entirely on the indefatigable Dr. Coke, although a nominal missionary committee occasionally sat in London to transact business in his absence. But when the Conference sanctioned his departure for India, it was deemed necessary to make new arrangements for carrying on the work, to which he could no longer attend as formerly. It is believed that the idea of forming a Methodist Missionary Society originated with the late Rev. George Morley. It was not till 1817 that the connectional society was formally inaugurated, with a code of 'Laws and Regulations,' having the express sanction and authority of Conference; but 1813 and the Leeds meeting are regarded as the true commencement of the society. At this time Wesleyan foreign missions had been successfully carried on for forty-four years, and upwards of one hundred missionaries were usefully employed in foreign fields of labor. Thus it will be seen that Methodist missions do not owe their origin to the Missionary Society, but that, on the other hand, the Missionary Society owes its origin to the missions.

"When the Wesleyan Missionary Society had been fully organized, and auxiliaries and branches established in various parts of the United Kingdom, the early foreign missions of the connection were not only maintained in their wonted efficiency and good working order, but they were extended to other countries from year to year as openings presented themselves, and men and means were found available for the work. In 1811 a mission was commenced in Western Africa, and the work was extended to Southern Africa in 1814, to Australia in 1815, to Tasmania in 1821, to New Zealand in 1822, to the Friendly Islands in 1826, to China in 1845, and to Italy in 1860. In all these countries congregations have been gathered, churches organized, schools established, and places of worship erected on a scale more or less extensive, according to circumstances, and the Wesleyan Missionary Society has endeavored to take its full share in the work of evangelizing the inhabitants of those and other distant regions of the globe.

"According to the report for the year 1871, the Wesleyan Missionary Society has now, in connection with the various fields of labor occupied by its agents in Europe, Africa, Asia, America, and Australia, 1029 ordained missionary ministers and assistants, including supernumeraries; 779 central or principal stations, called circuits; 4366 chapels and other preaching-places; 95,924 full and accredited Church members, and 144,733 scholars receiving instruction in the mission schools. The total amount of income from all sources for the year was £149,767 5s. 11d. Of this sum, £39,698 1s. 6d. was contributed by affiliated conferences and foreign districts.

"*Ladies' Committee for Ameliorating the Condition of Heathen Women.*—In the year 1858 the degraded condition of heathen women was brought to the notice of a few eminent Christian ladies in London connected with the Wesleyan Missionary Society, who at once formed themselves into a committee to devise the means of promoting their welfare. The first measure decided upon was to send out female teachers to assist missionaries' wives in the schools already formed, and up to the present time 27 teachers have been sent abroad: to the West Indies, 3; continental India, 10; Ceylon, 3; South Africa, 7; China, 3; and Italy, 1. The committee also supports nine Bible women in Mysore, Bangalore, Canton, and Jaffna. Important assistance has also been rendered by grants of pecuniary aid or materials to 13 schools in continental India, 17 in Ceylon, 3 in China, 17 in South Africa, 1 in Italy, 1 in Honduras, and 5 in the Hudson's Bay Territory. In this good work about £1000 has been collected and spent annually, and Christian counsel and encouragement have often been communicated to female teachers and missionaries' wives abroad of more value than any material aid.

"*Wesleyan Home Missions.*—Methodism was professedly missionary in its character from the beginning, and it has ever sought to spread scriptural holiness throughout the land. But of late years the Wesleyan Conference has organized a systematic plan of home missionary work to supply and maintain earnest ministers for the benefit of the neglected population of our large cities and rural districts, as well as to afford aid to the poor, dependent circuits of the United Kingdom. Seventy-six missionary ministers are now employed in home mission work in England, Scotland, and Wales, besides eight as chaplains to minister to soldiers and sailors in the British army and royal navy. About £30,000 are annually contributed and expended in carrying on this good work, with gratifying results, and much more good might be done if funds were available for the purpose. Since the commencement of the work under its present organization, to the Conference of 1870, there had been an increase in the home mission circuits of 14,686 persons. In connection with that increase, and springing from it, the higher work of spiritual conversion to God was everywhere manifested. Last year more than 800 excellent people, constrained by the love of Christ, aided the home missionary ministers in the work in which they were engaged.

"*Primitive Methodist Missionary Society.*—Its missions may be divided into Home, Colonial, and Foreign, all of which are prosecuted with vigor. Besides supplying many neglected districts in England, Wales, Scotland, and Ireland with plain, faithful preachers of the Gospel, it has sent forth foreign missionaries to British North America, Australia, Western and Southern Africa, and some other distant lands. The success which has already attended the efforts of the society is very encouraging, and it bids fair to take its full share of labor in seeking to evangelize the heathen at home and abroad. The number of missionaries employed in England is 92; in Wales, 8; in Ireland, 7; in Scotland, 7; in circuits, 9; in Victoria, 7; in New South Wales, 15; in Queensland, 4; in Tasmania, 4; in New Zealand, 4; in Canada, 51; in Western Africa, 2; in Southern Africa, 1; total, 211. The total number of stations is 143, and of members, 13,898.

"*Minor British Missionary Societies.*—In addition to the leading missionary societies of the United Kingdom which carry on the work of propagating the Gospel in heathen countries on a large scale in various parts of the globe, there are several minor institutions which have been made very useful, notwithstanding the comparatively limited sphere of their influence. These associations have generally been organized for special objects or single missions, and have been conducted with varied results, according to circumstances. Of these the following may be mentioned:

"*Welsh Calvinistic Methodist Foreign Missionary Society.*—The first foreign mission of the Welsh Calvinistic Methodists was to the north-east district of Bengal, among the Kassias, one of the hill-tribes of natives. This work was undertaken soon after the formation of the society (1840), and about ten years subsequently, in 1850, another station was commenced at Sythet. The missionaries did not confine their labors to preaching and teaching; they also turned their attention to those literary studies which are so necessary to success in all evangelical efforts in India. Messrs. Jones and Lewis succeeded in translating the four Gospels and the Acts of the Apostles into the Kassia language; nor did they labor without success in their direct efforts to turn the heathen from dumb idols to serve the true and living God. The Calvinistic Methodists have also established a mission in Brittany, the language of that part of the European continent being similar, it is said, to the Welsh. They have also a mission to the Jews, which has been prosecuted with as much success as could be expected considering the peculiar difficulties of the enterprise.

"*Evangelical Continental Society.*—The object of this institution is to disseminate the saving truths of the Gospel among the various nations of the European continent. Its principal fields of labor are France, Belgium, Spain, Italy, and Bohemia. About £4000 per annum is raised and expended in carrying on this work, and the results have so far been encouraging.

"*The Foreign Aid Society.*—This association exists, not for the purpose of supporting and managing foreign missions, but to aid such as have been established and are carried on by other societies, and especially for the maintenance of Christian schools for the training of the rising generation. Its principal spheres of labor have hitherto been on the continent of Europe. In France the work formerly aided by this society was interrupted during the prevalence of the late war, but in Italy the work of evangelization was vigorously prosecuted. At Naples no fewer than 500 children are receiving instruction in schools to which this society has regularly contributed assistance. In Madrid the church under the care of Señor Carraso has been substantially assisted, and 350 persons have been admitted to Church membership.

"*Vernacular Education Society for India.*—This society was instituted in 1858 as a memorial of the mutiny, and has for its object the providing of Christian vernacular education and literature for India. It has 118 schools, with 5122 scholars, who are instructed in 113 different languages, at a cost of about £8000 per annum, and bids fair to be a powerful and useful auxiliary to the various missionary societies which are laboring for the spread of the Gospel throughout the Indian empire.

"III. *American Missionary Societies—American Board of Foreign Missions.*—This useful institution was organized Sept. 10, 1810, under circumstances which clearly show the superintending providence of God in the interests of missionary work. A few years before a theological seminary had been established at Andover, Mass., for the support of which a Mr. Norris, of Salem, had presented a donation of $10,000, to be devoted to the education of missionaries. At the same time a gracious influence descended upon several of the students, turning their hearts especially to the subject of Christian missions. One of these, Samuel Mills, called to mind with feelings of deep emotion the words of his beloved mother with reference to him: 'I have consecrated this child to the service of God as a missionary.' This young man shortly afterwards engaged with Gordon Hall and James Richmond in conversation and prayer upon the subject of

missions in the retirement of a lonely glen, and was delighted to find that their hearts also were drawn to the same subject. These three were soon joined by Messrs. Judson, Newell, Nott, and Hall, the whole of whom offered themselves for mission work, and the American Board of Foreign Missions was forthwith established.

"As it was proposed to found the institution on a broad and unsectarian basis, after the plan of the London Missionary Society, Mr. Judson was despatched to England to inquire into the working of that institution. The board was at first appointed by the General Association of Massachusetts, which is Congregational; but since the first election there has been no preference given to any Christian sect. In 1831, of 62 corporate members, 31 were Presbyterians, 24 Congregationalists, 6 Reformed Dutch, and 1 Associate Reformed. Of the 79 ordained missionaries of that period, 39 were Presbyterians, 2 Reformed Dutch, and the others Congregationalists. The missions are not under the control of ecclesiastical sects, but are governed as communities, where the majority of the votes of the missionaries is decisive. Nor are they regarded as permanent, but as established to plant churches, and to train them to self-support, with a view to a still wider diffusion of the Gospel. Hence, at an early period, seminaries were opened for the training of native teachers and preachers, and also for the education of girls who might engage actively in foreign service, or prove suitable partners to missionaries. From the very commencement this society was liberally supported, and proved very successful.

"The first field of labor occupied by the agents of the American Board of Foreign Missions was India. The Rev. Messrs. Judson, Nott, Newell, Hall, and Rice arrived in Calcutta in June, 1812, and were followed by other laborers in a few months afterwards. Numerous difficulties met them on the very threshold of the enterprise. The country was involved in war; no missionary operations were allowed by government; Messrs. Judson and Rice joined the Baptists, and Mr. Newell proceeded to Mauritius, where his wife and child found an early grave. At length, however, after many discouragements and delays, the way opened for the commencement of missionary labor in India, and a station was formed by Messrs. Hall and Nott in Bombay in 1814. Afterwards the work was extended to Ahmednuggur, Satara, Kolapur, Madura, Arcot, Madras, and other places, with a measure of success which more than compensated for the early trials and bereavements which were endured. In 1817 a mission was commenced by this society among the Cherokee Indians, in the state of Georgia, by the appointment of the Rev. Mr. Kingsbury, who was joined a few months afterwards by Messrs. Hall and Williams. The first station was called Brainerd, and the second Eliot, in honor of the celebrated missionaries of former times. To these several other stations were ultimately added, and a good work was carried on for many years among the Cherokees, Choctaws, Osages, Chicasaws, Creeks, Ottawas, Ojibwas, Dakotas, Abenaquis, Pawnees, and other tribes of North American Indians. In 1820 the good work was commenced in Syria. The first missionaries were the Rev. Messrs. Parsons and Fisk, who arrived in Smyrna on Jan. 15. They were followed by other zealous laborers, who, amid many difficulties, succeeded in their literary and evangelical labors among the Armenians, Nestorians, and others, as well as could be expected. In 1828 the missionaries extended their labors to Greece, and shortly afterwards missions were commenced in China and India. In 1833 the Rev. J. L. Wilson was appointed to Cape Palmas, in Western Africa, and in the following year the Rev. Messrs. Grout, Champion, and Adams were sent out to labor among the Zulus, on the south-eastern coast of the great African continent. But perhaps the most remarkable and successful of the society's missions was that which was established in the Sandwich Islands in 1819. The Rev. Messrs. Bingham and Thurston were the first who were sent out to the Pacific, but they were accompanied by a farmer, a physician, a mechanic, a catechist, and a printer, with their wives, the band in all amounting to seventeen souls, including John Honoree, Thomas Hoper, and William Temoe, native youths who had been educated in America. On their arrival they found that the native idols had already been destroyed and abolished by public authority, and the people were thus in a measure prepared to receive the Gospel, untrammelled by those attachments to long-cherished systems which in other instances have proved such a serious barrier to the dissemination of divine truth. From that day to this the mission to the Sandwich Islands has continued to advance in all its departments. The Scriptures have been translated into the native language of the people, schools have been established for the training of the rising generation, and thousands of converted natives have been united in Church fellowship, so that the whole population of those beautiful islands are now at least nominally Christian.

"*American Baptist Missionary Society.*—This society was established as early as 1814, but it did not receive its present name till 1846. It was first called the Baptist Triennial Convention for Missionary Purposes, and was commenced in Philadelphia, but afterwards transferred to Boston. It belongs to and is almost exclusively supported by the Calvinistic Baptists of the Northern States. There were some interesting circumstances connected with the early history of this institution which deserve a passing notice. The Revs. A. Judson and L. Rice, of the American Board of Foreign Missions, underwent a change of views with regard to the subjects and mode of baptism when on their voyage to India, and having resolved to join the Baptist denomination, they were immersed by the Rev. Mr. Ward at Serampore, soon after their arrival in Calcutta. This circumstance was the means of stirring up the missionary spirit among the Baptists in America, and of the formation of a society for the support of the new converts in their foreign labors, and for the propagation of the Gospel in heathen lands. The loss thus sustained by one society was gain to another, and resulted in a large increase of missionary agency and in a wide extension of the means of religious instruction. This society, which originated in the manner described, ultimately extended its labors from Rangoon, where they were commenced, through the Burman empire, to Siam, China, and Assam, to the Teloogoos in India, to Western Africa, to Greece, Germany, and France, and to various tribes of Indians on the American continent. Both in the character, extent, and results of its labors, this institution has proved itself worthy of the high commendation and liberal support with which it has been favored, and it bids fair to maintain its honorable position among the leading American missionary societies of the present day.

"*Methodist Episcopal Missionary Society.*—The Methodist Episcopal Church in America was itself the offspring of the missionary zeal of English Methodism, the first Wesleyan missionaries ever sent abroad having been appointed to New York and Philadelphia in 1769. Within half a century from this period the work had spread over the whole continent, reaching even to California and Oregon, and in 1819 the missionary society was provisionally organized in New York, and was formally adopted as an authorized institution of the Church by the General Conference the following year. It has for its object the spread of the Gospel at home and abroad, among all ranks and classes of men. The bishop in charge of the foreign missions appoints the agents to their respective spheres of labor, and places a superintendent over each station. The pecuniary interests of the society are managed by a board, which is constituted in the usual way, and which meets at stated periods for the transaction of business. Its first field of labor, after arrangements had been made to supply the spiritual wants of German and other European immigrants, was among the North American Indians. In 1832 the Rev. Melville B. Cox was appointed as the first Methodist missionary to Liberia, in Western Africa. Before he had been six months in the country, however, he had been cut down by malignant fever, and the people were left as sheep having no shepherd. Other zealous laborers followed, and a good work has ever since been carried on in the small republic of Liberia by this society, chiefly through the agency of colored missionaries, who are found by experience to be best adapted to the climate. The work in Western Africa has since been organized into a separate Conference, over which a bishop has been ordained of African descent, and himself the fruit of missionary labor. In 1847 a mission was commenced in China, and soon afterwards in India, to the great advantage of vast numbers of the dark, benighted heathens of these densely-populated regions. Nor has the continent of Europe been neglected by the Missionary Society of the Methodist Episcopal Church of America. By a remarkable providence, some of the German immigrants converted in America were made the means of conveying the blessings of the Gospel back to their native land, where a blessed work was commenced through their instrumentality, which soon extended from Germany to Sweden, Norway, Scandinavia, and other countries in the North of Europe. By their genuine missionary spirit the Methodists of America prove themselves worthy of their noble and honored ancestry.

"*Protestant Episcopal Board of Missions.*—The Missionary Society of the Protestant Episcopal Church of the United States of America was organized by the General Convention of 1820, with the seat of operations in Philadelphia. In 1835 an entire change was made in the constitution of the society, when the title given above was adopted by general consent. The first scene of labor entered upon by the missionaries of this institution was Greece, the Revs. J. J. Robertson and J. W. Hill, and Mr. Bingham, a printer, being sent out towards the close of 1830. They first settled at Tenos, but subsequently removed to Athens, where they were very successful in their educational labors. Their principal object was not to proselytize, but to revive and reform the Greek Church, and their labors were not without fruit. Stations were also formed in Syria and Crete, but afterwards abandoned. In 1836 the board extended their labors to Western Africa, by the commencement of a station at Cape Palmas, among a dense population speaking the Grebo language. The first missionaries were the Rev. Messrs. Paine, Minor, and Savage, the last of whom was a medical man, and his skilful services were highly valuable in a country noted for its insalubrious climate. Considerable success was real-

ized in this part of the mission field, several converted natives being gathered into Church fellowship, Christian schools established, and a small newspaper published in English and Grebo, called the *Cavalla Messenger.* In 1834 missionaries were sent to Bavaria and China by this society, and about ten years afterwards Dr. Boone was consecrated missionary bishop, and went out with a large staff of laborers to Shanghai. Nor were the heathen nearer home neglected by this institution. Mission stations were commenced among various tribes of North American Indians; and, notwithstanding numerous difficulties which had to be encountered, arising from the wandering habits of the people and other causes, 300 native children were soon reported as being under Christian instruction. In 1837 bishop Kemper consecrated a new church at Dutch Creek, and appointed Solomon Davis, a converted native, as pastor over it, whose ministry was made a blessing to many of his fellow-countrymen.

"*American Society for Ameliorating the Condition of the Jews.*—The primary object of this society, which was organized in 1820, was the temporal relief of persecuted converts. It was not until 1849 that anything like missionary effort was put forth for the benefit of the lost sheep of the house of Israel. It was found in 1851 that there was a Jewish population stately residing within the United States amounting to 120,000, in addition to which there were hundreds and thousands constantly moving from place to place. In this wide field of labor the society at an early period employed ten missionaries and seven colportors, who visited forty towns, in which they endeavored to sow the good seed of the kingdom, with some visible proofs of spiritual success.

"*Freewill Baptist Foreign Missionary Society.* — The founders of this institution conceived the idea, after the plan of the eccentric Gossner, of sending forth missionaries to the heathen without any guaranteed support, expressing great aversion to what they called the hireling system. Their principles were lacking in true missionary power; but at length the Rev. Amos Sutton, of the English Baptist Mission in Orissa, succeeded in awakening a few earnest spirits out of their deep slumber—first of all by a letter, and secondly by a personal address while on a visit to the States for the benefit of his health in 1833. The result was that the Revs. Eli Noyes and Jeremiah Phillips left for Orissa in September, 1835, accompanied by Mr. Sutton, with whom they passed the first six months of their foreign residence. The society has only occupied this one mission; and, although their agents have suffered much from the climate, their labors have not been without success, especially in dispensing medicine and establishing Christian schools. Some time ago there were 17 missionaries employed, with 16 native preachers, 11 churches, and 654 members.

"*Board of Foreign Missions of the Presbyterian Church in the United States of America.*—The Presbyterians of the United States were engaged in missionary work at a very early period. The Scottish Society for Promoting Christian Knowledge secured a board of correspondence in 1741, and appointed a minister to the Indians on Long Island, and in the following year sent the distinguished David Brainerd to the Indians in Albany. John Brainerd succeeded his brother David in 1747, and they were both partly sustained by the American Presbyterians. In 1765 the Presbytery of New York made a collection in all the churches for the mission to the Indians. In 1796 the 'New York Missionary Society' was instituted. This was followed in 1797 by the organization of the 'Northern Missionary Society;' and in 1831 these were merged in the Board of Missions of the Presbyterian Church, which established and conducted several interesting stations among the American Indians, in addition to those which had been previously commenced. In 1832 this society sent out a mission to Liberia, in Western Africa, and the work was afterwards extended to the island of Corisco and other places on the coast, where it has been carried on with a varied measure of success amid many difficulties incident to the climate and a deeply-debased heathen population. In 1833 the Rev. Messrs. Reed and Lowrie were sent out to India, and succeeded in establishing a mission station in the city of Lodiana, on the River Sutlez, one of the tributaries of the Indus—a place far distant from any other scene of missionary labor. The first band of missionaries suffered much from the inroads of sickness and death, but were soon aided or followed by a reenforcement of laborers, who succeeded in forming a native Church in 1825, the first two members of which became eminently useful as preachers of the Gospel to their fellow-countrymen. In 1838 the American Presbyterians commenced a mission at Singapore; and after the Chinese war three stations were formed at Canton, Amoy, and Ningpo, to which a fourth was afterwards added at Shanghai. The society suffered a severe blow in the death of the Rev. W. M. Lowrie, who was murdered by a party of pirates. The board has also sent missionaries to labor among the Chinese in California, and in every department of the work considerable success has been realized. Corea was entered in 1884.

"*Evangelical Lutheran Church Mission.*—The Evangelical Lutheran Church of Nova Scotia is a religious community which numbers only four or five thousand members, chiefly of German extraction, and yet it has shown a most praiseworthy zeal in the cause of missions. This Church entered upon its foreign missionary labors in 1837, and a few years afterwards it reported 5 ordained and 2 unordained native preachers as engaged in the good work in India, with 86 Church members and 355 scholars under their care.

"*Seventh-day Baptist Missionary Society.*—This institution was organized in 1842, and has been engaged ever since chiefly in Western Africa and China, where three or four agents have been usefully employed. The Chinese mission was begun in 1847 in Shanghai by the Rev. Messrs. Carpenter and Worden, who secured a house within the walls, fitted up a portion of it as a chapel, and commenced public worship in it soon afterwards. A few converts have been gathered into the fold of Christ as the result of their evangelistic labors.

"*American Indian Mission Association.*—This society was founded also in 1842, and is connected with the Baptist churches in the south-west, having its executive in Louisville. The agents of this society, numbering about thirty, have labored among different tribes of American Indians with a considerable measure of success, notwithstanding the difficulties which they have had to encounter. They report upwards of 1000 converted natives as united in Church fellowship on their respective stations.

"*Free Baptist Missionary Society*—This small but useful institution was organized in 1843 at Utica, in the State of New York, on the broad Christian ground of having no connection with slavery. For several years it has had a successful mission in Hayti, with 1 missionary, 3 female assistants, 1 native pastor, and 4 native teachers.

"*Associate Reformed Presbyterian Church.*—This organization dates from 1844, and has sent forth three missionaries to India, two to Turkey, and three to the Pacific; but we have been unable to gather any very definite information with reference to the history or the results of their labors.

"*Southern Baptist Convention's Missions.*—The Foreign Missionary Society of the Southern Baptists was formally instituted in 1845, missionaries having been sent out to China the year before. Important stations were formed at Macao, Hong-Kong, and Shanghai, which were very prosperous. In 1848 a gloom was cast over the mission by the loss of Dr. and Mrs. James, who were drowned by the upsetting of a boat when on their way to Shanghai; but the places of the dear departed were soon supplied by other laborers, and the good work continued to advance. The next field of labor occupied by this society was Western Africa. Soon after a station had been established in Liberia the work was extended to the Yarriba country, where several colored missionaries were usefully employed, who, from their being of African descent, could better endure the climate. According to the last returns, this society had 40 missionaries, 26 native assistants, 1225 Church members, and 633 scholars in the mission schools.

"*American Missionary Association.*—This society was formed at Albany, N. Y., in the year 1846, by those friends of missions who declared themselves aggrieved by the countenance given by some other philanthropic institutions to slavery, polygamy, and kindred forms of evil. Their avowed object was to secure a broad, catholic basis for the co-operation of Christians, but to exclude from their organization all persons living in or conniving at the flagrant forms of iniquity alluded to. The formation of this society was no sooner made known than it was joined by other smaller institutions, as the 'West India Mission,' the 'Western Evangelical Missionary Association,' and the 'Union Missionary Society,' who transferred their influence and their agencies to it, and thus gave to the new organization laborers in the West Indies, among the North American Indians, and in Western Africa. The labors of the society were subsequently extended to Siam, the Sandwich Islands, California, and Egypt. In 1867 it supported over 200 missionaries at home and abroad. Since that time the pressing needs of the freedmen of the Southern States have absorbed almost all the means at the disposal of the board, which they withdrew from other work to do this duty which lay nearest to them. This association have their schools and churches scattered through the former slave and border states. The whole number of missionaries and teachers commissioned during the last ten years amount to 3470; and schools have been established in 343 localities, the pupils under instruction numbering 23,324, who, as a rule, make rapid progress in learning. The interest and zeal of the colored people in urging their children's education increases every year, and every year they also become more able to assist in the work. In a short time both schools and churches are expected to become self-supporting.

"*American and Foreign Christian Union.*—This institution was organized in New York in 1849. It was, in fact, the union of three other small societies—the 'Foreign Evangelical Society,' the 'American Protestant Society,' and the 'Philo-Italian Society'—which was afterwards called the Christian Alliance. The principal fields of labor cultivated by these associations, both before and after their union, were the papal countries of France, Belgium, Sweden, Canada, Hayti, and South America. In 1854, the fifth year of the new organization, it numbered 140 missiona-

ries of all grades, one half of whom were ordained, and belonged to seven different nations, and a proportionate number of converted natives united in Church fellowship, and scholars in the mission schools.

"*French Canadian Missionary Society.*—This society was organized in 1839. Its object is to evangelize the French Canadian Roman Catholics, of whom there are nearly a million in the province of Quebec. It is conducted by a committee in Montreal, and employs a threefold agency—education, evangelization, and colportage. Above 240 scholars are supported in whole or in part by the mission; eight small French Protestant churches have been organized, and about 1300 copies or portions of the Scriptures are annually circulated, in addition to other religious works which have been translated for the purpose.

"*Board of Foreign Missions of the Presbyterian Church of Nova Scotia.*—The board was organized in 1844 in consequence of an overture on foreign missions by the Presbytery of Prince Edward's Island. The principal promoter of the enterprise, the Rev. John Geddie, was the first missionary who proceeded to Polynesia, accompanied by Mr. Isaac Archibald as catechist. On reaching their destination, they were kindly received by the agents of the London Missionary Society, and proceeded to establish a station at Anetteum, one of the New Hebrides group, where they arrived in July, 1848. The entire population of the island soon renounced their pagan practices, and became professing Christians. An anxious desire for religious instruction was manifested, and a goodly number of the natives were brought under gracious religious influences.

"*Minor Associations.*—There are several minor missionary associations, both in Europe and America, concerning which our limited space prevents a separate description."

In order to make the above list complete, it would be necessary to add the numerous Bible societies [see BIBLE SOCIETIES], and also Tract and Book publication societies, which are in constant and intimate co-operation with the regular missionary societies, together with a constantly-increasing number of smaller organizations contemplating missionary results. Some of the above will be included in the subjoined tabular exhibit on pages 368 and 369.

Notwithstanding the numerous points of interest shown in our tabular exhibit, it is utterly impossible to reduce to statistics anything like a full showing of the work accomplished and in progress by modern missions. Indeed, as human language cannot fully set forth the horrors of heathenism, so no form of description can adequately portray the actual and possible results of missionary efforts earnestly and perseveringly put forth in harmony with the divine plan for evangelizing the world.

VI. *General Views suggested by the Present Period of Missionary History as compared with Preceding Periods.*—1. *The field of missionary operations is now more comprehensive than ever before, and more nearly illustrative of the Gospel design of evangelizing the whole world.* In the apostolic period the Roman empire comprised the then known world. Up to the end of the mediæval period, the world formerly known to the Romans was chiefly enlarged by the addition of the northern countries of Europe. Now, every continent and island of the globe is not only known by discovery, but accessible to Christian influence. In fact, all the important and many of the unimportant nations of the earth have been actually made the subjects of missionary instruction, in accordance with the fullest literal meaning of the Saviour's precepts, "Go ye into all the world and preach the Gospel to every creature;" "Go teach *all* nations."

2. *The Church of modern times has returned to the apostolic idea of Christian missions.* Hence missionary operations now throughout the world are peaceful. No more crusades, no more inquisitions and *autos da fé* are employed for the pretended advancement of Christianity, but rather preaching and teaching generally of the pure Word of God as a means of persuading men to become followers of Christ.

3. *The number of workers for this object is greater than ever before, and is rapidly increasing by the enlistment of native converts in almost every land.*

4. *The appliances and advantages of Christian civilization, such as the press and general education, are everywhere brought to the aid of missionary effort.*

5. *The sympathies of the Christian Church at large are extensively, though as yet far from fully, enlisted in the grand enterprise of Christianizing the human race.* In this enterprise unity of idea is to a large extent neutralizing diversity of action, and making even the rivalries of different Christian organizations conducive to a common advantage.

6. *The progress and results, especially of Protestant missions within the current century, not only justify all the efforts of the past, but give most hopeful signs of promise for the future.* These results comprise not only the conversion and salvation of individuals of every race and condition of humanity, but the actual Christianization of whole nations, and the initial steps by which whole races of men may be expected at no distant period to receive the Gospel. Of necessity, a large share of the work of modern evangelical missions has thus far been preparatory; such as the acquisition of languages, the translation and printing of the Scriptures, and the education of native ministers in heathen lands. If, therefore, what has been done shall by the blessing of the Head of the Church be made to act as leaven, according to our Saviour's promise, we may in due time expect the whole mass of human populations to be leavened with the influence of Christian truth.

"The social and moral advantages which the missionary enterprise has conferred on the heathen are before the world. What vast tracts has it rescued from barbarism, and with what creations of benevolence has it clothed them! How many thousands whom ignorance and selfishness had branded as the leavings and refuse of the species, if not actually akin to the beasts that perish, are at this moment rising under its fostering care, ascribing their enfranchisement, under God, to its benign interposition; taking encouragement from its smiles to assume the port and bearing of men; and by their acts and aspirations retrieving the character and the dignity of the slandered human form! When did literature accomplish so much for nations destitute of a written language? or education pierce and light up so large and dense a mass of human ignorance? When did humanity save so many lives, or cause so many sanguinary 'wars to cease?' How many a sorrow has it soothed; how many an injury arrested; how many an asylum has it reared amid scenes of wretchedness and oppression for the orphan, the outcast, and the sufferer! When did liberty ever rejoice in a greater triumph than that which missionary instrumentality has been the means of achieving? or civilization find so many sons of the wilderness learning her arts, and agriculture, and commerce? or law receive so much voluntary homage from those who but yesterday were strangers to the name? By erecting a standard of morality, how vast the amount of crime which it has been the means of preventing! By asserting the claims of degraded woman, how powerful an instrument of social regeneration is it preparing for the future! And by doing all this by the principle and power of all moral order and excellence—the Gospel of Christ—how large a portion of the world's chaos has it restored to light, and harmony, and peace!

"But great as are the benefits enumerated, most of which can in a sense be seen and measured and handled, we venture to affirm that those which are at present comparatively impalpable and undeveloped are greater still. The unseen is far greater than that which appears. The missionary has been planting the earth with principles, and these are of as much greater value than the visible benefits which they have already produced as the tree is more valuable than its first year's fruit. The tradesman may take stock and calculate his pecuniary affairs to a fraction; the astronomer may count the stars, and the chemist weigh the invisible element of air; but he who in the strength of God conveys a great truth to a distant region, or puts into motion a divine principle, has performed a work of which futurity alone can disclose the results. At no one for-

mer period could either of our missionary societies have attempted to 'number Israel'—to reduce to figures either the geographical extent or the practical results of its influence, without having soon received, in the cheering events which followed, a distinct but gracious rebuke. How erroneous the calculation which should have set down the first fifteen years of fruitless missionary labor in Greenland, or the sixteen in Tahiti, or the twenty in New Zealand, as years of entire failure! when, in truth, the glorious scene which then ensued was simply that which God was pleased to make the result of all that had preceded—the explosion, by the divine hand, of a train which had been lengthening and enlarging during every moment of all those years. Therefore were the whole field of missions to be suddenly vacated, and all its moral machinery at once withdrawn, we confidently believe that the amount of temporal good arising from what has been done will be much greater twenty years hence than it is at present" (Harris's *Great Commission*, p. 185, 186).

But happily there is no prospect that the field of missionary effort will soon be vacated. The thirty years that have elapsed since the above paragraph was written have proved to be the most productive of missionary results of any similar period since the days of the apostles. During their lapse the "moral machinery" of the Protestant Church in particular has become vastly augmented in volume and in power, and has been set to working with great efficiency in many important localities which were then wholly inaccessible. The records of even that period fill numerous volumes, and yet the half has not been written.

VII. *Missionary Aspect of the World, with the Literature appropriate to each Region.*—So vast is the field of modern missions, so numerous are the workers, and so various are the departments of effort, that it is difficult, though very important, to form an adequate idea of the enterprise as *a whole*. In order to do so even approximately, an inquirer has to glean from many sources, and to combine into one view all the various lines and successive phases of action which focalize towards the contemplated result. The proper mode of studying this subject may be indicated by a comprehensive grouping of the different sections and countries of *the world* in reference to missionary occupation and progress, coupled with such references to the literature of missions as will enable a student to prosecute thorough inquiry into the history, condition, and prospects of each particular field.

It may here be remarked that the literature of modern missions is already very extensive. It embraces two distinct classes of publications, of which the first may be denominated auxiliary, the second descriptive. To the first belong versions of the Scriptures, and all tracts and books designed for circulation in mission fields, whether educational, apologetic, or devotional. To the second belong accounts of countries, peoples, and systems of false religion, also missionary explorations, experiences, biography, and history. Publications of the latter class are specially interesting and valuable to Christian workers in all lands. As there is a common brotherhood in humanity, which is greatly strengthened by the ties of Christian relationship, so the experiences of foreign mission life become not only interesting but instructive to the agents and supporters of Christian work in Christian lands. The converse of this proposition is equally true, and thus it is that home missions and regular Church work in Christian countries practically blend together with missionary work in foreign and pagan countries, forming one great system of effort for the evangelization of the world.

In proceeding to a brief panoramic survey of the principal divisions of the earth in reference to missions, it seems proper to begin with the earlier scenes of Christian occupation and labor, and pass around to the American continent and islands, thus completing the circuit of the habitable globe.

TABULAR VIEW OF FOREIGN MISSIONARY ORGANIZATIONS IN 1889.

Society Organized.	Names.	Ordained Missionaries.	Church Members.	Scholars.	Approximate Annual Income.	Field.
	I. CONTINENTAL.					
1732.	Moravian Missionary Society.................	135	84,201	18,280	$250,000	{ Greenland, Labrador, West Indies, Australia, Thibet.
1822.	Paris Evangelical Missionary Society............	33	8,254	4,931	72,500	S. Africa, S. E. Africa, Polynesia.
1815.	Basle Evangelical Missionary Society...........	92	9,803	8,513	180,000	India, China, W. Africa, Australia.
1824.	Berlin Missionary Society...................	56	10,218	3,542	77,500	South Africa, China.
1828.	Rhenish Missionary Society.................	71	9,671	5,435	96,250	South Africa, China, Polynesia.
1836.	Gossner's Missionary Society, Berlin...........	13	12,200	2,100	40,000	India.
1836.	North German Missionary Society of Bremen.....	8	409	321	22,500	New Zealand, West Africa.
1836.	Leipsic Evangelical Lutheran Missionary Society........	22	14,014	3,653	75,500	South India.
1849.	Hermannsburg Evangelical Lutheran Missions.....	70	13,424	443	72,280	{ South Africa, India, New Zealand, Australia.
1797.	Netherland Missionary Society...............	18	20,000	10,000	35,000	Polynesia.
1858.	Dutch Missionary Society, Rotterdam..........	7	737	102	17,500	West Java.
1859.	Dutch Reformed Missionary Society, Amsterdam....	3	5,048	..	7,000	Java.
1859.	Utrecht Missionary Society.................	8	490	125	15,000	New Guinea, Almahera, Boeroe.
1849.	{ Mennonite Society for the Propagation of the Gospel in the Dutch Colonies..........	3	213	125	..	Java, Sumatra.
1721.	Danish Government Mission.................	3	3,874	1,982	15,000	Greenland.
1853.	Danish Missionary Society, Lutheran..........	4	114	92	13,000	India.
1842.	Norwegian Missionary Society...............	40	20,660	30,620	100,000	Africa.
1835.	Swedish Missionary Society.................	3	..	130	..	Lapland.
1868.	Missionary Committee of the Swedish Church.....	3	12	68	13,015	Natal.
1878.	Swedish Missionary Union..................	..	50	11	13,750	N. Africa, Alaska, Russia, Lapland.
1856.	Swedish Evangelical Missionary Society.........	10	109	498	44,000	East Africa, India.
1860.	Jönköping Missionary Union for Home and Foreign Missions	1	..	..	..	China.
1880.	The Friends of the Mission to the Laplanders.....	1	..	..	2,940	Lapland.
1850.	{ The Ladies' Committee at Stockholm for the Furtherance of the Gospel among the Women of China............	..	..	41	940	China.
1859.	Finland Missionary Society.................	6	75	300	7,050	Southwest Africa.
1874.	Missions of the Free Churches of French Switzerland........	7	133	330	12,000	South Africa.
	II. BRITISH.					
1649.	New England Company.....................	3	238	702	10,500	Ontario, British Columbia.
1701.	Society for the Propagation of the Gospel in Foreign Parts...	460	66,593	32,092	693,334	{ E. & W. Indies, China, Japan, Africa, Europe, N. & S. Amer., Austr.
1792.	Baptist Missionary Society.................	118	19,776	7,822	378,894	{ India, China, Japan, Palestine, W. Indies, Congo.
1795.	London Missionary Society.................	152	78,618	115,176	624,300	Polynesia, China, India, Africa.
1799.	Church Missionary Society.................	282	47,531	77,451	1,106,654	{ Africa, Palestine, Persia, India, Japan, China.
1816.	Wesleyan Missionary Society...............	152	37,031	64,092	659,335	{ Europe, India, China, Africa, British Honduras.
1816.	General Baptist Missionary Society...........	9	1,344	1,330	40,535	India.
1821.	United Presbyterian.....................	61	13,342	13,387	282,674	{ Jamaica, Trinidad, Africa, India, China, Japan.
1821.	Bible Christian Missionary Society...........	4	..	..	35,473	Australia, China.
1824.	Methodist New Connection.................	6	1,245	187	30,422	China.
1824.	Church of Scotland Missions...............	17	750	6,058	144,030	India, China, Africa.
1837.	{ United Methodist Free Churches Home and Foreign Missionary Society.	21	6,670	3,793	105,130	China, E. and W. Africa, Jamaica.
1840.	Foreign Missions of the Irish Presbyterian Church..........	13	313	3,449	65,270	India, China.
1843.	Free Church of Scotland Mission.............	49	5,771	19,129	419,065	Ind., Afr., Melanesia, Syria, Arab.
1840.	Welsh Calvinistic Methodist Missionary Society..........	9	1,389	3,833	25,000	India.
1843.	Primitive Methodist Missionary Society.........	5	426	356	74,643	South Africa.
1844.	South American Missionary Society...........	10	411	512	67,500	South America.
1847.	Presbyterian Church of England Missions.......	15	3,553	716	81,800	China, India.
1859.	Universities Mission.....................	98	529	674	87,500	Central Africa.
1862.	China Inland Mission....................	153	2,105	220	169,620	
1861.	Strict Baptist Mission...................	1	353	509	3,440	India.
1865.	Friends' Foreign Mission Association...........	..	2,970	14,600	47,500	India, Madagascar, China.
1867.	Friends' Syrian Mission..................	..	..	420	11,675	
1872.	Scottish Episcopal Church.................	..	..	..	2,500	South Africa.
1878.	Salvation Army........................	..	..	..	250,000	India, South Africa, St. Helena.
	Women's Societies.					
1834.	Society for Promoting Female Education in the East........	..	..	2,300	..	India, the Levant.
1837.	{ Church of Scotland Ladies' Association for Foreign Missions and Zenana Work.	..	..	2,460	38,300	India, East Africa.
1852.	Indian Female Normal School and Instruction Society.......	..	..	3,637	5,500	India.
1859.	Wesleyan Missionary Society Ladies' Auxiliary.............	..	..	9,313	38,000	India, China, Africa.
1860.	British Syrian Schools and Bible Mission.........	..	..	2,861	25,000	
1866.	Ladies' Association, S. P. G...............	..	..	..	31,755	India, Japan, Africa.
1866.	Ladies' Association, Baptist Missionary Society.........	..	..	1,650	31,930	India.
1873.	Ladies' Association, Irish Presbyterian.........	..	..	1,098	14,020	India, China.
1878.	{ Woman's Mission Association Presbyterian Church of England.	..	..	155	11,330	China, India.
1880.	Church of England Zenana Missionary Society.............	..	..	6,916	116,340	India, China, Japan.
..	United Presbyterian Church of Scotland Zenana Mission....	..	..	..	17,875	India, China, Africa.
1880.	Zenana Medical College, London.............	..	..	..	5,875	
	Miscellaneous Foreign Societies.					
1836.	Christian Faith Society...................	..	..	..	11,450	Jamaica.
1838.	Coral Missionary Fund...................	..	..	..	..	
1870.	Missionary Leaves Association...............	..	..	..	..	
	The Net Collections in Aid of the S. P. G...........	..	..	..	11,810	
	Lebanon Schools Committee................	1	..	30	3,750	
1876.	Cambridge Mission to Delhi................	6	..	660	..	
1874.	Mission to Lepers in India.................	..	..	..	10,165	India, Burmah.
1854.	Turkish Missions' Aid Society...............	..	..	..	13,980	Turkey, Egypt.
1887.	Mission to the Chinese Blind...............	..	..	..	15,385	
..	English Egyptian Mission.................	..	..	600	10,000	
1881.	North Africa Missions...................	..	6	50	20,000	
1872.	E. London Institute for Home and Foreign Missions..........	..	..	..	55,000	
	Medical Missions.					
1841.	Edinburgh Medical Missionary Society.........	..	..	..	26,010	Syria.
1866.	Delhi Medical Mission to Women and Children.....	..	..	..	2,725	
1878.	Medical Missionary Society, London...........	..	..	..	5,000	
..	Children's Medical Mission................	..	..	..	1,000	
1881.	Friends' Medical Missions among the Armenians...........	..	..	..	1,825	
1878.	Jaffa Medical Mission and Hospital...........	..	..	120	6,000	
	Publication Societies Interested in Foreign Mission Work.					
1804.	British and Foreign Bible Society............	..	..	..	125,912	
1861.	National Bible Society of Scotland............	..	..	..	171,945	
1831.	Trinitarian Bible Society.................	..	..	..	7,605	
1840.	Bible Translation Society.................	..	..	..	14,085	
1799.	Religious Tract Society..................	..	..	..	158,250	
1698.	Society for Promoting Religious Knowledge.......	..	..	..	201,450	
1858.	Christian Vernacular Education Society for India.........	..	..	..	48,230	
1874.	Association for the Free Distribution of the Scriptures.......	..	..	..	8,500	
1793.	Religious Tract and Book Society of Scotland.......	..	..	..	3,800	
1884.	Book and Tract Society of China.............	..	..	..	2,000	

TABULAR VIEW OF FOREIGN MISSIONARY ORGANIZATIONS IN 1889.—(Continued.)

Society Organized.	Names.	Ordained Missionaries.	Church Members.	Scholars.	Approximate Annual Income.	Field.
	II. BRITISH.—(Continued.)					
	Missions to the Jews.					
1809.	London Society for Promoting Christianity among the Jews..	..	..	..	$169,625	Syria, &c.
1842.	British Society for the Propagation of the Gospel among the Jews.....................	..	..	..	40,910	
1843.	Free Church of Scotland's Mission to the Jews...............	6	256	704	40,875	
1876.	Mildmay Mission to the Jews........................	..	..	..	32,655	
1842.	Church of Scotland Mission to the Jews..................	..	..	1,792	..	
1843.	Church of Scotland Ladies' Association...............	..	..	480	5,920	
	III. AMERICAN.					
1810.	American Board of Commissioners for Foreign Missions......	158	29,795	41,736	667,289	Africa, Turkey, India, China, Japan, Micronesia.
1814.	American Baptist Missionary Society...................	262	61,062	17,504	418,792	Burmah, India, China, Japan, Afr.
1833.	Free-Will Baptist Missionary Association............	8	654	3,058	24,885	India.
..	Baptist General Association (Colored).................	3	..	..	5,000	Liberia.
1884.	Consolidated American Baptists (Colored)..............	4	50	..	..	Africa.
1842.	Seventh-Day Baptist Missionary Society...............	2	23	..	12,680	China, Holland, Austria.
1881.	German Baptist Brethren (Dunkers)...................	..	150	..	5,587	Denmark.
1842.	Southern Baptists................................	33	2,050	..	24,885	Africa, China, India, Bulgaria, Japan, Corea.
1819.	Methodist Episcopal Missionary Society...............	260	21,048	18,646	1,206,581	
1870.	Methodist Protestant Board.........................	2	232	401	20,000	Japan.
1878.	Mission Board of the Evangelical Church.............	8	150	280	30,397	Japan.
..	Wesleyan Methodist Connection.....................	2	300	..	2,000	West Africa.
1845.	Home and Foreign Missionary Society of the M. E. Church.	21	1,044	666	130,000	Africa, Hayti, Indian Territory.
	Methodist Episcopal Church, South...................	18	652	1,279	275,000	China, Japan.
1821.	Domestic and Foreign Missionary Society of the Protestant Episcopal Church.........................	16	2,115	2,838	189,932	Africa, China, Japan, Hayti.
1853.	United Brethren.................................	5	1,306	..	14,162	
1837.	Board of Foreign Missions of the Presbyterian Church.......	132	18,354	20,602	901,180	Africa, India, China, Japan, Corea, Persia, Syria.
1861.	Presbyterian Board (South).........................	19	1,022	750	81,000	China, Greece, India, Japan.
1856.	Reformed Presbyterian Church......................	2	171	1,279	16,691	Syria.
1836.	Reformed Presbyterian (General Synod)...............	1	17	26	4,500	India.
1876.	Cumberland Presbyterian..........................	6	524	..	17,475	
1858.	United Presbyterian Church.........................	19	6,878	9,942	100,323	Egypt, India.
1857.	Board of Missions of the Reformed Church in America (Dutch)	25	4,559	3,524	109,946	China, India, Japan.
1837.	Board of Foreign Missions of the General Synod of the Evangelical Lutheran Church in the United States............	2	5,316	3,336	82,404	India, Liberia.
1880.	Mennonites......................................	3	6	..	6,000	
1869.	General Council Evangelical Lutheran...............	5	..	700	10,000	India.
1838.	Foreign Missions Reformed (German) Church in the U. S...	7	1,202	719	20,000	Japan, India.
1875.	Foreign Christian Missionary Society...............	22	394	..	40,559	Turkey, India, China.
1886.	American Christian Convention.....................	1	64	..	2,000	Japan.
	Women's Societies.					
1861.	Woman's Union Missionary Society...................	..	..	..	37,346	India, China, Japan.
1868.	Woman's Board (Congregational, 4 Boards)............	..	..	..	201,685	
1870.	Woman's Board (Presbyterian, 5 Boards).............	..	..	..	312,286	
1874.	Presbyterians (Southern)..........................	..	..	..	20,732	
1879.	United Presbyterians.............................	..	..	..	15,619	Egypt.
1879.	Woman's Board, Cumberland Presbyterian.............	..	..	..	7,658	Japan, Mexico.
1875.	Reformed (Dutch) Church..........................	..	..	..	17,544	China, Japan, India.
1879.	Evangelical Lutheran.............................	..	..	..	14,197	India.
1876.	Woman's Baptist Missionary Society, 2 Boards............	..	..	3,850	120,215	India, Liberia, &c.
1888.	Southern Baptists................................	..	..	..	15,554	
1871.	Woman's Board, Protestant Episcopal...............	..	..	..	25,000	
1869.	Woman's Foreign Missionary Society, M. E. Church........	..	..	..	206,308	Same as the Parent Board.
1878.	Woman's Foreign Missionary Society, M. E. Church (South)	..	..	..	37,000	Mexico, Brazil, China.
1879.	Woman's Foreign Missionary Society, Methodist Protestant	..	..	60	5,000	Japan.
1881.	Friends' Missionary Society........................	..	..	241	11,288	Japan, Mexico, Syria.
1873.	Baptists, Free....................................	..	..	..	7,200	
1877.	Woman's Missionary Association, United Brethren..........	..	706	192	..	Africa.
1875.	Christian Woman's (Disciples)......................	..	..	..	26,226	Jamaica, India.
..	Woman's Missionary Society Evangelical Association......	..	..	..	1,854	Germany, Japan.
1816.	American Bible Society............................	..	..	..	557,340	
1825.	American Tract Society............................	..	..	..	140,000	
	Canada.					
1873.	Missionary Society of the Methodist Churches...........	10	1,283	..	..	Japan.
1872.	Presbyterian Committee...........................	..	2,658	..	..	China, India.
1866.	Canadian Baptists................................	9	1,330	..	15,219	India.
..	Baptist Convention, Maritime Provinces...............	7	2,039	2,965	8,825	India.
1883.	Church of England in Canada.......................	..	..	..	13,236	
	Women's.					
1876.	Woman's Foreign Miss. Soc., Presbyterian, Canada (East)...	..	..	..	25,657	
1877.	Woman's Foreign Miss. Soc., Presbyterian, Canada (West)..	..	..	..	5,091	
1879.	Baptists, Ontario, etc.............................	..	..	..	6,182	
1870.	Baptists, Maritime Provinces.......................	..	..	..	4,493	
1881.	Methodist, Canadian..............................	..	..	252	14,197	

HOME MISSIONARY ORGANIZATIONS IN 1889.

Society Organized.	Names.	Missionaries.	Members.	Scholars.	Approximate Annual Income.
	I. ENGLAND.				
1803.	Wesleyan Home Missions...........................	97	..	..	$138,700
1779.	Baptist Home Missions (England and Ireland)..........	..	..	..	32,315
1816.	Baptist Home Missions (Scotland)..................	22	..	..	9,690
1819.	Congregational Church Aid and Home Missionary Society..........	121	35,554	63,165	51,000
1835.	London City Missions.............................	500	..	..	283,690
..	Open-Air Mission................................	11	1,064	..	7,290
1837.	Country-Towns Mission............................	58	..	..	14,435
..	Army Scripture-Readers' Society....................	85	..	..	58,835
1825.	Christian Instruction Society......................	..	..	..	..
1818.	British and Foreign Sailors' Society................	..	..	..	83,930
1867.	Children's Special Service Mission..................	..	..	..	..
1859.	Midnight Meeting Movement.......................	..	..	..	..
	II. AMERICA.				
1832.	American Baptist Home Missionary Society...........	790	..	4,183	375,254
1846.	American Home Missionary Society..................	449	..	11,607	323,147
1845.	Lutheran Home Missionary Board...................	..	..	..	..
..	Presbyterian Board Home Missions..................	1,592	93,188	6,785	885,518
	Methodist Episcopal Missionary Society.............	3,632	242,386	..	591,412
1877.	Woman's Baptist Home Missionary Society (Western).....	71	..	..	5,094
1877.	Woman's American Baptist Home Missionary Society (Eastern)......	37	..	..	28,346
1880.	Woman's Home Missionary Society, Methodist Episcopal............	42	..	..	109,604

1. *The Continent of Europe* presents at this time the interesting spectacle of active missionary labor prosecuted not only by British but also by American Protestants in most of those old countries where a ceremonious or a nominal Christianity has long held sway. In Northern Europe, especially in Germany, Denmark, Sweden, and Norway, the missionaries are in many cases natives of those countries, who as emigrants to the United States of America became experimental Christians, and who have returned to preach the doctrines of vital godliness to their fatherlands. Protestant missions are also established in France, Switzerland, Austria, Portugal, Spain, and Italy. In all these countries the Scriptures and Christian tracts are circulated more freely and more numerously than ever before.

With some correspondence to the activity of Protestants in the Roman Catholic countries of Europe, the Church of Rome has become very zealous for the reconversion of England to mediæval Christianity. The Jesuits expelled from Germany and the monks disfranchised in Italy are sent there in great numbers. These measures have a tendency to stimulate greater activity among British Christians in home missions, and thus, so long as peaceful measures are employed on both sides, it is to be hoped that mutually good results will follow. Thought will be stimulated, liberality increased, watchfulness will be awakened, and Christ will be preached, even though of contention. As the movements now referred to are for the greater part quite recent, the latest information respecting them must be sought in the current reports and correspondence of the societies engaged in them, inclusive of the Bible and Tract societies. In this field comparatively little has been required in the matter of Bible translations, but much attention has been given to the revision of versions to make them as perfect as possible for popular circulation. See Rule, *Mission to Gibraltar and Spain;* Arthur, *Italy in Transition;* Scott, *Telström and Lapland; Reports of Missionary Societies;* Toase, *Wesleyan Mission in France;* Mrs. Peddie, *Dawn of the Second Reformation in Spain;* Ellis, *Denmark and her Missions; Henderson's Life and Labors.* See also the articles BAPTISTS; METHODISTS; PRESBYTERIANS; PROTESTANT EPISCOPALIANS; WESLEYANS.

2. *Greece, Turkey, Asia Minor, and Western Asia.*—The modern populations of the northern shores of the Mediterranean are greatly mingled. The Moslem races predominate, but nominal Christians are found in every country and under all the governments. They constitute more than a third part of the inhabitants of Constantinople, and are found in every province of the Turkish empire, while in Persia they are supposed to number twelve millions. Hence a wise plan for the conversion of the Mohammedans of those lands involved the primary necessity of evangelical missions to the nominal Christians of the East. To this task, as a republication of the Gospel in Bible lands, the American Board of Foreign Missions has addressed itself energetically and perseveringly. It has in so doing established missions in Greece, in Palestine, in Syria, among the Jews, Mohammedans, and Bulgarians of Turkey, the Armenians, the Nestorians, and the Druses. A very interesting history of these missions and their adjuncts has recently been published by Dr. Anderson, from which it appears that, notwithstanding many difficulties, great and encouraging results have been attained, not only in the direct experience of the Christian life, but in the awakening of a general spirit of inquiry, the improvement of education, increased toleration, and the diffusion of the Word of God throughout the various regions that have been occupied and permeated by the influence of the missions. The printing of the board has been on a very extensive scale, including the issue of the Scriptures and other publications in the following languages, viz. Italian, modern Greek, Græco-Turkish, ancient Armenian, modern Armenian, Armeno-Turkish, Osmanli-Turkish, Bulgarian, Hebrew, Hebrew-Spanish, modern Syriac, and Arabic. The printing of the whole Bible in Arabic, at the expense of the American Bible Society, was completed in 1865. The great work of its translation and conduct through the press was accomplished by the zeal and energy of sixteen years' labor on the part of two learned missionaries of the American Board, Drs. Smith and Van Dyck. This one publication offers the Word of God to the Arabic reading world, comprising a population (though largely uneducated) of 120,000,000 of people. See Anderson, *Oriental Missions;* Smith and Dwight, *Missionary Researches in Armenia;* Hartley, *Researches in Greece and the Levant;* Perkins, *Eighteen Years in Persia;* Grant, *Nestorians;* Wortabet, *Syria and the Syrians;* Dwight, *Christianity in Turkey;* Churchill, *Residence in Mount Lebanon;* Ewald, *Mission in Jerusalem;* Thomson, *The Land and the Book;* Wilson, *Greek Mission;* Yeates, *Gospel in Syria;* Wilson, *Lands of the Bible.*

3. *Missions among the Jews.*—For more than eighteen centuries the Jews have been a cosmopolitan people. The very first missions of the apostles were to the Jews "scattered abroad." In subsequent ages the once chosen but now dispersed race was in many countries made the object of cruel and wasting persecution. Still as a peculiar people the Jews have continued "among all nations" to maintain their own beliefs and customs, and especially an inveterate prejudice against Christianity. See JEWS; JUDAISM. As such they could not be reached by missionary efforts of the usual type. Hence at an early period of the missionary movement of the current century it was deemed important to organize special missions to the Jews in the various countries where they resided in the greatest numbers. Indeed, some beginnings of this character were made in Holland and Germany during the preceding century, and not without good results. August Hermann Francke took a lively interest in this subject. One of the ablest workers raised up under him was professor Callenberg, who in 1728 founded an *institute* for the education of Christian theologians in Hebrew antiquities and the Rabbinic theology. Feb. 15, 1809, the London Society for promoting Christianity among the Jews was organized. In 1820 the American Society for ameliorating the condition of the Jews was begun. In 1849 it was greatly enlarged in its scope. In 1842 the British Society for the propagation of the Gospel among the Jews was organized by the Dissenting churches. In 1839 the Church of Scotland commenced missionary efforts in behalf of the Jews. In 1845 the Scottish Society for the conversion of Israel was organized. Besides these principal organizations, there have been various local societies for the same object both in Great Britain and on the continent of Europe, and also various missionary societies, e. g. the American Board, the Presbyterian Board, and that of the Reformed Presbyterian Church, have maintained special missions to Jewish populations. The aggregate result of these efforts is impossible of indication by figures, and yet it is no small thing to be able to say that many thousands of copies of the Scriptures of both the Old and New Testaments have been circulated among the 5,000,000 of Jews accessible to Christian effort. The versions used have been Hebrew, Hebrew-Spanish, German, French, Portuguese, and those of other European languages. The number of missionary stations established is over 130, missionaries employed over 350, mostly converted Jews, and an aggregate of probably 70,000 confessed converts. Many of these converts have given the best proofs of their sincerity and faithfulness by the endurance of bitter persecution from their kindred; and many who have not identified themselves with the Christian Church are believed to have accepted the vital truths of Christianity, and to have received to their hearts Jesus as the true Messiah. An intelligent writer says, "If all things be taken into consideration, we have no doubt that the results of these labors (missions to the Jews) exceed *in proportion* rather than fall short of those of other valued missionary societies."

Missions to Jews have been prosecuted in the following countries: Great Britain, Holland, Poland, Germany, France, Italy, North Africa, Smyrna, Hungary, Moldavia, Wallachia, Turkey, Egypt, Palestine, Persia, Abyssinia, and the United States of America. While it must be admitted that the results of these efforts have not been as great as might have been hoped, yet they must not be undervalued in their past influence nor in their promise for the future. Great changes are now taking place among the Jews, especially those inhabiting the more enlightened countries, and although certain forms of rationalism seem to be most popular with many who have relinquished the faith of their ancestors, yet when the insufficiency of these shall have been proved they may be found to have served as stepping-stones to evangelical truth. Should this be the case, the beginnings of missionary effort in behalf of Israel in so many lands may ere long prove to be of inestimable value in hastening the grand consummation of the world's conversion. See Steger, *Die Evangelische Judenmission, in ihrer Wichtigkeit u. ihren gesegeneten Fortgange* (1847); Hausmeister, *Die Judenmission* (Heidelb. 1852), an address read at the Paris meeting of the *Evangelical Alliance*; id., *Die evangel. Mission unter Israel* (1861); Harens, *Ueber Judenmission* (Altona, 1862); Kalkar, *Israel u. die Kirche* (Hamburg, 1869); Halsted, *Our Missions* (Lond. 1866); Anderson, *Oriental Missions; Reports* of societies.

4. *Egypt.*—A form of Christianity has long existed among the Copts of Egypt. But they, together with the followers of Mohammed, are sunk in a state of deplorable ignorance and moral depravity. The United Brethren were the first to form a mission in Egypt, but, meeting with little or no success, it was relinquished in 1783. The missionary societies now operating are the American Association, United Presbyterian Church, Kaiserswerth Deaconesses' Institute, and Jerusalem Union, at Berlin. The Bible versions in use are the Coptic and Ethiopic. The mission of the United Presbyterian Church of America has been particularly successful. They have stations both in Cairo and Alexandria, together with a number of minor stations. A Church has been organized with a large and increasing membership. The customs that doom women to a life of seclusion and degradation have been gradually invaded. The Sabbath is more and more sacredly revered, and the vicious and idle habits so common among the people are somewhat abandoned. See Boaz, *Egypt;* Lansing, *Egypt's Princes;* Thompson, *Egypt, Past and Present;* Miss Whately, *The Huts of Egypt.*

5. *Northern Africa*, with the exception of Egypt, seems abandoned to Moslem predominance. Owing to its vast deserts of sand, it is in fact but thinly inhabited —indeed only traversed occasionally by tribes of wandering and savage Arabs. The French occupation of portions of Algeria, including the locality of the churches of Tertullian, Cyprian, and Augustine, has done little towaras restoring the Christianity taught by those fathers, and for the present the prospect of a re-evangelization of Northern Africa is in no sense hopeful. See Davies, *Voice from North Africa; Carthage and her Remains.*

6. *Western Africa.*—This title includes Senegambia, the British colony of Sierra Leone, the American settlement of Liberia, and the country of Guinea. In the latter are included the kingdoms of Ashantee and Dahomey. A large proportion of the people are pagans; among the remainder a very corrupt form of Mohammedanism exists. The earliest efforts made by the Protestant Church to Christianize them were made by the Moravian Brethren in 1736. The missionary societies now in the field are the Church, Wesleyan, Baptist, North German, Society of Bremen, Evangelical Mission at Basle, Free United Methodists, United Presbyterian Church, American Southern Baptist, American Episcopal Board, American Methodist Episcopal, and American Presbyterian. Some of the Bible versions in use are

the Berber, Mandingo, Grebo, Yarriba, Haussa, Ibo, and Dualla. In all, twenty-five dialects have been mastered. There are now many thousands of hopeful converts to Christianity; also above 200 schools, with more than 20,000 scholars under instruction. A very important result has been achieved in the success of native agency. See Wilson, *Western Africa;* East, *Western Africa;* Mrs. Scott, *Day-dawn in Africa;* Schön and Crowther, *Expedition up the Niger;* Beecham, *Ashantee and the Gold Coast;* Randolph, *The People of Africa;* Tucker, *Abeokuta;* Walker, *Sierra Leone;* Bowen, *Central Africa;* Cruikshank, *Eighteen Years on the Gold Coast;* Fox, *Western Coast of Africa; Liberia and its Resources; Life of Daniel West; Memoirs of M. B. Cox;* Waddell, *Twenty-nine Years in the West Indies and Central Africa;* Freeman, *Ashantee.*

7. *Southern Africa.*—The section of Africa now under consideration comprises the six provinces of Cape Colony, British Kaffraria, Kaffraria Proper, the sovereignty beyond the Orange River, Natal, and Amazula. The ideas of the people about God were very confused and indefinite, and there appeared to be no particular form of worship among them. The first mission to the tribes of Southern Africa was established by the Moravian Church in 1737. The missionary societies now in the field are the American Board of Commissioners, Propagation, London, Wesleyan, Free Church of Scotland, United Presbyterian, and Evangelical Moravian Brotherhood, with six Continental societies. The Bible versions in use are the Benga, Namacqua, Bechuana, Sesuto, Zulu, Pedi, and Kaffir. There are nearly a quarter of a million of communicants. Numerous schools have been opened, with a large average attendance of scholars. As a Hottentot has expressed it, the missionaries have given them a religion where formerly they had none: taught them morality, whereas before they had no idea of morality; they were given up to profligacy and drunkenness, now industry and sobriety prevail among them. See Moffat, *Missionary Labors in South Africa;* Livingstone, *Missionary Travels;* Philips, *Researches;* Campbell, *Travels in South Africa;* Holden, *Kaffir Races;* Shaw, *Memorials of South Africa;* Broadbent, *Martyrs of Namaqualand;* Taylor, *Adventures in South Africa.*

8. *Abyssinia* was formerly divided into three independent states; now, however, there is but one. The Christianity of the Abyssinians is so impure as to be little better than heathenism. Thus far it has proved a discouraging field for missionary effort. The Bible versions in use are the Amharic and Ethiopic. See Salt, *History of Abyssinia;* Hotten, *Abyssinia and its People* (Lond. 1868); Gobat, *Three Years' Residence in Abyssinia;* Flad, *Abyssinia;* Isenberg and Stern, *Missionary Journals;* Stern, *The Captive Missionary;* Krapf, *Eighteen Years in Eastern Africa.* See ABYSSINIAN CHURCH.

9. *Madagascar* is one of the largest islands in the world, with a population of five millions. The native religion is idolatrous, but no public worship is offered to the idols. The London Missionary Society introduced the Gospel into Madagascar in the year 1818. The work of that society has been very successful, having largely secured the Christianization of the island. The other missionary societies are the Church and Propagation. The Bible version in use is the Malagasy. The native Church passed through a terrible persecution in 1849. Two thousand persons suffered death rather than renounce Christ. So plentiful has been the ingathering since that Madagascar is now in an important sense counted a Christian country. See Ellis, *History of Madagascar;* id., *Martyr Church of Madagascar;* Freeman, *Persecutions in Madagascar;* Reports of the London Missionary Society.

10. *Mauritius.*—This island has a population of 300,000, three quarters of whom represent the races of India. The missionary societies in this field are the London, Propagation, and Church. An extensive and

promising work is carried on among the Tamils and Bengali-Hindustani-speaking coolies, and also by the London Society among the refugees and other emigrants from Madagascar. See Bond, *Brief Memorials of the Rev. J. Sarjant*; Backhouse, *Visit to Mauritius*; Le Brun, *Letters*.

11. *Ceylon* is an island situated off the south-west coast of Hindustan. The inhabitants are divided into four classes: the Singhalese, who are Buddhists; the Tamils, who profess Hinduism; the Moormen, and the Whedahs. A form of Christianity was introduced into Ceylon by the Jesuits as early as 1505. Protestant missions were commenced by the Dutch in 1656, by the London Missionary Society in 1804, by the Baptists in 1812, and by the American Board in the same year. The Wesleyans of England commenced their important mission in the same island in 1813. Glorious triumphs have been wrought in this field during the last half-century, and a steady advance now characterizes the work. The Wesleyan mission has been very successful. It reports 1535 members. The missionary societies are the Baptist, Church, Propagation, and American Board. The Bible versions in use are the Pali, Singhalese, and Indo-Portuguese. See Tennent, *Christianity in Ceylon*; Hardy, *Buddhism in Ceylon*; Echard, *Residence in Ceylon*; Harvard, *Mission in Ceylon*; Selkirk, *Recollections of Ceylon*; Hardy, *Jubilee Memorials of the Wesleyan Mission in South Ceylon*.

12. *India* has been divided by the British into the three presidencies of Bengal, Bombay, and Madras; these again are subdivided into districts. Its entire extent is about 1,357,000 square miles, with a population of 250,000,000. The religions may be divided into four classes: Hinduism, Buddhism, Mohammedanism, and that taught by Zoroaster. Under their individual and united influence the condition of the people was deplorable. Children were thrown into the River Ganges as offerings to imaginary deities; widows were burned with the dead bodies of their husbands, and numbers destroyed themselves by throwing their bodies under the wheels of the cars of their bloodthirsty idols. The pioneers of Protestant missions in this country were two Danes, who arrived in 1706. There are now twenty-seven missionary societies laboring in the field. The following are a few: Church, Propagation, London, Baptist, Wesleyan, Church of Scotland, American Presbyterian, American Baptist, and American Methodist Episcopal. A few of the Bible versions in use are the Bengali, Hindui, Urdu Telinga, Tamil, Mahratti, and Punjabi. The number of native Christians at the close of 1871 was 224,161. Within the preceding ten years an increase of 85,430 took place. The system of caste, which has proved a great barrier to the triumph of the Gospel, is becoming lax, and showing signs of its coming dissolution. Widows are often remarried. Females for the first time are under education. There is a better appreciation of justice, morality, and religion than ever there was. The native Church promises to become gradually self-supporting. The number of towns and villages scattered over the country inhabited by Protestant Christians is 4657. Statistical facts, however, can in no way convey an adequate idea of the work which has been done in any part of India. The Gospel has been working like leaven, and the effect is very great even in places where there are but few avowed conversions. Even Keshub Chunder Sen, the leader of the new Theistic school, has been constrained to use the following language: "The spirit of Christianity has already pervaded the whole atmosphere of Indian society, and we breathe, think, feel, and move in a Christian atmosphere. Native society is aroused, enlightened, and reformed under the influence of Christian education." Sir Bartle Frere, who was thirty years in India in various official positions, says: "I speak simply as to matters of experience and observation, and not of opinion, just as a Roman prefect might have reported to Trajan or the Antonines, and I assure you, whatever you may be told to the con-

trary, the teaching of Christianity among one hundred and sixty millions of civilized, industrious Hindûs and Mohammedans in India is effecting changes—moral, social, and religious—which, for extent and rapidity of effect, are far more extraordinary than anything which you or your fathers have witnessed in modern Europe. It has come to be the general feeling in India that Hinduism is at an end—that the death-knell has been rung of that collection of old superstitions which has been held together so long." Similar testimony has been borne by lord Lawrence in his famous letter to the London *Times*; also by lord Napier, Sir William Muir, colonel Sir Herbert Edwards, and others in the civil and military service in India. The general opinion, not only of the missionaries, but of thoughtful and intelligent laymen, is that India is much in the condition of Rome just previous to the baptism of the emperor Constantine. Idolatry now in India, as then in Rome, is falling into disgrace—men are becoming wiser. Truth in its clearness and power is gradually entering their minds and changing their habits and lives. An intelligent Hindû said to a missionary on one occasion: "The story which you tell of him who lived, and pitied, and came, and taught, and suffered, and died, and rose again —that story, sir, will overthrow our temples, destroy our ritual, abolish our shastras, and extinguish our gods." The preaching of Christ crucified, and the proclaiming of him who is the way, the truth, and the life, is already accomplishing in some measure what this Hindû said it would, and we may hope, with the divine blessing, to see in the near future a great turning of the people unto the Lord, and the utter destruction of all idols. See Thornton, *India, its State and Prospects*; Duff, *India and Indian Missions*; Kay, *History of Christianity in India*; Butler, *Land of the Veda*; Hough, *Christianity in India*; Hoole, *Madras and Mysore*; Clarkson, *India and the Gospel*; Massie, *Continental India*; Tinling, *Early Roman Catholic Missions in India*; Weitbrect, *Missions in Bengal*; Wylie, *Bengal*; Storrow, *India and Christian Missions*; Stirling, *Orissa*; Arthur, *Mission to Mysore*; Long, *Bengal Missions*; Mullen, *Missions in South India*; *Memoirs of Carey, Marshman, Ward, and Schwartz*; Rev. E. J. Robinson, *The Daughters of India*; Mary E. Leslie, *The Zenana Mission*; J. F. Garey, *India*.

13. *Indo-China* comprises the kingdoms between India and China. The whole district may be divided into four parts: the British territories, Burmah, Siam, and Cochin China, including Cambodia and Tonquin. Buddhism is the leading religion. The missionary societies are the American Baptist, American Presbyterian, American Missionary Association, and Gossner's Evangelical. The Bible versions in use are the Burmese, Bghai-Karen, Sgau-Karen, Pwo-Karen, and Siamese. The Baptists have achieved great success in these regions. Heathen customs are loosened, prejudices are dissolved. The king of Burmah sends his son to the mission school. The late king of Siam sought his most congenial associates among European Christians. Evangelization is going on with great vigor among the Karens of Burmah. Though poor, they support their own pastors. See Mrs. Wylie, *Gospel in Burmah*; Mrs. Judson, *American Baptist Mission to the Burman Empire*; *Life of Judson*; Malcom, *Travels*; Gutzlaff, *Notices of Siam, Corea, and Loo Choo*; Gammell, *Baptist Missions*.

14. *The Indian Archipelago.*—This vast extent of islands forms a bridge as it were to Australia, and from thence northward to China. The outer crescent begins with the Nicobar and Andaman Islands, followed by Sumatra and Java, and then by the Lesser Sunda Islands. Northward of these are the Moluccas, which are followed by the Philippines, and lastly by Formosa. The superficial area is estimated at 170,000 square miles. The population is 20,000,000. The most ancient inhabitants were the Papoos; they were supplanted by the Malays; these in turn are threatened with the same fate by the Chinese coolies. The religions are numerous: Hindûs, Buddhists, and Mohammedans form the larger

proportion of the populations. The missionary societies are the Netherland Society of Rotterdam (1797), Java Society of Amsterdam, Separatist Reformed Church, Utrecht, Netherland Society of Rotterdam (1859), Netherland Reformed, Church of England, and Rhenish. The Bible versions in use are the Malay, Javanese, Dajak, and Sundanese. Considerable good has been accomplished among the Saribas tribes and the Land Dyaks of Borneo. Both their moral and social state testify to the civilizing power of Christianity. See Wigger, *Hist. of Missions*; *Memoirs of Munson and Lyman*; *Hist. of the Missions of the American Board*.

15. *China.*—This is an extensive country of Eastern Asia. Its superficial area is equal to about one third that of Europe, and its population is estimated at 434,000,000. The empire is divided into eighteen provinces. The religions of China are chiefly Buddhism and Confucianism. The first Protestant mission in China was that of the London Missionary Society, founded by Dr. Morrison in the year 1807. The missionary societies now in the field are twenty-two in all, a few of which are the following: London, American Board of Commissioners, American Baptist, American Methodist Episcopal, American Episcopal, American Presbyterian, Baptist, Wesleyan, and Presbyterian. The Bible versions in use are the Chinese, Mandarin, Ningpo, Canton, Hakka, and other local dialects of China. For several years there was little or no visible fruit of the missionary's labor, but at length the tide of success set in, and a large ingathering of converts took place. All the open ports are occupied by mission stations, and some places that are not open by treaty stipulations are occupied on sufferance. There are now one hundred ordained missionaries, and one hundred and eighty native catechists and teachers. The result of their united labors is encouraging as to the past and full of promise for the future. A review of the results which have been accomplished in India (see above), and of the spiritual revolution which is in progress there, is in a high degree encouraging to those who are laboring for the conversion of the still more populous empire of China. Missions in China have been established only about half the period that they have in India, and there have been only about half as many laborers. When they shall have been continued for as long a time, and with as many missionaries, the prospect is that there will be an equal or greater number of converts, and the prospect for the utter overthrow of the religious systems of China will be equally bright. The obstacles to the conversion of the Chinese people are many and great, but they are not more numerous or formidable than those which are now successfully encountered in India. If the Chinese are a more materialistic people than the Hindûs, and their leading men more sceptically inclined, there is, on the other hand, an absence of the immense obstacle of caste; nor is there any set of men in China that are looked up to with such awe and reverence, and wield such immense power, as the Brahmins of India. Moreover, there is not the same diversity of races in the Chinese empire, and the number of languages is but about half the number of those in India. There is, too, this advantage in China, that, whatever the mother-tongue may be, all who have received a good education can read books understandingly, which are in the general written (unspoken) language. The Chinese also are becoming a ubiquitous people, and of the multitudes who come to our own and other Christian lands, we have good reason to believe that not a few will return to China prepared in heart and mind to aid in spreading the Gospel of Christ. The number of Chinese converts at the present time is 35,000, which is about the number there were in India thirty years ago, and the stage of progress of the missions in other respects is about the same as it was in the latter country at that period; but the outlook in China now is much more encouraging than it was in India then, and all those who are seeking the spiritual conquest of the most ancient and most

populous nation of the world have abundant encouragement to press forward in their efforts. See Medhurst, *China*; Huc, *Christianity in China, Tartary, and Thibet*; *Morrison's Life*; Abeel, *Residence in China*; Kidd, *China*; Williams, *Middle Kingdom*; Doolittle, *China*; Williamson, *Journeys in North China, Manchuria, and Mongolia*; Lockhart, *Medical Missionary in China*; Milne, *Life in China*; Matheson, *Presbyterian Mission in China*; Dean, *China Mission*; Wiley, *Fuh-Chau and its Missions.*

16. *Japan.*—This empire consists of three large islands and several smaller ones, which have a superficial area of 90,000 square miles, and a population of 40,000,000. The Japanese are divided into two religious sects, called Sinto and Budso, or Buddhists. The missionary societies are the American Episcopal, American Presbyterian, American Reformed (Dutch) Church, and American Methodist Episcopal Church. The Bible version in use is the Japanese. This peculiar country, which, following the expulsion of the Jesuits in the 17th century, could not be brought under missionary influence from being closed to foreigners, has now become so freely open, and brought into such favorable relations with Christian nations, as to encourage the hope that as a nation it will be entirely Christianized at no distant period. See Smith, *Visit to Japan*; Caddell, *Missions in Japan*; recent *Reports* of missionaries; Mori, *Education in Japan.*

17. *Australia* is the largest island in the world, being nearly the size of the whole of Europe. The aborigines, a race more degraded than either the Hottentot or Bushmen of South Africa, are fast diminishing in numbers. The missionary societies are the Colonial Presbyterian, Gossner's Evangelical, Evangelical Moravian Brotherhood, and Wesleyan Propagation. The migratory habits of the native tribes have stood in the way of any great success of missionary labors. Some, however, have been reached by localizing them on mission reserves. The colonization and occupation of Australia by Great Britain has introduced Christian civilization and English institutions throughout its vast extent, and made it the subject of evangelical labor in modes peculiar to all Protestant Christian countries. See Young, *Southern World*; Jobson, *Australia*; Strachan, *Life of Samuel Leigh*; *Memoirs of Rev. B. Carvosso, D. J. Draper, and Nathaniel Turner*; Angus, *Savage Life in Australia.*

18. *New Zealand* comprises a group of islands in the Pacific Ocean, the principal of which, three in number, are distinguished as the Northern, Middle, and Southern Islands. The natives were savage cannibals, without any fixed idea of worship, but believers in a great spirit called Atua and an evil spirit called Wiro. The first missions to this people were commenced in 1814 by the Church and Wesleyan missionary societies. The missionary societies now in the field are the Propagation, Church, North German, and Wesleyan. The Bible versions in use are the Maori and New Caledonian. The natives are now chiefly professed Christians. The Christian Sabbath and Christian ordinances are observed all over the islands, and this triumph of Christianity, in rescuing such a nation from the depths of heathenism, and even from the practice of the bloodiest cannibalism, is indeed glorious. See Yates, *New Zealand*; Thompson, *Story of New Zealand*; Miss Tucker, *The Southern Cross and Southern Crown*; Brown, *New Zealand and its Aborigines*; *Memoirs of J. H. Bumby.*

19. *Tonga and Fiji.*—Although embraced in the generic title of Polynesia, and even in the minor term South Sea Islands, yet the insular groups known as Tonga and Fiji deserve special notice as having exhibited some peculiar features of savage life, and correspondingly wonderful triumphs of Christian labor. The population of the Tonga, frequently called the Friendly Islands, is estimated at 50,000; that of Fiji, 127,000, scattered over not less than eighty different islands. Cannibalism is a characteristic practice of the heathen of Polynesia. In Fiji it was an institution of the people

interwoven in the elements of society, forming one of their pursuits, and regarded by the mass as a refinement. But even this revolting crime has yielded before the mild influence of Christianity, and is for the most part abolished. Perhaps it may be still secretly practiced by a few in some of the islands. The triumphs of the Gospel in these remote parts of the earth have been in every sense wonderful. Cruel practices and degrading superstitions have given way before Christian teaching. "Thousands have been converted, have borne trial and persecution, well maintained good conduct, and died happy. Marriage is sacred; the Sabbath regarded; family worship regularly conducted; schools established generally; slavery abolished or mitigated; the foundation of law and government laid; many spiritual churches formed, and a native ministry raised up for every branch of the Church's work." The missionary societies are the London, Wesleyan, and a few smaller organizations. The Bible versions are the Fijian and Rotuman. See Williams and Calvert, *Fiji and the Fijians*; Miss Farmer, *Tonga and the Friendly Isles*; West, *Ten Years in South Central Polynesia*; Martin, *Tonga Islands*; Lawry, *Visits to the Friendly Islands*; Seemann, *Mission to the Fiji Islands*; Turner, *Nineteen Years in Polynesia*; Waterhouse, *King and People of Fiji*; Memoirs of Mrs. Cargill.

20. *The South Sea Islands.*—The above term is popularly applied to the islands of the Pacific south of the equator, including the Marquesas, the Austral, the Society, the Georgian, the Harvey, the New Hebrides, and the Solomon Islands, as well as the groups above noticed. A mission was begun in that distant and degraded region as early as 1797, but the difficulties were so great that it came near being abandoned. But in 1812 the night of heathenism seemed to be suddenly illuminated by the Sun of Righteousness. It has since been followed by a glorious awakening. Up to that time a native Christian in Polynesia was unknown. Two generations later it was difficult to find a professed idolator in all Eastern or Central Polynesia where Christian missions had been established. "The hideous rites of their forefathers have ceased to be practiced. Their heathen legends and war-songs are forgotten. Their cruel and desolating tribal wars appear to be at an end. The people are gathered together in peaceful village communities, and live under recognised codes of law. On the Sabbath a large proportion of them attend the worship of God. In some instances more than half the adults are members of Christian churches. They educate their children, they sustain their native ministers, and send their noblest sons as missionaries to heathen lands farther west." In fact, those islands are no longer to be regarded as heathen. See Ellis, *Polynesian Researches*; Williams, *Missionary Enterprises in the South Sea Islands*; *Martyr of Erromanga*; *Life of John Williams*; Gill, *Gems from the Coral Islands*; Lundie, *Mission in Samoa*; Pritchard, *Missionary's Reward*; Murray, *Missions in Western Polynesia*; *History of the London Missionary Society.*

21. *Sandwich Islands.*—The Sandwich or Hawaiian Islands constitute the most important Polynesian group north of the equator. They have been the locality of one of the most important missions of the American Board. That mission was commenced in 1820. Its history for forty years following is one of struggle, trial, perseverance, and encouraging success. The report of the mission in 1857 said, "When we contrast the present with the not very remote past, we are filled with admiration and gratitude in view of the wonders God has wrought for this people. Everywhere and in all things we see the marks of progress. Instead of troops of idle, naked, noisy savages gazing upon us, we are now surrounded by well-clad, quiet, intelligent multitudes, who feel the dignity of men. Instead of squalid poverty, we see competence, abundance, and sometimes luxury. Instead of brutal howlings and dark orgies, we hear the songs of Zion and the supplications of

saints." The year 1860 was distinguished for revivals of religion over a large part of the islands. As a result, nearly 1500 were received into the churches during that year, and 800 the year following. So great had been the success of this mission that the American Board, as early as 1848, incepted measures for creating an independent and self-supporting Church in the islands. Carefully and slowly following the leadings of Providence, the native churches were by degrees educated up to this idea, which was happily consummated in 1863, and has since been put in practice with excellent results. Thus, following about fifty years of missionary labor, not counting the good intermediately accomplished, the world witnesses the grand result of a nation converted from barbarism, and a native Christian community supporting its own pastors and maintaining foreign missions in islands and regions beyond. See Stewart, *Missions to the Sandwich Islands*; Dibble, *Sandwich Islands Mission*; Bingham, *Twenty-one Years in the Sandwich Islands*; Jarves, *History of the Hawaiian Islands*; Anderson, *History of the Mission of the American Board to the Sandwich Islands.*

22. *North America.*—The aboriginal races of the North American continent have, to a greater or less extent, been the subjects of missionary labor almost from the period of the first settlements by Europeans. Eliot's mission to the Indians of Massachusetts was begun in 1646. The French Catholic mission to the natives of Canada dates back to 1613. Spanish missions were commenced in Florida in 1566, in New Mexico in 1597, and in California in 1697. The vast extent of the continent, the lack of national affiliation among the numerous native tribes, the imperfection and multiplicity of languages, together with the extreme unsusceptibility of American Indians to the influences and habits of civilized life, have rendered this class of missions peculiarly difficult. Nevertheless they have been prosecuted by Christians of various denominations with a zeal and perseverance that have not been without encouraging results, both as to individuals and communities. A full history of these missions has never been written, yet many volumes have been filled with sketches embodying material for such a history. In no part of the world have there been greater personal sacrifices or more diligent toil to Christianize savages with results less proportioned to the efforts made. Without enumerating or discussing causes, the fact must be recognised that throughout the whole continent the aboriginal races are dying out to an extent that leaves little present prospect of any considerable remnants being perpetuated in the form of permanent Christian communities. Still missions are maintained in the Indian territories and reservations, and the government of the United States is effectively co-operating with them to accomplish all that may be done for the Christian civilization of the Indians and Indian tribes that remain. The Canadian government also maintains a similar attitude towards the Indian missions within its boundaries. See Tracy, Eliot, and Mayhew, *Gospel among the Indians*; *Lives of Eliot and Brainerd*; Mather, *History of New England*; Gookin, *Christian Indians of New England*; Shea, *Catholic Missions*; Kip, *Early Jesuit Missionaries*; Winslow, *Progress of the Gospel in New England*; Hallet, *Indians of North America*; Heckewelder, *Missions among the Delawares and Mohicans*; Latrobe, *Moravian Missions in North America*; Loskiel, *Moravian Missions in North America*; Hawkins, *Episcopal Missions in North American Colonies*; M'Coy, *Baptist Indian Missions*; Finley, *Wyandot Mission*; Hines, *Indian Missions in Oregon*; Pitezel, *Mission Life on Lake Superior*; Jones, *Ojibway Indians*; West, *Mission to the Indians of the British Provinces*; Marsden, *Mission to Nova Scotia*; Churchill, *Missionary Life in Nova Scotia*; Ryerson, *Hudson's Bay Mission*; Tucker, *Rainbow in the North*; De Schweinitz, *Life of Zeisberger.*

23. *The United States and Canada.*—In no part of the world is there more enlightened and persevering activ-

ity in missionary effort than in these great Christian countries. To them the tide of emigration has been flowing from Europe for a hundred years, and of late it has set in from Asia. Hence, in addition to the providential call upon American Christians for efforts to evangelize the Indians of their forests, there has been even a louder call upon them to teach the Gospel to the foreign populations in their midst, including the African slaves and their descendants. In recognition of this call, missions have been prosecuted with great effect among the German and Scandinavian populations, the fruits of which are already seen in the American missions to Europe. Missions have also been prosecuted to some extent among the French in America and their descendants, but with less success. But, as the tendency is strong towards the mingling of all nationalities in a homogeneous American population, the greatest results have been secured in the normal spreading of the various churches on the ever-enlarging frontier, and in the accumulating masses of our ever-growing cities. In this work of home evangelization, Sunday-schools [see SUNDAY-SCHOOLS] have served as a most efficient auxiliary. In addition to the various general and local home missionary societies, there have been missions to seamen in the ocean ports and along the inland waters of the nation, and also especially, since the extinction of slavery, to the freedmen of the South. Recently efficient missions have been established among the Chinese in California.

24. *Mexico and Central America.*—These countries were favorite fields of the Spanish Roman Catholic missionaries, and by them were pronounced Christianized at a comparatively early period in the settlement of America. The intermediate history of those countries, however, illustrates in a striking manner the defectiveness of that form of Christianization which contents itself with ceremonious conversion, and the exclusion of the Word of God from the people. Within a recent period, and more particularly since the extinction of the empire of Maximilian, there has been a reaction in favor of religious liberty, in consequence of which Protestant missions have been established in the city of Mexico, and in several of the more important provinces. The Scriptures in the Spanish language are now freely circulated throughout Mexico, and to some extent in the republics of Central America. The greatest obstacles to their influence on the public mind are found in the prevailing ignorance and superstition of the people. It may be hoped, however, that these will gradually pass away. See Robertson, *History of America;* Prescott, *Conquest of Mexico; History of the British and Foreign and American Bible Societies;* Bishop Haven, *Letters from Mexico;* recent *Reports* of the American Christian Union, the Presbyterian Board, the American Board, and the Missionary Society of the Methodist Episcopal Church; Crowe, *Gospel in Central America, Honduras, and Guatemala;* Griffin, *Mexico of To-day.*

25. *South America.*—With the exception of Brazil, which was settled by the Portuguese, the several countries of South America were populated by colonies from Spain. The entire continent was long ago Christianized after the Roman Catholic type. It was in Paraguay, the centre of the continent, that the Jesuits planted and developed the most remarkable mission known to their history, and yet by Roman Catholic power they were summarily expelled both from Paraguay and Brazil. The aboriginal races of South America have to some extent become mingled with the European and African races that have come to be occupants of their territory, but to a large extent they have declined in numbers, giving omen of ultimate extinction. The tribes that have been pronounced Christianized resemble in superstition and their low grade of intelligence the native races of Mexico, and their religious aspirations are equally hopeless. Most of the South American governments maintain a limited toleration, under which Protestant missions have been established

in Guiana, Guatemala, Brazil, Montevideo, Buenos Ayres, Peru, and Chili. Most of these missions have met with encouraging success, which, although as yet on a limited scale, may prove the beginning of great results hereafter, especially in elevating the standard of Christianity hitherto prevailing in those vast regions. Patagonia is still wholly abandoned to a sparse population of cruel savages. An unsuccessful mission to them was attempted in 1848 by captain Allen Gardiner, of the English navy, and several associates. Nevertheless efforts for the evangelization of the Patagonians are still kept up by English Christians. See Robertson, *History of America;* Prescott, *Conquest of Peru;* Southey, *History of Brazil;* Kohl, *Travels in Peru;* Muratori, *Missions in Paraguay;* Bernan, *Missionary Labors in British Guiana;* Brett, *Indian Missions in Guiana;* Kidder, *Sketches of Brazil; Reports* of the Presbyterian Board and of the Methodist Episcopal Missionary Society; Marsh, *Memoir of Captain Gardiner;* Hamilton, *Life of R. Williams.*

26. *West Indies.*—The West India Islands are divided into three principal groups: 1, the Bahamas; 2, the Greater Antilles; 3, the Lesser Antilles. The population is estimated at about 3,400,000. Of these, about two thirds are negroes, one fifth white men, and the remainder mixed races. Through cruel oppression on the part of the early European emigrants to these islands, the native races, with a few exceptions, have long been extinct. To supply their place as laborers, African slaves were imported. The religion of the negroes was a mixture of idolatry, superstition, and fanaticism. Obeism and myalism, species of witchcraft, were commonly practiced. The first missionary efforts among the negroes were made by the Moravian Brethren in 1732. Since then the following missionary societies have entered the field: the Wesleyan, American Free Baptist, Propagation, Baptist, American Missionary, London, Church, and United Presbyterian. Since the abolition of slavery in 1838 the negroes have given increasing heed to the precepts and practices of Christianity, and thus secured a higher degree of moral improvement and social elevation. The most prosperous society, the Wesleyan, numbers 44,446 Church members. See Coke, *History of the West Indies;* Duncan, *Wesleyan Mission to Jamaica;* Phillippo, *Jamaica, Past and Present;* Samuel, *Missions in Jamaica and Honduras;* Horsford, *Voice from the West Indies;* Candler, *Hayti;* Knibb, *Memoirs; Memoirs of Jenkins, Bradnack, and Mrs. Wilson;* Trollope, *West Indies.*

27. *Greenland and Labrador.*—The arrival of Hans Egede on the shores of Greenland in 1721 marked an epoch in the history of modern missions, and the whole subsequent history of Moravian missionary effort among the inhabitants of Greenland and the coasts of Labrador is full of intense though sometimes of melancholy interest. In several instances both the missionaries and the people for whom they labored were decimated alike by disease and famine. But, notwithstanding all discouragements, the missionaries toiled on. By them it was effectually demonstrated that the one agency adapted to elevating degraded savages was the preaching of Christ and him crucified. By this appointed agency, first one and subsequently many of the Greenlanders were awakened and converted, after which civilization and education followed. From the original nucleus of Christian effort at Disco, Christianity has been effectively disseminated by missionary settlements in other parts of the island. Five such settlements are now occupied, and nearly two thousand souls are under the direct care of the missionaries. About one fifth of the population of West Greenland receive Christian instruction at the mission settlements, and there are scarcely any unbaptized Greenlanders on the whole west coast up to the seventy-second degree of north latitude. On the east coast the inhabitants are still heathen; but they are very few in number, and practically inaccessible to foreigners. The peninsula of Lab-

rador is sparsely inhabited by Esquimaux, a race of natives similar in language and customs to the Greenlanders. To that land, therefore, the Moravians extended their efforts successfully in 1771, since which time they have been extending Christian influence by means of mission stations, of which there are now four—Nain, Okak, Hopedale, and Hebron. At these stations thirty-five missionary agents are employed, and about twelve hundred natives are under Christian instruction. The Gospel has triumphed in frozen Labrador as well as in Greenland. See Crantz, *History of Greenland;* Egede, *Greenland Mission;* Holmes, *United Brethren;* Histories of Moravian missions in Greenland and Iceland.

VIII. *Missionary Geography.*—From the above survey it may be seen that in an important sense the world is already occupied as the field of active missionary enterprise. A few brief statements of results accomplished by it during the current century may serve as a just indication of still greater results that may now be safely anticipated in time to come from its increasing and maturing agencies.

The mission to Tahiti in 1793–4 was the first attempt in modern times to carry the Gospel to an isolated and uncivilized people. It was commenced at a period when the greater heathen nations of the world were wholly inaccessible. In the islands of the southern seas, as upon a trial-ground, all the great problems of humanity have since been wrought out. The densest ignorance has been enlightened, the fiercest cannibalism has been confronted, the lowest conditions of humanity have been elevated, and the most abominable idolatries overthrown and substituted by a pure worship. The various languages and dialects of the islands of the Pacific have been committed to writing. Dictionaries, grammars, translations of the Scriptures, and many other books, have been printed and introduced to the daily use of the populations, a large proportion of whom have been taught by schools to read and write in their own languages. The civil condition of the various communities has also been improved by modifications of their laws and customs adapted to the new and improved state of public feeling and knowledge.

It is hardly possible for the processes of elevating nations from pagan barbarism to Christian civilization to be better stated than in the language of John Williams, the renowned missionary martyr of Erromanga. "I am convinced," wrote he, forty years ago, "that the first step towards the production of a nation's temporal and social elevation is to plant among them the tree of life, when civilization and commerce will en-

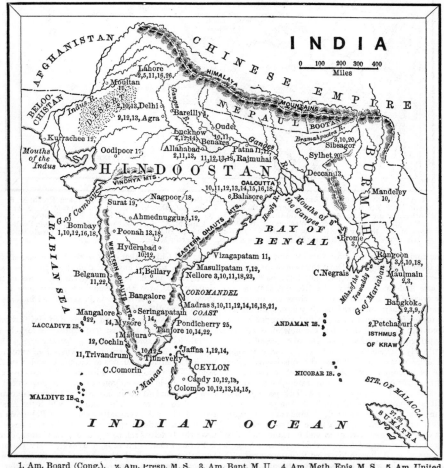

1. Am. Board (Cong.). 2. Am. Presb. M. S. 3. Am. Bapt. M. U. 4. Am. Meth. Epis. M. S. 5. Am. United Presb. M. S. 6. Am. Free Bapt. M. S. 7. Am. Luth. M. S. 8. Am. Ref. (Dutch) M. S. 9. Am. Miss. Assoc. 10. Eng. Soc. Prop. Gospel. 11. Eng. London M. S. 12. Eng. Church M. S. 13. Eng. Bapt. M. S. 14. Eng. Wesleyan M. S. 15. Eng. Presb. M. S. 16. Scotch Estab. Ch. M. S. 17. Scotch United Presb. M. S. 18. Scotch Free Ch. M. S. 19. Irish Presb. Ch. M. S. 20. Welsh Calv. Meth. M. S. 21. Leipsic M. S. 22. Basle M. S. 23. Hermannsburg M. S. 24. Gossner's M. S. 25. Danish M. S. 26. Moravian M. S. 27. Rhine M. S. 28. Dutch Zending M. S.

1. Am. Board (Cong.). 2. Am. Presb. M. S. 3. Am. United Presb. M. S. 4. Am. Southern Presb. M. S. 5. Am. Meth. Ep. M. S. 6. Am. Southern Meth. M. S. 7. Am. Ref. (Dutch) M. S. 8. Am. Bapt. M. U. 9. Am. Southern Bapt. M. S. 10. Am. Seventh-Day Bapt. M. S. 11. Am. Prot. Ep. M. S. 12. Eng. London M. S. 13. Eng. Church M. S. 14. Eng. Wesleyan M. S. 15. Eng. Bapt. M. S. 16. Eng. Presb. M. S. 17. Eng. United Meth. M. S. 18. Eng. Meth. New Con. M. S. 19. Eng. China Inland M. S. 20. Scotch United Presb. M. S. 21. Irish Presb. M. S. 22. Basle M. S. 23. Rhine M. S. 24. Berlin M. S.

twine their tendrils around its trunk, and derive support from its strength. Until the people are brought under the influence of religion they have no desire for the arts and usages of civilized life, but that invariably creates it." "While the natives are under the influence of their superstitions, they evince an inanity and torpor from which no stimulus has proved powerful enough to arouse them but the new ideas and the new principles imparted by Christianity. And if it be not already proved, the experience of a few more years will demonstrate the fact that the missionary enterprise is incomparably the most effective machinery that has ever been brought to operate upon the social, the civil, and the commercial, as well as the moral and spiritual interests of mankind." At the present time the mission field of the South Sea Islands presents every variety of communities, from those of the coral islets, just emerging from barbarism and learning their first lessons of Christianity, to those that have been longest taught and most thoroughly tried by intercourse with the outer world, which has sometimes been as destructive as their original paganism. It has been thought by some that the first experiments of modern missions to the heathen were providentially directed to the small islands of Polynesia, among an impressible people, rather than to the great and ancient nations of

India and China; that comparatively the easiest work was given to the churches at first, in the process of which they might solve the great problems of missionary measures and economies preparatory to the greater work awaiting them in larger and in some respects more difficult fields.

The marvellous rise and progress of civilization in Australia during the last half-century is largely due to missionary effort. Three generations ago there was not a civilized man on the Australian continent, nor in the adjacent islands of Tasmania and New Zealand. Now there are two millions of English-speaking Protestants, in the enjoyment of a good government, a free press, and all the immunities of liberty, education, art, and commerce. The influence which the Australian colonies will eventually exert upon Polynesia and the Asiatic nations, from Japan to India, as well as upon the Indian Archipelago and New Guinea, cannot fail to be great. There is, moreover, every reason to hope that it may be both good and Christian. In no communities does there exist a greater desire for the spread of education and the circulation of sound literature. In Sydney, Melbourne, and Adelaide there are excellent public libraries. Whatever disadvantages were fastened upon those regions by the original plan and effort of England to populate them with trans-

1. Am. Board (Cong.). 2. Eng. Church M. S. 3. Eng. Soc. Prop. Gospel. 4. Eng. Wesleyan M. S. 5. Eng. London M. S. 6. Eng. Moravian M. S. 7. Scotch Free Church M. S. 8. Scotch United Presb. M. S. 9. Berlin M. S. 10. Rhine M. S. 11. Hermannsburg M. S. 12. French Evan. M. S. 13. Norwegian M. S. 14. Holland Ref. of Natal M. S.

ported criminals, have now been largely if not wholly counteracted. Indeed, it is asserted by English writers that there is on the whole a larger proportion of well-informed, educated people in the Australian colonies than among the same number of people in Great Britain, while the religious feeling is fully equal. The proportion of the aboriginal population is now not only small, but, notwithstanding all influences, growing relatively less, so that the missionary activity of Australian Christians may be expected to seek fields in the surrounding countries in the midst of which they are placed.

As the voyage of Columbus, by which America was discovered, and many of the expeditions by which the New World was opened up to settlement, were in a certain sense missionary in their character, so from that day down to the present, missionary effort has been making geographical explorations, and increasing both the extent and thoroughness of geographical knowledge. Of this the expeditions and journeys of Livingstone in Africa are a striking proof and illustration. Moreover, the influence which missions have exerted, and are now more than ever promising to exert over vast portions of the earth, renders the subject of *missionary occupation* in various countries one of peculiar interest. For a full illustration of this subject nothing less than a missionary map of the world is requisite; nevertheless, very suggestive indications are practicable on a condensed scale, like those herewith presented to the reader. Without any attempt to show the island world of the southern hemisphere, to which reference has been made above, a miniature outline of India is first introduced, followed by similar outlines of other important fields, to which, for lack of space, we cannot further allude.

It would be difficult, even with the largest map, to impress the mind adequately with the extent and importance of India. That ancient country embraces a territory twenty-three times as large as England, and, leaving out Russia and Scandinavia, equal in extent to all Europe. It contains twenty-one races and thirty-five nations, while its inhabitants speak fifty-one different languages and dialects. Its population, according to the census of 1872, is 237,552,958, of which number 191,300,000 are directly governed by British rulers, and 46,250,000 by native governments dependent upon the British.

Notwithstanding some praiseworthy efforts to introduce the Gospel into India during the 18th century, all such efforts were opposed, and to a great extent neutralized, by the East India Company, which then practically ruled the country in the name of Great Britain. It was not till 1815 that toleration was obtained for missions in India from the British Parliament. Since that period diligent efforts have been made, both by English and American Christians, to antagonize idolatry, and introduce Christian truth and worship by all appropriate means. Yet the government connection with idolatrous worship was not fully withdrawn till 1849.

A most interesting exhibit of the work and influence of missions in India may be found in a Parliamentary Blue-book ordered to be printed by the House of Commons, April 2, 1873. From it the following facts are abridged and copied:

"The Protestant missions of India, Burmah, and Ceylon are maintained by 35 missionary societies, in addition to local agencies. They employ the services of 606 foreign missionaries. They occupy 522 principal stations and 2500 subordinate stations. A great impulse was given to these societies by the changes in public policy inaugurated by the charter of 1833, and since that period the number of missionaries and the outlay on their missions have continued steadily to increase."

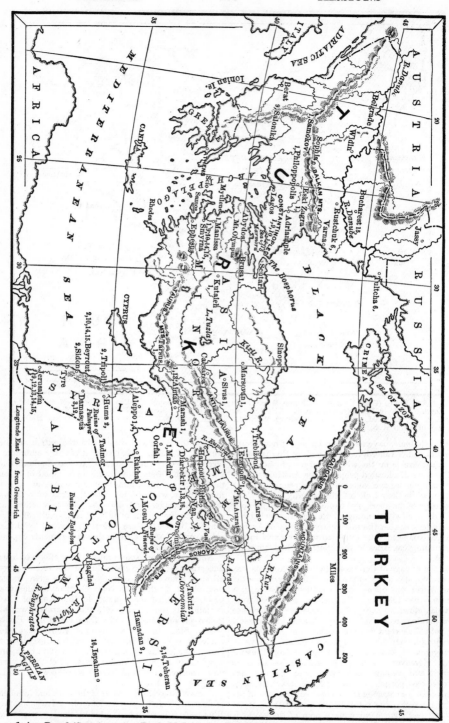

1. Am. Board (Cong.). 2. Am. Presb. M. S. 3. Am. United Presb. M. S. 4. Am. Ref. Presb. M. S. 5. Am. Southern Presb. M. S. 6. Am. Meth. Epis. M. S. 7. Am. Prot. Epis. M. S. 8. Am. Bapt. M. S. 9. Eng. Church M. S. 10. Scotch Estab. Ch. M. S. 11. Scotch Free Ch. M. S. 12. Irish Presb. M. S. 13. Bishop Gobot's M. 14. Jerusalem Verein. 15. Kaiserswerth Deaconesses. 16. Independent Missions.

Co-operation of Missionary Societies.—"This large body of European and American missionaries bring their various moral influences to bear upon the country with the greater force because they act together with a compactness which is but little understood. From the nature of their work, their isolated position, and their long experience, they have been led to think rather of the numerous questions on which they agree than of those on which they differ, and they co-operate heartily together. Localities are divided among them by friendly arrangements; and, with few exceptions, it is a fixed rule among them that they will not interfere with each other's converts and each other's spheres of duty. The large body of missionaries resident in each of the presidency towns form conferences, hold periodic meetings, and act together on public matters. They have frequently addressed the Indian government on important social questions involving the welfare of the native community, and have suggested valuable improvements in existing laws."

Various Forms of Labors.—"The labors of the foreign missionaries in India assume many forms. Apart from their special duties as public preachers and pastors, they constitute a valuable body of educators. They contribute greatly to the cultivation of the native languages and literature, and all who are resident in rural districts are appealed to for medical help for the sick."

Knowledge of the Native Languages.—"No body of men pays greater attention to the study of the native languages. The missionaries, as a body, know the natives of India well. They have prepared hundreds of works, suited both for schools and for general circulation, in the fifteen most prominent languages of India, and in several other dialects. They are the compilers of several dictionaries and grammars; they have written important works on the native classics and the system of philosophy; and they have largely stimulated the great increase of the native literature prepared in recent years by native gentlemen."

Mission Presses and Publications.—"The mission presses in India are 25 in number. During the ten years between 1862 and 1872 they issued 3410 new works in thirty languages. They circulated 1,315,503 copies of books of Scripture, 2,375,040 school-books, and 8,750,129 Christian books and tracts."

Schools and Training Colleges.—"The missionary schools in India are chiefly of two kinds, purely vernacular and Anglo-vernacular. In addition to the work of these schools, several missions maintain training colleges for their native ministers and clergy, and training institutions for teachers of both sexes. An important addition to the efforts made on behalf of female education is seen in the Zenana schools and classes, which are maintained and instructed in the houses of Hindû gentlemen. The great progress made in the missionary schools and the area they occupy will be seen from the following fact. They now contain 60,000 scholars more than they did twenty years ago. In 1872 the scholars numbered 142,952."

Christian Communities.—"A very large number of the Christian communities scattered over India are small, and they contain severally fewer than a hundred communicants and three hundred converts of all ages. At the same time some of these small congregations consist of educated men, have considerable resources, and are able to provide for themselves. From them have sprung a large number of the native clergy and ministers in different churches, who are now taking a prominent place in the instruction and management of an indigenous Christian Church. Taking them together, the rural and aboriginal populations of India which have received a large share of the attention of the missionary societies now contain among them *a quarter of a million* native Christian converts."

General Influence of Missions.—"The missionaries in India hold the opinion that the winning of these converts, whether in the city or in the open country, is but a small portion of the beneficial results which have sprung from their labors. No statistics can give a fair view of all that they have done. They consider that their distinctive teaching, now applied to the country for many years, has powerfully affected the entire population. The moral tone of their preaching is recognised and highly approved by multitudes who do not follow them as converts. Insensibly a higher standard of moral conduct is becoming familiar to the people; the ancient systems are no longer defended as they once were, many doubts are felt about the rules of caste, and the great festivals are not attended by the great crowds of former years. This view of the general influence of their teaching, and of the greatness of the revolution which it is silently producing, is not taken by missionaries only. It has been accepted by many distinguished residents in India and experienced officers of the government, and has been emphatically endorsed by the high authority of Sir Bartle Frere. Without pronouncing an opinion upon the matter, the government of India cannot but acknowledge the great obligation under which it is laid by the benevolent exertions made by these six hundred missionaries, whose blameless example and self-denying labors are infusing new vigor into the stereotyped life of the great populations placed under English rule, and are preparing them to be in every way better men and better citizens of the great empire in which they dwell."

The following is the testimony of Sir Bartle Frere, governor of Bombay:

"I speak simply as to matters of experience and observation, and not of opinion—just as a Roman prefect might have reported to Trajan or the Antonines—and I assure you that, whatever you may be told to the contrary, the teaching of *Christianity among the one hundred and sixty millions of civilized, industrious Hindûs and Mohammedans in India is effecting changes, moral, social, and politi-* *cal, which, for extent and rapidity of effect, are far more extraordinary than anything you or your fathers have witnessed in modern Europe.*"

To the above may be fitly added the following similar authoritative testimonies:

"I believe, notwithstanding all that the English people have done to benefit India, *the missionaries have done more than all other agencies combined.*
"Lord Lawrence, viceroy and governor-general."

"In many places an impression prevails that the missions have not produced results adequate to the efforts which have been made; but I trust enough has been said to prove that there is no real foundation for this impression, and *those who hold such opinions know but little of the reality.* Sir Donald M'Leod,
"Lieutenant-governor of the Punjaub."

In the light of such competent and unequivocal testimony it would seem impossible for any reasonable mind to doubt the grandeur or the beneficence of the results accomplished by Christian missions during the current century, or to question their still greater promise in time to come. The above notices of missionary work in India may serve as a sample of similar testimony which might be adduced from various other countries. In nearly all cases the most that has been done is to be regarded as in a large measure preparatory to greater efforts and successes hereafter.

The great empire of China affords another remarkable example. That most populous country of all the earth had for ages maintained a rigid system of non-intercourse with the people of foreign nations, whom it indiscriminately stigmatized as outside barbarians. Until within a little more than thirty years all Christian efforts in behalf of China had to be made outside of the empire, or stealthily if within its borders. On the opening of the "Five Ports" to commerce in 1842 missions also entered, and, notwithstanding multiplied obstacles, have since made wonderful progress. Already there are 34,000 native Christians in China. The principal great cities of the empire have become recognised centres of missionary effort, from Canton on the south to the old Tartar capital, Peking, on the north. What is perhaps most interesting of all is the demonstrated fact that, nothwithstanding the peculiarities of the Chinese character, the power of the Gospel has proved itself adequate to its complete transformation and renewal after the New-Testament model. Many ministers of the Gospel have already been raised up. The native churches are also developing both the capacity and the disposition for self-support. Thus all the elements of a successful and progressive establishment of Christianity throughout the empire of China seem now to be happily at work.

In Japan a few recent years have witnessed extraordinary changes in favor of Christianity. Not less than 527 Protestant missionaries, of whom half are American, are now energetically but peacefully at work within the empire, from whose borders, owing to passions and prejudices, excited by the Jesuit missionaries of the 16th century, Christianity had long been excluded by the most barbarous decrees. Native churches have already been formed, and converted Japanese are becoming apostles to their countrymen, while a system of education, indirectly under Christian influence, promises to elevate the general intelligence and character of the nation at an early day. The old edicts against Christians, if not formally repealed, are practically set aside, and a favorable sentiment towards Christianity has become very general in various grades of society.

In South Africa a mission was commenced by the Moravians as early as 1737; but it was withdrawn in 1744, and not effectively resumed till 1792. In 1798 the London Missionary Society entered the field, in 1812 the Wesleyan, and since various others. Although Hottentots and Kaffirs are not promising subjects for missionary influence, yet the Gospel, through missionary agency, has not been wanting in glorious triumphs among them, as well as other native tribes of South Africa, while it has made substantial progress among the Dutch and English colonists who now permanently occupy that portion of the African continent.

In 1815 the Church of England Missionary Society first turned its attention to the countries on the eastern border of the Levant. In 1819 the American Board commenced its work in the same regions. The missions in Greece, Turkey, and Persia have been mainly addressed to the nominal Christians of those lands. As a result, thousands have been converted, and a large number of evangelical congregations have been established both in European and Asiatic Turkey. Most interesting and promising also have been the results of the educational efforts made in connection with the Protestant missions in the Orient.

IX. *General Missionary Literature.*—Notwithstanding the numerous references in this article to books relating to the several fields of missionary effort throughout the world, the subject of missions as a whole would be but imperfectly delineated without allusion to its general literature, which embraces several classes of valuable works not heretofore named, and which can now be but briefly indicated.

1. *General Histories of Missions,* by Wiggers, Steger, Klumpp, Blumhardt, Brown, Callenburg, Clarkson, Huie, Choules and Smith, Pearson (*Propagation of the Gospel*).

2. *Cyclopædias, Gazetteers, etc.*—Newcombe, Aikman, Hassel (*Pole to Pole*), Moister (*Missionary World*), Edwards (*Gazetteer*), Hoole (*Year-book*), Grundemann (*Missions-Atlas,* Gotha, 1867–71); Bliss, *Miss. Year-book,* 1890.

3. *Histories of Missionary Societies.*—*Annales de la Propagation de la Foi; Lettres Edifiantes;* Anderson, *Hist. of the Colonial Church;* Alder, *Wesleyan Missions;* Moister, *Wesleyan Missions;* Bost, *Moravians;* Cox, *Baptist Missionary Society;* Gammell, *Baptist Missionary Society; Jubilee of the Church Missionary Society;* Ellis, *London Missionary Society;* Kennett, *Accounts of the Society for the Propagation of the Gospel; Jubilee of the Religious Tract Society; Jubilee of the British and Foreign Bible Society; American Bible Society;* Tracy, *Hist. of the American Board;* Strickland, *American Methodist Missions;* Green, *Presbyterian Missions;* Lowrie, *Presbyterian Missions;* Reid, *Missions of the M. E. Ch.*

4. *Missionary Biographies.* — Morison, *Lives of the Fathers;* Pierson, *American Missionary Memorial;* Tarbox, *Missionary Patriots;* Yonge, *Pioneers and Founders;* Eddy, *Daughters of the Cross;* Lives of Schwartz, Carey, Marshman, Coke, Morrison, Phillips, Shaw, Judson, Hall, and many others.

5. *Discussions of Missionary Principles.* — Harris, *Great Commission;* Duff, *Missions the Chief End of the Church:* Hamilton, *End and Aim of Missions;* Campbell, *Philosophy of Missions;* Kingsmill, *Missions and Missionaries;* Müller, *On Missions,* a lecture delivered at Westminster Abbey, Dec. 3, 1873, with an introductory sermon by dean Stanley; Beecham, *Christianity the Means of Civilization;* Maitland, *Prize Essay;* Stowell, *Missionary Church;* Stowe, *Missionary Enterprises;* Wayland, *Moral Dignity of Missions; Liverpool Conferences on Missions;* Richard Watson, *Sermons;* Macfarlane, *The World's Jubilee;* Seelye, *Chr. Missions;* the addresses on *Missions* delivered at the New York meeting of the Evangelical Alliance; and many others. The following periodicals contain valuable articles on the subject of missions: *English Rev.* vii, 42 sq.; xviii, 354 sq.; *Western Rev.* Jan. 1855; July, 1856; *Christian Rev.* i, 325 sq.; ii, 449 sq.; vi, 285; x, 566 sq.; vol. xiv, Nov.; *Amer. Bibl. Repository,* 3d series, iv, 453; vi, 161 sq.; Jan. 1867, p. 58; *Bibl. Repos. and Princet. Rev.* Oct. 1870, p. 613; *New-Englander,* viii, 489; ix, 207; *Princet. Rev.* v, 449; x, 535; xv, 349; 1858, p. 436; xvii, 61; xxxvi, 324; July, 1867; *Christian Examiner,* i, 182; iii, 265, 449; xxix, 51; xliv, 416; *Biblioth. Sacra,* Oct. 1867; *Brit. and For. Evangel. Rev.* April, 1871; *Evangel. Qu. Rev.* Oct. 1870, p. 373; *Meth. Qu. Rev.* vii, 269; viii, 165 sq.; *Baptist Qu.* Oct. 1873, art. vii; April, 1874, art. vi; *Theol. Medium,* July, 1873, art. ii; Oct. art. ii; *Catholic World,* 1870, p. 114. See also Malcom, *Theol. Index,* s. v.

6. *Missionary Periodicals.*—Their number is legion. Every country interested in missionary enterprises is publishing one or more. Germany, England, and America have them by the score. Among the most valuable are the *Missionary Chronicle* (Lond.), the *Missionary Magazine* (Lond.), and the *Missionary Herald* (Boston); *Missionary Review of the World* (N. Y.); also *Mission Life* (Lond. 1866 sq.), a magazine consisting chiefly of readings on foreign lands with reference to the scenes and circumstances of mission life; the Basle *Evang. Missions-Magazin* (established in 1816); Burkhardt, *Missionsbibliothek.* A *General Missionary Periodical,* a monthly, is just starting at Gütersloh, Germany. Its editors are Christlieb, Grundemann, and Warneck. It is to be published in English, and its contributors are to be of the world at large.

The above outline will serve at least as an indication of the great extent and value of a species of Christian literature which is obviously destined to increase in volume and in interest from year to year and from age to age. Whoever, by means of the authentic information now accessible, will acquire a full and just comprehension of the grand enterprise of missions, as it stands embodied in the active movements and growing successes of Christian missionaries and churches, can hardly fail to recognise with wonder and gratitude the rapid and substantial progress that is now made towards the fulfilment of the Saviour's great command, "Go teach all nations." (D. P. K.)

Misson, FRANÇOIS MAXIMILIEN, an eminent French lawyer, distinguished himself by his pleadings before the Parliament of Paris in behalf of the Protestants during the persecution of the Huguenots in the 17th century. He retired to England on the revocation of the Edict of Nantes, and afterwards travelled as tutor to an English nobleman. He published *A Voyage to Italy* (3 vols.):—*A Tour in England:*—and *Le Théâtre sacré des Çevennes,* in which the author betrayed his credulity and fanaticism by espousing the cause of the French prophets. He died in London in 1701.

Missy, CÉSAR DE, a writer of French parentage, was born June 2, 1703, at Berlin, and studied theology at Frankfort-on-the-Oder; but for his persistent refusal to sign the official formula of creed he was excluded from the ministry in Prussia. He went to Holland, where he allied with his duties of a minister the pursuits of a literary critic and poet. In 1731 he was appointed minister at the church of Savoy, London; in 1762, at St. James's Chapel. He died at London, Aug. 10, 1775. His judgment was very good, his taste refined, and his love of study passionate. He numbered among his friends several distinguished men of learning, as Beausobre, Formey, Jordan. His rich library, together with his manuscripts, went to the library of the duke of Sussex. He left a work in verse, *Paraboles ou fables et outres narrations d'un citoyen de la république Chrétienne du dix-huitième siècle* (Londres, 1769, 1770, 1776, 8vo):—*Sermons sur divers textes* (ibid. 1780, 3 vols. 8vo). Missy was also one of the editors of the *Bibliothèque Britannique,* of the *Journal Britannique,* and of the *Magasin Français,* of London. Other poetical productions and critical articles of his were published in the *Mercure de France* and in English newspapers.

Mist (אֵד, *ed,* Gen. ii, 6) signifies a rising vapor, a fog, or cloud, which again distils upon the ground (Job xxxvi, 27). The Chaldee paraphrase renders it עֲנָנָא, *the cloud.*

Mistletoe (Anglo-Sax. *misteltan,* Ger. *mistel;* the *tan* of the Anglo-Saxon name means a tine or prong, a shoot of a tree; *mistel* is of uncertain etymology, but probably the same, in meaning at least, as the Latin *viscus*), a genus (*Viscum*) of small parasitical shrubs of the natural order *Loranthaceæ.* This order is exogenous, and contains more than four hundred known species, mostly tropical and parasites. The leaves are entire, almost nerveless, thick and fleshy, and without stipules. The flowers of many species are showy. The calyx arises from a tube or rim, which sometimes assumes the appearance of a calyx, and is so regarded by many botanists; what others deem the colored calyx being viewed by them as a corolla of four or eight petals or segments. Within this are the stamens, as numerous as its divisions, and opposite to them. The ovary is one-celled, with a solitary ovule; the fruit one-seeded, generally succulent. The stems are dichotomous (i. e. divide by forking); the leaves are opposite, of a yellowish-green color, obovate-lanceolate, obtuse. The flowers are inconspicuous, and grow in small heads at the ends and in the divisions of the branches, the male and the female flowers on separate plants. The berries are about the size of currants, white, translucent, and full of a very viscid juice, which serves to attach the seeds to branches, where they take root when they germinate, the radicle always turning towards the branch, whether on its upper or under side. The mistletoe derives its nourishment from the living tissue of the tree on which it grows, and from which it seems to spring as if it were one of its branches.

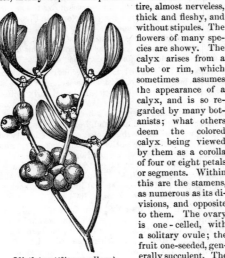

Mistletoe (*Viscum album*).

Superstitious Use. — The mistletoe was intimately connected with many of the superstitions of the different branches of the Aryan race. In the Northern mythology, Baldur is said to have been slain with a mistletoe. Among the Celts the mistletoe which grew on the oak was in peculiar esteem for magical virtues. Traces of the ancient regard for the mistletoe still remain in some old English and German customs, as kissing under the mistletoe at Christmas. The British Druids are said to have had an extraordinary veneration for it, and that mainly because its berries as well as its leaves grow in clusters of three united to one stock, and, as is well known, they had a special veneration for the number three (comp. Vallancey, *Grammar of the Irish Language*). Stukeley (*Medallic History of Carausius*, ii, 163 sq.), speaking of the Druids' festival, the Jul (q. v.), and the use of the mistletoe, relates as follows: "This was the most respectable festival of our Druids, called Yule-tide, when mistletoe, which they called *all-heal* (because used to cure disease), was carried in their hands, and laid on their altars, as an emblem of the salutiferous advent of Messiah. . . . The custom is still preserved in the north, and was lately at York. On the eve of Christmas-day they carry mistletoe to the high altar of the cathedral, and proclaim a public and universal liberty, pardon, and freedom to all sorts of inferior and even wicked people at the gates of the city, towards the four quarters of heaven." See Brand, *Popul. Antiquities of Great Britain*, i, 521–4.

Mitâksharâ is the name of several Sanscrit commentatorial works of the Hindûs. One of these is a commentary on the text-book of the Vedânta philosophy; another, a commentary on the Mîmânsâ work of Kumârila; a third, a commentary on the Brihadâranyaka, etc. See VEDA. The most renowned work, however, bearing this title is a detailed commentary by Vijnâneswara (also called Vijnânanâtha) on the lawbook of Yâjnavalkya (q. v.); and its authority and influence are so great that "it is received in all the schools of Hindû law from Benares to the southern extremity of the peninsula of India as the chief groundwork of the doctrines which they follow, and as an authority from which they rarely dissent" (comp. *Two Treatises on the Hindû Law of Inheritance*, translated by H. T. Colebrooke, Calcutta, 1810). Most of the other renowned law-books of recent date, such as the Smriti-Chandrikâ, which prevails in the south of India, the Chintâmani, Vîramitrodaya, and Mayûkha, which are authoritative severally in Mithilâ, Benares, and with the Mahrattas, generally defer to the decisions of the Mitâksharâ; the Dâyabhâga of Jimûtavâhana alone, which is adopted by the Bengal school, differs on almost every disputed point from the Mitâksharâ, and does not acknowledge its authority.

The Mitâksharâ, following the arrangement of its text-work, the code of Yâjnavalkya, treats in its first part of duties in general; in its second, of private and administrative law; in its third, of purification, penance, devotion, and so forth; but, since it frequently quotes other legislators, expounding their texts, and contrasting them with those of Yâjnavalkya, it is not merely a commentary, but supplies the place of a regular digest. The text of the Mitâksharâ has been edited several times in India. An excellent translation of its chapter *On Inheritance* was published by Colebrooke in the work above referred to; and its explanation of Yâjnavalkya is also followed by the same celebrated scholar in his *Digest of Hindû Law* (Calcutta and London, 1801, 3 vols.).

Mitchell, Alfred, a Congregational minister, was born May 22, 1790, at Wethersfield, Conn. He graduated at Yale College in 1809; was ordained pastor in Norwich Oct. 1814; and died Dec. 19, 1831. He published five occasional sermons.—Sprague, *Annals*, ii, 601.

Mitchell, Donald, a Scotch missionary to India, flourished in the first half of our century. Of his early history nothing is known to us. He was the first missionary sent out by the Scottish Missionary Society. He settled at Bombay, where he labored with zeal, and saw his efforts crowned with much success. His plan was to convert the people by influencing the young, and, to secure their confidence, he established schools for their mental training. He succeeded in starting, in connection with his mission, eight schools, which were attended by some three thousand pupils. More fully to fit himself for the important work in which he was engaged, Mr. Mitchell mastered the difficult Morathi language. He preached to the people, not only in the immediate neighborhood of the station which he occupied, but also for many miles along the coast and in the interior, with very encouraging results for several years, till called to rest from his labors. See *The Missionary World* (N. Y. 1873, 12mo), p. 493.

Mitchell, Elisha, D.D., an American scientist in early years, and later a popular preacher, was born at Washington, Conn., Aug. 19, 1793, and was educated at Yale College (class of 1813). From 1816–18 he taught in his alma mater. In 1817 he was elected professor of mathematics in the North Carolina University, whither he removed at once. In 1825 he was transferred to the chair of chemistry, and in this position he greatly distinguished himself. In 1831 he turned towards the ministry, was ordained by the Presbytery of Orange, and became noted as an able preacher and a good Biblical scholar. He died at Black Mountain, N. C., June 27, 1857. Dr. Mitchell contributed frequently to the *Journal of Science.*

Mitchell, John, a Congregational minister, editor, and author, was born at Chester, Conn., Dec. 27, 1794; was educated at Yale College (class of 1821) and at Andover Theological Seminary; edited the *Christian Spectator* from 1824 to 1829; was then licensed to preach;

in 1830 became pastor of the First Congregational Church in Fair Haven, Conn.; and of the Edwards Church, Northampton, Mass., in 1836. In 1842 he went abroad for his health, and after his return spent most of his remaining years at Stamford, Conn., engaged, as far as his strength allowed, in literary work. He died in April, 1870. Mr. Mitchell published *Principles and Practice of the Congregational Churches of New England* (Northampton, Mass., 1838, 16mo) :—*Notes from Over Sea* (New York, 1844, 2 vols. 8vo):—*Letters to a Disbeliever in Revivals* (32mo); and occasional sermons and contributions to periodicals and newspapers. See Sprague, *Annals of the American Pulpit* (see Index); Drake, *Dict. of Amer. Biog.* s. v.; Allibone, *Dict. of Brit. and Amer. Authors*, s. v.

Mitchell, John Thomas, a minister of the Methodist Episcopal Church, was born near the village of Salem, Roanoke County, Va., Aug. 20, 1810, and enjoyed the advantages of a good common-school education. In 1817 the family moved to Illinois, and settled near Belleville, St. Clair County. At a conference camp-meeting he was converted, and shortly after united with the Church, but afterwards became careless and indifferent. In 1830 he commenced teaching school. About the same time he was appointed assistant superintendent of the Sabbath-school, and becoming deeply impressed with a clear sense of duty, he entered the ministry, April 13, 1831, at Hillsborough. In 1832 he set out for Indianapolis, Indiana; in 1837 preached at Jacksonville Station, and in 1838–39 at Springfield. In 1840 he was transferred to Rock River Conference, and by the General Conference of 1344 was elected assistant book-agent of the Western Book Concern. He died May 30, 1851. Mr. Mitchell possessed great and growing powers, combining in a very marked manner social, intellectual, and moral qualities. He was well read in theology, and had an excellent knowledge of philosophy, mathematics, and the classic languages. See *Annual Minutes of the M. E. Church*, 1863, p. 144.

Mitchell, Jonathan, a Presbyterian divine of note, was born in England in 1624. He came to this country in 1635. Jonathan was afforded all the advantages of education within reach. After due preparation, he was entered at Harvard College, and graduated in 1647. He was ordained at Cambridge, Aug. 21, 1650, and settled as minister in that place. Soon after this president Dunstar embraced the principles of the Baptists. This was a peculiar trial to Mitchell; but, though he felt it to be his duty to combat the principles of his former tutor, he did it with such meekness of wisdom as not to lose his friendship. Mitchell's controversy resulted in the removal of president Dunstar from the college. In 1662 he was a member of the synod which met in Boston to discuss and settle a question concerning Church-membership and Church discipline, and the report was chiefly written by him. The determination of the question relating to the baptism of the children of those who did not approach the Lord's table, and the support thus given to what is called the half-way covenant, was more owing to him than to any other man. See HALF-WAY COVENANT. Time has shown that the views which this good man labored so hard to establish on this point cannot be sustained without ruining the purity of the churches. Jonathan Mitchell was eminent for piety, wisdom, humility, and love. He possessed a retentive memory, and was a fervent and energetic preacher. He died July 9, 1668. He published several letters and sermons, for which consult Justin Winsor's *Catalogue of the Prince Library* (Boston, 1870, royal 8vo). See *Life*, by C. Mather; *Magnalia*, iii, 158–185; *Hist. Soc.* vii, 23, 27, 47–52. (J. H. W.)

Mitchell, Orin, a minister of the Methodist Episcopal Church, was born in Granville, Licking Co., Ohio, Jan. 18, 1809; was converted in 1829; licensed to preach in 1833; received on trial in the Ohio Annual Conference in 1834, and appointed to Danville Circuit. He

travelled on Plymouth, Grand River, and Lapier circuits, in Michigan. In Ohio he received appointments to the station of Maumee and Perrysburgh; to the circuits of Portland, Mexico, Bucyrus, Norwich. Frederick, Clarksfield, Amity, Jeromeville, and Fairfield. In 1854 he took a superannuated relation, and died in August, 1869. Orin Mitchell excelled as a pastor, and his labors resulted in much good for the Christian cause.

Mitchell, Samuel C., a Presbyterian minister, was born in Overton Co., East Tennessee, April 20, 1806. He received a careful Christian training, early united with the Cumberland Presbyterian Church, and was soon after elected ruling elder. He subsequently left Tennessee and settled in Indiana, and, becoming deeply impressed with a call to the ministry, in 1841 he placed himself under the care of the Wabash Presbytery, and immediately commenced preparation for the ministry. He was licensed to preach in 1843, and ordained at Limestone, Indiana, in 1846. He died Aug. 6, 1862. Mr. Mitchell was a plain, earnest, and impressive preacher. See Wilson, *Presb. Hist. Almanac*, 1863, p. 415.

Mitchell, Thomas W., a minister of the Methodist Episcopal Church, South, who labored as a missionary among the North American Indians, was born in Indiana April 15, 1816. His father removed to East Tennessee when Thomas was but two years old. Here he was educated. He professed religion in his eleventh year; joined the Methodist Episcopal Church; removed to Missouri, with his parents, in 1835; was licensed to preach in 1857; admitted into the Missouri Conference the same year, and filled the following appointments: New Madrid Circuit in 1837, and Weberville Circuit in 1838. In 1840 he was located; removed to the Cherokee Nation in 1845, and taught a public school until 1846, when he was readmitted into the Indian Mission Conference. From that time to 1851 he filled different appointments, and was then appointed to preside over the Creek District. In 1855 he was appointed superintendent of Fort Coffee and New Hope seminaries, and continued until 1858. Then he was transferred to the St. Louis Conference, where he labored until 1862. During the war-storm he retreated to Texas, and, after the opening of brighter days, in 1866 he entered the Trinity Conference, where he labored until 1869, when he took a superannuated relation. In 1871 he obtained a transfer and removed to the Indian Mission Conference, and was appointed presiding elder of the Creek District. He died in the midst of his work, March 17, 1872, in Ocmulgee, Creek Nation. See *Minutes of Conferences*, 1872, p. 745.

Mitchell, William B., a minister of the Methodist Episcopal Church, was born in 1815. He was converted in 1843, and, though engaged in a lucrative business, turned aside to the ministry, to which he felt called of God. In 1845 he was licensed to preach; in 1846 was stationed at the Delaware Mission, Delaware County, N. Y., under his presiding elder; in 1847 joined the New York Conference, and was successively appointed to Windham, Lexington, Jefferson, Prattsville, and Kortright circuits, and subsequently to Coxsackie and Hyde Park stations. He died Oct. 27, 1858. "His life was useful and consistent; his zeal for the interests of the Church untiring; his anxiety for the salvation of souls earnest and abiding." See Smith, *Sacred Memories* (N. Y. 1870), p. 99 sq.

Mitchell, William H., D.D., an American divine and educator of the Presbyterian communion, was born Sept. 7, 1812, at Monoghan, Ireland. His early training he received in his native town, and even then distinguished himself by superior abilities and unwearied application. In his early manhood he was a practitioner in law. In his twenty-seventh year, a little more than a year after his marriage, he came to this country, and settled at Montgomery, Alabama. For a number of years after this he was engaged as teacher. In 1843 he was licensed to preach by the presbytery of East Alabama, and shortly after he was installed pastor of the Presbyterian Church at Wetumpka, Alabama. Possessing abilities of a high order, and being in all respects exemplary and pious, faithful, untiring, and devoted to his ministerial and pastoral duties, he enjoyed the confidence and esteem of all who knew him. In August, 1850, Mitchell removed to Florence, Alabama, and became the pastor of the church in that place. He remained in this pulpit till June, 1871, when the onerous and accumulating duties and cares of the Synodical Female College of that place, of which he had become president, in connection with his pastoral responsibilities, rendered it necessary that he should devote himself more entirely to the care and interests of the college. He died Oct. 3, 1872, after having held the presidency of the synodical college for over sixteen years. Personally, Dr. Mitchell was a fine-looking man, rather low of stature, pleasing in his address, and courteous and dignified in his deportment; sometimes grave and serious, and at other times humorous and entertaining. When among his most intimate acquaintances and friends, he was free and unreserved, and abounded in anecdote and wit. In ecclesiastical bodies he was usually a calm and quiet listener, speaking but seldom, and modest and diffident in advancing his opinions, but always wise, prudent, and conservative, yet decided and firm in his convictions. His sermons were written with care, and preached almost always from his manuscript; but his delivery was fluent and easy, and his oratory, without very much action, was earnest, solemn, tender, and impressive. See *Memphis Presbyterian*, Nov. 9, 1872. (J. H. W.)

Mitchell, William Luther, a Presbyterian minister, was born in Maury County, Tenn., July 11, 1828; was converted at the age of twelve; graduated in 1854, with honor, at Jefferson College, Pa., and in 1857 at Princeton Theological Seminary; was licensed in 1857 by the presbytery of Lafayette, Mo.; in 1857 and 1858 supplied the First Presbyterian Church, Burlington, Iowa; and in 1859 was ordained and installed pastor of the church at Hillsborough, Ill., where he died, Feb. 23, 1864. Mr. Mitchell was a minister of more than ordinary ability and attainments. As a Christian, his life was religion exemplified; as a preacher, he was earnest and instructive, and often eloquent and impressive. His sermons were doctrinal, and at the same time intensely practical. See Wilson, *Presb. Hist. Almanac*, 1864, p. 102.

Mitchell, William W., a minister of the Methodist Episcopal Church, was born in Virginia Feb. 16, 1815. He was educated with a view to the legal profession, and was afforded the best advantages within reach. While a student at Yale he was converted, and he became convinced that his place was in the pulpit. After much opposition at home, he joined the Illinois Conference in 1834, and was appointed to Lebanon Circuit, where he continued about six months, and was then removed to Vandalia Station. He afterwards filled many important appointments on circuits, stations, and districts, all in Illinois, except one year in Kentucky. William W. Mitchell was a good rather than a great preacher. His last appointment was to Edwardsville Station. During his second year in this station he became severely afflicted, so as to disqualify him for pulpit labors. He consequently resigned his charge and removed to Richview, Illinois, where, after severe suffering for almost a year, he died, March 7, 1869. See *Minutes of Conferences*, 1869, p. 204.

Mite is the rendering in the Auth. Vers. (Luke xii, 59; xxi, 2; Mark xii, 42) of the Greek term λεπτόν (*thin, like a scale*), a minute coin (Alciphr. i, 9; Pollux, *On.* ix, 92), of bronze or copper (see Smith's *Dict. of Class. Antiq.* s. v. Æs), two of which made a quadrans (Mark xii, 42), and which was, therefore, the eighth part of the Roman *as*, i. e. equal originally to a little over one mill, but in the time of Christ about half a mill. At Athens it was reckoned as one seventh of the χαλκοῦς (Suidas,

s. v. ταλαντίον). From Mark's explanation, "two mites, which make a farthing" (λεπτὰ δύο, ὅ ἐστι κοδράντης, ver. 42), it may perhaps be inferred that the κοδράντης or "farthing" was the commoner coin, for it can scarcely be supposed to be there spoken of as a money of account, though this might be the case in another passage (Matt. v, 26). See FARTHING.

Cavedoni (*Bibl. Num.* i, 76) has supposed that Mark meant to say "*one lepton* was of the value of *one quadrans*," for had he intended to express that two of the small pieces of money were equal to a *quadrans*, then he must have written ἃ ἐστι instead of ὅ ἐστι κοδράντης; and the Vulg. has also translated *quod est*, but not *quæ sunt*. This argument, however, is too minute to be of much force. Another argument adduced is that the words of our Lord in the parallel passages of Matthew (v, 26) and Luke (xii, 59) prove that the *quadrans* is the same as the *lepton*. In the former passage the words are ἔσχατον κοδράντην, and in the latter ἔσχατον λεπτόν. This argument, again, hardly merits an observation, for we might as well assume that because we say such a thing is not worth a *penny*, or not worth a *farthing*, therefore the *penny* and the *farthing* are the same coin. A third argument, deemed by Cavedoni to be conclusive, assumes that the *quadrans* only weighed 30 grains, and that if the *quadrans* equalled *two lepta*, there would be coins existing at the time of our Saviour of the weight of 15.44 grains. This argument is sufficiently answered by the fact that there are coins of the ethnarch Archelaus and of the emperor Augustus struck by the procurators weighing so low as 18 to 15 grains,

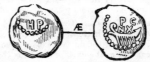

Copper Coin (λεπτον or "mite") of Archelaus.
(*Obverse*—H P [ΗΡΩΔΟΥ] within beaded circle.
Reverse—PC NX [ΕΘΝΑΡΧΟΥ!] above a galley.)

and by comparing them with others of the same period a result can be obtained proving the existence in Judæa of three denominations of coinage—the *semis*, the *quadrans*, and the *lepton*. There is no doubt that the *lepton* was rarely struck at the time of the evangelists, yet it must have been a common coin from the time of Alexander II to the accession of Antigonus (B.C. 69–B.C. 40), and its circulation must have continued long in use. The extreme vicissitudes of the period may only have allowed these small copper coins to be struck. They were formerly attributed to Alexander Jannæus, but are now given to Alexander II. They average in weight from 20 to 15 grains. See MONEY.

It may be as well to notice that Schleusner (*Lex. N. T.* s. v. κοδράντης), after Fischer, considers the *quadrans* of the N. T., of which the *lepton* was the half, not to have equalled the Roman *quadrans*, but to have been the fourth of the Jewish *as*. The Jewish *as* is made to correspond with the half of the half-ounce Roman *as*, and as, according to Jewish writers, the פרקטה or פרוטה was the eighth part of the *assar*, or Jewish *as* (Buxtorf, *Lex. Talm.* s. v. אסיר), and as the evangelists have understood this word פרוטה to be the *lepton*, it follows that the *quadrans* equalled δύο λεπτά. This theory, however, is quite out of the question, and a comparison of the coins of Judæa with those struck at Rome clearly proves that the *quadrans* in Judæa was the same as the *quadrans* in Rome. Moreover, as the Romans ordered that *only Roman coins, weights, and measures* should be used in all the provinces of the Roman empire (Dion. Cass. lii, 20), it is certain that there can have been no *Jewish as* or *Jewish quadrans*, and that all the coins issued by the Jewish princes, and under the procurators, were struck upon a *Roman standard* (F. W. Madden, *Hist. of Jewish Coinage and of Money in O. and N. T.* p. 296–302).

VI.—13

Mitelli, GIUSEPPI MARIA, a noted Italian painter, was born at Bologna in 1634. He received instruction from his father, who was an eminent fresco painter of Bologna, and afterwards entered the school of Flaminio Torre. He painted a number of works for the churches of Bologna, among which may be mentioned *St. Reniero healing the sick*, in S. Maria della Vita, a *Pietà*, in the Nunziato, and *Christ taken in the Garden*, at the Cappuccini. He was more distinguished as an engraver, and etched a number of plates of the most celebrated masters, as well as many of his own designs—among the latter the set of twenty-six plates illustrating the *Twenty-four Hours of Human Felicity*. Bartsch has credited him with one hundred and sixty-two prints, but Nagler increases the list. He died in 1718. See Lanzi's *History of Painters*, transl. by Roscoe (Lond. 1847, 3 vols. 8vo), iii, 138; Spooner, *Biog. History of the Fine Arts* (N. Y. 1865, 2 vols. 8vo), ii, 569.

Mith'cah (Heb. *Mithkah'*, מִתְקָה, *sweetness*, prob. of the water found there; Sept. Μαθεκκᾶ), the twenty-ninth station of the Israelites in the desert, between Tarah and Hashmonah (Numb. xxxiii, 28, 29); perhaps at the intersection of Wady el-Ghamr with Wady el-Jerafeh. See EXODE.

Mith'nite (Heb. *Mithni'*, מִתְנִי, patronymic or gentile apparently from מֶתֶן, *Me'then, firmness;* Sept. Μαθθανί v. r. Βαιθανί, Vulg. *Mathanites*, as if from מַתָּן, *Mat'tan*), an epithet of Joshaphat, one of David's body-guard (1 Chron. xi, 43); either from his ancestor or native place, of neither of which, however, is there any other mention, or further means of determination.

Mithra or **Mithras** (Greek Μίθρας; Sanscrit *Mitra* or *Mitras*), the highest of the twenty-eight second-class divinities of the ancient Persian Pantheon, is generally regarded as the chief of the *Izeds* (Zend. *Yazata*), the ruler of the universe. He is spoken of as the god of the sun; but he is more properly the god of day, and, in a higher and more extended sense, the god of light, presiding over the movements and influence of the principal heavenly bodies, including the five planets of the sun and moon. The primary signification of the word *Mitra* is *a friend*, and Mithra would therefore convey the representation of light as the friend of mankind, and as the mediator (μεσίτης) between heaven and earth. Protector and supporter of man in this life, he watches over his soul in the next, defending it against the impure spirits, and transferring it to the realms of eternal bliss. He is all-seeing and all-hearing, and, armed with a club—his weapon against Ahriman and the evil *Devs*—he unceasingly "runs his course" between heaven and earth. In this character of mediator, as well as in some other respects, he would seem to approach the character of *Agni*.

From Persia the cultus of Mithra and the mysteries were imported into Asia Minor, Syria, Palestine, etc., and it is not unlikely that in some parts human sacrifices were connected with this worship. In the days of the emperors the worship of Mithra found its way into Rome, and thence into the different parts of the Roman empire, and the mysteries of Mithra (*Hierocoracica, Coracica Sacra*), which fell in the spring equinox, became famous even among the many Roman festivals. The ceremonies observed in the initiation to these mysteries—symbolical of the struggle between Ahriman and Ormuzd (the Good and the Evil)—were of the most extraordinary and, to a certain degree, even dangerous character. Baptism and the partaking of a mystical liquid, consisting of flour and water, to be drunk with the utterance of sacred formulas, were among the inaugurative acts. The seven degrees—according to the number of the planets—were, 1, Soldiers; 2, Lions (in the case of men) or Hyænas (in that of women); 3, Ravens; 4, Degree of *Perses;* 5, of *Oromios;* 6, of *Helios;* 7, of Fathers—the highest—who were also called Eagles and Hawks. At first of a merry character—thus the king of Persia was allowed to get drunk only on the Feast of the Mysteries—the solemnities gradually assumed a severe and rigorous aspect. Through Rome, where this worship, after many vain endeavors, was finally suppressed in A.D. 378, it may be presumed that it found its way into the west and north of Europe; and many tokens of its former existence in Germany are still to be found, for instance, such as the Mithra monuments at Heidenheim, near Frankfort-on-the-Main, and at other places.

Among the Persians Mithra is pictured as a young man, clothed with a tunic and a Persian cloak, and having on his head a Persian bonnet or tiara. He kneels upon a prostrate bull, and while holding it with the left hand by the nostrils, with the right he plunges into the shoulder a short sword or dagger. The bull is at the same time vigorously attacked by a dog, a serpent, and a scorpion. The ancient monuments represent him as a beautiful youth, dressed in Phrygian garb, kneeling upon an ox, into whose neck he plunges a knife; several minor, varying, allegorical emblems of the sun and his course surrounding the group. At times he is also represented as a lion, or the head of a lion. The most important of his many festivals was his birthday, celebrated on the 25th of December, the day subsequently fixed—against all evidence—as the birthday of Christ. In the early days of the Church it was not an uncommon occurrence to find an apologist of the inspired teacher laying undue stress on some points of resemblance between Mithraism and Christianity, and thus the triumphant march of the latter was much re-

Mithra.

tarded. In modern times Christian writers have been again induced to look favorably upon the assertion that some of our ecclesiastical usages (e. g. the institution of the Christmas festival) originated in the cultus of Mithraism. Some writers, who refuse to accept the Christian religion as of supernatural origin, have even gone so far as to institute a close comparison with the founder of Christianity; and Dupuis and others, going even beyond this, have not hesitated to pronounce the Gospel simply *a branch of Mithraism.* The ablest reply to these theories we have from Creuzer and Hardwick.

Among the chief authorities on this subject are Sainte-Croix, *Recherches historiques et critiques sur les mystères du paganisme,* edited by Sylvestre de Sacy (Paris, 1817); Burnouf, *Sur le Yaçna,* p. 351 sq.; Lajard, *Recherches sur le culte public et les mystères de Mithra* (Paris, 1847–8); O. Müller, *Denkmäler d. alten Kunst;* Creuzer, *Mythologie u. Symbolik* (2d ed.), i, 238, 261, 341, 714 sq.; id. *Das Mithreum* (Heidelb. 1838); Schwenk, *Mythologie der Perser* (Frankf. 1850); Seel, *Die Mithrasgeheimnisse* (Aarau, 1823); Hammer, *Mithriaka* (Vienna, 1834); Dupuis, *Origine de tous les cultes,* i, 37; Hardwick, *Christ and other Masters,* ii, 431–438. See PARSEES; ZENDAVESTA.

Mith'redath (Heb. *Mithredath',* מִתְרְדָת, from the Pers. *given by Mithras,* see Gesenius, *Thesaur. Heb.* p. 832, and comp. the Gr. form of the name Μιϑριδάτης, Lat. *Mithridates;* Sept. Μιϑριδάτης and Μιϑραδάτης), the name of two Persian officers after the exile.

1. The "treasurer" (גִּזְבָּר) of king Cyrus, commissioned by him to restore the sacred vessels of the Temple to Sheshbazzar, the Jewish chief (Ezra i, 8). B.C. 536.

2. One of the governors of Samaria, who wrote to king Artaxerxes, or Smerdis, charging the Jews with rebellious designs in rebuilding Jerusalem (Ezra iv, 7). B.C. 522.

Mithrida'tès (Μιϑριδάτης or Μιϑραδάτης), the Græcized form (*a.* 1 Esdr. ii, 11; *b.* 1 Esdr. ii, 16) of the Heb. name MITHREDATH (q. v.)

Mitre is the rendering in the Auth. Vers. of the Hebrew word מִצְנֶפֶת (*mitsne'pheth,* something *rolled* around the head), spoken especially of the *turban* or head-dress of the high-priest (Exod. xxviii, 4, 37, 39; xxix, 6; xxxix, 28, 31; Lev. viii, 9; xvi, 4; for its form, see Josephus, *Ant.* iii, 7, 3; Braun, *De Vestitu sacerd. Heb.* p. 624 sq.; Töppffer, *De tiaris summi et minorum sacerdotum,* Vitemb. 1722; Funcke, *De tiara pontif. Ebr.* Gies. 1728), once of a royal crown ("diadem," Ezek. xxi, 26); also צָנִיף (*tsaniph',* from the same root), spoken of a *tiara* or head-band, e. g. of men (Job xxix, 14, "diadem"), of women (Isa. iii, 23, "hood"), of the high-priest (Zech. iii, 5), and once of the king (Isa. lxii, 3, "diadem," where the text has צָנוֹף or צָנוֹף). See BONNET; CROWN; PRIEST.

MITRE is the name given also to the head-dress worn in solemn Church services by the pope, the bishops, abbots, and certain other prelates of the Church of Rome. The name, as probably the ornament itself, is borrowed from the Orientals, although, in its present form, it is not in use in the Greek Church, or in any other of the churches of the various Eastern

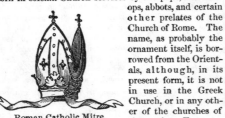

Roman Catholic Mitre.

rites. The Western mitre is a tall, tongue-shaped cap, terminating in a twofold point, which is supposed to symbolize the "cloven tongues," in the form of which the Holy Ghost was imparted to the apostles, and is furnished with two flaps, which fall behind over the shoulders.

Opinion is much divided as to the date at which the mitre first came into use. Eusebius, Gregory of Nazianzum, Epiphanius, and others speak of an ornamented head-dress worn in the church; but there is no very early monument or pictorial representation which exhibits any head-covering at all resembling the modern mitre. A statue of St. Peter, said to have been erected in the seventh century, bears this mark of distinction in the shape of a round, high, and pyramidal mitre, such as those which the popes have since worn, and offers, perhaps, one of the earliest instances of its usage in churches. The most ancient mitres were very low and simple, being not more than from three to six inches in elevation, and they thus continued till the end of the thirteenth century. Since the 9th century the mitre is found to have been in use quite extensively. From the time of Leo IX until Innocent IV the mitre was worn by cardinals, and instances are recorded in which the popes granted permission to certain bishops to wear the mitre; as, for example, Leo IV to Anschar, bishop of Hamburg, in the ninth century. In the fourteenth century, when the mitre had come into general use, they gradually increased in height to a foot or more, and became more superbly enriched; their outlines also presented a degree of convexity by which they were distinguished from the older mitres.

The mitre, as an ornament, seems to have descended in the earliest times from bishop to bishop. Among the Cottonian MSS. is an order, dated July 1, 4 Henry VI, for the delivery to archbishop Chichely of the mitre which had been worn by his predecessor. It was in some cases a very costly ornament. Archbishop Pecheham's new mitre, in 1288, cost £173 4s. 1d. The material used in the manufacture of the mitre is very various, often consisting of the most costly stuffs, studded with gold and precious stones. The color and material differ according to the festival or the service in which the mitre is used, and there is a special prayer in the consecration service of bishops, used in investing the new bishop with his mitre. The mitre of the pope is of peculiar form, and is generally called by the name of *tiara* (q. v.). There are four different mitres which are now used by the pope. These are more or less richly adorned, according to the nature of the festivals on which they are to be worn. The two horns of the mitre are generally taken to be an allusion to the cloven tongues of fire which rested on each of the apostles on the day of Pentecost.

At first the mitre was by special favor conferred on certain bishops; gradually it became the common right of every bishop to wear the mitre, and later its use was also permitted by special privilege to certain abbots, to provosts of some distinguished cathedral chapters, and to a few other dignitaries. (Compare Walcott, *Archæology,* p. 383 sq.; Binterim, *Denkwürdigkeiten der Kirche,* i, pt. ii, p. 348).

In some of the Lutheran churches (as in Sweden) the mitre is worn; but in the Church of England, since the Reformation, the mitre is no longer a part of the episcopal costume; it is simply placed over the shield of an archbishop or bishop instead of a crest. The mitre of a bishop has its lower rim surrounded with a fillet of gold; but the archbishops of Canterbury and York are in the practice of encircling theirs with a ducal coronet, a usage of late date and doubtful propriety. The bishop of Durham surrounds his mitre with an earl's coronet, in consequence of being titular count palatine of Durham and earl of Sedburgh. Before the custom was introduced of bishops impaling the insignia of their sees with their family arms, they sometimes differenced their paternal coat by the addition of a mitre.

Mittarelli, NICOLAS-JACQUES (also known as JEAN-BENOÎT), an Italian theologian and bibliographer, and a learned historian, was born at Venice Sept. 2, 1707. At an early age he entered the order of the Camaldules, and prosecuted his theological studies at Florence and at Rome, where he secured the friendship of the cardinal Rezzonico, subsequently Clement XIV. Appointed to the professorship of philosophy, and afterwards to that of theology, in the convent of Saint-Michel, at Murano, near Venice, Mittarelli banished from his teaching the scholastic method, and all the idle questions to which it gives rise. Nine years later he was sent to Treviso as confessor to the monastery of Saint-Parisio; here he was occupied in arranging the archives of that house, acquired a taste for ecclesiastical antiquities, and gave himself to researches in this direction. His nomination in 1747 to the office of chancellor of his order gave him the opportunity of visiting the libraries and archives of a great number of convents. He then conceived the idea of writing a history of his congregation. The renown which this well-executed enterprise gained for him caused his election in 1760 as abbot of the convent of Saint-Michel at Murano, and in 1765 as general of his order. In 1770 he resumed the government of the monastery of Saint-Michel, which he kept until his death. He died Aug. 14, 1777. Endowed with a prodigious memory and a nice critical sense, Mittarelli acquired a thorough knowledge of Italian ecclesiastical history. To all the virtues he united an exemplary modesty, which many times caused him to refuse the honors offered him. From his pen we have *Memorie della vida di S. Parisio, monaco Camaldolese e del monastero de SS.-Cristina e Parisio di Treviso* (Venice, 1748, 8vo) :—*Memorie del monastero della S.-Trinità di Faenza* (Faenza, 1749, 8vo) :—*Annales Camaldulenses, quibus plura inseruntur tum cæteras Italico-monasticas res, tum historiam ecclesiasticam remque diplomaticam illustrantia* (Venice, 1755–1773, 9 vols, fol.) ; this important work, drawn up after the model of the *Annales ordinis S.-Benedicti* of Mabillon, extends to the year 1764 :—*Ad Scriptores rerum Italicarum Cl. Muratorii accessiones historiæ Faventinæ* (Venice, 1771, fol.) :— *De Litteratura Faventinorum* (Venice, 1775, fol.) :— *Bibliotheca codicum manuscriptorum monasterii S.-Michaelis de Muriano Venetiarum, cum appendice librorum impressorum sæculi xv* (Venice, 1769, fol.). See Fabroni, *Vitæ Italorum ;* Tipaldo, *Biographia degli Italiani illustri*, x, 140 ; Jagemann, *Magazin der italiänischen Literatur*, vol. iv ; Hirsching, *Histor.-liter. Handbuch.*

Mityle'nè (Μιτυλήνη, Acts xx, 14 ; written also *Mytile'ne*, Μυτιλήνη, which is the older and more accurate form [see Tzchucke, *ad Mel.* II, ii, 484] ; of uncertain etymology), the capital of the isle of Lesbos (Ptolemy, iv, 2, 29), in the Ægæan Sea, about seven and a half miles from the opposite point on the coast of Asia Minor. It was a well-built town, with two harbors, but unwholesomely situated (Vitruvius, *De Architect.* i, 6). It was the native place of Pittacus, Theophanes, Theophrastus, Sappho, Alcæus, and Diophanes, and was liberally supplied with literary advantages (Strabo, xiii, 617 ; Senec. *Helv.* ix ; Pliny, v, 37 ; comp. Vell. Paten. ii, 18). The town was celebrated for the beauty of its buildings ("Mitylene pulchra," Horace, *Epist.* I, xi, 17 ; see Cicero, *Rull.* ii, 16). It had the privileges of a free city (Pliny, *N. H.* v, 39). The apostle Paul touched at Mitylene overnight between Assos and Chios, during his third apostolical journey, on the way from Corinth to Judæa (Acts xx, 14). It may be gathered from the circumstances of this voyage that the wind was blowing from the N.W.; and it is worth while to notice that in the harbor or in the roadstead of Mitylene the ship

Coin of Mitylene.   (In the British Museum.)

would be sheltered from that wind. Moreover, it appears that Paul was there at the time of dark moon, and this was a sufficient reason for passing the night there before going through the intricate passages to the southward (see Conybeare and Howson's *Life of St. Paul*, ii, 210). It does not appear that any Christian Church was established at this place in the apostolic age. No mention is made of it in ecclesiastical history until a late period; and in the 2d century heathenism was so rife in Mitylene that a man was annually sacrificed to Dionysus. In the 5th, 6th, 7th, and 8th centuries, however, we find bishops of Mitylene present at several councils (Magdeburg, *Hist. Eccles. Cent.* ii, 195 ; v, 6 ; vi, 6 ; vii, 4, 253, 254 ; viii, 6). Mitylene still exists, under the designation of *Metelin*, and has given its name, in the form of *Mytilni*, to the whole island ; but it is now a place of no importance (Tournefort, *Trav.* ii, 115 ; Olivier, *Voyage*, ii, 93 ; Sonnini, *Travels in Greece*, p. 366). The town contains about 700 Greek houses, and 400 Turkish ; its streets are narrow and filthy (Turner, *Tour in the Levant*, iii, 299). See, generally, Pauly's *Realencyklop.* v, 372 sq. ; Anthon's *Class. Dict.* s. v. ; Smith's *Dict. of Class. Geography*, s. v. ; M'Culloch's *Gazetteer*, s. v.

Mixed marriages, i. e. marriages between Jews and Gentiles, were strictly prohibited by the Mosaic law. The New Testament, if it be thought to contain no positive prohibition of the intermarriage of Christians and heathens, yet, to say the least, strongly represents such a proceeding as inconsistent with a Christian profession (1 Cor. vii, 39 ; 2 Cor. vi, 14). The early fathers denounced the practice as dangerous and even criminal (Tertullian, *Ad.Uxor.* lib. ii, c. 2–9 ; *De Coron. Mil.* c. 13 ; Cyprian, *Ad Quirin*, lib. iii, c. 62 ; Ambrosius, *De Abrahamo*, lib. i, c. 9 ; *Ep.* lib. ix, ep. 70 ; *De Fide et Oper.* c. 19 ; Jerome, *In Jovin.* lib. i, c. 10) ; and it was afterwards positively prohibited by the decrees of councils and the laws of the empire (*Conc. Chalced.* c. 14 ; *A relat.* i, c. 11 ; *Illiberit.* c. 15, 16, 17 ; *Aurelian*, ii, c. 18 ; *Cod. Justin.* lib. i, tit. 9, 1, 6 ; *Cod. Theodos.* lib. iii, tit. 7, 1, 2 ; lib. ix, tit. 7, 1, 5 ; lib. xvi, tit. 8, 1, 6). These prohibitions extended to the marriage of Christians with Jews, Pagans, Mohammedans, and certain heretics, namely, those whose baptism was not admitted as valid by the Church. The first interdiction of marriage with heretics on record is one which was made about the middle of the fourth century (*Conc. Laodic.* c. 10, 31 ; see also *Conc. Agath.* c. 67 ; *Chalced.* c. 14). It does not appear that such marriages, although prohibited, were declared null and void whenever they had actually taken place : and we read of some illustrious examples of the breach of the rule, as in the case of Monica, the mother of Augustine (Augustine, *Confess.* lib. ix, c. 9), and Clotildis, the queen of Clovis (Gregorius Turon. *Hist. Franc.* lib. ii, c. 28), who became instrumental in the conversion of their respective husbands to Christianity. See Riddle, *Christ. Antiquities*, p. 745–749. See DIVORCE ; MARRIAGE.

Mixed multitude (עֵרֶב, *e'reb* ; Sept. ἐπίμικτος, Vulg. *promiscuum*), the designation of a certain class who went with the Israelites as they journeyed from Rameses to Succoth, the first stage of the exodus from Egypt (Exod. xii, 38). In the Targum the phrase is vaguely rendered "many foreigners," and Jarchi explains it as "a medley of outlandish people." Aben-Ezra goes further, and says it signifies "the Egyptians who were mixed with them, and they are the 'mixed multitude' (אֲסַפְסֻף, Numb. xi, 4) who were gathered to them." Jarchi, on the latter passage, also identifies the "mixed multitude" of Numbers and Exodus. During their residence in Egypt marriages were naturally contracted between the Israelites and the natives, and the son of such a marriage between an Israelitish woman and an Egyptian is especially mentioned as being stoned for blasphemy (Lev. xxiv, 11), the same law holding good for the resident or naturalized foreigner as for the native Israelite (Josh. viii, 35). This hybrid race is evidently alluded to by Jarchi and Aben-Ezra, and is most probably that to which reference is made in Exodus. Knobel understands by the "mixed multitude" the remains of the Hyksos who left Egypt with the Hebrews. Dr. Kalisch (Comm. on Exod. xii, 38) interprets it of the native Egyptians who were involved in the same oppression with the Hebrews by the new dynasty, which invaded and subdued Lower Egypt; and Kurtz (Hist. of Old Cov. ii, 312, Eng. tr.), while he supposes the "mixed multitude" to have been Egyptians of the lower classes, attributes their emigration to their having "endured the same oppression as the Israelites from the proud spirit of caste which prevailed in Egypt," in consequence of which they attached themselves to the Hebrews, "and served henceforth as hewers of wood and drawers of water." That the "mixed multitude" is a general term including all those who were not of pure Israelitish blood is evident; more than this cannot be positively asserted. In Exodus and Numbers it probably denotes the miscellaneous hangers-on of the Hebrew camp, whether they were the issue of spurious marriages with Egyptians, or were themselves Egyptians or belonging to other nations. The same happened on the return from Babylon, and in Neh. xiii, 3 a slight clew is given by which the meaning of the "mixed multitude" may be more definitely ascertained. Upon reading in the law "that the Ammonite and the Moabite should not come into the congregation of God forever," it is said "they separated from Israel all the mixed multitude." The remainder of the chapter relates the expulsion of Tobiah the Ammonite from the Temple, of the merchants and men of Tyre from the city, and of the foreign wives of Ashdod, of Ammon, and of Moab, with whom the Jews had intermarried. All of these were included in the "mixed multitude," and Nehemiah adds, "Thus cleansed I them from all foreigners." The Targ. Jon. on Numb. xi, 4 explains the "mixed multitude" as proselytes, and this view is apparently adopted by Ewald, but there does not seem to be any foundation for it. See MINGLED PEOPLE.

Mi'zar (Heb. Mutsar', מִצְעָר, smallness, i. e. a little of anything, as in Gen. xix, 20, etc.; Sept. μικρός, Vulg. modicus, Auth. Vers. margin "little"), apparently the name of a summit on the eastern ridge of Lebanon or some contiguous chain, not far from which David lay after escaping from the rebellion of Absalom (Psa. xlii, 7). Others (with the versions above) understand it merely as an appellation, "the small mountain;" but this is a more harsh construction, and mention is made in the context of the trans-Jordanic region of Hermon, not very far from which was Mahanaim, whither David retired (see Tholuck's Comment. ad loc., who nevertheless renders "the little hill"). If any particular spot is intended, it must doubtless be sought in some eminence of the southern part of this general range, perhaps in the present Jebel Ajlun, which may have properly been so styled (i. q. "the little") in contrast with the greater elevation of Lebanon, Hermon, and Gilead.

Miz'pah (Heb. Mitspah', מִצְפָּה, Gen. xxxvi, 49; Josh. xi, 3; Judg. x, 17; xi, 11, 34; xx, 1, 5, 8; 1 Sam. vii, 6, 11, 12, 16; x, 17; 1 Kings xv, 22; 2 Kings xxv, 23, 25; 2 Chron. xvi, 6; Neh. iii, 7, 15, 19; Jer. xl, 6-15; xli, 1, 3, 6, 10, 14, 16; Hos. v, 1; always [except in Hos. v, 1] with the art. הַמִּצְפָּה; Sept. Μασσηφά, Vulg. Maspha; but in Gen. xxxi, 49, Sept. ὅρασις, Vulg. omits; 1 Sam. vii, 5-13; Vulg. Masphath; 1 Kings xv, 22, Sept. σκοπιά; 2 Chron. xvi, 6, Μασφά; Neh. iii, 19, Μασφὲ v. r. Μασφαι; Hos. v, 1, σκοπιά, speculatio), or **Miz'peh** (Heb. Mitspeh', מִצְפֶּה, Josh. xi, 8; Judg. xi, 29; 1 Sam. vi, 5, 6, 7; xxii, 3; with the art. Josh. xv, 38; xviii, 26; 2 Chron. xx, 24; Sept. Μασσηφά, but σκοπιά in Judg. xi, 29; Μασσηφάς in 1 Sam. xxii, 3; Vulg. Maspha, but Masphe in Josh. xi, 8; Mesphe in Josh. xviii, 26), the name of several places (in the Auth. Vers. "Miz-

pah" in Gen. xxxi, 49; 1 Kings xv, 22; 2 Kings xxv, 23, 25; 2 Chron. xvi, 6; Neh. iii, 7, 15, 19; Jer. xl, xli; Hos. v, 1; elsewhere "Mizpeh"), signifying properly a beacon or watch-tower (as in Isa. xxi, 8); hence also a lofty place, whence one can see far and wide over the country, whether furnished with a castle or not (as in 2 Chron. xx, 24). (Mizpeh becomes Mizpah "in pause.")

1. A place in Gilead, so named (in addition to its other names, GALEED and JEGAR-SAHADUTHA, both signifying the "heap of witness") in commemoration of the compact formed by Jacob with Laban, who overtook him at this spot on his return to Palestine (Gen. xxxi, 49, where the word הַמִּצְבָּה has apparently fallen out of the text by reason of its similarity to the name itself, so that we should read "and he called the obelisk Mizpah" [see Gesenius, Thes. p. 1179]. It would seem that the whole of verse 49 is the language of Jacob, for it contains a play upon the Heb. [רָצֶּף, yitseph] basis of the name Mizpeh, and also appeals to Jehovah; whereas Laban spoke Aramæan, and his language is resumed with ver. 50). This cannot be the Mizpeh of Gilead (see below), for it lay north of Mahanaim, on Jacob's route, which was southward towards the Jabbok (xxxii, 2, 22). We are therefore to look for it in some of the eminences of that vicinity. It probably never became an inhabited locality.

2. Another place east of Jordan, called MIZPAH OF GILEAD (Auth. Vers. "Mizpeh"), where Jephthah assumed his victorious command of the assembled Israelites (Judg. x, 17; xi, 11), and where he resided (Judg. xi, 34), is probably the same with the RAMATH-MIZPEH of Gad (Josh. xiii, 26), and may be identified with RAMATH-GILEAD (q. v.). Eusebius names it as a Levitical city in the tribe of Gad (Onomast. s. v. Μασφά).

3. Another place in Gilead, apparently a district inhabited by a branch of the Hivites, at the foot of Mount Hermon (Josh. xi, 3), and so named from a valley east of Misrephoth-maim and opposite Zidon (Josh. xi, 8); possibly the tract immediately west of Jebel Heish (see Keil, Comment. ad loc.). The idolatries practiced in this vicinity are alluded to in Hos. v, 1 (see Schwarz, Palest. p. 60). Pressel (in Herzog's Real-Encyklop. s. v.), ingeniously conjecturing that Mizpah (the fem. Heb. form of the name) is properly the country in general, and Mizpeh (the masc.) an individual place or town, understands in this case the land to be the entire plain of Paneas or Cæsarea Philippi, now called the Ard el-Hûleh, and the valley to be that of the eastern source of the Jordan from Jebel Heish. Not much different is the view of Knobel and others in their commentaries, thinking of the country from Hasbeiya southward, and westward from Tell el-Kâdy, the ancient Dan. They refer in confirmation of their views to Robinson's account (Researches, iii, 373) of a Druse village, built on a hill which rises 200 feet above the level of the plain, and commands a noble view of the great basin of the Hûleh; it bears the name of Mutulleh or Metelleh, an Arabic word of the same meaning as Mizpah, and employed to render it in Gen. xxxi, 49 by Saadias. Comp. Seetzen, Reisen durch Syrien (Berl. 1857-59), i, 393 sq.; Ritter, Die Sinai-Halbinsel, Palästina u. Syrien (Berl. 1850-51), vol. ii, pt. i, p. 1121 sq.

4. A city of Benjamin (Josh. xviii, 26), where the people were wont to convene on national emergencies (Judg. xx, 1, 3; xxi, 1, 5, 8: 1 Sam. vii, 5-16; x, 17 sq.). It was afterwards fortified by Asa, to protect the borders against the kingdom of Israel (1 Kings xv, 22; 2 Chron. xvi, 6). In later times it became the residence of the governor under the Chaldæans (2 Kings xxv, 23, 25; Jer. xl, 6 sq.: xli, 1), and was inhabited after the captivity (Neh. iii, 7, 15, 19). In the Jewish traditions it was for some time the residence of the ark (see Jerome, Qu. Hebr. on 1 Sam. vii, 2; Reland, Antiq. i, vi); but this is possibly an inference from the expression "before Jehovah" in Judg. xx, 1. Josephus frequently mentions it (Μασφάτη, Ant. vi, 2, 1; Μασφαθά, vi, 4, 4; x, 9, 2, 4, 5), once identifying it with Ramah (Μασφά, viii, 13, 4). From the account in 1 Sam. vii, 5–16, it appears to have been near Gibeah, and it could not have been far from Ramah, since king Asa fortified it with materials taken from that place; and that it was situated on an elevated spot is clear from its name. On these grounds Dr. Robinson (Researches, ii, 144) inclines to regard the modern village of Neby Samwil ("the prophet Samuel") as the probable site of Mizpah, especially as in 1 Macc. iii, 46 it is described as "over against Jerusalem," implying that it was visible from that city. This place is now a poor village, seated upon the summit of a ridge, about 600 feet above the plain of Gibeon, being the most conspicuous object in all the vicinity. It contains a mosque, now in a state of decay, which, on the ground of the apparently erroneous identification with Ramah, is regarded by Jews, Christians, and Moslems as the tomb of Samuel (see Schwarz, Palest. p. 127). The mosque was once a Latin church, built in the form of a cross, upon older foundations, and probably of the time of the Crusaders. There are many traces of former dwellings. The modern hamlet clusters at the eastern side of the mosque. The houses, about twelve in number, are either ancient or composed of ancient materials. Their walls are in places formed of the living rock hewn into shape, and some of the little courts are excavated to the depth of several feet. There is thus an air of departed greatness and high antiquity about the place, which, added to its commanding situation, gives it an inexpressible charm (Porter, Hand-book, p. 216; comp. Tobler, Zwei Bücher Topagraphie von Jerusalem u. seine Umgebungen [Berl. 1853, 1854], ii, 874 sq.). Mr. Williams (in Smith's Dict. of Greek and Roman Geog. s. v.) doubts this location, urging that Jer. xli, 5, 6 appears to require a position more directly on the great route from Jerusalem to Samaria; and Neby Samwil is exactly on the route by which Johanan overtook the murderer of Gedaliah (Jer. xli, 12; comp. 2 Sam. ii, 13). He suggests the modern village Shaphat, lying upon the ridge anciently called Scopus, as more likely to have been Mizpah; and Stanley (Sinai and Palestine, p. 222) argues for a similar identity on the ground of the common signification of these latter (i. q. look-out). This last place, however, is described by Josephus (Ant. xi, 8, 5) in very different terms from Mizpah (ut sup.), and Jerusalem is not visible from Shaphat (for which Dr. Bonar likewise contends, Land of Promise, Append. viii). See RAMAH.

5. A town in the plains of Judah (Josh. xv, 38). Eusebius and Jerome identify it with a place which in their time bore the name of Maspha (Onomast. s. v. Μασφά), on the borders of Eleutheropolis, northward, on the road to Jerusalem; perhaps the present Tell es-Safieh (Schwarz, Palest. p. 103), the Alba Specula of the Crusaders (Robinson, Researches, ii, 362–367), which was probably the GATH (q. v.) of later Biblical times.

6. A town of Moab to which David took his parents, lest they might be involved in Saul's persecution of himself (1 Sam. xxii, 3). His placing them there under the protection of the Moabitish king implies that it was the chief city, or royal residence of the Moabites; and under that view we may, perhaps, identify it as an appellative (i. q. the acropolis or stronghold of Moab) with KIR-MOAB (q. v.) or Kerak.

Miz'par (Heb. Mispar', מִסְפָּר, number, as often; Sept. Μασφάρ), one of the leading Israelites who accompanied Zerubbabel on the return from Babylon (Ezra ii, 2), in the parallel passage (Neh. vii, 7) called by the equivalent name MISPERETH. B.C. 536.

Miz'peh. See MIZPAH; RAMATH-MIZPEH.

Miz'raïm (Heb. Mitsra'yim, מִצְרַיִם, if of Heb. origin, meaning two mounds or fortresses [see MAZOR]; but the word is, perhaps, of foreign [Egyptian or even Arabic] derivation; Sept. Μεσραΐν; but usually in all the versions, "Egypt" or "Egyptians"), the name by which the Hebrews generally designated Egypt, appar-

ently from its having been peopled by Mizraim, the second son of Ham (Gen. x, 6, 13). B.C. post 2513. See also ABEL-MIZRAIM. The name is in the dual form, double Egypt, and seems to have originally among the Hebrews at least, denoted lower and upper Egypt by zeugma, as we now say the two Sicilies, for Sicily and Naples (Gen. xlv, 20; xlvi, 34; xlvii, 6, 13). This origin appears to have been afterwards left out of view, and the dual form is sometimes so employed as not to include Pathros or Upper Egypt (Isa. xi, 11; Jer. xliv, 15). Some writers ineptly refer the dual form of Mizraim to the two parts of Egypt as divided by the Nile. Lower Egypt appears to have been designated by the name Mazor (2 Kings xix, 24; Isa. xxxvii, 25). The ancient Hebrew name Mizraim is still preserved in the abbreviated form Muzr, the existing Arabic name of Egypt. See EGYPT.

Miz'zah (Heb. Mizzah', מִזָּה, despair; Sept. Μοζέ, in Chron. Μοχέ), the last named of the four sons of Reuel, the son of Esau by Bashemath (Gen. xxxvi, 13; 1 Chron. i, 37), and a petty chieftain of the Edomites (Gen. xxxvi, 17). B.C. considerably post 1927. The settlements of his descendants are believed by Mr. Forster (Hist. Geog. of Arab. ii, 55) to be indicated in the μεσανίτης κόλπος, or Phrat-Misan, at the head of the Persian Gulf.

Mna'son (Μνάσων, perh. reminding), a Christian with whom Paul lodged during his last visit at Jerusalem (Acts xxi, 16). A.D. 55. He seems to have been a native of Cyprus, but an inhabitant of Jerusalem, like Barnabas (comp. Acts xi, 19, 20). He was well known to the Christians at Cæsarea, and may have been a friend of Barnabas (Acts iv, 36), but appears not to have been before this acquainted with Paul. Some think that he was converted by Paul and Barnabas while at Cyprus (Acts xiii, 9); but the designation "an old disciple" (ἀρχαῖος μαθητής) has more generally induced the conclusion that he was converted by Jesus himself, and was perhaps one of the seventy (see Kuinöl, Comment. ad loc.).

Mo'äb (Heb. Moäb', מוֹאָב, water [i. e. seed] of her father, with allusion to his incestuous origin [see below]; Sept. Μωάβ), the son of Lot and his eldest daughter, and founder of the Moabitish people (Gen. xix, 30–38). B.C. 2063. Moab is also used for the country or territory of the Moabites (Jer. xlviii, 4); and also for the people of Moab (Numb. xxii, 3–14; Judg. iii, 30; 2 Sam. viii, 2; 2 Kings i, 1; Jer. xlviii, 11, 13). The "Plains of Moab," near Jericho, was the last station of the Hebrews in their journey to Canaan (Numb. xxi, 33; xxii, 1; xxxiii, 48). The proper territory of the Moabites, more fully called the field of Moab (Ruth i, 1, 2, 6; ii, 6; iv, 3), lay on the east of the Dead Sea and the Jordan, strictly on the south of the torrent Arnon (Numb. xxi, 13, 26; Judg. xi, 18); but in a wider sense it included also the region anciently occupied by the Amorites over against Jericho, usually called the plains (deserts) of Moab (Numb. xxii, 1; xxiv, 3; xxxi, 12; xxxiii, 49, 50; xxxv, 1; Deut. xxxiv, 1); or elsewhere simply the land of Moab (Deut. i, 5; xxviii, 69; xxxii, 49; xxxiv, 5); which latter region was afterwards assigned to the Reubenites, but during the captivity was again occupied by the Moabites (see Isa. xv, xvi; Jer. xlviii). It is now called the district of Kerak, from the city of that name, anciently Kir-Moab. See MOABITE; PAHATH-MOAB.

As to the etymology of the name, "various explanations have been proposed. (1.) The Sept. inserts the words λέγουσα· ἐκ τοῦ πατρός μου, saying 'from my father,' as if מֵאָב. This is followed by the old interpreters; as Josephus (Ant. i, 11, 5), Jerome's Quæst. Hebr. in Genesim, the gloss of the Pseudo-Jon. Targum; and in modern times by De Wette (Bibel), Tuch (Gen. p. 370), and J. D. Michaelis (B. für Ungelehrten). (2.) By Hiller (Onom. p. 414) and Simon (Onom. p. 479) it is derived from מוֹבָא אָב, 'ingressus, i. e. coïtus, patris.' (3.) Rosenmüller (see Schumann, *Genesis*, p. 302) proposes to treat מוֹ as equivalent for מַיִם, *water*, in accordance with the figure employed by Balaam in Numb. xxiv, 7 (as above adopted). This is countenanced by Jerome—'aqua paterna' (*Comm. in Mic.* vi, 8)—and has the great authority of Gesenius in its favor (*Thes.* p. 775 a); also of Fürst (*Handwb.* p. 707) and Bunsen (*Bibelwerk*). (4.) A derivation, probably more correct etymologically than either of the above, is that suggested by Maurer from the root רָאַב, 'to desire'—'the desirable land'—with reference to the extreme fertility of the region occupied by Moab (see also Fürst, *Hwb.* p. 707 b). No hint, however, has yet been discovered in the Bible records of such an origin of the name."

MOAB, PLAINS OF (עַרְבוֹת מוֹאָב, *Arboth' Moab'*, *Deserts of Moab*), a plain east of the Jordan, opposite Jericho (Numb. xxii, 1; xxvi, 13; Josh. xiii, 32), where the Israelites under Moses pitched their encampment on their way into Canaan (Numb. xxxi, 12; xxxiii, 48 sq.; Deut. i, 1, 5), in the vicinity of Nebo (Deut. xxxiv, 1, 8). It is the level spot in the great depression of the Ghôr into which Wady Hesbân opens, between Wadys Kefrein and Jerîfeh, a part of it being called the Valley of Shettim (q. v.). It then belonged to the Amorites (Numb. xxi, 22 sq.), but earlier to the Moabites, whence it had its name. In the division of the country it fell to the Gadites and Reubenites (Numb. xxxii, 33 sq.; Josh. xiii, 32). See MOABITE.

Mo'äbite (Heb. *Moäbi'*, מוֹאָבִי, a Gentile from *Moab*, Deut. xxiii, 24; Neh. xiii, 1; fem. מוֹאָבִית, 2 Chron. xxiv, 26; or מוֹאָבִיָּה, Ruth i, 22, etc.; plur. מוֹאָבִיּוֹת, Ruth i, 4; 1 Kings xi, 1, a *Moabitess*, or "woman of Moab;" once rendered "Moabitish," Ruth ii, 6), the designation of a tribe descended from Moab the son of Lot, and consequently related to the Hebrews (Gen. xix, 37). In the following account of them we treat the subject at large.

I. *Locality and Early History.*—Zoar was the cradle of the race of Lot. Although the exact position of this town has not been determined, there is no doubt that it was situated on the south-eastern border of the Dead Sea. From this centre the brother-tribes spread themselves. Ammon (q. v.), whose disposition seems throughout to have been more roving and unsettled, went to the northeast and took possession of the pastures and waste tracts which lay outside the district of the mountains; that which in earlier times seems to have been known as Ham, and inhabited by the Zuzim or Zamzummim (Gen. xiv, 5; Deut. ii, 20). The Moabites, whose habits were more settled and peaceful, remained nearer their original seat. The rich highlands which crown the eastern side of the chasm of the Dead Sea, and extend northwards as far as the foot of the mountains of Gilead, appear at that early date to have borne a name, which in its Hebrew form is presented to us as Shaveh-Kiriathaim, and to have been inhabited by a branch of the great race of the Rephaim. Like the Horim before the descendants of Esau, the Avim before the Philistines, or the indigenous races of the New World before the settlers from the West, this ancient people, the Emim, gradually became extinct before the Moabites, who thus obtained possession of the whole of the rich elevated tract referred to—a district forty or fifty miles in length by ten or twelve in width, the celebrated Belka and Kerak of the modern Arabs, the most fertile on that side of Jordan, no less eminently fitted for pastoral pursuits than the maritime plains of Philistia and Sharon, on the west of Palestine, are for agriculture. With the highlands they occupied also the lowlands at their feet, the plain which intervenes between the slopes of the mountains and the one perennial stream of Palestine, and through which they were enabled to gain access at pleasure to the fords of the river, and thus to the coun-

try beyond it. Of the valuable district of the highlands they were not allowed to retain entire possession. The warlike Amorites—either forced from their original seats on the west, or perhaps lured over by the increasing prosperity of the young nation—crossed the Jordan and overran the richer portion of the territory on the north, driving Moab back to his original position behind the natural bulwark of the Arnon. The plain of the Jordan valley, the hot and humid atmosphere of which had perhaps no attraction for the Amoritish mountaineers, appears to have remained in the power of Moab. When Israel reached the boundary of the country, this contest had only very recently occurred. Sihon, the Amoritish king under whose command Heshbon had been taken, was still reigning there—the ballads commemorating the event were still fresh in the popular mouth (Numb. xxi, 27–30).

Of these events, which extended over a period, according to the received Bible chronology, of not less than 500 years, from the destruction of Sodom to the arrival of Israel on the borders of the Promised Land, we obtain the above outline only from the fragments of ancient documents, which are found embedded in the records of Numbers and Deuteronomy (Numb. xxi, 26– 30; Deut. ii, 10, 11).

The position into which the Moabites were driven by the incursion of the Amorites was a very circumscribed one, in extent not so much as half that which they had lost. But on the other hand its position was much more secure, and it was well suited for the occupation of a people whose disposition was not so warlike as that of their neighbors. It occupied the southern half of the high table-lands which rise above the eastern side of the Dead Sea. On every side it was strongly fortified by nature. On the north was the tremendous chasm of the Arnon. On the west it was limited by the precipices, or more accurately the cliffs, which descend almost perpendicularly to the shore of the lake, and are intersected only by one or two steep and narrow passes. Lastly, on the south and east it was protected by a halfcircle of hills, which open only to allow the passage of a branch of the Arnon and another of the torrents which descend to the Dead Sea.

It will be seen from the foregoing description that the territory occupied by Moab at the period of its greatest extent, before the invasion of the Amorites, divided itself naturally into three distinct and independent portions. Each of these portions appears to have had its name, by which it is almost invariably designated. (1) The enclosed "corner" or canton south of the Arnon was the "field of Moab" (Ruth i, 1, 2, 6, etc.). (2) The more open rolling country north of the Arnon, opposite Jericho, and up to the hills of Gilead, was the "land of Moab" (Deut. i, 5; xxxii, 49, etc.). (3) The sunk district in the tropical depths of the Jordan valley, taking its name from that of the great valley itself—the Arabah—was the Arboth-Moab, the dry regions—in the A. V. very incorrectly rendered the "plains of Moab" (Numb. xxii, 1, etc.).

II. *Connection with the Israelites.*—Outside of the hills, which enclosed the "field of Moab," or Moab proper, on the south-east, and which are at present called the Jebel Uru-Karaiyeh and Jebel el-Tarfuyeh, lay the vast pasture-grounds of the waste, uncultivated country, or "Midbar," which is described as "facing Moab" on the east (Numb. xxi, 11). Through this latter district Israel appears to have approached the Promised Land. Some communication had evidently taken place, though of what nature it is impossible clearly to ascertain. For while in Deut. ii, 28, 29 the attitude of the Moabites is mentioned as friendly, this seems to be contradicted by the statement of xxiii, 4; while in Judg. xi, 17, again, Israel is said to have sent from Kadesh asking permission to pass through Moab—a permission which, like Edom, Moab refused. At any rate, the attitude perpetuated by the provisions of Deut. xxiii, 3—a provision maintained in full force by the latest of the Old-Testament reformers (Neh. xiii, 1, 2, 23)—is one of hostility. See Nöldeke, *Die Amalekiten*, etc. (Gött. 1864), p. 3.

1. But whatever the communication may have been, the result was that Israel did not traverse Moab, but, turning to the right, passed outside the mountains through the "wilderness," by the east side of the territory above described (Deut. ii, 8; Judg. xi, 18), and finally took up a position in the country north of the Arnon, from which Moab had so lately been ejected. Here the head-quarters of the nation remained for a considerable time while the conquest of Bashan was taking effect. It was during this period that the visit of Balaam took place. The whole of the country east of the Jordan, with the exception of the one little corner occupied by Moab, was in possession of the invaders, and although at the period in question the main body had descended from the upper level to the plains of Shittim, the Arboth-Moab, in the Jordan valley, yet a great number must have remained on the upper level, and the towns up to the very edge of the ravine of the Arnon were still occupied by their settlements (Numb. xxi, 24; Judg. xi, 26). It was a situation full of alarm for a nation which had already suffered so severely. In his extremity the Moabitish king, Balak—whose father Zippor was doubtless the chieftain who had lost his life in the encounter with Sihon (Numb. xxi, 26)—appealed to the Midianites for aid (Numb. xxii, 2-4). With a metaphor highly appropriate both to his mouth and to the ear of the pastoral tribe he was addressing, he exclaims that "this people will lick up all round about us as the ox licketh up the grass of the field." What relation existed between Moab and Midian we do not know, but there are various indications that it was a closer one than would arise merely from their common descent from Terah. The tradition of the Jews (*Targum Pseudo-Jonathan* on Numb. xxii, 4) is that up to this time the two had been one nation, with kings taken alternately from each, and that Balak was a Midianite. This, however, is in contradiction to the statements of Genesis as to the origin of each people. The whole story of Balaam's visit and of the subsequent events, both in the original narrative of Numbers and in the remarkable statement of Jephthah—whose words as addressed to Ammonites must be accepted as literally accurate—bears out the inference already drawn from the earlier history as to the pacific character of Moab.

The account of the whole of these transactions in the book of Numbers, familiar as we are with its phrases, perhaps hardly conveys an adequate idea of the extremity in which Balak found himself in his unexpected encounter with the new nation and their mighty Divinity. We may realize it better (and certainly with gratitude for the opportunity) if we consider what that last dreadful agony was in which a successor of Balak was placed, when, all hope of escape for himself and his people being cut off, the unhappy Mesha immolated his own son on the wall of Kir-haraseth; and then remember that Balak in his distress actually proposed the same awful sacrifice—"his first-born for his transgression, the fruit of his body for the sin of his soul" (Mic. vi, 7)—a sacrifice from which he was restrained only by the wise, the almost Christian (Matt. ix, 13; xii, 7) counsels of Balaam. This catastrophe will be noticed in its proper place.

The connection of Moab with Midian, and the comparatively inoffensive character of the former, are shown in the narrative of the events which followed the departure of Balaam. The women of Moab are indeed said (Numb. xxv, 1) to have commenced the idolatrous fornication which proved so destructive to Israel, but it is plain that their share in it was insignificant compared with that of Midian. It was a Midianitish woman whose shameless act brought down the plague on the camp, the Midianitish women were especially devoted to destruction by Moses (xxv, 16-18; xxxi, 16), and it was upon Midian that the vengeance was taken. Except in the passage already mentioned, Moab is not once

named in the whole transaction. The latest date at which the two names appear in conjunction is found in the notice of the defeat of Midian "in the field of Moab" by the Edomitish king Hadad ben-Bedad, which occurred five generations before the establishment of the monarchy of Israel (Gen. xxxvi, 35; 1 Chron. i, 46). By the Jewish interpreters—e. g. Solomon Jarchi in his commentary on the passage—this is treated as implying, not alliance, but war between Moab and Midian (comp. 1 Chron. iv, 22).

It is remarkable that Moses should have taken his view of the Promised Land from a Moabitish sanctuary, and been buried in the land of Moab. It is singular, too, that his resting-place is marked in the Hebrew records only by its proximity to the sanctuary of that deity to whom in his lifetime he had been such an enemy. He lies in a ravine in the land of Moab, facing Beth-Peor, i. e. the abode of Baal-Peor (Deut. xxxiv, 6).

2. After the conquest of Canaan the relations of Moab with Israel were of a mixed character. With the tribe of Benjamin, whose possessions at their eastern end were separated from those of Moab only by the Jordan, they had at least one severe struggle, in union with their kindred the Ammonites, and also, for this time only, the wild Amalekites from the south (Judg. iii, 12-30). The Moabitish king, Eglon, actually ruled and received tribute in Jericho for eighteen years, but at the end of that time he was killed by the Benjamitish hero Ehud, and the return of the Moabites being intercepted at the fords, a large number were slaughtered, and a stop put to such incursions on their part for the future. A trace of this invasion is visible in the name of Chephar-ha-Ammonai, the "hamlet of the Ammonites," one of the Benjamitish towns; and another is possibly preserved even to the present day in the name of Mukhmas, the modern representative of Michmash, which is by some scholars believed to have received its name from Chemosh, the Moabitish deity. The feud continued with true Oriental pertinacity to the time of Saul. Of his slaughter of the Ammonites we have full details in 1 Sam. xi, and among his other conquests Moab is especially mentioned (1 Sam. xiv, 47). There is not, however, as we should expect, any record of it during Ishbosheth's residence at Mahanaim, on the east of Jordan.

But while such were their relations to the tribe of Benjamin, the story of Ruth, on the other hand, testifies to the existence of a friendly intercourse between Moab and Bethlehem, one of the towns of Judah. Jewish tradition (*Targum Jonathan* on Ruth i, 4) ascribes the death of Mahlon and Chilion to punishment for having broken the commandment of Deut. xxiii, 3, but no trace of any feeling of the kind is visible in the book of Ruth itself—which not only seems to imply a considerable intercourse between the two nations, but also a complete ignorance or disregard of the precept in question, which was broken in the most flagrant manner when Ruth became the wife of Boaz. By his descent from Ruth, David may be said to have had Moabitish blood in his veins. The relationship was sufficient, especially when combined with the blood-feud between Moab and Benjamin, already alluded to, to warrant his visiting the land of his ancestress, and committing his parents to the protection of the king of Moab, when hard pressed by Saul (1 Sam. xxiii, 3, 4). But here all friendly relation stops forever. The next time the name is mentioned is in the account of David's war, at least twenty years after the last-mentioned event (2 Sam. viii, 2; 1 Chron. xviii, 2). The abrupt manner in which this war is introduced into the history is no less remarkable than the brief and passing terms in which its horrors are recorded. The account occupies but a few words in either Samuel or Chronicles, and yet it must have been for the time little short of a virtual extirpation of the nation. Two thirds of the people were put to death, while the remainder became bondmen, and were subjected to a regular tribute. An incident of this war is probably recorded in 2 Sam. xxiii, 20, and 1 Chron. xi, 22. The spoils taken from the Moabitish cities and sanctuaries went to swell the treasure acquired from the enemies of Jehovah, which David was amassing for the future Temple (2 Sam. viii, 11, 12; 1 Chron. xviii, 11). It was the first time that the prophecy of Balaam had been fulfilled—"Out of Jacob shall come he that shall have dominion, and shall destroy him that remaineth of Ar," that is of Moab. So signal a vengeance can only have been occasioned by some act of perfidy or insult, like that which brought down a similar treatment on the Ammonites (2 Sam. x). But as to any such act the narrative is absolutely silent. It has been conjectured that the king of Moab betrayed the trust which David reposed in him, and either himself killed Jesse and his wife, or surrendered them to Saul. But this, though not improbable, is nothing more than conjecture.

It must have been a considerable time before Moab recovered from so severe a blow. Of this we have evidence in the fact of its not being mentioned in the account of the campaign in which the Ammonites were subdued, when it is not probable they would have refrained from assisting their relatives had they been in a condition to do so. Throughout the reign of Solomon they no doubt shared in the universal peace which surrounded Israel; and the only mention of the name occurs in the statement that there were Moabites among the foreign women in the royal harem, and, as a natural consequence, that the Moabitish worship was tolerated, or perhaps encouraged (1 Kings xi, 1, 7, 33). The high place for Chemosh, "the abomination of Moab," was consecrated "on the mount facing Jerusalem," where it remained till its "defilement" by Josiah (2 Kings xxiii, 13), nearly four centuries afterwards.

3. At the disruption of the kingdom, Moab seems to have fallen to the northern realm, probably for the same reason that has been already remarked in the case of Eglon and Ehud—that the fords of Jordan lay within the territory of Benjamin, who for some time after the separation clung to its ancient ally, the house of Ephraim. But, be this as it may, at the death of Ahab, eighty years later, we find Moab paying him the enormous tribute, apparently annual, of 100,000 rams, and the same number of wethers with their fleeces; an amount which testifies at once to the severity of the terms imposed by Israel, and to the remarkable vigor of character and wealth of natural resources which could enable a little country to raise year by year this enormous impost, and at the same time support its own people in prosperity and affluence. This affluence is shown by the treasures which they left on the field of Berachoth (2 Chron. xx, 25), no less than by the general condition of the country, indicated in the narrative of Joram's invasion; and in the passages of Isaiah and Jeremiah which are cited further on in this article. It is not surprising that the Moabites should have seized the moment of Ahab's death to throw off so burdensome a yoke; but it is surprising that, notwithstanding such a drain on their resources, they were ready to incur the risk and expense of a war with a state in every respect far their superior. Their first step, after asserting their independence, was to attack the kingdom of Judah in company with their kindred the Ammonites, and, as seems probable, the Mehunim, a roving semi-Edomitish people from the mountains in the south-east of Palestine (2 Chron. xx). The army was a huge, heterogeneous horde of ill-assorted elements. The route chosen for the invasion was round the southern end of the Dead Sea, thence along the beach, and by the pass of En-gedi to the level of the upper country. But the expedition contained within itself the elements of its own destruction. Before they reached the enemy dissensions arose between the heathen strangers and the children of Lot; distrust followed, and finally panic; and when the army of Jehoshaphat came in sight of them they found that they had nothing to do but to watch the extermination of one half the huge host by the other half, and to seize the prodigious booty which was left on the field. Dis-

VI.—13*

astrous as was this proceeding, that which followed it was even still more so. As a natural consequence of the late events, Israel, Judah, and Edom united in an attack on Moab. For reasons which are not stated, but one of which we may reasonably conjecture was to avoid the passage of the savage Edomites through Judah, the three confederate armies approached, not, as usual, by the north, but round the southern end of the Dead Sea, through the parched valleys of Upper Edom. As the host came near, the king of Moab, doubtless the same Mesha who threw off the yoke of Ahab, assembled the whole of his people, from the youngest who were of age to bear the sword-girdle (2 Kings iii, 21), on the boundary of his territory, probably on the outer slopes of the line of hills which encircles the lower portion of Moab, overlooking the waste which extended below them towards the east (comp. Numb. xxi, 11—"towards the sun-rising"). Here they remained all night on the watch. With the approach of morning the sun rose suddenly above the horizon of the rolling plain, and as his level beams burst through the night-mists they revealed no masses of the enemy, but shone with a blood-red glare on a multitude of pools in the bed of the wady at their feet. They did not know that these pools had been sunk during the night by the order of a mighty prophet who was with the host of Israel, and that they had been filled by the sudden flow of water rushing from the distant highlands of Edom. To them the conclusion was inevitable: the army had, like their own on the late occasion, fallen out in the night; these red pools were the blood of the slain; those who were not killed had fled, and nothing stood between them and the pillage of the camp. The cry of "Moab to the spoil!" was raised. Down the slopes they rushed in headlong disorder. But not, as they expected, to empty tents; they found an enemy ready prepared to reap the result of his ingenious stratagem. Then occurred one of those scenes of carnage which can happen but once or twice in the existence of a nation. The Moabites fled back in confusion, followed and cut down at every step by their enemies. Far inwards did the pursuit reach, among the cities and farms and orchards of that rich district; nor when the slaughter was over was the horrid work of destruction done. The towns, both fortified and unfortified, were demolished, and the stones strewed over the carefully-tilled fields. The fountains of water, the life of an Eastern land, were choked, and all timber of any size or goodness felled. Nowhere else do we hear of such sweeping desolation; the very besom of destruction passed over the land. At last the struggle collected itself at Kir-haraseth, apparently a newly-constructed fortress, which, if the modern Kerak—and there is every probability that they are identical—may well have resisted all the efforts of the allied kings in its native impregnability. Here Mesha took refuge with his family and with the remnants of his army. The heights around, by which the town is entirely commanded, were covered with slingers, who—armed partly with the ancient weapon of David and of the Benjamites, partly perhaps with the newly-invented machines shortly to be famous in Jerusalem (2 Chron. xxvi, 15)—discharged their volleys of stones on the town. At length the annoyance could be borne no longer. Then Mesha, collecting round him a forlorn hope of 700 of his best warriors, made a desperate sally, with the intention of cutting his way through to his special foe, the king of Edom. But the enemy were too strong for him, and he was driven back. And then came a fitting crown to a tragedy already so terrible. An awful spectacle amazed and horrified the besiegers. The king and his eldest son, the heir to the throne, mounted the wall, and, in the sight of the thousands who covered the sides of that vast amphitheatre, the father killed and burned his child as a propitiatory sacrifice to the cruel gods of his country. It was the same dreadful act to which, as we have seen, Balak had been so nearly tempted in his extremity. But the danger, though perhaps not really greater than his, was more imminent; and Mesha had no one like Balaam at hand to counsel patience and submission to a mightier Power than Chemosh or Baal-Peor. See MESHA.

Hitherto, though able and ready to fight when necessary, the Moabites do not appear to have been a fighting people; perhaps, as suggested elsewhere, the Ammonites were the warriors of the nation of Lot. But this disaster seems to have altered their disposition, at any rate for a time. Shortly after these events we hear of "bands"—that is, pillaging, marauding parties—of the Moabites making their incursions into Israel in the spring, as if to spoil the early corn before it was fit to cut (2 Kings xiii, 20). With Edom there must have been many a contest. One of these marked by savage vengeance—recalling in some degree the tragedy of Kir-haraseth—is alluded to by Amos (ii, 1), where a king of Edom seems to have been killed and burned by Moab. This may have been one of the incidents of the battle of Kir-haraseth itself, occurring perhaps after the Edomites had parted from Israel, and were overtaken on their road home by the furious king of Moab (Gesenius, *Jesaia*, i, 504); or, according to the Jewish tradition (Jerome, on Amos ii, 1), it was a vengeance still more savage because more protracted, and lasting even beyond the death of the king, whose remains were torn from his tomb, and thus consumed.

In the "Burden of Moab" pronounced by Isaiah (ch. xv, xvi) we possess a document full of interesting details as to the condition of the nation at the time of the death of Ahaz, king of Judah, B.C. 726. More than a century and a half had elapsed since the great calamity to which we have just referred. In that interval Moab has regained all, and more than all, of his former prosperity, and has besides extended himself over the district which he originally occupied in the youth of the nation, and which was left vacant when the removal of Reuben to Assyria, which had been begun by Pul in B.C. 770, was completed by Tiglath-pileser about the year 740 (1 Chron. v, 25, 26). This passage of Isaiah cannot be considered apart from that of Jeremiah, ch. xlviii. The latter was pronounced more than a century later, about the year B.C. 600, ten or twelve years before the invasion of Nebuchadnezzar, by which Jerusalem was destroyed. In many respects it is identical with that of Isaiah, and both are believed by the best modern scholars, on account of the archaisms and other peculiarities of language which they contain, to be adopted from a common source—the work of some much more ancient prophet. Isaiah ends his denunciation by a prediction—in his own words—that within three years Moab should be greatly reduced. This was probably with a view to Shalmaneser, who destroyed Samaria, and no doubt overran the other side of the Jordan in B.C. 725, and again in 723 (2 Kings xvii, 3; xviii, 9). The only event of which we have a record to which it would seem possible that the passage, as originally uttered by the older prophet, applied, is the above invasion of Pul, who, in commencing the deportation of Reuben, very probably at the same time molested Moab. The difficulty of so many of the towns of Reuben being mentioned as at that early day already in the possession of Moab may perhaps be explained by remembering that the idolatry of the neighboring nations—and therefore of Moab—had been adopted by the trans-Jordanic tribes for some time previously to the final deportation by Tiglath-pileser (see 1 Chron. v, 25), and that many of the sanctuaries were probably, even at the date of the original delivery of the denunciation, in the hands of the priests of Chemosh and Milcom. If, as Ewald (*Gesch.* iii, 588) with much probability infers, the Moabites, no less than the Ammonites, were under the protection of the powerful Uzziah (2 Chron. xxvi, 8), then the obscure expressions of the ancient seer as given in Isa. xvi, 1-5, referring to a tribute of lambs (comp. 2 Kings iii, 4) sent from the wild pasture-grounds south of Moab to Zion, and to protection and relief from op-

pression afforded by the throne of David to the fugitives and outcasts of Moab, acquire an intelligible sense. On the other hand, the calamities which Jeremiah describes may have been inflicted in any one of the numerous visitations from the Assyrian army, under which these unhappy countries suffered at the period of his prophecy in rapid succession.

But the uncertainty of the exact dates referred to in these several denunciations does not in the least affect the interest or the value of the allusions they contain to the condition of Moab. They bear the evident stamp of portraiture by artists who knew their subject thoroughly. The nation appears in them as high-spirited, wealthy, populous, and even to a certain extent civilized, enjoying a wide reputation and popularity. With a metaphor which well expresses at once the pastoral wealth of the country and its commanding, almost regal position, but which cannot be conveyed in a translation, Moab is depicted as the strong sceptre (Isa. xvi, 6; Jer. xlviii, 29), the beautiful staff, whose fracture will be bewailed by all about him, and by all who know him. In his cities we discern a "great multitude" of people living in "glory," and in the enjoyment of great "treasure," crowding the public squares, the housetops, and the ascents and descents of the numerous high places and sanctuaries where the "priests and princes" of Chemosh or Baal-Peor minister to the anxious devotees. Outside the town lie the "plentiful fields," luxuriant as the renowned Carmel—the vineyards, and gardens of "summer fruits"—the harvest is in course of reaping, and the "hay is stored in its abundance," the vineyards and the presses are crowded with peasants, gathering and treading the grapes, the land resounds with the clamor of the vintagers. These characteristics contrast very favorably with any traits recorded of Ammon, Edom, Midian, Amalek, the Philistines, or the Canaanitish tribes. And since the descriptions we are considering are adopted by certainly two, and probably three prophets—Jeremiah, Isaiah, and the older seer—extending over a period of nearly 200 years, we may safely conclude that they are not merely temporary circumstances, but were the enduring characteristics of the people. In this case there can be no doubt that among the pastoral people of Syria, Moab stood next to Israel in all matters of material wealth and civilization.

It is very interesting to remark the feeling which actuates the prophets in these denunciations of a people who, though the enemies of Jehovah, were the blood-relations of Israel. Half the allusions of Isaiah and Jeremiah in the passages referred to must forever remain obscure. We shall never know who the "lords of the heathen" were who, in that terrible night, laid waste and brought to silence the prosperous Ar-Moab and Kir-Moab; nor the occasion of that flight over the Arnon, when the Moabitish women were huddled together at the ford, like a flock of young birds, pressing to cross to the safe side of the stream—when the dwellers in Aroer stood by the side of the high-road which passed their town, and eagerly questioning the fugitives as they hurried up, "What is done?"—received but one answer from all alike—"All is lost! Moab is confounded and broken down!" Many expressions also, such as the "weeping of Jazer," the "heifer of three years old," the "shadow of Heshbon," the "lions," must remain obscure. But nothing can obscure or render obsolete the tone of tenderness and affection which makes itself felt in a hundred expressions throughout these precious documents. Ardently as the prophet longs for the destruction of the enemy of his country and of Jehovah, and earnestly as he curses the man "that doeth the work of Jehovah deceitfully, that keepeth back his sword from blood," yet he is constrained to bemoan and lament such dreadful calamities to a people so near him both in blood and locality. His heart mourns—it sounds like pipes—for the men of Kir-heres; his heart cries out, it sounds like a harp for Moab. Isaiah recurs to the subject in another passage of extraordinary force, and of fiercer character than before, viz. xxv, 10–12. Here the extermination, the utter annihilation of Moab is contemplated by the prophet with triumph, as one of the first results of the re-establishment of Jehovah on Mount Zion: "In this mountain shall the hand of Jehovah rest, and Moab shall be trodden down under him, even as straw—the straw of his own threshing-floors at Madmenah—is trodden down for the dunghill. And he shall spread forth his hands in the midst of them—namely, of the Moabites—as one that swimmeth spreadeth forth his hands to swim, buffet following buffet, right and left, with terrible rapidity, as the strong swimmer urges his way forward; and he shall bring down their pride together with the spoils of their hands. And the fortress of Misgab—thy walls shall he bring down, lay low, and bring to the ground, to the dust." If, according to the custom of interpreters, this and the preceding chapter (xxiv) are understood as referring to the destruction of Babylon, then this sudden burst of indignation towards Moab is extremely puzzling. But, if the passage is examined with that view, it will perhaps be found to contain some expressions which suggest the possibility of Moab having been at least within the ken of the prophet, even though not in the foreground of his vision, during a great part of the passage. The Hebrew words rendered "city" in xxv, 2—two entirely distinct terms—are positively, with a slight variation, the names of the two chief Moabitish strongholds, the same which are mentioned in xv, 1, and one of which is in the Pentateuch a synonyme for the entire nation of Moab. In this light ver. 2 may be read as follows: "For thou hast made of Ar a heap; of Kir the defenced a ruin; a palace of strangers no longer is Ar, it shall never be rebuilt." The same words are found in ver. 10 and 12 of the preceding chapter, in company with chutsôth (A. Vers. "streets"), which we know from Numb. xxii, 39 to have been the name of a Moabite town. See KIRJATH-HUZOTH. A distinct echo of them is again heard in xxv, 3, 4; and, finally, in xxvi, 1, 5 there seems to be yet another reference to the same two towns, acquiring new force from the denunciation which closes the preceding chapter: "Moab shall be brought down, the fortress and the walls of Misgab shall be laid low; but in the land of Judah this song shall be sung, 'Our Ar, our city, is strong. . . . Trust in the Lord Jehovah, who bringeth down those that dwell on high: the lofty Kir, he layeth it low,'" etc. It is perhaps an additional corroboration of this view to notice that the remarkable expressions in xxiv, 17, "Fear, and the pit, and the snare," etc., actually occur in Jeremiah (xlviii, 43), in his denunciation of Moab, embedded in the old prophecies out of which, like Isa. xv, xvi, this passage is compiled, and the rest of which had certainly, as originally uttered, a direct and even exclusive reference to Moab.

Between the time of Isaiah's denunciation and the destruction of Jerusalem we have hardly a reference to Moab. Zephaniah, writing in the reign of Josiah, reproaches them (ii, 8–10) for their taunts against the people of Jehovah, but no acts of hostility are recorded either on the one side or the other. From one passage in Jeremiah (xxv, 9–11), delivered in the fourth year of Jehoiakim, just before the first appearance of Nebuchadnezzar, it is apparent that it was the belief of the prophet that the nations surrounding Israel—and Moab among the rest—were on the eve of devastation by the Chaldæans, and of a captivity for seventy years (see ver. 11), from which, however, they should eventually be restored to their own country (ver. 12, and xlviii, 47). From another record of the events of the same period, or of one just subsequent (2 Kings xxiv, 2), it would appear, however, that Moab made terms with the Chaldæans, and for a time acted in concert with them in harassing and plundering the kingdom of Jehoiakim.

Four or five years later, in the first year of Zedekiah (Jer. xxvii, 1), these hostilities must have ceased, for there was then a regular intercourse between Moab and the court at Jerusalem (ver. 3), possibly, as Bunsen suggests (Bibelwerk, Propheten, p. 536), negotiating a combined resistance to the common enemy. The brunt of the storm must have fallen on Judah and Jerusalem. The neighboring nations, including Moab, when the danger actually arrived, probably adopted the advice of Jeremiah (xxvii, 11), and thus escaped, though not without much damage, yet without being carried away as the Jews were. That these nations did not suffer to the same extent as Judæa is evident from the fact that many of the Jews took refuge there when their own land was laid waste (Jer. xl, 11). Jeremiah expressly testifies that those who submitted themselves to the king of Babylon, though they would have to bear a severe yoke—so severe that their very wild animals would be enslaved—yet by such submission should purchase the privilege of remaining in their own country. The removal from home, so dreadful to the Shemitic mind, was to be the fate only of those who resisted (Jer. xxvii, 10, 11; xxviii, 14). This is also supported by the allusion of Ezekiel, a few years later, to the cities of Moab, cities formerly belonging to the Israelites, which, at the time when the prophet is speaking, were still flourishing, "the glory of the country," destined to become at a future day a prey to the Bene-kedem, the "men of the East"—the Bedouins of the great desert of the Euphrates (Ezek. xxv, 8–11).

III. Later History.—After the return from the captivity, it was a Moabite, Sanballat of Horonaim, who took the chief part in annoying and endeavoring to hinder the operations of the rebuilders of Jerusalem (Neh. ii, 19; iv, 1; vi, 1; etc.). He confined himself, however, to the same weapons of ridicule and scurrility which we have already noticed Zephaniah resenting. From Sanballat's words (Neh. ii, 19) we should infer that he and his country were subject to "the king," that is, the king of Babylon. During the interval since the return of the first caravan from Babylon the illegal practice of marriages between the Jews and the other people around, Moab among the rest, had become frequent. So far had this gone that the son of the high-priest was married to an Ammonitish woman. Even among the families of Israel who returned from the captivity was one bearing the name of PAHATH-MOAB (Ezra ii, 6; viii, 4; Neh. iii, 11; etc.), a name which must certainly denote a Moabitish connection, though to the nature of the connection no clue seems to have been yet discovered. By Ezra and Nehemiah the practice of foreign marriages was strongly repressed, and we never hear of it again becoming prevalent.

In the book of Judith, the date of which is laid shortly after the return from the captivity (iv, 3), Moabites and Ammonites are represented as dwelling in their ancient seats, and as obeying the call of the Assyrian general. Their "princes" (ἄρχοντες) and "governors" (ἡγούμενοι) are mentioned (v, 2; vii, 8). The Maccabees, much as they ravaged the country of the Ammonites, do not appear to have molested Moab proper, nor is the name either of Moab or of any of the towns south of the Arnon mentioned throughout those books. Josephus not only speaks of the district in which Heshbon was situated as "Moabitis" (Ant. xiii, 15, 4; also War, iv, 8, 2), but expressly says that even at the time he wrote they were a "very great nation" (Ant. i, 11, 5). (See 5 Macc. xxix, 19.) Nöldeke, in his recent work, Ueber die Amalekiter und einige andere nachbarvölker der Israeliten (Göttingen, 1864), p. 3, insists that the final extinction of Ammonites and Moabites dates from the appearance of the Yemen tribes Salib and Gassan in the eastern districts of the Jordan. This would bring them down to about A.D. 200.

In the time of Eusebius (Onomast. Μωάβ), i. e. cir. A.D. 380, the name appears to have been attached to the district, as well as to the town of Rabbath—both of which were called Moab. It also lingered for some time in the name of the ancient Kir-Moab, which, as Charakmoba, is mentioned by Ptolemy (Reland, Palæst. p.

463), and as late as the Council of Jerusalem, A.D. 536, formed the see of a bishop under the same title (*ibid.* p. 533). Since that time the modern name Kerak has superseded the older one, and no trace of Moab has been found either in records or in the country itself.

IV. *Geography and Characteristics.*—Like the other countries east of Jordan, Moab has until recently been very little visited by Europeans, and beyond its general characteristics hardly anything is known of it. Of the character of the face of the country travellers only give slight reports, and among these there is considerable variation even when the same district is referred to. Thus between Kerak and Rabba, Irby (p. 141 *a*) found "a fine country," of great natural fertility, with "reapers at work and the corn luxuriant in all directions;" and the same district is described by Burckhardt as "very fertile, and large tracts cultivated" (*Syr.* July 15); while De Saulcy, on the other hand, pronounces that "from Shihan (six miles north of Rabba) to the Wady Kerak the country is perfectly bare, not a tree or a bush to be seen" (*Voyage*, i, 353); which, again, is contradicted by Seetzen, who not only found the soil very good, but encumbered with wormwood and other shrubs (Seetzen, i, 410). These discrepancies are no doubt partly due to difference in the time of year and other temporary causes, but they are not essentially contradictory; for while the whole region has been denuded of all habitations and larger forms of vegetation, it is still a rich pasture-ground for the Bedouins who roam in every direction over it, and who likewise till its extensive fields of wheat and barley. In one thing all writers agree—the extraordinary number of ruins which are scattered over the country, and which, whatever the present condition of the soil, are a sure token of its wealth in former ages (Seetzen, i, 412). Some of the most remarkable of these have recently been described by Tristram. The whole country is undulating, and, after the general level of the plateau is reached, without any serious inequalities; and in this and the absence of conspicuous vegetation has a certain resemblance to the downs of the southern counties of England.

Of the *language* of the Moabites we know nothing or next to nothing. In the few communications recorded as taking place between them and the Israelites no interpreter is mentioned (see Ruth; 1 Sam. xxii, 3, 4; etc.). From the origin of the nation and other considerations we may perhaps conjecture that their language was more a dialect of Hebrew than a different tongue. This, indeed, would follow from the connection of Lot, their founder, with Abraham. It is likewise confirmed by the remarkable inscription recently discovered. See MESHA. The narrative of Numb. xxii–xxiv must be founded on a Moabitish chronicle, though in its present condition doubtless much altered from what it originally was before it came into the hands of the author of the book of Numbers. No attempt seems yet to have been made to execute the difficult but interesting task of examining the record with the view of restoring it to its pristine form. The following are the names of Moabitish persons preserved in the Bible—probably Hebraized in their adoption into the Bible records; of such a transition we seem to have a trace in Shomer and Shimrith (see below): Zippor, Balak, Eglon, Ruth, Orpah (עָרְפָּה), Mesha (מֵישַׁע), Ithmah (1 Chron. xi, 46), Shomer (2 Kings xii, 21), or Shimrith (2 Chron. xxiv, 26), Sanballat. Add to these—Emim, the name by which they called the Rephaim who originally inhabited their country, and whom the Ammonites called Zamzummim or Zuzim; Chemôsh, or Chemish (Jer. xlviii, 7), the deity of the nation. Of names of places the following may be mentioned: Moab, with its compounds, Sedê-Moab, the fields of Moab (A. V. "the country of Moab"); Arboth-Moab, the deserts (A. V. "the plains") of Moab, that is, the part of the Arabah occupied by the Moabites; ham-Mishor, the high undulating country of Moab proper (A. V. "the plain"); Ar, or Ar-Moab (עָר)—this Gese-

nius conjectures to be a Moabitish form of the word which in Hebrew appears as Ir (עִיר, a city); Arnon, the river (אַרְנֹן); Bamoth Baal, Beer Elim, Beth-diblathaim, Dibon or Dimon, Eglaim, or perhaps Eglath-Shelishiya (Isa. xv, 5), Horonaim, Kiriathaim, Kirjath-huzoth (Numb. xxxii, 39; comp. Isa. xxiv, 11), Kir-haraseth, -haresh, -heres; Kir-Moab, Luhith, Medeba, Nimrim, or Nimrah, Nobah, or Nophah (Numb. xxi, 30), hap-Pisgah, hap-Peor, Shaveh-Kariathaim (?), Zophim, Zoar. It should be noticed how large a proportion of these names end in *im*.

For the *religion* of the Moabites, see CHEMOSH; MOLECH; PEOR.

Of their *habits* and customs we have hardly a trace. The gesture employed by Balak when he found that Balaam's interference was fruitless—"he smote his hands together"—is not mentioned again in the Bible, but it may not on that account have been peculiar to the Moabites. Their mode of mourning, viz., cutting off the hair at the back of the head and cropping the beard (Jer. xlviii, 37), is one which they followed in common with the other non-Israelitish nations, and which was forbidden to the Israelites (Lev. xxi, 5), who indeed seem to have been accustomed rather to leave their hair and beard disordered and untrimmed when in grief (see 2 Sam. xix, 24; xiv, 2).

V. *Literature.*—As above remarked, through fear of the predatory and mischievous Arabs that people it, few of the numerous travellers in Palestine have ventured to explore it (see Büsching's *Asia*, p. 507, 508). Seetzen, who, in February and March, 1806, not without danger of losing his life, undertook a tour from Damascus down to the south of the Jordan and the Dead Sea, and thence to Jerusalem, was the first to shed a new and altogether unexpected light upon the topography of this region. He found a multitude of places, or at least of ruins of places, still bearing the old names, and thus has set bounds to the perfectly arbitrary designations of them on the old charts (see U. I. Seetzen's *Reisen*, etc., von Prof. Kruse, etc., i, 405–26; ii, 320–77; also the editor's notes thereon in vol. iv). From June to September, 1812, Burckhardt made the same tour from Damascus beyond the Jordan down to Kerak; whence he advanced over Wady Mousa, or the ancient Petra (which he was the first European traveller to visit), to the bay of Aila, and thence went to Cairo (*Travels in the Holy Land and Syria*, Lond. 1822; see also the notes of Gesenius to the German translation [Weimar, 1824], ii, 1061–64). A party of English gentlemen — captains Irby and Mangles, Mr. Bankes and Mr. Legh—passed through the land of Moab in returning from Petra in 1818 (*Travels in Egypt*, etc. [1822, 8vo; 1847, 12mo], ch. viii; see also Legh's Supplement to Dr. Macmichael's *Journey from Moscow to Constantinople* [1819]). The northern parts of the country were visited by Mr. Buckingham, and more lately by Mr. George Robinson and by lord Lindsay (see also the plates to Laborde's new work, *Voyage en Orient*). Kerak, the capital of the country, was penetrated by the party in command of Lieut. Lynch (*Expedition to the Dead Sea* [1849]); and the region was partially examined by M. De Saulcy, January, 1851 (*Voyage autour de la Mer Morte*, Paris, 1853; also translated into English, Lond. and N. York, 1853). Tristram, however, was the first who really explored it accurately (*Land of Moab*, Lond. and N. York, 1873), and the American engineers of the Palestine Exploration Society have triangulated the northern portion of it. Several parties of tourists have also traversed it in various directions lately. See generally Gesenius, *Comment. on Isa.* xv, xvi, *Introduct.* translated by W. S. Tyler, with *Notes* by Moses Stuart, in *Biblical Repos.* for 1836, vii, 107–124; Keith, *Evidence from Prophecy*, p. 153–165; and *Land of Israel*, p. 279–295; Kitto, *Pictorial Bible*, Notes to Deut. ii, 2; Isa. xvi, xvii; Jer. xliii; H. Scharban, *Parerga philol. theol.* (Lubeck, 1723 sq.), pt. iii and iv; G. Kohlreiff, *Gesch. d. Philist. u. Moab*

(Ratzeb. 1738). See also the *Quarterly Rev.* Oct. 1873, art. vi; *Brit. and For. Ev. Rev.* Jan. 1874, p. 195; *Meth. Qu. Rev.* Jan. 1874, p. 174; *Luth. Ev. Rev.* Jan. 1874, p. 140. For a singular endeavor to identify the Moabites with the Druses, see Sir G. H. Rose's pamphlet, *The Affghans the Ten Tribes*, etc. (Lond. 1852); especially the statement therein of Mr. Wood, late British consul at Damascus (p. 154–157).

Mo'abitess (Heb. *Moabiyah'*, מוֹאֲבִיָּה, fem. of *Moabite;* Sept. Μοαβῖτις), a Moabitish woman (Ruth i, 22; ii, 2, 21; iv, 5, 19; 2 Chron. xxiv, 26). See MO-ABITE.

Moädi'ah (Neh. xiii, 17). See MAADIAH.

Mobley, WILLIAM H., a minister of the Methodist Episcopal Church, South, was born in Kentucky in 1830; removed to Missouri in 1852; was licensed to preach in 1854, and shortly after joined the St. Louis Conference; continued to travel and preach regularly till 1861, when the troubles of war compelled his removal to Arkansas, where he remained till 1865. He then returned to Kentucky, his native state, and died in Hickman County, July 27, 1865. Mr. Mobley was a good man and an efficient preacher. See *Minutes of the M. E. Church, South,* 1866, s. v.

Mocetto, GIROLAMO, a painter and engraver of the Venetian school, and sometimes called *Hieronymus Mocetus,* was a native of Verona, according to Lanzi, or of Brescia, according to Vasari, and was probably an early disciple of Bellini. Lanzi mentions an altar-piece in the church of S. Nazario-e-Celso bearing his name, and dated 1493. Mocetto was chiefly known, however, as an engraver, and his works in this line are extremely scarce and valuable. Among others may be mentioned engravings of the *Resurrection;* the *Sacrifice,* with many figures; the *Virgin and Child,* with St. John the Baptist and another saint, which is now in the British Museum; the *Virgin and Child seated on a Throne,* and a wood-cut of the *Entry of Christ into Jerusalem.* He died about 1500. See Spooner, *Biog. Hist. of the Fine Arts* (N. Y. 1865, 2 vols. 8vo), ii, 590; Lanzi, *Hist. of Painting,* transl. by Roscoe (Lond. 1847, 3 vols. 8vo), ii, 107; *Revue des Beaux Arts,* Juin 15, 1859.

Mocha OF TIBERIAS, or PALESTINE, a noted rabbi, who flourished shortly after the middle of the 8th century, is said to have been one of the world's greatest savans. Unfortunately but little is known of his personal history. He established, or at least amplified, the interlineary system of vocalization, called the *Tiberian,* or *Palestinian,* which has for centuries been generally adopted both by Jew and Gentile in pointed editions of the O.-T. Scriptures, to the exclusion of the superlineary system, called the *Babylonian,* or *Assyrian,* which was invented or extended by Acha of Irak (in the first half of the 6th century). Like his predecessor R. Acha, the author of the opposite system, R. Mocha also compiled a large and small Masorah, in which are discussed the writing of words with or without the vowel letters (מלא וחסר), the affixing of certain accents (נגינות), accented syllables, *Dagesh* and *Raphe,* rare forms, archaic words, homonymes, etc., as is evident from an ancient MS. of the Pentateuch by Firkowitzsch, where the following Masoretic gloss frequently occurs: "Rabbi Mocha writes this with and that without the vowel letters." These Masoretic glosses he wrote in Aramaic, and in the Tiberian dialect—the language of the Palestinian Jews—in order to make his labors both accessible and intelligible to all his people. Not unfrequently, however, these Masoretic glosses are intermixed with notes written in Hebrew. See Pinsker, *Likuti Kadmonijot* (Vienna, 1860), p. 62, Appendix; Grätz, *Gesch. d. Juden,* v, 552; Fürst, *Gesch. des Karäerthums,* i, 15 sq., 134 sq.

Moch'mur, THE BROOK (ὁ χειμάρρος Μοχμούρ; Alex. omits Μοχ.; Vulg. omits), a torrent, i. e. a *wady* —the word "brook" conveys an entirely false impres-

sion—mentioned only in Judith vii, 18; and there as specifying the position of Ekrebel—"Near unto Chusi, and upon the brook Mochmur." Ekrebel has been identified, with great probability, by Mr. Van de Velde in Akrabeh, a ruined site in the mountains of Central Palestine, equidistant from Nablûs and Seilûn, south-east of the former and north-east of the latter; and the torrent Mochmur may be either the *Wady Makfuriyeh,* on the northern slopes of which Akrabeh stands, or the *Wady Ahmar,* which is the continuation of the former eastwards. The reading of the Syriac (*Nachol de-Peor*) possibly points to the existence of a sanctuary of Baal-Peor in this neighborhood, but is more probably a corruption of the original name, which was apparently מַחְמוּר (Simon, *Onomasticon N. T.* p. 111).

Modalism is a term applied to the heretical views regarding the Trinity first espoused by Sabellius, a presbyter of Ptolemais, who flourished about the middle of the 3d century. Adopting the notions of the earlier *Monarchians,* he maintained, in opposition to the doctrine propounded by Origen and his school, that the appellations of Father, Son, and Holy Ghost were only so many different manifestations and names of one and the same divine being. He thus converted the objective and real distinction of persons (a trinity of essence) into a merely subjective and modalistic view (the trinity of manifestation). See, however, MONARCHIANS; SABELLIANISM. Compare also the articles HYPOSTA-SIS and TRINITY.

Modality (from Lat. *modus*), a philosophical term applied by Kant, who, in treating of our judgments, reduced them to the four heads of quantity, quality, relation, and *modality.* In reference to modality, he teaches, they are either problematic, or assertory, or apodictical. Hence the category of *modality* includes possibility and impossibility, existence and non-existence, necessity or contingency. But existence and non-existence should have no place; the contingent and the necessary are not different from being. Kant was not, however, the first to use the term modality. Aristotle may not have used it himself in the four *modal* propositions which he defined and opposed (Περὶ ἑρμηνείας, c. 12–14), but it is to be found among his commentators and the scholastic philosophers. See Krauth's Fleming, *Vocabulary of Philos.* (N. Y., Sheldon & Co.) p. 320, 321; *Dict. des Sciences Philosoph.* s. v.

Modena, formerly a sovereign duchy of Upper Italy, and now a part of the united kingdom, is situated between Parma, Lombardy, Venice, the Papal States, Tuscany, and the Adriatic Ocean, and covers an area of about 966 square miles, with 273,231 inhabitants in 1885).

The ancient history of Modena affords evidence that it enjoyed at an early period a considerable degree of prosperity; the splendor, wealth, and arts of its capital of like name, being mentioned by Cicero, Pliny, and Strabo. In modern times Modena has shared, more or less, the various vicissitudes which befell Italy, and participated in the great internecine feuds of the country. In 960 a member of the great house of Este was proclaimed marquis of Modena, and in 1452 the then reigning marquis was created duke by the emperor Frederick III. In 1797 Modena formed part of the Cisalpine Republic, but was restored in 1814 by the congress of Vienna to the reigning family. The duchy had at that time an area of 2310 square miles, and a population of 586,000. In 1848 the duke of Modena was temporarily deprived of his rights; and in 1859 the population definitively expelled their unpopular ruler, who carried off all the property and valuables within his reach, including the silver handles of the palace doors. In the beginning of March, 1860, a plebiscitum declared in favor of annexation to the kingdom of Sardinia, which is now included in Italy as a united kingdom.

In ecclesiastical history, Modena figures quite prominently during the Reformatory movement of the 16th century. The learned Sicilian, Paola Ricci, labored there successfully in 1540, and the Roman bishop of the diocese, cardinal Morone, at one time gave the country up as Lutheran. The duchess herself, Renata de Ferrara, a sister of Francis I of France, greatly distinguished herself as a promoter of the new doctrines. But the Inquisition came, and from its introduction dates the wane of Protestantism in Modena. See INQUISITION; ITALY.

Modena, Barnaba da, an esteemed Italian painter of the school of Modena, who flourished in the 14th century, was among the first artists who obtained any reputation in Piedmont. Two pictures exist in the Conventuals of Pisa by this master, one in the church and the other in the convent; both portray the *Virgin*. In the second the coronation is represented, and the Virgin is seen surrounded by St. Francis and other saints of his order. Della Valle speaks in high terms of a third picture of the *Virgin*, remaining in the possession of the Conventuals of Alba, which he says is in a grander style than any contemporary works; and he states that it bears the date 1357. Morrona extols the beauty of his heads and the delicacy of his coloring, and prefers him to Giotto. Hardly anything is known of his personal history. See Lanzi, *Hist. of Painting*, transl. by Roscoe (Lond. 1847, 3 vols. 8vo), ii, 345; iii, 292; Spooner, *Biog. Hist. of the Fine Arts* (N. Y. 1865, 2 vols. 8vo), ii. 370.

Modena, Leon da. See LEON.

Modena, Niccoletto da, an old Italian painter and engraver, flourished at Modena about the beginning of the 16th century. He is principally known as one of the first engravers of Italy. His plates are well designed, but are rudely executed. The principal productions are, *The Adoration of the Shepherds; St. Sebastian*, with Niccoletto on a tablet; *St. Jerome; St. George*; a full-length figure of *Christ; St. Sebastian*, with his arms tied over his head to a column, and his body pierced with six arrows. Another *St. Sebastian*, larger than the preceding, and pierced with three arrows. *David with the head of Goliath; St. Anthony; The vestal Lucca carrying water in a sieve to prove her virginity; St. Catharine*, and a *Saint* bearing a large bag on his back. The date of his death is unknown. See Jameson and Eastlake, *Hist. of our Lord* (Lond. 1864, 2 vols. 8vo), ii, 57; Lanzi, *Hist. of Painting*, transl. by Roscoe (Lond. 1847, 3 vols. 8vo), i, 107; ii, 346; Spooner, *Biog. Hist. of the Fine Arts* (N. Y. 1865, 2 vols. 8vo), ii, 571.

Modena, Pellegrino da, an Italian painter, the most eminent of the Modena school, was born about the middle of the 15th century. He is often called *Pellegrino Munari*, and sometimes *Aretusi*, but is commonly known by the title prefixed to this notice. According to Lanzi, he first studied with his father, who was also an artist of considerable repute, and in 1509 painted an *altar-piece* for the church of St. Giovanni at Modena, which gained him no little reputation. At this time the fame of Raphael reached Modena, and Pellegrino at once journeyed to Rome, and placed himself under the instruction of that sublime master, who, perceiving the remarkable talent of his pupil, employed him as assistant in the famous works in the Vatican. At first Pellegrino painted in the open galleries, but afterwards executed from the designs of Raphael the *History of Jacob* and the *History of Solomon* in the Vatican, which Lanzi says were painted entirely after the manner of his master, and in a style almost incomparable. After the death of Raphael he continued to paint at Rome from his own designs, and executed some admirable works for the different churches, particularly a work in fresco in the church of St. Giacomo, entitled the *History of St. James*. After its completion he returned to Modena. Here he painted his most celebrated picture of the *Nativity of our Lord*, in the church of St. Paolo, which is characterized by Lanzi as "breathing in every part the

graces of him of Urbino." Pellegrino met with a tragic death at the hands of some Modenese, who turned their fury against him because his son had slain an antagonist in a quarrel, in 1523. See Lanzi, *Hist. of Painting*, transl. by Roscoe (Lond. 1847, 3 vols. 8vo), i, 397; ii, 350; Spooner, *Biog. Hist. of the Fine Arts* (N. Y. 1865, 2 vols. 8vo), ii, 570.

Moderate. To *moderate a call*, in the Church of Scotland, is, under the presidency of one of the clergy, to publicly announce and give in an invitation to a minister or licentiate to take the charge of a parish; which announcement or invitation, thus given in the hearing of the assembled parishioners, is regarded as the first legal step towards a settlement.

Moderates is a name applied to those theologians of the Church of Scotland who favor patronage (prohibited by the Parliament of 1692, and in the Books of Discipline) and a *moderate* orthodoxy, i. e. a mitigation of the strictness of the old confessions. The first Moderates flourished in the middle of the last century, under the Robertsonian administration (1752–82). As early as 1720, however, the Moderate party had its influence in the Church, as is apparent from the five propositions which were condemned in a council held at that time to suppress Antinomianism [see MARROW CONTROVERSY]; and the secession of 1734 was no doubt provoked by the ascendency of the Neonomians, afterwards leaders in the party of the *Moderates*. In many respects the Moderates are the "Latitudinarians" of the Church of Scotland. Many of them adopted the ethical principles of Francis Hutcheson (q. v.). The leading pulpit orator among the Moderates—Dr. Hugh Blair—deficient in evangelical thought and feeling, actually defended Hume against the Assembly; and well he might, for had not his party declared (in 1720) that *holiness is not necessary to salvation?* There were, however, many Moderates of an evangelical spirit, and these prepared the way for the *Free-church movement*. See SCOTLAND, CHURCH OF. (J. H. W.)

Moderation imports a proper government of passion and pleasure, preventing extremes of any kind. The presence of moderation is manifest in the exhibition of a calm and temperate frame of mind. "Moderation," says Blair, "ought to take place in our wishes, pursuits, expectations, pleasures, and passions."

(1.) We should be moderate in our *wishes*. The active mind of man is seldom or never satisfied with its present condition, how prosperous soever. Originally formed for a wider range of objects, for a higher sphere of enjoyments, it finds itself, in every situation of fortune, straitened and confined. Sensible of deficiency in its state, it is ever sending forth the fond desire, the aspiring wish after something beyond what is enjoyed at present. Assuredly there is nothing unlawful in our wishing to be freed from whatever is disagreeable, and to obtain a fuller enjoyment of the comforts of life. But when these wishes are not tempered by reason they are in danger of precipitating us into extravagance and folly. If we suffer our fancy to create to itself worlds of ideal happiness; if we feed our imagination with plans of opulence and splendor far beyond our rank; if we fix to our wishes certain stages of high advancement, or certain degrees of uncommon reputation or distinction, as the sole stations of felicity, the assured consequence will be that we shall become unhappy in our present state, unfit for acting the part and discharging the duties that belong to it; we shall discompose the peace and order of our minds, and foment many hurtful passions. Here, then, let moderation begin its reign, by bringing within reasonable bounds the wishes that we form. As soon as they become extravagant, let us check them by proper reflections on the fallacious nature of those objects which the world hangs out to allure desire.

(2.) We should be moderate in our *pursuits*. When the active pursuits in which we engage rise beyond moderation, they fill the world with great disorders, often with flagrant crimes. Yet all ambition is not to be condemned, nor ought high purposes on every occasion to be checked. Some men are formed by nature for rising into conspicuous stations of life. In following the impulse of their minds, and properly exerting the talents with which God has blessed them, there is room for ambition to act in a laudable sphere, and to become the instrument of much public good. But this may safely be pronounced, that the bulk of men are ready to overrate their own abilities, and to imagine themselves equal to higher things than they were ever designed for by nature. We should therefore be sober in fixing our aims and planning our destined pursuits. We should beware of being led aside from the plain path of sound and moderate conduct by those false lights which self-flattery is always ready to hang out. By aiming at a mark too high we may fall short of what it was in our power to have reached. Instead of attaining to eminence, we may not only expose ourselves to derision, but bring upon our heads manifold disasters.

(3.) We should be moderate in our *expectations.* When our state is flourishing, and the course of events proceeds according to our wish, we ought not to suffer our minds to be vainly lifted up. We ought not to flatter ourselves with high prospects of the increasing favors of the world and the continuing applause of men. By want of moderation in our hopes we not only increase dejection when disappointment comes, but we accelerate disappointment; we bring forward with greater speed disagreeable changes in our state. For the natural consequence of presumptuous expectation is rashness in conduct. He who indulges in confident security of course neglects due precautions against the dangers that threaten him; and his fall will be foreseen and predicted. He not only exposes himself unguarded to dangers, but he multiplies them against himself. By presumption and vanity he either provokes enmity or incurs contempt. A temperate spirit and moderate expectations are the best safeguard of the mind in this uncertain and changing state. They enable us to pass through the world with most comfort. When we rise in the world they contribute to our elevation, and if we fall they render our fall the lighter.

(4.) We should be moderate in our *pleasures.* It is an invariable law of our present condition that every pleasure which is pursued to excess converts itself into poison. What was intended for the cordial and refreshment of human life, through want of moderation, we turn to its bane. No sooner do we pass the line which temperance has drawn than pernicious effects succeed. Could the monuments of death be laid open to our view, they would read a lecture in favor of moderation much more powerful than any that the most eloquent preacher can give. We should behold the graves peopled with the victims of intemperance; we should behold those chambers of darkness hung round on every side with the trophies of luxury, drunkenness, and sensuality. So numerous should we find those martyrs of iniquity that it may safely be asserted where war or pestilence has slain its thousands intemperate pleasure has slain its ten thousands.

(5.) We should be moderate in all our *passions.* This exercise of moderation is the more requisite because every passion in human nature has of itself a tendency to run into excess. All passion implies a violent emotion of mind. Of course it is apt to derange the regular course of our ideas, and to produce confusion within. Of some passions, such as anger and resentment, the excess is so obviously dangerous as loudly to call for moderation. He who gives himself up to the impetuosity of such passions without restraint is universally condemned. Of the insidious growth of passion, therefore, we have great reason to beware. Let us be persuaded that moments of passion are always moments of delusion; that nothing truly is what it then seems to be; that all the opinions which we then form are erroneous; and that all the judgments which we then pass are ex-

travagant. Let moderation accustom us to wait till the fumes of passion are spent; till the mist which it has raised begins to be dissipated. On no occasion let us imagine that strength of mind is shown by violence of passion. It is the strength of one who is in the delirium of a fever, or under the disease of madness. True strength of mind is shown in governing and resisting passion, and acting on the most trying occasions according to the dictates of conscience and right reason. See Blair, *Sermons,* vol. ii, serm. xlii.

Moderator is the name of an ecclesiastical officer in the Presbyterian churches. His duty is to preside over a meeting or an assembly of ministers, to regulate their proceedings in session, and to declare the vote (see *Presbyt. Confession,* p. 366 sq.). *To moderate in a call* is to preside over the election of a minister. When the attempt was made to introduce episcopacy into Scotland, one plan was to have *perpetual moderators* for presbyteries—a bishop or his vicar to be chosen to the office.

Moderatus OF GADES (*Moderatus Gaditanus*), a distinguished exponent of the neo-Pythagorean school of philosophy, surnamed after his native place, flourished during the reign of the emperor Nero (A.D. 54–68). He collected all the MSS. extant on the philosophical views of Pythagoras, and embodied them in his works: Lib. xi, *De placitis sectæ Pythagoricæ;* Lib. v, *Scholarum Pythagoricarum,* which are unfortunately no longer extant. (Simply a fragment of his is preserved by Stobæus, *Eclog.* p. 3.) According to Porphyry (*Vita Pythag.* § 32 et 53), Moderatus sought to justify the incorporation into Pythagoreanism of Platonic and neotheological doctrines, through the hypothesis that the ancient Pythagoreans themselves intentionally expressed the highest truths in signs, and for that purpose made use of numbers. The number *one* was the symbol of unity and equality, and of the cause of the harmony and duration of all things, while *two* was the symbol of difference and inequality, of division and change, etc. See NEO-PYTHAGOREANISM. Moderatus is reputed to have been a man of considerable eloquence, and not only to have been popular in his day, but to have found an imitator, to some extent, in Iamblichus (q. v.). See Schoell, *Histoire de la littérature Grecque,* vi, 54; Ueberweg, *Hist. Philos.* i, 232 sq. (J. H. W.)

Modern Question, The, is a term used by some to designate a controversy on the doctrine of *salvation.* The question raised is, "Whether it be the duty of all to whom the Gospel is preached to repent and believe in Christ?" It is called the *Modern* question because it is supposed never to have been agitated before the early part of the last century. The following is an abstract of Dr. Ryland's history of the controversy, which he considers as having originated in Northamptonshire, England, in the Baptist churches in which Mr. Davis, of Rothwell, preached; though it does not appear that the latter took an active part in it. Mr. Maurice, his successor, even strenuously opposed the negative side of the question, which had been maintained by some of Mr. Davis's admirers, particularly by Mr. Lewis Weyman, of Kimbolton, to whom Mr. Maurice wrote a reply, which, Mr. Maurice dying before it was completed, was published by the celebrated Mr. Bradbury. This was between 1737 and 1739. Mr. Gutteridge, of Oundle, also took the affirmative side; and in 1743 Mr. Brine the negative; as did also the learned Dr. Gill, though he did not write expressly on the subject. The question thus started agitated the Baptists down to the time of Andrew Fuller, who very ably supported the positive side, viz., that "faith is the duty of all men, although, through the depravity of human nature, men *will not* believe till regenerated by the Holy Spirit." On the other side it was contended that "faith was not a duty, but a grace," the exercise of which was not required till it was bestowed. Mr. Fuller, holding that it is both, published *The Gospel worthy of all Acceptation, or the Duty of all Men to believe in Jesus*

Christ. "The leading design of this performance (says Mr. Morris) is to prove that men are under indispensable obligations to believe whatever God says, and to do whatever he commands; and a Saviour being revealed in the Gospel, the *law* in effect requires those to whom he is made known to believe in him, seeing it insists upon obedience to the whole will of God; that the inability of man to comply with the divine requirements is wholly of a *moral* nature, and consists in the prevalence of an evil disposition, which, being *voluntary*, is in the highest degree criminal." On this subject Mr. Fuller was attacked by Mr. Button, a supralapsarian, on the one hand, and by Mr. Daniel Taylor, an Arminian, on the other; to whom he replied by *A Defence* of his former tract, and thus ended the controversy. The late Mr. Robinson shrewdly remarks that those ministers who will not use *applications*, lest they should rob the Holy Spirit of the honor of *applying* the Word, should, for the same reason, not use *explications*, lest they should deprive him of the honor of *illustrating* it. See Ryland, *Life of Fuller*, p. 6–11; Morris, *Life of Fuller*, ch. ii; Wilson, *Dissenting Churches*, ii, 572; Ivimey, *English Baptists*, iii, 262. See SALVATION.

Modestus (1), ST., an apostle of the Church in Carinthia, flourished in the 8th century. He was one of six whom bishop Vigilius of Salzburg sent to Carinthia to preach the glad tidings. Modestus lived but a short time after his arrival in Carinthia, but the success of his mission is manifest in the conversion of the princes of the country, who are said to have espoused the cause of Christianity at this time. See CARINTHIA. Modestus is commemorated in the Latin Church as a saint. (2.) Another Modestus flourished in the 7th century (616–626) as patriarch of the Church of Jerusalem. He is reputed as the restorer of the holy church at Jerusalem, which was destroyed by the Persians under Chosroes II in 614.

Modesty (Lat. *modestia*, from *modus*, a measure) is sometimes used to denote humility, and sometimes to express chastity. The Greek word *kosmios* signifies neat, or well arranged. It suggests the idea of simple elegance. Modesty, therefore, consists in purity of sentiment and manners, inclining us to abhor the least appearance of vice and indecency, and to fear doing anything which will justly incur censure. An excess of modesty is called bashfulness or diffidence, and the want of it impertinence or impudence. There is also a false or vicious modesty, which influences a man to do anything that is ill or indiscreet; such as, through fear of offending his companions, he runs into their follies or excesses; or it is a false modesty which restrains a man from doing what is good or laudable, such as being ashamed to speak of religion, and to be seen in the exercises of piety and devotion.

Modi or **Mode** (i. e. *courageous*, from a root cognate with the Danish *mod*, and the German *muth*, "courage") is in northern mythology the name of a son of Thor, who, the legend goes, is to survive the destruction of the world at Ragnaröck, and in the renovated world will share with Mogni the possession of their father's hammer, and engage in the extermination of all strife. See Thorpe, *Northern Mythology*, vol. i; Keyes, *Religion of the Northmen*.

Modigliana, FRANCISCO, a Bolognese painter, flourished about the beginning of the 17th century. Lanzi says he "was not remarkably powerful, nor always consistent with himself, but very graceful and beautiful, and deserving a place in our lexica." His works at Urbino, where he is known under the name of Francisco da Forli, are a picture of *Christ taken down from the Cross*, in oil, at St. Croce, and some *Angels*, in fresco, at St. Lucia. His finest works, however, are in the churches at Forli and Rimini, among which are *Adam driven from Eden*, the *Deluge*, and the *Tower of Babel*. He died suddenly, leaving his work imperfect, but it was afterwards continued by Arrigoni, who painted the *Death of Abel* in the same place. See Lanzi,

Hist. of Painting, transl. by Roscoe (Lond. 1847, 3 vols. 8vo), iii, 57.

Mo'din (Μωδεῖν v. r. Μωδεείμ, Μωδιείμ, Μωδαείμ, and in ch. ii Μωδεείν; Josephus, Μωδιείμ, and once Μωδεείν; Vulg. *Modin*: the Jewish form is, in the Mishna, המודיעים, in Joseph ben-Gorion, ch. xx, המודעית; the Syriac version of Maccabees agrees with the Mishna, except in the absence of the article, and in the usual substitution of *r* for *d*, *Mora'im*), a place not mentioned in either the Old or New Testament, though rendered immortal by its connection with the history of the Jews in the interval between the two. It was the native city of the Maccabæan family (1 Macc. xiii, 25), and as a necessary consequence contained their ancestral sepulchre (τάφος) (ii, 70; ix, 19). Hither Mattathias removed from Jerusalem, where up to that time he seems to have been residing, at the commencement of the Antiochian persecution (ii, 1). It was here that he struck the first blow of resistance, by slaying on the heathen altar which had been erected in the place both the commissioner of Antiochus and a recreant Jew whom he had induced to sacrifice, and then demolishing the altar. Mattathias himself, and subsequently his sons Judas and Jonathan, were buried in the family tomb, and over them Simon erected a structure which is minutely described in the book of Maccabees (xiii, 25–30), and, with less detail, by Josephus (*Ant.* xiii, 6, 6), but the restoration of which has hitherto proved as difficult a puzzle as that of the mausoleum of Artemisia.

At Modin the Maccabæan armies encamped on the eves of two of their most memorable victories—that of Judas over Antiochus Eupator (2 Macc. xiii, 14), and that of Simon over Cendebæus (1 Macc. xvi, 4)—the last battle of the venerable chief before his assassination. The only indication of the position of the place to be gathered from the above notices is contained in the last, from which we may infer that it was near "the plain" (τὸ πεδίον), i. e. the great maritime lowland of Philistia (ver. 5). By Eusebius and Jerome (*Onomast.* Μηδεείμ, Modim) it is specified as near Diospolis, i. e. Lydda; while the notice in the Mishna (*Pesachim*, ix, 2), and the comments of Bartenora and Maimonides, state that it was fifteen (Roman) miles from Jerusalem. At the same time the description of the monument seems to imply (though for this see below) that the spot was so lofty as to be visible from the sea, and so near that even the details of the sculpture were discernible therefrom. All these conditions, except the last, are tolerably fulfilled in either of the two sites called *Latrûn* and *Kubâb*. The former of these is, by the shortest road—that through Wady Ali—exactly fifteen Roman miles from Jerusalem; it is about eight English miles from Lydd, fifteen from the Mediterranean, and nine or ten from the River Rubin, on which it is probable that Cedron—the position of Cendebæus in Simon's battle—stood. Kubâb is a couple of miles farther from Jerusalem, and therefore nearer to Lydd and to the sea, on the most westerly spur of the hills of Benjamin. Both are lofty, and both apparently—Latrûn certainly—command a view of the Mediterranean. In favor of Latrûn are the extensive ancient remains with which the top of the hill is said to be covered (Robinson, *Bib. Res.* iii, 151; Tobler, *Dritte Wand.* p. 186), though of their date and particulars we have at present no accurate information. The foundations of the fortress appear to be of the Roman age, or perhaps earlier, though the upper parts exhibit pointed arches and light architecture of a much later date. The view from the summit is commanding, and embraces the whole plain to Joppa and the Mediterranean beyond. The name Latron appears to have arisen in the 16th century, from the legend which made this the birthplace of the penitent thief—"Castrum boni *Latronis*" (Quaresmius, ii, 12; Porter, *Hand-book*, p. 285; Reland, p. 901; Thomson, *Land and Book*, ii, 308). Kubâb appears to possess no ruins, but, on the other hand, its name may retain a trace of the monument. Ewald (*Gesch.* iv, 350, note) suggests that the name Modin may be still surviving in *Deir Ma'in.* But this is questionable on philological grounds; and the position of Deir Ma'in is less in accordance with the facts than that of the two named in the text. The mediæval and modern tradition (see Robinson, ii, 7) places Modin at *Soba,* an eminence south of Kuriet el-Enab; but this being not more than seven miles from Jerusalem, while it is as much as twenty-five from Lydd and thirty from the sea, and also far removed from the plain of Philistia, is at variance with every one of the conditions implied in the records. It has found advocates in our own day in M. de Saulcy (*L'Art Judaïque,* etc., p. 377 sq.) and M. Salzmann (*Jérusalem, Étude,* etc., p. 37, 38; where the lively account would be more satisfactory if it were less encumbered with mistakes), the latter of whom explored chambers there which may have been tombs, though he admits that there was nothing to prove it. A suggestive fact, which Dr. Robinson first pointed out, is the want of unanimity in the accounts of the mediæval travellers, some of whom, as William of Tyre (viii, 1), place Modin in a position near Emmaus-Nicopolis, Nob, and Lydda. M. Mislin also—usually so vehement in favor of the traditional sites—has recommended further investigation. If it should turn out that the expression of the book of Maccabees as to the monument being visible from the sea has been misinterpreted, then one impediment to the reception of Soba will be removed; but it is difficult to account for the origin of the tradition in the teeth of those which remain.

The descriptions of the tomb by the author of the book of Maccabees and Josephus, who had both apparently seen it, will be most conveniently compared by being printed together:

1 Macc. xxiii, 27-30.	Josephus, *Ant.* xiii, 6, 6.
"And Simon made a building over the sepulchre of his father and his brethren, and raised it aloft to view with polished stone behind and before. And he set up upon it seven pyramids, one against another, for his father and his mother and his four brethren. And on these he made engines of war, and set great pillars round about, and on the pillars he made suits of armor for a perpetual memory; and by the suits of armor thus carved, so that they might be seen by all that sail on the sea. This sepulchre he made at Modin, and it stands unto this day."	"And Simon built a very large monument to his father and his brethren of white and polished stone. And he raised it up to a great and conspicuous height, and threw cloisters around, and set up pillars of a single stone, a work wonderful to behold: and near to these he built seven pyramids to his parents and his brothers, one for each, terrible to behold both for size and beauty. And these things are preserved even to this day."

The monuments are said by Eusebius (*ut sup.*) to have been still shown when he wrote—A.D. cir. 320. Any restoration of the structure from so imperfect an account as the above can never be anything more than conjecture. Something has been already attempted under MACCABEES (q. v.). But in its absence one or two questions present themselves.

(1.) The "ships" ($\pi\lambda o \tilde{i} a$, *naves*). The sea and its pursuits were so alien to the ancient Jews, and the life of the Maccabæan heroes who preceded Simon was—if we except their casual relations with Joppa and Jamnia and the battle-field of the maritime plain—so unconnected therewith, that it is difficult not to suppose that the word is corrupted from what it originally was. This was the view of J. D. Michaelis, but he does not propose any satisfactory word in substitution for $\pi\lambda o \tilde{i} a$ (see his suggestion in Grimm, ad loc.). True, Simon appears to have been to a certain extent alive to the importance of commerce to his country, and he is especially commemorated for having acquired the harbor of Joppa, and thus opened an inlet for the isles of the sea (1 Macc. xiv, 5). But it is difficult to see the connection between this and the placing of ships on a monument to his father and brothers, whose memorable deeds had been of a different description. It is perhaps more

feasible to suppose that the sculptures were intended to be symbolical of the departed heroes. In this case it seems not improbable that during Simon's intercourse with the Romans he had seen and been struck with their war-galleys, no inapt symbols of the fierce and rapid career of Judas. How far such symbolical representation was likely to occur to a Jew of that period is another question.

(2.) The distance at which the "ships" were to be seen. Here again, when the necessary distance of Modin from the sea—Latrûn, fifteen miles; Kubâb, thirteen; Lydda itself, ten — and the limited size of the sculptures are considered, the doubt inevitably arises whether the Greek text of the book of Maccabees accurately represents the original. De Saulcy (*L'Art Judaïque,* p. 377) ingeniously suggests that the true meaning is, not that the sculptures could be discerned from the vessels in the Mediterranean, but that they were worthy to be inspected by those who were sailors by profession. Hitzig (*Gesch. des Volkes Israels,* p. 449) insists upon it (1869) that Modin is recognised in the modern little village *el-Burjh* (comp. Robinson, iii, 272), but the exact location is by recent excavations determined to be in *el-Mediyeh,* two and a quarter hours east of Lydda (*Quar. Statement* of "Palestine Exploration Fund," 1870, p. 245 sq.; 1874, p. 58 sq.).

Modius. See BUSHEL.

Modius (from Greek μόδιος, *a measure*) designates, in the language of archæological sculpture, a kind of basket frequently found in representations of heathen divinities. It was placed on their heads in imitation of the practice prevailing among the ancients, among whom the women carried in baskets on their heads sacrifices for the gods.

Modoin, or **Mautwin,** a noted early French ecclesiastic, was born towards the latter part of the 8th century. In his early manhood he was a priest connected with St. George's church at Lyons. Later he was bishop of Autun. The first mention of his name in the Church records of Autun occurs in 815. Soon afterwards he was recognised as one of the leading prelates in the empire. Louis "le Debonnaire," in his disgrace and adversity, had no adherent more faithful than Modoin, whose credit at the court of Charles the Bald was equally high. When Pepin was driven out of Aquitaine, Charles the Bald divided that kingdom into three governments, the designated capitals of which were, respectively, Limoges, Clermont, and Angoulême. The ecclesiastical district of Clermont was then assigned to bishop Modoin. Later, after the deposition of Agobard, archbishop of Lyons, Modoin took an active part in the administration of the archiepiscopal see. Florus reproaches him with undue firmness in his treatment of the Lyonnese clergy. The reverend Rouvier mentions Modoin as being numbered among the abbés of Moutier-Saint-Jean, in the diocese of Langres. In the 9th century it was not uncommon to meet bishops engaged in the same pursuits with abbés. When Theodulfe, bishop of Orleans, was in prison at Angers, he sent a poetical composition to Modoin, begging him to interfere in his favor. Modoin, in reply, indited a short poem, his only literary work extant. He died about 842. See *Gallia Christ.* vol. iv, col. 359; *Hist. Littér. de la France,* iv, 547.

Modus, in ecclesiastical law, signifies an exemption from the payment of tithes, and is of two kinds: first, a partial exemption, when it is called a *modus decimandi;* secondly, a total exemption, when it is called a *modus de non decimando.* There is a third species of exemption, called a *real composition,* where an agreement is made between the owner of lands and the parson or vicar, with the consent of the patron and ordinary, that the lands specified shall be exempt from tithes on such considerations as are contained in the stipulation, such as land or other real recompense given in lieu and satisfaction of the tithes to be relinquished. The *modus* *decimandi* is that which is generally meant when the term *modus* is used. It is defined to be a custom of tithing in a particular manner, different from that which the general law prescribes; and the custom must have existed from time immemorial. The modes of tithing established by these customs are exceedingly various: sometimes it is a compensation in work and labor, as that the incumbent shall have only the twelfth cock of hay, and not the tenth, in consideration of the landowner making it for him; sometimes it is a less quantity of tithe in a more perfect, in lieu of a larger quantity in a crude and imperfect state, as a couple of fowls in lieu of tithe eggs; sometimes, and more frequently, it consists in a pecuniary compensation, as twopence an acre for the tithe of land.

The *modus de non decimando* is an absolute exemption from tithes. It exists in four cases: 1. The ruler may prescribe that he and his progenitors have never paid tithes for ancient crown lands, and this prescription will be good. 2. One Church officer does not pay tithes to another officer his superior, nor the superior to the inferior, according to the rule that *ecclesia ecclesiæ decimas solvere non debet*. 3. An ecclesiastical person, as a bishop, may prescribe to be exempt from paying tithes on the ground that the lands belong to the bishopric, and that neither he nor his predecessors have ever paid them. 4. The abbeys and monasteries at the time of their dissolution were possessed of large estates of land, a great part of which was held tithe-free, either by prescription or by unity of possession, which was, in fact, no more than prescription, or by the pope's bull of exemption, or by a real composition. Thus in England, for example, the statute of 31 Henry VIII, c. 13, which dissolved the larger abbeys, enacted that all persons who should come to the possession of the lands of an abbey then dissolved should hold them tithe-free, in as ample a manner as the abbeys themselves had formerly held them. The lands which belonged to the Order of the Knights of St. John of Jerusalem and to the Order of the Cistercians are within the protection of this statute; and those of them, consequently, which were tithe-free before they came into the hands of the king still continue tithe-free, in whosesoever hands they may now be. Some lands have been made tithe-free by special legislative acts. See Blackstone, *Commentaries*, ii, 28; Selden, *History of Tithes*, ch. xiii; Burton, *Compendium of the Law of Real Property*, p. 367 sq.

Moebius (or Möbius), GEORG, a Lutheran divine, was born at Laucha, Thuringia, Dec. 18, 1616; studied at Jena and Leipsic; became rector of the gymnasium at Mercersburg in 1647; professor and doctor of theology at Leipsic in 1668; and died Nov. 28, 1697. He edited and enlarged Crusius's *Grammatica Græca*, and was the author of numerous essays in Latin on Biblical and theological topics, which were afterwards published in a collective edition (Leips. 1699, 4to). See Jöcher, *Gelehrten Lexikon*, s. v.

Moëd. See TALMUD.

Moedsognir, in Norse mythology, is the name of the highest class of pigmies who dwell in stones.

Moehler. See MÖHLER.

Moelart, JACOB, a Dutch painter, was born at Dort in the year 1649. He was a pupil of Nicholas Maas, and gained an enviable reputation as a historical painter, though he is better known by his portraits. Spooner mentions two religious works by this artist — *Pharaoh and his Host drowned in the Red Sea*, and *Moses striking the Rock*. He died in 1727.

Moeller. See MÖLLER.

Mœso Gothic Version. See GOTHIC VERSION.

Mo'ëth (Μωίθ, Vulg. *Medius*), a Levite, "son of Sabban," who aided Ezra in conveying the bullion from Babylon (1 Esdr. viii, 63); evidently the "NOADIAH (q. v.) son of Binnui" of the Heb. text (Ezra viii, 33).

Moffatt, JOSIAH, a Presbyterian minister, was born in Chester County, S. C., May, 1836. His parents were godly people, and reared their children in the nurture and admonition of the Lord. He prosecuted his classical studies privately for two years, entered Erskine College, Due West, S. C., in 1852, and graduated with honor in 1859. The next two years he spent in general reading at the libraries of his alma mater. He was received by the Second Presbytery as a student of theology in April, 1861; licensed in 1864; and subsequently preached in congregations in the First and Second Presbyteries, making Due West his home. In 1865 he returned to his former home in Chester County, where he remained until his death, March 18, 1867. Mr. Moffatt was a man of solid intellect. His writings were excellent specimens of composition, and full of the marrow of divinity. Benevolence and humility were prominent features of his character. See Wilson, *Presb. Hist. Almanac*, 1868, p. 393.

Mogila(s), PETER, a distinguished Russian prelate, was born in Moldavia very near the close of the 16th century (about 1597). He studied at the University of Paris and other high schools, afterwards entered the Polish army, and greatly distinguished himself. Becoming sober-minded, he decided to devote himself to the service of the Church, was made a monk at Kief in 1625, and rapidly rose in favor. In 1629 he was elected archimandrite of his monastery, and in 1633 was elevated to the rank of metropolitan of Kief, Galicia, and Little Russia. Mogila was the first to introduce at the study of theology at Kief the developments which it had acquired in the European universities. Indeed, Mogila is to-day honored annually by a panegyrical oration at the Academy of Kief, in recognition of his services to that institution of learning. He arranged and improved the courses of study in every particular; established, among other advantages, three classes in philosophy and theology in the Latin and Polish languages; obtained from the Polish government permission to erect a printing-press, invited many learned men to the academy, and settled upon them sources of revenue which had formerly gone to the metropolitan; and, besides affording all these advantages, gave them his own library, which was considered a very rare and valuable collection of books. He died Dec. 31, 1646. To confirm the views and feelings of the Oriental Church in opposition to the encroachments of Roman and Protestant elements, Mogila wrote a *Confession of Faith* (Ὀρθόδοξος ὁμολογία τῆς καθολικῆς καὶ ἀποστολικῆς ἐκκλησίας τῆς ἀνατολικῆς), which occupies an important place in the history of the Russian Church. In this the doctrines of the Church are presented in the simple manner and style of the ancient Church, but in accordance also with the latest developments they had gradually attained; and as the reception of the work was ranked among the three cardinal theological virtues, it has become prominent in the practical system of the Church (Hase, *Ch. Hist.* p. 481). "The Eastern churches," says M. Boulgakof, bishop of Vinitzi, "had heretofore no symbolic books of their own in which they could find, on matters of faith, sufficient authoritative information and direction; no systematic exposition and apology of their dogmas; they had to be satisfied with short definitions, given by œcumenical and local councils, and with the rules of the fathers named in the council *in Trullo*. For anything further they had to refer to the other writings of the fathers, which did not possess the same authority. The *Confession of Faith* of Peter Mogila, examined and approved by two councils—that of Kief in 1640, and that of Jassy in 1643—and further endorsed by the four œcumenical patriarchs, and by the Russian patriarchs Joachim and Adrian, became the first symbolic book of the Eastern Church." This work, which remains to this day the text-book of the Russo-Greek Church in dogmatic theology, went through numerous editions in Russian, was translated into Greek (Amst. 1662), Latin (Leips. 1695), and German (Berlin, 1727, and Breslau, 1751), and has furnished the basis for several catechisms in different Greek churches. See CONFESSIONS OF FAITH. Mogila published also a *Catechism* (Kief, 1645), and some pamphlets. A work containing biographical sketches of the saints, in the Slavonic language, he undertook, but did not bring to completion. But Mogila gained some distinction also as a poet, and made dramas, which were acted by the pupils of his academy; one of them, on the *Nativity of Christ*, was for a long time very popular. See *Hist. de la Hiérarchie Russe*, iii, 735; *Dictionnaire des Auteurs Ecclésiastiques Russes*, s. v.; Otto, *Hist. of Russian Literature* (Oxf. 1839, 8vo), p. 321 sq.; Brühl, *Russische Studien zur Theologie u. Gesch.* (Münst. 1857–58); Gerebtzof, *Essai sur l'Histoire de la Civilisation en Russie*; Haag, *Hist. des Dogmes Chrétiens*, i, 458; Kimmel, *Libri symbolici ecclesiæ Orientalis* (Jena, 1843, 8vo), p. 56. See GREEK CHURCH; RUSSIA. (J. H. W.)

Mogtasilah (i. e. *those who wash themselves*) is a name which mediæval Arabic writers gave to a sect of Christians said to have flourished on the eastern shore of the Dead Sea. Recent investigations render it probable that they were the *Zabians* (from צבע = טבע, βαπτίζειν, to wash), or *Mendæans* (q. v.) of the present day.

Mogul, GREAT, the popular designation of the emperor of Delhi, as the impersonation of the powerful empire established in Hindustan by the Mongols, who were called *Moguls* by the Persians. The first Great Mogul was Baber, the great-grandson of Timûr, who founded the Mongul empire in Hindustan in 1526. In 1803 the Great Mogul was deprived of his throne; in 1827, of even the appearance of authority, becoming a mere pensioner of the British; and in 1858, Mohammed Bahadûr, the last of the dynasty, was condemned, and transported for complicity in the Indian mutiny. See MONGOLS.

Mohammed or **Mahomet** (written also *Mahommed* or *Mahommet*, and *Muhamed* or *Muhamet*, an Arabic word meaning *the predicted Messiah*; applied to him in allusion to Hag. ii, 7; but formerly called, according to a tradition quoted by Halabi, *Kotham*) was a great Arabian legislator, who not only completely changed the face of the world in his own age, but still continues to exercise a powerful influence in the civilization of the Eastern world, being best known as the founder of a religious system which has spread extensively among men, and is denominated *Islam*, or, more properly, after its founder, *Mohammedanism* (q. v.).

Sources for his Life.—Arabian literature is very rich in sources for a biography of Mohammed. Besides the Koran, which records the most important events of his life, there exist numerous collections of traditions in which the expressed views of the Arabian prophet on various incidents and relations of life are introduced; then there are biographies proper, some of which extend as far back as the first century of the Mohammedan æra. They are, it is true, written with a religious prejudice, and more or less spiced with legends, but in most cases the historical part worthy of credit is easily discerned. It must not be believed that these biographies were allowed too free a rein to fancy, or were permitted to distort facts or pass them over in perfect silence; for they had to fear being convicted of mendacity and negligence by no less an authority than the Koran itself, already collected by the contemporaries of the prophet. Still another circumstance helps the historian in determining truth, namely, that the Mohammedans rarely try to conceal the frailties of their founder, for their judgment is guided by a standard different from that of non-Mohammedans—they praise some of his deeds

and words as virtuous which we brand as infamous. They even proceed generally on the principle that Mohammed, as a privileged individual, was exempt from the common laws. Hence, notwithstanding the abundance of historical accounts on the rise of *Islam* (the proper name for the religion established by Mohammed, while its professors are called *Moslems*), and the continued lively intercourse between Mohammedans and Christians in Syria and Palestine, as well as in Egypt and Spain, the most perverted opinions on Mohammedanism and its author came to prevail among the non-Mohammedans, even in the Occident. He was represented either as a sorcerer or as an idol; some believed him the Antichrist, others a renegade cardinal. And in proportion as the later Mohammedans—especially the Persians, greedy of miracles and mysteries—rendered the historical Mohammed of the ancient Arabians scarcely recognisable by over-much adoration and proximity to the supernatural, and the more Mohammedanism spread in the Occident and threatened to become dangerous to Christianity, hatred and fear exerted themselves to disfigure Mohammed and his creed by ridiculous and absurd calumnies. Even in modern times, after several translations of Arabian biographies of Mohammed had been published, his true character was little understood. As late as 1829 a work appeared in London demonstrating, or rather aiming to demonstrate, that Mohammed was foreshadowed by the little horn which issued from the fourth monster described by the prophet Daniel. In a still later publication, the author endeavors, at a great expense of learning, to prove that Mohammed was an instrument of the devil's device and handling. But, as observed in Weil's work, *Mohammed der Prophet*, the advance of knowledge in these days requires the historical characters handed down to us from remote periods to be re-examined by the light of new and of better-classified authorities, and to be recast upon a surer and more truthful basis. See *Meth. Review*, Jan. 1889.

Among characters of world-wide celebrity, there is none other that calls more loudly for a reinvestigation of the "original sources" than that of Mohammed. Born in an obscure age, among a people whose antecedents are dimly shadowed out to us, in a country of all famous regions the least explored, his own career was a series of marvels and contradictions. While searching earnestly for truth, he taught millions of men to believe a gigantic fable; and, while tormented with doubts agonizing to his own breast, he inspired others with an invincible faith in his infallibility. With too little energy or too little ambition to support himself, except by the despised employment of a shepherd, he withstood for years the ridicule, the malice, and the furious opposition of the leaders of his own family and of the nation, and finally vanquished all their efforts. Over this extraordinary and seemingly unfathomable character the disciples and the opponents of his doctrines have alike combined to draw an additional veil of uncertainty. The first Mohammedans piously encompassed their prophet with a cloud of miracles—"the mythology," as Dr. Sprenger calls it, of Islam. Romish prelates foolishly distorted history to calumniate him; and philosophers, more impartial but equally unjust, endowed him with crimes of their own invention, such as they thought congenial to the character of an impostor. Thus, while Khadijah beheld him shaded by angels on his journey to Syria, Prideaux accuses him of robbing orphans of their patrimony, and Voltaire depicts him as yielding to the indulgence of his passions on his triumphal return to Mecca—a triumph of which the greatest glory was his clemency and forbearance. Of those who have pretended to describe this singular being, one party has studiously disguised or perverted what they knew, and another has sedulously invented what they did but suspect or hope. In fact, the great difficulty of the Arabic language, and the rarity and inaccessibility of the MSS. of early Mohammedan writers, were sufficient of themselves, if not to deter Europeans from undertaking the biography of the apostle of Islam, at least to cover the attempt, until a comparatively recent date, with the disgrace of failure. The earliest and most authentic chronicles of the rise of Mohammedanism were not known, even by name, to those who aspired to guide the opinions of Europe on that great event. Gibbon, for example, appeals to Gagnier's translation of Abulfeda, a prince who wrote in the fourteenth century, as his "best and most authentic guide." But to consider so late a historian as Abulfeda an authority at all would convict an Orientalist of the most culpable ignorance in Arabic literature. Yet before we can turn from the Mohammed as pictured by enthusiastic Musselmen, or the monks of the Middle Ages and their successors among modern writers, to the true historical Mohammed, as he comes before us after a profound and unprejudiced study of the original documents, it is necessary that we take a hasty glance at the condition of Arabia, the country that claims him as her own, at the time and previous to the birth of Mohammed.

State of Arabia previous to the Introduction of Islam. —From time immemorial the aboriginal inhabitants of the peninsula had been divided into a great number of free and wandering clans, limited communities, and petty states, whose peculiarities of character, mode of life, and political institutions, as they were mostly dependent upon local circumstances, were for centuries stamped with the same unalterable features, and had been preserved almost unchanged even from the time of the patriarchs of the book of Genesis. The mountainous table-land of central Arabia, abounding in rich pasturage and fertile valleys, but at the same time intersected and skirted with dreary wastes and sandy plains, was occupied by those roving tribes who, in opposition to the settled inhabitants, are proud of the name of Bedouin, or people of the plains. Most of them were addicted to a wandering pastoral life, but from being strongly disposed to war and chivalrous adventures, their peaceable occupations were interrupted, either by conducting a caravan of merchants, or still oftener by assailing and robbing their fellow-tribes. Every tribe was governed by the most aged or worthy sheik of that family which had been exalted above its brethren by fortune and heroic deeds, or even by eloquence and poetry. For as the heroic bards were at once the historians and moralists by whom the vices and virtues of their countrymen were impartially censured or praised, a noble enthusiasm for poetry animated those Arabs, and at an annual fair at Okhad thirty days were consecrated to poetical emulation, after which the successful poem was written in letters of gold and suspended in the temple of Mecca. These meetings, however, formed but a very feeble bond of union among the independent and hostile tribes, who only occasionally, and in times of danger and warfare, submitted to a supreme chief, or emir of emirs, and had never yet been united into one body. And the tie was still less binding on those inhabitants who, being collected in flourishing towns and cities on the coasts of the peninsula, and mostly employed in trade and agriculture, were regarded with supreme contempt by the free Bedouin as a weak and degenerate race of slaves.

Concerning the religious condition of the Arabs before the promulgation of Mohammed's doctrines, we have but scanty information. The Mohammedans themselves disdained inquiry into the idolatrous worship of their ancestors. For what we do know about it we are indebted to accidental notices of some of their deities mentioned in the Koran (q. v.), and to sundry not always trustworthy accounts diffused through the more ancient works, and not to any connected treatise upon the pagan religions of Arabia. The scanty notices of the Greeks and Romans concerning this topic are very uncertain. We must not, however, fail to mention the genealogical records, to which the Arabs attribute great importance, as auxiliary sources for the religious faith of the ancient Arabians. From these genealogical tablets we learn the names of some of their idols and the distribution of their worship; for many

personal names relate to the worshipped deities or the places where they were worshipped. Thus we are not altogether without some clew respecting Arabian polytheism, and secure the information that no one religious system prevailed throughout all Arabia, or at any given time.

Their religious worship, it would appear, consisted chiefly in the adoration of the heavenly luminaries, which were considered as so many tutelar deities of the different tribes; and among these, after the sun and moon, the planet Venus had acquired such peculiar preeminence that even to the pious Moslem Friday ever after remained the sacred day of the week. These deities, with many other images of the personified powers of nature, rudely represented by idols of every variety of shape, were principally gathered round the ancient Kaaba—the Pantheon of Arabian idolatry; and their worship was accompanied, not only with the most horrid rites and shocking ceremonies of a degraded paganism, but even with human sacrifices and cruelties of every description. Even children were immolated by some of the ruder clans to the idols, while others, as the Kendites, buried their daughters alive (*Sur.* vi, 137; xvi, 58; lxxxi, 8); and we need scarcely remark that, except a vague belief of the soul becoming transformed into an owl, and hovering round the grave, there is no indication that the Arabian idolaters believed in a future life and final retribution. (Comp. Pococke, *Specimen Historiæ Arabum*, ed. White, 1806.)

Arabian idolatry centred in Mecca, whither annual pilgrimages were made by all Arabians. See MECCA. Its temple, which tradition claimed to have been founded by Abraham and Ishmael, was, so to speak, the hotel (khan), where the most diverse idols of the various Arabian tribes were lodged. It was the object of high veneration for the whole Arabian peninsula. Every tribe had its particular deity represented here, as well as its own chief. See KAABA. But there were also many Arabs who acknowledged a supreme being, and regarded all idols as subordinate to this principal being. Some were even converts to Judaism or to Christianity, especially those who had much intercourse with Jews and Christians. As a rule, however, religious life occupied but little the minds of the Bedouin, so much engrossed with their material wants and affairs, and to this day religious fanaticism is rarely found among the children of the desert. The particular wishes of the votaries were brought before the idols and their priests, and their advice was desired; but if expectation were disappointed, the idols were broken to pieces and their priests insulted and maltreated. Besides the idolaters, in a literal sense of the word, there lived in Arabia single tribes, who worshipped the sun, moon, and other celestial bodies, or inclined to the religion of the Magians; vestiges of hero-worship, and worship of trees and stones are also traceable.

Among the foreign settlers in Arabia, we pass over in silence the few adherents of Zoroaster, scattered along the Persian Gulf, and the Sabæans, on the southern coast of the peninsula, who, even from the time of David and Solomon, stored their rich emporiums of Ophir, Saba, and afterwards Aden, with Indian merchandise, and who, as is clear from many good arguments, were undoubtedly of Hindû origin. The Christian religion had long been established in several parts of Arabia, but the Christianity of the Oriental Church at that time almost resembled paganism, being associated with monachism, and with the worship of martyrs, relics, and images. Among the heretical sectaries who, absorbed in their monophysitical and other abstruse dogmatical controversies, looked upon each other with the utmost hatred, we find particularly mentioned the Nestorians, Jacobites, Marcionites, and Manichæans, besides some other obscure sects, such as the Collyridians, who, deifying the mother of Christ, and adoring her as the third person in the Trinity, probably gave rise to the Christian tritheism so often dwelt on by the author of the Koran. The Jews were at this time in Arabia in great numbers. After the destruction of Jerusalem many of them had retired hither, where, owing to the loose connection and the jealousy of the aboriginal tribes, they had gained considerable power. Some of them, adopting the fierce manners of the desert, chose a wandering life, connected with all its dangers and adventurous strife, and a poem composed by a Jewish Bedouin has been preserved in the Hamâsa, which breathes the true spirit of Arabian chivalry (*Hamâsa*, p. 49, ed. Freytag). But in general the Jews were peacefully settled in towns and fortified castles, principally along the coast, or dispersed among the inhabitants of large cities. (Comp. Krehl, *Vorislamitische Religionen* [Leips. 1863]; *Zeitschrift d. deutsch. Morgenl. Gesellsch.* x, 61 sq.; xix, 262; xx, 284; Malcom, *History of Persia*, i, 168 sq., 180 sq.) See ARABIA.

Early Life.—Since Mohammed was by birth anything but a prince, nothing certain is known about its time, and even the oldest sources do not agree as to the date. According to the most probable reckoning, he was born in April, A.D. 571, at Mecca. This city was at that time a considerable commercial centre, where caravans from Southern Arabia, Abyssinia, Persia, and India crossed those from Egypt, Syria, and Mesopotamia, and exchanged their agricultural and industrial products. This happened particularly at the time of the pilgrimage. By descent Mohammed belonged to the aristocracy of Mecca, but the branch of which he was an offspring was very much impoverished. His mother, Amînah, possessed, it is said, a peculiarly nervous temperament, and used to fancy, while between sleeping and waking, that she was visited by spirits. It is probable that Mohammed inherited from her his constitutional tendency to epilepsy, as well as his most remarkable mental peculiarities. Mohammedan authors have labored to endow the birth of their prophet with miraculous events, and in consequence many marvellous stories are told. It is related, among other things, that his mother experienced none of the pangs of travail. As soon as her child was born, he raised his eyes to heaven, exclaiming, "There is no God but God, and I am his prophet!" That same night, it is related, also with the same inclination to extravagance, that the fire of Zoroaster, which, guarded by the Magi, had burned uninterruptedly for more than a thousand years, was suddenly extinguished, and all the idols in the world fell down. When only two months old, Mohammed's father died (according to some accounts, he died two months before the birth of Mohammed). Amînah for a short time nursed the infant herself; but sorrow soon dried the fountains of her breast, and the young child, after much exertion to meet this extra expenditure, was committed to the care of a nurse, with whom he remained about five years. It is related by Mohammedans that when the nurse, who was a shepherd's wife, showed the child to a celebrated soothsayer, who was an idolater, the latter exclaimed, "Kill this child!" Halîmah snatched away her precious charge and fled. Afterwards the soothsayer explained to the excited multitude: "I swear by all the gods that this child will kill those who belong to your faith; he will destroy your gods, and he will be victorious over you." When Mohammed was six years old he lost his mother, and the poor orphaned child fell to the care of relatives. He was taken charge of by his grandfather, Abdul Mutalib, who was then the chief priest of the Kaaba. Upon his decease the care of the child fell to his uncle, Abu-Talib; but he was so indigent that he could not long afford to keep his nephew, and Mohammed was obliged to earn his livelihood as a shepherd—an occupation to which only the lower class of the population resorted, while the more opulent engaged in trade. Later (in his twenty-fifth year) he entered the service of a rich widow (Kadijah), attended to her affairs in Southern Arabia, according to some accounts also in Syria, where he is said to have become conversant with

monks, who gave him information regarding Christianity. Mohammed soon gained Kadijah's confidence to such a degree that she offered him her hand in matrimony, which he accepted, though she was much his senior—she was forty years old.

Preparation for his Mission.—Placed in affluent circumstances by marriage, Mohammed gradually abandoned commercial enterprises and gave himself up to religious contemplation, to which he may have been induced by a cousin of his consort, who, like many Arabs of his time, had relinquished idolatry, and had been converted first to Judaism, then to Christianity, but had failed to find satisfaction in either. Mohammed was no scholar—it is even doubtful whether he acquired reading and writing in later years—his education had certainly been neglected in his earlier years by reason of circumstances. Chirography had only been introduced into Arabia a short time previously, though poetry was highly cultivated—for this, however, in spite of his oratorical talent, he had little aptitude. On the whole, his visionary character and piety formed a great contrast to the sober and robust Arabs of his time, who indulged in wine, gambling, and sensuality as the main objects of life; while he, though not insensible to terrestrial enjoyments, was more disposed to religious reflection. Retired in solitude, he made God, the future life, and revelation the themes of his thoughts, and reviewed the various systems of religion known to him by oral tradition, in order to form from them a new religion adapted to Arabia. There were at this time Ebionitish Christians in the country—the *Rakusi* and the *Hanifs*. To the first belonged, according to Sprenger's conjecture (*Leben u. Lehre des Mohammed*, i, 43 sq.), Koss, who preached at Mecca the unity of God and the resurrection of the dead, and for this purpose also visited the fair at Okhad, where Mohammed had heard him. The Hanifs were (as Sprenger will have it) Essenes, who had lost nearly all knowledge of the Bible, and had submitted to various foreign influences, but professed a rigid monotheism. Their religious book was called the "Roll of Abraham." In the time of Mohammed several members of this sect were living at Mecca and Medina, and Mohammed himself, who originally had worshipped the gods of his people, became a Hanif. The doctrine of the Hanifs was "Islam"—i. e. submission to the one God; they were themselves "Moslem"—i. e. men characterized by such submission. Besides his knowledge from such connections, Mohammed enjoyed the instruction of Jewish scholars, among whom are particularly mentioned a celebrated rabbi, Abdallah Ibn-Salaam, and Waraka, the nephew of his wife. (Comp. Abrah. Geiger, *Was hat Mohammed aus dem Judenthume aufgenommen*, Bonn, 1833.) The Arabs, Mohammed knew, were ready for a new faith, and he desired the establishment of a religious system which should embody the essentials of all that his countrymen were acquainted with. Idolatry was already on the wane. The idols were considered by the poets and other intelligent Arabs as powerless beings, at most as mediators between the supreme God (Allah) and mankind; and there were some who even accepted the belief in a future life, as entertained among the Jews and Christians of Arabia. The greatest opposition he had reason to fear was from religious indifference, scepticism, and selfishness. According to the Koran, from which alone we can correctly gather Mohammed's religious views, he laid down the following fundamental doctrines: The existence of a monotheistic divinity, a being superior to all; a revelation, but only by special inspiration (by which alone the prophets were distinguished, while in all other respects on an equality with the rest of mankind); and, finally, a life hereafter, in which the virtuous were to be rewarded and the vicious punished. In his opinion, this was the religion of Abraham, who, as the Koran says, was neither Jew nor Christian, but a pious, God-fearing man. Moses and Christ were prophets; but their revelation had been distorted by Jews and Christians. He therefore determined that some of the laws and ordinances of the Old Testament, not suitable for Arabia, should be set aside; and of the New, many dogmas, which were looked upon by him and his contemporaries as bordering on idolatry, should be revoked, in order to successfully convert his people to monotheism.

Mohammed having arrived at these results by reflection and tradition, notwithstanding the prejudices of his time, from which he was by no means himself free, and endowed with a nervous constitution and a lively imagination, it was not at all unnatural for him to come, after a time, to regard himself as actually called of God to build up his people in a new faith. Mohammed, as we gather from the oldest and most trustworthy narratives, was an epileptic, and as such was considered to be possessed of evil spirits. At first he believed the same; but gradually he came to the conclusion, confirmed by his friends, that dæmons had no power over so pure and pious a man as he was, and he conceived the idea that he was not controlled by evil spirits, but that he was visited by angels, whom he, disposed to hallucinations of vision and audition, and afflicted with a morbid state of body and mind, saw in dreams, or even while awake conceived he saw. What seemed to him good and true, after such epileptic attacks, he esteemed revelation, in which he, at least in the first stage of his prophetic course, firmly believed, and which imparted to his pensive, variable character the necessary courage and endurance to brave all mortifications and perils.

Mohammed as a Religious Teacher. — Mohammed was, according to Mohammedan reports, forty years of age when he began to act the part of a prophet, and this he did first among his nearest relatives and friends. He claimed to have been "moved" to teach a new faith by a special "divine" communication which he had received in the solitude of the mountain Hîra, near Mecca. Gabriel, he asserted, had appeared to him, and in the name of God commanded him to "read"—i. e. to preach—the true religion, and to spread it abroad by committing it to writing (*Sur.* xcvi). In three years he made only fourteen converts; but among these were the high-spirited, devoted, and indomitable Ali, who was afterwards surnamed the "ever-victorious Lion of God," and Abu-Bekr, whose character for good-sense, benevolence, and straightforward integrity contributed not a little to the respectability and ultimate success of the new religion. In the fourth year of his mission, in obedience, as he alleges, to an express command from heaven, he resolved to make a public declaration of his faith. He addressed himself to the Koreish and others, asking them, "If I were to tell you that there is an army on the other side of that mountain, would you believe me?" "Yes," they answered, "for we do not consider thee to be a liar." He then said, "I come to warn you; and if you do not believe me, a great punishment will befall you;" he told them they must renounce idolatry, and make a profession of the one true God; that unless they did so they could have no true happiness in this life nor salvation in the life to come.

The people listened to the precepts of the moralist, and though they were enraptured by the force of his eloquence, very few were yet inclined to desert their hereditary and long-cherished ceremonies, and to adopt a spiritual faith the internal evidence of which they were unable to comprehend. Mohammed was repeatedly urged by them to confirm his divine mission by miracles, but he prudently appealed to the internal truth of his doctrine, and expressly declared that wonders and signs would depreciate the merit of faith and aggravate the guilt of infidelity. The only miraculous act which Mohammed professed to have accomplished, and which has been greatly exaggerated by his credulous adherents, is a nocturnal journey from the temple of Mecca to Jerusalem, and thence through the heavens, which he pretended to have performed on an imaginary animal like an ass, called Borak (lightning); but we need scarcely remark that the simple words of

the Koran (*Sur.* xvii) may as well be taken in the allegorical sense of vision. The few converts he made were of the lowest class, the aristocracy in the mean time growing more decided in their opposition to the enthusiast and innovator. Hitherto they had contented themselves by mocking him and deriding him as a sorcerer and dæmoniac, but as the number of converts was gradually increasing, and there seemed danger that the sacredness of Mecca might be disturbed by the new religionists, and thus the city be deprived of her chief glory and the aristocracy of the ample revenues of the pilgrimages, they rose in fierce opposition against the new prophet and his adherents, who dared to call their ancient gods idols, and their ancestors fools. Many of the converted slaves and freedmen had to undergo terrible punishments, and others suffered so much at the hands of their own relatives that they were fain to revoke their creed; so that the prophet himself advised his followers to emigrate to Abyssinia. Mohammed himself now belonging to the aristocracy, and further protected by the strong arm of Abu-Talib, had of course nothing personal to fear; but yet he became so low-spirited and fearful lest his attempt should fail altogether that he decided to appeal once more to the prejudices of the aristocracy, and he even went so far as to raise the idols, which hitherto he had represented as naught, to intermediate beings between God and man—a dictum, however, which he soon revoked, as an inspiration of Satan, thereby increasing the hatred of his adversaries, at whose head stood two members of the family of Machzûm, Al-Walid and Abulhakam Amr (called by Mohammed "Father of Foolishness"), and who in every way tried to throw ridicule on him.

Several years elapsed in this unsettled state, Mohammed all the while actively engaged in the propagation of his new doctrines. Apparently but little progress had been made, when he suddenly received vigorous support by the conversion of several of the noblest citizens, such as Abu-Obeida, Hamza, an uncle of Mohammed, Othman, and the stern and inflexible Omar, who were successively gained by the moderation and influence of Abu-Bekr, with whom, by marrying his only daughter Ayesha, the prophet had become more nearly allied after the death of his wife Kadijah. With this revival of the new faith hostility against its author became more decided, and the jealous leaders of the Koreishites, directing their animosity and violence against the whole line of Hashem, now demanded that Mohammed should be delivered into their hands for punishment; and when compliance with this request was refused them, they finally pronounced excommunication against the whole tribe of the Hashemites. The feud thus kindled between the different parties also obliged the few adherents of the prophet who had thus far remained to quit Mecca, and the new religionists spread through the country. Mohammed's enemies now came forth in open revolt, and it was formally and publicly resolved that he should be slain. In order to baffle the vengeance of the Hashemites, and to divide the guilt of his death, it was agreed that one man from every family should at the same moment plunge his sword into the heart of their victim. Nothing now remained for Mohammed but death or instant flight. At the dead of night, accompanied by his faithful friend Abu-Bekr, he took his flight to Yatreb, afterwards known by the name of Medina (Medinat al-nabi), or the City of the Prophet.

About a league from Mecca, at the cave of Thor, the fugitives halted, and there they remained hiding for three days from their Meccan pursuers. According to one account, these, after exploring every hiding-place in the vicinity, came to the mouth of the cave. But a spider having providentially spread her web over the entrance, the Koreishites, deeming it impossible that Mohammed could have entered there, turned back from their pursuit. Perhaps a more probable explanation is that as the Koreishites knew Medina to be the destination of the fugitives, they never suspected that they could be concealed in the cave of Thor, which lay in an opposite direction. While they were in the cave, the legend goes, Abu-Bekr, contrasting their weakness with the strength of their enemies, said, trembling, "We are but two." "No," replied Mohammed, "there is a third: it is God himself." On the fourth night the prophet and his companion left their hiding-place, and, riding on camels which the servant of Abu-Bekr had brought, arrived safely at Medina sixteen days after their flight from Mecca.

Mohammed's reason for turning his face towards Medina may be found in the sympathy which the Medinans had frequently manifested towards the prophet. They had been moved to this by various causes. Mohammed's mother was a Medinan, on account of which her clansmen considered themselves under obligation to take sides with him. There was another motive still: the Medinans, jealous of the authority of Mecca as a place of pilgrimage, might have hoped to attain the ascendency over Mecca by the aid of Mohammed and his followers. There were, moreover, many adherents to the new cause among the inhabitants of Medina, who had paid homage to the prophet while he was yet at Mecca. There were some who looked to him as perchance the Messiah expected by the Jews. Accordingly a considerable part of Medina was enthusiastic in the new cause, and when Mohammed's approach was made known to them, hundreds of its citizens advanced in procession to meet the coming prophet, welcoming him with loud acclamations; and he who a few days before had left his native city as a fugitive, with a price upon his head, now entered Medina more like a king returning victorious from battle than an exile seeking a place of refuge. This separation or flight of Mohammed from the city of his nativity, called in Arabic *Hejrah*, or anglicized *Hegira* (q. v.), formed not only an auspicious turning-point in the prophet's own life, but became the point of departure in the Mohammedan movement.

His earliest attention after his arrival at Medina was given towards the consolidation of the new worship and the minor arrangements in the congregation of his flock. At this time Mohammed endeavored, by various concessions, to gain the Jews over to his faith. He selected Jerusalem as the point of direction in prayer, appointed the tenth day of the first month as a day of fasting, and allowed the new converts to celebrate their Sabbath. But when the Jews, notwithstanding these advances, would not acknowledge him as prophet, ridiculed his pretension to be the Messiah, and enraged him by their constant taunts, he soon abrogated his concessions, became their bitterest enemy, sought closer alliance with the heathenish Arabs, and substituted practices likely to please them. In prayer the worshipper was now directed to turn towards Mecca, the month Ramadan was henceforth fixed upon as a fasting-time, and Friday as the day of rest.

Gradually Mohammed now appears in a new character. His internal arrangements perfected, his followers increased, and his allies concluding to yield him armed assistance, he was no longer content to convert his adversaries by words; he was no longer come to give peace, but to make war; where the warnings of the prophet had failed to convince, the strong arm of the conqueror must compel, and the persecuted apostle appears suddenly transformed into the triumphant soldier. He who had formerly insisted upon liberty of conscience for himself, and had opposed religious violence, now maintained that Islam should, if necessary, be defended and propagated by the sword. "The sword," said he, "is the key of heaven and of hell: a drop of blood shed in the cause of God, or a night spent in arms, is of more avail than two months of fasting and prayer; whoever falls in battle, his sins are forgiven him, and at the day of judgment the loss of his limbs shall be supplied by the wings of cherubim." This was a sort of manifesto, directed mainly against the Meccans, and he was not

long in carrying his new principles into practice. Not powerful enough to warrant an open fight with his enemies, he determined to weaken their strength by attacks and pillage upon the caravans of the Meccans, which on their commercial expeditions to Syria passed in the neighborhood of Medina, and ere long plunder and robbery were sanctioned, even during the sacred months —yea, many an assassination, consequent upon these attacks, was instigated by Mohammed himself.

Henceforth Mohammed ceases to be a religious leader in the eyes of the impartial biographer; he cannot possibly have, at this time, fancied himself inspired of God, and as acting according to divine pleasure; for, aside from the circumstance that some pretended revelations concerned only his own advantage, or even sometimes solely the gratification of his lust, he frequently withheld them, and waited for the temper of his adherents to manifest itself before he dared to proclaim them. Thus, to mention one instance of his irresolution and trickery, he commanded one of his votaries to waylay a caravan which he was cognizant could be reached only in a sacred month; and when the order had been complied with, and great dissatisfaction prevailed on account of this desecration of the holy month, he maintained not to have arranged the same, for he had given the order in so ambiguous a manner that he could clear himself of the responsibility of an act execrated by all Arabia.

Mohammed as an Impostor.—While at Mecca the prophet had kept unflinchingly in his path, through mockery and persecution. No threats, no injuries, had hindered him from preaching to his people the unity and the righteousness of God, and exhorting to a far purer and better morality than had ever been set before them. He had claimed no temporal power, no spiritual domination; he had asked but for simple toleration, for free permission to win men by persuasion into the way of truth. He claimed to be sent neither to compel conviction by miracles, nor to constrain outward profession by the sword. He was but a preacher, sent to warn men that there is one God, and that there is no other; that all that He requires is that men should do justice and love mercy, and walk humbly with their God, and as the sanction of all, that there will be a resurrection of the dead, as well of the just as of the unjust. Such had been his teachings at Mecca, and in his own person he had fulfilled the duties urged upon others—a thoroughly good and righteous man, according to his light, with nothing to be alleged against his life, even if judged by a higher morality than that of the Koran. His virtues *may* have been hypocrisy, his mission *may* have been imposture, but as a resident of Mecca all his actions outwardly had created a presumption in his favor. With his arrival at Medina, however, the scene shifts, and with the days of power and victory of the propagandist opens a dark and bloody page in the history of the East. From the moment when the formerly despised "madman and impostor" was raised to the position of highest judge, lawgiver, and ruler of Medina, and of the two most powerful Arabic tribes—thus opening a vast theatre to the enthusiasm and ambition of Mohammed—his revelations assumed a much higher claim. He now inculcated as a matter of religion and of faith the waging of war against the infidels; and the sword once drawn at the command of heaven, from that time remained unsheathed until the tribes of all Arabia and the adjacent countries had joined in the profession that there is no God but Allah, and that Mohammed is his apostle.

Acts of such character, Mohammed, even if not endowed with a very delicate ethic sense, must have known to be wrong, and could have approved solely for a selfish end. Even before his emigration to Medina he had, in several instances, deviated from the truth, where it seemed to answer his purpose best. Thus he had related the whole history of the Old and New Testament prophets, spiced by Jewish and Christian traditions, and had claimed them as communicated to him by the angel Gabriel—an assertion which was of course discredited by the Meccans, who guessed rightly that he owed this knowledge to his conversations with foreign scriptural scholars. Revelations also concerning his own person, and which he can certainly not have believed himself, abound in the Koran. Thus he had restricted the number of legitimate wives to four, but exempted himself from that restraint, and after the death of his first wife married twelve others. Another time he fell in love with a female slave, and when his consorts expressed their displeasure he swore that he would forsake her. A few months subsequently he had himself released from his oath by some verses of the Koran, and threatened his women with divorce if they should continue to stand in the way of his voluptuousness. His relation to Zeineb or Zaid, the spouse of his former slave and later adopted son, throws a still worse light on his revelations. Zaid, observing that Mohammed paid undue attention to his wife, caused himself to be divorced from her. Mohammed took her in matrimony. But when this marriage was found very reprehensible, because he had shown so little regard to Zaid's feelings, and because an adopted son with the Arabs was deemed equal to a son german, wherefore matrimony contracted with his wife, even after divorce, was considered illegal, Mohammed, in the name of God, branded as absurd, first, the usage hitherto in vogue calling an adopted male child a son, and in future declared such procedure even sinful, by actual proof drawn from the Koran, and announced that, far from having advised Zaid to separate himself from his wife, he had rather tried to dissuade Zaid from such a course; and, in the second place, that he (Mohammed), even after the separation, afraid of men's judgment, had hesitated to marry her, until God commanded him, in order to demonstrate that he who acted according to the Lord's will need not care for the talk of men, and in order that he might add, by the force of his own example, more vigor to the law respecting adopted sons.

But to return to the external history of Mohammed and his votaries. First of all our attention is claimed by the first battle proper, fought near Badr, situated between Mecca and Medina, which, though insignificant as to the numbers of the combatants, was of material consequence. The original object was the pillage of a Meccan caravan. The Meccans, having been advised of this intention, despatched succor to their people, and, as was supposed, were thus prepared to meet the Hashemites and Medinans. Yet the Meccans, although superior in number, were nevertheless defeated by Mohammed's adherents. Some Moslem writers will have it that 3000 angelic warriors, on white and black steeds, guided and assisted the faithful. The prophet himself, during the fight, was engaged in prayer. In most of the later wars, also, Mohammed generally kept at a distance from the melée. He obtained many a victory, to be sure, by skilful disposition of his forces, but he distinguished himself by no means as a brave warrior. This is especially manifest in the expedition immediately following, and undertaken by the Meccans to take revenge for the defeat, by which they had suffered not only severe loss of lives and property, but had added booty, glory, and increase to the new religionists. Mohammed, namely, when the Meccans, a few thousand strong, advanced against Medina, wanted to retire to the city and to confine himself to its defence, and only when his disciples declared this plan dishonorable, he unwillingly turned out against the enemy, and was vanquished near Mount Ohod. Many of the faithful covered the battle-field with their corpses. Mohammed himself was wounded slightly; he wore a double coat of mail and a closed helmet, so that the Meccans did not recognise him, and his companions promptly secured his safety. When the Meccans advanced a second time with a superior force, Mohammed's advice to his own to fortify themselves in the city was promptly complied with, and the

Meccans, inexperienced in siege operations, and by Mohammed's intrigues having fallen out with their confederates, were obliged after a few weeks to retire without accomplishing anything.

We pass over the wars waged by Mohammed against the Jews in Medina and in other parts of Arabia, all of which were marked by great cruelty on his side, also the conflicts which he waged against several Arabian tribes allied with the Meccans, and remark only that, in spite of many a failure, in the sixth year of the Hegira (A.D. 628) he felt sufficiently confident to venture at the head of his votaries on a pilgrimage to Mecca. Yet, though he exhorted to this pilgrimage in the name of God, it was not participated in to the degree expected, and nothing remained to him but the hope that the Meccans would be afraid to shed blood in the holy month, though he himself had violated it long ago by robbery and murder. When he arrived at the boundary of the Meccan territory, he was bidden to stop, and threatened with force in case he should attempt to penetrate into the city. After protracted negotiations, however, many Meccans being desirous of peace on account of their commercial interests, concluded it, and, among other terms, it was fixed that Mohammed should be allowed to partake of the pilgrim celebration the ensuing year. This treaty of peace, by which Mohammed was recognised as an equal power, increased his authority, and permitted him to despatch his emissaries to all parts of Arabia, to make proselytes and enter into alliances. Soon he felt strong enough to avail himself of an opportune pretext to break the peace, and on a sudden surprised Mecca, without any formal declaration of war, at the head of 10,000 men. The chief magistrates of the city were obliged (A.D. 630) to make their submission, and acknowledged him not only as secular ruler, but as a plenipotentiary of the Deity. See KOREISH. With this the victory of the new religion was secured in all Arabia. While, however, employed in destroying all traces of idolatry in the besieged city, and fixing the minor laws and ceremonies of the true faith, Mohammed heard of new armies which several warlike Arabic tribes had sent against him, and which were concentrated near Taïf (630). He went forth to encounter the enemy, was again victorious, and his dominion and creed extended further and further every day. From all parts flocked the deputations to do homage to him in the name of the various tribes, either as the messenger of God, or at least as the Prince of Arabia, and the year 8 of the Hegira was therefore called the year of the Deputations.

Even before the capture of Mecca, Mohammed had been bold enough to summon the princes of the countries antiguous to Arabia—Chosroes (of Persia), the emperor Heraclius (of Constantinople), the king of Abyssinia, and several Byzantine and Persian provincial governors—to be converted to his faith. His letter to the king of Abyssinia has been discovered on a leaf of parchment, which served as a cover to a manuscript, in a Coptic monastery in Upper Egypt, and accords tolerably with what we know from Arabian biographers. It reads as follows: "In the name of God, the all-gracious and all-merciful, from Mohammed, the servant and ambassador of God, to Almucaucas, the prefect of the Copts. Hail to him who follows the divine guidance! I summon thee to confess the Islam. If thou compliest with this summons, thy salvation is secured, and God will give thee a double reward for thy devotion. But if thou refusest, the guilt of the Copts rests on thee. Oh, ye men of the Scriptures! approach and become our equals by professing that we adore only Allah, unassociated with terrestrial beings, and own as Lord none beside him. If you will not agree to this, testify that we are God-resigned and faithful." The governor of Egypt was no more converted than Heraclius and Chosroes. He, however, received the delegates of Mohammed hospitably, and sent him, besides other valuable presents, two Abyssinian female slaves, one of whom (Mariam or

Maria) charmed the prophet to such a degree that he neglected his other wives on her account.

The execution of one of Mohammed's emissaries by Amru, the chief of the Christian Arabs on the Syrian frontier, occasioned the first war between Mohammed and the Byzantines, terminating unfavorably to the former. Nor had a second campaign the desired success, for he did not secure the wished-for participation of the pagan allies, and he had to be satisfied with the homage of a few minor princes on his way to the frontiers, and returned without having carried out his intention.

Towards the end of the 10th year of the Hegira he undertook, at the head of at least 40,000 Moslems, his last solemn pilgrimage to Mecca, and there (on the Mount Arafat) instructed them in all the important laws and ordinances, chiefly of the pilgrimage; and the ceremonies observed by him on that occasion were recorded in the Koran and fixed for all time. He again solemnly exhorted his believers to righteousness and piety, and chiefly recommended them to protect the weak, the poor, and the women, and to abstain from usury. Among the most important of his ordinances at this time are to be noticed the abolishment of the leap-year, which the Arabs, in common with the Jews, had been accustomed to observe, and in its place introduced the pure lunar year, by which alone the sacred months as well as the pilgrimage and the month of fasting were fixed. Another very important commandment which he gave at this time was that thenceforth the sacred city of Mecca was to be entered only by Mohammedans, and that even outside of it idolaters were to be entirely exterminated. Jews and Christians were to be tolerated, if they would humbly submit and pay a capitation tax. His caliph—Omar—added to the commandment, in order to humiliate those of another faith, several oppressive restrictions for the nations conquered by him, and the succeeding caliphs, according to the degree of tolerance or fanaticism actuating them, mitigated or aggravated the same. Non-Mohammedans, in order to be easily recognised as infidels, were obliged to distinguish themselves by the color of their turbans, the Jews being enjoined to wear black, the Christians blue ones. They were forbidden to carry arms, were ordered to ride on asses (not on horses), on the streets to yield the way to the Mohammedans, and in public assemblies to rise before them. Their houses must not be higher than those of the faithful; nor were they permitted to hold public processions nor ring bells, nor make proselytes, nor keep any Moslem slaves, nor acquire any captives or other military persons, nor possess any seal with Arabic letters, nor have any intimacy with Moslem females. Jews and Christians should not be employed in offices of chancery—an interdiction enacted by Omar, but rarely observed because of the ignorance of the primitive Arabians as well as later Turks, who, for want of knowledge of state affairs, found the services of Jews and Christians in various administrative branches indispensable.

After his return from Mecca, Mohammed busily applied himself to the fitting-out of a new expedition against the Byzantines. In the very midst of his warlike preparations he was suddenly taken dangerously ill with fever. One night, while severely suffering, we are told by Mohammedan chroniclers, Mohammed went to the cemetery of Medina, and prayed and wept upon the tombs, praising the dead, and wishing that he himself might soon be delivered from the storms of this world. For a few more days he went about; at last, too weak further to visit his wives, he chose the house of Ayesha, situated near a mosque, as his abode during his sickness. He continued to take part in the public prayers as long as he could; until at last, feeling that his hour had come, he once more preached to the people, recommending Abu-Bekr and Usâma, the son of Zaid, as the generals whom he had chosen for the army. He then asked, like Samuel, whether he had wronged any one, and read to them passages from the Koran, preparing the minds of his hearers for his death, and exhorting them to peace among themselves, and to strict obedience to the tenets of the faith. A few days afterwards he asked for writing materials, probably in order to fix a successor to his office as chief of the faithful; but Omar, fearing he might choose Ali, while he himself inclined to Abu-Bekr, would not allow him to be furnished with them. In his last wanderings he only spoke of angels and heaven. He died in the lap of Ayesha, about noon of Monday, the 12th (11th) of the third month, in the year 11 of the Hegira (June 8, 632). Mohammedan biographers maintain that their prophet died of the consequences of eating roast mutton poisoned by a Jewess, who is said to have sought the revenge of a brother whom the Islamites killed in the campaign of Cheibar. But, as this campaign took place four years previous to Mohammed's death, it might have been a difficult task to the contemporary Arabian physicians to prove it, even if the attempt at poisoning were verified. It is much more probable (what also occurred in the case of Abu-Bekr, the later caliph) that such a story was concocted to have him die a martyr's death; for the Arabs regard as martyrs those who perish in a holy war, i. e. in a war carried on against infidels.

Many fictions were resorted to in the first century of the Mohammedan æra to glorify their deceased prophet. Fanatic Moslems represent him to have enjoyed special favors from on high from the day of his birth. We recur to the exclamation he is said to have uttered as he made his appearance in the world; as a man, we are told the desert was covered with shade-trees as he wandered through the same, and even rocks saluted him as the apostle of the Lord. A man created before all created beings, as tradition has it (at whose birth there were supernatural manifestations), must not die of a common illness: he must perish at least as a martyr. It is difficult to decide how much Mohammed himself has contributed to these legends; certain it is that he frequently, in order to attain his ends, did not despise any means of imposture and delusion, and made the angel Gabriel play a part as bearer of divine revelations in which he did not himself believe. He probably feared the destruction of his whole work—a work which, after naive credulity and religious enthusiasm had been succeeded by sober sense, he cannot possibly have considered salutary for his people, certainly not if his new doctrines were to be forced upon them by the sword and persecution. The inconsistency of his course is certainly marvellous, for he introduced those very measures against which he had himself declaimed so loudly until suddenly transformed from the subject to the ruler. It may be granted even that he frequently played the deceiver for the good of a cause which he believed just and worthy of his best strength, and for which he judged his people ill prepared unless he could claim the authority of a divine messenger; but it is to be regretted that if Mohammed actually strove to elevate his people, as we believe he did at first, he continued the deceiver after he had attained power sufficient to enforce his dicta, and that he not unfrequently did so to further his own personal purposes, often only for a transient accommodation, as, for instance, when he represented God as commanding that nobody should enter his house unless invited, and to retire immediately after taking a meal. "The Prophet hesitates to dismiss you, even if you are tedious; but God does not hesitate to tell you the truth."

As much as his public life and his appearance as prophet and legislator may be liable to censure, his private life, excepting his sensuality, if his biographers report the truth, was exemplary. He was affable, conversed with everybody, was plain in dress and diet, and so little pretentious as to forbid external reverence from his companions, and to refuse from his slaves a service which he could perform himself. He was often seen in the market buying provisions, and at home milking goats and mending clothes. He visited the sick, and was in sympathy with sufferers; he was generous and forbearing, if policy did not dictate a contrary course. His benevolence and liberality were especially marked; and indeed they must have been great, for he left no riches, though the war-booty which he shared, and the presents which flowed to him from all sides, must have placed large means at his command. Upon the whole, it cannot be denied that Mohammed improved and elevated the political and religious condition of Arabia. He united the dispersed, mutually inimical, idolatrous Arabian tribes into a great nation, allied by a faith in God and a belief in a future life. In place of bloody vengeance for murder and of rude force, he instituted an inviolable code, which, in spite of deficiencies, still forms the fundamental law of the Islamitic kingdoms. On the women he bestowed, in spite of some restrictions, many rights which they had not enjoyed before him. He mitigated the lot of the slaves, as far as the spirit of his age permitted, and declared emancipation to be a work agreeable to the Deity. He cared like a father for the poor, the widows, and orphans; condemned the vices which degrade humanity and have a disturbing influence on social life, and exhorted to the virtues recommended in the Old and New Testaments.

This, in briefest outline, is the history of Mohammed's career. We have not been able to dwell, as we could wish, at any length, either on the peculiar circumstances of his inner life, which preceded and accompanied his "prophetic" course, nor on the part which idolatry, Judaism, Christianity, and his own reflection respectively, bore in the formation of his religion; nor have we been able to trace the process by which his "mission" grew upon him, as it were, and he, from a simple admonisher of his family, became the founder of a faith to which above 130,000,000 are said to adhere.

Personal Characteristics.—In appearance, Mohammed was of middling size, had broad shoulders, a wide chest, and large bones; and he was fleshy, but not stout. The immoderate size of his head was partly disguised by the long locks of hair, which in slight curls came nearly down to the lobe of his ears. His oval face, though tawny, was rather fair for an Arab, but neither pale nor high-colored. The forehead was broad, and his fine and long but narrow eyebrows were separated by a vein, which you could see throbbing if he was angry. Under long eyelashes sparkled bloodshot black eyes through wide slit eyelids. His nose was large, prominent, and slightly hooked, and the tip of it seemed to be turned up, but was not so in reality. The mouth was wide; he had a good set of teeth, and the fore-teeth were asunder. His beard rose from the cheek-bones, and came down to the collarbone; he clipped his mustaches, but did not shave them. He stooped, and was slightly hump-backed. His gait was careless, and he walked fast but heavily, as if he were ascending a hill; and if he looked back, he turned round his whole body. The mildness of his countenance gained him the confidence of every one; but he could not look straight into a man's face: he turned his eyes usually outwards. On his back he had a round fleshy tumor of the size of a pigeon's egg; its furrowed surface was covered with hair, and its base was surrounded by black moles. This was considered as the seal of his prophetic mission, at least during the latter part of his career, by his followers, who were so devout that they found a cure for their ailings in drinking the waters in which he had bathed; and it must have been very refreshing, for he perspired profusely, and his skin exhaled a strong smell. He bestowed considerable care on his person, and more particularly on his teeth, which he rubbed so frequently with a piece of wood that a Shiah author was induced to consider it as one of the signs of his prophetic mission. He bathed frequently, washed several times a day, and oiled his head profusely after washing it. At times he dyed his hair and beard red with henna, in imitation of his grandfather, who imported this habit from Yemen. Though he did not comb himself regularly, he did it now and

then. At first he wore his hair like the Jews and Christians; for he said, "In all instances in which God has not given me an order to the contrary, I like to follow their example;" but subsequently he divided it, like most of his countrymen. Every evening he applied antimony to his eyes; and though he had not many gray hairs even when he died, he concealed them by dyeing or oiling them, in order to please his wives, many of whom were young and inclined to be giddy, and whose numbers he increased in proportion as he became more decrepit. The prophet was usually dressed in a white cotton shirt, or blouse, with pockets, and sleeves which reached to his wrists. He had a skull-cap and a turban on his head, the extremities hanging down the back; and sandals, with two leather straps over the instep, on his feet. In the house he wore merely a piece of cloth tied round his temples, leaving the crown of the head uncovered. Sometimes he wore, instead of the shirt, a "suit of clothes," which consisted of an apron—that is to say, a piece of cloth tied round the waist and hanging in folds down to the legs, like a woman's petticoat—and a sheet, or square shawl, which was thrown over the left shoulder and wrapped round the body under the right arm. Sometimes he wrapped himself in a blanket. In temperament, Mohammed was melancholic, and in the highest degree nervous. He was generally low-spirited, thinking, and restless; and he spoke little, and never without necessity. His eyes were mostly cast to the ground, and he seldom raised them towards heaven. The excitement under which he composed the more poetical Súrahs of the Koran was so great that he said that they had caused him gray hair; his lips were quivering and his hands shaking while he received the inspiration. Any offensive smell made him so uncomfortable that he forbade persons who had eaten garlic or onions to come into his place of worship. In a man of semi-barbarous habits this is remarkable. He had a woollen garment, and was obliged to throw it away when it began to smell from perspiration, "on account of his delicate constitution." When he was taken ill, he sobbed like a woman in hysterics; or, as Ayesha says, he roared like a camel; and his friends reproached him for his unmanly bearing. During the battle of Badr his nervous excitement seems to have bordered on frenzy. The faculties of his mind were extremely unequally developed; he was unfit for the common duties of life, and even after his mission he was led in all practical questions by his friends. But he had a vivid imagination, the greatest elevation of mind, refined sentiments, and a taste for the sublime.

The articles KORAN and MOHAMMEDANISM contain some further details on his doctrine and its history.

Mohammed Abd-el-Wahab, the founder of the Mohammedan sect named after him *Wahabites*, was born in Nejed or Nejd, Central Arabia, about the close of the 17th century, in the tribe of Temim, and claimed descent from Mohammed the prophet. Like his prototype, the great Mohammed, he spent the early part of his life in trading expeditions to Bassora, Bagdad, and Damascus. Tradition even claims for him extensive journeys, reaching to India on the east and to Constantinople on the west. He was a prudent and sagacious young man, and greatly devoted to his studies in the law and the Koran; and, like a faithful Moslem, he made a pilgrimage to Mecca and Medina. There he became fired with such an ascetic fanaticism that on his return he was compelled to quit his native village for Deraijeh, in the central highlands of Arabia, soon to become the capital of the new theocracy. Like the prophet of the crescent, when he looked abroad over the degenerate state of his countrymen, Abd-el-Wahab saw that his co-religionists had fallen away from the purity of life and belief which made Islam master of all the civilized world save a corner of Europe, and he resolved to bring them back to the truth. He scouted the traditions which had buried the pure Koran under their mass, he condemned the idolatry which regarded Mohammed as more than a mere man inspired by the one God, and he enforced with a fanatical earnestness fasting, alms-giving, prayer, and the pilgrimage to Mecca, while he forbade the gratification of all vice and luxury, whether drinking, gambling, smoking, debauchery, usury, false witnesses, fine dresses, or grand tombs. Being a man of talent and eloquence, he soon gained followers. At first his progress was slow, but gradually his doctrines became popular, and he ultimately succeeded in spreading them widely, and in establishing his power likewise. He died near the close of the 18th century; but the *Wahabites* have continued to grow in strength and numbers all over Asia, particularly India, until there is now scarcely a city of any size in Northern India in which followers of his are not to be found. For the last ten years the Wahabites have been subject to rigorous searching on the part of the British government, and it would now appear that they have joined to their religious a political creed which is dangerous to the welfare of Western society in the East. See MOHAMMEDAN SECTS; WAHABEES. (J. H. W.)

Mohammed Aben-Kerram, founder of a Mohammedan sect, was born at Serenj about A.D. 820. After teaching in his native city, he came to Khorassan, where he met a celebrated hermit, Ahmed ben-Harb, who induced him to visit the Kaaba. On his return to Khorassan, after a five years' sojourn in Mecca, he taught his new doctrines in Nichapûr. He was imprisoned by Mohammed ben-Thaher, but finally escaped and found refuge in Jerusalem. He is the founder of the Anthropomorphites, or *Mochebihes.* He died in Jerusalem in 868.

Mohammed al-Darazi, one of the founders of the sect of the Druses, was born near Bokhara about A.D. 960. In 1010 he came to Egypt, where he was converted to the doctrines of Hakim al-Mokanna. This doctrine admitted incarnation consecutive with divinity in different persons. He was the first to regard Hakim al-Mokanna, then ruling in Egypt, as the last of these incarnates. He published a book in which he set forth the successions of incarnation since Adam. The caliph Hakim was so influenced by him as to intrust to him virtually the management of all government affairs. Darazi, having published his work, read it in a mosque at Cairo, whereupon the people, greatly displeased with his innovations, attempted to slay him. Hakim appeared to disapprove of the conduct of Darazi, but secretly furnished him with money to quietly advance his cause, and advised him to preach his doctrines in the mountains of Syria, where he successfully taught his dogmas, permitting his followers the use of wine, fornication, and incest. Mohammed afterwards returned to Egypt, where he set himself up as the true imam, brought about a revolt against authority, and in the conflict lost his life in 1019. See works referred to in the article DRUSES; ISMAELITES.

Mohammed Hakim Ispahani (*Haji*), a Parsee doctor, was born at Ispahan about 1790. He was the mollah of a religious sect known as the *Rasmians,* or old orthodox Parsees. His writings reveal interesting facts concerning what is left at Bombay of the Parsees, or fire-worshippers. For the good of his sect, Mohammed wrote, in Persian and in English, *Kathib fi bilan Asbat al-Kabiseh,* or "Selections of Mohammed from History, forming a perfect Illustration of the present Theological Discussions of the Parsees" (Bombay, fol. 1827), in which he aims to prove that the old Persian intercalary æra is of the remotest antiquity, and, in fact, originated in the days of Zoroaster. The believers of other Parsee sects, however, such as the Chahinchahmians, Kodmians, and Churigarians, would have it date only from Yezdegerd III, the last of the Sassanide kings. In answer to certain books written by his opponents on religious matters, Mohammed wrote *Dafakh al-Hazl,* being a refutation of mollah Firuz's work, entitled *Ressana Moussumal badallah,* etc. (Bom-

bay, 1832, 4to). Mohammed Hakim Ispahani died at Bombay about 1846. See Zenker, *Bibl. Orient.* u. v.; Spiegel, *Chrestomathia Persica.*—Hoefer, *Nouv. Biog. Générale,* xxxv, 759.

Mohammedanism, called by its professors *Islam,* meaning "resignation" or "entire submission" (i. e. to the will of God), in accordance with the Koran, which, as we have already seen in the article under that heading, is the Bible of the Mohammedan, and in the days of the Prophet was the only sacred book in use, the sole exponent of duty and privilege to the *Moslem,* as the Mohammedan calls himself. The Koran, however, being a miscellaneous collection of hymns, prayers, dogmas, sermons, occasional speeches, narratives, legends, laws, orders for the time in which they were given, without any chronological arrangement, and full of repetitions and contradictions, owing to the manner of its collection, which took place subsequent to Mohammed's death, soon proved too disconnected to be continued, even by the most ardent disciple of Islam, as the sole guide of authority. Neither dogmas nor laws are here reduced to a system; they had been inserted by piecemeal just as they had been written down, or even afterwards discovered in the reminiscences of Mohammed's companions. But, aside from these imperfections of contradictions, repetitions, and the want of system, it was manifest also that the Koran was lacking in instruction on many important theological questions, in which light the Mohammedan is accustomed to regard all ritual, dogmatic, and juridical matters. The Moslem therefore resorted, in the first place, to oral *tradition,* and by the aid of reported expressions of the Prophet, and examples in his public and private life (*Hadith* and *Sunnah*), supplemented the deficiencies and elucidated the obscure passages of the Koran (q. v.). When this resource failed to meet all wants, the decrees of the imams, i. e. of the caliphs as spiritual heads, were raised to the authority of divine laws and doctrines. Thus a religious structure, extended by analogy and induction, supported by the Koran, by tradition, and by decrees of the imams, comprising juridical, ritualistic, and dogmatic doctrines, was gradually completed into a systematic whole, sufficient for all purposes as a guide to the Moslem. But we need hardly add that into such a peculiar construction contradictions in theory and practice have found their way, according to the different traditions and decisions of the imams or expounders of the law, besides the various interpretations put upon the Koran itself within the pale of the different Mohammedan sects that have arisen since the days of the Prophet. See MOHAMMEDAN SECTS. For the historical and ethical circumstances that conduced to the origin and progress of Mohammedanism, see the article MOHAMMED.

Moslemism consists of a dogmatical or theoretical part, called "Imân" (i. e. *faith*), and a practical part, called "Dîn" (i. e. *religion*.) (See Vambéry, *Der Islam im neunzehnten Jahrhundert* [Leips. 1875]).

I. *Dogmas.*—The doctrines of Islam, as originally instituted upon its foundation, may be reduced to three leading propositions, viz.: (1) the doctrine of one Deity, (2) of the revelation or prophetic vision of Mohammed, and (3) the immortality of the soul, the latter being closely interlinked with the doctrine of the resurrection of the dead, of paradise, and of hell, the day of judgment, and the rewarding of the good and faithful, as well as the punishment of the wicked and of infidels. Though these doctrines are plain and simple, they became, nevertheless, even in the first century of the Mohammedan æra, subjects of the most violent polemics. A man like Mohammed, in whom not the least trace of scholarly education is to be found, was unable to set up a systematic structure of doctrines. True, we find in sundry passages of the Koran that God is the creator and preserver of the world; that he is One, omniscient, omnipotent, eternal, just, and gracious. But the Arabs, after becoming acquainted with Persian religions and ideas, and with Grecian philosophy, would not be satisfied with such simplicity. Their desire for knowledge led them to further inquiries, for which they found no solution in the Koran, and which therefore gave occasion to dissensions, the more irremediable as they were in part connected with political differences. At the very earliest epoch reflective minds among the faithful took offence and exception to many dogmas, particularly on the essence of the Deity and its relation to mankind, as well as to the irrational doctrines concerning the Koran itself. Thus the orthodox taught that the divine attributes existed, so to speak, by the side of Deity; while the Motazelites, i. e. the Separatists, considered the Deity itself as the essence of wisdom, beneficence, power, and other qualities. The doctrine of the justice of God led the latter (i. e. the dissenters) further to accept the dogma of human free will, while the orthodox inclined more or less to the Augustinian doctrine of predestination and grace. This same doctrine induced the liberal Mohammedans to assume a gradation of sin and punishment; while, according to the opinion of the strictly orthodox, every Moslem who commits only one sin, and departs this life without repentance, is consigned to eternal punishment. (See below.) Thus also the absolute unity of the Deity induced the Separatists to maintain that the Koran was created, since otherwise two (things) beings must have existed from eternity; the orthodox, on the contrary, regard the Koran as something uncreated, lest, God being immutable, it be viewed as not belonging to his being, and thereby the whole doctrine of revelation become undermined. The latter dogma was fiercely disputed under the caliph Mamun, who instituted a formal inquisition, and persecuted to the utmost the adherents of the doctrine of the eternity of the Koran.

Much controversy arose also concerning the dogma of divine foreordination, and both contending parties found no difficulty in bringing proof from the Koran, which is especially rich in contradictions on this point. In one passage it reads: "To him who wants this world we give directly according to our pleasure; but he will be rejected and derided in the future state, and burned in hell." In another passage it is said: "Follow the most beautiful sent to you from your Lord, before punishment befalls you, and you find no more assistance; before the soul exclaims, Woe to me! I have sinned and was of the mockers; or, If God would have guided me, I would have feared him; or, Could I return to the earth, I would practice the good. Not so; my signs (the verses of the Koran) have come to thee, thou hast declared them lies, thou wast haughty and unbelieving." While these and similar passages, as well as the continual threats and promises, speak clearly in favor of a dogma of human free will, there are others which make the acts of man dependent on the divine will, and render man, as to virtue and vice, a blind instrument of divine arbitrariness. Thus we read: "For those who are unbelievers, it is the same whether thou (God is speaking to Mohammed) admonishest them or not; they believe not. God has sealed their hearts, and over their eyes and ears there is a covering." And further: "The infidels say, Why does God not send any miracles to him (Mohammed)? Say, The Lord leaves in error whom he chooses, and guides those who turn to him who believe, and whose hearts find rest at the thought of Divinity." Very frequently we meet in the Koran with the phrase: "God guides whom he pleases, and leaves in error whom he pleases." These and similar verses, however, if we survey the whole without any bias, can be interpreted as meaning that God in his wisdom appoints at what time and which people he will bless by his revelation, and that he strengthens by faith the men who desire the good and true in their aspirations, while he abandons those in whom the propensity for evil predominates, to their more and more increasing corruption, and thus measurably hardens their hearts. Again: if the doctrine of predestination is stiffly adopted, not to come in conflict with divine justice, the doctrine of original sin—i. e. of an internal corruption of mankind in consequence of the sin of Adam—must also be assumed. But such a dogma is not mooted in the Koran; on the contrary, in several places the idea of accountability for the sins of others is controverted. There is, to be sure, in the Koran, as in the Old Testament, the narrative of the first human couple residing in paradise, of their disobedience against God's interdiction, and of their expulsion from it; however, when Adam repented of his sin, God pardoned him, and said to him: "Leave the paradise, but my guide (revelation) will come to you; he who follows it has nothing to fear and never will know sorrow, but the infidels who declare our signs lies will be eternal inmates of hell." Thus it is evidently taught that the curse which rested on the human race by Adam's sin is averted; divine grace manifests itself by revelation, and every prophet from Adam to Mohammed, who designated himself as the last one for the seal of prophecy, is a Saviour for every one who believes in revelation, and acts according to its precepts. Of a further grace to purify mankind from original sin, and enable them to regain the beatitude of paradise, no mention is made, consequently the idea of being predestined to damnation would not be compatible with divine justice.

The history of the prophets also occupies a very large space in the Koran. Besides the Old Testament, several other prophets are named, who are said to have been sent to the extinct tribes of Arabia. The history of all these so-called divine messengers is embellished with many legends, partly to be found in the Talmud and in the Midrash, but by Mohammed fashioned to suit his purpose, in order to inspire his antagonists with fear and his votaries with consolation. He likes to identify himself with the Biblical prophets, puts into their mouth such words as he addressed to the Meccans, represents also those messengers of God as disregarded by their contemporaries, and that hence God's wrath is inflamed, and infidels are caused to perish with ignominy, until finally, however, truth comes to prevail, and the persecuted prophet triumphs, surrounded by the few who believed in him previous to the divine punishment. In pursuance of this system, Mohammed, to be consistent, cannot accept the crucifixion of Christ; for no man ought to atone for the sins of others, nor ought a prophet to be forsaken by God. Therefore the Koran teaches it was not Christ who was crucified, but an infidel Jew whom God invested with the form of Christ, whom the Jews crucified in his stead. "Verily, Christ Jesus, the son of Mary, is the apostle of God, and his word, which he conveyed unto Mary, and a spirit proceeding from him, honorable in this world and in the world to come; and one of those who approach near to the presence of God. Yet Jesus was a mere mortal, and not the son of God; his enemies conspired against his life, but a phantom was substituted for him on the cross, while he was translated to heaven" (Sur. iii, 54; iv, 156, 159). There is also other mention and estimate expressed in the Koran concerning Christ. He is called the living Word and Spirit of God. The miraculous birth of Christ has nothing offensive to Mohammed, for Adam had also been created by the breath of God. Neither does he hesitate to receive all miracles related in the Gospels, since similar ones had been performed by Abraham and Moses. Even the ascension is to him neither new nor incredible, as the same is reported of Elijah and Enoch. Besides the crucifixion, he abhors in the Christian dogmas the supposition that a prophet with his mother are placed next to the Deity, and declares the Trinitarian view to be an impious fiction of the priests. The Mohammedan doctrine of God's nature and attributes coincides with the Christian, inasmuch as he is by both taught to be the creator of all things in heaven and earth, who rules and preserves all things, without beginning, omnipotent, omniscient, omnipresent, and full of mercy. Yet, according to the Mohammedan belief, he has no offspring: "He begetteth not, nor is he begotten." Nor is Jesus called anything but a prophet and an apostle, although Mohammed goes so far as to say that the birth of Christ was due to a miraculous divine operation. But after all it is taught that, as the Koran superseded the Gospel, so Mohammed supersedes Christ, and he is declared to be by far the most illustrious apostle (Sur. xxiii, 40). Of particular importance for Mohammed is the annunciation of a Paraclete, which he applied to himself, either pretending or even actually believing it to be himself. Of equal significance for him, and therefore treated by him with great predilection, is Abraham, first, because of his simple doctrines, to which Mohammed himself adhered in the early period of his prophetic mission; and, secondly, on account of the sacred places and relics in Mecca of which he (Abraham) is called the founder; and, thirdly and finally, because he was the father of Ishmael, from whom Mohammed and his race claim descent. The Sunnites look in quite a different light upon the prophets. They regard them, as a class, as the simple carriers of revelation, but in all other respects declare them to be common men, liable to human infirmities; while the Shiites pronounce them perfectly pure and sinless, like the angels, instruments of God, who only execute and always have executed his orders, except Iblis, who on account of his disobedience was rejected, and, as Satan, tries to seduce men. An important dogma with the Shiites is that of the Imamat, or hereditary succession of descendants of the Prophet by his daughter Fatima, consort of Ali—a doctrine which the Sunnites do not acknowledge. Many of them see in the caliphate merely a political institution, which ought to have the welfare of the nations for its foundation and supreme end.

A prominent dogma in Islam is the belief in angels, whom they thus picture: Created of fire, and endowed with a kind of uncorporeal body, they stand between God and man, adoring or waiting upon the former, or interceding for and guarding the latter. The four chief angels are "The Holy Spirit," or "Angel of Revelations" —Gabriel; the special protector and guardian of the Jews—Michael; the "Angel of Death"—Azraël (Raphael, in the apocryphal gospel of Barnabas), and Israfil—Uriel, whose office it will be to sound the trumpet at the resurrection. It will hardly be necessary, after what we have said under MOHAMMED, to point out, in every individual instance, how most of his "religious" notions were taken almost bodily from the Jewish legends; this angelology, however, the Jews had themselves borrowed from the Persians, only altering the names, and, in a few cases, the offices of the chief angelic dignitaries. Besides angels, there are good and evil genii, the chief of the latter being Iblis (Despair), once called Azazil, who, refusing to pay homage to Adam, was rejected by God. These Jin are of a grosser fabric than angels, and subject to death. They, too, have different names and offices (Peri, Fairies; Div, Giants; Takvins, Fates, etc.), and are, in almost every respect, like the Shedim in the Talmud and Midrash. A further point of belief is that of certain God-given Scriptures, revealed successively to the different prophets. Four only of the original one hundred and four sacred books, viz. the Pentateuch, the Psalms, the Gospel, and the Koran, are said to have survived; the three former, however, in a mutilated and falsified condition. Besides these, a certain apocryphal gospel, attributed to St. Barnabas, and the writings of Daniel, together with those of a few other prophets, are taken notice of by the Moslems, but not as canonical books. The number of prophets, sent at various times, is stated variously at between two and three hundred thousand, among whom 313 were apostles, and six were specially commissioned to proclaim new laws and dispensations, which abrogated the preceding ones. These were Adam, Noah, Abraham, Moses, Jesus, and Mohammed—the last the greatest of them all, and the propagator of the final dispensation.

The belief in the resurrection and the final judgment is another important article of faith. The dead are received in their graves by an angel announcing the coming of the two examiners, Monker and Nakir, who put questions to the corpse respecting his belief in God and Mohammed, and who, in accordance with the answers, either torture or comfort him. This, again, is the Jewish "Chibbut hak-keber," the Beating of the Grave, a hyperbolical description of the sufferings during the intermediate state after death. The soul, awaiting the general resurrection, enters according to its rank, either immediately into paradise (prophets), or partakes, in the shape of a green bird, of the delights of the abode of bliss (martyrs), or—in the case of common believers—is supposed either to stay near the grave, or to be with Adam in the lowest heaven, or to remain either in the well of Zem-Zem, or in the trumpet of the resurrection. According to others, it rests in the shape of a white bird under the throne of God. The souls of the infidels dwell in a certain well in the province of Hadramaut (Heb. Courts of Death), or, being first offered to heaven, then offered to earth, and rejected by either, become subject to unspeakable tortures until the day of resurrection.

Mohammedan theologians are very much divided in regard to the doctrine of the resurrection. Mohammed himself seems to have held that both soul and body will be raised, and the "Bone Luz" of the Jewish Haggadah was by him transformed into the bone Al-Ajb, the rump-bone, which will remain uncorrupted until the last day, and from which the whole body will spring anew, after a forty-days' rain. Among the signs by which the approach of the last day may be known—nearly all taken from the legendary part of the Talmud and Midrash, where the signs of the coming of the Messiah are enumerated—are the decay of faith among men, the advancing of the meanest persons to highest dignities, wars, seditions, and tumults, and consequent dire distress, so that a man passing another's grave shall say: "Would to God I were in his place!" Certain provinces shall revolt, and the buildings of Medina shall reach to Yahâb. Again: the sun will rise in the west; the Beast will appear; Constantinople will be taken by the descendants of Isaac; the Antichrist will come, and be killed by Jesus at Lud. There will further take place a war with the Jews, Gog and Magog's (Jajug and Majuj's) eruption, a great smoke, an eclipse, the Mohammedans will return to idolatry, a great treasure will be found in the Euphrates, the Kaaba will be destroyed by the Ethiopians, beasts and inanimate things will speak, and, finally, a wind will sweep away the souls of those who have faith, even if equal only to a grain of mustard seed, so that the world shall be left in ignorance.

The time of the resurrection even Mohammed could not learn from Gabriel: it is a mystery. Three blasts will announce it: that of consternation, of such terrible powers that mothers shall neglect the babes on their breasts, and that heaven and earth will melt; that of examination, which will annihilate all things and beings, even the angel of death, save paradise and hell, and their inhabitants; and, forty years later, that of resurrection, when all men, Mohammed first, shall have their souls breathed into their restored bodies, and will sleep in their sepulchres until the final doom has been passed upon them. The day of judgment, lasting from one to fifty thousand years, will call up angels, genii, men, and animals. The trial over, the righteous will enter paradise, to the right hand, and the wicked will pass to the left, into hell; both, however, have first to go over the bridge Al-Sirât, laid over the midst of hell, being finer than a hair, and sharper than the edge of a sword, and beset with thorns on either side. The righteous will proceed on their path with ease and swiftness, but the wicked will fall down headlong to hell below. Paradise is divided from hell by a partition (Orf), in which a certain number of half-saints will find place. The blessed, destined for the abodes of eternal delight (Jannat-Aden; Heb. Gan-Eden)—of which it is, however, not quite certain whether it is already created— will first drink of the Pond of the Prophet, which is supplied from the rivers of paradise, whiter than milk, and more odoriferous than musk. Arrived at one of the eight gates, they will be met by beautiful youths and angels; and their degree of righteousness (prophets, religious teachers, martyrs, believers) will procure for them the corresponding degree of happiness. It may, however, not be superfluous to add that, according to the Mohammedan doctrine, it is not a person's good works or merits which gain his admittance, but solely God's mercy; also that the poor will enter paradise five hundred years before the rich; and that the majority of the inhabitants of hell are women.

As to the various felicities which await the pious (and of which there are about a hundred degrees), they are a wild conglomeration of Jewish, Christian, Magian, and other fancies on the subject, to which the Prophet's own exceedingly sensual imagination has added very considerably. Feasting in the most gorgeous and delicious variety, the most costly and brilliant garments, odors and music of the most ravishing nature, and, above all, the enjoyment of the Hûr Al-Oyûn, the black-eyed daughters of paradise, created of pure musk, and free from all the bodily weaknesses of the female sex, are held out as a reward to the commonest inhabitants of paradise, who will always remain in the full vigor of their youth and manhood. For those deserving a higher degree of recompense, rewards will be prepared of a purely spiritual kind—i. e. the "beholding of God's face" (Shechinah) by night and by day. A separate abode of happiness will also be reserved for women; but there is considerable doubt as to the manner of their enjoyment. That they are not of a prominently spiritual nature is clear from the story of the Prophet and the old woman. The latter solicited Mohammed to intercede with God that she might be admitted into paradise, whereupon he replied that old women were not allowed in paradise; which dictum—causing her to weep—he further explained by saying that they would first be made young again.

Regarding the punishment of the wicked, the Moslem has received detailed information from the Prophet. According to him, hell is divided into seven stories or apartments, one below another, designed for the reception of as many distinct classes of the damned. The first, which is called *Jehenam*, is the receptacle of those who acknowledged one God, that is, the wicked Mohammedans, who, after having been punished according to their demerits, will at length be released; the second, named *Ladha*, they assign to the Jews; the third, named *al-Hotama*, to the Christians; the fourth, named *al-Sair*, to the Sabians; the fifth, named *Sakar*, to the Magians; the sixth, named *al-Jahin*, to the idolaters; and the seventh, which is the lowest and worst of all, and is called *al-Hawyat*, to the hypocrites, or those who outwardly professed some religion, but in their hearts were of none. Over each of these apartments they believe there will be set a guard of angels, nineteen in number, to whom the damned will confess the just judgment of God, and beg them to intercede with him for some alleviation of their pain, or that they may be delivered by being annihilated. Mohammed has, in his Koran and traditions, been very exact in describing the various torments of hell, which, according to him, the wicked will suffer both from intense heat and excessive cold. We shall, however, enter into no detail of them here; but only observe that the degrees of these pains will also vary in proportion to the crimes of the sufferer, and the apartment he is condemned to; and that he who is punished the most lightly of all will be shod with shoes of fire, the fervor of which will cause his skull to boil like a caldron. The condition of these unhappy wretches, it is taught, cannot be properly called either life or death; and their misery will be greatly increased by their despair of being ever delivered from that place, since, according to that frequent expression in the Koran, "they must remain therein forever." It must be remarked, however, that the infidels alone will be liable

to eternity of damnation; for the Moslems, or those who have embraced the true religion, and have been guilty of heinous sins, will be delivered thence after they shall have expiated their crimes by their sufferings. The time which these believers shall be detained there, according to a tradition handed down from their Prophet, will not be less than nine hundred years, nor more than seven thousand. As to the manner of their deliverance, they say that they shall be distinguished by the marks of prostration on those parts of their bodies with which they used to touch the ground in prayer, and over which the fire will therefore have no power; and that, being known by this characteristic, they will be released by the mercy of God, at the intercession of Mohammed and the blessed; whereupon those who shall have been dead will be restored to life, as has been said; and those whose bodies shall have contracted any sootiness or filth from the flames and smoke of hell will be immersed in one of the rivers of paradise, called the River of Life, which will wash them whiter than pearls.

II. *Practical Duties.*—Our consideration is next required for an examination of that part of Islam called the "Din," or practical part, which Mohammedan jurists and theologians divide into two principal sections: (*a*) the religious or *ceremonial law* (parts of which, however, according to our Western notions, belong to the category of state rights); and (*b*) the civil law, including police and special laws.

(*a*) The ceremonial law, or Ritual of Islam, contains (1) the various regulations concerning *purification*, which is to precede, especially, prayer and other religious obligations, or the approach to or touch of sacred things. Here is taught what is to be considered as impure, and requires a purification after touching; what kind of water is to be used for ablution, or how, in want of water, sand is to be applied; what parts of the body are to be washed; what conditions of body require a second ablution; how women, after parturition or during menstruation, have to conduct themselves. Religious purifications are of two kinds: the *Ghusl*, or total immersion of the body, required as a religious ceremony on some special occasions; and the *Wudu*, a partial ablution, to be performed immediately before the prayer. This is of primary importance, and consists of the washing of hands, face, ears, and feet up to the ankles—a proceeding generally accompanied at each stage by corresponding pious sentences, and concluded by the recital of the 97th chapter of the Koran. "The practice of religion being founded on cleanliness, it is not sufficient that the believer himself should be purified, but even the ground or the carpet upon which he prays must be clean; hence the use of a special prayer-carpet" (Segaddeh).

(2) The precepts which have for their object the performance of prayer—"the key of paradise." They refer to the time at which the five daily devotions are to be held; to the prayers on Fridays and festival days; at eclipses of the sun and moon, or in seasons of drought; and to the position of the body in prayer. They treat further of the prayer of women, of things which invalidate prayer, of the abbreviation of prayer during travel or in peril of life, of the direction while praying, and the places where prayers must not be said. In this section the Shafiites adduce the prohibition for men to wear silk clothing, or gold and silver ornaments, as well as the various ceremonies to be observed at funerals: how the corpse is to be washed, dressed, and placed in the grave; how the dead is to be prayed for; how the tomb is to be constructed; how the deceased is to be lamented for, the family of the departed to be comforted, etc.

The prayers (Salah) performed by every Mohammedan five times daily consist partly of extracts from the Revealed Book, the Koran (Fard), partly of pieces ordained by the Prophet, without allegation of a divine order (Sunnah). The first time of prayer commences at the Maghrib, or about sunset; the second at the Eshè, or nightfall; the third at Subh, or daybreak; the fourth at the Duhr, or about noon; the fifth at the Asr, or afternoon. The believers are not to commence their prayers exactly at sunrise, or noon, or sunset, lest they might be confounded with the infidel sun-worshippers. These several times of prayer are announced by the muezzins (q. v.) from the minarets or madnehs of the mosques. Their chant, sung to a very simple but solemn melody, sounds harmoniously and sonorously down the height of the mosque, through the mid-day din and roar of the cities; but its impression is one of the most strikingly poetical in the stillness of night; so much so that even many Europeans cannot help congratulating the Prophet on his preferring the human voice to either the Jewish trumpet-call of the time of the Temple, or the Christian church-bells. The day-call (the Adan) consists chiefly of the confession of faith (God is most great; Mohammed is God's apostle; come to prayer; come to security), repeated several times; the nightcalls (Ula, the first; Ebed, the second), destined for persons who desire to perform supererogatory acts of devotion, are much longer. The believer often changes his posture during his prayers; and a certain number of such inclinations of head and knees, prostrations, etc., is called a Rekah. It is also necessary that the face of the worshipper should be turned towards the Keblah (q. v.), that direction being marked in the exterior wall of the mosque by a niche (Mehrab). All sumptuous and pompous apparel is laid aside before the believer approaches the sacred place; and the extreme solemnity and decorum, the unaffected humility, the real and allabsorbing devotion which pervade it, have been unanimously held up as an example to other creeds. The Moslems, it may be remarked here, do not pray to Mohammed, but simply implore his intercession, as they do that of the numerous saints, the relatives of the Prophet, and the first propagators of Islam. For the particulars of the service in the *mosque*, the reader is referred to that heading. It may be remarked in passing that Mohammedanism has no clergy in our sense of the word, the civil and religious law being bound up in one. See also MOLLAH; MUFTI.

(3) Instructions about the *taxes* of property to be paid to the state, and the manner of their application. Taxable articles are fruits of the field, domestic animals, silver, gold, and merchandise, lying with the owner a year. The taxes (the varying amounts we pass by) are to be used to aid the poor, for the conversion of infidels, for the redemption of slaves and prisoners, for the payment of the debts of the indigent, for the aid of travellers in distress, and in general for purposes pleasing to God; as, for instance, the erection of mosques, schools, hospitals, and the like.

(4) The precepts about *fasting*, particularly in the month of Ramadan. Here is specified what is commanded and forbidden to the one who fasts, how fasting is interrupted, who is entitled to be dispensed from fasting, and what must be done in expiation for not fasting. In this section are mentioned also the various regulations for an individual who during the Ramadan wishes to retire from the world and pass his time in devotion in the mosque, and thus to lead a kind of monastic life. It was Mohammed's special and express desire that no one should fast who is not quite equal to it, lest it might prove injurious to health. But there are very few Moslems who do not keep the Ramadan—the Mohammedan Lent—even if they neglect their other religious duties; at all events, they all pretend to keep it most strictly, fasting being considered "one fourth part of the faith," nay, "the gate of religion."

(5) The precepts concerning the *pilgrimage*, an obligation which a Moslem has to meet at least once in his life. He who neglects to perform this duty "might as well die a Jew or a Christian." Various preparations are necessary for pilgrimage. Certain holy places are to be visited, mostly such as were sacred even before Mo-

hammed, and are connected with legends about Abraham and Hagar; certain prayers and ceremonies are to be performed, and sacrifices to be slaughtered, the meat of which is in part to be distributed among the poor. It is forbidden to wear sewed dresses during the journey. Men are not allowed to cover their heads nor women their faces; the nails of the fingers and toes are not to be cut; the hair is not to be combed nor shorn; the use of unguents and perfumes is forbidden; the contracting of marriage is forbidden, as well as the gratification of sexual passion. Finally, it is explained how the pilgrimage is considered interrupted, or as not performed, and how the transgression of any prohibition is to be atoned for.

(6) There are various regulations referring to *food.* Wine and intoxicating beverages are not allowed; also the drinking of the blood even of clean animals is interdicted. Quadrupeds and birds must be killed according to certain fixed rules, God being invoked before the slaughter; but game shot by a hunter may be eaten. The eating of carnivorous animals of prey, quadrupeds as well as birds, is prohibited; and particularly the flesh of swine, dogs, cats, mice, etc. Of fish, such as have no scales, and those resembling serpents, are forbidden. As the same laws are in force also among the Jews, a Moslem may partake of a Jew's meal; with Christians he can dine only if he know that he conforms to the laws of Islam; but with pagans he must not eat at all, even when the food has been prepared in a proper manner, because it has been prepared without the religious ceremonies that make it fit for the believer's table.

(7) Among the "positive" ordinances of Islam may also be reckoned the "Saghir," or minor, and the "Kebir," or great festivals. The first (Al-Fetr, or breaking the fast), following immediately upon the Ramadan, begins on the 1st day of the month of Shawâl, and lasts three days. The second (Eed Al-Kurban, or sacrifice) begins on the 10th of Dsu'l Heggeh, when the pilgrims perform their sacrifice, and lasts three or four days. Yet, although intended to be the most important of the two, the people have in most places changed the order, and, by way of compensation for the previous fast, they make the lesser festival which follows the Ramadan the most joyful and the longest of the two. The day set aside for the weekly day of rest is Friday—not, as is generally supposed, because both the Jewish Sabbath and the Christian Sunday were to be avoided, but because, from times long before Mohammed, the people used to hold public assemblies for civil as well as religious purposes on that day. The celebration of the Moslem days of religious solemnity is far less strict than is the custom with the other Shemitic religions. Service being over, the people are allowed to return to their worldly affairs, if they cannot afford to give themselves up entirely to pleasure or devotion for the rest of the sacred period.

(8) One of not the least important duties laid upon the Moslem by the Koran is that of giving alms. These are twofold—legal (Zekah) and voluntary (Sadakah; Heb. Zedekah, piety, righteousness); but the former (Sur. ii, 3), once collected by the sovereign and applied to pious uses, has now been practically abrogated. The Sadakah is, according to the law, to be given once every year, of cattle, money, corn, fruits, and wares sold, at about the rate of two and a half up to twenty per cent. Besides these, it is usual to bestow a measure of provisions upon the poor at the end of the sacred month of Ramadan.

(9) Before we quit this department of Mohammedan law, it may not be inappropriate to mention the procedure against apostates. To prevent the faithful from ever falling back into idolatry, the laws relating to images and pictures have been made very stringent. Whoever makes an imitation of any living being in stone, wood, or any other material, shall on the day of judgment be asked to endow his creation with life and

soul, and on his protesting his inability to do so, shall undergo the punishment of hell for a certain period.

(b) The *civil law* of the Mohammedans comprises the following main sections:

(1) *Commercial relations*, including rules to govern relations of commerce, of various contracts, of pawn and mortgage, of power of attorney, of debt obligations, and other property rights; excepting, however, hereditary and matrimonial claims. We cannot, of course, enter into details here, but we may remark that the law of trade contains many restrictions very burdensome for modern conditions of society. Thus, for instance, it is not permitted to make a difference whether the price is paid immediately or only in instalments. The re-sale of articles not yet in possession of the purchaser is invalid; nor can objects of value which are not the undivided property of single persons be subjects of trade. Further, trade in things whose use is forbidden to the Moslem, e. g. liquors and unclean animals, is prohibited. A bargain concluded on a Friday, at the time of the noon prayer, is void. The buying up of merchandise, especially of victuals, in order to produce a rise of prices, is unlawful. In lending money, it is forbidden to receive interest. In case of insolvency, or refusal to pay a debt, the creditor can require the arrest of the debtor's person. A pledge is not, as according to European law, a means of security for the payment of debt, but only a proof that such a debt exists. Only when a pledge has been given in a condition of decided insolvency does the creditor acquire the right to secure redemption of the pledge.

(2) The law of *inheritance* and the *testament*. We pass over the details of the first, and only observe that the law of primogeniture does not exist in the Mohammedan code, and that, as a rule, brothers or sons, and male heirs generally, enjoy many advantages over females. A testament, in order to be valid, must not contain allusions to any articles prohibited by law, such as swine, blood, wine, and the like. A legacy in favor of strangers, if persons able to succeed legal inheritance exist, must not go beyond the amount of one third; among the relatives themselves the division is at pleasure. A testament, whether written or oral, must be executed before two witnesses of the male sex. A testament in favor of minors, bondmen, and infidels is not valid in law.

(3) The *marriage* law. A man is allowed to see but the hands and the face of the maiden or widow whom he intends to wed; then follows the courting in person or by proxy; a marriage-contract is concluded, in which the nuptial gift is fixed, i. e. what is allotted to the wife in case the husband dies or has himself divorced; and the ecclesiastic consecrates the marriage. A free man can marry four free women; a female slave he is only allowed to marry if he have not the means to contract marriage with a free person. Polygamy is allowed among Mohammedans, we see, then, surrounded by a number of restrictions. Hear the Koran on this point: "Take in marriage of the women who please you, two, three, or four; but if ye fear that ye cannot act equitably, one, or those whom your right hand has acquired"—i. e. slaves (Sur. iv, 3). Minor girls can be forced by their father or grandfather to enter into matrimony as long as they are single; if widows, they have their own choice. Marriage of near relatives, among which niece, nurse, and milk-sister are enumerated, is prohibited. A Moslem may, if urged by excessive love, or if unable to obtain a wife of his own creed, marry a Christian woman or a Jewess, but a Mohammedan woman is not, under any circumstances, to marry an unbeliever. In all cases, however, the child born of a Moslem, whatever the mother's faith, is a Moslem; nor does the wife, who is an unbeliever, inherit at her husband's death. See also MARRIAGE. Matrimony is annulled by insanity, apostasy from Islam, impotence of the male, or corporeal disability for sexual intercourse of the female. See DIVORCE. The husband is to treat his wives equally; only newly-married women are privileged for

a few days. The Shiites sanction also temporary marriage. The free man can give a divorce to his wife twice and retake her, even without her consent, if three menstruations or three months have not elapsed, and then only if in the mean while she had contracted another marriage which has been dissolved by death or divorce. On this point the Mohammedan law differs from the Mosaic law, by which a divorced woman who has contracted another marriage is forever forbidden to the first husband. According to the Mosaic law, the marriage between uncle and niece is permitted, but not between aunt and nephew. Pregnant women are allowed to remarry only after their confinement; if not pregnant, after four months and ten days. If a man accuses his wife of adultery, he must either bring witnesses to confirm his statement, or he must himself swear four times in the mosque before a number of men that he speaks the truth, adding, "The curse of God may strike me if I speak false." The woman is then considered an adulteress, the marriage is dissolved, and can never be renewed. But if the woman afterwards swear four times against the accusation, declaring at the same time that God's wrath may strike her if her husband have spoken true, the marriage is annulled, but the woman is not considered an adulteress. Children of divorced wives must be cared for by the mother to the seventh year; later, the child can choose whether it will live with the father or the mother. The woman has a right to ask for divorce if the husband cannot support her.

(4) The *penal* law and procedure. An intentional murder is punished by death; the relatives of the murdered, however, possessing the right to avenge his blood, may take a ransom instead. (Modern practices in Turkey deviating from these laws are in harmony with those of Christian countries.) Manslaughter not intentional is expiated by a ransom, estimated according to the intent of the slayer to injure the slain. For the murder of a woman only half price is paid; for that of a Jew or a Christian, a third; for that of a pagan, a fifteenth part. In case of mutilation, revenge or ransom may satisfy. Adultery is punished by death, if the marriage between adulterer and adulteress be forbidden on account of consanguinity; or if the adulterer marry the adulteress without having previously atoned for his crime according to precepts; or if a non-Moslem is the criminal. Other cases of adultery are punished by one hundred lashes and one year of banishment. He who charges another with adultery without being able to prove his accusation is punished by eighty lashes. Drinking wine is punished by forty lashes. Pederasty and sodomy are punishable with death, like adultery. He who steals for the first time is to have his right hand cut off; for the second time, his left; for the third time, his right foot; for the fourth time, the left foot. (The Turkish government has substituted the ordinary punishments of imprisonment, hard labor, and the bastinado.) Highway robbers, if they have committed a murder, are to be crucified; if they only threatened to murder, they are to receive corporeal punishment and to be imprisoned. A Moslem apostatizing from his faith, and persevering in his apostasy, or denying only one of the obligations of Islam, is to be punished with death.

Of the Mohammedan procedure, we mention only the peculiarity as regards witnesses. In civil suits the testimony of two men, or of one man and two women, or of one man in conjunction with the plaintiff, is required. In affairs of tutelage, as testament, divorce, guardianship, and the like, the testimony of two men only is accepted. In affairs which concern only women, as, for instance, birth, female infirmities, nurses, the testimony of four women is necessary. In crimes of sodomy and pederasty and adultery, four male witnesses are required; in other crimes, as theft, partaking of forbidden food and drink, apostasy from the faith, the testimony of two men is sufficient. Non-Moslems, or Moslems known as hardened sinners, are not admitted as witnesses.

(5) *War on Infidels.*—The Koran abounds in contradictions respecting the right and duty of the faithful to make war on infidels; for Mohammed, while he was the weaker party, showed himself very tolerant, and commanded to convert only by the power of the word; but later, when he became more potent, he issued severer ordinances against those who would not submit to his faith. His successors, therefore, have established the following doctrines, and declared null and void the passages of the Koran adverse to them. Every major Moslem fit for military service is in duty bound to participate in holy wars against infidels who will not submit to the dominion of Moslems, and against the faithful who refuse obedience to the legitimate prince, or adhere to dogmas contrary to the faith. In a war against Moslemite rebels or heretics it is not allowed to kill prisoners of war, nor to attack the wounded or pillage property. As for infidel prisoners of war, who do not adopt the Islam before their capture, women and children are made slaves; men can, according to the pleasure of the prince or political exigency, either be killed, ransomed, or exchanged for Moslem prisoners; or even, as circumstances may dictate, be released or be made slaves. Children of infidels will be educated as Moslems, if their father or mother have been converted to Islam, if they have been captured without parents, or if they are found on Islamitic territory. We omit the direction for the distribution of booty and conquered lands, as we have already alluded to the treatment to be accorded to Jews and Christians. We only remark that, in accordance with the letter of the Koran, as well as the principles of the early imams, war against non-Mohammedans is declared permanent; if it is carried on against pagans, to extinction; against Christians, to subjection; and that, therefore, in earlier times, when the Islamitic powers decided to discontinue hostilities, they simply concluded a truce. In the precepts of this kind, the Moslems come to realize that their sacred scripture contains laws and ordinances not applicable and practicable for all times and circumstances, nor to all countries and people; for the most orthodox ulemas cannot think of urging the sultan to declare war against Russia or Austria, or to forbid Europeans living in Constantinople to ride on horseback or dwell in palaces surpassing in height the houses of the Moslems. Again, in spite of Koran and Sunnah, the idolaters and fire-worshippers were no more exterminated than the Christians were humbled and made to pay capitation tax. Many fire-worshippers in Persia retained not only their lives, but preserved in several places also their pyres. It even occurred that the Mohammedan government corrected ecclesiastics because they wished to transform temples of the Guebers into mosques. The strict execution of the religious precept would have compelled them to massacre all, since their character is very tenacious—a proceeding which would prove of great injury to the Islamitic state, and apparently be regarded as too cruel even for execution by bloodthirsty Arabs. The government was not unmerciful against those who remained true to their faith, but it knew no bounds against those converted to the Islam who, abhorring it in their heart, conspired secretly against the Islam and the State, and tried to undermine the first by old Parsee doctrines and philosophic speculation, and the latter by the revival of Persian nationality.

(6) *Slave Laws.*—According to the fundamental doctrines of Islam, only captives of war made in an infidel country are slaves; in all Moslem countries, however, negroes and Abyssinian slaves also are kept in bondage by ruse or force. If slaves of an infidel become converts to Islam, the master is obliged to sell them to a Moslem for a price customary in the country. The Koran enunciates distinctly their equality with the freemen before God; and a tradition worthy of credit says: "He who manumits a faithful slave is delivered from the torments of hell." Female slaves, by whom their master has begotten children, at his death obtain their liberty, pro-

VI.—14

vided one of the children is alive; the children are born free, and even over the mother the master has a restricted control; he is not permitted to sell or marry her to another. There are in the Koran still other precepts favorable to the slaves.

III. *Ethics.*—The moral law of the Koran may be considered as the most perfect part of this remarkable book. The ethics of the Koran, an element of Islam which (because not to be circumscribed and defined by doctors) has undergone the least change in the course of time, most distinctly reveals the mind of its author. It is, to be sure, as disconnected and unsystematically arranged as other matters, but the most beautiful moral principles and precepts permeate like a thread of gold this whole texture of religion, enthusiasm, superstition, and delusion. Injustice, falsehood, pride, revenge, calumny, mockery, avarice, prodigality, debauchery, mistrust, and suspicion are inveighed against as ungodly and wicked; while benevolence, liberality, modesty, forbearance, patience and endurance, frugality, sincerity, straightforwardness, decency, love of peace and truth, and, above all, trusting in God, and submitting to his will, are considered as the pillars of true piety, and the principal signs of a true believer. Thus, e. g. the Koran contains passages like the following, which is in a sort of dialogue form: "Speak (thus God addressed Mohammed): Approach! I will read to thee what God has forbidden thee. Thou shalt not associate with him any other being; thou shalt honor father and mother; thou shalt not kill thy children for fear of poverty, for we feed thee and them; thou shalt not live unchaste, neither privately nor publicly; thou shalt not kill any being which Allah has commanded to hold sacred, unless thou art (legally) empowered to do so; further, thou shalt not stretch out thy hand after the property of orphans, unless it be for their benefit, till they are of age; thou shalt give good measure and weight; thou shalt not lay on anybody a burden heavier than he can perform. If thou give judgment, be just even if the person concerned be a relation, and hold fast to the covenant of God." By the prohibition of gambling and drinking wine and other intoxicating beverages, many an excess and vice is of course prevented, and quarrel and enmity avoided. Particularly mockery, haughtiness, and slanderous talk are warned against: "O ye faithful (says the Koran), deride not one another; for it might happen that those on whom ye look contemptuously are better than yourself. Do not insult each other, and do not give each other ignominious bynames! Such words are abominable in the mouth of the faithful. He who does not correct this habit is counted with malefactors. O ye faithful! beware of too great suspiciousness, for many a suspicion is sinful. Be not eavesdroppers, and do not speak ill of each other. Would ye fain eat the flesh of your brother, if he be dead? As ye abhor this, do not soil his honor to his back! O ye people, we have created you of one wife and one man, and divided you in different nations and tribes (think of that!), that you may know that only the most pious is the most notable before God." In another passage it is said: "Do not strut this earth in self-conceit! Thou canst not perforate the earth, nor attain the height of the mountains (i. e. the lifeless earth extends farther in depth and in height than thou)." In conclusion we read: "Piety does not consist in turning your face towards the east or west; but he is pious who believes in the Deity, in the day of judgment, in the angels, in the scripture and the prophets; who, though fond of property, disposes of the same to relatives, the poor, orphans, travellers, and other indigent persons, or uses it for the delivery of slaves and prisoners; who prays to God and pays his poor-tax (alms); who complies with every bargain entered into, and bears patiently distress, oppression, and all kinds of war-calamities: these are the really pious, these are the God-fearing."

Mohammed was, to a certain extent, obliged to proclaim equality and fraternity of all believers as a religious principle; for he himself, as already mentioned, belonged not to the ruling party in Mecca, and his first adherents were for the most part of the lower class, so that the Meccans retorted on him : "If God had pleased to send a prophet, he would have selected him from a more prominent family." Mohammed was frequently censured for being surrounded by slaves, freedmen, and a promiscuous crowd. It is, therefore, natural that he combated with all his might prejudices of birth and rank of every description. If, on the other hand, Mohammed is reported to have said : "He who was of the nobility in paganism remains so in Islam, if he bow before true wisdom;" this sentence is probably to be placed in that time when he was inclined to all sorts of concessions, in order to make proselytes also among the higher classes. At any rate, he revoked it when the Meccan nobility persisted in their opposition against his doctrine; as he retracted, for a similar reason, his opinion which represented the idols as mediators between God and man, and in a measure representatives of spirits or angels, and branded it even as a sentiment of Satan. But however decidedly Mohammed pronounced in favor of equality of all men, i. e. all the faithful, he failed in the attempt to abolish slavery altogether, though he mitigated its lot in many respects. Nor was he more successful in emancipating woman, albeit he protected her against the arbitrariness of man, and granted her many rights which she had not enjoyed in Arabia before his time. While he prescribed to the faithful to take not more than four women, and allowed intercourse with female slaves only to the unmarried, he proclaimed revelations by which God relieved him of restrictions binding upon others. He had the right to request every faithful to divorce his wife, if he desired marrying her himself. He claimed to contract for himself and others any matrimonial connection, without the consent of the girl or her protector. He was permitted to marry as many women as he pleased, and he indeed increased their number to thirteen, and felt not bound to treat them alike. The excessive jealousy of the legislator had the most grievous consequences for the women. It extended so far that his women not only remained excluded from all intercourse with other men during his life, but were also prohibited remarrying after his death. Later, all other faithful women were also ordered to wear a close veil, leaving only the eyes free, when going out, and even in the house not to show themselves unveiled except to their nearest relatives. Thus women who, with pagan Arabs, were the spice of public and social life, were by Mohammed's jealousy confined entirely to the home and the family circle. The fair sex, with the Bedouins as well as with the mediæval knights of the Occident objects of veneration and worship, was changed by the Islam into a subject of pity and mistrust. The place of their abode was, it is true, called Harem—i. e. sanctuary—but it was understood to be a sanctuary requiring veil and curtain, and finally lock and bolt and eunuchs to protect it against violation. This system of close confinement had, of course, the saddest consequences for the male sex. The husband found only sensual, but no cordial and mental enjoyment in his harem, and fell more and more into rudeness and unnatural vices. Mohammed, by his own life and by his ordinances concerning women, has impressed the character of transitoriness and human weakness on himself and his revelations. Here is manifest in the "reformer" himself the want of a strictly moral sentiment, and in his precepts sanctioning polygamy and seclusion of woman he has left a legacy which prevents the professors of his faith making any considerable progress in civilization, and raising themselves by a sound family life to a prosperous life of state. The Jews, on the other hand, to whom the Mosaic law allows a plurality of wives, have found a rabbi from whom they have accepted monogamy as a law, even in countries where polygamy is not forbidden. The Moslem may soon also, like the Jew of our times, learn to make a distinction be-

tween eternal truths and laws and ordinances enacted for transient external circumstances. The Moslem in general is not so firmly attached to his faith as the Jew. We observe this in those Arabs and Turks who have lived a few years in Christian countries, and have participated in European civilization. Should the political independence of the Moslems, which owes its existence only to the mutual jealousies of the European powers, cease, their religion, as it is founded on illusion, spread by the sword, and leaning on secular force, will not long survive it. The professors of Islam will then suffer great change. There will be some who will relapse into former indifferentism to religion, while others will adopt the faith of their conquerors, and probably the larger number. For a revival of the caliphate, i. e. a Mohammedan empire ruled by a head of a supremacy at once spiritual and secular, the necessary elements are lacking—unity of faith and nationality. Shiites and Sunnites are still as hostile towards each other as they were a thousand years ago; and to the old incompatibility of the Arabian and Persian element a third one is added, semi-Mongolian—the Osmanic—considerably increasing the rupture. A new universal blaze of fanaticism, even if it could prevail against rifled cannon and iron-plated frigates, is no more to be apprehended.

IV. *Mohammedanism and Christianity.*—The friends and advocates of Mohammedanism have repeatedly, especially in our day of comparative religious research, urged upon the Christian world a consideration of the claims Islam has in the advance of humanitarian principles and the propagation of civilizing influences. Islamism, it is declared, started as the outspoken foe of all creature-worship; with emphasis proclaimed the superiority and sublimity of God; and, like the Jew and the Christian, the Moslem based his faith upon the revealed book known as the Bible. It is further urged in defence of the Arabian religion that its successes and rapid spread over a vast portion of the then known world would stamp the religion of Moslem with the approval of the Most High. As a matter of history, we have to record that scarcely a century had elapsed after Mohammed's death when Islam reigned supreme over Arabia, Syria, Persia, Egypt, the whole of the northern coast of Africa, even as far as Spain; and, notwithstanding the subsequent strifes and divisions in the interior of this gigantic realm, it grew, and grew outwardly, until the Crescent was made to gleam from the spires of St. Sophia at Constantinople, and the cry "Allah il Allah" resounded before the gates of Vienna, and that but for the successful opposition of Charles Martel, the Moslems might not only have caused the downfall of the Romish hierarchy, but even extirpated Christianity itself. See SARACENS. If, however, we inquire into the causes of these successes of the Crescent, we find that Mohammed's law was artfully and marvellously adapted to the corrupt nature of man; and, in a most particular manner, to the manners and opinions of the Eastern nations, and the vices to which they were naturally addicted: for the articles of the faith which it proposed were few in number, and extremely simple; and the duties it required were neither many nor difficult, nor such as were incompatible with the empire of appetites and passions. It is to be observed, further, that the gross ignorance under which the Arabians, Syrians, Persians, and the greatest part of the Eastern nations labored at this time rendered many an easy prey to the artifice and eloquence of this bold adventurer. To these causes of the progress of Mohammedanism we may add that these victories of the Crescent were secured, not by the spread of the Koran, but by armies in hostile array, invading peaceful countries for spoil and devastation. It is an error even to place the first conquests and the rapid spread of Islam to the credit of Arabian religious fanaticism. We must reflect that military glory and booty to the Bedouins, who formed the flower of the first Arabian armies, were not less enticing than the pleasure-gardens with everblooming virgins [see HOURIS] vouchsafed to the faithful. Nor must it be forgotten that the state of the countries and nations conquered by the Arabs was decayed and rotten, falling to pieces at the first touch. In Persia and Syria, as well as in Egypt, in Barbary, in Sicily, and in Spain, the Arabs were victorious because the population was dissatisfied with their governments, and often in secret understanding with the enemy. Persia was weakened by long wars with Byzantium, and divided by the nobility ruling the court; while, besides, many of its inhabitants, of Arabian origin, especially in the Western provinces, sympathized with the kindred troops. A similar condition of things prevailed in Syria, where also the Shemitic population predominated, looking upon the Byzantines as their oppressors. In Egypt, to the antipathy between Copts and Greeks was added an ecclesiastical pressure against the Monophysites by the Byzantine court, which held to the doctrine of the double nature of Christ. For the subjugation of Sicily the Saracens were mostly indebted to the traitor Euphemius, and count Julian made way for the Arabs in the conquest of Spain, the more rapidly accomplished since a part of the maltreated people were indifferent spectators of the struggle, while another part even aided the enemy. Thus it is explained how the Islam, within a short century, victoriously raised its standard from the Guadalquivir to the Indus. But thus rapidly it also went to decline, when the caliphs became effeminate, and were controlled by foreign mercenaries; when rude force obstructed every scientific elevation; and internal feuds, in consequence of no appointed succession by Mohammed, consumed its best energies. If undisputed legitimate foundation was formerly wanting to strengthen monarchy, because the adherents of Ali believed only his descendants worthy of succession, this difficulty is still greater under the Osmanlis, who are not looked upon as legitimate dynasts even by the Sunnites, and hence it has happened twice in our day that Christian bayonets have had to defend the sultan against an Arabian army commanded by an ambitious Turk (Ali and Ibrahim Pasha). How long European diplomacy will succeed in nursing the sick empire cannot be predicted; but it is certain that if no other reforms than those hitherto introduced, and these mostly on paper, impart a fresh, vigorous spirit to the Mohammedan states and the Islam faith, both will verge on ruin.

The Christian must, moreover, refuse all credit to Islam as a civilizing influence, because it has failed to prove itself such after a trial of centuries. In the East, as we have already conceded, it has done some good. But let it not be forgotten that it scarcely accomplished as much as Judaism could have secured. Had Mohammedanism been confined to the limits of Arabia, it would have accomplished a mission, an appointment—possibly even divine—for it would have fitted that country for Christianity as such, as the Mosaic institutions fit for the higher laws of Christianity. And, as has been well said, "were it not for the all-important fact that Christianity had been preached in the interval, the mission of Mohammed would appear exactly analogous to that of Moses. If the religion of Mohammed was imperfect, so was that of Moses; if the civil precepts of Mohammed were adapted only to a single nation, so were those of Moses also. Indeed, in some respects, Mohammedanism is a clear advance upon Judaism. It more distinctly represents God as the God of the whole world, and not of one nation only; it preaches with more clearness the doctrines of God's general providence, of a resurrection, and of a final judgment. . . . In short, had Mohammedanism only preceded Christianity, it might have been accepted as another step towards it; the mosque might have been an appropriate and friendly halting-place between the synagogue and the church. As it is, Mohammedanism, coming after Christianity, has proved its deadliest enemy. Its claim to be to Christianity what Christianity was to Judaism is belied

by the fact that this supposed reformed and developed Christianity is in fact a retrogression, denying nearly all those points in which Christianity is a reformed and developed Judaism. . . . Mohammed saw that many Christians of his time were practical idolaters, and he too hastily confounded the worship of Christ with the worship of his mother and his servants. Christianity was distracted and confounded by unintelligible disputes as to the divine nature and attributes of Christ; Mohammed hastily cast them all aside as alike violations of the divine unity. Too many Christians had made themselves many mediators; Mohammed too hastily rejected the one true Mediator, and represented Jesus as a mere preacher like himself" (Freeman, Saracens, p. 60 sq.).

The effects of the Mohammedan conquests on the religion of the conquered have been very various. In Christian countries where the Moslem power has not been lasting, as in Spain, Sicily, and those parts of Eastern Europe conquered by the Turks, no trace of them is left except buildings, and some popular customs and superstitions. But where their dominion has endured, as in Western Asia and Northern Africa, Christianity, once supreme, has now almost perished. This has been caused partially by individual conversions—for no Christian population, except perhaps that of Crete, has ever in a body apostatized—but mainly by the substitution of a Moslem for a Christian population. Baptism and the teaching of Christianity were forbidden; Christian women were forced into the harems of Mohammedans; Christian children were forcibly brought up as Moslems; indignities, burdensome taxes, and personal duties were imposed on Christians; from time to time violent persecutions took place. Moreover, in many countries heresy largely prevailed, which is unable to furnish any firm ground of faith. Heretics frequently invited or combined with Mohammedans for the sake of overthrowing their orthodox rivals (comp. on Egypt, Lane, ii, 276; Gibbon, vi, 332, 428; Syria and North Africa, Finlay, Byzantine Empire, i, 159; Asia Minor, ib. i, 198).

One remarkable effect of the Mohammedan spirit of conquest must be noticed. Since it attacked Christianity as a religion, at first defence, and subsequently reprisals, on the part of the Church became a religious duty. The unwarlike spirit of the early Church entirely passed away, and in its stead appeared that military Christianity which is so conspicuous in the history of the Crusades (see Milman, Latin Christianity, ii, 220–222; Lecky, Hist. of European Morals, ii, 262–268). In heathen countries the inhabitants usually embraced, after a longer or shorter time, the Moslem faith. Persia, since its first conquest, has undergone many vicissitudes between heathenism (under the Mongols), Sunnism, and Shiism, the last of which is now the national faith, and has become in many points assimilated to the ancient Magianism. In India, during the Moslem dominion, Islam was confined to the ruling classes at the various courts, and found little acceptance with the natives. The emperor Akbar discarded Mohammedan peculiarities, and was a simple deist. In many points Islam has approximated to Brahminism. Persecution has done its work here also, even in modern times, especially by Tippu Saib of Mysore (Döllinger, p. 15, 16). The sword and persecution have ever been the means of propagating Islam; no missionary organization has at any time existed, and individual efforts for voluntary conversion have been rare and accidental. Yet instances are frequent—the Turks (11th century), the Mongols (13th century)—of whole heathen nations, brought in contact with Mohammedans, having voluntarily accepted Islam. Astonishing progress was thus made in Central Africa; while in China and the Asiatic islands also it made many converts (Döllinger, Muhammad's Religion, etc., p. 16–20; Möhler, Ueber das Verhältniss, etc., i, 386).

The causes of the success and rapid extension of Islam may be thus summarized: (1) The great power over nomadic and Eastern races—as were the Saracens and Turks—of Mohammed's personal character and religion. Even in his faults he nearly corresponds with their ideal; and his religion suits their habits and ways of thought. (2) Extension by the sword, as a religious principle, together with the intense and burning religious zeal of the Mohammedans, fanned by hopes of immediate bliss—sensual or spiritual, to suit different temperaments—to those who died fighting for the faith. (3) Want of religious depth and earnestness among the Christians to whom Islam was opposed. In early times this was in great measure the result of widespread heresy, which weakened faith, caused indifference through weariness of controversy, and created numerous divisions and discords; in later times, of discords between the Roman and Eastern churches and Protestants. Christendom was divided; Mohammedanism was, at the time of its successes, absolute unity, spiritual and temporal. (4) The outward character presented by Mohammedanism. The permission in this life, and promise in the next, of sensuality influenced low and coarse minds; asceticism in the long and strict fast, regular prayers and ablutions, almsgiving, abstinence from intoxicating liquors, and other burdensome precepts, and a generally austere and scrupulous spirit, suited higher characters (see Hallam, *Middle Ages* [ed. 1872], ii, 117). (5) The inward truth in the religion, namely, the intense acknowledgment of God's sole supremacy, hatred of idolatry, and of everything that trenched upon his prerogatives. (6) The military skill and wise policy of both Saracens and Turks in dealing with Christians, and the consequent strength of their government as opposed to the weakness and discords among Christian powers.

The cause of Mohammedan decline is mainly that Islam is especially designed for nomad and half-nomad races; hence when they settle they lose the strength which arises from their nomadic life, and their religion loses its purity and power. They degenerate, become luxurious and inactive; internal dissensions and divisions arise; the same doctrine (e. g. fatalism) that strengthened them in their success weakens them in their depression. Moreover, the opposition to progress innate in Islam tends to keep Mohammedan nations stationary, while Christian powers advance in strength and wealth. Says Mr. Palgrave, who has given the latest and best account of Mohammedanism in Central and Southern Arabia: "Islam is in its essence *stationary*, and was framed thus to remain. Sterile like its God, lifeless like its First Principle and Supreme Original, in all that constitutes true life—for life is love, participation, and progress, and of these the Koranic Deity has none—it justly repudiates all change, all advance, all development. To borrow the forcible words of lord Houghton, the 'written book' is the 'dead man's hand,' stiff and motionless, and whatever savors of vitality is by that alone convicted of heresy and defection. But Christianity, with its living and loving God, begetter and begotten, spirit and movement; nay, more —a Creator made creature, the Maker and made existing in one; a Divinity communicating itself by uninterrupted graduation and degree from the intimate union far off to the faintest irradiation, through all it has made for love and governs in love; One who calls his creatures, not slaves, not servants, but friends—nay, sons—nay, gods; to sum up, a religion in whose real secret 'God in man is one with man in God' must also be necessarily a religion of vitality, of progress, of advancement. The contrast between it and Islam is that of movement with fixedness, of participation with sterility, of development with barrenness, of life with petrifaction. The first vital principle and the animating spirit of its birth must, indeed, abide ever the same; but the outer form must change with the changing days, and new offshoots of fresh sap and greenness be continually thrown out as witnesses to the vitality with-

in; else were the vine withered and the branches dead. I have no intention here—it would be extremely out of place—of entering on the maze of controversy, or discussing whether any dogmatic attempt to reproduce the religious phase of a former age is likely to succeed. I only say that life supposes movement and growth, and both imply change; that to censure a living thing for growing and changing is absurd; and that to attempt to hinder it from so doing, by pinning it down on a written label, or nailing it to a Procrustean framework, is tantamount to killing it altogether. Now Christianity is living, must grow, must advance, must change, and was meant to do so; onwards and forwards is a condition of its very existence; and I cannot but think that those who do not recognise this show themselves so far ignorant of its true nature and essence. On the other hand, Islam is lifeless; and, because lifeless, cannot grow, cannot advance, cannot change, and was never intended so to do."

The *effects* of Mohammedanism, as shown in life and character, must be briefly noticed. The minuteness of the ritual and social rules, together with the hardness and coldness of the morality taught, produces a great amount of formalism. The name of God and pious ejaculations are constantly on the lips, even in the midst of the most indecent conversation. Mohammedans often say the "Bismillah" before committing a crime (Sprenger, ii, 206). Hence the most scrupulous observance of outward duties is not unfrequently united with the grossest habitual immorality and crime (Döllinger, p. 26-29); religion and morality seem completely sundered. Another great evil results from the minuteness of the laws concerning marriage and divorce. Many volumes have been written to explain them, entering into the closest and most disgusting details, forming "a mass of corruption, poisoning the mind and morals of every Mohammedan student" (Muir, iii, 302), and utterly defiling the very language. Hence arises the prevalence not only of the most indecent language and conduct, but also of extreme profligacy among both sexes. Unnatural vice is fearfully common. The pictures of the joys of paradise contribute in some degree to this profligacy; these come to be the object of their thoughts, and are anticipated, as far as possible, on earth. The doctrine of predestination, or, rather, fatalism, produces extreme apathy and want of energy in action; while the notion that all Mohammedans are God's chosen in a special sense, though causing a deep brotherly feeling among themselves, which is fostered by the precepts and almsgiving, leads them to a bitter contempt and hatred of all other religions.

It remains to sum up the good and evil sides of Mohammedanism. On the one hand, it is a rigid foe to idolatry, as it teaches the unity, perfection, providence, and government of God, and hence submission and resignation to his will, together with the great doctrine of a judgment and eternal retribution. It inculcates, moreover, brotherly love and union with fellow-believers, and many social virtues; with almsgiving, temperance, and a certain standard of morality. On the other hand, it perpetuates the great evils of the East—polygamy, slavery, and absolute despotism; it opposes all political and social progress, while the semi-civilized, arbitrary character of its law and justice renders property insecure. Its doctrine of propagation by the sword leads to constant wars and rebellions, with an utter contempt for human life. It is in fact a semi-barbarous religion. On its religious side it fails to satisfy the natural longing for some mediator between God and man, while yet it bows before God as an irresistible power; its morality, in itself defective, is dry, cold, hard, lifeless, without any amiable traits; and, finally, as substituting Mohammed for Christ, it is essentially anti-Christian. While it may be an advance on heathenism, it is an advance which almost excludes the further advance of Christianity, missionary efforts being well-nigh without result.

Christian and Mohammedan Polemics.—The contest of Christianity with Islam, so far as it has been a struggle of argument and not of the sword [see SARACENS], offers few remarkable points. In the first sweep of Mohammedan conquest, when the Christians succumbed not only in the East but even in the West, there was no field for a question of truth. But among nations which were removed from the peril, and yet sufficiently in contact to entertain the question of the claims of the Mohammedan religion, a consideration of its nature, regarded as a system of doctrine, naturally enough arose. Accordingly in Constantinople, and in Spain and the other parts of Western Europe which came into connection with the Moors, works of this character appeared. The history may be conveniently arranged in three periods, each of which is marked by works of defence, some called forth by danger, a real demand, but subsiding into or connected with inquiries prompted only by literary tastes. The first is from the 12th to the middle of the 16th century; the second during the 17th and 18th; the third during the present century.

1. A notice of the Mohammedan religion exists in a work of John of Damascus (q. v.), who flourished in the 8th century; and Euthymius Zigabenus (q. v.), a Byzantine writer of the 12th: but the first important treatise written directly against it was prepared in 1210 —*Richardi Confutatio*, edited in 1543 by Bibliander from a Greek copy. The refutation of Averroes by Aquinas, about 1250, can hardly be quoted as an instance of a work against the Mohammedan religion, being rather against its philosophy. The ablest Christian polemic who waged war against Islam in the 13th century was, however, the well-known Raymond Lully (q. v.), whose zeal could not fail to stir up many laborers for the mission-field, especially that branch of it aiming at the conversion of Mohammedans. Thus we read of a monk who penetrated the great mosque at Cairo in 1345 to require the sultan himself to become a follower of Christ crucified; and so powerful was his appeal that a renegade who had lapsed into Islam returned into the bosom of the Church. Then we find Ethier, the father confessor of the infanta of Aragonia, preaching Christ to the Moslems in 1370; and his example followed in 1439 by the papal legate Albert of Larzana and two assistants, etc.

But if we return to works aimed to defend Christianity against Mohammedanism, we meet with a treatise by John Cantacuzene, written a little after 1350, which is to be explained probably by the circumstance that the danger from Mohammedan powers in the East directed the attention of a literary man to the religion and institutions which they professed. Thus far the works were called forth by a real demand. A series of treatises, however, commences about the time of the expulsion of the Moors from Spain, the cause of the existence of which is not so easy of explanation. Such are those in Spain by Alphonso de Spina, 1487, and by Turrecremata (see Eichhorn, *Gesch der Lit.* vol. vi); by Nicholas de Cuza, published in 1543; in Italy about 1500 by Ludovicus Vives, and Volterranus; one by Philip Melancthon in reference to the reading of the Koran; and a collection of treatises, including those of Richardus, Cantacuzene, Vives, and Melancthon, published by Bibliander in 1543. Probably the first two of this list may have been a relic of the crusade of Christianity against the Moorish religion; the next two possibly were called forth by the interest excited in reference to Mohammedans by reason of their conquests, or, less probably, by the influence of their philosophy at Padua. The last two are hardly to be explained, except by supposing them to be an offshoot of the Renaissance, and called forth by the largeness of literary taste and inquiry excited by that event.

2. When we pass into the 17th century we find a series of treatises on the same subject, which must be explained by the cause just named—the newly acquired interest in Arabic and other Eastern tongues. We meet, however, with others, called forth by the missionary exertions which had brought the Christians into contact with Mohammedans in the East.

The treatise by Bleda (*Defensio Fidei Christianæ*, 1610) stands alone, unconnected with any cause. It was partly a defence of the conduct of Christians towards the Mohammedans. A real interest, however, belongs to the work of Guadagnoli, in 1631. A Catholic missionary, Hieronymo Xavier, had composed in 1596 a treatise in Persian against Mohammedanism, in which the general principle of theism was laid down as opposed to the Mohammedan doctrine of absorption; next, the peculiar doctrines of Christianity was stated; and, lastly, a contrast was drawn between the two religions. (See Lee's *Tracts on Christianity and Mohammedanism, Pref.* p. 5 sq.) This work was answered in 1621 by a Persian nobleman named Ahmed ibn-Zain Elebidin. The line adopted by him was—(1) to show that the coming of Mohammed was predicted in the O. T. (Hab. iii, 3); (2) to argue that Mohammed's teaching was not more opposed to Christ's than his was to that of Moses, and that therefore both ought to be admitted, or both rejected; (3) to point out critically the discrepancies in the Gospels; (4) to attack the doctrines of the Trinity and Christ's deity (Lee, *Pref.* p. 41 sq.). It was written in golden characters, and sent to pope Urban VIII, with a challenge to refute its contents. A person competent to deal with it was carefully selected, and the work was ably answered (1631) by a treatise in Latin by Philippo Guadagnoli, dedicated to pope Urban VIII. It is divided into four parts: (1) respecting the objections about the Trinity; (2) the Incarnation; (3) the authority of Scripture; (4) the claims of the Koran and of Mohammed (Lee, *Pref.* p. 108 sq.; who also gives references [p. 113] to a few other writers, chiefly in the 17th century).

The further works of defence produced in this century arose, as it were, accidentally. The lengthy summary of the Mohammedan controversy in Hoornbeek's *Summa Controversiarum* (1653, p. 75 sq.) was either introduced merely to give completeness to the work as a treatise on polemics, or was called forth by considerations connected with missions, as is made probable by his work *De Conversione Gentilium et Indorum.* Le Moyne's publication on the subject in the *Varia Sacra* (1685, vol. i) arose from the accidental discovery of an old treatise, *Bartholomæi Edess. Confutatio Hagareni.* A third work of this kind, Maraccio's *Criticism on the Koran* (1698), arose from the circumstance that the pope would not allow the publication of an edition of the Koran without an accompanying refutation of each part of it. This effort remains to our day the *chef-d'œuvre* in Christian polemics against the Koran. The work of Hottinger (*Hist. Orient.* bk. i), Pfeiffer's *Theol. Judaica et Mahom.*, and Kortholt's *De Relig. Mahom.* (1663), form the transition into an independent literary investigation; which is seen in the literary inquiries concerning the life of Mohammed, as well as his doctrine, in Pocock, Prideaux (1697), Reland (1707), Boulainvilliers (1730), and the translation of the Koran by Sale (1734). A slightly controversial tone pervades some of them. The materials collected by them were occasionally used by deist and infidel writers (e. g. by Chubb) for instituting an unfavorable comparison between Christ and Mohammed. The great literary historians of that period give lists of the previous writers connected with the investigation. (See J. A. Fabricius, *Bibliotheca Græca,* ed. 1715, vii, 136; Walch, *Biblioth. Theol. Sel.* vol. i, chap. v, § 9.) A summary of the arguments used in the controversy is given in J. Fabricius, *Delectus Argumentorum,* p. 41 sq.; and Stapfer's *Inst. Theol. Polem.* iii, 289 sq.

3. In the present century the literature in reference to Mohammedanism is, as in the former instances, twofold in kind. Part of it has been called forth by missionary contests in the East; part by literary or historic

tastes, and the modern love of carrying the comparative method of study into every part of history.

The first class is illustrated by the discussions at Shiraz, in 1811, between the saintly Henry Martyn (q. v.) and some Persian mollahs. The controversy was opened by a tract, sophistical but acute, written by Mirza Ibrahim (Lee, p. 1–39), the object of which was to show the superiority of the standing miracle seen in the excellence of the Koran over the ancient miracles of Christianity. Martyn replied to this in a series of tracts (Lee, p. 80 sq.), and was again met by Mohammed Ruza of Hamadan in a much more elaborate work, in which, among other arguments, the writer attempts to show predictions of Mohammed in the Old Testament and in the New, applying to him the promise of the Paraclete (Lee, p. 161–450). These tracts were translated in 1824, with an elaborate preface containing an account of the preceding controversy of Guadagnoli, by Professor S. Lee, of Cambridge (*Controversial Tracts on Christianity and Mohammedanism*, which is the work so frequently cited above). To complete the history, it is necessary to add that a discussion was held a few years ago between an accomplished Mohammedan and Mr. French, a learned missionary at Agra. Since then a very able defence of Christianity and an attack on Mohammedanism was published by Dr. Pfander, "a highly respected missionary of the English Church Missionary Society" (1864), which, though forbidden, found its way to Constantinople and to Mohammedan families, and was replied to by several Moslems. In 1865 a Moslem doctor of India, Syud Ahmed Khan, and P. Scudder Amin, actually brought out a bilingual commentary on the Holy Bible in English and Urdu, placing the Bible and Koran upon the same footing, and equally binding on the Moslems. The Rev. J. T. Gracey, in a review of this work, sent from Bareilly, India, September 26, 1866, and published in the *Methodist*, says : "A résumé of the relative bearings of this book might be interesting; but, as nothing is more baffling than the study of contemporaneous history, I dislike to venture my speculations about what is indicated in such a publication, or the probable influence it will exert. 1. Its bearings on the Mohammedan controversy with Christianity are important. The Mohammedan mind is thoroughly impregnated with the belief that the Jewish and Christian Scriptures have been corrupted, and hence are unworthy of credit. Accordingly, when we have urged that, since Mohammed based his claims on the Jewish and Christian Scriptures, Mohammedans were under obligation to regard these, and reconcile with them the Koran, they have always assented to the proposition abstractly, but have charged that interpolations of the Jewish and Christian Scriptures were the cause of the discrepancies in doctrine which appear. *Mohammedanism has, however, it is claimed, always had a philosophical school, which ignored many popular beliefs.* Syud Ahmed is of this class, and, after examining the Colenso controversy, asserts essential integrity for the record. His book is among the first attempts to popularize this belief, however esoterically it may have been held by a school; and as the book has had considerable circulation among the most influential persons in the various communities, it can scarcely fail in time to materially modify the popular notion of the lack of authenticity of the Scriptures. 2. In comparison with the Hindû, the Mohammedan mind of India has been roused but little from its wonted apathy by its contact with Western civilization. A heavy prize offered in Calcutta recently for the best essay on a subject familiar to the Mohammedan mind called forth less than half a dozen monographs, none of which merited the prize. A like offer to Hindûs would have met a very different fate. But this book is, I hope, a harbinger of a better state of affairs, and may do much to induce it, notwithstanding the fact, which the author assures me in personal correspondence, that the limited sale of this second volume does not justify his completing the series, though

he has the matter prepared. It is to be hoped that in this he may prove to be in error. 3. This volume clearly supports the opinion expressed in advance by me, that those who talked of this commentary as being about to furnish a refutation of Colenso were simply guilty of idle gossip. It contains on the Noachian deluge a respectable compilation, from archdeacon Pratt mainly, of certain arguments in favor of a partial deluge; but there is not an original respectable argument in it, so far as I know, bearing on the controversy with Colenso and the Reviewers. Nor is any one who knew the Mohammedan mind disappointed in this, simply because none such expected it to be otherwise than it is. It contains, true to the Mohammedan mind, an amount of mere puerilities, amid a mass of matter that shows a keen appreciation of nice points in a controversy. It adds nothing to European, though it does add much to Asiatic Biblical criticism."

The literary aspect of the subject — not, however, wholly free from controversy—was opened by White in the *Bampton Lectures* for 1784, and abundant sources have lately been furnished. Among them are a new translation of the Koran by the Rev. J. M. Rodwell, where the Suras are arranged chronologically. The following ought also to be added : Dr. Macbride's *Mohammedan Religion Explained* (1857); Arnold, *Koran and Bible* (1st edit. 1859; 2d edit. 1866); Tholuck, *Vermischte Schriften*, i, 1–27; *Die Wunder Mohammed's und der Charakter des Religionstifters;* Dr. Stanley's *Lectures on the History of the Eastern Church* (lect. viii, and the references there given); Maurice, *Religions of the World;* Renan, *Études d'Histoire Religieuse*, ess. iv. The modern study has been directed more especially to attain a greater knowledge of Mohammed's life, character, and writings, the antecedent religious condition of Arabia, and the characteristics of Mohammedanism when put into comparison with other creeds, and when viewed psychologically in relation to the human mind. The materials also for a study of the Mohammedan form of philosophy, both in itself and in its relation to the religion, have been furnished by Aug. Schmoelders, *Essai sur les Écoles Philosophiques chez les Arabes* (1842). See also Ritter's *Christliche Philosophie*, iii, 665 sq.; iv, 1–181.

V. *Statistics.*—It remains for us to consider the number of Islam's adherents in our day, and the countries that contain them. There are believed to be over 185,000,000 of Mohammedans in the world, and there are a number of countries, outside of Turkey and Egypt, in which Mohammedanism is the predominant religion, or at least a great power. Europe contains only 6,500,000 of the Crescent's adherents, but Asia is the home of nearly 80,000,000 Mohammedans, and Africa is asserted to have even many more. Islamism is still the predominant religion of the entire north of Africa, and its rule extends far down eastward, and into the centre of the continent; and it is believed that fully one half, or about 100,000,000 souls, may be set down as Mohammedans. It is a remarkable circumstance, however, that by far the most powerful Mohammedan ruler of the globe—the sultan of Turkey—resides in Europe, where the Islam has only a population of about 4,500,000 in the Turkish and 2,000,000 in the Russian dominions. Even the sultan himself has in the European division of his empire more Christian subjects than Mohammedan. In Asia, Mohammedanism strongly predominates in Asiatic Turkey, which has a Mohammedan population of at least 13,000,000. Persia, with its 5,000,000, is an almost exclusively Mohammedan country. The same is the case with Afghanistan, Beloochistan, and the khanates of Independent Tartary. In China the Mohammedans constitute a compact body, both in the north-west and in the south-western provinces. In both places they have endeavored to establish their independence. In the north-west they have so far succeeded that the new Mohammedan empire of Yakoob Kushbegi has for several years successfully maintained its independence, and is still extending its boundaries. On the other hand, the Mohammedan rebels in the south-west, the so-called Panthay, have during the present year succumbed to the victorious Chinese armies. The death of their sultan and the destruction of their capital, Talifu, and their other principal places, seem for the present to have put an end, not only to their rule in those regions, but even to their political influence. In the vast British empire of India the Mohammedan population is estimated at about 40,000,000, and predominates in a number of the native states which are British dependencies. The Mohammedans also constitute a majority of the population of the large and important island of Java, where they are rapidly increasing; and on the island of Sumatra they control, among others, the kingdom of Achin, which has recently attracted attention by its conflict with the Netherlands. Russia has in its Asiatic possessions a Mohammedan population of about 4,500,000. In Africa, Mohammedanism has, since the beginning of the present century, made great progress in the negro states, and has in particular become the controlling power of Central Africa, and advanced westward as far as Liberia. Morocco, Algeria, Tunis, Tripoli, Egypt, Zanzibar, are all Mohammedan states; in the south and south-west they do not anywhere predominate, although they are found everywhere in increasing numbers. But although Mohammedanism, since the beginning of the present century, has been making these advances in Central Africa, the number of real and thorough believers is infinitely small; and since it has left off conquering, it has lost also that energy and elasticity which promises great things. Its future fate will depend chiefly, we should say, on the progress of European conquest in the East, and the amount of Western civilization which this will, for good or evil, import into those parts.

Mohammedanism may be said, even in its most successful field—Africa—to be everywhere in a condition of steadily progressing decay. The most intelligent travellers of modern times show a remarkable agreement with regard to this point. H. von Maltzahn, who visited, in the disguise of a Mohammedan pilgrim, all the countries from Timbuctoo to Mecca, and the Hungarian, Vambéry, who in the same disguise travelled from Teheran to Samarcand; Henry Barth, who penetrated into Central Africa as far as Timbuctoo; and Palgrave, who in 1862 visited Central and Eastern Arabia, and in particular the empire of the Wahabites, all bear witness to this decay of the Islam. The baron of Maltzahn, in his book of the *Pilgrimage to Mecca*, which he joined in 1860, under the name of Sidi Abd'er Rahman ben-Mohammed es-Shikdi, says: "The Islam has long been undermined, but now it appears to be on the eve of a general collapse; all that formerly constituted its glory —science, scholarship, art, industry—has long left it; its political power has become a laughing-stock, its commerce has been reduced to zero; one thing only seems to stay for a time the impending collapse—religious fanaticism. A remarkable instance of this decline of Mohammedanism is shown in the decrease of the population of the large cities. Thus Bagdad, which at the time of the caliphate had 2,000,000 inhabitants, has now only 100,000; the population of Basrah has been reduced from 200,000 to 80,000; that of Aleppo from 200,000 to 90,000; that of Samarcand from 180,000 to 20,000; that of Katsena, which in the 17th century was the first city of Central Soudan, from 100,000 to 8000. Even the population of the holy city of Mecca, the most licentious city of the East, has been reduced from 100,000 to 45,000. The only country of the Mohammedan world which, during the last twenty years, has made real and important progress is Egypt; but its progress is clearly traceable to the influence of Christian countries. Most of the rulers of the house of Mehemet Ali have shown their appreciation of the superiority of Western civilization, and made earnest efforts to elevate Egypt to a level with it. All the

sons of the present khedive have received a European education: one has been instructed in Paris, a second one in England, and a third one is to enter the Prussian army. Industrial departments have been created, as in the constitutional monarchies of Europe, and a council of state has been created to advise the khedive in all the important affairs of the state. The most influential among the Egyptian ministers, and for many years the chief adviser of the khedive, is an Armenian Christian, Nubar Pasha. Even an assembly of deputies meets annually since 1866, which, as it is officially expressed, is to control the administration and to fix the budget. Sweeping reforms have, in particular, been effected in the department of public education. Since 1868 public schools have been established by the government in all the important places of the country. They numbered in 1870 about 4000 pupils, who received from the government not only gratuitous instruction, but their entire support, inclusive of clothing. These schools embrace both the primary and the secondary instruction. The former embraced Arabic reading and writing, arithmetic, drawing, French, or, according to the location of the place, some other foreign language. From the elementary school the pupils pass into the preparatory department of the secondary school. The course lasts three years, and embraces the study of the Arabic, Turkish, French, and English languages; mathematics, drawing, history, and geography. After completing this preparatory course, the pupil enters one of the special schools which are to finish his education for the service of the state. These special schools are: 1. The Polytechnic School, the course of which lasts four years. As in France, its pupils are permitted to choose between the civil and the military career. In the former case the pupil enters for two years the School of Administration, and afterwards the service of the state; in the latter case he enters the Military Academy of the Abbassieh at Cairo. The Polytechnical School had in 1871 seventy-one pupils. 2. The Law School. The students study the law of the Islam, especially that of Egypt, which is now in the course of a radical transformation, and also the Roman law and the present laws of the European countries. 3. The Philological School. 4. The School of Arts and Industry, founded at Bulak by Mehemet Ali, and greatly perfected by Ismail Pasha. 5. The Medical School, with which is connected a School of Midwifery, the only one which exists in the East. 6. The Naval School in Alexandria. Quite recently the Egyptian government has called the celebrated German Orientalist, H. Brugsch, of Göttingen, to Cairo, in order to organize there an academy for archæology, and, in particular, Egyptological studies. All these reforms are making wide breaches into the walls by which Mohammedan fanaticism has so long tried to isolate itself from the remainder of the world. Still more is this the case with the construction of the canal of Suez, which opens to the civilization of the Christian countries a new and wide road to the intellects and minds of the Egyptian Mohammedans, which, it is believed, no obstruction will ever be able again to block up. The results of this contact between Egypt and Christian Europe and America are already apparent. The fanatical customs which the Mohammedans, like those of other countries, used to indulge in with regard to Christians begin to disappear one by one. The growth of some of the Egyptian cities is marvellous. Alexandria, which at the close of the 18th century had only 6000, in 1820 only 15,000 inhabitants, has now over 200,000. The rule of the khedive has been extended far southward into Central Africa and on the coasts of the Red Sea, and it appears to be highly probable that his ambitious scheme of building up a vast civilized African empire has good prospects of being realized." Detailed accounts of the several national branches of Mohammedans are given under the articles treating of the respective countries. In an article under SARACENS we will consider the political history of the Moslems since the days of their great

Prophet to the present, especially their conquests in the Western world and the sacred places of the East.

VI. *Literature.*—(1) Among the Mohammedan biographies of the Prophet, those of Wackidi, Hishani, and Tabari are perhaps the most important. Dr. Ferdinand Wüstenfeld has edited and brought out in a European dress *The Life of Muhammed*, based on Muhammed Ibn Ishak, by Abd el-Malik Ibn Hisham (Lond. 1869, 8vo, pp. 1026), and the Rev. James L. Merrick has brought out in English *The Life and Religion of Mohammed*, as contained in the Shiite traditions of the Hyal-Ul-Kuloob (Bost. 1850, 8vo). Abulfeda's work, formerly considered an authority, is now ignored (see art. MOHAMMED, p. 397). Among European and American biographies of the Prophet of Islam are those of Maraccius (Padua, 1688); Gagnier (Gibbon's chief dependence; Amsterdam, 1732); Rampoldi (Rome, 1822); Bush (N. Y. 1832); Vergers (Paris, 1833); Hammer-Purgstall (Leips. 1837); Green (N. Y. 1840); Weil (Stuttgard, 1843); Caussin de Perceval (1847); Washington Irving (N. Y. 1852). But the three lives which probably present the greatest research are those by Sir William Muir (Lond. 1858), by Dr. Sprenger (Berlin, 1869 et sq., 6 vols. 8vo), and by Nöldeke (Lond. 1863). The last of these is popular in character, but rests substantially on original investigation, though the labors of Weil, Caussin, Muir, and Sprenger have been used. These works suggested a series of essays to M. Barthélemy St. Hilaire, *Mahomet et le Coran* (Paris, 1865), which are considered valuable. But none of these, though liberal in their judgments, are satisfactory to the Syud Ahmed, who has published some essays in English (Lond. 1870) on Mohammed and subjects subsidiary thereto, and who explains in his preface the reasons why he prefers some contemporary accounts that Europeans have less valued, and he writes with the express purpose of counteracting the effect of Muir upon young Mohammedan students of English. The fiftieth chapter of Gibbon's *Decline and Fall* (reprinted separately also) is probably the strongest vindication that Mohammed has received from a European. Carlyle, in his *Heroes and Hero-worship*, has also taken the palliative side, and he is followed by Kingsley in his *Alexandria and her Schools*, who assents to Carlyle's "true and just description of a much-calumniated man."

(2) Of the different works treating on Mohammedanism and its founder, or only the former, one of the oldest European works, by White (*Bampton Lectures*, 1784), treats of this faith in the usual derogatory way. Price's work (Lond. 1811-21, 4 vols. 4to), compiled from original Persian authorities, and tracing the history from the death of Mohammed to 1556, is generally commended. So also is Mill's *Hist. of Mohammedanism* (Lond. 1812), and likewise Sale's English version of the Koran, prefixed by a dissertation, regarded as "one of the best of the descriptive and historical surveys." De Tassy's works—*Doctrines et Devoirs de la Religion Musulmane, tirés du Coran*, and his *Mémoire sur des Particularités de la Religion Musulmane dans l'Inde*—are valuable. Neale's *Islamism, its Rise and Progress*, is an ordinary compilation simply, and Taylor, *Hist. of Mohammedanism*, treats mainly of the sects; but indispensable to every student of Mohammedanism is Von Hammer-Purgstall's *Gesch. des Osmanischen Reiches* (Pesth, 1827-35, 10 vols. 8vo). One of the best treatises is by Döllinger—*Muhammed's Religion nach ihrer innern Entwickelung u. ihrem Einflusse auf das Leben der Völker* (Ratisbon, 1838). Useful are Renan's *Mah. et les origines de l'Islamisme* (Par. 1857, 7th rev. ed. 1864), and Arnold's *Koran and Bible* (Lond. 1866; rewritten and published in 1874, entitled *Islam, its History, Character, and Relation to Christianity*). The *Islamisme* of the learned Dr. Dozy, of Leyden, is a superior work, and deserves an English dress. It is full in its account of the historical circumstances and preparations out of which Mohammedanism sprang, and gives a well-compiled account of its subsequent influence on the world, and of its sects and

actual position at the present day. A very interesting and valuable contribution is the work by Kremer—*Geschichte der herrschenden Ideen des Islams* (Leips. 1868, 8vo). Worth mentioning are also the *Lectures on Mohammedanism* by Freeman (Oxf. and Lond. 1870, 18mo), by Smith (Lond. 1874, 8vo), and Brown, *Mohammedanism, its present Condition and Influence in India* (Lond. 1873, 12mo). See also Hardwick, *Christ and other Masters*; Clarke, *Ten great Religions*, ch. xi; Milman, *Hist. of Latin Christianity*, ii, 108 sq.; Stanley, *Hist. of the Eastern Church*, lect. viii; Wright, *Early Christianity in Arabia*, p. 152 sq.; Neander, *Church History*, iii, 84 sq.; Cox, *Latin and Teutonic Christendom*; D'Herbelot, *Bibliothèque Orientale*; Malcom, *Hist. of Persia* (2 vols. 4to); Cazenove, *Mohammedanism* (Lond. 1855; reprinted from the *Christian Remembrancer*, Jan. 1855); Deutsch, *Literary Remains* (Lond. and N. Y. 1874; containing articles reprinted from the *Quarterly Review*, Lond. 1869, 1870). In many travels, especially those in Arabia, the condition and history of Mohammedanism are dwelt upon, as in Burckhardt; and Warburton gives a chapter to it in his *Crescent and the Cross*. See also Wellsted, *Travels to the City of the Caliphs* (Lond. 1840, 2 vols. 8vo); Lane, *The Moslem Egyptians* (5th edition, Lond. 1871); Zincke, *Egypt of the Pharaohs and the Khedive*; General Daumas, *La vie Arabe et la Société Musulmane*. See also *Harper's Monthly*, xiv, 1 sq.; *Christian Examiner*, 1830, iv, 360 sq.; *North Amer. Rev.* 1831, p. 257; *North Brit. Rev.* 1850, p. 101 sq.; Jan. and Aug. 1855; *Christian Remembrancer*, Jan. 1855, art. iii; *Free-will Baptist Qu.* Jan. 1855, art. i; *Edinburgh Rev.* Oct. 1857; July, 1866; *Nat. Qu. Rev.* March, 1861, art. vi; Sept. art. v; *Jahrb. deutscher Theologie*, x, 166; 1862, p. 385; *Revue des deux Mondes*, Sept. 1865; *Prospect. Rev.* ii, 159; *Journal of Sacred Lit.* vols. xxi and xxiv; (Lond.) *Quarterly Rev.* cxxvii, 293 sq.; Oct. 1869, p. 160; *Bibliotheca Sacra*, April, 1870; *Meth. Qu. Rev.* 1864, p. 141; 1865, p. 283; 1866, p. 602; 1871, p. 62; *Westm. Rev.* 1868, p. 245; Jan. 1873, p. 124; July, p. 115 sq.; *Brit. Qu. Rev.* Jan. 1872, p. 100 sq. On Mohammedan law are works by Muradgea, D'Ohsson, Knijzer, Von Tornaw, and Perron. See Osborn, *Islam* (Lond. 1878, 2 vols.).

Mohammedan Sects. "My community," the Prophet of Islam is reported to have said, "will separate itself into seventy-three sects; one only will be saved —all the others shall perish." This prophecy, if it were ever made, has in a large measure been fulfilled. The Mohammedans are divided into fifty-five orthodox and eighteen liberal sects. Probably the prophecy was made after the division had taken place. (A very important and instructive treatise on this subject was presented by Silvestre de Sacy to the Institute of France. It is based on the writings of the Mohammedan writer Sheristani, and also on Macrisi.) But, be this as it may, differences of opinion arose among the Prophet's followers even during his own lifetime, and multiplied rapidly after his death. A perusal of the articles KORAN and MOHAMMEDANISM will reveal clearly that the fundamentals of Islam were by no means unequivocal, and hence a great variety of interpretation of the Koran has resulted. To add to the poetical uncertainty of the Koranic principles, a vast number of oral traditions accumulated in Islam, and were circulated as an expansive corollary of the Koran. Political causes soon came to assist the confusion and contest, and religion was made the pretext for faction-fights, which in reality had their origin in the ambition of certain men of influence. Thus "sects" increased in far larger numbers even than the Prophet is said to have foretold, and though their existence was but short-lived in most instances, they yet deserve attention, were it only as signs and tokens of the ever-fresh life of the human spirit, which, though fettered a thousand times by narrow and hard formulas, will break these fetters as often, and prove its everlasting right to freedom of thought and action. The bewildering mass of these currents of controversy has by the Arabic historians been brought under four chief heads or fundamental bases. The first of these relates to the divine attributes and unity. Which of these attributes are essential or eternal? Is the omnipotence of God absolute? If not, what are its limits? Further, as to the doctrine of God's predestination and man's liberty—a question of no small purport, and one which has been controverted in nearly all religions— How far is God's decree influenced by man's own will? How far can God countenance evil? and questions of a similar kind belonging to this province. The third is, perhaps, the most comprehensive "basis," and the one that bears most directly upon practical doctrines—viz., the promises and threats, and the names of God, together with various other questions chiefly relating to faith, repentance, infidelity, and error. The fourth is the one that concerns itself with the influence of reason and history upon the transcendental realm of faith. To this chapter belong the mission of prophets, the office of Imam, or head of the Church, and such intricate subtleties as to what constitutes goodness and badness; how far actions are to be condemned on the ground of reason or the "law," etc.

I. One broad line, however, came to be drawn, in the course of time, among these innumerable religious divisions—a line that separated them all into orthodox sects and heterodox sects; orthodox being those only who adopted the oral traditions, or Sunna (q. v.). Of these Sunnites, i. e. traditionists, or believers in the Sunna, there are four divisions, which, though at issue on most points, are yet acknowledged by each other as *faithful*, and *capable of salvation*. They are severally designated by the name of the men who in leadership attained to greatest authority. Each of these guides also to this day continues the expounder of the sect by a manual which each left to his adherents as a compend of theology and jurisprudence.

1. The first of these sects are the *Hanefites*, founded by Abu Hanefa, who died 150 years after the Hegira. They are emphatically called "the followers of reason," while the other three are guided exclusively by tradition. They allow reason to have a principal share on decisions in their legal and other points. To this sect belong chiefly the Turks and Tartars.

2. The second sect are the *Malekites*, founded by Malek Ibn Ans, who died about 180 of the Hegira at Medina. As one of the chief proofs of his piety and humility, it is recorded that when asked for his decision on forty-eight questions, he would only decide on sixteen, freely confessing his ignorance on the others. In Barbary and other portions of Africa the greatest part of his adherents are found.

3. Mohammed al-Shâfeï, born in Palestine in 150 of the Hegira, but educated in Mecca, is the founder of the third sect, *Shafiites*. He was a great enemy to the scholastic divines, and seems altogether to have been of an original cast of mind. He never swore by God, and always took time to consider whether he should at all answer any given questions or hold his peace. The most characteristic saying recorded of him is, "Whosoever pretends to love both the work and the Creator at the same time is a liar." He is accounted of such importance that, according to his contemporaries, "he was as the sun to the world, and as health to the body;" and all the relations of the traditions of Mohammed were said to have been asleep until he came and awoke them. He appears to have been the first who reduced Moslem jurisprudence to a method, and thus made it, from a number of vague sayings, a science. His followers are now chiefly found in Arabia and Persia.

4. Ahmed Ibn Hanbal founded the fourth sect, the *Hanbalites*. He was born in 164 of the Hegira, and was a most intimate friend of Shâfeï. His knowledge of the traditions (of which he could repéat no less than a million) was no less famed than was his piety. He taught that the Koran was not created, but everlastingly subsisted in the essence of God—a doctrine for which he was severely punished by caliph Al-Motasena. On the

VI.—14*

day of his death, the Mohammedans would have us believe, no less than 20,000 unbelievers (Jews, Christians, and Magians) embraced the Mohammedan faith. Once very numerous, the Hanbalites are now but very rarely met with outside of Arabia.

5. In recent times a new orthodox Mohammedan sect has sprung up, called Wahabis or Wahabites, after their founder, Mohammed Abd-el-Wahab (q. v.). They are intent upon restoring the primitive and vigorous Mohammedanism which they claim does not now exist under the Turks and Persians, whom they call idolatrous. The Wahabis are a sort of Puritanic Iconoclasts, and their power is fast spreading. But their recent history is so mystified that we defer them for consideration under the heading WAHABITES.

II. Much more numerous than the orthodox divisions are the heterodox ones. Immediately after Mohammed's death, and during the early conquests, the contest was chiefly confined to the question of the Imamat. But no sooner were the first days of warfare over than thinking minds began to direct themselves to a closer examination of the faith itself, for which and through which the world was to be conquered, and to the book which preached it, the Koran. The earliest germs of a religious dissension are found in the revolt of the Kharegites against Ali, in the thirty-seventh year of the Hegira (see Ockley, *Hist. of the Saracens*, ii, 50); and several doctors shortly afterwards broached heterodox opinions about predestination and the good and evil to be ascribed to God. These new doctrines were boldly, and in a very advanced form, openly preached by Wâsil Ibn Atâ, who, for uttering a moderate opinion in the matter of the "sinner," had been expelled from the rigorous school of Basrah. He then formed a school of his own—that of the Separatists or *Motazilites*, who, together with a number of other "heretical" groups, are variously counted as one, four, or seven sects.

1. The first of these heretical groups, the *Motazilites* —also called *Moattalites*, i. e. those who divest God of his attributes; and *Kadarija*, i. e. "those who hold that man has a free will, and deny the strict doctrine of predestination"—is traced back even to Mabad, who, in the time of Mohammed himself, already began to question predestination, by pointing out how kings carry on unjust wars, kill men, and steal their goods, and all the while pretend to be merely executing God's decrees. The real founder of the sect, as such, however, is, as we have already indicated, Wâsil Ibn Atâ. He denied God's "qualities"—such as knowledge, power, will, life —as leading to, if not directly implying, polytheism. As to predestination itself, this he only allowed to exist with regard to the outward good or evil that befalls man, such as illness or recovery, death or life, but man's actions he held to be entirely in his own hands. God, he said, had given commandments to mankind, and it was not to be supposed that he had, at the same time, preordained that some should disobey these commandments, and that, further, they should be punished for it. Man alone was the agent in his good or evil actions, in his belief or unbelief, obedience or disobedience, and he is rewarded according to his deeds. (*a*) These doctrines were further developed by his disciple, Abul-Hudail, who did not deny so absolutely God's "qualities," but modified their meaning in the manner of the Greek philosophers, viz. that every quality was also God's essence. The attributes are thus not without, but within him, and, so far from being a multiplicity, they merely designate the various ways of the manifestations of the Godhead. God's will he declared to be a peculiar kind of knowledge, through which God did what he foresaw to be salutary in the end. Man's freedom of action is only possible in this world. In the next all will be according to necessary laws immutably preordained. The righteous will enjoy everlasting bliss; and for the wicked everlasting punishment will be decreed. Another very dangerous doctrine of his system was the assumption that before the Koran had been revealed man had

already come to the conclusion of right and wrong. By his inner intellect, he held, everybody must and does know—even without the aid of the divinely given commandments—whether the thing he is doing be right or wrong, just or unjust, true or false. He is further supposed to have held that, unless a man be killed by violent means, his life would neither be prolonged nor shortened by "supernatural" agencies. His belief in the traditions was also by no means an absolute one. There was no special security, he said, in a long, unbroken chain of witnesses, considering that one fallible man among them could corrupt the whole truth. (b) Many were the branches of these Motazilites. There were, apart from the disciples of Abul-Hudail, the Jobbaians, who adopted Abu Ali al-Wahhab's (Al-Jobbâi's) opinion, to the effect that the knowledge ascribed to God was not an "attribute;" nor was his knowledge "necessary;" nor did sin prove anything as to the belief or unbelief of him who committed it, who would anyhow be subjected to eternal punishment if he died in it, etc. (c) Besides these, there were the disciples of Abu Hashem—the Hashemites—who held that an infidel was not the creation of God, who could not produce evil. (d) Another branch were the disciples of Ahmed Ibn Hayet, who held that Christ was the eternal Word incarnate, and assumed a real body; that there were two gods, or creators, one eternal, viz. the Most High God, and the other not eternal, viz. Christ—not unlike the Socinian and Arian theories on this subject; that there is a successive transmigration of the soul from one body into another, and that the last body will enjoy the reward or suffer the punishments due to each soul; and that God will be seen at the resurrection with the eyes of the understanding, not of the body. (e) Four more divisions of this sect are mentioned, viz. the Jâhedhians, whose master's notion about the Koran was that it was "a body that might grow into a man, and sometimes into a beast, or to have, as others put it, two faces—one human, the other that of an animal, according to the different interpretations." He further taught them that the damned would become fire, and thus be attracted by hell; also, that the mere belief in God and the Prophet constituted a "faithful." (f) Of rather different tendencies was Al-Mozdar, the founder of the branch of the Mozdarians. He not only held the Koran to be uncreated and eternal, but, so far from denying God the power of doing evil, he declared it to be possible for God to be a liar and unjust. (g) Another branch was formed by the Pasharians, who, while they carried man's free agency rather to excess, yet held that God might doom even an infant to eternal punishment —all the while granting that he would be unjust in so doing. (h) The last of these Motazilite sectarians we shall mention are the Thamamians, who held, after their master, Thamâma, that sinners would undergo eternal damnation and punishment; that free actions have no producing author; and that, at the resurrection, all infidels, atheists, Jews, Christians, Magians, and heretics should be returned to dust.

We cannot in this place enlarge upon the different schools founded by the Motazilites, nor upon their subsequent fate (see for details, Steiner, Mutaziliten; Weil, Gesch. d. Islam. Völker, and his Gesch. d. Khalifen). The vast cyclopædic development, however, which their doctrines begot, and which resulted in the encyclopædic labors called "The Treatises of the Sincere Brethren and True Friends," will be considered in the article SINCERE BRETHREN (q. v.).

2. We now come to the second great heretical group, the Sefatians, or attributionists, who held a precisely contrary view to that of the Motazilites. With them God's attributes, whether essential or operative, or what they in more recent times have called declarative or historical, i. e. used in historical narration (eyes, face, hand), anthropomorphisms, in fact, were considered eternal. But here, again, lay the germs for more dissensions and more sects in their own midst. Some, tak-

ing this notion of God's attributes in a strictly literal sense, assumed a likeness between God and created things; others gave it a more allegorical interpretation, without, however, entering into any particulars beyond the reiterated doctrine that God had no companion or similitude. (a) The different sects into which they split were, first, the Asharians, so called from Abul Hasan al-Ashari, who, at first a Motazilite, disagreed with his masters on the point of God's being bound to do always that which is best. He became the founder of a new school, which held (1) that God's attributes are to be held distinct from his essence, and that any literal understanding of the words that stand for God's limbs in the Koran is reprehensible. (2) That predestination must be taken in its most literal meaning, i. e. that God preordains everything. The opinions on this point of man's free will are, however, much divided, as indeed to combine a predestination which ordains every act with man's free choice is not easy; and the old authors hold that it is well not to inquire too minutely into these things, lest all precepts, both positive and negative, be argued away. The middle path, adopted by the greater number of the doctors, is expressed in this formula: There is neither compulsion nor free liberty, but the way lies between the two; the power and will being both created by God, though the merit or guilt be imputed to man. Regarding mortal sin, it was held by this sect that if a believer die guilty of it without repentance, he will not, for all that, always remain a denizen of hell. God will either pardon him, or the Prophet will intercede on his behalf, as he says in the Koran: "My intercession shall be employed for those among my people who shall have been guilty of grievous crimes;" and further, that he in whose heart there is faith but of the weight of an ant shall be delivered from hell-fire. (b) From this more philosophical opinion, however, departed a number of other Sefatian sects, who, taking the Koranic words more literally, transformed God's attributes into grossly corporeal things, like the Mosshabehites, or assimilators, who conceived God to be a figure composed of limbs like those of created beings, either of a bodily or spiritual nature, capable of local motion, ascent or descent, etc. The notions of some actually went so far as to declare God to be "hollow from the crown of the head to the breast, and solid from the breast downward; he also had black curled hair." (c) Another subdivision of this sect were the Jabarians, who deny to man all free agency, and make all his deeds dependent on God. Their name indicates their religious tendency sufficiently, meaning "Necessitarians."

III. The third principal division of "heretical sects" is formed by the Kharegites, or "rebels" from the lawful prince—i. e. Ali—the first of whom were the 12,000 men who fell away from him after having fought under him at the battle of Seffein, taking offence at his submitting the decision of his right to the caliphate (against Moawiyyah) to arbitration. Their "heresy" consisted, first, in their holding that any man might be called to the Imamat though he did not belong to the Koreish, nor was even a freeman, provided he was a just and pious man, and fit in every other respect. It also followed that an unrighteous imam might be deposed, or even put to death; and further, that there was no absolute necessity for any imam in the world.

IV. The fourth principal sect are the Shiites, or sectaries, so called by the Sunnites, or orthodox Moslems, because of their heretical tendencies. The Shiites, as they are now generally called, were originated by Ali Ibn Abi Taleb, and prefer to call themselves Al-Adeliat, Sect of the Just Ones, or familiarly, "Followers of Ali," because they believe that the Imamat, or supreme rule, both spiritual and temporal, over all Mohammedans was originally vested in him whom they acknowledge as their founder, and that the Imamat now of right belongs to his descendants. In the opinion of the Shiites, the vicarship of the Prophet was not to be, like an earthly kingdom, the mere prize of craft or of valor. It was the inalienable heritage of the sacred descendants of the Prophet himself. They therefore consider the caliphs Abu Bekr, Omar, and Othman, the first three incumbents of the caliphate after Mohammed, unrighteous pretenders and usurpers of the sovereign power, which properly ought to have gone to Ali direct from the Prophet. For the same reason the Shiites abominate the memory of the Ommayad caliph who executed Hossein, a son of Ali, and still mourn his death at its anniversary. (This most pathetic story is perhaps generally remembered from the pages of Gibbon; it should be read in its full detail in those of Ockley and Price.) The Shiites likewise reject the Abbasside caliphs, notwithstanding their descent from Mohammed, because they did not belong to Ali's line. See KALIPH.

The Shiites have special observances, ceremonies, and rites, as well as particular dogmas of their own. They believe in metempsychosis and the descent of God upon his creatures, inasmuch as he, omnipresent, sometimes appears in some individual person, such as their imams. They are subdivided into five sects, to one of which, that of Haidar, the Persians belong—the present dynasty of Persia deriving its descent from Haidar. Their five subdivisions they compare to five trees, with seventy branches; for their minor divisions of opinions, on matters of comparatively unimportant points of dogma, are endless. The Shiites and Sunnites are, then, represented respectively by the two great Mohammedan powers, the former being upheld by the Persian dynasty, the latter by the Ottomans. This division between Turk and Persian on doctrine dates chiefly from the caliphate of Mothi Lilla, the Abbasside, in 363 of the Hegira, when political dissensions, which ended in the destruction of Bagdad and the loss of the caliphate of the Moslems, assumed the character of a religious war. But it may be stated here also that the Shiites are by no means confined to Persia. They have indeed, in greater or lesser numbers, been dispersed throughout all the countries of the empire of the Mussulmans. They have possessed several kingdoms both in Asia and Africa. They are now dominant, outside of Persia, in half the territory ruled over by the princes of the Uzbecks, and situated beyond the river Gihon; and there are some Mohammedan kings of the Indies who make profession of the Shiite faith. Mohammed's life, as represented by Shiite tradition, has been furnished in an English dress by the Rev. James L. Merrick (Bost. 1850).

V. It remains now only to mention a few of the more prominent of the many pseudo-prophets who have arisen in the bosom of Islam, drawing a certain number of adherents around them, and, as it would appear to us "outsiders," threatening by this decentralization the very life of Mohammedanism, but by the Moslems themselves alleged as a sign of the purity of their creed. Christianity, they say, an improvement on Judaism, can boast of more sects than Judaism; Islam, an improvement on Christianity, can boast of more sects than Christianity.

The pseudo-prophets who have arisen have invariably either declared themselves the great Prophet's legal successors, or, utterly renouncing his doctrines, have sought to build up on the ruins of Islam. The first and most prominent among these was *Mosaylima* (i. e. little Moslem), who was a rival of the Prophet in his lifetime. Mosaylima belonged to the clan Dûl, a division of the tribe of the Bani Hanifah, of Yamâma in Nejed. The traditions about his life and age appear to be extremely legendary. It is, however, tolerably clear that he had risen to a certain eminence in his tribe as a religious teacher before Mohammed assumed his prophetical office. The name he was known by among his friends was Rahmân, the Benignant or Merciful; a term which Mohammed adopted as a designation of God himself. This word, which is Aramaic, was a common divine epithet among the Jews, from whom Mohammed took it,

together with a vast bulk of dogmas and ceremonies and legends. If, however, as is supposed by some, Mosaylima assumed that name in the meaning of Messiah, Saviour, it would prove that he had anticipated Mohammed in the apostleship, which is commonly denied. It was in the ninth year of the Hegira that, at the head of an embassy sent by his tribe, he appeared before Mohammed, in order to settle certain points of dispute. The traditions are very contradictory on the circumstance whether or not Mosaylima was then already the recognised spiritual leader of his tribe. When they were introduced to Mohammed in the mosque, they greeted him with the orthodox salutation of Moslems, "Salâm alayk" (Peace upon thee), and, after a brief parley, recited the confession of faith. Shortly after this event, Mosaylima openly professed himself to be a prophet, like Mohammed. The latter sent a messenger to him, as soon as he heard of this, to request him to reiterate publicly his profession of Islam. Mosaylima's answer was a request that Mohammed should share his power with him. "From Mosaylima, the apostle of God," he wrote, according to Abulfeda, "to Mohammed, the apostle of God. Now let the earth be half mine, and half thine." Mohammed speedily replied: "From Mohammed, the apostle of God, to Mosaylima, the liar. The earth is God's: he giveth the same for inheritance unto such of his servants as he pleases, and the happy issue shall attend those who fear him." Yet notwithstanding these testimonies, of probably late dates, it seems, on the other hand, quite certain that Mohammed made very great concessions to his rival—concessions that point to his having secretly nominated Mosaylima his successor, and that he by this means bought Mosaylima's open allegiance during his lifetime. It was not a question of dogmas, though they each had special revelations, but a question of supremacy, which was thus settled amicably. "Mohammed," Mosaylima said, "is appointed by God to settle the principal points of faith, and I to supplement them." He further had a revelation, in accordance with Mohammed's: "We have sent to every nation its own prophet," to the effect: "We have given unto thee [Mosaylima] a number of people; keep them to thyself, and advance. But be cautious, and desire not too much; and do not enter into rival fights." When Mohammed was at the point of death, he desired to write his will. Whatever he may have wished to ordain is uncertain; it is well known, at all events, that his friends did not obey his order, and refused to furnish him with writing materials, very probably because they did not like to be bound by his last injunctions. Sprenger supposes that he wished formally to appoint Mosaylima his successor, and that it was just this which his surrounding relations feared. Mosaylima then openly declared against Islam, and many parodies of the Koran sprang up in the Nejed, ascribed to him. In the eleventh year of the Hegira it at last came to an open breach between the two rival powers. Abu Bekr, the caliph, sent Khalid, "the Sword of the Faith," with a number of choice troops, to compel Mosaylima to submission. Mosaylima awaited the enemy at Rowdah, a village in the Wadi Hanifah. So formidable indeed was Mosaylima's force that Khalid is said to have hesitated for a whole day and night before he undertook an assault unanimously disapproved of by his council. On the second morning, however, he advanced, and, in a battle which lasted until the evening, contrived, with fearful losses of his own, to gain the victory. Mosaylima fell by the hands of a negro slave, and his head was cut off by the conqueror, and placed at the head of a spear, to convince both friends and foes of his death. Khalid then advanced to the slain prophet's birthplace, in order to slay all its inhabitants. They, however, by a clever stratagem, contrived to conclude an honorable peace, and embraced Islam. The Mosayliman "heresy" was thus stamped out, and only a few scattered remnants of the new faith contrived to escape to Hasa and Basrah, where they may have laid the foundation of the later Karmathian creed. See KARMATHIANS. It is extremely difficult to come to any clear notion of Mosaylima's real doctrines, as all the accounts that have survived of them come from victorious adversaries—adversaries who have not hesitated to invent the most scandalous stories about him. Thus a love-adventure between Mosaylima and the prophetess Sajâh, the wife of a soothsayer of Yamâma, who is supposed to have stayed three days in his tent, is told with great minuteness, even to the obscene conversation that is supposed to have taken place between them during that time; the fact being that this story, which is still told with much relish by the natives, is without the slightest foundation. From the same source we learn that Mosaylima tried to deceive his followers by conjuring tricks. It seems, on the contrary, that he was of much higher moral standing than Mohammed himself. For it is said that Mosaylima enjoined the highest chastity even among married people: unless there were hope of begetting children, there should be restriction of conjugal duty. Even the nickname "Little Moslem" given to him seems to indicate that he, too, preached the unity of God, or Islam, as the fundamental doctrine of faith. How far his religion had a socialistic tendency, and offered less show of dignity and outward morality to its followers, or whether it rejected fatalism, contained an idea of incarnation, and invested its preachers and teachers with a semi-mediatorial character, as the latest explorer of the Nejed, Mr. Palgrave tells us, we have no means of judging. But we must receive these conclusions, probably drawn from the information of the natives, with all the greater caution, as that story of the prophetess Sajâh, whom he reports, after his informants, not only to have been properly married to Mosaylima, but to have become, after his death, a devout partisan of Islam, and to have entered an "orthodox alliance," does not, as we have said before, according to the best European authorities on Mohammedanism, deserve the slightest credence.

Next to Mosaylima figures prominently Al-Aswad, originally called Aihala, of the tribe of Ans, of which, as well as of that of a number of other tribes, he was governor. He pretended to receive certain revelations from two angels, Sohaik and Shoraik. Certain feats of legerdemain and a natural eloquence procured him a number of followers, by whose aid he made himself master of several provinces. A counter-revolution, however, broke out the night before Mohammed's death, and Al-Aswad's head was cut off; whereby an end was put to a rebellion of exactly four months' duration, but already assuming large proportions.

In the same year (11 of the Hegira), but after Mohammed's death, a man named Toleiha set up as a prophet, but with very little success. He, his tribe, and followers were met in open battle by Khalid, at the head of the troops of the Faithful, and, being beaten, had all finally to submit to Islam.

A few words ought also to be said regarding the "Veiled Prophet," Al-Mokanna, or Borkai, whose real name was Hakem Ibn Hashem, at the time of Al-Mohdi the third Abbasside caliph. He used to hide the deformity of his face (he had also but one eye) by a gilded mask, a circumstance which his followers explained by the splendor of his countenance being too brilliant (like that of Moses) to be borne by ordinary mortals. Being a proficient in jugglery besides, which went for the power of working miracles, he soon drew many disciples and followers around him. At last he arrogated the office of the Deity itself, which, by continual transmigrations from Adam downwards, had at last resided in the body of Abu Moslem, the governor of Khorassan, whose secretary this new prophet had been. The caliph, finding him growing more and more formidable every day, sent a force against him, which finally drove him back into one of his strongest fortresses, where he first poisoned and then burned all his family; after which he threw himself into the flames, which consumed him

completely, except his hair. He had left a message, however, to the effect that he would reappear in the shape of a gray man riding on a gray beast, and many of his followers for many years after expected his reappearance. They wore as a distinguishing mark nothing but white garments. He died about the middle of the 2d century of the Hegira. See MOKANNA.

Of the Karmathians and the Ismaelians we have spoken under their respective headings. We can scarcely enumerate among the prophets Abul Teyeb Ahmed al-Motanebbi, one of the most celebrated Arabic poets, who mistook, or pretended to mistake, his poetical inspiration for the divine afflatus, and caused several tribes to style him prophet, as his surname indicates, and to acknowledge his mission. The governor of his province, Lûlû, took prompt steps to stifle any such pretensions in the bud by imprisoning him, and making him formally renounce all absurd pretensions to a prophetical office. The poet did so with all speed. He was richly rewarded by the court and many princes for his minstrelsy, to which thenceforth he clung exclusively; but the riches he thus accumulated became the cause of his death. Robbers attacked him while he was returning to his home in Kufa, there to live upon the treasure bestowed upon him by Adado'ddawla, sultan of Persia.

The last of the new prophets to be mentioned is Baba, who appeared in Amasia, in Natolia, in 1221 of the Hegira, and who had immense success, chiefly with the Turcomans, his own nation, so that at last he found himself at the head of nearly a million men, horse and foot. Their war-cry was, God is God, and Baba—not Mohammed—is his prophet. It was not until both Christians and Mohammedans combined for the purpose of self-defence that this new and most formidable power was annihilated, its armies being routed and put to the sword, while the two chiefs were decapitated by the executioner. See BABISTS. See Weil, Geschichte der Khalifen; and his Geschichte des Mohammedanismus; Taylor, History of Mohammedanism; and the works referred to in the article MOHAMMEDANISM.

Moharram, any thing sacred or forbidden by the Mussulman law. It is likewise the name of the first month of the Arabic year, before the time of Mohammedanism, and was so called because the ancient Arabs were forbidden to make war against one another during this month. The first ten days of the month Moharram are called by the Mohammedans Aiam al-mâdulat, that is, the reckoned days, because they believe that during these ten days the Koran was sent down from heaven to be communicated to men. The last of these ten days is called Ashûr. See Broughton, Biblioth. Histor. Sacra, ii, 116.

Mohdi (i. e. the Director) is the title among the Mohammedans for that descendant of Mohammed whose coming is to be one of the signs of the general resurrection. Concerning this person, Mohammed prophesied that the world should not have an end till one of his own family should govern the Arabians, whose name should be like his own name, and whose father's name should also be like that of his own father. The Mohdi is to fill the earth with Righteousness. The Shiites (q. v.) believe the Mohdi to be now alive, and concealed in some secret place till the proper time of his manifestation; and they suppose him to be none other than the last of the twelve imâms, named Mohammed Abulkasem, and the son of Hassan al-Askeri, the eleventh of that succession. See Broughton, Biblioth. Histor. Sacra, ii, 116. See MOHAMMEDANISM.

Mohl, JULIUS VON, an eminent German Oriental scholar, was born at Stuttgard in 1800. After having studied at the gymnasium in that city, he entered the Protestant seminary in the University of Tübingen in 1818, received his diploma as doctor of philosophy in 1820, and won the prize in theology in 1822. His taste ιor Oriental languages, which he had pursued diligently amid all the duties of his college life, induced him to remove to Paris, where he studied under Sylvestre de Sacy and Remusat. In 1826 he was appointed professor of Oriental literature at Tübingen, but he never occupied that chair, preferring to continue his studies, which he pursued in 1826–7 and 1830–1 at London and Oxford. In 1840 he became assistant secretary of the Asiatic Society; in 1844 succeeded Burnouf, sen., as a member of the Academy of Inscriptions; the same year was installed professor of the Persian language and literature at the College of France; and in 1852 succeeded Burnouf, jun., as inspector of Oriental typography at the imperial printing-house. He died in 1874. Mohl constantly sought to improve the standard of Oriental philology. His philosophic views on the subject, together with his warm enthusiasm, have contributed not a little to facilitate and extend recent investigations in that science. His principal works are: *Fragments relatifs à la religion de Zoroaster* (Paris, 1829, 8vo), published anonymously:—*Confucii Chi-King, ex Latino P. Lacharme interpret.* (Stuttgard, 1830, 8vo):—*Y.-King, antiquissimus Sinarum liber, ex Latina interpret. P. Regis* (ibid. 1834–9, 2 vols. 8vo):—*Livre des Rois, par Abdoul Kasim Firdousi* (Paris, 1836–55, fol.):—*Firdousi's Schahnameh* (ib. 1838–66, 5 vols. 8vo); and many contributions of great value to different Oriental societies in France, England, and Germany, of which he had the honor to be a member. See Hoefer, *Nouv. Biog. Générale*, xxxv, s. v.; Brockhaus, *Conversations-Lexikon*, s. v.; Vapereau, *Dict. des Contemporains*, s. v. (J. H. W.)

Möhler, JOHANN ADAM, one of Germany's most distinguished Roman Catholic theologians—the Schleiermacher, as he has aptly been called, of his branch of the Christian Church—was born of humble parentage, May 6, 1796, at Igersheim, near Mergentheim, in Würtemberg. He received his preparatory training at the gymnasium in Mergentheim, and in his seventeenth year removed to Ellwangen and there studied at the lyceum until, in 1815, the faculty was transferred to Tübingen, and he repaired to that well-known high-school to continue his theological studies. He completed his course at the episcopal seminary in Rottenburg, and in 1819 was made priest, and became vicar of Riedlingen. He continued, however, but a short time in the pastorate. In 1820 he returned to Tübingen University, and there lectured and studied. Proffered a permanent position in the university, he decided, in order to fit himself the more thoroughly for it, to spend some time in making himself acquainted with the routine of the theological courses of other universities—as Göttingen, Berlin, Prague, Vienna, etc.; and in consequence of this thorough preparation, so successfully met his engagement that in 1826, though still very young, he was made extraordinary professor, and only two years later, shortly after receiving his doctorate in divinity, was honored with the full or ordinary professorship in Church history and patrology. This position afforded him a controlling influence over the Roman Catholic young men studying with a view to the priesthood, and he aimed to awaken among them, by the description of great ecclesiastical characters of the early Catholic Church, such as Athanasius and Anselm, a spirit of speculative inquiry in the sphere of faith and in connection with ecclesiastical fellowship; and he also renewed the old confessional controversy on the principles of the Protestant and Roman Catholic creeds by the publication of a work on Symbolism, in which the Reformation, though much of the Protestants' labors are recognised as relatively justifiable and worthy, is stamped, in contrast with an ideal Roman Catholicity, as a mistake. This book came not only to be regarded as a remarkable work, but actually fixed the attention of the whole theological world upon him; and it has been well said that "his reputation, both posthumous and among his own contemporaries, rests mainly on his

Symbolik" (in English entitled *Symbolism; or the Doctrinal Differences between Catholics and Protestants, as represented by their Public Confessions of Faith*, translated by J. R. Robertson, 2 vols. London, 1843; New York, 1844; and since republished). D'Aubigné pronounced it "one of the most important writings produced by Rome since the time of Bossuet" (*History of the Ref.* iv, 326). It was first published in 1832, passed through five large editions in the next six years, was translated into all the leading European languages, and drew forth numerous criticisms and rejoinders from the Protestant world, of which the most important are: Bauer, *Gegensatz des Katholicismus u. Protestantismus, nach den Principien u. Hauptdogmen der beiden Lehrbegriffe* (Tüb. 1834, 8vo); Nitzsch, *Prot. Beantwortung der Symbolik Möhlers* (in *Studien u. Kritiken*, 1834–35, and later separately reprinted); Marheineke, *Recension der Möhlerschen Symbolik* (in *Jahrbuch für wissenschaftliche Kritik*, Berlin, 1833). To these—particularly, however, the attack by Bauer—Möhler replied in his *Neue Untersuchungen der Lehrgegensätze* (Mayence, 1834; 2d edit. 1835). The polemical bitterness evoked by these controversies made it desirable that Möhler should leave Tübingen, where Bauer then also lectured; and after refusing various positions proffered him by different celebrated German universities, he accepted in 1835 a professorship at Munich, then in the first flush of its efficiency under king Louis. Möhler's first appointment was nominally the chair of Biblical exegesis, but he really devoted himself to the department of Church history, in which his opening course was eminently successful. His uninterrupted and severe labors, however, had taxed him to the utmost, and, after refusing to accept a renewed and very tempting offer from Bonn, he reluctantly consented to change his place at the university for the deanery of Würzburg, which the king had urged upon him. Shortly after appointment to this new position he was completely prostrated, and died of consumption April 12, 1838. Möhler is not only generally acknowledged to have been a good and pious man, but is universally recognised also as the greatest theologian the Roman Catholic Church has produced since Bellarmine and Bossuet. He was certainly the most acute and the most philosophical of the modern controversialists of his Church. He helped Romanism again to self-consciousness, and breathed into it a new polemic zeal against Protestantism; although he betrayed the influence which the study of Protestant theology, especially that of Schleiermacher, and of modern culture generally, had exercised on his own idealistic apprehension and defence of the Roman dogmas and usages. He did not, indeed, write a Church history, or discuss the scriptural or traditional evidences of the peculiar doctrines of Roman Catholicism, but rather devoted himself to the exposition of the points and the grounds of the doctrinal differences of modern sects; yet all his writings have more or less to do with the historical sphere, particularly with the history of doctrines, and are remarkable for their freshness of spirit and a vigorous and animated style. Says Hagenbach (*Ch. Hist. of the 18th and 19th Cent.* ii, 446), "Whatever vigorous vitality is possessed by the most recent Catholic theological science is due to the labors of this man, who was cut off early in the midst of his work." "He sent rays of his spirit," says Kurtz (*Ch. Hist. from the Reformation*, p. 391), "deep into the hearts and minds of hundreds of his enthusiastic pupils by his writings, addresses, and by his intercourse with them; and what the Roman Catholic Church of the present possesses of living scientific impulse and feeling was implanted, or at least revived and excited by him. . . . His 'Symbolik' combats Protestant doctrines with the weapons of Protestant science, and silently ennobles and sublimates those of the Roman Catholic Church. Did the Protestants up to this time generally despise or ignore the contributions of Roman Catholic theologians, here a scientific power of the highest significance approached them, to despise which would have been a sign of weakness. In fact, long as was the opposition which existed between both churches, no work from the camp of the Roman Catholics produced as much agitation and excitement in the camp of the Protestants as this." Yet no work produced by a Romanist has been of greater service than this polemic. Written after a thorough study of the subject, it has gathered a mass of material invaluable to the Protestant student, and in this *Cyclopædia* we have not unfrequently referred to Möhler's "Symbolik" with great pleasure. The other principal works from Möhler's pen are: *Die Einheit in der Kirche oder das Princip des Katholicismus* (Tübing. 1825, 8vo; translated into French by Ph. Bernard):—*Athanasius d. Grosse u. d. Kirche seiner Zeit im Kampfe mit dem Arianismus* (Mayence, 1827; 2d ed. 1844, 8vo; translated into French, Paris, 1841, 3 vols. 8vo):—*Patrologie oder christliche Literaturgeschichte* (Ratisb. 1839, 2 vols. 8vo; translated into French by Cohen, Paris, 1842, 2 vols. 8vo). His *Nachgelassene Schriften* were published by Döllinger (Ratisb. 1839–40), and his *Patrologie oder Christl. Literaturgesch.* by Reithmayer (Regensb. 1869). See Beda Weber, *Charakterbilder* (Frankf. 1853); D. F. Strauss, *Kleine Schriften*, etc. (Leips. 1862); Hare, *Vindication of Luther*, p. 167–169; Schaff, *Hist. of the Apostol. Ch.* p. 60; Ffoulkes, *Divisions in Christendom*, vol. i, § 53; Hase, *Protestantische Polemik; Werner, Gesch. d. Katholicismus;* and particularly the biographical sketch preceding the 5th edition of the "Symbolik." See also Hoefer, *Nouv. Biog. Générale*, xxxv, 734; Herzog, *Real-Encyklop.* ix, 662; *Bibl. Sacra*, Jan. 1850, p. 61; *English Rev.* ii, 7; *Christian Examiner*, xxxvii, 119; *Brit. and For. Ev. Review*, July, 1868, p. 591.

Mohnike, GOTTLIEB CHRISTIAN FRIEDRICH, a German divine of note, was born at Grimmen, in Pomerania, in 1781; studied theology at Greifswalde and Jena; in 1811 became rector of the city school at Greifswalde; in 1813 entered the pastorate, and gained a name universally honored and revered. He was made councillor of the Consistory after having removed to Stralsund about 1830, and died July 6, 1841. Besides several secular publications, we have from his pen *Ulrich Hutten's Jugendleben* (Greifsw. 1816):—*Hymnologische Forschungen* (ibid. 1831–32, 2 vols.).

Moine, ÉTIENNE LE, a very learned French Protestant minister, was born at Caen, in October, 1624, and became well skilled in the Oriental and classical languages, besides attaining great distinction as a theologian even while yet a student at the Protestant seminary in Sedan and the University of Leyden. After his graduation he was appointed pastor at Rouen, and rapidly rose in favor with his brethren. For political reasons he was imprisoned for a short time, and upon his release negotiated for an appointment at his Dutch alma mater, where he was finally appointed a professor, and successfully taught for some time. He was honored with the rectorate, and in various other ways, and his learning was acknowledged even in England. Oxford University conferred the doctorate of divinity on him in 1677. He died at Leyden April 4, 1689. Several dissertations of his are printed together, and entitled *Varia Sacra* (Leyden, 1685, 1694, 2 vols. 4to). He also wrote other works, but none of them are now of any value. See Hoefer, *Nouv. Biog. Gén.* s. v.

Moira ($Mo\tilde{\imath}\rho\alpha$, *a share*), the classical personification of that mysterious yet irresistible power whose invisible sceptre controls and directs human events, and assigns to each individual his fate or share. Homer, with a single exception (*Il.* xxiv, 29), speaks of but one Moira, a personification of fate, whom he represents as spinning the thread of each man's life, and though counselling with the other gods, yet as having supreme authority in directing and controlling the fate of each individual, and yielding obeisance only to Zeus. Hesiod, living a little later, distinguishes three Moiræ, and names them as *Clotho*, or the spinning fate; *Lachesis*, or the

one who assigns man his fate; and *Atropos*, or the fate that cannot be avoided. These he calls the daughters of Zeus and Thermis, a genealogy from which later writers differ. Other mythographers picture Clotho as holding the distaff, and ever furnishing the present; Lachesis, twirling the spindle, lays out the future; and Atropos severs the past by cutting the thread with her fatal scissors. The representations of the character and nature of the Moiræ, as varied as they are numerous, may, for our purpose, be classed in two divisions: 1st, those in which the Moiræ are but allegorical representations of the duration of human life; 2d, those in which the Moiræ are considered strictly as divinities of fate. As used in the first sense, it is supposed the Greeks originally conceived of but one Moira, but on further consideration of her nature and attributes adopted the idea of two, representing life's two boundaries of birth and death. Ultimately the number became three, and personified past, present, and future. Considering the Moiræ as strictly divinities of fate, they are viewed as independent, meting out individual destinies in accordance with eternal laws which know no variations or exceptions. The gods as well as mortals are subject to their authority, and even Zeus is sometimes represented as powerless to annul their decrees. Oftener, however, Zeus is pictured as in the background, weighing out power to them, and interfering with their decrees when disposed to save his favorites or destroy those with whom he is angry. This twofold view of the Moiræ, considering them sometimes as possessed of supreme power, and issuing irrevocable decrees, and at other times as interfered with and overruled by Zeus, is easily accounted for in the vain attempts of uninspired man to harmonize the seemingly inconsistent meting out of fate. By this means the ancients were enabled to interpret, satisfactorily to themselves, the varying freaks of fickle fortune, and account for apparent favoritism and injustice. It proved a magic key to open the mysteries of the dealings of Providence, and shifted the burden of human complaints from the shoulders of their beloved Zeus to those of the hated Moiræ, while all the praise for sudden prosperity or escape from danger and death was given to Zeus for his kindly interference with the will of the fates. Without the aid of this double view of the relationship existing between Zeus and the Moiræ, the Greeks could see in the strange events of national and personal history naught but the workings of an imperfect divinity; but with this explanatory means they were enabled to clothe Zeus with a robe interwoven with threads both of justice and mercy. For the sake of conceiving a blameless divinity, they were willing even to admit the occasional absence of supreme authority. Like the Erinyes, with whom they are often confounded, the Moiræ differ singularly from all the other gods in that they have no sympathy whatever for man, their iron sceptres never being wielded by the hands of mercy. Yet they were worshipped in many parts of Greece, and had sanctuaries at Corinth, Sparta, Olympia, and Thebes. The ancient artists and poets give us many fanciful pictures of the Moiræ. The earliest of the former represent them as goddesses holding staffs or sceptres in their hands as emblematic of their dominion. In later works of art they form a triplet of grave though beautiful maidens: Clotho holding a spindle or a roll (the book of fate); Lachesis pointing with her staff to the globe; while Atropos holds a pair of scales, a sun-dial, or some cutting instrument. By the poets they are sometimes pictured as aged and decrepit women, typical of the slow and often sorrowful march of fated events, and the various epithets applied to them are not so much the outburstings of human hate as poetical pencillings of the severity, inflexibility, and sternness of fate. See Vollmer, *Mythol. Wörterbuch*, s. v.; Smith, *Dict. Greek and Roman Biog. and Mythol.* s. v.; Dwight, *Classical Mythol.* s. v.; Grote, *Hist. of Greece*, iv, 197 sq. (H. W. T.)

Moïse, François Xavier, a French theologian, was born at Gras, in Franche-Comté, in 1742. He was professor of theology at Dôle when the Revolution broke out; and, taking the oath of loyalty to the civil constitution, in 1791 was elected bishop for the Jura district. During the reign of terror he had to conceal himself in the mountains. But being a learned canonist, and conversant with theology and the Levantine languages, his country needed his services, and he was called out to take a prominent part in the discussions which marked the national councils held in Paris during the years 1797 and 1801. At the expiration of the latter year he resigned his sacerdotal functions, together with abbé Grégoire, with whom he was intimately acquainted, left Paris soon thereafter, and retired to his farm at Morteau. Bishop Lecôz then bestowed upon him the title of honorary canon of Besançon. Moïse died at Morteau in 1813. He wrote: *Réponses critiques à plusieurs questions proposées par les incrédules modernes sur divers endroits des Livres Saints* (Paris, 1783, 18mo):—*De l'Opinion de M. Grégoire dans le procès de Louis XVI* (1801); together with some articles in the *Annales de la Religion, La Chronique Religieuse*, etc.

Mokanna (i. e. *the Concealed*) is the name of a Mohammedan prophet who flourished about A.D. 778. He was so called because, as the Mohammedans say, "he shrouded from his followers the excessive glory of his human face divine with a golden mask." He was the first who introduced into Islamism the doctrine of the transmigration of souls. Mokanna taught that God had assumed a human form, had commanded the angels to adore the first man, and from that time the divine nature had descended from prophet to prophet to Abu Moslem, the founder of the Abassides, and finally to himself. He afterwards added the Indian dogma of the incarnation of the human and divine nature, as well as the metempsychosis adopted by the Ghullats. See Madden, *Hist. of the Turkish Empire*, ii, 169. See MOHAMMEDAN SECTS.

Moket, RICHARD, an English theologian, was born in Dorsetshire in 1578, and was educated at Oxford University, of which he finally became fellow and doctor, distinctions that opened to him several prominent positions, of which he finally accepted that of provost of All-Souls' College, Oxford. He was also appointed one of the royal commissioners to supervise ecclesiastical affairs. He translated into Latin the Liturgy, sundry catechisms, the constitution, and several other instruments and documents relative to the Anglican Church, in order to distribute them as models worthy of imitation by foreign Church establishments. The collection was printed at London (1616, folio). But it had hardly been given to the public when theologians and schoolmen raised such a hue and cry against the work as finally consigned it to the fire. According to Heylin (*Life of Laud*, p. 70), this proscription was due solely to the unintentional omission on the part of the hapless translator of one of the prerogatives of the English Church. The whole edition of his work was utterly destroyed. One of the treatises which it contained—*De Polita Ecclesiæ Anglicanæ*—was reprinted at London, 1683, 8vo. Moket died at Oxford in 1618. See Wood, *Athenæ Oxon.;* Hoefer, *Nouv. Biog. Générale*, s. v.; Allibone, *Dict. of British and American Authors*, s. v.

Mol, PETER VAN, a Flemish painter, was born in Antwerp in 1590. He was a pupil of Rubens, and painted, in the style of his master, many noted works for the churches of Flanders and Brabant. In the cathedral of Antwerp is his *Adoration of the Magi*, which is a superior work. Another remarkable work by him was in the gallery of the Louvre, representing *Christ after the Crucifixion*, with the Marys, Joseph of Arimathæa, and John. The time of his death is unknown. See Spooner, *Biographical Hist. of the Fine Arts*, ii, 574.

Mola, a term derived from the sacramental immolation of Christ, alludes to the middle of an altar, signed with the dedication cross, and covering the sepulchre of relics.

Mola, Giovanni Battista, a French painter of the Bolognese school, was born about 1620, and was a scholar of Albano. He copied a vast work of Paul Veronese for cardinal Bichi. Lanzi gives but one example of his works from the collection of the marchesi Rinuccini, at Florence, the *Repose in Egypt*. Mrs. Jameson mentions a fine *Holy Family* by him in the Louvre, in which the Virgin watches with upturned eyes while Joseph and the Child sleep. Mola died in 1661. See Lanzi, *Hist. of Painting*, transl. by Roscoe, iii, 92; Mrs. Jameson, *Legends of the Madonna*, p. 241.

Mola, Pietro Francesco, an eminent Italian painter and architect, was born in the diocese of Como in 1612. He studied successively under Giuseppe Albano and Guercino. In his earlier life the works of the latter master were greatly admired by him, but subsequently he went to Venice, where he devoted himself to Titian and Veronese. From the result of this course of study he formed a style peculiar to himself, combining parts of all those from whom he had studied, and his fame spread throughout all Italy. He went to Rome in the pontificate of Innocent X, by whom he was immediately employed in executing numerous works, among which are *St. Peter delivered from Prison by the Angel* and the *Conversion of St. Paul*, in the chapel of the church Del Gesu. He was also patronized by pope Alexander VII, for whom he painted, in the pontifical palace of Monte Cavallo, his most celebrated work, *Joseph making himself known to his Brethren*. At Milan are two of his most admired productions, in the church of S. Maria della Vita, *St. John in the Wilderness* and *St. Paul the Hermit*. Mrs. Jameson mentions several works by this artist, among which are *Jacob wrestling with the Angel*, the *Meeting of Jacob and Rachel*, and the *Baptism of Christ*, in which an angel is disrobing the Saviour. Mola died suddenly at Rome in 1668, while preparing to set out for Paris, whither he had been invited by the king of France, who had appointed him court-painter, with a liberal pension. See Lanzi, *Hist. of Painting*, transl. by Roscoe, i, 462; ii, 535; iii, 92; Spooner, *Biographical Hist. of the Fine Arts*, ii, 574; Jameson and Eastlake, *History of our Lord*, i, 151, 153, 297.

Mola'dah (Heb. *Moladah'*, מוֹלָדָה [in Nehemiah מֹלָדָה], *birth;* Sept. Μωλαδά v. r. Μωδαδά, etc.), a city in the southern part of the tribe of Judah towards the Edomitish border (Josh. xv, 26), which fell within the portion set off to Simeon (Josh. xix, 2; 1 Chron. iv, 28). It was also occupied after the exile (Neh. xi, 26). Reland (*Palæst.* p. 901) thinks it was the *Malatha* (Μάλαθα) mentioned by Josephus (*Ant.* xviii, 6, 2) as a castle of Idumæa, to which Agrippa retired in chagrin after his return from Rome. Eusebius and Jerome (*Onomast.* s. v. Ἀραμά) allude to it (Μαλαθί) as a place four Roman miles distant from Arad, which latter they describe as an ancient city of the Amorites situated in the wilderness of Kadesh, and twenty miles from Hebron, on the road to Aila (see Reland, *Palæst.* p. 885). At a later period Malatha became a Roman colony (Reland, p. 231). Dr. Robinson (*Researches*, ii, 621) finds the locality in the present *el-Milh*, first observed by Schubert (*Reise*, ii, 454), consisting of extensive ruins with a well, situated at the required distance from the site of Arad (comp. Schwarz, *Palest.* p. 100). The present name, signifying "salt," has little affinity with the Heb. appellation, but may be a corruption of it (Wilson, *Lands of the Bible*, i, 346; Van de Velde, *Memoir*, p. 335; Ritter, *Pal. und Syr.* i, 124; Tristram, *Land of Israel*, p. 369 sq.; Stewart, *Tent and Khan*, p. 217).

Molans, PHILIBERT DE, founder of the *Order of St. George*, was born at Molans, France, and flourished in the 14th century. He belonged to one of the oldest families in the country. The duke of Burgundy, Philip the Bold, took him into his service as equerry. Molans followed his master to the Holy Land, and was very useful to him. In return for his efficiency, the duke appointed him general inspector of the ducal arsenals. Molans afterwards went again to Palestine, and is said to have brought back the remains of one St. George, presenting these relics to the church at Rougemont, which instituted special services in honor of them. In 1390 Molans established an order under the inspiration of the alleged martyr. In order to become a member of this association one had to be a native of the duchy or county of Burgundy, and show not less than sixteen quarterings on his shield. Each chevalier of St. George had to take a vow to devote his life and fortune to the vindication of the Roman Catholic religion, and the protection of the oppressed, the. virgins, and the orphans. The distinctive badge of the order was a gold image, suspended from a blue ribbon, and representing St. George smiting a dragon to the ground. Although this society had a purely moral aim, the Besançon Parliament persistently declined to legalize it. The Order of St. George continued in France until the Revolution. Historians are not agreed as to the place and date of Molans's death. The latter part of his life was shrouded in obscurity. Great Britain, Bavaria, Spain, and Russia have each, in turn, created an Order of St. George. See Thomas Varin, *Etat de l'illustre Confrérie de Saint-Georges en* 1663; Pointier de Gouhelans, *Statuts de l'Ordre de Saint-Georges, avec la liste des Chevaliers depuis* 1390 (Besançon, 1768, 8vo); John Milner, *Historical and Critical Inquiry into the Existence and Character of St. George;* Heylin, *History of St. George.*

Molanus, Gerhard Walther, a German Lutheran theologian, was born at Hameln, on the Weser, Nov. 1, 1633. He studied at the University of Helmstädt under Calixtus (q. v.). In 1659 he became professor of mathematics in the University of Rinteln, but in 1664 was made extraordinary, and soon after ordinary professor of theology in the same university, which position he retained until 1677. In the mean time he published various works, partly mathematical, partly theological. Among the latter we notice *De communicatione et prædicatione idiomatum, qua inter alia ostenditur humanam Christi naturam extrinsecus omnipotentem appellari posse* (Rinteln, 1665), quite in the manner and method of Calixtus. In 1674 duke John Frederick of Hanover appointed him director of the consistory for that province, and in 1677 he became abbot of the convent of Loccum. He was very active in promoting union conferences with the Reformed and Roman Catholic theologians, and, although without success, he acquired the well-earned reputation of a peace-maker. This was especially shown in his efforts in behalf of the French Reformed, whom the revocation of the Edict of Nantes had driven to seek refuge in Germany. Duke John Frederick, who had himself returned to Romanism, wished to induce Molanus to follow his example, but the latter withstood all his offers. Having, in his efforts for a union with the Romish Church, come in contact with Bossuet, Molanus conceded that the Eucharist "quodammodo proprie dici sacrificium;" also that "de conciliis œcumenicis legitime celebratis dico: Christus nunquam permittet ut ecclesia universalis in concilio aliquid fidei contrarium pronuntiet," etc. Yet he would not recognise as "legitime celebratum" the Council of Trent, which had condemned the Protestants without a hearing, and which was not universally recognised, for instance, in Germany. Molanus was accused of having gone over to Romanism, and therefore published in his defence *Migæ venales s. refutat. calumniar.* etc. (1698). He died Sept. 7, 1722. See J. v. Esinem, *Leben G. W. Molani* (Magdeb. 1724, 8vo); Kapp, *Sammlung einige Briefe über d. Vereinigung d. luth. u. ref. Theol.* (Leips. 1745, 8vo); Schlegel, *Kirchengesch.*

d. 18ten Jahrh. i, 559 sq.; ii, 213 sq.; Schröckh, *Kirchengesch.* vii, 83, 103 sq. (J. N. P.)

Molanus (Vermeulen), John, a Belgian theologian of some note, was born at Lille in 1533. He was educated at Louvain, and there obtained the doctorate in 1570, and then taught theology for several years. By different publications he called attention to his learning, and gradually gained favor at the court and at Rome. He was made a canon of the church of St. Peter, and director of a seminary then founded at Louvain. He died Sept. 18, 1585. Baronius pays him great homage in the preface to his *Martyrologe Romain.* Molanus published: *De Picturis et Imaginibus sacris* (Louvain, 1570, 1574, 1595, 8vo): — *De Historia sacrarum Imaginum et Picturarum,* lib. iv; *Theologie des peintres, sculpteurs, et dessinateurs* (Paris, 1765, 12mo): — *Annales urbis Louvaniensis ac obsidionis illius historia* (Louvain, 1572, 4to): — *Calendarium Ecclesiasticum* (Anvers, 1574, 12mo): — *De fide hæreticis servanda,* lib. iii; *quartus item de fide rebellibus servanda, et quintus de fide ac Juramento quæ a tyrannis exiquantur* (Cologne, 1584): — *De piis Testamentis* (Cologne, 1584, 1661, 8vo): — *Theologiæ practicæ Compendium* (Cologne, 1585, 1590, 8vo): — *Orationes III de agnis Dei, de decimis dandis et de decimis recipiendis* (Cologne, 1587, 8vo): — *De Canonicis,* lib. iii (Cologne, 1587, 8vo): — *Militia sacra Ducum ac Princium Brabantiæ cum annotat. Petri Lourvii* (Anvers, 1592, 8vo): — *Medicorum ecclesiasticum Diarium* (Louvain, 1595, 8vo): — *Bibliotheca materiarum Theologica quæ a quibus auctoribus, quum antiquis, tum recentioribus, sint pertractæ* (Cologne, 1618, 4to).

Molay, Jacques de, the last grand-master of the Knights Templars, was born about the year 1244 in Burgundy, of the families of Longvic and Raon. He was admitted to his order at Baune, in the diocese of Autun. Of his subsequent history but little is known until he was promoted to the grand-mastership about the year 1298. Pierre Dupuy, a French writer, insinuates that he did not obtain his election by his own merits, but through the intrigues of the nobility of France. If this were true it might account for the suspicions and fears which animated Philip IV. against the establishment of the Order of the Temple in France just at this time, when monarchy was endeavoring to rear itself on the political abasement of the Church and the feudal lordships. But there is nothing to prove this assertion, for it is difficult to conceive how the nobility of France could influence an election contested at such a distance. The affairs of Christianity in the East were at this time in a grievous condition. Several important towns had fallen into the hands of the Mohammedans. Many of the last defenders of the Cross had perished. One of the most illustrious grand-masters of the order had recently died. Syria was lost to the Christian arms, and the Templars and Hospitallers had taken refuge in Cyprus and Tortosa, whence they invoked the aid of the Holy See, the princes and people of Europe. All Europe being engaged in great internal contests — monarchy and feudalism and the Church arrayed against each other — help was looked for in vain by the poor Christians of the East. Besides, the Cross had not fallen in Palestine without embittering numbers against the cause, leading many to say that men should not persist in a contest which God himself had abandoned. Jacques de Molay, however, had no sooner been put at the helm than he went forward with his task. He did not wait for succor from Europe, but endeavored to derive some benefit from the projects of the Mogul Tartars of Persia against Egypt and Syria; so that in the spring of 1299, when the grand khan assembled a powerful force, Jacques de Molay commanded one of the wings of the Tartar army. With the troops confided to him he invaded Syria, and subsequently, under the conduct of the Tartar general, recovered Jerusalem from the infidels. This unexpected event was received with delight by the Christian world. The Mogul Tartars, counselled doubtless by some of the Christian chiefs, sent messengers to Europe, to the pope and the kings of France and England, urging them to engage in a new crusade, which should strike a final blow at the Mohammedan power in the East. But the Tartar messengers had scarcely returned before reverses and treason had destroyed the army of the grand khan. Jerusalem was lost in 1300, and the Templars under Jacques de Molay were obliged to retire to the island of Tortosa, near Tripoli, whence they could simply watch and harass the movements of the enemy. But in 1302 they were finally surprised and defeated, and the grand-master, with those that remained of the order, took refuge in Cyprus, now and then renewing the contest by sudden incursions upon the Mohammedans. The brother and successor of the grand khan still looked for aid from Europe, and even approached the pope, but the replies were evasive. Philip IV, in his attempt to check the feudal power and all ecclesiastical control, feared that the papacy might recover, in an institution like that of the Temple, the military force it needed to defend its theocracy. He dreaded leaving to the nobility an order so entirely filled with its members and benefits, and an organized constitution as a means of rallying and defence; for the Templars had become in almost every kingdom of the West a formidable republic, governed by their own laws, animated by the closest corporate spirit, under the severest internal discipline, and an all-pervading organization; independent alike of the civil power and of the spiritual hierarchy; possessing fifteen thousand of the bravest and best-trained soldiers in the world, armed and accoutred in the most splendid fashion of the time, ready at the summons of the grand-master to embark on any service, their one aim being the aggrandizement of the order. Philip, fearing the strength and the wealth of the order, claiming allegiance only to the pope, as the supreme head of the Church, and greatly desirous of possessing their lands, munitions, arms, ships, and treasures, determined upon its destruction; but, lest his influence might be overpowered in an open contest, he resolved to make the pope his instrument. A new crusade, he saw clearly, would only revive religious passions favorable to the Holy See, and render necessary, inviolable, more important, and more powerful still, these soldier-monks; consequently Philip promptly opposed the opening of a new crusade. June 6, 1306, Clement V summoned the grand-masters of the Templars and Hospitallers to Europe, under pretext of consulting them in regard to the proposed crusade, and some previously advanced plans for uniting the two orders of Templars and Hospitallers. Promptly Molay returned to Europe, but the manner in which he came was not of a nature to stifle the ambitious designs of his enemies. With sixty of the most distinguished knights of the order and a vast amount of treasure, he made an ostentatious entry into Paris, August, 1306, where he was received by the king with great courtesy. If De Molay had been of a less generous and unsuspicious character, he would have understood that every motive that influenced Philip was concentrated in great intensity against his order. The grand-master, lulled into security by the apparent kindness of the French king, proceeded to Poitiers to pay his allegiance to the pope, and to present two memorials drawn up by himself, relative to the state of affairs in the East, and the projected union of the different existent military orders, which he opposed on the ground that by such act their power would only be augmented, and thus consequently provoke greater envy, of which even now there was more than enough; and, so far from suppressing prevailing jealousies among the knights, it would only embitter the strife among the brethren, and cause more frequent collisions. He begged the pope to examine into the sinister rumors which had spread abroad concerning the faith, morals, and secret mysteries of the order;

for they had been accused of treachery, murder, idolatry, Islamism, and many other villainies; and demanded a rigid investigation, in order that, if proved innocent, they might receive public absolution; if culpable, suffer condemnation. Under these pretexts, Philip strongly urged the pope to proceed against the Temple, and the latter, finally yielding to the king's importunity and threats, inaugurated the investigation, and sent to Philip for all possible information. Philip affected to take the request for information as a permission to proceed against the order himself. Accordingly, on Oct. 13, 1307, every Templar in the realm was made a prisoner. Jacques de Molay was seized in the house of the Temple, and summoned before the Inquisition of France, Oct. 24, 1307. According to the report of his interrogatory, he made full confession of having denied Christ, and of having been guilty of other crimes. Confession was bribed out of some by offers of indulgence; wrung from others by the dread of torture, or by actual torture. The pope, enraged by the king's liberty, suspended the powers of the inquisitor, and forbade the bishops to continue their proceedings against the Temple. Philip IV simulated ready and complete submission; but at the same time he urged all the princes of Europe to follow his example, endeavored to embitter the French against the Templars, and finally invented a circular letter from the grand-master to all the brethren and subjects in prison, advising them to acknowledge the crimes he himself had confessed. Aug. 20, 1308, Jacques de Molay himself was subjected to a second examination by a special commission of cardinals and agents of the king; but as the commission proved very treacherous in their conduct towards him, he finally tired of the proceedings, and demanded that he be brought before the Roman pontiff; "for," said he, "to the pope alone belongs the power of judging the grand-master of the order, and to his judgment I refer." March 2, 1310, he was again summoned by the papal commission, but persisted in his determination to be judged by the pope only. While the papal commission was still in session, Philip IV, tiring of their slow progress, and fearing that the power of the Temple was not yet crushed, summoned fifty-four more of the Templars before a council at Paris, and caused them to be burned the same day, May 11, 1310. The pope now became anxious for his own authority, appointed a new commission to hasten a decision in the case of Jacques de Molay, and he was by it condemned to death. Just as the fatal sentence was about to be pronounced, De Molay arose, and in a calm, clear voice thus addressed his judges: "Before heaven and earth, on the verge of death, where the least falsehood bears like an intolerable weight upon the soul, I protest that we have richly deserved death, not on account of any heresy or sin of which we ourselves or our order have been guilty, but because we have yielded, to save our lives, to the seductive words of the pope and of the king; and so by our confessions brought shame and ruin on our blameless, holy, and orthodox brotherhood." The cardinals stood confounded, the people could not repress a profound sympathy, and the assembly was hastily broken up to meet another day. But the king, who had been informed of all, ordered the grand-master to be burned immediately. He was led forth to the flames, a feeble old man, loaded with fetters, bent and whitened by age and captivity. He sustained his sufferings with perfect firmness and resolution, protesting to the end in favor of the innocence of his order, and perishing bravely — the last champion of Christianity against the Orient, the last liberator of Jerusalem, the last grand-master of the Temple. See Porter, *History of the Knights of Malta*, i, 180, 190 sq.; Sutherland, *Achievements of the Knights of Malta*, vol. i, ch. ix; Milman, *History of Latin Christianity*, vol. vi, bk. xii, ch. i and ii; Hase, *Church History*, p. 319; and especially the excellent article in Hoefer, *Nouv. Biog. Générale*, xxxv, 79 sq. (J. P. L.)

Molcho, SOLOMON, or DIOGO PIRES, as he was called when a Marrano or Neo-Christian, was born about A.D. 1501 in Portugal. He not only received a liberal education, which enabled him to hold a state office as "escrivão aos ouvidores na casa da supplicação," but was probably also made acquainted in his childhood with Hebrew and Talmudic lore, as he is the author of a Hebrew work and a synagogal poem written in the Aramaic language (comp. Zunz, *Literaturgesch. d. synagog. Poësie*, p. 534). About this time a man named David Rëubeni appeared in the court of the king of Portugal. He announced that he had come from India, and was sent by his brother, the king of the Jews, to propose an alliance in order to recover the Holy Land from the sultan Solyman. Many of the Neo-Christians believed in him. He passed through Spain, where he made many proselytes; into France to Avignon, and into Italy. He inscribed banners with the holy name of God. In many cities—Bologna, Ferrara, Mantua—numbers believed that he was commissioned to be the leader of the army of Israel. He even had an interview with pope Clement VII. Coming to Portugal, Molcho sought his acquaintance in order to find out whether his visionary revelations, which had all Messianic background, were in harmony with Rëubeni's commission. The latter treated Molcho very coolly, and told him that his military commission had nothing to do with his cabalistic mysticism, being himself no adept in this branch of science. Molcho, however, misunderstood Rëubeni, believing as he did that this prince and would-be Messiah would have nothing to do with him since he had not the seal of the covenant, and he thus apostatized to Judaism, performing the rite of circumcision himself, which operation became to him the cause of a severe sickness. When Rëubeni was acquainted with this fact he was very angry, and feared that he might be suspected as the author of Molcho's apostasy. The Jews relate that Molcho was utterly ignorant while he was a Christian; but immediately on his circumcision "the Lord gave him wisdom, and he became wiser than all men in a very short time, and many wondered at him." His preaching was of such an inspiring eloquence that the Jews believed it to be dictated by angels. He preached Judaism before kings; even pope Clement VII admitted him to an audience, and gave him the privilege to dwell wherever he would. Solomon Molcho seems to have been permitted to pour out his apocalyptic rhapsodies (pages of them may be read in the *Chronicles of R. Joseph ben-Joshua ben-Meïr, the Sephardi*, ii, 152–189) without restraint. Bishops and princes—the bishop of Ancona and the duke of Urbino, Francesco Maria della Rovere I—from credulity, curiosity, or compassion, protected him against his enemies. Two of his prophecies, inundations of the Tiber in Rome and earthquakes in Lisbon, could hardly fail of accomplishment (the former took place October 8, 1530; the latter, January 26, 1531). But he came to a woful end. He attempted to convert the emperor Charles V. at Ratisbon; but Charles was hard-hearted, and ordered him to be put in prison with his friend Rëubeni, whom he met after he was obliged to leave Rome. When peace was restored with Solyman the Turk, the emperor betook himself to Italy, and both prisoners were conveyed to Mantua. Molcho, who was an object rather for a lunatic asylum than the stake, was condemned to be burned as an apostate Christian. "With a bridle on his jaw-bones to prevent his speaking to the people," as the Jewish chronicle relates, "they brought him out, and all the city was moved about him, and the fire burned before him. And one of the nobles of the emperor said, 'Take the bridle from between his teeth, for I have a message unto him from the king;' and they did so. And he said unto him, 'The emperor hath sent me unto thee, saying, "If thou turn from thy ways, shalt thou not be accepted and live?" And he will maintain thee, and thou shalt be before him; and if not, evil is determined against thee.' But he answered like a saint, like an angel of God, and said, 'Because I walked in that religion, my heart is bitter and grieved; and now what is good in your sight do, and my soul shall return unto the Father's house as in its youth, for then it will be better with it than now.' He was cast into the fire, and the Lord smelled the sweet savor, and took to him his spotless soul, and is with him as one brought up with him, rejoicing always before him." Molcho died in November or December, 1532; yet there were Jews who believed that the fire had no power over him, and that he departed—God only knows whither. Comp. Basnage, *Histoire des Juifs* (Engl. translation), p. 722; Lindo, *History of the Jews in Spain and Portugal*, p. 361 sq.; Milman, *History of the Jews*, iii, 367 sq.; *The Chronicles of Rabbi Joseph ben-Joshua ben-Meïr, the Sephardi* (transl. from the Hebrew into English by C. H. F. Bialloblotzky, London, 1836), ii, 150–192; Jost, *Geschichte d. Judenthums u. s. Sekten*, iii, 125; Kayserling, *Geschichte der Juden in Portugal*, p. 176 sq., 192 sq.; Cassel, *Leitfaden für jüdische Geschichte und Literatur* (Berlin, 1872), p. 92 sq.; Fürst, *Biblioth. Judaica*, ii, 387; Grätz, *Geschichte der Juden*, ix, 264–285; the same in Frankel's *Monatsschrift* (1856), p. 205, 241, 260 sq. (B.P.)

Moldavia and Wallachia, two states forming the so-called *Danubian Principalities*, but since December 23, 1861, united under one prince and administration, are now officially bearing the name *Roumania*. We treat them unitedly in this article, as this is the custom generally among geographers.

1. MOLDAVIA (Ger. *Moldau*, Turk. *Bogdan* or *Kera-Islak*) is bounded on the N. and E. by Russia, on the S. by Wallachia and the Danube, and on the W. by the Austrian empire. Greatest length from north-west to south-east, 280 miles; greatest breadth, 128 miles; area, 20,118 square miles; population about 1,300,000. The country forms, geographically, part of the great undulating pastoral plains or steppes of South Russia, except towards the west, where spurs from the Carpathians give it a somewhat mountainous character. It is watered by the Pruth, the Sereth, and the Danube, and is almost everywhere fertile. The forests of Moldavia are also of great extent and importance. But the riches of the country consist mainly in its cattle and horses, of which immense numbers are reared on its splendid and far-stretching pastures. Swine and sheep are also numerous; and the rearing of bees, owing to the multitude of lime-trees, is extensively carried on. The great plagues of the land are locusts and earthquakes. Minerals and precious metals are said to be abundant, but they have not as yet been worked. The capital is Jassy, but the great centre of trade is Galatz. The principal exports are wool, lambskins, hides, feathers, maize, tar, tallow, honey, leeches, cattle, and salt (in blocks); the imports are chiefly the manufactured products of Western Europe.

2. WALLACHIA, the larger of the united Danubian Principalities, is bounded on the N. by the Austrian empire and Moldavia, on the E. and S. by the Danube, and on the W. by the Austrian empire and the Danube. Length from the western frontier to Cape Kaliakra on the Black Sea, 305 miles; greatest breadth, 130 miles; area, 27,930 square miles; population about 4,000,000. The greater part of Wallachia is quite flat; but in the north, where it borders on Hungary and Transylvania, it gradually rises up into a great mountain-wall, impassable save in five places. It is destitute of wood throughout almost its whole extent, and (especially along the banks of the Danube) is covered with marshy swamps miles upon miles in breadth. The principal river flowing *through* the country is the Aluta, which joins the Danube at Nikopol. The climate is extreme; the summer heats are intense, while in winter the land lies under deep snow for four months. The soil is rich, and would leave nothing to be desired, were it not for the ravages of locusts and the calamitous summer droughts. The principal products are corn, maize, millet, wine, flax, tobacco, and olive-oil. The vast treeless heaths afford

sustenance to great herds of cattle, sheep, and horses. As in Moldavia, agriculture is an important branch of industry. In minerals—especially gold, silver, copper, and rock-salt—the soil is rich, but only the last of these is extensively worked. The imports and exports are the same as in Moldavia. In both countries they might be more than doubled, as scarcely one half of the soil, which is said to be everywhere good, is under cultivation.

3. *History.*—In ancient times what now constitutes Roumania formed an important part of Dacia. At the period of the migration of nations, and in the following centuries, it was the scene of the struggles between the Gothic, Hunnic, Bulgarian, and Slavic races, who left their traces among the Romanized Dacian inhabitants, and helped to form that composite people, the modern Wallachs, who in the 11th century were converted to the Christianity of the Eastern or Greek Church. Their incursions, however, frightfully devastated the country. In the 11th century the Kumans, a Turkish race, established in Moldavia a kingdom of their own. Two centuries later the great storm of Mongols broke over the land. It now fell into the hands of the Nogai Tartars, who left it utterly wasted, so that only in the forests and mountains was any trace left of the native Wallachian population. In the latter half of the 13th century a petty Wallach chief of Transylvania, Radu Negru of Fogarasch, entered Wallachia, took possession of a portion of the country, divided it among his nobles, founded a senate of twelve members and an elective monarchy, and gradually conquered the whole of Wallachia. Rather less than a century later (1354) a similar attempt, also successful, was made by a Wallach chief of the Hungarian Marmarosh, of the name of Bogdan, to repeople Moldavia. In the beginning of the 16th century both principalities placed themselves under the protection of the porte, and gradually the nobles or boyars lost the right of electing their own ruler, whose office was bought in Constantinople. After 1711 the Turks governed the countries by Fanariot princes, who in reality only farmed the revenues, enriched themselves, and impoverished the land. In 1802 the Russians wrested from Turkey the right of surveillance over the principalities. A great number of the nobles, through family marriages with the Fanariots, were now of Greek descent, the court tongue was Greek, and the religious and political sympathies of the country were the same; hence the effort of the principalities in 1821 to emancipate themselves from Turkish authority, which was only the prelude to the greater and more successful struggle in Greece itself. In 1822 Russia forced Turkey to choose the princes or hospodars of Wallachia and Moldavia from natives, and not from the corrupt Greeks of Constantinople, and after 1829 to allow them to hold their dignity for life. The principalities were united, as has been already mentioned, under one ruler in 1858, and under one administration in 1861. In 1866 the Wallachians refused to endorse the reign of Cusa, and, with the consent of Turkey and the great Powers, prince Charles of Hohenzollern was called to govern the united principalities. He was the first to call the country *Roumania.* To this day (1875) he remains its ruler.

4. *Social Condition.*—The Roumanians, claiming to be the descendants of the ancient Dacians, betray that origin largely in their language, which is a Latin dialect, three fourths of the words being Latin (the Dacian has disappeared), the other fourth being made up of words indicating a Grecian, Gothic, Slavic, or Turkish origin. A *Grammatica Daco-Romana* was published by Johann. Alexi (Vienna, 1826), and a *Historia Linguæ Daco-Romanæ* by Laurianus (Vienna, 1849). A large Latin-Romanic-Hungarian Dictionary was carefully executed by the bishop of Fogarasch, Joh. Bob (Klausenburg, 1839, 3 vols.). The nobles of the land generally speak French, and indeed French ideas and customs are in favor with the Roumanians, particularly the young. There is no middle class. The common people, though very poor, are on the whole good-hu-

mored, frugal, sober, and cleanly; murder and larceny are almost unknown. Their dwellings, however, are, as may be supposed, of the most wretched description; composed chiefly of interlaced willow-withes, covered with mud, cane, and straw; and often, even in the large towns, they are only of mud; a cloak serves for a bed, and the whole house-furniture is comprised in a few kitchen utensils. The education of the country is not in a very forward condition, but promises under the present administration to take advanced ground. The trade of the country is largely in the hands of foreigners, especially Jews, who fare badly. Gypsy communities are an important element in the population; upwards of 150,000 of this mysterious race are serfs belonging to the rich boyars and the monasteries. In 1844 about 30,000 were emancipated, and settled in colonies in different parts of the land; they are ruled by a *Bataf*, or king, of their own choice, of which every gypsy village has one: they call themselves *Romnitschel* or *Romni.*

5. *Religion.*—(1) *Ecclesiastical Status.*—The established religion of "Roumania" is that of the Greek Church, but all forms of Christianity are tolerated, and their professors enjoy equal political rights. At the head of the Greek clergy stands a metropolitan archbishop chosen by the general assembly of the different estates, confirmed in his office by the prince, and serving 4,275,000 members. Every bishop is assisted by a council of clergy, and has a seminary for priests; the superintendent of the preaching clergy is the *Proto-papa* of the diocese. In Moldavia there are 1795 churches, 3268 priests, and 491 deacons; also 7622 married secular clergy and 60 monasteries, of which the richest is that of Niamtz, with 1300 monks. In Wallachia there are 4171 churches (of which 2587 are wooden), 36,638 persons belonging to the families of married priests, 10,749 deacons, 9500 monks and nuns, and 202 monasteries and nunneries. The property belonging to the priesthood of the principalities is immense, and at present (1875) efforts are being made by the government to have it secularized. The Roumanians are very superstitious, and care little for human life. The catechism of their morals contains scarcely anything more than fasting and hospitality. They hate all foreigners except the Latin races, and are especially severe against the Jews, who are there in large numbers, and are invaluable for the commercial interests of the country. They number over 400,000. Public persecutions against Jews have continued until very recently, and in consequence the great powers have threatened armed intervention. The United States has pursued a humane policy in selecting a Jewish representative. (2) *Evangelism.*—Christianity must have early made its way to these parts, and been strengthened during Gothic invasion. St. Nicetas, who flourished about 400, is regarded as the apostle of Roumania. The barbarians in part removed Christian influences, and in 861 Cyril attempted anew the Christianizing of the people, especially the Bulgarians. In consequence the Slavonian language secured a foothold, and in the conflict between Constantinople and Rome this Danubian country sided with the Eastern Church. Rome made repeated efforts to regain her hold, but ineffectually. For political reasons princes now and then favored Rome, but in the 15th century, when it became a dependency of the Turks, the Greek Church gained absolute adherence. In the days of the Reformation Wallachia remained unmoved, but in Moldavia John Heraclides (Jacob Basilius), an adventurer who had gained the throne, favored Protestantism (1561–63). Twenty years later the prince was again Protestant — Janked Sass, "the Lutheran" († 1584). From that time but little was heard for Protestantism, and even to-day, though ruled by a Prussian prince, there is only 1 Protestant for 6 Armenians, 50 Romanists, 1450 Greek Catholics, and 280 Jews. Protestant societies exist at Bucharest (one Lutheran and one Reformed), at Crajona, in Wallachia, and at Jassy and

Galatz, in Moldavia. Besides these, Protestants live scattered in different places. See Michel de Koyalm'-tchan, *Histoire de la Valachie, de la Moldavie, et des Valaques Transdanubiens;* the *Reports* of the Gustavus Adolphus Society, St. John, in *Lond. Acad.* Aug. 15, 1874, p. 181; Prof. Wells, in *Meth. Qu. Rev.* Jan. 1873, art. i; Stanley, *East. Ch.* p. 104.

Moldenhawer, JOHANN HEINRICH DANIEL, a German theologian, was born at Halle, Oct. 29, 1709. He was educated at the "Collegium Fridericianum," and later at the University of Königsberg, where he was a diligent student in ancient languages, especially the Greek and Hebrew. He was appointed in 1733 deacon at Kreuzburg, and in 1737 to the Sackheinsche Kirche at Königsberg, but had very many difficulties in this new position, and did not live in harmony with his colleagues. He therefore gladly accepted a call to the University of Königsberg as professor of divinity in 1744. He published there in 1745 his *Introductio in libros sacros Veteris et Novi Testamenti,* of which Horne says that few treatises of the kind are more useful than this. He shows the canonical authority of the Bible in general, and treats of the author, time of writing, argument, scope, chronology, etc., of each book in particular. He was appointed in 1756 ecclesiastical counsellor, and also librarian of the Wallenrodsche library. He received a call in 1765 as minister to Hamburg, where he died, April 8, 1790. Besides several contributions to journals, he published *Diss. I et II Acta apostoli Pauli chronologice digesta* (Königsberg, 1744, 4to):—*Einleitung in die Alterthümer der Ægypten, Juden, Griechen, und Römer* (ibid. 1754, 8vo):—*Gründliche Erläuterungen der schweren Stellen der heiligen Bücher des neuen Testaments* (Leipzig und Königsberg, 1763-70, 4 vols.):—*Betrachtungen über das Vaterunser* (Hamburg, 1765, 8vo):—*Hauptinhalt der Betrachtungen über die Heilswahrheiten, welche in den Montags-Betstunden in der Domkirche 1766-68 vorgetragen worden sind* (Hamburg, 1768, 8vo):—*Der Brief Pauli an die Römer, nach dem Grundtext übersetzt, nebst Erklärungen und Anmerkungen* (ibid. 1770, gr. 8vo). He also translated and wrote commentaries on all the most important books of the New Testament. He was likewise the author of *Ausführliche Prüfung des fünften Fragments aus der Wolfenbüttelschen Bibliothek von der Auferstehung Jesu durch welche zugleich die Auferstehungsgeschichte Christi bestätigt und erläutert wird* (Hamburg, 1779, 8vo):—*Ausführliche Prüfung des dritten Fragments aus der Wolfenbüttelschen Bibliothek, von dem Durchgange der Israeliten durch's rothe Meer* (ibid. 1779, 8vo):—*Ausführliche Prüfung des zweiten Fragments aus der Wolfenbüttelschen Bibliothek von der Unmöglichkeit einer Offenbarung, die alle Menschen auf eine gegründete Art glauben können* (ibid. 1782, gr. 8vo):— *Der Hauptzweck des Leidens und Sterbens Jesu* (Köthen, 1787, 8vo). See Döring, *Gelehrte Theol. Deutschlands,* ii, 557-62.

Mole is the rendering in the Auth. Vers. of the Heb. תִּנְשֶׁמֶת, *tinshe'meth,* in Lev. xi, 30, where, however, it probably signifies some species of the *lizard* tribe; but in Lev. xi, 18; Deut. xiv, 16, it is rendered "swan," where it evidently refers to some kind of *bird.* It thus appears to denote two very different kinds of animal, but in neither case the mole. See CHAMELEON; SWAN. The mole is thought to be represented by the Heb. חֹלֶד, *cho'led,* rendered "weasel" in Lev. xi, 29. This is an animal very abundant in Palestine. See WEASEL. The word elsewhere occurs only in the difficult expression, Isa. ii, 20, לַחְפֹּר פֵּרוֹת, *lachphor' peroth'* (if regarded as two words, perhaps, *to the hole of the rats* or burrowers, Sept. τοῖς ματαίοις, Vulg. *talpas,* Auth. Vers. "to the moles"), which Gesenius (*Comment.* ad loc.) thinks should be pointed as one word, לַחֲפַרְפֵּרוֹת, *lachapharperoth',* indicating an animal, חֲפַרְפֵּרָה, *chapharperah',* so called from digging into

the walls of houses, probably the *rat,* a creature common in every habitable part of the world.

Many scholars "consider the ἀσπάλαξ of the Greeks to be the creature intended by at least the first of the above Hebrew words. Whether this was what modern zoologists would call a *mole* is, however, rather doubtful. Aristotle, in his history of the *aspalax,* evidently derived from personal and careful examination, describes it as absolutely blind. Now the eyes of our common mole (*Talpa Europœa*), though they are very minute, and so imbedded in the fur as to be readily overlooked by a cursory examiner, are distinctly open, and could not escape the detection of so accurate a physiologist as Aristotle Hence it has been supposed that the *aspalax* could not have been a *Talpa;* and another animal has been found to inhabit the east of Europe and west of Asia, which, while possessing much of the form, and even the peculiar structure of the moles, together with their burrowing powers, is absolutely and totally void of sight, the eyes, which are rudimentary specks, being completely covered by the skin of the face, which is quite imperforate. For a while it seemed certain that this was the creature intended; and accordingly the genus was technically named *Aspalax* by Olivier, the species receiving the appellation of *typhlus.* But still more recently a species of true mole, now called *Talpa cœca,* has been discovered inhabiting Greece, in which the eyes are as minute, and as useless, because as completely covered by the skin, as in the *aspalax.* As the *aspalax* is larger and more conspicuous than the blind *talpa,* which, moreover, appears to be rare, on the assumption that the former is the *tinshemeth* we here devote a few words to its appearance and habits. It belongs to the family *Muridæ* among the *Rodents,* and is in fact a rat under the guise of a mole. Hence it has been called the mole-rat. The animal is from eight inches to a foot in length, with a great round head, no external ears or eyes, the nostrils opening beneath, the limbs very short, with strong nails formed for digging; the body clothed with a short, thick, soft fur of an ashy hue, and the naked skin of the muzzle white. It is particularly abundant in the south of Russia, excavating the surface of the vast steppes or level plains, and forming long burrows beneath the turf, with many lateral ramifications. The object of its pursuit is not earthworms or subterraneous larvæ, which form the prey of the true mole; for the mole-rat is exclusively a vegetable feeder, and it drives

Blind Mole-rat—*Aspalax typhlus.*

its runs solely for bulbs and roots, especially for the fleshy root of an umbelliferous plant, the *chœrophyllum.* At frequent intervals the burrow comes to the surface of the soil, and here hillocks are cast up a couple of yards in circumference, and of proportionate height. Altogether its work closely imitates that of the mole, but on a somewhat larger scale. It is said to work energetically and rapidly, and on the approach of an enemy, of which it is warned probably by an acute sense of smell, it instantly turns downward and penetrates the earth perpendicularly. It is said to devour corn, and to gather large quantities, which it lays up in its deeper galleries for winter supply, in this respect agreeing with many other of the *Muridæ*. Like the mole, it can proceed forward or backward in its burrow with equal celerity. During the early hours of the day a pair may often be seen near the entrance of a hole, basking in the sun, but instantly disappearing on alarm. The least noise excites it; though it cannot see, it lifts its head to listen, in a menacing attitude, and if its retreat is cut off, it becomes animated with rage and ferocity, snorting and gnashing its teeth, and biting severely, yet uttering no cry, even when wounded. The superstitious peasants of the Ukraine believe that miraculous healing powers are communicated to the hand which has suffocated one of these creatures. The specimens which have been brought from Syria are smaller, and may possibly possess specific distinctness. Hasselquist testifies to their abundance on the plains of Sharon. He had never seen any ground so cast up by moles as in the region between Ramah and Jaffa. The molehills were scarcely a yard apart (*Trav.* p. 120).

" The other term, *chaphorperoth*, rendered 'moles' in Isa. ii, 20, is rather a descriptive periphrase than an appellative. It might be literally rendered 'the dig-holes.' The Sept. has adopted a different construction : '—— his idols . . . which he had made for the purpose of bowing down *to the vanities*, to the bats.' Perhaps the words may be taken generically, of any creatures which burrow in ruined and desolate places. Travellers describe the ruins of Babylon 'as perforated throughout with cavities which are inhabited by doleful creatures.' Buckingham speaks of the 'dens of wild beasts,' the 'quantities of porcupine quills' in the cavities, and the numbers of bats and owls (*Trav.* ii, 30). 'These souterrains,' observes Sir Robert Ker Porter, 'are now the refuge of jackals and other savage animals' (*Trav.* ii, 342). 'The mound,' says major Keppel, 'was full of large holes . . . strewed with the carcasses and skeletons of animals recently killed' (*Nar.* i, 180). The total and final degradation of idols, and their removal out of sight and remembrance, we may understand by the phrases employed."

Molé, FRANÇOIS RÉNÉ, a French comedian, demands our notice for his impious conduct during the great French Revolution. Molé, who was born at Paris in 1734, had made his début on the stage in 1754, and gained great notoriety as an actor after 1760. He had a kind heart and lovely disposition, and therefore became a favorite with all who knew him. But he was as blasphemous as he was kind-hearted; and, without a hope of a hereafter, he sought openly to bring reproach upon the cause of God. During the progress of the Revolution he became an associate of the Jacobins, and impiously officiated in the church of St. Roch as the priest of the goddess of Reason. He died in 1802.

Mo'lech (Heb. *Mo'lek*, מֹלֶךְ, *king*, always with the art. הַמֹּלֶךְ, except in 1 Kings xi, 7; Sept. ἄρχων in Lev. xviii, 21; xx, 2, 3, 4; Μελχών v. r. βασιλεύς in 1 Kings xi, 7; Μολὸχ ὁ βασιλεύς in Jer. xxxii, 35; and simply Μολόχ in 2 Kings xxiii, 10, as Aquila, Symmachus, and Theodotion everywhere render; Vulg. *Moioch*), called also MOLOCH (Amos v, 25; Acts vii, 43), MILCOM (1 Kings xi, 5, 33; 2 Kings xxiii, 13), MALCHAM (Zeph. i, 5), and MELCOM (marg. Jer. xlix, 1, 3, text "their king"), is chiefly found in the Old Testament as the national god of the Ammonites, to whom children were sacrificed by fire.

1. *The Name.*—The root of the word Molech is the same as that of מֶלֶךְ, *me'lek*, or "king," and hence he is identified with Malcham ("their king") in 2 Sam. xii, 30; Zeph. i, 5, the title by which he was known to the Israelites, as being invested with regal honors in his character as a tutelary deity, the lord and master of his people. Our translators have recognised this identity in their rendering of Amos v, 26 (where "your Moloch" is literally "your king," as it is given in the

margin), following the Greek in the speech of Stephen, in Acts vii, 43. Dr. Geiger, in accordance with his theory that the worship of Molech was far more widely spread among the Israelites than appears at first sight from the Old Testament, and that many traces are obscured in the text, refers "the king," in Isa. xxx, 33, to that deity : " For Tophet is ordained of old; yea, for *the king* it is prepared." Again, of the Israelitish nation, personified as an adulteress, it is said, " Thou wentest to *the king* with oil" (Isa. lvii, 9); Amaziah, the priest of Bethel, forbade Amos to prophesy there, "for it is *the king's* chapel" (Amos vii, 13); and in both these instances Dr. Geiger would find a disguised reference to the worship of Molech (*Urschrift*, etc., p. 299–308).

Traces of the root from which Molech is derived are to be found in the *Milichus, Malica*, and *Malcander* of the Phoenicians; with the last mentioned may be compared *Adrammelech*, the fire-god of Sepharvaim. The fire-god Molech, as the tutelary deity of the children of Ammon, was essentially identical with the Moabitish Chemosh. The Hebrew form, as an undoubted proper name, likewise occurs with some variety, as seen above. Solomon had in his harem many women of the Ammonitish race, who "turned away his heart after other gods," and, as a consequence of their influence, high places to Molech, "the abomination of the children of Ammon," were built on "the mount that is facing Jerusalem"—one of the summits of Olivet (1 Kings xi, 7). Two verses before, the same deity is called MILCOM, and from the circumstance of the two names being distinguished in 2 Kings xxiii, 10, 13, it has been inferred by Movers, Ewald, and others, that the two deities were essentially distinct. Movers (*Phönicier*, i, 358) is probably correct in regarding the latter as merely an Aramaic pronunciation. It is true that in the later history of the Israelites the worship of Molech is connected with the valley of Hinnom, while the high place of Milcom was on the Mount of Olives, and that no mention is made of human sacrifices to the latter. But it seems impossible to resist the conclusion that in 1 Kings xi, " Milcom the abomination of the Ammonites," in ver. 5, is the same as "Molech the abomination of the children of Ammon," in ver. 7. To avoid this Movers contends, not very convincingly, that the latter verse is by a different hand. Be this as it may, in the reformation carried out by Josiah, the high place of Milcom, on the right hand of the mount of corruption, and Tophet in the valley of the children of Hinnom were defiled, that "no man might make his son or his daughter to pass through the fire to Molech" (2 Kings xxiii, 10, 13). In the narrative of Chronicles these are included under the general term "Baalim," and the apostasy of Solomon is not once alluded to. Tophet soon appears to have been restored to its original uses, for we find it again alluded to, in the reign of Zedekiah, as the scene of child-slaughter and sacrifice to Molech (Jer. xxxii, 35). Kimchi, following the Targum, takes the word Milcom as an appellative, and not as a proper name, while with regard to *sikkuth* (סִכּוּת, A. V. "tabernacle") he holds the opposite opinion. His note is as follows : " *Sikkuth* is the name of an idol; and (as for) *malkekem* he speaks of a star which was made an idol by its name, and he calls it 'king,' because they thought it a king over them, or because it was a great star in the host of heaven, which was as a king over his host; and so 'to burn incense to the *queen* of heaven,' as I have explained in the book of Jeremiah." Gesenius compares with the "tabernacle" of Molech the sacred tent of the Carthaginians mentioned by Diodorus (xx, 65). Rosenmüller, and after him Ewald, understood by *sikkuth* a pole or stake on which the figure of the idol was placed. It was more probably a kind of palanquin in which the image was carried in processions, a custom which is alluded to in Isa. xlvi, 1; Epist. of Jer. 4 (Selden, *De Dis Syr.* synt. i, c. 6).

There remains to be noticed one passage (2 Sam. xii,

31) in which the Hebrew written text has מַלְבֵּן, *mal-kên*, while the marginal reading is מַלְבֵּן, *malbên*, which is adopted by our translators in their rendering "brick-kiln." Kimchi explains *malkên* as "the place of Molech," where sacrifices were offered to him, and the children of Ammon made their sons to pass through the fire. Milcom and Malken, he says, are one. On the other hand, Movers, rejecting the points, reads מַלְבֵּן, *malkân*, "our king," which he explains as the title by which he was known to the Ammonites.

2. *Biblical Account of this Deity.*—There is some difficulty in ascertaining at what period the Israelites became acquainted with this idolatry; yet four reasons render it probable that it was before the time of Solomon, the date usually assigned for its introduction. First, Molech appears—if not under that name, yet under the notion that we attach to it—to have been a principal god of the Phœnicians and Canaanites, whose other idolatries the Israelites confessedly adopted very early. Secondly, there are some arguments which tend to connect Molech with Baal, and, if they be tenable, the worship of Molech might be essentially as old as that of the latter. Thirdly, if we assume, as there is much apparent ground for doing, that, wherever human sacrifices are mentioned in the Old Testament, we are to understand them as being offered to Molech—the apparent exception of the gods of Sepharvaim being only a strong evidence of their identity with him—then the remarkable passage in Ezek. xx, 26 (comp. ver. 31) clearly shows that the Israelites sacrificed their first-born by fire when they were *in the wilderness.* Fourthly, the rebuke contained in Amos v, 26, as quoted in Acts vii, 43, appears to imply that some idol similar to this was secretly worshipped as early as the exodus. See CHIUN. Moreover, those who ascribe the Pentateuch to Moses will recognise both the early existence of the worship of this god and the apprehension of its contagion in that express prohibition of his bloody rites which is found in the Mosaic law. The offender who devoted his offspring to Molech was to be put to death by stoning; and in case the people of the land refused to inflict upon him this judgment, Jehovah would himself execute it, and cut him off from among his people (Lev. xviii, 21; xx, 2-5).

Nevertheless, it is for the first time directly stated that Solomon erected a high place for Molech on the Mount of Olives (1 Kings xi, 7); and from that period his worship continued uninterruptedly there, or in Tophet, in the valley of Hinnom, until Josiah defiled both places (2 Kings xxiii, 10, 13). Jehoahaz, however, the son and successor of Josiah, again "did what was evil in the sight of Jehovah, according to all that his fathers had done" (2 Kings xxiii, 32). The same broad condemnation is made against the succeeding kings, Jehoiakim, Jehoiachin, and Zedekiah; and Ezekiel, writing during the captivity, says, "Do ye, by offering your gifts, and by making your sons pass through the fire, pollute yourselves with all your idols *until this day,* and shall I be inquired of by you?" (xx, 31). After the restoration, all traces of this idolatry disappear.

Molech, "the king," was the lord and master of the Ammonites; their country was his possession (Jer. xlix, 1), as Moab was the heritage of Chemosh; the princes of the land were the princes of Malcham (Jer. xlix, 3; Amos i, 15). His priests were men of rank (Jer. xlix, 3), taking precedence of the princes. So the priest of Hercules at Tyre was second to the king (Justin, xviii, 4, § 5), and like Molech, the god himself, Baal Chamman, is *Melkart,* "the *king* of the city." The priests of Molech, like those of other idols, were called Chemarim (2 Kings xxiii, 5; Hos. x, 5; Zeph. i, 4).

Most of the Jewish interpreters, Jarchi (on Lev. xviii, 21), Kimchi, and Maimonides (*Mor. Neb.* iii, 38) among the number, say that in the worship of Molech the children were not burned, but made to pass between two burning pyres, as a purificatory rite. But the al-

lusions to the actual slaughter are too plain to be mistaken, and Aben Ezra, in his note on Lev. xviii, 21, says that "to cause to pass through" is the same as "to burn." "They sacrificed their sons and their daughters unto devils, and shed innocent blood, the blood of their sons and of their daughters, whom they sacrificed unto the idols of Canaan" (Psa. cvi, 37, 38). In Jer. vii, 31, the reference to the worship of Molech by human sacrifice is still more distinct: "They have built the high places of Tophet . . . *to burn* their sons and their daughters *in the fire,*" as "burnt-offerings unto Baal," the sun-god of Tyre, with whom, or in whose character, Molech was worshipped (Jer. xix, 5). Compare the statements in Deut. xii, 31; Ezek. xvi, 20, 21; xxiii, 37; the last two of which may also be adduced to show that the victims were slaughtered before they were burned. But the most remarkable passage is that in 2 Chron. xxviii, 3, in which the wickedness of Ahaz is described: "Moreover, he burned incense in the valley of the son of Hinnom, and burned (וַיַּבְעֵר) his children in the fire, after the abominations of the nations whom Jehovah had driven out before the children of Israel." Now, in the parallel narrative of 2 Kings xvi, 3, instead of וַיַּבְעֵר, "and he burned," the reading is הֶעֱבִיר, "he made to pass through," and Dr. Geiger suggests that the former may be the true reading, of which the latter is an easy modification, serving as a euphemistic expression to disguise the horrible nature of the sacrificial rites. But it is more natural to suppose that it is an exceptional instance, and that the true reading is וַיַּעֲבֵר, than to assume that the other passages have been intentionally altered. We may infer from the expression, "after the abominations of the nations whom Jehovah had driven out before the children of Israel," that the character of the Molech-worship of the time of Ahaz was essentially the same as that of the old Canaanites, although Movers maintains the contrary.

The sacrifice of children is said by Movers to have been not so much an expiatory as a purificatory rite, by which the victims were purged from the dross of the body and attained union with the deity. In support of this he quotes the myth of Baaltis or Isis, whom Malcander, king of Byblus, employed as nurse for his child. Isis suckled the infant with her finger, and each night burned whatever was mortal in its body. When Astarte, the mother, saw this she uttered a cry of terror, and the child was thus deprived of immortality (Plutarch, *Is. and Os.* ch. 16). But the sacrifice of Mesha, king of Moab, when, in despair at failing to cut his way through the overwhelming forces of Judah, Israel, and Edom, he offered up his eldest son a burnt-offering, probably to Chemosh, his national divinity, has more of the character of an expiatory rite to appease an angry deity than of a ceremonial purification. Besides, the passage from Plutarch bears evident traces of Egyptian, if not of Indian influence.

The worship of Molech is evidently alluded to, though not expressly mentioned, in connection with star-worship and the worship of Baal in 2 Kings xvii, 16, 17; xxi, 5, 6, which seems to show that Molech, the flame-god, and Baal, the sun-god, whatever their distinctive attributes, and whether or not the latter is a general appellation including the former, were worshipped with the same rites. Another argument might be drawn from Jer. iii, 24, in which *Hab-bosheth,* "the shame," is said to have devoured their flocks and herds, their sons and daughters. Now, as Bosheth is found, in the names Ishbosheth and Jerubbesheth, to alternate with Baal, as if it were only a contemptuous perversion of it, it would appear that human sacrifices are here again ascribed to Baal. Further, whereas Baal is the chief name under which we find the principal god of the Phœnicians in the Old Testament, and whereas only the two above-cited passages mention the human victims of Baal, it is remarkable that the Greek and Latin authors give abundant testimony to the human sacrifices which the Phœnicians and their colonies offered to their principal god, in whom the classical writers have almost always recognised their own $K\rho\acute{o}\nu o\varsigma$ and Saturn. Thus we are again brought to the difficulty [see BAAL] of reconciling Molech as Saturn with Baal as the sun and Jupiter. In reality, however, this difficulty is in part created by our association of classical with She-mitic mythology. When regarded apart from such for-eign affinities, Molech and Baal may appear as the per-sonifications of the two powers that give and destroy life, which early religions regarded as not incompatible phases of the same God of nature.

3. *Information from other Sources.*—Fire-gods appear to have been common to all the Canaanitish, Syrian, and other tribes, who worshipped the destructive element under an outward symbol, with the most inhuman rites. Among these were human sacrifices, purifications, and ordeals by fire, devoting of the first-born, mutilation, and vows of perpetual celibacy and virginity. To this class of divinities belonged the old Canaanitish Molech, as well as Chemosh, the fire-god of Moab, Urotal, Du-sares, Sair, and Thyandrites, of the Edomites and neigh-boring Arab tribes, and the Greek Dionysus, who were worshipped under the symbol of a rising flame of fire, which was imitated in the stone pillars erected in their honor (Movers, *Phön.* i, c. 9). Tradition refers the or-igin of the fire-worship to Chaldæa. Abraham and his ancestors are said to have been fire-worshippers, and the Assyrian and Chaldæan armies took with them the sa-cred fire accompanied by the magi.

As the accounts of this idol and his worship found in the Old Testament are very scanty, the more detailed notices which Greek and Latin writers give of the bloody rites of the Phœnician colonies acquire peculiar value. Münter has collected these testimonies with great completeness in his *Religion der Karthager.* Many of these notices, however, only describe late develop-ments of the primitive rites. Thus the description of the image of Molech as a brazen statue, which was heated red hot, and in the outstretched arms of which the child was laid, so that it fell down into the flaming furnace beneath—an account which is first found in Di-odorus Siculus, as referring to the Carthaginian $K\rho\acute{o}\nu o\varsigma$, but which was subsequently adopted by Jarchi and others—is not admitted by Movers to apply to the Mo-lech of the Old Testament.

According to Jewish tradition, from what source we know not, the image of Molech was of brass, hollow within, and was situated without Jerusalem. Kimchi (on 2 Kings xxiii, 10) describes it as "set within seven chapels, and whoso offered fine flour, they open to him one of them; (whoso offered) turtle-doves or young pig-eons, they open to him two; a lamb, they open to him three; a ram, they open to him four; a calf, they open to him five; an ox, they open to him six; and to who-ever offered his son, they open to him seven. And his face was (that) of a calf, and his hands stretched forth like a man who opens his hands to receive (something) of his neighbor. And they kindled it with fire, and the priests took the babe and put it into the hands of Molech, and the babe gave up the ghost. And why was it called Tophet and Hinnom? Because they used to make a noise with drums (*tophim*), that the father might not hear the cry of his child and have pity upon him, and return to him. Hinnom, because the babe wailed (מנהם, *menahem*), and the noise of his wailing went up." Another opinion (is that it was called) Hin-nom, because the priests used to say—"May it profit (יהנה) thee! may it be sweet to thee! may it be of sweet savor to thee!" All this detail is probably as fic-titious as the etymologies are unsound, but we have nothing to supply its place. Selden conjectures that the idea of the seven chapels may have been borrowed from the worship of Mithra, who had seven gates corre-sponding to the seven planets, and to whom men and women were sacrificed (*De Dis Syr.* synt. i, c. 6). Ben-

jamin of Tudela describes the remains of an ancient Ammonitish temple which he saw at Gebal, containing a stone image richly gilt seated on a throne. On either side sat two female figures, and before it was an altar on which the Ammonites anciently burned incense and offered sacrifice (*Early Travels in Palestine*, p. 79, Bohn). By these chapels Lightfoot explains the allusion in Amos v, 26; Acts vii, 43, to "the tabernacle of Molech;" "these seven chapels (if there be truth in the thing) help us to understand what is meant by Molech's taber-nacle, and seem to give some reason why in the prophet he is called *Sikkuth*, or the *Covert God*, because he was retired within so many *Cancelli* (for that word Kimchi useth) before one could come at him" (*Comm. on Acts* vii, 43). It was more probably a shrine or ark in which the figure of the god was carried in processions, or which contained, as Movers conjectures, the bones of children who had been sacrificed, and were used for magical pur-poses. The crown of Malcham, taken by David at Rabbah, is said to have had in it a precious stone (a magnet, according to Kimchi), which is described by Cyril on Amos as transparent and like the day-star, whence Molech has groundlessly been identified with the planet Venus (Vossius, *De Orig. Idol.* ii, c. 5, p. 331). A legend is told in Jerome's *Quæstiones Hebraicæ* (1 Chron. xx, 2) that, as it was unlawful for a Hebrew to touch anything of gold or silver belonging to an idol, Ittai the Gittite, who was a Philistine, snatched the crown from the head of Milcom, and gave it to David, who thus avoided the pollution.

Many instances of human sacrifices are found in an-cient writers, which may be compared with the de-scriptions in the Old Testament of the manner in which Molech was worshipped. The Carthaginians, accord-ing to Augustine (*De Civit. Dei*, vii, 19), offered children to Saturn, and by the Gauls even grown-up persons were sacrificed, under the idea that of all seeds the best is the human kind. Eusebius (*Præp. Ev.* iv, 16) col-lected from Porphyry numerous examples to the same effect, from which the following are selected. Among the Rhodians, a man was offered to Kronos on the 6th of July; afterwards a criminal condemned to death was substituted. The same custom prevailed in Salamis, but was abrogated by Diiphilus, king of Cyprus, who substituted an ox. According to Manetho, Amosis abol-ished the same practice in Egypt at Heliopolis sacred to Juno. Sanchoniatho relates that the Phœnicians, on the occasion of any great calamity, sacrificed to Saturn one of their relatives. Istrus says the same of the Cu-retes, but the custom was abolished, according to Pal-las, in the reign of Hadrian. At Laodicea a virgin was sacrificed yearly to Athene, and the Dumatii, a people of Arabia, buried a boy alive beneath the altar each year. Diodorus Siculus (xx, 14) relates that the Car-thaginians, when besieged by Agathocles, tyrant of Sic-ily, offered in public sacrifice to Saturn 200 of their no-blest children, while others voluntarily devoted them-selves to the number of 300. His description of the statue of the god differs but slightly from that of Mo-lech, which has been quoted. The image was of brass, with its hands outstretched towards the ground in such a manner that the child, when placed upon them, fell into a pit full of fire.

4. *Literature.*—E. F. Rivinus, *De τεκνοθυσία Judæo-rum* (Lips. 1735); M. F. Cramer, *De Molocho* (Viteb. 1720); N. W. Schroeder, *De tabernac. Molochi et stella dei Remphan* (Marb. 1745); P. Viret, *Des sacrifices d'en-fans faits à Moloch* (in his *Vraye et fausse religion*, 1682, p. 599); H. Witsius, *De cultu Molochi* (in his *Mis-cell. sacr.* i, 485); J. Braun, *Selecta Sacra*, p. 449 sq.; Deyling, *Observ. sacr.* ii, 444 sq.; Dietzsch and Ziegra, in Ugolini *Thesaur.* vol. xxiii; Movers, *Phönic.* p. 65 et al.; Creuzer, *Symbol.* ii, 431 sq.; Buttmann, *Mythol.* ii, 28 sq.; Buddei *Histor. eccl. V. T.* i, 609; Hug, in the *Freib. Zeitschr.* vii, 82 sq.; Gesenius, *Thes. Heb.* p. 794; J. G. Kotch, *Molocholatria Judæorum* (Lips. 1689); C. T. Zieger, *De immolatione liberorum* (Viteb. 1684);

Schwab, *De Moloch et Remphan* (Viteb. 1667; also in the *Thes. Theol. Philol.* ii, 444 sq.). See SATURN.

Molesworth, *Sir* WILLIAM, an English statesman and celebrated writer on philosophy and political economy, was born in Surrey in 1810. He was at an early age ready for college and sent to Cambridge University, where, however, he failed to complete his course of study, because of a quarrel in which he engaged with one of his tutors, whom he even challenged to a duel. He finally continued his studies at the University of Edinburgh, and subsequently went abroad, and studied for some time in the high-schools of Germany. In 1831 he became prominent in the political affairs of his native country, and soon rose to distinction in English parliamentary society. He also largely identified himself with literary labors, and in 1834 founded the *London Review*, shortly after merged into the *Westminster Review*, of which he was for many years an editorial associate with the late John Stuart Mill (q. v.). Sir William was also the intimate friend of James Mill and of Bentham, and was generally regarded as the parliamentary representative of the "philosophical Radicals." He is, however, of particular interest to us as the student of Hobbes, whom Sir William greatly admired. He accumulated materials for a life of the "Philosopher of Malmesbury," which remain in MS. uncompleted. He was more successful in the publication of an edition of Hobbes's works—which he commenced in 1839, and carried to completion at a cost of many thousand pounds—consisting of a reprint of the entire miscellaneous and voluminous writings of Hobbes (Lond. 1842-45, 11 vols. 8vo), and constituting a valuable contribution to the republic of letters. By Sir William's munificence the works of Hobbes were placed in most of the university and provincial public libraries. The publication, however, did him great disservice in public life, his opponents endeavoring to identify him with the freethinking opinions of Hobbes in religion, as well as with the great philosopher's conclusions in favor of despotic government; yet he continued a parliamentary career of the greatest energy and usefulness. Indeed, even for his political connections he deserves our notice. He was the first to call attention to the evils connected with the transportation of criminals, and as chairman of a parliamentary committee brought to light all the horrors of the convict system, and by untiring labors remedied this abuse, as well as the disorders generally in colonial administration. In 1855 he became secretary of state for the colonies, and no doubt would have greatly distinguished himself by his wholesome measures, but he died soon after, Oct. 22, 1855. The London *Times* called him the "liberator and regenerator of the colonial empire of Great Britain." See *English Cyclop.* s. v.; *Fraser's Magazine*, xvii, 338; *Lond. Gentleman's Magazine*, 1845, pt. ii, p. 645; *Blackwood's Magazine*, xxxviii, 506; xliii, 519; xliv, 625. See also HOBBES. (J. H. W.)

Mo'li (Μοολί, Vulg. *Moholi*), given (1 Esdr. viii, 47) instead of MAHLI (q. v.), the son of Levi (Ezra viii, 18).

Mo'lid (Heb. *Molid'*, מוֹלִיד, *begetter*; Sept. Μωλήδ v. r. Μωλάδ, Μωλίδ, and Μωήλ), the last named of the two sons of Abishur, of the tribe of Judah, by Abihail (1 Chron. ii, 29). B.C. long after 1612.

Molières, JOSEPH PRIVAT DE, a French philosophical writer of some note, was born at Tarascon in 1677. He became a member of the Congregation of the Oratory; but, having embraced the philosophical doctrines of Malebranche, he quitted the society after the death of Malebranche to devote himself wholly to physics and mathematics. He was made professor of philosophy at the royal college, and became a zealous advocate of the Cartesian views. He died May 12, 1742. His works range within the departments of mathematics, physical science, and philosophy. In the last-named field he published *Philosophical Lectures* (Paris, 1732, 4 vols.

8vo). See Saveriens, *Hist. des Philosophes Modernes*, vi, 217 sq.; *Revue Chrétienne*, 1869, p. 725.

Molin, LAURENT, a Swedish theologian, who flourished towards the close of the 17th century as a professor at Upsala, was born in 1657, and died Sept. 19, 1724. He published *De Clavibus Veterum* (Upsala, 1684, 4to):—*De Origine Lucorum* (ibid. 1689):—a translation of the Bible in the Swedish language (Stockholm, 1720, 12mo).

Molina, Antonio de, a Spanish theologian, was born at Villa-Nueva-de-los-Infantes, Castile, about the middle of the 16th century. He became a member of the Order of the Augustines, among whom he taught theology, and was promoted to the position of superior. The desire to lead a still more retired life led him to forsake his official connection, and take refuge in a small convent at Miraflores, where he died, Sept. 21, 1612. He wrote many works which have a considerable reputation; among others, *Instruccion de sacerdotes* (Barcelona and Madrid). This book had already passed through seven editions when it was translated into Latin by P. Nicolas Jassenboy (Anvers, 1618, 8vo). There existed also a French (1639), an English (1652), and an Italian version:—*Exercicios espirituales de las excelencias provecho* (Burgos, 1615, 4to; Madrid, 1653); also translated into Italian.

Molina, Luis, a distinguished Spanish theologian, was born at Cuença, in New Castile, in 1535. In 1553 he entered the Order of the Society of Jesus, studied at Coimbra, and afterwards served for twenty years as professor of theology in the University of Evora, in Portugal. He died at Madrid, Oct. 12, 1601. In his writings, which treat especially of grace and free-will, he propounded a system of doctrine which has since been called *Molinism*, after him. It was while writing a commentary on Thomas Aquinas (published at Cuença, 1593, 2 vols. fol.) that he was led to attempt the old *Pelagian Controversy* by a conciliation of free-will in man with the divine foreknowledge, and with predestination, and he finally advocated his system in his *De liberi arbitrii concordia cum gratiæ donis, Divina Præscientia, Providentia, Prædestinatione, et Reprobatione* (Lisbon, 1588, 4to). This book, dedicated to the grand Inquisition of Portugal, at once gave rise to a violent controversy. Molina rejects the sufficiency of grace, asserting that grace is sometimes sufficient, sometimes insufficient, according as the will is co-operating with or resisting it. According to his theory, the efficacy of grace is the result of the consent of the human will; not that this consent gives it any strength, but because this consent is requisite in order that grace should be efficient. He therefore says that man requires grace in order to do good, but that God never fails to grant this grace to those who ask it with fervor; he also asserts that man has it in his power to answer or not to the calling of grace. These opinions, which had found many followers, were first attacked by the Spanish Dominicans as being of a Pelagianizing tendency, while they themselves were firmly attached to the doctrine of Thomas Aquinas, and came hence to be named *Thomists* (q. v.). The innovation was afterwards attacked also by the Calvinists as opposing the theology of Augustine, and also by the Jansenists. Indeed, so much opposition had been encountered by the *Molinists*, as the propagators of this peculiar doctrine were called, that it was thought wise in 1594 to bring the matter to the consideration of pope Clement VIII, who enjoined silence on both parties, and promised to commit the decision of the dispute to a congregation of theologians. Upon this the Dominicans used their influence with Philip II to induce the pope to reopen the question at once; and, the king's persuasion prevailing, the pope in 1597 organized for that special purpose a congregation called *De Auxiliis*, consisting of a president, cardinal Malnici, the bishop of Trent, of three other bishops, and seven theologians of different fraternities. It was made their task to inquire into the nature of the assistance derived from grace, and its mode of operation. On Jan. 16, 1598, the opinions of Molina were thus summarized: (1) A reason or ground of God's predestination is to be found in man's right use of his free-will. (2) In order that the grace which God bestows to enable men to persevere in religion may become the gift of perseverance, it is necessary that they may be foreseen as consenting and co-operating with the divine assistance offered them, which is a thing within their power. (3) There is a mediate prescience which is neither the free nor the natural knowledge of God, and by which he knows future contingent events before he forms his decree.* (4) Predestination may be considered as either general (relating to whole classes of persons), or particular (relating to individual persons). In general predestination there is no reason or ground for it beyond the good pleasure of God, or none on the part of persons predestinated; but in particular predestination (or that of individuals) there is a cause or ground in the foreseen good use of free-will. In 1601, finally, the decision of the congregation was rendered. It pronounced in favor of the Thomistic opinions. But notwithstanding this decision, the Jesuits, who were almost en masse with the *Molinists*, succeeded in prevailing on Clement VIII to reopen the case; and a new congregation was appointed, consisting of fifteen cardinals, five bishops, and nine doctors, over whom the pope himself presided on seventy-eight different occasions between March 20, 1602, and Jan. 22, 1605; but when about to pronounce sentence he died, and the congregation's sittings had to be continued under his successor, Paul V, from September, 1605, until March, 1606. Yet even after the expiration of such a long period of deliberation, covering over two hundred sittings, a settlement of the question seemed less likely than ever; and pope Paul, not wishing to condemn or to approve either party, public policy requiring that the pope should not make an enemy of France by deciding against the Jesuits, nor of Spain by deciding against the Dominicans, quietly concluded to discontinue the sittings, simply announcing that he reserved to himself the right of giving his verdict when he should see fit. Only, in dismissing the contending parties, in 1607, he forbade their publishing anything more on the subject. This command, however, was but little regarded, and the *Scientia media* of Molina came to be substantially adopted by Jesuit theologians, while all his adversaries, the upholders of "efficacious grace," have protested against this system as semi-Pelagianism. Jansenius, for instance, accuses Molina of disregarding St. Augustine, and of misrepresenting his opinions, etc. Bossuet says, in answer to this reproach of semi-Pelagianism (see his answer to Jurieu, *Avertissement aux Protestants*), "As for M. Jurieu's objection of our Molinists being semi-Pelagians, if he had only opened their books he would have seen that they recognised in all the elect a gratuitous preference on the part of divine grace—a grace ever predisposing, ever necessary for all pious deeds. This we never find among the semi-Pelagians. Going further, or making grace to be preceded by some purely human acts with which it is then connected, I do not hesitate to assert that no Roman Catholic will contradict me when I say that this would be a fearful mistake, which would take away the very foundation of humility, and that the Church would never tolerate it, after having so often decided, and lately in the Council of Trent, that everything good, even to the first disposition of the sinner to be converted, comes from an impelling and predisposing grace, which is preceded by

* In Molina's theology the "natural" knowledge of God is that of what he effects by his direct power or by second causes. His "free" knowledge is that of what he purposes of his own free-will. His mediate "knowledge" ("scientia media") is that of what will depend on the free-will of his creatures, whose actions he foresees by a knowledge of all the forces by which those actions will be brought about and controlled.

no merit." Molina wrote also *De Justitia et Jure* (Cuença, 1592, 6 vols. fol.; Mayence, 1659). See Antonio, *Nova Bibliotheca Hispano;* Alegambe, *De Script. Soc. Jesu*, p. 314 sq.; *Abrégé de l'Hist. de la Congrégation de Auxiliis;* Bossuet, *Avertissement aux Protestants; Encycl. des Gens du Monde;* Fleury, *Eccl. Hist.* clxxxiii, 4; Le Clerc, *Bibl. Univ. et Hist.* vol. xiv; Aug. le Blanc, *Hist. Congreg. de Auxil. Gratiæ Divin.* (Domin.); Meyer, *Hist. Controv. de Divin. Gratia Auxil.* (Jesuit); Kuhn, *Kathol. Dogmatik*, i, 291 sq.; Ranke, *Hist. of the Papacy*, i, 587 sq.; ii, 90 sq.; Nicolini, *Hist. of the Jesuits*, p. 231, 232; Walch, *Religiöse Streitigkeiten ausser d. luther. Kirche*, i, 269 sq.; Schröckh, *Kirchengeschichte s. d. Ref.* iv, 295 sq.; Hagenbach, *Hist. Doctrines*, ii, 202, 278, 280, 288; Bickersteth, *Christian Student*, sec. iv, p. 233; Wetzer u. Welte (Roman Catholic), *Kirchen-Lexikon*, vii, 199 sq.

Molinæus. See MOULIN, DE.

Molinari, Antonio, a Venetian painter, who flourished in the early part of the 18th century, was a pupil of Antonio Zanchi, whose maxims he afterwards renounced, creating a style of his own. Molinari painted some excellent works for several of the Venetian churches, but his pictures were very unequal in merit. Lanzi says that in his best works, "as the *History of Hosea*, in the Corpus Domini at Venice, he displays a style no less solid than pleasing, which equally satisfies the judgment and the eye. There is a study of both design and expression, ample beauty of forms, richness of drapery, with a taste and harmony of coloring not surpassed by any artist of the time." See Lanzi, *Hist. of Painting*, transl. by Roscoe, ii, 295; Spooner, *Biog. Hist. of the Fine Arts*, ii, 575.

Molinari, Giovanni, an eminent painter of the school of Piedmont, was born at Savigliano in 1721. He was a pupil of Cavaliere Beaumont, and executed a number of works of art for the various churches at Turin and adjacent cities. A picture in the church of S. Bernardo di Vercelli, representing a number of saints, is, according to Lanzi, "well disposed, with good action, and conducted with great care." In Turin there is an *Addolorata* by him at the Regio Albergo della Virtu; in other places in the state are numerous religious works, among which a *St. John the Baptist*, in the abbey of S. Benigno, is worthy of mention. His character was naturally timid, reserved, and modest; and Lanzi says he did not paint history as much as he should. Lanzi does not give the date of his decease, but Spooner places his death in 1793. See Lanzi, *Hist. of Painting*, transl. by Roscoe, iii, 315; Spooner, *Biog. Hist. of the Fine Arts*, ii, 575.

Molinet, CLAUDE DU, a French ecclesiastical antiquary, was born at Chalons-sur-Marne in 1620, and during the greater part of his life occupied the position of canon regular and procurator general of the Congregation of St. Genevieve, Paris. He was the author of several works, based mainly upon his researches in ecclesiastical antiquities, the most prominent of which are an edition of *The Epistles of Stephen, Bishop of Tournay*, with notes, and *The History of the principal Popes, as taken from Medals.* The latter work extends from Martin V to Innocent XI, and includes a description of medals from 1417 to 1678. In addition to his labors in numismatics, he collected a great many rare curiosities and relics, and some very remarkable Greek and Oriental MSS. The library of St. Genevieve owes much to him for its present renown on account of its great collection and careful preservation of antiquities, which have not only proved of public interest, but of great historical value. He died Sept. 2, 1687. (H. W. T.)

Molinier, Étienne, a French Roman Catholic, born at Toulouse about the latter part of the 16th century, began life with the study of law, and became counsellor to the parliament of his native city; but subsequently took orders, and became doctor of theology and of civil and canon law. He preached with great success in the principal churches of Provence and Paris, and even preached before Louis XIII, when that monarch was crowned in 1610. He died in 1650. Molinier wrote *Sermons pour les dimanches de l'année* (Toulouse, 1631, 2 vols. 8vo) :— *Id. sur le mystère de la Croix* (1635, 8vo) :—*Id. pour l'Octave de Saint Sacrement* (Toulouse, 1640, 8vo) :—*Id. sur le symbole de la Croix* (Rouen, 1650, 8vo). These sermons evince much depth of thought as well as vast erudition. See *Biographie Toulousaine ; Dictionnaire portatif des Prédicateurs.*

Molinier, Jean-Baptiste, a French divine, was born at Arles in 1675, began his studies in his own country, and continued them at Pézenas, under the fathers of the Oratory; he then entered the army, but finally quitted the sword to take holy orders. He taught theology at Arles, and entered the Congregation of the Oratory in 1700. He was subsequently sent to the seminary of Saint-Magloire of Paris, and to Macon and Grenoble. He evinced remarkable talent for preaching, and was very successful at Toulouse, Lyons, Orleans, and at Paris. Massillon, hearing him, was impressed by his eloquence, but at the same time surprised at the inequality of his talent, which sometimes rose to the sublime, and again sank heavily to the obscure and commonplace. Biographers say that when Molinier devoted much labor to his discourses, he equalled the most celebrated French orators; but he relied too much upon his talent, and did not sufficiently moderate the impetuosity of his imagination. His discourses are the production of a happy genius, which expresses itself with much fire, energy, force, dignity, and ease. He only lacked taste; his style is incorrect, unequal, and marred by common phrases, which form a strange contrast to many parts full of life and grandeur. Molinier left the Oratory in 1720, and retired to the diocese of Sens, whence he returned to Paris to resume his preaching, but was prohibited from doing so by M. de Vintimille. No longer permitted to preach, Molinier wrote. He left the following works: *Traduction nouvelle* of the *Imitation de Jésus-Christ* (Paris, 1725, 12mo) :— *Sermons Choisis* (1732–34, 3 vols. 12mo); the sermon *Du Ciel* is considered his principal production :— *Panégyriques* (1732–34, 3 vols. 12mo) :—*Discours sur la vérite de la religion Chrétienne* (1732–34, 2 vols. 12mo) :—*Instructions et Prières propres à soutenir les âmes dans les voies de la pénitence,* etc. (12mo) ; a sequel to the *Directeur des âmes pénitentes* of Vauge :—*Exercice du pénitent,* with an *Office de la pénitence* (18mo) :—*Les Psaumes,* translated into French, with some *Notes littérales et morales* (12mo) :—*Paraphrase du psaume Miserere :—Sur l'Arianisme* (1718, 4to); very rare. He retired from public life but a short time before his death, which occurred in Paris, March 15, 1745. See Bougerel, *Histoire des Hommes illustres de Provence ;* Chaudont and Delandine, *Dict. hist.* s. v.

Molinism, the name given to the system of grace and election taught by Louis Molina (q. v.). The kind of prescience denominated in the Romish schools *Scientia media* is that foreknowledge of future contingencies which arises from an acquaintance with the nature and faculties of rational beings, of the circumstances in which they shall be placed, of the objects that shall be presented to them, and of the influence which their circumstances and objects must have on their actions. This system has been commonly taught in the Jesuit schools; but a modification of it was introduced by the celebrated Spanish divine, Suarez (q. v.), in order to save the doctrine of *special election.* Suarez held that although God gives to all men grace absolutely sufficient for their salvation, yet he gives to the elect a grace which is not alone in itself sufficient, but which is so attempered to their disposition, their opportunities, and other circumstances, that they infallibly, although yet quite freely, yield to its influence. This modification of Molina's system is called CONGRUISM. Molinism must not

be confounded either with Pelagianism or semi-Pelagianism, inasmuch as Molinism distinctly supposes the inability of man to do any supernatural act without grace (q. v.). See THOMISTS ; WILL, FREE.

Molinos, MIGUEL DE, a Spanish theologian, founder of the Quietists, was born of noble parentage near Saragossa, December 21, 1627. He studied at Pampeluna, and, after finishing his studies at the University of Coimbra, took holy orders, and in 1669 went to Rome, where his pious conduct and the purity of his life caused many to choose him for their spiritual director. He acquired great reputation, but steadily refused all ecclesiastical preferment. In 1675 he published his *Way* or *Guide* to what the Mystics call *a spiritual* or *contemplative life.* This book, written in Spanish, was supported by the recommendations of some of the greatest and most respectable men. In 1681 it was published at Rome in Italian, though it had appeared in that language some time before in other places. Afterwards it was translated into the Dutch, French, and Latin languages; and was very often printed in Holland, France, and Italy. The Latin translation, under the title of *Manuductio spiritualis,* was published by A. H. Franke (Halle, 1687, 12mo). In Italian it bore the title of *Guida Spirituale.* But though the work added greatly to Molinos's celebrity, it also became the subject of bitter opposition. It was soon attacked. There were not wanting many who in the specious but visionary principles of this work discovered the seeds of a dangerous and seductive error. Among these the celebrated preacher Segneri was the first who ventured publicly to call its orthodoxy into question; but his strictures were by Molinos's friends ascribed to jealousy of the influence which Molinos had acquired with the people. By degrees, however, reports unfavorable to the practical results of this teaching, and even to the personal conduct and character of its author, or of his followers, began to find circulation; and eventually the Jesuits took decided ground against him, and he was accused of heresy. The substance of his system, which his friends interpret in one way and his opponents in another, amounted to this: Christian perfection consists in the peace of the soul, in renouncement of all external and temporal things, in the pure love of God, free from all considerations of interest or hope of reward. Thus a soul which desires the supreme good must renounce not only all sensual pleasures, but also all material and sensual things; silence every impulse of its mind and will, and concentrate and absorb itself in God. Molinos's enemies accused him and some of his disciples of reviving the abuses of the Gnostics, and of teaching, both by their precepts and their example, the most objectionable principles of *Quietism.* According to the propositions which were condemned by the Inquisition, he pushed to such an extreme the contemplative repose which is the common characteristic of Quietism as to teach the utter indifference of the soul, in a state of perfect contemplation, to all external things, and its entire independence of the outer world, even of the actions of the very body which it animates; insomuch that this internal perfection is compatible with the worst external excesses, since these are of no importance so long as the soul remains in communion with God. See QUIETISM. It is very probable that the opposition to him, especially that of the Jesuits and others who watched over the interests of the Romish cause, was provoked because they perceived that Molinos's system tacitly accused the Romish Church of a departure from true religion. Molinos, though he had a vast number of friends, and though the pontiff himself, Innocent XI, was partial to him, was in 1685 cited before the Inquisition, and submitted to close imprisonment and examination. In addition to the opinions contained in his book, a prodigious mass of papers and letters, to the number, it is said, of 20,000, found in his house, were produced against him, and he was himself rigorously examined as to his opinions. The trial lasted two years; and in 1687 sixty-eight propositions contained in his book were solemnly condemned. By a decree of Aug. 28, 1687, he was declared to have taught false and dangerous dogmas, contrary to the doctrine of the Church and to Christian piety. On Sept. 3 following he was brought out in a yellow scapular, with a red cross before and behind, made to kneel on a scaffold in front of the church of the Dominicans, and there compelled to recant all he had taught in his books; after which he was compelled to pass the remainder of his life in prison. A bull of Innocent XII, of Nov. 19, confirmed the action of the Inquisition, and condemned, *in globo*, the sixty-eight propositions. A refutation of Molinos's doctrine is to be found in Fénelon's works (Versailles, 1820), and in Bossuet, *États d'Oraison*. See Moréri, *Dict. histor.; Pluquet, Diction. des hérésies; Recueil de diverses pièces concernant le Quietisme et les Quietistes, ou Molinos, ses sentimens et ses disciples* (Amsterd. 1688, 8vo); *Lettres écrits de Rome touchant le Quietisme; ou Molinos, ses sentiments*, etc. (Amsterd. 1688); Herzog, *Real-Encyklopädie*, ix, 698; Mosheim, *Eccles. Hist.* iii, 339 sq.; Bergier, *Dict. de Theologie*, iv, 420; Wetzer u. Welte, *Kirchen-Lexikon*, vii, 213 sq.; Scharling, in Niedner's *Zeitschrift*, 1854, p. 325 sq., 489 sq.; 1855, p. 3 sq.; Baumgarten-Crusius, *Compend. d. Dogmen Gesch.* i, 407 sq.; Hodgson, *Reformers and Martyrs;* Heinroth, *Gesch. u. Kritik d. Mysticismus*, pt. iii, ch. iii; Walch, *Religiöse Streitigkeiten ausser der luther. Kirche*, i, 293 sq.; ii, 982 sq.; Schröckh, *Kirchengeschichte s. d. Ref.* vii, 453 sq. See MYSTICISM.

Molkenbuhr, MARCELLIN, a German Roman Catholic theologian, was born at Münster, Sept. 1, 1741, and was educated in the convents of the Rhenish country. In 1758 he entered the Order of St. Francis at Hanau, but was ordained to holy orders Oct. 27, 1764, and for nine years taught philosophy and mathematics, and for twelve years divinity and moral theology at Paderborn. He then retired to the convent of St. Francis at Münster; but in 1811, when it was abolished, he lived for a while privately. In 1815 he re-entered monastic life in the convent of St. Francis at Paderborn, and died there in 1831. Some of his most important works are: *Das Zeitalter der Vernunft herausgegeben von Thomas Paine, widerlegt*, etc. (Paderborn, 1797, 2d edition; Münster, 1802):—*Neue Auslegungsart des alten Testaments von Wecklein, Prof. zu Münster, widerlegt* (Dorsten, 1806):—*Neue der Gottheit Jesu nachtheilige Auslegung des I Capitel des Evangel. Joh. von Muth, Prof. in Erfurt, widerlegt* (ibid. 1807):—*Wo ist die älteste und vornehmrste bischöfliche Kirche in der ganzen Christenheit? Bei den Griechen oder bei den Lateinern?* (Paderborn, 1815):—*Ueber die Ankunft des hl. Apostel Petrus nach Rom und Antiochia, und einige vorgebliche alte Streitigkeiten mehrerer Bischöfe wider die Päpste* (ibid. 1816):—*Anmerkungen über die neuen deutschen Uebersetzungen des N. T. durch Carl und Leander van Esz, auch besonders über den bestraften Cephas* (ibid. 1817):—*Historia religionis Christianæ in compendio et ordine chronico exhibita*, tom. i, ab anno 1–326 (ibid. 1818). See Waitzenegger, *Gelehrten- und Schriftsteller Lexikon der deutschen katholischen Geistlichkeit*, ii, 18 sq.

Mollah (Arab. *maula*, Turk. *meula*, i. e. ruler) is the name of a Turkish superior judge, who is an expounder of civil and criminal law, and of the religion of the state; he is therefore necessarily both a lawyer and an ecclesiastic. Under him is the cadi or judge, who administers the law, and superior to him are the kadhiasker and the mufti (q. v.). They all are, however, subject to the Sheik al-Islam, or supreme mufti. In Persia, the office of mollah is similar to what it is in Turkey; but his superior there is the "sadr," or chief of the mollahs. In the states of Turkestan, the mollahs have the whole government in their hands. See MULLAH.

Möller, Heinrich, popularly known as *Henry von Zütphen*, one of the early Protestant martyrs, was born in 1488, in the county of Zütphen, in the Netherlands. In 1504 he joined the Augustinians, and in 1515 went to the then newly-established University of Wittenberg. Here he became intimate with Luther. In 1516, on his return home, he was, notwithstanding his youth, made prior of the Augustinian convent of Dort, but was finally obliged to leave it in 1520 on account of his reformatory opinions, went to Antwerp, and there became sub-prior of the Augustinian convent. This place also he was obliged to leave in December, 1520, his favorable opinion of the Reformers having made him many enemies in the body, and in March, 1521, we find him back at Wittenberg, occupied in studies. But when, in consequence of the Edict of Worms, the evangelical party began to be persecuted in the Netherlands, he returned, in 1522, to Dort and to Antwerp, and there by his example encouraged the Augustinians to spread the principles of the Reformation. The Inquisition quickly recognised in him a leading spirit, and he was marked as one whose head should fall. On Sept. 29 he was arrested, but the people rallied and released him. Satisfied that safety could be found only in flight, he then bade adieu to his Christian friends, and went successively to Amsterdam and Zütphen, with the expectation of making his way back to Wittenberg. But he was stopped in Bremen, and entreated by the people to stay there and preach the new doctrines. Consenting, after much urgent solicitation, he was made pastor, and by his preaching soon gained the greater portion of the people to the cause of the Reformation. In November, 1524, when his friends felt satisfied that the cause had been so efficiently served as to make a falling away to Romanism well-nigh impossible, he left for Meldorf, in Denmark, where he was desired to introduce the Reformation. He encountered great opposition, and, though the authorities of the place were in his favor, he was seized on the 10th of December by the Roman Catholic clergy and their dupes, and burned the next day as a heretic. The news as it reached the different German Reformers caused great sorrow. The loss sustained seemed irreparable. Melancthon wrote a hymn of praise over him, Luther a letter of sympathy to the Christians of Bremen, and an account of his martyrdom. In the cemetery of Meldorf, where Möller's remains had been deposited after a severe struggle with the drunken rowdies who, fired by religious fanaticism, had caused his death, a monument was erected to his memory, June 25, 1830. See Luther, *Vom Bruder Heinrich*, etc., in *Werke*, vol. xxvi (Erlangen edition); Heckel, *Die Märtyrer in d. evangel. Kirche*, edited by Wichern (Hamb. 1845 and 1849); Rudelbach, *Christliche Biographie* (Leips. 1849); Fliedner, *Buch. d. Märtyrer*, vol. ii; Schlegel, *Kirchen u. Reformationsgesch. v. Norddeutschland*, vol. ii; Ranke, *Deutsche Gesch. im Zeitalter d. Reform.* vols. i and ii; *Hist. of the Reformation* (Austin's transl. Phila. 1844, 8vo), bk. i; Motley, *John of Barneveld* (N. Y. 1874), i, 283 sq.; *Zeitschr. f. hist. theol.* 1868, p. 485; Pierer, *Universal-Lexikon*, xi, 367; Herzog, *Real-Encyklopädie*, ix, 704. (J. H. W.)

Möller, Henry, a Lutheran minister, noted for his valuable labors in the Lutheran interests in the United States, was born in Hamburg, Germany, in 1749. When only a youth of fourteen he migrated to this country, and went to Philadelphia. There he was one day, shortly after his arrival, met in the street by the celebrated Dr. Muhlenberg, who had known his people, and who recognised in the young man so striking a family resemblance as to induce him to stop and inquire his name. Identified by the doctor, Henry was at once given a place in his own house, and everything was done to promote his welfare. The doctor also gave him an appointment as assistant in a school in which he himself was then teaching, while Möller's leisure hours were devoted to the study of theology, under the direction of his patron. Möller was licensed to preach the Gospel by the Synod of Pennsylvania, and was willing to share the privations and sufferings incident to those early days, when the members of churches were scattered through the wilderness, like sheep without a shepherd. He engaged in preaching the Gospel to the poor, in collecting congregations and rearing churches, in extending the principles of the Lutheran faith, and promoting the interests of the Redeemer's kingdom. During the Revolutionary War he was chaplain of a German regiment in the army commanded by general Washington. Möller's first regular pastoral charge was Reading, Pa. Thence he removed to Philadelphia, and later settled at Albany, N. Y., where he built the first Lutheran church, and promoted the interests of his sect. In 1788 he received and accepted a call to New Holland, Pa., and labored there until, in 1795, he was induced to take the Lutheran flock at Harrisburg, and he served them most acceptably for seven years. In 1802 Möller returned to Albany, and for six years more served the people to whom he had in his first connection so greatly endeared himself. He next accepted a call to the united churches of Sharon and New Rhinebeck, N. Y., where he labored until physical infirmities rendered him unable to attend to the active duties of his profession. Cheered by domestic affection and Christian hope, the last six years he lived were spent in retirement, "although," says a contemporary, "his whole life was devoted to the interests of his divine Master. Until the end he sought opportunity to do good, and to make himself useful to those around him." He died as he had lived, full of faith, calm and confident in the great truths of that blessed religion which he had faithfully preached, Sept. 16, 1829. As a preacher, Möller's talents were not brilliant, yet he accomplished greater things than the more highly gifted. As a man, his whole life was marked by integrity, truthfulness, and a contempt of everything mean or dishonorable. See (Lutheran) *Evangel. Qu. Rev.* (memoirs of deceased ministers), 1865, p. 273 sq.; Sprague, *Annals of the Amer. Pulpit*, vol. ix (Lutherans). (J. H. W.)

Mollius or **Mollio**, GIOVANNI, a distinguished Italian martyr in the Protestant cause, was a native of Montalcino, in the territory of Siena, and the descendant of a very respectable family. He was born near the opening of the 16th century. When only twelve years of age he was placed in the monastery of Gray Friars, where he made rapid progress in arts, sciences, and languages. He entered the order of *Minorites* while yet a youth, and took priest's orders when only eighteen. Every minute was improved in study of polite letters and theology, and he came soon to be noted for his learning and industry. After having pursued his studies six years longer at Ferrara, he was made theological lecturer in the university of that city. He subsequently lectured at the universities of Brescia, Milan, and Pavia, and was appointed professor of theology in the University of Bologna about 1533. There, on reading several treatises of the Reformers, he became at heart a zealous Protestant, and began to expound in its purity the Epistle to the Romans. Immense crowds soon attended his lectures, and, the report coming to Rome, he was seized by order of the pope, and, being denied a public trial, gave an account of his opinions in writing, confirming them by scriptural authority. Mollius defended himself with such ability and address that the judges appointed by Paul III to try the case were forced to acquit him, in the way of declaring that the sentiments which he had maintained were true, although they were such as could not be publicly taught at that time without prejudice to the apostolical see. He was therefore sent back to Bologna, with an admonition to abstain for the future from explaining the same doctrine (i. e. justification by faith). But continuing to expound the epistles of Paul as formerly, and with still greater applause from his hearers—even the monks of different convents, many of the nobility, and individuals of episcopal orders, attending them—cardinal Campeggio procured an order from the pope to remove him from the

university (Pontaleon, *Rerum in Eccl. Gest.* lib. ix, fol. 263). Mollius did not remain idle when relieved of his duties at the university, but continued his studies, and grew in strength among his fellows. He finally became lecturer to the monastery of St. Lorenzo at Naples. But even here he was persecuted; and in 1542 the opposition grew so decided that he was frequently in great danger. He was several times imprisoned, but always escaped until the time of the accession of pope Julius III, when he was hunted down at Ravenna, and transported to Rome. On Sept. 5, 1553, a public assembly of the Inquisition was held with great pomp, and Mollius was brought before that body, attended by six cardinals and their episcopal assessors. All the prisoners brought forward in this session recanted and performed penance except Mollius and another, a native of Perugio named Tisserano, who refused to do violence to their conscience. When the articles of accusation against Mollius were ready, permission was given him to speak. He defended the doctrines which he had taught respecting justification, the merit of good works, auricular confession, and the sacraments; pronounced the power claimed by the pope and his clergy to be usurped and antichristian; and addressed his judges in a strain of bold and fervid invective, which silenced and chained them to their seats, at the same time that it cut them to the quick; and when he had finished his address, he threw the flaming torch which he held in his hand on the ground and extinguished it, thus showing to his accusers that he would rather extinguish life than suffer them to force a lie from him. Of course mercy to such a criminal was not within the gift of Rome, and he was consequently condemned, together with his companion, to instant death. They were at once conveyed to the place of execution, first hung, and then burned to ashes. See *Hist. des Martyrs*, p. 264, 265; Gerdesius, *Ital. Reform.* p. 103; M'Crie, *Ref. in Italy*, p. 95, 124, 261; Young, *Life of Paleario*, ii, 113 sq. Fox, *Book of Martyrs*, p. 184, gives Mollius's history inaccurately. (J. H. W.)

Molloy, FRANCIS, an Irish divine of some celebrity, flourished in the College of St. Isidor at Rome, Italy, in the second half of the 17th century, as professor of theology. He wrote *Sacra Theologia* (Rome, 1666, 8vo): —*Lucerna Fidelium* (1676, 8vo), a Roman Catholic Catechism in Irish:—*Grammatica Latino-Hibernica compendiata* (1677, 12mo). Shingel, who gives an abstract of the last work in his *Archæological Britannica*, says that it was the most complete Irish grammar then extant, although imperfect as to syntax, etc. See Ware, *Writers of Ireland*, vol. ii.

Mo'loch (Heb. *Me'lek*, מֶלֶךְ, *king*, as often; Sept. and N. T. Μολόχ), the name of an Ammonitish idol (Amos iv, 26; Acts vii, 43); usually called MOLECH (q. v.).

Molokans. See MALAKANS.

Molten Image. See IDOL.

Molten Sea. See SEA, MOLTEN.

Moluccas (or ROYAL or SPICE ISLANDS), a number of islands of the Malay Archipelago, in the Indian Ocean. The term comprehends, in its most extensive sense, all the islands between Celebes and New Guinea, situated to the east of the Molucca passage, in long. 126°, particularly those of Gilolo; but, in a more limited sense, it is usually restricted to the Dutch Spice Islands: (1) Ternate, the most important, lies in 0° 48' N. lat. and 127° 8' E. long., and is 25 miles in circumference. It has a population of 9000, of whom only about 400 are Europeans. Its natives are mainly Mohammedans. It was formerly the residence of sultans, who ruled over large territories, and could call out 100,000 fighting-men. The island is fertile and well watered. Rice, cotton, tobacco, etc., are cultivated, and a trade is supported with the adjacent islands. (2) Tidore, south of Ternate, in 0° 40' N. lat. and 127° 25' E. long., is 18 miles in circumference, and rises towards the interior.

Of its population of 8000, the natives are less gentle but more industrious than those of Ternate and diligently cultivate the soil, weave, and fish. They are also Mohammedans, and have many mosques. The sultans of Ternate and Tidore are subsidized by and subject to the Netherlands, being appointed by the governor of the Moluccas, and exercising their authority under the surveillance of the resident. (3) Makian, in $0^\circ 18' 30''$ N. lat. and $127^\circ 30'$ E. long., is very fertile—yields much sago, rice, tobacco, canary-oil, etc., and has important fishings. (4) Farther north is the island of Motir, which is uninhabited, but formerly yielded a considerable quantity of cloves, and later sent much earthenware to all the Spice Islands. (5) Batjan, the only remaining Royal Island, situated between $0^\circ 13'$–$0^\circ 55'$ S. lat. and $127^\circ 22'$–128° E. long., is 50 miles in length and 18 in breadth, and has many mountain-peaks from 1500 to 4000 feet in height, the sources of numerous rivers. The greatest part of this beautiful island is covered with ebony, satin-wood, and other valuable timber-trees, which give shelter to numerous delicately-plumaged birds, deer, wild hogs, and reptiles. Sago, rice, cocoa-nuts, cloves, fish, and fowls are plentiful, and a little coffee is cultivated. Coal is abundant; gold and copper are found in small quantities. The inhabitants, who are lazy and sensual, are a mixed race of Portuguese, Spaniards, Dutch, and natives. All the above-named islands are volcanic, Ternate being a mountain, sloping upwards to 7000 feet, to which Tidore bears a striking resemblance. Makian is an active volcano, and, so late as December, 1861, threw forth immense quantities of lava and ashes, by which 326 lives were lost, and 15 villages in part or in whole destroyed. Motir is a trachyte mountain, 2296 feet in height; and Batjan a chain with lofty peaks. The total population of the Moluccas proper is 23,500. (6) To the south-west of Batjan lie the Obi group, consisting of Obi Major, Obi Minor, Typha, Gonoma, Pisang, and Maya. Obi Major, in $1^\circ 35'$ S. lat. and from 127° to 128° E. long., is by far the largest of these, it having an area of 598 square miles. It is hilly and fertile, being covered, like the smaller islands of the group, with sago and nutmeg trees. The Obi group are uninhabited, and serve simply as lurking-places for pirates and escaped convicts. In 1671 the Dutch built a block-house, called the Bril; and a few years later the sultan of Batjan sold them the group, but the unhealthy climate caused its abandonment in 1738.

The Moluccas, or Spice Islands, in the broad use of the term, lie to the east of Celebes, scattered over nearly eleven degrees of latitude and longitude, between 3° S.–8° N. lat. and 126°–135° E. long., including all the territories formerly ruled over by the sultans of Ternate and Tidore. They are now tributary to Holland, and are virtually under the jurisdiction of the governors appointed by the Dutch, and are divided into the residencies of Amboyna, Banda, and Ternate; a fourth residency, under the governor of the Moluccas, being Menado. Over the northern groups of the Spice Islands the Netherlands exercise an indirect government, the sultans of Ternate and Tidore requiring to have all their appointments of native officials ratified by the resident. The southern groups are directly under European rule. The residency of Amboyna contains that island—sometimes called Ley-Timor, or Hitu, from the two peninsulas of which it is formed—Buru, the Uliassers group, and the west part of Ceram. That of Banda includes the Banda, Keffing, Key, Arru, and other islands; also the eastern part of Ceram. Under the residency of Ternate are placed the Moluccas proper, Gilolo, the neighboring islands, and the north-west of Papua. The population ruled over by the governor of the Moluccas is 767,000. Amboyna, the Banda and Uliasser islands, chiefly supply the cloves, nutmegs, and mace which form the staple exports. The Banda Islands are Neira, or Banda-Neira, Great Banda, Ay or Way, Rhun, Rozingain, and Goenong-Api, containing an area of 588

square miles. Of the population, which is about 6000, 400 are Europeans; in the whole residency, the inhabitants number about 110,000, including the eastern part of Ceram. The principal island of the group is Neira, south-east from Amboyna, in $4^\circ 33'$ S. lat. and 130° E. long., separated by narrow straits from Goenong-Api on the west, and Great Banda on the east. The coast is steep, and surmounted by several forts and batteries, which command the straits and roadstead. The town of Neira, on the south side of the island, is the capital of the Dutch residency of Banda. It has a Protestant church, school, and hospital. The Banda Islands have a rich soil, and are planted with nutmeg-trees, producing upwards of a million pounds of nuts and over a quarter of a million pounds of mace. Pine-apples, the vine, banana, cocoa-nut, and other fruit-trees thrive, and are abundant. Ay is the prettiest and most productive of the group. Goenong-Api is a lofty volcano. The climate is not particularly healthy. The east monsoon begins in May, and the west in December, and both are accompanied with rain and storms. The Uliassers, which, with Amboyna, produce the cloves of commerce, are Saparoua, Oma or Haroukou, and Nousa-Laut. They lie to the east of Amboyna, in $3^\circ 40'$ S. lat. and $128^\circ 33'$ E. long., and have an area of $107\frac{1}{2}$ square miles. Saparoua is the largest, and is formed of two mountainous peninsulas, joined in the middle by a narrow strip of undulating, grassy land. The population amounts to 11,655, of whom 7340 are Christians, having twelve schools, with a very large attendance of scholars. Oma, separated from Saparoua by a strait of a league in width, has eleven villages, of which Harouka and Oma are the chief. It is mountainous in the south, and has several rivers and sulphurous springs. The beautiful village of Harouka, on the west coast, is the residence of the Dutch postholder, who is president of the council of chiefs. Here is the head office of the clove produce. There are two forts on Oma, several churches, and six schools, with 700 pupils. Population 7188; one half Christians, the other Mohammedans. Nousa-Laut lies to the south-east of Saparoua. It is planted with clove-trees, which in 1853 produced 120,283 pounds. There are upwards of 30,000 cocoa-nut-trees. The inhabitants, who were formerly pirates and cannibals, amount to 3479 souls, are all Christians, and have schools in every village—in 1859 they were attended by 870 pupils.

The Spice Islands generally are healthy both for Europeans and Asiatics; and, though the plains are sometimes very hot, mountains are always near, where it is pleasantly cool in the mornings and evenings. Besides the spice-trees, the bread-fruit, sago, cocoa-nut, banana, orange, guava, papaw, also ebony, iron-wood, and other valuable timber-trees, are abundant.

The natives of some of the islands are *Alfoers;* of others, *Malays* on the coasts, and *Alfoers* in the interior. In Ceram are also *Papuan* negroes, brought originally from Bali and Papua as slaves. These are harshly treated and poorly fed. The governor of the Moluccas has a salary of $8500, gold, and, with the secretary and other officials, resides in the city of Amboyna, the streets of which are broad, planted with rows of beautiful trees, and cut each other at right angles. There are two Protestant churches, a town-house, orphanage, hospital, and theatre, besides a useful institution for training native teachers, with which is connected a printing-press.

History, etc.—The Moluccas were first discovered by Europeans in 1511, when the Portuguese, under Antonio de Abreu and Francisco Serrao, landed there. They found, however, that the Arabians had already been there, and had made converts of the natives along the coast—the Malays. In the mountains they found the Papuans (q. v.), but these Oriental negroes were savages, and in a large measure remain so to this day. The king of Portugal claimed the island, and held undisputed sway until 1599, when the Netherlanders took Tidore. In 1623 they drove out the English from these islands, of which they had taken possession, and in 1663 the Netherlanders alone remained to lord it over the Moluccas. Though for a time the British got a hold in the island, the Dutch finally became its possessors. The islanders have frequently attempted to throw off the Dutch yoke, but have failed thus far. The wars with the Alfoers of Ceram, in 1859 and 1860, have brought them more fully under Dutch rule. Recently new sultans of Ternate and Tidore have been appointed, with less power than their predecessors. The natives along the coast speak a dialect of the Malay tongue, mixed with many foreign words; but the ancient Molucca or Tirnata language appeared to the eminent Asiatic linguist, Dr. Leyden, to have been an original tongue. They have adopted many of the tenets, or rather observances, of the Brahminical system; but many of them, named Sherifs, boast of their descent from Mohammed, and are held in great respect, especially if they have performed the pilgrimage to Mecca. The Papuans have been rapidly decreasing, and have wholly disappeared in most of the smaller islands. But they still exist in many of the more eastern islands, and hold undisturbed possession of New Guinea. The houses on these islands are generally raised on pillars eight or ten feet high, on account of the moisture, and are entered by means of a ladder, which is afterwards drawn up. The color of the natives is a deep mixture of black and yellow, and their dispositions uncivil. They subsist chiefly on sago. The men wear little covering, except a hat of leaves, and a piece of cloth round the middle; and the women are dressed in a large wide garment like a sack, with a remarkably broad hat on their heads. Their arms are a kind of light tough wood, arrows of reeds, pointed with hard wood, and bucklers of black hard wood, ornamented with designs in relievo, made with beautiful white shells. The Moluccans have themselves but little intercourse with natives of civilized countries; indeed they know considerably less of them than others in the archipelago. They seldom see a European vessel.

Missionary Labors.—The native tribes of the mountains remain very largely in heathen ignorance. Many of the Moluccans were made converts to Mohammedanism even before the appearance of Christians on the soil, and Islamism is gaining new adherents daily. Christianity, on the other hand, has thus far secured but few in number, as the first impression made by the Portuguese did not result very favorably. The Inquisition at Goa extended its power to these parts, and tried hard to carry the Moluccans into the Christian fold, but failed utterly.

The exchange of ownership imported the Protestant doctrines, but the natives have failed to see much difference between Romanism and the Reformed faith, and Islam is still ahead. All efforts until 1815 made by Protestants are hardly worth mentioning. In that year Jos. Kasse, in the employ of the *Rotterdam Missionary Society* (Zenddinggenootschap), inaugurated successful efforts for the conversion of the Moluccans, and for eighteen years apostolic labors were performed there. In 1819 missionary Jungmichel inaugurated successful labors at Ternate and in the Sangur Islands. At the same time valuable enterprises were inaugurated also at Timor and Amboyna. To the former Lebrun went. He settled at Cupang, the seat of the Dutch governor, on the south coast of Timor. For twenty years there had been no Christian minister among the natives there, who profess Christianity. With so much greater eagerness did they now crowd to the missionary's preaching; and in the very first year ninety pagans were admitted to the Church, which already consisted of 3000 professed Christians. Moreover, the rajah of Rotti submitted himself to Christ crucified; and in 1823 Lebrun baptized in Little Timor, Kissor, Letti, and Moa, 496 persons. The Friendly Society which he established was subscribed to even by some of the pagan princes. He everywhere formed

schools, and to the remote churches he addressed pastoral letters, after the manner of the apostles, of the good effect of which there are very pleasing testimonies. A few years before his death, which took place in 1829, eight missionaries more arrived, who distributed themselves among various stations, and made it one part of their business to establish more fundamentally in Christianity the churches and congregations that had been gained to it. Their work, indeed, is often exceedingly harassing and fatiguing. The centre, however, of missionary labors in the archipelago is, and always has been, Amboyna. Its inhabitants have since 1850 been regarded as Christians. The Rotterdam Society has a number of stations there, and a seminary for the education of native teachers. These stations are now subject to the Church at Batavia, and it is anticipated that the Dutch government will recognise the missionaries as stationed pastors, and contribute for their support. See Sonnerat, *Voyage to the Spice Islands;* Forrest, *Voyage to New Guinea;* Crawford, *Hist. of the Indian Archipelago,* i, 18 sq.; Earl, *Native Races of the Indian Archipelago,* ch. vi; Daniel, *Handbuch der Geographie,* i, 323 sq.; Grundemann, *Missions-Atlas,* pt. ii, No. 6; Newcomb, *Cyclop. of Missions,* p. 485 sq.

Molyneux, WILLIAM, an Irish mathematician and philosopher, who was born at Dublin April 17, 1656, was educated at the university of his native place, and afterwards studied law, is noted as one of the founders of the "Dublin Philosophical Society," of which he was first secretary (1683), and then president, and as the author of twenty-seven papers on miscellaneous subjects inserted in the "Philosophical Transactions" between 1684 and 1716, and of a *Translation of the six Metaphysical Dissertations of Descartes, together with the Objections against them by Thomas Hobbes* (Lond. 1671). Molyneux was a devoted Protestant, and during the political disturbances was obliged to seek refuge in England in 1688. After the battle of the Boyne he returned again to Ireland. Among the many persons of literary eminence with whom Molyneux maintained a correspondence, Locke was held by him in particular esteem, and in the last year of his life he went to England for the purpose of visiting that philosopher. Molyneux died in Dublin Oct. 11, 1698. (J. H. W.)

Mom′dis (Μομδείς v. r. Μόμδιος), given (1 Esdr. ii, 4) in place of MAADAI (q. v.) of the Heb. (Ezra x, 34).

Moment (רֶגַע, *re′ga,* the *wink* of an eye, i. e. an *instant; στιγμή,* a *point* of time, Luke iv, 5).

Momiers or **Mummers** (from the French word *momerie*—mummery, hypocrisy) is a name of contempt given to a sect of Calvinistic Methodists in French Switzerland. In the first part of the present century we find in Switzerland, as in Germany, a conflict between the old confessional faith and Rationalism. The Genevan school had broken loose from rigid Calvinism, and the heresies of Arianism and Socinianism were taught and believed. But after the great political events of the years 1813–15 we see the old evangelical faith beginning once more to assert itself, young theologians in Geneva and the canton Vaud declaring in favor of orthodox preaching, and avowing the then almost forgotten doctrines of Christ's divinity and of total human depravity. Their preaching caused great bitterness of feeling. Empaytaz, generally recognised as the first preacher of the Momiers at that time, was in 1816 obliged to quit Geneva, and in 1817 the "Vénérable Compagnie des Pasteurs" (i. e. the Presbytery of Geneva) issued a formal prohibition against preaching on those doctrines which had ever been held as the fundamental doctrines of the Reformed Church. This arbitrary action led to an open rupture between the evangelical and rationalistic parties. A number of preachers—among them, Malan (q.v.), Empaytaz, Gaussen, Bost, Galland, and Drummond (a British Methodist)—refused to obey, and actually separated from the state Church, organizing their own independent evangelical congregations. Their adherents were all more or less influenced by Methodist tendencies, and inclined to a sombre view of life. They were called by the people "Momiers," as if to say hypocrites, and exposed to the insults of the populace. Many vexatious occurrences took place; they were much disturbed in their worship, particularly at Geneva, where they had erected a church by funds secured in England; but they were at last officially tolerated. In the canton Vaud, however, where they had spread considerably, their assemblies were entirely forbidden by the authorities by special act (May 20, 1824), and in consequence the pastors Scheler, Olivier, Chavannes, Professor Monnard, and others, were obliged to leave their flocks or suffer heavy penalties. But the old experience that persecution only strengthens a persecuted cause proved true here also. The sect gladly took to itself the name given in reproach, and the "Momiers," in spite of interdict, continued to increase, and finally caused the formation of an independent Church (Église séparé). In 1834 the right of assembling together, and free exercise of their religious convictions, was granted them by the state, and they spread now more than ever. They found adherents also in German Switzerland. Thus in Berne a Württemberger named Möhrli, and a physician from Weimar named Valenti, actively proselyted for the new doctrines. In Neuenburg also, and in other Protestant cantons of the little European republic, this peculiar "Methodism" spread and flourished. A paper was also started, the Gazette Évangelique, and it rapidly gained a large circulation. While the Evangelical Society of Geneva [see the articles MALAN and HALDANE brothers] owes its origin and strength largely to the influence and zealous co-operation of this sect, the grand results of this schism are embodied in a free evangelical Church union, called the "Église libre," which was organized by the different nonconforming congregations in 1848. See Malan, Swiss Tracts, i, 20 sq.; Les Procès du Méthodisme en Genève (1835); Hagenbach, Ch. Hist. 18th and 19th Cent. ii, 406 sq.; Hist. véritable des Momiers de Genève (Paris, 1824); Schweizer, Die kirchl. Zerwürfnisse im Kanton Waadt; Mestral, Mission de l'Église libre (1848); Bost, Défense des fidèles de l'Église de Genève (Paris, 1825); Von Goltz, Die reform. Kirche Genfs im 19 Jahrh. (Basle and Gen. 1862); Chenevière, Quelques mots sur la Genève religieuse du baron de Goltz (Gen. 1863); Aschbach, Kirchen-Lex. iv, 259.

Mona ($\mu\delta\nu\eta$) is a term applied to females who assumed the monastic life. The common name applied to female recluses is nuns, from nonna; Gr. $\nu\acute{\alpha}\nu\nu\eta$, aunt. See NUNS.

Monacensis, Codex. See MUNICH MS.

Monachism. See MONASTICISM.

Monaco, Francisco-Maria del, an Italian theologian, a native of Sicily, was born in 1593. In 1618 he entered holy orders, but, instead of preaching, devoted himself to pedagogy. He taught for a time at Padua, and was subsequently employed in different offices. In 1644 he came to France, welcomed by cardinal Mazarin, who appointed him his successor. He preached successfully before the court and in the churches of Paris. He was appointed, through the influence of the prime minister, archbishop of Rheims, but died shortly after at Paris (1651). He wrote Il Sole, panegirico (Venice, 1618, 4to):—La Penna, panegirico (1620, 4to): —Patrum Clericorum regularium XIV Elogia (Padua; Milan, 1621, 8vo):—In actores et spectatores comœdiarum nostri temporis Parænesis (Padua, 1621, 4to):— Horæ subcesivæ (1625, 4to):—De Paupertate evangelica (Rome, 1644, folio); a work which his departure for France obliged him to leave unfinished:—De Fidei unitate, III, ad Carolum, Britanniarum regem. (Paris, 1648, folio):—In universam Aristotelis Philosophiam Commentaria (Paris, 1652, folio). Other works of his are

preserved in manuscript at Palermo. See Silos, Hist. Cleric. reg. part iii, bk. viii; L. Allatius, De Viris Illustr. p. 108; F. M. Maggi, De Vita Ursulæ Benincasæ; Mongitore, Bibl. sicula. i, 225; Uomini illustri della Sicilia, vol. iv.

Monaco, Lorenzo, a Genoese painter, sometimes called the "Monk of the Isole d'Oro," flourished in the 14th century. He was a favorite of the king and queen of Aragon, to whom he presented several illuminated missals. A beautiful Angel, with arms crossed over his bosom, and floating in the air, is credited to him in the Florence gallery; also The Flight into Egypt, in the Arena at Padua, in which picture Mary and Joseph are attended by Salome and three youths. But very little is known of this artist. He died, according to Lanzi, in 1408. See Lanzi's History of Painting, transl. by Roscoe (London, 1847, 3 vols. 8vo), iii, 233; Mrs. Jameson, Legends of the Madonna (ibid. 1857, 8vo), p. 231; Sacred and Legendary Art (ibid. 1857, 2 vols. 8vo), i, 120; ii, 796.

Monadology (from Gr. $\mu o\nu\acute{\alpha}\varsigma$, unity, and $\lambda\acute{o}\gamma o\varsigma$, discourse) is the term applied to the doctrine or science of Monads, which was fully developed by the German philosopher Leibnitz. "He conceived the whole universe, bodies as well as minds, to be made up of monads, that is, simple substances; each of which is, by the Creator, in the beginning of its existence, endowed with certain active and perceptive powers. A monad, therefore, is an active substance, simple, without parts or figure, which has within itself the power to produce all the changes it undergoes from the beginning of its existence to eternity. The changes which the monad undergoes, of what kind soever, though they may seem to us the effect of causes operating from without, are only the gradual and successive evolutions of its own internal powers, which would have produced all the same changes and motions although there had been no other being in the universe" (Reid, Intell. Powers, essay ii, ch. 15). "Monadology," says Cousin, "rests upon this axiom: every substance is at the same time a cause, and, every substance being a cause, has therefore in itself the principle of its own development; such is the monad—it is a simple force. Each monad has relation to all others; it corresponds with the plan of the universe; it is the universe abridged; it is, as Leibnitz says, a living mirror which reflects the entire universe under its own point of view. But every monad being simple, there is no immediate action of one monad upon another; there is, however, a natural relation of their respective development, which makes their apparent communication; this natural relation, this harmony, which has its reason in the wisdom of the supreme Director, is pre-established harmony" (Hist. of Mod. Philos. ii, 86). See Ueberweg, Hist. Philos. ii, 92 sq., 107 sq.; also p. 27, 54, 130, 145, 312, 316, 336, 507. See also LEIBNITZ; NEO-PLATONISM.

Monarchæ was the title occasionally bestowed in the Christian churches, especially in those of the East, instead of the more familiar metropolitan (q. v.). In the 6th canon of the Council of Sardica, which was held in 344, we find metropolitans distinguished by the title princeps provinciæ (ἔξαρχος τῆς ἐπαρχίας); but elsewhere, in references of those days, they are entitled monarchæ. See Riddle, Christian Antiquities, p. 224.

Monarchia is the term by which is designated the leading or opening statement in the orderly enunciation of the doctrine of the Trinity (q. v.), i. e. the doctrine that there is one and only one Ἀρχή, principle or fountain of Divinity, God the Father, the first person in the Trinity, who only is Αὐτόϑεος, "God of and from himself" (Pearson [Expos. of the Creed (1741, fol.), p. 39] is very particular on the form of this statement, and takes exception to Bull, who uses the word "from"—" of and from himself," which Pearson considers a contradiction). The doctrine of the Trinity assumes that the Son and the Holy Ghost derive their divinity from the Father as the one $A\rho\chi\eta$. The scriptural and only true idea of God involves in its development the idea of the trinity; and the doctrine of the Monarchia may be approached either from the side of the unity of God or from the side of the trinity of persons. Coming to it on the side of the unity, there is presented to the mind, first, the existence of God, then the unity of God, then the underived nature—that is, his self-existence. Coming to the doctrine on the side of the trinity of persons, Scripture reveals God the Son, who is $\Theta\epsilon\delta\varsigma$ $\dot\epsilon\kappa$ $\Theta\epsilon o\tilde v$ by an eternal generation; and God the Holy Ghost, who is $\Theta\epsilon\delta\varsigma$ $\dot\epsilon\kappa$ $\Theta\epsilon o\tilde v$ by an eternal procession. This refers us to the first person of the Trinity, as him from whom the second and third persons derive their divinity. The doctrine of the Monarchia, flowing as it does directly from the unity of God, in its expression guards that unity; while at the same time it renders it possible that the Son is God, and the Holy Ghost God, by a derivation of Godhead; the full doctrine of the Godhead of the second and third persons being maintained by the further doctrine of the perichoresis. It is to be remarked that as $\dot\alpha\rho\chi\eta$ has the meaning of "beginning" with reference to time, as well as the meaning of "principle" with reference to origin, so with regard to the former meaning the Son and the Holy Spirit are $\check\alpha\nu\alpha\rho\chi o\iota$ as well as the Father. $A\iota\tau\iota\alpha$, cause, is also used in the enunciation of this doctrine: the Father himself, $\alpha\iota\tau\iota\alpha$, is $\dot\alpha\nu\alpha\iota\tau\iota o\varsigma$; the Son and the Holy Spirit are $\alpha\iota\tau\iota\alpha\tau\delta\varsigma$ and $\alpha\iota\tau\iota\alpha\tau\delta\nu$. Scripture and the Church avoid the appearance of tritheism by tracing back (if we may so say) the infinite perfection of the Son and Spirit to him whose Son and Spirit they are. They are, so to express it, but the new manifestation and repetition of the Father; there being no room for numeration or comparison between them, nor any resting-place for the contemplating mind, till they are referred to him in whom they centre. On the other hand, in naming the Father, we imply the Son and Spirit, whether they be named or not. This is the key to much of the language of holy Scripture which is otherwise difficult to understand, as, e. g. 1 John v, 20; 1 Cor. xii, 4-6; John xiv, 16-18 (Newman's *Arians*, p. 192). Viewing this doctrine on the side of the second and third persons of the Trinity, it becomes the doctrine of their subordination to the Father. In nature, in perfection of substance, equal to the Father; in authority, in origin, the Son and Holy Spirit are subordinate. Bull expresses it thus: "Pater igitur minor est Filius $\kappa\alpha\tau'$ $\alpha\iota\tau\iota\alpha\nu$. Æqualis vero est Patri Filius $\kappa\alpha\tau\dot\alpha$ $\phi\upsilon\sigma\iota\nu$. Deus ac Dominus est Filius æque ac Pater; et in hoc solo discrepat a Patre Filius, quod Deus et Dominus sit a Patre Deo ac Domino; hoc est, Deus licet de Deo sit, de vero tamen Deo Deus verus est, ut definivit synodus ipsi Nicæna" (Bull's *Works*, Burton's ed., vi, 707). The like things may be said of the Holy Spirit. This subordination, and the ministrations of the Son and of the Holy Spirit in executing the counsels of the individual society of the Godhead, is styled the economy of the Holy Trinity. See Procession.

Monarchians is a name given to those Christians of the early Church who denied the distinction of *persons* in the divine nature. They insisted on the divine unity, which they thought was infringed by the common and orthodox doctrine of the Trinity. "Monarchiam tenemus" was their frequent assertion when comparing themselves with the orthodox fathers, whom they accordingly charged with Tritheism. Yet it is apparent that the Monarchians did not properly use the term $\mu o\nu\alpha\rho\chi\iota\alpha$—at least not in the catholic sense, as maintaining that there is only one $\dot\alpha\rho\chi\eta$, source or fountain of Deity, the Father, which sense implies the existence of the Begotten Son and Proceeding Spirit as distinct Persons; nor in the sense of unity, for unity can only be asserted when there is plurality (in which lies the misuse of the term by the Unitarians); nor, again, in the sense of God's sole government, which affirms nothing concerning the existence or non-existence of a distinction of Persons in the Godhead; but they used it in the sense of simple oneness, from which oneness they argued that the Godhead is so simple a being as to be $\mu o\nu o\pi\rho\delta\sigma\omega\pi o\varsigma$—a solitary, single Hypostasis. That this was the meaning in which they used the term $\mu o\nu\alpha\rho\chi\iota\alpha$ is apparent on the very face of the controversy. Thus Tertullian goes on to assert that monarchia means nothing else than "singulare et unicum imperium."

The Monarchians are generally credited as the adherents of Praxeas, a writer of the Grecian school. They were sometimes called *Patripassians*, because their views led to the conclusion that, if the union between God the Father and his Son Jesus were so intimate as they affirmed, then the former must be supposed to have suffered with the latter all the afflictions of his life and death. Praxeas held that the Word of God (Jesus Christ) meant nothing more than the word of his mouth —the emissions of his voice, to which distinct agency had been metaphorically ascribed. These heretics considered that the doctrine of the Church with respect to the personality of the Son was a disparaging representation of Christ, whom they held to be the supreme God himself, and who, in a way he had never done besides, had revealed himself in human nature, and had appeared in a human body. They taught that God was to be considered in two different relations: 1, the hidden Being, as he was before the Creation—*the Father*; and, 2, in so far as he revealed himself, the *Son of the Logos*; and it was only in virtue of these considerations that Christ, as the most perfect revelation of God the Father, was called the Son of God. They maintained that this doctrine was most eminently calculated to dignify Christ. (See, however, below.) The Monarchians received both the Old and New Testaments, and held doctrines somewhat resembling modern Unitarianism. This general class, however, comprehended many who differed more from each other than they did even from those reputed orthodox, and who, indeed, had nothing in common but a great zeal for Monotheism, and a fear lest the unity of God should be endangered by the hypostases of the Alexandrian fathers. Thus Theodotus, Artemon, and Paul of Samosata were placed by the side of Praxeas, Noëtus, Beryllus of Bostra, and Sabellius, between whom and themselves, on every essential point of Christian doctrine, there was an unmistakable opposition.

Monarchianism is generally supposed to have originated about the end of the 2d century. It seems to us, however, that this heresy may be traced to the very earliest times of Christianity. Justin Martyr expressly denounces it, and his notice guides us to its source, for he finds the heresy to exist both among Jews and Christians. He condemns the Jews for thinking that, when God was said to have appeared to the patriarchs, it was God the Father who appeared. Such, he says, are justly convicted of knowing neither the Father nor the Son; for they who say that the Son is the Father are convicted of neither understanding the Father nor of knowing that the Father of the universe has a Son, who, being the first-born Logos of God, is likewise God (*First Apol.* ch. lxiii). In the Dialogue with Trypho he handles the same topic, and extends the charge to Christians. "I am aware that there are some who wish to meet this by saying that the power which appeared from the Father of the universe to Moses, or Abraham, or Jacob, is called an Angel in his coming among men, since by this the will of the Father is made known to men; he is also called Glory, since he is sometimes seen in an unsubstantial appearance; sometimes he is called a Man, since he appears under such forms as the Father pleases; and they call him the Word, since he is also the bearer of messages from the Father to men. But they say that this power is unseparated and undivided from the Father, in the same manner that the light of the sun when on earth is unseparated and undivided from the sun in heaven, and when the sun sets the light is removed with it; so the Father, they say, when he wishes, makes his power go forth, and when he wishes he brings it back again to himself" (*Dial. c. Tryph.* cc. 127, 128). It appears, then, there were persons in Justin's time who called themselves Christians, but who believed that the Son was merely an unsubstantial energy or operation of the Father (see Bull, *Def. Fid. Nic.* can. ii, qu. iv, 4; Burton, *Bampt. Lect.* note 103). Now in this the Jews had deserted the better teachings of their earlier rabbins; for these ascribed a divine personality to the angel of the Presence, and the doctrine of the holy and undivided Trinity subsisted, though in a less developed form, in the synagogue of old (see Mill, *Panth. Prin.* pt. ii, p. 92 sq.). The cause of this declension in doctrine was, that opposition to the Incarnate Word, when he really appeared, seemed to have predisposed them to accept a heathen philosophy, and to represent the Logos as Philo did—as the manifest God not personally distinct from the concealed Deity. This error found its way into Christianity through the Gnostics, who were largely indebted to the Platonic school of Alexandria. It appears as the foundation of the system of Simon Magus, who taught that the originating principle of all (which he asserted to be Fire, for "God is a consuming fire") is of a twofold nature, having a secret part and a manifest part, corresponding, as Hippolytus remarks, to the potentiality and energy of Aristotle. If this be nothing else than Philo's representation of the Logos, there is some sure ground for the notion that Simon held the heresy afterwards called Sabellian. Burton rejects the notion, inasmuch as the doctrine of emanations is not to be confounded with the theory of Sabellius; but Hippolytus (whom Burton did not possess) shows that the Logos, in Simon's theory, employed certain portions of the divine fulness, which portions he called Æons; and that the Logos, although Simon uses the word Begotten, is really the manifest God not personally distinct from the concealed Deity (see Burton, *Bampton Lect.* note 46). Although, therefore, the doctrine of emanations is not to be confounded with the doctrine of Sabellius, it had in its original form, as constructed by Simon, a foundation of Sabellianism. Traces of Sabellianism are found even in the later schools of Gnostics, and the later Sabellianism approached to an emanation theory. A resemblance has been noticed between the tenets of Valentinus and those of Sabellius (Peturius, *Dogm. Theol.* II, i, 6; Wormius, *Hist. Sabel.* ii, 3), and Neander is inclined to think that Marcion may have adopted some of the Patripassian doctrines in Asia Minor (*Church Hist.* i, 796: Burton, *Bampton Lect.* note 103). The leading tenet of the Monarchians thus appears to have been introduced into Christianity principally through the Alexandrian Jews and the Gnostics. It may also have been derived immediately from heathen philosophers, as in the case of Noëtus it is ascribed by Hippolytus immediately to Heraclitus (see NOËTIANS).

But whatever its origin in its development, Monarchianism must be carefully distinguished among two opposite classes claiming to be Monarchians: the rationalistic or dynamic Monarchians, who denied the divinity of Christ, or explained it as a mere power ($\Delta\acute{v}\nu\alpha\mu\iota\varsigma$); and the patripassian Monarchians, who identified the Son with the Father, and admitted at most only a modal trinity, a threefold mode of revelation. "The first form of this heresy," says Schaff, "involved in the abstract Jewish monotheism, deistically sundered the divine and the human, and rose little above Ebionism. The second proceeded, at least in part, from pantheistic preconceptions, and approached the ground of Gnostic docetism. The one prejudiced the dignity of the Son, the other the dignity of the Father; yet the latter was by far the more profound and Christian, and accordingly met with the greater acceptance."

1. The Monarchians of the first class saw in Christ a mere man, filled with divine power; but conceived this divine power as operative in him, not from the baptism only, according to the Ebionitish view, but from the

beginning; and admitted his supernatural generation by the Holy Ghost. To this class belong:

(1) The *Alogians*, a heretical sect in Asia Minor about A.D. 170, of which very little is known. See ALOGIANS.

(2) The *Theodotians*, so called from their founder, Theodotus, who flourished near the close of the 2d century. He denied Christ in a persecution, with the apology that he only denied a man; but still held him to be the supernaturally begotten Messiah. He taught that Jesus was born of the Virgin according to the will of the Father, and that at his baptism the higher Christ descended upon him. But this higher Christ Theodotus conceived as the Son of him who was at once the Supreme God and the Creator of the world, and not (with Cerinthus and other Gnostics) as the son of a deity superior to the God of the Jews. See THEODOTIANS.

(3) The *Artemonites*, or adherents of Artemon, who came out somewhat later at Rome with a similar opinion, declaring the doctrine of the divinity of Christ an innovation, and a relapse to heathen polytheism. They asserted that until the time of Victor, bishop of Rome, their doctrine was the reigning one in the Roman Church, and that it was first proscribed by Victor's successor, Zephyrinus (after A.D. 200). This was an unreasonable charge, but may have been made possible by the indefiniteness of the earliest formulas of the Christian Church. The Artemonites were charged with placing Euclid and Aristotle above Christ, and esteeming mathematics and dialectics above the Gospel. See ARTEMONITES.

(4) *Paul of Samosata*, bishop of Antioch in the second half of the 3d century, who denied the personality of the Logos and of the Holy Ghost, and considered them merely powers of God, like reason and mind in man; but granted that the Logos dwelt in Christ in larger measure than in any former messenger of God; and taught, like the Socinians in later times, a gradual elevation of Christ, determined by his own moral development, to divine dignity (a $\vartheta\epsilon\sigma\pi\sigma\acute{\iota}\eta\sigma\iota\varsigma$ $\acute{\epsilon}\kappa$ $\pi\rho\sigma\kappa\sigma\pi\tilde{\eta}\varsigma$). His overthrow by the emperor Aurelius in 272 decided the fall of the Monarchians, though they still appear at the end of the 4th century as condemned heretics, under the name of *Samosatenians* (q. v.), *Paulianists* (q. v.), and *Sabellians* (q. v.).

2. The second class of Monarchians, called by Tertullian *Patripassians* (as afterwards a branch of the Monophysites was called Theopaschites), together with their unitarian zeal, felt the deeper Christian impulse to hold fast the divinity of Christ; but they sacrificed to it his independent personality, which they merged in the essence of the Father.

(1) The first prominent advocate of this class of Monarchians, rather than the founder of Monarchianism, was *Praxeas*, of whom we have already spoken above. *Noëtus* of Smyrna, who differed but little from Praxeas, is frequently recognised as the leader of a branch of this class; and *Callistus* (pope Calixtus I), who adopted and advocated the doctrines of Noëtus, as the leader of a third branch. Those who strictly followed him were called *Callistians*, in distinction from the direct followers of Noëtus, who were called *Noëtians* (q. v.). Noëtus taught (according to Hippolytus, *Philos.* ix, 7 sq.) that the one God who created the world, though in himself invisible, had yet from most ancient times appeared from time to time, according to his good pleasure, to righteous men; and that this same God had himself become also the Son, when it pleased him to submit to being born; he was consequently his own son, and in this identity of the Father and the Son consisted the "monarchia" of God. An associate and disciple of Noëtus was Epigonus, who brought the doctrine he professed to Rome; and *his* pupil, again, was Cleomenes, who defended the doctrine of Noëtus in the time of bishop Zephyrinus, the successor of Victor. With this Cleomenes, according to Hyppolytus, Callistus, the successor of Zephyrinus, was on terms of friendship, and was of

like opinions. Callistus declared the Son to be merely the manifestation of the Father in human form; the Father animating the Son, as the spirit animates the body (John xiv, 11), and suffering with him on the cross. "The Father," says he, "who was in the Son, took flesh and made it God, uniting it with himself, and made it one. Father and Son were therefore the name of the one God, and this one person ($\pi\rho\delta\sigma\omega\pi\sigma\nu$) cannot be two; thus the Father suffered with the Son." After the death of this pope, Patripassianism virtually disappeared from the Roman Church.

(2) The stepping-stone from simple Patripassianism to what we shall presently deal with as Sabellian modalism constitutes the doctrine advanced by *Beryllus* of Bostra, in Arabia. From him we have only a somewhat obscure and very variously interpreted passage in Eusebius (*H. E.* vi, 33). He denied the personal pre-existence ('Ιδία οὐσίας περιγραφή, i. e. a circumscribed, limited, separate existence), and in general the independent divinity ('Ιδία Θεότης) of Christ, but at the same time asserted the indwelling of the divinity of the Father ('Η πατρικὴ Θεότης) in him during his earthly life.

(3) The Sabellian modalism had its starting-point in the views evolved by *Sabellius* (q. v.), who flourished in the beginning of the 2d century. He differed from the orthodox standard mainly in denying the trinity of essence and the permanence of the trinity of manifestation; making the Father, Son, and Holy Ghost only temporary phenomena, which fulfil their mission and return into the abstract monad. He differed from the other Monarchians by embracing the Holy Ghost in his speculation, and thereby reached a trinity; not a simultaneous trinity of essence, however, but only a successive trinity of revelation. He starts from a distinction of the monad and the triad in the divine nature. His fundamental thought is that the unity of God, without distinction in itself, unfolds or extends itself ('Η μονὰς πλατυνθεῖσα γέγονε τριάς) in the course of the world's development in three different forms and periods of revelation ('Ονόματα, πρόσωπα—not in the orthodox sense of the term, however, but in the primary sense of mask, or part [in a play]), and, after the completion of redemption, returns into unity. The Father reveals himself in the giving of the law or the Old-Testament economy (not in the creation also; this, in his view, precedes the trinitarian revelation; the Son, in the incarnation; the Holy Ghost, in inspiration. He illustrates the trinitarian relation by comparing the Father to the disk of the sun, the Son to its enlightening power, the Spirit to its warming influence. His view of the Logos, too, is peculiar. The Logos is not identical with the Son, but is the monad itself in its transition to triad; that is, God conceived as vital motion and creating principle—the speaking God (Θεὸς λαλῶν), in distinction from the silent God (Θεὸς σιωπῶν). Each πρόσωπον is another διαλέγεσθαι, and the three πρόσωπα together are only successive evolutions of the Logos or the worldward aspect of the divine nature. As the Logos proceeded from God, so he returns at last into him, and the process of trinitarian development (Διάλεξις) closes (comp. Baur, *Gesch. d. Dreieinigkeitslehre*, on this point). Athanasius traced the doctrine of Sabellius to the Stoic philosophy; and it must be confessed that in the Pythagorean system also, in the Gospel of the Egyptians, and even in the pseudo-Clementine homilies, there are kindred ideas. But, notwithstanding these, it is now generally conceded that Sabellius was in all respects original in the propounding of his theory of the Trinitarian doctrine. Says Schaff (*Ch. Hist.* i, 293): "Sabellius is by far the most original, ingenious, and profound of the Monarchians. His system is known to us only from a few fragments, and some of these not altogether consistent, in Athanasius and other fathers. It was very fully developed, and has been revived in modern times by Schleiermacher (*Ueber den Gegensatz der Sabellianischen u. Athanasian-*

ischen Vorstellung v. d. Trinität) in a peculiarly modified form." Since the writing of the above by Dr. Schaff. the general Monarchian view of the incarnation has been revived by the Rev. Henry Ward Beecher, who in his *Life of Christ* (N. Y. 1871, 8vo), vol. i, denies the union of the human and divine nature in Christ, and asserts that he was God dwelling in and subject to the infirmities and limitation of the human flesh—a view which he supports largely from ch. ii of Hebrews. See ARIANS; INCARNATION; MONOPHYSITES; PATRIPASSIANS; SABELLIANS; UNITARIANS.

From this cursory glance at the history of Monarchianism, there is apparent an endeavor to escape from the revolting tenet of Patripassianism, and to retain or supply that which the nature of man almost instinctively requires—a superhuman mediation and atonement. The working of these two motives, as the Monarchian adopted either the Arian or the Patripassian alternative, is very remarkable; inasmuch as the return to catholicity appears to be much easier in the school which adopted the former alternative. Where Patripassianism was at once and decisively rejected, it was open to the Monarchian to satisfy the need for a mediator by magnifying the divine element in our Lord, which at first he considered to be only the highest degree of prophetic grace, and passing through stages of Arianism and semi-Arianism to approach nearer and nearer to the truth. Whereas, when Patripassianism had been adopted, and the need was felt for freeing the mind from a tenet at which one shudders, it was only done by diminishing the divine nature in Christ, through the stages of supposing it to be a portion of the divine fulness, then an emanation from the Godhead. The result was a deliberate Psilanthropism. Regarding the heresy itself of pseudo-Monarchianism, the main points for consideration are the following: First, an eternal mind must needs have in it from eternity an ἔννοια or λόγος, a notion or conception of itself, which the schools term *verbum mentis:* nor can it be conceived without it. "This Word in God cannot be, as it is in us, a transient, vanishing accident, for then the divine nature would indeed be compounded of substance and accident, which would be repugnant to its simplicity; but it must be a substantial, subsisting Word" (Bull, *Cath. Doct. concerning the blessed Trinity*). The Monarchians denied this (Τελειότατον καὶ ζῶντα καὶ αὐτοῦ τοῦ πρώτου νοῦ λόγον ἔμψυχον). Denying this, they denied also that substantial *vinculum caritatis* in which the Father and the Son are one ἑνότητι Πνεύματος. Secondly, thus is destroyed that αὐτάρκεια which we attribute to God, i. e. his self-sufficiency and most perfect bliss and happiness in himself alone, before and without all created beings. For this we cannot well conceive without acknowledging a distinction of persons in the Godhead. The Monarchians, it is clear, denied this individual society of the Trinity (comp. Blunt, *Dict. of Sects, Heresies*, etc., p. 332). See Möhler, *Athanasius der Grosse* (Mainz, 1827), bk. i (*Der Glaube der Kirche der drei ersten Jahrh. in Betreff der Trinität*, etc.), p. 1–116; Baur, *Die christl. Lehre von der Dreieinigkeit u. Menschwerdung Gottes in ihrer geschichtlichen Entwickelung* (Tüb. 1841–43, 3 vols.), i, 129–341; Meier, *Die Lehre von der Trinität in ihrer hist. Entwickelung* (Hamb. 1844, 2 vols.), i, 45–134; Dorner, *Entwickelungsgeschichte der Lehre von der Person Christi* (1839; 2d ed. Stuttg. u. Berl. 1845–56, 2 vols.), i, 122–747; Lange, *Gesch. d. Lehrbegriffes der Unitarier vor der nicänischen Synode* (Leips. 1831); Schleiermacher, *Werke*, i, 2, p. 485–574; Vogt, *Lehre des Athanasius von Alexandrius* (Bremen, 1861); Hagenbach, *Hist. of Doctrines*, i, 62 sq., 116 sq., 131 sq.; Mosheim, *Comment. Eccles. Hist.* (see Index); Milman, *Hist. of Christianity*, and *Latin Christianity*, i, 70–73; Pressensé, *Early Years of Christianity, Heresy, and Christian Doctrine* (N.Y. 1873, 12mo). ch. v; Neander, *Hist. Dogmas* (see Index in vol. ii), and *Ch. Hist.* vol. i; Ueberweg, *Hist. Philos.* ii, 306–11; Ebrard, *Dogmengesch.* vol. i; Hase, *Ch. Hist.* p. 98 sq., 196,704; Schaff, *Ch. Hist.* vol. i, § 81 and 83.

Monarchy, ISRAELITISH (see Kale, *De potestate regia ingente Hebr.* Havn. 1749). According to the sense of the Mosaic constitution, the Hebrews were erected into a kind of republic under the immediate dominion of Jehovah, forming a strict theocracy (q. v.); the law of the kingdom (Deut. xvii, 14–20) being partly expounded by the Pentateuch itself, which alludes to it as a future institution, and partly organized on a permanent basis by Solomon, largely independent of the Mosaic law (see Städlein in Bertholdt's *Theol. Journ.* iii, 259, 361 sq.; Hengstenberg, *Pentat.* ii, 246 sq.). It was inaugurated by Samuel in compliance with a general request of the people, which had grown out of the bitter experience of many years, rendering it an inevitable necessity sooner or later (Ewald, *Israel. Gesch.* ii, 140 sq.), as the order of judges was but a temporary and precarious safeguard against total anarchy. The king, however, was only empowered to administer the theocratic government as *a viceroy of Jehovah,* the heavenly sovereign (Psa. ii, 2), and was bound to this law as the highest authority, so as to exclude the idea of an independent and absolute monarch. In particular cases the Urim and Thummim, or a prophet, or some other medium of divine communication (1 Sam. xxviii, 6; xxx, 7 sq.; 2 Sam. ii, 1; 1 Kings xxii, 7 sq.; comp. John xi, 51), might be referred to in order to direct and confirm the theocratic regent as to the will of Jehovah, so that in this way the monarchical administration still retained the character of a divine government, and the kings were reminded of their dependency (see Kalkar, *Over de israel. Godesregering,* in his *Verhandling van het Haagsche Genootschap,* etc., ii, 3 sq.). But in practice the Israelitish kings assumed the right of declaring war and concluding peace (1 Sam. xi, 5 sq.), as well as of exercising judicial functions in the highest cases (2 Sam. xv, 2; 1 Kings iii, 16 sq.; comp. Jer. xxi, 12), and of pronouncing amnesty (2 Sam. xiv). The king was also the patron of the religious cultus (1 Kings viii; 2 Kings xii, 4 sq.; xviii, 4 sq.; xxiii, 1 sq.), and in war he was likewise the usual leader of his troops (1 Sam. viii, 20). Despotism was held in check sometimes by a sort of coronation-oath—a *Magna Charta,* as it were (1 Sam. x, 25; 2 Sam. v, 3; 1 Kings xii, 4 sq.; 2 Kings xi, 17; comp. Josephus, *War,* ii, 1, 2)—and sometimes by a mass meeting of the tribes (1 Chron. iv, 41 sq.; the heads of families formed a kind of popular representatives, 1 Chron. xxix, 1 sq.; comp. xiii, 2); and there even occurs an example of the direct intervention of the people (1 Sam. xiv, 45 sq.); but especially the prophets, who from the time of Samuel were set to guard the theocracy, and constituted a species of continually self-renewing order, often made the most unshrinking opposition to the prince, either by introducing themselves officially into the royal cabinet (Nathan, Isaiah), or by demanding a special audience (1 Kings xx, 22 sq., 38; 2 Kings i, 15, etc.), and even went so far as open resistance, by their severe invectives at least, to unlawful measures of government (compare 1 Sam. xxii, 17 sq.). See PROPHET.

The regular succession was confined to the house of David. Usually the first-born son (even when a minor [2 Kings xi, 21]—there is found no provision for a guardian or regent [yet see the Sept. at 1 Kings xii, 24]; the queen-dowager, however, seems to have a position as counsellor in such cases [Jer. xiii, 18; comp. 2 Kings xxiv, 12]) appears to have as a matter of course assumed the reins of government, but occasionally the father is stated to have designated a particular son to the throne (1 Kings i, 17, 20; 2 Chron. xi, 22); sometimes the people themselves interfered (2 Kings xxi, 24; xxiii, 30), and even foreign powers at length imposed rulers as their own vassals upon the nation (2 Kings xxiii, 34; xxiv, 17). In the kingdom of *Israel* the first king was inducted into office by a prophet (1 Kings xi, 31 sq.), and the succession was thenceforth hereditary (descending to the son, or, when the direct line failed, to the brother, 2 Kings iii, 1); but the brief dynasties followed

each other with many interruptions through extinction, conspiracy, or deposition (1 Kings xvi, 9, 16, 21), and several interregna occurred. An association in the throne, or rather viceroyship, of the successor in consequence of the disability of the ruling monarch is mentioned in 2 Chron. xxvii, 21; and numerous other instances are rendered probable by the discrepancies in the regnal years. See CHRONOLOGY. In the election of a king, ancient nations had great regard to personal size (1 Sam. x, 23) and beauty (1 Sam. xvi, 12; Ezek. xxviii, 12; comp. Psa. xl, 3; Homer, *Il.* iii, 166 sq.; Herod. iii, 20; Strabo, xv, 699; xvii, 822; Athen. xii, 566; Barhebr. *Chron.* p. 384; see also Dougtæi *Analect.* i, 131); and Hebrew kings were required to be native citizens (Deut. xvii, 15). Those who instituted a new dynasty sought to strengthen their power by the extinction of the previous reigning family (1 Kings xvi, 11; 2 Kings x, 11, 17; xi, 1; comp. Josephus, *Ant.* xv, 7, 10), as is customary still in the East (Tavernier, *Voyage,* i, 253). The first kings, Saul (1 Sam. ix, 16; x, 1; xv, 1, 17) and David (1 Sam. xvi, 12 sq.; 2 Sam. ii, 4; v, 3; xii, 7), also Solomon (1 Kings i, 34, 39; v, 1—so likewise Absalom unlawfully, 2 Sam. xix, 11), were regularly anointed by a prophet or the high-priest; but in later times this was done only in the case of Josiah, whom the priesthood restored to the throne in place of the usurping Athaliah (2 Kings xi, 12), and Jehoahaz his son, whom the people raised to the throne (2 Kings xxiii, 30), besides Jehu of the kingdom of Israel, who established a new dynasty (2 Kings ix, 1 sq.); the principle apparently being in these cases to supply the lack of the hereditary right. The *Anointed of Jehovah* (מְשִׁיחַ יְהֹוָה), or simply the *Anointed,* accordingly appears (in the sacred style) as the official title of the regular sovereign (1 Sam. ii, 10, 35; xvi, 6; xxiv, 6; xxvi, 16, 23; 2 Sam. xix, 22; xxii, 51; Psa. ii, 2; Lam. iv, 20, etc.). No other ceremony of investiture seems to have been enjoined; although we occasionally find a popular assembly (1 Sam. x, 24; 1 Kings i, 25, 39; 2 Kings ix, 13; xi, 13; 2 Chron. xxiii, 11; comp. Josephus, *War,* i, 33, 9), a coronation (2 Kings xi, 12), music (1 Kings i, 40), and thank-offerings (1 Kings i, 24). The royal beast of burden is also mentioned (1 Kings i, 38). See Fort. Scacchi *Dissert. de inaugurat. regum Israel.* in Ugolini *Thesaur.* vol. xxxii. Regal costumes, consisting of costly and elaborate garments, were also used (at least armlets, 2 Sam. i, 19; 1 Macc. x, 20, 62; xi, 5; xiv, 43), in accompaniment with the simple diadem (נֵזֶר, 2 Sam. i, 10; 2 Kings xi, 12), jewelled crown (עֲטָרָה, 2 Sam. xi, 30; Cant. iii, 11; comp. Ezek. xxi, 26; 1 Macc. x, 20), the sceptre (שֵׁבֶט), and the throne (כִּסֵּא). See each word. Later occurs the purple mantle (1 Macc. vi, 15; x, 20, 62; xiv, 43; comp. Acts xii, 21).

The income of the Israelitish kings, with which they defrayed the expenses of their court and administration, was derived from voluntary but (as still in the East; see Kämpfer, *Amœn.* p. 95) valuable presents from their subjects in Palestine and the dependencies (1 Sam. x, 27; xvi, 20; 2 Sam. viii, 2, 11; 1 Kings x, 25; comp. Herod. iii, 87, 97; Ælian, *V. H.* i, 31; Heeren, *Ideen,* I, i, 225 sq., 483), from public domains and royal possessions, consisting of lands, vineyards, and olive-yards (1 Sam. viii, 14; 1 Chron. xxvii, 26 sq.; 2 Chron. xxvi, 10; comp. Josephus, *Ant.* vi, 13, 10; xiv, 10, 6), which sometimes fell to the crown by confiscation of private property (1 Kings xxi, 16 sq.; comp. Ezek. xlvi, 18; see Kämpfer, *ut sup.* p. 96), from monopolies (1 Kings x, 11 sq., 26 sq.; Amos vii, 1), from public services (1 Kings v, 13; ix, 21; comp. 1 Sam. viii, 13), and from regular taxes in kind (comp. 1 Sam. viii, 15; xvii, 25), which were farmed by head collectors (Isa. xvi, 1; Eccles. ii, 8). At times there is mention of an extraordinary levy upon personal property (2 Kings xxiii, 35); and the king also claimed a share of the booty obtained in war (2 Sam. viii, 11 sq.). See ASSESSMENT. Hence came the at times so considerable royal treasures (1 Kings x, 21; xiv, 26; 2 Kings xiv, 14), the rich wardrobes (2 Kings x, 22), the palaces and parks (1 Kings vii, 9; xix, 2; 2 Kings xxi, 18; xxv, 4; Jer. xxxix, 4; lii, 7; Cant. viii, 11), the sumptuously served table (1 Kings iv, 22 sq.; comp. Dan. v, 1 sq.; Esth. i, 3 sq.), to which it was esteemed a great distinction to be invited as a regular guest (2 Sam. ix, 7; see Morier, *Second Journey*, p. 148; Rosenmüller, *Morgenl.* iii, 163; comp. 2 Kings xxv, 29; Dan. i, 5; Herod. iii, 132; Heeren, *Ideen*, I, i, 217). An especial mark of royal luxury was a well-stocked harem (2 Sam. v, 13; 1 Kings xi, 1 sq.; xx, 3; comp. Quint. Curt. iii, 3, 24; Athen. xii, 514; Plutarch, *Artax.* c. 43), which was guarded by eunuchs, and descended to the succeeding king (2 Sam. xii, 8; comp. Herod. iii, 68; the regulation in Deut. xvii, 17 was interpreted as a limit of eighteen wives, Schickard, *Jus. reg.* p. 175). See HAREM. To aspire to a connection with this was equivalent to being a pretender to the throne (2 Sam. xvi, 22; 1 Kings ii, 21 sq.; comp. Movers, *Phönic.* i, 491). See ABSALOM. Among the holidays, the day of the king's birth or ascension was prominent (Hos. vii, 5; Matt. xiv, 6; comp. Gen. xl, 20; Herod. i, 133; ix, 109; Josephus, *Ant.* vii, 3, 1). Music at court and table is early mentioned (2 Sam. xix, 35; Eccles. ii, 8). Kings expressed their favor by rich presents, especially of arms and apparel [see GIFT]; and on royal festive days malefactors were pardoned or their punishment was postponed (1 Sam. xi, 13; 2 Sam. xix, 22 sq.; comp. Gen. xl, 20; see Philo, ii, 529). It was, however, a still more distinguished honor when the king invited any one to sit at his right hand (1 Kings ii, 19; comp. Sueton. *Nero*, 13; Wetstein, *N. T.* i, 456). The reverence paid to the monarch was very great (Prov. xxiv, 21); persons fell prostrate in his presence, so as to touch the forehead to the earth (1 Sam. xxiv, 9; xxv, 23; 2 Sam. ix, 6; xix, 18; even females of royal rank did the same, 1 Kings i, 16), dismounted in the street on meeting him (1 Sam. xxv, 23), and greeted him with salvos in the streets and at audiences (Dan. ii, 4; iii, 9; comp. Josephus, *War*, ii, 1, 1; see Rosenmüller, *Morgenl.* iv, 350). A high notion was entertained of his sagacity (2 Sam. xiv, 17; xix, 27; comp. Rosenmüller, *Morgenl.* iii, 142 sq.). His entrance into a city was signalized by pomp (2 Kings ix, 13; 1 Sam. xviii, 6 sq.; comp. Josephus, *Ant.* xvi, 2, 1). Of the *rank* of the early Hebrew kings of course nothing can be particularly said; but in later times those created by the Romans held the honor of the senatorial order (comp. Josephus, *Ant.* xiv, 10, 6). Whether in their edicts the Israelitish monarchs, like the Persian (Ezra iv, 18; vii, 24), Syrian (1 Macc. x, 19; xi, 31; xv, 19), and Egyptian (3 Macc. iii, 14; vii, 2), issued their edicts in the *plural* number (see Fromann, *Opusc.* i, 202 sq.), is uncertain (comp. Theodoret, *Quæst. in Genes.* 19). Any infringement of the regal majesty was followed by the death penalty (1 Kings xxi, 10), or if perpetrated by a member of the royal family, it incurred an ignominious expulsion from court (2 Sam. xiv, 24, 25). In general Hebrew kings were quite as popular as other Oriental monarchs (Esth. i, 14; iv, 11; Herod. i, 99; iii, 140; Diod. Sic. ii, 21; iii, 47; Agatharch. ed. Hudson, i, 63; Strabo, xvii, 821; Harmer, ii, 95; Lüdecke, *Beschr. d. türk. Reichs*, p. 276), often exhibited themselves in the midst of their subjects (2 Sam. xix, 8: 1 Kings xx, 39; xxii, 10; 2 Kings vi, 26; vii, 17; Jer. xxxviii, 7), and were affable with them (1 Kings iii, 15; 2 Kings vi, 26 sq.; viii, 3 sq., etc.), even to the extent of personal intercourse (1 Kings xxi, 2 sq.; for later indications, see the Mishna, *Sanhedr.* ii, 2 sq.). After their death the kings were laid in royal sepulchres (those of Judah in Jerusalem) (1 Kings ii, 10; xi, 43; xiv, 31, etc.), but the wicked ones were sometimes denied this honor (2 Chron. xxviii, 27 [? xxvi, 23]), which, nevertheless, does not argue the adoption of a death-tribunal on the Israelitish monarchs (Rosenmüller,

Morgenl. iii, 269 sq.), after the Egyptian custom (Diod. Sic. i, 22). The consorts of deceased kings remained in high honor, and even held the title of queen-mother (גְּבִירָה, *mistress*, 1 Kings xv, 13; 2 Kings x, 13; Jer. xiii, 18; xxix, 2). The title "king" was applied to the princes of the royal house as well (Jer. xvii, 20; comp. 2 Chron. xxxii, 4). Monarchs expressed their regard for each other by rich presents (1 Kings x, 2) and diplomatic embassies, the latter to convey especially their well-wishes and compliments (2 Sam. xx, 2; 2 Kings xx, 12 sq.; comp. Herod, vi, 39). See SALUTATION.

The following *official courtiers* are mentioned: (1.) *Chief major-domo* or *head palace-marshal* (נָגִיד עַל הַבַּיִת or אֲשֶׁר עַל הַבַּיִת, 1 Kings iv, 6; xviii, 3; 2 Kings xxiii, 18; xix, 2; Isa. xxii, 15), who directed the court state (Kämpfer, p. 78), but was also occupied with civil duties. Among his subordinates were the palace doorkeepers (שֹׁעֲרִים, 2 Kings vii, 11). (2.) *Chief bailiff* (אֲשֶׁר עַל הַמַּס, 2 Sam. xx, 24; 1 Kings iv, 6; xii, 18; comp. xi, 28). (3.) *Chief warder of the wardrobe* (שֹׁמֵר עַל הַמֶּלְתָּחָה, 2 Kings x, 22, or שֹׁמֵר הַבְּגָדִים, 2 Kings xxii, 14; 2 Chron. xxxiv, 22). (4.) *Superintendent of the exchequer and lands* (שֹׁמֵר הָרְכוּשׁ, 1 Chron. xxvii, 25 sq.), who had the oversight of the royal herds and domains (perhaps the ἐπίτροπος of Luke viii, 3). Similar were the financial officers of Solomon in the twelve districts (נִצָּבִים, 1 Kings iv, 7 sq.). The *chamberlains* proper were usually eunuchs (2 Kings viii, 6; Jer. lii, 25); among whom probably was the cup-bearer (מַשְׁקֶה, 1 Kings x, 5; comp. Josephus, *Ant.* xv, 17, 4, xiv, 11, 4; xvi, 8, 1; see Kämpfer, p. 81 sq.). A kind of chamberlain or *valet* is apparently designated in Jer. lii, 25; 2 Kings xxv, 19 (אֲנָשִׁים מֵרֹאֵי פְנֵי הַמֶּלֶךְ), unless the expression indicates generally the highest officers of the court and state. What official is denoted in Jer. li, 60 (שַׂר מְנוּחָה) is doubtful; Hitzig has perhaps conjectured rightly, the *field-marshal*. Finally, here belong the royal life-guard, who had to keep watch of the castle or palace (2 Kings xi, 5), but also saw the royal mandates executed in cases of capital punishment (2 Sam. xv, 1). See CHERETHITE.

See generally W. Schickard, *Jus. regium Hebræor.* (Tübing. 1621, with notes by J. B. Carpzov, Lips. 1674; also in Ugolini *Thesaur.* vol. xxiv); Carpzov, *Appar. Crit.* p. 52 sq.; Michaelis, *Mos. Recht*, i, 298 sq.; Jahn, *Archäol.* II, ii, 218 sq.; Paulsen, *Regier. d. Morgenländ.* (Altona, 1755); Otho, *Lex. Rabb.* p. 575. See KING.

Monasteria is a term which was sometimes used in the early Church to designate the places of worship belonging to the Egyptian Therapeutæ. Thus Eusebius (*Hist. Eccles.* lib. ii, c. 177) uses it (Μοναστήριον). Afterwards, in the Middle Ages, it became usual to give this name (monasteria) to large parochial and cathedral churches; hence the word *minster* (q. v.). See Riddle, *Christian Antiquities*, p. 705.

Monastery (Latin, *Monasticum*; Greek, Μοναστήριον; from μοναστήρ, equivalent to μοναστής, a solitary, a *monk*; from μονάζειν, to be alone, to live in solitude; from μόνος, alone) is the name of a residence of persons, male or female, who have bound themselves by monastic vows. We confine this article to Christian monasteries of the Western world, and refer for pre-Christian monasticism to the article MONASTICISM; and for Oriental and Russian monasteries to the article MONKS, EASTERN.

1. Monasteries received various distinctive appellations, derived from the names of the founders of the order; from that of the patron or guardian saint to whom they were dedicated; from the site which they occupied; from the peculiar design of the foundation or occupation of the monks; from the particular color of the habit worn within the walls, and other circumstances. See MONK.

To one or other of the four leading orders a monastery was usually referred: (1) the Order of *Basil*, including all the Greek monks and Carmelites; (2) the Order of *Augustine*, in its three classes—canons regular, monks, and hermits, together with the congregations of nuns; (3) the Order of *Benedict*, with its various branches, male and female; (4) the Order of *Francis*, with its numerous ramifications.

The common appellation of monasteries are the following: (1) Μοναστήριον, *monastery*, as being the residence of *monasterium*, μονάζοντες, μοναχοί, μοναχαί, μόναι, or religious solitaries. (2) *Claustrum* or *claustra*, cloister; literally, a place of confinement. This was the prevailing name in the West, and the choice of the name indicates the strict seclusion which prevailed. (3) *Cœnobium*, a common dwelling-place. (4) *Laura*, λαῦρα or λάβρα, which is the old name for the residence of the anchorites. It appears to denote a narrow, confined, and inconvenient abode. According to Epiphanius (*Hæres.* p. 69), it was the name of a narrow, dirty street in Alexandria, whence it was applied to the wretched habitations of anchorites in the Thebaid, Palestine, and Syria. By Latin writers *laura* is usually employed in contradistinction from *cœnobia*. (5) Σεμνεῖον, which is the name applied by Philo to the abodes or places of resort of the Therapeutæ, and hence it was sometimes given to monasteries. The Latins retained the word *sumnium* (simnium, or scimnium). (6) Ἀσκητήριον, i. e. ἀσκητῶν καταγωγή, a place of religious exercise or contemplation. We find various words of similar form to the Latin *asceterium;* such as *archisterium*, *architerium*, *arcisterium*, *architrium*, etc. (7) Φοντιστήριον is the same as ἀσκήτηριον, but with special reference to meditation and spiritual exercises. Monasteries retained this name chiefly on account of their schools. (8) Ἡσυχαστήριον, *place of silence and repose.* This term was applicable to those monasteries in which silence was, to a certain extent, imposed on the members. (9) *Conventus*, a convent, in reference to the common life of the inmates. (10) Ἡγουμενεῖον, denoting properly the residence of the president (ἡγούμενος or ἡγουμένη), was used for the whole building. (11) Μάνδρα, a word which means *a pen*, or *sheepfold*, and refers to the residence of the anchorites in remote districts, or to their congregating together in flocks. Hence the president was sometimes called *archimandrite*. (12) Lastly, the Syrians and Arabians, almost without exception, used the word *daira, dairon* (Arab. *deir*), to denote a monastery. The word is derived from another, which is especially applied to the tents and other habitations of the nomadic tribes (see Du Cange, in the *Glossarium mediæ et infimæ Latinitatis*, under the respective words).

The word *monastery*, in a most strict acceptation, is confined in its modern and Western application to the residences of monks, or of nuns of the cognate orders (as the Benedictine), and, as such, it comprises two great classes, the *Abbey* and the *Priory*. The former name was given only to establishments of the highest rank, governed by an abbot, who was commonly assisted by a prior, sub-prior, and other minor functionaries. An abbey always included a church, and the English word *Minster*, although it has now lost its specific application, has its origin in the Saxon and German *Münster* (Lat. *monasterium*). A *Priory* supposed a less extensive and less numerous community. It was governed by a prior, and was generally, although by no means uniformly, at least in later times, subject to the jurisdiction of an abbey. Many priories possessed extensive territorial domains, and of these not a few became entirely independent. The distinction of abbey and priory is found equally among the Benedictine nuns. In the military orders, the name of *Commandery* and *Preceptory* corresponded with those of abbey and priory in the monastic orders. The establishments of the Mendicant, and, in general, of the modern orders, are sometimes, though less properly, called monasteries. Their

more characteristic appellation is *Friary* or *Convent*, and they are commonly distinguished into *Professed Houses* (called also *Residences*), *Novitiates*, and *Colleges*, or *Scholastic Houses*. The names of the superiors of such houses differ in the different orders. The common name is *Rector*, but in some orders the superior is called *Guardian* (as in the Franciscan), or *Master, Major, Father Superior*, etc. The houses of females—except in the Benedictine or Cistercian orders—are called indifferently *Convent* and *Nunnery*, the head of which is styled *Mother Superior* or *Reverend Mother*. The name *Cloister* properly means the enclosure; but it is popularly used to designate, sometimes the arcaded ambulatory which runs around the inner court of the building, sometimes in the more general sense of the entire building, when it may be considered as synonymous with *Convent*.

2. During the persecutions in the early ages of Christianity many believers sought shelter in the mountains and deserts, where they gradually acquired a taste for solitude and devotion. In process of time disorders arose among the various monastic orders, and it was found expedient to collect the monks into large societies, living under a common government, and within the walls of separate buildings, appropriated to the purpose. In the year 340 Pachomius built a large *cœnobium*, or monastery, on an island of the Nile, and the example was soon extensively followed. In these establishments, which in some places were very large, the members lived in strict subordination to their superiors.

The monastery was divided into several parts, and directors were appointed over each. Ten monks were subject to one who was called *decanus*, or dean, from his presiding over ten; every hundred had another superior, called *centenarius*, from his presiding over one hundred. Above these were *patres*, or fathers of the monasteries, called also *abbates*, abbot, from the Hebræo-Greek word ἀββᾶ, a father; and *hegumeni*, presidents, and *archimandrites*, from *mandra*, a sheepfold, they being, as it were, the keepers or rulers of these sacred folds in the Church. The business of the deans was to exact every man's daily task, and bring it to the *œconomus*, or steward of the house, who himself gave a monthly account to the father of them all (Bingham, *Origines Ecclesiasticæ*, bk. vii, ch. iii, § 11).

The rules and regulations of these houses varied according to the difference of the founders, and other circumstances. To give some impression of the routine of a conventual house, we recite the rule of St. Benedict as in operation: "The abbot represented Christ; called all his monks to council in important affairs, and adopted the advice he thought best: he required obedience without delay, silence, humility, patience, manifestation of secret faults, contentment with the meanest things and employments. *Abbot* selected by the whole society; his life and prudence to be the qualifications, and to be addressed *dominus* or *pater*. *Prior* appointed by the abbot; deposable for disobedience. A *dean* set over every ten monks in larger houses. The monks to observe general silence; no scurrility, idle words, or exciting to laughter; to keep head and eyes inclined downwards; to rise to church two hours after midnight; to leave the church together at a sign from the superior. No property; distribution according to every one's necessities. To serve weekly, and by turns, at the kitchen and table. On leaving their weeks, both he that left it and he that began it to wash the feet of the others; and on Saturday to clean all the plates and the linen which wiped the others' feet. To render the dishes clean and whole to the cellarer, who was to give them to the new hebdomary. These officers to have drink and food above the common allowance, that they might serve cheerfully. *Daily routine*—Work from prime till near ten o'clock, from Easter to October; from ten till near twelve, reading. After refection at twelve, the meridian or sleep, unless any one preferred reading. After nones, labor again till the evening. From October to

Lent, reading till eight A.M., then tierce, and afterwards labor till nones; after refection, reading or psalmody. In Lent, reading till tierce; doing what was ordered till ten: delivery of books at this season made. Senior to go around the house, and see that the monks were not idle. On Sunday, all reading except the officers. Workmen in the house to labor for the common profit. If possible—to prevent evagation—water, a mill, garden, oven, and all other mechanical shops, to be within or attached to the house. *Refection* in silence, and reading Scripture during meals: what was wanted to be asked for by a sign. Reader to be appointed for the week. Two different dishes at dinner, with fruit. One pound of bread a day for both dinner and supper. No meat but to the sick. Three quarters of a pint of wine per day. From Holyrood-day to Lent, dining at nones; in Lent, till Easter, at six o'clock; from Easter to Pentecost at six; and all summer, except on Wednesdays and Fridays, then at nones. Collation or spiritual lecture every night before compline (after supper); and compline finished, silence. [See BREVIARY; COMPLINE.] Particular abstinence in Lent from meat, drink, and sleep, and especial gravity. Rule mitigated to children and the aged, who have liberty to anticipate the hour of eating. *Dormitory*, light to be burning in. To sleep clothed, with their girdles on, the young and old intermixed. Monks travelling to say the canonical hours wherever they happened to be. When staying out beyond a day, not to eat abroad without the abbot's leave. Before setting out on a journey to have the previous prayers of the house, and upon return to pray for pardon of excesses on the way. No letters or presents to be received without the abbot's permission. Precedence according to the time of profession. Elders to call the juniors brothers; the seniors to call the elders *nonnos*. When two monks met, the junior was to ask benediction from the senior; and when he passed by the junior was to rise and give him his seat, and not to sit down till he bade him. Impossible things ordered by the superior to be humbly represented to him; but if he persisted, the assistance of God to be relied on for the execution of them. Not to defend or excuse one another's faults. No blows or excommunication without the abbot's permission. Mutual obedience, but no preference of a private person's commands to those of the superiors. Prostration at the feet of the superiors as long as they were angry. *Strangers* to be received with prayer, the kiss of peace, prostration, and washing their feet, as of Christ, whom they represented; then to be led to prayer; the Scripture read to them; after which the prior might break his fast (except on a high fast). Abbot's kitchen and the visitors' separate, that guests coming in at unseasonable hours might not disturb the monks. *Porter* to be a wise old man, able to give and receive an answer; who was to have a cell near the gate, and a junior for his companion. *Church* to be used only for prayer. *Admission*—Novices to be tried by denials and hard usage before admission. A year of probation. Rule to be read to them in the interim every fourth month. Admitted by a petition laid upon the altar, and prostration at the feet of all the monks. Parents to offer their children by wrapping their hands in the pall of the altar; promising to leave nothing to them (that they might have no temptation to quit the house); and if they gave anything with them, to reserve the use of it during their lives. Priests requesting admission to be tried by delays; to sit near the abbot; not to exercise sacerdotal functions without leave, and conform to the rule. *Discipline*—Upon successless admonition and public reprehension, excommunication; and, in failure of this, corporal punishment. For light faults, the smaller excommunication, or eating alone after the others had done. For great faults, separation from the table, prayers, and society, and neither himself nor his food to receive the benediction: those who joined him or spoke to him to be themselves excommunicated. The abbot to send seniors to persuade him to humility and

making satisfaction. The whole congregation to pray for the incorrigible, and if unsuccessful, to proceed to expulsion. No person expelled to be received after the third expulsion. Children to be corrected with discretion, by fasting or whipping" ("Sanctorum Patrum Regulæ Monasticæ," in Fosbrooke's *British Monachism*, p. 109). By the strict law of the Church, called the law of cloister or enclosure, it is forbidden to all except members of the order to enter a monastery; and in almost all the orders admission of females to the monasteries of men is denied. Yet must they have been at times admitted, if we may believe the accusations brought against the chastity of monastics, especially since the Middle Ages. In the Greek Church the law of enclosure is far more rigidly enforced than in the West. Thus in the celebrated enclosure of Mount Athos, not only women, but all animals of the female sex are rigorously excluded.

3. In the East monasteries are supposed to have existed about the time of Christ's stay on earth. See MONASTICISM. In the West the first monasteries were founded by St. Martin of Tours, about 360, at Ligugé, near Poictiers, and at Marmoutier. The chiefs only of these monasteries were in orders, and women who entered the monasteries were permitted to relinquish the monastic state and marry down to the 6th century. See CELIBACY. The regular life of the community was introduced by Eusebius of Vercelli about 350. Theodoret mentions a large number of monasteries, both in the East and West, some founded by St. Basil about 358, others by St. Augustine in Africa about 390, and some by St. Ambrose at Milan in 377. On British soil St. Patrick is supposed to have started the first monasteries near the opening of the 6th century, when he flourished as bishop of Ireland. During thirty-three years he worked at the conversion of the people to the Christian faith, and filled the island with schools and monasteries, the sites of which are still to be distinguished by the round towers that served as belfries for the conventual churches. The prefix "kill" is the Latin "cella," and marks the "religio loci" of innumerable localities in Ireland; and well has Macaulay said that "without these Christianizing institutions the population would have been made up of beasts of burden and beasts of prey." A missionary spirit has always distinguished the Irish Church. Its monks, as hardy navigators, established themselves in the Hebrides, with Iona for their capital, and passed over to the western districts of Britain; whence they settled upon the coasts of Brittany, together with the British population expelled by Saxon invasion in the 4th and 5th centuries. It was a province of Gaul that had remained comparatively free from Roman rule, and preserved old Celtic habits, while the rest of Gaul was Romanized. The missionary spirit of his race impelled Columban to settle in Gaul, and to found the monastery of Luxeuil, in Burgundy, the mother of numerous conventual establishments, and the capital of Monastic Gaul (Milman, *Latin Christianity*, iv, 5). He has been termed the Irish Benedict, and various legends are connected with his name, which are only reproductions of Benedictine fable. Though he treated the Roman see with respect, he never sacrificed his own independence of opinion to its authority; and he gave to the see of Jerusalem precedence in point of honor (*Ep.* v, sec. 18). He also gave his monks a rule, but its excessive severity prevented its extended use; and it was superseded by the Benedictine rule, which finally became the universal law of monasticism. The County Down monastery, on the north-west coast of Ireland, and Clonfert were towns of monks rather than monasteries. The former contained more than three thousand under religious vow in the time of Patricius. The founder having been accompanied by learned monks from Gaul and Lerin, these monasteries soon became renowned for their sound learning, as well as for a pure faith. In England all the most ancient sees have been established upon pre-existing monastic foundations. At

the close of the 5th century Dubricius, bishop of Caerleon, founded Llandaff monastery. St. David, his successor at Caerleon, built the monastery at St. David's, a site indicated to him by St. Patrick, the wild promontory on which the cathedral now stands. He also rebuilt the convent at Glastonbury; and it was in honor of St. David that the privilege of asylum was indulged to sites in any way connected with his name—a privilege that may occasionally have secured innocence against oppression and wrong, but which became intolerable from abuse in later years. St. Asaph, in its origin, was a convent of nine hundred and sixty-five monks, founded at the end of the 6th century by Kentigern, himself a monk and missionary bishop among the southern Scots and Picts. Bangor, on the Dee, was founded by Ittud, a fellow-disciple with St. David at St. Germain of Auxerre. It contained within its "wide precincts" a whole army of monks. Yet it was only a little more than half the size of the Irish establishment of the same name. The diocese of Bangor owes its origin to the foundation of Daniel, a disciple of Dubricius, at the commencement of the 6th century. Winchester, first established as a monastery by Cenwalch, king of Wessex, under a promise to his dying father, was made an episcopal see by the same king about the middle of the 7th century. Ripon was a monastery founded by Alfrid, king of Northumberland, having Wilfrid for its first abbot. He repaired and beautified the cathedral at York, of which see he became bishop, and built the priory of Hexham in the most elaborate style; the church was said to have been the most beautiful on this side of the Alps. Wilfrid was the first of a series of clerical and monastic architects who for several centuries made Anglican ecclesiastical buildings the glory of Europe. It is curious to find that the churchwarden's sovereign cure for all defects was also introduced by him: "Parietes lavans . . . alba calce mirifice dealbavit" (Montalembert, iv, 235). Ely was at first a double monastery for monks and nuns of the foundation of Ethelreda, queen of Northumberland: "virgo bis nupta." Columba, like Pelagius, is the classical equivalent for a Celtic name. He is not to be confounded with Columban, the Celtic founder of Luxeuil. Columba (born A.D. 521, died A.D. 597), after founding thirty-seven monasteries in Ireland, passed over to the Hebrides, selected Iona, the most desolate of those desolate islands, flat-lying and sandy, as the site of a monastery, and made it the "glory of the West," and the cradle of the civilization of North Britain. See IONA. From Iona, Aidan went forth as the apostle and bishop of the Northumbrians; and, having found a site as desolate and unattractive as Iona on Lindisfarne (since called Holy Island), there founded a monastery, which became the mother-church of all the provinces north of the Humber. The character of sanctity impressed upon it by St. Aidan long distinguished it; and its abbots, like himself, mostly became bishops of the northern provinces. His great and benevolent character has been nobly drawn by Bede (H. E. iii, 3, 5, 17). Hilda, foundress (A.D. 658) and abbess of Whitby, received the veil from him. The feminine love of whatever is beautiful in nature led to the selection of a most noble site for her abbey, and contrasts strongly with the masculine austerity and contempt for æsthetics that led the Celtic monks to choose Iona and Lindisfarne. The influence of Hilda was everywhere felt: kings and princes sought her counsel; she was a "mother" by endearment to the very poorest who received alms at the abbey gate. Bede (H. E. iv, 23) speaks in enthusiastic terms of her tender care and administrative tact. A convent for monks as well as nuns was under her rule, and Bede notes that six prelates, eminent for their piety and learning, received their training at Whitby under her eye. To Hilda also we are indebted for having drawn the earliest Saxon poet, Cædmon, from his obscurity. He was a common herdsman, but at her persuasion became a monk. He anticipated Milton in

taking as a theme for poetic song the fall of Satan and the sin of our first parents. The foundation of Wearmouth Abbey by Benedict Biscop, a monk of Lindisfarne (A.D. 665), was remarkable for the introduction of painted glass. Workmen were brought from the Continent, who instructed the Saxon monks in the mystery of their craft (Milman, Latin Christianity, iv, 4). The sister-foundation, Jarrow, endowed with a domain granted by Egfrid, was the monastery in which the venerable Bede had his cell. In South Britain the most ancient monastery was that founded by Augustine at Canterbury, and placed under Benedictine rule. The deed of gift whereby king Ethelbert conveyed the site (A.D. 605) is, according to Palgrave, the earliest existing document of the public records of England. Gregory followed up the mission with a colony of monks, who also imported all that could be required for the observance of the Romish ritual. Thus the subjugation of England to the see of Rome was the work of the Benedictine monks. One of their number, Mellitus, first bishop of London, founded Westminster Abbey. The first metropolitan recognised by all England was Theodore, an Oriental monk, a native of Tarsus, and placed in the see of Canterbury by pope Vitalianus, A.D. 668. The council held at Whitby on the subject of Easter (A.D. 664) showed that strong traces still remained of the Oriental tendencies of the British Church; and an African monk, Adrian, was sent with the bishop elect as a safeguard and trusty envoy: "ne quid ille contrarium veritati et fidei, Græcorum more, in ecclesiam cui præcesset, introduceret" (Bede, H. E. iv, 1). To him is due the creation of the parochial system, by persuading the territorial proprietors to build and endow churches, retaining the advowson in their own hands. The Church-rate is of co-ordinate date. Theodore was a laborious student, and, with the assistance of Adrian, he gradually made the monasteries of England schools of sound learning. The principal sees having sprung from monastic origin, the canons were naturally monks. After the Conquest disputes arose between the secular and the regular, i. e. between the parochial and monastic clergy; and an attempt was made by Walkelin, bishop of Winchester, to supersede the monastic chapter by a body of forty secular clergy. Lanfranc, however, vigorously opposed the change, and obtained from pope Alexander a constitution in confirmation of the capitular rights of the monasteries affected (Fleury, H. E. lxi, 53; comp. also Soames, Latin Ch. during the Anglo-Saxon Times [Lond. 1848, 12mo]; and Soames, The Anglo-Saxon Ch. [Lond. 1856, 12mo, 4th ed.]).

4. In 550 the rule of St. Basil, followed by all Greek monasteries, was introduced at Rome; but St. Benedict gradually absorbed all other monks into his great rule. In 585 St. Columban's rule of prayer, reading, and manual labor was founded in Gaul. In 649 the Monothelite persecution in the East transferred many monks to the Western Church, and in the 8th century the Iconoclasts were the cause of a still larger assimilation. In the 13th century St. Dominic prevailed on women to observe a stricter rule. The first written rule—that of St. Basil, bishop of Cæsarea in the 4th century, who embodied the traditional usages, was derived from that of Pachomius, and aimed at the combination of prayer and manual toil; it was modified by St. Benedict, the patriarch of Western monks, but in the 11th century was still vigorous in Naples. Polydore Vergil says that in 373 St. Basil first enacted the triple vows of chastity, poverty, and obedience. In 410 Lerins was founded. The Benedictine rule spread rapidly in Italy before his death in 543. Maurus and Placidus extended it in France and Sicily; others introduced it into Spain, where monasteries are said to have existed in 380; and in less than two centuries all the monastic orders in the West were affiliated to it. St. Columban built the first abbey in England in 563, as he had done in Ireland; in the latter instance it was preceded only by

the St. Bridget's cell at Kildare, which was famous in 521, being established probably by a pupil of St. Patrick. In 802 the Council of Aix-la-Chapelle decreed that the Benedictine rule should be universally adopted. From the 10th century it put forth branches: Clugny in 910, under its abbots, embraced the rule; so did the Camaldolesi in 1020, from St. Romuald; the Cistercians in 1098, from St. Robert; the Carthusians in 1080, from St. Bruno; the Valombrosans in 1060, from John Gualberte; the Celestines in 1294, from Peter di Merona; and the Olivetans in 1319. At Bangor in 603 there was a monastery with seven portions, each consisting of three hundred monks. with their provosts or rectors. Benedict Biscop in 677 built the monasteries at Wearmouth and Yarrow of stone; and in 1035 Lanfranc united all the English abbeys into one congregation. St. Maur in 1621 was the last instance of its reform. The lands possessed by monasteries were held under the same tenure as all other land; and, till a comparatively late period, the abbots themselves led their quota of troops into the field. In the time of Charlemagne fourteen monasteries of the empire furnished their proportion of soldiers. In 982 the bishop of Augsburg and the abbot of Fulda were killed in the same battle. Charles Martel was opposed by troops collected and headed by an abbot of Fontenelle.

Monasteries were called *ingenua* if exempt from their foundation, or *libera* if the grant or privilege had been made subsequently. Those which were not exempt were compelled to render to the bishop obedience; annual fees called jus synodale, or circadas; procurations, or the provision of entertainment; solemn processions, and the right of celebrating mass in their minsters. All abbots, however, despite their repugnance, certainly after the 9th century, were compelled to make the profession of canonical obedience to the diocesan when receiving his benediction, and this implied his right to give holy orders, consecrate churches, altars, and cemeteries, and grant chrism and dismissory letters when the abbots travelled out of the diocese.

5. In their first institution, and in their subsequent uses, there can be no doubt that monasteries were among the most remarkable instances of Christian munificence, and they certainly were, in the so-called Dark Ages, among the beneficial adaptations of the talents of Christians to pious and charitable ends. The foundation of the monastery was the dictate of religious motives in the youth of the Church, but the reward of piety was temporal also; the estates of the founder were improved, the vassals educated, order introduced, the sick and aged tended, and handicraft and useful arts taught. "The services," says Blunt, "that monasticism has rendered to civilization in the transition of society from ancient times to the Middle Ages have been most important. Monks were the skilled agriculturists of the period; and many terms in rural life, and in the fauna and botany of all Northern Europe, may be traced back through them to Greek and Latin terms; e. g. 'hawky,' οἶκι, harvest-home; and 'ranny,' *aranea*, a shrew-mouse; 'chervil,' χηρόφυλλον. The belladonna, which is now found indigenous, was introduced first among the pharmaceutical herbs of the convent-gardens, for the monks were the physicians of the period. As men of letters also and energetic missionaries they kept the lamp of knowledge and civilization from expiring in the very darkest periods; and whatever was done in the way of educating the young was carried on within the walls of the monastery." Monasteries, indeed, were the sole preservers of learning in the Dark Ages. The Benedictines, bound by the rules of their order to mental as well as bodily labor, performed a work that has been of priceless value. That anything at all has come down to us from classical antiquity is owing in great part to their diligence as transcribers. Gerbert, an abbot, and afterwards pope Silvester II (999), speaks of his care in collecting books, and of the host of copiers that were found in every town: "Tu sai con quanta premura io

raccolga da ogni parte libri; tu sai quanti scrittiri e nelle città e nelle ville d'Italia in ogni luogo s'incontrino" (Muratori, *Lit. It.* III, i, 29). Desiderius, abbot of Monte Casino, and subsequently pope Victor III, employed many copyists, "antiquarii," as they were called (Muratori, *Stor.* IV, ch. xxviii; Mabillon, *Act. Bened.*). Three offsets from the Benedictine stock have also rendered invaluable services to literature: the Clugniac monks, dating from the early part of the 10th century; the Carthusians (1084); and the Cistercians (1090). They created a craving for the luxury of books, beautifully written and sumptuously illuminated; and libraries, gradually increasing in size, soon grew up from their labors. "It was their pride to collect, and their business to transcribe books" (Hallam, *Literature of the Middle Ages*, i, 82); and their collections were the "germ whence a second and more glorious civilization" should in due time spring (Macaulay, *Hist. of England*, ch. i). But the evils which grew out of these societies more than counterbalanced the good. Being often exempted from all civil or foreign ecclesiastical authority, they became hotbeds of insubordination to the state and of corruption to the Church. The temptations arising out of a state of celibacy, too often enforced in the first instance by improper means, and always bound upon the members of these societies by a religious vow, were the occasion of great scandals. Moreover, the enormous wealth with which some of them were endowed brought with it a greater degree of pride and ostentation and luxury than was becoming in Christians; and still more in those who had vowed a life of religious asceticism. Thus it came that the intrigues of the friars, the accumulation of wealth, and the decay of discipline wrought the fall of the monasteries. See MONASTICISM; MONK. The monasteries of England were the first to feel the displeasure of the outside world. Corruption had become so apparent in the 8th century as to call for the founding of the Clugniac order on British soil. But this order, in turn, though beginning in the 10th century with a strict rule, sank into luxury in the 12th; the Cistercians then started to shame them, but soon lost all moral vigor; next the Franciscan mendicants appeared, but they degenerated more completely in the first quarter of a century after their introduction into England than other orders had in three or four centuries (comp. Matt. Paris, A.D. 1243; see Brakelond, *Chron. Abb. S. Edmundi; Tho. Elmham. Hist. Mon. St. Aug. Cantuar.;* Hugh de Poitiers, *Monastère de Vezelai*). No wonder, then, that an opposition found ready utterance and prompt organization, and, led successively by the greatest of Anglican scholars and divines, as Wykeham, Fisher, Alcock, Chichely, Beckington, the countess of Salisbury, and cardinal Wolsey, claimed the monastic endowments for university foundations. "What, my lord," said Oldham to Fox in 1513, "shall we build houses and provide livelihoods for a company of bussing monks, whose end and fall we may live to see?" See REFORMATION, ENGLISH. Thus it was not reserved for the period of the Reformation to inaugurate opposition to monasteries. Their dissolution was commenced in England as early as 1312, when the Order of Templars was suppressed, and a portion of their possessions given to the Knights of St. John of Jerusalem. During the 15th century many other houses were dissolved, and their revenues transferred to the universities of Oxford and Cambridge. Henry VIII obtained an act of Parliament for the dissolution of the monasteries, and the transfer of their revenues to the crown. Rome itself had furnished a precedent for Henry's attack on the monastic institutions. About the year 1517 cardinal Wolsey was desirous of building and endowing two splendid colleges—one at Ipswich, the place of his birth; the other at Oxford, the place of his academical education. For this purpose Clement VII granted him a bull, which empowered him to visit and suppress certain monasteries. A number of these, variously stated at from nineteen to forty, were consequently dissolved, and their revenues applied by Wolsey to the purpose contemplated.

The following calculation has been made as to the number and wealth of the religious houses in England dismantled and scattered at the period of the Reformation: "The number of houses and places suppressed from first to last in England, so far as any calculations appear to have been made, seems to be as follows:

Of lesser monasteries, of which we have the valuation	374
Of greater monasteries	186
Belonging to the Hospitallers	48
Colleges	90
Hospitals	110
Chantries and free chapels	2374
Total	3182

These are in addition to the friars' houses, and those suppressed by Wolsey, and many small houses of which we have no particular account. The sum total of the clear yearly revenue of the several houses at the time of their dissolution, of which we have any account, seems to be as follows:

Of the greater monasteries	£104,919 13 3
Of all those of the lesser monasteries of which we have the valuation	29,702 1 10
Knights Hospitallers, head house in London	2,385 12 8
We have the valuation of only twenty-eight of their houses in the country	3,026 9 5
Friars' houses, of which we have the valuation	751 2 0
Total	£140,784 19 2

If proper allowances are made for the lesser monasteries and houses not included in this estimate, and for the plate, etc., which came into the hands of the king by the dissolution, and for the valuation of money at that time, which was at least six times as much as at present, and also consider that the estimate of the lands was generally supposed to be much under the real worth, we must conclude their whole revenues to have been immense. It does not appear that any exact computation has been made of the number of persons contained in the religious houses.

Those of the lesser monasteries dissolved by 27 Henry VIII were reckoned at about	10,000
If we suppose the colleges and hospitals to have contained a proportionable number, these will make about	5,347
If we reckon the number in the greater monasteries according to the proportion of their revenues, they will be about 35,000; but as, probably, they had larger allowances in proportion to their number than those of the lesser monasteries, if we abate upon that account 5000, they will then be	30,000
One for each chantry and free chapel	2,374
Total	47,721

But as there was probably more than one person to officiate in several of the free chapels, and there were other houses which are not included within this calculation, perhaps they may be computed in one general estimate at about 50,000. As there were pensions paid to almost all those of the greater monasteries, the king did not immediately come into the full enjoyment of their whole revenues; however, by means of what he did receive, he founded six new bishoprics—viz. those of Westminster (which was changed by queen Elizabeth into a deanery, with twelve prebends and a school), Peterborough, Chester, Gloucester, Bristol, and Oxford. And in eight other sees he founded deaneries and chapters, by converting the priors and monks into deans and prebendaries—viz. Canterbury, Winchester, Durham, Worcester, Rochester, Norwich, Ely, and Carlisle. He founded also the colleges of Christ Church in Oxford and Trinity in Cambridge, and finished King's College there. He likewise founded professorships of divinity, law, physic, and of the Hebrew and Greek tongues, in both the said universities. He gave the house of Gray Friars and St. Bartholomew's Hospital to the city of London, and a perpetual pension to the poor knights of Windsor, and laid out great sums in building and fortifying many ports in the channel" (Baxter, *Hist. of the Church of England*). Compare Hook, *Lives of the Arch-*

bishops of Canterbury, vol i (Lond. 1868, 8vo); Fuller, *Church Hist.* i, 115 sq.; Burnet, *Hist. of the Reformation*; Soames, *Ref. Ch. of England*, vol. i, especially the Introd.; Fosbrooke, *Brit. Monachism*, ch. i–v, and lxii; Hill, *English Monasticism, its Rise and Influence* (Lond. 1867, 8vo), p. 488 sq., 515 sq.

It is hardly necessary to state that all the Reformed churches in the 16th century discarded the practice of monachism, and suppressed monasteries as useless. In some of the German states, however, the temporalities of the suppressed monasteries were retained, and were granted at pleasure by the sovereign, to be enjoyed together with the titular dignity. In Roman Catholic countries also, as, e. g., France, Spain, Austria, and Italy, the suppression of monasteries has been more or less general in more recent times. See MONASTICISM. But, as count Montalembert has well put it in his celebrated work on the *Monks of the West* (Edinb. 1861–7, 5 vols. 8vo), "this work of spoliation, which may be said to have fairly set in with the Reformation, is now proceeding with methodical gravity." In the five years from 1830 to 1835 no less than "3000 monasteries have disappeared from the soil of Europe." In Portugal some 300 were destroyed, 200 in Poland, and the number annihilated by queen Christina of Spain, though it has never been estimated, was certainly not much smaller than in Poland. The destruction, however, has proved greatest in the recent reforms in France, and especially in Italy. The great monastery of Clairvaux, which once held St. Bernard and his five hundred monks, is now a prison with five hundred convicts in it. The celebrated abbey at Clugny, which figures so largely in the history of the Middle Ages, has been turned into stud-stables, and in 1844 the place of the high-altar was "the starting-post of the stallions." The abbey of Le Bec, in Normandy, from which Lanfranc and Anselm came forth successively to fill the see of Canterbury, has been utilized in the same fashion, and horses fatten where monks once fasted and prayed. A china manufactory is carried on in the Chartreux of Seville, and swine have taken possession of the cells in the Cistercian abbey of Cadouin. Everywhere, as the count informs us, the work of ruin proceeds. "Sometimes," says he, "the spinning-mill is installed under the roof of the ancient sanctuary. Instead of echoing night and day the praises of God, these dishonored arches too often repeat only the blasphemies and obscene cries, mingling with the shrill voice of the machinery, the grinding of the saw, or the monotonous clank of the piston." Nor is this all. John Knox has been sometimes stigmatized as a barbarian for the encouragement which he is said to have given the populace in demolishing Christian edifices where the relics of idolatry were enshrined; yet even where the excited rabble did their worst, the ivied ruin still remains to tell of a grandeur which has passed away, and to mark, for the present and other generations, the spot where their fathers prayed. But in France, it appears, the work of demolition is done much more scientifically and thoroughly. They are not content there with confiscation, plunder, profanation; they overthrow, raze from the foundation, leave not a single stone standing on another. "The empire of the East," says the count, "has not been ravaged by the Turks as France has been and still is by the band of insatiable destroyers who, after having purchased these vast constructions and immense dominions at the lowest rate, work them like quarries for sacrilegious profit. I have seen with my own eyes the capitals and columns of an abbey-church which I could name employed as so much material for the neighboring road." And again: "What remains of so many palaces raised in silence and solitude for the products of art, for the progress and pleasure of the mind, for disinterested labor? Masses of broken wall inhabited by owls and rats, shapeless remains, heaps of stones, and pools of water. Everywhere desolation, filth, and disorder" (Introduction, ch. viii). The young and free kingdom of Italy has not been slow to perceive that a sacerdotal class, with interests alien, if not antagonistic, to society and to the family, is necessarily and logically a foe to civil and political liberty. By a law enacted June 28, 1866, all monasteries and similar religious corporations in the kingdom of Italy were suppressed, their members pensioned, and their property sold and funded for the maintenance of public schools. Monte Casino and San Marco, of Florence, were alone exempted. The former is left as a venerable monument of the past; the latter is spared in honor of Savonarola and the beautiful frescos of Fra Angelico da Fiesole. This law has been executed with great rigor: and in spite of allocutions, excommunications, and all the *brutum fulmen* of the Vatican, the work of secularization is already finished. Some of the monks have gladly seized the opportunity of bettering their condition by marriage; others have returned to their homes or accepted the refuge offered by charity; but the great majority of these unfortunates, whose only crime consists in having been misplaced in chronology by being born several centuries too late, and whose habits are too fixed and inveterate to be easily changed, hire houses and live in clubs on the subsidies of the government. While in Italy and France, the two most Catholic nations, the monastic system is thus rapidly disappearing, the tendency to introduce similar institutions in Protestant countries, especially the effort of the Ritualists of the Anglican communion, under the pretence (more or less honest) of promoting Christian charities, can only be regarded as a fatal retrogression and dangerous degeneracy.

In 1870 revelations of corruption, bestiality, and cruelty in a Polish convent contributed more than all else to quicken the Protestant, and we may well say general dislike for monastic institutions. The story of Barbara Ubryk, the Polish nun, however exceptional, could not but raise a sense of horror throughout Europe, and it is not to be denied that the prejudice such an instance excites is in a great degree just. It is one thing to hear of an exceptional instance of individual cruelty; it is another thing to know that such cruelty can be practiced in the name of religion, and in institutions which, under its shelter, claim peculiar immunities. There is great force in the plea that one such case substantiated justifies the public control of all similar establishments. In England, the famous trial of "Saurin *v.* Starr" revealed what spiritual tyranny and moral degradation might be concealed in conventual institutions under the most harmless exterior. The convent which Miss Saurin entered was one of those for which the plea is advanced that they do practical service in the cause of education and charity. It is not difficult to imagine that a hotheaded Protestant might have been for the time confused if he had been taken to see Miss Saurin and her fellow-sisters patiently devoting themselves to the instruction of their scholars. Yet, whatever the technical result of the trial, it left all impartial readers with a most painful impression of the degrading and demoralizing atmosphere of the convent. And in consequence Parliament was moved to appoint, March 29, 1870, a select committee to make inquiries concerning conventual or monastic institutions in Great Britain. The result of such investigation was unfavorable in that country, and has turned popular opinion against their existence. In Poland also the Russian government has in very recent times found itself faced with a most alarming spread of treason and corruption generated and fostered in monasteries, and the days of monasticism may be said to be numbered even there. As what is said of English Christianity is so well applicable to all other Protestant countries, we quote Mr. Blunt here in conclusion of this subject: "The day of monasticism has forever set. . . . There is no longer any need for its existence, even if it could be set up again in its best condition. More than Benedictine learning sheds a ray of glory on our colleges. Our

Poor-laws render unnecessary the alms for the monastery wicket; and such doles would become a positive evil now as an encouragement to idleness and sloth. Our clergy are welcome visitors at the cottage fireside, where the monk of later days was not, with his contributions for the house. The glory of monasticism was the fidelity with which it discharged its earlier mission; the self-sacrifice with which it taught men to rise superior to the trials and calamities of life; the unfeigned piety with which the monk resigned every earthly advantage that he might win a heavenly reward. But it survived its reputation, and there is more hope of recovering to life the carcass around which the eagles have gathered than of renovated monkdom. The ribaldry of Boccaccio and Rabelais, the *Ep. obscuror. vit.*, and the more measured terms of Piers Ploughman and Chaucer, were mainly instrumental in bringing about the downfall of monasticism; but this was after it had already been shorn of its splendor, and when scarcely a ray remained to it of its former glory" (comp. Murphy, *Terra Incognita, or the Convents of the United Kingdom* [Lond. 1873, 8vo]; Pauli, *Pictures of Old England* [Lond. 1861, 12mo], chap. iii).

6. In *architectural arrangement*, monastic establishments, whether abbeys, priories, or other convents, followed nearly the same plan. The great enclosure (varying, of course, in extent with the wealth and importance of the monastery), generally with a stream running beside it, was surrounded by a wall, the principal entrance being through a *gateway* to the west or north-west. This gateway was a considerable building, and often contained a chapel, with its altar, besides the necessary accommodation for the porter. The *almery*, or place where alms were distributed, stood not far within the great gate, and generally a little to the right hand: there, too, was often a chapel with its altar. Proceeding onwards, the west entrance of the church appeared. The church itself was always, where it received its due development, in the form of a Latin cross; i. e., a cross of which the transepts are short in proportion to the nave. Moreover, in Norman churches, the eastern limb never approached the nave or western limb in length. Whether or not the reason of this preference of the Latin cross is found in the domestic arrangements of the monastic buildings, it was certainly best adapted to it; for the nave of the church, with one of the transepts, formed the whole of one side and part of another side of a quadrangle; and any other than a long nave would have involved a small quadrangle, while a long transept would leave too little of another side, or none at all, for other buildings. How the internal arrangements were affected by this adaptation of the nave to external requirements we have seen under the head CATHEDRAL, to which also we refer for the general description of the conventual church. Southward of the church, and parallel with the south transept, was carried the western range of the monastic offices; but it will be more convenient to examine their arrangement within the court. We enter, then, by a door near the west end of the church, and passing though a vaulted passage, find ourselves in the *cloister court*, of which the nave of the church forms the northern side, the transept part of the eastern side, and other buildings, in the order to be presently described, complete the quadrangle. The *cloisters* themselves extended around the whole of the quadrangle, serving, among other purposes, as a covered way from every part of the convent to every other part. They were furnished, perhaps always, with lavatories, on the decoration and construction of which much cost was expended; and sometimes also with desks and closets of wainscot, which served the purpose of a scriptorium. Commencing the circuit of the cloisters at the north-west corner, and turning southward, we have first the *dormitory* or *dorter*, the use of which is sufficiently indicated by its name. This occupied the whole of the western side of the quadrangle, and sometimes had a

groined passage beneath its whole length, called the *ambulatory*, a noble example of which, in perfect preservation, remains at Fountains. The south side of the quadrangle contained the *refectory*, with its correlative, the *coquina* or *kitchen*, which was sometimes at its side, and sometimes behind it. The refectory was furnished with a pulpit, for the reading of some portion of Scripture during meals. On this side of the quadrangle may also be found, in general, the *locutorium* or *parlor*, the latter word being, at least in etymology, the full equivalent of the former. The *abbot's lodge* commonly commenced at the south-east corner of the quadrangle; but, instead of conforming itself to its general direction, rather extended eastwards, with its own chapel, hall, parlor, kitchen, and other offices, in a line parallel with the choir or eastern limb of the church. Turning northwards, still continuing within the cloisters, we come first to an open passage leading outwards, then to the *chapter-house* or its vestibule; then, after another open passage, to the south transept of the church. Immediately before us is an entrance into the church, and another occurs at the end of the west cloister. The parts of the establishment especially connected with *sewerage* were built over or close to the stream; and we may remark that both in drainage and in the supply of water great and laudable care was always taken. The stream also turned the *abbey mill*, at a small distance from the monastery. Other offices, such as *stables, brewhouses, bakehouses*, and the like, in the larger establishments usually occupied another court, and in the smaller were connected with the chief buildings in the only quadrangle. It is needless to say that, in so general an account, we cannot enumerate exceptional cases. It may, however, be necessary to say that the greatest difference of all, that of placing the quadrangle at the north, instead of the south side of the church, is not unknown; it is so at Canterbury and at Lincoln, for instance (comp. Hook, *Church Dict.* p. 414, 415). This branch of the subject may be followed out in the several plans of monasteries scattered among topographical works, and especially in Parker, *Glossary of Architecture*, p. 146 sq.

Literature.—The large number of works treating of *Monasticism* (q. v.) should be consulted by the student, especially the Church histories. See also Walcott, *Sacred Archæol.* s.v.; Blunt, *Theol. Dict.* s.v.; Eadie, *Eccl. Dict.* s. v.; Riddle, *Christian Antiquities*, p. 781-783. The best materials for a history of the series of confiscations that ensued in England are in *Three Chapters of Letters relating to the Suppression of Monasteries* (Lond., Camden Society, 1843).

Monasticism (Gr. μονάζειν, *to dwell apart* in solitude; whence μοναχός, a monk), a state of religious retirement, more or less complete, accompanied by contemplation and by various devotional, ascetical, and penitential practices, is in truth *Asceticism* (q. v.), with the elements of religious solitude superadded. Monasticism, until the beginning of the study of comparative religion, was regarded as a strictly Christian institution, but recent researches reveal it as having entered into various religious systems, both ancient and modern. Indeed, it is now clearly apparent that the Western theory of the ascetic life travelled from the East to the West, but the question of the time when it originated in the East is still clouded in mystery. "The origin of monasticism," writes Mr. Johnson in his little work on the *Monks before Christ*, "will always be enveloped in mystery. 'Its history is shrouded in the same obscurity as the source of the mighty stream upon the banks of which the first ascetics commenced the practice of their austerities'" (p. 51, 52). The probability is that monachism is a strictly Asiatic institution, and originated among heathen nations. We certainly do not think that monasticism can prove a Christian or even Jewish origin; it is not heavenly, but earthly. Yet do we not desire to have our development theorists infer that we agree with them that it is one of the early religious forms of man.

Says one, "The older the religion, the older its ascetic practices; for they were among the first forms assumed by the religious impulse, and not among the later and better ones. They belong to the religion of the passions and emotions, and not to the religion of reason;" and then he logically infers that therefore "monasticism is as old as religion itself; for it does not gain favor with the progress of new ideas, but is gradually falling in the estimation of all." We are far from believing that monasticism is a primitive institution, and is forsaken by modern civilization. Quite the contrary, we hold that ascetic practices prevail largely among semi-civilized or civilized nations, and only after a clear conception has been formed of man's dependence on a higher Being, and a desire is manifest for future existence. The inspired religion prepares the way for these, and from religious excesses or alienation spring the ascetic practices. In the far East the very notion of the supreme Lord faded for ages from the grasp of philosophy, and became too subtle and refined a conception for any to retain it in their knowledge; but the inherent evil of matter, of flesh, of sense, and of human life has remained to stimulate the curiosity, to exhaust the efforts of the melancholy victims of the grim delusion, and to shape in various forms the fact that man's incumbent duty has ever been to escape from the contamination, and rise above the conditions of the flesh. Indeed, we believe that ascetic tendencies in general, and monasticism in particular, are the outgrowth of a religious enthusiasm, seriousness, and ambition likely to be pursued only by those who have once believed in revealed religion and have retrograded, having gone from the presence of their God to the idol they reared to represent him. But, whatever may be the differences of opinion as to the relation of the heathen religions to the revealed, it is generally conceded that monasticism cannot prove its heavenly origin, nor honestly identify itself with the Christian religion, as it is known to be *much older than Christianity.* In times far anterior to the Gospel, prophets and martyrs, "in sheepskins and goatskins," wandered in the Oriental world over mountains and deserts, and dwelt in caves and dens of the earth, as have likewise evangelical monks.

I. *Pagan Monachism.* — 1. *Its Monumental History.* —In examining the inscriptions which have been discovered in South-western Asia and Egypt, we find an abundance of representations of priests and religious ceremonies. We learn from these that many of the priests shaved the head, and always wore a peculiar habit, which in historic times, we are told, was white. We learn furthermore that these priests taught that the body must be kept pure by fasting and other ascetic observances. No doubt, as our knowledge in hieroglyphics shall progress, our information on this subject will be greatly enriched. In Arabia and India the modern traveller comes across numberless "rock-cut temples." We now know that nearly 600 years B.C. the artificial caves of India were occupied by Buddhistical monks, and there is conclusive evidence that they had served the Brahmins for a like purpose long before that. (Comp. the occasional notices of the Indian gymnosophists in Strabo [lib. xv, c. 1, after accounts from the time of Alexander the Great], Arrian [*Exped. Alex.* lib. vii, c. 1-3; and *Hist. Ind.* c. 11], Pliny [*Hist. Nat.* vii, 2], Diodorus Siculus [lib. ii], Plutarch [*Alex.* c. 64], Porphyry [*De abstinent.* lib. iv], Lucian [*Fugit.* c. 7], Clemens Alex. [*Strom.* lib. i and iii], and Augustine [*De civit. Dei*, lib. xiv, c. 17: "Per opacas Indiæ solitudines, quum quidam nudi philosophentur, unde gymnosophistæ nominantur; adhibent tamen genitalibus tegmina, quibus per cætera membrorum carent;" and lib. xv, c. 20, where he denies all merit to their celibacy, because it is not "secundum fidem summi boni, qui est Deus"]. With these ancient representations agree the narratives of Fon Koueki [about A.D. 400, transl. by M. A. Rémusat, Paris, 1836], Marco Polo [1280], Bernier [1670], Hamilton [1700], Papi, Niebuhr, Orlich,

Sonnerat, and others.) The manner of the construction of these caves of India and Arabia leads to the supposition that they were *originally* intended for monkish abodes, and, if so, the exceeding great antiquity of monasticism can no longer be doubted. These temples and caves are the oldest monuments of the countries in which they are found.

2. *Earliest written History of Monachism.*—If from these monuments we descend to an examination of the written books of the ancients, and search in "The Nabatæan Agriculture," which is believed to have been written about the time of Nebuchadnezzar (or B.C. 600), we find in this history of Chaldæa, reaching back several thousands of years before the beginning of the Christian æra, that in the very earliest history of which this work gives any account there flourished Azada, an apostle of Saturn, who "founded the religion of renunciation or asceticism," and that "his partisans and followers were the subjects of persecution by the higher and cultivated classes; but that to the mass of the people, on the contrary, they were the objects of the highest veneration." Another ascetic whom it mentions flourished about B.C. 2000. He is said to have inveighed against the godliness of those who believed it possible to preserve the human body from decay, after death, by the employment of certain natural agents. "Not by natural means," warmly replies Dhagrit, "can man preserve his body from corruption and dissolution after death, but only through good deeds, *religious exercises*, and offering of sacrifices—by invoking the gods by their great and beautiful names—*by prayers during the night, and fasts during the day.*" Then Dhagrit goes on, in his monkish zeal, to give the names of various saints of Babylonian antiquity whose bodies had long been preserved, after death, from corruption and change, and says: "These men had distinguished themselves by piety, by abstemiousness, and by their manner of life, which resembled that of angels; and the gods, therefore, by their grace, had preserved the bodies of these men from corruption; whereby those of later times, in view of the same, were encouraged in piety, and in the imitation of those holy modes of life." See Chwolson, *Ueber die Ueberreste der altbabylonischen Literatur* (St. Petersburg, 1859); M. le Baron de St. Croix, *Recherches Historiques et Critiques sur les Mystères du Paganisme* (Paris, 1817).

Turning from these written sources, still the subjects of much discussion as to their authenticity, to the well-established records of India, Persia, and China, the oldest written records in existence aside from the sacred Scriptures (viz. the Veda [q. v.] and the Laws of Manu [q. v.]—the sacred books of the Brahmins; the Zend-Avesta [q. v.]—the sacred book of the Persians or Zoroastrians; and the Shu-King [see CONFUCIUS]—the sacred book of China), we find the hoary parent of monastic rule dwelling in the far East, and gathering obedient millions under her ample folds, long before the introduction of Christianity, even if we should trace Christian monasticism back to St. Bartholomew and St. Thomas.

Among the Hindûs (q. v.), we learn from the Brahminical writings—especially the Rig-Veda, portions of which are assigned to a period as far back as B.C. 2400, the Laws of Manu, which were certainly completed before the rise of Buddhism (that is, six or seven centuries before our æra), and the numerous other sacred books of the Indian religion—that there was enjoined by example and precept entire abstraction of thought, seclusion from the world, and a variety of penitential and meritorious acts of self-mortification, by which the devotee assumes a proud superiority over the vulgar herd of mortals, and is absorbed at last into the divine fountain of all being. Says Spence Hardy, "The practice of asceticism is so interwoven with Brahminism, under all the phases it has assumed, that we cannot realize its existence apart from the principles of the ascetic." (Compare Wilson, *Asiatic Researches*, xvi, 38; Pavie, in

Revue des deux Mondes, 1854; Hardwick, *Christ and other Masters*, i, 351.)

3. *Probable Origin of Eastern Monachism.*—"At an early period of the present æra of Brahminic manifestation," the legend goes, in the Rig-Veda, "Dhruva, the son of Uttanapada, the son of Manu Swayambhuva, who was 'born of and one with Brahma,' began to perform penance, *as enjoined by the sages*, on the banks of the Yamuna. While his mind was wholly absorbed in meditation, the mighty Hari, identical with all natures, took possession of his heart. Vishnu being thus present in his mind, the earth, the supporter of elemental life, could not sustain the weight of the ascetic. The celestials called Yamas, being excessively alarmed, then took counsel with Indra how they should interrupt the devout exercises of Dhruva; and the divine beings termed Kushmandas, in company with their king, commenced anxious efforts to distract his meditations. One, assuming the semblance of his mother, Suniti, stood weeping before him, and calling in tender accents, 'My son, my son, desist from destroying thy strength by this fearful penance! What hast thou, a child but five years old, to do with rigorous penance? Desist from such fearful practices, that yield no beneficial fruit. First comes the season of youthful pastime, and when that is over it is the time for study; then succeeds the period of worldly enjoyments; and, lastly, that of austere devotion. This is thy season of pastime, my child. Hast thou engaged in these practices to put an end to existence? Thy chief duty is love for me; duties are according to time of life. Lose not thyself in bewildering error—desist from such unrighteous actions. If not, if thou wilt not desist from these austerities, I will terminate my life before thee.' But Dhruva, being wholly intent on seeing Vishnu, beheld not his mother weeping in his presence, and calling upon him; and the illusion, crying out, 'Fly, fly, my child; the hideous spirits of ill are crowding into this terrible forest with uplifted weapons,' quickly disappeared. Then advanced frightful rakshasas, wielding terrible arms, and with countenances emitting fiery flame; and nocturnal fiends thronged around the prince, uttering fearful noises, and whirling and tossing their threatening weapons. Hundreds of jackals, from whose mouths gushed flame as they devoured their prey, were howling around to appall the boy, wholly engrossed by meditation. The goblins called out, 'Kill him! kill him!—cut him to pieces!—eat him! eat him!' and monsters, with the faces of camels and crocodiles and lions, roared and yelled with horrible cries to terrify the prince. But all these uncouth speeches, appalling cries, and threatening weapons made no impression upon his senses, whose mind was completely intent on Govinda. The son of the monarch of the earth, engrossed by one idea, beheld uninterruptedly Vishnu seated in his soul, and saw no other object." How like the legends of Christian monachism are these pagan descriptions! The desert has always been the abode of asceticism, whose devotees, in their struggle against the flesh, peopled its sands with horrible monsters of every kind—with devils, hobgoblins, and giants, who (in the minds of the people) have held possession ever since. The Vedas also command that the tonsure be performed, but, so far as known, they prescribed no rules with regard to the monastic life. Their teachings seem to be confined solely to asceticism. On the other hand, in the Laws of Manu rules are given for the conduct of monastics; and, as these rules were in the possession of the people of India long before they were committed to writing, it is no wonder that monasticism is believed to have been practiced for thousands of years before the time of Christ. Hardwick, by no means a superficial student, is led even, in the face of these conditions, to say that "India was the real *birthplace* of monasticism" (*Christ and other Masters*, i, 351).

A large portion of the Laws of Manu are taken up by regulations to be observed by those who wish to attain to the ultimate good by the practice of monastic observances. The rule of St. Benedict itself does not afford a more decided proof of the existence of the ascetic life. The work is divided into twelve books. The sixth book is entitled "Duties of the Anchorite and of the Ascetic Devotee." The subject of the eleventh book is "Penitences and Expiations." The Dwijas, for whom these rules are principally laid down, are described as a sort of monks, who practiced tonsure, wore girdle, carried staff, asked alms, fasted, lacerated the body, and dwelt for the most part in the deserts and forests. We have space but for a few illustrations, which will suffice, however, to show the character of this work. From the sixth book, "Duties of the Anchorite and of the Ascetic Devotee," we quote as follows:

" ¶ 24. The Dwija, who dwells alone, should deliver himself to austerities, increasing constantly in their severity, that he may wither up his mortal substance.

" ¶ 27. Let him receive from the Brahminical anchorites, who live in houses, such alms as may be necessary to support his existence." (The case was similar in early Christian times: Simon the Stylite, and a host of others, were thus provided for.)

" ¶ 49. Meditating with delight on the supreme soul, seated, wanting nothing, inaccessible to all sensual desire, without other society than his own soul, let him live here below in the constant expectancy of the eternal beatitude.

" ¶ 75. In subduing his organs, in accomplishing the pious duties prescribed by the Vedas, and in submitting one's self to the most austere practices, one is able to attain here below to the supreme end, which is to become identified with Brahma." ("Their whole doctrine of spirit, of the supreme Being, and the relation of man to God, must have made the Brahmins ascetics from the very first. So that, when the origin of this religion can be ascertained, we may say, without further examination, monasticism was there, and gave birth to it" [Johnson, Monks before Christ, p. 70].)

" ¶ 87. The novice, the married man, the anchorite, and the ascetic devotee form four distinct orders, which derive their origin from the superior of the house.

" ¶ 91. The Dwijas, who belong to these four orders, ought always to practice with the greatest care the ten virtues which compose their duty.

" ¶ 92. Resignation, the act of rendering good for evil, temperance, probity, purity, the subjugation of the senses, the knowledge of the Shastras, that of the supreme soul, veracity, and abstinence from choler—such are the ten virtues in which their duty consists."

From the eleventh book, "Penitences and Expiations," we make the following extracts:

" ¶ 211. The Dwija, who undergoes the *ordinary* penitence called Prajapatya, ought to eat during three days only in the morning; during the next three days, only at night; during the following three days, he should partake only of such food as persons may give him voluntarily, without his begging for it; and, finally, let him fast three days entirely.

" ¶ 214. A Brahmin, accomplishing the *severe* penitence (Taptakrichra), ought to swallow nothing but warm water, warm milk, cold clarified butter, and warm vapor, employing each of them three days in succession.

" ¶ 215. He who, master of his senses and perfectly attentive, supports a fast of twelve days, makes the penitence called Paroka, which expiates all of his faults.

" ¶ 216. Let the penitent who desires to make the Chandrayana, having eaten fifteen mouthfuls on the day of the full moon, diminish his nourishment by one mouthful each day during the fifteen days of obscuration which follow, in such a manner that on the fourteenth day he shall eat but one mouthful, and then let him fast on the fifteenth, which is the day of the new moon; let him augment, on the contrary, his nourishment by one mouthful each day during the next fifteen days, commencing the first day with one mouthful.

" ¶ 239. Great criminals, and all other men guilty of divers faults, are released from the consequences of their sins by austerities practiced with exactitude.

" ¶ 251. By reciting the Hovichyantiya or the Natamanha sixteen times a day for a month, or by repeating inaudibly the hymn Porucha, he who has defiled the bed of his spiritual master is absolved from all fault."

"The ascetic system," says Schaff, "is essential alike to Brahminism [see HINDUISM] and Buddhism (q. v.), the two opposite and yet cognate branches of the Indian religion, which in many respects are similarly related to each other as Judaism is to Christianity, or as Romanism to Protestantism. Buddhism is a later reformation of Brahminism. . . . But the two religions start from opposite principles. Brahminic asceticism proceeds from a pantheistic view of the world—the Buddh-

istic from an atheistic and nihilistic, yet very earnest view; the one is controlled by the idea of the absolute but abstract unity, and a feeling of contempt of the world—the other by the idea of the absolute but unreal variety, and a feeling of deep grief over the emptiness and nothingness of all existence; the one is predominantly objective, positive, and idealistic—the other more subjective, negative, and realistic; the one aims at absorption into the universal spirit of Brahma—the other constantly at an absorption into nonentity." "Brahminism," says Wuttke, "looks back to the beginning, Buddhism to the end; the former loves cosmogony, the latter eschatology. Both reject the existing world; the Brahmin despises it because he contrasts it with the higher being of Brahma; the Buddhist bewails it because of its unrealness; the former sees God in all, the other emptiness in all" (*Das Geistesleben der Chinesen, Japaner, und Indier*, 1853, p. 593, constituting pt. ii of his *History of Heathenism*). "Yet," adds Schaff, "as all extremes meet, the abstract all-entity of Brahminism and the equally abstract non-entity or vacuity of Buddhism come to the same thing in the end, and may lead to the same ascetic practices. The asceticism of Brahminism takes more the direction of anchoretism, while that of Buddhism exists generally in the social form of regular convent life." The Hindû monks, the Vanaprastha, or *Gymnosophists* (q. v.), as the Greeks called them, are Brahminical anchorites (q. v.), who live in woods or caves, on mountains or rocks, in poverty, celibacy, abstinence, contemplation: sleeping on straw or the bare ground, crawling on the belly, macerating the body, standing all day on tiptoe, exposed to the pouring rain or scorching sun with four fires kindled around them, presenting a savage and frightful appearance, yet greatly revered by the multitude, especially the women. As procreation of at least one child is strictly enjoined by Brahminism, some take their wives along, but never have intercourse with them except at such times as they are most likely to conceive. They are reputed to perform miracles, and not unfrequently complete their austerities by suicide on the stake or in the waves of the Ganges. Thus they are described by the ancients and by modern travellers (see Dubois, *Description of the Character, Manners, and Customs of the People of India* [Philadelphia, 1818]).

The Buddhist monks are less fanatical and extravagant than the Hindû *Yogis* (q. v.) and *Fakirs* (q. v.). They depend mainly on fasting, prayer, psalmody, intense contemplation, and the use of the whip, to keep their rebellious flesh in subjection. See BUDDHISM; GOTAMA. They have a fully developed system of monasticism in connection with their priesthood, and a large number of convents; also nunneries for female devotees. The laws of Buddha, it is true, are often purely moral, and they do not profess to be the transcript of a higher than a human mind. Yet they aimed at reducing the entire company of the faithful to strictly monastic rule, to the mortification of all human passion, to the separation and isolation of the sexes, to mendicancy, and to the cessation and relinquishing of all personal and individual rights. Hence India, though she expelled Buddhistic rule, and princes and professors from her soil, yet shows at a hundred points the deep furrow which Buddhist monasticism has drawn across the more hoary superstitions and more agonizing asceticism of Hindû philosophy; and her monuments and literature bear witness to the brave, self-sacrificing devotion of these sons and daughters of Buddha, and to the fact that they went into all Eastern lands to preach the faith of their sires, to build monasteries, to organize worship, to multiply their sacred books, to perform pilgrimage to holy shrines of their faith, to adore the relics of saints and martyrs, and work miracles by their aid, and to adapt themselves to such varying populations as the cultivated philosophers of Nepaul, the ingenious and susceptible Japanese, the Cingalese, and Burmese, to say nothing of the pontifical empire of Thibet (q. v.), where, to the present day, the monks still grasp a mighty sovereignty, where whole cities are filled with monastic populations, and where the temples, ritual, incense, tonsure, and vestments resemble the mediæval worship of the Romish Church so strongly as to deceive the unwary. At the present day the canonization of departed worth continually takes place in China, Tartary, and Thibet. Temples are erected in honor of meditative and hysteric damsels, who have gone through prodigies of self-sacrifice and communion with the gods, and have entered into their final rest. See LAMAISM. Up to the present century, the learning, the science, the art, and literature of China have been largely promoted by the priesthood. The conflict between a caste and a true priesthood, the victory of the "religious order" over the sacred tribe, the triumph of monkery over hereditary privilege, cannot be exclusively claimed for Christian recluses and Catholic corporations. Buddha commenced this mighty strife six centuries before Christ. Indeed, Buddhist monasticism bears such a remarkable resemblance to that of the Roman Catholic Church that Romish missionaries believed it necessary to brand the *older* as a diabolical imitation. But, as has been well said, "The original always precedes the caricature." (See the older accounts of Romish missionaries to Thibet in Pinkerton, *Collection of Voyages and Travels*, vol. vii, and also the recent work of Huc, a French missionary priest of the Congregation of St. Lazare—*Souvenirs d'un Voyage dans la Tartarie, le Thibet, et la Chine, pendant les années* 1844–1846, translated into English, and published by the Harpers [N. Y. 1855, 2 vols. 12mo]. Comp. also on the whole subject the two works of R. S. Hardy—*Eastern Monachism,* and *A Manual of Buddhism in its modern Development, translated from Cingalese MSS.* [Lond. 1850]. The striking affinity between Buddhism and Romanism extends, by the way, beyond monkery and convent life to the hierarchical organization, with the grand lama for pope, and to the worship, with its ceremonies, feasts, processions, pilgrimages, confessional, a kind of mass, prayers for the dead, extreme unction, etc. The view is certainly at least plausible, to which the great geographer Carl Ritter [*Erdkunde*, ii, 283–299, 2d ed.] has given the weight of his name, that the Lamaists in Thibet borrowed their religious forms and ceremonies in part from the Nestorian missionaries. But this view is a mere hypothesis, and is rendered improbable by the fact that Buddhism in Cochin China, Tonquin, and Japan, where no Nestorian missionaries ever were, shows the same striking resemblance to Romanism as the Lamaism of Thibet, Tartary, and North China. Respecting the singular tradition of Prester John, or the Christian priest-king in Eastern Asia, which arose about the 11th century, and respecting the Nestorian missions, see Ritter, *l. c.* See also Johnson, *Monks before Christ,* p. 100–108).

4. *Organization and Development of non-Christian Monachism.*—(1). *Indian.*—What St. Benedict became to the monks of Christendom, Gotama Buddha was to those of India. At least a thousand years before the former enunciated his law from the top of Mount Cassino—that Sinai of Western monasticism—Buddha, the Benedict of Eastern monachism, flourished at Kapilawastu. Up to this time Eastern asceticism appears to have been without a settled rule or organization. The Laws of Manu, it is true, specified the manner of conducting many austere observances, and contain rules for nearly all the monastic observances, such as the tonsure, fasting, celibacy, mendicancy, novitiate, etc.; but each monastery was accustomed to arrange its own inner life, and stood quite independent of any other.

The *growth of monasticism* must have been somewhat after this manner: First came austere practices without separation from society; then the devotee sought the solitude, like the Christian anchorite (q. v.). Some one who was particularly celebrated for the holiness of his life, or more inventive than others in methods of bodily torment, soon began to gather admirers and imitators about him. They came and dug their caves or built their huts in the neighborhood of his: and thus arose the second form of life corresponding to the Christian *Cœnobites* (q. v.). Sometimes the community was assembled under one roof; at other times, as in the Thebaid, they dwelt apart. As yet, however, their mode of life was by no means settled or uniform. Now was the time for a lawgiver; and the people of India found theirs in the person of Buddha (the Enlightened), who was born B.C. 624. He early manifested a love for contemplation, and was determined to the ascetic mode of life by seeing a monk who carried an alms-bowl, and whose external appearance spoke of inward peace and composure. His father was king of Kapilawastu, who, having detected the dreamer in his son, married him, while yet quite young, to a princess, who gave birth to a child before Buddha divorced himself from her. The circumstances which led him to take this step are thus narrated by J. Barthélemy Saint-Hilaire (*Le Buddha et sa Religion*): "One day when the prince, with a large retinue, was driving through the eastern gate of the city, on the way to one of his parks, he met on the road an old man, broken and decrepit. One could see the veins and muscles over the whole of his body; his teeth chattered; he was covered with wrinkles, bald, and hardly able to utter hollow and unmelodious sounds. He was bent on his stick, and all his limbs and joints trembled. 'Who is that man?' said the prince to his coachman. 'He is small and weak; his flesh and his blood are dried up; his muscles stick to his skin; his head is white; his teeth chatter; his body is wasted away; leaning on his stick he is hardly able to walk, stumbling at every step. Is there something peculiar in his family, or is this the common lot of all created beings?' 'Sir,' replied the coachman, 'that man is sinking under old age; his senses have become obtuse, suffering has destroyed his strength, and he is despised by his relations. He is without support and useless; and people have abandoned him, like a dead tree in a forest. But this is not peculiar to his family. In every creature youth is defeated by old age. Your father, your mother, all your relations, all your friends, will come to the same state: this is the appointed end of all creatures.' 'Alas!' replied the prince, 'are creatures so ignorant, so weak, and so foolish as to be proud of the youth by which they are intoxicated, not seeing the old age which awaits them? As for me, I go away. Coachman, turn my chariot quickly. What have I—the future prey of old age—what have I to do with pleasure?' And the young prince returned to the city without going to his park. Another time the prince was driving through the southern gate to his pleasure-garden, when he perceived on the road a man suffering from illness, parched with fever, his body wasted, covered with mud, without a friend, without a home, hardly able to breathe, and frightened at the sight of himself and the approach of death. Having questioned his coachman, and received from him the answer which he expected, the young prince said, 'Alas! health is but the sport of a dream, and the fear of suffering must take this frightful form. Where is the wise man who, after having seen what he is, could any longer think of joy and pleasure?' The prince turned his chariot and returned to the city. A third time he was driving to his pleasure-garden through the western gate, when he saw a dead body on the road, lying on a bier, and covered with a cloth. The friends stood about, crying, sobbing, tearing their hair, covering their heads with dust, striking their breasts, and uttering wild cries. The prince, again calling his coachman to witness this painful scene, exclaimed, 'Oh, woe to the youth which must be destroyed by old age! Woe to health which must be destroyed by so many diseases! Woe to this life, where a man remains so short a time! If there were no old age, no disease, no death; if these could be made captive forever!' Then, betraying for the first time his intentions, the young prince said, 'Let us turn back: I must think how to accomplish deliverance.' A last meeting put an end to his hesitation. He was driving through the northern gate, on the way to his pleasure-gardens, when he saw a mendicant, who appeared outwardly calm, subdued, looking downwards, wearing with an air of dignity his religious vestment, and carrying an alms-bowl. 'Who is this man?' asked the prince. 'Sir,' replied the coachman, 'this man is one of those who are called *bhikshus*, or mendicants. He has renounced all pleasures, all desires, and leads a life of austerity. He tries to conquer himself. He has become a devotee: without passion, without envy, he walks about asking for alms.' 'This is good and well said,' replied the prince. 'The life of a devotee has always been praised by the wise. It will be my refuge, and the refuge of other creatures: it will lead us to a real life, to happiness and immortality.' With these words, the young prince turned his chariot, and re-entered the city" (translated in Müller's *Essays on the Science of Religion*). Buddha then declared to his father and wife his determination to become a recluse, and soon after escaped from his palace in the night while the guards had fallen asleep. The religion which he established is now, after a lapse of 2000 years, professed by one third of the inhabitants of the entire globe. One king is said to have founded 84,000 monasteries for his order, that being the number of discourses which Buddha pronounced during his lifetime. The "Law" which he gave to his order is contained in the first of the three Pitakas, and was orally handed down until about B.C. 100, when it was committed to writing in the island of Ceylon. It is called the Winaya Pitaka, and contains rules for every conceivable monastic observance. It is composed of 42,250 stanzas. To alms-giving Buddha attached an extraordinary importance. He declares that "there is no reward either in this world or in the next that may not be received through alms-giving." Ten centuries later, Chrysostom wrote, "Hast thou a penny? purchase heaven. Heaven is on sale, and in the market, and yet ye mind it not! Give a crust, and take back paradise; give the least, and receive the greatest; give the perishable, and receive the imperishable; give the corruptible, and receive the incorruptible. Alms are the redemption of the soul. . . . Alms-giving, which is able to break the chain of thy sins. . . . Alms-giving, the queen of virtues, and the readiest of all ways of getting into heaven, and the best advocated there" (comp. Taylor, *Anc. Christianity*). According to the Winaya Pitaka, "The wise priest never asks for anything; he disdains to beg: it is a proper object for which he carries the alms-bowl; and this is the only mode of solicitation." Celibacy, poverty, the tonsure, a particular garb, confession of sins, etc., are made compulsory. The vows, however, are not taken for life; and a monk may retire from the order if he finds it impossible to remain continent. A novitiate is provided for; and there are "nuns" or "sisters" who live in houses by themselves. The novice usually begins her connection with the order in the school, where she is sent while yet quite young. Foundlings were often given to the early Christian monasteries, by whom they were reared for the ascetic life. *No Buddhist can attain to Nirvana unless he has served a time as an ascetic.* There are five modes of meditation specified by the Pitaka: 1, Maitri; 2, Mudita; 3, Karuna; 4, Upeksha; 5, Asubha. We read of a monk who was so profoundly sunk in contemplation that he did not wash his feet for thirty years; so that at last the divine beings called *dervas* could smell him a thousand miles off. The monk refrains from severely injuring his body, so that he may practice as long as possible his ascetic rites. Their mode of reasoning on this subject is illustrated by the following quotation from the *Milinda-prasna*, a work in Pali and Cingalese: "*Milinda.* Do the priests respect the body?—*Nagasena.* No.—*Milinda.* Then why do they take so much pains to preserve it? Do they not

by this means say, 'This is me, or mine?'—*Nagasena.* Were you ever wounded by an arrow in battle?—*Milinda.* Yes.—*Nagasena.* Was not the wound anointed? Was it not rubbed with oil? And was it not covered with a soft bandage?—*Milinda.* Yes.—*Nagasena.* Was this done because you respected the wound, or took delight in it?—*Milinda.* No; but that it might be healed.—*Nagasena.* In like manner, the priests do not preserve the body because they respect it, but that they may have the power required for the keeping of the precepts."

(2.) *Persian Monachism.*—The Zend-Avesta, written, it is generally agreed, about B.C. 500, contains no allusion to ascetic rites; but this fact would go no further to disprove the existence of monastic life among the Persians than the absence of such allusion from the N. T. would disprove the existence of Jewish monks. The Avesta is not of a historical character; and what was said about the Vedas is particularly true of it—prayers and hymns make up almost its entire contents. Zoroaster originally dwelt with the Brahminical or Sanscrit branch of the Aryan family; and we know that monasticism was rife among them before the separation took place. It is not likely that they ever shook off this institution, which is as universal as religion or intemperance. We are told that there was a class of "solitaries" among them. According to the Desatir, the Dobistan, and the old Iranian histories, "there was a great king of that branch of the Aryan people known as Kai-Khuero, who was a prophet and an ascetic. He had no children; and, after a 'glorious reign of sixty years,' he abdicated in favor of a subordinate prince, also an ascetic, who, after a long reign, resigned his throne to his son Gushtasp. It was during the reign of Gushtasp that Zoroaster appeared. Gushtasp was succeeded by Bohman, his grandson." These were not kings of Persia, but they reigned at Balkh, and lived many centuries before Persia became an independent kingdom. This would place the origin of asceticism anterior to Zoroaster, who lived, the Greeks said, 5000 years before the Trojan war, or 6000 before Plato—an antiquity greater than that assigned to it by the "Nabatæan Agriculture."

(3.) *Chinese Monachism.*—An examination of the Chou-King, the sacred book *par excellence* of China, is without fruit for our purpose. It is a significant fact, however, that the word "priest" is written in Chinese "Cha-men," or "Sang-men," which mean, respectively, one who exerts himself,* or one who restrains himself. The Chou-King was transcribed by Confucius (*Life and Teachings of Confucius*, by James Legge, D.D. [Phila. 1867]) about B.C. 480, and to him we owe its preservation. It is only one out of a large number of books upon religious topics which must have existed in his time. Lao-Kiün, who lived several generations before Confucius, was a great ascetic, advocated perfect freedom from passion, and passed much of his time in the mountains. Of Confucius, it is known that he taught no new doctrines, but insisted upon a more faithful observation of the ancient law. He flourished in the 5th century B.C. (551-479). At nineteen years of age he divorced himself from his wife, after she had given birth to a son, to devote himself to study and meditation; and his last days were passed in a quiet valley, where he retired with a few of his followers. He fasted quite frequently, and advocated many other monkish observances: such as retirement, contemplation, and agricultural employment. (See Schott, *Werke des chinesischen Weisen Kong-Fu-Dsü* [Halle, 1826]. Comp. also Meng Tseu, ed. Stanislaus Julien, lib. i, c. 5, par. 29; c. 6, p. 29; and article CONFUCIUS.) Mencius, an apostle of Confucius, who flourished in the 3d century B.C., says, "Though a man may be wicked, yet, if he adjust his thoughts, fast, and bathe, he may sacri-

---

* There is a remarkable similarity between the derivation of this word and that of *ascetic* (from ἀσκεῖν, to *exercise*, or practice gymnastics).

fice to God." (Compare Johnson, *Monks before Christ, their Spirit and their History* [Bost. 1870, 18mo], ch. ii.)

(4.) *Greek Monachism.*—The Hellenic heathenism was less serious and contemplative, indeed, than the Oriental. The first monastic society of which we have any knowledge are the *Pythagoreans* (q. v.), who, no doubt, are an importation from Egyptian or even from Indian soil (see Clement Alexandrinus, *Stromat.* lib. iii; Ueberweg, *Hist. Philos.* i, 42 sq.). "The mysteries of Bacchus and Ceres were copied after those of Osiris and Isis. These latter, in some respects, resembled Freemasonry more than they did monastic orders. They forbade, however, all sensuous enjoyment, enjoined contemplation, long-protracted silence, etc. Moreover, it is probable that Pythagoras found here many of those ascetic observances which he afterwards introduced into his own order" (Johnson, *Monks before Christ*, p. 87). Bunsen says that the rules for the conduct of Egyptian priests, as described by Chæremon and preserved by Porphyry, remind one of the Laws of Manu and the Vedas; so that if the conjectures of this Egyptologist be accepted, we are forced to conclude that Hellenic monasticism came from the Hindûs through the Egyptians, unless the theory be accepted that the Greeks borrowed it directly from the Indians during their intercourse in the 5th and 6th centuries B.C. But whatever our opinion on this point, certain is that more than 2000 years before Ignatius Loyola assembled the nucleus of his great "society" in a subterranean chapel in the city of Paris there was founded at Crotona, in Greece, an order of monks whose principles, constitution, aims, method, and final end entitle them to be called the "Pagan Jesuits" (see Zeller, *Pythagoras u. die Pythagora-Saga*, in his *Vorträge u. Abhandlungen* [Leips. 1865]; Johnson, *Monks before Christ*, p. 87, 88). The extinction of Pythagoreanism (soon after B.C. 400) by no means did away with asceticism in Greece. The philosophical mantle of the Pythagoreans fell upon a new school, among whom Epimenides and Plato are usually reckoned; and the Platonic view of matter and of body not only lies at the bottom of the Gnostic and Manichæan asceticism, but had much to do with the ethics of Origen and the Alexandrian school.

(5.) *Jewish Monachism.*—The origin and extent of Jewish monasticism is shrouded in much uncertainty and doubt. Yet it is clearly manifest from the records that have come down to us that Judaism was not altogether alien to asceticism. As far back as the days of Moses, while the Israelites were yet in the wilderness, a special law was made for those who should seek an ascetic life; and the *Nazarites* (q. v.), though they did not separate themselves from the other people, yet did set themselves *apart* for special divine worship (Numb. vi, 1–21; Judg. xiii, 5; 1 Sam. i, 11; Luke i, 15). Later, in Palestine, the Jews had their *Essenes* (q. v.), and in Egypt their *Therapeutæ* (q. v.), though it must be confessed that these betray the intrusion of foreign elements into the Mosaic religion, and so receive no mention in the New Test., unless the allusion in Matt. xix, 12 refers to these ascetics, which is believed, however, by only a few Biblical scholars. (See, besides the works quoted in the article ESSENES, Zeller, *Griech-Philos.* vol. iii, pt. ii, p. 589; and *Theol. Jahrb.* 1856, iii, 358; Keim, *Der Geschichtliche Christus* [Zurich, 1865], p. 15; Langen, *Das Judenthum in Palästina zur Zeit Christi* [Freib. 1866], p. 186.)

(6.) *Mohammedan Monachism.*—"The two most successful religious impostures," says Cunningham, "which the world has yet seen are Buddhism and Mohammedanism. Each creed owed its origin to the enthusiasm of a single individual, and each was rapidly propagated by numbers of zealous followers. But here the parallel ends; for the *Koran* of Mohammed was addressed wholly to the 'passions' of mankind, by the promised gratification of human desires both in this world and in the next; while the *Dharma* of Sákya Muni was addressed wholly to the 'intellect,' and sought to wean

mankind from the pleasures and vanities of this life by pointing to the transitoriness of all human enjoyment. . . . The former propagated his religion by the merciless edge of the sword; the latter by the persuasive voice of the missionary. The sanguinary career of the Islamite was lighted by the lurid flames of burning cities; the peaceful progress of the Buddhist was illuminated by the cheerful faces of the sick in monastic hospitals [for the crippled, the deformed, the destitute], and by the happy smiles of travellers reposing in Dharmasálas by the road-side. The one was the personification of bodily activity and material enjoyment; the other was the genius of corporeal abstinence and intellectual contemplation" (*Bhilsa Topes*, p. 53, 54). These words of Cunningham may apply to the early history of the two religions, but they are hardly in place in their history of more modern times. It is true, indeed, that Mohammedanism was the religion of the sword, but, its conquests over, it has studied the religions of the world, and to-day Islam embodies much from every creed in the universe. Its founder had been especially careful to rigidly exclude monasticism, and himself declared "*no monachism* in Islam," yet to-day the dervishes of the East are to be met almost wherever Islam has its adherents. See DERVISHES. Celibacy is not likely to get a great hold in Mohammedan nations, but ascetic practices, hermitage, and mendicancy prevail to a large extent among them. Mr. Ruffner, in his *Fathers of the Desert* (N. Y. 1850, 2 vols., a work popular in form, and full of valuable and curious information), has furnished an extended description of Mohammedan monasticism, and goes so far as to assert that the Christians derived it largely from them, who, in turn, borrowed from the Buddhists (see vol. i, ch. ii–ix); but such a view can hardly be reconciled with the great place of the phenomenon in history, and would, moreover, stamp as heretics many of the Christian fathers who were among the greatest and best representatives both East and West. (See below.) The probability is that monachism, so far as it exists in the Mohammedan world, was introduced either direct from the heathen world around it, or came from the Christians of the Post-Nicene age, especially the churches of Africa, and Egypt in particular.

II. *Christian Monachism.*—1. *Origin of Monasticism in the Church.*—The advocates of Christian monasticism claim for it an evangelical origin. They think they find at once its justification and primitive form in the Gospel exhortation to voluntary poverty (the instance in which Christ charged the rich young man to sell all he had, that, as a follower of his, he should receive a hundred-fold more, "with persecution," Matt. xix, 21). "But this monastic interpretation of primitive Christianity," as Dr. Schaff has well said, "mistakes a few incidental points of outward resemblance for essential identity, measures the spirit of Christianity by some isolated passages, instead of explaining the latter from the former, and is upon the whole a miserable emaciation and caricature. The Gospel makes upon all men virtually the same moral demand, and knows no distinction of a religion for the masses and another for the few." Monachism, in this light, is at variance with the pure spirit of Christianity, inasmuch as it impels men, instead of remaining as a salt to the corrupt world in which they live, outwardly to withdraw from it, and to bury the talent which otherwise they might use for the benefit of the many. "Jesus, the model for all believers, was neither a cœnobite nor an anchoret, nor an ascetic of any kind, but the perfect pattern man for universal imitation. There is not a trace of monkish austerity and ascetic rigor in his life or precepts, but in all his acts and words a wonderful harmony of freedom and purity, of the most comprehensive charity and spotless holiness. He retired to the mountains and into solitude, but only temporarily, and for the purpose of renewing his strength for active work. Amid the society of his disciples, of both sexes, with kindred and friends, in Cana and Bethany, at the table of publicans and sinners, and in intercourse with all classes of the people, he kept himself unspotted from the world, and transfigured the world into the kingdom of God. His poverty and celibacy have nothing to do with asceticism, but represent, the one the condescension of his redeeming love, the other his ideal uniqueness and his absolutely peculiar relation to the whole Church, which alone is fit or worthy to be his bride. . . . The life of the apostles and primitive Christians in general was anything but a hermit life; else had not the Gospel spread so quickly to all the cities of the Roman world. Peter was married, and travelled with his wife as a missionary. Paul assumes one marriage of the clergy as a rule, and notwithstanding his personal and relative preference for celibacy in the then oppressed condition of the Church, he is the most zealous advocate of evangelical freedom, in opposition to all legal bondage and anxious asceticism."

As little as we find in the life of Christ or his apostles any authority for the monastic life, so little do we find it represented in the life of primitive Christians generally. It is true in the infant Church, for a time, all things were in common, but even in this community of life, certainly the oldest or, rather, earliest phase of Christianity, monasticism finds no authority; for if it had been intended to serve as such, it would have been perpetuated. It failed because it was a social impossibility. "It gives a beautiful picture of what Christianity might be, when all are of one mind and one spirit;" but it was incompatible with the general course of human affairs, and it ceased to be. While, therefore, not even the Christian primitive communism can have been the germ from which monachism in the Church started, the theory of the monastic institution may possibly have been thereby suggested. Not even the asceticism of the infant Church can be made to account for this institution. Severe asceticism, it is true, was the religion of thousands throughout the Christian world, but those who practiced it neither separated themselves from the world nor from its social and political duties. They were simply a standing memorial of the solemn nature of the Christian baptismal vow in the heart of the families of the people. The most rigid monastic rule could have added neither severity to their self-discipline nor higher temper to their chastened spirit (see Neander, *Ch. Hist.* ii, 223 sq.).

But though monasticism was not a form of life that sprang originally and purely out of Christianity, yet there can be no doubt that by Christianity a new spirit was infused into this foreign mode of life, whereby with many it became ennobled and converted into an instrument of effecting much which could not otherwise have been effected by any such mode of living. Unless this view is taken, it would, as Dr. Schaff has well said, "involve the entire ancient Church, with its greatest and best representatives both East and West—its Athanasius, its Chrysostom, its Jerome, its Augustine—in apostasy from the faith." And, as he aptly adds, "no one will now hold that these men, who all admired and commended the monastic life, were antichristian errorists, and that the few and almost exclusively negative opponents of that asceticism, as Jovinian, Helvidius, and Vigilantius, were the sole representatives of pure Christianity in the Nicene and next following age" (comp. Kingsley, *Hermits,* p. 14, 15). We shall come to consider the good and evil influences in another part of this article. Here we have to deal simply with its origin and relation to primitive Christianity. In the article ASCETICISM it has been shown that a distinction must be made between it and the monastic life, which was not known until the 4th century. That class of ascetics known as *Hermits* flourished probably as early as the age succeeding Christ's stay on earth; indeed, it is barely possible that its origin may be traced to John the Baptist and his surroundings. There were, no doubt, many in the early Church who, with a view to more complete freedom from the cares, temptations, and

business of the world, withdrew from the ordinary intercourse of life, and took up their abode in natural caverns or rudely formed huts in deserts, forests, mountains, and other solitary places. The pagan depravation of manners must have in no small degree contributed to it. Then there must naturally have been multitudes of outwardly professing Christians, especially in large cities, who sickened the heart of those earnest souls whose spirit and disposition led to a nearness with Christ. Hence we find that hermits are generally spoken of as emanating from large cities, which were seats of corruption, thereby indicating clearly that in the primitive Church the ascetic desire was prompted by man's noblest impulses. In the writings of the Church fathers we can trace these germs of Christian monachism back to the middle of the 2d century. Thus writes Ricaut, when speaking of Mount Athos (*Present State of the Greek and Armenian Churches* [A.D. 1678], p. 218): "Though St. Basil was the first author and founder of the order of *Greek* monks, so that before his time there could be none who professed the strict way of living in convents and religious societies—I mean in Greece—yet certainly, before his time, the convenience of the place, and the situation thereof, might invite *Hermites,* and persons delighting in solitary devotions, of which the world, in the *first* and *second* century, did abound" (comp. Origen, *Ep. ad Rom.* c. iii; Möhler, *Gesch. d. Mönchthums in s. ersten Entstehung,* etc., in *Vermischte Schriften,* ii, 165 sq.). Yet it is as late as the middle of the 3d century, in which falls the Decian persecution (A.D. 249–251), that there are first brought to light numerous instances of a retirement of devoted Christians to the desert (comp. Sozomen, *Hist. Eccles.* lib. vi, cap. 43). But even these hermits were not monastics in the modern sense of the word. They were accustomed to live singly, each according to his own inclination, without any specific form of union, and that *within* the precincts of the Church to which they severally belonged, unless personal safety required removal to more distant parts. It was reserved for the 4th century—the very age which gave state aid and perpetuity to Christianity—to develop that branch of asceticism which has ever since continued to flourish in a part of the Church, and to this day figures in the history of Christian civilization, sometimes to advantage, and oftentimes to great disadvantage.

2. *Development of Monachism.* — In what has preceded it is clearly foreshadowed that the historical development of the monastic institution was neither sudden nor rapid, but that it passed through several stages before it finally took the shape under which it is now known to us. Dr. Schaff distinguishes *four* stages —the first three complete in the 4th century; the remaining one reaches maturity in the Latin Church of the Middle Ages. (*a*) The first stage covers the ascetic life, neither organized nor separated from the Church. It comes down from the ante-Nicene age, and is noticed in the article ASCETICISM (q. v.). In the 4th century it took the form, for the most part, of either hermit or cœnobite life, and continued in the Church itself, especially among the clergy, who might be called halfmonks. (*b*) The second stage, which is hermit-life or anchoretism [see ANACHORETS], arose in the beginning of the 4th century, gave asceticism a fixed and permanent shape, and pushed it even to external separation from the world. It took the prophets Elijah and John the Baptist for its models, and went beyond them (comp. *Lond. Qu. Rev.* April, 1855, p. 164). Not content with partial and temporary retirement from common life, which may be united with social intercourse and useful labors, the consistent anchoret secluded himself from all society, even from kindred ascetics, and came only exceptionally into contact with human affairs, either to receive the visits of admirers of every class, especially of the sick and the needy (which were very frequent in the case of the more celebrated monks), or to appear in the cities on some extraordinary occasion, as a spirit from

another world. His clothing was a hair shirt and a wild-beast's skin; his food bread and salt; his dwelling a cave; his employment prayer, affliction of the body, and conflict with satanic powers and wild images of fancy. They were, as Montalembert says, "naifs comme des enfants, et forts comme des géants;" though Villemain, forming a more unimpassioned estimate of monasticism and its results, says, "De cette rude école du desert il sortait des grands hommes et des fous;" heroes and madmen (Melanges Elog. Chrét. p. 356). The anchorets maintained from choice, after the cessation of the persecutions, the seclusion to which they had originally resorted as an expedient of security; and a later development of the same principle is found in the still more remarkable psychological phenomenon of the celebrated Pillar Saints (q. v.).

The founder of the anchoretic mode of life is supposed to have been one certain Paul of Thebes, but St. Anthony is generally looked upon as "the father of monasticism" (Neander, ii, 229); and though this is perhaps going a little too far, he must certainly be regarded as the principal influence in the anchoretic movement. Says Neander (Ch. Hist. ii, 228, 229), "In the 4th century men were not agreed on the question as to who was to be considered the founder of monasticism, whether Paul or Anthony. If by this was to be understood the individual from whom the *spread* of this mode of life proceeded, the name was unquestionably due to the latter; for if Paul was the first Christian hermit, yet he must have remained unknown to the rest of the Christian world, and without the influence of Anthony would have found no followers. (Before Anthony, there may have been many who, by inclination or by peculiar outward circumstances, were led to adopt this mode of life; but they remained, at least, unknown.) The first whom tradition—which in this case, it must be confessed, is entitled to little confidence, and much distorted by fable—cites by name is the above-mentioned Paul. He is said to have been moved by the Decian persecution, which no doubt raged with peculiar violence in his native land, the Thebaid, in Upper Egypt, to withdraw himself, when a young man, to a grotto in a remote mountain. By degrees he became attached to the mode of life he had adopted at first out of necessity. Nourishment and clothing were supplied him by a palm-tree that had sprung up near the grotto. Whether everything in this legend, or, if not everything, what part of it, is historically true, it is impossible to determine. According to the tradition, Anthony (q. v.) . . . having heard of Paul, visited him, and made him known to others. But as Athanasius, in his life of Anthony, is wholly silent as to this matter, which he certainly would have deemed an important circumstance—though he states that Anthony visited all ascetics who were experienced in the spiritual life—the story must be dismissed as unworthy of credit."

It was really Anthony who gave to his age a pattern, which was seized with love and enthusiasm by many hearts that longed after Christian perfection, and which excited many to emulate it. Like Paul, Anthony was a native of Egypt, and being himself of a noble family, his influence was considerable, and he persuaded many members of the old Egyptian families to join him, and spread his ascetic views and practices throughout all Egypt; even the deserts of this country, to the borders of Lybia, were sprinkled with numerous anachoretic societies. Hence the institution spread to Palestine and Syria, and Anthony, indeed, was visited not only by Egyptian ascetics, but also by those coming from Jerusalem (see Palladii *Lausiaca*, c. 26, *Biblioth. patrum Parisiensis*, t. xiii, fol. 939). Thus it was that Anthony, "*without any conscious design of his own*" (Neander), became the founder of this new mode of Christian living; for it in truth happened of its own accord, without any special efforts of his, that persons of similar disposition attached themselves to him, and, building their cells around his, made him their spiritual guide and

governor, and thus constituted the first societies of Anachorets, who lived scattered, in single cells or huts, united together under one superior — demonstrating, moreover, that in monasticism prevailed the same law as in every other intellectual movement. An idea exists long in a state of free solution, till the mastermind is revealed, destined to give it fixity and permanence; and from that time it becomes a nucleus around which system gathers and crystallizes. Thus the recluses of the desert continued to gain in strength and number until gathered by Anthony; the connecting tie being a triple vow of chastity, poverty, and manual labor for the common good. Thenceforth the attention of Christendom was attracted to the Thebaid; all who needed it found there an asylum. But it was, after all, only for the East, and not for the world. Christianity had proved itself adapted to the wants of all; this form of asceticism could prevail only where the climate favored a hermit's life. It was too eccentric and unpractical for the West, and hence less frequent there, especially in the rougher climates. To the female sex it was entirely unsuited. An order of widows, employed in charitable works, and supported from the offerings of the faithful, was apparently one of the primitive institutions of the apostles (Lea, *Celibacy*, p. 100); yet they were not separated from the world, but moved in it. See DEACONESSES. There was, to be sure, a class of hermits, the *Sarabaites* (q. v.) in Egypt, and the *Rhemoboths* (q. v.) in Syria; but their quarrelsomeness, occasional intemperance, and opposition to the clergy brought them into ill-repute.

(c) The third step in the progress of the monastic life brings us to *Cœnobitism* or *cloister life*—monasticism in the ordinary sense of the word. The necessities of the religious life itself—as the attendance at public worship, the participation of the sacraments, the desire for mutual instruction and edification—naturally enough led gradually to modifications of the degree and of the nature of the solitude. First came the simplest form of common life, which sought to combine the personal seclusion of individuals with the common exercise of all the public duties; an aggregation of separate cells into the same district, called by the name *Laura*, with a common church, in which all assembled for prayer and public worship. From the union of the common life with personal solitude is derived the name *cœnobite*, i. e. common life, by which this class of monks is distinguished from the strict solitaries, as the anchorets or eremites. In this, too, is involved, in addition to the obligations of poverty and chastity, which were vowed by the anchorets, a third obligation of obedience to a superior, which, in conjunction with the two former, has ever been held to constitute the essence of the religious or monastic life. See MONASTERY.

Like all the other ascetic institutions, the monastic life also found its home in Egypt. The country was certainly favorable to the production and expansion of just such an institution. "The land where Oriental and Grecian literature, philosophy, and religion, Christian orthodoxy and Gnostic heresy, met both in friendship and in hostility," was in every way adapted to be "the native land" of the monastic life. We may add also that "monasticism was favored and promoted here by climate and geographic features, by the oasis-like seclusion of the country, by the bold contrast of barren deserts with the fertile valley of the Nile, by the superstition, the contemplative turn, and the passive endurance of the national character, by the example of the Therapeutæ, and by the moral principles of the Alexandrian fathers; especially by Origen's theory of a higher and lower morality, and of the merit of voluntary poverty and celibacy." Even back in the days of Ælian we are told by him that the Egyptians bear the most exquisite torture without a murmur, and would rather be tormented to death than compromise truth. Such natures, once seized with religious enthusiasm, were certainly very eminently qualified for saints of the desert. No wonder, then, that the monastic life soon gained general favor. *Pachomius* (292–348), a disciple of Anthony, is recognised as the founder of this peculiar ascetic life. Palladius, himself a convert in these early days to this institution, furnishes an account of its progress in connection with an account of its author, which Neander thus presents: "Pachomius, at the beginning of the 4th century, when a young man, after having obtained his release from the military service, into which he had been forced, attached himself to an aged hermit, with whom he passed twelve years of his life. Here he felt the impulse of Christian love, which taught him that he ought not to live merely so as to promote his own growth to perfection, but to seek also the salvation of his brethren. He supposed—unless this is a decoration of the legend—that in a vision he heard the voice of an angel giving utterance to the call in his own breast—it was the divine will that he should be an instrument for the good of his brethren, by reconciling them to God (*Vita Pachom.* § 15). On Tabennæ, an island of the Nile, in Upper Egypt, betwixt the Nomes of Tenthyra and Thebes, he founded a society of monks, which during the lifetime of Pachomius himself numbered three thousand, and afterwards seven thousand members; and thus went on increasing until, in the first half of the 5th century, it could reckon within its rules fifty thousand monks (*Lauriaca*, vi, 1, c. 909; also c. 38, fol. 957; Hieronymi *Præfat. in regulam Pachomii*, § 7)." We are told that when Athanasius visited Pachomius three thousand monks passed before him in procession, chanting hymns, and exhibiting practical proofs of direct piety under the monastic rule. Nor was the new movement confined to the Tabennæ region. The development in the Nitrian and Thebaid deserts was equally rapid; so that Rufinus (*V. Patr.* ii, 7) affirms that the monastic population of Egypt equalled the inhabitants of the towns. In the single district of Nitria, we are told, there were no fewer than fifty monasteries (Sozomen, *Eccles. Hist.* vi, 31), and the civil authorities even found it expedient to place restrictions on their excessive multiplication. Neither was the movement confined to Egypt. Arabia, Syria, Palestine, and more especially the region of Mount Sinai, soon swarmed with recluses, and were thickly studded with monasteries. "We daily receive monks," says Jerome (346–420), writing at Bethlehem, "from India, and Persia, and Ethiopia." The entire Eastern Church gave this practice confidence, and the greatest teachers of the Church—as Gregory Nazianzen (329–389), Basil the Great (328–379), and the golden-tongued Chrysostom (342–407)—became its enthusiastic admirers and promoters. Nor did the desert remain the home of the new life. Monastic institutions were soon transplanted to the towns, and in agitated times these places became safe houses of refuge from the troubles of the world. Indeed, it must be conceded by all honest students of early ecclesiastical history that the example of the monasticism of the early Eastern Church had a powerful influence in forwarding the progress of Christianity; although it is also certain that the admiration which it excited occasionally led to its natural consequence among the members, by eliciting a spirit of pride and ostentation, and by provoking, sometimes to fanatical excesses of austerity, sometimes to hypocritical simulations of rigor. The abuses which arose, even in the early stages of monachism, are deplored by the very fathers who are most eloquent in their praises of the institution itself. These abuses prevailed chiefly in a class of monks called *Sarabaites* (q. v.), who lived in small communities of three or four, and sometimes led a wandering and irregular life. Yet though many took exception to any abuses growing out of the institution, but few were found, like Jovinian, to assail the principle. And even emperors, as, e. g., Valens and his suc-

cessors, sought in vain to arrest the too rapid increase of monachism. A picture is drawn by Theodoret, in his *Religious Histories*, of the rigor and mortification practiced in some of the greater monasteries, which goes far to explain the assertion of Protestant writers that the monks were commonly zealots in religion; and that much of the bitterness of the religious controversies of the East was due to their unrestrained zeal; and that the opinions which led to these controversies originated for the most part among the theologians of the cloisters. (Most famous among these was an order called *Acœmetæ* [Gr. *sleepless*], from their maintaining the public services of the Church day and night without interruption. See IMAGE-WORSHIP; MONOPHYSITES; MONOTHELITES; NESTORIANS.)

Under the growing influence of the Byzantine emperors, the Eastern Church, and with it Eastern monachism, lost all vitality and became petrified. No attempts were made to revive its declining vigor by creating new organizations, and though there have indeed been occasional examples of splendid benevolence in Oriental monachism, these are after all isolated instances. "As a general rule," says Stanley, "there has arisen in the East no society like the Benedictines (see below), held in honor wherever literature or civilization has spread; no charitable orders, like the Sisters of Mercy, which carry light and peace in the darkest haunts of suffering humanity" (*Eastern Church*, p. 114). Traditionally all the Eastern monks have followed up to the present day the so-called rule of Pachomius, or, as they prefer, of St. Anthony. They remain numerous in all the Eastern churches, and some of their establishments, as the convents of Mount Athos, are still celebrated for their literary treasures or political influence [see MONKS, EASTERN]; but they have ceased to be powerful agencies of religious influence. This is of course easily to be accounted for on general principles. The Eastern Church is by us of the West recognised as *stationary* and *immutable*, while our own motto is *progress* and *flexibility*. Hence active life is, on the strict Eastern theory, an abuse of the system. And while the monastic life, as we shall presently examine it in detail, in the Western world is characterized by literary and agricultural activity, the Eastern monks, whether in Egypt or Greece, have always passed a passive life, turning aside, and that only occasionally, simply to secure the necessaries for their subsistence. Some monks, it is true, devoted a portion of their time to mechanical trades, among which we find ship-building, and to agriculture; but all their occupations and rules were after all designed to overcome the desires of the body, and to make it a willing servant and instrument of the soul in its excessive religious aspirations. Annihilation of individualism was aimed at, in order to be wholly possessed and owned by God. The wildest individual excesses of a Bruno or a Dunstan seem poor beside the authorized national, we may almost say imperial, adoration of the pillar saints of the East. Thus also, e. g., amid all the controversies of the 5th century, on one religious subject the conflicting East maintained its unity—in the reverence of the hermit on the pillar. The West certainly has never had a Simeon Stylites (q. v.).

It is clearly apparent, then, to the careful student of ecclesiastical history that monasticism proper, in its first stage, was developed in the Eastern Church. But we shall see presently that monasticism was early transplanted to the West also. We will see it, however, in a modified form, really constituting the fourth and last stage of asceticism, or the second stage of monasticism proper. Before we pass to its consideration, it may not be amiss to regard here the third stage in its relation to the other two that preceded it. Pachomius himself, as we have seen, was originally a hermit. It will be found upon examination that all other ascetics who are marked as the most celebrated order-founders of later days were also originally hermits. Cloister life, indeed, is a regular organization of the ascetic life on a social basis, recognising as it does, at least in a measure, the social element of human nature, and representing it in a narrower sphere secluded from the larger world. Hence hermit life led to cloister life, and the cloister life became not only a refuge for the spirit weary of the world, but also in many ways a school for practical life in the Church. We must certainly confess that it formed the transition from isolated to social Christianity ; for it consists in an association of a number of anchorets of the same sex for mutual advancement in ascetic holiness. The cœnobites, living somewhat according to the laws of civilization, under one roof, and under a superintendent or abbot, divide their time between common devotions and manual labor, and devote their surplus provisions to charity ; except the mendicant monks, who themselves live by alms.

In this modified form monasticism became available to the female sex, to which the solitary desert life was utterly impracticable ; and with the cloisters of monks there appear at once cloisters also of nuns. Anthony and Pachomius, we are told by their biographers, were tended by their sisters ; Ammonius by his wife ; and crowds of heroic women confided their honor to the wilderness rather than to the caprices of fortune in times of trouble. Hence this germ of nunneries developed their growth even as rapidly as the monasteries, and, though the cause no longer exists, cloisters for female ascetics abound to this day in the East and in the West. See NUNNERIES.

(d) *Fourth Stage of Monasticism.*—The same social impulse, finally, which produced monastic congregations, led afterwards to monastic orders, unions of a number of cloisters under one rule and a common government. In this, the fourth and last stage, monasticism presents itself in the West, and played no little part, we gladly confess, for the diffusion of Christianity and the advancement of learning, becoming in one sense even the cradle of the German Reformation (comp. Schaff, *Ch. Hist.* ii, 158, 176).

We have seen above that Athanasius, one of the Western Church fathers, was in the East, and enjoyed a personal association with Anthony and Pachomius. When Athanasius returned to Rome (about A.D. 341), he determined to introduce the practice of the monastic life into the Western Church. He brought home with him some Egyptian monks for the purpose of initiating the Romans, and in order to exhibit to them living evidence of the sanctifying principles of the new "religio." Their uncouth and savage appearance, however, excited disgust and ridicule, and for a time the effort failed. But Athanasius, in nowise disconcerted, published a biographical account of St. Anthony, which, being early translated into Latin, had great influence on the people. Besides, respectable bishops of the West, who had been banished to the East during the Arian controversies, brought back with them, on their return, an enthusiasm for the monastic life. In Rome especially the feeling of ridicule gave way to enthusiastic admiration, and men and women of rank were impelled by the ascetic spirit which was spread by Jerome (346-420) during his residence in that city to retire from the great world, in which they had shone, and devote themselves to the monastic life. Patricians, rich merchants, and men of letters adopted the distinctive dress of the anchorite, and with it the three self-denying vows of the ascetic life. Senators and matrons transformed their palaces and country-seats. Villas, bearing the names of Gracchus, Scipio, Camillus, and Marcellus, were converted by the representatives of these great names into monasteries (the ruins of the Anician palace, of vast extent, were still to be seen in the middle of the 8th century at the gate of Nursia [comp. Montalembert, ii, 8] ; and the family from whence it had its name is renowned in the annals of monasticism as the stock of which Benedict and

Gregory the Great were descendants). From Rome the movement spread through the provinces, and established itself in the isles of the Mediterranean ; chiefly through the energetic action of Eusebius of Vercelli, who, like Athanasius, had obtained a temporary resting-place in the Thebaid when driven from his see. Men possessing such great influence as Ambrose of Milan, John Curianus, Martin of Tours, the presbyter Jerome (q. v.), also contributed subsequently, in the course of the 4th century, still further to awaken and diffuse this tendency of the Christian spirit in Italy and in Gaul.

Everywhere the institution now spread rapidly, in the same general forms in which the monasteries were built up in the East. Pachomius had started some of these and given them monastic shape, but it was reserved for Basil the Great (328-379) to give perfect organization to the vast army of monks, and to bind them by a formal vow of chastity, poverty (involving the duty of self-support by manual labor), and obedience to authority. But even Basil's work was vague and desultory, and St. Augustine was not a little tried in his endeavors to diffuse monasticism in North Africa and Italy. He condemned the idleness of the monks, ever fearing the danger which would spring from affording too great freedom to men who had been accustomed to severe corporeal labor and to rigid restraint. Many there were who would be right well disposed to exchange a needy, sorrowful, and laborious life for one free from all care, exempt from labor, and at the same time enjoy the pleasure of being looked up to with universal respect. Those who discarded the obligation to manual labor ventured, in defending their principles, to pervert many passages of the New Testament. When that precept of the apostle Paul in 2 Thess. iii, 12 was objected to them, they appealed, on the other hand, to those misconceived passages in the Sermon on the Mount in which all care for the wants of the morrow, hence all labor to acquire the means of sustenance for the morrow, were forbidden. Christian perfection was made to consist in this—that men should expect, without laboring for their support, to be provided for by the hand of God, like the fowls of the air. This precept of Christ, they contended, Paul could not mean to contradict ; the laboring, accordingly, as well as the eating, in those words of Paul, must be understood not in the literal, but in a spiritual sense—as referring to the obligation of communicating the nourishment of the divine Word, which men had themselves received, to others also—an example of the perversion of Scripture worthy to be noticed. But not only Augustine— other friends of monasticism soon came to apprehend the obstacles likely to face Christian activity, and a Church Council, that of Chalcedon (A.D. 451), found it necessary to pass canons for the regulation of monks. Yet these changes could affect only the East, the West having no part in its deliberations, and having as its representatives only four papal legates. Hence, while in the East some provisions were made for the safety of Christian asceticism, in the garb of monasticism, the Western Church was constantly and considerably modifying the Eastern practices, until the relaxations of Western monastics threatened apostasy and heresy unlimited. The inmates of different cells under the same head varied in their observance, each recluse retaining his accustomed usage when admitted into the community. And, in truth, no rule could well be universal. In Gaul the monks declaimed against the severe rule of fasting imported from the East. A discipline that was practicable under a burning Syrian sun required modification to suit the colder latitude of Gaul. Discontent and laxity were taking hold everywhere, and monachism would perhaps have been unable to withstand the destructive influences which, in this and the following times, were spreading far and wide ; and the irregularities prevailing in the spiritual order would have become more widely diffused in

Western monachism, which had a still laxer constitution, had not a remarkable man introduced into the monastic life a more settled order and a more rigid discipline, and given it the shaping and direction of a hierarchical religious order, by which it became so influential an instrument to Christianity, particularly for the conversion and the culture of rude nations (Neander, ii, 259). This remarkable man was *Benedict*, an Italian monk of the early part of the 6th century. His religious rules were at first intended and framed merely for the government of the convent Monte Cassino (q. v.), over which he presided, but they afterwards were adopted by or forced upon a very great number of monasteries. His rule was founded on that of Pachomius, though in many respects it deviated from it. His great object seems to have been to render the discipline of the monks milder, their establishment more solid, and their manners more regular than those of other monastic establishments. "Benedict," says Neander, "aimed to counteract the licentious life of the irregular monks—who roamed about the country, and spread a corrupting influence both on manners and on religion—by the introduction of a severer discipline and spirit of order." The dominant principles of Benedict's rule are obedience and labor; being administrative rather than creative in its origin, and presupposing the existing rules of chastity and poverty. The founder speaks of his rule as merely a beginning, a tentative ordinance—"Hanc minimam inchoationis regulam," etc. (c. 73). The principal of every establishment was enjoined to take counsel, either of the whole house in capitular assembly, or of the decanal body chosen from the different decades of the community. A candidate for the novitiate was long kept without the walls to try his constancy. When admitted within, he was placed for two months under the tuition and surveillance of an experienced monk, and warned daily with respect to the hardships and discipline of the monastery. If the novice still wished to take the vow, the laws of the society were read over to him, and permission given him to return to the world if he so pleased. The same opportunity was three times repeated during the year of novitiate, at the expiration of which time he was admitted as a member of the community. The sixty-three heads under which the rule is arranged refer to the relative duties of the principal and subordinate members—divine worship, discipline, household economy, and various ordinances referring to hospitality, missions, nursing, etc. The prescribed dress was in all probability that which had always been adopted by recluses, for it is almost the same coarse garb as that which Columella (*De Re Rustica*, xi, 1) recommends for the farm serf in all kinds of weather. The whole time of the monks of his order he directed to be divided between prayer, reading, the education of youth, and other pious and learned labors. All who entered his order were obliged to promise when they were received as novitiates, and to repeat their promise when they were admitted as full members of the society, that they would in no respect and on no account attempt to change or add to the rules which he had instituted. Doubtless aware that the ascetic severity of many of the monastic orders in the East was unsuited to the rude men of the West, and also to the more unfriendly climate, Benedict did not require of his monks many of the mortifications which were sometimes imposed upon those of the East, and allowed them several indulgences which were there sometimes forbidden. His rule was consequently embraced by nearly all the monks of the West. In some of the more isolated churches, as, for instance, that of Britain, it would seem that the reformations of St. Benedict were not introduced until a late period; and in the churches of that country, as well as those of Ireland, they were a subject of considerable controversy.

Benedict admitted both the learned and unlearned into his order; it was the duty of the first to assist at the choir, of the latter to attend to the household economy and temporal concerns of the monastery. At this period, it may be observed, the recitation of the divine office at the choir (as it is called by the Roman Catholics) was confined to the monks; afterwards it was established as the duty of all priests, deacons, and sub-deacons. The Benedictines at first admitted none into their order who were not well instructed how to perform it; but it was not necessary that they should be priests, or even in holy orders. Afterwards many were admitted who were ignorant of the duty of the choir; they were employed in menial duties: hence the introduction of *Lay Brothers* into the Benedictine order. When first introduced, they were not considered as a portion of the monastic establishment, but as merely attached and subordinate to it; but in course of time both the order and the Church acknowledged them to be, in the strictest sense of the word, professed religious. All other religious orders, both men and women, following the example of the Benedictines, have admitted lay brothers and sisters. In 1322 the Council of Vienna ordered all monks to enter into the order of priesthood. The monks of Vallombrosa, in Tuscany, are the first among whom lay brothers are found under that appellation. See LAY BROTHER; PRIESTHOOD. One of the most important modifications of monachism in the West, it will be noticed by the careful reader, regarded the nature of the occupation in which the monks were to be engaged during the times not directly devoted to prayer, meditation, or other spiritual exercises. In the East, manual labor formed the chief, if not the sole external occupation prescribed to the monks; it being held as a fundamental principle that for each individual the main business of life was the sanctification of his own soul. In the West, besides the labor of the hands, mental occupation was also prescribed, not, it is true, for all, but for those for whom it was especially calculated. From an early period, therefore, the convents of the West became schools of learning, and training-houses for the clergy and the missionary. At a later period, most monasteries possessed a *scriptorium*, or writing-room, in which the monks were employed in the transcription of MSS.; and though much of the work so done was, as might naturally be expected, in the department of sacred learning, yet it is to the scholars of the cloister we owe the preservation of most of those masterpieces of ancient classic literature which have reached our age (comp., however, Leckey, *Hist. Europ. Morals*, ii, 220 sq.). Thence also went out those who became founders of Christianity in heathen countries. In this way Germany and Switzerland were converted. In these, as well as in the Slavic countries, it was not only by preaching, but still more by the establishment of convents having the character of agricultural establishments, that conversion was advanced (comp. Maclear, *Hist. of Christian Missions in the Middle Ages*, p. 406 sq.).

3. *Degeneracy of Monachism, and its Extension.*— The irruption of the Lombards into Italy and of the Saracens into Spain, and the civil wars in France after the death of Charlemagne, as well as the many favors received from the Church, which had come to regard recluses as a higher class of Christians, having facilitated the growth of moral corruption among the monastics, and having introduced great disorder also among the Benedictines, several attempts at reform were made, and for many centuries the history of monachism now comes to present a continual struggle of reformers with the laxity, indifference, or immorality obtaining in a larger or lesser number of the convents of those times. The first and most noted of the reformers was Benedict of Aniane († 821), whose commentary on the rule of Benedict of Nursia obtained later an equally authoritative character. Next in order stands Berno, the founder of the *Clugny Congregation* (q. v.), afterwards reformed by his successor,

St. Odo. Several monasteries adopted Odo's reforms; but it was Clugny alone that enjoyed the greatest privileges, and it was generally looked upon as the main pillar of the reformatory party. It controlled nearly all the important convents of Gaul and Italy. In the 11th century the Benedictine order again fell from its original purity and strictness. This gave rise to many attempts to restore it to its pristine form and object; hence arose the *Carthusians*, the *Camaldules*, the *Celestines*, the *Cistercians*, the monks of *Grammont*, the *Congregation of St. Maur*, and the celebrated monks of *La Trappe*.

In the 8th century a kind of middle order between the monks and the clergy had been formed, called the canons regular of St. Augustine. Their dwellings and table were in common, and they assembled at fixed hours for the divine service. In these respects they resembled the monks; but they differed from them in taking no vows, and they often officiated in churches committed to their care. Having degenerated in the 12th century, pope Nicholas II introduced a considerable reformation among them. At this period they seem to have divided into several branches of the original order; some formed themselves into communities, in which there was a common dwelling and table, but each monk, after contributing to the general stock, employed the fruits of his benefices as he deemed proper. At the head of another union was the bishop of Chartres. They adopted a more rigid and austere mode of life, renounced their worldly possessions, all private property, and lived exactly as the strictest order of monks did. This gave rise to the distinction between the *secular* and *regular* canons. The former observed the decree of pope Nicholas II; the latter followed the bishop of Chartres, and were called the *regular canons of St. Augustine*, because they were formed on the rules laid down by St. Augustine in his Epistles. They kept public schools for the instruction of youth, and exercised a variety of other employments useful to the Church. A reform was effected in the Augustines by St. Norbert; and, as he presided over a convent at Primontre, in Picardy, those monks who adopted his rule were called *Premonstratenses*. They spread throughout Europe with great rapidity.

Other orders also arose, mainly devoted to special benevolent or religious purposes. Thus, e. g., the *Order of St. Anthony* (1095) and the *Hospitallers* (1078) devoted themselves to the nursing of the sick, the *Order of Fontévraud* (1094) to the correction of lewd women, and the *Trinitarians* (1198) to the redeeming of Christian prisoners. Even the warlike tendencies of those times sought a union with the monastic spirit by the establishment of several orders of knights, such as the Knights of St. John, the Templars, the Teutonic Knights, the orders of St. Jago, Calatrava, Alcantara, Avis, and St. Maurice. See KNIGHTHOOD. During this period convents of nuns were also established, the institutes and regulations of which were similar to those adopted by the Benedictines and Augustines, or to the reformed branches springing from those two great orders.

We see in all this that in the remarkable religious movement which characterized the Church of the 12th century the principle of monachism underwent considerable modification; and yet, however active and consistent these different orders might be, they were still too imperfectly adapted to the wants of the fast approaching 13th century. There was yet too much self-indulgence in the inhabitants of the cloister, and too little for the general want in the semi-monastic orders of the knights. The latter were too much confined to special wants in life only; the former, as men who had renounced the business of this world to make themselves another in the cloisters where they lived and died, kept too far aloof from secular concerns; and even where they had been most assiduous in the duties

of their convent, their attachment to it often indisposed them to stand forward and do battle with the numerous sects that threatened to subvert Christianity itself. Something ruder and more practical, less wedded to peculiar spots and less entangled by superfluous property, was needed if the Church was to retain its rigid and monastic form (comp. Hardwick, *Ch. Hist. M. A.* p. 230). The want was made peculiarly apparent when the *Albigenses* began to lay unwonted stress on their own poverty and to decry the self-indulgence of the monks; and the Church itself, fearing for its safety, declared against the further extension of the monastic power in the Lateran Council of 1215.

At this juncture arose the two *mendicant* orders, (1) the *Minors* or *Franciscans* (q. v.), and (2) the *Preachers* or *Dominicans* (q. v.), both destined for two centuries to play a leading part in all the fortunes of the Church. See MENDICANTS. They aimed at being the best soldiers of the Church militant, and they had therefore a marked influence on subsequent Church history. They renounced every kind of worldly goods, and founded what was termed an "order of penitence" (the third estate of friars), composed of the laity (especially the working classes), who, while pledged to do the bidding of the pope and to observe the general regulations of the institute, were not restricted by the vow of celibacy, nor compelled to take their leave entirely of the world. We thus see that the *spiritual egotism*, so to speak, of the early monachism, which in some sense limited the work of the cloister to the sanctification of the individual, gave place to the more comprehensive range of spiritual duty, and made the spiritual and even the temporal necessities of one's neighbor, equally with if not more than one's own, the object of the work of the cloister. But more than that. The mendicants thus created for themselves a numerous and influential party among the laity by these tertiaries, and the Church, prizing this hold on the community, stood ready to give place to such aids. They wandered over all Europe, instructing the people, both old and young, and exhibiting such an aspect of sanctity and self-denial that they speedily became objects of universal admiration. Their churches were crowded, while those of the regular parish priests were almost wholly deserted; all classes sought to receive the sacraments at their hands; their advice was eagerly courted in secular business, and even in the most intricate political affairs; so that in the 13th and two following centuries the mendicant orders generally, but more especially the Dominicans and Franciscans, were intrusted with the management of all matters both in Church and State. They also secured many of the chairs of the theological schools in spite of the secular clergy, and the most illustrious representatives of the 13th and 14th centuries (Thomas Aquinas, Bonaventura, Albertus Magnus, Alexander of Hales, etc.) were either Dominicans or Franciscans. Several of their number filled the highest ecclesiastical positions, even the papal chair. They certainly raised monachism to the zenith of its power, influence, and prosperity. Besides the Franciscans and the Dominicans, there were the *Carmelites* and the *Hermits of St. Augustine*, but both of these were much inferior in number, reputation, and influence to the Franciscans and Dominicans. Having thus become both important and powerful, the mendicants rapidly multiplied, and the most serious results were likely to arise, as they were generally independent of episcopal jurisdiction, and were rivals to bishops and priests. The high estimation, moreover, into which monachism had risen, more particularly through the wide-spread influence of the begging friars, awakened a spirit of bitter hostility, not simply in all orders of the clergy, but also in the universities. In England the University of Oxford, and in France the University of Paris, arduously labored to overthrow its now spreading power. Pope Gregory X, with a view to check the overgrown evil, went so far even as to issue a decree prohibiting all the orders which had originated since the time of Innocent III (A.D. 1200), and reduced the mendicants to four orders—the Dominicans, Franciscans, Carmelites, and Augustinians. The Church of Rome, says Butler, " has acknowledged only these four orders to be mendicant," and the reason given is that " an order is considered to be mendicant, in the proper import of that word, when it has no fixed income, and derives its whole subsistence from casual and uncertain bounty, obtained by personal mendicity. To that St. Francis did not wish his brethren to have recourse till they had endeavored to earn a competent subsistence by labor, and found their earnings insufficient. But soon after the decease of St. Francis, the exertions, equally incessant and laborious, of his disciples for the spiritual welfare of the faithful appeared, in the universal opinion of the Church, to be both incompatible with manual labor and much more than a compensation to the public for all they could possibly obtain from it by mendicity. This opinion was unequivocally expressed by St. Thomas Aquinas, and sanctioned by a bull of pope Nicholas III ; since that time the friars have not used manual labor as a means of subsistence, but resorted in the first instance to mendicity." Mendicity seems to have made no part of the original rules of the Dominicans, Carmelites, or Hermits of Augustine ; and, in consequence of the evils attendant on it, the Council of Trent confined mendicity to the Observantines and Capuchins, allowing the other Franciscan establishments, and almost all the establishments of the three other orders, to acquire permanent property.

In the 14th century, though partly checked by the mendicant orders, a general degeneracy of monachism commenced, and the corruption, from which hardly a single order kept itself entirely free, became so overwhelming that towards the close of the Middle Ages the name monk was often used by writers as synonymous with rudeness and ignorance. "The monks," says Hardwick, "gorged with the ecclesiastical endowments, lost the moral elevation they had shown throughout the early periods of the Church, and with it forfeited their hold on the affections of the people. Except the Order of Carthusians, none of them adhered to the letter of their institute. Their intellectual vigor at the same time underwent a corresponding deterioration, insomuch that few if any works of merit, either in the field of science or in that of theology, proceeded in this age from the cloisters of the West" (*Ch. Hist. M. A.* p. 343; comp. Gieseler, *Eccles. Hist.* iii, 85 sq., 286 sq.). The monks, like a swarm of locusts, covered all Europe, proclaiming everywhere the obedience due to the holy mother Church, the reverence due to the saints (and more especially to the Virgin Mary), the efficacy of relics, the torments of purgatory, and the blessed advantages arising from indulgences. Reformatory attempts were vainly made in every century. Different new orders—as the *Jesuits, Brigittines, Servites, Hieronymites,* and others — were founded ; but their influence was weak in comparison with that of their predecessors, and frequently, after an existence of fifty or one hundred years, they themselves were as far astray from the primitive standard of rigid asceticism. "The progress of monasticism," says Cramp, "was distinguished for several centuries by unexampled prosperity and its ordinary attendant, corruption. Replenished with wealth, which the ignorant and superstitious people lavished upon them, thinking to gain favor with God thereby, the monks indulged in every kind of licentious excess, till they were as infamous for vice as their predecessors had been renowned for piety. Reformation was frequently attempted, and many new orders arose, professing at first great zeal for purity, and adopting the strictest modes of discipline, verging sometimes to the extremity of human endurance. But these also soon shared the general fate, and sank to the same low level of

shameless sensuality" (comp. *Concil.*, Labbe et Cossart, ed. Mansi, tom. xviii, 270 ; Gieseler, *Eccles. Hist.* ii, 120). The councils of Constance (A.D. 1415) and Basle (A.D. 1431), in their endeavors to brace up monastic discipline afresh, devised reformatory measures ; but they produced only transitory changes, and those only in few places. As a whole, it was daily more apparent that monasticism was growing almost incorrigible, and was ripening daily for the scythe. One of the strongest evidences of such a tendency was the formation of four spiritual associations to take the place of the monastic orders. Thus flourished, in spite of the indiscriminate denunciation of pope and priest and persecution by the Inquisition, the *Beguards* or *Beguines,* who must be regarded as an offshoot of monasticism, though they exhibited a freer and less hierarchical spirit. They flourished mainly in Germany and the Netherlands ; but other groups, in which the Beguard influence was apparent, began to spread rapidly throughout the West. They were religious brotherhoods and sisterhoods, distinguished for their zeal in visiting the sick, or, as in the case of those to whom the name of *Lollards* (q. v.) was popularly given, for singing at funerals, and for otherwise assisting in the burial of the dead. This associational principle was further developed by the *Brethren of the Free Spirit,* a confraternity which owed their origin to Gerhard Groot (middle of the 14th century), and who for some time seemed to be preparing the way for an entirely new phase of monachism. In their reformatory labors they frequently came into collision with the highest Church authorities, especially the Inquisition, though this did not prevent their spread. Their numerous societies were equally distinguished for their mysticism and their usefulness. Some of the brethren were engaged in instruction, others employed themselves in various kinds of handicraft for their livelihood. One of their chief objects was always to advance the religious education of the common people, and especially to raise up from them a pious clergy, so that they soon became fruitful nurseries for monks. This activity, and the respect in which the brethren were held by the people, excited powerfully the envy of the mendicants, but they gradually slackened their opposition when they found their own numbers increasing through the labors of these *Fratres communis vitæ.* The most remarkable of the new orders established in this period was that of the *Minimi.* Their founder, Francis of Paula, a small town in Calabria, after having lived for a short time in an unreformed Franciscan convent, established himself as a hermit in the neighborhood of his native city, and from 1457 gathered around him a society of those who shared his views. The fame of his miraculous power soon extended his society, which was confirmed by Sixtus IV (1474), under the name of the Eremitæ s. Francisci, first in Italy, and afterwards in France, where the superstitious Louis XI had summoned the founder of the order to his aid in the last extremity (1482) ; and at a later period in Spain. The order, distinguished always from the rest of the Franciscans by the observance of the vita quadragesimalis, received afterwards a rule from its founder, and, to distinguish themselves from the Fratres Minores, and to go one step beyond them, assumed the name of "Ordo minimorum fratrum eremitarum Fratres Francisci de Paula." See MINIMS.

The Reformation of the 16th century may well be called the Revolutionary period in the history of monachism. The deep decline which this institution had suffered during and immediately following the Crusades, a period in which, as we have seen, even the knights and barons subjected their profession of warriors to the forms of monkish laws, had been, it is true, to a very great extent relieved by a period of spiritual activity, ushered in by the mendicants. At their commencement they undoubtedly contributed to the restoration of primitive simplicity, their avowed object, but gradually most of them also became disorderly and worldly; and a leading feature in the corruption of the Church was perceived to be in those very orders founded to promote apostolic simplicity in the Christian Church. The best and most influential men in the Church cordially joined in the demand for a thorough reformation; they willingly and frankly admitted that the crisis had been in part occasioned by the corruption of the clergy, secular as well as monastic, and they urged, in particular, the imperious necessity of a reformation of the religious orders (comp. Gieseler, *Eccles. Hist.* iv, 131-156). The protest of the Reformers met with a cordial response in the breasts of multitudes whose attachment to the Church of Rome was warm and almost inextinguishable. In Italy attempts were made to renovate their youth; but on the Continent, especially in Germany and the Netherlands, the people would be satisfied with nothing short of the dissolution of monkery (Ranke, *Papacy*, i, 129, 384): they were determined that no monasteries or convents should longer subsist. This opposition had been engendered partly by a gradual alienation of all monastics from the people, but even more by the attacks that had been made upon it by many of the leading Reformers, who sought reformation within the Church. Foremost among them was that declared foe of all superstition, the immortal Erasmus (q. v.). In his early days he had tasted, by constraint, something of monkish life, and his natural abhorrence of it was made more intense by his bitter recollection, and by the trouble it cost him, after he had become famous, to release himself from the thraldom to which his former associates were inclined to call him back. He was very competent, therefore, to bear testimony for or against the monkish life, and when he became its opponent his opinions commanded the attention of all the thoughtful. And not only became he now an opponent, but a lifelong warfarer against the monks and their ideas and practices. His tongue and his pen also were used freely. His *Praise of Folly*, and, in particular, the *Colloquies*, in which the idleness, illiteracy, self-indulgence, and artificial and useless austerities of "the religious" were handled in the most diverting style, were read with infinite amusement by all who sympathized with the new studies, and by thousands who did not calculate the effect of this telling satire in abating popular reverence even for the Church establishment as a whole. It is not to be wondered, then, that popes, bishops, and councils urged upon the reformers within the religious orders to speed the day of transformation. Indeed, the internal history of nearly every order records, at this point of time, strong resolutions in favor of an enforcement of the rigorous primitive rules. "As early as 1520," says Ranke, "and since, in proportion to the advances made by Protestantism in Germany, there arose in countries which had not yet been reached by it, a feeling of the necessity of a new amelioration of the hierarchical order. This feeling made its way even in the religious orders themselves; sometimes in one, sometimes in another of them." Even the Order of the Camaldoli, secluded as they were, owned themselves implicated in the general corruption, and instituted reforms, by founding in 1522 a new congregation, that of *Monte Corona* (comp. Helyot, *Hist. des ordres monastiques*, v, 271). Its leader, Paul Giustiniani, held, in order to the attainment of Christian perfection, three things to be essential, viz. solitude, vows, and the separation of the monks into separate cells. Those small cells and oratories, such as are yet to be found here and there, on the highest hills, in charming wilds, such as seem to conduct the soul at once to sublime flights and to more profound tranquillity, are spoken of by him in some of his letters with special satisfaction. The reforms of the hermits of Monte Corona extended to all parts of the world. But not only in the smaller orders did this spirit of reform bear fruit. In the most numerous and powerful order, that

of the Franciscans, who had perhaps become the most profoundly corrupt of any, yet another new effort at reformation was attempted, in addition to the many that had been made before. The more rigorous party achieved a complete success over those inclined towards laxity, and several new reformed congregations branched off from them, among which the Capuchins were the most prominent. These friars contemplated the restoration of the regulations of their original founder—divine service at midnight, prayers at appointed hours, discipline, and silence; in short, the whole severe rule of life laid down in the original institution. One cannot but smile at the importance which they attached to things of no consequence; but, setting that aside, it must be acknowledged that they again behaved with great courage, as, for example, during the pestilence of 1528.

Besides the reformation of the old orders, the Church showed itself most prolific in producing new ones, and the character of the times is clearly apparent in many of these new organizations. The monastic institutions of former days had been, as religious communities, essentially contemplative; the new ones were predominantly operative, the mendicant orders forming, so to speak, a connecting link between the two. Preaching, teaching, visiting the sick and poor, and similar objects, formed the chief occupations of the new orders, to which the greatest energy was directed. Thus arose the *Theatines* (q. v.) in 1524, started by Cajetan of Thiene; "a man," says Ranke, "of a peaceful, quiet, and soft temper, of few words, and prone to indulge in the ecstasies of a spiritual enthusiasm; of whom it was said that he wanted to reform the world, but without its being known that he was in the world" (*Papacy*, ii, 131). The Theatines did not call themselves monks, but regular clergy; they were priests bound by monkish vows, but expressly declared that neither in life nor worship should any mere custom oblige the conscience. Their desire, no doubt, was to prevent the spread of reformatory opinions leading to alienation from the Church of Rome; and, themselves Italians, they sought, in the resumption of clerical duties under the monastic vow, to raise up a new supply for the priesthood free from the objections of the times. They became pretty numerous, not only in Italy, but also in Spain, South Germany, and in France. Another of these orders was that of the *Barnabites* (q. v.), also founded in Italy in 1532, suggested at Milan by the ravages of war and the consequent sufferings of the people, which the order was intended to mitigate by active beneficence, as well as to remove the disorderly habits which it had brought in its train, by instruction, preaching, and good example. Somewhat later, St. Philip Neri, an active and remarkable devotee of the papacy at Florence, founded the order *Fathers of the Oratory*, which was confirmed by pope Gregory XIII in 1577, and spread not only in Italy, but to this day continues to flourish, especially in France.

But whatever might be accomplished by all these congregations in their own circles, either the limited extent of their object, as in the instance we have last mentioned, or that circumspection of their means, which was involved in the nature of the case, as on the part of the Theatines, hindered their exercising a general and thoroughly efficient influence. They are remarkable as signalizing, in the spontaneity of their origin, a powerful tendency, which contributed immensely to the restoration of Roman Catholicism; but other forces were requisite in order that the bold advance of Protestantism might be effectually withstood. These forces developed themselves in a similar, but in a very unlooked-for and extremely peculiar manner; and as heretofore, so even now, monasticism proved Rome's strongest ally, and the papacy once more leaned on the new-born babe of the monastic spirit. Leo X had died, leaving the fierce flame of insubordination untrammelled, and Paul III had vainly tried to subdue the indomitable will of that fierce monster, the Reformation, when suddenly there arose in the Iberian peninsula a semi-monastic organization, which, growing out of the Capuchin order, laid the foundation for the strongest religious society the world has ever known. The Society of Jesus, or *Jesuits*, as it is generally called, took a middle rank between monks and the secular clergy, approaching nearer to the regular canons than to any other order. They lived separate from the multitude, and were bound by religious vows; but they were exempt from stated hours of worship, and other strict observances, by which the monks were bound. In short, instead of spending their time in devotion and penance and fasting, they gave themselves to the active service of the Church. Their principal duty was to direct the education of youth and the consciences of the faithful, and to uphold the cause of the Church by their missions, and their pious and learned labors. They were divided into three classes, the first of which were the professed members. These, besides the ordinary vows of poverty, chastity, and obedience, bound themselves to go, without murmur, inquiry, deliberation, or delay, wherever the pope should think fit to send them: they were monastics without property. The second class comprehended the scholars: these were possessed of large revenues; their duty was to teach in the colleges of the order. The third class comprehended the novices, who lived in the houses of probation. (See, however, the article JESUITS.) The constitution of the Jesuits was controlled, more than that of any other order before or after, by the principle of an absolute submission to the Church and the pope. The order was to be an instrument in the hands of the Church; the individual, therefore, was advised to become, with regard to the commands of his superior, as destitute of self-will "as a corpse," or "as a cane in the hands of an old man." No order ever carried out its fundamental principle more faithfully, and in subsequent battles of the Roman Catholic Church the Jesuits stood in the front rank. Other orders also were founded which proved more or less valuable supports of the papacy. There arose even several female orders, among them the *Elizabethines* (q. v.), the *Ursulines* (q. v.), and the *Sisters of Charity*. See CHARITY, SISTERS OF. One of the strongest orders which arose in the 17th century was the *Lazarist* (q. v.).

The culture of literature, against which in the Middle Ages some founders of monastic orders had expressly warned their members, showed itself, after the 16th century, so great a necessity that it was practically observed by all orders, though but few gave it special attention. Among those orders which thus greatly distinguished themselves, the French Oratorians and the Benedictines of St. Maur hold by universal consent not only the most prominent position, but they are even assigned a distinguished place among the great literary societies of the world. Indeed the cause of education, especially the cause of primary instruction, became gradually a subject of more or less interest to all the religious orders. Many congregations, both male and female, were instituted for the special purpose of controlling primary instruction, especially in France, and a large number of schools have ever since been under the direction of monastics.

If the Romish Church sought to strengthen itself by the new measures adopted by monasticism in providing such education for the coming generations as the Church could endorse, another measure was still needed to give the Church strength abroad. Great loss of territory and numbers had been suffered in consequence of the Reformation. This want also the monastics soon provided for. They became very extensively missionary organizations. Instead of confining their labors, as was their wont to do, to the home work, they now directed their attention to the foreign missionary cause. Most of the larger orders, espe-

cially the mendicants and the Jesuits, engaged in it with great zeal and emulation. The latter even took, besides the usual three vows, a fourth obligation, viz. to go without hesitation as missionaries to any country where it might please the pope to send them. In consequence, the extent of their missionary operations in Europe, Asia, Africa, and America excelled anything the Roman Catholic Church had done in this field before. See MISSIONS. Indeed, the great majority of the Roman Catholic missions in all pagan countries have ever since been conducted by the members of religious orders (see *Harper's Monthly* for February, 1875).

4. *Present Condition of Roman Catholic Monachism.* —In the 17th century the attention of many monastics was more specially directed towards the necessity of bringing back their institutions, as far as possible, to the rules and laws of their order, and the monks of the Roman Catholic churches now became divided into the Reformed and the Unreformed, and some real effort to restore the monasteries and nunneries to their original state was attempted. But whatever necessity existed for these institutions in an age of barbarism and violence, it had now ceased. The printing-press was proving a more powerful preservative of the Bible and religious literature than the cells of the monks, and long experience had demonstrated that to shut one's self out from the world was but a sorry way to keep unspotted from it. Such a time was not likely to give life to new monastic institutions, and hence we find the productivity of the Church as regards monachism very greatly decreased. In the 18th century only one larger order, the *Redemptorists*, or the Congregation of the Most Holy Redeemer, founded by St. Alfonso di Liguori, sprang up. Most of the orders, indeed, in the second half of this century, relapsed either into torpor or corruption, and made but a very feeble resistance when the rationalistic views which became so prevalent among the educated classes in every European country, Catholic as well as Protestant, declared against them a war of destruction. Hence in many countries the state authorities interfered anew to destroy conventual life. In Austria, Joseph II suppressed as useless all convents of monks not occupied in education, pastoral duties, or the nursing of the sick; and many Roman Catholic writers demanded the extirpation of monasticism altogether, after stamping it as both an outgrowth and a promoter of fanaticism. Even the papacy was influenced, and the incumbent of St. Peter's at Rome had no other alternative left him than to yield to the general pressure. The consequence was the abolishment of the most powerful of the orders, the Jesuits. The French Revolution threatened the very life of monachism, and had that movement proved successful the monastic institutions would have passed out of existence probably in all Europe.

The downfall of the Napoleonic rule gave brighter prospects to the friends of monasticism, and as an evidence of its revival may be cited the re-establishment of the Jesuits by Pius VII in 1814. These now rapidly rose again to considerable strength and influence wherever they were not forcibly suppressed. See JESUITS. In the countries of the Latin races, both in Europe and America, the fate of monachism was closely allied with the political strife of the conservative and the liberal or progressive parties, the former patronizing it, together with all other ecclesiastical institutions; the latter subjecting it to prohibitive rules, or suppressing it altogether. In consequence of the successes of the liberals, monachism was greatly reduced in South America, and in Italy (in 1848, and again in 1859, 1860, 1866, and 1870, until it is now on the eve of complete suppression by law of the state, 1875). See MONASTERY. It was also wellnigh extinguished in Spain (1835), and especially in Portugal (1834). In France alone the vicissitudes of political rule have thus far failed to affect monasticism — indeed, the rapid growth of monastic institutions in that country have not been in point of zeal, activity, and general prosperity behind what they had been during the golden æra of their existence. Under the Bourbons, and under Louis Philippe, the liberal party occasionally demanded coercive measures against them; but since the establishment of the republic in 1848 even the liberals, having given a wider interpretation to religious liberty than Americans have ever dared to give, have accustomed themselves no longer to refuse the free right of association to the members of religious orders. Nearly every one of the old orders established itself in France, and a number of new congregations were formed, and there is at present a greater variety of monastic institutions in that country than any state has possessed at any previous period. In July, 1860, M. Dupin, in a speech before the senate of France, stated that there were then in the country 4932 authorized and 2870 unauthorized establishments, and since then their number has somewhat increased. Next to France, they are most numerous, wealthy, and influential in Belgium, where, as in France, public instruction is very largely under their control.

Among the Teutonic nations the monastic establishments have, throughout the British possessions, Holland, and North America (see below; see also *Sisters of Charity*), partaken more or less of the blessings of liberal institutions, and can hardly be accused of departure from their rules except in isolated instances. Public opinion, however, has provided for one measure in their constitution not known elsewhere, viz. that any member wishing to leave their establishments shall have liberty to do so. Austria protected monasticism, but kept the inhabitants of convents under a bureaucratic guardianship until 1848, when it was changed into a zealous support and encouragement. Since 1866, however, the monasteries have been under a shadow, and it is more than likely that ere long monastic institutions will be done away with in that Roman Catholic country. In many of the other German countries, the revolution of 1848 has procured for monasticism a favorable position; and in lands where formerly it was either proscribed or but barely tolerated, it has since flourished. Even those states whose codes retain laws against their admission in general, as Saxony and the neighboring countries of Sweden and Denmark, have admitted the Sisters of Charity. See DEACONESSES and SISTERHOODS. In Russia the monastics suffered severe losses, but in Turkey they have as missionaries done much to build up the Christian faith.

The number of monastic associations founded in our century is so considerably in advance of any former period of equal length, that to a superficial observer it would indicate a growth of the monastic spirit. This is, however, due solely to the concentration of Romanism in this direction, the papacy finding these its best and perhaps only never-failing support. A peculiar feature which characterizes them as the offspring of the present age, and distinguishes them from the preceding orders, is easily discovered in all of them; the marks which externally distinguish them from the non-monastic world are less visible, and the social wants of ecclesiastical and civil society stand pre-eminently forth as the primary cause of their origin and the chief object of their labors. A large number of them are devoted to the instruction of youth. Such are several congregations of school-brothers and school-sisters, Brothers and Sisters of St. Joseph, Brothers and Daughters of the Holy Cross, etc. Many others bind themselves to the service of the sick and the poor, as the Little Sisters of the Poor, the most numerous and popular among them. Not a few cultivate the mission field; either the foreign missions, as the *Picpus Society*, the *Oblates*, the *Brothers and Daughters of Zion* (both for the conversion of the Jews, the latter consisting exclusively of converts), or the home missions, as the *Paulists*.

In the United States, monachism, because modified to suit the nature and exigencies of the times, is a flourishing and important institution, and serves as the great feeder of the Roman Catholic Church. Most of the Roman Catholic schools are more or less directly connected with these institutions, and under the care of "fathers" or "sisters." The rigor which characterized the monasteries and nunneries when they were devoted wholly or chiefly to devotional uses is somewhat relaxed here, and they are simply working institutions. "In the schools connected with these monastic establishments, especially in those for girls," says a contemporary, "secular branches are taught, but commingled with the Romish theology; and the pupils are brought under influences, both strong and subtle, upon the imagination and the feelings, in favor of the Romish communion; while the effect of the education (we speak of the result both of personal observation and of inquiry among pupils in these schools) is to divert the mind from the more solid to the more superficial branches—from mathematics and the sciences, to painting, drawing, music, and needle-work; and to base such studies as are taught rather upon authority than upon any habits of personal and individual investigation. It is impossible to obtain the statistics of these conventual schools, for they are carefully concealed; we have, however, instituted some inquiries upon this point, with the following results: There are in the United States to-day, at the very least, 300 nunneries and 128 monasteries, besides 112 schools for the education of girls, and 400 for the education of boys. Of the nunneries and monasteries (as such) we have found it impossible to obtain any trustworthy information, either as to discipline or number of inmates; but the 112 girls' schools acknowledge the charge of 22,176 young women, and this we have excellent reasons for believing to be far below the real number, for the disposition to conceal the actual work done is so marked that even their own official organs admit the impossibility of obtaining statistics. Thus, there are known to be 400 Roman Catholic schools for boys; but there are only returns from 178 procurable. The archdiocese of Baltimore alone contains 21 convents—one of colored sisters—in all of which education is carried on. Besides these, there are in Baltimore at least a dozen colleges and young girls' seminaries under Roman Catholic spiritual direction; also 50 pay and free schools taught by the "brothers and sisters of Christian schools," "Sisters of Notre Dame," "Sisters of Mercy," etc., who also have charge of 13 orphan asylums, and various other charitable and pious sodalities. And the archdiocese of Baltimore only represents what is done all over the country. These figures —and they are far from complete—certainly underrate rather than overrate the work." The Rev. Samuel W. Barnum, a learned and careful writer, and the latest Protestant author on Romanism in this country (*Romanism as it is*, p. 332), has brought together the scattered and incomplete statistics of monasticism in the United States of America, and comes to the conclusion that there are "about 30 religious orders and congregations for men, and about 50 for women, the whole numbering more than 2500 males (including Jesuits) and more than 8000 females, and having under their care considerably more than 200,000 children and youth in the process of education. More than one. half of the male religious are priests, and more than 300 Jesuits."

In a literary point of view monastics do not at present share the reputation of their predecessors in former centuries, though men like Lacordaire, Ravigna, Gratry, and Hyacinthe in France, Rosmini and Secchi in Italy, and Haneberg in Germany, occupy a high place in the annals of contemporaneous literature. In respect to their present moral condition, Roman Catholics admit the existence in some places, particularly in Central and South America, of considerable corruption and ignorance in many convents of the older orders. In some of them, also, the ancient constitutions have fallen more or less into disuse. The regular connection of the general superiors with their subordinates has been in great part interrupted, and the holding of general assemblies has ceased. The present pontiff at the commencement of his reign proclaimed it as one of his chief tasks to carry out a thorough reform of monastic orders; and in some orders, as the Dominicans, an extensive reformation has since taken place. The whole number of monastic institutions in the Roman Catholic Church throughout the world was estimated by the *Catholic Almanac* for 1870 to be 8000 establishments for males, with an aggregate of 117,500 members, and 10,000 for females, with an aggregate membership of 189,000, making a grand total of 306,500 members. It is beyond the scope of this work to give in this place a list of all the monastic organizations; they are severally treated under their respective names. It may not be out of place, however, to call the reader's attention to the fact that the different monastic institutes of the West are almost all offshoots or modifications of the *Benedictines* (q. v.); of whom the most remarkable are the *Carthusians*, *Cistercians*, *Grammonites*, *Clugniacs*, *Præmonstratensians*, and above all the *Maurists*, or Benedictines of St. Maur (q. v.). Among the eremitical orders are the Hermits of St. Augustine, who trace their origin to the early father of that name, but are subdivided into several varieties, which had their rise in the 11th, 12th, and 13th centuries; also the Camaldolese, founded by St. Romuald in 1012; the Celestines, a branch of the Franciscans, established by Peter Murrone, afterwards pope Celestine V; the Hieronymites (q. v.), established first in Castile in the 14th century, and thence introduced into other parts of Spain and into Italy by Lope d'Olmeda in 1424; and the Paulites, so called from St. Paul, the first hermit, but an institute of the 13th century, which had its origin in Hungary, and attained to a wider extension and a greater popularity than perhaps any other among the eremitical orders.

5. *Monasticism in the Protestant Church.*—The Reformation of the 16th century rejected monachism, as supported by the papacy and the patriarchate, as being based on the false principle of the meritoriousness of good works. One small denomination, the Dunkers, have retained nearly the whole of the monastic organization. Solitary voices among the Protestant theologians of the 16th, 17th, 18th centuries, and even of our own more advanced age, have expressed a regret that, with the monachism of the old churches, the principle of forming religious communities of men and women for the more efficient fulfilment of the duties of charity had been altogether discarded. Since the beginning of this century both the "Evangelical" and "High Lutheran" schools of Germany have approved the establishment of houses of *deacons* (q. v.) and *deaconesses* (q. v.), also called brother-houses and sisterhouses, the inmates of which associate for the purpose of teaching, of attending the sick, of taking charge of public prisons, and for other works of Christian charity. Institutions of this kind are rapidly spreading in Germany and the adjacent countries. In the Church of England and the Protestant Episcopal Church of the United States, *sisterhoods* (q. v.) have been formed at various times, and have recently greatly multiplied. There have also started in England, under the auspices of what is commonly called the High-Church party, several male monastic organizations, but they have not found favor generally, and are not likely to continue long in existence. The principal leader in this Protestant monastic establishment in Britain is Mr. Lyne, better known as Father Ignatius, who assumes the monkish dress, and, with shaven crown and sandalled feet, reminds one of the monastics of the Middle Ages (see *St. James's Magazine*, March, 1870).

6. *Nature and Effect of Monasticism.*—We have al-

ready indicated in some measure the character of monachism, as we have traced its origin and progress. It remains to consider briefly the spirit as well as the results of monasticism. In surveying monasticism as an institution coming down from the 4th century till the Reformation, we freely admit that, in the circumstances in which the world found itself placed during that period of time, it was far from being an unmitigated evil. In its origin, at least, it was a great human effort to remedy the moral disorder by which mankind in all ages are infected. When children raise a ladder upon the hill-top with the design that upon it they may climb upwards, and thus draw near to God, we cannot make light of their motives, even though we should smile at their plans; and so every attempt of man to eradicate the selfishness of his nature, to turn back the tide of the world's corruption, and to elevate himself in the scale of morality, is so far praiseworthy, even though we have no faith that this is to be done by men and women entering voluntarily into a prison, shutting themselves up, and barring the world out. "It was the spirit of monachism," says Neander, "which gave special prominence to that Christian point of view from which all men were regarded as originally equal in the sight of God; which opposed the consciousness of God's image in human nature, to the grades and distinctions flowing out of the relations of the state. . . . The spirit of contempt for earthly show, the spirit of universal philanthropy, revealed itself in the *pure* appearances of monachism, and in much that proceeded from it" (ii, 251; comp. p. 238). In the darkest of the ages, souls truly pious, there can be no doubt, often withdrew to such places that they might without distraction prepare for another world. In times of lawless force and bloodshed, every one knows that the monastery was an asylum where weak and timorous spirits, ill able to cope with the rude society in which they found themselves, could retire for shelter and safety. The old monks, in their earliest and best days, before their indolence was fostered by wealth and luxury, were often the only examples of peaceful industry in a district, and taught their less skilful neighbors how to till the earth, and draw from the reluctant soil a more generous return for their labor. In their lonely cells they often spent their leisure in copying valuable manuscripts and producing original works, which, though seldom rising to the rank of classics, have preserved many valuable facts, and are true photographs of the bright and the dark, the comely and ungainly features of their times. "The cloisters, moreover," says Neander, "were institutions of education, and, as such, were the more distinguished on account of the care they bestowed on religious and moral culture, because education generally in this period . . . had fallen into neglect" (ii, 252). Perhaps it is not too much to say that in the deluge of barbarism that overflowed the civilization of Christendom in the early mediæval ages, the Scriptures and the classics must have perished had it not been that they were deposited in those monastic edifices, for which the wildest pagans, in many instances, entertained a superstitious respect. Moreover, in cases without number, the monastery was a missionary training-school, planted within the limits of some heathen land, from which the monks went forth courageously and devotedly to propagate the religion of the age, such as it was, in the surrounding districts—to be the pioneers of civilization and the advance-guard of Christianity among a rude and idolatrous population. The conversion of the pagan English, and particularly of the southern kingdoms, to the faith of Christ, was mainly due to the energy and sacrifice of the monks and bishops of Rome, and it was accompanied by a parallel conversion to the authority of St. Peter. It was at that time a vast and unspeakable blessing to England to be brought in this way into association with other people, and to become thus an integral part of the Christian commonwealth. The ideal of the divine life which was set before the young and crude converts was impressive, and upon the whole beneficial, even though it lacked the freedom and naturalness of true life, and cramped and resisted the grace of God. Dean Milman tells us that the calm example of the domestic virtues in a more polished, but often, as regards sexual intercourse, more corrupt state of morals, is of inestimable value, as spreading around the parsonage an atmosphere of peace and happiness, and offering a living lesson on the blessings of conjugal fidelity. But such Christianity would have made no impression on a people who still retained something of their Teutonic severity of manners, and required, therefore, something more imposing—a sterner and more manifest self-denial—to keep up their religious veneration. The detachment of the clergy from all earthly ties left them at once more unremittingly devoted to their unsettled life as missionaries. It is probable that the isolation and the self-torture of the monks did produce a deep impression on those who had neither moral energy nor mental concentration equal to such a task. It is possible that the claims of a hierarchy were more rapidly introduced by these means, so that it became more easy to create new institutions, to organize Christian worship, to build vast ecclesiastical edifices, to promote literature, to divide the labor of Christian workmen, as soon as the available strength of young Christendom was all brought under severe drill, taught to monopolize the highest grace, and invested with preternatural powers. In old feudal times, when the strong were so ready to domineer over the weak, and society had so little thought of providing for the unfortunate, in the monastery, spirits bruised and bleeding found advice, the sick found medicine, the hungry poor found bread, and the benighted and storm-stayed traveller entertainment and rest. It would be uncandid not to admit, with very little exception indeed, the statement of count Montalembert that the monasteries "were for ten centuries and more the schools, the archives, the libraries, the hostelries, the studios, the penitentiaries, and the hospitals of Christian society."

But while acknowledging the great services which the monks have rendered to the world in the mediæval period, there is another view of the case to which we cannot close our eyes. Monasticism, instead of being "one of the greatest institutions of Christianity," has no claim whatever to be divine in its origin; Christ and his apostles were not monks, neither did they enjoin upon their followers to renounce the society of their kind, and immure themselves in the solitude of a cloister. On the contrary, the leaven was to be put into the meal; the true religion was to come in contact with humanity, and strive to gain, to direct, to improve it. Asceticism is a mere human attempt to perform upon human nature a work which the Gospel has made ample provision for performing in a more effective way. "Monasticism," says Schaff, "withdrew from society many useful forces; diffused an indifference for the family life, the civil and military service of the state, and all public practical operations; turned the channels of religion from the world into the desert, and so hastened the decline of Egypt, Syria, Palestine, and the whole Roman empire. It nourished religious fanaticism, often raised storms of popular agitation, and rushed passionately into the controversies of theological parties; generally, it is true, on the side of orthodoxy, but often, as at the Ephesian 'council of robbers,' in favor of heresy, and especially in behalf of the crudest superstition. For the simple, divine way of salvation in the Gospel, it substituted an arbitrary, eccentric, ostentatious, and pretentious sanctity. It darkened the all-sufficient merits of Christ by the glitter of the over-meritorious works of man. It measured virtue by the quantity of outward exercises instead of the quality of the inward disposition, and disseminated self-righteousness and an anxious, legal, and mechan-

ical religion. Monasticism, indeed, lowered the standard of general morality in proportion as it set itself above it, and claimed a corresponding higher merit; and it exerted in general a demoralizing influence on the people, who came to consider themselves the *profanum vulgus mundi*, and to live accordingly" (comp. Neander, ii, 255-257). Grant that the cloister has often sheltered the helpless and unfortunate; it has often sheltered, too, the ignorant, the superstitious, the criminal, the polluted, the despot, the knave. Brigands have been known to use abbeys as the storehouse of their plunder, and kings have used their rich revenues for pensioning their mistresses, supporting their bastards, and rewarding the most unscrupulous of their tools. The education received in the cloisters was essentially of a narrow kind, dwarfing the intellect, and robbing it of that expansiveness and freedom essential to high culture and to real progress. If they opened their door to the feeble and innocent in days of oppression and danger, it cannot be pretended that there is the same need for them now, when law and order are established, when society provides ample means for alleviating every want and woe that it is possible to relieve, when the printing-press has given a perpetuity to literature which neither Goth nor Vandal can destroy, and when the claims of the poor and the defenceless meet with favorable consideration from every government in Christendom.

It is not, however, monasticism, as such, which has proved a blessing to the Church and the world; for the monasticism of India, which for three thousand years has pushed the practice of mortification to all the excesses of delirium, never saved a single soul, nor produced a single benefit to the race. It was *Christianity* in monasticism which has done all the good, and used this abnormal mode of life as a means for carrying forward its mission of love and peace. In proportion as monasticism was animated and controlled by the spirit of Christianity, it proved a blessing; while separated from it, it degenerated and became a fruitful source of evil. Monasticism, moreover, seems even to have lost its power of propagating Christianity in any type; there is no instance since the Reformation of any pagan nation being Christianized by monks. Indeed we cannot concede that it should be the aim of the Christian missionary to create a well-organized society under the dictation of one great ecclesiastical rule, such as monasticism, if it labored at all, would make its object and end. We indignantly repudiate the position that, in order to teach men to become Christians, to recommend the law of Christ, convert the untutored savage, stem the fierce passions of a pagan world, recreate the springs of national and social life, any such methods were necessary, or even peculiarly adapted to the purpose, as monasticism employed in its missionary work. The Western monks accepted, as the Eastern monks had done before them, an antisocial theory which strikes at the very heart of the providence of God, and which sprang first of all, and springs still, from a dualistic scepticism of the love of the supreme Father, from a jaundiced estimate of the world, from a grievous mistake as to the seat of evil and the nature of sin. They ennobled the theory; they consecrated it to higher issues than any of which paganism ever dreamed; they hallowed it as they hallowed other things, hiding its evil root with the influence of their virtues, but they did not change the character of the root. It always had led to spiritual pride, and fostered the very propensities it professed to hold in abeyance. True, it provided for ages an asylum for broken hearts; it stood in its corporate capacity and strength between forces of the state; it furnished opportunities for great intellectual and artistic feats; it quickened and subtilized the faculties of men to encounter the difficult problems of pure thought, and furnished various agencies of a civilizing character; but it contained within itself the seeds of its own dissolution.

It perished finally, not from sacrilegious hands nor Protestant animosities, but from its own inherent vices.

M. de Montalembert, the latest and perhaps ablest defender of monachism, breaks ground with a vindication of monasteries from the charge of being the asylums of broken hearts; for weak, exhausted, and disappointed energies; for men and women tired of the world, and unfit for the strife and battle of life; maintaining that they were peopled rather by the young and the brave, and by those who, as far as this world is concerned, had everything to lose in assuming monastic vows; by those who had a large surplusage of dauntless energy for the conquest of nature, for industrious grappling with the barrenness of the desert, or the riotous prodigality of the primæval forest. He also asserts that these mysterious precursors of civilization and order, these men of prayer and faith, solved the mystery of life, and showed to a barbaric and selfish world the secret of real happiness; and urges that, so far from wishing to escape from their vows, or from the fellowship of the cloister, they conceived a passionate attachment for each other and to their self-imposed restraints; that their mutual affection was stronger than death; and that, instead of morose and hopeless abnegation of humanity — benignitas, simplicitas, hilaritas—gayety and songs of joy transformed their exile from the world into the paradise of God. But "monasticism," Dr. Schaff has well said, "is not the *normal* form of Christian piety. It is an abnormal phenomenon, a humanly devised service of God (comp. Colos. ii, 16-23), and not rarely a sad enervation and repulsive distortion of the Christianity of the Bible. It is to be estimated, therefore, not by the extent of its self-denial, not by its outward acts of self-discipline (which may all be found in heathenism, Judaism, and Mohammedanism as well), but by the Christian spirit of humility and love which animated it. For humility is the groundwork, and love the all-ruling principle of the Christian life, and the distinctive characteristic of the Christian religion. Without love to God and charity to man, the severest self-punishment and the utmost abandonment of the world are worthless before God (comp. 1 Cor. xiii, 1-3). . . . Even in the most favorable case monasticism falls short of harmonious moral development, and of that symmetry of virtue which meets us in perfection in Christ, and next to him in the apostles. It lacks the finer and gentler traits of character, which are ordinarily brought out only in the school of daily family life and under the social ordinances of God. Its morality is rather negative than positive. There is more virtue in the temperate and thankful enjoyment of the gifts of God than in total abstinence; in charitable and well-seasoned speech than in total silence; in connubial chastity than in celibacy; in self-denying practical labor for the Church than in solitary asceticism, which only pleases self and profits no one else." Believing this, we are constrained to maintain further that, although the monastic orders have done much to promote the good of man, the ideal which they have proposed to themselves is no more that of genuine sacrifice than a collection of probable statements is history. The highest forms of self-surrender are those of which the world knows nothing, and whose beauty is derived not from the halo of sacerdotal sentiment, but from the quiet discharge of unromantic and, it may be, irksome duties.

Montalembert also makes light of the charges brought against monasticism, even in its decline, and repudiates the right of any layman to cast a stone at the accumulations of wealth and luxury under which at length it succumbed. In an introductory chapter on the decline of monastic institutions, he admits that their corruption and abuses were denounced by the monks themselves, that the shield which religion had thrown over them was pierced and shattered from within, and that the most effective instrument in their downfall was what he terms the infamous "com-

mende" by which the title of abbot was conferred on those who were ignorant of monastic institutions; albeit this step, so loathsome in his judgment, was the work of infallible popes and Catholic kings. Catholics have their own institutions and the great dignitaries of their own Church to blame for the most conspicuous illustrations and examples of spoliation and robbery. The enormous wealth accumulated by these monasteries was too tempting a prize to be resisted, first by rapacious abbots, then by bishops hungering for temporal power as well as ecclesiastical influence, then by needy kings, and at last by unprincipled popes. They turned from one to the other for protection, and found the spoiler rather than the friend. The utter and ignominious fall of more than three thousand monasteries in Europe, and the ruthless destruction even of their ruins in countries which had never repudiated the authority of the Roman See, is a startling fact, which, although our author recounts, he fails to explain on his own theory of the supreme and God-given claims of the Church; while the jeremiad that he wails over the base uses to which these gorgeous buildings have returned is out of harmony with his vivid appreciation of modern ideas of progress. One might suppose that on the fall of the monastery the spirit of humanity, all care for the sick and dying, all science, art, and literature, all brave adventure, all subjugation and replenishing of the earth, and missionary enterprise had utterly vanished; while, on the contrary, the fact of the case is that the mighty spirit generated by the contact of Christianity with modern thought was too strong to be retained in the crisp and worn-out skins of monastic orders; and when these burst, neither the spirit nor the fragrance was lost. New life demanded new institutions, and it is too late in the day to prove that modern civilization is only a feeble parody on that which we readily allow took its origin in the cloister. Grand and even worthy attempts, to be sure, have been made at various times to recover the ancient prestige of monasticism, and there is a kind of work that none perhaps can do so well as the Society of Jesus; but the fuel which even now promotes the flame of monastic piety is that morbid view of the nature of the human will which is fostered by materialistic science, that mischievous estimate of human life which proceeds from the scepticism of the Fatherhood of God, and that neo-Platonic or Gnostic repudiation of the true brotherhood of all mankind which is perpetual dishonor to the word and spirit of Jesus Christ. We do not wonder that in the light of these truths a celebrated English savant writes that the continued violation of the most distinctive attributes of human nature is the recorded secret of the failure of monachism. "Its principle of poverty has ever outraged man's original conception of property; as a celibate, it is directly opposed to the social nature of man; and its law of solitary striving for religious perfection is antagonistic to the first principle of Christian communion and spiritual intercourse. The profession of poverty frequently ended in the most insatiable avarice and cupidity, while vows of perpetual virginity resulted in unbounded licentiousness. That which began with a sincere desire for perfect purity, ended in the diffusion of licensed corruption." For these reasons we do not feel justified in dissenting from the general opinion, which is that, "however serviceable the monastery may have been as an institution in the mediæval ages, preserving, as in an ark, the treasures of religion and learning from the waves of barbarism which in rapid succession broke over Europe, it has lost to a great extent its beneficial power, and in the present state of society has no peculiar functions of a useful nature to discharge; and that the truly good of both sexes would better serve the end of their being by mixing in society, and trying to improve it, than by turning monks and nuns, and looking out on the world from behind the bars of a prison, within which they have by their own consent submitted to be encaged" (*Brit. and For. Rev.* 1868, p. 450).

Literature.—(1.) *Greek writers:* Socrates, *H. Eccles.* lib. iv, cap. 23 sq.; Sozomen, *H. E.* lib. i, cap. 12–14; iii, 14; vi, 28–34; Palladius, *Historia Lausiaca* (Ἰστορία πρὸς Λαῦσον, a court-officer under Theodosius II, to whom the work was dedicated), composed about 421, with enthusiastic admiration, from personal acquaintance, of the most celebrated contemporaneous ascetics of Egypt; Theodoret († 457), *Historia religiosa, seu ascetica vivendi ratio* (φιλόθεος ἱστορία), biographies of thirty Oriental anchorets and monks, for the most part from personal observation; Nilus the elder († about 450), *De vita ascetica, De exercitatione monastica, Epistolæ* 355, and other writings. (2.) *Latin writers:* Rufinus († 410), *Hist. Eremitica, s. Vitæ Patrum;* Sulpicius Severus (about 400), *Dialogi III* (the first dialogue contains a lively and entertaining account of the Egyptian monks, whom he visited; the two others relate to Martin of Tours); Cassianus († 432), *Institutiones cænobiatis, and Collationes Patrum* (spiritual conversations of Eastern monks). Also the ascetic writings of Athanasius (Vita Antonii), Basil, Gregory Nazianzen, Chrysostom, and Isidore of Pelusium among the Greek; Ambrose, Augustine, Jerome (his lives of anchorets, and his letters), Cassiodorus, and Gregory the Great among the Latin fathers. (3.) *Later literature:* Holstenius (a Roman convert), *Codex regularum monastic.* (Rom. 1661; enlarged, Paris and Augsb. 6 vols. fol.); the older Greek *Menologia* (μηνολόγια) and *Menæa* (μηναῖα), and the Latin *Calendaria* and *Martyrologia*—i. e. Church calendars or indices of memorial days (days of the earthly death and heavenly birth) of the saints, with short biographical notices for liturgical use; Herbert Rosweyde (Jesuit), *Vitæ Patrum, sive Historiæ Eremiticæ,* lib. x (Antwerp, 1628); *Acta Sanctorum, quotquot toto orbe coluntur* (Antwerp, 1643–1786, 53 vols. fol.; begun by the Jesuit Bollandus, continued by several scholars of his order, called *Bollandists,* down to October 11 in the calendar of saints' days, and resumed in 1845, after long interruption, by Theiner and others); D'Achery and Mabillon (Benedictines), *Acta Sanctorum ordinis S. Benedicti* (Paris, 1668–1701, 9 vols. folio [to 1100]); Helyot (Franciscan), *Histoire des ordres monastiques religieux et militaires* (Par. 1714–19, 8 vols. 4to; new ed., with an additional vol. on the modern history of monachism by Migne, 1849, 4 vols.); Butler (R. C.), *The Lives of the Fathers, Martyrs, and other principal Saints,* arranged according to the Catholic calendar, and completed to December 31 (1745, and often since; best ed. Lond. 1812–13, 12 vols.; another, Baltimore, 1844, 4 vols.); Gibbon, chap. xxxvii ("Origin, Progress, and Effects of Monastic Life;" very unfavorable, and written in lofty philosophical contempt); Henrion (R. C.), *Histoire des ordres religieux* (Par. 1835); Biedenfeld, *Ursprung sämmtlicher Mönchsorden im Orient u. Occident* (Weimar, 1837, 3 vols.); Schmidt (R. C.), *Die Mönchs-, Nonnen-, u. geistlichen Ritterorden nebst Ordensregeln u. Abbildungen* (Augsb. 1838 sq.); Paul Lacroix, *Military and Religious Life in the Middle Ages and at the Period of the Renaissance;* Day, *Monastic Institutions: their Origin, Progress,* etc. (Lond. 1846, 2d ed.); Milman (Anglican), *History of Ancient Christianity* (bk. iii, chap. xi), and his *Latin Christianity;* Ruffner (Presbyterian), *The Fathers of the Desert* (N. Y., 1850, 2 vols.), full of curious information, in popular form; Montalembert (R. C.), *Les Moines d'Occident depuis St. Bénoît jusqu'à St. Bernard* (Paris, 1860 sq.; translated into English, *The Monks of the West,* etc., Edinb. and Lond. 1861 sq.); another extensive work has been in preparation for some time by the Benedictine Dom Gueranger, of France; Zöckler, *Kritische Geschichte der Askese* (Frankfurt-am-Main, 1863); comp. also Hefele, *Conciliengeschichte* (the several volumes); Wessenberg, *Kirchen versammlungen,* i, 119 sq. (see Index in vol. iv); Ozanam, *Études Germaniques;*

Guizot, *Hist. Civilization,* ii, 279 sq.; and the relevant sections of Tillemont, Fleury, Schröckh (vols. v and viii), Neander, Schaff, and Gieseler. Regarding *Christian monasticism as compared with other forms of asceticism,* see Hospinian, *De origine et progressu monachatus,* lib. vi (Tig. 1588; enlarged, Geneva, 1669, folio); Möhler (R. C.), *Geschichte des Mönchthums in der Zeit seiner Entstehung u. ersten Ausbildung* (1836; collected works, Regensb. vol. ii, p. 165 sq.; Taylor (Independent), *Ancient Christianity* (Lond. 1844), i, 299 sq.; Vogel, "Ueber das Mönchthum" (Berlin, 1858), in the *Deutsche Zeitschrift f. christl. Wissenschaft,* etc.; Schaff, "Ueber den Ursprung und Charakter des Mönchthums," in Dorner's, etc., *Jahrbücher für deutsche Theologie* (1861), p. 555 sq.; Cropp, *Origines et Causæ monachatus* (Gött. 1863); Lea, *Hist. Sacerdotal Celibacy,* chap. vii, xxx; Lecky, *Hist. Rationalism* (see Index); id., *Hist. European Morals* (see Index); Gould, *Origin of Religious Belief* (N. Y., 1871, 2 vols. 8vo), i, 339 sq.; *Edinburgh Review,* Jan., 1849; *Eclectic Magazine,* April, 1849; *English Review,* ii, 77, 424; [Lond.] *Quar. Rev.* cxxvii, July, 1861; *Eclectic Review,* July, 1859; *Brit. and For. Ev. Rev.* July, 1868; *British Quar. Rev.* art. viii, July, 1868; *Edinb. Rev.* April, 1868; *St. James's Magazine,* March, 1870.

Monboddo, JAMES BURNET, *Lord,* a Scotch writer, noted for his eccentric speculations of primitive history, was born at the family seat of Monboddo, in Kincardineshire, Scotland, in 1714. He was educated at the University of Aberdeen, and at Groningen, Holland. On his return to Scotland in 1737, he was admitted to the bar, and succeeded in gaining considerable practice. In 1767 he was promoted to the judicial bench, and became titled as Lord Monboddo. But he by no means confined himself to the legal profession. He employed his pen in various departments of speculative philosophy, in which he displayed a profound rather than a useful learning. He was thoroughly versed in Greek literature, of which he became such an enthusiastic admirer as almost to scorn modern learning. His great work, *Origin and Progress of Languages,* first appeared in 1773. In this he affirms, and endeavors to demonstrate, the superiority of his favorite ancients over their present degenerate posterity, and discourses at large on the honor due the Greek language. This work met with no very marked success, being read more on account of its eccentricities than for its practical utility. Monboddo was in a certain sense, however, the forerunner of the now so well-known English naturalist, Charles Darwin. Like the latter, Monboddo expressed his belief in the theory that men were originally monkeys, and he went even so far as to insist that a nation still exists possessed of tails. His peculiar views were the subject of much merriment and ridicule by Dr. Johnson, who represents lord Monboddo as asking Sir Joseph Banks, who had made a visit to Botany Bay, whether he had met this strange race in his travels. On receiving a negative answer, he was much disappointed. Lord Monboddo's pen furnished the public also with a work on *Ancient Metaphysics,* in 6 vols., the first part of which appeared in 1778. In this he endeavors to dissect the philosophy of Sir Isaac Newton; and, as in the former work, he shows an extravagant fondness for Grecian learning and philosophy. He seems to lack the ability of placing these ideas within the easy grasp of modern thought, though he shows his own thorough knowledge, of Aristotle particularly. In this work he further explains and supports his Darwinian ideas. Sir James Edward Smith draws a pen-picture of this eccentric genius, and represents him as "a plain, elderly man, wearing an ordinary gray coat, leather breeches, and coarse worsted stockings, conversing with great affability about various matters—lamenting the decline of classical learning, and claiming credit for having adopted the Norfolk husbandry." Lord Monboddo resided in Edinburgh until his death, May 26, 1799. See *Edinb. Review,* lviii, 45; Cooper, *Biog. Dict.*

s. v.; Allibone, *Dict. of British and American Authors*, s. v.; Chambers, *Cyclopædia*, s. v.; *English Encyclop.* s. v.; *Gentleman's Magazine*, 1799; Tytler, *Life of Lord Karnes*. (H. W. T.)

Moncada, LOUIS-ANTOINE DE BELLUGA DE, a Spanish prelate, was born at Motril, in the kingdom of Granada, Nov. 30, 1662. He entered the Church, where his distinguished birth placed many ecclesiastical honors within his power, but, with pious modesty, he refused them all. Philip V appointed him bishop of Carthagena and Murcia in 1705. Soon after the archduke, who disputed the crown with Philip, invaded Spain. Moncada remained faithful to his sovereign, and so strongly evinced his devotion that Philip rewarded him with the titles of viceroy of Valencia and captain-general of Murcia in 1706. But, notwithstanding these royal favors, his zeal did not degenerate into servility, and he resisted the court when he thought the interests of the Church were compromised. Thus he obstinately opposed a duty placed on the property of the clergy. At the height of his quarrel with the king's party, he was included in a promotion of cardinals; but, believing in faithful submission to the administration of his country, though a prelate, he declared that he would not accept the purple without the king's consent. This permission had only been delayed to test the bishop's constancy, and, according to Saint-Simon, "the affair ended with unequalled glory for Belluga." "Subsequently," adds Saint-Simon, "Belluga, who had more zeal than discretion, wished to institute some reforms, which the bishops of Spain could not permit. They opposed his plans with great success, and Belluga, not being able to procure for his country the advantages he proposed, became greatly disgusted, and entreated the king to release him from the bishopric of Murcia, and permit him to retire to Rome." He was there, as in Murcia, a very faithful subject to his king, and still preserved an anxious interest in all his affairs. His virtue, which lifted him above all politics, acquired for him a veneration and consideration during the whole course of his long life. He died at Rome, Feb. 22, 1743. See Moréri, *Grand Dict. Histor.* s. v.; Saint-Simon, *Mémoires*, xi, 197-199 (edit. Chéruel).

Monceaux (*Moncæus*), FRANÇOIS DE, a French writer noted for his studies in comparative archæology, was a native of Arras, and flourished in the second half of the 16th century. He took quite an active part in the political affairs of France and Italy, but nevertheless found time to write: *De portis civitatis Judæ et fori judiciorumque in iis exercendorum prisco ritu* (Paris, 1587, 4to) :— *Bucolica Sacra, sive Cantici Canticorum poetica paraphrasis et in eamdem lucubrationum*, lib. ii (ibid. 1587, 4to; 1589, 8vo) :— *Apparitionum divinarum quæ de Rubo et quæ in Ægypto revertenti in diversorio Moysi facta Historia* (Arras, 1592, 12mo; 1597, 4to) :— *In Psalmum xliv Paraphrasis poetica* (Douai, 4to) :— *Aaron purgatus, seu de vitulo aureo*, lib. ii (Arras, 1606, 8vo; Leipsic, 1689, in *Antiquitates Biblicæ*, and in vol. ix of Pearson's *Critici Sacri*. The Church of Rome expurgated it in 1609) :— *Responsio pro vitulo aureo non aureo* (Paris, 1608, 8vo), a reply to Viseur's *Destruction du "Veaux d'or purgé"* (ibid. 1608, 8vo). See André, *Bibliotheca Belgica*, s. v.

Monclar, JEAN-PIERRE-FRANÇOIS DE RIPERT, *Marquis de*, a French religious writer, noted as a defender of the Huguenots, was born Oct. 1, 1711, at Apt, Provence. He was descended from the family of the dauphiness, and was the son of a magistrate whom the chancellor Daguesseau had surnamed L'Amour du bien. Dec. 19, 1732, he succeeded his father as procurator-general to the Parliament of Provence; he was then twenty-one years of age. He was a ready orator, a brilliant lawyer, and profoundly versed in public law. From 1749 he energetically declared himself in favor of the Protestants, and endeavored to obtain for them civil rehabilitation and liberty of conscience. In his article

on the clandestine marriages of the Reformed, he raised his voice, in the name of justice and humanity, against the iniquitous laws which condemned to ignominy and illegitimacy the fruits of their unions; and at the same time he demonstrated, by learned calculations, that it was greatly to the interest of the state to favor the progress of population. In 1752 the republic of Geneva, a prey to civil dissensions, rendered homage to the integrity of the magistrate by choosing him as arbiter for the two parties in collision. "At this time," says M. Villemain, "an event occurred which developed the talents of several men in the parliaments of the kingdom; this was the trial and expulsion of the celebrated society of the Jesuits. Monclar took a lively and active interest in this affair, and his exposé of their doctrines was a masterpiece of method and clearness, without exaggeration, and without false eloquence. In the remonstrances that he was charged to draw up in the name of those opposed to the Jesuits, Monclar knew how to unite a dignified firmness with the respect due to the sovereign, and to avoid that rather republican severity with which Voltaire reproaches Malesherbes." He was instrumental in restoring Venaissin to France (in 1768), and received for his services from Louis XV a pension and the title of marquis (October, 1769). Monclar, after forty years of active life, withdrew to his estate of Saint-Saturnin, where he died, Feb. 12, 1773. Romanists claim that Monclar in his dying hour made known to his confessor a regret for what he had said against the Holy See and the Society of Jesus. But there seems to be no ground for the declaration, as the whole life of the marquis speaks against any such change. He wrote *Mémoire théologique et politique au sujet des mariages clandestins des Protestants en France* (1755, 8vo); at the time of its appearance it aroused a warm discussion: more than twenty pamphlets were published for or against :— *Compte rendu des Constitutions des Jésuites* (1762, 2 vols. 12mo); reprinted since with the *Requisitoire du 4 Janvier*, 1763, and the *Conclusions du 5 Mars*, 1765, on the bull *Apostolicum pascendi* (Paris, 1769, 2 vols. 4to and 8vo). The complete works of Monclar, comprising 8 vols. 8vo, were published in 1855. See Borély, *Eloge de Monclar*, pronounced November, 1843; Achard, *Dict. de Provence*, s. v.; Villemain, *Tableau du dix-huitième siècle*, 9ᵉ leçon; Hoefer, *Nouv. Biog. Générale*, s. v.

Monçon, JEAN DE, a Spanish theologian, who advanced heretical opinions on the doctrine of the immaculate conception, was born at Monteson, Aragon, about 1360. He joined the brotherhood of St. Dominic, taught theology at Valentia, and in 1383 went to Paris, where he received the degree of doctor four years later. Having in his theses advanced some propositions contrary to the belief of the immaculate conception of the Virgin, he saw them condemned by the faculty, and Pierre d'Orgemont, then bishop, forbade their maintenance under pain of excommunication. This quarrel led to great trouble in the university; those partisans of the Spanish monk who refused to retract were thrown into prison, and he himself was excluded from all the Dominican courts. Monçon thereupon appealed to Clement VII, schismatic pope, residing at Avignon; but, perceiving that the commissioners given him were not favorable, he took to flight (January, 1389), and was found in Aragon, where he was excommunicated. In order to revenge himself for the persecution, he entered the service of pope Urban IV, and wrote against Clement VII. Peace was not concluded until 1408, and only by the intervention of many princes and of the pope of Avignon, Benedict XIII. In 1412 he was instructed by the duke Alfonso to sustain his right to the crown of Aragon. His works have never been printed. See Echard and Quetif, *Script. ord. Prædicatorum*.

Monconys, BALTHASAR, Dr., a French traveller, noted for his Oriental studies, was born at Lyons near the opening of the 17th century. After receiving a liberal education at the University of Salamanca, he visited the East, for the purpose of tracing the remains of the philosophy of Trismegistus and Zoroaster; but returned without accomplishing the object of his mission, and died in 1665. His travels were published by his learned friend, Jean Berthet, of the Society of Jesus (Paris, 1665-6, 3 vols. 4to; reprinted in Holland, 1696, 5 vols. 12mo). See Hoefer, *Nouv. Biog. Générale*, xxxv, 952.

Moncrieff, *Sir* HENRY, Bart., D.D., a Scottish divine, son of the Rev. Sir William Moncrieff, was born in Blackford, Perthshire, Feb. 6, 1750. After receiving an elementary education in his native place, he repaired to the University of Glasgow for the purpose of fitting himself for the pulpit. In the midst of his collegiate course he had the misfortune to lose his father. The patrons of the charge thus left vacant, moved by a strong affection for Sir William, and a confidence in the more than ordinary talent displayed by his son, reserved the pastorate for "Sir Harry," as he was familiarly called. He repaired to Edinburgh, and there entered upon a theological course, which he completed in August, 1771; was then ordained a minister of the Church of Scotland, and installed as successor to his father. His talents were too remarkable to allow of his remaining long in this humble position, and the attention he attracted soon caused him to be called to Edinburgh, where, in 1775, he became the officiating minister of St. Cuthbert's, the largest parochial charge in the Scottish capital. Though the numerical strength of his parish prevented him from coming into frequent personal contact with all, still he seems to have been dearly beloved as a pastor and friend. He had a commanding appearance, was gifted with a powerfully argumentative oratory, and was zealous as well as learned. In the pulpit his style was characterized by force more than by elegance. Avoiding flights of fancy and displays of rhetorical talent, he used his cultured intellectual strength to make truth strike the heart rather than please the brain. In his time the moderate party held the majority in the Scottish Church, but his hatred of intolerance and love of freedom led him to take a stand with the liberal and evangelical party, while his natural independence of character made his position one of boldness and prominence. The deliberations of the General Assembly, which met yearly at Edinburgh, were of a mixed political and religious nature. In these meetings Sir Harry took an active part, and his talents as a debater soon ranked him among the ablest of Scotland's platform orators. In 1785 he was unanimously chosen as moderator of the Assembly, an honor which was conferred on him several times thereafter. In these religious discussions he showed great abhorrence of everything savoring of bigotry or intolerance, and was ever ready to listen to and engage in any argument which aimed at the discovery of truth. Yet his religious beliefs were tenaciously adhered to and boldly advocated. Politically also he was active, and, to use his own expression, as "a Whig of 1688." He earnestly opposed all civil disabilities for religious creeds, and heartily supported "the constitution as founded upon the rock of lawful resistance by the patriots of the first James and Charles's time, and as finally purified by those of the Revolution." Indeed, it has been truly said that "in him Scotland found a warm-hearted lover of mankind, a strong advocate of political and religious freedom, and a zealous party leader." He continued to labor in this wide field of usefulness as pastor of St. Cuthbert's and leader of the liberal party until the time of his death, June 14, 1827. In the latter part of his life he adopted the additional surname of WELLWOOD; but he is better known as "Sir Harry," he being in his day the only man of noble rank who ministered in the Church of Scotland. He published several treatises concerning the ecclesiastical discussions of his time, also *Discourses on the Evidences of the Jewish and Christian Revelations*

(1815), and an *Account of the Life and Writings of Dr. John Erskine* (1818). His *Sermons*, with a memoir by his son, have also been published in three volumes (1829-31). "Those who read these sermons," says a critic in the *Edinb. Rev.* (vi, 112), "will never be disturbed with the author's admiration of himself or his misconception of the subject; nor will their impatience be excited by anything puerile, declamatory, verbose, or inaccurate. They will find everywhere indications of a vigorous and independent understanding ; and, though they may not always be gratified with flights of fancy or graces of composition, they can scarcely fail to be attracted by the unaffected expression of goodness and sincerity which runs through the whole publication." See *Edinb. Rev.* xlvii, 242; *Encyclop. Britannica*, s. v.; Chambers, *Biog. Dict. of Eminent Scotsmen*, iv, 456; *Blackwood's Magazine*, xxii, 530; Allibone, *Dict. of Brit. and Amer. Authors*, s. v. (H. W. T.)

Mondonville, JEANNE JULIARD, *Dame* TURLES DE, a French Roman Catholic woman, noted as the foundress of a pious order, was born at Toulouse in 1626. The daughter of a president of the Parliament of Toulouse, Jeanne Juliard was distinguished for her mind and her beauty. In 1646 she married Turles, lord of Mondonville, who left her a widow while still young, but endowed with a considerable fortune. Refusing many honorable offers of marriage, she determined to devote herself to the instruction of the poor and the relief of the sick. In order the more completely to effect her object, she founded in 1652, with the approbation of Marca, archbishop of Toulouse, the congregation called *Les Filles de l'Enfance*. This institution was authorized in 1663 by pope Alexander VII, and approved by letters patent of eighteen bishops and many doctors in theology. The congregation was progressing finely, and already counted many chapels, when it was suddenly and violently attacked by the Jesuits, on the ground that the constitution of the new congregation contained maxims dangerous to religion and morals. They obtained the nomination of commissioners to examine the criminated points, and exerted themselves so effectively that the congregation of the *Filles de l'Enfance* was suppressed by a decree of council in 1686. Madame de Mondonville was imprisoned at the Hospitalières of Coutances, where she died in 1703, after twenty years of the most rigorous confinement. The Jesuits did not wait for that event before they confiscated the property of the dissolved congregation, and established in its stead seminaries and houses of their own order. An old Jesuit and lawyer, Reboulet, in his *Histoire des Filles de la Congrégation de l'Enfance* (Avignon, 1734), accuses Madame de Mondonville of having given an asylum to men of treasonable views towards the state, that she had furnished some of them with means of leaving the kingdom, and that she had printed in her house many libels on the conduct of the king and his council; and the Jesuits as an order fought these unfortunate women as if they had been redoubtable enemies, and very soon despoiled them of all their goods. But when, subsequently, circumstances changed, and the credit of the Jesuits declined rapidly, the Parliament of Toulouse, at the request of the abbé Juliard, a relation of Madame de Mondonville, condemned Reboulet's work to the flames as calumnious and false. See *Nécrologe des Amis de la Vérité*.

Monegonde, SAINTE, a French Roman Catholic woman, noted as the foundress of a religious order, was born at Chartres in the early part of the 6th century. She was the descendant of a noble family, and was married, contrary to her own wishes, in obedience to her parents' will, and had two daughters, who died at an early age. The period of mourning having passed, she withdrew to a narrow cell, with no other opening than a shutter, where she received a little barley-flour, which she kneaded into bread. This was her sole nourishment, and even in this she indulged only when pressed by extreme hunger. After a considerable period, Sainte Monegonde left the city of Chartres in order to continue the same kind of life at Tours, near the tomb of St. Martin. The sensation produced by the miracles attributed to her aroused her husband and many of her friends, who took her back to Chartres; but, convinced by her urgent solicitations, they permitted her to return to Tours, where she formed a small religious order of women, called *Les Filles spirituelles*, with whom she continued her austerities until her death. St. Gregory of Tours refers to her so-called miracles, and aided her in building a monastery, called *Saint-Pierre-le-Puellier*. This edifice became a collegiate church for secular canons. It was burned in 1562 by the Calvinists, and Sainte Monegonde's body perished in the flames. She died at Tours, July 2, 570, and this day is still observed in her honor. See St. Grégoire, *De Gloria Confessorum; Martyrol. Rom.* (July 2); Baillet, *Vies des Saints*, vol. ii (July 2); Richard and Giraud, *Bibliothèque Sacrée.*

Monergism (from μόνος, *sole*, and ἔργον, *work*) is a term used to designate the doctrine that in regeneration there is but one efficient agent, viz. the Holy Spirit. It is held by monergists that "the will of sinful man has not the least inclination towards holiness, nor any power to act in a holy manner, until it has been acted upon by divine grace; and therefore it cannot be said with strictness to co-operate with the Holy Spirit, since it acts in conversion only after it is quickened by the Holy Spirit." The doctrine is opposed to *synergism*, which teaches that there are two efficient agents in regeneration—the human soul and the divine Spirit—co-operating together, a theory which accordingly holds that the soul has not lost all inclination towards holiness, nor all power to seek for it under the influence of ordinary motives. See SYNERGISM.

Monestier, BLAISE, a French philosopher, who did great service in combating the evil influences of the infidel schools which abounded in France towards the close of the 18th century, was born April 18, 1717, at Antezat, diocese of Clermont. After belonging to the Jesuits for some time, he abandoned that order to allow himself more liberty for the cultivation of his taste for study. He taught mathematics at Clermont-Ferrand and philosophy at Toulouse, where he died in 1776. He is the author of *Dissertation sur la Nature et la Formation de la Grêle* (Bordeaux, 1752, 12mo), which won a prize at the Academy of Bordeaux:—*Dissertations sur l'Analogie du Son et la Lumière, et sur le Temps*, which also drew a prize at the Academy of Nancy, and was printed in the collection of that company in 1754:—*Principes de la Piété Chrétienne* (Toulouse, 1756, 2 vols. 12mo):—*La vraie Philosophie*, par l'Abbé M—— (Bruxelles and Par. 1774, 8vo), a work directed against the philosophy of the Encyclopædists, and particularly against *Le Système de la Nature*, and published by Needham. "In order to gain an idea of *La vraie Philosophie*," says a reviewer, "we should not permit ourselves to be repelled by the violent declamations and bad taste presented by each page, above all in the preface, nor by the indecision of the plan and the disorder in the succession of ideas which result from it. The doctrine which it contains is an experimental and eclectical spiritualism, equally distant from the theory of innate ideas and from the system of transformed sensation, but where Cartesianism occupies the greatest place." After having placed sensations and sentiments in the heart, Monestier analyzes reason, which he divides into primitive ideas (ideas of unity, being, time, space, affirmation, negation, with the axioms of geometry and morals), the faculty of generalizing and abstracting, the idea of the infinite, and the faculties of induction and reasoning. The idea of the infinite, imprinted as it is on all nature's work, attests to us the existence of God and the immortality of the soul,

at the same time that it instructs us in regard to our own destiny. The author closes by a discussion of free will. See *Dict. des Sciences philos.* iv, 289–291, s. v.

Moneta, an Italian theologian and member of the order of the Dominicans at Cremona, flourished in the 13th century. He was, before entering the order, professor in the University of Bologna. He was noted for his sense and his zeal against the false teachers of his time. He died about 1240. Moneta left a *Summa contra Catharos et Waldenses* (Rome, 1643). He is also supposed to be the author of *Compendium logicæ propter minus eruditos*. See Arisius, *Cremona literata;* Echard, *Bibliotheca Prædicatorum* (Paris, 1719–31, 2 vols. fol.), i, 122.

Money (Heb. כֶּסֶף, *ke'seph, silver*, as often rendered, Chald. כְּסַף, *kesaph'*, Gr. ἀργυρίον, *silver*, or a piece of silver, as often rendered; also κέρμα, *coin*, i. q. νόμισμα, lit. a *standard* of valuation; χαλκός, *brass*, as sometimes rendered; and χρῆμα, lit. whatever is *used* in exchange). In the present article we shall confine our attention to the consideration of the subject in general, leaving the discussion of particular coins for the special head of NUMISMATICS. The *value* of the coins is a relative thing, depending, with respect to the several pieces and kinds of metal, in part upon the ascertained *weight* (i. e. *intrinsic* value, for which see METROLOGY), and in part upon the interchange of the mintage of various ages and countries prevalent in Palestine (i. e. *current* value; see COIN); but, in point of fact, still more upon the depreciation of the precious metals as a standard of value in comparison with purchasable articles, arising from the fluctuating balance of supply and demand (i. e. *mercantile* value). In the following discussion we give a general view of this extensive subject, referring to other articles for subsidiary points.

I. *Non-metallic Currency*. — Different commodities have been used as money in the primitive state of society in all countries. Those nations which subsist by the chase, such as the ancient Russians and the greater part of the North American Indians, use the skins of the animals killed in hunting as money (Storch, *Traité d'Economie Politique*, tome i). In a pastoral state of society cattle are chiefly used as money. Thus, according to Homer, the armor of Diomede cost nine oxen, and that of Glaucus one hundred (*Iliad*, vi, 235). The etymology of the Latin word *pecunia*, signifying money, and of all its derivatives, affords sufficient evidence that cattle (*pecus*) were the first money of the Romans. They were also used as money by the Germans, whose laws fix the amount of penalties for particular offences to be paid in cattle (Storch, *l. c.*). In agricultural countries corn would be used in remote ages as money, and even at the present day it is not unusual to stipulate for corn rents and wages. Various commodities have been and are still used in different countries. Smith mentions salt as the common money of Abyssinia (*Wealth of Nations*, i, 4). A species of *cypræa*, called the *coury*, gathered on the shores of the Maldive Islands, and of which 6400 constitute a rupee, is used in making small payments throughout India, and is the only money of certain districts in Africa. Dried fish forms the money of Iceland and Newfoundland; sugar of some of the West India Islands; and among the first settlers in America corn and tobacco were used as money (Holmes's *American Annals*). Smith mentions that at the time of the publication of the *Wealth of Nations* there was a village in Scotland where it was customary for a workman to carry nails as money to the baker's shop or the alehouse (i, 4).

II. *Bullion as a Circulating Medium.*—1. A long period of time must have intervened between the first introduction of the precious metals into commerce and their becoming generally used as money. The peculiar qualities which so eminently fit them for this purpose would only be gradually discovered. They would probably be first introduced in their gross and unpurified state. A sheep, an ox, a certain quantity of corn, or any other article, would afterwards be bartered or exchanged for pieces of gold or silver in bars or ingots, in the same way as they would formerly have been exchanged for iron, copper, cloth, or anything else. The merchants would soon begin to estimate their proper value, and, in effecting exchanges, would first agree upon the quality of the metal to be given, and then the quantity which its possessor had become bound to pay would be ascertained by weight. This, according to Aristotle and Pliny, was the manner in which the precious metals were originally exchanged in Greece and Italy. The same practice is still observed in different countries. In many parts of China and Abyssinia the value of gold and silver is always ascertained by weight (Goguet, *De l'Origine des Loix*, etc.). Iron was the first money of the Lacedæmonians, and copper of the Romans. See METAL.

In the many excavations which have been made in Egypt, Assyria, and Babylonia, no specimen of coined money has yet been discovered. Egyptian money was composed of rings of gold and silver; and in Assyria and Babylonia only clay tablets commemorating grants of money *specified by weight* have been found in considerable numbers;. while in Phœnicia no pieces of an antiquity earlier than the Persian rule have yet come to light (Rawlinson, *Herod.* i, 684). Nor, indeed, is coined money found in the time of Homer, but traffic was pursued either by simple barter (*Iliad*, vii, 472; xxiii, 702; *Odyss.* i, 430); or by means of masses of unwrought metal, like lumps of iron (*Iliad*, xxiii, 826; *Odyss.* i, 184); or by quantities of gold and silver, especially of gold (*Iliad*, ix, 122, 279; xix, 247; xxiii, 269; *Odyss.* iv, 129; viii, 393; ix, 202, etc.), which latter metal, called by Homer τάλαντον χρυσοῦ, seems to be the only one measured by weight. Before the introduction of coined money into Greece by Pheidon, king of Argos, there was a currency of ὀβελίσκοι, "spits" or "skewers," six of which were considered a handful (δραχμή). Colonel Leake thinks that they were small pyramidal pieces of *silver* (*Num. Chron.* xvii, 203; *Num. Hellen.* p. 1, appendix), but it seems more probable that they were nails of *iron* or *copper*, capable of being used as spits in the Homeric fashion. This is likely, from the fact that six of them made a handful, and that they were therefore of a considerable size (Rawlinson, *Herod.* App. i, 688). See WEIGHTS.

It is well known that ancient nations which were without a coinage weighed the precious metals, a practice represented on the Egyptian monuments, on which gold and silver are shown to have been kept in the form of rings (see cut under the art. BALANCES). The gold rings found in the Celtic countries have been held to have had the same use. It has indeed been argued that this could not have been the case with the latter, since they show no monetary system; yet it is evident from their weights that they all contain complete multiples or parts of a unit, so that we may fairly suppose that the Celts, before they used coins, had, like the ancient Egyptians, the practice of keeping money in rings, which they weighed when it was necessary to pay a fixed amount. We have no certain record of the use of ring-money or other uncoined money in antiquity excepting among the Egyptians. With them the practice mounts up to a remote age, and was probably as constant, and perhaps as regulated with respect to the weight of the rings, as a coinage. It can scarcely be doubted that the highly civilized rivals of the Egyptians—the Assyrians and Babylonians—adopted, if they did not originate, this custom, clay tablets having been found specifying grants of money by weight (Rawlinson, *Herod.* i, 684); and there is therefore every probability that it obtained also in Palestine, although seemingly unknown in Greece in the time before coinage was there introduced. There is no trace in Egypt, however, of any different size in the rings represented, so that there

is no reason for supposing that this further step was taken towards the invention of coinage.

2. The first notice in the Bible, after the flood, of uncoined money as a representative of property and medium of exchange, is when Abraham came up out of Egypt "very rich in cattle, in silver, and in gold" (Gen. xiii, 2; xxiv, 35). In the further history of Abraham we read that Abimelech gave the patriarch "a thousand [pieces] of silver," apparently to purchase veils for Sarah and her attendants; but the passage is extremely difficult (Gen. xx, 16). The Sept. understood shekels to be intended (χίλια δίδραχμα, *l. c.* also ver. 14), and there can be no doubt that they were right, though the rendering is accidentally an unfortunate one, their equivalent being the name of a coin. We next find "money" used in commerce. In the purchase of the cave of Machpelah it is said, "And Abraham weighed (וַיִּשְׁקֹל) to Ephron the silver which he had named in the audience of the sons of Heth, four hundred shekels of silver current with the merchant" (עֹבֵר לַסֹּחֵר; Sept. δοκίμου ἐμπόροις, Gen. xxiii, 16). Here a currency is clearly indicated like that which the monuments of Egypt show to have been there used in a very remote age; for the weighing proves that this currency, like the Egyptian, did not bear the stamp of authority, and was therefore weighed when employed in commerce. A similar purchase is recorded of Jacob, who bought a parcel of a field at Shalem for a hundred *kesitahs* (xxiii, 18, 19). The occurrence of a name different from shekel, and, unlike it, not distinctly applied in any other passage to a weight, favors the idea of coined money. But what is the *kesitah* (קְשִׂיטָה)? The old interpreters supposed it to mean a lamb, and it has been imagined to have been a coin bearing the figure of a lamb. There is no known etymological ground for this meaning, the lost root, if we compare the Arabic *kasat*, "he or it divided equally," being perhaps connected with the idea of division. Yet the sanction of the Sept., and the use of weights having the forms of lions, bulls, and geese, by the Egyptians, Assyrians, and probably Persians, must make us hesitate before we abandon a rendering so singularly confirmed by the relation of the Latin *pecunia* and *pecus*. Throughout the history of Joseph we find evidence of the constant use of money in preference to barter. This is clearly shown in the case of the famine, when it is related that all the money of Egypt and Canaan was paid for corn, and that then the Egyptians had recourse to barter (xlvii, 13–26). It would thence appear that money was not very plentiful. In the narrative of the visits of Joseph's brethren to Egypt, we find that they purchased corn with money, which was, as in Abraham's time, weighed silver, for it is spoken of by them as having been restored to their sacks in "its [full] weight" (xliii, 21). At the time of the exodus money seems to have been still weighed, for the ransom ordered in the law is stated to be half a shekel for each man—"half a shekel after the shekel of the sanctuary, [of] twenty gerahs the shekel" (Exod. xxx, 13). Here the shekel is evidently a weight, and of a special system of which the standard examples were probably kept by the priests. Throughout the law money is spoken of as in ordinary use; but only silver money, gold being mentioned as valuable, but not clearly as used in the same manner. This distinction appears at the time of the conquest of Canaan. When Jericho was taken, Achan embezzled from the spoils 200 shekels of silver, and a wedge (Heb. *tongue*) of gold (γλῶσσαν μίαν χρυσῆν) of 50 shekels' weight (Josh. vii, 21). Throughout the period before the return from Babylon this distinction seems to obtain: whenever anything of the character of money is mentioned the usual metal is silver, and gold generally occurs as the material of ornaments and costly works. Thus silver, as a medium of commerce, may be met with among the nations of the Philistines (Gen. xx. 16; Judg. xvi, 5, 18; xvii, 2 sq.), the Midianites (Gen. xxxvii, 28), and the Syrians (2 Kings

v, כ, 23). By the laws of Moses, the value of laborers and cattle (Lev. xxvii, 3 sq.; Numb. iii, 45 sq.), houses and fields (Lev. xxvii, 14 sq.), provisions (Deut. ii, 6, 28; xiv, 26), and all fines for offences (Exod. xxi, xxii), were determined by an estimate in money. The contributions to the Temple (Exod. xxx, 13; xxxviii, 26), the sacrifice of animals (Lev. v, 15), the redemption of the first-born (Numb. iii, 45 sq.; xviii, 15 sq.), the payment to the seer (1 Sam. ix, 7 sq.)—in all these cases the payment is always represented as silver. It seems probable from many passages in the Bible that a system of jewel currency or ring-money was also adopted as a medium of exchange. The case of Rebekah, to whom the servant of Abraham gave "a golden ear-ring of half a shekel weight, and two bracelets for her hands of ten shekels' weight of gold" (Gen. xxiv, 22), proves that the ancients made their jewels of a specific weight, so as to know the value of the ornaments in employing them as money. That the Egyptians kept their bullion in jewels seems evident from the plate given by Sir Gardner Wilkinson, copied from the catacombs, where they are represented as weighing rings of silver and gold; and is further corroborated by the fact of the Israelites having, at their exodus from Egypt, borrowed "jewels of silver and jewels of gold," and "spoiled the Egyptians" (Exod. xii, 35, 36). According to the ancient drawings, the Egyptian ring-money was composed of perfect rings. So, too, it would appear that the money used by the children of Jacob, when they went to purchase corn in Egypt, was also an annular currency (Gen. xlii, 35). Their money is described as "bundles of money" (Sept. δέσμοι), and when returned to them, was found to be "of [full] weight" (Gen. xliii, 21). The account of the sale of Joseph by his brethren affords another instance of the employment of jewel ornaments as a medium of exchange (Gen. xxxvii, 28); and that the Midianites carried the whole of their bullion wealth in the form of rings and jewels seems more than probable from the account in Numbers of the spoiling of the Midianites—"We have therefore brought an oblation for the Lord what every man hath gotten (Heb. found), of jewels of gold, chains, and bracelets, rings, ear-rings, and tablets, to make an atonement for our souls before the Lord. And Moses and Eleazar the priest took the gold of them, even all wrought jewels" (xxxi, 50, 51). The friends of Job, when visiting him at the end of the time of his trial, each gave him a piece of money (קְשִׂיטָה) and an ear-ring of gold (נֶזֶם זָהָב; Sept. τετράδραχμον χρυσοῦ καὶ ἀσήμου), thus suggesting the employment of a ring-currency. (For this question, see W. B. Dickinson in the *Num. Chron.* vols. vi to xvi, *passim*). A passage in Isaiah has indeed been supposed to show the use of gold coins in that prophet's time: speaking of the makers of idols, he says, "They lavish gold out of the bag, and weigh silver in the balance" (xlvi, 6). The mention of a bag is, however, a very insufficient reason for the supposition that the gold was coined money. Rings of gold may have been used for money in Palestine as early as this time, since they had long previously been so used in Egypt; but the passage probably refers to the people of Babylon, who may have had uncoined money in both metals like the Egyptians. Supposing that the above-quoted passages relative to a *gold* medium of exchange be not admitted, there is a passage recording a purchase made in *gold* in the time of David. ·The threshing-floor of Ornan was bought by David for 600 shekels of *gold* by weight (1 Chron. xxi, 25). Yet even this is rendered doubtful by the parallel passage mentioning the price paid as 50 shekels of *silver* (2 Sam. xxiv, 24).

It seems then apparent, from the several authorities given above, that from the earliest time *silver* was used by the Hebrews as a medium of commerce, and that a fixed weight was assigned to single pieces, so as to make them suitable for the various articles presented in trade. Unless we suppose this to be the case, many of the above-quoted passages (especially Gen. xxiii, 16; comp. 2 Kings xii, 4 sq.) would be difficult to understand rightly. In this latter passage it is said that the priest Jehoiada "took a chest and bored a hole in the lid of it, and set it beside the altar," and "the priests that kept the door put in all the money that was brought into the house of the Lord." These passages not only presuppose pieces of metal of a definite weight, but also that they had been recognised as such, either in an unwrought form or from certain characters inscribed upon them. The system of weighing (though the Bible makes mention of a balance and weight of money in many places—Gen. xxiii, 16; Exod. xxii, 17; 2 Sam. xviii, 12; 1 Kings xx, 39; Jer. xxxii, 9, 10) is not likely to have been applied to every individual piece. In the large total of 603,550 half-shekels (Exod. xxxviii, 26), accumulated by the contribution of each Israelite, each *individual half-shekel* could hardly have been weighed out, nor is it probable that the scales were continually employed for all the small silver pieces which men carried about with them. For instance, that there were divisions of the standard of calculation is evident from the passage in Exod. xxx, 13, where the *half-shekel* is to be paid as the atonement money, and "the rich shall not give *more*, and the poor shall not give *less*" (ver. 15). The *fourth part of the shekel* must also have been an *actual piece*, for it was *all the silver* that the servant of Saul had at hand to pay the seer (1 Sam. ix, 8, 9). If a quantity of pieces of various weights were carried about by men in a purse or bag, as was the custom (2 Kings v, 23; xii, 10; Gen. xlii, 35), without having their weight marked in some manner upon them, what endless trouble there must have been in buying or selling, in paying or receiving. From these facts we may safely assume that the Israelites had already, before the exile, known silver pieces of a definite weight, and used them in trade. By this is not meant *coins*, for these are pieces of metal struck under an authority. A curious passage is that in Ezekiel (xvi, 36), which has been supposed to speak of *brass* money. The Hebrew text has יַעַן הִשָּׁפֵךְ נְחֻשְׁתֵּךְ, which has been rendered by the Vulg. "quia effusum est æs tuum," and by the A.V. "because thy *filthiness* was poured out." As brass was the latest metal introduced for money into Greece, it seems very unlikely that we should have brass money current at this period in Palestine: it has, however, been supposed that there was an independent copper coinage in farther Asia before the introduction of silver money by the Seleucidæ and the Greek kings of Bactriana. The terms רַצֵּי כֶּסֶף (Psa. lxviii, 30) and אֲגוֹרַת כֶּסֶף (1 Sam. ii, 36) are merely expressive of any small denomination of money. See SILVER.

III. *Coined Money.*—1. *The Antiquity of Coinage.*—There are two generally received opinions as to who were the inventors of the coining of money. One is that Phidon, king of Argos, coined both gold and silver money at Ægina at the same time that he introduced a system of weights and measures (Ephor. ap. Strabo, viii, 376; Pollux, ix, 83; Ælian, *Var. Hist.* xii, 10; *Marm. Par.*). The date of Phidon, according to the Parian marble, is B.C. 895, but Grote places him between 770 and 730, while Clinton, Böckh, and Müller place him between 783 and 744 (Grote, *Hist. of Greece*, iv, 419, note). The other statement is that the Lydians "were the first nation to introduce the use of gold and silver coin" (Herod. i, 94). This latter assertion was also made, according to Pollux (ix, 6, 83), by Xenophanes of Colophon, and is repeated by Eustathius (ap. Dionys. Perieg. v, 840). The early coins of Ægina and Lydia have a device on one side only, the reverse being an incuse square (*quadratum incusum*). On the obverse of the Æginetan coins is a tortoise, and on the of the Lydian the head of a lion. The reverse, however, of the Æginetan coins soon shows the incuse square divided into four parts by raised lines, the fourth quarter being again divided by a diagonal bar, thus forming four compartments. Apart, however, from the history relative to these respective coinages, which decidedly is in favor of a Lydian origin (Rawlinson, *Herod.* i, 683; Grotefend, *Num. Chron.* i, 235) against the opinion of the late colonel Leake (*Num. Hell.* App.), the Lydian coins seem to be ruder than those of Ægina, and it is probable that while the idea of *impress* may be assigned to Lydia, the perfecting of the silver and adding a *reverse type*, thereby completing the art of coinage, may be given to Ægina (W. B. Dickinson, *Num. Chron.* ii, 128). It may be remarked that Herodotus does not speak of the coins of Lydia when a kingdom, which coins have for their type the heads of a lion and bull facing, and which in all probability belong to Crœsus, but of the *electrum* staters of Asia Minor. If we conclude that coinage commenced in European and Asiatic Greece about the same time, the next question is whether we can approximately determine the date. This is extremely difficult, since there are no coins of a known period before the time of the expedition of Xerxes. The pieces of that age are of so archaic a style that it is hard, at first sight, to believe that there was any length of time between them and the rudest, and therefore earliest, of the coins of Ægina or the Asiatic coast. It must, however, be recollected that in some conditions the growth or change of art is extremely slow, and that this was the case in the early period of Greek art seems evident from the results of the excavations on what we may believe to be the oldest sites in Greece. The lower limit obtained from the evidence of the coins of known date may perhaps be conjectured to be two, or at most three, centuries before their time; the higher limit is as vaguely determined by the negative evidence of the Homeric writings, of which we cannot guess the age, excepting as being before the first Olympiad. On the whole, it seems reasonable to carry up Greek coinage to the 8th century B.C. Purely Asiatic coinage cannot be taken up to so early a date. The more archaic Persian coins seem to be of the time of Darius Hystaspis, or possibly of Cyrus, and certainly not much older, and there is no Asiatic money, unless of Greek cities, that can be reasonably assigned to an earlier period. Crœsus and Cyrus probably originated this branch of the coinage, or else Darius Hystaspis followed the example of the Lydian king. Coined money may therefore have been known in Palestine as early as the fall of Samaria, but only through commerce with the Greeks, and we cannot suppose that it was then current there. The earliest coined money current in Palestine is supposed to be the Daric (see below).

2. *The principal Monetary Systems of Antiquity.*—This subject has already been ably treated by Mr. R. S. Poole (*Encyclopædia Britannica*, s. v. Numismatics), and in the present article it will be sufficient for our purpose to mention briefly the different talents (q. v.).

i. *The Attic talent* was that employed in most Greek cities before the time of Alexander, who adopted it, and from that time it became almost universal in Greek coinage. Its drachm weighed about 67.5 grains Troy, and its tetradrachm 270 grains. In practice it rarely reached this standard in coins after the Punic War; at Alexander's time its tetradrachm weighed about 264 grains.

ii. *The Æginetan talent,* which was used at as early a period as the Attic, was employed in Greece and in the islands. Its drachm had an average maximum weight of about 96 grains, and its didrachm about 192 grains. When abolished under Alexander, this weight had fallen to about 180 grains for the didrachm.

iii. *The Alexandrian* or *Ptolemaic talent,* which may also be called the *Earlier Phœnician,* and also *Macedonian,* as it was used in the earlier coinage of the cities of Macedon, and by the Macedonian kings before Alexander the Great, was restored during the sway of the Ptolemies into the talent of Egypt. In the former case its drachm weighed about 112 grains, and its so-called

tetradrachm about 224, but they gradually fell to much lower weights. In the latter case the drachm weighs about 50 grains, and the tetradrachm about 220.

Tetradrachm of Archelaus, king of Macedon.

iv. *The later Phœnician* or *Carthaginian talent* was in use among the Persians and Phœnicians. It was also employed in Africa by the Carthaginians. Its drachm (or hemidrachm) weighed, according to Mr. Burgon (Thomas, *Sale Cat.* p. 57), about 59 grains, and its tetradrachm (or didrachm) about 236.

v. *The Euboïc talent* in Greek money had a didrachm of 129 grains; but its system of division, though coming very near the Attic, was evidently different. The weight of its didrachm was identical with that of the Daric, showing the Persian origin of the system. The order of origin may be thus tabulated:

Macedonian,   224 didrachms.

Æginetan,   196   "

Attic-Solonian, 135   "   Euboïc, 129.
      Later Phœnician, 236.

Respecting the Roman coinage, we may here state that the origin of the weights of its gold and silver money was undoubtedly Greek, and that the denarius, the chief coin of the latter metal, was under the early emperors equivalent to the Attic drachm, then greatly depreciated. The first Roman coinage took place, according to Pliny (*Hist. Nat.* xxxiii, 3), in the reign of Servius Tullius, about 550 years before Christ; but it was not until Alexander of Macedon had subdued the Persian monarchy, and Julius Cæsar had consolidated the Roman empire, that the image of a living ruler was permitted to be stamped upon the coins. Previous to that

Early Roman Coin.

period heroes and deities alone gave currency to the money of imperial Rome. In the British Museum there is a specimen of the original Roman *as,* the surface of which is nearly the size of a brick, with the figure of a bull impressed upon it.

3. *Coined Money mentioned in the Bible.*—The earliest mention of coined money in the Bible refers to the Persian coinage. In Ezra (ii, 69) and Nehemiah (vii, 70) the word דַּרְכְּמֹנִים occurs, and in Ezra (viii, 27) and 1 Chron. (xxix, 7) the word אֲדַרְכֹּנִים, both rendered in the Sept. by χρυσοῦς, and in the Vulg. by *solidus* and *drachma.* Many opinions have been put forward concerning the derivation of the words *adarkon* and *darkemon;* but a new suggestion has recently been made, which, though ingenious, will not, we think, meet with much support. Dr. Levy (*Jüd. Münzen,* p. 19, note) thinks that the root-word is דָּרַךְ, "to stretch," "tread," "step forward," from the forward placing of

one foot, which a man does in bending the bow, and that from this word was formed a noun, דרכון, or with the *Aleph* prefixed אדרכון, "archer," which is the type upon these coins, especially as the ancients called the old Persian coins τοξόται. That the more extended form דרכמון could have been formed from the simple דרכון is very possible, as the *Mem* could easily have been inserted. All, however, agree that by these terms the Persian coin *Daric* is meant. This coin was a

Daric. (Obverse: King of Persia to the right, kneeling, bearing bow and javelin. Reverse: Irregular incuse square. British Museum.)

gold piece current in Palestine under Cyrus and Artaxerxes Longimanus. The ordinary Daric is not of uncommon occurrence; but Levy (*l. c.*) has given a representation of a *double piece*, thereby making the ordinarily received Daric a *half-Daric*. Of the *double piece*, he says, only three are known. In this he is mistaken, as Mr. Borrell, the coin-dealer, has a record of not less than eight specimens (F. W. Madden, *Hist. of Jewish Coinage*, etc., p. 272, note 4). Besides these gold pieces, a silver coin also circulated in the Persian kingdom, named the *siglos*. See DARIC. Mention is probably made of this coin in the Bible in those passages which treat of the Persian times (Neh. v, 15; comp. x, 32). Of these pieces twenty went to one gold Daric (Mommsen, *Geschichte des Röm. Münzwesens*, p. 13 and 855), which would give a ratio of gold to silver of one to thirteen (Herod. iii, 95). These coins also have an archer on the obverse. As long, then, as the Jews lived under Persian domination, they made use of Persian coins, and had no struck coins of their own. In these coins also were probably paid the tributes (Herod. iii, 89).

On the overthrow of the Persian monarchy in B.C. 333, by Alexander the Great, Palestine came under the dominion of the Greeks. During the lifetime of Alexander the country was governed by a vice-regent, and the high-priest was permitted to remain in power. Jaddua was at this time high-priest, and in high favor with Alexander (Josephus, *Ant.* xi, 8, 5). At this period only Greek coins were struck in many cities of Palestine. The coinage consisted of gold, silver, and copper. The usual gold coins were *staters*, called by Pollux Ἀλεξάνδρειοι. The silver coins mostly in circulation were tetradrachms and drachms. There are two specimens of the tetradrachms struck at Scythopolis (the ancient Bethshan), preserved in the Gotha and Paris collections. There are also tetradrachms with the initials ΙΟΠ struck at Joppa, which, being a town of considerable importance, no doubt supplied Jerusalem with money. Some of the coins bear the monograms of two cities sometimes at a great distance from each other, showing evidently some commercial intercourse between them. For instance, Sycamina (Hepha) and Scythopolis (Bethshan), Ascalon and Philadelphia (Rabbath-Ammon) (Müller, *Numismatique d'Alexandre le Grand*, 1464, pl. xx).

Shortly after the death of Alexander the Great, in B.C. 324, Palestine fell into the hands of Ptolemy I Soter, the son of Lagus, from whom Antigonus wrested it for a short time, until, in B.C. 301, after the battle of Ipsus, it came again into his hands, and afterwards was under the government of the Ptolemies for nearly one hundred years.

The same system of coinage was continued under the Seleucidæ and Lagidæ, and we find the same and other mints in Palestine. The history, from that time to B.C. 139, will be found under ANTIOCHUS, MACCABEES, and other names, and would be out of place in an article which more especially treats only of money.

The next distinct allusion to coined money is in the Apocrypha, where it is narrated in the first book of Maccabees that Antiochus VII granted to Simon the Maccabee permission to coin money with his own stamp, as well as other privileges (Καὶ ἐπέτρεψά σοι ποιῆσαι κόμμα ἴδιον νόμισμα τῇ χώρᾳ σου. xv, 6). This was in the fourth year of Simon's pontificate, B.C. 140. It must be noted that Demetrius II had in the first year of Simon, B.C. 143, made a most important decree granting freedom to the Jewish people, which gave occasion to the dating of their contracts and covenants—"In the first year of Simon, the great high-priest, the leader, and chief of the Jews" (xiii, 34–42), a form which Josephus gives differently—"In the first year of Simon, benefactor of the Jews, and ethnarch" (*Ant.* xiii, 6). This passage has raised many opinions concerning the Jewish coinage, and among the most conspicuous is that of M. de Saulcy, whose classification of Jewish coins has been generally received and adopted. It has been fully treated upon by Mr. J. Evans in the *Numismatic Chronicle* (xx, 8 sq.). See NUMISMATICS. The Jews, being the worshippers of the one only true God, idolatry was strictly forbidden in their law; and therefore their shekel never bore a head, but was impressed simply

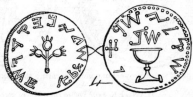

Early Jewish Shekel.

with the almond rod and the pot of manna. Later shekels of copper bore likewise other devices. See SHEKEL.

Hebrew-Samaritan Copper Coin, in the Cufico-Borgian Museum.

4. *Money in the New Testament.*—The coins mentioned by the evangelists, and first those of silver, are the following: the *stater* is spoken of in the account of the miracle of the tribute money. The receivers of *didrachms* demanded the tribute, but Peter found in the fish a *stater*, which he paid for our Lord and himself (Matt. xvii, 24–27). This stater was therefore a tetradrachm, and it is very noteworthy that at this period almost the only Greek imperial silver coin in the East was a tetradrachm, the didrachm being probably unknown, or very little coined.

The *didrachm* is mentioned as a money of account in the passage above cited, as the equivalent of the Hebrew shekel.

The *denarius*, or Roman penny, as well as the Greek *drachm*, then of about the same weight, is spoken of as a current coin. There can be little doubt that the latter is merely employed as another name for the former. In

Roman Denarius (from the British Museum).

the famous passages respecting the tribute to Cæsar, the Roman denarius of the time is correctly described (Matt. xxii, 15–21; Luke xx, 19–25). It bears the head of Tiberius, who has the title Cæsar in the accompanying inscription, most later emperors having, after their accession, the title Augustus: here again therefore we have an evidence of the date of the Gospels. See DENARIUS; DRACHM.

Of copper coins the farthing and its half, the mite, are spoken of, and these probably formed the chief native currency. See FARTHING; MITE.

From the time of Julius Cæsar, who first struck a living portrait on his coins, the Roman coins run in a continued succession of so-called Cæsars, their queens and crown-princes, from about B.C. 48 down to Romulus Augustulus, emperor of the West, who was dethroned by Odoacer about A.D. 475 (Quarterly Review, lxxii, 358). See COIN.

Copper Coin of Vespasian commemorating the Capture of Jerusalem.

MONEY-CHANGER (κολλυβιστής, Matt. xxi, 12; Mark xi, 15; John ii, 15). According to Exod. xxx, 13–15, every Israelite, whether rich or poor, who had reached or passed the age of twenty, must pay into the sacred treasury, whenever the nation was numbered, a half-shekel as an offering to Jehovah. Maimonides (Shekal. cap. 1) says that this was to be paid annually, and that even paupers were not exempt. The Talmud exempts priests and women. The tribute must in every case be paid in coin of the exact Hebrew half-shekel, about $15\frac{1}{2}d$. sterling of English money. The premium for obtaining by exchange of other money the half-shekel of Hebrew coin, according to the Talmud, was a κόλλυβος (collybus), and hence the money-broker who made the exchange was called κολλυβιστής. The collybus, according to the same authority, was equal in value to a silver obolus, which has a weight of 12 grains, and its money value is about $1\frac{1}{2}d$. sterling. The money-changers (κολλυβισταί) whom Christ, for their impiety, avarice, and fraudulent dealing, expelled from the Temple, were the dealers who supplied half-shekels, for such a premium as they might be able to exact, to the Jews from all parts of the world, who assembled at Jerusalem during the great festivals, and were required to pay their tribute or ransom money in the Hebrew coin; and also for other purposes of exchange, such as would be necessary in so great a resort of foreign residents to the ecclesiastical metropolis. The word τραπεζίτης (trapezites), which we find in Matt. xxv, 29, is a general term for banker or broker, so called from the table (τραπέζης) at which they were seated (like the modern "bank," i. e. bench). See EXCHANGER. Of this branch of business we find traces very early both in the Oriental and classical literature (comp. Matt. xvii, 24–27: see Lightfoot, Hor. Heb. on Matt. xxi, 12; Buxtorf, Lex. Rabbin. col. 2032).—Smith. It is mentioned by Volney that in Syria, Egypt, and Turkey, when any considerable payments are to be made, an agent of exchange is sent for, who counts paras by thousands, rejects pieces of false money, and weighs all the sequins either separately or together. It has hence been suggested that the "current money with the merchant" mentioned in Scripture (Gen. xxiii, 16), might have been such as was approved of by competent judges, whose business it

was to detect fraudulent money if offered in payment. The Hebrew word סוֹחֵר, socher', signifies one who goes about from place to place, and is supposed to answer to the native exchange-agent or money-broker of the East, now called shroff. See MERCHANT. It appears that there were bankers or money-changers in Judæa, who made a trade of receiving money in deposit and paying interest for it (Matt. xxv, 27). In the Life of Aratus, by Plutarch, there is mention of a banker of Sicyon, a city of Peloponnesus, who lived 240 years before Christ, and whose whole business consisted in exchanging one species of money for another. See CHANGER OF MONEY.

MONEY, LOVE OF (φιλαργυρία, 1 Tim. vi, 10, avarice or cupidity). See COVETOUSNESS.

MONEY, PIECE OF (קְשִׂיטָה, kesitah', Gen. xxxiii, 19; Job xlii, 11; "piece of silver," Josh. xxiv, 32; στατήρ, Matt. xvii, 27). See KESITAH; STATER.

Money, Ecclesiastical. See NUMISMATICS; USURY.

Money-stone is, in ecclesiastical language, the upper slab of a tomb, on which payments were made by or to ecclesiastics. There is one at Carlisle, at York. and at Dundry, in England.

Monfort, David, D.D., a Presbyterian divine, was born in Adams County, Pa., March 7, 1790. His ancestors were the Huguenot De Monforts of France, who were driven to Holland, and afterwards emigrated to this country about 1640. David Monfort was educated at Transylvania University, in Lexington, Ky., and graduated in the theological seminary at Princeton, N. J., in 1817; was licensed by Miami Presbytery in 1818, and continued all his life a missionary preacher, acting at different times as the stated supply of Bethel Church, in Oxford Presbytery; Terre Haute Church, Ind.; Sharon Church, at Wilmington, Ohio; and a church in Franklin, Ind., where he labored for twenty years. In 1854 he became stated pastor of the church at Knightstown, Ind.; and in 1857 he removed to Macomb, Ill., where he remained until his death, Oct. 18, 1860. Dr. Monfort was a thoroughly trained minister, an able expositor, an excellent linguist, and an eloquent preacher. He published two sermons on Baptism and one on Justification, which appeared in a volume called Original Sermons by Presbyterian Divines in the Mississippi Valley. See Wilson, Presb. Hist. Almanac, 1862, p. 104.

Monfort, Peter, a Presbyterian minister, was born in Adams County, Pa., March 14, 1784. He was, like the above, descended from the Huguenot De Monforts. He attained his education through great effort, pursuing his course with much difficulty for want of teachers and books. After several years of private tuition in the classics and theology, he was licensed in the spring of 1813, and ordained in 1814 by Miami Presbytery; was pastor four years at Yellow Springs, Ohio, and eleven years in Unity and Pisgah, near his early home; subsequently he undertook the work of a domestic missionary at Findlay, Ohio, where he labored for three years. In 1836 he transferred his relations from the Presbyterian to the Associate Reformed Church, and in that connection preached at Syracuse, in Hamilton County, Ohio; Jacksonburg, Quincy, and Middleburg, Ohio; and at College Corner. He died Nov. 13, 1865. Mr. Monfort showed much ability as an expositor of the Scriptures, and as an advocate of sound doctrinal theology. He was a man of deep religious experience, uniform life, and lowliness of mind. See Wilson, Presb. Hist. Almanac, 1867, p. 361.

Mongin, EDMONDE, a French Roman Catholic preacher, noted for his pulpit oratory, was born in 1668 at Baroville, diocese of Langres. At the age of nineteen he gave proofs of his talent for the pulpit, and in after-years the French Academy successively awarded him three different prizes for eloquence. He was intrusted with the education of Louis-Henri de Bourbon and of Charles de Charolais, princes of the house of Condé. Elected a member of the Academy in the place of the abbé Gallois, he was received March 1, 1708, and it was in this capacity he pronounced in the chapel of the Louvre the funeral oration of Louis XIV. He was appointed in 1711 abbé of Saint-Martin d'Autun, and became bishop of Bazas Sept. 24, 1724, devoting himself entirely to the administration of his diocese. In the midst of the unfortunate quarrels which troubled the Church of France he was as remarkable for his moderation as for his wisdom. "Believe me," said he to an over-zealous prelate, "we should speak much and write little." Mongin died at Bazas, May 6, 1746. He has left some sermons, some panegyrics, some funeral orations (among others, that of Henri de Bourbon, prince de Condé), and several different academical pieces, collected into one volume (Paris, 1745, 4to). D'Alembert says that "his works evince more taste than warmth, more thought than emotion, more wisdom than imagination; but there is found throughout all a noble and simple tone, a sweet sensibility, an elegant and pure diction, and that sound instruction which should be the basis of Christian eloquence" (*Hist. des Membres de l'Académie Française*, vol. v).

Mongitore, ANTONINO, an Italian ecclesiastic, noted mainly, however, for his literary labors, was born at Palermo, May 1, 1663, entered the priesthood, and was made dean of the cathedral of his native place, and finally became one of the papal counsellors. He died June 6, 1743. Besides his *Bibliotheca Sicula* (Palermo, 1708-14, 2 vols. fol.), which contains a history of Sicily and its writers, secular and ecclesiastic, we should note *Breve Compendio della Vita di S. Francisco di Sales* (1695, 12mo): — *Vite de' due Santi Mamiliani, arcivescovi di Palermo* (1701, 4to); and the biographies of other celebrated ecclesiastics, and also a history of the Teutonic order of knighthood. See Du Pin, *Biblioth. des Auteurs ecclésiast. du dix-huitième siècle.*

Mongolia, an Asiatic country, now a part of China, situated between lat. 35° and 52° N. and long. 82° and 123° E., is bounded by the Russian government of Irkutsk in Siberia, N.E. by Mantchuria, S. by the Chinese provinces of Chili and Shan-si and the Yellow River, S.W. by Kansu, and W. by Cobdo and Ili, and has an area of 1,400,000 square miles, with a population of 2,000,000. See CHINA.

Geographical Features.—It is chiefly a high plain, 3000 feet above the sea, almost destitute of wood and water. In the central part is the great sandy desert of Gobi, which stretches from N.E. to S.W., with an area estimated at 600,000 square miles. The chief mountain ranges of Mongolia are the Altai and its various subordinate chains, which extend eastward, under the names of Tangnu, Khangai, and Kenteh, as far as the Amur; and the Alashan and Inshan ranges, which commence in lat. 42° N. and long. 107° E., and run N.E. and N. to the Amur, in lat. 53° N. The rivers of Mongolia are chiefly in the north. The Selenga, Orkhon, and Tula unite their streams and flow into Lake Baikal. The Kerlon and Onon rise near each other, on opposite sides of the Kenteh range, and flow in a N.E. direction to the Amur. In the south, the Siramuren and its branches unite in the Lian River. Lakes are numerous, and some of them are large. South of the desert of Gobi are the Oling and Dzaring, and the Koko-nor or Blue Sea, which, according to the Chinese accounts, is 190 miles in length and 60 in breadth. In the N.W. part of the country lakes abound, the largest of which are the Upsa-nor, Altai-nor, Alak-nor, and the Iki-ural. Mongolia is divided into four principal re-

gions: 1, Inner Mongolia, lying between the great wall and the desert of Gobi; 2, Outer Mongolia, between the desert and the Altai mountains, and reaching from the Inner Hingan to the Tien-shan; 3, the country about Koko-nor; 4, Uliassutai and its dependencies. Inner Mongolia is divided into 6 corps and 24 tribes, which are again divided into 49 standards, each comprising about 2000 families and commanded by hereditary princes. The Kortchin and the Ortus are the principal tribes. Another large tribe, the Tsakhars, occupy the region immediately north of the great wall. Outer Mongolia is divided into 4 circles, each of which is governed by a khan, or prince, who claims descent from Genghis Khan. The Khalkas is the principal tribe, and their 4 khanates are divided into 86 standards, each of which is restricted to a particular territory, from which it is not allowed to wander. The country about Lake Koko-nor is occupied by Turguths, Hoshoits, Khalkas, and other tribes, arranged under 29 standards. Uliassutai is a town of 2000 houses, in the western part of Mongolia, and lies in a well-cultivated valley upon the River Iro. Its dependent territories comprise 11 tribes of Khalkas, divided into 31 standards (*Amer. Cyclop.*).

But little is accurately known of the natural history of Mongolia, except that its immense plains and gloomy forests are inhabited by multitudes of wild animals. The camel, double-humped or Bactrian, exists in both the wild and domesticated state. In the latter condition it is the cow and horse of that region. It gives milk excellent in quality, and from it butter and cheese are prepared, and at the same time it is the camel which serves the Mongolian frequently as a beast of burden, etc. Very little of Mongolian soil is fit for cultivation, rain or snow rarely falling in sufficient quantities, except on the acclivities of the mountain ranges. It is noticed, however, that wherever agriculture has been attempted the climate has been more or less influenced, and changes have been wrought; as e. g. in Southern Mongolia, where the Chinese, far advanced beyond the Mongols proper in culture, introduced agriculture, with the cultivation of cereals, which formerly did not grow. As a rule, the winter lasts nine months, and is suddenly succeeded by three months of intense heat.

Inhabitants.—The natives of Mongolia are a part of the Mongolian race, a division of mankind numerous and widely spread—according to Prof. Dieterici's estimate, in 1859, counting as many as 528,000,000 souls, or about half the human race; the second in the classification of Blumenbach, and corresponding in almost every respect with the branch designated as *Turanian* by more recent ethnologists. See ORIGIN OF MAN. Under the designation of Mongolians are included not only the Mongols proper, but the Chinese and Indo-Chinese, Thibetans, Tartars of all kinds, Burmese, Siamese, Japanese, Esquimaux, Samoieds, Finns, Lapps, Turks, and even Magyars. Collectively, they are the great nomadic people of the earth, as distinguished from the Aryans, Shemites, and Hamites. The *physical characteristics* of the Mongolians in their primitive state are thus described by Dr. Latham in his *Descriptive Ethnology:* "The face of the Mongolian is broad and flat. This is because the nasal bones are depressed and the cheekbones stand out *laterally;* they are not merely projecting, for this they might be without giving much breadth to the face, inasmuch as they might stand forward.... The distance between the eyes is great, the eyes themselves being oblique, and their carunculæ being concealed. The eyebrows form a low and imperfect arch, black and scanty. The iris is dark, the cornea yellow. The complexion is tawny, the stature low. The ears are large, standing out from the head; the lips thick and fleshy rather than thin, the teeth somewhat oblique in their insertion, the forehead low and flat, and the hair lank and thin." Of course, such a description as this cannot be understood as applying to the more civilized nations of Mongol origin, such as the Turks and Magyars, especially the latter, who in physical appearance differ but little, if at all, from other European nations.

The Mongols are, with a few exceptions, nomadic in their mode of life, living in tents and subsisting on animal food, the product of their flocks and herds. The Mongol tent, for about three feet from the ground, is cylindrical in form; it then becomes conical, like a pointed hat. Its wood-work is composed below of a trellis-work of crossed bars, which fold up and expand at pleasure. Above these a circle of poles, fixed in the trellis-work, meets at the top, like the sticks of an umbrella. Over the wood-work is stretched a thick covering of coarse felt. The door is low and narrow, and is crossed at the bottom by a beam which serves as a threshold. At the top of the tent is an opening to let out the smoke, which can at any time be closed by a piece of felt hanging above it, to which is attached a long string for the purpose. The interior is divided into two compartments—that on the left being for the men, while that on the right is occupied by the women, and is also used as a kitchen, the utensils of which consist chiefly of large earthen vessels for holding water, wooden pails for milk, and a large bell-shaped iron kettle. A small sofa or couch, a small square press or chest of drawers (the top of which serves as an altar for an idol), and a number of goats' horns fixed in the wood-work of the tent, on which hang various utensils, arms, and other articles, complete the furniture of this primitive habitation. The odor pervading the interior of the Mongol tent is, to those not accustomed to it, disgusting and almost insupportable. "This smell," says M. Huc, "so potent sometimes that it seems to make one's heart rise to one's throat, is occasioned by the mutton-grease and butter with which everything on and about a Tartar is impregnated. It is on account of this habitual filth that they are called Tsao-Ta-Dze ('stinking Tartars') by the Chinese, themselves not altogether inodorous, or by any means particular about cleanliness." Household and family cares among the Mongols are assigned entirely to the women, who milk the cows, make the butter and cheese, draw water, gather fuel, tan skins, and make cloth and clothes. The occupation of the men consists chiefly in conducting the flocks and herds to pasture, which, as they are accustomed from infancy to horseback, is an amusement rather than a labor. They sometimes hunt wild animals for food or for their skins, but never for pleasure. When not on horseback, the men pass their time in absolute idleness, sleeping all night and squatting all day in their tents, drinking tea or smoking. Their education is very limited. The only persons who learn to read are the lamas or priests, who are also the painters, sculptors, architects, and physicians of the nation. The training of the men who are not intended for priests is confined to the use of the bow and the matchlock, and a thorough mastery of horsemanship. M. Huc says: "When a mere infant, the Mongol is weaned, and as soon as he is strong enough he is stuck upon a horse's back behind a man, the animal is put to a gallop, and the juvenile rider, in order not to fall off, has to cling with both hands to his teacher's jacket. The Tartars thus become accustomed from a very early age to the movement of the horse, and by degrees and the force of habit they identify themselves, as it were, with the animal. There is perhaps no spectacle more exciting than that of Mongol riders in chase of a wild horse. They are armed with a long, heavy pole, at the end of which is a running-knot. They gallop—they fly after the horse they are pursuing, down rugged ravines and up precipitous hills, in and out, twisting and turning in their rapid course, until they come up with their game. They then take the bridle of their own horse in their teeth, seize with both hands their heavy pole, and, bending forward, throw by a powerful effort the running-knot around the wild horse's neck. In this exercise the greatest vigor must be combined with the greatest dexterity, in order to enable them to stop short

the powerful untamed animals with which they have to deal. It sometimes happens that the cord and pole are broken; but as to a horseman being thrown, it is an occurrence we never saw or heard of. The Mongol is so accustomed to ride on horseback that he is like a fish out of water when he sets foot on the ground. His step is heavy and awkward; and his bowed legs, his chest bent forward, and his constant looking about him, all indicate a person who spends the greater portion of his time on the back of a horse or a camel. The Mongols marry very young, and their marriages are regulated entirely by their parents, who make the contract without consulting the young people at all. No dowry is given with the bride, but, on the contrary, the bridegroom's family pay a considerable price for the maiden. A plurality of wives is permitted, but the first wife is always the mistress of the household. Divorce is very frequent, and is effected without the intervention of either the civil or the ecclesiastical authorities. The husband who wishes to repudiate his wife sends her back to her parents without any formality, except a message that he does not require her any longer. This proceeding does not give offence, as the family of the lady retain the cattle, horses, and other property given to them at the time of the marriage, and have an opportunity of selling her over again to a fresh purchaser. The women, however, are not oppressed, and are not kept in seclusion; they come and go at pleasure, ride on horseback, and visit from tent to tent. In their manners and appearance they are like the men—haughty, independent, and vigorous. The chiefs of the Mongol tribes and all their blood-relations form an aristocracy, who hold the common people in a mild species of patriarchal servitude. There is no distinction of manners nor of mode of living between these classes; and though the common people are not allowed to own lands, they frequently accumulate considerable property in herds and flocks. Those who become lamas are entirely free."

History.—The Mongolians, as a race, are supposed to be the same who, in remote antiquity, founded what is called the "Median empire" in Lower Chaldæa—an empire, according to Rawlinson, that flourished and fell between 2458 and 2234 B.C., that is, before Nineveh became known as a great city. Thus early did some of these nomadic tribes, forsaking their original pastoral habits, assume the character of a nation. Another great offshoot from this stock founded an empire in China, the earliest date of which it is impossible to trace, but which certainly had reached a state of high civilization at least 2000 years B.C. In early Greek history they figure as Scythians, and in late Roman as Huns, carrying terror and desolation over the civilized world. In the Middle Ages they appear as Mongols, Tartars, and Turks. In the beginning of the 13th century Genghis Khan, originally the chief of a small Mongol horde, conquered almost the whole of Central and Eastern Asia. His sons and grandsons were equally successful, and in 1240-41 the Mongol empire extended from the sea-board of China to the frontiers of Germany and Poland, including Russia and Hungary, and the whole of Asia, with the exception of Asia Minor, Arabia, India and the Indo-Chinese states, and Northern Siberia. This vast empire soon broke up into a number of independent kingdoms, from one of which, Turkestan, arose another tide of Mongol invasion, under the guidance of Timûr or Tamerlane, who in the latter part of the 14th century reduced Turkestan, Persia, Hindustan, Asia Minor, and Georgia under his sway, and broke for a time the Turkish power. On the death of his son, shah Rokh, the Mongol empire was subdivided, and finally absorbed by the Persians and Usbeks; but an offshoot of Timûr's family founded in the 16th century the great Mogul empire of Delhi. After the decline of Timûr's empire, the Turkish branch maintained the glory of the race, and spread terror to the very heart of Western Europe. In the 9th century the Magyars, a tribe of Ugrians, also of Mongol extraction, under their leader Arpad, established themselves in Hungary, where in process of time they became converted to Christianity, and founded a kingdom famous in European history. See GEORGIA; HUNGARY; TURKEY.

Religion.—(a) Heathenism.—The primitive religion of the Mongolians was no doubt largely influenced by the inspired faith, if it did not to some extent prevail among them for some time. The earliest traces reveal them as mostly adherents to *Shamanism* (q. v.). There are, however, among them, according to the different countries in which they reside, and to the several names of which the reader has been referred, various other religions, as *Buddhism, Confucianism, Taouism, fire-worship, paganism* of different kinds, *Mohammedanism,* and *Christianity.* In Mongolia proper, that species of Buddhism known as *Lamaism* (q. v.) was introduced in the 13th century of the Christian æra, and, like the Buddhists of Thibet, they recognise as their spiritual head the grand lama at Lassa. The people are very devout, and generous to a fault in their support of religious institutions, and hence the country abounds in well-endowed lamasaries, constructed of brick and stone with elegance and solidity, and ornamented with paintings, sculptures, and carvings. "The most famous of these monasteries is that of the great Kuren, on the banks of the river Tula, in the country of the Kalkas. Thirty thousand lamas dwell in the lamasary, and the plain adjoining it is always covered with the tents of the pilgrims who resort thither from all parts of Tartary. In these lamasaries a strict monastic discipline is maintained, but each lama is at liberty to acquire property by practicing as physician, by casting horoscopes, or by working as sculptor or painter, or in any occupation not inconsistent with his priestly character. Almost all younger sons of the free Mongols are devoted from infancy to the priesthood, and this tendency to monasticism is encouraged by the Chinese government, in order to keep down the growth of population among the Mongols. Almost every lamasary of the first class possesses a living Buddha, who, like the grand lama of Thibet, is worshipped as an incarnation of the deity. The influence of these personages is very great; and the Chinese emperors, who are constantly in dread of the Mongols, watch the living Buddhas with constant care, and spare no pains to conciliate them and win over to their interest those who manage these deities."

(b) Christianity.—The Nestorians (q. v.), who dwelt in large numbers among the Mongolians, seem to have exerted but little if any influence on this heathen people. What was by the early Christians regarded as an indication of their leaning towards the religion and culture of the Christian dispensation, proves to have been only a temporary accommodation. The Western or Roman Church has made repeated attempts to convert the Mongols. In the 13th century, when their invasion threatened to overthrow European society and civilization, the Western pontiff, Innocent IV (1245), sent two embassies, one to charge these sanguinary warriors to desist from their desolating inroads, the other to win them over to Christianity. The first of these, consisting of Dominicans, headed by one named Ascelin (Neander, *Kirchengeschichte,* vii, 66), approached the commander-in-chief of the Mongol forces in Persia, but was unsuccessful. The other, consisting of Franciscans, headed by an Italian, Johannes de Plano Carpini, a disciple and devoted friend of Francis d'Assisi, pushed quite to the Tartaric court, and approached the khan in person (1246); but though they secured a hearing before the Mongolian throne, they yet failed to accomplish more than that the Mongol chief, like Vladimir of Russia, gave a patient hearing to Romanist, Nestorian, Buddhist, and Mohammedan, who each in their turn sought his conversion and influence. In 1253 Louis IX, hearing of the Mongolian's tendency towards Christianity, despatched another Franciscan, William de Rubruiquis (Neander, vii, 69); but he reported that the

Mongolian chief listened patiently to Christian emissaries, "filled with the idea that the Mongol conquests would come to an end unless the gods of foreign countries were propitiated." Only one Christian Church had been founded. Rubruiquis, however, succeeded in baptizing about sixty persons; yet, after all, Rubruiquis's success was not flattering, and he finally returned to Europe disheartened. The removal, five years later, of the capital of the Mongol empire to China (q. v.), further obstructed the progress of Christianity in Mongolia. There developed, however, among its simple pastoral tribes an article of belief which promised much for the final establishment of Christianity, viz. the belief in the existence of one almighty Being. In their heathen views, of course, they could not content themselves with acknowledging an earthly ruler unless a supernatural origin could be assigned to him, and they made the khan the son of this one almighty Power, an earthly ruler whom all men were bound to obey. While thus there was room for the most comprehensive toleration, there was room also for every kind of superstition; and the desire to bring the one Supreme, living apart in awful isolation, into nearer communion with his feeble worshipper—to bridge over the awful chasm between them —predisposed the people to a composite religion of Buddhism and Lamaism (see Hardwick, *Christ and other Masters,* vol. ii, Append. 2; iii, 89; *Middle Ages,* p. 235). Still, "the son of Heaven" entertained a respect for all religions, and not least for Christianity. Marco Polo, who had been sent there by Gregory X in 1274, reports Kublai Khan as saying: "There are four great prophets who are reverenced by the different classes of mankind. The Christians regard Jesus Christ as their God; the Saracens, Mohammed; the Jews, Moses; the idolators, Sakyamuni Buddha, the most eminent among their idols. I honor and respect all the four" (*Travels,* p. 167, ed. Bohn, 1854). One of the most successful of the early Christian laborers from the West was John de Monte Corvino, who went to Pekin in 1292, and for eleven years kept alive the flickering spark of Christianity in the Tartar realm. He translated the Scriptures for its people, educated their youth, and trained a native ministry. Yet even his labors bore fruit only while he was on earth; for soon after the close of his life, in 1330, "every vestige of his work was obliterated" (Gieseler, *Eccles. Hist.* iv, 259, 260; Hardwick, *Ch. Hist. M. A.* p. 235, 237). This was caused no doubt in a large measure by the termination of the Mongolian rule in China, and the accession of the Ming dynasty in 1370, which, fearing everything foreign, banished Christianity as dangerous to their interests. It remained for the Jesuits to plant Christianity anew. The missionary work performed in Persia, and in the border lands of the Caspian Sea and in Middle Asia, was so insignificant that it is not even worth mentioning. See Maclear, *Hist. of Christian Missions in the M. A.* (Lond. 1863, 12mo), p. 370–77; Assemani, *Bibl. Orient.* iii, 2 sq.; Huc, *Journey through the Chinese Empire; Recollections of a Journey through Tartary and Thibet;* Schmidt, *Forschungen im Gebiete der älteren religiösen, politischen, u. literarischen Bildungsgeschichte der Mongolen u. Tibeter* (St. Petersb. 1824); Tumerelli, *Kazan, the ancient Capital of the Tartar Khans* (Lond. 1854, 2 vols. 12mo); Neumann, *Die Völker des südlichen Russlands* (Leipsic, 1847); Aboul-Ghâze Bîhâdour Khan, *Histoire des Mogols et des Tartares* (St. Petersb. 1874), vol. ii; Daniels, *Handb. d. Geogr.* i, 346 sq.; *Am. Cyclop.* s. v. See TARTARY.

Mongul, PETER. See MONOPHYSITES.

Monheim, JOHANNES, a follower of the great Desiderius Erasmus, and a noted teacher of the 16th century, was born of humble parentage at Claussen, near Elberfeld, in 1509. His father was a linen-draper, and Monheim entered his business when quite young. But his superior mental endowments soon led him into a different course; and, though not privileged with the advantages of a careful training, he yet managed to acquire a good classical education. It is said that he studied with Erasmus, but Hamelmann's assertion that Monheim studied at Münster and Cologne deserves more credit. When but twenty-three years old, he was elected rector of the school at Essen, and four years later he received a call to Cologne as rector of the *schola metropolitanæ ecclesiæ Coloniensis*. Here he enjoyed intimate connections with the leaders of Erasmianism, and in a short time became so popular as a teacher that he attracted students from every direction. In 1545 he received and accepted a very flattering call from duke Wilhelm of Cleve to take the rectorship of the newly founded institute at Düsseldorf, and only five years after his inauguration in this new position Monheim wrote to a friend that his scholars outnumbered most German universities, more than 2000 young men being just then matriculated (see Frid. Reiffenbergii e Soc. Jesu Presbyteri *Hist. Societatis Jesu*, i, 89). Monheim, in opposition to other humanists, insisted on a religious instruction, and published numerous catechisms, the best known of which is his *Catechismus in quo Christianæ religionis elementa sincere simpliciterque explicantur* (Düsseldorf, 1560, with an introduction; and, edited and revised, it was recently published by Dr. Sack, Bonn, 1847). Though, outwardly at least, Monheim belonged to the Church of Rome, his catechism proves beyond doubt that he taught and believed the evangelical doctrines as set forth in the teachings of Calvin. The book was severely attacked. The theological faculty of the University of Cologne issued a *Censura et docta explicatio errorum Catechismi Johannis Monheimii* (Cologne, 1560); and a number of other essays, partly in defence, partly in opposition to Monheim, were published. Monheim, however, himself remained quiet; but Martin Chemnitz, enraged at the open and secret attacks of the Cologne Jesuits on the learned man, edited his *Theologiæ Jesuitarum præcipua capita, ex quadam censura, quæ Coloniæ anno 1560 edita est* (Lips. 1563), which, together with his *Examen Concilii Tridentii*, so embittered pope Paul IV that he requested duke William to depose and banish "that arch-heretic" Johannes Monheim. Monheim was cited before the duke, and obliged to sign an agreement in which he promised to abstain from teaching Protestant doctrines, either openly or secretly (see *Zeitschrift d. bergischen Geschichtsvereins*, ii, 255). The pope, however, was not satisfied even with this. He insisted upon an open judgment on Monheim, especially as the pardoning of a heretic was not within the duke's jurisdiction—"nec princeps hæretico publico quicquam ignoscere potuit." Further steps of the papal court were made unnecessary by Monheim's sudden decease, Sept. 9, 1564. Monheim wrote a great number of learned books, but his most valued work is the above-mentioned catechism, which Theo. Strack calls *Catechismum orthodoxum, in quo Reformatorum doctrina, quæ hodie Luthero-Calvinismi nomine odiose traducitur, accurate confirmatur.* Monheim lacked strength of character to take a decided position in the great struggle of the Reformation. He preferred, although thoroughly Protestant in all his views, to remain in the Church of Rome. "He belonged," said one, "to that class of actors on the stage of life who have always appeared as the harbingers of great social men gifted with the power to discern and the hardihood to proclaim truths of which they want the courage to encounter the infallible result." See Möhler, *Symbolik*; Seck, *Protestant. Beantwortung der Symbolik Möhler's.*

Moniales. See NUNS.

Monica, St., the mother of St. Augustine, "counted," says Schaff, "among the most noble and pious women who adorn the temple of Church history," was born, according to tradition, of Christian parents, in Africa, about the year 332. Having attained to the age of womanhood she was married to Patrice of Tagaste, a heathen of Numidia, by whom she had two sons and

one daughter. She was instrumental in the conversion of her husband a year before his death, after having spent with him years in hardship and sore trial. He was of violent temperament, and unfaithful to her in conjugal duties, yet she met all his shortcomings by a Christian spirit of forgiveness and love, and thus at last conquered in the name of her Saviour, whom she adored and faithfully followed. "Her highest aim," says Schaff, "was to win him over to the faith—not so much by words as by a truly humble and godly conversation, and the most conscientious discharge of her household duties" (*Life of St. Augustine*, p. 10). The same earnestness which she displayed for the conversion of her husband she manifested also for the spiritual safety of her children. She was especially anxious for her son Augustine, who in his youth was given to dissipation, having inherited from his father strong sensual passions, and who had embraced the Manichæan heresy, which she feared would ultimately ruin his spiritual life. For thirty years she therefore uninterruptedly prayed for his conversion. "A son of so many prayers and tears," says Schaff, "could not be lost, and the faithful mother, who travailed with him in spirit with greater pain than her body had in bringing him into the world (Augustine, *Confess.* ix, c. 8), was permitted, for the encouragement of future mothers, to receive, shortly before her death, an answer to her prayers and expectations, and was able to leave this world with joy without revisiting her earthly home." Augustine had embraced Christianity at Milan, whither he had gone in 384. Hither his mother followed him, and together they worshipped under the ministration of St. Ambrose. In the spring of 387, shortly after his baptism, they had quitted Rome to return to Africa, and it was on this homeward journey that Monica died, in Ostia, at the mouth of the Tiber, in 387, in the arms of her son, after enjoying with him a glorious conversation that soared above the confines of space and time, and was a foretaste of the eternal Sabbath-rest of the saints. She regretted not to die, aye, not even in a foreign land, because she was not far from God, who would raise her up at the last day. "Bury my body anywhere," was her last request, "and trouble not yourselves for it; only this one thing I ask, that you remember me at the altar of my God, wherever you may be." Augustine, in his *Confessions*, has erected to Monica the noblest monument, and it can never perish. The Roman Catholic Church keeps May 4 in commemoration of her. Pope Martin V gives an account of the translation of her remains to Rome in 1430. See St. Augustine, *Confessions*; Godescard, *Vie des Saints*; Braune, *Monica u. Augustinus* (1846); Petet, *Histoire de Sainte-Monique* (1848); Schaff, *Life and Labors of St. Augustine* (N. Y. 1854), ch. i, iv, viii; Mrs. Jamieson, *Legends* (see Index); Schaff, *Ch. Hist.* iii, 991, 992; Neander, *Ch. Hist.* ii, 227. See AUGUSTINE. (J. H. W.)

Moniglia, TOMMASO-VINCENZO, an Italian theologian, was born August 18, 1686, in Florence. Having received his education at the University of Pisa, he returned to Florence, and entered the Order of St. Dominic. Very soon after he contracted a close friendship with the English ambassador, Henry Newton. Seduced by his promises, he fled from the convent and repaired to London. His pecuniary resources being exhausted, he was forced to support himself by teaching. After an absence of three years he succeeded, by the favor of the grand duke, in returning to his own country, where he was kindly received and his errors pardoned. From that time he devoted himself to preaching with indefatigable zeal, and taught theology at Florence and Pisa. Moniglia had an extensive knowledge of nearly all the sciences, and was well versed in sacred and profane literature. He was one of the first among the Italians to refute the opinions of Locke, of Hobbes, of Helvetius, and of Bayle, but not always to advantage. He died at Pisa, Feb. 15, 1767. He is the author of *De Origine sacrarum precum rosarii B. M.*

Virginis (Rome, 1725, 8vo); which dissertation he composed by order of his superiors and to refute the Bollandists, who do not believe that St. Dominic is the author of these prayers:—*De annis Jesu-Christi servatoris et de religione utriusque Philippi Augusti* (Rome, 1741, 4to):—*Contro i Fatalisti* (Lucca, 1744, 2 parts, 8vo):—*Contro i Materialisti e altri increduli* (Padua, 1750, 2 vols. 8vo):—*Osservazioni critico-filosofiche contro i materialisti* (Lucca, 1760, 8vo):—*La mente umana spirito immortale, non materia pensante* (Padua, 1766, 2 vols. 8vo). See Fabroni, *Vitæ Italorum,* vol. xi.

Monism. See MONADS.

Monita Secreta Societatis Jesu, or *secret instructions for the Jesuitic order,* is a work which has been the cause of much dispute, both as to its authenticity and as to the veracity of its contents. In Europe the book has attracted some attention, and, in consequence, some controversy; but in America it has been the subject of a very animated discussion, and we are therefore warranted in giving a detailed history of the book, and the position of the acknowledged authorities in such difficulties.

I. *History of its Origin, Editions, etc.*—The *Monita* was first printed in Latin, from the Spanish, at Cracow, the capital of Poland, with this title: *Monita Privata Societatis Jesu,* Notobirgæ, Anno 1612, by an unknown editor, with various "Testimonies of several Italian and Spanish Jesuits" confirmatory of the truth of the *Monita.* The "Constitutions of the Society," though printed as early as 1558, had never been published. Everything connected with the rules of the order had been carefully concealed from the public eye. The *Monita,* therefore, was rapidly bought and everywhere circulated, not only in Poland, but in Germany, Italy, and France. It gratified an intense curiosity, and was generally recognised at once as a faithful portraiture of Jesuitism. Claude Acquaviva. "the ablest and most profound politician of his time," and "the beau ideal of Jesuitism," was the general of the order, exercising over it a complete control. The *Monita* was regarded then, as it has been since by Van Mastricht and many other judicious scholars, as the product of his pen. The book certainly does not misrepresent him. The tactics are his, and may well have derived their inspiration from his wily brain. It does not appear that he ever denied them. He took no steps to prove the publication a forgery. Down to the day of his death (January 31, 1615), nearly three years, the book passed unmolested, though the Jesuits were all-powerful in Poland. The circulation of the *Monita* finally occasioned the appointment of a commission, July 11, 1615, by Peter Tylick, bishop of Cracow. His confessor was a Jesuit, as was the king's. Tylick admitted that "nothing is certainly known of its author; but," he affirmed, "it is reported, and the presumption is, that it was edited by the venerable Jerome Zaorowski, pastor of Gozdziec." The commission were instructed October 7th to inquire whether "at any time or place Zaorowski had been heard to speak approvingly of such a famous libel, or to affirm that the contents were true, or to say anything of the kind from which it can be gathered that he is the author, or, at least, an accomplice in the writing of this libel." The papal nuncio, Diotallenius, a few weeks after (November 14), added his sanction to the investigation. Yet the author was not found, and there remained no other step for the Papists than the condemnation of the book to prevent its circulation. It was therefore put on the "Index" May 10, 1616, and a professor of Ingolstadt, the learned Gretser, commissioned to prepare a refutation of the *Monita's* disclosures. This refutation, entitled *Libri Tres Apologetici contra Famosum Libellum,* was published August 1, 1617, and a second decree was issued by the "Index" in 1621 to make sure of suppressing the circulation of the *Monita.* Notwithstanding these efforts on the part of the Jes-

uits to disprove the authenticity of the work, their opponents continued to assert it genuine. Thus e. g. in 1633 Caspar Schoppe (Scioppius), a German scholar, himself a Roman Catholic, but a genuine hater of the Jesuits, published his *Anatomia Societatis Jesu,* in which, among other things, he presents a critique on a book that had come into his hands, which he calls "Instructio Secreta pro Superioribus Societatis Jesu." His analysis of the book proves it to have been the same, with slight differences, as the *Monita Privata.* But his copy could not have been of the 1612 edition, for he attributes the discovery of the work to the plundering of the Jesuit college at Paderborn, in Westphalia, by Christian, duke of Brunswick. That was in February, 1622, ten years later. If his copy had been of the Cracow edition, he could not have made so gross a mistake. This, then, was another source, independent of the first, from which the book was derived. It was credibly reported that another copy had been found at the capture of Prague in 1631, only two years before. The Jesuit Lawrence Forer thereupon pointed out the apparent anachronism in his *Anatomia Anatomiæ,* but he failed to convince Schoppe, nor could he shake the popular belief. This position now seems reasonable indeed, for there is in the British Museum Library a volume printed at Venice in 1596, and containing, at the end of the book, several manuscript leaves on which the whole of the *Monita Secreta* is inscribed, the writing being evidently of ancient date. The remote date would rather lead to the conclusion that this work came from some convent, probably Jesuitical, in which the *Monita* had been introduced for *service.* The book had now attracted the attention of people everywhere; not only all over the Continent, but even in England the *Monita* was sought after, and so great was the demand that an edition appeared in England in Oliver's time (1658). On the Continent several editions were sent forth. A French version, entitled *Secreta Monita, ou Advis Secrets de la Société de Jésus,* was published in 1661 at Paderborn, under the eaves of the Jesuit college. A second edition of Schoppe's *Anatomia* appeared in 1668. To aggravate the difficulty, the next year Henry Compton, canon of Christ Church, Oxford, and afterwards bishop successively of Oxford and London, published, in 9 sheets 4to, *The Jesuits' Intrigues, with the Private Instructions of that Society to their Emissaries.* The latter had been "lately found in MS. in a Jesuit's closet after his death, and sent, in a letter, from a gentleman at Paris to his friend in London." This, too, was the *Monita Secreta,* entirely independent of the others.

At Strasburg, in 1713, Henri de St. Ignace, under the pseudonym of "Liberius Candidus," a Flemish divine of the Carmelite order, published his *Tuba Magna,* addressed to the pope and all potentates, on the "necessity of reforming the Society of Jesus." In the appendix the *Monita Secreta* is reproduced in full. In proof of its authenticity, he gives these three reasons: "1. Common fame. 2. The character of the document—wholly Jesuitical. 3. Its exact conformity with their practices. Besides, its having been found in the Jesuit colleges." The Jesuit, Alphonso Huylenbrock, published his "Vindications" of the society in the following year. De Ignace could not be shaken from his belief in the authenticity of the book, and issued a second edition in 1714, in which he says that "nothing, or next to nothing, is contained therein that the Jesuits have not reduced to practice." A third edition of the *Tuba Magna* was published in 1717, and a fourth in 1760. In 1717 the *Monita* was published by John Schipper, at Amsterdam, from a copy purchased at Antwerp, with the significant title of *Machiavelli Mus Jesuiticus.* This was followed, in 1723, by an edition in Latin and English, published at London by John Walthoe, Jun., and dedicated to Sir Robert Walpole. A second edition was issued in 1749. Another edition in French (probably a reprint of the Paderborn edition of 1661) was issued at Cologne in 1727.

After the suppression of the order in 1773, several MSS. of the work were found in Jesuitic haunts, particularly in their colleges. A MS. was even found in Rome which was printed in 1782 under the title *Monita Secreta Patrun Societatis Jesu,* "nunc *primum* typis expressa." Evidently its editor had never heard of a published copy of the *Monita.* It contains numerous errors, such as are very likely to creep into a MS. The New York Union Theological Seminary possesses a copy of this printed edition. The early restoration of the order to power, in 1814, prevented the unearthing of copies direct from Jesuitic hands.

II. *Defenders of its Authenticity; recent Editors, etc.*— As far back as the 17th century, after the authenticity of the *Monita* had been a matter of dispute for more than a hundred years, we find that astute Lutheran theologian Dr. Johann Gerhard, whose familiarity with polemic divinity was perfectly marvellous, make mention of Schoppe's *Anatomia* in his great work *Confessio Catholica* (Frankfort and Leipsic, 1679), and refer to the *Monita Secreta* as a work of *undoubted authenticity.* This opinion has been generally quoted and endorsed by ecclesiastical historians, especially of the Protestant Church, with only one exception (Gieseler, *Kirchengesch.* vol. iii, pt. ii, p. 656 sq.). In 1831, after "careful investigation," an edition was published at Princeton, N. J., by the learned Dr. W. C. Brownlee, under the auspices of the "American Protestant Society," containing the original, an English translation based upon that of Walthoe (1723), and a "Historical Sketch." Dr. Hodge, in reviewing the case in the *Biblical Repository* (iv, 138), takes occasion to say that the authenticity of the work has never been disproved.. "Attempts," he says, "have been made to cry down this work as a forgery. . . . We cannot imagine that these doubts can be seriously entertained by those who peruse the historical essay which is prefixed to it. Facts and authorities are there adduced which we cannot help thinking ought to satisfy every mind, not only of the authenticity of the work, but also of the entire justice of the representations which it gives of the society whose official instructions it professes to exhibit." In 1843, shortly after an edition of the *Monita* had been issued by Seeley, Mr. Edward Dalton, the secretary of the "Protestant Association of Great Britain," took occasion thus to comment on it in his *The Jesuits; their Principles and Acts:* "If we weigh well the evidence which has been handed down to us by historians; if we peruse the writings of the Jesuits themselves, and maturely consider the doctrines therein promulgated, and their practical tendency, we can scarcely fail to be convinced of the authenticity of the *Secreta Monita.*" In 1844 an edition was again published in the United States, this time under the auspices of the "American and Foreign Christian Union." It then became the subject of considerable agitation, several Protestant writers of note taking the ground that the work had not a real basis in Jesuitism, and had been proved spurious. In consequence, the learned professor Henry M. Baird, of the New York University, contributed the following additional testimony: "In proof of the authenticity of the 'Secret Instructions,' we have the testimony of a gentleman who as a historical investigator has scarcely a peer—certainly no superior. I refer to M. Louis Prosper Gachard, the 'archiviste-general' of the kingdom of Belgium, to whose rare sagacity, profound erudition, and indefatigable industry our own distinguished historians, Prescott and Motley, pay such frequent and deserved compliments; the latter, in the preface to his *Dutch Republic,* remarking: 'It is unnecessary to add that all the publications of M. Gachard—particularly the invaluable correspondence of Philip II and of William the Silent, as well as the "Archives et Correspondance" of the Orange Nassau family, edited by the learned and distinguished Groen van Prinsterer—have been my constant guides through the tortuous labyrinth of Spanish and Netherland politics.' In M. Gachard's *Analectes Belgiques,* a volume

from which Mr. Prescott draws much of the material of the first chapter of his *Philip the Second,* I find a short article devoted to 'The Secret Instructions of the Jesuits' (p. 63). 'When the *Monita Secreta Societatis Jesu* were published, a few years since,' says M. Gachard, 'many persons disputed the authenticity of this book; others boldly maintained that it had been forged, with the design of injuring the society by ascribing to it principles which it did not possess. *Here are facts that will dissipate all uncertainty in this respect:* At the suppression of the order in the Low Countries in 1773, there were discovered in one of its houses, in the College of Ruremonde (everywhere else they had been carefully destroyed at the first tidings of the bull fulminated by Clement XIV), the most important and most secret papers, such as the correspondence of the general with the provincial fathers, and the directions of which the latter alone could have had cognizance. Among these papers were the *Monita Secreta.* A translation of them was made, *by order of the government,* by the "substitut procureur-general" of Brabant, De Berg. It still exists in the archives of the kingdom, and *I can vouch that it differs in nothing substantially* (quant au fond) *from that which has been rendered public.' "*

In 1869 the Rev. Dr. Edwin F. Hatfield ably reviewed the case of the "Secret Instructions" in the *New York Observer,* and since that time but little has been advanced either pro or con. Prof. Schem, well known for his ecclesiastical learning, and himself educated at the Jesuitical college in Rome, but now a Protestant in theology, in the article JESUITS in this *Cyclopædia* took ground against the authenticity of the *Monita,* and, as he is entitled to a hearing, we did not there dissent from his article. Our own judgment, however, is to accept the *Monita* as a Jesuitical production, containing the instructions of the order. In the article "Jesuits" in the *Encyclop. Britannica,* Dr. Isaac Taylor, its author, states that the *Monita* is "believed to be a spurious production," but he by no means anywhere indicates that he himself believed it spurious; on the contrary, it is more than likely that he held it to be genuine.

Monition, a term in ecclesiastical law, used now only in the Church of Rome and the Church of England and its dependencies, and the Protestant Episcopal Church. It designates a formal notice from a bishop to one of the subordinate clergy requiring the amendment of some ecclesiastical offence. The general admonition was anciently made publicly and solemnly, so that it could come to the knowledge of the person in fault, and when it expressed his name it was called "nominal." Lindewood defines canonical monition as requiring three several proclamations, or one for all, with a proper interval of time allowed. The name of the person should be distinctly mentioned, where law or custom demands it; this is called monition "in specie," a general monition being known as "in genere." A public monition in synod by the bishop is equivalent to three monitions otherwise given. If the offender did not comply after the third monition, he was formally subjected to excommunication; because the term, distinctly named, gave to the monition the character of an introductory sentence, and after its expiration no offer of explanation was admitted. No monition is required when the superior gives sentence of excommunication, or when an inferior does not submit to his superior in the discharge of his special right, as in the office of visitation; or, after he has been visited, when he refuses to pay procurations which are due, as these are cases of positive and manifest contumacy. But if the superior proceeds as judge, and punishes offences, past or present, monition is necessary before the fulmination of the ecclesiastical censure. Although three monitions were held to be fair, yet one would suffice, provided a suitable delay elapsed between it and the sentence. Any incumbent or curate allowing unauthorized persons to officiate in his church is liable to be called before the bishop in person, and to be publicly or privately mon-ished. When a living has been for one year sequestered, the person who holds it, if he neglect the bishop's monition to reside, is deprived; and so also for drunkenness or gross immorality, after monition. Sentence of monition ought not to be given without a previous admonition, unless where the offence is of such a nature as to require immediate suspension; and if in ordinary cases suspension should be given without monition, there may be cause of appeal. See Lea, *Studies in Church History*, p. 417, 443.

Monitoire or **Monitory**, the technical term for ecclesiastical censure, explained under MONITION, s. v.

Monk (derived from the Latin *monachus*, and that from the Greek μοναχός, i. e. solitary, which in its turn is derived from the word μόνος, Lat. *solus*, designating a person who lives sequestered from the company and conversation of the rest of the world) is a term applied to those who dedicate themselves wholly to the service of religion, in some building set apart for such ascetics, and known as a *monastery* (q. v.) or *religious house*, and who are under the direction of some particular statute or rule. Those of the female sex who lead such a life are denominated *Nuns* (q. v.).

Riddle (*Christian Antiquities*, p. 777 sq.) furnishes the following as the chief names by which monks have been designated: (1) 'Ασκητής, i. e. *ascetic*. This name, borrowed from the Greek profane writers, was originally applied to athletes, or prize-fighters in the public games. In early ecclesiastical writers it is usually equivalent to ἐγκρατής, continent; and Tertullian renders both words alike by *continens* (in a technical sense). Sometimes they use ἀσκητής in the sense of ἄγαμος, *cœlebs*, unmarried. (2) Μοναχοί, or (more rarely) μονάζοντες, i. e. solitaries, is a term which denotes generally all who addict themselves to a retired or solitary life; and it was usually applied, not merely to such as retired to absolute solitude in caves and deserts, but also to such as lived apart from the rest of the world in separate societies. Since the 3d and 4th centuries this name has been almost universally employed as the common designation of religious solitaries, or members of religious societies, and has passed into various languages of Europe. The Syrians translate it by *jechidoje* (*solitarii*). (3) The term ἀναχωρηταί, *anachoretæ* or *anachoritæ*, Engl. anchorite, is used in the rule of Benedict as synonymous with ἐρημίται, *eremitæ*, hermits. Other writers observe a distinction in conformity with the etymology of the two words, restricting the application of the term *anachoretæ* to those persons who led a solitary life, without retirement to a desert, and of *eremitæ* to those who actually retired to some remote or inhospitable region. The Syrians contracted the word *anachoreta* into *nucherite;* they translated *eremitæ* into *madberoje*. (4) The term *cœnobitæ*, cenobites, is evidently derived from the Greek κοινὸς βίος (vita communis), and refers at once to the monastic custom of living together in one place, hence called κοινόβιον, *cænobium*, and to that of possessing a community of property, and observing common rules of life. The term συνοδῖται, *synoditæ* (*Cod. Theodos.* lib. xi, tit. 31, l. 37), has the same signification, being derived from σύνοδος; so that it may be rendered *conventualis*. The Syrians express the same by the words *dairoje* and *oumroje*. (5) In the rule of Benedict we find mention of *gyrovagi*, certain wandering monks, who are there charged with having occasioned great disorder. (6) Στυλῖται, *stylitæ*, pillarists, a kind of monk so called from their practice of living on a pillar. Simeon Stylites and a few others made themselves remarkable by this mode of severe life, but it was not generally adopted (Evagr. *Hist. Eccl.* lib. i, c. 13; lib. vi, c. 23; Theodor. *Lect.* lib. ii). (7) We find also a large number of other classes of monks and ascetics, which are worthy of remark only as furnishing a proof of the high esteem in which a monastic life was held in the early Church. Such are: i. Σπου-

δαῖοι (*studiosi*), a sect of ascetics who practiced uncommon austerities (Euseb. *Hist. Eccl.* lib. vi, c. 11; Epiphan. *Expos. Fid.* c. 22). ii. 'Εκλεκτοί, or ἐκλεκτῶν ἐκλεκτότεροι, the elect, or elect of the elect (Clem. Alex. *Quis Dives Salv.* n. 36). iii. 'Ακοίμητοι, *insomnes*, the sleepless, or the watchers; a term applied especially to the members of a monastery (στούδιον) near Constantinople (Niceph. *Hist. Eccl.* lib. xv, c. 23; Baron. *Annal.* a. 459). iv. Βοσκοί, i. e. the grazers; so called because they professed to subsist on roots and herbs, like cattle (Sozomen, *Hist. Eccl.* lib. vi, c. 33; Evagr. *Hist. Eccl.* lib. i, c. 21). v. 'Ησυχασταί, *quiescentes*, or *quietistæ*, quietists, monks who lived by themselves in perpetual silence (Justin. *Novell.* v, c. 3; Suicer. *Thesaur. Eccl.* s. v. ἡσυχαστής). vi. 'Αποταξάμενοι, *renunciantes*, renouncers; so called from their formal renunciation of the world and secular enjoyments (Pallad. *Hist. Laus.* c. 15). vii. *Culdai*, Colidei, Keldei, Keledei, certain ancient monks in Scotland and the Hebrides, supposed to have been so called as *cultores Dei*, worshippers of God, because they were wholly occupied in preaching the Gospel. Some suppose that they were priests; others regarded them as canons regular; others, again, that they constituted a secret society, and were the forerunners of the modern Freemasons. viii. *Apostolici*, apostolicals, monks in England and Ireland, before the arrival of the Benedictines, with Augustine, at the latter end of the 6th century.

There were the following orders of monks: 1, those of Basil—Greek monks and Carmelites; 2, those of Augustine, in three classes—canons regular, monks, and hermits; 3, those of Benedict; and, 4, those of St. Francis: all of which names may be consulted in their respective places. Monks are now distinguished by the color of their habits into *black, white, gray*, etc. The ancient dress was the *colobium* or *lebitus*, a linen sleeveless dress; a *melotes* or *pera*, a goatskin habit; a cowl, covering the head and shoulders; the *maforta*, a smaller cowl, cross-shaped over the shoulders; and a black pall. St. Benedict introduced during manual labor the lighter scapular, reaching from the shoulders down the back, and the cowl became a habit of ceremony, and worn in choir. Borrowing the language of the regular and secular canons, the monks at length, when in their common habits they attended choir, called it ordinary service days, "dies in cappis," in distinction to "dies in albis," days in surplices or festivals, the cope being black like the frock. There are different classes of monks: some are called *monks of the choir*, others *professed monks*, and others *lay monks;* which latter are destined for the service of the convents, and have neither clericate nor literature. *Cloistered monks* are those who actually reside in the house, in opposition to *extra* monks, who have benefices depending on the monastery. Monks are also distinguished into *reformed*, whom the civil and ecclesiastical authority have made masters of ancient convents, and enabled to retrieve the ancient discipline, which had been relaxed; and *ancient*, who remain in the convent, to live in it according to its establishment at the time when they made their vows, without obliging themselves to any new reform.

Among the remarkable institutions of Christianity which have prevailed in the Roman Catholic and the Greek Church, there is none that makes a more conspicuous figure than the institution of monachism or monkery; and, if traced to its origin, it will be found strikingly to exemplify the truth of the maxim that, as some of the largest and loftiest trees spring from very small seeds, so the most extensive and wonderful effects sometimes arise from very inconsiderable causes. In times of persecution during the first ages of the Church, while "the heathen raged, and the rulers took counsel together against the Lord, and against his anointed," many pious Christians, male and female, married and unmarried, justly accounting that no human felicity ought to come in competition with their fidelity to Christ, and diffident of their own ability to persevere in resisting the temptations with which they were incessantly harassed by their persecutors, took the resolution to abandon their professions and worldly prospects, and, while the storm lasted, to retire to unfrequented places far from the haunts of men (the married with or without their wives, as agreed between them), that they might enjoy in quietness their faith and hope, and, exempt from the temptations to apostasy, employ themselves principally in the worship and service of their Maker. The cause was reasonable and the motive praiseworthy, but the reasonableness arose solely from the circumstances. When the latter were changed the former vanished, and the motive could no longer be the same. When there was not the same danger in society, there was not the same occasion to seek security in solitude. Accordingly, when persecution ceased, and the profession of Christianity was rendered perfectly safe, many returned without blame from their retirement and resumed their stations in society. Some, indeed, familiarized by time to a solitary life, at length preferred, through habit, what they had originally adopted through necessity. See ASCETICS ; HERMITS. They did not, however, waste their time in idleness : they supported themselves by their labor, and gave the surplus in charity. But they never thought of flattering themselves by vows or engagements, because by so doing they must have exposed their souls to new temptations and perhaps greater dangers. It was, therefore, a very different thing from that system of monkery which afterwards became so prevalent, though in all probability it constituted the first step towards it.

Egypt, the fruitful parent of superstition, afforded the first example, strictly speaking, of the monastic life. The first and most noted of the solitaries was Paul, a native of Thebes, who, in the time of Athanasius, distributed his patrimony, deserted his family and house, and took up his residence among the tombs and in a ruined tower. After a long and painful novitiate, he at length advanced three days' journey into the desert, to the eastward of the Nile, where, discovering a lonely spot which possessed the advantages of shade and water, he fixed his last abode. His example and his lessons infected others, whose curiosity pursued him to the desert ; and before he quitted life, which was prolonged to the term of one hundred and five years, he beheld a numerous progeny imitating his original. The prolific colonies of monks multiplied with rapid increase on the sands of Lybia, upon the rocks of Thebais, and the cities of the Nile. But there were no bodies or communities of men embracing this life, nor any monasteries built, until Pachomius, who flourished in the peaceable reign of Constantine, caused some to be erected [see MONASTERY]. Once the custom established, they soon multiplied, and even to the present day the traveller may explore the ruins of fifty monasteries which were planted to the south of Alexandria by the disciples of Pachomius. Inflamed by this example, a Syrian youth, whose name was Hilarion, fixed his dreary abode on a sandy beach, between the sea and a morass, about seven miles from Gaza. The austere penance in which he persisted for forty-eight years diffused a similar enthusiasm, and innumerable monasteries were soon distributed over all Palestine. Not long after, Eustathius, bishop of Sebastia, brought monks into Armenia, Paphlagonia, and Pontus. While Macarius, the Egyptian, peopled the deserts of Scethis with monks, Gregory, the apostle of Armenia, did the like in that country. But St. Basil is generally considered as the great father and patriarch of the Eastern monks. It was he who reduced the monastic life to a fixed state of uniformity ; who united the anchorets and cœnobites, and obliged them to engage themselves by solemn vows. It was St. Basil who prescribed rules

for the government and direction of the monasteries, to which most of the disciples of Anthony, Pachomius, Macarius, and the other ancient fathers of the deserts submitted ; and to this day all the Greeks, Nestorians, Melchites, Georgians, Mingrelians, and Armenians follow the rule of St. Basil. In the West, Athanasius (about A.D. 340) taught the anchorets of Italy to live in societies ; and a little later Martin of Tours, "a soldier, a hermit, a bishop, and a saint," established the monasteries of Gaul, and the progress of monkery is said not to have been less rapid or less universal than that of Christianity itself. Every province, and at last every city of the empire, was filled with their increasing multitudes. The disciples of Pachomius spread themselves wherever Christianity found a foothold. The Council of Saragossa, in Spain (A.D. 380), in condemning the practice of clergymen who affected to wear the monastical habits, affords proof that there were monks in that kingdom in the 4th century, before St. Donatus went thither out of Africa, with seventy disciples, and founded the Monastery of Sirbita. Augustine, sent into England by Gregory the Great, in the year 596, to preach the faith, at that time introduced the monastic state into British territory, and it made so great a progress there that, within the space of two hundred years, there were thirty kings and queens who preferred the religious habit to their crowns, and founded stately monasteries, where they ended their days in retirement and solitude. The monastery of Bangor, in Flintshire, a few miles south of Wrexham, contained above two thousand monks, and from thence a numerous colony was dispersed among the barbarians of Ireland, where St. Patrick is regarded as the founder of monasticism ; and so readily did the monasteries multiply there that it was called "the Island of Saints." Iona, also, one of the western isles of Scotland, which was planted by the Irish monks, diffused over all northern regions a ray of science and superstition.

The ancient monks were not, like the modern, distinguished into orders, and denominated from the founders of them ; but they had their names from the places which they inhabited, as the monks of *Scethis, Tabennesus, Nitra, Canopus,* in Egypt, etc., or else were distinguished by their different ways of living. Of these, the most remarkable were : 1. The anchorets, so called from their retiring from society and living in private cells in the wilderness. 2. The cœnobites, so denominated from their living together in common. All monks were originally no more than laymen ; nor could they well be otherwise, being confined by their own rules to solitary retreats, where there could be no room for the exercise of the clerical functions. Accordingly, St. Jerome tells us the office of monk is not to teach, but to mourn; and St. Anthony himself is reported to have said that "the wilderness is as natural to a monk as water to a fish, and therefore a monk in a city is quite out of his element, like a fish upon dry land." Theodosius actually enacted that all who made profession of the monastic life should be obliged by the civil magistrate to betake themselves to the wilderness, as their proper habitation. Justinian also made laws to the same purpose, forbidding the Eastern monks to appear in cities except to defend Christianity from heretics (as was done e. g. by Anthony, to confute Arianism), and to despatch their secular affairs, if they had any, through their *apocrisarii* or *responsales*—that is, their proctors or syndics, which every monastic company was allowed for that purpose. The Council of Chalcedon (A.D. 451) expressly distinguishes the monks from the clergy, and reckons them with the laymen. Gratian (A.D. 1150) himself, the noted Benedictine writer, who is most interested for the moderns, owns it to be plain from ecclesiastical history that, to the time of popes Siricius (A.D. 324–398) and Zosimus (died 418) the monks were only simple monks, and not of the clergy. In some cases, however, the clerical and monastic life were capable of being conjoined—as, first, when a monastery happened to be at so great a distance from its proper church that the monks could not ordinarily resort thither for divine service, which was the case with the monasteries in Egypt and other parts of the East; in this case, some one or more of the monks were ordained for the performance of divine offices among them. Then it also happened that some of the clergy, and even bishops themselves, embraced the monastic life by a voluntary renunciation of property, and enjoyed all things in common. This was, however, as late as the middle of the 4th century; until that time it was generally understood that not only should monks never enter the priesthood, but also that priests should never turn monastics. This appears clearly from the letters of St. Gregory [see below]. Eusebius of Vercillensis (A.D. 315-370) was the first who brought this way of living among the clergy of Hippo, and thus constituted what may be denominated the monastico-clerical condition.

The Church however, in her early days, recognised only one style of monastics, i. e. the cœnobites, and for them alone were certain laws and rules of government specially provided. They were in substance that every one should not be allowed to turn monk at pleasure, because there were certain classes so conditioned that they could not enter that state without damaging the interests of others. Thus, e. g., the civil law forbade any of those officers called *curiales* to become monks, unless they parted with their estates to others, who might serve their country in their stead. For the same reason servants were not admitted into any monastery without their masters' leave. Justinian, however, afterwards abrogated this law by an edict of his own, which first set servants at liberty from their masters under pretence of betaking themselves to a monastic life. The same precautions were observed in regard to married persons and children; the former were not to embrace the monastic life unless with the mutual consent of both parties. This precaution was afterwards set aside by Justinian, but the Church never approved of this innovation. As to children, the Council of Gangra (about the second half of the 4th century) decreed that if any such, under pretence of religion, forsook their parents, they should be anathematized; but Justinian enervated the force of this law likewise, forbidding parents to hinder their children from embracing the monastic or clerical life. And as children were not to turn monks without the consent of their parents, so neither could parents oblige their children to embrace a monastic life against their own consent—at least not until the fourth Council of Toledo (A.D. 633), which set aside this precaution, and decreed that whether the devotion of their parents, or their profession, made them monks, both should be equally binding, and there should be no permission to return to secular life again.

The *manner of admission to the monastic life* was usually by some change of habit or dress, not to signify any religious mystery, but only to express gravity and a contempt of the world. Long hair was always thought an indecency in men, and savoring of secular vanity; and, therefore, they polled every monk at his admission, to distinguish him from seculars; but they never shaved any, for fear they should look too like the priests of Isis. This, therefore, was the ancient tonsure, in opposition to both these extremes. As to their habit and clothing, the rule was the same: they were to be decent and grave, as became their profession. The monks of Tabennesus, in Thebais, seem to have been the only monks, in those early days, who were confined to any particular habit. St. Jerome, who often speaks of the habit of the monks, intimates that it differed from others only in this, that it was a cheaper, coarser, and meaner raiment, expressing their humility and contempt of the world, without any singularity or affectation. That father is very severe

against the practice of some who appeared in chains or sackcloth; and Cassian blames others who carried wooden crosses continually about their necks, which was only proper to excite the laughter of the spectators. In short, the Western monks used only a common habit, the philosophic pallium, as many other Christians did. Salvian seems to give an exact description of the habit and tonsure of the monks when, reflecting on the Africans for their treatment of them, he says, "they could scarce ever see a man with short hair, a pale face, and habited in a pallium, without reviling and bestowing some reproachful language on him." We read of no solemn vow or profession required at their admission; but they underwent a three years' probation, during which time they were inured to the exercises of the monastic life. If, after that time was expired, they chose to continue the same exercises, they were then admitted without any further ceremony into the community. This was the method prescribed by Pachomius. No direct promise of celibacy was at first made; nay, there appear to have been married monks. Nor yet was there any vow of poverty, though, when men renounced the world, they generally sold their estates for charitable uses, or keeping them in their own hands, made a distribution regularly of all the proceeds. The Western monks did not always adhere to this rule, as appears from some imperial laws made to restrain their avarice. But the monks of Egypt were generally just to their pretensions, and would accept of no donations but for the use of the poor.

As the monasteries had no standing revenues, all the monks were obliged to exercise themselves in bodily labor to maintain themselves without being burdensome to others. Monks therefore labored with their own hands at a great variety of occupations, and their industry is often commended. "A laboring monk," said they, "was tempted by one devil, but an idle monk by a legion." The Church would tolerate no idle mendicants. Sozomen tells us that Serapion presided over a monastery of 10,000 monks, near Arsinoë, in Egypt, who all labored with their own hands, by which means they not only maintained themselves, but had enough to relieve the poor. To their bodily exercises they joined others that were spiritual, viz., penitence, fasting, and prayer—all supposed to be more extraordinary in intensity and frequency than could be practiced in the world. The most important of these was perpetual repentance, whence the expression of Jerome that the life of a monk is the *life of a mourner*. In allusion to this, the isle of Canopus, near Alexandria, formerly a place of great lewdness, was, upon the translation and settlement there of the monks of Tabennesus, called *Insulæ Metanœœ*, the *Isle of Repentance*. Next in importance they regarded fasting. The Egyptian monks kept every day a fast till three in the afternoon, excepting Saturdays, Sundays, and the fifty days of Pentecost. Some exercised themselves with very great austerities, fasting two, three, four, or five days together; but this practice was not generally approved. They did not think such excessive abstinence of any use, but rather a disservice to religion. Pachomius's rule, which was said to be given him by an angel, permitted every man to eat, drink, and labor according to his bodily strength. Thus fasting was a discretionary thing, and matter of choice, not compulsion. Their fastings were accompanied with extraordinary and frequent returns of devotion. The monks of Palestine, Mesopotamia, and other parts of the East, had six or seven canonical hours of prayer; besides which they had their constant vigils, or nocturnal meetings. The monks of Egypt met only twice a day for public devotion; but in their private cells, while they were at work, they were always repeating psalms, and other parts of Scripture, and intermixing prayers with their bodily labor. St. Jerome's description of their devotion is very lively: "When they are assembled together," says that father, "psalms are sung and Scriptures read; then, prayers being ended, they all sit down, and the father begins a discourse to them, which they hear with the profoundest silence and veneration. His words make a deep impression on them; their eyes overflow with tears, and the speaker's commendation is the weeping of his hearers. Yet no one's grief expresses itself in an indecent strain. But when he comes to speak of the kingdom of heaven, of future happiness, and the glory of the world to come, then one may observe each of them, with a gentle sigh, and eyes lifted up to heaven, say within himself, 'O that I had the wings of a dove, for then would I flee away and be at rest!'" In some places they had the Scriptures read during their meals at table. This custom was first introduced in the monasteries of Cappadocia, to prevent idle discourses and contentions. But in Egypt they had no occasion for this remedy, for they were taught to eat their food in silence. Palladius mentions one instance more of their devotion, which was only occasional; namely, their psalmody at the reception of any brethren, or conducting them with singing of psalms to their habitation.

The laws forbade monks to participate in public affairs, either ecclesiastical or civil; and those who were called to any employment in the Church were obliged to quit their monasteries thereupon. Nor were they permitted to encroach upon the duties or rights and privileges of the secular clergy, unless the clerical and monastic life were united, as when the bishops took monastics for the service of the Church, which did not happen until the monasteries had become schools of learning. Such monastics when removed were by the Greeks styled ἱερομόναχοι, i. e. clergymonks. As the monks of the ancient Church were under no solemn vow or profession, they were at liberty to betake themselves to a secular life again. Julian himself was once in the monastic habit. The same is observed of Constans, the son of Constantine, who usurped the empire in Britain. The rule of Pachomius, by which the Egyptian monks were governed, has nothing of any vow at their entrance, nor any punishment for such as deserted their station afterwards. In process of time it was thought proper to inflict some punishment on such as returned to a secular life. The civil law excluded deserters from the privilege of ordination. Justinian added another punishment; which was that if they were possessed of any substance, it should be all forfeited to the monastery which they had deserted. The censures of the Church were likewise inflicted on deserting monks in the 5th century. Thus when a monk deserted and married, he was declared incapable ever after of holy orders. After the establishment of monasteries under the rule of St. Basil, the actions of a monk, his words, and even his thoughts, were determined by an inflexible rule and a capricious superior; the slightest offences were corrected by disgrace or confinement, extraordinary fasts or bloody flagellations; and disobedience, murmur, or delay were ranked in the catalogue of the most heinous sins. Whenever monastics were permitted to step beyond the precincts of the monastery, two jealous companions were the mutual guards and spies of each other's actions; and after their return they were condemned to forget, or at least to suppress, whatever they had seen or heard in the world. Strangers who professed the orthodox faith were hospitably entertained in a separate apartment; but their dangerous conversation was restricted to some chosen elders of approved discretion and fidelity. Except in their presence, the monastic slave might not receive the visits of his friends or kindred; and it was deemed highly meritorious if he afflicted a tender sister or an aged parent by the obstinate refusal of a word or look.

By their special addiction to an ascetic life, indicating superior sanctity and virtue, the monastics secured great favor with the multitude, and speedily acquired for themselves such popularity and influence that the clergy could not but find in them either powerful allies or formidable rivals. When they began to form large and regular establishments, it was needful that some members of their body should be ordained, in order to secure the regular performance of divine worship; and at length, not only was it usual for many members of a monastery to be in holy orders, but it came to be regarded as an advantage for the clergy to possess the additional character of monastics. From the 4th century, in the West, at the request of the people or their abbot, the monks very frequently took orders; and in the East at the instance of the bishops, the archimandrites being sometimes elevated to the episcopate, or acting as bishops' deputies at councils, and their monks ranking after priests and deacons, they frequently went to study in the cloister. It was not until the 6th century that the cœnobites left the desert for the suburbs of cities and towns, but as early as the close of that century they were known as monastics, having come to be distinguished from the populace, and, endowed with much opulence and many honorable privileges, found themselves in a condition to claim an eminent station among the pillars and supporters of the Christian community. The fame of their piety and sanctity was so great that bishops and presbyters were often chosen out of their order; and the passion for erecting edifices and convents, in which the monks and holy virgins might serve God in the most commodious manner, was at that time carried beyond all bounds. "So much was the world infatuated by the sanctimonious appearance of the recluses that men thought they could not more effectually purchase heaven to themselves than by beggaring their offspring, and giving all they had to erect or endow monasteries; that is, to supply with all the luxuries of life those who were bound to live in abstinence, and to enrich those who had solemnly sworn that they would be forever poor, and who professed to consider riches as the greatest impediment in the road to heaven. Large monasteries, both commodious and magnificent, more resembling the palaces of princes than the rude cells which the primitive monks chose for their abode, were erected and endowed. Legacies and bequests from time to time flowed in upon them. Mistaken piety often contributed to the evil, but oftener superstitious profligacy. Oppression herself commonly judged that to devote her wealth at last, when it could be kept no longer, to a religious house, was full atonement for all the injustice and extortion by which it had been amassed. But what set in a stronger light the pitiable brutishness to which the people were reduced by the reigning superstition, was that men of rank and eminence, who had shown no partiality to anything monastical during their lives, gave express orders, when in the immediate view of death, that their friends should dress them out in monkish vestments, that in these they might die and be buried, thinking that the sanctity of their garb would prove a protection against a condemnatory sentence of the omniscient Judge" (Cramp, *Text-book of Popery*, p. 323). Nevertheless, although many monastics greatly distinguished themselves, and established such a popular interest in monasticism as to cause eminent ecclesiastics to adopt the monastic life, yet it was not the custom to place monks, as such, on an equal footing with the clergy. They, indeed, were not then reckoned as *sæculares*, but were distinguished by the name of *religiosi* or *regulares* (canonici), and they were first regarded as part of the clerical body in the 10th century; but even then a distinction was carefully made between *clerici sæculares*, i. e. parish priests and all who were charged with the cure of souls, and *clerici regulares*, i. e. those belonging to monastic orders; and the former vehemently protested against the right of the latter to interfere with their own peculiar duties. In fact, no complete amalgamation of the two bodies ever took place; and all monasteries continued to include a certain number of lay brethren, or *conversi*, who, without discharging strictly spiritual functions, formed, as in the ancient Church, a middle order between the clergy and the laity. In the 9th century there existed also the *monachi sæculares*, who were members of religious fraternities, living under a certain rule and presidency, but without submitting to the confinement of a cloister. They were the forerunners of the religious fraternities which arose in France, Italy, and Germany, and greatly multiplied and extended during the 15th and 16th centuries. The members of these fraternities formed a class between the laity and clergy. However, their licentiousness, even in the 6th century, became a proverb; and they are said to have excited the most dreadful tumults and sedition in various places.

The monastic orders, as we have already indicated, were at first under the immediate jurisdiction of the bishops, but they were exempted from them by the Roman pontiff about the end of the 7th century (Boniface IV); and the monks, in turn, devoted themselves wholly to advancing the interests and to maintaining the dignity of the bishop of Rome. "The partiality of the popes for monastic orders," says Cramp, "is easily accounted for. They constitute a peculiar and distinct body, so estranged from society that they can give undivided attention and solicitude to any object that is presented to their notice. That object has uniformly been the aggrandizement of the Church—that is, the See of Rome. Incorporated by pontifical authority, exempted to a degree from episcopal jurisdiction, and endowed with many privileges and favors from which the rest of the faithful are excluded, they are bound in gratitude to make the pope's interest their own. History records that they have ever been ready to come forward in support of the most glaring enormities of the papal system, and that to their indefatigable diligence and adroit management the triumphant progress of that system was mainly indebted. They formed a sort of local militia, stationed in every country in Europe, always prepared to uphold the cause to which they had attached themselves, by aggression, defence, or imposture, as the case might require" (*Text-book of Popery*, p. 359). The immunity which the monks thus obtained was a fruitful source of licentiousness and disorder, and largely occasioned the vices with which they were afterwards so justly charged. In the 8th century the monastic discipline was extremely relaxed, and all efforts to restore it were ineffectual. Nevertheless, this kind of institution was in the highest esteem; and nothing could equal the veneration that was paid about the close of the 9th century to such as devoted themselves to the gloom and indolence of a convent. This veneration caused several kings and emperors to call monks to their courts, and to employ them in civil affairs of the greatest moment. Their reformation was attempted by Louis the Meek, but the effect was of short duration. In the 11th century they were exempted by the popes from the authority established; but this caused such laxity that in the Council of Lateran, in 1215, a decree was passed, by the advice of Innocent III, to prevent any new monastic institutions; and several were entirely suppressed. In the 15th and 16th centuries, it appears, from the testimony of the best writers, that the monks were generally lazy, illiterate, profligate, and licentious epicures, whose views in life were confined to opulence, idleness, and pleasure. "Whenever a general council was assembled," says Cramp, "the irregularities or usurpations of the monastic orders commonly occupied a large share of the proceedings. Canon after canon was issued, and still the interposition of ecclesiastical authority was constantly required. An abstract of the decree passed on this subject in the twenty-fifth session of the Council of Trent will place before the reader the then existing condition of that

portion of the Roman Catholic Church. It was enacted that care should be taken to procure strict observance of the rules of the respective professions; that no regular should be allowed to possess any private property, but should surrender everything to his superior; that all monasteries, even those of the mendicants (the Capuchins and friars minor Observantines excepted at their own request), should be permitted to hold estates and other wealth; that no monk should be suffered to undertake any office whatever without his superior's consent, nor quit the convent without a written permission; that nunneries should be carefully closed, and egress be absolutely forbidden the nuns, under any pretense whatsoever, without episcopal license, on pain of excommunication—magistrates being enjoined under the same penalty to aid the bishop, if necessary, by employing force, and the latter being urged to their duty by the fear of the judgment of God and the eternal curse; that monastics should confess and receive the eucharist at least once a month; that if any public scandal should arise out of their conduct, they should be judged and punished by the superior, or, in case of his failure, by the bishop; that no renunciation of property or pecuniary engagement should be valid unless made within two months of taking the vows of religious profession; that immediately after the novitiate, the novices should either be dismissed or take the vow, and that if they were dismissed, nothing should be received from them but a reasonable payment for their board, lodging, and clothing during the novitiate; that no females should take the veil without previous examination by the bishop; that whoever compelled females to enter convents against their will, from avaricious or other motives, or, on the other hand, hindered such as were desirous of the monastic life, should be excommunicated; that if any monk or nun pretended that they had taken the vows under the influence of force or fear, or before the age appointed by law, they should not be heard, except within five years after their profession—if they laid aside the habit of their own accord, they should not be permitted to make the complaint, but be compelled to return to the monastery, and be punished as apostates, being in the mean time deprived of all the privileges of their order. Finally, with regard to the general reformation of the corruptions and abuses which existed in convents, the council lamented the great difficulty of applying any effectual remedy, but hoped that the supreme pontiff would piously and prudently provide for the exigencies of the case as far as the times would bear" (*Text-book of Popery*, p. 359). However, the Reformation had a manifest influence in restraining these excesses, and in rendering monastics more circumspect and cautious in their external conduct. See MONASTERY and MONASTICISM; also MONKS, EASTERN.

Monk, George, *Duke of* ALBEMARLE, a noted British general of the days of the Commonwealth, celebrated for the services he rendered, first to the Protectorate and afterwards to the crown, causing the restoration of king Charles, was born in the parish of Merton, Devonshire, Dec. 6, 1608. He devoted himself early to military life, and had acquired some experience in the wars on the Continent when the war broke out (1638) between Charles and the Scotch. Monk enlisted in the English service, and was made lieutenant-colonel. In 1641 he served against the Irish rebels; and in the following year, upon the outbreak of the war between Charles and Parliament, he obtained a full colonelcy. He was very popular with his soldiers, and to the last remained their idol. For a while his loyalty to the king was questioned; but he soon regained the confidence of the throne, and was suffered to take the field. He rapidly acquired reputation as an able officer; but was made prisoner at Nantwich in January, 1644, by the Roundheads, and confined in the Tower of London more than a year. While himself immured, matters outside turned very much against the king, who was finally taken prisoner, thus terminating the civil war. Efforts were now made by Parliament to secure Monk's services. His known ability and favor with the soldiers made him a desirable acquisition. Clarendon insists upon it that Monk was bought by Parliament (vii, 382); but there is no proof for such an assertion, though his final acts in the scene of Restoration would point that way. In all probability Monk felt the king's cause lost, and was thus persuaded to serve Parliament. The silence which he ever after preserved would confirm such a belief. This seems reasonable also when it is considered that originally Monk must have been in sympathy with the people's cause, for he was suspected by the Royalists. Most likely, too, Monk was influenced by the condition of affairs. He liked to be with the winning side, and, though he had come to be an admirer of the splendor and attraction of court, he would yet fain resign all these rather than serve the minority. He finally in 1647 consented to take a commission in the Parliamentarian army. He first commanded for his new masters in Ireland, where he distinguished himself greatly. He afterwards acted as lieutenant-general under Cromwell in Scotland, where he aided much in gaining the victory of Dunbar. Cromwell finally left him with 6,000 men to complete the subjugation of Scotland, a work which Monk effectually performed. He was next employed as an admiral of the Commonwealth's fleet, and he shared in the perils and the glories of the desperate struggle with the Dutch navy, which Blake so successfully conducted. After being rewarded with many honors at the hand of Cromwell and the Parliament, Monk was sent back to his command in Scotland, where fresh troubles had broken out. He was at this time in a very embarrassing position, and yet he discharged himself of his task with satisfaction to all. His own soldiers were the most restless and fanatical of the army. Besides, he had to contend with lord Middleton, with whom the Royalists had risen in the Highlands, and the people generally, who were discontented and ready for rebellion. His vigilance, activity, and good sense in this position were remarkable. "The country," writes Guizot, "submitted; the army did not quit it till it had, by means of a certain number of garrisons, secured the payment of taxes, which the Highlanders had hitherto thought they could refuse with impunity; and order was established in those sanctuaries of plunder with such effect that the owner of a strayed horse, it is said, recovered it in the country by means of a crier" (p. 80). He was also instrumental in bringing about the union which was established under the Protectorate between England and Scotland; and thus likewise strengthened the Cromwellian efforts. Indeed, it is generally conceded that Monk was always attached to Cromwell from the moment he openly espoused the popular cause, and was never suspected of disloyalty while the Protector lived. This is manifest also from Monk's prompt action when importuned by Charles for his cause. The king sent Monk a letter expressive of confidence, and, instead of reply, Monk turned the letter over to Cromwell. In 1655 Monk was made one of the commissioners for the government of Scotland, and he largely, if not wholly, controlled the action of the council of state. That in this position also he pleased Cromwell is evident from the way in which he was remembered in the Protector's last hour. Cromwell on his death-bed is said to have recommended him to his son and successor, who as soon as installed likewise received Monk's support. But Richard's failure turned Monk away. Monk soon discovered the weakness of the new ruler, and determined to follow that policy by which he would both connect himself with the strongest party, and also lay that under the greatest possible obligation to him. He temporized for some months; listening to the advances of all sides, and saying little in return. He had, no doubt,

made up his mind that the Royalist cause was the strongest, and that Richard was not fitted to give stability to the government; and though when circumstances compelled him to act he declared for the Parliament against the army and decided upon marching to London, there were many, even at the time when he thus declared himself, who altogether discredited his sincerity, and believed him to be at heart a Royalist, seeking to restore the king as soon as it might be done with safety; and there is reason to suppose that he even then was determined to promote the Restoration. We give Mr. Hallam's opinion on this point: "I incline, upon the whole, to believe that Monk, not accustomed to respect the Rump Parliament, and incapable, both by his temperament and by the course of his life, of any enthusiasm for the name of liberty, had satisfied himself as to the expediency of the king's restoration from the time that the Cromwells had sunk below his power to assist them; though his projects were still subservient to his own security, which he was resolved not to forfeit by any premature declaration or unsuccessful enterprise" (Const. Hist. ii, 384). When Monk arrived in London he was lodged in the apartments of the prince of Wales. He addressed the Parliament, was invited to occupy his place there, was made a member of the council of state, and charged with the executive power. With his usual address, he continued to use the power of his army as a means of awing Parliament, and the assertion of duty owed to the Parliament as a means of controlling his army. At length in 1660 the "Rump" became so unpopular, and the cries for a free Parliament so loud, that the city of London refused the payment of taxes. Monk obeyed an order from the Parliament to march into the city and subdue it; but his subservience to them did not last long. He sent them a harsh letter, ordering them immediately to fill up the vacant seats, fixing a time for their dissolution, and the 6th of May for the election of a new and free Parliament. The restored members appointed him general of the forces of England, Scotland, and Ireland; and the Republicans, as a last resource, listened to his continued protestations against the king, the House of Lords, and the bishops, and allied themselves to him. Every day his personal power increased; he was offered the Protectorate, which he declined; continuing the line of conduct he had always followed—"that is to say, steadfast in varying his language according to the individual—he gave no handle to any definite opinions with respect to himself." The expectation of the Restoration daily increased, and some indications in the conduct of Monk, who was gradually dismissing persons and removing objects that might prove obnoxious to the king, showed plainly that the event was not far distant. Moreover, the Presbyterians were in constant communication with Monk, and this of itself speaks volumes. They were in favor of Charles's restoration, and in Monk they found a ready helper. He was warmly attached to them, and thus may have been easily persuaded to throw his influence in favor of the exiled king. That he preferred Presbyterianism to the Episcopal Church he had not feared to declare in one of his speeches in Parliament, when, after repeated declarations in favor of a republic, he yet dared to speak for Presbyterianism. Said he, "As to a government in the Church, moderate, not rigid, Presbyterianism appears at present to be the most indifferent and acceptable way to the Church's settlement" (Parl. Hist. iii, 1580). At length the farce was brought to a close, and Monk openly declared for the king. It was on the 19th of March when the royal requests for his assistance came, and to royal promises of high reward he yielded, agreed to the king's return, and directed the manner in which he wished it to be brought about. The king, by Monk's advice, went from Brussels to Breda, and on the 1st of May sent letters to the new Parliament drawn up as Monk desired, and the king was immediately acknowledged and proclaimed. On the 23d of May, Monk received him on the beach at Dover, was embraced by him, and addressed with great affection. Monk obtained many offices and titles, of which the principal was the duke of Albemarle. As such he changed again to be an Episcopalian, after he had in turn worshipped as Independent and Presbyterian, and by this change forever set at rest all hopes for the disestablishment of the Episcopal Church. The failure of the Independent and Presbyterian cause may thus be truly laid to Monk, and he therefore figures in no inconsiderable way in the ecclesiastical as well as political history of England, and even of Great Britain. From this time forth but little influence remained to him except as he wielded it through the king. He went to sea again in 1666, against his old enemies the Dutch, and maintained his reputation for courage and conduct. He died in 1670. "Monk," says one of his biographers, "had strong nerves, strong common-sense, a cold heart, an accommodating conscience, a careful tongue, an unchanging countenance, and an imperturbable temper. He showed considerable skill in civil government as well as in military affairs. He had shrewdness enough to see what was best for the nation's interest; and, if it also promoted his own, he had ability and vigor enough to bring it to pass. He was never unsettled by enthusiasm in determining his ends, and he was never checked by principle in choosing his means." M. Guizot would hardly concede all this. He acknowledges that Monk "was a man capable of great things," but confesses that "he had no greatness of soul." It certainly was not to England's interest to restore Charles, but he only brought him back because he was disappointed in Richard Cromwell, and dared not himself assume the reins of the government. See Clarendon, *Hist. Rebellion and Civil Wars of England*, vii, 373 sq.; Skinner, *Life of Monk*; Guizot, *Memoirs of Monk*, ably edited by the late lord Wharncliffe; Maseres's *Tracts*; Pepys and Evelyn, *Memoirs*; Stoughton, *Eccles. Hist. Church of England* (Restoration), i, 44 sq.; Hallam, *Const. Hist.* p. 393–406; Macaulay, *Hist. of England*, i, 143–146, 296; Stephen, *Hist. of the Church of Scotland*, ii, 350, 370, 376, 380; *State Papers of Charles II* (Lond. 1866); *Retrospective Review*, vol. xiii (1826). (J. H. W.)

Monk, James Henry, D.D., an English prelate, was born at Huntingford, Herts, in the early part of 1784. His preparatory education was received at the Charterhouse, and he then entered Trinity College, Cambridge, where he became a fellow in 1805. Two years later he occupied the position of assistant tutor, and in 1808 succeeded Porson as regius professor of Greek. While in this chair he applied himself faithfully to critical analyses of various Greek texts. He published, in conjunction with C. J. Bloomfield, D.D., *The Posthumous Tracts of Richard Porson.* During his professorship an exciting dispute arose concerning the occupancy of the chair of botany, and Sir James Edward Smith, president of the Linnæan Society, London, being disappointed in not securing the position, made bitter use of his pen concerning it. In reply, Monk published *A Vindication of the University of Cambridge* (1818), which, from the prominence of both parties, caused considerable stir in literary circles (*Lond. Quart.* xix, 434–446). In 1822 he resigned his professorship to ₂ccept the deanery of Peterborough, and eight years later was made bishop of Gloucester. During this year (1830) he published a *Life of Richard Bentley, D.D.* This work not only possesses literary excellence and biographical interest, but also comprises a large portion of the literary annals of the first half of the last century, besides valuable historical facts concerning the University of Cambridge. "The style is generally plain and masculine, and if sometimes negligent, and at others elaborate, its ordinary tone is that of a writer of strong sense and of elegant and scholarlike accomplishment" (*Lond. Quart.* xlvi, 120). Many minor inaccuracies

have been justly and severely criticised (*Edinb. Rev.* li, 321), but its general merit caused it to receive a hearty welcome by the literati. In 1836 Bristol was added to Gloucester, and he became the bishop of the united dioceses. This office he held until his death at Stapleton, near Bristol, June 6, 1856. See Stubbs, *Registrum Sacrum Anglicanum* (Oxf. 1858, 8vo); Allibone, *Dict. of Brit. and Amer. Authors*, s. v.; Hallam, *Hist. Lit.* ii, 275; and the Reviews quoted. (H. W. T.)

Monkey-god is a divinity of the Hindûs, very common in the temples of the Deccan. He is said to have been a favorite general of the god Rama, and was named *Hanuman*, but, being an aboriginal, the Puranas transformed him into a monkey. See Trevor, *India, its Natives and Missions*, p. 82.

Monks, Eastern. The Oriental Church differs in many respects from the Latin or Western, but in no particular more than in its paucity of monastic orders. In the early ages of the Church, these flourished especially in the East; indeed, that part of the world, as may be seen in the article MONASTICISM, was the home of Christian monks. But the downfall of the Roman empire despoiled the Church more or less, and the monastic institution became a part of the Western Church, while in the East it gradually degenerated and declined.

I. *Oriental Monks.*—The conflict with the Saracens contributed to the weakening of the monastic orders; and though there are remains of ancient monastic institutions in all the provinces of European Turkey and Greece, especially in Bulgaria, Thrace, Macedonia, Thessaly, the Morea, the islands of the Ægean, and the sea-borders of Asia Minor, those used as such in our day are comparatively few.

Among the monasteries still existing, the most remarkable are those of Mount Athos, Metcora, Mount Sinai, and of the Princes Islands. The first of these is under the control of both the Oriental and the Russo-Greek Church. The latter established a monastery on this mount, occupied by about twenty monks, during the reign of the empress Catharine. See below; compare also the article ATHOS. Two of the existing monasteries, on the west side, were founded by a king of Servia in the 12th century, and are occupied by Bulgarian monks, using the Slavonic tongue in religious worship. Most of the monasteries, however, were founded and richly endowed by the Greek emperors. There are about one hundred and twenty hermitages; and the number of chapels, oratories, and shrines, in a space not exceeding ten leagues in diameter, is estimated at nine hundred and thirty. The monasteries of Princes Islands were formerly the most flourishing in Turkey, but they are now nearly abandoned by monastics, and have become places of pleasure and recreation in the summer months. "The empty cloisters of one or two," says a recent visitor, "are trodden by a few pale and wretchedly poor monks, some deposed patriarchs and disgraced priors, or other subordinates of theirs, flitting through the sombre porches and gliding along the deserted churches like the ghosts of the former inmates." The nearly ruined monasteries of Metcora (seven in all), in Thessaly, are situated in the wildest part of Mount Pindus, many of them perched on the peaks of the mountain and on summits of precipitous rocks, the only access to which is by nets attached to ropes and pulleys, by means of which visitors are drawn up, or by ladders fixed to the rock. There are about sixty monks remaining in the ruins of those now dilapidated monasteries. The famous Greek monastery of Mount Sinai is exceedingly austere. It contains about one hundred monks, under a superior styled archbishop and head of Mount Sinai. He is chosen by election, but receives investiture from the patriarch of Jerusalem. See SINAI.

The rule of the Oriental monks has continued to be

Jacobite Monk.

Ethiopian Monk.

Maronite Monk.

Armenian Monk.

Coptic Monk.

Montolivetian Monk.
(A Western Order.)

Greek Monk.

Greek Monk.

Russian Monk.

that of Pachomius or of Basil. They are divided into two classes—cœnobites, or ordinary communities, and anchorets (idiorithmes), who live separately, unless on certain festivals (in recent times) when they eat in common. Each monastery is governed by a prior (hegumenos), whose office is for life, or in his absence (or the non-existence of one) by a provider or steward (epitropos), elected annually by the community. The brethren are divided into ordinary monks (monachi) and consecrated monks (hieromonachi); the latter are the learned portion of the community—but these are few indeed. In 1545, when Belon visited Mount Athos (less than a century after the conquest), he found six thousand caloyers, or monks, in the different monasteries, and of that number, he states, "it would be difficult to find more than two or three in each monastery who can read or write." Recent travellers find no change. Madden says: "This was the state of things in all the monasteries I have visited in the Greek islands, in European Turkey, in Syria, and in Egypt. But among the few—the very small minority of monks who could read and write in the monasteries I visited —there was generally one monk, sometimes two of the brotherhood, who were addicted to study, were acquainted with the ancient Greek, had a knowledge of ecclesiastical history and of the writings of the Greek fathers, and some acquaintance with the principal works or rarest MSS. of their several libraries" (Turkish Empire, ii, 83). The time of Oriental monastics is divided between religious duties and manual labor, providing food and other necessaries, tending cattle, and domestic affairs.

Down to the period of the Greek revolution and its termination in the Hellenic kingdom, but especially till 1821, the monasteries were unmolested by the Turks, and consequently the literary treasures remained uninjured, except by the ignorant members of their communities. But the successes of the Greeks in the Morea in 1821 led to irreparable mischief to the monastic libraries of several parts of Greece, and particularly of the monasteries of Mount Athos, at the hands of the infuriated Turks, and vast numbers of rare books and still more valuable and irreplaceable MSS. were destroyed. It is to be hoped that ere long the treasures still remaining will be in the hands of European scholars, and their contents become the possession of the world of letters.

II. *Russian Monks*.—Russian monasticism is so unlike that of the other Christian countries in which the institution has gained a footing, that we devote a special section to its orders. In the consideration of this subject we must dismiss from our minds all the Western ideas of beneficence, learning, preaching, etc., such as we attribute to the Benedictines or Franciscans; of statecraft, subtlety, and policy, such as we ascribe to the Jesuits. In the dark forests of Muscovy is carried out the same rigid system, at least in outward form, that was born and nurtured in the burning desert of the Thebaid. There is no variety of monastic orders in Russia. The one name of the Black Clergy is applied to all alike; the one rule of St. Basil (q. v.) governs them all. For convenience' sake they might be divided into two classes—the Hermits and the Monks.

1. *The Hermits*.—Even at the present day the influence of a hermit in Russia is beyond what it is in any other part of the world, and in earlier times their sanctity had acquired the strongest hold over all who came within their reach. Anthony and Theodosius, in the caves of Kief, were known far and wide for their piety and asceticism, and their dried skeletons still attract pilgrims from the utmost bounds of Kamtchatka. The pillar-hermits never reached the West, but were to be found in the heart of Russia. Fletcher, in his *Russian Commonwealth* (p. 117), describes them thus: "There are certain eremites who use to go stark naked, save a clout about their middle, with their hair hanging long and wildly about their shoulders, and many of them

with an iron collar or chain about their necks or middles, even in the very extremity of winter. These they take as prophets and men of great holiness, giving them a liberty to speak what they list without any controlment, though it be of the very highest himself. So that if he reprove any openly, in what sort soever, they answer nothing but that it is 'Po Grecum' (for their sins). The people liketh very well of them, because they are as pasquils [pasquins] to note their great men's faults, that no man else dare speak of. . . . Of this kind there are not many, because it is a very hard and cold profession to go naked in Russia, especially in winter." Of the numerous hermits, we mention *Basil of Moscow*, "that would take upon him to reprove the old emperor, the terrible Ivan, for all his cruelty and oppression done towards the people. His body they have translated into a sumptuous church near the emperor's house in Moscow, and have canonized him for a saint." That sumptuous church remains a monument of the mad hermit. It is the cathedral immediately outside the Kremlin walls, well termed "*the dream of a diseased imagination*." Hundreds of artists were kidnapped from Lübeck to erect it, and of all the buildings in Moscow it makes the deepest impression.

2. *Monks and Monasteries*.—The Russian monasteries sprang mostly out of the neighborhood of hermitages, like their Egyptian prototypes. Russian monachism was a modification of the Eastern system. In Russia, as in the East, the monks lived a solitary life, but in their own cells, which they themselves had built within the immediate surroundings of the monastery. With their own hands they worked for the means of subsistence, devoting the rest of their time to solitary spiritual exercises, and assembling only twice a day for common prayers. This solitary way of living was the original system of Russian monachism, while living together in convents was introduced in the 14th century only. It never was universally adopted, and both modes of living are practiced to this day. The Russian monasteries are controlled either by an *archimandrite* (q. v.) (i. e. abbot), a *hegumen* (i. e. prior), or a *stroitel* (i. e. superior). Convents with stroitels, or superiors, are usually under the care of a larger monastery. At first the monks elected their own superiors, but afterwards the bishop or regent nominated them. All monasteries were originally under the control of the bishop in whose diocese they were. This strict superintendence, however, soon became onerous; and already in early times, but especially in the 16th and 17th centuries, we find the more influential convents exempted from episcopal jurisdiction, and under the immediate care of the patriarch of Constantinople or of the Russian metropolitan. Those monasteries which are exempt from episcopal jurisdiction, and which are nowadays under the superintendence of the Synod of St. Petersburg, are called *lauropigia* or *laura*; while those under episcopal jurisdiction are named *cenobia, monasteria*, or *erorieka*.

Monachism in Russia has three degrees. The first degree comprises the *novitiate*. The *novice* does not take any vow upon himself, but has to live according to the monastic regulations; his dress is a black *rharso*, or coat with a black cape. After a preparation of three years the novice enters the second degree, and becomes a *monk*. He takes the solemn vows before the archimandrite, changes his name, and receives the tonsure. Men are not allowed to take these vows until they are thirty years old, while women are not admitted until they have reached their fiftieth year. The third degree comprises the *perfect* ones. They are dressed in a long black coat, with a wide hood which conceals the face entirely. The peculiarities of this class consist in very strict spiritual exercises, restraining of all bodily appetites for the purpose of mortifying the sensual nature, and allowing the spirit to be absorbed in the contemplation of divine things only.

They are not allowed to leave the convent, and must renounce all and every connection with the world. They are very highly esteemed, exempt from episcopal jurisdiction, and stand under the immediate care of the Synod of St. Petersburg. Monks of this third degree are very rare. Different from Western monachism, priests and deacons are found among the Russian monks. Very many enter the monasteries, not for inclination's or piety's sake, but simply to gain clerical influence and position. For the monks, although their learning is small, are looked up to as of superior education, and the monastery is therefore the only road in Russia to important clerical positions.

The income of the monasteries, which often was enormous, was at first under the care of the archimandrite. His administration, however, was subject to the inspection of the bishop. Ivan IV Vasilivitch was the first regent who seized the property of the monasteries at Novgorod in 1500. Peter the Great obliged the monasteries to take care of the invalids and poor. The empress Catharine I deprived the archimandrites of their ancient rights, and put the administration of monastic goods into the hands of a special committee (1725). This committee was subsequently abolished (1742), and the empress Elizabeth transferred the administration of monastic incomes to the holy synod. In 1762 Peter III tried to secularize all convents and monasteries; but the plan was not executed until 1764, when Catharine II secularized all monasteries with their pecuniary income and vassals, and thereby secured to the crown more than 900,000 peasants and enormous riches. The Russian monasteries at present are most of them very poor, and the monks live in apostolical poverty and simplicity. But though this be the rule, there are some remarkable exceptions. The St. Petersburg Gazette, late in 1871, furnished some interesting statistics as to the revenues of the most important monasteries in Russia, from which it is clearly apparent that some of the monasteries of Russia are well provided for in a temporal sense. The Gazette says that the receipts of the priors of the monasteries of the first class (lauras) vary from 40,000 to 60,000 rubles (£5000 to £7500), and of the other priors from 1000 to 10,000 rubles. The income of the monastery of Troilzki-Sergiev, near Moscow, which formerly contained about 100,000 persons, now amounts to 500,000 rubles (£62,500). That of the Kief monastery is even greater, as it derives a considerable profit from the sale of wax-lights. The Alexander-Nevski monastery at St. Petersburg has a special source of revenue, besides its ordinary one, in the shape of a share of all the corn imported into the capital. How large this revenue is may be inferred from the fact that a short time ago the city wished to compound for it by a yearly payment of a million rubles, and that the monastery declined the offer. Next to the monasteries of the first class, the largest revenue possessed by a monastery in Russia is that of the Iversk chapel in Moscow (a branch of the Perevinsk monastery), whose yearly receipts are calculated on an average at 100,000 rubles. In the ecclesiastical district of Novgorod the wealthiest monastery is that of Yuriev, whose bare capital alone is said to amount to 740,821 rubles.

The monasteries have really been a great help and advantage to the Russian nation, as all its bishops, artists, and scholars were educated in them. No schools or educational institutions were to be found outside of them until very recently. Their mission in Russian history was peculiar. Not only were they the nurseries of Christianity, transplanting with great struggles and dangers the benevolent doctrines of Christ among the heathen of the steppes and mountains, but, like the convent of Sinai and the convents of Greece, they are the refuges of national life, or "the monuments of victories won for an oppressed population against invaders and conquerors."

3. *Russian nunneries* existed in a very early period of that Church. The nuns are either virgins or widows. They adopt the rules of St. Basil. They mostly live together in a convent under the control of a hegumena, or prioress, elected by them. Their habit is a long black woollen dress, made after the Oriental fashion, a long black tunic or mantle, and a black veil. Formerly monks and nuns sometimes lived together in the same monastery; but as this gave rise to great immorality and disorder, it was strictly prohibited by the council in 1503.

4. *Monastery of Troitza.*—There is no more celebrated monastery in Russia than this monastery of Troitza (i. e. the Holy Trinity). It was founded A.D. 1338, when during the Tartar dominion the clergy showed themselves the deliverers of their country. About sixty miles from Moscow, in the midst of a wild forest, rises the immense pile of the ancient convent. Like the Kremlin, it combines the various institutions of monastery, university, palace, cathedral, and churches, planted within a circuit of walls. Hither from all parts of the empire stream innumerable pilgrims. No emperor comes to Moscow without paying his devotions there. The office of archimandrite, or abbot, of it is so high that for many years it has never been given to any one but a metropolitan of Moscow; and the actual chief, the hegumen, is one of the highest dignitaries of Russia.

The founder of it was St. Sergius (A.D. 1315-1392), whose career is encircled with a halo of legend. When the heart of the grand-duke Demetrius failed in his advance against the Tartars, it was the remonstrance, the blessing, and the prayers of Sergius that supported him to the field of battle on the Don (1380). No historical picture or sculpture in Russia is more frequent than that which represents the youthful warrior receiving the benediction of the aged hermit.

See Herzog, *Real-Encyklop.* ix, 675 sq.; Aschbach, *Kirchen-Lexikon,* iv, 251; Stanley, *Eastern Church,* p. 440 sq.; King, *Greek Church in Russia,* p. 24 sq.; Mouravieff, *History of the Russian Church,* trans. by Blackmore (Oxford, 1842); Fletcher, *Russian Commonwealth;* Curzon, *Ancient Monasteries of the East;* Eckhart, *Modern Russia* (Lond. 1870, 8vo), p. 210 sq.; Dixon, *Free Russia* (N. Y. 1870, 12mo), p. 29 et al.; Montalembert, *Monks of the West,* i, 38-133.

Monlezun, JEAN-JUSTIN, a Swiss ecclesiastic and historian, was born at Saramon, near Auch, in 1800. He studied at the College of Aire, consecrated his first labors to the instruction of youth destined for the service of the altar, and was subsequently appointed to the parish of Castelnau d'Arbieu, near Lictoure, and in 1833 to that of Barran (canton of Auch). The archbishop of Auch appointed him in 1847 titular canon of his metropolitan see. He died in 1859. Besides numerous articles published in different journals and historical collections, Monlezun wrote, *Histoire de la Gascoyne, depuis les temps les plus reculés jusqu'à nos jours* (Auch, 1846-50, 7 vols. 8vo); this begins with the 3d century before the Christian æra, and closes at the end of the last century:—*L'Église angélique, ou Histoire de l'Église de Notre-Dame du Puy, et des établissements religieux qui l'entourent* (Clermont, 1854, 18mo):—*Notice historique sur la ville de Mirande* (1856, 8vo):—*Vies des saints Évêques de la métropole d'Auch* (1857, 8vo).

Monmorel, CHARLES LE BOURG DE, a French preacher, was born at Pont-Audemar about the middle of the 17th century. In 1697 he became almoner to the duchess of Bourgogne, and was provided with the abbey of Lannoy, in Flanders, by the influence of Madame de Maintenon. He died in 1719, and left a highly esteemed collection of *Homélies sur les évangiles des dimanches, sur la passion, sur les mystères, et sur tous les jours du carême* (Paris, 1698, 10 vols. 12mo). The method he follows is very similar to that of the fathers of the Church, who familiarly explain the Holy Scriptures: he paraphrases all the verses, one after the other, draws from each some moral, and employs a simple and precise style. See *Dict. portatif des Prédicateurs*, s. v.; Hoefer, *Nouv. Biog. Générale*, s. v.

Monmouth, JAMES, *Duke of*, reputed natural son of king Charles II of England, deserves a place here for the part he had in the agitation provoked by the Romish Titus Oates plot, and for his relation to the Scotch Covenanters. He was born at Rotterdam in 1649, and was brought to England by his mother, Lucy Walters, in 1656, during the Commonwealth. They were both imprisoned for a time, but finally James was intrusted to the care of a nobleman, and on the Restoration was handsomely provided for by the court. He had scarcely completed his sixteenth year when he was married to a woman selected for him at court, and was then created duke of Monmouth. About 1670 he was put forward by lord Shaftesbury as the crown rival of the duke of York (later James II, q. v.), and during the revelations of the Titus Oates plot (1678), when the feeling against Romanists and all who favored them ran high, public opinion was so decidedly in his favor, and so indignant against the duke of York, that the latter was compelled to quit the kingdom; and a bill was brought forward by Parliament for excluding the duke of York from the succession; but Charles suddenly dissolved it, and a document was at the same time issued by the king, solemnly declaring that he had never been married to Lucy Walters. Monmouth himself was sent into Scotland in 1679 to quell the rebellion. He defeated the Covenanters at Bothwell Bridge; but his humanity to the fleeing and wounded was so conspicuous, and his recommendations to pardon the prisoners were so urgent, as to bring upon him the violent censures of the king and of Lauderdale. He thus became the idol of the English Nonconformists. The return of the duke of York and the exile of Monmouth having followed, the latter went to Holland, and allied himself with the leaders of the Nonconformist party, exiled like himself; and when he was allowed to return to London, he was received with such demonstrations of joy that Monmouth felt that he was the people's choice. In 1680 he made a semi-royal progress through the west of England, with the design, probably, of courting the Nonconformists, who were more numerous there than in any other part of the country, except London and Essex. In 1682 he traversed some of the northern counties. The king and his brother were alarmed; and Monmouth was arrested at Stafford, and bound over to keep the peace. He meanly confessed his participation in the Rye-House plot, accusing himself and others of a design to seize the king's person, and subvert his government. The king pardoned him, on his solemn promise to be a loyal subject to the duke of York, in case the latter should survive the king. In 1684 Monmouth fled to Antwerp, and remained abroad until the death of the king, when he embarked for England, landed (June 11, 1685) at Lyme-Regis, and issued a manifesto declaring James to be a murderer and usurper, charging him with introducing popery and arbitrary power, and asserting his own legitimacy and right by blood to be king of England. He was received with great acclamations at Taunton, where he was proclaimed as king. At Frome he heard the news of the defeat of Argyle, who, at the head of the Scottish exiles, had attempted to raise an insurrection in Scotland. Money and men were now abundant; but arms were lacking, and thousands went home for want of them. On July 5 he was persuaded, with only 2500 foot and 600 horse, to attack the king's forces, which, under the command of the earl of Feversham, were encamped at Sedgemoor, near Bridgewater. Monmouth lost ground, and, having himself set a cowardly example of flight, his troops were slaughtered like sheep. About 300 of his followers fell in the battle; but 1000 were massacred in the pursuit. Monmouth was found concealed in a ditch, and was brought to London. He made the most humiliating

submissions, and obtained a personal interview with James. "He clung," says Macaulay, "in agonies of supplication round the knees of the stern uncle he had wronged, and tasted a bitterness worse than that of death, the bitterness of knowing that he had humbled himself in vain." Even his prayer for "one day more," that he might "go out of the world as a Christian ought," was brutally refused. On July 15 he was brought to the scaffold, and beheaded on Tower Hill; the executioner performing his office so unskilfully that five blows were struck before the head was severed. See Robert, *Life of Duke of Monmouth* (1844); the histories of Macaulay, Hume, and Lingard; Stoughton, *Eccles. Hist. since the Restoration;* Chambers, *Cyclop.* s. v.; and the article JAMES II in this *Cyclopædia*.

Monnard, CHARLES, a noted Swiss literary character, deserves our attention specially on account of his humanitarian struggles in Switzerland. He was born at Berne in 1790, and was educated first at the academy in Lausanne, and then at Paris, where he enjoyed the friendship of the truly great, though himself a youth. In 1817 he returned to Lausanne, to become professor of French literature, and quickly rose to distinction for his great erudition, and the enthusiasm with which he approached his subject. He had taken orders, expecting to enter the service of the Church, but, turned aside by this appointment, he now devoted his leisure hours to the study of ecclesiastical and civil law. That Monnard largely profited by the knowledge thus acquired was manifest shortly after, when the obnoxious law passed, May 30, 1824, depriving men of the free exercise of the dictates of their conscience, intended, of course, mainly to stay the inroads which new Protestant doctrines were making in Switzerland, particularly those of the Momiers (q. v.). Monnard came forward as a defender of religious liberty, and declared the law unconstitutional. He enjoyed at this time the intimate association of the learned Swiss divine, Alexandre Rodolphe Vinet (q. v.), and brought out for this friend the treatises *De la liberté des cultes* (1826), and *Observations sur les sectaires* (1829). This action resulted in Monnard's suspension from his professorship and removal to Geneva, where, however, he soon found as warm friends as he had left at Lausanne, both among the learned and those seeking knowledge. Political changes finally permitted his return to Canton Vaud, and he was publicly honored, and called to fill several civic offices. After the revolution of 1845, Monnard retired altogether from political life. It was supposed by his friends that he would now enter the Church; but he, having found that much ill-feeling still existed against him among the clergy for the position he had taken in behalf of the Momiers, finally resolved to quit Switzerland, and accepted a chair in the University of Bonn, which he held until his death, Jan. 12, 1865. See *Journal de Genève*, Jan. 13, 1865; *Augsburger Allgemeine Zeitung*, Feb. 1865. (J. H. W.)

Monniotte, JEAN-FRANÇOIS, a French Benedictine monk, was born at Besançon in 1723. He early entered the Congregation of St. Maur, and subsequently taught philosophy and mathematics in the abbey of St. Germain-des-Prés, at Paris. After the suppression of his order, he withdrew to the village of Tigery, near Corbeil, where he died, April 29, 1797. He was the editor of the *Institutiones Philosophiæ* of François Rivard (Paris, 1778 and 1780, 4 vols. 12mo). It is an erroneous opinion which Courbier and other bibliographers have entertained that Monniotte should be considered the author of *L'Art du Facteur d'Orgues*, published, under the name of Bedos de Celles, in the *Description des Arts et Métiers* (1769, fol.). See Feller, *Dict. Biog.* s. v.; Hoefer, *Nouv. Biog. Générale*, s. v.

Monod, Adolphe, one of the distinguished divines of this century, was born at Copenhagen Jan. 21, 1802. He belongs to a family to which France is indebted for an uncommonly large number of celebrated clergymen. His father, Jean Monod, who was a native of Switzerland, born about 1760, was at the time pastor of a French Protestant church; but in 1808, having received a call from a church at Paris, he removed thither with his family, and there enjoyed much distinction. He was president of the Reformed Consistory until 1834, and died in 1836. Adolphe was educated at the College Bonaparte at Paris, and after the completion of his studies there he pursued a course in theology in the University of Geneva, where he remained until 1824. In 1825 he made a journey to Italy, during which he felt drawn nearer to God, and decided to preach the Gospel to the little Protestant congregation of Naples. There he remained until 1827. On his return he was appointed pastor of Lyons; here, however, his earnest Christian exhortations proved distasteful to a worldly congregation, and his removal was asked for and granted. Strengthened and encouraged by the spirit of the Lord, he now continued to preach and to teach. The Church of the state was locked for him. His congregation met in a private room, which was, however, soon exchanged for a spacious chapel, where numerous people were fed with the bread of eternal life. Thirty years have passed since, and at present the Evangelical Church of Lyons is a great association, with four pastors, many evangelists, and eight chapels. The government —either touched by the religious activity of Monod, or wishing to make good the wrong it had done to him —appointed him professor of theology at Montauban, where he remained eleven years. During this time he held prayer-meetings every Sunday, and in the vacations travelled in Southern France to preach and to instruct. Wherever he appeared, multitudes of people followed him, attracted by the spiritual power of his orations. In 1847 the Consistory of Paris appointed him minister of the Reformed Church there, the government confirming the selection and he accepting. He labored there with remarkable success for seven years. The churches where he preached, especially the large Oratoire, were filled every Sunday by pious people. In the smaller room of the Oratoire he gave Bible-lessons every Sunday; and a great many of his hearers, surprised by his beautiful, practical remarks on the Word of God, by his great knowledge of the Scriptures, and by his spiritual experience, preferred the Bible-lessons to his greater sermons. In 1856 he was suddenly stricken down by disease; but, with his Christian resignation, he acknowledged in sickness also the voice of God to his servant—"Lo, I come quickly." The physicians pronounced his disease incurable; Monod quietly heard the announcement, and prepared himself for departure to his Master. His faith grew stronger daily; not only a full resignation to the will of God, but a great joy filled his soul even in his greatest pain. Every Sunday, in the afternoon, his friends gathered around his bed. One of them read the Scriptures, preached, and prayed; after this he himself began to speak to them, teaching them, and bearing testimony to the Word of God. Never were his words so impressive as just before his death, occurring April 6, 1856, which was Sunday, while in all the churches of Paris prayers were ascending to the throne of God for his recovery, the Protestant Church of France fairly trembling under the great loss that was befalling it.

Adolphe Monod was possessed of more than ordinary intelligence, a kind, sympathizing heart, and a lofty imagination. He had allied to these a great taste for the beautiful, and a mind aspiring after Christian perfection in wisdom. His knowledge of the German, English, and Italian languages supplied him with the treasures of the literatures of those nations, which he esteemed very much. Concerning his theological knowledge, his earlier studies might have been imperfect; but this imperfection was afterwards fully repaired, especially in the eleven years of his professorship. The Bible, which he daily read in the original languages, was the fountain from which he drew most of his theological knowl-

edge. His Christian character was the foundation of his activity and his oratorical power. Of many a celebrated man it is said, "He was a perfect man;" all those who knew Monod say, "He was a perfect Christian." Since the moment when his heart was touched by Jesus, his whole life belonged to him. He saw and felt what he believed, and so he preached to others. Gifted with so many talents for the Christian ministry, he proved a perfect model as a preacher of the Gospel. One principle characterizes all his speeches—that is, to save immortal souls from destruction. His noble appearance, kind looks, classic style, combined with the purest pronunciation—his high seriousness, which impressed every hearer that his own heart was deeply touched by the feelings which he wished to awaken in them—his humility in confessing his own doubts and struggles, for the purpose of seeking together with his hearers the way of salvation and true happiness—all these qualities were combined for the one purpose, to gain souls for his Lord Jesus Christ.

The literary works of Adolphe Monod are few, being mainly sermons. In 1830 he published three of them, which bear evidence of his great talents. In the first of these sermons he speaks with a divine power about the relation of error and sin and that of virtue and truth. In his second and third sermons he treats of the wretchedness of sin and the great mercy of God. In 1844 he published a volume of sermons, the first of which (*La crédulité de l'incrédule*), covering 68 pages, is considered the most excellent apologetic of modern days. Before, as after his death, many other sermons of his were published; two of these about the duties of Christian women (*La femme*), and five about the apostle Paul, are especially celebrated. In these Monod answers the question, often heard, "Why has the preaching of the Gospel so little success in our century in comparison with the time of the apostles?" thus: "The Word of God is as living and powerful now as then, but our sinful example in life is the cause of the little success of our preaching. The *life* of the ancient Christians was the world-conquering power of their witness. Restore that life in the Church of Christ, and she will be able to perform wonders as of old." The apostle Paul was to him witness of this truth, which he unfolded in five sermons, entitled *The Work of Paul, His Christianity or his Tears, His Conversion, His Weakness, and his Example for us*. In the days of his sickness Monod gathered all his writings. Three volumes of sermons were published after his death, namely, two volumes containing those preached at Lyons and at Montauban, and a third volume containing the sermons preached at Paris. See *Christian Qu.* Oct. 1873, p. 565; *New-Englander*, July, 1873, p. 594; Herzog, *Real-Encyklopädie*, s. v.; Hase, *Ch. Hist.* p. 609; Vapereau, *Dict. des Contemporains*, s. v. (J. H. W.)

Monod, Frédéric, D.D., brother of the above, and, like him, celebrated for his great attainments as a divine, was born at Monnaz, Canton de Vaud, Switzerland, May 17, 1794. He entered the ministry in 1820, and was a pastor of the Reformed Church in Paris until 1849. In 1824 he began the publication of the *Archives du Christianisme*, a leading organ of the evangelical portion of French Protestantism, and he remained its editor while he lived. At the time of the French Revolution, in 1848, Frederic Monod was the leader of a movement which resulted in the establishment of the union of free evangelical churches. The original intention of the movement was to restore the synodical constitution of the Reformed State Church, and to readopt a rule of faith which would exclude the Rationalists. When this attempt failed, Monod, count de Gasparin, and some of their friends, left the state Church (1849) and organized independent congregations, which soon after formed the "Union of Evangelical Free Churches." See FRANCE. Monod was constantly reelected president of the different synods, and always remained one of the leading spirits of this new denomination, which, although small in comparison with the two Protestant state churches (the Lutheran and the Reformed), contains some of the best and most influential men of French Protestantism—as count de Gasparin, E. de Pressensé, and pastor Fisch, who attended the last general session of the Evangelical Alliance held in New York City in 1873. The hope of bringing over the majority of the French Protestants to the evangelical free churches was not realized; but the existence, spirituality, and prosperity of the Free Church greatly strengthened the evangelical party in the state Church, which has since steadily gained in influence, and appears to be at present in undisputed ascendency. (Comp. *Zeitschrift für historische Theologie* [1851], No. III.) Monod, like all the members of the free evangelical churches, was an ardent admirer of American institutions. He, with his friends, pointed to the separation of Church and State as it exists here, and to the great amount of civil liberty which Americans are enjoying, as model institutions which the people of Europe, and especially of France, would do well to follow as much as lies in their power. The favorable opinion which he had always held of the United States was greatly strengthened by a journey he made through this country about 1855. After the outbreak of the American rebellion, he showed himself one of the warmest European friends of the Northern cause. He took a prominent part in all the demonstrations which the Protestant clergy made in favor of the Union, and in which they manifested a greater unanimity than the Protestant clergy of any other country in the world. Monod was himself one of the originators of the address—signed by the great majority of Protestant French ministers, and objected to by not a single one—in which Protestant France, through her clergy, recorded her opinion that "the triumph of the rebellion would throw back for a century the progress of Christian civilization and of humanity, would cause angels in heaven to weep, and would rejoice dæmons in hell; would throughout the world probably raise the hopes of the favorers of slavery and the slave-trade, quite ready to come forth at the first signal, in Asia, in Africa, and even in our refined cities of Europe; would give a sad blow to the work of evangelical missions; and what a terrible responsibility would it impose upon the Church which should remain mute while witnessing the accomplishment of this triumph." The address is noted for the change of opinion it wrought, not only in France, but also in England. Frederic Monod died Dec. 30, 1863, mourned not only by his own country, but by the Protestant world, which recognised in him a zealous champion of the evangelical cause the world over. He was so busy with his pen for all humanity that he found but little time for extensive composition. Most of his writings are embodied in the *Archives* which he edited. He published, besides, a few pamphlets and several of his sermons. See *Archives du Christianisme*, Jan. 1864; and Dr. M'Clintock in the N. Y. *Methodist*, Jan. 30, 1864. (J. H. W.)

Monod, Jean. See MONOD, ADOLPHE.

Monod, Pierre, a learned Savoyard Jesuit, was born at Bonneville in 1586. He entered the Order of Jesuits in 1603, taught belles-lettres and philosophy in different colleges of his order, and finally became principal of that of Turin. Appointed confessor to the duchess Christine, sister of Louis XIII of France, he exercised much influence over that princess, and shared largely in the direction of political affairs. In 1636 he was sent to Paris to reclaim the honors of royalty for the house of Savoy, but he was unable to obtain an interview with Richelieu. Irritated by having his demands eluded, he allied himself with the enemies of the ministry, especially with Caussin, confessor to Louis XIII, with the object of overthrowing the cardinal. Richelieu, partly divining these intrigues, sent Monod back to Turin, when the latter endeavored to withdraw Christine from the French alliance. Then the cardinal attempted to remove him from the service of the duchess; but Monod knew how to preserve his authority over her. In 1640 he was arrested by the order of Richelieu, imprisoned first at Pignerol, and subsequently at Cunéo, but found means of escaping; and was finally retaken and transferred to Miolans, where, in spite of the interposition of the pope, he remained until his death, March 31, 1644. He is the author of *Recherches historiques sur les alliances de France et de Savoie* (Lyons, 1621, 4to):—*Amedeus pacificus, seu de Eugenii IV et Amedei Sabaudiæ ducis, in sua obedientia Felicis V nuncupati, controversiis* (Turin, 1624, 4to; Paris, 1626, 8vo); reproduced in the seventeenth volume of the *Annales* of Baronius:—*Apologie pour la Maison de Savoie contre les scandaleuses invectives de la Première et Seconde Savoysienne* (Chambéry, 1631, 4to); followed by a *Second Apologie,* which, translated into Italian by the author, appeared at Turin (1632, 4to):—*Trattato del titolo regio dovuto alla casa di Savoya, con un ristretto delle revoluzioni del Reame di Cipri e ragioni della casa di Savoya sopra di esso* (Turin, 1633, fol.); this work, published at the same time in Latin, was the cause of a quarrel between Savoy and Venice; it was attacked with violence by Graswinckel:—*Il Capricorno ossia l'Oroscopo d'Augusto Cesare* (Turin, 1633, 8vo); fictitious:—*Extirpation de l'Hérésie, ou Déclaration des motifs que le Roi de France a d'abandonner la protection de Genève;* the second part remains unedited, as well as the following works, preserved in MS. in the university library of Turin:—*Annales ecclesiastici et civiles Sabaudiæ; Vita B. Margaritæ Sabaudiæ, marchionissæ Montisferrati;* etc. See Rosetti, *Scriptores Pedemontii,* p. 470; Richelieu, *Memoirs,* vol. x; Le Vassor, *Hist. de Louis XIII;* Botta, *Storia d' Italia.*

Monogamy. See MARRIAGE.

Monogram (Greek μόνος, *single,* and γράμμα, *letter*), a character composed of two or more letters of the alphabet, often interlaced with other lines, and used as a cipher or abbreviation of a name, is found to be of frequent occurrence in the annals of early ecclesiastical history, and seems to have been introduced into the early Church from the heathen nations.

I. The use of monograms began at a very early date. They are found on Greek coins, medals, and seals, and are particularly numerous on the coins of Macedonia and Sicily. Both on coins and in MSS. it was the practice to represent the names of states and cities by monograms, of which above 500 are known, but some have not been deciphered. Monograms occur on the family coins of Rome, but not on the coins of the earlier Roman emperors. Constantine placed on his coins one of the earliest of Christian monograms, which is to be traced in the recesses of the catacombs, composed of the first and second letters of ΧΡιστός (*Christus*), a monogram which also appeared on the Labarum, and was continued on the coins of the succeeding emperors of the East down to Alexander Comnenus and Theodore Lascaris. We often find it combined with the first and last letters of the Greek alphabet (Rev. i, 8). Another well-known monogram is that of the name of Jesus, IHS, from the first three letters of 'ΙΗΣοῦς. (See below, *Monogram of Christ.*) Popes, emperors, and kings, during the Middle Ages, were in the practice of using a monogram, frequently replacing by it their signatures. Painters and printers used it; and, unintentionally on the part of its authors, the monogram has frequently served in modern times to determine the age of a MS., and even of early printed works. See Horne, *Introduction to Bibliography,* vol. ii; Brulliot, *Dict. des Monogrammes* (Munich, 1832–34). See also ICONOGRAPHY; ILLUMINATION, ART OF.

II. *Monogram of Christ.*—The sign used to represent the name of Christ. This name is usually given to the combination of the first two letters forming his name in Greek; but there is also a monogram of the name of

Jesus, which is of great antiquity, and of both names together. We will examine them successively.

(1) For the name of *Christ*. The monogram used in the primitive Church is communicated to us by the ancient ecclesiastical writers, and also by the numerous Christian monuments of that period which are still extant. We find it generally formed by one of the two combinations of the letters XP, the P being set inside of the X, which latter is either an erect X or reversed, giving the forms ☧ and ⳨. The first is the form described by Eusebius (*Vita Constant.* i, 31) and Paulinus of Nola (*Poem.* xix, *de Felic. Nat.* xi, *v. Orig. Opp.* ed. Muret. p. 481); the other is described by Lactantius (*De mort. persecut.* c. 44), for we can hardly make out his expression concerning the *transversa* X, the point of which is bent, to signify anything else than the ✝, the upright part of which is made into a P. These two forms give rise to two others, by merely turning the P the other way, thus, ⳨ and ⳨. There are also instances of other less usual combinations. For a description of all the various forms, see, besides the special works on the monograms of Christ, Mamachi, *Orig. et antiq. Christ.* liii, 62 sq.; Münter, *Sinnbilder*, pt. v, p. 34–37; Didron, *Iconogr. Chrét.* p. 401 sq.; Letronne, *Exam. archéol. de deux quest. sur la croix ansée Égypt.* (*Mém. de l'Acad. des Inscript.* vol. xvi, pt. ii, p. 284); Twining, *Symbols and Emblems*, pt. i, iii, iv. If we now inquire into the further significance of these two forms of the monogram, in order to see whether it contain some further meaning of importance, we must first consider whether it is indeed always a distinctive mark of Christian monuments. Here we find that the form ⳨ is exclusively used by Christians, and is the sign of the name of Christ. Yet it must be observed that it closely resembles the Egyptian hooped cross, ☥, the symbol of life, which is often represented in the hand of the Egyptian deities, and then, in consequence of little irregularities on both sides, the two monograms happen sometimes to be exactly alike; even the Egyptian Christians sometimes used the Egyptian sign for that of the cross (see Letronne, *Exam. archéol.* in *Mémoires de l'Acad. des Inscript.* xvi, 285 sq.). The other form, ☧, a combination of XP, is essentially of heathen origin. We find it on Greek money greatly anterior to Christ, namely, on the Attic tetradrachma (Eckhel, *Doctr. numm.* ii, 210), as also on the coins of Ptolemæus, a specimen of which, with the head of Zeus Ammon on the one side, and on the other an eagle holding the monogram ☧ in his claws, is to be seen in the collection of coins at Berlin (No. 428). It is also found in an inscription on a monument erected to Isis, in Egypt, in the year B.C. 137–8 (see Böckh, *Corp. Inscr. Gr.* n. 4713, b). At the same time such heathen monuments are very scarce; and where the sign is found on tombs, it may generally be taken for granted that it is there as the Christian emblem. In after-times the signification of this sign was altered, especially among the Greek writers, where we seldom find ☧ used to designate Christ. It most generally stands for Χρυσόστομος, and in the construction Πολὺ Πολυχρόνιος; it is also used as an abbreviation for χρύσεον (see Montfaucon, *Paleogr. Gr.* p. 344). On the other hand, in the Greek calendar, since the 11th century, ☧ πάσχα is used for Χριστιανῶν πάσχα, in opposition to νομικὸν πάσχα (see Piper, *Karl's des Grossen Kalendarium u. Ostertafel*, p. 130 sq.). It has long been a much controverted point to know whether this monogram were introduced only by the emperor Constantine, or whether it were in use anterior to his reign. It seems, however, pretty much established that the monuments which have been referred to in order to prove its greater antiquity are either spurious or doubtful (see Mamachi, *Orig. et antiq. Christ.* c. i, p. 54, n. 3); and the oldest monument of ascertained date which bears it is a grave-stone at Rome of the year

331, where the monogram ☧ stands between branches of palm, and preceded by the words IN SIGNO, which recall the apparition of Constantine (Piper, *Ueber den Christlichen Bilderkreis*, p. 4, 65, with a plate, fig. 1). Yet another inscription, lately discovered in the catacombs of Melos, and containing the monogram, is considered as belonging to the 2d century (see Ross, *Inscript. Gr. ined.* fasc. iii, n. 246, b, p. 8). It is further probable that, since in the early part of the 2d century the first two letters of the name of Jesus were already used in that manner, as we shall see hereafter, the same was already done also with the name of Christ; and also that, from the moment Constantine wished to adopt a general sign, he would more likely have adopted one previously in use than invented a new one. After Constantine it became very numerous in private monuments, and especially on the graves, and that in most Christian countries. In Germany we find many such inscriptions, with either the ☧ or the ⳨, at Trèves (Hersch, *Centralmuseum*, pt. iii, Nos. 56, 61; Le Blant, *Inscrip. Chrét. de la Gaule*, vol. i, No. 230, 244), and at Cologne (Hersch, p. i, No. 95, 96; Le Blant, vol. i, No. 355, 359). They are also found on things deposited in the graves, as, for instance, on lamps and glass vessels, and, finally, on things used in daily life, as on stones, rings, etc. (D'Agincourt, *Scult.* pl. ix, fig. 1, 24). Under Constantine the Great the monogram came to be used on public monuments. He caused it to be inscribed on the *Labarum* (q. v.), doubtless in the form ☧ (Eusebius, *Vit. Constant.* i, 28, speaks only of the cross; but the cross seen by Constantine was this very monogram), as also on his helmet, and on the shields of his soldiers. His vision is recalled in the Labarum by the monogram in the hand of the emperor, who is crowned by victory, and by the legend HOC SIGNO VICTOR ERIS on the coins of his son Constantius, and of the contemporary Vetranius (350) and Gallus (351–354). Of his own reign there is a celebrated coin with the monogram of the Labarum, placed on and piercing a snake, with the legend APES PUBLICA (Eckhel, *Doctr. numm.* viii, p. 88). Coins show it also on the helmet of Constantine, and on the shield of the emperor Majorianus (457–461). In the coins of the Eastern Roman empire, the monogram in its two principal forms is quite common until the time of Justinian I, with an interruption during the reign of the emperor Julian. Under Justinian († 565) the sign of the cross took the place of the monogram. Soon after Constantine, in the second half of the 4th century, we find it placed on buildings. The oldest monogram of that kind of which the date is known is an inscription of the year 377 at Sitten, in Switzerland, probably by the prætor of that place, and relating his restoration by the prætor Pontius (Momiesse, *Inscript. Helvet. Lat.* pl. 3, No. 10; Le Blant, *Inscript. Chrét.* p. 496, pl. 38, No. 231; Gelpke, *Kirchengesch. d. Schweiz.* pt. i, p. 86 sq.). It was especially used in Church architecture. The oldest, from the time of Constantine, is to be found in the mosaic of S. Constantia at Rome, where it is on a roll in the hand of Christ. In the Middle Ages it was especially placed on the top of the pulpit, as in the churches of S. Francesca Romana and of S. Maria Maggiore at Rome, both built in the 13th century. In the Lateran it is placed in the gable end, according to the orders given by Clement XII in 1735. This monogram, in funereal inscriptions, where it occurs at the beginning, in the middle, and at the end, may be considered in general as confessing Christ. It is sometimes used in connection with other words, but generally alone, as in an inscription at Vienna Faustina "in ☧" (Mai, *Sanct. ver. nov. coll.* v, 432, 433); one in the museum of the Vatican, on Gentianus, ends with the words "quia scimus te in ☧" (Marini, *Hist. Allan.* p. 37). In the images on the graves it is especially used to designate the person of Christ, particularly where there are any representations of him. Thus a lamb standing on a mountain, as represented in Rev. xiv, 1, pictured on a coffin in the Vatican grottoes, bears on its head the ☧ (Bottari, *Scult. e pitt. sacre*, vol. i, tav. xxi). It is also used with the bodily representations of Christ, either simply over his head, or in the nimbus around him, or one on each side of his head, as in a lately discovered painting in the cemetery of Prætextatus (Perret, *Les Catacombes de Rome*, t. i, H. L.). There is a gem of heathen origin representing the heads of Jupiter, Apollo, and Diana, with the inscription *Vivas in deo f(eliciter)*, in which the head of Jupiter is surmounted by the sign ☧. This was probably added to it in after-times by a Christian owner, either to give it a sort of Christian consecration, or, more probably, to transform the head of Jupiter into a likeness of Christ (Piper, *Mythol. u. Symb. d. christl. Kunst*. I, i, p. 115-117). Sometimes the monogram also appears alone in carvings, and is then intended to represent the person of Christ; for instance, on glass vessels, where it is placed between two persons, to signify that Christ is with them. An especially interesting instance of that kind recurs on several coffins, where a cross is represented, with those who watched at the grave at the foot of it, and on the cross the monogram ☧, in a wreath, borne by a soaring eagle. While the lower part is indicative of the crucifixion and burial, the crowned monogram held aloof is the emblem of the crucifixion and ascension. A drawing and explanation of it are to be found in the *Evang. Kalender* for 1857, p. 37, 45 sq. Finally, we find also the monogram used with a symbolical meaning. On a grave-stone of the year 355 the ☧ is placed by the side of the figure of a person who, with the outstretched right hand, takes hold of the name (Aringhi, *Roma subterran.* lib. ii, c. 23, t. ii, p. 570).

(2) For the name of *Jesus Christ* we have, first, in Greek, the monogram $\overline{\text{IC}}$ $\overline{\text{XC}}$. This is the usual abbreviation of the two names found in the oldest MSS. of the N. T., as in the *Codex Alexandrinus* of the 5th and the *Claromontanus* of the 6th century, and which is retained in the Minuskel MSS. It appears also on monuments, namely, in the inscription $\dfrac{\text{IC} | \text{XC}}{\text{NI} | \text{KA}}$, found in the catacombs of Naples, in a niche, at the place of an old well (Pellicia, *De eccles. Christ. polit.* ii, 414, ed. Bonn; Bellermann, *Ueber d. ältesten christlichen Begräbnissstätten*, p. 81), and is still used in the Greek Church, namely, on the bottom of the vases used for communion (Goar, *Eucholog.* p. 99). In sculptures and carvings, we find this monogram accompanying the figure of Christ: as in the Byzantine coin, first under J. Zimisces (969-975), whence it remained in use until the downfall of the Greek empire. There is yet extant a fine gold medal of the last emperor, Constantine XIV Palæologus, on the reverse of which is the figure of Christ standing, with the inscription $\overline{\text{IC}}$ $\overline{\text{XC}}$ (a specimen of it is to be seen in the imperial collection of coins at Vienna) (see Eckhel, *Doctr. numm.* viii, 273). It is also found on ancient Greek monuments, and on the ancient doors of the church of St. Paul at Rome of the year 1070. Byzantine paintings in which it is represented are to be found in the royal gallery of Berlin (Nos. 1044, 1048). The introduction of this monogram into the Latin Church is especially remarkable. The ancient church of St. Peter at Rome contained mosaics of the time of Innocent III, which represented Christ enthroned between the apostles Peter and Paul, with the inscription $\overline{\text{IC}}$ $\overline{\text{XC}}$ (see the *Evang. Kalender* for 1851, p. 50). The same is found in the still extant mosaic of Philip Dusuti of 1300, in the church of S. Maria Maggiore at Rome (Valentini, *Basil. Liber.* pl. ciii). There are also numerous easel pictures of Italian origin of the 14th and 15th centuries, which contain the likeness of Christ, together with this monogram, as, for instance,

the crucifixion of Taddeo Gaddi, of 1334, in the royal gallery at Berlin, No. 1080, and an apparition of Christ to Magdalena after his resurrection, by Donatus Bizamanus, in the Christian Museum at the Vatican (D'Agincourt, *Peint.* pl. xcii). Secondly, we have in Latin the monogram $\overline{\text{IHS}}$ $\overline{\text{XPS}}$. The Latin Church has also a special abbreviation of both names, which we find in the oldest Latin MS. copies of the Bible; for instance, in the Greek and Latin *Codex Claromontanus*. It is occasionally preserved in the Minuskel MSS., as in the *Sacramentarium* of Gellone at Paris, in the 8th century, where the Gospel of Matthew begins with the words "Liber generationis $\overline{\text{ihu}}$ $\overline{\text{xpi}}$" (fac-simile in Silvestre, *Paléogr.* t. iii). This mode of writing gave rise to numerous researches in the French Church in the 9th century. Amalarius, from Metz, author of the book *De Officiis Ecclesiasticis*, asks, in a letter to Jeremiah, archbishop of Sens, in the year 827, to know why the name of Jesus is written with an aspirate, an H, and expresses the opinion that, according to the Greek, it should be written with IH, and C or S (D'Achery, *Spicileg.* iii, 330); to which the other answers that it is not an aspirate, but a Greek H. He asked also bishop Jonas whether it were more correct to write $\overline{\text{IHC}}$ or $\overline{\text{IHS}}$, and was answered that the latter form was preferable, the first two letters being taken from the Greek and the last from the Latin, as had been done with the name Christ, XPS. The formula IhS XPS (and IhS XIS) REX REGNANTIVM occurs on Byzantine coins, according to the example of Justinian II, from Basilius Macedo (De Saulcy, *Essai de classificat. des suites monét. Byzantine*, pl. xix, 1), down to Romanus IV Diogenes (1068-1071); and it is only there that the other monogram, $\overline{\text{IC}}$ $\overline{\text{XC}}$, remained in use. In the West, we find the monogram $\overline{\text{IHS}}$ $\overline{\text{XPS}}$ in use at a very early period, both in inscriptions, carvings, and paintings, as, for instance, miniatures in the Carolinian MSS., and in pictures of the Middle Ages.

(3) For the name of *Jesus* alone, we find in Greek the monogram IH. It is the first form of which we have any knowledge, and occurs as early as in the Epistle of Barnabas (q. v.), e. g., where the number 318 of the men circumcised by Abraham (resulting from a comparison between Gen. xvii, 23 and xiv, 14) is found to be a sign of the name of Jesus and of the cross, for 318 is written with Greek letters, $\iota\eta\tau'$. This meaning was generally received, as also by the Latin Church (Coteler). This abbreviation, however, occurs but seldom on the more ancient monuments. In the West, the monogram IHS (q. v.) obtained great popularity in the Middle Ages through the preaching of Bernard of Sienna, who in divers cities, and especially at Viterbo, in 1427, was in the habit of exhibiting a tablet on which that monogram was painted in golden letters, surrounded by a halo of golden rays, and to which he directed their devotions. He was accused of innovation indeed, but succeeded in satisfying pope Martin V (Wadding, *Annal. minor.* T.V. a. 1427, p. 183 sq.). This monogram, to which the cross is sometimes added, remained in use in small Latin letters, and sometimes in Gothic. Thus, in the picture of the adoration of the three kings, by Raphael, in the royal gallery at Berlin, we find at the upper edge of a golden sun, written in golden letters, *ɤƒ᪲*, which, however, must not be understood, as some have made it out, to signify *in hoc signo*. The Jesuits also appropriated that monogram to their use. On the election of the first general of the order, in 1541, which resulted in the elevation of Ignatius, the latter had headed his vote with the name IHS, and the sign ihs was engraved on his seal, the same with which the election of the generals since Jacob Laynez has always been sealed (*Acta Sanct.* d. xxxi, mens. Jul. t. vii, p. 532 a). See, besides the authorities already referred to, Herzog, *Real-Encyklopädie*, ix, 738 sq.; Münter, *Sinnbilder u.*

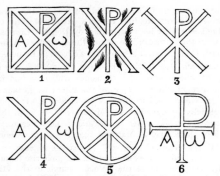

Various forms of the Constantinian Monogram.
(Figs. 1, 4, 6, with α and ω, as symbols of eternity; 2, with olive-branch, as an emblem of peace.)

Kunstvorstellungen d. alten Christen (Altona, 1825); Piper, *Mythologie u. Symbolik d. christl. Kunst*, vol. i (1847) and ii (1851); Withrow, *Catacombs of Rome* (N. Y. 1874), p. 264 sq. See CHRIST, MONOGRAM OF.

Monoimos, an Arabian heretic of the 2d century, who appears to have been a follower of Basilides. He is mentioned by Theodoret; but the particulars of his system, which was formed of strange geometrical and arithmetical speculations respecting the origin of the world, are given only by Hippolytus. The substance of these is that primal man is the universe; that the universe is the originating cause of all things, he himself being unbegotten, incorruptible, and eternal; that a son of the primal man was generated independently of time; that the Son of man is a monad represented by the iota and the tittle—that is, the Greek figure 10 (ι); that all things have emanated from the substance of this monad; that cubes, octahedrons, pyramids, and all such figures, out of which crystallize fire, water, and earth, have arisen from numbers which are comprehended in the number 10. In a letter from Monoimos to Theophrastus, which is quoted by Hippolytus, the former avows that he believed in no God separate from man's own self. See Hippolytus, *Refut. Hær.* viii, 5–8; x, 13; Theodoret, *Hær.-fab.* i, 18; Taylor. *Hippolytus*, p. 106.

Monomania (μόνος, *single*, and μανία, *madness*) has loosely been made to represent every form of partial insanity, but has been more rigidly defined as that mental condition in which a single faculty, or class of faculties or associations, become diseased, the mind generally remaining healthy. Slight and solitary aberrations — such as where a savage antipathy to cats coexists with a love for human kind; where there appears to be an incontrollable tendency to steal, to squander, to drink, to destroy—are of common occurrence, and are supposed to be compatible with the exercise of intelligence, and with the discharge of many of the ordinary duties of life. By a more strict limitation, the term has been confined to such affections as involve the emotions and propensities alone. It is, however, held that, notwithstanding its apparent integrity, the whole mind is involved or influenced by the presence of such morbid conditions, at least while they are predominant. It is undoubtedly difficult to point out in what manner the belief, e. g., that a particular organ has been transmuted into glass can interfere with or render the memory, or the power of instituting comparisons, defective and untrustworthy; yet it is legitimate to receive with caution *every* manifestation of powers so constituted that they fail to detect the incongruities and absurdities with which they are associated, or, having detected the real character of these errors, are unable or unwilling to cast them out or to disregard them. There is much countenance given to this theory by facts which indicate that even trivial forms of mental obliquity are connected with an unsound organization,

and that particular and rarely recognised monomanias are invariably associated with the *same* structural alteration. The unhealthy elevation of the sentiment of cautiousness, for example, especially where it amounts to fear of death, panic, or panphobia, is a symptom of disease of the heart and large blood-vessels, while the monomania of ambition (or optimism, as it has been styled) is the concomitant of the general paralysis of the insane. It will be obvious, from the definitions previously introduced, that the species or varieties of monomania must correspond to the faculties or phases of the human mind, and to their combinations. Several great divisions, however, have been signalized, both on account of their frequency and of their influence upon the individual and upon society. 1. Monomania of suspicion, comprehending doubts in the fidelity and honesty of friends and those around, belief in plots and conspiracies, the dread of poison; and where, as is often the case, it is conjoined with cunning, the propensity to conceal, mystify, and deceive. This malady has frequently been observed in intimate connection with cancer and malignant growths. 2. Monomania of superstition and unseen agencies, where credulity, mingled with religious awe, peoples the external world with spectres, omens, mysteries, magnetism, and the imagination with horrors or ecstatic reveries. Insensibility to pain, or indifference to external injuries, has been observed as a characteristic of individuals affected with this disease. 3. Monomania of vanity, or euphoria, where display and ostentation are indulged, without reference to the position and means of the patient. 4. Monomania of fear. 5. Monomania of pride and ambition. 6. Kleptomania (q. v.). 7. Dipsomania, or Oinomania (q. v.). If it can be proved that such morbid tendencies as have been here mentioned, and others still less prominent, are merely salient points of a great breadth and depth of mental disease, the plea of insanity may justifiably be employed more frequently in the consideration of criminal acts.—Chambers, s. v. Dr. Forbes Winslow, in *The Pall Mall Gazette*, holds that what is called partial insanity, or monomania, is not sufficient to prove of itself a testamentary incapacity. "I have often," he says, "witnessed among the insane the possession of delicate, just, and honorable ideas respecting their own social position, and the pecuniary claims of those most near and dear to them." He approves the action of ecclesiastical judges in former times, who, when a will was brought before them to be contested, inquired, first, if there were prima facie evidence in the wording, arrangement, etc., of the will that its author was insane; and, next, whether the testator's lunacy were visible in the distribution of his property. If neither of these points was established, the will generally stood against unquestionable evidence of mental unsoundness or eccentricity in other things. He quotes a case where the testator left a large fortune to his housekeeper, and directed in the same will that his executors should make fiddle-strings of part of his bowels and smelling-salts of others, and that the rest of his body be vitrified into lenses for optical purposes. He did this, he said, to mark his moral aversion to funeral pomp. It appeared that he had conducted his affairs with great shrewdness and ability. See Esquirol, *La Monomanie;* Bayle, *Maladies du Cerveau;* Stephens, *Criminal Law of England*, p. 92.

Monophysites (Greek, Μονοφυσῖται, from μόνος, *single*, and φύσις, *nature*) is the name of a Christian sect which took form under that name in the year 451, when the Eutychian heresy was condemned by the orthodox Eastern Church in the Council of Chalcedon. But though the name of the Monophysites first occurs in the acts of the Council of Chalcedon, Monophysitism must be regarded as of much older date, and is to be traced to *Eutychianism* (q. v.), from which it sprang, though by no means identical with it. Eutyches not only attributed but one nature to Christ after his incarnation, but held that Christ's body, being the body of God, was not identical with the human body. The Monophysites, in distinction, held that the two natures were so united that, although the "one Christ" was partly human and partly divine, his two natures became by their union only one nature (Μόνη φύσις). This modification of the Eutychian doctrine was taught by Dioscorus, the successor of St. Cyril as patriarch of Alexandria. He presided at the Council of Ephesus (A.D. 449), which considered the opinion of Eutyches, and from the murderous violence shown by his Egyptian partisans was called "Latrocinium," or "Robber Synod." Under the influence of Dioscorus, who wished to gain a victory over the patriarchs of Antioch and Constantinople, the chief opponents of Eutyches, the assembled bishops were persuaded to give their decision in favor of Eutyches, the key-note to that decision being struck by the passionate exclamation of Dioscorus: "Will you endure that two natures should be spoken of after the incarnation" (Mansi, Concil. vi, 583). "Partly thus terrified, partly ignorant, partly, perhaps, persuaded," says Neale, "the assembled fathers set their hands to the acquittal of Eutyches, and thus the Monophysite heresy was born in the Church" (Patriarchate of Alexandria, i, 295). The decision so given was not, however, accepted by the patriarchs of Antioch and of Constantinople, nor by the bishop of Rome, and another council was called by the new emperor Marcian in the following year, which assembled first at Nicæa, but eventually at Chalcedon, whence its name. This council condemned the doctrine of the Eutychians and Monophysites, and it was stated "that Christ was really divine and really human; in his divinity co-eternal, and in all points similar to the Father; in his humanity, son of the Virgin Mary, born like all others, and like unto us men in all things except sin; that after his incarnation his person contained two natures unmixed (ἀσυγκύτως) and unaltered (ἀτρέπτως), yet at the same time completely (ἀδιαιρέτως) and intimately (ἀκωρίσως) united." The adherents of the Alexandrian school saw themselves overpowered and withdrew from the council, and thus "started those violent and complicated Monophysite controversies which convulsed the Oriental Church, from patriarchs and emperors down to monks and peasants, for more than a hundred years, and which have left their mark even to our day." Dioscorus himself was deposed from the patriarchate, and a certain Proterius placed in his stead. The people, however, sympathized with the persecuted, and the Monophysites increased very rapidly. They spread especially in Palestine, mainly through the agency of the monk Theodosius, who was instrumental in the expulsion of the patriarch Juvenal from Jerusalem, and got himself appointed in his place. The conflict between the two parties was only quelled by force of arms. Egypt, and in particular Alexandria, proved, however, the greatest strongholds of Monophysite views, and constant troubles were there the result. The patriarch Proterius was frequently annoyed by his opponents, and public quarrels were a common occurrence. Finally, in the heat of passion, a few Monophysite partisans attacked the house of Proterius, and, driving him from it, followed him to the church, and there stabbed him to death, and disposed of his body in a most cruel manner. In Proterius's place was put a Monophysite, the presbyter Timotheus Ælurus, and henceforth there ruled in Alexandria an unbroken succession of Monophysite patriarchs. Under Ælurus's rule all who accepted the decisions of the Council of Chalcedon were excommunicated, especially pope Leo. But complaint being made against Ælurus to the emperor, he was banished to Gangra in 460. In many respects the rule of Ælurus was a profitable one to the Church, and had fanatics only stood aside the best results would have been assured. He was conciliatory in his nature, as may be seen from his acts. He evidently intended to draw his flock back into the orthodox fold. Thus Dioscorus had

followed Eutyches in denying Christ's human nature to be of the same kind as that of ordinary men; but when Timothy was on a visit to Constantinople, and Eutychian monks desired to join his communion, he took the opportunity of disclaiming this part of their belief, and declared the conviction of himself and his followers to be that the Saviour became consubstantial with men according to his human nature, as he had ever been consubstantial with the Father according to his divine nature. In this particular the Monophysite followers of Timothy, who were hence called "Timotheans," as the opposite party were called "Dioscorians," returned to the creed of St. Cyril, which his deacon and successor Dioscorus had forsaken.

Another patriarchate which the Monophysites appropriated was that of Antioch. Peter the Fuller (γναφεύς), an adherent of Eutyches, who had been driven out of two convents of Constantinople, having gone to Antioch with Zeno, a relation of the emperor, connected himself there with the remaining Apollinarists, and opposed the orthodox bishop Martyrius; the latter fled to ask help of the emperor, and in the mean time Fuller was appointed patriarch. He condemned the Council of Chalcedon, excommunicated all who held that God was not crucified, and introduced into the liturgy the formula Θεὸς ὁ σταυρωθεὶς δι' ἡμᾶς, which became subsequently the shibboleth of the Monophysites. He was finally deposed and exiled by the emperor.

The usurper Basiliscus, who succeeded Zeno on the throne in 476, protected Monophysitism, declaring it the religion of the state, and condemning the Council of Chalcedon and the epistle of Leo in an ἐγκύκλιον. But Acacius, bishop of Constantinople, having in the mean time organized a dyophysite counter-revolution, and gradually gaining strength, the orthodox succession was revived after the death of Ælurus (477), when Zeno, who had recovered the throne, appointed Timothy Salophakiolus as patriarch of Alexandria. At the death of the latter, who had ruled for twelve years, the Catholic party nominated John Talaia, and the Monophysites Peter Mongus, as his successor: the latter succeeded through the influence of the emperor. In 482 Zeno issued his Henotikon for the purpose of uniting the two parties: it aimed at satisfying both parties, but it did not please either. The stricter Monophysites of Egypt, who insisted on an unvarnished rejection of the Council of Chalcedon, separated from the others to form a Monophysite society of their own, which received the name of Ἀκέφαλοι. See ACEPHALI. The dyophysites also split into two parties, one of which accepted the Henotikon, while the other rejected it. At the head of the latter party stood Felix II of Rome, who excommunicated Acacius (484); thus this attempt at conciliation resulted only in making four parties instead of two, and in creating a schism between the Latin and the Greek churches which lasted thirty-five years (484–519). Zeno's successor, Anastasius, adhered strictly to the Henotikon, and even inclined somewhat to Monophysitism. In 513 Severus, one of the principal men among the Acephali, became patriarch of Antioch. His attempt to introduce the formula Θεὸς σταυρωθεὶς δι' ἡμᾶς in the churches of Constantinople created fresh troubles; the patriarch Macedonius, who opposed the innovation, was deposed, and the disorders which followed were hard to repress. But in consequence of the revolt of the general Vitalianus (514), the orthodox party were finally restored to the possession of their rights, and in 519 the unity with Rome was fully established. The partisans of the Henotikon were taken off the church lists, and all the Monophysite bishops deposed. Most of these withdrew to Egypt. Here they were soon divided among themselves. Julian, formerly bishop of Halicarnassus, affirmed that the body of our Lord was rendered incorruptible in consequence of the divine nature being blended with it. See APHTHARTODOCETÆ. Others maintained that it was corruptible. See AGNOETÆ and

PHTHARTODOCETÆ. The leader of the last named was Severus, the deposed patriarch of Antioch, who maintained the corruptibility of Christ's human nature, or its identity with that of ordinary pain-suffering, weak, and mortal manhood. This theology eventually became that of the Monophysites at large, hence he deserves special attention in this connection. With him Monophysitism receded another step from Eutychianism; and although it was still maintained that Christ, after his incarnation, was of one nature only, the doctrine came to be held in such a way as not to be extremely divergent from the Church. For "in the theology of Severus, the qualities of human nature were all retained in Christ after the incarnation, although the nature was in him so amalgamated with the divine Being that it could not be said to possess any being or identity of its own. Thus the Monophysite conception of Christ's person settled into that of a Theandric, or composite nature, analogous to that composite action of his person which later divines have called a Theandric operation ($\Im\varepsilon\alpha\nu\delta\rho\iota\kappa\dot{\eta}$ $\dot{\varepsilon}\nu\dot{\varepsilon}\rho\gamma\varepsilon\iota\alpha$). Yet belief in such a composite nature is inconsistent with the Nicene Creed, which asserts that Jesus Christ is 'of one substance with the Father,' and since the Father is not of such a composite nature, to declare the Son to be so is to declare him to be of a different substance from him." Thus the intellectual form which Severus gave to Monophysitism cannot escape from the charge of heresy any more than that earlier form of opinion which was condemned at Chalcedon. The instability of opinion, when disassociated from the safeguard of the Nicene Creed, was also strikingly illustrated in the case of this later monophysite school as it had been in the earlier. Severus himself "held views respecting the soul of the united natures of Christ which were not logically consistent with the theology respecting their oneness, and thus it was only one step forward for Themistius, his deacon, to invent the tenet of the Agnoëtæ, that the human soul of Christ was like ours in everything, even in the want of omniscience or ignorance." When, again, Severus maintained that the divine and the human wills in the united natures were also so united that there could be no volition of the one nature one way and of the other nature in the other direction, he was preparing the way for that development of his opinion which was made by the Monothelites (q. v.), who maintained that "there was only one will in Christ, as well as only one nature." After the death of Severus, his followers divided—the men of wealth and the clergy choosing as successor to Timothy a certain Theodosius, and the monks and lower classes choosing Gaianus, the leader of the Aphthartodocetæ, whose party took the name of the Gaianites [see GAIANITÆ]; the latter, viewing the body of Christ as created ($\kappa\tau\iota\sigma\tau\acute{o}\nu$), were also called Ktistolatræ (comp. Dorner, ii, 159 sq.; and Ebrard, Kirchen- u. Dogmengesch. i, 268 sq.). This division, and the energy of the emperor Justinian in supporting the orthodox cause, finally led to a revival of the orthodox patriarchate in the person of Paul (A.D. 539), and for a hundred years there were two lines in the patriarchate —one monophysite, the other orthodox. Many other sects arose also, such as the Tritheists, the Philoponists, the Conists, the Damianists. Indeed, the 6th century was an age of as great turbulence in the Church on account of monophysitism as any that preceded. Justinian was even moved to call a council, which, convening at Constantinople in A.D. 553, constituted the fifth œcumenical council, the result of whose deliberations was a partial victory for the Alexandrian monophysite doctrine, so far as it could be reconciled with the definitions of Chalcedon. But, notwithstanding the concessions of the fifth œcumenical council, the Monophysites remained separated from the orthodox Church, refusing to acknowledge in any manner the dyophysite Council of Chalcedon. Another effort of Justinian to gain them, by sanctioning the Aphthar-

todocetic doctrine of the incorruptibleness of Christ's body (564), threatened to involve the Church in fresh troubles; but his death soon afterwards, in 565, put an end to these fruitless and despotic plans of union. His successor, Justin II, in 565 issued an edict of toleration, which exhorted all Christians to glorify the Lord, without contending about persons and syllables. Since that time the history of the Monophysites has been distinct from that of the Catholic Church. A numerous body of Monophysites of Alexandria seceded from the communion of the patriarch of that city appointed by the emperor, and chose another spiritual chief; and thus they continue to the present day, under the name of Copts. The Ethiopian or Abyssinian Church was always in connection with them. The Christians in Armenia and Georgia, among whom also monophysitism had early gained acceptance, openly declared themselves in favor of this doctrine; and thus the Armenian and Georgian churches continue at this time, separated from the other monophysite churches merely by peculiar customs. In Syria and Mesopotamia the Monophysites had nearly become extinct, in consequence of persecution and the want of ministers, when Jacob Baradæus, an obscure monk, was the instrument of reviving them: after him the Syrian Monophysites are called Jacobites (q. v.). An attempt to reconcile the Monophysites with the orthodox party in the 7th century led to a modified form of the doctrine, and a new sect, the Monothelites, who attempted to compromise between the two factions by the hypothesis that after the union of the divine and human natures in Christ, though there continued to be two distinct natures, yet there was but one will. The only effect of this was to increase the controversy. See MONOTHELITES. Monophysitism still continued to be held in some parts of the East, and even by the Maronites (q. v.) until their final reconciliation with the Church of Rome in 1182, when it was renounced by them. The doctrine that Jesus Christ possesses only one simple nature, being not truly man, but the divine Spirit in a human body, has recently been revived by Henry Ward Beecher in his Life of Christ, and is also maintained by the Swedenborgians. See NEW JERUSALEM CHURCH. The union of the divine and human natures in Christ is maintained by Dr. Hovey (God With Us). See the Acta, in Mansi, vol. vii-ix; Mai, Scriptorum veterum nova collectio e Vaticanis codicibus edita (vol. vii); Gieseler, Commentat. qua Monophysitarum veterum variæ de Christi persona opiniones inprimis ex ipsorum effatis recens editis, illustrantur (1835-1838); Assemani, De Monophys. (in Bibl. Or. vol. ii); Le Quien, Oriens Christianus in IV patriarchatus digestus (Par. 1740); Renaudot, Hist. Patriarcharum Alex. Jacobitarum (Par. 1743); Makrizii Hist. Coptorum Christ., Arab. et Lat. ed. Wetzer (Solisbaci, 1828); Walch, Ketzerhistorie, vol. vi, vii, viii); Baur, Trinitätslehre, ii. 37-96; Dorner, Lehre v. d. Person Christi (2d ed.), vol. ii, pt. i; Hefele, Conciliengeschichte, ii, 545 sq.; Gfrörer, Allg. Kirchengesch. vol. ii, pt. ii; Schröckh, Kirchengesch. xviii, 433-636; Neander, Ch. Hist. ii, 524 sq.; and his Dogma, i, 337; Ebrard, Handbuch der Kirchen- u. Dogmengesch. i, 263 sq.; Schaff, Ch. Hist. iii, 143-145; Neale, Hist. East. Church (patriarchate of Alexandria), i, 278 sq.; ii, 3 sq.; Stanley, Lect. East. Ch. p. 92 sq.; Hagenbach, Hist. Doctrines, i, 277 sq.; Milman, Hist. Latin Christianity, p. 312 sq.; Princeton Review, xxxviii, 567 sq.; Princeton Repository, (January, 1867), art. iii. Compare also Cureton's edition of the Eccles. Hist. of John, Bishop of Ephesus (Oxf. 1853), pt. iii. See CHRISTOLOGY; INCARNATION.

Monotheism (from $\mu\acute{o}\nu o\varsigma$, one, and $\Im\varepsilon\acute{o}\varsigma$, God) is the belief in and worship of one only God, in opposition to polytheism, which acknowledges a plurality of gods. All the different mythologies have, among the host of gods with which they people heaven and earth, some superior or supreme deity, more or less defined, but in every case distinguished above the others; and in the history of all the different nations where polytheism has obtained we may trace a period when the idea of one God was more or less prevalent. The most ancient traditions concur with the testimony of sacred Scripture in representing this as the primary and uncorrupted religion of mankind. M. Rénan, in his *Histoire Générale et Système comparé des Langues Sémitiques* (Par. 1858, 2d ed.), and *Nouvelles Considérations sur le caractère général des Peuples Sémitiques et en particulier sur leur tendance au Monothéisme* (Par. 1859), takes the ground that the Shemitic nations of the world are the propagators of the doctrine of the unity of God — indeed, that "of all the races of mankind, the Shemitic race alone was endowed with the instinct of monotheism . . . a *religious instinct* analogous to the instinct which led each race to the formation of its own language" (p. 73). Max Müller, however, takes exception to this position, and insists upon it that the primitive intuition of God was in itself neither monotheistic nor polytheistic, but consisted solely in that simplest article of faith — that *God is God*. "This must have been the faith of the ancestors of mankind previously to any division of race or confusion of tongues. . . . It is too often forgotten by those who believe that a polytheistic worship was the most natural unfolding of religious life, that polytheism must everywhere have been preceded by a more or less conscious theism. In no language does the plural exist before the singular. No human mind could have conceived the idea of gods without having previously conceived the idea of a god. . . . There are, however, in reality two kinds of oneness which, when we enter into metaphysical discussions, must be carefully distinguished, and which for practical purposes are well kept separate by the definite and indefinite articles. . . . If an expression had been given to that primitive intuition of the Deity, which is the mainspring of all later religion, it would have been, 'There is a God,' but not yet 'There is but one God.' The latter form of faith, the belief in one God, is properly called monotheism, whereas the term *henotheism* would best express the faith in a single God" (*Chips*, i, 348–50). This kind of monotheism, according to Müller, "forms the birthright of every human being. . . . In some form or other, the feeling of dependence on a higher power breaks through in all the religions of the world, and explains to us the meaning of St. Paul, 'that God, though in times past he suffered all nations to walk in their own ways, nevertheless left not himself without witness, in that he did good, and gave us rain from heaven and fruitful seasons, filling our hearts with food and gladness.' This primitive intuition of God, and this ineradicable feeling of dependence on God, could only have been the result of a primitive revelation, in the truest sense of that word" (p. 346–8, see also p. 363, 374; comp. Gould, *Origin of Religious Belief*, i, 267–277). In this respect Judaism, Christianity, and Mohammedanism agree.

"Two facts," says Gould, "arrest our attention . . . the prevalence of monotheism, and the tendency of civilization towards it. Monotheism is at present the creed of a large section of the human race. The Christian, the Jew, and the Mohammedan hold the unity of the great cause with varying distinctness, according to their powers of abstraction" (*Origin of Religious Belief*, i, 238). But in regard to the Trinity they seriously differ, the Mohammedan and the Jew rejecting with vehemence the least approach to a trinitarian conception of the Deity. "The monotheism of the Mohammedan," says J. F. Clarke, "is that which makes of God pure will; that is, which exaggerates personality (since personality is in will), making the divine One an infinite Free Will or an infinite I. But will divorced from reason and love is wilfulness, or a purely arbitrary will. The monotheism of the Jews differed from this in that it combined with the idea of will the idea of justice. God not only does what

he chooses, but he chooses to do only what is right. Righteousness is an attribute of God, with which the Jewish books are saturated. Both of these systems leave God outside of the world; *above* all as its Creator and Ruler, *above* all as its Judge; but not *through* all and *in* all. The idea of an infinite love must be added and made supreme, in order to give us a Being who is not only above all, but also through all and in all. This is the Christian monotheism. . . . Mohammed teaches a God above us; Moses teaches a God above us, and yet with us; Jesus teaches God above us, God with us, and God in us" (*Ten Great Religions*, p. 481–83). See *Jahrb. deutsch. Theol.* (1860), iv, 669; *Brit. Quar. Rev.* (April, 1873), art. ii; *Lond. Quar. Rev.* vol. cxxvii. See also UNITY OF GOD.

Gould holds to a gradual development of monotheism. Recognising a Jewish, Mohammedan, and Christian monotheism, he traces first the development of the Jewish, which, under Moses, received "its final and complete form as a system, and embraced four leading doctrines: (1) the absolute being of God; (2) the absolute unity of his being; (3) the difference in kind of matter from God; (4) the subjection of matter to God" (i, 262; comp. MOSAISM). The Mohammedan's monotheism he recognises as "the offspring of Jewish monotheism." Yet has the pure deism proved inferior to the Jewish, for "as a working system it annihilates morality. Before the almighty power of God the creature is nothing. Man, ox, ass, are on a level; and if the notion be humbling to him, he may recover a little self-respect when he remembers that the archangels are in no better plight. Between man and God is a profound and wide abyss, and no bridge spans it. Too far above man to sympathize in any way with him, God can yet crush him with his jealousy. If man attempt to attribute to himself anything that is of God, and appear to encroach on his all-engrossing majesty by ever so little, the wrath of God is kindled and man is levelled with the dust" (i, 265). "It is," says Palgrave, "his singular satisfaction to let created beings continually feel that they are nothing else than his slaves, tools, and contemptible tools also, that thus they may the better acknowledge his superiority, and know his power to be above their power, his cunning above their cunning, his will above their will, his pride above their pride; or, rather, that there is no power, cunning, will, or pride save his own. But he himself, in his inaccessible height, neither loving aught save his own and self-measured decree, without son, companion, or counsellor, is no less barren for himself than for his creatures, and his own barrenness and lone egoism in himself is the cause and rule of his indifferent and unregarding despotism around" (*Aralia*, i, 366). See POLYTHEISM.

Christian monotheism Gould excludes from comparison with the Jewish and Mohammedan, because "its doctrines of the Trinity and the incarnation remove it from the class to which Mosaism and Islamism . . . belong" (i, 277). See, however, GOD; TRINITY. See besides Gould, Clarke, Max Müller, and Rénan; Hagenbach, *Hist. of Doctrines*, i, 330; Christlieb, *Modern Doubt and Christian Belief* (N. Y. 1875, 8vo), lect. iii and iv; Lewes, *Hist. Philos.* vol. ii (see Index); Liddon, *Divinity of Christ*, p. 67, 76, 95, 270, 307; and the literature appended to the article THEISM.

Monothelism (from μόνος, *single*, and Θέλημα, *will*), the doctrine of a Christian sect, maintains that Christ, though possessed of two natures, was yet subject only to *one* will; the human will being merged in the divine, or absorbed by it. The doctrine was given shape in an attempt on the part of the emperor Heraclius to unite the different factions of the Catholic Church, and to bring back to the fold the *Eutychians* and the *Monophysites*. There was near the beginning of the 7th century much controversy in the Eastern Church respecting the two wills in Christ, kindred to that concerning his nature. The Monophysites were at that time a most powerful sect, and the movement, especially in Egypt, threatened to assume a political character. In this difficulty the emperor Heraclius, hoping to reconcile the two parties, adopted the doctrine that there was in Jesus the Christ, after the union of the two natures, only *one* divine-human energy and *one* will ($\mu \acute{o} \nu o \nu$ $\vartheta \acute{e} \lambda \eta \mu a$); and when, in the course of a campaign against Persia, Heraclius passed through Armenia and Syria, he came to an understanding with the Monophysite leaders of the Severians and Jacobites, and induced Sergius (q. v.), the orthodox patriarch of Constantinople, to give his assent to the doctrine of $\check{e} \nu$ $\vartheta \acute{e} \lambda \eta \mu a$ $\kappa a \grave{\iota}$ $\mu \acute{\iota} a$ $\grave{e} \nu \acute{e} \rho \gamma \epsilon \iota a$, or of an $\grave{e} \nu \acute{e} \rho \gamma \epsilon \iota a$ $\vartheta \epsilon a \nu \delta \rho \iota \kappa \acute{\eta}$. Monothelism, it will be perceived, then, is nothing more nor less than a modification of Eutychianism (q. v.). It consisted in maintaining that, although Christ has two natures, yet these natures possessed or are acted on by but a single will, the divine will superseding or supplying the place of a human will. It will be observed also that in this way the controversy was removed from the province of pure metaphysics into the moral and practical sphere; and although the assertion of an independent nature without independent action was a *contradictio in adjecto*, it was yet hoped that the doctrine might be adopted by the Monophysites. The author of this doctrine was probably Sergius himself; he was, at least, its most active propagandist. The progress of the doctrine was materially forwarded by the relation which, at the instance of Sergius, and under his representations, pope Honorius (q. v.) was induced to maintain regarding the question. The Monophysite Cyrus, whom the emperor had promoted from the episcopate of Phasis to the patriarchate of Alexandria, promptly called a synod (A.D. 633), which by the seventh canon of its decrees solemnly approved of the monothelite doctrine (in the words $\tau \grave{o} \nu$ $a \grave{v} \tau \grave{o} \nu$ $\check{e} \nu a$ $X \rho \iota \sigma \tau \grave{o} \nu$ $\kappa a \grave{\iota}$ $v \grave{\iota} \grave{o} \nu$ $\grave{e} \nu \epsilon \rho \gamma o \tilde{v} \nu \tau a$ $\tau \grave{a}$ $\vartheta \epsilon o \pi \rho \epsilon \pi \tilde{\eta}$ $\kappa a \grave{\iota}$ $\grave{a} \nu \vartheta \rho \acute{\omega} \pi \iota \nu a$ $\mu \iota \tilde{a}$ $\vartheta \epsilon a \nu \delta \rho \iota \kappa \tilde{\eta}$ $\grave{e} \nu \epsilon \rho \gamma \epsilon \acute{\iota} a$, Mansi, *Concil.* xi, 565), thereby hoping to effect permanently a union between the different parties (Mansi, *Concil.* xi, 564 sq.; *Letters of Cyrus*, ibid. 561). As Cyrus was the principal mover in this attempt, he has been generally esteemed the founder of the Monothelites. The work of the council certainly proved salutary, at least for a time. By bringing the doctrine of the Council of Chalcedon nearer to the Eutychian system, numbers of the Eutychians, who were dispersed throughout Egypt, Armenia, and other remote provinces, returned to the bosom of the Church. The only dissenting leader proved a certain Sophronius, a monk of Palestine, who from the first opposed the decree of the Alexandrian Synod with violence, and when elevated to the vacant patriarchate of Jerusalem (635) was thus afforded ecclesiastical position and power, and now came forward to contest the question, notwithstanding that the patriarch of Constantinople approved of the Alexandrian decision, and the pope at Rome offered no remonstrance. Sophronius (q. v.) endeavored to show that this doctrine was inadmissible, since the doctrine of two natures set forth by the Synod of Chalcedon (q. v.) necessarily implied that of two wills (see *Sophronii Epistola Synodica*, which is given in Mansi, xi, 461). He finally summoned a council, and condemned monothelism as a branch of the Eutychian heresy. In order to terminate, if possible, the commotions to which this division was giving rise, the emperor Heraclius in 638 issued an edict, $\check{E} \kappa \vartheta \epsilon \sigma \iota \varsigma$ (so named because it contained an exposition of the faith), in which he confirmed the agreement made by the patriarchs for the preservation of ecclesiastical union, and in which all controversies upon the question whether in Christ there was a double operation were prohibited, though the doctrine of a unity of will was inculcated. A considerable number of the Eastern bishops declared their assent to the *Ecthesis*, and above all Pyrrhus, who

succeeded Sergius in the see of Constantinople. A similar acceptance was obtained from the metropolis of the Eastern Church; but at Rome the *Ecthesis* was differently received. John IV assembled a council, in which that exposition was condemned. See ECTHESIS. Neither was the monothelite system maintained in the Eastern Church any longer than during the life of Heraclius. In 648 the emperor Constans II issued the $T \acute{v} \pi o \varsigma$, i. e. an edict, by which the *Ecthesis* was suppressed, and the contending parties were prohibited from resuming their discussions on the doctrine in question (see Mansi, x, 992, 1029 sq.; Neander, *Church Hist.* [Torrey] iii, 186–192). Pope Honorius, as we have seen, appeared in favor of the union, and was probably himself inclined to monophysitism; but his successors, Severinus and John IV, thought and felt differently. The latter condemned the doctrine of the Monothelites, and Theodore excommunicated Paul, patriarch of Constantinople, till the doctrine of *two* wills and *two* energies was at last adopted at the first synod of the Lateran, held under Martin I, bishop of Rome, in the year 649 (see Mansi, x, 863 sq.). "Si quis secundum scelerosos hæreticos cum una voluntate et una operatione, quæ ab hæreticis impiis confitetur, et duas voluntates, pariterque et operationes, hoc est, divinam et humanam, quæ in ipso Christo Deo in unitate salvantur, et a sanctis patribus orthodoxe in ipso prædicantur, denegat et respuit, condemnatus sit" (see Gieseler, c. 1, § 128, note 11; Münscher v. Colla, ii, 78 sq.). The emperor was so indignant at this daring of Martin that he had him secured, carried to Constantinople, there treated for a time as a criminal, and then banished him to the Crimea, where he died in 655, to be numbered among the martyrs of the Western and the confessors of the Eastern Church. His great intellectual supporter at the council had been a Greek abbot named Maximus, and he, too, underwent a long persecution, being scourged, having his tongue cut out, and at last dying a death little short of martyrdom just as he had reached his place of exile, A.D. 662. The final and authoritative condemnation of the monothelite dogma took place at the sixth general council, held at Constantinople in the year 680, where it was decided that there are in Christ "two natural wills and two natural operations, without division, without conversion or change, with nothing like antagonism, and nothing like confusion, but at the same time the human will of Christ could not come into collision with his divine will, but is in all things subject to it." An anathema was also pronounced on Theodore, Sergius, Honorius, and all who had maintained the heresy, this anathema being confirmed by Leo II, who wrote to the emperor respecting his own predecessor in the see of Rome: "Anathematizamus . . . necnon et Honorium qui hanc apostolicam ecclesiam non apostolicæ traditionis doctrina lustravit, sed profana proditione immaculatam subvertere conatus est" (Mansi, *Concil.* xi, 631–637, 731). This anathema of pope Honorius was repeated by his successors for three centuries. See HONORIUS; INFALLIBILITY. The council (also called the First Trullan) was summoned by Constantinus Pogonatus. The decision of the synod was based upon the epistle of Agatho, the Roman bishop, which was itself founded upon the canons of the above-mentioned Lateran synod (Agathonis *Ep. ad Imperatores*, in Mansi, xi, 233 sq.). Baur says of this controversy (*Dogmengesch.* p. 211): "Its elements on the side of the Monothelites were the unity of the person or subject, from whose one will (the divine will of the incarnate Logos) all must proceed, since two wills also presuppose two personal subjects (the chief argument of bishop Theodore of Cara, in Mansi, xi, 567); on the side of the Dyothelites, the point was the fact of two natures, since two natures cannot be conceived without two natural wills, and two natural modes of operation. How far now two wills can be without two persons willing was the point from which they slipped away by mere supposition." See Combefis, *Hist. hær. Monothelit.* (Paris, 1648); Hagenbach, *Hist. of Doctrines*, i, 229, 241, 282; Schaff, *Church Hist.* iii, 752, 782; Neander, *Church Hist.* iii, 186 sq.; Gieseler, *Church Hist.* c. i, § 128; Baur, *Dogmengesch.* i, 211; and his *Trinitätslehre*, vol. ii; Ebrard, *Kirchen- u. Dogmengesch.* i, 279 sq.; Trench, *Hulsean Lect.* p. 200; Gregory, *Hist. of the Christ. Church*, i, 379; Dorner, *Doct. of the Person of Christ*, vol. ii, pt. i; Neale, *Hist. East. Church* (patriarchate of Alexandria), ii, 60 sq., 76 sq.; Stanley, *East. Church*, p. 94, 110; Knapp, *Christian Theology*, p. 366; Milman, *Hist. of Latin Christianity*, ii, 266 sq.; Walch, *Ketzerhistorie*, ix, 3–666; Gfrörer, *Kirchengesch.* vol. iii, pt. i, p. 36 sq.; Döllinger, *Kirchengesch.* i, 170 sq.; Schröckh, *Kirchengesch.* xx, 386 sq.; *Westminster Rev.* April, 1871, p. 247. See MONOPHYSITES. (J. H. W.)

Monothelites (Μονοϑελῆται), an ancient heretical sect which is first spoken of in the writings of St. John of Damascus, in the middle of the 8th century, but which may be traced back to Severus, the deposed patriarch of Antioch, who flourished in the first half of the 7th century. He founded *Monophysitism* (q. v.). In some fragments of his writings which have come down to us, Severus remarks that Christ's words, "Not my will, but thine, be done" (Luke xxii, 42), do not prove the existence of a will distinct from the divine will, nor that there was any struggle or resistance on the part of the Saviour's soul, as if he had a human fear of death or a human unwillingness to die; but that the words are so set down by way of accommodation, and for Christian instruction (Mai, *Coll. Nov.* vii, 288). The distinct formulation of monothelism is attributed, however, to Theodore, bishop of Cara, in Arabia. Although not a Monophysite, Theodore taught that all the acts of Christ proceeded from one principle, originating in the Word, and operating through the human soul and body. Hence, though the Logos and the manhood were distinct natures, they were both acted upon by one and the same ἐνέργεια; and there being one activity, there was one will, by which it was moved, that will being divine. (Αὐτοῦ γὰρ τὸ ϑέλημα ἕν ἐστι, καὶ τοῦτο ϑεϊκόν; Mansi, *Concil.* xi, 568.) Athanasius, the Monophysite patriarch of Antioch, was a zealous convert to the opinion of Theodore, and laid it before the emperor Heraclius as offering a basis for such a compromise between his sect and the Church as might enable them to reunite in one communion. The emperor most enthusiastically espoused the plan, and thus became the promoter of the monothelite dogma, and really the founder of the Monothelites. This emperor, Heraclius I, was born about A.D. 575, and was a son of Heraclius, governor of Africa. By the violent death of the tyrant Phocas in 610, Heraclius, who had served in the army with credit, obtained the imperial power, and soon afterwards married Eudoxia. In the early part of his reign the empire was ravaged by pestilence and the barbarian armies of Chosroes, king of Persia. In 622 he led an army against Persia, defeated Chosroes at Tauris, and fought several successful campaigns, in which he displayed great military talents and personal courage. In the course of his campaigns against Persia he passed through Armenia and Syria, and came to a peaceful understanding with the Monophysite leaders of the Severians and the Jacobites, who at this time had become a powerful and dangerous political party. Hoping to reconcile them, he, in connection with Sergius, patriarch of Constantinople, proposed to them the curious doctrine of monothelism, which satisfied the Monophysites, without apparently disturbing the decision of the Council of Chalcedon. Having made peace with Persia in 628, he returned to Constantinople, and abandoned himself to inglorious ease, sensual vices, and the subtleties of monothelism, of which he was the chief supporter, ignoring the victorious progress of the Mussulman arms, until the very

VI.—17

subversion of his empire was threatened. In 639, finally, he made an energetic attempt to establish monothelism by issuing his Ἔκϑησις, with what result may be seen in the article MONOTHELISM. Heraclius died in 641. His character is a puzzle, and presents surprising contradictions. Protected and nurtured by imperial approbation, the Monothelites became a very considerable sect. The decisions of the sixth Council of Constantinople determined that their opinions were not consistent with the purity of the Christian faith, and monothelism was formally condemned; and though its advocates were sometimes the objects of royal favor, yet they were in general condemned and depressed. In 711, when Philippicus Bardanes was Greek emperor, they became once more influential and powerful. He convened a new council at Constantinople, which reversed the decisions of the sixth council, and adopted monothelism as an orthodox doctrine. Some few bishops resisted, but were driven from the council. Two years later Anastasius II reinstituted dyothelism, and the same bishops who had two years before vetoed dyothelism now changed their mind, and adopted it as the only true exposition of faith! Thus persecuted, the Monothelites retired to the neighborhood of Mount Lebanon. After the Crusades (1291), and especially after 1596, they began to gradually go over to the Roman Church, although retaining the communion under both kinds, their Syriac missal, the marriage of priests, and their traditional fast-days, with some saints of their own, especially St. Maron. See MARONITES. The Monothelites have often been bitterly persecuted, but our concern for the cruelties they suffered cannot but be lessened by the consideration of the persecutions which in the day of their power they were tempted to commit against their orthodox brethren. See, besides the references in the article MONOTHELISM, Blunt, *Dict. of Heresies and Sects*, s. v.; Schaff, *Church Hist.* iii, 752 sq.; Gregory, *Hist. of the Christ. Church*, i, 397; Mosheim, *Ecclesiastical History*, ii, 36; Robinson, *Palestine*, iii, 744; Walch, *Geschichte der Ketzereien*, ix, 475; Baumgarten, *Geschichte der Religionspartheien*, p. 617.

Monrad, DITLER GOTHARD, a Danish prelate of note, was born at Copenhagen Nov. 24, 1811. In 1836 he passed his theological examinations, and was two years later honored by the title of D.D. In 1846 he was called to the pastorate of Vester Ulsler, in the diocese of Laaland. Having taken a prominent position in the national party, he was made chaplain March 24, 1848, but occupied the position only until the following November, when he retired, together with most of his colleagues. He continued to take an active part in political affairs until 1850, when he was created bishop of Laaland-Falster, and later figured as a cabinet officer until 1864. After the unsuccessful termination of the war against Prussia he migrated to New Zealand, where he died in 1874. He published valuable papers on the *Organization of Schools in many large Protestant Cities* (1844), besides which he issued mainly "Political Pamphlets" (1839–42). See Vapereau, *Dictionnaire Universel des Contemporains*, s. v.

Monro, ALEXANDER, D.D., an English prelate, was born in 1648, in the County of Ross. After having taught philosophy in the University of Aberdeen, he was principal of that of Edinburgh (1686), and had just been appointed bishop of the Orkney Islands when, refusing to take the oath of allegiance to William III, he lost that dignity. He was appointed in 1688 bishop of Argyle, but it is doubtful whether he ever were instituted. He died in 1713. Bishop Monro is the author of *XII Sermons* (London, 1673, 8vo):—*Letter to Sir Robert Howard*, occasioned by the *Twofold Vindication of Archbishop Tillotson* (1696):—*Inquiry into the New Opinions of the Presbyterians*, etc. (1696, 8vo). He was also the author of one of the four letters published as *An Account of the Present Persecution of the Church of*

Scotland (1690, 4to, 68 pages). See Allibone, *Dict. of Brit. and Amer. Authors*, vol. ii, s. v.

Monroe, Andrew, a minister of the Methodist Episcopal Church, South, called the patriarch of Missouri Methodism, was born in Hampshire County, Va., Oct. 29, 1792; was converted and joined the Church when but a youth. In March, 1815, he was licensed to preach, and sent to labor on the Fairfield Circuit. In the following year he was admitted on trial to the Ohio Conference. In 1824 he was transferred to Missouri, and stationed at St. Louis; he returned the next year, and was then placed over the St. Louis District, which embraced the entire state. He was a member of eleven General Conferences, and took an active part in the establishment of the Church, South. He died in Mexico, Mo., Nov. 18, 1871. His several appointments were: 1816, Jefferson Circuit; 1817, Franklin Circuit; 1818, Fountain Head Circuit; 1819, Bowling Green. In the Kentucky Conference: 1820, Hopkinsville; 1821 and 1822, Maysville; 1823, presiding elder of Augusta District. In the Missouri Conference: 1824 and 1825, St. Louis Station; 1826 and 1827, presiding elder of Missouri District; 1828 and 1829, St. Louis Station; 1830, St. Louis District; 1831, left, by request, without an appointment; 1832 to 1835, presiding elder of St. Louis District; 1836 and 1837, Missouri District; 1838, Columbia District; 1839 and 1840, agent of St. Charles College; 1841 and 1842, St. Charles Station, and agent of the college; 1843, presiding elder of St. Charles District; 1844 and 1845, presiding elder of St. Charles District, and agent of the college; 1846 to 1849, presiding elder of Columbia District; 1850 and 1851, Fayette Circuit; 1852 and 1853, presiding elder of Hannibal District; 1854, transferred to the St. Louis Conference, and appointed superintendent of Kansas Mission District; 1855, transferred back to the Missouri Conference, and appointed presiding elder of Fayette District; 1856 to 1859, presiding elder of St. Charles District; 1860, agent of Central College; 1861 and 1862, Fayette Circuit; 1863 and 1864, Brunswick District; 1865, Fayette District; 1866 and 1867, Conference missionary; 1869 to 1870, St. Charles District; 1871, Conference missionary. It is not within the scope of this sketch to enter into any exhaustive analysis of a life so protracted, aims so single and sublime, purposes so pertinaciously adhered to through a long, eventful course. His name is historic: scarcely a book of Methodist annals has appeared within half a century past that does not contain it. See McFerrin, *Hist. of Meth. in Tenn.* ii, 473; *Minutes of Conference of Meth. Episc. Ch., South* (1872); Elliott, *Hist. of the Meth. Episc. Ch. in the South-west*, p. 74 and sq.

Monroe, Jonathan, an American Methodist minister, was born in Annapolis, Md., June 11, 1801; joined the Baltimore Conference, and was appointed to Alleghany Circuit in 1825; in 1826, to Concord; in 1827 he was ordained deacon by bishop Soulé, and appointed to Shamoken; in 1828, to Lewistown; in 1829 he was ordained elder by bishop M'Kendree, and appointed to Concord; in 1830, to Gettysburg; in 1831, to Shrewsbury; in 1833, to Patapsco; in 1835, to Calvert; in 1837, to Lewistown; in 1839, to Warrior's Mark; in 1841, to Huntingdon; in 1843, to Bedford; in 1845, to Westminster; in 1847, to Liberty; in 1849, to Montgomery; in 1850, to Gettysburg; in 1852, to Mechanicsburg; in 1854, to Mercersburg; in 1856, to East Hartford; in 1858, to Great Falls; in 1859, to Hereford; in 1861, to Westminster; in 1863, to Emmitsburg; and in 1864 he became supernumerary, and retired to Westminster, Carroll County, Md., where he died, Dec. 4, 1869. His Christian virtues, uniform piety, and devotion to his calling demonstrated the power of divine grace in his life, and endeared him to all who knew him. See *Minutes of Baltimore Conference for* 1870.

Monroe, Samuel Yorke, D.D., an eminent minister of the Methodist Episcopal Church, was born at Mount Holly, New Jersey, July 1, 1816. He enjoyed the advantages of a thorough English training, and after his conversion, which occurred in 1833, decided to devote himself to the work of the Christian ministry. He labored for several years as a local preacher; was admitted on trial into the New Jersey Conference in 1843, and quickly rose to distinction among his brethren. His first appointment does not appear in the minutes. In 1844 he travelled the Sweedsborough Circuit. At the Conference held in Mount Holly in 1845 he was admitted into full connection, and stationed at Salem, N. J. He was returned to the same appointment in 1846. In 1847–48 he preached in Paterson; in 1849–50, in Newark; in 1851, at Princeton. He was next successively stationed at Newark, New Brunswick, Camden, Trenton, and Trinity Church, Newark (located in Newark Conference, to which he had been transferred). He served as presiding elder several years, first in the Bridgeton District, after he had preached at Camden; and in the Camden District after he had labored in Trenton. He was a member of the General Conference in 1856, 1860, and 1864, at which last time he was prominently named for the episcopacy. He was by this body then elected a member of the General Missionary Committee, and shortly afterwards was appointed by the bishops of the Church as recording secretary of the newly organized society for "Church extension." Upon this work he entered with his usual vigor and zeal, and was meeting with success beyond the highest expectation of the friends of the enterprise. On Sunday, the 27th of January, 1867, he had preached in St. Paul's Methodist Episcopal Church in New York City, for the cause of "Church extension," and was on his way from Camden, New Jersey, to New York, with the intention of occupying one of the city pulpits for the same object, when he was lost overboard a train, no one has ever found how, and was killed in the fall, February 9, 1867, as was declared by the verdict of a coroner's jury. Few men labored more earnestly for the Church than did Dr. Monroe. After his appointment to the secretaryship, besides attending to an extensive correspondence, he visited and addressed some fifty Conferences upon the subject of "Church extension;" preached once or twice nearly every Sabbath; organized his work almost over the whole Church; and raised and disbursed about $60,000 during the first year of the society's existence. During this period his labors were undoubtedly excessive; and, in the opinion of those who had the best opportunity for knowing, were beginning sensibly to impair his health and vigor. "Dr. Monroe," say the *Newark Conference Minutes* of 1867, "was in many respects a remarkable man. As a Christian, he was conscientious, without being morbidly sensitive; fervent in spirit, without being boisterous or fanatical; faithful, without being severe or censorious; and spiritual and pure in heart, without a profession of extraordinary religious attainments. . . . His success in winning souls to Christ proved that wherever he labored God was with him. As a preacher he was able, evangelical, and edifying; and as a pastor diligent, sympathetic, and faithful. But that which distinguished him more than anything else was his remarkably clear perception of the relations of things, his rapid mental comparisons and inductions, and his consequent seemingly intuitive and almost infallible judgment. In this respect he had probably no superiors, if, indeed, he had many equals, in our Church. Remarkably free from prejudice and selfishness, and ever cool and conscientious, and with a mind that could grasp a question, view it in all its relations, and at once deduce the appropriate conclusion, he was an eminently wise and safe counsellor in everything pertaining to the kingdom of God." The *N. Y. Methodist* (February 16, 1867), commenting on his death, says: "Dr. Monroe was one of the leading representatives of the American Methodist Church. . . . As secretary of the Church Extension Society, he displayed his characteristic good sense, rare executive ability, laboriousness, and eminent pulpit power. In all these elements of character he excelled." See also *Ladies' Repository*, March, 1868; Appleton's *Annual*, 1867; *N. Y. Christian Advocate*, February 8, 1872 (*MS. Sermons of the late Dr. Monroe*). (J. H. W.)

Monroe, William, a minister of the Methodist Episcopal Church, was born in Alleghany County, Ind., Sept. 8, 1783. He was converted when but a youth; was licensed to preach in 1809, and entered the Baltimore Conference in 1810. He was ordained deacon by bishop M'Kendree, and elder by bishop Asbury. His active ministerial life extended over a period of thirty-three years, during which time he labored on some of the most difficult circuits in the Baltimore Conference. Mr. Monroe was a man of Christian virtues and great piety, and his true devotion to Methodism has endeared him to the whole Church. His appointments were—Lyttleton Circuit, Huntington Circuit, Greenville Circuit, Randolph Circuit, Georgetown, D.C., Redstone Circuit, East Wheeling, Monongahela, Rockingham Circuit, Va.; Alleghany, Va.; Ebenezer, Washington, D.C.; Chambersburg; Winchester, Va.; Stafford, Va.; Rockingham, Va.; Staunton, Va.; Berkeley, Va.; Jefferson; Berkeley, Va.; South Branch; and Hillsborough. After this for two years (1837 and 1838) he was supernumerary. In 1839-40 he was stationed at Boonsborough, and in 1841 at Codorus Mission. In 1844 he was again supernumerary; in 1843-44, Mercersburg; and in 1845, Greencastle. This year closed his active service, and in 1846 he asked for and obtained a superannuated relation, which he sustained until removed to the Church triumphant. He died in Washington County, Md., May 29, 1871. See *General Minutes of the M.E. Church*, 1872, p. 17.

Monseigneur (*my lord*), a French title, once applied to saints, and subsequently to princes, nobles, certain high dignitaries of the Church, and other titled personages, is now only given to prelates. The Italian *monsignore* has a similar signification.

Monsignore. See MONSEIGNEUR.

Monster. See SEA-MONSTER.

Monstrance. See MONSTRANTIA.

Monstrantia (MONSTRUM, OSTENSORIUM) is a vessel used for the preserving of relics, and particularly for the consecrated host (*sanctissimum, venerabile, eucharistia*), and in which they are presented to the adoration of the people. When, in the 13th century, the doctrine of transubstantiation was established by the Church, the elevation of the host followed, as also its special exhibition, for instance, in the procession of Corpus-Christi Day (q. v.). For that purpose the host (q. v.) was placed on a curved surface (*lunula*), and introduced in a transparent vessel (*monstrantia, in qua sub vitro crystallino cruor inclusus* [Du Fresne, *Glossar.* s. h. v.]). This case (*phylacterium, arcula*) is enlarged by the addition of rays, forming an image of the sun, or the like, and provided with a stand. It is placed on the altar. Thus the monstrantia becomes a movable shrine for the sacrament (*tabernaculum gestatorium*), generally made of

Monstrance.

costly material, and richly decorated. "At first," says Walcott (*Sacred Archæology*, p. 390), "it took the shape of an ordinary reliquary, but at length was made like a tower of crystal, of cylindrical form, and mounted on a foot like that of a chalice, and covered by a spire-like canopy, with flying buttresses. Inside the cylinder was a crescent held by an angel, in which the host was set; in some cases the cylinder was replaced by a quarterfoil, or was surrounded by a foliage like a jesse-tree, and at a later date by the sun, a luminous disk, with rays alternately straight and wavy, set upon a stand. Upon the vessel itself the Doom was often represented, and relics were placed in it. The monstrance did not become common till the 15th, and is probably not earlier than the 14th century. It bore different forms: (1) a little tower, jewelled, and having apertures of glass or crystal; (2) the figure of a saint, or the Holy Lamb, with St. John the Baptist pointing to it; (3) a cross; (4) a crystal lantern, or tube, mounted on a pedestal of precious metal, and covered with a canopy in the 15th century; (5) a sun, with rays, containing in the centre a kind of pyx (this is found as early as the 16th century)." The ecclesiastical laws now regulate its construction. The statutes of the archbishopric of Prague of 1605, tit. xviii, command, for instance, "Monstrantia ad exponendam vel in processionibus deferendam hostiam magnam, si non ex auro, aut argento, saltem ex aurichalco bene aurato refulgeat, et velo vel peplo congruo ornata sit." The monstrantia is a sacred vessel, and not to be touched by an unconsecrated person; hence any one who stole it was to be burned to death. The high altar is always provided with a monstrantia, and often the side altars also. All evangelical churches have rejected the prayer *De venerabile* of the Romish Church, and Luther declared, "It is insulting and dishonoring to the holy sacrament to carry it about, and to make it an instrument of idle idolatry." See also Herzog, *Real-Encyklopädie*, ix, 757.

Montagioli, CASSIODORO, a learned Italian ecclesiastic, was born at Modena Feb. 5, 1698; entered the Benedictine Order in 1717, and successively filled several prominent offices in the order. He gave himself largely to the study of philosophy. His principal works are, *Esercizi di celesti affetti, tratti dal libro de' Salmi* (Rome, 1742) :—*Trattato practico della carita Cristiana in quanto è amor verso Dio* (Bologna, 1751, and Venice, 1761) : — *Enchiridio evangelico* (Mod. 1755) : — *Maniera facile di meditare con frutto le massime Cristiane* (Bologna, 1759, 2 vols.) : — *Detti pratiche e ricordi di S. Andrea Avellino* (Venice, 1771) :—*Parabole del figliuol di Dio* (Plaisance, 1772) :—*Il divino sermone nel monte* (Rome, 1779).

Montagnuoli, GIOVANNI DOMENICO, an Italian theologian, was born at Batignano (territory of Sienna) in the first half of the 17th century. As a Dominican monk, he was distinguished for his austere piety, as well as for his attachment to the doctrine of St. Thomas. He was the author of *Defensiones philosophicæ angelicæ Thomisticæ* (Venice, 1609, fol.). This work, enlarged and revised, appeared again under the same title at Naples in 1610). See Échard et Quétif, *Script. Ord. Prædicat.* ii, 337.

Montagu, WALTER, a Roman Catholic divine of note, was born at London in 1604. He was the son of Sir Henry Montagu, who afterwards became earl of Manchester. After being educated at Sidney College, Cambridge, he travelled abroad, and became a convert to Romanism, though opposed by his nearest friends. On returning to his native land, he attracted the attention and secured the favor of his queen, who appointed him her confessor. She also honored him by sending him on a confidential mission to Rome, where he met with a gracious reception by pope Urban VIII. The breaking out of the Civil War clouded his prosperity, and in 1643 he was imprisoned in the Tower, where he remained confined for several years. As soon as he was released he retired into France, where he became abbot of the Benedictine monastery at Nanteuil. He afterwards obtained the rich abbey of St. Martin's, near Pontoise, where he remained until the Restoration, when the queen-mother of England appointed him master of St. Catharine's Hospital, a position occupied by him till his death at Paris in 1677. As an author, the chief works of his pen are, *The Shepherd's Paradise*, a pastoral comedy possessing some merit, though ridiculed severely by Sir John Suckling in his "Sessions of the

Poets":—*Miscellanea Spiritualia*, published in two parts (1648–54), a series of religious essays or tracts:—a *Letter* from Paris to his father, in which he justifies the Church of Rome, and states his personal reasons for changing his belief. This letter was printed with lord Falkland's *Discourse on Infallibility* (1651). He also made an English translation of Bossuet's *Exposition of the Doctrines of the Catholic Church* (1672). (H. W. T.)

Montague, RICHARD, D.D. See MOUNTAGU.

Montaigne, MICHEL, *Seigneur de*, a distinguished French moralist, remarkable for his deep insight into the principles of our common nature, was born Feb. 28, 1533, and was a younger son of a nobleman, whose estate, from which the family name arose, was situated in the province of Perigord, near the river Dordogne. His father, an eccentric, blunt, feudal baron, placed him under the care of a German tutor who did not speak French, and the intercourse between tutor and pupil was carried on entirely in Latin; and even his parents made it a rule to address him in that language, of which they knew a sufficient number of words for common purposes. The attendants were enjoined to follow the same practice. "They all became Latinized," says Montaigne himself; "and even the villagers in the neighborhood learned words in that language, some of which took root in the country, and became of common use among the people." Thus, without the aid of scholastic teaching, Montaigne spoke Latin long before he could speak French, which he was afterwards obliged to learn like a foreign language. He studied Greek in the same manner, by way of pastime more than as a task. He was sent to the college of Guienne, at Bordeaux; and at the age of thirteen he completed his college education. He then studied law, and in 1554 he was made "conseiller," or judge, in the Parliament of Bordeaux. He repaired several times to court, and enjoyed the favor of Henri II, by whom, or, as some say, by Charles IX, he was made a gentleman of the king's chamber and a knight of the Order of St. Michael. When he was thirty-three years of age Montaigne married, to please his friends rather, as he says, than himself, for he was not inclined to a married life. He, however, always lived on good terms with his wife, by whom he had a daughter. He managed his own estate, on which he generally resided, and from which he derived an income of about 6000 livres. In 1569 Montaigne translated into French a Latin work of Raymond de Sebonde or Sebon, a Spanish divine, on *Natural Theology*, at the request of his then recently deceased father, who had feared for his son's apostasy to Protestantism (comp. Fisher, *Hist. Ref.* p. 6, note 2). France was at that time desolated by civil and religious war, and Montaigne, disapproving of the conduct of the court towards the Protestants, and yet being by education a Roman Catholic, and by principle and disposition loyal to the king, was glad to live in retirement, and take no part in public affairs except by exhorting both parties to moderation and mutual charity. By this conduct he became, as might be expected, obnoxious to both sides. The massacre of St. Bartholomew plunged him into a deep melancholy, for he detested cruelty and the shedding of blood. It was about this dismal epoch of 1572 that he began to write his *Essais*, which were published in March, 1580, and met with great success. (See below.) With a view to restoring his health, which was not good, Montaigne undertook a journey to Germany, Switzerland, and lastly to Italy. At Rome he was well received by several cardinals and other persons of distinction, and was introduced to pope Gregory XIII. and received the freedom of the city of Rome by a bull of the pope, an honor of which he appears to have been very proud. Montaigne was delighted with Rome; he there found himself at home among those scenes and monuments which were connected with his earliest studies and the first impressions of his boyish years.

He wrote a journal of his tour, evidently not intended for publication; but the manuscript, when discovered after nearly two centuries in an old chest in the chateau of his family, was published (in 1774) under the title of *Journal du Voyage de Michel de Montaigne en Italie, par la Suisse et l'Allemagne, en* 1580-81. It is one of the earliest descriptions of Italy written in a modern language. While he was abroad he was elected mayor of Bordeaux by the votes of the citizens, an honor which he would have declined had not the king, Henri III, insisted upon his accepting the office. At the expiration of two years Montaigne was re-elected for an equal period. On his retiring from office he returned to his patrimonial estate. The war of the League was then raging in the country, and Montaigne had some difficulty in saving his family and property from the violence of the contending factions. At this time the plague also broke out in his neighborhood (in 1586), and obliged him to leave his residence and wander about various parts of the country. He was at Paris in 1588, busy with a new edition of the *Essais*. It appears from De Thou's account that about this time Montaigne was employed in negotiations with a view to conclude a peace between Henri of Navarre, afterwards Henri IV, and the duke of Guise. At Paris he became acquainted with Mademoiselle de Gournay, a young lady who had conceived a kind of sentimental affection for him from reading his book. Attended by her mother she visited him, and introduced herself to him, and from that time he called her his "fille d'alliance," or adopted daughter, a title which she retained for the rest of her life, as she never married. Montaigne was then fifty-five years of age. This attachment, which, though warm and reciprocal, has every appearance of having been of a purely Platonic nature, is one of the remarkable incidents of Montaigne's life. At the time of his death, Mademoiselle Gournay and her mother crossed one half of France, notwithstanding the civil troubles and the insecurity of the roads, to repair to Montaigne's residence and mingle their tears with those of his widow and daughter. On his return from Paris in the latter part of 1588, Montaigne stopped at Blois with De Thou, Pasquier, and other friends. The States-General were then assembled in that city, in which the duke de Guise and his brother the cardinal were treacherously murdered, on the 23d and 24th of December of that year. Montaigne had long foreseen that the civil dissensions could only terminate with the death of one of the great party leaders. He had also said to De Thou that Henri of Navarre was inclined to adopt the Roman Catholic faith, but that he was afraid of being forsaken by his party; and that, on the other side, Guise himself would not have been averse to embracing the Protestant religion, if he could thereby have promoted his ambitious views. After the catastrophe Montaigne returned to his chateau. In the following year he became acquainted with Pierre Charron, a theological writer of considerable reputation, and formed an intimate friendship with him. Charron, in his book *De la Sagesse*, borrowed many ideas from Montaigne's *Essais*. Montaigne by his will empowered Charron to assume the coat of arms of his family, as he himself had no male issue. Montaigne's health was in a declining state for a considerable time before his death; he was afflicted with the gravel and the colic, and he obstinately refused to consult medical men, of whom he had generally an indifferent opinion. In September, 1592, he fell ill of a malignant quinsy, which kept him speechless for three days, during which he had recourse to his pen to signify his last wishes. He invited several gentlemen of the neighborhood, in order that he might take leave of them, and when they were all assembled in his room, a priest said mass, and at the elevation of the host, Montaigne, while half raised up in his bed, with his hands joined together as in prayer, expired, Sept. 13, 1592. His body was buried at Bordeaux in the church of the Feuillants. The character of Montaigne is amply delineated in his *Essais.* They contain much that an advanced Christianity can hardly approve, yet, notwithstanding these inconsistencies, it is impossible to avoid admiring the continued benignity and pensive gayety which distinguished his temper. The amiableness of his private life is attested by the fact that, under the five monarchs who during his time successively swayed the sceptre of a kingdom torn with fanatical divisions, his person and property were always respected by both parties; and few at an advanced age can say, like him, that they are yet untainted with a quarrel or a lawsuit.

Montaigne's *Essais* have been the subject of much conflicting criticism. If we reflect upon the age and the intellectual condition of the country in which the author lived, we must consider them a very extraordinary production, not so much on account of the learning contained in the work, although that is very considerable, as for the clear good-sense, philosophical spirit, and frank, liberal tone which pervades their pages, as well as for the attractive simplicity of the language. Literature was then at a very low ebb in France, the language was hardly formed, the country was disturbed by feudal turbulence, ignorant fanaticism, deadly intolerance, and civil factions, and yet in the midst of all this a country gentleman, living in a remote province, himself belonging to the then rude, fierce, feudal aristocracy, composed a work full of moral maxims and precepts, conceived in the spirit of the ancient philosophers of Greece and Rome, and founded on a system of natural ethics, on the beauty of virtue and of justice, and on the lessons of history; and this book was read with avidity amid the turmoil of factions, the din of civil war, and the cries of persecution and murder. "The *Essais* of Montaigne," says Hallam, "make in several respects an epoch in literature, less on account of their real importance than of their influence on the taste and opinions of Europe. . . . No prose writer of the 16th century has been so generally read, nor, probably, given so much delight. Whatever may be our estimate of Montaigne as a philosopher—a name which he was far from arrogating—there will be but one opinion of the felicity and brightness of his genius" (*Introduction to the Literature of Europe*, ii, 29). "The author of these *Essais*," says Leo Joubert, "is certainly the most independent spirit that ever existed—independent without revolt, and detached from the systems of others without having any system of his own. . . . We recognise in his *Essais* a nature well endowed, not heroic, perhaps, but generous, exquisitely sensible, not aspiring to the sublime, capable of devotion, and incapable of a base act—in fine, a model of what we may call average virtue" (*la vertu moyenne*) (*Nouvelle Biographie Générale*, s. v.). Sprightly humor, independence, *naïveté*, and originality are the characteristics of his mind; and his style is admired for its graceful simplicity. His works are highly seasoned with his own individuality, and afford much insight into his character. "The *Essais*," says Emerson, "are an entertaining soliloquy on every random topic that came into the author's head—treating everything without ceremony, yet with masculine sense. There have been men with deeper insight, but, one would say, never a man with such abundance of thoughts: he is never dull, never insincere, and has the genius to make the reader care for all that he cares for. . . . This book of Montaigne the world has endorsed by translating it into all tongues and printing seventy-five editions of it in Europe—and that, too, a circulation somewhat chosen, namely, among courtiers, soldiers, princes, men of the world, and men of wit and generosity" (*Representative Men*). John Morley, the eminent English writer and most recent biographer of Jean Jacques Rousseau (Lond. 1873, 2 vols. 8vo), frequently turns aside to pay a tribute to Montaigne, and acknowledges that the author of *Emile* had read Montaigne's *Essais* "with that profit and increase which attends the dropping of the good ideas of other men into fertile minds" (ii, 198; comp. i, 144).

The morality of the *Essais* has been called—and not unreasonably, though not correctly in the expression—a pagan morality: it is not founded on the faith and the hopes of Christianity, and its principles are in many respects widely different from those of the Gospel. Montaigne was a sceptic, but not a determined infidel; his philosophy is in a great measure that of Seneca and other ancient writers, whose books were the first that were put into his hands when a child. Accordingly Pascal, Nicole, and other Christian moralists, while they do justice to Montaigne's talents, and the many good sentiments contained in his work, are very severe upon his ethics, taken as a system. "Ancient scepticism," says Ueberweg, "was revived, and, in part, in a peculiar manner further developed by Montaigne. The scepticism of this clever man of the world was more or less directed to doctrines of Christianity, but was generally brought in the end, by a—whether sincere or merely prudent—recognition of the necessity of a revelation, on account of the weakness of human reason, into harmony with theology" (*Hist. Philos.* [N. Y. 1874, 2 vols, 8vo] ii, 14; comp. Fisher, *Hist. Ref.* [N. Y. 1873, 8vo] p. 251). One of the ablest of moralists of our own time, Prof. Vinet, has given, we think, a very fair analysis of the spirit of Montaigne's ethics (*Essais de Philosophie Morale Religieuse suivis de quelques Essais de Critique Littéraire*, Paris, 1828). In the fifty-fourth chapter of the first book of the *Essais*, Montaigne, after distinguishing two sorts of ignorance, the one which precedes all instruction, and the other which follows partial instruction, goes on to say that "men of simple minds, devoid of curiosity and of learning, are Christians through reverence and obedience; that minds of middle growth and moderate capacities are most prone to doubt and error; but that higher intellects, more clear-sighted, and better grounded in science, form a superior class of believers, who, through long and religious investigations, arrive at the fountain of light of the Scriptures, and feel the mysterious and divine meaning of our ecclesiastical doctrines. And we see some who reach this last stage through the second, with marvellous fruit and confirmation, and who, having attained the extreme boundary of Christian intelligence, enjoy their success with modesty and thanksgiving; unlike those men of another stamp, who, in order to clear themselves of the suspicions arising from their past errors, become violent, indiscreet, unjust, and throw discredit on the cause they pretend to serve." A few lines farther on Montaigne modestly places himself in the second class, namely, of those who, disdaining the first state of uninformed simplicity, have not yet attained the third and last exalted stage, "and who," he says, "are thereby rendered inept, importunate, and troublesome to society. But I, for my part, endeavor, as much as I can, to fall back upon my first and natural condition, from which I have idly attempted to depart." In his chapter on prayers (bk. i, 56) he recommends the use of the Lord's Prayer in terms evidently sincere; and in the journal of his travels, which was not intended for publication, he manifested Christian sentiments in several places. Montaigne has been censured for several licentious and some cynical passages in his *Essais*. This licentiousness, however, appears to be rather in the expressions than in the meaning of the author. He spoke plainly of things which are not alluded to in a more refined state of society, but he did so evidently without bad intentions, and only followed the common usage of his time. Montaigne combats earnestly the malignant feelings frequent in man—injustice, oppression, inhumanity, uncharitableness. His chapters on pedantry, on the education of children, and on the administration of justice, are remarkably good. He also throws much light on the state of manners and society in France in his time. The *Essais* have gone through very many editions, and been translated into most European languages: the edition of Paris (1725, 3 vols. 4to) was perhaps the most complete until the appearance of the recent edition, *Avec les notes de tous les commentateurs, choisies et complétées par M. J. V. Le Clerc, et une nouvelle étude sur Montaigne par Prévost-Paradol* (Paris, 1865). Cotton's, the best and oldest English translation, is somewhat coarse, though characteristic. It has frequently been revised, and in the form given it by the learned Hazlitt is pronounced a superior work. Very recently an edition of the *Complete Works of Montaigne*, etc., was brought out at London (1873). Vernier published in 1810 *Notices et Observations pour faciliter la Lecture des Essais de Montaigne* (Paris, 2 vols. 8vo). It is a useful commentary. Meusnier de Querlon published his journal under the title *Journal du Voyage de Michel de Montaigne* (Rome, 1774, 4to). Extracts from the *Essais* have at various times been published, as *Pensées de Montaigne, propres à former l'esprit et les mœurs*, par Artaud (Paris, 1700, 12mo); *L'Esprit de Montaigne, ou les maximes, pensées, jugements, et réflexions de cet auteur rédigées par ordre de matières*, par Pesselier (Berlin [Paris], 1753, 2 vols. 12mo); *Christianisme de Montaigne, ou pensées de ce grand homme sur la religion*, par M. l'Abbé L. (Labouderie) (Paris, 1819, 8vo). See De Thou, *Historia sui temporis*; E. Pasquier, *Lettres*; La Croix du Maine, *Bibliothèque Française*; J. Bouhier, *Mémoires sur la vie et les ouvrages de Montaigne, avec une comparaison d'Epictète et de Montaigne* (by B. Pascal); Talbert, *Éloge de Mich. de Montaigne* (Paris, 1775, 12mo); Dom Devienne, *Éloge historique de Mich. de Montaigne* (Paris, 1775, 12mo); La Dixmerie, *Éloge analytique et historique de Montaigne* (Paris, 1781, 8vo); Mme. de Bourdie-Viot, *Éloge de Montaigne* (Paris, 1800, 8vo); Jay, *Éloge de Montaigne* (1812, 8vo); Droz, *Éloge de Michel Montaigne* (1812, 8vo); Villemain, *Éloge de Montaigne* (*Journal des Savans*, July and October, 1855); Payen, *Notice bibliographique sur Montaigne* (new ed. Paris, 1856, 8vo); *Documents inédits ou peu connus sur Montaigne* (1847, 8vo); *Nouveaux documents* (1850, 8vo); *Documents inédits* (1855, 8vo); *Recherches sur Montaigne* (1856, 8vo); Grün, *La vie publique de Michel Montaigne* (Paris, 1855, 8vo); Vinet, *Essai de Philosophie morale*; Emerson, *Representative Men*; Sainte-Beuve, *Port-Royal*; *Causeries du lundi*, vol. iv; Clément, *Revue Contemporaine*, Aug. 31, 1855; Bayle St. John, *Montaigne, the Essayist* (Lond. 1858); De Laschamps, *M. de Montaigne* (2d ed. Paris, 1860, 12mo); Brinbenet, *Les Essais de Montaigne dans leurs rapports avec la législation moderne* (Orleans, 1864, 8vo); Mrs. Shelley, *Lives of the most eminent French Writers*; Tennemann, *Geschichte der Philosophie*, ix, 443; Church, in *Oxford Essays* (1857); Morell, *History of Modern Philosophy*, p. 199; Lewes, *History of Philosophy* (see Index in vol. ii); the Histories of France by Michelet and Martin; *English Cyclopædia*; Hoefer, *Nouv. Biog. Générale*, xxxvi, 55–71; *Retrospective Review*, vol. ii (1820); *Quart. Rev.* (Lond.) Oct. 1856; *Westm. Rev.* July, 1838.

Montaigu, Guillaume de, a French ecclesiastic, was born in the latter part of the 12th century. He was at first prior of Clairvaux, subsequently abbot of La Ferté, then of Citeaux. Gregory IX employed him in a very important negotiation. In 1229 he was sent to reconcile the kings of France and England, who were on the point of going to war. Montaigu first went to the king of France, calmed his resentment, and afterwards was similarly successful with the king of England, and consequently the impending war did not take place. Different letters of Gregory IX, published in the *Annales des Citeaux*, inform us that the court of Rome intrusted to Guillaume's sagacity the regulation of many other affairs of less general interest. In 1239, as he was proceeding to the Council of Rome, he fell into the hands of Frederick II, was taken captive, and loaded with chains. Towards the close of his life Montaigu abdicated the government of Citeaux, withdrew to the monastery of Clairvaux, and there died in the garb of a simple monk, May 19, 1246. See *Annales Cistercienses*, vol. iv, passim; *Hist. Littér. de la France*, xviii, 358; *Gallia Christiana*, vol. iv, col. 995.—Hoefer, *Nouv. Biog. Générale*, xxxvi, 72.

Montaigu, Pierre Guérin de, thirteenth grandmaster of the Knights Hospitallers of St. John of Jerusalem, was born at Montaigu-en-Combraille, near Riom, in Auvergne, France, about 1168. He was elevated to the grand-mastery in 1208, after having successively filled all the lower offices. His devotion and valor distinguished him everywhere during the second crusade (1186); but he refused to take part in the third (1188), though he had himself encouraged pope Gregory XIV to preach it, because this movement was headed by the German emperor Frederick Barbarossa, then under the major excommunication. Guérin de Montaigu died in 1230 in Palestine. See Bosio and Baudouin, *Hist. de l'ordre de Jérusalem*; Naberat, *Priviléges de l'ordre de Jérusalem.*

Montaigut, GILLES-AYCELIN DE, a French prelate, was born at Glaine-Montaigut, near Billom (Auvergne), about 1252; appointed provost of the cathedral of Clermont in 1285, and shortly after canon of Narbonne. He was finally chosen archbishop of that city, by a part of the chapter, in 1287. Ordained priest, March 17, 1291, by Simon de Beaulieu, archbishop of Bourges, he subsequently started for Rome, and cardinal Gérard Bianchi, bishop of Sabine, consecrated him at Viterbo in the following May. He is found in the number of counsellors of state present at the Louvre in 1296, when the chancellor, Pierre Flotte, read the letters by which Guy, count of Flanders, revoked the powers of his ambassadors commissioned to negotiate a peace with Philip the Fair. Gilles, in the name of the latter prince, signed, June, 1299, the truce concluded with the king of England at Montreuil. October 24, 1301, he was one of the assembly convoked at Senlis to judge Bernard Saisset, bishop of Pamiers, legate of the pope, and one of his suffragans. Called to Rome by this affair, Gilles was ordered by the king not to repair to that city, and he obeyed his royal master. He was one of the five prelates of the council at the Louvre, March 12, 1303, held against Boniface VIII, and labored for the election of Bertrand de Goth (Clement V), his friend. He was also the first of the French bishops appointed to proceed against the Templars. February 27, 1309, he was made keeper of the seals; and after having presided over a diocesan synod at Narbonne, and in 1310 over a council at Béziers, he exchanged his bishopric, May 5, 1311, for that of Rouen. Present at the council-general of Vienna, he was there persuaded that it was useless to allow the Templars to attempt to vindicate themselves. On his return to Rouen, he there presided at a provincial council, October, 1313; held two others at Rouen in 1315, and one at Pontoise, November 17, 1317. Montaigut died at Paris June 23, 1318. By his testament, December 13, 1314, he constituted his nephew, Albert Aycelin de Montaigut, bishop of Clermont, his heir, on the condition of maintaining in the houses belonging to him in Paris as many poor scholars as the number of times the sum of ten pounds should be contained in the annual revenue of these houses. Such was the origin of the College of Montaigut, on the site of which the Library of Saint-Geneviève now stands. See *Gallia Christiana,* vols. vi and xii; Du Chesne, *Histoires des Chanceliers de France; France Pontificale.*

Montalembert, CHARLES FORBES RENÉ, *Comte de,* one of the brightest lights in the history of modern France, noted for his attainments in ecclesiastical as well as secular learning, distinguished as statesman, orator, and writer, was born, of French extraction, at London, March 10, 1810. He was the descendant of one of the oldest noble families of France. One of his ancestors played an important part in the reign of Francis I. His own father served in the army of Condé, but quitted France during the Revolution, and, marrying a Scottish lady, entered the English service, and fought in Egypt and Spain against Napoleon, returning only to his native country after the restoration of the Bourbons in 1814. Charles was left in Britain in charge of his grandfather on his mother's side, an old gentleman who had evinced his interest in the child when yet only a one-year-old babe by dedicating to him a great work (*Oriental Memoirs*, 42 vols. 4to), by which the name of Forbes was to live for ages to come. Mr. James Forbes watched over his young charge with the fondest affection, training and educating the boy himself, until, at the age of eight, it was thought best to place him at school in Fulham. Charles remained there, however, only one year, for, his grandfather dying in 1819, he was sent for by his parents, who were then residing in Paris, and leading a most fashionable and gay life. This was hardly a proper sphere for a boy who had been accustomed to spend much of his time in reading and study in the well-filled library of his grandpa's retreat at Hanmore, near Harrow, or in intellectual conversations with his accomplished ancestor, for whom, if we may believe Mrs. Oliphant, Montalembert's biographer, this boy, with his early and precocious intelligence, had become a "companion." The count, his father, who had but recently returned from Stuttgard, where he had represented his country as minister plenipotentiary, was too much absorbed by political movements and intrigues to give any time to Charles, and his mother was still too young and too gay to assume parental cares and duties, sure to interfere with the exciting stir and bustle of her life, to which she had hitherto been left free by Charles's stay with his grandpa; hence the boy was largely left to his instructors or to himself. That he did not waste his opportunities is apparent from his diary, which he always kept. The life of mere amusement by which he saw himself surrounded had no attraction for his early developed sense of duty, and he marks the irksome demands frequently by a record of a "day lost, like so many others." His principal instructor at this time was Prof. Gobert, of the College Henri IV. In 1824 abbé Nicolle, head of the College of Sainte-Barbe, was brought into contact with the precocious young student, and finally, in 1826, induced his parents to place him under a regular course of study. It was while in this school, engaged in close mental application, that the great thought which never after ceased to animate him, which became, in fact, the motto of all his labors—"God and freedom" —first took shape. "He was seventeen," says Mrs. Oliphant, "when he wrote in his commonplace-book, 'God and liberty—these are the two principal motive-powers of my existence. To reconcile these two perfections shall be the aim of my life.'" "We call especial attention to this phenomenon," says a recent reviewer of Mrs. Oliphant's work, "for it is the best answer to the imputations so frequently levelled at his consistency. His probable liability to them even then dawned upon him: 'What shall I do? What will become of me? How shall I reconcile my ardent patriotism with religion?' He would neither have found nor feared any difficulty of the kind, if he had meant religion in the broad sense of the term. He was clearly speculating on the difficulty of reconciling love of country with ardent, uncompromising devotion to the Catholic Church. In August, 1828, he records a fixed determination to write a great work on the politics and philosophy of Christianity, and, with a view to its completion, to waste no more time on the politics or history of his own time. Three notes of admiration in red ink are set against this entry in the original journal. He attended the debates in the Chamber of Peers, and

found them *d'une médiocrité effrayante*. In fact, his thoughts, his plans, his subjects of interest were those of a matured intellect, of a formed man, who felt 'cabin'd, cribb'd, confined' within the walls of a lecture-room." Yet he quitted Sainte-Barbe in the following year (1829) with great regret, for he knew that before him lay much more of frivolous gayety than delightful interchange of heart and mind. Far, then, from looking forward with fervent expectations of enjoyment to his approaching introduction to society, he foresaw no gratification in mingling undistinguished in the crowd: "I can imagine Pitt or Fox coming out of the House of Commons, where they had struck their adversaries dumb by their eloquence, and enjoying a dinner-party. I can imagine Grattan amusing himself, after fifty years of glory, playing hide-and-seek with children. But for an obscure and unknown individual, lost in the crowd of other men, or at the best numbered only among the *élégants* who feel themselves obliged to wander every evening into three or four houses where they are half stifled under pretence of enjoying themselves, I see neither pleasure nor honor in it. I see only a culpable loss of time, and mortal weariness." In this mood he started to join his father, then French ambassador at Stockholm, *via* Belgium and Holland, lingering on the way to see everything worth seeing, and duly recording his impressions as they arose. Received at once into the gay circles of the Swedish capital, he was with difficulty induced to lay aside his stiffness and reserve; his manner naturally enough gave offence to the light-hearted and haply frivolous companions who were forced upon him; he was voted a prig; and it was not till some time that his really gentle and unassuming nature began to be recognised. But if Charles was formal on the surface at this time, in the consciousness of the grandeur of his youthful aims, he was yet sharply observant, as he always was, and his journal contains "an extremely lively sketch" of the Swedish court and its surroundings. He studied also carefully the institutions of Sweden, as may be seen from the article he published on the subject shortly after. He besides devoted himself to the study of philosophy, and by advice of Cousin spent much time in the reading of Kant, whom he found "terribly difficult," as he himself tells us, and not by any means a congenial study —a fact not to be wondered at, for Montalembert's mind, with all its noble and powerful impulses, had no affinity for philosophic studies. He was throughout life impatient of sifting principles to their last results, and holding them upon his mind in pure rational abstraction. "Metaphysics," says his biographer, "were never much to his taste, and he was wont to arrive at conviction by a shorter road than argument. Truths divine did not come to him sounded by the tongue of a theologian; they came by insight, by intuition, by inspiration; and they went forth from him with the lightning flash of genius, in spontaneous and irresistible bursts." His genius was poetic, rhetorical, but in no degree philosophical. Hence the speeches of the great Irish orators, Grattan and O'Connell, and the eloquence of Burke, were far more attractive than even "the great Schelling," of whom he speaks at this time "as being so ill understood in France." But yet foremost among all his thoughts came forth the great objects to which he had consecrated himself—religion and freedom. Roman Catholicism was now, and always to him, religion, and this Catholicism, in order to triumph, he saw clearly, "must have liberty as its ally and tributary." Every effort of his own, and those of his friends whom he believed fitted to take a part in this great work, he endeavored to make serviceable in this direction. In this spirit he wrote to his friend Rio, the future historian of Christian art, whom he numbered thus early among his most devoted associates: "Do not, I beseech you, abandon yourself to that political discouragement which Burke justly calls the most fatal of all maladies. Do not despair of the cause which you have adopted, or give up sound principles, because a generation without faith and without soul seem to dishonor them by pretended attachment." By a like spirit he was enthusiastically inspired for Roman Catholic Ireland, and resolved to make a journey to that country in order to fit himself properly as historian of the Green Isle; this, however, was prevented by the sudden illness of a sister, who died at Besançon, Oct. 29, 1829, in his arms but a few hours after he had reached her. He had been passionately attached to her, and this sudden removal threw him into a deep melancholic state. He was now more than ever interested in religious subjects, and was even inclined to take holy orders. But he finally forsook this plan, thought of studying law, and, under a passing impulse, even of joining the army of Algiers, a folly to which in after-life he thus pleasantly alluded: "Je suis le premier de mon sang qui n'ai guerroyé qu'avec la plume." He had no real military ardor, and the pen in his hand proved a far more trenchant weapon than the sword.

In this restless state, utterly unable to make a choice for life, he wrote an article on Sweden, and presented it to the learned Protestant Guizot for publication in the *Revue Française*, of which Guizot was editor. Though exception was taken to parts, and much erased that the young would-be *littérateur* thought his best, the article was printed, and at once established his fame as a good writer and careful observer. His literary friendships rapidly multiplied, and he counted among his most intimate associates Lamartine, Sainte-Beuve, and Victor Hugo, "then the poet of all sweet and virtuous things," cherishing the hope of "a universal religious restoration and rebirth of the world." He now also became a contributor to the *Correspondant*, a well-known Roman Catholic periodical, for which he continued to write all his life. But, restless as he was, he could not give up the plan of writing on Ireland, and at length, in the end of July, on the very eve of the Revolution, he set out for that country. The news of the re-overthrow of the Bourbons met him at London, and he went back to Paris; not to stay, however, for his father insisted upon his quitting the scene, and he resumed his journey. We cannot touch upon his Irish visit in detail, but we must at least allude to his call at Maynooth, for the scene he there beheld had no doubt a wonderful influence on his life-work. He himself describes a most striking scene of suffering and devotion which he enjoyed at a mass celebrated there, "the men kneeling in the mud, all uncovered, though the rain fell in torrents, and the mud quivered beneath them." No wonder that such a scene deepened his ardent devotion to Romanism, and confirmed in him the hitherto half-resolved purpose to give himself to the service of the Church and of Freedom! Mrs. Oliphant may well think that it was this visit to Ireland that decided the future of Montalembert. He had seen the Island of the Saints, the island in which liberty was making common cause with faith, in which the standard of patriotism was waved from the altar by the priest. In the Irish Church, then, the twin ideals of his young enthusiasm seemed to him united, sitting like "a dethroned queen" among her people, the guardian of their faith and of their rights, and all the more glorious in her rags and poverty to his dazzled vision. Here was an object worthy of all his ardor and labor. Here religion was the emblem, not of successful power, but of patient suffering. Here she was plainly on the side of the people. He returned to France, burning with eagerness to give a like noble place to the Church of his own country, that there also the Church might be the guardian of the people's faith and of their rights. Not only the peculiar condition of the country—the July Revolution had just ended—favored his project, but Lamennais had long dreamed of just such a work as Montalembert proposed, and, be-

ing brought in contact with him and his pupil Lacordaire, the three men together launched a paper, *L'Avenir*, by which to give circulation to their opinions. See LACORDAIRE; LAMENNAIS. And why should they not? France was in one of its fits of "Liberal" ecstasy. "The charter—the free institutions it guaranteed, the self-government which it held out to the hopes of the nation—was the popular idol. But in the midst of this impetuous rush towards political freedom the Church remained in bondage." Why should this be so? Why should the Church not be free as well as the State, with right to appoint her own bishops, and educate her own children as she wished? These were questions that demanded agitating, and for it *L'Avenir* came into existence. The first number of the paper appeared Oct. 15, 1830. In a little more than three months the country was ablaze because of the severe attacks made upon the government by the triumvirate of *L'Avenir*. Jan. 31, 1831, two of its editors were in criminal courts answering to charges of bitterly assailing the king for exercising his constitutional right in clerical appointments. This time they were lucky enough to secure acquittal. But, instead of profiting by their experience, they only drew from it encouragement to continue in their course, and, not content with the limited influence of *L'Avenir*, attempted a fresh and original enterprise. They formed a society called *Agence de la liberté religieuse*, which publicly announced that, *attendu que la liberté se prend et ne se donne pas*, three of their members would open a school, free and gratuitous, at Paris, for Catholic education, independent as well of the university as of all other state influence, by way of testing the right. The school was opened on May 1, 1831, after due notice to the prefect of police, by three members of the society, Lacordaire, M. de Coux, and Montalembert himself, who succinctly relates what followed: "The abbé Lacordaire delivered a short and energetic inaugurative discourse. We formed each a class for twenty children. The next day a commissary came to summon us to decamp. He first addressed the children: 'In the name of the law, I summon you to depart.' Lacordaire immediately rejoined: 'In the name of your parents, whose authority I have, I order you to remain.' The children cried out unanimously, 'We will remain.' Whereupon the police turned out pupils and masters, with the exception of Lacordaire, who protested that the schoolroom hired by him was his domicile, and that he would pass the night in it unless he was dragged out by force. 'Leave me,' he said to us, seating himself on a mattress he had brought there; 'I remain here alone with the law and my right.' He did not give way till the police laid hands upon him; after which the seals were affixed, and a prosecution was forthwith commenced against the schoolmasters."

Montalembert's father having died soon after the commencement of these proceedings, he was entitled, by successorship in the peerage, to trial before the Chamber of Peers; and before them he appeared on Sept. 19, 1831, and there made the event memorable by his first speech, one of the most brilliant upon record, and a clear foreshadowing, not alone of the eloquence, but of the bold and uncompromising earnestness in the cause of his Church and of the common interests of religious liberty which constantly characterized his later career. After a touching allusion to his great bereavement, and an exposition of the reasons which induced him to claim the judgment of his peers, he said: "It is sufficiently well known that the career on which I have entered is not of a nature to satisfy an ambition which seeks political honors and places. *The powers of the present age, both in government and in opposition, are, by the grace of Heaven, equally hostile to Catholics.* There is another ambition, not less devouring, perhaps not less culpable, which aspires to reputation, and which is content to buy that at any price; that, too, I disavow like the other. No one can be more conscious than I am of the disadvantages with which a precocious publicity surrounds youth, and none can fear them more. But there is still in the world something which is called faith; it is not dead in all minds. It is to this that I have early given my heart and my life. My life—a man's life—is always, and especially to-day, a poor thing enough; but this poor thing, consecrated to a great and holy cause, may grow with it; and when a man has made to such a cause the sacrifice of his future, I believe that he ought to shrink from none of its consequences, none of its dangers. It is in the strength of this conviction that I appear to-day for the first time in an assembly of men. I know too well that at my age one has neither antecedents nor experience; but at my age, as at every other, one has duties and hopes. I have determined, for my part, to be faithful to both." He thus, on the most solemn occasion of his life, deliberately took his stand upon the principles to which he persistently adhered to his dying day; and the nobility of thought, the moral courage, the spirit of self-sacrifice which actuated him are beyond cavil or dispute, whatever may be thought of the prudence or wisdom of his course. It must be borne in mind all the time that, inasmuch as in the infidel reaction following the great Revolution Roman-Catholic France had been allowed to sink into a withering and hopeless secularism, nipping its youthful national life at the root, and yielding a stunted harvest of many evils (the end of which is not even yet), the effort of Montalembert and his colleagues to vindicate a place for religion in the national life and government—to proclaim that society without God is a soulless and corrupting mass, never far from anarchy —was a manifestation of an enthusiasm such as all France could not but pronounce both noble and true, and therefore it is not surprising that the result of the trial was a simple fine of 100 francs. But then came also the question what step to take next. The circulation of $L'Avenir$ had not reached 3000; instead of being self-supporting, it had proved a drain on the scanty resources of the society, which, having to sustain also the expense of prosecutions and propagandism, broke down. As the little band had contrived to place themselves very much in the position of Ishmael, and the clergy, headed by the episcopacy, were among the fellest of their foes, further appeals to an enlightened public were voted nugatory, and they formed the extraordinary step of submitting the crucial questions in dispute to the pope. The great lawsuit was not to be at Paris, but at Rome. His holiness was to decide whether $L'Avenir$ was or was not entitled to the support of the Roman Catholic world, and the journal was to be suspended till his sovereign will and pleasure should be made known. The suggestion came from Lacordaire: "We will carry our protest, if necessary, to the City of the Apostles, to the steps of the Confessional of St. Peter, and we shall see who will stop the pilgrims of the God of Liberty." No one thought of stopping them; the more's the pity, for this expedition was a blunder of the first magnitude, conceived in utter ignorance or forgetfulness of that traditional policy of Rome which lord Macaulay deems a main cause of her durability and strength. "She thoroughly understood, what no other Church has ever understood, how to deal with enthusiasts. In some sects, particularly in infant sects, enthusiasm is suffered to be rampant; in other sects, particularly in sects long established and richly endowed, it is regarded with aversion. The Catholic Church neither submits to enthusiasm nor proscribes it, but uses it." She used Ignatius Loyola and St. Teresa; she would have used John Bunyan, John Wesley, Joanna Southcott, Selina, countess of Huntingdon, and Mrs. Fry. The founders of $L'Avenir$ were just the sort of enthusiasts she wanted, so long as they could be kept within bounds. But they had proved uncontrollable. If the pope and his advisers had been equally

confident that the Church of Rome owed no more to absolute power than the primitive Church of Christ, or would rise the higher if cut free from its temporalities, they would have wished nothing better than the support of an organ like $L'Avenir$. But they would have been unaccountably wanting in the sagacity for which Macaulay gives them credit "had they not penetrated to the fallacy of such arguments at a glance, and drawn a widely different moral from the history. They could not shut their eyes to the fact that spiritual supremacy attained its loftiest pitch in the Dark Ages, and has everywhere declined in proportion to the spread of knowledge." The three apostles of the new æra, which they hoped to inaugurate with the direct approval of an $infallible$ guide, knocked at the gate of the Vatican, were admitted into the presence of "his holiness," but completely failed in their mission. See LACORDAIRE; LAMENNAIS. The very Church they wished to serve—to whose cause they had consecrated, with such touching earnestness, all their gifts—repudiated their aid. The court of Rome understood its own mission better than they did. It admitted "their good intentions," but at the same time silenced them as inspired by a zeal without discretion in the treatment of "supremely delicate questions!" Indeed, this was but the only consistent course for Rome to take. It could not suffer severely orthodox followers to profess to hold upon essential points the doctrines of advanced modern liberalism without seeing them in direct antagonism with the teaching and practice of the Church in all ages; hence the encyclical of pope Gregory XVI, declaring the conviction of the writers of $L'Avenir$ "abominable," and fulminating anathema against the most sacred liberties, declaring that "freedom of conscience is a mortal pest." This was anything but a flattering and brilliant solution, yet the triumvirate meekly submitted. Outwardly all three were equally actuated by that sense of duty which Roman Catholics are wont to place as highest—of bowing reverentially and unqualifiedly before the wisdom of the papal incumbent, as "the voice of God in the flesh;" but in the inner camp there was a terrible struggle. To Montalembert the whole case was a matter of but little moment after all—certainly of much less moment than to the other two. True, his faith was not less sincere or ardent than theirs, but he was as yet merely a young writer; the other two were priests—Lamennais a preacher whose fame had already reached through the whole Catholic world, and had brought him back many distinctions. In vain did Lacordaire offer to submit quietly, and argue that they should act consistently, as there was only one alternative from the first—"Either we should not have come, or we should submit and hold our tongues." Montalembert and Lacordaire forever after acted on this plan, and held their peace; but Lamennais's submission was hollow and formal, and it wanted only (as was afterwards apparent) an opportunity to be disdainfully ignored. See LAMENNAIS. We as Protestants, unaccustomed to such "Catholic" submission, find it, of course, difficult even to conjecture by what process of reasoning these men contrived to reconcile absolute submission to the Romish Church with the defence of that which she has again and again emphatically denounced and condemned. "The conduct of Lamennais," as the $Brit. and For. Ev. Rev.$ (October, 1863, p. 726) has well said, "was at least more consistent than that of his two disciples. They, proclaiming themselves the faithful and obedient followers of an infallible Church—which says to its disciples, 'I am the truth; it is in me, in me alone; to seek it elsewhere is heresy and rebellion'—accepted a part of her doctrine and rejected a part. He, finding that his attempt to reconcile the Church with the tendencies of the age, to unite Republicanism and Romanism, was condemned by Rome herself, and that he must choose between the two, broke with Rome, and proclaimed himself ready to combat and to suffer for what he deemed, however erroneously, the cause of justice and humanity. He broke with a Church which had lost the germs of life and progress, and sought elsewhere the means of regenerating mankind, while they professed implicit submission. But his schism was at least logical and consistent; their submission partial and absurd. He and the Church were thenceforward in direct antagonism; while they, its submissive sons, for the rest of their lives went on endeavoring to carry out the plan which Lamennais had traced in the columns of *L'Avenir*, which Rome had emphatically condemned, and which its author had abandoned as impracticable. He gave up Rome because he found her claims inconsistent with those of humanity; they attempted to save her in spite of herself—to reconcile her with the wants and aspirations of the age—to put new cloth into old garments, new wine into old bottles. Yet we cannot but believe that both master and disciples were sincere and disinterested in their conduct: the former in his schism, the latter in their submission." No one certainly can be believed to know anything of either Lacordaire or Montalembert who would suppose for a moment that these men were influenced by any mere personal considerations. No men probably ever acted under a higher sense of duty, only they never thought of duty in the case apart from the pope. When they saw what the result was likely to be, they quietly and without struggle bowed the knee. "The position," says a writer in *Blackwood* (Nov. 1872, p. 603), "is intelligible, but hardly great or magnanimous. Submission may be heroic in a grave practical crisis which admits of no argument, but it is hardly so in questions of truth and right, which have roused the conscience as well as the judgment to vigorous action. We confess to following Lamennais in his disdainful retirement with far more interest than we contemplate the 'Catholic submission' of his colleagues. Duty loses its higher heroism when it loses individuality, and passes into blind self-surrender." Lamennais's publication of *Paroles d'un Croyant* caused Lacordaire to step forward in defence of the papacy, and this left Montalembert, who had stood by Lamennais through good and evil report, no alternative but to concur with Lacordaire in separating from him. Hereafter the three men stand apart, Lamennais the propagator of a socialist theory, Lacordaire the exponent of papal Christianity, and Montalembert the student of mediæval institutions.

His journalistic career being cut short by papal disapproval, and himself unable to enter political life for lack of age (the peerage begins at twenty-five), Montalembert now went abroad to travel, mainly in Germany, to study the preservation of Roman Catholicism as well as monuments of its history in that country. It was during one of his frequent tours of inspection of mediæval buildings and monuments that he was inspired with the conception of his first sustained and eminently successful effort in literature, the history of St. Elizabeth (*Hist. de Ste. Elisabeth de Hongrie* [1836]; transl. into English by Mary Hackett and Mrs. J. Sadlier, N. Y. 1854). The opening sentences of the introduction to this work are so characteristic that we quote them here: "On the 19th of November, 1833, a traveller arrived at Marbourg, a town in the electorate of Hesse, situated upon the beautiful banks of the Lahn. He paused to examine the church, which was celebrated at once for its pure and perfect beauty, and because it was the first in Germany where the pointed arch prevailed over the round in the great renovation of art in the 13th century. This church bears the name of St. Elizabeth, and it was on St. Elizabeth's day that he found himself within its walls. In the church itself (which, like the country, is now devoted to the Lutheran worship) there was no trace of any special solemnity, except that in honor of the day, and, contrary to Protestant custom, it was open, and children were

at play in it among the tombs. The stranger roamed through its vast, desolate, and devastated aisles, which are still young in their elegance and airy lightness. He saw placed against a pillar the statue of a young woman in the dress of a widow, with a gentle and resigned countenance, holding in one hand the model of a church, and with the other giving alms to a lame man. . . . The lady is there depicted, fairer than in all the other representations, stretched on her bed of death amid weeping priests and nuns; and, lastly, bishops exhume a coffin, on which an emperor lays his crown. The traveller was told that these were events in the life of St. Elizabeth, queen of that country, who died on that day six hundred years ago in that very town of Marbourg, and lay buried in that very church." After his first visit to the church, Montalembert with great difficulty sought out a copy of a "Life of St. Elizabeth," of which he possessed himself as a prize; and though he found it "the cold, lifeless composition of a Protestant," the sympathetic chord was struck, and he set about the study of her career with hourly increasing eagerness, consulting traditions, visiting every place that she had hallowed by her presence, and ransacking all the books, chronicles, and manuscripts in which mention was made of her, or which threw light on her contemporaries or her age. He spent his days and his nights in the preparation of the work, and it need not surprise us, therefore, that the book established his fame as an author. What is really most valuable and most characteristic in the book is that which elucidates her age, especially the Introduction (135 pages royal 8vo), in which he seeks to prove that the 13th century, in which she flourished, has been shamefully calumniated; that it was not merely the age in which the papacy attained its culminating point of pride and power, but the age in which Christian literature and art—that is to say, what he deems the best and purest literature and art—approached nearer to perfection than they have ever approached since or are likely to approach again. This clearly manifests that though his historic insight was fine, minute, and picturesque, he yet lacked depth of historic judgment, and strength and range of sympathy. Here as everywhere *fact*, with its complex variety of association and breadth of human interest, was not so attractive to him as sentiment, and the curious personation with which it can invest the most obvious realities. With all its beauty and grace of outline and charm of portraiture, Montalembert's life of St. Elizabeth does not gainsay this judgment.

On his return from Germany, Montalembert married, in the celebrated Flemish family De Merode, a sister of the now greatly renowned Monsignore de Merode, and selected for his wedding-trip an excursion into Switzerland and Italy. He then settled at Paris, and having succeeded to the peerage in 1835, he now fully entered upon his distinguished political career. Though not entitled to the right of voting until thirty, Montalembert was yet entitled to a seat, and in consequence to a participation in the debates, and in these he took a lively part, distinguishing himself very rapidly as an orator of no common rank, as well as a man of principle. He broke ground as a debater in September, 1835, in behalf of the liberty of the press, followed by other speeches, all of a liberal tendency. But his great aim at this time was the successful issue of the work which he had intended to bring about by the *Avenir*—viz. liberty of the Church; struggling mainly in behalf of an educational system free from the state and in alliance with the Church. In its behalf he dared to say anything which he felt to be the truth. "He could," says Sainte-Beuve, "utter with all freedom the most passionate pleadings for that liberty which was only the excess of his youth. He could develop without interruption those absolute theories which from another mouth would have made the Chamber shiver, but which pleased them from his. He could even give free course to his mordant and incisive wit, and make personal attacks with impunity upon potentates and ministers. . . . His bitterness—and he was sometimes bitter—from him seemed almost amenity, the harshness of the meaning being disguised by the elegance of his manner and his perfect good grace." "It was a sight full of interest," says another, "to see this ardent, enthusiastic, impetuous young man rise in the midst of the Chamber of Peers, composed almost entirely of the relics of past conditions of society—men grown gray in public business, conversant with politics, and among whom experience had destroyed enthusiasm—and disturb with the accents of an impassioned voice the decent calm, the elegant reserve, and the polite conventionalities of their habitual discussions, as he vindicated the rights and interests of that religion which was said to have no partisans but old men, and no life but in the past." Montalembert did not, indeed, shine by lofty sustained imagery, like Burke and Grattan, the objects of his early admiration; nor by polished rhetoric, flights of fancy, or strokes of humor, like Canning. His strength lay in earnestness, ready command of energetic language, elevation of thought and tone, rapidity, boldness, conviction, passion, heart. His vehemence, his *vis vivida*, was power: when he warmed to his subject, he carried all before him with a rush. He had all, or almost all, that is comprised in the *action* of Demosthenes.

But as an author also Montalembert was now greatly adding to his fame. He devoted a large share of his time to study, and as a result published a work on "Mediæval Art" (*Du Vandalisme et du Catholicisme dans les arts* [1840]) and a "Life of St. Anselm" (*Saint Anselme, fragment de l'introduction à l'histoire de St. Bernard* [1844]). In 1843 he began to develop an unusually great activity in the debates in the Chamber of Peers, and he delivered some masterly speeches on such general questions as the liberty of the Church, instruction and education, the theory and constitution of the monastic orders, and the affairs of Poland, in which he always took a deep interest. Towards the close of the same year, while staying at Madeira for the sake of his health, he published *Du Devoir des Catholiques dans la Question de la Liberté d'Enseignement.* This was followed by his celebrated *Letter to the Cambridge Camden Society,* designed to disprove the attempts made by that society to identify the Reformed Church of England with that of the Middle Ages and of continental Europe. In 1847 he delivered his celebrated speech on the affairs of Switzerland, in which he distinctly foretold the revolution which broke out among the continental nations in the year following; and his brilliant *Discours sur les affaires de Rome,* delivered shortly after the popular outbreak, was received with a triple salvo of applause by an audience which sympathized but coldly with his views. After the revolution of February, 1848, the department of Doubs, in which he held property, elected him its representative to the National Assembly, from which he passed into the Legislative Assembly, where he uniformly acted true to his professions as the exponent of the views and interests of the Roman Catholic Church. He worked hard as a member of the commission which, under many difficulties and compromises, prepared the new law of education known as the "Loi Falloux" (and which he might be excused from thinking ought to have been the "Loi Montalembert"); but his influence was even at this time due in the main to his powers as an orator. Like many other men of the oratorical temperament, he was not fitted for parliamentary diplomacy and intrigue, or the many acts behind the scenes by which political power is often acquired and maintained. It is thus that the estrangement of the extreme section of the clerical party from him after the passage of the educational law is to be accounted for. He called this settlement of the question the "Concordat d'Enseignement," and believed himself a

valuable servant of Rome. But the Ultramontanes designated it as a base compromise of the best interests of the Church. The very paper which he had been mainly instrumental in raising up—*L'Univers*—denounced him and all who had been instrumental in passing the law in most virulent language. Thus is it evermore in the Church of Rome. Her most devoted members, if happily they do the bidding of the Ultramontanes, are applauded, and they who, while seeking earnestly to serve the Church, should yet fail to accomplish all that is demanded, are condemned and ignored. See MAYNOOTH.

Although Montalembert lost the support of those upon whom he had reason to lean, he now found, as every honest man is sure to find, support from all classes, and he enjoyed further successes. Yet none of these elated or even satisfied him. He had dedicated himself to the interests of the Church, and failing to gain that support from the source to which he believed himself entitled, he finally in 1852 determined to close his political life. He was not superseded in the Legislature until 1857, yet his political activity may be said to have closed in 1852. And now that he was free to consider the past and the part he had played, the bitter truth broke upon him that he had been acting for Romanism against liberty, and for the remainder of his life he determined to struggle manfully to repair or atone for his mistake. That he failed utterly it will not be necessary to state here. But even in his failure there is yet apparent the striving for truth and right, as we shall see presently. At the outset of his political career under the republic he had avowed democratic sentiments, and voted against Napoleon's admission to the Assembly; but when the Bonapartists turned defenders of Rome, Montalembert's sympathy was enlisted, and he for some time favored the Imperialists. After the confiscation of the Orleans property he ignored the Bonapartists, and it was therefore no small mark of distinction which he received at this time from the Academy by election to its membership. In 1854 he was engaged in the publication of *L'Avenir politique de l'Angleterre* (transl. in 1856), which aims to show that the future prospects of England would be improved by a resumption of intercourse with Rome; and this leading idea he pursues through an infinity of digressions and speculations, interspersed with various particulars of English life as exhibited in its schools, its journalism, and its political institutions. He was bitterly assailed on both sides of the Channel, especially for what he said about the churches; and in a letter dated La Roche-en-Breny, Jan. 3, 1856, he wrote, "This act has been, and deserves to be, looked upon as an act of foolhardiness. I have to contend both in Europe and America with the whole weight of *religious* prejudice against Protestant England, and of *political* prejudice against English freedom or English ambition." What turned out an act of still greater foolhardiness was an article in the *Correspondant* of October, 1858 (published separately in England), entitled *Un Débat sur l'Inde au Parlement Anglais,* which he made the vehicle of such exasperating allusions to the Imperial *régime* that it provoked a prosecution. In brilliant and enthusiastically admiring pictures he drew the social and political institutions of Britain, for the purpose mainly of covertly contrasting them with the condition of his own native land. He was defended by Berryer, and gave his own evidence as to the exact meaning of the inculpated passages, which no English judge or jury could have held libellous, but he was found guilty, and the sentence on *him* was six months' imprisonment with a fine of 3000 francs: one month's imprisonment and a fine of 1000 francs on the publisher. The sentence, after being confirmed on appeal, was gladly remitted by the emperor; so that the prosecution proved a signal triumph to Montalembert in all respects, and had the singular advantage of presenting him for the last time before the world in the attitude which above all he would have probably most desired—of an advocate for the freedom of the press.

The remainder of this noble man's life was entirely devoted to literary labors. He had for twenty years earnestly inquired into the mediæval institutions and characters, and in 1860 brought out the first two volumes of *Les Moines d'Occident depuis Saint Bénoît jusqú à Saint Bernard* (transl. into English by Mrs. Oliphant, Edinb. 1861 and sq.). The whole Western world, Protestant as well as Roman Catholic, was attracted, and everybody who claimed a place for culture read what were a decade's studies—the mature conclusions of this brilliant Frenchman. Especially in England, where Montalembert had always been well known and much admired, the work was universally spoken of and freely commented upon by the press. (See *Blackwood's Magazine*, June, 1861.) The *British and Foreign Evangelical Review*, in July, 1868, reviewing the first five volumes, observes, " However mistaken we may think this gifted son and servant of the Church of Rome as to the importance of the object to which he has consecrated so large a portion of his life, it is impossible to withhold our admiration, either from the earnestness of spirit which prompted him to make the sacrifice, or from the fine conception and vigorous execution displayed in his attempt to teach the world what it owes to the monks, what it has gained by their existence, what it has lost by their overthrow. . . . He would disclaim—indeed, he does expressly disclaim—the work of the panegyrist; he even admits and deplores the errors and follies and abuses which the system has developed in the course of ages" (p. 450, 454, 476; compare *British Quarterly Review*, July, 1868, p. 202, 203). See MONASTICISM. Montalembert lived to bring out three more volumes of this work, making five in all, but did not complete it. Though, as we have seen, Protestants cannot in every particular endorse it, they have yet gladly assigned it a most important place in ecclesiastical literature. Of course Roman Catholics regard it as a chef-d'œuvre in all respects, and greatly lament that the author did not live to complete it. "This great monument of history, this great work interrupted by death," says M. Coclin, "is gigantic as an uncompleted cathedral." It is certainly a vast conception, a durable, if unfinished, monument of energy, zeal, literary skill, research, learning, eloquence, and (we must add) credulity. The most remarkable result of Montalembert's labors in this direction he reaped in his own household. "One day," says Mr. Coclin, "his charming and beloved child entered that library which all his friends know so well, and said to him, 'I am fond of everything around me. I love pleasure, wit, society and its amusements; I love my family, my studies, my companions, my youth, my country, but I love God better than all, and I desire to give myself to him.' And when he said to her, 'My child, is there something that grieves you?' she went to the bookshelves and sought out one of the volumes in which he had narrated the history of the monks of the West. 'It is you,' she answered, 'who have taught me that withered hearts and weary souls are not the things which we ought to offer to God.'" After describing the agony inflicted on both mother and father by this event, Montalembert exclaims, "How many others have undergone this agony, and gazed with a look of distraction on the last worldly appearance of a dearly beloved daughter or sister." Yet it never once occurred to this warm-hearted, noble-minded man that a system which inflicts such agony on so many innocent sufferers, which condemns to the chill gloom of a cloister what is meant for love and light—which runs counter to the whole course of nature—may be wrong.

In 1862 Montalembert published a sketch of the life of Lacordaire (q. v.), which abounds, like all his other productions, in loyal expressions to the Church of his

birth as well as of his choice. His motto was still, "Tout pour l'Église et par l'Église" (comp. *Brit. and For. Ev. Rev.* Oct. 1863, p. 722 sq.). In the same year he gave yet more emphatic expression to his devotion to Romanism in his oration before the Roman Catholic Congress held at Mechlin, and afterwards published in a separate form under the title of *L'Église Libre dans l'État Libre* (Paris, 1863, 8vo). As in the Chamber of Peers and in the Assembly, so also at this time count Montalembert's orations proved highly interesting, both on account of the eloquence of style and nobleness of sentiment, as well as because they contain so strong an advocacy of the principles of religious toleration. Yet it was not inappropriately said by a Protestant journal in 1864 that in these discourses he appeared not as the exponent of the doctrines of the Church of Rome, but rather as an opponent and impugner of her teaching and authority. No doubt this was not his intention; quite the contrary. Yet in these speeches we Protestants can only see that "he praises what she condemns. He affirms what she denies. He claims as a right for every man what she refuses to accord to any. He, a devout Roman Catholic, defends doctrines which the head of the Church denounces as 'fatal,' and as 'works of Satan;' and, so far at least as these doctrines are concerned, distinctly and unequivocally despises and denies the authority of the Church. In short, in these speeches count Montalembert has shown himself a good Protestant" (*Brit. and For. Ev. Rev.* April, 1864, p. 337).

The foolhardy move of 1869 to establish the infallibility dogma was the first occasion on which Montalembert rose in direct antagonism to the papacy. He clearly saw that the Jesuits were scheming the plot, and he boldly descended into the lists, and dealt vigorous sword-thrusts all around. Perhaps in his whole long and illustrious career Montalembert never committed a more courageous act, nor ever clothed lofty and noble thoughts in nobler and loftier language, than he did in his letter of Feb. 28, 1870, addressed to a friend in England, and published in the London *Times*, March 7, 1870, in which he declared himself against the absolute tendency in the Church; yes, he even boldly and uncompromisingly declared that he "gloried" in counting as his colleagues in the Académie Française two such great and good champions of truth as the bishop of Orleans and father Gratry, and he denounced the Jesuit intrigues at Rome as "idolatrous," quoting in support of the word "idol," as applied to the pope, a most remarkable letter written to him seventeen years ago by the (then) archbishop of Paris, Mgr. Sibour. "Nothing," said a correspondent of the *N. Y. Nation*, under date from Paris, March 11, 1870, "so strong, so decided, or so eloquent has yet appeared on this terrible Roman question as this letter of count Montalembert. It will be read wherever the French tongue is spoken, and it will support and console all right-thinking, high-minded Catholics—but the obloquy that will be cast upon M. de Montalembert by the Ultramontanes is indescribable. He perceives the bare truth when he says that the 'Litany of Abuse' will be lavished upon him. It will be so unlimitedly, and it will require all the genuineness of his faith and all the chivalry of his nature to bear what will be his inevitable fate." Of course such an act was enough to eclipse all the services of a lifetime. He had dared to act in harmony with the avowed opinions of his youth; he had supported the demands of the German Catholics, and he was to bear forever the sorrow of such a self-willed act, and it is most painful to reflect that not even his spirit was suffered to pass away in peace; that his dying hours were troubled by an imperative call to choose his side in a wantonly provoked schism. He died March 15, 1870, just sixteen days after writing his memorable letter on papal infallibility. In reply to a visitor who ventured to catechise him on his death-bed, he is reported to have given in his unconditional adhesion to what confessedly he did not understand. "And God does not ask me to understand. He asks me to submit my will and intelligence, and *I will do so*." This concession even failed to satisfy Rome. The atonement was not sufficient for the crime he had committed; and the highest tribute of ecclesiastical respect which the Church accords to a faithful son was denied to his memory; to the memory of him who had devoted his whole life to her cause, who had dared impossibilities for her sake, who had given up to her what was meant for mankind, and thereby abdicated that place among practical statesmen and legislators which, apart from her blighting influence, his birth, his personal gifts, his high and rare quality of intellect, his eloquence, his elevation of purpose, his nobility of mind and character, must have won for him (comp. Italian correspondence of the N. Y. *Tribune*, under date of March 25, 1870). No wonder that we are told by the *Tribune* correspondent that "the feelings awakened in society were very strong both among the clergy and the laity, one of the former, a bishop, saying, 'I would have gone to Paris to attend a service,' and another, speaking of prohibition, observed, 'Ce n'est pas un crime, mais c'est une faute.'" And well might the *Tribune* editorial add that "count de Montalembert filled too large a space in the esteem and admiration of his co-religionists, and of the political and literary world, not to be accorded a special chapter of remembrance."

Montalembert was a man whom title, gifts, accomplishments, fortune, united to make illustrious. The opposite in many respects of his great contemporary, Sainte-Beuve, who preceded him but a little while to the tomb, he laid down his life, with all its brilliancy and all its latter suffering, upon the altar of his faith. "We are dying of the same disease," Sainte-Beuve is said to have remarked; "only I trace it to nature, while Montalembert will ascribe it to Providence." The man was not shallow who saw in life religion and in death Providence; and it will not be difficult to say which of the two great men has left the most earnest example. Well has it been said that "a braver or more chivalrous spirit never passed from earth. He was a veritable '*miles Christi*'—*Chevalier de l'Église*—as he liked to describe his monastic heroes. He was much besides—a picturesque historian, an eloquent orator, a keen and in many respects enlightened politician; but his religious chivalry was the essence of his nature. No monk of old ever consecrated himself with a more cordial devotion to the service of God and the Church. No knight ever fought more gallantly for the cause dear to his heart. Shall we say, in the view especially of his last words on the doctrine of infallibility—which he struggled against to the last, and yet was prepared to accept when once proclaimed—no hero of the cloister ever offered as the sacrifice and service of his faith higher powers or a more entire——only too entire!—self-submission?" (*Blackwood's*, Nov. 1872, p. 609). On one thing the whole world, irrespective of religious difference of opinion, can unite in praise of Montalembert. "He was the very personification of candor. He had not a shadow of bigotry; he hated intolerance; he shuddered at persecution; he had none of the arrogance or unbending hardness of the dogmatist; he was singularly indulgent to what he deemed error; the utmost he would accept from the temporal power, from the state, was a fair field and no favor; the Church, he uniformly maintained, far from having any natural affinity with despotism, could only blossom and bear fruit in an atmosphere of freedom; while liberty, rational liberty, was never safer than under the protecting shadow of her branches—

> 'Nusquam Libertas gratior exstat
> Quam sub rege pio.'

If he waved the consecrated banner of St. Peter with the one hand, he carried *La Charte*, the emblem and guarantee of constitutional government, in the other; and his life and character would be well worth studying if no higher or more useful moral could be drawn from them than that it is possible to reconcile a dogmatic, damnatory, exclusive system of belief with generosity, liberality, Christian charity, patriotism, and philanthropy" (*Lond. Qu. Rev.* April, 1873, p. 219, 220).

Among publications of his not yet mentioned deserve to be alluded to his *Des Intérêts catholiques au dix-neuvième siècle* (Paris, 1852, 8vo), which gives a rapid and brilliant, though one-sided, review of Catholicism throughout the whole of Europe in that day as compared with what it was some fifty years previous, maintaining that upon the whole the progress made is deep, sound, and likely to be lasting: in the same work he expresses himself strongly on the political changes that had taken place in France, and on the language of the French press in their regard, and thus this publication largely resembles the *Political Future of England* spoken of above. It was translated and published in English in 1855. He also republished two articles from the *Correspondant—Pie IX et Lord Palmerston* and *La Paix et la Pairie*, and a review of the memoirs of the duke de St. Simon. He was a frequent contributor to the *Revue des deux Mondes* and the *Encyclopédie Catholique*.

See Sainte-Beuve, *Causeries du lundi*, vol. i; Nettement, *Histoire de la littérature Française*; De Loménie, *M. de Montalembert, par un Homme de Rien* (Paris, 1841); Mrs. Oliphant, *Memoir of Count de Montalembert*, etc. (Edinb. and Lond. 1872, 2 vols. 8vo); Duke d'Aumale's *Éloge sur Montalembert*, read in the Academy on April 4, 1873, and the periodicals quoted and referred to; *Lond. Qu. Rev.* April, 1856, July, 1861; *Edinb. Rev.* Oct. 1861; *North Brit. Rev.* Aug. 1861; *Blackwood's Magazine*, April, 1870; also *Le Temps* (Paris), March 15, 1870; *Le Journal des Débats*, March 15, 1870. The *catalogue raisonné* of Montalembert's published writings, including his pamphlets and contributions to reviews, in the *Revue Bibliographique Universelle*, fills five closely printed pages of small type.

Montalto, ELIAS, a Jewish savant, was born in Portugal in the second half of the 16th century, and, professing Christianity, went under the name of *Felipe* or *Filotheo*. About 1598 he went to Italy, where his medical skill and fame attracted the attention of Concino Concini, who caused his appointment as principal physician to Mary de Medici, queen of Henry IV of France, and this obtained for him the free exercise of his religion. He was subsequently physician and counsellor to Louis XIII, and died at Paris in 1616. The queen caused his body to be embalmed, and it was conveyed into Holland by some of his Jewish relations whom he had about him. Montalto not only wrote some esteemed medical works, but also a theologico-apologetical book in the Portuguese language, wherein he defends Judaism against Christianity—his *Livro Fayto*, ii, 388 sq. He also wrote a tract on Isa. liii, and on Daniel, which are still in MS. See Fürst, *Bibl. Jud.* ii, 388 sq.; De Rossi, *Dizionario* (Germ. transl.), p. 233; Cassel, *Leitfaden für jüd. Gesch. u. Literatur* (Berlin, 1872), p. 100; Basnage, *Histoire des Juifs* (Engl. transl.), p. 676; Lindo, *Hist. of the Jews in Spain*, etc., p. 362 sq.; Grätz, *Gesch. d. Juden*, ix, 521, 524; x, 10; Kayserling, *Gesch. d. Juden in Portugal* (Leipsic, 1867), p. 274 sq., 283, 308; *Sephardim*, p. 176, 201; his essay, "Drei Controversisten," in Frankel's *Monatsschrift*, 1858, p. 323 sq.; Zunz, *Die Monatstage des Kalenderjahres* (Berlin, 1872), p. 9; Geiger, *Jüd. Zeitschrift für Wissenschaft u. Leben*, 1867, p. 184 sq.; 1868, p. 158 sq. (B. P.)

Montani, GIOVANNI-GIUSEPPE, an Italian theologian, was born at Pesaro about 1685. He was descended from a noble family; joined the Society of Jesus at Rome, and taught in the schools of that order moral theology with so much success that persons came from distant parts to consult him. He revised and corrected a work of P. Pelizzari, made many additions to it, which he drew mostly from the decrees of the sacred congregation and from the bulls of Benedict XIV, and published it under the title *Tractatus de Monialibus* (Rome, 1755, 4to; 2d ed. Venice, 1761). He died in 1760. See Richard et Giraud, *Bibliothèque Sacrée.*

Montanism. See MONTANISTS.

Montanists, a Christian sect, is now generally believed to have arisen in Asia Minor, about the middle of the 2d century after Christ. But little if anything is known of their earliest history. It is apparent, however, that as a sect they embodied all the ascetic and rigoristic elements of the Church of the 2d century.

As Christianity had gradually become settled in humanity, "its supernatural principle being naturalized on earth," prophecy and miraculous manifestations were believed to be past. The Montanists, however, came forward to declare a continuance of the miraculous gifts of the apostolic Church, and proclaimed that the age of the Holy Ghost and the millennial reign had been established in the village of Pepuza, in Western Phrygia (Epiphan. *De Hœres.* xlviii, 14), which they termed the New Jerusalem. Those who followed the Holy Ghost, speaking through these new prophets, were held to be the only genuine Christians, and were to form the Church. They were the *pneumatici*, the spiritually-minded; and all the opponents of these new revelations were the *psychici*, the carnally-minded. As a sect they condemned second marriages, considering wedlock a spiritual union, sanctified by Christ, and intended to be renewed beyond the grave. They expelled from the Church all that were guilty of notorious crimes, imposed rigid fasts, advocated celibacy, encouraged martyrdom, allowed of divorce, and held it unlawful to fly in time of persecution. Such were their notions of their own sanctity that, while they did not directly separate from the rest of the Church, they esteemed others very imperfect Christians, and deemed themselves a spiritual Church within the carnal Church. The Christian life was by them not merely referred to a miraculous beginning, the intervention in history of a reparative and saving power, inaugurating a new and final historical development. No, there must be nothing less than a perpetual miracle; everything would be lost if the concurrence of natural activity, of patient labor, were for a moment admitted, if the conditions of a slowly progressive development were in any degree recognised. The Montanists thus conceived religion as a process of development, which they illustrated by the analogy of organic growth in nature, distinguishing in this process four stages: (1.) natural religion, or the innate idea of God; (2.) the legal religion of the Old Testament; (3.) the Gospel during the earthly life of Christ; and (4.) the revelation of the Paraclete; that is, the spiritual religion of the Montanists, and accordingly they called themselves the $\pi\nu\epsilon\upsilon\mu\alpha\tau\iota\kappa\omicron\iota$, or the spiritual Church, in distinction from the psychical Catholic Church. This is the first instance of a theory of development which assumes an advance beyond the New Testament and the Christianity of the apostles; misapplying the parables of the mustard seed and the leaven, and Paul's doctrine of the growth of the Church *in* Christ and his Word, not *beyond* them. In such a light, "the religion of the Spirit," says Pressensé aptly, therefore "is not a new sun which has arisen on the horizon of humanity, and which is to run its regular course after the primary miracle of its appearance; it is to retain ever the brilliancy of its lightning; it is to be one long flashing storm, rather than the quiet shining of the sun. The divine does not harmonize with the human element; it always descends upon it as on its prey, overcoming and subverting" (*Heresy and Christian Doctr.* p. 105). Such was the fundamental error of Montanism; it did not recog-

nise the supernatural as taking possession of the natural order, penetrating and transforming it; it marked out the two domains as in direct and constant opposition. The Montanists, then, believed in the constancy of supranatural phenomena *within* the Church. The miraculous element, particularly the prophetic ecstasy, was not removed; on the contrary, the necessity for it was greater than ever, and they considered those only to be true or perfect Christians who possessed the inward prophetic illumination of the Holy Spirit—they, indeed, were the true Church; and the more highly gifted were to be looked upon as the genuine successors of the apostles. They thus asserted a claim to universal validity, which the Catholic Church was compelled, for her own interest, to reject; since she left the effort after extraordinary holiness to the comparatively small circle of ascetics and priests, and sought rather to lighten Christianity, than add to its weight, for the great mass of its professors.

According to Apollinaris of Hierapolis (quoted by Eusebius in his *Ecclesiastical History*, ch. xvi), the earliest Montanists were exclusively Phrygians; but this is not correct, though it is easy to see, from what we have said in the article MONTANUS, why his views should have laid strong hold on that race of excitable and superstitious Asiatics. Gieseler and Milman remark that the national character of the Phrygians impressed itself on their Christianity, and led to a sensuous, enthusiastic worship of the Deity, and to a wild mysticism. But this cannot have been the cause of the Montanist movement; it can only have given a peculiar character to the heresy, and influenced its details. For "Montanism is but one of a number of similar movements in the Church. At intervals throughout the annals of Christianity, the Holy Ghost has been summoned by the hopes, felt as present by the enkindled imaginations, been proclaimed by the passionate enthusiasm of a few as accomplishing in them the imperfect revelation—as the third revelation which is to supersede and to fulfil the law and the Gospel." This notion appears not only thus early, but again in the Middle Ages, as the doctrine of the abbot Joachim, of John Peter de Oliva, and the Fratricelli; in a milder form it is that of George Fox and of Barclay (Milman, *Lat. Christianity*, i, 1), and in the Irvingites of to-day. In all these cases there is a striving, but a misguided striving, after a higher standard. Certain it is that, whatever doubt may exist as to the historical existence and consequent influence of Montanus, the heresy which bears his name spread not only in Phrygia, but throughout the bounds of the Catholic Church; and that if he existed, and taught Montanism, he was rather, as Neander observes, "the unconscious organ through which a peculiar mental tendency, which had developed itself in various parts of the Church, expressed itself with clearer intelligence and greater strength" (*Antignost.*). Indeed, there was much in the system which their pretended revelations were employed to establish, not only well adapted to take root and flourish among such a people as the Phrygians, but also sure to find in every country persons prepared to receive it by previous habits of mind. "It was attractive to the more rigid feelings, by holding out the idea of a life stricter than that of ordinary Christians; to weakness, by offering the guidance of precise rules where the Gospel had only laid down general principles; to enthusiasm and the love of excitement, by its pretensions to prophetical gifts; to pride, by professing to realize the pure and spotless mystical Church in an exactly defined visible communion; and by encouraging the members of this body to regard themselves as spiritual, and all other Christians as carnal" (Robertson, p. 71). It is said to have been chiefly among the lower orders that Montanism spread; but even in the powerful mind of Tertullian it found congenial soil; and his embracing their opinions is one of the most interesting events in the history of the sect, as it is also in the biography of Tertullian himself. It occuned about A.D. 200, and the treatises which he wrote after that important period in his life give us the clearest insight into the essential character of Montanism; for he carried the opinions of the sect to their utmost length of rigid and uncompromising severity, though at the same time on the great fundamental points in which the Montanists did not differ from the Church he continued, as he had before been, one of the ablest champions of scriptural truth, and one of the mightiest opponents of every form of heresy.

Montanism, it is apparent, then, must be treated as a doctrinal development of the 3d rather than of the 2d century; for though the history of the sect may be dated back to the middle of the 2d century, it remained for Tertullian to give definite shape to Montanism, and it is as a *separate* sect that we can first deal with the Montanists (or Tertullianists, as they were also called in Africa) in the 3d century, continuing to flourish as a sect until the close of the 6th century, and all this time being the subject of legal enactments under all the successors of Constantine down to Justinian (A.D. 530). As a doctrinal system, Montanism in its original inception agreed in all essential points with the most catholic teachings, and held very firmly to the traditional rule of faith. This was acknowledged even by those who were opposed to Montanism (compare Epiphanius, *Hær.* xxviii, 1). Nor is this to be wondered at. "For Montanism," as Dr. Schaff has well said, "was not originally a departure from the faith, but a morbid overstraining of the practical morality of the early Church. It is the first example of an earnest and well-meaning, but gloomy and fanatical hyperchristianity, which, like all hyperspiritualism, ends again in the flesh. . . . Its views were rooted neither (like Ebionism) in Judaism nor (like Gnosticism) in heathenism, but in Christianity, and its errors consist in a morbid exaggeration of Christian ideas and demands." It is true also that the Montanists combated the Gnostic heresy with all decision, and, through Tertullian, contributed to the development of the orthodox doctrine of the Trinity, in asserting against Patripassianism the personal distinctions in God, and the import of the Holy Ghost. Yet this orthodoxy in the substance of its doctrine did not give Montanism the right to claim its place in evangelical Catholicity, for it was itself a principle of implacable and irreconcilable exclusion. Though first seen and felt only in the field of practical life and discipline, this Montanistic movement, coming then into conflict with the reigning Catholicism, finally and consistently carried out, broke to some extent into the province of doctrine, and thus proved true the theory that "every schismatic tendency becomes in its progress more or less heretical" (Schaff).

The one thing by which Montanism came to be especially distinguished from the Church catholic was its assertion of the *continuance of prophecy*, and hence it went generally under the name of *nova prophetia.* Now there was nothing heretical in the simple doctrine that charismata had not ceased in the Church; but there was heresy in the doctrine, which the Montanists espoused, that these charismata introduced a new dispensation superior to that of Christ and his apostles. That Christ, who came to fulfil the law and the prophets, and promised his Holy Spirit to his apostles to guide them into all truth, bequeathed to his Church only an insufficient morality, and a dispensation which needed to be supplemented by the Paraclete of Montanus, is utterly inconsistent with a true reception of the doctrines of the Church catholic and of the Holy Ghost, who spake by the prophets. This distinction in Montanism between the Paraclete and the Holy Ghost is not a distinction (or difference, rather) of person or nature, but the distinction of a plenary bestowal for a complete revelation following a partial bestowal for an imperfect and temporary revelation. It may be compared, and is virtually compared by Tertullian in the passages cited above from the treatises *De Monog.* and *De Virg. Vel.*, to the distinction drawn by St. John when he says, "The Holy

Ghost was not yet given." It was the same Spirit in the Mosaic and the Christian dispensations, yet might be called another on account of the different and larger grace of the Christian dispensation. So the Paraclete is in person and being identified with the Holy Ghost, but the larger measure of the Spirit given for the completion of Christianity introduces a distinction by which the Holy Ghost bestowed on the apostles is inferior to the Paraclete. The Paraclete is undeniably identified with the promised Spirit of Truth—i. e. the promise of Christ, which the Church believes to have been fulfilled on the first Pentecostal day, was not fulfilled until the Spirit came on Montanus. Mosheim (cent. ii, pt. ii, ch. v, sect. 23, note), we must take the liberty of saying, entirely mistakes the nature of the distinction if his words imply, as we understand them to imply, a teacher other than the third person of the Christian Trinity. This heresy gave a character to the new disciplinary rules. It introduced also schism in its most aggravated form, asserting that the party of Montanus alone was the true Church, the pneumatici, all other nominal Christians being psychici.

Montanism manifestly claimed for itself a position above the organization and regular powers of the Church, asserting ·as its own monopoly the continuity of revelation. Anterior revelations, to be sure, are not set aside; they are, however, regarded simply as initiatory steps. The Old Testament retains its claims, but the New Testament suffers depreciation, inasmuch as it is no longer the final utterance of the divine teaching. It has not brought revelation to perfection; it has made, especially in the teaching of the apostles, more than one concession to human weakness, and, like Moses, it has allowed certain practices because of the hardness of men's hearts. "The Lord," says Tertullian, "has sent the Paraclete, because human weakness was not capable of receiving the truth all at once; it was necessary that the discipline should be regulated and progressively ordered, until it was carried to perfection by the Holy Spirit" (*De Virg. Veland.* pt. i). Paul gave certain instructions rather by permission than in the name of God; he tolerated marriage because of the weakness of the flesh, in the same manner as Moses permitted divorce. "If Christ has abolished that which Moses had commanded, why should not the Paraclete forbid that which Paul allows?" (*De Monog.* i, 4). "In fine, the Holy Spirit is rather a restorer than an innovator (ibid.). Was not the new development of the revelations given foreseen and declared by Jesus Christ? The final and glorious economy of the Paraclete may, indeed, have commenced at Pentecost, but it only reached its culminating point with the appearance of Montanus and the prophetesses of Phrygia; none can tell where its developments may end." Such were the principles of Montanism. Surely it were impossible to make a more serious assault than this upon apostolic Christianity. It clearly enough regarded revelation not as a fact, but rather as a doctrine or a law, and in consequence religion lost the definitive character which belongs to that which is absolute. "Inspiration," says Pressensé, "which thus had power to change everything, was exempted from the restraint of all the rules of reason, as well as from the authority of the Holy Scriptures. It was admitted to be a sort of ecstasy, and its great merit, according to the sect, consisted in its bringing man into a state of complete passivity. 'Ecstasy seized the inspired man; this is the power of the Holy Spirit which produces prophecy' (Tertullian, *De Anima*, pt. ii). It is a sort of God-sent madness, which constitutes the spiritual faculty called by us prophecy. The soul is no longer self-possessed when it prophesies; it is in a state of delirium; a power not its own masters it. *Dreams and visions occupy the principal place in the inspiration of the Montanists.* Inspiration is only the harp which vibrates as it is touched by the player's finger (Epiphanius, *Hær.* xlviii, 4). 'Man sleeps; I alone am walking,' says the Paraclete (ibid.). In such a conception of inspiration, flexible natures, susceptible of keen and rapid impressions, were the chosen organs of revelation. . . . Ambiguous and lying oracles could thus be substituted for the clear and exact prescriptions of the sacred books. It is obvious that the whole of Christianity was imperilled by this doctrine of the Paraclete (q. v.). This was the fundamental heresy of Montanism, and infinitely more serious than the particular errors into which it might be led" (*Heresy and Doctrine*, p. 114-115).

The view which the Montanists took of divine inspiration led them to ignore the demands of the ecclesiastical order, and to assert the universal prophetic and priestly office of Christians—even of females. They found the true qualification and appointment for the office of teacher in direct endowment by the Spirit of God, in distinction from outward ordination and episcopal succession. They everywhere proposed the supernatural element, and the free motion of the spirit, against the mechanism of a fixed ecclesiastical order. Now they were undoubtedly right in their resistance to the encroachments of the hierarchy, and to the relaxation of discipline; but they went too far on this point, as on every other—insisting upon a Church of saints and perfect men, a standard applicable only to the invisible Church. "The Church," said Tertullian, "is not constituted by the number of bishops; it is the Holy Spirit in the spiritual man" (*De Pudicit.* p. 21)—a false and dangerous theory for practice in the visible Church, where the secrets of the heart can never be judged of—where, as Pressensé has aptly said, "the tares grow with the good wheat, and their separation is impossible. For the evil is not excluded by making a profession of the faith the personal condition of membership; there is no guarantee that this profession will be in all cases sincere, and, even were it so, there is no religious community in which it is not incomplete. It follows that no one such community can claim to be itself, to the exclusion of all others, the temple of the Holy Ghost; else it becomes an exclusive sect like the Montanists, who called themselves the perfect, the spiritual men, speaking scornfully of all other Christians as carnal. Their conception of inspiration, as never final and complete, moreover rendered any fixed order impossible, and destroyed ecclesiastical authority. All the elements of the faith were daily liable to change. It was impossible to divine what strange answers to spiritual questions might fall from heaven" (*Heresy*, p. 116). Here, then, was the point where they necessarily assumed a schismatic character, and arrayed against themselves the episcopal hierarchy. They only brought another kind of aristocracy into the place of the condemned distinction of clergy and laity. They claimed for their prophets what they denied to the Catholic bishops. They put a great gulf between the true spiritual Christians and the merely psychical, and thus induced spiritual pride and false pietism. Their affinity with the Protestant idea of the universal priesthood is clearly more apparent than real; they go on altogether different principles. (Compare Schaff, i, 367.)

As to its matter, the Montanistic prophecy related— (1) to the approaching heavy *judgments of God*, a sort of visionary millenarianism; (2) the *persecutions;* (3) fasting and other *ascetic practices*, which were to be enforced as laws; and (4) as to the distinction to be made between *the various kinds of sins.*

One of the most essential and prominent traits of Montanism was its visionary millenarianism, founded, indeed, on the Apocalypse and on the apostolic expectation of the speedy return of Christ, but giving them extravagant weight and a materialistic coloring. The Montanists lived under a vivid impression of the great final catastrophe, and looked therefore with contempt upon the present world, and directed all their desires to the second advent of Christ, which they believed to be near at hand. "After me," exclaimed one of its prophetesses, "there is no more prophecy, but only the end of

the world" (Epiphanius, *Hær.* xlviii, 2). The failure of these predictions weakened, of course, all the other pretensions of the system; though, on the other hand, it must be confessed here that the abatement of faith in the near approach of the Lord was certainly accompanied with an increase of worldliness in the Catholic Church.

But besides the prominent traits of Montanism already indicated, there remain those questions of *discipline and morals*, which were made the subject of special revelation in order to impart to the system its legal character. The distinction between the two covenants was lost sight of. "The Church," says Tertullian, "blends the law and the prophets with the Gospels and the writings of the apostles" (*De Præscript.* § 6). The Gospel was a code, no less than Mosaism, especially with the amplifications given to it by the Paraclete. "The law of liberty," says Pressensé, "is replaced by precepts of the minutest detail. All that was not permissible was laid under a stern interdict (Tertullian, *De Corona Milit.* p. 2), and thus vanished that noble Christian liberty which enlarges the domain of the moral principle instead of narrowing it, and takes possession of the entire life, to bring it all under our direction, and to animate it with the inspiration of love as with the breath of life" (*Heresy*, p. 117). Montanism, indeed, tended to a system of growing severity; and Tertullian, moreover, gloried in that the restoration of this rigorous discipline was made the chief office of the new prophecy (*De Monog.* c. 2 and 4). Now it must be confessed that the Montanists raised a zealous protest against the growing looseness of the Catholic penitential discipline, which in Rome particularly, under Zephyrinus and Callistus, to the great grief of earnest minds, established a scheme of indulgence for the grossest sins, and began, long before Constantine, to obscure the line between the Church and the world; but, on the other hand, it must be remembered also that Montanism certainly went to the opposite extreme, and fell from evangelical freedom into Jewish legalism. It turned with horror from all the enjoyments of life, and held even art to be incompatible with Christian soberness and humility. Above all, it laid stress upon three points: first, it exalted martyrdom with solemn fervor. It courted blood-baptism, and condemned concealment or flight in persecution as a denial of Christ: "For if persecution proceeds from God, it is in no way their duty to flee from what has God for its author; it ought not to be avoided, and it cannot be evaded." The treatise of Tertullian, *Flight and Persecution*, clearly and perfectly expresses these ideas, and they were the ideas of the Montanists. The Church had given to martyrdom no niggardly honor, but in the spirit of its founder's teachings (Matt. x, 23) flight was considered proper. Montanism, however, severely condemned every measure of prudence in times of proscription (comp. Eusebius, *Hist. Eccles.* v, 16; Tertullian, *De Fuga*, § iv, p. 691-697).

The same extreme severity characterizes their practice of fasting. Kaye (in his *Tertullian*, p. 416) sums up the differences between the orthodox and Montanists on the subject of fasting thus: "With respect to the jejunium, or total abstinence from food, the orthodox thought that the interval between our Saviour's death and resurrection was only the period during which the apostles observed a total fast, and consequently the only period during which fasting was of positive obligation upon all Christians. At other times it rested with themselves to determine whether they would fast or not. The Montanists, on the contrary, contended that there were other seasons during which fasting was obligatory, and that the appointment of those seasons constituted a part of the revelations of the Paraclete. With respect to the Dies stationarii, the Montanists not only pronounced the fast obligatory on all Christians, but prolonged it until evening, instead of terminating it, as was the custom, at the ninth hour. In the observance of *Xerophagiæ* (q. v.), the Montanists abstained not only from flesh and wine, like the orthodox, but also from richer fruits, and omitted their customary ablutions." Apollonius (in Eusebius, *H. E.* v, 18), in this particular, simply notices of Montanus, "This is he who laid down laws of fasting," pointing out in these words that Montanus's offence was not the changing of one law for another, but the imposition of a law where there had been liberty. Tertullian has written an entire treatise in defence of fasting, and the objections brought against Montanism on this point show clearly the exaggerated legalism by which it was estranged from the true Christian tradition. The law and the prophets, it was said to the Montanists, were until John; fasting thenceforward should be a voluntary, not an enjoined act. The apostles themselves observed it, without laying it as a yoke upon any: we must not return to legal prescriptions. The prophets showed great contempt for all that is merely outward observance. Tertullian (*De jejuniis*, c. 2 and 3) replies that nothing is more adapted to give large license to the flesh than the reducing of the law to the great commandment of love. He maintains the necessity of fasting—first, on the ground that self-indulgence led to the fall. "It is necessary," he says, "that man should give satisfaction to God with the same element by which he offended, and that he should deny himself food, which caused his fall." That fasting is agreeable to God is proved by the words full of tenderness addressed to Elijah when he was fasting in the desert of Horeb, especially as compared with the severe tone of the call to Adam when he had been eating the forbidden fruit. Fasting facilitates holy visions, as is proved by sacred history from Daniel to Peter, and it prepares for martyrdom; while the neglect of such abstinence leads to apostasy, by fostering the love for material pleasures. To the objections drawn from Holy Scripture, Tertullian replies by the revelations of the Paraclete, which legitimately give expansion to its obligation, and refuses to recognise any distinction between the O. and N. T., as might be naturally enough expected from his strictly legal stand-point (comp. *De jejuniis*, c. 6–8).

Its strongest protests, however, Montanism, like all ascetic doctrines, entered against the union of the sexes. It not only prohibited second marriage as adultery, for laity as well as clergy, but even went so far as to distinctly impugn all marriage, urging its faithful ones to absolute continence. Tertullian does not hesitate to compare the conjugal union to adultery, forgetting his own beautiful words about the perpetuity of marriage after death (*Adv. Marc.* i, c. 29, p. 452), and brands the union of sexes as caused by an impulse of lust. "Thus, then," he suggests, as an objection urged, "you set a brand even on first marriages." "*And rightly*," he replies, "*since they consist in the same act as adultery. . . .* Thus it is good for a man not to touch a woman; virginity is the highest holiness, since it is furthest removed from adultery" (*De Virg. Veland.* p. 16). In his treatise on monogamy, however, Tertullian contents himself with prohibiting second marriages, taking his stand on Scripture, when he can make it sustain his view, appealing to the higher power of the Paraclete when he has to deal with the exact texts of St. Paul. The apostle, according to him, gave sanction to second marriages, but with a marked tone of antipathy, and simply in consequence of his knowledge and prophecy having been only in part. The Paraclete, however, in his new revelation, always acts in conformity with Jesus Christ and his promises. "We acknowledge," said Tertullian, "only one marriage, as we acknowledge only one God. Jesus Christ has had only one bride, which is the Church. By his example, and by the explicit command revealed by the Paraclete, he has restored the true nature; for monogamy dates from Eden. The priests were to have only one wife. Now, under the new economy, every Christian is a priest of Christ. No difference should be made in a moral point of view between the clergy and the laity, for the former are taken from among Christian people. Besides, how can marriage,

which makes of the man and woman one flesh, be renewed? Is such an assimilation capable of repetition? Besides, the bonds between husband and wife continue in death; they have only become more sacred by becoming more spiritual." Yet Tertullian's views, though extreme, do not in this instance clearly set forth the views of all Montanists. Indeed some of them insisted that their founder taught λύσεις γάμων—dissolution of marriage—and that Prisca and Maximilla, as soon as they recognised the spirit, abandoned their husbands. It is true Wernsdorf (see Routh's note, *Rel. Sac.* i, 473) observes that Montanus's teaching was on this point not by precept, but by the example of his two prophetesses, and yet the extreme asceticism must have had a far-reaching influence even for Tertullian to advocate celibacy on the strength of it, and in his *Exhortation to Chastity* he comes to recognise a morality of perfection which rises above the ordinary standard. "Permanent virginity is its highest point; abstinence from the sexual relations in marriage is akin to it in virtue." In an extreme ascetic tendency Montanism forbade women all ornamental clothing, and required virgins to be veiled. Thus Tertullian urges that it be done so as not to kindle the flame of passion. "I entreat thee, O woman, be thou mother, daughter, or virgin, veil thy head: as mother, veil it for the sake of thy son; as sister, for thy brother; as daughter, for thy father. For thou dost imperil men of every age. Put on the armor of modesty; encircle thee with a rampart of chastity. Set a guard over thine own eyes, and over those of others. Art thou not married to Christ?" (*De Virg. Veland.* p. 16).

The perversion of the doctrine of redemption, which is the source of all such legalism, casuistry, and extreme asceticism, as the Montanists taught, is more especially notable in the arbitrary disposition made by Montanism of various kinds of sins. In the same manner as it recognises two orders of perfection, and thus does violence to the true idea of good, so does it tamper with the idea of evil. In accordance with the words of John —"a sin not unto death," and "a sin unto death"—it made a difference between sins venial and mortal, and denied that the Church had power to pardon the latter, because, as it taught, there is no possibility of a second repentance for mortal sins, and therefore no power in the Church to restore the lapsed into fellowship. Tertullian's treatise on *Modesty*, called forth by the decree of the bishop of Rome, who had assumed the right to pardon the gravest sins, expresses the Montanist theory with perfect clearness. He does not dwell for an instant on the real difficulty of obtaining proof of true repentance, but speaks only of the comparative gravity of sins. "Some," he says, "are pardonable; others, on the contrary, are beyond remission; some merit punishment, others damnation. From this difference in the offences comes the difference in the penitence, which varies according as it is exercised on account of a pardonable or unpardonable sin." He held all mortal sins (of which he numbers seven) committed after baptism to be unpardonable (*De Pudicit.* c. 2 and 19), at least in this world; and a Church which showed such lenity towards gross offenders, as the Roman Church at that time did, according to the corroborating testimony of Hippolytus, he called worse than a "den of thieves," even a "spelunca moechorum et fornicatorum." At the head of the black catalogue of unpardonable or mortal sins the Montanists placed adultery and apostasy. They did not deny that God could pardon them directly, or through the medium of an exceptional revelation; but on this side the grave no restoration was possible for those who had been guilty of such sins, even though they gave the strongest pledges of their repentance. Here we have a clear departure from the grand Christian doctrine of the fulness of God's mercy, irrespective of the proportion of sin, and that the Church must suffer all to enter its fellowship who manifest "a desire to flee from the wrath to come." If Montanism taught truly, it follows that the work of redemption is insufficient, and that, in addition to repentance, a certain satisfaction is demanded of the sinner. We have here unquestionably reached the root of the error of Montanism, from which grows its legalism and its asceticism.

The religious earnestness which animated Montanism, and the fanatical extremes into which it ran, have frequently reappeared in the Church after the death of Montanism, under various names and forms, as in Novatianism, Donatism, Anabaptism, the Camisard enthusiasm, Puritanism, Pietism, Irvingism, and so on, by way of protest and wholesome reaction against various evils in the Church. And what may appear perhaps more strange, several of those very doctrines of the Montanists which in their earliest rise were pronounced heretical gradually made their way into the Church of Rome, and, with slight modifications, remain to this day a part of her creed. Thus it is to Montanism that it owes the idea of the infallibility of its councils, which attempt in the same way to add to revelation. From the same source, too, it has derived its "counsels of perfection," and the distinction between venial and mortal sins. Says Dr. Newman, in his *Essay on Development*, a work which he would hardly care to own now, "the prophets of the Montanists prefigure the Church's doctors, and their inspiration her infallibility; their revelations her developments" (p. 349–352). Since this was written a new significance has been given it by the proceedings of the last Vatican Council (1869), which has lodged in the individual head of the Church the infallibility formerly attributed to the Church as a whole. See, however, INFALLIBILITY; PAPACY.

We now return to the *external* history of Montanism. We have stated that it probably originated in Phrygia about the middle of the 2d century, and that it spread rapidly during the bloody persecutions under Marcus Aurelius. In Asia Minor, however, it met with opposition, and the bishops and synods almost universally declared against the new prophecy as the work of dæmons. Among its literary opponents in the East are mentioned Claudius Apollinaris of Hierapolis, Miltiades, Apollonius, Serapion of Antioch, and Clement of Alexandria. The Roman Church likewise, during the episcopate of Eleutherus (177–190) or of Victor (190–202), after some vacillation, set itself against it at the instigation of the presbyter Caius and the confessor Praxeas. Yet the opposition of Hippolytus to Zephyrinus and Callistus, and the later Novatian schism, shows that the disciplinary rigorism of Montanism found energetic advocates in Rome till after the middle of the 3d century. Indeed it was some time before the Montanists formed themselves into an independent sect in the Western Church (comp. Gieseler, *Eccles. Hist.* i, 125, note 6). The Gallic Christians, Irenæus at their head, took, it is now generally believed, a conciliatory posture, and sympathized at least with the moral earnestness, the enthusiasm for martyrdom, and the chiliastic hopes of the Montanists. They sent the bishop Irenæus to bishop Eleutherus at Rome to intercede in their behalf, and this mission may have induced him or his successor to issue letters of peace, which were, however, soon afterwards recalled. In North Africa they met with extensive sympathy, as the Punic national character leans naturally towards gloomy and rigorous acerbity. Here it secured Tertullian, who helped the gropers in the dark towards a twilight of philosophy. He is its proper and only theologian. Through him, too, its principles reacted in many respects on the Catholic Church; and that not only in North Africa, but also in Spain, as we may see from the harsh decrees of the Council of Elvira in 203. It is singular that Cyprian, who, with all his High-Church tendencies and abhorrence of schism, was a daily reader of Tertullian, makes no allusion to Montanism. Augustine (*De hæresibus*, § 6) relates that Tertullian left the Montanists and founded a new sect, which was called after him, but was through his (Augustine's) agency reconciled to the Catholic congrega-

tion at Carthage. As a sect, the Montanists run down into the 6th century; but, as has been remarked with much truth, although the actual number of the Montanists was at one period very considerable, the importance of the sect is really to be estimated by the extent to which their character became infused into the Church. Neander attributes much of this to the great influence which Tertullian exerted through the relation in which he stood to Cyprian, who called him his teacher. At the same time it is to be noticed that there was some tendency in the opposite direction in the introduction of a prophetical order superior in rank and importance to the order of bishops. The first order among the Montanists was that of *patriarch*, the second that of *cenones*, and the third that of *bishop*. The patriarch resided at Pepuza, in Phrygia, the anticipated seat of the millennial kingdom, and at that time almost exclusively inhabited by Montanists.

See Tertullian's works, especially his numerous Montanistic writings; Eusebius, *Hist. Eccles.* v, 3, 14–19; Epiphanius, *Hær.* p. 48, 49; Wernsdorf, *De Montanistis* (Dantsic, 1741); Münter, *Effata et oracula Montanistar.* (Copenh. 1829); Neander, *Antignosticus oder Geist aus Tertullian's Schriften* (Berl. 1825; 2d ed. 1849); Schwegler, *Der Montanismus u. die christl. Kirche des 2ten Jahrh.* (Tüb. 1841); Kirchner, *De Montanistis* (Jena, 1852, 8vo); Baur, *Das Wesen des Montanismus nach den neuesten Forschungen*, in the *Theol. Jahrbücher* (Tüb. 1851; comp. his *Christenth. der 3 ersten Jahrh.* p. 213–224); Niedner, *Kirchen-Geschichte*, p. 253 sq., 259 sq.; Ritschl, *Entstehung der altkathol. Kirche* (2d ed. 1857), p. 402–550; Pressensé, *Early Years of Christianity* (Heresy and Doctr.), iii, 101–124; Neander, *Ch. Hist.* i, 507, 526; *Hist. Christian Dogma* (see Index); Schaff, *Ch. Hist.* i, 362–469; Hagenbach, *Hist. Doctr.* i, 60 sq.; Walch, *Gesch. der Ketzereien*, i, 611 sq.; Killen, *Anc. Ch.* p. 436 sq.; Burton, *Eccl. Hist. First Three Cent.* p. 405 sq.; Ebrard, *Kirchen- u. Dogmengesch.* i, 137 sq.; Mossman, *Hist. Catholic Church* (Lond. 1873, 8vo), ch. v; Lipsius, in Hilgenfeld's *Zeitschr. für wissenschaftliche Theologie*, 1865 and 1866; *Lond. Qu. Rev.* Jan. 1869, p. 473; *Christian Examiner*, Sept. 1863, p. 157; *Brit. Qu. Rev.* Oct. 1873, p. 288.

Montano, LEANDRO, a Spanish theologian, a native of Murcia, flourished in the 17th century. He was also known under the name *Leandro of Murcia*. He was a Capuchin monk, ecclesiastical inspector of Castile, qualificator of the Inquisition, and preacher to the king. Among his numerous works may be mentioned, *Questiones regulares y regla de los menores* (Madrid, 1645, 4to):—*Commentaria in Esther* (ibid. 1647, fol):—*Explicacion de las bulas de Innocencio X* (ibid. 1650, 4to):—*Disquisitiones morales in primam S. Thomæ* (ibid. 1663–70, 2 vols. fol.). See Antonio, *Bibl. Nova Hispana;* Saint-Antoine, *Bibl. univ. Franciscana*, ii, 279.

Montānus, a celebrated heresiarch of the early Christian Church, the supposed founder of a sect named after him *Montanists* (q. v.), was a Phrygian by birth, and, according to Eusebius (*Hist. Eccles.* v, 16), made his first public appearance about A.D. 170, in the village of Ardabar, on the confines of Phrygia and Mysia, of which place he is believed to have been a native (comp., however, the bishop of Lincoln's [Kaye] *Tertullian*, p. 13 sq.). He was brought up in heathenism, but appears to have embraced Christianity (about 170) with all the fanatical enthusiasm for which his countrymen were noted. Neander endeavors to explain his character and tendencies on the supposition of his possessing an essentially Phrygian temperament, and the little we know concerning him renders this highly probable. The frenzy, the paroxysms, the fierce belief in the supernatural, that marked the old Phrygian priests of Cybele and Bacchus, are repeated under less savage, but not less abnormal conditions, in the ecstasies, somnambulism, and passion for self-immolation of the Montanists. According to some of the ancient writers, Montanus was believed by his followers to be the Paraclete, or Holy Spirit. But this is an exaggeration, for he, falling into somnambulistic ecstasies, came simply to consider himself the *inspired organ* of the Paraclete, the Helper and Comforter promised by Christ in these last times of distress. He, however, certainly claimed divine inspiration for himself and his associates. They delivered their prophecies in an ecstasy, and their example seems to have introduced into the Church the practice of appealing to visions in favor of opinions and actions, of which practice Cyprian and others availed themselves to a great extent (comp. Middleton, *Free Inquiry*, p. 98, etc.). His principal associates were two prophetesses, named Prisca, or Priscilla, and Maximilla. The doctrines which Montanus, if he taught at all as a leader of a sect, disseminated are now clearly seen to have been in general agreement with those of the Church catholic of the 2d century, and the fact that Tertullian at one time became the most brilliant exponent of the Montanists would go far to confirm such a position. But the austerity of manner, the strictness of discipline, and the doctrine of a permanent extraordinary influence of the Paraclete, manifesting itself by prophetic ecstasies and visions, opened wide the door to all manner of fanatical extravagances, and brought reproach upon the name of founder and sect alike. Ecclesiastical writers of succeeding centuries have in consequence brought more or less reproach upon the name of Montanus by accusations of immorality and crime, and he is even said to have ended his days violently. But there is no authority for such statements, if we may believe Schwegler, *Der Montanismus u. die christliche Kirche des zweiten Jahrh.* (Tüb. 1841, 8vo). He insists upon it that "there is nothing of historical value in the life of this man at our command" (p. 242), and believes that "the person Montanus is of no significance in the examination and elucidation of what is known as *Montanism*," and would go even so far as to "doubt the historical existence of this apocryphal character" (p. 243). There is certainly ground for such a position in the fact that in their earliest days the Montanists were never spoken of under that name, but were generally called, especially by Tertullian and Eusebius, after the name of the country in which they originated, *Cataphrygians*, or after the name of the place to which they assigned special sanctity, *Pepuzians* (comp. Epiphan. *Hær.* xlviii, 14). Bishop Kaye, in his *Tertullian* (p. 28 sq.), takes it for granted that Montanus was a historical character, and awards to him the dignity of founder of the Montanists. The learned bishop even believes, depending upon Tertullian's work, "that the effusions of Montanus and his female associates had been committed to writing," and that "Tertullian, believing that Montanus was commissioned to complete the Christian revelation, could not deem him inferior to the apostles, by whom it was only obscurely and imperfectly developed." See references to the article MONTANISTS.

Montanus, BENEDICT ARIAS. See ARIAS.

Montanus OF TOLEDO, a noted Spanish prelate of the early Christian Church, flourished in the 6th century. But little is known of his personal history. He succeeded Celsus in the see of Toledo A.D. 531; he presided at the council held in Toledo, and died in the year 540. There are two letters of his extant, one to the brethren of Palantia, and the other to Theodorius, bishop of Palantia. See Clarke, *Sacred Lit.* ii, 306.

Montanye, THOMAS B., a Baptist minister, was born in New York in 1769. He began preaching when quite young, and was in 1788 ordained pastor of the Baptist society in Warwick, N. Y., where he remained until 1801, when he accepted a call from the Church in Southampton, Bucks County, Pa., which situation he held until his death, Sept. 27, 1829. He was a truly popular preacher, and on account of his talents and piety

his services came to be much sought after for ordinations, councils, and especially religious anniversaries, yet none of his works have been published. See Sprague, *Annals*, vi, 265.

Montargon, ROBERT FRANÇOIS DE (*Hyacinthe de l'Assomption*), a French preacher and theologian, was born at Paris May 27, 1705. He assumed the vows of the Augustines of the strect Notre Dame of the Victoires at Paris (*les Petits Pères*), and very soon became remarkable for his oratorical talent. He was made court preacher by Louis XV, and received the title of almoner to Stanislaus I (ex-king of Poland), duke of Lorraine and of Bar. His life was consecrated to his ministry. Attacked by paralysis, he resorted in 1770 to the waters of Plombières for relief. An inundation of the Angronne destroyed that city, and Montargon found only death where he had expected recovery—July 25, 1770. He is the author of *Dictionnaire apostolique à l'usage de messieurs les curés de la ville et de la campagne qui se destinent à la chaire* (Paris, 1752–58, 13 vols. 8vo); this work has remained the vade mecum of the ecclesiastics. It has often been reprinted, and translated into different languages. The first six volumes treat of morals, the seventh and eighth of the mysteries of Jesus Christ, the ninth of the Virgin, the tenth of the saints, the eleventh of the homilies of Lent, the twelfth of different subjects, and the thirteenth is a general table of the subjects treated in the other twelve volumes. See *Recueils d'Éloquence sainte; Histoire de l'institution de la fête du Saint-Sacrement* (1753, 12mo); *Dictionnaire portatif des prédicateurs*, s. v.

Montazet, ANTOINE DE MALVIN DE, a French prelate, was born Aug. 17, 1713, in the castle of Quissac, near Agen. He belonged to a good family of the Agenais, and, embracing the ecclesiastical profession, obtained, among other benefices, the abbeys of Saint-Victor of Paris and of Monstier in Argonne. At the close of 1742 he became almoner to the king, and in 1748 was appointed bishop of Autun. March 31, 1759, he was raised to the archbishopric of Lyons in the place of cardinal de Tencin. "Zealously opposed to the philosophers," says Feller, "an ardent defender of the prerogatives of his see, which he claimed privileged even to the reformation of metropolitan judgments, a successful adversary to the customs and privileges of his chapter, which he succeeded in suppressing by civil authority, this prelate holds a distinguished place in the history of the Gallican Church of this century." He had numerous debates with M. de Beaumont, archbishop of Paris, relative to the religious quarrels of the time. He felt much inclined to side with the Jansenists, and did say much in their favor; yet he never became one of the number of the *Appellants*, and avoided any formal proceedings of opposition against the bull *Unigenitus*. He died May 2, 1788, at Paris. Montazet had a happy memory, a brilliant imagination, an active mind; his eloquence was lofty, energetic, and copious. In 1757 he was admitted to the French Academy. His principal writings are, *Lettre à l'Archevêque de Paris* (Lyons, 1760, 4to); he there takes the title of *Primate of France:—Mandement contre "L'Histoire du Peuple de Dieu" de Berruyer* (Lyons, 1762, 12mo):—*Instruction pastorale sur les sources de l'incredulité et les fondements de la religion* (Paris, 1775, 4to); this work was greatly praised up to the time when it was reprinted under the title of *Plagiats de M. l'Archevêque*, and with the passages drawn from the *Principes de la foi chrétienne* of Daguet; but there is reason for believing that the composition of the *Instruction pastorale* is by P. Lambert:—*Catéchisme* (Lyons, 1768):—*Rituel de diocèse de Lyon* (Lyons, 1788, 3 vols. 12mo). It was under his auspices that the *Institutiones Theologicæ* appeared (Lyons, 1782, 1784, 6 vols. 12mo); and the *Institutiones Philosophicæ* (Lyons, 1784, 5 vols. 12mo); this system of theology, proscribed in France, was introduced into Italy and Spain, where it was held in esteem for a short time. See *L'Ami de la*

Religion, xxii, 161, 172; Bachaumont, *Mémoires secrets*, passim; Migne, *Dict. des Jansénistes*, s. v.; Feller, *Dict. Hist.* s. v.; Hoefer, *Nouv. Biog. Générale*, s. v.; Jervis, *Hist. Ch. of France* (Lond. 1872, 2 vols. 8vo), ii, 325 sq.

Montbas, JEAN BARTON DE, a French prelate, a native of Guéret, flourished in the 15th century. He was abbot of the Dorat in 1446, and on April 1, 1457, was made bishop of Limoges, and counsellor to the Parliament. In 1465 he resigned his functions in favor of his nephew, Jean Barton de Montbas II, who put into print the *Breviarium Lemovicense* (Paris, 1500, 8vo) and the *Breviarium diœcesis Lemovicensis* (1504), *Manuscrit de* 1638, in the library of Limoges. He died in the castle of Isle, March 4, 1497, with the honorable title of archbishop of Nazareth. We owe to him the construction of the magnificent nave in the cathedral of Limoges, and the impression of the *Missale ad usum Lemovicensis Ecclesiæ: Parisiis, per Joannem de Prato* (1483, 4to). See *Gallia Christiana nova*, vol. ii, col. 536, 551; Bonaventura, iii, 166, 713, 729, 731.

Montboissier. See PETER THE VENERABLE.

Montbray, GEFFROI DE, a French prelate, was born at Montbray, near Saint Lò, in the early part of the 11th century. Descended from a noble family of Normandy, he was early devoted to the Church, and on April 10, 1049, was consecrated bishop of Coutances. He was present at the assembly held in 1066 by William, duke of Normandy, at Lillebonne, in which it was resolved to invade England. One of the principal promoters of that war, he followed the duke, his friend, to the conquest, and acquitted himself very courageously at the battle of Hastings. He accompanied William to London, and in the ceremony of the coronation at Westminster acted as chamberlain for the states of Normandy. When the Conqueror was recalled to his duchy, he left Geffroi de Montbray at the head of his soldiery. In 1067, when he had defeated the two Anglo-Saxon princes, Edmund and Godwin, Geffroi entered Dorset and Somerset, and there destroyed all who rose in arms, or who were suspected of having taken up arms. Some years after the earls of Northumberland, Norfolk, and Hereford, having rebelled against the Conqueror, Geffroi powerfully aided in the victory of Fagadon, obtained over them in 1074, and forced them to take refuge in Norwich, where he besieged and took them by capitulation. As a reward for these noble and numerous deeds, William gave to him in fief 280 manorial lands. After the death of that prince (1087) he was obliged to return to Normandy, where he died, Feb. 2, 1094. See Ordericus Vitalis, *Historia ecclesiastica; Gallia Christiana*, vol. xi; Thierry, *Hist. de la Conquête de l'Angleterre par les Normands;* Lecanu, *Hist. des Évêques de Coutances;* Fisquet, *France pontificale.*

Montbrun, Charles du Puy, a Huguenot warrior, and a zealous Protestant, was born in the diocese of Gap in 1530. He took an active part in the civil wars of his time, and rendered the Huguenots great service, performing several very daring deeds, and showing his bravery in an especial manner at Jarnac and Montcontour. He was at last captured and executed in 1575. See Allard, *Vie du brave Montbrun* (Grenoble, 1675, 12mo): Martin, *Hist. de Charles Dupuy* (2d ed. Paris, 1816, 8vo); Hoefer, *Nouv. Biog. Générale*, xxxvi, 141–43; Smiles, *Huguenots.*

Montbrun, Guillaume. See BRIÇONNET.

Montchal, CHARLES DE, a French prelate, was born in 1589 at Annonay (Vivarais). His mother was Anne of Guillon. At first abbot of Saint-Amand-de-Boisse, in the diocese of Angoulème, and of Saint-Sauveur-le-Vicomte, in the diocese of Coutances, he became archbishop of Toulouse in 1627 by the resignation of Louis de Nogaret, cardinal of La Villette. The cardinal of La Villette had not received holy orders, and was not even a simple clerk. As for Montchal, he had not only

been ordained, but he was that rare thing among ecclesiastics of quality, a theologian, and even an erudite theologian. He was consecrated in Paris Jan. 9, 1628, and subsequently repaired to his metropolitan town. Toulouse then had a prelate who, clothed in his sacerdotal robes, officiated and preached, which was a great novelty. Charles de Montchal returned to Paris in 1635, and assisted at the assembly of the clergy, where he was one of the principal orators. In 1641 he was present at the assembly of Mantes, the history of which he wrote. In 1645 he again took his seat in the assembly of Paris, where he energetically pleaded the cause of ecclesiastical franchise. Sept. 8, 1643, he consecrated the church of Sorèze. Under his administration the Church of Toulouse prospered greatly, and became enriched by a considerable number of monasteries and convents. He died at Carcassonne Aug. 22, 1651. The zeal of Montchal for religion was that of an enlightened mind. He thought that the Church should be powerful, and was sensible enough to seek for the elements of that power in the example of good morals, the progress of ecclesiastical studies, and the noble triumphs of eloquence. He was the patron of a multitude of learned men, who dedicated their works to him; among them may be mentioned Étienne Molinier, François Combéfis, Innocent Cironius, Casanova, Ravel, etc. He is the author of *Mémoires* (Rotterdam, 1718, 2 vols. 12mo); in these *Mémoires* is the *Journal de l'Assemblée de Mantes*. See *Gallia Christ.* vol. xiii, col. 61; Du Mége, *Hist. des Institut. de la ville de Toulouse*, iii, 126, 127.

Mont de Piété. See MONTES PIETATIS.

Monte, Cardinal del. See JULIUS II.

Monte, Andreas de (אנדריאס די מונטי), a celebrated Jewish convert to Christianity, so named after he had embraced the new faith (before his conversion he was called *R. Joseph Tsarpathi Ha-Alphasi*, רוסף צרפתי האלפסי), was born in the early part of the 16th century at Fez, in Africa (hence his second surname, האלפסי), of Jewish parents, who were natives of France, which is indicated by his first surname (צרפתי, *Gallus*). He emigrated to Rome, where, after exercising the office of chief rabbi for many years, and distinguishing himself as an expounder of the Mosaic law, he embraced Christianity about the year 1552, during the pontificate of Julius III. He at once consecrated his vast knowledge of Hebrew and rabbinical literature to the elucidation of the prophecies, with a view to bringing his brethren into the fold of the Romish Church, and wrote—(1) A voluminous work, entitled מבובת היהודים, *The Perplexity of the Jews*, demonstrating both from the Scriptures and the ancient rabbinical writings all the doctrines of the Christian religion. Bartolocci, who found the MS. in loose sheets in the Neophyte College at Rome, carefully collated it and had it bound. He did not know that it ever was printed, but Fürst (*Bibliotheca Judaica*, iii, 544, s. v. Zarfati) states that it was published in Rome, 16—, 4to. However, Fabiano Fiocchi, in his work called *Dialogo della Fede*, has almost entirely transcribed it, so that the Biblical student may derive all the advantages from it for Christological purposes. (2) An epistle to the various synagogues, written both in Hebrew and Italian, and entitled אגרת שלום, *Lettera di Pace*, dated Jan. 12, 1581. It treats of the coming of the true Messiah, and shows from the prophecies of the O. T., as well as from the works of the ancient rabbins, that he must have come long ago in the person of Jesus Christ (Rome, 16—, 4to). This learned work and the former one are very important contributions to the exposition of the Messianic prophecies, and to the understanding of the ancient Jewish views about the Messiah. Gregory XIII appointed Monte in 1576 preacher to the Hebrews of Rome in the oratory of the Holy Trinity; he was afterwards made Oriental interpreter to the pope, in which capacity he translated several ecclesiastical works from the Syriac and Arabic. He died in the beginning of the 17th century. See Bartolocci, *Bibliotheca Magna Rabbinica*, iii, 848 sq.; Wolf, *Bibliotheca Hebræa* i, 556 sq.; Ginsburg, in Kitto, *Cyclop. Bibl. Lit.* s. v.; Kalkar, *Israel u. die Kirche*, p. 71; Fürst, *Bibl. Jud.* i, 45 (s. v. Andreas).

Monte Cas(s)ino, the first Benedictine convent ever established, "the venerable mother of Western monachism," and for a thousand years the spot especially dear to the great Benedictine order, was so named after the place in which it was located.

Benedict of Nursia (q. v.) having been induced by the representations of the priest Florentius to settle in the Campania, near Naples, found on a mountain, near the old *Castrum Casinum*, a temple of Apollo and a shrine of Venus, which were still resorted to by the heathen inhabitants. He converted them, destroyed the temple and shrine, and in their place erected a chapel dedicated to St. Martin, and soon after commenced building a convent for himself and his followers, which subsequently received the name of Monte Cassino. The undertaking succeeded in spite of difficulties of all kinds (it is said the devil made the stones so heavy that it was impossible to lift them, etc.!), and was terminated in 529. The convent was, of course, subject to the rule of Benedict, who remained its abbot until his death, March 21, 543. He was succeeded by the abbots Constantine, Simplicius, and Vitalis, under whose government the convent, although often invaded by the barbarians, continued to prosper, owing chiefly to the miracles performed by the relics of its founder. In 580 Monte Cassino was stormed by the Lombards. The abbot and monks, taking with them their most valuable ornaments, and the original copy of their rule, fled to Rome, where they were well received by pope Pelagius II. They soon built a new convent by the side of the Quirinal Palace, and remained in possession of it during 140 years. Gregory the Great proved particularly well-disposed towards the order, inciting them to turn their attention towards missions, and particularly to England, from whence they spread to Scotland, Ireland, and Germany. St. Willibrod introduced the order in Friesland, and under St. Bonifacius it acquired supremacy throughout Germany. In 720 pope Gregory II appointed the Brescian Petronax to build a new convent and a church on the ruins of Monte Cassino, which was then only inhabited by hermits, and the church was consecrated by pope Zacharias himself in 748. Petronax was appointed abbot, and the pope confirmed all the donations made to the convent, exempting it at the same time from episcopal jurisdiction, and restoring to it the autograph rule of St. Benedict. But in the mean time the convent had met with an irreparable loss: a French monk, Aigulf de Fleury, had in 633 taken from the ruins the remains of the saint, and carried them to his own convent, which henceforth had taken the name of St. Benoit sur Loire. Abbot Petronax died May 6, 740. Under his successors Monte Cassino became a centre of learning. Prof. Leo, in his *Gesch. v. Italien*, says: "Benevento and the convent of Monte Cassino must be considered as having been for a time, in the beginning of the Middle Ages, the most important abode of scientific activity. Africa, Greece, and the Western German countries met there; and from the meeting of the distinguished men of these different countries resulted naturally a higher intellectual life than could be found anywhere else; for there neither trade nor the coarse enjoyments of immoderate eating or drinking, which engross all in the sea-towns and on the northern coasts, were the adversaries of science" (ii, 21). Among its eminent men we may mention Paulus, the son of Warnefried, the historian of the Lombards, whom, after in sorrow at the fate of his country he had retired to Monte Cassino, Charlemagne repeatedly invited to his court, and who wrote the *Homiliarium*, and taught Greek to the cler-

gy. Under his influence Charlemagne granted great privileges to the order, and subjected all the convents of his empire to their rule. The relations between Rome and Monte Cassino were always of the most friendly character; and while, down to the 8th century, it was Rome that encouraged and sustained the convent in its progress, the latter came in the troubled times of the 8th, 9th, and 10th centuries to be considered by the Romish clergy as the centre of scientific culture. However, in 884, the Saracens attacked the convent, slew the abbot, Bertharius, at the altar, and destroyed Monte Cassino and St. Salvator; and the monks had to flee with their treasures to the convent of Teano. In 886, monk Erchembert, at the head of some of the order, made an attempt to restore the convent; but they were driven off by Greek robbers, and remained until the death of abbot Leo in 915 at Teano, gradually losing their importance. The count of Teano was thus enabled to seize without opposition some of the property of the convent; those of Capua appropriated also a part, and, finally, after the death of Leo, the young archdeacon, John of Capua, a cousin of the duke of Capua, became the abbot of the remaining Cassinites, who now removed to Capua. There they built the church of St. Benedetto, together with a rich college of canons. But they now commenced gradually relaxing the severity of their rule, and we find pope Agapetus II complaining bitterly of their insubordination. In 949 abbot Aligernus succeeded by his zeal in restoring Monte Cassino; through the protection of the princes of Capua he regained the possessions taken from it in former times; he invited colonists, with whom he concluded a "placitum libellari statuto," and built for them in several places churches and chapels. He obliged the monks to devote themselves to agriculture and to literary labors, and enforced the discipline. He obtained also from the emperors Otto I and II the confirmation of the possessions and privileges of the convent, and used every exertion to restore it to its former splendor. He remained abbot thirty-five years, and is called the third founder of Monte Cassino. His successor, Manso (986), only sought to increase the temporal welfare of the convent, regardless of discipline. He led a princely life, and the disorder became so great during his administration that Nilus, visiting the convent, exclaimed: "Let us quickly, my brethren, leave this place, which will soon be visited by the anger of God." Manso, deceived by some of his own monks, died of grief in 996. Nothing particular occurred under the succeeding abbots Athenulph (1011–22), Theobald (1022–35), Richerius (1038–55), Frederick (1057–58). Under abbot Desiderius (1058–87) the order commenced to improve again; he was a son of a duke of Benevento, and had been educated in the convent De la Casa; Leo IX made him cardinal deacon of St. Sergius and Bacchus, and on March 26, 1059, Nicholas II appointed him cardinal priest of the title of St. Cecilia. The next day he was appointed abbot of Monte Cassino. He restored the building, the church was consecrated by pope Alexander II in person, and the number of the monks increased to two hundred. At the same time the discipline was strictly enforced, and scientific studies vigorously resumed (see Giesebrecht, *De litt. studiis apud Italos primis medii ævi sæculis* (Berol. 1845). Gregory VII himself designated Desiderius as his successor, and he was finally made pope, somewhat by force, in 1086, as Victor III. He ever regretted having left his convent, and finally returned to die in the place he loved so dearly, after reigning eight years. His successor as abbot was Oderisius I (1087–1105). Under him the convent received various valuable endowments, a hospital was added to the already existing buildings, and these completed in a very handsome manner. Pope Urban II confirmed by a bull all the donations which had been made to the convent, and replaced the abbey of Glanfeuil, in France, founded by St. Maurus, under the rule of Monte Cassino. Under the successors of Oderisius I the reputation of Monte

Cassino gradually declined again, and was never regained. Among those who inhabited it are yet to be mentioned bishop Bruno of Segni (abbot 1107–11), cardinal Giovanni Gaetano. afterwards pope Gelasius II, and especially the learned Petrus Diaconus. In 1239 the emperor Frederick II dispersed the monks, and occupied the convent with his soldiers. Urban IV then appointed the wise and learned Bernard Ayglerius of Lyons abbot and reformer of the convent. He succeeded in regaining some of its lost possessions, and in subjecting the monks to the discipline, for which purpose he composed the *Speculum Monachorum* (Venice, 1505), and a commentary on the rule of St. Benedict. Bernard died April 3, 1282. In 1294 pope Celestine V made an attempt to change the rule into that of the Celestines, and with that view appointed the Celestine Angelarius abbot of Monte Cassino; but Boniface VIII gave up the attempt. A bull of John XXII made the church of Monte Cassino a cathedral, the abbot bishop, and the monks cathedral canons. Still the order continued to sink, and in 1359 there remained but a few monks living in huts built on the ruins of their convent. Pope Urban V sought to revive an interest in the convent, became himself its abbot, invited the assistance of the other Benedictine convents, had well-disciplined Benedictines imported from two other convents, and finally in 1370 appointed Andreas de Faenza, a Benedictine of the Camaldula, abbot of Monte Cassino. But the political troubles which were then agitating Italy, and particularly Naples, prevented prosperity in the convent, and pope Julius II incorporated it with the Benedictine convent of St. Justina.

The services which have been rendered to science by the convent of Monte Cassino are related by Dom Luigi Tosti in his *Storia della Badia di Monte-Cassino, divisa in libri nove ed illustrata di note et documenti* (Naples, 1842–43, 3 vols.). He concludes with the words: "At present there are some twenty monks dwelling in the vast convent, attending with praiseworthy diligence to the singing of psalms and their devotions; they take much trouble in educating a school of fifteen boys, who wear the monks' garb, and they direct the seminary of the diocese of Cassino, containing some sixty pupils. They occupy themselves, besides, in publishing old works contained in the archives of the convent." See Tosti's *Archivi Casinese* (Naples, 1847); Maclear's, *Hist. Christian Missions*, p. 172. See MONASTERY.

Monte Catino, ANTONIO, an Italian philosopher, was born at Ferrara in 1536. Of noble extraction, he studied different sciences in his own country, and became professor of philosophy. He was particularly esteemed by duke Alfonso II, who chose him for his secretary, and sent him as ambassador to the court of France, and to that of Rome. According to Muratori, he repaid the family of his benefactor with ingratitude, and was the principal instrument in the overthrow of the duchy of Ferrara by the Holy See. He died at Ferrara in 1599. Monte Catino is the author of *Aristotelis Politicorum lib. iii* (Ferrara, 1587–97, 3 vols. fol.); this Latin version is accompanied by a commentary, which Naudé does not esteem very highly; and the second volume, which appeared in 1784, contains also the *Republic* and the *Laws* of Plato, as well as some fragments:—*In octavum librum Physicæ Aristotelis Commentarius* (Ferrara, 1591, fol.):—*In primam partem lib. iii Aristotelis de Anima.* Francesco Patrizi has dedicated to Monte Catino one of the volumes of his *Discussiones Peripateticæ*, and he has left a magnificent eulogy of the virtues of this philosopher. See Bayle, *Dict. Critique*, s. v.; Naudé, *Bibliogr. Polit.* vol. xxvii; Ag. Superbi, *Apparato degli Uomini illustri di Ferrara*; Muratori, *Antichità Estensi*, pt. ii, c. 14; Tiraboschi, *Storia della Letter. Ital.* vol. vii, pt. i.

Monte Corvino, JOHN DE (chiefly known on account of his wonderful missionary labors in the East), a native of France, was born in 1247. By papal authority Monte Corvino visited India in 1291, and thence proceeded to China, where he was kindly received by the emperor Kublai Khan, who permitted him to build a church at Peking, then called Cambalu. In spite of the opposition he met, not only from Pagans, but also from Nestorians, he seems to have been so successful that as a result of eleven years' labor he baptized nearly 6000 persons and gathered 150 children, whom he taught Greek and Latin, and for whom he composed sundry devotional works. He also translated into the Tartar language all of the N. T. and Psalms. The success which attended his labors caused Clement V to constitute him archbishop of Peking in 1307, and seven bishops were sent to him as suffragans. His death occurred in 1330, and scarcely forty years passed before the results of his life-work were almost annihilated by the Ming dynasty, which expelled his successors. See Williams, *Middle Kingdom* (see Index in vol. ii); Newcomb, *Cyclop. of Missions.* (H. W. T.)

Monte Oliveto, a rich and famous abbey in Italy, is the most noted place of this order. The Order of the Holy Sacrament, also known as the Congregation of the Body of Jesus Christ, united with the Olivetenses in 1582. See Brunel, *Hist. du Clergé seculier et regulier* (Amst. 1716, 18mo), ii, 288, 291.

Monte, Pietro dal, a celebrated Italian ecclesiastical canonist, was born at Venice in the latter part of the 15th century. After studying Greek and Italian under the direction of Guarino, he was made master of arts in Paris, and then obtained the rank of doctor in Padua. In 1433 he was made apostolic prothonotary, and in 1434 was sent by pope Eugenius IV to the council at Basle. He afterwards went to Rome to ask of her citizens, in the name of that council, a tax for liberating a nephew of the pope, whom cardinal Condolmieri had imprisoned. In 1434 he was sent to England to collect the taxes due the pontifical court. He remained in that country five years, during which time he became a favorite of the duke of Gloucester, uncle of the king. In 1442 he was made bishop of Brescia, a position which he held for two years. He was afterwards sent to France as legate of the Holy See. In 1447 he again visited Rome to assist in the ceremonies attending the ordination of pope Nicholas V. On his return to Brescia he founded many churches and a few religious institutions. Monte died in 1457, leaving a reputation worthy of a learned and pious man. His works are, *Repertorium Juris utriusque* (Bologna, 1465, 3 vols. fol.):—*Monarchia, in qua generalium conciliorum materia, de potestate et præstantia Romani Pontificis et Imperatoris discutitur* (Rome, 1496, 4to):—a Latin translation of the *Miraculum Eucharistiæ* of St. Epiphany (Rome, 1523, 8vo). Some fragments of his discourses and letters have been published by cardinal Quirini in his *Fr. Barbari Epistolæ*, t. ii, and in his *Epistolæ ad Benedictum*.

Montenat, BENOÎT, a French ecclesiastic, was born about the commencement of the 16th century; he was almoner to duke Charles of Bourbon, but he was so little known that his name cannot be found in the *Bibliothèque Française* of La Croix du Maine. At the request of Anne of France, daughter of Louis XI, he wrote in 1505 a treatise on the *Conformité des prophètes et Sibylles avec les douze articles de la foi;* this work remains unedited, and is preserved among the manuscripts of the Imperial Library, No. 7287. See Paulin. Paris, *Manuscrits Français de la bibliothèque du Roi*, vii, 310.

Montenegro, called by the natives *Tchernagora*, and by the Turks *Karadagh*, i. e. Black Mountains, in view of the dark appearance of the wooded hills of this remarkably mountainous country, is a semi-independent Slavish principality, between lat. 42° 10′ and 42° 56′ N., and long. 18° 41′ and 20° 22′ E.; bounded on the north by the Turkish provinces of Bosnia and Herzegovina, on the south and east by Albania, and on the west by the Dalmatian circle of Cattaro, and covering a territory of 3738 square miles, with a population of about 311,000.

General Description.—The country is very mountainous, and agriculture is therefore prosecuted to a moderate extent only, and in a very rude and primitive manner. The products are like those of other European lands of the same latitudes. "The general aspect of Montenegro," says Wilkinson, the celebrated English traveller, "is that of a succession of elevated ridges, diversified here and there by a lofty mountain-peak, and in some parts looking like a sea of immense waves turned into stone. Trees and bushes grow amid the crags, and in the rugged district of Ceoo the fissures in the rocks are like a glacier, which no horse could pass over without breaking its legs. The mountains are all limestone, as in Dalmatia; but in no part of that country do they appear to be tossed about as in Montenegro, where a circuitous track, barely indicated by some large loose stones, calling itself a road, enables a man on foot with difficulty to pass from the crest of one ascent to another. Some idea of the rugged character of the country may be formed from the impression of the people themselves, who say that 'when God was in the act of distributing stones over the earth, the bag that held them burst, and let them all fall upon Montenegro.' The chief productions cultivated there are Indian corn and potatoes; cabbages, cauliflowers, and tobacco are also grown in great quantities, and vegetables are among the principal exports of Montenegro. Potatoes, indeed, have been a most profitable acquisition to the poor mountaineers, as well for home consumption as for exportation, since their introduction in 1786" (*Dalmatia and Montenegro* [London, 1848, 2 vols. 8vo], i, 411-413). Besides agriculture, the chief occupation of the Montenegrins is fishing. There are few who exercise any trade, though some perform the offices of blacksmiths, farriers, or whatever else their immediate wants may require. They are knit together in clans and families, and have many feuds among themselves, which are perpetuated by the hereditary obligation of avenging blood. In their disposition towards strangers they are, like most mountaineers, hospitable and courteous, and bear a friendly feeling for those who sympathize with their high notions of independence and devotion to their country. They are cheerful in manner, and though very rude, yet by no means uncouth. Education among them is at a very low ebb; in fact, it is held in contempt, and many, even among the priests, are unable to read or write. In 1841 several schools were established, and the art of printing introduced; but the unsettled state of the country has hitherto prevented much improvement. Their language is a very pure Servian dialect, called by Krasinski "the nearest of all the Slavonian dialects to the original Slavonic tongue; that is, that into which the Scriptures were translated by St. Cyril and Methodius in the 9th century, and which still continues to be the sacred tongue of all the Slavonian nations who follow the Eastern Church."

There are no towns in Montenegro, and the largest village contains only 1200 inhabitants. Cettigne or Tzettinie, the seat of government, contains between twenty and thirty well-built houses, besides a convent and the palace of the prince of Montenegro. The villages are unwalled; the houses, or rather huts, which compose them are very rarely provided with chimneys, and in the elevated districts are more wretched in appearance than even the mud-hovels of Ireland. "The houses," says Wilkinson, "are of stone, generally with thatched roofs, but many are covered partly or entirely with wooden shingles, a mode of roofing very common in Slavonic countries. Some of the better kinds are roofed with tiles, on which large stones, the primitive nails of Montenegro, are ranged in squares, to keep them from being torn off by the wind. Each house generally con-

tains one or two rooms on the ground-floor, with a loft above, occupying the space between the gables, where they keep their Indian corn and other stores. The ascent to it is by a ladder, applied to a square hole in its floor, calling itself a door; and this floor, which performs the part of ceiling to the lower room, is frequently of wicker-work, laid on rafters running from wall to wall. The lower room is at once the parlor, the sleeping-room, and the kitchen; but in the small villages the houses have no loft, and their style of building is very primitive, the walls being merely of rude stones, without cement, and the roof of the coarsest thatch. In the better kind of houses is a bedstead, standing in one corner of the room. It may be styled a large bench, and generally consists of planks resting on a simple frame, having the head and one side to the wall; and a foot-board, with a post running up to the ceiling, completes the whole wood-work. Those who can afford it have a large mattress and quilt, or blankets; but no Montenegrin bed is encumbered with curtains or sheets, and the only extras seen upon it are intended for warmth, in which the struccha [somewhat like the Scotch plaid, and worn by both sexes over their shoulders] performs an essential part. Native visitors are satisfied to roll themselves up in their strucche and lie on the floor, which is the bare earth; and the poorer people, who cannot afford bedsteads, do the same at their homes, though this is no great hardship to the Montenegrin, who is accustomed, as long as the season will allow him, to sleep out of doors, upon the ground, or on a bench made of stones and mud. But whether in or out of the house, in a bed or on the ground, the Montenegrin always keeps on his clothes, his arms are close to his side, and when aroused by any alarm, or by the approach of morning, he is up at the shortest notice; and no toilet intervenes, on ordinary occasions, between his rising and his pipe. The embers of the fire, which had been covered up with ashes the night before, are then scraped up, and the usual habits of the day begin. The fireplace, which is in another corner of the room, is a raised hearth on the floor, with a caldron suspended from a ring above; it also serves as an oven, the Montenegrin bread being merely dough baked in ashes, as by the Arabs now and by the patriarchs of old, and without leaven. Chimneys are an unknown luxury in most Montenegrin houses, and the smoke escapes as it can. The furniture is not abundant, consisting of a bench, a few wooden stools, and a simple table; and the only brilliant-looking objects in the house are the arms and dresses of the inmates. Clocks or watches are also luxuries unknown to Montenegro, except at Tzettinie and the convents, and the only mode of ascertaining time is by watching the sun, or by common hour-glasses, and an occasional sundial. In some of the wildest mountain districts the houses or huts are of the meanest character, made of rough stones piled one on the other, or of mere wicker-work, and covered with the rudest thatch, the whole building being merely a few feet high. Few houses in Montenegro have an upper story, except at Tzettinie, Rieka, and some other places, where they are better built than in the generality of the villages, of solid stone, and roofed with tiles. Warm houses are indeed very requisite there in winter, when it is very cold, the level of the whole country being considerably above the sea, amid lofty peaks covered with snow during many months, and subject to stormy winds that blow over a long range of bleak mountains. The climate, however, is healthy, and these hardy people are remarkable for longevity.

"Both men and women are very robust, and they are known to carry as much as 200 funti (about 175 pounds) on their shoulders, over the steepest and most rugged rocks. All appear muscular, strong, and hardy in Montenegro; and the knotted trees, as they grow amid the crags, seem to be emblematic of their country, and in character with the tough, sinewy fibre of the inhabitants. But, though able, the men are seldom inclined to carry anything, or take any trouble that they can transfer to the women, who are the beasts of burden in Montenegro; and one sees women toiling up the steepest hills under loads which men seldom carry in other countries. They are therefore very muscular and strong, and the beauty they frequently possess is soon lost by the hard and coarse complexions they acquire, their youth being generally exhausted by laborious and unfeminine occupations. The sheaves of Indian corn, the bundles of wood, and everything required for the house or the granary are carried by women; and the men are supposed to be too much interested about the nobler pursuits of war or pillage to have time to attend to meaner labors. As soon as the tillage of the lands is performed, they think they have done all the duties incumbent upon men; the inferior drudgery is the province of the women, and the Montenegrin toils only when his inclination demands the effort. The men therefore (as often is the case in that state of society), whenever active and exciting pursuits are wanting, instead of returning to participate in or lighten the toils necessity had imposed on the women, are contented to smoke the pipe of idleness or indulge in desultory talk, imagining that they maintain the dignity of their sex by reducing women to the condition of slaves. The men wear a white or yellow cloth frock, reaching nearly to the knees, secured by a sash around the waist; under it is a red cloth vest, and over it a red or green jacket without sleeves, both richly embroidered, and the whole covered by a jacket bordered with fur. They wear a red Fez cap, and white or red turban, below which protrudes at the back of the neck a long lock of hair. The women wear a frock or pelisse of white cloth and open in front, but much longer than that of the men, and trimmed with various devices, and with gold ornaments in front as well as around the neck. The red cap of the girls is covered with Turkish coins arranged like scales. The red cap of the married women has, instead of coins, a black silk border, and on gala days a bandeau of gold ornaments. Women and men wear opanche (sandals), the soles of which are made of untanned ox-hide, with the hair taken off, and that side outward, and these enable them to run over the steepest and most slippery rocks with facility. The marriage ceremonies are celebrated with great signs of rejoicing. Eating and drinking form a principal part of the festivity, with the noisy discharge of guns and pistols, and the duration of the entertainment depends on the condition of the parties." When a young man resolves on marrying, he expresses the wish to the oldest and nearest relation of his family, who repairs to the house of the girl, and asks her parents to consent to the match. This is seldom refused; but if the girl objects to the suitor, he induces some of his friends to join him and carry her off; which done, he obtains the blessing of a priest, and the matter is then arranged with the parents. The bride only receives her clothes, and some cattle, for her dowry.

Political Divisions and Government.—Montenegro is divided into the districts of Montenegro Proper and Brda or Zjeta, each of these being subdivided into four "nahies" or departments, and these are further subdivided, each subdivision having its own hereditary chief. Some islands in the Lake of Scutari also belong to Montenegro. Until 1852 the head of the government was the *Vladika* ("metropolitan," or "spiritual chief"), who, besides his proper office of archbishop and ecclesiastical superior, was at the same time chief ruler, lawgiver, judge, and military leader. This theocratic administration became (1697) hereditary in the Petrovitch family, but as the vladika cannot marry, the dignity was inherited through brothers and nephews. (See below.) Since 1852 the two offices have been disjoined, and the vladika is restricted to his ecclesiastical office, while the cares of government devolve upon the "Gospodar" ("hospodar") or lord, though the common people still apply to him the title "sveti gospodar," which

properly belongs to the vladika alone. The vladika Pietro II (1830–51) established a senate of sixteen members, elected from the chief families of the country, and in this body the executive power is vested. The public officers, local judges, and public representatives are appointed by popular election. From time to time an *Assembly* of all the adult males of the country takes place in a grassy hollow near Cettigne, the capital; but the powers of this assembly are very undefined. For defraying the expenses of government, taxes are levied on each household. The prince also receives from Russia a subsidy of 8000 ducats (£3733), and from France one of 50,000 francs (£1980). As the Montenegrin, even when engaged in agricultural operations, is always armed with rifle, yataghan, and pistols, an army of

Military Costume of the "Hospodar."

26,000 men can be summoned on the shortest notice, and in desperate cases 14,000 more troops can be raised. Their intense love of independence and heroism in defence of their country are worthy of the highest respect; but out of their own country they are savage barbarians, who destroy with fire and sword everything they cannot carry off.

History.—Montenegro belonged in the Middle Ages to the great Servian kingdom, but after the dismemberment of the latter, and its conquest by the Turks at the battle of Kossovo (1389), the Montenegrins, under their prince, who was of the royal blood of Servia, maintained their independence, though compelled to relinquish the level tracts about Scutari, with their chief fortress of Zabliak, and confine themselves to the mountains (1485). In 1516 their last secular prince resigned his office, and transferred the government to the vladika. The Porte continued to assert its claim to Montenegro, and included it in the pachalic of Scutari; but the country was not conquered till 1719, and on the withdrawal of the Turks soon afterwards, it resumed its independence. In 1710 Montenegro sought and obtained the protection of Russia, the czar agreeing to grant an annual subsidy on condition of harassing the Turks by inroads, and this compact has, down to the present time, been faithfully observed by both parties. Another part of the agreement was that the vladika be consecrated by the czar, and this continues to be done even now, though this officer is at present only an ecclesiastical ruler. In 1796 the prince-bishop, Pietro I, defeated the pacha of Scutari, who had invaded Montenegro, with the loss of 30,000 men; and for the next quarter of a century we hear no more of Turkish invasions. The Montenegrins rendered important aid to Russia in 1803 against the French in Dalmatia, and took a prominent part in the attack on Ragusa, the capture of Curzola, and other achievements. Pietro II, who ruled from 1830 to 1851, made great efforts to civilize his people and improve their condition. He established the senate, introduced schools, and endeavored, though unsuccessfully, to put an end to internal feuds and predatory expeditions into the neighboring provinces. Some Turkish districts having joined Montenegro, the Turks attacked the latter in 1832, but were repulsed. A dispute with Austria regarding the boundary resulted in a war, which was terminated by treaty in 1840. In 1851 the last prince-bishop died, and his successor, Danilo I, separated the religious from the secular supremacy, retaining the latter under the title of gospodar. This step caused the czar Nicholas to withdraw his subsidy (which was renewed, and the arrears paid, by the czar Alexander II), and the imposition of taxes thus rendered necessary caused great confusion. This was taken advantage of by the Turks, who, under Omer Pasha, invaded the country; but the intervention of the great powers compelled a treaty, Feb. 15, 1853. Danilo, however, in vain endeavored to obtain the recognition of Montenegro as an independent power, though he repaired to the Paris Conference in 1857 for this purpose. He, moreover, greatly improved the laws and condition of the country. In 1860 the Montenegrins excited an insurrection against the Turkish rule in the Herzegovina, which was soon suppressed, and in return they themselves were so hard pressed by the Turks that they were glad to agree to a treaty (Sept. 13, 1862) by which the sovereignty of the Sublime Porte over Montenegro was recognised, though the word itself consigning such authority is not stated in the compact. The present ruler of the country is Nikita, a man of good education, secured in Paris and Berlin, and an excellent politician, who has been actively engaged in seeking support from Austria, Russia, and Germany to establish the complete independence of his realm. Since the commencement of the Pan-Slavic movement he has enjoyed many favors from Russia, and received from its emperor in 1869, while on a visit to St. Petersburg, a historical sword, with the Servian inscription "God save the king." In 1874 new complications arose with Turkey on account of murders committed on the Albanian borders, and Montenegro declared war in January, 1875; but a compromise was effected towards the end of the month. Since 1871 a political weekly has been published at Cettigne, and there are now telegraphic connections in the Montenegrin possessions. There is also a post-office department, which was established with the aid of the Austrian government in 1872. The most recent improvements are of a character indicating a very rapid progress in culture.

Religion.—The Montenegrins are members of the Non-united Greek Church, excepting only a few Roman Catholics and Jews. The czar of Russia is recognised as the highest authority, for to him belongs the ordination of the *Vladika*, the spiritual head of the Montenegrin Church. As we have seen above, the vladika was formerly both temporal and spiritual ruler. He is now prince-bishop, and next to him in authority stands the archimandrite of the convent of Ostrok. Priests, of whom there are about 200, are ordained by the vladika, and are charged thirty dollars for admission to holy orders, the money going to the state. They join in war and in the other occupations of the people. The priests must also be married before they can come up for con-

Pontifical Costume of the Montenegrins.

secration, but the vladika is not allowed to marry; and as the office must be kept within the family to which it has descended since 1516, the succession always falls to a nephew, or some other male relative. The vladika has an annual revenue of $10,000. The Montenegrin Greek Christians, who number, according to the *Statistical Year-book of the Russian Empire* (vol. ii, 1871), 125,000, hate the pope equally as the Turks. They reject images, crucifixes, and pictures, and will not admit a Romanist without rebaptizing him. Monasticism exists to a small extent. Their principal convents are those of Tzetinie, Ostrok, and St. Stefano. See Wilkinson, *Dalmatia and Montenegro*, vol. i, ch. vi; Krasinski, *Montenegro and the Slavonians in Turkey* (Lond. 1855); and the same author in the *Brit. and For. Qu. Rev.* July, 1840; Vaclik, *La Souveraineté du Montenegro* (Leipsic, 1858); Ubicini, *Les Serbes du Turquie* (Paris, 1865); Noe, *Montenegro* (Leipsic, 1870); Nightingale, *Religious Ceremonies*, p. 99–112; Daniels, *Geographie*, ii. 61 sq.

Montenses seems to have been a local name of the *Donatists*. St. Augustine says distinctly that in his time those heretics were called "Montenses" at Rome (Aug. *Hær.* lxix). Epiphanius and Theodoret both associate the name, on the other hand, with the *Novatians* (Epiph. *Hær.* lix; Theodor. *Hær.-fab.* iii, 5). In the early list of heresies which goes under the name of St. Jerome it is said that the Montenses were found chiefly at Rome, and that they were so named because they had concealed themselves in the hill-country during a time of persecution. This author speaks of them as distinct from the Donatists and Novatians, but as adopting the heresy of the one as to the rejection of penitents, and of the other as to rebaptism (Pseudo-Hieron. *Indicul. de Hæres.* xxxiv). In one of the canons of the African code, which directs the mode of receiving a person into the Church when coming "de Donatistis vel de Montensibus," the two names seem to be used as synonymous.

Montereuil, BERNARDIN, a learned Jesuit, was born in Paris in 1569, and died there in 1646. But little is known of his personal history. He is, however, distinguished for his works, of which *A History of the early State of the Church* and *A Life of Jesus Christ* are highly esteemed.

Montesar. See MONCON.

Montesino, ANTHONY, a noted Spanish Dominican, flourished in the 16th century. He entered the order at Salamanca, and died as a martyr in the West Indies in 1645. His only work is, *Informatio juridica in Judæorum defensionem.* See Echard, *Biblioth. Prædicatorum* (Par. 1719–21, 2 vols. fol.), ii, 123.

Montespan, FRANÇOISE ATHENAÏS, *Marquise de*, one of the mistresses of Louis XIV. noted for her profligacy and vices, deserves a place here because of the influence she exerted on the fate of the religion of France. She was born in 1641, married to the marquis de Montespan in 1663, but, supplanting the duchess de la Valliere in the affections of the king in 1668, the marquis was banished from court. The marchioness, freed from the authority of her husband, became the mistress of a ruler who claimed to be a faithful servant of the Church of Rome. In 1670 she accompanied him to Flanders, and unblushingly revealed her real position at court. She openly braved the queen and the whole kingdom. But, what is stranger still, she endeavored to reconcile imperious vice with humble piety, and formed a set of morals for herself which Christians would hardly care to endorse. She did not disdain to work for the poor, and, like many others, brought herself to believe that frequent alms and exterior practices of devotion would purchase a pardon for everything. She even presented herself at the communion-table, favored by absolutions, which she either purchased from mercenary or procured from ignorant priests. One day she endeavored to obtain absolution from the curate of a village who had been recommended to her on account of his flexibility. "What!" said this man of God, "are you that marchioness de Montespan whose crime is an offence to the whole kingdom? Go, madam, renounce your wicked habits, and then come to this awful tribunal." She went, not indeed to renounce her wicked habits, but to complain to the king of the insult she had received, and to demand justice upon the confessor. The king, naturally religious, was not sure that his authority extended so far as to judge of what passed in the holy sacraments, and therefore consulted Bossuet, preceptor to the dauphin and bishop of Condom, and the duke de Montauzier, his governor. The minister and the bishop both supported the curate, and tried upon this occasion to detach the king from Madame de Montespan. The strife was doubtful for some time, but the mistress at length prevailed. In 1675 she lost her hold on the king, who had fallen in love with Madame de Maintenon (q. v.), and she never regained her former position in the reign of her master and former lover. She retired to Paris for the winter, and in the summer visited watering-places. In 1707, while away at one of these places (Bourbon), she died, neither regretted by the king, her children, nor the nation. One half of her life was spent in grandeur, and the other half in contempt. She was rather ashamed of her faults than penitent for them. In a word, her reign was so intolerable and fatal that it was looked upon in France as a judgment from heaven. See *General Biographical Dictionary*, s. v.; Saint-Simon, *Mémoires;* Voltaire, *Siècle de Louis XIV;* Houssaye, *Mlle. de la Vallière et Mme. de Montespan;* see also LOUIS XIV. (J. H. W.)

Montes Pietātis (Fr. *Mont de Piété,* Ital. *Monte di Pietá*) is the name of charitable institutions, thoroughly Christian in origin and purpose, the object of which is to lend money to the very poor at a moderate rate of interest. They date from the close of the mediæval period, when all such transactions were in the hands of usurers, to whom the necessities of the poor were but an inducement to the most oppressive extortion. The principle was to advance small sums, not ordinarily exceeding $100, on the security of pledges, but at a rate of interest barely sufficient to cover the working expenses of the institution, any surplus to be expended for charitable purposes. The earliest of these charitable banks is believed to have been that founded by the Minorite Barnabas at Perugia in 1464, and was confirmed by pope Paul III. Another was founded at Padua in 1491, and a third (the first in Germany) was established in 1498 at Nuremberg. The first opened at Rome was under Leo X; and the Roman Monti di Pietá are confessed to have been at all times the most successful and the best managed in Italy. The institution extended to Florence, Milan, Naples, and other cities. The Mont-de-Piété system has been generally intro-

duced into France and Germany, the state now controlling its affairs, and not the Church. It has also been introduced into Spain, and into the Spanish provinces of the Netherlands. It formed the model of the *Loan-Fund Board* of Ireland, established by the administration of queen Victoria.

Montesquieu, CHARLES DE SECONDAT, *Baron de la Brède et de,* one of the most noted moralists of the world, and a celebrated French writer, was born Jan. 18, 1689, at the Chateau de la Brède, in the immediate neighborhood of Bordeaux. He was descended from a

Montesquieu's Birthplace.

noble and otherwise distinguished family of the province of Guienne. Even as a youth he gave the promise of his future fame. His habits were most studious, and his desire for learning was encouraged in every way by a fond and judicious father. While engaged in a most laborious study of the civil law, with a view to the profession for which he was destined, young Montesquieu was also much devoted to the study of general literature and philosophy, and even found time to prepare a work on a theological subject, namely, *Whether the Idolatry which prevailed among the Heathen deserved eternal Damnation?* His love of the writers of antiquity had led him to enter the lists in defence of pagan writers, pronouncing them worthy of salvation. The book was favorably received, but did not create much stir. In 1714 Montesquieu attained the rank of "conseiller" in the Parliament of Bordeaux, and three years afterwards, on the death of a paternal uncle, he succeeded at the same time to his fortune and to his post of "président à mortier" in the same Parliament. With the most assiduous and conscientious discharge of his duties as a judge, he yet continued the pursuit of literature. His most favorite studies were historical and moral sciences. But he also loved the study of the natural sciences, and even joined in 1716 the Academy of Bordeaux, zealous to direct the attention of this body to physical science. He seems at this time to have been very much impressed with the importance of physical science. He wrote about this time his *Physical History of the Ancient and Modern World,* which was published in 1719. He shortly returned, however, and allowed the academy likewise to return, to literature and morals; and he now wrote several small essays on literary and moral subjects, which were read at meetings of the academy. In 1721, just six years after the death of Louis XIV, when France had outlived the lethargy of the last years of the great reign, and the orgies of the regency were in full swing, Montesquieu appeared with the work which first brought him fame, the *Lettres Persanes,* which was published anonymously. The author, however, was soon recognised, and his name was in everybody's mouth. The book, in which, in the character of a Persian, he ridicules with exquisite humor and clear, sharp criticism the religious, political, social, and literary life of his countrymen, secured him a place in the "Academy," though he had even levied his attacks against it. It is supposed that the *Siamois* of Dufresny, or the *Espion Turc,* suggested the plan of this work, but, be this as it may, its execution is entirely original. "The delineation of Oriental manners," says D'Alembert, "real or supposed, of the pride and the dulness of Asiatic love, is but the smallest of the author's objects; it serves only, so to speak, as a pretext for his delicate satire of our customs, and for other important matters which he fathoms, though appearing but to glance at them." Some censures which Montesquieu in his *Persian Letters* bestowed upon the conduct of Louis XIV caused the work to be regarded with an evil eye at court; and one or two sarcasms levelled at the pope awakened the zeal of such as were rigidly devout Romanists, or found it convenient to seem so, and Montesquieu was industriously represented as a man equally hostile to the interest of religion and the peace of society. Those calumnies reached the ear of cardinal de Fleury; and when Montesquieu, sustained by the public opinion of his talents, applied for the place which M. Sacy's death had left vacant in the French Academy, that learned body was made to understand that his majesty would never give his consent to the writer of the *Lettres Persanes;* because, though his majesty had not read the work, persons in whom he placed confidence had pointed out its poisonous tendency. Without feeling too much anxiety for literary distinction, Montesquieu perceived the fatal effect that such an accusation might produce upon his dearest interests. According to D'Alembert, Montesquieu waited upon Fleury, therefore, and signified that, although for particular reasons he had not acknowledged the *Lettres Persanes*, he was very far from wishing to disown that work, which he believed to contain nothing disgraceful to him, and which ought at least to be read before it was condemned. Struck by these remonstrances, the cardinal perused the work, the objections were removed, and France avoided the disgrace of forcing this great man to depart, as he had threatened, and seek among foreigners, who invited him, the security and respect which his own country seemed little inclined to grant. This story of D'Alembert is by some discredited, and, instead of it, Voltaire's version is accepted. According to him, "Montesquieu adopted a skilful artifice to regain the minister's favor: in two or three days he prepared a new edition of his book, in which he retrenched or softened whatever might be condemned by a cardinal and a minister. M. de Montesquieu himself carried the work to Fleury—no great reader—who examined a part of it. This air of confidence, supported by the zeal of some persons in authority, quieted the cardinal, and Montesquieu gained admission to the Academy" (*Ecrivains du Siècle de Louis XIV*, sec. *Montesquieu*). The authenticity of this statement, however, appears to rest solely on Voltaire's evidence, not altogether unexceptionable in the present case. D'Alembert's account is generally preferred. Shortly after his admission to the Academy, Jan. 24, 1728, Montesquieu set out for a journey to qualify himself for the arduous task of investigating and appreciating the different political or civil constitutions of ancient or modern times, and in order to study, as far as possible, the manners and character, the physical and moral condition, of the European nations by actual inspection. He first visited Vienna, along with lord Waldegrave, the English ambassador. From this city, after conversing with the celebrated prince Eugene, and surveying all that seemed worthy of notice, he passed into Hungary, and afterwards to Italy, where he met with lord Chesterfield, and travelled in his company to Venice. While examining the singular institutions of this republic, and canvassing the subject with eager frankness in places of public resort, he learned that he had incurred the displeasure of the authorities, and was in danger of persecution. He instantly embarked for Fucino, next visited Rome, and, having surveyed Switzerland and the United Provinces, he repaired in 1730 to Great Britain. Newton and Locke were dead, but the philosophical traveller found men in England qualified to estimate his talents. He was respected and patronized by queen Caroline, and enjoyed the intimacy of Pope, Bolingbroke, and many other eminent characters of that

period. He spent there two years, and collected much material for his future literary labors. He was made aware of the great esteem in which the English held him by being chosen a fellow of the Royal Society. After his return to Brède, Montesquieu published his *Considérations sur les Causes de la Grandeur et de la Décadence des Romains* (Paris, 1734), a masterly view of Roman history, expressed in a sententious, oracular, and vigorous style. "In attempting to derive the grandeur and downfall of Rome from the admitted principles of human nature, he gave a new turn to such investigations. If some elements of a problem so complex have been omitted, and others rated too high or too low, the work must be allowed to exhibit views of political society, at all times specious, often equally just and profound: the vivid pictures, the acute and original thoughts, with which it everywhere abounds, are to be traced in many succeeding speculations. It deserves praise also for the manly and liberal tone of feeling that pervades it." But by far his greatest work, on which he had been engaged for twenty years, the *Esprit des Lois*, he published in 1748 (Geneva, 2 vols.). In it Montesquieu attempts to exhibit the relation between the laws of different countries and their local and social circumstances. It was immensely popular. No fewer than twenty-two editions were published in eighteen months, and it was translated into various European languages. "The *Esprit des Lois*," says a contemporary, "is a wonderfully good book, considering the age in which it appeared. Without adopting Voltaire's hyper-eulogistic criticism, that 'when the human race had lost their charters, Montesquieu rediscovered and restored them,' it may be said that it was the first work in which the questions of civil liberty were ever treated in an enlightened and systematic manner, and to Montesquieu, more than to any other man, is it owing that the science of politics has become a favorite subject of study with the educated public." "The *Esprit des Lois*," says another, "is one of the most laborious books ever written. It had an immense influence on the literature of the age, and founded that method of philosophizing and finding out facts to justify opinion which characterized his followers of the French school, and entered in a great measure into the spirit of the Scottish school of philosophy. Like most original-minded men, he brought to his work a degree of genius and knowledge which his imitators could not cope with, and which concealed, in his hands, the defects of the system." "Notwithstanding," says Villemain, "some expressions here and there inexact, according to our ideas, from their very materialism, the character of his writing is generally metaphysical. Succeeding the light and brilliant epicureanism and scepticism of the 18th century, the *Esprit des Lois* began the spiritualist reaction which Rousseau carried on" (*Cours de Littérature*, vol. i, ch. iv). The work rendered great service to humanitarianism by the respect it paid to human life. Pascal, indeed, in his letter on homicide, had preceded him in this, but we know how indifferent on this subject were the courtly and elegant Frenchmen of that day; how little they troubled themselves about "those Breton peasants who were never tired of being hanged." Montesquieu did not wish absolutely to restrain the utmost penal power of the law, but he recommended clemency and equity, and in his own century Tuscany abolished capital punishment. As Dr. Vinet has well said, we may further commend the author of the *Spirit of Laws* for his "respect for human nature; his love for justice; his true philanthropy; his reverence for all the virtues which ennoble man and his destiny; and, in short, for his attachment to the principles which form the basis of human society." But, though the work found many friends, there were yet some who took decided exception to many of its doctrines. Thus the editor of the *Gazette Ecclesiastique*, long deeply engaged in the Jansenist quarrels which then agitated France, assailed the author of the *Esprit des Lois* in two pamphlets with the charge of deism, and the weightier though contradictory one of following the doctrines of Spinoza. The defence which Montesquieu published, admirable for its strain of polite irony, candor, and placid contempt, was entirely triumphant. Indeed, abilities of a much lower order than his would have sufficed to cover with ridicule the weak and purblind adversary who discovered the source of the *Esprit des Lois* in the *Bull Unigenitus*, and blamed his opponent for neglecting to examine the doctrines of grace and original sin. It is to be wished that Montesquieu had employed means so legitimate to counteract Dupin's criticism. His admirers would willingly forget that when a copy of the latter's work, ready for circulation, fell into his hands, he carried it to the royal mistress, Madame Pompadour, and allowed her to inform Dupin that, as the *Esprit des Lois* enjoyed her special favor, all objections to it must be instantly suppressed. It must be borne in mind, however, that Montesquieu held a place peculiarly his own, and quite apart from the Christian writers. He was a moralist to be sure, but he did not claim to be a theologian, nor even a devoted or enthusiastic Christian, but simply a cold and calculating philosopher, and as such it was much for him to turn aside and pay the high tributes and warm encomiums to Christianity which he did pay in all his writings; and it may indeed be asserted that "among the laymen of the 18th century no one has spoken so admirably of Christianity." Says he, in the *Spirit of Laws*, "How admirable the Christian religion, which, while it seems only to have in view the felicity of the other life, constitutes the happiness of this" (bk. xxiv, ch. iii). This is very unlike the sneering infidelity of Bayle or Voltaire.

Montesquieu's moral doctrine is, perhaps, best gleaned from his *Pensées Diverses*, collected from his MSS., and published in 1758. From this work it appears that he differed little from the ancient stoicism, though he has not laid it down in a systematic form. His own nature was his true system. Nevertheless he loses no opportunity of boasting of stoicism in general: "No philosopher has ever made men feel the sweetness of virtue and the dignity of their nature better than Marcus Aurelius; he affects the heart, enlarges the soul, and elevates the mind." "If I could for a moment cease to think that I am a Christian, I could not possibly avoid ranking the destruction of the sect of Zeno among the misfortunes that have befallen the human race." The stoicism of Montesquieu is softened and restrained by a certain feeling of religion. Stoicism alone could not satisfy this loving mind. In the picture which he draws of human virtues, the idea of God constantly returns, not as something useless, but as its necessary completion. He several times took the opportunity of expressing the very lively aversion that he felt to atheism: "The pious man and atheist always talk of religion: the one speaks of what he loves, and the other of what he fears." This aversion, which had its principle in the uprightness of his mind, was strengthened by his acquaintance with the real necessities and true condition of society. He defended with no less warmth the immortality of the soul: "Although the immortality of the soul were an error, I should be sorry not to believe it: I confess I am not so humble as the atheists. I know not how they think, but, for myself, I would not exchange the idea of my immortality for the happiness of a day. I delight in believing that I am immortal as God himself. Independently of revelation, metaphysics give me a very strong hope of my eternal happiness, which I would not willingly renounce. Indifference about a future life leads us to be soft and easy with regard to the present, and renders us insensible and incapable of everything which implies an effort." Montesquieu knew that all religion is social, while atheism is eminently anti-social. Montesquieu felt this, and more than once expressed it. Not only does he admit that "all religions contain precepts useful to society," but he declares that religion is the best guarantee that

we can have for the morals of mankind;" and he goes so far as to say that "all societies require a religion." No one has shown better than he the intimate relation between religion and social life; and it is interesting to observe that it is in the *Persian Letters*, namely, in the work into which he has introduced the rashest statements, and in which he has conceded most to the ideas and manners of his time, that we find this remarkable passage, which explains so well what we have merely indicated: "In any religion which we profess, the observance of laws, love to men, devotedness to parents, are always the first religious acts. . . . For, whatever religion a man professes, the moment any religion is supposed, it must also necessarily be supposed that God loves mankind, since he establishes a religion to render them happy; that, if he loves men, we are certain of pleasing him in loving them also; that is, in exercising towards them all the duties of charity and humanity, and not breaking the laws under which they live." In the *Spirit of Laws*, and in the *Thoughts*, we meet with passages much stronger in favor of Christianity, proving that Montesquieu understood it far better than the moralists of his time, at least in the philosophical view. But for further development of these criticisms we must refer the reader to Vinet, *Hist. of French Lit. 18th Century* (Engl. by the Rev. James Bryce, Edinb. 1855, 8vo), p. 199 sq. Montesquieu died at Paris, Feb. 10, 1755. The private character of Montesquieu was such as the tendency of his works might lead us to anticipate. Possessing that calm independence which secured him respect, he possessed also that mildness and benignity of character which displayed itself in a cheerful temper, and obtained for him universal love. He was distinguished by the readiness which he always manifested to use his influence with the government in behalf of persecuted men of letters; and strict frugality frequently enabled him, without impairing the property of his family, to mitigate the wants of the indigent. Burke characterizes him as "a genius not born in every country or every time; a man gifted by nature with a penetrating, aquiline eye; with a judgment trained by the most extensive erudition; with a herculean robustness of mind, and nerves not to be broken with labor." The most complete edition of his works is that by D'Alembert and Villemain (Paris, 1827, 8 vols. 8vo). Nugent's translation of the *Spirit of the Laws*, together with D'Alembert's biographical sketch of Montesquieu, were published at Cincinnati in 1873. See Voltaire, *Siècle de Louis XIV et Louis XV*; D'Alembert, *Éloge de Montesquieu*; Villemain, *Éloge de Montesquieu* (1820); Riaux, *Notice sur Montesquieu* (1849); Maupertuis, *Éloge de Montesquieu* (1755); Bersot, *Montesquieu* (Paris, 1852); Burs, *Montesquieu u. Cartesius*, in *Philos. Monatshefte*, Oct. 1, 1869; Sainte-Beuve, *Causeries du Lundi*, vii, 41 sq.; Mennechet, *Littérature Moderne* (Paris, 1857, 12mo), iv, 125–143; and the excellent article in the *Edinburgh Cyclop.* s. v.

Montesquieu-Fezensac, DE, FRANÇOIS XAVIER MARC ANTOINE, *abbé*, a French ecclesiastic, was born near Auch in 1757. He was a deputy from the clergy of Paris to the States-General in 1789, and was twice elected president of the National Assembly. During the Reign of Terror he took refuge in England, but after the second Restoration returned to his native country and was made a duke, receiving the title of minister of state. He died in 1832. See Guizot, *Mémoires*.

Monteth (or **Monteith**, or even **Montieth**), ROBERT, a Scotch priest, who was chaplain of cardinal de Retz and a canon of Notre Dame, flourished near the middle of the 17th century. He wrote mainly works on secular history. See Allibone, *Dict. of British and American Authors*, s. v.

Monteverde, CLAUDIO, an Italian composer, was born at Cremona about 1565, and died at Venice in 1649. He composed both secular and ecclesiastical music, but was particularly celebrated for his motets and madrigals; of the latter he produced five books.

Montfaucon, BERNARD DE, one of the learned Benedictines of Saint-Maur, noted for his valuable antiquarian labors, was born Jan. 17, 1655, of a high family of Soulage, in Languedoc. He early evinced great facility for acquiring languages, and a remarkable love of study. He was educated at the College of Limoux, but threw aside his books, and in 1672 entered the army, and served in several campaigns under Turenne. After the death of his parents, he joined the Benedictines at Toulouse in 1675. His time was now largely employed in correcting the Latin translations of the Greek Church historians. Dom Claude Martin, to whom he communicated his work, pointed him out to his superiors as a man of great capacity, and particularly fitted to take a part in the publication of the Greek fathers contemplated by the Congregation of St. Maur. He was consequently called to Paris in 1687. The following year he published his *Analecta sive varia opuscula Græca* (Paris, 1844, 4to), which contains also some lives of saints. In 1690 he published *La vérité de l'histoire de Judith* (2d ed. Paris, 1692, 12mo), in which, with a great deal of historical talent, he attempts to establish the authenticity of the facts related in that narrative against the opinion of those who consider it as a fable or a parable. But his reputation rests chiefly on the part he took in the publication of the works of the fathers. He first gave Athanasius (Paris, 1698, 3 vols. folio), revised by means of the MSS. of Paris and of the Vatican, with a new Latin translation; the third volume contains the doubtful and spurious works. With this is connected the *Collectio nova patrum et scriptorum Græcorum* (Par. 1707, 2 vols. fol.). In this work Montfaucon gives, besides an excellent biography of Athanasius, some newly discovered works of that father, those of Eusebius of Cæsarea, and the *Topographia Christiana* of the Egyptian monk Cosmas Indicopleustes. The critical tact and acumen, the extensive learning, and the thorough linguistic knowledge which Montfaucon evinced in these works, led his superiors to intrust him also with the publication of the works of Chrysostom. As the MSS. at Paris were insufficient, he was sent to Rome to consult the codices of that city. Innocent XII showed him the greatest regard, while one of the librarians of the Vatican, out of jealousy, defamed and persecuted him. He refused high offices which were opened to him at Rome, and devoted himself exclusively to his studies. The pope and cardinals were lavish in their attentions, and Montfaucon, during the intervals of his ecclesiastical functions, gave frequent and unequivocal proofs of the learning which he possessed and was anxious to augment. It is related that Zacagni, then sublibrarian of the Vatican, feeling his vanity wounded by the praise bestowed on this accomplished foreigner, laid several schemes to lower him in the public estimation. One day while Montfaucon, among a crowd of distinguished persons, happened to be sauntering in the library, Zacagni, with affected politeness, requested the antiquary to favor him with the date of a Greek manuscript which he spread out before him. Montfaucon replied that apparently it was written about 700 years ago. His antagonist, with a triumphant sneer, desired him to observe the name of Basil, the Macedonian, written at the top. The Frenchman asked if it were not Basil Porphyrogenitus, later by 150 years; and as this, upon examination, proved to be the case, Zacagni retired with his manuscript, and thenceforth left the stranger at peace. After his return to Paris Montfaucon published the *Hexapla* of Origen (1713, 2 vols. fol.), with variations, notes, and introductory remarks not only on the work itself, but on the general history of the Greek versions of the Bible. His next publication was an edition of the works of Chrysostom (Par. 1718 sq., 13 vols. fol.; Venice, 1780, 14 vols. 4to). Montfaucon had consulted the French, Roman, English, and German codices; the text was accompanied by a new Latin transla-

tion, a biography of Chrysostom, numerous notes, and an introduction to each separate work. This is universally pronounced one of the chef-d'œuvres of the Maurines, and the best edition of this Church father. Some time previous to this Montfaucon had published another valuable work, *Le Livre de Philon de la Vie Contemplative* (Par. 1709, 12mo), with notes, and an attempt to prove that the Therapeutæ of whom Philo speaks were Christians; and in 1710 an *Epistola* on the fact mentioned by Rufinus that St. Athanasius baptized children when himself a child. In 1719 he gave to the world a great work on the history of art, entitled, *L'Antiquité expliquée et Representée en Figures;* and in 1729 *Les Monuments de la Monarchie Française.* His last but not least important work is his *Bibliotheca Bibliothecarum MSS. nova* (Par. 1739, 2 vols. fol.). He died suddenly at the abbey of Saint-Germain-des-Près, Dec. 21, 1741. He was chosen a member of the Academy of Inscriptions in 1719, and contributed many papers to this and other learned bodies. Montfaucon was celebrated for the mildness and benignity of his character. Neither the favors which he had received from an emperor, nor the honors with which he was decorated by two successive popes, could at all abate his humility; and strangers who conversed with him returned not more surprised at the amazing extent of his information than at the unpretending simplicity of his manners. Of an author who has left 44 vols. folio, it may be expected that elegance will not be a characteristic; and, accordingly, Montfaucon's writings are blamed for their cumbrous style and defective arrangement. But his erudition, a quality more befitting such pursuits, has never been called in question; and his works are still looked up to as guides through that obscure and intricate department of knowledge which he devoted his life to study. See *Edinburgh Cyclop.* s. v.; Tassin, *Histoire littéraire de la Congrégation de St. Maur,* p. 591 sq.; Fabricius, *Bibl. Græca,* xiii, 849; *Éloge de Montfaucon,* in the *Hist. de l'Acad. des Inscriptions,* vol. xvi; *Gentleman's Magazine* (Dec. 1855), p. 572. (J. H. W.)

Montferrat, formerly an independent duchy of Italy, between Piedmont, Milan, and Genoa, and consisting of two separate portions, Casale and Acqui, lying between the Maritime Alps and the Po, and having an area of over 1300 square miles, with its capital at Casale, is now incorporated in the kingdom of Italy. Montferrat, after the downfall of the Frankish empire, was ruled by its own margraves till the beginning of the 14th century. This illustrious house for a long time disputed the sovereignty of Piedmont with the house of Savoy, and sent to the Crusades more heroes than any other sovereign house in Europe. Members of the family ruled simultaneously in Montferrat, Thessaly, and Jerusalem. On the death of the marquis John I in 1305, his sister, Iolande or Irene, who was empress of Constantinople, succeeded to Montferrat; and her second son became the founder of the family of Montferrat-Palæologus, which became extinct in 1533, when Montferrat passed to the Gonzagas of Mantua. In 1631 the dukes of Savoy obtained possession of a portion of the territory, and in 1703, with the consent of the German emperor, the remaining portion passed under their sway, and was incorporated with their own dominions. The cession of Savoy to France after the war of 1869 placed Montferrat for a while under French rule, but after the conflict between Germany and France in 1870 Italy gained back this territory, and it now forms a part of the united kingdom. The ecclesiastical history is detailed in the article ITALY.

Montfiquet, RAOUL DE, a noted French writer on asceticism, was born in the village of Montfiquet, near Bayeux, towards the close of the 15th century. He was a doctor of theology, and enjoyed great distinction among his fellows. He died about 1520. His works, which are much sought after by bibliographers on account of their antiquity, are, *Tractatus de vera, reali* *atque mirabili existentia totius Christi* (Paris, 1481, fol.): —*Le Livre ou Traicté du sainct sacrement de l'autel* (Paris, 1500, 4to):—*Exposition de l'Oraison Dominicale* (Paris, 1485, 4to):—*Exposition de l'Ave Maria* (Paris, 4to):—*Le Guidon et Gouvernement des gens mariez, traitié singulier du sainct sacrement, estat et fruit du mariage* (Paris, about 1520, 4to). See Hoefer, *Nouv. Biog. Générale*, s. v.

Montfort, SIMON DE, a bold, merciless, and superstitious, but devoted follower of the papacy, was descended from the counts of Montfort, near Paris. He was born about the middle of the 12th century. His career dates from the year 1199, when he appears as a leader in the Crusade of Cery, where he was associated with Rainald de Montmirail, Garnier, bishop of Troyes; Walther of Brienne, and the marshal of Champagne, Geoffroy of Villehardouin, and others. The crusade set forth Oct. 8, 1202. A bargain had been previously made with the Venetians, by which the latter agreed to furnish "ships and other conveniences to pass the sea." When the time for embarkation arrived, the Crusaders were lacking 34,000 marks of the stipulated price. The "wise old doge" saw his advantage, and proposed that Venice would fulfil her part of the treaty if, in discharge of the 34,000 marks of silver, the Crusaders would lend their aid in the conquest of Zara. After much hesitation, the plan was acceded to by all but De Montfort. "We are Christians; we war not against our brother Christians," said he. "His object in assuming this position," says Villehardouin, "was to break up the misguided army." After the capture of Zara, the Crusaders advanced to Constantinople for the purpose of placing young Alexius on the throne. The pope denounced the design. He excommunicated the Venetians; but of this no one took the slightest heed, except De Montfort. He, with his brother and a few French knights, separated themselves from the camp of the Crusaders, passed over to the king of Hungary, and, amid many difficulties, made for the Holy Land to fulfil his vows to the Church. He finally, however, returned home, and after a short rest took up arms again at the summons of pope Innocent III, and in the summer of 1209 he was made leader of the crusade against the Albigenses. Under his guidance and that of the pope's legate, Amaury, abbot of Citeaux, the crusading army marched into Languedoc and besieged the town of Béziers, which was stormed July 22, 1209. A horrible massacre ensued. One of the superior officers inquired of the abbot of Citeaux how they were to distinguish the heretics from the faithful: "Slay them all!" returned the savage Churchman, "for the Lord knoweth those that are his." Not a living soul was spared. It is said that fifteen thousand people were thus mercilessly slaughtered in this one place. Carcassone was scarcely better treated; and at Lavaur the ferocious deeds of Montfort made his name a byword of tyranny and cruelty. In 1210 De Montfort was invested by Peter of Aragon with the viscounty of Béziers and Carcassone. Peter designed, no doubt, in this way to conciliate De Montfort, and protect his (Peter's) kinsmen from the rapacity and savagery of De Montfort. He was, however, disappointed, and in 1213 Peter crossed the Pyrenees with a force superior to that of Simon to protect his own. Yet Simon, impressed with a fanatical conviction that God would give him the victory, confessed his sins, made his will, placed his sword upon the altar, and declared that he took it back from God to fight his battles, and at the battle of Muret defeated and slew Peter and the larger part of his army. After the battle of Muret, the progress

and success of the Crusaders were uninterrupted. Toulouse was taken in 1215. De Montfort was chosen prince of the whole subjugated territory; a strict inquisition after heretics was ordered, and the Church of Rome, pleased with the faithfulness of her servant Simon, at a Council of the Lateran, November, 1215 (styled the twelfth General Council), confirmed him in all his conquests. On his return to Northern France, he was received with the greatest honor as the champion of the faith, and hailed with acclamations: "Blessed is he that cometh in the name of the Lord!" The remaining years of the life of De Montfort were consumed in a bloody struggle to maintain his ascendency over the territory he had subdued. During the year 1216 the people, under the leadership of the younger count Raymond, broke out in general insurrection. But success still followed De Montfort. He with his army sacked Toulouse, and plundered the inhabitants to the very last piece of cloth or measure of meal. "Oh, noble city of Toulouse!" exclaims the troubadour, "thy very bones are broken!" The ensuing year the war with the young count Raymond continued to the advantage of De Montfort, till suddenly the old count Raymond appeared before Toulouse. The city received him with the utmost joy. New walls were built and new fortifications raised. It was in the siege of this place that De Montfort lost his life, June 25, 1218; when heading an attack, a stone from an engine struck on the head the champion of Jesus Christ (as he was called by his admirers), and he died on the spot. His fanatical followers reproached God with his death. A monkish historian adds also that he received five wounds from arrows; and in this respect likens him to the Redeemer, "in whose cause he died, and with whom we trust he is in bliss and glory." A daring and skilful leader; chivalric, affable, and popular; enthusiastically devout and fanatically attached to Romanism; ambitious, unscrupulous, and remorseless, he naturally rose to the position of guiding spirit in the turbulent times in which he lived and the cruel war in which he engaged. See Milman, *Hist. of Latin Christianity*; *Chronique de Simon, Comte de Montfort* (printed in Guizot's *Mémoires relatifs à l'Histoire de France*); Hoefer, *Nouv. Biog. Générale*, xxxvi, 246–257; and the histories of the *Albigenses* (q. v.).

Montfort Manuscript (CODEX MONTFORTIANUS, known as MS. 61 of the Gospels, 34 of the Acts, 40 of the Pauline Epistles, and 92 of Revelation), so named from a Cambridge divine of the 17th century, who gave it to archbishop Usher, by whom it was presented to Trinity College, Dublin, in the library of which it still remains (there designated as G. 97); an octavo cursive Greek MS. of the entire N. T., written in the 15th or 16th century, on 455 paper leaves, and famous as containing the text of "the three heavenly witnesses" (1 John v, 7, that leaf being *glazed* to preserve it from in-

Specimen of the *Codex Montfortianus*—containing the noted text 1 John v. 7. A strict translation, line for line, is as follows:

for—[there] are three that bear—
witness in the heaven, father, word, and holy spirit,
And these the three, are one. And [there] are three that bear—
witness in the earth, spirit, water, and blood, if we
receive the witness of men, the witness of
god is greater, for—this is the witness of god, that—
he hath testified concerning his son.

jury). An earlier owner was William Clap, once a fellow of Cambridge, who derived it from Thomas Clement, and originally it belonged to one Froy, a Franciscan friar. It is apparently the work of three or four successive scribes, perhaps in part at first independent of each other; and the Apocalypse bears marks of having been copied from the Codex Leicestrensis. It is doubtless the "Codex Britannicus" referred to by Erasmus as his sole authority for inserting the above disputed text in his edition of 1522, in accordance with a promise he had made to his detractors that if a single Greek MS. could be found containing it he would add it. See WITNESSES, THE THREE HEAVENLY. It has the Ammonian sections, and the number of verses noted at the end of the MS., with the Latin division of chapters. There are many corrections by a more recent hand, erasures of the pen, etc. An imperfect collation of it, while in Usher's hands, was printed in Walton's *Polyglot*. Dr. Banet collated the remainder for his edition of the Dublin palimpsest Z, and more recently Dr. Dobbin has published a complete collation (*The Codex Montfortianus*, etc., Lond. 1854). See Tregelles, in Horne's *Introd.* iv, 218 sq.; Scrivener, *Introd. to N. T.* p. 149. See MANUSCRIPTS, BIBLICAL.

Montgaillard, Bernard de, also known as *Petit Feuillant*, a Roman Catholic ecclesiastic noted for his great talent in pulpit oratory, but especially for the part he bore in the Roman Catholic intrigues against the Huguenots, was born at Montgaillard, in the diocese of Toulouse, in 1563. He commenced as a Feuillant, or mendicant friar, in 1579, and began to preach immediately, though he had not studied divinity. He preached at Rieux, Rhodes, and Toulouse with so much success that they applied to him this passage in Holy Writ, "Happy is the womb which bare thee." He went to France at the time when Henry III drew the Feuillants thither, and so charmed the French court with his sermons that the king and queen-mother appointed him to preach upon several particular occasions. Here he acquired the reputation of the most eminent preacher that had been known in the memory of man —so great were his talents for the pulpit, especially in moving the passions and subduing the heart. He condemned himself to so austere a way of life among the Feuillants that the pope commanded him to quit that order, lest he should shorten his days by it. He behaved himself furiously in supporting the interest of the League, and bore a considerable part in the horrible crimes of that villainous combination. "The preachers," says Maimbourg (*Hist. de la Ligue*, liv, iii, 295), "of whom the most noted were father Bernard de Montgaillard, surnamed the Petit Feuillant, and the famous Cordelier Feuardent, who preached in the parishes of Paris during the Christmas holidays, changed their sermons into invectives against the sacred person of the king," etc. Montgaillard is charged with having been instrumental in inflaming the rebellious elements of his day, and with having suborned an assassin to murder Henry IV. Montgaillard died in 1628. He was at that time abbé of Orval. Such a saint as Montgaillard, and one who had done such singular services to the holy Church must needs have possessed qualities above the usual standard, and therefore the writers of his life have not hesitated to assert that God performed great miracles both in his favor and by his means. See Bayle, *Dict. Hist.* s. v.; *Gen. Biogr. Dict.* s. v.

Montgaillard, Jean Jacques de, a French monastic, noted as a writer on religious topics, was born in 1633 at Toulouse, and early entered the Dominican order in his native place. He died there March 21, 1711. He is the author of a curious work entitled, *Monumenta Conventus Tolosani ordinis F. F. Prædicatorum* (Toul. 1693, fol.), which contains much valuable material for the history of the Inquisition in that district of France. Himself a devoted Romanist, and believing the harshest measures of the Inquisition justifiable in

behalf of religion, he does not withhold anything, however barbarous or outrageous, and his work contains many a page presenting a most ghastly spectacle of inhumanity perpetrated by misguided fanatics.

Montgaillard, Pierre Jean François de, a French prelate, brother of the preceding, was born at Toulouse, March 29, 1633, and was educated at Paris, where he entered the Sorbonne, by which high school he was created doctor. He entered holy orders, and soon rose to positions of ecclesiastical distinction. In 1664 he was made bishop of Saint-Pons, and distinguished himself by great liberality of sentiment as well as religious devotion. He was one of the nineteen bishops who signed a petition to pope Clement IX for the pardon of the bishops of Alet, Passiers, Beauvais, and Angers, who had opposed the doctrines espoused in the papal bull issued by Alexander VII to defend the Jesuits and their tenets and practices. He also afterwards defended persecuted ecclesiastics against the Jesuits, whose immorality he unhesitatingly denounced. He was so severe that he was branded as a Jansenist, but there is proof extant that he freed himself from the imputation of disloyalty to the Church of Rome. He died March 13, 1713. He was well versed in archæological studies, and noted for his valuable attainments in ancient ecclesiastical history. His works are of a controversial nature, and of value only to those interested in the Jansenist controversy. A list of them is given by Hoefer, *Nouv. Biog. Générale*, xxxvi, 265, 266.

Montgomery, Alexander, a Presbyterian minister, was born in Westfield, N. Y., in 1808. He graduated at Amherst College, Mass., in 1837; studied theology first in Union Seminary, New York City, and afterwards in Auburn Seminary, N. Y.; was licensed by Hampden Congregational Association, Mass., and ordained in 1839 as pastor of Maryville Church, N. Y., where he remained until he removed West, and joined the Presbytery of Chicago, and was agent for some time. He finally settled at Beaver Dam, Wisconsin, where he labored until his death, Feb. 18, 1859. Mr. Montgomery was an earnest Christian, a good theologian, and a fervent preacher. See Wilson, *Presb. Hist. Almanac*, 1868, p. 121.

Montgomery, Henry Eglinton, D.D., a noted clergyman of the Protestant Episcopal Church, was born in Philadelphia Dec. 9, 1820; was educated at the University of Pennsylvania, class of 1839; studied law for two years; travelled in Europe, and then continued his studies in Nashotah College, in Wisconsin. After remaining there two years, he entered the general theological seminary at New York. He was ordained for the holy ministry by bishop Alonzo Potter, and in 1846 assumed charge of All-Saints' Church of Philadelphia, then a small organization. His labors were very successful; the Church-membership rapidly increased, and the pastor became highly respected and beloved. In 1855 he received and accepted a call to the Church of the Incarnation of New York, which was an offshoot of and dependent upon Grace Church, and which worshipped in the edifice at the corner of Madison Avenue and Twenty-eighth Street. During the earlier years of his ministry in New York he was able to separate his church from Grace Church; and so efficient and satisfactory was his work that in 1864 a new church building was erected at Madison Avenue and Thirty-fifth Street. His labors were identified with it until his sudden decease, Oct. 15, 1874. Dr. Montgomery was a man of acknowledged ability, and of more than ordinary endurance. He was always a hard worker; he had no assistant in his ministry, and, besides the constant demands upon his strength made by a growing Church, he had for years been a prominent member of nearly all the missionary and home societies for the advancement of the Gospel. The Missionary Society, which was in session when his death occurred, paid him a very warm and merited tribute through bishop Vail on Oct. 15, 1874. See *The Church Journal and Gospel Messenger*, Oct. 22, 1874.

Montgomery, James (1), D.D., a clergyman of the Protestant Episcopal Church, was born in Philadelphia Nov. 25, 1787, and was educated at Princeton College, where he graduated in 1815. After practicing law for a short time, he prepared for holy orders; was ordained in 1816, and elected rector of St. Michael's, N. J. In 1818 he became rector of Grace Church, New York, and subsequently removed to St. Stephen's, Philadelphia, where he held several important offices, and devoted himself to his ministry with much earnestness till his death, March 17, 1834. His works are five *Sermons*, issued at different times. See Sprague, *Annals of the Amer. Pulpit*, v, 596.

Montgomery, James (2), one of the greatest of English hymnologists, was born at Irvine, in Ayrshire, Scotland, Nov. 4, 1771. His parents were Irish—his father a Moravian preacher. James was designed for the same office, and in his sixth year was placed in the Moravian establishment at Fulneck, near Leeds, England. While here his parents went as missionaries to the West Indies, where they soon died. To their fate he thus beautifully alludes:

"My father—mother—parents, are no more!
  Beneath the lion-star they sleep,
  Beyond the Western deep:
And when the sun's noon glory crests the waves,
He shines without a shadow on their graves."

Left to himself, he refused to study for the ministry, and the Brethren placed him as an apprentice to a grocer in Mirfield. He disliked the drudgery of the shop, wrote verses, and at length ran away, with three shillings and sixpence in his pocket. He was soon compelled by necessity to engage as a shopboy in the village of Wath, in Yorkshire. He remained there but a year, and then, intent upon publishing a volume of verses, went up to London, and introduced himself to one of the Brethren in Paternoster Row, and gained employment as clerk and general assistant; but he could get no one to undertake publishing his poetry. In eight months we find him back again at Wath. In his twenty-first year he went to Sheffield as clerk to the editor of the *Sheffield Register;* and when, two years afterwards, a political prosecution was instituted against the editor, Montgomery succeeded him in the management of the paper, changing its name to that of *The Iris*. The tone of his paper was very temperate, but firm. At that time the quailing cause of arbitrary power and divine right was making its last struggles against freedom and commonsense. Notwithstanding the moderation of our poet-editor, it was not long before the hands of the officers of the law were upon him. The publication of a song written by a clergyman to commemorate the destruction of the Bastile, which had been printed in half the newspapers in the kingdom, was made the pretence of fining Montgomery £20 and imprisoning him three months in the Castle of York. On his deliverance from his incarceration he resumed his editorial labors, and avoided every extreme in politics; but in giving a narrative of the circumstances attending the death of two men killed in a riot in the streets of Sheffield by the military, a volunteer officer, who was also a magistrate, feeling his honor wounded by the statement, presented him for libel. The result was another fine of £30, and imprisonment for six months. During his confinement, in 1796, he wrote his poems entitled *Prison Amusements*. He now became a regular contributor to magazines, and, despite adverse criticism in the *Edinburgh Review* (Jan. 1807, p. 347–355; comp. however, July, 1835, p. 473), established his right to rank as a poet. (See the defence by Southey in [Lond.] *Qu. Rev.* vi, 405 sq., and by Wilson in *Blackwood's Magazine*, Sept. 1831, p. 476.) In 1805 he issued *The Ocean;* in 1806, *The Wanderer of Switzerland, and other Poems;* and the next year *The West Indies*—this last meeting in its

various editions with a most extraordinary patronage. In 1813 appeared *The World before the Flood;* in 1819, *Greenland;* and in 1827 *The Pelican Island*, the most original and powerful of all Montgomery's works. He now also collected two volumes of his sketches from periodicals, entitled *Prose by a Poet*. *A Poet's Portfolio* appeared in 1835. In 1830–31 he delivered a course of lectures on poetry and general literature, which were afterwards published in one volume. His collected works appeared in 1851 (1 vol. 8vo).

But it is with the poet as a writer of hymns and sacred songs that we have most to do, as it is by these that he has most endeared himself to his age, and will be longest and most favorably remembered. In 1822 he published his *Songs of Zion, being Imitations of Psalms*. This work consisted of sixty-seven pieces, being versions of fifty-nine Psalms, closely as well as beautifully rendered. In 1828 he published his *Christian Psalmist*, containing 103 original hymns; in 1853, *Original Hymns for Public, Private, and Social Devotion*. Judged by the use made of these hymns by the Christian world, Montgomery takes his place next to Watts and Wesley, in company with Doddridge. This place we think he has well earned. What Advent song surpasses for comprehensiveness, appropriateness of expression, force, and elevation of sentiment, this one beginning "Angels from the realms of glory?" What a glorifying of God and his work from eternity to eternity is found in this hymn, "Songs of praise the angels sang!" Will the time ever come on earth when the Church will not respond to "Stand up and bless the Lord, ye people of his choice?" or cease to look forward with anticipations of victory in the "Hark, the song of jubilee?" or forbear to encourage one another with "Daughter of Zion, from the dust?" or fail to use "Oh, where shall rest be found?" What a spirit of Christian love, mingled with hope drawn from the deepest truths of our faith, flows through the invitation, "Come to Calvary's holy mountain;" and a reaching out of the right hand of fellowship in this, "Come in, thou blessed of the Lord!"

In a letter written in 1807 Montgomery gives us the history of his hymnological efforts. "When I was a boy," he says, "I wrote a great many hymns; indeed, the first-fruits of my mind were all consecrated to Him who never despises the day of small things, even in the poorest of his creatures. But as I grew up, and my heart degenerated, I directed my talents, such as they were, to other services; and seldom indeed, since my fourteenth year, have they been employed in the delightful duties of the sanctuary. Many conspiring and adverse circumstances that have confounded, afflicted, and discouraged my mind, have also compelled me to forbear from composing hymns of prayer and praise, because I found that I could not enter into the spirit of such divine themes with that humble boldness, that earnest expectation and ardent feeling of love to God and truth which were wont to inspire me when I was an uncorrupted boy, full of tenderness and zeal and simplicity." We have indicated here the main ground of the excellence and usefulness of his hymns. They are the offspring not only of a heart naturally sensitive to religious themes, but of a deep, rich, and varied Christian experience. They were lived before they were sung. From the experiences of the Christian life came their expression in Christian song; hence they are applicable to every believer's feelings, and touch unexpectedly the most secret springs of joy and sorrow, faith, fear, hope, love, despondency, and triumph. This was the reason for their success given by the author himself. When advanced in life and seriously ill, he placed in the hands of his friend, Dr. Holland, "transcripts of his original hymns to be read to him. But as the poet was much affected, the doctor was about to desist, when Montgomery said, 'Read on; I am glad to hear you. The words recall the feelings which first suggested them, and it is good for me to feel affected and humbled by the terms in which I have endeavored to provide for the expression of similar religious experience in others. As all my hymns embody some portion of the joys or sorrows, the hopes and fears of this poor heart, so I cannot doubt but that they will be found an acceptable vehicle of expression of the experience of many of my fellow-creatures who may be similarly exercised during the pilgrimage of their Christian life.' "

From the fact that he was a layman in active and laborious business, he was less likely than some of his clerical brothers in song to make the hymn simply a doctrine in rhyme. While evangelical in faith, his hymns are always far more than doctrinal statement in verse. The rules which he laid down in the " Introductory Essay" to his *Christian Psalmist*, which should be adhered to in writing hymns, he has seldom failed to regard. "There should be," he says, " unity, gradation, and mutual dependence in the thoughts, a conscious progress, and at the end a sense of completeness," and he insists that hymns ought to be easy to understand. It may be said of his hymns without exception that there is nothing in them to offend the taste, and much to gratify it. The most precious truths of Scripture and the richest experiences of the Christian find in them simple but poetic expression; and they are made suitable for the use of congregations by a poet who was quite familiar with the requirements of an assembly of worshippers. As expressive of how important Mr. Montgomery deemed his last work, and of his high appreciation of the works of others, may be quoted part of the closing paragraph of his preface. He says: "Having on three former occasions expatiated freely on hymnology and sacred poesy, I will close this egotistical preamble to the most serious work of my long life (now passing fourscore years) with a brief quotation from what may be esteemed a sainted authority on such a subject. Bishop Ken somewhere says, beautifully, humbly, and poetically:

'And should the well-meant song I leave behind
  With Jesus' lovers some acceptance find,
  'Twill heighten even the joys of heaven to know
  That in my verse saints sing God's praise below.'"

His last years were passed in ease and comfort, he enjoying, besides the frugal earnings of an industrious life, from 1835 a pension from the government of £150 per annum. He died at his own residence near Sheffield, April 30, 1854. The London *Athenæum*, shortly after his death, thus spoke of him: "Montgomery held a place in the eyes of the English public—universal as well as sectarian—not far behind Campbell, by the side of Lisle Bowles and Milman, and before such lesser lights as Carrington and Crowe. This generation knows less than its predecessor of the poems of James Montgomery, of Sheffield. Some have adopted Pollok as their religious poet elect; others have taken Keble as their bosom friend. But the author of 'The West Indies,' 'The World before the Flood,' and 'Greenland,' is still not forgotten, in spite of these shiftings of the shrine at which religious fashion chooses to burn its incense; and his vogue may one day return—the sooner because it was merited by the genuine gifts of the poet as well as by the eloquence of the class-preacher." *Memoirs of the Life and Writings of James Montgomery, with Extracts from his Correspondence*, etc., were published in 1855–6 (7 vols. 8vo) by two of his friends, John Holland and James Everett. An abridgment of these Memoirs was published by Mrs. Helen C. Knight at Boston in 1857 (12mo, 416 pages). See *British and For. Ev. Rev.* vol. xxii; xliii, 248; [*Lond.*] *Qu. Rev.* vol. xi, art. ix; *North Amer. Rev.* (Oct. 1857) p. 563; *Living Age*, xlv, 370; xlvii, 282; Howitt, *Homes and Haunts of British Poets*; Wilson, *Essays, Crit. and Imag.* (1856) ii, 238; and especially the excellent article in Allibone's *Dict. of Brit. and Amer. Auth.* ii, 1345–47.

Montgomery, Robert, an Anglican clergyman, very noted especially as a writer of sacred poetry, was born at Bath, England, in 1807, and was educated at

Lincoln College, Oxford, where he secured his A.B. in 1833, and A.M. in 1838. He took holy orders in 1835; became curate of Whittington, subsequently (1836) removed to London as minister of Percy Street Episcopal Chapel; afterwards went to Glasgow, where he preached for four years, but returned to London, and resumed functions at Percy Street Chapel in 1843, and there preached until his death, December 3, 1855. Montgomery's works comprise a large number of volumes in prose and verse, on themes more or less sacred. He is best known by his poem *The Omnipresence of the Deity* (1828), which has passed through twenty - eight editions, and *The Christian Life: a Manual of Sacred Verse* (1848, 12mo; 6th edition, 1853, 24mo). The former of these provoked unusual severity of criticism—even lord Macaulay unmercifully poured his invectives against it: " His works have received more enthusiastic praise, and have deserved more unmixed contempt, than any which, as far as our knowledge extends, have appeared within the last three or four years. . . . The circulation of this writer's poetry has been greater than that of Southey's *Roderick*, and beyond all comparison greater than that of Cary's *Dante*, or of the best works of Coleridge" (Macaulay, *Essays*, i, 257, 265–7, 269, 276). Nevertheless, as has been well said, the book must have pleased, or people would not have bought it in the face of such unfavorable comments. It must be stated also that the work on its appearance met with the high commendations of those illustrious writers, Southey, Wilson, Alison, and Sharon Turner. Montgomery's *Christian Life* was generally commended; and some Anglican writers were most enthusiastic in its praise. The *Church of England Quarterly* (April 9, 1849, No. 50, p. 286) pronounced it "far superior to anything else from the author; and, of all the uninspired collections of religious poetry which any poet has ever produced in any Church or age or country, there is none which, in our opinion, can venture a comparison — intellectual or poetical — with Montgomery's *Christian Life*." A writer in the *Scottish Magazine* goes even further: "To eulogize this divine *now* as a successful Christian poet would be to offer an indignity to all who have the slightest knowledge of what is passing in the literary world. His *Omnipresence* long ago stamped him as one of our greatest poets. . . . We must, however, express our honest conviction that the present volume manifests higher and more intrinsic beauties and excellences than any one of his previous poetic works. And what will very much enhance it in the opinion of all true Churchmen is the fact that it is a thoroughly *Church* volume—breathing and inculcating her scriptural and catholic verities, exhibiting her in the thrilling and beautiful expression of a fond and sacred mother, who lovingly cares and unweariedly provides for the spiritual wants and comforts of her children. While all these poems are fraught with deep truth and lofty sentiments, portraying in poetical form the Church's creed and character, the duties and dangers, the hopes and fears, the faults, privileges, and final destinies of a believer in the religion of Christ, . . . we must declare that we have not read anything more beautiful and heavenly, more eloquent and pathetic, than the poems on 'Baptism,' 'Visitation of the Sick,' 'Burial of the Dead,' 'Commination,' and the 'Eucharist.' Nothing like this volume has appeared since the 'Christian Year,' whether we consider its style and tone, its sentiments, the variety of its metres, or the harmony of its verse. It is a 'Voice of the Church,' a kind of second 'Christian Year.'" A list of all his works is given by Allibone (*Dict. of Brit. and Amer. Auth.* ii, 1348–9). We have room only for mention of his other religious works. Of those in verse: *A Universal Prayer, Death, Heaven, Hell* (1828, 4to, and often):—*Satan: or Intellect without God* (1830):—*The Messiah* (1832):—*Luther; or the Ideal of the Reformation* (1842):—*The Sacred Gift: a Series of Meditations upon Scripture Subjects* (1842):—*The Sanctuary: a Companion in Verse for the English Pray-*

er-book (1855). Of those in prose: *The Gospel in Advance of the Age: a Homily for the Times, with an Introduction on the Spirit of the Bible and the Spirit of the Age* (1st ed. 1847; 3d ed. revised and rearranged, with additional matter, etc., 1848, and often since):—*The Ideal of the English Church* (1845):—*Christ our All in All* (1845):—*Eight Sermons: being Reflective Discourses on some Important Texts* (1843, 8vo):—*The Great Salvation, and our Sin in Neglecting it: a Religious Essay, in Three Parts* (1846):—*The Scottish Church, the English Schismatics* (1846; 3d ed. with documentary evidence, 1847, 12mo). A collected edition of his poetical works (in 6 vols. 8vo) was published in 1839–40, and his *Christian Poetry*, by Ed. Farr, in 1854 (12mo). Selections from them were also made under the title, *Religion and Poetry, with an Introductory Essay by Archer Gurney* (1847, 8vo); and *Lyra Christiana* (1851, 32mo). See *Fraser's Magazine*, i, 95, 721; iv, 672; *Westm. Rev.* xii, 355; *Lond. Month. Rev.* cxvii, 30; cxxi, 313; *Blackwood's Magazine*, xxiii, 751–71; xxvi, 241 sq.; *Lond. Gentleman's Mag.* 1856, pt. i, 313; [Lond.] *Athenæum*, 1832, p. 348; *South. Qu. Rev.* ii, 290; *N. Y. Lit. and Theol. Review*, i, 688; Breen, *Mod. Eng. Lit.: its Blemishes and Defects* (1857), p. 206; Koenen, *Voorlozing over den Engelschen Dichter Rob. Montgomery* (Amst. 1853, 8vo); and the excellent and very full article in Allibone's *Dict. of Brit. and Amer. Auth.* s. v. (J. H. W.)

Montgomery, William B., a missionary to the Osage Indians, who flourished in the early half of this century, died in 1834. He published a translation into the Osage language of various portions of Scripture.

Month (usually חֹדֶשׁ, *cho'desh*, i. e. *new* moon; later also יֶרַח, *ye'rach*, Chald. יְרַח, *yerach'*; Gr. μήν, etc.). The terms for "month" and "moon" have the same close connection in the Hebrew language as in our own and in the Indo-European languages generally; we need only instance the familiar cases of the Greek μήν and μήνη, and the Latin *mensis*; the German *mond* and *monat*; and the Sanscrit *mâsa*, which answers to both month and moon. The Hebrew *chodesh* is perhaps more distinctive than the corresponding terms in other languages; for it expresses not simply the idea of a *lunation*, but the recurrence of a period commencing definitely with the *new moon*; it is derived from the word *chadásh*, "new," which was transferred in the first instance to the "new moon," and in the second instance to the "month," or, as it is sometimes more fully expressed, חֹדֶשׁ יָמִים, "a month of days" (Gen. xxix, 14; Numb. xi, 20, 21; comp. Deut. xxi, 13; 2 Kings xv, 13). The term *yerach* is derived from *yaréach*, "the moon;" it occurs occasionally in the historical (Exod. ii, 2; 1 Kings vi, 37, 38; viii, 2; 2 Kings xv, 13), but more frequently in the poetical portions of the Bible.

1. The most important point in connection with the month of the Hebrews is its length, and the mode by which it was calculated. The difficulties attending this inquiry are considerable, in consequence of the scantiness of the *data*. Though it may fairly be presumed from the terms used that the month originally corresponded to a lunation, no reliance can be placed on the mere verbal argument to prove the exact length of the month in historical times. The word appears even in the earliest times to have passed into its secondary sense, as describing a period approaching to a lunation; for in Gen. vii, 11; viii, 4, where we first meet with it, equal periods of 30 days are described, the interval between the 17th days of the second and the seventh months being equal to 150 days (Gen. vii, 11; viii, 3, 4). We have therefore in this instance an approximation to the solar month, and as, in addition to this, an indication of a double calculation by a solar and a lunar year has been detected in a subsequent date (for from viii, 14, compared with vii, 11, we find that the total duration of the flood exceeded the year by eleven days; in other words, by the precise difference between the lunar year of 354 days and the solar one of 365 days), the passage has attracted considerable attention on the part of certain critics, who have endeavored to deduce from it arguments prejudicial to the originality of the Bible narrative. It has been urged that the Hebrews themselves knew nothing of a solar month, that they must have derived their knowledge of it from more easterly nations (Ewald, *Jahrbüch.* 1854, p. 8), and consequently that the materials for the narrative and the date of its composition must be referred to the period when close intercourse existed between the Hebrews and the Babylonians (Von Bohlen's *Introd. to Gen.* ii, 155 sq.). It is unnecessary for us to discuss in detail the arguments on which these conclusions are founded; we submit in answer to them that the *data* are insufficient to form any decided opinion at all on the matter, and that a more obvious explanation of the matter is to be found in the Egyptian system of months. To prove the first of these points, it will be only necessary to state the various calculations founded on this passage: it has been deduced from it (1) that there were 12 months of 30 days each [see CHRONOLOGY]; (2) that there were 12 months of 30 days, with 5 intercalated days at the end to make up the solar year (Ewald, *l. c.*); (3) that there were 7 months of 30 days, and 5 of 31 days (Von Bohlen); (4) that there were 5 months of 30 days, and 7 of 29 days (Knobel, *in Gen.* viii, 1–3); or, lastly, it is possible to cut away the foundation of any calculation whatever by assuming that a period might have elapsed between the termination of the 150 days and the 17th day of the 7th month (Ideler, *Chronol.* i, 70). "The year being lunar, the interval is, in fact, but 148 days; the discrepancy, however, is of no account" (Browne, *Ordo Sæclorum*, p. 326): both extremes are included, as is usual in Hebrew computations. See DELUGE. But, assuming that the narrative implies equal months of 30 days, and that the date given in viii, 14 does involve the fact of a double calculation by a solar and a lunar year, it is unnecessary to refer to the Babylonians for a solution of the difficulty. The month of 30 days was in use among the Egyptians at a period long anterior to the period of the exodus, and formed the basis of their computation either by an unintercalated year of 360 days or an intercalated one of 365 (Rawlinson's *Herodotus*, ii, 283–286). Indeed, the Bible itself furnishes us with an indication of a double year, solar and lunar, in that it assigns the regulation of its length indifferently to both sun and moon (Gen. i, 14). See YEAR.

From the time of the institution of the Mosaic law downward the month appears to have been a lunar one. The cycle of religious feasts, commencing with the Passover, depended not simply on the month, but on the moon (Josephus, *Ant.* iii, 10, 5); the 14th of Abib was coincident with the full moon (Philo, *Vit. Mos.* iii, p. 686); and the new moons themselves were the occasions of regular festivals (Numb. x, 10; xxviii, 11–14). The statements of the Talmudists (Mishna, *Rosh Hash.* i–iii) are decisive as to the practice in their time, and the lunar month is observed by the modern Jews. The commencement of the month was generally decided by observation of the new moon, which may be detected about forty hours after the period of its conjunction with the sun: in the later times of Jewish history this was effected according to strict rule, the appearance of the new moon being reported by competent witnesses to the local authorities, who then officially announced the commencement of the new month by the twice-repeated word "Mekuddash," i. e. *consecrated* (see Cudworth's *Intellectual System*, ii, Append. p. 528). According to the rabbinical rule, however, there must at all times have been a little uncertainty beforehand as to the exact day on which the month would begin; for it depended not only on the appearance, but on the announcement: if the important word *Mekuddash* were not pronounced until after dark, the following day was the first of the month: if before dark, then that day (*Rosh*

Hash. iii, 1). But we can hardly suppose that such a strict rule of observation prevailed in early times, nor was it in any way necessary; the recurrence of the new moon can be predicted with considerable accuracy by a calculation of the interval that would elapse either from the last new moon, from the full moon (which can be detected by a practiced eye), or from the disappearance of the waning moon. Hence David announces definitely "To-morrow is the new moon," that being the first of the month (1 Sam. xx, 5, 24, 27), though the new moon could not as yet have been observed, and still less announced. Jahn (*Arch.* iii, 3, § 352) regards the discrepancy of the dates in 2 Kings xxv, 27, and Jer. lii, 31, as originating in the different modes of computing by astronomical calculation and by observation. It is more probable that it arises from a mistake of a copyist, substituting ו for ה, as a similar discrepancy exists in 2 Kings xxv, 19 and Jer. lii, 25, without admitting a similar explanation. The length of the month by observation would be alternately 29 and 30 days; nor was it allowed by the Talmudists that a month should fall short of the former or exceed the latter number, whatever might be the state of the weather. The months containing only 29 days were termed in Talmudical language *chasêr* (חָסֵר), or "deficient," and those with 30 *malê* (מָלֵא), or "full."

The usual number of months in a year was twelve, as implied in 1 Kings iv, 7; 1 Chron. xxvii, 1–15; but inasmuch as the Hebrew months coincided, as we shall presently show, with the seasons, it follows as a matter of course that an additional month must have been inserted about every third year, which would bring the number up to thirteen. No notice, however, is taken of this month in the Bible. We have no reason to think that the intercalary month was inserted according to any exact rule; it was sufficient for practical purposes to add it whenever it was discovered that the barley harvest did not coincide with the ordinary return of the month of Abib. In the modern Jewish calendar the intercalary month is introduced seven times in every 19 years, according to the Metonic cycle, which was adopted by the Jews about A.D. 360 (Prideaux's *Connection*, i, 209, note). At the same time the length of the synodical month was fixed by R. Hillel at 29 days, 12 hours, 44 minutes, and 3¼ seconds, which accords very nearly with the truth.

2. The usual method of designating the months was by their numerical order, e. g. "the second month" (Gen. vii, 11), "the fourth month" (2 Kings xxv, 3); and this was generally retained even when the names were given, e. g. "in the month Zif, which is the second month" (1 Kings vi, 1); "in the third month, that is, the month Sivan" (Esth. viii, 9). An exception occurs, however, in regard to Abib in the early portion of the Bible (Exod. xiii, 4; xxiii, 15; Deut. xvi, 1), which is always mentioned by name alone, inasmuch as it was necessarily coincident with a certain season, while the numerical order might have changed from year to year. We doubt indeed whether Abib was really a proper name. In the first place, it is always accompanied by the article, "*the* Abib," as an appellation (=the season of the new ears of grain); in the second place, it appears almost impossible that it could have been superseded by Nisan if it had been regarded as a proper name, considering the important associations connected with it. The practice of the writers of the post-Babylonian period in this respect varied: Ezra, Esther, and Zechariah specify both the names and the numbered order; Nehemiah only the former; Daniel and Haggai only the latter. The names of the months belong to two distinct periods: in the first place we have those peculiar to the period of Jewish independence, of which four only, even including Abib, which we hardly regard as a proper name, are mentioned, viz.: Abib, in which the Passover fell (Exod. xiii, 4; xxiii, 15; xxxiv, 18; Deut. xvi, 1), and which was established as the first

month in commemoration of the exodus (Exod. xii, 2); Zif, the second month (1 Kings vi, 1, 37); Bul, the eighth (1 Kings vi, 38); and Ethanim, the seventh (1 Kings viii, 2)—the three latter being noticed only in connection with the building and dedication of the Temple, so that we might almost infer that their use was restricted to the official documents of the day, and that they never attained the popular use which the later names had. Hence it is not difficult to account for their having been superseded. In the second place we have the names which prevailed subsequently to the Babylonian captivity; of these the following seven appear in the Bible: Nisan, the first, in which the Passover was held (Neh. ii, 1; Esth. iii, 7); Sivan, the third (Esth. viii, 9; Bar. i, 8); Elul, the sixth (Neh. vi, 15; 1 Macc. xiv, 27); Chisleu, the ninth (Neh. i, 1; Zech. vii, 1; 1 Macc. i, 54); Tebeth, the tenth (Esth. ii, 16); Sebat, the eleventh (Zech. i, 7; 1 Macc. xvi, 14); and Adar, the twelfth (Esth. iii, 7; viii, 12; 2 Macc. xv, 36). The names of the remaining five occur in the Talmud and other works; they were Iyar, the second (Targum, 2 Chron. xxx, 2); Tammuz, the fourth (Mishna, *Taan.* iv, 5); Ab, the fifth, and Tisri, the seventh (*Rosh Hash.* i, 3); and Marchesvan, the eighth (*Taan.* i, 3; Josephus, *Ant.* i, 3, 3). The name of the intercalary month was Veadar, i. e. the *additional* Adar, because placed in the calendar after Adar and before Nisan. The opinion of Ideler (*Chronol.* i, 539) that the first Adar was regarded as the intercalary month, because the feast of Purim was held in Veadar in the intercalary year, has little foundation.

The first of these series of names is of Hebrew origin, and has reference to the characteristics of the seasons—a circumstance which clearly shows that the months returned at the same period of the year; in other words, that the Jewish year was a solar one. Thus Abib (אָבִיב) was the month of "ears of corn," Zif the month of "blossom" (זִו or זִיו, or, more fully, as in the Targum, זִו נִצָּנַיָּא, "the bloom of flowers;" another explanation is given in Rawlinson's *Herodotus*, i, 622; viz. that Ziv is the same as the Assyrian *Giv*, "bull," and answers to the zodiacal sign of Taurus), and Bul the month of "rain" (בּוּל; the name occurs in a recently discovered Phœnician inscription [Ewald, *Jahrb.* 1856, p. 135]. A cognate term, מַבּוּל, is used for the "deluge" [Gen. vi, 17, etc.]; but there is no ground for the inference drawn by Von Bohlen [*Introd. to Gen.* ii, 156] that there is any allusion to the month Bul). With regard to Ethanim there may be some doubt, as the usual explanation, "the month of violent or, rather, *incessant* rain," is decidedly inappropriate to the seventh month. Thenius, on 1 Kings viii, 2, suggests that the true name was אֶתָנִים, as in the Sept. 'Aθανίμ, and that its meaning was the "month of gifts," i. e. of fruit, from תָּנָה, "to give." There is the same peculiarity in this as in Abib, viz. the addition of the definite article (הָאֵיתָנִים). In the second series, both the origin and the meaning of the terms are controverted. It was the opinion of the Talmudists that the names were introduced by the Jews who returned from the Babylonian captivity (Jerusalem Talmud, *Rosh Hash.* i, 1), and they are certainly used exclusively by writers of the post-Babylonian period (see Benfey and Stern, *Monatsnamen einiger alter Völker*, Berlin, 1836). It was therefore perhaps natural to seek for their origin in the Persian language, and this was done some years since by Benfey (*Monatsnamen*) in a manner more ingenious than satisfactory. The view, though accepted to a certain extent by Gesenius in his *Thesaurus*, has since been abandoned, both on philological grounds and because it meets with no confirmation from the monumental documents of ancient Persia. The names of the months, as read on the Behistun inscriptions, *Garmapada, Bagayadish, Atriyata*, etc., bear no resemblance to the Hebrew names (Rawlinson's *Herodotus*, ii, 593–6). The names are probably borrowed from the Syrians, in whose regular calendar we find names answering to Tisri, Sebat, Adar, Nisan, Iyar, Tammuz, Ab, and Elul (Ideler, *Chronol.* i, 430). The names of the Syrian months appear to have been in many instances of *local* use: for instance, the calendar of Heliopolis contains the names of Ag and Gelon (Ideler, i, 440), which do not appear in the regular Syrian calendar, while that of Palmyra, again, contains names unknown to either. Chisleu and Tebeth appear on the Palmyrene inscriptions (Gesenius, *Thesaur.* p. 702, 543). The resemblance in sound between Tebeth and the Egyptian Tobi, as well as its correspondence in the order of the months, was noticed by Jerome (*ad Ezek.* xxxix, 1). Sivan may be borrowed from the Assyrians, who appear to have had a month so named, sacred to Sin or the moon (Rawlinson, i, 615). Marchesvan, coinciding as it did with the rainy season in Palestine, was probably a purely Hebrew term. Von Bohlen connects it with the root *râchásh* (רָחַשׁ), "to boil over" (*Introd. to Gen.* ii, 157). The modern Jews consider it a compound word, *mar*, "drop," and *Cheshvan*, the former betokening that it was wet, and the latter being the proper name of the month (De Sola's *Mishna*, p. 168, note). With regard to the meaning of the Syrian names we can only conjecture from the case of Tammuz, which undoubtedly refers to the festival of the deity of that name mentioned in Ezek. viii, 14, that some of them may have been derived from the names of deities. We draw attention to the similarity between Elul and the Arabic name of Venus Urania, *Alil-at* (Herod. iii, 8); and again between Adar, the Egyptian Athor, and the Syrian Atargatis. Hebrew roots are suggested by Gesenius for others, but without much confidence. The Hebrew forms of the names are: אָב, תַּמּוּז, אִיָּר, סִיוָן, נִיסָן, אֲדָר, שְׁבָט, טֵבֵת, כִּסְלֵו, מַרְחֶשְׁוָן, תִּשְׁרִי, אֱלוּל, and וַאֲדָר.

Subsequently to the establishment of the Syro-Macedonian empire, the use of the Macedonian calendar was gradually adopted for the purpose of literature or intercommunication with other countries. Josephus, for instance, constantly uses the Macedonian months, even where he gives the Hebrew names (e. g. in *Ant.* i, 3, 3, he identifies Marchesvan with Dius, and Nisan with Xanthicus, and in vii, 7, 6, Chisleu with Appellæus). The only instance in which the Macedonian names appear in the Bible is in 2 Macc. xi, 30, 33, 38, where we have notice of Xanthicus in combination with another named Dioscorinthius (ver. 21), which does not appear in the Macedonian calendar. Various explanations have been offered with respect to the latter. Any attempt to connect it with the Macedonian Dius fails on account of the interval being too long to suit the narrative, Dius being the first and Xanthicus the sixth month. The opinion of Scaliger (*Emend. Temp.* ii, 94) that it was the Macedonian intercalary month rests on no foundation whatever, and Ideler's assumption that that intercalary month preceded Xanthicus must be rejected along with it (*Chronol.* i. 399). It is most probable that the author of 2 Macc. or a copyist was familiar with the Cretan calendar, which contained a month named Dioscurus, holding the same place in the calendar as the Macedonian Dystrus (Ideler, i, 426), i. e. immediately before Xanthicus, and that he substituted one for the other. This view derives some confirmation from the Vulgate rendering, *Dioscorus*. We have further to notice the reference to the Egyptian calendar in 3 Macc. vi, 38, Pachon and Epiphi in that passage answering to Pachons and Epep, the ninth and eleventh months (Wilkinson, *Anc. Egyp.* i, 14, 2d ser.).

3. The identification of the Jewish months with our own cannot be effected with precision on account of the variations that must inevitably exist between the lunar and the solar month, each of the former ranging over portions of two of the latter. It must therefore be understood that the following remarks apply to the general identity on an average of years. As the Jews still retain the names Nisan, etc., it may appear at first sight needless to do more than refer the reader to a modern almanac, and this would have been the case if it were not evident that the modern Nisan does not correspond to the ancient one. We are indebted to J. D. Michaelis for discovering the true state of this case, after the rabbinical writers had so universally established an erroneous opinion that it has not even yet disappeared from our popular books. His dissertation, "De Mensibus Hebræorum" (in his *Commentationes per annos 1763–68 oblatæ* [Bremen, 1769], p. 16; translated by W. Bowyer, Lond. 1773; also in the *Critica Biblica* [London, 1827], iii, 324–340), proceeds on the following chief arguments: First, that if the first month began with the new moon of *March*, as was commonly asserted, the climate of Palestine would not in that month permit the oblation of the sheaf of barley, which is ordered on the second day of the Paschal Feast (Lev. xxiii, 10); nor could the harvest be finished before the Feast of Weeks, which would then fall in May; nor could the Feast of Tabernacles, which was after the gathering of all fruits, accord with the month of September, because all these feasts depend on certain stages in the agricultural year, which, as he shows from the observations of travellers, solely coincide with the states of vegetation which are found, in that climate, in the months of April, June, and October. This has been confirmed by later accounts; for the barley harvest does not take place even in the warm district about Jericho till the middle of April, and in the upland districts not before the end of that month (Robinson's *Researches*, i, 551; iii, 102, 145). Secondly, that the Syrian calendar, which has essentially the same names for the months, makes its Nisan absolutely parallel with our April. Lastly, that Josephus (*Ant.* ii, 14, 6) synchronizes Nisan with the Egyptian Pharmuth, which commenced on the 27th of March (Wilkinson, *l. c.*), and with the Macedonian Xanthicus, which answers generally to the early part of April, though considerable variation occurs in the local calendars as to its place (comp. Ideler, i, 435, 442). He further informs us (iii, 10, 5) that the Passover took place when the sun was in Aries, which it does not enter until near the end of March. Michaelis concludes that the later Jews fell into this departure from their ancient order either through some mistake in the intercalation, or because they wished to imitate the Romans, whose year began in March. Ideler says, "So much is certain, that in the time of Moses the month of ears cannot have commenced before the first days of our April, which was then the period of the vernal equinox" (*Handbuch der Chronologie*, i, 490). As Nisan, then, began with the new moon of April, we have a scale for fixing the commencement of all the other months with reference to our calendar; and we must accordingly date their commencement one whole month later than is commonly done: allowing, of course, for the circumstance that, as the new moon varies in its place in our solar months, the Jewish months will almost invariably consist of portions of two of ours. For the details of each month, see CALENDAR, JEWISH. See, in addition to the treatises above noticed, Langenberg, *De mense veterum Hebræorum lunari* (Jen. 1713). Compare CHRONOLOGY.

Monthly Meeting. See MEETING.

Montholon, JEAN DE, a French ecclesiastic, was born at Autun near the middle of the 15th century. At an early age he received the degree of doctor of laws, and was registered among the regular canons of St. Victor, at Paris. His theological learning and his superior attainments in jurisprudence rapidly advanced his name among his fellows, and he was finally promoted to the cardinalship by pope Clement VII. Montholon died in Paris in 1528. His works are: *Promptuarium* *seu Breviarium Juris divini et utriusque humani* (Paris, 1520, 2 vols. fol.) : — *De sacramento altaris* (ibid. 1517, 8vo).

Month's Mind is the name by which is designated an office performed for the period of one month, in the Romish Church, for her dead. "Mind" in that case is used in its old sense of *memory*, as in the phrases "to call to mind," "time out of mind."

Monthyon (or **Montyon**), ANTOINE JEAN BAPTISTE ROBERT AUGET, a French baron, celebrated for his great philanthropic labors and munificent endowments of humanitarian institutions, was born at Paris Dec. 23 or 26, 1733. He was successively intendant of the provinces of Provence, Auvergne, and Aunis ; and, as a member of the royal council, opposed the unlawful proceedings resorted to in the case of Lachalotais, and protested against the dissolution of ancient parliaments decreed by chancellor Maupeon. In consequence of this latter act he was deprived of his office. Soon after the accession of Louis XVI he was appointed councillor of state ; became, in 1780, chancellor of the count d'Artois (afterwards Charles X) ; emigrated to England on the breaking out of the French Revolution, and did not return to France until the second restoration. He possessed a princely fortune, and devoted the larger portion not only of his income, but also of his capital, to philanthropic purposes. He generously assisted his exiled countrymen, and bequeathed to French hospitals over 3,000,000 francs. As early as 1782 he had founded a prize for virtue, and several other prizes, to be awarded by the French Academy and the Academy of Sciences. These having been suppressed by order of the Convention, were renewed by the donor on his return to France in 1816, and afterwards increased. Every year the French Academy distributes two Monthyon prizes of 10,000 francs each : one to the poor person who has performed the most meritorious deed of virtue, the other to the author of the work which has been judged the most useful for the improvement of public morals. Two others, of equal amount, are awarded by the Academy of Sciences : one to him who shall have found during the year some means of improvement of the medical and surgical art, the other to him who shall have discovered the means of rendering some mechanical art less unhealthy. Monthyon died in 1820.

Monti, Filippo Maria, an Italian prelate, was born March 23, 1675, at Bologna, of an illustrious and noble family ; studied at the high school of his native place ; then went to Rome, where by his superior talent and acquisitions he quickly rose to eminent favor with popes Clement XI and XII. In 1743 Benedict XIV created Monti a cardinal. He died Jan. 17, 1754, at Rome. His library of over 12,000 volumes was given, by his request, to the library of his native place ; also other valuable treasures, among them a fine collection of paintings. He wrote: *Roma tutrice delle belle arti, scultura ed architettura: — Prose degli Arcadi: — Elogia cardinalium pietate, doctrina, legationibus ac rebus pro Ecclesia gestis illustrium a pontificatu Alexandri III ad Benedictum XIII* (Rome, 1751. 4to).

Monti, Vincenzo, a noted Italian ecclesiastic, who wrote poetry of a superior order, and only used his position in the Church as a general passport into society, flourished in the second half of the 18th century. He was a native of Ferrara (born in 1753), and studied in the university of that place. He was made abbé in 1776, and became secretary to the pope's nephew. He soon found favor in the eyes of Roman celebrities, and was generally noticed by prelates and cardinals as a fit subject for promotion in the Church. He was especially popular when, in 1792, he wrote a poem commemorating the efforts of Pius II against the Austrian court, which then, in the person of Joseph II, was fast breaking away from the papacy. The poem which Monti wrote

on this occasion of Pius's visit to Vienna is entitled *Il Pellegrino Apostolico*. He died at Milan, October, 1828.

Montignot, HENRI, a French ecclesiastic, was born about 1715, at Nancy. He was a doctor of theology, canon of the cathedral, and member of the academy in his native place, where he died about the close of the 18th century. He wrote: *Remarques théologiques et critiques sur l'Histoire du Peuple de Dieu du P. Berruyer* (1755, 12mo) :—*Dictionnaire diplomatique, ou Étymologie des termes de la basse Latinité pour servir à l'intelligence des archives, des chartes*, etc. (Nancy, 1787, 8vo) :—*Réflexions sur les immunités ecclésiastiques* (Paris, 1788, 8vo) :—*État des Étoiles fixes au second siècle par Cl. Ptolémie, comparé à la position des mêmes étoiles en 1786, avec le texte Grec à la traduction Française* (Nancy, 1786 ; Strasburg, 1787, 4to).

Montigny, JEAN DE, a French prelate of some note, was born in Bretagne in 1637, of parents highly esteemed in the best social circles of France ; and thus, surrounded with superior advantages, was especially fitted for the highest literary culture. He entered the ecclesiastic life, and soon attained to eminence. In 1670 he was made bishop of Léon, and in the same year was admitted to membership in the French Academy. He died Sept. 28, 1671, at Vitré. He wrote: *Lettre à Éraste pour reponse à son libelle contre La Pucelle de Chapelain* (Paris, 1656, 4to) :—*Oraison funèbre d'Anne d'Autriche* (Rennes, 1666, 4to) :—*Lettre contenant le voyaye de la cour en 1660 ; dans le Recueil de quelques pièces nouvelles et galantes.*

Montjoy is the name given to mounds serving to direct the travellers on a highway, probably often originally tumuli, or funeral-mounds of an elder people— heaps of stones, overgrown with grass, which have been piled over a dead chieftain. They often were crowned with a cross. Montjoie St. Denis was the French war-cry ; Montjoie St. Andrew, that of Burgundy ; Montjoie Notre Dame, of the dukes of Bourbon ; and Montjoie St. George, of England.

Montlaur, JEAN DE, a French prelate, was born near Montpellier about 1120 ; entered the ecclesiastical life while yet quite a youth, and rapidly advanced to positions of prominence and responsibility. In 1158 he was made bishop, and everywhere gained friends by his generous and open-hearted life. He was particularly devoted to his diocesan work, and built up the people in holy and consistent living. He died Feb. 24, 1190, in his native place, with whose history his whole life was interwoven. His works remain in MS. See *Histoire littéraire de la France*, vol. xiv, s. v. ; *Gallia Christiana*, vol. vi.

Montluc, Blaise de, a French marshal, noted for his cruelty towards Protestants ; one of the "two personages who obtained by their enormities a notoriety so hideous that the history of cruelty would be imperfect if they were passed over in silence" (Smedley, i, 211). He was a brother to the succeeding, and was born in Gascony in 1501. When only a youth of twenty, he entered military life, and soon distinguished himself by his bravery as well as his brutality. He was universally severe with his enemies, and would give no quarter. In the contest with the Huguenots, he advised their absolute extermination, and actually wrote a memoir (in 1562) showing how easily it might be done (see *Mémoires de Condé*, iii, 184 sq.). Placed in charge of his native province, he used his unlimited power to destroy every one who appeared to be tainted with the heresy, and instituted a strict inquisition "into the strange names of overseers, deacons, consistories, synods, and conferences," "food of which kind," he adds, "never yet had furnished me with a breakfast" (*Comment*. lib. v, tom. ii, p. 3). The number of persons who fell victims to his rage is legion, and he appears to us in the role of a modern Nero. We have not room to enter here into detail, but refer to Smedley (*Hist. of the Ref. Religion in*

France, i, 211 sq.; ii, 25). Montluc fought also against the imperialists, commanded by Charles V, and assisted at the siege of La Rochelle and Calais. For his services against the Protestants he was in 1573 made " marshal" by Henry III. Montluc died in 1577, leaving the *Mémoires* of his military life (1592), which are not an honor to any man's memory nor to any man's country. See Brantôme, *Vies des Hommes illustres Français;* Mézeray, *Abrégé de l'histoire de France;* Sainte-Beuve, in the *Moniteur* (Paris), Oct. 1854; Browning, *Hist. of the Huguenots,* i, 118, 136, 280; ii, 4. (J. H. W.)

Montluc, Jean de, brother of the preceding, a distinguished French prelate, noted both for his attainments in ecclesiastical and political life, was born about 1508. He entered in boyhood days the Dominican Order of Gray Friars, and soon made himself the favorite of his associates. The outer world also took a liking to him, and even at court he had many friends. Francis I reposed much confidence in him, and he was intrusted with diplomatic missions. He was successful especially in efforts for a peaceful solution of the differences between his native country and the Ottoman power, concluding for Francis an advantageous peace with Soliman. In 1553 he was made bishop of Valence and of Die, and gained great popularity as a pulpit orator. He was not unfrequently invited to preach at court during the rule of Catharine de Medici. However, after the Conference of Poissy (1561), Montluc seems to have fallen into disrepute at court, for he was believed to have been one of the bishops whom Beza's argument had "almost persuaded to be a Protestant" (Browning, *Huguenots,* i, 108) ; and two years later he was one of the prelates excommunicated by pope Pius IV (Browning, i, 180). Montluc was finally restored to his former influence and position by the French Parliament; but he never thereafter exerted himself much in ecclesiastical labors, and because of his shrewdness, wisdom, and learning, he was selected by the government of his country for several diplomatic missions, the most important of which was to Poland (in 1572), where he zealously exerted himself to secure the crown for the duke of Anjou. It is generally conceded that Montluc's conduct in this affair was anything but honorable and manly. He persuaded the Poles to believe that the duke had had no part in the massacre of St. Bartholomew. On his return to France he lived at Toulouse, where he died April 13, 1579. His theological writings are : *Deux instructions et deux épistres au clergé et peuple de Valence* (Avignon, 1557, 8vo) :—*Cleri Valentii et Diensis Reformatio* (Paris, 1557, 8vo) :—*Recueil des lieux de l'Écriture servant à découvrir les fautes contre les dix commandemants de la loi* (ibid. 1559, 8vo) :—*Sermons* (ibid. 1559, 8vo) :—*Familière Explication des articles de la foi* (ibid. 1561, 8vo) :—*Sermons sur les articles de la foi et de l'Oraison dominicale* (ibid. 1561, 8vo). See De Thou, *Hist. sui temporis ;* Sismondi, *Hist. des Français,* chap. xvii, xviii, xix; Smedley, *Hist. of the Ref. Religion in France,* i, 122 sq., 189; ii, 82; De Felice, *History of the Protestants of France,* p. 142 sq. (J. H. W.)

Montmignon, JEAN BAPTISTE, a French theologian, was born at Lucy in 1737, prepared in his studies for holy orders, and finally became successively secretary of the bishopric of Soissons, canon, vicar, grand-vicar, and archdeacon. In 1786 he accepted the editorship of the *Journal Ecclésiastique ;* but as early as January, 1788, abandoned this work, and took part in the publications which were preparing at the outbreak of the Revolution under the bishop of Soissons. Obliged to quit France in 1793, he went to Belgium, and remained there until the government of the Directory made his return possible. He was then nominated grand-vicar of Poitiers; in 1811 was made canon of the metropolis, and then grand-vicar of this diocese. He was also made censor of all ecclesiastical publications at Paris. He died at Paris Feb. 21, 1824. He wrote:

Crime d'apostasie; lettre d'un religieux à un de ses amis (1790, 8vo) :—*Vie édifiante de Benoit-Joseph Labre, mort à Rome, en odeur de Sainteté, le 16 Avril, 1783, composée par ordre du Saint-Siège, etc., par M. M——(Marconi), lecteur du collége Romain, confesseur du serviteur de Dieu; traduit de l'Italien* (Paris, 1784, 12mo) :—*Préservative contre le fanatisme, ou les nouveaux millénaires rappelés aux principes fondamentaux de la foi Catholique* (Paris, 1806, 8vo) :—*Exposition des prédictions et des promesses faites à l'Église, pour les derniers temps de la Gentilité* (1806, 2 vols. 12mo) :—*Choix de Lettres édifiantes, écrites des missions étrangères,* etc. (1808, 8 vols. 12mo) :—*De la Règle de vérité et des Causes du fanatisme* (1808, 8vo).

Montmorency is the name of one of the oldest noble families of France, which figures both in secular and ecclesiastical history, though oftentimes its celebrity was purchased at the expense of all humanitarian principles. The name of the family was derived from the village in which its several members lived, and dates from the 10th century. Oftentimes the house of Montmorency has been styled "the first barons of France," and in recognition of their services to Romanism, "the first *Christian* barons." They furnished officers of state and generals for the French army, distinguished ecclesiastics for the Church of Rome, some of whom rose even to the cardinalate, besides a number of grand-masters and knights of the different European orders. One of the branches established in the Netherlands furnished count of Horn (Philip II de Montmorency-Neville), who, together with Egmont, was executed in Brussels during the bloody reign of the Spanish general Alva. But we have room here only for those chiefly concerned in the Huguenot movement.

1. ANNE, first duke of Montmorency, marshal and grand-constable of France, noted for his alliance with the Guises [see HUGUENOTS], was born in March, 1493. His Christian name, *Anne,* it is said, he received from his godmother, Anne of Brittany. He distinguished himself by his gallantry and military skill in the wars between Francis I and the emperor Charles V, and was taken prisoner along with his sovereign in the battle of Pavia, which was fought against his advice. He afterwards became the leader of the French government, showing great ability in matters of finance and diplomacy, and was made constable in 1538; but his rough manners made him an object of dislike to many ; and the suspicions of the king having been aroused against him, he was suddenly banished from court in 1541, and passed ten years on his estates, till the accession of Henry II, when he came again to the head of affairs. In 1548 he suppressed the insurrection in Guienne, but was less successful in 1557 in his contest with the celebrated general of Philip II, duke Philibert Emmanuel of Savoy, which resulted in the, to France, disadvantageous peace of Chateau-Cambrésis; and hence, with the accession of the youthful king, Francis II, there came a decline of the power of the house of Montmorency, and the ascendency of the house of the Guises, who had Francis entirely under their control. Fortunately for Montmorency, the widow of the late king, Catharine de Medici, ambitious to rule the kingdom, cast her influence with constable Montmorency, who had retired from court, though apparently she coveted the friendship of the Guises (Martin, viii, 362). An alliance was now formed among disaffected courtiers, bourgeoisie, and Protestants against the Guises, and him who, ruling over the nation, had submitted to their guidance; and though it is not believed that Montmorency had any part in it, it is certain that some of his house—three brothers of the house of Chatillon (Obet, cardinal of Chatillon, admiral Coligny, and Dandelot, colonel of the Cisalpine infantry), sons of Louisa of Montmorency, the sister of the constable—were more or less intimately associated with all Protestant movements in France, and that possibly two of these three had actually a part in, or at least a knowledge of, the conspiracy of Amboise (see HUGUENOTS; and comp. Ranke, *Französ. Gesch.* i, 147; Mrs. Marsh, *The Protest. Ref. in France,* i, 142; Brantôme, *Vie des Hommes illustres,* iii, 20). The sudden termination of the reign of Francis II (1560) brought forward the minor, Charles IX, and with him the regency of Catharine. Her object was to effect a fusion of parties, or, rather, to hold the balance evenly between them, and, by allowing neither to preponderate, to preserve the paramount authority in her hands. By the advice of the sagacious counsellor L'Hôpital (q. v.), the king of Navarre was made lieutenant-general, and Montmorency was again given the direction of military affairs, while the Guises kept their places in the council, and duke Francis retained the post of master of the royal household. The Guises, perceiving the intent of the queen, now denominated "apostate," labored earnestly for an alliance with Montmorency, in order to foil the queen in her designs. The constable finally separated from his nephews, who had reappeared at court, and were enjoying many favors, and allied himself with the duke of Guise and the marshal St. André, composing the famous triumvirate which resisted Catharine de Medici, and proceeded in most stringent measures against the Huguenots (q. v.). The colloquy at Poissy had softened the heart of Catharine, and the Protestants were given many privileges. The triumvirate opposed all such concessions, and finally brought on the massacre at Vassy—"the St. Bartholomew of 1562" (March). The queen-mother and king were seized, and forced to inaugurate a new policy. Montmorency himself signalized the new departure by various open attacks on the Huguenots. Thus he led a mob to storm a Protestant church in the suburbs of Paris called "the Temple of Jerusalem." "Bursting in the doors of the empty place, they tore up the seats, and, placing them and the Bibles in a pile upon the floor, they set the whole on fire, amid great acclamation." He returned to Paris as if a victor fresh from battle, and, flushed with success, he rested not until other churches had been submitted to a like treatment, and he was given the nickname of "Captain Burnbenches." In 1562 he commanded the royal army against the Huguenots, but at the battle of Dreux was wounded and taken prisoner by the Protestants. Released by the peace of Amboise in 1563, he plotted a massacre of the Protestants; but the court not only refused to approve his proposal, but also caused his retirement finally. In 1567 he again appeared on the stage of public affairs, and again took part in the warfare against the Huguenots; but he did not long remain in the field, for he received a fatal wound at St. Denis, and died at Paris on the following day, Nov. 12, 1567. His death was in many respects a blessing to France. From a neutral, if not a friend of the Huguenots, he had turned to a most deadly enemy, because, after he had espoused the Guises' interest, and had been placed in command of the army, he had never been able to gain a victory over the Huguenot armies. Even the duke of Guise, who had fallen in 1563 (when returning from his outposts he was mortally wounded by a fanatical Huguenot, Poltrot [q. v.] de Méré), had counselled in his dying hour that the queen-regent should make peace with her revolted subjects, but Montmorency insisted on their destruction, and counselled their massacre in open battle and by private means. His last hours were spent in a most deadly struggle, and yet even then he failed to be the victor; for, though he sacrificed himself, the contest remained undecided, the Huguenots, if anything, having the vantage-ground, as they had saved their leader. It is generally asserted that Montmorency's death was welcome news to Catharine de Medici and the courtiers, whom he had frequently offended by his overbearing manners. See Lescouvel, *Anne de Montmorency* (1696); Davila, *Hist. of the Civil Wars of France;* Martin, *Hist. of France,* vol. ix; Ranke, *Französische Gesch. vornehmlich im 16 u. 17 Jahrh.* (Engl. transl. *Hist. of Civil Wars and Monarchy*

in France), i, 164–212; Sir J. Stephen, *Lect. Hist. France* (3d ed. Lond. 1857, 2 vols. 8vo), vol. ii, lects. xvi and xvii; Student's *Hist. of France,* p. 311, 316, 319, 324, 337; Jervis, *Hist. of the Church of France* (Lond. 1872, 2 vols. 8vo), vol. i, ch. ii; Fisher, *Hist. of the Ref.* p. 258 sq.; and the works referred to in the article HUGUENOTS.

2. HENRI, second *Duc de Montmorency,* grandson of the famous constable de Montmorency, but more honorable and consistent in his conduct, though he also warred against the Huguenots, was born at Chantilly April 30, 1595. His godfather was the great Henri Quatre, who always called him his "son." Louis XIII made him admiral when he was but a youth of seventeen. He succeeded his father in the governorship of Languedoc, and took an active part in the wars against the Huguenots, distinguishing himself on the royal side in the sieges of Montauban and Montpellier, and in 1625 by taking the Isle of Ré from the Huguenots of Rochelle. He afterwards gained other victories over them, and in 1629 was mainly instrumental in bringing about the peace of Alais, which terminated the religious civil wars in France. In 1630 he received the chief command of the French troops in Piedmont, where he defeated the Spaniards, for which he received a marshal's baton. Unfortunately for himself, he ventured to oppose Richelieu, who had always been his enemy, and espoused the cause of Gaston, duke of Orleans; for this he was declared guilty of high-treason, and marshal Schomberg being sent against him, defeated him at Castelnaudary, and took him prisoner. Although almost mortally wounded, Montmorency was carried to Toulouse, sentenced to death by the Parliament, and notwithstanding his expressions of penitence, and the most powerful intercession made for him—for example, by king Charles I of England, the pope, the Venetian republic, and the duke of Savoy—was beheaded, Oct. 30, 1632. He was distinguished for amiability and courtesy of manners, as well as for his valor. His life was written by one of his officers (1663, 4to). See also the works cited above.

Montolivetenses, a name given to the monks of Mount Olivet, because living in a residence so called. The Montolivetenses dress in white serge, and profess the rule of St. Benedict. They sprang up in the 14th century, were approved by pope John XXI, and confirmed by Gregory XI in 1371. They trace their origin to St. Bernard Ptolomei of Sienna, and their first monastery was at Ancona; but the order soon spread through Italy and Sicily. See MONKS, EASTERN.

Montorsoli, FRA GIOVANN' ANGELO, a celebrated Italian sculptor, largely engaged on sacred and ecclesiastical subjects, was born about the beginning of the 16th century at Montorsoli, near Florence. His first instruction in art he received from Andrea de Fiesole, with whom he lived three years. He then found employment at Rome, at Perugia, and at Volterra. He was next employed by Michael Angelo on the church of San Lorenzo at Florence, and gained the admiration and lasting friendship of the great Florentine. In 1527 Montorsoli had a strong disposition to turn, as it appeared to him, to the only life in which peace was to be obtained; but after trying in vain several convents, he fixed in 1530 upon the brotherhood of the Nunziata at Florence, and became a friar of the Order Dei Servi della Nunziata. Shortly after he had taken up his abode in this convent, having been recommended to the pope by Michael Angelo, he was called to Rome by Clement VII to restore several ancient monuments, much to the dissatisfaction of his brothers of the Nunziata. When the tasks assigned him by the pope were finished, he returned to Florence with Michael Angelo to complete the statues and other sculptures of the sacristy and library of San Lorenzo. After the death of Clement, Montorsoli again joined Michael Angelo at Rome, and assisted him in the works of the monument of Julius II; but while engaged on this work he was invited by cardinal Turnone, and advised by Michael Angelo to go with the cardinal to Paris. Owing, however, to difficulties with the treasury and servants of the French court, Montorsoli left Paris and returned to Florence. After completing there several works, he went by Rome to Naples, and there constructed the tomb of Jacopo Sanazzaro. He next went to Genoa, and ornamented the church of San Matteo there, besides many other works, and upon their completion returned to Michael Angelo at Rome; but departed again soon afterwards, in 1547, for Messina, where he was employed to make a grand fountain for the place in front of the cathedral, and designed the church of San Lorenzo, etc. In 1557, by a decree of pope Paul IV, all religious persons, or all who had taken holy orders and were living at large in the world without respect to their religious character, were ordered to return to their convents and reassume their religious habits; and Montorsoli was accordingly obliged to leave many works unfinished, which he intrusted to his pupil Martino, and he returned to his convent at Florence. He was, however, shortly afterwards called to Bologna to construct there the high altar of the church of his own order, Dei Servi, which he completed with great magnificence in twenty-eight months. He returned to Florence in 1561, and being rich he built a common sepulchre for artists in the chapter-house of the convent of the Nunziata, with the requisite endowment for regular masses at appointed times, and gave the whole sepulchre, chapter, and chapel to the then almost decayed society of St. Luke, or company of painters, etc., which, upon the completion of the sepulchre, was at a solemn feast celebrated by forty-eight of the principal artists of Florence, re-established by the consent and authority of the duke Cosmo I upon a firmer and permanent basis; and the society still subsists as the Academy of Florence, though since that time it has been considerably enriched and endowed by successive dukes of Tuscany. Montorsoli died, says Vasari, on the last day of August, 1563. See Cicognara, *Storia della Scultura*; Valery, *Voyages historiques et littéraires en Italie*; Spooner, *Biographical Hist. of the Fine Arts*, s. v.; *English Cyclop.* s. v.

Montpellier (Lat. *Mons pessulanus* or *puellarum*), a city of France, in the department of Hérault, in 43° 36' N. lat. and 3° 50' E. long., with a population (1881) of 52,673, is noted as the seat of several Church councils held there in the 12th and 13th centuries. At the *first* of these, held in 1162, by pope Alexander III, assisted by ten bishops, the antipope Victor (Octavianus) was excommunicated (Labbé, *Conc.* x, 1410). At the *second* council, held in 1195, indulgences were granted to those who marched into Spain to fight against the infidels (Moors), and interdicts were intrusted to the bishops in whose dioceses the Albigenses were gaining ground (Labbé, *Conc.* x, 1796). At the *third* council, held in 1215, by the papal legate, Peter of Beneventum, the question was the disposition of the city of Toulouse, and the other cities conquered by the Crusaders, count Simon of Montfort claiming them. Montfort (q. v.) was granted his demand. There were also forty-six canons passed relating to the dress of monastics and the clergy (Labbé, *Conc.* xi, 183, and Append. p. 2330). At the *fourth* council, held in August, 1224, and composed of all the bishops of the province, under the archbishop of Narbonne, the propositions of peace made by Raymond, count of Toulouse, and the Albigenses were considered. Raymond promised to keep the Catholic faith, and to cause it to be held throughout his territories, to purge out from them all heretics, to restore the Church to her rights, to preserve her liberties, and to pay within three years 15,000 marks as an indemnification for what she had suffered, upon condition that the count of Montfort should relinquish his pretensions to the lands of the county of Toulouse; but Amauri, who pretended to be count of Toulouse, in virtue of a decree of Innocent III given in the Council of

Lateran, wrote to the bishops, and represented to them that, as he hoped to be able to bring the Albigenses into subjection, it would be a scandal to the whole Church should they enter into any agreement with Raymond. The council appear to have acquiesced in his view of the matter, and the offer of Raymond was rejected (*Conc.* xi, 289, and Append. p. 2334). The *fifth* council was held September 6, 1258, by James, archbishop of Narbonne. Eight statutes were published: 1, excommunicates *ipso facto* all who usurp the property of the Church and insult the persons of the clergy; 2, forbids bishops to give the tonsure or holy orders to persons not of their own diocese; 3, declares that clerks not living as clergymen ought to do so, or carrying on any business, they shall lose their privileges; 5, forbids Jews to exact usury; 6, forbids bishops to give letters to mendicant friars to authorize their begging before the friars have obtained leave of the metropolitan (Labbé, xi,778). See Hefele, *Conciliengeschichte*, vol. v and vi (see Index); Landon, *Manual of Councils*, s. v.

Montpellierians, a fanatical sect which, under the religious garb, committed all manner of excesses, and became guilty of most immoral conduct, but which, fortunately, was only short-lived, the people soon becoming disgusted with the licentiousness of its members. It arose at Montpellier, France, about the year 1723. Its founder, master, and high-priest took the name of *Jacob Prophetus*, and designated his meeting as the "New Sion." They held nightly meetings, in which the grossest licentiousness was indulged in under cover of religion. Their place of assembly contained numerous apartments, carpeted with white, and furnished with beds and mattresses. In the farthest apartment, considered as the sanctum sanctorum, stood an altar, a pulpit, a candlestick with seven branches, and a gazophylakion. There were also some priests dressed in the garb of the Hebrew priests. They circumcised and baptized their children, but in the latter ceremony brandy was used instead of water. Louis XV commissioned the marquis de Roquelaure to put an end to their abomination, and the sect was speedily suppressed. See P. I. von Huth, *Versuch einer Kirchengesch. d. 18ten Jahrh.* i, 543 sq.

Montredon (also called **Montrond**), RAIMOND DE, a French prelate of some note, was born at Nismes near the beginning of the 12th century. He was in 1130 archdean of Beziers, when he was promoted to the bishopric of Agde. He was made archbishop of Arles in 1143. He died about 1155. He figured prominently in the civil affairs of France, but gave little time to theological studies, and left no works of value in that field of knowledge. See *Gallia Christiana*, vol. i, col. 560; *Hist. littér. de la France*, xiii, 236.

Montrélais, HUGUES DE, a French cardinal, was born at Montrélais, near Ancenis, about 1315. He early entered the service of the Church, and was made canon, and later archdeacon, of St. Peter's at Nantes. In 1354 he was elected bishop of Nantes, but the year after he was transferred by pope Innocent VI to the see of Tréguier, and in 1358 to that of Sainte-Brienne. Devoted to Charles the Bald, Hugues accompanied that prince in 1364 to Poitiers to assist in diplomatic conferences. He also performed other diplomatic services. The troubles which agitated Brittany in 1371 caused Hugues's retirement to Avignon, where pope Gregory XI created him cardinal (Dec. 20, 1375). He died there, Feb. 28, 1384. See *Gallia Christiana*, vol. iii, col. 71.

Montreuil, BERNARDIN DE, a French theologian, was born in Paris in 1596. He joined the Jesuits in 1624, and taught philosophy and moral theology. He died in Paris in 1646. His works are: *Vie de Jésus-Christ, tirée des quatre Évangélistes* (1637, 4to):—*La Vie glorieuse de Jésus-Christ et l'établissement de son Église par le ministère des Apôtres, ou les Actes des Apôtres et l'Histoire de l'Église naissante* (Paris, 1640 and 1799, 2 vols. 12mo):—*Les derniers Combats de l'Église, dans l'explication de l'Apocalypse* (Paris, 1645, 4to).

Montrocher (*Guido de Monte-Rocheri*), GUI DE, a Spanish theologian of some note, who flourished in the first half of the 14th century at Valencia, is noted as the author of *Manipulus Curatorum*, a work regarded of so much value that it was among the very first books issued after the invention of the art of printing, and passed through over fifty editions in the first thirty years of the 15th century. The oldest edition is entitled *Manipulus Curatorum, liber utilissimus, per Christophorum Bugamum et Johannem Glim* (Savigliano, 1471, folio). See Du Pin, *Biblioth. des Auteurs Ecclés. du quartorzième siècle;* Fabricius, *Biblioth. Græca*, x, 786; *Biblioth. Hispana vetus*, ii, 155, 156.

Montrose, JAMES GRAHAM, *Marquis of*, a Scotch soldier, noted for the part he took in the contests between the Covenanters and king Charles I, was a member of a celebrated noble family, and born at the family estate of Auld Montrose in 1612, and on the death of his father in 1626 became earl of Montrose. He was educated at the University of St. Andrews; and after having married a lady who lived only four years before death separated them, leaving him a child, he went abroad and travelled for several years in France and Italy, devoting much of his time to study in general literature and army tactics. Introduced on his return to England to king Charles, he was so coldly received that he at once left for his native country, and there allied himself with the Covenanters, who were just then arrayed against the king. It was the year 1637 when the tumults broke out in Edinburgh on the attempt to introduce the Prayer-book. Montrose, to all appearances, became heart and soul enlisted in the movement to resist the introduction of episcopacy in the Scottish Church, and was one of the four noblemen selected to compose the "table" of the nobility, which, along with the other tables of the gentry, of the burghs, and of the ministers, drew up the famous National Covenant [see COVENANT and COVENANTERS] sworn to by all ranks at Edinburgh in the spring of 1638. He was likewise sent on a mission to Aberdeen, to secure the support of its citizens also; was instrumental in bringing many of them to join the national cause, and in 1639 went there with an army to overawe those who had refused to join his side. Encountering finally the army of king Charles, he gave it battle at Meagra Hill, near Stonehaven (June 15), and obtained a complete victory. When the temporary peace of Berwick was made, Charles invited several of the Covenanting nobles to meet him at Berwick, where he was then holding his court, and to consult with him about Scottish affairs. Among those who went was Montrose, and his party dated what they regarded as his apostasy from that interview. Be that as it may, his political position was certainly much modified after his return. In the General Assembly which met August 13, 1639, under the presidency of the earl of Traquair as royal commissioner, he showed symptoms of toleration towards the Royalists, and was the object of much popular obloquy. One night he is said to have found affixed upon his chamber-door a paper bearing these words, *Invictus armis, verbis vincitur*. The dissolution of the Parliament, in June, 1640, led to an open rupture between the king and the Covenanters, and both parties prepared to decide their quarrel by force of arms. The former assembled at York an army of 21,000 horse and foot; the latter another of 26,000, which, under the command of Leslie, crossed the Tweed August 21, 1640. Montrose was the first man who forded the stream. The successes of the Scots, as is well known, soon forced Charles to summon a new Parliament for the settlement of the national grievances. But though Montrose had fought, he had, along with several other influential nobles, entered into a secret engagement at Cumbernauld, for the purpose of frus-

trating what they regarded as the factious designs of *extreme* Covenanting leaders. His conduct in England, too, had been questionable. It was accidentally discovered that he had been communicating with the king; and when the Parliament assembled (November, 1640), he was cited to appear before a committee. The affair of the Cumbernauld Bond, discovered by the ingenuity of Argyle, was brought up; but Montrose defended his conduct and that of his colleagues, and nothing came of it, though some fiery spirits among the clergy, says Guthrie, "pressed that their lives might go for it." In the following June, Montrose and some others were accused of plotting against Argyle, and were confined in Edinburgh Castle, where they remained till the beginning of 1642, when they were set at liberty in return for the concessions which Charles had made his Scottish subjects. Although they had frequently been examined, nothing definite had been proved against them. The accusation that Montrose had proposed to the king to assassinate Argyle is not historically substantiated, and is intrinsically improbable. During the next year or two Montrose kept aloof, at least outwardly, from public affairs, and became alienated from the Covenanters. He went to York to wait on the king some time in 1643, but failed to meet him. He finally joined the queen, but did not secure any open alliance with the king; the Covenanters all this time trying to win him over to their side again. The civil war which had broken out in England determined Charles and his advisers to crush the Presbyterian leaders in Scotland, who were abetting the efforts of the English Parliamentarians. In the spring of 1644 Montrose finally entered into the king's service, and was raised to the rank of marquis. He left Oxford, where he had been residing with his sovereign, and proceeded to Scotland to raise the Royalists in the North. The battle of Marston Moor for a moment paralyzed him, but his resolution speedily returned. He threw himself into the Highlands, and, after skulking about the hills for some time in disguise, met at Blair-Athol some Irish auxiliaries and a body of Highlanders, who had forced their way thither from the Western Isles in hopes of joining him, and with these enforcements he marched south, fell suddenly (September 1) on the Covenanting army commanded by lord Elcho at Tippermuir, near Perth, and gained a complete victory. Not a single Royalist was slain. After a three-days' stay at Perth, he set out for the North, defeated a force of Covenanters under lord Burleigh at Aberdeen (September 13), and took possession of the city, which was abandoned for four days to all the horrors of war. The approach of Argyle, at the head of 4000 men, compelled Montrose, whose forces were far inferior in numbers and discipline, to retreat into the wilds of Badenoch, whence he recrossed the Grampians, and suddenly appeared in Angus, where he wasted the estates of more than one Covenanting nobleman. With fresh supplies, he then once more returned to Aberdeenshire, with the view of raising the Gordons; narrowly escaped defeat at Fyvie in the end of October, and again withdrew into the fastnesses of the mountains. Argyle, baffled in all his attempts to capture or crush Montrose, returned to Edinburgh and threw up his commission. His opponent, receiving large accessions from the Highland clans, planned a winter campaign, marched southwestward into the country of the Campbells, devastated it frightfully, drove Argyle himself from his castle at Inverary, and then wheeled north, intending to attack Inverness, where the Covenanters were posted in strong force under the earl of Seaforth. The "Estates" at Edinburgh were greatly alarmed, and, raising a fresh army, placed it under the command of general Baillie, a natural son of Sir William Baillie of Lamington. After consulting with Argyle, it was arranged that he should proceed by way of Perth, and take Montrose in front, while Argyle should rally his vast array of vassals and attack him in the rear. The Royalist leader was in the great glen of Albin—the basin of the Caledonian Canal—on his way to Inverness, when he heard that Argyle was following him. He instantly turned on his pursuer, fell upon him unexpectedly at Inverlochy, February 2, 1645, and utterly routed his forces. Fifteen hundred of the Campbells were slain, and only four of Montrose's men. He then resumed his march northwards, but did not venture to assault Inverness—his wild mountaineers being admirably fitted for rapid irregular warfare, but not for the slow work of beleaguerment. Directing his course to the east, he passed, with fire and sword, through Elgin and Banff into Aberdeenshire, which suffered a similar fate. On the 9th of May he attacked and routed Hurry at Auldearn, near Nairn; and after enjoying a short respite with his fierce veterans in Badenoch, again issued from his wilds, and inflicted a still more disastrous defeat on Baillie himself at Alford, in Aberdeenshire (July 2). There was now nothing to prevent his march south, and about the end of the month he set out with a force of from 5000 to 6000 men. He was followed by Baillie, who picked up reinforcements on his way, and on the 15th of August again risked a battle at Kilsyth, but was defeated with frightful loss—6000 of the Covenanters being slain. The cause of Charles was for the moment triumphant, and Montrose, who was virtually master of the country, was made lieutenant-governor of Scotland, and commander-in-chief of the royal forces. All the principal cities in the west hastened to proclaim their fidelity, and laid the blame of the recent troubles on the unfortunate Presbyterian clergy. But gradually affairs took a turn. Great numbers of the Highlanders, having become restless, returned home, and Montrose was obliged to seek safety near the borders. On the 4th of September he broke up his camp at Bothwell, and marched for the eastern counties, where Charles had informed him that the earls of Traquair, Home, and Roxburgh were ready to join him. In this he was disappointed, and on the 13th of the same month he was surprised at Philiphaugh, near Selkirk, by David Leslie, who fell upon the relics of Montrose's army and his raw levies with 6000 cavalry, and completely annihilated them. Escaping from the field of battle, he made his way to Athol, and again endeavored, but in vain, to arouse the Highlands; and at last Charles, now beginning to get the worst of it in the civil war, was induced to order him to withdraw from the kingdom. On the 3d of September, 1646, Montrose sailed for Norway, whence he proceeded to Paris, where he endeavored, but unsuccessfully, to enlist queen Henrietta Maria in aid of her husband; and at last Montrose, in despair, betook himself to Germany, in hope of service under the emperor. He soon after returned to Holland, and entered into communication with the prince of Wales, afterwards Charles II. It was here that news of Charles I's execution reached him. Montrose fainted on receipt of the dreadful intelligence, and gave way to the most passionate regrets. Charles II reinvested him with the dignity of lieutenant-governor of Scotland, and Montrose undertook a fresh invasion on behalf of the exiled monarch. In March, 1650, he arrived at the Orkneys with a small force, and after the lapse of three weeks proceeded to Caithness; but neither the gentlemen nor the commons would rise at his call. He forced his way as far south as the borders of Ross-shire, where his dispirited troops, not over 1500 strong, were attacked and cut to pieces at a place called Corbiesdale, near the pass of Invercarron, by a powerful body of cavalry under colonel Strachan. Montrose fled into the wilds of Assynt, where he was nearly starved to death, when he fell into the hands of M'Leod of Assynt, who delivered him up to general Leslie, by whom he was brought to Edinburgh. Condemned to death as a traitor to the Covenant, he was executed May 21, 1650. His demeanor in his last moments was dignified, but that of the Covenanters open to condemnation, for they were cruel, and heaped indignities upon him even on the gallows. His head was placed on the Tolbooth, and his limbs were sent to different parts of Scotland. After

the Restoration his remains were collected and given a public funeral. See Napier, *Montrose and the Covenanters* (Lond. 1838, 2 vols. 8vo); Grant, *Life of Graham, Marquis of Montrose* (1859); Wishart, *Memoirs of Graham*, etc.; Sir Edward Cust, *Lives of the Warriors of the Civil Wars* (1867); Clarendon, *Hist. of the Rebellion*, vol. ii; Hetherington, *Hist. Ch. of Scotland*, p. 175, 178, 191; Russell, *Hist. Ch. of Scotland*, vol. ii, chap. xii, xiii; Stephen, *Hist. Ch. of Scotland* (Anglican view), i, 576, 641; ii, 6, 17, 34, 44, 50, 61, 63, 96, 111, 144, 156, 167, 316, 317; and the works referred to under COVENANTERS.

Mon(t)serrat, one of the smallest of the West India Islands, belonging to Great Britain, situated 43 miles N.W. of Guadeloupe, and at a similar distance from Antigua and St. Kitts, about 11 miles in length and 7 in breadth, contains an area of 47 English square miles, with a population of a little over 8500, the females exceeding the males by 735. About two thirds of the surface is mountainous and barren; the rest is well cultivated. The chief products are sugar, rum, and molasses; but cotton, arrow-root, and tamarinds are also exported. The island forms a portion of the government of the Leeward Isles, and is directly ruled by a president, aided by a council and house of assembly. The chief town is Plymouth, on the south coast. The revenue of Montserrat in 1860 amounted to £3333, and the expenditure to £3243. In the same year 203 vessels of 7825 tons entered, and 194 vessels of 7450 tons cleared its port; and the total values of imports and exports were respectively £20,060 and £17,043. The religion of the country is Christian, Protestants predominating now; though many Roman Catholics have sprung from those Irish settlers who entered the island in 1632, and the French, who owned it from 1712 till 1746.

Montyon. See MONTHYON.

Monument is the incorrect rendering in Isa. lxv, 4 for נָצוּר, *natsur'*, a *guarded* place ("hidden thing," as in Isa. xlviii, 6; elsewhere "besieged," etc.), such as *caves* (so the Sept. σπήλαιον), or the adyta or shrines of heathen temples (so the Vulg. *delubra*), as places of idolatrous or illicit devotion. It was anciently a practice in most nations for persons to resort to the sepulchres for the purpose of magic or necromancy, and this still holds its ground in India and other Oriental countries. See SUPERSTITION.

In the Apocrypha, "monument" is the correct rendering in Wisd. x, 7 for μνημεῖον, but inexactly in 1 Macc. xiii, 27 for ᾠκοδόμησε, and in 2 Macc. xv, 6 for τρόπαιον. See TOMB.

For the monuments of Egypt and Assyria, see those countries respectively.

Monumental Theology, a term of late employed to designate the scientific presentation of the notions and doctrines of theology as they are found in and taught by monuments. It aims to interpret the life and thought of the Christian Church as these are *unconsciously* recorded in monumental remains. It goes out of the ordinary course of historic investigation, and searches for the isolated and fragmentary. Indeed, wherever Christian peoples have left a monumental trace of their life this discipline directs its inquiries.

Relation to other Departments.—Since these monumental remains are mostly of the nature of art-works, monumental theology is very intimately connected with Art Criticism, Art History, Archæology, Epigraphics, and Numismatics. What have usually been regarded as only auxiliaries to Historical Theology have been recently elevated to an independent science. Art and written language differ entirely, both in their scope and in their modes of expression. Art appeals to the *whole race;* not, indeed, through the faculty of the understanding, but through the higher faculty of the intuition, to which physical sight is only a medium or instrument. The difference is this: while in thought the subject under consideration is resolved into its constituent elements by the discursive faculty, and, therefore, such knowledge is connected with a *series* of elements that are apprehended successively, an art-work, as an object in space, may be understood at once in the totality of its elements, without division and without succession. In this respect the theology of art differs from dogmatics, for example, since the former would have to do chiefly with *intuitive* truth, the latter with results of the exercise of the *discursive faculty*.

But since the Christian Church was founded in the midst of two great opposing systems of religion and philosophy—viz. Heathenism and Judaism—these so-called Christian monuments will often appear of a *mixed* character. Likewise, in the course of the history of the Church she has been subjected to various attacks of error from within and without. Heresies within the Church, the hostile spirit of philosophy, and the persecuting spirit of the temporal powers, have been potent moulding influences. Hence the complete discussion of " Monumental Theology" would demand a careful estimate of the reciprocal influence of these opposing elements. It would therefore include the examination of those heathen monuments that testify, by their monotheistic character, either of lingering traces of an original divine revelation, or of an expectation of an approaching deliverance, as well as that class of monuments that clearly show the presence and influence of heretical systems in the Church itself.

Chronological Limits.—The principles of Christianity, from its institution to the present time, have evidently exerted a most powerful influence on human thought and life. Art has likewise been affected. While at different periods (e. g. in the Western Church during the invasion of the Northern tribes, and in the iconoclastic struggle of the East) art has suffered terrible catastrophes, it has, nevertheless, ever had a more or less intimate connection with the Christian Church. Hence it is with no sufficient reason that a class of writers (Bingham, Rheinwald, Böhmer, Guericke, and Neander) have limited ecclesiastical monuments and Christian archæology to the chronological bounds of Patristics, i. e. to the first six centuries. More scientific is the view of another class of writers (Baumgarten, Augusti, etc.), who regard the Reformation of the 16th century as a modern boundary; since by the revival of classical studies, and the introduction of new elements of life, Art was liberated from its servitude to the Church, and found its subjects and inspiration more in nature and the affairs of common life. Nevertheless the highest art must ever find its truest inspiration in the Christian religion, and therefore art monuments must continue to embody much of the Christian thought and spirit of an age. Hence the more recent writers on Theological Encyclopædia (Hagenbach, Rosenkranz, etc.) extend the study of Christian monuments to the present time.

Synoptical View of the Science.—Piper, the chief defender of monumental theology as an independent discipline, presents the following scheme in his *Einleitung in die Monumentale Theologie:* Since inscriptions and art monuments are the chief subjects examined by monumental theology, these demand a twofold treatment: (*a.*) *An ontological;* (*b.*) *a historical.* In other words, the subject must be discussed partly according to its *essence*, as it is a product of intellectual activity exerted on a given material; and partly according to its *historical development.* And since Christianity is recognised as the chief inspiring motive of these Christian art monuments, another closely related division is necessary, viz. the systematic arrangement and representation of the ideas that have found expression in Christian monuments. Expanded, there would result the following outline:

A. Of the essential nature of Christian art.
  1. Of the art faculty.
    a. The relation of the Church to art *per se.*
      Rise of a Christian art.

    b. Relation of Christian art to the art of classical antiquity.
    c. Emancipation of art from the Church at the end of the Middle Ages.
      Relation of Protestantism to art.
  2. The artist.
    a. Relation of the artist to the Church office: (1) In Christian antiquity; (2) in the Middle Ages; (3) since the close of the Middle Ages.
    b. The training of the artist: (1) His relation to the antique; (2) his relation to nature; (3) schools and guilds.
    c. The individuality of the artist.
  3. Art works.
    a. The *synthetical* division: (1) The material and its treatment; (2) the idea and its embodiment.
      aa. The language of art. Symbolism.
      bb. Art composition.
    b. The *analytical* division: (1) Antoptics; (2) criticism and hermeneutics of art-works.
B. History of Christian art and art-works.
  1. Chronology and geography of art.
  2. The various species of art.
    a. History of architecture.
    b. History of the graphic arts.
  3. Art monuments.
    a. Civil monuments with Christian characters: (1) Coins; (2) consular diptychs.
    b. Private monuments: (1) Monuments of domestic life—gems, rings, etc.; (2) sepulchral monuments.
    c. Ecclesiastical monuments: (1) Architecture, cemeteries, churches, cloisters; (2) vessels of the churches; (3) ornamentation of churches—mosaics, paintings, etc.
    d. Monuments of ideal or free creative art.
C. Christian art ideas.
  1. In architecture: symbolism of architecture.
  2. In the graphic arts.
    a. The development of the scope and range of Christian representation.
    b. The content of Christian representation: (1) Monumental exegesis; (2) monumental history of the kingdom of God; (3) monumental dogmatics and ethics.
    c. Practical utility of Christian representations.

Explanation and Justification of the foregoing Synopsis.—(I.) In the first branch. 1. If we discuss the harmony of art with the Christian Church, and its realization therein, the first thing to be examined is *the essential nature of that art itself*, both generally as a necessary subject of the activity of the *human mind*, as well as specially how it accords with the *genius of Christianity* itself. However, the problem here is not the same as in the art archæology of classical antiquity, since early Christianity holds an entirely different relation to art. It is similar to its relation to philosophy. Neither art nor philosophy was originated by the Church, but both had already passed through all stages of a great development. The Church found art already occupying human thought, and its rise and history are presupposed. By this art the early Christians were as much attracted as repelled. This conditions the *dependence* of the earliest Christian art on the antique—most especially in technical treatment, but also to some extent in spirit and motive; so that this comes to be a constitutive element in the discussion, just as in the earliest history of doctrines we must carefully note the influence of the Greek (specially the Platonic) philosophy. On the other hand, the *independence* of Christian art is shown even in the presence of the antique. Specially those peoples who subsequently appeared upon the stage of history, and received contemporaneously their culture with Christianity, have developed from the first a characteristically Christian art; since the final grounds of art antiquity are found in the nature of man itself, and to these we must at last return. This art activity likewise takes direction among a people to that extent that the period of the perfection of Christian art may be delayed by means of its connection with a development so influenced by the models of antiquity. At the same time another sphere of art life of universal interest will be liberated, and attain to an independent value. According to this view, the subjects that pertain to the essence of Christian art, as springing from a general art susceptibility, demand a preliminary discussion.

2. The essential nature of art from its *objective* side discussed, it is necessary to pass to the *subjective* element, the interest in which part will depend upon the personality—specially the gifts and endowments—of him who devotes himself to the service of art and the Church. In this connection, the first question that meets us is the personal and official relation of the artist to the Church. At the beginning we find the strange contrasts that heathen artists became interested in Christian works of art, while also Christian artists became martyrs. After a period of untrammelled art development had elapsed, at length, during the Middle Ages, both science and art fell under the exclusive superintendence of monks and priests, until the transference of art to the laity introduced the new æra. In this connection must also be discussed the question of the culture of artists, and the diffusion of those important guilds, partly industrial, partly ecclesiastical, by whose means the flourishing period of art in the later mediæval period was ushered in. Here, as elsewhere, progress is connected with the *individual* and his work, and the measure of this progress is determined by investigation of the condition of the individual. In the study of the development of doctrines and the organization of the early Church an acquaintance with the Christian fathers is of fundamental importance. In monumental theology, the history of artists corresponds to patristics in the history of doctrines and ecclesiastical polity; yet in an inverse chronological order, since the most noted names of the Christian fathers are found at or near the organization of the Church, while the names of the most renowned masters of art are associated with the conclusion of the Middle Ages and the dawning of the modern epoch. With the exception of a few noted architects, the names of artists hardly appear at all in Christian antiquity. So completely was art merged in the *general* interest of the Church that *individual* service is almost forgotten. In the later Middle Ages the guilds effected a like result, so that the names of the architects of those most wonderful works that stand at the very acme of perfection are entirely wanting. Subsequently to the 13th and 14th centuries, however, in the departments of sculpture and painting, the individuality of the artist again asserted itself, and art pursued its high mission in a most noteworthy union of free endowment and the observance of organic æsthetic laws.

3. The third division has reference to art-creation. An art-work presupposes a *material* as well as an *idea*. Each is to be examined by itself, as well as in its combination in the production of a work of art. On the one side is such a moulding of the material as to breathe into it a living soul, and create in it a spiritual presence. This leads to the discussion of the laws of Technics. On the other hand, there is the projection of the idea into form—its embodiment in the material. This gives rise to questions of art composition. This latter involves the laws of the grouping in space of art representations. The first question pertains to the conception of the idea in space, to the successive stages of the transition from spiritual life to corporeity; or, according to the language of art, through what means, and by what law, art *expresses* thought and feeling. If we examine painting and sculpture, we find this occurs in part *directly* through *historic* composition; in part, *indirectly* through *symbolic* composition. In symbolic representation, the entire visible world is laid under contribution to aid in this transition to the unseen. When this method is practiced, as in delineations within the sphere of the Church, such means are perfectly legitimate. Hence arise the doctrines of Christian art symbolism, that occupies so wide a field, and, theologically considered, is of such vast significance.

Here is also naturally connected a department to which no certain and well-defined position has hitherto been assigned (since notice has only been taken of it in

connection with the art archæology of *classical* antiquity); we refer to Christian archæological criticism and hermeneutics. This is the very reverse of art composition: the latter treating of the transition from the thought and the person of the artist to the execution of his work; the former leading from the art-work back to the thought, purpose, and character of the artist, and to the discovery of the circumstances under which the work was produced.

(II.) The second chief division of the subject—the history of art—treats of the different kinds of art. It remains an open question whether the subject of monuments should be connected directly with this division of the subject or receive an independent treatment. Authorities are divided. To both, however, must there be a preliminary section that shall describe art as a whole in its *chronological* development. With this also is naturally connected an account of the *geographical* distribution of monuments. This would include a description of those *in situ*, as well as of those that have been artificially distributed or gathered into art collections, both public and private.

(III.) The third division, that treats of art ideas, corresponds in some extent to that which is embraced in the archæology of classical art, under the head "Subjects of Formative Arts." For theological purposes this is the chief difficulty, and to illustrate this all the other portions are preliminary and subordinate. Architecture, from its very nature, furnishes to this department but a meagre contribution, since here symbolism has not a wide range or application. Much more copious in materials are painting and sculpture, inasmuch as since the 16th century the history of images has been a subject of theological literature.

For a methodical treatment of this subject we must carefully observe the distinction between the *historical course* that the representation of images has generally taken (in which connection would be discussed the questions what, by what means, and in what spirit such representation has taken place), and the *content* of such representation (in which latter case the whole range of image representation is to be canvassed and carefully estimated). This subject, being Christian in its nature, has reference partly to the sacred history in its entire extension with Church history, and partly to the supersensuous subjects of faith, as well as the phenomena and motives of moral life. Hence would arise two further divisions, viz. 1, the monumental history of the kingdom of God; 2, monumental dogmatics and ethics. For the illustration of these two departments the whole wealth of monuments that have been preserved would be useful, and their connection as well with the course of history as of dogma would be shown.

At this point would arise yet two other themes of discussion: (1.) The return from this range of Biblical representations to the text of the Holy Scriptures themselves. Since the subjects of the Bible, in whole or in part, are found in numerous works of art in all periods of the history of the Church, we are thereby furnished a kind of translation and commentary of the same. This pictorial representation frequently proves more impressive than an oral or written exegesis, since the speaker or writer can pass by what is difficult in the Scriptures or let it remain undetermined, while the artist cannot, but must bring whatever topic he treats distinctly before the perception of himself and others. As, therefore, the artist has to practice a most searching exegetical avocation, monuments of art are exceedingly rich original sources of information for the interpretation of the Word of God, and also for the related questions of Biblical introduction, viz. the doctrines of the canon and of linguistic usage. Here rests the claim of "Monumental Exegesis."

(2.) The other theme has reference to practical theology. Through the contemplation of a sacred subject present to the beholder, and through the interpenetrating genius of a gifted artist, there is doubtless in Christian art representations a grand power to enkindle and exalt devotional feeling. An art-work, equally with the fleeting word, has its language of eloquence, and is able to convince and to inspire. Hence there is in monuments a *practical* power that has been used by the Church in all ages for purposes of moral and religious training. The "Lay-Bible," for example, illuminated as it was most copiously, became a most efficient means of the moral education of the masses, who were unable to read the text of the Scripture; and even the cultured have derived almost equal pleasure and profit from these sources. Practical theology, however, does not receive such helpful and constant illustration from monuments as the other chief divisions of theology.

The foregoing are among the chief reasons urged by Piper in justification of the term "Monumental Theology," and for regarding it as an independent discipline equally with "Patristics," "the History of Doctrines," etc. This claim to independence of treatment has been controverted by many eminent modern encyclopædists, and the question must be regarded as still unsettled.

Literature.—Since "Monumental Theology" includes under it archæology, art history, epigraphics, and numismatics, its literature would include the literature of these subjects. Specially, see Piper, *Einleitung in die Monumentale Theologie* (Gotha, 1867, 8vo), who gives the literature from the earliest time; also his article in Herzog's *Real-Encyklopädie*, xv, 752 sq., which is a copious summary. See also Bennett, in the *Methodist Quarterly Review* (Jan. 1871), p. 5 sq., for a brief estimate of some of the most important works on this subject. One of the most interesting fields of monumental theology is found in the early Christian catacombs of Rome, and the results of explorations have been succinctly presented by Withrow, *The Catacombs of Rome, and their Testimony relative to primitive Christianity* (N. Y. 1874, 12mo). See also *Lond Academy*, October 1, 1873, p. 370; *Brit. and For. Ev. Rev.* Jan. 1874, art. vi; *Bibliotheca Sacra*, vol. xciv; *Meth. Qu. Rev.* Oct. 1874, art. iv. (C. W. B.)

Moody, Joseph, an American divine of the Congregational Church, was born in 1701. But little is known of his early life. As a minister he was noted for his many eccentricities, but also for his piety, and as a remarkably useful preacher of the Gospel. In his younger years he often preached beyond the limits of his own parish, which was in Maine, and wherever he went the people hung upon his lips. In one of his excursions he went as far as Providence, R. I., where his exertions were the means of laying the foundation of a church. Such was the sanctity of his character that it impressed the irreligious with awe. He also with importunate earnestness pleaded the cause of the poor, and was very charitable himself. It was by his own choice that he derived his support from a free contribution, rather than a fixed salary; and in one of his sermons he mentions that he had been thus supported twenty years, and yet had been under no necessity of spending one hour in a week in care for the world. Some remarkable instances of answers to his prayers, and of correspondence between the event and his faith, are not yet forgotten in York. The hour of dinner once came, and his table was unsupplied with provisions; but he insisted upon having the cloth laid, saying to his wife he was confident that they should be furnished by the bounty of God. At this moment some one rapped at the door, and presented a ready-cooked dinner. It was sent by persons who on that day had made an entertainment, and who knew the poverty of Mr. Moody. He published several of his discourses. See Sullivan, *Maine*, p. 238; Allen, *Biographical Dictionary*, s. v.; Sprague, *Annals of the Amer. Pulpit*, vol. ii.

Moody, Joshua, a Congregational minister, was born in Wales in 1633. His father migrated to this country, and settled at Newbury, Mass., in 1635, and Joshua was educated at Harvard College, class of 1653.

There had been no regular clergyman in Portsmouth, N. H., previous to 1658, in which year he began to preach, and a church being formed in 1671, he was ordained pastor. In 1684 Cranfield, the governor, had him unjustly imprisoned for nonconformity with the Church of England rites, and after a confinement of thirteen weeks he was set free, but commanded to cease preaching in the province. Going to Boston, he became the assistant in the First Church, and was also invited to take charge of Harvard University, but he declined the last-named offer, and in 1692 returned to his charge at Portsmouth. During the witchcraft troubles in 1692 he had opposed the unjust and violent measures towards the imagined offenders, and aided Philip English and his wife to escape from prison. His zeal in this matter caused his dismissal from his church, and he retired from the ministry. He died in 1697. He published, *A practical Discourse concerning the choice Benefit of Communion with God in his House, witnessed unto by the Experience of Saints as the best Improvement of Time, being the Sum of several Sermons on Psalm lxxxiv*, 10, *preached at Boston on Lecture Days* (Boston, 1685 and 1746, 12mo):—*A Sermon on the Sin of Formality in God's Worship, or the Formal Worshipper proved a Liar and Deceiver, preached on the Weekly Lecture in Boston from Hosea ii*, 12; and two or three occasional sermons. See Cotton Mather's *Funeral Sermon, Magnolia*, iv, 192-199; Sprague, *Annals of the Amer. Pulpit*, i, 160; Drake, *Dict. of Amer. Biog.* s. v.

Moody, Samuel, an American divine of some note, was born at Newbury, Mass., Jan. 4, 1676; was educated at Harvard College, where he graduated in 1697; then entered upon the special study of theology, and Dec. 29, 1700, was ordained to the sacred ministry in the Congregational Church at York, Me., where he died, Nov. 13, 1747. Like his namesake, Joseph, who flourished very near his time, he was eccentric, though also a very useful man. He also refused a stated salary, and depended altogether upon voluntary contributions, many of which were spent upon the poor and the needy. He published, *The Doleful State of the Damned* (1710):—*Judas Hung up in Chains* (1714):—*Election Sermon* (1721):—*Life and Death of Joseph Quasson, an Indian* (1729). See Allibone, *Dict. of Brit. and Amer. Authors*, s. v.; Drake, *Dict. of Amer. Biog.* s. v.; Sprague, *Annals of the Amer. Pulpit*, vol. ii.

Moody, Samuel S., a minister of the Methodist Episcopal Church, South, was born in Powhattan County, Va., May 1, 1810; was converted in 1828, joined the ministry in the Tennessee Conference, and held the following appointments: 1831, Lebanon Circuit; 1832, Sandy Circuit; 1833, Nashville Station; 1834, Memphis Station; 1835, Florence Station; 1836, Montgomery Circuit; 1837, Lebanon District; 1839, Murfreesborough District; was transferred to the Memphis Conference in 1841, and appointed to Jackson District; in 1842 to Memphis Station; in 1843 to Jackson Station; was transferred back to the Tennessee Conference in 1844, and appointed to Murfreesborough Station; in 1845, 1846, and 1847, to Huntsville District, and in 1848 to Nashville District. In the fall of 1850 failing health obliged him to take a supernumerary relation, and, after years of wasting affliction, he died May 5, 1863. "The older members of this Conference will long cherish the memory of his many virtues, and class him among the brightest and best and most beloved of its members. Perhaps no man of our Conference was more universally beloved; indeed, the virtues of this holy man will live in the memories of thousands as long as life shall last. He never had an enemy. Our Church has seldom produced so pure a specimen of our holy religion." See *Min. Ann. Conf. M. E. Church, South*, ii (1858-65), 546.

Moon (יָרֵחַ, *yare'ach*, so called from its *paleness*; Chald. יְרַח, *yerach'*, Ezra vi, 15; Dan. iv, 26; poetical לְבָנָה, *lebanah'*, the *white*, Cant. vi, 10; Isa. xxiv, 23;

xxx, 26; Gr. σελήνη), the lesser of the two great celestial luminaries. See ASTRONOMY.

1. It is worthy of observation that neither of the terms by which the Hebrews designated the moon contains any reference to its office or essential character; they simply describe it by the accidental quality of color. Another explanation of the second term is proposed in Rawlinson's *Herodotus*, i, 615, to the effect that it has reference to *lebenâh*, "a brick," and embodies the Babylonian notion of *Sin*, the moon, as being the god of architecture. The strictly parallel use of *yarêach* in Joel ii, 31 and Ezek. xxxii, 7, as well as the analogy in the sense of the two words, seems a strong argument against the view. The Greek σελήνη, from σέλας, expresses this idea of brilliancy more vividly than the Hebrew terms. The Indo-European languages recognised the moon as the measurer of time, and have expressed its office in this respect, all the terms applied to it—μήν, moon, etc.—finding a common element with μετρεῖν, *to measure*, in the Sanscrit root *ma* (Pott's *Etym. Forsch.* i, 194). The nations with whom the Hebrews were brought into more immediate contact worshipped the moon under various designations expressive of its influence in the kingdom of nature. The exception which the Hebrew language thus presents would appear to be based on the repugnance to nature-worship which runs through their whole system, and which induced the precautionary measure of giving it in reality no name at all, substituting the circuitous expressions "lesser light" (Gen. i, 16), the "pale," or the "white." The same tendency to avoid the notion of personality may perhaps be observed in the indifference to gender, *yarêach* being masculine, and *lebanâh* feminine. See below.

2. The moon held an important place in the kingdom of nature as known to the Hebrews. In the history of the creation (Gen. i, 14–16) it appears simultaneously with the sun, and is described in terms which imply its independence of that body as far as its light is concerned. Conjointly with the sun, it was appointed "for signs and for seasons, and for days and years;" though in this respect it exercised a more important influence, if by the "seasons" we understand the great religious festivals of the Jews, as is particularly stated in Psa. civ, 19 ("He appointed the moon for seasons"), and more at length in Ecclus. xliii, 6, 7. Hence, as a measure of time among the Israelites, a lunation was the period of their month; and many of their festivals were on the new moon, or on one of its quarterly phases (Ecclus. xliii, 6 sq.; comp. Sohar *in Gen.* fol. 236). See MONTH. This was especially the case with the Passover, their chief festival (see Bähr, *Symbol.* ii, 639). See PASSOVER. Besides this, the moon had its special office in the distribution of light; it was appointed "to rule over the night," as the sun over the day, and thus the appearance of the two founts of light served "to divide between the day and between the night." In order to enter fully into this idea, we must remember both the greater brilliancy of the moonlight in Eastern countries, and the larger amount of work, particularly travelling, that is carried on by its aid. The appeals to sun and moon conjointly are hence more frequent in the literature of the Hebrews than they might otherwise have been (Josh. x, 12; Psa. lxxii, 5, 7, 17; Eccles. xii, 2; xxiv, 23, etc.); in some instances, indeed, the moon receives a larger amount of attention than the sun (e. g. Psa. viii, 3; lxxxix, 37). The inferiority of its light is occasionally noticed, as in Gen. i, 16; in Cant. vi, 10, where the epithets "fair" and "clear" (or, rather, *spotless*, and hence extremely brilliant) are applied respectively to moon and sun; and in Isa. xxx, 26, where the equalizing of its light to that of the sun conveys an image of the highest glory. Its influence on vegetable or animal life receives but little notice; the expression in Deut. xxxiii, 14, which the A. V. refers to the moon, signifies rather *months* as the period of ripening fruits. The coldness of the night-dews is prejudicial to the health, and particularly to the eyes of those who are ex-

posed to it, and the idea expressed in Psa. cxxi, 6 ("The moon shall not smite thee by night") may have reference to the general or the particular evil effect: blindness is still attributed to the influence of the moon's rays on those who sleep under the open heaven, both by the Arabs (Carne's *Letters*, i, 88) and by Europeans. If this extreme (comparative) cold is considered in connection with the Oriental custom of sleeping *sub divo*, out of doors, *à la belle étoile*, on the flat roofs of houses, or even on the ground, without in all cases sufficient precautionary measures for protecting the body, we see no difficulty in understanding whence arose the evil influence ascribed to the moon. In the East Indies similar effects result from similar exposure. The connection between the moon's phases and certain forms of disease, whether madness or epilepsy, is expressed in the Greek σεληνιάζεσθαι (Matt. iv, 24; xvii, 15), in the Latin derivative "lunatic," and in our "moon-struck." The various influences anciently attributed to the moon in her different phases (Pliny, ii, 102), not only in changes of the weather (Varro, *R. R.* i, 37; Virgil, *Georg.* i, 275, 427; comp. Hos. v, 7; Isa. xlvii, 13), but also in physical effects upon the human system (Macrob. *Sat.* vii, 16; comp. Psa. cxxi, 6), is a superstition (Horat. *Ars Poet.* v, 454; Virgil, *Æn.* iv, 512) still very prevalent in the East (Rosenmüller, *Morgenl.* iv, 108), and has not even ceased among modern Occidentals (comp. Hone, *Every-day Book*, i, 1509; Shakespeare, *Mids. N. D.* ii, 2; *Othello*, v, 2), although science has shown that this planet has no specific influence either upon meteorology or health. See Hayn, *De Planetar. in Corp. hum. Influxu* (Frckf. 1805); Kretschmar, *De Astror. in Corp. hum. Imperio* (Jena, 1820); Raschig, *De lunæ imperio in valetud. corp. hum. nullo* (Vit. 1787); Krazenstein, *Einfluss des Mondes in d. m. Körp.* (Halle, 1747); Reil, *Archiv. f. Physiol.* i, 133 sq. See LUNATIC.

3. The clearness of the Oriental atmosphere early led to the worship of the heavenly bodies (Herod. ii, 47; Strabo, xii, p. 557; Pliny, viii, 1, etc.), among which the moon received special honors (Job xxxi, 26; comp. Julian, *Orat. in Salem.* p. 90), as the most conspicuous object of the nocturnal firmament (comp. Deut. iv, 19; xvii, 3; 2 Kings xxiii, 5; Jer. viii, 2; see Selden, *Dii Syr.* i, 239 sq.). If the sun "rules the day," the moon has the throne of night, which, if less gorgeous than that of the sun, is more attractive, because of a less oppressively brilliant light, while her retinue of surrounding stars seems to give a sort of truth to her regal state, and certainly adds not inconsiderably to her beauty. There is to the same effect a remarkable passage in Julian (*Orat. in Salem.* p. 90): "From my childhood I was filled with a wonderful love for the rays of that goddess; and when, in my boyhood, I directed my eyes to her ethereal light, I was quite beside myself. By night especially, when I found myself under a wide, pure, cloudless sky, I forgot everything else under her influence, and was absorbed in the beauties of heaven, so that I did not hear if addressed, nor was aware of what I did. I appeared solely to be engaged with this divinity, so that even when a beardless boy I might have been taken for a star-gazer." Accordingly the worship of the moon was extensively practiced by the nations of the East, and under a variety of aspects. In Egypt it was honored under the form of Isis, and was one of the only two deities which commanded the reverence of all the Egyptians (*Herod.* ii, 42, 47). In Syria it was represented by that one of the Ashtaroth (i. e. of the varieties which the goddess Astarte, or Ashtoreth, underwent) surnamed "Karnaim," from the horns of the crescent moon by which she was distinguished. See ASHTORETH. In Babylonia it formed one of a triad in conjunction with Æther and the sun, and, under the name of *Sin*, received the honored titles of "Lord of the month," "King of the gods," etc. (Rawlinson's *Herodotus*, i, 614). There are indications of a very early introduction into the countries adjacent to Palestine of a species of worship distinct from any that

we have hitherto noticed, viz. of the direct homage of the heavenly bodies—sun, moon, and stars—which is the characteristic of *Sabianism* (q. v.). The first notice which we have of this is in Job (xxxi, 26, 27), and it is observable that the warning of Moses (Deut. iv, 19) is directed against this nature-worship, rather than against the form of moon-worship which the Israelites must have witnessed in Egypt. At a later period, however, the worship of the moon in its grosser form of idol-worship was introduced from Syria: we have no evidence indeed that the Ashtoreth of the Zidonians, whom Solomon introduced (1 Kings xi, 5), was identified in the minds of the Jews with the moon, but there can be no doubt that the moon was worshipped under the form of an image in Manasseh's reign, although Movers (*Phöniz.* i, 66, 164) has taken up the opposite view; for we are distinctly told that the king "made an *asherah* (A. V. 'grove'), i. e. an *image* of Ashtoreth, and worshipped all the host of heaven" (2 Kings xxi, 3), which *asherah* was destroyed by Josiah, and the priests that burned incense to the moon were put down (xxiii, 4, 5). At a somewhat later period the worship of the "queen of heaven" was practiced in Palestine (Jer. vii, 18; xliv, 17). The title has generally been supposed to belong to the moon (comp. Horace, *Carm. Sæc.* 35; Apuleius, *Metam.* ii, p. 254), but some think it more probable that the Oriental Venus is intended, for the following reasons: (1) the title of *Urania* "of heaven" was peculiarly appropriate to Venus, whose worship was borrowed by the Persians from the Arabians and Assyrians (*Herod.* i, 131, 199); (2) the votaries of this goddess, whose chief function was to preside over births, were women; and we find that in Palestine the married women are specially noticed as taking a prominent part; (3) the peculiarity of the title, which occurs only in the passages quoted, looks as if the worship were a novel one; and this is corroborated by the term *kavvân* (כַּוָּן) applied to the "cakes," which is again so peculiar that the Sept. has retained it (χαυών), deeming it to be, as it not improbably was, a foreign word. Whether the Jews derived their knowledge of the "queen of heaven" from the Philistines, who possessed a very ancient temple of Venus Urania at Ascalon (*Herod.* i, 105), or from the Egyptians, whose god Athor was of the same character, is uncertain. See QUEEN OF HEAVEN.

The moon was regarded in the old Syrian superstition as subject to the sun's influence, which was worshipped as the active and generative power of nature, while the moon was reverenced as the passive and producing power. The moon, accordingly, was looked upon as feminine. Herein Oriental usage agrees with our own. But this usage was by no means universal. The gender of *mond* in German is an exception in modern days, which may justify the inference that even among the Northern nations the moon has masculine qualities ascribed to it. By the people of Carran, in Mesopotamia, the moon was worshipped as a male deity, and called *Lunus.* Spartian tells us these people were of the opinion that such as believe the moon to be a goddess, and not a god, will be their wives' slaves as long as they live; but, on the contrary, those who esteem her to be a god will ever be masters of their wives, and never be overcome by their artifices. The same author tells us that there were remaining several medals of the Nysæans, Magnesians, and other Greek nations, which represented the moon in the dress and under the name of a man, and covered with an Armenian bonnet. The Egyptians also represented their moon as a male deity, *Ihoth*; and Wilkinson (*Anc. Egypt.* v, 5) remarks that "the same custom of calling it male is retained in the East to the present day, while the sun is considered feminine, as in the language of the Germans. Ihoth, in the character of Lunus, the moon, has sometimes a man's face, with the crescent of the moon upon his head supporting a disk." Plutarch says the Egyptians "call the moon the mother of the world, and hold it to be of both sexes:

female, as it receives the influence of the sun; male, as it scatters and disperses through the air the principles of fecundity." In other countries also the moon was held to be hermaphrodite. Another pair of dissimilar qualities was ascribed to the moon—the destructive and the generative faculty—whence it was worshipped as a bad as well as a good power. The Egyptians sacrificed to the moon when she was at the full. The victims offered to her were swine, which the Egyptians held to be impure animals, and were forbidden to offer them to any other deities but that planet and Bacchus. When they sacrificed to the moon, and had killed the victim, they put the end of the tail, with the spleen and fat, into the caul, and burned them on the sacred fire, and ate the rest of the flesh on the day of the new moon. Those whose poverty would not admit of the expense of this sacrifice moulded a bit of paste into the shape of a hog, and offered up that (Herodotus, i, 2). In India this goddess bore the name of *Maja;* among the Syrians, *Mylitta;* among the Phœnicians, *Astarte* or *Ashtoreth;* among the Greeks, *Artemis;* and among the Romans, *Diana* (see Bähr, *Symbol.* i, 436 sq., 478; ii, 222, 232). In these nations, however, the moon was usually the representative of the benign or prolific power of nature. See Carpzov, *Apparat.* p. 510; Frischmuth, *De Melecheth Cœli* (Jen. 1663); A. Calov, *De Selenolatria* (Vit. 1680). See ASTROLOGY.

In the Western world also the moon has been, and continues even now to be worshipped or superstitiously regarded. In Europe there are several countries in which untold superstitious acts are performed, depending upon the moon's rotation (see Brand, *Popular Antiquities of Great Britain*, Index in vol. iii). In Great Britain and the Northern wilds the moon is placed highest in the scale of nature-worship. In America the wild man, like other heathen, both of civilized and barbarous races, has been long accustomed to the thought that all the heavenly bodies are possessed of animation, and even gifted with some measure of intelligence. To each, accordingly, has been ascribed an independent, vitalizing soul. The sun-god, for example, is the living sun itself, and worship is never paid to it symbolically, as if it were the representative of some invisible or absent spirit, but because it is an actual depository of the supersensuous, an embodiment of the divine. As the sun stands for the Creator, so the moon is connected, as in Babylonian mythology, with the thought of some evil principle. Says Müller (*Amerikanische Urreligionen*), "The rude American was haunted by the thought of some co-equal and co-ordinate array of hostile deities, who manifested their malignant nature by creating discord, sickness, death, and every possible form of evil. These were held in numerous cases to obey the leadership of the moon, which, owing to its changeful aspects, have become identical with the capricious, evil-minded spirit of American Indians" (p. 53; comp. 170, 272; comp. also Brinton, *Myths of the New World*, p. 130–140). In Africa moon-worship prevails to a considerable extent, and is spoken of by Livingstone (*Travels in South Africa*, p. 235).

4. In the figurative language of Scripture the moon is frequently noticed as presaging events of the greatest importance through the temporary or permanent withdrawal of its light (Isa. xiii, 10; Joel ii, 31; Matt. xxiv, 29; Mark xiii, 24): in these and similar passages we have an evident allusion to the mysterious awe with which eclipses were viewed by the Hebrews in common with other nations of antiquity (comp. Jer. xiii, 16; Ezek. xxxii, 7, 8; Rev. viii, 12). With regard to the symbolic meaning of the moon in Rev. xii, 1, we have only to observe that the ordinary explanations, viz. the sublunary world, or the changeableness of its affairs, seem to derive no authority from the language of the O. T., or from the ideas of the Hebrews.

. MOON or LUNETTE (Isa. iii, 18). See TIRE.

MOON, NEW. See NEW MOON.

Moor, Michael, a Roman Catholic divine, who flourished in England from 1640 to 1726, was a native of Dublin, Ireland, and spent some time in France, at one time filling the post of principal of the College of Navarre. In England he was regius professor of philosophy, Greek, and Hebrew. He wrote, *De Existentia Dei et Humana Immortalitate* (Paris, 1692, 8vo):—*Hortatio ad Studium Linguæ Græcæ et Hebraicæ* (1700, 12mo):—*Vera Sciendi Methodus* (Paris, 1716, 8vo); against the philosophy of Des Cartes. See Harris's Ware's *Ireland*, s. v.; Allibone, *Dict. of Brit. and Amer. Authors*, s. v.

Moor, Thoroughgood, a missionary of the Anglican establishment to the "Iroquois or Praying Indians," flourished near the opening of the 18th century, in the vicinity of the place now known as Albany, the capital of the state of New York. Mr. Moor arrived in New York from England in 1704, and, after a stay at Albany long enough to acquire the Indian tongue, he at once set out upon his work, and for many years labored among the Iroquois. His success was limited because of the opposition manifested by lord Cornbury, at that time governor of the New York and New Jersey colonies. Moor for some time braved all opposition, but, encountering the ill-will of the governor, he was incarcerated, and after his escape from prison went to sea, and was lost on his homeward voyage. See Anderson, *Hist. Col. Ch.* iii, 415 sq.; Hawkins, *Hist.* p. 264 sq., 271, 281.

Moore, Aaron, a minister of the Methodist Episcopal Church, South, was born in Ohio April 2, 1813; joined the Church when about twenty years old, was admitted into the Louisville Conference in 1846, and remained a regular minister of the Gospel, filling many important appointments with great acceptability until the fall of 1859, when, his health failing him, he accepted a superannuated relation, and retained it till the time of his death, which occurred in Madisonville, Ky., Oct. 15, 1863. See *Min. Ann. Conf. M. E. Church, South*, ii (1858-65), 481.

Moore, Benjamin, D.D., a bishop of the Protestant Episcopal Church, was born at Newton, N. J., and was educated at King's (now Columbia) College, New York, where he graduated in 1768, and then devoted his time to the study of theology, supporting himself by private instruction in Greek and Latin. In May, 1774, he went to England to enter into holy orders, and in June of that year was ordained deacon and priest by the bishop of London, and on his return to America officiated in Trinity Church, New York, of which he became rector, Dec. 22, 1800. The extent of Dr. Moore's labors, and his popularity in this position, were beyond all precedent, and when, in 1801, the diocese needed a bishop, he was elected and consecrated. He was also made president of Columbia College in this year, and so remained until 1811, continuing all the while the duties of his ministry, and even until his death, Feb. 27, 1816. From 1811 to the hour of his death, Dr. Hobart, who afterwards succeeded him, acted as his assistant bishop, bishop Moore having been struck with paralysis, and thus disabled from discharging any longer the duties of his office. Bishop Moore was an accomplished scholar and an able pulpit orator. He was, with one single exception, the last of the venerable men in the diocese of New York who had derived their ordination from the parent Church of England. He published two sermons in the *American Preacher* (vols. i and ii, 1791):—*A Sermon before the General Convention* (1804):—*A Pamphlet in Vindication of Episcopal Services* (2 vols. 8vo). His *Posthumous Sermons* were published under the direction of his son, Clement C. Moore, LL.D. (N. Y. 1824, 2 vols. 8vo). See Sprague, *Annals of the Amer. Pulpit*, v, 299; Bishop White, *Memoirs of the Episcopal Church* (1836), p. 32; Moore, *Hist. of Columbia College*; Anderson, *Hist. of the Colonial Church*, iii, 611 sq.; Drake, *Dict. of Amer. Biog.* s. v. (J. H. W.)

Moore, Charles, a clergyman of the English Es-

tablishment, eldest son of archbishop Moore, was educated first at Westminster School, and next at Trinity College, Cambridge, where he took his degrees and obtained a fellowship. He flourished in the second half of the last century, first as rector of Cuxton, in Kent, then as vicar of St. Nicholas at Rochester, and later as one of the six preachers of the cathedral of Canterbury. He wrote, *A Visitation Sermon preached before his Father* (1785, 4to):—*A full Inquiry into the Subject of Suicide* (1790, 2 vols. 4to):—*The good Effects of a united Trust in the Arm of the Flesh and the Arm of the Lord, a Sermon* (1804, 8vo):—*Female Compassion illustrated, a Sermon* (1806, 8vo):—*Personal Reform the only effectual Basis of National Reform, a Sermon* (1810, 8vo). See *Biog. Dict. of Living Authors* (Lond. 1816, 8vo), p. 239.

Moore, Clement Clarke, LL.D., an American scholar, noted for his knowledge of exegetical theology, son of Benjamin Moore, was born in New York July 15, 1779; was educated at Columbia College, class of 1798; then entered on the special study of Hebrew, and after a while secured the appointment as professor of Biblical literature in the Protestant Episcopal Seminary, New York; in 1821 was transferred to the chair of Hebrew and Greek literature, and later to Oriental and Greek literature. While in connection with the "General Seminary" of his Church, as it came finally to be known, he donated to it the large plot of ground upon which its buildings now stand. In 1850 he received the title of emeritus professor, and lived to take an interest in the institution he had served so many years, and so acceptably, until July 10, 1863, his death occurring at Newport, R. I., whither he had gone to spend the summer recreating. To Dr. Moore belongs the honor of having published the first American contributions to Hebrew philology, viz. a *Hebrew Lexicon, with Notes, a Grammar, and a complete Vocabulary of the Psalms* (N. Y. 1809, 2 vols. 8vo). He also published his father's sermons, and contributed valuable works to the department of belles-lettres (for which see Allibone, *Dict. of Brit. and Amer. Authors*, s. v.). See Drake, *Dict. of Amer. Biog.* s. v.

Moore, Franklin, D.D., a minister of note of the Methodist Episcopal Church, was born Feb. 14, 1822, in Beaver, Pa. In quite tender years he was converted, and though his father, who was a lawyer and eminent at the bar, wished him to choose the legal profession as his life-calling, his mind drifted beyond all persuasion towards the ministry. In preparing for this work he studied at Washington College, in Washington, Pa., and also at the Presbyterian Theological Seminary in Alleghany City, and graduated from both institutions with honor. In 1845 the Pittsburgh Conference held its annual session in the place of his nativity, and during the session he, having shortly after his conversion joined the Methodist Church, was received into the travelling connection, and appointed to Chartiers Circuit. The next year he was sent to Steubenville, and in 1847 he was received into full connection and ordained deacon. He was stationed at New Lisbon, Ohio. In 1849 he was ordained elder, and stationed at Uniontown, Pa.; in 1851 and 1852 he was in Washington, Pa.; and in 1853 and 1854 on Uniontown District. He was transferred in 1855 to the West Virginia Conference, then called Western Virginia Conference, and stationed for two years at Fourth Street, in Wheeling. At the close of his term of service in that station he was transferred to the Philadelphia Conference, and there filled the following appointments: in 1857 and 1858, Trinity Church, Philadelphia; in 1859 and 1860, Wharton Street Church, Philadelphia; in 1861 and 1862, Harrisburg; in 1863 and 1864, Union Church, Philadelphia; in 1865 a supernumerary, but doing work a part of the year; in 1866 in Thirty-eighth Street Church, but still a supernumerary; in 1866 and 1867, Pottsville; and in 1869 he was finally placed on the superannuated list, his failing health making further duties in the ministry impossible. He was suffering from *laryngytis*, and was counselled by physicians to go South. He visited Florida, but, finding no relief, then went to California, and died there Jan. 22, 1870, in the city of Sacramento. Dr. Moore was widely known among Methodists for his sweetness of spirit, his devout and genial life, and his earnest services in the ministry of the Church. "His life," says the *Pittsburgh Christian Advocate*, "embraced more of excellences than usually falls to the lot of man. Unassuming, gentle, loving, true as steel, thoroughly conscientious, he moved through society a centre and source of the very best Christian influences. Around him grew up, as one result, some of the most enduring affections." During his travels he wrote for the Church papers, and filled the place of corresponding editor of the *Philadelphia Home Journal*. His letters were largely circulated, and much admired for their beauty of description. His love of nature was such that he revelled in woodland scenes, in quiet dells and unbroken forests, in towering hills and mountains, in broad and picturesque valleys, in the changing hues of foliage and flowers; and no weariness did he ever seem to know in descanting upon these themes. See *Minutes of Annual Conferences*, 1870, p. 48; *Methodist Home Journal*, Jan. 29, 1870; *Pittsburgh Christian Advocate*, Feb. 5, 1870. (J. H. W.)

Moore, George C., a Presbyterian minister, was born in Barre, Vt., in 1832. He was educated in the State University, Burlington, Vt., and became a member of the legal profession. In 1858 he removed to Texas, commenced teaching at Goliad, and soon after was called to take charge of Aranama College in that city. Becoming very much impressed with the spiritual desolation of Texas, he removed to Clinton in that state, and entered upon the study of theology under the care of the Rev. Joel T. Case; was licensed and ordained in 1865, and became pastor of the churches in Victoria and Lavaca, Texas. He was a member of the General Assembly which met in Memphis, Tenn., in 1866. On his return he continued his labors until his death, Sept. 3, 1867. Mr. Moore was remarkable for his piety, general intelligence, and impressive manner of preaching. His sermons were rich in thought and unction, and he was quite successful as an educator. See Wilson, *Presb. Hist. Almanac*, 1868, p. 345.

Moore, George W., a minister of the Methodist Episcopal Church, South, was born in Charleston, S. C., Sept. 27, 1799. He was converted in 1819, was licensed to preach in 1823, and continued in the itinerancy until about 1855, when he entered the mission-field, and labored among the colored population of South Carolina. He died in the Anderson District, S. C., Aug. 16, 1863. See *Min. Ann. Conf. M. E. Church, South*, ii (1858–65), 449.

Moore, Hannah. See MORE, HANNAH.

Moore, Henry (1). See MORE, HENRY.

Moore, Henry (2), a Wesleyan preacher and writer of considerable note, and an associate of the founder of Methodism, was born in Dublin, Ireland, in 1751. He had heard Wesley in his childhood, and had at once become impressed with the preacher's bearing and earnestness. On removing to London he often attended the preaching of Madan and Charles Wesley, and the religious impressions of his early childhood were renewed; yet he failed to identify himself with the Methodists until, after his return to Ireland, he heard Smyth, a nephew of an archbishop, who had left friends and position to preach the simple Methodist theology. This "good man," as Moore himself delighted to call him, persuaded Moore finally to cast his lot with the Wesleyans. His family opposed the step, but Moore persisted, and he was even permitted to introduce domestic worship among them. He at once gave himself to the work. He visited the prisons, braving fever and pestilence, and the still harder trial of agonizing sympathy with felons condemned to the gallows. After a while

he was induced to exhort, and in a short time to preach. His audience gathered in a deserted weaver's shop, which was furnished for the purpose with seats and a desk. He soon gathered the masses, and in a very brief period had an organized society of twenty-six members. He was zealous in good works, and rich in his personal religious experiences. Wesley's attention was called to Moore, and in 1780 he ordered him to take the field as an itinerant of the Londonderry Circuit. He soon progressed in his work, and finally Wesley called him to London, where he became the constant companion of the great religious reformer of the 18th century. The two men of God met together in the morning at five o'clock to answer letters; they travelled together, and Moore became the counsellor of the Connection. Wesley himself had so high an estimation of Moore's talents and character that he endeavored to procure him ordination in the national Church; and, when disappointed in this, he himself set Moore aside for the sacred work, assisted by two presbyters of the establishment, Peard Dickinson and James Creighton. Visiting Ireland now and then, he helped to build up the interests of Methodism in that country. Indeed, one of the principal Methodist chapels in Dublin now stands a monument of his successful labors in the Irish capital. Like the other Methodist preachers, Moore frequently addressed the people in the open air, and shared the usual persecutions of his ministerial brethren. When the controversies arose in the Wesleyan Connection on Church polity, Moore proved himself worthy of the trust reposed in him by Wesley. Conservative by nature, he had so carefully cultivated his judgment as to make a competent counsellor for the Methodist body, and to his untiring efforts the successful issue of the conferences and controversies from 1791 to 1797, resulting in the definite outlines of a Wesleyan polity, are largely due (see *Wesleyan Magazine*, 1845, p. 314; Smith, *History of Wesleyan Methodism*, vol. ii, Append. 9; *Life*, by Mrs. Smith, ann. 1794, p. 164). Wesley's estimate of Moore is especially manifest in the fact that he suffered Moore to be a witness to his conference with the lady of his early affection, who, when the Christian laborer in his eighty-fifth year happened to be near her, had sent word for his presence (Stevens, *Hist. of Methodism*, ii, 406); and also in his appointment of this companion of his youth as one of the trustees of his manuscripts and books. Moore's love for Wesley is manifest in the biography which he furnished of the founder of Methodism in conjunction with Dr. Coke (q. v.). Henry Moore lived to be "the last survivor of the men whom Wesley had ordained;" and by his pen and his preaching "promoted Methodism through nearly seventy years, and died in his ninety-third year April 27, 1843, its most venerable patriarch" (Stevens). Besides a *Life of John and Charles Wesley and the Family* (1824, 8vo), Moore published, *Private Life and Moral Rhapsody* (1795, 4to): —*Reply to a Pamphlet entitled "Considerations on a Separation of the Methodists from the Established Church"* (1794, 8vo):—*Memoir of Henry Fletcher*. See *Life of Rev. Henry Moore*, by Mrs. Richard Smith (daughter of Adam Clarke) (Lond. 1844, 8vo); Stevens, *History of Methodism*, ii, 190 sq.; iii, 52, 56, 75; Smith, *History of Wesleyan Methodism*, vol. i, bk. ii, ch. v–vii; Tyerman, *Life of Wesley*, vol. iii (see Index). (J. H. W.)

Moore, Henry Eaton, an American composer of music, both sacred and secular, was born at Andover, N. H., July 21, 1803, and took up the study of music while engaged in the printing business. In 1826 he began to teach it, and then published several valuable contributions to the science of this fine art, among which are of interest to us, *N. H. Coll. of Ch. Music:—Collect. of Anthems, Choruses, and Set Pieces:—The Northern Harp, a Collection of Sacred Harmony*. He died at East Cambridge, Mass., October 23, 1841. A brother of his, John Weeks Moore, who was born at Andover April 11, 1807, has published *A Cyclop. of Music:—Sacred Minstrel;* etc. See Drake, *Dict. of Amer. Biog.* s. v.

Moore, Humphrey, D.D., a Congregational minister, was born in Princeton, Mass., about the year 1779; graduated at Harvard College in 1799; in 1802 was ordained pastor of the Congregational Church in Milford, where he preached for a period of more than thirty years. He died April 8, 1871. Dr. Moore was a man of more than ordinary ability, and his influence extended widely throughout the southern portion of New Hampshire. Appleton's *Annual Cyclop.* 1871, p. 572.

Moore, Jacob, a minister of the Methodist Episcopal Church, was born in Sussex Co., Del., in 1791; was converted while young; entered the Philadelphia Conference in 1815; was presiding elder of the West Jersey District in 1823–4; on Chesapeake District in 1825–6; and died at Dover, Del., April, 1828. He was a pious and exemplary minister, a vigorous and successful student, and abounded in labors and usefulness, in spite of ill-health and great discouragements. See *Minutes of Annual Conferences,* ii, 39.

Moore, James, an early minister of the Methodist Episcopal Church, was born in Tyrone Co., Ireland, in 1760; joined the Methodists in 1786; migrated to America in 1792, and joined the Philadelphia Conference in 1794. For forty-eight years he was a faithful and useful minister, particularly gifted in exhortation. He died at Medford, N. J., May 11, 1842. See *Minutes of Annual Conferences,* iii, 355.

Moore, James G., a Presbyterian minister, was born near Johnsonburg, N. J., Nov. 30, 1813. At the age of eleven years he was apprenticed to a tailor in Newton, N. J.; during his apprenticeship was converted, and, through the influence of his pastor, was persuaded to turn his attention to the ministry. He graduated at Lafayette College, Easton, Pa.; studied theology at Princeton, N. J.; was licensed and ordained pastor of the church at Beaver Meadow, Pa., in 1845; shortly after resigned this charge for a Dutch Reformed Church at Montague, N. J., where he remained until 1849, when he took charge of the academy at Blairstown, N. J., under the patronage of the Presbyterian Church. Close confinement broke down his health, and in 1851 he removed to Croton Falls, N. Y., and took charge of a small select school. In 1853 he moved West, to try a change of climate, but all in vain; he died near Philadelphia, Marion County, Mo., May 28, 1858. Mr. Moore was a man of decided piety. The great desire of his soul was to preach the Gospel. See Wilson, *Presb. Hist. Almanac,* 1860, p. 76.

Moore, James Lovell, a clergyman of the Church of England, who flourished near the beginning of this century, was successively master of the free school at Hertford and vicar of Benger, in Hertfordshire, also incumbent of the perpetual curacy of Denham, Suffolk. He wrote, *View of the External Evidence of the Christian Religion* (1791, 8vo):—*On the Plenary Inspiration of the New Testament* (1793, 8vo):—*The Columbiad, a Poem* (1793, 8vo):—*Commentaries on the Corruptions of the Roman Catholic Religion* (1811, 12mo). See *Biog. Dict. of Living Authors* (London, 1816, 12mo), p. 239.

Moore, John (1), D.D., a noted prelate of the Anglican communion, was born at Market Harborough, Leicestershire, near the middle of the 17th century. He was educated at Clare Hall, Cambridge, where he graduated in 1665, and became a fellow of the college. Afterwards he was appointed chaplain to the earl of Nottingham, whose interest secured Moore the first prebendal stall in the cathedral church of Ely. His next preferment was the rectory of St. Austin's, London, to which he was admitted in 1687. Two years later he was presented by William and Mary (to whom he was then chaplain in ordinary) to the rectory of St. Andrew's, Holborn, vacated by Dr. Stillingfleet's promotion to the episcopate; and in 1691, on the deposition of the bishop of Norwich, Dr. Moore was appointed to that see, from which he was in 1707 transferred to the see of Ely. He

died in 1714. Debary (*Hist. of Ch. of Engl. from the Accession of James II* [Lond. 1860, 8vo], p. 235) speaks of Dr. Moore as "a man of considerable celebrity in his day, but now better remembered for his connection with the fortunes of Dr. Samuel Clarke and Bentley than for his once famous discourses from the pulpit." His *Sermons,* which were published after his death by his chaplain, Dr. Samuel Clarke (Lond. 1715–16, 2 vols. 8vo; 2d ed. 1724), were translated into the Dutch. His library, which was a very valuable collection, was purchased by king George I and presented to the University of Cambridge. See Burnet, *Reformation;* id. *His Own Times;* Bentham, *Ely;* Birch, *Life of Tillotson; Blackwood's Mag.* xxviii, 455; Hook, *Eccles. Biog.* s. v. (J. H. W.)

Moore, John (2), D.D., a noted prelate of the Church of England, was born of very humble parentage, at Gloucester, in 1733, and was educated at Pembroke College, Oxford. He took holy orders; and after filling various minor appointments in the Church, he became chaplain to the duke of Marlborough, and tutor to one of his sons, and obtained by that interest a prebendal stall in the cathedral of Durham; in 1771 he was installed into the deanery of Canterbury; in 1776 was awarded the bishopric of Bangor; and in 1783 was raised to the metropolitan see, recommended to this great distinction by bishops Lowth and Hurd, both of whom had been offered the place, but preferred that it be assigned to bishop Moore, whom they esteemed as a superior man, particularly fitted "by his business-like habits and affable manners." It does not appear, says Perry (*Hist. of Ch. of Engl.* iii, 444, 445), that he possessed any special literary or theological claims, nor yet can it be believed that his advancement was due to strong family interest, for he had none to commend him. He died in 1804 or 1805. He published several *Sermons* (Lond. 1777, 4to; 1781, 4to; 1782, 8vo). (J. H. W.)

Moore, John (3), a clergyman of the Church of England, who flourished about the opening of this century, was minor canon of St. Paul's, lecturer of St. Sepulchre's, rector of St. Michael Barrisham, London, and of Langdon Hills, Essex. He in vain endeavored to secure public aid for the publication of an edition of bishop Waldon's *Ecclesiastical History of London.* He was a learned man and an excellent preacher. He published, *Case of the London Clergy* (1802, 8vo):—*Attempt to Recover the Reading of* 1 Sam. *xiii,* 1, *with Inquiry of the Duration of Solomon's Reign* (1797, 8vo):—*Prophetiæ de LXX Hebdomadis ap. Danielum explicatio* (1802, 8vo): —*Prophecy of Isaiah vii,* 14, 15 (1809, 8vo). See *Biog. Dict. of Living Auth.* s. v.

Moore, John Weeks. See MOORE, HENRY EATON.

Moore, Martin, a Congregational minister of some note as a religious journalist, was born at Sterling, Mass., April 22, 1790; was educated at Brown University, where he graduated in 1810; and for nearly thirty years served in the ministry at Natick, Mass., and afterwards at Cohasset; and then was for some twenty years editor of the *Boston Recorder.* He was also from 1861 to 1866 vice-president of the "New England Historical and Genealogical Society." Moore died at Cambridge, Mass., March 12, 1866. He wrote, *Life of John Eliot* (1842):— *Hist. of Natick* (1817). See Drake, *Dict. of Amer. Biog.* s. v.

Moore, Nathaniel F., LL.D., an American educator of note, was born at Newtown, L. I., Dec. 25, 1782, and was the nephew of bishop Benjamin Moore (q. v.). Educated at Columbia College, class of 1802, he turned to the bar as his life-work; but in 1817 was induced to take the adjunct professorship in Greek and Latin, and in 1820 was given the full chair, which he held until 1835, when he went to Europe. On his return, in 1837, he was made librarian. In 1839 he again went to Europe, and this time travelled also in the Orient. In 1842 he was made president of his alma mater; and he served in that capacity until 1849, when he retired to private life. His works are of a secular character, and do not concern us here; but his life-work was eminently Christian, and greatly enriched American Christian culture. He died April 27, 1872. Dr. Moore was a man of rare scholarly attainments, and was greatly beloved for his gentle nature and purity of character. See Duyckinck, *Cyclopædia of American Literature*, i, 380–383.

Moore, Philip, a clergyman of the Anglican communion, noted for his pulpit oratory and his scholarship, flourished in the second half of the 18th century. He was born about 1709, was for some time rector of Kirkbridge, and chaplain of Douglas, Isle of Man, and died Jan. 22, 1783. He is noted as the reviser of the translation of the Bible into Manks, in which task he had the counsel of bishop Lowth and Dr. Kennicott, and also as the translator of the Book of Common Prayer, and several theological works. See Butler, *Memoirs of Bp. Hildesby*, p. 186; *General Biog. Dict.* (Lond. 1798), xi, 61.

Moore, Richard Channing, D.D., an early bishop of the Episcopal Church in America, was born in New York Aug. 21, 1762; was educated at King's College, and then practiced medicine for four years, when he suddenly turned towards the ministry, and was ordained by bishop Provoost of New York in 1787. He preached at Rye, Westchester Co., N. Y., and then at St. Andrew's, Richmond, Staten Island (the parish embracing the whole of the island), where he labored successfully for twenty-one years. In 1808 he represented the diocese of New York at the General Conference in Baltimore, and aided in making a selection of hymns for the Church. In 1809 he succeeded to St. Stephen's Church, New York; in 1814, to the rectorship of the Monumental Church at Richmond, and to the episcopate of Virginia, for which he proved himself pre-eminently qualified. "Bishop Hobart hesitated not to express the conviction of his thankful heart that the 'night of adversity' had passed, and that a long and splendid day was dawning on the Church" (Anderson, *Hist. Ch. of Engl. in the Colonies*, iii, 277). The efforts of bishop Moore were "unremittingly exerted to build up the nearly exhausted diocese committed to his care; and so well directed were his labors, and so beneficial his example and influence, that at the time of his death the number of the Episcopal clergymen in Virginia had increased to upwards of one hundred. During the last twelve years of his life his episcopal duties were shared by bishop Meade, who had been appointed his assistant, and who succeeded him in office. He was a prominent leader in the evangelical branch of the Church." He died Nov. 11, 1841. He published many *Charges:—A Sermon on "the Doctrines of the Church"* (1820). A *Memoir* appeared shortly after his death, by Rev. J. P. K. Henshaw (1843, 8vo). See also Sprague, *Annals of the Amer. Pulpit*, v, 367; Bishop Wilberforce, *Hist. Am. Ch.* p. 286, 293; Hawks, *Eccl. Hist. of Virginia*, p. 251–260. (J. H. W.)

Moore, Sir Thomas. See MORE, THOMAS.

Moore, Thomas Jefferson, a minister of note of the Methodist Episcopal Church, South, was born in Franklin, Ky., March 2, 1824. His parents were useful and devoted members of the Methodist Church. His father died when Thomas was but twelve years of age, and he was obliged to shift for himself. He learned the art of printing, and thus earned a livelihood. In his eighteenth year (1841) he was converted and joined the Church, and soon after felt that his calling was to preach the Gospel. He was licensed, and appointed to the Owensboro' Circuit in 1843. In 1845 he was ordained deacon, and appointed to Litchfield, and the next year to Henderson Circuit. In 1847 he was ordained elder, and appointed to Salem Circuit. The next year he travelled on the Lafayette Circuit, and the following year on the Hopkinsville Circuit. After a year's rest he resumed his labors on the Lebanon Circuit, where he remained for two years; he then went to the Jefferson Circuit for one year, and afterwards preached

two years with great success on the Logan Circuit. He was next appointed agent of the Southern Methodist Book Concern and Tract Society, and he so ably discharged the obligations of his office as to largely increase the influence of the institution. He met with great success — preaching, raising funds, or circulating books. The next year he was appointed to the Franklin Circuit, and the following year he was made presiding elder of the Glasgow District. His last work was on the Logan District. He died Sept. 14, 1867. Mr. Moore was a preacher of no ordinary ability. He was a diligent student, possessing a clear perception and a retentive memory. He was well versed in the doctrines and history of the Bible and of the Church. See *Min. Ann. Conf. M. E. Church, South*, 1867, p. 163.

Moore, Zephaniah Swift, D.D., a noted American educator and Congregational minister, was born Nov. 20, 1770, in Palmer, Mass.; graduated at Dartmouth College in 1793; entered the ministry Feb. 3, 1796, and was made pastor at Leicester, Mass. He was elected professor of languages at Dartmouth College in 1811, and president of Williams College in 1815. In 1821 he was chosen first president of Amherst College, then just founded, and he occupied this position until his death, June 30, 1823. He published an *Oration at Worcester, July 5*, 1802:—*An Address to the Public in respect to Amherst College* (1823); and two occasional *Sermons*. See Sprague, *Annals of the Amer. Pulpit*, ii, 392; Drake, *Dict. of Amer. Biog.* s. v.

Mooring, CHRISTOPHER S., an early Methodist Episcopal minister, was born in Surrey County, Va., in 1767; entered the Virginia Conference in 1789; and died Sept. 30, 1825, having preached with excellent success until called to his future home. He was distinguished for modesty, gravity, and faithfulness; always ready to teach and to preach, and many souls were converted through his labors. See *Minutes of Annual Conferences*, i, 507.

Moors (Lat. *Mauri*, meaning *dark*; Span. *Moros*), the original designation of the inhabitants of the ancient *Mauritania* or *Morocco* (q. v). The Arabs, who entered and conquered this country in the 7th century, denominated the native population *Moghrebins*, i. e. "Westerners," or "men of the West," but they called themselves *Berbers*, while to the Europeans they were known as *Moors*. The Arabic language, customs, and manners soon came to prevail among the Berbers; and the Arab conquerors, who gave them the Mohammedan faith, freely amalgamating with them, their character was totally changed, and they became hardly distinguishable from their conquerors; and under Moors we now generally understand the mixed races that arose in the 7th century, when the Saracens wrested North Africa from the Byzantine empire, and incorporated it with the caliphate of Damascus. The Moors were distinguished by the warlike spirit which was then common among the Mohammedan nations, and at an early period began to make inroads for plunder into Spain. A battle with the Visigoths of that country took place in A.D. 672, in which they were defeated with considerable loss; but an opportunity which favored their designs occurred when, during a rebellion which in A.D. 710 placed Roderic, duke of Cordova, on the Spanish throne, the defeated party called in the aid of the Moors. A force of them, led by Taric, entered in the following year, and at the battle of Xeres de la Frontera, near Cadiz, July 11, 711, the army of the Goths, under king Roderic, was almost entirely destroyed, while the death of Roderic himself, who was killed in the battle, put an end to the dominion of the Goths. Muza, the governor of North Africa, jealous of the success of Taric, now advanced with a new army, and took Cordova and Toledo, and within five years subdued the greater portion of the peninsula to his power. Receiving re-enforcements from Africa, he even crossed the Pyrenees, twenty years later, and advanced as far as Bordeaux and Tours. Here, however, the invaders were defeated by Charles Martel in the battle of Poitiers, and they recrossed the Pyrenees, never to return. The defeat not only drove the Moors from the Continent, but forever after confined them to the Iberian peninsula; and even here the inhabitants of Asturia, Galicia, and the Basques successfully resisted their dominion. Also in the parts in which the African invaders had successfully established themselves, internal divisions, which soon arose among the chiefs, together with insubordination towards the caliph of Africa, often brought them near an overthrow, until after the extinction of the family of the Ommiades, when Abderahman I, the last representative of the Ommiade caliphs, who had escaped from Damascus on the subversion of that dynasty in A.D. 752, brought about the consolidation of the government with the caliphate of Cordova, and annulled its previous dependence on the caliphate of Damascus. Under this new government order and prosperity revived. Abderahman changed the laws, regulated the administration, built a fleet, and provided for the instruction of the people. His residence was established at Cordova, where he built a magnificent mosque. His successors, and particularly Abderahman III and Alhakem II, followed his example; and under the dynasty of the Ommiades Spain became the equal in civilization and learning of any country in Europe. It seemed as if the Arabs had only been transplanted to Spain to enable them to acquire the high intellectual culture which was unknown in the East. But while they advanced in civilization, they gradually lost the warlike qualities which had enabled them to make their conquest, and the oppressed Spanish Christians came to look forward to the time when they could throw off the yoke and regain their nationality. The flourishing period of the reign of the Ommiades lasted until the 10th century, the whole period covering the brightest page of Moorish history. After holding for 282 years the caliphate of Cordova, the Ommiade family became extinct in 1037 in the person of Hesham III, who, on account of the insubordination of his subjects, retired from the government in 1031, to devote himself to science and literature. With his retirement the caliphate of Cordova also ended; and the territory was divided into a number of little states, the governors erecting themselves into hereditary and independent princes, and they severally wasted their strength in internecine wars, interrupted only occasionally by an alliance for mutual defence when the Christians threatened their very existence. The latter had not in the mean time remained stationary. By A.D. 801 Charlemagne had definitely incorporated the territory north of the Ebro with the Frankish dominions, and the Moors were driven out of Catalonia. They then retained simply the provinces of Leon and Castile. But even there the Arab population was greatly diminishing; and when in 1085 the Castilians succeeded in taking Toledo, and the Tagus became the frontier of Christian Spain, the Arabs clearly saw their dominion seriously threatened, and, for centuries broken up and scattered, now became more united, and finally resolved to call Jussuf, of the family of the Almoravides, who had established a great empire in Africa, to assist them against the king of Castile. Jussuf arrived in 1086 with a numerous army, and promptly defeated the Christians at Zalacca, but was obliged to return to Africa to defend his possessions there. He came back soon afterwards, however, and all the Moors of Spain remained united under his government. After his death, in 1106, a second period of internal ruptures followed. Abdelmumen, chief of the Almohades, a family opposed to the Almoravides, came from Africa with a large army, and, taking Cordova and Granada in 1157, established for a while its supremacy. Whenever the Arabs were at peace with each other, the surrounding Christian princes thought it their duty to attack these enemies of the cross. Unity having been in a measure restored by the Almoravides, the

archbishop Martin of Toledo invaded Andalusia in 1194, and laid the country waste; the following year king Alphonso III of Castile sent a challenge to Africa to the governor, Jacob Almansor, who, in return, came to Spain with a large army, and defeated Alphonso, July 19, 1195. Thirty thousand Christians, including the most distinguished Spanish knights, were left slain on the field of battle. Almansor fortunately died soon after, and his successors had neither the spirit nor the means to follow up his advantage. The Christians now perceived the necessity of combined action on their part also, and pope Innocent III caused a crusade to be preached against the Moors, both in Spain and in France. In the wars which ensued the Christians proved successful, and completely routed their adversaries in the battle of Las Naves de Tolosa, on the Sierra Morena, July 16, 1212, and by this result brought about the termination of the rule of the Moors in Spain; so that a tract of land, comprising 430 square miles, in the vicinity of Granada, alone remained free from Christian rule. The Aragonians took Valencia, a part of Murcia, and the Balearic Islands; the Castilians took Estremadura, Cordova, and the remaining part of Murcia; even Granada was compelled in 1246 to surrender to king Ferdinand of Castile. Yet this province retained a sort of independence on account of its position, and its almost completely Moorish population. The position of the Arabs varied greatly in the different conquered provinces; but to the shame of the so-called Christians of the Iberian peninsula be it said that generally it was much worse than had been that of the Christians under the rule of the Moors. The Goths, after the conquest, under Moorish rule, had remained in possession of their lands; their taxes were made no higher than those which rested on the Moors subject to military services; they retained their religion, their worship, their laws, and their judges. The bishops, with their chapters, occupied their former position, and were allowed to call together councils. They were only forbidden building new churches, ringing bells, and having processions. The civil government was intrusted to a civil magistrate appointed by the people, who was to act with the bishop. Lawsuits between Christians were to be adjusted by the cadi according to the Gospel and the Gothic laws, and only disputes between Christians and Arabs were judged by the Koran. The Christians who under these circumstances had endured Mohammedan rule received the name of Mozarabic Christians. See MOZARABIC LITURGY. The military classes ever remained entirely distinct, and in constant communication with their brethren at the north, acting secretly as their allies whenever they invaded the Moorish provinces. The Arabs under Christian rule, on the other hand, were in quite different conditions, and even the concessions granted them were seldom conscientiously observed. They were generally allowed to follow their own mode of worship, but often excessive proselytizing zeal created exceptions, and converted the mosques into churches. They were allowed to retain possession of their estates, but were seldom permitted to sell them, or to change their residence. They were suffered to elect their own judges, and only disputes with Christians were decided by Christian judges. They were obliged to pay tithes of all their income to the state, besides the poll-tax levied by their feudal lords. They were forbidden having slaves or Christian servants; but this was the fate only of those who had *submitted* to the Christians. Those whose cities had resisted and been conquered were all reduced into slavery in its severest form. The master could sell, punish, or kill them at his pleasure, and all their earnings were his by law. They could, however, obtain their freedom by becoming Christians; but in after-times even this was restricted to the case when the master was either a Mohammedan or a Jew. By their conversion the Arabs were indeed endowed with all political rights, but by no means could they attain to the same social position as the old Christians; they were everywhere despised, and could seldom enter into other Christian families. A relapse into Islamism was punished with the greatest severity, the penalty being, according to the circumstances, death by fire, spoliation, and inability to inherit. Occasionally, however, the relations between Moors and Christians were more friendly, especially in the country, where landowners fully appreciated the skill and activity of the Arabs as agriculturists. Among the nobility, the Arab nobles, by their courage and skill, as well as by their learning—much superior to that of their Spanish conquerors—knew also how to command respect.

All the Arab learning, art, industry, and fortune gradually centred in Granada, which succeeded in maintaining its political autonomy until about the end of the 15th century. A small sea-coast province of not over 430 square miles, it arrived—partly owing to its situation, and more particularly to the zeal and industry of its inhabitants—at a degree of prosperity which other and larger countries might well have envied. But its principal glory was the city of Granada, its capital, which in the 14th century counted 200,000 inhabitants. It contained the world-renowned palace of the Alhambra —a sort of fortress in which 40,000 people might find refuge. (See a popular and accurate account in Prime, *Alhambra and Kremlin*, 1874, 12mo.) Its principal feature is the so-called Lions' Court, built in 1213–38, which is considered as the finest specimen of Moorish architecture. It was the residence of the kings of Granada, which vied in splendor with those of the most favored European monarchs, and where many a Christian prince was entertained with bountiful hospitality. Next in rank to Granada were the sea-towns of Almeria and Malaga, distinguished for their manufacturing and commercial importance as well as for the beauty and richness of their palaces. There the finest kinds of silken fabrics and steel-work were produced as far back as the 12th century, and from thence exported to Italy and to the East. But its very prosperity only increased the greed of the neighboring Christian princes, and especially of Ferdinand and Isabella; and, unfortunately for the Moors, one of their own rulers—the reigning king of Granada, Muley-Abul-Hakem — himself voluntarily broke the peace with Castile by refusing to pay the tribute. At first he haughtily declared that the mint of Granada no longer coined gold, but only steel. A few years afterwards he went so far as to seize on the frontier fortress of Zahara by treachery, and took the whole population as slaves to Granada. In reprisal, a Spanish knight, with a determined band of warriors, stormed the city of Alhama, the summer residence of the king of Granada. The king of Granada himself left for Fez, and died soon after in battle in the service of another prince, showing a courage which he had not exhibited in the defence of his own country. In the mean time a revolution broke out in Granada, occasioned by the jealousy of the queen against a rival, and resulted in Muley's oldest son being called to the throne, while Muley himself was obliged to retire to Malaga. A younger brother of his, El Zagal (the courageous), having surprised the Christian army in a narrow pass and destroyed it entirely, king Ferdinand now determined to wage war for the extermination of both. He improved this opportune moment of their dissensions, and first marched against Granada with all his forces, and in 1487 besieged Malaga, which was compelled by famine to surrender on the 18th of August. El Zagal, looking upon the fall of Malaga as an omen, surrendered Almeria, and left for Africa. The young king, Abdallah (generally named Boabdil), had promised to submit when Almeria was taken, but the inhabitants of Granada would not hear of submitting; they trusted to the strength of their fortifications, consisting of strong walls and 1030 towers. The summer of 1491 was spent by both armies in single combats, which have been the subject of numerous romances and tales. But Granada was destined to fall—the more after the

Christians had erected opposite Granada a rival fortified city, Santa Fe. The king, certain of being unable to resist, began secretly to negotiate with the Spaniards, and the terms of surrender were settled Nov. 25, 1491. The conditions were such as might have satisfied the inhabitants of Granada had they been observed. They were to retain possession of their mosques, and to be allowed to follow their own religious worship; their own laws were to be administered by their own cadis, under the oversight of the Spanish governor; they were to retain their own customs, language, and dress, and to have the free and unlimited use of all their property; those who preferred leaving the country were to be furnished ships to take them to Africa. The taxes to which they would be subjected should not exceed those which they paid under their own government. King Abdallah was to retain his estates, and to administer them under the supervision of the Spanish authorities. The city was on these terms surrendered (Jan. 2, 1492) to the Spaniards, who made a triumphal entry; but shortly after the capitulation the Moors found that they had surrendered their rights to the conquerors, and were in danger of losing much more than they had granted. The finest houses in Granada were occupied by the Spanish noblemen; a converted Moor (such, according to the terms of surrender, were not to hold any official situation) was made chief alguazil, and the largest mosque was changed into a church. The most zealous members of the Romish Church were advising that the Moors should be made to choose between baptism and banishment. But this unwise counsel did not at first prevail. Count de Tendilla and the archbishop Fernando de Talavera, who were at the time governors of the province, sought by mild treatment to unite the Moors with the Spaniards; the archbishop especially was so successful with them by his kindness that large numbers consented to be baptized by him.

This system of conversion, however, appeared too slow to the fanatical party, and the archbishop of Toledo, cardinal Ximenes (q. v.), obtained from the grand inquisitor an authorization to establish an Inquisition among the Elches (Christians who had embraced Islamism; most of them were baptized Moors), and this gave him the means of gradually monopolizing the work of converting the Moors. He set to work, not only by preaching, but also by bribery, and he was at first so successful that thousands were baptized. But this awakened the opposition of the most earnest believers in Mohammedanism. This opposition Ximenes thought to subdue by imprisonment and other severities against their priests; and, in order to strike at the root, he caused all the copies of the Koran and all Arab works of theology to be seized. It is said that he thus collected 80,000 (?) works. He then caused them to be publicly burned. These proceedings led, as he had expected, to an outbreak, directed chiefly against himself. Count Tendilla and the archbishop of Talavera, however, succeeded in quelling the insurrection by promising that the grievances complained of would be inquired into. A capitulation was drawn up, which needed only the royal sanction. Ximenes, whose conduct had at first been sharply blamed by Isabella, had, however, succeeded in converting both her and the king to his views; and the capitulation, for which count Tendilla had given both his wife and children as hostages, was rejected by the king. A royal edict was even proclaimed leaving the Moors to choose between being baptized and punishment for high-treason. Some 50,000 of the inhabitants of Granada sought peace by submitting to baptism; others sold their possessions and emigrated to Africa. The Moors who became Christians received now the name of *Moriscoes*. But the manner in which the inhabitants of Granada had been treated led to an insurrection in the mountains of the district of Alpujarras. The energetic measures taken to repress that outbreak seemed at first successful; but an attack, in 1500, on the mountains of Serrena de Bonde, almost entirely inhabited by Moors, proved disastrous to the Spaniards; one of their best generals, Alonso de Aguilar, was killed, and his army destroyed. The Moors, however, were at last obliged to submit. A large number emigrated to Africa; others were baptized, stipulating for nothing of their former rights but their dress, language, and exemption from the Inquisition for forty years. This was granted them, but soon evaded; no tribunal of the Inquisition was, indeed, established at Granada, but that of Cordova extended its jurisdiction over Granada. Nine years later another remnant of Mohammedan Moors were forcibly Christianized in the same manner, and baptized en masse in 1526. In the same year a tribunal of the Inquisition was finally established at Granada, and on the 7th of December a proclamation appeared forbidding the Moors from wearing their national dress, or using their national language and their Arab names. But the very next day the Moors purchased the recall of that decree for a sum of 260,000 ducats; this was subsequently several times renewed. The Moors were also, in spite of the treaties concluded with them, subjected to several heavy taxes; so that, besides paying tithes to the Church, they had to pay tithes to the king, and a tax for breeding silk-worms.

Aside from their outward compulsatory profession of Christianity, which the vexatious treatment they experienced at the hands of the Christians did not tend to make them like any the more, they were at heart firmly attached to the old religion, and grew more attached to it in proportion as they suffered for it. They retained the mosque beside the church, had their alfaki as well as their Romish priests, circumcised their children after they were baptized, celebrated their marriages according to Mohammedan customs, etc. At times this was winked at. Thus in the latter part of the reign of Charles V the Moriscoes were left in peace; Philip II expressly commanded the Inquisition to show great mildness and toleration towards them, and even a papal bull was promulgated to that effect. But when, during the war with the piratical Moors of Barbary, it was found out that the Moriscoes had always remained in communication with their African brethren, they became again the objects of persecution. They were forbidden to carry arms without a special authorization, under a penalty of six years of hard labor in the galleys. This gave rise to numerous insurrections, which finally settled into a war of ambush and assassination, and the government was thereby forced to restore the former more rigorous system. After trying other means, Philip II was finally brought to issue a proclamation (November 13, 1556), in which the use of Arabic either in speaking or writing, that of Arab names, and of the national costume of the Moors, even that of their usual baths, was forbidden them; three years were given them to learn Spanish, and those who after that time should contravene these commands were to be punished, according to circumstances, by imprisonment or banishment. This proclamation, against which the Spanish governor of Granada and many Spanish statesmen (among them the duke of Alba) emphatically protested, was nevertheless enforced by the advice of a cardinal and an archbishop. The first result was an insurrection, organized in secret, with the aid of the Moors of Africa, which broke out in the spring of 1568, and at once assumed the character of a war of extermination. The war continued with various vicissitudes — the Moors rising up again when they were thought to have been thoroughly subjected—for several years, until finally, after the assassination of the second leader of the insurgents, Aben-Abû (March 18, 1571), the war ended.

The kingdom of Granada, previously the most populous and richest province of Spain, had now become a desolate desert, with here and there a few bands of Moors supporting themselves by robbery amid the ruins of its former splendor. The greater number of Moors were transplanted into other provinces, where they were strictly watched. The use of the Arabic lan-guage or of any article of their national dress, the dancing an Arab dance or playing on an instrument suspected to be of Arab origin, were punished as crimes. Only those Moors more anciently settled in Valencia were allowed a little more liberty. Yet, in spite of oppression and watching, the Moriscoes after a few years began to contemplate again a revolt—the more as Spain was then weakened by her war in the Netherlands, and threatened both by France and England. They opened negotiations with France, and in 1605 a vast conspiracy was organized, relying on the assistance of the French. It was, however, betrayed, and the grand inquisitor now clamored that the Moriscoes should either be sent out of Spain or destroyed by the sword. Although Philip III, who was then on the throne, did not wish to accede to so general a measure, and even the pope declined to favor it, yet, as this step seemed to be the only possible means of securing tranquillity to the state, the king issued a proclamation (Aug. 4, 1609) banishing the Moriscoes of Valencia to Africa. The landed nobility, who foresaw the loss of their best farmers, and the clergy that of their tenants, protested in vain, and grand preparations were made to secure the execution of the edict. A delay was granted the Moors for the regulation of their affairs; they were not allowed to sell their land, and could only take away so much of their personal property as they could carry off themselves. At first the Moors offered to pay enormous sums to obtain the recall of that edict; but afterwards, when they had time to reflect, and saw that nothing was to be done, their sorrow changed to joy; they looked upon their exile as a liberation from slavery, in which they could cast aside their mask of Christianity. The emigration proceeded well at first, the nobility even helping the poor people by purchasing their property at a fair price. But this did not suit the viceroy, who forbade such purchases being made. The Moors now became again frightened, and those of the south of Valencia, who had not yet emigrated, rose in arms. Many were killed, the others very cruelly treated. The emigration from Murcia and Andalusia succeeded better, most of the Moriscoes from those provinces taking refuge in Fez. Those of Aragon, Castile, and Estremadura were ordered to Navarre, but on the frontiers were informed by the French that they had strict orders not to allow them to penetrate into the country. Exasperated, they either fought their way through or purchased permission to enter. Those of Catalonia were directed to Africa. A small remnant of about 30,000, who had been permitted to stay on exhibiting certificates from their bishops testifying to their sound Christianity, were also driven away a few years later, and left Spain in 1612 and 1613. The whole number of persons thus forced to emigrate is generally reckoned at about a million, and consisted largely of the most active and industrious among the inhabitants of Spain. Those who had emigrated to Africa were at first well received, but subsequently persecuted also by their own coreligionists, whom their European views and habits displeased, and who were jealous of their skill as workmen; so that they were driven out of Algiers and Fez. Only at Tunis, whose inhabitants were mostly descendants of the Moors of Granada, did they find a really hospitable shelter. A small remnant of Moriscoes, some 60,000 in number, remained concealed in the valleys of the Alpujarras, and have to this day retained their peculiar manners and customs, but they have long since become earnest Roman Catholics. See Conde, *Historia de la Dominacion de los Arabes en Espanna* (Madrid, 1820–21, 3 vols.; Engl. transl., *Hist. of the Dominion of the Arabs in Spain*, by Mrs. Jonathan Foster [London, 1855, 3 vols. 12mo, Bohn's Library]); Moron, *Curso de historia de la Civilizacion de Espanna* (Madrid, 1841–3, 3 vols.); Aschbach, *Gesch. d. Ommajaden in Spanien* (Frankf.-am-Main, 1829, 2 vols.); id. *Gesch. Spaniens u. Portugals z. Zeit d. Herrschaft d. Almoraviden u. Almohaden* (Frankf. 1833–7, 2 vols.); Von Rochau, *Die Moriskos in Spanien* (Leips. 1853); Herzog,

Real-Encyklopädie, ix, 183 sq.; Wetzer u. Welte, *Kirchen-Lexikon*, vi, 933 sq.; Prescott, *Reign of Ferdinand and Isabella*; Dozy, *Gesch. der Mauren in Spanien bis zur Eroberung Andalusiens durch die Almoraviden* (711–1110) (Leips. 1873–5); Hallam, *History of the Middle Ages* (student's ed.), p. 237–43; Ticknor, *Spanish Literature*, iii, 389 sq.; *Southern Review* (Jan. 1874), art. ii; and especially the seventeen articles by Prof. Coppee on the "Moorish Conquest of Spain," in the *Penn Monthly* of 1873 (Phila.). See also MOROCCO.

Moösi'as (Μοοσίας, Vulg. *Moosias*), a Græcized form (1 Esdr. ix, 31) of the MAASEIAH (q. v.) of the Heb. text (Ezra x, 30).

Moph. See MEMPHIS.

Mopinot, SIMON, a learned French ecclesiastic, was born at Rheims in 1685; took the vows of a Benedictine in 1703 at the monastery of St. Farom, where he had been educated, and largely devoted himself to literary labors. After having assisted Didier in his edition of Tertullian, he was summoned to Paris about the year 1715 by his superiors, and was there associated with father Peter Constant in preparing his collection of the *Lettres des Papes*. The first volume of this work was published in 1721 (fol.), with a dedication to Innocent XIII, and a preface by Mopinot; and he was preparing to print a second volume when he was attacked by a violent dysentery, of which he died in 1724.

Mopsuestia, CHURCH COUNCIL OF (*Concilium Mopsuestanum*), was held June 17, 550, by order of the emperor Justinian, on account of the troubles excited by the Three Chapters (q. v.). There were in attendance nine bishops. Examination was made whether the name of Theodore of Mopsuestia was to be found in the diptychs of that church, and, if not, whether it had been there within the memory of man. It appeared from the testimony of irreproachable witnesses far advanced in years that his name had either never been inserted, or had been erased before their time. Notice of this was sent to the pope and the emperor.

Moquamo, a designation of the temples or chapels of the inhabitants of the island of Socotra, on the coast of Africa. These islanders are idolaters, and worship the moon as the parent of all things. The moquamos are very small and low. They have three little doors, and in order to enter any one of them a person must stoop almost to the ground. In each of them is an altar, on which are deposited several sticks formed like flower-de-luces, which have something of the resemblance of a cross. Every moquamo has a priest, called *hodamo*, who is annually chosen, and the general insignia of office are a staff and cross, which he must not presume to give away on any pretence whatever, or suffer any person to touch on pain of losing one of his hands. The usual time set apart for divine service in these chapels is when the moon sets, or when she rises. They then strike a certain number of blows on a long staff with a shorter one, and walk around the chapel three times. This ceremony is accompanied with an oblation of some odoriferous wood, put in an iron basin, which hangs by three chains over a large fire. After this the altar is incensed three times, and the doors of the temple as often, and the devotees make the most solemn vows and earnest supplications to the moon. In the mean time the hodamo sets on the altar a lighted taper made of butter, and besmears the crosses and other utensils with this favorite grease. On certain days they make a solemn procession around the temple, when one of the chief men of the country carries a sacred staff. After the procession is over very singular honors are paid him. See Broughton, *Biblioth. Historica*, s. v. See SOCOTRA.

Mor. See MYRRH.

Moral Ability. See INABILITY.

Moral Agency. See WILL.

Moral Attributes. See GOD.

Moral Faculty. See MORAL SENSE.

Moral Inability. See INABILITY.

Moral Intuitions. See MORAL SENSE.

Moral Law may be contemplated under three aspects: first, as a branch of the Decalogue [for this, see LAW OF MOSES]; secondly, in a practical point of view [see ETHICS]; and, thirdly, in a metaphysical light, as a department of theology or theosophy, which is the only relation under which we here propose to treat it. Under the head MORAL SENSE, we suggest that a law emanating from a beneficent Creator for the government of responsible intelligences can be essentially no other than a transcript of his own benignant nature, hence the deep philosophy as well as cogent value of the Gospel axiom that love is the one essential requirement of the law (Matt. xxii, 36–40; Rom. xiii, 8–10; 1 John iv, 21); and this applies no less to angelic than to human creatures, and extends through time and through eternity. It is proper to consider more distinctly these questions of the origin, universality, permanence, and sanction of the divine law.

1. *Its Source.* — Some philosophers have been in the habit of representing — either expressly or by implication — the basis of morality as independent of, if not prior to and externally stringent upon the divine Being himself. They have used such expressions as "the eternal principles of right," "God was absolutely bound to do so and so," "he could not have done otherwise," etc.; and although these phrases are usually accompanied with some caveat of reverence or disclaimer of limiting the Almighty's perfection, they yet savor of fatalism, or at least of dualism, and do not attribute the moral system of the universe to its precise cause. That origin is no other than God himself, simply and purely. To his sovereign will everything that exists owes its being, with all the qualities that relate to it; and this grand postulate includes the Deity himself, with all the laws that he has promulged and now administers. He is *self-existent,* the "I am," the "one that is, and was, and is to be;" and he is what he is and as he is merely because he pleases it himself. In the same absolutely autocratic yet unconstrained manner he has produced the substance, mechanism, organic forces, and mutual relations — which we call *laws*—of the material and spiritual creation; and they are all, therefore, intrinsically copies of his own nature. This view differs essentially from pantheism, which confounds the universe with God himself; and at the same time from atheism, which dissevers it from his being or control. That this is the true doctrine of Scripture may be easily and abundantly proved (Gen. i, 1; Isa. xlv, 6; John i, 3; Col. i, 16, 17, etc.). Both sides of this universal proposition—the self-constitution of the Infinite, and the externality of the finite—are necessarily and impenetrably mysteries to our mind; yet we can sufficiently comprehend them by a comparison with our own microsmic nature—in which our wills are self-conditioned, and our bodies are extrinsic to our spirit—to enable us to receive them as intelligible truth. There is, therefore, no essential difference between the "moral laws" of God and the so-called *laws of nature:* they are both neither more nor less than his own will as expressed in the material and spiritual departments of his dominion. Human nature, in so far as it is a just reflection of this will, is a correct transcript of these laws; and is generally recognised as such, wherever not perverted by the effects of free agency. This latter is but an extension of the externality of creation, adding merely—and a very important increment it is — the godlike productive power, to be exercised within a certain range ever subordinate to the divine agency. It is thus that God retains full jurisdiction, without incurring the responsibility of human conduct. The divine law, of course, continues its claims over the accountable creature, whether he acknowledge or sub-

mit to them or not; for it would be the height of absurdity to make his puny rebellion or insolent disregard operate their abrogation. The penalty may be suspended at the divine pleasure, but it is sure in the end to overtake every transgressor with a complete vindication.

2. *Its Extent.*—This likewise is self-evident. As the "natural" laws of God are coextensive with the universe, so his "moral" laws are obligatory upon all his moral creatures, i. e. those endowed with a capacity for understanding the relations of right and wrong. Hence the enactments of the Decalogue have been essentially accepted in all ages and countries as the foundation of the civil code, and religious usages have generally conformed to the prescriptions of the first table (those relating to God and his worship, the family, etc.), not excepting even the seeming conventionality of a stated day of rest. But the two fundamental principles underlying these Mosaic statutes, so admirably summed up in the New Testament as *fealty to God* and *equity to man,* have never failed to be admitted, theoretically at least, as the only secure basis of social organization. How it is with other worlds, if such exist, we are not called upon to speculate; but this fact of the universality of the divine law on the globe is so emphatically attested by all history and legislation that we need dwell no further upon it.

3. *Its Duration.*—It follows from the above views of the cause and character of moral law that it must forever remain essentially the same, and of permanent obligation on all its legitimate subjects throughout their being. It is a peculiar trait of the divine creations that while their *form* changes to suit the varied circumstances of diversified beauty and harmonious co-operation, their substance ever remains, imperishable except by the fiat which first called it into existence. Annihilation is not God's method; he never absolutely extinguishes any light of his own kindling. Man's works, as they are not real creations, pass away into a nonentity that leaves only their memory; but God builds for eternity. Especially is this true of the divine administration: amid all the variety of his different and successive dispensations the same fundamental principles, as we have seen, prevail; and even in the future world the obligations of supreme allegiance to God and mutual regard for each other will beatify the inhabitants of bliss by their spontaneous and full discharge, or torment the denizens of hell by their relentless and irksome grasp. The joy of conscious rectitude is the greatest bliss of which a rational soul is capable, and the remorse for an irremediable violation of clearly known duty we may well imagine to be the most poignant ingredient in the cup of endless damnation.

4. This brings us, lastly, to the *penalty* of moral law. Statutes without awards attached to their observance or neglect are valueless and ineffectual. The rewards and punishments of moral law are, as its nature implies, and as we have already seen, chiefly and properly of a moral character. Yet we see no impropriety in the current belief—sanctioned by the figurative language of Scripture—that the immunities and penalties experieneed in the other world are likewise—at least after the resurrection state (which by its renewed bodily organism furnishes at once the means and the pledge of corporeal enjoyments and sufferings)—of a physical nature, suited to the new conditions of being then entered upon. Precisely what will be the form of either kind of award, beyond the presumed—and indeed promised—emotions from the genial or uncomfortable society and surroundings, we can only conjecture; but this much we may safely argue from the well-known consequences of obedience or transgression in this life, that they will be of the highest pungency of which the human spirit is susceptible; and we may infer from God's justice and impartiality—no less than from the express statements of the Bible (Prov. xvi, 5; Eccles. xii, 14; John v, 29; Rom. ii, 6; Gal. vii, 7)—that they will be exactly meted

out in accordance with the real merits or demerits of each individual. In this life we know that this retribution or compensation does not in all cases precisely occur—virtue often lies oppressed, and vice stalks about triumphant; hence the greater presumption that in the coming world all this will be balanced (Luke xvi, 25), and a necessity indeed arises for such a state in order to the proper adjudication (Psa. lxxiii). There remain under this head three points of much importance to be briefly discussed.

(1.) *Each class of laws is in the main administered separately yet co-ordinately with the rest.*—Thus a violation of or a compliance with any physical law is invariably followed by its corresponding penalty or disadvantage, and this without regard to the religious character of the subject himself (Matt. v, 45); on the other hand, moral delinquency or exemplariness will ensure its appropriate meed or degradation, whatever be the care or negligence of the actor in temporal concerns. A good child is as likely to be burned if it thrust its finger into the flame as a bad one, and a pious traveller is as liable as a wicked one to lose his life by venturing on board an insecure train or vessel. Yet the practice of virtue tends to habits of thrift, economy, and prudence, thus naturally promoting earthly welfare (1 Tim. iv, 8), and a special divine blessing may also be expected upon the good man's affairs (Psa. xxxvii, 25). On the other hand, since great prosperity is inimical to piety, the Lord often afflicts his children with temporal reverses for their spiritual benefit (John xvi, 33). It thus appears that while physical laws regularly have their own course, and the physical effects duly follow, yet Providence specially watches over those who commit their ways to the divine keeping, and they are accordingly saved from many of the consequences which their own inadvertence might bring upon them. This, however, is not effected by miracle (except in a few anomalous cases), nor by extraordinary interference with the usual operation of law, but by those secret and delicate connections which pervade the whole economy of nature, and perhaps by an unseen touch of the divine hand directly upon the inscrutable springs of human intercourse. Indeed, as it is the same Being who administers both series of laws, we might reasonably expect that he would make them co-operate in harmony for the higher—i. e. moral—ends (Rom. viii, 28). See PROVIDENCE.

(2.) *The effects of transgression are not always confined to the individual offender.*—This is evidently true of the violation of physical laws, for the children, friends, and neighbors of the person erring are frequently involved in calamity consequent upon his blunders. How often does a mistake or a careless act spread conflagration, disaster, and even death, in a community. The same takes place to a certain extent with regard to the temporal results from a violation of moral laws, as in cases of inherited disease, murder, and crimes generally, in which the family or victims innocently suffer. Nor is this all: a continued course of immorality is sometimes propagated through successive generations, mostly, no doubt, by the force of vicious example and defective or erroneous training, but partly also perhaps by a certain congenital taint or bias to the same vices. With regard to social sins, these forms of retribution are especially illustrated—for national wrongs and crimes are as certain to be visited by the appropriate penalty as personal ones. But the punishment that falls upon the nation is of course shared by its individual members in common, some of whom, however, and frequently those most guilty, escape in whole or in part by reason of their exalted position and peculiar advantages (2 Sam. xxiv, 17), while in other instances the blow falls most heavily upon eminent individuals as representative characters (2 Sam. xxi, 1–9). Nor does the retribution always come upon the same generation or the same portion of the community that has sinned (Matt. xxiii, 35). These are but specimens of that inequality in the penalty of wrong-doing that prevails in the present life (Jer. xxxi, 29); but they do not extend to the other world. There the account will be strictly personal, and the settlement rigidly just. As we have already indicated, it is this final award that vindicates the sentence of the supreme Judge. The vicarious sufferings of the Redeemer as a ransom from this ultimate adjudication have been considered under the article MEDIATION.

(3.) We thus finally reach the question of the alleged *disproportion between human guilt and endless punishment*. We do not seek, with many, to justify the everlasting doom of the wicked by magnifying their crime as having been committed against infinite authority, majesty, and forbearance, however much we may conceive these features as aggravating its enormity. We base our theodicy upon simpler and more palpable ground, namely, the continued and hopelessly incorrigible sinfulness of the condemned themselves. We may presume that none are cut off from probation till they have evinced a desperate moral condition (Luke xiii, 8); but whether this be so or not, it follows inevitably from the above line of reasoning, and from the character of the depraved heart bereft of the probationary aids to reform, that the impenitence, unbelief, and rebellion for which the sentence is at first pronounced will but harden and intensify as the ages of eternity advance. Unless the fable of purgatory be true—and its absurdity is not less than its mendacity—there can be no improvement in the fate of the finally lost, because there can be no amendment in their moral character. Their destiny is eternally fixed, not so much by the arbitrary decree of omnipotent vengeance as by their own determined resistance of sovereign law. Perdition is but another name for self-destruction ($\dot{a}\pi\acute{o}\lambda\lambda\upsilon\mu a\iota$, in the middle voice). See Pye-Smith, *First Lines of Christian Theology*, p. 177 sq.; Müller, *Christian Doctrine of Sin;* Howarth, *Abiding Obligation of the Moral Law;* Watts, *Uses of the Moral Law;* Cobbin, *View of Moral Law;* Cudworth, *Eternal and Immutable Morality; Cumberland Presb. Qu.* Jan. 1873, art. ii; *New-Englander*, July, 1872; *Academy*, Sept. 1, 1873, p. 328.

Moral Obligation. See MORAL LAW; MORAL SENSE.

Moral Philosophy. Nearly every system of philosophy broached in ancient or modern times has impinged more or less closely upon the domain of morals. Indeed, this part of the field has usually been the most hotly contested, as the theosophical problems which it presents have afforded more occasion for philosophical as well as theological polemics than all other themes. The paramount importance of the subjects mentioned—the relation of the finite to the Infinite, and the consequent duties and destiny of man at the hands of God—have given the most intense interest to the reasonings, teachings, and controversies respecting them. But as these have been so commonly mentioned in the intellectual or metaphysical branches of the investigation, we will here content ourselves with referring to PHILOSOPHY in general for the history of their development, and to the article ETHICS for their more systematic classification. We shall therefore in the present article discuss, in a brief and practical manner, only a few points upon which every scheme of moral philosophy worthy of the name must hinge.

1. *Human Responsibility.*—Were man a mere animal, endowed with locomotion, instinct, and perception, or could we conceive of him as possessing simply emotion and will, such as brutes seem to evince—nay, even as capable of the boldest stretch of reason and the highest flights of fancy, yet destitute of the power of appreciating the difference between right and wrong, and therefore unable to recognise the fundamental relation of allegiance subsisting on his part toward his Maker, and the common bond of brotherhood between himself and his fellows, we could not justly hold him amenable for his moral conduct, since this entirely depends upon a due ob-

servance of these twofold claims. It is the faculty of *conscience*, sitting as a viceroy of heaven and a representative of earth within his breast, urging the rights of all outside himself, that constitutes him an accountable being; and though this interior light may become dim through the mists of passion and the clouds of ignorance, it yet shines sufficiently clear to show him his essential duties, or, if utterly eclipsed, the fault will generally be found to be his own—the few cases of congenital paralysis being thereby removed from the category of responsibility. See MORAL SENSE. His first obligation, therefore, and his prime measure of safety, is to cultivate this faculty by information and prompt obedience, that it may the more surely guide him through the labyrinths of life to the portals of endless day. The beginning and the termination of his personal responsibility, as well as its boundaries on either hand throughout his mortal pilgrimage, are exactly marked by the development of this faculty—one peculiar to him of all the occupants of the globe. This accountability is, in the nature of the case, an individual one, each for himself alone, and it is due in the threefold aspect above indicated to the several classes of beings with whom he has here to do in the order and degree named below. This sums up all his duty, even under the perfect code of Christianity, and is the staple—the core and substance—of every ethical system devised for human conduct.

2. *Duty to God.*—This is obviously paramount. In this the Holy Scriptures do but enforce, by an authoritative mandate, what all pagan religions have more feebly demanded—namely, the unconditional and primary obligation of obedience to the divine behests. These have been promulged in different ways—sometimes more expressly, at other times more enigmatically and imperfectly; but when once fairly understood, the common-sense of mankind has declared that they must be unflinchingly and peremptorily obeyed. This claim is universally grounded on an admitted creatorship, supported by the avowed dependence of the creature; the Bible adds a third most touching argument to those of natural religion, namely, redemption, thus forming a triple cord—paternity, providence, and grace. The foremost and generic duty that grows out of this obligation is that of *reverence*—so all the older dispensations conceive it, but Christianity terms it *love*, taking a nearer and more privileged position. See ADOPTION. This reverential regard is chiefly expressed in *worship*, which accordingly occupies the prominent place in all religions, standing at the very head of the Decalogue. The devotion thus due is unique as well as supreme, because no other being can possibly occupy this relation, nor any higher; worship is therefore due exclusively to our Maker. Idolatry is consequently reckoned as the most odious and damning of all sins, because it virtually overthrows the throne of heaven itself, and thus destroys the very basis of all moral law. Jehovah brooked every transgression of his chosen people but this; and when the captivity had burned away its exterior manifestation, the final excision affirmed his detestation of its still cherished spirit, which incited Israel to the culminating apostasy of the Crucifixion. The same crime in essence has reappeared in the mummeries of Christian churches; and even Protestants may be guilty of it under another name, for any undue love of earthly objects is tantamount to idolatry (Col. iii, 5; 1 John ii, 15). Under the Christian economy, again, the worship due to God is to assume a purely spiritual form, in distinction from the typical and ceremonial guise of Mosaism (John iv, 24); but this, of course, does not exclude all exterior observances—it rather requires them, at least for congregational concert. See WORSHIP. We mention here but one other specific duty under this head, because it is inclusive of all others—namely, *regard for God's revealed word*. The respect we show to any one naturally extends to his communications; and in the case of an invisible sovereign or an absent friend, our reverence is often measured chiefly by this mark. How much more

highly should we prize and cheerfully heed the words of our God and Saviour! Nor is the Bible to be fondly cherished merely as a memento of dying love, or as a token of kindly concern, nor yet is it to be valued simply as a useful guide-book in ancient lore, but still more as a practical directory to regulate our hearts and our lives: it must become our *vade-mecum* in every-day concerns of the most vital moment, for by it shall we be finally adjudged. As prayer, therefore, is the central act of divine worship, so is searching the Scriptures the most direct method of ordering our behavior aright in all respects; the two are the complete counterparts, internal and external; one fortifies and purifies the heart, the other moulds and directs the life. The devout Bible-student cannot fail of becoming a strong, earnest, consistent fulfiller of all the claims of God upon him.

3. *Duties to one's Fellow-beings.*—These spring immediately out of the above relation of the common fatherhood of God, and they can never be successfully met except by bearing this thought constantly in mind. Selfishness, the most common and baleful besetment of every association of life, is most effectually counteracted by this consideration; and Scripture, no less than conventional politeness, and even statute law, everywhere holds forth teachings grounded on this principle. We hazard nothing in affirming that all the disorders of society have their root in a violation or neglect of this truth—the universal brotherhood and consequent essential equality of all human beings. We may therefore be spared, after the enunciation of this one general clew to the multiform and complex duties of life, from entering upon a discussion of these in detail, simply observing that they may all be classified under two divisions: 1, the *domestic,* including the relations of parent and child, of husband and wife, of brother and sister, and of near consanguinity or affinity; 2, the *social,* embracing the relations of neighbor, fellow-citizen, church-member, and voluntary association for literary, benevolent, or commercial purposes. For all these, see the appropriate titles in this *Cyclopædia.* We here dismiss this branch of the subject, with the remark that our duty in all these regards is not fully discharged by the mere rendering of *justice* to these various classes of persons connected with us; we owe them likewise the offices of courtesy, charity, and sympathy. This is true, not only in the family and the Church, but also in the community and the world at large; the twofold obligation extends to every ramification of the social fabric. The question of Cain, "Am I my brother's keeper?" expresses the first and most wide-spread heresy against the mutual rights and well-being of the race. It is here, as everywhere else, that the doctrine of the Gospel shows its transcendent excellence—as wise as it is beautiful—doctrine appropriate to the lips of him who was both God and man; namely, the inculcation of love for all mankind as such, and as the common offspring of the one Being to whom we all owe supreme allegiance. The sublime extension of this precept to our very enemies (Rom. xii, 14) is a peculiar trait of Christianity (Matt. v, 43-48); not a mere fancy sketch (Matt. xviii, 23-35), as an offset to our own shortcomings (Matt. vi, 14, 15), or as a noble revenge (Rom. xii, 20), but a life-likeness (1 Pet. ii, 19-24) of the heroism of the faultless Master (Luke xxiii, 34), realized (Acts vii, 60) by saints (1 Cor. iv, 12): so faithfully are the divine lineaments (Exod. xxxiii, 18-23; xxxiv, 5-7) mirrored (Heb. i, 3) in the enduring (1 Pet. i, 25) Word (Rev. xix, 13), whose command (Luke vi, 36) is a promise of performance (1 Thess. v, 24). This is the only effectual motive, as well as the sole general bond, in the eager rush of men, each for the maintenance of himself and his. The natural instincts of home affection, and the ties of mutual advantage, may go far to soften the asperities of intimate association; but a wide-reaching and generous philanthropy can never be attained, nor can even the sweetest amenities of closely domestic and social intercourse be

steadily secured, without the habitual recognition of this fellowship in the divine sight.

4. *Duties towards one's Self.*—These are properly and advisedly placed last, although in the perversity and suicidal folly of human nature they are usually promoted to a front rank, and, indeed, enhanced almost to the exclusion of all the preceding. But no maxim was ever more profoundly true in its application to this subject than our Lord's paradox: "He that seeketh his own life [i. e. personal gratification as his foremost aim], shall lose it." There is no joy equal to that of making others happy; and he who is willing to forego his own ease, comfort, and emolument for the sake of blessing, consoling, and enriching his fellow-creatures, will find himself repaid a thousand-fold even in the satisfaction he experiences in this life, to say nothing of the rewards of that life which is to come. Selfishness always misses its mark, and is therefore sure to be miserable, whereas generosity invariably succeeds in its noble purposes. We need not here enter upon the metaphysical question of purely disinterested benevolence; God has not required us to scan our motives so closely as to detect and eject a thought of the reflex influence of our philanthropy upon our minds in the bliss of doing good and the retrospect of usefulness. On the contrary, he encourages us to a beneficent course by such considerations; and the Son of God himself did not disdain, in his consummate act of self-devotion for the rescue of a fallen world, to contemplate the fruit of his redeeming love (Isa. liii, 11; Heb. xii, 2). We may preliminarily remark, as a confirmation and parallel of this secret of the most successful happiness, that all the proclivities of the heart (especially the passions and the appetites) tend not only to excess, and therefore require, even for their own best ends, to be held in check by counter influences of a higher character, but they likewise are set upon the most *immediate* gratification possible; and as this is not always, nor even usually, the safest or the most complete, the prudent and experienced habitually restrain and defer them till the time and object are ripe for full and wholesome enjoyment. For this reason, all the more do we need to keep the love and pursuit of self in the background, till our nobler sentiments have acquired such strength and discipline that we may securely give to self-love the rein, and guide it to its most successful and harmonious results; otherwise we shall be likely to grasp only the present shadow, and lose the more remote substance. It is precisely this most egregious and irreparable folly of which the mass of mankind are guilty, in pursuing the pleasures of time and sense to the hazard of spiritual and eternal joys. We devote the remainder of this article to a few practical suggestions, under the head of personal duties to one's self, specifically calculated to guard against so lamentable an error, and secure the highest accomplishment of each one's destiny as a subject of moral government.

(1.) *The harmonious development of all one's native faculties.*—The gift of reason, and still more of a moral faculty, carries with it the obligation to exercise and improve it; we owe this no less as a debt of gratitude to the Giver than as a means of extracting the full value for ourselves. Hence, while a sense of self-preservation naturally and justly leads us to care for and cultivate our physical powers, the neglect of our intellect in any of its glorious capacities is a self-stultification that entitles one to the contempt of his fellows; but the crushing out of conscience or the dwarfing of any of our godlike moral capabilities is a literal suicide of the soul. Such a dereliction defeats the very end of probation, and turns it into a curse forever. Because we are surrounded by and filled with temptation in this scene of trial, all the more diligent do we need to be in rousing and confirming and intensifying every moral power that may aid us in the life-long struggle with our desperate inward and outward foes. Most of all have we occasion to lay hold on the alliance with almighty grace which is proffered us as a restorer to the full image of Deity (Phil. ii, 13).

(2.) *The careful culture of any particular aptitude that each may possess.*—Variety within certain limits of uniformity is evidently God's law as expressed in nature, and the same rule is observed in the human constitution—bodily, mental, and spiritual. Hence the obvious propriety, and indeed necessity, of noting and turning to account the peculiar genius of every individual, in order to its perfection by judicious practice. In this way the economy and skill of that ingenious modern contrivance the "division of labor" have their higher results. The idea that all are reduced by piety to the same Procrustean bed, either here or hereafter, is preposterous. The facile dexterity of the expert, as compared with the clumsy slowness of the tyro in art, is but a type of the excellence of one saint above another (1 Cor. xv, 41), or even of the same in successive stages of growth (Luke viii, 18); and this superiority on earth furnishes a vantage-ground by reason of which the moral distance must be forever widening in heaven. The same is true in this life of all the human powers, especially of the mind and heart; and doubtless a like perpetually increasing pre-eminence in these endowments, so akin with the spiritual, will hold good in the other world. From this we see the transcendent importance of cultivating in the present state of existence every power of the soul, before eternity shall fix the plastic ductile condition that pertains to probation. This thought again suggests, on the other hand, the mistaken policy of altogether neglecting even the less marked talent; for a feeble indication may lead to the discovery of a precious treasure, many unpromising beginnings having eventuated in brilliant eminence. And it is the common virtues—like the ordinary acquirements—that are most generally useful; as we approve the necessity of teaching every child, however dull, at least the simple rudiments of education, while we deem it worth while to expend years at the piano or the easel only upon those who evince extraordinary artistic tact. Once more, let no one excuse himself from the everyday duties of life on the ground of his small natural ability (Luke xix, 15–26), nor plead his peculiar indisposition or special hinderances to any form of morality, for all really experience the same difficulties and insufficiency in one form or another; this very reluctance, arduousness, opposition, calls for redoubled zeal and effort (Eccles. x, 10), for it is an omen, or rather symptom, of moral death the more imminent and total.

(3.) *The earnest and constant application to practical results of all one's time, powers, and resources.*—It is not enough to possess, enlarge, and employ wealth, influence, learning, skill, health, or longevity; we have not yet reached the just standard of requirement till we fully direct them towards useful ends—till they positively redound to the glory of God and the benefit of mankind. We should not be so absorbed in the luxury of their acquisition, increase, or exercise as to forget their ultimate design. In short, we must everywhere, at all times, and in all things, bear in mind that we are but *stewards* in the occupancy of these endowments, and hold ourselves constantly in readiness to give to the great Proprietor a satisfactory account of their appropriation (1 Cor. vi, 20).

(4.) *The sober but cordial and devout enjoyment of whatever blessings Providence has conferred upon us.*—Asceticism and epicureanism are equally removed from sound godliness (Eccles. xi, 9, 10). A morose piety is next to none at all, but a cheerful moderation is the best recommendation of saintliness, and thankfulness sweetens the homeliest morsel. Stoicism can never teach us to be content with our lot. Distrust of God's mercies is as atheistic as their abuse. The moral philosophy of the Bible is alike guarded against all extremes, because it begins, centres, and ends in a true theism (Eccles. xii, 13): "He hath showed thee, O man, what is good; and what doth the Lord require of thee,

but to do *justly,* and to love *mercy,* and to walk *humbly* with thy God?" (Mic. vi, 8). In our lapsed estate, to regain the lofty completeness we must trace our way back by the same steps; for *penitence* is the fit condition to our restoration to moral rectitude through divine *clemency* and *fidelity* (1 John i, 9).

Literature.—One of the earliest treatises on the subject in English is Paley's *Moral Philosophy* (Lond. 1785; often reprinted with extensive modifications by later editors); but it essentially ignores conscience, and has generally been reprobated by sound moralists. See Blakey, *Hist. of Morals* (4 vols. 8vo); Garve, *Different Principles of Moral Philos.* (from Aristotle to 1798); Channing's Jouffroy, *Introd. to Moral Philos.* (includes a critical survey of modern systems); Doddridge, *Lectures;* Belsham, *Moral Philos.;* Gisbourne, *Principles of Moral Philos.* (1789); Grove, *Moral Philos.;* Pearson, *Theory of Morals* (1800); Beattie, *Moral Science* (Edinburgh, 1816, 2 vols.); Taylor (J.), *Sketch of Moral Philos.;* Turnbull, *Principles of Moral Science;* Smith (J. S.), *Lectures on Moral Philos.;* Stewart, *Outlines of Moral Philos.;* and his *Active and Moral Powers;* and *Progress of Ethical Philos. in Europe;* Merivale, *Boyle Lectures,* 1864; Calderwood, *Hand-book of Moral Science* (Lond. 1872, 8vo); Gillett (E. H.), *The Moral System* (N. Y. 1874, 8vo), the latest and best work on the subject. Among express treatises on the general subject, we may name, as being best known and most accessible in this country, Wayland, *Elements of Moral Science* (Bost. 1835, 12mo); Whewell and Henry, *Morals* (Bost. 1839); Alexander, *Outlines of Moral Science* (N. Y. 1852); Hickock, *Moral Science* (N. Y. 1853); Upham, *Moral Philos.* (N. Y. 1857, 12mo); Winslow, *Elements of Moral Philos.* (N.Y. 1857, 12mo); M. Hopkins, *Lectures on Moral Science* (Bost. 1862, 12mo); ibid., *Law of Love* (N. Y. 1869, 12mo). The periodicals which contain valuable articles on this topic are: *Christian Examiner,* viii, 265; xviii, 101; xix, 1, 25; xxviii, 137; xxix, 153; xxx, 145; xli, 97; xlix, 215; lii, 188; *Christian Rev.* vii, 321; *Princeton Rev.* v, 33; vii, 377; xviii, 260; xx, 529; *Meth. Qu. Rev.* v, 220; *New-Englander,* Oct. 1870, p. 549; *Brit. and For. Ev. Rev.* Jan. 1874, p. 183; *Lond. Qu. Rev.* iii, 1; vi, 407; xi, 494; xlviii, 83; Oct. 1873, art. v; *Bib. Sacra,* April, 1873, art. ix; *Edinb. Rev.* vii, 413; lxi, 195; xci, 86; *Prospect. Rev.* i, 577; ii, 400; *North Brit. Rev.* xiv, 160; *Westm. Rev.* i, 182; ii, 254; xii, 246; *North Amer. Rev.* lx, 293; *Contemp. Rev.* July, 1872, art. vii. See MORALS.

Moral Science. See MORAL PHILOSOPHY.

Moral Sense is a term frequently used to designate the *conscience.* It is believed to have originated with lord Shaftesbury, who contended for the existence of disinterested affections in man, as against Hobbes (q. v.), and in anticipation of what Hutcheson (q. v.) afterwards advocated. Whatever we may think of the principles involved, the term *Moral Sense* itself is incorrect, however, in at least two essential particulars in which that faculty differs from the characteristics of the senses. In the first place, these latter are exercised upon *external* objects, whereas the conscience (συνείδησις, *consciousness,* or self-knowledge) is exclusively introversive or subjective, and passes in review only the acts or states of the individual himself. Secondly, the senses give us absolute and invariable information of the real properties or relations of things, and when acting normally they never mislead or deceive any one as to the facts in the case; while conscience is so subjective that it conveys to us intimation only of a relative character, and hence affects different persons quite variously in respect to the same act or condition of things, according to the habit of mind, or education, or preconceived notions. In short, conscience is a *sense* only in the general signification of an impression or influence of an emotive nature. It has usually been defined as that faculty of the mind by which we become aware of the moral quality of an act (purpose, sentiment, etc.), and are suitably (i. e. agreeably or painfully) affected by it. Only the latter part of this definition is accurate; for the apprehension of the agreement or contrariety between the given subjects of thought (the act, purpose, etc.) is a purely intellectual exercise of the judgment, comparing the thing contemplated or reviewed with some previously acquired or adopted standard or principle of right. Hence the importance of a correct and true rule by which to try all moral questions; and hence, too, the exceeding diversity and even opposition of views on moral points between persons of different religions and associations. The tendency of the passions, moreover, to warp the judgment is proverbial; and as human nature is constitutionally corrupt, the unaided and untrained conscience cannot be relied upon to give a just verdict. It is chiefly at this point that a divine revelation becomes necessary in order to furnish a perfect norm to the erring judgment, as well as to reinforce the sanction of the conscience in its conflict with the depraved inclinations. On the other hand, the emotional function of conscience, which is benumbed by nature as well as by habitual sin, needs quickening, so that it may become a clearer and more emphatic monitor in advance, as well as a more effectual penalty or reward after the performance of a praiseworthy or the commission of a guilty act, and thus stimulate—by its twofold action—to virtue in the future. It is revelation, again, that furnishes this aid, not only by the motives which the light that it sheds upon the rewards and punishments of a future state supplies, but likewise by the supernatural influences of the Holy Spirit promised to all who humbly seek and encourage them. As this double culture of the natural conscience—its habitual exercise in accordance with a heavenly standard of duty, and its alliance with Almighty power—ensures its sound development and steady action, so, on the contrary, the repeated violation of its behests, and the incorrigible rejection of the proffered assistance from above, must eventually lead—as we find to be actually the case with many hardened wretches—to an apparent obliteration of the faculty itself, or at least a total suppression of its admonitions and awards. The latter state is one of hopeless impenitence [see JUDICIAL BLINDNESS], and the former that of assured salvation. Yet even in an unfallen condition man's conscience was not of itself adequate for his moral guidance, and hence an objective law—the prohibition of the single tree as a prescriptive sample only—was given to supplement and direct its energy; and still Eve's judgment seems to have been incompetent, under that non-redemptive economy, despite her moral perfection, to detect the mortal error that lurked in the tempter's suggestions: the actual "knowledge of good and evil" by bitter experience alone was effectual to awaken the full power of this faculty. So, on the other hand, in the world of perdition we are wont to imagine that the seared and blunted conscience will rouse itself to chastise the soul with retributive agony. But the pangs of guilt, at least in this probationary existence, are not strictly the measure or criterion of wrong-doing; for then the self-complacent Pharisee would be acquitted, and the tender penitent would be condemned. The most atrocious crimes have been committed under the plea of conscience, and that not hypocritically, but in self-delusion (Acts xxvi, 9); while the first steps in transgression are visited by a degree of remorse which gradually lessens as the offender progresses in his downward career. This leads us back once more to the main proposition of this discussion, namely, the insufficiency of conscience as a moral light. Nothing is right simply because our conscience approves it. The appeal must be to a higher authority than man's nature affords. He is not an absolute "law unto himself." It is his Creator who retains supreme jurisdiction over him, and who has reserved the prerogative of prescribing what he may innocently do, and what he is morally bound to do. See MORAL LAW. Yet when an individual has availed himself of the best means

within his reach for ascertaining his Maker's will, and has scrupulously followed that light, he is not culpable for any error of faith or practice into which he may fall by reason of his fallible judgment, or for any other consequence of his naturally defective or even depraved condition. He must and he ought to obey his reason and conscience, however imperfect; but if sincere and docile, he will not long remain in serious misapprehension of moral truth; and in any case his responsibility is exactly proportioned to the measure of light he enjoys or might have attained (Luke xii, 47, 48). While therefore a *mistake*, be it ever so grievous or closely related to moral subjects, is not in itself a sin, yet every man's conduct should be tried—both by himself and others, as it certainly is and finally will be by the unerring Judge—according to that standard of rectitude which the divine law as vouchsafed to him enjoins. To the heathen, walking by the dim light that tradition reflects upon his path from the primeval revelations, supplemented only by the uncertain flickerings of the lamp of experience, or perchance by a few rays that occasionally break through the embrasure of his shrouded pilgrimage from the radiance of more favored dispensations, the office of conscience is all-important in aiding him to grope his way out of the thraldom of nature to a sense of the divine acceptance; and we may charitably hold that in rare examples he has thus been enabled to reach the day of moral purity, and emerge at last into the serene glory of the heavenly abode; but the melancholy facts of past history and present observation seem only to justify the fear that the mass of paganism, even in the cultured instances of Greece and Rome, of India or China, have but grovelled in the mire of sensuality, and quenched their higher aspirations and better convictions in the absurdities of a beastly idolatry. Even Islamism, setting out with much of borrowed truth to reform a polytheistic faith, rapidly degenerated into puerile fanaticism, and aims no higher than a licentious Paradise; while Judaism, disciplined by a direct contact with the supernatural to the sternest regimen that the race has ever known, has generally resulted in heartless Pharisaism and puerile formalism. Under the Redemptive scheme a simpler and profounder maxim—that of universal benevolence—has supervened for the resuscitation and tuition of the believer's conscience, stunned and bewildered by the burdensome technicalities of previous systems; yet we find, alas! a large share of Christendom either reverting to the obsolete methods of salvation by asceticism and ritualism and ecclesiasticism, or abusing the liberty of the Gospel by fanaticism and humanitarianism and rationalism. Yet, amid these vagaries and inconsistencies, the one cardinal principle of "faith that works by love and purifies the heart" must be recognised by the candid and thoughtful of all times and all climes as the sole test of genuine piety and philanthropy. Selfishness is the bane of all morality, and in proportion as the carnal self is crucified the spiritual self is resurrected out of the ruins of the fall, until at length the ideal man—God's own image—becomes transfigured in its permanent beauty; for "God is love" (comp. 1 John iv).

Literature.—Abercrombie, *Philos. of the Moral Feelings;* Brown, *Lect. on the Mind;* Butler, *Analogy of Religion and Nature;* Hutcheson, *Inquiry into Beauty and Virtue;* and his *Essay on the Passions;* Necker, *On Religious Opinions;* Witherspoon, *Lectures,* Lect. iv; Bentham, *Morals and Legislation;* Smith (Southwood), *On Divine Government;* Mackintosh, *Preliminary Dissertation* (1832); Dymond, *Essay on Morality* (1832); Hall (Robert), *Sermon on Mod. Infidelity;* Sedgwick (Adam), *Discourse on the Studies of the University of Cambridge* (1834); Dwight (T.), *Sermon* 99, and many others; Wainwright, *Vindication of Paley's Theory of Morals,* etc. (1830); Edwards, *Works* (see Index); Bautain, *Moral Qualifications of Man;* Fürst, *Moral des Evangeliums mit den verschiedenen philos. Moral-systemen;* Knapp, *Christian Theol.* p. 31; Pye-Smith, *Outlines of*

Christian Theol. (see Index); Hopkins, *Outline Study of Man* (N. Y. 1874, 12mo), Lect. ix and sq.; Ueberweg, *Hist. Philos.* ii, 319 sq., 446, 494; Leckey, *Hist. Europ. Morals* (N. Y. 1870, 2 vols. roy. 8vo), i, 93, 123; *Contemporary Rev.* Jan. 1872, art. v (Savages); Appleton, *Works*, Lects. xv and xvii; Jenkins, *Reasonableness of Christianity*; Law, *Theory of Religion*, pt. ii; Pearson, *Rem. on Morals*; Liddon, *Bampton Lecture on the Divinity of Christ*; Blackie, *Four Phases of Christian Morals*; Spalding, *Philos. of Morals, with a Review of Ancient and Modern Theories*; Lewes, *Hist. Philos.* vol. ii (see Index); *Old and New*, April, 1870; *Brownson's Rev.* Jan. 1853; *Presb. Rev.* April, 1870; *Bib. Sacra*, April, 1870; *Studien und Kritiken*, Jan. 1866; *Lond. Qu. Rev.* Jan. 1871, p. 26; *Westminster Rev.* xlii, 286 sq.; *Brit. and For. Ev. Rev.* 1843, p. 293; 1844, p. 412; Oct. 1872, art. iii; *Journal of Speculat. Philos.* Jan. 1870, art. iv; April, 1870, art. vii; Jan. 1871, art. v; *New-Englander*, Jan. 1871, p. 160; *Princeton Rev.* Oct. 1871, p. 634; *Theol. Presb.* (*Cumberland Presb. Qu.*) July, 1871, art. ix; *Univ. Qu.* Oct. 1873, art. v (German and Anglo-American Morals); *Revue Chrétienne*, Jan. 1867; *Contemporary Rev.* Aug. 1868, art. vii. See also MORAL PHILOSOPHY.

Moral Theology is only another name for the science of ETHICS (q. v.). Under the last-named heading we have considered as much of the subject as can be encompassed from a strictly philosophical and Protestant theological stand-point. Only the views of Romanists remain to be treated here. These are in many respects radically different from those of the other classes referred to. The Protestant view, as we have seen in the article *Ethics*, is that Christianity is essentially an ethical religion; that, while it is true that other religions favor certain virtues, or give a certain sanction to all virtues, Christianity is truly morality, for it aims at moral *regeneration*, and that is itself religion. Says Blackie (*Four Phases of Morals*), "It is a religion; by its mere epiphany it forms a Church; in its starting-point, its career, and its consummation, it is 'a kingdom of heaven upon earth'" (p. 207 sq.; comp. p. 219 sq., 266 sq.). As the sources of this science, we pointed out, "Christ, his person and teaching; also the writings of the apostles as shown in the N. T., as objective and as subjective to the influence of the Holy Spirit in the faithful." The Roman Catholic Church, however, recognises no standard of morality except that of her own construction, and insists upon it that not only the Scriptures, but also the tradition and declarations of the Church must control any effort, even in the domain of speculative philosophy. Says Dr. Fuchs, in the Roman Catholic Cyclopædia of Wetzer and Welte: "The traditions of the Church, *together* with the Scriptures, constitute the source of ethical knowledge. Tradition serves partly to complement the moral precepts of the Bible by further demands and institutions, and partly to elucidate and more clearly to interpret their sense and purpose." Not even does he rest here. Lest he be misunderstood as to the extent of the domain of ecclesiastical tradition, he continues: "From the domain of ecclesiastical tradition we regard especially as important for moral purposes: (1) the rules and canons of the general ecclesiastical councils; (2) the decisions and declarations of the holy chair; (3) the infallible (?) utterances of the Church fathers." Not content yet, he goes even so far as to declare that "into the circle of moralistic sources we most naturally and properly admit also ecclesiastical customs and the lives of the saints, for in the life of the Church and her saints is reflected the life of our divine Lord and Master." In quoting Dr. Fuchs we do not by any means wish to be understood as citing only one writer; as a contributor to the standard Roman Catholic Cyclopædia of Germany, he speaks most assuredly the opinions of the Church for which he writes, and his views are those of the Romish Church at large. It is apparent, then, that by an outward law of the Church Romanists have modified the

ethics of the N. T., and controlled the ethical consciousness of Christendom down to the period of the Reformation. The Protestant regards this modification as adulterous, and insists that notably sacerdotalism played no unimportant part; the clergy interpreting as they saw fit, and the people being taught by them as they were themselves influenced by the ascetic notions which invaded the Church in the 4th century, and have ever since continued to exert their authority among papists. See ASCETICISM; MONASTICISM; SACERDOTALISM. In our references in the article *Ethics* we have inserted the works of writers who deal carefully with the early teaching of the Church on this subject, and we here give only a brief résumé of the views of ecclesiastical writers from the apostolic period down, in order to furnish the names most prominently connected with Roman Catholic ethics from the foundation of Christianity to the present.

1. *Apostolic Period.*—As regards the extent of apostolic ethics, it encompasses pretty much all departments of life, and the duties and virtues corresponding with them. Yet in this province such are made particularly conspicuous and praiseworthy as are natural to the spirit of Christianity. For while all antiquity had made the sovereign good consist in escape from pain, either by virtue or by pleasure, Christianity, by the mystery of the passion, announced the divinity of sorrow, and the most characteristic element in Christian virtue to be love. Hence the apostolic writers gave special prominence to those Christian ideals of faith, hope, love, prayer, mercy, chastity, martyrdom, and the like, which are the characteristic elements of perfect charity, and which, if realized, must absorb like ethics and politics in a higher science. The vacillation on some single moral questions and principles observable in the writings of these early Christian fathers gradually died out as a more profound and comprehensive Christian consciousness spread in the Church. As regards the manner of treatment of this subject, most apostolic writings deal with it in a way serviceable mainly to devotional purposes. "Their basis," it has been well said, "remained from the first rather religious than speculative, notwithstanding the persuasion that in the reason enlightened by the Word there was given a ground of union between objective revelation and subjective knowledge." Even among those contributions to this field, in that period, which rise above the sphere then usually occupied, only a few maintain a strictly scientific character. Earliest among the productions of that age stand the writings of the celebrated disciple of the apostle Paul, Clement of Rome, whose epistle to the Christian congregation at Corinth is one of the finest monuments of Christian antiquity. Its especial object was, however, to reconcile the dissensions and factions which had arisen in that congregation, and it contains therefore mainly admonitions to concord and peace. More noteworthy in this department of Christian ethics are the productions of Ignatius (q. v.), who wrote six epistles to diverse congregations, and one to Polycarp; they were penned on his way to the lions of the Colosseum, and breathe the spirit of a man who had beheld John, and, full of faith, is ready to meet his Lord and Master. The moral precepts and admonitions of the Ignatian epistles are mostly passages quoted from the N. T., or sentiments in accord with its contents, expressed with fervency as well as simplicity. A remarkable feature in them is the emphasis with which their author insists on the propriety to belong publicly and externally to the Church, though he by no means forgets its value in the sight of God as consisting in the communion with Christ and in the sincere search for union with God. We learn to recognise ecclesiastical consociation, the alliance of so many thousands by unity of faith and love, as something grand, the true obedience to the officers of the Church (elders) as something inseparable from Christian life. This decidedly ecclesiastical disposition is also shared by Poly-

carp (q. v.) himself in his epistle to the congregation at Philippi. Above all things, he desires that attachment to pure unadulterated faith be strengthened; like Ignatius, he establishes Christian ethics on Christian Church creed. His moral precepts are rightly denominated "apostolic grains of gold." But really the most eminent attempt to reconcile Christian ideas with the forms and views of ancient philosophy, especially those of its latest efflorescence—New Platonism—was made in the mystic speculations of the Areopagite Dionysius, in which the Christian scientific spirit aims at an innermost comprehension of itself, for this end calling in the support of traditional knowledge. No other product of mind has exercised a deeper or more powerful influence upon the development of Christian mysticism—the culminating-point of ecclesiastical ethics—than his writings, in which the several dispersed rays of mystical ideas and views, such as here and there glimmer in Clemens Alexandrinus, Augustine, Macarius, and others, converge as in a focus, and form one of the strongest links connecting the period of which we are speaking with the subsequent ones. To these relics of spiritual treasures of the apostolic fathers we join three compositions, two of which plainly show spurious authorship, and a third gives no clew at all. They are the Epistle of Barnabas, the Shepherd of Hermas, and the Epistle to Diognetus. The author of the first-named work calls his moral precepts the road of light, in contrast with the crooked road of darkness, as he designates sinful life. The Shepherd is divided into three sections, the second of which deals entirely with ethics. The letter to Diognetus, as already stated, comes from an unknown hand. The principal interest which attaches to this ancient Christian memorial lies in the excellent description which the author gives of the life and morals of the early Christians. Here, also, two other writings adorned with the name of apostles deserve to be mentioned—namely, "The Apostolic Constitutions" and "The Apostolic Canons." Both collections, as to their origin, it is true, come far short of reaching up to the apostolic age, but they deserve a place here because Romanists assert "that they exhibit a picture of the most primæval condition of Christian manners and ecclesiastical discipline." They are certainly worthy of attention on account of the treasure of tradition they furnish; still more, the peculiarity of their moral character renders them notable and significant, this character being wholly catholic, mingling severity with mildness, keeping the right medium between laxity and rigor.

2. *Patristic Period.*—We now reach the period in which we deal with the writings of the fathers of the Church. The series opens with Justin Martyr (q. v.), "the evangelist wearing the mantle of a philosopher." It was his mind, trained by ancient ethical philosophy, which placed in the ground of Christian ethics the first seed of scientific treatment. He clothed the Christian ideas in the scientific forms of antique wisdom, and showed that the classic must bend before the higher light of the Gospel. Particularly noticeable is his conception of reason as identical with knowledge and conscience. One of the fundamental Christian ideas—liberty of human will — in contraposition to fatalism, sustained by pagan views, he vindicated by an argumentation as acute as striking. He tried to elucidate the relation of Christian principles to the Mosaic law, and defended the Christian ethics against objections raised both from the Jewish and from pagan stand-points. Next we place the two apologists, Athenagoras (q. v.) and Theophilus (q. v.), bishop of Antioch. Their writings furnish a rich store for ethics. After them we meet that great disciple of Polycarp, St. Irenæus (q. v.). In opposition to the transcendental speculations of the Gnostics, he urges with emphasis to a practical life. But in thus giving prominence to the practical part of Christianity, he is far from falling into a "moralizing" tendency. Far greater services than those named were rendered in the scientific elaboration of Christian ethics by Clement

of Alexandria. His three principal writings form a tripartite entity, in which he successively imparts the Christian doctrine of life in its fundamental features. His first work ($\Lambda \acute{o} \gamma o \varsigma$ $\pi \rho o \tau \rho \epsilon \pi \tau \iota \kappa \grave{o} \varsigma$ $\pi \rho \grave{o} \varsigma$ $"E\lambda \lambda \eta \nu a \varsigma$) is polemico-apologetic; he combats what is morally injurious in popular religions and in the philosophical systems of heathendom, and compares with it the beneficial influence which Christianity exercises on its professors; he shows the absurdity of the pagan legends of gods, and demonstrates how the religious mysteries of the pagans so often most deeply offend the moral sentiments, while the Christian doctrines and mysteries have the advantage of harmonizing with reason and moral purity; he admits that the writings of pagan philosophers contain seeds of morality, but reminds us that they owe their origin to the $\Lambda \acute{o} \gamma o \varsigma$, the source of all vital truth in the world. The second treatise ($\acute{o}$ $\pi a \iota \delta a \gamma \omega \gamma \acute{o} \varsigma$) is divided into several books. The first treats of moral life in general; it may be considered an introduction to Christian ethics. The second treats of Christian ethics in its main features. The remaining books, corresponding to special morals, expatiate on the particular duties and virtues, and discuss conduct, in the several relations and occurrences of external life, from the Christian stand-point. The third essay ($\sigma \tau \rho \acute{\omega} \mu a \tau a$, miscellanies) leads to a higher degree of moral knowledge and action. The difference of the two degrees lies in $\gamma \nu \widetilde{\omega} \sigma \iota \varsigma$. On the foundation of the ideas gained by a deeper and increased knowledge a higher religio-moral culture is constructed, the culmination of which is love assimilating and uniting with the Deity. In conclusion of the whole, Clement sketches the image of the $\gamma \nu \omega \sigma \tau \iota \kappa \acute{o} \varsigma$, and thus presents the Christian ideal of a moral personage. The $\gamma \nu \widetilde{\omega} \sigma \iota \varsigma$ Clement deduces from no other source than from the idea of the divine Logos which personally appeared in Christ; an idea which, supporting and illustrating, pervades all his definitions of morality. In his smaller address, $T\acute{\iota} \varsigma$ $\acute{o}$ $\sigma \omega \zeta \acute{o} \mu \epsilon \nu o \varsigma$ $\pi \lambda o \acute{u} \sigma \iota o \varsigma$ ("Who is the rich man saved?"), he discusses a practical question of the time concerning the use of earthly valuables and possessions. It may not be too much to assert that Clement, by his literary activity, is of no less significance for the department of Christian ethics than his worthy disciple Origen, by his celebrated work $\Pi \epsilon \rho \grave{\iota}$ $\acute{a} \rho \chi \widetilde{\omega} \nu$, became to that of Christian dogmatics. To these two Alexandrian Christians science is indebted for the most profound and lasting stimulus. The merits of Origen about Christian apologetic ethics we need but allude to here, and can speak only of his two practical treatises—$\Pi \epsilon \rho \grave{\iota}$ $\epsilon \grave{\upsilon} \chi \widetilde{\eta} \varsigma$ (on prayer) and $E\acute{\iota} \varsigma$ $\mu a \rho \tau \acute{u} \rho \iota o \nu$ $\pi \rho o \tau \rho \epsilon \pi \tau \iota \kappa \grave{o} \varsigma$ $\lambda o \gamma \acute{o} \varsigma$ (exhortation to martyrdom). One feature to which we have alluded in the writings of these Church fathers—the leaning on the definitions of the ethics of classical antiquity—need of course hardly excite surprise. For it must be apparent to every well-read student of antiquity that the fathers, in order to be understood, had to speak the language of the then prevailing scientific consciousness; they could not break at one stroke the barriers of the surrounding cultured circle, and they felt the less obliged to do this as they were thoroughly convinced that in reason, enlightened by the *Logos*, was given a point of intermediation between the classical and Christian consciousness, between the objective basis of revelation and the subjective principle of cognizance. This definition of unity is by no one more emphasized than by Justin Martyr, Clement of Alexandria, and Origen. They agree in the view that reason is the source and measure of morality, consequently that what is rational is moral, what is irrational is immoral or sinful, and therefore that Christian ethics, as the most rational, because derived from absolute reason personified in Christ, must also be the most complete and perfect. The writings of Tertullian (q. v.), which come next, are marked by a dark rigor, growing more prominent in proportion as he inclined to Montanism (q. v.). The moral earnestness of Christianity, under Montanist direction, was aggravated into unnatural severity; the moral advice of the Gospel was made a command, and extended to all Christians. With this theory, if it had prevailed, Christian principle would have failed of its mundane victory, and must have ultimately perished. In the use, then, of Tertullian's moralistic writings we must distinguish the ante-Montanistic period of the author's life from his later. Of the first class are *De Patientia, De Oratione, De Pœnitentia, Ad Martyres, Ad Uxorem.* Next stands Cyprian. Though in general he shared the strictly moral view of Tertullian, highly spoken of by him, and though, in contrast with Alexandrian speculation, he was strenuously attached to practical ecclesiasticism, yet he was never carried away to the rigid, excessive severity of his exemplar, and by his more spiritual manner of contemplation he inclined to the ideal, thus offering points for reconciling the Alexandrian and North African schools. (See, however, this *Cyclopædia*, iii, 321, col. 2.) Cyprian's writings belonging to the department of ethics are *De zelo et livore*, distinguished by its psychological tenor, the third book of his *Libri testimoniorum*, which gives an outline of moral rules for life; *De Bono Patientiæ; De Opere et Eleomosynis; De Oratione Dominica; De Lapsis*, etc. We find in his letters also specimens of casuistry—decisions on difficult cases presented to him by bishops. Next Lactantius (q. v.), the Christian Cicero, spreads over the morals of the Gospel the splendor of rhetoric, and proves by comparison the insufficiency and perversity of pagan ethics. His *Institutiones Divinæ*, in which he performs that task, can be looked upon as an exemplar of a development tending to reconcile speculative and practical elements. The Christian religion, which teaches man to find his supreme happiness in God, is pronounced by him the true philosophy of life. If some obliquity and error have crept into his ethical statements, they must be attributed to the circumstance that at the time of his authorship the moral doctrines of the Church were not yet so fixed as they were after the Pelagian disputes. Of not equal, yet of considerable importance, are the writings of Athanasius, the pillar of orthodoxy in the Arian controversy. One would naturally suppose that he, busy with an attempt to solve the great dogmatic problem, had no time for moralistic discussion; nevertheless we find in his numerous dogmatic writings many moral reflections disseminated. Almost exclusively devoted to moral subjects are the writings of Ephraem (q. v.) the Syrian, whose edifying compositions contain a rich store of moral ascetic thoughts. A condign pendant to the writings of the *propheta Syrorum* are the ethical writings of Macarius (q. v.); they are especially important for mysticism, containing as they do the germs of the ecclesiastic traditional form later represented by the great mystics of the Middle Ages. Cyril (q. v.) of Alexandria is too well known as the zealous advocate of Christian ethics against the assaults of Julian to need special consideration here. Beside him stands Cyril (q. v.) of Jerusalem, who distinguishes between the dogmatic and ethic in the later usual manner, designating what concerns faith, δόγμα, and what has moral action for its purpose, πρᾶξις. Ὁ τῆς Θεοσέβειας τρόπος ἐκ δύο τούτων συνέστηκε, δογμάτων εὐσεβῶν καὶ πράξεων ἀγαθῶν. The dogmas he regards as the roots of moral motives. We turn next to that bright triple constellation of Cappadocia—Basil the Great and the Gregories —those great influential theologians of the 4th century. The sublime moral earnestness which animated them, their warm attachment to the Church, the superior culture which they had gained by industrious study, are mirrored in their literary products, spirit, learning, and eloquence. The main merit about Christian ethics is undoubtedly due to Basil the Great; yet also his brother, Gregory of Nyssa (in his writings on the life of Moses, on perfection, on virginity, as well as in his homilies), and his theological friend, Gregory of Nazianzum (in his poems and homilies), labored in the department zealously and successfully. The ἠθικά of

Basil contain the main features of Christian moral doctrine continuously based on sentences of Holy Writ. His ἀσκητικά have the higher morality and the perfection of monastic orders for their principal topic. Three of his letters addressed to Amphilochius, the bishop of Iconium, which contain regulations of Church discipline, have acquired canonical authority in the Roman Catholic Church. At the confines of the 4th century we are met by the grave and venerable form of Ambrose, the bishop of Milan, whose writings introduce us into a green and flowery garden of moral meditations. In his three books, *De Officiis*, he furnishes a counterpiece to Cicero's treatise of the same title. It aims to bring the purity, sublimity, and sanctity of Christian ethics to a conscious and clear recognition. After him we come to three men—(347–407) Chrysostom, Jerome, and Augustine—all more or less connected with the Pelagian controversy. The first of them discourses on the question of free-will and grace, and in a most practical manner. Soon after his death we see the same raised as an issue of controversy full of moral interest by Pelagius, a British monk. Until the commencement of the 5th century strictly doctrinal questions had been the topics of ecclesiastical disputes; now the Pelagian contest, an eminently moral question, engaged public attention. The contrast of liberty and grace must have been recognised at the first awakening of reflection. It found, however, no final equitable solution, and remained in continual vacillation, sometimes grace, at other times liberty, preponderating, at the expense of the adverse. (Compare the view of the Grecian fathers of the Church of ἑκούσιν, Petavius, *De theol. dogm.* tom. i, lib. v, cap. 2.) Pelagius, however, asserted the freedom of will to such lengths that the divine influence of grace was nearly reduced to a nullity. Pelagius, in referring man to the power of his will, wished to rouse him to energetic action. This intention is ingenious, and deserving of respect. But, as Neander (*Joh. Chrysostomus u. die Kirche*, ii, 134 sq.) correctly observes, man should be brought not only to the consciousness of his originally divine nature, but at the same time to the recognition of his internal corruption unlike it, and to the ideal of sanctity to be obtained: he ought to have cheered man, bowed down, by proclaiming what the infinite love of the Deity has done in Christ to deliver him from this corruption; he ought to have led him to the inexhaustible spring of divine life, by which the faithful may be renewed in heart, in order to impart to him confidence in moral exertions, not liable to be deceived, but rather confirmed, by self-knowledge and experience, which, according to his needs, humiliate and elevate him. Jerome (q. v.) preceded Augustine in coming forth to the conflict; he had already retired when the latter made his appearance, and by the momentum of speculative talent, mental profundity, and Christian knowledge and experience, turned and decided the contest. See PELAGIANISM. Of the three, however, Augustine deserves by far the most important place. Except perhaps Clement of Alexandria and Ambrose, St. Augustine is certainly the ablest moralist of all the patristic writers. He was among the first to be distinguished by reduction to principles, by clear statement, dialectic progress of ideas, and systematic organization in general. The sovereign genius of Augustine, moreover, succeeded best in emancipating himself from classical influences. Nowhere is the Christian vital principle of love (caritas) more exactly defined and carried out more consequentially than in his excellent treatise, *De moribus ecclesiæ catholicæ et Manichæorum*, c. 15, 21–24 (comp. also his *De civit. Dei*, xiv, 9, p. 54, 167; *Enchirid.* c. 121; *De fide et operibus*, c. 7). It is true he does not exhibit in his writings a strictly ethical system, but wherever and whenever he treats moral subjects, he is always led by a scientific dialectic spirit, and never loses sight of the spiritual ideal unity floating before his clear and comprehensive mind. Among his ethical works, besides the one mentioned above, the following are especially worthy of note: *Enchiridion ad Laurentium s. de fide, spe et caritate; De fide et operibus; De vita beata; De agone Christiano; De mendacio; De bono conjugali; De sancta virginitate; De continentia; De patientia.* See, however, the article AUGUSTINE. In the further lapse of this period a number of men, partly of the Greek, partly of the Latin Church, have rendered service to ethics. Among these is Isidore of Pelusium, whose moral writings breathe the spirit of Chrysostom, and plainly show the love devoted by him to this great master, so influential in the Greek Church. Nilus also must be considered as being in spiritual connection with this illustrious exemplar. Both clothed their ethic definitions, precepts, counsels, and casuistic decisions in epistolary form. Even in the Occident we meet with a disciple of the "Gold-mouthed," John Cassian, who was actively engaged in the Pelagian movement by an attempt at mediation, which, however, miscarried. For ethics, not only his *De octo capit. vitiis* is worthy of mention, but also his *Collationes Patrum,* and his twelve books, *De institutis cœnobiorum.* Among the moralistic authors of the Greek Church, the series of the fathers hitherto enumerated is worthily concluded by John the Scholastic, author of that moral-ascetic treatise, *Climax Paradisi,* and by Anastasius Sinaita, whose writings are mainly of an ascetic description. In the Western Church, Gregory the Great closes the period by his *Moralia,* a work which he skilfully introduces by some passages from Job, disseminating many suggestive thoughts, the abundant fruits of which will not escape the attentive observer in subsequent periods of ethic history.

3. *Scholastic Period.*—The men whom we meet from the beginning of the 7th until the end of the 11th century, with few exceptions, made it their main task to collect from the patristic mines all moralistic material, and to distribute and group it under definite rubrics and titles. Among these collectors archbishop Isidore of Hispalis deserves first mention. His principal ethical work is *Sententiarum s. de summo bono libri iii.* The maxims gathered from older fathers treat of virtue and sin in general, the auxiliaries of virtue, and particular duties. The main source from which he draws are Augustine and Gregory the Great. In his *De Differentiis Spiritualibus* also a moralistic tendency predominates, while his *Synonyma* and *Soliloquia* are entirely pervaded by it. With perspicuity he develops in them etymologically moral ideas, and reduces them to logical connection. He is surpassed, if not in learning, in mental productiveness by the abbot Maximus (the Confessor), whose Κεφάλαια on love contain the most profound ideas, and are extremely valuable for scientific ethics. He besides has well deserved by the interpretation of the mystic writings of the Areopagita. Maximus enunciates the proposition that the incarnation of the Λόγος had to be renewed in us spiritually; the human and divine must penetrate vitally. He distinguishes between the law of nature, the written law, and the law of grace, and attempts to develop the three elements in their single and in their interchanging relations. The collections of moral maxims by the Palestinian monk Antiochus in his *Pandects of Holy Writ,* and Beda the venerable in his *Scintillæ Patrum,* are surpassed by John of Damascus in his extensive work Τὰ ἱερά. This ample collection of materials, surpassing all previous ones as regards completeness, is arranged alphabetically; the single articles are divided into a Biblical and a Patristic part. Also his still more renowned work, Ἔκδοσις ἀκριβὴς τῆς ὀρθοδόξου πίστεως, contains moral sections, the more significant the higher they stand in a scientific point of view. Alcuin's writing, *De Animæ Ratione,* is allied to Platonic doctrines, as they are stated by Augustine. It descants on virtue in general, and the cardinal virtues and principal vices. His other work, *De Virtute et Vitiis,* is less scientific, and more remarkable for diligence in collecting. The thread of ethical writings, without enriching

its particular sphere, was continued through the darkest times of the Middle Ages by Smaragdus (*Via Regia* and *Diadema Monachorum*), by bishop Halitgar of Cambray (*De Pœnitentia libri v*), by Jonas, bishop of Orleans (*Libri iii de Institutione Laicali* and *Libri de Institutione Regia*), by Rabanus Maurus (*De Vitiis, De Pœnitentia, De Institutione Clericorum*), by Pascharius Radpertus (*Tract. de Fide, Spe et Caritate*), by Hincmar (*Epp. de Canendis Vitiis et Virtut. Exercend.*), by Ratherius (*Medit. Cordis libri vi*), and by Peter Damiani. The next writer, Anselm of Canterbury, really opens up the most auspicious outlook of the scholastic field. His writings, which in greater part belong to the department of morals, indicate a decided advance in a well-cultured spirit; and there are foreshadowed in them the tendencies of the moralists of the latter part of the Middle Ages, by whom were brought forth those extravagances which successively held sway in the theological world under the name of mysticism, scholasticism, and casuistry. We come here upon Bernard of Clairvaux and Hugo of St. Victor, who were truly the coryphæi of Middle Age ethics, and the leading representatives of mysticism (see Helfferich, *Die Christl. Mystik* [Gotha, 1842], i, 349 sq., 430 sq.). Bernard is surpassed by no author in his delineations of the worth and power of love. From him proceeded that passionate inspiration which the monastery of St. Victor perpetuated through the Middle Ages, and which remains embodied in the *Imitation of Christ.* The two pre-eminent Christian sentiments, according to him, are humility and love; both spring from the knowledge of ourselves. A sense of humiliation is the first experience when we duly regard ourselves, and this prepares for intensity of love, which in its highest degree is felt only in reference to God. We come next to the great masters of scholastic theological ethics. These are Peter Lombard, Thomas Aquinas, and Duns Scotus. Their aim is to harmonize Aristotelianism and Christianity. The first completed, in his *Magister Sententiarum,* the list of the seven cardinal virtues by adding faith, hope, and charity to the ancient series of justice, fortitude, temperance, and wisdom. His scholars, Alexander of Hales and Albert the Great, still further perfected his system. Thomas's task is to fully develop, in his *Summa Theol.* pt. ii, the mediæval philosophy of virtue. He makes the intellect the highest principle, and distinguishes between universal and special ethics, the former being that of perfect beings in heaven, the latter that of imperfect beings on earth. This work is by all critics conceded to be the most magnificent of all ethical structures of the Middle Ages. Duns Scotus, in his *Quæstiones in iv libb. sentt.,* opposes the primacy of the will to that of the intellect, and thus introduces a subjective element in place of the objective knowledge to which Aquinas has given prominence. Besides these great writers of this period, there are many others who have greatly distinguished themselves as contributors to the department of ethics. Among these, above all others of the Christian writers of these times whom we have just passed in review, towers the revered Bonaventura, the conciliator of the dialectico-scholastic and mystical forms of the Middle Age spirit. He commented upon Lombard's writings, and wrote in a scholastic manner his *Breviloquium* and his *Centiloquium;* in a mystical tendency he composed his *Itinerarium mentis in Deum,* and smaller works. A pretty exhaustive epitome of Christian ethics was furnished by William Perault (Peraldus) in his *Summa de Virtutibus et Vitiis.* A still richer and more thorough treatise of moral theology came from the pen of the Dominican Antoninus, archbishop of Florence, who, after Thomas, performed the greatest service in this field. He deserves to stand by the side of Bonaventura, as the author of *Summa Theologiæ in iv partes distributa.* The *Speculum Morale* of Vincence of Beauvais stands in intimate relation to Thomas's writings, many regarding Thomas as its author even, because of the similarity to the *Secunda Se-*

cundæ; yet there seems to be little ground for this supposition, and Vincence should be counted here as a writer of merit. Gerson also deserves mention here for his valuable contributions to scholastic morals (as contained in vol. iii of the Antwerp edition of his works).

Mysticism, during the quarrels of the scholastics, developed and flourished more than ever in the latter part of this (14th) century, and brought forth much valuable fruit. Prominent among those who at this time gave to mysticism a popular, practical tendency were John Tauler (q. v.) and Henry Suso (q. v.). On the borders of the objective ecclesiastical and subjective unecclesiastical mysticism we meet John Ruysbroech, who is by Gerson ruled out of the Church writers as a heretic (see Ullmann, *Reformers before the Reformation*). But the greatest influence by far was exerted by Thomas à Kempis, who, breaking away altogether from speculation, entered the practical popular road in his *Imitation*, to which we have already referred. But while thus gradually by this new mystical method morality was referred to inner feelings, aspirations, and conflicts, and by the scholastic method it was founded on systems of intellectual principles, prominence was given to the casuistical method, which limits itself to the determination of duty in particular cases (casus conscientiæ) in practical life. Numerous works on casuistry, some of them designed for the use of the confessional, were produced from the 13th to the 16th century, the principal of which are the *Astesana*, by a Minorite of Asti; the *Angelica*, by Angelus de Calvasio; the *Pisanella*, also called the *Magistruccia*, by Bartholomeo de Sancta Concordia, in Pisa; the *Rosella*, by the Genoese Minorite Trouamala; and the *Monaldina*, by archbishop Monaldus, of Benevento. The *Astesana* treats, in eight books, of the divine commandments, of virtues and vices, of covenants and last wills, of the sacraments, of penance and extreme unction, of ordination, of ecclesiastical censures, and of marriage. The tendency of casuistry is to dissipate the essential unity of the Christian life in the technical consideration of a diversity of works.

4. *Modern Period.* — Casuistry had begun to decline when it was revived and zealously improved by the Order of Jesuits, and became their peculiar ethics. The doctrine of probabilities was developed by them in connection with it. The number of writers who devoted themselves to this task is very large. We can only make room here for the more noted. Though rather a polemic than a moralist, Bellarmine († 1621) deserves to be first mentioned here because of the Jesuitic moral sentiments contained in his *Disputationes de controversiis Christianæ fidei*. He has, moreover, played his part as a mystico-ascetic writer. His *Libri iii de genitu Columbæ* (Antw. 1617), and his *De ascensione mentis in Deum per scalas rerum creatarum* (Par. 1606), are greatly valued by Romanists. But little less noted is Peter Canisius († 1597), author of *Summa doctrinæ Christianæ*, a work which, though intended as an aid to catechetics, is yet much valued by Roman moralists because of the many important hints which it furnishes them. Other Jesuitical moralists who deserve mention here are Francis of Toledo († 1596), *Summa casuum conscientiæ s. Instructorium sacerdotum in libb. viii distinctum* (Rome, 1602); Immanuel Sa († 1596), *Aphorismi confessariorum ex doctorum sententiis collecti* (ed. ult. Duac. 1627); John Azor († 1600), *Institutiones Morales* (Rome, 1600 sq.); Gregory of Valentia († 1603), *Commentt. theol. et disputt. in Summam Thomæ Aquinatis;* Gabriel Vasquez († 1604), *Commentt. et disputt. in Thom.* (Ingolst. 1606); Thos. Sanchez († 1630), *Opus Morale in præcepta Decalogi* (Mad. 1613); *Disputationes de legibus ac Deo legislatore in decem libros distributæ* (Lugd. 1613, et *Opp.* t. xi); *De Triplici virtute theologica, Fide, Spe et Caritate* (Aschaffenb. 1622; *Opp.* xii); *De Ultimo hominis Fine, voluntario et involuntario, humanorum actionum Bonitate et Malitia, Passionibus, Habitibus, Vitiis et Peccatis* (Mogunt. 1613; t. vi et

VI.—19

vii); Paul Laymann († 1635), *Theologia Moralis* (Monach. 1625); Vincence Filliatius († 1622), *Quæstiones morales de Christianis officiis et casibus conscientiæ ad formam cursus, qui prælegi solet in Societate Jesu Collegio Rom.* (Lugd. 1622 sq.); Leonhard Less († 1623), lib. iv, *De Justitia et Jure cæterisque virtutibus cardinalibus ad Secundam Secundæ Thomæ* (Lugd. 1630); Ferdinand de Castro Palao († 1633), *Opus Morale de Virtutibus et Vitiis* (Lugd. 1633 sq.); John de Lugo († 1660), *Disputt. de Sacramentis*, etc.

Pascal, and others with him, though not so ably as he, assailed the indefiniteness and ambiguity of casuistical principles as espoused by many of these Jesuitic moralists [see PROBABILISM]: as the adequate type of whom it should, however, be stated here that the *Medulla* of Hermann Busenbaum, which is the basis of the *Theologia Moralis* of Liguori, attained the highest reputation. Busenbaum's work is truly the embodiment of Jesuitical ethics. It appeared first in 1645 at Munster, and passed through fifty editions, enjoying a circulation like that of no other moral compend; and yet this was not the end, for its embodiment into the *Theologia Moralis* of Liguori gave it another lease of life, and thus the *Medulla* may be said to have enjoyed a two-hundred-years' rule. See, however, our article LIGUORI. The *Medulla* was also used and commented upon by Claude Lacroix and Francis Anth. Zacharia. Of like tendency are the writings of Taberna, Viva, Mazotta, Francolinus, and Edm. Voit. The casuistico-moral treatise of the last named is now, after Liguori's, the great favorite of Romanists, especially of Jesuits and Ultramontanes, and has in recent years been repeatedly published at Rome and Paris.

Among the writers of the Roman Catholic Church who have stood aloof in a great measure from the casuists, as well as the reformers led by Pascal, the first place in this period belongs to bishop Louis Abelly († 1691), whose *Medulla Theologica* has passed through several editions (last, Regensb. 1839). A favorite text-book for theological students, because of its brevity and clearness, is the *Examen theologiæ Morale*, by Marianus at Angelis. It has been exceeded in popularity only by Sobiech's *Compend. theologiæ Moralis,* and more recently by Liguori's *Homo Apostolicus.*

5. *Recent Period.*—Among those who in more recent days have led the Romanists on moral subjects, none deserve so high a place as Hirscher, whose *Christl. Moral* (Tüb. 1835, 3 vols. 8vo, and often) is really a work of more than ordinary merit. Perhaps equal merit is accorded to Sailer (*Christkatholische Moral*, Ratisbon, 1831), also a scholar and a clear thinker. These two men were liberal in sentiment, and accommodated themselves to the spirit of the age; but for this reason they are well known only in Germany and among the Gallican clergy of France. Everywhere else Liguori still holds sway. Ambrose Joseph Stapf may in many respects be counted a disciple of Sailer and Hirscher. His *Christliche Sittenlehre* was published at Innsbruck in 1850, edited by J. B. Hofmann. Other works of like tendency and worth are from the distinguished Roman Catholic theologians Filser, Martin, Propst, and especially Werner. Danzer, Mutschelle, and Schreiber may be pointed out as principal organs of a negative tendency. They are Pelagian in their interpretation of Christianity, and betray the modern rationalistic leaning in their moral systems. Among those who have closely allied themselves with the sceptical philosophic schools of our day the following are worthy of mention: Aug. Isenbiehl († 1800), *Tugendlehre nach Grundsätzen der reinen Vernunft u. des praktischen Christenthums* (Augsb. 1795); Jos. Geishüttner († 1805), *Theol. Moral in einer wissenschaftlichen Darstellung* (Augsb. 1805). The last named is a disciple of Fichte, and, together with Maurus Schenkl († 1816), who published *Ethica Christiana* (5th ed. Vienna, 1830), indicates a passing over to a more positive tendency. One of the more recent and noted works on the subject is Prof.

Paul Palasthy's *Theologia Morum Catholica* (1861, 4 vols.). Though the author is a Hungarian, the work has been brought out in Germany, and there enjoys a wide circulation, and is acknowledged superior to the German works (comp. *Literarischer Handweiser f. d. kath. Deutschland*, Sept. 18, 1867). It is based on the labors of Suarez, Billuart, Less, Laymann, and Leander. Another work of about the same date is Prof. F. Friedhoff's *Allgem. Moraltheologie* (Mayence, 1860). Later he wrote another work on the subject, entitled *Specielle Moraltheologie* (1865), but neither of them compares favorably with the Hungarian production. Of greater value even than Palasthy's work, and more recent in origin, is Prof. Simar's *Lehrb. d. kathol. Moraltheologie* (Bonn, 1867, 8vo), which is fast gaining ground in the theological schools of Germany. In his introduction he furnishes a valuable résumé of the history of Roman Catholic moral theology, which we have freely consulted in writing this article. See Wetzer u. Welte, *Kirchen-Lexikon*, vii, 294-308; Aschbach, *Kirchen-Lexikon*, s. v. Moral Theologie; *Dublin Rev.* Oct. 1853; *Brownson's Rev.* Jan. 1853; and for Protestant criticisms, Manning and Meyrick, *Moral Theology of the Church of Rome, or certain Points in S. Alfonso de Liguori's Moral Theology considered, in* 19 *Letters* (1855); *Presbyterian Quarterly*, April, 1873, p. 367; *North British Review*, July, 1870, p. 266; *Westminster Review*, Jan. 1873, p. 118 sq.; *Christian Remembrancer*, Jan., July, and Oct. 1854.

Morales, Ambrosio, a learned Spanish Dominican, the best authority on early Spanish history, was born at Cordova in 1513. His parents and relatives were people eminent in literary circles, and Ambrosio enjoyed all the advantages his country could afford him. One of his uncles, Fernan Perez de Oliva, who was a professor of philosophy and theology at Salamanca, took a prominent part in his education, and greatly influenced his tendency to theological study. He was also indebted to Juan de Medina and to Melchior Cano, two great writers and eloquent professors of divinity of that time, the former at Alcala, the latter at Salamanca, where he was the great antagonist of his eminent colleague Bartholomeo Carranza, and a still greater opponent of the Jesuits. This Cano, or Canus, is the author of the excellent treatise *De Locis Theologicis*, and was a great reformer of the schools, from which he banished many futile and absurd questions. While yet a youth Morales produced a translation of the *Pinax* or *Table of Cebes*. But religious enthusiasm arose far above all his literary aspirations, and pervaded all his actions. At the age of nineteen Morales became a Jeronymite, when, his religious fervor being no longer controllable, in order to secure himself against temptation, he attempted to follow the precedent of Origen. The excruciating pain inseparable from this self-mutilation drew from him a shriek which brought a brother monk to his cell in time to give him effectual relief. In order to obtain a papal dispensation for his conduct, he set out for Rome, but fell into the sea, and was saved, according to his own account, by a miracle. Considering this accident as a warning not to proceed, he joined his friends at court, and lived thenceforward as a secular priest. After the death of his father he became a professor at Alcala, where he had, among others, Guevara, Chacon, Sandoval, and the first Don Juan of Austria, among his pupils. He sustained the high literary credit of his family by his investigations into the antiquities of Spain. He also devoted himself to belles-lettres, and did much to cultivate among the Spanish of his day a taste for literature. His services were recognised at court, and he was made historiographer to Philip II, king of Spain. Morales died in 1590. He was the author of several works on the secular as well as religious history and antiquities of Spain; but his extreme credulity greatly deteriorates the value of his writings. See Bouterweck, *Hist. of Spanish Lit.* (see Index); Ticknor, *Hist. of Spanish Lit.* iii, 129.

Morales, Juan Bautista, a Spanish moralist, was born at Montella, Andalusia, and flourished in the first half of the 17th century. Scarcely anything is known of his personal history. He is, however, noted as the author of *Jardin de Suertes morales y civitas* (Seville, 1616, 16mo). See Antonio, *Bibliotheca Hispana nova*, s. v.

Morales, Luis de, a Spanish artist, noted for his paintings of sacred subjects, was born in Badajoz in 1509. Either from his constant choice of sacred subjects, or (less probably) from the merits of his works, he received the surname of *El Divino*, "the divine." His pictures were nearly all heads, generally of Christ or the Virgin; some authorities believe that there are no instances of his painting the figure at full length. His *Ecce Homo* and *Mater Dolorosa* are the best types of his paintings. In spite of his acknowledged ability, the prices he received for his works are said not to have been enough to compensate him for the great labor and time he spent upon them; and he lived in the greatest want until his old age, when he was supported by Philip II. His chief works are at Toledo, Valladolid, Burgos, and Granada. He died in Badajoz in 1586.

Moralities, a term used for the theatrical representations made by the monks in the Middle Ages, designed to exhibit virtue and vice, so as to make the former look desirable, the latter detestable. This word is classed with two others of similar meaning—*miracles* and *mysteries*. See MYSTERIES.

Morality is that relation which human actions bear to a given rule of rectitude. Says Whately, "To lay down in their universal form the laws according to which the conduct of a free agent ought to be regulated, and to apply them to the different situations of human life, is the end of *morality*" (*Lessons on Morals*). It is the opposite of legality, as that expresses only conformity with justice, while morality is applied to the *tendency in the mind or heart* towards harmonious action with the law. It is the doctrine, in short, which treats of actions as right or wrong. It does not cover so vast a field as religion, but is, nevertheless, the outgrowth of it. "Morality," it has been aptly said, "is a studious conformity of our actions to the relations in which we stand to each other in civil society. Morality comprehends only a part of religion; but religion comprehends the whole of morality. Morality finds all its motives here below; religion fetches all its motives from above The highest principle in social morals is a just regard to the rights of men; the first principle in religion is the love of God." While religion, then, covers the whole life both in its present and future relations, morality confines itself virtually to the temporal, or better civil life. "Morality," says Coleridge, "commences with and begins in the sacred distinction between thing and person. On this distinction all law, human and divine, is grounded" (*Aids to Reflection*, i, 265). "There are in the world," says Sewell, "two classes of objects, persons and things; and these are mutually related to each other. There are relations between persons and persons, and between things and things; and the peculiar distinctions of *moral* actions, *moral* characters, *moral* principles, *moral* habits, as contrasted with the intellect and other parts of man's nature, lies in this, *that they always imply a relation between two persons*, not between two things" (*Christian Morals*, p. 339). Now the Christian Church holds that so much of the glory of man's origin remains in him, that even when farthest from the light and grace of Christ's presence in the Church he retains some spark of that divine conscience which is derived from him—"the true light, which lighteth every man that cometh into the world" (John i, 9). "Morality," argues Culverwell aptly, "is founded in the divine nature. It is an eternal ordinance made in the depth of God's infinite wisdom and counsel for regulating and governing the whole world, which yet had not its binding virtue in respect of God himself, who has always the full and unrestrained liberty of his cwn essence that it cannot bind itself" (*Light of Nature*). Hence a knowledge of good and evil, some sense of responsibility to God, and some capacity for practical virtue, may be possessed even by persons not Christians; those of them at least who have not been brought within reach of the Church, with its revelation of truth and its sacraments of grace. Of such St. Paul speaks in Rom. ii, 14; or at least his words respecting the Gentiles who had not the Jewish "law" may be fairly interpreted as extending also to those who have not the Christian law. They may do by nature some of those duties which are extended and heightened by grace, and may thus be "not far from the kingdom of God." To what extent such natural morality now exists (after eighteen centuries of Christianity) it is impossible to say; probably to a very small extent. In his epistle to the Romans, St. Paul clearly distinguishes between that conformity with the letter of the law springing from a Christian heart, and that external conformity prompted simply by a desire to evade the odium or punishment of the transgressor. The latter the apostle does not recognise as true morality; the δικαιοσύνη νομική is in its simple legality, and for want of a real inwardness of a moral or better spiritual life, only an *apparent* morality. The ἔργα νόμου are not by any means the ἔργα ἀγαθά which the spirit of Christianity elicits; they want that life-giving spirit which is none other than the spirit of divine love, of the fullest, inmost, and truly unconditional surrender to God and his most holy purposes. The germ, the life or essence, of Christian morality is *love*, itself the principle of union in and with God, the fountain and original of all good. It is to Christian morality, then, that the highest standard and the noblest place must be assigned; indeed, it is Christian morality which must not only precede, but supersede, all other systems of morality. "What the duties of morality are," says Coleridge, "the apostle instructs the believer in full, comprising them under the two heads of negative and positive: negative, to keep himself pure from the world; and positive, beneficence from loving-kindness—that is, love of his fellow-men (his kind) as himself. Last and highest come the spiritual, comprising all the truths, acts, and duties that have an especial reference to the timeless, the permanent, the eternal, to the sincere love of the true as truth, of the good as good, and of God as both in one. It comprehends the whole ascent from uprightness (morality, virtue, inward rectitude) to godlikeness, with all the acts, exercises, and disciplines of mind, will, and affections that are requisite or conducive to the great design of our redemption from the form of the evil one, and of our second creation or birth in the divine image. It may be an additional aid to reflection to distinguish the three kinds severally, according to the faculty to which each corresponds, the part of our human nature which is more particularly its organ. Thus, the prudential corresponds to the sense and the understanding; the moral to the heart and the conscience; the spiritual to the will and the reason, that is, to the finite will reduced to harmony with and in subordination to the reason, as a ray from that true light which is both reason and will, universal reason and will absolute" (*Aids to Reflection*, i, 265, also 22, 23). On the near coincidence of this scriptural division with the Platonic, see Prudence. See Bishop Horsley's *Charge* (1790); Paley's and Grove's *Moral Philosophy;* Beattie's *Elements of Moral Science;* Evans's *Sermons on Christian Temper;* Watts's *Sermons on Christian Morals;* Mason's *Christian Morals;* More's *Hints*, ii, 245; Gisborne's *Sermons designed to illustrate and enforce Christian Morality;* Meysenburg, *De Christianæ religionis vi et effectu in jus civile* (Gott. 1828, 8vo); Hoffbauer, *Das allgem. oder Naturrecht u. die Moral* (Halle, 1816); Schleiermacher, *Grundlinien einer Kritik der bisherigen Sittenlehre* (Berl. 1813), p. 465; Brend, *Difference between the*

Morality of Jesus and that of the Jews; Ensor, *Principles of Morality;* Hildreth, *Theory of Morals;* Kames, *Principles of Morality;* Whewell, *Morality*, § 76; Maurice, *Lectures on Social Morality* (1873); Smith, *Characteristics of Christian Morality* (Bampton Lects. 1873); *Contemp. Rev.* April, 1872, art. vi and viii; March, 1872, art. v; *Westminster Rev.* April, 1871, p. 243, 260, 261; and literature in Malcom, *Theol. Index*, s. v.

Morals, a term usually employed to designate the aggregate of the moral principles of an individual or a community as evinced in its conduct in comparison with the acknowledged rules of morality. The various general relations of this subject are so fully discussed in the articles Ethics, Moral Law, etc., that we here bring together only some special distinctions under the head of *duty*, the fulfilment of which is the ultimate criterion of public and private morals.

Baumgarten defines duties to be actions which one is bound to perform, and Christian August Crusius coincides with this opinion when he defines duty as the application of the principles of morality to individual cases, and with Opitz, who calls it the inward knowledge of what one must do or abstain from doing in order to lead a religious life. Reinhard defines duty as the moral necessity of doing or not doing a certain thing, resulting from our perception of right (*System d. christl. Moral*, pt. ii, § 196). This is the view taken by many others, even by Roman Catholic moralists (see Riegler, *Christl. Moral*, pt. i, § 124 sq.). This, however, considers only the outward part of duty, as manifested in action; its scope was afterwards enlarged by connecting it with the conscience (see Moral Sense), which Crusius understands to be the inborn impulse by which we recognise the obligation of subjecting all our thoughts and actions to the will of God. Paley stands almost alone in making virtue consist in *utility*, and those who resolve it into "the fitness of things" do but indirectly refer it to the will of God, who has ordained the constitution of the universe. All our duties to God are comprised in the expression, *honor God* (Walch), or, *love God*. For to fear God and keep his commandments is the whole duty of man (Eccles. xii, 13). It was already presented as such in the O. T., but in the N. T. this is put in the first place, as the one important principle: unlimited love towards God, and to one's neighbor as the image of God, as well as of one's self (Matt. xxii, 37 –40; Rom. xiii, 8–10; Deut. vi, 4–9; Lev. xix, 14, 17, 18, etc.). As the Kantian philosophy, abandoning the cognition of a thing *per se*, placed the power of truth entirely in the consciousness of obligation (categorical imperative), duty, as that commanded by it, acquired in that system an extraordinary significance. Will nothing, and do nothing which it cannot be lawful for entire mankind to do; or, As ye would that men should do to you, do ye also to them likewise (Matt. vii, 12; Luke vi, 31). The total submission to the categoric imperative arising from pure regard for the law is the highest morality; while that arising from love, a sort of subjective satisfaction in it, is less pure, since the motive is akin to egotism. Thus morality resolved itself into the doctrine of law and duty, while previously it was considered as almost exclusively a question of good. Indeed, Paley made morality itself consist in seeking the highest good, a theory not far removed from the purer form of ancient Epicureanism. The modern philosophy, however, has justly repudiated this utilitarian text, and thrown the subject back for solution upon the deeper convictions of mankind as expressed in the instinctive discriminations of conscience. See also Moral Philosophy.

Morand, St., a Clugny monk, was born in Germany, and flourished in the 11th century. He was educated at Worms, and then went to Burgundy, in France, and joined the Congregation of Clugny. Falling in with Hugo of Samur, a severe ascetic, Morand was enlisted in behalf of monasticism, and he preached in its favor wherever he went. He roamed all over France and Switzerland, restoring as far as possible the former interest in monastic institutions, and creating new ones where they had never been. His austerity and piety secured for him a place in the list of saints; and it is claimed by Romanists that he worked many miracles. See *Vita S. Morandi* in *Biblioth. Cluniacensis*, col. 501; Montalembert, *Monks of the West*, vol. iii (see Index).

Morando, PAOLO, a Veronese painter, sometimes called Cavazzuola, was born in 1491. He died young, and consequently left but few works to perpetuate his name; these, however, are of a high order of merit. *Christ bearing his Cross*, now in the gallery of Verona, is attributed to him, and is one of the best compositions on the subject which can be found among the old painters. Mrs. Jameson says: "This conception is one of the few which realize the scriptural and historical picture to the mind. Simon is here in his suitable character, and no superadded incident diverts the eye from the chief figure." See Mrs. Jameson and Eastlake, *Hist. of Our Lord* (Lond. 1864, 2 vols. 8vo), ii, 113.

Morange, BEDION, a French theologian, was born at Paris about 1635, and was educated at the Sorbonne, where he received the doctorate. In 1660 he became canon of Lyons, and later vicar-general of that diocese. He died there in 1703. He wrote, *Libri de præadamitis brevis Analysis* (Lyons, 1656, 8vo): — *Primatus Lugdunensis Apologeticon* (1658, 8vo): — *Summa universæ Theologiæ Catechistæ* (1670, 4 vols. 8vo).

Morant, PHILIP, a British antiquary and divine, was born in the island of Jersey in 1700; was educated at Pembroke College, Oxford; then entered the sacred ministry, and became, first, rector of St. Mary's, Colchester, afterwards of Aldham, Essex. He died in 1778. Morant edited several works, and wrote a *History of Colchester* (Lond. 1748, fol.); also enlarged, and incorporated in a later work of his, *Hist. and Antiquities of the County of Essex* (1768, 2 vols.). He also wrote all the biographies marked with the letter C and the life of Stillingfleet in the *Biog. Brit.* (1st ed. 17 vols. fol.). See Allibone, *Dict. of Brit. and Amer. Authors*, ii, 1359.

Mo'rasthite (Heb. *Morashti'*, מוֹרַשְׁתִּי, gentile from *Moresheth;* Sept. Μωραϑίτης, Μωρασϑεί), a native of MORESHETH-GATH (Jer. xxvi, 18; Mic. i, 1). See MICAH.

Morata, Olympia Fulvia, an Italian lady of great genius and learning, noted for her piety and faithful service to Italian Protestantism, and spoken of by the biographer of the duchess Renée as "a woman whose history may be pondered in silent compassion, yet in silent admiration—a saint so tried in life, so blessed in death," was born at Ferrara in 1526. Her father, preceptor to the young princes of Ferrara, sons of Alphonso I, observing her genius, took great pains in cultivating it; and when Olympia was called to court for the purpose of instructing the princess Anna d'Este, daughter of the duchess of Ferrara, and of herself studying belles-lettres with the princess of Ferrara, under the tutelage of her father, she astonished the Italians by declaiming in Latin and Greek, explaining the paradoxes of Cicero, and answering any question that was put to her. The example of Renée de France, duchess of Ferrara, who was much interested in the religious controversies of the times, had a great influence upon Olympia's mind. Men like Jamet, Marot, Peter Martyr, Lælio Giraldi, and Celius Calcagnini were received at court, and formed a select circle. Calvin, who went in disguise from France to Italy to see her, brought her over to his opinions, and her court became the refuge of all those suspected of heresy. Peregrino Morata, Olympia's father, became himself converted, but Olympia showed little inclination as yet for a devout, religious life. Her whole mind was taken up with her own literary works and the court gayeties. "If Olympia," says Young, the biographer

of Palerio, "learned anything at court of true religion, she also found much to distract her attention. The extreme precocity of her talents had early called forth her reasoning and reflective powers, but she herself owns that at this time she did not duly relish the sacred Scriptures. They were to her a holy, but a sealed book; her intellect revelled with greater delight in the mazes of human learning and philosophy." She wrote several essays at this time, the best known of which is a eulogy on Mucius Scævola. But the year 1548 brought a decided change. Her friend, the princess Anna of Ferrara, married and went to Lorraine, and shortly afterwards her father died. His death, and the ill-health of her mother, withdrew her from court, and she devoted herself to household affairs, the education of three sisters and a brother, and especially to spiritual contemplation and devotion. In communing with her own heart she began to perceive her need, and from that moment resolved to live and die a follower of the Gospel. In this her hour of greatest happiness she made the acquaintance of a young German named Andrew Grunthler, who had studied medicine, and taken his doctor's degree at Ferrara. He was a Protestant, and the day when she was married to him (in 1549) she followed her father's example and embraced Protestantism. Her husband, unprepared to depart at once with his bride, advanced to Germany to prepare the way for her, and over a year elapsed before he was ready to return for her. Together with her little brother and her husband she now left for Germany. They went to Schweinfurt, in Franconia, which was soon after besieged and burned, and they barely escaped with their lives. They suffered many hardships in consequence, until Grunthler in 1554 received a call to Heidelberg as professor of medicine. Now at last it was hoped that better days had come for poor Olympia, but the fearful hardships she had suffered during the siege of Schweinfurt had undermined her health. In December, 1554, she was taken sick, and never left her bed again. She died Oct. 26, 1555. A few months later her husband and brother died also. Several of her works were burned at Schweinfurt, but the remainder were collected and published at Basle in 1558 by Cœlius Secundus Curio. They consist of orations, dialogues, letters, and translations, and are known as *Olympiæ Fulviæ Moratæ, mulieris omnium eruditissimæ Latina et Græca, quæ haberi potuerunt, monumenta* (Basle, 1558). They are distinguished for a deep religious conviction and great refinement of language and thought. See Bonnet, *Vie d'Olympie Morata* (Paris, 1850; in English, *Life of O. Morata, with a Historical Sketch of the Ref. in Italy* [Edinb. 1854, 18mo]); Turnbull, *O. Morata, her Life and Times* (Bost. 1846, 12mo); Mrs. Smith, *Life, Times, and Writings of O. Morata; Some Memorials of Renée of France, Duchess of Ferrara* (2d ed. Lond. 1859, 12mo), p. 62 sq.; Trollope, *Decade of Italian Women*, vol. ii; Colquhoun, *Life in Italy and France in the Olden Time;* Young, *Life and Times of Palerio*, ii, 90 sq.; M'Crie, *Hist. of the Ref. in Italy*, p. 54: *Littell's Living Age*, March 13, 1852, p. 510. (J. H. W.)

Morata, Peregrino Fulvio, an Italian writer, noted as the father of the foregoing, and also for his defence of the Reformatory movement, which made him a Protestant, was born at Mantua near the close of the 15th century. During the early half of the 16th century he was professor of belles-lettres at the university of his native place, and later at Ferrara, whither the fame of his learning and virtue had brought him. He now taught not only in the high schools, but was also employed by duke Alphonso d'Este as preceptor of his two sons. He frequently appeared in the receptions at court, but he remained nevertheless an alien to the gayeties of its surroundings, and devoted himself largely to sacred meditations, in which he was assisted by his pious wife, Lucrezia. As a result of these studies, he brought out finally an exposition of the Lord's Prayer in 1526 (*Expozitione dell' orazione Dominicale della*

"Pater Noster"), and shortly after he published a book taking ground favorable to the Reformed opinions (see Calcagnini, *Opera*, p. 156). He was on this account obliged to leave Ferrara in 1533, and only after a six-years' stay abroad secured permission to return. He died in 1548. See Young, *Life of Paleario*, ii, 96 sq.; Bonnet, *Life of Olympia Morata*, p. 69 sq.

Moravia (German *Mähren*, Slavic *Morawa*), a margraviate of the Austrian empire, especially interesting as being the chief seat of the Church of the United Brethren.

General Description.—Moravia, situated in 48° 40'–50° N. lat., and 15° 10'–18° 28' E. long., is bounded N. by Prussian and Austrian Silesia, E. by Hungary and Galicia, S. by the duchy of Austria, and W. by Bohemia, and contains in superficial area about 8555 square miles, with a population in 1882 of 1,997,897, divided about as follows: 450,000 are Germans, upwards of a million and a quarter Slavonians, and 50,000 belonging to other nations. The Slavonians of Moravia are composed of Zechs and Poles, the former of whom are inferior to their brethren in Bohemia, being an incorrigibly lazy, dirty people. The Moravian Poles, although less industrious and cultivated than the Germans, are a physically well-developed, courageous, and enterprising people. Moravia is a very mountainous country, and except in the south, where are extensive plains, the level above the sea is about 800 feet. Not more than half of the territory is arable. The more elevated parts are not fertile, and the climate is severe; but in the mountain valleys and on the southern plains the soil is remarkably rich, and the temperature more genial than in other European countries lying in the same parallel. Moravia produces largely for export fine crops of grain, also hops, mustard, potatoes, clover-seed, beet-root; and in the south, maize, grapes, chestnuts, and many other of the less hardy fruits and vegetables. The breeding of cattle and sheep, and the making of cheese from sheep's milk, constitute an important branch of industry; in the southern districts of the Hanna (a plain famous for its fertility), horses are bred for exportation. Geese and fowls are reared in large numbers for the sake of their feathers, and the keeping of bees is conducted with great success. The mineral products, which include gold, silver, iron, alum, saltpetre, coal, graphite, whetstones, sulphur, vitriol, pipe-clay, marble, topazes, garnets, and other precious stones, have not been made as available as they might have been. Some of the mines have been known since the 8th century. No gold or silver has been extracted since the 16th century, and the iron and coal mines are but little worked. The principal branches of industry are the manufacture of linen and thread, which now enjoy a European reputation, and leather goods, cotton, flannels and other woollen fabrics. Brünn, the capital, is the chief emporium for the manufacturing trade, and Olmütz the principal cattle-mart.

Religion and Education.—Christianity was introduced among the Slavic nations as early as the reign of Charlemagne [see SLAVES], but the conversions then made were only transitory. In 863 the Holy Scriptures, the preaching of the Gospel, and the service of the Christian religion as then practiced, were introduced to the *Moravians* in the Slavonic tongue by the Greek monks Cyrillus (Constantine) and Methodius, who became connected with Rome, but did not relinquish their peculiar Greek forms of worship. Methodius was consecrated at Rome archbishop of Moravia, and the Slavish forms of worship received the papal sanction (880), on the ground that God understood all languages, and should be worshipped by all nations. The efforts, however, to erect a distinct national Church met with continual opposition on the part of the German bishops, and finally, in 908, the Moravian kingdom was divided by the swords of the Hungarians and Bohemians. The Slavish ritual was kept up under these new rulers in only a few churches, and gradually the Romish practices were here

the same as elsewhere (comp. Dobrowsky, *Cyrill u. Methodius, der Slaven Apostel* [Prague, 1823]). The Reformation made some inroads into the country, but as conformity to the Romish worship was enforced by law, many of the people holding the doctrine of the Reformation had to meet secretly for worship, and as opportunity offered fled into the Protestant states of Germany. This was especially the case with the *Moravian Brethren* (q. v.). The bulk of Moravians remain Romanists to this day, the Protestants only counting about 57,000, among whom the Lutherans and Reformed, who are the most numerous, have each a superintendent appointed by the state. There are also about 30,000 Jews, who, since 1848, have been freed from all oppressive obligations and restrictions. The Romanists have an archbishop, who resides at Olmütz, and a bishop, whose episcopal head-quarters are at Brünn. Both of these ecclesiastics are admitted to the provincial diet as members. The educational advantages of the country are exceptionally good. Until recently there was a university at Olmütz. There are now twelve Catholic gymnasia, besides numerous parish schools, and about ninety-nine per cent. of the children of proper age attend school.

History.—Moravia was anciently occupied by the Quadi, who, on their migration in the 5th century to Gaul and Spain, were replaced first by the Rugii, next by the Heruli and Longobardi, and finally by a colony of Slavonians, who, on their settlement in the country, took the name of Moravians, from the river Morava. Charlemagne, who brought the people under nominal subjection after they had spread themselves over a territory greater than the present Moravia, constrained their king, Samoslav, to receive baptism. Moravia was made tributary to the German empire before the close of the century; but in 1029 it was incorporated with Bohemia, after having for a time been a prey to the incursive attacks of its Slavonic and Teutonic neighbors. At the close of the 12th century, Moravia was erected into a margraviate, and declared a fief of Bohemia, to be held from the crown by the younger branches of the royal house. On the death of Lewis II, at the battle of Mohacz, in 1526, Moravia, with all the other Bohemian lands, fell to Austria, in accordance with a pre-existing compact of succession between the royal houses. Since then it has shared the fortunes of the empire, and in 1849 was formally separated from Bohemia, and declared a distinct province and crown-land. See Dudik, *Mähren's allgem. Gesch.* (Brin, 1860–65, 4 vols. 8vo); Pilaret Morawitz, *Moravian. Hist. Eccles. et Pol.* (Brin, 1785 sq. 3 vols. 8vo).

Moravian Brethren, the designation of a body of Christians, will be considered under two heads.

1. THE ANCIENT MORAVIAN BRETHREN, or, more properly, "THE BOHEMIAN BRETHREN," an evangelical Church which flourished before the Reformation of the 16th century, and which was overthrown in the beginning of the Thirty-Years' War of Germany.

I. *History.*—John Huss (q. v.) was the precursor of the Brethren. They originated in that national Church of Bohemia into which the two factions of his followers, the Calixtines and the Taborites, were formed at the close of the Hussite War, and which was based upon the *Compactata of Basle.* These compactata were certain concessions, particularly the use of the cup in the Lord's Supper and of the vernacular in public worship, granted (1433) to the Bohemians by the council which met in that city. In 1456, some members of the Theyn parish at Prague, who recognised the corruptness of the national Church, and wished to further their own personal salvation, withdrew to a devastated and sparsely inhabited estate, called Lititz, on the eastern frontier, by permission of George Podiebrad, the regent of Bohemia, and through the intervention of John Rokyzan, their priest. He had eloquently inveighed against the degeneracy of the age, but lacked courage to inaugurate reforms such as these parishioners longed for, although they entreated him to do so, and promised their support even to death. Their object in retiring to Lititz was not to found a new sect, but to carry out, on the basis of the Articles of Prague, and of the Compactata of Basle, the reformation begun by Huss, confining their work, however, to their own circle, and forming a society within the national Church, pledged to accept the Bible as the only rule of faith and practice, and to maintain a scriptural discipline. Accordingly, in 1457, they adopted a formal declaration of principles, which was committed to the keeping and administration of twenty-eight elders. The association took the name of the "Brethren and Sisters of the Law of Christ." But as this title induced the belief that they were a new monastic order, it was changed into that of "The Brethren." At a later time the expressive name of "Unity of the Brethren" came into vogue, and was used indiscriminately both in its Bohemian and Latin forms, namely, *Jednota Bratrska*, and *Unitas Fratrum*. The latter has remained the official denomination of the Moravians to the present day. At the head of the Brethren stood Gregory the Patriarch (q. v.); while Michael Bradacius (q. v.), and some other priests of the national Church, ministered to them in holy things. The association at Lititz soon began to exercise a great influence throughout Bohemia and Moravia. Its elders disseminated its principles, and received hundreds of awakened souls into its fellowship. The first persecution, which broke out in 1461, did not stop its growth; and in 1464, at a synod held in the open air, among the mountains of the domain of Reichenau, three of the twenty-eight elders were chosen to assume a more special management of its affairs. In the discharge of this duty they were guided by a document drawn up at that synod, and containing the doctrinal basis of the society; as well as rules for a holy life. This document, which is the oldest record of the Brethren extant, opens as follows: "We are, above all, agreed to continue, through grace, sound in the faith of our Lord Jesus Christ; to be established in the righteousness which is of God, to maintain the bond of love among each other, and to have our hope in the living God. We will show this both in word and deed, assist each other in the spirit of love, live honestly, study to be humble, quiet, meek, sober, and patient, and thus to testify to others that we have in truth a sound faith, genuine love, and a sure and certain hope." This extract sets forth the tendency of the Brethren, to which they remained true throughout their history. The great object which they had in view was Christian life. They strove to be a body of believers who showed their faith by their works. They tenaciously upheld a scriptural discipline as an essential feature of a true Church. Although, in the course of time, they defined their doctrines in regular Confessions of Faith, they always made practical Christianity prominent, and required personal piety, and not merely an adhesion to a creed, as a condition of Church-membership. The Synod of Reichenau not only gave expression to this tendency, but also decided a grave question. The Brethren felt the necessity of separating entirely from the national Church, and of establishing a ministry of their own. Yet they were so anxious to avoid a schism, and to do nothing contrary to the will of God, that they spent several years in debating this step, and, in view of it, frequently appointed special days of fasting and prayer. The result to which they were led was to leave the decision to the Lord, by the use of the lot. This directed the Brethren to organize a Church of their own. Three years more were passed in praying to God for his Holy Spirit; and then in 1467, at a synod held in the village of Lhota, on the domain of Reichenau, three men, Matthias of Kunwalde, Thomas of Prelouc, and Elias of Chrenovic, were appointed to the ministry, again by the lot. For the particulars, see MATTHIAS OF KUNWALDE. Thereupon the subject of their ordination was discussed. The synod believed that presbyterial

ordination had been practiced in the times of the apostles, but recognised the episcopacy as a very ancient institution. It was deemed important, moreover, to secure a ministry whose validity both the Roman Catholics and the national Church would have to acknowledge. On the other hand, a primitive usage must not thereby be condemned. It was therefore determined to remain true both to the practice of the apostolical Church and to that of the Church immediately following the days of the apostles. Hence the nominees were ordained, on the spot, by the priests present at the synod; and then three of the latter, Michael Bradacius and two others, were sent to a colony of Waldenses, who were living on the confines of Austria, and who had secured the episcopal succession. For a history of this succession, see MICHAEL BRADACIUS. The Waldensian bishops consecrated the three delegates to the episcopacy, who "returned to their own with joy," as the old record says. Another synod was called, at which they, first of all, reordained Matthias, Thomas, and Elias to the priesthood, and then consecrated Matthias a bishop. A well-matured ecclesiastical government was instituted, and the Church soon spread into every part of Bohemia and Moravia. But it had to contend with two evils. The one threatened it from within. This was an extravagant tendency to press the discipline to anti-scriptural extremes. It occasioned disputes which continued for fourteen years, from 1480 to 1494, and which were finally settled in the interests of the liberal party. For an account of these disputes, as well as of the exploratory journeys of the Brethren, see GREGORY, LUKE OF PRAGUE, and MATTHIAS OF KUNWALDE. The other evil approached from without. Two terrible persecutions occurred (1468 and 1508). The Roman Catholics and the national Church united in a bloody determination to root out the Brethren from the land. Imprisonment, confiscation, tortures, and death were the means employed. Many of the Brethren suffered martyrdom. But their blood was the seed of the Church. In both instances the persecution gradually came to an end; and the Unitas Fratrum renewed its strength and increased its numbers. A full history of these and subsequent persecutions is found in the *Historia Persecutionum Ecclesiæ Bohemicæ*, published anonymously in 1648. This work was written by Amos Comenius (q. v.) and other exiled ministers of the Brethren, and has been translated into many languages. The English version is very rare. It came out in London in 1650, and was entitled "The History of the Bohemian Persecution." The latest German version is by Czerwenka, with notes: *Das Persekutionsbüchlein*. (Gütersloh, 1869).

When Martin Luther began his Reformation, in 1517, the Church of the Brethren was prospering greatly. It counted 400 parishes; had at least 200,000 members, among whom were some of the noblest and most influential families of the realm; used a hymn-book and catechism of its own; had a Confession of Faith; and employed two printing-presses, in order to scatter Bohemian Bibles and evangelical books throughout the land. Hence the Brethren deservedly bear the name of the "Reformers before the Reformation." This position, however, did not prevent them from cordially fraternizing with the movement which Luther inaugurated. They corresponded with him, and sent several deputations to Wittenberg. It is true a personal estrangement between him and bishop Luke of Prague (q. v.) put an end for a time to this friendly intercourse; but it was soon resumed, and extended to the Swiss Reformers. Such fellowship was mutually beneficial. It purified the doctrinal system of the Brethren, who dropped some dogmas that still savored of scholasticism, and defined others more clearly. It gave the Reformers new ideas with regard to a scriptural discipline, and taught them the importance of union among themselves. These were the two points which the Brethren steadfastly urged in all their negotiations with other Protestants. Touching the first, they entreated Luther to apply himself to a reform of Christian life, and not merely of doctrine; and they gave to Calvin some important principles, which he subsequently introduced in his disciplinary system at Geneva. On the occasion of the last deputation to Luther, bishop Augusta warned him, almost like a prophet, of the evil which would result in the Protestant Church if the discipline were neglected. This prediction was fulfilled by the dead orthodoxy into which the Church was subsequently petrified in Germany, and by the Socinianism which ate out the vitals of that in Poland. Touching the second point, the Brethren were a standing protest against the controversies which rent Protestantism; they strove to promote peace, and succeeded in bringing about an alliance among the Polish Protestants at Sandomir, where in 1570 the Unitas Fratrum, the Lutherans, and the Reformed conjointly issued the celebrated *Consensus Sandomiriensis*. The Brethren had established themselves in Poland in 1549, in consequence of the fourth great persecution which broke upon them in the reign of Ferdinand I, who falsely ascribed the Bohemian League, which had been formed against him during the Smalcald War, to their influence. In the course of this persecution a large number of them were banished from Bohemia and emigrated to East Prussia. Thence came George Israel to preach the Gospel in Poland, and met with such success that at the General Synod of Slecza, held in 1557, the Polish churches were admitted as an integral part of the Unitas Fratrum. During the reign of Maximilian II (1564–1576) the Brethren enjoyed peace, and united with the Lutherans and Reformed in the presentation of the *Confessio Bohemica* to this monarch (1575). His successor, Rudolph II, was constrained by his barons to grant a charter which established religious liberty in Bohemia and Moravia (1609). An Evangelical Consistory was formed at Prague, in which body the Brethren were represented by one of their bishops. They were now a legally acknowledged Church. But the Bohemian revolution in 1619, caused by the accession of Ferdinand II, a bigoted Romanist, to the throne, brought about a change in the religious affairs of the kingdom. The Protestants and their rival king, Frederick of the Palatinate, were totally defeated at the battle of the White Mountain, near Prague, in 1620; the Bohemian revolution developed into a European war of thirty terrible years; and Bohemia and Moravia fell wholly into the power of the Roman Catholic Church. In 1621, Ferdinand II began the so-called "anti-Reformation" in those countries, after having executed a number of the leading Protestant nobles. Commissioners, accompanied by Jesuits and soldiers, were sent from place to place to force the inhabitants to embrace Romanism. Many were put to death; more than 30,000 families emigrated; the rest were driven into an outward subjection to the Catholic faith. The Unitas Fratrum, as well as the Lutheran and Reformed churches, were swept from the kingdom (1627). But the Brethren reappeared as a Church in exile. The contingent which they furnished to the emigration was, in proportion to the whole number of members in each body, three or four times larger than that either of the Lutherans or of the Reformed. About one hundred new parishes were organized, chiefly in Prussia, Hungary, and Poland; and the executive council which governed the Church was set up at Lissa, in the country last named. The hope of returning to Bohemia and Moravia at the close of the Thirty-Years' War was generally entertained by the Brethren; but the Peace of Westphalia (1648) painfully undeceived them. Their native land was excluded from the benefits of religious liberty. Eight years later, the colony which had been gathered at Lissa was broken up (1656) in the war between Poland and Sweden. The members of the council scattered; the Polish parishes united with the Reformed Church; while some sort of a superintendence over the rest was kept up by bishop Amos Comenius (q. v.), who had found an asylum at Amsterdam. This eminent

divine hoped and prayed for the resuscitation of the Unitas Fratrum. To this end he published its history and a new catechism, republished the *Ratio Disciplinæ*, which had been adopted in 1616, and which was an official account of its constitution and discipline, and cared for the perpetuation of the episcopacy. After his death, in 1670, the scattered parishes of the Brethren were gradually absorbed by other Protestant churches. But the episcopal succession was maintained in the midst of that union between the Reformed and the Brethren which had been brought about in Poland; while in Bohemia and Moravia a remnant secretly worshipped God according to the custom of their fathers, and never relinquished the hope of a renewal of their Church. This state of affairs continued for half a century; and then their expectations were fulfilled. See MORAVIAN BRETHREN, THE RENEWED (No. 2 below).

II. *Ministry, Constitution, Worship, Ritual, and Discipline.*—The ministry of the Brethren consisted of three orders: bishops, priests, and deacons. In the course of time assistant bishops were associated with the bishops. These latter were often called *Seniors*, also *Antistites;* and the assistants *Conseniors*. Acolytes were young men preparing for the ministry, who performed certain inferior functions in connection with public worship, but were not ordained. The deacons instructed the young, occasionally preached, baptized, when directed to do so by a priest, and assisted at but never administered the Lord's Supper. A priest stood at the head of each parish, and exercised all the duties usually connected with the priesthood. In the bishops was vested the power to ordain, to appoint pastors to the various parishes, to hold visitations, to superintend the printing-offices, and in general to oversee the Church. Each bishop had a diocese of his own, but all of them together—their number varying from four to six—were associated with from six to eight assistant bishops as a council. Of this council the primate among the bishops was president. He enjoyed certain prerogatives, but could undertake nothing of importance without consulting his colleagues. Another of the bishops was secretary of the council. It was his duty to care for the records of the Church, and to examine and answer, if necessary, the publications which appeared against it. Bishops and assistant bishops were elected by the ministers, and the council was responsible to the General Synod, which met every three or four years. In this synod all the bishops, assistant bishops, and priests of the Bohemian, Moravian, and Polish provinces, into which the Unitas Fratrum was gradually divided, had seats. The deacons and acolytes, as also lay patrons of the churches, likewise attended, but without a vote. The bishops and their assistants constituted the upper house, and the priests the lower. Each house met by itself. Diocesan synods were held in order to legislate for a particular diocese, but their acts were reported to the council, and by it to the General Synod. Owing to the frequent persecutions that occurred, and to the idea that the cares of a family would interfere with the usefulness of the ministers, they were, for the most part, unmarried. There was no law enjoining celibacy; it was a usage, which gradually fell into desuetude. Towards the end of the 16th century an unmarried priest or bishop was the exception.

The membership of a parish was divided into *beginners*, that is, children and new converts from Romanism; *proficients*, or full members; and *perfect*, or such as were "so established in faith, love, and hope as to be able to enlighten others." From this last class were elected the *civil elders*, who constituted the advisers of the priest in spiritual things; the *ædiles*, who managed the external affairs of a parish; and the *almoners*, who administered the poor fund. Turning to worship and ritual, we find that four regular services were held every Sunday; the second one in the morning being "the great service," when a sermon on the Gospels was delivered. In the early service the prophets, and in the afternoon service the apostolic writings, were explained; while the evening was devoted to the reading of the Bible in order, with instructive remarks. Throughout the summer, the young were taught the Catechism at noon. The Holy Communion was celebrated four times a year, but could be held more frequently. Confirmation took place generally at the time of the bishop's annual visitation. The principal festivals of the ecclesiastical year were observed, and special days for fasting and prayer appointed. There were three degrees of discipline. Private admonition and reproof constituted the first, public reproof and suspension from the Lord's Supper the second, and total exclusion from the Church the third. The official account of the constitution and discipline of the Brethren opens with the following general principles: "There are in Christianity some things *essential* (essentialia), some things *auxiliary* (ministerialia), and some things *accidental* (accidentalia). Essentials are those in which the salvation of man is immediately placed," i. e. cardinal doctrines; "auxiliaries are means of grace, the Word, the keys, and the sacraments; accidentals are the ceremonies and external rites of religion." For a more thorough study of this subject, consult Lasitii *Historiæ de Origine et Rebus Gestis Fratrum Bohemicorum, Liber Veterus*, edited by Comenius in 1649, and containing a full description of the constitution and discipline—a very rare work; J. A. Comenii *Ecclesiæ Fratrum Bohemorum Episcopi, Historia Fratrum Bohemorum, eorum Ordo et Disciplina Ecclesiastica* (republished at Halle in 1702, by Buddæus); Köppen, *Kirchenordnung u. Disciplin der Hussit. B. Kirche in B. u. M.* (Leipsic, 1845); Seifferth, *Church Constitution of the Boh. and Morav. Brethren, the original Latin, with a Translation and Notes* (Lond 1866).

III. *Schools and Literary Activity.*—The Brethren devoted themselves to education. Their earliest schools were found in the parsonages of the priests. Many of these, instead of families, had classes of young acolytes living with them, whom they trained for the ministry. Next were instituted parochial schools, in which a thorough elementary education was given, including Latin, and which were frequented by large numbers of pupils not connected with the Church. In 1574 a classical school or college, with professor Esrom Rüdinger, from Wittenberg, as its rector, was founded at Eibenschütz, in Moravia; soon after another at Meseritsch, in the same country; and in 1585 a third at Lissa, in Poland. Of this last Amos Comenius subsequently became the rector. These colleges were attended by many young nobles, not excepting such as were of the Catholic faith. In 1585 three theological seminaries were opened at Jungbunzlau, in Bohemia, and at Prerau and Eibenschütz, in Moravia. The training of acolytes in the parsonages was, however, not given up.

By the side of such efforts to promote education may well be put the literary activity of the Brethren. This was extraordinary, far surpassing that of the national and Roman Catholic churches, and competing even with that of the Reformers. The Unitas Fratrum had four publication offices: three in Bohemia, the first established in 1500, and one in Poland. From these offices, and from several public presses, which were often used, came forth a multitude of publications in Bohemian, Polish, German, and Latin, comprising the Holy Scriptures, hymn-books and catechisms, confessions of faith, exegetical and doctrinal works, books and tracts of a devotional character, polemical writings, and in the time of Comenius school-books, didactic works, and philosophical treatises. In addition to this prolific author, whose works numbered over ninety, the principal writers were Luke of Prague (eighty works), Augusta, Blahoslav (twenty-two works, among them a Bohemian Grammar, still in use), Lorenz, Æneas, Turnovius, Ephraim, Aristo, Rybinski, etc. Their Latin diction was often rough, but their Bohemian style pure, elegant, and forcible. In this respect they reached a standard which has never been surpassed. Excepting the writings of Comenius, the literature of

the Brethren was mostly lost in the anti-Reformation, when evangelical books of every kind were committed to the flames. The most important of those works which have been preserved are the Kraliz Bible (q. v.), the catechisms, the confessions of faith, and the hymnbooks. The first Catechism in Bohemian appeared in 1505; the second, in Bohemian and German, in 1522 republished by Zezschwitz in 1863, translated into English by Schweinitz in 1869; the third, in German, by J. Gyrck, in 1554 and 1555; the fourth, the "Greater Catechism," in Latin, in 1616; the fifth, the "Shorter Catechism," in German and Polish; and the sixth, the Catechism of Comenius, in German, in 1611. Several others are mentioned, of which, however, little is known, except that one of them was a tetraglot—in Greek, Latin, Bohemian, and German—published in 1615. There were twelve different confessions of faith, in Bohemian, German, Latin, and Polish. Gindely counts up thirty-four, but of these the majority were merely new editions of the same Confession. The most important are, the Confession of 1533, printed in German at Wittenberg, preface by Luther, presented to the margrave of Brandenburg—very rare, a copy in the Bohemian Museum at Prague; the Confession of 1535, in Latin, with a historical introduction, presented by a deputation of bishops and nobles to Ferdinand II at Vienna, found in Niemeyer's *Collectio*, p. 771-818, published in a revised form at Wittenberg in 1538, together with a Latin version of the Confession of 1533, both in one volume, under the supervision of Luther, who supplied the work with a preface, found in Lydii *Waldensia*, ii, 344, etc.; and the Confession of 1573, in Latin and German, based upon all the previous confessions, giving the matured doctrines of the Church, embracing a historical proœmium by Rüdinger, and printed at Wittenberg, under the direction of the theological faculty of the university, the Latin Confession found in Lydii *Waldensia*, iii, 95–256, and the German in Köcher, p. 161–256. The hymnology of the Brethren was one of the chief means which they used for spreading the Gospel and promoting spirituality. They gave to the national fondness for song a sacred direction. Their hymns were doctrinal; the German versification was hard, the Bohemian soft and smooth; the tunes, which were printed out in the hymn-books, were in part the old Gregorian, in part borrowed from the German, and in part popular melodies adapted. In spite of their roughness, the German hymns, whose simplicity and devotion, fervor and loving spirit, Herder highly commends, found favor in the churches of the Reformation, while the Bohemian expressed, says Chlumecky, "the deep religious feelings of the people, and were a blossom of the national life, showing forth the Slavonic ideal of a sanctified mind." The first Bohemian Hymn-book appeared in 1504; the second, which was the masterpiece of the Brethren's hymnology, containing 743 hymns, in 1661. This latter passed through a number of editions. The first German Hymn-book was published in 1531; the second in 1543; the third and best in 1566. This was dedicated to Maximilian II, contained 411 hymns, and was frequently republished. Polish hymn-books came out in 1554 and 1569.

IV. *Doctrines.* — For an exposition of the cardinal views of the Christian faith, as taught by the Brethren, the reader is referred to the works cited below. These doctrines agreed, in the main, with those of the Reformers. Gindely (R. C.), Zezschwitz (Luth.), and some other writers, try to show that the Unitas Fratrum did not hold to justification by faith. Gindely asserts that its stand-point in this respect was altogether Romish; but this is disproved by the standards, although some of the private and polemical writings of Luke of Prague produce such an impression. In order to promote holy living, the Brethren strongly insisted on good works; but they taught that men are saved by faith, which they never understood in the Romish sense, and they utterly rejected an *opus operatum*. In their earlier confessions and catechisms, following Huss, they distinguished between *credere de Deo, credere Deo*, and *credere in Deum*. The first is faith in God's existence; the second faith in his revelation through his Word; the third that faith by which a man appropriates to himself God's grace in Christ, and consecrates himself to Christ's service. Prior to the Reformation, the Brethren accepted the seven sacraments of the Roman Catholic Church; after that, about 1530, they repudiated all but baptism and the Lord's Supper. Up to that time, moreover, their views of baptism were peculiar. They rebaptized converts from the Roman Catholic and national churches, because they deemed both to be idolatrous; and they extended this practice to the young, because they considered personal faith an essential condition of the baptismal covenant. But they did not on this account reject infant baptism. Children were baptized soon after their birth, and thus dedicated to God; then they were rebaptized, after a thorough course of instruction in the Catechism, when old enough to exercise personal faith, and thus brought into full communion with the Church. This practice, however, was relinquished by a formal act of the General Synod of 1534, and confirmation substituted in the place of rebaptism. Touching the Lord's Supper, the Brethren taught that it is to be received in faith, to be defined in the language of Scripture, and every human explanation of that language to be avoided, except in so far that the spiritual, and not the real, presence is to be held. To this view they remained faithful, and were consequently often misunderstood both by the Catholics and the Utraquists on the one part, and by the Lutherans and the Reformed on the other. The great aim of the Brethren was to discountenance speculations and controversies with regard to this point. Finally, from the earliest times, they rejected purgatory, the adoration of the saints, and the worship of the Virgin Mary. For a further investigation of their doctrinal system, the following works are specially important: Balthasar Lydii *Waldensia* (tom. i, Rotterdam, 1616; tom. ii, Dordrecht, 1617), containing a number of their confessions; Köcher, *Glaubensbekenntnisse der Böhm. Brüder* (Frankfort and Leipsic, 1741); Ehwalt, *Alte u. neue Lehre der Böhm. Brüder* (Dantzic, 1756); Köcher, *Katechetische Geschichte* (Jena, 1768); Niemeyer, *Collectio Confessionum in ecclesiis reformatis publicatarum* (Leipsic, 1840); Gindely, *Ueber die dogmat. Ansichten d. Böhm. Brüder*, in the 13th vol. of the *Transactions of the Akademie der Wissenschaften* (Vienna, 1854, from the Roman Catholic stand-point); Zezschwitz, *Katechismen d. Waldenser u. Böhm. Brüder* (Erlangen, 1863, from the ultra-Lutheran stand-point); *The Catechism of the Boh. Brethren*, translated from the old German by E. de Schweinitz (Bethlehem, 1869); *Die Lehrweise d. Böhm. Brüder*, by Dr. Plitt, in the *Theol. Stud. u. Krit.* of 1868.

V. *Literature.*—Until comparatively recent times the only sources of the history of the Bohemian Brethren were the following: *A History in Latin, in Eight Books*, by J. Lasitius, a Pole, written in 1560-70, but never published—two MSS. extant, at Herrnhut and Göttingen; *Historica Narratio de Fratrum Orthodoxorum ecclesiis in Bohemia, Moravia, et Polonia*, written between 1570 and 1574, by Joachim Camerarius, published, after his death, at Heidelberg, 1605; Regenvolscii (Adrian Wengersky) *Systema historico-chronologicum ecclesiarum Slavonicarum* (Utrecht, 1652; Amsterd. 1679); J. A. Comenii *Ratio Disciplinæ*, etc. (Lissa, 1632; Amsterdam, 1660; Halle, 1702). On these sources were based, Cranz, *Ancient Hist. of the Brethren* (Lond. 1780); *Gedenktage d. alten Brüderkirche* (Gnadau, 1821); Holmes, *Hist. of the Prot. Church of the U. B.* (London, 1825, 2 vols.); Rieger, *Die alten u. neuen Böhm. Brüder* (St. Züllich, 1734); Lochner, *Entstehung, etc., d. Brüdergemeine in Böhmen u. Mähren* (Nürnb. 1832); Carpzov, *Religions-Untersuchung d. Böhm. Brüder* (Leipsic, 1742; a bitter enemy of the Brethren); Bost, *Hist. of the Boh. and Morav. Brethren* (Lond. 1848). In 1842 a Moravian clergyman

discovered, in one of the churches at Lissa, thirteen folio volumes of MSS., which proved to be the long-lost archives of the Bohemian Brethren, and which were purchased by the Moravian Church, and removed to Herrnhut. They are known and cited as the *Lissa Folios*. The 14th volume was subsequently discovered at Prague. About the same time other original records were found: Jaffet's Hist. MSS. in the library at Herrnhut, Blahoslaw's MSS. at Prague, etc. These various documents have thrown an entirely new light upon the history of the Bohemian Brethren, and have been used particularly by Professor A. Gindely, a Roman Catholic, who has produced: *Geschichte der Böhmischen Brüder* (Prague, 1857, 2 vols.); *Quellen zur Geschichte d. B. B.* (Vienna, 1859; very important, containing many of the documents of the Lissa Folios); *Dekreten d. Brüder Unität* (Prague, 1865, being the enactments of the General Synod, in the original Bohemian); *Rudolph II u. seine Zeit* (Prague, 1868, 2 vols.); *Gesch. d. 30 jährigen Krieges* (Prague, 1869, 2 vols.); *Ueber des J. A. Comenius Leben* (Vienna, 1855, in the 15th vol. of the *Transactions of the Akademie*). Other works based upon the new sources are: Palacky, *Geschichte v. Böhmen* (Prague, 1844-67, 10 vols.); J. Fiedler, *Todtenbuch der Geistlichkeit der Böhm. Brüder* (Vienna, 1863, being the official necrology of the ministers of the U. F., in Bohemian; transl. into German in 1872); H. L. Reichel, *Geschichte d. alten Brüderkirche* (Rothenb. 1850); Cröger, *Geschichte d. alten Brüderkirche* (Gnadau, 1865, 2 vols.; reviewed in *The Moravian* Feb. 14, 1867); Benham, *Origin and Episcopate of the Bohemian Brethren* (Lond. 1867); Schweinitz, *Moravian Episcopate* (Bethlehem, 1865); Schweinitz, *Moravian Manual* (ibid. 1869); Benham, *Life of Comenius* (Lond. 1858); Czerwenka, *Geschichte d. Evang. Kirche in Böhmen* (Bielefeld and Leipsic, 1869 and 1870, 2 vols., containing the best history of the Brethren that has yet been written); Pescheck, *Ref. and Anti-Reformation in Bohemia* (Lond. 1845, 2 vols., from the German). Consult the following periodicals: *Lond. Qu. Rev.* April, 1857, art. x; *Amer. Presb. Qu.* July, 1858; July, 1864, art. ii; *Ch. Rev.* July, 1865; April, 1866; *Meth. Qu. Rev.* July, 1863, p. 516; April, 1870, p. 265; *Princeton Rev.* vii, 77; *Christian Examiner*, lxvi, 1 sq. Compare also the works cited in the body of this article. Sources for the history of the Brethren in Poland are: Jablonski, *Hist. Consensus Sandomiriensis* (Berlin, 1731); Krasinski, *Reformation in Poland* (Lond. 1840, 2 vols.); Fischer, *Geschichte der Ref. in Polen* (Grätz, 1856, 2 vols.). The article in Herzog's *Encyklopädie*, by Dieckhoff, entitled "Böhmische Brüder," was written without any knowledge of the new sources. It was consequently supplemented by Zezschwitz, in the article "Lukas v. Prag," vol. xx, conceived from an ultra-Lutheran point of view. (E. de S.)

2. THE RENEWED MORAVIAN BRETHREN, so called because they form the resuscitated Church of the Ancient Moravian Brethren (see No. 1, above). They are commonly known as "The Moravians," and "The Moravian Church," inasmuch as they originally came from Moravia. Their official title is "THE UNITED BRETHREN," or *Unitas Fratrum*.

I. *History.*—At the close of the Bohemian anti-Reformation (1627), a remnant of the Brethren remained concealed in Bohemia and Moravia, and for many years kept up religious services in secret according to the faith and usages of the fathers. This "hidden seed," as it is generally called, was revealed in 1722, when two families, named Neisser, escaped from Moravia under the guidance of Christian David, "the servant of the Lord," and settled on the domain of Berthelsdorf, in Saxony, by the invitation of its young owner, count Nicholas Lewis de Zinzendorf (q. v.). In the course of the next seven years (1722-29), about three hundred other Brethren from Moravia and Bohemia emigrated in little companies to the same place, leaving their houses and lands to be confiscated by the Austrian government, and braving the punishments which were inflicted on those refugees who fell into its hands. They built a town called Herrnhut, or "The Watch of the Lord," to which godly men from various parts of Germany were soon attracted, so that its population rapidly increased. In the midst of this colony the Church of the Brethren was renewed, through the introduction of the ancient discipline, preserved in the *Ratio Disciplinæ* of Amos Comenius, and through the transfer of the venerable episcopate, which had been kept up with such care, *in spem contra spem*, even after the ancient Church, as a visible organization, had ceased to exist. This transfer was made at Berlin, March 13, 1735, on which day David Nitschmann was consecrated as the first bishop of the Renewed Church, by Daniel Ernst Jablonski and Christian Sitkovius, the two surviving bishops of the ancient line.

In considering this renewal, two points are important. First, it was not a scheme of man, but altogether a work of God. Hence it bears a reality, and assumes its place in history with an authority, for both of which we would look in vain had a mere human plan been carried out. When Zinzendorf offered his estate as a refuge for the Brethren, he had not the remotest idea of renewing their Church, of which he knew little or nothing. Long before they came to his domain his aims in the interests of the Gospel had received an entirely different direction through the pietism of Spener. Nor did the Moravians themselves, when they began to emigrate, agree to reorganize in some other land. They left the issue of their flight in the hands of God. It was only by degrees that both parties were led to understand the divine will. The failure of his own plans, and other circumstances beyond his control, at last induced Zinzendorf to identify himself with the Brethren, and to labor for the resuscitation of their Church; while the gradual increase of their number at Herrnhut, and the opportunity which they there had to consult and to tell each other of the pious hopes of their fathers, gave them courage to maintain their independence, and to look for a new *Unitas Fratrum.* Secondly, this renewal involved a union of the German element of pietism with the Slavonic element of the ancient Brethren's Church. Thus arose some principles which were not found in the latter, and a polity of exclusivism that gave a peculiar tendency for more than a century to the Moravians of the modern period. Zinzendorf was a Lutheran by birth, education, and conviction. He was devoted to the system of Spener, who had been one of his sponsors at his baptism, and especially to the project of establishing "little churches in the Church" (*ecclesiolæ in ecclesia*), in other words, unions or associations of converted persons within a regular parish, for the purpose of personal edification. Hence the great aim which shaped his course was not to interfere with the State Church, but to develop Spener's idea in such a way that the Brethren would constitute, on the one hand, an independent Church, and yet, on the other, be a union of believers within the ecclesiastical establishments of the various countries in which they might settle. Accordingly, wherever they spread, exclusive towns were founded, in which religion controlled not only spiritual, but also social and industrial interests; from which the vices and follies of the world were banished, and where none but Brethren were allowed to hold real estate. That the Church could not, with such a system, enlarge its borders to any great extent in its home-field is evident. That its avowed purpose was to remain small is equally clear. The Moravian element, indeed, which drew its life from the old *Unitas Fratrum*, struggled for a time to gain free scope and expand. But Zinzendorf's views prevailed in the end, and were consistently carried out. Here and there Moravian villages were planted, as a leaven in Christendom. Such villages were to know nothing of a mere nominal Church-membership. All their inhabitants were to be true followers of Christ; and within their secure retreats they were to cultivate simplicity and lowly-mindedness, to foster holiness and love, to show forth a guile-

less spirit and a beautiful brotherhood. This constituted Zinzendorf's ideal, which was crowned with wonderful success.

At the time of Zinzendorf's death (1760), the Brethren were established in most of the Protestant states of Germany, in Holland, Great Britain, and North America, and after his decease they spread to Russia, Denmark, and Baden. In all of these countries they were represented by exclusive settlements; in Great Britain and America they had, besides, a number of churches in which their peculiar system did not prevail. The various governments granted them liberal concessions, and made them independent of the State Church; the Parliament of Great Britain, with the full concurrence of the bench of bishops, acknowledged them in 1749 as "an ancient episcopal Church," and passed an act encouraging them to settle in the North American colonies. On the part of the theologians of the day, however, the same fraternal spirit was not always manifested. Lutheran divines, especially, began to publish bitter attacks upon the Brethren. That these, in this early period of their history, gave just cause of offence, at least to some extent, cannot be denied. In the first place, the controlling influence of the Church was carried to unreasonable extremes, particularly as regards the sacred rights of the marriage relation and of the family. These were interfered with. In order to educate a chosen generation for work in the kingdom of God, the Church undertook the training of the children almost to the exclusion of parental rule. In the second place, about the year 1745 there began to appear in the churches of Middle Germany a spirit of fanaticism, which spread to some other Moravian towns on the Continent, and even to Great Britain. Those in America were not affected. It was a fanaticism which grew out of a one-sided view of the relation of believers to Christ. The Brethren spoke of him in a fanciful and antiscriptural style. A new religious phraseology, unwarranted by the Bible, gained the supremacy. The wounds of Jesus, and particularly the wound in his side, were apostrophized in the most extravagant terms. Images were used more sensuous than anything found in the Song of Solomon. Hymns abounded that poured forth puerilities and sentimental nonsense like a flood. This state of affairs, which in Moravian history is designated "the time of sifting," continued for about five years, reaching its climax in 1749. When Zinzendorf and his coadjutors awoke to a sense of the danger which was threatening the Church, they adopted the most energetic measures to bring back the fanatics to the true faith. By the blessing of God they succeeded; the Church was fully restored to sound doctrine and scriptural practice. This is an experience without a parallel in ecclesiastical history, and shows how firmly it was founded upon Christ as its chief corner-stone. This, too, is the sufficient answer to those assaults which were then made upon it by Rimius, by the author of *The Moravians Detected,* and by a legion of other writers, whose publications have been collected by the librarian of the archives at Herrnhut, where they fill up a large book-case, and are examined as literary curiosities by the visitor of the present day.

The best evidence of the entire suppression of fanaticism is the fact that the Moravian settlements, subsequent to 1750, not only continued to be centres of a widely spread influence for good, but also exercised such influence in an ever-increasing degree throughout the world. However exclusive their system, they were not market-places in which the people stood idle all the day; on the contrary, there were various ways in which these towns made their power to be felt. They gave a direction to chosen men of God, who became illustrious leaders in other parts of Christendom—as, for instance, to John Wesley, to Schleiermacher, and to Knapp; they were cities of refuge for the pure Gospel during the long reign of rationalism in Germany; they educated in their boarding-schools thousands of young people not connected with the Moravian Church; they originated a vast home missionary work, which will be described below, under the head of "Diaspora;" and they sent out so large an army of missionaries into heathen lands that by common consent the Moravians are recognised as the standard-bearers in the foreign missionary work of modern times.

Since the beginning of the present century various modifications have been introduced in the Church, especially such as set aside any undue interference on its part with the rights of the family. The General Synod of 1857 undertook a thorough revision of the Constitution, on the basis of local independence in the three "provinces" of the *Unitas Fratrum*.

II. *Moravian Towns*.—There still exist fifteen exclusively Moravian settlements on the Continent of Europe, and four in Great Britain. In such settlements the membership is divided into seven classes, called "choirs," from the Greek χορός. These classes are: the married couples, the widowed, the unmarried men, the unmarried women, the boys, the girls, and the little children. Each class is committed to the supervision of an elder. Growing out of this system, we find in every Moravian town a *Brethren's*, a *Sisters'*, and a *Widows' House*. In a Brethren's House, unmarried men live together and carry on trades, the profits of which go to support the establishment, as also the enterprises of the Church in general. A Sisters' House is inhabited by unmarried women, who maintain themselves by work suited to their sex. In each house there is a prayer-hall, where daily religious services are held. A common kitchen supplies the inmates with their meals. There is nothing monastic in the principles underlying these establishments, or in the regulations by which they are governed. The inmates are bound by no vow, and can leave at their option. A Widows' House is a home for widows, supplying them with all the comforts which they need at moderate charges, and enabling the poorest to live in a respectable manner. Each house has a spiritual and a temporal superintendent. The settlements in general are governed by two boards: the one, called the "Elders' Conference," with the senior pastor at its head, attends to the spiritual affairs; the other, called the "Board of Overseers," with the "warden" as its president, to financial and municipal matters. On business of importance, a general meeting of the adult male members is convened. These towns at present count among their inhabitants not a few who are not members of the Moravian Church. Such residents, until recently, were not permitted to own real estate. This fundamental principle is now undergoing a change which will, without doubt, gradually lead to the abolition of the entire system of exclusivism.

III. *The American Moravian Church*.—The Moravians settled in Georgia in 1735, but left that colony in 1740, on account of the war which had broken out with Spain. In the following year they founded Bethlehem, and subsequently Nazareth, in Pennsylvania. These towns, together with several smaller settlements, not only adopted exclusive principles, but also instituted a communism of labor. "The lands were the property of the Church, and the farms and various departments of mechanical industry were stocked by it and worked for its benefit. In return, the Church provided the inhabitants with all the necessaries of life. Whoever had private means, retained them. There was no common treasury, such as we find among the primitive Christians." This peculiar social system, which bore the name of "Economy," and which has given rise to the erroneous idea that there prevailed at one time a community of goods among the Moravians, existed for twenty years (1742-62). It accomplished great results. Each member of the "Economy" was pledged "to devote his time and powers in whatever direction they could be most advantageously applied for the spread of the Gospel." Hence, while there proceeded from the Moravian settlements an unbroken succession of itinerants, who traversed the colonies and the Indian country in every

direction, preaching Christ Jesus and him crucified, there labored at home a body of farmers and mechanics in order to maintain this extensive mission. After the abrogation of the "Economy," the Church for eighty years continued to uphold its foreign exclusive polity. It is true there were a number of organizations not exclusive, but these were looked upon as of secondary importance, and were characterized as mere "city and country congregations." Consequently the Moravians of the United States could expand as little as their brethren in Europe. From 1844 to 1856, however, the old system was gradually relinquished, and has now ceased to exist. There no longer are any Moravian towns in this country. The American Moravian Church now stands on the same footing as the other Protestant denominations of the land, and is pursuing the same policy of extension. In the last twenty years it has nearly doubled its membership, and flourished in other respects.

IV. *The Constitution*.—The *Unitas Fratrum* is distributed into three *provinces*, the German, British, and American, which are independent in all provincial affairs, but form one organic whole in regard to the fundamental principles of doctrine, discipline, and ritual, as also in carrying on the work of foreign missions. Hence we find a provincial and a general government. Each province has a Provincial Synod, which elects from time to time a board of bishops and other ministers, styled the "Provincial Elders' Conference," to administer the government in the interval between the synods. To this board is committed the power of appointing the ministers to their several parishes. It is responsible to the synod. The Provincial Board of the American Province consists of three members, has its seat at Bethlehem, Pa., and is elected every six years. The American Provincial Synod, composed of all ordained ministers and of lay delegates elected by the churches, meets triennially; and the province is divided into four districts, in each of which a District Synod is annually held. Every ten or twelve years a General Synod of the whole *Unitas Fratrum* is convened at Herrnhut, in Saxony. It consists of nine delegates from each province, elected by the Provincial Synod; of representatives of the foreign missions; and of such other members as are entitled to a seat by virtue of their office. This synod elects a board of twelve bishops and other ministers, styled the "Unity's Elders' Conference," which oversees the whole Church in so far as general principles come into question, and superintends the foreign missionary work. At the present time the same Conference acts as the Provincial Board of the German Province. It has its seat in the castle of Berthelsdorf, the former residence of count Zinzendorf.

V. *Doctrines*.—The Renewed Moravian Church does not, as was the case in the ancient Church of the Brethren, set forth its doctrines in a formal confession of faith, nor does it bind the consciences of its members to any which are not essential to salvation. Such essential doctrines, however, it publishes in its Catechism, its Easter-morning Litany, and its *Synodical Results*, or code of statutes, drawn up and published by each General Synod. From this latter work, as issued by the Synod of 1869, we quote the following extract:

"The points of doctrine which we deem most essential to salvation are:

"1. The doctrine of the total depravity of human nature: that there is no health in man, and that the fall absolutely deprived him of the divine image.

"2. The doctrine of the love of God the Father, who has 'chosen us in Christ before the foundation of the world,' and 'so loved the world that he gave his only-begotten Son, that whosoever believeth in him should not perish, but have everlasting life.'

"3. The doctrine of the real godhead and the real manhood of Jesus Christ: that God, the Creator of all things, was manifested in the flesh, and has reconciled the world unto himself; and that 'he is before all things, and by him all things consist.'

"4. The doctrine of the atonement and satisfaction of Jesus Christ for us: that he 'was delivered for our offences, and was raised again for our justification;' and that in his merits alone we find forgiveness of sins and peace with God.

"5. The doctrine of the Holy Ghost, and the operations of his grace: that it is he who works in us the knowledge of sin, faith in Jesus, and the witness that we are children of God.

"6. The doctrine of the fruits of faith: that faith must manifest itself as a living and active principle, by a willing obedience to the commandments of God, prompted by love and gratitude to him who died for us.

"In conformity with these fundamental articles of faith, the great theme of our preaching is Jesus Christ, in whom we have the grace of the Lord, the love of the Father, and the communion of the Holy Ghost. We regard it as the main calling of the Brethren's Church to proclaim the Lord's death, and to point to him, 'as made of God unto us wisdom, and righteousness, and sanctification, and redemption.'"

An authorized manual of doctrine is bishop Spangenberg's *Exposition of Christian Doctrine as taught in the Church of the U. B.* (Lond. 1784); a systematic work for theologians, although not authorized by the synod, is *Evangelische Glaubenslehre nach Schrift und Erfahrung* (Gotha, 1863), by Dr. Plitt, president of the German theological seminary. See also Zinzendorf's *Theologie* (Gotha, 1869-74, 3 vols.), by the same author.

VI. *Ministry, Ritual, and Usages.*—The ministry consists of bishops, presbyters, and deacons. The episcopal office is not provincial, but represents the whole *Unitas Fratrum.* Hence bishops have an official seat, not merely in the synods of the provinces in which they are stationed, but also in the General Synod; hence, too, they can be appointed only by this body, or by the Unity's Elders' Conference, although the American Province has secured the right of nomination. From all this it is evident that the Moravian episcopacy is not diocesan, and that bishops are not rulers of the Church *ex officio*, as was the case among the ancient Brethren. They are, however, almost invariably connected with the government by election to the Unity's Elders' Conference, or to the Provincial Boards. The president of the former is always a bishop; the presidents of the latter are, as a general thing, the same. The contrary is the exception. In the episcopate is vested exclusively the power of ordaining; it constitutes, moreover, a body of men whose duty it is to look to the welfare of the entire *Unitas Fratrum*, in all its provinces and missions, and especially to bear it on their hearts in unceasing prayer before God. At present there are eleven bishops in active service: four in America, two in England, and five in Germany. Of these, seven are members of the governing boards.

The ritual is liturgical in its character. A litany is used every Sunday morning; free prayer is allowed in connection with the litany, and at other times. There are prescribed forms for baptism, the Lord's Supper, confirmation, ordination, marriage, and the burial of the dead; special offices of worship for parochial, boarding, and Sunday schools; liturgical services for the various festivals of the ecclesiastical year, such as Advent, Christmas, Epiphany, etc., which are all observed; and a particular litany for Easter morning, prayed annually at sunrise, and, wherever practicable, amid the graves of them that sleep. Certain days commemorating important events in Moravian history are celebrated, and in those churches in which the division of the membership into "choirs" has been retained, which is the case not only in the exclusive settlements, each class observes an annual day of praise and covenanting, the festival closing with the Holy Communion. *Love-feasts* are held, in imitation of the ancient "agapæ," preparatory to the Lord's Supper, and on other occasions. At all liturgical services sacred music forms a prominent feature. Foot-washing (pedilavium) was formerly practiced on certain occasions within the limited circles of some of the "choirs," but has been universally discontinued since the beginning of the present century. The statement in this *Cyclopædia*, vol. iv, p. 616, taken from Herzog's *Real-Encyklopädie*, iv, 630, that the Moravians still practice foot-washing, is therefore incorrect. At one time the lot was employed in the appointment of

ministers, and in connection with marriages. Its use in the former case has been greatly restricted, and is left to the discretion of each provincial board. In the American Church it is scarcely ever resorted to, except when a minister receiving an appointment requests its use. Touching marriages by lot, they were abolished, as a rule, by the General Synod of 1818. Since that time they have been almost unknown in the American Province. This usage, which has been so generally misunderstood and ridiculed outside of the Church, was a legitimate result of its controlling influence in all the relations of its members, and constituted, moreover, a wonderful example of the childlike faith of the early Moravians. They gave themselves entirely into the hands of God. He was to lead them in all respects. In view of the loose ideas that prevail in our day with regard to the marriage contract, an intelligent mind cannot but admire such a spirit. That God did not put the confidence of the Brethren to shame is evident from the results of this practice. While it continued, there were fewer unhappy marriages among them than among the same number of people in any other denomination of Christians. This is a well-known fact, which can be established by statistics. Not a single divorce ever occurred. Without going into the details of this usage, we will merely add that any woman was at liberty to reject an offer of marriage even when sanctioned by the lot.

VII. *Schools and Missions.*—The Moravians have 35 flourishing boarding-schools: 17 in the German Province, 14 in the British, and 4 in the American. They are intended for young people not connected with the Church, and educate annually about 2500 pupils of both sexes. The schools in the American Province are the following: Moravian Seminary for Young Ladies, at Bethlehem, Pa., founded in 1785 (200 pupils); Nazareth Hall, for boys, at Nazareth, Pa., founded in 1785 (125 pupils); Linden Hall, at Litiz, Pa., founded in 1794 (75 pupils); Salem Female Academy, at Salem, N. C., founded in 1802 (200 pupils); Hope Academy, for girls, founded in 1866 (75 pupils). This province, moreover, has a flourishing theological seminary, with a classical department, at Bethlehem. It was founded in 1807; reorganized in 1858. The British theological seminary is located at Fulneck, Yorkshire, England; and the German seminary at Gnadenfeld, in Silesia. The German Province has a prosperous college at Nisky, in Prussia.

The work of foreign missions was begun in 1732, only ten years after the first house had been built at Herrnhut, and when that settlement counted but 600 inhabitants. Leonhard Dober and David Nitschmann were the pioneers, and established the first mission among the negro slaves of St. Thomas. Since that time the home Church has sent out 2171 missionaries, male and female. The following missions proved unsuccessful: Lapland (1734-35); among the Samoyedes, on the Arctic Ocean (1737-38); Ceylon (1738-41); Algiers (1740); Guinea, West Africa (1737-41, and 1767-70); Persia (1747-50); Egypt (1752-83); East Indies (1759-96); among the Calmucks (1768-1823); Demerara, South America (1835-40). At the present time the work embraces the following fields, called "Mission Provinces:" Greenland (begun 1733); Labrador (1771); Indian Country of North America (1734); St. Thomas and St. John (1732); St. Croix (1732); Jamaica (1754); Antigua (1756); St. Kitt's (1775); Barbadoes (1765); Tabago (1790, renewed in 1827); Mosquito Coast (1848); Surinam (1735); South African Western Province (1736, renewed in 1792); South African Eastern Province (1728); Australia (1849); Thibet (1853). This extensive work is supported by the contributions of the members of the Church, by the interest of funded legacies, by the donations of missionary associations, and by such revenue as the missions themselves can raise through voluntary gifts and the profits accruing from mercantile concerns and trades. The annual cost of the foreign missions is about $250,000. On retiring from the field in consequence of sickness or old age, missionaries are pensioned. Their widows also receive a pension, and their children are educated at the expense of the Church. In other respects they are satisfied with a bare support. The converts are divided into four classes: *New People*, or applicants for religious instruction; *Candidates for Baptism; Baptized Adults; Communicants*. The principal missionary associations are the following: *The Society of the United Brethren for Propagating the Gospel among the Heathen*, founded in 1787, at Bethlehem, Pa.; *The Wachovia Society of the United Brethren for Propagating the Gospel among the Heathen*, founded in 1823, at Salem, N. C.; *The Brethren's Society for the Furtherance of the Gospel among the Heathen*, founded in 1741, in England, supporting the mission in Labrador, and owning "The Harmony," a missionary ship annually sent out to supply the missionaries with the necessaries of life; *The London Association in Aid of the Missions of the United Brethren*, founded in 1817, and composed chiefly of members not connected with the Moravian Church; *The Missionary Society of Zeist*, in Holland, founded in 1793; and *The Missionary Union of North Sleswick*, founded in 1843.

In addition to these foreign missions, the last General Council inaugurated a work in Bohemia (1870), in the midst of the ancient seats of the Brethren, which promises to be successful. It already numbers four churches.

Independently of the other provinces, the German Province carries on its *Diaspora*. This is a mission which receives its name from the Greek $\delta\iota\alpha\sigma\pi\circ\rho\acute{\alpha}$ in 1 Pet. i, 1, and which has for its object the evangelization of the European state churches, without depriving them of their members. Hence missionaries itinerate through Protestant Germany, Switzerland, Denmark, Norway, Sweden, Poland, Livonia, Esthonia, and some other parts of Russia, and organize "societies" for the purpose of prayer, of expounding the Scriptures, and of edification in general. The members of such societies do not leave the communion of the state churches. In the event of their disestablishment, however, which seems to be approaching, it is more than probable that the members of such "societies" will fully join the Moravian Church, whose membership will thus be increased by thousands. Indeed such a change is now taking place in Switzerland, where, since the adoption of the new ecclesiastical laws (1873), three independent Moravian churches have grown out of the Diaspora.

VIII. *Statistics.—German Province:* churches, 26, of which 15 are in Moravian towns; ministers, 113; members, 8067. *British Province:* churches, 38; ministers, 55; members, 5575; number in Sunday-schools, 3994. *American Province:* churches, 70; ministers, 80; members, 16,698; number in Sunday-schools, 8212. *Foreign Missions:* mission provinces, 16; stations, 114; out-stations, 8; preaching-places, 307; ordained missionaries from Europe and America, 161; female assistants from Europe and America, 172; total of laborers from Europe and America, 333; native ordained missionaries, 41; native assistants, 1575; normal schools, 7; day-schools, 217; scholars, 16,590; teachers (natives), 290; monitors, 623; Sunday-schools, 92; scholars, 13,604; teachers, 944; total number of converts, 79,021. *Bohemian Mission:* stations, 4; missionaries, 4; members, 259. *Diaspora:* central stations, 61; ordained missionaries, 33; unordained missionary assistants, 32; members, about 100,000. *Totals in home provinces of the Unitas Fratrum:* ministers, 248; members, 27,906. *Totals in missions:* laborers, 1454; members, 69,473. *Totals in Diaspora:* laborers, 65; members of societies, 100,000. The *Unitas Fratrum* therefore has in all 1767 laborers engaged in the work of the Gospel, numbers 110,130 members, and has besides 100,000 souls in its Diaspora societies.

IX. *Publications and Literature.*—Periodicals of the German Province: *Herrnhut* (weekly); *Der Brüder-Bote* (every alternate month); *Nachrichten aus der Brüdergemeine* (monthly); *Journal de l'Unité des Frères* (monthly); *Berigten uit de Heiden-Wereld* (monthly);

Missionsblatt (monthly); *Brüdermissionsblatt für Kinder* (monthly). British Province: *The Messenger* (monthly); *The Missionary Reporter* (monthly); *Periodical Accounts* (quarterly). American Province: *The Moravian* (weekly); *Der Brüderbotschafter* (weekly); *The Little Missionary* (monthly). South African Mission Province: *De Bode* (monthly); *De Kinder-Vriend* (monthly). Besides these periodicals, there is an annual published by the Unity's Elders' Conference, entitled *The Text-book*, containing two passages from the Bible—one from the Old, the other from the New Testament—each with a corresponding stanza from the Hymn-book, and arranged for every day in the year. This annual has appeared since 1731; it is published in German, English, French, Swedish, Esquimau, and Negro-English; and thousands of copies are circulated every year outside of the Moravian Church.

The denominational literature is very extensive. We mention only the most important works: Cranz, *Ancient and Modern History of the Brethren* (Lond. 1780); Holmes, *History of the United Brethren* (Lond. 1825, 2 vols.); *A concise History of the Unitas Fratrum* (Lond. 1862); *The Moravian Manual* (Bethlehem, Pa., 2d ed.), giving a short but complete account of the Church; Bp. Cröger, *Geschichte der Erneuerten Brüderkirche* (Gnadau, 1852–54, 3 vols.); Schrautenbach, *Zinzendorf und die Brüdergemeine* (Gnadau, 1851); Burckhardt, *Zinzendorf und die Brüdergemeine* (Gotha, 1865); *Memorial Days of the Renewed Church of the Brethren* (Lond. 1822); *Results of the General Synod of 1869* (Lond. 1870); Plitt, *Gemeine Gottes in ihrem Geist u. ihren Formen* (Gotha, 1859). The principal works relating to the foreign missions are: Holmes, *Missions of the United Brethren* (Lond. 1827); Cranz, *Greenland* (Lond. 1767, 2 vols.); *The Moravians in Greenland* (Edinb. 1839); Oldendorp, *Mission der Brüder auf den Karaïbischen Inseln* (Barby, 1777); *The Moravians in Jamaica* (Lond. 1854); Loskiel, *Hist. of Indian Missions* (Lond. 1794); Heckewelder, *Hist. of the Indian Mission* (Phila. 1817); *Moravian Missions among the Indians* (Lond. 1838); Schweinitz, *Life and Times of David Zeisberger* (Phila. 1870). Works not emanating from the Church are: Bost, *Hist. of the Moravian Brethren* (Lond. 1848; an abridged translation of *Hist. de l'Église des Frères de Bohème et Moravie*, Paris, 1844, 2 vols.); Schaaf, *Evangelische Brüdergemeinde* (Leipsic, 1825); Tholuck, *Vermischte Schriften*, i, 433; Müller, *Selbstbekenntnisse merkwürdiger Männer*, vol. iii; Schröder, *Zinzendorf und Herrnhut* (Nordhausen, 1857); Bengel, *Abriss d. Brüdergemeinde* (1751; reprinted in 1859; written against the Church); Litiz, *Blicke in d. Vergangenheit u. Gegenwart d. B. K.* (Leipsic, 1846); Nitzsch, *Kirchengeschichtliche Bedeutung d. Brüdergemeine* (Berlin, 1853); Kurtz, *Text-book of Church History* (Phila. 1862). This last work contains a chapter on the Moravians, dictated by the personal animosity of the author to their mission in Livonia, where he resides, and full of gross misstatements, as is shown in *The Moravian Manual*, p. 11–14. (E. de S.)

Moravians. See MORAVIAN BRETHREN.

Morcelli, STEFANO ANTONIO, a celebrated Italian archæologist, of the Order of Jesus, was born at Chiari Jan. 17, 1737: studied at Rome, then joined the Jesuits; was sent to Ragusa, and afterwards returned to Rome, and was made professor in the Roman College. After the suppression of the order in 1773, Morcelli became librarian to cardinal Alessandro Albani, and while thus employed wrote his *De Stilo Inscriptionum Latinarum*, libri iii (Rome, 1780, 4to). In 1790 he was elected provost of the chapter in his native town, and so interesting became this work to him that he refused the proffered see of Ragusa. He died in 1821. Few men lived more unselfishly than Morcelli. He liberally bestowed of his own to the poor, and abounded in philanthropic labors. Among other provisions, he founded an institution for the gratuitous education of young girls. Besides the work mentioned above, he wrote *Inscripti-*

ones Commentariis subjectis (Rome, 1783, 4to):—*Parergon Inscriptionum Novissimarum* (Padua, 1818, 4to):—*Kalendarium Ecclesiæ Constantinopolitanæ cum Commentariis illustratum* (Rome, 1785, 2 vols. 4to), from an ancient MS. anterior to the schism between the Eastern and Western churches. Morcelli translated the MS. from Greek into Latin, adding his own commentaries, and rendering it a valuable work on Church history:—*Explanatio Ecclesiastica Sancti Gregorii.* This Gregory was one of the earliest bishops of Agrigentum:—*Africa Christiana* (Brescia, 1816, 3 vols. 4to). This is another important work on Church history, from A.D. 197 till A.D. 697. It may be styled the Fasti of the Christian churches in Northern Africa. Morcelli's works on inscriptions have been collected and published together—*Opera Epigraphica* (Padua, 1818-25, 5 vols.). Professor Schiassi has added to them a *Lexicon Epigraphicum Morcellianum*, in Latin and Italian. Morcelli wrote also a book of epigrams—*Electorum Libri ii*—and various dissertations on Roman antiquities. See Baraldi, *Notizia di Morcelli* (Mod. 1825); Tipaldo, *Biogr. degli Ital.* x, 102.

Mor'decai (Heb. *Mordekay'*, מָרְדְּכַי, either from the Persian, *little man*, see Gesenius, *Thes. Heb.* p. 818; comp. Benfey, *Monatsnamen*, p. 201; or from MERODACH, i. q. *worshipper of Mars*, Simon, *Onom.* p. 558; Sept. Μαρδοχαῖος v. r. in Neh. Μαρδοχέος), the name of one or two men during the Babylonian exile.

1. One of the principal Israelites who returned from Babylon with Zerubbabel (Ezra ii, 2; Neh. vii, 7). B.C. 536. He was perhaps identical with the following.

2. The son of Jair, of the tribe of Benjamin, and of the lineage of king Saul; apparently one of the captives transported to Babylon with Jehoiachin (Esth. ii, 5). B.C. 598. He was resident at Susa, then the metropolis of the Persian empire, and had under his care his niece Hadassah, otherwise Esther, at the time when the fairest damsels of the land were gathered together, that from among them a fitting successor to queen Vashti might be selected for king Xerxes. Among them was Esther, and on her the choice fell; while, by what management we know not, her relationship to Mordecai, and her Jewish descent, remained unknown at the palace. B.C. 479. The uncle lost none of his influence over the niece by her elevation, although the seclusion of the royal harem excluded him from direct intercourse with her. He seems to have held some office about the court, for we find him in daily attendance there; and it appears to have been through this employment that he became privy to a plot of two of the chamberlains against the life of the king, which through Esther he made known to the monarch. This great service was, however, suffered to pass without reward at the time. On the rise of Haman to power at court, Mordecai alone, of all the nobles and officers who crowded the royal gates, refused to manifest the customary signs of homage to the royal favorite. Some think that this refusal arose from religious scruples, as if such prostration (προσκύνησις) were akin with idolatry (see Theune's two monographs, Sorau, 1747, Brieg, 1750). It would be too much to attribute this to an independence of spirit which, however usual in Europe, is unknown in Eastern courts. Haman was an Amalekite; and Mordecai brooked not to bow himself down before one of a nation which from the earliest times had been the most decided enemies of the Jewish people. The Orientals are tenacious of the outward marks of respect, which they hold to be due to the position they occupy; and the erect mien of Mordecai among the bending courtiers escaped not the keen eye of Haman. He noticed it, and brooded over it from day to day: he knew well the class of feelings in which it originated, and, remembering the eternal enmity vowed by the Israelites against his people, and how often their conquering sword had all but swept his nation from the face of the earth, he vowed by one great stroke to exterminate the Hebrew nation, the fate of which he believed to be in his hands. The temptation was great, and to his ill-regulated mind irresistible. He therefore procured the well-known and bloody decree from the king for the massacre of all the Israelites in the empire in one day. When this decree became known to Mordecai, he not only felt impelled to exert himself to save his countrymen, as he was himself the cause of their meditated destruction, but he found his own safety involved, as well as that of his royal niece. Accordingly he covered himself with sackcloth and ashes, and rent the air with his cries. This being made known to Esther through the servants of the harem, who now knew of their relationship, she sent Hatach, one of the royal eunuchs, to demand the cause of his grief; through that faithful servant he made the facts known to her, urged upon her the duty of delivering her people, and encouraged her to risk the consequences of the attempt. She was found equal to the occasion. She hazarded her life by entering the royal presence uncalled, and having by discreet management procured a favorable opportunity, accused Haman to the king of plotting to destroy *her* and her people. His doom was sealed on this occasion by the means which in his agitation he took to avert it; and when one of the eunuchs present intimated that this man had prepared a gallows fifty cubits high on which to hang Mordecai, the king at once said, "Hang him thereon." This was, in fact, a great aggravation of his offence, for the previous night the king, being unable to sleep, had commanded the records of his reign to be read to him; and the reader had providentially turned to the part recording the conspiracy which had been frustrated through Mordecai. The king asked what had been the reward of this mighty service, and being answered, "Nothing," he commanded that any one who happened to be in attendance without should be called. Haman was there, having come for the very purpose of asking the king's leave to hang Mordecai upon the gallows he had prepared, and was asked what should be done to the man whom the king delighted to honor? Thinking that the king could delight to honor no one but himself, he named the highest and most public honors he could conceive, and received from the monarch the astounding answer, "Make haste, and do even so to Mordecai that sitteth in the king's gate!" Then was Haman constrained, without a word, and with seeming cheerfulness, to repair to the man whom he hated beyond all the world, to invest him with the royal robes, and to conduct him in magnificent cavalcade through the city, proclaiming, "Thus shall it be done to the man whom the king delighteth to honor." After this we may well believe that the sense of poetical justice decided the perhaps till then doubtful course of the king, when he heard of the gallows which Haman had prepared for the man by whom his own life had been preserved (Esth. iii–viii). B.C. 474. See HAMAN. Mordecai was invested with power greater than that which Haman had lost, and the first use he made of it was, as far as possible, to neutralize or counteract the decree obtained by Haman. It could not be recalled, as the kings of Persia had no power to rescind a decree once issued; but, as the altered wish of the court was known, and as the Jews were permitted to stand on their defence, they were preserved from the intended destruction, although much blood was, on the appointed day, shed even in the royal city. The Feast of Purim was instituted in memory of this deliverance, and is celebrated to this day (Esth. ix, x). See PURIM. He was probably the author of the book of Esther, which contains the narrative. His name is freely introduced into the apocryphal additions to that book, to which, however, it is unnecessary to pay attention. See ESTHER, BOOK OF. There are some questions connected with Mordecai that demand further consideration.

1. His *date.* This is pointed out with great particularity by the writer himself, not only by the years of the king's reign, but by his own genealogy in Esth. ii,

5, 6. Most interpreters, indeed, have understood this passage as stating that Mordecai himself was taken captive with Jehoiachin. But that any one who had been taken captive by Nebuchadnezzar in the eighth year of his reign should be vizier after the twelfth year of any Persian king among the successors of Cyrus is not very easy to believe. Besides, too, the difficulty of supposing the ordinary laws of human life to be suspended in the case of any person mentioned in Scripture, when the sacred history gives no such intimation, there is a peculiar defiance of probability in the supposition that the cousin-german of the youthful Esther, her father's brother's son, should be of an age ranging from 90 to 170 years at the time that she was chosen to be queen on account of her youth and beauty. But not only is this interpretation of Esth. ii, 5, 6 excluded by chronology, but the rules of grammatical propriety equally point out, not Mordecai, but Kish, as being the person who was taken captive by Nebuchadnezzar at the time when Jehoiachin was carried away. Because, if it had been intended to speak of Mordecai as led captive, the ambiguity would easily have been avoided by either placing the clause הַגְלָה אֲשֶׁר, etc., immediately after הַבִּירָה בְּשׁוּשַׁן, and then adding his name and genealogy, מ' וּשְׁמוֹ, or else by writing וְהוּא instead of אֲשֶׁר at the beginning of ver. 6. Again, as the sentence stands, the distribution of the copulative וֹ distinctly connects the sentence אֹמֵן וַיְהִי in ver. 7 with הָיָה in ver. 5, showing that three things are predicated of Mordecai: (1) that he lived in Shushan; (2) that his name was Mordecai, son of Jair, son of Shimei, son of Kish the Benjamite, who was taken captive with Jehoiachin; (3) that he brought up Esther. This genealogy does, then, fix with great certainty the age of Mordecai. He was great-grandson of a contemporary of Jehoiachin. Now four generations cover 120 years— and 120 years from B.C. 598 brings us to B.C. 479, i. e. to the sixth year of the reign of Xerxes; thus confirming with singular force the arguments which led to the conclusion that Ahasuerus is Xerxes. See AHASUERUS. This carrying back of the genealogy of a captive to the time of the captivity has an obvious propriety, as connecting the captives with the family record preserved in the public genealogies before the captivity, just as an American would be likely to carry up his pedigree to the ancestor who emigrated from England (see Bertheau, *Exeg. Handb.* ad loc.). Furthermore, it would seem entirely possible (though it cannot be certainly proved) that the Mordecai mentioned in the duplicate passage, Ezra ii, 2; Neh. vii, 7, as one of the leaders of the captives who returned from time to time from Babylon to Judæa [see EZRA], was the same as Mordecai of the book of Esther. It is not unlikely that on the death of Xerxes, or possibly during his lifetime, he may have obtained leave to lead back such Jews as were willing to accompany him, and that he did so. His age need not have exceeded fifty or sixty years, and his character points him out as likely to lead his countrymen back from exile if he had the opportunity. The name Mordecai not occurring elsewhere makes this supposition the more probable. We may add that in a passage of Josephus (*Ant.* xi, 4, 9), which gives an account of troubles excited by the Samaritans against the Jews about that time, as they were rebuilding the Temple, the names of Ananias and Mordecai (Μαρδοχαῖος) are given along with that of Zerubbabel as ambassadors from the Jews to king Darius.

2. As regards Mordecai's place in *profane* history, the domestic annals of the reign of Xerxes are so scanty that it would not surprise us to find no mention of this Jew. But there is a person named by Ctesias, who probably saw the very chronicles of the kings of Media and Persia referred to in Esth. x, 2, and whose name and character present some points of resemblance with Mordecai, viz. *Matacas* or *Natacas* (as the name is variously written), described by him as Xerxes's chief favorite, and the most powerful of them all. His brief notice of him in these words, ἡμιαρρένων δὲ μέγιστον ἠδύνατο Νατακᾶς, is in exact agreement with the description of Mordecai (Esth. ix, 4; x, 2, 3). He further relates of him that when Xerxes, after his return from Greece, had commissioned Megabyzus to go and plunder the temple of Apollo at Delphi (perhaps, rather, the temple of Apollo Didymæus, near Miletus, which was destroyed by Xerxes after his return, Strabo, xiv, cap. 1, § 5), upon his refusal, he sent Matacas the eunuch to insult the god and to plunder his property; which Matacas did, and returned to Xerxes. It is obvious how grateful to the feelings of a Jew, such as Mordecai was, would be a commission to desecrate and spoil a heathen temple. There is also much probability in the selection of a Jew to be his prime minister by a monarch of such decided iconoclastic propensities as Xerxes is known to have had (Prideaux, *Connect.* i, 231–233). Xerxes would doubtless see much analogy between the Magian tenets of which he was so zealous a patron and those of the Jews' religion; just as Pliny actually reckons Moses (whom he couples with Jannes) among the leaders of the Magian sect, in the very same passage in which he relates that Osthanes the Magian author and heresiarch accompanied Xerxes in his Greek expedition, and widely diffused the Magian doctrines (lib. xxx, cap. 1, § 2); and in § 4 he seems to identify Christianity also with Magic. From the context it appears highly probable that this notice of Moses and of Jannes may be derived from the work of Osthanes, and, if so, the probable intercourse of Osthanes with Mordecai would readily account for his mention of them. The point, however, here insisted upon is that the known hatred of Xerxes to idol-worship makes his selection of a Jew for his prime minister very probable, and that there are strong points of resemblance in what is thus related of Matacas and what we know from Scripture of Mordecai. Again, that Mordecai was, what Matacas is related to have been, a eunuch, seems not improbable from his having neither wife nor child, from his bringing up his cousin Esther in his own house (to account for this, the Targum says that he was seventy-five years old), from his situation in the king's gate, from his access to the court of the women, and from his being raised to the highest post of power by the king, which we know from Persian history was so often the case with the king's eunuchs. With these points of agreement between them, there is sufficient resemblance in their names to add additional probability to the supposition of their identity. The most plausible etymology usually given for the name *Mordecai* is that favored by Gesenius, who connects it with Merodach the Babylonian idol (called Mardok in the cuneiform inscriptions), and which appears in the names Mesessi-Mordacus, Sisi-Mordachus, in nearly the same form as in the Greek, Μαρδοχαῖος. But it is highly improbable that the name of a Babylonian idol should have been given to him under the Persian dynasty (Rawlinson [*Herod.* i, 270] points out Layard's conclusion [*Nin.* ii, 441], that the Persians adopted generally the Assyrian religion as "quite a mistake"), and it is equally improbable that Mordecai should have been taken into the king's service before the commencement of the Persian dynasty. If, then, we suppose the original form of the name to have been Matacai, it would easily in the Chaldee orthography become Mordecai, just as פַּרְסָא is for פַּסָא, שַׂרְבִיט for שֵׁבֶט, דַּרְמֶשֶׂק for דַּמֶשֶׂק, etc. In the Targum of Esther he is said to be called Mordecai because he was like לְמִירָא דַכְיָא, "to pure myrrh."

3. As regards his place in *rabbinical* estimation, Mordecai, as is natural, stands very high. The interpolations in the Greek book of Esther are one indication of his popularity with his countrymen. The Targum (of late date) shows that this increased rather than dimin-

ished with the lapse of centuries. There Shimei in Mordecai's genealogy is identified with Shimei the son of Gera, who cursed David, and it is said that the reason why David would not permit him to be put to death then was that it was revealed to him that Mordecai and Esther should descend from him; but that in his old age, when this reason no longer applied, he was slain. It is also said of Mordecai that he knew *the seventy languages*, i. e. the languages of all the nations mentioned in Gen. x, which the Jews count as seventy nations, and that his age exceeded 400 years (*Juchasin* ap. Wolf, and Stehelin, *Rabb. Liter.* i, 179). He is continually designated by the appellation צְדִיקָא, "the Just," and the amplifications of Esth. viii, 15 abound in the most glowing descriptions of the splendid robes, and Persian buskins, and Median scimitars, and golden crowns, and the profusion of precious stones and Macedonian gold, on which was engraved a view of Jerusalem, and of the phylactery over the crown, and the streets strewed with myrtle, and the attendants, and the heralds with trumpets, all proclaiming the glory of Mordecai, and the exaltation of the Jewish people. Benjamin of Tudela mentions the ruins of Shushan and the remains of the palace of Ahasuerus as still existing in his day, but places the tomb of Mordecai and Esther at Hamadan, or Ecbatana (p. 128). Others, however, place the tomb of Mordecai in Susa, and that of Esther in or near Baram in Galilee (note to Asher's *Benj. of Tud.* p. 166). With reference to the above-named palace of Ahasuerus at Shushan, it may be added that considerable remains of it were discovered by Mr. Loftus's excavations in 1852, and that he thinks the plan of the great colonnade, of which he found the bases remaining, corresponds remarkably to the description of the palace of Ahasuerus in Esth. i (Loftus, *Chaldæa*, ch. xxviii). It was built or begun by Darius Hystaspis. The so-called tomb of Esther and Mordecai at Hamadan has

General View of the Tomb of Mordecai and Esther. (The cut under ESTHER gives a somewhat different view of the central dome, without the adjoining structures.)

no claim, as Flandin remarks, to a very remote antiquity, for the dome and the general style of architecture correspond with those commonly found in Mussulman sepulchres in Persia. Although the tomb now standing is more ancient than that of Ezra, it is on essentially the same plan, both in its exterior and interior appearance, with such differences as proceeded from the difference of situation, one being in the midst of a town, and the other on the borders of the desert. The bell-shaped dome is also in an older taste than that which the other tomb

exhibits. The stork's nest by which it is surmounted frequently appears upon the highest points of public buildings in that country. The tomb stands on ground somewhat more elevated than any in the immediate neighborhood, and is in rather a decayed condition. It occupies a small space in the midst of ruins, in the quarter appropriated to Jewish families. The entrance to the building is by a stone door of small dimensions, the key of which is always kept by the chief rabbi. This door conducts to the antechamber, which is small, and contains the graves of several rabbies. A second door, of still more confined dimensions than the first, leads to the tomb-chamber, which is larger than the outer apartment. In the midst of this stand the two sarcophagi of Mordecai and Esther, of dark and hard wood, like that of Ezra. They are cenotaphs, standing beside each other, distinguished only by the one (Mordecai's) being a little larger than the other. They are richly carved, and have a Hebrew inscription along the upper ledge, taken from Esth. ii, 5, and x, 3. The wood is in good preservation, though evidently very old. The present building is said to occupy the site of one more magnificent, which was destroyed by Timur Beg, soon after which this humble building was erected in its place, at the expense of certain devout Jews; and it is added that it was fully repaired about 160 years since by a rabbi named Ismael. If this local statement be correct, some of the inscriptions which now appear must, as the resident Jews state, have belonged to the preceding building, which, however, could not have been the *original* mausoleum, since one of these inscriptions describes it as having been finished posterior to the Christian æra (see R. K. Porter's *Travels in Persia*, ii, 107). See ACHMETHA.

Mordecai BEN-HILLEL, of Austria, a pupil of the famous Meir of Rothenburg (q. v.), son-in-law of R. Jechiel of Paris, and brother-in-law of R. Jacob of Corbeil, flourished towards the end of the 13th century, and was martyred in 1310 at Nuremberg. He is the author of the book מרדכי, *Mordecai*, also called סֵפֶר הַמָּרְדְּכִי, the *Book of Mordecai;* a treatise on the legal code (סֵפֶר הַהֲלָכוֹת), embodying all the laws of the Talmud, which was compiled, revised, corrected, annotated, and supplemented by Isaac Alfasi (q. v.). The *Sepher Mordecai* has been printed with the *Sepher Ha-Halachoth* (Constantinople, 1509; Venice, 1521–22; Sabionetta, 1524, etc.). It has also been published separately (Venice, 1558; Cracow, 1598, etc.).—Fürst, *Bibl. Jud.* ii, 324 sq.; De Rossi, *Dizionario* (Germ. transl.), p. 234; Steinschneider, *Catalogus libr. Hebr. in Bibliotheca Bodleiana*, 1659, etc.; Basnage, *Hist. des Juifs* (Taylor's transl.), p. 685; Ginsburg, in Jacob ben-Chajim ibn-Adonijah's *Introduction to the Rabbinic Bible* (Lond. 1867), p. 76 sq.; Cassel, *Leitfaden für jüd. Gesch. u. Literatur* (Berlin, 1872), p. 87; Grätz, *Gesch. d. Juden* (Berlin, 1873), vii, 252 sq.; Zunz, *Literaturgeschichte der synagogalen Poesie* (Berlin, 1865), p. 364; *Die Monatstage des Kalenderjahres* (Berlin, 1872), p. 44. (B. P.)

Mordvins is the name of a people inhabiting Eastern Russia. They form a subdivision of the Bulgaric or Volgaic family of the Finnic branch of the Suranian, Uralo-Altaic, or Mongolian races, and are related to the Tcheremisses and Tchuvashes. Their number has been estimated at 400,000, and their territory lies principally between the rivers Oka and Volga, in the Russian governments of Nishni Novgorod, Tambov, Pensa, Simbrisk, and Saratov, extending also into Samara and Astrachan. Dialectically they may be subdivided into Mokzhas, chiefly dwelling on the banks of the Sura and Mokzha, and Ersas, occupying the shores of the Oka.

More, Alexander, a very noted preacher of the French Protestants, who flourished in the 17th century in France and Switzerland, was born at Castres, Languedoc, Sept. 25, 1616, of Scottish parents. He received his preparatory training under his father at Castres.

and went from home at the age of twenty to study divinity at Geneva. But it so happened that the chair of Greek was vacant at this time, and though so young a man and a stranger, More was chosen to fill it. He promptly accepted the proffered honor, and three years later had the pleasure of being promoted to a professorship in divinity, he having improved his time in the study of that department. His rapid advance made him many enemies, and he was accused of heresy. But, notwithstanding much and able opposition, More advanced, and in 1645 was made rector of the high school with which he was connected. He was, however, destined soon to decline, for he was very arrogant and proud, and some even dared to assert that he was immoral. He was wise enough to perceive the near approach of his fall, and he therefore decided to quit Geneva. In 1649 he secured the divinity professorship and pastoral office at Middleburg, in Zealand, and there also he won a reputation for his learning and ability, which opened to him in 1652 the university at Amsterdam. He had been proffered before a position in that noble high school, but had refused it; now he accepted, and removed thither. In 1654 he vacated his chair, and went on a visit to Italy, and became well acquainted with the men of note and of rank in that country. He enjoyed a personal intercourse with the duke of Tuscany, and was a favorite at Venice. Returning to his charge, he encountered decided opposition, many of his congregation doubting his sincerity, and declaiming against the unholiness of his life. Charges were brought against him, and he was condemned by the Synod of Torgau. He quitted his parish, and accepted a call from a Church in Paris, and though there was great variety of opinion as to his trustworthiness, he was confirmed in the position. He had not, however, occupied it long before he was openly attacked. Though his manner of preaching procured him applause from a crowd of hearers, his character was generally acknowledged to be ambiguous, and he had the mortification to see his reputation attacked by persons of merit, who accused him anew to the synod. He escaped further condemnation by quitting France in December, 1661. He returned again in the summer following, and, finding that the opposition had not subsided, he sickened at heart, as it is generally believed, declined rapidly in health, and died at Paris in September, 1670. By the confession of his friends, he was proud, vindictive, imperious, satirical, contemptuous; not to say that his character was not quite unblemished in point of chastity, although there is no occasion to believe all that Milton has said of him. Milton had had a quarrel with More, and this may have provoked much that was far from the truth, though the great English bard was not given to falsifying. The trouble had been produced by a publication of More in 1652, addressed under the printer's name to the king of Great Britain, entitled *Regii sanguinis clamor ad cœlum adversus parricidas Anglicanos*. It is a very violent invective against the Parliament party; and Milton, in particular, is extremely abused in it. He is no better used in the epistle dedicatory than in the book itself. Milton therefore wrote a reply, in which he considered More as the author as well as the editor of the book. He is treated upon the footing of a dog, or rather of a goat; for he is accused of a thousand lewd tricks, particularly of several acts of debauchery. He was also charged with having been convicted of heresies at Geneva, and of having shamefully abjured them with his lips, though not with his heart. Milton accused him of having for many months been deprived of his salary at Geneva, and suspended from his offices as a professor and a minister on account of a process of adultery which had been entered against him; and for which, says he, he would have been condemned, if he had not avoided the decisive sentence by declaring that he would leave the place. But, whatever Milton's opinion, the pious Huetius favored More, and wrote in his be-

half. He even praised him in song (*Pœnit*, p. 30 and 77, ed. 1700). More published some works: there is a treatise of his, *De gratia et libero arbitrio* (Geneva, 1644, 4to; Middleburg, 1652); and another, *De Scriptura Sacra, sive de causa Dei* (Middleburg, 1653, 4to):—*A Comment on the 53d Chapter of Isaiah:—Notæ ad loca quædam Novi Fœderis* (Lond. 1661, 8vo):—a reply to Milton, with the title of *Alexandri Mori fides publica* (La Haye, 1654, 12mo):—some *Orations and Poems in Latin*. See Senebier, *Hist. littér. de Genève*; Haag, *La France Protestante*, vii, 543 sq.; Bayle, *Hist. Dict.* s. v. (J. H. W.)

More, Hannah, one of the most brilliant female ornaments of Christian literature, was born at the village of Stapleton, in Gloucestershire, Feb. 2, 1745, and was the daughter of a clergyman of the Church of England, a man eminent for his classical attainments, and at that time employed as a village schoolmaster in charge of a charity school. Some time after the birth of his daughter Hannah he removed to Bristol, where he kept a private school. There were other daughters, and the family soon began to be taken notice of as one in which there was a display of talent that was unusual; so that some exertions were made by persons to whom they were known, and the sisters became early in life established in a school for the education of girls, which continued for many years the most flourishing establishment of the kind in the west of England. Hannah was from the beginning the most remarkable of the group. She wrote verse at a very early age, and though these compositions were highly thought of in the family circle, they were never allowed to go beyond the precincts of their own house. And yet, in ways and by circumstances almost unnoticed, the fame of her literary talent was widely spread, and in 1773 she was prevailed upon to publish a pastoral drama, which was entitled *The Search after Happiness*. It was brought out under the direction of her pastor, Dr. Stonehouse, a learned clergyman of the Church of England. He it was also who introduced Hannah to the great literati. In 1774 she published a regular tragedy on the story of Regulus, and two tales in verse; and her turn being then thought by her friends to incline to the drama, means were taken to obtain an introduction for her to Garrick, by whom she was very kindly received. He, in turn, introduced her to Dr. Johnson, Burke, Sir Joshua Reynolds, and other persons, who at that time formed what was considered the best literary society of London. Her manners and conversation confirmed the good impression elicited by her talents, and the position in society originally conceded as a favor was soon acknowledged as a well-established right. During this period of her life she produced two tragedies, *Percy* (1777) and *The Fatal Falsehood* (1779), and other poems. These attempts at dramatic composition, and the consequent connection with the stage, seem to indicate that she was then, in a great measure, if not altogether, a stranger to evangelical views of Christian duty. But the death of David Garrick (1779), to whom she had become very much attached, produced a great change in her character. Educated as she had been with a deep impression of the truths of the Christian religion, the life which she now led began to appear to her as unbefitting a creature with the glorious prospects which Christianity opens to man. She therefore determined on forsaking the drama and retiring from the gay circles of fashion and of literature, and even quitted London in order the better to devote herself to the life befitting, as she thought, a child of God and an heir of immortality. She established her residence at a little rural retreat in the vicinity of Bristol, named Cowslip Green, where she enjoyed a freshness of feeling and a sweet mental tranquillity to which she had previously been a stranger. In her transitive state she had produced her *Sacred Dramas* (1782), a publication more favorably received perhaps than her former works. But she finally resolved to devote herself to a treatment of subjects surer of good results, and to write with careful preparation. She felt obliged to confess, to quote her own words from the Preface of the third volume of her works, that she did not "consider the stage in its present state as becoming the appearance or countenance of a Christian; on which account she thought proper to renounce her dramatic productions in any other light than as mere poems." Having become sensible of the follies of the world and the reigning defects of modern society, she resolved to embody the results of her observations and experience in the form of earnest and solemn admonitions against them. The first in this series of contemplated works was of a didactic nature, and was entitled *Essays to Young Ladies*. This was almost immediately followed by *Thoughts on the Manners of the Great*, a little volume which was issued in 1788 anonymously, and the object of which was to expose, in order to amend, the low morality — the loose and licentious principles — of fashionable society. Having excited a considerable degree of interest and curiosity, the work was attributed to the pen of more than one person of official dignity in the Church as well as the State. But the real author was ere long discovered, and the éclat which the discovery gave to her name encouraged her to persevere in the course of moral instruction she had contemplated. Almost every successive year brought out some new production from her pen; and such was the power as well as the charms of her eloquent composition that her works were universally applauded, and by none more than by the very classes whose faults many of them were designed to expose and censure. Thus, immediately after the last-mentioned popular work, appeared *An Estimate of the Religion of the Fashionable World* (1791), and this enjoyed as great a measure of success as its predecessor. To counteract the principles of the French Revolution, which had unsettled every European nation, and introduced a wild and turbulent spirit among some classes even of Great Britain, she conferred an incalculable benefit on her country by publishing, first, *Village Politics*, by Will Chipp, and next a periodical work, "The Cheap Repository Tracts"—a series of admirable tales of a moral and religious nature for the common people, one of which is the well-known *Shepherd of Salisbury Plain*. The influence which both these publications had over the popular mind is almost beyond conception. They were circulated by hundreds of thousands in all parts of the United Kingdom, and were more than anything else instrumental in maintaining the cause of order and of true religion against the torrent of infidel philosophy which had set in so strongly from France. The next work which came from her pen was entitled *Strictures on the Modern System of Female Education* (1799). Exceptions were taken by some to the "high Calvinistic principles" of this work; but it amounted to little after all, for she was known to do so much good that the opposition soon died out. Testimony was borne to its merits by bishop Porteus, in that he recommended the authoress as a competent person to superintend the education of the young princess Charlotte; and although an absurd etiquette, it seems, prevented that responsible office being held by any lady beneath the ranks of the aristocracy, she showed her fitness for the task by the publication of *Hints towards Forming the Character of a Young Princess* (1805). After the lapse of some years she published *Cœlebs in Search of a Wife*, one of the best of novels in respect to principle and moral tendency; and this was followed by *Practical Piety* (1811), *Christian Morals* (1812), *The Spirit of Prayer* (1813), *An Essay on the Character and Writings of St. Paul* (1815), and *Modern Sketches* (1819). But though these literary labors demanded much of her time, she yet found a portion for philanthropic labor; and having built a pleasant home and received her sisters there, she devoted herself with them to the people of her vicinity, especially the poor, of whom there were many — it being a mining district — who "had grown up

Hannah More's Cottage.

coarse, brutal, ferocious, utterly neglected by their clergy, without any means of education or hopes of improvement" (Perry). Determined to elevate these downtrodden and forlorn people, the three sisters attempted the appalling task of alleviating all suffering and of educating the laboring classes. They devised various schemes of benevolence and usefulness, not the least of which was the erection of schools, which, though at first confined to the children of their immediate surroundings, soon extended their operations over no less than ten parishes where there were no resident clergymen, and in which upwards of 1200 children were thus provided with the benefits of a moral and religious education. Miss Hannah More's numerous writings, which produced her upwards of $150,000, enabled her to do much, but she was by no means dependent upon her own resources. Her high character had impressed itself on her friends and associates, and these freely poured out their treasures for the promotion of the More schemes. Bibles were distributed, prayer-books given away, and instruction provided for all who came to study, whether adult or child. In short, so unremitting were they in their labors and measures that what had been a moral desert was changed into a garden, which brought forth in rich abundance the excellent fruits of wide-spread intelligence, of elevated morality, and genuine religion. But at last age came upon Hannah More, and brought along some of its infirmities. In 1828 she was moved therefore to quit Barleywood, the place in which many years had been spent, and she now took up her abode at Clifton. Here she continued amid a painful and protracted illness until relieved by death on the 7th of September, 1833, surrounded by many to honor her and many also to love her; who looked up to her as one of the great reformers of the manners of English society; one who had asserted very successfully the right of Christianity, or, in other words, the right of the Christian Scriptures to have a larger share than it had been the wont to allow them in forming the character and directing the course of human beings while in this state of their probation. She bequeathed £10,000 for pious and charitable purposes. The best edition of her works is in 11 vols. 16mo (Lond. 1853). See *The Memoirs and Correspondence of Hannah More*, by William Roberts (Lond. 1834, 4 vols. 8vo; N. Y. 1836, 2 vols. 12mo, abridged in "Christian Family Library"); *Life*, by Rev. H. Thompson (Lond. 1838, 8vo); *Correspondence of Hannah More with Zachary Macaulay* (Lond. 1860); Mrs. Hall's visit to Mrs. Hannah More in *Pilgrimage to English Shrines; Lives* of Bishop Wilberforce; Perry, *Hist. Church of England*, iii, 480 sq.; Clissold, *Lamps of the Church* (Lond. 1863, 12mo), p. 167 sq.; Jamieson, *Cyclop. Religious Biog.* s. v.; and the literature appended to the excellent article in Allibone, *Dict. Brit. and Amer. Auth.* s. v.

More, Henry, an English Arminian divine and moralist, noted as a leader of that class of English philosophers who arose in the 17th century to exorcise the spirit of Calvinism from the English high schools, was born at Grantham, Lincolnshire, Oct. 12, 1614. He was educated at Eton, where, aside from his regular studies, he bestowed much time on the reading of the philosophical works of Aristotle, Julius Scaliger, etc., poring, immature as he was, over the doctrine of predestination. His parents were Calvinists, and they had reared him with like notions, but he early became distrustful as to the real ground of Calvinism, and finally turned sceptic. In 1631 he went to Christ College, Cambridge, and graduated in 1635. More all his years at college was most diligently employed in metaphysical studies. He says himself, "I immersed myself over head and ears in the study of philosophy, promising a most wonderful happiness to myself in it." Dissatisfied with all other systems, he found rest for his mind only when he came to the writings of the Platonic school; whence, as he tells us, he learned that something better and higher than the knowledge of human things constitutes the supreme happiness of man, and that this is attainable only through that purity of mind and divine illumination which raise man to a union with God. But yet, he adds himself, that though the Platonic writings attracted and benefited him, there was "among all the writings of this kind none which so pierced and affected" him "as that golden little book with which Luther is also said to have been wonderfully taken, viz. *Theologia Germanica*. This book More prized next to the Bible, and studied it until he could say that he was free from all scepticism, and once more truly devoted to Christian interests. He had taken his M.A. in 1639, and had been made also a fellow of his college. With these honors he contentedly rested, and, insisting upon refusal of all Church preferments, he withdrew to retirement for a course of "spiritual discipline." He in short gave himself up to a life of most devout spiritual exercise, and would suffer nothing to stand in his way to eternal happiness as it had been taught him by the mystical work he so fondly read. "From this time," says More's biographer, "he had a wonderful sense of God, sacred and ineffable, and of his unconceivable attributes, and he soon found all things to his satisfaction, and himself not unsuitable to them. And that there may be a 'turning after righteousness' (as he speaks) as well as a 'running after knowledge,' More now actually came forward to demonstrate with great care the principles both of revealed and natural religion, and to recommend to all at the same time, with the greatest seriousness possible, the practice of morality and virtue; or, rather, what is justly called the Christian or divine life." "It would seem, therefore," adds his biographer, "that Henry More was raised by a special Providence in those days of freedom, as a light to those that may be fitted or inclined to high speculations, and a general guide to all that want it, how they are to mix the Christian and philosophic genius together, and make them rightly to accord in one common end, viz. the glory of God with the highest felicity and perfection of man." The depth and originality of his metaphysical theories, and the remarkable combination of great argumentative abilities, extensive learning, and ardent piety with which he set them forth, occasioned his being looked up to as a person of an extraordinary character by the greatest and best of his contemporaries. Indeed, he himself admitted, with frankness and simplicity natural to his temper, that the talents and dispositions lavished upon him were such as brought him into singular responsibilities; that, to adopt his own expression, he had "as a fiery arrow been shot into the world, and he hoped that it had hit the mark." After his election to a fellowship by his college he took charge of several pupils, some of them persons of rank, whose studies he directed with great fidelity and application—his management of them being distinguished from that of ordinary tutors chiefly by unusual gentleness, and by the deep tone of piety which pervaded his instructions. He has recorded his opinion that "the exercise of love and goodness, of humanity and brotherly kindness, of prudence and discretion, of unfeigned religion and devotion, in the plain

and undoubted duties thereof is, to the truly regenerate soul, a far greater pleasure than all the fine speculations imaginable." It was life, not notions, which he chiefly valued; and he preferred "a single-heartedness of temper beyond any theories." He had no ambition to play the part of a leader in society, and steadily declined every attempt to draw him into a public position. He was content in the youthful circle which he gathered about himself as private tutor, and preferred to address the masses by his pen. The deanery of Christ Church in Dublin, with the provostship of Trinity College, and also the deanery of St. Patrick's, were proposed for his acceptance, as a step to either of the two bishoprics when a vacancy should occur; but he could not be persuaded to accept these preferments. It is said that after the failure of these attempts, a very good English bishopric was procured for him, and that his friends had actually brought him, on some pretence or other, as far as Whitehall, designing to introduce him to the king to kiss the hands of his royal master for the appointment; but when More understood on what business he had been brought thither, nothing could induce him to enter the royal grounds. Once, late in life (in 1675), he accepted a prebend in the cathedral of Gloucester; this, however, as the event proved, only with the view of serving his friend, Dr. Fowler, afterwards bishop of that diocese, into whose hands, with the chancellor's permission, he resigned it, refusing at the same time repayment of the expenses he had incurred. In the same manner, he for a short time kept possession of the rectory of Ingoldsbury, in Lincolnshire, which his father had purchased for him, and then presented it to several friends in succession. He had the satisfaction of providing in this way for his friend, Dr. Worthington, when that accomplished divine, in common with many other clergymen, lost his church in the fire of London. When the mastership of his college fell vacant, it was proposed to him, in preference to Cudworth, as a piece of preferment likely, if any could do so, to suit his wishes; he declined it as he had done everything else, "passing otherwise his time within those private walls, it may be as great a contemplator, philosopher, and divine as ever did or will hereafter visit them." In fact, he believed that by a life of contemplation, and by laying the results of it before the world in his writings, he followed the course appointed him by Providence as best suited to his disposition and abilities, and likely to be serviceable to that and succeeding generations. Yet so humble were his notions of what he had accomplished by the employment of many years in earnest pursuit of those august theories which filled his mind, that he would say he "had lived a harmless and childish life in the world." His works, he remarked to a person who was speaking in commendation of them, "were such as might please some solitary men that loved their Creator." In his later years Dr. More was sorely tried by the separation of his friend and former pupil, lady Conway, from the communion of the Church which was his ideal in the form "as it existed before the times of disturbance—the Church of the Reformation and of Hooker." To popery in every form he was violently opposed, as is evinced by a work of his on *The true Idea of Antichristianism* (see below), and also to the sects he was opposed: "Both his reason and his love of quietness and order were opposed to what he considered the excesses of Puritanism—the dismal spectacle of an infinity of sects and schisms." Yet it should not be thought that More loved the ecclesiastical organization of England rather than the cause of Christ. "His main concern," says his biographer, "is that neither one order of the Church government nor another usurp the place which only religion itself should hold. He is for the 'naked truth of Christianity,' and nothing more; willing even to be called a Puritan, 'if *this* be to be a Puritan.'" Such was his liberality, and yet he sought earnestly to recall lady Conway to the Church communion. She had been a favorite of his in her girlish days, and much of his time he had passed at Ragley, in Warwickshire, her country-seat after marriage to lord Conway. She was a person of enthusiastic piety and great accomplishments, and by her More and his opinions were known to be held in high veneration. Indeed, her husband is said to have been hardly less enthusiastic, and to have treasured everything of More's "with as much reverence as if it were Socrates's." Among such friends it was but natural that More should frequently pass his time, and it was among the shades of Ragley that he composed some of his writings, among them his *Conjectura Cabalistica*, his *Philosophicæ Teutonicæ Censura*, and his *Divine Dialogues* (see below). He often counselled with lady Conway, and is believed to have been urged into authorship by her. She was particularly attracted by his mystical studies. Her consultations with him ultimately led her to turn aside and make her life one of most intense mystical devotion. She thus came to admire the patient quietude of the Quakers, as well as the opinions of that sect, at that time flushed with all the fervor attendant on novelty, persecution, and success, and finally she was induced to join them. Perhaps the doctor was conscious that his own religious views, characterized as they are by a degree of subjectiveness which unfits them for general reception (when eagerly adopted by a person of her peculiar temperament, not fortified by the counteraction of those healthier and more robust attainments which prevented any very evil consequences in his own case), might have prepared the way to this unfortunate result. At all events, he received the account of it with unfeigned affliction, and labored many years with all the earnestness of a faithful friend to reclaim the fair proselyte for the Church establishment of which he was a most devout adherent. He was thus led into a controversy with William Penn, both by writing and conversation. An admirable letter on *Baptism* and the *Lord's Supper*, addressed on this occasion to Penn, is printed in the appendix to his life. He encountered also George Fox, and has left a description of the interview on his own feelings little flattering to that ill-used religious enthusiast. More failed to reconvert his pupil, but he retained her friendship. He continued to spend much of his time, as before, at Ragley "and its woods," and there composed several of his books at lady Conway's "own desire and instigation." After her death he drew her portrait under another name, and with so much address that "the most rigid Quaker would see everything they could wish in it, and yet the soberest Christian be entirely satisfied with it." At Ragley, More formed several valuable acquaintances; of these we shall come to speak hereafter. But it is only there that he was surrounded by any associates. In his own "paradise," as he called his home at Christ College, he lived very much alone. Yet if he thus kept himself retired from the world, this life of solitude greatly stimulated his productivity as an author.

More began authorship in 1640 by the publication of his *Psychozoia, or the First Part of the Song of the Soul, containing a Christiano-Platonical Display of Life* (reprinted in 1647, and, together with some additional pieces, published under the title of *Philosophical Poems*). It was a most singular effort in the literary line, for it seeks to turn metaphysics into poetry. It is an early attempt on his part to express in verse the Platonic principles which he afterwards so clearly and forcibly expressed in prose. These poems are now hardly known. His first prose work was published in 1652—*Antidote against Atheism* (new ed. 1655; also in coll. of philos. writings, 1662). In the following year he sent forth *Conjectura Cabalistica, or Attempt to Interpret the first three Chapters of Genesis in a threefold Manner—literal, philosophical, and mystical, or divinely moral*. His next work of importance appeared in 1659, being an essay on the *Immortality of the Soul* (also 1662), accompanied by a valuable preface on the

general subject of his philosophy. The leading principle of More's ethical system is that "moral goodness is simple and absolute, and that right reason is the judge of its nature, essence, and truth; but its attractiveness and beauty are felt by a special capacity, *in boniformi animæ facultate*, not unlike the *moral sense* of later writers. Therefore all moral goodness is properly termed intellectual and divine. To affect this as supreme gives supreme felicity. By the aid of reason we state the axioms or principles of ethics in definite propositions, and derive from them special maxims or rules." In his philosophical views More espouses Descartes in the main, stating at great length and with much minuteness the doctrine of innate ideas, and defending it against misconceptions and objections. He qualifies Descartes's opinion that the soul has its seat in the pineal gland, and contends for the extension or diffusion of the soul, at the same time arguing that this does not involve its discerptibility. He contends at times for the reality of space as an entity independent of God, and again makes space to be dependent on God (anticipating the argument of Samuel Clarke). He argues the existence of God from the moral nature of man. He also ably defends the doctrine of free-will "as the basis of morality." "Against the theological Necessitarians, who deny contingency, More argues clearly that God himself can alone know what events are necessary and what contingent. Prescience of such events either implies a contradiction or not. But to suppose a contradiction is virtually to say that the prescience is not divine. Contradictory objects cannot come within the sphere of the divine omniscience. And if there is no contradiction, we may recognise in this very fact that there is no inconsistency betwixt the divine prescience and free-will. Either way no solid argument can be drawn against moral liberty from the idea of divine prescience. Again, the whole force of the objections as to the will always following what appears for the moment best, More supposes to be met by the simple experience that the good we know we frequently do not do. Our works are not determined by our knowledge of what is best. We may have fine ideas of virtue, and yet never put them in practice. Our freedom in this sense is only too real; and it is the very object of morality to bring the idea and the will into unison, and so enlighten the one and discipline the other that they may attain to the highest good." Hobbes is said to have entertained a very high opinion of More's philosophical views, and to have declared that if his "own philosophy was not true, he knew none that he should sooner like than Henry More's, of Cambridge." In 1660, finally, More came out again, and this time with one of the ablest productions we have from his pen, being an extended treatise on the *Mystery of Godliness*, "written after an illness in which he had vowed, if spared, to write a book demonstrative of the truth of the Christian religion—so far as concerns the person and offices of Christ, he would attempt to construct the Christian theology after those subjective ethical relations and beliefs which were taught by Plato and Plotinus, and at the same time to recognise the reality of the supernatural in the Christian history—to the confusion of fanatics and infidels alike." He here reverently discusses the incarnation of Christ in all its bearings, and illustrates it with many curious and interesting thoughts derived from philosophy and history. Notwithstanding the Platonic dress in which he loves to array everything, More holds firmly and expounds reverently and lovingly all the great doctrines of Christianity. He protests most energetically against the tendency to spiritualize away the reality of the Gospel history. "That the human person of Christ," he says, "is not to be laid aside is evident from the whole tenor of the epistle to the Hebrews. For he that there is said to be a high-priest forever is that very man who was crucified on the cross at Jerusalem." Again he says, "I have with all earnestness and endeavor, and with undeniable clearness of testimony from reason and Scripture, demonstrated the truth and necessity of both Christ within and Christ without." It would appear that he did not altogether relish the phrase "imputative righteousness," yet his views on justification did not really differ from those of other divines of the period; but he was perhaps fonder of laying stress upon this, that "the end of the Gospel was to renovate the spirits of men in true and real inherent righteousness and holiness," and he spoke of the phrase in question as a "great scandal and effectual counterplot against the power of the Gospel, the nullifying and despising of moral honesty by those that are great zealots and high pretenders of religion." "For what an easy thing it is," he exclaims, "for a man to fancy himself an Israelite, and then to circumvent his honest neighbors under the notion of Egyptians." As for the Roman Catholic Church, he says that the economy of that Church "naturally tends to the betraying of souls to eternal destruction;" but adds, nevertheless, "not that it is possible for me (who cannot infallibly demonstrate to myself that all who lived under paganism are damned) to imagine that all who have gone under the name of papists have tumbled down into hell." The *Mystery of Godliness* enjoyed great popularity, and so did his *Inquiry into the Mystery of Iniquity*, a work directed chiefly against popery. But of all his writings, the only one which can be said to have retained any lasting popularity, or to be commendable to the modern reader, is his *Divine Dialogues*, which he brought out in 1668, containing "Disquisitions concerning the Attributes and Providence of God." This is pronounced by Tulloch the period which "may be said to mark the apex of More's intellectual activity." Of the book itself, Dr. Blair speaks in his lectures on rhetoric (lect. xxxvi) as "one of the most remarkable in the English language." "Though the style," he adds, "be now in some measure obsolete, and the speakers be marked with the academic stiffness of those times, yet the dialogue is animated by a variety of character and a sprightliness of conversation beyond what are commonly met with in writings of this kind." What is recounted in the *Dialogues* under the name of *Bathynous* is believed to be his own peculiar experience, and gives an admirable picture of his clear, confiding, and enthusiastic spirit. The third dialogue is regarded as the best, for it is strikingly illustrative of the dreamy ideal enthusiasm with which the young Platonist (More) pursued his studies and inquiries. The *Divine Dialogues* are certainly, upon the whole, the most interesting and readable of all of More's works. They possess, moreover, the advantage of condensing his general views on philosophy and religion. More's authorship continued far beyond this time (to 1687, making a period of thirty-five years in all), and he composed after this his *Manual of Metaphysics* (1671, 4to), and attacked both Jacob Böhme (in *Philosophiæ Teutonicæ Censura* [1670]), and Spinoza (*Duarum præcipuarum Atheismi Spinoziani columnarum subversio* [1672]) in elaborate treatises. But the elasticity and temper of his philosophical genius are less buoyant in these efforts. "His *Metaphysics*," says Tulloch, "elaborate though they be, are in the main only a systematic and somewhat desultory expansion of views regarding the nature and proof of incorporeal substances, which he had already more than once expressed; while his cabalistical and prophetical studies have acquired a stronger hold of his mind." Within the next ten years he issued no fewer than five publications taken up with mystical subjects—some of them of the most curious technical character—including a *Cabalistic Catechism*. Two of these writings are addressed to his friend Knorr (q. v.), the learned German Orientalist, whose speculations on the cabalistic art at this time considerably influenced More. After this we find him deeply engaged in prophetical studies. The theosophic elements, already so apparent in his philosophical poems, had been for some time held in check by his higher life of reason and healthy appreciation of natural

and moral facts. But gradually they acquired a more marked ascendency, as his mental habits became fixed, and the elasticity of natural feeling and thought began to decay. The balance, which had long been trembling, began at length to decline on the unhealthy side. *Ezekiel's Dream* and the *Synchronous Method of the Apocalyptic Visions* received elaborate transcendental explanation. He was himself apparently conscious of an undue confidence in this sort of study. Yet he was unable to resist its fascinations. In allusion it is supposed to himself, he makes one of the speakers in his fifth dialogue say: "The greatest fanaticism I know in him is this, that he professeth he understands clearly the truth of several prophecies of the mainest concernment, which yet many others pretend to be very obscure." His latest work, which he left incomplete, is a practical treatise entitled *Medela Mundi, or the Cure of the World*. There is no trace of this work except allusions to it in his correspondence, and it is probably the work which he mentions in one of his letters under the name of *The Safe Guide*. It was, to judge from what can be gleaned from his correspondence, intended to vigorously advocate the rights of reason, and one of its chief objects was to show how the "Christian and philosophic genius" should "mix together." "The Christian religion, rightly understood," appeared to him to be "the deepest and choicest piece of philosophy that is." It was "the main, if not the only scope" of his long and anxious studies to demonstrate the rationality of the Christian religion throughout. "For to heap up a deal of reading and notions and experiments, without some such noble and important design, had but been to make his mind or memory a shop of small wares." He adopted, therefore, without hesitation the generous resolution of Marcus Cicero—"Rationem quo ea me cunque ducet, sequor." He was proud to adorn himself as a writer with "the sacerdotal breastplate of the Λόγιον, or *Rationale*." "Every priest," he adds," quoting Philo, "should endeavor, according to his opportunity and capacity, to be as much as he can a *rational* man, or *philosopher*." Again, "to take away *reason*, under what fanatic pretence soever, is to dissolve the priest, and despoil him of this breastplate, and, which is worst of all, to rob Christianity of that special prerogative it has above all other religions in the world—viz. *that it dares appeal unto reason*, which as many as understand the true interest of our religion will not fail to stick closely to; the contrary betraying it to the unjust suspicion of falsehood, and equalizing it to every vain imposture. For, take away reason, and all religions are alike true; as, the light being removed, all things are of one color" (*Pref. to Antidote*, p. vi).

Though More's strength was displayed rather in what he could elaborate by thought than in the immediate use of his reading, he was nevertheless a laborious student. He devoted himself to the study of the best authors only. "He was wont to say that he was no wholesale man." It was with the weightiest matters that his mind was mostly engaged; though there was no part of learning, laudable and worthy, for which he had not a due esteem. For about a year before his death he was visibly sinking. His mind, sympathizing with his body, was, says his biographer, "'in sort out of tune.' I speak as to that deep and plastic sense (to use his own terms) he had been under usually in divine matters." His progress towards the close of life was nevertheless marked by humble piety and cheerful resignation. "Never," he said, "any person thirsted more for his meat and drink than he, if it pleased God, after a release from the body." "Yet," says Tulloch, "it is pleasant to reflect that his active mind remained full of thoughts for others to the last, and that those great questions in which he had spent all his time—What is good? and What is true?—were apparently as fresh and important with him at the end as at the beginning." He frequently in his last days expressed the hope that when he was called out of the present life his writings would be of use to the Church of God and to the world. Short-ly before his death he expressed his view of what awaited him by repeating the first words of Cicero's famous exclamation, "O præclarum illum diem," etc.; intimating, as he had also done before, his conviction that at his release from this painful world he would be admitted to converse with blessed and congenial spir-its. He expired calmly, and almost imperceptibly, Sept. 1, 1687, and lies buried in the chapel of the college of which he had been for so many years an admired orna-ment. In person Henry More was tall and thin, but of a "serene" and vivacious countenance—rather pale than florid in his later years—yet was it clear and spirituous, and his eye hazel, and vivid as an eagle's. There is, indeed, as all who have seen his portrait by Loggan will admit, a singularly vivid elevation in his countenance, with some lines strongly drawn around the mouth, but with ineffable sweetness, light, and dignity in the gen-eral expression. As he is the most poetic and tran-scendental, so he is, upon the whole, the most spiritual-looking of all the Cambridge divines. He was from youth to age evidently gifted with the most happy and buoyant religious temper. "He was profoundly pious, and yet without all sourness, superstition, or melan-choly." His habitual cast of mind was a serene thought-fulness, while his "outward conversation" with his friends was for the most part "free and facetious." Re-ligion was in practice with him clearly what he con-ceived it to be in theory—the consecration and perfec-tion of the natural life—the brightest and best form which it could attain, under the inspiration and guidance of the Divine Spirit. Although he chose for himself a secluded life, and so far suffered in consequence from a lack of that comprehensive experience which is more than all other education to the wise and open mind, he yet was not actuated in doing so by any indifference to the lighter and more active interests of humanity. It was remarked that his very air had in it something an-gelic. He seemed to be full of introversions of light, joy, benignity, and devotion at once, as if his face had been overcast with a golden shower of love and purity. Strangers even noticed this "marvellous lustre and ir-radiation" in his eyes and countenance. "A divine gale," as he himself said, breathed throughout all his life as well as his works; but, however far it lifted him, it never inflated him. Ward, in his life of this remark-able man, repeats some extraordinary encomiums passed upon him while living by eminent persons who knew him well. One of them averred that he looked upon Dr. More as "the holiest man on the face of the earth;" another that "he was more of an angel than a man." More substantial proofs, however, than words of the re-spect felt for him by his contemporaries were offered in the attentions paid to him by the learned world. Yet it would be difficult indeed to name a Christian grace in which he did not excel. His charity and humility were not less conspicuous than his piety. "His very cham-ber door was a hospital to the needy." Self-denial he regarded as the practical ground of moral virtue; and in his own heart and behavior he evinced his obser-vation that humility is the most precious part of pi-ety. The fervor of his direct approaches to and inter-course with God in prayer could not be surpassed. When the winds were ruffling about him, he made the utmost endeavor to keep low and humble, that he might not be driven from that anchor. So intense were his acts of worship, and accompanied with such a joyful sense of the divine presence, that his friends, when sometimes coming upon him unexpectedly while en-gaged in prayer, were surprised by indications of peace and joy in his countenance truly angelic. His tem-per was serene and cheerful, his discourse serious, yet lighted up with playful coruscations of wit and humor. "Few were of a cheerfuller spirit than he; none of a more deep felicity and enjoyment. In short, he pos-sessed in as great purity perhaps as it has existed in any man of modern times the light, sanctity, and bless-edness of the divine life." It is truly said by Tulloch that, "while More was no hero, either in thought or in deed—his speculations were too transcendental and his life too retired for this—he yet comes before us a singu-larly beautiful, benign, and noble character—one of those higher spirits who help us to feel the divine pres-ence on earth, and to believe in its reality." His works were published in 1679, in 3 vols. folio; his philosophi-cal writings in 1662, folio (4th ed. 1712); his theological works in 1675, folio. An analytical catalogue of all his works may be found in Cattermole's *Literature of the Church of England*, and also in Tulloch's *Rat. Theology*, from which we extract this view of More as a writer: "More, still more than Cudworth, repeats himself, add-ing prefaces and appendices to what he has already written, and returning again and again upon the same track of thought. The germ, in fact, of most of his speculations may be traced in his early *Philosophical Poems*. His genius in one sense was singularly fecund. Work after work sprang with easy luxuriance from his pen. But his writings do not exhibit any clear growth or system of ideas, unfolding themselves gradually, and maturing to a more comprehensive rationality. This lack of method is more or less characteristic of the school. Not only so, in his later productions there is rather a decay than an increase and enrichment of the rational element. To enter into any exposition of his cabalistical studies, of his discovery of Cartesianism in the first chapters of Genesis, and his favorite notion of all true philosophers descending from Moses through Pythagoras and Plato; and, still more, to touch his pro-phetical theories—the divine science which he finds in the dream of Ezekiel or the visions of the Apocalypse—would be labor thrown away, unless to illustrate the weakness of human genius, or the singular absurdities which beset the progress of knowledge, even in its most favorable stages. The supposition that all higher wis-dom and speculation were derived originally from Mo-ses and the Hebrew Scriptures, and that it was confir-matory both of the truth of Scripture and the results of philosophy to make out this traditionary connection, was widely prevalent in the 17th century. It was warmly supported and elaborately argued by some of the most acute and learned intellects. Both Cudworth and More profoundly believed in this connection. But this was only one of many instances of their lack of critical and historical judgment. Historical criticism, in the modern sense, was not even then dreamed of; and it is needless to consider forgotten delusions which have perished, rather with the common growth of reason than by the force of any special genius or discovery" (ii, 351–353). See his *Præfatio Generalissima* prefixed to his *Opera Omnia* (1679); Ward, *Life of Henry More* (Lond. 1710, 8vo); Burnet, *Hist. of his own Times;* Tulloch, *Rational Theol. and Christian Philos. in England in the 17th Century* (Lond. 1872, 2 vols. 8vo), ii, 303–409; Mul-linger, *Cambridge Characteristics in the 17th Century* (Lond. 1867, 8vo), ch. iv; Tennemann, *Hist. Phil.* p. 302, 321; Morell, *Hist. Mod. Philos.* p. 208, 211 sq.; Stough-ton, *Eccles. Hist.* ii, 385, 454, 482–485; Hallam, *Introd. to Lit.* (see Index in vol. ii, Harper's edition); Enfield, *Hist. Phil.* bk. viii, ch. iii, sec. 3; Theodore Parker, in *Christian Examiner*, vol. xxvi, art. 1; xxvii, 48 sq.; *Ret-rospective Rev.* vol. v (1822).

More, *Sir* **Thomas,** the noted chancellor of king Henry VIII of England, celebrated for the part he played in the political and ecclesiastical history of his country and for the philosophical views he espoused, was the son of Sir John More, one of the justices of the Court of King's Bench. Thomas was born in London in 1480 (some say 1479, others again 1484), and was edu-cated at St. Anthony's School in Threadneedle Street until about his fifteenth year, when he was placed, ac-cording to the custom of the times, in the house of car-dinal Morton, archbishop of Canterbury, where he be-came known to Colet, dean of St. Paul's, who used to say "there was but one wit in England, and that was young

Thomas More." In 1497 More went to Oxford. He had rooms in St. Mary's Hall, but carried on his studies at Canterbury College (afterwards Christ Church). Here he became intimately acquainted with Erasmus, who resided there during the greater part of 1497 and 1498, and formed a friendship which continued during life. It was also at Oxford that More composed the greater number of his English poems, which, though deficient in harmony and ease of versification, are spoken of by Ben Jonson as models of English literature. After More left Oxford he prosecuted the study of the law, and soon acquired great celebrity for his legal knowledge. He was appointed reader at Furnival's Inn, where he delivered lectures on law for three years; and about the same time he also delivered lectures at St. Lawrence's church in the Old Jewry, on the work of St. Augustine, *De Civitate Dei.* It must be remembered that religion, morals, and law were then taught together without distinction; yet More, in his lectures, did not so much discuss the points of divinity as the precepts of moral philosophy and history. It is, however, well known that More also did delight to touch on questions of theology, for he was always fond of it, and for some time thought of taking orders. "He manifested," says Mackintosh, "a predilection for monastic life, and is said to have practiced some of those austerities and self-inflictions which prevail among the gloomier and sterner orders" (Life, in *Works,* i, 405). He resolved indeed at one time to turn monk, and actually became a lay-brother of the Carthusian convent (the Charter-House) in London, where he is said to have passed several years. But he finally relinquished the ecclesiastical life, influenced perhaps by the general corruption of the priestly orders, or, as Erasmus has it, he preferred to be a chaste husband rather than an impure priest. More was called to the bar, though at what time is uncertain. He appears to have acquired an extensive practice. He came to be generally regarded as one of the most eloquent speakers of his day; indeed, his reputation became so great towards the latter part of the reign of Henry VII that it is said that there was no case of consequence before any court of law in which he was not engaged as counsel. About 1502 he first entered upon public office. He was then made an under-sheriff of London, an office at that time of great legal responsibility. Only two years later he was elected to Parliament, in which he opposed a subsidy which had been demanded by Henry VII for the marriage of his eldest daughter. In consequence of this opposition More incurred the displeasure of Henry VII, a prince who never forgave an injury; and had not the king died soon afterwards, More would have been obliged to leave the country. Notwithstanding all opposition at court, More flourished, and gained constantly in reputation and friends. His graceful and varied learning, coupled as it was with sprightly, inexhaustible wit, so that Erasmus could write of him that "with More you might imagine yourself in the Academy of Plato," no doubt contributed in a large measure to his rapid advancement. "His professional practice became so considerable," says Mackintosh, "that about the accession of Henry VIII (1509) it produced £400 a year, probably equivalent to an annual income of £5000 in the present day." With the accession of Henry VIII to the English throne More's most auspicious days began. He became a favorite of his royal master, always so quick to detect in his surroundings whatever and whoever was likely to prove serviceable to him. King "Harry" remarked More's talents, and not only gladly consulted him on affairs of state, but sought him as the companion of his amusements and convivial hours. According to the account of Erasmus, the circle there collected must have been one of the most brilliant and engaging that the world has ever seen, and it was adorned by virtues which to other associations, high in intellect, have often been wanting. More was appointed to several important civil offices, and even employed as envoy

on foreign missions. Thus, in 1514, he was sent to Flanders, to secure favors from the prince afterwards known as emperor Charles V. More was also employed by his king on various public missions to France, and so interested did Henry VIII become in More that he ordered cardinal Wolsey, then his chancellor, to engage More in the service of the court. Accordingly More was made treasurer of the exchequer in 1520, and not only acceptably performed his public functions, but also grew in popularity with the courtiers and the king, by reason of his sweet temper and great conversational power. The king frequently met More, and enjoyed many hours with him, not only socially, but intellectually. Indeed, in 1521, when king Harry was working up his reply to the German Reformer, More assisted his royal friend by casting that celebrated treatise against the Protestant effort into a proper method. It was published in 1521, under the title of *Assertio septem sacramentorum adversus M. Lutherum,* etc., and in 1523 More himself published *Responsio ad convitia M. Lutheri congesta in Henricum regem Angliæ.* "In this *Answer to Luther,*" says Atterbury, "More has forgot himself so as to throw out the greatest heap of nasty language that perhaps ever was put together; and that the book throughout is nothing but downright ribaldry, without a grain of reason to support it, and gave to the author no other reputation but that of having the best knack of any man in Europe at calling bad names in good Latin, etc. The like censure do his English tracts against Tindal, Barnes, etc., deserve" (*Epistolary Correspondence,* iii, 452). And though this criticism is rather harsh, it was yet in a large measure deserved (comp., however, More's *Apology,* in which he denies these charges of overzeal against heresy). In 1523 More was chosen speaker of the House of Commons, and now entered upon a career in which for a time he alienated both his royal master and the chancellor. The cardinal had taken the liberty of asking a greater subsidy for the king than he was entitled to, and was inclined to be generally lavish in his expenditures for the crown, as well as very unmindful of the ancient liberties and privileges of the house. More valiantly defended the people's cause, and hesitated not to speak out, though it endangered his popularity with the king. Indeed, More had never deceived himself as to the extent of his favor with the king, though his friend Erasmus had dared to assert that "the king would scarcely ever suffer the philosopher to quit him," and though Henry visited him uninvited at Chelsea, and walked with him by the hour in his garden, "holding his arm about his neck." More had a true insight into Henry's character, and clearly revealed this in an answer which he once gave when congratulated by his son-in-law, Roper, on the king's favor: "If my head would win him a castle in France, when there was war between us, it should not fail to go." Henry's faithfulness, was, however, more lasting in More's case than it was wont to be, for he clung to him notwithstanding this waywardness, and shortly after caused his appointment as chancellor of Lancaster, and on the death of the cardinal in 1529 More was even more strongly impressed with his royal friend's affection by his appointment to the high chancellorship of all England, vacated by the disgrace of Wolsey. Here was more than usual expression of confidence and affection. The favor was, moreover, the more extraordinary as he was a layman, and it was wont to be the custom to invest an ecclesiastic with the office of lord chancellor. But it was afterwards revealed why this apparent warmth and fervor. Henry had simply advanced More to the chancellorship with the hope that he would assist him in his divorce, and marriage with Anne Boleyn, and no sooner had he been elevated to the high chancellorship than the king pressed him strongly for his opinion on the subject. But More was sincerely attached to the Roman Catholic Church; he looked with a certain degree of horror upon a project which was denounced by the pontifical head of

English Chancellor's Costume in Sir Thomas More's time.

the Church, and therefore begged Henry to excuse him from giving an opinion. This was granted for a time; but as it was evident that Henry had determined to effect the divorce, and would soon require the active co-operation of his chancellor, More, who determined not to be a party to the transaction, finally asked and obtained permission to retire from the office, May 16, 1532. From this time Henry, who never seems to have recollected any former friendship when his purposes were in the least degree thwarted, appears to have resolved upon the destruction of his old favorite. Anne Boleyn's coronation being fixed for May 31, 1533, all fair means were used to win him over; and when these proved ineffectual, recourse was had to threats and terrors. More was included in the bill of attainder which was passed against Elizabeth Barton, the celebrated nun of Kent, and her accomplices for treasonable practices, on the ground that he had encouraged Elizabeth; but his innocence in the case was made so clear that his name had to be withdrawn from the bill of accusation. He was then accused of other crimes, but with the same effect. Yet the court party soon found an opportunity of gratifying their vindictive master. By a law passed in the session of 1533–34 it was made high-treason, by writing, print, deed, or act, to do anything to the prejudice, etc., of the king's lawful matrimony with queen Anne; and it was also provided that all persons should take an oath to maintain the whole contents of the statute. At the end of the session commissioners were appointed to administer the oath, and on April 15, 1534, More was summoned before them to take it. This More declined doing, but at the same time offered to swear that he would maintain the order of succession to the throne as established by Parliament. In consequence of his refusing to take this oath, More was committed to the Tower; and in the same year two statutes were passed to attaint More and Fisher [see FISHER, JOHN] of misprision of treason, with the punishment of imprisonment and loss of goods. More remained in prison for thirteen months, during which time several efforts were made to induce him to take the oath, and also to subscribe to the king's ecclesiastical supremacy. His reputation and credit being very great in the kingdom, and much being apprehended from his conduct at that critical conjuncture, all arguments that could be devised were alleged to him by archbishop Cranmer and others to persuade him to a compliance, and many fair promises were made from the king to induce him thereto; but, as nothing could prevail, he was finally brought to trial for high-treason. He appears to have been indicted under the statute alluded to above, which made it high-treason to do any-

thing to the prejudice of Henry's lawful marriage with queen Anne, and also for refusing to admit the king's ecclesiastical supremacy; and although the evidence against him completely failed, he was found guilty and condemned to death. He was beheaded July 6, 1535, and met his fate with intrepidity and even cheerfulness. In the words of Addison: "The innocent mirth which had been so conspicuous in his life did not forsake him to the last. When he laid his head on the block, he desired the executioner to wait until he had removed his beard, 'for that had never offended his highness.' He did not look upon the severing of his head from his body as a circumstance which ought to produce any change in the disposition of his mind; and as he died in a fixed and settled hope of immortality, he thought any unusual degree of sorrow and concern improper" (*Spectator*, No. 349). His body was first interred in the Tower, but was afterwards begged and obtained by his daughter, Margaret Roper, and deposited in the chancel of the church at Chelsea, where a monument, with an inscription written by himself, had been some time before erected, and is still to be seen. His head was placed on London Bridge, but was taken down and preserved also by his daughter in a vault belonging to the Roper family, under a chapel adjoining St. Dunstan's church in Canterbury. The story of Margaret's tenderness and devotion to her father should live as long as the English language endures.

More was the author of many and various works, which were mostly in defence of Romanism, and directed against the revolutionary tendencies of the Church of his day. They have no value now as literary productions. There is, however, one work of his which deserves special notice. It is entitled *De optimo rei-publicæ statu deque nova insula Utopia* (Lovanni, 1566, 4to), the first communistic writing by an English author. It criticises the English government and European politics, and is an account of an imaginary commonwealth on the island of Utopia, feigned to have been discovered by a companion of Amerigo Vespucci, and from whom More learns the tale. Society is represented there as an ideal system, in which opinions are expressed with great boldness and originality, and especially favorable to freedom of inquiry even in religion. In it all its members would labor for the public good, all being equally obliged to contribute, and the only difference being in the nature of the labor; all its members would thus be on a footing of absolute equality, all property be in common, all forms of religion perfectly free, etc. "Many questions of the highest importance to the citizen," says Lieber, "are discussed in a spirit far in advance of his time. He recommended perfect freedom of conscience, which was a thing absolutely unknown then, and for centuries afterwards" (*Political Ethics*, pt. i, p. 332). Of the work as a whole, lord Campbell says that "since the time of Plato there had been no composition given to the world which, for imagination, for philosophical discrimination of men and manners, and for felicity of expression, could be compared to the *Utopia*" (*Lives of the Lord Chancellors; Life of Sir Thomas More*). Hallam pronounces it "the only work of genius that England can boast in this age" (*Lit. Hist. of Europe* [4th ed. 1854], p. 276). Yet, though Sir Thomas advocated such lofty principles in his *Utopia*, it must be admitted that he was not himself altogether free from the religious bias of the times, being not only a most strenuous advocate of the power of the pope, but also a vehement opponent and persecutor of heretics. It is true Erasmus cites as proof of More's clemency "that while he was chancellor no man was put to death for these pestilent dogmas;" but Froude contradicts this statement, and implicates Sir Thomas in the persecutions for conscience' sake. There is, however, a solemn declaration by the chancellor himself in his *Apology* (published in 1533), in which he expressly denies that he was guilty of any cruel treatment of the heretics. It was never contradicted in his own time, and therefore should be well considered before Froude's statement is accepted.

If now, from his works, we turn to the personal character of Sir Thomas More, we find that he is generally acknowledged to have been, "for justice, contempt of money, humility, and a true generosity of mind, an example to the age in which he lived." His Christian temper, too, we may add, was such as made him an honor to the Christian cause in general. It is true he declared upon the scaffold that he died in and for the faith of the Church of Rome, but any Church might have wished him theirs; and therefore that Church has placed him, not without reason, among the brightest of her martyrs. "More," says bishop Burnet, "was the glory of his age; and his advancement was the king's honor more than his own, who was a true Christian philosopher. He thought the cause of the king's divorce was just, and as long as it was prosecuted at the court of Rome, so long he favored it; but when he saw that a breach with that court was likely to follow, he left the post he was in with a superior greatness of mind. It was a fall great enough to retire from that into a private state of life, but the carrying matters so far against him as the king did was one of the justest reproaches of that reign. More's superstition seems indeed contemptible, but the constancy of his mind was truly wonderful" (*Hist. Reformation*, iii, 100). A British writer of considerable note thus summarizes upon More: "The terseness and liveliness of his sayings, his sweet temper and affectionate disposition, his blameless life, his learning and probity, combine to make a union of perfect simplicity with moral and intellectual greatness which will forever endear his memory to his countrymen of every sect and party." The English works of Sir Thomas More were collected and published at London in 1557, and his Latin works at Louvain in 1556. His letters to Erasmus are printed in the collection of Erasmus's letters published at London in 1642. His *Utopia*, which has been translated into many European languages, and has had a world-wide circulation, was given an English dress by Robynson (Lond. 1551), by bishop Burnet, and more recently by Arthur Cayley (Lond. 1808). The Life of Sir Thomas More has been written by his son-in-law, Roper, who married his favorite daughter Margaret (Lond. 1626); by his great-grandson, T. More (1626); by Hoddesden (Lond. 1652); by Cayley (1808); by Walter [R. C.] (Lond. 1840); and by Sir James Mackintosh, in *Lives of Eminent British Statesmen*, published in Dr. Lardner's *Cabinet Cyclop.*, and in *Miscell. Works* (Lond. 1854, 18mo), i, 393 sq. See also lord Campbell, *Lives of the Lord Chancellors*; Froude, *Hist. of Engl.* vol. ii, ch. ix, reviewed in *North Brit. Rev.* 1859; Burnet, *Own Times*, i, 155 sq.; Wordsworth, *Eccles. Biog.* ii, 49 sq.; Soames, *Reformed Ch. of Eng.* vol. i and ii; Macaulay, *Crit. and Hist. Essays*, ii, 543; Seebohm, *The Oxford Reformers of* 1498 (Lond. 1869); *Edinburgh Rev.* xiv, 360; *Westminster Rev.* xi, 193; *Foreign Rev.* v, 391; *Retrospective Rev.* (1822), v, 249; *North American Rev.* viii, 181; lxvi, 272; *National Qu. Rev.* June, 1863, art. iii.

Morea. See GREECE, KINGDOM OF.

Moreau, Gabriel François, a French prelate, was born at Paris Sept. 24, 1721. Descended from a lawyer's family, he became council scribe in the Parliament of Paris, and was in 1737 provided with a sinecure canonship in the metropolitan church, but rapidly rose to distinction, and in 1759 was made bishop of Vence. In 1763 he was transferred to the see of Macon. After the concordat of 1801 he obtained the bishopric of Autun, where he died, Sept. 8, 1802. The first consul (Napoleon Bonaparte) esteemed him highly, and demanded from the pope the cardinal's hat for him. His literary remains, however, are scanty, consisting mainly of a few funeral sermons on distinguished individuals, viz. *Oraison funèbre de Ferdinand VI et Marie de Portugal, roi et reine d'Espagne* (1760), and *Oraison funèbre*

de M. le Duc de Bourgogne (1761). See Hoefer, *Nouv. Biog. Générale*, xxxvi, 479.

Moreau, Jean, a French theologian, was born at Laval near the opening of the 16th century. He was educated at Paris, and when about thirty years of age was appointed professor of theology at the University of Paris. He next became canon at the cathedral of Meaux. He died about 1584. His work, *Nomenclatura seu Legenda aurea pontificum Cenomanensium, ab anno Verbi incarnati* 902 *usque ad annum* 1572, is still preserved in MS.

Moreau, Macé, a French martyr to Protestant Christianity, was born in the first half of the 16th century, and flourished at Troyes, in Champagne. He was reared in the Roman Catholic faith, but about 1547 accepted the Reformed faith, and went to Geneva to study theology. In 1550 he returned to France, going about the country distributing tracts that might turn men's attention from this world's affairs to spiritual things. While at Troyes he was entrapped by Romanists, and after a short imprisonment brought to trial before the Inquisition, and condemned to death at the stake unless he should recant. This he refused to do; and he continued steadfast even at the stake, "until he was smothered by the flames, and his voice on earth forever hushed." See Hurst, *Martyrs to the Tract Cause* (N. Y. 1872, 18mo), p. 111.

Mo'reh (Heb. *Moreh'*, מוֹרֶה, an *archer*, as in 1 Sam. xxxi, 3, etc., or *teaching*, as in Isa. ix, 14), an old title that appears in the designation of two localities of central Palestine.

1. Apparently a Canaanite (perhaps a chief, like Mamre), B.C. 2088, owning or inhabiting the region south of Shechem, from whom the grove (אֵלוֹן, *oak* [also in the plur.], Auth. Vers. "plain") of Moreh derived its name as early as the time of Abraham, who made this his first tarrying-place in the land (Gen. xii, 6, where the Sept. has ἡ δρῦς ἡ ὑψηλή, Vulg. *convallis illustris*), a designation that continued till the exode (Deut. xi, 30, Sept. ἡ δρῦς ἡ ὑψηλή, Vulg. *vallis tendens et intrans procul*)—"the first of that long succession of sacred and venerable trees which dignified the chief places of Palestine, and formed not the least interesting link in the chain which so indissolubly united the land to the history of the nation. See OAK. Here Jehovah 'appeared' to Abraham, who here built the first of the series of altars (it may be roughly said that Abraham built altars, Isaac dug wells, Jacob erected stones) which marked the various spots of his residence in the Promised Land, and dedicated it 'to Jehovah, who appeared (נִרְאָה, again, as if a play upon the name of the place) unto him' (Gen. xii, 7). It was at the 'place of Shechem' (ver. 6), close to (אֵצֶל) the mountains of Ebal and Gerizim (Deut. xi, 30), where the Samar. Cod. adds 'over against Shechem.' Ecclus. l, 26 perhaps contains a play on the name Moreh— 'that foolish people (ὁ λαὸς ὁ μωρός) who dwell in Sichem.' If the pun existed in the Hebrew text, it may have been between Sichem and Sichor (drunken). A trace of this ancient name, curiously reappearing after many centuries, is probably to be found in *Morthia*, which is given on some ancient coins as one of the titles of Neapolis, i. e. Shechem, and by Pliny and Josephus as *Mamortha* or *Mabortha* (Reland, *Diss.* III, § 8). The latter states (*War*, iv, 8, 1) that 'it was the name by which the place was called by the country people' (ἐπιχώριοι), who thus kept alive the ancient appellation, just as the peasants of Hebron did that of Kirjath-arba down to the date of Sir John Mandeville's visit." From the notices given, the grove of Moreh appears to have been a forest occupying the ridge afterwards known as the mountains of Ephraim. (The treatise of Chr. J. Grabener, *De Allon Moreh*, Lips. 1737, is valueless.)

2. An eminence (hill of Moreh, גִּבְעַת הַמּוֹרֶה, i. e.

teacher's hill; Sept. βουνὸς τοῦ ᾿Αμορέ v. r. Γαβαω-Ͻαμοραί, Vulg. *collis excelsus*) in the valley of Jezreel, on the north side of the well of Harod, near which the Midianitish host was encamped when attacked by Gideon (Judg. vii, 1); probably identical with that known as *Little Hermon*, the modern *Jebel ed-Duhy* (see Bertheau, *Comment.* ad loc.), or, rather, one of the lower southern spurs of this mountain (where ruins are still extant), since it is itself too lofty (1839 feet, Van de Velde, *Memoir*, p. 178) for a military encampment. It is a bare gray ridge parallel to Mount Gilboa on the north, and between them lay the battle-field. No doubt —although the fact is not mentioned—the enemy kept near the foot of Mount Moreh, for the sake of some spring or springs which issued from its base, as the Ain-Charod did from that on which Gideon was planted. See HAROD. The hostile camp probably extended from the village of Shunem on the west down to the strong city of Bethshan on the east, for we are told that "the Midianites and the Amalekites, and all the children of the east, lay along the valley like grasshoppers for multitude" (ver. 12). The mountain is the site not only of Shunem, but also of Endor and Nain (see Porter, *Hand-book*, p. 357 sq.). Whether this place has any connection with the preceding is doubtful; and it is still more unlikely that either is related to Moriah, as thought by Stanley (*Sin. and Pal.* p. 141, 232). Van de Velde locates the battle too far south (*Syr. and Pal.* ii, 341). See GIDEON.

Morehead, ROBERT, D.D., an English divine of some note, flourished in the first half of this century. But little is known of his personal history. He was for some time rector of St. Paul's in Edinburgh, and there attained to distinction as a pulpit orator. Subsequently he became rector of Easington, Yorkshire, and died in 1840. He was one of the early and most valued contributors to the *Edinburgh Review*. His works are, *Tour to the Holy Land* (18mo) :—*Discourses on Religious Belief* (Edinb. 1809, 8vo; 4th ed. 1811–16, 2 vols. 8vo); commended by lord Jeffrey in the *Edinburgh Review*, xiv, 82–95:—*Sermons* (1816, 8vo):—*Dialogues on Natural and Revealed Religion* (1830, 12mo); praised by Lowndes's *Brit. Lib.* p. 941, the *Edinb. Rev.*, and the British contemporary press generally, in most unqualified terms:— *Explanation of St. Paul's Epistles* (1843, fcp. 8vo):—*Philosophical Dialogues* (1845, 8vo).

Morel, Claude, a French theologian and preacher of note, flourished in the 17th century. He was a doctor of the Sorbonne and court preacher, but is best known as a passionate adversary of the Jansenists. He published against them *La conduite de Saint Augustin contre les Pelagiens* (1658), and *L'Oracle de la Verité, ou l'Église de Dieu contre toutes sortes d'hérésies* (1666). The Jansenists failed not to answer him, as four pieces still attest, viz. a Latin epistle in prose, two pieces in Latin verse inveighing against him, and a French sonnet. In 1659 the council of state instituted proceedings against these Jansenistic opponents and sentenced them.

Morel, Guillaume, a learned French printer, noted for the valuable editions he published of the writings of distinguished ecclesiastical writers, was born at Le Tilleul, near Mortain, in 1505. He was the successor of Turnebius (1550) in the office of director of the royal printing-office, and died in 1561. Besides his editions of Greek and Latin authors (Aristotle, Strabo, Dio Chrysostomus, Cicero, etc.), he published a French translation of the treatise on the use of images approved by the seventh Nicene Council, and of John Damascenus's *Treatise on Images*.

Morel, Jean, a French martyr to the cause of Protestant Christianity in its earliest days in France, was born in 1538 near Lisieux, of a poor and obscure family in Normandy. He sought the capital, and though without means contrived to pursue and finish

a scholarly education, during this period earning his living partly by instruction, partly by work in a printing-office. Thereafter, it is not known from what motive, he made a journey to Geneva, and returned full of enthusiasm for the new religious doctrines. He then entered the service of the (Calvinistic) minister, Antoine de Chandieu, both as domestic and secretary. While in this position the police came to seize the books written in favor of the new religion, and he, along with his master, was arrested. Chandieu, at the reclamation of the king of Navarre, was soon set at liberty; but Morel was placed in one of the most dismal dungeons of the Chatelet, and thence transported to Fort l'Evêque, where he had to undergo numerous interrogatories. He resisted the entreaties of his judges and the urgent requests of his relatives, who tried to make him abjure his creed, and Feb. 16, 1559, was declared a heretic, expelled from the Church, and surrendered to the secular power. Four days later he was found dead in the Conciergerie—rumor reported poisoned. Like the condemned dying in prison, his body was buried the day following; but by order of the procureur-général it was disinterred, brought back to the Conciergerie, carried in a rubbish-cart to the arca before the church of Notre Dame, and publicly burned, Feb. 27, 1559.

Morel, Robert, a French Benedictine monk, was born in 1653 at La Chaise Dieu, in Auvergne. He took holy orders at the abbey of Saint Faron de Meaux in 1671; was sent to the abbey of Saint Germain des Prés to finish his studies, and in 1680 became its librarian. He was afterwards appointed superior (prior) of a convent at Meulan, and at Saint Crespin de Soissons, and secretary to the visiting officer of France. Deafness, with which he became afflicted, obliged him to resign these offices, and he retired in 1699 to Saint Denis, near Paris, where he divided the rest of his life between pious religious exercises and the editing of several ascetic works. He died Aug. 19, 1731, in the odor of sanctity. He was a man of a clear, well-balanced, fertile mind; his words breathed charity and righteousness; but great modesty, joined to simplicity, served to conceal his talents. His publications are: *Effusions de cœur, ou entretiens spirituels et affectifs d'une âme avec Dieu sur chaque verset des Psaumes et des Cantiques de l'Église* (Paris, 1716) :— *Méditations sur la règle de Saint-Benoit* (Paris, 1717): —*Entretiens spirituels sur les Évangiles* (Paris, 1720) :— *Entretiens spirituels pour servir de préparation à la mort* (Paris, 1721):—*Imitation de Jésus-Christ*, a translation, with additional pieces (Paris, 1723) :— *Méditations Chrétiennes sur les Évangiles* (Paris, 1726) : —*Du bonheur d'un simple Religieux et d'une simple Religieuse, qui aiment leur état et leurs devoirs* (Paris, 1728):—*De l'espérance Chrétienne* (Paris, 1728) :—*Effusion de cœur sur le Cantique des Cantiques* (Paris, 1730).

Morell, Samuel, an Irish Presbyterian minister, flourished in the second half of the 18th century. He was born about 1744, and was educated at Dublin. He was a young man of rare promise, and was very much liked as a minister. He began preaching when not more than twenty-five years old at Tullylish, in the Synod of Ulster, but during the civil disturbances of 1772 he was persecuted for the part he took in behalf of law and order, and in a riot which occurred on the 6th of March of that year he was shot down in the streets, and died from the effects of the wound. See Reid and Killen, *Hist. Presbyt. Ch. in Ireland*, iii, 370.

Morell, Thomas, D.D., an eminent English critic and lexicographer, was born at Eton in 1703. He studied first at Eton, then at Cambridge, where he became a fellow of King's College. He was noted, however, not as a theologian, but as a classical scholar. He published valuable editions of Ainsworth's Latin Dictionary and Hedericus's Greek Lexicon, and was the author of *Annotations on Locke's Essay on the Human Understand-*

ing (1794). He edited the plays of Euripides and Æschylus, translated the *Epistles* of Seneca, assisted Hogarth in writing his *Analysis of Beauty*, and selected the passages of Scripture for Handel's oratorios. Several of his best sermons were also published; among these, one on the death of queen Caroline (1739, 8vo). He died in 1784.

Morellet, ANDRÉ, a celebrated French abbot, noted for his literary labors, was born at Lyons in 1727, and educated in the Sorbonne, at Paris. He became a friend of Voltaire, Rousseau, Diderot, and D'Alembert, to whose *Encyclopédie* he also contributed. He translated into French Beccaria's treatise *On Crimes and Penalties* (1766), and wrote several treatises on political economy, and many others, among which is *Mélanges de la Littérature et de la Philosophie du dix-huitième siècle* (Paris, 1818, 4 vols. 8vo). In 1785 he was admitted to the French Academy, and concealed its archives at the risk of his life during the reign of terror. He died in 1819. See Lemontey, *Éloge de Morellet*, prefixed to Morellet's *Mémoires* (1821, 2 vols.); *Nouv. Biog. Générale*, s. v.; "Morellet and his Contemporaries," in the *North Amer. Rev.* Oct. 1822, by A. H. Everett.

Morelli, Cosimo, an Italian architect of considerable note among those of the last century, deserves a place here because his life-labors were very largely devoted to ecclesiastical architecture. He was born at Imola in 1732, and was the son of Domenico Morelli (also an architect), and studied under Domenico Trifogli, who executed several works of merit at Imola. It was Cosimo's good fortune to obtain powerful patronage at the very outset of his professional career—first, that of Giovan-Carlo Bandi, bishop of Imola, for whom he made designs for rebuilding the cathedral of that city, and through him that of his nephew Giovanni Antonio Braschi, who was elevated to the papal throne in 1775, with the name of Pius VI. The new pontiff, who entertained a personal regard for Morelli, obtained for him the appointment of city architect at Cesena (the pope's native town), and various other commissions. He died, after a severe paralytic attack, in February, 1812. The principal structures executed by him in the line in which we are interested are the cathedral of Imola, the metropolitan church at Fermo, the duomo at Macerata, and the conventual church at Fossombrone, St. Petronio at Castel Bolognese, a church at Barbiano, that of the nuns of St. Chiara at Imola, and St. Maria in regola in the same city, and another church at Lugo; also some alterations in the metropolitan church at Ravenna. See Tipaldo, *Biogr. degli Italiani illustri; Engl. Cyclop.* s. v.; Spooner, *Biog. Dict. of the Fine Arts*, ii, 588.

Morelli, Giacomo, *Abbé*, an Italian ecclesiastic, noted for his antiquarian labors, and one of the most distinguished librarians of modern times, was born at Venice, April 14, 1745. He was the son of poor parents, who were unable to give him a liberal education. It was against their will that he resolved to enter the Church, although in all other respects he always showed the greatest deference to their wishes. He afterwards supplied the deficiencies of his education by private study, and the knowledge which he thus acquired was more substantial and extensive than that of any of his Italian contemporaries, though it was not till late in life that he became acquainted with the Greek and French languages. His love of independence induced him to refuse several very advantageous offers that were made to him both by the Church and by wealthy collectors of books at Venice, and he continued to live as a simple abbé. He formed, however, an intimate friendship with the patrician Farsetti, of whose rich collection of MSS. he published a catalogue, under the title of *Bibliotheca Manuscritta del bali T. G. Farsetti* (Venice, 1771–80, 2 vols. 12mo). While this work was in course of publication, he also wrote *Dissertazione Storica intorno alla Publica Libreria di S. Marco* (Venice, 1774), in which he discussed and solved a great many

questions connected with the history of literature. He then prepared a similar work on the history of the library of the academy at Padua, whither he had accompanied his friend Farsetti; but the materials which he collected for that purpose were unfortunately left in the hands of Colle, the historiographer of that institution, through whose carelessness they were lost. In 1776 he published a catalogue of the MSS. of ancient writers which were in the library of the Narni family; and somewhat later a catalogue of the MSS. of Italian works contained in the same library. These works alone would have sufficed to secure to Morelli an honorable place among the eminent bibliographers of modern times; but he acquired a still greater reputation as librarian of the library of St. Mark—an office which he received in 1778, and which he held until his death, which occurred May 5, 1819. In 1795 he discovered a considerable fragment of the 55th book of Dion Cassius, which he published at Bassano, together with new various readings of other books of the same historian. The work which exhibits his extensive knowledge and his critical acumen in the strongest light is his *Bibliotheca Manuscripta Græca et Latina*, of which, however, only one volume was published at Bassano (1802), although he had collected materials for several more volumes. His last production was *Epistolæ septem variæ eruditionis* (Padua, 1819). After his death there appeared *Operette ora insieme con Opuscoli di Antichi Scrittori* (Venice, 1820, 3 vols. 8vo). See Zendrini, *Elogio di Morelli* (Mil. 1821); reproduced in the *Galleria du Letterati ed artisti illustri della provincii Veneziane nel Secolo XVIII* (Venice, 1822–24); Bettio, *Orazione recitata nelle solenne Esequie nella Chiesa Patriarcale di Venezia* (Venice, 1819).

Morelstshiki (i. e. *self-immolators*), also called the "*Voluntary Martyrs*," a Russian sect of fanatics, whose wild and savage practices are more like those of ancient Scandinavians than of professing Christians of the 19th century. It is difficult to know what are the dogmas of these voluntary martyrs, because they have no printed books, and they do not confide to foreigners the mysteries of their sect. Regarding the Old and New Testament as having been corrupted, it is said that they give themselves the right to change it. They recognise God the Father, manifested to men under the double form of Jesus Christ and the Holy Ghost. They reject the true death and resurrection of Jesus, maintaining that the body placed in the sepulchre by Joseph of Arimathea was not the Lord's body, but that of an obscure soldier. They think that Christ will soon return, and make his triumphant entrance into Moscow, and that thither his disciples will hasten from every part of the earth. They do not observe the Sabbath. Their only religious holiday is Easter. They then celebrate the Lord's Supper with bread which has been buried in the tomb of some saint, supposing that it thus receives a kind of mysterious consecration. Their meetings are held on Saturday night. The following are a few lines of one of their hymns: "Be firm, mariners! Triumph over the tempest! Fear neither fire nor whirlwind. Christ is with us. He will collect the faithful in his vessel. His masts will not break; his sails will never be rent; and he will hold the helm firmly, and land us in a safe haven. The Holy Spirit is with us; the Holy Spirit is in us." Their custom is to meet together on a certain day in the year in some retired place, and, having dug a pit, to fill it with wood, straw, and other combustibles, while they are singing weird hymns, like that of which we have given an extract, relating to the ceremony. Fire is then applied to the piled fuel, and numbers leap into the midst of it, stimulated by the triumphant hymns of those around, to purchase a supposed martyrdom by their suicidal act. Others, without sacrificing life, cruelly mutilate their bodies, like the fanatics of India, who throw themselves beneath the triumphal car of their idol. These sectarians are to be found chiefly in the north of Russia, especially Siberia, but they are also represented on the banks of the Volga. There are a few at Moscow, St. Petersburg, Riga, Odessa, etc. They try to make proselytes in the army, but the imperial police pursue their missionaries, and when they are discovered punish them most cruelly. The Russian government has endeavored to suppress them by means of very severe measures, but has thus far failed in doing so. See Marsden, *Hist. of Christian Churches and Sects*, ii, 231, 232.

Morely (or **Morelly**) (Lat. *Morelius*), JEAN BAPTISTE, a French Protestant divine, noted for his attempts to introduce into the Church a democratic organization such as it had in apostolic times, was born at Paris about 1510. But little is known of his early personal history. He suddenly became noted by his criticism of the fourth book of Calvin's *Institution Chrétienne*, in an essay on ecclesiastical discipline, in which he tried to prove that the laity ought to have power to decide on all important questions of doctrine, morals, election of pastors, etc., privileges assigned by the Geneva Reformer to a Consistory, and fortified his theory by declarations of Scripture and the usages of the primitive Church. He submitted the same in manuscript to Calvin; but Calvin returned it with the excuse that he had not time to peruse so long a treatise on a subject already settled by the Word of God. Morely then had it printed under the title, *Traité de la discipline et police Chrétienne* (Lyons, 1561). The moderation, the force of argument, the clearness of exposition displayed in it found little countenance with the Calvinistic churches, and when in 1562 he presented it to the National Synod held at Orleans it was rejected. This condemnation appeared rather strange to a large number of the Reformed; among others, Soubise expressed himself strongly against this proceeding to Theodore de Beza, who, however, succeeded in quieting him. Morely retired to Tours, where he found a violent adversary in the pastor of Saint-Germain, and thence to Geneva (Nov. 1562). Here he was ere long summoned before the Consistory, and asked to retract. This he refused to do, but proposed to submit the matter to the judgment of Farel, De Viret, and Calvin. The latter would not accept the part of arbiter, saying he would not place himself above the synod, which had condemned his book. Even Morely's request to give him permission to defend himself in writing was not granted; on the contrary, the Consistory treated him as an obstinate heretic, and (Aug. 31, 1563) excommunicated him; his book, referred to the council, was condemned to be burned (Sept. 17), and all bookstores were forbidden to expose it for sale, all citizens and inhabitants of Geneva warned not to purchase it for reading, and all who possessed copies of it were ordered to bring them, and those who knew where there were any, to denounce them within twenty-four hours at the risk of severe punishment in case of non-compliance. Morely left Geneva, but the passion of the Calvinistic clergy ceased not to manifest itself against him. When in 1566 he acted as tutor to the son of Jeanne d'Albret, the Consistory did not rest satisfied until he was dismissed from that family. The National Synods of Paris (1565) and Nîmes (1572) also condemned his *Traité de la Discipline*, as well as his *Réponse*, which he published against *An Apology of the Calvinistic Doctrine*, variously attributed to Chandieu and Viret. On the other hand, a goodly number of persons of rank, several churches of Languedoc, those of Sens, Meaux, and others, approved and shared his opinions concerning church organization, and demanded with him that the laity should have a vote in the election of elders, pastors, etc. Ramus, too, became interested, and insisted upon that right. The author of all this agitation in 1572 dropped out of sight. He is supposed to have died towards the end of the 16th century in London, England. His plan of congregational lay representation in ecclesiastic government is now realized essentially in most Protestant churches, after three hundred years of controversy. Be-

sides the two principal works mentioned, two other publications are ascribed to him, viz. *Verborum Latinorum cum Græcis Anglicisque conjunctorum locupletissimi Commentarii* (1583), and *De Ecclesia ab antichristo per ejus excidium liberanda* (Lond. 1589); the latter was dedicated to queen Elizabeth, and translated into German. See Bayle, *Hist. Dict.* s. v.; Haag, *La France Protestante*, s. v.; Nicéron, *Mémoires*, vol. xxxvi; Hoefer, *Nouv. Biog. Générale*, xxxvi, 546, 547.

Moréri, LOUIS, a French ecclesiastic noted for his literary labors, was born at Bargemont, in Provence, in 1643. He first studied the classics in the Jesuitical college at Aix, and finally theology at Lyons, and was there ordained for the priesthood. When only eighteen years of age he made himself noted as the author of an allegorical composition, and later by a collection of his poems. He applied himself diligently to the study of the Italian and Spanish languages, and translated Rodriguez's book on *Christian Perfection*, which he published under the title *Pratique de la perfection Chrétienne et religieuse, traduite de l'Espagnol* (Lyons, 1677, 3 vols. 8vo). Moréri preached for five years at Lyons with great success, and while there formed his plan for his *Historical Dictionary*. He so applied himself to this stupendous work, of which the first edition appeared at Lyons in 1674, that his health was impaired and his strength exhausted. In 1680 appeared the first volume of the second edition. He died in the same year, July 10. But though Moréri had lived only so few years, he had yet accomplished the work of a common lifetime, and secured a name among posterity for centuries. His *Historical Dictionary* contains whatever is curious and noteworthy in sacred and profane history; hence everybody was amazed to see so prodigious a work from so young a man. He was at once, after the publication of the book in 1674, surrounded by the learned of his country, taken from his charge, and made welcome into the family of the bishop of Apt, in Provence, whom he attended the year following to Paris; he was there soon introduced to the prelates, who held their assembly in St. Germain en Laye, and the learned men in the metropolis. His friends also recommended him to M. de Pompone, secretary of state, who invited him to his house in 1678; and he might have expected great advantages from the patronage of that minister had not his intense application cut short his life. Indeed, he may be said to have sacrificed both his fortune and his life for the public when he undertook so laborious a work. Besides the writings above alluded to, he put the *Lives of the Saints* into more elegant French, and added methodical tables for the use of preachers, with chronological tables; and in 1671 he published at Lyons the following book, *Relations nouvelles du Levant, ou traités de la religion, du gouvernement, et des coutumes des Perses, des Arméniens, et des Gaures, composés par le P. G. D. C. C.* (that is, P. Gabriel du Chinon, capuchin), *et donnés au public par le sieur L. M. P. D. E. T.* (that is, Louis Moréri, prêtre, Docteur en Théologie). The *Historical Dictionary* has passed through many editions, and has from one vol. fol. been extended constantly until in its 19th edition (Paris, 1759) it made 10 vols. fol. Both the well-informed Bayle and the scholarly Du Pin have enlarged and enriched the work as its editors. See *Gen. Biog. Dict.* s. v.; Nicéron, *Mémoires*, s. v.; Hoefer, *Nouv. Biog. Générale*, s. v.; Péricaud, *Moréri à Lyon* (Lyons, 1837, 8vo). (J. H. W.)

Mores, EDWARD ROWE, an English Roman Catholic noted for his antiquarian labors, was born of Protestant parents Jan. 13, 1730, at Tunstall, in Kent, where his father was rector for nearly thirty years. He was educated at Merchant Taylor's school and at Queen's College, Oxford. Even while yet a student at the university he was noted for his attainments, and assisted in antiquarian labors. Being intended for orders by his father, he took the degrees of B.A. May 12, 1750, and M.A. Jan. 15, 1753, before which time he had formed considerable collections relative to the antiquities, etc., of Oxford, and particularly to those of his own college, whose archives he arranged, and made large extracts from, with a view to its history. He also gathered some collections for a history of Godstow Nunnery and of Iffley church. His MSS. relative to his own college, with his collections about All Souls' College, are still unpublished, but are treasured in the Bodleian Library. In 1752 he printed in half a 4to sheet some corrections made by Junius in his own copy of his edition of *Cædmon's Saxon Paraphrase of Genesis, and other parts of the Old Testament* (Amstelod. 1655), and then went to the Continent, where he seems to have fallen in with Roman Catholics, and to have secretly joined their communion. He is even reported to have taken orders, but there is no clear record of this. He was favored by the Sorbonne with the degree of D.D., indicating that he must have made strong friends among the French Romanists. On his return to England he entered into deacon's orders in the Establishment, but never held any preferments, as he was universally disliked for his peculiar religious opinions. Thus he avowed a preference for the Latin language in religious worship, and composed a creed in it, with a kind of mass, of which he printed a few copies in his own house, under the disguised title of *Ordinale Quotidianum* (1685), *Ordo Trigintalis* (1685). That Mores, however, had forsaken his Roman Catholic notions, at least in part, in later life, is apparent from his conduct in the case of his daughter, who, while under the tuition of French Romanists, was surrounded by influences of such a character as might secure her conversion. He no sooner gained knowledge of it than he had her removed, besides severely remonstrating against the breach of good faith of the friends he had trusted. He died in 1778, leaving many works and collections of great value to the antiquarian. A curious work which he left in MS. in Latin, entitled *De Ælfrico Archiepiscopo Dorovernensi Commentarius Auctore Edwardo Rowe Mores, A.M., Soc. Antiq. Lond. Soc.*, seems to have been intended for publication. It contains ten chapters; and the first seven relate to archbishop Ælfric; cap. 8 is entitled "De Ælfrico Bata;" cap. 9, "De Ælfrico Abbate Meildunensi;" cap. 10, "De aliis Ælfricis." An appendix is subjoined, containing transcripts of Saxon charters and extracts from historians concerning archbishop Ælfric. It is now preserved in the Lambeth Library. See *Gen. Biog. Dict.* s. v.; and the *Memoirs* prefixed to his history of Tunstall. (J. H. W.)

Mor'esheth-gath (Heb. *More'sheth-Gath*, מוֹרֶשֶׁת גַּת, *possession of Gath*; Sept. κληρονομία Γέθ, Vulg. *hæreditas Geth*), a town of Palestine (perhaps so named from its vicinity to Gath), where the prophet Micah appears to have been born or to have resided (Mic. i, 14), who was hence called a MORASTHITE (Mic. i, 1; Jer. xxvi, 18). It is named by that prophet (Mic. i, 13-15) in company with Lachish, Achzib, Mareshah, and other towns of the lowland district of Judah. His words, "Therefore shalt thou give presents to Moresheth-gath," are explained by Ewald (*Propheten*, p. 330) as referring to Jerusalem, and as containing an allusion to the signification of the name Moresheth, which, though not so literal as the play on those of Achzib and Mareshah, is yet tolerably obvious: "Therefore shalt thou, O Jerusalem, give compensation to Moresheth-gath, itself only the possession of another city." Hitzig (*Comment.* ad loc.) lately insists upon the old Jewish interpretation of the name as an appellative for some dependency of the Philistines (but see Maurer, *Comment.* ad loc.). Jerome (*Onomast.* s. v. Morasthi) places it a short distance east of Eleutheropolis, and remarks (*Comment. in Mic.* prol.) that it was still a moderately sized village ("haud grandis viculus"), containing a church over the tomb of Micah (*Ep. ad Eustach.* p. 677). From these intimations Dr. Robinson (*Researches*, ii, 423) concludes that it must have been near Mareshah, perhaps at the site of the church of *Santa*

Hanneh, twenty minutes S.S.E. of Beit-Jibrin, close by which are the ruined foundations of a village possibly ancient. Thomson inclines to identify it with Mareshah (*Land and Book*, ii, 360); but the sacred writer clearly distinguishes them (Mic. i, 15). See GATH; MICAH.

Moretto DA BRESCIA, a distinguished Italian artist of Titian's school, and sometimes called *Bonvicino*, was born, according to Lanzi, in 1514, and was the first to introduce Titian's style to his native district. His picture of *St. Niccolo*, painted for the Madonna de Miracoli, is in Titian's best manner. He was mostly employed in his native province, distinguishing himself more by his delicacy than by his grandeur of handling. A fine specimen of this last qualification, however, may be seen in his terrific picture of *Elias* in the old cathedral. His picture of *St. Lucia*, in the church of St. Clemente, is not so much studied as that of *St. Catharine*, and even this yields to his painting of the great altar, representing *Our Lady* in the air, with the titular and other saints seen below. An altar-piece, consisting of various saints, at St. Andrea, in Bergamo, another at St. Giorgio, in Verona, with the *Fall of St. Paul*, at Milan, are all of the most finished composition. A work entitled the *Flagellation*, in the Museo Tosi at Brescia, is remarkably fine; also the *Murder of the Innocents*, in the church of St. Giovanni Evangelista at Brescia. The time of his death is unknown. See Lanzi, *History of Painting* (transl. by Roscoe), ii, 180; Mrs. Jameson and Eastlake's *History of Our Lord*, i, 271; ii, 98.

Morgan, Abel, a Baptist minister of some note, was born in Wales in 1637, emigrated to this country in 1711, and settled at Pemupek, Pa., where he preached until his death, Dec. 16, 1722. He was a good man, well beloved by his people, and did efficient service for the Christian cause among the Welsh who were settled in Pennsylvania in his day. He compiled a folio Concordance to the Welsh Bible, which was printed at Philadelphia, and also translated *The Century Confession* into Welsh, with original additions. See Benedict, *Hist. Bapt.* i, 583; *Bapt. Quar.* July, 1874, art. v.

Morgan, Asbury, a minister of the Methodist Episcopal Church, was born in Mecklenburg County, Va., Aug. 25, 1797; converted in 1812; entered the South Carolina Conference in 1818; was stationed in Charleston in 1828, and died there, Sept. 25th of the same year, of the "stranger's fever." He was a good man, had been successful on former appointments, and promised usefulness to the Church. See *Minutes of Conferences.* ii, 36.

Morgan, Cæsar, D.D., an English divine of some note, flourished in the second half of last century as canon of Ely. But little is known of his personal history. His works, however, show that he was a man of much erudition and a close student. He published several of his sermons (1780, 4to; 1781, 4to); also a work on *Philosophy and Revelation* (1789, 8vo); and another, *The Trinity of Plato and Philo-Judæus*, etc. (1797, 8vo), universally commended as an able work from an orthodox standpoint. See Allibone's *Dict. of Brit. and Amer. Authors*, s. v.

Morgan, Erasmus B., a minister of the Methodist Episcopal Church, was born at Wilmington, Vt., in 1806. He was converted when about twenty-five years of age, and immediately began to preach. For two years he was employed by the presiding elder, and in 1833 joined the New Hampshire Conference. He was stationed successively at Athens, Putney, Claremont, Peterborough, Westmoreland, and Chesterfield, Keene, Landaff, East Haverhill, Lancaster, Canaan, and South Reading. In 1846 he was superannuated, and continued in that and the supernumerary relation for seven years, after which, in 1853, he was stationed at Chesterfield, Mass., within the bounds of the New England Conference. Afterwards he was stationed at Palmer, Three Rivers, Brookfield, and Dudley. In 1857 he was superannuated, after which time he never resumed an effective relation. During 1871, while supplying the Church at North Blandford, his health failed, and he removed his residence to Williamsburgh, Mass., where he died, June 10, 1872. "Morgan was a man of strong, clear mind. . . . He was a decided man—uncompromising in hostility to the powers of darkness, and in his advocacy of every movement calculated to elevate humanity, and reveal more of the glory of Deity." See *Minutes of Conferences*, 1872, p. 47.

Morgan, Gerard, a minister of the Methodist Episcopal Church, was born in Baltimore County, Md., June 8, 1784; was converted in 1801; entered the Baltimore Conference in 1806, and died March 17, 1846. He possessed a clear intellect, a penetrating judgment, and his life was equable, evangelical, and eminently useful. See *Minutes of Conferences*, iv, 10.

Morgan, Gilbert, D.D., a noted minister of the Southern Presbyterian Church, was born at Salem, N. Y., May 23, 1791, received his collegiate training at Union College, Schenectady, and pursued his theological studies at Princeton, N. J. At an early age he engaged in Central and Western New York in the foundation of churches and institutions of learning, one of his co-laborers being Dr. Archilaus G. Smith. In 1836 Dr. Morgan became president of the Western University of Pennsylvania at Pittsburgh, and at the invitation of the Legislature drew up a report, which finally was substantially introduced into the educational system of Pennsylvania. He afterwards became connected with the Hampden Sidney College in Virginia, later removed to North Carolina, and finally made South Carolina his permanent home, and there preached as a member of the Southern Presbyterian Church. Failing health and advanced age finally induced his return North. He died in New York City May 27, 1875. Dr. Morgan was highly esteemed by his brethren, and greatly beloved among those to whom he ministered in spiritual things. Few men in the Church South could claim the superior scholarship to which he had attained. He was an ornament to his own denomination and to the Christian Church. (J. H. W.)

Morgan, Hector Davies, an English divine, noted for his sociological studies, was born in 1768, and was educated at Cambridge University. After taking holy orders he at once rose to positions of prominence, and finally became canon of Trallong. In 1819 he had the honor to be selected Bampton lecturer, and his sermons preached that year were published (1819, 8vo). He also published several other theological treatises of minor value. But he is best known as the author of *Doctrine and Law of Marriage, Adultery, and Divorce* (Oxford, 1826, 2 vols. 8vo). This valuable work exhibits a theological and practical view of the divine institution of marriage, the religious ratification of marriage, the impediments which preclude and vitiate the contract of marriage, the reciprocal duties of husbands and wives, the sinful and criminal character of adultery, and the difficulties which embarrass the principle and practice of divorce, etc. See *Lond. Gent. Mag.* 1851, pt. i, p. 562; Allibone, *Dict. of Brit. and Amer. Authors*, vol. ii, s. v.

Morgan, Homer Bartlett, a missionary of the Presbyterian Church, was born at Watertown, N. Y., May 31, 1827. He was educated at Hamilton College, N. Y., studied theology at Auburn Seminary, N. Y., was licensed by Cayuga Presbytery, and ordained by Watertown Presbytery in 1850. He entered upon the foreign missionary work under the American Board of Commissioners for Foreign Missions, and was by them, in 1851, sent to Salonica, in Greece, and afterwards transferred to Antioch, in Syria. He thus completed nearly fourteen years of missionary life, when it was decided by the committee and the Central Turkish Mission to which he belonged that he should return with his family to this country. When they were about ready for their journey his youngest son sickened and

died. This event, with his responsibility at his post, and official cares as treasurer of the mission, devolved upon him an amount of labor which brought on typhoid fever, and after proceeding on his journey as far as Smyrna he died, Aug. 25, 1865. Mr. Morgan, writes the Rev. Dr. Hamlin, then president of Robert College, Constantinople, "was a noble missionary, a man of right judgment, of executive power, and of self-denying devotion to his work. He has finished it early, but done it well." See Wilson, *Presb. Hist. Almanac*, 1866, p. 218.

Morgan, Joseph, a minister of the (Dutch) Reformed Church, was born of Welsh parentage in 1674, and ordained in 1697 in Connecticut. After settlements at East Chester, N. Y., from 1699 to 1704, and Greenwich, Conn., from 1704 to 1708, he became pastor at Freehold and Middletown, N. J., where he served both the Dutch and Presbyterian churches (1709-31). He gave to the former church about three fourths of his services, although he was a member of the Philadelphia Presbytery. A revival of religion followed his labors in 1721. His last settlement was at Hopewell and Maidenhead, N. J., where he preached from 1732 to 1737. Although his library was very small, he seems to have been a studious man and a voluminous author. He was a correspondent of Cotton Mather. One of his Latin letters to Mather, dated in 1721, is still preserved at Worcester, Mass. In addition to several printed sermons, he published treatises on *Baptism, Original Sin, Sin its own Punishment, Election*, etc. His latter years were sadly overcast with trials and sorrow. In 1728 he was charged with having "practiced astrology, countenanced promiscuous dancing, and transgressed in drink." These charges were not proved. In 1736 he was suspended from the ministry for intemperance, but was restored in 1738. He died in 1740. See Webster, *Hist. Presb. Ch.*; Corwin, *Manual Ref. Ch.* s. v. (W. J. R. T.)

Morgan, Morgan, a prominent lay-worker of the early days of the Protestant Episcopal Church, was a native of Wales, but had come to this country while yet a youth, and settled in Pennsylvania. In 1726 he removed to the south of the Potomac, in Virginia, and there built in 1740 the first Episcopal church, now known as the Mill Creek Church, and situated in the parish of Winchester. He lived to an advanced age, pursuing to the last a course of ardent and active piety, which made him a light and a blessing to all within his influence. Under the direction also of the clergymen, whether present or absent, Morgan fulfilled the duties of lay-reader, which enabled him the more intimately to know the people's wants and cares, and to direct them along the path of duty. In the exercise of these duties he was succeeded by a son, who prosecuted them with the same affectionate, diligent, and humble spirit. See *Episc. Recorder*, vol. i, No. 5, quoted in Hawk's *Eccles. Hist.* p. 111-113.

Morgan, Nicholas J. B., D.D., a minister of the Methodist Episcopal Church of some note, was born in Bath County, Va., Nov. 23, 1811. He was the oldest son of the Rev. Gerald Morgan, also a preacher of the same body, who died in March, 1846, closing a forty-years' ministerial service of honor and usefulness long to be remembered among those for whom he labored. Nicholas's early educational advantages were secured at the common school, and under private tutorship at Harrisonburg, whither his parents removed when he was ten years old. He was converted in 1825, and shortly after believed himself called to preach. He taught school a while to prepare for the work before entering upon it, and in 1829 was admitted into the Baltimore Conference, and appointed to the Fincastle Circuit. After this he successively served in this Conference as follows: in 1830, Pendleton; 1831, Liberty; 1832, Jefferson; 1833-34, Winchester Circuit; 1835-36, Warrenton; 1837, Loudon; 1838-39, East Baltimore Station; 1840-41, Harper's Ferry; 1842-45, Rockingham District; 1846-47, Foundry, Washington City; 1848-50, Baltimore District; 1851-54, North Baltimore District; 1855-56, Fayette Street Station; 1857, Winchester Station; 1858-59, Baltimore City Station; 1860-61, Georgetown; 1862-65, Baltimore District; 1866-69, Washington District; 1870-71, Baltimore City Station; and in 1872, First Charge, Annapolis. On the morning of his second Sabbath (March 24) in this charge he was taken with a chill while preaching. This resulted in pneumonia, and he died April 6, 1872, in Anne Arundel County, Md. From this list of appointments it is apparent that Dr. Morgan was deemed fitted to fill the best stations in the Conference, and nineteen years out of the forty-three in which he preached he had the honor to be presiding elder, and in length of service in this office was exceeded only by Peter Cartwright. The esteem in which he was held by his ministerial brethren is best judged when it is known that he was regularly chosen to represent them in the highest ecclesiastical council of the Church. He was elected to the General Conference in 1844, and to every succeeding one but the last, to which he declined an election. On account of ill-health, he did not attend the session of 1868. Dr. Morgan certainly lived in an eventful period of Methodism. He had some knowledge of the agitation that produced the Methodist Protestant Church, and was an actor in the scenes through which the Methodist Episcopal Church, South, came into being. Though his district in 1844 was in Virginia, and literally upon the border, he stood by the Methodist Episcopal Church, and the Church South met with but little success in its bounds during his term upon it. It is true that while in General Conference in 1844 he voted for the so-called plan of separation, a step which he afterwards regretted, yet to his fidelity may largely be attributed the adherence of nearly that whole section to the Methodist Episcopal Church. In the great trouble which came to his Conference from the action of the General Conference of 1860, incorporating a new chapter in the Discipline against slavery, he stood faithfully for the Northern Church, and led the minority of the Baltimore Conference in 1860-61 opposed to the efforts made to take the Conference from under the jurisdiction of the Church; though, notwithstanding his efforts, it resulted in the secession of a number of preachers and a large number of members from it to the Church South. But for the efforts of himself, his brother, Dr. L. F. Morgan, and a few others, very little of the old Baltimore Conference would have remained in the Northern Church. Like a true man and patriot, Virginian though he was, he stood by the government in the dark days of the Rebellion. He was antislavery in his convictions, Methodistic in doctrine, experience, and practice. All in all, Dr. Morgan's career was not that of a brilliant man, but rather that of a faithful and devoted man, endowed with more than ordinary capacity for work, and born to be a leader of his associates. "With strong intellectual endowments, there were blended in him those stanch moral qualities which made him the man he was. Mental power and moral force characterized him in the pulpit and on the Conference floor. As a preacher, he was a man of one work. To this he gave the study of life." See *Minutes of Annual Conferences*, 1873, p. 28-30; Dr. M'Cauley, in *New York Methodist*, May 18, 1872.

Morgan, Thomas (1), a Scotch Presbyterian divine of the Unitarian cast, who flourished near and after the opening of this century as pastor of a congregation in London, is noted, in conjunction with some others of his persuasion, as the editor of a mutilated edition of Dr. Watts's psalms and hymns, which, from being Calvinistic, they perverted to Socinianism. He was also the coadjutor of Dr. Aikin in compiling the work entitled *General Biography* (1799-1814, 10 vols. 4to), and was besides editor of the *New Annual Register* after the demise of Dr. Kippis. See *Dict. Liv. Auth. Gr. Britain and Ireland* (Lond. 1816, 8vo), s. v.

Morgan, Thomas (2), a distinguished English deist, noted for his attempt to make moral excellence the only test of every system of religion, and for his rejection of a historic revelation of positive duties as inadmissible, flourished about the middle of last century. Of his life we know but very little, and the following meagre facts are taken from *Memoirs of the Life and Writings of Mr. William Whiston* (1749, p. 318). "Morgan ministered for some time to an orthodox Presbyterian congregation, but in 1726 was deposed for Arianism by the presbytery. He then seems to have practiced medicine among the Quakers at Bristol, but finally devoted himself entirely to literary labors, and died at London Jan. 14, 1743" (see Baumgarten, *Hall. Bibl.* v, 331 sq.; vi, 181). Morgan published a number of works against the Holy Scriptures, the best known of which is *The Moral Philosopher, in a Dialogue between Philalethes, a Christian Deist, and Theophanes, a Christian Jew* (Lond. 1737). This work was supplemented by a second volume, *Being a further Vindication of Moral Truth and Reason*, in 1739, and by a third, *Superstition and Tyranny inconsistent with Theocracy*, in 1740. This work elicited many answers, for a list of which see Lowndes, *Brit. Libr.* p. 1203; see also the references at the end of this article. Morgan acknowledges himself a firm believer in God as the almighty creator and ruler of the universe. He lays especial stress on God's continued presence, power, and agency. "God governs the natural and moral worlds by his constant, uninterrupted presence, power, and incessant action upon both, and not by any such essential, inherent powers or properties in the things themselves as might set aside the continued presence, power, and agency of God as unnecessary, or as having nothing to do in the government of either the natural or moral world" (*Moral Philosopher*, i, 186). Like his predecessors, Hobbes (q. v.), Blount (q. v.), and Toland (q. v.), Morgan refuses, however, to acknowledge any revelation of the divine will. He asserts the supremacy of reason, or, as bishop Van Mildert expresses it (*Boyle Lectures*), "Morgan allows the possibility and even the utility of revelation, but artfully destroys the effect of the admission by confounding revelation with man's natural reason."

In his examination of Judaism, Morgan rejects its claims wholly on grounds similar to those explained by Chubb, as incompatible with the moral character of God. According to his view, there exists an irreconcilable opposition between the Jehovah of the Jews and the God of the Christians, or, in other words, between the two religious systems—the Law and the Gospel. The O. T. and the N. T. he considered essentially antagonistic. The love and charity which are manifested in the Gospel of Christ he is unable to find in the O. T. He calls Moses "a more fabulous, romantic writer than Homer or Ovid" (*Moral Philosopher*, i, 251; iii, 94 sq.). The moral law of the O. T., he argues, was but national, and has reference to this life only; "none of its (the law's) rewards or punishments relating to any future state, or extending themselves beyond this life" (*Moral Philosopher*, i, 27). The old dispensation was, according to his view, the reign of a "national tutelar God," but not of the almighty Jehovah who chose the Jews for his own people." Their God was an "idol, after the manner of the Egyptians." The Israelites, from the days of Moses, believed their national tutelar God to be Jehovah, or the supreme God, but no other nation upon earth ever believed it (*Moral Philosopher*, i, 315). In short, he looked upon the O. T. as a religious system not only differing from, but entirely opposed to Christianity. Lechler (*Gesch. d. Englischen Deismus*, p. 383) calls Morgan the modern Marcion; and in reality the system of Morgan bears a close resemblance to that of Marcion. In examining the New Testament, he, like his deistical predecessors, attacked the evidence of miracles and prophecy, and asserted the necessity of moral right and wrong as the ground of the interpretation of Scripture. Morgan wrote against religion, wishing to set up morality in its stead. Leland judges him thus (*Deistical Writers*, p. 107): "By a prevarication and a disingenuousness which is not easily paralleled except among some of those that have appeared on the same side, under all his fair pretences and disguises he hath covered as determined a malice against the honor and authority of the Christian revelation as any of those that have written before him." Morgan's writings all created quite a sensation, and called forth numerous refutations. Among his opponents were Hallet, Leland, Chapman, Chandler, and bishop Warburton. The last named was provoked by Morgan to write his celebrated treatise, *On the Divine Legalism of Moses* (1737–38). See Walch, *Bibl. Theol.* i, 773 sq., 807–810; Mosheim, *Eccl. Hist.;* Leland, *Deistical Writers;* Von Mildert, *Boyle Lect.;* Schlosser, *Hist. of the 18th Cent.* (Davison's transl.) i, 47; Lechler, *Gesch. d. Englischen Deismus*, p. 380 sq.; Farrar, *Crit. Hist. of Free Thought*, p. 140 sq.

Morgan, William, a learned British prelate, was born at Gwibernant, in Carnarvonshire, Wales, in the second half of the 16th century, and was educated at St. John's College, Cambridge. We know but little of his progress in the Church, but we find that in 1595 he was elevated to the episcopate of Llandaff, and in 1601 was transferred to the see of St. Asaph. He died in 1604. Bishop Morgan is worthy of immortal honor as the author of the translation of the Scriptures into Welsh, published in 1588; also the translation of the Psalms in the same year. See Soames, *Elizabethan Rel. Hist.* p. 611.

Morgan, William N., a minister of the Methodist Episcopal Church, South, was born in Mecklenburg County, Va., June 1, 1806. His early educational advantages were limited. In 1836, being impressed with a call to preach, he joined the Memphis Conference of the then Methodist Episcopal Church, and in 1844 went over with the Separatists into the Church South. He was actively engaged in the work for twenty years, preaching in Tennessee and Mississippi. For thirteen years he sustained a supernumerary relation, and finally died Oct. 18, 1869, in Sommerville, Tenn., where he had settled because of impaired health. He occupied an important position in the Conference. He was a good preacher, sound in doctrine, clear and practical in the exhibition of divine truth, and earnest and forcible in his appeals to the Church and to the world. Many gracious revivals were the result of his pastoral visitations of the people and the faithful preaching of the Word. See *Minutes of Conf. of M. E. Ch., South*, 1869, p. 344, 345.

Morganatic marriage (Goth. *morgjan*, to curtail, limit), sometimes called *left-handed marriage*, a lower sort of matrimonial union, which, as a civil engagement, is completely binding, but fails to confer on the wife the title or fortune of her husband, and on the children the full status of legitimacy or right of succession. See CONCUBINE. The members of the German princely houses were for centuries in the practice of entering into marriages of this kind with their inferiors in rank. Out of this usage has gradually sprung a code of matrimonial law by which the union of princes with persons of lower rank in other than morganatic form involves serious consequences, especially towards the lady. In the 16th and 17th centuries a fashion began among German princes of taking a morganatic wife in addition to one who enjoyed the complete matrimonial status—landgrave Philip of Hesse setting the example, with a very qualified disapprobation on the part of the leading Reformers. In the present century morganatic marriages are on the decline among the German reigning houses. They are recognised not only among the princely families, but among the higher aristocracy of the empire; and in Prussia even the "Niedere Adel," or inferior gentry, may contract unions of this kind. There is, however, a strong public opinion against the practice, and as the people begin to enter into the control of state affairs, the practice is sure

to be opposed by special legislation. No such alliance is now permitted to any one having another wife, and the State as well as the Church hold the parties as having entered the strictly matrimonial state. A sort of left-handed or "hand-fasted" marriage was recognised in early times in the Highlands of Scotland and in Ireland: the hand-fasted bride could be put away, and a fresh union formed, with the full status of matrimony. Unlike the case of German morganatic marriages, the issue were often accounted legitimate, even to the prejudice of the children of the more regular union that followed. The Royal Marriage Act, 12 Geo. III, c. 11, reduces to a position somewhat like that of morganatic unions every marriage in the royal family of Great Britain not previously approved by the sovereign under the Great Seal, provided the prince entering into it is under twenty-five, and every such marriage of a prince above twenty-five which is disapproved by Parliament. In the United States no such marriages are lawful. See MARRIAGE.

Morghen, RAFFAELLE SANZIO, *Cavaliere*, one of the most celebrated engravers of modern times, who devoted himself largely to sacred art, was born at Florence, Italy, June 19, 1758. His father, Filippo Morghen, was also an engraver, and instructed his son in the principles of the art with such success that at the age of twelve Raffaelle could engrave a very tolerable plate. At twenty his father, believing his son's genius worthy a more cultivated master, sent him to the celebrated Volpato at Rome, whose daughter he afterwards married. In 1771 he engraved Raphael's allegorical figures of Poetry and Theology, from the Vatican. In 1792 the Neapolitan court, wishing him to reside in Naples, offered him a salary of 600 ducats; but he accepted in preference an invitation from the grand-duke of Tuscany to Florence, where he established himself in 1793, with a salary of 400 scudi and free apartments in the city, under the condition that he might found a public school for engraving, and the privilege of engraving what he deemed fit, also retaining all his prints as his individual property. His first work in Florence was the *Madonna della Seggiola*. In 1795 he commenced the celebrated *Madonna del Sacco*, after Andrea del Sarto, and Raphael's *Transfiguration*. The first picture is in Florence, but the *Transfiguration* he engraved from a drawing by Tofanelli; the latter was completed in 1812, and dedicated to Napoleon I, by whom Morghen was invited to Paris and honored with valuable presents. This print was originally sold at four guineas, or twenty scudi, but the price afterwards realized for some impressions was £20 and £30. The engraving is a work of immense labor and great skill, and though not altogether satisfactory in the way of aerial perspective, being in parts hard and metallic, is highly valued as a work of art. Morghen's masterpiece, upon which he was engaged three years, is a copy of Leonardo da Vinci's *Last Supper*, the early impressions of which (1800) are among the most precious engravings of the work. He died at Florence April 8, 1833, having engraved, according to a list published by his pupil, Palmerini, 73 portraits, 47 Biblical and religious pieces, 44 historical and mythological pieces, 24 views and landscapes, and 13 vignettes and crests. See *Engl. Cyclop.* s. v.; Spooner, *Biog. Hist. of the Fine Arts*, s. v.; Nagler, *Künstler Lex.* s. v.

Morgians, a Mohammedan sect, hold that faith without good works is sufficient to salvation. Gazali, a Mohammedan doctor, tells us that the Morgians expect that God will work everything in them, and affirm that sin does not hurt believers; works without faith signifying nothing. Shabi, another Mohammedan doctor, in his allusions to this sect, exhorts his disciples to be afraid of the threatenings of God, and not to behave like those who defer doing anything that is good, and hope to be saved notwithstanding. See Broughton, *Hist. of Religion*, ii, 141; D'Herbelot, *Biblioth. Orientale*, s. v.

Morgues, MATTHIEU DE, *Sieur de St. Germain,* a noted French Roman Catholic pulpit orator of the 16th century, was born at Vellai, in Languedoc, in 1582, of no inconsiderable family. He turned Jesuit at first, and had several pupils at Avignon, in the Jesuits' college there, but afterwards got disgusted with the Jesuits and quitted their order. He preached at Paris with great success, and in 1613 was made preacher to queen Margaret. He was nominated to the bishopric of Toulon by Louis XIII, but never could obtain his bulls from Rome. Some impute this to his talking too freely about the liberties of the Gallican Church; but others are of opinion that his grant was stopped by the secret artifices of Richelieu. Upon the imprisonment of Mary de Medici he retired from court to his father's house, where Richelieu took measures to seize him. The commission bore "that they should take St. Germain dead or alive; that they should seize him without making an inventory of the papers they should find, and that they should send the said papers to bishop Beaucaire, while the prisoner should be conducted to Mande to be put into the bishop's hands." It is believed that Beaucaire, who had been a domestic of the cardinal, would have caused him to be quietly strangled, if secured. But fortunately Morgues was apprised of the design of his persecutors, and he retired into the most uncultivated parts of France, where he lay concealed for six weeks under all the inconveniences his health could be exposed to. "What was the most insupportable circumstance," says he, "of this whole proceeding, was the uneasiness which the presence of the officers gave my father and mother, who were much advanced in years; for by this time I, the youngest of eight children, was beginning to have gray hairs." It is very probable that the cardinal, who had the weakness to be infinitely sensible of satire, was afraid of St. Germain's pen, and aware of the severities it would inflict; for we see that in all the negotiations for recalling the queen-mother, he made it a condition "that St. Germain, who by his defamatory libels had forgotten nothing to ruin his reputation, should be delivered up to the king." Meanwhile the queen-mother, coming from Compiègne, and being desirous to publish an apology for herself, sent in quest of St. Germain, and ordered him to write an answer to a pamphlet entitled *La Défense du Roi et de ses Ministres,* whose author, it seems, had taken great freedom with that princess's honor. In 1631 he published an answer to the queen's satisfaction, but afterwards wrote several pieces against the creatures of Richelieu. This obliged him to quit the kingdom when Mary left France, and he did not dare to return until after the death of the cardinal. Morgues died in 1670. He left in MS. a complete history of Louis XIII, by him surnamed "the Just." See *Gen. Biog. Dict.* s. v.; Bayle, *Hist. Dict.* s. v.

Mori'ah (Heb. *Mcriyah'*, מוֹרִיָּה, 2 Chron. iii, 1; and מֹרִיָּה, Gen. xxii, 2; as to the etymology, Gesenius remarks [*Thesaur. Heb.* p. 819] that the sacred writers themselves derive it from רָאָה, *to see,* and understand it as for מַרְאִיָּה, *chosen* or *shown by Jehovah ;* but the form may be readily made as the part. fem. of מָרָה, *to be bitter,* i. e. *obstinate,* and thus signifying the *resisting,* i. q. castle; comp. Fuller, *Miscell.* ii, 14; Sept. in Gen. ὑψηλός, Vulg. *visio ;* in Chron. Ἀμορία v. r. Ἀμωρία, Vulg. *Moria*), one of the hills of Jerusalem, on which the Temple was built by Solomon, on the spot that had been occupied by the threshing-floor of Ornan the Jebusite (2 Chron. iii, 1). See TEMPLE. The name seldom occurs (not even in 1 Kings vi, 1), being usually included in that of Zion, to the north-east of which it lay, and from which it was separated by the valley of Tyropœon (Josephus, *Ant.* viii, 3, 9; *War,* v, 4, 1; see Robinson, *Researches,* i, 393, 413, 416). See JERUSALEM. The land of Moriah, whither Abraham went to offer up Isaac (Gen. xxii, 2), is generally supposed to denote the

same place, and may at least be conceived as describing the surrounding district (comp. Josephus, τὸ Μώριον ὄρος, *Ant.* i, 13, 1). The Jews themselves believe that the altar of burnt-offerings in the Temple stood upon the very site of the altar on which the patriarch purposed to sacrifice his son (see Michaelis, *Suppl.* v, 1551; Jänisch, in Hamelsveld, ii, 39 sq.; Bleek, in the *Theol. Stud. u. Krit.* [1831], p. 530 sq.; comp. Hengstenberg, *Pentat.* ii, 195 sq.; Ewald, *Israel. Gesch.* i, 358; iii, 35). The force of the tradition is impaired by the mythic addition that here also Abel offered his first sacrifice, and Noah his thank-offering (Munster, Fagius, and Grotius, ad loc.). The following disquisition treats of certain disputed points. See ABRAHAM.

Before considering the geographical and other diffi, culties in the way of this identification, it is desirable to investigate the derivation of the word מֹרִיָּה. Various etymologies supplied by Jews all proceed on the supposition of the identity of the Moriah of Genesis with that on which the Temple was built. The oldest, that of Onkelos and Gerundensis, was that it was derived from מוֹר, *myrrh,* as in Canticles iv, 6, "I will go to the mountains of myrrh." Fuller (in *Misc. Sacra,* ii, 15) maintains that the הַמּוֹר of Canticles was an abbreviation of הַמּוֹרִיָּה, and referred to the holy mount where the great king had just erected his Temple. Rabbi Solomon supposes it to be derived from הוֹרָאָה, *instruction,* because thence the word of the Lord went forth into all Israel. Kalisch (*Comment. on Gen.* ad xxii, 2) approaches this interpretation by saying that it springs in all probability from מֹרִירִיָּה, "Jehovah is my instructor," from יָרָה, the root of the great derivative תּוֹרָה. Jonathan derives it from מוֹרָא, *fear* or *reverence,* and imagines that the word was used anticipatory of the worship and fear of God there solemnized (Lightfoot, *Opera, Descriptio Templi,* i, 553). Fuller (*Misc. Sacra,* ii, 15) maintains that the word represents an abbreviation of מוֹרָאֶה-יָּה, *conspicietur Jehovah,* because there eventually the Son of God would appear in human flesh. Knobel insists that it is a compound of מָרְאֶה (a dual form of רָאָה, *to see*) and יָּה; and Hengstenberg (*Dissert. on Gen. of Pentateuch,* ii, 159–163, Clark's transl.), Kurtz (*Old Covenant,* i, 272), Gesenius (*Thesaurus,* p. 819), Fürst (*Lex.*), all agree as to the presence in the word of the elements of the name of Jehovah. Vatke, Vater, Van Bohlen, the early opponents of the genuineness of the Pentateuch, even based a portion of their antagonism on this proof of a later date. Bishop Colenso (*Pentateuch and Joshua,* pt. ii, ch. ix, x) labors to demolish the etymology, but without much success. The existence of a proper name *Moriah* would be a proof of the existence of the name and worship of Jehovah before some of the modern documentists would find it at all satisfactory. Hengstenberg states that the word הַמּוֹרִיָּה is a compound of מָרְאֶה, the Hophal participle of רָאָה, *to see,* and means *that which is shown,* or *the appearance of Jehovah.* Colenso objects to the sense of the interpretation, and maintains that there is no explanation of the disappearance of the characteristic radical א. Gesenius accounts for the form מָרִיָּה by a combination of the Hophal participle of רָאָה and the *jod-compaginis* common in derivatives from verbs of the form of ל"ה. Thus מָרְאֶה, combined with יָּה, would suffer the following change, מֹרִיָּה=מָרְאִי-יָּה. There is another proper name, derivable from the same root, which has lost its characteristic radical א—viz. רוּת, from רָאוּת, *beautiful to look upon* (Ruth). But whatever may be the precise nature of the contraction, the obvious interpretation of the writer is given in ver. 8: יְהוָה יִרְאֶה, which is the name given by Abraham to the place where Jehovah *saw* his agony and provided a victim in place of his son. Here it was that the proverb was originated, "In the mountain Jehovah shall be seen." *Moriah* was the name permanently attaching itself to the place, just as קָרָן had been the abbreviation of Eve's exclamation, קָנִיתִי אִישׁ; and it was used by the narrator 400 years afterwards to describe a district, a *land*, a mountain which had always gone by that name ever since the proverb had first been uttered, amid the very circumstances he was then proceeding to describe. It would be presumptuous to assert to what extent the knowledge and worship of Jehovah was diffused, on the ground of the mere presence of the name Jehovah in this proper name; still, there is nothing to shake the conclusion. It is curious that the Sept. translates the אֶרֶץ־הַמּוֹרִיָּה by εἰς τὴν γῆν ὑψηλήν; and it also renders by some similar expression the various references to the *oak or plains of* MOREH, near Sichem (Gen. xii, 6); where the Hebrew text has אֵלוֹן מוֹרֶה the Sept. reads τὴν δρῦν τὴν ὑψηλήν (see also Deut. xi, 30). The translation of Aquila in Gen. xxii, 2 is εἰς τὴν γῆν τὴν καταφανῆ; and Symmachus has εἰς τὴν γῆν τῆς ὀπτασίας, closely resembling the *in terram visionis* of the Vulgate.

Dr. Davidson (in *Introduction to the O. T.* vol. i) conjectures that *Moreh* was the original reading; but neither Kennicott, De Rossi, nor Dr. Davidson himself (in his *Printed Text of the O. T.*) give any diplomatic authority for such a reading. The translations of Aquila and Symmachus may have originated with some reading resembling that in the Samaritan text, מוראה, and signifying "far seeing" or "conspicuous." But when Josephus wrote (*Ant.* i, 13, 2), it is quite clear that the reading in Gen. xxii, 2 and 2 Chron. iii, 1 must have been identical, as he speaks of the place of Abraham's sacrifice as τὸ ὄρος ἐφ' οὗ τὸ ἱερὸν Δαβίδης ὁ βασιλεὺς ὕστερον ἱδρύεται. In 2 Chron. iii, 1 the Sept. does not attempt to translate the proper name הַמּוֹרִיָּה, but writes ἐν ὄρει τοῦ Ἀμωρία. It is true that there is no reference to the original manifestation of God on this site to the patriarch, and express mention is made of second and additional reasons for this hill being called Moriah (see 1 Chron. xxi, 16; xxii, 1; 2 Sam. xxiv, 1; 2 Chron. iii, 1). This was in perfect harmony with the law of God that forbade the offering of burnt sacrifices in any place which the Lord had not consecrated by his visible manifestation (Hengstenberg, *Diss.* ii, 32 sq.). The geographical conditions supplied by the narrative in Genesis are not inconsistent with the Samaritan tradition (see Robinson, *Biblical Researches*, iii, 100) that *Gerizim* was the scene of the sacrifice, and that the mountains of Gerizim and Ebal, from their neighborhood to *Moreh*, a spot well known to Abraham, were the mountains in the land of Moriah (Colenso, pt. ii, ch. x). They have led dean Stanley (*Syr. and Pal.* p. 250 sq.; *Hist. of Jewish Church*, i, 48, 49) to decide on Gerizim as the scene of the event. His arguments are weighty, but not conclusive. (1.) The distance from Beersheba to the plain of Sharon, from which Gerizim might be seen "afar off," corresponds with the two-days' journey of Abraham; while the third day, which would be occupied by the great event, would be sufficient for the journey to the summit and the return. The same thing, however, may be said with greater certainty of Jerusalem itself. (2.) Stanley objects that there is no spot from which the "place" where the sacrifice was to be offered could be seen from "afar off;" that the hill of Moriah is not visible at all until the traveller *is close upon it*, at the southern edge of the valley of Hinnom, from whence he looks down upon it, as on a lower eminence. Now the narrative informs us that Abraham lifted up his eyes and saw the *place* of which the Lord had spoken to him. That "place" was the אֶרֶץ הַמּוֹרִיָּה, or, as Gesenius translates it, the land about Moriah, just as אֶרֶץ הָעַי is the land about Ai. It is very possible

to see from the ridge *Mar Elias* the heights about Jerusalem, if not the hill of Moriah itself; and we are expressly told that Abraham did not see the place until he was fairly within a walk of the spot, and could leave the young men and the ass while he and Isaac proceeded, personally laden with the materials for the sacrifice. (3.) A formidable difficulty urged by others is that the fortress of Zion must at that time have been occupied by the king of the Jebusites, some forerunner of Adonizedek, or by Melchizedek himself, and therefore Abraham must have prepared to perform this awful sacrifice under the walls of the city. To obviate the great apparent improbability of this, it may be said that sometimes the outside of fenced cities—where a deep ravine runs between the wall and the suburb—is often one of the loneliest spots in the world. The name *Moriah* is unquestionably given by the chronicler to the Temple hill, but this passage is a solitary one. The more ordinary name, even for the entire city of Jerusalem and for the holy mountain, is *Mount Zion*, and various psalms and prophecies speak of the dwelling-place of Jehovah under this old and honored name. It cannot be true that any writer of the time of Solomon composed the narrative of Abraham's sacrifice to do honor to the Temple hill, as was suggested by De Wette; for, if that had been his intention, he would have called it *Zion*, and not Moriah. Great stress has been laid by bishop Colenso and by the writer in Smith's *Dictionary*, ii, 423, on the absence of other reference besides that of the chronicler to the name of Moriah as the site of the Temple hill, and also on the impropriety of associating the name and career of Abraham so vitally with Jerusalem. In the same article, however, Jerusalem is spoken of as the city of Melchizedek. For the shape of Moriah, its relations with Bezetha and Acra, the bridge that connected it with Zion across the valley of the Tyropœon, see JERUSALEM. Notwithstanding the various and variously motived endeavors to disturb the old Hebrew tradition, it has not been proved necessary to deny the identification of the two sites; nor to denounce the old etymology; nor to cease perceiving the interesting link of connection supplied by it between the sacrifice of Isaac, the vision of God's judgment and mercy, the erection of the Temple, and the offering up of God's only-begotten Son. See SOLOMON.

Moriarty, PETER, an early and very useful minister of the Methodist Episcopal Church, was born in Baltimore Co., Md., April 27, 1758, and educated a papist; was converted through Methodist influence about 1776; entered the itinerancy in Virginia in 1781, but subsequent to 1787 his labors were mostly at the North, in the bounds of what has since become the New York Conference. He died at Hillsdale, N. Y., June 23, 1814. Mr. Moriarty was one of the oldest and most widely known ministers in the connection at the time of his death, a man who had labored long and ardently in the work of saving men. Although not eloquent, he was among the most useful men and successful preachers of his time, and an excellent presiding elder. Many souls were converted through his labors, and he died honored and beloved in all the churches. See *Minutes of Annual Conferences*, i, 240; Stevens, *Memorials of Methodism*, vol. ii, ch. x. (G. L. T.)

Morice de Beaubois, *Dom Pierre Hyacinthe*, a French scholar, was born Oct. 25, 1693, at Quimperlé, Basse Bretagne, of noble and wealthy parentage. He studied at the College of Rennes, and made his vows in 1713 at the abbey Saint Melaine, which belonged to the Order of the Benedictines of Saint Maur, where he was intrusted with several offices, and also with the instruction of novices. In 1731 he was called to Paris to elaborate the genealogy of the family Rohan, and lived there in the monastery of "Notre Dame of the White Robes." After the completion of this work, which procured for him a pension of 800 livres, he engaged, at the solicitation of the authorities of Bretagne, on a new history of that province, but death surprised him at Paris, Oct. 14, 1750, before the entire publication of this work (afterwards revised and completed by Dom Taillandier). Morice edited Lobineau's *Mémoires pour servir de preuves a l'Histoire ecclésiastique de Bretagne* (Paris, 1742–46, 3 vols. fol.), and himself published *L'Histoire ecclésiastique et civile de Bretagne* (Paris, 1750–56, 2 vols. fol.), which is considered superior to Lobineau's by the additions and explanations, as well as by its style and exactness of details, and very valuable to the French ecclesiastical student. A new edition of the two works in 20 vols. 8vo (Guincamp, 1836–37) leaves much to wish for.

Morid is the Arabic name which the Mohammedans give to those who aspire to a life of uncommon spirituality and devotion, and for this purpose they are put under the direction of another, whom they call *Morsbid*, that is "director." They have a famous book, entitled *Adab al-Moridin*, which treats of the qualifications those ought to have who put themselves under the direction of one of those spiritual guides. See Broughton, *Hist. of Religion*, ii, 142.

Morier, JAMES, noted as the author of a series of novels descriptive of Eastern life and manners, and also for his accurate observations of the East as recorded in his books of travel, was born in England in 1780. When still very young he made an extensive tour through the East, the main incidents of which he described in his *Travels through Persia, Armenia, Asia Minor, to Constantinople* (Lond. 1812). In 1810 he was appointed British envoy to the court of Persia, where he remained till 1816, and soon after his return he published *A Second Journey through Persia*, etc. (ibid. 1818). During his stay in the East Morier made great use of his opportunity of studying the character of the people; and the knowledge thus acquired was turned to excellent account in his *Adventures of Hajji Baba of Ispahan* (1824–28, 5 vols.) (a species of Gil Blas, like Hope's *Anastasius*), whose "adventures in England" he described in a second series (1834); *Zohrab the Hostage; Ayesha, or the Maid of Kars; Abel Alnutt; The Banished*, etc.; in all of which, but especially in the first three, the manners, customs, and modes of thought prevalent in the East are portrayed with a liveliness, skill, and truthfulness to nature attained by few. He died in 1848. See the references in Allibone's *Dict. of Brit. and Amer. Authors*, ii, 1368, 1369.

Morigia, Jacobo Antonio de (1), an Italian monastic, noted as the founder of a religious order, was born in November, 1497, at Milan. Up to the age of twenty-five he indulged in all the pleasures of the world, but at that period experienced a change of heart, and enrolled himself directly in a brotherhood of penitents which existed in Milan under the name of "Brotherhood of Eternal Wisdom." Admitted into the Franciscan Order of the Minorites, he refused the rich abbey of San Victor, and performed ministerial functions of charity during the plague which in 1525 devastated Milan. A few years later he joined Antonio Maria Zacharia of Cremona and Barthelemi Ferrari of Milan, noblemen like himself, and the three together founded the *Congregation of the Regular Clericos of St. Paul*, so named after their first chapel, taking subsequently the appellation of *Barnabites*, from the church of San Barnabas. By a decree of Feb. 18, 1533, Clement VII approved the institution, and Morigia, after he had become formally a priest, was appointed its first provost, April 15, 1536. These regulars, established for missions and other sacerdotal functions, lived in their beginning only upon alms, and were not allowed any fixed revenues; but all this has since changed. Morigia undertook missions to Vicenza, Verona, and several other cities of Italy. He resigned his office in November, 1542, after he had governed wisely his congregation; but his colleagues re-elected him June 30, 1545, and on Oct. 20 following he took possession of the church of San Barnabas. He

died April 14, 1546. At present the Barnabites have a general in Rome and a house at Paris, and are spread through almost all Roman Catholic countries. See BARNABITES.

Morigia, Jacobo Antonio de (2), an Italian prelate of note, was born at Milan Feb. 23, 1632, entered the Order of the Barnabites when only seventeen years of age, taught philosophy at Macerata and at Milan, and preached with success in the principal churches of Italy. Cosmo III of Medici, grand-duke of Tuscany, chose him for theologian, and made him tutor of Ferdinand, his oldest son. The influence of this same prince procured for him in 1681 the bishopric of San Miniato, whence he was transferred, Jan. 11, 1683, to the archbishopric of Florence. In the promotion of Dec. 12, 1695, he was made cardinal "in petto" by pope Innocent XII, but this nomination was not published until the Consistory of 1698, simultaneously with the declaration that Morigia should have precedence of all the cardinals created in 1695, because he had been reserved for that very purpose. Archpriest of the Basilica Liberiana, it was he who at the jubilee of 1700 was charged to open the holy gate. Vacating his bishopric of Florence in 1699, he refused in the same year, after the death of Federigo Cacua, the appointment as archbishop of Milan, became a titular official of two abbeys, and finally in 1701 bishop of Pavia, where he died, Oct. 18, 1708. Literary remains of his are *Orazione funebre nelle obsequie di Filippo Visconte, vescovo di Cantanzano* (1664, 4to):— *Pietosi tributi resi alla grand' anima di Filippo IV* (Milan, 1666, 4to):— *L'Aquila volante, orazione funebre, per la stessa occasione* (Milan, 1666, 4to):—*Lettere pastorali al popolo di Firenze* (fol.).

Morin, Étienne, a learned French Protestant, noted for his attainments in Orientalia, was born at Caen Jan. 1, 1625. His father, who was a merchant, died when he was only three years of age, and his mother, though designing him for trade, suffered his vehement inclination to books, until she found him so greatly drawn to study as to make any attempt for his conversion to trade futile. He went through the classics and philosophy at Caen, and then removed to the Huguenot seminary at Sedan, to study theology under Peter du Moulin, who conceived a great friendship for him. Morin afterwards continued his theological studies under Andrew Rivet, and joined to them that of the Oriental tongues, in which he made a great proficiency under Golius. Returning to his country in 1649, Morin became a minister of two churches in the neighborhood of Caen. He was distinguished by uncommon tact and learning, and had several advantageous offers from abroad; but he did not care to stir from his own country. In 1664 he was chosen minister of Caen, and his merits soon connected him in friendship with several learned men who were then in that city, such as Huetius, Segrais, Bochart, and others. The revocation of the Edict of Nantes in 1685 obliging him to quit Caen, he retired with his family into Holland. He went at first to Leyden, but soon after was called to Amsterdam to be professor of the Oriental tongues in the university there, to which employment was joined, two years after, that of minister in ordinary. He died May 5, 1700. Morin wrote considerably. His most important works are, *Dissertationes octo, in quibus multa sacræ et profunæ antiquitatis monumenta explicantur* (Geneva, 1683, 8vo; a 2d ed., enlarged and corrected, Dort, 1700, 8vo):— *Oratio inauguralis de linguarum orientalium ad intelligentiam Sacræ Scripturæ utilitate* (Ludg. Bat. 1686):— *Explanationes sacræ et philologicæ in aliquot V. et N. Testamenti loca* (ibid. 1698, 8vo):— *Exercitationes de lingua primæva ejusque appendicibus* (Ultraj. 1694, 4to):—*Dissertatio de paradiso terrestri* (printed in Bochart's works, the 3d ed. of which was published at Utrecht in 1692, with Bochart's life by Morin prefixed):—*Epistolæ duæ, seu responsiones ad Ant. Van Dale de Pentateucho*

Samaritano (printed with Van Dale's *De origine et progressu idolatriæ*, Amst. 1696, 4to):—*Lettre sur l'origine de la langue Hebraïque*, with an answer of Huetius; printed in vol. i of *Dissertations sur diverses matières de Religion et de Philologie* recueillis par Tilladet (Paris, 1712, 12mo). In this work he argues boldly that Adam was inspired with a knowledge of the Hebrew tongue by the Almighty. See Nicéron, *Mémoires*, vol. xii; Haag, *La France Protestante;* Hoefer, *Nouv. Biog. Générale*, s. v.; *Gen. Biog. Dict.* s. v.   (J. H. W.)

Morin, Frédéric, a French philosopher, was born at Lyons June 18, 1823. After preliminary studies he entered the Normal School in 1844; received a fellowship in philosophy in 1848, and lectured on this branch successively at the lyceums of Macon and Nancy, and at the Lycée Bonaparte. When, after the coup d'état of 1852, he had refused the oath to the usurper, Louis Napoleon, he was considered as having resigned his professorship. He devoted himself henceforth to private instruction, and published works on religious philosophy, seeking to harmonize democratic principles with Christian beliefs. We have of him, *Saint François d'Assisses et les Franciscains* (1853, 12mo):—*De la Genèse et des Principes métaphysiques de la société moderne* (1856, 8vo):—*Dictionnaire de Philosophie et de Théologie scolastique* (1857–58, 3 vols. large 8vo). Besides, he has furnished articles to the journal *L'Avenir*, to the *Correspondant* (first period), to the *Revue de Paris*, to the *Revue de l'Instruction publique*, and to the *Biographie Générale*. He died in 1874.

Morin, Jean, a most learned French writer on theological subjects, and a convert to the Romanists, was born at Blois in 1591. His parents were members of the Reformed faith, but at Leyden, where he was studying philosophy and theology, the violent discussions between Calvinists and Arminians estranged him for a time from all religious connection, and he finally, falling under the influence of Romanists, accepted their creed, at Paris, under cardinal Perrone. Some time after his conversion to Romanism he entered into the Congregation of the Oratory, then but recently established, and began to make himself known by his learning and his works. In 1626 he published *De Patriarcharum et Primatum Origine* (Paris, 4to), dedicating the work to pope Urban VIII. In 1628 he undertook an edition of the *Septuagint Bible*, with the version made by Nobilius, supplying it with a preface, in which he treats of the authority of the Septuagint. He commends the edition of it that had been made at Rome by order of Sixtus V in 1587, which he followed, and maintained that we ought to prefer this version to the present Hebrew text, because that has been, he says, corrupted by the Jews. Having gone from the Protestant to the Romish fold, Morin very naturally, like all apostates, became a most enthusiastic adherent of Romanism, and therefore now engaged upon a systematic defence of those versions which the Church had approved by weakening the texts which passed for original (Simon, *Einleitung*, p. 522). Before this work was ready to appear, he published in 1629 *Histoire de la deliverance de l'Église Chrétienne par l'Empereur Constantin, et de la grandeur et souveraineté temporelle donnée à l'Église Romaine par les rois de France* (Paris, fol.); but this book was not well received at Rome, and Morin was forced to promise that he would retrench and correct it. Soon after he published *Exercitationes ecclesiasticæ in utrumque Samaritanorum Pentateuchum* (Paris, 1631, 4to), for the sake of establishing which, he, as we have already seen above, also now stoutly attacked the integrity of the Hebrew text. As there was then preparing an edition of the Polyglot at Paris, Morin took upon himself the care of the Samaritan Pentateuch. His endeavors to exalt this, together with the Greek and Latin versions of the Bible, at the expense of the Hebrew, made him very obnoxious to many savans, especially Hebraists; and he was attacked by Hottinger and Buxtorf in particu-

lar. Simon and Kennicott, however, countenance Morin's position. The opposition which Morin encountered only enhanced his merit at the court of Rome, insomuch that cardinal Barberini invited him thither by order of the pope, who received him very graciously, and intended to employ him in the communications that were then passing between the Eastern and Western churches looking towards reunion. He was greatly caressed at Rome, and intimate with Holstenius, Allatius, and all the learned there. After having remained nine years at Rome, he was recalled by order of cardinal Richelieu to France, where he spent the remainder of his life in learned labors, and died at Paris in 1659. Morin's works are very numerous, and some of them much valued by Protestants as well as Romanists on account of the Oriental learning contained in them. The writer of a sketch of his life and labors in Kitto's *Cyclopædia* pronounces Morin "the restorer of the ancient Samaritan language," but takes exception, like most Hebraists, to "his anti-Masoretic zeal as not according to knowledge, as later investigations in the same field have abundantly proved." The most important works not yet mentioned are, *Exercitationes Biblicæ de Hebraici Græcique textus sinceritate* (Paris, 1633, 4to, and greatly enlarged and improved in 1699, fol.; prefaced with a life of the author by father Constantine, of the Oratory). But also in positive theology Morin exerted himself as an author. Thus he wrote *Commentarius historicus de disciplina in administratione sacramenti pœnitentiæ xiii primis sæculis in Ecclesia occidentali et huc usque in orientali observata* (Paris, 1651, fol.; Anvers, 1682, fol.; Bruxelles, 1687, fol.), a work on which he is said to have spent thirty years of hard mental labor, but which, nevertheless, failed to gain much admiration. He attacks in it both the Port Royalists and the Jesuits:—*Commentarius historico-dogmaticus de sacris Ecclesiæ ordinationibus secundum antiquos recentiones Latinos, Græcos, Syros, et Babylonicos, in quo demonstratur orientalium ordinationes conciliis generalibus et summis pontificibus ab initio schismatis in hunc usque diem fuisse probatæ* (Paris, 1655, fol.), which is generally praised, and pronounced among his best efforts:—*Opera posthuma de catechumenorum expiatione, de sacramento confirmationis, de contritione et attritione* (Paris, 1703, 4to):—*Antiquitates Ecclesiæ Orientalis* (Lond. 1682, 12mo), treating of ecclesiastical antiquities as gleaned from his correspondence with the savans of Europe. Several of his works remain unedited and unpublished. Among these we notice *De Sacramentoi Matrimonii*, and *De Basilicis Christianorum et de Paschale et de vetustissimis Christianorum paschalibus ritibus.* See Nicéron, *Mémoires*, ix, 30–48; Du Pin, *Bibl. des Auteurs Ecclésiastiques;* Schröckh, *Kirchengesch. seit der Reformation*, iv, 123 sq.; Marsh, *Lect. Divinity;* Wolf, *Bibliotheca Hebraica*, pt. iv, p. 7; pt. ii, p. 25 and 270. Simon's biography is a mere satire, and unworthy of credit.   (J. H. W.)

Morin, Pierre, a French scholar, was born at Paris in December, 1531. He was a man of great attainments in languages, belles-lettres, and ecclesiastic antiquity. From France passing into Italy, he stopped at Venice, where Paulus Manucius secured him for his printing establishment. He lectured as professor of Greek and cosmography at Vicenza and Ferrara. By recommendation of San Carlo Borromeo he went to Rome in 1575, and there popes Gregory XIII and Sixtus V employed him on the editions of the Septuagint (1587), the Vulgate (1590, fol.), the Bible translated from the Septuagint into Latin (Rome, 1591, 3 vols. fol.), the Decretals till Gregory VII (Rome, 1591, 3 vols. fol.), and on the collection of the general councils (Rome, 1608, 4 vols.). He died before the completion of this his last work, some time in 1608. He bears the reputation of a pious, modest, and learned man. Besides the works enumerated, we possess of him, *Traité du bon Usage des Sciences*, published with some others of his writings by Quetif in 1675; a

Latin translation from St. Basil's discourses on the forty martyrs, and of a dozen selected sermons of St. Chrysostom.

Morin, Simon, a celebrated French religious visionary and fanatic of the 17th century, was born at Richemont, near Aumale. He was a very illiterate person, yet notwithstanding the want of all educational facilities he entered the field of authorship, and gave the world his extreme views on religion and philosophy. He meddled much in spiritual matters, and fell into great errors. His first book, which he caused to be privately printed in 1647, under the title of *Pensées de Morin dediées au roy,* is a medley of conceit and ignorance, and contains the most remarkable errors, which were afterwards condemned in the Quietists; but Morin carries them to a greater length than any one else had done, for he affirms that "the most enormous sins do not remove a sinner from the state of grace, but serve, on the contrary, to humble the pride of man." He says "that in all sects and nations God has a number of the elect, true members of the Church; that there would soon be a general reformation, all nations being just about to be converted to the true faith; and that this great reformation was to be effected by the second coming of Jesus Christ, and Morin incorporated with him." About the middle of the 17th century Morin was civilly prosecuted and for a time incarcerated, but he was finally set at liberty as a visionary, and suffered to continue so till 1661, when Des Marets de St. Sorlin, who, though a fanatic and visionary himself, with intent to injure, entered, under pretence of accepting all the views of Morin, into his whole scheme, only to have him taken up. Marets, in his treachery and dissimulation, went so far as to acknowledge Morin as "the Son of Man risen again," and thereby so pleased Morin that he conferred upon him as a particular grace the office of being his harbinger, calling him "a real John the Baptist revived." Then Des Marets impeached him and became his accuser, and Morin, after due trial, was condemned to be burned alive at Paris, March 14, 1663. He was burned, together with his book entitled *Pensées de Morin,* as also all his own papers and those of the trial. His ashes were thrown into the air, as a punishment for his having assumed the title of the "Son of God." His accomplices were obliged to assist at his execution, and then to serve in the galleys for life, after having been whipped and branded by the hangman. Morin in his last hours gave out that he would rise again the third day, which made many of the mob gather together at the place where he was burned. It is said that when De Lamoignon asked him whether it was written in any part of the Scriptures that the great prophet or new Messiah should pass through fire, he cited this text by way of answer, "Igne me examinasti, et non est inventa in me iniquitas" (Thou hast tried me in the fire, and no wickedness has been found in me). See Nicéron, *Mémoires,* vol. xxvii; Bayle, *Hist. Dict.* s. v.; *General Biog. Dict.* s. v.; Hoefer, *Nouv. Biog. Générale,* s. v. (J. H. W.)

Morison, John, D.D., a Scottish Presbyterian divine of some distinction, was born at Millseat, Aberdeenshire, July 8, 1791. But little is known of his personal history. He was for many years pastor of the Independent Chapel at Brompton, and in 1816 removed to London as pastor of Tower Chapel. In 1824 he was appointed editor of the *Evangelical Magazine,* and held this position for thirty-two years. He died July 13, 1859. He wrote an *Exposition of the Psalms* (1819, 8vo), of which Horne speaks favorably, though it is far from being an independent and thorough work. His other works, which are mainly in the department of *Practical Religion,* are too numerous to be mentioned here. But noteworthy among his different publications are an *Exposition of Part of the Epistle to the Colossians* (1829, 8vo):— *Lectures on the Reciprocal Obligations of Life* (1822, 12mo), of a practical and useful character:—*Protestant*

Reformation in all Countries (1843, and often):—*Protestantism in Great Britain:—The Fathers and Founders of the Lond. Miss. Soc.* (1844, 8vo, and often):—*Christianity in its Power* (1847, fcp. 8vo), a work which received the unqualified commendation of the English press and the Church. Said one: "The friends of vital Christianity may regard it as an appropriate sequel to the well-known work James's *Anxious Inquirer.*" See *Metropolitan Pulpit,* 1839, ii, 152–161; Allibone, *Dict. Brit. and Amer. Auth.* ii, 1369; Steele, *Burning and Shining Lights* (1864), ch. vi; Kitto, *Journal Sacred Lit.* 1852, Oct. (J. H. W.)

Morisonianism, a term which has been much used in Scotland since about the year 1841, and to some extent in the north of England, to designate a system of religious doctrine strongly opposed to the Calvinism of the Scottish Presbyterian churches, and exhibiting in the highest degree many distinctive features of Arminianism. It derives its name from a minister named JAMES MORISON, suspended from his office by one of the Scottish Presbyterian churches in 1841, and now a professor of theology in the academy of the *Evangelical Union* (q. v.). The doctrinal views stated by him prior to 1841 were far from having that complete development which they soon after received from himself and his followers. The point to which prominence was first given was the universal extent of the atonement —that Christ died for the sins of all men equally; with which was naturally connected the opinion that saving faith consists simply in a man's belief that Christ died for him, inasmuch as he died for the sins of the whole world; this further leading to the opinion that a believer must know the reality of his own faith in Christ; and to the opinion that every man possesses a sufficient ability to believe the Gospel, without any aid of grace but what is vouchsafed to all who hear it, and in the very fact of its being preached or presented to them; and so verging on the tenets which have long received the designation *Pelagian.* The opposition to the standards of the Scottish Presbyterian churches is very complete regarding the fall of man, the work of the Holy Spirit, election, and kindred subjects; while on the subject of justification the doctrine of imputation stated in the standards is repudiated, and the atonement is represented as a satisfaction of "public justice," not securing the salvation of any man, but rendering the salvation of all men possible.

The following summary of the Morisonian views is taken from the tract of the Rev. F. Ferguson on the denomination (London and Glasgow, 1852), p. 10: "That God the Father regarded mankind-sinners with an eye of compassion, and wished 'all men to be saved;' that God the Son became 'a propitiation for the sins of the whole world;' that God the Spirit has been 'poured out upon all flesh,' and 'strives' with all the irregenerate, and 'dwells' in all believers; that all those who, 'led by the Spirit,' 'yield themselves unto God,' are his chosen people, 'elect according to foreknowledge;' and that those who remain finally unsaved, and are thus the non-elect and reprobate, have themselves to blame for their infatuated 'resistance' of the Holy Ghost; that for the conversion of any soul all the glory is to be given to God, who 'quickens' the dead, while over every soul that perishes Jehovah complainingly cries, 'Why will ye die?' that although all men in their natural state are depraved and love sin, yet they possess the power to obey the command to believe the Gospel—a power bestowed by God, and not destroyed by the fall; that every sinner who believes the good news of salvation is conscious of the act, and, 'being justified by faith, has peace with God through Jesus Christ our Lord;' that Christ is 'made' to every believer 'wisdom, righteousness, and sanctification and redemption;' and that before the finally impenitent and 'the faithful unto death' there lies, respectively, either a miserable or glorious immortality." The same paper adds that "a printing and publishing establishment was commenced by private parties connected with the movement in 1846, in Glasgow, and from it there are issued a weekly newspaper entitled *The Christian News,* which was commenced in 1846, and a small monthly magazine called *The Day-Star,* which was started the year preceding, and has a large circulation, besides other periodicals, and an immense number of tracts and minor treatises, exhibiting in various forms the distinctive tenets of the denomination."

Moritz, JOHANN CHRISTIAN, a Jewish missionary of the Christian Church among his people, was born at Bernstein, in Pomerania, Jan. 1, 1786. He received a careful instruction according to the fashion of that time. The study at home of history, geography, poetry, and philosophy, more especially the works of Mendelssohn, greatly strengthened his mind. When sixteen years of age Moritz went to Berlin, where he was taken care of by his uncle. Here he met with free-thinking Jews, who, although they could not draw him into the fatal meshes of infidelity, yet exercised for a time a baneful influence upon his conversation and conduct. When Prussia suffered much humiliation in the wars of the first Napoleon, Moritz determined to go to England until the dawning of better days. With a letter of introduction to the chief rabbi of England of that time, Dr. Herschell, he reached London in July, 1807, and was kindly received by that divine. Moritz obtained a scanty living by teaching French and German, until the summer of 1808, when he made the acquaintance of Dr. Steinkopff, whose ministry he regularly attended, and by whom he was publicly baptized on the 31st of December, 1809, according to the forms of the Lutheran Church. He then laid aside his original Jewish name, *Moses Treitel,* and received the above Christian name, by which he has always since been known. In 1811 he went to Gottenburg, where he married, and where he stayed until 1817, when in a wonderful manner the way was opened for him to labor among his brethren in Russia. At St. Petersburg he met the Rev. Lewis Way, and formed a friendship which lasted for life. He labored in Russia under the sanction of the emperor Alexander, until by an official mandate he was compelled to abandon the labors of the last eight years. In May, 1820, Mr. Moritz was accepted by the London Society for Propagating Christianity among the Jews, which sent him to labor at Hamburg. He next labored at Copenhagen, Neuwied, Frankfort, and Stockholm, returning to Hamburg in 1834. He then removed to Dantzic, until, in 1843, his residence was finally fixed at Gottenburg, and Norway and Sweden assigned him for his field of labor. On Jan. 1, 1868, he retired from active service, after forty-two years' faithful labor for his Master in the society's ranks, and died on Feb. 17, at Gottenburg, rich in peace and joyful in hope. See *Jewish Intelligencer,* 1868. (B. P.)

Mörl, Gustav Philipp, a German theologian, was born at Nuremberg Dec. 26, 1673, and was educated first in the schools of his native place and then at the university in Altdorf, where he studied philosophy and philology from 1690 to 1692, when he was removed to Jena to study theology and the ancient languages. He travelled through Holland, and visited its most important universities. After his return home he was appointed assistant of the philosophic faculty at Halle, and in 1698 became professor and ecclesiastical inspector at Altdorf. He resigned this position in 1703, and was appointed dean of St. Sebald's church at Nuremberg. In 1706 he was appointed minister of the St. Aegidien church, and inspector of the gymnasium; in 1714 minister at St. Lawrence, in connection with which he had the supervision of the ecclesiastical seminary. In 1724 he was appointed minister of the church of St. Sebald, superintendent of the consistory of Nuremberg, city librarian, and professor of divinity of the Aegidische gymnasium. He died May 7, 1750. Besides several dissertations in journals, he published *Diss. de distinc-*

tione essentiali agnoscenda et attributis (Jenæ, 1694, 4to): —*Diss. continens theses miscellaneas* (Halæ, 1694, 4to): —*Diss. continens vindicationem regularem methodi Cartesianæ* (ibid. 1694, 4to): —*Diss. i et ii de mense humana* (ibid. 1696, 1697, 4to): —*Repetitio doctrinæ orthodoxæ de fundamento fidei, occasione disputationis Halensis de questione: An hæresis sit crimen?* (ibid. 1696, 4to): —*Defensio repetitionis hujus adversus Chr. Thomasium* (ibid. 1697, 4to): —*Disquisitio de fide, occasione epistolæ ad Chr. Thomasium scriptæ* (ibid. 1698, 4to): —*Diss. de modo dirigendi omnes actiones nostras ad gloriam Dei* (Altdorf, 1701, 4to): —*Vindiciæ doctrinæ Lutheranæ de gratia prædestinationis* (Norimb. 1702, 8vo): —*Die Lehre von der Busse, in* 122 *Predigten, nach den Lehrsätzen und Texten entworfen* (Nürnberg, 1711, 4to): —*Ordnung der Könige in Juda und Israel, in einer Tabelle* (ibid. 1740, fol.): —*Sterbeschule; eine Sammlung von Predigtentwürfen* (ibid. 1743, 1744, 2 vols. fol.).

Mörl, Johann Sigmund, a German theologian, son of the preceding, was born at Nuremberg March 3, 1710, and was educated in his native place until ready for the university at Altdorf, where he studied theology after 1727. In 1735 he was appointed dean of a church at Nuremberg. He preached until 1759, when he was appointed minister and inspector of the "Ægidianum." In 1765 he was elected in this gymnasium to the professorship of Greek. Towards the close of 1770 he was called to the position of minister of St. Lawrence's church. In 1773 he accepted the position of first minister at St. Sebald's church, the superintendency of the consistory of Nuremberg, the office of city librarian, and also a professorship of positive divinity and moral philosophy. He died Feb. 22, 1791. Besides several contributions to the *Hallische Allgemeine Welthistorie* and the *Antideistische Bibel* (Erlangen, 1768), to which he contributed a new computation of time from the exodus of the Jews to the time of Solomon, he published *Scholia philologica et critica ad selecta S. Codicis loca* (Norimb. 1737, 8vo; improved ed. by Wilder, ibid. 1793, 8vo): —*Schediasma philologico-geographicum, in quo Jo. Harduini disquisitio de situ Paradisi terrestris examinatur* (ibid. 1750, fol.): —*Oratio de meritis Norimbergensium in Geographiam* (ibid. 1750, 8vo).

Morlaks or **Morlachians** (Slav. *Primortzi,* i. e. "adjoining the sea"), the name of a rude people of uncertain origin, inhabiting the mountainous coast-land of Dalmatia, the Croatian military frontier, and the maritime districts of Austro-Hungary. They speak a south Slavic dialect, and are mostly Roman Catholics. They are skilful mariners. The strait which separates the islands of Veglia, Arbe, and Pago from the same coast is generally called from them the Strait of Morlacca.

Morley, George, D.D., a learned English prelate, noted for his able polemics against Romanism and his faithful adherence to king Charles II in the face of all opposition, was born in London in 1597. He lost his parents when very young, and also his patrimony. However, at fourteen he was elected a king's scholar at Westminster School, and became a student of Christ Church, Oxford, in 1615, where he took the first degree in arts in 1618, and the second in 1621. Then he entered holy orders, and in 1628 became chaplain to Robert, earl of Caernarvon, and his lady, with whom he lived till 1640, without having or seeking any preferment in the Church. After that he was presented to the rectory of Hartfield, in Sussex, which he exchanged for the rectory of Mildenhall, in Wiltshire; but before this exchange, Charles I, to whom he had been appointed chaplain in ordinary, had given him a canonry of Christ Church, Oxford, in 1641. This is said to be the only preferment he ever desired. In 1642 he was admitted to the degree of D.D. About that time also he preached before the House of Commons, then largely made up of Nonconformists, but so little to their liking that he was not commanded to print his sermon, as all the other preachers had been. Nevertheless he was nominated one of the assembly of divines at Westminster because of his strong leaning to Calvinism, but he never appeared among them; on the contrary, he always remained with the king, and did him what service he could. Dr. Morley also used his influence at Oxford University to incline its professors to opposition against the Visitation Bill which had been enacted by the anti-royalists in Parliament; and as the Cromwellian party gained the ascendency he was marked out for punishment. In 1648, the Presbyterians having in the mean time gained the control of state affairs, Dr. Morley was deprived of all his preferments, and imprisoned for some little time. The length of his imprisonment is not exactly known, but in 1649 we find him preparing to quit England to join his royal master in Holland. Dr. Morley met the king at the Hague, and was for some time a constant companion of Charles II. In 1650, when the king set out on his expedition to Scotland, Dr. Morley went first to the Hague and then to Antwerp, where he resided, together with his friend, Dr. John Earle, in the house of Sir Charles Cotterell, and a year later in the house of Sir Edward Hyde. While thus retired from home and public life, he yet remained a most faithful adherent of the royal and episcopal cause, and even held Church services daily, "catechized once a week, and administered the communion once a month to all the English who would attend" (Hook). About 1654 he became chaplain to the queen of Bohemia at the Hague, but about 1656 he removed to Breda with the family of Sir Edward Hyde, and there continued the same practice as at Antwerp.

During the protectorate of Richard Cromwell, while the royalists were preparing for the Restoration, Charles employed Dr. Morley as a messenger to the Presbyterians. He quickly gained their confidence, because he was known to be a strong Calvinist. He was, moreover, a fit person to instil the Presbyterians with a desire for moderation, for he had been a prominent party in the treaty agreed to by Charles I in the Isle of Wight, which favored the Presbyterians in many respects. See PRESBYTERIANS. It is true Baxter did not very much like Dr. Morley, because, as he complains, Morley "talked of moderation in the general, but would come to no particular terms" (*Autobiography*, p. 218). Yet Morley himself must have been persuaded of the successful issue of his mission if we judge him by his letter of May 4, 1660, in which he writes: "I have reason to hope that they (i. e. the Presbyterians) will be persuaded to admit of and submit to episcopal government, and to the practice of the liturgy in public, so they may be permitted, before and after their sermons, and upon occasional emergencies, to use such arbitrary forms as they themselves shall think fit, without mixing of anything prejudicial to the government of the Church and State as they shall be settled" (Clarendon, *State Papers*, vi, 738, 743). Upon the royalists, particularly, Dr. Morley had a good influence. They, as soon as they saw the approach of victory, manifested a too forward zeal, and made uncomfortable threatenings of revenge upon the republican party. Dr. Morley checked these evil tendencies, and thus softened down all opposition on both sides. Dr. Morley also, though incorrectly, represented the king's religious views, and refuted the statement that Charles II was a convert to popery. Of course Dr. Morley was duped by the king, and could never have served Charles had he known that man to have been a hypocrite. Morley was a diplomatist, seeking to gain the ascendency of the episcopal party in the English realm, but he was also an honest Christian, and would not have suffered himself to be the tool of an apostate. Indeed his position later in life against papists makes this plainer still. (See below.)

Upon the restoration of Charles II, Dr. Morley was rewarded for his faithfulness to his royal master by elevation to the bishopric, besides being restored to his canonry, and appointed dean of Christ Church. He was consecrated bishop of Worcester in 1660. In 1661 bishop Morley played a prominent part in the *Savoy Conference* (q. v.), commissioned to bring about such changes in the liturgy as might enable the Presbyterians and Episcopalians to unite once more. Though the archbishop of York was present, Morley appeared as the chief speaker of the bishops, and was for the Episcopalians what Baxter was for the Covenanters. Stoughton puts Morley next to Sheldon, yet acknowledges that the latter acted chiefly as adviser, "taking little share in the viva-voce discussions," while Morley appeared constantly as leader in the debates (i, 163). In 1662 bishop Morley was made incumbent of the deanery of the royal chapel, and shortly after was transferred from the see of Worcester to that of Winchester. In 1673, when the royalists made a desperate attempt to introduce severe measures against the Nonconformists, bishop Morley figured prominently in the effort, and thus brought reproach upon himself for intolerance and stubbornness. He especially favored the modification of the "Test Act" in such a manner that it became necessary for every English subject to be faithful to "the Protestant religion as established by law in the Church of England." Yet Morley's position at this time may be satisfactorily explained. "His main policy was to protect the Establishment, on the basis of the Act of Uniformity, against papists on the one hand and dissenters on the other. He shared in the alarm which conversions to Rome and the encroachments of that Church inspired throughout England at the time; and partly from that cause he was induced to support the bill, ... thinking by the new oath, which established the Church, to prevent an invasion by the enemy. ... Strength was wasted by internecine warfare at a moment when Episcopalians and Presbyterians stood before a common foe. It was the story of the Crusaders repeated. Why not gather the forces of the Church and of the sects, and concentrate them upon the great enemy of the country's liberty and peace? Such impressions, under the circumstances, were not unnatural in the mind of a man like Morley" (Stoughton, i, 439, 440). In his old age Morley is reputed to have become more tolerant again, for it is related that he stopped proceedings against an ejected minister, and invited him to dinner, endeavoring to soften down the terms of conformity; but, better still, it is said that in Morley's last days he drank to an intermeddling country mayor in a cup of Canary, advising him to let dissenters live in quiet, "in many of whom, he was satisfied, there was the fear of God"—and he thought they were "not likely to be gained by rigor or severity." The bishop died in 1684. Burnet says that he "was in many respects a very eminent man, very zealous against popery, and also very zealous against dissent; considerably learned, with great vivacity of thought; soon provoked, and with little mastery over his temper" (i, 590). His zeal against the doctrines of popery is apparent in his writings, and not less so his zeal against dissent; in connection with his opposition to both, he avows the doctrine of passive obedience, declaring in terms the most unequivocal "the best and safest way for prince, state, and people is to profess, protect, cherish, and allow of that religion, and that only, which allows of no rising up against or resisting sovereign power—no, not in its own defence, nor upon any other account whatsoever" (Morley's *Treatises*, sermon before the king, p. 38). Indeed, he maintains, again and again, the principle of intolerance in the government of the Church, and the principle of despotism in the government of the State; holding the king to be sole sovereign, while Parliament is only a concurring power in making laws, and the bishops the only legitimate ecclesiastical rulers. Bishop Morley was a very generous man, and freely expended his income for the good of his benefices. He was a benefactor to Oxford University by granting Christ Church £100 per annum, and by establishing several prizes at Pembroke and other colleges. He spent much money in repairing the buildings in the see of Winchester, bequeathed a considerable sum to St. Paul's, London, and left £1000 to purchase lands for the support of small vicarages. The bishop also bore a high reputation for theological learning before the civil wars, as well as after the establishment of the episcopacy, and was acknowledged as well versed in the logic of the schools, and as a formidable controversialist. He wrote *A Sermon at the Coronation of Charles II, April* 23, 1661. In the dedication to the king, by whose command it was published, he says that he was now past his great climacteric, and this was the first time that ever he appeared in print:—*Vindication of himself from Mr. Baxter's Calumny*, etc. (1662):—*Epistola apologetica et parœnetica ad theologum quendam Belgam scripta* (1663, 4to; written at Breda, June, 1659; reprinted in 1683, under this title, *Epistola, etc., in qua agitur de seren. regis Car. II erga reformatam religionem affectu*). In this letter he attempts to clear Charles II from the imputation of popery, and urges the Dutch to lend their utmost assistance towards his restoration; but he was mistaken in his master's religion, and perhaps lived long enough to know it:—*The Sum of a Conference with Darcey, a Jesuit, at Brussels* (1649):—*An Argument drawn from the Evidence and Certainty of Sense against the Doctrine of Transubstantiation:—Vindication of the Argument*, etc.:—*Answer to Father Cressy's Letter*, written about 1662:—*Sermon before the King*, Nov. 5, 1667: —*Answer to a Letter written by a Romish Priest* (1676): —*Letter to Anne, duchess of York* (1670). This lady, the daughter of Sir Edward Hyde, was instructed in the Protestant religion by our subject while he lived at Antwerp, but she afterwards forsaking the faith of her family, Dr. Morley wrote this defence of Protestantism: —*Ad Virum Janum Ulitium Epistolæ duæ de Invocatione Sanctorum* (1659). All the above pieces, except the first and second, were printed together in 1683, 4to: —*A Letter to the Earl of Anglesey concerning the Means to keep out Popery*, etc., printed at the end of *A true Account of the whole Proceedings betwixt James, duke of Ormond, and Arthur, earl of Anglesey* (1683):—*Vindication of himself from Mr. Baxter's injurious Reflections*, etc. (1683):—he made also *An Epitaph for James I* (1625), which was printed at the end of Spottiswood's *History of the Church of Scotland*, and is said to have been the author of *A Character of King Charles II* (1660, in one sheet 4to). In his polemics against Romanism bishop Morley discusses only three important points. The treatment of these indicates deep learning and great skill. He plies with much success the argument against transubstantiation, "drawn from the evidence and certainty of sense," maintaining his convincing argument with the dexterity of a practiced logician, so as to parry most successfully all the objections of Roman Catholic antagonists. He decidedly opposes the popish doctrine of purgatory; but he vindicates prayers for the dead in the way in which they were offered in the early Church, and as by modern Anglicans they are still encouraged to be offered; that is, for the rest of the soul, the resurrection of the body, and the plenitude of redemption at the last day. Whatever may be the propriety of praying for the dead in such a qualified sense as this, Morley contends there is no ground on which to rest the doctrine of the invocation of saints. That doctrine he overthrows by an appeal to Scripture; and then he proceeds, after the Anglican method, to examine the writings of the fathers, and to show that they do not justify the popish dogma and its associated practices. The bishop enjoyed the association of some of the most distinguished literati of his day. He was an intimate friend of Falkland, and mixed much with Ben Jonson and Edmund Waller. He was strict and exemplary in his life, though much given to witticisms, and surrounded by a host of gay courtiers and literati; and was acknowledged by all as truly abstemious and laborious in his habits. See *Chambers's Magazine*, viii, 69; Stoughton, *Eccles. Hist. of England (Church of the Restoration*) (see Index in vol. ii); Perry, *Eccles. Hist.* vol. ii (see Index in vol. iii); Wood, *Athenæ Oxon.;* Neal, *Hist. Puritans* (Harper's ed.), ii, 230; Burnet, *Hist. of his own Times*, i, 590; Salmon, *Lives of the English Bishops*, p. 346. (J. H. W.)

Morley, Thomas, one of the most distinguished of England's early composers of sacred and profane music, and author of the first regular English treatise on the art of music, was born probably about the middle of the 16th century, but the exact time is not determined. All that is known of this eminent professor is gathered from Wood, who, in his *Athenæ Oxoniensis*, tells us that he was a disciple of Birde, to whom he dedicated his book in very reverential and affectionate terms; that he obtained a bachelor's degree in 1588, and was sworn into his place as gentleman of the royal chapel in 1592. He died, Dr. Burney supposes, in or near the year 1604. Morley produced many compositions that are still well known, among which are canzonets of different kinds, particularly for two voices, madrigals for five voices, and services and anthems, including the fine *Funeral Service* published in Dr. Boyce's collection, the first that was set to the words of the Anglican Reformed Liturgy. See *Engl. Cyclop.* s. v.; Burney, *Hist. of Music*.

Mörlin, Joachim, a well-known German Lutheran theologian, and one of the most zealous defenders of the great German Reformer and his views, was born at Wittenberg April 6, 1514. His father, Jodocus Mörlin, professor of metaphysics at the Wittenberg University, and afterwards pastor at Westhausen, in Franconia, gave Joachim a careful training intellectually and morally, and in 1527 he entered the newly-founded University of Marburg, but soon left for his native city, where, under Luther's and Melancthon's special guidance, he devoted himself to the study of theology. When not quite twenty-three years of age he was chosen dean of a church at Wittenberg, and in 1539 accepted a call to the church of Eisleben. At Luther's request he returned in the following year to Wittenberg; but, hardly arrived, left it again for Arnstadt, whence he had received a call as its first ecclesiastical superintendent. He was now but twenty-six years old, and by far too young and inexperienced to fill such an influential position. Zealous in his religion, and of rather coarse and contentious disposition, he soon came into serious difficulties with some powerful church members, who persecuted him mercilessly. In 1543 he was deposed, without having been allowed the benefit of a trial. Though the citizens appealed for his retention, Mörlin had to leave Arnstadt, and removed to Göttingen, where he remained until 1549. About this time he, together with many other Lutheran theologians, openly declared against the Augsburg Interim, alleging that it re-established popery; thereupon duke Erich was deposed and Mörlin banished. A few months later he received a pastoral call to Kneiphof, one of the main quarters of Königsberg, in Prussia, which he accepted. Greatly favored by duke Albrecht, Mörlin was at first universally esteemed and beloved. But he soon became involved in the Osiandrian controversy. See OSIANDER; JUSTIFICATION. In his strict Lutheranism he opposed Osiander's views on the nature of justification and its relation to sanctification. According to the manner of the times, Osiander's departure from the grand Lutheran doctrine of *Justification* (q. v.), and especially of views approximating the Roman Catholic doctrine, were therefore made the subject of severe comment by Mörlin in a rather coarse and abusive way. The duke of Prussia, anxious to restore peace between the contending parties, issued an edict to all Prussian clergymen and professors of theology, in which slanders and denunciations of their respective opponents was threatened with severe bodily punishment. But the quarrel, in spite of the ducal edict, grew more and more bitter, and after Osiander's death Mörlin attacked and persecuted his followers. Several of them, among them Johann Funk, were beheaded because they refused to recant. Uncharitable against all opponents, and of a naturally contentious and passionate disposition, Mörlin grew so violent and abusive in his language that he called the ducal edict an inspiration of the devil, to which he refused to submit. In consequence he was dismissed (1553), and, notwithstanding his numerous and influential followers, had to leave Königsberg. He went to Dantzic, and lived there for some time, supported by voluntary contributions of his Königsberg friends, until he received a call to Brunswick as ecclesiastical superintendent and first city-preacher. Here, in connection with his friend, Martin Chemnitz, late librarian of duke Albrecht, Mörlin devoted himself to a closer study of the Bible and the fathers, and took a prominent part in all the theological controversies of the time. When in 1556 Albrecht Hardenberg attempted to introduce into the republic of Bremen Calvin's doctrine respecting the Lord's Supper, Mörlin, together with Chemnitz, opposed him most violently, and after his dismission caused the issue of that bigoted Bremen edict (Oct. 6, 1561) "against the sacramental enthusiasts and Anabaptists" (*Gegen die Sacraments-Schwärmer u. Wiedertäußer*). At this occasion he published his *Erklärung aus Gottes Wort u. kurzer Bericht d. Herren Theologen*, and *Von der Condemnation streitiger Lehr* (Magdeburg, 1563). These works are a not overlucid exposition of the strict Lutheran view on the Lord's Supper, and are far inferior to Chemnitz's work, *Repetitio sanæ doctrinæ de vera præsentia corporis et sanguinis Domini in cœna sacra*. In 1557 he went to Wittenberg, vainly endeavoring to put a stop to the *Adiaphoristic* controversies. He subsequently separated himself from Flacius, writing against him in his usual abusive and violent style. He was also present at the Worms Colloquy, which, like most such disputations, led to no result whatever. After the death of Melancthon, he grew, if possible, still more zealous in his strict Lutheranism, ample proof of which is to be found in the numerous works which he published about this time. We mention here his *Historia Prutenici:—Treue Warnung und Trost an die Kirchen in Preussen:—Sendschreiben an den Vogel:—Apologia auf die vermeynte Widerlegung dess Osiandrischen Schwarms*. Things meanwhile had changed materially in Prussia. Osiander and his followers had been entirely suppressed, and duke Albrecht, yielding to the repeated appeals of the citizens, recalled Mörlin in 1566 to Königsberg, nominating him bishop of Samland. Chemnitz, who always had been a great favorite with the duke, accompanied Mörlin to Königsberg, and became associated with him in the preparation of the *Corpus doctrinæ Prutenicum*, designed as the symbolical text-book of Prussia. July 7, 1567, the work was approved by the duke, and on the following day Mörlin left for Brunswick, choosing not to accept the proffered position (see *Biblioth. Lubec.* xii, 607 sq.). Owing to his contentious disposition, he came into a new difficulty with the city council of Brunswick, and was now glad to accept duke Albrecht's offer. As bishop of Samland, Mörlin took a very prominent part in the Majoristic controversy, and published his *Disputatio contra novam corruptilam, qua asseritur, operum præsentiam in actu justificationis necessariam esse* (Jenæ, 1567), and his *Verantwortung wider die falschen Auflagen der neuen drei Wittenberger in ihrer Grundfeste Königsberg*. He died May 23, 1571, at Königsberg, before the Majoristic controversy was concluded. Besides the works already named, Mörlin wrote also *Disputatio de communicatione idiomatum* (1571):—*Postilla:—Psalter-Predigten:—A new Catechism* (Eisleben, 1565):—*Vom Berufe der Prediger, sammt zwei Briefen Lutheri* (ibid. 1565, 4to). Mörlin was evidently a tenacious man, and born to be a polemic. His opponents charged him, and perhaps not unjustly, with assuming to be the guardian of the Church. He was evidently sincere and deeply in earnest, asserting that he became involved in these various controversies as a faithful son of the Church, doing only what every one was bound to do, namely, guarding its

VI.—20*

purity with all the power and skill at command. See Adam, *Vitæ Theol. Germ.* p. 457 sq.; Rettemeyer, *Kirchen-historie*, iii, 207; Salig, *Historie der Augsburg Confession*; Naton, *Gesch. der Concordienformel*; Schröckh, *Kirchengesch. seit d. Reformation*; Planck, *Protest. Lehrbegriff*, iv, 291; v, pass.; and his *Gesch. Protestantischer Theologie*, vi, 60 sq.; Kurtz, *Ch. Hist.* ii, 134; Döllinger, *Die Reformation*, ii, 453 sq.; Gieseler, *Eccles. Hist.* vol. iv (Harper's ed.); Erdmann, *Biog. sämmtlicher Pastoren zu Wittenberg* (Elberf. 1869, 8vo). (J. H. W.)

Mörlin, Maximilian. a younger brother of the preceding, was born at Wittenberg Oct. 14, 1516. He received his classical education at the Wittenberg Gymnasium, and studied theology under Luther and Melancthon, both of whom esteemed him highly, though subsequently he was one of Melancthon's most determined opponents. After his ordination he preached at Pegau and Zeitz, and in 1543 received a call to Schelkau, in Franconia, where he was so universally beloved for his piety and eloquence that the people would not let him go when in 1544 he was called to Coburg as court-preacher. In 1546 the theological faculty of his alma mater conferred the honorary degree of S.T.D. upon him, and two years later he was nominated superintendent of the churches and schools of Coburg. Like his brother Joachim, he was very decided in all his peculiar religious views, and the words which he inscribed (1530) on a copy of the Augsburg Confession give an insight into his strict Lutheranism: "Huic sacrosanctæ confessioni et indubitatæ assertioni ex verbo Dei toto pectore assentior et subscribo et Deum oro, ut in illius constanti confessione et immutabile professione per spiritum S. me perpetuo servet," etc. Everything outside of Lutheranism he considered heresy, and treated as such. In the same copy of the Augsburg Confession we find the following marginal note, which is significant of his character: "Ad hanc subscriptionem impulit me impia profanatio, corruptio et mutatio præcipuorum hujus confessionis articulorum per ipsum autorem in corpore suæ doctrinæ, quam ut hujus confessionis negationem detestor et abjicio et damno in articulis mutatis." His strict Lutheran views led him to subscribe the so-called *Censuræ* passed upon Andreas Osiander by the Saxon theologians at Weimar and Coburg, and with the same zealotism he fought against Justus Menius (q. v.) at the Synod of Eisenach (1556), determined to have him cut off from the Church for heresy. When this plan failed, he, nothing daunted, drew up a paper in which Menius's heretical views were set forth and his condemnation called for, and then travelled with Stolz, of Weimar, through all Saxony, to gather subscriptions thereto. As an undoubted champion of the genuine theology of Saxony, as taught by Luther, he, by order of his prince, went to the Worms Colloquy (q. v.), and so strictly followed the instructions of Flacius (q. v.) that the conference had to be abandoned as hopeless. Like Flacius, he was sincere and deeply in earnest, and as a true follower of Luther espoused the cause of his deceased teacher, showing by the severest logic that the Lutheran Church was, under Melancthon's guidance, drifting away from its moorings. Like a great many Lutherans of this period, he was mercilessly, though conscientiously, contentious. He was a born polemic. In connection with Flacius, Stössel, and Musäus, he published the *Sächsische Confutationsschrift* (1559), which was afterwards declared law by the prince of Saxony, and as such proved injurious both to the university and Flacius. About this time the elector Frederick prepared to introduce the doctrines of the Reformed Church into his territory. His zealous Lutheran son-in-law, prince Frederick of Saxony, tried his best to prevent him, and in 1560 went with Mörlin and Stössel to Heidelberg to meet Peter Boguin and other Reformed clergymen in open conference. The disputation, which was afterwards published under the title of *Propositiones, in quibus vera de cœna Domini sententiis juxta confessionem Augustanam, etc., propositæ* 1560 *in Academia Heidelb.* (Magdeb. 1561), led to no result. Shortly after his return, Mörlin separated from Flacius, who had made himself odious by the rash statement (in his discussion with Strigel at Weimar in 1560) that original sin is the very substance of man in his fallen state, thus laying himself open to the charge of Manichæism. Mörlin openly denounced Flacius, and the duke established a censorship, of which Mörlin was made a member. Flacius and his followers were deposed. March 3, 1562, he signed Strigel's declaration, and in his official visits tried to prevail upon the different ministers to sign the same, and to desist in future from all public denouncements of the Synergistic heretics. In 1569, when the government of Saxony was placed into the hands of John William, than whom there was no more ardent friend of Flacius, Mörlin was deposed, but yet in the same year was called as court-preacher to Dillenburg. His strict Lutheranism did not, however, prove acceptable to the count of Dillenburg; and when in 1572 John William extended a call to him to resume his former position, he gladly accepted it. But the clergy of Coburg, mostly followers of Flacius, with Musäus at their head, opposed him so decidedly that he had to leave Coburg again. At last (in 1573) Musäus and all the clergymen opposed to Mörlin were dismissed, and Mörlin resumed his former position. He died April 20, 1584. It cannot be denied that Mörlin was a consistent upholder of the doctrines which he originally learned from Luther. In his theological views he opposed Melancthon, asserting that if that reformer was great, truth was greater. He seemed to consider it his special mission to call every man to account who either openly or secretly attempted to destroy what Luther had built up. See Beck, *Johann Friedrich der Mittlere*, i, 94, 213 sq.; ii, 12 sq.; Steubing, *Biog. Nachrichten aus d. 16ten Jahrhundert*, 1790, p. 57; Jöcher, *Gelehrten-Lexikon*, s. v.; Gieseler, *Ecclesiastical History*, vol. iv (Harper's edition); Kurtz, *Church History*, ii, 134.

Morlot, FRANÇOIS NICOLAS MADELEINE, a French prelate of note, was born at Langres (department Haute-Marne) Dec. 28, 1795. His father, a modest mechanic, sent him to the college of his native town. Having afterwards passed through the course of theological studies at Dijon, before reaching the age required for priesthood, young Morlot was for some time private tutor. In 1825 he was appointed vicar of the diocese of Dijon, where, after the revolution of 1830, he made himself conspicuous by his resistance to bishop Rey, who was obnoxious to the clergy and legitimist party for having accepted his see from Louis Philippe. Discarded from the grand vicariate, but supported by the *Ami de la Religion* and other papers of the same party, he repeatedly refused an appointment as curate, and accepted only the place of canon. He published, under the title of *Remonstrance*, a censure of his bishop's acts, and was foremost in the attacks which at last forced the bishop to resign in 1838. In 1839 Morlot was appointed bishop of Orleans. He was also for his valuable services decorated with the cross of the Legion of Honor on the occasion of the baptism of the comte de Paris, and in 1842 was elevated to the archiepiscopal see of Tours. Created cardinal March 7, 1853, he took as such his seat in the senate of the new empire, and Jan. 24, 1857, he was promoted to the archbishopric of Paris. The same year he was also put at the head of the grand Aumônerie, and at the beginning of 1858 he was called to the counsel of regency and to the private council. Cardinal Morlot died in 1870. His literary activity was very limited. Besides his *Mandements* and *Circulaires*, or *Lettres Pastorales*, all of them written with great simplicity, he edited *Explication de la doctrine Chrétienne, en forme de lectures* (2 vols. 12mo):—*Catéchisme du diocèse de Dijon* (18mo):—the *Heures choisies de la Marquise d'Andelarre* (1825, 12mo). See *Dict. des Cardinaux*, s. v.; Hoefer, *Nouv. Biog. Générale*, xxxvi, 614-15; Vapereau, *Dict. des Contemporains*, s. v.

Mormons, the usual name of a religious sect which was founded in this country A.D. 1830, and claims to be called of God to gather within its fold the people of this universe, by authority of a new dispensation, which is to be the last given to man in his present existence. They style themselves "The Church of Jesus Christ of Latter-day Saints," or briefly, "Latter-day Saints," and object to the popular designation, Mormons, derived from the name of one of their sacred books (i. e. *The Book of Mormon*). Though this word is derived from the Greek (μορμών), and literally signifies a lamia, maniola, female spectre (the mandrill for its ugliness was called Cynocephalus Mormon), the Saints, according to Joseph Smith, the first prophet and originator of Mormonism, treat its etymological origin thus extravagantly: "We say from the Saxon *good*, the Dane *god*, the Goth *goden*, the German *gut*, the Dutch *goad*, the Latin *bonus*, the Greek καλός, the Hebrew טוב, and the Egyptian *mon*. Hence, with the addition of *more*, or the contraction *mor*, we have the word *mormon*, which means literally *more good*." According to anti-Mormons, the name Latter-day Saints was assumed in 1835 by the Mormons, at the suggestion of one of their leaders, Sidney Rigdon, and the word "Mormon" is more distasteful to them than is the word "Mohammedan" to the Muslim or "Jew" to the Hebrew. In accordance with our general practice to let each religious body speak for itself in these pages, we insert here the history of the organization of the Church of these "Saints" as furnished by their apostle Orson Pratt, the ablest living exponent of Mormonism, and George A. Smith, the first counsellor of president Brigham Young.

I. *History.*—The Church of Jesus Christ of Latter-day Saints was founded by Joseph Smith, who was born in the town of Sharon, Windsor County, Vt., Dec. 23, 1805. When ten years old his parents, with their family, moved to Palmyra, N. Y., in the vicinity of which he resided for about eleven years, the latter part in the town of Manchester. He was a farmer by occupation. His advantages for acquiring scientific knowledge were exceedingly small, being limited to a slight acquaintance with two or three of the common branches of learning. He could read without much difficulty, and write a very imperfect hand, and had a very limited understanding of the elementary rules of arithmetic. These were his highest and only literary attainments, while the rest of those branches so universally taught in the common schools throughout the United States were entirely unknown to him. When about fourteen or fifteen years old, he began seriously to reflect upon the necessity of being prepared for a future state of existence; but how or in what way to prepare himself was a question as yet undetermined in his own mind: he perceived that it was a question of infinite importance, and that the salvation of his soul depended upon a correct understanding of it. He saw that if he understood not the way, it would be impossible to walk in it except by chance, and the thought of resting his hopes of eternal life upon chance or uncertainty was more than he could endure. If he went to the religious denominations to seek information, each pointed to its own particular tenets, saying, "This is the way—walk ye in it;" while at the same time the doctrines of each were in many respects in direct opposition to the rest. It also occurred to his mind that God was the author of but one doctrine, and therefore could acknowledge but one denomination as his Church, and that such denomination must be a people who believe and teach that one doctrine (whatever it may be) and build upon the same. He then reflected upon the immense number of doctrines now in the world, which had given rise to many hundreds of different denominations. The great question to be decided in his mind was: If any one of these denominations be the Church of Christ, which one is it? Until he could become satisfied in relation to this question he could not rest contented. To trust to the decisions of fallible man, and build his hopes upon them, without any knowledge of his own, would not satisfy the anxious desires that pervaded his breast. To decide without any positive and definite evidence on which he could rely upon a subject involving the future welfare of his soul was revolting to his feelings. The only alternative that seemed left to him was to read the Scriptures and endeavor to follow their directions. He accordingly began perusing the sacred pages of the Bible with sincerity, believing the things that he read. His mind soon caught hold of the following passage: "If any of you lack wisdom, let him ask of God, that giveth to all men liberally and upbraideth not, and it shall be given him" (James i, 5). From this promise he learned that it was the privilege of all men to ask God for wisdom, with the sure and certain expectation of receiving liberally, without being upbraided for so doing. This was cheering information to him—tidings that gave him great joy. It was like a light shining forth in a dark place to guide him to the path in which he should walk. He now saw that if he inquired of God, there was not only a possibility but a probability, yea more, a certainty, that he should obtain a knowledge which of all the doctrines was the doctrine of Christ, and which of all the churches was the Church of Christ. He therefore retired to a secret place in a grove but a short distance from his father's house, and knelt down and began to call upon the Lord. At first he was severely tempted by the powers of darkness, which endeavored to overcome him; but he continued to seek for deliverance until darkness gave way from his mind, and he was enabled to pray in fervency of the spirit and in faith; and while thus pouring out his soul, anxiously desiring an answer from God, he saw a very bright and glorious light in the heavens above, which at first seemed to be at a considerable distance. He continued praying, while the light appeared to be gradually descending towards him; and as it drew nearer it increased in brightness and magnitude, so that by the time that it reached the tops of the trees the whole wilderness, for some distance around, was illuminated in a most glorious and brilliant manner. He expected to see the leaves and boughs of the trees consumed as soon as the light came in contact with them; but perceiving that it did not produce that effect, he was encouraged with the hope of being able to endure its presence. It continued descending slowly until it rested upon the earth, and he was enveloped in the midst of it. When it first came upon him it produced a peculiar sensation throughout his whole system, and immediately his mind was caught away from the natural objects with which he was surrounded, and he was enwrapped in a heavenly vision, and saw two glorious personages who exactly resembled each other in their features or likeness. He was informed that his sins were forgiven. He was also informed upon the subjects which had for some time previously agitated his mind, namely, that all religious denominations were believing in incorrect doctrines; and, consequently, that none of them was acknowledged of God as his Church and kingdom. He was expressly commanded not to go after them; and he received a promise that the true doctrine—the fulness of the Gospel—should at some future time be made known to him; after which the vision withdrew, leaving his mind in a state of calmness and peace indescribable. Some time after having received this glorious manifestation, being young, he was again entangled in the vanities of the world, of which he afterwards sincerely and truly repented. It pleased God, on the evening of Sept. 21, 1823, again to hear his prayers; for he had retired to rest as usual, except that his mind was drawn out in fervent prayer, and his soul was filled with the most earnest desire " to commune with some kind messenger who could communicate to him the desired information of his acceptance with God," and also unfold the principles of the doctrine of Christ, according to the

promise which he had received in the former vision. While he thus continued to pour out his desires before the Father of all good, endeavoring to exercise faith in his precious promises, " on a sudden, a light like that of day, only of a purer and far more glorious appearance and brightness, burst into the room—indeed the first sight was as if the house were filled with consuming fire. This sudden appearance of a light so bright, as must naturally be expected, occasioned a shock or sensation that extended to the extremities of the body. It was, however, followed with a calmness and serenity of mind and an overwhelming rapture of joy that surpassed understanding, and in a moment a personage stood before him." Notwithstanding the brightness of the light which previously illuminated the room, " yet there seemed to be an additional glory surrounding or accompanying this personage, which shone with an increased degree of brilliancy, of which he was in the midst; and though his countenance was as lightning, yet it was of a pleasing, innocent, and glorious appearance—so much so that every fear was banished from the heart, and nothing but calmness pervaded the soul." " The stature of this personage was a little above the common size of men in this age; his garment was perfectly white, and had the appearance of being without seam." This glorious being declared himself to be an angel of God, sent forth by commandment to communicate to him that his sins were forgiven, and that his prayers were heard; and also to bring the joyful tidings that the covenant which God made with ancient Israel concerning their posterity was at hand to be fulfilled— that the great preparatory work for the second coming of the Messiah was speedily to commence—that the time was at hand for the Gospel in its fulness to be preached in power to all nations, that a people might be prepared with faith and righteousness for the millennial reign of universal peace and joy. He was informed that he was called and chosen to be an instrument in the hands of God to bring about some of his marvellous purposes in this glorious dispensation. It was also made manifest to him that the " American Indians" were a remnant of Israel; that when they first emigrated to America they were an enlightened people, possessing a knowledge of the true God, enjoying his favor and peculiar blessings from his hand; that the prophets and inspired writers among them were required to keep a sacred history of the most important events transpiring among them, which history was handed down for many generations, till at length they fell into great wickedness. The greatest part of them were destroyed, and the records (by commandment of God to one of the last prophets among them) were safely deposited to preserve them from the hands of the wicked who sought to destroy them. He was informed that these records contained many sacred revelations pertaining to the gospel of the kingdom, as well as prophecies relating to the great events of the last days; and that to fulfil his promises to the ancients who wrote the records, and to accomplish his purposes in the restitution of their children, etc., they were to come forth to the knowledge of the people. If faithful, he was to be the instrument who should be thus highly favored in bringing these sacred things to light. At the same time he was expressly informed that it must be done with an eye single to the glory of God—that no one could be intrusted with those sacred writings who should endeavor to aggrandize himself by converting sacred things to unrighteous and speculative purposes (see *Book of Mormon*, ch. iv, § 2, p. 510). After giving him many instructions concerning things past and to come, which would be foreign to our purpose to mention here, he disappeared, and the light and glory of God withdrew, leaving his mind in perfect peace, while a calmness and serenity indescribable pervaded his soul. But before morning the vision was twice renewed, instructing him further and still further concerning the great work of God about to be performed on the earth. In the morning he went out to his work as usual, but soon the vision was renewed—the angel again appeared, and having been informed by the previous visions of the night concerning the place where those records were deposited, he was instructed to go immediately and view them.

Accordingly he repaired to the place, a brief description of which was best given by Oliver Cowdery [Joseph Smith's scribe and first follower by baptism], who shortly after this event visited the spot:

"As you pass on the mail-road from Palmyra, Wayne County, to Canandaigua, Ontario County, New York, before arriving at the little village of Manchester, about four miles from Palmyra, you pass a large hill on the east side of the road. Why I say large is because it is as large, perhaps, as any in that country. The north end rises quite suddenly until it assumes a level with the more southerly extremity, and I think I may say an elevation higher than at the south a short distance, say half or three fourths of a mile. As you pass towards Canandaigua it lessens gradually, until the surface assumes its common level, or is broken by other smaller hills or ridges, watercourses, and ravines. I think I am justified in saying that this is the highest hill for some distance around, and I am certain that its appearance, as it rises so suddenly from a plain on the north, must attract the notice of the traveller as he passes by. The north end (which has been described as rising suddenly from the plain) forms a promontory, without timber, but covered with grass. As you pass to the south you soon come to scattering timber, the surface having been cleared by art or wind; and a short distance farther left you are surrounded with the common forest of the country. It is necessary to observe that even the part cleared was only occupied for pasturage, its steep ascent and narrow summit not admitting the plough of the husbandman with any degree of ease or profit. It was at the second-mentioned place where the record was found to be deposited, on the west side of the hill, not far from the top, down its side; and when myself visited the place in the year 1830 there were several trees standing—enough to cause a shade in summer, but not so much as to prevent the surface being covered with grass, which was also the case when the record was first found. How far below the surface these records were anciently placed I am unable to say; but from the fact that they had been some fourteen hundred years buried, and that, too, on the side of a hill so steep, one is ready to conclude that they were some feet below, as the earth would naturally wear, more or less, in that length of time. But being placed towards the top of the hill, the ground would not remove as much as at two thirds, perhaps. Another circumstance would prevent a wearing of the earth: in all probability, as soon as timber had time to grow the hill was covered, and the roots of the same would hold the surface. However, on this point I shall leave every man to draw his own conclusion and form his own speculation; but, suffice to say, a hole of sufficient depth was dug. At the bottom of this was laid a stone of suitable size, the upper surface being smooth. At each edge was placed a large quantity of cement, and into this cement, at the four edges of this stone, were placed erect four others, *their* bottom edges resting *in* the cement, at the outer edges of the first stone. The four last named, when placed erect, formed a box; the corners, or where the edges of the four came in contact, were also cemented so firmly that the moisture from without was prevented from entering. It is to be observed, also, that the inner surfaces of the four erect or side stones were smooth. This box was sufficiently large to admit a breastplate, such as was used by the ancients to defend the chest, etc., from the arrows and weapons of their enemy. From the bottom of the box, or from the breastplate, arose three small pillars, composed of the same description of cement used on the edges, and upon these three pillars were placed the records. This box containing the records was covered with another stone, the bottom surface being flat, and the upper crowning. When it was first visited by Mr. Smith, on the morning of the 22d of September, 1823, a part of the crowning stone was visible above the surface, while the edges were concealed by the soil and grass; from which circumstance it may be seen that however deep this box might have been placed at first, the time had been sufficient to wear the earth, so that it was easily discovered when once directed, and yet not enough to make a perceivable difference to the passer-by. After arriving at the repository, a little exertion in removing the soil from the edges of the top of the box, and a light lever, brought to his natural vision its contents. While viewing and contemplating this sacred treasure with wonder and astonishment, behold! the angel of the Lord, who had previously visited him, again stood in his presence, and his soul was again enlightened as it was the evening before, and he was filled with the Holy Spirit, and the heavens were opened, and the glory of the Lord shone round about and rested upon him. While he thus stood gazing and admiring, the angel said, 'Look!' and as he thus spake he beheld the Prince of Darkness, surrounded by his innumer-

able train of associates. All this passed before him, and the heavenly messenger said, 'All this is shown—the good and the evil, the holy and the impure, the glory of God and the power of darkness—that you may know hereafter the two powers, and never be influenced or overcome by the wicked one. Behold, whatsoever enticeth and leadeth to good, and to do good, is of God; and whatsoever doth not, is of that wicked one. It is he that filleth the hearts of men with evil, to walk in darkness and blaspheme God; and you may learn from henceforth that his ways are to destruction, but the way of holiness is peace and rest. You cannot at this time obtain this record, for the commandment of God is strict; and if ever these sacred things are obtained, they must be by prayer and faithfulness in obeying the Lord. They are not deposited here for the sake of accumulating gain and wealth for the glory of this world; they were sealed by the prayer of faith, and because of the knowledge which they contain; they are of no worth among the children of men only for their knowledge. On them is contained the fulness of the Gospel of Jesus Christ, as it was given to his people on this land; and when it shall be brought forth by the power of God it shall be carried to the Gentiles, of whom many will receive it, and after will the seed of Israel be brought into the fold of their Redeemer by obeying it also. Those who kept the commandments of the Lord on this land desired this at his hand, and through the prayer of faith obtained the promise that if their descendants should transgress and fall away a record should be kept, and in the last days come to their children. These things are sacred, and must be kept so, for the promise of the Lord concerning them must be fulfilled. No man can obtain them if his heart is impure, because they contain that which is sacred. . . . By them will the Lord work a great and marvellous work; the wisdom of the wise shall become as naught, and the understanding of the prudent shall be hid; and because the power of God shall be displayed, those who profess to know the truth but walk in deceit shall tremble with anger; but with signs and with wonders, with gifts and with healings, with the manifestations of the power of God and with the Holy Ghost shall the hearts of the faithful be comforted. You have now beheld the power of God manifested, and the power of Satan: you see that there is nothing desirable in the works of darkness—that they cannot bring happiness—that those who are overcome therewith are miserable; while, on the other hand, the righteous are blessed with a place in the kingdom of God, where joy unspeakable surrounds them. There they rest beyond the power of the enemy of truth, where no evil can disturb them. The glory of God crowns them, and they continually feast upon his goodness and enjoy his smiles. Behold, notwithstanding you have seen this great display of power, by which you may ever be able to detect the Evil One, yet I give unto you another sign, and when it comes to pass, then know that the Lord is God, and that he will fulfil his purposes, and that the knowledge which this record contains will go to every nation, and kindred, and tongue, and people under the whole heaven. This is the sign: When these things begin to be known—that is, when it is known that the Lord has shown you these things—the workers of iniquity will seek your overthrow. They will circulate falsehoods to destroy your reputation, and also will seek to take your life: but remember this, if you are faithful, and shall hereafter continue to keep the commandments of the Lord, you shall be preserved to bring these things forth; for in due time he will give you a commandment to come and take them. When they are interpreted, the Lord will give the holy priesthood to some, and they shall begin to proclaim this gospel and baptize by water, and after that they shall have power to give the Holy Ghost by the laying on of their hands. Then will persecution rage more and more: for the iniquities of men shall be revealed, and those who are not built upon the Rock will seek to overthrow the Church; but it will increase the more opposed, and spread farther and farther, increasing in knowledge till they shall be sanctified and receive an inheritance where the glory of God will rest upon them; and when this takes place, and all things are prepared, the ten tribes of Israel will be revealed in the north country, whither they have been for a long season; and when this is fulfilled will be brought to pass that saying of the prophet, "And the Redeemer shall come to Zion, and unto them that turn from transgression in Jacob, saith the Lord." But notwithstanding the workers of iniquity shall seek your destruction, the arm of the Lord will be extended, and you will be borne off conqueror if you keep all his commandments. Your name shall be known among the nations, for the work which the Lord will perform by your hands shall cause the righteous to rejoice and the wicked to rage; with the one it shall be had in honor, and with the other in reproach—yet with these it shall be a terror, because of the great and marvellous work which shall follow the coming forth of this fulness of the Gospel. Now go thy way, remembering what the Lord hath done for thee, and be diligent in keeping his commandments, and he will deliver thee from temptations and all the arts and devices of the wicked one. Forget not to pray that thy mind may become strong, that when he shall manifest unto thee thou mayest have power to escape the evil and obtain these precious things.'"

The above quotation is an extract from a letter written by elder Oliver Cowdery, which was published in one of the numbers of the *Latter-day Saints' Messenger and Advocate.*

Although many more instructions were given by the mouth of the angel to Mr. Smith, for which we have not space here, yet the most important items are contained in the foregoing relation. During the period of the four following years he frequently received instructions from the mouth of the heavenly messenger. On the morning of the 22d of September, A.D. 1827, the angel of the Lord delivered the records into his hands. These records were engraved on plates which had the appearance of gold. Each plate was not far from seven by eight inches in width and length, being not quite as thick as common tin. They were filled on both sides with engravings in Egyptian characters (see *Book of Mormon*, Mormon, chap. iv, § 8, p. 515), and bound together in a volume as the leaves of a book, and fastened at one edge with three rings running through the whole. This volume was something near six inches in thickness, a part of which was sealed. The characters or letters upon the unsealed part were small and beautifully engraved. The whole book exhibited many marks of antiquity in its construction, as well as much skill in the art of engraving. With the records was found "a curious instrument, called by the ancients the Urim and Thummim, which consisted of two transparent stones, clear as crystal, set in the two rims of a bow. This was in use in ancient times by persons called seers. It was an instrument by the use of which they received revelation of things distant or of things past or future." (See *Biogr. Sketches*, p. 101; *Book of Mormon*, Ether, ch. i, § 7–11, p. 520 sq. See also Nephi, § 20, p. 5 sq.) In the mean time the inhabitants of that vicinity, having been informed that Mr. Smith had seen heavenly visions, and that he had discovered sacred records, began to ridicule and mock at those things. After having obtained those sacred things, while proceeding home through the wilderness and fields, he was waylaid by two ruffians, who had secreted themselves for the purpose of robbing him of the records. One of them struck him with a club before he perceived them; but being a strong man and large in stature, with great exertion he cleared himself from them and ran towards home, being closely pursued until he came near his father's house, when his pursuers, for fear of being detected, turned and fled the other way. Soon the news of his discoveries spread abroad throughout all those parts. False reports, misrepresentations, and base slanders flew as if upon the wings of the wind in every direction. The house was frequently beset by mobs and evil-designing persons. Several times he was shot at, and very narrowly escaped. Every device was used to get the plates away from him. Being continually in danger of his life from a gang of abandoned wretches, he at length concluded to leave the place and go to Pennsylvania; and accordingly packed up his goods, putting the plates into a barrel of beans, and proceeded upon his journey. He had not gone far before he was overtaken by an officer with a search-warrant, who flattered himself with the idea that he should surely obtain the plates; after searching very diligently, he was sadly disappointed at not finding them. Mr. Smith then drove on, but before he got to his journey's end he was again overtaken by an officer on the same business, and after ransacking the wagon very carefully, he went his way as much chagrined as the first at not being able to discover the object of his research. Without any further molestation Smith pursued his journey until he came into the northern part of Pennsylvania, near the Susquehanna River, in which part his father-in-law resided. Having provided himself with a home, he commenced translating the record, as he himself tells us in his *Autobiography*, "by the gift and power of God, through the means of the Urim and Thummim;" and being a poor writer, he was under the necessity of em-

ploying a scribe to write the translation as it came from his mouth. (See, for criticism, editorial appendix below, and Stenhouse, p. 23.)

Mr. Smith continued the work of translation, as his pecuniary circumstances would permit, until he finished the unsealed part of the records. The part translated is entitled the *Book of Mormon*, which contains nearly as much reading as the Old Testament. This volume purports to be a history of ancient America, from its early settlement by a colony who came from the Tower of Babel at the confusion of languages, to the beginning of the fifth century of the Christian æra. By these records we are informed that America, in ancient times, was inhabited by two distinct races of people. The first, or more ancient race, came directly from the great Tower, being called Jaredites. The second race came directly from the city of Jerusalem, about six hundred years before Christ, being Israelites, principally the descendants of Joseph. The first nation, or Jaredites, were destroyed about the time that the Israelites came from Jerusalem, who succeeded them in the inheritance of the country. The principal nation of the second race fell in battle towards the close of the fourth century. The remaining remnant, having dwindled into an uncivilized state, still continue to inhabit the land, although divided into a "multitude of nations," and are called by Europeans the "American Indians." We learn from the same history that at the confusion of languages, when the Lord scattered the people upon all the face of the earth, the Jaredites, being a righteous people, obtained favor in the sight of the Lord, and were not confounded. Because of their righteousness, the Lord miraculously led them from the Tower to the great ocean, where they were commanded to build vessels, in which they were marvellously brought across the great deep to the shores of North America. The Lord God promised to give them America, which was a very choice land in his sight, for an inheritance; and he swore unto them in his wrath that whoso should possess this land of promise, from that time henceforth and forever should serve him, the true and only God, or they should be swept off when the fulness of his wrath should come upon them, and they were fully ripened in iniquity. Moreover, he promised to make them a great and powerful nation, so that there should be no greater nation upon all the face of the earth. Accordingly in process of time they became a very numerous and powerful people, occupying principally North America; building large cities in all quarters of the land, being a civilized and enlightened nation. Agriculture and machinery were carried on to a great extent. Commercial and manufacturing business flourished on every hand; yet, in consequence of wickedness, they were often visited with terrible judgments. Many prophets were raised up among them from generation to generation, who testified against the wickedness of the people, and prophesied of judgments and calamities which awaited them if they did not repent, etc. Sometimes they were visited by pestilence and plagues, and sometimes by famine and war, until at length (having occupied the land some fifteen or sixteen hundred years) their wickedness became so great that the Lord threatened by the mouth of his prophets to utterly destroy them from the face of the land. But they gave no heed to these warnings; therefore the word of the Lord was fulfilled, and they were entirely destroyed—leaving their houses, their cities, and their land desolate; and their sacred records also, which were kept on gold plates, were left by one of their last prophets, whose name was Ether, in such a situation that they were discovered by the remnant of Joseph, who soon afterwards were brought from Jerusalem to inherit the land. This remnant of Joseph were also led in a miraculous manner from Jerusalem, in the first year of the reign of Zedekiah, king of Judah. They were first led to the eastern borders of the Red Sea; then they journeyed for some time along the borders thereof, nearly in a south-east direction; after which they altered their course nearly eastward, until they came to the great waters, where, by the command of God, they built a vessel, in which they were safely brought across the great Pacific Ocean, and landed upon the western coast of South America. In the eleventh year of the reign of Zedekiah, at the time the Jews were carried away captive into Babylon, another remnant were brought out of Jerusalem, some of whom were descendants of Judah. They landed in North America, soon after which they emigrated into the northern parts of South America, at which place they were discovered by the remnant of Joseph, something like four hundred years after. The same records inform us that this remnant of Joseph, soon after they landed, separated themselves into two distinct nations. This division was caused by a certain portion of them being greatly persecuted, because of their righteousness, by the remainder. The persecuted nation emigrated to the northern parts of South America, leaving the wicked nation in possession of the middle and southern parts of the same. The former were called Nephites, being led by a prophet whose name was Nephi. The latter were called Lamanites, being led by a very wicked man whose name was Laman. The Nephites had in their possession a copy of the Holy Scriptures, viz. the five books of Moses and the prophecies of the holy prophets down to Jeremiah, in whose days they left Jerusalem. These Scriptures were engraved on plates of brass in the Egyptian language. They themselves also made plates soon after their landing, on which they began to engrave their own history, prophecies, visions, and revelations. All these sacred records were kept by holy and righteous men, who were inspired by the Holy Ghost, and were carefully preserved and handed down from generation to generation. The Lord gave them the whole continent for a land of promise, and he promised that they and their children after them should inherit it, on condition of their obedience to his commandments; but if they were disobedient they should be cut off from his presence. The Nephites began to prosper in the land, according to their righteousness; and they multiplied and spread forth to the east, and west, and north—building large villages, cities, synagogues, and temples, together with forts, towers, and fortifications to defend themselves against their enemies. They cultivated the earth, and raised various kinds of grain in abundance. They also raised numerous flocks of domestic animals, and became a very wealthy people, having in abundance gold, silver, copper, tin, iron, etc. Arts and sciences flourished to a great extent. Various kinds of machinery were in use. Cloths of various kinds were manufactured; swords, scimitars, axes, and various implements of war were made, together with head-shields, arm-shields, and breastplates to defend themselves in battle with their enemies. In the days of their righteousness they were a civilized, enlightened, and happy people. But, on the other hand, the Lamanites, because of the hardness of their hearts, brought down many judgments upon their own heads; nevertheless they were not destroyed as a nation; but the Lord God sent forth a curse upon them, and they became a dark, loathsome, and filthy people. Before their rebellion they were white and exceedingly fair, like the Nephites; but the Lord God cursed them in their complexions, and they were changed to a dark color; and they became a wild, savage, and ferocious people, being great enemies to the Nephites, whom they sought by every means to destroy. Many times they came against them with their numerous hosts to battle, but were repulsed by the Nephites and driven back to their own possessions, not, however, generally speaking, without great loss on both sides; for tens of thousands were very frequently slain, after which they were piled together in great heaps upon the face of the ground, and covered with a shallow covering of earth, which will account

for these ancient mounds, filled with human bones, so numerous at the present day both in North and South America.

The second colony, which left Jerusalem eleven years after the remnant of Joseph left that city, landed in North America, and emigrated from thence to the northern parts of South America; and about four hundred years after they were discovered by the Nephites, as stated above. They were called the people of Zarahemla. They had been perplexed with many wars among themselves, and having brought no records with them, their language had become corrupted, and they denied the being of God. At the time they were discovered by the Nephites they were very numerous, and only in a partial state of civilization; but the Nephites united with them and taught them the Holy Scriptures, and they were restored to civilization, and became one nation with them. In process of time the Nephites began to build ships near the Isthmus of Darien, and launch them forth into the western ocean, in which great numbers sailed a great distance to the northward, and began to colonize North America. Other colonies emigrated by land, and in a few centuries the whole continent became peopled. North America at that time was almost entirely destitute of timber, it having been cut off by the more ancient race who came from the great Tower at the confusion of languages; but the Nephites became very skilful in building houses of cement; also much timber was carried by the way of shipping from South to North America. They also planted groves and began to raise timber, that in time their wants might be supplied. Large cities were built in various parts of the continent, both among the Lamanites and Nephites. The law of Moses was observed by the latter. Numerous prophets were raised up from time to time throughout their generations. Many records, both historical and prophetical, which were of great size, were kept among them; some on plates of gold and other metals, and some on other materials. The sacred records, also, of the more ancient race who had been destroyed were found by them. These were engraved on plates of gold. They translated them into their own language by the gift and power of God, through the means of the Urim and Thummim. They contained a historical account from the creation down to the Tower of Babel, and from that time down until they were destroyed, comprising a period of about thirty-four hundred or thirty-five hundred years. They also contained many prophecies, great and marvellous, reaching forward to the final end and consummation of all things, and the creation of a new heaven and new earth. The prophets also among the Nephites prophesied of great things. They opened the secrets of futurity—saw the coming of Messiah in the flesh—prophesied of the blessings to come upon their descendants in the latter times—made known the history of unborn generations—unfolded the grand events of ages to come—viewed the power, glory, and majesty of Messiah's second advent—beheld the establishment of the kingdom of peace—gazed upon the glories of the day of righteousness—saw creation redeemed from the curse, and all the righteous filled with songs of everlasting joy. The Nephites knew of the birth and crucifixion of Christ by certain celestial and terrestrial phenomena, which at those times were shown forth in fulfilment of the predictions of many of their prophets. Notwithstanding the many blessings they had received, they had fallen into great wickedness, and had cast out the saints and the prophets, and stoned and killed them. Therefore at the time of the crucifixion of Christ they were visited in great judgment: thick darkness covered the whole continent — the earth was terribly convulsed — the rocks were rent into broken fragments, and afterwards found in seams and cracks upon all the face of the land — mountains were sunk into valleys, and valleys raised into mountains—the highways and level roads were broken up and spoiled—many cities were laid in ruins; others were buried up in the depths of the earth, and mountains occupied their place; while others were sunk, and waters came up in their stead; and others still were burned by fire from heaven. Thus the predictions of their prophets were fulfilled upon their heads. Thus the more wicked part, both of the Nephites and Lamanites, were destroyed. Thus the Almighty executed vengeance and fury upon them, that the blood of the saints and prophets might no longer cry from the ground against them.

Those who survived these terrible judgments were favored with the personal ministry of Christ; for after he arose from the dead, finished his ministry at Jerusalem, and ascended to heaven, he descended in the presence of the Nephites, who were assembled round about their temple in the northern parts of South America. He exhibited to them his wounded hands, side, and feet; commanded the law of Moses to be abolished; introduced and established the Gospel in its stead; chose twelve disciples from among them to administer the same; instituted the sacrament; prayed for and blessed their little children; healed their sick, blind, lame, deaf, and those who were afflicted in any way; raised a man from the dead; showed forth his power in their midst; expounded the Scriptures, which had been given from the beginning down to that time; and made known unto them all things which should take place down until he should come in his glory, and from that time down to the end, when all people, nations, and languages should stand before God to be judged, and the heaven and the earth should pass away, and there should be a new heaven and a new earth. These teachings of Jesus were engraved upon plates, some of which are contained in the *Book of Mormon;* but the greater part are not revealed in that book, but hereafter are to be made manifest to the saints. After Jesus had finished ministering unto them, he ascended into heaven; and the twelve disciples whom he had chosen went forth upon all the face of the land preaching the Gospel, baptizing those who repented for the remission of sins, after which they laid their hands upon them, that they might receive the Holy Spirit. Mighty miracles were wrought by them, and also by many of the Church. The Nephites and Lamanites were all converted unto the Lord, both in South and North America, and they dwelt in righteousness above three hundred years; but towards the close of the fourth century of the Christian æra they had so far apostatized from God that he suffered great judgments to fall upon them. The Lamanites at that time dwelt in South America, and the Nephites in North America. A great and terrible war commenced between them, which lasted for many years, and resulted in the complete overthrow and destruction of the Nephites. This war commenced at the Isthmus of Darien, and was very destructive to both nations for many years. At length the Nephites were driven before their enemies a great distance to the north and north-east; and having gathered their whole nation together, both men, women, and children, they encamped on and round about the hill Cumorah, where the records were found, which is in the State of New York, about two hundred miles west of the city of Albany. Here they were met by the numerous hosts of the Lamanites, and were slain, hewn down, and slaughtered, both male and female— the aged, middle-aged, and children. Hundreds of thousands were slain on both sides; and the nation of the Nephites were destroyed, excepting a few who had deserted over to the Lamanites, and a few who escaped into the south country, and a few who fell wounded, and were left by the Lamanites on the field of battle for dead, among whom were Mormon and his son Moroni, who were righteous men.

Mormon had made an abridgment from the records of his forefathers upon plates, which abridgment he entitled the *Book of Mormon;* and (being commanded of God) he hid in the hill Cumorah all the sacred records of his forefathers which were in his possession, except the abridgment called the *Book of Mormon,* which he gave to his son Moroni to finish. Moroni survived his nation a few years, and continued the writings, in which he informs us that the Lamanites hunted those few Nephites who escaped the great and tremendous battle of Cumorah until they were all destroyed, excepting those who were mingled with the Lamanites, and that he was left alone, and kept himself hid, for they sought to destroy every Nephite who would not deny the Christ. He furthermore states that the Lamanites were at war one with another, and that the whole face of the land was one continual scene of murdering, robbing, and plundering. He continued the history until the four hundred and twentieth year of the Christian æra, when (by the commandment of God) he hid the records in the hill Cumorah, where they remained concealed until by the ministry of an angel they were discovered to Mr. Smith, who, by the gift and power of God, translated them into the English language by the means of the Urim and Thummim, as stated in the foregoing. (See editorial criticisms below.)

After the book was translated the Lord raised up witnesses to bear testimony to the nations of its truth, who at the close of the volume send forth their testimony, which reads as follows:

"Be it known unto all nations, kindreds, tongues, and people unto whom this work shall come, that we, through the grace of God the Father and our Lord Jesus Christ, have seen the plates which contain this record, which is a record of the people of Nephi, and also of the Lamanites, their brethren, and also of the people of Jared, who came from the Tower of which hath been spoken; and we also know that they have been translated by the gift and power of God, for his voice hath declared it unto us; wherefore we know of a surety that the work is true. And we also testify that we have seen the engravings which are upon the plates; and they have been shown unto us by the power of God, and not of man. And we declare, with words of soberness, that an angel of God came down from heaven, and he brought and laid before our eyes, that we beheld and saw the plates and the engravings thereon; and we know that it is by the grace of God the Father and our Lord Jesus Christ that we beheld and bear record that these things are true, and it is marvellous in our eyes; nevertheless, the voice of the Lord commanded us that we should bear record of it; wherefore, to be obedient unto the commandments of God, we bear testimony of these things. And we know that if we are faithful in Christ we shall rid our garments of the blood of all men, and be found spotless before the judgment-seat of Christ, and shall dwell with him eternally in the heavens. And the honor be to the Father, and to the Son, and to the Holy Ghost, which is one God. Amen.

"OLIVER COWDERY,
DAVID WHITMER,
MARTIN HARRIS."

Then follows the testimony of eight witnesses:

"Be it known unto all nations, kindreds, tongues, and people unto whom this work shall come, that Joseph Smith, Jr., the translator of this work, has shown unto us the plates of which hath been spoken, which have the appearance of gold; and as many of the leaves as the said Smith has translated we did handle with our hands; and we also saw the engravings thereon, all of which has the appearance of ancient work and of curious workmanship. And this we bear record with words of soberness, that the said Smith has shown unto us, for we have seen and hefted, and know of a surety that the said Smith has got the plates of which we have spoken. And we give our names unto the world, to witness unto the world that which we have seen; and we lie not, God bearing witness of it.

"CHRISTIAN WHITMER,
JACOB WHITMER,
PETER WHITMER, Jr.,
JOHN WHITMER,
HIRAM PAGE,
JOSEPH SMITH, Sr.,
HYRUM SMITH,
SAM. H. SMITH."

In the year 1829, Mr. Smith and Mr. Cowdery, having learned the correct mode of baptism from the teachings of the Saviour to the ancient Nephites, as recorded in the *Book of Mormon,* had a desire to be baptized; but knowing that no one had authority to administer that sacred ordinance in any denomination, they were at a loss to know how the authority was to be restored; and while calling upon the Lord with a desire to be informed on the subject, a holy angel appeared and stood before them, and laid his hands upon their heads, and ordained them priests of the order of Aaron, and commanded them to baptize each other, which they accordingly did. In the year 1830 a large edition of the *Book of Mormon* first appeared in print. "As some began to peruse its sacred pages, the spirit of the Lord bore record to them that it was true; and they were obedient to its requirements, by coming forth humbly repenting before the Lord, and being immersed in water for the remission of sins, after which, by the commandment of God, hands were laid upon them in the name of the Lord for the gift of the Holy Spirit. And on the 6th of April, in the year of our Lord one thousand eight hundred and thirty, the 'Church of Jesus Christ of Latter-day Saints' was organized in the town of Fayette, Seneca County, State of New York, North America. Some few were called and ordained by the spirit of revelation and prophecy, and began to preach and bear testimony, as the spirit gave them utterance; and although they were the weak things of the earth, yet they were strengthened by the Holy Ghost, and gave forth their testimony in great power, by which means many were brought to repentance, and came forward with broken hearts and contrite spirits, and were immersed in water confessing their sins, and were filled with the Holy Ghost by the laying on of hands, and saw visions and prophesied. Devils were cast out, and the sick were healed by the prayer of faith and the laying on of hands. Thus was the word confirmed unto the faithful by the signs following. Thus the Lord raised up witnesses to bear testimony of his name, and laid the foundation of his kingdom in the last days. And thus the hearts of the saints were comforted and filled with great joy."

Editorial Appendix and Criticisms.—Mr. Pratt's account stops with the organization of the Saints as an ecclesiastical body. We supplement it with the later history.

Joseph Smith seems at first to have had vague and confused ideas as to the nature and design of the Church he was about to establish until he found a convert in Sidney Rigdon, an able Campbellite preacher, then residing in Ohio. He was inclined to teach Millenarianism and bring his flock over to the new faith. This settled Smith, and together they worked out a sort of Millenarian faith, in which at that time Western New York was largely interested. It was by these two religionists declared that the millennium was close at hand, that the Indians were to be speedily converted, and that America was to be the final gathering-place of the Saints, who were to assemble at New Zion or New Jerusalem, somewhere in the interior of the American continent. With the *Book of Mormon* as their text and authority, they began to preach this new gospel; and Smith's family and a few of his associates, together with some of Rigdon's former flock, were soon enough in numbers to constitute a Mormon Church, which, as we have learned from Mr. Pratt's account, was organized April 6, 1830, at Fayette, N. Y. Though exposed to ridicule and hostility, the Saints continued to gather disciples. The publication of the *Book of Mormon*, and some alleged miracles and prophecies, attracted the people to the preaching of Smith and his companions, and at the first Conference of the Church, June 1, 1830, held at Fayette, N. Y., thirty members were present. Missionaries were now set apart, and every member was utilized, and in consequence the Saints were soon met with everywhere. Their missionaries were full of zeal, and converts gathered rapidly. Among them were Brigham Young, the two brothers Pratt, and Sidney Rigdon, the Campbellite preacher, who all became most efficient workers in Mormondom. Churches also were established in Ohio, Pennsylvania, New York, and even so far west as Indiana and Illinois. But with their growth persecution intensified, and the Saints finally turned their eyes westwards

for a permanent home. In the beginning of 1831 they established their head-quarters at Kirtland, Ohio, and everything pointed to it as the seat of the "New Jerusalem." Indeed, Smith advised the Saints to gather there. In a short time, however, opposition was strengthening also at Kirtland, and Smith urged the people to pray to the Lord "that he would in due time reveal unto them the place where the New Jerusalem should be built, and where the Saints should eventually be gathered in one." Smith's eyes were now turned to the far West— to the region of the great prairies—hoping there to work out his religious system in peace and freedom. In the autumn of 1831 a successful work was inaugurated at Independence, Jackson County, Mo.; and shortly after the revelation came that "it was appointed by the finger of the Lord" that a colony of the Saints should be established in that part of Missouri, it being "the land of promise and the place for the city of Zion." In a very short time nearly 1200 persons gathered in the place "where Christ would shortly reign in person." Land was largely bought; preaching was vigorously carried on; a printing-press was established; a monthly periodical (*The Morning and Evening Star*) and a weekly newspaper (*The Upper Missouri Advertiser*) were started to propagate the doctrines of the new sect; and it is only fair to the Mormons to state that a spirit of industry, sobriety, order, and cleanliness was everywhere visible. Account for it how we may, the Mormons were in many important respects, morally, socially, and industrially, far in advance of their neighbors. Smith himself, with such of the Saints as preferred to stay in Ohio until forced from it, continued to reside there, though, as we shall see presently, he was by no means stationary there, and was now in Ohio, now in Missouri, as the state of affairs required. In 1838 unsuccessful financial speculations obliged the Prophet also to withdraw, after having besides encountered persecutions from mobs.

In Missouri also the Mormons early engendered opposition. Secret societies were formed a short time after their settlement to expel them from that region; their periodicals were stopped, their printing-press confiscated, their ministers tarred and feathered, and numberless other outrages were committed. Finally, in 1833 the hapless Saints were compelled to flee across the Missouri River, and men, women, and children had to encamp in the open wilderness on a winter night (see Parley P. Pratt, *Hist. of the Missouri Persecutions*). The cruelty with which they were treated is a disgraceful page in American colonization history, and every true man has reason to regret the outrages perpetrated against these religionists. They subsequently settled in Clay County, in the same state. Smith, when informed of these outrages, at once set out for Missouri; and now assumed, besides the role of "prophet, seer, revelator, and translator," that of military leader of his people. A lengthened revelation was given in February, 1834, to raise "the strength of the Lord's house," and go up to Missouri to redeem Zion, and the Prophet became, by the election of a council of elders, "commander-in-chief of the armies of Israel." With a band of 150 men, the "Prophet" set out from Kirtland for Missouri. By the time he reached Missouri the little band had increased to 205; but they were intercepted by the settlers before they could effect a junction with the Saints in Clay County, and were so badly defeated in their schemes that the few faithful ones who were left, together with the Prophet himself, gladly enough returned to their home at Kirtland. Here, while recruiting from the trials of this warfare, Smith determined upon a more perfect organization of his adherents. In 1833 he had published for their spiritual guidance *The Book of Doctrine and Covenants*, and in May, 1834, had adopted as the formal title of his ecclesiastical body "The Church of Jesus Christ of Latter-day Saints." He now instituted the hierarchical organization to which the Mormons owe in so large a measure their success and perpetuity. As heads of the Church he appointed a presidency of three (and this remains the practice of the Mormons), assigning to himself the first place, and associating with himself the Rigdon of whom we have had occasion to speak before, and one Frederick G. Williams, a "revelation" from the Lord having declared that the sins of Rigdon and Williams were forgiven, "and that they were henceforth to be accounted as equals with Joseph Smith, jun., in holding the keys of his last kingdom." His own superiority the Prophet had declared to his followers as early as 1830 by special "revelation," which, after appointing him "seer, translator, prophet, apostle of Jesus Christ, and elder of the Church," also demands that "the Church shall give heed to all his words and commandments which he shall give unto you; for his word shall ye receive as if from my own mouth, in all patience and faith." On Feb. 4, 1835, Smith selected his high council of twelve, and delegated these his apostles "to go unto all nations, kindreds, tongues, and people, to preach the Gospel of the New Covenant." They departed into the Eastern States, and later into Europe; the first in 1837 to England, where the first Conference of converts was held at Preston, Lancashire, on Dec. 25th of that year. Everywhere the Saints now gained adherents. In March, 1836, when the Temple at Kirtland was dedicated, over 1000 Mormons were gathered in that little town to witness the "sacred ceremony," and "to receive great blessings."

The year 1837 was a most auspicious one for the Saints, though for a time it threatened their very life as an ecclesiastical body. In Ohio they lost the confidence and support of their "Gentile" associates by the mismanagement of mercantile affairs, so that the Prophet laid himself open to the suspicion of deceit, double-dealing, and fraud. They also sustained several important apostasies from their ranks, one seceder being one of Joseph's councillors, and three others apostles in the "kingdom." But while these trials awaited them at their own "Zion," the New Covenant was rapidly spreading in England, under the preaching of the apostles Orson Hyde and Heber C. Kimball, and the Saints received large accessions to their numbers, especially from the masses in the great manufacturing and commercial towns—Manchester, Liverpool, Leeds, Birmingham, Glasgow; and above all from the mining districts of South Wales, where Mormonism, in some places, almost competed for popularity with Methodism itself. Since then they have extended their strange evangelization to the East Indies, Australia, the islands of the Pacific, Egypt, Palestine, Turkey, and almost every country on the continent of Europe. In 1838 Kirtland was finally altogether abandoned, for, luckily for the Prophet, just at the moment of his indictment for swindling, etc., a new "revelation" ordered his immediate departure for Missouri, which he promptly obeyed, with all the more alacrity as internal disorders had painfully manifested themselves also in Missouri, resulting in the expulsion of several influential members, among them David Whitmer, the second witness to the *Book of Mormon*, and Oliver Cowdery, the first convert by baptism. Smith's presence soon healed all internal disorders, but the conflict between the Saints and the other Missourians became daily fiercer. The organized religionists, though guilty of fanatical extravagance in their faith, were yet so perfectly united in all their material undertakings as to make their prosperity almost a necessity, and this success annoyed the other settlers to such a degree that a constant warfare was maintained. The rapid increase of the Saints made them, moreover, a subject of suspicion, especially as they had declared it to be their intention to take Missouri as their earthly portion for an "everlasting possession." The Prophet, it was said, had declared that he would yet trample on the necks of his enemies, and these had therefore every reason to fear his growing strength. Besides, it was known that a band of men had secretly organized to defend the first presidency by any means, fair or foul; and it is

therefore not to be wondered that there was constant quarrelling and fighting between Saints and Gentiles, until the contest amounted to civil war, and called for the interference of the state authorities. That such a step was really necessary became clearly apparent when on Oct. 24, 1838, Thomas B. March, himself the president of the Mormon Apostolical College, and Orson Hyde, one of the twelve apostles, and now (1875) again a faithful "Saint," made before a justice of the peace in Ray County, Mo., an affidavit in which it is declared that "They (i. e. the Mormons under Smith) have among them a company consisting of all that are considered true Mormons, called the Danites, who have taken an oath to support the heads of the Church in all things that they say or do, whether right or wrong. . . . The plan of said Smith, the Prophet, is to take this state; and he professes to his people to intend taking the United States, and ultimately the whole world. This is the belief of the Church, and my own (i. e. March's) opinion of the Prophet's plan and intentions. The Prophet inculcates the notion, and it is believed by every true Mormon, that Smith's prophecies are superior to the law of the land. I have heard the Prophet say that he would yet tread down his enemies and walk over their dead bodies; that if he was not let alone he would be a second Mohammed to his generation, and that he would make it one gore of blood from the Rocky Mountains to the Atlantic Ocean." Coming from the Saints' own fellow-worshippers, this statement was of course credited by the "Gentiles." It was, moreover, confirmed by the published utterances of Sidney Rigdon, who, in a sermon on July 4, 1838, preached at Far West, had said: "We take God and all the holy angels to witness this day that we warn all men in the name of Jesus Christ to come on us no more for war. The man or the set of men who attempts it does it at the expense of their lives. And that mob that comes on us to disturb us, it shall be between them and us a war of extermination, for we will follow them till the last drop of their blood is spilled, or else they will have to exterminate us. For we will carry the seat of war to their own houses and their own families, and one party or the other shall be utterly destroyed." Near the close of 1838 the state militia was finally called out, nominally to establish peace, really to crush the Mormons. After much loss and suffering, especially at a place called Hawn's Mill, where several Mormons were massacred, the Saints were driven in the depth of winter across the Mississippi into Illinois. The Prophet, his brother Hyrum, and other leading Mormons, were seized, and sentenced by court-martial to be shot; but the sentence was not carried out, and after some months' close confinement they all escaped into Illinois (April, 1839).

The number of Saints who at this time gathered in Illinois is estimated at no less than 15,000, notwithstanding the defections which the Saints sustained by their expulsion from the land of promise. The people of Illinois treated the new-comers very kindly, and gave them a grant of land on the east bank of the Mississippi, forty miles above Quincy, and twenty miles below Burlington, Iowa. Here, on the bend of the river, upon rising ground that commands a magnificent view of the Mississippi for many miles, they established themselves a new home, which, in obedience to a "revelation" given to Smith, was called *Nauvoo*, or the "City of Beauty." The country was a mere wilderness when the Mormons settled in it; it soon, however, began to rejoice and blossom as the rose. The foundation of the first house was laid in 1839, and in less than two years over 2000 dwellings, together with school-houses and public edifices, were erected, besides other evidences manifesting the great prosperity of their body. The Legislature of the state was induced to grant a charter to Nauvoo; a body of Mormon militia was formed under the leadership of the Prophet, who, as we have seen before, hesitated not to assume also the part of a military leader, and he besides assumed such civil offices as gave him entire control of the place, and made him safe from all persecution of the Missourians, in case they should attempt to take him back into their own state for punishment. He enjoyed, moreover, making military displays. Thus, on April 6, 1841, when the cornerstone of the grand Temple was laid, the Prophet appeared at the head of his military legion, and in the local papers of that time is only spoken of in his military capacity. A special revelation had demanded the building of the Temple, which was to be on a far grander scale than the edifices in Ohio or Missouri (see *Doctrines and Covenants*, sec. 103). Another revelation had summoned all converts to Nauvoo, bringing with them "their gold, their silver, and their precious stones" (see *Doctr. and Cov.* sec. 103). Still another revelation now ordered a mansion-house to be begun, where the Prophet and his family were to be lodged and maintained at the public cost. "Let it be built in my name, and let my servant Joseph Smith and his house have place therein

Nauvoo Temple.

from generation to generation, saith the Lord; and let the name of the house be called the Nauvoo House, and let it be a delightful habitation for man" (*Doctr. and Cov.* sec. 103). Thus the spiritual and temporal power of Smith increased until he found himself absolute ruler of over 20,000 persons, besides having many spiritual adherents in the different parts of this vast country, and no less than 10,000 in Great Britain. Smith's head was so far turned by his success that in 1844 he offered himself as a candidate for the Presidency of the Union. Probably, however, this proceeding was only meant as a bravado. In Nauvoo itself he reigned supreme. The contributions of his votaries and the zeal of their obedience fed his appetite for riches and power. But opposition gradually sprang up; and though it was obliged to hide itself for a while, and could only be nourished secretly, it was yet growing, and it soon was rumored among the Saints that Smith failed to restrain himself from the indulgence of more sensual passions, which ease and indolence had bred. As early as 1838 the Prophet, it is affirmed, had commenced to practically carry out his doctrine of the "Celestial Marriage" (see below, p. 627 sq.), or of a "Plurality of Wives;" but it was not till July, 1843, that he formally received a revelation on the subject authorizing polygamy. When the "revelation" became public, considerable indignation was felt even in Nauvoo, and serious disturbances took place. Several women whom Joseph and his apostles had taken a fancy to, and sought to win over under the new revelation, declined their proposals, and disclosed them to their relatives. These circumstances roused into activity a latent spirit of resistance which had for some time been secretly gathering force. The malcontents felt themselves strong enough to beard the lion in his own den; they renounced Mormonism, and even ventured to establish an opposition paper, called the *Expositor*, and published in its first number the affidavits of sixteen women, who alleged that Smith, Rigdon, Young, and others, had invited them to enter into a secret and illicit connection under the title of *spiritual marriage*. This open and dangerous rebellion was put down forthwith by the application of physical force. Joseph Smith ordered a body of his disciples to "abate

the nuisance," and they razed the office of the *Expositor* to the ground. The proprietors fled for their lives, and when they reached a place of safety sued out a writ from the legal authorities of Illinois against Joseph and Hyrum Smith as abettors of the riot. The execution of the warrant was resisted by the people and troops of Nauvoo, under the Prophet's authority. On this the governor of the state called out the militia to enforce the law; and the ultimate result was that the Prophet and his brother Hyrum were thrown into prison at Carthage. After a short time it began to be rumored, however, that the governor of the state was desirous of letting the two Smiths escape, and thereupon a band of "roughs," about 200 in number, broke into the jail, June 27, 1844, and shot them (see accounts of eye-witnesses in Burton, appendix iii; Mackay, p. 189 sq.).

The sudden removal of their leader and the manner of his death caused great agitation among the Mormons, and they were much confused for a while. This status led the people of Illinois to the belief that the sect would rapidly be broken up. The opinion seemed at first reasonable. There was much disputing as to the successorship, and it seemed very likely that the Church would thus be shattered into fragments. There were four claimants, and it was doubted whether any one of them could be persuaded to yield. And yet order was soon brought out of all this chaos, and disastrous as this termination of his career was to Smith himself, it proved a most fortunate thing for the system which he founded. "The blood of the martyrs is the seed of the Church." A halo of solemn and tender glory now encircles the memory of one who, whatever were his virtues or vices, stood greatly in need of this spiritual transfiguration. As Burton tells us, the Saints came to revere the name of Smith beyond that of any other name. They speak of him "with a respectful veneration, *sotto voce*, as Christians name the founder of their faith." Brigham Young had been Joseph's favorite. He was known to have been such by the apostolical college, of which he was chairman, and he was therefore chosen Joseph's successor by a unanimous vote of that body. The choice made by the highest council, the Mormons had been taught, no one should gainsay;

and consequently it was accepted by the great majority of the inhabitants of Nauvoo, and approved of by a general Council of the Church, summoned about six weeks after Joseph's death. The other pretenders were excommunicated, and the council even ventured to "deliver over to Satan" the great Rigdon himself, one of the aspirants, although their sacred books declared him equal with the Prophet; who had, however, latterly shown a disposition to slight and humble him. The Mormons throughout the world acquiesced in all these decisions, and Brigham Young was established in the post of "seer, revelator, and president of the Latter-day Saints."

This manifestation of complete organization aroused the people of Illinois once more to a sense of the danger of constant strife with the settlers at Nauvoo. In 1845 the state Legislature revoked the charter given to the city of Nauvoo, while the citizens banded together for possible contingencies. Open and severe hostility against the Mormons was frequent, and henceforward it was evident that while they continued to inhabit Nauvoo they must live in a perpetual state of

January 20, 1846. It was also communicated to their hostile neighbors, who agreed to allow the Mormons time to sell their property, on condition that they should leave Nauvoo before the ensuing summer. A pioneer party of sixteen hundred persons started before the conclusion of winter, in the hope of reaching their intended settlement in time to prepare a reception for the main body by the close of autumn. Agricultural operations were commenced almost the instant they reached the shores of the Salt Lake. "The cheerfulness, intelligence, and zeal exhibited on all sides," it has been justly said, "were truly admirable. The world has never seen swifter, more active, more glad-hearted colonists than these singular Saints. It would be unfair to shut our eyes to such facts. In judging Mormonism, we must keep these constantly in view to prevent us from forming mere abstract and theoretical decisions, which will not in the least affect the future of Mormonism." Brigham himself arrived in the valley July 24, 1847, and the main body of the Mormons in the autumn of 1848. The Salt Lake City was soon founded; public buildings, including a tabernacle, or temporary place for

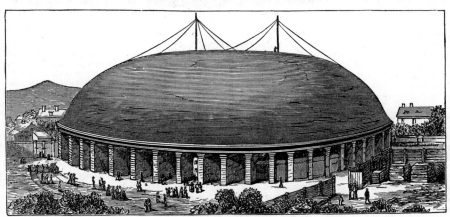

The Tabernacle.

siege, and till their fields with a plough in one hand and a rifle in the other. Moreover, experience had shown that elements of disunion existed even among themselves. So long as they were established in any of the settled states they could not exclude unbelievers from among them. There must always be Gentile strangers who would intrude among the Saints for lucre's sake, and form a nucleus around which disappointed or traitorous members might rally and create internal conflict. This could only be avoided by the transplantation of the Mormon commonwealth beyond the reach of foreign contact. Actuated by these reasons, the leaders who met to deliberate on the steps demanded by the crisis came to a decision which, adventurous as it then seemed, has since proved no less wise than bold. They resolved to migrate in a body far beyond the boundaries of the United States, and to interpose a thousand miles of wilderness between themselves and the civilized world. In the fastnesses of the Rocky Mountains, the Alps of North America, they determined to seek that freedom, civil and religious, which was denied them by their countrymen. In a hymn composed for the occasion, they express this Phocæan resolution as follows:

"We'll burst off all our fetters, and break the Gentile yoke;
For long it has beset us, but now it shall be broke.
    No more shall Jacob bow his neck;
    Henceforth he shall be great and free
    In Upper California.
    Oh, that's the land for me!
    Oh, that's the land for me!"—(*Hymns*, 353.)

Their decision was announced to the Saints throughout the world by a General Epistle, which bears date

public worship, promptly built; manufactories and shops were also soon reared, an emigration fund established, and in a little while settlers poured in from all parts of Europe and America; and perhaps a greater amount of physical comfort was enjoyed here than in any part of the world. As early as March, 1849, a convention was held at Salt Lake City, and a state organized under the name of *Deseret*, a word understood by the Mormons to signify "the land of the honey-bee" (Ether, *Book of Mormon*, ch. i, § 3, p. 518). A Legislature was elected, and a Constitution framed and sent to Washington. Congress, however, refused to recognize the new state, and in September organized the country occupied by the Mormons into the Territory of Utah, of which Brigham Young was appointed governor by president Fillmore. District judges were also appointed by the federal government, but these were looked upon with great suspicion and mistrust by the Saints, who finally drove them out of the country in 1851, and openly defied and subverted the laws of the United States. In 1852 the "celestial law of marriage," authorizing polygamy, was promulgated and at once acted upon, notwithstanding that in 1845 the heads of this self-same religious body had deemed it prudent to put forth a formal denial of any such phase of faith or practice in the following words: "Inasmuch as this Church of Christ has been reproached with the crimes of fornication and polygamy, we declare that we believe that one man should have but one wife, and one woman but one husband, except in the case of death, when either is at liberty to marry again." In 1853 the corner-stone of the great Temple, the plan of which, with all its details, was "revealed" to president

Young, was laid, so sure felt the Mormons that they had finally reached a spot where they could defy all opposition, and enjoy unmolested their most extravagant religious or social notions. The United States government had no disposition to interfere with these, but it felt itself outraged in the removal of its officers, and in 1854 a United States colonel arrived at Salt Lake City to become the successor of president Young as governor of the territory. This officer, however, encountered so much

Ruins of the Nauvoo Temple.—[From Stenhouse.]

opposition that he found it expedient, after wintering in Salt Lake City without receiving the governorship, to formally resign his post, and he removed with his battalion of troops to California. No wonder that Young declared in a sermon to his people, "I am and will be governor, and no power can hinder it until the Lord Almighty says, 'Brigham, you need not be governor any longer.'" During the next three years the collisions between the United States officers and the Saints became more and more frequent, and in the spring of 1856 the whole of the former were forced to flee from the territory. A new appointment was finally made in 1857 by the Washington government, and the appointee, accompanied by 2500 picked United States troops, sent to enforce order and submission to the United States laws. The Mormons were greatly exasperated against the federal government by this action, but were finally overawed; and after a proclamation granting pardon to all Mormons guilty of treachery, etc., the Saints submitted, and permanent peace was established. In 1871 some of the Mormon leaders were indicted under the United States laws against bigamy, in order to force the Mormons to abandon the institution of polygamy. More recently president Young himself has been indicted, and mainly for the self-same purpose, though avowedly on a charge of conspiracy and murder, and has escaped trial only because of some informality or uncertainty respect-

ing the constitution of the court. By the Saints this result is looked upon as of providential interference. The proposition, it is asserted, has been semi-officially made, as from him, to abandon polygamy, on condition that the United States government recognize the legitimacy of children heretofore born of polygamous marriages. This does not seem, however, in harmony with their printed declarations in very recent times. The Mormons in these assert their resolve to resist to the death all attempts to put down polygamy, and their firm belief that God will work miracles for them, as for his ancient saints, the Jews. (See *Millennial Star*, vol. xxxii, *passim*, esp. p. 328. Comp. Rae, *Westward by Rail*, p. 116.) Mr. T. B. H. Stenhouse, formerly a Mormon elder and missionary, and editor of a Mormon paper, has issued a history of Mormonism, whose revelations of the internal workings of Mormonism are made impressive by the calmness and moderation of his language, and the official and indisputable evidence which he has with assiduity gathered to sustain his revelations. He insists upon it that the Mormons are not really in favor of polygamy, and will gladly give it up if they can be made to see that it is not an essential religious ordinance. By others, however, equally well informed, it is rumored that Brigham Young is preparing for another exodus of the entire community to regions yet more remote from the incursion of civilization, which has so completely changed the character of Salt Lake City in the last five years. It will be borne in mind that in 1869 the Pacific Railroad opened up the country, so that it is no longer cut off from civilization. Gentiles take up their residence in Salt Lake City freely, and have not the fear of their lives which was formerly, justly or unjustly, entertained; missionaries are preaching the Gospel of Jesus Christ in the midst of the people, and there is no dread of any power able to stop them. Sev-

Mormon Head-quarters at Salt Lake City.
Fig. 1. The "Tithing" Office.   Fig. 2. The "Prophet's" Mansion.

eral Protestant Christian churches have been organized there (1872), and a recent movement among the Mormons themselves, begun in 1869, and denominated as a body the "Church of Zion," and recently re-christened "The Liberal Institute," repudiates the authority of Brigham Young and the hierarchy; and though, like all reactions from priestly authority, its tendency is unmistakably towards flagrant infidelity, for it advocates freedom of thought and action, it is nevertheless a sign of the weakening of the entire system. See Rae, *Westward by Rail*, p. 157 sq.; Ollivant, *A Breeze from the Great Salt Lake*, p. 82–90; Stenhouse, ch. lv sq.

II. *Sacred Writings of the Mormons.*—(1.) Their most important publication is of course the *Book of Mormon*, a work which, as it professes to be a new and more recent revelation than the Bible, is placed above the latter in import and value. Indeed, it really constitutes the *Mormon Bible*. In its published form it is a duodecimo volume of 563 pages of small print. (The edition here referred to came to us from Mr. Young himself, and was printed at Salt Lake City in 1871.) It is divided, in imitation of the Old Testament, into fifteen books, of unequal length, bearing the names of their supposed authors—Nephi (comp. 2 Macc. i, 36), Jacob, Enos, and the like—and professing to have been written (see p. 619) at different periods, each book being divided into chapters and numbered paragraphs. We insert a list of contents for fuller information:

FIRST BOOK OF NEPHI.

Language of the Record.	Promises to the Gentiles.
Nephi's Abridgment.	Two Churches.
Lehi's Dream.	The work of the Father to
Lehi departs into the wilderness.	commence.
Nephi slayeth Laban.	A man in white robes (John).
Sariah complains of Lehi's Vision.	Nephites come to knowledge.
Contents of the brass plates.	Rod of Iron.
Ishmael goes with Nephi.	The sons of Lehi take wives.
Nephi's brethren rebel, and bind him.	Director found (ball).
Lehi's dream of the tree, rod, etc.	Nephi broke his bow.
	Directors work by faith.
Messiah and John prophesied of.	Ishmael died.
	Lehi and Nephi threatened.
Olive Branches broken off.	Nephi commanded to build
Nephi's Vision of Mary.	a ship.
Do. the Crucifixion of Christ.	Nephi about to be worshipped by his brethren.
Do. darkness and earthquake.	
Great abominable church.	Ship finished and entered.
Discovery of the promised land.	Dancing in the ship.
	Nephi bound; ship driven back.
Bible spoken of.	Arrived on the promised land.
Book of Mormon and Holy Ghost promised.	Plates of ore made.
Other books come forth.	Zenos, Neum, and Zenock.
Bible and Book of Mormon one.	Isaiah's Writings.
	Holy One of Israel.

SECOND BOOK OF NEPHI.

Lehi to his sons.	Christ shall show himself.
Opposition in all things.	Signs of Christ, birth and death.
Adam fell that men might be.	
Joseph saw our day.	Whisper from the dust, book
A choice seer.	sealed up.
Writings grow together.	Priestcraft forbidden.
Prophet promised to the Lamanites.	Sealed book to be brought forth.
Joseph's prophecy on brass plates.	Three witnesses behold the book.
Lehi buried.	The words [read this, I pray thee].
Nephi's life sought.	
Nephi separated from Laman.	Seal up the book again.
Temple built.	Their priests shall contend.
Skin of blackness.	Teach with their learning and deny the Holy Ghost.
Priests, etc., consecrated.	
Make other plates.	Rob the poor.
Isaiah's words (by Jacob).	A Bible, a Bible.
Angels to a devil.	Men judged of the Books.
Spirits and bodies reunited.	White and a delightsome people.
Baptism.	
No kings upon this land.	Work commenced among all people.
Isaiah prophesieth.	
Rod of the stem of Jesse.	Lamb of God baptized.
Seed of Joseph perish not.	Baptism by water and Holy Ghost.
Law of Moses kept.	

BOOK OF JACOB.

Nephi anointed a king.	A righteous branch from Joseph.
Nephi died.	
Nephites and Lamanites.	Lamanites shall scourge you.

More than one wife forbidden.	Another branch.
	Wild fruit had overcome.
Trees, waves, and mountains obey us.	Lord of the vineyard wept.
	Branches overcome the roots.
Jews looked beyond the mark.	Wild branches plucked off.
Tame olive-tree.	Sherem the Antichrist.
Nethermost part of the vineyard.	A sign, Sherem smitten.
	Enos takes the plates from his father.
Fruit laid up against the season.	

THE BOOK OF ENOS.

Enos, thy sins are forgiven.	Records threatened by Lamanites.
	Lamanites eat raw meat.

THE BOOK OF JAROM.

Nephites waxed strong.	Fortify cities.
Lamanites drink blood.	Plates delivered to Omni.

THE BOOK OF OMNI.

Plates given to Amaron.	Coriantumr discovered.
Plates given to Chemish.	His parents came from the Tower.
Mosiah warned to flee.	
Zarahemla discovered.	Plates delivered to King Benjamin.
Engravings on a stone.	

THE WORDS OF MORMON.

False Christs and Prophets.	

BOOK OF MOSIAH.

Mosiah made king, and received.	Beggars not denied.
	Sons and daughters.
The plates of brass, sword, and director.	Mosiah began to reign.
	Ammon, etc., bound and imprisoned.
King Benjamin teacheth the people.	Limhi's proclamation.
Their tent-doors towards the temple.	Twenty-four plates of gold.
	Seer and Translator.
Coming of Christ foretold.	

RECORD OF ZENIFF.

A battle fought.	King Limhi baptized.
King Laman died.	Priest and teachers labor.
Noah made king.	Alma saw an angel.
Abinadi the prophet.	Alma fell (dumb).
Resurrection.	King Mosiah's sons preach to the Lamanites.
Alma believed Abinadi.	
Abinadi cast into prison and scourged with fagots.	Translation of Records.
	Plates delivered by Limhi.
Waters of Mormon.	Translated by two stones.
The daughters of the Lamanites stolen by King Noah's priests.	People back to the Tower.
	Records given to Alma.
Records on plates of ore.	Judges appointed.
Last tribute of wine.	King Mosiah died.
Lamanites' deep sleep.	Alma died.
	Kings of Nephi ended.

THE BOOK OF ALMA.

Nehor slew Gideon.	Anti-Nephi-Lehies removed to Jershon, called Ammonites.
Amlici made king.	
Amlici slain in battle.	
Amlicites painted red.	Tremendous battle.
Alma baptized in Sidon.	Antichrist, Korihor.
Alma's preaching.	Korihor struck dumb.
Alma ordained elders.	The devil in the form of an angel.
Commanded to meet often.	
Alma saw an angel.	Korihor trodden down.
Amulek saw an angel.	Alma's mission to Zoramites.
Lawyers questioning Amulek.	
	Rameumptom (holy stand).
Coins named.	Alma on hill Onidah.
Zeezrom the lawyer.	Alma on faith.
Zeezrom trembles.	Prophecy of Zenos.
Election spoken of.	Prophecy of Zenock.
Melchizedek's priesthood.	Amulek's knowledge of Christ.
Alma and Amulek stoned.	
Records burned.	Charity recommended.
Prison rent.	Same spirit possess your body.
Zeezrom healed and baptized.	
	Believers cast out.
Nehor's desolation.	Alma to Helaman.
Lamanites converted.	Plates given to Helaman.
Flocks scattered at Sebus.	24 plates and directors.
Ammon smote off arms.	Gazelem, a stone (secret).
Ammon and King Lamoni.	Liahona, or compass.
King Lamoni fell.	Alma to Shiblon.
Ammon and the Queen.	Alma to Corianton.
King and Queen prostrate.	Unpardonable sin.
Aaron, etc., delivered.	Resurrection.
Jerusalem built.	Restoration.
Preaching in Jerusalem.	Justice in punishment.
Lamoni's father converted.	If Adam took the tree of life.
Land Desolation and Bountiful.	Mercy rob justice.
	Moroni's stratagem.
Anti-Nephi-Lehies.	Slaughter of Lamanites.
General council.	Moroni's speech to Zerahemnah.
Swords buried.	
1005 massacred.	Prophecy of a soldier.
Lamanites perish by fire.	Lamanites' covenant of peace.
Slavery forbidden.	

Alma's prophecy 400 years after Christ.
Dwindle in unbelief.
Alma's strange departure.
Amalickiah leadeth away the people, destroyeth the church.
Standard of Moroni.
Joseph's coat rent.
Jacob's prophecy of Joseph's seed.
Fevers in the land, plants and roots for diseases.
Amalickiah's plot.
The king stabbed.
Amalickiah marries the Queen, and is acknowledged king.
Fortifications by Moroni.
Ditches filled with dead bodies.
Amalickiah's oath.
Pahoran appointed judge.
Army against king-men.
Amalickiah slain.
Ammoron made king.
Bountiful fortified.
Dissensions.
2000 young men.
Moroni's epistle to Ammoron.

Ammoron's answer.
Lamanites made drunk.
Moroni's stratagem.
Helaman's epistle to Moroni.
Helaman's stratagem.
Mothers taught faith.
Lamanites surrendered.
City of Antiparah taken.
City of Cumeni taken.
200 of the 2000 fainted.
Prisoners rebel, slain.
Manti taken by stratagem.
Moroni to the governor.
Governor's answer.
King Pachus slain.
Cords and ladders prepared.
Nephihah taken.
Teancum's stratagem; slain.
Peace established.
Moronihah made commander.
Helaman dies.
Sacred things; Shiblon.
Moroni died.
5400 emigrated north.
Ships built by Hagoth.
Sacred things committed to Helaman; Shiblon died.

THE BOOK OF HELAMAN.

Pahoran died.
Pahoran appointed judge.
Kishkumen slew Pahoran.
Pacumeni appointed judge.
Zarahemla taken.
Pacumeni killed.
Coriantumr slain.
Lamanites surrendered.
Helaman appointed judge.
Secret signs discovered, and Kishkumen stabbed.
Gadianton fled.
Emigration northward.
Cement houses.
Many books and records.
Helaman died.
Nephi made judge.
Nephites become wicked.
Nephi gave the judgment-seat to Cezoram.
Nephi and Lehi preached to the Lamanites.
8000 baptized.

Alma and Nephi surrounded with fire.
Angels administer.
Cezoram and son murdered.
Gadianton's robbers.
Gadianton's robbers destroyed.
Nephi's prophecy.
Gadianton's robbers are judges.
Chief judge slain.
Seantum detected.
Keys of the kingdom.
Nephi taken away by the spirit.
Famine in the land.
Gadianton's band destroyed.
Famine removed.
Samuel's prophecy.
Tools lost.
Two days and a night, light.
Sign of the crucifixion.
Samuel stoned, etc.
Angels appeared.

BOOK OF NEPHI.

Lachoneus chief judge.
Nephi receives the Records.
Nephi's strange departure.
No darkness at night.
Lamanites became white.
Giddianhi to Lachoneus.
Gidgiddoni chief judge.
Giddianhi slain.
Zemnarihah hanged.
Robbers surrendered.
Mormon abridges the Records.
Church began to be broken up.
Government of the land destroyed.
Chief judge murdered.
Divided into tribes.
Nephi raised the dead.
Sign of the crucifixion.
Cities destroyed, earthquakes, darkness, etc.
Law of Moses fulfilled.
Christ appeared to Nephites.
Print of the nails.
Nephi and others called.
Baptism commanded.
Doctrine of Christ.
Christ the end of the law.
Other sheep spoken of.
Blessed are the Gentiles.
Gentile wickedness on the land of Joseph.
Isaiah's words fulfilled.
Jesus healed the sick.
Christ blessed children.
Little ones encircled with fire.
Christ administered the sacrament.
Christ taught his disciples.
Names of the Twelve.

The Twelve taught the multitude.
Baptism, Holy Ghost, and fire.
Disciples made white.
Jesus came, second time.
Faith great.
Christ breaks bread again.
Miracle, bread and wine.
Gentiles destroyed (Isaiah).
Zion established.
From Gentiles, to your seed.
Sign, Father's work commenced.
He shall be marred.
Gentiles destroyed (Isaiah).
New Jerusalem built.
Work commenced among all the tribes.
Isaiah's words.
Saints did arise.
Malachi's prophecy.
Faith tried by the Book of Mormon.
Children's tongues loosed.
The dead raised.
Baptism and Holy Ghost.
All things common.
Christ appeared third time.
Moses's Church.
Three Nephites tarry.
The Twelve caught up.
Change upon their bodies.
Disciples raise the dead.
Zarahemla rebuilt.
Other disciples ordained in their stead.
Nephi died; Amos kept the Records in his stead.
Amos died, and his son Amos kept the Records.
Prisons rent by the three.
Secret combinations.
Amaron hid Records.

Three disciples taken away.
Mormon forbidden to preach.
Mormon appointed leader.
Samuel's prophecy fulfilled.
Mormon makes a Record.
Lands divided.
The Twelve shall judge.
Desolation taken.
Women and children sacrificed.
Mormon took the Records hid in Shim.

BOOK OF MORMON.

Mormon repented of his oath and took command.
Coming forth of Records.
Records hid in Cumorah.
230,000 Nephites slain.
Shall not get gain by the plates.
These things shall come forth out of the earth.
The state of the world.
Miracles cease, unbelief.
Disciples go into all the world and preach.
Language of the Book.

BOOK OF ETHER.

Twenty-four plates found.
Jared cried unto the Lord.
Jared went down to the valley of Nimrod.
Deseret, honey-bee.
Barges built.
Decree of God, choice land.
Free from bondage.
Four years in tents at Moriancumer.
Lord talked three hours.
Barges like a dish.
Eight vessels, sixteen stones.
Lord touched the stones.
Finger of the Lord seen.
Jared's brother saw the Lord.
Two stones given.
Stones sealed up.
Went aboard of vessels.
Furious wind blew.
344 days' passage.
Orihah anointed king.
King Shule taken captive.
Shule's son slew Noah.
Jared carries his father away captive.
The daughter of Jared danced.
Jared anointed king by the hand of wickedness.

Jared murdered, and Akish reigned in his stead.
Names of animals.
Poisonous serpents.
Riplakish's cruel reign.
Morianton anointed king.
Poisonous serpents destroyed.
Many wicked kings.
Moroni on Faith.
Miracles by Faith.
Moroni saw Jesus.
New Jerusalem spoken of.
Ether cast out.
Records finished in the cavity of a rock.
Secret combinations.
War in all the land.
King Shared murdered by his High-priest; the High-priest was murdered by Lib.
Lib slain by Coriantumr.
Dead bodies cover the land, and none to bury them.
2,000,000 of men slain.
Hill Ramah.
Cries rend the air.
Slept on their swords.
Coriantumr slew Shiz.
Do. fell to the earth.
Records hid by Ether.

BOOK OF MORONI.

Christ's words to the Twelve.
Manner of Ordination.
Order of Sacrament.
Order of Baptism.
Faith, Hope, Charity.
Baptism of little children.
Women fed on their husbands' flesh.
Daughters murdered and eat.

Sufferings of women and children.
Cannot recommend them to God.
Moroni to the Lamanites.
420 years since the Sign.
Records sealed up (Moroni).
Gifts of the Spirit.
God's Word shall hiss forth.

With the history, as will be noted from the synopsis furnished above, are mixed up long exhortations, visions, parables, religious meditations. These are in language imitating that of the English Bible, and some 300 passages, including large portions of Isaiah, the Sermon on the Mount, and some verses of St. Paul's Epistles, bear such strong resemblance that non-Mormon critics claim these passages to be directly copied, sometimes with slight variations which do not improve the sense (see Stenhouse, p. 538–543). The narrative, as a whole, is most tedious; there is not a trace of elevated, poetic, or religious feeling. The style is that of an uneducated person, glaring grammatical errors appearing on nearly every page, besides gross absurdities and anachronisms. Beyond the assertions that the book is the work of inspired writers teaching true religion, and that revelations, miracles, and gifts of tongues are ever with the faithful, few of the doctrinal peculiarities of Mormonism can be gleaned from it. Materialistic notions of the Deity are hinted at (*Ether*, ch. i, § 8, p. 521, 522), and infant baptism is forbidden (*Moroni*, ch. viii, § 2, p. 557), but with these exceptions it is free from heretical statements or novel dogmas. It asserts the perpetuity of miracles in the Church, and on this account the Irvingites were induced to send a deputation in the early stages of Mormonism to express their sympathy with Joseph Smith. It is also most explicit in its condemnation of polygamy and free-masonry. It will be remembered from the account furnished by Mr. Pratt of the early history of this strange work, that the original copy, engraved on golden plates, was in a tongue then unknown to the world, and that by the aid of the "Urim and Thummim" the English version was obtained. According to the Mormon authority, the book was placed in Smith's hands in the reformed Egyptian language, and we are also told that the way in which Smith translated was as follows: He sat behind a blanket hung across the room to keep the sacred records from profane eyes, and read off, by the help of his "Urim and Thummim," to Oliver Cowdery, of whom we have had occasion to speak before, who wrote down what the invisible "Prophet" gave as a translation, Smith himself being, as he confesses, but a "poor writer." A farmer by the name of Martin Harris supplied Smith with the necessary funds to get the work printed. But before he so supplied Smith he went to New York to consult the late Prof. Anthon regarding the correctness of the Prophet's translation, and took with him a copy of the characters on one of the plates. The Mormons assert that the professor declared the characters to be Egyptian, Chaldaic, Assyrian, and Arabic, and asked to see the original (*Pearl of Great Price*, p. 45). But, according to Gentile authority, Prof. Anthon pronounced the extract furnished him to consist "of all kinds of crooked characters, disposed in columns, and evidently prepared by some person who had before him at the time a book containing various alphabets. Greek and Hebrew letters, crosses and flourishes, Roman letters, inverted or placed sideways, were arranged and placed in perpendicular columns, and the whole ended in a rude delineation of a circle divided into various compartments decked with various strange marks, and evidently copied after the Mexican calendar given by Humboldt, but copied in such a way as not to betray the source whence it was derived," and warned Harris against being the victim of roguery (*Letter* in Mackey, p. 32–34). A fac-simile, alleged to be identical with that shown to Prof. Anthon, is published in the *Millennial Star* (xv, 540), and is here reproduced. It will be noticed by the philological student that these characters have no resemblance to any existing ones, and are like nothing else but the scratches made by children for amusement when they begin to learn writing. Harris, however, lost not his faith by Prof. Anthon's persuasions, and, returning to Smith, continued to assist the preparation of the English version of the *Book of Mormon* until about 116 pages had been completed. The MS. of these Harris one day took to his house to show to his wife, probably to satisfy her that the money which he was furnishing for Smith's support, and which he was expecting to supply for its publication, was well-spent. Herself a non-believer, she connived with others for the secret removal of the MS. On this the "Prophet" produced a "revelation" ordering him not to retranslate the portion lost in the English version, lest the wicked, finding the two translations to differ, should scoff at God's work (*Doctr. and Cov.* xxxvi, p. 178 sq.). Shortly after Harris was moreover superseded in his position as scribe by Oliver Cowdery, but he remained faithful to Smith; and when the work was ready for publication he furnished, as we have stated, all needed pecuniary aid, having even, in obedience to a revelation (*Doctr. and Cov.* xliv, 3, p. 194–5), sold his farm to procure means for this purpose. In 1830, finally, the *Book of Mormon* appeared, accompanied, as has been stated above by Mr. Pratt, with a declaration from eleven persons that they had seen the original plates from which this version had been prepared. This statement was necessary, as these were the only persons so privileged. No other human being has ever seen them. Like Macpherson's Ossianic MSS., they have never been forthcoming, however loudly demanded, and of late years all knowledge of them has become traditional. The Mormons declare that no one else was allowed to see them; and Joseph himself informs us that after he had "accomplished by them what was required at his hand," . . . "*according to arrangements, the messenger called for them, and he [the angel] has them in his charge until this day*" (*Autobiog.* ch. xiv).

Fac-simile of a portion of the Gold Plates, as said to be represented on the Paper which Joseph Smith gave to Martin Harris, and which he submitted to Prof. Anthon.

Controversial writers against Mormonism are unanimous in discarding this whole story of angel visits and gold plates as a pure invention, and brand Joseph Smith as an impostor. Yet there seems to be no ground for such a harsh judgment. That Smith had at one time in his possession metallic plates of some kind, with engraved characters upon them, there appears no reason to doubt, if human testimony be accepted as evidence. Where and how he got the plates which he exhibited to a number of persons, and whether the *Book of Mormon* is a veritable interpretation of the characters on those plates, are very different questions. Again, whether or not the narrative presented is true and of any importance to the world as a subject of faith, are still different questions. Certain it is that Mormon apologists have thus far failed to account on reasonable principles for the close resemblance of portions of their inspired writings which they claim to be taken from speeches, exhortations, and sermons said to have been delivered by ancient American prophets and apostles, who of course never saw, or could see, the English Bible as it now exists in its modern translation, and for the still more strange appearance in their writings of the errors of translation existing in the English version made 1200 years after the death of the last of these American seers (comp. Stenhouse, p. 538-545). Besides, Gentile polemics have brought forward evidence to show that, with the exception of certain illiterate and ungrammatical interpolations bearing on religious matters, the so-called *Book of Mormon* was really borrowed or copied nearly verbatim from a MS. romance written by an ordained minister named Solomon Spaulding, who was born at Ashford, Conn., in 1761, and was educated at Dartmouth College (class of 1785), who died in 1816 at Amity, Pa. It is unnecessary to go over the arguments pro and con. Suffice it to say, that *anti*-Mormons generally think them conclusive, while the "Saints" consider the whole story of Spaulding's MS. romance a scandalous fabrication. There is unquestionable evidence that the said Spaulding did write something about the ancient inhabitants of America; that his MS. was intrusted for publication in 1812 to a bookseller named Paterson at Pittsburgh, Pa.; and that Spaulding dying before publication, the MS. remained in Pittsburgh, where a copy of it was made by Sidney Rigdon, then one of Paterson's compositors, but afterwards the associate of Joseph Smith in the promulgation of Mormon doctrines; and it is furthermore asserted by one of Spaulding's brothers, from his recollection of portions of the MS., that it was identical with the *Book of Mormon*, and that the latter was indeed the bona-fide work of his deceased brother; this statement being sustained by several of Mr. Spaulding's friends from their remembrance of the readings to which they had frequently listened. It is therefore conjectured by anti-Mormonists that Rigdon (into whose hands Spaulding's romance is supposed to have fallen for some time) gave it to his new associate to further his purposes when he joined him in 1829, and that the latter—in whose soul there may have been some rude and gross religious notions and feelings—devised the ungrammatical interpolations. This theory acquires some probability from the fact that these religious passages do not refer to the Old-World faiths and the practices of an ancient ritual, but to quite modern questions, such as interested the people of Western New York about 1830. Calvinism, Universalism, Methodism, Millenarianism, Roman Catholicism are discussed, if not in name, yet in reality. But those who accept such statements as the true solution of the origin of this book must necessarily conclude that Joseph Smith was "a deliberate falsifier and wilful impostor." The most incisive writer on this subject—John Hyde, jun. (*Mormonism, its Leaders and Disciples*), formerly a Mormon elder—unhesitatingly announces this as his own conclusion. Yet there is no good ground for such a position if it be considered that the *Book of Mormon* was in preparation for publication when Smith first met Rigdon, and that he was already noted as the discoverer of the gold plates. We cite the comments on this great question by Mr. Stenhouse, who, as he was himself once a believer, is most likely to know whereof he speaks. He says:

"To conclude that there was 'wilful' imposture in the origin of Mormonism is, in an argumentative sense, to 'take arms against a sea of troubles' to which there is no limit. There is, however, an easy solution of the difficulty respecting the origin of the book—i. e., to admit honest credulity in Joseph Smith, in the persons who 'witnessed unto the world' of that which they saw, and in all that follows in the history of the Mormon movement. Probably, if Mr. Hyde were now to write on the subject, while he would undoubtedly preserve the same powerful arguments against the divinity of the book, he would conclude that Joseph Smith was after all only an extraordinary 'spirit medium,' and had been subjected to all the vagaries and caprices of that peculiar condition. In this solution of the difficulty respecting Joseph's claims there is a perfect consistency, and it harmonizes completely with the testimony both of the orthodox and the heterodox. It admits the claim of honesty in Joseph Smith and in his 'witnesses,' and equal honesty in those who have rejected their testimony and denounced the folly of their assertions. In brief, when Joseph Smith said that he had visions, dreams, and revelations, it is best to allow that he probably had all that experience; but when he clothed his communications with the sanctity of absolute and di-

vine truth, the acceptance or rejection of which was to be 'the salvation or damnation of the world,' it was simply the operation and assertion of that yet uncomprehended mysterious influence that has been experienced by both good and bad men in all ages and in all countries within the historical ken of man. With the developments which have followed, the life of the Mormon Prophet is easily understood. He was but the vehicle of 'spirit communication,' and when he erred it was *not intentional imposture or deliberate fraud*, but in the native honesty of his simple nature he believed too much. ... It does not seem possible that he could have borne up through his whole life of persecution, and have lived and died maintaining the truth of his story, if the book had been a fraud. ... That some of those ancient inhabitants may have made and engraved plates, and that they did so for a purpose—whatever that might be—is very possible. The relics of sculpture and painting suggest also the probability of engraving. Other persons besides Joseph Smith have discovered in the ground similar plates, bearing evidence of a great antiquity, and as time rolls on there may yet be many similar discoveries. There need be no difficulty, then, in accepting Joseph's story of finding the plates; it is what is claimed to be the contents of the plates that is incredible. If no living person fabricated for Joseph Smith the *Book of Mormon*, and if Joseph did not use the manuscript of Solomon Spaulding, the Mormon may very properly ask, 'Who, then, was the author of the book?' To this query the *Book of Abraham* is the answer. (See below, 3.) In the preceding chapter, the Prophet's 'translation' of the papyrus found with the Egyptian mummies is evidently untrue; yet Joseph Smith sat with his amanuensis, and, by 'the gift of God,' believed he was giving a truthful translation. The scientist says that the whole story is untrue; that the Prophet's version of the hieroglyphics is a perfect romance; that the hieroglyphics had no more allusion to the Abraham of Mosaic history than they had to do with Abraham the martyred president of the United States. When Joseph Smith translated the *Book of Mormon* by the means of his Urim and Thummim, the 'reformed Egyptian' was evidently not transformed before his eyes into the translated text, or 'the gift and power of God' used peculiarly bad English. He gazed upon that Urim and Thummim until his mind became psychologized, and the impressions that he received he dictated to his scribe. With such a conclusion, the anachronisms of the book, the quotations from the Old and New Testaments, and the language of modern preachers and writers are accounted for. That there is such a mental condition in human life as clairvoyance, in which persons are strangely operated upon, and can mentally perceive what to the natural eye is unseen, is a belief as old as the history of man; and that, when the mind is psychologized by a condition of its own, or by the operation of external influences, singular impressions or revelations are had, few people to-day dispute. That Joseph Smith was in these experiences one of the most remarkable men that ever lived, those outside of Mormonism altogether, who knew him intimately, testify. He believed that his gifts were divine, and his impressions were revelations from the Almighty Creator. To insist that there were deliberate imposture and deliberate falsehood at the origin of Mormonism is to challenge the veracity and honesty of the hundreds and thousands of persons who accept that faith and who testify that *they know* of its truth. It is more rational and consistent to admit that what such a body of people allege that they have experienced is probably true in statement, than to deny it and brand it as imposture; but it does not follow that the interpretation which any of them put upon their experience is itself true. They may be fully persuaded that they have had visions, dreams, the ministering of angels, and have heard the 'voice of God,' all witnessing to the truth of the divinity of Mormonism, for all this has been asserted again and again by very many others besides Joseph Smith—men, and women too, who have claimed to have received divine missions. Outside of all religious enthusiasm, also, there are tens of thousands of men and women—sober, reliable, and truthful in every relation and business of life—with as unchangeable convictions as ever the Mormons had that they have personally experienced all these extraordinary phenomena. The trouble with the Mormons and with all this class of believers is, not in what they have experienced, but the after-interpretation that they may have put upon it. ... There have been multitudes of persons in the world who have believed and asserted that to them, and to them only, God gave visions, dreams, angel-visits, the power of healing the sick and 'casting out devils;' and they have declared that these were proofs of the heavenly origin of the faith which they proclaimed, and this it is that the Saints have been taught by the modern apostles to regard as special and particular to them, while it has been a peculiarity common to the religious experience of all the world, and is an evidence of nothing more than a certain condition of mind that renders such manifestations possible with persons adapted naturally to receive them. ... That Joseph thought Moroni and some of those ancient personages whom he mentions in his biography appeared to him is no doubt true; that they used him for their purposes Spiritualists all believe; and when the origin of some of the great religions of the world is considered, there is not much cause for wonder that those persons who have accepted Mormonism, with all its crudities, should have honestly believed it. Millions have accepted Mohammed and his visions; many millions more have lived and died in the faith of Buddha; Confucius has swayed a spiritual empire from ages long before the Christian æra; and by these and other founders of religious systems, and by many of their disciples, visions and revelations, gifts and miraculous powers, have all been claimed" (*Rocky Mountain Saints*, p. 546–555).

To this solution of the question we are disposed substantially to accede, with this exception, that we would refer the mental impression of visions, revelations, etc., to the hallucinations of an excited imagination rather than to clairvoyance or any other so-called spiritual influence or communication.

It may not be out of place here to add that Joseph Smith, while discredited among his own townsmen, elicited the testimony that from an early period he was regarded as a visionary and a fanatic. This fact is of the utmost importance as affording a clew to his *real* character, and an explanation of that otherwise unaccountable tenacity of purpose and moral heroism displayed in the midst of fierce persecution. A *mere* impostor—i. e. a person who did not, in some sense or other, partly believe in his own mission, but who, on the contrary, felt that he was simply the liar and cheat that people called him—would have broken down under such a tempest of opposition and hate as Smith's course excited.

(2.) The chief authority on Mormon doctrine is *The Book of Doctrine and Covenants of the Church of Jesus Christ of Latter-day Saints, selected from the Revelations of God*, by Joseph Smith, president. "This work is to the Mormon Bible," says Burton (p. 447 sq.), "what the Vedanta is to the Vedas, the Talmud to the O. T., the Traditions to the Gospel, and the Ahadis to the Koran —a necessary supplement of amplifications and explanations." The first edition, published in 1833, differs much from the later ones, and was subsequently suppressed. The work consists of two distinct parts: p. 1–64 contain seven lectures on faith, originally delivered before a class of elders at Kirtland, and it seems probable that they were written by Rigdon, who was really the theological founder, though he is only recognised as the literary assistant (*Doctr. and Cov.* sec. ii). In them are some very curious statements; and it is believed that

whatever there is in it of materialism was introduced by Rigdon, and with it many other strange departures from the theology of the *Book of Mormon*. Thus, e. g., it is inferred in the *Doctr. and Cov.*, from Heb. xi, 3, that faith is "the principle of power existing in the bosom of God by which the worlds were framed, and that if this principle or attribute were taken from the Deity, he would cease to exist" (Lect. i, 13–17, p. 3). Again: "When a man works by faith, he works by mental exertion instead of physical force. It is by words, instead of exerting his physical powers, with which every being works by faith" (Lect. vii, 3, p. 55). Many other peculiar doctrines are here set forth. The second part, entitled *Covenants and Commandments*, consists of the revelations given to Smith at various times, and is evidently by a different hand from the *Lectures*. The style and grammar betray the editor of the English version of the *Book of Mormon*. The *Covenants and Commandments* resemble in form the Koran: both works contain divine revelations; much in both is only of temporary interest, and both afford undesigned materials for the life of their authors. But all the merits of the Koran are absent and all its defects present in the work of Joseph Smith. The revelations were given to a great number of persons, but always through the medium of Joseph Smith. They refer to various subjects: the organization, worship, and hierarchy of the Church; instructions in faith and morals, prophecies, visions, parables, interpretations of Scripture, directions to individuals about their acts, preachings, journeyings, for the promotion of the faith, and concerning the affairs and needs, spiritual and temporal, of the Church. There are also two addresses of the Prophet to the Saints in Nauvoo, delivered in writing only; minutes of the High Council (February 17, 1834); declarations of the Church on marriage and governments, and an account of the martyrdom of Joseph Smith and his brother. Those sections relating to the organization of the Church and the duties of the ministry are placed first, then the portions chiefly treating of faith and practice; lastly, those that relate mainly to individuals and to temporary circumstances.

(3.) Many other revelations, translations, prophecies, addresses, etc., of Smith were published in the periodicals of the sect, all of which are regarded as of authority. Some of these have been collected into a pamphlet, entitled *The Pearl of Great Price, being a choice Selection from the Great Revelations, Translations, and Narrations of Joseph Smith* (Liverpool, 1851). In this book is set forth the theory that Mormonism is the revival of the primitive religion revealed to Adam (see also *Doctr. and Cov.* Lect. ii, p. 8 sq.; *Covenants and Comm.* iii, 18–29, p. 78). A similar theory is found in the Koran. There also appears a translation, with facsimiles, of some Egyptian papyrus rolls, procured from a travelling showman. Smith declared these rolls to be written by Abraham, narrating his stay in Egypt. An eminent French Egyptologist, M. Devéria, of the Museum of the Louvre at Paris, before whom the facsimiles were laid, showed that they represent the

Interior of the Mormon Tabernacle.—[From Stenhouse.]

resurrection of Osiris, a funerary disk, and a painting from a funerary MS. This deviation of M. Devéria's translation from Smith's would naturally again lead to the supposition that the would-be prophet intentionally played off a fictitious translation as an exact rendering of the original papyri. This theory need not, however, be espoused, as has been well shown by Mr. Stenhouse : "With the Prophet's story of the supposed *Book of Abraham* placed side by side with the translation of the papyrus by the scientist, the reader may possibly conclude that Joseph Smith imposed upon the credulity of the Saints, and hence that the claim throughout this work that Joseph was sincere is here unsupported. The author, notwithstanding, still clings to the assertion that Joseph believed sincerely that he was inspired, and the pride with which he gave this translation to the world supports that conclusion. Had he ever doubted the correctness of his translation, he never would have given to the public the fac-simile of the characters and his translation of them. Joseph Smith at this time was over thirty years of age, and had passed through too rough an experience to have risked his reputation upon anything about which he had the slightest doubt. If the translation of the scientist is correct, and it bears upon its face evidence to that effect, then Joseph was as much deceived as many others have been before and since who have laid claim to the possession of divine and supernatural powers and the receiving of revelations." Those who may be interested in these Egyptian antiquities and the variability of the two translators will do well to consult Stenhouse, p. 512 to 519. The *Pearl of Great Price* contains also two different accounts of the creation, both made up out of Gen. i. A translation is given of Matt. xxiii, 39, and xxiv, differing from the Authorized Version in containing additions to the extent of one third, entirely unsupported by any MS. or version. There are some other fragments, absurd but unimportant, except as showing the audacity of the author. The "translations" are portions of a translation of the whole Bible, said to exist in MS., in the hands of the Mormon leaders. Some further extracts have appeared in periodicals; the text is altered to suit Mormon doctrines, and large additions made. It is asserted by the Mormons that the Authorized Version has been fraudulently corrupted, and that this "translation" alone represents the original and true form. Other revelations are also said to exist in MS., to be published when the world is ripe for them.

III. *Mormon Doctrines.*—The creed of the Mormonists would naturally be supposed to be embodied in the *Book of Mormon.* This is not the case, however. The theology as there embodied differs but little from orthodox Trinitarianism. But this is by no means the real creed of the Latter-day Saints. Indeed, it is not an easy matter to set forth exactly and clearly the principles of Mormon theology. First, there is the theory of continuous revelation abiding in the Church (see Preface to *Hymn-book* [1856]; *Compendium of the Faith and Doctrines*, p. 43-47). Secondly, Mormon theology abounds in such an extraordinary admixture of truth and superstition, of philosophy and fanaticism, that it is difficult to disentangle them and reduce them to anything like an orderly system. The only document at all resembling a creed is published in the *Pearl of Great Price*, p. 55 sq., and in the pamphlet entitled *The Rise, Progress, and Travels of the Church of Jesus Christ of Latter-day Saints; being a series of Answers to Questions*, by Bro. George A. Smith (Salt Lake City, 1872, 8vo), p. 40, 41. It is from the pen of Joseph Smith, and was compiled by him in 1842. We insert it here in full :

"First. We believe in God, the Eternal Father, and in his Son Jesus Christ, and in the Holy Ghost.

"We believe that men will be punished for their own sins, and not for Adam's transgression.

"We believe that through the atonement of Christ all mankind may be saved by obedience to the laws and ordinances of the Gospel.

"We believe that these ordinances are: 1, Faith in the Lord Jesus Christ; 2, Repentance; 3, Baptism by immersion for the remission of sins; 4, Laying on of hands for the gift of the Holy Ghost.

"We believe that a man must be called of God, by 'prophecy, and by laying on of hands' by those who are in authority, to preach the Gospel and administer in the ordinances thereof.

"We believe in the same organization that existed in the primitive Church, viz. apostles, prophets, pastors, teachers, evangelists, etc.

"We believe in the gift of tongues, prophecy, revelation, visions, healing, interpretation of tongues, etc.

"We believe the Bible to be the Word of God, as far as it is translated correctly; we also believe the Book of Mormon to be the Word of God.

"We believe all that God has revealed, all that he does now reveal, and we believe that he will yet reveal many great and important things pertaining to the kingdom of God.

"We believe in the literal gathering of Israel and in the restoration of the Ten Tribes; that Zion will be built upon this continent; that Christ will reign personally upon the earth, and that the earth will be renewed and receive its paradisaic glory.

"We claim the privilege of worshipping Almighty God according to the dictates of our conscience, and allow all men the same privilege, let them worship how, where, or what they may.

"We believe in being subject to kings, presidents, rulers, and magistrates; in obeying, honoring, and sustaining the law.

"We believe in being honest, true, chaste, benevolent, virtuous, and in doing good to *all men;* indeed, we may say that we follow the admonition of Paul, 'We believe all things, we hope all things;' we have endured many things, and hope to be able to endure all things. If there is anything virtuous, lovely, or of good report, or praiseworthy, we seek after these things."

A more perfect and complete copy is furnished by Mr. Orson Pratt, which we also insert, as it is now seldom to be reached in this detailed and explanatory form, and on many points clearly elucidates the strange views of these Saints. (See, however, Burton, p. 467-480.)

"We believe in God, the Eternal Father, and in his Son Jesus Christ, and in the Holy Ghost, who bears record of them, the same throughout all ages and forever.

"We believe that all mankind, by the transgression of their first parents, and not by their own sins, were brought under the curse and penalty of that transgression, which consigned them to an eternal banishment from the presence of God, and their bodies to an endless sleep in the dust, never more to rise, and their spirits to endless misery under the power of Satan; and that, in this awful condition, they were utterly lost and fallen, and had no power of their own to extricate themselves therefrom.

"We believe that through the sufferings, death, and atonement of Jesus Christ all mankind, without one exception, are to be completely and fully redeemed, both body and spirit, from the endless banishment and curse to which they were consigned by Adam's transgression; and that this universal salvation and redemption of the whole human family from the endless penalty of the original sin is effected without any conditions whatsoever on their part: that is, that they are not required to believe, or repent, or be baptized, or do anything else, in order to be redeemed from that penalty; for whether they believe or disbelieve, whether they repent or remain impenitent, whether they are baptized or unbaptized, whether they keep the commandments or break them, whether they are righteous or unrighteous, it will make no difference in relation to their redemption, both soul and body, from the penalty of Adam's transgression. The most righteous man that ever lived on the earth, and the most wicked wretch of the whole human family, were both placed under the same curse without any transgression or agency of their own, and they both alike will be redeemed from that curse without any agency or conditions on their part. Paul says (Rom. v, 18), 'Therefore, as by the offence of one, judgment came upon *all men* to condemnation; even so, by the righteousness of one, the free gift came upon *all men* unto the justification of life.' This is the reason why *all men* are redeemed from the grave. This is the reason that the spirits of *all men* are restored to their bodies. This is the reason that *all men* are redeemed from their first banishment and restored into the presence of God. And this is the reason that the Saviour said (John xii, 32), 'If I be lifted up from the earth, I will draw *all men* unto me.' After this full, complete, and universal redemption, restoration, and salvation of the whole of Adam's race, through the atonement of Jesus Christ, without faith, repentance, baptism, or any other works, then all and every one of them will enjoy eternal life and happiness, never more to be banished from the presence of God *if they themselves have committed no sin;* for the penalty of the original sin can have no more power over them at all, for Jesus hath destroyed its power, and broken the bands of the first death, and obtained the victory over the grave, and delivered all its captives, and restored them from their banishment into the presence of his Father; hence eternal life will then be theirs, *if they themselves are not found transgressors of some law.*

"We believe that all mankind, in their infant state, are incapable of knowing good and evil, and of obeying or disobeying a law; and that therefore there is no law given to them, and that where there is no law there is no transgression; hence they are innocent, and if they should all die in their infant state they would enjoy eternal life, not being transgressors themselves, neither accountable for Adam's sin.

"We believe that all mankind, in consequence of the fall, after they grow up from their infant state and come to the years of understanding, know good and evil, and are capable of obeying or disobeying a law, and that a law is given against doing evil, and that the penalty affixed is a second banishment from the presence of God, both body and spirit, *after* they have been redeemed from the *first banishment* and restored into his presence.

"We believe that the penalty of this second law can have no effect upon persons who have not had the privilege in this life of becoming acquainted therewith; for although the light that is in them teaches them good and evil, yet that light does not teach them the law against doing evil, nor the penalty thereof. And although they have done things worthy of many stripes, yet the law cannot be brought to bear against them and its penalty be inflicted, because they can plead ignorance thereof. Therefore they will be judged, not by the revealed law which they have been ignorant of, but by the law of their conscience, the penalty thereof being a few stripes.

"We believe that all who have done evil, having a knowledge of the law, or afterwards in this life coming to the knowledge thereof, are under its penalty, which is not inflicted in this world, but in the world to come. Therefore such in this world are prisoners, shut up under the sentence of the law, awaiting with awful fear for the time of judgment, when the penalty shall be inflicted, consigning them to a *second banishment* from the presence of their Redeemer, who had redeemed them from the penalty of the *first* law. But, inquires the sinner, is there no way for my escape? Is my case hopeless? Can I not devise some way by which I can extricate myself from the penalty of this *second law*, and escape this *second banishment?* The answer is—If thou canst hide thyself from the all-searching eye of an omnipresent God, that he shall not find thee, or if thou canst prevail with him to deny justice its claim, or if thou canst clothe thyself with power and contend with the Almighty, and prevent him from executing the sentence of the law, then thou canst escape. If thou canst cause repentance, or baptism in water, or any of thine own works to *atone* for the least of thy transgressions, then thou canst deliver thyself from the awful penalty that awaits thee. But be assured, O sinner, that thou canst not devise any way of thine own to escape, nor do anything that will *atone* for thy sins. Therefore thy case is hopeless unless God hath devised some way for thy deliverance; but do not let despair seize upon thee, for though thou art under the sentence of a broken law, and hast no power to atone for thy sins and redeem thyself therefrom, yet there is hope in thy case, for he who gave the law has devised a way for thy deliverance. That same Jesus who hath atoned for the original sin, and will redeem all mankind from the penalty thereof, hath also atoned for thy sins, and offereth salvation and deliverance to thee on certain conditions to be complied with on thy part.

"We believe that the first condition to be complied with on the part of sinners is to *believe* in God, and in the sufferings and death of his Son Jesus Christ to atone for the sins of the whole world, and in his resurrection and ascension on high to appear in the presence of his Father to make intercession for the children of men, and in the Holy Ghost, which is given to all who obey the Gospel.

"That the second condition is to *repent*—that is, all who believe according to the first condition are required to come humbly before God and confess their sins with a broken heart and contrite spirit, and to turn away from them, and cease from all their *evil deeds*, and make restitution to all they have in any way injured, as far as it is in their power.

"That the third condition is to be *baptized* by immersion in water, in the name of the Father, Son, and Holy Ghost, *for remission of sins*; and that this ordinance is to be administered by one who is called and authorized of Jesus Christ to baptize; otherwise it is illegal and of no advantage, and not accepted by him; and that it is to be administered only to those persons who believe and repent according to the two preceding conditions.

"And that the fourth condition is to receive the *laying on of hands* in the name of Jesus Christ for the gift of the Holy Ghost; and that this ordinance is to be administered by the apostles or elders whom the Lord Jesus hath called and authorized to lay on hands; otherwise it is of no advantage, being illegal in the sight of God; and that it is to be administered only to those persons who believe, repent, and are baptized into this Church, according to the three preceding conditions. These are the first conditions of the Gospel. All who comply with them receive

forgiveness of sins and are made partakers of the Holy Ghost. Through these conditions they become the adopted sons and daughters of God. Through this process they are born again, first of water and then of the Spirit, and become children of the kingdom—heirs of God—saints of the Most High—the Church of the first-born—the elect people, and heirs to a celestial inheritance eternal in the presence of God. After complying with these principles, their names are enrolled in the book of the names of the righteous.

"They are then required to be humble, to be meek and lowly in heart, to watch and pray, to deal justly; and inasmuch as they have the riches of this world, to feed the hungry and clothe the naked, according to the dictates of wisdom and prudence; to comfort the afflicted, to bind up the broken-hearted, and to do all the good that is in their power; and, besides all these things, they are required to meet together as often as circumstances will admit and partake of bread and wine, in remembrance of the broken body and shed blood of the Lord Jesus; and, in short, to continue faithful to the end in all the duties enjoined upon them by the word and Spirit of Christ.

"'It is the duty and privilege of the saints thus organized upon the everlasting Gospel to believe in and enjoy all the gifts, powers, and blessings which flow from the Holy Spirit. Such, for instance, as the gifts of revelation, prophecy, visions, the ministry of angels, healing the sick by the laying on of hands in the name of Jesus, the working of miracles, and, in short, all the gifts as mentioned in Scripture, or as enjoyed by the ancient saints.' We believe that inspired apostles and prophets, together with all the officers as mentioned in the New Testament, are necessary to be in the Church in these days.

"We believe that there has been a general and awful apostasy from the religion of the New Testament, so that all the known world have been left for centuries without the Church of Christ among them; without a priesthood authorized of God to administer ordinances; that every one of the churches has perverted the Gospel, some in one way and some in another. For instance, almost every Church has done away '*immersion for remission of sins*.' Those few who have practiced it *for remission of sins* have done away the ordinance of the '*laying on of hands*' upon baptized believers for the gift of the Holy Ghost. Again, the few who have practiced the last ordinance have perverted the first, or have done away the ancient gifts, powers, and blessings which flow from the Holy Spirit, or have said to inspired apostles and prophets, We have no need of you in the body of these days. Those few, again, who have believed in and contended for the miraculous gifts and powers of the Holy Spirit have perverted the ordinances or done them away.

"We believe that there are a few sincere, honest, and humble persons who are striving to do according to the best of their understanding; but in many respects they err in doctrine because of false teachers and the precepts of men; and that they will receive the fulness of the Gospel with gladness as soon as they hear it.

"The gospel in the *Book of Mormon* is the same as that in the New Testament, and is revealed in great plainness, so that no one who reads it can misunderstand its principles. It has been revealed by the angel to be preached as a witness to all nations; first to the Gentiles and then to the Jews; then cometh the downfall of Babylon—thus fulfilling the vision of John, which he beheld on the Isle of Patmos (Rev. xiv, 6-8).

"Many revelations and prophecies have been given to this [i. e. the Mormon] Church since its rise, which have been printed and sent forth to the world. These also contain the gospel in great plainness, and instructions of infinite importance to the Saints. They also unfold the great events that await this generation; the terrible judgments to be poured forth upon the wicked, and the blessings and glories to be given to the righteous. We believe that God will continue to give revelations by visions, by the ministry of angels, and by the inspiration of the Holy Ghost, until the Saints are guided into all truth; that is, until they come in possession of all the truth there is in existence, and are made perfect in knowledge. So long, therefore, as they are ignorant of anything past, present, or to come, so long, we believe, they will enjoy the gift of revelation. And when in their immortal and perfect state—when they enjoy 'the measure of the stature of the fulness of Christ'—when they are made perfect in one, and become like their Saviour, then they will be in possession of all knowledge, wisdom, and intelligence; then all things will be theirs, whether principalities or powers, thrones or dominions; and, in short, then they will be filled with all the fulness of God. Then they will no longer need revelation.

"We believe that wherever the people enjoy the religion of the New Testament, there they enjoy visions, revelations, the ministry of angels, etc.; and that wherever these blessings cease to be enjoyed, there they also cease to enjoy the religion of the New Testament.

"We believe that God has raised up this Church in order to prepare a people for his second coming in the clouds of heaven, in power and great glory; and that then the saints who are asleep in their graves will be raised, and reign with him on earth a thousand years.

"We believe that great and terrible judgments await the nations of the wicked, and that after the message of the *Book of Mormon* has been sufficiently sounded in their ears, if they reject it, they will be overthrown and wasted away until the earth shall no longer be encumbered with them. New and unheard-of plagues will sweep through the nations, baffling the skill of the most experienced and learned physicians, depopulating whole cities and towns, and carrying off millions of wretched beings in every quarter of our globe. Nations, no longer restrained by the Spirit of God, which will cease striving in them, will rise against nations, till the whole earth, comparatively speaking, shall be filled with blood and carnage. Thrones and empires shall be cast down—new governments will be erected but to meet with the same fate. Peace shall be taken from among the nations, and it shall happen as with the Papists so with the Protestants, as with their ministers so with the people whom they have deceived—they shall all fall into the ditch and perish together because they reject the voice of the Lord from the heavens, and the voice of his servants whom he hath sent to testify against their wickedness and prepare the way of the Lord for his second coming.

"But the righteous shall escape, for the Lord shall gather them from all nations unto a land of peace, and his arms shall be stretched out over them, and his glory shall be upon them for a defence, and 'they shall be the only people under heaven that shall not be at war with one another,' for thus hath the Lord spoken.

"We believe that in this generation a house of the Lord shall be built by the Saints upon Mount Zion, and a cloud of glory shall rest upon it by day and the shining of a flaming fire by night, and that the face of the Lord will be unveiled, and the pure in heart shall see him and live. O Zion, how glorious are thy habitations, and how blessed are thy children! Many people shall come unto thee to be taught in the ways of the Lord and instructed in his paths; for out of thee shall proceed forth a perfect law which shall establish righteousness in the earth.

"We believe that the ten tribes of Israel, with the dispersed of Judah, shall soon be restored to their own lands, according to the covenants which God made with their ancient fathers, and that when this great work of restitution shall take place the power of God shall be made manifest in signs and wonders, and mighty deeds far exceeding anything that took place in their exodus from Egypt. Jerusalem will be rebuilt, together with a glorious temple, and the Lord shall visit them also, as well as his saints in Zion. In that day the name of the Lord shall become great unto the ends of the earth, and all nations shall serve and obey him, for the wicked shall have perished out of the earth.

"We believe that all persons who wish to escape the judgments of great Babylon must come out from among both the Papists and the Protestants, for they are the whore of all the earth, and have made the nations drunk with their abominations, and are to be burned by fire; therefore woe unto that man or woman that shall stand in connection with them, for the hour of their judgment is at hand.

"And we now bear testimony to all, both small and great, that the Lord of Hosts hath sent us with a message of glad tidings—the everlasting gospel, to cry repentance to the nations, and prepare the way of his second coming. Therefore *repent*, O ye nations, both Gentiles and Jews, and cease from all your *evil deeds*, and come forth with broken hearts and contrite spirits, and be *baptized* in water, in the name of the Father, Son, and Holy Ghost, *for remission of sins*, and ye shall receive the gift of the Holy Spirit, by the *laying on of the hands* of the apostles or elders of this Church; and signs shall follow them that believe, and if they continue faithful to the end they shall be saved. But woe unto them that hearken not to the message which God has now sent, for the day of vengeance and burning is at hand, and they shall not escape. Therefore *remember*, O reader, and *perish not !*"

The reader will notice that Mr. Pratt does not dwell at any length upon the first article, but simply restates in other words what is embodied in the Confession. Yet this very article has given rise to a most materialistic tendency, developing in some points into pantheism. The explanatory statements which they have from time to time given to this article warrant the assertion that, while they profess belief in the Trinity, their Godhead is formed on Buddhistic principles, and develops a system of anthropomorphism which has never been equalled by any heretic sect of the Christian Church, though it was approached by the Egyptian monks whom Theophilus (q. v.) anathematized in the fourth century. The Mormons explain that God was once a man, who has, however, so advanced in intelligence and power that he may now be called (comparatively speaking) perfect, infinite, etc., but that he has still the form and figure of a man; he has even "legs," as is evident (according to

Mr. Orson Pratt's utterances in sermons, etc.) from his appearance to Abraham; though he has this advantage over his creatures that "he can move up or down through the air without using them." The following is an extract from one of their popular catechisms bearing on the subject: "*Q*. 28. What is God? *A*. He is a *material* intelligent personage, possessing both body and parts.—*Q*. 38. Doth he also possess passions? *A*. Yes; he eats, he drinks, he loves, he hates.—*Q*. 44. Can this being occupy two distinct places at once? *A*. No" (*Latter-day Saints' Catechism*, quoted in *Morm. Illust.* p. 43). To the same effect we read in the Mormon Hymn-book (p. 349):

"The God that others worship is not the God for me:
He has no parts nor body, and cannot hear nor see."

A local residence is assigned to this anthropomorphic deity: he lives, we are told, "*in the planet Kolob*" (*Seer*, p. 70, and *Millen. Star*, xiv, 531). Moreover, as he possesses the body and passions of a man, so his relations to his creatures are purely human. St. Hilary of Poitiers asserts that some Arians attacked orthodoxy by the following argument: "Deus *pater* non erat, quia neque ei *filius;* nam si filius, necesse est ut et *fœmina* sit" (Hil. *adv. Const.*). The conclusion thus stated as an absurdity in the 4th century the Mormons embrace as an axiom in the 19th. "*In mundi primordiis, Deo erat fœmina*," is an article of their creed (*Patr. Order*, p. 1, and p. 15; also *Seer*, i, 38, 103). No existence is "created;" all beings are "begotten." The superiority of the Mormon God over his creatures consists only in the greater power which he has gradually attained by growth in knowledge. He himself originated in "the union of two elementary particles of matter" (Gunnison, p. 49), and by a progressive development reached the human form. Thus we read that "God, *of course*, was once a man, and from manhood by continual progression became God; and he has continued to increase from his manhood to the present time, and may continue to increase without limit. And man also may continue to increase in knowledge and power as fast as he pleases." And again: "If man is a creature of eternal progression, the time must certainly arrive when he will know as much as God now knows" (*Millen. Star*, xiv, 386). This is in strict accordance with the following words of Joseph Smith: "The weakest child of God which now exists upon the earth will possess more dominion, more property, more subjects, and more power and glory than is possessed by Jesus Christ or by his Father; while at the same time they will have their dominion, kingdom, and subjects increased in proportion" (*Mill. Star*, vol. vi, quoted in *Morm. Illust.*). An apostle carries this view into detail as follows: "What will man do when this world is filled up? Why, he will *make more worlds*, and swarm out like bees from the old world. And when a farmer has cultivated his farm, and raised numerous children, so that the space is beginning to be too strait for them, he will say, *My sons, yonder is plenty of matter, go and organize a world and people it*" (P. Pratt, in *Millen. Star*, xiv, 663, and *Seer*, i, 37). This doctrine of indefinite development naturally passes into polytheism. Accordingly, the Mormon theology teaches that there are gods innumerable, with different degrees of dignity and power. It was revealed to Joseph Smith that the first verse of Genesis originally stood as follows: "The *Head God* brought forth *the Gods*, with the heavens, and the earth" (*Millen. Star*, xiv, 455). The same prophet also tells us (*ibid.*) that a hundred and forty-four thousand of these gods are mentioned by St. John in the Apocalypse. Moreover, "each God is the God of the spirits of all flesh pertaining to the world which he forms" (*Seer*, i, 38). Young claims that it was revealed to him that the God of our own planet is Adam, who (it seems) was only another form of the archangel Michael: "When our father Adam came into the garden of Eden, he brought Eve, *one of his wives*, with him. He helped to make and organize this world. He is Michael the

Archangel, the *Ancient of Days*. He is our Father and our God, *and the only God with whom we have to do* (from *Discourses of the Presidency*, in vol. xv, p. 769, preached in the Tabernacle, April 9, 1852). It is curious to observe, from such examples, how easily the extremes of materialism and immaterialism may be made to meet. For here we have the rudest form of anthropomorphism connected with a theory of emanation which might be identified with that of some Gnostic and Oriental idealists. There can be no doubt that, under its present intellectual guides, Mormonism is rapidly passing into that form of practical atheism which is euphemistically termed *pantheism*. Thus we read in the Washington organ of the presidency that the only thing which has existed from eternity is "an infinite quantity of *self-moving intelligent matter*. Every particle of matter which now exists existed in the infinite depths of past duration, and was then capable of self-motion" (*Seer*, i, 129). "There is no substance in the universe which feels and thinks, but what has *eternally* possessed that capacity" (*ibid*. p. 102). "Each individual of the *vegetable* and animal kingdom contains a living spirit, possessed of intelligent capacities" (*ibid*. p. 34). "Persons are only tabernacles, and *truth* is *the God* that dwells in them. When we speak of only one God, and state that he is eternal, etc., we have no reference to any particular person, but to *truth dwelling in a vast variety of substances*" (*ibid*. p. 25; comp. also Stenhouse, p. 484 sq.).

again, is declared to be the "god" of Jesus Christ; Jesus Christ the god of Joseph Smith; and Joseph Smith is now the god of this generation: but the whole affair is a mass too wild and mystical to be explained intelligently. The human intellect probably never sank into more abysmal nonsense; all that can be definitely set before the mind is that Mormons believe that by faith, obedience, holiness, any man may rise into a deity, and acquire the power of making, peopling, and ruling a "world" forever! (See Stenhouse, p. 486.)

The third article, which teaches universal salvation, is strangely elucidated regarding the future state. Thus, according to Mormon teaching, not only will the body, but all the habits, occupations, and necessities of life, be the same in the future world as in the present. One of their chief pillars tells us that "the future residence of the Saints is not an ideal thing. They will need houses for their persons and for their families as much in their *resurrected* condition as in their present state. In this identical world, where they have been robbed of houses and lands, and wife and children, they shall have a hundredfold" (Spencer, p. 174). Another "apostle" calculates the exact amount of landed property which may be expected by the "*resurrected* Saints:" "Suppose that, out of the population of the earth, one in a hundred should be entitled to an inheritance upon the new earth, how much land would each receive? We answer, they would receive over a hundred and fifty acres, which would be quite enough to raise manna, and to build some splendid mansions. It would be large enough to have our flower gardens, and everything the agriculturist and the botanist want" (P. Pratt, in *Millen. Star*, xiv, 663). They also venture directly to contradict the words of Christ himself, by affirming that, *in the resurrection, men both marry and are given in marriage*. Thus the author above quoted tells us that "Abraham and Sarah will continue to mul-

THE ETERNAL GOD.

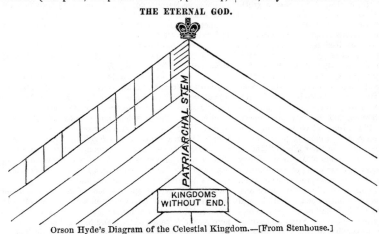

Orson Hyde's Diagram of the Celestial Kingdom.—[From Stenhouse.]

Christ is the offspring of the "material" union, on the plains of Palestine, of God and the Virgin Mary— the latter being duly married after betrothal by the angel Gabriel. Yet he is believed to have had a previous existence, to have even made the universe out of "unformed chaotic matter as old as God," and his worship is enjoined as Lord of all (*Doct. and Cov.* Lect. v, 2, p. 45, 47). The Paraclete is vaguely described. He is also a member of the Godhead, being the mind of the Father and the Son; but while the other two persons have bodies of flesh and bones, the Holy Ghost has not, but is a personage of Spirit (*Compend*. p. 154). Yet his substance is material, and subject to the necessary laws which govern matter. He has therefore parts which are infinite and spread through all space, and so is he virtually omnipresent. The Father and the Son, as persons, are not omnipresent, but only through the Spirit (*Compend*. p. 140–148). He may properly be called God's minister, to execute his will in immensity. He is therefore the worker of miracles, the source of grace, and even the cause of increase, being in every person upon the face of the earth; for the "elements that every individual is made of and lives in possess the Godhead" (Young, in *Compend*. p. 148). It would appear, however, that there is an older Trinity, that of "Elohim, Jehovah, and Michael, which is Adam." Adam,

tiply, not only in this world, but in all worlds to come. ... Will the resurrection return you a mere *female acquaintance*, that is *not* to be the wife of your bosom in eternity? No; God forbid. But it will restore you the wife of your bosom immortalized, who shall bear children from your own loins in all worlds to come" (see Spencer, p. 6; and compare Stenhouse, p. 480).

We desire to call special attention also to the Mormon doctrine regarding miraculous gifts, as embodied in the seventh article of their Confession. This doctrine of the discerning of spirits led Smith into a variety of curious speculations. He teaches that the soul of man was not created, but "coexisted" equal with God. "God," he says in one of his sermons in 1853 (p. 62), "never did have power to create the spirit of man at all. The very idea lessens man in my estimation. I *know better!*" He also holds to the transmigration of souls. Rebellious spirits descend into brute tabernacles till they yield to "the law of the everlasting gospel." The eighth article may be declared decidedly liberal; it expresses a belief that the Word of God is recorded, not only in the Bible and the *Book of Mormon*, but in "all other good books." As for the contradictions that exist in the first, Smith admits them, but alleges that they are "corruptions," and that they can be removed by his or any other prophet's inspired explanations. It is said that he has left an "inspired translation" of the whole Bible in MS.; but as it has never been published, we can judge it only by the occasional extracts which have been made by prophets and elders, and from these we have quoted in appropriate places.

The tenth article, though it affirms the literal gathering of Israel, the restoration of the Ten Tribes (the American Indians, who are in consequence treated with considerable humanity by the Saints), and the personal reign of Christ for one thousand years, does not, as has always been supposed, make the in-gathering at the Zion of the East, but at that New Zion on the Western continent which has been appointed under this new dispensation ushered in by Joseph Smith. And as the Jews were bidden to separate themselves from the Gentiles, and the early Christians (the ancient Saints) from the heathen, so the Latter-day Saints are now called forth from a wicked world, doomed to almost immediate destruction (before the close of this century), which is indeed already beginning, to the Zion of this continent. When the Gospel has been preached to all the world, and the elect have been assembled at Zion, then all unbelievers will be destroyed; the kingdom of heaven will be set up on the earth, and the formal reign of Christ commence in the Western Zion. Surely no one need wonder that Joseph Smith, when he first promulgated his new faith, maintained that "one of the grand fundamental principles of Mormonism is to receive truth, come whence it may" (Sermon preached July 9, 1843) Indeed their faith, if we have but distantly reached their true position, consists of a spontaneous agglomeration of tenets which, were its disciples of a more learned and philosophical body, would suggest extensive eclecticism. And Mr. Burton has well said that "the Mormons are like the Pythagoreans in their procreation, transmigration, and exaltation of souls; like the followers of Leucippus and Democritus in their atomic materialism; like the Epicureans in their pure atomic theories, their summum bonum, and their sensuous speculations; and like the Platonists and Gnostics in their belief of the Æon, of ideas, and of moving principles in element. They are Fetichists in their ghostly fancies, their Avestra, which became souls and spirits. They are Jews in their theocracy, their ideas of angels, their hatred for Gentiles, and their utter segregation from the great brotherhood of mankind. They are Christians, inasmuch as they base their faith upon the Bible, and hold to the divinity of Christ, the fall of man, the atonement, and the regeneration. They are Arians, inasmuch as they hold Christ to be 'the first of God's creatures; a perfect creature, but still a creature.' They are Moslems in their views of the inferior status of womankind, in their polygamy, and in their resurrection of the material body; like the followers of the Arabian Prophet, they hardly fear death, because they have elaborated 'continuation.' They take no leap in the dark—they spring from this sublunary stage into a known, not into an unknown world; hence also their worship is eminently secular, their sermons are political or commercial, and —religion being with them not a thing apart but a portion and parcel of every-day life—the intervention of the Lord in their material affairs becomes natural and only to be expected. Their visions, prophecies, and miracles are those of the Illuminati, their mysticism that of the Druses, and their belief in the millennium is a completion of the dreams of the Apocalyptic sects. Masonry has entered into their scheme, the Demiurgus whom they worship is 'as good at mechanical inventions as at any other business.' With their later theories, Methodism, Swedenborgianism — especially in its view of the future state—and Transcendentalism are curiously intermingled. Finally, we can easily discern in their doctrine of affinity of minds and sympathy of souls the leaven of that faith which, beginning with Mesmer and progressing through the Rochester Rappers and the Poughkeepsie Seer, threatens to extend wherever the

susceptible nervous temperament becomes the characteristic of the race."

The ethical teachings of Mormonism are not distinguished by any other remarkable peculiarities than we have already had occasion to point out. The chief duty impressed upon the Saints is the prompt payment of tithings. Their official publications are strenuous in their exhortation to the fulfilment of that indispensable obligation (see Stenhouse, p. 578). Next to this cardinal virtue seems to be rated the merit of abstinence from fermented liquors and tobacco. This, however, is not absolutely insisted upon, but is only urged as a "precept of wisdom." It was enforced by Joseph, but under the present head of the Church it is asserted that intemperance is rapidly invading the Saints' households. The virtue of patriotism is also a frequent theme of Mormon eulogy. The national colors are exhibited on every public occasion, and there seems to be every endeavor to refute the charges that Mormonism seeks secular power, and is antagonistic to the United States government, and that if statehood is ever secured to Utah, "Brigham Young's theocracy will be triumphant over the republic and the national laws." The practice of dancing must also be included in the ethical system of Mormonism. Indeed, when the Temple is completed, public dances are to form a part of the regular worship. In saltatorial as in military movements the priesthood occupy the foremost place. The president leads off, and bishops, patriarchs, and elders are to be seen figuring enthusiastically — "not," says colonel Kane, "in your minuets or other mortuary processions of Gentiles, but in jigs and reels."

IV. Ordinances and Practices.—1. The ordinances of the Mormon Gospel are five: (1) Faith, which is very strangely described in the Doctr. and Cov., as already quoted. What is really required of a Saint in this respect is "faith in Joseph and his successors," and not absolute acceptance of the Scriptures, i. e. the Bible and the Mormon writings, but a "reverence" for them, and "absolute obedience" to the president and priesthood. (See § V, below.) (2) Repentance, i. e. sorrow for sin and resolution to lead a good life. (3) Baptism, which is administered by immersion, to none younger than eight years, that being regarded as the age at which responsibility begins (Doctr. and Cov. ch. xxii, § 4, p. 160). Infant baptism is declared to be a "solemn mockery, because little children have no sins to repent of, and are not under the curse of Adam" (Book of Mormon: Moroni, ch. viii, § 2, 3, p. 557). The rite is administered as follows: "The person who is called of God, and has authority of Jesus Christ, shall go down into the water with the person who has presented him or herself for baptism, and shall say, calling him or her by name, 'Having been commissioned of Jesus Christ, I baptize you in the name of the Father, and of the Son, and of the Holy Ghost. Amen.' Then shall he immerse him or her in the water, and come forth again out of the water" (Book of Mormon: Nephi, ch. v, § 8, p. 457; Doctr. and Cov. ch. ii, § 21, p. 73). The effect of baptism, when administered to and by a qualified person, is declared to be the remission of sins, the gift of the Holy Ghost, and a title of eternal life. It is regarded as absolutely necessary to salvation; without it neither repentance nor faith avail (Doctr. and Cov. ch. iv, § 12, p. 87). A most peculiar tenet of their creed is the necessity of baptism for the dead. To supply the deficiency of those who through ignorance or other involuntary defect have died unbaptized in the Mormon faith, the practice of baptism for the dead was ordained at a very early period of Mormonism, and is incorporated as a necessary ordinance into the Book of Doctr. and Cov. (§ 105, 106). The faith is preached to the dead in Hades by departed Saints; and the benefit of baptism is obtained for them by proxy. Any believer may and should be baptized for his departed friends, relations, and ancestors to the most remote ages; and, in the perfect state, those for whom a person has been thus baptized will be added to his family and subjects (Spencer, *Letters*, p. 162–164; *Millen. Star*, v, 87 sq.; Stenhouse, p. 476 sq.). To this effect the Mormon hymnist sings:

"I am Zionward bound, where a
    Seer is our head,
We'll there be baptized for our
    friends that are dead;
By obeying this law we may set
    them all free,
And *saviours we shall upon Mount
    Zion be.*"
                    (*Millen. Star*, xv, 143.)

The chancellor of the University of Deseret informs us that " unless this is done for the dead *they cannot be redeemed*" (Spencer, p. 166). The same learned authority announces that " Peter tells how the devout and honorable dead may be saved, who never heard the Gospel on earth. Says he [St. Peter!], 'else why are they baptized for the dead?'" (Spencer here refers incorrectly to 1 Cor. xv, 29 as the work of St. Peter.) A careful record of the persons vicariously baptized is kept by duly appointed registrars. These records are the books spoken of by St. John (Rev. xx, 12), the Book of Life being a record kept in heaven to verify those kept on earth

A Mormon Baptism.

(*Doctr. and Cov.* ch. cvi, § 6, 7, p. 319). (4) *Laying on of hands* for the gift of the Holy Ghost, sometimes called baptism by fire as distinguished from baptism by water. It is usually administered immediately after baptism, of which it is regarded as the completion. By it the spirit of prophecy, the gift of tongues, and the power to work miracles are given. There have been multitudes of persons in the world who have believed and asserted that to them, and to them only, God gave visions, dreams, angel-visits, the power of healing the sick and " casting out devils;" and they have declared that these were proofs of the heavenly origin of the faith which they proclaimed, and this it is that the Saints have been taught by the modern apostles to regard as special and particular to them, while it has been a peculiarity common to the religious experience of all the world. (5) *The Sacrament of the Lord's Supper* was originally administered in bread and wine, as Christ himself ordained when he appeared to the Nephites (*Book of Mormon: Nephi*, ch. viii, § 6, p. 469). But in 1833 it was revealed to Smith that " strong drinks are not for the belly, but for the washing of your bodies," and that wine was only to be used in this ordinance if it was the pure juice of the grape, and made by Mormons (*Doctr. and Cov.* ch. lxxxi, § 1, p. 240). Water only, therefore, is now used. The rite is administered every Sunday. The water, having been blessed, is handed around in tin cans, together with the bread (Rae, p. 106).

2. *Marriage* is not a civil contract with the Latter-day Saints, but a sacrament of the Church, and a sacred tenet of the faith. Matrimony, moreover, as practiced by the Mormons, is an institution so peculiar to themselves, they having introduced into the modern social system the polygamic system, that their marriage service is a most important rite. Mormons are in every possible way encouraged to be polygamists, and are reminded of the revelation given to the Prophet that " the rank and dignity given to the Saints in the other world is proportioned to the number of their wives and children." It is true that polygamy is not, as many suppose, essential to their religious system, yet it has entered so largely into the marital relations of the Latter-day Saints of Utah as to give them a most obnoxious record in the sight of all other Christian religious sects. As we have seen above, in their early his-

tory the Mormons clearly rebuked polygamy (*Book of Mormon: Jacob*, ch. ii, p. 118 sq.). From 1830 to 1843 they were monogamists; but in the latter of these years, as we have also seen, Smith obtained a revelation permitting, and even recommending, a plurality of wives. (They reject the word " polygamy," and prefer the term *pluralism*.) Still, pluralism does not appear to have become the general practice among the Mormons till their journey across the prairies to the valley of the Salt Lake. Since then it has been openly avowed, and defended against other sects by an appeal to Scripture. Tracts, dialogues, and hymns are circulated in its behalf. Says Stenhouse, " Tens of thousands of sermons have been preached on its divine origin; voluminous treatises have been published in its exposition, and the Mormon press has teemed with articles in its defence" (p. 183). And even the " pluralistic" marriage ceremony has been published. To afford our readers a fuller understanding of the Mormon vice of " pluralism," we here insert in full the special " revelation" which they claim to have had.

" CELESTIAL MARRIAGE:

" A REVELATION ON THE PATRIARCHAL ORDER OF MATRIMONY, OR PLURALITY OF WIVES.

" *Given to Joseph Smith, the Seer, in Nauvoo, July* 12, 1842.

" 1. Verily, then saith the Lord unto you, my servant Joseph, that inasmuch as you have inquired of my hand to know and understand wherein I, the Lord, justified my servants Abraham, Isaac, and Jacob, as also Moses, David, and Solomon, my servants, as touching the principle and doctrine of their having many wives and concubines: Behold! and lo, I am the Lord thy God, and will answer thee as touching this matter: Therefore prepare thy heart to receive and obey the instructions which I am about to give unto you; for all those who have this law revealed unto them must obey the same; for behold! I reveal unto you a new and an everlasting covenant, and if ye abide not that covenant, then are ye damned; for no one can reject this covenant and be permitted to enter into my glory; for all who will have a blessing at my hands shall abide the law which was appointed for that blessing, and the conditions thereof, as was instituted from before the foundations of the world; and as pertaining to the new and everlasting covenant, it was instituted for the fulness of my glory; and he that receiveth a fulness thereof must and shall abide the law, or he shall be damned, saith the Lord God.

" 2. And verily I say unto you that the conditions of this law are these: All covenants, contracts, bonds, obligations, oaths, vows, performances, connections, associations, or expectations that are not made and entered into and sealed by the Holy Spirit of promise, of him who is anointed, both as well for time and for all eternity, and that, too, most holy, by revelation and commandment, through the medium of mine anointed, whom I have appointed on the earth to hold this power (and I have appointed unto my servant Joseph to hold this power in the last days, and there is never but one on the earth at a time on whom this power and the keys of the priesthood are conferred), are of no efficacy, virtue, or force in and after the resurrection from the dead: for all contracts that are not made unto this end have an end when men are dead.

"3. Behold! mine house is a house of order, saith the Lord God, and not a house of confusion. Will I accept of an offering, saith the Lord, that is not made in my name? Or will I receive at your hands that which I have not appointed? And will I appoint unto you, saith the Lord, except it be by law, even as I and my Father ordained unto you before the world was? I am the Lord thy God, and I give unto you this commandment, that no man shall come unto the Father but by me, or by my word, which is my law, saith the Lord; and everything that is in the world, whether it be ordained of men by thrones or principalities or powers, or things of name, whatsoever they may be that are not by me or by my word, saith the Lord, shall be thrown down, and shall not remain after men are dead, neither in nor after the resurrection, saith the Lord your God; for whatsoever things remaineth are by me, and whatsoever things are not by me shall be shaken and destroyed.

"4. Therefore if a man marry him a wife in the world, and he marry her not by me nor by my word, and he covenant with her so long as he is in the world, and she with him, their covenant and marriage is not of force when they are dead, and when they are out of the world; therefore they are not bound by any law when they are out of the world; therefore when they are out of the world they neither marry nor are given in marriage, but are appointed angels in heaven, which angels are ministering servants, to minister for those who are worthy of a far more and an exceeding and an eternal weight of glory; for these angels did not abide my law, therefore they cannot be enlarged, but remain separately and singly, without exaltation, in their saved condition, to all eternity, and from thenceforth are not gods, but are angels of God forever and ever.

"5. And again, verily I say unto you, if a man marry a wife, and make a covenant with her for time and for all eternity, if that covenant is not by me, or by my word, which is my law, and is not sealed by the Holy Spirit of promise, through him whom I have anointed and appointed unto this power, then it is not valid, neither of force, when they are out of the world, because they are not joined by me, saith the Lord, neither by my word; when they are out of the world, it can not be received there, because the angels and the gods are appointed there, by whom they cannot pass: they cannot, therefore, inherit my glory, for my house is a house of order, saith the Lord God.

"6. And again, verily I say unto you, if a man marry a wife by my word, which is my law, and by the new and everlasting covenant, and it is sealed unto them by the Holy Spirit of promise, by him who is anointed, unto whom I have appointed this power and the keys of this priesthood, and it shall be said unto them, Ye shall come forth in the first resurrection; and if it be after the first resurrection, in the next resurrection; and shall inherit thrones, kingdoms, principalities and powers, dominions, all heights and depths, then shall it be written in the Lamb's Book of Life, that he shall commit no murder whereby to shed innocent blood; and if ye abide in my covenant, and commit no murder whereby to shed innocent blood, it shall be done unto them in all things whatsoever my servant hath put upon them, in time and through all eternity, and shall be of full force when they are out of the world; and they shall pass by the angels and the gods which are set there, to their exaltation and glory in all things, as hath been sealed upon their heads, which glory shall be a fulness and a continuation of the seeds forever and ever.

"7. Then shall they be gods, because they have no end; therefore shall they be from everlasting to everlasting, because they continue; then shall they be above all, because all things are subject unto them. Then shall they be gods, because they have all power, and the angels are subject unto them.

"8. Verily, verily I say unto you, except ye abide my law ye cannot attain to this glory; for strait is the gate and narrow the way that leadeth unto the exaltation and continuation of the lives, and few there be that find it, because ye receive me not in the world, neither do ye know me. But if ye receive me in the world, then shall ye know me, and shall receive your exaltation, that where I am ye shall be also. This is eternal life, to know the only wise and true God, and Jesus Christ whom he hath sent. I am he. Receive ye, therefore, my law. Broad is the gate and wide the way that leadeth to the death; and many there are that go in thereat; because they receive me not, neither do they abide in my law.

"9. Verily, verily I say unto you, if a man marry a wife

according to my word, and they are sealed by the Holy Spirit of promise, according to mine appointment, and he or she shall commit any sin or transgression of the new and everlasting covenant whatever, and all manner of blasphemies, and if they commit no murder, wherein they shed innocent blood—yet they shall come forth in the first resurrection and enter into their exaltation; but they shall be destroyed in the flesh, and shall be delivered unto the buffetings of Satan unto the day of redemption, saith the Lord God.

"10. The blasphemy against the Holy Ghost, which shall not be forgiven in the world nor out of the world, is in that ye commit murder, wherein ye shed innocent blood, and assent unto my death after ye have received my new and everlasting covenant, saith the Lord God; and he that abideth not this law can in nowise enter into my glory, but shall be damned, saith the Lord.

"11. I am the Lord thy God, and will give unto thee the law of my holy priesthood, as was ordained by me and my Father before the world was. Abraham received all things, whatsoever he received, by revelation and commandment, by my word, saith the Lord, and hath entered into his exaltation and sitteth upon his throne.

"12. Abraham received promises concerning his seed and of the fruit of his loins—from whose loins ye are, viz. my servant Joseph—which were to continue so long as they were in the world; and as touching Abraham and his seed, out of the world, they should continue; both in the world and out of the world should they continue as innumerable as the stars; or if ye were to count the sand upon the sea-shore, ye could not number them. This promise is yours also, because ye are of Abraham, and the promise was made unto Abraham; and by this law are the continuation of the works of my Father, wherein he glorifieth himself. Go ye, therefore, and do the works of Abraham; enter ye into my law, and ye shall be saved. But if ye enter not into my law, ye cannot receive the promises of my Father which he made unto Abraham.

"13. God commanded Abraham, and Sarah gave Hagar to Abraham to wife. And why did she do it? Because this was the law, and from Hagar sprang many people. This, therefore, was fulfilling, among other things, the promises. Was Abraham, therefore, under condemnation? Verily I say unto you, Nay; for I, the Lord, commanded it. Abraham was commanded to offer his son Isaac; nevertheless it was written, Thou shalt not kill. Abraham, however, did not refuse, and it was accounted unto him for righteousness.

"14. Abraham received concubines, and they bare him children, and it was accounted unto him for righteousness, because they were given unto him for righteousness, because they were given unto him, and he abode in my law: as Isaac, also, and Jacob did none other things than that which they were commanded; and because they did none other things than that which they were commanded, they have entered into their exaltation, according to the promises, and sit upon thrones, and are not angels, but are gods. David also received many wives and concubines, as also Solomon, and Moses my servant, and also many others of my servants, from the beginning of creation until this time; and in nothing did they sin, save in those things which they received not of me.

"15. David's wives and concubines were given unto him of me, by the hand of Nathan my servant, and others of the prophets who had the keys of this power; and in none of these things did he sin against me, save in the case of Uriah and his wife; and therefore he hath fallen from his exaltation and received his portion; and he shall not inherit them out of the world, for I gave them unto another, saith the Lord.

"16. I am the Lord thy God, and I gave unto thee, my servant Joseph, an appointment, and to restore all things; ask what ye will, and it shall be given unto you according to my word; and as ye have asked concerning adultery, verily, verily I say unto you, if a man receiveth a wife in the new and everlasting covenant, and if she be with another man, and I have not appointed unto her by the holy anointing, she hath committed adultery, and shall be destroyed. If she be not in the new and everlasting covenant, and she be with another man, she has committed adultery; and if her husband be with another woman, and he was under a vow, he hath broken his vow, and hath committed adultery; and if she hath not committed adultery, but is innocent, and hath not broken her vow, and she knoweth it, and I reveal it unto you, my servant Joseph, then shall you have power, by the power of my holy priesthood, to take her and give her unto him that hath not committed adultery, but hath been faithful, for he shall be made ruler over many: for I have conferred upon you the keys and power of the priesthood, wherein I restore all things, and make known unto you all things in due time.

"17. And verily, verily I say unto you, that whatsoever you seal on earth shall be sealed in heaven; and whatsoever you bind on earth, in my name and by my word, saith the Lord, it shall be eternally bound in the heavens; and whosoever sins you remit on earth shall be remitted eternally in the heavens; and whosoever sins ye retain on earth shall be retained in heaven.

"18. And again, verily I say, whomsoever you bless I will bless, and whomsoever you curse I will curse, saith the Lord; for I, the Lord, am thy God.

"19. And again, verily I say unto you, my servant Joseph, that whatsoever you give on earth, and to whomsoever you give any one on earth, by my word and according to my law, it shall be visited with blessings, and not cursings, and with my power, saith the Lord, and shall be without condemnation on earth and in heaven; for I am the Lord thy God, and will be with thee even unto the end of the world and through all eternity: for verily I seal upon you your exaltation, and prepare a throne for you in the kingdom of my Father, with Abraham your father. Behold, I have seen your sacrifices, and will forgive all your sins; I have seen your sacrifices in obedience to that which I have told you: go, therefore, and I make a way for your escape, as I accepted the offering of Abraham of his son Isaac.

"20. Verily I say unto you, a commandment I give unto mine handmaid, Emma Smith, your wife, whom I have given unto you, that she stay herself, and partake not of that which I commanded you to offer unto her: for I did it, saith the Lord, to prove you all, as I did Abraham, and that I might require an offering at your hand, by covenant and sacrifice: and let mine handmaid, Emma Smith, receive all those that have been given unto my servant Joseph, and who are virtuous and pure before me; and those who are not pure, and have said they are pure, shall be destroyed, saith the Lord God; for I am the Lord thy God, and ye shall obey my voice: and I give unto my servant Joseph that he shall be made ruler over many things, for he hath been faithful over a few things, and from henceforth I will strengthen him.

"21. And I command mine handmaid, Emma Smith, to abide and cleave unto my servant Joseph, and to none else. But if she will not abide this commandment, she shall be destroyed, saith the Lord; for I am the Lord thy God, and will destroy her if she abide not in my law; but if she will not abide this commandment, then shall my servant Joseph do all things for her, even as he hath said; and I will bless him, and multiply him, and give unto him a hundredfold in this world, of fathers and mothers, brothers and sisters, houses and lands, wives and children, and crowns of eternal lives in the eternal worlds. And again, verily I say, let mine handmaid forgive my servant Joseph his trespasses, and then shall she be forgiven her trespasses wherein she has trespassed against me; and I, the Lord thy God, will bless her and multiply her, and make her heart to rejoice.

"22. And again, I say, let not my servant Joseph put his property out of his hands, lest an enemy come and destroy him, for Satan seeketh to destroy; for I am the Lord thy God, and he is my servant; and behold! and lo, I am with him, as I was with Abraham thy father, even unto his exaltation and glory.

"23. Now, as touching the law of the priesthood, there are many things pertaining thereunto. Verily, if a man be called of my Father, as was Aaron, by mine own voice, and by the voice of him that sent me, and I have endowed him with the keys of the power of this priesthood, if he do anything in my name, and according to my law and by my word, he will not commit sin, and I will justify him. Let no one, therefore, set on my servant Joseph, for I will justify him; for he shall do the sacrifice which I require at his hands for his transgressions, saith the Lord your God.

"24. And again, as pertaining to the law of the priesthood: If any man espouse a virgin, and desire to espouse another, and the first give her consent; and if he espouse the second, and they are virgins, and have vowed to no other man, then he is justified; he cannot commit adultery, for they are given unto him; for he cannot commit adultery with that that belongeth unto him, and to none else: and if he have ten virgins given unto him by this law, he cannot commit adultery, for they belong to him, and they are given unto him: therefore is he justified. But if one or either of the ten virgins, after she is espoused, shall be with another man, she has committed adultery, and shall be destroyed; for they are given unto him to multiply and replenish the earth, according to my commandment, and to fulfil the promise which was given by my Father before the foundation of the world, and for their exaltation in the eternal worlds, that they may bear the souls of men; for herein is the work of my Father continued that he may be glorified.

"25. And again, verily, verily I say unto you, if any man have a wife who holds the keys of this power, and he teaches unto her the law of my priesthood as pertaining to these things, then shall she believe, and administer unto him, or she shall be destroyed, saith the Lord your God; for I will destroy her; for I will magnify my name upon all those who receive and abide in my law. Therefore it shall be lawful in me, if she receive not this law, for him to receive all things whatsoever I, the Lord his God, will give unto him, because she did not believe and administer unto him, according to my word; and she then becomes the transgressor, and he is exempt from the law of Sarah, who administered unto Abraham according to the law, when I commanded Abraham to take Hagar to wife. And now, as pertaining to this law: Verily, ver-

VI.—21

ily I say unto you, I will reveal more unto you hereafter; therefore let this suffice for the present. Behold, I am Alpha and Omega. Amen."

Following the revelation is this explanation:

"Plurality of wives is a doctrine very popular among most of mankind at the present day. It is practiced by the most powerful nations of Asia and Africa, and by numerous nations inhabiting the islands of the sea, and by the aboriginal nations of the great western hemisphere. The one-wife system is confined principally to a few small nations inhabiting Europe, and to those who are of European origin inhabiting America. It is estimated by the most able historians of our day that about four fifths of the population of the globe believe and practice, according to their respective laws, the doctrine of a plurality of wives. If the popularity of a doctrine is in proportion to the numbers who believe in it, then it follows that the *plurality system* is four times more popular among the inhabitants of the earth than the *one-wife* system.

"Those nations who practice the plurality doctrine consider it as virtuous and as right for one man to have many wives as to have one only. Therefore they have enacted laws, not only giving this right to their citizens, but also protecting them in it, and punishing all those who infringe upon the chastity of the marriage covenant by committing adultery with any one of the wives of his neighbor. Those nations do not consider it possible for a man to commit adultery with any one of those women to whom he has been legally married according to their laws. The posterity raised up unto the husband through each of his wives are all considered to be legitimate, and provisions are made in their laws for those children, the same as if they were the children of one wife. Adulteries, fornications, and all unvirtuous conduct between the sexes are severely punished by them. Indeed, plurality among them is considered not only virtuous and right, but a great check or preventative against adulteries and unlawful connections, which are among the greatest evils with which nations are cursed, producing a vast amount of suffering and misery, devastation and death; undermining the very foundations of happiness, and destroying the framework of society and the peace of the domestic circle.

"Some of the nations of Europe who believe in the one-wife system have actually forbidden a plurality of wives by their laws; and the consequences are that the whole country among them is overrun with the most abominable practices; adulteries and unlawful connections prevail through all their villages, towns, cities, and country places to a most fearful extent. And among some of these nations these sinks of wickedness, wretchedness, and misery are licensed by law; while their piety would be wonderfully shocked to authorize by law the plurality system as adopted by many neighboring nations.

"The Constitution and laws of the United States, being founded upon the principles of freedom, do not interfere with marriage relations, but leave the nation free to believe in and practice the doctrine of a plurality of wives, or to confine themselves to the one-wife system, just as they choose. This is as it should be: it leaves the conscience of man untrammelled, and so long as he injures no person, and does not infringe upon the rights of others, he is free by the Constitution to marry one wife or many, or none at all, and becomes accountable to God for the righteousness or unrighteousness of his domestic relations.

"The Constitution leaves the several states and territories to enact such laws as they see proper in regard to marriages, provided that they do not infringe upon the rights of conscience and the liberties guaranteed in that sacred document. Therefore if any state or territory feels disposed to enact laws guaranteeing to each of its citizens the right to marry many wives, such laws would be perfectly constitutional; hence the several states and territories practice the one-wife system out of choice, and not because they are under any obligations so to do by the National Constitution. Indeed, we doubt very much whether any state or territory has the constitutional right to make laws prohibiting the plurality doctrine in cases where it is practiced by religious societies as a matter of conscience or as a doctrine of their religious faith. The first article of the Amendments to the Constitution says expressly that 'Congress shall make no law respecting an establishment of religion, or *prohibiting the free exercise thereof*.' Now if even Congress itself has no power to pass a law 'prohibiting the free exercise of religion,' much less has any state or territory power to pass such an act.

"The doctrine of a plurality of wives was believed and practiced by Abraham, the father of the faithful; and we find that while in this practice the angels of God frequently ministered to him, and at one time dined with him; and God manifested himself to him, and entered into familiar conversation with him. Neither God nor his angels reproved Abraham for being a polygamist, but on the contrary the Almighty greatly blessed him, and made promises unto him concerning both Isaac and Ishmael, clearly showing that Abraham practiced what is called polygamy under the sanction of the Almighty. Now if the father of the faithful was thus blessed, certainly it should not be considered irreligious for the faithful, who are called his children, to walk in the steps of their father Abraham. Indeed, if the Lord himself, through his holy prophets, should give more wives unto his servants, as he gave them unto the prophet David, it would be a great sin for them to refuse that which he gives. In such a case it would become a matter of conscience with them and a part of their religion, and they would be bound to exercise their faith in this doctrine, and practice it, or be condemned; therefore Congress would have no power to prohibit the free exercise of this part of their religion; neither would the states or territories have power, constitutionally, to pass a law 'prohibiting the free exercise thereof.' Now a certain religious society, called Shakers, believe it to be wrong for them to marry even one wife; it certainly would be unconstitutional for either the Congress or the states to pass a law compelling all people to marry at a certain age, because it would infringe upon the rights of conscience among the Shakers, and they would be prohibited the free exercise of their religion.

"From the foregoing revelation, given through Joseph the seer, it will be seen that God has actually commanded some of his servants to take more wives, and has pointed out certain duties in regard to the marriage ceremony, showing that they must be married for time and for all eternity, and showing the advantages to be derived in a future state by this eternal union, and showing still further that if they refused to obey this command, after having the law revealed to them, they should be damned. This revelation, then, makes it a matter of conscience among all the Latter-day Saints; and they embrace it as a part and portion of their religion, and verily believe that they cannot be saved and reject it. Has Congress power, then, to pass laws 'prohibiting' the Church of Jesus Christ of Latter-day Saints '*the free exercise*' of this article of their religion? Have any of the states or territories a constitutional right to pass laws 'prohibiting the free exercise of the religion' which the Church of the Saints conscientiously and sincerely believe to be essential to their salvation? No; they have no such right.

"The Latter-day Saints have the most implicit confidence in all the revelations given through Joseph the Prophet; and they would much sooner lay down their lives and suffer martyrdom than to deny the least revelation that was ever given to him. In one of the revelations through him we read that God raised up wise men and inspired them to write the Constitution of our country, that the freedom of the people might be maintained, according to the free agency which he had given to them; that every man might be accountable to God and not to man, so far as religious doctrines and conscience are concerned. And the more we examine that sacred instrument framed by the wisdom of our illustrious fathers, the more we are compelled to believe that an invincible power controlled, dictated, and guided them in laying the foundation of liberty and freedom upon this great western hemisphere. To this land the Mohammedan, the Hindâ, the Chinese can emigrate, and each bring with him his score of wives and his hundred children, and the glorious Constitution of our country will not interfere with his domestic relations. Under the broad banner of the Constitution, he is protected in all his family associations; none have a right to tear any of his wives or his children from him. So, likewise, under the broad folds of the Constitution, the legislative assembly of the territory of Utah have the right to pass laws regulating their matrimonial relations, and protecting each of their citizens in the right of marrying one or many wives, as the case may be. If Congress should repeal those laws, they could not do so on the ground of their being unconstitutional. And even if Congress should repeal them, there still would be no law in Utah prohibiting the free exercise of that religious right; neither do the citizens of Utah feel disposed to pass such an unconstitutional act which would infringe upon the most sacred rights of conscience.

"Tradition and custom have great influence over nations. Long-established customs, whether right or wrong, become sacred in the estimation of mankind. Those nations who have been accustomed from time immemorial to the practice of what is called polygamy would consider a law abolishing it as the very height of injustice and oppression; the very idea of being limited to the one-wife system would be considered not only oppressive and unjust, but absolutely absurd and ridiculous: it would be considered an innovation upon the long-established usages, customs, and laws of numerous and powerful nations; an innovation of the most dangerous character, calculated to destroy the most sacred rights and privileges of family associations—to upset the very foundations of individual rights, rendered dear and sacred by being handed down to them from the most remote ages of antiquity.

"On the other hand, the European nations who have been for centuries restricted by law to the one-wife theory would consider it a shocking innovation upon the customs of their fathers to abolish their restrictive laws, and to give freedom and liberty, according to the plurality system. It is custom, then, in a great degree, that forms the conscience of nations and individuals in regard to the marriage relationships. Custom causes four fifths of the population of the globe to decide that polygamy, as it is called, is a good and not an evil practice; custom causes the balance, or the remaining fifth, to decide in opposition to the great majority.

"Those individuals who have strength of mind sufficient to divest themselves entirely from the influence of custom, and examine the doctrine of a plurality of wives under the light of reason and revelation, will be forced to the conclusion that it is a doctrine of divine origin; that it was embraced and practiced under the divine sanction by the most righteous men who ever lived on the earth: holy prophets and patriarchs, who were inspired by the Holy Ghost—who were enwrapt in the visions of the Almighty—who conversed with holy angels—who saw God face to face, and talked with him as a man talks with his friend—were 'polygamists,' that is, they had many wives, raised up many children by them, and were never reproved by the Holy Ghost, nor by angels, nor by the Almighty, for believing in and practicing such a doctrine; on the contrary, each one of these 'polygamists' received by revelation promises and blessings for himself, for his wives, and for his numerous children born unto him by his numerous wives. Moreover, the Lord himself gave revelation to different wives belonging to the same man, revealing to them the great blessings which should rest upon their posterity; angels also were sent to comfort and bless them; and in no instance do we find them reproved for having joined themselves in marriage to a 'polygamist.' Indeed, the Lord himself gave laws, not to prohibit 'polygamy,' but showing his will in relation to the children raised up by the different wives of the same man; and, furthermore, the Lord himself actually officiat. ed in giving David all the wives of Saul; this occurred, too, when David already had several wives which he had previously taken: therefore, as the Lord did actually give into David's own bosom all the wives of Saul, he must not only have sanctioned 'polygamy,' but established and instituted it upon a sure foundation by giving the wives himself, the same as he gave Eve to Adam. Therefore those who are completely divested from the influence of national customs, and who judge concerning this matter by the Word of God, are compelled to believe that the plurality of wives was once sanctioned, for many ages, by the Almighty; and by a still further research of the divine oracles, they find no intimations that this divine institution was ever repealed. It was an institution not originated under the law of Moses, but it was of a far more ancient date; and, instead of being abolished by that law, it was sanctioned and perpetuated: and when Christ came to fulfil that law, and to do it away by the introduction of a better covenant, he did not abolish the plurality system: not being originated under that law, it was not made null and void when that law was done away. Indeed, there were many things in connection with the law that were not abolished when the law was fulfilled; as, for instance, the Ten Commandments, which the people under the Gospel covenant were still obliged to obey; and until we can find some law of God abolishing and prohibiting a plurality of wives, we are compelled to believe it a divine institution: and we are, furthermore, compelled to believe that if this institution be entered into now, under the same principles which governed the holy prophets and patriarchs, that God will approbate it now as much as he did then; and that the persons who do thus practice it conscientiously and sincerely are just as honorable in the sight of God as those who have but one wife. And that which is honorable before God should be honorable before men; and no one should be despised when he acts in all good conscience upon any principle of doctrine; neither should there be laws in any of these states or territories to compel any individual to act in violation to the dictates of his own conscience; but every one should be left in all matters of religion to his own choice, and thus become accountable to God, and not to his fellow-man.

"If the people of this country have generally formed different conclusions from us upon this subject, and if they have embraced religions which are more congenial to their minds than the religion of the Saints, we say to them that they are welcome to their own religious views; the laws should not interfere with the exercise of their religious rights. If we cannot convince you by reason nor by the Word of God that your religion is wrong, we will not persecute you, but will sustain you in the privileges guaranteed in the great charter of American liberty: we ask from you the same generosity—protect us in the exercise of our religious rights—convince us of our errors of doctrine, if we have any, by reason, by logical arguments, or by the Word of God, and we will be ever grateful for the information, and you will ever have the pleasing reflection that you have been the instruments in the hands of God of redeeming your fellow-beings from the darkness which you may see enveloping their minds. Come, then, let us reason together, and try to discover the true light upon all subjects connected with our temporal or eternal happiness; and if we disagree in our judgments, let us impute it to the weakness and imperfections of our fallen natures, and let us pity each other, and endeavor with patience and meekness to reclaim from error, and save the immortal soul from an endless death."

This document was not officially promulgated at Salt Lake City until August 29, 1852 (Rémy, ii, 112-130), when it was given to a great conference, to be thereafter as a possession unto all the Saints (Stenhouse, p. 182 sq.). The Prophet's widow at once denounced it as a forgery, and with four of her sons declaimed against it as gravely unjust to the memory of their husband and father. There seems to be, however, no ground for this protest. Mormons who knew Smith and afterwards apostatized, as well as more recent apostate Saints, insist, after a most searching inquiry, that Smith must have been the author, or the supposed "seer," of this "revelation." Says Stenhouse: "The sons of the Prophet have been very restive under the imputation of polygamous practices being attributed to their father. They have labored indefatigably in decrying polygamy, and have devoted a large share of their time, talent, ink, and paper in hostility to it, as they evidently believe it is both a great error and a great sin. But as the facts of Joseph's marital relations with 'sisters' who claim to be his 'wives,' in the Mormon sense, are overwhelming, the sons, in denying their sire's polygamy, are driven to the alternative of silently allowing the inevitable charge of practical 'free love,' 'adultery,' or whatever others may choose to call it. At the present time there are probably about a dozen 'sisters' in Utah who proudly acknowledge themselves to be the 'wives of Joseph,' and how many others there may have been who held that relationship 'no man knoweth.' . . . Mrs. Emma Smith may feel justified in denying that her husband was a polygamist; for she may neither assent to the use of the term nor acknowledge the principle. But there is to the author's mind the most satisfactory evidence that Joseph Smith had 'sealed' to him a large number of women some time before his death, many of whom have stated to the author that they were 'the wives of Joseph Smith;' that 'Mrs. Emma Smith was aware of the fact,' and that it was the trouble growing out of the discovery of such relationship that called forth the revelation" (p. 185-188). We have not room here to quote further from the writings and sayings of the Saints on the subject of "pluralism." In the article on POLYGAMY the Mormon position will be carefully considered. Suffice it to say here that the practice of pluralism is now carried to great lengths among the Saints, their leading men having from fifteen to forty wives each. Mr. Young is known to have nineteen "real, living wives." "How many spiritual wives he has had," says Mrs. Stenhouse (*Tell it All*), "it would be impossible to say. Probably he himself does not know their number. Lately, I believe, he has been making his will, and, if so, I suppose he has 'taken count of all.' He has besides in various parts of Utah many other wives, who are all more or less provided for; but they are of little account, and he seldom or never sees them. The nineteen whom I have named form his family at home, as I may say— are all under his own roof, or, at least, they live in Salt Lake City, and are known to every one of his wives" (p. 290). The universal testimony of all travellers is that if the effect of polygamy has not been to corrupt the morals and deteriorate the character of the people, it has certainly degraded their physical condition. It is believed that the women submit to a yoke which they abhor because they see no escape, or that they bend to it from a mistaken sense of duty. The wives generally live apart, in some instances in separate houses. The first wife is practically recognised as the head, though not always the favorite of the husband.

We quote from Mr. Bowles's pages, who epitomizes in a paragraph the common testimony of all observers against the polygamous practices of the Mormons of Utah: "It is a dreadful state of society to any of fine feelings and true instincts; it robs married life of all its sweet sentiment and companionship; and while it degrades woman, it brutalizes man, teaching him to despise and domineer over his wives, over all women. It breeds jealousy, distrust, and tempts to infidelity; but

the police system of the Church and the community is so strict and constant that it is claimed and believed the latter vice is very rare. As I have said, we had little direct communication with the women of the Saints, but their testimony came to us in a hundred ways—sad, tragic, heart-rending. One woman, an educated, handsome person, as yet a single wife, said, with bated breath and almost hissing fury, to one of our party in some aside discussion of the subject, 'Polygamy is tolerable enough for the men, but it is hell for the women!'" Even stronger and more heart-rending is the testimony of Mr. and Mrs. Stenhouse. The latter's book, *Tell it All* (Hartford, Conn., 1875, 12mo, pp. 623), gives the story of a woman's life experience in Mormondom in such detail that it really constitutes the fullest review of pluralistic life. Her husband's work is, however, more valuable to the inquirer, as it is written more impartially and considerately. And his picture of pluralism has enough to sadden the most cold-hearted. Says he: "To assert that any true woman living in polygamy is in heart and soul satisfied and happy, is to simply libel her nature. . . . The women are, however, not alone the sufferers by polygamy. The intelligent of the fair sex among the Mormons will readily admit this, and some even go so far as to pity their husbands, and to extend to them the genuine sympathy of their hearts, though polygamy has been their own curse. Whatever else it has achieved, polygamy has at least been impartial with the sexes, and while it has martyred the woman, it has not failed to enslave the man. . . . No man ever regained his senses after the act of sealing without feeling that he had fatally wounded the wife of his youth. It is a cruelty that he realizes as well as his wife, and he, the nominal but innocent cause of her wrong, seeks to assuage her sufferings by greater kindness and tenderness. But no smooth words, nor the soul-speaking affection of his eye, can heal the wound. It steals her life away, and in her true heart she curses the day she ever heard of Mormonism. For the man who realizes and shares the misery of his wife, the future life is but 'a living lie.' Were the man an angel, it would be impossible for him to act justly towards two or twenty wives, and divide to each the full measure of her rights. . . . Polygamy may be the marital relation of the sexes in heaven; it may be the 'celestial law' of the gods —of that there is no discussion or dreaming; but one thing is certain, that it is not the true marital relation of the sexes upon the earth, and thirty years of its practice under the most favorable circumstances have stamped it as a withering curse" (p. 584–588).

Pluralism, then, which has thus far failed to gain the hearty support of the more intelligent Mormons, if we may accept Mr. Stenhouse's statement, and there seems to be no reason to gainsay that it has, reacted against the Church of the Latter-day Saints, not only socially, but also numerically; for since the promulgation of this tenet many of its converts have quitted them, and their progress has been stayed in a great measure. Says Mr. Stenhouse: "On the 1st of January, 1853, it was published in the *Star*. It fell like a thunder-bolt upon the Saints, and fearfully shattered the mission. The British elders, who in their ignorance had been denying polygamy, and stigmatizing their opponents as calumniators, up to the very day of its publication, were confounded and paralyzed, and *from that time to the present the avenues of preaching have closed one after another, and the mission that was once the glory of the Mormon Church has withered and shrivelled into comparative insignificance.* The outside world misjudges the Mormon people when it imagines that polygamy was ever a favorite doctrine. Doubtless to some few it was a pleasant revelation; but it was not so to the mass of the people, for they resisted it until they were compelled to yield their opposition, or else abandon the Church in which they had faith. The statistical reports of the mission in the British Islands (June 30, 1853) show that the enormous number of 1776 persons were excommunicated there during the first six months of the preaching of polygamy. The entire Church then numbered, men, women, and children over eight years of age, 30,690. There were forty 'seventies' and eight 'high-priests' [see § V, below, for explanation of these terms] from Utah in Britain at that time, carrying with them a powerful personal influence to help the Saints to tide over the introduction of this doctrine. These Utah missionaries were aided by a native priesthood of 2578 elders, 1854 priests, 1416 teachers, 834 deacons; and yet no less than 1776 recusants were excommunicated. That tells its own tale. That all these persons withdrew from the fellowship of the Mormon Church on account of polygamy would be an unfair inference. Still, doubtless polygamy was the great contributing cause of apostasy then, and more persons have left the Mormon communion on account of polygamy and Brigham's favorite deity, Adam (which he first preached in October of the same year), than all else put together. Few of the Mormon women have ever accepted polygamy from the assent of their judgments. They have first been led by their teachers to consider the doctrine true, and afterwards have been afraid to question it. Their fears have counselled submission. ... Brigham Young, with all the commanding influence of his position, could not silence the murmuring within his own domicile until he threatened to divorce all his wives, and told them that, if they despised the order of heaven, he would pray that the curse of the Almighty might be close to their heels, and follow them all the day long (*Sermon*, July 14, 1855, in the Bowery, Provo), and even all that violent language has not attained the end; their hearts revolt as much to-day, though they have schooled themselves into submission and silence" (p. 201, 202, 588).

We append the preparations and the wedding ceremony for a marriage in "pluralism" as sketched by the apostle Pratt:

"When the day set apart for the solemnization of the marriage ceremony has arrived, the bridegroom and his wife, and also the bride, together with their relatives and such other guests as may be invited, assemble at the place which they have appointed. The scribe then proceeds to take the names, ages, native towns, counties, states, and countries of the parties to be married, which he carefully enters on record. The president, who is the prophet, seer, and revelator over the whole Church throughout the world, and who alone holds the 'keys' of authority in this solemn ordinance (as recorded in the 2d and 5th paragraphs of the Revelation on Marriage), calls upon the bridegroom and his wife and the bride to arise, which they do, fronting the president. The wife stands on the left hand of her husband, while the bride stands on her left. The president then puts this question to the wife:
" 'Are you willing to give this woman to your husband to be his lawful and wedded wife for time and for all eternity? If you are, you will manifest it by placing her right hand within the right hand of your husband.'
"The right hands of the bridegroom and bride being thus joined, the wife takes her husband by the left arm, as if in the attitude of walking: the president then proceeds to ask the following question of the man:
" 'Do you, brother' (*calling him by name*), 'take sister' (*calling the bride by her name*) 'by the right hand, to receive her unto yourself, to be your lawful and wedded wife, and you to be her lawful and wedded husband, for time and for all eternity, with a covenant and promise on your part that you will fulfil all the laws, rites, and ordinances pertaining to this holy matrimony in the new and everlasting covenant, doing this in the presence of God, angels, and these witnesses, of your own free-will and choice?'
"The bridegroom answers, 'Yes.' The president then puts the question to the bride:
" 'Do you, sister' (*calling her by name*), 'take brother' (*calling him by name*) 'by the right hand, and give yourself to him to be his lawful and wedded wife for time and for all eternity, with a covenant and promise on your part that you will fulfil all the laws, rites, and ordinances pertaining to this holy matrimony in the new and everlasting covenant, doing this in the presence of God, angels, and these witnesses, of your own free-will and choice?'
"The bride answers, 'Yes.' The president then says:
" 'In the name of the Lord Jesus Christ, and by the authority of the holy priesthood, I pronounce you legally and lawfully husband and wife for time and for all eternity; and I seal upon you the blessings of the holy resur-

rection, with power to come forth in the morning of the first resurrection, clothed with glory, immortality, and eternal lives; and I seal upon you the blessings of thrones, and dominions, and principalities, and powers, and exaltations, together with the blessings of Abraham, Isaac, and Jacob; and say unto you, Be fruitful and multiply and replenish the earth, that you may have joy and rejoicing in your posterity in the day of the Lord Jesus. All these blessings, together with all other blessings pertaining to the new and everlasting covenant, I seal upon your heads, through your faithfulness unto the end, by the authority of the holy priesthood, in the name of the Father, and of the Son, and of the Holy Ghost. Amen.'
"The scribe then enters on the general record the date and place of the marriage, together with the names of two or three witnesses who were present" (*The Seer*, p. 32).

"The reader will observe that, in this ordinance of polygamic sealing, the husband and the young bride are each asked the question, are you 'doing this in the presence of God, angels, and these witnesses, *of your own free-will and choice*,' while the question put to *the wife* carefully avoids the issue that would instantly arise between her wounded, bleeding heart and the falsehood that would be forced from her trembling lips if she essayed to utter that it was of her 'own free-will and choice.' That poor 'victim' is but asked if she has been subdued and is 'willing to give this woman' to her husband" (Stenhouse, p. 587). It should be added that the Mormon president possesses the papal prerogative of annulling all marriages contracted under his sanction (Mrs. Stenhouse, p. 554 sq.); a prerogative which cannot fail to prove a source of wealth and power. As to marriages celebrated without his authority, they are *ipso facto* void, *in foro conscientiæ*. Consequently either man or woman is at liberty to desert an unbelieving spouse and take another. Marriage, it may be stated here also, is allowed within near degrees; a man may marry two sisters, a niece, and mother and daughter, and even a half-sister.

3. *Other Practices.*—There appears to be no prescribed ritual for the burying of the dead, and there is but little of the true devotional element in any of the religious exercises of the Mormons. Their ordinary worship consists of prayers, with addresses, often of a very homely character, and hymns. The duties of private prayer, meditation, communion with God, self-examination, are seldom or never spoken of. "Every household," says Stenhouse, "is instructed to have morning and evening prayers. The father gathers his children around him, and all kneeling, he prays for revelation, the gifts of the Spirit for himself and family; then in turn comes every order of priesthood. 'Bless Brigham Young, bless him; may the heavens be opened unto him, angels visit and instruct him; clothe him with power to defend thy people, and to overthrow all who rise up against him; bless him in his basket and in his store, multiply and increase him in wives, children, flocks and herds, houses and lands—make him very great,' etc. After Brigham has been properly remembered, then come his councillors, the apostles, the high-priests, the seventies, the elders, the priests, the teachers, the deacons, and the Church universal. Another divergence is made in remembrance of the president of the Conference, and the president of that particular 'branch' where the family resides, and every officer in it. All are prayed for—if the father does his duty. The power and the greatness of the 'kingdom' that is to roll on till it fills the whole earth, and subjugates all earthly and corrupt man-made governments, are specially urgent. All nations are to weaken and crumble to pieces, and Zion is to go forth in her strength, conquering and to conquer, till the priesthood shall . . . 'reign and rule and triumph, and God shall be our king'" (p. 557, 558). Very gross irreverence is often shown during public worship. There is in their chief town, Salt Lake City, an immense tabernacle, where their religious services are held, and where one or more of their prophets preach to them every Sabbath. "The gatherings and services," says Mr. Bowles, describing a service which he attended (*Our New West*, p. 243), "both in speaking and singing, reminded me of

the Methodist camp-meetings of fifteen or twenty years ago. The singing, as on the latter occasions, was the best part of the exercises—simple, sweet, and fervent. 'Daughter of Zion,' as sung by the large choir one Sunday morning, was prayer, sermon, song, and all. The preacher that day was apostle Richards; but beyond setting forth the superiority of the Mormon Church system, through its presidents, councils, bishops, elders, and seventies, for the work made incumbent upon Christians, and claiming that its preachers were inspired like those of old, his discourse was a rambling, unimpressive exhortation. . . . The rite of the sacrament [of the Lord's Supper] is administered every Sunday, water being used instead of wine, and the distribution proceeds among the whole congregation, men, women, and children, numbering from three to five thousand, while the singing and the preaching are in progress. The prayers are few and simple, undistinguishable, except in these characteristics, from those heard in all Protestant churches, and the congregation all join in the Amen." (Comp. *Qu. Rev.* cxxii, 486–488; Ollivant, p. 54, and Appendix A, p. 119, 147; Rae, p. 106 sq.) When the Temple is completed, it is intended, as the founder ordered, to establish sacrifices and every ordinance belonging to the priesthood as they existed prior to Moses's day (*Compend.* p. 177). There are also some secret ceremonies, of which very different accounts have been given. The most important of these are the "mysteries of the *Endowment*

House," where the marriage ceremony is performed. Stenhouse tells us that "within its portals are performed all the rites and ceremonies that hold Mormonism together," but he reveals nothing, probably because he is bound by oaths to terrestrial secrecy. He indicates, however, that the importance of these secrets has been overestimated. Mrs. Stenhouse gives a detailed description of her own experience in the Endowment House, and it confirms the statement of an intelligent gentleman who, when interrogated shortly after passing through the house by one who had been there—"I went in expecting everything; I came out with nothing." (Those desiring full details may consult Mrs. Stenhouse, *Tell it All*, ch. xxv.)

V. *Hierarchical Organization.*—Mormonism is a pure theocracy; its priesthood, who rule in matters temporal and ecclesiastical, make up about one fifth of the male members. They are recognised because of the declaration made by prophet Smith as "the channel through which the Almighty commenced revealing his glory at the beginning of the creation of this earth, and through which he has continued to reveal himself to the children of men to the present time, and through which he will make known his purposes to the end of time" (*Compend.* p. 176). They are divided into various orders. The highest is the *First Presidency*, composed of three, harmonious in representation upon the earth with "the Father, the Son, and the Holy Ghost" in heaven, and the successors of Peter, James, and John in

Design of Salt Lake Temple.—[From Stenhouse.]

the Gospel Church. Of these, the first is *primus inter pares.* He is elected by the whole body of the Church, and possesses supreme authority. "Throughout all Mormondom," says Stenhouse, "the highest rank of the priesthood is sacred, and all councillors are but aids. The theory is that a president is nearer to 'the throne' than his councillors, and though the latter may speak and diffuse their measure of light, at the moment the president is ready to decide what should be done, the Lord will give him direction" (p. 560). The second office in point of dignity is that of *Patriarch,* whose sole duty is to administer blessings. He is appointed by the Church for life. Then follows the council of "The Twelve," whose functions are of great practical importance. They ordain all other officers, elders, priests, teachers, and deacons; they baptize, administer the sacraments, and take the lead in all meetings. Next come the *Seventies* (of whom there are many). They are under the direction of the "Twelve Apostles," and are the great propagandists, missionaries, and preachers of the body. The fifth order is that of *High-priests,* composed usually of men advanced in years. Their duty is to officiate in all the offices of the Church when there are no higher officers present. After these come the *Bishops,* who are "overseers" of the Church chiefly in secular matters, attending to the registration of births, marriages, and deaths, the support of "literary concerns" (such as newspapers and magazines, house-visiting, and the settlement of private grievances. The duties of the *Elders* are not very precise; they are charged with the conduct of meetings, and exercise a general surveillance over the *Priests,* who correspond to the "fixed ministry" of other sects; i. e. they preach, exhort, and expound the Scriptures. The lowest orders are the *Teachers* and *Deacons;* the former are simply assistants to the priests, elders, and bishops, and act as catechists; the latter are Church-collectors, treasurers, etc. The whole priesthood is divided into two classes, the Melchizedek and the Aaronic. To the first belong the offices of apostle, seventy, patriarch, high-priest, and elder; to the second, those of bishop, priest, teacher, and deacon. The latter can be held only by "literal descendants of Aaron," who are pointed out by special revelation. Besides these office-bearers, there is also the Standing High Council, to settle difficulties among believers. This consists of eighteen (at first twelve) high-priests, appointed by ballot, with one or three presidents, being the first president alone, or with his assessors. After the evidence has been heard, and the accusers, accused, and a certain number of councillors, from two to six, according to the gravity of the case, have spoken, the president gives his decision, and calls on the other members to sanction it. Sometimes a case is re-heard; in special difficulties recourse is had to revelation. Every "stake" and separate church is governed by its own "High Council," with a similar constitution and procedure, and with an appeal to the Supreme High Council. General affairs are managed by Conferences, held April 6 in each year. At these, which sometimes last several days, the first presidency and other office-bearers are sustained in office by vote, always unanimous, of the meetings; vacancies are filled, reports on various subjects are read, prayers are offered, addresses delivered, hymns and anthems sung, etc. (see *Mill. Star,* passim; Burton, p. 367 sq.; *Qu. Rev.* cxxii, 488). "This great net-work of priesthood, which covers everything, and the influence of which permeates everything," says Stenhouse, "is the key to the power of their president over the Saints in Zion. Through the priesthood he can sway them at his will. . . . As seen in all the Conference minutes, the people are, by their own free voting, made responsible for everything that is done, and when once they have [as they are obliged to do by fear of persecution or excommunication], by uplifted hand before heaven, expressed their wish, it becomes their duty and obligation to sustain it" (p. 566). In theory, the Mormons recognise the right of private judgment; in fact, the attempt to exercise that right has always been hazardous. The whole duty of a Mormon consists in thinking and doing as he is told, even as regards his most private and personal affairs. The president may order or forbid a man to marry; a bishop may at any time enter any Mormon's house, and issue what orders he pleases. All Saints are compelled to deal only at the authorized shops and stores, which are managed on the co-operative principle for the benefit of the Church. By means of a constant system of espion-

Mormon Coin.

age any breach of rules is promptly noticed, and if it be persisted in the offender is cut off from the Church. Persons are even excommunicated without any reason assigned, and, on complaining, are told that their crime will in due time come to light; it being held that if any man fails in obedience to the priesthood in any respect he must have committed some great crime, whereby he has lost the Spirit of God (Ollivant, p. 86, 87). Indeed, all the arrangements at Utah are admirably suited to maintain obedience. Every means are adopted to prevent any but the chief men from accumulating money; so that while a man can live from hand to mouth in some comfort, he cannot save anything. The majority, therefore, are virtually dependants in Utah (Ollivant, p. 47, 101). If any man secedes, or is cast out, all Mormons are forbidden to have any intercourse with him, even to give him food or shelter; and sometimes violence, even to death, has been used. All "Gentiles" are suspected, and every means are used to keep them away (see Rae, p. 118–120; *Fraser's Mag.* June, 1871, p. 692).

VI. *Propagandism, etc.*—Missions are a great feature of Mormonism. Any member of the priesthood is liable to be sent, at the will of the president on a sudden impulse, at short notice to "preach the gospel to the Gentiles." "Joseph Smith, the prophet," says Pres. George A. Smith, "enjoined upon the twelve apostles that they should preach the gospel to all the nations of the earth, and wherever they could not go to send the same, that all nations might be faithfully warned of the restoration of the everlasting gospel in all its purity and fulness for the salvation of mankind, and the near advent of the Messiah, preparatory to the introduction of his reign of righteousness upon the earth" (*Ans. to Questions,* p. 30). The zeal and activity of these emissaries, though it has been much exaggerated, is still remarkable. The Mormon presidents are good judges of character, and it seems to be their plan to select the restless and enterprising spirits, who, perhaps, may threaten disturbance at home, and to utilize their fanaticism, while they flatter their vanity, by sending them as representatives of the Church to distant fields of labor. "From the youth in his teens," says Stenhouse, "to the elder in hoary age, all the brethren are subject to be 'called on mission' at any time, and in such calls no personal conveniences are ever consulted. Should a merchant be wanted for a 'mission,' his business must be left in other hands, and his affairs be conducted by other brains; so with the artisan, the mechanic, the farmer, and the ploughboy—they must in their way do the best they can. Seed-time or harvest, summer or winter, pleasure or important work—nothing in which they are engaged is allowed to stand in the way. If poor, and the family is dependent upon the outgoing missionary, that must be no hinderance—the mission is given, he has to go, and the family 'trusts in the Lord,' and in the tender mercies of the bishop!" (p. 568). Their method of establishing a mission in a foreign country is as follows.

Among their converts, taken at random from the mixed population of the Union, there are natives to be found of every nation in Europe. They select a native of the country they wish to attack, and join him as interpreter to the other emissaries whom they are about to despatch to the land of his birth. On arriving at their destination, the missionaries are supported by the funds of the Church till they can maintain themselves out of the offerings of their proselytes. Meanwhile they employ themselves in learning the language and circulating tracts in defence of their creed, and then sit down to the weary task of translating the *Book of Mormon.* By this process they have formed churches in Great Britain, France, Denmark, Sweden, Norway, Iceland, Germany, Palestine, the Pacific Isles, Italy, Switzerland, Malta, Gibraltar, South Africa, Australia, and the Sandwich Islands; and, besides these, they have also sent missionaries to Siam, Ceylon, China, Hindostan, the West Indies, Guiana, and Chili. The *Book of Mormon* has been published in French, German, Italian, Danish, Polynesian, and Welsh. Besides various tracts which are circulated by these missionaries, they have established regular periodicals in English, German, French, Welsh, and Danish. We should observe, however, that of the missions above enumerated, those to Great Britain, the Icelandic countries, and the Sandwich Islands have alone been really successful. In England they preached first in the summer of 1837, and at their April Conference in 1841 there was represented a total of 5184 persons baptized. Of these, 106 were ordained elders, 303 priests, 169 teachers, and 63 deacons. Besides these, 800 souls had emigrated to "build up Zion at Nauvoo." In Denmark, at the beginning of 1853, they possessed 1400 baptized converts, and had also despatched 297 more to Utah. In the Sandwich Islands they baptized thousands before their mission had been established twenty months. These proselytes were all previously Christians, converted from heathenism. The other foreign missions have as yet only succeeded in making a very small number of proselytes. In Great Britain, as we have seen above, the promulgation of the doctrine of "pluralism" has seriously checked the progress of Mormonism. Of the converts made from 1840 to 1854 in the different missions, 17,195 emigrated to this country to "strengthen Zion." Up to 1860 about 30,000 Mormons had come, and from that time to the present there have probably been 25,000 more, making a contribution to America of a round 55,000 souls. And yet these figures do not even distantly convey the spread of Mormonism in Europe. The very sons of the apostles and prophets testify, on their return to Utah from European missions, that "they never knew what Mormonism was . . . till they went abroad to preach. . . . It is especially the British mission, with latterly the Scandinavian, that has built up Utah" (Stenhouse, p. 11). The Mormons, the world over, are estimated at no less than 300,000 souls, 125,000 of whom live in Utah Territory.

Several schisms have taken place, but they have thus far but very inconsiderably affected "the Church of the Latter-day Saints." The first departure from the main body was occasioned in 1852 by the widow and sons of the founder of Mormonism on the publication of the revelation authorizing polygamy, the genuineness of which they denied. They bear the title of "The Reorganized Church of Jesus Christ of Latter-day Saints," and have their head-quarters at Nauvoo. Their chief feature is the rejection of "pluralism," and all that gathers about that practice. Neither do they approve of the political schemes of Brigham Young and the leaders of the Church in Utah. Joseph Smith, the son of the Prophet, is regarded by them as the *true* living head of the Church, and under his direction they have established themselves in the place pointed out by their founder as the site of the "New Zion." Their number, which is inconsiderable, will probably be largely increased soon, if polygamy is not abandoned in Utah.

"Young Joseph" is peculiarly "favored" with "visions," and "visits of angels," and "gifts of tongues," "interpretations," and "powers of healing;" and these worshippers "cast out" all the devils that come in their way. Some of their elders and prophets have been in Utah, and there "added numbers to the New Church, and shook the faith of many more in Brigham" (Stenhouse, p. 629). Another branch of the Church has recently established itself at Independence, Mo., they regarding this place as the supposed site of the New Jerusalem. But this branch only counts an insignificant membership. The most powerful opposition to Mormonism came out of its own midst in the beginning of 1869, when a large number of influential Saints quitted the main body, and formed themselves into an independent organization in Utah, and right in Salt Lake City itself. They first assumed the name of "Church of Zion," and have been holding religious services in a hall built by Young for his own disciples, beginning Dec. 19, 1869. "Of all the apostasies from the Mormon Church," says Stenhouse, "this was the most formidable, and has done more damage to the position of Brigham Young than all of them put together. The preaching of the 'reformers' [as they were called] first shook the people's confidence in the Prophet; and, as they travelled further, it has led many of them out of Mormonism altogether" (p. 643; comp. p. 630 sq.). The leading "reformers," who were originally distinguished as advocates of freedom of thought and action, as opposed to the despotism of the priesthood, have since become zealous propagators of spiritualistic views; but, as they are all of a superior class, they have had liberality enough not to seek to carry their companions with them, and, while the movement has been subject to more or less change since it first started, there still remains enough to characterize it as the beginning of a "liberal" Christian Church. The Church institute which they have erected, first christened "Church of Zion," has been changed to "The Liberal Institute," and there lecturers, male and female, of every shade of opinion in religion, politics, or science, can speak for the edification of Saint and sinner. "The Liberal Institute," says Stenhouse, "is the Faneuil Hall of Utah, and from its platform will go forth facts of history and science that will work in a few years a grander revolution among the Saints than would the presence of ten thousand troops, or any other movement that could possibly be construed into 'persecution.'"

VII. *Literature.*—The publications of the Saints are very numerous. A pretty full account of their work in this direction is furnished by Mr. Stenhouse in an Appendix (ii) to his work, p. 741 sq. Mr. Burton has also compiled a list, and both these should be consulted by any seeking detailed information regarding Mormonism. See, however, especially, *A Compendium of the Faith and Doctrines of the Church of Jesus Christ of Latter-day Saints* (1857); *Letters exhibiting the most prominent Doctrines of the Church,* etc., by Elder Orson Spencer (5th ed. 1866); *Sacred Hymns and Spiritual Songs for the Church,* etc. (12th ed. 1863); *Tracts,* chiefly those by Orson Pratt; *The Millennial Star,* a periodical published for a while at Liverpool (15 vols. up to 1853); *The Evening and Morning Star,* edited by W. W. Phelps (1832, 1833); *Times and Seasons,* founded and published at Nauvoo (1843 sq.); *The Seer,* edited by Orson Pratt, and published at Washington; *Deseret News,* published at Salt Lake City, being the official paper of Mormondom; *Voice of Warning to all Nations,* by Parly P. Pratt; Bennet, *Mormonism Exposed* (Boston, 1842); Kane, *The Mormons* (1850); Mackay, *The Mormons* (4th ed. Lond. 1851); Chandlers, *A Visit to Salt Lake;* Burton, *City of the Saints; an Expedition to the Valley of the Great Salt Lake of Utah, etc., with an authentic Account of the Mormon Settlement,* etc., by Howard Stansbury, of the U. S. A. (Phila. 1852); Lieut. Gunnison, *History of the Mormons* (Phila. 1852); Ferris, *Utah and the Mormons*—unfavorable to the Saints, but full of valuable information (N. Y. 1854); Hyde, *Mormonism, its Leaders and Designs* (N. Y. 1857), an exposé by a former Mormon elder; Tucker, *Origin, Rise, and Progress of Mormonism* (N. Y. 1867); and the latest and best, Stenhouse, *The Rocky Mountain Saints* (N. Y. 1873), whose book we have had occasion to refer to so frequently. See also travels like Rémy's *Journey to Great Salt Lake City*, Dixon's *New America*, Rae's *Westward by Rail*, and Ollivant's *Breeze from the Great Salt Lake*. Among periodical articles, see *Revue des deux Mondes*, Sept. 1853, Feb. 1856, Sept. 1859, April, 1861; *Edinb. Rev.* of 1854, p. 185 sq.; *Quart. Rev.* April, 1867; *Fraser's Mag.* vols. iii and iv, new series, June and July, 1871; *Good Words*, June, 1866; *Blackwood's Mag.* 1867; *Brit. Qu. Rev.* Jan. 1862; *London Rev.* March, 1854, art. iv; July, 1862, art. iii; *North British Rev.* Aug. 1863, vol. viii; *Princeton Rev.* Jan. 1862, art. ii; *Christian Examiner*, Jan. to May, 1858; *Littell's Living Age*, 1852, 1854, and 1856. See *Additional Note* on p. 991 of this vol.

Mornay, PHILIP DUPLESSIS DE. See DU PLESSIS.

Morning (properly בֹּקֶר, *bôker*, Gen. i, 5; πρωΐα, Matt. xxi, 18), the early part of the day, after sunrise. The break of day, שַׁחַר, *sháchar*, was at one period of the Jewish polity divided into two parts, in imitation of the Persians; the first of which began when the eastern, the second when the western division of the horizon was illuminated. The authors of the Jerusalem Talmud divided it into four parts, the first of which was called in Hebrew אַיֶּלֶת הַשַּׁחַר, *aijeleth ha-shachar*, or "the dawn of day," which is the title of Psalm xxii. The Hebrews, like most simple people, were accustomed to early rising (הַשְׁכִּים, Gen. xix, 27, etc.), as is still the Oriental custom (Hackett, *Illustrations of Scripture*, p. 115 sq.). See AFTERNOON; DAY; HOUR.

Morning Lecture. See LECTURE.

Morning Sacrifice. See DAILY OFFERING.

Morning Service, it would appear from the Apostolic Constitutions, was regularly performed in the early Christian Church. The order observed was as follows: "It began with the sixty-third psalm (according to our arrangement), 'O God, thou art my God; early will I seek thee.' After this followed the prayers for the several orders of catechumens, energumens, candidates for baptism, and penitents. When these were sent away, there followed the prayers which on the Lord's-day began the communion service. After the prayer for the whole state of the Church was ended, the deacon exhorted the people to pray, thus: 'Let us beg of God his mercies and compassions, that this morning and this day, and all the time of our pilgrimage, may be passed by us in peace and without sin; let us beg of God that he would send us the angel of peace, and give us a Christian end, and be gracious and merciful unto us. Let us commend ourselves, and one another, to the living God, by his only-begotten Son.' Immediately after this common prayer of the deacon and people together, the bishop offered 'the morning thanksgiving,' in the following words: 'O God, the God of spirits and of all flesh, with whom no one can compare, and who art above all need, that givest the sun to govern the day, and the moon and the stars to govern the night, look down now upon us with the eyes of thy favor, and receive our morning thanksgivings, and have mercy upon us. For we have not spread forth our hands to any strange god. We have not chosen unto ourselves any new god among us, but thou, the eternal and immortal God: O God, who hast given to us our being through Christ, and our well-being through him also, vouchsafe by him to make us worthy of everlasting life, with whom unto thee be glory, honor, and adoration, in the Holy Ghost, world without end. Amen.' After this the deacon bade them bow their heads, and receive the bishop's benediction in the following form: 'O God, faithful and true, that showest mercy to thou-

sands and ten thousands of them that love thee; who art the friend of the humble and defender of the poor; whose aid all stand in need of, since all things serve thee; look down upon this thy people, who bow their heads unto thee, and bless with thy spiritual benediction; keep them as the apple of an eye; preserve them in piety and righteousness, and make them worthy of everlasting life, through Jesus Christ thy beloved Son, with whom with thee be glory, honor, and adoration, in the Holy Ghost, now and forever, world without end. Amen.' The deacon then dismissed the congregation with the usual form—'Depart in peace.'"

Morocco (or MAROCCO), called by the natives *Maghreb-el-Aksa*, i. e. "the extreme west," an empire or sultanate in the north-west of Africa, is bounded on the E. by Algeria, on the N. and W. by the Mediterranean Sea and Atlantic Ocean, and on the S. by a line which runs from Cape Nun (Lat. 28° 45' 43" N.) in an easterly direction through the Sahara to the Algerian frontier, in long. 2° E. It includes at the present day the former kingdoms of Maghrib, Fez, and Tafilelet, covering 190,560 English square miles, with a population of about 6,000,000, according to Behm (*Geographisches Jahrbuch*, 1866).

The *inhabitants*, like those of Barbary (the entire country of North Africa, from Egypt to the Atlantic Ocean, and from the Mediterranean to the Greater Atlas) in general, consist of Moors, Berbers, Arabs, Negroes, and Jews, with various intermixtures between these races. The Arabians, who have kept their identity notwithstanding the long period of time they have dwelt in the country, are mostly given to cultivation of the land; indeed, they are about the only agriculturists of the country. They dwell mainly in the valleys. The Moors (q. v.) are the most numerous in the cities, and are the dominant race in Morocco, numbering about 4,000,000; next to them are the Berbers, or Amaziyehs, who amount to about 3,000,000, and include the Berbers of the Riff coast and the Shelluks of the Great Atlas. Very few Europeans reside in Morocco. The state of civilization is very low, and many of the Amaziyehs are complete savages. Excepting the Jews and the few Europeans, the whole population is Mohammedan. The negroes, numbering only about 20,000, were generally brought into the country as slaves from Soudan, until the abolition of the African slave-trade.

The country is generally mountainous, the Atlas range traversing it in several parallel chains from the south-west to north-east, and sending numerous spurs to both the coast country and the desert. There are, however, many level tracts throughout Morocco, especially at its western and eastern extremities, and on the borders of the desert. Morocco is divided into four territories—Fez, Morocco, Suse, and Tafilelet. For convenience of administration, the empire is subdivided into thirty-three governments or districts ("ammala"), each under the superintendence of a "caid," whose chief duty it is to collect the imposts; but the semi-independent tribes are ruled by their own chiefs, and scarcely acknowledge the authority of the sultan. The government is purely despotic, and in the absence of written laws the will of the sultan and his subordinates decides everything. The public officials eke out their allowances by practicing extortion on those under their charge, and are in turn plundered by their superiors. The sovereign of Morocco, called by Europeans emperor, is known among his subjects as sultan, and assumes the titles of *Emir-ul-mumenín*, or "Prince of the Believers," and *Khalifet-allah-fi chalkihi*, or "Vicegerent of God upon Earth." The title is hereditary in the male line, but does not necessarily descend to the eldest son. The revenue of the emperor consists of a tenth upon every article of consumption, as allowed by the Koran; an annual tax upon the Jews; custom-house and excise duties; tributes exacted from his own subjects, foreign states, and European merchants, in the form of presents; which last articles form the chief source of his income. The duties and tributes are so frequently changed that it is impossible to estimate their annual amount with any degree of certainty.

Among the chief *products* of the country are wheat, barley, rice, maize, durra, and sugar-cane; and among fruits, the fig, pomegranate, lemon, orange, and date are common; while cotton, tobacco, hemp, etc., are largely produced both for home use and export. Morocco is rich in mineral treasures; plentiful supplies of copper are obtained at Teseleght, near the source of the Assaker, and gold and silver occur in several places. Iron, antimony, lead, tin, and rock-salt, the last three in considerable quantity, are also found. Owing to the character of the country and its thin population (thirty-five to the English square mile), the country is much infested with wild animals. Lions, panthers, hyenas, wild-boars, and various kinds of deer, gazelles, etc., abound in suitable localities, and occasional devastations are committed by locusts. Ostriches are found in Tafilelet. The Moorish horses, formerly so famous, are now much degenerated. The breeding of sheep, oxen, goats, camels, mules, and asses forms an important item of national industry. Oxen and bulls are chiefly employed in field labor.

The only industrial arts prosecuted to any considerable extent are the manufacture of caps, fine silk, and leather. In the production of the last article the Moroccans far surpass Europeans. There is an important caravan trade between Morocco and Soudan, and also with Mecca and the Levant. The intercourse with Algiers has in very recent times become a source of great trouble, and there is danger of war between France and Morocco unless the emperor's subjects shall hereafter prove more considerate of French interests. The Jews of Algeria, who largely control the caravan trade, have been very unkindly treated, and their complaints have been made the subject of special diplomatic service, the end of which is not yet (April, 1875). Education consists in learning to read, write, and recite portions of the Koran, and this quantum of education is pretty generally diffused among the people; but the art of printing is unknown, and the arts and sciences are at a very low ebb.

The *religion* of Morocco was no doubt Christian until, in the 7th and 8th centuries, the Saracens overran it, and made converts of the native population. See AFRICA, in vol. i, p. 94. Since this changed condition Morocco has been faithful to the Moslem faith. Yet toleration is granted in some measure to any sect which does not teach a plurality of gods; and on proper application is permitted to appropriate a place for public worship. There are Roman Catholic establishments in Morocco, Mequinez, Mogadore, and Tangier, but the number of communicants is not much over 200. Protestants are scarcely known in the country, and thus far no missionary efforts have been made in this part of Africa. Until 1814 Christians were frequently held as slaves, but since the power of France asserted itself on the African coast this abuse has terminated. Some of the practices of the natives are very peculiar. Thus through all the country there are buildings of an octagonal form called Zawiat, or sanctuaries, with an unenclosed piece of ground attached to each for the interment of the dead. In these places is a priest or saint, who superintends divine service and the burial of the dead, and who is often applied to as arbiter in disputes. In these consecrated places the wealthy inhabitants often deposit their treasures for security, and criminals find protection against the hands of justice. Polygamy is practiced in the country generally. The emperor himself supports a large harem, but has one superior wife, who is sultaness, and three other wives. Besides these he has a large number of concubines. Many of these are Moorish women, as the Moors consider it an honor to have their daughters in the harem; some of them European slaves; several are negresses: in all there are usually from sixty to one hundred,

VI.—21*

besides their slaves and domestics. Priestesses, who are so far learned as to read and write, are employed to teach the younger part of the harem to repeat their prayers, and to instruct the older females in the principles of their religion. The other religious institutions of the empire are so similar to those of most Mohammedan countries as to render a separate account of them altogether superfluous. See MOHAMMEDANISM.

The *history* of Morocco is, generally speaking, similar to that of the rest of Northern Africa (q. v.) down to the end of the 15th century. About that time it was formed into a monarchy, and, notwithstanding internal divisions, enjoyed considerable prosperity, and the confines of the empire were extended as far as Timbuctoo. This empire fell to pieces, and was succeeded in 1647 by that of the Sherifs of Tafilelet, who conquered both Morocco Proper and Fez, and united the whole country under one government. This is the present ruling dynasty. In the middle of the 17th century the empire of Morocco embraced part of the present province of Algeria, and extended south as far as Guinea, where it came into collision with the Portuguese settlements. Since the commencement of the 19th century the rebellions of the wild mountain tribes, the disturbances in Algeria, and difficulties with foreign states, caused by the aggressions of the Riff pirates, have greatly retarded the well-conceived measures of the various rulers for the development of the resources and increase in the civilization of Morocco. In 1817 piracy was prohibited throughout Morocco. In 1844 Morocco took part in the war of Abd-el-Kader against the French, in the course of which Tangier was bombarded and Mogadore occupied; but peace was concluded in the same year. In 1851 and 1856 complications took place with France concerning some French vessels which had been plundered by the Riff pirates, but in each case compensation was given by the sultan. In 1859 the Spanish government, smarting under a series of similar outrages, demanded compensation, and also an apology for an insult to the Spanish flag at Ceuta; and on the sultan's disclaiming all responsibility for these acts, war was declared by Spain Oct. 22, 1859. A short invasion brought the sultan to terms on March 25, 1860, and a treaty was accordingly signed April 27, 1860, by which the sultan ceded great commercial and social advantages to Spaniards. Christianity was by special treaty afforded many advantages also, but of course they are confined to Roman Catholics. As a consequence of these treaties a mission-house was opened at Fez, which promises to do something, but has as yet accomplished very little for the conversion of natives to Christianity. See *Specchio geografico e statistico dell' imperio di Marocco* (Genoa, 1833); Calderon, *Cuadro geografico, stadistico, historico, e politico del imperio de Marrucos* (Madrid, 1844); Renou, *Description géographique de l'empire de Maroc* (Paris, 1846); Augustin, *Marokko in seinen geographischen, historischen, religiösen, politischen, etc., Zuständen* (Pesth, 1845); Rohlf, "Reiseberichte" in Petermann's *Mittheilungen* (1863–65).

Morocco, SAMUEL ISRAELI OF, a Jewish convert to Christianity, and an author of considerable distinction, who lived at the close of the 11th century, is said to have come to Toledo from Fez, in Africa, about the year 1085, where he became a convert to Christianity. Before his conversion was completed he addressed a letter to rabbi Isaac, a Jew in the kingdom of Morocco, in which he says, "I would fain learn of thee, out of the testimony of the law and the prophets, and other Scriptures, why the Jews are thus smitten. Is this a captivity wherein we are, which may be properly called the perpetual anger of God, because it has no end; for it is now above a thousand years since we were carried captive by Titus? And yet our fathers, who worshipped idols, killed the prophets, and cast the law behind their back, were punished only with a seventy-years' captivity, and then brought home again. But now there is no end of our calamities, nor do the prophets promise any." This famous epistle, אגרת, which was originally written in Arabic, and gives in twenty-seven chapters an ample refutation of Jewish objections to the Christian faith, was translated from the Hebrew into the Latin by the Dominican Alfonso de Buen Hombre in 1329, under the title, *Tractatulus multum utilis ad convincendum Judæos de errore suo, quem habent de Messia adhuc venturo, et de observantia legis Mosaicæ*, and often since, and has been inserted in the *Bibliotheca Patrum*, xviii, 1519; into Italian by G. A. Brunati (Trident. 1712); into German by W. Link (Altenburg, 1524), and inserted in Luther's works, v, 567–583; and often since; by E. Trautmann (Goslar, 1706); by F. G. Stieldorff (Trier, 1833); into English by Th. Calvert, under the title, *Demonstration of the true Messiah*, by R. Samuel, a converted Jew (s. l. e. a.). A Spanish translation of this letter still remains in MS. in the library of the Escurial. Soon after his conversion rabbi Samuel appears to have returned to Morocco, whence his surname, and there to have held a conference on religion with a learned Mohammedan, of which his account, still in MS., is also to be found in the library of the Escurial. Comp. Fürst, *Bibl. Judaica*, ii, 152 sq.; De Rossi, *Dizionario storico degli autori Ebrei*, p. 208 (Germ. transl. by Hamberger); Wolf, *Bibl. Hebr.* iii, 1100–1106; Da Costa, *Israel and the Gentiles*, p. 311; Adams, *History of the Jews*, ii, 40. (B. P.)

Morone, GIOVANNI, an Italian prelate of considerable note for the illustrious part he took in the Reformatory movement of the 16th century, and for the noble efforts he made to uphold the lustre of the Roman Catholic Church, was born at Milan, Jan. 25, 1509, and descended from a noble family. His father, count Girolamo Morone, is of historic celebrity from the efforts he made to free his country (Milan) from the yoke of Charles V, and for his subsequent devotion to imperial interests. During his younger years Giovanni Morone was carefully instructed at home, and afterwards sent to the University of Padua to pursue his more serious studies. There his talents and assiduous application procured him honors which enrolled his name among the chief philosophers and jurists. In 1529 Morone finally took orders, and, though yet a youth, his unusual attainments rapidly secured him friends and position, and in the year following he was elevated to the bishopric of Modena. He was also in the same year selected by Paul III as papal nuncio to the emperor Ferdinand, and in that capacity did most excellent service to the Romish cause. He was instrumental in preparing the way for a council of the German princes for a final settlement of all religious differences, and did everything in his power to prevent a rupture in the Church. Yet it must not be inferred that he was so conciliatory as to ignore his own personal convictions. Determined to sustain the papal cause, he was yet in favor of reformatory measures, and succeeded in persuading both parties to give him their confidence because he acted conscientiously. He never feared to do or say what he thought right. Thus in 1540, when, on account of the plague, the Diet was to be removed from Spires to Hagenau, Morone hesitated not to make a most energetic protest, and in consequence was finally recalled to give an account of himself at Rome. His explanations must have been satisfactory to Paul III, for in 1541 Morone was again on his way to Germany to attend the Spires Diet, and in 1542 he attended the Diet at Ratisbon, where all hope of union between Protestants and Romanists was entirely extinguished. Yet, notwithstanding the failure of reconciliation, Morone's services found acknowledgment at Rome, and he was this same year presented with the red hat. He was also sent, together with Parisio and Pole, as papal representative to the nominal opening of the Council of Trent (November, 1542). His consummate knowledge of affairs pointed to him as the proper person for papal envoy when, the Tridentine Council having failed to

secure the support of the German princes and theologians, another Diet was called at Spires by the emperor in 1544. This was a most difficult task. Charles V, just returned from the Low Countries, seeing clearly that the successful issue of his war against Francis I of France was possible only if he had the German princes unitedly in his favor, graciously yielded everything in ecclesiastical matters, and this conciliatory position made of course no light work for the papal representative. Cardinal Morone was too sagacious not to perceive how the Protestant princes would take courage now, and move forward to a platform from which it would hereafter be difficult to dislodge them. He failed to influence the emperor as he desired, yet his faithfulness to the papal cause was universally acknowledged, and when he returned to Rome the legation of Bologna, then become vacant by the death of Contarini (q. v.), was conferred on Morone. In 1550 he gave up the bishopric of Modena, that diocese having during his absence become greatly distracted by the spread of Reformatory opinions. Whatever secret modifications his own views had undergone, he was not prepared, nor had he ever intended, to contaminate himself with the odious name of heretic; and therefore, rather than suffer his diocese to be spoken of as one alien to the faith, he promptly gave it up altogether. He had earnestly tried, immediately on his return from Germany, to rally his clergy around a common confession of faith, so liberal in its inception and construction that all might endorse it; but he had failed to unite them by this measure. Several of the most learned theologians deserted the territory rather than perjure themselves in any manner. The academicians were specially remiss in submission, and Morone finally wrote to Rome for permission to withdraw the paper, "as they had assured him of the sincerity of their devotion to the Roman Catholic Church, and had entreated that suspicion might not be cast on their faith by obliging them to subscribe" (*Life of Paleario*, ii, 28). The papal answer proved unfavorable in more than one respect. The pope, thinking Morone too indulgent, which no doubt was true, for he himself believed the doctrine of justification as held by the Lutherans, had appointed six cardinals to examine the condition of this Italian diocese. Morone, naturally enough offended at such a want of confidence in his integrity and competency, had almost then resolved to withdraw altogether from the diocese, had not the governor's entreaties prevailed, and he been induced to continue its spiritual head at least for a while longer. But the continued spread of Reformatory opinions, and his own indisposition to punish men for conscience' sake, so long as they avowed obedience to the pope of Rome as their spiritual head, finally led him to forsake the diocese altogether, and Foscarari, a Dominican friar, and a man of great talent and virtue, became his successor. The latter did not live to quit the diocese under such favorable auspices, but was taken from the episcopal mansion to the heretic's prison (*Life of Paleario*, ii, 45). Morone, however, lost nothing by forsaking the diocese of Modena, for he was by the duke of Milan presented with the bishopric of Novara. In 1549 Morone's friend at Rome, pope Paul III, died, and the next incumbent of the papal chair became Julius III. He was not warmly attached to our cardinal, yet at least esteemed him, and in 1555, when the Diet of Augsburg was to convene to discuss important religious topics, Morone was selected as the representative of Rome. Scarcely, however, had the cardinal reached Augsburg when the news of the sudden death of his pope was brought him, and he was obliged to turn back to Rome. He was now instrumental in elevating Marcello II, and hoped for reformation and purification in the Church. But this good man lived only a short time, and again the papal conclave was convened. The most prominent candidate was Caraffa, the inquisitor: a man of harshness of character, and not highly esteemed by Morone. The two had not been on very favorable terms for some time. Caraffa had suspected Morone of heresy, and the cardinal, in turn, had thought the inquisitor hypercritical and inhumane in the exercise of his official functions. Yet, moved by the sentiments of a generous mind, Morone, after all, cast his influence in the conclave for Caraffa (believing thereby to disarm his enmity), and thus helped to create him Paul IV. No sooner, however, was Caraffa elevated to the papal dignity than he at once conspired with Morone's enemies, and the cardinal was accused of leaning to the doctrines of the Reformers, and imprisoned in San Angelo to pass examination on his religious opinions. The only proofs of the heretical opinions of Morone are to be found in the articles of accusation drawn up against him. Vergerio, bishop of Capo d'Istria, who had left Italy, published these articles, with *scholia* on each article. No one was better acquainted than Vergerio with the facts treated of under the several heads. Though this little book came out anonymously, it bears marks of its origin. Printing being then comparatively in its infancy, each printer and the place of his habitation were pretty well known by the form of his types. Vergerio lived a good deal at Tübingen after he left Italy, and it is thought that these articles were sent to him, and that he printed them in despite of the Church of Rome. (A copy of these articles may be found in the *Life of Paleario*, ii, 309–312.) Notwithstanding the ready acuteness of the inquisitors, the answers of Morone prevented their finding any proof against him of heresy, and he was declared innocent. But after the inquisitors had pronounced cardinal Morone free from all heretical taint, and Paul IV had given orders for his liberation, he refused to go out of prison unless the pope publicly declared he had been unjustly accused. This Paul could not be persuaded to do, and Morone remained in prison till the death of that pope in 1559. On this occasion, after some discussion among the cardinals, he was liberated, and allowed to sit in the conclave which elected cardinal De' Medici pope, who took the name of Pius IV, and after the elevation of this prelate to the papal chair Morone was reinstated in his former influential position. In 1562 the cardinal was sent as papal legate to the emperor Ferdinand, and in the year following Morone became the presiding officer of the Council of Trent, and continued as such during all the important sessions of this ecclesiastical council. From the very beginning of his work at Trent he played a most important part, and exerted a most salutary influence for the Romish cause. He was conciliatory in speech and action, and intimated to the council that he came by orders of the pope "to establish the articles of faith, correct abuses, and promote the peace of nations, in so far as was consistent with the dignity and authority of the Holy See." This position seems not to have been warranted, however, by the views entertained at Rome; for it is now quite clearly revealed that the pope was determined to refuse the reforms desired by the common clergy and the people of Germany, and that Pius IV was at the time enjoying the promise of Spain's support in case Ferdinand ignored the papacy, and went over to the Protestants. Yet Morone must certainly have had the appearance of truth in his own dealings with the emperor, as that sovereign, in a meeting with Morone at Innsbruck in 1563, granted nearly all the favors he asked for, and even gave his sanction to an early discontinuance of the council, which was brought about this very year, Dec. 4. See TRENT, COUNCIL OF. Morone's services could not be too highly estimated at Rome. He had brought the council which threatened so much mischief to the papal cause to a close without any diminution of the pontifical authority, and had even left the Inquisition in a more enviable position than it had occupied previously. "All," says Ranke, "ended at last in a prosperous issue. That council which had been so vehemently called for and so long avoided; after being twice dissolved, shaken by so many of this world's storms, and when convened for the third time, anew beset with perils, was now closed amid the general concord

of the Roman Catholic world." On his return to the Eternal City the cardinal was therefore made dean of the cardinal college, and intrusted with diplomatic missions whenever the services of an acute and trustworthy messenger were needed. Upon the death of Pius IV, in 1566, Morone came very near being elected Pope. Unfortunately for Italy, sterner counsels prevailed, and the inquisitor, cardinal Alessandrino, was raised to the papal chair. We have no means of ascertaining what were Morone's feelings when he saw the power of the Inquisition, from which he had suffered so much, again seated on the papal throne. Morone died Dec. 1, 1580, at Rome, and was buried in the church of the Minerva. His peculiar life prevented much literary activity, and there remain from his pen only some letters to cardinals Pole and Cortese, and some of his orations. See Schelhorn, *Amœnitates Literariæ*, xii, 537 sq.; Tiraboschi, *Lett. Ital.* vii, 260; Young, *Life and Times of Paleario* (Lond, 1860, 2 vols. 8vo), ii, 307–314; Fisher, *Hist. Ref.* p. 393, 406; Wessenberg, *Die Grossen Kirchenversammlungen des 15 u. 16 Jahrh.* iii, 147 sq.; *North Brit. Rev.* Jan. 1870, art. viii, p. 284 sq.; Ranke, *Hist. of the Papacy*, i, 109 sq., 227, 247 sq. (J. H. W.)

Moroni (ANNA). See JESUS, HOLY CHILD, *Congregation of the Daughters of.*

Morosino, GIULIO (originally *Samuel Nachmias*), a Jewish convert to Romanism, was a native of Thessalonica. In Venice, where he settled, he first received a favorable impression of the truth of Christianity by being present at a public dispute between two of his nation, one of whom had renounced Judaism, respecting the accomplishment of Daniel's prophecy of the seventy weeks. In this dispute Simone Luzzatto (q. v.), the celebrated rabbi of Venice, was chosen arbitrator. Luzzatto's explanation was, "I beseech you to permit us to be silent and shut up our books, for if we proceed to examine the prophecies any further we shall all become Christians. It cannot be denied that in the prophecy of Daniel the coming of the Messiah is so clearly manifested that the time of his appearance must be allowed to be already past; but whether Jesus of Nazareth be the person, I cannot determine." This speech closed the debate, and made such a deep impression upon Samuel and his brother Joseph that they both formed the design of renouncing Judaism. Grätz, the Jewish historian, says that Nachmias either misunderstood or perverted Luzzatto's expression (sic!), but the fact is that a few months after, upon reconsidering the subject seriously and calmly, both brothers embraced Christianity, and were openly baptized Nov. 22, 1649, Nachmias assuming the name of *Giulio Morosino*, while his brother took the name of *Ottavio*. Ten years later he was called to Rome by pope Clement IX, who invested him with the office of librarian at the Vatican library, and this position he held until his death in 1687. Morosino wrote, *Via delle fide monstrata a gli Ebrei* (Rome, 1683), in which he appeals to the Jews no longer to be bound to observe the ceremonies, but to embrace the doctrines of the Gospel. See Kalkar, *Israel u. d. Kirche* (Hamburg, 1869), p. 82 sq.; Basnage, *Histoire des Juifs* (Engl. transl. by Taylor), p. 725; Adams, *History of the Jews*, ii, 76 sq. (Boston, 1812); Wolf, *Bibl. Hebr.* iii, 1128; Grätz, *Gesch. d. Juden*, x, 164; Bartolocci, *Biblioth. Rabbin.* iii, 756; Fürst, *Bibl. Jud.* ii, 391; iii, 8. (B. P.)

Morozzo, GUISEPPE, an Italian prelate, descended from an ancient and noble family, was born in March, 1758, at Turin. Under the tuition of the abbot of Aligre, who later became bishop of Pavia, Morozzo was made doctor of theology in 1777, and finished his studies at Rome in the ecclesiastical academy, where Litta, Caracioli, Pacca, and Emmanuele di Gregori were his fellow-students. Pope Pius VI nominated him successively apostolic prothonotary, vice-legate of Bologna, governor of Perugia and Civita Vecchia. He was a competitor for the papal see in the conclave which resulted in the election of Pius VII, and after the accession of the new pope was by him sent as ambassador to the king of Etruria. In 1802 Morozzo received the title of archbishop of Thebes in partibus, and was appointed secretary of the Congregation of Bishops. In 1808 he went to Paris with the difficult mission of adjusting the contentions which had arisen between the pope and the emperor (Napoleon I); but, becoming aware that his efforts were futile, he retired to Turin. In 1816 he was created cardinal, and in 1817 made bishop of Novara. He died March 22, 1842. He published *Statistics* of the patrimony of St. Peter (Rome, 1797), and a *Eulogy* on cardinal Bobba (Turin, 1799, 4to).

Morpurgo, SIMEON BEN-JOSHUA-MOSES, a Jewish writer of note, was born at Gradiska in 1681; studied at Padua, and graduated as doctor of medicine. In 1709 he was ordained by Leon Briele rabbi of Mantua, and in 1721 he was called to the rabbinate at Ancona, where he died in 1740. He wrote, שו"ת שמש צדקה, a collection of legal decisions (2 parts, Venice, 1742, 1743):— עיץ הדעת, *The Tree of Knowledge*, a commentary on the ethical work of Jedaja Penini, entitled *Bechinat Olam* (Venice, 1704):—an approbation to Isaac Norzi's עטור בכורי קצדד (ibid. 1715, 1717). Comp. Fürst, *Bibl. Jud.* ii, 391; Wolf, *Biblioth. Hebr.* iii, 1160; Jöcher, *Allgem. Gelehrten Lex.* s. v.

Morrell, THOMAS, one of the fathers of that branch of American Methodism known as the Methodist Episcopal Church, was born at New York Nov. 22, 1747. His mother was a devout follower of Mr. Wesley, and a member of the pious band led by Philip Embury. Thomas lived in most exciting times, and when the war for freedom broke out he early took to arms for republican life. He held successively the commissions of captain and major, and gained honorable distinction on the field. In 1785 Thomas Morrell was deeply impressed with his relation to God and the Church, and determined to enter the ministry. He joined Conference in 1787, and was stationed at Trenton Circuit, N. J. In 1788 he was preacher in charge in New York, with Robert Cloud as associate, and the following year their labors were blessed with a great revival. The same year he was ordained elder, and continued in that city five years. He was sent to Philadelphia in 1794-5; here taken sick, and not entirely well until 1799; next to Baltimore for two years; and in 1802-3 restationed at New York for two years. After this Mr. Morrell was never stationed out of Elizabethtown, N. J., but continued to labor regularly sixteen years until 1822, when he preached usually every Sabbath, and at least once a day, until January, 1833. After this failing health obliged him to desist from pulpit labor, and he only preached occasionally. He died Aug. 9, 1838. Father Morrell was a man of vigorous mind, and well endowed naturally for the work to which he felt himself called. He had fine preaching talents, and discharged the duties of his office with great acceptability and success. He was bold, earnest, and scrupulously faithful in all things. His name, usefulness, and devotedness to Christ's Church are remembered and honored. See *Meth. Quar. Rev.* 1841, p. 325; Sprague, *Annals of the Amer. Pulpit*, vol. vii; *New Jersey Conf. Memorial; Minutes of Ann. Conf.* ii, 669.

Morren, NATHANIEL, a Presbyterian divine, noted as the author of valuable Biblical works, flourished in the first half of our century at Edinburgh, Scotland. He was born in 1798, and died in 1847. Morren published, *Annals of the Church of Scotland from 1739 to 1776* (Edinb. 1835, 2 vols. 8vo):—*Biblical Theol.* vol. i:—*Rule of Faith* (1835); and a translation of Rosenmüller's *Biblical Geog. of Central Asia Minor, Phoenicia*, and *Arabia* (1836-37, 2 vols. 12mo). After his death his *Sermons* were published with a *Memoir* (1848, cr. 8vo). See Lowndes, *Brit. Lib.* p. 711; Allibone, *Dict. of Brit. and Amer. Auth.* s. v.

Morrill, DAVID LAWRENCE, a noted American phy-

sician, who distinguished himself also as a politician, figured at one time as minister of the Gospel and religious author. He was born in Epping, N. H., June 10, 1772. After receiving a good academic and medical education, he established himself in practice at Epsom in 1793; but in 1800 began to study theology, and in 1802 accepted a call to the Congregational Church in Goffstown, N. H., where he preached for nine years. He then resumed the practice of medicine from 1807 to 1830. He was at the same time also engaged in political life, and played no unimportant part in the passing history of New Hampshire. From 1817 to 1823 he was United States senator; and was governor from 1824 to 1827. He died at Concord, Jan. 28, 1849. Dr. Morrill was connected with many of the charitable, medical, and agricultural associations of his time. He published several sermons, orations, and controversial pamphlets, and was for some years after abandoning public office editor of the *New Hampshire Observer*, a religious newspaper.

Morris, Anthony, a Quaker preacher of some note, was born about 1654 in England, and emigrated to this country about 1680. He settled in New Jersey, and finally removed to Philadelphia, Pa. In 1701 he began to preach, and through fidelity in the exercise of his gift his communications were sound and edifying. Having a prospect of much religious labor, he circumscribed his worldly affairs, and devoted his time chiefly to the holy cause he had espoused. He travelled in the work of the ministry in most of the North American provinces, and in the year 1715 he visited Great Britain. He died August 23, 1721. See Janney, *Hist. of Friends*, iii, 202.

Morris, Francis M., a minister of the Methodist Episcopal Church, South, was born in Middle Tennessee about the year 1830; came to Kentucky in the fall of 1851, and was licensed to preach in 1852. He joined the Kentucky Conference in 1853, and was sent to Murray Circuit; in 1854, to Obion Circuit; in 1855, to Brynansburg Circuit; in 1856, to Ripley Circuit; in 1857, to Maury Circuit; in 1858, to Wesley Circuit; in 1859, to La Grange Circuit; in 1860 and 1861, to Brownsville Circuit; in 1862 and 1863, to Mount Zion Circuit; in 1864, to Salem Circuit, but was prevented from going to his work by the troubles of war then existing; in 1865, to Dresden Circuit, but was prevented from reaching it by the great floods, which swelled all the rivers of West Tennessee at that time; in 1866, to Fulton Station, where he died, Feb. 13, 1867. Mr. Morris was a man beloved and useful, and a fervent and zealous preacher, his ministry being greatly blessed to the Church and the world. See *Minutes of the Meth. Epis. Ch., South*, 1867, s. v.

Morris, Gouverneur, an eminent statesman and orator, who was born at Morrisania, near the city of New York, in 1752, was educated at Columbia (then King's) College, and licensed to practice law in 1771; and thereafter held several prominent civic positions, among these, in 1777, representing the people of New York in the Continental Congress, and in 1787 was a member of the convention which framed the Constitution of the United States. He also represented the American republic in France. He is stated by Thomas Jefferson to have been a disbeliever in Christianity. But this is a mistake; or, if at one time true, his views altered. He delivered two months before his death (which occurred in 1835) an address to the Historical Society, in which he points out the superiority of scriptural history to all other history. He regarded religious principle, indeed, as necessary to national independence and peace. "There must be something more to hope than pleasure, wealth, and power. Something more to fear than poverty and pain. Something after death more terrible than death. There must be religion. When that ligament is torn, society is disjointed and its members perish." See Allen, *Biog. Dict.* s. v.; Sparks, *Amer. Biog.* s. v.

Morris, John G., D.D., an American Lutheran divine of note, was born at York, Pa., in 1803, and was educated at Dickinson College, Pa. (class of 1823); then studied theology at Princeton Theological Seminary, and in 1826 entered the Lutheran ministry. He was at once called as pastor to the First Lutheran Church in Baltimore, and for six years (1859–65) of another Lutheran Church in the same city. He was the first librarian of the Peabody Institute at Baltimore; he founded a seminary for young ladies at Lutherville, and was active in several other public enterprises. He was editor of the *Lutheran Observer* from 1831 to 1832, and co-editor of the *Year-book of the Reformation* (1844). He published several translations of German theological works (1824–26), and wrote himself, *Popular Exposition of the Gospels* (Balt. 1840, 2 vols. 8vo):—*Life of John Arndt* (1853):—*The Blind Girl of Wittenberg* (1856, 12mo):—*Catharine de Bora; or Social and Domestic Scenes in the House of Luther* (1856, 12mo), etc. Dr. Morris also gave much time to studies in natural science, especially entomology, and became quite prominent in this field. He was acknowledged as an American authority, and was honored in various ways by the Smithsonian Institute and other associations. See Allibone, *Dict. of Brit. and Amer. Authors*, s. v.; *Putnam's Magazine*, Feb. 1856, p. 217. (J. H. W.)

Morris, John Piper, a minister of the Methodist Episcopal Church, South, was born in Devon, England, Jan. 30, 1846. His early life was spent in Canada under the pious training of his father, who was himself a local minister of the Wesleyan Church. Young Morris was converted at seventeen, and soon after became convinced that he was called of God to preach. While preparing for the ministry his health was impaired, and he was advised to go South. After his arrival at Charleston, S. C., he decided at once to enter the ministry, and supplied a vacancy in the village of Summerville. In 1862 he was received on trial in the South Carolina Conference, and appointed to Aiken. In 1867 he was ordained deacon, and appointed to Darlington; but his health failing, he was obliged to give up all work. He died Jan. 24, 1868. See *Min. of Ann. Conf. of the Meth. Epis. Church, South*, 1868, p. 214.

Morris, Joseph, an English Baptist divine, flourished as pastor of a London congregation in the first half of the eighteenth century. He is believed to have been born about 1685. He died in 1755. Ivimey speaks of him as "a sensible, pious, and learned man," and that he was "in habits of intimacy with the excellent Dr. Johnson, who esteemed him for his modesty and ability" (*History of the English Baptists*). He published several of his *Sermons* (Lond. 1722, 8vo; 1743, 8vo; 1757, 8vo), which were admired for their solidity, and prove him to have been a man of more than ordinary talent. His influence in the English metropolis was considerable in his day and generation.

Morris, Judah, a Jewish convert to Protestant Christianity, was a native of Italy, and emigrated to this country about 1835. He was for a time instructor in Harvard University. He died in 1855. He published a *Hebrew Grammar*, and some religious books.

Morris, Samuel, a Presbyterian lay worker in colonial days, flourished near the middle of last century in Hanover, Va. He was a man of singularly earnest and devoted spirit, and did much to advance the interests of Presbyterianism in Virginia. His house was a resort for those "who were dissatisfied with the preaching of the parish incumbents, and anxious to enjoy the privilege of listening on the Sabbath to the reading of instructive and devotional works on religion." He was himself reared in the Anglican establishment, but by accident becoming acquainted with Presbyterian works —among them Boston's *Fourfold State*—he embraced that Calvinistic confession, and soon gathered about him others who, like him, chose rather to subject them-

selves to the payment of the fines imposed by law than to attend church where they felt that they could not be profited. The little band of lay workers, as yet never under the instruction of a Presbyterian pastor, but nevertheless greatly interested in Presbyterian doctrine, and unconsciously its adherents even, first met every Sabbath alternately at each other's houses to read and pray. But as their number increased they regularly gathered at Mr. Morris's house, until at length that dwelling-house was too small to contain the people, and it was determined "to build a meeting-house," "merely for reading," as Mr. Morris himself adds. This house of worship was afterwards designated "Morris's Reading-room," and was the starting-point of Presbyterianism in Virginia. From Hanover Mr. Morris was frequently called to different places in the state to instruct the inquiring, and, complying with their invitations, went out and spread the interest in distant parts. As they increased in numbers the Established Church made complaint against them to the governor, and they were called up for trial, but they were promptly discharged when it was found that their creed was that of the Kirk. See PRESBYTERIANISM. See also Gillett, *Hist. of the Presbyterian Church in the United States of America*, i, 111–120; Anderson, *Hist. of the Colonial Church*, iii, 229 sq. (J. H. W.)

Morris, Sarah, a Quaker preacher, the daughter of Anthony Morris, himself a Quaker preacher, was born at Philadelphia in 1704; preached in New Jersey, Maryland, and Long Island; went to Rhode Island in 1764; and travelled through Great Britain, preaching in many places, in 1772–73. She died in Philadelphia Oct. 24, 1775. Possessing a superior mind, combined with a social and cheerful disposition, she proved an efficient helper to her people.

Morris, Susanna, a Quakeress noted as an efficient preacher of the doctrines of her sect, was born about 1682. But little is accessible to us regarding her personal history. She labored in the work of the ministry for nearly forty years both in this country and in Europe, where she visited England, Ireland, and Scotland. She died April 28, 1755. She was a devout Christian, and a firm adherent to her people, whom she dearly loved. See Janney, *Hist. of the Religious Society of Friends*, iii, 336.

Morris, Thomas Asbury, D.D., a bishop of the Methodist Episcopal Church, and for many years the senior officer of the episcopal cabinet, a man of indomitable energy and great love for the Christian cause, in which he proved a most efficient workman, was born in Kanawha County, Va., April 28, 1794. His parents, while he was yet a youth, removed to Charlestown, W. Va., and it was for some time his home. The educational facilities of that period, and especially of that region, were extremely limited. It was the good fortune of the Morris family, however, to enjoy the advantages of a good grammar-school, organized by William Paine, an educated Englishman, near the homestead, when Thomas was about sixteen years of age. His oldest brother, Edmund, held the clerkship of Cabell County, in which the family resided, and Thomas, at the age of seventeen, became a deputy in the office, a position which he held until he was about twenty years of age. While discharging the duties of this office, and when greatly broken down in health, and somewhat depressed in spirits, he was drafted into a company of militia, to perform a six-months' tour in the North against the British and Indians. They met at the court-house, shouldered their muskets, and took up their line of march to join a regiment forming at Point Pleasant, to re-enforce the main army near the Canada line. The father of Young Morris was so affected by his son's frail and youthful appearance and his feeble health that after the company had started he procured a substitute, overtook the young soldiers their second day out, and procured a discharge for his slender and delicate boy. The early religious training of bishop Morris was in the Baptist Church, of which both his parents were pious and exemplary members. He grew up, however, without giving much thought to the subject of personal religion until he was about eighteen years of age. In his twentieth year he made a profession of religion, and at the same time began to ponder seriously the question whether Providence was not leading him to cast in his lot with the people called Methodists. Against this course many considerations pleaded powerfully: he had been trained in another communion, his prejudices were deeply rooted, the Methodists in that region were feeble and persecuted, but the result of a careful comparison of their doctrines and polity with the New Testament which he instituted at this time was a fixed, unalterable determination to unite with them as the people of his choice. He was shortly after admission to membership in the Church licensed to preach, and was received as a travelling preacher into the Ohio Conference in 1816. In 1818 he was ordained deacon by bishop George, and elder in 1820 by bishop Roberts. Though in a large measure self-educated, because an affliction of the eye restricted his studies in early manhood, he yet labored most acceptably in the pastoral work in various parts of Kentucky, Tennessee, and Ohio till 1834, when he was deemed cultured enough to be intrusted with the literary management of a paper, and was placed in the editorial chair of the then newly-established *Western Christian Advocate*, a religious and literary weekly, which two years after its commencement numbered 8000 subscribers—certainly a successful enterprise for the times. In 1836 the General Conference, held that year at Cincinnati, where he resided, elected him to the episcopal office. He now really entered a field for which he was specially fitted, and gained a most enviable reputation not only in his own denomination, but throughout the Christian Church. In 1864 declining health and the infirmities of age obliged him to ask for relief, and he was less heavily taxed. In 1868, at the General Conference in Chicago, he sought and obtained permission to be withdrawn from episcopal visitation duties, and led a rather quiet life until his death, Sept. 2, 1874. Only a few days before this he had addressed a loving missive to the members of the Cincinnati Conference (bearing date August 27), saying, among other noble Christian words, "I am no longer able to go in and out before you, to sit in your councils and take part in your deliberations, yet my heart and sympathy are with you, and for Zion's prosperity my tears shall fall and my prayers ascend until my release is signed, and I go to join the Church triumphant in the skies." Bishop Morris was a man of great uniformity and simplicity. He was noted in his Church for the quiet power and prudent skill with which he discharged the episcopal duties. His death occurring about the same time as that of the bishop of Winchester—Dr. Charles Sumner (q. v.)—the *New York Methodist* took occasion to institute a comparison between the two bishops, and thus concludes in favor of bishop Morris: "This man had done more in his time for the extension of Christianity than a whole bench of English prelates. He had assigned to their places of labor not less than 30,000 ministers, had traversed this country to the outer edge of its civilization over and over again; had preached sermons innumerable, and only ceased to labor when labor became physically impossible. Nor was his pen idle. He was one of the founders of a great paper, which is still in existence. He issued volumes from the press, which are models of vigorous, idiomatic English. And all this fruitful work was done in the most unpretending way. Bishop Morris never thought of himself as a great actor in the world's affairs, a great preacher, or a great writer. The beauty of his character was that he never appeared to think of himself at all; his work was before him, and he did it; and that was the end of the matter." Bishop Morris's only works of any special import are a vol-

ume of sermons, and a miscellany, consisting of essays, biographical sketches, and notes of travel. Of the former, about 15,000 copies have been sold; the latter has been but sparsely circulated. "His style was epigrammatic, clear, and forcible. His printed sermons were characterized by simplicity, pith, directness, lucid arrangement, and earnest and practical enforcement of the truth. They have been useful and popular. As a presiding officer he was the *beau ideal* of a Methodist bishop. He had rare practical wisdom, quick and accurate judgment, and inflexible decision. He acted no superiority, put on no prelatical airs, and never felt that his office lifted him above the fellowship and sympathy of his brethren" (Marlay). As a pulpit orator, the bishop was quite noted in the prime of his life. His delightful evangelical discourses abounded in pithy sentences, and gratified thousands of hearers as they fell from his lips. See Marlay, *Life of Bishop Morris* (N. Y. 1875, 12mo); *Meth. Qu. Rev.* July, 1875, art. iii; *Minutes of Annual Conferences*, 1874; *N. Y. Christian Advocate*, Sept. 1874; *Men of the Time*, s. v.; Drake, *Dict. of Amer. Biog.* s. v.

Morris-dance, a peculiar and fantastic species of dance, constituting the chief enjoyment at parochial festivals in England, was commonly practiced in the Middle Ages, and continues to the present day among the country people in different parts of England. Its origin is ascribed to the Moors, though the genuine Moorish dance (the *fandango* of the present day) bears little resemblance to it. The chief performer was the *hobby-horse*, so called from the light frame of wicker-work which was fastened around its body, and supplied with a pasteboard head and neck, so as to give it the appearance of a man on horseback. Bells were also attached to its ankles, and the great art consisted in so moving the feet as to produce a rude kind of concord. The other principal actors, after a fashion, personified the characters of Maid Marian, the Queen of the May, Robin Hood, Friar Tuck, the Fool, etc.; and the performance was accompanied by rude music and the clashing of swords and staves.

Morrison, John, D.D., a Scotch divine, noted as a hymnologist also, was born in the County of Aberdeen in 1749. He studied for the ministry, and in 1780 entered upon his pastoral duties over the parish of Canisbay, Caithness-shire. He was one of the committee of the General Assembly for revising the Church Paraphrases, and himself contributed some of the best renderings. Of these, the 19th, "The race that long in darkness pined," and the 30th, "Come, let us to the Lord our God," have been generally adopted by the churches. In his early life he contributed verses to the *Edinburgh Weekly Magazine*, over the signature of "Musæus." He also published the second and fourth books of Virgil's *Æneid*, translated into English verse (1787). He died at Canisbay, June 12, 1798.

Morrison, John W., a Presbyterian minister, was born in Chester County, South Carolina, in 1811; was educated in the Indiana University, Bloomington, Ind.; studied theology under the late Rev. Hugh MacMillan, of Xenia, Ohio, and was licensed and ordained in 1841, as pastor of the Thorn Grove Presbyterian Church, in Bloom, Cook Co., Indiana. This was his only charge. At the close of twenty-five years of pastoral duty he resigned this position to accept the agency in behalf of the freedmen, feeling, as he expressed it, "that the education of that people was the work to which God now calls the Church and the nation." He continued to labor as an agent until he died, Jan. 5, 1867. Mr. Morrison was a man of great integrity, of noble disposition, and of untiring effort in the service of Christ. He was an accurate classical scholar, a critical and profound expositor of Scripture, and an earnest and affectionate preacher. See Wilson, *Presb. Hist. Almanac*, 1868, p. 391.

Morrison, Jonas S., a minister of the Methodist

Episcopal Church, was born in Plattsburg, N. Y., March 11, 1836; was converted at the age of sixteen years; licensed to preach in 1857, and in the same year joined the Southern Illinois Annual Conference; was appointed junior preacher on Collinsville Circuit; next year he was stationed at Main Street, Alton City; and thereafter successively at Chester, Gillespie, two years; Litchfield, Brighton, Highland, Carlyle, two years; Greenville, Gillespie; and, lastly, as presiding elder of Alton District. He died October 18, 1871. "The traits of his character were strongly marked. As a Christian and a minister of the Lord Jesus Christ, he exemplified the purity of the one and the fidelity of the other. He rather lived than professed religion, and proved his ministry by the practical sympathy that carries the consolations of Christ to the abodes of poverty, of sickness, and of bereavement. His pulpit ministrations were characterized by clearness, by fidelity to the Scriptures, by an adaptation of the truth to his hearers, and by a manner which demonstrated his own interest in his theme. Love for the Church was with him an absorbing passion." See *Minutes of Annual Conferences*, 1872, p. 137.

Morrison, Levi R., a Presbyterian minister, was born in Mecklenburg County, North Carolina, July 3, 1805. His early educational advantages were very limited, and he had to struggle with poverty and its attendant trials and perplexities. He studied his Bible and such books as he was able to secure, and exercised his gifts as a speaker; was licensed in 1831, and began his labors in Spring Creek and Smyrna churches, Tennessee. In 1836 he was ordained, and became pastor of the churches at Sparta and McMinnville, Tenn. He subsequently labored at Mars Hill, Tenn., Glade Spring, Va., North Prairie and Springfield, Mo. His life was that of a toiling pastor and home missionary. He died Dec. 28, 1867. Mr. Morrison was a man of most amiable character, of strong and vigorous intellect, a very acceptable preacher, and greatly blessed in his labors. See Wilson. *Presb. Hist. Almanac*, 1868, p. 346.

Morrison, Robert, D.D., a distinguished English missionary to China, the first Protestant missionary to that country, and holding the same relation to it as Vanderkemp to Africa or Williams to the South Seas, was born of humble but respectable parentage at Morpeth, Northumberland, Jan. 5, 1782. After receiving some elementary instruction in English, writing, and arithmetic, in a school conducted by a maternal uncle at Newcastle, he was apprenticed at a very early age to his father, who was then engaged in last-making. But so devoted had the boy become to his books that he spent his leisure in close study. "For the purpose of securing a greater portion of quiet retirement," says his widow, "he had his bed removed to his workshop, where he would often pursue his studies until one or two in the morning. Even when at work, his Bible or some other book was placed open before him, that he might acquire knowledge or cherish the holy aspirations of spiritual devotion while his hands were busily occupied in the labors of life." Amid such disadvantages Morrison hesitated not to commence a course of religious reading and study, and in 1801 was ready to study Hebrew, Latin, and theology under the superintendence of a Presbyterian minister of the town, by whom he was so much liked that Morrison was, in 1803, introduced by him to the committee and tutors of the Independent Theological Academy at Hoxton, as a fit person to be received into that institution to study theology. Morrison was admitted, and had not long been an inmate of the institution before he decided to devote himself to the missionary cause in heathen lands. Though his friends dissuaded him from such a step, he yet felt it his duty to devote the talent given him as Providence seemed unmistakably to point it out to him; and in May, 1804, he offered his services as a missionary to the London Missionary Society, was promptly ac-

cepted, and now removed from Hoxton to the Mission College at Gosport. In August, 1805, he commenced the study of Chinese under a native teacher. In January, 1807, he was ordained as a missionary, set out at once for China, and in September of the same year arrived at Canton. Before leaving England, Mr. Morrison had procured from the British Museum a *Harmony of the Gospels* and the *Pauline Epistles*, translated into Chinese by an unknown Roman Catholic missionary; and the Royal Asiatic Society lent him a manuscript Latin and Chinese dictionary. His moderate knowledge of Chinese inclined him to mingle at once among the natives, and having perhaps studied the customs of Roman Catholic missionaries, adopted, like them, the prevailing usages of diet, dress, and manners. He handled chop-sticks, coiled up his hair in form, and let his nails grow. But he soon saw the folly of this extreme conformity, and assumed a distinctive European character and aspect. He rapidly acquired the mastery of the Chinese, and how greatly his knowledge of the language was esteemed is apparent in that, though a minister, he was in 1808 appointed translator to the East India Company's factory at Canton. In 1810 the Acts of the Apostles in Chinese, which he had brought with him, were printed, after he had carefully revised and amended the text. In 1811 a Chinese grammar, which he had prepared about three years before, was sent to Bengal to be printed; but, after many delays, it did not issue from the press until 1815, when it was printed at Serampore, at the expense of the East India Company. In 1812 the Gospel of St. Luke in Chinese was printed; and by the beginning of 1814, the whole of the New Testament being ready for the press, the East India Company sent out a press and materials and a printer to superintend the printing of the work. In 1813 the London Missionary Society had sent out the Rev. (afterwards Dr.) Milne to assist Morrison, and together these two Christian scholars now proceeded with the translation of the Old Testament. In 1815 the Book of Genesis and Psalms were printed, and by 1818 this great work of translating the Bible into Chinese was completed. The translation of the Scriptures, the great object of Dr. Morrison's life, was given to the world "not as a perfect translation." Dr. Morrison says he studied "fidelity, perspicuity, and simplicity;" "common words being preferred to classical ones." The authorized English version was followed. Dr. Morrison always explicitly stated that the Chinese manuscript in the British Museum was "the foundation of the New Testament;" which, he says, "I completed and edited." It is no disparagement of Dr. Morrison to assert that his work required revision; it was a first version into the most difficult language in the world. The translators contemplated the improvement of their work at some future period, "expecting that they should be able to sit down together and revise the whole." This expectation was never realized; Dr. Milne died in 1822, and the correction of errors and the verbal alterations made by Dr. Morrison were not of great importance. Towards the latter part of his life Dr. Morrison became more and more confirmed in the necessity of a thorough revision, and he anticipated the probability of this being effected by his son, who, however, on the death of his father, was selected to succeed him as the translator to the Superintendents of British Trade at Canton, and could not therefore devote his time to this object. From 1810 to 1818 the British and Foreign Bible Society had voted the sum of £6000, at seven different times, to assist in the printing and publication. The Old Testament formed 21 vols. 12mo. The Book of Job and the historical books were translated by Dr. Milne, and the other portions by Dr. Morrison. Of the New Testament, Dr. Morrison translated the four Gospels, and from Hebrews to the end. Besides this great work, Dr. Morrison was also engaged on a *Chinese Dictionary*, which he completed in 1816, and it was printed by the East India Company, at a cost of £15,000, in 1821. Nor must it be supposed that he ever lost sight of the great missionary work intrusted to his charge while assuming so many other engagements. He constantly preached, and in every way possible sought out the native population, and in 1814 was gratified with his first convert, Tsae-ako, who died in 1818. Believing that the Chinese could be reached better through educational channels, he caused an Anglo-Chinese college to be founded at Malacca; gave £1000 for the erection of buildings, and £100 annually for its support. In 1824 he visited England, and remained home nearly two years. He was received everywhere with great distinction, and was even honored with a reception by king George IV, to whom Morrison presented a copy of the Scriptures in Chinese. He had brought home with him a Chinese library of 10,000 volumes, and labored earnestly to awaken an interest among his countrymen for Chinese literature. In this he moderately succeeded. In 1826 he again set sail for China, and now even more assiduously devoted himself to the missionary work. His time he mainly occupied in preaching, translating, and superintending the distribution of printed works for the conversion of the Chinese. In 1832 he felt so encouraged with the prospects of an early harvest for his many years of toil as to write to his friends in England: "I have been twenty-five years in China, and am beginning to see the work prosper. By the press we have been able to scatter knowledge far and wide." In the midst of these occupations Dr. Morrison died at Canton, Aug. 1, 1834, preserving unimpeached until death the consistency, efficiency, and benevolence of the Christian missionary.

Dr. Morrison certainly achieved great things in China. The compilation of his dictionary in the vernacular language of that country was a Herculean task, which none but a man of the greatest strength of intellect and energy of purpose could have accomplished. Along with that he completed a Chinese version of the Old and New Testaments, which, in the opinion of all the learned men of Europe, was deemed utterly beyond the power of any single person. Nor were his exertions for the Chinese confined solely to literary works. He went about doing good. "He endeavored," says his biographer, "in the employment of such expedients as he could command, to relieve the wants, to mitigate the sufferings, and heal the diseases of the poor and suffering Chinese around him. In order to secure to the natives the means of a liberal and religious education, as well as to furnish facilities to foreigners to prosecute the study of the Chinese language, he projected the establishment of the Anglo-Chinese college." His whole life and works snow the activity and energy and comprehensiveness of his mental endowments, as well as the Christian benevolence of his heart. His office was that only of a pioneer who prepared the way for the evangelization of China. But with the instruments which his zeal and indefatigable industry put into the hands of the Evangelical churches, the preliminary obstacles have been removed, and the way prepared for carrying on the work of direct Christian instruction. His coadjutor, Dr. Milne, who died some time before, said of Morrison that "his talents were rather of the solid than the showy kind; adapted more to continued labor than to astonish by sudden bursts of genius; and his well-known caution fitted him for a station where one false step at the beginning might have delayed the work for ages." It may serve to give an idea of the exertions of Dr. Morrison and his colleagues to state that from 1810 to 1836, 751,763 copies of works, consisting of 8,000,000 pages, were printed in the Chinese and Malay languages at Canton, Malacca, Batavia, Penang, and Singapore. This includes 2075 complete Chinese Bibles, 9970 New Testaments, and 31,000 separate portions of Scripture in Chinese. See *Memoirs of the Life and Correspondence of Robert Morrison, D.D., compiled by his Widow*, to which is appended *A Critical Essay on the Literary Labors of Dr. Morrison*, by the Rev. S. Kidd, professor of Chinese in the University College

(Lond. 1839, 2 vols. 8vo); Aikman, *Cyclop. of Christian Missions*, p. 102 sq.; *Eclectic Review*, 4th series, vii, 176; *Philadelphia Museum*, xxxvii, 94; Rémusat, in *Journal des Savans* for 1824.

Morrison, Robert E., a minister of the Methodist Episcopal Church, was born in Lancaster County, Pa., Oct. 12, 1800. When seventeen years of age he united with the Presbyterian Church; but eight years afterwards, being brought into intimate relations with Methodists, he united with the Methodist Episcopal Church. He preached under the presiding elder for three years, and in 1833 was received into the Philadelphia Conference, and appointed to Chester Circuit, Pa., where he labored very acceptably for two years. In 1835 he was appointed to Tuckerton Circuit, N. J. The necessities of the case requiring it, he was removed and appointed to Haddonfield. In 1836-7 he travelled Swedesborough Circuit. Here great success crowned his efforts. In 1838-9 he labored in Pemberton; in 1840-1 in Long Branch; in 1842-3 in Pennington; in 1844-5 in Allentown; and in 1846 at Crosswicks. A throat difficulty compelled him to take a supernumerary relation, and locating at Hightstown, N. J., he became one of its most respected citizens. For a number of years he was president of Hightstown Bank. He died Aug. 30, 1873. Mr. Morrison, being studious, acquired a large store of knowledge, and became a good thinker. Though not a graduate of any literary institution, he read Latin, Greek, and Hebrew, and was quite at home in mathematics. He was also a thorough student of divinity. See *Minutes of Annual Conferences*, 1874, p. 37.

Morrow (מָחָר, *machar'*, αὔριον). See PROCRASTINATION.

Morrow-Mass Priest is the name of the priest who said early mass, *morrow* being equivalent to *morning.*—Walcott, *Sac. Archæol.* s. v.

Morrow, RICHARD H., a Presbyterian minister, was born in Huntingdon Co., Pa., Jan. 13, 1823. In early youth he was hopefully converted, and determined to preach the Gospel. He obtained his preparatory education in the academy at Academia, and graduated at Jefferson College, Pa., in 1851, after which he engaged for some time as teacher in the Milnwood Academy at Shade Gap, Pa. He studied theology at Alleghany and Princeton seminaries, graduating at the latter in 1854; was licensed by the Presbytery of Huntingdon, and in 1855 ordained and installed pastor of the church at Cedar Rapids, Iowa, where he continued to labor until compelled by declining health to resign his charge, in April, 1859. He died June 10, 1859. Mr. Morrow was a plain and practical preacher, his style giving evidence of fine culture. He was humble, consistent, devoted, possessing in an eminent degree the happy faculty of gaining the friendship and esteem of all who knew him. See Wilson, *Presb. Hist. Almanac*, 1861, p. 98.

Mors Peccatōrum (*the death of sins*), an expression used by Tertullian and other writers to describe the efficacy of baptism, in allusion to Rom. vi, 4; Col. ii, 12.

Morse is the technical term for the *clasp* of a cope or pectoral.

Morse, Abner, a Congregational minister, was born at Medway, Mass., Sept. 5, 1793, and was educated at Brown University, class of 1816. He decided to enter the ministry, and sought further preparation for this important work at Andover Seminary, where he graduated in 1819. He then became pastor at Nantucket, Mass.; subsequently at Bound Brook, N. J., and later removed to Indiana, where he became a professor of natural science, a department of study in which he had greatly interested himself. He attained to considerable distinction as a scientist, and published several genealogical works. He died at Sharon, Mass., May 16, 1865. See *New England Hist. and Genealog. Register*, xix, 371; Drake, *Dict. of Amer. Biog.* s. v.

Morse, Asahel, a minister of the Baptist Church in America, who distinguished himself in the Revolutionary period of this country's history, was born in the north parish of New London, now called Montville, Conn., Nov. 10, 1771. He received his early educational training from his father, Joshua Morse, also a minister, who preached in the vicinity where Asahel was born until death cut short his ministrations in 1795. At nineteen Asahel had progressed sufficiently in his studies to teach country schools and earn sufficient to defray the expenses of his education at more advanced institutions of learning. In 1782 he was converted, and decided to enter the ministry, feeling himself specially called to the work. He preached a while near his own home, then labored in Winsted. In 1802 the Baptist church in Stratfield, Conn., called him as their pastor, and he removed thither in 1803. In 1807 he accepted an appointment as missionary to the Upper Canada Indians, and while in this position endured many hardships. He was faithful to his task, and made converts not only among the Indians, but also among the white people of that region, and greatly strengthened his denomination there. In 1810 he was invited and went to preach at Suffield, Conn., one of the best Baptist churches in New England. But Mr. Morse by no means confined his labors to this church. He went much about the country, and everywhere endeavored to encourage religious life and to secure followers for the Baptist society. In 1832 he became pastor of the Second Baptist Church in Colebrook, Conn. In 1836 he returned to Suffield, and there died, June 10, 1838. During his illness he manifested the utmost confidence in the doctrines he had preached, and frequently said that he relied upon Christ for salvation. See *Baptist Memorial*, iii (1844), 234 sq., 272 sq., 293 sq.

Morse, David Sanford, a Presbyterian minister, was born about the year 1793. He first chose the legal profession, but was converted at the age of twenty-five, turned aside to the ministry, and devoted the remainder of his life to this sacred work. He died in Austerlitz, Columbia County, N. Y., Dec. 21, 1871. See Appleton's *Annual Cyclop.* 1871, p. 592.

Morse, Frank Currier, a minister of the Methodist Episcopal Church, was born in Hopkinton, N. H., Feb. 23, 1835. His youth was spent in Newbury, N. H., till the age of seventeen, when he was sent to the Baptist Academy in New London, N. H. He afterwards went to study at Lowell, and while there was converted. Feeling called to the ministry, he entered the Wesleyan University in 1857, and graduated in the regular course in 1861, and at once joined the New England Conference. He was stationed at Blanford. In 1862 he enlisted in the army, and held the position of chaplain during his three years of service. In 1865 he acted as "supply" in Leyden, Mass., and filled this charge for two years. His health failing him, he moved West, hoping a change might benefit him, but died in Kansas, Jan. 14, 1871.

Morse, Jedediah, D.D., a Congregational minister of note, was born Aug. 23, 1761, in Woodstock, Conn. He graduated at Yale College in 1783, entered the ministry in 1785, and was chosen tutor in Yale in 1786. In October he changed places with the Rev. Abiel Holmes, pastor in Midway, Ga., where he preached about six months, when he returned North, and, after preaching in several places, was ordained pastor of the First Congregational Church in Charlestown, Mass., April 30, 1789, and held this charge till 1820, when, having received a commission from J. C. Calhoun, secretary of war, to visit several Indian tribes, he spent two winters in his observations, the report of which was published in 1822. He died in New Haven, June 9, 1826. Dr. Morse published the first American work on geography, in 1784 (passing through many editions in this country and abroad, and after his death it was enlarged and improved by his son). He also wrote *A Compendious*

History of New England, in company with E. Parish, D.D. (1804):—a pamphlet, *The true Reasons on which the Election of a Hollis Professor of Divinity in Harvard College was opposed at the Board of Overseers* (1804):—*An Appeal to the Public on the Controversy respecting the Revolution in Harvard College* (1814); and a number of occasional sermons and addresses. From 1790 to 1821 he published twenty-five of his sermons and addresses. Dr. Morse was also much occupied in religious controversy; in upholding the orthodox faith of the New England churches against the assaults of Unitarianism, and was so earnest in these labors as to seriously impair his health. In 1804 he was active in enlarging the Massachusetts General Association of Congregational Ministers. He was also a prominent actor in the establishment of the theological seminary at Andover, especially by his successful efforts to prevent the threatened establishment of a rival institution at Newbury, projected by the Hopkinsians, and to effect a union between them and other Calvinists on their common symbol, the Assembly's Catechism. The articles of this union, which still constitute substantially the basis of the Andover Seminary, were signed in his own study in Charlestown, in the night of Nov. 30, 1807, by himself, Dr. Samuel Spring, and Dr. Eliphalet Pearson. Morse participated in the organization of the Park Street Church in Boston in 1808, when all the Congregational churches in the city, except the Old South Church, had abandoned the primitive faith of the fathers of New England. In 1805 he started a religious magazine, *The Panoplist*, of which he was the sole editor for five years. Dr. Morse was universally esteemed for his piety and learning, and is acknowledged to have been one of the most eminent ministers of his day in New England. He was distinguished alike for the versatility of his powers and the wide extent of his influence, and was almost equally well known on both sides of the Atlantic. See Sprague, *Annals of the Amer. Pulpit*, ii, 247; Allibone, *Dict. of Brit. and Amer. Authors*, s. v.

Morse, Joshua. See MORSE, ASAHEL.

Morse, Richard Cary, an American Presbyterian minister, noted as a religious journalist, and son of Jedediah Morse, was born June 18, 1795, at Charlestown, Mass. At the age of nine he was sent to Phillips's Academy, Andover, to prepare for admission to college, and entered Yale College in 1808. He graduated in 1812, the youngest member of his class. The year immediately following his graduation he spent in New Haven, being employed as the amanuensis of president Dwight, and living in his family, and thus enjoyed an association invaluable to any man, and by which, no doubt, Mr. Morse was greatly profited. In 1814 he entered the theological seminary at Andover, and, having passed through the regular three-years' course, was licensed to preach in 1817. The winter immediately succeeding his licensure he spent in South Carolina as a supply of the Presbyterian church on John's Island. He became, however, early impressed with the idea that he had not the requisite natural qualifications for the ministry, and therefore silently retired from it, though his whole life was a continued act of devotion to the objects which the ministry contemplates. On his return to New England he became associated with his father for some time in a very successful geographical enterprise; and in the spring of 1823 enlisted with his brother in another enterprise still more important—the establishing of the *New York Observer*, of which he was associate editor and proprietor for the remainder of his life, and during this long period contributed largely to its columns, especially by translations from the French and German. He died, while abroad on a visit to recuperate his health, at Kissingen, Germany, Sept. 22, 1868. Under the ordering of a wise and gracious Providence, his circumstances from the very beginning of life acted upon him as a benign influence. What his early training was may be inferred from his distinguished parentage, and his intimate association with Dr. Dwight. And, indeed, during his whole life his associations, whether viewed in respect to near relationship or general acquaintance, were fitted to develop and mature both the intellectual and moral man. His Christian character shone conspicuously in all his life. He not only had a strong conviction of the truth of the Gospel, but a high appreciation of the system of evangelical doctrine. He became at an early period a communicant in the Church, and his whole subsequent life was worthy of his Christian profession. See *New York Observer*, Nov. 5, 1868; and the *Jubilee Year-book* of that paper for 1873. (J. H. W.)

Morse, Sidney Edwards, an American religious journalist, brother of the preceding, was born at Charlestown, Mass., Feb. 7, 1794, and was educated at Yale College, which he entered at eleven years of age, and was graduated at fourteen, with a class many of whom lived to a great age and became famous in various departments of professional life. He studied theology at Andover and law at Litchfield, but at sixteen began his apparently predestinated life-work by writing for a Boston newspaper. Afterwards, when a number of clergymen about Boston, among them his own father, determined to try the experiment of a religious newspaper, and the *Boston Recorder* was projected, young Morse was chosen to conduct it. A few years later (in 1823) he established, in connection with his brother Richard, the *New York Observer*, which perhaps during the whole of Sidney E. Morse's administration as its senior editor, that is, till 1858, was the ablest religious paper in the country, as it was the pioneer of its class of periodicals. He died Dec. 23, 1871, at his residence in New York. Mr. Morse had a clear and logical mind, wide culture, and a tireless spirit of investigation. He was acknowledged to be a man of broad and catholic views, though eminently conservative in his temperament, and of strong convictions, to which he rendered the most complete loyalty. He was uniformly calm and kind, and not without charity for those with whom he differed on many of the great moral movements of the age, and lived and died having faith in humanity and in God. Few men have had so long a career—for he was engaged in public life sixty years—and fewer yet have ever enjoyed in so rich a measure the reverence of associates and the respect of the great public. He will be especially remembered in coming time as the founder of the *New York Observer*, in the conduct of which he was for nearly forty years actively engaged. From his mind and spirit, probably more than from any other, the religious press of the present day has received its best characteristics, and if new papers now surpass their venerable predecessor—which but few do—they owe their success in no small degree to the inspiration of his genius. Like his distinguished brother, Prof. S. F. B. Morse, he always took an active interest in science, and especially in those branches which relate to geography and exploration, and was engaged until interrupted by his last illness in perfecting an invention for exploring the depths of the ocean. He had been writing on this favorite subject until a late hour a week before his death. His best-known works are *A New System of Modern Geography* (1823), *A North American Atlas,* and a series of general maps. For several years the sales of the two first-mentioned works averaged 70,000 copies annually, and more than 500,000 copies of the first-named have been printed. See *Appleton's Annual Cyclopædia*, 1871, p. 532; *New York Observer*, Dec. 1871; *North Amer. Rev.* Jan. 1823, p. 176–181; *Observer Jubilee Year-book*, 1873. (J. H. W.)

Morsel (prop. פַּת, a *bit*, especially of food, Ruth ii, 14, etc.; βρῶσις, Heb. xii, 16; in the plur. *crumbs*, Lev. ii, 6, etc.; and so of a piece of ice or *hail*, Psa. cxlvii, 17; once [1 Sam. ii, 36] incorrectly for כִּכָּר, *kikkar'*, a *circle* or "loaf" of bread, as elsewhere). See BREAD.

Morta(i)gne, WALTER OF, a noted scholastic of the 12th century, who embraced the realistic views in philosophy, flourished as bishop of Laon, and died in 1174. He is best known as a logician, and is mentioned by John of Salisbury as the chief representative of the doctrine that "the same objects, according to the different condition (status) in which they are considered—i. e. according as our attention is desired to their differences or to their likeness, to the *indifferences* or the *consimile* in them—were either individuals, or species, or genera" (*Metalog.* ii, 17). This doctrine is spoken of by the same author as no longer maintained by any one in his time. See Ueberweg, *Hist. Philos.* i, 387, 398.

Mortal (or DEADLY, as the Anglican theologians prefer to call it) **sin** is, according to Roman Catholicism, the worst form of sin, thus distinguishing in grade of sin, and recognising as moderate and pardonable sin, under the name of *venial*, all such acts of transgression as are not likely to bring eternal punishment on the sinner. According to Peter Dens, the eminent Roman Catholic theologian, whose dicta the Church has accepted as authoritative, mortal sin (Lat. *peccatum*) is that which of itself brings spiritual death to the soul, inasmuch as of itself it deprives the soul of sanctifying grace and charity, in which the spiritual life of the soul consists; and venial sin (Lat. *vitium*) that which does not bring spiritual death to the soul, or that which does not turn it away from its ultimate end, or which is only slightly repugnant to the order of right reason.

Protestants dissent from this view, and indeed visit it with their condemnation, on the ground that this distinction respecting sins tends to immorality and laxity of life. That sins differ in magnitude they concede to be the doctrine of the Scriptures (e. g. Christ declared the sin of Judas to be greater than that of Pilate. This appears also in the case of the servant who knew the will of his master and did it not. This difference, indeed, is conspicuous in the judgment of the degrees and expressions of anger in calling men Raca, "vain," or μωρέ, "fool," and also in Christ's comparing some sins to gnats and others to camels; and in his mention of the "many stripes," and in the "greater condemnation" spoken of by James). Yet the Scriptures also declare that "the wages of sin is death." Therefore, though Protestants, like the Christians of the apostolic and patristic Church, distinguish between greater and less sins (*graviora et leviora*), and hold that a knowledge of this distinction is important in considering the discipline which the early Christians exercised, they yet hold that the early Church did not think any sins to be venial, but deemed all to be mortal (whenever we find the expressions *venial* and *mortal* applied to sins by Augustine and others, these appear to be simply a reference to such sins as require penance and such as do not); and therefore now maintain on this question that all sins are punishable as God may determine, even with everlasting destruction from the presence of God and the glory of his power. They assign for such view the following reasons:

"(i.) Every sin is an offence against God's law, and therefore is deadly and damnable on account of the claims of divine justice; for though sins may be divided into greater and less, yet their proportion to punishment is not varied by their temporal or eternal consequences, but by greater and less punishments.

"(ii.) The law of God never threatens, nor does the justice of God inflict, punishment on any except the transgressors of his law; but the smallest offences are not only threatened, but may be punished with death; therefore they are transgressions of divine law.

"(iii.) Every sin, even that apparently insignificant, is against charity, which is the end of the commandment.

"(iv.) When God appointed expiatory sacrifices for sin, though they were sufficient to show that there existed a difference in the degree of it, yet, because 'without shedding of blood there is no remission,' all manner of sin has rendered the offender guilty and liable to punishment; for 'cursed is every one that continueth not in all things written in the book of the law to do them.' No sin was recognised as venial in the covenant which God entered into with our first parents, for there was no remission; and without the death of Christ there could be none afterwards; therefore, if any sin be venial or pardonable, it is only through the death of Christ and the grace of God; and as God pardons all upon the condition of faith and repentance, and none otherwise, it must follow that, although sins differ in degree, they vary not in their essential character. The man who commits sin at all must die, if he repent not; and he who repents in time and effectually will be saved. 'The wages of sin is death;' of sin indefinitely, and consequently of all sin." See Elliott, *Delin. of Roman Catholicism*, p. 229.

There is, however, a class of Protestants who go so far as to teach that, "while mortal sins are punishable eternally, venial or deadly sins are punishable by God's fatherly chastisements in this life;" and in the same way, as regards the pardon of sin, that "while mortal sins are only forgiven through a direct act of absolution, venial sins are forgiven by renewal of grace (especially in the Eucharist); each mode of pardon presupposing a degree of penitence conformable to the degree of sin." Such is the teaching of the High-Churchmen of the Anglican establishment, the Ritualists of the Protestant Episcopal Church, and the High Lutherans. See the articles SATISFACTION; SIN.

Mortality, subjection to death, is a term not only thus used, but signifies also a contagious disease which destroys great numbers of either men or beasts. *Bills of mortality* are accounts or registers specifying the numbers born, married, and buried in any parish, town, or district; and these are kept in Great Britain generally, and its colonial possessions. In general, they contain only these numbers; and even when thus limited are of great use, by showing the degrees of healthiness and prolificness and the progress of population in the place where they are kept. They should become common also in this country, the clergy keeping really the only trustworthy account of a town's people.

Mortar [for *building*] stands in the Auth. Vers. for two Heb. words: חֹמֶר (*cho'mer*, prop. *red* "clay," as sometimes rendered), *cement*, of lime and sand (Gen. xi, 3; Exod. i, 14), also potter's *clay* (Isa. xli, 25; Nah. iii, 14); עָפָר (*aphar'*, prob. *whitish* "dust," as usually rendered), *mud* or clay, used as a cement in the walls of buildings (Lev. xiv, 42, 45). In Ezek. xiii, 10 the expression occurs, "One built up a wall, and lo, others daubed it with untempered *mortar*" (there is no word in the original answering to this last), which the Targum and the Vulgate seem to understand not of plaster, but of the cement used in uniting the materials of a wall, rendering it "clay without straw," clay and straw, well mixed together, being understood to have been the ordinary cement of Eastern buildings. There is no doubt that the Hebrews sometimes plastered their walls; and that kind of plaster now most common in the East is made with the same materials as the cob-walls, sun-dried bricks and mortar, namely, clay and straw mixed together, the straw such as they give to their cattle, chopped and beaten small, and serving the same purpose as the ox-hair which our plasterers mix with their plaster. This requires to be well tempered, which is generally done by long-continued treading or beating (Kitto, *Pict. Bible*, note ad loc.). See BRICK. Mr. Rich, speaking of the Birs Nimroud at Babylon, says, "The fire-burned bricks of which it is built have inscriptions on them, and so excellent is the cement, which appears to be lime-mortar, that it is nearly impossible to extract one whole." See DWELLING. "Omitting iron cramps, lead [see HANDICRAFT], and the instances in which large stones are found in close apposition without cement, the various compacting substances used in Oriental buildings appear to be: (1) bitumen, as in the

Babylonian structures; (2) common mud or moistened clay; (3) a very firm cement compounded of sand, ashes, and lime, in the proportions respectively of 1, 2, 3, well pounded, sometimes mixed and sometimes coated with oil, so as to form a surface almost impenetrable to wet or the weather. See PLASTER. In Assyrian, and also Egyptian brick buildings, stubble or straw, as hair or wool among ourselves, was added to increase the tenacity (Shaw, *Trav.* p. 206; Volney, *Trav.* ii, 436; Chardin, *Voy.* iv, 116). If the materials were bad in themselves, as mere mud would necessarily be, or insufficiently mixed, or, as the Vulgate seems to understand (Ezek. xiii, 10), if straw were omitted, the mortar or cob-wall would be liable to crumble under the influence of wet weather. (See Shaw, *Trav.* p. 136, and Gesenius, *Thesaur.* p. 1515, s. v. תָּפֵל: a word connected with the Arabic *tafal*, a substance resembling pipe-clay, believed by Burckhardt to be the detritus of the felspar of granite, and used for taking stains out of cloth; Burckhardt, *Syria*, p. 488; Mishna, *Pesach*, x, 3.) Wheels for grinding chalk or lime for mortar, closely resembling our own

Lime-grinding Mill at Cairo.

machines for the same purpose, are in use in Egypt (Niebuhr, *Voy.* i. 122, pl. 17; Burckhardt, *Nubia*, p. 82, 97, 102, 140; Hasselquist, *Trav.* p. 90)." See MASON. Modern Orientals have several materials for mortar superior to bitumen. These consist of three kinds of calcareous earth found abundantly in the desert west of the Euphrates. The first, called *nûra*, is, in present use, mixed with ashes, and employed as a coating for the lower parts of walls in baths and other places liable to dampness. Another, called by the Turks *karej*, and by the Arabs *jus*, is also found in powder mixed with indurated pieces of the same substance and round pebbles. This forms even now the common cement of the country, and constitutes the mortar generally found in the burned brickwork of the most ancient remains. When good, the bricks cemented by it cannot well be detached without being broken, while those laid in bitumen can easily be separated. The third sort, called *borak*, is a substance resembling gypsum, and is found in large lumps of an earthy appearance, which, when burned, form an excellent plaster or whitewash. Pure clay or mud is also used as a cement; but this is exclusively with the sun-dried bricks (Kitto, *Pict. Bible*, note on Gen. xi, 3). See CLAY; LIME.

Mortar [for *pulverizing*] is the rendering of מְדֹכָה (*medokah'*, something for *beating*), Numb. xi, 8; also of מַכְתֵּשׁ (*maktesh'*, lit. a *pounder*, applied also to a "hollow" or socket, e. g. of a tooth, Judg. xv, 19), Prov. xxvii, 22, an instrument for comminuting grain or other substances, by means of a pestle, in place of the later invention or mill (q. v.). In the representation of the various processes of preparing bread on the paintings of the tombs of ancient Egypt, it will be found that the

Ancient Egyptians pounding various substances in mortars with metal pestles.—From Thebes.
a g i, mortars. *d d*, pestles. Figs. 1 and 2, alternately raising and letting fall the pestles into the mortar. Figs. 3 and 4, sifting the substance after it is pounded ; the coarser parts, *h*, being returned into the mortar to be again pounded.

mortar was similarly employed, and the form of the pestle and mortar is there given, and the manner of using them in pounding articles in large quantities. Their mortars were probably blocks of wood, similar to those employed in India. The pestles were different from those now generally employed, but the manner of use, by men striking them alternately, was the same. "Certain persons were also employed in the towns of Egypt, as at the present day in Cairo and other places, to pound various substances in large stone mortars; and salt, seeds, and other things were taken in the same manner by a servant to these shops, whenever it was inconvenient to have it done in the house. The pestles they used, as well as the mortars themselves, were precisely similar to those of the modern Egyptians; and their mode of pounding was the same; two men alternately raising ponderous metal pestles with both hands, and directing their falling point to the centre of the mortar, which is now generally made of a large piece of granite, or other hard stone, scooped out into a long, narrow tube to a little more than half its depth. When the substance was well pounded, it was taken out and passed through a sieve, and the larger particles were again returned to the mortar, until it was sufficiently and equally levigated; and this, and the whole process here represented, so strongly resembles the occupation of the public pounders at Cairo that no one who has been in the habit of walking in the streets of that town can fail to recognise the custom, or doubt of its having been handed down from the early Egyptians, and retained without alteration to the present day" (Wilkinson, *Anc. Eg.* ii, 166). "The simplest and probably most ancient method of preparing corn for food was by pounding it between two stones (Virgil, *Æn.* i, 179). Convenience suggested that the lower of the two stones should be hollowed, that the corn might not escape, and that the upper should be shaped so as to be convenient for holding. The pestle and mortar must have existed from a very early period. The Israelites in the desert appear to have possessed mortars and handmills among their necessary domestic utensils. When the manna fell they gathered

Modern Oriental Mortar and Pestle.

it, and either ground it in the mill or pounded it in the mortar till it was fit for use (Numb. xi, 8). So in the present day stone mortars are used by the Arabs to pound wheat for their national dish *kibby* (Thomson, *Land and Book*, i, 134). Niebuhr describes one of a very simple kind which was used on board the vessel in which he went from Jidda to Loheia. Every afternoon one of the sailors had to take the *durra*, or millet, necessary for the day's consumption, and pound it 'upon a stone, of which the surface was a little curved, with another stone which was long and rounded' (*Descr. de*

l'Arab. p. 45). Among the inhabitants of Ezzehhoue, a Druse village, Burckhardt saw coffee-mortars made

Eastern Coffee-mortar.

out of the trunks of oak-trees (*Syria*, p. 87, 88). The spices for the incense are said to have been prepared by the house of Abtines, a family set apart for the purpose, and the mortar which they used was, with other spoils of the Temple, after the destruction of Jerusalem by Titus, carried to Rome, where it remained till the time of Hadrian (Reggio, in Martinet's *Hebr. Chrest.* p. 35). Buxtorf mentions a kind of mortar (פּוּתָשׁ, *kuttâsh*) in which olives were slightly bruised before they were taken to the olive-presses (*Lex. Talm.* s. v. כתשׁ). From the same root as this last is derived the *maktêsh* of Prov. xxvii, 22, which probably denotes a mortar of a larger kind in which corn was pounded: 'Though thou bray the fool in the *mortar* among the bruised corn with the pestle, yet will not his folly depart from him.' Corn may be separated from its husk and all its good properties preserved by such an operation, but the fool's folly is so essential a part of himself that no analogous process can remove it from him. Such seems the natural interpretation of this remarkable proverb. The language is intentionally exaggerated, and there is no necessity for supposing an allusion to a mode of punishment by which criminals were put to death by being pounded in a mortar. A custom of this kind existed among the Turks, but there is no distinct trace of it among the Hebrews. The Ulemas, or body of lawyers, in Turkey had the distinguished privilege, according to De Tott (*Mem.* i, 28, Eng. tr.), of being put to death only by the pestle and the mortar. Such, however, is supposed to be the reference in the proverb by Mr. Roberts, who illustrates it from his Indian experience. 'Large mortars are used in the East for the purpose of separating the rice from the husk. When a considerable quantity has to be prepared, the mortar is placed outside the door, and two women, each with a pestle of five feet long, begin the work. They strike in rotation, as blacksmiths do on the anvil. Cruel as it is, this is a punishment of the state: the poor victim is thrust into the mortar, and beaten with the pestle. The late king of Kandy compelled one of the wives of his rebellious chiefs thus to beat her own infant to death. Hence the saying, "Though you beat that loose woman in a mortar, she will not leave her ways;" which means, Though you chastise her ever so much, she will never improve' (*Orient. Illustr.* p. 368)." "We do not infer from the above passage in Proverbs that the wheat was pounded to meal instead of being ground, but that it was pounded to be separated from the husk. The Jews probably had no rice, but there are several passages from which we may gather that they used wheat in the same way that rice is now used—that is, boiled up in pillaus, variously prepared. In fact, we have partaken of wheat thus employed in the remote mountains where rice could not be obtained, or only at a price which the villagers could not afford; and it is also so used among the Arabs, forming a very palatable and nutritive food. For this purpose it is necessary that, as with rice, the husk should be previously disengaged from the grain; and if we suppose that this object was attained with wheat, by a similar treatment with that to which rice is now subjected, the present text may be very satisfactorily explained. There are men, and even women, who gain their bread by the labor of husking rice, which they generally perform in pairs. Their implements consist of a rude wooden mortar, formed of a block hollowed out; pestles, about five feet long, with a heavy block of wood at the upper end; and a sieve for sifting the pounded grain. They carry these utensils to the house where their services are required, and, if men, strip to the skin (except their drawers), and pursue their labor in a shady part of the court-yard. When two work together, they commonly stand opposite each other, and strike their pestles into the mortar alternately, as blacksmiths strike their iron. Sometimes, however, one pestle alone acts, and the laborers relieve each other, the relieved person taking the easier duty of supplying the mortar, and removing and sifting the cleaned grain. From the weight of the pestle, the labor of pounding is very severe, and the results of the process are but slowly produced" (Kitto, *Pict. Bible*, note on Prov. xxvii, 22). See PESTLE.

Mortar, HOLY, the term applied to mortar used in cementing altar stones in churches and in Roman Catholic establishments, is made with holy water.

Mortera, SAUL HA-LEWI, a Jewish divine of note, was born about 1596 in Germany; studied at Venice and France; and settled at Amsterdam as rabbi of the Sephardim, or Spanish Jews, where he founded in 1643 the academy *Keter Tora*. When Elias Montalto died, Mortera was sent to Paris to convey the corpse of Montalto for interment in Amsterdam. He died in 1660. Mortera is noted, moreover, as having been the teacher of the famous Baruch Spinoza. Of his works the following are worthy of notice: his *Gibeath Shaul* (גִּבְעַת שָׁאוּל), a collection of *Sermons* (Amst. 1645), and a polemical work, entitled תּוֹרַת מֹשֶׁה, *The Divine Providence of God towards Israel*, impugning Romanism so severely that it could never be printed. See Fürst, *Bibl. Jud.* ii, 391; De Rossi, *Dizionario* (Ger. transl.), p. 284 sq.; *Bibl. Jud. Antichr.* p. 72 sq.; Rodriguez de Castro, *Bibl. Rabb. Span.* i, 573; Lindo, *Hist. of the Jews in Spain*, p. 368; Kayserling, *Sephardim*, p. 201, 206, 254; *Gesch. d. Juden in Portugal*, p. 275–310; Jost, *Gesch. d. Juden. u. s. Sekten*, iii, 232 sq.; Grätz, *Gesch. d. Juden*, ix, 525; x, 9, 10, 11, 141, 169, 176; Zunz, *Monatstage* (Berlin, 1872), p. 7. (B. P.)

Mortgage (עָרַב, *arab'*, Neh. v, 3, *to pawn* anything), a lien upon real estate for debt (Gesenius reads the passage, "we must pawn our houses"); in 1 Sam. xvii, 18 rendered "pledge," and in Prov. xvii, 18 "surety," whence עֲרָבוֹן, *arabôn*, "anything given as a pledge or promise" (Gen. xxxviii, 17, 18, 20). Gesenius thinks the word was probably introduced as a commercial term, from the Hebrew or Phœnician language, into the Greek and Latin, as ἀῤῥαβών, and *arrhabo*, in the signification of *earnest*, or purchase-money. See LOAN.

Mortification (1), is a term generally applied, in theological parlance, to certain voluntary inflictions of pain or acts of self-denial, which are supposed by those that employ them to have a meritorious efficacy, or at least a salutary moral influence on the sufferer. Wherever these austerities have been practiced, it is easy to trace erroneous views of Christian truth. This is apparent in the system of monkery and asceticism which at so early a period overspread the Church. Every religion of man's devising, or mixed and modified by man's corruptions, will be found to place religious excellence more in self-inflicted sufferings than in moral duties; to prize more that mortification which consists in voluntary endurance of pain and privation than that which consists in the habitual subjugation of sinful passions. It will ordinarily be found that the prevalence in any religion of general laxity of morals and of severe austerities will keep pace with each other. The greater the merit attached to self-inflicted sufferings by certain devotees, the greater will be the indulgence for neglect of moral duties; and the stricter the requirement of fasts and mortifications at certain seasons, according to prescribed regulations, the less the general restraint at other times. The religion of Christ inculcates habitual self-control, a readiness and firmness in the discharge of each appointed duty, however painful; which is a self-denial more difficult to the natural man than even habitual austerities. The mortification of sin in believers is a duty enjoined in the sacred Scriptures (Rom. viii, 13: "For if ye live after the flesh, ye shall die [μέλλετε ἀποθνήσκειν]; but if ye through the Spirit do mortify [θανατοῦτε] the deeds of the body, ye shall live;" Col. iii, 5: "Mortify [νεκρώσατε] therefore your members which are upon the earth"). It consists in breaking the league with sin, declaration of open hostility against it, and strong resistance to it (Eph. vi, 10, etc.; Gal. v, 24; Rom. viii, 13). The means to be used in this work are not macerating the body, seclusion from society, or our own resolutions; but the Holy Spirit is the chief agent (Rom. viii, 13), while faith, prayer, and dependence are subordinate means to this end. The evidences of mortification are not the cessation from one sin, for that may be only exchanged for another, or it may be renounced because it is a gross sin, or there may not be an occasion to practice it; but if sin be mortified, we shall not yield to temptation; our minds will be more spiritual; we shall find more happiness in spiritual services, and bring forth the fruits of the Spirit. See Owen *On the Mortification of Sin, and on the Holy Spirit*, ch. viii, bk. 4; Charnock's *Works*, ii, 1313; Bryson's *Sermons on Rom. viii*, p. 97, etc.; Farrar, *Eccles. Dict.* s. v. See SELF-DENIAL.

Mortification (2), in Scotch law, is a term used to denote lands given for charitable or other public uses. When lands are so given, they are in general formally conveyed to the trustees of the charity, to be held blench, or in feu. When mortifications are given in general to the poor, without naming particular trustees, they fall under the administration of the Court of Session. By the statute of 1633, c. 6, it was declared unlawful to alter any mortifications, and the managers were rendered liable to be called to account for malversation. Any person entitled to the benefit of the fund can pursue actions of this kind.

Mortimer, John Hamilton, an English artist of high repute in his day, who gave himself largely to ecclesiastical and Biblical subjects, was born in 1741 of humble parentage, and was the youngest of four children. Having acquired a taste for drawing from an uncle who was an itinerant portrait-painter, he was at about the age of eighteen placed under Hudson, who had been the instructor of Reynolds. With him, however, he did not continue long; but, after having studied a while in the gallery of the duke of Richmond, Mortimer began to make himself known by his productions. One of his earliest works, founded on an incident in the life of Edward the Confessor, painted in competition with Romney, obtained from the Society for the Encouragement of Arts a premium of fifty guineas, and another, presenting *St. Paul preaching to the Britons,* one hundred guineas. He was further distinguished by the notice and friendship of Reynolds, which friendship has been attributed, not to the sympathy, but to the opposition of their tastes in art. Mortimer was no colorist, and but an indifferent portrait-painter, although he produced many admirable heads and likenesses in black and white chalk. His talent lay in design, and in wild and fantastic quite as much as in historical subjects. He designed *The Brazen Serpent* in the great window of Salisbury Cathedral, and the cartoons for that in Brazenose College. He died Feb. 4, 1779, and was buried in the church at High Wycombe, near the altar, where is his painting of *St. Paul preaching to the Britons.* See *Engl. Cyclop.* s. v.; Spooner, *Dict. of the Fine Arts,* s. v.

Mortimer, Thomas, D.D., an English divine, who was born near the opening of our century, flourished at London as minister of Gray's Inn, and died in 1849. He published *Lectures on the Influence of the Holy Spirit* (Lond. 1824, 8vo), which Bickersteth pronounces "evangelical, practical, and edifying," and several series of his *Sermons* (Lond. 1822, 8vo; 1825, 8vo). See Allibone, *Dict. of Brit. and Amer. Auth.* s. v.

Mortmain (from French *mort,* "dead," and *main,* "hand," which in turn from Latin *mortua manu,* i. e. in the *dead hand*) is the technical term of a series of Anglican statutes dealing with the lands of corporate bodies, especially ecclesiastical. The most probable origin of the term is that given by Coke, that "the lands were said to come to dead hands as to the lords, for that by alienation in mortmain they lost wholly their escheats, and in effect their knights' services, for the defence of the realm, wards, marriages, reliefs, and the like, and therefore was called a dead hand, for that a dead hand yieldeth no service." In the latter part of the Middle Ages the Roman Catholic Church, which had acquired a strong hold in England, came to own very largely the real estate of the country, until at one time it owned fully one third of all the English landed estate, which thus paid no taxes. By 1215 it had obtained so large a part of the real estate that it practically disabled the government from raising the necessary means to pay its expenses. To put a stop to this evil, a clause was introduced into the *Magna Charta* forbidding gifts of land to religious houses. This was the first statute of mortmain, and declares "that if any one shall give land to a religious house, the grant shall be void, and the land forfeited to the lord of the fee." But when the Romish Church, which had no interest in state affairs, saw itself thus suddenly cut short in its expansion of power and wealth, it found a way to evade the law by taking, instead of a fee-simple title to the land, leases for a thousand years. To meet this evasion of the intent of the law, the state, in the reign of Edward I, passed the statute *De Religiosis,* which restrained people at the time of their death, or otherwise, from giving or making over any lands or rents to churches or religious houses without the king's leave being first obtained. This was rendered extremely necessary by the fact that the king's exchequer had been impoverished to the utmost by the

accumulation of landed property in the hands of ecclesiastical bodies, and protection of the state interests, especially in view of the evasions of the Church. But even this provision failed to meet the case. The wily churchmen found a way to evade compliance with this law by a collusive action brought in court for each piece of real estate the Church wished to get title of. In this way an individual entirely under control of the Church would take the title to the property and occupy it; then the religious corporation would bring a suit of ejectment against him, claiming that the title in the property was in the Church, and that he was illegally keeping the Church out of it. The tenant, being in collusion with the Church, would make no defence, and a decree on default would be taken, adjudging the property to the Church; then they would hold it by a decree of court called a recovery. Thus the statute of the 7 Edward I was completely evaded and the state circumvented. Another statute, the 13 Edward I, was passed, prohibiting religious corporations from taking either by gift, purchase, lease, or recovery. Priestly ingenuity, however, in a short time succeeded in meeting also this provision, and for its evasion introduced into England from the Roman law the doctrine of uses, by which the title of real estate would be in another; but he would hold it to the uses of a religious house, so that the religious corporation would get all the benefit of the real estate, the naked title standing only in the individual. This practice was shielded under a royal charter of license, which (as e. g. by 17 Car. II, c. 3) enacted, "Every owner of any impropriations, tithes, or portions of tithes, in any parish or chapelry, may give and annex the same, or any part thereof, unto the patronage or vicarage of the said parish church or chapel where the same do lie or arise; or settle the same in trust for the benefit of the said parsonage or vicarage, or of the curate or curates there successively, where the parsonage is impropriate and no vicar endowed, without any license or mortmain." The evil became so oppressive that finally the 15 Richard II was enacted to head off the priests from swallowing up the fruits of the lands under their new doctrine imported from Italy of uses and trusts. But again priestcraft gained the upper hand, and by the 23 Henry VIII, c. 10, it was enacted, "That if any grants of lands or other hereditaments should be made in trust to the use of any churches, chapels, churchwardens, guilds, fraternities, etc., to have perpetual obits, or a continual service of a priest forever, or for sixty or eighty years, or to such like uses and intents, all such uses, intents, and purposes shall be void; they being no corporations, but erected either of devotion or else by the common consent of the people; and all collateral assurances made for defeating this statute shall be void, and the said statute shall be expounded most beneficially for the destruction of such uses as aforesaid." Even this provision failed to cover the case; and at last, in 1736, the celebrated statute of George II was passed, which effectually put an end to all evasions of ecclesiastical taxation. Perhaps even it would have been insufficient to cope with Romish cunning, but the dethronement of the Roman Catholics from their former predominance as an ecclesiastical body no doubt greatly contributed to a successful issue in the question. It was the confiscation of Church property in the reign of Henry VIII that paved the way for a successful issue of the provisions sought for in the statutes of mortmain. The statute of mortmain as enacted under George II, which is entitled, "An Act to restrain the Disposition of Lands, whereby the same become inalienable," is now the leading English act. It forbids the gift of money or lands to charitable uses except by deed operating *immediately,* and without power of revocation, formally executed and enrolled in chancery at least six months before the donor's death. This provision was made especially to prevent priests and others from importuning a dying man to convey his land for charitable purposes. Hence, though a person can, in England, up to the last hour of his life, if possessing sufficient knowledge of what he does, devise by will all his land to individuals absolutely, it is otherwise if he intend to give the land to trustees for a charitable purpose, as to build a church, or school, or hospital. The statute of mortmain, 9 George II, c. 36, reciting that public mischief had greatly increased by many large and improvident dispositions made by languishing and dying persons to charitable uses, to take place after their deaths, to the disinheritance of their lawful heirs, enacts that in future no lands or sums of money to be laid out in land shall be given to any person or body, unless such gift or conveyance shall be made or executed in presence of two witnesses twelve months before the death of the donor or grantor, and be enrolled in the Court of Chancery within six months after the execution. Therefore a person on death-bed cannot in England give land, or money to buy land, for a charitable purpose. It can only be done in the life of the donor, at least twelve months before his death; and the property must be completely alienated, so that he has no further control over it. The deed must have a present operation, and must not reserve any life-interest to the donor; it must be done at once and forever. The policy of this statute has sometimes been questioned, and several well-known modes of evading the statute have been adopted from time to time. The act has been held to apply only to land locally situated in England: and hence, if the land is situated in Scotland, or the colonies, or abroad, a will conveying it for charitable purposes will receive effect. In Scotland the mortmain act has no application; but the reason for this is that the common law of Scotland contains a similar check on the alienation of land on death-bed, and which, in some respects, has a universal application. Several acts have been passed since 9 George II, c. 36, as already stated, for exempting various bodies from the operation of that act. These acts chiefly apply to the Established Church. The statute 58 George III, c. 45, amended by 59 George III, c. 134, and 2 and 3 William IV, c. 61, is intended to promote the building of new churches in populous places in England and Wales. The law 43 George III, c. 107, was passed to exempt decrees and bequests to the governors of Queen Anne's Bounty. By 12 and 13 Victoria, c. 49, § 4, grants of land for sites of schools, not exceeding five acres, are voted; and there are other more recent modifications.

In the United States the English mortmain laws have not in general been adopted or recognised, except in Pennsylvania; and in that state, by an act passed in 1855, bequests, devises, or conveyances, for religious or charitable uses, may be valid if made by deed or will at least one calendar month before the death of the testator or alienor. In New York, by a statute enacted in 1848, gifts to charitable corporations by will must be made two months before the testator's death; and by another enacted in 1860 any person having a husband, wife, child, or parent, is precluded from bequeathing more than one half of his clear estate to any society, association, or corporation. In Georgia, in like manner, a gift to charitable uses by will is made void if the testator has a wife or issue living, unless made ninety days before his death. In other states the checks to the acquisition of real estate by corporate bodies are such as are imposed by their charters, or by the general laws under which they have become incorporated. These limit their property to an amount sufficient for their natural uses, and whenever corporations come into the possession of more than is thus demanded or authorized, a special act of legislation is necessary to legalize such possessions; excepting, however, the transfer of landed estate in liquidation of indebtedness by the grantor, yet such possessions can be held only until they can be properly disposed of by sale. Roman Catholics generally evade the statues by holding their property in the bishop's name, thus constituting it his own estate, though they use it for ecclesiastical purposes. See Collier, *Eccles. Hist.* (see Index in vol. ix); Milman, *Lat.*

Christianity (see Index in vol. viii); Baxter, *Ch. Hist.* p. 283; Elliott, *Delineation of Romanism*, p. 173, 296; Chambers, *Cyclop.* s. v.; *Amer. Cyclop.* s. v.; Eadie, *Eccles. Cyclop.* s. v.; Coke, *First Part of the Institutes of the Laws of England* (Phila. 1853, 2 vols. 8vo), i, 99, 112; Blackstone, *Commentaries on the Laws of England* (Phila. 1863, 2 vols. 8vo), bk. i, 479; bk. ii, 268; bk. iv, 108, 424, 426, 441.

Morton, Charles, an early New England divine, was born in Cornwall, England, in 1626; was educated at Oxford University, of which he was a fellow; entered holy orders, and was at first a Royalist, but becoming a Puritan, was ejected from Blisland for his nonconformity in 1662. He had established an academy at Newington Green, and continued at its head for twenty years. Among his pupils was Defoe, the author of *Robinson Crusoe.* Being much annoyed by the bishop's court, Morton felt obliged to leave the country, and in 1686 emigrated to New England, and settled in Charlestown, Mass., where he held a position till his death, which occurred April 11, 1698. He was well esteemed by his contemporaries, and acknowledged to be a man of eminent learning. He wrote a number of religious works, among which is *The Ark, its Loss and Recovery.* See Drake, *Dict. of Amer. Biogr.* s. v.

Morton, James Douglas, *Earl of,* a Scotch nobleman, who figures quite notably in the secular as well as ecclesiastical history of his country, was the second son of Sir George Douglas of Pittendriech, and in 1553 succeeded, in right of his wife, Elizabeth, daughter of the third earl, to the title and estates of the earldom. His father was a most ardent adherent to the cause of the Reformation, and very early he also favored the same cause, and was a friend of king Henry VIII in the designs of that monarch in reference to Scotland. His name, however, does not often appear in the public transactions of the period; and although in 1557 he was one of the original Lords of the Congregation, he seems yet to have been afraid of the consequences, in a personal point of view, of casting off the queen-regent, from whom he had already received considerable favors, and therefore held a rather doubtful and irresolute course. It was for this reason that Sadler, the English envoy, describes Morton as "a simple and fearful man." The death of the queen-regent, however, completely changed the man. He now boldly came forward and avowed himself unequivocally a Protestant. Sworn a privy councillor in 1561, he was appointed lord high chancellor of Scotland, Jan. 7, 1563, in the place forfeited by the earl of Huntly, who had been the great head of the Roman Catholic party in Scotland. He had, however, only been in office a few years when he was obliged to quit it; for, having been one of the chief conspirators against Rizzio, the Italian secretary of queen Mary, on his assassination, March 9, 1566, he fled with his associates to England, and remained there until, through the interest of the earl of Bothwell, he obtained his pardon from the queen. Bothwell, unprincipled as he was, no doubt helped Morton because he hoped, in turn, to be obliged; and no sooner was the earl reinstated in favor with the queen than Bothwell opened to him the plot which he meditated for the murder of Darnley, expecting, of course, Morton's ready acquiescence. In this, however, Bothwell was mistaken; Morton refused to concur. But neither did he inform Darnley of the plot, nor take any measures to prevent its being executed; and he was one of those who subscribed the famous bond to protect Bothwell against the charge of being concerned in the murder, and to use every endeavor to promote his marriage with the queen. Yet when this latter event took place, and when Bothwell became odious to the nation, Morton was the great leader in opposition to him; and it was to the castle of his relative, the lady of Lochleven, that Mary was conducted when she delivered herself up at Carbery Hill. When Mary was securely lodged in this place of confinement, the earl of Murray was made regent of the kingdom, and Morton reinstated in the office of lord chancellor. He continued in this situation during the regencies of Murray, Lennox, and Mar, and was indeed a principal actor in all matters of importance which took place in their time; and on Mar's death, at the end of the year 1572, Morton was himself appointed regent of the kingdom. While in the regency Morton played an important part for the ecclesiastical history of Scotland. The court and the Kirk were at this time involved in much controversy, because the former was bent upon the introduction of the episcopacy. The conflict had begun previous to the death of Knox (November, 1572), for the purpose of securing to the Church the revenues of the episcopal sees; and a convention of superintendents and other ministers favorable to the design had been held in Leith in August, 1572, and had declared that the titles of bishop and archbishop should be restored, provided that with the restoration of *titles* no greater authority was delegated than was possessed by the superintendents, and that they be elected by the ministers of the respective dioceses. The primary object was to prevent the property passing into the hands of the nobles and courtiers. But the General Assembly, which convened shortly after the convention, condemned the innovation, and hence arose a conflict with the regent, who favored the action of the convention which he had been instrumental in calling. He had himself an interest in the successful issue of this movement; he cared less for the Church's interest than he did for his own, his object being ostensibly to place these bishops in positions to draw the income of the benefice, but really to secure for himself and other nobles a larger part of the revenues from those ecclesiastics whom he should help to elevate to such stations; and hence these episcopal incumbents were called *tulchan bishops*—a *tulchan* being a calfskin stuffed with straw, which the country people set up beside a cow to induce her to give her milk. The bishop, it was said, had the title, but my lord had the milk. This conflict between the tulchan episcopacy and the Church establishment, supported by legal enactments, continued until the close of the earl's regency, when it was brought to a successful termination for the Kirk's interests by the efforts of that worthy follower of John Knox, the learned and resolute and noble-souled Andrew Melville (q. v.). See SCOTLAND, CHURCH OF. In this struggle with the Kirk, as well as in secular affairs, Morton displayed great vigor and ability, yet at the same time his ambition, his avarice, and rapacity, and his general want of principle, became apparent to all; he was now at once feared and hated; and finding himself becoming odious to the nation, and knowing that the young king, James VI, desired to assume the reins of government, Morton finally resigned the regency in March, 1578. Subsequently obtaining possession of the castle of Stirling, with the person of the king, he recovered his authority, and by the help of queen Elizabeth retained it for some time; but at length the king's new favorite, captain Stewart, who, as Robertson says, shunned no action, however desperate, if it led to power or favor, charged him in the king's presence with being accessory to the murder of Darnley, and thus procured Morton's incarceration. Elizabeth used every endeavor in favor of Morton, but the greater the solicitude which she showed for his safety, the more eagerly did his enemies urge his destruction; and being carried by captain Stewart, then earl of Arran, into Edinburgh, he was, on June 1, 1581, brought to trial, found guilty, and condemned to death. When that part of the verdict was read which, besides finding that he had concealed, found that he was also accessory to the murder, he repeated the words with vehemence, and then exclaimed, "God knows it is not so." The next morning, speaking of the crime for which he was condemned, he admitted that on his return from England, after the death of Rizzio, Bothwell had informed him of the conspiracy against Darnley, which the queen, as he told him, knew

of and approved, but he had no hand in it. And as to revealing the plot, "To whom," said he, "could I reveal it? To the queen? She was aware of it. To Darnley? He was such a babe that there was nothing told to him but he would tell to her again; and the two most powerful noblemen in the kingdom, Bothwell and Huntly, were the perpetrators. I foreknew and concealed the plot, but as to being art and part in its execution, I call God to witness I am wholly innocent." When his keepers told him that the guards were attending, and all was in readiness, he replied, "I thank my God, I am ready likewise." On the scaffold his behavior was calm, his countenance and voice unaltered, and after some time spent in acts of devotion, he was beheaded by the instrument called the Maiden, June 3, 1581. See Froude, *Hist. of England*, vii, 306 sq.; viii, 250 sq.; x, 53 sq.; xi, 96, et al.; Burke, *Peerage of England*; Burton, *Hist. of Scotland*; Robertson, *Hist. of Scotland*; Spottiswood, *Hist. of the Church of Scotland*, ii, 171–195; Butler, *Manual of Eccles. Hist.* ii, 550–553; *English Cyclopædia* (Biographical Department, vol. iv, s. v.).

Morton, John, an English cardinal and archbishop, one of the most noted characters of the history of England during the Middle Ages, figuring prominently in the political history of Europe, was eldest son of Richard Morton, of Milbourne St. Andrews, in Dorsetshire, and was born at Bere in that county in 1410. He received his primary education at the Benedictine abbey of his native place, and thence went to Baliol College, Oxford, to study canon and civil law; and after having become master of arts, went to London, and practiced law in the Court of Arches, retaining, however, all the time his connection with the university. In 1453 he was made principal of Peckwater Inn, having been previously ordained. In 1450 he was appointed subdean of Lincoln, and in 1458 he was collated to the prebend of Fordington with Writhlington, in the cathedral of Salisbury, which he resigned in 1476. In the same year he was installed prebendary of Covingham, in the cathedral of Lincoln. In 1472 he was collated by archbishop Bourchier to the rectory of St. Dunstan's-in-the-East, London; and the same year also to the prebend of Isledon, in the cathedral of St. Paul, which he exchanged in the following year for that of Chiswick. In 1473 he was appointed master of the rolls, and in 1474 archdeacon of Winchester and Chester. In the following year he became archdeacon of Huntington and prebendary of St. Decuman, in the cathedral of Wells. In April, 1476, he was installed prebendary of South Newbald, in the metropolitan church of York, and archdeacon of Berkshire; and in January following he was made also archdeacon of Leicester. Rarely were appointments bestowed so liberally upon any one as upon Morton. But the reason is easily found. While yet practicing as an advocate in the Court of Arches, his eminent qualities were a matter of general comment, and brought him to the notice of cardinal Bourchier, who, besides conferring many of the above preferments on him, had introduced him to Henry VI, by whom he was made one of the privy council. To this unfortunate prince Morton adhered with so much fidelity, while others deserted him, that even his successor, Edward IV, admired and recompensed his attachment, took him into his council, and was principally guided by his advice. He also in the same year, 1478, made him bishop of Ely and lord chancellor of England; and at his death he appointed him one of his executors. On this account, however, he was considered in no favorable light by the protector, afterwards Richard III, and he was marked as one whose life was required to give peace to the sovereign. Accordingly, when Morton and others assembled in the Tower, June 13, 1483, to consult about the coronation of Edward V, the bishop, with archbishop Rotheram and lord Stanley, were taken into custody, as known enemies to the measures then in agitation. Morton's execution was expected by everybody. His numerous friends, however, made bold, particularly those at the University of Oxford, and these learned men addressed king Richard "in the most courteous language of which their Latinity was capable in behalf of their imprisoned patron; and praised him and apologized with such success that the king relented so far as to direct his being sent to Brecknock, in Wales, to be in charge of the duke of Buckingham" (Williams). He was accordingly sent to the castle of Brecknock, but thence made his escape to the Isle of Ely, and soon after, disguising himself, went to the Continent, to Henry, earl of Richmond. It is said that the plan of marrying Elizabeth, the eldest daughter of Edward IV, to Henry, and thus, by joining the white rose with the red, effecting a coalition between the jarring parties of York and Lancaster, was originally suggested by Morton. In 1485 the word came to Morton, then in Flanders, that his enemy had been dethroned, and with it an invitation for his attendance upon the coronation of the new king, afterwards Henry VII. He returned forthwith, easily got his attainder reversed, and was at once admitted into the confidence of his new royal master, who was no sooner seated on his throne than he made Morton one of his privy council; and on the death of cardinal Bourchier in 1486, secured his election to the archbishopric of Canterbury, a position which he honored, and in which he accomplished much for the good of his country.

Williams thus sums up his official character and conduct (*Lives of the English Cardinals* [Lond. 1862, 2 vols. 8vo], ii, 167 sq.):

"In the performance of his ecclesiastical duties Morton took high ground. To a considerable extent he favored the pretensions of the papal court, but while doing so exercised a vigilant superintendence over the Anglican establishment, and maintained a severe discipline. The objects with which the principal religious houses of a mixed charitable and religious order had been founded were gradually lost sight of; and the great abbeys and priories throughout the country, with a few honorable exceptions, had become so notorious for the luxurious and depraved living of the fraternities, as to excite satirical attacks from both clergy and laity. The archbishop of Canterbury, knowing the scandalous practices that existed in his own diocese, as well as in others, was anxious to remedy so grave an evil. He heard the reports of various persons likely to be well informed on the subject, and then sent to Rome for instructions. He was well aware that without due support from the highest quarter no amelioration of the disease, which he knew to be eating like a leprosy into the Church, could be effected. The immorality of the English clergy had become so flagrant in the last quarter of the fifteenth century that the primate readily procured the pope's authority for a visitation. He proceeded from one to another of the monasteries and abbeys, and laid the result before a provincial synod. His exposure of folly and profligacy produced no great effect upon the assembly; admonitions and cautions were bestowed upon the great offenders, but the swarm of clerical roysterers, sportsmen, and swashbucklers were scarcely at all interfered with judicially. The severest thing done was the sending around to religious houses a written address dilating on the scandalous lives that many priests were living, and exhorting them to reform.

"The state of things was atrocious enough apparently to have caused the bones of the English pope to stir in his grave with indignation. Ample provocation had been given for the extreme exercise of the powers granted by the head of the Church thus disgraced and outraged; but archbishop Morton presently found that he had commenced a task which he had neither the power nor the courage to complete. Probably he was made aware that the abbot William had influential friends in England as well as in Rome, as such delinquents could always secure, and that his proper punishment was impossible; or discovered that St. Alban's was only one of the many establishments in England in which prodigality and profligacy flourished—in short, that the evil was too formidable to be grappled with successfully by him. So no further step was taken in the reformation that even then had become imperative in the opinion of right-minded Catholics. Several attempts had previously been made to check clerical foppery, but with scarcely any result. The archbishop made a strenuous effort at reform in this direction, threatening with sequestration those who offended by assuming the extravagances of fashion adopted by the laity. Priests were prohibited wearing hoods, with fur or without, doubled with silk, or adorned with a horn or short tail, or having camlet about the neck. They were not to array themselves with sword or dagger, or with decorated belts, but were to walk abroad in their proper crowns and tonsures, showing their ears.

"A most remarkable document was the bull of Pope Innocent VIII, published in 1489, stating that the English clergy were for the most part dissolute and reprobate, and giving authority to the primate for their correction and reformation. The latter was earnest in the cause, for he got the pope's bull backed by an act of Parliament for the sure and likely reformation of priests, clerks, and religious men, culpable, or by their demerits openly reputed of incontinent living in their bodies, contrary to their order, and directed punishment to be awarded to fornication, incest, or any other fleshly incontinency (*Statutes at Large*, ii, 65). The king took special interest in this praiseworthy movement, and encouraged the primate to go through with his work. With the co-operation of pope, king, and Parliament, he increased his exertions, and proceeded with all the state he could assume, in accordance with his exalted spiritual and temporal offices, to make visitation after visitation—at Rochester, Worcester, and Salisbury, twice; Lichfield and Coventry, Bath and Wells, Winchester, Lincoln, and Exeter. While he corrected abuses, he collected money, as he found the offenders ready to

"'Compound for sins they were inclined to,
By damning those they had no mind to.'"

That Morton found favor in the eyes of his king is evident, inasmuch as he made this archbishop also lord chancellor. In a council of his suffragans, which the archbishop held in February, 1486, at St. Paul's, in London, the corruptions in the Anglican Church were further considered, and measures adopted to deepen the religious fervor of the people. It was also provided that "every bishop of the province shall cause a service and six masses to be said for the soul of a departed bishop, within a month from the time of their hearing of his death." Some measures adopted by this council were made the subjects of attack. Among other arrangements it was provided that ecclesiastics should not preach against the papacy or against any ecclesiastical officers before the lay people. Morton's intent, no doubt, was to favor and please the papacy in so far as was at all consistent with the end he desired to attain. He certainly did not mean to check any reforms. Thus he provided that if any spiritual person behaved himself wickedly, the ordinary was to be informed; and if the ordinary did not correct such offender, the archbishop was to be appealed to; and, finally, if he did not punish the delinquent, then it was the said prelate's will that the preachers generally should declaim against him.

In 1493 Morton, after repeated and urgent requests of the English king, was created a cardinal by pope Alexander VI. The few years that remained him for activity he employed in the work to which he had dedicated his life. He instituted and promoted reforms in the Church wherever his keen eye could detect their need. He also labored assiduously to advance the interests of his royal master, and even went so far as to urge upon the pope the canonization of Henry VI. He failed in this, but succeeded in securing the canonization of Anselm, which he had also desired. He died, according to the Canterbury Obituary, Tuesday, 16 kal. Oct.; but according to the Register of Ely, Sept. 15, 1500. Leland says that cardinal Morton employed the fortune he possessed in building and repairing Church property at Canterbury, Lambeth, Maidstone, Allington Park, Charing, Ford, and Oxford; it is said also that he repaired the canon-law school, assisted in the building of the divinity school, and the rebuilding of St. Mary's Church. In Feb., 1494, he was elected chancellor of the University of Oxford, in which year, Fuller says, he greatly promoted the rebuilding of Rochester bridge. Among other public-spirited enterprises which his liberality conduced to execute, was the famous cut or drain from Peterborough to Wisbeach, a tract of upwards of twelve miles across a fenny country, which proved a great benefit to his diocese and to the public, and was completed entirely at his expense. This is still known by the name of Morton's Leame. "Cardinal Morton," says Williams, "has left solid claims on the respect of posterity; but more enduring than his benevolent bequests, and his useful buildings and improvements, have been his labors to effect a reformation in the Church. They were not productive of much immediate result, but helped materially to bring about the vigorous movement which was successful in the following reign. His investigations proved beyond the possibility of doubt that the evils of the papal system had nearly reached their limit" (p. 190). Cardinal Morton was the patron of Sir Thomas More, who eulogized him in his *Utopia.* The *Life of King Richard III*, sometimes attributed to More, is believed to have been written by Morton; and if Morton did not himself write the *Life*, it seems to be quite clear that More (who was in early life a page in Morton's house) must have derived part of his information directly from the archbishop. See Tanner, *Bibl. Brit. Hib.* p. 532, 533; Bentham, *Hist. of Ely* (Cambr. 1771), p. 179–181; Budden, *Life of John Morton* (1607); Hook, *Lives of the Archbishops of Canterbury*, vol. v; Williams, *Lives of the English Cardinals*, vol. ii, chap. vii; Collier, *Eccles. Hist.* (see Index in vol. viii).

Morton, Nathaniel, an American writer on ecclesiastical history, and one of the Plymouth colonists, was born in England in 1612, and came to this country with his father in 1623. In 1645 he was made secretary of the colony, and continued to hold that office until his death, June 28, 1685. He is noted as the author of *New England's Memorial, or a brief Relation of the most memorable and remarkable Passages of the Providence of God manifested to the Planters of New England*, etc., compiled chiefly from the MSS. of his uncle, William Bradford, and the journals of Edward Winslow, and including the period from 1620–1646 (Cambridge, 1669, 4to; 2d ed. Boston, 1721, 12mo; 3d ed. Newport, 1772; 5th ed., with notes by Judge Davis, 1826; 6th ed., with notes by the Congregational Board, 1855, 8vo). He also wrote in 1680 a brief *Eccles. Hist. of the Plymouth Church*, in its records, preserved in Ebenezer Hazard's *Historical Collections.* See Chancellor Kent, *Course of English Reading* (1853), p. 15; *North Amer. Rev.* xlvi, 481 sq.; Winthrop, *New England* (1853), i, 94; Bacon, *Genesis of the New England Churches* (1875), p. 199, 475.

Morton, Thomas, an English prelate noted for his learning and prudence, was born at York in 1564. He was a relative of cardinal Morton, but a Protestant. In 1582 he was sent to St. John's College, Cambridge University, and after graduation was chosen a fellow (in 1592). He lectured for a while at his alma mater on logic, and about 1599 became chaplain to the earl of Huntingdon, and made himself conspicuous in attempts for the recalling of such of the Protestants as had become recusants during the reign of bloody Mary. During the plague of 1602 also Morton distinguished himself by great charity and resolution. In 1603 he went abroad as chaplain to lord Eure, ambassador to Germany and Denmark, and while in those countries availed himself of the valuable literary advantages brought within his reach. In 1606 he was made chaplain to king James I, and given the preferment of the deanery of Winchester. He was also at this time made a fellow of the newly-established college at Chelsea, whose aim was to defend Protestantism from the assaults of the Romanists. In 1615 Morton was elevated to the episcopate, and given the see of Chester; was transferred to that of Lichfield and Coventry in 1618, and in 1632 to that of Durham, which he held with great reputation until the opening of the Long Parliament, when the strong prejudices against the episcopate vented themselves also against Morton, and he had to endure many annoyances and trials. He was finally deposed from his office when the bishoprics were dissolved, but was granted a pension of £800, which he never enjoyed. He removed to the house of the earl of Rutland, and later to the seat of Sir Henry Yelverton, at Easton Mauduit, in Northamptonshire, and there he died, Sept. 22, 1659. His funeral sermon was preached by Dr. John Barwick, afterwards dean of St. Paul's, and printed at

London in 1660, under the title ΙΕΡΟΝΙΚΗΣ, *or the Fight, Victory, and Triumph of St. Paul, accommodated to the Right Rev. Father in God, Thomas, late Lord Bishop of Duresme.* Morton was a man of very great learning, piety, hospitality, charity, liberality, temperance and moderation. He converted several persons of learning and distinction from the Romish religion. He published several works, chiefly controversial, and written against the papists, from 1603 to 1653. Among these, the best are *Apologia Catholica* (Lond. 1605–6, 2 pts. 4to):—*An exact Discovery of Romish Doctrine in the Case of Conspiracy and Rebellion* (ibid. 1605, 4to); deals with the Powder Plot conspiracy:—*A Catholicke Appeale for Protestants out of the Confessions of the Romane Doctrines* (ibid. 1610, fol.):—*Causa regia* (1620, 4to); this is a refutation of Bellarmine's treatise, *De officio principis Christiani:—Of the Institution of the Sacrament by some called the Mass* (1631 and 1635, fol.): —*Confessions and Proofs of Protestant Divines* (Oxf. 1644, 4to):—*Ezekiel's Wheels* (1653, 8vo). He had an intimate acquaintance and correspondence with most of the learned men of his time, and was a great friend and patron of the noted Swiss savant Casaubon, who spent some time in England under king James. Shortly before his death, the bishop was engaged in a lively controversy on his position regarding the episcopal succession. In 1657 there had been published a book at Rome, entitled *A Treatise of the Nature of Catholic Faith and Heresy*, in which it was asserted that "in the beginning of the Long Parliament, when some Presbyterian lords presented to the upper house a certain book to prove that the Protestant bishops had no succession nor consecration, therefore were no bishops, and had no right to sit in Parliament; bishop Morton replied against the book in behalf of himself and his brethren, and endeavored to prove succession from the last Roman Catholic bishops, who ordained the first Protestant bishops at the Nag's Head, in Cheapside." The bishop took decided exception to such a version, and insisted that he had no faith in the verity of the Nag's Head consecration, and preferred not to endorse it. See *Life of Thomas, bishop of Durham*, by Dr. John Barwick (1660, 4to); also Richard Baddily and John Naylor, *Life of Thomas Morton* (1669, 8vo); *Biogr. Brit.* s. v.; *Gen. Biogr. Dict.* s. v.; Soames, *Ch. Hist. Elizabethan Period;* Perry, *Ch. Hist.* (see Index in vol. iii). (J. H. W.)

Mortuarian. See MORTUARY.

Mortuary (derived from *mors*, death) is, in British ecclesiastical law and usage, a gift which is offered to the minister upon the death of one of the parishioners. It was anciently the usage, Selden tells us, to bring the mortuary to the church with the corpse; whence it took the name of *corse-present*, a name which shows that the payment of the mortuary was once voluntary, though so early as in the reign of Henry III we find that the custom was established. The mortuary was given by way of compensation for the tithes and offerings which the deceased had failed to pay in his lifetime, and for the salvation of his soul. In the reign of Henry VIII the custom was found to be the cause of great exactions on the part of the clergy, and of expensive litigation. Accordingly the statute 21 Henry VIII, c. 6, was passed, by which it is enacted that mortuaries shall be taken in the following manner, unless where less or none is due by the custom, viz.: for every person who does not leave goods to the value of ten marks, nothing; for every person who leaves goods to the value of ten marks and under thirty pounds, 3s. 4d.; if above thirty and under forty pounds, 6s. 8d.; if above forty pounds, of what value soever the goods may be, 10s., and no more. It is enacted further that no mortuary shall be paid on the death of a married woman, nor for any child, nor for any one that is not a housekeeper, nor for any wayfaring man; but such wayfaring man's mortuary shall be paid in the parish to which he belonged. This is the statute which regulates mortuaries at the present day (see Blackstone, *Commentaries*, ii, 424; Burns, *Ecclesiastical Law*, title "Mortuary"). The purpose and mode of paying mortuaries anciently are given by Spelman. He says, "A mortuary was thus paid: the lord of the fee had the best beast of the defunct, by way of a heriot, for the support of his body against secular enemies; and the parson of the parish had the second, as a mortuary for defending his soul against his spiritual adversaries.

Prior to the Reformation in Scotland, the popish priest, after a parishioner's death, claimed a cow and the corpse-cloth, or uppermost cloth — apparently the coverlet of the bed of the deceased. Forret, vicar of Dollar, had gained some new light, and began to preach to the people, and refuse also this customary present. Being summoned on suspicion of Lutheranism before the bishop of Dunkeld, the following colloquy took place:

"*Bishop.* 'My joy dean Thomas! I am informed that you preach the epistle or gospel every Sunday to your parishioners, and that you take not the cow nor the uppermost cloth from your parishioners, which thing is very prejudicial to the churchmen; and therefore, my joy dean Thomas, I would you took your cow and your uppermost cloth, as other churchmen do, or else it is too much to preach every Sunday, for in so doing you may make the people think that we should preach likewise. But it is enough for you, when you find any good epistle or any good gospel that setteth forth the liberty of the Holy Church, to preach that and let the rest be.'

"*The Martyr.* Thomas answered, 'My lord, I think that none of my parishioners will complain that I take not the cow nor the uppermost cloth, but will gladly give me the same, together with any other thing that they have; and I will give and communicate with them anything that I have; and so, my lord, we agree right well, and there is no discord among us. And whereas your lordship saith it is too much to preach every Sunday, indeed I think it is too little, and also would wish that your lordship did the like.'

"*Bishop.* 'Nay, nay, dean Thomas,' saith my lord, 'let that be, for we are not ordained to preach.'

"*Martyr.* Then said Thomas, 'Whereas your lordship biddeth me to preach when I find any good epistle or a good gospel, truly, my lord, I have read the New Testament and the Old, and all the epistles and the gospels, and among them all I could never find an evil epistle or an evil gospel: but if your lordship will show me the good epistle and the good gospel, and the evil epistle and the evil gospel, then I shall preach the good and omit the evil.'

"*Bishop.* Then spake my lord stoutly, and said, 'I thank God that I never knew what the Old and New Testament was [and of these words rose a proverb which is common in Scotland, Ye are like the bishop of Dunkeldene, that knew neither new nor old law]; therefore, dean Thomas, I will know nothing but my portnese and my pontifical. Go your way, and let be all these fantasies; for if you persevere in these erroneous opinions, ye will repent it when you may not mend it.'

"*Martyr.* 'I trust my cause to be just in the presence of God, and therefore I pass not much what do follow thereupon.'"

Forret was burned at Edinburgh in 1539. See Fox, *Book of Martyrs*; Eadie, *Eccles. Cyclop.* s. v.; Hook, *Eccles. Dict.* s. v.; Walcott, *Sacred Archæology*, s. v. See TAXES.

Morus, Samuel Frederic Nathaniel, a distinguished German Lutheran divine, was born at Lauban, in Upper Lusatia, Nov. 30, 1736. He received his first education from his father, who was professor in the grammar-school at Lauban, and in 1754 Samuel went to study philosophy and theology in the University of Leipsic, where he was a devoted pupil of Ernesti, and under the guidance of this celebrated master of exegetical theology laid the foundations of his future usefulness and renown. He soon distinguished himself by his learning and his sound judgment, and became successively at his alma mater professor of philosophy in 1768, and of the Greek and Latin languages in 1771. After the death of his beloved teacher, Ernesti, in 1782, Morus was appointed to fill his place as professor of theology. His learning, activity, and sound judgment rendered him eminently fitted for that position, which he retained until his death, Nov. 11, 1792. It was as a teacher rather than as a writer that the influence of

Morus was chiefly felt. His works are mostly posthumous publications, issued under the editorship of men who had been his pupils, one of whom fairly estimates the position of Morus when he says that the science of hermeneutics "ab Ernestio reformata," was "a Moro exculta et dilucidius explicata." He left valuable editions of various classical authors, commentaries on most of the books of the N. T., and other books of value. Among these, the most important are *Vita J. J. Reiskii* (Leips. 1776, 8vo):—*Epitome Theologiæ Christianæ* (Leips. 1789, 8vo; transl. into German by Schneider, 1795). This manual of theology went through several editions, and was long used as a text-book of dogmatics in several universities. It is a work highly commended by Hagenbach in his *Hist. of Doctrines*, ii, 383; and by J. Pye Smith, *First Lines of Christian Theology*, p. 39 sq.:—*Commentarius exegetico-historicus in Mori Epitomen* (Halle, 1797–98, 2 vols. 8vo), published after his death by C. A. Hempel:—*Prælectiones in Lucæ Evangelium*, ed. C. A. Donat (Leips. 1795, 8vo):—*Recitationes in Evangelium Joannis*, ed. Th. J. Dindorf (Leips. 1808, 8vo):—*Versio et explicatio Actorum Apostolorum*, ed. G. J. Dindorf (Leips. 1794):—*Prælectiones in Epistolam Pauli ad Romanos; cum ejusdem versione Latina, locorumque quorundam N. T. difficiliorum interpretatione*, ed. I. T. T. Holzapfel (Leips. 1794, 8vo):—*Acroases in Epistolas Paulinas ad Galatas et Ephesios* (Leips. 1795):—*Prælectiones in Jacobi et Petri epistolas*, ed. C. A. Donat (Leips. 1794):—*Prælectiones exegeticæ in tres Joannis epistolas cum nova earundem paraphrasi Latina*, cura C. A. Hempel (Leips. 1797, 8vo):—*Akademische Vorlesungen über die theologische Moral* (Leips. 1794–95, 3 vols. 8vo), published by F. T. Voigt:—*Dissert. theologicæ et philologicæ* (Leips. 1787–94, 2 vols. 8vo; transl. into German by Rüchel, Leips. 1793–94):—*Super hermeneutica Novi Testamenti Acroases academicæ* (Leips. 1797–1802, 2 vols. 8vo), published by H. K. A. Eichstaedt. This work may be best described as lectures upon the *Institutes* of Ernesti. A collection of his sermons was published at Leipsic in 1786. See *Autobiographie von Morus*, in Beyer, *Magazin für Prediger*, vol. v, art. ii; *Recitatio de Moro, habita a Christiano Dan. Beckio* (Leips. 1792); Höpfner, *Ueber d. Leben u. d. Verdienste d. verewigten Morus* (1793); Weisse, *Museum für sächsische Gesch.* i, 26 sq.; Kahnis, *Hist. German Protestantism*; Schlichtegroll, *Nekrolog. d. Deutschen*, 1792, i, 304 sq.; Hoefer, *Nouv. Biog. Générale*, xxxvi, 697; Herzog, *Real-Encyklopädie*, x, 19; Meusel, *Gelehrten-Lexikon*, s. v. (J. H. W.)

Morus, Thomas. See MORE, *Sir* THOMAS.

Morvillier, JEAN DE, a French prelate, was born of noble and distinguished parentage at Blois Dec. 1, 1506. He early decided to enter holy orders, and therefore received careful training, and after filling various minor positions, was made successively dean of Bourges and Evreux, abbot of St. Pierre de Melun and Bourge-Moyen, and was finally designated by king Henry II for the bishopric of Orleans, and confirmed in this see by the pope, April 21, 1552. This is, however, not the complete list of his benefices; he possessed many others, the functions of these being performed by vicars or proxies. Entirely taken up with service to the king, he appeared rarely even in his bishopric. One of his few visits to Orleans gave occasion to a strange controversy; it was in November, 1552. He was more of a gentleman than of an ecclesiastic, and, according to court fashion, wore a long beard. This exercised the canons of Orleans to such an extent that in a chapter they resolved unanimously that the lord bishop must divest himself of this uncanonical ornament at the earliest moment possible. He received the summons, but did not comply. Hence new complaints, another refusal of obedience, judicial pleadings, quotations from the common law, and great tumult in Orleans. This grave and stormy dispute lasted nearly four years. Finally, thinking that the cause of his beard was lost, he appealed to the king for intervention. In 1556 the king notified the canons of Orleans in writing that he had the intention of sending J. Morvillier to foreign countries, "in quibus necessaria erat barba," and thus the contest terminated. It was J. Morvillier who in 1560 received Francis II and his consort, Mary Stuart, in Orleans. In 1561 he attended the colloquy at Poissy, and in 1562 the council at Trent. In 1564 he resigned the bishopric of Orleans in favor of his nephew, Mathurin de la Saussaye. From 1568 to 1570 we find him keeper of the seals of France, succeeding the celebrated L'Hôpital. On his return from a journey to Poitiers he was at Tours attacked by a sickness, which cut short his life, Oct. 23, 1577. During thirty-five most turbulent years Morvillier stood in high esteem and favor at the French court, where his moderation and suavity, no less than his skill in transacting diplomatic affairs, won and retained him friends and adherents. See *Gallia Christiana*, viii, col. 1485; Martin, *Hist. of France*; Jager, *Hist. de l'Église Catholique en France depuis son origine jusq'au Concordat de Pie VII* (Paris, 1863–66, 13 vols.), vol. xi; Wessenberg, *Gesch. d. Kirchl. Conferenzen*, iii, 483; *North Brit. Rev.* Jan. 1870, p. 266.

Morzillo, SEBASTIAN FOX, a Spanish philosopher, was born about 1523 at Seville; and, after studying at the high schools of his own country, went to France, and finally finished his studies at the University of Louvain (Belgium), and applied himself with particular care to the history of the quarrels of the Platonicans and Peripatetics. At the early age of nineteen he published a treatise on philosophy. Philip II called him home as preceptor for his son Don Carlos, but on his voyage to enter on his charge of the infante the vessel was wrecked and he perished (1560). Contemporary authors have bestowed on him great praise. Vossius calls him "philosophum præstantissimum et doctissimum." Notwithstanding his untimely death, we have several valuable works from him: *In topica Ciceronis Paraphrasis et scholia* (Anvers, 1550, 8vo):—*De Imitatione, sive de informandi styli ratione* (ibid. 1554 8vo):—*In Platonis Timæum commentarius* (Basle 1554, fol.):—*Compendium ethices philosophiæ ex Platone, Aristotele aliisque autoribus collectum* (ibid. 1554, 8vo):—*De natura Philosophiæ, seu de Platonis et Aristotelis consensione lib. v.* (Louvain, 1554, 8vo; Paris, 1560, 1589, 8vo; Lyons, 1622, 8vo), which latter work, according to Boivin, "is perhaps the best and most solid that has been written on this subject," though he adds that the subject has not been treated exhaustively:—*De Usu et Exercitatione Dialecticæ*; *De Demonstratione*; *De Juventute, De Honore* (Basle, 1556, 8vo):—*De Regno et regis Institutione lib. iii* (Antwerp, 1556, 8vo):—*In Phædonem* (Basle, 1556, fol.):—*De Historiæ Institutione* (Antwerp, 1557, 1564, 8vo).

Mosaic (Lat. *Musivum*), ornamental work formed by inlaying small pieces, usually cubes, of glass, stone, etc. It was much used by the Romans in floors and on the walls of houses, and many specimens which have been discovered are rendered exceedingly beautiful by the introduction of different-colored materials, and are made to represent a variety of subjects with figures and animals; others are of coarser execution, and exhibit only such patterns as frets, guilloches, foliage, etc.

In the Middle Ages this kind of work continued to be used in Italy and some other parts of the Continent, and was applied to walls and vaults of churches; in England it was never extensively employed, though used in some parts of the shrine of Edward the Confessor, on the tomb of Henry III, and in the paving of the choir at Westminster Abbey, and Becket's crown at Canterbury, where curious patterns may be seen. Mosaic-work is still executed with great skill by the Italians.

Mosaism, a term of late used to designate the system of religion instituted by Jehovah through the agency of Moses, and maintained by the subsequent theocracy of the Old Testament. This, so far as its *history* is concerned, has been treated under the heads JUDAISM and MOSES, and as formulated in the sacred *code*, it has been analyzed and summed up under LAW OF MOSES. It remains to consider it as regards its essential *purpose*, its interior *spirit*, and its practical *operation*. With this view we shall here briefly discuss it.

I. *As a Sequel to the Patriarchal Dispensation*.—We pass over the divine economy of Eden as a brief and ideal scheme, adapted only to a state of moral perfection no longer existing, and proved to be inadequate to resist even outward temptation to wrong. We likewise dismiss the antediluvian probation as having equally demonstrated the incompetency of human nature to retain traditional piety, or even to preserve a tolerable degree of virtue. The race born of the germ rescued from the deluge must be trained under closer restrictions and by a more palpable embodiment of divine authority. This was measurably secured by the successive heads of the Shemitic family, each in his turn acting as a representative of heaven in his twofold function of priest and medium of revelation. In the Abrahamic Church it was more fully realized by a formal recognition of the several patriarchs as special plenipotentiaries of God to his chosen people. Many important defects, however, still existed under that arrangement for religious discipline, which Mosaism was intended to supply.

1. *A written constitution* was required to prevent uncertainty, discrepancy, and oblivion of the principles of moral truth and practice. This was furnished by the Pentateuch, with its historical introduction and statutory detail.

2. *A prescribed form of worship* was needed to obviate the casual and irregular methods hitherto prevalent, and ever prone to recur, and especially in order to preclude all human contrivances and corrupt observances. This was effected by the Levitical cultus, with its hereditary caste, imposing apparatus, and solemn festivals.

3. *A territorial patrimony* was essential to give "a local habitation and a name" to the favorites of heaven, and to preserve their lineage from contamination and disintegration, as well as from the dissipation of migratory habits. This was attained by the permanent title in the Promised Land, where their Hebrew forefathers had been merely nomadic tenants. This, too, was calculated to develop the refining influences of home, neighborhood, and clan, with all their literary, social, and domestic amenities.

4. *A living ministry* was continuously provided in the person of the *prophets*, to keep alive the idea of theocratic sovereignty, to fan the flame of national devotion, and to guard against the varying dangers and degeneracies to which any polity, however well devised and balanced, must be exposed in the lapse of centuries.

These are the main provisions of Mosaism as distinguished from the dispensation that immediately preceded it, and to these all the particulars of miracle and vision, and angelic and political machinery, were subordinate. While it possessed these advantages, it yet exhibited the following marked deficiencies as compared with the more perfect æra that was to follow.

II. *Mosaism an Introduction to Christianity*.—The apostle Paul, who was pre-eminently qualified to judge of this relation, in a single term emphatically characterizes it as that of a *pædagogue* (παιδαγωγός, not "schoolmaster" or tutor, but the servant who took the children to school), to lead us to Christ (Gal. iii. 24). This was, indeed, the legitimate function of Mosaism, as the same apostle makes clear in numerous other passages (see especially Rom. x, 4; Heb. x, 9). The first and most necessary inference from this fact, of course, is the comparative imperfection of the earlier as compared with the later dispensation. But before we proceed to detail the defects which called for this super-sedure, we invite attention to another inference not so frequently noted, but equally significant. It is this, that as Judaism contained the *germ* of Christianity, it was essentially identical with it in at least the rudimentary principles. Indeed, true religion everywhere and in all ages is substantially the same, however it may differ in its manifestation and development. It consists in earnest devotion to God, and is more or less pure according to the direction and intensity which circumstances give to the sincere worshipper. All else is accessory or subordinate. Hence the Psalms have retained under Christianity their place as a manual of religious experience which they held under Judaism; and the Christian Church has adopted all the deeper and more central elements of the Hebrew Scriptures. The Lord's Sermon on the Mount is an admirable commentary on this point, showing how the Gospel is but an extension and refinement of the Law; and on more than one other occasion he summarized the latter as but a crystallization around the core of *love* (Matt. xix, 19; xxii, 37), an exposition which his apostles universally followed (Rom. xiii, 9; Gal. v, 14; James ii, 8; 1 John iv, 21).

A writer in the *Christian Review* for January, 1874, in noticing Paul's view of Mosaism as compared with Christianity, reduces the characteristics of the former to the following points:

"1. Governmental authority expressed in statute.
2. The authority so expressed a rule of life.
3. Penalty following infraction.
4. Its entire force is from without. It seeks to accomplish nothing by establishing a principle within.
5. It is utterly inflexible, and knows no mercy.
6. Its righteousness is perfect obedience to the things which are written."

The writer "does not claim for this analysis that it is exhaustive, or that the points are so well put as they might have been." It would be easy, we think, to criticise them. But we give them with the general remark, that while they are in the main correct, they relate to Mosaism simply as a scheme of *law*. This is doubtless the most important aspect of that dispensation; but it has other traits, especially in its practical workings, and as modified or supplemented by the prophetical teachings (comp. 1 Sam. xv, 22; Prov. xxi, 3; Isa. lviii, 3-6; Hos. vi, 6, etc.). To some of these we may recur; but under this head we propose to take a view of certain marked features in which it resembled while yet it differed from Christianity. This will particularly illustrate the mission of Jesus as a prophet like Moses (Deut. xviii, 18).

1. *Doctrinally.*—We need not here recapitulate the tenets of Mosaism in detail; it will be sufficient to note the salient points of its belief, especially those in which Christianity is most conspicuously an advance upon it.

(1.) *The Trinity.*—This is perhaps the greatest doctrinal stumbling-block in the way of the reception of the Gospel among the Jews from the earliest times (John viii, 58, 59; x, 33; Matt. xxvi, 65) to the present day. Yet not a few hints, at least, of the plurality of persons in the Godhead are afforded in the Old Testament. Not to dwell upon the doubtful sense of the plural form of *Elohim* [see GOD], or the conferences in the divine *consessus* implied in the frequent use of the plural *we* by the Deity (Gen. i, 26; iii, 22; xi, 7, etc.), we may fairly cite in evidence of our position the plain allusions not seldom made to the divinely eternal and omnific Spirit (Gen. i, 2; vi, 3, etc.), and to the still more palpable theophanies of the Logos, common under the older dispensation, as the angel Jehovah (Gen. xviii, 17 sq.; xix, 16; xxii, 15, 16; xxxii, 24 sq.; Josh. v, 15; Judg. xiii, 15 sq.; Dan. iii, 25, etc.). We have not space to develop at length this important distinction between the Jewish and the Christian creeds, but the above facts will suggest its fundamental and undeviating import.

(2.) *Mediation.*—This under the Mosaic system was effected only by the intervention of a human priesthood, with a vast array of ceremonial apparatus and parade. Under the Christian economy, on the other hand, the human soul is taught to come directly to God for pardon of its sins. Yet here likewise there is a close analogy in the person of the Redeemer, who is at once Victim and Intercessor. The practical influence, however, of the recourse by the Jewish penitent to the Levitical arrangements, with the necessity of a prescribed sacrifice, at a special place in a particular manner, and above all by the instrumentality of a public functionary, must have been immense in keeping out of the popular mind the immediate responsibility of each human being to its offended Maker and God. In this respect Romish and Greek Catholicism has gone back to "the weak and beggarly elements" of Judaism, and the exaltation of prelatical and priestly authority invariably tends in the same direction. The apostle Paul everywhere enters his most vigorous and emphatic protest against these assumptions as a corruption of the whole evangelical scheme. The *Epistle to the Hebrews*, especially, is a prolonged argument on this topic.

(3.) *Immortality.*—The survival of the soul after the dissolution of the body is not expressly taught in the Old Testament, but it is continually implied, and not obscurely intimated in the references to the spirits of the departed (e. g. "gathered unto his fathers," i. e. in the world of shades), and in the anticipation of meeting in the other world (e. g. 2 Sam. xii, 23; Eccles. xii, 7). Jesus proved this point to the confusion of the Jewish sceptics of his day (Matt. xxii, 32). But the doctrine of the resurrection of the body likewise is so allied to that of the immortality of the soul, that the later Jews appear to have inferred it from the few hints dropped to that effect in their Scriptures (especially, perhaps, from Job xix, 25-27; Psa. xvi, 10; Isa. xxvi, 19; Dan. xii, 2), for the Pharisees and Talmudists entertained it as a settled portion of the orthodox faith. Yet it was so far reserved for Christ to establish and illustrate this glorious truth by his own revival from the grave, and his explicit declarations (e. g. John xi, 25), that he may justly be said to have "brought life and immortality to light."

2. *Socially and Politically.*—Here, too, a few points must suffice by way of characterization.

(1.) *Marriage.*—In no particular, perhaps, is modern civilization more distinguished from the cultured nations of antiquity, as well as from modern Paganism and Mohammedanism, than in the delicate regard for woman which it has enforced. But this is chiefly due to the moral influence of Christianity, and is directly traceable to the restoration by our Saviour of marriage to its pristine monogamic condition (Matt. xix, 3-12). Here likewise the Gospel appears as much superior to the Mosaic law as the latter does to heathenism. The last tolerated almost indiscriminate licentiousness, and the mythologies of Greece and Rome added the example of a profligate religion with indescribable orgies. But Mosaism, although it restrained, still did not abolish concubinage, and thus left the female sex measurably enthralled by traditionary degradation. To its credit, however, it must be said that it never (except in the limited and late example of the Essenes) ran into the morbid prurience of celibacy, which has entailed severe evils upon corrupt forms of Christianity.

(2.) *Exclusiveness.*—The Jew was hereditarily a bigot. Territorially, ecclesiastically, and commercially his position by the Mosaic economy was an isolated one, and that reserve and suspicion of foreigners which was originally a safeguard against idolatry, became at length a turbulent, odious, and anti-humanitarian trait of national character. The Hebrew word for the outside nations (גּוֹי) acquired a sense of proscription, and "Gentile" was regarded by the Israelite as nearly synonymous with "dog." Christianity, on the contrary, "broke down this middle wall of partition," and taught that all men are brethren, alike made by the common

Father, and equally redeemed by the one Saviour. Zerubbabel encouraged sectarianism (Ezra iv, 3); Jesus rebuked it (Luke ix, 55). With the Hebrews circumcision was a test of caste, and is hence contrasted with the essence of Christianity (Gal. v, 2). So liberal is the genuine spirit of the latter, that no greater reproach or inconsistency, perhaps, in modern times is found among its professors than a similar refusal of fraternity on the ground of some ceremonial or ordinational peculiarity.

(3.) *Patriotism.*—This partook largely of the above clannish feeling engendered by Mosaism. Rome was not more jealous of the rights of citizenship than was Judaism. "Thou shalt love thy fellow [Jew], and hate thy enemy [the Gentile]," was the interpretation put by the Israelites in general upon the Mosaic code. True, this was a perversion of its spirit, which repeatedly enjoins the largest charity towards aliens (Exod. xxiii, 9; Lev. xix, 33; Deut. x, 18, etc.), but it was the natural result of the Hebrews' history and training. Hence the Jewish passion for independence, and hence, too, the ambition that nurtured a literal interpretation of the glowing pictures in the Old-Testament prophecies concerning the ultimate aggrandizement of the nation. Christianity, on the other hand, renounced at the outset all pretensions to political power (John xviii, 36), and enjoined an absolute humility and submission little calculated to awaken patriotic ardor. Indeed, the early Christians were compelled to regard themselves as "pilgrims and strangers" on earth, and they transferred to the Church and to heaven their former attachment to countrymen and fatherland. At the same time their philanthropy became both more intense and more cosmopolitan; and this depth as well as expansion of patriotism in the truest sense has ever since, with the most earnest Christians, refused to be limited to the accidents of birthplace. The essential brotherhood of all mankind is a principle with which Christianity is slowly leavening the world, and the millennial glory will be but the universal realization of the idea.

3. *Spiritually.*—The analogy between Mosaism and Christianity, as we have sketched it, has, it will be perceived, been gradually opening into contrast. This is most apparent in this the highest range of significance of either economy. It is here that the earlier structure intended to serve but as the scaffolding for the final edifice is seen to be but an obstruction that needed to be removed when the grand temple was finished. We name, as before, but a few leading particulars.

(1.) *Regeneration.* — The absolute necessity of this change of the moral affections, when propounded by our Lord to Nicodemus, as a prime condition at the very entrance of the Christian career, struck the Jewish ruler as a novelty, if not absurdity. Yet, as the Great Teacher's retort of equal surprise at his hearer's ignorance implies, there are intimations, neither few nor indistinct, of such a change in Old-Test. characters (1 Sam. x, 6; Psa. li, 10, etc.). Even the sense of divine adoption, attendant upon the new birth, is plainly indicated, though under a different name (Gen. v, 24; comp. Heb. xi, 5). Nevertheless there can be no doubt that the mass of saints under the Jewish economy knew little about the spiritual experience which is the privilege of every child of God since the fuller dispensation of the Holy Spirit (Matt. xi, 11). The improvement in the religious state and conduct of the apostles after the memorable Pentecost is of itself an evidence and exemplification of this. The highest possible difference in the attitude and sentiments of believers towards God before this event is expressed by our Lord in one word as an advance from *service* to *friendship* (John xv, 15; comp. James ii, 23); thenceforth it was a transition to *sonship* (John i, 12), with all the perquisites of the immediate pledge (Gal. iv, 6), and the future reversion (Rom. viii, 16, 17). It is to be feared that too many professing Christians of the present day rest in the con-

dition of legalism (Rom. viii, 15), without rising to the privilege of spiritual liberty (Gal. iv, 7). A religion of forms, however sincere and consistent, without the regenerating power, is but a relapse to Mosaism (Gal. v, 1)

(2.) *Worship.*—In nothing, perhaps, was the revolution from the Mosaic law to that of Christianity more striking than in the abandonment of the pompous ritual of the former for the simple devotion of the latter. True, the services of the Synagogue had prepared the way for those of the Church, and indeed formed their model. But so strong a hold upon the imagination and the heart of the Jews had the Temple and its pageantry made, that even after the adoption of the Christian faith most of the Hebrew converts of the apostolic age continued to maintain the Mosaic observances in addition to those of their new relation. The great axiom propounded by our Lord at Jacob's well, that God's nature requires a spiritual worship (John iv, 24), struck the key-note of a fundamental reform in the very basis act of all religion. Alas that this truth should ever have been again overlaid by the mummeries of form! The bane of true worship is formalism. Not alone amid the gorgeousness of Catholicism, or of semi-Romish ritualism, does this insidious influence display itself; the baleful tendency lurks likewise in the sanctimonious tones of Puritanism and the cant of Pietism, and even under the demure garb of Quakerism. An effort is constantly required to keep from reverting to the deadness of the letter (Rom. vii, 6).

(3.) *Holiness.*—This, the crowning purpose of both the Mosaic and the Christian schemes, was very differently expressed and effected by them respectively. In the former it meant simply an external and formal dedication (קָדַשׁ) of a person or animal, or a valuable article, objectively considered, to Jehovah, as a token of its separation and interdiction thenceforth from secular uses. In the latter it signified an internal and actual consecration ($\ddot{\alpha}\gamma\iota o\varsigma$) of the human spirit, subjectively regarded, to the glory of God, but yet to be employed in all the legitimate words and works of useful life. There was thus a cardinal, if not radical distinction in the nature and manifestation of sanctity as sought and attained by the Jew and the Christian. No mere form of words, like a magical spell, no *opus operatum*, can avail to free the heart from the sense and love of sin (Heb. x, 1). Indeed, the Mosaic law provided no sacrifice as an atonement for spiritual offences, such as pride, anger, selfishness, lust, etc.; but only for outward infractions of certain ceremonial prescriptions. It is a fact not commonly understood, that wilful and presumptuous sins have no remedy or means of expiation under the Levitical code. Heart sins, and even outbreaking crimes—violations, for instance, of any of the Ten Commandments—were purposely excluded from the category of compoundable misdemeanors. Hence, after David had committed adultery he did not offer a sacrifice to ease his conscience of the guilt (Psa. li, 16, 17). There was no way in such cases for relief but by an extra-Mosaic recourse to the general mercy of God, directly dispensed to the penitent—in short, by an anticipation of the Gospel scheme of gratuitous pardon for the sake of Another (Psa. li, 1–3). In like manner Mosaism of itself made no provision for the effectual reformation of the sinner by the removal, or even the control, of his depraved nature and wicked tendencies. This was too sacred a precinct for even the unsandalled foot of the great lawgiver to venture upon. It was silently reserved as the province of the Holy Spirit, whose function as the Sanctifier was even then proleptically recognised (Psa. li, 11). Yet with all this borrowed light added to the boasted vantage of the only written revelation hitherto vouchsafed to man (Rom. ii, 17–24; iii, 1, 2), Pharisaism and Rabbinism, the final twin offspring of Mosaism, were such a mockery of righteousness, though claiming superlative saintship, as alone could stir the gentle spirit of the Redeemer to indignant protest (Matt. xv, 3-14) and bitter invective (Matt. xxiii). The tender-hearted Revelator, too, found no language to describe the central seat of its worship but as "the city which is spiritually called Sodom and Egypt" (Rev. xi, 8), and branded its expatriated sanctuary as "the synagogue of Satan" (Rev. ii, 9; iii, 9). No man knew better by sad experience the hollowness of its pretensions than the apostle who had been "a Hebrew of the Hebrews;" for amid the glare which its Sinaitic flashes threw upon his natural conscience he cried out in an agony of despair, "O wretched man that I am, who shall deliver me from this body of death?" and he ever afterwards characterized it as "a yoke of bondage," and applied to it not only severe refutation, but likewise caustic irony (e. g. "the concision," Phil. iii, 2). Once more we are compelled to repeat the lament that a nominal Christianity should have reproduced the same spurious sainthood and the same blind truckling to an assumed oral law. The 19th century of our Lord has witnessed the insane blasphemy of a pseudo-infallibility as a culmination of abominations that have emanated from the "mother of harlots." Drunk with the blood of the saints, she is the melancholy and shocking successor of the adulterous apostasy (Matt. xvii, 39) which was not content till it had entailed upon itself (Matt. xxvii, 25) the guilt of the murder of its greatest Benefactor. Such is the outcome of all "Holiness" not grounded in a radical renewal of the moral nature by the Spirit of Christ which first breathed the conscious soul into man.

III. *In Contrast with Heathenism.*—In this aspect, which is the really just point of view, Mosaism shines with its true lustre. We name under this head likewise a few only of the most prominent particulars.

1. *Monotheism.*—The whole Judaic system was a standing protest against polytheism, as the most stringent of its precepts were against the idolatry constantly associated with the heathen multiplication of divinities. It may safely be averred that the doctrine of the unity of God was original with the Abrahamic, and specially the Jewish race. Mohammedanism, the only form of false faith that holds it, borrowed it directly from the Jews. We have not space to develop the multiform influences growing out of this cardinal tenet of all true religion; some of them are specified below, and for others we refer to POLYTHEISM. See also MONOTHEISM.

2. *Scrupulousness.*—The vast moral superiority of Mosaism over heathenism is seen most conspicuously, perhaps, in the stern sense of right which it cultivated. The Greeks and Romans, with all their philosophical acumen, can hardly be said to have possessed or been actuated by a *conscience*, as we understand the term. There was a frivolity, a deep-seated scepticism, which led them to look upon sin as a venial affair, and to hold in contempt that tenderness of moral sensibility upon which conscientiousness depends. Among Oriental nations, with all their veneration for various deities, the case was, if possible, still worse; for the perception of right and wrong was so blunted by the grossness of their religions as to preclude any consistent probity or even virtue. The picture which Paul draws (Rom. i, 21 sq.) of the degraded immorality of the heathen world in its ripest day reveals a reeking rottenness revolting to common decency; but shocking as are the disclosures, his pen blushed to tell even half the abominations. The licentiousness, debauchery, drunkenness, violence, cruelty, and treachery of the age were absolutely beyond description in any page fit for the public eye. The word utterly *abandoned* is the only one that at all approaches the depth of depravity into which the whole Gentile world was sunk. The Jews, it is true, were not universally pure. Many sad rebukes by our Saviour, as earlier many severe castigations from the prophets, attest the prevalence of but too much corruption in every age. Yet a high sense of loyalty to God, of personal accountability to him, of public and private honor, of obligation to truthfulness and integrity generally prevailed as a distinguishing trait of the Hebrew nation. Above all they prized and clung to their creed and institutions with a tenacious conviction that nerved them to brave all obloquy and opposition. Few if any heathen thought enough of their religion to die for it, or cared enough for its sanctions to forego any considerable gratification in order to meet its prohibitions. The Jew, on the contrary, gloried in martyrdom for his faith, and submitted to the most onerous privations in the observance of its requirements. The very stiffness of its unæsthetic simplicity, the coldness and sternness of its behests, the multiplicity and minuteness of its enactments, and the rigidity of its penalties, schooled its votaries into a Puritanic conscientiousness, which, indeed, often degenerated into morbid punctilio and puling casuistry, but in more robust and generous spirits has never been excelled in moral heroism, at least in the line of fortitude (Heb. xi, 33-38). Even amid the convulsive throes of their expiring commonwealth, sublime examples of daring and devotion, actuated by a mistaken but intense zeal for their imperilled polity, are recorded by Josephus. This *esprit du corps*, if we may so style it, for which the adherents of Mosaism have ever been proverbial, differs from the mere bravery of heathendom in being sustained by a *religious* fervor based upon the most earnest conviction that it was heaven's cause for which they were contending. The paradox of a misguided but superlatively dominant conscience (Rom. x, 2) was exhibited in the case of Saul of Tarsus, who thought he was doing God service (Acts xxvi, 9) while he was perpetrating acts for which, when enlightened by the halo from the skies, which taught him that *love* is the highest duty (1 Cor. xiii), he ceased not to his dying day to feel the keenest remorse (1 Cor. xv, 9; 1 Tim. i, 15).

3. *Freedom from Superstition.*—As a result of this single eye to the glory of a supreme God, Mosaism was calculated to deliver its followers from those chimerical fears and goblin doubts which continually haunt the votaries of polytheism and dæmonism. The Jew was not distracted by uncertainty at which of many often contradictory shrines he should pay his homage, nor any uncertainty as to whether his God was able or willing to heed and answer his petition. No ghostly horrors veiled his cultus, nor mystic rites overshadowed his introduction into the divine presence. There were no subordinate imps or questionable demi-gods that might thwart the higher designs, nor any petty envy in the bosom of a jealous deity. True, there was Satan and his host of fallen angels against him; but he believed that these were mere creature powers, tethered (Job i, 12; ii, 6) by the Almighty with whom he was in covenant, and therefore harmless while he maintained that allegiance. There was no peopling by his imagination of every brook and dale and hill and wood with naiads and nymphs and fauns and satyrs of superhuman power and antihuman whim. There were for him no lucky and unlucky days, no capricious auguries and enigmatic oracles, no conjuring spells and omens of fortune. There was no blind *fate*, but everything was in the hand of an all-wise, beneficent Creator, Upholder, and Ruler. This gave a nobility, a magnanimity, an expansiveness to his views of life and destiny, which raised him out of the puerile calculations and belittling aspirations, the undefined guesses and terrors that took up so large a share of the heathen's time and attention. True, he had his festal and his fasting seasons, his routine of sacrifice and ceremony; but these were all fixed and conclusive, and were grounded on some clear historical or prophetical principle, so that they enlisted his intelligent interest. It was the hair-splitting technicalities of the rabbins that introduced bewilderment of mind and morals into the later Judaism. The drivelling trash of the Talmud is an excrescence upon Mosaism. Such fables and endless distinctions were a fashion worthier of heathenism (Tit. iii, 9).

4. *Sublime Views of the Future World.*—We have al-

ready touched upon this theme, but for another purpose; its importance and pertinence here call for a special notice. To a thoughtful mind, the destiny of the soul beyond the grave is a most momentous consideration. Hence pagan philosophy has exercised its most earnest efforts to solve the problem, but in vain. The pall that covers the bier was to them an impenetrable veil. Socrates and his most spiritual disciples, Plato, and Cicero, could only conjecture the fate of the human spirit. True, all religions hold to a future retribution, and this implies a survival of the soul after death. Yet this view was so beclouded with mythological poetry and metaphysical speculation, that the passage into eternity was truly "a leap in the dark" even to the most cultivated heathen. The light of revelation alone could pierce the gloom that shrouded the spirit as it passed away from consciousness and observation. The bare *fact* of immortality might indeed be guessed — or rather, perhaps, the surmise was a trace of the pristine truth of Eden. But the *circumstances* of that state, especially the possibility and conditions of happiness in the future world, were even a more absorbing question; for continued existence without this assurance would hardly be deemed a real boon. On this point it is evident that the Jew never had any doubt; and hence he was ready to meet death cheerfully and even gladly. We repeat that martyrs could not have been possible without the faith which the Bible—whether of the Old or the New Testament—inspired. Mosaism, so far as we know, furnished the first *written* revelation of God's will to man, and the first authentic clew to man's origin, moral relations, and final destiny. This gave the believer in the Mosaic code, with its concomitants and sequents, an immense advantage over Gentile theosophists and religionists of however high a grade. He could not only walk more securely in the path well-pleasing to heaven, but he knew assuredly that it would, if persevered in, at length conduct him thither in everlasting bliss. Even the dawning beams of that celestial illumination enabled Enoch, Noah, Melchizedek, Job, and doubtless many other ante-Mosaic, but not extra-Hebraic saints to tread with firm and elastic step that sacred road, and Christianity is but the noontide blaze of the same effulgence from the one great Sun of Righteousness which shone with a clear and steady, but not yet full lustre, on the horizon of Mosaism (Psa. lxxxiv, ii).

Mosaylima. See MOHAMMEDAN SECTS, in this vol., p. 424.

Moscato, JUDAH, a noted physician and rabbi at Mantua, where he died in the year 1580, is the author of an important commentary on the Kozari of the celebrated Jehudah ha-Levi ben-Samuel (q. v.), entitled קוֹל יְהוּדָה, *The Voice of Judah* (Venice, 1594). He also wrote, under the title of נְפוּצוֹת יְהוּדָה, *The Dispersed of Judah*, fifty-two lectures on diverse matters (Venice, 1589; republished at Warsaw, 1871). See Fürst, *Bibl. Jud.* ii, 391 sq.; De Rossi, *Dizionario storico degli autori Ebrei*, s. v.; Zunz, *Gottesdienstliche Vorträge* (Berlin, 1832), p. 432.

Moschabeans is the name of a Mohammedan sect who believe that God is literally what the Koran describes him to be. They are a sort of Anthropomorphites. It is certain that the vulgar Mohammedans are ignorant enough to imagine that God has hands, feet, eyes, and ears; some of them even hold that he has a thick, black beard, with a great many other imaginary attributes. See Broughton, *Bibliotheca Historico-Sacra*, p. 143.

Moschampar, GEORGIUS (Γεωργιός ὁ Μοσχάμπαρ), a noted Eastern ecclesiastic, flourished towards the close of the 13th century. He was a friend and contemporary of George of Cyprus, patriarch of Constantinople. Moschampar took a leading part in opposition to the doctrine of the Latin Church on the procession of the Holy Spirit, and to the distinguished advocate of that Church, Joannes Beccus or Veccus. He seems, however, to have had little weight with his own party. He published several treatises in opposition to Veccus, to which the latter ably replied; but neither the attacks of the one nor the answers of the other seem to be preserved. There is a letter of Moschampar to his friend George of Cyprus, printed in the life of the latter, which was published by J. F. Bernard de Rubeis (Venice, 1753). See Pachymerius, *Hist.* i, 8; Allatius, *Græc. Orthodox.* ii, 3, 9, 10; Fabricius, *Bibl. Græc.* iii, 46, 47, comp. viii, 53, 54; Smith, *Dict. of Greek and Roman Biog. and Mythol.* s. v.

Moschi is the name given to an ancient people of Asia, south of the Caucasus, whose territory at the time of Augustus was divided between Colchis, Tiberia, and Armenia, and from whom a mountain range, extending from the Caucasus to the Antitaurus, received the name of the Moschi Mountains. Their name, in the early classical writers, frequently appears coupled with that of the Tibareni, and the two tribes are generally identified with the *Meshech* (q. v.) and *Tubal* (q. v.) of Scripture.

Moscholatry. See CALF-WORSHIP.

Moschus (Μόσχος), or, as Photius calls him, *Joannes, the son of Moschus,* surnamed Ἐγκρατής, or, what appears to be a corruption rather than translation of that epithet, *Eviratus,* was born about 550, and was at first a monk in the monastery of St. Theodosius of Jerusalem. He afterwards lived among the anchorites in the desert on the banks of the Jordan, and subsequently filled the office of canonarchus in the convent of St. Saba. After visiting a large number of monasteries in Syria and Egypt, he, together with his friend Sophronius, afterwards patriarch of Jerusalem, came to Alexandria, where they enjoyed the sincere friendship of John the Almsgiver (q. v.), one of the best of the patriarchs of the Eastern Church, who esteemed them as fathers in Christ, obeying them in all things. After preaching at Alexandria for some time, Moschus travelled to Cyprus, Samos, and finally to Rome, attacking everywhere the heresy of Severus Acephalus. At Rome he applied himself, in connection with his friend and co-laborer, Sophronius, to the composition of a work giving an account of the life of the monks of that age down to the time of Heraclius. It is dedicated to Sophronius and John of Damascus; and Nicephorus assigned Sophronius himself as the author, from which it has been supposed that it was in reality mainly his work, though the name of Joannes Moschus was allowed to stand as that of the writer. It is, however, more probable that Moschus and Sophronius were co-laborers in this work as well as in their missionary journeys. The work was entitled Λειμών or Λειμωγάριον, or Νέος παράδεισος, and is still better known under the title of *Pratum Spirituale.* In that edition it is divided into 219 chapters. Photius speaks of it as consisting of 304 διηγήματα, but mentions that in other manuscripts it was divided into a larger number of chapters. In compiling it Moschus did not confine himself to giving the results of his own observations, but availed himself of the labors of his predecessors in the same field. His narratives contain a plentiful sprinkling of the marvellous. "The style of the work," as Photius says, "is mean and unpolished;" but nevertheless it contains some valuable facts in regard to doctrines, heresies, Church-discipline, and especially monachism of those times. Moschus died at Rome, and Bollandus gives A.D. 620 as the date of his decease. The above-mentioned work was first published in an Italian translation, and incorporated in several collections of lives of the saints. The Latin translation of Ambrosius Camaldulensis is in the seventh volume of Aloysius Lipsomannus (Venice, 1558). It appeared in Greek and Latin in the second volume of the *Auctarium Bibl. Patrum Ducæanum* (Paris, 1644, 1654). See Smith, *Dict. of Greek and Roman Biogr. and Mythol.* s. v.; Fleury, *Hist. Eccles.* ad an. 614 sq.; Sardagne,

Indic. P. P. (Ratisb. 1772); Photius, *Cod.* p. 199; Fabricius, *Bibl. Græca*, v, cap. 16; viii, 201 sq.; x, 124; Voss, *De Hist. Græc.* ii, 220; Hamburger, *Zuverlässige Nachrichten*, iii, 469; Saxe, *Onomast. litt.* ii, 67; Kurtz, *Handbuch d. allgem. Kirchengesch.* i, 2, 499; Basse, *Grundriss d. christ. Litt.* i, 190 sq.; Du Pin, *Nouvelle Bibl. des Auteurs Ecclés.* xi, 57 sq.; Ceillier, *Hist. des Auteurs Sacrés*, xvii, 610 sq.

Moscorovius, HIERONYMUS, a Polish Unitarian writer of note, flourished towards the close of the 16th or about the opening of the 17th century. He was a nobleman and a lay worker in the Church. He is supposed to have died about 1625. He is distinguished especially as the joint author (with Valentine Schmalz, a Socinian minister) of the larger *Socinian Catechism*, which was published in the Polish tongue (1605, 12mo). It was translated into Latin under the title: *Catechesis Ecclesiarum, quæ in regno Polon. et magno ducatu Lithuaniæ et aliis ad istud regnum pertinentibus provinciis affirmant, neminem alium præter patrem domini nostri J. C. esse illum unum Deum Israelis, hominem autem illum, Jesum Naz., qui ex virgine natus est, nec alium præter aut ante ipsum, Dei filium unigenitum et agnoscunt et confitentur* (Ravoc. 1609, 12mo): a new edition, together with a refutation, was published by G. L. Oeder (Francf. and Leips. 1739, 8vo); here the questions are for the first time numbered. This Catechism was ordered to be burned by the Parliament of England in 1652. It was translated, with notes and illustrations, and a sketch of the history of Unitarianism, by Thomas Rees (Lond. 1818). See extracts in Gieseler, *Eccl. Hist.* iv, 367 sq. Concerning other editions, which also contain other confessions of faith adopted by the Socinians (the *Confessio Fidei* drawn up by Joh. Schlichting, 1646, 8vo), comp. Winer, *Handbuch der theol. Literatur*, ii, 25 sq. See also Hagenbach, *Hist. Doct.* ii, 212.

Moscow (Russ. *Moskwá*), the ancient capital of Russia, and formerly the residence of the czars, and situated in a highly cultivated and fertile district on the Moskva, 400 miles south-east of St. Petersburg, is not only "the very personification of the ecclesiastical history of Russia," as Stanley speaks of it (*East. Ch.* p. 424), but has acquired a stronger hold over the religious mind of a larger part of Christendom than is probably exercised by any other city except Jerusalem and Rome. It must, therefore, be briefly considered here. Just as the Jew delights to call Jerusalem "the holy Zion," the Russian points with pride to this central city of his empire as "our holy mother Moscow;" and the lower classes, not content with this, even go so far as to name the road which leads to it "our dear mother, the great road from Vladimir to Moscow" (Haxthausen, *Researches in Russia*, iii, 151). In one word, Moscow is a very Russian Rome. Not that Christianity was first proclaimed here for the Russians (this was done at Kief), but because it is the ultimate and permanent seat of the Russian primates (since 1325), and contains within its walls the Kremlin (Russ. *Kreml*), "that fortress surrounded by its crusted towers and battlemented walls," in which are united all the elements of the ancient religious life of Russia. The city abounds in churches and convents. Of the former it is said to have 400, all of the orthodox Greek faith, with the exception of the English and Roman chapels, a German and a French chapel, two or three Armenian chapels, and a Turkish mosque. It has convents also by the hundreds, counting many of the "white clergy." See Scheutzler, *Moscow* (St. Petersb. and Par. 1834); Prime, *The Alhambra and the Kremlin* (N. Y. 1874, 12mo); Clarke, *Travels in Russia, Tartary, and Turkey* (Aberd. 1848, 12mo), ch. iv-ix; Ackerman, *Historical Sketch of Moscow; Harper's Monthly*, vol. xxvi; *Blackwood's Magazine*, 1855, Jan. p. 8. See RUSSIA. (J. H. W.)

MOSCOW, COUNCIL OF (*Concilium Moscoviense*). Several of these were held in the interests of the Russian Church from time to time, ever since the estab-

lishment of the metropolitan see of Moscow in 1320. (See below.) Of these councils, the most important are the following:

I. Held about 1500, and presided over by the metropolitan Simon, when it was decreed that monasteries for men and for women should be separated; monks were forbidden to perform divine service, and widower clerks to consecrate the holy mysteries in the latter; unworthy clerks were sentenced to be degraded; and all payments on account of ordination were forbidden.

II. Held in 1551, under czar John the Terrible. It was attended by all the Russian bishops and the metropolitan of Moscow; Macarius presided. The czar himself opened the synod by a speech, in which he exhorted the bishops to use all the understanding, knowledge, and ability each one possessed in their deliberations; promising that he would be ready to join and support them in correcting what was amiss, or in confirming what was well established, according as the Holy Spirit should direct them. He then put them in mind that in the year in which he was crowned he had charged all bishops and hegumens to collect the lives of the saints of their various dioceses or monasteries, and that twenty new names had been in consequence glorified as saints in the Church. The council then repeated and confirmed the decree, ordering that the memory of these saints should be celebrated in the Church. After this the czar required of the council a reply to various questions relating to the external and internal discipline of the Church; whereupon they delivered a long answer, divided into one hundred chapters, which caused this assembly to be known ever after by the name of "the Council of the Hundred Chapters." These chapters appear not to have been signed by any Russian bishop, nor to have been submitted to the œcumenical patriarch for approval; and it is curious that Macarius himself, who presided at the council, makes no mention of it in his *Books of the Genealogies*, in which he relates the history of affairs both in Church and State. These chapters give countenance to some superstitious customs and local errors, which in after-years produced lamentable schisms. In this council, moreover, the correction of the Church books, which was afterwards actually performed by the patriarch Nikon, was first proposed.

III. Held in the palace of the czar at Moscow in 1655, by the czar Alexis; Nikon, the patriarch of Moscow, presiding. The object of the council was the correction of the liturgy, etc., of the Russian Church. Nikon, soon after his appointment to the patriarchate, had his attention drawn to the great alterations which had crept into the service-books then in use, which in many places, and even in the creed itself, differed from the ancient Greek and Slavonic copies; he therefore induced the czar to convoke this council, at which the following metropolitans, Macarius of Novgorod, Cornelius of Kazan, Jonah of Rostoff, Silvester of the Steppes, and Michael of Servia, were present, together with three archbishops and one bishop. The unanimous decision of the council was that "the new books should be corrected by the old Slavonic and Greek MSS., and that the primitive rule of the Church should in all things be adhered to." This decision confirmed in a council of Greek bishops, convened at Constantinople by the patriarch Paisius, whose judgment the Russian bishops had requested. Upon this the czar and the patriarch procured an immense number of MSS. and books from Mount Athos, by means of which and other assistance the revision of the Russian service-books was completed.

IV. Held in 1677 to select a successor to Nikon, the patriarch, who, having by intrigues of his enemies fallen into disgrace with the czar Alexis, who had formerly been his great friend and patron, had in a moment of irritation abruptly renounced the patriarchate, and by this step had given rise to such disorders in the Church that Alexis, in order to re-establish peace, was obliged to invite the Eastern patriarchs to form a court for his

The Kremlin.

trial, and if possible for his dismissal, in order to make legal the appointment of a new incumbent in the patriarchate. Besides the Eastern patriarchs, Macarius of Antioch and Paisius of Alexandria, there were present at this council four Russian metropolitans, viz. Pitirim of Novgorod, Laurentius of Kazan, Jonah of Rostoff, and Paul of the Steppes; six Greek metropolitans, viz. those of Nicæa, Amasia, Iconium, Trebizond, Varna, and Scio; the metropolitans of Georgia and Servia; six Russian and two other archbishops; and, lastly, five bishops, and fifty archimandrites, hegumens, and archpriests, besides monks and others. Before this council

Nikon was solemnly cited to appear, "and thus it came to pass," says Stanley, "that the most august assembly of divines which Russia had ever witnessed met for the condemnation of the greatest man whom the Eastern hierarchy had produced in modern times." The trial was in the hall of Nikon's own palace. He appeared before the council like a person having made every preparation as for death, yet would he not brook treatment as a cast-out, and went in his character of patriarch, with his cross borne before him; and finding no place prepared for him upon a level with the seats of the Eastern patriarchs, he refused to sit at all, and during all his trial remained standing. His accusation was read, with tears, by Alexis himself; it was to the effect that he had, by his unlawful retirement and capricious conduct, been the cause of grievous evils and disorders in the Church. A week was spent in deliberating upon his case, and in searching for precedents which had occurred in the Church of Constantinople; after which Nikon was summoned before the council in its third session. Having heard his accusation read, sentence was passed upon him, to the effect that he should be degraded, retaining only the rank of a monk, and that he should pass the rest of his life in penance in a remote monastery. One voice only, that of an excellent bishop, Lazarus of Chernigoff, was raised in opposition to this cruel judgment. See Blackmore's Mouravieff, *Hist. of the Russian Church*, p. 92, 103, 204, 227; Stanley, *Lect. on the East. Church*, p. 480 sq.; Strahl, *Beiträge zur Russischen Kirchengesch.* vol. iii and iv; Landon, *Dict. of Councils*, s. v. See NIKON.

MOSCOW, METROPOLITAN SEE OF, was established by St. Peter, the 25th metropolitan of Russia, in 1320. As early as 891 a metropolitan had been appointed to that country, and until 1240 their episcopal centre was at Kief. But the terrible invasion of the Tartars, which burst over the country at the beginning of the 13th century, caused the metropolitan see to be established at Vladimir in 1299, whence its final removal to Moscow. All this time the metropolitan was confirmed by the Oriental Church; yet until the middle of the 15th century almost all the metropolitans of Moscow were members of the Church of Rome, and favorable towards a reunion of the Eastern and Western churches. Peter (1318-26), Theognost (1326-53), and Alexis (1354-78) zealously labored for this end. Indeed, Alexis was originally within the Romish communion, united himself with it, and edited a liturgy and form of service which obtained the endorsement of the pope. In 1380, however, the metropolitan Pimen (called the pseudo-metropolitan) made strong efforts against the possibility of union with Rome, but failed to carry his point. His successor, Cyprian (1380-1406), than whom there was no more ardent friend of the Roman Church, undertook to unite the whole Russian Church with Rome. He had several conferences with Jagello, the king of Poland, and Witout, the grand-duke of Lithuania, the result of which was the reunion of the Lithuanian churches with the Roman Church. This reunion, however, never obtained the assent of the people. After Cyprian's death, Photias tried again to dissever the Russian Church from Rome. But grand-duke Witout and the bishops of Southern Russia opposed him energetically, and at a meeting of a synod (1414) they denounced him as a heretic, and nominated Gregory Jamblak metropolitan of Moscow. At this same time also the metropolitan seat of Russia was divided into the metropolitanate of Kief and of Moscow, Kief ruling the southern episcopacies and Moscow the northern ones. The real reason for this division was the leaning of the Kief party to Rome; and while in later years Moscow was decidedly opposed to the Church of Rome, Kief was its warm friend and ally. This division was brought to an end in 1437, when Joseph, patriarch of Constantinople, consecrated the learned Isidore of Thessalonica metropolitan of all Russia. Isidore is well known in Church history as one of the principal movers of the Council of Florence

(1439), whose sole object was the reunion of the Greek with the Latin Church. He was highly esteemed by pope Eugenius IV, who created him cardinal of Russia in 1441. He returned to Moscow, but miserably failed in his zealous efforts of reunion. The people were so enraged against him that the grand-duke Wasilj III had to imprison him. In 1443 he escaped and fled to Rome, where he died in 1463. This persecution of Isidore led to a new division between Kief and Moscow, and the Roman Catholic bishops of Lithuania in 1474 elected Michael, bishop of Smolensk, as metropolitan of Kief, and henceforth the two metropolitan sees remained intact. The northern part stood again under the metropolitan of Moscow, while the southern part belonged to the metropolitan of Kief. They were, moreover, divided in sentiment, the former favoring strict adherence to the Eastern Church, the latter leaning strongly towards Rome; and thus matters remained until 1520, when the Kief party abandoned the hope of union with Rome. The seeds of dissension, however, took root in the Russian Church, and the fruits were manifest in the following century, finally resulting in the establishment of the independent metropolitanate. See Strahl, *Russ. Kirchengesch.* vol. ii; Neale, *Introd. Hist. Holy East. Ch.* i, 55 sq., 283 sq.; Stanley, *Lect. on the East. Ch.* p. 435 sq. Compare RUSSIAN CHURCH.

Mosellanus, PETER, an eminent German scholar of the time of the Reformation, was born in the little village of Proteg, on the Moselle, in 1493. His family name was *Schade*, but after the literary fashion of the age he changed it to *Mosellanus*. His parents were honest and pious, and in easy circumstances. He was educated at Cologne, and distinguished himself by uncommon precocity of mind, and graduated as master of arts in 1514. In the following year he began to lecture at Freiberg, and published several learned works. He took rank at once among the very first Greek and Latin scholars of the age, and in 1517, after the death of Richard Crocius, was called to Leipsic as professor of Greek and Latin literature. The year following he applied to Luther and Spalatin for the then vacant professorship of Greek at the Wittenberg University, but Melancthon was chosen in preference to him, and Mosellanus remained at Leipsic. With the study of Greek and Roman literature he combined a careful and reverent study of the Bible in the original. This, in connection with the influence of his friends, Luther, Camerarius, Melancthon, Hessus, and others, predisposed him favorably to the great movement of the Reformation. He was decidedly the most popular teacher of the university, and attracted students from every direction, and was twice chosen rector. At the personal request of prince George, he opened the Leipsic Disputation (1519) between Eck and Luther with a most excellent address—"*Oratio de ratione disputandi, præsertim in re theologica.*" With the leaders of the Reformation he remained ever after in constant communication, and was greatly beloved by them for his scholarship and suavity of manners. Luther called him an Erasmian, because of his close application to classical studies notwithstanding the excitement of the time in which he flourished. These labors of Mosellanus in behalf of the revival of classical literature in Europe were arduous and extremely important, and a full list of his philological works may be found in *Vitæ Germanorum philosophorum* a Melchiore Adamo (Francf. 1705), p. 26 sq. He died, while yet scarcely more than a youth in age though hoary with learning, Feb. 17, 1524. See Hallam, *Introd. to the Literature of Europe*, i, 188; De Wette, *Luther's Briefe*, ii, 542; *Viti Lud. A. Seckendorf Commentarius historicus et apologet. de Lutheranismo* (Leips. 1694, 1696); Löscher, *Vollständige Reformations-Acta et Documenta* (Leips. 1729), iii, 567 sq.

Möser, JUSTUS, a great German statesman and author, whose writings have had much moral influence upon the general public mind, was born in Osnabrück Dec. 14, 1720. In 1740 he entered the university at Jena, and there and at Göttingen studied jurisprudence. In 1746 he became an attorney, and was soon noted for his ability and integrity. He resisted the arbitrary arrogance of the vicegerent of Osnabrück, in consequence of which the citizens elected him *advocatus patriæ*. For twenty years during the minority of the duke Frederick of York, who came into possession of Osnabrück in 1763, he was the principal adviser of the regent, and enjoyed the full confidence of George III, king of England. From 1762 to 1768 he officiated as a magistrate in the criminal court, and afterwards until his death as one of the superior officers of justice. His services were as disinterested as they were important. "I enjoyed," he once said, "many things; was sorrowful about a few; defamed by none." He enjoyed excellent health, and died quietly, with hardly a struggle, Jan. 8, 1794.

In his writings, which take high rank in German literature, Möser often presents his ideas in a humorous garb, which, suiting the tastes of the people, made him deservedly popular. His most important contribution to literature is his *Geschichte von Osnabrück* (2 vols. 1768; 2d and improved ed. 1780; 3d ed. 1820; a 3d vol. published from his literary remains by Herbert von Bär, 1824), a work which for critical research and popularity of diction still stands unsurpassed. His celebrated short essays, which originally appeared from 1766–1782, in the Osnabrück *Intelligenzblätter*, and were afterwards published under the title of *Patriotische Phantasien* (3d ed. prepared by his daughter, in 4 vols. [Berl. 1804]), relate mostly to local subjects, but are to this day calculated to enlighten the mind and improve the character of German officials. In his work on the German language and literature, he attacks the Gallomania and infidelity of Frederick the Great, and in a letter addressed to Jean Jacques Rousseau he opposes the theories of that philosopher. Rousseau had gained many followers even in Germany, and the public burning of his works (1765), instead of harming him, had gained him new admirers. The burning of his works proved nothing. Möser, knowing that writings have to be refuted by writings, undertook the task of opposing Rousseau with his own weapons. He issued his letter *To the Vicar in Savoy, to be had of J. J. Rousseau*, in which he maintained the necessity of a positive religion for the people. He ridiculed the impractical character of a merely natural religion with plain mother-wit. In order to meet Rousseau on his own stand-point, he adopted a very moderate idea of religion, such as even Hume might have shared. "It is of the greatest necessity to have certain fortified articles of faith, which comfort the unfortunate, restrain the fortunate, humble the proud, bind kings, and keep tradesmen within limits. It is impossible for the rough masses to be affected by the preaching of mere nature." "The preaching of God's works, that we have daily before our eyes, is like the singing of a canary bird, which its possessor has long since ceased to hear." "Natural religion," he argues, "is not only insufficient for those classes which are commonly called 'the populace' (*der Pöbel*), but for all." "We are all populace, and God has done better in putting a bridle on our soul instead of on our noses; for at least in one place, I think, it was very necessary for us, in order to be led to certain ends. Our religion was made for us populace, and not for angels." "The sentiment that men can be saved in all religions," he says, "stifles the very germ of true religion. I have found that the Christian religion is perfectly sufficient for all purposes which God can have for man, and I draw therefrom this conclusion, that we act foolishly in weakening or breaking so perfect a bond." These outspoken, manly views of the eminent jurist had a great influence on the German mind, and his efforts proved most beneficent to men like Schleiermacher and others. A complete edition of his works was published by R. B. Abeken (Berl. 1842, 10 vols.).

See Herzog, *Real-Encyklop.* xx, 170; Jöcher, *Gelehrten-Lex.*; Bechstein, *Deutsche Männer*; Hurst's Hagenbach, *Hist. of the 18th and 19th Centuries*, i, 220.

Moser, JOHANN JACOB, a distinguished German Protestant jurist and hymnologist, noted for his efforts in behalf of the Church in her relation with the State, was born at Stuttgard, Jan. 18, 1701. He studied law in the University of Tübingen, where he graduated in 1720, and was the very same year appointed extraordinary professor. As he had, however, but a small audience there, he went in 1721 to Vienna. The emperor and the vice-chancellor, count of Schönborn, offered him a very prominent position on condition that he should abjure the Lutheran doctrines, but he steadfastly refused. On his return to his country, he was accused of having given to the emperor information concerning affairs which the duke of Würtemberg desired should remain secret. In 1724 he returned to Vienna, and was still better received than the first time, the count of Schönborn presenting him a pension, and intrusting him with divers works concerning jurisprudence. Recalled to Stuttgard in 1726, Moser was appointed counsellor of the regency, and the following year professor of jurisprudence in the ducal college of Tübingen. Annoyed, however, by the jealousy of several of his colleagues, he resigned in 1732. In 1733, duke Charles Alexander taking the reins of government, he was again made counsellor. In 1736 the king of Prussia made him privy counsellor and professor of jurisprudence at the University of Frankfort-on-the-Oder. In 1739 he resigned also this position in consequence of some disputes with his colleagues, and retired into private life at Ebersdorf. During the eight years he stayed there he was employed by several princes on highly important missions; thus in 1741 he represented the elector of Trèves in the long discussions which preceded the election of emperor Charles VII. In 1747, after refusing to approve the religious changes introduced by count Zinzendorf, he accepted the arch-chancellorship of Hesse-Homburg, on the condition that he should be allowed to carry out his liberal views concerning government and political economy; and when this privilege was subsequently taken from him, he resigned his office and settled at Hanau, where he founded, in 1749, a professional school for young men destined for administration service. He afterwards became the legal adviser of Würtemberg; and having in that capacity opposed the arbitrary measures of the prime minister, he was arrested July 12, 1759, and retained five years in prison, without judgment. Liberated by the Aulic Council in September, 1764, he resumed his functions, in which he continued six years longer, and then retired from official life. He died at Stuttgard Sept. 30, 1785. Among his works and pamphlets, numbering over five hundred volumes, covering, besides legal subjects, also the department of practical religion, especially hymnology, those of his writings deserve special mention which have more or less relation to ecclesiastical law and humanitarian objects; such are: *Merkwürdige Reichshofrath Conclusa* (Francf. 1726, 8 vols. 8vo): — *Bibliotheca juris publici* (Stuttg. 1729–1734, 3 vols. 8vo): — *Miscellanea juridico-historica* (Francf. 1729–1730, 2 vols. 8vo): — *Grundriss d. heutigen Staatsverfassung von Deutschland* (Tübing. 1731, 8vo; six editions since): — *Einleitung in den Reichshofraths-Process* (Francf. 1733–1737, 4 vols. 8vo): — *Syntagma dissertationum Jus publicum Germanicum illustrantium* (Tübing. 1735, 4to): — *Corpus juris evangelicorum ecclesiasticum* (Zullichau, 1737–1738, 2 vols. 4to): — *Altes deutsches Staatsrecht* (Nuremb. 1737–1754, 53 parts, 4to): — *Alte u. neue Reichshofraths Conclusa in causis illustribus* (Francf. 1743–1746, 3 parts, 8vo): — *Opuscula academica selecta Juris capita explicantia* (Francf. 1745, 4to): — *Deutsches Staatsarchiv* (Francf. 1751–1757, 13 parts, 4to): — *Neues deutsches Staatsrecht* (Stuttg. 1766–1772, 20 vols. 4to, with 3 vols. of supplement [Francf. 1781–1782, 3 vols. 4to], and an Index, 1775): — *Vermischte Nachrichten v. reichsritterschaftlichen Sach-*

en (Nuremb. 1772, 6 parts, 8vo) :—*Beiträge zu reichsrit-terschaftlichen Sachen* (Ulm, 1775, 4 parts, 8vo) :—*Ab-handlungen über verschiedene Reichsmaterien* (Ulm, 1772-1778, 5 vols. 4to) :—*Reichsstädtisches Magazin* (Ulm, 1774-1775, 2 vols. 8vo) :—*Neueste Geschichte der unmit-telbaren Reichsritterschaft* (Ulm, 1775-1776, 2 vols. 8vo); *Erläuterung des Westphälischen Friedens* (Erlangen, 1775-1776, 2 parts, 4to) :—*Versuch des neuesten europä-ischen Völkerrechts in Friedens- und Kriegszeiten* (Francf. 1777-1780, 10 vols. 8vo) :—*Betrachtungen über die Wahl-capitulation Josephs II* (Francf. 1778, 2 vols. 4to) :—*Beiträge zu dem neuesten europäischen Völkerrechte* (Tü-bing. 1787, 5 parts, 8vo), etc. See *Lebensgeschichte Mosers* (autobiography [Francf. 1777-1783], 4 parts, 8vo); Ledderhose, *Aus dem Leben J. v. Moser's* (2d ed. 1852); Grüneisen, in Piper's *Kirchen-Kalender*, 1852; Weidlich, *Nachrichten von jetztlebenden Rechtsgelehrten*, vol. ii; Hirsching, *Hist. lit. Handbuch;* Herzog, *Real-Encyklop.* x, 32; Hoefer, *Nouv. Biog. Générale*, xxxvi, 719; *Bullet. Theol.* Oct. 1869, p. 310. (J. H.W.)

Mose'ra (Heb. *Moserah'*, מוֹסֵרָה, prob. i. q. מֵאָסַר, a *band* [but the final ה is not local, as it has the tone; it is apparently fem.]; Sept. Μοσερά v. r. Μισαδαί), the thirty-ninth station of the Israelites in the desert, between Jaakan and Gudgodah (Deut. x, 6); evidently at the foot of Mount Hor, since Aaron is said to have died there (comp. Numb. xxxiii, 37, 38). The name appears in the plur. form MOSEROTH, as an earlier station of the Israelites, in the inverse order (Numb. xxxiii, 30, 31). See EXODE. It may probably be identified with the small fountain *et-Tayibeh*, at the bottom of the pass er-Rubay, leading to the western ascent of Mount Hor (Robinson's *Researches*, ii, 583). This spring in the wady is quite choked with sand, but there is fine water in the ravines higher up the hill-side, where the Bedouin pitch their tents. Schwarz is entirely astray in locating it (*Palest.* p. 213) at *Wady el-Muzeiriah*, in the heart of the western cesert (Robinson, i, 277). Burckhardt vaguely suggested *Wady Musa*, or the valley of Petra; but this has no probability. Rowlands, in Fairbairn's *Dictionary*, contends at length for *Jebel Madurah*, near-ly in the middle of the desert plateau; but in this he is evidently influenced by his theory of the location of Kadesh.

Mose'roth (Heb. *Moseroth'*, מוֹסֵרוֹת, prob. fem. plu. for מֵאָסַר, a *band;* Sept. Μασουρού-ϑ), the thirty-first station of the Israelites, between Hashmonah and Bene-jaakan (Numb. xxxiii, 30, 31); doubtless the same elsewhere (Deut. x, 6) called MOSERA (q. v.).

Mo'ses, the great Jewish prophet and lawgiver, and the founder, we may say, under God, of the Hebrew na-tion and religion (Euseb. *Præp. Ev.* vii, 8; comp. Philo, *V. Mos.* i, 80). His importance in Biblical history justi-fies a somewhat extended biography here. In prepar-ing it, we have to depend chiefly upon the Scriptural notices and references.

I. *The Name.*—This in Heb. is מֹשֶׁה, *Mosheh'*, signi-fying, according to Exod. ii, 10, *drawn out*, i. e. from the water, as if from מָשָׁה, to *draw* out; but in that case the form would be active, *drawing* out; and it is hardly probable that the daughter of Pharaoh would have giv-en him a Hebrew name. This, therefore (as in many other instances, *Babel*, etc.), is probably the Hebrew form given to a foreign word. Hence the Alexandrine Jews (Philo, *Vit. Mos.* i, 4) assigned it an Egyptian or-igin, from *mo, water* (*mou*, or *mos;* Copt. *mo*), and *ouses* (Copt. *ushe*), *saved*, i. e. "water-saved;" see Jablonski, *Opusc.* i, 152. This is the explanation given by Jose-phus (*Ant.* ii, 9, 6; *Apion*, i, 31), and confirmed by the Greek form of the word adopted in the Sept. and other writings, and thence in the Vulgate. Brugsch, however (*L'Histoire d'Egypte*, p. 157, 173), renders the name *Mes* or *Messon*=child, being that borne by one of the princes of Ethiopia under Rameses II. In the Arabic

traditions the name is derived from his discovery in the water and among the trees; "for in the Egyptian lan-guage *mo* is the name of water, and *se* is that of a tree" (Jalaladdin, p. 387). Clem. Alex. (*Strom.* i, p. 343) de-rives *Moses* from "drawing breath." In an ancient Egyptian treatise on agriculture cited by Chwolson (*Ueberreste*, etc., p. 12, note) his name is given as *Mo-nios.* For other etymologies, see Gesenius, *Thes.* Heb. p. 824. His original Hebrew name is said to have been *Joachim* (Clem. Alex. *Strom.* i, p. 343). The Sept., Jo-sephus, Philo, and the most ancient MSS. of N. T., give the Greek form as Μωϋσῆς (declined Μωϋσέως, Μωϋσεῖ or Μωϋσῇ, Μωϋσέα or Μωϋσῆν); other editions, how-ever, have Μωσῆς, as in Strabo, xvi, 760 sq. (see Winer, *Grammat. N. T.* p. 52); the Vulg. gives *Moyses* (declined *Moysi*, gen. and dat.; *Moysen*, acc.); the Rec. Text of the N. T. and Protestant versions, *Moses*—Arabic, *Músa;* Numenius (ap. Euseb. *Præp. Ev.* ix, 8, 27), Μουσαῖος; Artapanus (*ibid.* 27), Μώϋσος; Manetho (ap. Joseph. *c. Ap.* i, 26, 28, 31), *Osarsiph*, i. e. (Osiri-tef?) "saved by Osiris" (Osburn, *Monumental Egypt*); Chæremon (*ib.* 32), *Tisithen.* In Scripture he is entitled "the man of God" (Psa. xc, title; 1 Chron. xxiii, 14); "the slave of Jehovah" (Numb. xii, 7: Deut. xxxiv, 5; Josh. i, 1; Psa. cv, 26); "the chosen" (Psa. cvi, 23).

II. *His Biography.*—The materials for this are the following: *a.* The details preserved in the last four books of the Pentateuch. *b.* The allusions in the proph-ets and Psalms, which in a few instances seem indepen-dent of the Pentateuch. *c.* The Jewish traditions pre-served in the N. T. (Acts vii, 20-38; 2 Tim. iii, 8, 9; Heb. xi, 23-28; Jude 9); and in Josephus (*Ant.* ii, iii, iv), Philo (*Vita Moysis*), and Clemens Alexandrinus (*Strom.*). *d.* The heathen traditions of Manetho, Ly-simachus, and Chæremon, preserved in Josephus (*c. Ap.* i, 26-32), of Artapanus and others in Eusebius (*Præp. Ev.* ix, 8, 26, 27), and of Hecatæus in Diod. Sic. xl; Stra-bo, xvi, 2. *e.* The Mussulman traditions in the Koran (ii, vii, x, xviii, xx, xxviii, xl), and the Arabian legends, as given in Weil's *Biblical Legends;* D'Herbelot (s. v. Moussa), and Lane's *Selections*, p. 182. *f.* The frag-mentary apocryphal books of Moses (Fabricius, *Cod. Pseud. V. T.* i, 825): (1) Prayers of Moses, (2) Apoca-lypse of Moses, (3) Ascension of Moses. *g.* In modern times his career and legislation have been treated by Warburton, Michaelis, Ewald, Bunsen, and others.

The life of Moses, in the later period of the Jewish history, was divided into three equal portions of forty years each (Acts vii, 23, 30, 36). This agrees with the natural arrangement of his history into the three parts of his Egyptian training, his exile in Arabia, and his government of the Israelitish nation in the wilderness and on the confines of Palestine.

1. *His Parentage, Birth, and Education.*—The imme-diate pedigree of Moses is as follows:

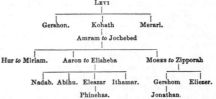

In this genealogy, as in all the others given of the same period, there is an interval of four to six generations (Browne, *Ordo Sæclorum*, p. 301 sq.). In the Koran, by a strange confusion, the family of Moses is confounded with the Holy Family of Nazareth, chiefly through the identification of Mary and Miriam, and the third chap-ter, which describes the evangelical history, bears the name of the "Family of Amram." Although little is known of the family except through its connection with this its most illustrious member, yet it was not without influence on his after-life. The fact that he was of the tribe of Levi no doubt contributed to the selection of that tribe as the sacred caste. The tie that bound them to Moses was one of kinship, and they thus naturally rallied around the religion which he had been the means of establishing (Exod. xxxii, 28) with an ardor which could not have been found elsewhere. His own eager devotion is also a quality, for good or evil, characteristic of the whole tribe. The Levitical parentage and Egyptian origin both appear in the family names. *Gershom, Eleazar*, are both repeated in the younger generations. *Moses* and *Phinehas* (see Brugsch, *Hist. de l'Egypte*, i, 173) are Egyptian. The name of his mother, Jochebed, implies the knowledge of the name of Jehovah in the bosom of the family. It is its first distinct appearance in the sacred history. Miriam, who must have been considerably older than himself, and Aaron, who was three years older (Exod. vii, 7), afterwards occupy that independence of position which their superior age would naturally give them.

Moses was born B.C. 1738, and, according to Manetho (Josephus, *Ap.* i, 26; ii, 2), at Heliopolis, in the time of the deepest depression of his nation in the Egyptian servitude. Hence the Jewish proverb, " When the tale of bricks is doubled, then comes Moses." His birth (according to Josephus, *Ant.* ii, 9, 2, 3, 4) had been foretold to Pharaoh by the Egyptian magicians, and to his father Amram by a dream—as respectively the future destroyer and deliverer. The pangs of his mother's labor were alleviated so as to enable her to evade the Egyptian midwives. The story of his birth is thoroughly Egyptian in its scene. The beauty of the new-born babe— in the later versions of the story amplified into a beauty and size (Josephus, *ib.* 1, 5) almost divine (ἀστεῖος τῷ Θεῷ, Acts vii, 20; the word ἀστεῖος is taken from the Sept. version of Exod. ii, 2, and is used again in Heb. xi, 23, and is applied to none but Moses in the N. T.)— induced the mother to make extraordinary efforts for its preservation from the general destruction of the male infants of Israel. For three months the child was concealed in the house. Then his mother placed him in a small boat or basket of papyrus—perhaps from a current Egyptian belief that the plant is a protection from crocodiles (Plutarch, *Is. and Os.* p. 358)—closed against the water by bitumen. This was placed among the aquatic vegetation by the side of one of the canals of the Nile. See NILE. The mother departed as if unable to bear the sight. The sister lingered to watch her brother's fate. The basket (Josephus, *ib.* 4) floated down the stream. The Egyptian princess came down (after the custom of her country, which allowed more freedom to females than is now common in the East) to bathe in the sacred river, or (Josephus, *Ant.* ii, 9, 5) to play by its side. Her attendant slaves followed her (see Wilkinson, *Anc. Eg.* ii, 389). She saw the basket in the flags, or (Josephus) borne down the stream, and dispatched divers after it. The divers, or one of the female slaves, brought it. It was opened, and the cry of the child moved the princess to compassion. She determined to rear it as her own. The child refused the milk of Egyptian nurses (Josephus). The sister was then at hand to recommend a Hebrew nurse. The child was brought up as the princess's son, and the memory of the incident was long cherished in the name given to the foundling of the water's side—whether according to its Hebrew or Egyptian form. (See above.) The child was adopted by the princess. Tradition describes its beauty as so great that passers-by stood fixed to look at it, and laborers left their work to steal a glance (Josephus, *Ant.* ii, 9, 6). His foster-mother (to whom the Jewish tradition gave the name of *Thermuthis*, Josephus, *Ant.* ii, 9, 5; Artapanus, *Praep. Ev.* ix, 27, the name of *Merrhis*, and the Arabian traditions that of *Asiat*, Jalaladdin, p. 387) was (according to Artapanus, Eusebius, *Praep. Ev.* ix, 27) the daughter of Palmanothes, who was reigning at Heliopolis, and the wife of Chenephres, who was reigning at Memphis. In this tradition, and that of Philo (*V. M.* i, 4), she has no child, and hence her delight at finding one. Many attempts have been

made in modern times to identify the Pharaoh into whose family Moses was thus introduced, but different Egyptologists have varied widely as to his name and relative position, according to their several chronological and historical schemes. See EGYPT. The latest and most plausible effort in this direction is that of Osburn (in the *Jour. of Sac. Lit.* July, 1860, p. 257 sq.), who argues from a number of striking coincidences with the monumental records that it must have been no less than Sesostris-Rameses, the famous architectural monarch of the 19th dynasty, whose son Amenephthis, dying soon after his accession, was succeeded by a sister, Thonoris (in that case the foster-mother of Moses), who again, after a long reign, was succeeded by her nephew, Sethos II, the latter having already been associate king in Upper Egypt. This last then, if we might trust these precarious synchronisms, would be the Pharaoh of the exode (q. v.).

From this time for many years Moses must be considered as an Egyptian. In the Pentateuch this period is a blank, but in the N. T. he is represented as "educated (ἐπαιδεύθη) in all the wisdom of the Egyptians," and as "mighty in words and deeds" (Acts vii, 22). The following is a brief summary of the Jewish and Egyptian traditions which fill up the silence of the sacred writer. He was educated at Heliopolis (comp. Strabo, xvii, 1), and grew up there as a priest, under his Egyptian name of Osarsiph (Manetho, ap. Josephus, *c. Ap.* i, 26, 28, 31) or Tisithen (Chaeremon, *ib.* 32). He was (according to these accounts) taught the whole range of Greek, Chaldee, and Assyrian literature. From the Egyptians especially he learned mathematics, to train his mind for the unprejudiced reception of truth (Philo, *V. M.* i, 5). "He invented boats and engines for building—instruments of war and of hydraulics—hieroglyphics—division of lands" (Artapanus, ap. Euseb. *Praep. Ev.* ix, 27). He taught Orpheus, and was hence called by the Greeks Musaeus (*ib.*), and by the Egyptians Hermes (*ib.*). He taught grammar to the Jews, whence it spread to Phœnicia and Greece (Eupolemus, ap. Clem. Alexand. *Strom.* i, p. 343). He was sent on an expedition against the Ethiopians. He got rid of the serpents of the country to be traversed by turning basketfuls of ibises upon them (Josephus, *Ant.* ii, 10, 2), and founded the city of Hermopolis to commemorate his victory (Artapanus, ap. Euseb. ix, 27). He advanced to Saba, the capital of Ethiopia, and gave it the name of Meroe, from his adopted mother Merrhis, whom he buried there (*ib.*). Tharbis, the daughter of the king of Ethiopia, fell in love with him, and he returned in triumph to Egypt with her as his wife (Josephus, *ib.*). See D. W. Moller, *De Mose philosopho* (Altorf, 1707); Adami, *Exerc. exeg.* p. 92 sq.; Brucker, *Hist. phil.* i, 78; J. G. Walch, *Observ. in N. T.* (Jen. 1727), p. 62 sq.

2. *Period of Moses's Retirement.*—The nurture of his mother is probably the unmentioned link which bound him to his own people, and the time had at last arrived when he was resolved to reclaim his nationality. Here again the N. T. preserves the tradition in a more distinct form than the account in the Pentateuch. "Moses, when he was come to years, refused to be called the son of Pharaoh's daughter; choosing rather to suffer affliction with the people of God than to enjoy the pleasures of sin for a season; esteeming the reproach of Christ greater riches than the treasures"—the ancient accumulated treasure of Rhampsinitus and the old kings—" of Egypt" (Heb. xi, 24–26). In his earliest infancy he was reported to have refused the milk of Egyptian nurses (Josephus, *Ant.* ii, 9, 5), and when three years old to have trampled under his feet the crown which Pharaoh had playfully placed on his head (*ib.* 7). According to the Alexandrian representation of Philo (*V. M.* i, 6), he led an ascetic life, in order to pursue his high philosophic speculations. According to the Egyptian tradition, although a priest of Heliopolis, he always performed his prayers, in conformity with the custom of his fathers, outside the walls of the city, in the open air,

turning towards the sun-rising (Josephus, *Apion*, ii, 2). The king was excited to hatred by the priests of Egypt, who foresaw their destroyer (*ib.*), or by his own envy (Artapanus, ap. Euseb. *Præp. Ev.* ix, 27). Various plots of assassination were contrived against him, which failed. The last was after he had escaped across the Nile from Memphis, warned by his brother Aaron, and when pursued by the assassin he killed him (*ib.*). The same general account of conspiracies against his life appears in Josephus (*Ant.* ii, 10). All that remains of these traditions in the sacred narrative is the simple and natural incident that seeing an Israelite suffering the bastinado from an Egyptian, and thinking that they were alone, he slew the Egyptian (the later tradition, preserved by Clement of Alexandria, said, "with a word of his mouth"), and buried the corpse in the sand (the sand of the desert then, as now, running close up to the cultivated tract). The fire of patriotism which thus turned him into a deliverer from the oppressors, turns him in the same story into the peace-maker of the oppressed. See J. F. Mayer, *Utrum Moses Ægyptium juste interfecit* (Viteb. 1685); Hoffmann, *Moses just. Ægyptii percussor* (Hal. 1776). It is characteristic of the faithfulness of the Jewish records that his flight is there occasioned rather by the malignity of his countrymen than by the enmity of the Egyptians. So in St. Stephen's speech it is this part of the story which is drawn out at greater length than in the original, evidently with a view to showing the identity of the narrow spirit which had thus displayed itself equally against their first and their last Deliverer (Acts vii, 25–35). But his spirit was yet too rash and vindictive to fit him for being the meek and patient instrument of the Divine purposes. The discovery, too, of the servile and treacherous temper of his own compatriots disheartened him. He needed the bracing as well as the purifying discipline which years of calm reflection and peaceful self-culture alone could give in order to make him the cool, firm, and independent leader of a popular movement.

Moses fled into Midian, B.C. 1698. Beyond the fact that it was in or near the peninsula of Sinai, its precise situation is unknown. Arabian tradition points to the country east of the Gulf of Akaba (see Laborde). Josephus (*Ant.* ii, 11, 1) makes it "by the Red Sea." There was a famous well ("the well," Exod. ii, 15) surrounded by tanks for watering the flocks of the Bedouin herdsmen. By this well the fugitive seated himself "at noon" (Joseph. *ib.*), and watched the gathering of the sheep. There were the Arabian shepherds, and there were also seven maidens, whom the shepherds rudely drove away from the water. The chivalrous spirit (if we may so apply a modern phrase) which had already broken forth in behalf of his oppressed countrymen, broke forth again in behalf of the distressed maidens. They returned unusually soon to their father, and told him of their adventure. Their father was a person of whom we know but little, but of whom that little shows how great an influence he exercised over the future career of Moses. It was Jethro, or Reuel, or Hobab, chief or priest ("Sheik" exactly expresses the union of the religious and political influence) of the Midianitish tribes. Moses, who up to this time had been "an Egyptian" (Exod. ii, 19), now became for a long period, indicated by the later tradition as forty years (Acts vii, 30), an Arabian. He married Zipporah, daughter of his host, to whom he also became the servant and shepherd (Exod. ii, 21; iii, 1).

The blank which during the stay in Egypt is filled up by Egyptian traditions can here only be supplied from indirect allusions in other parts of the O. T. The alliance between Israel and the Kenite branch of the Midianites, now first formed, was never broken. See KENITE. Jethro became their guide through the desert. If from Egypt, as we have seen, was derived the secular and religious learning of Moses, and with this much of their outward ceremonial, so from Jethro was derived the organization of their judicial and social ar-

rangements during their nomadic state (Exod. xviii, 21–23). Nor is the conjecture of Ewald (*Gesch.* ii, 59, 60) improbable, that in this pastoral and simple relation there is an indication of a wider concert than is directly stated between the rising of the Israelites in Egypt and the Arabian tribes, who, under the name of "the Shepherds," had recently been expelled. According to Artapanus (Euseb. *Præp. Ev.* ix, 27), Reuel actually urged Moses to make war upon Egypt. Something of a joint action is implied in the visit of Aaron to the desert (Exod. iv, 27; comp. Artapanus, *ut sup.*); something also in the sacredness of Sinai, already recognised both by Israel and by the Arabs (Exod. viii, 27; comp. Joseph. *Ant.* ii, 12, 1).

But the chief effect of this stay in Arabia was on Moses himself. It was in the seclusion and simplicity of his shepherd-life that he received his call as a prophet. The traditional scene of this great event is in the valley of Shoeib, or Hobab, on the north side of Jebel Mûsa. Its exact spot is marked by the convent of St. Catharine, of which the altar is said to stand on the site of the Burning Bush. The original indications are too slight to enable us to fix the spot with any certainty. To judge from the indications given in the Bible (Exod. iv, 27; Numb. x, 30), Jethro must have resided southeast of that mountain (Keil, ii, 325; Antonini Placent. *Itinerar.* c. 37; *Acta Sanct.* Maji, ii, 22). It is remarkable that the time of the calling of Moses in the mount of God was contemporaneous with the extraordinary spirit of prayer among the oppressed nation in Egypt (Exod. ii, 23). The call itself was at "the back" of "the wilderness" at Horeb (Exod. iii, 1); to which the Hebrew adds, while the Sept. omits, "the mountain of God." Josephus further particularizes that it was the loftiest of all the mountains in that region, and the best for pasturage, from its good grass; and that, owing to a belief in its being inhabited by the Divinity, the shepherds feared to approach it (*Ant.* ii, 12, 1). Philo (*V. M.* i, 12) adds that it was "a grove" or "glade." Upon the mountain was a well-known briery shrub or tree (הַסְּנֶה, *the senéh*, A. V. "a bush"—the definite article may indicate either "the particular celebrated tree," sacred perhaps already, or "the tree" or "vegetation peculiar to the spot"), usually thought to have been the acacia or the thorn-tree of the desert, spreading out its tangled branches, thick set with white thorns, over the rocky ground; but perhaps only a bramble, or some one of the bristly plants with which the desert abounds. Comp. Reichlin-Meldeg, *Mos. Gesch. v. brennenden Dornbusch* (Frieb. 1831). See SHITTIM; THORN. It was this bush which became the symbol of the divine Presence, in the form of a flame of fire in the midst of it, in which the dry branches would naturally have crackled and burned in a moment, but which played around it without consuming it. In Philo (*V. M.* i, 12) "the angel" is described as a strange but beautiful creature. Artapanus (Euseb. *Pr. Ev.* ix, 27) represents it as a fire suddenly bursting from the bare ground, and feeding itself without fuel. But this is far less expressive than the Biblical image. Like all the visions of the divine Presence recorded in the O. T. as manifested at the outset of a prophetical career, this was exactly suited to the circumstances of the tribe. It was the true likeness of the condition of Israel—in the furnace of affliction, yet not destroyed (comp. Philo, *V. M.* i, 12). The place too, in the desert solitude, was equally appropriate, as a sign that the divine protection was not confined either to the sanctuaries of Egypt or to the Holy Land, but was to be found with any faithful worshipper, fugitive and solitary though he might be. The rocky ground at once became "holy," and the shepherd's sandal was to be taken off no less than on the threshold of a palace or a temple. It is this feature of the incident on which St. Stephen dwells as a proof of the universality of the true religion (Acts vii, 29–33). The call or revelation was twofold—(1.) The declaration of the Sacred Name expressed the eternal self-existence of the one God. The name itself, as already mentioned, must have been known in the family of Aaron. But its grand significance was now first drawn out. See JEHOVAH. (2.) The mission was given to Moses to deliver his people. The two signs are characteristic—the one of his past Egyptian life, the other of his active shepherd life. In the rush of leprosy into his hand is the link between him and the people whom the Egyptians called a nation of lepers (Josephus, *Apion*, i, 26). (The Mussulman legends speak of his white shining hand as the instrument of his miracles [D'Herbelot]. Hence "the white hand" is proverbial for the healing art.) In the transformation of his shepherd's staff is the glorification of the simple pastoral life, of which that staff was the symbol, into the great career which lay before it. The humble yet wonder-working crook is, in the history of Moses, as Ewald finely observes, what the despised cross is in the first history of Christianity. In this call of Moses, as of the apostles afterwards, the man is swallowed up in the cause. Yet this is the passage in his history which, more than any other, brings out his external and domestic relations.

Moses returned to Egypt from his exile, B.C. 1658. His Arabian wife and her two infant sons were with him. She was seated with them on the ass (the ass was known as the animal peculiar to the Jewish people from Jacob down to David). He apparently walked by their side with his shepherd's staff. (The Sept. substitutes the general term $\tau\grave{a}$ $\dot{v}\pi o\zeta\dot{v}\gamma\iota a$.) On the journey back to Egypt a mysterious incident occurred in the family, which can only be explained with difficulty. The most probable explanation seems to be that at the caravansary either Moses or Gershom (the context of the preceding verses [iv, 22, 23] rather points to the latter) was struck with what seemed to be a mortal illness. In some way, not apparent to us, this illness was connected by Zipporah with the fact that her son had not been circumcised—whether in the general neglect of that rite among the Israelites in Egypt, or in consequence of his birth in Midian. She instantly performed the rite, and threw the sharp instrument, stained with the fresh blood, at the feet of her husband, exclaiming, in the agony of a mother's anxiety for the life of her child—"A bloody husband thou art, to cause the death of my son." Then, when the recovery from the illness took place (whether of Moses or Gershom), she exclaimed again—"A bloody husband still thou art, but not so as to cause the child's death, but only to bring about his circumcision." So Ewald explains the narrative (*Geschichte*, vol. ii, pt. ii, p. 105), taking the sickness to have visited Moses. Rosenmüller makes Gershom the victim, and makes Zipporah address Jehovah, the Arabic word for "marriage" being a synonym for "circumcision." It is possible that on this story is founded the tradition of Artapanus (Euseb. *Pr. Ev.* ix, 27), that the Ethiopians derived circumcision from Moses. It would seem to have been in consequence of this event, whatever it was, that the wife and her children were sent back to Jethro, and remained with him till Moses joined them at Rephidim (Exod. xviii, 2-6), which is the last time that she is distinctly mentioned. In Numb. xii, 1 we hear of a Cushite wife who gave umbrage to Miriam and Aaron. This may be—(1) an Ethiopian (Cushite) wife, taken after Zipporah's death (Ewald, *Gesch.* ii, 229); (2) the Ethiopian princess of Josephus (*Ant.* i, 10, 2; but that whole story is probably only an inference from Numb. xii, 1); (3) Zipporah herself, which is rendered probable by the juxtaposition of Cushan with Midian in Hab. iii, 7. The two sons also sink into obscurity. Their names, though of Levitical origin, relate to their foreign birthplace. Gershom, "stranger," and Eli-ezer, "God is my help," commemorated their father's exile and escape (Exod. xviii, 3, 4). Gershom was the father of the wandering Levite Jonathan (Judg. xviii, 30), and the ancestor of Shebuel, David's chief treasurer (1 Chron. xxiii, 16; xxiv, 20).

Eliezer had an only son, Rehabiah (1 Chron. xxiii, 17), who was the ancestor of a numerous but obscure progeny, whose representative in David's time—the last descendant of Moses known to us—was Shelomith, guard of the consecrated treasures in the temple (1 Chron. xxvi, 25-28).

After this parting Moses advanced into the desert, and at the same spot where he had had his vision encountered Aaron (Exod. iv, 27). From that meeting and co-operation we have the first distinct indication of Moses's personal appearance and character. The traditional representations of him in some respects well agree with that which we derive from Michael Angelo's famous statue in the church of St. Pietro in Vinculi at Rome. Long, shaggy hair and beard is described as his characteristic equally by Josephus, Diodorus (i, p. 424), and Artapanus ($\kappa o\mu\dot{\eta}\tau\eta\varsigma$, ap. Euseb. *Præp. Ev.* ix, 27). To this Artapanus adds the curious touch that it was of a reddish hue, tinged with gray ($\pi v\rho\rho\acute{a}\kappa\eta\varsigma$, $\pi o\lambda\iota\acute{o}\varsigma$). The traditions of his beauty and size as a child have already been mentioned. They are continued to his manhood in the Gentile descriptions. "Tall and dignified," says Artapanus ($\mu\acute{a}\kappa\rho o\varsigma$, $\dot{a}\xi\iota\omega\mu a\tau\iota\kappa\acute{o}\varsigma$)—"Wise and beautiful as his father Joseph" (with a curious confusion of genealogies), says Justin (xxxvi, 2). But beyond the slight glance at his infantine beauty, no hint of this grand personality is given in the Bible. What is described is rather the reverse. The only point there brought out is a singular and unlooked-for infirmity: "O my Lord, I am not eloquent, neither heretofore nor since thou hast spoken to thy servant; but I am slow of speech and of a slow tongue. . . . How shall Pharaoh hear me, which am of uncircumcised lips?" (i. e. slow, without words, stammering, hesitating; Sept. $\iota\sigma\chi\nu\acute{o}$-$\phi\omega\nu o\varsigma$ $\kappa a\grave{\iota}$ $\beta a\rho\acute{v}\gamma\lambda\omega\sigma\sigma o\varsigma$); his "speech contemptible," like St. Paul's—like the English Cromwell (comp. Carlyle's *Cromwell*, ii, 219)—like the first efforts of the Greek Demosthenes. In the solution of this difficulty which Moses offers we read both the disinterestedness, which is the most distinct trait of his personal character, and the future relation of the two brothers. "Send, I pray thee, by the hand of him whom thou wilt send" (i. e. "make any one thy apostle rather than me"). In outward appearance this prayer was granted. Aaron spoke and acted for Moses, and was the permanent inheritor of the sacred staff of power. But Moses was the inspiring soul behind; and so as time rolls on, Aaron, the prince and priest, has almost disappeared from view, and Moses, the dumb, backward, disinterested prophet, is in appearance what he was in truth—the foremost leader of the chosen people.

3. *Moses's Public Career.*—Thus, after the solitude of pastoral life, where he was appointed to ripen gradually for his high calling, he was now unexpectedly and suddenly sent back among his people, in order to achieve their deliverance from Egyptian bondage. Overruled and encouraged by the above remarkable interview with Jehovah, he resumed his journey into Egypt, where neither the dispirited state of the Israelites nor the obstinate opposition and threatenings of Pharaoh were now able to shake the man of God. Supported by his brother Aaron, and commissioned by God as his chosen instrument, proving, by a series of marvellous deeds, in the midst of heathenism, the God of Israel to be the only true God, Moses at last overcame the opposition of the Egyptians (Exod. v–xii). According to a divine decree, the people of the Lord were to quit Egypt, under the command of Moses, in a triumphant manner. The punishments of God were poured down upon the hostile people in an increasing ratio, terminating in the death of the firstborn, as a sign that all had deserved death. See Bauer, *Hebr. Myth.* i, 274 sq., and *Ausführl. Erklär. der ältest. Wundergeschichte*, ii, 174 sq.; Rosenmüller, *Morgenl.* i, 275 sq., and *Schol.* i, ii; J. Bryant, *Observ. on the Plagues inflicted on the Egyptians* (Lond. 1794); L. Bertholdt, *De reb. a Mose in Ægypt. gestis* (Erl. 1795); Eichhorn, in the *Comment. Soc. Gott*

reg. iv, 35 sq. The formidable power of paganism, in its conflict with the theocracy, was obliged to bow before the apparently weak people of the Lord. The Egyptians paid tribute to the emigrating Israelites (Exod. xii, 35), who set out laden with the spoils of victory. See Harenberg, in the *Biblioth. Brem.* vii, 624 sq.; Kanne, *Biblische Untersuch.* ii, 267 sq.; Hengstenberg, *Pent.* ii, 520 sq.; Justi, *Ueb. die den Aegypt. abgenommenen Geräthe* (Frckf. 1771); Augusti, *Theol. Blätter,* i, 516 sq.; Zeibich, *Vern. Betracht.* II, i, 20 sq.). B.C. 1658. The enraged king vainly endeavored to destroy the emigrants. Moses, firmly relying upon miraculous help from the Lord, led his people through the Red Sea into Arabia, while the host of Pharaoh perished in its waves (Exod. xii–xv). See RED SEA, PASSAGE OF.

After this began the most important functions of Moses as the lawgiver of the Israelites, who were destined to enter into Canaan as the people of promise, upon whom rested the ancient blessings of the patriarchs. By the instrumentality of Moses, they were appointed to enter into intimate communion with God through a sacred covenant, and to be firmly bound to him by a new legislation. Moses, having victoriously repulsed the attack of the Amalekites, marched to Mount Sinai, where he signally punished the defection of his people, and gave them the law as a testimony of divine justice and mercy. From Mount Sinai they proceeded northward to the desert of Paran, and sent spies to explore the Land of Canaan (Numb. x–xiii). On this occasion broke out a violent rebellion against the lawgiver, which he, however, by divine assistance, energetically repressed (Numb. xiv–xvi). The Israelites frequently murmured, and were disobedient during about forty years. In a part of the desert of Kadesh, which was called Zin, near the boundaries of the Edomites, after the sister of Moses had died, and after even the new generation had, like their fathers, proved to be obstinate and desponding, Moses fell into sin, and was on that account deprived of the privilege of introducing the people into Canaan (Numb. xix, 12). He was appointed to lead them only to the boundary of their country, to prepare all that was requisite for their entry into the land of promise, to admonish them impressively, and to bless them. It was according to God's appointment that the new generation also, to whom the occupation of the country had been promised, should arrive at their goal only after having vanquished many obstacles. Even before they had reached the real boundaries of Canaan they were to be subjected to a heavy and purifying trial. It was important that a man like Moses should have been at the head of Israel during all these providential dispensations. His authority was a powerful preservative against despondency under heavy trials. Having in vain attempted to pass through the territory of the Edomites, the people marched around its boundaries by a circuitous and tedious route. Two powerful kings of the Amorites, Sihon and Og, were vanquished. Moses led the people into the fields of Moab over against Jericho, to the very threshold of Canaan (Numb. xx–xxi). The oracles of Balaam became, by the instrumentality of Moses, blessings to his people, because by them they were rendered conscious of the great importance of having the Lord on their side. Moses happily averted the danger which threatened the Israelites on the part of Midian (Numb. xxv–xxxi). Hence he was enabled to grant to some of the tribes permanent dwellings in a considerable tract of country situated to the east of the River Jordan (Numb. xxxii), and to give to his people a foretaste of that well-being which was in store for them. Moses made excellent preparations for the conquest and distribution of the whole country, and concluded his public services with powerful admonitions and impressive benedictions, transferring his government to the hands of Joshua, who was not unworthy to become the successor of so great a man. B.C. 1618. For details of these incidents, see EGYPT; Ex-

VI.—22*

ODE; LAW; PASSOVER; PLAGUE; SINAI; WANDERINGS; WILDERNESS.

4. *Moses's Death.*—In exact conformity with his life is the account of his end. The book of Deuteronomy describes, and is, the long, last farewell of the prophet to his people. It took place on the first day of the eleventh month of the fortieth year of the wanderings, in the plains of Moab (Deut. i, 3, 5), in the palm-groves of Abila (Josephus, *Ant.* iv, 8, 1). See ABEL-SHITTIM. He is described as 120 years of age, but with his sight and his freshness of strength unabated (Deut. xxxiv, 7). The address from ch. i to ch. xxx contains the recapitulation of the law. Joshua was then appointed his successor. The law was written out, and ordered to be deposited in the ark (ch. xxxi). The song and the blessing of the tribes conclude the farewell (ch. xxxii, xxxiii).

Then came the mysterious close. As if to carry out to the last the idea that the prophet was to live not for himself, but for his people, he is told that he is to see the good land beyond the Jordan, but not to possess it himself. The sin for which this penalty was imposed on the prophet is difficult to ascertain clearly. It was because he and Aaron rebelled against Jehovah, and "believed him not to sanctify him," in the murmurings at Kadesh (Numb. xx, 12; xxvii, 14; Deut. xxxii, 51), or, as it is expressed in the Psalms (cvi, 33), because he spoke unadvisedly with his lips. It seems to have been a feeling of distrust. " *Can* we (not, as often rendered, can *we*) bring water out of the cliff?" (Numb. xx, 10; Sept. μὴ ἐξάξομεν, "surely we cannot"). The Talmudic tradition, characteristically, makes the sin to be that he called the chosen people by the opprobious name of "rebels." He ascends a mountain in the range which rises above the Jordan valley. Its name is specified so particularly that it must have been well known in ancient times, though, owing to the difficulty of exploring the eastern side of the Jordan, the exact location has until recently been unidentified. See NEBO. Hence it is called by the specific name of *the Pisgah* (q. v.). It was one of those summits apparently dedicated to different divinities (Numb. xxiii, 14). Here Moses took his stand, and surveyed the four great masses of Palestine west of the Jordan—so far as it could be discerned from that height. The view has passed into a proverb for all nations. In two remarkable respects it illustrates the office and character of Moses. First, it was a view, in its full extent, to be imagined rather than actually seen. The foreground alone could be clearly discerned: its distance had to be supplied by what was beyond, though suggested by what was within, the actual prospect of the seer. Secondly, it is the likeness of the great discoverer pointing out what he himself will never reach. To English readers this has been made familiar by the application of this passage to lord Bacon, originally in the noble poem of Cowley, and then drawn out at length by lord Macaulay.

"So Moses, the servant of Jehovah, died there in the land of Moab, according to the word of Jehovah, and he buried him in a 'ravine' in the land of Moab, 'before' Beth-peor—but no man knoweth of his sepulchre unto this day. . . . And the children of Israel wept for Moses in the plains of Moab thirty days" (Deut. xxxiv, 5–8). This is all that is said in the sacred record. Jewish, Arabian, and Christian traditions have labored to fill up the detail. "Amid the tears of the people—the women beating their breasts, and the children giving way to uncontrolled wailing—he withdrew. At a certain point in his ascent he made a sign to the weeping multitude to advance no farther, taking with him only the elders, the high-priest Eliezar, and the general Joshua. At the top of the mountain he dismissed the elders—and then, as he was embracing Eliezar and Joshua, and still speaking to them, a cloud suddenly stood over him, and he vanished in a deep valley. He wrote the account of his own death [so also Philo, *V. M.* iii, 39] in the sacred books, fearing lest he should be deified" (Josephus, *Ant.* iv, 8, 48). "He died in the last month of the Jewish year"—in the Arabic traditions, the 7th of Adar (Jala-laddin, p. 388). After his death he is called "*Melki*" (Clem. Alex. *Strom.* i, p. 343).

The grave of Moses, though studiously concealed in the sacred narrative, in a manner which seems to point a warning against the excessive veneration of all sacred tombs (see Jude 9), and though never acknowledged by the Jews, is shown by the Mussulmans on the *west* (and therefore the wrong) side of the Jordan, between the Dead Sea and St. Saba (Stanley, *S. and P.* p. 302). There is some reason, however, to conclude from the appearance of Moses with Elijah on the Mount of Trans-figuration (Luke ix, 30, 31) that he was honored with an anticipatory resurrection. See Bauer, *Hebr. Gesch.* i, 337 sq.; J. A. Schmid, *De Morte M.* (Helmst. 1703); Abbt, *Ob Gott Moses begraben* (Hal. 1757); J. G. Drasde, *De morte ac sepultura Mosis* (Viteb. 1784); *Recherches sur la sepulture de Moïse*, in the *Bibl. raisonn.* p. 302, 243 sq.; Donauer, *De corpore Mosis* (Ratisb. 1682); Hech, *De Mosis corpore* (Jen. 1653); Reusmann, *Moses resuscitatus* (Gotting. 1747); Rohling, *Moses' Abschied* (Jena, 1867); J. J. Müller, *De morte Mosis* (Jena, 1710); Rathlef, *De corpore Mosis* (Hann. 1733); Zeibich, *Von dem Grabe Mosis* (Gera, 1758); Heyden, *De Mosis re-surrectione* (Hal. 1723); *Dansville Review*, Sept. 1861.

III. *Character, Work, and Writings of Moses.*—It will be best to confine ourselves here to such indications of these as transpire through the general framework of the Scripture narrative, or appear in traditions and pro-fane accounts.

It is important to trace his relation to his immediate circle of followers. In the exodus he takes the decisive lead on the night of the flight. . Up to that point he and Aaron appear almost on an equality; but after that Moses is usually mentioned alone. Aaron still held the second place, but the character of interpreter to Moses which he had borne in speaking to Pharaoh withdraws, and it would seem as if Moses henceforth became altogether, what hitherto he had only been in part, the prophet of the people. Another who occupies a place nearly equal to Aaron, though we know but little of him, is Hur, of the tribe of Judah, husband of Miriam, and grandfather of the artist Bezaleel (Josephus, *Ant.* iii, 2, 4). He and Aaron are the chief supporters of Mo-ses in moments of weariness or excitement. His adviser with regard to the route through the wilderness, as well as in the judicial arrangements, was, as we have seen, Jethro. His servant, occupying the same relation to him as Elisha to Elijah, or Gehazi to Elisha, was the youthful Hoshea (afterwards Joshua). Miriam always held the independent position to which her age entitled her. Her part was to supply the voice and song to her brother's prophetic power.

But Moses is incontestably the chief personage of the history, in a sense in which no one else is described be-fore or since. In the narrative, the phrase is constantly recurring, "The Lord spake unto Moses," "Moses spake unto the children of Israel." In the traditions of the desert, whether late or early, his name predominates over that of every one else: "The Wells of Moses"— on the shores of the Red Sea;. "the Mountain of Moses" (Jebel Mûsa)—near the convent of St. Catharine; the Ravine of Moses (Shuk Mûsa)—at Mount St. Catharine; the Valley of Moses (Wady Mûsa)—at Petra. "The Books of Moses" are so called (as afterwards the Books of Samuel), in all probability, from his being the chief subject of them. The very word "Mosaism" has been in later times applied (as the proper name of no other saint of the O. T.) to the whole religion. Even as applied to tessellated pavement ("Mosaic," *Musivum*, μουσεῖον, μουσαϊκόν) there is some probability that the expres-sion is derived from the variegated pavement of the later Temple, which had then become the representa-tive of the religion of Moses (see an essay of Redslob in the *Zeitschrift der Deutsch. Morgenl. Gesells.* xiv, 663).

It has sometimes been attempted to reduce this great character into a mere passive instrument of the divine

Will, as though he had himself borne no conscious part in the actions in which he figures, or the messages which he delivers. This, however, is as incompatible with the general tenor of the scriptural account as it is with the common language in which he has been de-scribed by the Church in all ages. The frequent ad-dresses of the Divinity to him no more contravene his personal activity and intelligence than in the case of Elijah, Isaiah, or Paul. In the N. T. the Mosaic legis-lation is expressly ascribed to him : "*Moses* gave you circumcision" (John vii, 22). "*Moses*, because of the hardness of your hearts, suffered you" (Matt. xix, 8). "Did not *Moses* give you the law?" (John vii, 19). "*Moses* accuseth you" (John v, 45). Paul goes so far as to speak of him as the founder of the Jewish religion : "They were all baptized *unto Moses*" (1 Cor. x, 2). He is constantly called "a prophet." In the poetical lan-guage of the O. T. (Numb. xxi, 18; Deut. xxxiii, 21), and in the popular language both of Jews and Christians, he is known as "the Lawgiver." The terms in which his legislation is described by Philo (*V. M.* ii, 1-4) are decisive as to the ancient Jewish view. He must be considered, like all the saints and heroes of the Bible, as a man of marvellous gifts, raised up by divine Provi-dence for a special purpose; but as led, both by his own disposition and by the peculiarity of the revelation which he received, into a closer communion with the invisible world than was vouchsafed to any other in the Old Testament.

Such a marvellous character was not exempted from the most virulent attacks of that criticism called the *Rationalismus vulgaris*, which at one time threatened to devour every fragment of antiquity. The history of Moses was considered merely a tissue of contradictory statements, till Voltaire (in *Questions sur l'Encyclopé-die*, § 127) boldly called his very existence in question. The exodus of Israel, of which Moses was the sole in-strument, was deprived of its strictly historical basis. Goethe wantonly reduced the forty years' wandering to two years. Most of the halting-places named in the books of Exodus and Numbers were deemed unhistor-ical, and the whole chain of events was said to be pure-ly mythical. De Wette (*Kritik der israelitischen Ge-schichte*), Gramberg (*Religionsideen*), Vatke (*Biblische Theologie*), Von Bohlen (*Commentar zum Buche Gen-esis*), and George (*Jüdische Feste*) combine to reduce the whole to a fable. Even the best substantiated acts of Moses—such as the construction of the taber-nacle, the founding of an hereditary priesthood, the ap-pointment of cities of refuge—were assumed to have been stripped of every vestige of historical veracity. The finding of the Law (2 Kings xxii, 8) was said to prove nothing of its Mosaic authorship, because the Egyptian priests pretended to have become possessed of the books of Hermes in the same way. The tables of stone, as evidence of the historical activity of Moses, were said to be no evidence, because no mention is made of them at the revelation of the Decalogue (Exod. xx), but only on a later occasion, in chap. xxii. The testi-mony of their existence (1 Kings viii, 9) in the days of Solomon was thought not worthy to be depended upon, because the author lived after the destruction of Jeru-salem! By such frivolous assertions Nork finds him-self authorized (see *Hebräisch-chaldäisch-rabbinisches Wörterbuch*) to resolve the character of Moses into a mythical personage; and to reduce the marvellous exo-dus, and the subsequent journey through the wilderness, to a level with the mythological conquests of Osiris or those of Bacchus, in each of whom personifications of the solar year were recognised. Moses is contrasted with Bacchus, whose grandfather Kadmus placed him in an ark and exposed him to the ocean (see J. J. Mül-ler, *De Mose in Bacchum converso* [Jena, 1667]). The 600,000 fighting men in Israel are assumed to be so many stars, which ancient astronomers believed to ex-ist. The wonder-working rod of Moses was considered to be as pure a fiction as the serpent-rod of Hermes.

The passage of the Red Sea by Moses and his followers was regarded as a striking parallel to some of the details of Bacchus's expedition to India (Nonnus, xx, 253). Bacchus also smites the Hydaspes with a rod, and passes over dry-shod (Nonnus, xxiii, 115, 124, 156-188; xxiv, 41). Even the smiting of the rock by Moses is compared to a myth recorded in Euripides (*Bacch.* v, 703); to Bacchus smiting a rock—not indeed in his own person, but by the instrumentality of his priestess, who wielded the thyrsus-rod—with a similar result of water flowing from it. These attempts to neutralize history are quoted simply as literary curiosities, and they show by what methods it was thought possible to establish the mythical origin of the Jewish commonwealth. But as the historical veracity of the Gospel history can alone account for the existence and subsistence of Christianity, so the past and present influence of the Mosaic constitution can only be explained by the strictly historical character of its beginnings.

1. There are two main characters in which Moses appears, namely, as a Leader and as a Prophet. The two are more frequently combined in the East than in the West. Several remarkable instances occur in the history of Mohammedanism : Mohammed himself, Abd-el-Kader in Algeria, Shamyl in Circassia.

(*a.*) As a Leader his life divides itself into the three epochs of the march to Sinai, the march from Sinai to Kadesh, and the conquest of the transjordanic kingdoms. Of his natural gifts in this capacity we have but few means of judging. The two main difficulties which he encountered were the reluctance of the people to submit to his guidance and the impracticable nature of the country which they had to traverse. The patience with which he bore their murmurs is often described—at the Red Sea, at the apostasy of the golden calf (the eccentric Beke contends that the idol was a *cone*, and not a calf [*The Idol in Horeb*, Lond. 1871]), at the rebellion of Korah, at the complaints of Aaron and Miriam (see below). The incidents with which his name was specially connected both in the sacred narrative and in the Jewish, Arabian, and heathen traditions were those of supplying water when most wanted. This is the only point in his life noted by Tacitus, who describes him as guided to a spring of water by a herd of wild asses (*Hist.* v, 3). In the Pentateuch these supplies of water take place at Marah, at Horeb, at Kadesh, and in the land of Moab. That at Marah is produced by the sweetening of waters through a tree in the desert; those at Horeb and at Kadesh by the opening of a rift in the "rock" and in the "cliff;" that in Moab by the united efforts, under his direction, of the chiefs and of the people (Numb. xxi, 18). (See Philo, *V. M.* i, 40.) An illustration of these passages is to be found in one of the representations of Rameses II (contemporary with Moses), in like manner calling out water from the desert rocks (see Brugsch, *Hist. de l'Eg.* i, 153). Of the first three of these incidents, traditional sites, bearing his name, are shown in the desert at the present day, though most of them are rejected by modern travellers. One is Ayûn Mûsa, "the wells of Moses," immediately south of Suez, which the tradition (probably from a confusion with Marah) ascribes to the rod of Moses. Of the water at Horeb, two memorials are shown : one is the Shuk Mûsa, or "cleft of Moses," in the side of Mount St. Catharine; and the other is the remarkable stone, first mentioned expressly in the Koran (ii, 57), which exhibits the twelve marks or mouths out of which the water is supposed to have issued for the twelve tribes (Stanley, *Syr. and Pal.* p. 46, 47; also Wolff, *Travels*, p. 125, 2d ed.). The fourth is the celebrated "Sik," or ravine, by which Petra is approached from the east, and which, from the story of its being torn open by the rod of Moses, has given his name (the Wady Mûsa) to the whole valley. The quails and the manna are less directly ascribed to the intercession of Moses. The brazen serpent that was lifted up as a sign of the divine protection against the snakes of the desert

(Numb. xxi, 8, 9) was directly connected with his name down to the latest times of the nation (2 Kings xviii, 4; John iii, 14). Of all the relics of his time, with the exception of the ark, it was the one longest preserved. See NEHUSHTAN.

The route through the wilderness is described as having been made under his guidance. The particular spot of the encampment was fixed by the cloudy pillar; but the direction of the people, first to the Red Sea and then to Mount Sinai (where he had been before), was communicated through Moses, or given by him. According to the tradition of Memphis, the passage of the Red Sea was effected through Moses's knowledge of the movement of the tide (Euseb. *Præp. Ev.* ix, 27). In all the wanderings from Mount Sinai he is said to have had the assistance of Jethro. In the Mussulman legends, as if to avoid this appearance of human aid, the place of Jethro is taken by El Khudhr, the mysterious benefactor of mankind (D'Herbelot, s. v. Moussa). On approaching Palestine the office of the leader becomes blended with that of the general or the conqueror. By Moses the spies were sent to explore the country. Against his advice took place the first disastrous battle at Hormah. To his guidance is ascribed the circuitous route by which the nation approached Palestine from the east, and to his generalship the two successive campaigns in which Sihon and Og were defeated. The narrative is told so shortly that we are in danger of forgetting that, at this last stage of his life, Moses must have been as much a conqueror and victorious soldier as Joshua.

(*b.*) His character as a Prophet is, from the nature of the case, more distinctly brought out. He is the first as he is the greatest example of a prophet in the O. T. The name is, indeed, applied to Abraham before (Gen. xx, 7), but so casually as not to enforce our attention. But in the case of Moses it is given with peculiar emphasis. In a certain sense he appears as the centre of a prophetic circle, now for the first time named. His brother and sister were both endowed with prophetic gifts. Aaron's fluent speech enabled him to act the part of prophet for Moses in the first instance; and Miriam is expressly called "the Prophetess." The seventy elders, and Eldad and Medad also, all "prophesied" (Numb. xi, 25-27). But Moses (at least after the exodus) rose high above all these. The others are spoken of as more or less inferior. Their communications were made to them in dreams and figures (Deut. xiii, 1-4; Numb. xii, 6). But "Moses was not so." With him the divine revelations were made "mouth to mouth, even apparently, and not in dark speeches, and the similitude of Jehovah shall he behold" (Numb. xii, 8). In the Mussulman legends his surname is *Kelim Allah*, "the spoken to by God." Of the especial modes of this more direct communication four great examples are given, corresponding to four critical epochs in his historical career, which help us in some degree to understand what is meant by these expressions in the sacred text. See PROPHET.

(1.) The appearance of the divine Presence in the flaming acacia-tree has already been noticed. The usual pictorial representations of that scene—of a winged human form in the midst of the bush—belong to Philo (*V. M.* i, 12), not to the Bible. No form is described. "The angel" or "messenger" is spoken of as being "in the flame." On this it was that Moses was afraid to look, and hid his face in order to hear the divine voice (Exod. iii, 2-6). See BURNING BUSH.

(2.) In the giving of the Law from Mount Sinai, the outward form of the revelation was a thick darkness, as of a thunder-cloud, out of which proceeded a voice (Exod. xix, 19; xx, 21). The revelation on this occasion was especially of the name of Jehovah. Outside this cloud Moses himself remained on the mountain (Exod. xxiv, 1, 2, 15), and received the voice, as from the cloud, which revealed the Ten Commandments, and a short code of laws in addition (Exod. xx-xxiii). On two occasions he is described as having penetrated within the darkness, and remained there successively for two periods of forty days, spent in seclusion and fasting (Exod. xxiv, 18; xxxiv, 28). On the first occasion he received instructions respecting the tabernacle, from "a pattern showed to him" (xxv, 9, 40; xxvi, xxvii), and respecting the priesthood (xxviii–xxxi). Of the second occasion hardly anything is told us (see Ortlob, *De jejunio Mosis* [Lips. 1702]). But each of these periods was concluded by the production of the two slabs or tables of granite containing the successive editions of the Ten Commandments (Exod. xxxii, 15, 16). On the first of the two occasions the ten moral commandments are undoubtedly those commonly so called (comp. Exod. xx, 1–17; xxxii, 15; Deut. v, 6–22). On the second occasion some interpreters (taking the literal sense of Exod. xxxiv, 27, 28) hold that they were the ten (chiefly) ceremonial commandments of Exod. xxxiv, 14–26; but they were evidently the same as before. The first are expressly said to have been the writing of God (Exod. xxxi, 18; xxxii, 16; Deut. v, 22); with respect to the second, the phraseology is ambiguous ("he wrote," Exod. xxxiv, 28), and hence some have held them to be merely the writing of Moses—contrary, however, to the language of Exod. xxxiv, 1. See LAW OF MOSES.

(3.) It was nearly at the close of those communications in the mountains of Sinai that an especial revelation was made to him personally, answering in some degree to that which first called him to his mission. In the despondency produced by the apostasy of the molten calf, he besought Jehovah to show him "his glory." The wish was thoroughly Egyptian. The same is recorded of Amenoph, the Pharaoh preceding the exodus. But the divine answer is thoroughly Biblical. It announced that an actual vision of God was impossible. "Thou canst not see my face; for there shall no man see my face and live." He was commanded to come absolutely alone. Even the flocks and herds which fed in the neighboring valleys were to be removed out of the sight of the mountain (Exod. xxxiii, 18, 20; xxxiv, 1, 3). He took his place on a well-known or prominent rock ("the rock") (xxxiii, 21). The cloud passed by (xxxiii, 22; xxxiv, 5). A voice proclaimed the two immutable attributes of God, Justice and Love, in words which became part of the religious creed of Israel and of the world (xxxiv, 6, 7). The importance of this incident in the life of Moses is attested not merely by the place which it occupies in the sacred record, but by the deep hold that it has taken of the Mussulman traditions and the local legends of Mount Sinai. It is told, with some characteristic variations, in the Koran (vii, 139), and is commemorated in the Mussulman chapel erected on the summit of the mountain, which from this incident (rather than from any other) has taken the name of the Mountain of Moses (Jebel Mûsa). A cavity is shown in the rock as produced by the pressure of the back of Moses when he shrank from the divine glory (Stanley, *S. and P.* p. 30). See Stemler, *De Mose Jehovam a tergo vidente* (Lips. 1730). See SINAI.

(4.) The fourth mode of divine manifestation was that which is described as commencing at this juncture, and which continued with more or less uniformity through the rest of his career. Immediately after the catastrophe of the worship of the calf, and apparently in consequence of it, Moses removed the chief tent outside the camp, and invested it with a sacred character under the name of "the Tent or Tabernacle of the Congregation" (xxxiii, 7). This tent became henceforth the chief scene of his communications with God. He left the camp, and it is described how, as in the expectation of some great event, all the people rose up and stood every man at his tent door, and looked—gazing after Moses until he disappeared within the tent. As he disappeared the entrance was closed behind him by the cloudy pillar, at the sight of which the people prostrated themselves (xxxiii, 10). The communications

within the tent are described as being still more intimate than those on the mountain. "Jehovah spake unto Moses face to face, as a man speaketh unto his friend" (xxxiii, 11). He was apparently accompanied on these mysterious visits by his attendant Hoshea (or Joshua), who remained in the tent after his master had left it (xxxiii, 11). All the revelations contained in the books of Leviticus and Numbers seem to have been made in this manner (Lev. i, 1; Numb. i, 1).

It was during these communications that a peculiarity is mentioned which apparently had not been seen before. It was on his final descent from Mount Sinai, after his second long seclusion, that a splendor shone on his face, as if from the glory of the divine Presence. It is from the Vulgate translation of "ray" (קרן), "*cornutam* habens faciem," that the conventional representation of the *horns* of Moses has arisen. See Zeibich, *De radiante Mosis facie* (Gera, 1764). The rest of the story is told so differently in the different versions that both must be given. (1.) In the A. V. and most Protestant versions Moses is said to wear a veil in order to hide the splendor. In order to produce this sense, the A. V. of Exod. xxxiii, 34 reads, "and [till] Moses had done speaking with them"—and other versions, "he *had* put on the veil." (2.) In the Sept. and the Vulgate, on the other hand, he is said to put on the veil, not during, but after, the conversation with the people—in order to hide, not the splendor, but the vanishing away of the splendor; and to have worn it till the moment of his return to the divine Presence in order to rekindle the light there. With this reading agrees the obvious meaning of the Hebrew words, and it is this rendering of the sense which is followed by Paul in 2 Cor. iii, 13, 14, where he contrasts the fearlessness of the apostolic teaching with the concealment of that of the O. T.: "We have no fear, as Moses had, that our glory will pass away."

(5.) There is another form of the prophetic gift in which Moses more nearly resembles the later prophets, namely, *as a writer*. We need not here determine (what is best considered under the several books which bear his name, PENTATEUCH, etc.) the extent of his authorship, or the period at which these books were put together in their present form. He is also traditionally connected with the first draft at least of the book of Job (q. v.). Eupolemus (Euseb. *Præp. Ev.* ix, 26) makes him the author of letters. But of this the Hebrew narrative gives no indication. There are two portions of the Pentateuch, and two only, of which the actual *writing* is ascribed to Moses: 1st, the second edition of the Ten Commandments (Exod. xxxiv, 28); 2d, the register of the stations in the wilderness (Numb. xxxiii, 1). But it is clear that the prophetical office, as represented in the history of Moses, included the poetical form of composition which characterizes the Jewish prophecy generally. These poetical utterances, whether connected with Moses by ascription or by actual authorship, enter so largely into the full Biblical conception of his character that they must here be mentioned.

[1.] "The song which Moses and the children of Israel sung" (after the passage of the Red Sea, Exod. xv, 1–19). It is unquestionably the earliest written account of that event; and, although it may have been in part, according to the conjectures of Ewald and Bunsen, adapted to the sanctuary of Gerizim and Shiloh, yet its framework and ideas are essentially Mosaic. It is probably this song to which allusion is made in Rev. xv, 2, 3: "They stand on the sea of glass mingled with fire . . . and sing the song of Moses, the servant of God."

[2.] A fragment of a war-song against Amalek (Exod. xvii, 16):

> "As the hand is on the throne of Jehovah,
> So will Jehovah war with Amalek
> From generation to generation."

[3.] A fragment of a lyrical burst of indignation (Exod. xxii, 18):

"Not the voice of them that shout for mastery,
Nor the voice of them that cry for being overcome,
But the noise of them that sing do I hear."

[4.] Probably, either from him or his immediate prophetic followers, the fragments of war-songs in Numb. xxi, 14, 15, 27–30, preserved in the "book of the wars of Jehovah," Numb. xxi, 14; and the address to the well, xxi, 16, 17, 18.

[5.] The song of Moses (Deut. xxxiii, 1–43), setting forth the greatness and the failings of Israel. It is remarkable as bringing out with much force the idea of God as the Rock (xxxii, 4, 15, 18, 30, 31, 37). The special allusions to the pastoral riches of Israel point to the transjordanic territory as the scene of its composition (xxxii, 13, 14).

[6.] The blessing of Moses on the tribes (Deut. xxxiii, 1–29). If there are some allusions in this psalm to circumstances only belonging to a later time (such as the migration of Dan, xxxiii, 22), yet there is no one in whose mouth it could be so appropriately placed as in that of the great leader on the eve of the final conquest of Palestine. This poem, combined with the similar blessing of Jacob (Gen. xlix), embraces a complete collective view of the characteristics of the tribes. See Vöck, *Mosis canticum cygneum* (Nordl. 1861); Kamphausen, *Das Lied Mosis erklärt* (Leips. 1862).

[7.] The 90th Psalm, "A prayer of Moses, the man of God." The title, like all the titles of the Psalms, is of doubtful authority—and the psalm has often been referred to a later author. But Ewald (*Psalmen*, p. 91) thinks that, even though this be the case, it still breathes the spirit of the venerable lawgiver. There is something extremely characteristic of Moses in the view taken, as from the summit or base of Sinai, of the eternity of God, greater even than the eternity of mountains, in contrast with the fleeting generations of man. One expression in the psalm, as to the limit of human life (seventy, or at most eighty years), in ver. 10, would, if it be Mosaic, fix its date to the stay at Sinai. Jerome (*Adv. Ruffin.* i, 13), on the authority of Origen, ascribes the next eleven psalms to Moses. Cosmas (*Cosmogr.* v, 223) supposes that it is by a younger Moses of the time of David.

How far the gradual development of these revelations or prophetic utterances had any connection with Moses's own character and history, the materials are not such as to justify any decisive judgment. His Egyptian education must, on the one hand, have supplied him with much of the ritual of the Israelitish worship. The coincidences between the arrangements of the priesthood, the dress, the sacrifices, the ark, etc., in the two countries, are decisive. On the other hand, the proclamation of the unity of God, not merely as a doctrine confined to the priestly order, but communicated to the whole nation, implies distinct antagonism, almost a conscious recoil against the Egyptian system. The absence of the doctrine of a future state (without adopting to its full extent the paradox of Warburton) proves at least a remarkable independence of the Egyptian theology, in which that great doctrine held so prominent a place. Some modern critics have supposed that the Levitical ritual was an after-growth of the Mosaic system, necessitated or suggested by the incapacity of the Israelites to retain the higher and simpler doctrine of the divine unity—as proved by their return to the worship of the Heliopolitan calf under the sanction of the brother of Moses himself. There is no direct statement of this connection in the sacred narrative; but there are indirect indications of it sufficient to give some color to such an explanation. The event itself is described as a crisis in the life of Moses, almost equal to that in which he received his first call. In an agony of rage and disappointment he destroyed the monument of his first revelation (Exod. xxxii, 19). He threw up his sacred mission (ib. 32). He craved and he received a new and special revelation of the attributes of God to console him (ib. xxxiii, 18). A fresh start was made in his career

(ib. xxxiv, 29). His relation with his countrymen henceforth became more awful and mysterious (ib. 32–35). In point of fact, the greater part of the details of the Levitical system were subsequent to this catastrophe. The institution of the Levitical tribe grew directly out of it (xxxii, 26). The inferiority of this part of the system to the rest is expressly stated in the prophets, and expressly connected with the idolatrous tendencies of the nation. "Wherefore I gave them statutes that were not good, and judgments whereby they should not live" (Ezek. xx, 25). "I spake not unto your fathers, nor commanded them in the day that I brought them out of the land of Egypt, concerning burnt-offerings or sacrifices" (Jer. vii, 22). Other portions of the law, such as the regulations of slavery, of blood-feud, of clean and unclean food, were probably taken, with the necessary modifications, from the customs of the desert-tribes. But the distinguishing features of the law of Israel, which have remained to a considerable extent in Christendom, are peculiarly Mosaic—the Ten Commandments; and the general spirit of justice, humanity, and liberty that pervades even the more detailed and local observances is equally indicative of a new æra in legislation.

The prophetic office of Moses, however, can only be fully considered in connection with his whole character and appearance. "By a prophet Jehovah brought Israel out of Egypt, and by a prophet was he preserved" (Hos. xii, 13). He was, in a sense peculiar to himself, the founder and representative of his people; and in accordance with this, complete identification of himself with his nation is the only strong personal trait which we are able to gather from his history. "The man Moses was very meek, above all the men that were upon the face of the earth" (Numb. xii, 3). The word "meek" is hardly an adequate reading of the Hebrew term עָנָו, which should be rather "much enduring;" and, in fact, his onslaught on the Egyptian, and his sudden dashing of the tables on the ground, indicate rather the reverse of what we should call "meekness." It represents what we should now designate by the word "disinterested." All that is told of him indicates a withdrawal of himself, a preference of the cause of his nation to his own interests, which makes him the most complete example of Jewish patriotism. He joins his countrymen in their degrading servitude (Exod. ii, 11; v, 4). He forgets himself to avenge their wrongs (ii, 14). He desires that his brother may take the lead instead of himself (Exod. iv, 13). He wishes that not he only, but that all the nation were gifted alike: "Enviest thou for my sake?" (Numb. xi, 29). When the offer is made that the people should be destroyed, and that he should be made "a great nation" (Exod. xxxii, 10), he prays that they may be forgiven—"if not, blot me, I pray thee, out of thy book which thou hast written" (xxxii, 32). His sons were not raised to honor. The leadership of the people passed, after his death, to another tribe. In the books which bear his name, Abraham, and not himself, appears as the real father of the nation. In spite of his great pre-eminence, they are never "the children of Moses."

2. In the O. T. the name of Moses does not occur so frequently after the close of the Pentateuch as might be expected. In the Judges it occurs only once—in speaking of the wandering Levite Jonathan, his grandson. In the Hebrew copies, followed by the A. V., it has been superseded by "Manasseh," in order to avoid throwing discredit on the family of so great a man. See MANASSEH, 2. In the Psalms and the Prophets, however, he is frequently named as the chief of the prophets.

In the N. T. he is referred to partly as the representative of the law—as in the numerous passages cited above—and in the vision of the transfiguration, where he appears side by side with Elijah. It is possible that the peculiar word rendered "decease" (ἔξοδος)—used only in Luke ix, 31, and in 2 Pet. i, 15, where it may have been drawn from the context of the transfiguration—was suggested by the exodus of Moses. As the author of the Law, he is contrasted with Christ, the Author of the Gospel: "The law was given by Moses" (John i, 17). The ambiguity and transitory nature of his glory is set against the permanence and clearness of Christianity (2 Cor. iii, 13–18), and his mediatorial character ("the law in the hand of a mediator") against the unbroken communication of God in Christ (Gal. iii, 19). His "service" of God is contrasted with Christ's sonship (Heb. iii, 5, 6). But he is also spoken of as a likeness of Christ; and as this is a point of view which has been almost lost in the Church, compared with the more familiar comparisons of Christ to Adam, David, Joshua, and yet has as firm a basis in fact as any of them, it may be well to draw it out in detail.

[1.] Moses is, as it would seem, the only character of the O. T. to whom Christ expressly likens himself— "Moses wrote of me" (John v, 46). It is uncertain to what passage our Lord alludes, but the general opinion seems to be the true one—that it is the remarkable prediction in Deut. xviii, 15, 18, 19—"The Lord thy God will raise up unto thee a prophet from the midst of thee, from thy brethren, like unto me; unto him ye shall hearken. . . . I will raise them up a prophet from among their brethren, like unto thee, and will put my words in his mouth; and he shall speak unto them all that I shall command him. And it shall come to pass that whosoever will not hearken unto my words which he shall speak in my name, I will require it of him." This passage is also expressly quoted by Stephen (Acts vii, 37), and it is probably in allusion to it that at the transfiguration, in the presence of Moses and Elijah, the words were uttered, "Hear ye him." It suggests three main points of likeness:

(a.) Christ was, like Moses, the great Prophet of the people—the last, as Moses was the first. In greatness of position none came between them. Only Samuel and Elijah could by any possibility be thought to fill the place of Moses, and they only in a very secondary degree. Christ alone appears, like Moses, as the Revealer of a new name of God—of a new religious society on earth. The Israelites "were baptized unto Moses" (1 Cor. x, 2). The Christians were baptized unto Christ. There is no other name in the Bible that could be used in like manner. See PROPHET.

(b.) Christ, like Moses, is a Lawgiver: "Him shall ye hear." His whole appearance as a Teacher, differing in much besides, has this in common with Moses, unlike the other prophets, that he lays down a code, a law, for his followers. The Sermon on the Mount almost inevitably suggests the parallel of Moses on Mount Sinai.

(c.) Christ, like Moses, was a Prophet out of the midst of the nation—"from their brethren." As Moses was the entire representative of his people, feeling for them more than for himself, absorbed in their interests, hopes, and fears, so, with reverence be it said, was Christ. The last and greatest of the Jewish prophets, he was not only a Jew by descent, but that Jewish descent is insisted upon as an integral part of his appearance. Two of the Gospels open with his genealogy. "Of the Israelites came Christ after the flesh" (Rom. ix, 5). He wept and lamented over his country. He confined himself during his life to its needs. He was not sent "but unto the lost sheep of the house of Israel" (Matt. xv, 24). It is true that his absorption into the Jewish nationality was but a symbol of his absorption into the far wider and deeper interests of all humanity. But it is only by understanding the one that we are able to understand the other; and the life of Moses is the best means of enabling us to understand them both.

[2.] In Heb. iii, 1–19; xii, 24–29; Acts vii, 37, Christ is described, though more obscurely, as the Moses of the new dispensation—as the Apostle, or Messenger, or Mediator of God to the people—as the Controller and Leader of the flock or household of God. No other person

in the O. T. could have furnished this parallel. In both the revelation was communicated partly through the life, partly through the teaching; but in both the prophet was incessantly united with the Guide, the Ruler, the Shepherd. See MEDIATOR.

[3.] The details of their lives are sometimes, though not often, compared. Stephen (Acts vii, 24–28, 35) dwells, evidently with this view, on the likeness of Moses in striving to act as a peacemaker, and in being misunderstood and rejected on that very account. The death of Moses, especially as related by Josephus (ut sup.), immediately suggests the ascension of Christ; and the retardation of the rise of the Christian Church till after its Founder was withdrawn gives a moral as well as a material resemblance. But this, though dwelt upon in the services of the Church, has not been expressly laid down in the Bible.

In Jude 9 is an allusion to an altercation between Michael and Satan over the body of Moses. It has been endeavored (by reading Ἰησοῦ for Μωϋσέως) to refer this to Zech. iii, 2. But it probably refers to a lost apocryphal book, mentioned by Origen, called the "Ascension or Assumption of Moses." The substance of this book is given by Fabricius, *Cod. Pseudoepigraphus Vet. Test.* i, 839–844. The "dispute of Michael and Satan" probably had reference to the concealment of the body to prevent idolatry. Gal. v, 6 is by several later writers said to be a quotation from the "Revelation of Moses" (Fabricius, *ibid.* i, 838). See REVELATIONS, SPURIOUS.

In later history the name of Moses has not been forgotten. In the early Christian Church he appears in the Roman catacombs in the likeness of St. Peter, partly, doubtless, from his being the leader of the Jewish, as Peter of the Christian Church, partly from his connection with the rock. It is as striking the rock that he appears under Peter's name. In the Jewish, as in the Arabian nation, his name has in later years been more common than in former ages, though never occurring again (perhaps, as in the case of David, and of Peter in the papacy, from motives of reverence) in the earlier annals, as recorded in the Bible. Moses Maimonides, Moses Mendelssohn, Mûsa the conqueror of Spain, are obvious instances. Of the first of these three a Jewish proverb testifies that "from Moses to Moses there was none like Moses." Numerous traditions, however, as might have been expected, and as has repeatedly been indicated above, have been current respecting so celebrated a personage. Some of these were known to the ancient Jews, but most of them occur in later rabbinical writers (comp. Philo, *De Vita Mosis*, c. iii; Joseph. *Ant.* ii, 9 sq.; Bartolocci, *Bibliotheca Rabbinica*, iv, 115 sq.). The name of Moses is celebrated among the Arabs also, and is the nucleus of a mass of legends (comp. Hottinger, *Historia Orientalis*, p. 80 sq.; Abulfeda, *Anteislam.* p. 31). These Mussulman traditions are chiefly exaggerations of the O.-T. accounts. But there are some stories independent of the Bible. One is the striking story (Koran, xviii, 65–80) on which is founded Parnell's *Hermit*. Another is the proof given by Moses of the existence of God to the atheistic king (Chardin, x, 836, and in Fabricius, p. 836). The Greek and Roman classics repeatedly mention Moses (see Grotius, *De verit. rel. Chr.* i, 16; Hase, in the *Biblioth. Brem.* vi, 769 sq.), but their accounts contain the authentic Biblical history in a greatly distorted form. See the collection of Meier, *Judaica, seu veterum Scriptorum profanorum de Rebus Judaicis Fragmenta* (Jenæ, 1832); also those from Tacitus, by Müller, in the *Stud. u. Krit.* 1843, p. 893–8. There are, likewise, as above intimated, traditionally ascribed to Moses several apocryphal books, as "an Apocalypse, or Little Genesis," the "Ascension or Assumption of Moses," and the "Mysterious Books of Moses," supposed to have been fabricated in the early ages of Christianity (see Fabricius's *Codex Pseudoepigraphus Vet. Testamenti*, and Whiston's *Collection of Authentic Records*, i, 449-65). Lauth (*Moses der Ebrä-*

er, Munich, 1859) thinks he has discovered traces of the history and name of Moses in two of the Leyden papyri written in the hieratic character (comp. Heath, *The Exodus Papyri*, Lond. 1855).

Concerning the life and work of Moses, compare also Warburton, *On the Divine Legation of Moses;* Hess, *Geschichte Mosis* (Zurich, 1778); Niemeyer, *Charakteristik der Bibel*, iii, 23 sq.; Hufnagel, *Moseh wie er sich selbst Zeichnet* (Frckf. 1822); Nork, *Leb. Mos.* (Lips. 1838); Ewald, *Isr. Gesch.* ii, 32 sq.; Schreiber, *Allgem. Religionslehre*, i, 166; Kitto, *Daily Bible Illustrations*, vol. ii; Hunter, *Sacred Biography;* T. Smith, *Hist. of Moses* (Edinb. 1859); Breay, *Hist. of Moses* (Lond. 1846); Townsend, *Character of Moses* (Lond. 1813, 2 vols. 4to); Ross, *Hist. of Moses* (Edinb. 1837); Anderson, *Life of Moses* (Lond. 1834); Plumtre, *Hist. of Moses* (Lond. 1848); Drasde, *Comparatio Mosis et Homeri* (Viteb. 1788); Hagel, *Apologie des Moses* (Sulzbach, 1828); Moller, *De Mose Philosopho* (Alt. 1701); Schumann, *Vita Mosis* (Lips. 1826); Reckendorf, *Das Leben Mosis*, (Leips. 1867); Clarke, *Ten Great Religions* (Bost. 1871), p. 409 sq.; also the dissertations referred to by Fürst, *Bib. Jud.* ii, 393 sq.

MOSES, ASCENSION or ASSUMPTION OF. See REVELATIONS, SPURIOUS.

MOSES, BOOKS OF. See PENTATEUCH.

MOSES, LAW OF. See LAW OF MOSES.

Moses is the name of several patriarchs of the Armenian Church.—**1**, was born about 400 at Manazgerd. After entering the service of the Church he rose rapidly to distinction, and in 457 became patriarch. He was very much disliked for his extreme abnegation of all patriotic feelings, and complete submission to Feroze, king of Persia, who then ruled Armenia. Moses was severe upon those who took exception to his rule, and imprisoned many ecclesiastics and episcopal dignitaries. He died in 465.—**2**, surnamed *Eghivartetsi*, after his native place, was born in 510. He also made his way rapidly to ecclesiastical distinctions after entering the service of the Church, and finally, in 551, mounted the throne of St. Gregory. He is the founder of a new calendar, which was used by the Armenians for several centuries. Nothing else of importance is to be noted during his rule of the Armenian Church. He died in 594 at Tovin.—**3**, surnamed *Dathevatse*, was born at Khodaran about 1580. In his youth he chose a secluded life, and entered the monastery of Dathev, whence his surname. He was chosen to the patriarchate in 1629. He died in 1633 at Echmiajin. See St. Martin, *Mémoires historiques sur l'Arménie;* Neale, *Hist. of East. Ch.* (Armenia).

Moses Albelda (called also BEN-JACOB), a Jewish theologian of some note, flourished in the beginning of the 16th century as rabbi of the Jews of Salonica in Thessalonica. He wrote a number of works in the department of dogmatic and Biblical theology, among which special mention is due to his דְּרַשׁ מֹשֶׁה, a homiletical Commentary on the Pentateuch, accompanied by several occasional homilies (Ven. 1603, folio):—עוֹלַת תָּמִיד, or *Disquisitions on the Books of the Law, partly exegetical and partly philosophical* (Ven. 1526, 1601, fol.).

Moses Botarel (or **Botarelo**), a Jewish writer of Spanish birth, who flourished in the 15th century, is the author of a commentary on the famous *Book Jezirah* (q. v.), entitled פֵּרוּשׁ סֵפֶר יְצִירָה, which he wrote for a Christian scholar, Maestro Juan, in 1409, and wherein he praises philosophy, speaks of Aristotle as of a prophet, and maintains that philosophy and the Kabbalah propound exactly the same doctrines, and that they only differ in language and in technical terms. In this commentary Moses Botarel shows how, by fasting, ablutions, prayer, and invocation of divine and angelic names a man may have such dreams as shall disclose to him the secrets of the future, and quotes in confirmation of his opinions such ancient authorities as Rab. Ashi, Saadia

Gaon, Hai Gaon, etc., whom the Kabbalah claims as its great pillars. Botarel's commentary was first published with the text of the *Book Jezira* and other commentaries (Mantua, 1562; Zolkiew, 1745; and in Grodno, 1806, 1820). Moses also wrote a work entitled עֲרָךְ מִשְׁפָּט, on astrology, redemption, and prophecies. See Fürst, *Bibl. Jud.* i, 128; Grätz, *Gesch. d. Juden*, viii, 106, 107; Ginsburg, *The Kabbalah*, p. 122; Jellinek, *Biograph. Skizzen.* vol. ii; *Mose Botarel*, in *L. B. des Or.* 1846, No. 12; Joh. Steudner, *Mos. Botarel de mysterio Trinitatis* (Lat. vers. et illustr. [reprinted in his *Die jüdische ABC-Schule*, p. 27]); Cassel, *Leitfaden für jüd. Gesch. u. Literatur.* p. 75. (B. P.)

Moses bar-Cepha, an Eastern prelate distinguished as an author, flourished as bishop of Bethchino, near Mosul, towards the close of the 9th century. According to Assemani (*Bibl. Orient.* ii, 218–19) Moses bar-Cepha died Feb. 12, 903. He is noted for his compilation of the long Syro-Jacobite Liturgy, which Neale speaks of as "not without its beauty, especially in the intercessory portions." See Cave, *Hist. Lit.* ii, 91; Renaudot, *Hist. Lit.* ii, 390; Neale, *Introd. East. Church*, i, 329.

Moses ben-Chanoch, a Hebrew savant who flourished in Spain in the second half of the 10th century, although not known in Jewish literature by his writings, holds, nevertheless, a very prominent place in the history of Jewish learning, since he must be regarded as its propagator on Spanish soil. While the famed Jewish academies of Persia and Pumbedita existed, the Jews of Spain respected them as the head of the Hebrew nation, and referred every weighty point or legal difference to their decision. Notwithstanding the distance and the dangers of the voyage, they sent their sons to them for the study of the law and for education. But as soon as the Persian dynasty had gained the caliphate, it commenced persecuting the Jews, and, without regard to the flourishing state which literature had attained in those academies, it expelled the Jews from Babylon, closed the renowned Jewish colleges, and dispersed their illustrious teachers. Four of these learned men, of whom R. Moses was one, fell into the hands of a Spanish corsair about the year A.D. 950, who was despatched by Abderahman from Cordova to cruise in the sea of the Grecian Archipelago. The wife of Moses accompanied him in his voyage. The high-minded woman, dreading defilement, looked to her husband for advice, asking in Hebrew whether those drowned at sea would be resuscitated at the resurrection. He answered her with the verse of the psalm. "The Lord said, I will bring again from Bashan, I will bring again from the depths of the sea." On hearing this, to save her honor, she plunged into the sea and perished. Moses was brought as a slave to Cordova, and redeemed, though his quality was unknown, by a Jew. One day he entered the college clad as a slave, in a scanty sackcloth. The discussion was on a difficult passage of the treatise *Joma* (day of atonement). After listening for some time, he explained it so satisfactorily to all the students present that R. Nathan, the president of the college, rose from his seat, and said, "I am no more judge; yon slave in sackcloth is my master, and I am his scholar." The very same day Moses was installed by acclamation as head of the community, and with him the foundation of Jewish learning was laid in Spain. The fame of his acquirements spread throughout Spain and the West. Numbers flocked from all parts to receive instruction from him, and thus through this man "the light of learning, which, by the rapid progress of the iron age of Judaism in Babylonia, by the extinction of the authority of the Prince of the Captivity, the dispersion of the illustrious teachers, and the final closing of the great schools, seemed to have set forever, suddenly rose again in the West in renewed and undiminished splendor." Moses ben-Chanoch died in 1104. See Grätz, *Geschichte d. Juden*, v, 310 sq.; Jost, *Geschichte d. Juden u. s. Sekten*, ii, 400; Dessauer, *Ge-*

schichte d. Israeliten, p. 281 sq.; Braunschweiger, *Geschichte d. Juden in den romanischen Staaten*, p. 22 sq.; Basnage, *Hist. of the Jews*, p. 606 (Engl. transl. by Taylor); Milman, *Hist. of the Jews*, iii, 156 sq.; Da Costa, *Israel and the Gentiles*, p. 250 sq.; id. *Hist. of the Jews in Spain*, p. 55 (Engl. transl. by E. D. G. M. Kirwan, Cambridge, 1851); Lindo, *Hist. of the Jews in Spain and Portugal*, p. 45 sq.; Smucker, *Hist. of the Modern Jews*, p. 112; Etheridge, *Introduction to Hebrew Literature*, p. 244 sq.; Finn, *Sephardim*, p. 150 sq.; S. Seckler, in *Jewish Messenger*, 1874 (" Some Jewish Rabbis"), art. xv. (B. P.)

Moses Chorenensis, surnamed "the father of poets and savans," an Armenian theologian, flourished in the 5th century. He was a nephew of *Mesrop* (q. v.), and besides being trained by that learned man, enjoyed all the educational advantages which he could secure at Alexandria, where he spent seven years in study under Cyril Alexandrinus, and others equally renowned. He next visited Rome, Athens, and Constantinople, and returned home after years of closest application in those great centres of learning. He entered the service of the Church, and was shortly promoted to the bishopric of Bagrevand. During the rule of the Persians over his native country he refused to occupy any ecclesiastical positions, and retired to the wilderness. He died at the advanced age of 120. His works are numerous. Among his ablest are the *History of Armenia*, written in 481 by request of prince Sabak, which covers the history of that country down to A.D. 441, and a *Manual of Rhetoric*. He also devoted much time to the writing of hymns, and many of these are still retained in the divine service of the Armenian Church. An edition of his works, excepting only fragments and hymns, was published at Venice in 1843. See Neale, *Hist. of the Eastern Church* (Armenia); Aschbach, *Kirchen-Lexikon*, iv, 278; *Jahrbuch deutsch. Theol.* 1868, vol. iv. (J. H. W.)

Moses ha-Cohen BEN-SAMUEL GIKATILLA (also called *Ibn-Gikatilla*), a noted Jewish writer, flourished at Cordova near the opening of the 12th century. He was a pupil of the celebrated Ibn-Ganach, and is known to have been one of the most extensive commentators and grammarians, though, unfortunately for Biblical learning, none of his works seem to be extant. Only fragments of his are preserved in the writings of other commentators, which reveal him to have been a superior scholar and master of Biblical lore. Unlike most of the interpreters of his time, he endeavored to explain away all the Messianic prophecies of the O. T. (comp. Aben-Ezra on *Isa. xi*), and assigned the authorship of some psalms to the Babylonian captivity (comp. Aben-Ezra on *Psa. xlii*), at the time when both the Synagogue and the Church believed that the whole Psalter proceeded from David. Like Ibn-Saadia, he frequently departed from the Masoretic division of the text. Thus למכביר, at the end of ver. 31, in Job xxxvi, he took over to על כפרם, in the following verse; i. e. " He giveth meat in abundance, covering the hands with light" (comp. also Habak. iii). The influence which this critic must have exercised upon contemporary and subsequent expositors of the Bible may be judged of from the fact that the eminent Aben-Ezra quotes his work so largely. He is generally quoted by Aben-Ezra as ר׳ משה הכהן הספרדי, R. Moses ha-Cohen ha-Sephardi, i. e. the Spaniard: or ר׳ משה הכהן, R. Moses ha-Cohen; or ר׳ משה הספרדי, R. Mose ha-Sephardi; or simply ר׳ משה, R. Mose. These different appellations must be borne in mind by the student of Hebrew exegesis to identify this celebrated commentator. Dr. Ginsburg, in his article on Gikatilla in Kitto, ii, 129, gives a list of the places where his writings are quoted by commentators. It is more complete than the list furnished by Dukes, *Beiträge zur ältesten Auslegung* (Stuttg. 1844), ii, 180 sq.

Moses Cordovero BEN-JACOB (also called *Remak* = רמ׳׳ק, from the acrostic of his name, קורדואיררו, *R. Moses Cordovero*), a Jewish savant, was born at Cordova in 1522, studied the Cabala under his brother-in-law, Solomon Alkâbaz, and very soon became so distinguished as a Cabalist and author that his fame travelled to Italy, where his books were greedily bought. Cordovero represents the Cabala in its primitive state, since he is chiefly occupied with its scientific speculations, or the *speculative Cabala* (קבלה עיונית), as can be seen from the following specimen of his lucubrations on the nature of the Deity. "The knowledge of the Creator is different from that of the creature, since in the case of the latter knowledge and the thing known are distinct, thus leading to subjects which are again separate from him. This is described by the three expressions— cogitation, the cogitator, and the cogitated object. Now the Creator is himself knowledge, knowing, and the known object. His knowledge does not consist in the fact that he directs his thoughts to things without him, since in comprehending and knowing himself he comprehends and knows everything which exists. There is nothing which is not united with him, and which he does not find in his own substance. He is the archetype of all things existing, and all things are in him in their purest and most perfect form; so that the perfection of the creatures consists in the support whereby they are united to the primary source of his existence, and they sink down and fall from that perfect and lofty position in proportion to their separation from him" (*Pardes Rimmonim*, 55 a). He died in 1570. Moses wrote an introduction to the Cabala, entitled *A Sombre or Sweet Light*, or אור נערב (first published in Venice, 1587, then in Cracow, 1647, and in Fürth, 1701):—*The Book of Retirement*, or ספר גרושין, Cabalistic reflections and comments on ninety-nine passages of the Bible (Venice, 1543):—*The Sacrifices of Peace*, or זבחי שלמים, a Cabalistic exposition of the Prayer-book (Lublin, 1613):—*The Plant of Deborah*, or תמר דבורה, ten chapters on ethics in the Cabalistic style (Venice, 1589; Livorno, 1794); but his principal work is the *Garden of Pomegranates*, or פרדס רמונים, which consists of thirteen sections or gates (שערים), subdivided into chapters, and discusses the *Sephiroth*, the divine names, the import and signification of the letters, etc. (Cracow, 1591). Excerpts of it have been translated into Latin by Bartolocci, *Bibl. Magna Rabbin.* iv, 231 sq.; and Knorr von Rosenroth, *Tractatus de Anima ex libro Pardes Rimmonim*, in his *Cabala Denudata* (Sulzbach, 1677). For the other works of Cordovero, see Fürst, *Bibl. Jud.* i, 187 sq. See also Steinschneider, *Catal. Libr. Hebr. in Bibl. Bodleiana*, col. 1793, etc.; De Rossi, *Dizionario* (Germ. transl.), p. 87 sq.; Etheridge, *Introd. to Hebr. Literat.* p. 359; Ginsburg, *The Kabbalah*, p. 132 sq. (Lond. 1865); Finn, *Sephardim*, p. 307 sq.; Lindo, *The Jews in Spain*, p. 359; Basnage, *Hist. of the Jews* (Taylor's transl.), p. 703; Jost, *Gesch. d. Juden u. s. Sekten*, iii, 137 sq.; Grätz, *Gesch. d. Juden*, ix, 444; Zunz, *Zur Gesch. u. Literatur*, p. 294; *Die Monatstage*, p. 35 (Berlin, 1872). (B. P.)

Moses de Coucy BEN-JACOB BEN-CHAYIM (*hak-Kohen ben-Chananel*), the most celebrated Jewish preacher of the Middle Ages, was born at Coucy, not far from Soissons, cir. A.D. 1200. He severely reprobated a custom then prevalent of marrying strange women. He often preached on that subject, and at last had the good fortune to be heard, for many sent away the Gentile wives they had married. He travelled much in Spain and France, and taught the law, which seemed to have been neglected by a good many of his co-religionists. He died in 1260. Moses is the author of a very highly esteemed work, called the *Major Book of the Commandments* (ספר מצות גדול), called סמ׳׳ג, *Semag*, from its initials). This work on the commandments and prohibitions consists of sermons which he delivered on his journeys through the south of France and Spain (1235–1245), the design of which was to confirm his brethren in the ancient faith, since the orthodox religion of the Jews was at that time undermined by the philosophy of Maimonides. The work which propounds the six hundred and thirteen precepts was first printed before 1480; then in Soncino, 1488; and in Venice, 1522, 1547, etc. An abridgment of the *Major Book* was made by Isaac de Corbeil, A.D. 1277, entitled ס' מִצְוֹת קָטָן (called סמ"ק, *Semak*, from the initials of its title), the *Minor Book of the Commandments*, and is divided into seven parts, for the seven days of the week. It was first published at Constantinople, 1510, then at Cremona, 1556, with glosses, etc., and at Cracow, 1596, etc. See Fürst, *Bibl. Judaica*, i, 189 sq., 186; De Rossi, *Dizionario* (Germ. transl.), p. 172; Steinschneider, *Catalogus Libr. Hebr. in Bibl. Bodleiana*, col. 1795–1798, col. 1103; Lindo, *Hist. of the Jews in Spain*, p. 80 (where the name is written "Micozzi"); Basnage, *Hist. of the Jews* (Eng. transl.), p. 659; Ginsburg, in Levitas, *Massoreth ha-Massoreth*, p. 249 sq., note (Lond. 1867); Grätz, *Gesch. d. Juden*, vii, 54, 62–64, 105, 119; Jost, *Gesch. d. Juden u. s. Sekten*, iii, 33; Carmoly, *La France Israélite*, p. 100 sq.; Da Costa, *Israel and the Gentiles*, p. 255; Zunz, *Zur Gesch. u. Literatur*, p. 83, 127, 143. (B. P.)

Moses ha-Darshan (i. e. *the Expositor*) OF NARBONNE, a rabbi noted as a pulpit orator of more than usual influence and power as well as an exegete of the O.-T. Scriptures, flourished in France in the second half of the 11th century. He was the teacher of Nathan the Jew, who is noted as another great light of the Jewish pulpit, and wrote a number of valuable commentaries, among which a commentary on the Pentateuch, resting largely on the Midrashic lore, is the most widely circulated and esteemed. His greatest work is a commentary on the Hebrew Scriptures, which is alternately quoted by the respective names of פרושי ר' משה הדרשן, *Expositions of R. Moses the Expositor*, בראשית רבה, *the Great Bereshith, Bereshith Rabba Major*, and *Bereshith Rabba R. Mose ha-Darshan*, and which has not as yet come to light. Copious and numerous fragments of it, however, are given by Rashi in his commentaries on Gen. xxxv, 8; xlviii, 7; Numb. viii, 7; vii, 18–23; xi, 20, 21; xv, 14; xix, 22; xxvi, 24, 36; xxviii, 19; xxxii, 24, 42; xxxiii, 1; Deut. xxi, 14; xxvii, 24; Josh. v, 9; Psa. xl, 2; lx, 4; lxii, 12; lxviii, 17; lxxx, 6; Prov. v, 19; xxvi, 10; Job xxxvi, 1; by Raymond Martin in his *Pugio Fidei* (Par. 1651, Leips. 1687), both in the original Hebrew and in a Latin translation; by Porchert in his *Victoria adversus impios Hebræos* (Paris, 1520); by Joshua Lorki, or Hieronymus de Santa Fide, as he was called after embracing Christianity, in his *Hebræomastix* (Frankfort-on-the-Main, 1602); and by Galatin in his *De Arcanis Catholicæ veritatis* (Basle, 1550). These fragments, which are exceedingly important contributions to the history of interpretation in the Middle Ages, show that R. Moses strove to explain the words and the context, and that he interspersed his literal expositions with ancient *Haggadas*, as well as with the interpretations of the sages of olden days. See Zunz, *Die Gottesdienstlichen Vorträge der Juden*, p. 286–293; Ginsburg, in Kitto, *Bibl. Cyclop.* s. v.; Etheridge, *Introd. to Hebrew Lit.* p. 248; Jost, *Gesch. d. Judenthums*, ii, 388; Grätz, *Gesch. d. Juden.* vol. viii.

Moses ibn-Ezra BEN-JACOB OF GRANADA, a Jewish writer of note, was born in Spain about 1070, and was descended from a family which once held noble rank in Jerusalem. He was equally celebrated as a learned Talmudist and a professor of Greek philosophy. Although, like his brother poets, he excelled in sacred song, he also tuned his lyre as an inhabitant of the West, and sang at times of love, but more often in praise of the beauties of nature. He was a contemporary of the celebrated rabbi Jehudah ben-Samuel ha-Levi (q. v.), who bestowed due meed of praise upon him and some other members of his noble and learned family. As a poet, Moses ibn-Ezra won the honor of being considered one of the most finished Hebrew writers. His works are remarkable not only for the intrinsic excellence of the matter, but for the purity, sweetness, and æsthetic grace of their style. Alexander von Humboldt, in his *Cosmos*, ii, 119, praises Moses ibn-Ezra's sublime description of natural scenery. The *Selichoth*, or penitential hymns, are greatly esteemed by the Jews, who give to Ibn-Ezra the epithet of *Hassalach* (הַסַּלָּח), or "the Selichoth poet" par excellence. He died about 1139. Moses ibn-Ezra wrote זְמִרוֹת וְתַחֲנוּנִים, *Hymns for Festival and other Occasions*, in the *Sephardim Ritual:—Dirvan R. M. ben-Ezra*, a collection in 2 parts, miscellaneous and religious:—ס' הַתַּרְשִׁישׁ, also ס' עֲנָק; this poem is called *Tarshish* from the number of its stanzas, 1210, expressed by the numerical value of the letters תרשיש:—ס' עֲרֻגַת הַבֹּשֶׂם, *The Garden of Spices*, on the philosophy of religion, in 7 parts:—תּוֹכָחָה, a penitential poem. He also wrote on eloquence and poetry, with an Arabic paraphrase; also a philosophical treatise, still unprinted. Extensive specimens of his writings are given in L. Dukes's *Moses ibn-Ezra* (Altona, 1839). See also Sachs, *Religiöse Poesie der Juden in Spanien*, p. 69–82, 310–319; Kämpf, *Nichtandalusische Poesie Andalusischer Dichter* (Prague, 1858), p. 213–240; Zunz, *Synagogal Poesie*, p. 21, 133, 228–230. See also Fürst, *Biblioth. Judaica*, i, 257 sq.; Grätz, *Gesch. der Juden*, vi, 123–127; Braunschweiger, *Die Juden in den roman. Staaten*, p. 62–64; Finn, *Sephardim*, p. 174; Lindo, *Jews in Spain*, p. 55; Da Costa, *Israel and the Gentiles*, p. 291; Margoliouth, *Modern Judaism Investigate I*, p. 243; Etheridge, *Introd. to Hebrew Literature*, p. 201 sq.; Zunz, *Literaturgesch. z. Synagogalen Poesie*, p. 210, 412, 585, 614; *Nachtrag* dazu, p. 8, 33; Jost, *Geschichte d. Judenthums u. s. Sekten*, ii, 414 sq.; Dukes, *Rabbinische Blumenlese*, p. 58; Delitzsch, *Zur Gesch. d. Jüd. Poesie*, 45, 168; Grätz, *Leket Schoschanim Blumenlese neuhebr. Dichtungen* (Breslau, 1862), p. 56 sq.; De Rossi, *Dizionario* (Germ. transl.), p. 11; Kimchi, *Liber Radicum* (ed. Biesenthal et Lebrecht, Berlin, 1847), p. 36. (B. P.)

Moses ben-Jacob. See MOSES ALBELDA.

Moses de Leon (*ben-Shem-Tob*), a Jewish philosopher, poet, and theologian of repute, was born at Leon about 1250, and died at Arevolo, A.D. 1305. He is best known as the author of the Cabalistic book called the *Sohar*, which he first published and sold as the production of R. Simon b.-Jochai. We do not agree with Etheridge, who states that "the opinion that ascribes it (viz. the *Sohar*) as a *pseudo*-fabrication to Moses de Leon in the 13th century has, I imagine, but few believers among the learned on this subject in our own day," for Moses's wife and daughter admitted that he was the author of it, as will be seen from an account of it in the *Book Juchassin* (p. 88, 89, 95, ed. Filipawski, London, 1857), which Ginsburg (*Kabbalah*, p. 99) gives in the following abridged form: When Isaac of Akko, who escaped the massacre after the capture of this city (A.D. 1291), came to Spain and there saw the *Sohar*, he was anxious to ascertain whether it was genuine, since it pretended to be a Palestinian production, and he, though born and brought up in the Holy Land, in constant intercourse with the disciples of the celebrated Cabalist, Nachmanides, had never heard a syllable about this marvellous work. Now Moses de Leon, whom he met in Valladolid, declared to him with a most solemn oath that he had at Avila an ancient copy, which was the very autograph of Rabbi Simon ben-Jochai, and offered to submit it to him to be tested. In the mean time, however, Moses de Leon was taken ill on his journey home, and died at Arevolo, A.D. 1305. But two distinguished men of Avila, David Rafen and Joseph de Avila, who were determined to sift the matter, ascertained the falsehood of this story from the widow and daughter of Moses de Leon. Being a rich man, and knowing that Moses de Leon left his family without means, Joseph de Avila promised that if she would give him the original MS. of the *Sohar* from which her husband made the copies, his son should marry her daughter, and that he would give them a handsome dowry; whereupon the widow and daughter declared that they did not possess any such MS.; that Moses de Leon never had it, but that he composed the *Sohar* from his own head, and wrote it with his own hand. Moreover, the widow candidly confessed that she had frequently asked her husband why he published the production of his own intellect under another man's name, and that he told her "that if he were to publish it under his own name nobody would buy it, whereas under the name of R. Simon ben-Jochai it yielded him a large revenue." Now this account is confirmed by the fact that the *Sohar* contains whole passages which Moses de Leon translated into Aramaic from his other works, as the learned Jellinek has clearly proved in his very elaborate and learned essay, *Moses ben-Shem-Tob de Leon, und sein Verhältniss zum Sohar*, p. 21–36. Moses de Leon also wrote a book on the soul and its destiny, entitled נֶפֶשׁ הַחָכְמָה, i. e. the *Soul of Wisdom* (Basle, 1608): —the *Weight of Wisdom*, מִשְׁקַל הַחָכְמָה, which contains the sayings of various philosophers, which he ably criticises:—סֵפֶר הַשֵּׁם, on the ten Sephiroth and the thirty-two ways of Wisdom:—מִשְׁכַּן הָעֵדוּת, *On Hell and Paradise:*—רִמּוֹן 'ס, *The Book of Pomegranates*, composed in 1287, which is a Cabalistic explanation of the Mosaic precepts. See Fürst, *Bibl. Judaica*, ii, 232; De Rossi, *Dizionario* (Germ. transl.), p. 177; Grätz, *Gesch. d. Juden* (Leips. 1873), vii, 216–234; Lindo, *Hist. of the Jews in Spain*, p. 113; Finn, *Sephardim*, p. 303 sq.; Steinschneider, *Jewish Literature*, p. 113; Etheridge, *Introd. to Hebr. Literature*, p. 276, 314; Ginsburg, *The Kabbalah*, p. 90 sq.; Ueberweg, *Hist. of Philosophy* (Morris's transl. N. Y. 1872), i, 417; A. Jellinek, *Moses ben-Shem-Tob, u. s. Verhältniss zum Sohar* (Leips. 1851); Jost, *Gesch. d. Juden. u. s. Sekten*, iii, 78; Cassel, *Leitfaden zur jüd. Gesch. u. Literatur* (Leips. 1872), p. 71. (B. P.)

Moses ben-Mocha OF PALESTINE, or Tiberias, a Jewish writer of some note, flourished towards the close of the 6th century. He developed and amplified *the interlineary* system of vocalization (טבסהתחחון, מנוקד, (לְמִשָׁה), called the *Tiberian* (נקוד טיברני), which has for centuries been adopted both by the Synagogue and the Church in all the pointed editions of the Hebrew Scriptures. Like his father, R. Moses also wrote Massoretic glosses both in the margin of the *Codd.* and in separate works, entitled ספרי נקוד.

Moses ben-Nachman. See NACHMANIDES.

Moses THE PUNCTUATOR (ר' משה הנקדן), or *the Cantor* (חזן), a Jewish exegetist, lived in London about the middle of the 13th century, and is noted as the author of the well-known *Treatise embodying the rules about the points of the Hebrew Scriptures*, called כללי הניקוד, or דרכי הניקוד והנגינות, also in the MSS. הוריית הקורא. Excerpts of this treatise, made by Jacob ben-Chayim, were first printed with the Massora in *the Rabbinic Bible* (Venice, 1524–25), and since in all the editions of the Rabbinic Bible. The treatise has also been published separately with a short commentary by Zebi ben-Menachem (Wilna, 1822), and with corrections and German notes by Frensdorff (Hanover, 1847). Those who recognise the real importance of the Hebrew vowel-points and accents will find in this unpretentious treatise a useful guide. R. Moses was thoroughly acquainted with and quotes the grammatical and exegetical writings of his predecessors, as Chayug,

Rashi, Ibn-Ganach, Ibn-Ezra, Parchon, etc. See Steinschneider, *Bibliographisches Handbuch*, p. 95; Zunz, *Zur Geschichte und Literatur*, p. 111; Ginsburg, in Kitto, *Bibl. Cyclop.* s. v.

Moses OF SATANOW. See SATANOW.

Moses ben-Shesheth, a Jewish interpreter of the Bible, who deserves to be ranked among the ablest exegetists of his people, flourished during the 12th century in Spain and Italy. But little is accessible regarding his personal history. His works, however, remain, and they are masterpieces, whether treating of Hebrew grammar, Old-Testament lexicography, or the Jewish Scriptures. His ablest and most valuable work, *A Commentary upon the Books of Jeremiah and Ezekiel*, was recently brought out in England from a Bodleian MS., with an English translation and notes by S. R. Driver (Lond. 1872, cr. 8vo). In this work Moses ben-Shesheth confines himself almost exclusively to the discussion of grammatical and lexicographical difficulties, and avoids all haggadic exposition. His interpretations are mostly rational, sometimes novel, and show throughout the independent thinker, guided only by grammatical rules. The great value of such old grammarians is now more and more appreciated; and the remark of Munk, "that the profound works of Gesenius and Ewald may still be improved by the dicta of such a man as Ibn-Ganach," may be applied also to our author. The work before us consists rather of notes on the prophets, and seems to have been originally an extra-commentary to another more extended one, as many difficult passages and words in Jeremiah and Ezekiel are passed over without any remark, which could not have escaped the attention of rabbi Moses. The author knew the works of Ibn-Ganach, R. Jehudah Chayug, and Moses Kimchi, whom he often quotes; but he never alludes to R. David Kimchi, more celebrated than his brother Moses, nor to Rashi, although he frequently agrees with them. It is to be hoped that Mr. Driver will continue the good work begun thus auspiciously, and give us any other of rabbi Moses's works now buried in MS. form in the Bodleian Library. A sketch of his life also will be appreciated.

Moshabbehites, or *Assimilators*, a heretical sect of the Mohammedans; so called because they hold to a resemblance between God and his creatures, supposing him to be a figure composed of members or parts, each spiritual or corporeal, and capable of local motion, of ascent and descent, etc. Some of this sect believe that the divine nature may be united with the human in the same person, for they grant it possible that God may appear in a human form, as Gabriel did; and to confirm this opinion, they allege Mohammed's words "that he saw the Lord in a most beautiful form, and Moses talking with God face to face." See Broughton, *Bibliotheca Historico-Sacra*, ii, 144.

Mosheim, Johann Laurenz von, a German theologian noted as an ecclesiastical historian of great merit, was born of a noble family at Lubeck, Oct. 9, 1694. He was educated at the Gymnasium of Lubeck and the University of Kiel, where, shortly after the completion of his studies in 1718, he succeeded Albert zum Felde as professor of philosophy in 1719. In 1723, at the invitation of the duke of Brunswick, he became professor of theology in the University of Helmstädt, where he remained until 1747; when, after having at various times refused several tempting offers from the high schools of Leipsic, Dantzic, Kiel, and others, he was appointed to the professorship of theology at Göttingen and the chancellorship of the university. Here his lectures on theology attracted all classes of students. He died September 9, 1755. He was thrice married. By his first wife he had two sons and one daughter, and by his third wife one daughter, afterwards duchess of Noailles. Mosheim is regarded as the most learned Lutheran theologian of his time. With a superior classical education he combined a thorough knowledge of the English,

French, and Italian languages and their literature, and was such a master of the purest German that he was esteemed one of the founders of modern German pulpit literature. The whole number of Mosheim's works is 161. He himself printed at Helmstädt in 1731 a catalogue raisonnée of the works which he had brought out up to that time. Among his theological works, special attention is due to one on Bible morality, entitled *Sittenlehre der Heiligen Schrift* (new ed. continued by J. P. Miller, Helmst. 1770–78, 9 vols. 8vo). But his most important contributions to theological literature are his ecclesiastical histories, of which his best known work is the *Institutiones Historiæ Ecclesiasticæ, Antiquioris et Recentioris, libri iv*. It is written in Latin, and was first published in 2 vols. 12mo in 1726, and the enlarged edition, in composing which he examined the original authorities, was published in 4to in 1755, just before his death. Another edition was published in 1764, with an account of Mosheim's writings by Miller, one of his pupils. It was translated into German by Von Einem and by J. R. Schlegel. Schlegel's translation is the better, and is enriched with valuable notes. It has also been translated into French, Dutch, and English. The first English version was made in 1764 by Dr. Maclaine, but is very unfaithful. Dr. Maclaine's professed object was to improve Mosheim's style, by adding words and rounding off periods. His alterations and additions constantly express his own sentiments instead of Mosheim's, and sometimes flatly contradict the author. (See, however, MACLAINE.) In 1832 a faithful translation, with valuable notes, was published by Dr. Murdock, of New Haven, Conn., of which there are many reprints; revised, N.Y. 1839. Mosheim's *Ecclesiastical History* extends from the birth of Christ to the beginning of the 18th century. Each century is treated separately, under the two heads of external and internal history. The internal history comprises "prosperous events," or the extension of the Church by the efforts of its public rulers and private members, and "calamitous events," such as persecutions and infidel attacks. The internal history includes the history, 1, of the Christian doctors; 2, of the doctrines and laws of the Church; 3, of its ceremonies and worship; 4, of heresies. This arrangement is open to several objections, of which the chief are—that it is too artificial; that what Mosheim calls external and internal history constantly run into each other (and indeed it is not easy to understand how any part of the history of a community can be said to be "external" to it); and, lastly, it imposes on the historian the necessity of deciding what no human mind can decide, namely, what events are prosperous and what calamitous to the Church. But the work of Mosheim is open to a graver objection. He has not treated his subject with the proper spirit of pious interest, though his own orthodoxy is undoubted. Nevertheless, his deep knowledge, his patient research, his general candor and impartiality, and his philosophical spirit, entitle Mosheim to a place among the best Church historians. His works gave an impulse to the study of Church history in Germany, which has produced, among other works, those of Pfaff, Baumgarten, Walch, Semler, Schröckh, Henke, Schmidt, Neander, etc. Of these, that of Schröckh, a pupil of Mosheim, is the fullest, extending to 45 vols. 8vo. "In his *Ecclesiastical History*," says Hagenbach—certainly a most competent critic—"Mosheim has labored with a candor which grants to all who differ from him an impartial presentation of their views, and insures justice to all; he has subjected their systems to a thoroughly scientific treatment, and in this he has been very happily likened to Melancthon." The most discriminating estimate of Mosheim seems to us to be that of Hase, who says: "Mosheim, conscious of historical talents, with a power of combination always bold, and sometimes extravagant, and an acquaintance with men in various and friendly relations, is universally acknowledged to have been a master of ecclesiastical historical writing" (*Ch. Hist.* p. 9).

Mosheim's other important works on Church history are his tract, *De Rebus Christianorum ante Constantinum* (Helmst. 1753), and *Institutiones Historiæ Christianæ Majores* (1739), which is a full Church history of the first century:—*Dissertationes ad Hist. Ecclesiasticam pertinentes* (new ed. Altona, 1767, 2 vols.):—and *Versuch einer unparteiischen Ketzergeschichte* (Helmst. 1746–48, 2 vols.). Among his other works are a Latin translation, with notes, of Cudworth's *Systema Intellectuale* (Jena, 1738):—six volumes of *Sermons* (1747). Mosheim's interpretations of Scripture are found in his *Observationes Sacræ* (Amsterdam, 1721); his *Cogitationes in N. T. locc. select.* (Hannov. 1726); his *Erklärung des I. Br. an d. Corinther* (1741, new ed. by Windheim, 1762); his *Erkl. d. beyden Br. an d. Timoth.* (1755); and in his volumes of sermons, *Heilige Reden.* His exegesis is usually broad and learned, and betokens good-sense and sound erudition. Mosheim was greatly distinguished as a preacher. His style was formed on the model of the English and French preachers, Tillotson and Watts, Saurin, Massillon, and Fléchier. He has been compared to Fénelon for the graces of his style. His talents were of a very high order, his learning was immense, and his character was exemplary. Says one: "In depth of judgment, in extent of learning, in purity of taste, in the passion of eloquence, and in a laborious application to all the various branches of erudition and philosophy, he had certainly very few superiors." "Mosheim's *noble character*," says Hagenbach (*German Rationalism*, p. 75), "*is just as lovely as his learning was thorough and comprehensive.* There is almost no domain of theology which he did not live to adorn and bless. . . . In the study of morals he, for a time at least, created an epoch, and in the history of German pulpit eloquence a new period dates from him. He has been termed the German Tillotson, the German Bourdaloue. What Michaelis wanted in fine taste was largely present in Mosheim, and gave to all his learned works, as well as to his sermons, an indescribable charm. Mosheim in faith was thoroughly orthodox, yet mild and patient towards others, and in this respect really unlike many of that school." We think Hagenbach, however, goes too far when he calls Mosheim also "the father of modern Church history;" as such no one deserves to be named except the learned and sainted Neander. He it was who first treated ecclesiastical history as it should be treated. See NEANDER. See Döring, *Gelehrte Theol. Deutschl. d. 18ten u. 19ten Jahrh.* vol. ii and iv; Gessner, *Memoria J. L. Moshemii* (1755); Lücke, *Narratio de Moshemio* (1837); Rössler, *Ueber Mosheim als Prediger*; Sachs, *Geschichte der Predigt. v. Mosheim bis Schleiermacher* (Heidelberg, 1866); Dowling, *Introd. Eccles. Hist.* p. 192, 193; Schaff, *Ch. Hist.* i, 22, 223, ad passim; Kahnis, *German Protestantism*, p. 118; *Bibl. Sacra*, Jan. 1851, p. 68; *Christ. Remembr.* 1862, p. 46.

Mosheim, Ruprecht von, a German religious enthusiast, was born in the first half of the 15th century. He believed himself commissioned of God to unite the four systems of religion—Papacy, Lutheranism, Zwinglianism, and Anabaptism—prevalent during the Reformatory period, and to lay the foundation of a new Jerusalem. He rejected all prevailing creeds as anti-Christian, and prayed for another reformatory movement that might unite all followers of Jesus. To further this end he also entered into negotiations with the evangelical theologians, Osiander and Venatorius, in 1539. But these negotiations were soon broken off. On the part of Romanists he was disliked from the first, for he was severe upon the immoral conduct of the clergy, the withholding of the cup, and the sale of indulgences. This brought him into conflict also with the emperor Ferdinand, in whose presence he hesitated not to deliver an oration against the papacy. He also went to Vienna to speak to the papal nuncio Morone, in order to get an interview with the pope; but instead of being afforded an opportunity to go to Rome, he was called by order of emperor Ferdinand before the authorities of the convent at Hazenau, and accused of heresy. The prince elector of Mentz had his work *De monarchia et renascentia Christianæ fidei* examined, and the ecclesiastical judge condemning him guilty of heresy, Mosheim was put into prison, and there died in 1544.

Moshier, ABSALOM, a minister of the Methodist Episcopal Church, was born in the early part of the present century. He was first employed in secular occupations, but after his conversion he preached for many years under the presiding elder, and in 1857 entered the Black River Conference, and was stationed at Antwerp; in 1858 and 1859, at De Peyster; in 1860–61, at Rensselaer Falls; in 1862–63, at Waddington; in 1864, at Richville; in 1865–66, at Redfield. In 1867, his health failing him, he was superannuated. He died in Hampden, Ohio, June 9, 1869. See *Minutes of Annual Conferences*, 1870, p. 136.

Mosol′lam (Μοσόλλαμος, Vulg. *Bosoramus*), a Græcized form (1 Esdr. ix, 14) of the MESHULLAM (q. v.) of the Heb. text (Ezra x, 15).

Mosol′lamon (same as preced. Μοσόλλαμος v. r. Μεσολάβων, Vulg. *Mosolamus*), a Græcized form (1 Esdr. viii, 44) of the MESHULLAM (q. v.) of the Heb. text (Ezra viii, 16).

Mosque (Spanish *mesquida*, French *mosquée*, Arabic *masjéd*, "a house of prayer," from *sajada*, "to bend, bow, adore") is the name applied in English to any Mohammedan house of worship; the larger houses of worship are called by Moslem "jami" (places of assembling) or "culliyet" (cathedrals). The first mosque was founded by Mohammed at Medina, part of the work be-

mihrab is the menber, or preacher's chair or pulpit; at one or more corners of the court rise minarets (q. v.), from which the faithful are called to prayers. The form of the oldest mosques, which next to those mentioned are supposed to be those located at Jerusalem (known as Omar's mosque) and Cairo, is evidently derived from that of the Christian Basilica, the narthex being the origin of the court with its arcade, and the eastern apse, representing the principal buildings of the mosque, facing Mecca. The original forms, however, became obliterated in the progress of Mohammedan architecture, and the mosques, with their arcaded courts, gateways, domes, and minarets, became the most characteristic edifices of Saracenic art. Wherever the Mohammedan faith prevailed, from Spain to India, beautiful examples of these buildings exist. The architectural notions of the different countries seem to have exerted an influence upon the Moslems, for these mosques differ in the various countries. Thus in India the mosques have many features in common with the temples of the Jainas, while in Turkey they resemble the Byzantine architecture of Constantinople.

Since the Turkish domination was established in Constantinople, the mosques have generally been built after the general type of Santa Sophia (q. v.), having a Greek cross as the basis of their plan, and being enclosed instead of hypæthral. Everywhere the dome is one of the leading and most beautiful features of the mosques, which commonly consist of porticos surrounding an open square, in the centre of which is the tank or fountain for ablution. In the south-east is a kind of pulpit (menber) for the imâm; and in the direction in

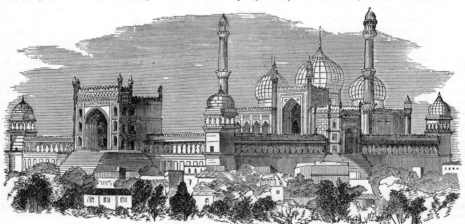

Great Mosque at Delhi, from the North-east.—From Fergusson's *Hand-Book of Architecture.*

ing done by his own hands. The site was a grave-yard shaded by date-trees, which was selected by the Prophet because his camel knelt opposite to it on his public entry into the city. The edifice was square and capacious, the walls of earth and brick, and the roof supported by the trunks of palm-trees and thatched with palm-leaves. It had three doors. A part of the building was assigned as a habitation to the poor among the faithful who had no other homes. In this mosque Mohammed was buried; and though the original edifice was long ago replaced by a larger structure, the temple still bears the name of *Masjéd el-Nebi*, "the Mosque of the Prophet" (see Wellsted, *City of the Caliphs*, i, 257 sq., 303 sq.). The most sacred mosque is the great temple of El-Hamram at Mecca, enclosing the Kaaba (q. v.). For many centuries the mosques were fashioned after this one. It consists of a large court enclosed by colonnades, with a fountain in the centre, where ablutions are made before prayer. On the side towards Mecca the colonnade is deeper. In the centre of this side is a niche (mihrab), surmounted by a vaulted arch; by the side of the

which Mecca lies (see KEBLAH) there is a niche (mihrab), towards which the faithful are required to pray. Opposite the pulpit there is generally a platform (dikkeb) surrounded by a parapet, with a desk bearing the Koran, from which portions are read to the congregation. In the imperial mosques at Constantinople there is a tribune (makswra), at the opposite side from the menber and the mihrab, reserved for the sole use of the sultan. In front of the mihrab is often another tribune (khûtab), from which the Imâm (q. v.) pronounces prayer, and an elevated square platform (mastabah) from which criers repeat the calls to prayer. The imperial mosque of Achmed in Constantinople is the only mosque that has six minarets, except the temple of El-Hamram in Mecca, to which Achmed built a seventh minaret. to quiet the complaint that he was attempting to outvie that holy sanctuary.

Many of the mosques are adorned with all the charms of the Saracenic and Moorish architecture, having texts and passages from the Koran intertwined among the delicate ornamentation, to lead the minds of the faithful while waiting for the hour of public prayer. The Turkish mosques are generally quite plain in their interior ornamentation, though often very stately and grand in their exterior architectural effect. It is not customary for women to visit the mosques, and if they do they are separated from the male worshippers. The utmost solemnity and decorum are preserved during the service, although in the hours of the afternoon (when there is no worship) people are seen lounging, chatting, even engaged in their trade, in the interior of the sacred building. On entering the mosque, the Moslem takes off his shoes, carries them in his left hand, sole to sole, and puts his right foot first over the threshold; he then performs the necessary ablutions, and finishes by putting his shoes and any arms he may have with him upon the matting before him. The congregation generally arrange themselves in rows parallel to that side of the mosque in which is the niche, and facing that side. The chief officer of a mosque is the Nazir (q. v.), under whom are two imâms. There are, further, many persons attached to a mosque in a lower capacity, as Mueddins (q. v.), Bowwabs (door-keepers), etc., all of whom are paid, not by contributions levied upon the people, but from the funds of the mosque itself. The revenues of mosques are derived from lands. With

their treasures, the sacredness of the place alone being sufficient protection. The former rigor by which unbelievers were excluded from mosques under penalty of death has been of late years relaxed in some places.

The finest specimens extant of Moslem architecture are thought to be the mosque at Mecca, the mosque of Omar at Jerusalem (see Spencer's *Egypt and the Holy Land*, Letter X), and the mosque at Medina, which three are considered also as peculiarly holy. The Jami Masjéd, or Great Mosque, at Delhi (see preceding page), built by Shah-Jehan in 1631-37, is generally considered the noblest building ever erected for Mohammedan worship. (G. F. C.)

Mosquito Territory (or **Mosquitia**). See NICARAGUA.

Moss, Charles, an Anglican prelate of some note, nephew of the following, flourished in the second half of the last century. He was educated at Caius College, Oxford, where he was afterwards fellow, and entered holy orders about the middle of last century. After filling many important livings, among them the rectory of St. James's and St. George's, London, the archdeaconry of Colchester, etc., he was finally elevated to the episcopate in 1766, and appointed to the see of St. David's, from which he was transferred to the see of Bath and

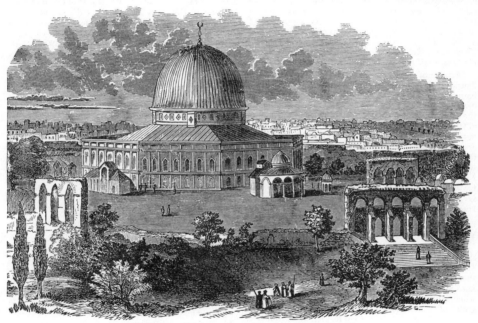

The Mosque of Omar at Jerusalem, from the South-east.

many of the larger mosques there are hospitals connected, and public kitchens, in which food is prepared for the poor.

To every mosque is also attached a school, in which reading of the Koran, at least, is taught; to every imperial mosque is attached a college, and to the mosque of El-Azhan, in Cairo, is attached the great Mohammedan university of the world, which is attended by several thousand students from all parts of the Mohammedan world. To the imperial mosques in Constantinople are attached not only colleges, but also libraries, hospitals, asylums for the poor, khans for travellers, baths, and a small cemetery, with the tomb of the founder. The spacious courts containing these extensive benevolent and charitable establishments are adorned with trees and shrubbery and fountains. The whole is supported by endowments left by the sultan whose name they bear. Travellers, orphans, widows, and minors also find here a refuge, where they can leave

Wells in 1774. He died in 1802. He wrote, *Evidence of the Resurrection Cleared* (Lond. 1744 and 1749, 8vo); and published many of his sermons in several series (Lond. 1750, 4to; 1756, 4to; 1764, 4to; 1769, 8vo; 1769, 4to; 1772, 4to; 1776, 4to). A son of his, of like name, also figured prominently in the Church. He was bishop of Oxford from 1807 until his death in 1811. He published only a *Fast Sermon* (Lond. 1798, 4to).

Moss, Robert, D.D., an English divine of distinction, was born of estimable parentage at Gillingham, in Norfolk, in 1666. He was educated first at Norwich school, then at Benet College, Cambridge, in 1682; made there B.A. and fellow in 1685, and B.D. in 1690; and entering holy orders, acquired great reputation both as a disputant and preacher. He was preacher to the Society of Gray's Inn, London, in 1698, and assistant preacher to Dr. Wake at St. James's, Westminster, in 1699. He was also sworn chaplain, in three succeeding reigns, to king William, queen Anne, and George I; and being one of the chaplains in waiting when queen Anne visited the University of Cambridge, April 5, 1705, he was then created D.D. In 1708 he was invited by the parishioners of St. Lawrence Jewry, on the resignation of dean Stanhope, to accept their Tuesday lecture, which he held till 1727, and then resigned it on account of his growing infirmities. In 1712, on the death of Dr. Roderick, he was nominated by the queen to the deanery of Ely, which was the highest but not the last promotion he obtained in the Church; for in 1714 he was collated by Robinson, bishop of London, to Gliston, a small rectory on the eastern side of Hertfordshire. The gout deprived him of the use of his limbs for some of the last years of his life, and he died March 26, 1729. His character may be seen in the preface to the eight volumes of his *Sermons*, which has usually been attributed to Dr. Snape, and has even been ascribed to him by Mr. Masters in his *History of Benet College;* but the credit of it has lately been transferred to Dr. Zachary Grey, who is now definitely known to have been the editor, and to have also written a *Life* of the dean, which has, however, never been published. He left no works of interest to us besides his sermons. He wrote a number of poems, among which the best are, *In doctissimi Sherlocci librum nuper editum de usu ac fine doni prophetici, necnon prædictionum maxime memorabilium per continuatum ab initio usque sæculorum seriem* (1726):—*A brief and easy Paraphrase upon the triumphal Song of Moses, Exodus, chap. xv, from ver.* 1 *to ver.* 20:—*A Lenten Thought.* See *Gener. Biog. Dict.* s. v.; Hook, *Eccles. Biogr.* s. v.; Nichols, *Anecdotes of Bowyer*, p. 78; *Lond. Gentleman's Magazine*, lxxiii, 1138. (J. H. W.)

Mossom, ROBERT, a learned Irish prelate, who flourished in the second half of the 17th century, was born about the opening of that æra; entered holy orders, and, being a stanch royalist, suffered much in the civil wars; but on the Restoration was made dean of Christ-church, Dublin, with which he held the bishopric of Londonderry, where he died in 1679. His works are, *The Preacher's Tripartite* (Lond. 1637, 1657, 1685, fol.):—*Variæ colloquendi Formulæ:—Narrative of George Wild, Bishop of Derry* (Lond. 1665, 4to):—*Zion's Prospect in its First View.* He also published some of his sermons, of which Bickersteth (*Christian Student*) says that they are "spiritual and evangelical." See Harris's Ware's *Ireland.*

Motazilites. See MOHAMMEDAN SECTS, in this volume, p. 423, col. 2.

Mote (κάρφος, something *dry*), any small dry particle, as of chaff, wood, etc. (Matt. vii, 3–5; Luke vi, 41, 42). Small faults or errors in others, discovered through the magnifying medium of prejudice, are likened by our Lord in these passages to a speck or splinter in the eye, which the censorious are fond of detecting, though guilty of more serious offences themselves, aptly compared to a beam (δοκός) (see Winckler, in *Animadvers. Philol.* iii, 803 sq.). The proverb was a familiar one with the Hebrews (see Buxtorf, *Lex. Rabb.* col. 2080). See EYE.

Motett, a term applied to two different forms of Church musical composition. 1. A sacred cantata, consisting of several unconnected movements, as a solo, trio, chorus, fugue, etc. 2. A choral composition, generally also of a sacred character, beginning with an introduction in the form of a song, perhaps with figurative accompaniment; after which follow several fugue subjects, with their expositions, the whole ending either with the exposition of the last subject, a repetition of the introduction, or a special final subject. A motett 'differs in this respect from a double or triple fugue, that the subjects never appear simultaneously, but are introduced one after the other. In one form of the motett, the successive phrases of an entire chorale are treated as so many fugal subjects. The subject is taken from the psalms or hymns of the Church. "Motett" seems to have been originally synonymous with *anthem*, and was

then probably accompanied only by the organ, which is now no longer the case in Roman Catholic churches, all kinds of musical instruments being used in it.

Moth (עָשׁ, *ash*, so called from its causing garments to *fall* in pieces, Job iv, 19; xiii, 28; xxvii, 18; Psa. xxxix, 11; Isa. l, 9; li, 8; Hos. v, 12; Sept. and Vulg. everywhere [except in the Psalms, where they have ἀράχνη, *aranea*] render σής, *tinea;* like the N. T., Matt. vi, 19, 20; Luke xii, 23; with which may be compared the Heb. סָס, *sas*, from its *leaping*, Isa. li, 8; Sept. σής, Vulg. *tinea*, Auth. Vers. "worm;" the word σής also occurs in the term σητόβρωτος, "moth-eaten," Jas. v, 2), the name of a well-known insect, which, in its caterpillar state, is very destructive to clothing. The tribe of moths is called by naturalists *Phalæna*, and is said to contain more than 1500 species. Linnæus, under the order Lepidoptera, genus Phalæna, gives the species of moths—*Tinea tapetzella, T. pellionella*, and *T. recurvaria sarcitella*—as peculiarly destructive to woollen clothes, furs, etc. The egg of the moth, being deposited on the fur or cloth, produces a very small, shining insect, which immediately forms a house for itself by cuttings from the cloth. It eats away the nap, weakens or destroys the thread, and finally ruins the fabric. Moths fly abroad only in the evening and night, differing in this respect from the tribe of butterflies, which fly only by day. Some of the species of moths feed on the leaves of plants. The "moth" *par eminence* is an insect of the order *Lepidoptera*, which possess four wings covered with minute tessellated scales, and of the tribe *Nocturna*, in which the antennæ (or "horns") are drawn out to a fine point. The genus *Tinea* in this division consists of small species, with the fore-wings long and narrow, and the head covered with coarse hairs. It includes a large number of species, several of which are noted for their destructiveness to clothes, woollen stuffs, furs, specimens of natural history in museums, and corn in granaries. The most pertinacious are *T. pellionella* and *T. tapetzella*, which feed on cloth; and these, from their abundance, and from their minuteness enabling them to penetrate into drawers and

Moth (enlarged view and actual size).

wardrobes, are but too well known in every household. The identity of this with the Biblical insect is apparent from the terms by which it is rendered in the Sept. (comp. Theophrast. *Hist. plant.* i, 16) and Vulg. (comp. Pliny, *Nat. Hist.* xi, 41). "The following allusions to the moth occur in Scripture—to its being produced in clothes: 'For from garments cometh a moth' (Ecclus. xlii, 13); to its well-known fragility: 'Mortal men are crushed *before* the moth' (Job iv, 19), which words really mean (so the Sept.) '*Like as* (לִפְנֵי, comp. 1 Sam. i, 10) the moth is crushed' (comp. Plautus, *Cistell.* i, 1, 73); but others take the phrase actively, 'As a moth consumes clothing' (so the Vulg.). The allusion to 'the house of the moth' (Job xxvii, 18) seems to refer plainly to the silky, spindle-shaped case, covered with detached hairs and particles of wool, made and inhabited by the larva of the *Tinea sarcitella;* or to the felted case or tunnel formed by the larva of the *Tinea pellionella;* or to the arched gallery formed by eating through wool by the larva of the *Tinea tapetzella.* References occur to the destructiveness of the clothes-moth: 'As a garment that is moth-eaten' (Job xiii, 28); 'The moth shall eat them up' (Isa. l, 9); 'The moth shall eat them up like a garment' (li, 8); 'I will be to Ephraim as a moth,' i. e. will secretly consume him (Hos. v, 12); comp. Matt. vi, 19, 20; Luke xii, 33; Jas. v, 2, metaphorically; and Ecclus. xix, 3—'Moths and worms shall have him that cleaveth to harlots,' but the better reading is $\sigma\acute{\eta}\pi\eta$, 'rottenness.' Since the 'treasures' of the Orientals, in ancient times, consisted partly of 'garments, both new and old' (Matt. xiii, 52; and comp. Josh. vii, 21; Judg. xiv, 12), the ravages of the clothes-moth afforded them a lively emblem of destruction. Their treasures also consisted partly of corn laid up in barns, etc. (Luke xii, 18, 24); and it has been supposed that the $\beta\rho\tilde{\omega}\sigma\iota\varsigma$, translated 'rust,' joined with the $\sigma\acute{\eta}\varsigma$ in Matt. vi, 19, 20, refers also to some species of moth, etc., probably in the larva state, which destroys corn. Kuinöl says the 'curculio, or corn-worm,' the larva of the *Tinea granella*, is injurious to corn. Compare the Roman phrase *blatta et tinea*. Moths, like fleas, etc., amid other more immediate purposes of their existence, incidentally serve as a stimulus to human industry and cleanliness; for, by a

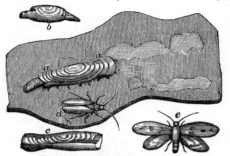

The Clothes-moth (*Tinea Pellionella*).

a. Larva in a case constructed out of the substance on which it is feeding. *b.* Case cut at the ends. *c.* Case cut open by the larva for enlarging it. *d, e.* The perfect insect.

remarkable discrimination in her instinct, the parent moth never deposits her eggs in garments frequently overlooked or kept clean. Indeed, the most remarkable of all proofs of animal intelligence is to be found in the larvæ of the water-moth, which get into straws, and adjust the weight of their case so that it can always float: when too heavy they add a piece of straw or wood, and when too light a bit of gravel (*Transactions of the Royal Society of Edinburgh*, i, 42)." "The *Tinea pellionella*, the larva of which constructs a portable case out of the substance on which it feeds, and is very partial to feathers, certainly occurs in Asia Minor, and we may safely conclude that it and *biselliata* (an abundant species often found in horse-hair linings of chairs) will be found in any old furniture - warehouse at Jerusalem." A detailed account of the habits of these insects may be found in Rennie's *Insect Architecture* (Lond. 1857), p. 220 sq. See WORM.

Mothe, PIERRE LAMBERT DE LA. See LAMOTHE.

Mothe le Vayer, FRANÇOIS DE LA, a French sceptical philosopher, was born at Paris in 1586, was so well educated that he was a favorite of the great cardinal ministers Richelieu and Mazarin, and was appointed through their favor counsellor of the state and tutor to the duke of Anjou, brother of king Louis XIV. La Mothe was a moral and temperate man—by no means a common case at the French court of that period. He became so interested in the study of history that he abandoned everything for it, and so generally esteemed was he that he was crowned with distinctions in all circles which he entered. In 1639 he was made a member of the Academy. La Mothe was nearly fifty years old before he published his first work: yet, once entered into the authors' lists, he contributed something regularly every year until his death in 1672. He fought with wit and satirical humor against the life led by the court, and the licentiousness to which the people of that century gave their sanction. In his philosophy he inclined to scepticism, applying the arguments of the ancient sceptics especially to theology, limiting the latter to the sphere of simple faith. He exemplified his views in his work *De la Vertu des Païens, ou Cinq dia-*

logues faits à l'imitation des anciens par Horatius Turbero (Mons, 1671, 12mo; 1673, 8vo; and a new edition, *Augmentée d'une refutation de la philos. sceptique ou préservatif contre le Pyrrhonisme par Mr. J. M. Kahle* [Berlin, 1704, 2 vols. 8vo]). In the first dialogue he defends scepticism in the style of Sextus with much show of learning. He treats of the variety and contradictions of human opinions, morals, and habits, wherefrom he comes to deduct the doctrine that there is nothing certain, and for the welfare in common not even a common binding law of morals. In his second dialogue he speaks about the variety of nourishment and beverage, and the different customs at repasts; of the conception of love, and takes ground in favor of what would now amount to the doctrine of free love, which he calls his sacred and divine philosophy. He recommends in his third dialogue a philosophic solitary life. The fourth dialogue contains a satirical praise of the ass, aiming thus sarcastically to reprimand the folly of his century. His fifth dialogue treats of the several religions, and he comes therein to the conclusion that there cannot be anything certain obtained by it; but he speaks here only in regard to the religion of reason, and says that positive religion possesses the principles of faith in revelation, which can be only gotten by God's grace, and must ever be above all reason. Mr. Arnauld, the learned theologian, answered La Mothe in a tract entitled *De la Necessité de la Foi en Jésus Christ*, which ably refutes the foolish reasonings of La Mothe, and yet treats the author with great consideration, as he deserved. La Mothe died in 1672. The rest of his works are of very little importance; they were published by his son at Paris in 1653; 2d ed. 1669; 3d ed. (3 vols. fol.) in 1684. This last edition is the most complete. Yet the best edition was got up in Germany at Dresden (1756–59, 14 vols. 8vo). See Étienne, *Essai sur La Mothe le Vayer* (1849); Bayle, *Hist. Dict.* s. v.; Hallam, *Introd. to Lit. Hist.* (see Index in vol. ii, Harper's edition). (J. H. W.)

Mother (אֵם, *em*, a primitive word; Gr. $\mu\acute{\eta}\tau\eta\rho$; but mother-in-law is חֲמוֹת, *chamoth'*; once חֹתֶנֶת, *chothe'-neth*, Deut. xxvii, 23; Gr. $\pi\epsilon\nu\theta\epsilon\rho\acute{\alpha}$). "The superiority of the Hebrew over all other contemporaneous systems of legislation and of morals is strongly shown in the higher estimation of the mother in the Jewish family, as contrasted with modern Oriental, as well as ancient Oriental and classical usage. See WOMAN. The king's mother, as appears in the case of Bathsheba, was treated with especial honor (1 Kings ii, 19; Exod. xx, 12; Lev. xix, 3; Deut. v, 16; xxi, 18, 21; Prov. x, 1; xv, 20; xvii, 25; xxix, 15; xxxi, 1, 30)" (Smith). "When the father had more than one wife, the son seems to have confined the title of 'mother' to his real mother, by which he distinguished her from the other wives of his father. Hence the source of Joseph's peculiar interest in Benjamin is indicated in Gen. xliii, 29 by his being 'his mother's son.' The other brethren were the sons of his father by other wives. Nevertheless, when this precision was not necessary, the step-mother was sometimes styled mother. Thus Jacob (Gen. xxxvii, 10) speaks of Leah as Joseph's mother, for his real mother had long been dead. The step-mother was, however, more properly distinguished from the womb-mother by the name of 'father's wife.' The word 'mother' was also, like FATHER, BROTHER, SISTER, employed by the Hebrews in a somewhat wider sense than is usual with us. It is used of a grandmother (1 Kings xv, 10), and even of any female ancestor (Gen. iii, 20); of a benefactress (Judg. v, 7), and as expressing intimate relationship (Job xvii, 14). In Hebrew, as in English, a nation is considered as a mother, and individuals as her children (Isa. l, 1; Jer. l, 12; Ezek. xix, 2; Hos. ii, 4; iv, 5); so our 'mother-country,' which is quite as good as 'father-land,' which we seem beginning to copy from the Germans. Large and important cities are also called mothers, i. e. 'mother-cities' (comp. *me-*

tropolis, from the Greek), with reference to the dependent towns and villages (2 Sam. xx, 19), or even to the inhabitants, who are called her children (Isa. iii, 12; xlix, 23). 'The *parting* of the way, at the head of two ways' (Ezek. xi, 21), is in the Hebrew 'the mother of the way,' because out of it the two ways arise as daughters. In Job i, 21 the earth is indicated as the common 'mother, to whose bosom all mankind must return.'" The term is also applied to a city as the parent or source of wickedness and abominations; as "Babylon the Great, the mother of harlots" (Rev. xvii, 5). The Church, as the Bride, is spoken of as the mother of believers (Isa. xlix, 14–22; lvi, 8–13; Psa. lxxxvii, 5, 6; Gal. iv, 22, 21); and the sentiment, at once so mild and so tender, which unites the mother to her child is often alluded to in the sacred volume to illustrate the love of God to his people (Isa. xliv, 1–8; lvi, 6–14; 1 Cor. iii, 1, 2; 1 Thess. ii, 7; 2 Cor. xi, 2). See CHILD.

Mother-Church (Latin, *Matrix Ecclesia*) is a term which has been used in various significations. The ancient Christians used this denomination of a Church in different senses. First, they understood by it an original Church, planted immediately by some one of the apostles, and from which others were afterwards derived and propagated. In this sense the Church of Jerusalem is called the mother of all churches in the world by the second General Council of Constantinople; and Arles was the mother-church of France, because supposed to be planted by Trophimus, the apostles' missionary; and first bishop of that place. Secondly, a mother-church denotes a metropolis, or the principal church of a single province; as in some of the African canons, where *matrix* is sometimes used for the primate's see, to which the other bishops were to have recourse for judgment and decision of controversies. But, thirdly, most commonly it signifies a cathedral, or bishop's church, which was usually termed the Great Church, the Catholic Church, and the Principal See, in opposition to the lesser tituli, or parish churches, committed to simple presbyters. *Ecclesia matrix*, or mother-church, is opposed to *diœcesana*, or diocesan church; though by their ambiguity they are often confounded, and mistaken for one another. See Broughton, *Bibliotheca Historico-Sacra*, ii, 145.

Mother of God. The *Virgin Mary* is sometimes so styled by Christians of all denominations. There is, however, a disinclination to the use of this expression because Romanists have given to Mary a place which the Scriptures do not warrant us in assigning her. "The Virgin Mary," says Pearson (*On the Creed*), "is frequently styled the Mother of Jesus in the language of the evangelists, and by Elisabeth, particularly, the mother of her Lord, as also by the general consent of the Church, because he that was born of her was God (*Deipara*); which, being a compound title, begun in the Greek Church, was resolved into its parts by the Latins, and so the Virgin was plainly named the Mother of God." Protestants admit that the Virgin Mary is the mother of God, but protest against the conclusion that she is on that account to be treated with peculiar honor, or to be worshipped; for this expression is used not to exalt her, but to assert unequivocally the divinity of her Son: he whom she brought forth was God, and therefore she is the bringer forth or mother of God. The term was first brought prominently forward at the Council of Ephesus, when it was deemed necessary by the Church to prevent giving Mary a station above that of her Son Jesus the Christ. In the Protestant world there is among the common people a hesitancy to the use of it, "because," as Hook has well put it, "by the subtlety of the Romish controversialists, it has been so used, or rather misused, as to make it seem to confer peculiar honor and privileges upon the Virgin Mary. The primitive Christians, like ourselves, were contented with speaking of the Virgin as 'the mother of my Lord;' and this phrase sufficed until, as we have seen, heretics

arose who understood the word Lord in an inferior sense, and then it became necessary to assert that God and Lord, as applied to our blessed Saviour, are synonymous terms. And sound theologians will still occasionally use the term *Mother of God*, lest Nestorianism should be held unconsciously by persons who wish to be orthodox; and people forget the great truth expressed by Paul that 'God purchased the Church with his own blood; and that Christ is over all, God blessed forever.'" See, however, the article MARIOLATRY in this *Cyclopædia*, vol. v.

Mother of God, Congregation of the, a monastic order instituted about 1574 at Lucca, in Tuscany, by John Leonardi. Their purpose is to save the lost of all conditions by any and all spiritual means, as the preaching of the Gospel, catechetical instruction, and visiting. They especially aim to reach the sick and the dying, and make the hospitals their principal fields of labor. Their founder was particularly devoted to the mother of Christ, and he provided in the constitution of the order that every day at 1 P.M. the litanies of the Holy Virgin be recited, and other like religious devotions be paid to her memory. The order was approved by pope Clement VIII in 1595, and confirmed by pope Paul V. Pope Gregory XV, anxious to spread the order throughout Italy, permitted its members to take the three monastics vows. Their dress is very much like the common monastic garb. See *Hist. du Clergé seculier et regulier* (Amst. 1716), iii, 123–125.

Habit of a Monk of the "Congregation of the Mother of God."

Mother Goddess (Latin, *Mater dea*). The pagans gave the name of *mother* to certain goddesses of the first rank, particularly to Cybele, Ceres, Juno, and Vesta. Cicero speaks of a famous temple erected in the city of Engyum, in Sicily, to the Great Mother, or simply The Mothers. Concerning this temple, the Engyans entertained a strange superstition. It was confidently affirmed that certain goddesses, called The Mothers, frequently appeared there. They relate a story of one Nicius, a man of wit, and a considerable person of the city, who had frequently laughed at this pretended apparition. One day, as he was haranguing in public, he fell down, roared like a madman, and rent his clothes in pieces. Upon this he was thought possessed by the furies, and every one acknowledged the vengeance of the injured goddesses. However, it was found afterwards that this was only a pretended delirium, and an expedient to deliver himself out of the hands of his persecutors, who had thoughts of destroying him, under pretence of punishing him for his impiety in denying the apparition of The Mothers; for, being suffered to go out of the city, he made his escape to the Roman general Marcellus. In that temple were shown javelins and brazen helmets, with inscriptions which made some believe that Murunes and Ulysses had consecrated these to the goddesses styled The Mothers. See Broughton, *Bibliotheca Historico-Sacra*, ii, 145.

Mothering Sunday (or Midlent Sunday), supposed to be the day on which, in popish times, people visited the mother-church and made their annual offering. In more recent times children and servants in England obtain leave to visit their parents on this day. This custom, according to some, originated in this Sunday being the *Dominica Refectionis*, or Sunday of Refreshment, the gospel for the day being the record of the miraculous banquet to the five thousand in the desert. On that day the guests used to eat frumenty, consisting of whole grains of wheat, boiled in milk, and sweetened and spiced.

Motive, that which *moves*, excites, or invites the mind to volition. It may be one thing singly, or many things conjointly. Some call it a faculty of the mind, by which we pursue good and avoid evil. Aristotle defines *motive* thus: "The deliberate preference by which we are moved to act, and not the object for the sake of which we act, is the principle of action; and desire and reason, which is for the sake of something, is the origin of deliberate preference" (*Ethic.* lib. vi, cap. 2). Kant distinguishes between the subjective principle of appetition, which he calls the mobile or spring (*die Triebfeder*), and the objective principle of the will, which he calls motive or determining reason (*beweggrund*); hence the difference between *subjective ends*, to which we are pushed by natural disposition, and *objective ends*, which are common to us with all beings endowed with reason (Willm, *Hist. de la Philosoph. Allemande*, i, 357). This seems to be the difference expressed in French between *mobile* and *motif*. "A motive is an object so operating upon the mind as to produce either desire or aversion" (lord Kames, *Essay on Liberty and Necessity*). "By *motive*," says Edwards (*Inquiry*, pt. i, § 2), "I mean the whole of that which moves, excites, or invites the mind to volition, whether that be one thing singly, or many things conjunctly. Many particular things may concur and unite their strength to induce the mind; and when it is so, all together are, as it were, one complex *motive*. . . . Whatever is a *motive*, in this sense, must be something that is *extant in the view or apprehension of the understanding, or perceiving faculty*. Nothing can induce or invite the mind to will or act anything any further than it is perceived, or is in some way or other in the mind's view; for what is wholly unperceived, and perfectly out of the mind's view, cannot affect the mind at all." Hence it has been common to distinguish *motives* as *external* or *objective*, and as *internal* or *subjective*. Regarded *objectively*, motives are those external objects or circumstances which, when contemplated, give rise to views or feelings which prompt or influence the will. Regarded *subjectively*, motives are those internal views or feelings which arise on the contemplation of external objects or circumstances. In common language, the term *motive* is applied indifferently to the external object and to the state of mind to which the apprehension or contemplation of it may give rise. The explanation of Edwards includes both. Dr. Reid (*Correspondence* prefixed to his *Works*, p. 87) said that he "understood a *motive*, when applied to a human being, to be that for the sake of which he acts, and therefore that what he never was conscious of can no more be a *motive*

to determine his will than it can be an argument to determine his judgment." "This is Aristotle's definition (τὸ ἕνεκα οὗ) of *end* or *final cause*; and as a synonyme for end or final cause the term *motive* had been long exclusively employed" (Sir Wm. Hamilton). In Dr. Reid's *Essays on the Active Powers* he says, "Everything that can be called a *motive* is addressed either to the animal or the rational part of our nature." Here the word *motive* is applied *objectively* to those external things which, when contemplated, affect our intelligence or our sensitivity. But in the very next sentence he has said, "*motives* of the former kind are common to us with the brutes." Here the word *motive* is applied *subjectively* to those internal principles of our nature—such as appetite, desire, passion, etc.—which are excited by the contemplation of external objects, adapted and addressed to them. But, in order to a more precise use of the term *motive*, let it be noted that, in regard to it, there are three things clearly distinguishable, although it may not be common nor easy always to speak of them distinctively. These are, the external object, the internal principle, and the state or affection of mind resulting from the one being addressed to the other. For example, bread or food of any kind is the external object, which is adapted to an internal principle which is called appetite, and hunger or the desire for food is the internal feeling, which is excited or allayed, as the circumstances may be, by the presentment of the external object to the internal principle. In popular language, the term *motive* might be applied to any one of these three; and it might be said that the *motive* for such an action was *bread, appetite*, or *hunger*. But, strictly speaking, the feeling of hunger was the *motive*; it was that, in the preceding state of mind, which disposed or inclined the agent to act in one way rather than in any other. The same may be said of *motives* of every kind. In every case there may be observed the external object, the internal principle, and the resultant state or affection of mind; and the term *motive* may be applied, separately and successively, to any one of them; but, speaking strictly, it should be applied to the determining state or affection of mind which arises from a principle of human nature having been addressed by an object adapted to it; because it is this state or affection of mind which prompts to action. The *motive* of an agent, in some particular action, may be said to have been *injury*, or *resentment*, or *anger*—meaning by the first of these words the wrong behavior of another; by the second, the principle in human nature affected by such behavior; and by the third, the resultant state of mind in the agent. When it is said that a man acted *prudently*, this may intimate that his conduct was in accordance with the rules of propriety and prudence; or that he adopted it after careful consideration and forethought, or from a sense of the benefit and advantage to be derived from it. In like manner, when it is said that a man acted *conscientiously*, it may mean that the particular action was regarded not as a matter of interest, but of duty, or that his moral faculty approved of it as right, or that he felt himself under a sense of obligation to do it. In all these cases the term *motive* is strictly applicable to the terminating state or affection of mind which immediately precedes the volition or determination to act. To the question, therefore, whether *motive* means something in the mind or out of it, it is replied that what moves the will is something in the preceding state of mind. The state of mind may have reference to something out of the mind. But what is out of the mind must be apprehended or contemplated—must be brought within the view of the mind, before it can in any way affect it. It is only in a secondary or remote sense, therefore, that external objects or circumstances can be called *motives*, or be said to move the will. *Motives* are, strictly speaking, *subjective*—as they are internal states or affections of mind in the agent. *Motives* may be called *subjective*, not only in contradistinction to the external objects and circumstances which may be the occasion of them, but also in regard to the different effect which the same objects and circumstances may have, not only upon different individuals, but even upon the same individuals, at different times. A man of slow and narrow intellect is unable to perceive the value or importance of an object when presented to him, or the propriety and advantage of a course of conduct that may be pointed out to him, so clearly or so quickly as a man of large and vigorous intellect. The consequence will be that, with the same *motives (objectively* considered) presented to them, the one may remain indifferent and indolent in reference to the advantage held out, while the other will at once apprehend and pursue it. A man of cold and dull affections will contemplate a spectacle of pain or want without feeling any desire or making any exertion to relieve it; while he whose sensibilities are more acute and lively will instantly be moved to the most active and generous efforts. An injury done to one man will rouse him at once to a frenzy of indignation, which will prompt him to the most extravagant measures of retaliation or revenge; while in another man it will only give rise to a moderate feeling of resentment. An action which will be contemplated with horror by a man of tender conscience will be done without compunction by him whose moral sense has not been sufficiently exercised to discover between good and evil. In short, anything external to the mind will be modified in its effect according to the constitution and training of the different minds within the view of which it may be brought. Not only may the same objects differently affect different minds, but also the same minds, at different times or under different circumstances. He who is suffering the pain of hunger may be tempted to steal in order to satisfy his hunger, but he who has bread enough and to spare is under no such temptation. A sum of money which might be sufficient to bribe one man would be no trial to the honesty of another. Under the impulse of any violent passion, considerations of prudence and propriety have not the same weight as in calmer moments. The young are not so cautious, in circumstances of danger and difficulty, as those who have attained to greater age and experience. Objects appear to us in very different colors in health and in sickness, in prosperity and in adversity, in society and in solitude, in prospect and in possession. It would thus appear that *motives* are in their nature *subjective*, in their influence *individual*, and in their issue *variable*.

There are two points which render this interesting topic of metaphysical philosophy or psychology also an important one in theology. See WILL.

1. *The Extent to which Motives control Volition.*—On this question there are essentially two theories. (*a*) That the *will itself* determines the force or prevalence of the motives. This is not done by any previous volition, but in the act of choosing among the various motives, i. e. in selecting between the different courses to which these motives prompt. This is the only theory that leaves the will absolutely free, and fully vindicates moral character. For Cicero has long since observed that "if the things which move the will are not in our own power, then neither our actions nor our volitions are free, and there is no room for praise or blame." See LIBERTY. (*b*) That the motives control the will, so as to produce volitions according to their relative force. This is argued, either (1) on the *materialistic* (i. e. physical or mechanical) ground alleged by Hobbes, Collins, and others, that there is a natural law regulating unerringly and necessarily these processes, external and oftentimes independent of the subject himself; or (2) on the basis of a *moral* necessity, assumed by Edwards and his followers, whereby the actual mental condition of the subject (i. e. his desires, etc.) dictates the direction of the volitions. On the other hand, consciousness, no less than Scripture (e. g. especially Rom. vii, 15–23), most unequivocally declares that we are capa-

ble of selecting a course contrary to our most urgent inclinations, and conscience pronounces us guilty because we suffer our evil passions to overcome our will. Did not our judgment (otherwise called conscience or the moral sense) thus step in to cast a weight into the scale, and, moreover, were not the prevenient grace of God ever ready to aid us "both to will and to do" what is right, it might indeed remain doubtful whether the will of fallen creatures at least could freely determine in the presence of violent emotion or habitual predilection. See INABILITY.

The phrase "the strongest motive" contains an ambiguity which has led to great confusion in this controversy. If those who use it merely mean those inducements which are usually most efficacious in moving men, then it is irrelevant to the present issue, because some persons at all times, and all persons at some times, are proof against those influences which are most sure to incite other individuals or under other circumstances. So proverbially is this the case that human conduct is of all things the most uncertain to predict in particular cases. If, on the other hand, as is more exact, the phrase is employed to designate those considerations which are so peculiarly adapted to the mental state of the person at the time as to effect an inclination of the will accordingly, then there still remains this fallacy in the expression, namely, that the *strength* of the motives really depends upon the moral condition of the subject himself, of which condition the will itself forms a large (indeed a preponderating) element. Hence we term persons "obstinate," "stubborn," "headstrong," "self-willed," etc., or the reverse. See VOLITION.

2. The doctrine that "*the character of the motives determines the moral quality of an act*" would be more correctly stated thus: "The *purpose* of the actor determines his moral character in any given case." There is hardly any specific act (unless perhaps we except idolatry) which may not be praiseworthily performed under certain circumstances and for right ends. Thus homicide may be murder or execution in altered cases; sexual connection is the legitimate privilege of matrimony or the illicit indulgence of licentiousness; the use of the name of God may be either a lawful oath, or devout prayer, or profanity, according to the intent of the invocation. Nor is this axiom tantamount to the maxim condemned in Scripture (Rom. iii, 8), and justly scouted under the popular name of "Jesuitism," that "*the end justifies the means.*" Not only the end in view, but all the means employed to accomplish that end, must be tested with the same scrupulous care by a comparison with the identical standard of rectitude, the revealed will of God, by which alone the moral quality of the motive of him who seeks to effect the one or make use of the other is to be ultimately and surely determined. Thus while the intention of the party acting vindicates or condemns him in the act, the propriety of the act itself is to be tried by a more unerring external tribunal. Hence also a crime or good act meant, but (through unavoidable hinderance) not executed, is, in the eye of divine justice, accounted as guilt or virtue (Matt. v, 22, 28; 2 Cor. iii, 12; 1 John iii, 15). See MORALS.

See Edwards, *On the Will*, p. 7, 8, 124, 259, 384; Toplady, *Works*, ii, 41, 42; Buck, *Theol. Dict.* s. v.; Hamilton, *Metaphysics*, p. 692 sq., 129, 556 sq.; Watson, *Theological Institutes*, ii, 439 sq.; Krauth's Fleming's *Vocabulary of Philos.* s. v.

Mott, WILLIAM F., an American philanthropist of some note, was born in New York City in 1818. Mr. Mott commenced life with moderate means, but, being honest and of frugal habits, amassed an ample fortune, which he spent for the relief of the poor and needy. He made large contributions to the philanthropic institutions of his native place; among them, to the City Dispensary, the House of Refuge, the Colored Orphan Asylum, and Woman's Hospital. He was an active member of the Society of Friends. He died in New York in 1867.

Motzer, DANIEL, a Presbyterian minister, was born in Perry County, Pa., Aug. 16, 1817. He graduated at Jefferson College, Pa.; studied theology in the Western Seminary, Alleghany, Pa.; was licensed by Carlisle Presbytery in 1848, and in 1849 was ordained and installed pastor of the church at Cold Spring, N. J. He subsequently served the churches of Madison and Adams's Mill, Muskingum County, Ohio, and near Warrenton, Fauquier County, Va., and lastly the Nealsville and Darnestown churches, in Montgomery County, Md. He died Nov. 1, 1864. Mr. Motzer was a scriptural and edifying preacher, an untiring and affectionate pastor, and a kind and true friend. He felt a deep interest in the mental and religious training of the young, and the interests of the parochial school were very dear to his heart. See Wilson, *Presb. Hist. Almanac*, 1866, p. 131.

Moulding, a general term applied to all the varieties of outline or contour given to the angles of the various subordinate parts and features of buildings, whether projections or cavities, such as cornices, capitals, bases, door and window jambs and heads, etc. The regular mouldings of *Classical* architecture are, the *Fillet*, or *list*; the *Astragal*, or *bead*; the *Cyma reversa*, or *ogee*; the *Cyma recta*, or *cyma*; the *Cavetto*; the *Ovolo*; the *Scotia*, or *trochilus*; and the *Torus*: each of these admits of some variety of form, and there is considerable difference in the manner of working them between the Greeks and Romans. (See those terms.) The mouldings in classical architecture are frequently enriched by being cut into leaves, eggs, and tongues, or other ornaments, and sometimes the larger members have running patterns of honeysuckle or other foliage carved on them in low relief; the upper moulding of cornices is occasionally ornamented with a series of projecting lions' heads.

In mediæval architecture the diversities in the proportions and arrangements of the mouldings are very great, and it is scarcely possible to do more than point out a few of the leading and most characteristic varieties.

In the *Norman* style the plain mouldings consist al-

Binham, Norfolk.

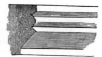

Norwich Cathedral.

Peterborough Cathedral.

Peterborough Cathedral.

most entirely of rounds and hollows, variously combined, with an admixture of splays, and a few fillets. The rich mouldings, however, are very various, one of the most marked being the constant recurrence of mouldings broken into zigzag lines, and forming what is called the *Zigzag* or *Chevron* moulding: it has not been very clearly ascertained at what period this kind of decoration was first introduced, but it was certainly not till some considerable time after the commencement of the style; when once adopted, it became more common than any other ornament. A series of grotesque heads placed in a hollow moulding, called *Beak-heads*, with their tongues or beaks lapping over a large bead or torus, was also very common. The *Hatch* moulding

Westminster Hall, A.D. 1097.

is also not uncommon, and is found early in the style, as it can be cut conveniently without the aid of a chisel, with the pick only. The other favorite mouldings of the Norman style are the *Billet* mouldings, both square and round, the *Lozenge*, the *Nail-head*, the *Pellet*, the *Chain*, the *Cable*, and the *Rose*, of all which illustrations are here given. There may also be mentioned the *Star*,

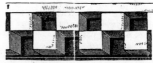

Square Billet.—St. Augustine's, Canterbury.

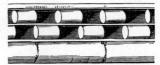

Round Billet.—Binham Priory, Norfolk.

Lozenge.—Tickencote, Rutland.

Nail-head.—Ely Cathedral.

Pellet.—Iffley, Oxford.

Chain.—St. William's Chapel, York.

Cable.—Romsey, Hants.

Rose.—Iffley Church, Oxfordshire.

the *Billeted Cable*, the *Nebule*, the *Studded*, the *Indented*, the *Scalloped*, the *Fir-cone*, the *Double Cone*, the *Dovetail*, the *Embattled*, the *Open Heart*, and the *Antique*.

In the *Early English* style the plain mouldings become lighter, and are more boldly cut than in the Norman; the varieties are not very great, and in arches, jambs of doors, windows, etc., they are very commonly so arranged that if they are circumscribed by a line drawn to touch the most prominent points of their contour it will be found to form a succession of retangular recesses. They generally consist of alternate rounds and hollows, the latter very deeply cut, and a few small fillets; sometimes also splays are used: there is considerable inequality in the sizes of the round mouldings, and the larger ones are very usually placed at such a distance apart as to admit of

Salisbury Cathedral.

several smaller between them; these large rounds have frequently one or more narrow fillets worked on them, or

are brought to a sharp edge in the middle, the smaller rounds are often undercut, with a deep cavity on one side (e e), and the round and hollow members constantly unite with each other without any parting fillet or angle. The ornamental mouldings in this style are not numerous, and they are almost invariably placed in the hollows; the commonest and most characteristic is that which is known by the name of *Dog-tooth ornament*, which usually consists of four small plain leaves united so as to form a pyramid; these ornaments are commonly placed close together, and several series of them are frequently introduced in the same suite of mouldings; the other enrichments consist chiefly of single leaves and flowers, or of running patterns of the foliage peculiar to the style.

Peterborough Cathedral.

The plain mouldings in the *Decorated* style are more diversified than in the Early English, though in large suites rounds and hollows continue for the most part to prevail; the hollows are often very deeply cut, but in many instances, especially towards the end of the style, they become shallower and broader; ovolos are not very uncommon, and ogees are frequent; splays also are often used, either by themselves or with other mouldings;

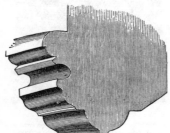

Door, Kiddington, Oxford.

fillets placed upon larger members are abundant, especially in the early part of the style, and a round moulding, called the *Scroll-moulding*, with a sharp projecting edge on it, arising from one half being formed from a smaller curve than the other, is frequently used, and is characteristic of Decorated work; when used horizontally the larger curve is placed uppermost: there is also another moulding, convex in the middle and concave at each extremity, which, though sometimes found in the Perpendicular style, may be considered as generally characteristic of the Decorated. Fillets are very frequently used to separate

other members, but the rounds and hollows often run together, as in the Early English style. The enrichments consist of leaves and flowers, either set separately or in running patterns, figures, heads, and animals, all of which are generally carved with greater truth than at any other period; but the *ball-flower*, which belongs

Kiddington, Oxford.

especially to this style, and a variety of the *four-leaved flower*, are the commonest.

In the *Perpendicular* style the mouldings are generally flatter and less effective than at an earlier period. One of the most striking characteristics is the prevalence of very large and often shallow hollows; these sometimes occupied so large a space as to leave but little room for any other mouldings: the hollows and round members not unfrequently unite without any line of separation, but the other members are parted either by quirks or fillets.

Baliol College, Oxford.

The most prevalent moulding is the ogee, but rounds, which are often so small as to be only beads, are very abundant; and it is very usual to find two ogees in close contact, with the convex sides next each other. There is also an undulating moulding, which is common in the abacus

Deddington Church, Oxford.

and dripstones, peculiar to the Perpendicular style, especially the latter part of it; and another indicative of the same date, which is concave in the middle and round at each extremity, is occasionally used in door-jambs, etc. In Perpendicular work small fillets are not placed upon larger members, as in Decorated and Early English; splays also are much less frequent. The ornaments used in the mouldings are running patterns of foliage and flowers; detached leaves, flowers, and bunches of foliage; heads, animals, and figures, usually grotesque; shields, and various heraldic and fanciful devices; the large hollow mouldings, when used in arches or the jambs of doors and windows, sometimes contain statues with canopies over them.

Mouldy. The word נִקֻּדִּים, *nikkudim'* (Josh. ix, 5), refers, as Gesenius remarks, rather to crumbs of bread, and, instead of, as in our version, "all the bread of their [the Gibeonites'] provision was dry and mouldy," he reads, "all the bread of their travelling provision was dry, and had fallen into crumbs." See BREAD.

Moulin (Lat. *Molynæus*), **Charles du,** a celebrated French lawyer, and a convert to Protestantism, was born of a noble family at Paris, in 1500, and studied at the University of Paris and at Poictiers and Orleans. He became advocate of Parliament in 1522. He embraced the Protestant religion, first as a Calvinist, and afterwards became a Lutheran. He was imprisoned at the instigation of the Jesuits, became equally obnoxious to the Calvinists, and ultimately returned to the communion of the Church of Rome. He died in 1566. His works were published in 5 vols. fol. (Paris, 1681); among them are *Collatio et unio quatuor evangelistarum, eorum serie et ordine* (1596, 4to).

Moulin (Lat. *Molinæus*), **Pierre du** (1), a French Protestant divine of great note for his opposition to the

Romanists, especially the Jesuits, was born at Buhy, in the Vexin, Oct. 18, 1568. He studied first at the Protestant school in Sedan, and next at the English high school at Cambridge, from which university he removed, after a four-years' stay, to accept the professorship of philosophy at Leyden. This professorship he held for five or six years, and had several disciples who afterwards became famous; among the rest, Hugo Grotius. He read lectures upon Aristotle, and disciplined his scholars in the art of disputing, of which he made himself so great a master that he was always the scourge and terror of the papists. Scaliger was very much his patron, and when Du Moulin published his *Logic* at Leyden in 1596 was so gracious as to say of the epistle prefatory, "Hæc epistola non est hujus ævi." In the divinity schools he also taught Greek, in which he was extremely well skilled, as appears from his book entitled *Novitas Papismi*, in which he exposes cardinal Perron's ignorance of that language. In 1599 he returned to France, and became minister at Charenton, near Paris, and chaplain to Catharine of Bourbon, the king's sister, and then the wife of Henry of Lorraine. It is generally believed that Catharine's faithfulness to the Protestant cause is due to Du Moulin's influence. On the assassination of Henry IV, Du Moulin charged the guilt of that detestable deed upon the Jesuits, which produced a violent controversy between him and some of that society. Cotton, a Jesuit, then chaplain at court, was vainly struggling to free the Society of Jesus from the imputation which had been generally placed upon it that Ravaillac had been incited by them and their doctrines to this bloody deed, and finally even published a book in defence of the order. Du Moulin. however, believing the Jesuits guilty, replied in his *Anti-Cotton, or a Refutation of Father Cotton*, wherein is proved that the Jesuits were the real authors of that execrable parricide. In 1615, James I, who had long been in correspondence with Du Moulin by letters, invited him to England; but his Church would not suffer him to go till he had given a solemn promise in the face of his congregation that he would return to them at the end of three months. The king received him with great affection; took him to Cambridge at the time of the commencement, where he was honored with a doctor's degree; and at his departure from England presented him with a prebend in the church of Canterbury. On his return to France, Du Moulin had again innumerable disputes with the Jesuits; and when they found that nothing was to be done with him in this way, they made use of others. They tried to bring him over to them by the promise of great rewards; and they attempted more than once his life, so that he was obliged at length always to have a guard. In 1617, when the United Provinces desired the Reformed churches of England, France, and Germany to send some of their ministers to the Synod of Dort, Du Moulin and three others were deputed by the Gallican Church, but were forbidden to go by the king upon pain of death. In 1618 he had an invitation from Leyden to fill the divinity chair, which was vacant, but he refused it. In 1620, when he was preparing to go to the National Synod of the Gallican Church, baron Herbert of Cherbury, then ambassador from Britain at the court of France, asked him to write to king James, and to urge him, if possible, to undertake the defence of his son-in-law, the king of Bohemia. Du Moulin declined the office; but the ambassador, knowing his interest with James, would not admit of any excuse. This brought him into trouble, for it was soon after decreed by an order of Parliament that he should be seized and imprisoned for having solicited a foreign prince to take up arms for the Protestant churches. Apprised of this, he secretly betook himself to the ambassador Herbert, who, suspecting that his letters to the king were intercepted, advised him to fly, as the only means of providing for his safety. Du Moulin finally went to Sedan, and there accepted the divinity professorship and the ministry of the Church, both which he held till the time

of his death, which occurred March 10, 1658. In 1623, when cardinal Perron's book was published against king James, Du Moulin took a journey into England, and at the king's instigation answered it in a work published at Sedan, after the death of James, under the title of *Novitus Papismi, sive Perronii confutatio, regisque Jacobi, sed magis sacræ veritatis defensio*. A list of Du Moulin's works, to the number of seventy-five, is given by Aymon (*Synodes de France*, ii, 273). He also published many of his sermons. He was a violent opponent of Arminianism, and attacked Amyraldus (q. v.) bitterly in his *De Moses Amyraldi Libro judicium*. His most important works are, *The Buckler of the Faith, or a Defence of the Confession of the Reformed Churches in France against M. Arnoux, the Jesuit* (3d ed. Lond. 1631, 4to):—*Le Combat Chrétien* (8vo):—*Anatomie de la Messe* (Sedan, 1636, 12mo). See Nicholls, *Calvinism and Arminianism compared*, i, 224; Bates, *Vitæ*, p. 697 sq.; Sax, *Onomasticon*, iv, 179; Haag, *La France Protestante*, iv, 420; Schweizer, *Centraldogmen*, ii, 225 sq., 564 sq.; Ebrard, *Dogmatik*, vol. i, § 43; Vinet, *Histoire de la Prédication parmi les Réformés en France au 17ᵐᵉ siècle* (Par. 1860).

Moulin, Pierre du (2), son of the preceding, and noted as a most enthusiastic Calvinist, was born in 1600 at Paris, and graduated at Leyden; but going afterwards to England, obtained, like his father, a prebend at Canterbury, and was one of the chaplains to king Charles II. He died in 1683. He was the author of *The Peace of the Soul:—Clamor Regii Sanguinis*, which, being anonymous, was attributed by Milton to Alexander More:—and *A Defence of the Protestant Church*. See Allibone, *Dict. of Brit. and Amer. Authors*, s. v.; Haag, *La France Protestante*, iv, 430.

Moullah. See MULLAH.

Mound (Lat. *mundus*) is a term in heraldry, designating a globe surmounted with a cross (generally) pattée. As a device, it is said to have been used by the emperor Justinian, and to have been intended to represent the ascendency of Christianity over the world. The royal crown of England is surmounted by a mound, which first appears on the seal of William the Conqueror, though the globe without the cross was used earlier.

Heraldic Mound.

Mount or **Mountain** (properly הַר, *har*, from its *swelling* form; with its cognate forms, הֶרֶר, *he'rer*, and הָרָר, *harar'*; Gr. ὄρος; also Chald. טוּר, *tur*, from their *rocky* nature, Dan. ii, 35, 45: but סֹלְלָה, *solelah'*, "mount," Jer. vi, 6; xxxii, 32; xxxiii, 4; Ezek. iv, 2; xvii, 17; xxi, 22; xxvi, 8; Dan. xi, 15; elsewhere "bank," 2 Sam. xx, 15; 2 Kings xix, 32; Isa. xxxvii, 33, is a *mound* or rampart, such as is thrown up by besiegers against a city; and מַצָּב, *mutsab'*, "mount," in Isa. xxix, 3, is a *station* of troops or military post, as occupied for purposes of besieging or a campaign. See WAR. "In the New Testament the word *mount* or *mountain* is confined almost exclusively to representing ὄρος. In the Apocrypha the same usage prevails as in the N. T., the only exception being in 1 Macc. xii, 36, where 'mount' is put for ὕψος, probably a mound, as we should now say, or embankment, by which Simon cut off the communication between the citadel on the Temple mount and the town of Jerusalem. For this Josephus [*Ant*. xiii, 5, 11] has τεῖχος, a wall" [Smith]. See FORTIFICATION. Another term, designating an individual mountain, is בָּמָה, *bamah'*, a *height* or "high place;" generally a lesser eminence, like גִּבְעָה, *gibah'*, a "hill," etc.). The term often occurs in connection with a proper name, or as the specific title of some particular mountain, e. g. Mount Sinai, Mount Tabor, Mount Lebanon,

Mount of Olives, etc., which see in their alphabetical order. The phrase "mountain of God" (הַר הָאֱלֹהִים) is spoken of Mount Sinai, as the place where the law was given (Exod. iii, 1; iv, 27; xviii, 5); of Mount Zion (Psa. xxiv, 2; Isa. ii, 3), which is also often called *God's holy mountain* (mostly הַר קָדְשִׁי and קָדְשׁוֹ, "mountain of my" or "his holiness," the suffix referring to God, as if immediately annexed to the former noun, or perhaps to be rendered correctly, "mountain of my *sanctuary*") (Isa. xi, 9; lvi, 7; lvii, 13; Psa. ii, 6; xv, 1; xliii, 3; Obad. 16; Ezek. xx, 40), more fully "mountain of the Lord's house" (Isa. ii, 2); of the mountain of Bashan (Psa. lxviii, 16), as being very high; also in the plur. of the Holy Land itself, as being generally mountainous (Isa. xiv, 25; xlix, 11; lxv, 9). See Walch, *De deo Ebræorum montano* (Gen. 1746). The term is also used collectively, "mountains," i. q. *mountainous region*, e. g. of Seir (Josh. xiv, 12), of Judah (Josh. xv, 48), etc.; and especially (with the art. הָהָר, *the mountain, κατ' ἐξοχήν*) of the high mountainous tract extending nearly through Palestine, between the plain on the sea-coast and the valley of the Jordan (Gen. xii, 8; Josh. ix, 1); or more specifically "the mountains of Judah," i. e. the same tract south of Jerusalem (Numb. xiii, 29; Deut. i, 2); the "hill-country" (ὀρεινή) of Luke i, 39; also the mountainous region east of the Dead Sea (Gen. xiv, 20; xix, 17, 19, 30). See Macfarlane, *Mountains of the Bible* (Lond. 1848, 1856). See HILL.

Palestine is a hilly country (Deut. iii, 25; xi, 11; Ezek. xxxiv, 13; comp. Exod. xv, 17; 1 Kings xx, 23; see Hasselquist, *Trav.* p. 148), divided into two natural portions by the deep depression of the Jordan from north to south. The mountain ranges which overspread it are connected on the north with Lebanon. *East* of the Jordan, Antilebanon terminates with the spur called Jebel Heish, a fruitful hilly district extending westward thence to the abrupt margin of the Sea of Gennesareth; while south of the intersection of the country from east to west by the river Hieromax the hills rear themselves afresh for several leagues, being traversed by wadys (watercourses) which run towards the Jordan, and interrupted by ravines and narrow passes, and continue in the form of moderately high, fertile plateaus, that do not clearly descend to a level till they reach the River Arnon, the boundary of the ancient transjordanic territory; southward of the deep, rocky vale of this stream, which was the key of Palestine in this region from the east, they still stretch away in connection with the mountains of Arabia Petræa, this entire chain sloping eastward, first into the fruitful meadows of the modern Hauran, and farther south into the Arabian desert, but westward bounded by rocky steeps along the Jordan (Volney, *Trav.* i, 226). *West* of the Jordan, a mountainous region extends from Lebanon and Antilebanon far down southwesterly into Galilee, where in the south-west, opposite Ptolemais, it ends in a ridge, terminating beyond the Kishon in the promontory of Carmel; while in the interior among the highlands it forms the high plain of Jezreel, and on the east descends by a series of terraces to the Sea of Gennesareth: this portion contains its most fruitful districts, endowed with a rich Alpine vegetation, for although the northern and north-western parts are mostly inclement, and their cultivation almost impossible, especially in the rocky tracts, yet the south-western section is an alternation of fine valleys and choice pasture-lands (Hasselquist, p. 176). From the elevated plain of Jezreel, or Esdraelon, rises the almost isolated peak of Tabor, as a limit of the northern mountain-chain on this side of Jordan. Southerly this plain is shut in by hills, which, in moderate heights and in directions only lately accurately investigated by Robinson, overspread the greater part of ancient Samaria; beyond this growing more precipitous and rocky (Maundrell, *Trav.* p. 88; Volney, *Trav.* ii, 225 sq.), although they are everywhere interspersed with fruitful valleys and plains. The moun-

tain ranges, which only admit communication with the sea-side by means of the intersecting passes and ravines, extend into Judæa several miles north of Jerusalem, and cover the greater part of this division of Palestine likewise, the hills becoming higher south of the metropolis. Stretching towards the south-east, they terminate in steep walls near the Dead Sea, and so join the sides of the deep Arabah; but in the south-west they somewhat abruptly bound the (tolerably high) hilly plain el-Tîh, which connects Palestine with Arabia Petræa. Westerly the mountains of middle and southern Palestine nowhere extend to the sea, but gently slope into plains, which grow continually wider farther south; towards the Jordan, however, they fall off ruggedly into the Ghor (Volney, *Trav.* i, 226), only at Jericho leaving a large amphitheatre-like level. Their greatest expansion from east to west is nowhere more than ten to fifteen miles, and in the vicinity of Hebron scarcely more than seven miles (Volney, *Trav.* ii, 243). The principal composition of all the Palestinian hills is limestone (of the Jura formation), occasionally with strata of chalk (whence the numerous caves), and, as is a frequent accompaniment of this latter, the hilly levels, especially in the east, are strewn with flint stones (see Schubert, *Reise,* iii, 108). Only in the north-east, from the boundaries of the Lebanon formation to the Hieromax, extends a basaltic region (Seetzen, xviii, 335), which has scattered its columns and blocks as far as the western shore of the Sea of Gennesareth (comp. Ritter, *Erdk.* ii, 315; Richter, *Wallfahrt,* p. 60; Schubert, *Reise,* iii, 222, 237, 260). At the southern extremity of the Dead Sea a salt-mountain uplifts itself, about three leagues in extent. The height of the mountains of Palestine is not great (Hasselquist, *Trav.* p. 148), but has only been measured by the barometer. The southern hills rise to a perpendicular elevation of about 2400 feet, and run at this elevation as far northward as Shechem; above this they sink to about 1750 feet, and grow still more insignificant towards the plain of Jezreel. Northward of this, the land of Galilee becomes again more lofty, especially in comparison with the Sea of Gennesareth, which lies 535 feet below the level of the Mediterranean (Schubert, iii, 231). The altitude of Lebanon is estimated at 10,000 feet. The mountains of Gilead are higher than the cisjordanic, being about 3000 to 4000 feet in height. (See Raumer, *Beiträge z. bibl. Geographie,* p. 12 sq.; Reland, *Palæst.* p. 346.) For particular hills, see CARMEL; EPHRAIM; LEBANON; OLIVET; TABOR, etc. The mountainous regions of Palestine not only served the inhabitants as places of defence against hostile incursions and of refuge from oppressive masters, but the hills by careful cultivation and terracing nearly doubled the arable soil (Prov. xxvii, 25; Psa. cxlvii, 8; Cant. viii, 14; Jer. xxi, 5; 2 Chron. xxvi, 10; Ezek. xxxiv, 14; Joel iii, 18, etc.); although quarries were but seldom opened in them for building-stone, and as it seems never mined for the supply of metals. See PALESTINE.

The frequent occurrence throughout the Scriptures of personification of the natural features of the country is very remarkable. With perhaps four exceptions, all these terms are used in our own language; but, in addition, we speak of the "crown," the "instep," the "foot," the "toe," and the "breast" or "bosom" of a mountain or hill. "Top" is perhaps only a corruption of *kopf,* "head." Similarly we speak of the "mouth" and the "gorge" (i. e. the "throat") of a ravine, and a "tongue" of land. Compare, too, the word *col,* "neck," in French. The following are, it is believed, all the words used with this object in relation to mountains or hills:

1. HEAD, רֹאשׁ, *rôsh,* Gen. viii, 5; Exod. xix, 20; Deut. xxxiv, 1; 1 Kings xviii, 42; (A. V. "top").

2. EARS, אַזְנוֹת, *aznôth,* in Aznoth-Tabor, Josh. xix, 34; possibly in allusion to some projection on the top

of the mountain. The same word is perhaps found in UZZEN-SHERAH.

3. SHOULDER, כָּתֵף, kathêph, in Deut. xxiii, 12; Josh. xv, 8, and xviii, 16 ("side"); all referring to the hills on or among which Jerusalem is placed. Josh. xv, 10, "the side of Mount Jearim."

4. SIDE, צַד, tsad (see the word for the "side" of a man in 2 Sam. ii, 16; Ezek. iv, 4, etc.), used in reference to a mountain in 1 Sam. xxiii, 26; 2 Sam. xiii, 34.

5. LOINS or FLANKS, כְּסָלֹת, kislôth, in Chisloth-Tabor, Josh. xix, 12. It occurs also in the name of a village, probably situated on this part of the mountain, Hak-Kesulloth, הַכְּסֻלּוֹת, i. e. the "loins" (Josh. xix, 18). See CHESULLOTH.

6. RIB, צֵלָע, tsêla, only used once, in speaking of the Mount of Olives, 2 Sam. xvi, 13, and there translated "side," ἐκ πλευρᾶς τοῦ ὄρους.

7. BACK, שְׁכֶם, shekém, probably the root of the name of the town Shechem, which may be derived from its situation, as it were on the back of Gerizim.

8. THIGH, יַרְכָּה, yerkeáh (see the word for the "thigh" of a man in Judg. iii, 16, 21), applied to Mount Ephraim, Judg. xix, 1, 18; and to Lebanon, 2 Kings xix, 23; Isa. xxxvii, 24; used also for the "sides" of a cave, 1 Sam. xxiv, 3.

9. The word translated "covert" in 1 Sam. xxv, 20 is סֵתֶר, séther, from סָתַר, "to hide," and probably refers to the shrubbery or thicket through which Abigail's path lay. In this passage "hill" should be "mountain."

The Chaldee טוּר, túr, is the name still given to the Mount of Olives, the Jebel et-Túr.

See the Appendix to professor Stanley's Sinai and Palestine, § 23, also p. 249 and 338, note. See TOPOGRAPHICAL TERMS.

In the symbolical language of Scripture, if the allegory or figurative representation is taken from the heavens, the luminaries denote the governing body; if from an animal, the head or horns; if from the earth, a mountain or fortress—and in this case the capital city or residence of the governor is taken for the supreme power. (See Wemyss, Clavis Symbolica, p. 309–316.) When David says, "Lord, by thy favor thou hast made my mountain to stand strong" (Psa. xxx, 7), he means to express the stability of his kingdom. In like manner the kingdom of the Messiah is described under the figure of a mountain (Isa. ii, 2; xi, 9; Dan. ii, 35), and its universality by its being the resort of all nations, and by its filling the whole earth. The mystic mountains in the Apocalypse denote kingdoms and states subverted to make room for the Messiah's kingdom (Rev. vi, 14; xvi, 20; comp. Psa. xlvi, 2). The Chaldæan monarchy is described as a mountain in Jer. li, 25; Zech. iv, 7; and the Targum illustrates the idea by substituting the word "fortress" in the former text. In this view, then, a mountain is the symbol of a kingdom, or of a capital city with its domains, or of a king, which is the same. Mountains are frequently used to signify places of strength, of what kind soever, and to whatsoever use applied (Jer. iii, 23). Eminences were very commonly chosen for the sites of pagan temples: these became places of asylum, and were looked upon as the fortresses and defenders of the worshippers, by reason of the presence of the false deities in them. On this account mountains were the strongholds of paganism, and therefore in several parts of Scripture they signify idolatrous temples and places of worship (Jer. ii, 23; Ezek. vi, 2–6; Mic. iv, 1; comp. Deut. xii, 2; Jer. ii, 20; iii, 16; Ezek. vi, 3). These temples were also built like forts or towers, as appears from Judg. ix, 46; xlviii, 49. (See Gesenius, Comment. on Isa. ii, 316 sq.; Gramberg, Die Religionsideen des A. T. pref. p. xv sq.) See HIGH PLACE. For the various eminences or mountain districts to which the word har is applied in the O. T., see ABARIM; AMANA; OF THE AMALEKITES; OF THE AMORITES; ARARAT; BAALAH; BAAL-HERMON; BASHAN; BETHEL; BETHER; CARMEL; EBAL; EPHRAIM; EPHRON; ESAU; GAASH; GERIZIM; GILBOA; GILEAD; HALAK; HERES; HERMON; HOR; and for those to which tor is prefixed, see HOREB; ISRAEL; JEARIM; JUDAH; MIZAR; MORIAH; NAPHTALI; NEBO; OLIVET, or OLIVES; PARAN; PERAZIM; SAMARIA; SEIR; SEPHAR; SHAPHER; SINAI; SION, SIRION, or SHENIR (all names for Hermon); TABOR; ZALMON; ZEMARAIM; ZION.

MOUNT (Isa. xxix, 3; Jer. vi, 6, etc.). See SIEGE.

MOUNT OF THE AM'ALEKITES (הַר הָעֲמָלֵקִי; Sept. ὄρος τοῦ Ἀμαλήκ; Vulg. Mons Amalech), a place near Pirathon, in the tribe of Ephraim (Judg. xii, 15), apparently so called from some branch of that Canaanitish clan settled there (comp. Judg. v, 14, מִנִּי אֶפְרַיִם שָׁרְשָׁם בַּעֲמָלֵק, from Ephraim [came those] whose seat [was] by Amalek, A.V. "out of Ephraim was there a root of them against Amalek"). See AMALEKITE.

MOUNTAIN OF THE AM'ORITES (הַר הָאֱמֹרִי; Sept. ὄρος τοῦ Ἀμορραίου; Vulg. Mons Amorrhæi), specifically mentioned, Deut. i, 19, 20 (comp. 44), in reference to the wandering of the Israelites in the desert. It seems to be the range which rises abruptly from the plateau of et-Tih, running from a little S. of W. to the N. of E., and of which the extremities are the Jebel Araif en-Nakah westward, and Jebel el-Mukrah eastward, and from which line the country continues mountainous all the way to Hebron. See AMORITE. The particular spot where the Israelites encountered it seems to have been at the present Nukb es-Sufeh. See EXODE.

MOUNT OF THE CONGREGATION (הַר מוֹעֵד, mountain of the assembly, namely, of the gods), a place mentioned in the words of the king of Babylon, Isa. xiv, 13, called "mount of the congregation," is prob. the Persian mountain el-Burj (comp. Gr. πύργος, a town, Germ. burg), called by the Hindûs Meru, situated in the extreme north, and, like the Greek Olympus, regarded by the Orientals as the seat of the gods (see Asiat. Researches, vi, 448; viii, 350 sq.; Hyde, De relig. Persar. p. 102). See CONGREGATION.

MOUNT OF CORRUPTION (2 Kings xxiii, 13). See CORRUPTION.

MOUNT EPHRAIM. See EPHRAIM.

MOUNT LEBANON, CHRISTIANS OF. See MARONITES.

MOUNT OLIVET, CONGREGATION OF. See MONT-OLIVETIANS.

MOUNT OF PIETY. See MONTES PIETATIS.

MOUNT OF THE VALLEY (הַר הָעֵמֶק; Sept. ὁ ὄρος Ἐνάθ v. r. Ἐνάκ; Vulg. Mons convallis), a district on the east of Jordan, within the territory allotted to Reuben (Josh. xiii, 19), containing a number of towns, such as Heshbon, Dibon, etc. The "valley" in question appears to have been the Ghor, or that of the Jordan (ver. 27); and hence the "mount" indicated was doubtless the hilly region immediately adjoining the northern end of the Dead Sea, where the towns mentioned were situated.

Mountagu(e) [or Montagu(e)], RICHARD, a learned English prelate, distinguished for his knowledge of primitive Christianity, was born at Dorney, Buckinghamshire, April 13, 1578, and was educated at Eton and at King's College, Cambridge University, of which he was afterwards a fellow. He took holy orders, and quickly rose to distinction. In 1617 he was made archdeacon of Hereford, in 1620 canon of Windsor, and in 1628 was elevated to the episcopate and made bishop of Chichester. In 1638 he was transferred to the see of Norwich. He was an ardent friend of archbishop Laud, and thus was led to write against the Puritans, and to defend the cause of the king and his sacerdotal companion. He therefore became a favorite at court, and the transfer to Norwich is said to have been prompted by Laud, who wished to acknowledge the valuable services of Mountague. Unfortunately, however, this prelate was not only an opponent to Puritanism, but a leaner towards Romanism; and it was even asserted by the moderate churchmen who opposed Laud's course that Mountague was aiming to carry the king, his court and his primate, bodily over to Rome, and to go there himself. He was also a devoted Arminianist, and thus the Calvinists likewise upbraided him, and left no opportunity unimproved against him. He died at Norwich, April 13, 1641. Bishop Mountague's literary labors are valuable, especially in the field of ecclesiastical antiquities. He assisted Savile in his edition of St. Chrysostom; edited Gregory Nazianzen's *In Julianum Invectivæ Duæ*, etc., also *Photi Epistolæ*, and *Eusebii Demonstratio*, and published several learned theological works and controversial tracts. Among the former are, *Analecta Ecclesiasticarum Exercitationum* (Lond. 1622):—*Apparatus ad Origines Ecclesiasticas* (Oxf. 1635, fol.):—*De Originibus Ecclesiasticis*, etc. (Lond. 1636, fol. 1641):—*De Vita Christi Originum Ecclesiasticarum, pars posterior* (1640): —*The Acts and Monuments of the Church before Christ Incarnate* (1642, fol.)—contents: State of the Church before Christ Incarnate; the Prophecies of Jacob and Daniel concerning Messias; the Sibyls; Reign of Herod in Judæa; State of Judæa under the Romans; the Succession of the High-priesthood; State of the Jews in Spirituals; their Heroes; the Ancestors and Parents of our Saviour. In 1841, 12mo, appeared bishop Mountague's *Articles of Inquiry*, with a *Memoir* (q. v.). See *Gen. Dict.* s. v.; *Biog. Brit.* s. v.; Fuller's *Worthies* and his *Church Hist.* bk. xi; Heylin, *Life of Archbishop Laud*, bk. ii; Harwood, *Alumni Etonenses*; Hallam, *Constit. Hist. of Eng.* (7th ed. 1854), ii, 62, 69, 70; Collier, *Eccles. Hist.* viii, 7 sq. (J. H. W.)

Mountain. See MOUNT.

Mountain, George Jehoshaphat, a noted American ecclesiastic, son of the following, was born in Norwich, England, July 27, 1789, and was educated at Trinity College, Cambridge, where he graduated in 1810. He entered holy orders in 1813, and was appointed evening lecturer in his father's cathedral. In 1814 he was nominated rector of Fredericton, New Brunswick, and in 1817 rector of Quebec and bishop's official. In 1821 he became archdeacon, and in 1825, during a mission to England, he received the degree of D.D. On his return, bishop Stuvard appointed him his examining chaplain, and in 1835 he was sent to England on business connected with the question of the clergy reserves. While there he was appointed bishop of Montreal, and given the entire charge of the Episcopal Church in Lower Canada. He continued to administer the dioceses of Quebec and Montreal till 1850, when he assumed the title of bishop of Quebec. In 1844 he visited the missions on Red River, and furnished a description of his journeys in *Songs of the Wilderness* (Lond. 1846). He died in Quebec, Jan. 8, 1863. He was the founder of Bishop's College, Lennoxville, and of the Church Society, spending most of his income for these institutions and for charitable purposes. Some time before his death he declined the dignity of metropolitan of Canada. He published *Sermons* and *Addresses*, and a *Journal of a North-west American Mission* (Lond. 1843). See *Am. Church Rev.* 1863, p. 156.

Mountain, Jacob, an Anglican prelate, was born in Norfolk, England, in 1750. He was a descendant of the celebrated Montaigne; his own grandfather was a great-grandson of the French essayist, and was exiled from France during the revocation of the Edict of Nantes. Mountain was educated at Caius College, Cambridge, class of 1774, became fellow in 1779, and, entering holy orders, held important livings in England, among them those of St. Andrew's, Norwich, of Buckden, and of Holbeach, as well as a stall in Lincoln Cathe-

dral. Mr. Pitt was intimately acquainted with him, and that statesman interested himself in the ecclesiastical promotion of his friend, so that in 1793 Mr. Mountain was made bishop of Quebec. He was the first Protestant prelate in the Canadas. He died near Quebec, June 16, 1825. "Bishop Mountain promoted the formation of missions and the erection of churches in all the more populous townships, which he regularly visited—even when age and infirmity rendered so vast and fatiguing a circuit a most arduous and painful undertaking."

Mountain-Men. See MEN, THE; SCOTLAND, CHURCH OF.

Mourges, MATHIEU. See MORGUES.

Mourgues, MICHEL, a French Jesuit noted for his profound erudition, was born at Auvergne about 1642. He became royal professor of mathematics and rhetoric in the Academy of Toulouse, and died there in 1713. Among his best works are, *A Parallel between Christian Morality and that of the Ancient Philosophers:—An Explanation of the Theology of the Pythagoreans;* and others of a secular character. See Feller, *Dict. historique*, s. v.; Moréri, *Grand Dict. Hist.* s. v.

Mourn (represented by numerous Heb. and several Gr. words). Orientals are much more demonstrative in the signs of grief than natives of Western countries, as is evinced especially by two marked features: *a.* What may be called its studied *publicity*, and the careful observance of the prescribed ceremonies. Thus Abraham, after the death of Sarah, came, as it were in state, to mourn and weep for her (Gen. xxiii, 2). Job, after his misfortunes, "arose, and rent his mantle (*meil*), and shaved his head, and fell down upon the ground on the ashes" (Job i, 20; ii, 8); and in like manner his friends "rent every one his mantle, and sprinkled dust upon their heads, and sat down with him on the ground seven days and seven nights" without speaking (ii, 12, 13). We read also of high places, streets, and house-tops as places especially chosen for mourning, not only by Jews, but by other nations (Isa. xv, 3; Jer. iii, 21; xlviii, 38; 1 Sam. xi, 4; xxx, 4; 2 Sam. xv, 30). *b.* The comparative *violence* of Oriental mourning—oftentimes, indeed, assumed for effect, and even at times artificial or venal, is evident in several of the forms which Eastern grief assumes. Many of these acts, of course, as being natural, are common to all times and countries, but others are somewhat peculiar. Most of them are spontaneous, being simply the uncontrollable language of emotion; others are purely matters of habit. Yet both these classes of manifestation have their significance and uses, and are not therefore altogether arbitrary. It is not difficult, however, to ascertain the philosophy of mourning. Potter thinks that it consisted in receding as much as possible from ordinary customs and manners, in token that an extraordinary event had happened, and observes that such is the diversity of human customs that the signs of mourning in some nations coincide with those of joy in others (*Archæologia Græca* [Lond. 1775], ii, 194, 195). Although, no doubt, many modes of mourning are conventional, and originated in caprice, yet there would seem to be physical reasons for certain forms which have so widely and permanently prevailed. We will endeavor to digest the information furnished on this subject by the Scriptures, and contemporaneous as well as modern writers, referring to other articles for details on minor or collateral particulars. See Geier, *De Ebræorum Luctu* (2d ed. Lips. 1666). Comp. GRIEF.

I. Occasions.—1. Instances of mourning for the *dead* are most numerous in Scripture. Abraham mourns for Sarah (Gen. xxiii, 2); Jacob for Joseph (Gen. xxxvii, 34, 35); the Egyptians for Jacob (Gen. l, 3–10); the house of Israel for Aaron (Numb. xx, 29), for Moses (Deut. xxxiv, 8), and for Samuel (1 Sam. xxv, 1); David for Abner (2 Sam. iii, 31, 35); Mary and Martha for their brother Lazarus (John xi); and "devout men" for Stephen (Acts viii, 2). These are a few examples out of many. See BURIAL.

2. Instances of mourning on account of *calamities* are not few; for example, Job under his multiplied afflictions (Job i, 20, 21; ii, 8); Israel under the threatening of the divine displeasure (Exod. xxxiii, 4); the Ninevites in view of menaced destruction (Jonah iii, 5); the tribes of Israel when defeated by Benjamin (Judg. xx, 26), and many others. The Lamentations of Jeremiah are illustrative of this point.

3. Mourning in *repentance* is illustrated by the case of the Ninevites adduced above; by the Israelites on the day of atonement, latterly called the fast (Lev. xxiii, 27; Acts xxvii, 9), and under the faithful preaching of Samuel (1 Sam. vii, 6); by many references in the Psalms, and the predicted mourning in Zechariah (Zech. xii, 10, 11). On the mourning for Adonis (Ezek. viii, 14), see TAMMUZ.

II. *Modes.*—1. *Weeping* appears either as one chief expression of mourning, or as the general name for it. Hence when Deborah, Rebecca's nurse, was buried at Bethel under an oak, the tree was then at least called Allon-bachuth, the oak of weeping (Gen. xxxv, 8). The children of Israel were heard to weep by Moses throughout their families, every man in the door of his tent (Numb. xi, 10; comp. xiv, 1; xxv, 6). So numerous are the references to tears in the Scriptures as to give the impression that the Orientals had them nearly at command (comp. Psa. vi, 6). The woman washed our Lord's feet with her tears (Luke vii, 38; comp. Ecclus. xxviii, 17). Men, as well as women, wept freely, and even aloud. "Lifted up his voice and wept" is an ordinary mode of expression. Giving vent to them is well known to be one of the physical alleviations of profound sorrow. It is so universal a sign of mourning that we need not detain the reader with further instances or illustrations, except to remark that the Egyptian monuments have not failed to depict the tears upon the faces of mourners. See WEEPING.

2. *Loud lamentation* is usually and naturally associated with weeping as a sign of grief (Ruth i, 9; 1 Sam. ii, 4; 2 Sam. iii, 31; xiii, 36). Nor are Orientals content with mere sobs: their excitableness appears in howls for grief, even amid the solemnities of worship (Joel i, 13; Mic. i, 8, etc.). The Egyptians have ever been renowned for the vociferation of their grief; "there was a great cry in Egypt at the death of the first-born" (Exod. xii, 30). Crying aloud certainly diverts the attention from anguish of mind or body, and the value of moans and shrieks is well known in severe surgical operations. But in addition to the wail of woe by the immediate bereaved, hired performers were often engaged to swell the lamentation with screams and noisy utterances; and this not merely at the funeral, but immediately after the decease. The first reference to professional mourners occurs in Eccles. xii, 5: "The mourners (הַסּוֹפְדִים) go about the streets." (The root of this word, observes Gesenius, signifies "a mournful noise," and he adduces Mic. i, 8; Jer. xxii, 18; xxxiv, 5). They are certainly alluded to in Jer. ix, 17–20: "the mourning women" (probably widows; comp. Psa. lxxviii, 64; Acts ix, 39). Another reference to them occurs in 2 Chron. xxxv, 25 (comp. Josephus, *War*, iii, 9, 5). The greater number of the mourners in ancient Egypt were women, as in the modern East. Mourning for the dead in the East was conducted in a tumultuous manner (Mark v, 38). Even devout men made great lamentations (Acts viii, 2). Akin to this usage was the custom for friends or passers-by to join in the lamentations of bereaved or afflicted persons (Gen. l, 3; Judg. xi, 40; Job ii, 11; xxx, 25; xxvii, 15; Psa. lxxviii, 64; Jer. ix, 1; xxii, 18; 1 Kings xiv, 13, 18; 1 Chron. vii, 22; 2 Chron. xxxv, 24, 25; Zech. xii, 11; Luke vii, 12; John xi, 31; Acts viii, 2; ix, 89; Rom. xii, 15). So also in times of general sorrow we find large numbers of persons joining in passionate expressions of grief (Judg.

ii, 4; xx, 26; 1 Sam. xxviii, 3; xxx, 4; 2 Sam. i, 12; Ezra iii, 13; Ezek. vii, 16; and the like is mentioned of the priests—Joel ii, 17; Mal. ii, 13). Clamor in grief is referred to by Job (xix, 7; xx, 28): it is considered a wicked man's portion that his widow shall not weep at his death (xxvii, 15). Upon Job's recovery from his afflictions, all his relatives and acquaintances bemoan and comfort him concerning his past sufferings; which seems to have been a kind of congratulatory mourning, indulged in order to heighten the pleasures of prosperity by recalling associations of adversity (xlii, 11). See LAMENTATION.

3. *Personal Disfigurement.*—In all the other acts expressive of grief the idea of self-mortification seems to prevail, whether by injuries to the person or neglect of it, by mean clothing, by unusual and humiliating attitudes, or other marks of individual abasement, intended chiefly for the public eye. Some of the more violent forms have perhaps a natural, if not a remedial or alleviating character. Shaving the head may be a dictate of nature to relieve the excited brain. Plucking the hair is well calculated to assuage the action of some particular organs, to which the sensations of the individual may be a sufficient guide. Beating the breast may relieve the heart, oppressed with a tumultuous circulation. Cutting may be the effect of nature's indication of bleeding. Tearing and rending seem to palliate nervous irritation, etc. But the greater part of the practices under this head have their origin in custom, or some supposed fitness to a state of grief. Among the particular forms observed the following may be mentioned:

a. Rending the clothes (Gen. xxxvii, 29, 34; xliv, 13; 2 Chron. xxxiv, 27; Isa. xxxvi, 22; Jer. xxxvi, 24 [where the absence of the form is to be noted]; xli, 5; 2 Sam. iii, 31; xv, 32; Josh. vii, 6; Joel ii, 13; Ezra ix, 5; 2 Kings v, 7; xi, 14; Matt. xxvi, 65, ἱμάτιον; Mark xiv, 63, χιτών). See CLOTHING.

b. Dressing in sackcloth (Gen. xxxvii, 34; 2 Sam. iii, 31; xxi, 10; Psa. xxxv, 13; Isa. xxxvii, 1; Joel i, 8, 13; Amos viii, 10; Jonah iii, 8, man and beast; Job xvi, 15; Esth. iv, 3, 4; Jer. vi, 26; Lam. ii, 10; 1 Kings xxi, 27). See SACKCLOTH.

c. Ashes, dust, or earth sprinkled on the person (2 Sam. xiii, 19; xv, 32; Josh. vii, 6; Esth. iv, 1, 3; Jer. vi, 26; Job ii, 12; xvi, 15; xlii, 6; Isa. lxi, 3; Rev. xviii, 19). See ASHES.

d. Black or sad-colored garments (2 Sam. xiv, 2; Jer. viii, 21; Psa. xxxviii, 6; xlii, 9; xliii, 2; Mal. iii, 14, marg.). See COLOR.

e. Removal of ornaments or neglect of person (Deut. xxi, 12, 13; Exod. xxxiii, 4; 2 Sam. xiv, 2; xix, 24; Ezek. xxvi, 16; Dan. x, 3; Matt. vi, 16, 17). See NAIL.

f. Shaving the head, plucking out the hair of the head or beard (Lev. x, 6; 2 Sam. xix, 24; Ezra ix, 3; Job i, 20; Jer. vii, 29; xvi, 6). See HAIR.

g. Laying bare some part of the body: Isaiah himself naked and barefoot (Isa. xx, 2), the Egyptian and Ethiopian captives (ib. ver. 4; xlvii, 2; 1, 6; Jer. xiii, 22, 26; Nah. iii, 5; Mic. i, 11; Amos viii, 10). See NAKED.

h. Fasting or abstinence in meat and drink (2 Sam. i, 12; iii, 35; xii, 16, 22; 1 Sam. xxxi, 13; Ezra x, 6; Neh. i, 4; Dan. x, 3; vi, 18; Joel i, 14; ii, 12; Ezek. xxiv, 17; Zech. vii, 5, a periodical fast during captivity; 1 Kings xxi, 9, 12; Isa. lviii, 3, 4, 5; xxiv, 7, 9, 11; Mal. iii, 14; Jer. xxxvi, 9; Jonah iii, 5, 7 [of Nineveh]; Judg. xx, 26; 2 Chron. xx, 3; Ezra viii, 21; Matt. ix, 14, 15). See FASTING.

i. In the same direction, diminution in offerings to God, and prohibition to partake in sacrificial food (Lev. vii, 20; Deut. xxvi, 14; Hos. ix, 4; Joel i, 9, 13, 16).

k. Covering the "upper lip," i. e. the lower part of the face, and sometimes the head, in token of silence; specially in the case of the leper (Lev. xiii, 45; 2 Sam. xv, 30; xix, 4; Jer. xiv, 4; Ezek. xxiv, 17; Mic. iii, 7).

l. Cutting the flesh (Jer. xvi, 6, 7; xli, 5). See CUTTING (in the flesh).

m. The sitting or lying posture in silence indicative of grief (Gen. xxiii, 3; Judg. xx, 26; 2 Sam. xii, 16; xiii, 31; Job i, 20; ii, 13; Ezra ix, 3; Lam. ii, 10; Isa. iii, 26); also bowing down the head (Lam. ii, 10), and lifting up the hands (Psa. cxli, 2; Lam. i, 17; Ezra ix, 5). See ATTITUDE.

Mourning at Grave, with uplifted hands.

Some of these outward expressions of mourning were usual among the heathen, but forbidden to the Israelits, e. g. making cuttings in the flesh (Lev. xix, 28), which seems to have been a custom of the votaries of Baal (1 Kings xviii, 28); "making baldness between the eyes for the dead" (Deut. xiv, 1), i. e. shaving the eyebrows and eyelids, and the fore-part of the head, which was, no doubt, an idolatrous custom. The priests were forbidden to "defile themselves for the dead" by any outward expression of mourning, except for their near relatives (Lev. xxi, 1); and the high-priest even for these (Lev. xxi, 10, 11), under which restriction Nazarites also came (Numb. vi, 7).

4. *Formal Celebrations.* — Besides and in connection with the funeral there were certain still more public usages indicative of grief, as noticed in the Scriptures:

(1.) Mourning for the dead in the earliest times was confined to the relatives and friends of the deceased; but in later times hired mourners, both men and women, were employed. Thus we are told that the "singing men and singing women spake of Josiah in their lamentations" (2 Chron. xxxv, 25). In accordance with this the Lord says to the Jews, when threatening heavy judgments for their sins—judgments calling for universal mourning: "Call for the mourning women that they may come, . . . let them make haste, and take up a wailing for us" (Jer. ix, 17). At first, most probably, hired mourners were called in to help to swell the tide of real sorrow, but afterwards they became a mere formal pageant, demanded by pride and custom rather than sorrow. (See above.) Mourning for the dead became a profession, learned and paid for, like any other; and the practice of it often became very boisterous and tumultuous. Hence we read of the "minstrels and people making a noise" in the house of Jairus (Matt. ix, 23), giving one the idea of a scene resembling an "Irish wake." See MINSTREL.

(2.) On such occasions neighbors and friends provided food for the mourners (2 Sam. iii, 35; Jer. xvi, 7; comp. Ezek. xxiv, 17); this was called "the bread of bitterness," "the cup of consolation." See Garman, *De pane lugentium* (Vitemb. 1708). In later times the Jews had a custom of giving bread to the poor at funerals, and leaving it for their use at tombs, graves, etc., which resembles the Roman *visceratio* (Tobit iv, 17; Ecclus. xxx, 8). Women went to tombs to indulge their grief (John xi, 31).

(3.) The period of mourning varied. In the case of Jacob it was seventy days (Gen. l, 3); of Aaron (Numb. xx, 29) and Moses (Deut. xxxiv, 8), thirty; a further period of seven days in Jacob's case (Gen. l, 10); seven days for Saul, which may have been an abridged period in time of national danger (1 Sam. xxxi, 13).

Excessive grief in the case of an individual may be noticed in 2 Sam. iii, 16; Jer. xxxi, 15; and the same hypocritically in Jer. xli, 6.

The first complete description of mourning for the dead occurs in 2 Sam. iii, 31–35, where David commands Joab and all the people that were with him to rend their clothes, gird themselves with sackcloth, and mourn for Abner; and David himself followed the bier, and they buried Abner in Hebron; and the king lifted up his voice and wept at the grave of Abner, and all the people wept, and David fasted two days, and wrote a lamentation for the deceased. Elegies were composed by the prophets on several disastrous occasions (Ezek. xxvi, 1–18; xxvii, 1–36; Amos v, 1, etc.). The incident of Jephthah's daughter is too uncertain to afford any index to the modes of mourning at that æra. It appears that she was allowed two months to bewail her virginity with her companions, and that the Jewish women of that country went somewhere yearly to lament or celebrate her (Judg. xi, 37–40). See JEPHTHAH.

III. *Illustrations of these Scriptural Usages from Contemporary and Later Sources.*—1. Similar practices are noticed in the Apocryphal books:

a. Weeping, fasting, rending clothes, sackcloth, ashes or earth on head (1 Macc. ii, 14; iii, 47; iv, 39; v, 14; xi, 71; xiii, 45; 2 Macc. iii, 19; x, 25; xiv, 15; Judith iv, 10, 11; viii, 5, 6; ix, 1; xiv, 19 [Assyrians]; x, 2, 3; 3 Macc. iv, 6; 2 Esdr. x, 4; Esth. xiv, 2);

b. Funeral feast with wailing (Bar. vi, 32: also Tob. iv, 17; see in reproof of the practice, Augustine, *Civ. D.* viii, 27);

c. Period of mourning (Judith viii, 6; Ecclus. xxii, 12 [seven days, so also perhaps 2 Esdr. v, 20]; Bel and Dragon, ver. 40);

d. Priests ministering in sackcloth and ashes, the altar dressed in sackcloth (Judith iv, 11, 14, 15);

e. Idol priests with clothes rent, head and beard shorn, and head bare (Bar. vi, 31).

2. In Josephus's writings, these notices are in the main confirmed, and in some cases enlarged:

a. Tearing hair and beating breast (*Ant.* xvi, 7, 5; xv, 3, 9);

b. Sackcloth and ashes (*Ant.* xx, 6, 1; xix, 8, 2; *War*, ii, 12, 5); clothes rent (ii, 15, 4);

c. Seven days' mourning for a father (*Ant.* xvii, 8, 4; *War*, ii, 1, 1); for thirty days (*War*, iii, 9, 5);

d. Those who met a funeral required to join it (*Ap.* ii, 26; see Luke vii, 12, and Rom. xii, 15);

e. Flute-players at a funeral (*War*, iii, 9, 5).

3. The Mishna prescribes seven days' mourning for a father, a mother, son, daughter, brother, sister, or wife (Bartenora, on *Moed Kat.* iii, 7). Rending garments is regularly graduated according to the degree of relationship. For a father or mother the garment was to be rent, but not with an instrument, so as to show the breast; to be sewn up roughly after thirty days, but never closed. The same for one's own teacher in the law, but for other relatives a palm breadth of the upper garment to suffice, to be sewn up roughly after seven days and fully closed after thirty days (*Moed Kat.* iii, 7; *Shabb.* xiii, 3; Carpzov, *App. Bib.* p. 650). Friendly mourners were to sit on the ground, not on the bed (see Lightfoot, *Hor. Heb.* on John xi, 19). On certain days the lamentation was to be only partial (*Moed Kat.* l. c.). For a wife there was to be at least one hired mourner and two pipers (*Ketuboth*, iv, 4).

4. When we turn to heathen writers we find similar usages prevailing among various nations of antiquity. Herodotus, speaking of the Egyptians, says, "When a man of any account dies, all the womankind among his relatives proceed to smear their heads and faces with mud. They then leave the corpse in the house, and parade the city with their breasts exposed, beating themselves as they go, and in this they are joined by all the women belonging to the family. In like manner the men also meet them from opposite quarters, naked to the waist and beating themselves" (Herod. ii, 85). He also mentions seventy days as the period of embalming (ibid. 86). This doubtless includes the whole mourning period. Diodorus, speaking of a king's death, mentions rending of garments, suspension of sacrifices, heads smeared with clay, and breasts bared, and says men and women go about in companies of 200 or 300, making a wailing twice a day, εὐρύθμως μετ' ᾠδῆς. They abstain from flesh, wheat bread, wine, the bath, dainties, and in general all pleasure; do not lie on beds, but lament as for an only child during seventy-two days. On the last day a sort of trial was held of the merits of the deceased, and, according to the verdict pronounced by the acclamations of the crowd, he was treated with funeral honors, or the contrary (Diod. Sic. i, 72). Similar usages prevailed in the case of private persons (ibid. 91, 92). The Egyptian paintings confirm these accounts as to the exposure of the person, the beating, and the throwing clay or mud upon the head; and women are represented who appear to be hired mourners (Long, Eg. Ant. ii, 154–159; Wilkinson, Anc. Eg. ii, 356–387). Herodotus also mentions the Persian custom of rending the garments with wailing, and also cutting off the hair on occasions of death or calamity. The last, he says, was also usual among the Scythians (Herod. ii, 66; viii, 99; ix, 24; iv, 71).

Lucian, in his discourse concerning Greek mourning, speaks of tearing the hair and flesh, and wailing, and beating the breast to the sound of a flute, burial of slaves, horses, and ornaments as likely to be useful to the deceased, and the practice for relatives to endeavor to persuade the parents of the deceased to partake of the funeral-feast (περίδειπνον) by way of recruiting themselves after their three days' fast (De Luctu, ii, 303, 305, 307, ed. Amsterdam). Plutarch mentions that the Greeks regarded all mourners as unclean, and that women in mourning cut their hair, but the men let it grow. Of the Romans, in carrying corpses of parents to the grave, the sons, he says, cover their heads, but the daughters uncover them, contrary to their custom in each case (Quœst. Rom. vii, 74, 82, ed. Reiske). Greeks and Romans both made use of hired mourners, prœficœ, who accompanied the funeral procession with chants or songs (Horace, Ars Poet. 429). Flowers and perfumes were also thrown on the graves (Ovid, Fast. vi, 660; Trist. v, 1, 47; Plato, Legg. vii, 9). The prœficœ seem to be the predecessors of the "mutes" of modern funerals.

5. With the practices above mentioned, modern Oriental customs in great measure agree. D'Arvieux says Arab men are silent in grief, but the women scream, tear their hair, hands, and face, and throw earth or sand on their heads. The older women wear a blue veil and an old abba by way of mourning garments. They also sing the praises of the deceased (Trav. p. 269, 270). Niebuhr says both Mohammedans and Christians in Egypt hire wailing women, and wail at stated times (Voy. i, 150). Burckhardt says the women of Atbara, in Nubia, shave their heads on the death of their nearest relatives, a custom prevalent also among several of the peasant tribes of Upper Egypt. In Barbary on a death they usually kill a sheep, a cow, or a camel. He also mentions wailing women, and a man in distress besmearing his face with dirt and dust in token of grief (Nubia, p. 176, 226, 374). Speaking of the Arab tribes of Upper Egypt, he says, "I have seen the female relations of a deceased man dance before his house with sticks and lances in their hands, and behaving like furious soldiers" (Notes

on Bed. i, 280). Shaw says of the Arabs of Barbary, after a funeral the female relations during the space of two or three months go once a week to weep over the grave and offer eatables (see Ecclus. xxx, 18). He also mentions mourning women (Trav. p. 220, 242). "In Oman," Wellsted says, "there are no hired mourning women, but the females from the neighborhood assemble after a funeral and continue for eight days, from sunrise to sunset, to utter loud lamentations" (Trav. i, 216). In the Arabian Nights are frequent allusions to similar practices, as rending clothes, throwing dust on the head, cutting off the hair, loud exclamation, visits to the tomb, plucking the hair and beard (i, 65, 263, 297, 358, 518; ii, 237, 354, 409). They also mention ten days and forty days as periods of mourning (i, 427; ii, 409). Sir J. Chardin, speaking of Persia, says the tombs are visited periodically by women (Voy. vi, 489). He speaks also of the tumult at a death (ibid. 482). Mourning lasts forty days: for eight days a fast is observed, and visits are paid by friends to the bereaved relatives; on the ninth day the men go to the bath, shave the head and beard, and return the visits, but the lamentation continues two or three times a week till the fortieth day. The mourning garments are dark-colored, but never black (ibid. 481). Russell, speaking of the Turks at Aleppo, says, "The instant the death takes place, the women who are in the chamber give the alarm by shrieking as if distracted, and are joined by all the other females in the harem. This conclamation is termed the wulwaly (Heb. יָלַל, Gr. ὀλολύζω, ἀλαλάζω, Lat. ejulo, ululo, an onomatopoetic word common to many languages. See Gesen. p. 596; Schoebel, Anal-Constit. p. 54; and Russell, vol. i, note 83, chiefly from Schultens): it is so shrill as to be heard, especially in the night, at a prodigious distance. The men disapprove of and take no share in it; they drop a few tears, assume a resigned silence, and retire in private. Some of the near female relations, when apprised of what has happened, repair to the house, and the wulwaly, which had paused for some time, is renewed upon the entrance of each visitant into the harem" (Aleppo, i, 306). He also mentions professional mourners, visits to the grave on the third, seventh, and fortieth days, prayers at the tomb, flowers strewn, and food distributed to the poor. At these visits the shriek of wailing is renewed; the chief mourner appeals to the deceased, and reproaches him fondly for his departure. The men make no change in their dress; the women lay aside their jewels, dress in their plainest garments, and wear on the head a handkerchief of a dusky color. They usually mourn twelve months for a husband and six for a father (ibid. 311, 312). Of the Jews he says the conclamation is practiced by the women, but hired mourners are seldom called in to assist at the wulwaly. Both sexes make some alteration in dress by way of mourning. The women lay aside their jewels, the men make a small rent in their outer vestment (ibid. ii, 86, 87). Lane, speaking of the modern Egyptians, says, "After death the women of the family raise cries of lamentation called welweleh or wilwal, uttering the most piercing shrieks, and calling upon the name of the deceased, 'Oh, my master! Oh, my resource! Oh, my misfortune! Oh, my glory' (see Jer. xxii, 18). The females of the neighborhood come to join with them in this conclamation: generally, also, the family send for two or more neddábehs, or public wailing women. Each brings a tambourine, and beating them they exclaim, 'Alas, for him.' The female relatives, domestics, and friends, with their hair dishevelled, and sometimes with rent clothes, beating their faces, cry in like manner, 'Alas, for him!' These make no alteration in dress, but women, in some cases, dye their dress, head-veils, and handkerchiefs of a dark-blue color. They visit the tombs at stated periods" (Mod. Eg. iii, 152, 171, 195). Wealthy families in Cairo have in the burial-grounds regularly furnished houses of mourning, to which the females repair at stated periods to bewail their dead.

The art of mourning is only to be acquired by long practice, and regular professors of it are usually hired on the occasion of a death by the wealthier classes (Mrs. Poole, *Englishw. in Egypt*, ii, 100). Dr. Wolff mentions the wailing over the dead in Abyssinia (*Autobiog.* ii, 273). Pietro della Valle mentions a practice among the Jews of burning perfumes at the site of Abraham's tomb at Hebron (see 2 Chron. xvi, 14; xxi, 19; Jer. xxxiv, 5; P. della Valle, *Viaggi*, i, 306).

The customs of the North American Indians also resemble those which have been described in many particulars, as the howling and wailing, and speeches to the dead; among some tribes the practice of piercing the flesh with arrows or sharp stones, visits to the place of the dead (Carver, *Travels*, p. 401; Bancroft, *Hist. of the United States*, ii, 912; Catlin, *N. A. Indians*, i, 90). The former and present customs of the Welsh, Irish, and Highlanders at funerals may also be cited as similar in several respects, e. g. wailing and howling, watching with the corpse, funeral entertainments ("funeral baked meats"), flowers on the grave, days of visiting the grave (Brand, *Pop. Antiq.* ii, 128, etc.; Harmer, *Obs.* iii, 40).

One of the most remarkable instances of traditional customary lamentation is found in the weekly wailing of the Jews at Jerusalem at a spot as near to the Temple as could be obtained. See JERUSALEM. This custom, noticed by St. Jerome, is alluded to by Benjamin of Tudela, and exists to the present day. (Jerome, *Ad Sophon.* i, 15; *Ad Paulam*, Ep. xxxix; *Early Trav. in Pal.* p. 83; Raumer, *Palästina*, p. 293; Martineau, *Eastern Life*, p. 471; Robinson, i, 237.) See FUNERAL.

MOURNING, CHRISTIAN.—Among the early Christians all immoderate grief for the dead was considered inconsistent with Christian hope; and hence the custom which prevailed among the Jews and Romans of hiring women to make lamentation at funerals was severely reprobated. There was not, however, the indulgence of any stoical apathy, but a becoming sorrow was evinced by Christians. Strong disapprobation of the practice of wearing black is expressed by some of the fathers; nevertheless it became prevalent, especially in the East. Some Christians imitated the heathen custom of repeating the mourning on the third, seventh, and ninth days, and some even added others. In the *Apostolical Constitutions*, the author takes notice of the repetition of this funeral-office on the third, ninth, and fortieth days; he says: "Let the third day be observed for the dead with psalms and lessons and prayers, because Christ on the third day rose again from the dead; and let the ninth be observed in remembrance of the living and the dead; and also the fortieth day, according to the ancient manner of the Israelites' mourning for Moses forty days." On the anniversary days of commemorating the dead they were accustomed to make a common feast or entertainment, inviting both clergy and people, but especially the poor, the widows and orphans, that it might be not only a memorial to the dead, but, according to Origen, "an odor of a sweet smell to God." See FUNERAL.

MOURNING-WEEDS, a particular dress worn during a certain period to express grief, especially for the decease of friends. The usages in this respect have varied much at different times and in different countries. Among the Jews, the duration of mourning for the dead was generally seven, but sometimes protracted to thirty days; and the garments were torn or squalid, or consisted of sackcloth (q. v.). The Jews of our day observe mourning ceremonies to a very considerable extent prescribed by the traditions of the rabbins. On the loss of a very near relative they seclude themselves from society for eight days, praying all waking hours for the safety of the soul of the departed friend, and every year the day of decease is observed as a day on which prayer for the departed must be observed. Among the Greeks, the period was thirty days, except in Sparta, where it was limited to ten. The relatives of the deceased secluded themselves from the public

eye, wore a coarse black dress, and in ancient times cut off their hair as a sign of grief. Among the Romans, the color of mourning for both sexes was black or dark blue under the republic; under the empire, the women wore white, black continuing to be the color for men, who did not cut off the hair or beard as in Greece. Men wore their mourning only a few days; women a year, when for a husband or parent. The time of mourning was often shortened by a victory or other happy public event, the birth of a child, or the occurrence of a family festival. A public calamity, such as a defeat, or the death of an emperor or person of note, occasioned a public mourning, which involved a total cessation of business, called Justitium. In modern Europe, the ordinary color for mourning is black; in Turkey, violet; in China, white; in Egypt, yellow; in Ethiopia, brown. It was white in Spain until 1498. White is supposed to denote purity; yellow, that death is the end of all human hopes, as leaves when they fall, and flowers when they fade, become yellow; brown denotes the earth, whither the dead return; black, the privation of life, as being the privation of light; blue expresses the happiness which it is hoped the deceased enjoys; and purple or violet, sorrow on the one side and hope on the other, as being a mixture of black and blue. Mourning is worn of different depth, and for different periods of time, according to the nearness of relationship of the deceased. On the death of a sovereign or member of the reigning house, a court mourning is ordered; and in many countries it is usual at the same time to recommend the adoption of a general mourning. In Scotch law, if a husband die, whether solvent or insolvent, the widow will be entitled to a preferred payment out of the assets for mournings suitable to his rank. The same privilege applies to mournings for such of the children as are to assist at the funeral (Chambers). The propriety of following the customs prevalent on this point has been of late very extensively called in question by Christians. Many individuals and religious bodies have objected against it: 1, that it is a useless ceremony; 2, that it involves needless expense, especially to the poor; 3, that the bustle of preparing it interferes with the moral and religious purposes of affliction. See GRIEF.

Mourners. See FLENTES; PENITENTS.

Mouse (עַכְבָּר, *akbar'*, according to Bochart, *Hieroz.* i, 1017, a compound of the Chald. עֲכַב, *to devour*, and בַּר, *a field*, from its ravages; but according to Gesenius, *Thes. Heb.* p. 508, from the Arab. for *swift digger;* Gr. μῦς), by which especially the field-mouse (Mishna, *Moed Katon*, i, 4)—a species, on account of its voracity and rapid increase, very injurious to crops (Aristotle, *Anim.* vi, 37; Strabo, iii, 165; Ælian, *Anim.* vi, 41; Pliny, x, 85; comp. Russell, *Aleppo*, ii, 59)—appears to be designated in 1 Sam. vi, 4 sq. See HÆMORRHOID. It was an unclean animal (Lev. xi, 29), in which passage, however, all the species of the genus *mus* are doubtless included (Bochart, *Hieroz.* ii, 429 sq.). But in Isa. lxvi, 77, a different creature seems to be denoted, apparently some esculent species of *glis*, or dormouse (see Varro, *R. R.* ii, 15); or perhaps the leaping variety of mouse, *mus jaculus*, or jerboa, which is designated in Arabic by a name corresponding to the Heb. *akbar*, although this animal has often been identified with the Heb. *shaphan*, or "coney." See also MOLE.

It is likely that the Hebrews extended the acceptation of the word *akbar* in the same manner as was the familiar custom of the Greeks, and still more of the Romans, who included within their term *mus* insectivora of the genus *sorex*, that is "shrews;" carnivora, among which was the *Mustela erminea*, "stoat" or "ermine," their *Mus ponticus;* and in the systematic order Rodentia, the *muridæ* contain *Myoxus glis*, or fat dormouse; *Dipus jaculus*, or Egyptian jerboa; *Mus*, rats and mice properly so called, constituting several modern genera; and *cricetus*, or hamster, which includes the marmot or Roman *Mus Alpinus*. In the above texts, those in 1 Sam. vi apparently refer to the short-tailed field-mouse, which is still the most destructive animal to the harvests of Syria (see William of Tyre, *Gesta Dei*, p. 823), and is most likely the species noticed in antiquity and during the crusades; for, had they been *jerboas* in shape and resembled miniature kangaroos, we would expect William of Tyre to have mentioned the peculiar form of the destroyers, which was then unknown to Western Europe; whereas, they being of species or appearance common to the Latin nations, no particulars were required. But in Leviticus and Isaiah, where the mouse is declared an unclean animal, the species most accessible and likely to invite the appetite of nations who, like the Arabs, were apt to covet all kinds of animals, even when expressly forbidden, were no doubt the hamster and the dormouse; and both are still eaten in common with the *jerboa* by the Bedouins, who are but too often driven to extremity by actual want of food. The common field-vole, often called the short-tailed field-mouse, is the *campagnol* of the French, and the *Arvicola agrestis* of modern zoologists. It is about the size of the house-mouse, to which it bears a general resemblance, but is easily distinguished by its larger head, its short ears and tail, its stouter form, and its reddish color, no less than by its habits (Fairbairn). "Of all the smaller rodentia which

Field-mouse (*Arvicola Agrestis*).

are injurious, both in the fields and in the woods, there is not," says Prof. Bell (*Hist. Brit. Quad.* p. 325), "one which produces such extensive destruction as this little animal, when its increase, as is sometimes the case, becomes multitudinous." The ancient writers frequently speak of the great ravages committed by mice. Herodotus (ii, 141) ascribes the loss of Sennacherib's army to mice, which in the night-time gnawed through the bow-strings and shield-straps. See generally Bochart, *Hieroz.* ii, 448 sq.

Mouskes, PHILIPPE (called also *Philippe Mus* and *Philippe Mussche*), a Belgian prelate and historian, was born about 1215 at Ghent, in East Flanders, and, after having taken holy orders, successively became canon (1242) and chancellor of the cathedral of Tournay, and in 1274 bishop of that city. He died at Tournay, Dec. 24, 1281 or 1283. Mouskes is the author of a rhymed chronicle, containing in 31,286 French verses the whole history of France, from the elopement of the fabulous Greek Helen with the Trojan prince Paris (the then usual beginning of such a narrative) up to the year A.D. 1242. There is only one MS. of this poem known, and it is at present preserved in the National Library at Paris, marked as No. 9634, small folio, written on parchment in two columns. It was published at Brussels (1836-38, 2 vols. 4to) under the auspices of the baron De Reiffenberg, who enriched the work with an introduction, a commentary, and appendices, all of which show much research and scholarship.—Hoefer, *Nouv. Biog. Générale*, s. v.

Mouson, ECCLESIASTICAL COUNCIL OF (*Concilium Mosomense*). Two such were held in the 10th century. The first, held Jan. 13, 948, was composed of Ruotbert, archbishop of Trèves, his suffragans, and some other bishops, who, when thus assembled, decreed that Artaud should keep possession of the see of Rheims; and that Hugo, who refused to appear at the council, as he had previously refused at Verdun, should be deprived of it until he should appear before the general council (appointed to be held Aug. 1) and justify himself. See *Conc. Verdua*, 947; Labbé, *Conc.* ix, 622.

Another was held June 2, 995. It was called by pope John XV, who was offended at the deposition of Arnulphus and the election of Gerbert (afterwards pope Sylvester II) to the see of Rheims, and therefore sent Leo, abbot of St. Bonifacius, into France as his legate, who assembled this council. No other prelates, however, attended but the archbishop of Trèves, and the bishops of Verdun, Liege, and Münster, all of them from Germany. The legate took his seat in the midst of them, and archbishop Gerbert, being the party accused, was placed opposite to him. Gerbert defended himself with eloquence, and declared that he had been raised to the archbishopric without his own concurrence. The sentence of the council was that he should abstain from the exercise of his archiepiscopal and sacerdotal functions until the matter should have been brought before the Synod of Rheims, convoked for the following July. It, however, was not held so early, and while Hugh Capet lived Gerbert remained archbishop, and Arnulphus a prisoner at Orleans. See Labbé, *Conc.* ix, 747.

Mouth (prop. פֶּה, *peh;* Gr. στόμα), besides its ordinary applications, was used in the following idiomatic phrases by the Hebrews (see Gesenius, *Heb. Lex.* s. v.): "Heavy-mouthed," that is, slow of speech, and so translated in Exod. iv, 10; "smooth mouth" (Psa. xxvi, 28), that is, a flattering mouth; so also "a mouth of deceit" (Psa. cix, 2). The following are also remarkable phrases: "To speak with one mouth to mouth," that is, in person, without the intervention of an interpreter (Numb. xii, 8; comp. 1 Kings viii, 15; Jer. xxxii, 4); "With one mouth," that is, with one voice or consent (Josh. ix, 2; 1 Kings xxii, 13; 2 Chron. xviii, 12); "With the whole mouth," that is, with the utmost strength of voice (Job xix, 16; Psa. lxvi, 17); "To put words into one's mouth," that is, to suggest what one shall say (Exod. iv, 15; Numb. xxii, 38; xxiii, 5, 12; 2 Sam. xiv, 19, etc.); "To be in one's mouth" is to be often spoken of, as a law, etc. (Exod. xiii, 9; comp. Psa. v, 10; xxxviii, 15). The Hebrew also says, "*upon* the mouth," where we say, and indeed our translation says, *in* or *into* the mouth (e. g. Nah. iii, 12); that which is spoken is also said to be "*upon* the mouth," where we should say, "upon the lips" (as in 2 Sam. xiii, 32). "To lay the hand upon the mouth" is to be silent (Judg. xviii, 19; Job xxi, 5; xl, 4; comp. Prov. xxx, 32), just as we lay the finger on the mouth to enjoin silence. "To write from the mouth of any one" is to do so from his dictation (Jer. xxxvi, 4, 27, 32; xlv, 1). The word of God, or, literally, "the word that proceeds out of his mouth," signifies the actions of God's providence, his commands, whereby he rules the world, and brings all things to his purpose (Isa. lv, 11). To "inquire at the mouth of the Lord" is to consult him (Josh. xix, 14). To "set their mouth against the heavens" is to speak arrogantly, insolently, and blasphemously of God (Psa. lxxiii, 9). "He shall smite the earth with the rod of his mouth, and with the breath of his lips shall he slay the wicked," are expressions which denote the sovereign authority and absolute power of the Messiah (Isa. x, 4). (See Wemyss, *Clavis Symbolica*, s. v.) The mouth, as the organ of speech, also signifies the words that proceed out of it, which in the sacred style are the same as commands and actions, because they imply the effects of the thoughts; words and commands being the means used to communicate decrees to those who are to execute them. Instances of this abound in Scripture, in various shades of application; but few of them are preserved in translation. Thus (Gen. xlv, 12), "according to the commandment of Pharaoh," is in the original, "according to the *mouth* of Pharaoh" (comp., among numerous other examples, Numb. iii, 16; Job xxxix, 27; Eccles. viii, 2). Hence, for a person or thing to come out of the mouth of another is to be constituted or commanded to become an agent or minister under a superior power; this is frequent in the Apocalypse (Rev. xvi, 13, 14; i, 16; xi, 4, 5; xii, 15; ix, 19). The term *mouth* is not only applied to a speech or words, but to the speaker (Exod. iv, 16; Jer. xv, 19), in which sense it has a near equivalent in our expression "mouthpiece."

Mouton, Jean, a French composer of Church music, flourished in the 16th century. He was first brought into notice about the opening of that age under the reign of Louis XII. Under Francis I he enjoyed royal protection and support, and as musical director of the royal chapel Mouton was encouraged to bring out his own compositions. He wrote considerably, and some of his productions were suffered dedication to pope Leo X. Mouton died before 1532. His *Masses* are justly celebrated. Five of these were published by Petrucci in 1508. Several of his compositions are preserved at Rome and Munich. His motets and madrigals are also circulated. As a composer, Mouton possessed more than the usual attainments. He was master of music as a science. His compositions are simple and natural, and betray the hand of a skilful artist. See Burney, *Gen. Hist. of Music;* Forkel, *Gesch. d. Musik;* Fites, *Biographie Universelle des Musiciens;* Patria, *Hist. de l'Art musical en France.*

Mouton, Jean Baptiste Sylvain, a noted French ecclesiastic and devoted adherent to the Jansenistic movement, was born in 1740 at Charité-sur-Loire. Having entered the service of the Church, he ardently devoted himself to bring about ecclesiastical reforms, and zealously embraced the Jansenistic cause as one sure to result favorably for the purity of the Church. He was, however, persecuted on that account, and finally quitted his native country and went over to Holland, and there labored with the Jansenists until his death, June 13, 1803, at Utrecht. He published *Nouvelles Ecclésiastiques*, first at Paris and afterwards at Utrecht. See Quérard, *La France Littéraire*, s. v.; Moréri, *Dict. Hist.* s. v.

Movable (and IMMOVABLE) **Feasts.** The feasts kept in the Christian Church are called movable and immovable, according as they fall, always on the same day in the calendar in each year, as the saints' days; or depend on other circumstances, as Easter, and the feasts calculated from Easter. The Book of Common Prayer contains several tables for calculating Easter, and the following rules to know when the movable feasts and holydays begin: Easter Day, on which the rest depend, is always the first Sunday after the full moon which happens upon or next after the twenty-first day of March; and if the full moon happens upon a Sunday, Easter Day is the Sunday after. Advent Sunday is always the nearest Sunday to the feast of St. Andrew, whether before or after.

Septuagesima		Nine Weeks	
Sexagesima	Sunday	Eight Weeks	before
Quinquagesima	is	Seven Weeks	Easter.
Quadragesima		Six Weeks	
Rogation Sunday		Five Weeks	
Ascension Day	is	Forty Days	after
Whit Sunday		Seven Weeks	Easter.
Trinity Sunday		Eight Weeks	

See FEASTS.

Movers, FRANZ KARL, a German Roman Catholic theologian and Orientalist, was born, of humble but honorable parentage, at Kösfeld, Rhenish Prussia, July 17, 1806. Franz Karl studied Orientalia and theology at Münster; was ordained priest; in 1830 became vicar

at Rath, near Deutz; in 1833 priest at Berkum, near Godesberg, and there remained until 1839, when he was appointed professor of Old-Testament theology in the Roman Catholic faculty of Breslau University, which office he held till his death, Sept. 28, 1856. His principal work, *Die Phönizier*, presents a comprehensive view of Phœnician history. The first volume (Breslau, 1840) treats of the religion and the divinities of the Phœnicians; the second volume bears the title of *Das Phönizische Alterthum*, and is divided into parts, embracing the political history (1849) and the colonial history (1850) of that nation. He further enriched this field of knowledge by the publication of two volumes of Phœnician texts (1845–47), and wrote the article *Phönicier* for Ersch u. Gruber's *Encyklopädie* (§ 3, vol. xxiv). Among his other works worth mentioning are, *Kritische Untersuchungen ü. d. Alttestamentliche Chronik* (Bonn, 1834) : *—De utriusque recensionis vaticiniorum Jeremiæ indole et origine* (Hamb. 1837) :—*Loci quidam historiæ Veteris Testamenti illustrati* (Bresl. 1843) :—*Zustand der katholisch-theol. Facultät an der Universität Breslau* (1847). He was also a frequent and esteemed contributor to the periodical literature of Germany, especially the philosophical and theological quarterlies; among which that of his own Church, the *Zeitschrift für Philosoph. u. Katholische Theologie*, enjoyed a very large number of valuable articles. (J. H. W.)

Möwes, HEINRICH, a Lutheran clergyman who flourished in Germany in the early part of this century, was settled near Magdeburg, Prussia. His life was marked by severe afflictions, which he bore with heroic faith. He died in 1831. He will be known to the English reader principally from his triumphant hymn, "Hallelujah! I believe," translated in *Hymns from the Land of Luther.*

Mowing (גֵּז, *gez*, Vulg. *tonsio*, Amos vii, 1; the Sept. reads Γὼγ ὁ βασιλεύς, either from a various reading or a confusion of the letters ז and נ), a word signifying also a shorn fleece, and rendered in Psa. lxxii, 6, "mown grass." As the great heat of the climate in Palestine and other similarly situated countries soon dries up the herbage itself, hay-making in our sense of the term is not in use. The term "hay," therefore, in the Prayer-book version of Psa. cvi, 20, for עֵשֶׂב, is incorrect; A. V. "grass." So also Prov. xxvii, 25, and Isa. xv, 6. The corn destined for forage is cut with a sickle. The term קָצִיר, A. V. "mower," Psa. cxxix, 7, is most commonly in A. V. "reaper," and once, Jer. ix, 22, "harvestman." See REAPING.

The "king's mowings," Amos vii, 1, i. e. mown grass, Psa. lxxii, 6, may perhaps refer to some royal right of early pasturage for the use of the cavalry. Comp. 1 Kings xviii, 5. See Shaw, *Trav.* p. 138; Wilkinson, *Anc. Eg.* abridgm. ii, 43, 50; *Early Trav.* p. 305; Pietro d. Valle, *Viaggi*, ii, 237; Chardin, *Voy.* iii, 370; Layard, *Nin. and Bab.* p. 330; Niebuhr, *Descr. de l'Arab.* p. 139; Harmer, *Obs.* iv, 386; Burckhardt, *Notes on Bed.* i, 210. See GRASS.

Moya, Don MATTHEO, a Spanish theologian, was born in 1607 at Moral, in the diocese of Toledo. Admitted into the Society of Jesus, he taught theology in Alcala and Madrid, became confessor to the duke of Ossuna, when the same was sent to Sicily, and received a like position with queen Mary Anne of Austria, widow of Philip IV. He became somewhat notorious by his *Opusculum singularia universæ fere theologiæ moralis complectens adversus quorumdam expostulationes contra nonnullas Jesuitarum opiniones morales* (Palermo, 1657, 4to), published under the pseudonyme of "Amadeus Guimenius," in which he attempted to justify the Jesuits for the laxity of their morals. This treatise was subsequently reprinted in Valentia, Madrid, and Lyon (the latter edition, 1664, in 4to). The Sorbonne, Feb. 5, 1665, denounced it as shameful, scandalous, imprudent, detestable, and as containing propositions which should be entirely eliminated from the Church and human memory. Pope Alexander VII annulled this condemnation in 1666; but when the Parliament appealed from it as error and abuse, and the Sorbonne maintained its right to pass censure on the books, and forbade the Jesuits to teach any of Moya's maxims, the pope changed his tactics, and reproved the Spanish theologian, and delivered his work to the Inquisition, which put it into the Index. Innocent XI, in 1688, condemned it to be burned. Pater Moya not only submitted to the pontifical authority, but even furnished himself a reprint of his book with refutations, and died in old age, probably satisfied with the mischief he had done. Among the writings which it provoked, an anonymous publication, *La morale des Jésuites justement condamnée dans le livre du P. Moya Jésuite* (Paris, 1681, 12mo), contains an almost complete summary of the controversial arguments. See Richard et Giraud, *Biblioth. Sacrée*, s. v.; Antonio, *Biblioth. Nova Hispaña*, s. v.

Moyer, *Lady* REBECCA, is noted as the foundress of a course of lectures in defence of the orthodox view of the Trinity. See LECTURES, MOYER'S. She was the wife of Sir Samuel Moyer, of the parish of St. Andrew, Holborn, in the County of Middlesex, England, who died in 1716. Lady Moyer herself died about 1720, and the foundation of the lectures she thus provided for in her will:

"My now dwelling-house in Bedford Row, or Jockey Field, I give to my dear child Eliza Moyer, that out of it may be paid twenty guineas a year to an able minister of God's Word, to preach eight sermons every year on the Trinity and divinity of our ever blessed Saviour, beginning with the first Thursday in November, and to the first Thursday in the seven sequal months, in St. Paul's, if permitted there, or, if not, elsewhere, according to the discretion of my executrix, who will not think it any incumbrance to her house. I am sure it will bring a blessing on it, if that work be well and carefully carried on, which in this profligate age is so neglected. If my said daughter should leave no children alive at her death, or they should die before they come to age, then I give my said house to my niece, Lydia Moyer, now wife to Peter Hartop, Esq., and to her heirs after her, she always providing for that sermon, as I have begun, twenty guineas every year."

There is a list of the preachers of this lecture, down to the year 1740-1, at the end of Mr. John Berriman's *Critical Dissertation on* 1 *Tim. iii,* 16 (which is the substance of the lectures he preached), and it is regarded as the ablest in the course. There is also in a copy of that book in Sion College Library a continuation of the list in MS., by Mr. John Berriman, to the year 1748. In the year 1757 they were preached by Mr. William Clements, librarian of Sion College, but he did not publish them till 1797. In the year 1764, or thereabouts, the preacher was Benjamin Dawson, LL.D., who printed them under the title of *An Illustration of several Texts of Scripture, particularly wherein the Logos occurs* (1765). Dr. Thomas Morell, author of the *Thesaurus Græcæ Poeseos,* is supposed to have been the last. One of these lectures Dr. Morell published *without his name* in April, 1774. It was written against Lindsay, and entitled *The Scripture Doctrine of the Trinity Justified.* Mr. Watts, recently librarian of Sion College (to whom the reader is indebted for the information here given), says Hook (*Ch. Dict.* s. v.), heard him preach one of them in January, 1772. As we have already stated under LECTURES, the Moyer foundation was only supported for about half a century. (J. H. W.)

Moyne, LE. See LEMOINE.

Moysey, CHARLES ABEL, an English divine quite noted as an able defender of the Trinitarian doctrine, flourished in the first half of this century. He was archdeacon of Bath, and enjoyed other clerical distinctions. In 1818 he held the appointment of Bampton lecturer, and treated of *Unitarianism* (Oxf. 1818, 8vo). He died about 1870. He published several of his sermons (Bath, 1822, 8vo), and lectures on *Romans* (Lond. 1820, 8vo) and *St. John's Gospel* (Oxf. 1821-23, 2 vols. 8vo).

Moza (Heb. *Motsa'*, מוֹצָא, a *going* forth, as often), the name of two men.

1. (Sept. Μοσά v. r. Ἰωσά.) The second of the three sons of Caleb by one of his concubines, Ephah (1 Chron. ii, 46). B.C. ante 1618.

2. (Sept. Μαισά, also Μασά v. r. Μασσά.) The son of Zimri and father of Binea, among the posterity of king Saul (1 Chron. viii, 36, 37; ix, 42, 43). B.C. considerably post 1037.

Mozah (Heb. *Motsah'*, מֹצָה, i. q. *Moza*, an *issuing* of water, but with the art.; Sept. Μωσά v. r. Ἀμωσά, Ἀμώκη), a city of the tribe of Benjamin, mentioned between Chephirah and Rekem (Josh. xviii, 26). A place of this name is mentioned by the rabbins (Mishna, *Sukkah,* iv, 5) as situated "below Jerusalem," at a spot whither the worshippers went down for the willow-branches used at the feast of Tabernacles (Reland, *Palæst.* p. 903). To this the Gemara adds, "the place was a Colonia (קילניא), that is, exempt from the king's tribute" (Buxtorf, *Lex. Talm.* col. 2043), which other Talmudists reconcile with the original name by observing that Motsah signifies an outlet or liberation, e. g. from tribute. Bartenora, who lived at Jerusalem, and now lies in the "valley of Jehoshaphat" there, says (in Surenhusius's *Mishna,* ii, 274) that Motsah was but a short distance from the city, and in his time retained its name of Colonia. Hence Schwarz infers (*Palest.* p. 127, 128) that the site is that of the modern *Kulonieh,* a village about three miles west of Jerusalem (Robinson, *Res.* ii, 146), containing ancient walls (Scholz, *Reise,* p. 161). "Interpreting the name according to its Hebrew derivation, it may signify 'the spring-head'—the place at which the water of a spring gushes out (Stanley, *S. and P.* App. § 52). The interpretations of the rabbins, just quoted, are not inconsistent with the name being really derived from its having been the seat of a Roman *colonia.* The only difficulty in the way of the identification is that Kulonieh can hardly be spoken of as 'below Jerusalem'—an expression which is most naturally interpreted of the ravine beneath the city, where the Bîr-Eyub is, and the royal gardens formerly were. Still there are vestiges of much vegetation about Kulonieh, and when the country was more generally cultivated and wooded, and the climate less arid than at present, the dry river-bed which the traveller now crosses may have flowed with water, and have formed a not unfavorable spot for the growth of willows. See CULON.

Mozambique, a territory on the east coast of South Africa, nominally belonging to Portugal, and placed under a governor-general, although the actual possessions of Portugal consist only of a few stations, and her authority in the country is inconsiderable. It extends from Cape Delgado, in lat. 10° 41' S., to Delagoa Bay, 26° S., and is estimated to have an area of 380,000 square miles, settled by a population of about 350,000. The chief river, the Zambesi, divides it into two portions—Mozambique proper on the north, and Sofala on the south. The coasts, which comprise large tracts of cultivated soil, yielding rich harvests in rice, are fringed with reefs, islands, and shoals, and between Delagoa Bay and Cape Corrientes, and from Mozambique, the principal station, to Cape Delgado, the shores are high and steep. The forests yield valuable ornamental woods; ivory is obtained from the hippopotami that haunt the marshes; and gold and copper are found and worked. The elephant, deer, and lion inhabit the jungle; crocodiles are found in the rivers, and numerous flamingoes on the coasts. The rainy season lasts from November to March. The summer heat is very great, and the climate, which is fine in the elevated tracts, is unhealthy on the low shores and the swampy districts. Besides numerous fruits and vegetables, the grains are rice, millet, maize, and wheat. Fish and turtle are caught in great quantities on the islands and reefs; pearl-fishing is a source of considerable profit;

cattle, sheep, and goats are numerous, and the principal exports are grain, gold-dust, honey, tortoise-shell, cowries, gums, and amber. The natives of this country are mainly *Kaffirs* (q. v.), and but very few of them have any inclination to accept Christianity as exemplified by the Romanists, who are its only exponents there. In the capital of Mozambique, of like name, with a population of 8522, there are only 270 Christians reported in the census. The natives who live along the coast are called Makooas or Makoonas. They are an athletic and ugly race of people, of the most ferocious aspect and savage disposition. They are fond of tattooing their skins, and draw a stripe down the forehead along the nose to the chin, which is crossed in a direct angle by another line from ear to ear, so as to give the face the appearance of being sewed together in four parts. They file their teeth to a point, so as to resemble a coarse saw; and suspend ornaments of copper or bone from a hole in the gristle of the nose. Their upper lip protrudes in a very remarkable degree, and this they consider as so principal a point of beauty that they endeavor to make it still longer by introducing into the centre a small circular piece of ivory, wood, or iron. They dress their hair in a very fantastic manner, some shaving one side of the head, others both sides, leaving a kind of crest from the front to the nape of the neck, while a few of them wear simply a knot of hair on their foreheads. Their females greatly resemble the Hottentot women in the curvature of the spine and protrusion of the hinder parts, and when past the prime of life are said to present the most disagreeable appearance that can be conceived. The natives are fond of music and dancing, but their tunes and motions are unvaried and monotonous. Their favorite instrument is called *ambira*, which is formed by a number of thin bars of iron of different lengths, highly tempered, and set in a row on a hollow case of wood, about four inches square, and closed on three sides. It is played upon with a piece of quill; and its notes, though simple, are sufficiently harmonious, sounding to the ear, when skilfully managed, like the changes upon bells. They are armed with spears, darts, and poisoned arrows, and possess also a considerable number of muskets, which they procure from the Arabs in the northern districts, and sometimes even from the Portuguese dealers. They are formidable enemies to the settlement, and have been rendered desperate in their hostilities by the nefarious practices of the traders who have gone among them to purchase slaves. There are also many Arabs in Mozambique, but they remain steadfast in their faith to the Koran and its Prophet.

This coast had been known to the Arabs, and its ports frequented by their traders, for centuries before its discovery by Europeans, and all the information possessed by the latter on the subject was chiefly drawn from the vague accounts of Ptolemy and the Periplus of the Erythrean sea. It was first discovered by the Portuguese in the year 1497, who found the whole of the coast in the possession of the Arabs; but the fame of its goldmines and the convenience of its ports, as resting-places for the Indian trade, led them to attempt the expulsion of the original settlers. This the Portuguese easily accomplished by their superiority in arms; and in 1508 they had conquered Quiloa, gained a footing in Sofala, and built the fort which still stands on the island of Mozambique. They gradually encroached on the Mohammedan possessions on the River Zambesi, and about the year 1569 they completely cleared that part of the river from Arabs by putting the whole of them to death. In their attempts to reach the gold-mines of the interior, the Portuguese were not very scrupulous as to the means which they employed, and have furnished, in the history of the East, a parallel to the atrocities of their Spanish neighbors in the West. But theirs was a harder task, and the natives of Africa maintained a nobler struggle for the independence of their country than the feebler South American race; and after nearly four

centuries of possession the Portuguese content themselves with acting on the defensive, occupying the coast along the line of the River Zambesi, and maintaining their influence in the country by exciting the native powers against one another. The government of Mozambique is even now in a most inefficient state, being, in most places, more in the hands of native chiefs than of the Portuguese. In former times the slave-trade was carried on here extensively; and from 1846 to 1857 four governors-general were removed by their government for countenancing, if not actively engaging in it. The principal settlements are Mozambique, Quilimane, Sena, and Tete. The colony is divided into six districts, and is ruled by the governor-general and his secretary, assisted by a *junta*. The country being in the hands of a Roman Catholic government, religion and education are supervised by about twelve Roman Catholic priests, and no Protestants are tolerated in the diffusion of their creeds. It is a matter of general comment that the morality of Mozambique is at the lowest ebb, and that the Romanists are responsible for this condition. In 1873 Sir Bartle Frere visited Mozambique and the adjoining countries, and negotiated for the suppression of the slave-trade (see Livingstone, *Last Journals*).

Mozarabian Liturgy is the name of a Christian liturgy originally in use among those Christian inhabitants of Spain [see MOZARABIANS] who remained faithful to their religion after the Arabic conquest. It is not apparent yet how the liturgy came to be called Mozarabian, for if the word itself were a nickname, it is not at all likely that these Christians would themselves have adopted that byname. In all probability it was connected with it at a much later date than the original introduction of this liturgy itself into Spain. Walcott (*Sacred Archæol*. p. 393) thinks that "it received its present title possibly from the right being a concession within the Moorish pale." Its origin is traced by some to Isidore of Seville (q. v.). See LITURGY, in vol. v, p. 459 (3). Recent researches, however, would make it almost certain that it is of much more ancient origin, and that it was only completed, or, at least, established by him and the fathers of the fourth Council of Toledo (633). Roman Catholic writers go so far as to ascribe it to the apostles themselves who converted Spain (comp. Migne's *Patrologia*, vol. lxxxiv [Paris, 1850]). Though closely resembling the Gallican liturgy, it cannot, on the other hand, have come into Spain from Gaul, for there are differences between the two which could not be accounted for in such a case. It is consequently most likely that it originated among the Christians of Spain, but the name of its author cannot be ascertained. The uniformity of style and singleness of plan show that the greatest part at least, if not the whole, was the work of one writer. This liturgy remained in use in Spain throughout the Middle Ages, to the exclusion of the Roman Catholic form, which liberty may be accounted for by the isolated, independent position of these communities, as otherwise they would soon have been brought to yield to the influence of Rome. As it was, they succeeded in obtaining the recognition of their liturgy by two popes—by John X in 918, and by Alexander II in 1064. About the same time, however, that the last recognition was secured at Rome the Mozarabic liturgy was silenced in Aragon to spread the Roman liturgy, and in 1074 it was suppressed for the same reason, by Sancho III of Navarre, in Navarre, Castile, and Leon, to the great regret of the people, who consoled themselves characteristically with the proverb, "Quo volunt reges vadunt leges" (Roderic, *De Reb. Hisp.* vi, 26). From Rome the first authoritative word for the exclusion of the Mozarabic liturgy came in the pontificate of Gregory VII (11th century). He compelled most of the Spanish churches and convents to adopt the common uniform liturgy of the Romish Church. Six Mozarabic congregations, chiefly in Leon and Toledo, were, however, permitted to retain their ancient ritual, and though it soon fell into disuse among them also, it was yet preserved long enough to save it from final destruction; and when the learned cardinal Ximenes, for the correction of the liturgies then in use, consulted all the ancient MSS. of liturgies extant, and thus came across the Mozarabic also, he became so much interested in its preservation that he caused a careful copy to be made, and it was printed for the first time in 1500. Two years later a Breviary was prepared to complete it. Both works were printed at Toledo by a German, Peter Hagenbach, and were approved by pope Julius II. The title of this compilation is, *Missale Mistum secundum Regulam Beati Isidori Dictum Mozarabicum,* which has, however, by some unfortunate accident, remained incomplete. A whole third of the Church-year is left out entirely. Ximenes, in the mean time, the more surely to preserve the Mozarabic liturgy, expressly founded a chapel at Toledo, with a college of thirteen chaplains, whose duty he made it to say mass according to the Mozarabic manner. This institution is still in existence.

The principal characteristics of the Mozarabic liturgy are:

1. Its festivals, which are different from those of the Roman Catholic Church; for instance, its Advent contains six Sundays, as in the ancient Milanese and in the Greek Church: this indicates a certain connection with these. There are two festivals of the Annunciation, one on March 24, as in the Roman Catholic liturgy, and the other on Dec. 18, which they designate by the peculiar name of "Sancta Maria de la O," because at the close of this festival both clergy and laity "sine ordine voce clara O longum proferunt ad flagrans illud desiderium significandum, quo sancti omnes in limbo, in cœlo angeli totusque orbis tenebatur nativitatis Redemptoris" (see the Preface to Migne's *Patrologia,* p. 170, D).

2. With regard to the lessons, the evangelists in this liturgy are not entirely similar; thus the lesson containing the parable of the rich man and Lazarus is placed before Lent as a sort of admonition against the riotousness prevailing at that period. But a point of much greater importance is the fact that there were not only two lessons, namely, the epistle and gospel, appointed for each great festival, but three; a lesson from the Old Testament being read before the epistle. This was taken not only from the poetical and historical books, but even from Jesus Sirach. Another remarkable fact is that between Easter and Pentecost the lesson from the Old Testament was replaced by portions of Revelation, and that from the epistles by the Acts.

3. The principal characteristic of this *missale* is the strong homiletic element it contains besides the liturgical. Thus, after the three Biblical lessons, and before the real offering, there was always an address to the people, specially appointed for each day of worship. These addresses are short, their tone familiar, but at the same time exegetical (as when treating of the allegorical character of Lazarus's resurrection, on the third Sunday in Lent [Migne, p. 341]), while a certain rhetorical elegance (as in the mass for Easter and Ascension-day) bespeaks one who was familiar with homiletic expressions. On this point there is a resemblance to the Gallican liturgy; although the latter, as given in Mabillon's edition (Paris, 1729), contains no such elements, yet the publisher says (p. 29): "Et Salvianus Massiliensis presbyter clarissimus homilias episcopis factas, Sacramentorum vero, quantas nec recordor, ait Gennadius, composuit. Quo in loco sacramentorum homiliæ intelliguntur vel sermones de mysteriis sacris, inter missarum solemnia quondam *ex more Gallicano* recitari soliti; vel orationes seu præfationes ad missam." The part, moreover, which is specially called *præfatio* is, in the Western *missale,* called *inlatio.*

4. Some parts of this liturgy recall the Eastern Church, as, for instance, the repetition of three *Agios* after the *Benedictus,* while in the Roman liturgy the word *Sanctus* precedes it (although the Greek word occurs also in the Roman hymns of Palestrina); also the formula in the Communion, *Sancta Sanctis;* but par-

ticularly the division of the host into nine parts, which, like the leaves in the Greek rite, have special names and significations, and are also to be laid and used in a certain order.

5. The Mozarabic chant has great similarity to the Gregorian, yet it is clear that here also the Spanish Church preserved some national characteristics, as is shown by the specimens contained in Migne's edition (Preface, p. xxxiii–xxxvi). These indicate a greater tendency to melody and a figurative style than is found in the Gregorian chant. It is named the *Eugenian* chant, from its author, the third archbishop of Toledo, Eugene, who, in regard to hymnology, occupies the same place in the Mozarabic Church, in opposition to Gregory, as does Isidore in the liturgical part. Further comparison between the two rites, implying that of the Breviaries, would be out of place here; we will merely remark that, as a whole, the Mozarabic liturgy is one of the most precious monuments of ancient Christianity, and is not inferior to any other liturgy in point of rich illustrations from Scripture, liturgical application of passages, nobleness of thought, etc. See Palmer, *Origin. litur.* vol. i, § x, p. 166 sq.; Bona, *Res. Liturg.* i, 11 sq.; Pinius, *De Lit. Mos.;* Lesleius, *Mis. Mos. Præf.;* Martene, *De Antiqu. Eccl. Ritibus,* i, 457 sq.; *Christian Remembrancer,* Oct. 1853.

Mozarabians (MUZARABIANS, MOSTARABIANS, or MUSTARABIANS), which properly designates a people living among the Arabs, but not of the same blood, and by the latter therefore looked upon with distrust, and even with contempt, was applied as a sort of nickname to those Christians of Spain who, under Mohammedan rule, remained faithful to their holy religion. The word is derived from Arabic *Estarab,* i. e. to *Arabize,* and as a participle (*Mostarab*) signifies one who has adopted the Arab mode of life. The Christians of Africa and Spain, as well as the Jews, deserved to be called Mozarabians, for they all, from fear of persecution, adopted the ways and customs of their conquerors, and in outward appearances gave themselves the air of conformity with Mohammedan life and practice. They abstained from meat, and submitted to the rite of circumcision. The modern form has lost the *t* (Mos*t*arab), but has substituted *z* for *s,* thus preserving the sound, notwithstanding the change of orthography (see Ticknor, *Span. Lit.* iii, 393).

Mozart, JOHANNES CHRYSOSTOMUS WOLFGANG AMADEUS, one of the greatest musical composers, if not the greatest, deserves a place here for his many and valuable contributions to sacred music. He was born at Salzburg (then in Bavaria, but soon after transferred to Austria), Jan. 17, 1756. From the earliest age Wolfgang evinced the strongest predilection for music, which induced his father, who was organist of the prince's chapel, to discontinue the instruction of others, in order to devote himself to his tuition and that of a sister about four years older. After studying the harpsichord during a year, the flights of his genius were so rapid that he exercised his own invention in original composition at the age of only five, and attempted notation, which could hardly be deciphered. When only six years of age, his performances were so remarkable that his father took him and his sister, who possessed similar gifts, to Munich and Vienna, where they obtained every kind of encouragement from the elector of Bavaria and the emperor Francis I. In 1763 the Mozart family visited Paris; and, though now only at the age of seven, Mozart surprised a party of musicians, including his father, by taking part, at sight, in a trio for stringed instruments. He also earned a great reputation as performer on the organ, and during his stay at Paris performed on the organ in the Chapelle du Roi before the whole court. While at the French capital Mozart also entered upon his career as musical author, for he there published his first two works. From Paris the Mozart family went to London in 1764, and there, according to Holmes, "the boy exhibited his talents before the royal family, and underwent more severe trials than any to which he had been before subjected, through which he passed in a most triumphant manner. So much interest did he excite in that country that the Hon. Daines Barrington drew up an account of his extraordinary performances, which was read before the Royal Society, and declared by the council of that body to be sufficiently important to be printed in the *Philosophical Transactions*, in the 60th volume of which it appears." In the 69th volume of the same work Dr. Burney remarks: "Of Mozart's infant attempts at music I was unable to discover the traces from the conversation of his father, who, though

House of Mozart.

an intelligent man, whose education and knowledge of the world did not seem confined to music, confessed himself unable to describe the progressive improvements of his son during the first stages of infancy. However, at eight years of age I was frequently convinced of his great knowledge in composition by his writings; and that his invention, taste, modulation, and execution in extemporary playing were such as few professors are possessed of at forty years of age." Symphonies of his own composition were produced in a public concert in London; and while there he composed and published six sonatas, and made acquaintance with the works of Handel, recently deceased. In 1765 the Mozarts returned to the Continent, and, passing through Paris, went to Holland, and at the Hague, when not more than eight years old, young Wolfgang composed a symphony for a full orchestra, on occasion of the installation of the prince of Orange. On their return to Germany shortly after, he again produced a sensation by his compositions for the religious service, and for a trumpet concert at the dedication of the Orphan House Church in Vienna, himself conducting the music in presence of the imperial court. After this the Mozarts went home to Salzburg, and Wolfgang was afforded every advantage for his musical training. He devoted himself most assiduously to the study of his art, and evinced his mastery of the subject in 1768, when, at the request of the emperor Joseph II at Vienna, he composed music to the opera-buffa *La Finta Semplice*, which, though never performed, was approved of by all the masters and cognoscenti of the period. In 1769 young Mozart was nominated concert-master to the archbishop of Salzburg, and thus gained a small compensation and a somewhat independent position. We do not know exactly what his salary was when first appointed, but in his twentieth year, we learn from his biographer, Mozart earned the trifling sum of $5 per annum. We do not wonder, therefore, that the artist occasionally strayed from home to earn a few additional dollars. Thus in the very year of his appointment we find him starting for Italy, where he was most rapturously welcomed. His first performance in Italy was given at Milan, where he was engaged to return and compose

the first opera for the carnival of 1771. At Bologna and Florence the reception he met with was equally flattering to the young musician. At Rome Mozart arrived in Passion Week, and on Wednesday went to the Sistine Chapel, where he heard for the first time the celebrated *Miserere*, which was prohibited to be copied, or in any manner published, on pain of excommunication. On Good Friday the same *Miserere* was again performed, when Mozart was present with the MS. copy he had made from memory concealed in his hat, that he might have an opportunity of making corrections. This circumstance created an immense excitement at Rome, because the peculiarities of the *Miserere* were thought impossible to be expressed by musical notation; and when young Mozart, in presence of some Sistine choristers, sang the composition in the very manner in which it was sung by those who had acquired it only after long practice, the professional singers expressed their astonishment in terms of unmeasured admiration. The fame of Mozart after this event was spread far and wide. His wonderful musical talents and power of performing on the organ were attributed to a charm which it was supposed he carried in his ring. When the pope first heard him perform he conferred upon him the order of the Golden Spur; and at Bologna he was unanimously elected a member of the Philharmonic Society, which was at that time an honor rarely conferred even upon the greatest musicians, but yet well earned by this marvellous youth, who, at the age of sixteen, was acknowledged the first claveçinist in the world, and had produced two requiems and a stabatmater, numerous offertories, hymns, and motets, 4 operas, 2 cantatas, 13 symphonies, 24 piano-forte sonatas, not to speak of a vast number of concertos for different instruments, trios, quartets, marches, and other minor pieces. In 1773 Mozart produced, among numerous other works, two Masses for the chapel of the elector of Bavaria, etc. In 1775, at the desire of the archduke Maximilian, he composed the cantata *Il Re Pastore;* and from that period till the year 1779 he continued to labor with his pen, though but few of its products then obtained, or ever will obtain, a celebrity at all equal to that which his subsequent productions have so justly acquired. In 1775 his fame was so completely established and so widely known that he could have made choice of engagements in all the capitals of Europe. His father preferred Paris, and therefore, in 1777, he, with his mother, set out for a second journey towards that city. The death of his mother made Paris insupportable, and he returned to his father at the beginning of the year 1779. Some time after this Mozart went to Munich, whence he went to Vienna; and in Nov., 1779, he finally settled in the latter city, the inhabitants and manners of which were very agreeable to him; and now, having reached his 24th year, he exhibited the rare example of one who had been astonishing as a child, had disappointed not even the most sanguine hopes, and became proportionately great as a man. Whatever the precocity of the child—and in that respect as well as in any other he was unlike other noted musical composers, for though Handel and Haydn and Beethoven all gave proofs of their musical powers in boyhood, none of them showed as children that full maturity of mind which distinguished Mozart, and which only a few of those who witnessed it could appreciate—it was now in the maturity of life that he began his career as composer, and gained that celebrity which will last to all time. Mozart was now in the service of the emperor as composer to the court; but his office was rather honorary than lucrative, and he lived by concerts, musical tours, teaching music, and the small profits derived from the sale of his published works, till an offer of a large salary made to him by the king of Prussia led the emperor to give him 800 florins a year; and though several tempting offers came to him after this time, and Mozart's pecuniary condition would have made greater compensation very desirable, he refused to quit his emperor's side. His great opera of *Idomeneo* was composed in 1780, with a view to induce the family of Mademoiselle Constance Weber, afterwards his wife, to consent to the marriage, which they had declined on the ground that his reputation was not sufficiently established. This opera forms an epoch not in the composer's life only, but in the history of music. In construction, detail, instrumentation, and every imaginable respect, it was an enormous advance on all previous works of the kind, and established his reputation as the greatest musician whom the world had seen. His other principal works, composed about and after this time, are *Cosi Fan Tutti:—L'Enlèvement du Sérail: —Nozze de Figaro:—Don Giovanni:—Zauberflöte:— Clemenza di Tito:*—and last, but not least, his world-renowned *Requiem*—one of the most perfect sacred musical compositions, if not the most perfect—in which, while the sacred character is maintained throughout, the airs have all the requisite grace and freedom, the instrumentation all the resources of modern refinement, and the whole exhibits in a perfect manner the blending of the varied powers of the orchestra with the voice, without ever allowing the former to encroach on the latter. The story of his composing the *Requiem* deserves mentioning here. Mozart's intense application to keep the wolf from his doors, and to avoid trouble on account of the many papers that came to him showing "res angusta domi" (warrants for debt), had brought on a state of melancholy from which nothing could arouse him, and he was full of terror at his approaching end. One day, while plunged in a profound reverie, a stranger of dignified manners was announced, who communicated the wishes of some unknown person of exalted rank that he should compose a solemn mass for the repose of the soul of one tenderly beloved, whom he had just lost. An air of mystery pervaded the interview; the composer was exhorted to exercise all his genius; and he engaged to finish his work in a month, when the stranger promised to return. He disappeared, and Mozart instantly commenced writing. Day and night were uninterruptedly occupied; but he was consumed by gloomy presages, and at length exclaimed abruptly to his wife, in great agitation, "Certainly I am composing this requiem for myself—it will serve for my own funeral." Though his strength continued to fail, his assiduity was unabated, and at length he was obliged to suspend the undertaking. At the appointed time the stranger returned. "I have found it impossible to keep my word," said Mozart; to which the stranger answered, "Give yourself no uneasiness. What longer time do you require?" Mozart replied, "Another month." The stranger now insisted on doubling the covenanted price, which he had paid down at the outset, and retired. It was in vain that Mozart endeavored to trace him, and this, conjoined with other circumstances, corroborated his belief that he was some supernatural being sent to announce the close of his mortal career. Nevertheless his labors were renewed, and the work at last was nearly completed within the stipulated period, when the mysterious stranger again returned; but Mozart was no more. He died Dec. 5, 1791. In the intervals of his greater works, Mozart composed the majority of the orchestral symphonies, quartets, and quintets which are an almost indispensable part of the programme of every concert in the present day, besides masses as familiar in England and America as in Catholic Europe, innumerable piano-forte concertos and sonatas and detached vocal compositions, all of the most perfectly finished description. "The genius of Mozart in music," says Hogarth, "was sublime. By the number, variety, combination, and effect of his works he ranks in the highest class of modern masters. An air of delicacy and sentiment pervades the whole. Full and harmonious, they are altogether free from that meagreness and those capricious eccentricities which betray the sterility of invention too common among musicians. The taste which they exhibit shows

that vulgar images were incompatible with his mind; it seems as if he knew that such a deformity is alike pernicious to science and the arts. . . . Mozart has been most successful in gloomy passages, or those of rising grandeur; they according better with the ordinary train of his feelings. On almost all occasions he is more serious than comic in endeavoring to portray the passions; and his love, it has been remarked, is rather sentimental than sportive. However simple the theme, however intricate its variations, his return is always natural, and the finale appropriate. Perhaps the celebrity of Mozart's music partly arises from the skilful management of his finales, for they invariably leave an agreeable impression. No one has surpassed him in the suitable distribution of the parts of his concerted pieces; for, understanding the precise qualities of every different instrument, nothing is appointed to any which is inconsistent with its character." "No composer has ever combined genius and learning in such perfect proportions; none has ever been able to dignify the lightest and tritest forms by such profound scholarship, or at the moment when he was drawing most largely on the resources of musical science, to appear so natural, so spontaneous, and so thoroughly at his ease" (Hullah). To Haydn Mozart always acknowledged his obligations; but Haydn's obligations to Mozart are at least as great. Haydn, though born twenty-four years earlier, survived Mozart eighteen years, and all his greatest works written after Mozart's death bear manifold traces of his influence. Mozart is the first composer in whose works all signs of the old tonality disappear; he is the father of the modern school. "Mozart," says Prof. J. K. Paine, "is rightly considered as the universal master. This universality is not only evinced in his complete mastery of every form of music, from a song to a symphony, from a simple dance to a solemn requiem, but in the rare adaptation of the national peculiarities of style—Italian, French, and German—to his own individuality. It was his mission to unite harmoniously and beautify these national elements. In his immortal works European music attained its concentration for the first and only time in history" (Lectures on Music, at the Boston University, in 1874). In person Mozart did not exceed the middle size; he was thin and pale, and his health was always delicate. The expression of his countenance, without anything striking, was exceedingly variable, and rather that of an absent-minded man. His habits were awkward, and his hands had been accustomed so incessantly to the piano that they seemed incapable of application to anything requiring address. He was of a mild and affectionate disposition: his mind was not uncultivated, and the number of his works is a sufficient proof of his industry. His opinions of other composers were liberal, and he entertained the highest respect for Haydn in particular. "Believe me, sir," said he to an officious critic, who sought to demonstrate certain errors of that great master—"believe me, sir, were you and I amalgamated together, we should not afford materials for one Haydn." He was not insensible of the beauties of his own compositions; and on the very day of his decease, calling for the *Requiem*, he had some parts of it performed by his bedside. See Holmes, *The Life of Mozart, including his Correspondence* (Lond. 1845, 2 vols. 8vo); Jahn, *Mozart's Leben* (Leips. 1856, 4 vols. 8vo; 2d ed. 1867); Döring, *Mozart* (Leips. and Paris, 1860); Nohl, *Mozart's Briefe* (Salzb. 1865; English version by Lady Wallace [Lond. and N. Y. 1865, 2 vols. 18mo]); Oubilicheff, *Mozart's Leben u. Werke* (Leips. 1873, 3 vols. 8vo); Hogarth's *Musical History, Biography, and Criticism* (Lond. 1835, 12mo); Jäger, *Gallery of German Composers, with Biographical and Critical Notices* by E. F. Rimbault, LL.D. (Lond. 1875); *For. Qu. Rev.* Jan. 1846; *Blackwood's Magazine*, Nov. 1845, art. v; *Edinb. Rev.* Apr. 1836, art. ii; *Edinb. Cyclop.* s. v.; *Chambers's Cyclop.* s. v.; *English Cyclop.* s. v.

Mozdarians, a heretical sect of the Mohammedans, followers of Isa ebn-Sobeih al-Mozdâr, who held it possible for God to be a liar and unjust, pronounced as infidels those who took upon themselves the administration of public affairs, and condemned all who did not embrace his opinions as guilty of infidelity. See Broughton, *Biblioth. Historico-Sacra*, ii, 146.

Mozetta, the technical term for a tippet worn by cardinals over a mantlet, or short cloak, showing only a chain of a breast-cross. At Pisa in summer a red mozetta is worn over a rochet; at Catania the mozetta of black cloth is worn over the rochet; at Syracuse the mozetta is violet, as at Malta, where it is used with a rochet and cope; at Ratisbon it is of red silk.

Mozier, JOSEPH, an American sculptor, noted for his contributions to sacred art, was born in Burlington, Vt., Aug. 22, 1812. He removed to New York in 1831, and was engaged in mercantile pursuits till 1845, when he retired from business, and shortly after visited Europe. Having devoted several years to the study of sculpture in Florence, he went to Rome, where he long resided. He died in Switzerland in October, 1870. His principal works on sacred and ethical subjects are statues of *Truth* and *Silence*, in possession of the New York Mercantile Library Association; *Rebecca at the Well; Esther;* a group illustrating the parable of *the Prodigal Son;* and *Jephthah's Daughter.* See *The American Cyclopædia*, s. v.

Mozzi, Luigi, a learned Italian ecclesiastic, was born at Bergamo May, 26, 1746. Of a patrician family, he was admitted (1763) into the Society of Jesus. He was professor at the college of the Nobili at Milan when (1773) that order was dissolved by pope Clement XIV. Returning to Bergamo, he was charged with the examination of candidates for holy orders, and became canon and archpriest. The piety and zeal which he manifested against the Jansenists in Italy gave him high repute; he was called to Rome, nominated apostolic missionary, and member of the Academy degli Arcadi. In 1804 he joined his confrères in the kingdom of Naples; but the Jesuits were again soon dispersed, and Mozzi found a refuge at the villa of the marquis Scotti, situated in the environs of Milan, where he died, June 24, 1813. Of the numerous writings left by him, his most important refer to the Jansenist controversy. Thus he wrote, *Jansenism by Daylight, or the Idea of Jansenism* (Venice, 1781, 2 vols. 8vo) :—*Brief History of the Schism of the New Church of Utrecht* (Ferrara, 1785, 8vo; Ghent, 1829, 8vo) :—*The Fifty Reasons why the Catholic Church should be Preferred* (Bassano, 1789). He published also *The Plans of the Unbelievers to Ruin Religion, as Revealed in the Works of Frederick, King of Prussia* (3d ed. Assisi, 1791, 8vo) :— *Historical and Chronological Abridgment of the most important Decrees of the Holy See regarding Brianism, Jansenism, and Quesnellism.*

Mozzi, Marco Antonio, an Italian literateur, was born at Florence, January 17, 1678; studied law and theology there, and at the same time devoted much attention to poetry and music. His skill on the mandoline procured for him frequent invitations to the ducal court of Tuscany. In 1700 he received a canonicate in his native city, and two years afterwards a position as lecturer on Tuscan literature. He was elected a member of the Academy de la Crusca, and became its archconsul. As a renowned preacher he delivered before the court in 1701 the funeral sermon on Charles II, king of Spain, and in 1703 did the like on archbishop Leon Strozzi before the metropolitan chapter. We possess of him, *Sonetti sopra i nomi dati al alcune dame Fiorentine dalla principessa Violanta* (Florence, 1705) :—*Istoria di S. Cresci et de' santi martyri suoi compagni, come pure della chiesa del medesimo santo posta in Volcava di Mugello* (Florence, 1710, fol., with illustrations) :—*Discorsi sacri* (Florence, 1717) :—*Vita di Lorenzo Bellini,* in the *Vite degli Arcadi; Orazione funerale del abate A.*

M. Salvini, in the *Prose Toscane* of Salvini. See Hoefer, *Nouv. Biog. Générale*, s. v.

Muciānus, or **Mutianus,** surnamed SCHOLASTICUS, an early ecclesiastic of some note, flourished near the middle of the 6th century A.D. He is celebrated as the translator of the 34 homilies of St. Chrysostom on the Epistle to the Hebrews, a task performed at the request of Cassiodorus, by whom he is called "vir disertissimus." This translation is still in existence; it was published for the first time at Cologne in 1530 (8vo), and has been inserted in the Latin editions of the works of St. Chrysostom, though in the Græco-Latin editions the translation by Hervet is generally preferred. He had previously furnished also a Latin translation of Gaudentius's *Treatise on Music.* See Fabricius, *Biblioth. Græca*, viii, 558, 559; Cassiodorus, *Divin. Lect.* 8.

Mucker, a German epithet applied to Christian sects who make much outward display of piety, has come to be applied especially to a class of modern *Adamites* (q. v.) who arose at Königsberg, East Prussia, about 1830. Their origin is attributed to the theosoph Johann Heinrich Schönherr (born at Memel in 1771, died at Königsberg in 1826), who held dualistic and Gnostic views concerning the origin of the universe, teaching that it was caused by the mingling of two primordial beings of a spiritual and sensuous nature as Eloahs. But Schönherr was himself too good a man to stand accused of having caused the formation of a sect so fanatic and immoral as the Muckers. In truth, the philosophic fancy of this pious but eccentric student was taken hold of by two Königsberg Lutheran clergymen named Diestel and Ebel (q. v.), who, after making profession of the exclusive kind of Christianity, gathered a circle of like-minded fanatics, and introduced shameless mysteries under the color of pietism. They elevated sexual connection into an act of worship, and designated it as the chief means of the sanctification of the flesh by which the paradisaic state was to be restored. Women of high standing in the community, some of noble birth, belonged to the Mucker circle. Three of them lived in Ebel's house, and were popularly regarded as his wives. Dixon (*Spiritual Wives*) tells us that Ebel held one to represent to him the principle of light (*Licht-Natur*), the second the principle of darkness (*Finsterniss-Natur*), and the third the principle of union (*Umfassung*). The last only was his legal wife; but it was discovered during a public trial of Ebel for the offence of immorality that she only held a subordinate place in his extraordinary household. This and like odious, licentious excesses were practiced by the Muckers generally, especially in their religious meetings, and the scandal concerning them became so great in Königsberg that a garden which they were wont to frequent acquired the name of the Seraphs' Grove. The subject was brought before the courts in 1839, and the result, in 1842, was that Ebel and Diestel were degraded from their offices; but upon appeal the higher court reversed the decision, and discharged the case for want of clear proof against the accused; and it is even alleged by some who have examined the whole evidence produced that the decisions of the first court did not proceed upon a calm judicial inquiry, but were dictated by strong prejudice against the accused on account of their religious views and peculiar eccentricities; and, in particular, that the evidence gives no support whatever to the charge of licentiousness (comp. Kanitz, *Aufklärung nach Acten, Quellen, etc., für Welt u. Kirchengesch.* [Basle and Ludwigsburg, 1862]). Mr. Dixon has directed attention to the similarity of the Mucker movement with that of the Princeites (q. v.) in England, and that of the Bible Communists or Perfectionists (q. v.) in this country, popularly known as Oneida Communists; all of which took place about the same time and in connection with revival excitement, although it may almost be regarded as certain that the originators of these movements had not even heard of each other. A class of religious enthusiasts who originated under Stephen in Saxony, and then emigrated to this country, will be treated in the article STEPHENITES. See *Zeitschrift für historische Theologie*, 1832; Hagenbach, *Kirchengesch.* vol. vii (2d ed. 1872), Lect. xxvi. (J. H. W.)

Mudge, Enoch, a Methodist Episcopal minister, and one of the pioneers of Methodism in New England, was born of religious parents at Lynn, Mass., June 21, 1776. He was converted at fifteen, under the ministry of Jesse Lee; entered the itinerancy in 1793, and labored assiduously; in 1796 he travelled, instead of the presiding elder, in Maine; in 1799 poor health obliged him to locate at Orrington, Maine, where he resided till 1816. While there he was twice chosen state representative, and had much to do with the passage of the "Religious Freedom Bill." At the end of this time he re-entered the itinerancy, and was stationed in Boston. He filled various charges until 1832, when he was appointed to the Seaman's Bethel at New Bedford, and there labored with signal success until 1844, when he was obliged by paralysis to retire from the active work of the ministry. He lived beloved at Lynn, and labored as his strength permitted until his death, April 2, 1850. He was the first minister that Methodism produced in New England, and his long and useful life was full of successful labor for God. He was an able and interesting preacher, and commanded universal respect and love. His published works are "a volume of excellent *Sermons*, and many poetical pieces of more than ordinary merit." See *Minutes of Conferences*, iv, 538; Stevens, *Memorials of Methodism*, vol. i, ch. x; Sprague, *Annals of the Amer. Pulpit*, vol. vii.

Mudge, John A., a minister of the Methodist Episcopal Church, was born in Ohio, Oct. 27, 1829. His parents being poor, his early education was greatly neglected. He was converted when quite young, and determined to enter the ministry. Feeling his need of a more thorough preparation, he studied for a while at the college in Berea. He joined the North Ohio Conference in 1850, and held several important positions in that Conference. He was a man eloquent in the pulpit, clear in his judgment, and diligent in his studies. He was secretary of the Conference for some time, and a delegate to the General Conference in 1872. He died Oct. 27, 1873. See *Minutes of Annual Conferences*, 1874, p. 110.

Mudge, Thomas Hicks, a minister of the Methodist Episcopal Church, was born in Orrington, Me., Sept. 28, 1815. His parents removed to Lynn, Mass., in his childhood; and being early brought under religious influence, he was converted, and united with the Church in 1829. Soon after his conversion he was seized with the desire to preach the Gospel, and in order to qualify himself for this work prepared for college at Wilbraham Academy. After going through the college course at the Wesleyan University in Middletown, Conn., where he graduated in 1840, and at the Union Theological Seminary at New York (class of 1843), he joined the New England Conference, and remained a member of it till 1857, when he became professor of sacred literature at M'Kendree College, Lebanon, Ill. In 1859 he was transferred to the Missouri Conference, and stationed successively at Pilot Knob, Simpson Chapel, St. Louis, and Independence. At the outbreak of the rebellion he was obliged to leave the state, and sought refuge in Manhattan, Kan., where he filled an appointment for a year; but joining the Kansas Conference, at the earnest solicitation of the Church was sent to Baldwin City. His health, however, failed, and he died there, July 24, 1862. Mr. Mudge was a close student, especially of the Word of God, and possessed much critical knowledge of the sacred text. For the exposition and illustration of it he collected, from American and foreign publishers, one of the most valuable private libraries of sacred literature in this country. His preaching was rich in

thought, and pervaded by a spirit of deep piety. Many of his brief expositions of the Scripture lessons, before his sermons, were of themselves pithy discourses of great value. He had devised large plans of usefulness through the application of his ripe scholarship to the exposition of God's Word, but the little he had written was never considered of sufficient importance for publication. See *Minutes of Annual Conferences*, 1863, p. 23.

Mudge, Zachary, an eminent clergyman and educator of the Anglican communion, was born near the close of the 17th century. About 1716 he became master of a free-school at Bideford, and about 1736 rector of St. Andrew's, in Plymouth. He was after this prebend of Exeter. He died in 1769. Mr. Mudge was an intimate friend of Dr. Johnson, and is highly spoken of as a scholar and clergyman. He published *A Specimen of a new Translation of the Book of Psalms* (1733, 4to): —*Essay towards a new English Version of the Book of Psalms* (1744, 4to); of these, Horne says, "Some of his notes are more ingenious than solid:"—*Church Authority* (a sermon, 1748, 4to), answered in *The Claims of Church Authority considered* (1749, 8vo):—and several others of his sermons (Lond. 1731, 8vo; 1739, 8vo). See Boswell, *Life of Johnson* (ed. 1848), p. 679, 686; Allibone, *Dict. of Brit. and Amer. Authors*, s. v.

Mudita, one of the five kinds of Bhawna or meditation in which the Buddhist priests are required to engage. The *mudita* is the meditation of joy, but it is not the joy arising from earthly possessions. It feels indifferent to individuals, and refers to all sentient beings. In the exercise of this mode of meditation the priest must express the wish, "May the good fortune of the prosperous never pass away; may each one receive his own appointed reward."

Mudo, el (*the Mute*), an eminent Spanish painter who attained great celebrity because of his masterly delineations of sacred subjects, was born at Logrono in 1526. His real name was *Juan Fernandez Navarette*, or *Juan Fernandez Ximenes de Naverette*. He was called "*el Mudo*," after he had acquired distinction as a painter, from his having been deaf and dumb from his infancy. He showed a talent for art early in life, and first studied under Foy Vicente de Santo Domingo, a monk of the Order of Geronomytes, under whom he made such rapid progress, and exhibited so much genius, that thy parents, by the advice of his instructor, sent him to Italy to study with Titian, with whom he remained several years, and thoroughly imbibed his principles and manner of coloring, so that he was called by his countrymen the Spanish Titian. He remained in Italy twenty years, visiting all the principal cities— Rome, Florence, Naples, etc.—studying the works of the most eminent painters, who entertained for him the highest respect on account of his eminent abilities, perhaps heightened by his infirmity. He had already acquired a distinguished reputation in Italy when, in 1568, he was summoned to Madrid by Philip II to paint in the Escurial, and on his arrival he was appointed painter to the king, with a pension of two hundred ducats, in addition to the price of his works. He was naturally of a delicate constitution, and he had hardly commenced his labors when a severe malady compelled him to retire, with the permission of his royal patron, to his native place, Logrono, where he remained three years, during which time he painted four magnificent pictures, and carried them with him to Madrid in 1571. These were the *Assumption of the Virgin*, the *Martyrdom of St. James the Great*, a *St. Philip*, and a *St. Jerome*, which were placed in the Escurial, while the artist was rewarded with five hundred ducats, besides his pension. The head of the Virgin in the *Assumption* is supposed to be a portrait of his mother, the Donna Catalina Ximenes, who in her youth was very beautiful. In 1575 he added four more pictures, the *Nativity*, *Christ at the Pillar*, the *Holy Family*, and *St. John writing the*

Apocalypse, for which he received eight hundred ducats. In the *Nativity* El Mudo successfully overcame a formidable difficulty in painting—the introducing of three lights into the picture, as in the famous *Notte* of Correggio; one from the irradiation proceeding from the infant Jesus, another from a glory of angels above, and a third from a flaming torch. It is related that Pellegrino Tibaldi, on seeing it, exclaimed, "Oh, i belli pastori!" This exclamation gave name to the picture, and it continues to be known to this day as "*The beautiful Shepherds.*" In 1576 he painted his famous piece of *Abraham entertaining the three Angels,* for which he received five hundred ducats. He now undertook a stupendous work, and was engaged to paint thirty-two pictures for the Escurial, twenty-seven of which were to be seven feet and a half in height and seven feet and a quarter in breadth, and the other five thirteen feet high and nine broad. He did not live to complete this vast undertaking; he painted eight, representing the apostles, the evangelists, and St. Paul and St. Barnabas; the others were finished by Alonso Sanchez Cællo and Luis de Carovajal. El Mudo died in 1579. His pictures are extremely inaccessible; except a small picture of the baptism of Christ in the museum at Madrid, they are buried in the royal solitude of the Escurial.

There were two other Spanish painters, of little note, called *El Mudo*—one PEDRO EL MUDO, and the other DIEGO LOPEZ, who must not be confounded with the illustrious Navarette.

Mueddin. See MUÉZZIN.

Muësis. See MYESIS.

Muëzzin (*Mueddin*) is the Arabic name of the Mohammedan official attached to a mosque, whose duty it is to summon the faithful to prayer at five different times of day and night. Stationed on one of the minarets, he chants in a peculiar manner the form of proclamation. Before doing so, however, the muezzin ought to repeat the following prayer: "O my God! give me piety; purify me: thou alone hast the power. Thou art my benefactor and my master, O Lord. Thou art towards me as I desire; may I be towards thee as thou desirest. My God! cause my interior to be better than my exterior. Direct all my actions to rectitude. O God! deign in thy mercy to direct my will towards that which is good. Grant me at the same time true honor and spiritual poverty, O thou, the most merciful of the merciful." His chant (Adan) consists of these words, repeated at intervals: "Allah is most great. I testify that there is no God but Allah. I testify that Mohammed is the apostle of Allah. Come to prayer. Come to security." ("Prayer is better than sleep" is added in the morning, at the Subh or Fegr.) "Allah is most great. There is no deity but Allah!" Besides these regular calls, two more are chanted during the night for those pious persons who wish to perform special nightly devotions. The first (Ula) continues, after the usual Adan, in this manner: "There is no deity but Allah! He hath no companion—to him belongeth the dominion—to him belongeth praise. He giveth life, and causeth death. And he is living, and shall never die. In his hand is blessing, and he is almighty," etc. The second of these night-calls (Ebed) takes place at an hour before daybreak, and begins as follows: "I extol the perfection of Allah, the Existing forever and ever: the perfection of Allah, the Desired, the Existing, the Single, the Supreme," etc. According to an Arab tradition, the office was instituted by Mohammed himself, and the words quoted for the morning prayer were added by the first muezzin on an occasion when the Prophet overslept himself. Mohammed approved of them, and they were ever afterwards retained in the morning call. The office of a muezzin is generally intrusted to blind men only, lest they might, from their elevation [see MINARET], have too free a view over the surrounding terraces and harems. The harmonious and sonorous voices

The Muezzin.

of the singers, together with the simplicity and solemnity of the melody, make a strikingly poetical impression upon the mind of the hearer in the daytime; much more, however, is this the case whenever the sacred chant resounds from the height of the mosque through the moonlit stillness of an Eastern night. See Trevor, *India under Moh. Rule* (see Index).

Muffler (רָעַל, *ra'al,* a *reeling,* as in Zech. xii, 2; Sept. and Vulg. undistinguishable), a term occurring in Isa. iii, 19, among articles of female apparel or ornament, and thought by Gesenius (*Heb. Lex.* s. v.) to signify a *veil,* from its tremulous motion, the corresponding Arabic word denoting a similar article of dress. See VEIL. The margin of the Auth. Vers. has "spangled ornaments," a mere conjecture. Roberts explains the ornaments spoken of by reference to the costume of the women of India: "The 'chains,' as consisting first of one most beautifully worked with a pendant ornament for the neck; there is also a profusion of others, which go round the same part, and rest on the bosom. In making curious chains, the goldsmiths of England do not surpass those of the East. The 'bracelets' are large ornaments for the wrists, in which are sometimes enclosed small bells. The 'mufflers' are, so far as I can judge, not for the face, but for the breasts." Kitto, however, accedes to the opinion of Gesenius that the last are a species of outdoor veil (see *Daily Bible Illustra.* ad loc.). See ATTIRE.

Mufti (Arabic, *expounder of the law*) is the name of the chief of the Turkish ecclesiastical and judicial order. There is a mufti in every large town of the Ottoman empire. In his religious capacity he administers the property of the Church, and watches over the due observance and preservation of its rites and discipline. In his civil capacity he pronounces decisions in such matters of dispute as may be submitted to him. The Turkish grand mufti is the supreme head of the *Ulemas* (servants of religion and laws), and has, together with the grand vizir (Vizir Azim), the supreme guidance of the state, nominally ruled by the sultan. He is the chief spiritual authority, and in this capacity he is also denominated Sheik-al-Islam (Lord of the Faith). The imáms (priests), however, chosen from the body of the ulemas, are, from the moment of their official appointment, under the authority of the Kislar-Aga, or Chief of the Black Eunuchs. The better class of the ulemas are the teachers and expounders of the law, from among whom the mollahs and cadis are elected. The Turkish laws have their basis in the Koran; the mufti thus, as head of the judges, acquires a spiritual authority, and so great is the popular regard for the mufti that even the sultan himself, if he will preserve any appearance of religion, cannot, without first hearing his opinion, put any person to death, or so much as inflict any corporeal punishment. In all actions, especially criminal ones, his opinion is required by giving him a writing, in which the case is stated under feigned names, which he subscribes with the word *Olur* or *Olmuz*, i. e. he shall or shall not be punished, accompanied with these emphatic words, in which he repudiates all claims to infallibility, "God knows better." Such outward honor is paid to the grand mufti that the grand seignior himself rises up before him, and advances seven steps towards him when he comes into his presence. He alone has the honor of kissing the sultan's left shoulder, while the prime vizir kisses only the hem of his garment. When the grand seignior addresses any writing to the grand mufti, he gives him the following titles: "To the *esad*, the wisest of the wise; instructed in all knowledge: the most excellent of excellents; abstaining from things unlawful; the spring of virtue and true science; heir of the prophetic doctrines; resolver of the problems of faith; revealer of the orthodox articles; key of the treasures of truth; the light to doubtful allegories; strengthened with the grace of the Supreme Legislator of mankind. May the Most High God perpetuate thy favors." The election of the grand mufti is vested solely in the sultan, who presents him with a vest of rich sables, and allows him a salary of a thousand aspers a day, which is about five pounds sterling. Besides this, he has the disposal of certain benefices belonging to the royal mosques, which he makes no scruple of selling to the best advantage; and on his admission to his office he is complimented by the agents of the bashas, who make him the usual presents, which generally amount to a very considerable sum. It is the grand mufti's prerogative generally to gird the sultan with the sword

The Grand Mufti.

at his ascension to the throne, a ceremony which takes place at the Mosque of Eyub, and which is equal to the ceremony of coronation. In modern days the position of mufti has lost much of its former dignity and importance. His fetwa, or decision, although attached to the imperial decrees, imparts to it but little additional weight. Nor is his own dictum in things spiritual always considered as finally binding. The only prerogative of muftis and ulemas which has hitherto remained untouched is their being exempt from bodily or otherwise degrading punishments; nor can their property ever be confiscated, but descends to their successors.

Muggleton. See MUGGLETONIANS.

Muggletonians, a sect that arose in England about the year 1651, and of which the founders were John Reeve and Ludovic Muggleton (the latter born 1607, died March 14, 1697), both until 1651 obscure men. The former's profession is not at all known, and he lived but a little while after their public declaration as religionists. Muggleton was a journeyman tailor, and is depicted by his contemporaries with long, thin hair, low forehead, protruding brow, broad high cheek-bones, and what physiognomists would call the aggressive nose. These men claimed to have the spirit of prophecy, and that they had been appointed by an audible voice from God as the last and greatest prophets of Jesus Christ, and affirmed themselves to be the *two witnesses* of Rev. xi. Muggleton professed to be the "mouth" of Reeve, as Aaron was of Moses. They asserted a right to bless all who favored and to curse all who opposed them, and did not hesitate to declare eternal damnation against their adversaries. They favored the world with a number of publications. In 1650 Muggleton published his first paper, in which it was asserted "that he was the chief judge in the world in passing sentence of eternal death and damnation upon the souls and bodies of men; that in obedience to his commission he had already cursed and damned many hundreds to all eternity; that in doing this he went by as certain a rule as the judges of the land do when they pass sentence according to law; and that no infinite Spirit of Christ, nor any God, could or should be able to deliver from his sentence and curse." In another paper, published later, he insisted "that he was as true an ambassador of God, and judge of all men's spiritual estate, as any ever was since the creation of the world." He also declared himself above ordinances of every kind, not excepting prayer and preaching, rejecting all creeds and Church discipline and authority. The most remarkable of his papers is the one particularly directed to the Parliament and commonwealth of England, and to his excellency the lord-general Cromwell, which was entitled *A Remonstrance from the Eternal God.* The consequence was that the prophets were declared "nuisances," and imprisoned in "Old Bridewell." Another remarkable publication was *A general Epistle from the Holy Spirit*, dated from "Great Trinity Lane, at a chandler's shop, over against one Mr. Millis, a brown baker, near Bow Lane End, London." A pretty full exposition of their doctrines they furnished in 1656 in their publication entitled *The divine Looking-glass of the Third Testament of our Lord Jesus Christ*, which makes the chief articles of their creed to have been confused notions of Gnostic heresies. Thus they taught that God has the real body of a man; that the Trinity is only a variety of names of God; that God himself came down to earth, and was born as a man and suffered death; and that during this time Elias was his representative in heaven. They also held very singular and not very intelligible doctrines concerning angels and devils. The Evil One, they taught, became incarnate in Eve, and there is no devil at all without the body of man or woman; and that the devil is man's spirit of unclean reason and cursed imagination, and that this is the only devil we have now to fear. According to them the soul of man is inseparably united with the body, with which it dies and will rise again. The works of Ludovic Muggleton, with his portrait prefixed. were published in 1756, and *A complete Collection of the Works of Reeve and Muggleton, together with other Muggletonian Tracts,* was published by some of their modern followers in 1832 (3 vols. 4to). A list of books and general index to Reeve's and Muggleton's works was published in 1846, royal 8vo. Among the works written against them are the following: *The New Witnesses proved Old Heretics,* by William Penn (1672, 4to); *A true Representation of the absurd and mischievous Principles of the Sect commonly known by the Name of Muggletonians* (Lond. 1694, 4to). Muggleton succeeded in gathering a large number of followers, and at the time of his death (1697) the Muggletonians, as they called themselves, were largely scattered all over England. They subsisted in good numbers until the end of the first quarter of this century; but the census of 1851 showed no trace of them, and they are supposed to be now wellnigh extinct. In 1868 one of the most eminent of the sect in modern times, Mr. Joseph Gander, died, and the London papers then announced that with him expired the Muggletonians. He had sustained a place of worship for a few of like mind with himself. Mr. Gander is spoken of as a "sincere member of the sect called Muggletonians for upwards of sixty years." Muggleton himself lies buried in Spinningwheel Alley, Moorfields, with the following inscription over his tomb:

"While mausoleums and large inscriptions give
    Might, splendor, and past death make potents live,
It is enough briefly to write thy name.
Succeeding times by that will read thy fame;
Thy deeds, thy acts, around the world resound,
No foreign soil where Muggleton's not found."

See Chamberlain, *Present State of England* (1702), p. 258; *Transact. of the Liverpool Lit. and Phil. Society,* 1868–70; Stoughton, *Eccles. Hist. of England* (*Ch. of the Restor.*), ii, 208, Evans, *Dict. of Sects,* etc.; Hunt, *Religious Thought of England,* i, 241.

Muhle (or *Muhlius*), HEINRICH, a German theologian, was born at Bremen, March 7, 1666. He was educated at the gymnasium of his native city, but went in 1686 to Hamburg to study ancient languages, and from there to the university at Giessen, where he studied theology. He then spent a year at Frankfort-on-the-Oder; in 1688 attended lectures at Kiel, in 1689 at Leipsic, and in 1690 at Wittenberg. He was appointed in 1691 professor of the Greek and Oriental languages, of poetry and ecclesiastical elocution, at the University of Kiel. In 1692 he made a voyage through England and Holland, and thus secured in 1695 the position of professor of theology and inspector of schools of Schleswig-Holstein. In 1697 he was appointed pastor of the city church at Kiel; but as that place did not suit him, he accepted a call in 1698 as general superintendent, chief court-preacher, and provost at Gottorf, with the title of chief counsellor of the Consistory, but had to resign this position on account of some difficulties at the court; he returned to Kiel, and was appointed in 1724 senior of the university. He died Dec. 7, 1733. Muhle had a dispute with the Danish superintendent-general Schwarz, who accused him of being a millenarian and a disciple of Cocceius, who had tried to cause a schism in the Schleswig-Holstein Church. Muhle was even obliged to go into court, where he reprimanded Schwarz severely; but the dispute did not end until Schwarz died. His most important works are: *De Messia sedente ad dextram Dei; Dissertatio philologico-theologica ad vindicandum locum Psa. cx,* 1 *contra ψευδερμένειαν Judæorum, sub moderamine D. Clodii* (Gissæ, 1687, 4to): —*Disquisitio de origine linguarum stirpeque ac matre Græcæ, Latinæ, et Germanicæ Hebræa* (Kilon, 1692, 8vo):—*Daphnis, sive de obitu C. Alberti, βουκολικὸν sacræ Divi Musagetæ memoriæ religioso, quo par est, affectu cultuque dicatum* (ibid. 1695, fol.):—*Kurze Anzeige der falschen Beschuldigungen des Dr. Josua Schwarz gegen ihn* (Schleswig, 1702, 8vo):—*Erörterung verschie-*

dener, jetziger Zeit erregten Materca in drei Ordinationsreden kürzlich abgehandelt, nebst einem Vorbericht von D. Schwarz'ens neulichst wider ihn herausgegebenen Tract. Chiliastischer Vorspiele, Principia und Chiliasmus selbst genannt, an das sämmtliche Schleswig-Holsteinische Ministerium (ibid. 1705, 8vo):—*De sectæ studio in ecclesia orthodoxa vitando, invitatio ad lectiones publicas in libros orthodoxæ ecclesiæ symbolicos universe ac sigillatim rite instituendas* (Kilon, 1712, 4to):—*M. Lutheri propositiones pro declaratione virtutis indulgentiarum, qua ostenditur, quantum illæ et reipublicæ et ecclesiæ nocuerint, quamque vere ac merito cum reformationi evangelicæ, tum schismati in evidente enato causam ac occasionem suppeditarint* (Hamburg, 1717, 4to):—*De variis pontificum iisque iniquissimis adversus Cæsares, reges ac principes molitionibus et ab Christi vicariis, quales se jactant, longe alienissimis, dissertatio* (Kilon, 1729, 4to): —*Hymnus A. Clarenbachii in Henr. Zütphaniensis, Martyris apprime celebrati, locum Meldorffium in Dithmarsiam vocati, ac Coloniæ Agrippinæ d. 28 Sept. 1529, concremati, memoriæ solenniter renovandæ* (ibid. 1733, fol.). See Döring, *Gelehr. Theol. Deutschlands,* iv, 618–629.

Mühlberg, BATTLE OF. See THIRTY-YEARS' WAR.

Muhlenberg, Friederich August, a minister of the Lutheran Church, noted in the Revolutionary history of this country, was the second son of Dr. H. M. Muhlenberg, and was born at the Trappe, Montgomery Co., Pa., Jan. 26, 1750. He was educated at Halle, in Saxony, and was ordained to the work of the ministry before his return to this country. He was pastor for a time in Lebanon Co., also at New Hanover and Reading, Pa. Thence he removed to the city of New York, where he continued to reside, as pastor of the Lutheran Church, until the British entered the city. In consequence of his devotion to American principles, it was supposed if he fell into the hands of the enemy he would be the victim of cruel and vindictive treatment; he therefore removed to Pennsylvania, and took charge for a season of the Lutheran congregation in New Hanover. Having been called by the people into political life, he laid aside the duties of the ministry. In 1779 he was elected a member of the Continental Congress. He was also sent as a delegate to the state convention which assembled to ratify the new Federal Constitution, and was selected by his colleagues to preside over their deliberations. He was repeatedly chosen as a representative to Congress under the new constitution, and on two different occasions served as Speaker of the House. He was a prominent and useful statesman. He was universally esteemed, and died, greatly lamented, at Lancaster in 1812. (M. L. S.)

Muhlenberg, Gotthilf Henry Ernest, D.D., the youngest son of Dr. H. M. Muhlenberg, was born at the Trappe, Pa., Nov. 17, 1753. He spent several years at the University of Halle in the prosecution of his studies for the sacred office. On his return to this country in 1770 he was ordained to the work of the ministry, and immediately became assistant to his father, and third minister of the United Lutheran churches in Philadelphia. He continued to occupy this position until the British obtained possession of the city. As he was threatened with the halter, because of his zealous attachment to the cause of the Revolution, he found it necessary to flee from the scene of danger. Disguised under a blanket, and with a rifle on his shoulder, he had nearly fallen into hostile hands through the treachery of a Tory innkeeper, who had intentionally directed him to take the road by which the British were approaching. Warned, however, in season, he succeeded in making his escape, and reached New Hanover in safety. Relieved for a time from professional duties, he engaged with great zest in the study of botany, and acquired that love for this favorite pursuit which afterwards so strongly manifested itself. On the election of his brother to a civil office he succeeded him as pastor. In the year 1780 he removed to Lancaster, where he labored in the ministry with great efficiency, enjoying the uninterrupted regard of his congregation, and exercising an influence in the community which it is rarely the privilege of the most highly favored to enjoy, until his death, which occurred May 23, 1815. He was a man of vigorous intellect and extensive attainments. He was an able theologian, a good linguist, and was distinguished as an Oriental scholar. His acquisitions in medicine, chemistry, and mineralogy were also considerable. As a botanist he had a European reputation, and was in correspondence with the most distinguished savans of the Continent. His *Catalogus Plantarum* and *Descriptio Uberior Graminum* are well known. His *Flora Lancastriensis* is still in manuscript, as well as several treatises in the department of theology and ethics. (M. L. S.)

Muhlenberg, Henry Augustus, a minister of the Lutheran Church, noted, however, more as a statesman than as a theologian, was the son of the preceding, and was born at Lancaster, Pa., May 13, 1782. He was largely educated by his father; and, after studying theology, was ordained for the ministry, and became pastor at Reading, Pa., in 1802. Poor health obliged him to resign in 1828, and he retired to live on a farm. He was, however, not suffered long to enjoy this life, for he was chosen member of Congress in 1829, and so continued until 1838, when he was made minister to Austria, a position which he held until 1840. He also held other political offices. He was a candidate for governor of his state in 1835, and declined in 1837 the secretaryship of the navy and the mission to Russia. He published the life of his uncle, Gen. Muhlenberg (Phila. 1849).

Muhlenberg, Henry Melchior, D.D., the patriarch of the Evangelical Lutheran Church in America, was born Sept. 6, 1711, at Einbeck, in Hanover, then a free city of Germany. He was the son of Nicolas Melchior and Anna Maria Kleinschmidt, originally Saxon, but who, like many of the earlier followers of the great Reformer, having suffered severely during the Thirty-years' War, which for a time threatened the extermination of the Protestant religion in Europe, removed to Einbeck. His father was well known in the community, and highly esteemed. He was a member of the city council, and also held a judicial appointment, from which he derived the necessary means for the support of his family. His mother was the daughter of a retired officer, and is represented as a woman of sterling good-sense, great energy, and devoted piety. Henry was early dedicated to God in Christian baptism, and was carefully instructed by his parents in the principles and duties of the Christian religion. These influences were never effaced from his mind. In his youth he laid the foundation of that character which proved so valuable in his future life. In consequence of the death of his father his studies were interrupted, and he was thrown upon his own resources for a support; but his leisure hours were faithfully devoted to the acquisition of knowledge. Nothing could repress his love of study. His early life was years of privation and toil, yet without this preparatory discipline he would probably never have acquired those habits of self-reliance and systematic effort, that strength of purpose and heroic determination, which so prominently marked his subsequent career, and contributed so much to his usefulness in this Western World. From his twelfth till his twenty-first year young Muhlenberg toiled incessantly in his efforts to assist in the maintenance of the family, yet during the intervals of repose he improved every opportunity afforded him for mental culture. On reaching his manhood he secured the position of tutor in the school of Raphelius at Zellerfeld, and the time not officially employed he devoted to study. In the spring of 1735 he entered the University of Göttingen, where he remained for three years, triumphing over all the difficulties he encountered, and

winning the confidence of his instructors. The pious teachings of Dr. Oporin, who had kindly received him into his family and employed him as an amanuensis, exerted over him a most favorable influence, awakening in him a deeper insight into his own character, and a clearer apprehension of the plan of salvation. "By his lectures," he says, "on the total depravity of our nature I was much moved, and so convinced of my sinfulness that I loathed myself on account of my folly. I was convinced by the Word of God that till this period my understanding in spiritual things was dark; that my will was disinclined to that new life which proceeds from God; that my memory had been employed only in collecting carnal things, my imagination in discovering sinful objects for the gratification of my perverted affections, and my members by habitual use had become weapons of unrighteousness. But as I learned to recognise sin as sin, then followed sorrow, repentance, and hatred of it—shame and humiliation on account of it—hunger and thirst for the righteousness of Jesus Christ. In this state of mind I was directed to the crucified Saviour; the merits of his death gave me life; my thirst was quenched by him, the Living Spring." From this period he became a most earnest Christian. He burned with an ardent desire to do good. On his graduation at Göttingen he repaired to Halle. There he continued his studies, and taught in the Orphan House. He lived on the most intimate terms with Franke, Cellarius, and Fabricius. By their advice he was led to prepare himself for the missionary work, and Bengal was the point selected as the field of his operations. While arrangements were making to send him to India, and just after he had been solemnly set apart to the work of the ministry, a most importunate application from congregations in Pennsylvania reached Germany for some one to supply the great spiritual destitution that existed. The attention of the faculty was immediately directed to Muhlenberg, then in his thirty-first year, as a most suitable person for the position. Cheerfully yielding to the call, and with unshaken confidence in God, he was ready to abandon the comforts of home and the society of friends, as well as the prospects of future distinction to which a mind so highly gifted might have aspired, and to settle in this remote and, at that time, wild and inhospitable region as a humble instrument for the advancement of Christ's kingdom. He reached this country in 1742. His arrival was an occasion of great joy and inexpressible gratitude to his German brethren. The Church he found in a most wretched condition; in his own language, it was not *plantata*, but *plantanda*. There had been numerous settlements in different parts of the country, and some of them had been furnished with able and faithful ministers, but as a general thing the Lutheran population had been sadly neglected. Muhlenberg's advent therefore marks a new æra in the history of the Lutheran Church in this country. Its character soon changed; its condition gradually improved; its position was at once strengthened, and permanence given to its operations. Frequent accessions were made to the ranks of the ministry—men educated at Halle, imbued with the spirit of their Master, and wholly devoted to their work, upon whose labors the blessing of Heaven signally rested. Entering upon the discharge of his duties, Muhlenberg assumed the pastoral care of the associated churches of Philadelphia, New Hanover, and Providence, which had united in a call for a minister. These three congregations continued to form the more prominent scenes of his ministerial labors, although there was probably not an organized Lutheran church in his day in which he did not preach; and when a difficulty occurred in any congregation, his aid was always invoked, and seldom did he fail in reconciling differences and restoring confidence. His duties, in many respects, resembled those of an itinerant bishop whose diocese extended over a large territory. Often he undertook distant and irksome journeys for the purpose of gathering together the scattered flock, preaching the Word and administering the sacraments, introducing salutary discipline for the government of the churches, and performing other kind services, in his desire to repair the waste places of Zion and promote the cause of genuine piety. The care of the churches rested upon him. He had the confidence of the people; his presence everywhere inspired hope. His opinions were valued; his influence was boundless and unprecedented. The first three years of his ministry in this country, Dr. Muhlenberg resided in Philadelphia; the next sixteen at Providence. In 1761 he returned to Philadelphia, and remained fifteen years, the condition of things in the congregation there requiring his presence. In 1776 he resumed his charge in the country. During the War of the American Revolution, because of his devotion to the principles involved in the struggle, he excited against him the most violent opposition, and his life was often exposed to imminent peril. He was warned and entreated to remove farther into the interior from the scene of hostilities, but he always refused. He was extensively known, and his relations to the Revolution were well understood. Many took advantage of his position, and persons of all classes resorted to his house. "His home," says a contemporary, "was constantly filled with fugitives, acquaintances and strangers, with the poor and hungry, noble and common beggars. The hungry never went away unsatisfied, nor the suffering uncomforted." The last few years of his life Dr. Muhlenberg's health gradually declined. His mind, in prospect of death, was calm, sustained by a humble yet firm reliance upon the Saviour of sinners. When the summons came, with entire composure, and in confident expectation of a blissful immortality, he yielded up his spirit, and rested in the bosom of his God. His active and useful career terminated Oct. 7, 1787. His death was the occasion of wide-spread and unaffected sorrow. The people grieved that they should no longer see his face and listen to his paternal counsels. He was the friend and father of all, and all regarded it as their duty and privilege to mourn "their father, friend, example, guide removed." In many places the bells were tolled, the churches enshrouded in mourning, and funeral sermons delivered, in grateful remembrance of the departed, and as testimonials of the respect his worth everywhere inspired. The honored remains of the patriarch peacefully rest near the church which was so long the scene of his earnest labors, and in which he so often dispensed the symbols of the Saviour's love among the people of God, and animated them in their Christian pilgrimage by the hopes and consolations of the Gospel. The history of Dr. Muhlenberg's life is the history of one of the noblest minds, consecrating its learning, its affections, its influence, its energies, to all the interests of the Church and of humanity, to the glory and service of that Saviour who redeemed him with his own precious blood. He possessed a combination of qualities which peculiarly fitted him for the duties he was called to perform. Gifted by nature with the highest powers, which had been brought under the influence of the best culture; endowed with a noble heart, which had been sanctified by divine grace and disciplined in the school of affliction; and in the possession of a physical constitution which in early life had been inured to labor; with an ardent, active piety, an earnest and enthusiastic devotion to the work, nothing seemed wanting for the successful accomplishment of his mission. He was the man kindly raised up by Providence for the particular emergency required at the time in this western hemisphere. The most sanguine expectations of his success were entertained by those who selected him for the mission. These expectations were more than realized. His praise is deservedly in all the churches. He has left a name fragrant with the richest honor attainable in this life—that of a good man, sincere in his professions and upright in his conduct, widely esteemed and greatly beloved. His society was sought and his influence courted by the learned

men of the day. By the special invitation of the faculty he attended the Commencement exercises of Princeton College, and from the University of Pennsylvania he received the doctorate in divinity, a distinction in those days rarely conferred, and only upon those whose claims to the honor were unquestionable. See Helmuth, *Denkmal der Liebe u. Achtung*, etc. (Phila. 1788); Stoever, *Life of H. M. Muhlenberg* (Phila. 1856); *Evang. Qu. Rev.* (Luth.) i, 390, 590. (M. L. S.)

Muhlenberg, John Peter, a Lutheran minister, was the oldest son of Henry Melchior Muhlenberg, and was born at the Trappe, Montgomery County, Pa., Oct. 1, 1746. His early education was conducted by his father and Dr. Smith, of Philadelphia. In the sixteenth year of his age he, with his two brothers, was sent to Germany to be educated at the University of Halle. On his return to this country, in 1768, he was ordained a minister of the Lutheran Church, and was for a season pastor of churches in New Germantown and Bedminster, N. J. In 1772 he removed to Woodstock, Dunmore County (now Shenandoah), Va., where many Germans from the Middle States had settled, and, forming themselves into a congregation, requested Dr. Muhlenberg to send them his son as their rector. These Lutherans, in consequence of the laws then existing in Virginia on the subject of Church establishment, had organized as members of the Swedish branch of the Lutheran Church, and in order that their minister might enforce the payment of tithes, it was necessary that he should be invested with episcopal ordination. Accordingly Mr. Muhlenberg repaired to England for the purpose, and in connection with Mr. White, afterwards the venerable bishop of Pennsylvania, was ordained as priest by the lord bishop of London. He continued his labors in Virginia till 1775, when his ardent patriotism and military spirit induced him, at the solicitation of general Washington, with whom he was on the most intimate terms, to accept a colonel's commission in the army. It is said that after he had received his appointment he preached a valedictory to his congregation, in the course of which he eloquently depicted the wrongs our country had suffered from Great Britain, and then added that "there was a time for all things; a time to preach and a time to pray; but there is also a time to fight, and that time has now come." Then, pronouncing the benediction, he deliberately laid aside his gown, which had thus far concealed his military uniform, and, proceeding to the door of the church, ordered the drums to beat for recruits. Nearly three hundred men enlisted under his banner, with whom he immediately marched to the protection of Charleston, South Carolina. He was present at the battle of Sullivan's Island, and performed a conspicuous part in all our Southern campaigns. Having been promoted in 1777 to the rank of brigadier-general, he held command in the battles of Brandywine and Germantown, and shared the dangers and responsibilities of Monmouth, Stony Point, and Yorktown. He continued in the service until the close of the war, and was then promoted to the rank of major-general before the army was disbanded. After the war, under the old constitution of Pennsylvania, he was elected vice-president of the state, with Benjamin Franklin as president. He was chosen for several terms as a representative in Congress, and also served as a presidential elector. In 1801 he was selected by the Legislature of Pennsylvania as United States Senator. He was likewise honored with several executive appointments. Jefferson appointed him supervisor of the revenue for Pennsylvania, and afterwards collector of the port of Philadelphia, which office he continued to hold during Madison's administration. He retained the confidence of the government till his death, and enjoyed the esteem of the community. He died at his residence near Gray's Ferry, Philadelphia, Oct. 1, 1807, and was buried by the side of his father at the Trappe. See Anderson, *Hist. of the Colonial Churches of Great Britain*, iii, 269. (M. L. S.)

Mühlhausen, Jom-Tob, of. See Lipmann.

Muhlius. See Muhl.

Muis, Simeon Marotte de, a French Hebraist, was born in 1587 at Orleans. Of his earlier personal history it is only known that he was canon and archdeacon of Soissons. Four years after Cayet's death (1614) he was installed professor of Hebrew in the royal college, and kept that chair until removed by death in 1644. Muis combined with the knowledge of this language solid judgment, fine discrimination, a pure, elegant, and easy style, and very extensive acquaintance with sacred history and the groundwork of religion. He had the reputation of being one of the most learned interpreters of the Scriptures. We possess of him, *R. Davidis Kimchi Commentarius in Malachiam, Heb. et Lat.* (Paris, 1618, 4to):—*In Psalmum xix trium rabbinorum Commentarii Hebraici cum Lat. interpretat.* (Paris, 1620, 8vo):—*Annotationes in Psalmum xxxiv,* printed in Bellarmine's *Institut. Hebraicæ* (1622, 8vo):—*Commentarius litteralis et historicus in omnes Psalmos et selecta V. T. cantica, cum versione nova ex Hebræo* (Par. 1630, fol.; Lovan. 1770, 2 vols. 4to); this commentary is considered one of the best in existence, and was so pronounced by Bossuet, Godeau, Gassendi, Voisin, and other Roman Catholic authorities:—*Assertio Veritatis Hebraicæ adversus Joannis Morini exercitationes in utrumque Samaritanorum Pentateuchum* (Par. 1631, 8vo): —and, in answer to Morin's repeated charge, *Exercitationes Biblicæ* (Par. 1633), a second defence of the Hebrew text entitled *Assertio Veritatis Hebraicæ altera* (Par. 1634), accompanied with a *Specimen variorum sacrorum,* containing notes of rabbins on the most difficult passages in the Pentateuch, the book of Joshua, and the first chapters of Judges:—*Castigatio Animadversionum ad Pentateuchum* (Par. 1639, 8vo). The most of De Muis's writings have, after his death, been collected and published by Claude d'Auvergne (Par. 1650, fol.). See Hoefer, *Nouv. Biog. Générale,* s. v.; Dupin, *Biblioth. des Auteurs Ecclésiastiques;* Nicéron, *Mémoires,* vol. xxxii, s. v.

Mulberry stands in the Auth. Vers. as the rendering of the Heb. בָּכָא, (*baka'*, regarded by Gesenius, *Heb. Lex.* s. v., as if from בָּכָה, *to weep*), or in the plur. בְּכָאִים (*bekaïm'*); which occurs, the first in Psa. lxxxiv, 6, "Who passing through the valley of *Baca* make it a well; the rain also filleth the pools;" the second in 2 Sam. v, 23, 24, and in 1 Chron. xiv, 14, 15, where the Philistines having spread themselves in the valley of Rephaim, David was ordered to attack them from behind, "And let it be, when thou hearest the sound of a going in the tops of the *mulberry-trees,* that thou shalt bestir thyself." In the former of these passages the term is usually regarded as an appellative, i. q. "the valley of *tears*" (so the Sept. ἡ κοιλὰς τοῦ κλαυθμῶνος, Vulg. *vallis lachrymarum;* see Baca); but in the latter two it undoubtedly designates some tree or shrub (the Sept. has also κλαυθμῶν in 2 Sam., but ἄπιος in 1 Chron.; the Vulg. *pyrus* in both places). The Jewish rabbins, with several modern versions, understand the mulberry-tree; others retain the Hebrew word. Neither 'the *mulberry* nor the *pear* tree, however, satisfies translators and commentators, because they do not possess any characters particularly suitable to the above passages. With regard to the mulberry, Rosenmüller justly observes (*Alterth.* IV, i, 247 sq.; *Bibl. Bot.* p. 256) that this interpretation "is countenanced neither by the ancient translators nor by the occurrence of any similar term in the cognate languages"—unless we adopt the opinion of Ursinus, who (*Arbor. Bib.* iii, 75), having in view the root of the word *bakah,* "to weep," identifies the name of the tree in question with the mulberry, "from the blood-like tears which the pressed berries pour forth." The mulberry-tree, moreover, appears to have another name in Scripture, namely, the "sycamine." Though there is no evidence to show that the

mulberry-tree occurs in the Hebrew Bible, yet the fruit of this tree (μόρον) is mentioned in 1 Macc. vi, 34 as having been, together with grape-juice, shown to the elephants of Antiochus Eupator, in order to irritate these animals and make them more formidable opponents to the army of the Jews. It is well known that many animals are enraged when they see blood or anything of the color of blood. See Sycamine.

Celsius (i, 339) quotes Abu'l Fadli's description of a shrub of Mecca called *baca,* with abundant fruit, distilling a juice from its branches when cut (whence the name, i. q. *tear*), and of a warming property; apparently some species of *Amyris* or *Balsamodendron.* Most lexicographers are satisfied with this explanation. That plant is probably the same with the one referred to by Forskål (p. 198) among the obscure plants without fructification which he obtained from Jobbæ, and which he says was called *baka,* or *ebka,* with a poisonous milky sap. If this be the same as the former, both are still unknown any further, and we cannot therefore determine whether they are found in Palestine or not. As to the tree of which Abu'l Fadli speaks, and which Sprengel (*Hist. rei herb.* p. 12) identifies with *Amyris Gileadensis,* Lin., it is impossible that it can denote the *baka* of the Hebrew Bible, although there is an exact similarity in form between the Hebrew and Arabic terms; for the *Amyridaceæ* are tropical shrubs, and never could have grown in the valley of Rephaim, the scriptural locality for the *bekaïm.*

"The tree alluded to in Scripture, whatever it is, must be common in Palestine, must grow in the neighborhood of water, have its leaves easily moved, and have a name in some of the cognate languages similar to the Hebrew *baka.* The only one answering to these conditions is that called *bak* by the Arabs, or rather *shajrat-al-bak*— that is, the *fly* or *gnat* tree. It seems to be so called from its seeds, when loosened from their capsular covering, floating about like gnats, in consequence of being covered with light, silk-like hairs, as is the case with those of the willow. In Richardson's Arabic dictionary the *bak-tree* is considered to be the elm; but from a passage of Dioscorides, preserved by Plempius, the *dirdar* of the Arabians seems to be another kind of bak-tree, probably the *arbor culicum* (tree of gnats) of the Latin translators of Avicenna. Now in other Arabic authors the dirdar is said to be a kind of *ghurb,* and the ghurb is ascertained to be the Lombardy poplar (*Illust. Himal. Bot.* p. 344). As it seems therefore tolerably clear that the bak-tree is a kind of poplar, and as the Arabic *bak* is very similar to the Hebrew *baka* [but in the Heb. the *k* in the name is כ, while in the Arabic it is that which corresponds to ק], so it is probable that one of the kinds of poplar may be intended in the above passages of Scripture. And it must be noted that the poplar is as appropriate as any tree can be for the elucidation of the passages in which the name occurs. For the poplar is well known to delight in moist situations, and bishop Horne, in his *Comm.* on Psa. lxxxiv, has inferred that in the valley of Baca the Israelites, on their way to Jerusalem, were refreshed by plenty of water. It is not less appropriate in the passages in 2 Sam. and 1 Chron., as no tree is more remarkable than the poplar for the ease with which its leaves are rustled by the slightest movement of the air; an effect which might be caused in a still night even by the movement of a body of men on the ground, when attacked in flank or while unprepared. That poplars are common in Palestine may be proved from Kitto's *Palestine,* p. 114: 'Of poplars we only know, with certainty, that the black poplar, the aspen, and the Lombardy poplar grow in Palestine. The aspen, whose long leaf-stalks cause the leaves to tremble with every breath of wind, unites with the willow and the oak to overshadow the watercourses of the Lower Lebanon, and, with the oleander and the acacia, to adorn the ravines of Southern Palestine; we do not know that the Lombardy poplar has been noticed but by lord Lindsay, who describes it as growing with the walnut-tree and weeping-willow under the deep torrents of the Upper Lebanon.'" See POPLAR.

Mulcaster, RICHARD, an English divine and teacher noted for his scholastic attainments, was a native of Carlisle, and of an old family in Cumberland. He received his earliest education on the foundation at Eton, under the celebrated Udal, whence, in 1548, he was elected scholar of King's College, Cambridge. From Cambridge he removed to Oxford, and in 1555 was chosen student of Christ Church. In the next year he was licensed to proceed in arts, and about the same time became known for his proficiency in Eastern literature. He began to teach in 1559; and on September 24, 1561, for his extraordinary attainments in philology, was appointed the first master of Merchant Tailors' School in London, then just founded. Here he continued till 1586, when he resigned; and some time after he was appointed upper master of St. Paul's School. Here he remained twelve years, and then retired to the rectory of Stanford Rivers, in Essex, to which he had been presented by the queen. He held this place until his death, April 15, 1611. Several of his smaller compositions, commendatory verses, etc., are prefixed to works of his contemporaries; and Gascoigne has printed some Latin verses of his composition which were spoken before the queen at Kenilworth in 1575. His separate works were, his *Positions, wherein those primitive circumstances be examined which are necessarie for the training up of Children, either for skill in theire book or health in their bodie* (Lond. 1581 and 1587, 4to); to which a second part was promised:—*The first part of the Elementarie, which entreateth chefely of the right writing of the English tung* (Lond. 1582, 4to); a book which Warton (*Hist. English Poetry*) says contains many judicious criticisms and observations on the English language:—*Catechismus Paulinus, in usum Scholæ Paulinæ conscriptus, ad formam parvi illius Anglici Catechismi qui pueris in communi Precum Anglicarum libro ediscendus proponitur* (1601, 8vo). This is in long and short verse, and, though now forgotten, was once esteemed. Mulcaster was a firm adherent to the Reformed religion; a man of piety, and a "priest in his own house as well as in the temple." See *Gentleman's Magazine*, vol. xxx; Hook, *Eccles. Biog.* vii, 388, 389; *English Cyclop.* s. v.; Fuller, *Worthies of England*, s. v.

Mulcìber (i. e. *the Softener*), a surname of VULCAN, the Roman god of fire. This euphemistic name of Mulciber is frequently applied to him by the Latin poets.

Mulder, ISRAEL, a Jewish writer of note, and celebrated also for his philanthropic labors among his people, flourished in Holland in recent times. He died at Amsterdam Dec. 29, 1862. He contributed largely for the dissemination of culture among his co-religionists, and did everything in his power to elevate the Jewish people in their literary life. He also wrote much himself, and among other works published a Hebrew-German dictionary and many essays on various subjects.

Mule (פֶּרֶד, *pe'red*, 2 Sam. xiii, 29, and often elsewhere; fem. פִּרְדָּה, *pirdah'*, 1 Kings i, 33, 38, 44; so called from their *quick* pace, or from *carrying* loads; but רֶכֶשׁ, *re'kesh*, Esth. viii, 10, 14, denotes a *steed* or nobler horse; "swift beast" in Mic. i, 13; "dromedary" in 1 Kings iv, 28), a hybrid animal, the offspring of a horse and an ass (comp. Varro, *De re rustica*, ii, 8; Pliny, viii, 69; Colum. vi, 36; Æsop, *Fab.* 140; Ælian, *Anim.* xii, 16; Strabo, v, 212). Of this animal there are two kinds: one is the produce of a he-ass with a mare; the other the produce of a she-ass and a stallion. The former is the *mule*, commonly so called. That in respect to swiftness the hybrid between the ass and the mare is much superior to the hybrid between the horse and the she-ass is abundantly attested (Aristot. *Rhetor.* iii, 2; Pliny,

Hist. Nat. viii, 44, etc.), which is in favor of Bochart's hypothesis that mules are meant by the אֲחַשְׁתְּרָנִים, A. V. "camels" of Esth. viii, 10, 14. See CAMEL. A mule is smaller than a horse, and is a remarkably hardy, patient, obstinate, sure-footed animal, living ordinarily twice as long as a horse. These animals are mostly sterile; as distinct species of animals do not freely intermix their breed, and hybrid animals do not propagate their kind beyond at most a very few generations, and no real hybrid races are perpetuated. The claim of Anah, son of Zibeon, to the discovery of breeding mules, as asserted in the Talmuds, may be regarded as an expression of national vanity (see Bochart, *Hieroz.* i, 221 sq.; Dougtæi *Anal.* i, 41 sq.). It rests on Gen. xxxvi, 24, where יֵמִם, *yemim'*, is rendered *mules;* but it more probably means *water*—meaning the warm springs of Callirrhoë on the eastern shore of the Dead Sea. See ANAH. There is no probability that the Hebrews bred mules, because it was expressly forbidden by the Mosaic law to couple animals of different species (Lev. xix, 19). But they were not forbidden to use them (Philo, *Opp.* ii, 307); and we find under the monarchy that mules were common among the Hebrews (see also Josephus, *Life*, 26), and they were probably known much earlier. Even the kings and most distinguished nobles were accustomed to ride upon mules (and apparently they only), although at first they used only male and female asses (2 Sam. xviii, 9; 1 Kings i, 33, 38, 44; xviii, 5; 2 Kings v, 17; 2 Chron. ix, 24; Psa. xxxii, 9). "It is an interesting fact that we do not read of mules till the time of David (as to the *yemim*, A. V. 'mules,' of Gen. xxxvi, 24, see above), just at the time when the Israelites were becoming well acquainted with horses. After this time horses and mules are in Scripture often mentioned together. After the first half of David's reign, as Michaelis (*Comment. on Laws of Moses*, ii, 477) observes, they became all at once very common. In Ezra ii, 66, Neh. vii, 68, we read of two hundred and forty-five mules; in 2 Sam. xiii, 29, 'all the king's sons arose, and every man gat him up upon his mule.' Absalom rode on a mule in the battle of the wood of Ephraim, at the time when the animal went away from under him, and so caused his death. Mules were among the presents which were brought year by year to Solomon (1 Kings x, 25). From the above-cited Levitical law we must suppose that the mules were imported, unless the Jews became subsequently less strict in their observance of the ceremonial injunctions, and bred their mules. We learn from Ezekiel (xxvii, 14) that the Tyrians, after the time of Solomon, were supplied with both horses and mules from Armenia (Togarmah), which country was celebrated for its good horses (see Strabo, xi, 13, 7, ed. Kramer; comp. also Xenoph. *Anab.* iv, 5, 36; Herod. vii, 40). Michaelis conjectures that the Israelites first became acquainted with mules in the war which David carried on with the king of Nisibis (Zobah) (2 Sam. viii, 3, 4). In Solomon's time it is possible that mules from Egypt occasionally accompanied the horses which we know the king of Israel obtained from that country; for though the mule is not of frequent occurrence on the monuments of Egypt (Wilkinson's *Anc. Egypt.* i, 386 [Lond. 1854]), yet it is not easy to believe that the Egyptians were not well acquainted with this animal. That a friendship existed between Solomon and Pharaoh is clear from 1 Kings ix, 16, as well as from the fact of Solomon having married the daughter of the king of Egypt; but after Shishak came to the throne a very different spirit prevailed between the two kingdoms: perhaps, therefore, from this date mules were obtained from Armenia." In latter times (eventually, at all events) the Hebrews appear to have obtained the more valuable mules from Assyria and Persia (Isa. lxvi, 20; Esth. viii, 10, 14; comp. Ctes. *Pers.* 44; see Host, *Marohk*, p. 292). We do not read of mules at all in the N. T.; perhaps, therefore, they had ceased to be imported. See HORSE.

Representations of Mules on the Monuments.

Fig. 1. Egyptian Mules (painting from Thebes in British Museum). Fig. 2. Assyrian Mule carrying Nets, etc. (Sculpture in British Museum).

Mules are represented on some of the ancient Assyrian bass-reliefs; they are seen in procession, belonging to a captured people (Layard's *Nineveh*, ii, 323, 324). They were also ridden in battle and by kings (*ibid.* 2d ser. p. 446, 449). There are various breeds of mules in Syria. Some very beautiful animals are produced from high-blood Arab mares, but they are few in number, and can only be possessed by the wealthy. Burckhardt states that the breed of the Baalbek mules is highly esteemed, and that he had seen some which were worth from thirty to five-and-thirty pounds (*Trav.* i, 57). The more ordinary sort of mules, which are capable of carrying heavy loads, are employed in the caravans; and they are of great service for the mill and water-wheels. The domestic trade with the maritime towns and the mountains is not only carried on chiefly by mule caravans, but they are sent even to Erzerûm, Constantinople, and other remote towns (Russell, *Aleppo*, ii, 50 sq.). In these caravans the male travellers are mounted on mules lightly laden, generally the mere personal luggage of the rider. Persons of rank travel in a kind of litter, carried by two mules. Within the towns, and in short excursions, asses are generally preferred, and the mules bear the luggage. In modern times the breeding of mules in Southern Europe and Western Asia has been greatly increased. Those of Persia are described as of large size, and of amazing strength and power of endurance. They will travel the stony and steep roads over rocky mountains, day after day, at the rate of from twenty-five to fifty miles per diem, loaded with a weight of 300 pounds. They require more food than the horse. The muleteers never remove the pack-saddles from their backs, except when cleaning or currying them. If the men find that the back has been galled, they take away some of the stuffing from the pack-saddle, where it presses on the sore part, and then put the saddle on again, experience having taught them that such sores, unless healed under the saddle, are apt to break out again. See Ugolino, *De re rustica Hebr.*, in his *Thesaur.* xxix, pt. iv, 10; Bochart, *Hieroz.* i, 209 sq.; Robinson, *Researches*, passim. See Ass.

Mulier-Subintroducta (γυνή συνείσακτος) is a term which was used by the great Nicene Synod in a sense synonymous to the "fœmina extranea," and near-

ly to the "focaria" and "concubina" of later times, as well as to the "agapeta" and "dilecta" of earlier date, and is by Protestants held to be simply an expression of the council against the improper female companionship of unmarried priests. Roman Catholics, however, interpret it to carry the desire for the separation from all female companionship, even the wife. See Lea, *Historical Sketch of Sacerdotal Celibacy in the Christian Church*, p. 51-53. See also CELIBACY.

Mullah (a title merely; see MOLLAH) **Firûz** BEN-KAWÛS, a modern Persian ecclesiastic, noted as a poet, was born at Bombay in 1759. When only a youth he accompanied his father to Persia, and became acquainted with the rich poetical literature of that country. He then conceived the idea of composing an epic poem like Ferdûsi's *Chah-Nameh*, taking, however, his subject from modern history. He called it *George-Nameh*. It treats of the conquest of the East Indies by the English, and elevates poor George III to the character of a hero. Containing 110,000 verses, it was to extend to the battle of Pûnah (1816), but the author died in his native city in 1831 before he had completed it. His nephew, Mullah Rustem ben-Kaikobad, published (Bombay, 1837, 4to) a part of the first volume, with a prospectus of the whole work. The poem has since appeared complete at Calcutta (1839, 3 vols. 4to). But these poetical labors did not only not interfere with the performance of Firuz's duties as high-priest of the Parsees, but he also devoted himself to ecclesiastical studies, and published an edition of the *Desatir*, or sacred writings of the ancient Persian prophets in the original tongue, etc., together with an English translation of the *Desatir*, and a commentary by M. Erskine (Bombay, 1818, 2 vols. 8vo). He published two essays in response to Hachem of Ispahan, to prove that the Persian intercalar æra dates not from Zoroaster, but is of more modern origin. They were both printed at Bombay, one in 1828 (1 vol. fol.), the other in 1832 (4to). All his books and manuscripts Mullah Firûz bequeathed to the grand library of the Parsees.

Mullens, WILLIAM, a minister of the Methodist Episcopal Church, South, was born in Virginia in 1804. He removed with his parents to Bedford County, Tenn., when a youth, and settled on Duck River. He joined the Church in 1820, and was licensed to preach shortly afterwards. In 1822 he joined the Tennessee Conference, and labored two years in West Tennessee. He afterwards travelled Bigbee, Duck River, Bedford, Dickson, Chapel Hill, and Lynnville circuits. His health failing him, he located for a while; but he had no sooner re-entered the work than his health gave way the second time, and he was granted a supernumerary relation, in which he continued until his death, March 18, 1870. "By nature he was a nobleman, and ever preserved his integrity of character. His sympathies were always with the afflicted, and his liberality in relieving the sufferings of others was proverbial." See *Minutes of Conferences of the M. E. Church, South*, 1870.

Müller, Adam Heinrich, a German statesman, noted for his efforts to give the secular laws a Christian basis, was born at Berlin June 30, 1779, and studied philosophy at the University of Göttingen, where in 1800 he spoke publicly against the French Revolution. In his journeys in later years he came to Vienna, where he turned Roman Catholic. He returned to Berlin; but not receiving an office there, he went again to Vienna, and entered the state service of Austria. He was intrusted with political missions. He went to Paris with Metternich, was afterwards consul-general in Leipsic, and was finally recalled to Vienna with the title of Counsellor of the Court. His favorite study being the fathers of the Church, he tried to give to all political and secular relations a Christian coloring. He died Jan. 17, 1829. His works are, *Vorlesungen über die deutsche Literatur und Wissenschaft* (1807):—*Von der Nothwendigkeit einer theologischen Grundlage der Staats-*

wissenschaft und Staatswirthschaft (Leipsic, 1819):—*Die Elemente der Staatskunst* (Berlin, 1809):—*Ueber Friedrich II* (Berlin, 1810):—*Die Theorie der Staatshaushaltung* (Vienna, 1812):— *Vermischte Schriften über Staat, Philosophie und Kunst* (Vienna, 1812). See Hurst's Hagenbach, *Ch. Hist. 18th and 19th Centuries,* ii, 296, 324, 448; and the references in Wetzer und Welte, *Kirchen-Lexikon,* xii, 814, 815.

Müller, Andreas, a German divine and Oriental scholar, greatly distinguished for his labors in illustration of the Chinese language, was a native of Pomerania, and was born in 1630. But little is known of his personal history. He assisted Walton in his *Polyglot Bible* and contributed to Castell's *Lexicon.* He also published a *Treatise on Cathay; Japanese Alphabet; Chinese Basilicon,* and other works. He died in 1694.

Müller, Daniel, a German religious enthusiast of low origin and condition of life, was born in Nassau in 1716, the time of the Pietist movements, when various indications of an inward religious life made their appearance in Germany, and many opposing circumstances excited a longing for a new development of the Church. At first he attached himself to the secondary effects of pietism, and busied himself with Jacob Böhme and other Mystics. For a long time also he was engaged in historical studies, and his mysticism became connected with a historical scepticism. At this juncture also there was the commencement of a rationalistic reaction, especially hastened on by the appearance of the *Wolfenbüttel Fragments.* But neither of the two parties—neither the Church nor the rationalistic—suited him. He wished to maintain the authority of the Bible against the new scepticism, and to insist on its inspiration in the most unqualified sense. But, on the other hand, he was not satisfied with orthodoxy; he was led to a peculiar religious idealism, by which he wished to establish a harmony of all religions. An original revelation was at the basis of all of them, the symbols of which had been misunderstood. Everything in the Old Testament and the New was to be understood symbolically; it was the garb of God's inner revelation, and of the eternal revelation of the divine Logos. Everything historical, as such, is untrue; it is only the clothing of ideal truth. In this view of the life of Christ, although proceeding on quite different principles, he was the forerunner of the modern mythic school, and combated the belief in the historical miracles of Christ on grounds very similar to those brought forward by Strauss. If such miracles, he says, as feeding the five thousand had actually happened, all the Jews would have received Christ, and would not have crucified him. Indeed, Müller went so far as to give any religion the authority for man's ultimate conversion to the state of eternal bliss, and Adam and Christ were to him simply the same human formation of the all-pervading Deity, the same divinity pervading the sacred writings of all nations. Later in life Müller himself claimed to be an Elias, called to redeem the world from the yoke of the letter. He travelled through the whole northern part of Germany to announce that the external Church was about to be subverted; and although he died in 1782, under an impression that God had deceived him, he had yet made such an impression on his fellows that even now there are followers of his in Germany. They reject the historical Christ, look upon infidels as their brethren, and are expecting Müller's return to set up a universal kingdom. See Keller, *Daniel Müller, Religiöse Schwärmer des Achtzehnten Jahrh.* (Leipsic, 1834); *Zeitschr. für Histor. Theologie* (1834); Neander's *Hist. Christian Dogmas,* p. 634, 635; Hase, *Ch. Hist.* p. 508.

Müller, Friedrich Theodosius, a German theologian, born at Ilmenau, Sept. 10, 1716; was educated at the gymnasium at Zittau, and entered the University of Jena in 1735, where he studied theology, philosophy, and ancient languages. He was appointed in 1742 deacon of the Stadt Kirche at Jena; in 1745, assistant of the philosophic faculty; in 1754, assessor of the consistory; in 1761, professor of theology; and in 1765, archdeacon of the Stadt Kirche at Jena, where he died in 1766. He published in 1745 a new theory of the Hebrew accents, in Latin. His most important works are, *Diss. de memoriæ amplitudine et diversitate* (Jenæ, 1735, 4to):—*Diss. Specimen sapientiæ divinæ ex neglecta in Scriptura. S. methodo demonstrativa* (ibid. 1739, 4to):—*Diss. Particulas Hebræorum esse nomina* (ibid. 1740, 4to):—*Diss. Theoria accentuum apud Hebræos nova, qui legati, vicarii et barones appellari consueverunt* (ibid. 1745, 4to):—*Progr. Anima hominis substantia in completa argumentum pro resurrectione carnis expectanda* (ibid. 1761, 4to).

Müller, Georg Christian, a German theologian, was born in 1769 at Mülhausen; received his preparatory education at his native place, then went to the university at Halle; entered the ministry in 1814, and became pastor at Neumark, near Zwickau, where he died about 1830. His most noteworthy works are, *Entwurf einer philosophischen Religionslehre* (Halle, 1797, 8vo): —*Protestantismus und Religion; ein Versuch zur Darstellung ihres Verhältnisses* (Leipsic, 1809, 8vo):—*Ueber Wissenschaft und System in der Ethik,* published in vol. ii of *Zeitschrift für Moral* (Jena, 1819, 8vo).

Müller, Heinrich (1), *Dr.,* a noted German divine, was born Oct. 18, 1631, at Lubeck, a place which his parents were obliged to quit because of Wallenstein's hordes. His earliest religious impressions he received from his mother Elizabeth, to whom he was indebted, like Augustine to his mother Monica, or Chrysostom to Anthusa. Although of a feeble constitution, Müller made such progress in the school of his native place that when, in 1644, his parents returned to Rostock he was matriculated as a student of philosophy, though only thirteen years of age. For three years he attended the lectures of Lütkemann (q. v.), went in 1647 to Greifswalde to study theology, and was honored with the degree of *magister artium.* Having travelled for some time in order to enrich his store of knowledge, he returned in 1651 to Rostock, where he commenced a series of lectures, which were so highly spoken of that the magistrate appointed him archdeacon of St. Marien Kirche when hardly twenty years of age. A year later the University of Helmstädt conferred upon him the degree of doctor of divinity, his own university not acknowledging him worthy until seven years afterwards. In 1659 he was appointed professor of Greek, in 1662 he became a member of the theological faculty and pastor, and in 1671 the whole clergy unanimously appointed him as their superintendent, and this position he held until his death, which occurred Sept. 13, 1675. Müller belonged to those men whom Providence had called to sow the seed of a new and fresh evangelical life in a soil which was enriched with the blood of the Thirty-Years' War, Lutheran orthodoxy, which had become weakened through constant controversies, not being sufficiently strong to successfully supplant error by truth in life as well as in faith. Christianity was to Müller not a dogma, but life, and thus he may be regarded, in connection with Joh. Arndt (q. v.), Val. Andreä (q. v.), and Chr. Scriver, as the predecessor of Spener; and like the writings of Arndt and Scriver, his own writings are read by the German people up to this day. Müller was a voluminous writer, and wrote not only in German, but also in Latin. The best known of his works are, *Apostolische Schlusskette und Kraftkern* (Frankfort, 1633, and often):—*Evangelische Schlusskette* (ibid. 1763, and often):—*Evangelischer Herzensspiegel* (ibid. 1679):—*Himmlischer Liebeskuss* (Rostock, 1659): —*Kreuz-, Buss- u. Betschule* (ibid. 1651, and often):— *Geistliche Erquickungsstunden* (ibid. 1663, and often):— *Orator ecclesiasticus,* etc. (ibid. 1659):—*Conjugii clericorum patrocinium* (ibid. 1665):—*Harmonia Veteris Novique Test. chronologica* (ibid. 1668):—*Theologia scholastica* (ibid. 1656). For a list of his writings, see Witte,

Memoriæ theologorum nostri sæculi clarissimorum renovatæ, decas xv (Frankfort, 1684), p. 1891; Rottermund, *Supplement zu Jöcher's Gelehrten-Lexikon,* v, 57. See also Koch, *Geschichte des deutschen Kirchenliedes* (Stuttgard, 1868), iv, 66 sq.; J. G. Russwurm, in his edition of Müller's *Erquickungsstunden* (Reutlingen, 1842); Bittcher, in Tholuck's *Liter. Anzeiger,* 1844, No. 15–18; *Dr. H. Müller, eine Lebensbeschreibung* von Aichel (Hamburg, 1854); Wild, *Leben u. Auswahl von Müller's Schriften,* in Klaiber's *Evang. Volksbibliothek* (Stuttgard, 1864), vol. iii; Niedner, *Lehrbuch der christl. Kirchengeschichte* (Berlin, 1866), p. 788; *Bibliotheca Sacra,* July, 1868, p. 587; Kitto, Oct. 1853, p. 208; Hase, *Church Hist.* p. 449. (B. P.)

Müller, Heinrich (2), a German theologian, was born at Joel, near Flensburg, Feb. 25, 1759. He studied theology and philosophy at the University of Kiel, and was called in 1786 to the position of deacon to the city church at Kiel. In 1789 he became also professor of theology and first teacher of the seminary. He finally resigned his position as minister, and became director of the seminary. He resigned the position as director of the seminary in 1805, and died Feb. 9, 1814. A monument by his scholars was erected in 1818 in the cemetery at Kiel. His most important works are, *Sammlung von Evangelien und Episteln, nebst Gebeten für die kirchliche und häusliche Andacht. Ein Anhang zum Schleswig-Holsteinischen Gesangbuche* (Kiel, 1813, 8vo) : —*Lehrbuch der Katechetik* (Kiel, 1816) :—*Handbuch der Katechetik; ein Commentar über das Lehrbuch: Herausgegeben von C. Carstensen* (Altona, 1821–23, 2 vols. 8vo). See Döring, *Gelehrte Theol. Deutschlands,* s. v.

Müller, Heinrich Daniel, a German theologian, was born at Buchenau, in Hesse-Darmstadt, Sept. 24, 1712. He was educated at Giessen, Marburg, Halle, and Jena. In 1742 he was appointed city minister and definitor at Giessen, and in 1748 professor extraordinary of theology. In 1749 he followed a call to Echzell, in Hesse-Darmstadt, as metropolitan and pastor primarius; became in 1777 inspector of the convent of the same place, and died March 22, 1797. His most important works are, *Diss. de Christo Deo magno vero et benedicto ad Tit. ii,* 13 ; 1 *Joh. v,* 20 ; *Rom. ix,* 5 (Jenæ, 1736, 4to) : —*Diss. inaug. de existentia Dei et revelationis ejusque criteriis* (Gissæ, 1739, 4to) :—*Disquisitio philosophica de quantitate* (ibid. 1746, 4to) :—*Theses philosophicæ* (ibid. 1746, 4to) :—*Commentatio philosophica de systemate harmoniæ præstabilitæ, qua comprimis quæritur, an libertatem tollat hoc systema?* (ibid. 1746, 4to) :—*Progr. de Philosopho practico* (ibid. 1748, 4to) :—*Diss. theologica de absoluto electionis et reprobationis decreto* (ibid. 1749, 4to) :—*Diss. de incredulitate finali* (ibid. 1749, 4to) : —*Commentatio de Messia Doctore justitiæ ad Joël ii,* 23, *qua exercitium disputatorium cum selectis theologiæ cultoribus instituendum significat* (ibid. 1750, 4to). See Döring, *Gelehr. Theol. Deutschlands,* iv, 580 sq.

Müller, Johann Baptist, a celebrated German painter of sacred subjects, was born at Gerartsried, in Bavaria, and studied art at the Academy of Munich under Eberhard, and later under Hess. The latter he assisted in the frescos of the All Saints' Chapel, and painted independently *The Baptism of Christ.* From 1842 to 1849 he painted for the king of Prussia, and these works were afterwards presented to the Cologne cathedral. Later he painted many sacred subjects on altars and church windows. He died at Munich in 1869. *Jeremiah upon the ruins of Jerusalem* is regarded as his best oil-painting. Many of his works have been reproduced in lithography, engravings, and chromos. See Nagler, *Allgemeines Künstler-Lexikon,* s. v.

Müller, Johann Caspar, a German Roman Catholic theologian, was born at Naumburg Feb. 26, 1749, and was educated at Fritzlar. In 1766 he entered the gymnasium at Mentz, and afterwards studied philosophy and theology. After being admitted to the theological seminary, he was ordained, and appointed chaplain at Hep-

penheim, and one year later professor at Worms, also prefect of the gymnasium, and vicar of the churches of St. Mary's and of the Holy Cross; assistant of the theological faculty, and minister of the court military hospital of St. John the Baptist. It was his pleasure to give his time entirely to study and to the duties of the Church; but the French war compelled him to leave Mentz. He returned to Mentz after the Prussians had taken possession of that place. He, however, now resigned his ecclesiastical offices, only soon after to be appointed canon of the chapter of the church of St. Peter at Fritzlar, and also of the St. John of the Amöneburg. Later he was removed to Aschaffenburg, as principal of the gymnasium and provost of the prince-electoral grammar schools. In 1804 he was appointed professor extraordinary of ecclesiastical law at Marburg; in 1806 principal of the seminary for teachers of the three Christian confessions. He died November 3, 1810. Müller had a thorough knowledge of Church history, patristic theology, and exegesis, which he evinced by his *Dissertatio de Socinianis* and *Harmonie der vier Evangelisten,* and similar works. He contributed often to the *Mainzer theologische Monatsschriften, Schuderoff's Journal zur Veredlung des Prediger- und Schullehrerstandes* (Jahrgang 5, Bd. 1, St. 1), and several other journals. His most important works are in the department of the classics. Among these are, *Titi Livii Patav. Historiarum liber primus et selecta quædam capita, scholis Moguntinensibus adornavit* (Mentz, 1780, 8vo) :—*Eutropii Breviarium historiæ Romanæ, scholis Moguntiacis in quibus Latinitatis initia docentur adornavit* (ibid. 1781, 8vo) :— *Quinti Horatii Flacci Odæ selectæ, scholis Moguntiacis edidit* (ibid. 1784, 8vo) :—*Diss. historico-theologica de ortu, vero religionis systemate, progressu, statu hodierno sectæ Unitariæ seu Socinianæ, ac de prono e secta Protestantium ad illam transitu, quam cum thesibus ex universa theologia selectis defendit* (ibid. 1784, 8vo; 2d edit. ibid. 1787, 8vo) :—*M. T. Ciceronis orationes selectæ ix, scholiis adornavit. Editio secunda aucta et emendata* (ibid. 1787, 8vo) :—*Der Triumph der Philosophie im 18ten Jahrhundert* (Frankf. a. M. 1803, 2 vols. 8vo) :— *Geschichte der Römer, für studirende und gebildete Leser, aus den Quellen dargestellt.* 1ste *Abtheilung vom Anfange des kleinen Staats bis zum Ende der grossen Republik* (ibid. 1805, 8vo). See Döring, *Gelehr. Theol. Deutschlands,* s. v.

Müller, Johann Christian Friedrich Wilhelm von, a noted German engraver of sacred subjects, was born at Stuttgart in 1782. He was carefully educated by his father, Johann Gotthard (see below), in all those branches of the arts which, by his own experience, he knew to be requisite to constitute an excellent engraver; and in 1802 went to complete his studies at Paris, where at that time the majority of the finest works of art in Europe were collected together in the Louvre. Here, in 1808, Müller engraved the *St. John about to write his Revelation,* after Domenichino, in which the eagle brings him his pen ; and *Adam and Eve under the Tree of Life,* after Raphael. He was commissioned shortly afterwards by Rittner, a printseller of Dresden, to engrave his last and greatest work, the *Madonna di San Sisto* of Raphael, in the Dresden Gallery. He was wholly occupied for the remainder of his short life on this plate, which he just lived to complete, but he never saw a finished print from it. He removed to Dresden in 1814, and was appointed professor of engraving in the academy there. His existence seems almost to have been wrapped up in the execution of this plate : he was occupied with it day and night, and, always of a sickly constitution, the infallible result of such constant application and excitement soon made its appearance. He was, however, in vain advised to desist for a while from his work. He completed the plate and sent it to Paris to be printed ; but with his plate the artificial excitement which supported him departed also; he had just strength enough left to admit of his being carried to the Sonnenstein, near Pirna, where he died in 1816, only a few days before the proof of his plate arrived from Paris. It was suspended over the head of his bier as he lay dead, thus reminding one of the similar untimely fate of the great master of the original, above whose head, as he lay in state, was hung also his last work, *The Transfiguration.* Müller engraved only eighteen plates, but the *Madonna di San Sisto* is in itself a host, and exhibits him at least the equal of Raphael Morghen, to whose *Transfiguration* it serves as a good pendant. There are several lithographic copies of it. An index of his plates and those of his father was published by Andresen at Leipsic in 1865. At Harvard College there are nineteen fine copies of his plates in the "Gray Collection." See Nagler, *Allgemeines Künstler-Lexikon,* s. v.; Spooner, *Biog. Hist. of the Fine Arts,* s. v.

Müller, Johann Daniel, a German theologian, was born at Allendorf May 22, 1721, and was educated at Giessen, where he studied theology, philosophy, and ancient languages. In 1740 he was appointed rector at his native place, and acted at the same time as assistant minister of a church. In 1768 he took the position of professor of divinity at the University of Rinteln, and there died, April 30, 1794. Besides numerous dissertations in journals, he published several works, of which the most important are, *Diss. in qua immortalitas animæ ex principiis rationis, methodo mathematicorum demonstratur* (Gissæ, 1743, 4to):—*Der rechte Gebrauch und Missbrauch der Vernunft bei Geheimnissen der Auferstehung der Todten insbesondere* (Frankf. a. M. 1747, 8vo):—*Possibilitas et certitudo resurrectionis mortuorum ex principiis rationis excitatæ, methodo mathematicorum demonstrata; cum præfatione J. G. Canzii* (Marburg, 1752, 8vo):—*Diss. theologica de Providentia Dei ex confusione mundi demonstrata* (Rinteln, 1771, 4to):—*Entdeckter Kunstgriff unserer Zeiten, die Religion durch die Bibel und die Bibel durch die Religion-zu bestreiten* (Brunsw. 1777, 8vo):—*Progr. de mutilatione Dei, Scripturæ, mundi et animæ violatæ rationis et revelationis teste* (Rinteln, 1784, 4to). See Döring, *Gelehr. Theol. Deutschlands,* iv, 585–587.

Müller, Johann Georg, D.D., brother of the famous historian J. v. Müller, was born at Schaffhausen Sept. 3, 1759. His early religious as well as secular education he received from his father, who was the minister of that place. The writings of Young and Lavater impressed him so deeply that he decided to devote himself to the study of theology. To this end he first went to Zurich and afterwards to Göttingen, which latter place, however, he soon left on account of the then prevailing neological tendency. He longed for truth, but Göttingen could not satisfy his thirst for it, and he sought for a teacher who could remove his doubts and ease his oppressed spirits. About this time Herder's name became known to the world, and Müller betook himself to Weimar, then celebrated as the Athens of Germany. Herder received Müller very kindly, and even took him into his house. In 1794 Müller returned to his native place, and accepted the professorship of the Greek and Hebrew languages at the *collegium humanitatis,* because of his feeble constitution, which prevented him from taking charge of a church. In the time of the revolution he held some high political positions, all of which he abandoned, only retaining his professorship until his death, Sept. 20, 1819. In him the Church lost a true divine, a faithful witness, whose main object was to propagate principles akin to those of Herder, but in a more orthodox sense. His writings, which have mainly an apologetical value, are as follows, *Philosophische Aufsätze* (Breslau, 1789):—*Unterhaltungen mit Serena* (Winterthur, 1793–1803):—*Bekenntnisse merkwürdiger Männer von sich selbst* (1791, 1795, 3 vols.):—*Briefe über das Studium der Wissenschaften,* etc. (1798; 2d ed. 1807):—*Theophil, Unterhaltungen über die christl. Religion* (1801), which treats of religion, mythology, revelation, the Old and New Testaments, and reading and explanation of

the holy Scriptures:—*Reliquien alter Zeiten, Sitten und Meinungen* (1803–1806, 4 vols.):—*Vom Glauben des Christen* (1816, 2 vols.; 2d ed. 1823):—*Blicke in die Bibel* (1830, 2 vols., ed. by Prof. Kirchofer, etc.). See Herzog, *Real-Encyklop.* s. v.; *Theol. Universal-Lexikon,* s. v.; Hurst's Hagenbach, *Hist. of the Church in the 18th and 19th Cent.* ii, 22, 47, 409. (B. P.)

Müller, Johann Gottgetreu, a German theologian, was born in 1701 at Calbe, in Prussia. He was educated first at his native place, then at Klosterbergen, and at the University of Halle, where he studied theology. He was appointed minister at the penitentiary at Halle in 1727, but was discharged, as he would not sanction the union of the Lutheran and Reformed churches, which was brought about by king Frederick William I of Prussia. Müller now went to Leipsic, and became there bachelor of divinity and minister of the university church. In 1739 the chief consistory secured for him a place at the "Kreuz Kirche" at Suhl. In 1745 he was appointed superintendent at Schleusingen, also assessor of the consistory. In 1750 he was appointed ephorus of the gymnasium, and died August 16, 1787. Müller possessed a thorough knowledge of ancient languages, which he shows in his programmes *De scholis purgatoriis* (1761, 4to) and *De animantibus apocalypticis s. emblematibus ministrorum Evangelii in scholis et ecclesiis* (1777, 4to). One of his most important works is *Progr. τὰ Urim et Thumim scholarum* (Schleusingiæ, 1748, 4to). See Döring, *Gelehr. Theol. Deutschlands,* s. v.

Müller, Johann Gotthard von, a celebrated German engraver of sacred subjects, was born at Bernhausen, near Stuttgard, in 1747. His father, who held an official situation under the government of his native country, wished to educate Müller for the Church, but the youth showed so much ability for art in the newly-established (1761) Academy of Fine Arts at Stuttgard that the prince himself urged him to follow art as his profession. Accordingly, in 1764, Müller, under court patronage, entered the school of the court-painter, Guibal, who recommended him to follow engraving, which he pursued for six years (1770–76) at Paris under Wille, with such success that in 1776 he was elected a member of the French Academy. He was called home in the same year by duke Carl to found a school of art at Stuttgard, which, under his guidance, produced many excellent artists. In 1785 Müller was invited to return to Paris to engrave the portrait of Louis XVI, painted in 1774 by Duplessis. In 1802 Müller was made professor of engraving in the academy at Stuttgard, where he instructed several of the best engravers of Germany during the earlier part of the 19th century, among whom his own son, Christian Friedrich, is the foremost. He was elected successively a member of the principal German academies, was presented in 1808 by the king Frederick of Würtemberg with the Order of Civil Merit, and in 1818 was made a Knight of the Würtemberg Crown by Frederick's successor, king William. He died at Stuttgard in 1830, and in the same year a biography of him was published in the *Schwäbische Merkur,* No. 71. Müller engraved only thirty-three plates—a small number—but some of them are large and elaborate works; they are, however, chiefly portraits. His principal sacred subjects are the *Madonna della Seggiola,* for the Musée Français, engraved in 1804, by many considered superior to the print of the same subject by Raphael Morghen; a *St. Catharine, with two Angels,* after Leonardo da Vinci. See Nagler, *Allgemeines Künstler-Lexikon,* s. v.; Spooner, *Biog. Hist. of the Fine Arts,* s. v.

Müller, Johann Gottlieb, a German theologian, who labored largely for the elevation of the masses and the spreading of holiness among the rural population of Germany, was born at Waldorf, near Löbau, Oct. 30, 1760. He was educated at the University of Wittenberg. He was appointed in 1784 minister at Podrosche, near Muskau; in 1802 minister at Jänkendorf and Ullersdorf, near Niesky; and in 1809 minister at Neukirch, near Bautzen, where he died, Jan. 11, 1829. His most important works are, *Ueber die schrecklichen Folgen oder Wirkungen des Aufruhrs* (Görlitz, 1793, 8vo): — *Oberlausitzische Reformationsgeschichte* (ibid. 1801, 8vo): —*Christoph Fromman zu Lobethal, oder: Der Landmann als Christ, wie er sein sollte und ist. Ein Christliches Sittenbuch für den lieben Bauernstand* (ibid. 1803, 8vo). See Döring, *Gelehrte Theol. Deutschlands*, iv, 590, 591.

Müller, Johann Stephan, a German theologian, was born at Smalobuch, in the Black Forest, July 20, 1730, and was educated at the gymnasium at Rudolstädt and the University of Jena. In 1756 he was appointed an assistant of the philosophical faculty, and became also a member of the Latin Society at Jena, and in 1758 assessor of the consistory at Rudolstädt. In 1759 he was appointed professor extraordinary of philosophy at Jena, and in 1763 he was made professor at Giessen. He became a member of the academies of sciences at Erfurt, Frankfort-on-the-Oder, and at Giessen. In 1768 he was honored with the superintendency of the diocese of Marburg, in which place he died, Oct. 24, 1768. His most important works are, *Dubiorum utrique modo, quo procedunt Theologi in explicanda imputatione peccati Adamitici oppositorum, brevis et modesta resolutio ac utriusque istius conciliatio* (Jena, 1752, 4to): —*Diss. utrum doctrina de mentis materialitate hypothesis philosophica possit vocari, et quo ostenso, an illa probabilior doctrina de simplicitate animi?* (ibid. 1753, 4to): —*Diss. philosophica de hominis obligatione ad utendum mediis revelationis vel ante admissam illius veritatem divinam* (ibid. 1755, 4to): — *Diss. sententias Protestantium juris naturæ doctorum de lege naturali a vituperationibus cel. P. Desingii defendens* (ibid. 1756, 4to): — *Diss. metaphysica sententiam Philosophorum Christianorum de mundi et substantiarum origine nova quadam hypothesi contra systemata Aristotelis defendens* (ibid. 1757, 4to): —*Die Unschuld Luther's in der Lehre von dem Zustande der Seele nach dem Tode, wider die in unsern Tagen erregte Beschuldigung, als ob derselbe ein Seelenschläfer gewesen sei, gerettet* (ibid. 1757, 4to): —*Dass Luther die Lehre vom Seelenschlafe nie geglaubt habe, weiter und mit den stärksten Gründen erwiesen* (ibid. 1759, 4to): —*Diss. Quid Reformati? ab eo vix Pontificii deflectunt in doctrina de S. Cœna, quod offendunt Reformati* (ibid. 1776, 4to): —*De novis inter Regem Gallorum et Magistratum dissensionibus quid mihi videtur* (ibid. 1766, 8vo). See Döring, *Gelehrte Theol. Deutschlands*, s. v.

Müller, Karl Ottfried, one of the most distinguished classical scholars of recent times, is noted for his labors in the department of comparative religion, having furnished works very valuable on Grecian mythology and religion. He was born Aug. 28, 1797, at Brieg, in Silesia, and received a careful education. He devoted himself, at the universities of Breslau and Berlin, to philological and archæological studies, and the first fruit of his learning was the publication of the *Ægineticorum Liber* (Berlin, 1817). Shortly after he received an appointment to the *Magdalenum* in Breslau, where his leisure hours were devoted to a grand attempt to analyze the whole circle of Greek myths. In 1819 he obtained an archæological chair in Göttingen; and to thoroughly prepare himself for it, visited the collections in Germany, France, and England. His great design was to embrace the whole life of ancient Greece, its art, politics, industry, religion, in one warm and vivid conception—in a word, to cover the skeletons of antiquity with flesh, and to make the dry bones live. With this view he lectured and wrote with a fine, earnest animation, until the political troubles in Hanover made his position uncomfortable. He obtained permission to travel, and made tours in Greece and Italy, but unfortunately died of an intermittent fever at Athens, Aug. 1, 1840. Müller's literary and scholarly activity stretched over the whole field of Greek antiquity, furnishing many new and striking elucidations of the geography and to-

pography, literature, grammar, mythology, manners and customs of the ancients. The work of special interest to us is his *Prolegomena zu einer wissenschaftlichen Mythologie* (Göttingen, 1825, 8vo; Engl. by Leitch, Lond. 1844, 8vo). His work on the *Dorians* is also valuable to the student of comparative religion, as well as his work on the *Etruscans.* "Müller," says a contemporary, "was a man of the most extensive and varied acquirements, and of a keen and penetrating judgment. He acquired a European reputation at a comparatively early age. His numerous works, however, are not all of equal merit, and the two faults more particularly to be noticed are his great haste in the composition of his works and a tendency to theorize and generalize on insufficient grounds. But in extent of knowledge and reading there scarcely ever was a scholar who surpassed him." See *Neuer Nekrolog der Deutschen für* 1841; Lücke, *Erinnerungen an Karl Ottfried Müller* (Götting. 1841, 8vo), which contains an admirable delineation of Müller's personal character.

Müller, Peter Erasmus, a Danish prelate, noted as a theological and antiquarian writer, was born at Copenhagen May 29, 1776. He studied at the university of that city, where in 1791 he passed his theological examination. He afterwards spent a year and a half at some of the German universities, and paid a visit of eight months to France and of three to England. After his return he attained to eminence as a scholar, wrote numerous works, was appointed professor of theology at the university in 1801, was raised to the rank of bishop in 1822, and in 1830 was appointed to the bishopric of Zealand, the highest ecclesiastical dignity in Denmark. He died Sept. 16, 1834. His theological works on the *Christian Moral System* (1808), on the *Grounds for Belief in the Divinity of Christianity* (1810), on the *Creeds of the Christian Church* (1817), all in Danish, are in high esteem, but his literary reputation is chiefly founded on his essays in the department of Danish and Norse antiquarian studies. Among these, his best are, *On the Importance of the Icelandic Language:—On the Rise and Decline of Icelandic Historiography:—On the Authenticity of the Edda of Snorro: —Critical Examination of the Traditional History of Denmark and Norway:—Critical Examination of the last Seven Books of Saxo Grammaticus:*—and, above all, his *Sagabibliothek, or Library of the Sagas* (Copenh. 1817–20, 3 vols.). Bishop Müller was also the editor of a literary journal (*Dansk Literatur Tidende*) for many years. See Kraft og Nycrup, *Altnindeligt Literaturlexicon*, s. v.

Müller, Philipp Jacob, a noted German-French (Alsace) theologian and philosopher, was born at Strasburg in March, 1732. He studied at the high school of his native place and at the celebrated German universities. In 1782 he became professor of philosophy at his alma mater and canon of St. Thomas, as well as president of the assembly of Strasburg pastors. He died in 1795. Müller was well versed in the Greek and Hebrew antiquities, and was a student of the exact sciences. His travels had extended his knowledge of men and things, and he therefore became a person of influence. His writings, which were mainly in the department of metaphysics and morals, helped only to confirm the reputation secured. The most interesting of his writings are, *De pluralitate mundorum* (1750, 4to):—*De commercio animi et corporis* (1761, 4to):—*Psychologia Pythagorica* (1773):—*De legibus naturæ* (1775).

Mullion or Monyall, the upright division between the lights of windows, screens, etc., in Gothic architecture. Mullions are rarely met with in Norman architecture, but they become more frequent in the Early English style, and in the Decorated and Perpendicular are very common. They have sometimes small shafts attached to them, which carry the tracery of the upper part of the windows. In late domestic architecture they are usually plain. The cut shows mullions

($a\,a$) supporting tracery. See Chambers, *Cyclop.* s. v.; Parker, *Glossary of Architecture*, p. 155, 157.

Mullion.—Window from Carlisle Cathedral.

Mumbo Jumbo, a mysterious personage frightful to the whole race of African matrons. According to the description of Mr. Wilson, "he is a strong, athletic man disguised in dry plantain leaves, and bearing a rod in his hand, which he uses on proper occasions with the most unsparing severity. When invoked by an injured husband, he appears about the outskirts of the village at dusk, and commences all sorts of pantomimes. After supper he ventures to the town-hall, where he commences his antics, and every grown person, male or female, must be present, or subject themselves to the suspicion of a guilty conscience. The performance is kept up until midnight, when Mumbo, with the agility of the tiger, suddenly springs upon the offender, and chastises her most soundly, amid the shouts and laughter of the multitude, in which the other women join more heartily than anybody else, with the view, no doubt, of raising themselves above the suspicion of such infidelity."

Mummy is a name derived from an Arabic word, *mum*, signifying *wax*, and is now applied not only to those dead bodies of men and animals in the preparation of which wax or some similar material was used, but to all those which are by any means preserved in a dry state from the process of putrefaction. The art of embalming, by which the greater part of the mummies now existing were prepared, was practiced by the Assyrians, Persians, Ethiopians, Egyptians, and to some extent also by the Hebrews, Greeks, Romans, and on this continent by the Mexicans and Peruvians. But with greatest skill it was practiced by the inhabitants of ancient Egypt, of whom whole generations still remain preserved from decay in the vast hypogæa or catacombs in the neighborhood of Thebes and the other great cities of that country. It has been estimated that more than 400,000,000 human mummies were made in Egypt from the beginning of embalming until its discontinuance in the 7th century. The mummies which are filled with aromatics only are olive-colored; their skin is dry, flexible, and like tanned leather, and contracted; their features are distinct, and appear to be like those that existed in life; the resins which all their cavities contain are dry, light, brittle, and aromatic; the teeth, hair, and eyebrows are generally perfect; some of them are gilded all over the body, or on the most prominent parts. The mummies which are filled with bitumen are reddish; their skins are hard and polished, as if they had been varnished; they are dry, heavy, inodorous, and difficult to unroll; their features are but slightly altered; the hard, black, resinous substance with which they are filled possesses little odor, and they are scarcely alterable by exposure to the air. Those which have been salted, as well as thus prepared, differ little in their general appearance from those just described, but they are usually less perfect, the features being altered, and their hair having commonly fallen off. When they are uncovered and exposed to the air, a slight saline efflorescence forms upon them, which consists of different salts of soda. Those mummies which have been only salted and dried are even less perfect than the preceding. Their features are entirely destroyed; all their hair has fallen off; and both the body and the bandages by which it is enveloped fall in pieces when brought to the air, or may very easily be broken up. In many of these adipocere is formed; but in general they are hard, dry,

Mummy Cases and Marble Sarcophagi.

and whitish, like dirty parchment. The bandaging, to which all the Egyptian mummies were subjected, was one of the most remarkable parts of the process. Their envelopes are composed of numerous linen bands, each several feet long, applied one over the other fifteen or twenty times, and surrounding first each limb and then the whole body. They are applied and interlaced so accurately that one might suppose they were intended to restore to the dry, shrivelled body its original form and size. The only difference in the bandages of the different kinds of mummies is in their greater or less fineness of texture; they are applied on all in nearly the same manner. All the bandages and wrappings which have been examined with the microscope are of linen. The body is first covered by a narrow dress, laced at the back and tied at the throat, or it is all enveloped in one large bandage. The head is covered by a square piece of very fine linen, of which the centre forms a kind of mask over the features. Five or six such pieces are sometimes put one over the other, and the last is usually painted or gilded in representation of the embalmed person. Every part of the body is then separately enveloped with several bandages impregnated with resin. The legs, extended side by side, and the arms, crossed over the chest, are fixed by other bandages which surround the whole body; and these last, which are commonly covered with hieroglyphics, are fixed by long, crossing, and very ingeniously applied bands, which complete the envelope. Most of the bodies are placed in this state in the catacombs; those of the rich only are enclosed in cases. The cases are usually double, the interior being composed of boards made of several portions of linen glued together, and the exterior cut from a piece of cedar or sycamore wood. See EMBALMING.

The body, after being embalmed, was thus completely swathed with strips of linen (some think cotton) cloth, of various lengths and breadths, and was then enclosed in an envelope of coarse, or sometimes of fine, cloth. In Mr. Davidson's mummy, the weight of the bandages, including the outer sheet, was 29 lbs., and their total length 292 yards; and in another, Mr. Pettigrew's, the cloth weighed $35\frac{1}{2}$ lbs.; and the one examined at Leeds was in no part covered with less than forty thicknesses of the cloth. The mummy as prepared presents the appearance of a large mass of cloth, somewhat resembling the general outline of the human figure. The mummy was thus prepared by the embalmers, and in this state consigned to the coffin-makers, who, in the first instance, enclosed it in a case of a strong but flexible kind of board, somewhat like *papier-maché*, made by gumming well together several layers of hempen or linen cloth. This was formed into the shape of the swathed mummy, which was inserted into it by means of a longitudinal slit on the under side, reaching from the feet to the head, and stitched up after the insertion of the mummy. This case is, in most instances, lined, and covered with a thin coating of plaster, with the representation of a human face on the upper part. This was then introduced into a coffin of sycamore wood, made sometimes out of one piece of wood, and either plain or ornamented within and without with representations of sacred animals or mythological subjects. Besides this there is often yet another wooden coffin, still more highly ornamented, and covered with paintings secured by a strong varnish. The upper part of both these cases is made to represent a human figure, and the sex is clearly denoted by the character of the head-dress, and by the presence or absence of the beard. The last covering of all was a sarcophagus of stone, which, from its heavy additional expense, could only, it may be supposed, be used for kings and wealthy people. These stone coffins consist of two parts—a case to contain the body, formed of one piece of stone, open at the top, and a lid to fit the opening. Some of them are comparatively plain, while others—of which there are examples in the British Museum, and one, of alabaster, in the

museum of Sir John Soane—are elaborately sculptured with hieroglyphics and figures of men and animals, forming not the least astonishing monuments which we possess of Egyptian industry and art. See Wilkinson, *Ancient Egyptians*, ii, 393 sq.; Hardwick, *Christ and other Masters*, ii, 297; *Blackwood's Magazine*, 1870, ii, 229 sq., 317 sq. See COFFIN; MECHANIC.

Mumpelgart, COLLOQUY OF. A conference between Beza and Andreä, with a view to bring about the union of the Lutheran and Reformed churches, but which loses much of its importance from the fact that the two theologians acted here of their own accord, and not as representatives of their respective churches. The occasion of it was the incorporation of the territory of Mumpelgart into the duchy of Würtemberg by inheritance. Farel had preached the Gospel there as early as 1526, but had been driven away. In 1535 duke George of Würtemberg had caused the Reformation to be introduced into Mumpelgart by Tossanus, a French minister. The Würtemberg authorities afterwards sought to introduce the Lutheran form of worship. But when, in consequence of persecution, many French Calvinists sought a refuge at Mumpelgart, they found great difficulty in being allowed to take part in the Lord's Supper, and in order to put an end to this state of things demanded a colloquy. Neither of the two theologians appointed entertained much hope of the result. Beza had been forewarned that all such attempts had heretofore served only to embitter the strife, yet he did not consider himself free to reject the application of the exiles, while Andreä felt the less opposed to take part in a discussion presided over by a Lutheran prince. On the Lutheran side appeared Andreä and Lucas Osiander, assisted by the two political counsellors, Hans Wolf von Anweil and Frederich Schütz; on the part of the Reformed, Beza, Abraham Musculus (pastor at Berne), Anton Fajus (deacon at Geneva), Peter Hybner (professor of the Greek language at Berne), Claudius Alberius (professor of philosophy at Lausanne), and the two counsellors, Samuel Meyer, of Berne, and Anton Marisius, of Geneva. The colloquy took place at the castle of Mumpelgart, March 21–26, 1586. Beza did not succeed in arranging that a protocol of the discussion should be drawn up, and the accounts of the proceedings led subsequently to a lengthy controversy. The points of the controversy were: 1, the Lord's Supper; 2, the person of Christ; 3, images and ceremonies; 4, baptism; 5, election. Beza, who had only intended to argue on the first point, was, in spite of all his efforts, obliged to discuss them all to the last, on which, as he had foreseen, the possibility of a compromise was still less than on the others. He declared himself ready to yield on all these points if he could be shown by Scripture to be in the wrong. Andreä, it is said, declared from the first—like Luther at Marburg—that he would yield nothing, and that the pure doctrine was forever established by the Confession of Augsburg. Both parties afterwards gave different versions of the colloquy. The Lutherans published the *Acta Colloquii Montisbelligartensis* (Tübingen, 1587), and also a German translation of it, and an *Epitome colloquii* in 1588. Beza defended himself in the *Responsio ad acta coll. M.* (Geneva, 1587 and 1588; German, Heidelberg, 1588), etc. At this colloquy both parties gave each other their doctrines and principles in writing. See Schweizer, *Gesch. der reformirten Centraldogmen*, i, 402 sq., 501 sq.; Herzog, *Real-Encyklopädie*, x, 89. (J. N. P.)

Mumpsimus is a nickname given to persons obstinate in religious matters; used by Henry VIII in Parliament, and founded on a story, related by Pace, of a priest who refused to abandon the practice of saying "quod ore mumpsimus," on the plea that he could not give up the usage of thirty years for any correction.

Muncer. See MÜNZER.

Munda cor meum (*cleanse my heart*) is the

technical form designating a prayer said in the high mass of Roman Catholics, after the reading of the epistle and its accompaniment. The position of the priest before the altar celebrating solemn mass is seen in the engraving below. The upper part represents Christ before Pilate. See the article MASS, and for full description of the service at mass, Barnum's *Romanism*, ch. xiv.

Antique picture of "*Munda cor Meum.*"

Münden, CHRISTIAN, a German Lutheran divine, was born at Burg, on the isle of Femern, Aug. 13, 1684. He was educated at the gymnasium at Lübeck; entered in 1701 the University of Kiel, where he studied theology, and returned home in 1704; but his desire for knowledge carried him in June, 1705, to Leipsic, where he was permitted to lecture. A rumor that Saxony might become the seat of war between Sweden and Poland drove him finally to Hanover, and he was appointed in 1708 teacher of Greek and Latin at the Gymnasium of Göttingen. In 1716 he got a position as pastor of the St. Nicholas Church in Göttingen. In 1725 he was appointed licentiate of theology at the University of Helmstädt, and in 1727 was made professor of theology at that high school. In 1731 he was called to the pastorate of the "Barfüsser Kirche" in Frankfort-on-the-Main, and there he died, Aug. 9, 1741. He greatly distinguished himself as a pulpit orator, but made many enemies by his opposition to the Reformed Church. He was also in constant warfare with the Roman Catholics, whom he greatly weakened at Frankfort by the frequent examination of their doctrines and practices. Münden's most important works are, *Diss. de הודיעה הא*, *sive de ה demonstrativo* (Lipsiæ, 1706, 4to):—*Progr. de litteris Hebræis et Græcis justo habendis pretio* (Gottingæ, 1708, 4to):—*De columna nubis et ignis commentatio, in qua primum Mosis de ea oraculum ex veris exegeseos sacræ principiis παρεμμενείᾳ, recens inventa, modeste vindicatur, nec non varia Scripturæ S. loca subinde illustrantur* (Gosl. 1712, 8vo):—*Regiæ et Electoralis Hannoveranæ Ecclesiæ ministri Epistola ad Io. Fr. Buddeum de pietistarum characteribus* (Götting. 1724, 4to):—*Progr. de incrementis studii exegetici adhuc sperandis* (Helmst. 1727, 4to):—*Progr. de quæstione, an operæ pretium sit, theologiam, quam dicunt casuisticam, singulari studio in Academiis tradere?* (ibid. 1727, 4to):—*Diss. exegetica moralis de ἀκριβείᾳ Christianorum practica*, ad Ephes. v cum xv (ibid. 1728, 4to):—*Diss. exegetica prior de dedicatione Evangelii S. Lucæ*, cap. i cum i–iv (ibid. 1728, 4to):—*Progr. in fest. pasch. de virtute resurrectionis Christi ex Phil. iii*, cap. x (ibid. 1729, 4to):—*Disquisitio de theologia morali in institutionibus theologicis a dogmatica theologia non divellanda* (ibid. 1730, 4to):—*Evangelische Lehrer, als Nachfolger Christi* (Frankf. a. M., 1730, 4to):—*Die Schmalkaldischen Arti-*

kel, mit einem Vorberichte (ibid. 1740, 4to). See Döring, *Gelehrte Theol. Deutschlands*, s. v.

Munger, PHILIP, a minister of the Methodist Episcopal Church, was born in South Brimfield, Mass., in 1780; was converted in 1796; entered the New England Conference in 1802; preached in the itinerancy thirty-four years; from 1836 to 1846 was either supernumerary or superannuated, and died Oct. 19, 1846. He was a man of energy and method, very studious, and a gifted and successful preacher. He preached more than nine thousand sermons, and wrote considerably for the Church literature. He was for many years an active trustee of the Maine Conference Seminary; and as a man, Christian, and minister was in all respects very exemplary and useful. See *Minutes of Conferences*, iv, 150; Stevens, *Memorials of Methodism*, vol. i, ch. xv. (G. L. T.)

Mûnî, a Sanscrit title, denoting a holy sage, and applied to a great number of distinguished personages, supposed to have acquired, by dint of austerities, more or less divine faculties.

Munich Manuscript (CODEX MONACENSIS, designated as X of the Gospels) is a valuable folio MS. of the end of the 9th or early in the 10th century, containing the four Gospels, with serious defects, and a commentary (chiefly from Chrysostom), surrounding and interspersed with the text of all but Mark, in early cursive letter. The very elegant uncials are small and upright; though some of them are compressed, they seem to be partial imitations of very early copies. Each page has two columns of about 45 lines each. There are no divisions by τίτλοι or sections. The ink of the MS. has much faded, and its general condition is bad. From a memorandum in the beginning we find that it came from Rome to Ingolstädt, and that it was at Innspruck in 1757; from Ingolstädt it was taken to Landshut, thence to Munich. Griesbach obtained some extracts from it through Dobrowsky; Scholz first collated it, Tischendorf more thoroughly, and Tregelles completely. See Scrivener, *Introd. to N. T.* p. 118 sq.; Tregelles, in Horne's *Introd.* iv, 195 sq. See MANUSCRIPTS, BIBLICAL.

Specimen of the *Codex Monacensis* (Luke vii, 25, 26: τίοις ἡμφιεσμένον· ἰδου ὁι | ἐν ἱματισμῷ ἐνδόξῳ και τρυφῇ ὑπάρχοντεσ ἐν τοῖς βασιλεί|οισ εἰσιν· ἀλλα τί ἐξεληλύθα.

Muniment Chamber, i. e. an *Ecclesiastical Register-house* or *Treasury*, is a room used for the preservation of charters, fabric and matriculation rolls, terriers, and registers. At Salisbury it is detached, on the south side of the cathedral. At Chichester it was over a chapel of the transept, dedicated to the Four Virgins, and at a later date next to the chapter-house, and furnished with a sliding panel. At Winchester and New College, Oxford, it is in a tower, as at St. Martin des Champs, Clugny, and Vaux des Sernay. At Fontenelle it was over the church-porch, as now at Peterborough. Where there was a provost, that officer kept the key. Muniments are, as it were, the defences of Church property.

Munition (מְצָד, *metsad'*, Isa. xxiii, 16; usually rendered "stronghold"), a fortress on a rocky eminence, such as those to which David resorted for safety from Saul (1 Sam. xxiii, 14); especially a "castle" or acropolis, as of Mount Zion (1 Chron. xi, 7). See FORT. In ancient times every city was located upon a naturally strong position [see CITY; HILL], and served itself for a stronghold (עִיר הַמִּבְצָר, עִיר בְּצוּרָה); yet in the period before the exile among the Hebrews particular strategic points, especially on the frontier and in low and level tracts, were more strongly and systematically fortified (1 Kings xv, 17, 22; 2 Chron. viii, 3; xi, 5 sq.; xiv, 6 sq.; xxvi, 6; xxvii, 4), in anticipation of sieges (2 Chron. xvii, 2), which, by reason of the more strenuous warfare, still oftener took place in post-exilian times (see 1 Macc. iv, 61; xii, 35; xiii, 30; xiv, 33 sq. [xv, 39]), when the residences of Palestine were distributed in citadels, walled towns, and open villages. First of all, strongholds were surrounded by one or more (2 Chron. xxxii, 5) walls (חוֹמָה), which were sometimes very thick (Jer. li, 58), and were furnished with battlements (פִּנּוֹת, 2 Chron. xxvi, 15; Zeph. i, 16; or שְׁמָשׁוֹת, Isa. liv, 12), parapet, and towers (מִגְדָּלִים, 2 Chron. xiv, 7; xxxii, 5; 1 Macc. v, 65; comp. Ezek. xxvi, 4; xxvii, 11; Jer. li, 12; Zeph. ii, 14; Judith i, 3), and were closed by powerful (in Babylon iron-bound, Isa. xlv, 2; Herod. i, 179) and strictly guarded (1 Kings iv, 13) gates (q. v.). Over these last were placed watch-towers (2 Sam. xiii, 34; xviii, 24, 33; 2 Kings ix, 17; 2 Chron. xxvi, 9; comp. Homer, Il. iii, 145, 154). See, generally, 2 Chron. xiv, 7. Around the wall lay the חֵיל (2 Sam. xx, 15; Isa. xxvi, 1; Nah. iii, 8; 1 Kings xxi, 23), apparently a moat with a rampart, but according to Kimchi a small outer wall (בַּר שׁוּרָה). See TRENCH. There were also watch-towers and forts (בִּירָנִיּוֹת) in the open field (2 Kings xviii, 8, 2 Chron. xxvii, 4), as well as castles in and at the cities for a final refuge (Judg. ix, 51 sq.). The most important fortress of Palestine in all ancient times was Jerusalem (q. v.). Other strong castles, especially for the protection of the borders, were, in the closing period of Jewish history, Alexandrium (Josephus, Ant. xiii, 16, 3), Machærus, Masada, Hyrcania (comp. Josephus, Ant. xiii, 16), Herodium (ib. xv, 9, 4; War, i, 21, 10), etc. They were usually located on hills (Ant. xiv, 6, 2). Caves and chasms in rocks were the first natural fastnesses (Judg. ix, 2). See CAVE.

The reduction (comp. צוּר, נצר) of strong places, to which the inhabitants retreated on the invasion of an enemy (Jer. viii, 14), began, after a demand to capitulate (Deut. xx, 10; comp. 2 Kings xviii, 17 sq.), with the demarcation of a line of circumvallation (מָצוֹר, בָּנָה, Eccles. ix, 14; בָּנָה דָיֵק, 2 Kings xxv, 1; Jer. vi, 6; lii, 4; Ezek. iv, 2; xvii, 17, etc.), and throwing up a bank (שָׁפַךְ סוֹלְלָה, 2 Sam. xx, 15; 2 Kings xix, 32; Isa. xxvii, 33; Hab. i, 10; Jer. vi, 6; Ezek. iv, 2; xvii, 17; xxvi, 8; 1 Macc. xi, 20; xiii, 43; comp. Josephus, Ant. xiii, 10, 2), and next proceeded by the employment of beleaguering engines (μηχαναί, 1 Macc. xi, 20, i. e. battering-rams, כָּרִים, Ezek. iv, 2; xxi, 27; comp. Josephus, War, iii, 9; Vitruv. x, 19), with which a breach was effected (Ezek. xxi, 27. A description of the customary Roman machinæ obsidionales, which Titus used—but for a long time in vain—in the siege of Jerusalem [Josephus, War, v, 6, 2 sq.; 9, 2; vi, 2, 3, etc.], is given by Ammian. Marcel. xxiii, 4. On the Roman aries especially, see Josephus, War, iii, 7, 19). A simpler operation was to set the fort on fire, and thus destroy at once both it and the besieged (Judg. ix, 49). As an example of undermining the walls, Jer. li, 58 is adduced only by a gloss in the Sept. and Vulg.; in later times this process becomes clearer (Josephus, War, ii, 17, 8; comp. Dio Cass. lxix, 12; Veget. Mil. iv, 24). The demolition of the aqueducts is once mentioned (Judith vii, 6). For defence the besieged were accustomed not only to shoot darts from the walls (2 Sam. xi, 24), but also to hurl large stones and beams (Judg. ix, 53; 2 Sam. xi, 21; Josephus, War, v, 3, 3; 6, 3), and even to pour down boiling oil (Josephus, War, iii, 7, 28); in later times they used slinging-machines (חִשְּׁבֹנוֹת, 2

Chron. xxvi, 15; Dio Cass. lxvi, 41). Also by skilfully managed sorties, which were disguised by mines (Josephus, Ant. xiv, 16, 2; War, v, 11, 4, etc.), they strove (especially by burning the siege-works) to break the siege (1 Macc. vi, 3; Josephus, War, v, 6, 6; 11, 5; vii, 6, 4), and for this purpose they watched the enemy by sentinels posted on the walls (Josephus, War, v, 2, 5). The Israelites were enjoined to spare fruit-trees when they laid siege to a city (Deut. xx, 19 sq.; yet see 2 Kings iii, 25; comp. Michaelis, Mos. Recht, i, 378 sq.). The beleaguering of strongholds was sometimes carried on for a long time (so Hyrcanus was able to reduce Samaria only after an investment of a whole year, Josephus, Ant. xiii, 10, 3), and brought upon the besieged (even when they had provisioned themselves beforehand, 1 Macc. xiii, 3) so severe a famine (2 Kings vi, 25 sq.; 1 Macc. vi, 53 sq.—but of a lack of water in besieged places there is seldom any mention [see Josephus, War, iii, 7, 12; Ant. xiv, 14, 6], probably owing to the copious cisterns usually at hand) that they were often obliged to resort to very unusual (comp. Judith xi, 11) and even nauseous means of subsistence (2 Kings vi, 25, 29; xviii, 27; Lam. iv, 10; Josephus, Ant. xiii, 10, 2; War, v, 10, 3; 13, 7; vi, 3, 3; comp. Barhebr. Chron. p. 149, 488). But the garrison sometimes contrived ingeniously to conceal from the besiegers the food and provisions brought into the city (Josephus, War, iii, 7, 12). Obstinate fortresses were taken by storm (comp. 1 Macc. v, 51), and the houses were razed to the ground (Judg. ix, 45; 1 Macc. v, 52; Josephus, Ant. xiii, 10, 3. Occasionally the plough was passed over the site of a captured town laid in ashes, Horace, Od. i, 16, 21; Senec. Clement. i, 26; but Mic. iii, 12 has no such allusion), the inhabitants massacred, manacled, and reduced to slavery (Judg. i, 25; 1 Macc. v, 52; comp. 2 Macc. v, 13 sq.; x, 17, 23). See SIEGE. On the other hand, the enemy usually spared such places as surrendered (1 Macc. xiii, 43 sq.). Citadels which had never been captured were called in Oriental phrase virgins (see Gesenius, Jesa. i, 736). See FORTIFICATION.

Munk, SALOMON, a Jewish writer of great celebrity, one of the most famous Shemitic scholars and Orientalists of our century, was born at Gross-Glogau, in Prussian Silesia, probably in 1802, though some put it 1805 and 1807. When fifteen years of age he left his native place for Berlin, where he studied under the famous philologist Buttmann at the gymnasium of the "Gray Cloister," and then attended lectures at the university. From Berlin he went to Bonn, where the Arabic scholar Freytag lectured, and under his guidance he took up the study of Arabic. In order to complete his studies he went in the autumn of 1829 to Paris, to attend the lectures of Sylvestre de Sacy, Abel Rémusat, Eugène Bournouf, and Chézy, who soon became his friends, and by whose assistance he completed his studies in the Arabic, Persian, and Sanscrit. In 1835 he visited England, and spent some time at the University of Oxford, collecting materials for an edition of Maimonides's celebrated work, Moreh Nebuchim (Guide of the Erring). Some essays which he wrote for the Journal Asiatique and the Dictionnaire des Sciences philosophiques attracted the attention of the learned world, and in 1840 he was appointed deputy-keeper of the Oriental MSS. in the Royal Library of Paris. In the same year Munk was invited to accompany Sir Moses Montefiore and M. Cremieux to the East, in behalf of the persecuted Jews of Damascus, to which he gladly consented, and secured while in Egypt many interesting MSS. in Arabic relating to the early literature of the Karaites, and other subjects of early Arabic literature. On his return he devoted himself so assiduously to his Arabic studies that he eventually lost his eyesight, and from 1852 was entirely blind. He had to relinquish his office in the library, and lived in retirement until 1865, when he succeeded M. Rénan as professor of Shemitic languages in the College of France. On Feb. 1 he delivered his inaugural address, *Cours de langues, Hebraïque, Chaldaïque, et Syriaque.* All scholars of France were elated at the appointment, even those who regretted the deposition of Rénan. The clergy also, Protestants as well as Roman Catholics, hailed the choice with joy. The *Union*, well known for its ultramontane tendencies, which could hardly have been supposed to favor a Jewish incumbent in the chair just made vacant by a Rationalist, thus commented: "A weak, blind man, who only by the sense of touch can build up the world of his thoughts, traverses the centuries of nations, cities, idioms. What a spiritual power! He is an ornament to science, for he teaches the scholar how to love. France possesses in him the greatest philologist, and though a mysterious decision of a kind Providence has robbed him of his physical light, the renown which he has gained, and the greater name which he will yet earn, are sure to shine in splendor for all times, and the light which he has shed into the darkness of Phœnician knowledge will never die out." But he soon after died, Feb. 6, 1867, lamented by all who knew him. Munk was an authority in the field of Oriental languages, and his works will always be highly esteemed. His principal publications are, *Réflexions sur le culte des anciens Hébreux, dans ses rapports avec les autres cultes de l'antiquité* (Reflections upon the worship of the ancient Hebrews, in its connection with the other worships of antiquity) (Paris, 1833):—*Notice sur Rabbi Saadia Gaon et sa version Arabe d'Isaie*, etc. (ibid. 1838):—*Notice sur Joseph ben-Jehoudah*, etc. (ibid. 1842):—*Commentaire de R. Tanhoum de Jérusalem sur le livre de Habakkuck*, etc. (ibid. 1843):—*L'Inscription Phœnicienne de Marseille*, etc. (ibid. 1847):—*Palestine, description géographique, historique, et archéologique* (ibid. 1845; Germ. transl. by Prof. M. A. Levy, Leipsic, 1871–72, 2 vols.): — *Notice sur Aboul-walid Merwan ibn Djana'h*, etc. (ibid. 1850):—*Mélanges de philosophie Juive et Arabe* (ibid. 1849); a part of which, the *Esquisse historique de la philosophie chez les Juifs*, has been transl. into German by B. Beer (Leipsic, 1852):— but Munk's *chef-d'œuvre* is his *Moreh Nebuchim* of Moses Maimonides (q. v.) in Arabic and French, with critical, literary, and explanatory notes, under the title *Le guide des égarés, traité de théologie et de philosophie* (vol. i–iii, Paris, 1856–66). See Fürst, *Bibl. Jud.* ii, 407; Frankel, *Monatsschrift*, 1867, p. 120–123, 453–459; Geiger, *Jüd. Zeitschrift*, 1867, p. 1–16; *Journal Asiatique*, July, 1867; Etheridge, *Introduct. to Hebr. Literat.* p. 482 sq.; Grätz, *Gesch. d. Juden*, xi, 538, 540, 545; Jost, *Gesch. d. Juden. u. s. Sekten*, iii, 363, 364; Cassel, *Leitfaden für Gesch. u. Literat.* p. 115, 117; Erentheil, *Jüdische Charakterbilder* (Pesth, 1867, 8vo), p. 94–106; *Jüdisches Athenæum*, p. 168 sq.; Lewes, *Hist. of Philos.* vol. ii; Ueberweg, *Hist. of Philos.* i, 109 sq., 421. (J. H. W.)

Munkhouse, RICHARD, D.D., an English divine of some note, flourished near the opening of this century. He was vicar of Wakefield, and died about 1811. He was noted as a pulpit orator, but his sermons, of which several series have been published (Lond. 1799, 8vo; 1802, 8vo; *Twenty-six Occas. Discourses*, 1805, 3 vols. 8vo; 1808, 3 vols. 8vo; 1813, 8vo), indicate that he was not a powerful speaker, but an able writer and a good Biblical scholar. See *London Monthly Review*, lvi, 233; Allibone, *Dict. of Brit. and Amer. Authors*, s. v.

Muñoz, Ægidius, Anti-pope, was born at the beginning of the 14th century. In consequence of the election of pope Martin V by the Council of Constance, the Church had again a chief, but notwithstanding Peter de Luna continued to play at the castle of Peniscola the part of pope. He only counted, however, a small circle of adherents. When Peter de Luna died in 1424, Ægidius Muñoz was elected anti-pope under the name of Clement VIII, and he continued in his office till July 26, 1429, when he resigned. In return for his resignation, the bishopric of Majorca was given to him. See CLEMENT VIII; MARTIN V.

Muñoz, Juan Baptista, a Spanish historian and philosophical writer, was born in 1745 at Muleros, near Valencia. He was appointed professor of philosophy at the university, and disestablished Aristotelian philosophy, which had hitherto reigned supreme in Spain. Later he became cosmographer of the Indies, and undertook by order of the king a history of America, of which he lived to publish only one volume. He died in 1799. His works of interest to the theological student are, *De recto Philosophiæ recentis in Theologia Usu Dissertatio:—De Scriptorum Gentilium Lectione:—Institutiones Philosophicæ.*

Munro, JOHN, a Scotch minister, who did much to advance in the "Far North" the interests of the Free Church of Scotland, was born in Ross-shire, about 1768, of humble but honorable parentage. John's father died while he was yet a lad, and the care of a large household was his early prospect. His mother, a pious woman, was anxious that John should follow his father's footsteps in all Christian work, and therefore devoted much of her time to his religious training. His secular educational advantages were few, and he was early obliged to learn a trade for his own and his family's support. When working as a journeyman carpenter he conceived the plan of entering the work of the holy ministry, and while residing at Aberdeen he spent his evenings in study, acquiring especially some knowledge of the languages. He finally entered the university, and after going through a course in literature and divinity was licensed to preach. In 1806 he went to Caithness to take charge of the Achreny mission, at that time including the three preaching stations of Achreny, Halsary, and Halladale, and extending over about twenty miles of hill country destitute of roads. He had labored here for ten years with great success when he was called to the Edinburgh Gaelic chapel, and, accepting the place, he occupied it until 1825, when he was presented to the parish church of Halkirk, and there he distinguished himself by great devotion to his people and close application to pulpit preparation, so that his sermons attracted all classes of society, even the most cultured, notwithstanding the deficiencies in his own culture for want of early advantages. Said one of his contemporaries: "His ministrations were highly acceptable to his hearers. They could not fail to recognise in them the instructions and exhortations of a man of God, who knew and felt the truth and loved their souls. He evidently spoke from the heart—spoke what he believed—what his own soul was full of, and was daily feeding on with delight." He died April 1, 1847, at Thurso, while in attendance on a meeting of the Presbytery of Caithness, to which he belonged. "Munro in personal appearance was not above the middle height, but of portly figure, and fair complexioned, his countenance beaming with benevolence. That his mental power—although not his predominant feature—was uncommon was evident from the position, weight, and influence he attained in the ministerial office." See Auld, *Ministers and Men of the Far North* (1868), p. 74–99.

Münscher, WILHELM, an eminent German theologian, was born at Hersfeld March 11, 1766, where his father was metropolitan and first preacher. After studying in the gymnasium in his native city, he continued his studies at Marburg. In 1785 he became his father's assistant, and in 1789 succeeded him as preacher at Hersfeld. In 1792 he was appointed professor of theology at Marburg, and member of the consistory, which positions he held for the remainder of his life. He died July 28, 1814. Dr. Münscher was classed by his countrymen with Michaelis, Döderlein, Planck, and others who stood on middle ground between the ancient, pure Lutheranism and the modern neology of Germany. He wrote, *Handbuch der christlich. Dogmengeschichte* (1797, 4 vols.), which went through three editions, and was republished under the editorship of Cöln and Neudecker in 1832–38, at Cassel:—*Lehrbuch der christlichen*

Kirchengesch. (Marburg, 1804): — *Abriss der Dogmengeschichte* (1811, and often since; published also in this country in an English dress [New Haven, 1830]): —also numerous historical articles in Henke's *Magazin*, Stäudlin's *Beiträge*, and Gabler's *Journal:—Predigten* (Marb. 1803):—*Politische Predigten* (Marb. 1813). Münscher's great work (*Dogmengeschichte*) is thus spoken of by C. F. L. Simon, in his *Continuation* of Nösselt's *Guide to the Literature of Theology* (§ 299): "The author has happily combined the chronological order with that of the relations of things; and the whole work is distinguished alike for the persevering, learned, and critical industry manifested in collecting the materials, and for the solidity and independence of judgment with which they are methodically arranged and agreeably expressed." He adds, "The same commendation is due to the author's *Elements of Dogmatic History*." Brettschneider, in his *Entwickelung der Dogmatik* (p. 99, 2d ed.), says of the *Manual*, "It is to be regarded as the *best work* on the subject." See Wachler, *Ueb. Dr. Wilhelm Münscher* (Frankf. 1814); *Christian Examiner and General Review*, 1830 (iv), p. 182. (J. H. W.)

Munsey, THOMAS K., a minister of the Methodist Episcopal Church, South, was born in Giles County, Va., Sept. 7, 1816. He was converted and joined the Church when eighteen years old, and had a strong desire to enter the ministry at once, but his education was so limited that he found it necessary to prepare himself for the great work. He spent one year in Emory and Henry college, and taught one year to pay his expenses. At the age of twenty-four he joined the Holstein Conference, and continued an acceptable member till his death. His first charge was the Rogersville Circuit, which contained twenty-eight appointments. His labors continued for six years, when failing health compelled him to seek rest. From this time he became a sufferer, but whenever sufficiently strong he was found laboring in the cause he loved so well. While he was on the Athens District in 1867 his health gave way entirely, and he was obliged to give up all work. He held a superannuated relation to the Conference till his death, which occurred July 4, 1872. See *Minutes of Ann. Conferences of the Methodist Episcopal Church, South,* 1873.

Munsinger, JOHANN, a German theologian of the 14th century, is noted in ecclesiastical history on account of the part he took in the Sacramentarian controversy of his time. He was rector of the school in Ulm in A.D. 1385, but was ejected because of his declarations, "Corpus Christi non est Deus. Nulla creatura est adoranda adoratione qua Deus debet adorari, adoratione scil. latriæ: *hyperdulia* debetur creaturæ excellenti, sicut est caro Christi, b. Virgo," etc. He maintained further, "Hostia consecrata non est Deus; Deus est *sub* hostia consecrata, corpus ejus, sanguis et anima;" namely, "per hostiam intelligo accidentia quæ sunt in pane, rotunditatem videlicet, saporem et gravitatem." He denied the propriety of calling the *hostia* the *corpus Christi*, "quia accidentia visa non sunt corpus Christi, licet intus sit corpus Christi;" therefore it was better to say, "hic esse corpus Christi sub specie panis." Munsinger, it is seen then, only objected to considering the visible bread to be Christ himself; but by no means denied that Christ should be prayed to, *sub specie panis*, and hence his propositions were approved by both the universities, notwithstanding that the Dominicans had ousted him as a heretic. See Flacius, *Catal. testium veritatis*, No. 315, and elsewhere; Schelhorn, *Amœnitates literariæ*, viii, 511; l. c. xi, 222; Gieseler, *Eccles. Hist.* iii, 136, note.

Munson, Eneas, M.D., a Christian physician, was born in New Haven June 24, 1734; graduated at Yale College in 1753; and, after having been a tutor, became a chaplain in the army in 1755 on Long Island. Ill-health induced him to study medicine. He practiced physic at Bedford in 1756, and removed in 1760 to New

Haven, where he died, June 16, 1826, in high repute as a physician. Of the medical society of Connecticut he was the president. He was a man of piety from an early period of his life. At the bedside of his patients he was accustomed to commend them to God in prayer. It was with joyous Christian hope that this venerable old man went down to the dead.

Munson, John, a Presbyterian minister, was born in New Jersey in 1783. But little is known of his early history, save that in 1808 the family removed west of the Alleghany Mountains, and settled near Greensburg, Westmoreland Co., Pa. In the academy of that place he received a fair education; studied theology privately; was licensed and ordained in 1817; and in 1818 installed pastor of the congregations of Plain Grove and Centre, Pa. In 1838 he was relieved from the former, and gave all his attention to the latter charge, where he labored till 1859, when he resigned. He subsequently removed to London, Mercer Co., Pa., where he died, Dec. 18, 1866. Mr. Munson was a man of superior intellect. He was a great reader, especially of standard works, such as Bates, Edwards, etc. As a theologian he was able, being familiar with all the great questions in controversy between the Calvinists and Arminians. His preaching was mostly textual. See Wilson, *Presb. Hist. Almanac*, 1867, p. 183.

Munson, Samuel, a Congregational minister, was born March 23, 1804, at New Sharon, Me. He graduated at Bowdoin College in 1829; and having entered the ministry with the intention of becoming a missionary, offered his services to the American Board, and was sent with the Rev. Henry Lyman to Sumatra and the neighboring isles. They sailed for Batavia June 10, 1833, in which place they remained until April, 1834, when they sailed to Nyas, thence to Tappanooly. Having obtained servants and guides, they started to visit the Batta region, but were murdered by the natives, April 28, 1834. See Sprague, *Annals Amer. Pulpit*, ii, 747; *American Missionary Memorial*, s. v.

Münster, PROTESTANT REVOLT AT. See ANABAPTISTS.

Münster, SEBASTIAN, a German theologian and Hebraist, who identified himself with the Reformers, but exerted an influence only as a scholar, was born in 1489 at Ingelheim, in the Palatinate. At sixteen years of age he went to Tübingen, where Stapfer and Reuchlin became his teachers. He then joined the Order of the Franciscans; but, brought in contact with Luther, he quitted the convent and embraced Protestantism. He was elected professor of Hebrew and theology at the University of Heidelberg, and subsequently at that of Basle, where he died of the plague in 1552. Besides being an eminent Hebraist, he was also an excellent mathematician; yet his erudition is hardly more praised by his contemporaries than his modesty. His tombstone bears the inscription, "Germanorum Esdras hic Straboque conditur." He was a sweet-tempered, pacific, studious, retired man, who wrote a great number of books, but never meddled in controversy; all which considered, his going early over to Luther must seem somewhat extraordinary. And yet he was one of the first who attached himself to Luther; but he seems to have done it with little or none of that zeal which distinguished the early Reformers, for he never concerned himself with their disputes, but shut himself up in his study, and busied himself in such pursuits as were most agreeable to his humor; and these were the Hebrew and other Oriental languages, the mathematics, and natural philosophy. His works are, *Biblia Hebraica Charactere Singulari apud Judæos Germanos in usu recepto, cum Latina planeque Nova Translatione, adjectis insuper e Rabbinorum Commentariis Annotationibus*, etc. (Basle, 1534–35, fol.; reprinted in 2 vols. fol. in 1546, with considerable additions and corrections). This version is considered much more faithful and exact than those of Pagninus and Arias Montanus, and his notes are generally approved, though he dwells a little too long upon the comments of the rabbins. For this version he received the appellation of "the German Esdras:"—*Grammatica Chaldaica* (4to):—*Dictionarium Chaldaicum non tam ad Chaldaicos interpretes, quam ad Rabbinorum intelligenda Commentaria necessarium* (4to):—*Dictionarium Trilingue* (Latin, Greek, and Hebrew, fol.):—*Captivitates Judæorum incerti autoris* (Hebrew and Latin, 8vo):—*Calendarium bibl. Hebr., ex Hebræorum penetralibus editum:*—*Higgaïon, logica R. Simeonis, Latine versa:*—*Institutiones Grammaticæ in Hebr. linguam:*—*Grammatica Ebræa:*—*Institutio elem. Gramm. Hebr.:*—*Hebraicæ Institutiones:*—*Catalogus omnium præceptorum legis Mosaicæ, quæ ab Hebræis sexcenta et octodecies numerantur, cum succincta Rabbinorum expositione et additione traditionum,* etc. (Hebrew and Latin, 8vo):—*Organum Uranicum; theorica omnium planetarum motus, canones* (fol.):—*Cosmographia Universalis* (1544, fol., translated into German, French, Italian, English, Bohemian, and other languages). It is one of the first universal geographies published in modern times, and is remarkably well executed considering the age in which it was written. The author is most diffuse in treating of Germany and Switzerland. He gives a description of the principal towns, their history, the laws, manners, and arts of the people; the remarkable animals of the country; the productions of the soil, the mines, etc.; and the whole is illustrated by wood-cuts, with a portrait of the author. Münster mentions several learned men of his time who furnished him with an account of their respective countries, of Sardinia, the Illyricum, etc. He also gives specimens of several languages:—*Rudimenta mathematica in duos libros digesta:*—*Horologiographia* (being a treatise of gnomonics). Münster also translated into Latin several works of the learned Hebrew grammarian, Elias Levita, on the Massorah and on Hebrew grammar. He also wrote notes on Pomponius Mela and Solinus. His commentaries upon several books of the Old Testament are inserted among the *Critici Sacri.* See Brucker, *Ehrentempel der teutschen Gelehrsamkeit,* p. 137 sq.; Schröckh, *Kirchengesch. s. d. Ref.* v, 72, 92 sq.; Adam, *Vitæ Philos. Germ.* p. 66 sq.; Rosenmüller, *Handb. f. d. Lit. d. bibl. Kritik u. Exegese,* v, 224 sq.; Gieseler, *Eccles. Hist.* (Harper's ed.) vol. iv. (J. H. W.)

Munster, SYNOD OF, is the name of an independent body of Irish Presbyterians, consisting of a few congregations in Dublin and the south of Ireland, who seceded from the main body of that country. They are mainly Unitarians in creed. See Killin's Reid, *Hist. Presb. Ch. in Ireland,* iii, 468–9, 488.

Münter, Balthasar, a German theologian, noted as a pulpit orator and scholar, was born at Lübeck March 24, 1735. He studied theology at Jena, was for a time preacher at Gotha, and eventually became celebrated as a pulpit orator in the German Church of Copenhagen, Denmark, where he removed in 1765, and as the editor of the *Bekehrungsgeschichte* of count Struensee, whom he had attended on the scaffold (Copenhagen, 1772; English translation, entitled *A Faithful Narrative of the Conversion and Death of Count Struensee,* etc., by the Rev. Mr. Wendeborn [2d ed. Lond. 1774]). Münter wrote also a series of hymns (1772 and 1774). He died in 1793.

Münter, Friedrich Christian Karl Heinrich, a theologian, Orientalist, and archæologist who gained great celebrity in Denmark, which became his country by adoption (see preceding article), was the son of Balthasar, and born at Gotha, Germany, Oct. 14, 1761. He studied at Copenhagen and Göttingen, and in 1786 went to Italy. After his return, towards the end of 1788, he was appointed professor of theology at Copenhagen. He became successively co-director of the Orphan House in 1805 and bishop of Zealand in 1808. He died April 9, 1830. Münter wrote a number of works of great interest to the student of ecclesiastical

archæology, and yet he must be regarded really as more important as a savant than as a theologian. He founded the Museum of Northern Antiquities at Copenhagen, and left a valuable collection of coins and archæological works. He wrote, *Metrische Uebersetzung der Offenbarung Johannis* (Copenh. 1784; 2d ed. 1806):—*Nachrichten ü. Sicilien* (Danish, 1788; German, 1790, 2 vols.):—*Die Kirchlichen Alterthümer der Gnostiker* (Ausb. 1790):—*Magazin für Kirchengesch. u. Kirchenrecht des Nordens* (Altona, 1792–96, 2 vols.):—*Statutenbuch d. Tempelherrn* (Berl. 1794):—*Vermischte Beiträge z. Kirchengeschichte* (1798):—*Handbuch der ältesten christlichen Dogmengeschichte* (Göttingen, 1801; by Evers, 1802, 2 vols.):—*Untersuchungen ü. d. Persepolitan. Inschriften* (1800, 1802):—*Versuch ü. d. Keilförmigen Inschriften in Sicilien* (Copenh. 1802):—*Spuren ägyptischer Religionsbegriffe in Sicilien u. d. benachbarten Inseln* (Prague, 1806):—*Religion d. Carthager* (Copenh. 1816; 2d ed. 1821):—*Antiquarische Abhandlungen* (Copenh. 1816):—*Miscellanea Hafnensia theologici et philologici argumenti* (Copenh. 1816–25, 2 vols.):—*Recherches sur l'origine des Ordres de chevalerie de Danemarc* (Copenh. 1822):—*Kirchengesch. v. Dänemark u. Norwegen* (Leips. 1823–34, 3 vols.):—*Sinnbilder u. Kunstvorstellungen d. alten Christen* (Altona, 1825):—*Der Stern der Weisen (Untersuchung über das Geburtsjahr Christi)* (Copenh. 1827):—*Religion d. Babylonier* (Copenh. 1827). See his life by Mynster, first in *Studien u. Krit.* 1833, i, 13–53; and later in book form (Copenh. 1834).—Herzog, *Real-Encyklop.* x, 98; Hoefer, *Nouv. Biog. Générale,* xxxvi, 954; Pierer, *Universal-Lex.* xi, 544; *Biblical Repos.* iv, 533. (J. N. P.)

Munthe, CASPAR FRIEDRICH, a Danish scholar noted for his researches in the original of the N. T. Scriptures, flourished at Copenhagen as professor of Greek in the first half of the 18th century. He died in 1762. He wrote, *Observationes philologicæ in Sacros Novi Testamenti Libros, ex Diodoro Siculo collectæ* (Copenh. and Leips. 1755, 8vo).

Muntinghe, HERMAN, a Dutch theologian of some note, flourished as professor of theology at the University of Groningen near the opening of this century. He died April 24, 1824. He was for some time pastor of the Reformed Church in Holland, but this is all we know of his personal history. As an author, however, he is well known by his *Pars Theologiæ Christianæ Theoretica* (Groning. 1801; 2d ed. 1818–22, 2 vols. 8vo). The first volume contains a compendious system of theology; the second a succinct account of the leading controversies with regard to religious doctrine, with copious references in each to Dutch, German, and English writers. Of Dr. Muntinghe's other works, it may be sufficient to mention a Latin *Outline of Church History,* on the basis of Schröckh's *Compendium,* and a voluminous *History of Mankind,* to which frequent reference is made in his *Theology.*

Munton, ANTHONY, an English divine, flourished near the middle of the 18th century as curate of St. Andrew's church, Newcastle. He died in 1755. He was noted in his day as a pulpit orator of great excellence and power. "Some of his sermons," says a contemporary, "would be pronounced truly excellent by every dispassionate judge." A volume of Munton's *Sermons* was published shortly after his death (Newcastle, 1756, 8vo).

Muntras, mystic verses or incantations which form the grand charm of the Hindû Brahmins. They occupy a very prominent place in the Hindû religion. The constant and universal belief is that when the Brahmin repeats the Muntras the deities must come obedient to his call, agreeably to the Sanscrit verse: "The universe is under the power of the deities, the deities are under the power of the Muntras, the Muntras are under the power of the Brahmins; consequently the Brahmins are gods." The Muntras are the essence of the Vedas, and the united power of Brahma, Vishnu, and Siva.

Munus Christi. See CHRIST, OFFICES OF.

Münzer, THOMAS, a religious enthusiast and fanatic of the great Reformation period, was born at Stolberg, in the Harz, about 1490. Of his youth we know little beyond what he stated himself to his judges at the time of his death (Walch, *Luther's Werke*, xvi, 158), namely, that he had resided at Aschersleben, and had studied at the university in Halle, and had taken part in a conspiracy against Ernest II, then archbishop of Magdeburg. As the archbishop died in 1513, this indicates how early Münzer began to be connected with secret associations. He also manifested early a great tendency to wandering from place to place in pursuance of visionary plans. He appears to have entered the University of Leipsic soon after he left Halle; at least we find him in 1515 with the degree of "magister artium" and bachelor of theology. He then acted as head of a school at Frohsen, near Aschersleben. In 1517 he appears as teacher in a gymnasium at Brunswick, then at Stolberg in the same year, and again at Leipsic in 1519. Next he was made chaplain and confessor of the Bernardine nunnery of Beutitz, near Weissenfels. This he left in 1520, and was made preacher of the church of St. Mary, at Zwickau, the principal church in the place. His very first sermon there (Rogation Sunday, 1520) made a deep impression, and brought him a large number of enemies as well as friends. At the breaking out of the Reformation, his unquiet spirit made him side at once with the movement. He entered into communication with Luther, and was looked upon as one of the sturdiest champions of reform. But he only understood the negative view of the Reformer's doctrines, that which overthrew the existing form of clerical life. Münzer now fearlessly attacked the mendicant orders, which were in a state of great prosperity at Zwickau, and soon found himself involved in a bitter controversy with their defender, brother Tiburtius of Weissenfels. Both parties had adherents among the population; yet Münzer succeeded in getting the ascendency by enlisting the sympathies of the most influential citizens, who had often suffered from the pride and arrogance of the monks. Münzer, however, still showed some moderation, as he declared himself ready to submit to the decision of the bishop of Naumburg, and also addressed letters of justification to Luther. Hardly was this quarrel over (towards the middle of 1520), when Münzer became involved in another. In the same church of St. Mary to which he was attached was another priest having the same functions, and who had been installed some years before Münzer. This priest was Dr. Johann (Sylvius) Wildenauer, a native of Eger, and generally known as Egranus. He inclined also to the doctrines of the Reformation, but only accepted their humanistic conclusions, and went no further with Münzer than condemning the ignorance of the monks. On other points he sided with the aristocracy of the town, and his private life was not above reproach. He was vain, conceited, and much given to advancing paradoxical theories. He and Münzer soon began to quarrel, and in November, 1520, they had already arrived at the point of exhibiting their differences in the pulpit. The population sided with Münzer, seeing in him not only the reformer of the Church, but their defender against clerical oppression. Münzer now gave full scope to his talents as a popular orator, and, helped on by the events of the times, had great success. Among his adherents was a weaver, Nicholas Storch, who subsequently obtained some reputation. Being either already connected with the sect of Böhme, or led on by Münzer alone, Storch soon became the head of a band of fanatics who boasted of supernatural communication, and spread by means of secret conventicles. Twelve apostles and seventy-two disciples were elected, and Münzer and Storch became the heads of the society. This movement made steady progress, and by its influence Egranus was finally obliged to leave Zwickau for Joachimsthal. This, however, did not suffice to restore peace to the town. Münzer, probably dissatisfied with his subordinate position as preacher of St. Mary's, succeeded in being appointed to the church of St. Catharine. Here, in connection with a master of arts, Loner, he excited the people against a priest of Marienthal, Nicholas Hofer, who had openly attacked him. Hofer was obliged to seek safety in flight, December, 1520. Being called to account by the official of the bishop, Münzer denounced the official in the pulpit, summoning him to appear at Zwickau (January 13, 1521). In spite of the admonitions of his friends, and in simple trust to the support of the lower classes, Münzer now cast off all restraint. He caused libels against Egranus to be posted up at the doors of the churches, and was therefore dismissed by the civil authorities after they had inquired into the whole affair. He remained in town nevertheless, and caused a rising of the weavers. The authorities were obliged to take vigorous measures; fifty-five of the ringleaders were apprehended, and a large number of the others hurriedly left the town, Münzer among them. Peace was now restored in the city, the more readily as the authorities, following Luther's advice, appointed Nicholas Hausmann, previously pastor of Schneeberg, as pastor of St. Mary's church. Still Storch and his followers stayed at Zwickau, and remained undisturbed until Christmas, 1521, when the zealous Hausmann caused them to be exiled from the city. Their subsequent career, under the name of "Prophets of Zwickau," in Wittenberg, is well known (on Münzer's stay at Zwickau, see Laurentius Wilhelm, *Descriptio urbis Cygneæ* [published by Tobias Schmidt, Zwickau, 1633], p. 90, 215, 217). Münzer left Zwickau in April, 1521, in company with Marcus Thomä, and travelled for a while through Central Germany (see Seidemann, *Thomas Münzer*, p. 122). His former career had given him some reputation, and the dissatisfied portion of the population everywhere rallied around him. In September, 1521, we find him at Saatz, where he met a large number of Moravians. The works of Luther were by that time known in Bohemia, and had awakened ardent sympathies. Münzer was warmly received, and in November, 1521, he openly published at Prague a proclamation to the Bohemians (printed in the *Anabaptisticum et enthusiasticum Pantheon*, 1702, and with additions in Seidemann, p. 122). This proclamation affords an early glimpse of the doctrines which Münzer subsequently unfolded in his publications. But Prague was not a suitable field for such attempts at a radical reform, and Münzer was exiled. In the early part of 1522 he went to Wittenberg, where, under the influence of Carlstadt and the prophets of Zwickau, a complete subversion of all existing ecclesiastical relations was daily progressing (see Salig, *Historie d. Augsburgischen Confession*, iii, 1099). Although connected with Melancthon and Bugenhagen, Münzer's feelings inclined him more towards Carlstadt's views. When Luther came to Wittenberg, Münzer felt that his labors would not be longer profitable there, and left. He appears to have soon after gone to Nordhausen, and in 1523 was married and succeeded in being appointed pastor of Alstedt, in Thuringia. The community at that place appears to have been entirely devoted to Münzer, as was also his colleague, Simon Haseritz (on the latter, see Hagen, *Deutschland's litterar. u. relig. Verf. im Reformationszeitalter*, 1844, iii, 114), and he conducted worship according to his own views. A work which he published on the subject at that time still shows some moderation (*Ordnung u. berechunge des Teutschen ampts zu Alstadt durch Tomam Müntzer*, etc., 1523). He retained the practice of infant baptism, with some ceremonies not commanded in Scripture. Soon after, however, he advanced further in his liturgical changes (in the *Deutsch-Evangelisch Messje*, Alstedt, 1524, and *Deutzsch Kirchenampt*, etc., Alstedt). He was the first preacher to substitute the German language for the Latin in the public prayers and singing, and composed a directory for worship which was in harmony with his ideas of the Reformation. The quiet duties of a pastor not satisfying Münzer, and being desirous to contest with Luther the leadership in the reformatory movement, Münzer determined to use all means to destroy the latter's influence; but his conduct displeased the princes who favored the Reformation under Luther, and finally, at the request of Frederick of Saxony and John of Weimar, Münzer was obliged to leave Alstedt in 1524. He now went successively to Nuremberg, Schaffhausen, and finally to Mühlhausen in Thuringia. In the latter place he acquired great influence over the people, which he hesitated not to use for his own purposes. He had adopted mystical views, and declaiming against what he called the "servile, liberal, and half" measures of the Reformers, required a radical reformation both in Church and State, according to his "inward light." He resolved on recourse to violent means, and his cry became, "We must exterminate with the sword, like Joshua, the Canaanitish nations." He caused the authorities of this place to be superseded, the convents and richest houses of the city to be plundered, and communism to be proclaimed. "Münzer," Luther wrote to Amsdorff, April 11, 1525, "Münzer is king, and emperor of Mühlhausen, and no longer is pastor." The lowest classes ceased to work. If any one wanted a piece of cloth or a supply of corn, he asked his richer neighbor; if the latter refused, the penalty was hanging. Mühlhausen being at that time a free town, Münzer exercised his power unmolested. He was, moreover, encouraged in his course by being joined about this same time by another band of fanatics under Pfeiffer. This, and the rumor that forty thousand peasants were arming in Franconia, decided Münzer to go still further and make himself master of the situation by an appeal to the peasants of Thuringia, promising them the spoils taken from their lords. The revolt of the peasants of Southern Germany led him to imagine that the time had come to extend his new kingdom. He had cast some large guns in the convent of the Franciscans, and now exerted himself to raise the peasantry and miners. "When will you shake off your slumbers," said he, in a fanatical address: "Arise and fight the battle of the Lord! The time is come—France, Germany, and Italy are up and doing. Up and at it!—Dran (at it!), dran, dran! Heed not the cries of the ungodly. They will weep like children—but be you pitiless.—Dran, dran, dran! Fire burns—let your swords be ever tinged with blood!—Dran, dran, dran! Work while it is day." The letter was signed "Münzer, God's servant against the ungodly," or "Thomas Münzer, with the sword of Gideon." Leaving Pfeiffer as governor at Mühlhausen, he marched towards Frankenhausen, and committed all manner of excesses in the country which he traversed. The country people, eager for plunder, flocked in crowds to his standard. Throughout the districts of Mansfeld, Stolberg, Schwarzburg, Hesse, and Brunswick the peasantry rose en masse. The convents of Michelstein, Ilsenburg, Walkenried, Rossleben, and many others in the neighborhood of the Hartz mountains or in the plains of Thuringia, were plundered. At Reinhardsbrunn, the place which Luther had once visited, the tombs of the ancient landgraves were violated, and the library destroyed. Terror spread far and wide. Even at Wittenberg some anxiety began to be felt—the doctors who had not feared emperors nor pope trembled in presence of the madman. Curiosity was all alive to the accounts of what was going on, and watched every step in the progress of the insurrection. Melancthon wrote: "We are here in imminent danger. If Münzer be successful, it is all over with us; unless Christ should appear for our deliverance. Münzer's progress is marked by more than Scythian cruelty. His threats are more dreadful than I can tell you." The elector John, duke George of Saxony, the landgrave Philip of Hesse, and duke Henry of Brunswick finally united their forces, and sent fifteen hundred horsemen and some companies of infantry against the rebels. Münzer's men then numbered about eight thousand. A battle was fought May 15,

1525, and the insurgents were completely defeated; according to some accounts they lost five thousand men, according to others seven thousand. Frankenhausen was taken and plundered. Münzer, discouraged, hid in a bed, feigning to be sick. He would have escaped, but a soldier having found in his travelling-bag a letter by count Mansfeld, Münzer was recognised and arrested. Being put to the torture, he revealed the names of his accomplices; was then taken to Mühlhausen, where Pfeiffer, who had sought to escape, was also a prisoner, and the two, together with twenty-four other rebels, were beheaded. His numerous writings, all of which are still extant, indicate a more than ordinary mind and will, but they betray also a great lack of sound judgment and a want of common-sense. His language is often forcibly eloquent, but all his utterances are tinged with coarseness and vulgarity. See Melancthon, Die Historie v. Thome Müntzer, etc. (1525); Christ. Guil. Aurbachii Dissertationes oratoriæ de eloquentia inepta Thomæ Munzeri (Wittenb. 1716); Löscher, Dissertatio de Muntzeri doctrina et factis (Leips. 1708); Strobel, Leben, Schriften u. Lehren Thomä Müntzer's (Nürnb. and Altdorf, 1795); Baczko, Thomas Münzer (Halle and Leips. 1812); Seidemann, Thomas Münzer (Dresden and Leipsic, 1842); Leo, Thomas Münzer (Berlin, 1856); Evangel. Kirchenzeit. 1856, p. 293; Kapp, Nachlese nützlich. Reformations-Urkund. ii, 613; Cyprian, Reformations-Urkunden, ii, 339; Walch, Luther's Werke, xvi, 4 sq., 171 sq.; Frank, Ketzer-Chronik, p. 187; Seckendorf, Hist. Lutheranismi, i, 118, 156, etc.; Sleidanus, De statu, etc., lib. v, 1; Arnold, Kirchen- u. Ketzerhistorie, 1740, i, 629, 674; Otting, Annales Anabaptist. 1672, p. 4, 6, 16, 42; Ranke, Deutsche Gesch. im Zeitalter d. Reform. ii, 187, 192, 215, 225; D'Aubigne, Hist. of the Ref. in Germany and Switzerland, iii, 207 sq.; Hardwick, Hist. Church of the Reformation, p. 252 sq., p. 40, n. 1; Hagenbach, Kirchengesch. iii (4th ed. Leips. 1870), Lect. 20; Gieseler, Eccles. Hist. vol. iv (Harper's ed.); Seebohm, Hist. Prot. Revolution, p. 136, 141 sq., 150; Blackwood's Magazine, Feb. 1847, p. 385 sq.; Zeitschr. f. hist. Theologie, 1858, 1860. See also PEASANT's WAR.

Mup'pim (Heb. Muppim', מֻפִּים, perh. contracted from מְצֻפִּים in the sense of flights; Sept. Μαμφίμ, v. r. 'Οφμίν and 'Οφιμίμ, Vulg. Mophim), a person named in Gen. xlvi, 21 as one of the sons of Benjamin born before the migration into Egypt; but really a grandson born much later, being a son of Becher (q. v.), as it would seem from parallel accounts. See BENJAMIN. He is doubtless the same elsewhere called SHEPHUPHAM (1 Chron. viii, 5), SHUPHAM (Numb. xxvi, 30), or SHUPPIM (1 Chron. vii, 12). See JACOB.

Muratori, LUDOVICO ANTONIO, a distinguished Italian theologian, archæologist, and historian, was born at Vignola, near Modena, Oct. 21, 1672. His family being in moderate circumstances, his early education was neglected. In 1685, however, he entered the college of the Jesuits, where he distinguished himself by his rapid progress. From a very early period his predilection for historical and literary pursuits began to manifest itself; and having entered into holy orders in 1688, without, however, accepting any ecclesiastical office, his life was devoted partly to the literature of his profession, but mainly to researches in history, both sacred and profane, especially the history of his native country. He took the degree of doctor in 1692; and his reputation for learning attracting the notice of Joseph Orsi and Felix Marsigli, he was on their recommendation appointed by Charles Borromeo sub-librarian of the Ambrosian Library at Milan. In that collection Muratori discovered several inedited MSS. He made extracts from these, and published them with notes and comments, under the titles of Anecdota Latina and Anecdota Græca (Milan, 1697–1713, 4 vols. fol.). Some years after he was recalled to Modena by the duke Rinaldo, who gave him the situation of librarian of the rich library of the house of Este, a place which he retained for the rest of his life. After this appointment Muratori devoted himself entirely to the study of the Italian records of the Middle Ages; and after many years of assiduous labor he produced his great work, *Rerum Italicarum Scriptores, ab anno æræ Christianæ* 500 *ad* 1500 (28 vols. fol.). The first volume of this immense collection was published at Milan in 1723, and the last appeared in 1751. Several princes and noblemen defrayed the expenses of the publication; sixteen of them contributed $4000 each. In this collection Muratori has inserted all the chronicles of Italy during the Middle Ages which he could discover, most of which were inedited, and has accompanied them with valuable commentaries. Some of the texts had already been published by Grævius in his *Thesaurus Antiquitatum et Historiarum Italiæ*, but they were mostly confined to the last century or two of the period of a thousand years embraced by Muratori. While engaged in these prodigious labors, he also carried on an active literary correspondence with the scholars of the various countries of Europe, and contributed essays not unfrequently to the principal historical and literary academies, of most of which he was a member. Muratori, however, held opinions not always in harmony with those of his contemporaries, and became involved in a quarrel with several writers by an attack upon the learned institutions of the time, and by an advocacy of the plan of a republic of the learned in a series of letters printed at Venice in 1703, under the name of Lamindo Britanio. In theology also he attempted to open a new path by his *De ingeniorum moderatione in religionis negotio* (first published at Paris, 1714; German, Coblentz, 1837). It is in the interests of Hermesianism (see HERMES, GEORG), and was republished in Germany. Muratori endeavors to show in this work that freedom of thought in religious matters may be tolerated, and to what degree this liberty may be exercised. But he excited the greatest tumult by his attacks against a society whose members pledged their lives to uphold the doctrine of the immaculate conception. A Jesuit, Francis Burgi, having entered into a controversy with him on this point, Muratori wrote his *De superstitione vitanda, sive censura voti sanguinarii in honorem immaculatæ conceptionis Deiparæ*. No printer dared publish this work, which appeared only in 1740 at Venice, pretending to have been printed at Milan. He followed it up by similar writings, under the alias of Ferdinandus Valdesius. Soon after, however, he reconciled himself with the Jesuits by writing the history of their missions in Paraguay, for which they showered honors upon him. He also published a collection of the Roman liturgy (Rome, 1748, 2 vols. fol.), and opposed the principles of the Reformation in his *Regolata divozioni de' Cristiani*, published under the name of Lamindo Britanio (Venice, 1747, and often reprinted). This work met with great success. Muratori wrote also an abridgment of his dissertations in Italian, which was published after his death: *Dissertazioni sopra le Antichità Italiane* (1766, 3 vols. 4to). He also wrote in Italian, *Annali d'Italia dal principio dell' era volgare sino all' anno* 1750 (1762, 12 vols. 4to). It is the first general history of Italy that was published, and is a useful book of reference. It has been continued by Coppi down to our own times: *Annali d'Italia in continuazione di quelli del Muratori, dal* 1750 *al* 1819 (Rome, 1829, 4 vols. 8vo). Another work of Muratori is his *Novus Thesaurus veterum Inscriptionum* (1739, 4 vols. fol.), in which he has inserted many inscriptions unknown to Gruter, Spon, Fabretti, and other archæologists who had preceded him. In seeking after the historical records of the Middle Ages, Muratori collected also a vast number of documents concerning the social, civil, intellectual, and political condition of Italy during that long period whose history he transcribed and commented upon, and he published the whole in seventy-five dissertations, *Antiquitates Italicæ medii ævi, sive Dissertationes de moribus Italici populi, ab inclinatione*

Romani Imperii usque ad annum 1500 (1738–42, 6 vols. fol.). "I have treated first," says the author in his preface, "of the kings, dukes, marquises, counts, and other magistrates of the Italian kingdom; after which I have investigated the various forms of the political government, and also the manners of the private citizens; the freedom and franchises of some classes and the servitude of others; the laws, the judicial forms, the military system; the arts, sciences, and education; the progress of trade and industry; and other matters of social and civil history." His work, entitled *Antichità Estensi* (Modena, 1710–40, 2 vols. fol.), treats of the Fasti of the house of Este in its various branches. He also wrote several historico-political treatises in support of the rights of his sovereign, the duke of Modena, over the towns of Ferrara and Comacchio, which had been seized by the court of Rome: *Questioni Comacchiesi* (Modena, 1711): — *Piena esposizione dei Diritti della Casa d'Este sopra la Citta di Comacchio* (1712):—*Ragioni della serenissima Casa d'Este sopra Ferrara* (1714). Among Muratori's other works we must mention, *Governo politico, medico, ed ecclesiastico della Peste* (1720), written on the occasion of the plague of Marseilles, and showing the methods required to counteract it :—*Difetti della Giurisprudenza* (1742), in which he shows the defects of judicial forms in most countries:—*Morale Filosofia* (1735): — *Instituzioni di publica felicità* (1749):—*Della regolata divozione dei Fedeli*. In this last treatise Muratori, who, though sincerely pious, was too enlightened to be superstitious, combated several popular devotional practices which were merely external, and recommended in preference internal habits of self-examination and prayer. His enemies accused him of heresy. Muratori wrote to the pope, Benedict XIV, explaining his meaning, and asking for his judgment on the matter of contention. That enlightened pontiff wrote him a kind letter in answer, telling him that "those passages in his works which were not found acceptable to Rome did not touch either the dogma or the discipline of the Church; but that had they been written by any other person the Roman Congregation of the Index would have forbidden them; which, however, had not been done in the case of Muratori's works, because it was well known that he, the pope, shared in the universal esteem in which his merit was held," etc. Muratori has been truly called the "father of the history of the Middle Ages." Subsequent historians, such as Sismondi and others, are greatly indebted to Muratori, without whose previous labors they could not have undertaken or completed their works. The character of Muratori is clearly seen in his works. Modest, though learned, indefatigable, intent upon the improvement of mankind, charitable and tolerant, sincerely religious and strictly moral, he was one of the most distinguished and yet most unobtrusive among the learned of Italy. In the studies of his own profession, as well liturgical and historical as dogmatical and even ascetical, Muratori, although he did not follow the method of the schools, was hardly less distinguished than if he had made these the pursuit of his life. Some of his opinions were regarded with disfavor, if not directly condemned, but his honesty stands unquestioned alike by Jesuits and Ultramontanes or radical Protestants. All pay homage to his scholarship and industry and integrity. Muratori was also rector of the parish of Pomposa at Modena, but his literary occupations did not make him neglect his flock; he assisted his parishioners with his advice and his money; he founded several charitable institutions, and rebuilt the parish church. He died at Modena in 1750. All his writings collected make up 46 vols. in folio, 34 in 4to, 13 in 8vo, and many more in 12mo. His minor works were collected and published at Arezzo in 1787, in 19 vols. 4to. The best uniform edition of Muratori's works is that published at Venice (1790–1810, 48 vols. 8vo). His tomb is in the church of St. Agostino at Modena, near that of his illustrious countryman, Sigonio. His life has been written by his nephew, G. F. Muratori, *Vita del celebre L. A. Muratori* (1756). See Scheldoni, *Elogio di L. A. Muratori* (1818); Tipaldo, *Biografia degli Italiani illustri*, s. v.; Abbé Gouget, in Ant. Gachet d'Antigny, *Mémoires d'histoire*, etc. (Par. 1756), vol. vi; *English Cyclop.* s. v.

Muratorian Fragment, also spoken of as CANON OF MURATORI, is a treatise on Biblical MSS. of great importance to the history of the N.-T. canon. It is believed to have been composed shortly after the production of the *Shepherd* of Hermas (q. v.), and therefore belongs to the second half of the 2d century. It is important, first, because of its remote antiquity, and also as an evidence as to what writings passed for canonical in the Catholic Church of that time. It enumerates as such the Gospel of Luke (as the third, the two others being presupposed), the Gospel of John, the Acts of the Apostles, thirteen Pauline epistles, a letter of Jude, two epistles of John, the Apocalypses of John and Peter, the latter, however, with contradiction asserted. The Epistles of Jacob (James) and Peter are therein omitted, also the one to the Hebrews. The epistles to the Laodicæans and Alexandrians are rejected. The fragment was noticed by Muratori in his *Antiq. Ital. medii ævi*, iii, 854, and has been reprinted in the *Introductions to the N. T.* of Eichhorn and Guericke, also by Kirchhofer and Credner. An exhaustive treatise on the subject, with the original text, and a translation of it into Greek, by Hilgenfeld, is found in the *Zeitschrift für wissenschaftliche Theologie*, 1872, p. 560. See also Gieseler. in *Studien u. Kritiken*, 1847 and 1856; Hesse, *Das Muratorische Fragment untersucht u. erklärt* (Giessen, 1873); Westcott, *Canon of N. T.* (2d ed.), p. 184 sq.; *Bapt. Quar.* April, 1868, p. 282; *Amer. Pres. Rev.* Jan. 1869, p. 100.

Murcot, JOHN, an English divine of some note, was born near the opening of the 17th century, and was educated at the University of Oxford. He wrote largely, and yet but little is known of his personal history. He died in 1654. His most important writings were collected and published as *Theolog. Treatises* (1657, 4to). Wood, in his *Athenæ Oxon.*, speaks of Murcot as characterized by "a forward, prating, and pragmatical precision." Thomas Manton held him highly in esteem, and speaks of him thus as a preacher: "It were pity that the sermons coming from such a warm, affectionate spirit should die away with the breath in which they were uttered: as his fruit remaineth (I hope) in the hearts of many that heard him, so is it wrapt up in these papers to preserve it from perishing and forgetfulness." See Allibone, *Dict. Brit. and Amer. Auth.* s. v.

Murder (properly קֶטֶל, which, however, is rendered "slaughter" in the Auth. Ver., from קָטַל, to "kill," φόνος). The criminal law of the Israelites naturally recognised the distinction between wilful murder and accidental or justifiable homicide (Numb. xxv, 16 sq.), although in the legislative language itself the word רָצַח is used for both kinds of manslaughter (see especially Numb. xxv, 26; Deut. xix, 3, etc.). Murder was invariably visited with capital punishment (Lev. xxiv, 17; comp. Gen. ix, 6), without the possibility of expiation. Mere homicide (the act of מַכֵּה נֶפֶשׁ בִּשְׁגָגָה, Numb. xxxv, 15, or רֹצֵחַ אֶת־רֵעֵהוּ בִּבְלִי דַעַת, Deut. iv, 42) was, however, liable to a forfeiture of life according to all ancient national observances.—Winer, ii, 105. (See Ewald, *Alterthümer des V. Israel*, p. 146–154.) See BLOOD-REVENGE. The principle on which the act of taking the life of a human being was regarded by the Almighty as a capital offence is stated on its highest ground as an outrage—Philo calls it sacrilege—on the likeness of God in man, to be punished even when caused by an animal (Gen. ix, 5, 6, with Bertheau's note; see also John viii, 44; 1 John iii, 12, 15; Philo, *De Spec. Leg.* iii, 15, vol. ii, p. 313). Its

secondary or social ground appears to be implied in the direction to replenish the earth which immediately follows (Gen. ix, 7). The exemption of Cain from capital punishment may thus be regarded by anticipation as founded on the social ground either of expediency or of example (Gen. iv, 12, 15). The postdiluvian command, enlarged and infringed by the practice of blood-revenge, which it seems to some extent to sanction, was limited by the Law of Moses, which, while it protected the accidental homicide, defined with additional strictness the crime of murder. It prohibited compensation or reprieve of the murderer, or his protection if he took refuge in the refuge-city, or even at the altar of Jehovah, a principle which finds an eminent illustration in the case of Joab (Exod. xxi, 12, 14; Lev. xxiv, 17, 21; Numb. xxxv, 16, 18, 21, 31; Deut. xix, 11, 13; 2 Sam. xvii, 25; xx, 10; 1 Kings ii, 5, 6, 31; see Philo, *l. c.*; Michaelis, *On Laws of Moses*, § 132). Bloodshed even in warfare was held to involve pollution (Numb. xxxv, 33, 34; Deut. xxi, 1, 9; 1 Chron. xxviii, 3). Philo says that the attempt to murder deserves punishment equally with actual perpetration; and the Mishna, that a mortal blow intended for another is punishable with death; but no express legislation on this subject is found in the Law (Philo, *l. c.*; Mishna, *Sanh.* ix, 2).

No special mention is made in the Law (*a*) of child-murder, (*b*) of parricide, nor (*c*) of taking life by poison, but its animus is sufficiently obvious in all these cases (Exod. xxi, 15, 17; 1 Tim. i, 9; Matt. xv, 4), and the third may perhaps be specially intended under the prohibition of witchcraft (Exod. xxii, 18; see Joseph. *Ant.* iv, 8, 34; Philo, *De Spec. Leg.* iii, 17, vol. ii, p. 315).

It is not certain whether a master who killed his slave was punished with death (Exod. xxi, 20; Knobel, ad loc.). In Egypt the murder of a slave was punishable with death as an example *à fortiori* in the case of a freeman; and parricide was punished with burning; but child-murder, though regarded as an odious crime, was not punished with death (Diod. Sic. i, 77). The Greeks also, or at least the Athenians, protected the life of the slave (Müller, *Dorians*, iii, 3, § 4; Wilkinson, *Anc. Eg.* ii, 208, 209).

No punishment is mentioned for suicide attempted (comp. 1 Sam. xxxi, 4 sq.; 1 Kings xvi, 18; Matt. xxvii, 5; see 2 Macc. xiv, 41 sq.), nor does any special restriction appear to have attached to the property of the suicide (2 Sam. xvii, 23); yet Josephus says (*War*, iii, 8, 5) that suicide was dealt with as crime by the Jews.

Striking a pregnant woman so as to cause abortion was punished by a fine; but if it caused her death it was punishable with death (Exod. xxi, 23; Joseph. *Ant.* iv, 8, 33).

If an animal known to be vicious caused the death of any one, not only was the animal destroyed, but the owner also, if he had taken no steps to restrain it, was held guilty of murder (Exod. xxi, 29, 31; see Michaelis, § 274, vol. iv, p. 234–5).

The duty of executing punishment on the murderer is in the Law expressly laid on the "revenger of blood;" but the question of guilt was to be previously decided by the Levitical tribunal. A strong bar against the licence of private revenge was placed by the provision which required the concurrence of at least two witnesses in any capital question (Numb. xxxv, 19–30; Deut. xvii, 6–12; xix, 12, 17). In regal times the duty of execution of justice on a murderer seems to have been assumed to some extent by the sovereign, as well as the privilege of pardon (2 Sam. xiii, 39; xiv, 7, 11: 1 Kings ii, 34). During this period also the practice of assassination became frequent, especially in the kingdom of Israel. Among modes of effecting this object may be mentioned the murder of Benhadad of Damascus by Hazael by means of a wet cloth (1 Kings xv, 27; xvi, 9; 2 Kings viii, 15; see Thenius, ad loc.: Jahn, *Hist.* i, 137; comp. 2 Kings x, 7; xi, 1, 16; xii, 20; xiv, 5; xv, 14, 25, 30).

It was lawful to kill a burglar taken at night in the act, but unlawful to do so after sunrise (Exod. xxii, 2, 3).

The Koran forbids child-murder, and allows blood-revenge, but permits money-compensation for blood-shed (ii, 21; iv, 72; xvii, 230, ed. Sale).—See MAN-SLAYER.

MURDER, CHRISTIAN LAWS CONCERNING. In civil law murder is termed the killing of a human being *of malice aforethought*, and the crime thus committed is in most countries punishable by death. In the United States there are several states in favor of life imprison-ment, and in Sweden capital punishment is no longer meted out. Murder is defined by Coke thus: "When a person of sound memory and discretion unlawfully killeth any reasonable creature in being, and under the king's peace, with malice aforethought, either express or implied." Almost every word in this definition has been the subject of discussion in the numerous cases that have occurred in the law-courts. The murderer must be of sound memory or discretion; i. e. he must be at least fourteen years of age, and not a lunatic or idiot. The act must be done unlawfully, i. e. it must not be in self-defence, or from other justifiable cause. The person killed must be a reasonable creat-ure, and hence killing a child in the womb is not mur-der, but is punishable in another way. See INFANTI-CIDE. The essential thing in murder is that it be done maliciously and deliberately; and hence in cases of hot blood and scuffling the offence is generally manslaugh-ter only. Killing by duelling is thus murder, for it is deliberate. It is not necessary, in order to constitute murder, that the murderer kill the man he intended, provided he had a deliberate design to murder some one. Thus if one shoots at A and misses him, but kills B, this is murder, because of the previous felonious in-tent, which the law transfers from one to the other. So if one lays poison for A, and B, against whom the poi-soner had no felonious intent, takes it and is killed, this is murder. The murderer is here regarded as *hostis humani generis.* "Anciently," Blackstone says, "the name of murder, as a crime, was applied only to the se-cret killing of another, which the word *moerda* signifies in the Teutonic language." Among the ancient Goths in Sweden and Denmark the whole vill or neighborhood was punished for the crime, if the murderer was not dis-covered. The Roman Catholic Church stands accused of encouraging murder in various instances. Though no doubt the Church has frequently been held responsible where the individual acted of his own will and accord, it is yet apparent, from various ecclesiastical actions, that the Church of Rome has taken a peculiar view of this subject. Thus the clergy (q. v.) were at times exempt-ed from severe punishment for this crime. In England the statute for the "Benefit of Clergy" was only abol-ished by George IV (7 and 8, c. 28). The murder of heretics has frequently been encouraged in the Romish Church, as witness the slaughter of St. Bartholomew (q. v.). Pope Urban II stands accused beyond dispute of having encouraged murder; and in the 15th century, when those of the Romanists who desired reform urged the Council of Florence and of Constance in vain to condemn the monstrous teachings of Jean Petet (see Monstrelet, *The Eight Principles of J. Petet*, li, c. xxxix), who in ambiguous writing had vindicated as just and lawful most foul and treacherous murder, and in this vindication laid down "principles utterly subversive of human society; principles which would let loose man-kind upon each other, like wild beasts; principles in direct violation of one of the commandments of God, and in plain, bold opposition to every principle, and to the whole religion of Christ"—the council not only did not condemn these monstrous tenets, but declared them simply "moral and philosophical opinions, not of faith," and therefore out of the province of the Church and of the council (Milman, *Hist. of Latin Christianity*, vii, 508). In the 16th century indulgences were freely

granted the clergy for murder committed, and the price fixed at $20 to the dean, and $55 to a bishop or abbot (see Barnum, *Romanism*, p. 566). Statisticians have prepared comparative lists of the crime of murder com-mitted in Roman Catholic and Protestant countries. We insert here one of these, as these statistics exhibit plainly the moral *results* of the Romish and Protestant systems. The Rev. M. Hobart Seymour gives in his *Evenings with the Romanists* an introductory chapter on "the moral results of the Romish system," which em-bodies various statistics respecting crime drawn directly from official returns in the several countries named. Thus the comparative numbers of committals (or trials) for murder as given by Mr. Seymour for each million of the population, according to the censuses next pre-ceding 1854, were these:

Protestant England		4 to the million.
Roman Catholic Belgium	18	" " "
" " Ireland	19	" " "
" " Sardinia	20	" " "
" " France	31	" " "
" " Austria	36	" " "
" " Lombardy	45	" " "
" " Tuscany	56	" " "
" " Bavaria	68	" " "
" " Sicily	90	" " "
" " Papal States	113	" " "
" " Naples	174	" " "

The *New-Englander* for July, 1869, and January, 1870, contains some additional statistics and later statements on this subject from official returns. These give the following proportion of convictions for murder and at-tempts at murder, and for infanticide, in England and France in the year 1865-6:

England, 1¼ convictions to the million for murder, etc.
France, 12 convictions to the million.
England, 5 convictions to the million for infanticide.
France, 10 convictions to the million.

The returns of suicides in England and France for the four years 1862-5 give the following yearly average:

England, 64 suicides to the million.
France, 127 suicides to the million.

There were in the Papal States in 1867, according to official (French) returns, 186 murders to each million of the population. Mr. Seymour furnishes also various statistics showing the immorality of Roman Catholic cities and countries in Europe to be decidedly greater than that of similar Protestant cities and countries, and often twice, thrice, etc., as great, and says: "Name any Protestant country or city in Europe, and let its depths of vice and immorality be measured and named, and I will name a Roman Catholic country or city whose depths of vice and immorality are lower still." Mr. Seymour's statistics, though widely published, have stood for years unimpeached. In April, 1869, it is true, *The Catholic World* attempted to break the force of his argument by citing the case of Protestant Stockholm, which it alleged that Mr. Seymour wilfully suppressed, and where, according to it, the rate of illegitimate births to the whole number of births "is over fifty to the hun-dred—quite equal to that of Vienna." To this the *New-Englander* of January, 1870, replies: "It seems to us suf-ficient to say, first, that the statement of the *Catholic World* is untrue. At the time of Mr. Seymour's state-ment the official return of illegitimacy in Stockholm was twenty-nine per cent., which is considerably less than 'over fifty to the hundred.' Secondly, that the following *eleven* Roman Catholic cities were worse than the notoriously worst of all Protestant cities: Paris, 33 per cent.; Brussels, 35; Munich, 48; Vienna, 51; Lai-bach, 38; Brunn, 42; Lintz, 46; Prague, 47; Lemberg, 47; Klagenfort, 56; Grätz, 65." The official statistics of Germany, as given in the *New-Englander* for Janu-ary, 1870, show an average of 117 illegitimate births in every 1000 births in the Protestant provinces, and of 186 in 1000 in the Roman Catholic provinces; those of Austria gave for the Roman Catholic provinces in 1866 an average of 215 illegitimate births in every 1000 births, and in the mixed provinces (containing 9 up to 83 per cent. of Roman Catholics, the remainder Protestants, Greeks, etc.) an average of 60 in every 1000. The average number of illegitimate births in every 1000 births for the various nations of Europe is as follows:

PROTESTANT.		ROMAN CATHOLIC.	
Denmark	110	Baden	162
England, Scotland, and		Bavaria	225
Wales	67	Belgium	72
Holland (35 per c. R. C.)	40	France	75
Prussia, with Saxony and		German Austria	181
Hanover	83	Italy [defective]	51
Sweden, with Norway	96	Spain [defective]	55
Switzerland (41 per c. R. C.)	55		
Würtemberg (between R.		Average	117
C. Baden and Bavaria)	164	or, rejecting Italy and	
Average	88	Spain	145

Taking the average birth-rate in Europe—1 a year for every 28 of the population—the returns in Italy show that more than one fourth of the births fail to be registered; and the official returns for Spain are notoriously untrustworthy. It has been said that the official returns for Ireland gave only 3.8 per cent. of illegitimate births, and most of this in the Protestant counties; but the registrar-general complains that many births and deaths are not registered; and the comparison of 1 birth only for every 42 of the population as returned, with the average European birth-rate of 1 in 28, would imply that nearly one third of the births in Ireland are unregistered. The percentage of illegitimate births in Italy, Spain, and Ireland may therefore be much larger than the imperfect official returns indicate, and is of course untrustworthy. Other statistics of immorality are also given in the *New-Englander*, but we have not room to quote here further, and refer our readers interested in a comparative statement of the moral influences of Protestantism and Romanism to the periodicals cited.

Murdock, David, D.D., a Presbyterian divine, was born in the village of Bonhill, in Dumbartonshire, Scotland, in 1801. His father was a stone-cutter, who often labored with the friends of Hugh Miller. David possessed indomitable energy, and obtained for himself a thorough and accomplished education. He graduated at Glasgow University; studied theology in the theological school of the Scottish Independents; and was licensed and ordained in Glasgow, according to the forms of the Scottish Congregationalists, about the year 1831. His first charge was the parish of Cambuslang, near Glasgow, a place memorable for the wonderful preaching of Whitefield. In 1834 he accepted an appointment from the Colonial Missionary Society as a missionary to Canada, and on his arrival in that country he resided principally at Bath, preaching as a supply to the destitute and feeble churches of that region. In 1837, about the time of the Patriot War, he left Canada, and was settled as the successor of Dr. McMaster at Ballston Centre, N. Y.; in 1842 he accepted a call to Catskill as successor to the Rev. Dr. Porter. In 1851 he accepted a call to the First Presbyterian Church in Elmira, N. Y., where he labored until his death, June 13, 1861. Dr. Murdock was emphatically a man of the people. In the pulpit, in the lecture-room, on the platform, he was indeed pre-eminent. He was a great reader, and especially a profound scholar in the sciences. He was eminently successful as an essayist. An article by him on *Canning and Chalmers*, in the *Presb. Quart. Review*, is one of power. See Wilson, *Presb. Hist. Almanac*, 1862, p. 189.

Murdock, James, D.D., one of the profoundest religious and ecclesiastical scholars of the United States, a bright ornament of the Congregational body, was born at Westbrook, Conn., Feb. 16, 1776, of Irish descent. He was left an orphan at the age of fourteen; but he struggled with his fate, and finally succeeded in making his way to Yale College, where he graduated in 1797. He then took up the study of theology under the well-known Congregational theologian, Dr. Timothy Dwight. Instead of entering at once the ministry, he decided to

teach for a while, and became successively preceptor of Hopkins grammar school in New Haven, and of the Oneida Academy, now Hamilton College, at Clinton, N. Y. In January, 1801, he was admitted to the ministry, and June 23, 1802, was ordained pastor over the congregation at Princeton, Mass. In 1815 he removed from that place to become professor of languages in the University of Vermont. In 1819 he exchanged this position for the Brown professorship of sacred rhetoric and ecclesiastical history in the theological seminary at Andover, Mass., and this post he held until 1822, when he removed to New Haven to devote himself altogether to special studies in ecclesiastical history and Oriental literature, which he prosecuted with a youthful zest beyond his fourscore years. He died at Columbus, Miss., Aug. 10, 1856. Dr. Murdock did the literary world great service by his superior English version of Mosheim's *Church History*. He published likewise, with great acceptance, Mosheim's *Commentaries on the Affairs of the Christians before Constantine.* See MOSHEIM. Dr. Murdock published a translation of the Peshito-Syriac N. T. (N. Y. 1851, 8vo). His miscellaneous productions were numerous and able. It was his temper to make fundamental researches, and to press his investigations into original sources. While at Andover he published *Two Discourses on the Atonement.* Later he brought out an English version of Münscher's *Elements of Dogmatic Hist.* (1830), and *Sketches of Modern Philos.* (1842). He also edited Milman's *Hist. of Christianity* (N. Y. 1841), and brought out a collection of his *Sermons*, one of which, on the atonement, attracted much attention. He was also a frequent contributor to periodicals, especially to the *Church Review*, and this well-known quarterly did itself the honor to ignore its denominational boundaries (Protestant Episcopal) and furnish a pretty full account of the doctor shortly after his decease (see below). Dr. Murdock was president of the "Connecticut Academy of Arts and Sciences," vice-president of the "Connecticut Philosophical Society," and one of the founders of the "American Oriental Society." See *Brief Memoirs of the Class of* 1797 (Yale), by Thomas Day; *Church Rev.* Jan. 1857, art. ii.

Muret(us), MARC ANTHONY, a celebrated Roman Catholic scholar, best known by his philosophical writings, was born at Muret, a village near Limoges, in France, April 11, 1526, of a good family. But little beyond this is known of his early life. When about eighteen we find him studying at Agens, under Scaliger, who interested himself in Muretus, and ever cherished the highest opinion of his pupil. In 1552 he delivered in the church of the Bernardins his first oration, *De dignitate ac præstantia studii theologici.* He was at this time teaching philosophy and law at Paris, but evidently leaning towards the sacred ministry. Accused of immoral practices, he was finally obliged to quit Paris, and he led for some time a roaming life. He went to different places, everywhere commanding for a time the respect of his followers by his vast and varied erudition, but his immoral tendencies would ever compromise him, and he was soon ignored by his associates. About 1560 Muretus found employment under cardinal Este at Rome, and from that time he is believed to have led a more regular life. In 1562 he attended his patron on a visit to Paris, and there remained, and was prevailed upon to lecture on Aristotle's *Ethics*, which he did with singular applause up to 1567. After that he taught civil law. In 1576 he entered holy orders, and is believed to have become both priest and Jesuit. He died June 4, 1585. He was made a citizen of Rome, probably by pope Gregory XIII, who esteemed him very highly. Muretus's theology is questioned, and he is believed to have cherished deistical views. See Nicéron, *Mémoires*, vol. xxvii, s. v.; Bèze, *Hist. Eccles.* iv, 534; Vitrac, *Éloge de Muret; New Gen. Biog. Dict.* (Lond. 1798), xi, 138, 141; Hallam, *Introd. to the Literature of Europe* (Harper's ed.), i, 247, 257, 356; Pye Smith, *Outlines of Theol.* p. 111. (J. H. W.)

Murillo, BARTOLOMÉ ESTÉBAN, the Titian of Spanish art, was born Jan. 1, 1618, at Pilas, a small hamlet about five leagues from Seville. Developing at an early age a wonderful proficiency in drawing, he was placed under the instruction of his maternal uncle, Juan del Castillo, a distinguished historical painter of Seville, who was the preceptor of some of the greatest artists of the Spanish school. In 1642, Murillo, having heard of the fame of Diego Velasquez of Madrid, which at this period had reached its zenith, was filled with a desire to study under that master, and consequently journeyed to Madrid, where he presented himself before Velasquez, who, perceiving his merit, not only took Murillo into his academy, but procured for him the privilege of copying the masterpieces of Rubens, Titian, and Vandyck in the royal collection. Here he passed three years in hard study; and in 1645 he returned to Seville, where his first work was painted in fresco for the convent of St. Francis. It was a picture consisting of sixteen compartments, in one of which is his celebrated production of *St. Thomas de Villanueva distributing Alms to the Sick and the Poor.* At the principal altar of the same convent is a large picture of the *Jubilee of the Porciuncula,* representing Christ bearing his cross, and the Virgin interceding for the supplicants, with a group of angels of most extraordinary beauty. These pictures created so much enthusiasm among his countrymen that his fame was at once established, and he immediately received a commission from the marquis of Villamansique to paint a series of five pictures from the life of David, the landscape backgrounds of which were to be executed by Ignacio Iriate, an eminent landscape-painter of Seville. There was a dispute between the two artists as to which part of the pictures should be first completed, Murillo holding very rightly that the backgrounds should be first painted; to this Iriate demurred, and the consequence was Murillo undertook to do the whole himself, which he did, changing the life of David to that of Jacob, and producing the famous pictures now in the possession of the marquis de Santiago at Madrid. In the same collection are two others of his finest works, *St. Francis Xavier,* and *St. Joseph with the young Saviour.* The cathedral of Seville contains several of his great pictures, among which are *St. Antonio with the Holy Infant,* a glory of angels and a remarkably fine architectural background, the *Immaculate Conception,* and portraits of several archbishops of Seville. From the St. Anthony picture the figure of the saint was cut in 1874, and brought for sale to this country; but, falling into the hands of a well-informed party, it was returned, and placed where it properly belongs. The Hospital of Charity contains three admired works, *Moses striking the Rock; Christ feeding the five thousand,* and one of *St. John* supporting a poor old man, aided by an angel, upon whom the saint looks with a beautiful expression of reverence and gratitude. The altar-piece of the *Conception,* in the church of San Felipe Neri at Cadiz, and a picture of *St. Catharine* at the Capuchins, are not only noteworthy for their beauty, but the latter is considered by many as his finest work, although Murillo himself always preferred his *St. Thomas de Villanueva* at Seville. In the chapel of the Nuns of the Angel at Granada is one of his most celebrated pictures, representing the *Good Shepherd.* Space does not admit of a full list of Murillo's works, but as a painter of religious subjects he ranks hardly second to Raphael. His pictures of the Virgin, saints, Magdalens, and of Christ, are all so characteristically beautiful and refined, so pure and chaste, that he can be said to have followed no given style, though the coloring of Titian is perceptible in his works. It is a curious fact that in all Murillo's pictures of the Virgin he has never displayed her feet, which in every instance are covered with almost faultless drapery, as if the charms of the holy Mother were too sacred to be made the subject of illustration. This can be said of no other religious painter, and evinces a proof of the purity with

which Murillo looked upon his art. In 1660 Murillo founded an academy of art in Seville, and was appointed its president, in which office he continued until April 3, 1682, when he died; his death having been hastened by a fall from a scaffold while engaged in painting the *St. Catharine* at Cadiz. In the National Gallery of Great Britain are a *Holy Family,* and a *St. John and the Lamb.* Dulwich Gallery contains, among others, *Christ with the Lamb; Mystery of the Immaculate Conception; Jacob and Rachel; Adoration of the Magi; Two Angels;* and a small *Immaculate Conception.* The Louvre contains a considerable number; the Pinakothek of Munich has some, and in the United States there are supposed to be a few of his works also. See *Engl. Cyclop.* s. v.; Scott, *Murillo and the Spanish School of Painting* (Lond. 1873, 1 vol. 4to); Stirling, *Annals of the Artists of Spain;* Mrs. Jameson, *Legends of the Madonna* (Lond. 1857, 1 vol. 8vo), p. 34, 36, 43, 46, 49, etc.; Jameson and Eastlake, *History of Our Lord* (Lond. 1864, 2 vols. 8vo), i, 138, 153, 155, 167, 273, 285, 292, etc.; ii, 93, 343, 380; Spooner, *Biog. Hist. of the Fine Arts,* s. v.; Davies, *Life of B. E. Murillo* (1819); *Biographies of Eminent Men from the 13th Century,* vol. ii; Tytler (Miss), *The Old Masters* (Bost. 1874), p. 230; *Fraser's Magazine,* April, 1846; *Blackwood's Magazine,* 1845, ii, 420; 1849, i, 73, 184; 1853, ii, 103; 1870, ii, 133.

Murimuth (or **Merimuth**), ADAM, an English divine of note, flourished in the second half of the 14th century successively as canon and prebend of St. Paul's, canon of Exeter, and prebend of Lincoln. He died about 1380. He published *Chronica in Temporibus* in two parts (pt. i, 1303–6; pt. ii, 1336–80). See Allibone, *Dict. of Brit. and Amer. Authors,* s. v.

Muris, JEAN DE, a learned French ecclesiastic who flourished in the first half of the 14th century (about 1310–45), is noted as the author of a valuable treatise on music, which is entitled *Speculum Musicæ.* An abridgment of this work was also published.

Murmuring (תְּלוּנָה, Exod. xvi, 7 sq.; γογγυσμός), a complaint made for wrong supposed to have been received. Paul forbids murmuring (1 Cor. x, 10), as did also the wise man in the Apocrypha (Wisd. i, 11). God severely punished the Hebrews who murmured in the desert, and was more than once on the point of forsaking them, and even of destroying them, had not Moses appeased his anger by earnest prayer (Numb. xi, 33, 34; xii; xiv, 30, 31; xvi, 3; xxi, 4–6; Psa. lxxviii, 30). See RESIGNATION.

Murmuring, "as a sign of disapproval or pleasure," says Walcott, "was once common in British churches." Bishop Burnet and bishop Spratt were both hummed when preaching at St. Margaret's, Westminster. Burnet sat down and enjoyed it, rubbing his face with his handkerchief; but Spratt, stretching out his hand, cried, "Peace, peace; I pray you, peace." At Cambridge a witty preacher, in the time of queen Anne, addressed his congregation at St. Mary's as "Hum et hissimi auditores." At Hereford this unseemly practice, which greeted every person arriving late in the choir, was prohibited (*Sacred Archæology,* p. 394).

Murner, THOMAS, a noted German satirist and most decided opponent of the Reformation, was born in Strasburg Dec. 24, 1475. He early entered a Franciscan monastery, and then studied at the principal universities of Europe, devoting himself particularly to theology and philosophy, and quickly gained a reputation for ability, marred, however, by a want of earnestness and a quarrelsome disposition. At Paris he acquired the degree of A.M., and in 1506 the emperor Maximilian nominated him *poeta laureatus.* He lost a place in the conventual Latin school of Strasburg by his invective against Wimpfeling, and afterwards led an unsteady life, preaching for some time at Frankfort-on-the-Main (1512). At this time he battled against the clerical crimes and abuses, generally incurring the displeasure of his congregation by the coarse personalities of his sermons. He was successively expelled from Freiburg, Trèves, and Venice. In 1512 he edited his *Narrenbeschwörung*, of which his *Der Schelmen Zunft* (Frankfort, 1512) may be regarded as a continuation. These works, which show considerable satirical talents, are remarkable imitations of Sebastian Brandt's celebrated poem, called *Narrenschiff*. In his *Gäuchmatt* (Basle, 1519) he ridicules the effeminate manhood of some of his contemporaries; and in his *Logica memorativa*, or *Chartiludium logicæ*, and in his *Ludus studentium Friburgensium* he proves himself a predecessor of the renowned pedagogue, Basedow, trying to show how logic and prosody may be studied to advantage at different games. In 1519 he seems to have resumed his functions in the conventual school of Strasburg, and made himself conspicuous as one of the most virulent opponents of the Reformation. When Hedio and Capito were preaching at Strasburg, Murner opposed them violently (see Hottinger, *Helvetische Kirchengesch.* iii, 145). As ambassador of the bishop of Strasburg, he afterwards attended the Diet at Nuremberg to accuse the Council of Strasburg (Sleidan, vol. iv). He opposed Luther's book, *An den Adel deutscher Nation*, by a work of similar title, *An den grossmächtigsten und durchlauchtigsten Adel deutscher Nation, dass sie den christlichen Glauben beschirmen wider den Zerstörer des Glaubens Christi, Martinum Luther, einen Verführer der einfältigen Christen*. Although he translated Luther's *Letter against Henry VIII*, and his *Babylonische Gefangenschaft* from Latin into German, he rejected all his teachings entirely. He called Luther a *Catilina*, and received himself the name of *Lutheromastix*. According to a letter of Luther to Brismann, Murner left the monastery (De Wette, ii, 58). This statement, however, is incorrect. In 1523 Murner repaired to England, in compliance with an invitation from Henry VIII, but troubles in his convent compelled him to return. Some of his writings against the Reformation had already been burned by order of the Diet of Worms. To elude the vigilance of the authorities he established a press of his own, which, however, was destroyed by a mob, together with his house. He was compelled to flee to Switzerland, whence he was in time likewise expelled. His most celebrated satirical work is entitled *Von dem grossen Lutherischen Narren* (Strasburg, 1522; new edition by Henry Kurtz, Zurich, 1848), which was answered by *Murnarus Leriethus vulgo dictus Halbnarr oder Gansprediger*. The latter part of his personal history is not known, although he is supposed to have lived in misery, and to have died at Heidelberg about 1536. See Waldau, *Nachricht. v. Thom. Murner Leben und Schriften;* Panzer, *Annales d. deutsch. Litt.;* Ruchat, *Histoire de la Réform. de la Suisse;* Yung, *Gesch. d. Reform. ü. Strasburg*, p. 238 sq.; Hagen, *Deutschland's liter. und relig. Verhältnisse im Reformations-zeitalter*, ii, 61, 183 sq.; Hagenbach, *Kirchengesch.* vol. iii; *For. Qu.* xx, 74.

Murphy, JAMES, D.D., a minister of the (Dutch) Reformed Church, was born near Rhinebeck, N. Y., in 1788; graduated at New Brunswick Theological Seminary, 1814; and was pastor of several Reformed churches, chiefly in the valley of the Mohawk and in Herkimer County, N. Y.; and died in 1857 at Frankfort, where he was then pastor. He was an evangelical preacher of superior abilities, fond of study, and particularly of classical and scientific pursuits. His volume entitled *Geology consistent with the Bible* is a creditable monument of his proficiency in that department of natural science, up to the period of its date. He was prominent in the councils of the Church, and for many years was an active trustee of Union College. (W. J. R. T.)

Murrain (דֶּבֶר, *de'ber, destruction*, especially by a "pestilence," as the word is elsewhere rendered; plur. "plagues" in Hos. xiii, 14), the fifth plague with which the Egyptians were visited when they held the Hebrews in bondage (Exod. ix, 3). See PLAGUES OF EGYPT. This consisted in some distemper that resulted in a sudden and dreadful mortality among the cattle in the field, including horses, asses, camels, oxen, and sheep. It was, however, confined to the Egyptian cattle, and to those that were in the field; for though the cattle of the Hebrews breathed the same air, and drank the same water, and fed in the same pastures, not a creature of theirs died (Exod. ix, 6). The Egyptian cattle that survived in the sheds, and were afterwards sent into the fields, were destroyed by the succeeding storm of fire and hail. Wilkinson has observed (*Anc. Eg.* i, 48, 49) that "the custom of feeding some of their herds in sheds accords with the scriptural account of the preservation of the cattle which had been 'brought home' from the field; and explains the apparent contradiction of the destruction of '*all* the cattle of Egypt' by the murrain, and the subsequent destruction of the cattle by the hail (Exod. ix; 3, 19, 20); those which 'were in the field' alone having suffered from the previous plague, and those in the stalls or 'houses' having been preserved." In the grievous murrain, and in the grievous hail, many, if not all, the war-horses must have escaped, as they were not 'in the field,' but in the 'stables or houses' (Exod. xiv, 27, 28; xv, 21)." See STALL. In the *Description de l'Égypte* (xvii, 126), it is said that murrain breaks out from time to time in Egypt with so much severity that they are compelled to send to Syria or the islands of the Archipelago for a new supply of oxen. It is also stated (*ib.* p. 62) that, since about the year 1786 a disease very much diminished the number of oxen, they began to make use of the buffalo in their place for watering the fields, and the practice is continued in later times. See PESTILENCE.

Murray, Alexander (1), D.D., an eminent Scotch divine, noted as an Orientalist, was born at Dunkitterick, Oct. 22, 1775, of very humble parentage, and therefore enjoyed scarcely any educational advantages in early life. It was not till he had reached his sixth year that he was taught the alphabet of his mother-tongue. "His father" (a shepherd), says his biographer, "in that year laid out a halfpenny in the purchase of a catechism, and from the letters and syllables on the face of the book he began to teach his son the elements of learning. It was however emphatically 'a good book,' and only to be handled on Sundays or other suitable occasions; it was therefore commonly locked up, and throughout the winter the old man, who had himself been taught reading and writing in his youth, drew for his son the figures of the letters in his written hand on the board of an old wool-card with the black end of a burned heatherstem. In this way young Murray was initiated into literature; and working continually with his board and brand, he soon became a reader and writer. The catechism was at length presented, and in a month or so he could read the easier parts of it. In the summer of 1782 he got a Psalm-book, then a New Testament, and at last a Bible, a book which he had heard read every night at family worship, which he often longed to get hold of, but which he was never allowed to open or even touch. He now read constantly, and having a good memory, he remembered well and would repeat numerous psalms and large portions of Scripture. In 1783 his reading and memory had become the wonder of the rustic circle in which he lived, and a wish began to be generally entertained that he should be sent to school." An uncle of the boy, attracted by the precocity of the youth, finally sent him to Galloway school in his ninth year. He remained there for a while only, and was then obliged to return home to help his father in the fields. In 1790, however, he found means to resume his studies, and he made his way rapidly thereafter. In 1794, being then already master of the Greek, Latin, Hebrew, and French, which he had mainly acquired without an instructor, he was brought to the notice of the Rev. Dr. Baird, of Edinburgh. This learned gentleman interested himself in Murray, and his subsequent progress was made comparatively easy. In the course of two years he obtained a bursary, or exhibition, in the University of Edinburgh; and never relaxing in his pursuit of knowledge, he soon made himself acquainted with all the European languages, and having formed the design of tracing up all the languages of mankind to one source, he began a work by which he will be known in the literary world. But though it is distinguished by profound and various learning, it is both imperfect and posthumous. It appeared under the auspices of the Rev. Dr. Scot of Corstorphine, and is entitled *A History of the European Languages, or Researches into the Affinities of the Teutonic, Greek, Celtic, Sclavonic, and Indian Nations* (1813). An extensive acquaintance with these languages convinced Murray that all the European languages were closely connected; and in the work now named it was his object to show that they all derive from and may be traced to nine euphonic primitives, which primitives he states to be "ag, bag, dwag, gwag, lag, mag, nag, rag, and swag." "By the help of these nine words and their compounds," he says, "all the European languages have been formed." The work was, however, nothing but a most desperate and unsuccessful attempt at generalization. Dr. Noah Webster says that "it presents one of the most singular medleys of truth and error, of sound observation and visionary opinions, that has ever fallen under my (Webster's) notice" (Pref. to his *Dict.* [ed. 1852], p. lxxiv). By the advice of his friends he prosecuted the studies necessary for the Church; was finally ordained; and in Dec., 1806, Murray was appointed assistant and successor to Dr. Muirhead, minister of Urr, in the stewartry of Kirkcudbright, a charge to which he in 1808 succeeded as full stipendiary. He still, however, continued his philological pursuits. In 1811 an incident occurred which brought him into prominent notice as a linguist: on the recommendation of Mr. Salt, envoy to Abyssinia, he was applied to by the marquis Wellesley as perhaps the only person in the British dominions qualified to translate a letter, written in Geez, from the governor of Tigrè to his Britannic majesty; and he performed the task in the most satisfactory way. The following year a vacancy occurred in the chair of Oriental languages in the University of Edinburgh, and, as suited to Murray's tastes and habits, he was invited to fill it in order to bring him to Edinburgh, where his literary labors could be both estimated and enjoyed. He was elected on the 8th of July, 1812; on the 15th the university conferred on him the degree of doctor in divinity; and on the 26th of August he was formally inducted to the chair. He began to lecture on the 31st of October following. Soon after that he published, for the use of his students, a small work entitled *Outlines of Oriental Philology* (1812), which is known to have been both composed and prepared for publication after his arrival in Edinburgh: the subject indeed was perfectly familiar to him. He continued to teach his class with little interruption till the end of February or the beginning of March, his health then failing him; and he lived but a little while to enjoy the distinctions which had just come in recognition of his industry and talent. He died April 15, 1813. His body was interred in the Gray Friars' church-yard, at the north-west corner of the church. His acquirements as a linguist pointed him out to Constable, the well-known publisher, as a fit person to superintend a new edition of Bruce's *Travels;* and in the preparation of that work he was employed for about three years, from September, 1802, Murray residing during that time chiefly at Kinnaird House, where he had access to the papers left by the traveller. He was also at different times employed in contributing to the *Edinburgh Review*, and other periodicals, evincing by his writings not only a superior linguistic knowledge, but also much reading and study in other fields of learning. It has been well said that, laboring under so many difficulties in early life, his acquirements were simply preparatory to the work which he might have accomplished, and that he was taken away just as he had completed the preparation for valuable work. See Chambers, *Biog. Dict. of Eminent Scotchmen*, div. vi, p. 72–77; *Pursuit of Knowledge under Difficulties*, vol. i; *Scot. Magazine*, July, 1812; *Engl. Cyclop.* s. v.; Lord Cockburn, *Memoirs of his Own Time* (1856), ch. iv.

Murray, Alexander (2), a Presbyterian minister, was born in the State of New York Sept. 2, 1806. He received a good academical education; graduated at the Associated Reformed Seminary at Canonsburgh, Pa., in 1842; was licensed and ordained in 1844 as pastor of Ohio church, and subsequently of Kerr's Creek church, in the Presbytery of the Lakes. Here he died, Oct. 8, 1860. Mr. Murray was a man of the most ardent piety and sincerity. As a preacher he stood high in the estimation of the brethren. See Wilson, *Presb. Hist. Almanac*, 1861, p. 209.

Murray, Daniel, a noted Roman Catholic prelate, was born in Ireland in 1768, and educated at Salamanca, where he was ordained priest in 1790. He filled various eminent positions in the Church, and finally was elevated to the archbishopric of Dublin in 1823. During the agitation for Roman Catholic emancipation in Ireland, he supported that measure by his influence, after which he took no part in political questions. In 1831 he was joined with archbishop Whately and others in the commission for Irish education, and sanctioned the institution of the queen's colleges. He withdrew, however, on knowing the contrary pleasure of the pope. He died in 1852. He wrote *The Douai and Rhenish Bible and the Bordeaux Testament Examined* (Lond. 1850, 18mo). See *Notice of the Life and Character of Archbishop Murray*, by Rev. W. Meagher (1853, 8vo); *Dublin University Magazine*, viii, 493.

Murray, Edward, an eminent English divine of recent times, was born near the opening of this century, and flourished successively as rural dean and chaplain to the bishop of Rochester; vicar of Hinsford in 1823, and of Northbolt in 1836. He died in 1852. He published, *Prayers and Collects translated from Calvin* (Lond. 1832, 8vo):—*Enoch Restitutus, or an attempt to separate from the Book of Enoch the Book quoted by St. Jude* (Dublin, 1836, 8vo), a work which "displays much learning, research, and diligent inquiry" (*British Magazine*, July, 1836, p. 57).

Murray, James (1), a Scotch divine of some note, flourished in the first half of the 18th century. He was born at Dunkeld in 1702, and educated at the Marischal College, Aberdeen; after taking his degree he was licensed for the ministry. He died in 1758. He is supposed to have preached for a time at Westminster. He published *Aletheia, or a General System of Moral Truths and Natural Religion* (London, 1747, 2 vols. 12mo). See Chalmers, *Biog. Dict.* s. v.; Wilson, *Dissenting Churches.*

Murray, James (2), an English divine, who flourished near the middle of the last century at Newcastle, where he died in 1782, devoted himself largely to the study of secular and ecclesiastical history, and published *Hist. of the Churches of England and Scotland* (Newcastle, 1771, 3 vols. 8vo):—*Impartial Hist. of the present War in America* (1778–80, 3 vols. 8vo). He also collected some of his sermons, and they were published in 1819 under the title of *Sermons to Asses, to Doctors in Divinity, to Lords Spiritual, and to Ministers of State* (Lond. 8vo). A copy of this curious collection, which is very rare, is in the Drew Theological Seminary library (Madison, N. J.). It betrays much disaffection with the National Church establishment.

Murray, James Stuart, *Earl of,* a natural son of James V, king of Scotland, deserves our attention for the part he played in the disposition of Scottish ecclesiastical affairs. He was born in 1531, and educated in France with his sister Mary, but joined the Reformers soon after her marriage with the dauphin, and became almost immediately chief of the Protestant party in Scotland. His political history is connected with the fortunes of the queen, after whose imprisonment in Lochleven castle in 1567 he was proclaimed regent, and defeated her troops at the battle of Langside, March 13, 1568. His personal history, in so far as it affects the political, social, and religious history of Scotland during the eventful reign of queen Mary Stuart, has been noticed in our articles on KNOX and MARY STUART. See also SCOTLAND. He was shot by James Hamilton, on the accusation that he had seduced (1570) his wife. But this accusation seems groundless; and there is every reason to believe that Hamilton acted as the executioner of a doom pronounced on him (Murray) by his enemies in secret conclave. Earl Murray was beloved by the people, and acknowledged by his contemporaries as a pious and lofty character who labored to promote the interests of the Church, and especially of Protestantism. The Romanists, of course, hated him, and he was slandered. See Butler, *Eccles. Hist.* ii, 550; Fisher, *Hist. of the Reformation*, p. 359, 367, 369, 373, 377, 380; Froude, *Hist. of England*, vol. viii, ix.

Murray, John (1), an eminent divine, regarded as the founder of the Universalist denomination of Christians in America, was born in Alton, Hampshire, England, December 10, 1741. He received the careful religious training of sincerely pious parents. When he was about eleven years of age, the family removed to Ireland, and settled near Cork. His father, a member of the Established Church, a Calvinist in sentiment, but an early convert to the religious views of John Wesley, infused his own sentiments and zeal into the mind of his child. His extreme anxiety for the spiritual welfare of his son—who, very young, became the subject of hopeful conversion—and his unwillingness to allow him to pass from under his immediate guardianship, induced him to reject a proffered opportunity to give him a liberal education. The earnestness, devotion, and ability of young Murray gave him, as he grew up, position and influence in religious circles, and he became an occasional preacher in Wesley's connection. At a later period, he formed an acquaintance with Mr. Whitefield—with whom he agreed touching the doctrine of election—and became greatly interested in his teachings. About the year 1760 Murray returned to England. Here his experiences were varied, trying, and sometimes humiliating. In a controversy with one who had embraced the religious views of James Relly, a teacher of Universalism, his own theological positions were somewhat disturbed. At length he allowed himself to read Relly's *Union;* and entered upon a careful re-examination of the sacred Scriptures. He afterwards attended regularly upon Mr. Relly's preaching, and received joyfully the doctrines of Universalism as taught by him. His faith soon became decided "that Christ Jesus died for all, and that every one for whom Christ died must finally be saved" (*Life*, new ed. 1870, p. 161). Excommunication from Mr. Whitefield's tabernacle in London naturally followed. Persecutions for opinion's sake, pecuniary embarrassments, and grief for the death of his wife and infant child, rendered him wretched. Having by a temporary devotion to business discharged all pecuniary obligations, he resolved to leave his native land and to seek retirement and relief in America. Yet on his first arrival in the New World, led, as he undoubtingly believed, by a superintending and special Providence, he was constrained to preach, and gave his first discourse in America September 30, 1770. The service was held in a small church in an obscure place—called "Good Luck"—in New Jersey. Thenceforward he regarded himself as called of God to teach the universal redemption of the human race through Christ, and gave himself devotedly to the work of his ministry. He labored first in New Jersey and New York. Afterwards, as he found opportunity, he preached—though often opposed and sometimes bitterly persecuted—in New-

port, Providence, Boston, Portsmouth, Norwich, and other places in New England. In Gloucester, Mass., where, in December, 1774, he had fixed his residence, whence "to go, a preacher of the Gospel," he was falsely represented as a papist, and as a secret emissary of lord North, sent out to the rebellious colonies in the interest of an obnoxious ministry in England. Anathemas and stones followed him in the streets, and by a vote, surreptitiously obtained, he was ordered to leave the town. The interference of influential friends saved him. In May, 1775, he was appointed chaplain of the Rhode Island brigade, encamped near Boston. The other chaplains petitioned for his removal, but, in utter disregard of this petition, he was confirmed by a general order, and the commander-in-chief, general Washington, honored him with marked and uniform attention. Ill-health soon obliged him to leave the army, and he returned to Gloucester, where, distinguished as a religious teacher and as a philanthropist, he was settled over a society of Universalists. In 1783 he became plaintiff in an action at law, brought to recover property belonging to individuals of his society, but taken for the use of the original parish of the town. After many delays, a final verdict was rendered for the plaintiff in June, 1786. This decision was of great significance and importance, and he afterwards rejoiced that he had been the "happy instrument to give a death wound to that hydra, parochial persecution" (*Life*, p. 331). Believers increased, and he was largely instrumental in securing a general meeting and organizing a convention of Universalists. They met in September, 1785, in Oxford, Mass., and organized under the denominational name, *Independent Christian Universalists.* Early in 1787 he visited his native land, where, during a brief stay, he preached in various places with great acceptance and power. He returned before the close of the year, and, in view of certain questions raised by his opponents involving his civil standing and position as an ordained minister, his ordination, regarded by some as informal, was publicly and solemnly renewed in the Gloucester church, on Christmas-day. In October, 1788, he married Mrs. Judith S. Stevens, a widow lady of estimable character, and of considerable literary ability. In 1790 he attended a convention of Universalists in Philadelphia, and was a member of a committee to present at that time an address to general Washington, president of the United States. He improved the opportunity to visit and hold service in the little church in New Jersey, where he first delivered in America the glad message of a full and free salvation. October 23, 1793, he was installed over a society of Universalists in Boston, and became the pastor of a united and devoted people, with whom he remained during the rest of his life. October 19, 1809, he was prostrated by paralysis, which rendered him helpless, and from which he never recovered. He lived several years, a patient and hopeful sufferer, and died with the assuring words of faith on his lips, September 3, 1815. His remains were buried September 4, in the "Granary burying-ground" in Boston. From this place, on June 8, 1837, they were removed, with solemn and interesting ceremonies, to Mount Auburn, where an appropriate monument is erected to his memory. The theological opinions of Murray show the impress of early training, as well as the moulding influence of Relly's teaching. He believed in God as the "*One Indivisible First Cause;*" that the Creator was enrobed in humanity and became God, the Son; and that he was manifested also as a Holy Spirit of Consolation. He believed in holy angels of different orders, in fallen angels, and in a personal devil (*Works*, ii, 320). It was a cardinal doctrine with him that every member of the entire human family was mysteriously united to the Creator, and so to Christ, who was made the head of every man. He held in especial abhorrence the doctrine that Christ was a mere man, and taught that "God the Father, God the Son, and God the Holy Ghost are no more than different exhibitions of the same self-existent, omnipresent Being" (*Works*, iii, 223). His fundamental doctrine, as a Universalist, was that Christ literally put away the sin of the whole world by the *sacrifice* of himself (*Works*, ii, 243, 270). He distinguished carefully between *universal salvation* and *universal redemption*, believing that *all* were redeemed, and would finally be taught of God and come to Christ; but that those who died unconverted would continue unhappy wanderers till the general judgment and restitution of all things, when the fallen angels would be placed on the left hand, the world of mankind be judged, and after all were found guilty before God, the *book of life* would be opened, in which all the members of the Redeemer, that is, every individual of the human family, would be found written, and, as members of Christ's body, *purged by him*, as the sole means, from their sins. He taught, moreover, that an *elect* few embraced the truth before death, and, as saints of God, will surround the Redeemer at his second coming (*Life*, p. 400 sq.). His published works consist of *Letters and Sketches of Sermons* (Bost. 1812, 3 vols.), and an *Autobiography*, with a continuation by Mrs. Judith Sargent Murray (1 vol., 18th edition, Bost. 1860). The first edition of the *Life* was published in Boston, 1816. The last and ninth, edited by Rev. G. L. Demarest, was issued in Boston as a centenary offering in 1870. Murray is described by a contemporary as a person of middling height, with a speaking countenance and masculine features, naturally rough and stern; as having a poetical imagination, a retentive memory, warm affections, a love for all mankind, but especially for those of a religious turn of mind. In his public discourses he was artless and unaffected, but spoke with great grace of oratory, with an astonishing volubility, a good choice of words, and a great variety of expression. He had a wonderful command of the feelings of his auditors; could arouse and animate them at pleasure, or depress them with a peculiarly soft eloquence even to tears (*Life*, new ed. p. 11). In private life he was genial and social. See *Meth. Quar. Rev.* Oct. 1874, art. v; *Univer. Quar.* July, 1872, art. ii; Oct. 1872, art. i, vi. See UNIVERSALISM. (J. P. W.)

Murray, John (2), an Irish Presbyterian minister, was born at Antrim May 22, 1742. He was educated at the university in Edinburgh, and then migrated to this country (1763), and settled first as pastor in Philadelphia in 1766; removed to Boothbay, Me., in 1767, and remained there until 1779, when he settled as pastor over a congregation at Newburyport, Mass., and there he died, March 13, 1793. He was a man of powerful eloquence, and exerted himself zealously for the Revolutionary cause. Indeed, he acquired great ascendency over the people of his vicinity by his powers as a preacher and his patriotic activity. He published *Three Sermons on Justification* (1780), and *Three Sermons on the Original Sin Imputed* (1791). See Drake, *Dict. of Amer. Biog.* s. v.

Murray, Lindley, an American writer on morals and education, who flourished near the opening of this century, was born at Swatara, Lancaster County, Pa., in 1745. He was educated at an academy of the Society of Friends, and on his father's removal to New York was placed in a counting-house, from which he escaped to a school in New Jersey. He then studied law, and was admitted to the bar at the age of twenty-one, and commenced a good practice. During the Revolutionary War he engaged in mercantile pursuits with such success as to accumulate a handsome fortune. His health failing, he went over to England and purchased the estate of Holdgate, near York, where he devoted himself to literary pursuits, chiefly the composition of books intended for the instruction of youth. In 1787 he published anonymously his *Power of Religion on the Mind*, which passed through seventeen editions. It is a selection of passages from various authors. In 1795 he issued a *Grammar of the English Language*, followed by *English Exercises*, the *Key*, the *English Reader*, *In-*

troduction and Sequel, and a *Spelling-book*. There can be no stronger indication how entirely the systematic study of the English language was, until recent years, neglected by scholars than the fact that Murray's Grammar was for half a century the standard text-book throughout Britain and America. Far better books are his later publications: *Selections from Horne's Commentary on the Psalms* (12mo), and *On the Duty and Benefit of a Daily Perusal of the Holy Scriptures* (1817). Mr. Murray wrote an autobiography to the year 1809, which was published after his death, which occurred at his residence, near York, England, Feb. 16, 1826. The Friends thought much of Lindley Murray, for he devoted himself to their interests, and as a member of their body did all in his power to give influence and power to them. "The humility of his deportment, and the Christian spirit that breathed through his whole conduct, endeared him to the members of York Monthly Meeting, where he served in the station of an elder, and proved to be eminently useful. His charities, both public and private, but particularly the latter, were extensive. He was deeply interested in promoting the education of the poor and the elevation of the African race." See Janney, *Hist. of the Friends*, iv, 55.

Murray, Nicholas, D.D., an eminent Presbyterian divine, was born in Armagh County, Ireland, Dec. 25, 1802. Both his parents and all his relatives were Roman Catholics, and trained up their families in that belief. His father dying while he was quite young, he lived with an aunt, and at eight years of age was sent from home to attend a village school, where his proficiency in the rudiments of an English education were such that in his twelfth year he was apprenticed as a merchant's clerk. In 1815 he emigrated to America, where he entered the publishing house of Harper and Brothers, New York. In 1820 he was converted, and became a member of the Old Brick Church, then under the pastoral care of the venerable Gardiner Spring, D.D. His pastor, attracted by Murray's intellectual superiority, soon suggested his studying for the ministry. This at first was not encouraged by Murray; but in 1821 he commenced to make preparation, though still in the employ of the Harpers, and, after due fitting for a higher course of study, entered Williams College, Mass.; there graduated in 1826, and then accepted an agency from the American Tract Society in Washington Co., N. Y., which arrangement lasted for some time. Of his services at this period, Dr. Aydelotte says: "He was indefatigable in application to the duties of his office, perfectly methodical, of rare prudence, always kind, and yet ever firm and faithful to his convictions and the interests of the society. . . . The labors of the board were exceedingly lightened; indeed he left them little to do beyond approving his proceedings and measures." Dr. Aydelotte also speaks of his frequent manifestations of an anti-Romish spirit. He next entered Princeton Theological Seminary, where he remained until he graduated. He was licensed in 1829, and began his labors at Norristown, Pa.; but afterwards accepted a commission from the Board of Domestic Missions for the valley of Wyoming, Pa., where he labored until he was ordained and installed pastor of the united congregation of Wilkesbarre and Kingston. His remarkable pulpit talents and his high promise attracted attention, and in 1833 he was given and accepted a call to the First Presbyterian Church, Elizabethtown, N. J., and there he continued to perform his life-work, declining calls to New York, Brooklyn, Boston, Cincinnati, St. Louis, and Natchez, and rejecting offers of two theological professorships. During this time, with persistent and untiring industry, he wrote much for the press, among which was a series of articles for *The New York Observer*, over the signature of "*Kirwan*," constituting those famous letters to bishop Hughes, the Roman Catholic prelate, noted as a polemic, which have made the name of "Kirwan," the nom-de-plume under which Murray wrote, a household word throughout the whole Protestant world, his writings having been translated into nearly all the living languages of the day. They present the history of the writer's progress from Romanism to Protestantism, and examine the reasons for not adhering to the Church of Rome. Luminous and sound in their expositions of truth, they not only uncover the evils of the Romish system, but present a perfectly impregnable defence of Protestantism. The vivacious style, the genial humor, biting sarcasm, anecdotes, incidents, illustration, argument, and appeals, are blended so harmoniously that they obtained a hold on the people at large, instead of being confined to the theological student, and thus enjoyed a circulation unparalleled in religious literature. Bishop Hughes essayed to reply to the series, but broke down in the attempt, and never resumed the effort. See HUGHES. Dr. Murray died at Elizabethtown, N. J., Feb. 4, 1861. His writings are, *Notes, Historical and Biographical, concerning Elizabethtown, N. J., its eminent Men, Churches, and Ministers* (1844) : — *Letters to Bishop Hughes by Kirwan* (1847–48); these have been translated into French, Spanish, Italian, German, and Tamul:—*The Decline of Popery, and its Causes,* pamphlet:—*Romanism at Home—Letters to the Chief-Justice R. Taney* (1852):—*Men and Things as I saw them in Europe* (1851–53):—*Parish and other Pencillings* (1857):—*The Happy Home* (1858); a delineation of the moral training which is essential in a home:—*Thoughts on Preachers and Preaching,* a work which tends to elevate the standard both of preaching and hearing:—*American Principles on National Prosperity,* a Thanksgiving sermon preached in the First Presbyterian Church, Elizabethtown, Nov. 23, 1854:—*Dr. Murray's Dying Legacy to the People of his beloved Charge—Things Unseen and Eternal* (1861). He also published many occasional sermons and addresses, and in early life contributed to *The New York Literary and Theological Journal, The Christian Advocate,* and other periodicals. Dr. Murray's intellect was decidedly of a marked character—clear, comprehensive, logical, and eminently practical. His style was luminous, simple, and in the highest degree sententious. He reasoned with great power and admirable clearness. His influence pervaded the entire Presbyterian Church, and was felt especially in her various judicatories and boards, and in the theological seminary at Princeton, which he cherished with a filial affection. In 1849 he was elected moderator of the General Assembly, one of the highest honors in the gift of the Church. As a man, his winning manner, rich stores of varied information, inexhaustible fund of pertinent and striking anecdotes, and ability to accommodate himself to every variety of character, made him the master-spirit of the social circle. In person Dr. Murray was a model of manly vigor; of middle height, broad chest and shoulders, with a round, ruddy face, a broad, high forehead, and benevolent, pleasant expression of countenance, his appearance was at once attractive and commanding. As a pastor he was always at work, ready at every call; in the chamber of sickness, in the homes of the poor, among the young—everywhere he was found, and always a welcome guest. His preparations for the pulpit were made with the greatest care, his sermons being completed as if for the press, and often far in advance of the time when they were to be delivered. His funeral was attended with every demonstration of respect and affection that could be paid to a national character. His remains were laid in the yard adjoining the church, in the midst of his children and his beloved flock. The Presbytery of which he was a member thus gave expression to its estimate of him whom they had come to look upon as its "father:" "His name, his character, and his works are already on record, wide as the limits of the Church at home and abroad. His greatness was not in one grace or one idea, but in the breadth of his heart and in the scope of his powers. He was a preacher and a pastor, a presbyter and a citizen, the patron of education, the ready advocate of benevolence, and the dread-

ed antagonist of popery. An author of wide fame, a writer for the weekly press—all of these, with an untold correspondence, literary, fraternal, and advisory. Few men had more calls outside of his pastoral and presbyterial duties; still he was a model pastor and presbyter, always in advance in his pulpit preparation—frequent in his pastoral visitations—abounding in his visits to the sick and the poor—ever ready to help his brethren —meeting calls abroad, and side issues of benevolence. He had time for every good work, and for every duty and occasion he was competent." See Wilson, *Presb. Hist. Almanac,* 1862, p. 105; Rev. Samuel A. Clark, *Hist. of St. John's Church, Elizabethtown, N. J.,* p. 387, 388; *Prot. Episc. Quar. Rev. and Church Reg.* April, 1855, p. 315; Allibone, *Dict. of Brit. and Amer. Authors,* s. v.; *Princeton Rev.* Jan. 1863; *Meth. Qu. Rev.* July, 1863, p. 527; 1861, p. 517; *Harper's Weekly,* Feb. 23, 1861; *Presbyterian Reunion Memorial,* vol. 1837–71 (N. Y. 1870), p. 172–178; *Memoirs of the Rev. Nich. Murray, D.D.,* by Sam. Irenæus Prime (Harpers, 12mo).

Murray, Richard, D.D., an Irish divine of some note, flourished near the opening of this century at Dublin. He is the author of *An Introduction to the Study of the Apocalypse,* to which was added *A Brief Outline of Prophetic History, from the Babylonish Captivity to the Commencement of the 19th Century* (Dublin, 1826, 8vo).

Murray, William, an English divine of Scottish parentage, was born in 1691, and received his education in Scotland, but then went to England, and studied for some time at the English high schools. He entered the ministry, and preached some time at Founder's Hall, whence he removed to Birmingham, where he became pastor of a dissenting congregation. He wrote several tracts in defence of the dissenters, and likewise against the deists; but his principal and best esteemed work is his *Closet Devotions.* He died in Birmingham in 1753.

Murrhone, PETER DE. See CELESTINE V.

Mursinna, SAMUEL, a German theologian, was born at Stolpe, in the province of Pomerania, East Prussia, Nov. 12, 1717. He received his preparatory training at Stolpe; then studied in Berlin in the Joachimsthal'sche Gymnasium, and was also a member of the theological seminary combined with that institution; and then studied theology at Halle for three years. He next assumed the work of a tutor at Berlin; was the year after appointed inspector of the seminary of the Joachimsthal'sche Gymnasium; in 1750 prorector of this institution; and in 1758 professor of divinity at the University of Halle, and died in that place February 15, 1795. His most prominent works are, *Diss. historico-philologica de hebdomade gentilium et dierum a planetis denominatione, qua Georgio Jacobo Pauli munus Rectoris Gymnasii, quod Halæ floret, gratulatur Societas amicorum litterariæ* (Berl. 1747, 4to):—*Polyæni stratagematum Libri viii recensuit, Justi Vulteji versionem Latinam emendavit et indicem Græcum adjecit* (ibid. 1756, 4to):—*Diss. philosophico-theologica de origine generis humani* (Halle, 1759, 4to):—*Diss. exegetica de ecclesia, columna et firmamento veritatis, ad 1 Timoth. iii, 13* (ibid. 1763, 4to):—*Primæ lineæ Encyclopædiæ theologicæ* (ibid. 1764, 4to):—*Homiletica, s. de recta eloquentiæ ecclesiasticæ ratione libellus* (ibid. 1766, 8vo):—*Diss. de institutione scholastica ad diversa discentium ingenia accommodanda* (ibid. 1767, 4to):—*Allgemeine theologische Biblioth.* 11ᵗᵉʳ bis 14ᵗᵉʳ *Band* (Mittau, 1778–1780, large 8vo; the first four volumes were published by C. F. Bahrdt; from the 5th to the 10th by J. C. F. Schulz):—*Biographia selecta, s. Memoriæ aliquot virorum doctissimorum, cum commentationibus quibusdam aliis ad historiam litterariam spectantibus, edidit et præfatus est* (Halle, 1782, large 8vo). See Döring, *Gelehrte Theol. Deutschlands,* s. v.

Murtia or **Museia Murtia,** a surname of Venus at Rome, supposed to be identical with *Myrtea,* because the myrtle was consecrated to this goddess.

Musæus. See MUSÄUS.

Musafia, BENJAMIN DIONYSE BEN-IMMANUEL, a Jewish savant, celebrated also as a physician, was born about 1619. He practiced medicine with great repute at Hamburg and Glückstadt. As an author he is noted for his treatise on *Potable Gold* (מֵי זָהָב). He also made additions to the Hebrew Lexicon of Nathan ben-Jechiel (q. v.) under the title of מוּסַף הֶעָרוּךְ. Besides, he compiled a dictionary entitled זֵכֶר רָב, giving the Hebrew words in seven poems for all the days of the week (Amst. 1635; Wilna, 1863). He also wrote the disputes between R. Jacob Sasportas and himself, entitled עֵדוּת בְּיַעֲקֹב, *the Testimony in Jacob* (Amst. 1672). He commented on the Jerusalem Talmud, and studied a subject that was still more obscure and intricate, since he tried to explain the *Flux and Reflux of the Sea*, a treatise which he dedicated to king Christian IV of Denmark, under the title מֵי חַיִּם (*Epistola Regia de maris reciprocatione* [Amst. 1642]). See Fürst, *Bibl. Jud.* ii, 408 sq.; Grätz, *Gesch. d. Juden*, x, 24, 26, 202, 227, 243, 244; Jost, *Gesch. d. Juden. u. s. Sekten*, iii, 170; Kayserling, *Gesch. d. Juden in Portugal*, p. 298; Lindo, *Hist. of the Jews in Spain*, etc., p. 368; Basnage, *Hist. of the Jews* (Taylor's transl.), p. 741; De Barrios, *Vida de Ishac Uziel*, p. 48; Cassel, *Leitfaden für Jüd. Geschichte u. Literatur*, p. 102; Steinschneider, *Bibliog. Handbuch*, p. 98; Delitzsch, *Zur Gesch. d. Jüd. Poesie* (Leips. 1836), p. 76; Etheridge, *Introd. to Heb. Literature*, p. 389. (B. P.)

Musaph Prayer (תְּפִלָּה מוּסָף) is the name of the evening prayer of the Jewish liturgy. The sacerdotal office of the Jews is closely connected with sacrificial service. It is indeed to be regarded partly as its accompaniment, partly as its substitute during the exile. The sacrifices (תמיד) which were offered twice a day find a correspondent usage in the morning and evening prayer. Already in the Old Testament this connection is clearly manifest, especially in the psalms dating from the exile, e. g. Psa. cxli, 2, "Let the lifting up of my hands be as an evening sacrifice." As on festival days, besides the daily morning sacrifice, a particular one was offered for the feast, it was consequent that the matins of Sabbaths and festival days in the ritual of prayers should be followed by such prayers as correspond to the special festival sacrifices. These are the Musaph prayers. They may be compared to the proprium of the church *officium*. In the Musaph prayer of the ordinary Sabbath express reference is made to the Mosaic ordinance regarding the special Sabbath sacrifice (see Arnheim, *Vollständiges Gebetbuch der Israeliten* [Glogau, 1839], p. 205). The same applies to the Musaph prayer on the day of Reconciliation (Machsor von Heidenheim, *Jom Kipurim* [Sulzb. 1842], p. 113), etc. There the מוּסָפִים are placed opposite to the תְּמִידִים. Liturgic rules concerning the Musaph prayer are given in the tract *Sopherim*, c. 20; fol. xl, c. 2; farther in *Orach Chajim*, viz., פו' ר' (Sabbath); תקפ' (New-year), etc. See MACHZOR; TEPHILLA; LITURGY.

Musäus, Johann, a Lutheran divine, was born at Langenwiesen, in Thuringia, February 7, 1613. His early education he received from his father, who was the minister of that place. Having been duly prepared at the gymnasium of Arnstadt, he went to Erfurt and Jena, where he first studied philosophy and humaniora, and afterwards theology. In 1642 he was appointed professor of history, and in 1646 professor of theology at Jena, which position he held until his death in 1681. Everywhere Musäus was acknowledged as a very learned man, the greatest Lutheran divine of his century, after Gerhard (q. v.) and Calixtus (q. v.). He distinguished between theology and confession, and favored the liberty of scientific theological. researches. On this account he withstood, in connection with the

theologians of Jena, the pretensions of Calovius (q. v.) to subscribe the *Consensus repetitus fidei vere Lutheranæ* of 1655, but rather wrote against it. When he had finally yielded to the representations of the duke to abjure all and every syncretism (q. v.) in 1680, he published his opinion against Calovius (*Hist. Syncr.* p. 999-1089), which the latter answered with his curse. Musäus's writings are all distinguished by a philosophical acumen, hence he was accused of *magis philosophari, quam quod loquatur eloquia Dei.* Besides his defence of Christianity against Herbert of Cherbury, under the title of *De luminis naturæ et ei innixæ theologiæ naturalis insufficientia ad salutem* (Jena, 1667), and against Spinoza, *Tractatus Theologico-politicus*, etc., ad veritatis lancem examinatus (ibid. 1674), he wrote *Disputatio de cultu divino Enochi* (Erfurt, 1634; against the Jesuit G. Holzhagen):—*De barbarismis N. T. contra Grossium* (Jena, 1642):—*De usu principiorum rationis et philosophiæ in controversiis theologicis contra Vedelium* (ibid. 1644):—*Bedencken ob gute Werke nöthig seien zur Seligkeit* (ibid. 1650):—*De resurrectione Christi ex mortuis* (ibid. 1653):—*Unbeweglicher Grund der Augsburgischen Confession* (ibid. 1654), etc. These are all cited in Rottermund's *Supplement* to Jöcher's *Gelehrten-Lex*. See Herzog, *Real-Encyklop*. x, 112 sq.; Buddei, *Isagoge in Theol.* p. 1076 sq.; Gass, *Gesch. der Protest. Dogmatik*, ii, 202, 212; Tholuck, 17ten *Jahrh.* pt. ii, p. 66. (B. P.)

Musäus, Johann Karl August, an eminent German writer, was born in 1735 at Jena, and studied at that university. He was appointed minister at Eisenach, but the peasants refused to receive him as their pastor because they had seen him dance. He died in 1788. His works are all of a secular character, but are valuable in the field of belles-lettres.

Musäus, Peter, brother of Johann, was born in 1620. He studied at Jena and Helmstädt, and also under George Calixtus at Rinteln in 1648. He became successively professor of philosophy and, in 1653, professor of theology. As such he took part in the Colloquy of Cassel in 1661. In 1663 he was appointed professor at Helmstädt, and in 1665 accepted a call in the same capacity to the newly established University of Kiel. He died in 1671. See Witten, *Mem. theol.* p. 1840-1852; Chrysander, *Professores acad. Juliæ*, p. 187-193; Dolle, *Lebensbeschreibung aller Professoren d. Theologie zu Rinteln*, pt. ii, p. 275-296; Moller, *Cimbria literata*, pt. ii, p. 565-573.

Musäus, Simon, a Lutheran divine, great-grandfather of Johann Musäus, was born in 1529. He studied at Frankfort and Nüremberg, and when twenty years of age he was called as pastor to Fürstenwalde, and three years later, in 1552, to Crossen, and in 1554 to Breslau. In the same year the University of Wittenberg conferred upon him the degree of doctor of divinity. In 1559 he was called as superintendent to Gotha, where he remained until 1561, when he was called as professor of theology to Jena, where, however, he did not stay long on account of his collisions with Victor Strigel. In 1565 we see him at Bremen and at Schwerin; in 1566 at Gera and Thorn; in 1570 at Coburg, which place he had to leave because of his zeal against the Crypto-Calvinists. He died at Mansfeld, July 11, 1582. He wrote, *Auslegung des 1 Psalms* (against Schwenkfield) (Breslau, 1556):—*Nützlicher Unterricht zum ersten Gebot* (Erfurt, 1557, and after):—*Auslegung des 91 Psalms* (ibid. 1565):—*De Bremensi editione excitata a Sacramentariis vera narratio*, etc. (1562):—*Katechismus-Examen* (Thorn, 1569):—*Predigten vom h. Abendmahl* (1568):—116 *Predigten über Genesis* (Magdeburg, 1576):—*Postille oder Auslegung der Episteln* (1587, etc.). See Jöcher, *Gelehrten-Lex.*, *Supplement*, by Rottermund, s. v.; Will, *Nürnbergisches Gelehrten-Lex*. pt. ii, p. 700 sq.; Strieder, *Hessische Gelehrten-Gesch.* pt. 9, p. 321; Kurtz, *Lehrbuch der Kirchengeschichte*, ii, 112 sq.

(Mittau, 1874); Niedner, *Lehrbuch d. Kirchengesch.* p. 712. (B. P.)

Muscat. See PERSIA.

Musculus, Andreas, originally *Meusel,* a German theologian, was born in 1514 at Schneeberg, in Saxony. Having graduated in the gymnasium of his native place, he went to Leipsic, where he studied, besides the scholastics, the ancient languages and Hebrew. Here he became acquainted with the writings of the Reformation, and the study of these estranged him from his Church. Having completed his studies, he returned to his native place, where he openly declared himself for the Lutheran doctrine. In 1538 he went to Wittenberg, where he very closely joined Luther, for whose doctrine he soon developed a great zeal. "For my part, I say it openly, there has never been a greater man on earth since the times of the apostles than Luther. In this one man all the gifts of God are concentrated. Whosoever will, let him put side by side the gifts, light, reason, and knowledge of the old teachers and those of Luther respecting spiritual things, and he will soon perceive that there is as much difference between the old teachers and Luther, as between the light of the sun and that of the moon." At the suggestion of Agricola (q. v.), the preacher to the elector of Brandenburg, he went to Frankfort in 1540, where he lectured, preaching at the same time in the church which formerly belonged to the Franciscans. In the year 1544 he was appointed *pastor primarius* and *professor ordinarius,* which positions he held until his death, September 26, 1581. He belonged to those theologians who in 1576 and a year later wrote the *Torgau Book* and the *Concordia Formula* (q. v.), and was one of the most orthodox on this point, as he was formerly one of the most zealous against those who did not strictly adhere to Luther's doctrines. Thus he had a bitter controversy with Staniarus and Staphylus regarding the mediatorship of Christ, and especially with his colleague Prætorius, who rather followed Melancthon. He defended the doctrine "that the law is necessary for repentance before faith, but is unnecessary to him who is born again." Besides these theological controversies, which were rather necessitated by the circumstances of those times, he had a constant fight with the magistrate of Frankfort. He published an extract of Luther's works, under the title *Thesaurus* (Frankf. 1573). Altogether we have of him about forty-six writings, which are all given by Spieker, *Lebensgesch. des Andreas Musculus* (Frankf.-on-the-Oder, 1858), p. 310. See Herzog, *Real-Encyklop.* s. v.; *Supplement* to Jöcher's *Gelehrten-Lex.* by Rottermund, s. v.; Gieseler, *Church Hist.* (New York, 1863, Smith's transl.), iv, 439, 483. (B. P.)

Musculus, Wolfgang. See MEUSEL.

Museia, a festival with contests celebrated in honor of the Muses every fifth year at Thespiæ, in Bœotia. See Gardner, *Faiths of the World,* p. 499.

Muserni, an atheistical sect among the Mohammedans who endeavored to conceal from all except the initiated their gross denial of the existence of a God. They attempted to account for the existence and growth of all things by referring to the inherent power of nature.

Muses was the name employed to designate in the classic mythology those divinities originally included among the Nymphs, but afterwards regarded as quite distinct from them. To them was ascribed the power of inspiring song, and poets and musicians were therefore regarded as their pupils and favorites. They were first honored among the Thracians, and as Pieria around Olympus was the original seat of that people, it came to be considered as the native country of the Muses, who were therefore called *Pierides.* In the earliest period their number was three, though Homer sometimes speaks of a single Muse, and once,

at least, alludes to nine. This last is the number given by Hesiod in his *Theogony,* who also mentions their names: Clio, Euterpe, Thaleia, Melpomene, Terpsichore, Erato, Polyhymnia, Urania, and Calliope. Their origin is differently given, but the most widely-spread account represented them as the daughters of Zeus and Mnemosyne. Homer speaks of them as the goddesses of song, and as dwelling on the summit of Olympus. They are also often represented as the companions of Apollo, and as singing while he played upon the lyre at the banquets of the immortals. In the most ancient works of art we find only three Muses, and their attributes are musical instruments, such as the flute, the lyre, or the barbiton; it was not until the more modern ideal of Apollo Musagetes, in the garb of the Pythian musicians, was developed that the number nine was established by several famous artists in regard to these virgins, who were in like manner clad for the most part in theatrical drapery, with fine intellectual countenances, distinguished from one another by expression, attributes, and sometimes also by attitudes. 1. Calliope, the Muse of epic poetry, is characterized by a tablet and stylus, and sometimes by a roll of papers. 2. Clio, the Muse of history, is represented either with an open roll of paper or an open chest of books. 3. Euterpe, the Muse of lyric poetry, is given a flute, and sometimes two flutes. 4. Melpomene, the Muse of tragedy, is characterized by a tragic mask, the club of Hercules, or a sword, her head is surrounded with vine-leaves, and she wears the cothurnus. 5. Terpsichore, the Muse of choral dance and song, appears with the lyre and the plectrum. 6. Erato, the Muse of erotic poetry and mimic imitation, is also characterized by a lyre. 7. Polymnia, the Muse of the sublime hymn, is usually represented leaning in a pensive or meditating attitude. 8. Urania, the Muse of astronomy, bears a globe in her hand. 9. Thalia, the Muse of comedy and idyllic poetry, is characterized by a comic mask, a shepherd's staff, and a wreath of ivy. Various legends ascribed to them victories in musical competitions, particularly over the Sirens (q. v.), and they are sometimes represented with plumes on their heads, supposed to typify such victory. In the later classic times, particular provinces were assigned to the Muses in connection with different departments of literature, science, and the fine arts; but the invocations addressed to them appear to have been, as in the case of modern writers, merely formal imitations of the early poets. Their worship among the Romans was a mere imitation of the Greeks, and never became truly national or popular. Among the places sacred to them were the wells of Aganippe and Hippocrene on Mount Helicon, and the Castalian spring on Mount Parnassus. See *Chambers's Cyclopædia,* s. v.; Smith, *Dict. Greek and Roman Biogr.* ii, 1124 sq.; Westropp, *Hand-book of Archæology,* p. 190 sq.

Museum (Gr. μουσεῖον), originally the name given by the ancients to a temple of the Muses, and afterwards to a building devoted to science, learning, and the fine arts. The first museum of this kind was the celebrated Alexandrian Museum. See ALEXANDRIA. After the revival of learning in Europe, the term museum was sometimes applied to the apartment in which any kind of philosophical apparatus was kept and used; but it has long been almost exclusively appropriated to collections of the monuments of antiquity, and of other things interesting to the scholar and man of science. In this sense it began to be first used in Italy, and probably in the case of the famous Florentine Museum, founded by Cosmo de' Medici, which soon became a great and most valuable collection of antiquities. Nothing analogous to the museums of modern times existed among the ancients, the greatest collections of statues and paintings which were made in the houses of wealthy Romans having been intended for splendor rather than for the promotion of art. The name soon ceased to be limited to collections of antiquities and sculptures and paintings; collections illustrative of natural history and other sciences now form a chief part of the treasures of many of the greatest museums, and there are museums devoted to particular branches of science. Of the museums of Britain, the British Museum is the greatest; that of Oxford, founded in 1679, is the oldest. The museum of the Vatican, in Rome, contains immense treasures in sculptures and paintings, and also in books and manuscripts. The museum of the Louvre, in Paris, that of St. Petersburg, and those of Dresden, Vienna, Munich, and Berlin, are among the greatest in the world. The usefulness of a museum depends not merely upon the amount of its treasures, but perhaps even in a greater degree upon their proper arrangement; and while great collections in the chief capitals of the world are of incalculable importance to science, its interests are also likely to be much promoted by those local museums, still unhappily not numerous, which are devoted to the illustration of all that belongs to particular and limited districts. Museums appropriated to the illustration of the industrial arts—their raw material, their machines, and their products—and of everything economically valuable, are of recent origin, but their importance is unquestionably very great. Pre-eminent among institutions of this kind in Britain are the South Kensington Museum and the Industrial Museum in Edinburgh. In recent times missionary museums have been started in the United States for the purpose of collecting all that is valuable for the proper interpretation of heathen religions, and to commemorate Christian victories over pagan idolatry.

Musgrave, THOMAS, D.D., an English prelate of note, was the son of a draper in Cambridge, where he was born in 1788. After an elementary education he entered as student Trinity College, Cambridge, in 1806, and was fourteenth wrangler in 1810. He was then elected a fellow of his college, which position he held up to 1837. He obtained the master's degree in 1813; became lord almoner's professor of Arabic in 1821; and was senior proctor in 1831. He was also incumbent of St. Mary-the-Great, Cambridge, and bursar of his college. In 1837 Dr. Musgrave was appointed by the late viscount Melbourne bishop of Hereford, and on the death of the venerable Dr. Harcourt was translated to the archiepiscopal see of York, and thus became primate of England, a governor of the Charter-house and of King's College, Oxford, a commissioner for building churches, and elector of St. Augustine's College, Canterbury. In his patronage as archbishop were ninety-six livings, which he dispensed most impartially and with credit to his exalted position. Archbishop Musgrave died May 5, 1860, at his residence in London. He published only several of his *Sermons* (1839 and 1849, 8vo).

Mu'shi (Heb. *Mushi'*, מוּשִׁי, once [1 Chron. vi, 19] מֻשִׁי, *receding;* Sept. Ὁμουσεί, ὁ Μουσί, Ὁμουσί), the second of the two sons of Merari, son of Levi (Exod. vi, 19; Numb. iii, 20; 1 Chron. vi, 19, 47; xxiii, 21; xxiv, 26); he had three sons (1 Chron. xxiii, 23; xxiv, 30), whose descendants were called in common MUSHITES (Numb. iii, 33; xxvi, 58). B.C. post 1856.

Mu'shite (Heb. same as *Mushi;* Sept. Ὁμουσί and ὁ Μουσί; Vulg. *Musites* and *Musi*), a descendant of the Levite MUSHI (Numb. iii, 33; xxvi, 58).

Music [HEBREW] (שִׁיר, *shir, singing,* 1 Chron. xv, 16; 2 Chron. v, 13; vii, 6; xxxiv, 12; Eccles. xii, 4; Amos vi, 5; a *song*, as it is usually elsewhere rendered; Chald. זְמָר, *zemar', the striking* of musical instruments, Dan. ii, 5, 7, 10, 15; Gr. συμφωνία, *symphony* of sound, Luke xv, 25; but נְגִינָה, *neginah',* Lam. v, 14, or מַנְגִּרְנָה, *manginah',* Lam. ii, 63, is a satirical "song;" comp. Job xxx, 9. See NEGINOTH). This is the oldest and most natural of all the fine arts, and therefore is found among all nations, however ignorant of every other art. In elucidating the subject in this and a following article (that on MUSICAL INSTRUMENTS) we give a general

treatment, referring to other heads for details on particular points.

The Hebrews were an eminently musical people. Their history is full of illustrations of this feature of their national character and life. Their literature is a monument of it; for a large portion of their poetry was conceived in the form of psalmody or sacred lyric song; and though exaggerated representations have sometimes been put forward of the perfection which musical science and art attained among them, it cannot be doubted that their musical progress and attainments went much beyond the narrow limits which some eminent modern writers of the history of music have thought themselves warranted to assign.

1. *Antiquity of Hebrew Music.*—The Hebrew nation made no claim to the invention of music or musical instruments, but assigned to it an antiquity as remote as the antediluvian days of Jubal, who "was the father of all such as handle the harp and organ" (Gen. iv, 21). The inventor of musical instruments, therefore, like the first poet and the first forger of metals, was a Cainite. Chardin relates that the Persians and Arabians call musicians and singers *Kayne,* or "descendants from Cain." From the occurrence of the name Mahalaleel, third in descent from Seth, which signifies "giving praise to God," Schneider concludes that vocal music in religious services must have been still earlier in use among the Sethites (*Biblischgesch. Darstellung der Hebr. Musik*, p. xi). It has been conjectured that Jubal's discovery may have been perpetuated by the pillars of the Sethites mentioned by Josephus (*Ant.* i, 2), and that in this way it was preserved till after the Flood; but such conjectures are worse than an honest confession of ignorance.

The first mention of music in the times after the Deluge is in the narrative of Laban's interview with Jacob. Moses has recorded words of Laban, the father-in-law of Jacob, from which it appears that instruments of various kinds were already in use among the ancient family beyond the Euphrates from which the Hebrews sprang: "Wherefore didst thou flee away secretly, and steal away from me, and didst not tell me, that I might have sent thee away with mirth and with songs, with tabret and with harp?" (Gen. xxxi, 27). Whatever else, then, the posterity of Jacob may have learned from "the wisdom of the Egyptians" during their long stay in Egypt—that ancient cradle of the arts and sciences—it may be assumed as certain that they were familiar with at least the rudiments of music before they went down to sojourn there, although it is reasonable to suppose that they were indebted to that ingenious and inventive people for some further progress in the art. It is a remarkable and interesting fact that their exodus from Egypt, which was their birthday as a nation, was an event celebrated by an outburst both of poetry and song. But whatever may have been its origin, and in whatever way it was preserved, the practice of music existed in the upland country of Syria; and of the three possible kinds of musical instruments, two were known and employed to accompany the song. The three kinds are alluded to in Job xxi, 12.

On the banks of the Red Sea, Moses and the children of Israel sang their triumphal song of deliverance from the hosts of Egypt; and Miriam, in celebration of the same event, exercised one of her functions as a prophetess by leading a procession of the women of the camp, chanting in chorus the burden to the song of Moses, "Sing ye to Jehovah, for he hath triumphed gloriously; the horse and his rider hath he thrown into the sea." Their song was accompanied by timbrels and dances, or, as some take the latter word, by a musical instrument of which the shape is unknown, but which is supposed to have resembled the modern tambourine (see DANCE), and, like it, to have been used as an accompaniment to dancing. The expression in the A. V. of Exod. xv, 21, "and Miriam *answered* them," seems to indicate that the song was alternate, Miriam leading off with the solo, while the women responded in full chorus. But it is probable that the Hebrew word, like the corresponding Arabic, has merely the sense of singing, which is retained in the A. V. of Exod. xxxii, 18; Numb. xxi, 17; 1 Sam. xxix, 5; Psa. cxlvii, 7; Hos. ii, 15. The same word is used for the shouting of soldiers in battle (Jer. li, 14), and the cry of wild beasts (Isa. xiii, 22), and in neither of these cases can the notion of response be appropriate. All that can be inferred is that Miriam led off the song, and this is confirmed by the rendering of the Vulg., præcinebat. The triumphal hymn of Moses had unquestionably a religious character about it, but the employment of music in religious service, though idolatrous, is more distinctly marked in the festivities which attended the erection of the golden calf. With this may be compared the musical service which accompanied the dedication of the golden image in the plains of Dura (Dan. iii), the commencement of which was to be the signal for the multitude to prostrate themselves in worship. The wild cries and shouts which reached the ears of Moses and Joshua as they came down from the mount sounded to the latter as the din of battle, the voices of victor and vanquished blending in one harsh chorus. But the quicker sense of Moses discerned the rough music with which the people worshipped the visible representation of the God that brought them out of Egypt. Nothing could show more clearly than Joshua's mistake the rude character of the Hebrew music at this period (Exod. xxxii, 17, 18), as untrained and wild as the notes of their Syrian forefathers. Comp. Lam. ii, 7, where the war-cry of the enemy in the Temple is likened to the noise of the multitude on a solemn feast-day: "They have made a noise in the house of Jehovah as in the day of a solemn feast." The silver trumpets made by the metal workers of the tabernacle, which were used to direct the movements of the camp, point to music of a very simple kind (Numb. x, 1–10), and the long blast of the jubilee horns, with which the priests brought down the walls of Jericho, had probably nothing very musical about it (Josh. vi), any more than the rough concert with which the ears of the sleeping Midianites were saluted by Gideon's three hundred warriors (Judg. vii). The song of Deborah and Barak is cast in a distinctly metrical form, and was probably intended to be sung with a musical accompaniment as one of the people's songs, like that with which Jephthah's daughter and her companions met her father on his victorious return (Judg. xi).

2. Golden Age of Hebrew Music.—The period of Samuel, David, and Solomon forms a new æra in Hebrew music, as well as in Hebrew poetry (see Delitzsch, Commentar über den Psalter, 1859 – 60). The simpler impromptu with which the women from the cities of Israel greeted David after the slaughter of the Philistine was apparently struck off on the spur of the moment, under the influence of the wild joy with which they welcomed their national champion, "the darling of the songs of Israel." The accompaniment of timbrels and instruments of music must have been equally simple, and such that all could take part in it (1 Sam. xviii, 6, 7). Up to this time we meet with nothing like a systematic cultivation of music among the Hebrews, but the establishment of the schools of the prophets appears to have supplied this want. Whatever the students of these schools may have been taught, music was an essential part of their practice. At Bethel (1 Sam. x, 5) was a school of this kind, as well as at Naioth in Ramah (1 Sam. xix, 19, 20), at Jericho (2 Kings ii, 5, 7, 15), Gilgal (2 Kings iv, 38), and perhaps at Jerusalem (2 Kings xxii, 14). Professional musicians soon became attached to the court; and though Saul, a hardy warrior, had only at intervals recourse to the soothing influence of David's harp, yet David seems to have gathered around him "singing men and singing women," who could celebrate his victories and lend a charm to his hours of peace (2 Sam. xix, 35). Solomon did the same (Eccles. ii, 8), adding to the luxury of his court by his patronage of art, and obtaining a reputation himself as no mean composer (1 Kings iv, 32).

But the Temple was the great school of music, and it was consecrated to its highest service in the worship of Jehovah. Before, however, the elaborate arrangements had been made by David for the Temple choir, there must have been a considerable body of musicians throughout the country (2 Sam. vi, 5); and in the procession which accompanied the ark from the house of Obededom, the Levites, with Chenaniah at their head, who had acquired skill from previous training, played on psalteries, harps, and cymbals, to the words of the psalm of thanksgiving which David had composed for the occasion (1 Chron. xv, xvi). It is not improbable that the Levites all along had practiced music, and that some musical service was part of the worship of the tabernacle; for unless this supposition be made, it is inconceivable that a body of trained singers and musicians should be found ready for an occasion like that on which they make their first appearance. The position which the tribe of Levi occupied among the other tribes naturally favored the cultivation of an art which is essentially characteristic of a leisurely and peaceful life. They were free from the hardships attending the struggle for conquest and afterwards for existence, which the Hebrews maintained with the nations of Canaan and the surrounding countries, and their subsistence was provided for by a national tax. Consequently they had ample leisure for the various ecclesiastical duties devolving upon them, and among others for the service of song, for which some of their families appear to have possessed a remarkable genius. The three great divisions of the tribe had each a representative family in the choir: Heman and his sons represented the Kohathites, Asaph the Gershonites, and Ethan (or Jeduthun) the Merarites (1 Chron. xv, 17; xxiii, 6; xxv, 1-6). Of the 38,000 who composed the tribe in the reign of David, 4000 are said to have been appointed to praise Jehovah with the instruments which David made (1 Chron. xxiii, 5), and for which he taught them a special chant. This chant for ages afterwards was known by his name, and was sung by the Levites before the army of Jehoshaphat, and on laying the foundation of the second temple (comp. 1 Chron. xvi, 34, 41; 2 Chron, vii, 6; xx, 21; Ezra, iii, 10, 11); and again by the Maccabæan army after their great victory over Gorgias (1 Macc. iv, 24). Over this great body of musicians presided the sons of Asaph, Heman, and Jeduthun, twenty-four in number, as heads of the twenty-four courses of twelve into which the skilled minstrels were divided. These skilled or "cunning" (מֵבִין, 1 Chron. xxv, 6, 7) men were 288 in number, and under them appear to have been the scholars (תַּלְמִיד, 1 Chron. xxv, 8) whom, perhaps, they trained, and who made up the full number of 4000. Supposing 4000 to be merely a round number, each course would consist of a full band of 166 musicians, presided over by a body of twelve skilled players, with one of the sons of Asaph, Heman, or Jeduthun as conductor. Asaph himself appears to have played on the cymbals (1 Chron. xvi, 5), and this was the case with the other leaders (1 Chron. xv, 19), perhaps to mark the time more distinctly, while the rest of the band played on psalteries and harps. The singers were distinct from both, as is evident in Psa. lxviii, 25, "the singers went before, the players on instruments followed after, in the midst of the damsels playing with timbrels;" unless the singers in this case were the cymbal-players, like Heman, Asaph, and Ethan, who, in 1 Chron. xv, 19, are called "singers," and perhaps while giving the time with their cymbals led the choir with their voices. The "players on instruments" (נֹגְנִים, nogenim), as the word denotes, were the performers upon stringed instruments, like the psaltery and harp, who have been alluded to. The "players on instruments" (חֹלְלִים, cholelim), in Psa. lxxxvii, 7, were different from these last, and were properly pipers or performers on perforated wind-instruments (see 1 Kings i, 40). "The damsels playing with timbrels" (comp. 1 Chron. xiii, 8) seem to indicate that women took part in the Temple choir; and among the family of Heman are specially mentioned three daughters, who, with his fourteen sons, were all "under the hands of their father for song in the house of Jehovah" (1 Chron. xxv, 5, 6). The enormous number of instruments and dresses for the Levites provided during the magnificent reign of Solomon would seem, if Josephus be correct (*Ant.* viii, 3, 8), to have been intended for all time. A thousand dresses for the high-priest; linen garments and girdles of purple for the priests, 10,000; trumpets, 200,000; psalteries and harps of electrum, 40,000; all these were stored up in the Temple treasury. The costume of the Levitical singers at the dedication of the Temple was of fine linen (2 Chron. v, 12).

3. *The Silver Age of Hebrew Music.*—So we may perhaps fitly designate the period of the captivity and the restoration, as denoting that the national music was still preserved and cultivated by considerable numbers of the people, especially of the Levitical families, although much of its ancient glory and splendor had passed away. In the first anguish and dejection of their captivity, it was natural that the tribes should feel what is so touchingly expressed in Psa. cxxxvii: that by the rivers of Babylon they should hang their harps upon the willows; and that, when required by their captors to sing them one of the songs of Zion, they should exclaim, with patriotic disdain, "How shall we sing the Lord's song in a strange land?" But by and by they would take down their harps again from the willow-boughs, and seek solace for the sorrows of their long exile in recalling the loved melodies of their native land, and the sacred psalmody of their desolated Temple. The Babylonians, besides, were a people as fond of music as themselves. Many of their instruments are mentioned in the book of Daniel (ch. iii, 7, 10, 15); and in the long period of seventy years the Hebrew exiles must have been able to enrich their own national music by many new ideas and new instruments. It is at least certain that when "the Lord turned again the captivity of Judah," there was a fresh inspiration and outburst of sacred poetry and song: "Then was our mouth filled with laughter and our tongue with singing" (Psa. cxxvi, 2). Not a few of the later parts of the Psalter are of that age, some of which are not much inferior to the best compositions of David himself; and in proof of the extent to which musical gifts were spread among the returned exiles, it may suffice to refer to the fact stated in Neh. vii, 67, that "they had two hundred forty and five singing men and singing women," by whom we are no doubt to understand professional as distinguished from amateur performers. Nor were the musical traditions of the Temple forgotten, or their official depositaries extinct. The Levitical families of Asaph, Heman, and Jeduthun were still numerous, and still devoted to their choral art and office. "The children of Asaph alone—the singers—were a hundred twenty and eight" (Ezra ii, 41). At the foundation of the second temple, "they set the priests in their apparel with trumpets, and the Levites, the sons of Asaph, with cymbals, to praise the Lord after the ordinance of David, king of Israel" (Ezra iii, 10); and when, after many interruptions, the house was at last finished and dedicated, the whole liturgical service of David's and Solomon's reigns was as far as possible restored. "They set the priests in their divisions and the Levites in their courses for the service of God which is at Jerusalem" (Ezra vi, 18).

In the apocryphal book of Ecclesiasticus (ch. i) we find an interesting reference to the musical service of the second temple in the days of Simon the high-priest, the son of Onias, "who in his life repaired the house again and took care of the Temple that it should not fall." When Simon "finished the service of the altar, by stretching out his hand to the cup and pouring out

the blood of the grape at the foot of the altar, a sweet-smelling savor," "then shouted the sons of Aaron, and sounded the silver trumpets, and made a great noise to be heard for a remembrance before the Most High. Then all the people together hasted and fell down to the earth upon their faces to worship their Lord God Almighty. The singers also sang praises with their voices, with great variety of sounds was there made sweet melody, and the people besought the Lord till the solemnity of the Lord was ended and they had finished his service."

The Talmud also contains some notices of the liturgical music of the Herodian temple. The ordinary Levitical orchestra (according to *Erachin*, 10a, and *Tamid*, vii, 3), consisted of only twelve performers, provided with nine lyres, two harps, and one cymbal, with the addition, on certain days, of flutes. These musicians were stationed upon the דּוּכָן (*dukán*), or the ascent of several steps which led from the outer court to the court of the priests, and were placed under the leadership of the chief musician, who gave the time with "the loud-sounding cymbals." Below the steps, and at the foot of the Levites, stood the chorister boys of the same tribe who sang the refrain. The daily week-day psalm (שִׁיר הַקָּרְבָּן) was sung in nine parts or strophes, and the pauses were marked by the trumpet-blasts of the priests. The musical service of the Herodian temple was by no means the same as that of earlier times; and if the present accentuation of the Psalter be regarded as representing the manner in which the psalms were sung or cantilated in the time of Herod, it would not suffice to give us any notion of the usage which prevailed in the days of the first temple, before the exile. Innovations upon ancient usage were from time to time introduced; and among these mention is made in the Talmud of the use of an instrument in the later temple, which would seem to have been of the nature of a wind-organ, provided with as many as a hundred different keys, and the power of which was such, according to Jerome, that it could be heard from Jerusalem to the Mount of Olives, and even farther. (See Saalschütz, *Archäologie*, i, 281–284; also Appendix to the same author's *Geschichte und Würdigung der Musik bei den Hebräern.*)

4. *The Uses and Characteristics of Hebrew Music.*—Sacred music, as in the above liturgical examples, was the most important application of the art among the Hebrews. The trumpets, which are mentioned among the instruments played before the ark (1 Chron. xiii, 8), appear to have been reserved for the priests alone (1 Chron. xv, 24; xvi, 6). As they were also used in royal proclamations (2 Kings xi, 14), they were probably intended to set forth by way of symbol the royalty of Jehovah, the theocratic king of his people, as well as to sound the alarm against his enemies (2 Chron. xiii, 12). A hundred and twenty priests blew the trumpets in harmony with the choir of Levites at the dedication of Solomon's temple (2 Chron. v, 12, 13; vii, 6), as in the restoration of the worship under Hezekiah, in the description of which we find an indication of one of the uses of the Temple music: "And Hezekiah commanded to offer the burnt-offering upon the altar. And when the burnt-offering began, the song of Jehovah began also, with the trumpets and with the instruments of David, king of Israel. And all the congregation worshipped, and the singers sang, and the trumpeters sounded; all until the burnt-offering was finished" (2 Chron. xxix, 27, 28). The altar was the table of Jehovah (Mal. i, 7), and the sacrifices were his feasts (Exod. xxiii, 18); so the solemn music of the Levites corresponded to the melody by which the banquets of earthly monarchs were accompanied. The Temple was Jehovah's palace, and as the Levite sentries watched the gates by night they chanted the songs of Zion; one of these it has been conjectured with probability is Psa. cxxxiv.

In the private as well as in the religious life of the Hebrews music held a prominent place. The kings had their court musicians (Eccles. ii, 8), who bewailed their death (2 Chron. xxxv, 25); and in the luxurious times of the later monarchy the effeminate gallants of Israel, reeking with perfumes and stretched upon their couches of ivory, were wont at their banquets to accompany the song with the tinkling of the psaltery or guitar (Amos vi, 4-6), and amused themselves with devising musical instruments while their nation was perishing, as Nero fiddled when Rome was in flames. Isaiah denounces a woe against those who sat till the morning twilight over their wine, to the sound of "the harp and the viol, the tabret and pipe" (Isa. v, 11, 12). But while music was thus made to minister to debauchery and excess, it was the legitimate expression of mirth and gladness, and the indication of peace and prosperity. It was only when a curse was upon the land that the prophet could say, "The mirth of tabrets ceaseth, the noise of them that rejoice endeth, the joy of the harp ceaseth: they shall not drink wine with a song" (Isa. xxiv, 8, 9). In the sadness of captivity the harps hung upon the willows of Babylon, and the voices of the singers refused to sing the songs of Jehovah at their foreign captors' bidding (Psa. cxxxvii). The bridal processions as they passed through the streets were accompanied with music and song (Jer. vii, 34), and these ceased only when the land was desolate (Ezek. xxvi, 13). The high value attached to music at banquets is indicated in the description given in Ecclus. xxxii of the duties of the master of a feast. "Pour not out words where there is a musician, and show not forth wisdom out of time. A concert of music in a banquet of wine is as a signet of carbuncle set in gold. As a signet of an emerald set in a work of gold, so is the melody of music with pleasant wine." And, again, the memory of the good king Josiah was "as music at a banquet of wine" (Ecclus. xlix, 1). The music of the banquets was accompanied with songs and dancing (Luke xv, 25). So at the royal banquets of Babylon were sung hymns of praise in honor of the gods (Dan. v, 4, 23), and perhaps on some such occasion as the feast of Belshazzar the Hebrew captives might have been brought in to sing the songs of their native land (Psa. cxxxvii). The triumphal processions which celebrated a victory were enlivened by minstrels and singers (Exod. xv, 1, 20; Judges v, 1; xi, 34; 1 Sam. xviii, 6; xxi, 11; 2 Chron. xx, 28; Judges xv, 12, 13), and on extraordinary occasions they even accompanied armies to battle. Thus the Levites sang the chant of David before the army of Jehoshaphat as he went forth against the hosts of Ammon and Moab and Mount Seir (2 Chron. xx, 19, 21); and the victory of Abijah over Jeroboam is attributed to the encouragement given to Judah by the priests sounding their trumpets before the ark (2 Chron. xiii, 12, 14). It is clear from the narrative of Elisha and the minstrel who by his playing calmed the prophet's spirit till the hand of Jehovah was upon him, that among the camp-followers of Jehoshaphat's army on that occasion there were to be reckoned musicians who were probably Levites (2 Kings iii, 15). Besides songs of triumph, there were also religious songs (Isa. xxx, 29; Amos v, 23; James v, 13), "songs of the Temple" (Amos viii, 3), and songs which were sung in idolatrous worship (Exod. xxxii, 18). In like manner the use of music in the religious services of the Therapeutæ of later times is described by Philo (De Vita contempl. p. 901 [ed. Frankf.]). At a certain period in the service one of the worshippers rose and sang a song of praise to God, either of his own composition or one from the older poets. He was followed by others in a regular order, the congregation remaining quiet till the concluding prayer, in which all joined. After a simple meal the whole congregation arose and formed two choirs, one of men and one of women, with the most skilful singer of each for leader; and in this way sang hymns to God, sometimes with

the full chorus, and sometimes with each choir alternately. In conclusion, both men and women joined in a single choir, in imitation of that on the shores of the Red Sea, which was led by Moses and Miriam. In the Scriptures love-songs are alluded to in Psa. xlv, title, and Isa. v, 1. There were also the doleful songs of the funeral procession, and the wailing chant of the mourners who went about the streets, the professional קִינָה of those who were skilful in lamentation (2 Chron. xxxv, 25; Eccles. xii, 5; Jer. ix, 17-20; Amos v, 16). Lightfoot (Hor. Heb. on Matt. ix, 23) quotes from the Talmudists (Chetubh. c. 4, h. 6) to the effect that every Israelite on the death of his wife "will afford her not less than two pipers and one woman to make lamentation." The grape-gatherers sang as they gathered in the vintage, and the wine-presses were trodden with the shout of a song (Isa. xvi, 10; Jer. xlviii, 33); the women sang as they toiled at the mill, and on every occasion the land of the Hebrews during their national prosperity was a land of music and melody. There is one class of musicians to which allusion is casually made (Ecclus. ix, 4), and who were probably foreigners —the harlots who frequented the streets of great cities, and attracted notice by singing and playing the guitar (Isa. xxiii, 15, 16). (See below.)

There are two aspects in which music appears, and about which little that is satisfactory can be said: the mysterious influence which it had in driving out the evil spirit from Saul, and its intimate connection with prophecy and prophetical inspiration. Miriam "the prophetess" exercised her prophetical functions as the leader of the chorus of women who sang the song of triumph over the Egyptians (Exod. xv, 20). The company of prophets whom Saul met coming down from the hill of God had a psaltery, a tabret, a pipe, and a harp before them, and smitten with the same enthusiasm he "prophesied among them" (1 Sam. x, 5, 10). The priests of Baal, challenged by Elijah at Carmel, cried aloud, and cut themselves with knives, and prophesied till sunset (1 Kings xviii, 29). The sons of Asaph, Heman, and Jeduthun, set apart by David for the Temple choir, were to "prophesy with harps, with psalteries, and with cymbals" (1 Chron. xxv, 1); Jeduthun "prophesied with the harp" (1 Chron. xxv, 3), and in 2 Chron. xxxv, 15 is called "the king's seer," a term which is applied to Heman (1 Chron. xxv, 5) and Asaph (2 Chron. xxix, 30) as musicians, as well as to Gad the prophet (2 Sam. xxiv, 11; 1 Chron. xxix, 29). The spirit of Jehovah came upon Jahaziel, a Levite of the sons of Asaph, in the reign of Jehoshaphat, and he foretold the success of the royal army (2 Chron. xx, 14). From all these instances it is evident that the same Hebrew root (נָבָא) is used to denote the inspiration under which the prophets spoke and the minstrels sang. Gesenius assigns the later as a secondary meaning. In the case of Elisha, the minstrel and the prophet are distinct personages, but it is not till the minstrel has played that the hand of Jehovah comes upon the prophet (2 Kings iii, 15). This influence of music has been explained as follows by a learned divine of the Platonist school: "These divine enthusiasts were commonly wont to compose their songs and hymns at the sounding of some one musical instrument or other, as we find it often suggested in the Psalms. So Plutarch . . . describes the dictate of the oracle anciently, . . . 'how that it was uttered in verse, in pomp of words, similitudes, and metaphors, at the sound of a pipe.' Thus we have Asaph, Heman, and Jeduthun set forth in this prophetical preparation (1 Chron. xxv, 1). Thus R. Sal. expounds the passage, 'When they played upon their musical instruments they prophesied after the manner of Elisha.' And this sense of this place, I think, is much more genuine than that which a late author of our own would fasten upon it, viz. that this prophesying was nothing but the singing of psalms. For it is manifest that these prophets were not mere singers, but composers, and such as were truly called prophets or enthusiasts" (Smith, *Select Discourses*, vi, ch. 7, p. 238, 239 [ed. 1660]). All that can be safely concluded is, that in their external manifestations the effect of music in exciting the emotions of the sensitive Hebrews, the frenzy of Saul's madness (1 Sam. xviii, 10), and the religious enthusiasm of the prophets, whether of Baal or Jehovah, were so nearly alike as to be described by the same word. The case of Saul is the most difficult. We are not admitted to the secret of his dark malady. Two turning-points in his history are the two interviews with Samuel, the first and the last, if we except that dread encounter which the despairing monarch challenged before the fatal day of Gilboa. On the first of these Samuel foretold his meeting with the company of prophets with their minstrelsy, the external means by which the spirit of Jehovah should come upon him, and he should be changed into another man (1 Sam. x, 5). The last occasion of their meeting was the disobedience of Saul in sparing the Amalekites, for which he was rejected from being told king (1 Sam. xv, 26). Immediately after this we are told the Spirit of Jehovah departed from Saul, and an "evil spirit from Jehovah troubled him" (1 Sam. xvi, 14); and his attendants, who had perhaps witnessed the strange transformation wrought upon him by the music of the prophets, suggested that the same means should be employed for his restoration. "Let our lord now command thy servants before thee to seek out a man, a cunning player on a harp: and it shall come to pass, when the evil spirit from God is upon thee, that he shall play with his hand, and thou shalt be well. ... And it came to pass when the spirit from God was upon Saul, that David took a harp and played with his hand. So Saul was refreshed, and was well, and the evil spirit departed from him" (1 Sam. xvi, 16, 23). But on two occasions, when anger and jealousy supervened, the remedy which had soothed the frenzy of insanity had lost its charm (1 Sam. xviii, 10, 11; xix, 9, 10). It seems, therefore, that the passage of Seneca, which has often been quoted in explanation of this phenomenon, "Pythagoras perturbationes lyra componebat" (*De Ira*, iii, 9), is but generally applicable.

On the scientific character of Hebrew music much has been written, but to very little purpose, and with extremely meagre results. The truth is that no adequate data exist to enable us to arrive at any satisfactory conclusions upon it. The Hebrews never were in possession of any system of notation, by which their musical traditions might have been fixed, and handed down to posterity; and in the absence of this it is hopeless to attempt to determine more than a very few points of a quite general kind. Several attempts, however, have been made by ingenious and learned men to overcome this insuperable barrier by converting the accentual system of the Psalter into a musical notation. One of the earliest of these writers was Speidel (*Unverwerfliche Spuren von der alten Davidischen Singkunst* [1704]). Another was Anton (in Paulus's *Neues Repertorium für biblisch. und morgenländ. Literatur* [1790-91]). The latest is Haupt (1854), who discovers in the accents viewed as marks of number, when combined with the arithmetical values of the Hebrew letters, all the notes of the diatonic scale, and sees in the series of notes thus indicated the original psalm-melodies. But however ingenious all these attempts may be, they all issue, as Delitzsch remarks, in self-illusion. For the accents, as Saalschütz urges, were not designed to serve any such musical use. "It is plain that the Masoretes had no other object in view in devising them than the preservation of the right pronunciation and understanding of the text. If the accents set forth a melody, it was only the melody of declamation, which among southern nations approaches nearer to proper singing than among the northern peoples. It was not the Temple music which the accents set forth, the communication of which could have no interest to the Masoretes, who were mere linguists. It would have been strange, besides, if they had made use of so many musical notes as the accents, when seven might have sufficed. Of the ancient Temple music not a trace remains, either in the text of Holy Scripture or anywhere else" (Saalschütz, *Von der Form der Hebräischen Poesie, nebst einer Abhandlung über die Musik der Hebräer*, 1825). Proceeding on the same false assumption that the poetical accents were of the nature of a musical notation, Forkel, the German historian of music, drew a conclusion very different from those of the authors now referred to. He inferred from the manifest imperfection and inadequacy of such a musical language how extremely rude and imperfect must have been the musical science and art which it represented. He concluded, in fact, that the Hebrew music was nothing more than a species of cantilation or intoned recitative, and that it never was able to advance beyond this rudimentary stage (*Geschichte der Musik*, i, 148). This was an absurd extreme; for how is it conceivable that a people who made such splendid progress in the art of lyric poetry, i.e. of poetry expressly designed to be married to music—to music expressive of the same emotions which were expressed in the poetry—should have lagged so far behind the other nations of antiquity in the sister science and art? See Saalschütz. On such a subject it is not safe to argue from the practice of the modern Jews (*Shilte hag-gib.* ii); and as singing is something so exceedingly simple and natural, it is difficult to believe that in the solemn services of their religion they stopped at the point of cantilation (Ewald, *Hebr. Poesie*, p. 166).

The nature of the Hebrew music was doubtless of the same essential character as that of other ancient nations, and of all the present Oriental nations; consisting not so much in harmony (in the modern sense of the term) as in unison or melody (Volney, *Trav.* ii, 325). This is the music of nature, and for a long time after the more ancient period was common among the Greeks and Romans. From the Hebrews themselves we have no definite accounts in reference to this subject; but the history of the art among other nations must here also serve as our guide. It was not the harmony of differing or dissonant sounds, but the voice formed after the tones of the lyre, that constituted the beauty of the ancient music (see Philo, *Opp.* ii, p. 484 sq.). This so enraptured the Arabian servant of Niebuhr that he cried out, in contempt of European music, "By Allah, that is fine! God bless you!" (*Reisebeschreib. nach Arabien*, p. 176). The whole of antiquity is full of stories in praise of this music. By its means battles were won, cities conquered, mutinies quelled, diseases cured (Plutarch, *De Musica*). Effects similar to these occur in the Scriptures, and have already been indicated. The different parts which we now have are the invention of modern times. See ALAMOTH; GITTITH; SHEMINITH, etc. Respecting the base, treble, etc., very few discriminating remarks had then been made. The old, the young, maidens, etc., appear to have sung one part. The beauty of their music consisted altogether in melody. The instruments by which, in singing, this melody was accompanied occupied the part of a sustained base; and, if we are disposed to apply in this case what Niebuhr has told us, the beauty of the concerts consisted in this, that other persons repeated the music which had just been sung three, four, or five notes lower or higher. Such, for instance, was the concert which Miriam held with her musical fellows, and to which the "toph," or tabret, furnished the continued base; just as Niebuhr has also remarked of the Arabian women of the present day, "that when they dance or sing in their harem they always beat the corresponding time upon this drum" (*Reisebesch.* i, 181). To this mode of performance belongs the 24th Psalm, which rests altogether upon the varied representation; in like manner, also, the 20th and 21st Psalms. This was all the change it admitted; and although it is very possible that this monotonous, or rather unisonous music, might not be interesting to ears tuned to musical progressions, modulations, and cadences, there is something in it with which the Orientals are well pleased. They love it for the very reason that it is monotonous or unisonous, and from Morocco to China we meet with no other. Even the cultivated Chinese, whose civilization offers so many points of resemblance to that of the ancient Egyptians, like their own music, which consists entirely of melody, better than ours, although it is not wholly despised by them (Du Halde's *China*, iii, 216). A music of this description could easily dispense with the compositions which mark the time by notes; and the Hebrews do not appear to have known anything of musical notation; for that the accents served that purpose is a position which yet remains to be proved. At the best, the accent must have been a very imperfect means for this purpose, however high its antiquity. Europeans had not yet attained to musical notes in the 11th century, and the Orientals do not profess to have known them till the 17th. On the other hand, the word סֶלָה, *selah*, which occurs in the Psalms and Habakkuk, may very possibly be a mark for the change of time, or for repeating the melody a few tones higher, or, as some think, for an accompaniment or after-piece of entirely instrumental music (see De Wette, *Comment. üb. d. Psa.* p. 32 sq.; Saalschütz, *Form der Hebr. Poesie*, p. 353 sq.; Ewald, *Hebr. Poesie*, p. 178 sq.). See SELAH. The Hebrew music is judged to have been of a shrill character (see Redslob, in Illgen's *Zeitschr.* 1839, ii, 1 sq.), for this would result from the nature of the instruments—harps, flutes, and cymbals—which were employed in the Temple service (comp. Mishna, *Erach.* ii, 3, 5, and 6).

The manner of singing single songs was, it seems, ruled by that of others in the same measure, and it is usually supposed that many of the titles of the Psalms are intended to indicate the names of other songs according to which these were to be sung (see Vensky, in Mitzler's *Musikal Biblioth.* iii, 666 sq.; Eichhorn, *Einl.* i, 245; Jahn, *Einl.* i, 353; Gesenius, *Gesch. d. Hebr. Sprache*, p. 220 sq.). See PSALMS.

Engel (*Music of the most Ancient Nations, particularly of the Assyrians, Egyptians, and Hebrews* [1864]) observes that the Hebrews had various kinds of sacred and secular musical compositions, differing according to the occasions on which they were employed. These he enumerates as follows: (a) *Sacred music in divine worship*, which was evidently regarded as of the highest importance; (b) *Sacred songs*, and instrumental compositions, which were performed also in family circles (Isa. xxx, 29; James v, 13); (c) *Military music*, sacred as well as secular (2 Chron. xx, 21; xiii, 12, 14); (d) *Triumphal songs* (Exod. xv; Jude v; 2 Chron. xx, 27, 28); (e) *Erotic songs*, alluded to in title of Psa. xlv, "A song of loves" (Isa. v, 1); (f) *Music at bridal processions* (Jer. vii, 34); (g) *Funeral songs* (2 Chron. xxxv, 25; Eccles. xii, 5; Amos v, 16; 2 Sam. i, 19); (h) *Popular secular songs*, such as the songs of the vintners (Isa. xvi, 10; Jer. xlviii, 33); (i) *Convivial songs* (Isa. xxiv, 8, 9; Luke xv, 25; Isa. v, 11, 12; Amos vi, 4, 5); (j) *Performances of itinerant musicians* (Isa. xxiii, 15, 16; Eccles. ix, 4).

For the literature of the subject, see MUSICAL INSTRUMENTS.

Music, CHRISTIAN. Music (from μοῦσα, a *muse*) is produced by the human voice, and by a variety of artificial instruments. For the application of the voice to musical purposes, see SINGING. Musical instruments are classified as stringed instruments, wind instruments, and instruments of percussion. In some stringed instruments, as the piano-forte, the sounds are produced by striking the strings by keys; in others, as the harp and guitar, by drawing them from the position of rest. In a third class, including the violin, viola, violoncello,

and double bass, the strings are put into vibration with a bow. In wind instruments the sound is produced by the agitation of an enclosed column of air; some, as the flute, clarionet, oboe, bassoon, flageolet—instruments of wood, and the trumpet, horn, cornet-a-piston, etc., of metal, are played by the breath; in others, as the organ, harmonium, and concertina, the wind is produced by other means. In the two last-named instruments the sound is produced by the action of wind on free vibrating springs or reeds. Instruments of percussion are such as the drum, kettle-drum, cymbals, etc. Musical compositions are either for the voice, with or without instrumental accompaniment, or for instruments only. Instrumental music may be composed for one or for more instruments. The rondo, the concerto, the sonata, and the fantasia generally belong to the former class; to the latter, symphonies and overtures for an orchestra, and instrumental chamber music, including duets, trios, quartets, and other compositions for several instruments, where each takes the lead in turn, the other parts being accompaniments. Of vocal music, the principal forms may be classed as church music, chamber music, dramatic music, and popular or national music. Vocal chamber music includes cantatas, madrigals, and their modern successors, glees, as also recitatives, arias, duets, trios, quartets, choruses, and generally all forms, accompanied or unaccompanied, which are chiefly intended for small circles. Dramatic music comprehends music united with scenic representation in a variety of ways, in the ballet, the melodrama, the vaudeville, and the opera, in which last music supplies the place of spoken dialogue. And finally we come to consider church music, with which alone we have to deal here. It includes plain song, faux-bourdon, the chorale, the anthem, the sacred cantata, the mass and requiem of the Roman Catholic Church, and the oratorio.

Among all nations music has always formed a part of public worship. "Praise," it has been aptly said, "is the appropriate language of devotion. A fervent spirit of devotion instinctively seeks to express itself in song. In the strains of poetry, joined with the melody of music, it finds an easy and natural utterance of its elevated emotions." Among the pagan nations of antiquity the singing of songs constituted indeed a great part of the religious worship. In all their religious festivals and in their temples they sang to the praise of their idol gods (comp. Gerbert, *Musica Sacra*, vol. i. Præf.; Burney, *Hist. of Music*). Yet no nation of antiquity made such extensive use of music in their worship as did the Hebrews (see the preceding article), especially in the time of their prosperity (Saalschütz, *Gesch. u. Würdigung d. Tempel-Musik d. Hebräer* [Berl. 1829]). Not only in the Temple, but in their synagogues and in their dwellings the Jews celebrated God with sacred hymns. See PSALM. From them the use of music and choral singing was adopted by the primitive Christians (see 1 Cor. xiv, 15, 26; Col. iii, 16). Says Coleman, "The singing of spiritual songs constituted from the beginning an interesting and important part of religious worship in the primitive Church" (*Prel. and Rit.* p. 321).

I. *Early Christian Usages.*—Grotius insists that we have in Acts iv, 24–30 an epitome of an early Christian hymn; and it would appear from a close examination of other N.-T. Scripture passages that even Christ himself, in his final interview with his disciples before his crucifixion, sung with them the customary paschal songs at the institution of the sacrament, and by his example sanctified the use of sacred songs in the Christian Church (Matt. xxvi, 30). In the opinion of Münter, the eminent Biblical archæologist, the gift of the Holy Spirit on the day of Pentecost was accompanied with poetic inspiration, to which the disciples gave utterance in the rhapsodies of spiritual songs (Acts ii, 4, 13, 47). There are also many other N.-T. passages which clearly indicate the use of religious songs in the worship of God. Paul and Silas, lacerated by the cruel scourging which they had received, and in close confinement in the inner prison, prayed and sang praises to God at midnight (Acts xvi, 25). The use of psalms and hymns and spiritual songs is moreover directly enjoined upon the churches by the apostle as an essential part of religious devotions (Col. iii, 16; Eph. v, 14, 19; James v, 13). The latter epistle was a circular letter to the Gentile churches of Asia, and therefore in connection with that to the Church at Colosse is explicit authority for the use of song in the religious worship of the apostolic churches (comp. Walch, *De Hymnis Ecclesiæ Apostolicæ*).

As the Hebrews worshipped God in their homes by sacred song, so the N.-T. people also did not restrict these acts of devotion to their public places of worship. In their social circles and around their domestic altars they worshipped God in sacred song; and in their daily occupations they were wont to relieve their toil and refresh their spirits by renewing their favorite songs of Zion. Persecuted and afflicted—in solitary cells of the prison, in the more dismal abodes of the mines to which they were doomed, or as wandering exiles in foreign countries—they forgot not to sing the Lord's song in the prison or the mine or the strange lands to which they were driven. In connection with the passage from Ephesians, the apostle warns those whom he addresses against the use of wine and the excesses to which it leads, with reference to those abuses which dishonored their sacramental supper and love-feasts. In opposition to the vain songs which, in such excesses, they might be disposed to sing, they are urged to the sober, religious use of psalms and hymns and spiritual songs. The phraseology indicates, too, that they were not restricted to the use of the psalms of David, as in the Jewish worship, but were at liberty to employ others of appropriate religious character in their devotions. Says Coleman, "The Corinthians were accustomed to make use of songs composed for the occasion (1 Cor. xiv, 26). And though the apostle had occasion to correct their disorderly proceedings, it does not appear that he forbade the use of such songs. On the contrary, there is the highest probability that the apostolic churches did not restrict themselves simply to the use of the Jewish Psalter. Grotius and others have supposed that some fragments of these early hymns are contained not only, as above mentioned, in Acts, but perhaps also in 1 Tim. iii, 16. Something like poetic antithesis they have imagined to be contained in James i, 17; 1 Tim. i, 1; 2 Tim. ii, 11–13. The expression in Revelation, 'I am Alpha and Omega, the first and the last,' has been ascribed to the same origin, as has also Rev. iv, 8, together with the song of Moses and the Lamb (Rev. xv, 3), and the songs of the elders and the beasts (Rev. v, 9–14). Certain parts of the book itself have been supposed to be strictly poetical, and may have been used as such in Christian worship, such as Rev. i, 4–8; xi, 15-19; xv, 3, 4; xxi, 1–8; xxii, 10–18. But the argument is not conclusive; and all the learned criticism, the talent, and the taste that have been employed on this point leave us little else than uncertain conjecture on which to build an hypothesis" (p. 325).

The earliest authentic record on this subject is the celebrated letter from Pliny to Trajan, just at the close of the apostolic age (A.D. 103, 104). In the investigations which he instituted against the Christians of his period, he discovered, among other things, that they were accustomed to meet before day to offer praise to Christ (*Epist.* x, 97). The expression used is somewhat equivocal, and might refer to the ascription of praise in prayer or in song. But it appears that these Christians rehearsed their "*carmen invicem*" *alternately*, as if in responsive songs, according to the ancient custom of singing in the Jewish worship. Tertullian, only a century later, evidently understood the passage to be descriptive of this mode of worshipping God and Christ, for he says that Pliny intended to express nothing else than assemblies before the dawn of the morning for singing praise to Christ and to God (*Apolog.* c.

2). Eusebius also gives the passage a similar interpretation, saying that Pliny could find nothing against them save that, arising at the dawn of the morning, they sang hymns to Christ as God (*Hist. Ecclesiast.* iii, 32). Viewed in this light, in which it is now generally viewed, it becomes evidence of the use of song in Christian worship immediately subsequent to the age of the apostles (comp. Münter, *Metrisch. Offenbar.* p. 25). Tertullian himself also distinctly testifies to the use of songs to the praise of God by the primitive Christians. Every one, he says, was invited in their public worship to sing unto God, according to his ability, either from the Scriptures or *de proprio ingenio*, "*one indited by himself*," according to the interpretation of Münter. Whatever may be the meaning of this phrase, the passage clearly asserts the use of Christian psalmody in their religious worship. Again, he speaks of singing in connection with the reading of the Scriptures, exhortations, and prayer (*De Anima*, c. 9). Justin Martyr also, who lived within half a century of the apostles, and is himself credited with being the author of a work on Christian Psalmody, mentions the songs and hymns of the Ephesian Christians: "We manifest our gratitude to him by worshipping him in spiritual songs and hymns, praising him for our birth, for our health, for the vicissitudes of the seasons, and for the hopes of immortality" (*Apol.* v, 28). Eusebius, moreover, furnishes this important testimony of an ancient historian at the close of the 2d century: "Who knows not the writings of Irenæus, Melito, and others, which exhibit Christ as God and man? And *how many songs and odes of the brethren there are*, written from the beginning ($\dot{\alpha}\pi'$ $\dot{\alpha}\rho\chi\tilde{\eta}\varsigma$) by believers, which offer praise to Christ as the Word of God, ascribing divinity to him!" (*Eccles. Hist.* v, 28). Here we have not only testimony to the use of spiritual songs in the Christian Church from the remotest antiquity, but also that there were hymn writers in the apostolic Church, and that their songs were collected for use at a very early date of the Christian Church (comp. Fabricius, *Biblioth. Græca* [ed. Harl.], vii, 67). These spiritual songs of the primitive Christians were almost exclusively of a doctrinal character. "In fact," says Augusti, "almost all the prayers, doxologies, and hymns of the ancient Church are nothing else than prayers and supplications to the triune God or to Jesus Christ. They were generally altogether doctrinal. The prayers and psalms, of merely a moral character, which the modern Church has in great abundance, in the ancient were altogether unknown" (*Denkwürdigkeiten*, v, 417; comp. Neander, *Allgem. Kirchengesch.* i, 523; Engl. ed. i, 304).

One such composition of the primitive Church—a hymn—has come down to us entire. It is found in the *Pædagogue* of Clement of Alexandria, a work bearing date about one hundred and fifty years from the time of the apostles; but it is ascribed to another, and assigned to an earlier origin. It is wanting in some of the manuscripts of Clement. It contains figurative language and forms of expression which were familiar to the Church at an earlier date; and, for various reasons, is regarded by Münter (*Metrische Offenbar.* p. 32) and Bull (*Defensio fidei Nicænæ*, § iii, ch. 2, p. 316) as a venerable relic of the early Church, which has escaped the ravages of time, and still remains a solitary remnant of the Christian psalmody of that early age. It is certainly very ancient, and the earliest that has been transmitted to us (see HYMNOLOGY, in vol. iv, p. 434, col. 2). A translation of it is furnished in Coleman's *Ancient Christianity*, p. 334–35.

Sacred music must, in the primitive Church, have consisted only of a few simple airs which could easily be learned, and which, by frequent repetition, became familiar to all. An ornate and complicated style of music would have been alike incompatible with the circumstances of these Christian worshippers and uncongenial with the simplicity of their primitive forms (comp. Augusti, *Denkwürdigkeiten*, v, 288). In their songs of Zion, both old and young, men and women, bore a part. Their psalmody was the joint act of the whole assembly in unison. Such is the testimony of Hilary, A.D. 355 (*Comment. in Psa. xxv*, p. 174). Ambrose remarks that the injunction of the apostle, forbidding women to speak in public, relates not to singing, "for this is delightful in every age and suited to every sex" (in *Psa. i, Præf.* p. 741; comp. *Hexæmeron,* lib. iii, c. 5, p. 42). The authority of Chrysostom is also to the same effect. "It was the ancient custom, as it is still with us, for all to come together, and unitedly to join in singing. The young and the old, rich and poor, male and female, bond and free, all join in one song. . . . All worldly distinctions here cease, and the whole congregation form one general chorus" (*Hom.* xi, vol. xii, p. 349; *Hom.* xxxvi, in 1 Cor. vol. x, p. 340; comp. Gerbert, *Musica Sacra,* lib. i, § 11, for other authorities). Each member was invited, at pleasure and according to his ability, to lead their devotions in a sacred song indited by himself. Such was the custom in the Corinthian Church. Such was still the custom in the age of Tertullian, to which reference has already been made. Augustine also refers to the same usage, and ascribes to divine inspiration the talent which was manifested in this extemporaneous psalmody.

Such was the character of the psalmody of the early Church, consisting in part of the psalms of David, and in part of hymns composed for the purpose of worship, and expressive of love and praise to God and to Christ (Neander, *Allgem. Kirchengesch.* i, 523; Engl. ed. i, 304). Few in number, and sung to rude and simple airs, they yet had wonderful power over those primitive saints. The sacred song inspired their devotions both in the public and private worship of God. At their family board it quickened their gratitude to God, who gave them their daily bread. It enlivened their domestic and social intercourse; it relieved the weariness of their daily labor; it cheered them in solitude, comforted them in affliction, and supported them under persecution. "Go where you will," says Jerome, "the ploughman at his plough sings his joyful hallelujahs, the busy mower regales himself with his psalms, and the vine-dresser is singing one of the songs of David. Such are our songs —our love-songs, as they are called—the solace of the shepherd in his solitude and of the husbandman in his toil" (*Ep. xvii, ad Marcellum*). Fearless of reproach, of persecution, and of death, they continued in the face of their enemies to sing their sacred songs in the streets and market-places and at the martyr's stake. Eusebius declares himself an eye-witness to the fact that, under their persecutions in Thebais, "they continued to their latest breath to sing psalms and hymns and thanksgivings to the God of heaven" (*Hist. Eccles.* viii, 9; comp. Herder, *Briefe zur Beförderung der Humanität* 7 *Samml.* p. 28 sq.; Augusti, *Denkwürdigkeiten,* v, 296– 97; Coleman, *Manual,* p. 331–33).

II. *Innovations.*—From the 4th century onward the Christian Church greatly modified the mode of performing this part of public worship.

1. The first innovation occurred in the Syrian churches, where *responsive singing* was introduced, probably very early in the 4th century. Soon after it became the practice of the Eastern churches generally, and finally was transferred to the West also by St. Ambrose of Milan (A.D. 370), and was called there the Ambrosian style of music. Some critics believe responsive singing to have been practiced at a very early date. Thus it would seem from the epistle of Pliny that the Christians of whom he speaks sang *alternately in responses.* The ancient hymn from Clement, too, above mentioned, seems to be constructed with reference to this method of singing. There is besides an ancient but certainly groundless tradition extant in Socrates (*Hist. Eccles.* vi, 8) that Ignatius was the first to introduce this style of music in the Church of Antioch. It was certainly familiar to the Jews, who often sang responsively in the worship of the Temple. In some instances the

same style of singing may have been practiced too in the primitive Church. But responsive singing is not generally allowed to have been in frequent use during the first 300 years of the Christian æra. This mode of singing was then common in the theatres and temples of the Gentiles, and for this reason was generally discarded by the primitive Christians (Augusti, *Denkwürdigkeiten,* v, 278).

2. The appointment of *singers* as a distinct class of officers in the Church for this part of religious worship, and the consequent introduction of *profane music* into the church, marks another alteration in the psalmody of the Church. These innovations were first made in the 4th century; and though the people continued for a century or more to enjoy their ancient privilege of all singing together, it is conceivable that it gradually was forced to die, as a promiscuous assembly could not well unite in theatrical music which required in its performers a degree of skill altogether superior to that which all the members of a congregation could be expected to possess. An artificial, theatrical style of music, having no affinity with the worship of God, soon began to take the place of those solemn airs which before had inspired the devotions of his people. The music of the theatre was transferred to the church, which accordingly became the scene of theatrical pomp and display rather than the house of prayer and of praise, to inspire by its appropriate and solemn rites the spiritual worship of God. The consequences of indulging this depraved taste for secular music in the church are exhibited by Neander in the following extract: "We have to regret that both in the Eastern and the Western Church their sacred music had already assumed an artificial and theatrical character, and was so far removed from its original simplicity that even in the 4th century the abbot Pambo of Egypt complained that heathen melodies [accompanied as it seems with the action of the hands and the feet] had been introduced into their Church psalmody" (*Kirchengesch.* ii, 681; comp. *Scriptores Ecclesiastici, De Musica,* i [1784], 3). Isidore of Pelusium also complained of the theatrical singing, especially that of the women, which, instead of inducing penitence for sin, tended much more to awaken sinful desires (in *Biblioth. Patr.* vii, 543). Jerome also, in remarking upon Eph. v, 19, says: "May all hear it whose business it is to sing in the church. Not with the voice, but with the *heart,* we sing praises to God. Not like the comedians should they raise their sweet and liquid notes to entertain the assembly with theatrical songs and melodies in the church, but the fire of godly piety and the knowledge of the Scriptures should inspire our songs. Then would not the voice of the singers, but the utterance of the divine word, expel the evil spirit from those who, like Saul, are possessed with it. But, instead of this, that same spirit is invited rather to the possession of those who have converted the house of God into a pagan theatre" (*Comment. in Ep. Eph.* lib. iii, c. 5, tom. iv, p. 387 [ed. Martianæ]). Until the 6th or 7th century the people were not entirely excluded from participation in the psalmody of the Church, and many there were who continued to bear some part in it even after it had become a cultivated theatrical art, for the practice of which the singers were appointed as a distinct order of the Church, but it was mainly in the chorus or in responses that the people could have their part. Thus it soon came about that the many, instead of uniting their hearts and their voices in the songs of Zion, could only sit coldly by as spectators.

3. Heresy largely pervading the Church, and making rapid headway by incorporation into hymns which were the laity's property, various restrictions were from time to time laid upon the use of hymns of *human composition* in distinction from the inspired psalms of David; and finally the Church authorities, in order more effectually to resist all encroachments of heresy, were driven to the necessity either of cultivating and improving their own psalmody, or of opposing their authority to stay the

progress of this evil. The former was the expedient of Ambrose, Hilary, Gregory Nazianzen, Chrysostom, Augustine, etc. But the other alternative in turn was also attempted. The churches by ecclesiastical authority were restricted to the use of the Psalter and other canonical songs of the Scriptures. All hymns of merely human composition were prohibited as of a dangerous tendency and unsuitable to the purposes of public worship. The Synod of Laodicea (A.D. 344–346, c. 59) felt itself compelled to pass a decree to that effect. The decree was not, however, fully enforced; the clergy eventually claimed the right of performing the sacred music as a privilege *exclusively their own*. And finally, the more effectually to exclude the people, the singing was in Latin. Where that was not the vernacular tongue, this rule was of necessity an effectual bar to the participation of the people in this part of public worship. Besides, the doctrine was industriously propagated that the Latin was the appropriate language of devotion, which became not the profane lips of the laity in these religious solemnities, but only those of the clergy, who had been consecrated to the service of the sanctuary. This expedient shut out the people from any participation in this delightful part of public worship. The Reformation again restored to the people their ancient and inestimable right. At that time the greater part of the services of the Romish Church was sung to musical notes, and on the occasion of great festivals the choral service was performed with great pomp by a numerous choir of men and boys. That abuses of the most flagrant kind had found their way into this department of Romish worship is beyond a doubt, as the Council of Trent found it necessary to issue a decree on the subject, in which they plainly state that in the celebration of the mass, hymns, some of a profane and others of a lascivious nature, had crept into the service, and given great scandal to professors of the truth. But by this decree the council, while it arranged the choral service on a proper footing, freeing it from all extraneous matter, gave choral music also a sanction which it had hitherto wanted. From that time the Church of Rome began to display that profound veneration for choral music which it has continued to manifest down to the present day.

The Protestants at the Reformation differed on the subject of sacred music. The Lutherans in great measure adopted the Romish ritual, and retained the choral service. Some of the Reformed churches varied more widely from Rome than others. Calvin introduced a plain metrical psalmody, selecting for use in churches the version of the Psalms by Marot, which he divided into small portions, and appointed to be sung in public worship. This Psalter was bound up with the Geneva Catechism. When the Reformation was introduced into England, Henry VIII, himself a musician of considerable celebrity, showed his partiality for the choral service by retaining it. The cathedral musical service of the Reformed Church of England was framed by John Marbeck of Windsor, in a form little different from that which is at present in use. It is a curious fact that the ancient foundations of conventual, collegiate, and cathedral churches make no provision for an organist, but simply for canons, minor canons, and choristers. The first Act of Uniformity, passed in the reign of Edward VI, allowed the clergy either to adopt the plain metrical psalmody or to preserve the use of the choral service. The musical part of queen Elizabeth's liturgy is said to have been arranged by Parker, archbishop of Canterbury. The Puritans, however, objected strongly to the cathedral rites, particularly "the tossing the Psalms from one side to the other," as Cartwright sarcastically describes the musical service; and it was regarded as inconsistent with that beautiful simplicity which ought ever to characterize the ordinance of divine worship. The assaults made by Puritans upon the musical as well as other portions of the cathedral service were answered with great ability and power by Richard Hooker in his fa-

mous work on *Ecclesiastical Polity*, the first four books of which appeared in 1594, and the fifth in 1597. From the date of that masterly defence of the polity of the Church of England down to the present day no material change has taken place in the musical service of that Church. The Lutheran and Episcopal churches, both in Europe and America, have also a solemn service, while the Reformed Church, including the Presbyterian and Independent, have a plain selection of melodies to which the metrical Psalms, Paraphrases, and Hymns are set. There is almost universally a precentor or leader of the sacred music in the congregation, and in some cases a select choir or band of male and female voices, while the whole congregation is expected to join in this solemn part of the devotional exercises of the sanctuary. For a number of years past, while Romish churches in Europe and America have made a gorgeous display of their musical service, which is still divided between the chants of the priests and the theatrical performances of the choir, made up altogether, as a rule, of regularly trained musicians, vocal and instrumental, who have thus perverted most effectually the devotional ends of sacred music, the Protestant churches have aroused to a more careful training of their whole congregation in the art of sacred music, that this interesting and impressive part of divine worship may be conducted both with melody of the voice and of the heart unto the Lord. See, however, for details, especially on the innovations in the Protestant churches, the influence of sacred song as exhibited in recent times in revivals, the articles PSALMODY and REVIVAL.

III. *Use of Instruments in the Church.*—The Greeks as well as the Jews were wont to use instruments as accompaniments in their sacred songs. The converts to Christianity accordingly must have been familiar with this mode of singing; yet it is generally believed that the primitive Christians failed to adopt the use of instrumental music in their religious worship. The word $\psi\alpha\lambda\lambda\epsilon\hat{\imath}\nu$, which the apostle uses in Eph. v, 19, has been taken by some critics to indicate that they sang with such accompaniments. The same is supposed by some to be intimated by the golden harps which John, in the Apocalypse, put into the hands of the four-and-twenty elders. But if this be the correct inference, it is strange indeed that neither Ambrose (in *Psa. i, Præf.* p. 740), nor Basil (in *Psa. i,* vol. ii, p. 713), nor Chrysostom (*Psa. xli,* vol. v, p. 131), in the noble encomiums which they severally pronounce upon music, make any mention of instrumental music. Basil, indeed, expressly condemns it as ministering only to the depraved passions of men (*Hom.* iv, vol. i, p. 33), and must have been led to this condemnation because some had gone astray and borrowed this practice from the heathens. Thus it is reported that at Alexandria it was the custom to accompany the singing with the flute, which practice was expressly forbidden by Clement of Alexandria in A.D. 190 as too worldly, but he then instituted in its stead the use of the harp. In the time of Constantine the Great the Ambrosian chant (q. v.) was introduced, consisting of hymns and psalms sung, it is said, in the four first keys of the ancient Greek. The tendency of this was to *secularize* the music of the Church, and to encourage singing by a choir. The general introduction of instrumental music can certainly not be assigned to a date earlier than the 5th and 6th centuries; yea, even Gregory the Great, who towards the end of the 6th century added greatly to the existing Church music, absolutely prohibited the use of instruments. Several centuries later the introduction of the organ in sacred service gave a place to instruments as accompaniments for Christian song, and from that time to this they have been freely used with few exceptions. The first organ is believed to have been used in Church service in the 13th century. Organs were, however, in use before this in the theatre. They were never regarded with favor in the Eastern Church, and were vehemently opposed in some of the Western churches. In Scotland no organ is allowed to this day, except in a few Episcopal churches. See MUSIC, INSTRUMENTAL. In the English convocation held A.D. 1562, in queen Elizabeth's time, for settling the liturgy, the retaining of organs was carried only *by a casting vote.* See ORGAN.

IV. *Sacred Music as a Science.*—A certain sort of music seems to have existed in all countries and at all times. Even instrumental music is of a very early date; representations of musical instruments occur on the Egyptian obelisks and tombs. The Hindû, Chinese, and Japanese music is probably what it was thousands of years ago. The Chinese, whose music practically is unpleasant to refined ears, have some sweet-toned instruments, and a notation for the melodies played on them which is sufficiently clear. Their history and fables touching the art antedate by many centuries those of classic nations. The higher style of Oriental music, which has a limited degree of melodious merit, with rhythms logically and distinctly drawn from consociation with poetry as refined and liquid as the Italian, may be found in that of India, dating also from remotest antiquity. The poetical legends of Hindostan, and indeed of all Southern Asia, rival those of China and Greece in ascribing fabulous effects to music. The Hindûs consider every art as a direct revelation from heaven, and while their inferior deities communicated other arts, it was Brahma himself who presented music to mortals. The music of the Hebrews is supposed to have had a defined rhythm and melody. The Greeks numbered music among the sciences, and studied the mathematical proportions of sounds. Their music, however, was but poetry sung, a sort of musical recitation or intoning, in which the melodic part was a mere accessory. The Romans borrowed their music from the Etruscans and Greeks, and had both stringed instruments and wind instruments.

The music of modern Europe is a new art, to which nothing analogous seems to have existed among the nations of antiquity. We look therefore to the early music of the Christian Church, to whose fostering influence through several centuries the preservation and progress of art was due, for the foundation upon which the modern system is built. The early music of the Christian Church was probably in part of Greek and in part of Hebrew origin. The choral was at first sung in octaves and unisons. St. Ambrose and Gregory the Great (590–604) directed their attention to its improvement, and under them some sort of harmony or counterpoint seems to have found its way into the service of the Church. The latter was the father of the Gregorian chant, upon the broad foundation of which the music of the Church rested for several centuries. Further advances were made by Guido of Arezzo, to whom notation by lines and spaces is due; but the ecclesiastical music had still an uncertain tonality and an uncertain rhythm. Franco of Cologne, in the 13th century, first indicated the duration of notes by diversity of form. He and John of Muris in the following century contributed greatly to the more rapid progress of sacred music. It is during their period of Christian ecclesiastical life that modern music first attained the character of an art, by which the devout heart gives utterance to its emotions. Its style was at that time serious, grand, and full of expression only when taken as a whole; and as the Church would not renounce the few melodies which had long been used, art could exert its power only on the harmonies by which they were embellished. The consequence was that many imitators adopted an artificial, dry, and learned kind of music, which derived all its life from some secular airs mingled with it. The Synod of Trent entreated the pope that he would devise some plan by which this state of things might be improved. Marcellus II accordingly disclosed his views to an enthusiastic young man, and soon after, under the papacy of Paul IV, Palestrina presented to the world his *Missa Marcelli* (1555). This was the commencement of a revolution in sacred music, which by

his influence became simple, thoughtful, aspiring, sincere, and noble, but destitute of passion and tenderness. The most spiritual of all arts, it raised the heart into immediate communion with the Infinite, and, while celebrating the mystery of the divine sacrifice in the different parts of the mass to which it was especially set, it found opportunity to express and to elevate, by its various combinations of sounds, every kind of Christian feeling. The centre of this school was the papal chapel, and its last creative master was Gregorio Allegri († 1640), whose *Miserere*, composed for a double choir, expresses with wonderful simplicity all the calm and profound sufferings of a Christian heart beneath the Saviour's cross.

The invention of the organ, and its use in accompanying the choral, had a large share in the development of harmony. Along with the music of the Church, and independently of it, secular music was making gradual advances, guided more by the ear than by science; it seems to have had a more decided rhythm, though not indicated as yet by bars. The airs which have become national in different countries were developments of it, but it had its chief seat in Belgic Gaul; and the reconciliation of musical science with musical art, begun in Flanders by Josquin Deprès in the 15th century, was completed in the 17th century by Palestrina and his school at Rome, and reacted eventually on the ecclesiastical style. "Mediæval Church music," says Prof. Paine, "did not fulfil the entire mission of the art, for it failed to embrace within its scope of expression all the nature of man, leaving out an important element of artistic representation—his earthly acts and passions. It was reserved for secular music to supply this want. Music can also express outside of the Church the highest principles of religion and morality, as they influence the sentiments and actions of men. The Reformation of the 16th century was undoubtedly the means of giving a new impulse to the cultivation of secular music, which previously had been ignored and held in contempt by the educated musicians and ecclesiastics; and in Germany the Reformation was also the source of a new style of sacred music of popular origin. During the absolute reign of mediæval counterpoint the sense of melody which existed later in the songs of the troubadours and minnesingers, and other popular melodies of a very early date, was almost wholly lost, and consequently melody had to be discovered again, so to speak, about the year 1600. It was not the learned musicians, but mere dilettanti, who took these first steps on a new path. In Italy the increasing interest in ancient literature and art led to an ardent desire on the part of cultivated men to restore Greek tragedy. Enthusiasts painted its splendors in glowing colors. They believed that modern counterpoint could not compare with ancient music, either with respect to the simple beauty of the melody or the comprehensive clearness and rhetorical expression of the words. This idea of restoring the ancient drama and music was first advocated at the meetings of a society of scholars and artists at Florence. The names of Vincenzio Galilei, Caccini, Cavaliere, and Peri have come down to us as associated with these feeble beginnings of the musical drama. As the result of their efforts they unfolded a new element in music, the modern *recitative*, out of which the *air* was gradually developed. It is true the heavy and monotonous recitative which the Florentine dilettanti had introduced remained for a time a doubtful experiment; yet the love for dramatic representations helped to sustain the novelty until the advent of original masters, like Monteverde, Carestini, and, above all, Alessandro Scarlatti. Under their guidance the *recitative* grew more flexible and expressive; the dramatic action and lyric passion of the play were heightened by means of the orchestral accompaniment, and the true *arioso* style of singing was formed. Finally, the *air* sprang into life, and the æra of beautiful and sensuous melody was fairly inaugurated." The opera, which thus appeared nearly contemporaneously with the Reformation and revival of letters (about 1600), greatly enlarged the domain of music. Italy advanced in melody, and Germany in harmony. Instrumental music in this way came to occupy a more and more prominent place. Upon sacred music the influence of the opera was very marked. It brought about the introduction of solo singing and instrumental accompaniment into sacred music, and in consequence the strict ecclesiastical style was greatly modified. In the course of the 18th century Italian Church music had wandered so far away from the chaste ideal of Palestrina as to lose its sacred style almost wholly. These innovations in the field of music brought about a conflict with the old ecclesiastical style, which struggled in Rome to maintain its ground. The consequence was that the school of music founded by Neri began to perform in the oratorium pieces relating to subjects from sacred history. In this way came into existence the *oratorio*, intermediate between the ancient and modern styles of music, and more distinctly expressive of precise characters and situations, more agreeable in its melodies, and richer in its instrumental accompaniments (comp. Hase, *Ch. Hist.* p. 465). Not only on the Continent, but also in England, this species of sacred music made its way. During the changes introduced there in ecclesiastical music at the Restoration the school of Purcell (q. v.) had arisen. This paved the way for the oratorio, and a little later England adopted the German Handel, who was the precursor of Haydn, Mozart, Beethoven, Spohr, and Mendelssohn. These masters, though they exercised their gifts in almost every noble form of musical composition, dedicated their genius especially to the pure and sublime themes of religion. Handel's forty operas are almost forgotten; his long career as a dramatic composer, however, served as an excellent school for his faculties, and his triumphs in the field of oratorio music were but the natural fruits of his previous discipline. Handel's strength of character and sincere faith rendered him fully worthy as a man, as well as an artist, to create such works as the *Messiah* and *Israel in Egypt*. These masterpieces are not mere lyric and dramatic works; they possess a grand objective and ideal character, comparable only to the greatest works of art; to the Greek drama or the romantic tragedies of Shakespeare. But the oratorio we do not care to see regarded as the highest type and expression of modern Church music. As such the cantatas and passion music by Bach express more intensely and vividly than any other compositions a profound religious conviction. The *Passion to St. Matthew* has no rival in its special form. It is the most dramatic and vivid conception in art of the trial and death of Christ. Among hundreds of similar works, this is the only music that has lived.

Here it may most appropriately be stated that all sacred music since the 16th century must be divided into two general divisions, *choral* and *figurate* music. Choral music is, in its original form, Church singing only, in which the melody is solemnly slow. It is devoid of ornament, and not bound to a strict observance of time. Figurate music is the execution of religious pieces with accompaniment of instruments, and arose from the choral melodies arranged for four or more voices, and having for their theme hymns, psalms, or passages of Scripture. From the signs or figures used in the different parts, and which were not used in choral music, this style received the name of figurate. The organ was generally used in it to conduct and assist the voice, and subsequently stringed and wind instruments were gradually added. At first the instruments were used only to give the tone to the singers. At the Reformation the Calvinistic Church entirely rejected the use of instruments. The ancient Italian masters, such as Palestrina and Orlando di Lasso, composed no instrumental music. Yet Luther introduced the custom of having chorals executed by instruments. The general use of the organ for accompaniment dates from

about the year 1640. Figurate music and choir singing, as distinguished from congregational singing, appears already in the fugues and motets of the 14th century, in which, after one part had commenced the singing, it was taken up by a second, then by a third, a fourth, and finally taken up again by the first, and so on to the end. We find it also in many compositions of the times of the Reformation, as, for instance, in the festive songs of John Eccard († 1611). Hammerschmidt († 1675) gave to this style a fuller development, and entitled it by the name of madrigal. In Italy, in the 16th century, the appearance of the opera, as we have seen above, was not without influence on sacred music, which gradually acquired a more secular style. Besides, this also led to the use of musical instruments in the churches. From Italy the custom was introduced into Germany by John Prætorius († 1621) and Henry Schütz († 1762), and thus gave rise to the *cantate*, in which John Sebastian Bach particularly distinguished himself, and of which we have spoken above. By all these innovations it is believed the old solemn style of sacred music lost ground, and the oratorio itself gradually turned more to the opera. Mozart and Beethoven wrote sacred music in precisely the same style as operas. On the other hand, the Romish clergy did not better the position by returning to the ante-Palestrinan mode of chanting mass, and this was not without a certain influence again in making the sacred music of the Protestant churches more secular. The importance of instrumental music was also on the increase; overtures and dancing-tunes were often played on the organ before and after service. It is only with the revival of evangelical piety that a change commenced to be perceptible in sacred music: it was brought about mainly by the efforts of such composers as C. F. Becker, J. C. H. Rück, G. W. Körner, and by the collection of classical pieces for the organ published by Kocher, Silcher, and Frech in 1851. The ancient figurate pieces were also remodelled by such composers as Rück, A. W. Bach, C. G. Reissiger, Silcher, Frech, Palmer, etc. In this country Lowell Mason (q.v.) may be said to be the father of Christian Church music. He is certainly the founder of the American school of sacred song, though it should be borne in mind that our musicians, especially composers, are very largely influenced by European culture, particularly German. See Hawkins, *General Hist. of the Science and Practice of Music* (Lond. 1776; new ed. 1853, 2 vols. 4to); Burney, *Hist. of Music* (Lond. 1776–89, 4 vols. 4to); Forkel, *Geschichte d. Musik* (Leips. 1788, 2 vols.); Hullah, *Hist. of Mod. Music* (Lond. 1862); Fétis, *Hist. générale de la Musique* (Paris, 4 vols. out, but yet unfinished); Chappell, *Hist. of Music* (Lond. 1874 and sq., 4 vols.); Naumann, *Umgestaltung der Kirchenmusik* (1852); *Psalmengesang in der Evangel. Kirche* (1856); *Tonkunst in der Culturgesch.* (1869–70); Riddle, *Christian Antiquities*, p. 384–391; Bingham, *Origines Ecclesiasticæ*, p. 315 sq.; Thibaut, *Ueber Reinheit der Tonkunst* (Heidelb. 1826); Laurenzin, *Geschichte der Kirchenmusik bei d. Italienern u. Deutschen* (Leips. 1856); Mansi, xxix, 107; Wiseman, *The Offices of Holy Week* (Lond. 8vo); Fink, in *Zeitschrift. f. hist. Theologie*, 1842; Pierer, *Universal Lexikon*, ix, 507; Milman, *Hist. of Christianity* and *Latin Christianity*; Neander, *Ch. Hist.*; Schaff, *Ch. Hist.*; Baxter, *Eccles. Hist. of England*, p. 263; *Ch. and World*, 1867, art. ix; Brand, *Pop. Antiquities in Great Britain*, ii, 267 sq.; Hardwick, *Hist. of the Reformation*, p. 387–389; Hase, *Hist. of the Christian Church*, p. 153, 465, 675; and especially Coleman, *Man. of Prelacy and Ritualism*, ch. xii; *Lond. Qu. Rev.* April, 1861, art. ii; July, 1871, art. v.; Oct. 1872, art. i; *Cath. World*, March, 1870, art. iii; *For. Qu. Rev.* xx, 29 sq.; xxiii, 121-248; Grove, *Dict. of Music and Musicians* (Lond. 1872–88, 2 vols. 8vo.).

Music, INSTRUMENTAL. As there are many Christians who hold that the use of instrumental music in the sacred services of the Church does not find its warrant in the New-Testament Scriptures, we here append an article on this negative position. We add a few arguments on the affirmative. Following so closely after the historical discussion furnished above, the inquiring student will be the better able to judge for himself whether instrumentals can be used in *Christian* worship.

I. Against the use of instruments in Christian churches the following reasons may be urged:

1. *There is no warrant in the New Testament for their use.* (*a*) There is no example of such by Peter, Paul, John, James, or the Master himself, nor by any others in the apostolic age; nor have we any in the first three centuries; nor until the mystery of iniquity was strongly at work. (*b*) We have no command either to make or to use them. It is claimed that $\psi\acute{a}\lambda\lambda o\nu\tau\epsilon\varsigma$ in Eph. v, 19 requires playing on strings; but that is expressly declared to be done in the heart. (See in a following paragraph.) (*c*) We find no directions, formal or incidental, for their use; while we have line upon line about singing—what to sing, when to sing, how to sing.

2. *Instruments were not used in the worship of the ancient synagogue.* They belonged to the tabernacle and the Temple, especially the latter; but were never in the congregational assemblies of God's people. The trumpet and other loud instruments were used in the synagogue, not to accompany the psalm, but in celebrating certain feasts (Lev. xxv, 9; Numb. x, 10; Psa. lxxxi, 3). There was a feast of trumpets (Lev. xxiii, 24; Numb. xxix, 1). They were used for proclamation, in going to war, in moving the camps, in assembling the congregations, as well as in triumphs, coronations, and other extraordinary occasions (Numb. x, 1–10; Lev. xxv, 9; 1 Kings i, 34; Joel ii, 1; Jer. vi, 1, et al.). Such celebrations resembled our day of Independence, but were much more devotional, and withal ceremonial in their meaning. Conrad Iken tells us that the Sabbath-day was introduced with blowing trumpets at the synagogues six times. At the first blast they dropped the instruments of husbandry, and returned home from the field. This was on Friday evening, as we call it. At the second blast they closed all offices, shops, and places of business. At the third blast pots were removed from the fire, and culinary occupation was suspended. The other three blowings were to designate the line between common and sacred time. All of these uses, though connected with the worship, were entirely different from the psalmody in which they were used at the Temple: but (*a*) No hint is given in Old Testament or New that instruments were ever used in the synagogue worship. (*b*) Orthodox Jews do not allow the organ or any other instrument in their synagogues; only Reformed or Liberal Jews have introduced the organ and many other innovations. (*c*) Archæologists (Prideaux, Jahn, Calmet, Townsend, etc.) make no mention of instruments in the worship, while they describe minutely the furniture of the synagogue; and Hahn particularly notices the singing of the doxologies, such as Psa. lxxii, 18; lxviii, 1; xcvi, 6; and cxiii, 1. Iken gives four doxologies for the Sabbath, but no organ or harp.

3. *The early Reformers, when they came out of Rome, removed them as the monuments of idolatry.* Luther called the organ an ensign of Baal; Calvin said that instrumental music was not fitter to be adopted into the Christian Church than the incense and the candlestick; Knox called the organ a kist [chest] of whistles. The Church of England revived them, against a very strong protest, and the English dissenters would not touch them.

4. *The instruments of the former economy were ceremonial.* This is probably the chief reason for their use in the Temple. They were not merely figurative, like bread, water, wine, light; nor merely typical, like Isaac, David, Solomon, and the manna; they were figurative, typical, and ceremonial, as appears thus: (*a*) They depended largely on the priesthood. The trumpet was the leading instrument—master of the whole; this belonged exclusively to the priests (Numb. x, 8, 9; xxxi, 6; Josh. vi, 4; 2 Chron. xiii, 12, 14). The smaller in-

struments belonged to the Levites, whose station was adjoining the priests (1 Chron. xxiii, 28; xxv, 1–8). In the worship, as well as in celebrations, both were combined (1 Kings i, 39, 40; 1 Chron. xv, 14–28; 2 Chron. v, 12, et al.). Thus all were made to depend on the priesthood. (*b*) They were combined over the sacrifices (see especially Numb. x, 10; xxix, 1, 2, etc.; 1 Chron. xv, 26; 2 Chron. vii, 5, 6; xxix, 26–28; xxx, 21, etc.; Ezra iii, 4, 5, 10, 11; Neh. xii, 43; comp. ver. 27, 35, 36, 41, 45–47). (*c*) They belonged to the national worship of the peculiar people (Exod. xv, 20; 2 Sam. vi, 5, 15): "All the house of Israel" (1 Chron. xiii, 5, 8; xv, 3, 28; 2 Kings iii, 13–15; Psa. lxviii, 25). So it had been arranged from the first (1 Chron. xxv, 1–8), and so carried out to the last (Neh. xii, 45). Incidental events, as well as set forms, show the same connection: the "company" in 1 Sam. x, 5 were coming down from the high-place, and those in Isa. xxx, 29 are going up to it. David's individual harp was like his songs, a preparation for the Temple; and the incident of 2 Kings iii, 15 was a national affair. Hence (*d*), even when introduced as symbols in the Apocalypse, they are grouped with their usual ceremonial accompaniments. Trumpets are not there presented as part of the music, though prominent for other uses. The "harpers" have their "vials full of odors," stand with the Lamb that had been slain, are on the sea of glass, and sing the song of Moses and the Lamb. They have their Mount Zion, their twelve tribes, their city of Jerusalem, their Temple and its pillars, their seven candlesticks, ark of the covenant, altar of incense, golden censer, pot of manna, cherubim, white robes, palm-branches, with other things which have passed away together; according to Heb. vii, 12, "The priesthood being changed, there is made, $\dot{\epsilon}\xi\ \dot{a}\nu\acute{a}\gamma\kappa\eta\varsigma$ (of necessity), a change also of the law." The use—valid use—of all these things ceased when Christ yielded up his spirit on the cross. The very sanctum sanctorum was thrown open when the veil was rent. The Christian Church carried her singing not from the Temple, but from the synagogue. See SYNAGOGUE.

5. *Instrumental music is incompatible with directions for singing given in the N. T.* (*a*) Heb. xiii, 15: "Let us offer the sacrifice of praise, that is, the fruit of the lips." This exhortation is given in terms of the O. T. (Psa. l, 14; lxix, 30, 31; cxvi, 17; Hos. xiv, 2, Sept.), yet the formal definition of praise makes it the production of the lips, not of the organ. (*b*) Eph. v, 19: "Singing and making melody ($\psi\acute{a}\lambda\lambda o\nu\tau\epsilon\varsigma$, *touching the chords*) in the heart to the Lord." Praise requires more than the mere "talk of the lips" (Prov. xiv, 23); but the accompaniment is not an instrument in the hand, but a living organ of some sort. (*c*) Col. iii, 16: "Singing with grace in your hearts to the Lord." In this passage "grace" answers exactly to $\psi\acute{a}\lambda\lambda o\nu\tau\epsilon\varsigma$— "touching the chords" in the heart; both passages harmonize in requiring something besides the voice, as do many others. But that something is not a machine in the hand. What is it? What was symbolized by all these cymbals, organs, harps, trumpets—these "things without life giving sound?" The general idea of Christian people is that they all were intended to represent grace in the heart—the working of a regenerated soul in gratitude to God. Hence the martyr's exclamation, "O for a well-tuned harp!" and the prayers of godly people for their hearts to be put in "tune." John Bunyan's account of Mr. Fearing, who was always playing on the base, with many such allusions, chime in exactly with the whole idea of acceptable worship (John iv, 24, "in spirit and in truth;" 1 Cor. xiv, 15, "I will sing with the spirit").

This idea is supported by the following considerations: (*a*) In the passages above cited "grace" in one answers to "melody" in the other, and both are in the heart. (*b*) This "melody," this "grace," is different from the "singing"—superadded to the "fruit of the lips." (*c*) The "harps" hold the same relation to praise that the vials of "odors" do to prayer. 1 Cor. xiv, 15: "I will pray with the spirit" (Psa. cxli, 2; Rev. v, 8; viii, 3, 4). (d) They are eminently adapted to represent "grace" in a variety of aspects. Take the following (with the trumpet as used in proclamation we have no concern here, but with the instruments of praise): (1) They represent grace as it deals with the deepest moving of the affections, both in sorrow and joy. In Isa. xv and xvi we have the workings of pity, even to hopeless commiseration, winding up with this: "My bowels shall sound like a harp for Moab;" and like expressions, lxiii, 15; Jer. iv, 19; xlviii, 36; xxxi, 20, margin; comp. Jer. xxxi, 4 with Job xvii, 6. They combine the deepest mixture of sorrow and joy (Gen. xxxi, 27; Ezra iii, 10). The change of feeling is sometimes very sudden (Job xxx, 31; 1 Chron. xiii, 8–11; Rev. xviii, 19–22). The same sound will give sorrow to one and joy to another at the same time (1 Sam. xviii, 6–9; Psa. xcvi, 9–13; xcviii, 6–9, with Rev. i, 7). (2) They represent the countless variety of gracious experiences, with their wide range of degrees and imperfections, from Bunyan's "Mr. Fearing" up through tenor, alto, and treble, with leger-line above the clouds (2 Tim. iv, 6–8). The combinations of musical notes amount to millions of millions. The harp of a thousand strings is a low approximation to playing on the chords of the heart to the Lord. (3) They represent grace especially in its pleasurable aspects—pleasing and being pleased (Psa. xcii, 1–4). Godly sorrow is real sorrow; the harp has a solemn sound when played on the base. Still the power predominating, both in music and in grace, is joy (Rev. xiv, 3; xv, 3). During the battle, long before the triumph, the tabret and harp are heard amid the din of war (Isa. xxx, 32). The believer is sometimes a captive, and then he suspends his harp on the willow, because for the time he has no joy (Psa. cxxxvii, 2). In every case short of this he can joyfully touch the chords in the heart (Isa. xxxviii, 20; Hab. iii, 17–19). (4) They represent all this grace in the heart as something that has been put there (Psa. iv, 7). The natural melody of the soul is lost in the fall—the strings are broken: "Ye must be born again." The Ethiopian treasurer, when born of water and of the Spirit, went on his way rejoicing. Spiritual joy is not natural, but gracious; neither is it unnatural, it fits the place; it is supernatural, restoring the soul to its original, and with greater security (Isa. xxxv, 10, "Everlasting joy upon their heads"). Ezek. xxviii, 13 gives some insight into this matter: "The workmanship of thy tabrets and of thy pipes," etc. There is textual difficulty here of no ordinary breadth; but whether the personage addressed be Ithobal, or Adam, or Abaddon, it illustrates the case in hand; each had the power of music concreated with him—especially Lucifer, son of the morning. There was a time when the morning-stars sang together, Apollyon with the rest. Such tabrets and pipes must have been of a spiritual nature, as they were of exquisite "workmanship" (Eph. ii, 10, "We are his workmanship, created in Christ Jesus unto good works;" so also Gal. vi, 15; v, 6). The new creation produces the faith which works by love, and harmonizes the music of Moses and the Lamb (Psa. cxix, 54; xl, 8; Rom. vii, 22; Heb. x, 9). The renewed soul sings that song which no other can learn. Such a one has the melody belonging to instruments of very honorable name (1 Chron. xvi, 42; 2 Chron. vii, 6; Rev. xv, 2; Isa. xxxviii, 20; Hab. iii, 19; Psa. lvii, 7, "My heart is prepared—I will sing and $\psi \alpha \lambda \tilde{\omega}$," Sept.). (5) They represent grace in its perfection—the sublimity of heavenly joy. Light has its own kind of sublimity; hence we read of "the inheritance of the saints in light." Light reveals objects at a distance; music carries us away. Music is incomplete unless voice and harp go together. Ezekiel's mellifluous oratory could not be illustrated by the one without the other (Ezek. xxxiii, 32). The Temple music represented very fitly the joy of that house where the sweet Singer will preside, the glory of which eye hath not seen nor ear heard; it is "reserved;" yet it is "prepared" for them that love him; where song and harp and organ blend with sweet odors; while they sweep the chords of the heart to the Lord.

II. *In favor of Instrumental Music for Churches*, it may be replied that the above considerations, however plausible in general and often beautiful in sentiment, are rather speculative than logical. But more particularly, it is not sufficient to show that such performances were not customary or known in the sacred services of the primitive Christians; if we would authoritatively exclude them, it must be proved that the N. T. positively forbids, or by direct implication discountenances them. There are many practices of modern times which are perfectly lawful, proper, expedient, and edifying, which were not known in the earliest days of Christianity. Such an argument would reprobate Sunday-schools and numerous well-approved institutions of the present day. Our Saviour and his apostles purposely left all these immaterial questions and detailed arrangements discretionary with the Church, and it is best they should so remain. Times change, and religious observances, where not absolutely prescribed, must be modified accordingly.

We might justly add, under this head, that there is no positive proof, after all, that instrumental music did not in any case accompany the songs of the early Christians. The evidence *a silentio* is always insecure. Indeed the reasoning above is not altogether conclusive on this very point. The presumption is certainly the other way, for it can hardly be presumed that persons who had always been accustomed to associate instrumental music with the services of the sanctuary—as was the case at least with the Hebrews, who formed the nucleus and dominant element of the infant Church—would have suddenly and totally abjured this delightful and inspiring part of divine worship under a new economy, unless there had been some express prohibition or absolute incompatibility respecting it. On the contrary, such an accompaniment has been found in all ages a decided stimulus to devotion, and a powerful auxiliary to the strains of vocal melody. It is so congenial with the spirit of Christianity that the most remarkable and sublime efforts of genius in this field have been those of Christian composers and Christian performers.

Finally, therefore, to interdict these concomitants of congregational worship is a mistake savoring of asceticism and iconoclasm. It is, moreover, a scientific blunder, as well as an æsthetic degeneration. If the O.-T. saint could profitably employ instrumental music as a means of grace, why should it be denied the Christian? If David's soul took wing with celestial vigor as he strung his lyre in accord with his devout lays, why may not the modern saint refresh his soul with the ravishing harmonies of the organ? The immortal productions of Mozart and others require the full orchestra to bring out their grandest effects, and even the ordinary songs of the Church are greatly enhanced in their power over the heart when properly accompanied from the choir. The human voice itself is but one instrument of music; and the experience of the truest and purest believers in every age, whether in high or low condition, has attested the healthful and edifying influence of instrumental symphony, when duly subjected as a handmaid to sacred lyrics and vocal execution.

Musical Instruments OF THE HEBREWS. The obscurity attaching to this subject has long been felt and complained of. The rabbins themselves know no more of this matter than other commentators who are least acquainted with Jewish affairs. The older writers on the subject had no means of assisting their speculations by examining any representations of the actual instruments in use, either among the Hebrews themselves or in the neighboring nations. But much light has of late been thrown, by the discovery of Egyptian and Assyrian monuments, upon the instruments which were used by these two great peoples—the nearest neighbors of the Hebrews, and with whom, at different periods of their history, they came into close and long-continued contact; and we have now the advantage of being able to infer, with a high degree of probability, if not with absolute certainty, from these collateral examples what were the forms and powers of at least the principal instruments referred to in the Hebrew Scriptures. This recent enlargement of our knowledge, however, still leaves much room for further light, especially in regard to the precise instruments intended by particular Hebrew words. There is yet much difference of opinion among Hebrew scholars and antiquarians upon this point of primary importance; and indeed, in the absence of all direct means of identification, and of any clear and steady tradition among the Jews themselves upon the matter, it is hardly to be expected that the obscurity which still encumbers this part of the subject can ever be entirely removed. We see certain instruments different from our own in use among the modern Orientals, and we infer that the Hebrew instruments were probably not unlike these, because the Orientals change but little, and we recognise in them the peoples, and among them the habits and the manners described in the Bible. We find also many instruments presented in the sculptures of Greece and Rome, and we need not refuse to draw inferences from them, for they derived their origin from the East, and the Romans distinctly refer then to Syria (Juvenal, *Sat.* iii; Livy, *Hist.* xxxix, 5). When, however, we endeavor to identify with these a particular instrument named by the Hebrews, our difficulty begins, because the Hebrew names are seldom to be recognised in those which they *now* bear, and because the Scriptures afford us little information respecting the form of the instruments which they mention.

I. *Stringed Instruments.*—We begin with these, because upon almost all occasions of the use of instrumental music, either in public or private, we find them occupying the principal place; while in point of antiquity of date they were not inferior apparently to other instruments of a simpler and ruder character

chief varieties of this class of instruments may be arranged as follows:

1. The כִּנּוֹר, *kinnôr*, commonly translated in our version *harp;* in the Sept. κιθάρα; Chald. כִּתָּרָא; Dan. iii, 5, 10, קִיתָרֹס. This is the stringed instrument ascribed to the invention of Jubal, and the only one referred to by Laban in his remonstrance with Jacob (Gen. xxxi, 27). It is mentioned among the instruments used by the sons of the prophets in their schools (1 Sam. x, 5); and it was the favorite instrument of David, of which he became so celebrated a master. In the first ages the *kinnor* was consecrated to joy and exultation, hence the frequency of its use by David and others in praise of the divine Majesty. It is thought probable that the instrument received some improvements from David (comp. Amos vi, 5). In bringing back the ark of the covenant (1 Chron. xvi, 5), as well as afterwards at the consecration of the Temple, the *kinnor* was assigned to players of known eminence, chiefly of the family of Jeduthun (1 Chron. xxv, 3). Isaiah mentions it as used at festivals along with the *nebel;* he also describes it as carried round by Bayaderes from town to town (xxiii, 16), and as increasing by its presence the joy of vintage (xxiv, 8). When Jehoshaphat obtained his great victory over the Moabites, the triumphal entry into Jerusalem was accompanied by the *nebel* and the *kinnor* (2 Chron. xx, 27, 28). The sorrowing Jews of the captivity, far removed from their own land and the shadow of the sanctuary, hung their *kinnors* upon the willows by the waters of Babylon, and refused to sing the songs of Zion in a strange land (Psa. cxxxvii, 2). Many other passages of similar purport might be adduced in order to fix the uses of an instrument, the name of which occurs so often in the Hebrew Scriptures. They mostly indicate occasions of joy, such as jubilees and festivals. Of the instrument itself the Scripture affords us little further information than that it was composed of the sounding parts of good wood, and furnished with strings. David made it of the *berosh* wood, or cypress ("fir"); Solomon of the more costly *algum* (2 Sam. vi, 5; 2 Kings x, 12); and

Various forms of Egyptian Harps.—Rosellini.

(Gen. iv, 21). The common name for all such instruments in Hebrew is נְגִינוֹת (*neginóth*), from a root denoting *to strike*, like the Greek root ψάλλω, *to strike*, which yields in like manner ψαλτήριον, with a like general meaning. But in this genus were included a great variety of species of stringed instruments, some of which are of constant occurrence in the Old Testament; while others are limited to those books which belong to the period of the Babylonish captivity, and are to be regarded rather as Babylonian than Hebrew instruments. Keeping this distinction in view, the

Josephus mentions some composed of the mixed metal called electrum. He also asserts that it was furnished with ten strings, and played with a plectrum (*Ant.* xi, 12, 3), which however is not understood to imply that it never had any other number of strings, or was always played with the plectrum. David certainly played it with the hand (1 Sam. xvi, 23; xviii, 10; xix, 9), and it was probably used in both ways, according to its size.

Kitto (*Pict. Bible*, note on Psa. xliii, 4) demurs to its being regarded as a *harp*, and argues at great length in favor of its being a *lyre*; the chief difference of these two being that, while in the harp the strings were free on both sides throughout their whole length, in the lyre they were carried in part over the face of the sounding-board, and could in that part of their length only be struck on one side with one of the hands. But it is obvious that a difference of this kind was only a modification of form, and did not involve any essential difference in the principles of construction. The main principle of construction was the same in both instruments, viz. the production of differences of sound by differences in the length of the strings, whatever modifications of form might be used in order to obtain this difference of length, and whatever modifications of size and shape might be called for, when the instrument was to vary in power, and according as it was to be employed either in solo or in choir. The lyre was only a modification of the harp. Even in Greek the words κιθάρα and λύρα were anciently used convertibly, as Dr. Kitto admits; and it is highly improbable that the Hebrew word *kinnor* did not originally include all instruments of the harp kind, whatever might be their differences in size or shape, or subordinate arrangement. Harps for single use would usually be made portable and light. Those intended for choral performances in the Temple service would probably be made large and powerful, so as to stand upon the ground when played instead of being carried. Some would have a larger, some a smaller number of strings, according to the degree of perfection wanted. In point of fact all these varieties are actually to be found upon the Egyptian monuments, and we see no good reason why the same generic name might not be applied to them all. The most eminent lexicographers are clearly of this mind. While Gesenius defines *kinnor* to be a species of harp or lyre, and Fürst renders it by the single word harp, Winer expresses himself in such a way as to indicate an opinion that the Hebrew instrument so named might be either harp, lyre, or lute. Engel leans to the same opinion as Dr. Kitto, but does not appear to have added anything to the arguments by which the latter has sought to support it. "It is uncertain," he thinks (p. 281), "which of the Hebrew names of the stringed instruments occurring in the Bible really designates the harp." Still he thinks also that the *kinnor*, the favorite instrument of king David, was most likely a lyre; although he owns in another place (p. 310) "that the reasons which can be given in support" of this opinion "are certainly far from conclusive." When he urges that the *kinnor* was a light and very portable instrument; that king David, according to the rabbinic records, used to suspend it during the night over his pillow; and that all its uses mentioned in the Bible are especially applicable to the lyre rather than to the harp—these considerations are all such as have already been fully met in the observations made above; and it is answer enough to them to refer the reader to the accompanying monumental illustrations, which make it plain and certain that the harps of ancient nations were extremely various in size and power, and that some of their varieties were as light and portable as the lyre itself.

The approximate illustrations of the *kinnor*, or harp, supplied by the Egyptian and Assyrian monuments are very copious and interesting, and we cannot err far in supposing the various modifications of the Hebrew instrument to have been substantially the same as those in use among their neighbors. The most ancient form of the *kinnor* was probably the bent or curved form, agreeably to the etymology of the name, which according to Fürst (*Hebräisches und Chaldäisches Handwörterbuch*) is derived from a root signifying to make in the shape of a bow or curve. Egyptian harps of this shape are represented in the first of the accompanying illustrations (p. 764), and are remarkable for their differences of size, arrangement, and power, two of the specimens having as many as thirteen strings, one nine, and one

only three; while one is light and portable, and the rest so large and heavy as to require to rest on the ground. It was by a natural transition that the curved form gave way in many cases to the triangular, such as we see in our next series of illustrations. Nearly resembling these ancient Egyptian forms of the portable

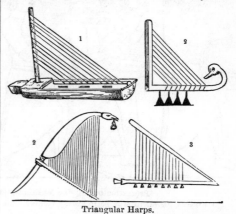

Triangular Harps.
Fig. 1. Ancient Egyptian Harp (from instrument in Egypt. Mus., Florence). Fig. 2, 2. Ancient Egyptian Harps (Wilkinson). Fig. 3. Persian *Chang* (from Persian MS. 410 years old).—Lane's *Arabian Nights.*

harp is the shape of the ancient Persian *chang* and the Arabic *junk* of the present day; and we are disposed to agree with Engel that this triangular instrument is most likely the *trigonon*, or triangle, mentioned by several classical authors. "Burney," he remarks, "in his *History of Music*, gives a drawing of a trigonon with ten strings. He observes that it is called by Sophocles a Phrygian instrument, and that a certain musician, of the name of Alexander Alexandrinus, was so admirable a performer upon it, that when exhibiting his skill in Rome he created the greatest *furore*. Burney further remarks, 'The performer being a native of Alexandria, as his name implies, makes it probable that it was an Egyptian instrument upon which he gained his reputation at Rome'—an opinion which is corroborated by the discovery of the instrument shown in our engraving. The representations, it is true, of the Grecian trigonon, given in our histories of music, exhibit it in the shape of a Greek *delta*, with three bars. In the Egyptian instruments the third bar, it will be observed, is wanting; but no ancient examples have been produced of the trigonon with three bars, and the representations referred to are probably only imaginary." Perhaps we have a still nearer approximation to the Hebrew harp in the two triangular instruments from the Assyrian sculptures. These harps are of very frequent occurrence on these Oriental monuments, showing that this form of the instrument was a favorite one. One of the two represented on the following page has twenty-one strings, the other has twenty-two strings; and it is a remarkable difference of construction as compared with the Egyptian specimens that the sounding-board forms the upper part of the instrument instead of the lower, while the reader will also observe openings for the escape of the sound. The ancient harp was sometimes played with a plectrum; but in all the Egyptian and Assyrian specimens now given it will be noticed that no plectrum occurs, but the instruments are all played with the hands, as we always figure to ourselves David handling his favorite harp. This Assyrian harp is probably the nearest approximation to the harp of the royal psalmist which we shall ever be able to reach. Remembering that the *kinnor* is one of the instruments mentioned by Laban as in common use in the country of Aram, we cannot but suppose that the harp which was used by the descendants of Jacob bore a closer resemblance to those which are figured upon the monuments of Mesopotamia than to those of the Egyptian monuments. See HARP.

Procession of Assyrian Musicians, their followers clapping hands in time.

Figs. 1 and 4. Assyrian Harps; 2. Double Flute; 3. Dulcimer. (Bass-relief of triumph of Sardanapalus over the Susians, British Museum.)

2. The נֵבֶל, *nébel*, probably the Greek ναβλίον (νά-βλα, νάβλη, ναύλα, or νάβλας) and the Latin *nablium* (*nablum* or *nabla*). The word is rendered "psaltery" in the A. V., in imitation of the Sept. translation of the Psalms and Nehemiah, which renders it by ψαλτήριον, with the exception of ψάλμος in Psa. lxxi, 22, and κιθάρα in Psa. lxxxi, 2. The Septuagint in the other books in which the word occurs renders it by νάβλα or, with a different ending, νάβλον. The Greek rendering ψαλτήριον evidently connects this instrument with the Chaldee פְּסַנְתְּרִין of Dan. iii, 5, 7. The first mention of it is in the reign of Saul (1 Sam. x, 5), and from that time forward we continue to meet with it in the O. T. It is, however, not found in the 2d chapter of Daniel, where mention is made of so many instruments; whence we may infer either that it did not exist among the Babylonians, or was known among them by another name. It was played upon by several persons in the grand procession at the removal of the ark (1 Chron. xv, 16; xvi, 5); and in the final organization of the Temple music it was intrusted to the families of Asaph, Heman, and Jeduthun (1 Chron. xxv, 1–7); Asaph, however, was only the overseer of the nebelists, as he himself played on a different instrument. Out of the worship of God it was employed at festivals and for luxurious purposes (Amos vi, 5). In the manufacture of this instrument a constant increase of splendor was exhibited. The first we meet with were made simply of the wood of the *berosh* (2 Sam. vi, 5; 1 Chron. xiii, 8), others of the rarer *algum* tree (1 Kings x, 12; 2 Chron. ix, 11), and some perhaps of metal (Josephus, *Ant.* i, 8, 3), unless the last is to be understood of particular parts of the instrument.

The *nebel* was an instrument apparently much resembling the *kinnor* in its nature and properties, though considerably different in form. According to Josephus (*Ant.* vii, 12, 13) it had twelve strings, which were played upon with the hand. One variety of it had only ten strings, and was distinguished as נֵבֶל עָשׂוֹר; and from an expression in Isa. xxii, 24 — כָּל־כְּלֵי־הַנְּבָלִים, all manner of *nebel* instruments—we gather that the instrument, like the harp, was used in various sizes and shapes. What its distinctive form was—preserved, no doubt, in the main, in all its varieties—cannot be determined with certainty. The etymology of the name, like that of *kinnor*, suggests a curved shape like that of a leathern bottle; but whether it was so called because the whole instrument was of this shape—

like the lyre, which is occasionally described by the Latin poets as the *lyra curva*—or because only a part of it was thus curved, viz. the sounding-board, as in the lute or guitar, it is impossible to decide. It is here we begin to feel the difficulty before referred to of identifying the Hebrew names with particular instruments. Kitto, as already noticed, pleads strongly for identifying it with the harp, while assigning the name *kinnor* to the lyre; but ancient authorities are opposed to this view, and he lands himself in the difficulty of being unable to find any Hebrew name at all for the lute or guitar, which he notwithstanding admits to have been in common use along with the lyre and harp. We cannot see, moreover, that anything is gained or any difficulty removed by adopting this opinion. We prefer to leave it a doubtful question whether the *nebel* was a lyre or a lute, or even some other form of stringed instrument, like that, for example, represented in the above illustration, derived from the Assyrian monuments. The only certain proof we possess of a lyre-like instrument having been in use among the Hebrews is the adjoining figure upon a coin of the times of the Maccabees. That either lutes or stringed instruments resembling the Assyrian ones just alluded to were employed by the Hebrews is a matter only of probable inference, from the fact that such instruments

Jewish Lyre. (British Museum.)

were in common use among the neighboring nations; we have no direct proof of it. Examples of lyres of various shapes and capabilities are shown on the monu-

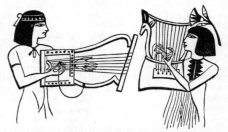

Egyptian Lyres: Fig. 1. Played with plectrum; 2. Played with fingers. (Paintings at Thebes.)

ments of Egypt and Assyria. To these we may add illustrations of Assyrian and Egyptian lutes or guitars. It need only be added that the *nebel* of Palestine and

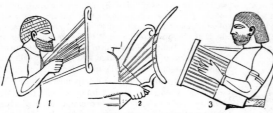

Assyrian Lyres: Figs. 1, 2. Sculptures from Kouyunjik (British Museum); 3. From Botta's *Nineve*.

the East must have had some considerable differences in form and properties from either the classical lyre or lute, as it was known and distinguished among the Greeks and Romans by its Oriental name, which the Greeks slightly altered into $\nu\acute{\alpha}\beta\lambda\alpha$ or $\nu\acute{\alpha}\beta\lambda\iota o\nu$, and the Romans into *nablium*. See PSALTERY.

3. The סַבְּכָא, *sabbekâ*, or "sackbut" of our version, is the third instrument in the list in Dan. iii, 5, 7. That this was a stringed instrument is certain, for the name passed over into Greek and Latin in the forms $\sigma\alpha\mu\beta\acute{\nu}\kappa\eta$ and *sambuca;* female performers on it from the East, called $\sigma\alpha\mu\beta\acute{\nu}\kappa\alpha\iota$, *sambucinæ*, and *sambucistriæ* by the classical authors, visited the cities of Europe, and found their way as far as Rome; and the instrument is de-

Assyrian Lute. (Terra-cotta figure in British Museum.)

Egyptian Lutes. (Painting from a tomb at Thebes, British Museum.)

scribed by Athenæus (iv, 175; xiv, 633) as a harp-like instrument of four or more strings, and of a triangular form. Now it is remarkable that one of the musical instruments most frequently occurring in the Assyrian sculptures answers very closely to this description. On comparing the instrument here represented with that

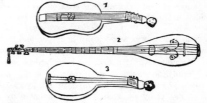

Sackbut. (Assyrian bass-relief, British Museum.)

exhibited in the procession above, a difference of structure will be observed, viz. that in the latter the strings seem to be carried over a *bridge*, which is not the case

with the former. In other respects the two forms are exactly the same; and the instrument was evidently a peculiarly Assyrian one, as there is nothing resembling it to be found on the Egyptian monuments or in the sculptures of Greece and Rome. This appears to us a decisive consideration in favor of identifying it with the sackbut of Dan. iii, 5, rather than with the same list, the word סוּמְפֹּנְיָה (*symphonia*) the word translated *dulcimer* in our version. This latter name is evidently borrowed from the Greek, and as such was no doubt the name of a Greek and not a native instrument; whereas the name and the nature of the sackbut were both probably Oriental, as the instrument figured in these Assyrian sculptures indubitably was. What the *symphonia* itself was it is impossible to say. It is worth mentioning that one of the musicians performing upon what we thus presume to have been the sackbut, is distinguished from the rest by a peculiar head-dress, which may probably have been a mark of distinction assigned to "the chief of the musicians" at the Assyrian court, an officer who was the counterpart of the Hebrew מְנַצֵּחַ, such as Asaph or Jeduthun. See SACKBUT.

Chief of Musicians. (Assyrian sculptures, British Museum.)

4. The גִּתִּית, *gittîth*, a word which occurs in the titles to Psa. viii, lxxxi, lxxxiv, and is generally supposed to denote a musical instrument. From the name it has been supposed to be an instrument which David brought from Gath; and it has been inferred from Isa. xvi, 10 that it was in particular use at the vintage season. If an instrument of music, it is remarkable that it does not occur in the list of the instruments assigned by David to the Temple musicians; nor even in that list which appears in verses 1 and 2 of Psa. lxxxi, in the title of which it is found. The supposition of Gesenius, that it is a general name for *a stringed instrument*, obviates this difficulty. The Sept. renders the title by $\acute{\nu}\pi\grave{\epsilon}\rho$ $\tau\tilde{\omega}\nu$ $\lambda\eta\nu\tilde{\omega}\nu$, "upon the wine-press;" and Carpzov, Pfeiffer, and others follow this in taking the word to denote a song composed for the vintage or for the Feast of Tabernacles (Carpzov, *Observ. Philol. super Psalmos Tres* עַל־הַגִּתִּית [Helmst. 1758]; Pfeiffer, *Ueber die Musik*, p. 32). See GITTITH.

5. מִנִּים, *minnim*, which occurs in Psa. xlv, 8 and cl, 4, is supposed by some to denote a stringed instrument, but it seems merely a poetical allusion to the *strings* of any instrument. Thus in Psa. xlv, 8 we would read, "Out of the ivory palaces *the strings* (i. e. concerts of music) have made thee glad;" and so in Psa. cl, 4, "Praise him with strings (stringed instruments) and *ugabs*." See STRING.

6. מַחֲלַת, *machaláth*, which occurs in the titles of Psa. liii and lxxxviii, is supposed by Gesenius and others to denote a kind of lute or guitar, which instrument others find in the *minnim* above noticed. The preva-

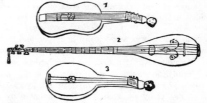

1. A kind of guitar; 2. Ancient lute; 3. Arabian *tanbur*.

lence in the East of instruments of this sort would alone suggest the probability that the Jews were not without them; and this probability is greatly increased by the evidence which the Egyptian paintings offer that they were equally prevalent in ancient times in neighboring

Ancient Egyptians playing on the lute or guitar: 2 is dancing; 3 has the instrument slung across the shoulders.

nations. The Egyptian guitar consisted of two parts: a long, flat neck or handle, and a hollow, oval body, composed wholly of wood, or covered with leather, whose upper surface was perforated with several holes to allow the sound to escape; over this body, and the whole length of the handle, extended three strings of catgut secured at the upper extremity. The length of the handle was sometimes twice, sometimes thrice that of the body, and the whole instrument seems to have

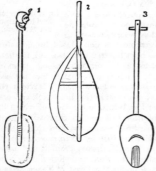

Egyptian stringed instruments with necks: 1 has an ornamental head; 3 approaches nearly to the lute.

measured three or four feet. It was struck with a plectrum, and the performers usually stood as they played. Both men and women used the guitar; some danced while they touched its strings (Wilkinson, *Anc. Eg.* i, 84–86, 123–125). See MAHALATH.

II. *Wind Instruments.*—1. The most ancient of these was the עוּגָב, *ugâb*, mentioned along with the *kinnôr* as the invention of Jubal (Gen. iv, 21). It is twice alluded to (Job xxi, 12; xxx, 31), and in both cases in connections which show that it was used on occasions of domestic festivity and joy. The only other place where it occurs is in Psa. cl, 4, where it is referred to among other instruments suitable to be employed in the praises of God. Opinion has been, and is still, much divided as to the instrument denoted by the name. Winer and Leyrer (in Herzog's *Real-Encyklopädie*) favor the idea that it was a species of bagpipe; and in this view they are supported by the authority of Jerome, the Targums (אֲגוּבָא), and some rabbinical writers. The Septuagint varies in its translation of the word; in Genesis rendering it by κιθάρα, in Job by ψαλμός, and in Psa. cl by ὄργανον, the term adopted by the Vulgate, Syriac, Arabic, and most other versions, as

well as by our own. But by ὄργανον we are by no means to understand the *organ*, which is an instrument of no great antiquity, even if we are to suppose, as some do, that there was a rudiment of the modern organ in use in the Temple of Jerusalem in the time of Christ, an invention of which strange and evidently fabulous things are told us by the Talmud, under the name of the מַגְרֵפָה (*magrephah*). The *organum* meant by the word was as old as the days of Jubal; it must, therefore, have been of a rude and simple construction, and is best understood of the so-called Pandean pipe, formed by a combination of reed-pipes of different lengths and thicknesses. In support of this view is the fact that the Pandean pipe was an instrument of Syrian or Oriental origin, and that it was of such high

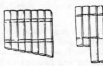

Pan Pipes. (Statues, British Museum.)

antiquity that the profane writers do not know to whom to ascribe it. Some refer it to Pan (Virgil, *Ecl.* ii), others to Mercury (Pind. *Od.* xii, *de Pallade*), others to Marsyas and Silenus (Athenæus, iv, 182). This antiquity corresponds with the Scriptural intimation concerning the *ugab*, and justifies us in seeking for it among the more ancient instruments of the Orientals, especially as it is still common in Western Asia. Niebuhr saw it in the hands of a peasant at Cairo (*Reisebeschr.* i, 181); and Russell, in his *Nat. Hist. of Aleppo* (i, 155, 156), says that "the *syrinx* or Pan's pipe is still a festival instrument in Syria; it is known also in the city, but very few performers can sound it tolerably well. The higher notes are clear and pleasing, but the longer reeds are apt, like the dervise flute, to make a hissing sound, though blown by a good player. The number of reeds of which the *syrinx* is composed varies in different instruments from five to twenty-three." The classical *syrinx* is usually said to have had seven reeds (Virg. *Ecl.* ii); but we find some on the monuments with a greater number, and the shepherd of Theocritus (*Id.* viii) had one of nine reeds. See ORGAN.

2. Of almost equal antiquity was the קֶרֶן, *kéren*, or horn, which sometimes, but not often, occurs as the name of a musical instrument (Josh. vi, 5; 1 Chron. xxv, 5; Dan. iii, 5, 7, 10, 15). Of natural horns, and of instruments in the shape of horns, the antiquity and general use are evinced by every extensive collection of antiquities. It is admitted that horns of animals were at first used, and that they at length came to be imitated in metal, but were still called horns. See HORN. This use and application of the word are illustrated in our "cornet." It is generally conceived that rams' horns were the instruments used by the early

Trumpets.
1. Curved (Cornu).—Trajan's Column.
2. Bronze.—British Museum.
3. Straight, of the Jews.—Arch of Titus.

Hebrews; and these are, indeed, expressly named in our own and many other versions as the instruments used at the noted siege of Jericho (Josh. vi, 5); and the horns of the ram are those which Josephus assigns to the soldiers of Gideon (*Ant.* v, 6, 5; comp. Judg. vii, 16). See also SHOSHANNIM.

3. שׁוֹפָר, *shophâr*, which is a far more common word than *keren*, and is rendered "trumpet" in the Auth. Ver. This word seems, first, to denote horns of the straighter kind, including probably those of neat cattle, and all the instruments which were eventually made in imitation of and in improvement upon such horns. It is, how-

ever, difficult to draw a distinction between it and the keren, seeing that the words are sometimes used synonymously. Thus that which is called "a jobel-horn" in Josh. vi, 5, is in the same chapter (ver. 4, 6, 8, 13) called "a jobel-horn trumpet" (shophar). See JUBILEE. Upon the whole, we may take the shophar, however distinguished from the keren, to have been that kind of horn or horn-shaped trumpet which was best known to the Hebrews. The name shophar means bright or clear, and the instrument may be conceived to have been so called from its clear and shrill sound, just as we call an instrument a "clarion," and speak of a musical tone as "brilliant" or "clear." In the service of God this shophar or trumpet was only employed in making announcements, and for calling the people together in the time of the holy solemnities, of war, of rebellion, or of any other great occasion (Exod. xix, 13; Numb. x, 10; Judg. iii, 7; 1 Sam. xiii, 3; xv, 10; 2 Chron. xv, 14; Isa. xviii, 3). The strong sound of the instrument would have confounded a choir of singers rather than have elevated their music. At feasts and exhibitions of joy horns and trumpets were not forgotten (2 Sam. vi, 15; 1 Chron. xvi, 42). There is no reason to conclude that the trumpet was an instrument peculiar to the Levites, as some have supposed. If that were the case we should be unable to account for the three hundred trumpets with which Gideon's men were furnished (Judg. vii, 8), and for the use of trumpets in making signals by watchmen, who were not always Levites. See TRUMPET.

4. The חֲצוֹצְרָה, chatsotserâh, or straight trumpet, is occasionally mentioned along with the shophar, showing that these two kinds of trumpets were sometimes used together, as in Psa. xcviii, 6, "with trumpets and sound of cornet make a joyful noise before the Lord the King" (comp. 1 Chron. xv, 28; 2 Chron. xv, 14). The two silver trumpets appointed by Moses to be made for

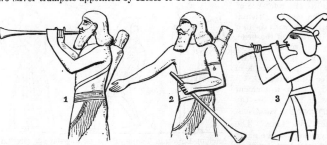

Straight Trumpets: 1, 2. Assyrian (Sculptures, British Museum); 3. Egyptian (Painting at Thebes).

the use of the priests of the tabernacle were of this construction, and were used for announcing to the people the advent of the different feasts, for signalling "the journeying of the camps," and for sounding alarms in time of war (Numb. x, 1–10). Their use in the sacrificial rites as a musical accompaniment was limited (ver. 10) to certain occasions, to "their solemn days, the beginnings of their months, and the day of their gladness;" but in the age of David and Solomon their sacrificial use was much extended, and the number provided for the use of the priests was correspondingly increased. At the dedication of the Temple as many as a hundred and twenty priests "sounded with trumpets;" and in the immensely developed ritual then introduced the part of the musical service assigned to the priests was to blow with the sacred trumpets during the offering of sacrifice, while the Levites accompanied on the other instruments of all kinds. There has been various speculation on the name; but we are disposed to assent to the conclusion of Gesenius that it is an onomatopoetic word, imitating the broken pulse-like sound of the trumpet, like the Latin taratantara, which this word would more resemble if pronounced as in Arabic, hadâderah. By many it has been identified with the mod-

VI.—25

ern trombone, on the assumption that the description in Numb. x, 2 implies that it was turned back at the end. But straight trumpets are to be seen upon the monuments both of Egypt and Assyria, and the straight silver trumpet of the Jewish Temple is distinctly figured upon the arch of Titus at Rome and on extant Jewish coins (Frölich, Anal. Syr. Proleg.). See CORNET.

5. The חָלִיל, halil, flute, the meaning of which is bored through, and denotes a pipe, perforated and furnished with holes. The Sept. always renders it by αὐλός, a pipe or flute. There are but five places where it occurs in the Old Testament (1 Sam. x, 5; 1 Kings i, 40; Isa. v, 12; xxx, 29; Jer. xlviii, 36); but the Greek αὐλός occurs in the New Testament (Matt. ix, 23) and in the Apocryphal books (1 Macc. iv, 54; ix, 39; Judith iii, 8). It was originally formed from the reed, by the

Egyptian Single Pipes: 1. From tomb at Thebes; 2. From tomb near the Pyramids (Wilkinson).

simple contrivance of cutting a larger or smaller number of holes in one of its lengths; but it was afterwards, in the progress of the arts, more artificially made of wood, bone, horn, and ivory. It was sometimes single, and at other times double, the two pipes uniting at top in a single mouthpiece. It would seem to have come rather late into use among the Hebrews, and probably had a foreign origin. The passages to which we have referred will indicate the use of this instrument or class of instruments; but of the form we can only guess by reference to those of the ancient Egyptians and Assyrians, which are very similar to those still in use in Western Asia. The pipe is, however, rarely introduced in the Egyptian sculptures, and does not seem to have been held in much estimation. The single pipe of the Greeks is allowed to have been introduced from Egypt (J. Pollux, Onom. iv, 10; Athenæus, Deipnos. iv), from which the Jews probably had theirs. It was a straight tube, without any increase at the mouth, and when played was held with both hands. It was usually of moderate length, about eighteen inches, but occasionally less, and sometimes so exceedingly long and the holes so low that the player was obliged to extend his arms to the utmost. Some had three holes, others four, and actual specimens made of common reed have been found (Wilkinson, Anc. Egypt. ii, 309). The double pipe was formed with two such tubes, of equal or unequal lengths, having a common mouthpiece, and each played with the corresponding hand. They were distinguished as the right and left pipes, and the latter, having but few holes and emitting a deep sound, served as a base; the other had more holes, and gave a sharp sound (Pliny, Hist. Nat. xvi, 36). This pipe is still used in Palestine. The Scottish missionary deputation overtook, among the hills of Judah, "an Arab playing with all his might upon a shepherd's pipe made of two reeds. This was the first time we had seen any marks of joy in the land" (Narrative, p. 118). See PIPE.

From the references which have been given it will be seen that the pipe was, among the Jews, chiefly consecrated to joy and pleasure. So much was this the case that in the time of Judas Maccabæus the Jews complained "that joy was taken from Jacob, and the pipe with the harp (κιθάρα) ceased" (1 Macc. iii, 45). It was particularly used to enliven the periodical journeys to Jerusalem to attend the great festivals (Isa. xxx, 29); and this custom of accompanying travelling in companies with music is common in the East at this day (Harmer, *Observatt.* ii, 197; to which add Tournefort, *Voyage du Levant*, iii, 189). Athenæus (iv, 174) tells us of a plaintive pipe which was in use among the Phœnicians. This serves to illustrate Matt. ix, 23, where our Saviour, finding the flute-players with the dead daughter of the ruler, ordered them away, because the damsel was not dead; and in this we also recognise the regulation of the Jews that every one, however poor he might be, should have at least two pipes (חליליכ) at the death of his wife (Lightfoot, *Hor. Hebr. ad Matt. ix,* 23). See MOURNING.

6. סוּמְפֹּנְיָה, *sumponyâh*, is evidently the Chald. form of the Gr. συμφωνία, rendered "dulcimer" (Dan. iii, 5; x, 15). It is described by the rabbins as a *bagpipe* consisting of two shrill-toned fifes pressed through a leathern bag. Servius, in his Commentary on the *Æneid*, describes the *symphonia* as a sort of bagpipe, which agrees

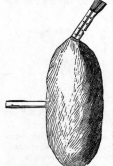
Oriental Bagpipe.

with the representations of Jewish writers. The bagpipe bore the same name among the Moors of Spain, and it is still called in Italy *zampogna*. The known antiquity of this instrument, together with its present existence in the East, appear to confirm the reference of the *sumponyah* to the bagpipe. The modern Oriental bagpipe is composed of a goat-skin, usually with the hair on, and in the natural form, but deprived of the head, the tail, and the feet. The pipes are usually made of reeds, terminated with tips of cows' horns, slightly curved. The entire instrument is primitively simple in its materials and construction. See DULCIMER.

7. There remains to be noticed a wind-instrument mentioned along with the others in Dan. iii, 5 — the מַשְׁרוֹקִיתָא, *mashroki-thâ*, A. V. "flute." The etymology of the name indicates that it was an instrument of the pipe class; but whether a bagpipe, a Pandean pipe, or a flute-pipe, single or double, it is impossible to determine. All these identifications have found supporters, and some have even inclined to the opinion that it was of the nature of a rudimentary wind-organ, such as was afterwards imitated and somewhat improved upon by the Temple organ before alluded to— the *magrephah* of the Talmud. See FLUTE.

Egyptian Double Pipe, and clapping hands. (Painting, British Museum.)

III. *Instruments of Percussion and Agitation.*—1. The most ancient pulsatile instrument mentioned in the O. T. is the תֹּף, *tôph*, consisting of a narrow circle or hoop of wood or metal covered with a tightened skin, and struck with the hand. The Sept. renders the word by τύμπανον, a drum. The "timbrel" of our own version is preferable, as there can be no doubt that the instrument intended was of the same nature and form as the timbrel or tambourine still in use in Oriental coun-

Assyrian Tambourine and Drums.   (Bass-reliefs, British Museum.)

tries. The Arabs still call it *dof*, and the Spaniards *adufe*. It is mentioned as early as the days of Laban (Gen. xxxi, 27), where our version has "tabret;" and it was the instrument with which Miriam and the women of Israel accompanied and beat time to their song and dance when they sang responsively the song of Moses (Exod. xv, 20). Here the name in the original is the same as in Gen. xxxi, 27, though the rendering varies to "timbrel." It is also mentioned by Job (xxi, 12). Isaiah adduces it as the instrument of voluptuaries, but left in silence amid wars and desolations (Isa. xxiv, 8). The occasions on which it was used were mostly joyful, and those who played upon it were generally females (Psa. lxviii, 25), as was the case among most ancient nations, and is so at the present day in the East. It is nowhere mentioned in direct connection with battles or warlike transactions; but it is mentioned on occasions when it was more probably performed on by

Ancient Egyptian Tambourines (1, angular; 2, circular) and Tabret-drum.

men (as in the bringing up of the ark, 1 Chron. xiii, 8; in worship, 1 Sam. x, 5; Psa. cxlix, 3; cl, 4), although this is by no means certain. It frequently occurs on the Egyptian monuments (Wilkinson, *Anc. Egypt.* ii, 240). There were three kinds, differing, no doubt, in sound as well as form : one was circular, another square or oblong, and the third consisted of two squares separated by a bar. They were all beaten by the hand, and often used as an accompaniment to the harp and other instruments. The imperfect manner of representation does not allow us to see whether the Egyptian tambourine had the same movable pieces of metal let into the wooden frame which we find in the tambourines of the present day. Their presence may, however, be inferred from the manner in which the tambourine is held up after being struck; and we know that the Greek instruments were furnished with balls of metal attached by short thongs to the circular rim (Wilkinson, *Ancient Egypt.* ii, 314). At mournings for the dead the tambourine was sometimes introduced among the Egyptians, and the "mournful song" was accompanied by its monotonous sound. This is still a custom of the East, and probably existed among the Jews. See MOURNING.

The *toph* was thus an instrument of the *drum* kind; and it is highly probable that, as other varieties of the drum, some of them much resembling the drums of modern times, were in use among both the Assyrians and Egyptians, they were also introduced among the Hebrews. If so, they must be included under the general name of *toph.* The ancient Egyptians had a long drum, very similar to the *tomtom* of India. It was about two feet or two feet and a half in length, and was beaten with the hand. The case was of wood or copper, covered at both ends with parchment or leather, and braced with cords extended diagonally over the exterior of the cylinder (figs. 1, 2). It was used chiefly in war. There

Drums.

1. Ancient Egyptian (Thebes); 2. Carried on back during march (Rosellini); 3. Modern *tarabúka* (*Descript. de l'Égypte*); 4. Ancient Egyptian, with sticks (Wilkinson).

was another larger drum, less unlike our own: it was about two feet and a half long by about two feet broad, and was shaped much like a sugar-cask (fig. 4). It was formed of copper, and covered at the ends with red leather, braced by catgut strings passing through small holes in its broad margin. This kind of drum was beaten with sticks. It does not appear on the monuments, but an actual specimen was found in the excavations made by D'Athanasi in 1823, and is now in the museum at Paris. Another species of drum is represented in the Egyptian paintings, and is of the same kind which is still in use in Egypt and Arabia under the name of the *tarabuka* drum. It is made of parchment stretched over the top of a funnel-shaped case of metal, wood, or pottery. It is beaten with the hand, and when relaxed the parchment is braced by exposing it for a few moments to the sun or the warmth of a fire (fig. 3, above). This kind of drum claims particular attention from its being supposed to be represented on one of the coins ascribed to Simon Maccabæus (fig. 5 of the second cut under No. 3, below). When closely examined, this instrument will appear to be the same in principle with our kettle-drum, which, indeed, has been confessedly derived from the East, where other instruments on the same principle are not wanting. One of them (fig. 4 of the second cut under No. 3, below) is just the same as the instrument we have derived from it; others are smaller in various degrees, are of different forms, and are tapped lightly with the fingers. Such drum-tabrets were not unknown to the ancient Egyptians (fig. 3 of the cut next but one preceding). The rabbins speak obscurely of a sort of drum, or *magrephah,* which may have been of this kind. It stood, they say, in the Temple court, and was used to call the priests to prayer, the Levites to singing, and leprous persons to their purification. They venture to add that its sound could be heard from Jerusalem to Jericho (Buxtorf, *Lex. Rabbin.* s. v. מגרפה). See TABRET.

2. פַּעֲמוֹן, *paamón.* This name nowhere occurs but with reference to the small golden appendages to the robe of the high-priest (Exod. xxviii, 33; xxxix, 25),

which all versions agree in rendering "bells," or "little bells." These bells were attached to the hem of the garment, and were separated from each other by golden knobs, shaped like pomegranates. They obviously produced their tinkling sound by striking against the golden knobs which were appended near them. There is no trace of bells among the ancient Egyptians or in classical antiquity, and we call these such for want of a better term to describe sonorous pieces of metal used in this manner. See BELL.

3. The צְלְצְלִים, *tseltselim,* or מְצִלּוֹת, *metsillôth,* or מְצִלְתַּיִם, *metsiltáyim.* In Zech. xiv, 20 only is this term rendered "*bells*"—the "bells of the horses." If the words, however, denote cymbals in other places, they cannot well denote a different thing here. It is true that camels, and sometimes horses, wear bells in the East at present; and it is probable that the Hebrews had something similar, in the shape of small cymbal-shaped pieces of metal, suspended under the necks of the animals, and which struck against each other with the motions of the animal. The Romans attached metallic pendants of this kind, called *phalarea,* to their war-horses, in order to produce a terrific effect when shaken by the rapid motions of the animals. These were certainly not bells, but might without any violent impropriety be called cymbals, from the manner in which they struck against each other. This name, being found only in the plural or dual forms, implies an instrument consisting of more parts than one and of not more than two. It is accordingly interpreted by the Sept. to mean κύμβαλα, or cymbals, and this is no doubt correct. Josephus describes the two parts of the instrument as πλατέα καὶ μεγάλα χάλκεα (*Ant.* vii, 12, 3), which were held in either hand and dashed sharply together, yielding a powerful and penetrating metallic sound. They are first mentioned in 2 Sam. vi, 5, as used by direction of David in the bringing up of the ark; and in 1 Chron. xvi, 5 the remarkable fact is recorded that when David organized the musical service which was to be carried on before the ark when brought up to Mount Zion, and "appointed certain of the Levites to thank and praise the Lord God of Israel," while the rest performed their office "with psalteries and with harps," Asaph, the chief musician, or conductor of the choir, "made a sound with cymbals." It thus appears that this was the instrument by which the conductor beat time to the whole Levitical choir. It further appears, from Psa. cl, 5, "Praise him upon the loud cymbal, praise him upon the high-sounding cymbals," that these cymbals, as used in the service of praise, were of two kinds, although the difference between them is very imperfectly indicated in our version of the passage. The rendering, "Praise him with the *clear* cymbals, praise him with the *resounding* cymbals," would be a very fair equivalent for the Hebrew שָׁמַה and תְּרוּעָה; and the first cymbals alluded to were probably finger cymbals, or castanets, which were small round plates of metal fastened upon the thumb and middle finger, and struck against each other by a motion of the hand, yielding a clear and sharp, though not a loud sound; while the *resounding* cymbals were a much larger and more powerful sort, played with both hands; and this view is all the more likely to be correct as cymbals of both kinds were in use among the Egyptians. It is worth noticing that the epithet applied

1. Ancient Egypt. Cymbals. (Brit. Museum.)
2. Modern Egypt. Castanets. (Lane.)

by Paul to the cymbal in 1 Cor. xiii, 1 is ἀλαλάζον ("without speech"), which is very happily selected, inasmuch as the music of such an instrument was necessarily more noisy than expressive or articulate. But our version, "tinkling," is a very poor equivalent for the apostle's word. It suggests the sound of a small bell rather than the clanging resonance of the cymbals. It should have been rendered *clanging* or *clashing.* The sound of these instruments is very sharp and piercing, but it does not belong to fine, speaking, expressive music. The Hebrew instruments were probably similar to those of the Egyptians. These were of mixed metal, apparently bronze, or a compound of copper and silver, and of a form exactly resembling those of modern times, though smaller, being only seven inches or five inches and a half in diameter. The same kind of instrument is still used by the modern inhabitants of

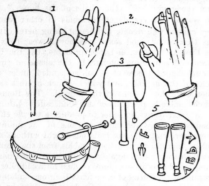

Instruments of Percussion.

Fig. 1. Mallet used in striking suspended boards. 2. Castanets. 3. Tabretdrum, struck by attached balls. 4. Oriental Kettle-drum. 5. Supposed ancient Jewish coin representing drums.

Egypt, and from them, says Wilkinson, "have been borrowed the very small cymbals, played with the finger and thumb, which supply the place of castanets in the *almeh* dance" (*Ancient Egyptians*, iii, 255). The modern castanet, introduced into Spain by the Moors, is to be referred to the same source. See CYMBAL.

4. מְנַעַנְעִים, *menaanim.* This instrument is only once mentioned in Scripture (2 Sam. vi, 5), where it stands next before cymbals in an enumeration of several instruments, and is strangely translated *cornets* in our version. It is singular that the example of the Vulg., which renders by the Latin *sistra,* was not followed by our translators in this instance, especially as the etymology of the name (rad. נוּעַ, *to shake*) suggests that it was an *instrument of agitation* which was denoted, the Greek σεῖστρα having an analogous derivation from σείω. It was generally from eight to sixteen or eighteen inches long, and entirely of bronze or copper; movable rings and bars of the same metal being inserted in the frame, by the sharp impact of which upon the frame, when shaken in the hand, a piercing metallic sound was produced. It was sometimes inlaid with silver, gilt, or otherwise ornamented, and the rings were frequently made to imitate snakes, or simply bent at each end to

Sistra.

Fig. 1, in the Louvre, Paris; 2, 3, in the British Museum; 4, Painting at Thebes.

secure them from slipping through the holes. Several actual specimens of these instruments have been found, and are deposited in the British, Berlin, and other museums (Wilkinson, *Anc. Egypt.* i, 131–133). They are mostly furnished with sacred symbols, and were chiefly used by the priests and priestesses in the ceremonies of religion, particularly in those connected with the worship of Isis (Plut. *De Isid.* c. 63; Juven. xiii, 93; Jablonsky, *Opusc.* i, 306). Instruments of the same rude principle, though different form, are still in use in the military music of some modern nations.

5. שָׁלִישִׁים, *shalishim.* This instrument is only once

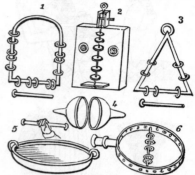

Instruments of Percussion.

Figs. 1, 3, 6. Triangular and other rods of metal charged with rings. 2. A supposed Hebrew instrument, regarded by some as the *menaanim.* 4. A kind of Eastern Cymbals. 5. A pan of sounding metal.

mentioned, viz. in 1 Sam. xviii, 6, where it is spoken of as used by the women of Israel when they came out to meet king Saul and David. Our translators render vaguely "instruments of music," but insert in the margin "three-stringed instruments." The word more probably denoted an instrument with *three sides;* and as some harps were of that shape, it may probably have meant such harps. (See above, under *kinnor.*) We insert the name in this place because it is generally thought by recent scholars that it meant what is understood by a *triangle,* an instrument of percussion which Athenæus (*Deipnos.* iv, 175) says was derived from Syria. If so, it was possibly in use among the Hebrews, and may have been the instrument referred to in 1 Sam. xviii, 6. But, on the other hand, no figure of such an instrument of percussion has been found on any of the monuments either of Assyria, Egypt, or Greece. Like the cymbals and sistra, it is still in use in military music, especially in the Turkish army.

6. The word "dance" is used in the A.V. for the Heb. term *machôl,* מָחוֹל, a musical instrument of percussion, supposed to have been used by the Hebrews at an early period of their history. Some modern lexicographers, who regard *machôl* as synonymous with *rakôd,* רָקוֹד (Eccles. iii, 4), restrict its meaning to the exercise or amusement of dancing; but according to many scholars it also signifies a musical instrument used for accompanying the dance, which the Hebrews therefore called by the same name as the dance itself. The Sept. generally renders *machôl* by χορός, "dancing;" occasionally, however, it gives a different meaning, as in Psa. xxx, 11 (Heb. Bible, ver. 12), where it is translated χαρά, "joy," and in Jer. xxxi, 4 and 14, where it is rendered Συναγωγή, "assembly." The Shemitic versions of the O. T. almost invariably interpret the word as a musical instrument. On the joyous occasion when the Israelites escaped from their Egyptian pursuers, and reached the Arabian shore of the Red Sea in safety, Miriam is represented as going forth striking the תֹּף, and followed by her sisters in faith, who join in "with timbrels and dances" (Exod. xv, 20). Here the sense of the passage seems to be, agreeably to the A. V., that the Hebrew women came forth to dance, and to accompany their

diance by a performance on timbrels; and this is the view adopted by the majority of the Latin and English commentators. Parkhurst and Adam Clarke do not share this opinion: according to the former, *machôl* is 'some fistular wind-instrument of music, with holes, as a flute, pipe, or fife, from חל, to make a hole or opening;" and the latter says, "I know no place in the Bible where *machôl* and *machalath* mean *dance* of any kind—they constantly signify some kind of pipe." The Targumists very frequently render *machôl* as a musical instrument. In Exod. xv, 20, Onkelos gives for *machalath* the Aramaic word חנגין, which is precisely the same employed by him in Gen. xxi, 27 for *kinnôr* (A. V. "harp"). The Arabic version has for *machôl* in most places *tablun*, pl. *tubulun*, translated by Freytag, in his Arabic Lexicon, "a drum with either one or two faces;" and the word ובמחלות (Judg. xi, 34, A.V. "and with dances") is rendered by *inaun*, "songs." Gesenius, Fürst, and others adopt for the most part the Sept. rendering; but Rosenmüller, in his commentary on Exod. xv, 20, observes that, on comparing the passages in Judg. xi, 34; 1 Sam. xviii, 6; and Jer. xxxi, 4, and assigning a rational exegesis to their contexts, *machôl* must mean in these instances some musical instrument, probably of the flute kind, and principally played on by women.

In the grand hallelujah psalm (cl) which closes that magnificent collection, the sacred poet exhorts mankind to praise Jehovah in his sanctuary with all kinds of music; and among the instruments mentioned at the 3d, 4th, and 5th verses is found *machôl*, which cannot here be consistently rendered in the sense of dancing. Joel Brill, whose second preface (הקדמה שניה) to Mendelssohn's Psalms contains the best treatise extant on the musical instruments mentioned in the Hebrew Bible, remarks: "It is evident from the passage, 'Praise him with the *toph* and the *machol*,' that machol must mean here some musical instrument, and this is the opinion of the majority of scholars." Mendelssohn derives *machol* from חלול, "hollow," on account of its shape; and the author of *Shilte Haggibborim* denominates it סיסטרוס, which he probably intends for κι-θάρα, rather than *sistrum.* Some modern critics consider *machalath* the same with *machol.* Gesenius, however, translates the latter "dancing," while the former he renders "a stringed instrument," from the root חלל, "to sing."

The musical instrument used as an accompaniment to dancing is generally believed to have been made of metal, open like a ring: it had many small bells attached to its border, and was played at weddings and merry-makings by women, who accompanied it with the voice. According to the author of *Shilte Haggibborim*, the *ma-chol* had tinkling metal plates fastened on wires, at intervals, within the circle that formed the instrument, like the modern tambourine; according to others, a similar instrument, also formed of a circular piece of metal or wood, but furnished with a handle, which the performer might so manage as to set in motion several rings strung on a metal bar, passing from one side of the instrument to the other, the waving of which produced a loud, merry sound. See DANCE.

Musical instruments accompanying the dance. (Mendelssohn.)

IV. The following are general or miscellaneous terms:
1. דחון, *dachavân*, Chald., rendered "instruments of music" in Dan. vi, 18. The margin gives "or *table*, perhaps lit. *concubines*." The last-mentioned rendering is that approved by Gesenius, and seems most probable. The translation, "instruments of music," seems to have

originated with the Jewish commentators, R. Nathan, R. Levi, and Aben-Ezra, among others, who represent the word by the Hebrew *neginoth*, that is, stringed instruments which were played by being struck with the hand or the plectrum.

2. שדה, *shiddâh*, is found only in one very obscure passage (Eccles. ii, 8), "I gat me men-singers and women-singers, and the delights of the sons of men, *musical instruments, and that of all sorts*" (שדה ושדות, *shid-dâh ve-shiddôth*). The words thus rendered have received a great variety of meanings. They are translated "drinking-vessels" by Aquila and the Vulgate; "cup-bearers" by the Sept., Peshito-Syriac, Jerome, and the Arabic version; "baths" by the Chaldee; and "musical instruments" by David Kimchi, followed by Luther and the A. V., as well as by many commentators. By others they are supposed to refer to the women of the royal harem. But the most probable interpretation to be put upon them is that suggested by the usage of the Talmud, where שידה, *shidah*, denotes a "palanquin" or "litter" for women. The whole question is discussed in Gesenius's *Thesaurus*, p. 1365.

V. *Literature.*—On the general subject of the music and musical instruments of the Israelites, see Martini, *Storia della Musica* (Bologna, 1757), i, 4 sq.; Burney, *General Hist. of Music* (Lond. 1776), i, 217 sq.; Schröter, *De Musica Davidica* (Dresd. 1716); Hawkins, *Hist. of Music*; Forkel, *Gesch. der Musik*, i, 99 sq.; Calmet, *Dissert. sur la Musique des Hebreux*, annexed to his *Commentary on the Psalms*; Bedford, *Temple Music* (Bristol, 1706); Pfeiffer, *Ueber die Musik der Alten Hebr.* (Erl. 1799; transl. in the *Amer. Bible Repository*, 1835); Saalschütz, *Form der Hebr. Poesie*, p. 329 sq.; also *Gesch. und Würdigung d. Musik bei den Hebr.* (Berl. 1829); Harenberg, *Comm. de Re Musica Vetus.* in *Misc. Lips.* ix, 218 sq.; Sonne, *De Musica Judæor. in sacris* (Hafn. 1724); Tal, *Dicht Sing und Spielkunst bes. der Hebr.* (Frankf. 1706); Jahn, *Biblische Archäologie*; Reland, *De Spoliis Temp. Hieros.*; Anton, *Die Melodie u. Harmonie der Alt. Hebr.* in Paulus, *N. Repert.* i, 160 sq.; ii, 80 sq.; iii, 1 sq.; *Shilte Haggibborim*, in Ugolini *Thesaur.* vol. xxxii; Contant, *Traité sur la Poésie et la Musique des Hébreux* (Paris, 1781); Beck, *De accentuum Hebr.* in Mencken, *Thesaur.* p. 563 sq.; Abicht, *Vindiciæ accentuum* (Lips. 1713); *Excellentia musicæ antiq. Hebr.* (Munich, 1718); Schneider, *Bibl.-gesch. Darstellung d. Hebr. Musik* (Bonn, 1834); De Wette, *Commentar. über die Psalmen*; Rosellini, *Monumenti dell' Egitto*; Wilkinson, *Anc. Egyptians*; Villoteau, *Sur la Musique des Orientaux*, in *Descript. de l'Égypte*; Lady M. W. Montague, *Letters*; Volney, *Voyage en Syrie*; Tournefort, *Voyage au Levant*; Niebuhr, *Reisebeschreibung*; Russell, *Nat. Hist. of Aleppo*; Lane, *Modern Egyptians*, ii, 69 sq.; Thomson, *Land and Book*; Engel, *Music of the most Ancient Nations* (Lond. 1864); Hutchinson, *Music of the Bible* (Bost. 1863).

Musician, CHIEF (מנצח, *menatstse'âch*, i. e. the most *conspicuous*, i. q. leader), an officer indicated in the titles of many (53) of the Psalms and in Hab. iii, 10, and to be interpreted, according to Kimchi, Rashi, Aben-Ezra, and many other authorities, the *precentor* of the Levitical choir or orchestra in the Temple. In one late instance the name of this officer seems to be indicated (1 Chron. xv, 21); but the first who held it appears to have been Jeduthun, in connection with his three brothers (1 Chron. xvi, 41, etc.); and the office seems to have been hereditary in the family (1 Chron. xvi, 1, 3), or else the name Jeduthun became a patronymic title for the incumbents afterwards (2 Chron. xxxv, 15). In this capacity Jeduthun's "office was generally to preside over the music of the Temple service, consisting of the *nebel*, or nablium, the *kinnor*, or harp, and the cymbals, together with the human voice (the trumpets being confined to the priests). But his peculiar part, as well as that of his two colleagues, Heman and Asaph, was 'to sound with cymbals of brass,' while the others played on the nablium and the harp. This appointment to the office was by election of the chiefs of the Levites (שֹׁרְרִים) at David's command, each of the three divisions probably choosing one. The first occasion of Jeduthun's ministering was when David brought up the ark to Jerusalem. He then took his place in the procession, and played on the cymbals. But when the division of the Levitical services took place, owing to the tabernacle being at Gibeon and the ark at Jerusalem, while Asaph and his brethren were appointed to minister before the ark, it fell to Jeduthun and Heman to be located with Zadok the priest, to give thanks 'before the tabernacle of the Lord in the high-place that was at Gibeon,' still by playing the cymbals in accompaniment to the other musical instruments (comp. Psa. cl, 5). In the account of Josiah's Passover in 2 Chron. xxxv reference is made to the singing as conducted in accordance with the arrangements made by David, and by persons representing Asaph, Heman, and Jeduthun, *the king's seer* (חֹזֵה הַמֶּלֶךְ). See HE-MAN. Perhaps the phrase rather means the king's ad-viser in matters connected with the musical service. The triple division of the Levitical musicians seems to have lasted as long as the Temple, and each appears to have been called after its respective leader. At the dedication of Solomon's Temple, 'the Levites which were the singers, all of them of Asaph, of Heman, of Jeduthun,' performed their proper part. In the reign of Hezekiah, again, we find the sons of Asaph, the sons of Heman, and the sons of Jeduthun, taking their part in purifying the Temple (2 Chron. xxix, 13, 14); they are mentioned in Josiah's reign, and so late as in Ne-hemiah's time we still find descendants of Jeduthun employed about the singing (Neh. xi, 17)." See JEDUTHUN.

Musimoes, festivals celebrated in honor of the dead among the native tribes of Central Africa. See Gardner, *Faiths of the World,* p. 503.

Musius, CORNELIUS, an eminent Dutch scholar of Roman Catholic proclivities, was born at Delft in 1503. He flourished as pastor of St. Agatha during the contest between the prince of Orange and the Spanish throne for the possession of the Netherlands. He was equally esteemed for his learning and for his amiable qualities, when, on account of his religious faith, he was put to the torture, which caused his death in 1575, by De la Marck. The Romanists have charged the wicked deed to the prince of Orange and his Reformed friends. This, however, is cruel and unjust. The prince himself, who highly esteemed Musius, shed many tears when he heard of the atrocious deed, and while the Estates of Holland were aroused to an indignation scarcely con-trollable, De la Marck was obliged to leave the coun-try, notwithstanding his powerful connections. Mu-sius wrote several religious poems, which are remarkable for their elegance and purity of style. See Brandt, *Gesch. der Ref.* x, 538–540; Hoofd, *De Neederlandsche Histo-rien,* vii, 281 sq.; Motley, *Hist. of the Rise of the Dutch Republic,* ii, 474, 475.

Musonius Rufus, CAIUS, a Stoic philosopher of the 1st century of the Christian æra, is mentioned with praise by Tacitus (*Ann.* xiv, 59), and also by Pliny the younger, Philostratus, Themistius, and others. He was a native of Volsinii, in Etruria, and belonged to the equestrian order. He was a friend of Thrasea Pætus, Barea Soranus, Rubellius Plautus, and other Stoics, who were the victims of Nero's suspicion and cruelty. Mu-sonius was banished to the island of Gyaros in A.D. 66, where he is said to have been visited by many Greeks for the purpose of listening to his lessons. Being re-called by Galba after Nero's death, he lived at Rome under Vespasian, who excepted him from the sentence of exile pronounced by that prince against the Stoic philosophers. This scanty information is all that we have concerning the biography of Musonius Rufus

(Nieuwland, *Dissertatio de Musonio Rufo, Philosopho Stoico*). The time of his death is not mentioned, but he was not alive in the reign of Trajan, when Pliny speaks of his son, Artemidorus. Musonius wrote vari-ous philosophical works, which are spoken of by Suidas as λόγοι διάφοροι φιλοσοφίας ἐχόμενοι. He reduced philosophy to the simplest moral teachings. One of his finest sayings is: "If thou doest good painfully, thy pain is transient, but the good will endure; if thou doest evil with pleasure, the pleasure will be transient, but the evil will endure." Fragments of his works are found in Stobæus, and have been collected and pub-lished, with the above dissertation and copious notes, under the title of *C. Musonii Rufi, Philosophi Stoici, Reliquiæ, et Apophthegmata, cum Annotatione, edidit T. Venhuizen Peerlkamp, Corrector Gymnasii Harlemensis* (Haarlem, 1822, 8vo). These fragments of Musonius are full of the purest morality and wisdom. See Fabri-cius, *Bibl. Græca,* iii, 566 sq.; Ritter and Preller, *Histo-ria Philosophiæ,* p. 438–441; Ueberweg, *Hist. Philosoph.* i, 185, 190; *English Cyclop.* s. v.; Smith, *Dict. of Gr. and Rom. Biogr. and Mythol.* s. v. Rufus; Lardner, *Works* (see Index in vol. x).

Musorites, a superstitious sect of Jews, who are said to have reverenced rats and mice. The origin of this peculiarity is to be found in an event which is nar-rated in 1 Sam. vi. The Philistines had taken away the ark of the covenant and detained it in their country seven months, during which time the Lord in anger sent a plague of mice, which destroyed the fruits of the ground. Under the dread inspired by this divine judgment upon their land they restored the ark, and by the advice of their priests and diviners they pre-pared as a trespass-offering to the God of Israel five golden emerods and five golden mice. Perverting the solemn incident of O.-T. history, the sect seems to have entertained a superstitious veneration for mice and rats.

Muspel(1) or **Muspel(1)heim** is, in Norse mythology, the world of light and heat, situated in the south part of the universe; Niflheim, the habi-tation of mist and cold, being situated in the north. The inhabitants of this world are called "the sons of Muspell," among whom Sturt or Surtur is chief, and the ruler of Muspellheim, who sits on its bor-ders bearing a flaming falchion, and at the end of the world he shall issue forth to combat, and shall vanquish all the gods, and consume the universe with fire.

Musserin is the name given to a sect of atheists in Turkey. The word signifies those who keep a se-cret, from the verb *aserra,* to conceal. Their secret is flatly to deny a deity. Many of the cadis and other educated classes in Turkey are believed to be Musserin. But mainly they are Christian renegades, who, having for pecuniary reasons abjured the faith of their fathers, seek refuge in blank atheism, under a public profession of Mohammedanism.

Musso, CORNELIUS, a famous Italian pulpit orator, was born at Placentia in 1511, and, after entering holy orders, rose rapidly to distinction in the Church. He was made bishop of Bertinoro, then of Bitonto, towards the close of the 16th century. He distinguished him-self at the Council of Trent, and seems to have enjoyed popular favor to an unusual degree, for medals were struck in his honor, and other distinctions of like char-acter were paid him. He died at Rome Jan. 9, 1574. He is the author of *Sermons on the Creed* (Venice, 1590, 4to). See Bayle, *Hist. Dict.* s. v.; *Gen. Biog. Dict.* xi, 154; Musso, *Vita di Cornelio Musso* (1586); Blackwood, 1869, i, 211; Wessenberg, *Die Grossen Kirchenversamm-lungen d.* 15 *u.* 16 *Jahrh.* iii, 160, 161.

Mussulman or **Mosleman** (from Arab. *Salama*), the proper term for a *Mohammedan.* The word is equivalent to *Moslem* (q. v.), of which it is, properly speaking, the plural; used in Persian fashion for the singular. We need hardly add that this Arabic plural termination of "án" has nothing whatever to do with our word *man*, and that a further English plural in *men* is both barbarous and absurd.

Mustapha (i. e. *the chosen one*) is the name by which Mohammedan tradition designates the greatest of their prophets. See MOHAMMED.

Mustard (σίναπι, Matt. xiii, 31; xvii, 20; Mark iv, 31; Luke xiii, 19; xvii, 6; in Talmudic Chaldee חַרְדָּל, *chardál*, Mishna, *Shabb.* xx, 2, from the Syriac *chardâl*,), a well-known pod-bearing shrub-like plant (genus *Sinapis*, of thirteen species, five of which are indigenous in Egypt, *Descript. de l'Egypte*, xix, 96) that sometimes grows wild, and at other times is raised from the seed, which is employed as a condiment, being usually of the two kinds, the black and the white (see *Penny Cyclopædia*, s. v. Sinapis). The Jews likewise cultivated mustard in their gardens (Mishna, *Maaser.* iv, 6). The round kernels (Matt. xiii, 31; xvii, 20), which were used also by the ancients as a spice (Pliny, xix, 54), passed in Jewish phrase as an emblem for a small, insignificant object (Buxtorf, *Lex. Talm.* col. 822); being the smallest seed commonly gathered in Palestine, although not literally the most diminutive known. "The Lord in his popular teaching," says Trench (*Notes on Parables*, p. 108), "adhered to the popular language" (see also the Koran, *Sur.* 31). The statements in Matt. xiii, 32, that when fully grown it is the greatest of plants, and becomes a tree under which the fowls may find shelter, has been supposed to indicate a larger growth than ordinary in Western countries (see Margrave, *Hist. nat. Brasil.* p. 291; Bauhin, *Hist. Plant.* ii, 855); but is confirmed by the statements of the Talmudists, one of whom describes it as a tree of which the wood was sufficient to cover a potter's shed (Talm. Hieros. *Peah*, vii, 4), and another says that he was wont to climb into it, as men climb into a fig-tree (ib. *Ketuboth*, fol. iii, 2; comp. Rosenmüller, *Alterth.* iv, 105). Mr. Buckham (*On the Mustard-tree of the Scriptures*, 1829) cites the following from Alonzo de Orvallo's *Travels in Chili* (as given in Awnshaw and Churchill's *Collection*): "The mustard-plant thrives so rapidly that it is as big as one's arm, and so high and thick that it looks like a tree. I have travelled many leagues through mustard-groves which were taller than horse and man; and the birds built their nests in them as the Gospel mentions." The statement of Irby and Mangles has also been referred to (Lambert, in the *Linnæan Transactions*, xvii, 450), that they found the mustard-plant (*Sinapis nigra*) growing wild between Beisan and Ajlun as high as their horses' heads. (See further in Celsii *Hierobot.* ii, 253 sq.; Billerbeck, *Flora class.* p. 172.) Prof. Hackett states that he was for a long time disappointed in his search for any specimens of the mustard answering to the requirements of the above texts of Scripture; but that while on his way across the plain of Akka, towards Carmel, he had the satisfaction of seeing a little forest-like field of these plants, in full blossom, from six to nine feet in height, with branches from each side of a trunk an inch or more thick; and that he actually witnessed the alighting of birds upon the stems (*Illustra. of Script.* p. 124). Dr. Thomson also (*The Land and the Book*, ii, 100) says that he has seen the wild mustard on the rich plain of Akkar as tall as the horse and the rider.

Even these descriptions, however, seem hardly to come up to the ancient accounts of the plant in question. Hence the conclusion of Dr. Royle (in a paper read before the Royal Asiatic Society, March 16, 1844) has been preferred, who shows that there is a plant still known in the East by the name of *khardal* (which corresponds to the rabbinical title, and is indeed the modern Arabic for "mustard"), growing near Jerusalem, but most abundantly on the banks of the Jordan and round the sea of Tiberias; its seed being employed as a substitute for mustard. The plant is the *Salvadora Persica* of Linnæus (the *Cissus arborea* of Forskål), a large shrub, or tree of moderate size, a native of the hot and dry parts of India, of Persia, and of Arabia. Dr. Roxburgh (*Flor. Ind.* i, 389 sq.) describes the berries as much smaller than a grain of black pepper, having a strong aromatic smell, and a taste much like that of garden cresses. The plant has a small seed, which produces a large tree with numerous branches, in which the birds of the air may take shelter. It is probably the tree which Irby and Mangles themselves suppose to be the mustard-tree of Scripture, rather than the ordinary shrub. They met with it while advancing towards Kerak, from the southern extremity of the Dead Sea. It bore its fruit in bunches resembling the currant; and the seeds had a pleasant, though strongly aromatic taste, nearly resembling mustard. A specimen of the tree had been brought home by Mr. W. Barker, and it had been ascertained by Messrs. Don and Lambert to be the *Salvadora Persica* of botanists; but both had

Oriental Mustard (*Sinapis Nigra*).

Salvadora Persica.

written against its claim to be the mustard-tree of Scripture, while Mr. Frost, hearing a conversation on the subject, had supposed the tree to be a *Phytolacca*, and had hence maintained it to be the mustard-tree of Scripture, but without adducing proofs of any kind (*Remarks on the Mustard-tree of the N. T.* [Lond. 1827]; *Bulletin des sciences nat.* Mai, 1826, p. 74; *Journal of the Royal Asiatic Society*, ut sup.).

On the other hand, "Hiller, Celsius, Rosenmüller, who all studied the botany of the Bible, and older writers, such as Erasmus, Zezerus, Grotius, are content to believe that some common mustard-plant is the plant of the parable. The objection commonly made against any *Sinapis* is that the seed grew into 'a tree' ($\delta\acute{\epsilon}\nu\delta\rho o\nu$), or, as Luke has it, 'a great tree' ($\delta\acute{\epsilon}\nu\delta\rho o\nu$ $\mu\acute{\epsilon}\gamma a$), in the branches of which the fowls of the air are said to come and lodge. Now, in answer to the above objection, it is urged with great truth that the expression is figurative and Oriental, and that in a proverbial simile no literal accuracy is to be expected; it is an error, for which the language of Scripture is not accountable, to assert, as Dr. Royle and some others have done, that the passage implies that birds 'built their nests' in the tree; the Greek word $\kappa a\tau a\sigma\kappa\eta\nu\acute{o}\omega$ has no such meaning, the word merely means 'to settle or rest upon' anything for a longer or shorter time; the birds came, '*insidendi et versandi causa*,' as Hiller (*Hierophyt.* ii, 63) explains the phrase; nor is there any occasion to suppose that the expression 'fowls of the air' denotes any other than the smaller *insessorial* kinds—linnets, finches, etc.—and not the 'aquatic fowls by the lake-side, or partridges and pigeons hovering over the rich plain of Genesareth' which Prof. Stanley (*S. and P.* p. 427) recognises as 'the birds that came and devoured the seed by the way-side'—for the larger birds are wild and avoid the way-side—or as those 'which took refuge in the spreading branches of the mustard-tree.' Hiller's explanation is probably the correct one; that the birds came and settled on the mustard-plant for the sake of the seed, of which they are very fond. Again, whatever the $\sigma\acute{\iota}\nu a\pi\iota$ may be, it is expressly said to be an herb, or, more properly, 'a garden herb' ($\lambda\acute{a}\chi a\nu o\nu$, *olus*). As to the plant being called a 'tree' or a 'great tree,' the expression is not only an Oriental one, but it is clearly spoken with reference to some other thing; the $\sigma\acute{\iota}\nu a\pi\iota$, with respect to the other *herbs* of the garden, may, considering the size to which it grows, justly be called '*a great tree*,' though, of course, with respect to trees properly so named, it could not be called one at all. Now it is clear from Scripture that the $\sigma\acute{\iota}\nu a\pi\iota$ was cultivated in our Lord's time, the seed a 'man took and sowed in his field;' Luke says, 'cast into his garden:' if, then, the wild plant on the rich plain of Akkar grows as high as a man on horseback, it might attain to the same or a greater height when in a cultivated garden; and if, as lady Callcott has observed, we take into account the very low plants and shrubs upon which birds often roost, it will readily be seen that some common mustard-plant is able to fulfil all the scriptural demands. As to the story of the rabbi Simeon ben-Calaphtha having in his garden a mustard-plant into which he was accustomed to climb as men climb into a fig-tree, it can only be taken for what Talmudical statements generally are worth, and must be quite insufficient to afford grounds for any argument. But it may be asked, Why not accept the explanation that the *Salvadora Persica* is the tree denoted?—a tree which will literally meet all the demands of the parable. Because, we answer, where the commonly received opinion can be shown to be in full accordance with the scriptural allusions, there is no occasion to be dissatisfied with it; and again, because at present we know nothing certain of the occurrence of the *Salvadora Persica* in Palestine, except that it occurs in the small tropical low valley of Engedi, near the Dead Sea, whence Dr. Hooker saw specimens, but it is evidently of rare occurrence. Mr. Ameuny says he had seen it all along the banks of the Jordan,

near the lake of Tiberias and Damascus; but this statement is certainly erroneous. We know from Pliny, Dioscorides, and other Greek and Roman writers, that mustard-seeds were much valued, and were used as a condiment; but it is more probable that the Jews of our Lord's time were in the habit of making a similar use of the seeds of some common mustard (*Sinapis*) than that they used to plant in their gardens the seeds of a tree which certainly cannot fulfil the scriptural demand of being called 'a pot-herb.'" Dr. Tristram likewise (*Nat. Hist. of the Bible*, p. 472 sq.) takes strong ground in favor of the common black mustard and against the *Salvadora Persica*. See Kitto, *Pict. Bible*, note on Luke xvii, 6.

Mustitani is the name of a small and obscure sect of Donatists, condemned by the three hundred and ten bishops of that schism who met at Bagai or Vaya, in Numidia, A.D. 398. See Augustine, *Contra Epist. Parmeniani*, lib. iii, cap. 29.

Musūrus, MARCUS, a learned Italian ecclesiastic, was a native of the island of Candia; emigrated to Venice about the end of the 15th century, and taught Greek in that city with great success. Afterwards he proceeded to Rome, where Leo X showed him great favor, and nominated him bishop of Epidaurus, in the Morea. He had been just invested with this distinction when he died at Rome in 1517. He published the first edition of Athenæus, printed by Aldus (Venice, 1514). Musurus published also the *Etymologicum Magnum Græcum* (Venice, 1499, fol.; reprinted in 1549, in 1594, and in 1710), and some Greek epigrams and other poetry, among them a poem in praise of Plato, prefixed to his edition of that philosopher's works, and translated into Latin verse by Zenobio Acciaioli, *Carmen in Platonem* (Cambridge, 1797).

Mutevel, the president or chief ruler of a Mohammedan mosque in Turkey, into whose hands the revenue is regularly paid.

Muth, Placidus, a German Roman Catholic theologian, was born at Poppenhausen, near Schweinfurt, Dec. 30, 1753; received his education at Würzburg and Erfurt; then entered, at the age of twenty-four, a convent near Erfurt, and was ordained to the priesthood in 1783. In 1794 he was elected abbot of Bischofsrode and Frankenrode, under the title of Placidus the Second, and also provost at Celle. In 1797, after introducing to the prince-elector of Mentz the idea of a more thorough education in convents, he was appointed archiepiscopal counsellor; but his idea was never carried out, and he went, after the secularization of his convent, to Erfurt, where he was appointed chief counsellor of schools and government, and also director of the gymnasium at that place. He died in 1821. His most important works are, *Disquisitio historico-critica in bigamiam Comitis de Gleichen, cujus monumentum est in ecclesia S. Petri Erfordiæ; una cum systematica theologiæ catholicæ synopsi* (Erfordiæ, 1788, 8vo) :—*Ueber die Verhältnisse der Philosophie und Theologie nach Kantischen Grundsätzen* (ibid. 1791, 8vo) :—*Progr. de novis perantiquæ Universitatis incrementis, de castris Thuringicis, quæ vulgo Comitum de Gleichen dicuntur, nec non de pluribus simulacris Universitati litterarum Erfordiensi dono datis. Particula i et ii* (ibid. 1812–13, 4to) :—*Gedächtnissfeier der Befreiung Pius VII aus der Gefangenschaft zu Fontainebleau und seine Rückkehr in seine Staaten* (ibid. 1814, 8vo). See Döring, *Gelehrte Theol. Deutschlands*, s. v.

Muth, Rufus. See MUTIANUS.

Muth-lab'ben (Hebrew, fully, *al muth labben'*, עַל־מוּת לַבֵּן, *upon the death to the son*; Sept. $\dot{v}\pi\grave{\epsilon}\rho$ $\tau\tilde{\omega}\nu$ $\kappa\rho v\phi\acute{\iota}\omega\nu$ $\tau o\tilde{v}$ $v\acute{\iota}o\tilde{v}$; Vulg. *pro occultis filii*; Auth. Ver. "upon Muth-labben"), a phrase occurring only in the title of Psa. ix. The following are conjectures that have been made regarding its import: 1. Perhaps the favorite opinion of modern critics, of Gesenius and De

Wette among the rest, is to connect the Hebrew words so as to read 'almuth labben, "with the voice of virgins [to be sung] by boys." But, granting the lawfulness of this critical effort, there is considerable difficulty in extracting the translation desiderated. The word 'ala-moth does occur in probably some such meaning (Psa. xlvi, title; 1 Chron. xv, 20); and it has been preferred by critics who modify the opinion now under considera-tion, to the extent of arriving at this word by altering the vowel-points as well as the division of the words. See ALAMOTH. Yet, after doing so, they have to face an awkward difficulty, arising from the absence of the preposition 'al, " upon ;" since they require this little word to become the first syllable of their noun. It is evident that the Sept. and Vulgate must have read עַל עֲלָמוֹת, " concerning the mysteries," and so the Arabic and Ethiopic versions. The Targum, Sym-machus (περὶ θανάτου τοῦ υἱοῦ), and Jerome (super morte filii), in his translation of the Hebrew, adhered to the received text, while Aquila (νεανιότητος τοῦ υἱοῦ), retaining the consonants as they at present stand, read al-muth as one word, עֲלְמוּת, " youth," which would be the regular form of the abstract noun, though it does not occur in Biblical Hebrew. In support of the reading עלמות as one word, we have the authority of twenty-eight of Kennicott's MSS., and the assertion of Jarchi that he had seen it so written, as in Psa. xlviii, 14, in the Great Masorah. If the reading of the Vulgate and Sept. be correct with regard to the con-sonants, the words might be pointed thus, עַל עֲלָמוֹת, 'al 'alamôth, " upon Alamoth," as in the title of Psa. xlvi; and לבן is possibly a fragment of לִבְנֵי קֹרַח, lib-néy Kôrach, " for the sons of Korah," which appears in the same title. 2. It has been very common to suppose that there is here the name of a person. The Jewish commentator Kimchi, according to Gesenius, mentions that some explained it, " upon the death of Labben," a person wholly unknown. But commonly the first syl-lable of labben has been taken to be the ordinary He-brew prefix preposition, " to, for, concerning." The Targum renders the title of the psalm, " On the death of the man who came forth from between (בְּרֵין) the camps," alluding to Goliath, the Philistine champion (אִישׁ הַבֵּינַיִם, 1 Sam. xvii, 4). That David composed the psalm as a triumphal song upon the slaughter of his gigantic adversary was a tradition which is mentioned by Kimchi merely as an on dit. An old opinion, main-tained at present by Fürst, is that it should be trans-lated " upon the death of Ben," who is named among the Levites appointed to preside over the music at the removal of the ark to its resting-place (1 Chron. xv, 18), while he is not named in the narrative of the actual re-moval ; indeed, his place seems to be filled by another, Azaziah (ver. 20, 21) ; and we are reminded of the sud-den death of Uzzah, when the removal was attempted on an earlier occasion. Hengstenberg, however, has re-vived an old opinion of Grotius—originally mentioned, but not adopted, by Jarchi—that Labben is transposed for Nabal, yet not so much with reference to the indi-vidual man as with reference to " the fool," which is em-phatically noticed as the meaning of his name ; and he thinks the psalm refers a good deal to the end of the wicked. Donesh supposes that Labben was the name of the man who warred with David in those days, and to whom reference is made as " the wicked" in verse 5. Arama (quoted by Dr. Gill in his Exposition) identifies him with Saul. Jarchi says that some regarded Labben as the name of a foreign prince who made war upon the Israelites, and upon whose overthrow this song of praise was composed. 3. The word ben being the common Hebrew word for " son," and so translated in this title by the ancient versions generally, the translation has been offered, " upon the death of the son," or " upon dying in reference to the son," viz. David's son Ab-

salom, for whom it is recorded that he wept and mourn-ed passionately (2 Sam. xviii, 33). The renderings of the Sept. and Vulgate induced the early Christian com-mentators to refer the psalm to the Messiah. Augustine understands " the son" as " the only-begotten Son of God." The Syriac version is quoted in support of this interpretation, but the titles of the Psalms in that ver-sion are generally constructed without any reference to the Hebrew, and therefore it cannot be appealed to as an authority. 4. As in the case of other titles of the Psalms, this has been taken to be a musical instrument, or more commonly and probably the name of an air to which the psalm was sung. This title might then be translated, " upon dying [which has happened] to the son," or " upon 'Die for the son.'" So Hupfeld, that it was the commencement of an old song, signifying "death to the son." Delitzsch adopts this sort of ex-planation, but translates differently, " upon 'Death makes white.'" Hitzig and others regard it as an ab-breviation containing a reference to Psa. xlviii, 14. Ac-cording to Jarchi, " this song is of the distant future when the childhood and youth of Israel shall be made white (רתלבן), and their righteousness be revealed and their salvation draw nigh, when Esau and his seed shall be blotted out." He takes עֲלְמוּת as one word, signify-ing " youth," and לְלַבֵּן = לַבֵּן, " to whiten." Menahem, a commentator quoted by Jarchi, interprets the title as ad-dressed " to the musician upon the stringed instruments called Alamoth, to instruct," taking לַבֵּן as if it were לְבוֹנֵן or לְהָבִרין. The difficulty of the question is suffi-ciently indicated by the explanation which Gesenius him-self (Thes. p. 741 a) was driven to adopt, that the title of the psalm signified that it was " to be chanted by boys with virgins' voices," i. e. in the soprano. (Comp. the briefer form, " unto death," Psa. xlviii, 9). See PSALMS.

Mutianus, Rufus Conradus, a distinguished German scholar, and head of the Erfurt humanists, was born at Homburg Oct. 15, 1471. His family name was Mudt, or Muth, but according to the literary fash-ion of the age he changed it to Mutianus. His parents lived in easy circumstances, and gave him a careful education. He entered the celebrated school of Alex. Hegius at Deventer, where he had for schoolfellow a youth named Gerhardus Gerhardi, who afterwards be-came celebrated throughout Europe as Desiderius Eras-mus. Mutianus displayed so much talent at Deventer that it was predicted that some day he would be reck-oned among the most learned men in Germany. When fifteen years old he entered the University of Erfurt, and in 1492 graduated as magister artium. Desirous of enjoying the best educational advantages, he then went to Italy, and took his degree as doc. jur. can. at Bologna. In 1502 he returned home, and was appointed to a very lucrative position at the ducal court of Hesse. But he soon resigned, preferring a small position at Go-tha, which gave him ample time for study. He re-ceived an annual salary of sixty florins (about twenty dollars), but was so well satisfied with this modest remu-neration that he could not be prevailed upon to accept another position. The inscription, " Beata tranquilli-tas," which he placed outside, and " Bonis cuncta pate-ant," which he placed inside of his house, is significant. He preferred not to publish anything except a few epi-grams; but his letters, directed to his friends, are of great historic value, and show the superior critical mind of the man. They are preserved in manuscript at the Frankfort City Library, and have been in part edited by W. E. Tetzel in Supplem. historiæ Gothanæ (Jenæ, 1704), vol. i. Mutianus was a humanist, but hu-manism was, in his opinion, only a means to the end. It served him as an introduction into the study of moral philosophy and theology, and, like his great contempo-rary, Erasmus, he placed himself in decided opposition to scholastic theology and Church abuses generally. He was one of the literary precursors of the Reformation,

VI.—25*

and as such contributed largely to prepare the minds of literary men throughout Germany for a rupture with Rome. The modest George Spalatin, jun., was an intimate friend and pupil of his; and when Spalatin was called to Wittenberg in 1508, he dismissed him thus:

"Ito bonis avibus dextro pede sidere fausto,
 Felix optatum carpe viator iter.
Aula patet, Spalatine! tibi tribuntur honores,
 Ito prætereant quæ nocitura putas."

Mutiánus came into intimate connections with the Erfurt humanists, and the Erfurt scholars visited him frequently (see C. Krause, *Euric. Condus.* [Hanau, 1863]), esteeming him as their head and leader. He outran his generation in thought, but lagged behind it in action. He at first hailed Luther with joy, but in 1521 he withdrew his support from the Reformers. He decided to remain in the Church of Rome, and is said to have lived in such poverty that he was obliged to beg for bread. He died on Good-Friday, 1526. It has been well said that Mutianus was a Reformer until the Reformation became a fearful reality. He was a learned, ingenious, amiable, timid, irresolute man, whose soul did not partake of the energy of his intellectual faculties. See Strauss, *Ulrich v. Hutten*, i, 42 sq.; ii, 336 sq.; Kampfschulte, *Die Universität Erfurt in ihrem Verhältniss zu d. Humanismus und d. Reformat.* (Trèves, 1858) i, 74 sq.; ii, 227 sq.

Mutianus, Scholasticus. See MUCIANUS.

Mutiles de Runic. See SKOPSIS.

Mutschelle, SEBASTIAN, a German Roman Catholic theologian, was born Jan. 18, 1749, at Altershausen, Bavaria. He was educated at Munich, entered in 1765 the Order of Jesus, and completed his education at Ingolstadt in 1776. He was then appointed vicar at Mattigkofen, and in 1779 canon of the convent of St. Veit at Freysingen, and ecclesiastical counsellor of the consistory, also school commissioner at the same place. Several difficulties into which he was drawn by publications of his made it agreeable to him to resign his clerical position, and he gave himself up to literary labors, especially the preparation of several works. He also taught privately Latin, French, and the fine arts. In this period (1784–86) he published *Geschichte Jesu aus den vier Evangelisten*, also *Kenntniss und Liebe des Schöpfers aus der Betrachtung der Geschöpfe*, and *Bemerkungen über die sämmtlichen Evangelien* (of this a second edition was published in 1790). In the midst of all his literary work he was surprised by the renomination to his former positions by Max Procop, count of Törring; but he yet found leisure time for literary work, and published in 1791 and 1792, *Unterredung eines Vaters mit seinen Söhnen über die ersten Grundwahrheiten der christlichen Religion*, and *Christkatholischer Unterricht, wie man gut und selig werden könne.* The first fruit of his thorough knowledge of Kant was his work, *Ueber das sittliche Gut* (1788). But again his enemies were at work to get him out of his position, and found a good opportunity to work against him, as he asked the different convents for contributions towards a continual fund for his remodelled schools. Mutschelle again resigned his position in 1793, but was appointed pastor at Baumkirchen, near Munich. This position afforded much leisure time, which he filled up by literary work. He then published *Bemerkungen über die festtäglichen Evangelien ;* also *Kritische Beiträge zur Metaphysik.* In 1799 he was also appointed professor at the university at Munich, which position he assumed with an oration: *Was soll die Schule für die Welt sein?* He died Nov. 28, 1800. He has published, besides the works already mentioned, *Geburts und Jugendgeschichte Jesu* (Munich, 1784, 8vo) :—*Ueber das sittliche Gut* (ibid. 1786, 2 vols. 8vo) :—*Oratio ante electionem neo-Episcopi ac Principis cathedralis Ecclesiæ Frisingensis, die 26 Maji habita* (Frisingæ, 1788, 4to) :—*Die heiligen Schriften des Neuen Testaments, übersetzt* (Munich, 1789–90, 2 vols. large 8vo) :—*Vermischte Schriften* (ibid. 1793–98, 4 vols. sm.

8vo) :—*Kritische Beiträge zur Metaphysik, in einer Prüfung der Stattlerisch-Anti-Kantischen* (ibid. 1795, 8vo) : —*Moraltheologie oder theologische Moral, vorzüglich zum Gebrauch für seine Vorlesungen* (ibid. 1801–2, 2 vols. large 8vo) :— *Ueber Kantische Philosophie* (Munich, 1799–1803). See Krug, *Philosophisches Lexikon,* s. v.; Döring, *Gelehrte Theologen Deutschlands,* ii, 636–644.

Mu-tsoo-po, the Chinese tutelary goddess both of women and of sailors, and worshipped with great reverence among them. This worship was introduced some centuries ago into the Celestial empire, and so strikingly does Mu-tsoo-po resemble the Virgin Mary of the Romanists that the Chinese at Macao call her *Santa Maria di China*—Holy Mother of China. The sailors especially make her an object of adoration, and there are very few junks that have not an image of her on board. She is also accompanied by very dismal satellites, the executors of her behests. See Gardner, *Faiths of the World,* p. 504 ; Doolittle, *Social Life of the Chinese* (Index in vol. ii).

Mutter (מַהְגִּים, *mahgím, mutterers*), in Isa. viii, 19, refers to the murmuring or indistinct enunciation of wizards and soothsayers in uttering their spells. See DIVINATION.

Muttra, a sacred town of the Hindûs, is the capital of a district of the same name, ninety-seven miles south-south-east of Delhi, on the right bank of the Jumna. Access is had to the river—which is considered by the Hindûs to have special sanctity—by numerous ghâts, ornamented with little temples ; and its banks are every morning and evening crowded by devotees of all ages and both sexes to perform their religious exercises. In Hindû mythology it is regarded as the birthplace of Krishna (q. v.). In honor of the monkey-god Hanuman, monkeys are here protected and fed, being allowed to swarm everywhere. There are also a great number of sacred bulls at large without owners.

Mutūnus, a deity among the ancient Romans who averted evil from the city and commonwealth of Rome. He was identical with the *Phallus* or *Priapus,* who chiefly delivered from the power of dæmons. Mutunus had a temple inside the walls of Rome, which existed until the time of Augustus, when it was removed outside.

Mutzenbecher, ESDRAS HEINRICH, a German theologian, was born at Hamburg March 23, 1744. He was educated at Hamburg and Göttingen, then acted for a while as tutor of the children of the baron of Steinberg. In 1774 he was appointed assistant of the ecclesiastical faculty and second minister of the university church at Göttingen, and while there he published his *Philologische Bibliothek.* In 1775 he was called as pastor to the evangelical church at the Hague, and in 1778 was appointed chief minister of all evangelical Lutheran congregations at Amsterdam, and in 1789 general superintendent and counsellor of the consistory of Oldenburg, where he died, Dec. 21, 1801. His most important works are, *J. C. Biel Novus Thesaurus philologicus sive Lexicon in lxx et alios interpretes et scriptores apocryphos Veteris Testamenti* (Hagæ Comitum, 1779–80, 3 vols. large 8vo) :—*Gesangbuch zur öffentlichen und häuslichen Andacht für das Herzogthum Oldenburg, nebst einem Anhange von Gebeten* (Oldenburg, 1791, 8vo) : —*Der Kleine Katechismus Dr. Martin Luther's nach den fünf Hauptstücken, mit kurzen Anmerkungen für Lehrer und Schüler* (ibid. 1797, 12mo) :—*Gebete* (Bremen, 1801, 8vo). See Döring, *Gelehrte Theol. Deutschlands,* s. v.

Muza, IBN-NOSEIR. See SPAIN.

Muziano, GIROLAMO, a distinguished Italian painter, was born at Acquafredda, near Brescia, in 1528. He painted a number of Biblical and religious subjects, one of which, the *Resurrection of Lazarus,* was greatly admired by Michael Angelo, who pronounced him one of the greatest painters of his time. Muziano is chiefly celebrated by his efforts to advance the art of working in mosaics, which, up to this period, was merely an ornamental art of inlaying stones, but which he perfected almost to a rivalry with painting. He was a great favorite with pope Gregory XIII, who employed him to paint a picture of St. Paul the hermit, and another of St. Anthony, for the church of St. Peter. Sixtus V also held Muziano in esteem, and intrusted to him the designs for the bass-reliefs of the column of Trajan. At the instance of this artist, pope Gregory founded the Academy of St. Luke, which Sixtus confirmed by a brief; and Muziano gave two houses to the institution. He also built the *Capella Gregoriana* at Rome. He died at Rome in 1590, and was buried in the church of Santa Maria Maggiore, near the spot where his picture of the *Resurrection of Lazarus* was placed. Many of his pictures have been engraved. His celebrated picture, *Christ Washing the Feet of his Disciples*, which is in the cathedral at Rheims, has been engraved by Desplaces. See Lanzi, *Hist. of Painting*, transl. by Roscoe (Lond. 1847, 3 vols. 8vo), i, 417; ii, 184; Spooner, *Biog. Hist. of the Fine Arts* (N. Y. 1865, 2 vols. 8vo); Jameson and Eastlake, *Hist. of Our Lord* (Lond. 1864, 2 vols. 8vo), i, 361.

Muzio (or **Mutio**), GIROLAMO NUZIO, an Italian writer, noted for his opposition to the Reformation and its adherents, and hence surnamed "*Malleus Hereticorum*," was born at Padua in 1496 and died in 1576. He wrote several polemical treatises against Luther, and various other works in prose and verse, none of which are of any value in our day except as literary curiosities. See Tiraboschi, *Storia della Litterature Italiana*, s. v.

Muzzarelli, ALPHONSO, an Italian theologian, was born in 1749, and was educated at the college at Prato. He was then ordained, and entered the Order of Jesus, but was compelled to leave it five years after, as he was appointed canon at Ferrara; he was afterwards director of the college at Parma, and finally was called by pope Pius VII to Rome to take the position as theologian of the Pœnitentiaria. He published while there several works against the irreligiousness of his time. He was in 1809 transported to Paris by the French, on account of his opposition to the Bonapartists, and there he died in 1815. His most important works are, *Il buon uso della Logica in materia della Religione*, transl. into French and Latin: — *L'Emilio disingannato contra Rousseau:— Influenza de' Romani Pontefici nel governo di Roma avanti Carlo Magno: — Memorie del Giacobinismo :—Dissertationes selectæ de auctoritate Romani Pontificis in Conciliis Generalibus, etc.*

Muzzle (מֹסֹם, *chasam'*, to *stop* the nostrils, as in Ezek. xxxix, 11). In the East grain is usually thrashed by sheaves being spread out quite thick on a level spot, over which oxen, cows, and younger cattle are driven, till by continued treading they press out the grain. One of the injunctions of the Mosaic code is, "Thou shalt not muzzle the ox when he treadeth out the corn" (Deut. xxv, 4). From the monuments we learn that the ancient Egyptians likewise suffered the ox to tread out the corn unmuzzled. "The origin of this benevolent law," says Michaelis, "with regard to beasts, is seemingly deducible from certain moral feelings or sentiments prevalent among the people of the early ages. They thought it hard that a person should be employed in the collection of edible and savory things, and have them continually before his eyes, without being permitted once to taste them; and there is in fact a degree of cruelty in placing a person in such a situation; for the sight of such dainties is tormenting, and the desire to partake of them increases with the risk of the prohibition. Add to this that, by prohibitions of this nature, the moral character of servants and day-laborers, to the certain injury of their masters' interests, seldom fails to become corrupted, for the provocation of appetite at the sight of forbidden gratification will, with the greater number, undoubtedly overpower all moral suggestions as to right or wrong. They will learn to help themselves without leave. Therefore when Moses, in the terms of this benevolent custom, ordained that the ox was not to be muzzled while thrashing, it would seem that it was not merely his intention to provide for the welfare of that animal, but to enjoin with the greater force and effect that a similar right should be allowed to human laborers. He specified the ox as the lowest example, and what held good in reference to him was to be considered as so much the more obligatory in reference to man." Comp. Hos. x, 11; 1 Cor. ix, 9-11; 1 Tim. v, 18. This ancient Mosaic law, allowing the ox, as long as he is employed in thrashing, to eat both the grain and the straw, is still observed in the East. Prof. Robinson, when at Jericho, in 1838, observed the process of thrashing by oxen, cows, and younger cattle. He says, "The precept of Moses, 'Thou shalt not muzzle the ox when he treadeth out the corn,' was not very well regarded by our Christian friends; many of their animals having their mouths tied up; while among the Mohammedans I do not remember ever to have seen an animal muzzled. This precept serves to show that of old, as well as at the present day, only neat cattle were usually employed to tread out the grain." See THRESHING.

Mwetyi, a Great Spirit venerated by the Shekani and Bakële people in Southern Guinea. The following account of him is given by Mr. Wilson in his *Western Africa :* "He is supposed to dwell in the bowels of the earth, but comes to the surface of the ground at stated seasons, or when summoned on any special business. A large, flat house, of peculiar form, covered with dry plantain-leaves, is erected in the middle of the village for the temporary sojourn of this spirit, and it is from this building that he gives forth his oracular answers. The house is always kept perfectly dark, and no one is permitted to enter it except those who have been initiated into all the mysteries of the order, which includes, however, almost the whole of the adult male population of the village. Strange noises issue forth from this dark den, not unlike the growling of a tiger, which the knowing ones interpret to suit their own purposes. The women and children are kept in a state of constant trepidation; and, no doubt, one of the chief ends of the ceremonies connected with the visits of this mysterious being is to keep the women and children in a state of subordination. He is the great African Bluebeard, whom every woman and child in the country holds in the utmost dread. Every boy, from the age of fourteen to eighteen, is initiated into all the secrets pertaining to this Great Spirit. The term of discipleship is continued for a year or more, during which period they are subjected to a good deal of rough treatment—such, undoubtedly, as makes a lasting impression both upon their physical and mental natures, and prevents them from divulging the secrets of the order. At the time of matriculation a vow is imposed, such as refraining from a particular article of food or drink, and is binding for life. When Mwetyi is about to retire from a village where he has been discharging his manifold functions, the women and children, and any strangers who may be there at the time, are required to leave the village. What ceremonies are performed at this time is known, of course, only to the initiated. When a covenant is about to be performed among the different tribes, Mwetyi is always invoked as a witness, and is commissioned with the duty of visiting vengeance upon the party who shall violate the engagement. Without this their national treaties would have little or no force. When a law is passed which the people wish to be specially binding, they invoke the vengeance of Mwetyi upon every transgression; and this, as a general thing, is ample guarantee for its observance. The Mpongwee people sometimes call in the Shekanis to aid them, through the agency of this Great Spirit, to give sanctity and authority to their laws."

Mycalessia, a surname of the goddess *Demeter,* or Ceres, derived from Mycalessus, in Bœotia, where she was worshipped.

Myconius, Friedrich, an intimate friend of Luther, and one of the Reformers of the 16th century, was born at Lichtenfels, Franconia, Dec. 26, 1491, of religious parents, and was educated at Annaberg. He joined the Franciscans at that place in 1510. While in that body he vainly strove to satisfy the yearnings of his heart by diligent application to his monastic duties and the study of such works as Peter Lombard's *Magister Sententiarum,* the writings of Alexander of Hales, Bonaventura, Gabriel Biel, and even Lyra's Biblical commentaries. Finally, Luther's ninety-five theses fell into his hands. He at once adopted the principles therein contained. In the mean time he was successively sent to the convents of Leipsic and of Weimar in 1512, and was ordained priest in 1516. But, since he had openly declared himself in favor of the evangelical doctrines, he had to undergo all sorts of annoyances from his superiors. He remained steadfast, however, strengthening himself by secretly reading the works of Luther in company with his convent associate Voit. Finally, his superiors contemplating his removal to Annaberg, he fled, and soon after (in 1524) appeared at Zwickau as an evangelical preacher. In the same year he was sent to Gotha by duke Johann to introduce the Reformation, and met with great success in this difficult task. He paid particular attention to the schools. In connection with Melancthon, Justus Menius, Christopher von Planitz, Georg von Wangenheim, and Johann Cotta, he made two visitations to Thuringia, in 1528 and in 1533, to improve the organization of the churches and schools. He took part also in the conferences of Marburg (1529), Wittenberg (1536), Smalcald (1537), Nuremberg, Frankfort (1539), and Hagenau (1540), in which he was often in contact with Melancthon. He was attached as theologian to the embassy sent by the elector to king Henry VIII in 1538 for the purpose of introducing the Reformation into England. On the death of duke George, Myconius, together with Cruciger, Pfeffinger, and M. Balthasar, was intrusted with the mission of introducing the Reformation into Saxony, and particularly into Leipsic. Yet he always remained especially attached to Gotha and Thuringia. In the former city he founded the afterwards celebrated gymnasium, and he used every exertion to procure for institutions of learning the necessary endowments. His health failing in 1541, he wrote to Luther that he was "sick, not unto death, but unto life." But he recovered, and, according to Luther's prayer, outlived him several months. He died April 7, 1546. Myconius was an active writer, but most of his productions were pamphlets and letters; his chronicle of Gotha was published by S. Cyprian under the title *Fr. Myconii historia Reformationis* (1715). Biographies of Myconius are to be found in Melchior Adam, *Vitæ Theologorum* (Frankf. 1705, vol. i); Sagittarii *Historia Gothana* (Jena, 1700); Junker, *Redivivus Myconius* (Waltershausen, 1730); Brückner, *Kirchen- u. Schulestaat d. Herzogthums Gotha* (1753, I, i, 41 sq.); Ledderhose, *Mykonius* (Gotha, 1854); Herzog, *Real-Encyklopädie,* x, 137; Middleton, *Evangel. Biog.* i, 250; Hardwick, *Church History, Reformation,* p. 110, 114, 119. (J. N. P.)

Myconius (also known as *Geisshüsler,* his name before he joined the Protestants), **Oswald,** a Swiss Protestant theologian, was born at Lucerne in 1488, and was educated at Basle. He taught for a while, accepting first a call to Zurich as director of a school; but he was only three months there when he was recalled to his native place to take charge of the high school. Taking a leading part in the new doctrine, which had just made its appearance, he was in 1523 again discharged, and

returned to Zurich to his old position. When Zwingle was killed at the battle of Kappel, and the citizens of Zurich became rather careless towards theological science, Myconius returned to Basle, where he was appointed deacon at St. Alban, chief minister of the city of Basle, and professor of the New Testament. He resigned the latter position in 1541, and died Oct. 14, 1552. Myconius was a true confessor of Zwingle's doctrine. He was largely instrumental in the publication of the Basle Confession, and for the sake of a union of all Protestant interests favored the Helvetian Confession of 1536. His tolerance towards Lutherans on their consubstantiation doctrine subjected him to many trials from the Zwinglians, who often, though unjustly, questioned his faithfulness to them. His most important works are, *Narratio de vita et obitu Zwingli :—Tractatus de liberis rite educandis :—De crapula et ebrietate.* See Melchior Adam, *Vitæ Theolog. German.* (Heidelberg, 1620), p. 223 sq.; Merle d'Aubigné, *Hist. of the Ref. in Switzerland;* Kirchhofer, *Leben O. Myconius des Reformators* (1814); Hagenbach, *Leben u. Schriften der Väter u. Begründer der reform. Kirche* (Elberf. 1857, 8vo), ii, 309–447. (J. H. W.)

Myers, Benjamin F., a minister of the Methodist Episcopal Church, was born in Chillicothe, Ohio, April 19, 1801. He was converted at the early age of nine years, and identified himself with the Methodists. In 1833 he was admitted into the Ohio Conference, and for ten years filled charges respectively in Wooster, Somerset, Cambridge, Newark, Granville, and Hebron. His health failing, he retired from ministerial life, and became judge of Licking County, Ohio. In 1850 he migrated to California, and in 1857 joined the California Conference, where for the next twelve years he was actively engaged in Christian work in Suttee County, Weaverville, Jackson, Coloma, Cacheville, Bodeya-Vallejo, Centreville, Woodbridge, and Linden. He was superannuated in 1869, and from that time until his death, which occurred in Stockton, Cal., July 18, 1874, gave himself to the work of re-examining the structures of the Christian Church against the attacks of infidelity and scientific research. See *Minutes of Annual Conferences,* 1874, p. 112.

Myers, Lewis, a minister of the Methodist Episcopal Church, was born in the vicinity of Indian Fields, Colleton District, S. C. He was of German extraction. He obtained his education in an academy near Washington, Ga., and became an itinerant preacher in 1799 in South Carolina, preaching on the Little Peedee and Anson Circuit. In 1800 he was appointed to the Orangeburg Circuit. In 1801 he was appointed to the Bush River and Cherokee Circuit, having been ordained deacon by bishop Asbury. In 1802 he was stationed in the Broad River Circuit. In 1803 he was ordained elder, and changed to the Little River Circuit. In 1804 and 1805 he was respectively at Ogeechee and Bladen circuits. In 1806 he was at Charleston. In 1807, 1808, and 1809 he was presiding elder of the Seleuda District; in 1810, 1811, 1812, and 1813, of the Ogeechee District; and in 1814, 1815, 1816, and 1817, of the Oconee District. In 1818 and 1819 he was stationed at Charleston. In 1820, 1821, 1822, and 1823 he was presiding elder of the Edisto District. In 1824 he was stationed at Georgetown. Having labored incessantly for a quarter of a century, he was appointed in 1825 as supernumerary on the Effingham Circuit, a spasmodic asthma rendering him unfit for more active work. He was finally made superannuate, and settled at Goshen, Effingham County, Ga., where he died, Nov. 16, 1851. From the time of his retirement from active service until his death he was busily engaged with a school, and occasionally preached. Lewis Myers was well known among the Methodists for his wise, pithy, and practical remarks. His style of preaching was direct and forcible, with very little ornament of gesture; his illustrations often bordered on the humorous, from the quaintness with which the subject was represented. See Dr. James Osgood Andrew, in Sprague, *Annals of the Amer. Pulpit*, vii, 321 sq.

Myēsis ($\mu\acute{\upsilon}\eta\sigma\iota\varsigma$, *initiation*), a designation of *baptism* among the Greek fathers, because they considered it to be the admittance of men to all the sacred rites and mysteries of the Christian religion. This term, as well as $\mu\upsilon\sigma\tau\alpha\gamma\omega\gamma\acute{\iota}\alpha$, of frequent occurrence in the writings of Cyril of Jerusalem, was intimately connected with the secret discipline, and fell into disuse with the termination of that system.

Myiagros, a hero who was invoked at the festival of Athene, celebrated at Aliphera, as the protector against flies.

Myles, JOHN, a minister of the Anglican establishment, who flourished during the colonial period of this country, was born in England about the latter half of the 17th century. He migrated to America, and in 1689 succeeded Mr. Radcliff as rector of the Episcopal church that is now known as King's Chapel, Boston. In 1692 he returned to England for aid for his people. In 1696 he again came to America, bringing with him much Church furniture, and several costly gifts from queen Mary and king William. He died about 1726. See Anderson, *Hist. of the Colonial Church*, ii, 681, 682; iii, 539, 540, 582, 594.

Mylitta (perhaps = מילדת, *Genitrix*, "who causes to bear"), a name which, according to Herodotus (i, 131), was given by the Assyrians to the goddess Aphrodite as the generative principle in nature. "She was apparently worshipped among the Babylonians, who gradually spread her worship through Assyria and Persia. She was originally, like almost every other mythological deity, a cosmic symbol, and represented the female portion of the twofold principle through which all creation bursts into existence, and which alone, by its united active and passive powers, upholds it. Mylitta is to a certain degree the representative of Earth, the mother, who conceives from the Sun Bel or Baal. Mylitta and Baal together are considered the type of the Beneficent. Procreation thus being the basis of Mylitta's office in nature, the act itself became a kind of worship to her, and was hallowed through and for her. Thus it came to pass that every Babylonian woman had once in her life to give herself up to a stranger, and thereby considered her person consecrated to the great goddess. The sacrifice itself seems, especially in the early stage of its introduction among the divine rites of the primitive Babylonians, to have had much less of the repulsiveness which, in the eyes of highly-cultivated nations, must be attached to it; and it was only in later days that it gave rise to the proverbial Babylonian lewdness. Herodotus's account of this subject must, like almost all his other stories, be received with great caution" (Chambers). In Babylonia this goddess was called *Beltis* or *Bilit*, i. e. "the Lady." She is commonly represented as the wife of Bel Nimrod (Belus), and the mother of his son Nin, though she is also called the wife of her son Nin. She united the characteristics of the classical divinities Juno, Venus, and Diana. Mylitta had temples at Nineveh, Ur, Erech, Nipur, and Babylon. The *Baaltis* of the Phœnicians was the same in name and character. The young women of Byblus, like those of Babylon, sacrificed in her service their virginity, and gave the price they received to the temple of the goddess. The *Derceto* of Ascalon, the *Ashera* of the Hebrews, and the *Ishtar* of the Babylonians were kindred divinities. See ASHTORETH.

Mylius, Ernst Friedrich, a German theologian, was born at Lühe June 10, 1710. He was educated by his uncle Mushard, afterwards at the gymnasium at Bremen, and at the university at Helmstädt, and finished his education in 1734 at Jena. He was appointed in 1738 minister at the "Johannes Kirche" at Verden,

with which position the conrectorship of the school was combined. He accepted in 1742 a call as minister of St. Peter's Church at Hamburg, where he died, Dec. 15, 1774. His most important works are, *Entwurf heilsamer Unterweisungen oder Dispositiones der Evangelien* (Hamburg, 1745–74, 8vo) :—*Friedenspredigt* (ibid. 1750, 4to) :—*Der Ruf Gottes an die Sünder aus dem Feuer; eine Buszpredigt* (ibid. 1750, 4to) :—*Auszug der Hauptsätze und Eintheilungen aus den Entwürfen heilsamer Unterweisungen für die Jahre* 1745–59 (ibid. 1759, 8vo). See Döring, *Gelehrte Theol. Deutschlands*, s. v.

Mylius, Georg (1), a noted German Lutheran divine, was born at Augsburg in 1548; studied at the universities of Strasburg, Marburg, and Tübingen, and in 1571 became pastor at Augsburg, and later was made superintendent and rector of the evangelical college. In 1584 his opposition to the Gregorian calendar made him very unpopular, and he was finally driven from the place. He went to Ulm, where he was kindly received; but he remained there only a short time, accepting in 1585 a call to Wittenberg University as professor of theology. When the Philippists gained supremacy at that high school Mylius removed to Jena, soon, however, to turn back to Wittenberg, where he died, May 28, 1603. Mylius was an industrious student, and prepared numerous exegetical works. See Adam, *Vitæ Theol. Germ.* (1620).

Mylius, Georg (2), a German Lutheran divine, flourished in the first half of the 17th century as pastor in Brandenburg, near Königsberg, East Prussia. He died in 1640. Mylius is noted as a German hymnologist. He was a true follower of the poetical school whose head was Dach (q. v.). Mylius is the author of the well-known German funeral dirge, "Herr, ich denk, an jene Zeit," etc.

Mylne, ROBERT, an English architect, was born in 1734 at Edinburgh. His father was of the same profession. While he was studying at Rome he gained the chief architectural prize at the Academy of St. Luke. Of that academy, and of the academies of Florence and Bologna, he was chosen a member. Blackfriars' Bridge, which was begun in 1760, and completed in ten years, is his great work. He finally became surveyor of St. Paul's Cathedral, London. He died May 5, 1811.

Mynchery is the Saxon name for a nunnery, nuns being called *mynche*. See MYNICENS.

Myn'dus ($M\acute{\upsilon}\nu\delta o\varsigma$), a town on the coast of Caria, between Miletus and Halicarnassus, the convenient position of which in regard to trade was probably the reason why we find in 1 Macc. xv, 23 that it was the residence of a Jewish population. Its ships were well known in very early times (Herod. v, 33); and its harbor is specially mentioned by Strabo (xiv, 658). It was originally a Dorian colony of Trœzene, and was protected by strong walls (Pausan. ii, 30, 8), so that it successfully resisted Alexander the Great (Arrian, *Alex.* i, 21). Its wine was famous as an aid to digestion (Athen. i, 32). Diogenes Laertius (vi, 2, 57) records a *bon mot* of Diogenes, the cynic, of which it is the theme. Seeing its huge gates, while the city itself was but small, he exclaimed, "Men of Myndus, shut the gates, lest the city walk out of them!" The name still lingers in the modern *Mentesche*, though the remains of the city are probably at *Gumishlu*, where admiral Beaufort found an ancient pier and other ruins (Smith, *Dict. of Class. Geog.* s. v.).

Coin of Myndus.

Mynecena. See MYNICENS.

Mynicens (Lat. *mynecena*, fem. of *munuc*; allied to *moniales*) is the name of a class of English monastics who flourished in 1009 and 1017, and were probably Benedictines. They differed from nuns in being of younger age, and under a rule more strict. See Walcott, *Sacred Archæology*, s. v.; Lea, *Sacerdotal Celibacy*, p. 179, note.

Mynster, JACOB PEDER, a Danish theologian, was born at Copenhagen Nov. 8, 1775. He was educated at the university of his native city, was employed some time in teaching, and became in 1801 pastor in Seeland. In 1811 he was appointed assistant minister of the principal church of Copenhagen, in 1828 preacher to the court and the royal family, and in 1834 bishop of Seeland. His writings comprise a great number of sermons, dissertations introductory to the study of the New Testament, and on other Biblical subjects, and several works on doctrinal theology. His admirable *Ordination Sermons* and other of his works have been translated into German. An edition of his miscellaneous publications, *Blandede Schrifter*, begun in 1852, was completed in 6 vols. in 1856. He died in Copenhagen Jan. 30, 1854.

My'ra (τὰ Μύρα), one of the chief towns of Lycia, in Asia Minor (Ptol. v, 3, 6). It is "interesting to us as the place where Paul, on his voyage to Rome (Acts xxvii, 5), was removed from the Adramyttian ship which had brought him from Cæsarea, and entered the Alexandrian ship in which he was wrecked on the coast of Malta. See ADRAMYTTIUM. The travellers had availed themselves of the first of these vessels because their course to Italy necessarily took them past the coasts of the province of Proconsular Asia (ver. 2), expecting in some harbor on these coasts to find another vessel bound to the westward. This expectation was fulfilled (ver. 6). It might be asked how it happened that an Alexandrian ship bound for Italy was so far out of her course as to be at Myra. This question is easily answered by those who have some acquaintance with the navigation of the Levant. Myra is nearly due north of Alexandria, the harbors in the neighborhood are numerous and good, the mountains high and easily seen, and the current sets along the coast to the westward (Smith's *Voyage and Shipwreck of St. Paul*). Moreover, to say nothing of the possibility of landing or taking in passengers or goods, the wind was blowing about this time continuously and violently from the N.W., and the same weather which impeded the Adramyttian ship (ver. 4) would be a hinderance to the Alexandrian (see ver. 7; Conybeare and Howson, *Life and Epistles of St. Paul*, ch. xxiii). Some unimportant MSS. having Λύστρα in this passage, Grotius conjectured that the true reading might be Λίμυρα (Bentleii *Critica Sacra* [ed. A. A. Ellis]). This supposition, though ingenious, is quite unnecessary. Both Limyra and Myra were well known among the maritime cities of Lycia. The harbor of the latter was strictly Andriace, distant from it between two and three miles, but the river was navigable to the city (Appian, *B. C.* iv, 82)."

Coin of Myra.

Myra lay about a league from the sea (in N. lat. 36° 18', E. long. 30°), upon rising ground, at the foot of which flowed a navigable river with an excellent harbor (Andriace) at its mouth (Strabo, xiv, p. 665; Pliny,

Hist. Nat. xxxii, 8). In later times the emperor Theodosius raised it to the rank of the capital of Lycia (*Hierocl.* p. 684). The town still exists, although in decay, and bears among the Greek inhabitants the ancient name of *Myra*; but the Turks call it *Dembre* (see Forbiger, *Alte Geogr.* ii, 256). It is remarkable for its fine remains of antiquity (Leake, *Asia Minor*, p. 183), which have been minutely described by Fellows (*Discoveries in Lycia*, p. 169 sq.) and Texier (*Descrip. de l'Asie Mineure*; comp. Spratt and Forbes, *Travels in Lycia*, i, 131 sq.). "The tombs, enriched with ornament, and many of them having inscriptions in the ancient Lycian character, show that it must have been wealthy in early times. Its enormous theatre attests its considerable population in what may be called its Greek age. In the deep gorge which leads into the mountains is a large Byzantine church, a relic of the Christianity which may have begun with Paul's visit. It is reasonable to conjecture that this may have been a metropolitan church, inasmuch as Myra was the capital of the Roman province. In later times it was curiously called the port of the Adriatic, and visited by Anglo-Saxon travellers (Bohn's *Early Travels in Palestine*, p. 33, 138). Legend says that St. Nicholas, the patron saint of the modern Greek sailors, was born at Patara, and buried at Myra, and his supposed relics were taken to St. Petersburg by a Russian frigate during the Greek revolution." See ASIA MINOR.

Myrrh is the rendering in the Auth. Ver. of two Heb. and one Gr. term. The following account is a collective view of the subject:

1. מֹר or מֹור, *môr*, σμύρνα, doubtless from a Shemitic root (signifying to *flow*, or else from another expressive of its *bitterness*), though some of the ancients traced it to the mythological *Myrrha*, daughter of Cinyras, king of Cyprus, who fled to Arabia, and was changed into this tree (Ovid, *Art. Am.* i, 288). Myrrh formed an article of the earliest commerce, and was highly esteemed by the Egyptians and Jews, as well as by the Greeks and Romans (Pliny, xiii, 2; Athen. xv, 688; Dioscor. i, 73), as it still is both in the East and in Europe. The earliest notice of it occurs in Exod. xxx, 23, "Take thou also unto thee principal spices, of *pure myrrh* five hundred shekels." It is afterwards mentioned in Esth. ii, 12, as employed in the purification of women; in Psa. xlv, 8, as a perfume, "All thy garments smell of *myrrh* and aloes and cassia;" also in several passages of the Song of Solomon, "I will get me to the mountain of *myrrh*, and to the hill of frankincense" (iv, 6); "My hands dropped with *myrrh*, and my fingers with *sweet-smelling myrrh*" (v, 5); so in ver. 13, in both which passages, according to Rosenmüller, it is *profluent myrrh*. We find it mentioned in Matt. ii, 11 among the gifts presented by the wise men of the East to the infant Jesus, "gold and frankincense and *myrrh*." It may be remarked as worthy of notice that myrrh and frankincense are frequently mentioned together. In Mark xv, 23 we learn that the Roman soldiers "gave him (Jesus) to drink wine mingled with *myrrh*, but he received it not" (see Hutten, *De potu felleo*, etc. [Guben. 1671]; Pipping, *De potu Christo prodromo* [Leips. 1688]). See GALL. The apostle John (xix, 39) says, "Then came also Nicodemus, and brought a mixture of *myrrh* and aloes, about a hundred-pound weight," for the purpose of embalming the body of our Saviour. Herodotus (iii, 107) mentions Arabia as the last inhabited country towards the south which produced frankincense, myrrh, etc.; Theophrastus (*Plant.* ix, 4) describes it as being produced in Southern Arabia, about Saba and Adramytta; so Pliny (xii, 33), Dioscorides (i, 77), and several other Greek authors (Strabo, xvi, 769, 782; Diod. Sic. v, 41; xix, 95). But others have not so limited its production. Celsius (*Hierobot.* i, 523) says it was produced in Syria, Gedrosia (Arrian, *Exped. Al.* vi, 421),

India, Ethiopia, Troglodytica, and Egypt; in which last country it was called bal ($\beta\dot{\alpha}\lambda$), according to Plutarch, $De\ Iside\ et\ Osiride$, p. 383 (Kircher, $Prod.\ Copt.$ p. 175). Plutarch, however, was probably in error, and has confounded the Coptic sal, "myrrh," with bal, "an eye" (Jablonski, $Opusc.$ i, 49 [ed. te Water]). Accordingly bol is the name by which it is universally known throughout India in the present day; and the Sanscrit name is $bola$, which occurs at least before the Christian æra, with several other names, showing that it was well known. But from the time of the ancients until that of Belon we were without any positive information respecting the tree yielding myrrh: he supposed it to be produced in Syria (so also Propertius [i, 2, 3] and Oppian [$Halieut.$ iii, 403]), and says ($Observat.$ ii, 80) that near Rama he met with a thorny shrub with leaves resembling acacia, which he believed to be that producing myrrh ($Mimosa\ agrestis$, Spr.). Similar to this is the information of the Arabian author, Abu'l-Fadli, quoted by Celsius, who says that mur is the Arabic name of a thorny tree resembling the acacia, from which flows a white juice, which thickens and becomes a gum. The Persian authors state that myrrh is the gum of a tree common in the Mughrub, that is, the West or Africa, in Room (a general name for the Turkish empire), and in Socotra. The Arabian and Persian authors probably only knew it as an article of commerce: it certainly is not produced in Socotra, but has undoubtedly long been exported from Africa into Arabia. It is reported that myrrh is always to be obtained cheap and abundant on the Sumali coast. Bruce had indeed long previously stated that myrrh is produced in the country behind Azab. Mr. Johnson, in his $Travels\ in\ Abyssinia$ (i, 249), mentions that "Myrrh and mimosa trees abounded in this place" (Koranhedudah, in Adal). The former he describes as being "a low, thorny, ragged-looking tree, with bright green trifoliolate leaves; the gum exudes from cracks in the bark of the trunk near the root, and flows freely upon the stones immediately underneath. Artificially it is obtained by bruises made with stones. The natives collect it principally in the hot months of July and August, but it is to be found, though in very small quantities, at other times of the year. It is collected in small kid-skins and taken to Errur, whence the Hurrah merchants, on their way from Shoa, convey it to the great annual market at Berberah, whence great quantities are shipped for India and Arabia." When the Portuguese first entered these seas, gold dust, ivory, myrrh, and slaves formed the staple commerce of Adal. As early as the time of Arrian, in his $Periplus\ of\ the\ Erythræan\ Sea$, we find myrrh one of the articles of export, with frankincense, from the coast of Adal, styled Barbaria. The $Periplus$ mentions the myrrh of this coast as the finest of its kind, and specifies the means of conveying it to Yemen, or Sabea. There the first Greek navigators found it, and through their hands it was conveyed into Europe under the name of Sabean myrrh. Though there is no doubt that the largest quantity of myrrh has always been obtained from Africa, yet it is equally certain that some is also procured in Arabia. This seems to be proved by Ehrenberg and Hemprich, who found a small tree in Arabia, near Gison, on the borders of Arabia Felix, off which they collected pieces of myrrh, which, when brought home and analyzed, was acknowledged to be genuine (Nees v. Eisenbeck, $Plant.$ $officin.$ tab. 357). This is the $Balsamodendron\ myrrha$ of botanists, which produces the myrrh of commerce; it belongs to the natural order $Terebinthaceæ$, and is a small tree found in Arabia Felix, allied to the $Amyridaceæ$ or incense-trees, and closely resembling the $Amyris\ Gileadensis$, or $Balsamodendron\ Gileadense$. See BALM. Its stunted trunk is covered with a light gray bark, which, as well as the wood, emits a strong balsamic odor. The characteristic gum-resin exudes in small, tear-like drops, at first oily, but drying and hardening on the bark, and its flow is increased by wounding the tree. When collected it is a brittle substance, trans-

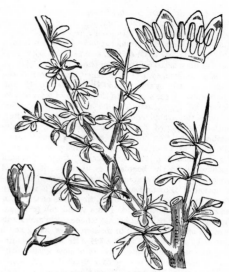

Myrrh ($Balsamodendron\ Myrrha$).

lucent, of a rich brown color, or reddish yellow, with a strong odor and a warm, bitter taste. Myrrh, it is well known, was celebrated in the most ancient times as a perfume and a fumigator (Martius, $Pharmakogn.$ p. 382 sq.), as well as for its uses in medicine. Myrrh was burned in temples, and employed in embalming the bodies of the dead. The ancients prepared a $wine$ $of\ myrrh$, and also an $oil\ of\ myrrh$, and it formed an ingredient in many of the most celebrated compound medicines (see $Penny\ Cyclopædia$, s. v. Balsamodendron). We read in Cant. i, 13 of a "bundle of myrrh," as our Auth. Ver. has it; but the word צְרוֹר ($tzerôr$), used for a purse or bag of money (Gen. xlii, 35; Prov. vii, 20, etc.), may rather indicate a scent-bag, or smelling-bottle, such as is sold by modern perfumers. Mason Good, who has "casque of myrrh," observes that a casket of gold or ivory, containing some costly perfume, is still worn by the ladies of Persia suspended from their necks by an elegant chain. The terms "pure myrrh" (מָר־דְּרוֹר, $mor\ deror'$, Exod. xxx, 23) and "sweet-smelling myrrh" (מֹר עֹבֵר, $mor\ ober'$, Cant. v, 5) probably represent the best, or self-flowing kind (Sept. σμύρνα ἐκλεκτή; comp. Plin. xii, 35; see Döpke, $Comment.\ v.$ Hopest. p. 165). (For the ancient notices, see Celsii $Hierob.$ i, 520 sq.; Bodæi a. Stapel, $Comment.\ ad$ $Theophrast.$ p. 796 sq., 974).

2. לֹט or לוֹט, $lôt$ (so called, perhaps, from $covering$, being used as a cosmetic or pomatum; Gesen. $Thesaur.$ p. 748; Sept. στακτή, and Vulg. $stacte$), occurs only in Gen. xxxvii, 25, "Behold, a company of Ishmaelites came down from Gilead with their camels bearing spicery ($nekôth$), and balm ($tsorî$), and $myrrh$ ($lôt$), going to carry it down to Egypt;" and in ch. xliii, 11 Jacob directs his sons to take into Egypt "of the best fruits in the land in your vessels, and carry down the man a present, a little balm ($tsori$), and a little honey, spices ($nekôth$), and $myrrh$ ($lôt$), nuts ($botnim$), and almonds ($shekadim$)." In this enumeration, in one case of merchandise, and in the other of several articles intended for a present, and both destined for Egypt, at that time a highly civilized nation, it is evident that we are to look only for such substances as were likely to be acceptable in that country, and therefore not such as were produced there, or as were more easily procurable from elsewhere than from Syria, as was the case with myrrh, which was never produced in Syria, and could not have been an article of export from thence. This difficulty has been felt by others, and various translations of $lôt$

have been proposed, as *lotus* (comp. Burckhardt, *Arab. Sprüchen*, p. 334), chestnuts, mastich, stacte, balsam, turpentine, pistachio nuts (Michaelis, *Suppl.* iv, 1424 sq.). Junius and Tremellius render it *ladanum*, which is suitable, and appears to be correct, as an etymological connection may be traced between the words. *Ladanum*, or *gum ladanum*, as it is often called, was known to the Greeks as early as the times of Herodotus (iii, 112) and Dioscorides (i, 128), and bore the names of *ledos* and *ledanon* (λῆδος, λῆδανον), which are very closely allied to *ladun*, the Arabic name of the same drug. A Hebrew author, as quoted by Celsius (*Hierobot.* i, 281), describes it as "an aromatic substance, flowing from the juice of a certain tree." *Ladanum* is described by Herodotus (iii, 112) as particularly fragrant, though gathered from the beards of goats, where it is found sticking. This is explained by referring to the description of Dioscorides (i, 128), from which we learn that goats, after browsing upon the leaves of the *ladanum* plants, necessarily have this viscid substance adhering to their hair and beards, whence it is afterwards scraped off. Tournefort, in modern times, has given a detailed description (*Voyage*, i, 79) of the mode of obtaining *ladanum*, and relates that it is now gathered by means of a kind of rake with whiplike thongs, which is passed over the plants. When these thongs are loaded with the odoriferous and sticky resin, they are scraped with a knife, and the substance rolled into a mass, in which state it is called *ladanum* or *labdanum*. It consists of resin and volatile oil, and is highly fragrant, and stimulative as a medicine, but is often adulterated with sand in commerce. The *ladanum* which is used in Europe is collected chiefly in the Greek isles, and also in continental Greece. It is yielded by the *Cistus*, known in Europe by the name of Rock Rose. It is a native of the south of Europe, the Mediterranean islands (especially Candia or Crete, whence the principal kind has derived its modern name), and the north of Africa. There are several species of *Cistus*, all of which are believed to yield the gum *ladanum;* but the species mentioned by Dioscorides is in all probability identical with the one which is found in Palestine, viz. the *Cistus Creticus* (Strand, *Flor. Palæst.* No. 289). The *C.*

Rock-rose (*Cistus Creticus*).

ladaniferus, a native of Spain and Portugal, produces the greatest quantity of the *ladanum;* it has a white flower, while that of the *C. Creticus* is rose-colored. Species are also found in Judæa; and *C. Creticus* in

some parts of Syria. Some authors have been of opinion that one species, the *Cistus roseus*, is more likely than any other to be the Rose of Sharon, as it is very common in that locality, while nothing like a true rose is to be found there. *Ladanum* seems to have been produced in Judæa, according to writers in the Talmud (Cels. *l. c.* p. 286). It is said by Pliny (xii, 37), as long before by Herodotus (iii, 112), to be a produce of Arabia, and as by this is probably meant Syria (comp. Pliny, xxvi, 20), it was very likely to have been sent to Egypt both as a present and as merchandise. See Celsius, *Hierobot.* i, 280 sq.; Rosenmüller, *Bib. Bot.* p. 158; Pococke, *Morgenl.* ii, 333 sq.; *Penny Cyclopædia*, s. v. Ladanum.

Myrtle (הֲדַס, *hadas'*, so called, perhaps, from its *springing* up rapidly) occurs in Isa. xli, 19; lv, 13; Neh. viii, 15; Zech. i, 8, 10, 11; and is identical with the Arabic *hadas*, which in the dialect of Arabia Felix signifies the myrtle-tree (Richardson, *Pers. and Arabic Dict.*). The myrtle is, moreover, known throughout Eastern countries under the name *As*, by which it is described in Arabic works; and its berries are sold in the bazaars of India under this name (*Illust. Himal. Bot.* p. 217). The name *Esther* is supposed by Simon (*Bibl. Cabinet*, xi, 269) to be a compound of *As* and *tur*, and so to mean a *fresh myrtle;* and hence it would appear to be very closely allied in signification to *Hadassah*, the original name of Esther. Almost all translators unite in considering the myrtle as intended in the above passages; the Sept. has μυρσίνη, and the Vulg. *myrtus*. The myrtle has from the earliest periods been highly esteemed in all the countries of the south of Europe, and is frequently mentioned by the poets (Virg. *Ecl.* ii, 54). By the Greeks and Romans it was dedicated to Venus (Virg. *Georg.* iv, 124; Ovid, *Met.* ix, 334; xi, 232; *Amor.* i, 1, 29), and employed in making wreaths to crown lovers (Pliny, xv, 36; Diod. Sic. i, 17); but among the Jews it was the emblem of justice. The note of the Chaldee Targum on the name Esther, according to Dr. Harris, is, "they call her Hadassah because she was *just*, and those that are just are compared to *myrtles*." The repute which the myrtle enjoyed in ancient times it still retains, notwithstanding the great accession of ornamental shrubs and flowers which has been made to the gardens and greenhouses of Europe. This is justly due to the rich coloring of its dark-green and shining leaves, contrasted with the white starlike clusters of its flowers, affording in hot countries a pleasant shade under its branches, and diffusing an agreeable odor from its flowers or bruised leaves. It is, however, most agreeable in appearance when in the state of a shrub, for when it grows into a tree, as it does in hot countries, the traveller looks under instead of over its leaves, and a multitude of small branches are seen deprived of their leaves by the crowding of the upper ones. This shrub is common in the southern provinces of Spain and France, as well as in Italy and Greece; and also on the northern coast of Africa, and in Syria. The poetical celebrity of this plant had, no doubt, some influence upon its employment in medicine, and numerous properties are ascribed to it by Dioscorides (i, 127). It is aromatic and astringent, and hence, like many other such plants, forms a stimulant tonic, and is useful in a variety of complaints connected with debility. Its berries were formerly employed in Italy (Pliny, xv, 35), and still are so in Tuscany, as a substitute for spices, now imported so plentifully from the far East. A wine was also prepared from them, which was called myrtidanum (Pliny, xv, 37), and their essential oil is possessed of excitant properties (Pliny, xxiii, 44). In many parts of Greece and Italy the leaves are employed in tanning leather. The myrtle, possessing so many remarkable qualities, was not likely to have escaped the notice of the sacred writers, as it is a well-known inhabitant of Judæa. Hasselquist and Burckhardt both notice it as occurring on the hills around Jerusalem. It is also found in the valley of Lebanon. Capt. Light, who visited the country of the Druses in 1814, says he "again proceeded up the mountain by the side of a range of hills abounding with myrtles in full bloom, that spread their fragrance around," and, further on, "we crossed through thickets of myrtle." Irby and Mangles (p. 222) describe the rivers from Tripoli towards Galilee as generally pretty, their banks covered with the *myrtle*, olive, wild vine, etc. Savary, as quoted by Dr. Harris, describing a scene at the end of the forest of Platanea, says, "Myrtles, intermixed with laurel-roses, grow in the valleys to the height of ten feet. Their snow-white flowers, bordered with a purple edging, appear to peculiar advantage under the verdant foliage. Each myrtle is loaded with them, and they emit perfumes more exquisite than those of the rose itself. They enchant every one, and the soul is filled with the softest sensations." When the Feast of Tabernacles was celebrated by the Jews on the return from Babylon, the people of Jerusalem were ordered to "go forth unto the mount and fetch olive branches, and pine branches, and myrtle branches, and to make booths." The prophet Isaiah foretells the coming golden age of Israel, when the Lord shall plant in the wilderness "the shittah-tree, and the myrtle-tree, and the oil-tree." The modern Jews still adorn with myrtle the booths and sheds at the Feast of Tabernacles. Myrtles (*Myrtus communis*) will grow either on hills or in valleys,

Myrtle (*Myrtus Communis*).

but it is in the latter locality where they attain to their greatest perfection. Formerly, as we learn from Nehemiah (viii, 15), myrtles grew on the hills about Jerusalem. "On Olivet," says Prof. Stanley, "nothing is now to be seen but the olive and the fig tree," but Dr. Hooker says the myrtle is not uncommon in Samaria and Galilee. See Celsii *Hierobot.* ii, 17 sq.; Bodæi *Comm. ad Theophr.* p. 375 sq.; Billerbeck, *Flora class.* p. 122; Loudon, *Arboreticum Britannicum*, iii, 962; Tristram, *Nat. Hist. of the Bible*, p. 365 sq.

Mys'ia (Μυσία, according to some, from the abundance of the beech-tree, μυσός, in the neighborhood; according to others, from the Celtic *moese*, a marsh, showing a connection with the Danubian marshy district of *Moesia;* comp. Eustath. *Ad Dion. Per.* 809; Schol. *Ad Apoleon. Rhod.* i, 145), a province occupying

the north-west angle of Asia Minor, and separated from Europe only by the Propontis and Hellespont; on the south it joined Æolis, and was separated on the east from Bithynia by the river Æsopus. Latterly Æolis was included in Mysia, which was then separated from Lydia and Ionia by the river Hermus, now Sarabad or Jedis (Strabo, xii, 562; xiii, 628; Pliny, *Hist. Nat.* vi 32; Ptol. *Geog.* v, 2). It was usually divided into five parts: Mysia Minor, Mysia Major, Troas, Æolis, and Tenthrania. The greater part of Mysia was unproductive, being covered with mountains and marshes; but it was celebrated for the fine wheat of Assus, for quarries of the lapis Assius (which had the power of decomposing dead bodies), and for its oyster beds. It was inhabited by various tribes, mostly barbarous, until, as a part of the kingdom of Pergamus, it was ceded to the Romans, by whom it was eventually formed into a province. Paul passed through this province, and embarked at its chief port, Troas, on his first voyage to Europe (Acts xvi, 7, 8). "They had then come κατὰ τὴν Μυσίαν, and they were directed to Troas, παρελθόντες τὴν Μυσίαν; which means either that they skirted its border, or that they passed through the district without staying there. In fact, the best description that can be given of Mysia at this time is that it was the region about the frontier of the provinces of Asia and Bithynia. The term is evidently used in an ethnological, not a political sense." See generally Rosenmüller, *Bibl. Geog.* iii, 32; Smith's *Dict. of Class. Geogr.* s. v.; Mannert, *Geogr.* VI, iii, 403; Forbiger, *Handb.* ii, 110; Richter, *Wallfahrten*, p. 460; Cramer, *Asia Minor*, i, 30. See ASIA MINOR.

Mysia, a surname of the ancient Grecian goddess *Demeter*, or Ceres, under which she was worshipped near Sparta. The term Mysia is also applied to a festival celebrated by the inhabitants of Pellene in honor of Demeter. This feast lasted for seven days. During the first two days the solemnities were observed by both men and women; on the third day the women alone performed certain mysterious rites throughout the night; and on the last two days the men returned to the festival, and the remainder of the time was passed in raillery and merriment.

Mysore. See INDIA.

Mystæ, those who were initiated into the lesser Eleusinian mysteries (q. v.).

Mystagogue (Gr. Μυσταγωγός, from μύστης, an initiated person, and ἄγω, *to lead*), the name in the Greek religious system of the priest whose duty it was to direct the preparations of the candidates for initiation in the several mysteries, as well as to conduct the ceremonial of initiation. It was sometimes applied by a sort of analogy to the class of professional *ciceroni*, who in ancient as in modern times undertook to show to strangers newly arrived in a city the noteworthy objects which it contained (Cicero, act. ii, *In Verrem*, liv, c. 59); but the former meaning is its primitive one, and formed the ground of the application of the same name in the Christian Church to the catechists or other clergy who prepared candidates for the Christian *mysteries*, or sacraments, of baptism, confirmation, and the eucharist, especially the last. In this sense the word is constantly used by the fathers of the 4th and 5th centuries; and in the well-known lectures of St. Cyril of Jerusalem, although they were addressed to candidates for the mysteries, some for baptism, and some for the eucharist, it is only to the lectures addressed to the latter that the name *mystagogic* is applied. This distinction was connected with the well-known Discipline of the Secret; and it appears to have ceased with the abolition or gradual disuse of that discipline. See Du Cange, *Glossarium ad scriptores mediæ et infimæ Græcitatis*, s. v.; Suicer, *Thesaurus Ecclesiasticus*, s. v.; see also MYSTAGOGY.

Mystagogy ($\mu\nu\sigma\tau\alpha\gamma\omega\gamma\acute{\iota}\alpha$, *introduction to the mysteries*) is a term used in the early Christian churches of the Orient to designate either the Lord's Supper or baptism. To designate the former it is frequently found in the writings of Cyril of Jerusalem and of Theodoret. It was intimately connected with the secret discipline, but fell into disuse with the termination of that system. See Riddle, *Christian Antiquities*, p. 485, 547; Bingham, *Antiq. of the Christian Church* (see Index). See also MYSTAGOGUE.

Mysteries, CHRISTIAN, otherwise called MIRACLES AND MORALITIES, or simply "*Miracle Plays*," were shows in the Middle Ages representing in rude dramatic form scenes from the Scriptures and from the apocryphal gospels. They were performed first in churches, and afterwards in the streets on fixed or movable stages. The actors were in the earliest times to which we can trace these shows generally monks, friars, and other ecclesiastics, and the aim was the religious instruction of the people by means of amusement. An examination of the inanimate fragments that remain to us of these plays is profitable only to those who can enter into the spirit of the age that called them forth, for it must be borne in mind by the intelligent inquirer that the coarse details in which they abound, and which shock our literary taste, were necessary to bring home to the people of those times the objects of their most serious and constant meditations—judgment, heaven, hell, the miracles and passion of their Lord, and the future of the soul of man. Nor must it be forgotten that the Church of the Middle Ages was not the first religious body to plant and promote religious sentiments by these means. The theatre, though the fact be singular, has taken its rise, wherever we can trace its origin, in religious sentimentalism. In Greece, from the very earliest ages to the days of Solon, religious feasts were accompanied by dances and performances. In the early Christian Church there was no doubt a strong tendency tc perpetuate the levity of the heathen practices; and to prevent the introduction of the pagan theatre in its entirety the Church may have felt itself forced to abolish these relics of an abhorred practice by providing dramatic entertainment in which subjects derived from the Old or New Testament took the place of those of mythology—means less apparent than outspoken opposition, but then believed, no doubt, equally sure to effect the purpose. This accounts for the custom which prevailed at an early date of the reading to the congregation in the time of Easter the narrative of Christ's passion, the various parts distributed among different parties. Later these readings came to be accompanied by dialogue and gestures, and probably the readers officiated in a suitable costume. Other festal days were gradually taken up with representations of these mysteries. Indeed, some curious proofs of the transition from the narrative form of the Bible to the dramatic form of the mysteries are still extant. They consist of dialogues in verse between several speakers, bound together by a narration, also in verse, which formed a part analogous to the Greek chorus. They were evidently accompanied in some degree by music, for in most ancient manuscripts each line is surmounted by its musical notation.

In time ecclesiastical dramatic representations were separated from the divine offices, and, though still performed in churches, formed a distinct part of priestly teaching, and under the name of *Mysteries* were acted after the sermon. Mysteries were probably taken from Biblical, and miracle plays from legendary subjects, but this distinction in nomenclature was not always strictly adhered to. The general character of all early religious plays, whether called *miracles* or *mysteries*, was about the same. If any distinction was made, the *miracles* were distinguished as those which represented the miracles wrought by the holy confessors, and the sufferings by which the perseverance of the martyrs was manifested; of which kind the first specified by name is a scenic representation of the legend of St. Catharine. The *mys-*

teries, strictly so called, were representations often oi great length, and requiring several days' performance, of the Scripture narrative, or of several parts of it, as, for instance, the descent of Christ into hell. We have an extant specimen of the religious play of a date prior to the beginning of the Middle Ages in the *Christos Paschōn*, assigned, somewhat questionably, to Gregory Nazianzen, and written in the 4th century in Greek. Next come six Latin plays on subjects connected with the lives of the saints, by Roswitha, a nun of Gandersheim, in Saxony; these, though not very artistically constructed, possess considerable dramatic power and interest; they have been lately published at Paris, with a French translation. The performers were at first the clergy and choristers; afterwards any layman might participate. The earliest recorded performance of a miracle play took place in England. Matthew Paris relates that Geoffroy, afterwards abbot of St. Albans, while a secular, exhibited at Dunstable the miracle play of *St. Catharine*, and borrowed copes from St. Albans to dress his characters. This must have been at the end of the 11th or beginning of the 12th century. Fitzstephen, in his *Life of Thomas à Becket* (A.D. 1183), describes with approval the representation in London of the sufferings of the saints and miracles of the confessors. Le Bœuf gives an account of a mystery written in the middle of the 11th century, wherein Virgil is introduced among the prophets that came to adore the Saviour; doubtless in allusion to the fourth eclogue. But there is a mystery earlier than this in the Provençal dialect, a curious mixture of Latin and the dialect of Southern France. It is on the subject of *The Wise and Foolish Virgins*, and probably belongs to the early part of the 11th century (comp. Demogeot, *Histoire de la Littérature Française*). Another mystery, entitled the *Jeu de St. Nicholas*, also of like antiquity, belongs to Northern France. Fitzstephen, in the reign of Henry II of England (born 1133, died 1189), dwells on the sacred plays acted in London representing the miracles or passions of martyrs. These plays, according to M. Raynouard (*Journal des Savans* [1828], p. 297), were the earliest dramatic representations, and gave rise to the mysteries. This is not probable, however, as they were even then denominated mysteries or miracles both in England and on the Continent. The truth is, as Mr. Hallam has said, that "it is impossible to fix their first appearance at any single æra" (*Introd. Europ. Lit.* i, 123). The fact is that in the 11th century these plays are found in favor within the walls of convents, and on public occasions and festivals, both in England and on the Continent. Thus, in the 11th century, Hilarius, a disciple of Abelard, substituted for the prose of the old ritual for the Feast of St. Nicholas a dialogue in Latin rhyme, with refrains in the *Langue d'oil*. A monk of St. Bénoit-sur-Loire, who flourished at a later period, treated the same history in simple Latin. Both these pieces were acted in the churches for nearly a century, when Jean Bodel, of Arras, founded upon them a drama, which was written entirely in French, and which was probably acted in the public squares of Arras, or in the hall of some large dwelling. This was, in all probability, the first instance of the emancipation of the drama from the Church. The trouvères of the 13th century followed readily in the lead of Jean Bodel. Among others we may mention Adam de la Halle, the fellow-townsman of Bodel, nicknamed *Le Bossu d'Arras*, and the witty enemy of the monks, the satirical Rutebœuf.

The clergy were soon altogether superseded by the laity, who formed themselves into companies and guilds to act these pieces, and every considerable town had a fraternity for the performance of *mysteries*. Such associations, it should be stated, however, were established in a serious spirit of piety and beneficence, without any thought of antagonism to the Church; and that the Church failed to recognise any opposition is apparent in the fact that, on the establishment of the Corpus Christi festival by Pope Urban IV, in 1264, miracle plays were made its adjuncts. The change from clergy to laity was very desirable, for one reason especially. Hitherto the plays had usually been written in Latin, and the greater part was made intelligible to the people only through pantomime. But as this was unsatisfactory, and the spectators could not always get at the player's intent, there was an obvious inducement to make use of the vernacular language. This gave import to the people's tongue, and in this way the mysteries of the 14th and succeeding centuries play no unimportant part in the development of the modern languages (comp. Schlegel, *Lect. Hist. of Mod. Lit.* lect. ix–xi). The most celebrated, though one of the latest founded (1350), of these fraternities was the *Confrérie de la Passion et Résurrection de notre Seigneur*. It was composed of Paris citizens, master masons, locksmiths, and others. The first scene of their representations was the village of St. Maur, near Vincennes. The provost of Paris refusing his license, the Confrérie applied to and received the authorization of Charles VI, who by letters patent, in 1402, gave permission to them to act "any mystery whatsoever either before the king or before his people, in any suitable place, either in the town of Paris itself or in its suburbs." Upon this they established themselves in the Hospital of the Holy Trinity, outside the Porte St. Denis. There on public holidays they gave representations of pieces drawn from the New Testament. Crowds both of clergy and laity flocked to them. *The Church did all in its power to further their success, altering the hour of vespers to facilitate the attendance of the faithful at them.* The Præmonstratensians, owners of the Hospital of the Holy Trinity, gladly let for them their spacious hall. The spectators sat on unwearied often until the night fell, and then the assembly broke up to meet again on the next Sunday for the continuation of the interrupted drama, which sometimes lasted for months at a time. The stage consisted of tiers of scaffolding raised one above another, the topmost tier, with its gilt balustrade, representing Paradise, and holding "*chaire parée*," which did duty as the throne of the Most High. "In pomp of show they far excelled our English mysteries," says Hallam; and the mixture of tragedy and comedy in the poetry appealed powerfully to the quick susceptibilities of an impressionable nation, which delights in nothing so much as in extremes and contrasts.

We have said that the laity intended no opposition to the Church, and that the clergy recognised no such opposition, and did not anticipate it; yet by or even before the end of the 13th century the laity had robbed the clergy of a great part of their influence, and in the course of the 14th became the means of paralyzing it entirely. The length, too, to which these performances were carried surpasses credence. No subject was deemed too sacred to be chosen as a theme, no subject too holy to be represented. Heaven was depicted, in which the Father was surrounded by his holy angels. Hell was portrayed by a dark and yawning cavern, from which issued hideous howlings, as of tormented souls; but whence also, with a curious inconsistency, came the jesters and buffoons of the sacred drama. Not only were all the Scripture characters freely introduced, but angels, archangels, Lucifer, Satan, Beelzebub, Belial, and even the three persons of the Holy Trinity. Some of these dramas lasted for a number of days, one of them covering the whole period of time from the creation of the world to the last judgment. No wonder, then, that these plays, which were originally designed as a means of instructing the people, and were performed in the churches, rapidly degenerated until they turned into a species of scandalously irreverent buffoonery. From being employed as a means of instruction, they were thus converted into a means of amusement; from being enacted in the churches and by the clergy, they came to be performed by strolling and vagabond players on temporary and portable stages constructed on wheels. Thenceforth the theatre took a wider scope;

art labored to supply the ever-increasing weakness of religious impressions; creations of the poet's fancy appeared side by side with scriptural characters; popular scenes became by degrees more common, and hence little by little arose the drama of our own day—a light amusement intended for the pastime of an idle crowd.

The 14th and 15th centuries were fertile of religious dramas in many parts of Europe, and throughout the centuries immediately following they continued in full force. In Germany they were very popular. In France they did not prevail largely after the 15th century. In Italy they were very congenial to the people, whose delight in sensible objects is so intense, and societies for their performance were formed as in France. They were largely popular in the 15th century (comp. Roscoe, *Life of Lorenzo*, i, 402; Hallam, *Lit.* i, 124, 125), and they have in some of their forms been continued for the edification and amusement of the populace quite down to our own times (Ticknor, *Hist. of Spanish Lit.* i, 229, foot-note 3). In Spain they were likewise common, and their origin is so remote that "it can no longer be determined" (Ticknor, i, 230). There, however, the clergy were left to play these mysteries, as is apparent from the code of Alfonso X, which was prepared about 1260, and in which, after forbidding the clergy certain gross indulgences, the law goes on to say: "Neither ought they to be makers of buffoon plays, that people may come to see them; and if other men make them, clergymen should not come to see them, for such men do things low and unsuitable. Nor, moreover, should such things be done in churches; but rather we say they should be cast out in dishonor, without punishment to those engaged in them; for the church of God was made for prayer, and not for buffoonery; as our Lord Jesus Christ declared in the Gospel that his house was called the house of prayer, and ought not to be made a den of thieves. But exhibitions there be that clergymen may make, such as that of the birth of our Lord Jesus Christ, which shows how the angel came to the shepherds, and how he told them Jesus Christ was born; and, moreover, of his appearance when the three kings came to worship him, and of his resurrection, which shows how he was crucified and rose the third day. Such things as these, which move men to do well, may the clergy make, as well as to the end that man may have in remembrance that such things did truly happen. But this must they do decently, and in devotion; and in the great cities where there is an archbishop or bishop, and under their authority, or that of others by them deputed, and not in villages, nor in small places, nor to gain money thereby." But though these earliest religious representations in Spain, whether pantomimic or in dialogue, were thus given, not only by churchmen, but by others, certainly before the middle of the 13th century, and probably much sooner, they passed entirely out of the control of those who intended them for religious and moral purposes, and though they were continued for several centuries afterwards, still no fragment of them, and no distinct account of them, now remain to us (see Ticknor, i, 231; and compare below).

In England they continued in full force for above four hundred years—a longer period than can be assigned to the English national drama as we now recognise it. Their height of popularity was in the 15th century. Of these mysteries, two complete series, which are supposed to belong to the 15th century (Hallam, *Lit.* i, 124 [105]), have lately been published from ancient manuscripts, *the Townley Mysteries*, performed by the monks of Woodchurch, near Wakefield, and the different leading companies of that town; and *the Coventry Mysteries*, performed with like help of the trades in Coventry, by the Gray Friars of that ancient city. Both of these collections begin with the creation, and carry on the story in different pageants or scenes until the judgment-day. The first two have been published by the Shakespeare Society, and the other by the Surtees Society. The Townley mysteries are full of the burlesque element, and contain many curious illustrations of contemporary manners. The Coventry mysteries were famous in England. Of these, Dugdale relates, in his *History of Warwickshire*, published in 1656, that, "Before the suppression of the monasteries this city was very famous for the pageants that were play'd therein, upon Corpus Christi day (one of their ancient fairs), which occasioning very great confluence of people thither from far and near, was of no small benefit thereto; which pageants being acted with mighty state and reverence by the Grey Friers, had theatres for the several scenes, very large and high, placed upon wheels, and drawn to all the eminent parts of the city, for the better advantage of spectators, and contain'd the story of the Old and New Testament, composed in the old Englishe rithme, as appeareth by an ancient MS. (in Bibl. Cotton. Vesp. D. VIII), entituled, *Ludus Corporis Christi*, or *Ludus Coventriæ*." The celebrity of the performances may be inferred from the rank of the audiences; for at the festival of Corpus Christi in 1483 Richard III visited Coventry to see the plays, and at the same season in 1492 they were attended by Henry VII and his queen, by whom they were highly commended. Of them it is said, "Every company had his pagiante, or parte, which pagiantes were a highe scaffolde with two rowmes, a higher and a lower, upon four wheeles. In the lower they apparelled themselves, in the higher rowme they played, being all open on the tope, that all behoulders might heare and see them. The places where they played them was in every streete. They begane first at the Abay Gates, and when the pagiante was played, it was wheeled to the High Cross before the mayor, and so to every streete; and so every streete had a pagiante playing before them, till all the pagiantes for the daye appointed were played; and when one pagiante was neere ended, worde was broughte from streete to streete, that soe the mighte come in place thereof, exceedinge orderlye, and all the streetes had their pagiante afore them, all at one time, playing together, to se which playes was great resorte, and also scafoldes, and stages made in the streetes, in those places wheare they determined to playe their pagiantes." The first mystery performed in Scotland was at Aberdeen, in 1445, and was called the *Haly Blade*. One was called Candlemas Day, and another Mary Magdalene. The records of the town council of Edinburgh, in 1554, contain an order to pay Walter Bynning for making, among other theatrical implements, a mitre, a fool's hood, a pair of angel's wings, two angels' hair, and a chaplet of triumph. Other and coarser scenes were enacted by the Boy-bishop (q. v.), and at the Feast of Asses (q. v.).

Out of the mysteries and miracle plays sprang a third class of religious plays called *Moralities*, in which allegorical personifications of the Virtues and Vices were introduced as dramatis personæ. These personages at first only took part in the play along with the scriptural or legendary characters, but afterwards entirely superseded them. This change from mysteries to moralities corresponded to a remarkable modification of the public mind. Reason, eager to produce and combine ideas, had been substituted for the simple, unquestioning faith of the Middle Ages. Allegory, no longer the concrete and material rendering of undisputed facts, became a work of intelligence, abstraction, and analysis. Nature, her high and undying loveliness unguessed, appeared commonplace and insipid, and in need of the fictitious combinations of imagination. The mind of man having shaken itself free from its old trammels, sometimes in its pride and joy abused its new-found freedom. The *moralities* were perhaps best promulgated in France, where a guild was established by Philip the Fair about 1303, with special privileges for their representations. In one of such dramas, of which Demogeot furnishes an extract, the gay boon companions *Eat-all*, *Thirst*, *Drink-to-you*, and *Sans Water*, are politely invited by the rich and splendid *Banquet*. The ladies of the party

are *Daintiness*, *Gluttony*, and *Lust*. The feast is all that can be desired, the guests are more than satisfied; when suddenly a band of enemies — *Colic*, *Gout*, *Jaundice*, *Quinsy*, and *Dropsy*—rush in and seize the assembled revellers by the leg or the throat or the stomach, as the case may be. Some are overwhelmed—some rush for succor to *Sobriety*, who calls *Cure* to help him. *Banquet* is condemned to death by the judge, *Experience*, and *Diet* is his executioner. The oldest-known English compositions of this kind are of the time of Henry VI; they are more elaborate and less interesting than the miracle plays. Moralities continued in fashion in England till the time of Elizabeth, and were there the immediate precursors of the regular drama. In France they were the precursors of the light play known as *farce*, which "may be reckoned a middle link between the extemporaneous effusions of the mimes and the legitimate drama" (Hallam, *Lit.* i, 26 [109]). And this seems the more natural result of the two. From such pieces as the one of which we give a synopsis above the step to farces was but a short one. Moralities could not long enchain a people on whom refinement of satirical wit is generally thrown away. The mysteries no longer made them weep — it would be well to make them laugh, and farce was invented. In Germany, especially in the Alpine districts, they were composed and acted by the peasants. These peasant-plays had less regularity in their dramatic form, were often interspersed with songs and processions, and in their union of simplicity with high-wrought feeling were most characteristic of a people in whom the religious and dramatic element are both so largely developed. In the early part of the sixteenth century they began to partake in some degree of the comic character which has been their frequent tendency; and thus, although designed at first for the religious instruction of the people, they had long before the Reformation so far departed from their original character as to be mixed up in many instances with buffoonery and irreverence, intentional or unintentional, and to be the means of inducing contempt rather than respect for the Church and religion.

It is a mistake to suppose that the hostility of the Reformers was what suppressed these popular exhibitions of sacred subjects. The fathers of the Reformation showed no unfriendly feeling towards them. Luther is reported to have said that they often did more good and produced more impression than sermons. The most direct encouragement was given to them by the founders of the Swedish Protestant Church, and by the earlier Lutheran bishops, Swedish and Danish. The authorship of one drama of the kind is assigned to Grotius. In England, the greatest check they received was from the rise of the secular drama; yet they continued to be occasionally performed in the times of James I and Charles I, and it is well known that the first sketch of Milton's *Paradise Lost* was a sacred drama, in which the opening speech was Satan's address to the sun. A degenerate relic of the miracle play may yet be traced in some remote districts of England, where the story of St. George, the dragon, and Beelzebub is rudely represented by the peasantry. "In Spain," says Ticknor, "as late as 1840, something resembling a *mystery* of the earliest time was represented at Valencia during the shows of the Corpus Christi (comp. Lamarca, *Tentro de Valencia*, 1840, p. 11). This, I suppose, is the dramatic entertainment which Julius von Minutoli witnessed in the Feast of the Sacrament at Valencia in 1853, and which he not only describes, but prints entire in the dialect of the country just as he heard it" (*Hist. of Spanish Literature*, iii, 347, foot-note). In Mexico, too, the mysteries have been kept up to this day. Thus Bayard Taylor, during his travels in that country, witnessed the performance of such a religious play.

But though the mysteries may still continue to be performed in Roman Catholic countries, it is nevertheless a fact that a Roman Catholic country struck the first blow for their extinction—this was done in the

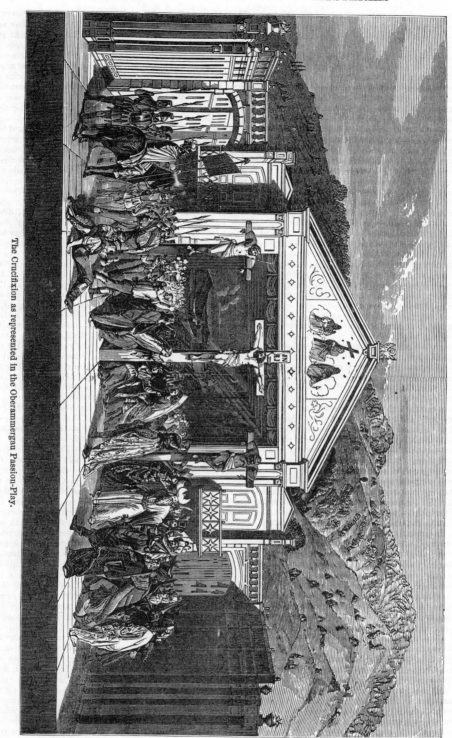

The Crucifixion as represented in the Oberammergau Passion-Play.

Roman Catholic south of Germany, where these miracle plays and mysteries had preserved most of their old religious character. They had begun to be tainted there, too, though only to a limited extent, with the burlesque element, which had brought them into disrepute elsewhere. In 1799 a manifesto was issued by the prince-archbishop of Salzburg condemning them, and prohibiting their performance on the ground of their ludicrous mixture of the sacred and the profane, the frequent bad acting in the serious parts, the distraction of the lower orders from more edifying modes of instruction, and the scandal arising from the exposure of sacred subjects to the ridicule of free-thinkers. This ecclesiastical denunciation was followed by vigorous measures on the part of the civil authorities in Austria and Bavaria. One exception was made to the general suppression. In 1633 the villagers of Oberammergau, in the Bavarian highlands, on the cessation of a plague which desolated the surrounding country, had vowed to perform every tenth year Christ's passion, out of gratitude, and as a means of religious instruction—a vow which has ever since been regularly observed. The pleading of a deputation of Ammergau peasants with Max Joseph of Bavaria saved this mystery from a general condemnation, on condition of everything that could offend good taste being expunged. It was then and afterwards somewhat remodelled, and is perhaps the only mystery or miracle play which has survived to the present day. The last performance took place in 1870 (see its photographic representation in the *Album of the Passion-play of Ober-Ammergau*, by J. P. Jackson, Lond. and Mun. 1873, 4to). The inhabitants of this secluded village, long noted for their skill in carving in wood and ivory, have a rare union of artistic cultivation with perfect simplicity. Their familiarity with sacred subjects is even beyond what is usual in the Alpine part of Germany, and the spectacle seems still to be looked on with feelings much like those with which it was originally conceived. What would elsewhere appear impious is to the Alpine peasants devout and edifying. The personator of Christ considers his part an act of religious worship; he and the other principal performers are said to be selected for their holy life, and consecrated to their work with prayer. The players, about five hundred in number, are exclusively the villagers, who, though they have no artistic instruction except from the parish priest, act their parts with no little dramatic power, and a delicate appreciation of character. The New-Testament narrative is strictly adhered to, the only legendary addition to it being the St. Veronica handkerchief. The acts alternate with tableaux from the Old Testament and choral odes. Many thousands of the peasantry are attracted by the spectacle from all parts of the Tyrol and Bavaria, among whom the same earnest and devout demeanor prevails as among the performers. The following are some of the principal scenes given by a late eye-witness: "1. The triumphal entry of Christ into Jerusalem; the children and people shouting 'Hosanna!' and strewing clothes and branches. This introduced the Saviour and the apostles, and formed in itself an admirable introduction to the whole. There were certainly no less than two hundred persons in the crowd, including seventy or eighty children. 2. The long and animated debates in the Sanhedrim, including the furious evidence of the expelled money-changers, and later the interview with Judas, when the contract was ratified between him and the priests by the payment of the thirty pieces of silver. Nothing could be more characteristic, real, and unaffected than these. 3. The Last Supper, and the washing of the apostles' feet. Here the table was arranged on the model of the well-known picture of Leonardo da Vinci. 4. All the scenes in which Christ was brought successively before Annas, Caiaphas, Pilate, and Herod; the 'Ecce Homo' (copied, it struck me, from Van Dyck), the scourging, etc. In some of these as many as two hundred and fifty persons were at once on the scene—infuriated mobs of priests, money-changers, Roman soldiers, etc.—and, violent as were the passions personified, there was not the least approach to rant, nor the slightest transgression into irreverence or improbability. In the course of these scenes a striking occurrence was the contrast of Barabbas—a brutal and squalid figure—with the noble form and countenance of the sacred sufferer—the latter formed more after the model of those of Albert Dürer than of any other painter; at least such was my impression. Both Pilate and Herod were admirably represented, but especially the former. 5. The whole long procession, at the slowest pace, from Pilate's

house to Golgotha; our Lord and the thieves carrying their huge crosses; his interview with his mother and the other women of Jerusalem. This contained the legendary or traditional incident of the wiping of Christ's face by St.Veronica; but there was no attempt to show the miraculous impression of the sacred countenance on the handkerchief, which forms the point of the legend. 6. The last dreadful scene—the uprearing of the three crosses with their living burdens, and all the cruel incidents of that most cruel and lingering death" (Eadie, *Eccles. Cyclop.* s. v.). Plays of an humble description, from subjects in legendary or sacred history, are not unfrequently got up by the villagers around Innspruck, which show a certain rude dramatic talent, though not comparable to what is exhibited at Ammergau. Girls very generally represent both the male and female characters. See, besides the authorities quoted in the article, Onésime le Roy, *Études sur les Mystères* (Paris, 1837, 8vo), ch. i; Edelstand du Meril, *Origines du Théâtre moderne* (Paris, 1849, 8vo); Wright, *Early Mysteries*, etc. (Lond. 1838, 8vo); Collier, *Hist. of Engl. Dramat. Poetry*; Magnin, *Les Origines du Théâtre moderne* (Paris, 1838); Devrient, *Geschichte d. Schauspielkunst* (Leipsic, 1848); Hone, *English Mysteries* (Lond. 1823); Marriott, *English Miracle-plays* (Basle, 1856). The *libretto* has been published (Lond. 1890, 8vo). For monographs, see Volbeding, *Index Programmatum*, p. 172.

Mystery ($\mu\nu\sigma\tau\eta\rho\iota\nu$), a term employed in the Bible (N. T.), as well as in some of the pagan religions, to denote a *revealed secret*. See Grossmann, *De Judæorum arcani disciplina* [see Essenes] (Lips. 1833-4); and on the Christian "secret discipline," the monographs cited by Volbeding, *Index Programm.* p. 138 sq.

I. *Etymology of the Word.*—Some have thought to derive the Greek $\mu\nu\sigma\tau\eta\rho\iota\nu$, from which the English *mystery* is plainly a transfer, from a Hebrew source, but sound philology forbids this. It is clearly a derivation, through $\mu\nu\sigma\tau\eta\varsigma$, an *initiated* person, from $\mu\nu\epsilon\iota\sigma\vartheta\alpha\iota$, *to initiate*, and thus ultimately from $\mu\nu\omega$, *to close* the eyes or mouth, i. e. to keep a secret. The derivative $\mu\nu\sigma\tau\eta\rho\iota\nu$ had always a reference to secrets of a *religious* character, and this sense is retained in the Bible.

II. *Pagan Mysteries in general.*—These were ceremonies in which only the initiated could participate. The practice may be obscurely traced to the early Orient, in the rites of Isis (q. v.) and Osiris (q. v.) in Egypt, in the Mithraic solemnities of Persia, and in the Greek festivals connected with the worship of Bacchus and Cybele, and may be even faintly recognised in our day in the ceremonies of freemasonry. They consisted in general of rites of purification and expiation, of sacrifices and processions, of ecstatic or orgiastic songs and dances, of nocturnal festivals fit to impress the imagination, and of spectacles designed to excite the most diverse emotions—terror and trust, sorrow and joy, hope and despair. The celebration was chiefly by symbolical acts and spectacles; yet sacred mystical words, formulas, fragments of liturgies, or hymns, were also employed. There were likewise certain objects with which occult meanings that were imparted to the initiated were associated, or which were used in the various ceremonies in the ascending scale of initiation. The sacred phrases, the $\dot{\alpha}\pi\dot{\rho}\rho\rho\eta\tau\alpha$, concerning which silence was imposed, were themselves symbolical legends, and probably not statements of speculative truths. The most diverse theories have been suggested concerning the origin, nature, and significance of the Hellenic mysteries. As Schönemann remarks (*Griechische Alterthümer*, 3d ed., Berlin, 1873), the very fact that it was not permitted to reveal to the uninitiated wherein these cults consisted, what were the rites peculiar to them, for what the gods were invoked, or what were the names of the divinities worshipped, has been the cause of our extremely incomplete information in regard to them.

The oldest of the Hellenic mysteries are believed to be the *Cabiric*, in Samothrace and Lemnos, which were renowned through the whole period of pagan antiquity.

Though they were only less august than the Eleusinian, nothing is certain concerning them, and even the names of the divinities are known to us only by the profanation of Manaseas. (See below.) The *Eleusinian* were the most venerable of the mysteries. "Happy," says Pindar, "is he who has beheld them, and descends beneath the hollow earth; he knows the end, he knows the divine origin of life." They composed a long series of ceremonies, concluding with complete initiation or perfection. The fundamental legend on which the ritual seems to have been based was the search of the goddess Demeter, or Ceres, for her daughter Proserpine, her sorrows and her joys, her descent into Hades, and her return into the realm of light. The rites were thought to prefigure the scenes of a future life. The same symbol was the foundation of the Thesmophoria, which were celebrated exclusively by married women, rendering it probable that initiation was designed to protect against the dangers of childbirth. (See below.) The *Orphic* and *Dionysiac* mysteries seem to have designed a reformation of the popular religion. Founded upon the worship of the Thracian Dionysus, or Bacchus, they tended to ascetic rather than orgiastic practices. Other mysteries were those of Zeus, or Jupiter, in Crete; of Hera, or Juno, in Argolis; of Athene, or Minerva, in Athens; of Artemis, or Diana, in Arcadia; of Hector in Ægina, and of Rhea in Phrygia. The worship of the last, under different names, prevailed in divers forms and places in Greece and the East, and was associated with the orgiastic rites of the Corybantes.

More important were the Persian mysteries of *Mithra*, which appeared in Rome about the beginning of the 2d century of the Christian æra. They were propagated by Chaldæan and Syrian priests. The austerity of the doctrine, the real perils of initiation which neophytes were obliged to encounter, the title of soldier of Mithra which was bestowed on them, and the crowns which were offered them after the combats preceding every grade of advancement, were among the peculiarities which gave to these rites a military and bellicose character; and Roman soldiers eagerly sought initiation into them. The fundamental dogma of the Mithraic doctrine was the transmigration of souls under the influence of the seven planets, over whose operations Mithra presided. The whole fraternity of the initiated was divided into seven classes or grades, which were named successively soldiers, lions, hyænas, etc., after animals sacred to Mithra. The sacrifice of the bull was characteristic of his worship. On the monuments which have been found in Italy, the Tyrol, and other parts of Europe, inscribed *Deo Mithræ Soli Invicto*, Mithra is usually represented as a young man in a flowing robe, surrounded with mystical figures, seated on a bull, which he is pressing down, or into which he is plunging the sacrificial knife. A dog, a serpent, a scorpion, and a lion are arranged near him. Nothing is certain concerning the signification of this scene. After the adoption of some of the ideas connected with other religious systems, as those of the Alexandrian Serapis, the Syrian Baal, and the Greek Apollo, the Mithra worship disappeared in the 5th or 6th century. See MITHRA.

See Creuzer, *Symbolik Mythologie* (1810–12), translated into French, with elaborate annotations, by Guigniant and others (1825–36); Sainte-Croix, *Recherches historiques et critiques sur les Mystères du Paganisme*, edited by Sylvestre de Sacy (1317); Seel, *Die Mithra-Geheimnisse während der vor- und christlichen Zeit* (1823); Limbourg-Brouwer, *Hist. de la Civilization morale et religieuse des Grecs* (1833–41); Lajard, *Recherches sur le Culte public et les Mystères de Mithra* (1847–8); Maury, *Hist. des Religions de la Grèce antique* (1857); Preller, *Römische Mythologie* (2d ed. 1865); and *Griechische Mythologie* (3d ed. 1872); Enfield, *Hist. of Philosophy*, p. 20, 39, 50, 65; Puffendorf, *Religio gentilium arcana* (Lips. 1772); Osiander, *De mysteriis Eleusiniis* (Stuttgard, 1808); Ousvaroff, *Sur les mystères d'Eleusis* (Paris, 1816).

III. *The Grecian Mysteries in particular.* — These mysteries certainly were always *secret*; but all Greeks, without distinction of rank or education—nay, perhaps even slaves—might be *initiated* ($\mu\nu\epsilon\tilde{\iota}\sigma\vartheta\alpha\iota$); such was the case, for instance, in the Eleusinian mysteries. It is the remark of Josephus that "the principal doctrines of each nation's religion were made known, among heathens, only to a chosen few, but among the Jews to the people no less than to the priests." It appears that in many of these mysteries certain *emblems* or symbols (thence called themselves mysteries) were displayed either to the initiated, in the course of their training, or to the people; and that the *explanation* of these to the initiated was the mode in which they were instructed.

The names by which mysteries or mystic festivals were designated in Greece are $\mu\nu\sigma\tau\acute{\eta}\rho\iota\alpha$, $\tau\epsilon\lambda\epsilon\tau\alpha\acute{\iota}$, or $\check{o}\rho\gamma\iota\alpha$. The name $\check{o}\rho\gamma\iota\alpha$ (from $\check{\epsilon}o\rho\gamma\alpha$) originally signified only sacrifices accompanied by certain ceremonies, but it was afterwards applied especially to the ceremonies observed in the worship of Bacchus, and at a still later period to mysteries in general. $T\epsilon\lambda\epsilon\tau\acute{\eta}$ signifies, in general, a religious festival, but more particularly a lustration or ceremony performed in order to avert some calamity, either public or private. $M\nu\sigma\tau\acute{\eta}\rho\iota o\nu$ signifies, properly speaking, the secret part of the worship; but it was also used in the same sense as $\tau\epsilon\lambda\epsilon\tau\acute{\eta}$, and for mystic worship in general.

These mysteries in brief may be defined as sacrifices and ceremonies which took place at night or in secret within some sanctuary, which the uninitiated were not allowed to enter. What was essential to them were objects of worship, sacred utensils, and traditions with their interpretation, which were withheld from all persons not initiated.

The most celebrated mysteries in Greece were of three kinds, chiefly those of Samothrace and Eleusis, which may be briefly described as follows:

1. The *Cabiria* ($\kappa\alpha\beta\epsilon\acute{\iota}\rho\iota\alpha$) were mysteries, festivals, and orgies solemnized in all places in which the Pelasgian Cabiri were worshipped, but especially in Samothrace, Imbros, Lemnos, Thebes, Anthedon, Pergamus, and Berytus. Little is known respecting the rites observed in these mysteries, as no one was allowed to divulge them. The most celebrated were those of the island of Samothrace, which, if we may judge from those of Lemnos, were solemnized every year, and lasted for nine days. Persons on their admission seem to have undergone a sort of examination respecting the life they had led hitherto, and were then purified of all their crimes, even if they had committed murder.

2. The *Thesmophoria* ($\vartheta\epsilon\sigma\mu o\phi\acute{o}\rho\iota\alpha$) were a great festival and mysteries, celebrated in honor of Ceres in various parts of Greece, and only by women, though some ceremonies were also performed by maidens. It was intended to commemorate the introduction of the laws and regulations of civilized life, which was universally ascribed to Ceres. The Attic thesmophoria probably lasted only three days, and began on the 11th of Pyanepsion, which day was called $\check{\alpha}\nu o\delta o\varsigma$ or $\kappa\acute{\alpha}\vartheta o\delta o\varsigma$, because the solemnities were opened by the women with a procession from Athens to Eleusis. In this procession they carried on their heads sacred laws ($\nu\acute{o}\mu\iota\mu o\iota$ $\beta\acute{\iota}\beta\lambda o\iota$ or $\vartheta\epsilon\sigma\mu o\acute{\iota}$), the introduction of which was ascribed to Ceres ($\Theta\epsilon\sigma\mu o\phi\acute{o}\rho o\varsigma$), and other symbols of civilized life. The women spent the night at Eleusis in celebrating the mysteries of the goddess. The second day, called $\nu\eta\sigma\tau\epsilon\acute{\iota}\alpha$, was a day of mourning, during which the women sat on the ground around the statue of Ceres, and took no other food than cakes made of sesame and honey. On this day no meetings either of the senate or the people were held. It was probably in the afternoon of this day that the women held a procession at Athens, in which they walked barefooted behind a wagon, upon which baskets with mystical symbols were conveyed to the thesmophorion. The third day, called $\kappa\alpha\lambda\lambda\iota\gamma\acute{\epsilon}\nu\epsilon\iota\alpha$, from the circumstance that

Ceres was invoked under this name, was a day of merriment and raillery among the women themselves, in commemoration of Iambe, who was said to have made the goddess smile during her grief.

3. But far more important, so much so indeed as almost to monopolize the term "mystery" among the Greeks, were the *Eleusinian mysteries* ($\dot{\epsilon}\lambda\epsilon\nu\sigma\dot{\iota}\nu\iota\alpha$), a festival and mysteries, originally celebrated only at Eleusis in Attica, in honor of Ceres and Proserpina. The Eleusinian mysteries, or *the* mysteries, as they were sometimes called, were the holiest and most venerable of all that were celebrated in Greece. Various traditions were current among the Greeks respecting the author of these mysteries; for, while some considered Eumolpus or Musæus to be their founder, others stated that they had been introduced from Egypt by Erechtheus, who at a time of scarcity provided his country with corn from Egypt, and imported from the same quarter the sacred rites and mysteries of Eleusis. A third tradition attributed the institution to Ceres herself, who, when wandering about in search of her daughter, Proserpina, was believed to have come to Attica, in the reign of Erechtheus, to have supplied its inhabitants with corn, and to have instituted the mysteries at Eleusis. This last opinion seems to have been the most common among the ancients, and in subsequent times a stone was shown near the well Callichorus at Eleusis on which the goddess, overwhelmed with grief and fatigue, was believed to have rested on her arrival in Attica. All the accounts and allusions in ancient writers seem to warrant the conclusion that the legends concerning the introduction of the Eleusinia are descriptions of a period when the inhabitants of Attica were becoming acquainted with the benefits of agriculture and of a regularly constituted form of society. In the reign of Erechtheus a war is said to have broken out between the Athenians and Eleusinians; and when the latter were defeated, they acknowledged the supremacy of Athens in everything except the mysteries, which they wished to conduct and regulate for themselves. Thus the superintendence remained with the descendants of Eumolpus, the daughters of the Eleusinian king Celeus, and a third class of priests, the Ceryces, who seem likewise to have been connected with the family of Eumolpus, though they themselves traced their origin to Mercury and Aglauros. At the time when the local governments of the several townships of Attica were concentrated at Athens, the capital became also the centre of religion, and several deities who had hitherto only enjoyed a local worship were now raised to the rank of national gods. This seems also to have been the case with the Eleusinian goddess, for in the reign of Theseus we find mention of a temple at Athens called Eleusinian, probably the new and national sanctuary of Ceres. Her priests and priestesses now became naturally attached to the national temple of the capital, though her original place of worship at Eleusis, with which so many sacred associations were connected, still retained its importance and its special share in the celebration of the national solemnities.

We must distinguish between the greater Eleusinia, which were celebrated at Athens and Eleusis, and the lesser, which were held at Agræ on the Ilissus. The lesser Eleusinia were only a preparation ($\pi\rho\omega\kappa\dot{\alpha}\vartheta\alpha\rho\sigma\iota\varsigma$ or $\pi\rho\omega\dot{\alpha}\gamma\nu\epsilon\nu\sigma\iota\varsigma$) for the real mysteries. They were held every year in the month of Anthesterion, and, according to some accounts, in honor of Proserpina alone. Those who were initiated in them bore the name of *Mystæ* ($\mu\dot{\nu}\sigma\tau\alpha\iota$), and had to wait at least another year before they could be admitted to the great mysteries. The principal rites of this first stage of initiation consisted in the sacrifice of a sow, which the mystæ seem to have first washed in the Cantharus, and in the purification by a priest, who bore the name of *Hydranus* ($\dot{Y}\delta\rho\alpha\nu\dot{o}\varsigma$). The mystæ had also taken an oath of secrecy, which was administered to them by the *Mysta-*

gogus ($\mu\nu\sigma\tau\alpha\gamma\omega\gamma\dot{o}\varsigma$, also called $\dot{\iota}\epsilon\rho\omega\phi\dot{\alpha}\nu\tau\eta\varsigma$ or $\pi\rho\omega\phi\dot{\eta}\tau\eta\varsigma$), and they received some kind of preparatory instruction, which enabled them afterwards to understand the mysteries that were revealed to them in the great Eleusinia.

The great mysteries were celebrated every year in the month of Boedromion during nine days, from the 15th to the 23d, both at Athens and Eleusis. The initiated were called $\dot{\epsilon}\pi\dot{o}\pi\tau\alpha\iota$ or $\dot{\epsilon}\phi\nu\rho\omega\iota$. On the first day those who had been initiated in the lesser Eleusinia assembled at Athens. On the second day the mystæ went in solemn procession to the sea-coast, where they underwent a purification. Of the third day scarcely any thing is known with certainty; we are only told that it was a day of fasting, and that in the evening a frugal meal was taken, which consisted of cakes made of sesame and honey. On the fourth day the $\kappa\dot{\alpha}\lambda\alpha\vartheta\omega\varsigma$ $\kappa\dot{\alpha}\vartheta\omega\delta\omega\varsigma$ seems to have taken place. This was a procession with a basket containing pomegranates and poppy-seeds; it was carried on a wagon drawn by oxen, and women followed with small mystic cases in their hands. On the fifth day, which appears to have been called the torch day ($\dot{\eta}$ $\tau\tilde{\omega}\nu$ $\lambda\alpha\mu\pi\dot{\alpha}\delta\omega\nu$ $\dot{\eta}\mu\dot{\epsilon}\rho\alpha$), the mystæ, led by the $\delta\alpha\delta\omicron\tilde{\nu}\chi\omicron\varsigma$, went in the evening with torches to the temple of Ceres at Eleusis, where they seem to have remained during the following night. This rite was probably a symbolical representation of Ceres wandering about in search of Proserpina. The sixth day, called *Iacchus*, was the most solemn of all. The statue of Iacchus, son of Ceres, adorned with a garland of myrtle and bearing a torch in his hand, was carried along the sacred road amid joyous shouts and songs, from the Ceramicus to Eleusis. This solemn procession was accompanied by great numbers of followers and spectators. During the night from the sixth to the seventh day the mystæ remained at Eleusis, and were initiated into the last mysteries ($\dot{\epsilon}\pi\omicron\pi\tau\epsilon\dot{\iota}\alpha$). Those who were neither $\dot{\epsilon}\pi\dot{o}\pi\tau\alpha\iota$ nor $\mu\dot{\nu}\sigma\tau\alpha\iota$ were sent away by a herald. The mystæ now repeated the oath of secrecy which had been administered to them at the lesser Eleusinia, underwent a new purification, and then they were led by the mystagogus in the darkness of night into the lighted interior of the sanctuary ($\phi\omega\tau\alpha\gamma\omega\gamma\dot{\iota}\alpha$), and were allowed to see ($\alpha\dot{\nu}\tau\omicron\psi\dot{\iota}\alpha$) what none except the epoptæ ever beheld. The awful and horrible manner in which the initiation is described by later, especially Christian writers, seems partly to proceed from their ignorance of its real character, partly from their horror of and aversion to these pagan rites. The more ancient writers always abstained from entering upon any description of the subject. Each individual, after his initiation, is said to have been dismissed by the words $\kappa\dot{o}\gamma\xi$, $\ddot{o}\mu\pi\alpha\xi$, in order to make room for other mystæ.

On the seventh day the initiated returned to Athens amid various kinds of raillery and jests, especially at the bridge over the Cephisus, where they sat down to rest, and poured forth their ridicule on those who passed by. Hence the words $\gamma\epsilon\phi\nu\rho\dot{\iota}\zeta\epsilon\iota\nu$ and $\gamma\epsilon\phi\nu\rho\iota\sigma\mu\dot{o}\varsigma$. These $\sigma\kappa\dot{\omega}\mu\mu\alpha\tau\alpha$ seem, like the procession with torches to Eleusis, to have been dramatical and symbolical representations of the jests by which, according to the ancient legend, Iambe or Baubo had dispelled the grief of the goddess and made her smile. We may here observe that probably the whole history of Ceres and Proserpina was in some way or other symbolically represented at the Eleusinia. The eighth day, called *Epidauria* ($\dot{E}\pi\iota\delta\alpha\dot{\nu}\rho\iota\alpha$), was a kind of additional day for those who by some accident had come too late, or had been prevented from being initiated on the sixth day. It was said to have been added to the original number of days when Æsculapius, coming over from Epidaurus to be initiated, arrived too late, and the Athenians, not to disappoint the god, added an eighth day. The ninth and last day bore the name of $\pi\lambda\eta\mu\omicron\chi\omicron\alpha\dot{\iota}$, from a peculiar kind of vessel called $\pi\lambda\eta\mu\omicron\chi\omicron\dot{\eta}$, which is described as a small kind of $\kappa\dot{o}\tau\nu\lambda\omicron\varsigma$. Two of these vessels were on this day filled with water or wine, and the contents of the one thrown to the east, and those of the other to the west, while those who performed this rite uttered some mystical words.

The Eleusinian mysteries long survived the independence of Greece. Attempts to suppress them were made by the emperor Valentinian; but he met with strong opposition, and they seem to have continued down to the time of the elder Theodosius.

Respecting the secret doctrines which were revealed in them to the initiated, nothing certain is known. The general belief of the ancients was that they opened to man a comforting prospect of a future state. But this feature does not seem to have been originally connected with these mysteries, and was probably added to them at the period which followed the opening of a regular intercourse between Greece and Egypt, when some of the speculative doctrines of the latter country and of the East may have been introduced into the mysteries, and hallowed by the names of the venerable bards of the mythical age. This supposition would also account, in some measure, for the legend of their introduction from Egypt (Smith, *Dict. of Class. Antiq.* s. v.). It does seem, indeed, as if the vague speculations of modern times on the subject were an echo of the manifold interpretations of the various acts of the mysteries given by the priests to the inquiring disciple—according to the lights of the former or the latter. Some investigators, themselves not entirely free from certain mystic influences (like Creuzer and others), have held them to have been a kind of misty orb around a kernel of pure light, the bright rays of which were too strong for the eyes of the multitude; that, in fact, they hid under an outward garb of mummery a certain portion of the real and eternal truth of religion, the knowledge of which had been derived from some primeval, or, perhaps, the Mosaic revelation; if it could not be traced to certain (or uncertain) Egyptian, Indian, or generally Eastern sources. To this kind of hazy talk, however (which we only mention because it is still repeated every now and then), the real and thorough investigations begun by Lobeck, and still pursued by many competent scholars in our own day, have, or ought to have, put an end. There cannot be anything more alien to the whole spirit of Greek and Roman antiquity than a hiding of abstract truths and occult wisdom under rites* and formulas, songs and dances; and, in fact, the mysteries were anything but exclusive, either with respect to sex, age, or rank, in point of initiation. It was only the speculative tendency of later times, when Polytheism was on the wane, that tried to symbolize and allegorize these obscure and partly imported ceremonies, the bulk of which had undoubtedly sprung from the midst of the Pelasgian tribes themselves in prehistoric times, and which were intended to represent and to celebrate certain natural phenomena in the visible creation. There is certainly no reason to deny that some more refined minds may at a very early period have endeavored to impart a higher sense to these wondrous performances; but these can only be considered as solitary instances. The very fact of their having to be put down in later days as public nuisances in Rome herself speaks volumes against the occult wisdom inculcated in secret assemblies of men and women (Chambers, *Cyclop.* s. v.).

IV. *Biblical Use of the Term "Mystery."*—A most unscriptural and dangerous sense is too often put upon the word, as if it meant something absolutely unintelligible and incomprehensible; whereas in every instance in which it occurs in the Sept. or New Testament it is applied to something which is *revealed*, declared, explained, spoken, or which may be known or understood. 1. It is sometimes used to denote the meaning of a symbolical representation, whether addressed to the mind by a parable, allegory, etc., or to the eye by a vision, etc. Thus our Lord, having delivered to the multitude the parable of the sower (Matt. xiii, 3–9), when the disciples asked him (ver. 10) why he spoke to them in parables, replied, "Unto you it is given to know the mysteries of the kingdom of heaven, but unto them which are without it is not given" (Mark iv, 11); "Therefore I speak to them in parables" (Matt. xiii, 13); "But *your* eyes see, and your ears understand" (ver. 16): here our Lord applies the term *mysteries* to the *moral* truths couched under that parable, that is, to its figurative meaning. Again, the mystery or symbolical vision of the "seven stars and of the seven golden candlesticks" (Rev. i, 12, 16) is explained to mean "the angels of the seven churches of Asia, and the seven churches themselves" (ver. 20). Likewise the mystery or symbolical representation "of the woman upon a scarlet-colored beast" (Rev. xvii, 3–6) is explained, "I will tell thee the mystery of the woman," etc. (xvii, 7). When St. Paul, speaking of marriage, says "this is a great mystery" (Eph. v, 32), he evidently treats the original institution of marriage as affording a figurative representation of the union between Christ and the Church (Campbell, *Dissert.* p. 10, pt. iii, § 9). 2. The word is also used to denote anything whatever which is hidden or concealed, till it is explained. The Sept. uses it to express רז, *a secret* (Dan. ii, 18, 19, 27, 28, 29, 30, 47; iv, 6), in relation to Nebuchadnezzar's dream, which was a secret till Daniel explained it, and even from the king himself, for he had totally forgotten it (ver. 5, 9). Thus the word is used in the New Testament to denote those doctrines of Christianity, general or particular, which the Jews and the world at large did not understand till they were revealed by Christ and his apostles: "Great is the mystery of godliness," i. e. the Christian religion (1 Tim. iii, 16), the chief parts of which the apostle instantly proceeds to adduce—"God was manifest in the flesh, justified by the Spirit, seen of angels," etc.—facts which had not entered into the heart of man (1 Cor. ii, 9) until God visibly accomplished them, and revealed them to the apostles by inspiration (ver. 10). The apostle is generally thought here to compare the Gospel with the greater Eleusinian mysteries (for which see Diod. Sic. iv, 25; Dem. xxix, *ult.* Xen. *H. G.* i, 4, 14; or Leland's *Advantage and Necessity of the Christian Revelation*, pt. i, ch. viii, ix; or Macknight's *Preface to the Ephesians*, § 7). Thus also the Gospel in general is called "the mystery of the faith," which it was requisite the deacons should "hold with a pure conscience" (1 Tim. iii, 9), and "the mystery which from the beginning of the world had been hid with God, but which was now made known through means of the church" (Eph. iii, 9); the mystery of the Gospel which St. Paul desired "to make known" (Eph. vi, 19); "the mystery of God, and of the Father, and of Christ," to the full apprehension or understanding of which (rather than "the acknowledgment") he prayed that the Colossians might come (Col. ii, 2; comp. the use of the word ἐπίγνωσις, 1 Tim. ii, 4; 2 Tim. iii, 7); which he desired the Colossians to pray that God would enable himself and his fellow-apostles "to speak and to make manifest" (Col. iv, 3, 4); which he calls "the revelation of the mystery that was kept secret since the world began, but now is made manifest and known to all nations" (Rom. xvi, 25); which, he says, "we speak" (Cor. ii, 7), and of which the apostles were "stewards" (1 Cor. iv, 1). The same word is used respecting certain particular doctrines of the Gospel, as, for instance, "the partial and temporary blindness of Israel," of which mystery "the apostle would not have Christians" ignorant (Rom. xi, 25), and which he explains (ver. 25–32). He styles the calling of the Gentiles "a mystery which in other ages was not made known unto the sons of men, as it is now revealed unto the holy apostles and prophets by the Spirit" (Eph. iii, 4–6; comp. i, 9, 10, etc.). To this class we refer the well-known phrase, "Behold, I show you a mystery (1 Cor. xv, 51): we shall all be changed;" and then follows an explanation of the change (ver. 51–55). Even in the case of a man speaking in an unknown tongue, in the absence of an interpreter, and when, therefore, no man understood him, although "by the Spirit he was speaking mysteries," yet the apostle supposes that the man so doing himself understood what he said (1 Cor. xiv, 2-4). In the prophetic portion of his writings, "concerning the mystery of iniquity" (2 Thess. ii, 7), he speaks of it as being ultimately "revealed" (ver. 8). (See below.) Josephus applies nearly the same phrase, μυστήριον κακίας, a mystery of wickedness, to Antipater's crafty conduct to ensnare and destroy his brother Alexander (War, i, 24, 1); and to complete the proof that the word "mystery" is used in the sense of knowable secrets, we add the words, "Though I understand all mysteries" (1 Cor. xiii, 2). The Greeks used the word in the same way. Thus Menander, μυστήριον σου μὴ κατείπης τῷ φιλῷ, "Tell not your secret to a friend" (p. 274, line 671, ed. Clerici). Even when they apply the term to the greater and lesser Eleusinian mysteries, they are still mysteries into which a person might be initiated, when they would, of course, cease to be mysteries to him. The word is used in the same sense throughout the Apocrypha as in the Sept. and New Testament (Tobit xii, 7; Judith ii, 2; Ecclus. xxii, 22; xxvii, 16, 17, 21; 2 Macc. xiii, 21); it is applied to divine or sacred mysteries (Wisd. ii, 33; vi, 22), and to the ceremonies of false religions (Wisd. xiv, 15, 23). See Bibliotheca Sacra, Jan. 1867, p. 196; Whately, St. Paul, p. 176; Contemp. Rev. Jan. 1868, p. 182.

V. Ecclesiastical Use of the Term.—The word "mysteries" is repeatedly applied to the Lord's Supper by Chrysostom. The eucharist was the last and the highest point of the secret discipline [see ARCANI DISCIPLINA]; and the name which it received on this account was retained so long as the superstitious doctrine of the miraculous presence of the body and blood of Christ gained ground. By the usage of the Christian Church it denotes the inscrutable union in the sacrament of the inward and spiritual grace with the outward and visible sign. In the early Church the term derived a still greater force from the secrecy which was observed in the administration of those ordinances. See SACRAMENT.

MYSTERY OF INIQUITY (τὸ μυστήριον τῆς ἀνομίας), an expression that occurs in Paul's description of the workings of an antichristian power in his own day (1 Thess. ii, 7), and the meaning of which is not clear. The attributive genitive (ἀνομίας) does not seem to be that of the agent (Theodoret), nor that of apposition (Lünemann and Alford), but simply of definition, or of the characterizing quality, i. e. the mystery of which the characterizing feature, or the active principle, was ἀνομία, or lawlessness—the antithesis of order and legality. This "mystery of iniquity" was no personality, i. e. Antichrist, or any real or assumed type of Antichrist (as Chrysostom), but all that mass of uncombined and, so to speak, unorganized lawlessness which, though as yet seen only in detail and not revealed in its true proportions, was even then (ἤδη) aggregating and energizing, and would eventually (ἐν τῷ ἑαυτοῦ καιρῷ) find its complete development and organization in the person and power of Antichrist (Ellicott, note ad loc.). See ANTICHRIST.

Mystic Veils (ἀμφίθυρα, a folding door, because they opened in the middle) were hanging veils used in Eastern churches to conceal the chancel from the catechumens and unbelievers. They were also designed to conceal the eucharist at the time of consecration. As Christian churches were constructed after the type of the Jewish Temple, the ἀμφίθυρα represents the veil which separated the holy of holies from other parts of the Temple.

Mystical INTERPRETATION, otherwise termed spiritual, figurative, is either tropological or anagogical, i. e. according to it words having a distinct literal sense receive either a moral or heavenly reference. Some include the allegorical under the mystical. The mystical

differs from the literal sense in this, that the meaning cannot at once be derived from the words; but the literal sense being assumed from it, and from the things signified by it, the meaning wrapped up in the words is disclosed.—Blunt, Dict. Doct. and Histor. Theol. For example, "Babylon" signifies literally a city of Chaldæa, the habitation of kings who persecuted the Hebrews, and who were overwhelmed in idolatry and wickedness. But John, in the Revelation, gives the name of Babylon, mystically, to the city of Rome. So "Jerusalem" is literally a city of Judæa, but mystically the heavenly Jerusalem, the habitation of the saints, etc. The "serpent" is literally or naturally a venomous reptile, but mystically the devil, the old serpent, etc. See INTERPRETATION.

Mystical Pantheism. See PANTHEISM.

Mystical Table, a name applied by Chrysostom to the communion-table (q. v.).

Mystical Theism. See THEISM.

Mysticism (Gr. μυστικόν), according to the strict meaning of the word, signifies a special knowledge and understanding of the mysteries from which the uninitiated are excluded. "Mysticism," says Cousin, "is the belief that God may be known face to face, without anything intermediate. It is a yielding to the sentiment awakened by the idea of the Infinite, and a summing up of all knowledge and all duty in the contemplation and love of him" (Hist. de la Philos. 1st ser. vol. ii, leçon 9, 10). Mysticism, therefore, properly defined, is the science of the supernatural state of the human soul manifested in the body and in the order of visible things by equally supernatural effects. "Mysticism," as one has well said, "despairs of the regular process of science; it believes that we may attain directly, without the aid of the senses or reason, and by an immediate intuition, to the real and absolute principle of all truth, God. It finds God either in nature, and hence a physical and naturalistic mysticism; or in the soul, and hence a moral and metaphysical mysticism." Thus mysticism should be divided into two distinct branches: esoteric, or inner mysticism, and exoteric, or outward mysticism. The first is the study of this supernatural state of the human soul, such as it has been described by saints and mystics. The obscure, unintelligible, and even absurd descriptions given by Mystics of these phenomena, reproduced even by modern theological writers, make mysticism synonymous with quietism (q. v.), and all forms of fanaticism and enthusiasm, etc. Thus, Bretschneider says, "Mysticism is the belief in a continuous, immediate action of God on the soul, produced by special religious exercises, the effect of which is to enlighten, sanctify, and strengthen the soul. It is therefore the faith in an inward light, the neglect of the written revelation, continence, contemplation, etc." Wegscheider considers enthusiasm as a branch of mysticism, differing only in degree from fanaticism: "Omnino mysticismum præ se ferre dicuntur ii, qui neglectis aut repudiatis sanæ rationis legibus sensibus acrioribus et phantasiæ ludibriis in religione describenda et colenda indulgentes immediatam quandam rerum divinarum perceptionem jactant. Mysticismus haud raro abit in fanaticum errorem." According to Hase, the common and principal defect of mysticism is its rejection from the domain of religious life of all human knowledge and general laws, by which indeed it does not lose its intensity of feeling, but its liberty, and, becoming liable to every kind of error, is gradually more inclined to superstition. Under the influence of the strange fancies of the imagination, it leads to enthusiasm; under that of a strong will, to fanaticism; and under that of the recognition of a spiritual sphere, apart from the medium of human experimental knowledge, to theosophy. The writers of the rationalistic period give ample evidence of the confusion often made between mysticism and pietism. This error has in modern times been corrected, especially by the efforts of Nitzsch, in his *System d. christlichen Lehre.* Mysticism, then, in the objective sense, is the divine element imparted to man by external or internal communication (for instance, in the sacraments), and in the subjective sense it is special experience, visions, etc., subject to particular conditions and processes; for although man is by nature susceptible of and intended for the reception of divine communications, yet a certain conduct, sometimes an ascetic self-renouncement, an abstraction of partly the sensual and partly the spiritual identity, is requisite in order to render us capable of receiving and understanding these supernatural communications in this natural state of existence. It follows that, strictly speaking, every religious person, as such, is a Mystic, etc. Says Mill, "Whether in the Vedas, in the Platonists, or in the Hegelians, mysticism is neither more nor less than ascribing objective existence to the subjective creations of our own faculties, to ideas or feelings of the mind; and believing that, by retaining and contemplating those ideas of its own making, it can read in them what takes place in the world without" (*Logic,* bk. v, ch. iii, § 5). The inner life of religion is always mystical. Mysticism is a one-sided manifestation of this force. Sack also, in his *Polemik* (p. 288), considers true mysticism as the inner portion of the Christian spiritual life, and fanatical mysticism as an exaggeration and a misconception of the reasonable views of the Church. We concede that mysticism in the proper sense, as the immediate life of the very essence of religion, is to be found in the mystery of revelation, and is in so far the very truth of religion. The soul's yearning for the invisible finds the object of its aspiration in a sacramental union with objects of its desire. Jacob's realization of the divine presence at Bethel was as the mystic ladder of communication on which the angels of God passed to and fro between earth and heaven. By a deeper generalization, Solomon saw in the wisdom of God the bond of union that connects the spirit of the universe with the Spirit of God. The religious idea had at that early date its obverse side of mystic impress. In the cognate theology of St. John the Word is the middle term between earth and heaven, and being God from the beginning, he is still the Light that lighteth every man that cometh into the world. Hence the mystic principle is inseparable from true religion, so far as it sets the Invisible before the eye of faith and enables the soul to anticipate the future for which it was created. Hence, also, the less true forms of religion have one and all embodied the mystic principle as involving the very essence of religion. Therapeutic contemplation was the obverse of Mosaic ordinance; the Cabala refined upon the Talmud; and Persian Sufism is as the spirit of which the Koran is the letter. In the Church of the 6th century the pseudo-Dionysian mysticism was a reaction upon the dogmatic ruling forced upon the Church by heresy; much as the mysticism of the *Alombrados,* or Illuminati, of Spain in the 16th century was called forth by the rigid orthodoxy of the Inquisition, and Jansenistic and Quietistic tenets by Jesuitism. Mysticism has been the most usual form in which the expiring flame of religion has flickered up from its embers.

We must not forget, however, that mysticism, as a special and historical religious manifestation, is an exceptional form of the inner religious life, even indicating a certain one-sided tendency in it, from which real mysticism is to be distinguished. If we consider the essence and life of religion in its general manifestation, we find it to appear as a healthy reciprocal action of the objective consciousness of the existence of God and of self-consciousness. Thus we give the name of *mysticism* to the predominating relation of subjective life to God revealing himself in it, and of *pietism* to the predominating relation of God in the subjective life. The Mystic aims at becoming absorbed in God by contemplation, the Pietist at imparting the divine character to all his actions. In the former, the consciousness of moral per-

sonality is cast in the shade; in the latter, the rest in God, the solemn contemplation of his objective majesty, predominates. Hence the former inclines to pantheism. Where the personality is not simply spiritually sacrificed, but great importance is attached to transcendent contemplation of God, man loses with the clear perception of his own personality that also of the personality of God. The other tendency, on the contrary, inclines to dualism, and even to polytheism, although never degenerating so far where monotheism is recognised. When man reflects in a one-sided, methodical manner on the exhibition of the divine in its subjective action, instead of acting before God with a simple consciousness of God, he is led to a lasting disunion of his consciousness; i. e. to a distinction between the idea of the divine and his life. This partiality, degenerating into morbidness, leads on the one side into mysticism, on the other into pietism. The Mystic loses his clear self-consciousness in obscure, arbitrary, ascetic, and ecstatic conceptions, or rather in a passive experience of the divine; moral piety would be the remedy. Pietism, on the contrary, loses itself in self-made subjective religious laws and self-torments; its natural remedy would be a healthy mysticism. The Mystic loses himself in God, and cherishes the desire to passively suffer God to act in him, instead of giving himself personally over to a personal God, and thus finding himself glorified; while the Pietist loses the inward presence of God because he does not liberate the feeling of his personality from subjective, egotistical limits and religious self-contemplation by subjecting it to the personality of God. Thus, dogmatically defined, mysticism would be religion with an excessive objective tendency, or religion in the form of a central life of feeling, of immediate thought, of contemplative and intuitive knowledge, which, accompanied by an ascetic tendency, seeks principally to lose itself *via negationis* in the Deity. Compared with the religious and the ethical element in human life, or with the consciousness of night and that of day time, mysticism is a leaning towards the first form of consciousness. "If we were required to define mysticism," says Stowell, "we should call it the setting up of personal thoughts and feelings as the standard of truth or as the rule of action. By mystical views of the spiritual life we understand such views of that life as are adjusted by this standard or ordered by this rule. The relation of such views to our present theme will be found in the fact that men ascribe this inward standard of truth and rule of action to the direct inspiration of the Holy Spirit. The mystical views may be regarded under different aspects, as (1) speculative, (2) contemplative, (3) imaginative, or (4) practical. Speculative mysticism has found its place in the schools of philosophy and of morals; contemplative mysticism has been the resource of the meditative, the tranquil, or the enthusiastic; imaginative mysticism deludes the visionary; practical mysticism misleads the fanatic." For a historical development of mystical views, see MYSTICS.

Mystics are religionists who profess a pure and sublime devotion, accompanied with a disinterested love of God, free from selfish considerations; and who believe that the writings which reveal to them the story of the supernatural have a *mystic* and *hidden* sense, which must be sought after in order to comprehend their true import. Under this name some understand all those who profess to know how they are inwardly taught of God. Mystics have existed from the time when men's thoughts began to be turned inward upon themselves. "In all religious writings in which the affections come in," says a writer in the *Saturday Review,* "there must be, if it is real, an element more or less of what must bear the name of mysticism. It is simply the same thing as saying that there cannot be poetry without feeling, or art without insight, or affection and friendship without warmth of heart." Yet as there are false poetry and false art, and extravagant and false affections, so there is a false and mistaken direction, as well as a true and right one, of the religious affections; and it seems hardly saying too much to affirm that the mischief done to religion and to human society by the misdirection of the religious affections is, as far as we can see, out of all proportion greater than that done by intellectual error, and by the divisions created by what has been deemed intellectual error. Perhaps it is only to be paralleled in the mischief done by misdirected social affections. Intellectual error at least does not directly sap men's strength; and often, in the earnest conflict to which it leads, it provokes the force which is to overthrow it or keep it in check. But the disasters arising out of the misdirection of the religious affections have been of a more fatal nature. They include not merely all the train of evils attending on what is forced, unreal, and hollow, but the irreparable exhaustion, and weakness, and failure of tone, which succeeds the fever of minds wound up to overstrained states of exaltation; the credulity, the mad self-conceit, and the perverse crookedness which never can be cured; and in opponents and lookers-on, influenced by the reaction of disgust, there result the scepticism, the hardness, and the mocking and cruel temper, which the sight of folly, and possibly selfishness, clothing themselves with the most august claims and taking the holiest names in vain, must inevitably call forth and confirm.

Christian mysticism declares, in the language of Pascal, that the head has reasons of its own which the reason knows not of; or, in the words of Paul, that the wisdom of God is a mystery which the natural man receiveth not (1 Cor. ii, 6–16). In this general sense nearly all Christians now recognise an element of mysticism in the Gospel; i. e. they recognise that Christian experience has depths which the natural reason cannot sound; that there are truths which the spiritual sense perceives, but which the natural sense, or reason, cannot recognise or demonstrate, though it may perceive that they are consonant with, or at least not antagonistic to, reason. It will be readily seen, however, from what we have said above, that this doctrine is liable to perversion; and, historically, it has been perverted. In a historical survey of the Mystics, we find that they embrace various classes, from those who held the orthodox doctrines of the Church, but in the form of an experience rather than as a dogma or system of philosophy, to those who not only undervalue but actually repudiate all doctrinal theology, and reduce theology from a system of truth to a dream. Yet all of them, however widely apart in many respects, agree in this, that they seek to develop in the human heart disinterestedness of love, without other motives, and profess to feel, in the enjoyment of the temper itself, an abundant reward, while passive contemplation is the state of perfection to which they aspire. They lay little or no stress upon the outward ceremonies and ordinances of religion, but dwell chiefly upon the *inward operations* of the mind. It is not uncommon for them to allegorize certain passages of Scripture; at the same time they do not deny the literal sense as having an allusion to the inward experience of believers. Thus, "according to them, the word Jerusalem, which is the name of the capital of Judæa, signifies, *allegorically*, the Church militant, *morally*, a believer, and, *mysteriously*, heaven." That sublime passage also in Genesis, "Let there be light, and there was light," which is, according to the letter, physical light, signifies, *allegorically*, the Messiah, *morally*, grace, and, *mysteriously*, beatitude, or the light of glory. All this appears to be harmless, yet we must be careful not to give way to the sallies of a lively imagination in interpreting Scripture. Thus Woolston is said to have been led to reject the Old Testament by spiritualizing and allegorizing the New. That among this class of devout men there was often genuine piety, with a living faith which realized Christ within them the hope of glory, is not to be doubted. But delusion soon sprang up, and men, given to mental introversion, mistook the dreams of their own distempered imagina-

tion for realities. Sudden impressions were cherished as the illapse of the Spirit, and pictures of morbid fancy were hailed as exhibiting the odors, hues, and riches of a spiritual paradise.

The forms of thought and modes of action in which mysticism has been developed in different periods and among different nations are almost infinitely varied. Mysticism has appeared in the loftiest abstract speculation, and in the grossest and most sensuous idolatry. It has allied itself with theism, atheism, and pantheism. Vaughan, in his *Hours with the Mystics*, divides Mystics into three classes: the *Theopathic*, the *Theosophic*, and the *Theurgic*. Under the first class, or the Theopathists, are included all those who resign themselves, in a passivity more or less absolute, to an imagined divine manifestation. The Theosophists, again, are those who form a theory of God, or the works of God, which has not reason, but an inspiration of their own for its basis. Finally, the Theurgists include all who claim supernatural powers generally through converse with the world of spirits.

Minds predisposed to mysticism have been found in every age and in every country. The earliest mysticism, that of India, as exhibited in the Bhagavat Gita [see HINDUISM], appears not in a rudimental and initial form, but fully developed, and as complete as it has ever manifested itself in modern Christendom. The Jewish Mystics are to be found at an early period among the ascetic *Therapeutæ*, a sect similar to the Essenes. "The soul of man," said they, "is divine, and his highest wisdom is to become as much as possible a stranger to the body, with its embarrassing appetites. God has breathed into man from heaven a portion of his own divinity. That which is divine is indivisible. It may be extended, but it is incapable of separation. Consider how vast is the range of our thought over the past and the future, the heavens and the earth. This alliance with an upper world of which we are conscious would be impossible were not the soul of man an indivisible portion of that divine and blessed Spirit. Contemplation of the Divine Essence is the noblest experience of man; it is the only means of attaining to the highest truth and virtue, and therein to behold God is the consummation of our happiness here." Jewish mysticism, combined with the profound philosophy of Plato, gave rise to the Neo-Platonic school, which, as shown in the teaching of Plotinus, its founder, was thoroughly mystical. The Mystic, according to this sect, contemplates the divine perfections in himself; and in the ecstatic state, individuality, memory, time, space, phenomenal contradictions and logical distinctions, all vanish.

In the Church, Mystics sprang up in its earliest days. They were to be met with in large numbers in the 2d and 3d centuries. But little is known of them historically. Their existence and influence, however, is manifest from the strange theological coloring of the writings of some Church fathers. The principles from which Christian mysticism sprang are more readily ascertained, and we are enabled to trace it back to the allegorizing exegesis of the Alexandrian school of theology, the remote source of which may be found in the writings of Philo (q. v.). The historical treatises of this writer were evidently composed for Hellenistic readers, and set forth such facts of Jewish history as were known to every child under synagogal discipline. His allegorizing treatises were addressed to that particular phase of the Jewish mind which is dimly indicated in the Proverbs of Solomon, more clearly in the writings of the Son of Sirach, and which became a rule of life in the Therapeutæ of Alexandria. At Alexandria the literary Jew added the study of Plato to the teachings of the Law, and learned to qualify the anthropomorphism of the latter by the transcendental notions of the Deity conveyed in the purest form of Greek philosophy. By a natural progression the anthropopathic descriptions of the Sacred Book were spiritually interpreted as divine allegory, and in time the whole letter of the Law was regarded only as a veil that screened deep mystical truths from the vulgar gaze; σχεδὸν τὰ πάντα ἀλληγορεῖται are the words of Philo. This is the true origin of the allegorizing school of exegesis that was developed in the catechetical school of Alexandria by Clement and Origen, and continued elsewhere by Theophilus of Antioch, Hilary, Cyril of Alexandria, Ephraem Syrus, and the elder Macarius.

The number of the Mystics was not large in the Church until the 6th century, when they rapidly increased, under the influence of the Grecian writings of the pseudo-Dionysius the Areopagite (q. v.), the then supposed and reputed disciple of St. Paul. It was at this time—that is, shortly after the Constantinopolitan Council of A.D. 533—that the Dionysian mystical views freely circulated, and made many converts. The Dionysians, by pretending to higher degrees of perfection than other Christians, and practicing great austerities, rapidly advanced their cause, especially in the Eastern provinces. Dionysian opinions were set forth in the works entitled *Mystical Theology*, the *Divine Names*, the *Heavenly Hierarchy*, and the *Ecclesiastical Hierarchy*. The object of the author of these writings was to give a Platonic development and coloring to the deep mysteries of the Christian faith, and to lead the soul on by contemplative energy to adunation with the Deity. The highest attainment in Christian philosophy he teaches is to behold in spirit and to become one with God, who is neither darkness nor light, neither negative nor positive. Three steps lead to this blissful consummation: purification, illumination, and vision (ἐποπτεία)—terms adopted from the various grades of Eleusinian initiation (Plut. *Demetr.* 26). A more direct application of the terminology of heathen mysticism was made by this writer when he gave its title to the work *De Mystica Theologia*. A copy of the pretended works of Dionysius was sent by Balbus to Louis the Meek in the year 824, which kindled the flame of mysticism in the Western provinces, and, filling the Latins with the most enthusiastic admiration of these new opinions, considerably influenced the thought of the Western Church of the Middle Ages. John Scotus Erigena translated the writings of Dionysius into Latin by the command of Charles the Bald, and left them as a model, of which the St. Victoire schoolmen afterwards made use. We have seen in the article DIONYSIUS that these writings are believed to be the work of the 5th or 6th century. One of the most recent critics on this subject, Dr. Westcott (*Contemp. Rev.* May, 1867), attributes the authorship to some writer of the Edessene school at the latter end of the 5th or commencement of the 6th century. The immediate source of Dionysian mysticism was certainly the *Symposium* of Plato, in which the function of Eros is described as the medium of intimate communication between God and man; filling every void place throughout the universe, and binding together all its parts, celestial and mundane, in one compact body of love (*Symposium*, 202, E). Says one, the Mystics of the early Church, led on by Dionysius, "proceeded upon the known doctrine of the Platonic school, which was also adopted by Origen and his disciples, that 'the divine nature was infused through all human souls;' or that the faculty of reason, from which proceed the health and vigor of the mind, was an emanation from God into the human soul, and comprehended in it the principles and elements of all truth, human and divine." "All that exists," says Vaughan, in describing the Dionysian sentiments, "this Mystic regards as a symbolical manifestation of the superexistent. What we call creation is the divine allegory. In nature, in Scripture, in tradition, God is revealed only in figures. This sacred imagery should be studied, but in such study we are still far from any adequate cognizance of the divine nature. God is above all negation and affirmation; in him such contraries are at once identified and transcended. But by negation we approach most nearly to

a true apprehension of what he is. Negation and affirmation, accordingly, constitute the two opposed and yet simultaneous methods he lays down for the knowledge of the Infinite. These two paths, the *Via Negativa* (or Apophatica) and the *Via Affirmativa* (or Cataphatica), constitute the foundation of his mysticism. They are distinguished and elaborated in every part of his writings. The positive is the descending process. In the path downwards from God, through inferior existences, the Divine Being may be said to have many names: the negative method is one of ascent; in that God is regarded as nameless, the inscrutable Anonymous. The symbolical or visible is thus opposed, in the Platonist style, to the mystical or ideal. To assert anything concerning a God who is above all affirmation is to speak in figure—to veil him. The more you deny concerning him, the more of such veils do you remove. He compares the negative method of speaking concerning the Supreme to the operation of the sculptor, who strikes off fragment after fragment of the marble, and progresses by diminution." These early Mystics, it may be added, denied that man could by labor or study excite this celestial flame in his breast; and therefore they disapproved highly of the attempts of those who, by definitions, abstract theorems, and profound speculations, endeavored to form distinct notions of truth, and discover its hidden nature. On the contrary, they maintained that silence, tranquillity, repose, and solitude, accompanied with such acts as might tend to extenuate and exhaust the body, were the means by which the hidden and internal word was excited to produce its latent virtues, and to instruct men in the knowledge of divine things. They reasoned as follows: Those "who behold, with a noble contempt, all human affairs, who turn away their eyes from terrestrial vanities, and shut all the avenues of the outward senses against the contagious influences of a material world, must necessarily return to God when the spirit is thus disengaged from the impediments which prevent that happy union; and in this blessed frame they not only enjoy inexpressible raptures from that communion with the Supreme Being, but are invested also with the inestimable privilege of contemplating truth undisguised and uncorrupted in its native purity, while others behold it in a vitiated and delusive form." Dante, himself an exponent of Plato's *Symposium*, perhaps drew from thence the inspiring thought of his Beatrice. The further development of the Platonic idea by the Neo-Platonists—Plotinus, Porphyry, and Proclus—is closely copied in the abstraction of the mundane from the grosser thought, and the unity of divine contemplation to which Dionysius aspired. He ploughed, as Fabricius says (*In Vit. Procli.* Proleg. xii), with the Neo-Platonic heifer (comp. Lupton, *Introd. to Dean Colet's two Treatises on Dionys.* xlii). The great end at which he aimed was to show how, by means of an intermediate mediatorial hierarchy, man may hold communion with these celestial powers, order above order, until he reposes on the immediate contemplation of God himself. But he seems to wander beyond the pale of the Church. The celestial hierarchy in this scheme replaces the mediatorial functions of the Redeemer of mankind; he himself defines this hierarchy (*Cæl. Hier.* iii, 1) as a divine order, science and energy standing in closest connection with the attributes of the Deity; it is, in fact, an exact reflex of those attributes. The works of Dionysius were explained as genuine in a commentary by Maximus, the monk, of Constantinople, who composed also an allegorizing work on the Liturgy, with the title of *Mystagogia*, very much in the spirit of the Dionysian views. This work still has a value as exhibiting the Liturgy of the Greek Church of the 7th century.

Maximus forms a middle term between the so-called Areopagite and Erigena. We find in his *Scholia* on Gregory of Nazianzum the same transcendental notions of the Deity and of the divine immanence in the world of matter, which only *is* by virtue of that immanence.

As supra-substantial ($\dot{v}\pi\epsilon\rho o\dot{v}\sigma\iota o\varsigma$), God has nothing in common with any known thing, but so far as the one is manifested in being it is multiform; and conversely, the multiform, by involution, is substantially one. It anticipates the Spinozist "Alles ist Eins, und Eins ist Alles." Man having had an eternal existence in the ideality of the Divine Being, partakes of that Being. From the divine substance he comes forth, and into that substance he returns, a consummation apparently but little removed from the Nirwâna (q.v.) of the Indian theosophy. Man, both in his origin and in his future destiny, is impersonal. As uniting in one the material and intellectual, he is a microcosmic representation of the universe; as the crowning effort of creation, he embodies in himself the future recapitulation of all things in God. Substantial union with the Deity is only possible in human nature; and it was made possible to all by the union of manhood and Godhead in Christ. Thereby man's spirit soars up to God through the energy of the will, and the incarnation of the Word is perpetuated in the individual. By means of his own free will man may be raised more and more above the trammels of the body, and be formed in God. As God is man by incarnation, so man through grace is divinely formed, and is one with God. God through love became man; man through love, and by virtue of the incarnation, becomes God. It is not once for all, but by an indefectible continuance in all and through all, the whole mass of humanity, that the mystery of the incarnation is perfected. These opinions were not held only by their author. The writings of Maximus, with Erigena's translation of Dionysius, circulated freely, and among the theologians of the West helped to raise scholastic thought from its dry dialectics, and to create a taste for spiritual contemplation. They even reached the secluded monks in their cells, and led them to speculate so boldly that they fell into the wildest extravagances. One of the most favorable examples of this mediæval monastic tendency is to be found in St. Bernard, of Clairvaux, who, in his deep appreciation of things unseen, stands forth in strong contrast with the materialism of Abelard and Gilbert de la Porée, for he went so far as to identify his own thoughts with the mind of God. Full of monastic prepossessions, Bernard spurned the flesh, and sought to rise by abstraction into the immediate vision of heavenly things. He denounced reason and the dialectics of the schools. Two canons of St. Victoire, selected apparently for their kindred tone of mystic thought—Hugo de St. Victoire being of Saxon, Richard of Irish extraction—did not, however, like St. Bernard, oppose scholasticism, but rather threw a fervor into the theology of the schools, the cold reasoning of which was seen by them to chill down religious warmth. The conception of Hugo on every other subject was "moulded by his theology, and that theology is throughout sacramental" (Maurice, *Medieval Philosophy*, iv, 74). Mysticism, as applied to this school, means a deep appreciation of the things of faith, a realization by the spirit of the unseen world, and is very far from implying the unintelligible musings of the enthusiast, or an other "cold, formal generalization of a later period" (Maurice, *Mediæv. Phil.* iv, 41). Fuller, in his *Church History*, speaking of this period of mysticism, quaintly says: "The schoolmen principally employed themselves in knotty and thorny questions of divinity; indeed, as such who live in London and like populous places, having but little ground for their foundations to build houses on, may be said to enlarge the *breadth* of their houses in *height*, so the schoolmen of this age, lacking the latitude of general learning and language, thought to enlarge their active minds by mounting up, so improving their small bottom with towering speculations—thought some of things mystical that *might* not, more of things difficult that *could* not, most of things curious that *need* not be known to us." Indeed, the schoolman and the Mystic were at this time generally regarded as formidable antagonists.

Yet it is apparent now that the schoolman and the Mystic are not so constantly antagonistic as has been supposed, and are assuredly alike in one respect—for the buildings of the latter, with foundations both very small and very insufficient, rise into the very clouds. We wish that the architectural analogy could be carried further, and that a Theological and Scientific Building Act could forbid the erections of theories above a certain height without a proportionate solidity of foundation. At the head of the Mystics of this time stands Hugo. Yet it was not his but Walter's mysticism which was in direct antagonism with the scholastic system, his *Contra quatuor Labyrinthos Galliæ* being a running invective against the principles developed by the four principal Gallican schoolmen — Peter Abelard, Gilbert de la Porée, Peter Lombard, and Peter of Poictiers. Joachim à Floris opposed an apocalyptic mysticism to the dialectical theology of the school. In Bonaventura and Gerson the mystic and dialectic elements flowed on once more in harmonious action. In the 14th century the mystic tone given by the Hesychast monks of Mount Athos to the Greek Church was approved by three councils held on the subject at Constantinople— A.D. 1341, 1347, and 1350. They drew their inspiration from the writings of Maximus, the annotator of the *Celestial Hierarchy*. In the controversy that arose in the Greek Church, Nicholas Cabasilas (archbishop of Thessalonica, A.D. 1354) stood forth as the Hesychast champion, and his *Seven Discourses of Life in Christ* is one of the most effective works that mystical theology has produced. The mysticism of St. Hildegard in the 12th century, of the Swedish saint Brigitta and of Catharine de Sienna in the 14th, all form part of the same wave of thought. Paulicianism, the remote germ of the Waldensian and Albigensian sects, was rooted in a dualistic mysticism; and the Quietists of the 17th century were still true to the Alombrado stock from which they sprang.

Asceticism not unfrequently issued from the mystical religious life, its highest instances being that of St. Francis of Assisi, the founder of the Franciscan Order. The Fratricelli of the 13th century were an offshoot from this stock. The Beguine establishments, originally asylums for the widows and daughters of Crusaders, became convents of mystical devotees, with more or less of heretical taint. See BEGHARDS.

Mysticism, which had been training men in the West for a great religious revolution, sprang up and spread rapidly also in the East. No sooner had the doctrines of Islam been proclaimed by the Arabian prophet than a class of Mystics appeared who revolted against the letter of the Koran in the name of the spirit, and boldly urged their claims to a supernatural intercourse with the Deity. For several centuries Persia was the chief seat of a body of Mohammedan Mystics, who are known by the name of Sufis; and the writings of their poets during the 13th and 14th centuries are deservedly admired by every student of Oriental literature. These Eastern Mystics sought, and in some cases claimed, an immediate knowledge of God by the direct exercise of the intuitive faculty, which is a ray of Deity, and beholds Essence. Hence the indifference which they uniformly exhibited to the various forms of positive religion. Self-abandonment and self-annihilation formed the highest ambition of the Sufi. He was bound wholly to lose sight of his individuality; by mystical death he began to live. The most extravagant among these Persian Mystics claimed identity with God, and denied all distinction between good and evil. They held the sins of the Sufi to be dearer to God than the obedience of other men, and his impiety more acceptable than their faith. The Sufism of the East has continued unmodified in its character down to the present day, and is actually at this moment on the increase in Persia, notwithstanding the inveterate hatred which the other Mohammedans bear to its adherents.

In the West, Germany has been the special seat of

mysticism before and since the Reformation period. In the fellowships and spiritual associations which existed in Germany and the Netherlands throughout the 13th century and part of the 14th, mysticism was the predominant element; chiefly, however, in the form of mystical pantheism. This, indeed, was the common basis of the doctrine espoused on the Rhine, in the 13th century, by the "Brotherhood of the Free Spirit." Their fundamental principle, that God is the Being of all beings, the only real existence, unavoidably led them to consider all things, without exception, as comprised in him, and even the meanest creature as participant of the divine nature and life. God is, however, chiefly present where there is mind, and consequently in man. In the human soul there is an uncreated and eternal principle, namely, the intellect, in virtue of which he resembles and is one with God. Such mystical doctrines are partially a revival of the tenets of the Amalricians and of David of Dinanto, who elaborated the doctrines of the Beghards into a regular speculative system. The following brief epitome of his doctrines is given by Dr. Ullman in his *Reformers before the Reformation:* "God is the Being, that is, the solid, true, universal, and necessary Being. He alone exists, for he has the existence of all beings in himself; all out of him is semblance, and exists only in as far as it is in God, or is God. The nature of God, exalted above every relation or mode (aveiro), and for that reason unutterable and nameless, is not, however, mere abstract being (according to the doctrine of Amalric), or dead substance; but it is spirit, the highest reason, thinking, knowing and making itself known. The property most peculiar to God is thinking, and it is by exerting it upon himself that he first becomes God; then the Godhead—the hidden darkness—the simple and silent basis of the Divine Being actually is God. God proceeds out of himself, and this is the eternal generation of the Son, and is necessarily founded in the divine essence. In the Son, or creative Word, however, God also gives birth to all things, and as his operation, being identical with his thinking, is without time, so creation takes place in an 'everlasting now.' God has no existence without the world, and the world, being his existence in another mode, is eternal with him. The creatures, although they be in a manner set out of God, are yet not separated from him; for otherwise God would be bounded by something external to himself. Much more, the distinction in God is one which is continually doing itself away. By the Son, who is one with God, 'all things are in God,' and that which is in God is God himself. In this manner it may be affirmed that 'all things are God as truly as God is all things.' In this sense also every created object, as being in God, is good. 'According to this the whole creation is a manifestation of the Deity; every creature bears upon it a "stamp of the divine nature," a reflection of the eternal Godhead; indeed, every creature is full of God. All that is divine, however, when extraneous to the Divine Being, necessarily strives to return to its source, seeks to lay aside its finitude, and from a state of division to re-enter into unity. Hence all created things have a deep and painful yearning after union with God in untroubled rest. It is only when God, after having, by the Son, passed out of himself into a different mode of existence, returns by love, which is the Holy Spirit, into himself once more, that the Divine Being is perfected in the Trinity, and he rests with himself and with all the creatures.' "

To this pantheistic mysticism was opposed a less noxious kind of mysticism, which reared itself on the basis of Christian theism. The chief representative of this theistical mysticism is Ruysbroek, by whose efforts the mystical tendency in the Netherlands and Germany underwent a complete revolution. The system of this able and excellent writer, in so far as it affects life, is thus sketched by Ullman: "Man, having proceeded from God, is destined to return and become one with him again. This oneness, however, is not to be understood as meaning that we become wholly identified with him, and lose our own being as creatures, for that is an impossibility. What it is to be understood as meaning is that we are conscious of being wholly in God, and at the same time also wholly in ourselves; that we are united with God, and yet at the same time remain different from him. Man ought to be conformed to God, and bear his likeness. But this he can only do in so far as it is practicable, and it is practicable only in so far as he does not cease to be himself and a creature. For God remains always God, and never becomes a creature; the creature is always a creature, and never loses its own being as such. Man, when giving himself up with perfect love to God, is in union with him, but he no sooner again acts than he feels his distinctness from God, and that he is another being. Thus he flows into God, and flows back again into himself. The former state of oneness with and the latter state of difference from him are both enjoined by God, and between the two subsists that continual annihilation in love which constitutes our felicity." Gerson, himself a Mystic, attempted to involve Ruysbroek in the same charge of pantheistical mysticism which attaches to Henry Eckhart. The accusation, however, is without foundation. The mysticism of Ruysbroek, which had the double advantage of being at once contemplative and practical, was thoroughly theistical in its character, and its influence was widely felt.

In the 14th century the pantheistic theory of J. Scotus Erigena was revived by Eckhart, provincial of the Dominican Order in Saxony—the "Doctor Ecstaticus"—a man of unquestioned purity of life and great earnestness of character. The boldest metaphysical speculations were united in his system with a severe asceticism. His was a period that particularly favored the development of mystical or spiritual theology. The distraction of party warfare in state matters, the hostile attitude of the emperor towards the court of Rome, and the increasing divergence of religious opinion, gave an opportunity that was not thrown away by this Mystic theologian. Without adopting any party in particular, the Mystic devotee could combine his higher spiritual aspirations with the most opposite political and religious theories, and gain a willing ear from all. The whole heart of the people was open to him. Hence the success of Tauler as a preacher in the 14th century. He was termed "Doctor Illuminatus," as being the most enlightened preacher of his age. A living faith in the pure Word of God, he said, was better than mass attendance or bodily mortification; the sincerely pious man alone was free, the friend of God, over whom the pope had no spiritual power, for God had enfranchised and sanctified him to his free service; the spiritual and political powers were essentially distinct; neither, if the former was ever on ill terms with the civil governor, had it authority to lay its subjects under a ban. In Tauler the mystic principle was exhibited on its most practical side, and in many of his views he was the harbinger of that school of thought which brought about the Reformation of the 16th century, and which was represented by Wycliffe in England, Huss in Bohemia, Savonarola in Italy, and John Wessel in Holland, more ubiquitously throughout the continent. See FRIENDS OF GOD. With Tauler must be associated the name of Henry Suso, his friend and ardent admirer, a pupil of Eckhart (A.D. 1300–1365). Mysticism with him was a matter of feeling rather than of speculation. Wisdom as personified by Solomon was his theme, identified at one time with Christ, at another with his Virgin Mother. To make himself worthy of the object of his adoration, he practiced severe austerities, and claimed to be frequently favored with divine visions. His was no connected system, but a tissue of rhapsodical applications of the mystical theology of the preceding period, which he invested with fantastic and visionary forms. He adopted the view which led the schools so closely to the verge of pantheism, namely, that all created nature is a mirror in which Deity is reflected. Creation was eternally in God as the universal exemplar. No name can sufficiently declare the Deity. As Basilides termed the divine Principle οὐκ ὤν, and as Hegel in modern times has said the same thing, so Suso declared that the Deity might with as great propriety be termed an eternal nothing as a self-existent entity. He is a circle whose centre is everywhere, whose circumference is nowhere. Imitation of Christ's sufferings is the true meaning of man's regeneration. Three principal steps lead on to unity with the Deity : purification, or expulsion of all mortal desire; illumination, which fills the soul with divine forms; and perfection, to which is accorded the fullest enjoyment of heavenly good. If Eckhart was the philosophic Mystic, and Tauler the more practical devotee, Suso was more poetical in his enthusiastic adoration of eternal Wisdom.

In all ages a yearning for more spiritual forms of religion has driven ardent spirits into mysticism. The period heralding the approach of the Reformation was by far the most fruitful for the propagation of mystic views and life. Greatest among the Mystics of those days was Thomas à Kempis (q. v.), who in his *Hortulus Rosarum, Vallis Liliorum, De Tribus Tabernaculis*, and, above all, in his *De Imitatione Christi*, gives sufficient indication of the mystic spirit. Molinos of Saragossa, a resident of Rome from A.D. 1669, published *Guida Spirituale* (A.D. 1675), of a similarly mystical cast. Father La Chaise, the confessor of Louis XIV, brought it under the notice of the pope as a production of a kindred spirit to the Beghards of the Netherlands or Spanish Alombrados, who laid the whole work of religion in silent prayer, to the neglect of external ritual. Sixty-eight heretical propositions were found in it, and the book was condemned by Innocent XI (A.D. 1677). Molinos, notwithstanding his confession of error, was confined in a Dominican cell under a tedious course of life-long penance. His followers were termed "Quietists," and as the "Pietism" of Germany was copied from them, they may be considered as a link of connection between Romanism and Protestantism. Pope Innocent, before the denunciation of père La Chaise, had received much edification from the work of Molinos which he afterwards condemned. Fénelon also, archbishop of Cambray (A.D. 1694), was more consistent in his appreciation of the mystic principle, as shown in his *Reflections and Meditations on the Inner Life of the Christian*. His rival, Bossuet, bishop of Meaux, complained of this metropolitan to the king, and the matter was referred to the court of Rome, where twenty-three propositions of doubtful character were declared to be erroneous. Fénelon submitted with humility to the papal decree; himself published the judicial bull, and proscribed his own writing. But there was nothing about him of the Protestant Pietist; one must be either Deist or Romanist, was rather his theory. There was also an unsuspected strain of mysticism about Pascal, the scourge of Jesuitism; for after his death an iron belt, rough with nails, was found to encircle his body, and a folded parchment sewn within his dress—Pascal's "amulet"—on which was a figure of the cross and the following writing : "In the year of grace 1654, Monday, Nov. 23d, feast of St. Clement, pope and martyr, and others of the martyrology; vigil of St. Chrysogonus, martyr, and others; from about half-past ten in the evening till about half-past twelve at night, fire; God of Abraham, God of Isaac, God of Jacob (Exod. iii, 6; Matt. xxii, 32), not of wise men and philosophers. Certainty, certainty; feeling joy, peace. The God of Jesus Christ, 'My God and your God' (John xxii, 17). Thy God shall be my God (Ruth i, 16). Forgetfulness of the world and of all besides. He is found only in ways taught of the Gospel. Dignity of the human soul. Righteous Father, the world hath not known thee, but I have known thee (John xvii, 25). Joy, joy, joy—tears of joy. I have separated myself from him. 'Dereliquerunt me fontem aquæ vivæ' (Jer. ii, 13). O God, wilt thou forsake me? (Matt. xxvii, 46). May I

not be separate eternally ! 'This is true life, that they may know thee, the only true God, and Jesus Christ, whom thou hast sent.' Jesus Christ! Jesus Christ! I have separated myself from him; I have fled from him—renounced, sacrificed. May I never be separated from him. Safety is alone in the ways taught by the Gospel. Self-renunciation, total and sweet; total submission to Jesus Christ and my guide. Everlastingly in joy for one day of trial upon earth. 'Non obliviscas sermones tuos' (Psa. cxix, 16). Amen." If this be mysticism, it may find its parallel in the conversion of St. Augustine (*Conf.* vii, 11, 12). Both sought peace in philosophy—the father in Plato, the Jansenist in Descartes; if their respective masters could demonstrate the existence of Deity, they could not lead the soul to the Eternal; the revelation of the way, the truth, and the life was in either case attended with the same effects—tears, vision, light, joy, peace. They were Mystics, according to Montesquieu's definition, " Les dévots qui ont le cœur tendre."

The mediæval mysticism, in its gradual progress from a mere poetical sentiment to a speculative system, and thence to a living, practical power, led men steadily forward towards the Reformation. In the view of scholasticism, Christianity was an objective phenomenon, but in the view of mysticism it was an inward life. The former pointed to the Church as the only possible means of salvation, but the latter pointed directly to God, and aimed at being one with him. The one concerned itself chiefly with a gorgeous hierarchy, outward forms, and necessarily efficacious sacraments; the other was mainly occupied with having Christ formed in the soul, the hope of glory. The Reformers therefore could not fail to sympathize far more deeply with the teachings of the Mystics than with those of the schoolmen. Though an exceptional class, the Mystics possessed, with all their extravagances, more of the truth of God than could be found within the wide domains of the Roman Church. But while Luther and his brother Reformers learned much from the Mystics, their theology went far beyond the doctrines of mysticism. During the 15th century, indeed, the Scripture element had gradually supplanted the mystical in the religion of the times. The Bible began to displace the schoolmen at the universities. Both in Germany and the Netherlands several able and orthodox divines had arisen, by whom the Word of God was brought into greater prominence than it had been for centuries as the standard of their teaching. No sooner was the great Protestant principle announced by Luther that the Scriptures are the sufficient standard of Christian truth than traditionalism and mysticism alike fell before it. Oral tradition and individual intuition were both of them rejected as infallible guides in an inquiry after truth. But while such was the general fate of mysticism among the Reformed, it broke forth in the most extravagant forms among the Zwickau prophets and the various sects of Anabaptists who appeared in the Low Countries and different parts of Germany. Thus, as Mr. Vaughan has well said, " By the Mystic of the 14th century the way of the Reformation was in a great measure prepared; by the Mystic of the 16th century it was hindered and imperilled." The wild fanaticism of the Anabaptists was alleged to be a practical refutation of the asserted right of every man to the exercise of private judgment; and though Luther, Melancthon, Zwingli, and Bullinger exposed the fallacy of such an objection, yet for a time the work of reform was undoubtedly retarded thereby.

The "*German Theology*" had a great effect on the inner religious life of Germany at the time of the Reformation, and gave to it a mystic tone. It is the title of a work that was first brought under public notice by Luther, and published by him (A.D. 1518) as "eyn edels Buchlein, von rechtem Verstand was Adam und Christus sey, und wie Adam zu uns sterben und Christus erstehen soll." Since that time it has frequently been translated and republished, and has been a great favorite in

Lutheran Germany. All that is known of the author is that he was custos of the Deutsch Herren Haus at Frankfort, or rather across the Main at Sachsenhausen, and a member of the society of " God's Friends," Romanists of mystical principles, who disappeared from the scene at the close of the 14th century. See FRIENDS OF GOD. The style of the book is quite similar to that of Tauler and Suso. The book inculcates the necessity of completely merging the will of man in the will of God, and of practicing the most complete self-denial and mortification of natural inclinations. It is self-will that stands as a wall of separation between God and man; it converted angels into devils, and is as the fire that never can be quenched; voluntary humiliation is its remedy. Of the high conceit and lax morals of the Brethren of the Free Spirit it speaks with much severity as the very spirit of Antichrist. Enlightenment, in which mysticism has always professed to initiate its votaries, is not to be attained by talk or study; but by steady acts of self-devotion, and the practice of active virtue. Love, and no taint of self-seeking, must be the spring of all one's actions; and he can only hope to attain perfection who renounces as unworthy all wish for earthly reward. The same mind must be in him which was in Christ Jesus—self-devoting and self-sacrificing. The tone of the book shows no symptom of disrespect for the Church; but its free application of Bible principles in a neoterizing spirit scarcely failed to prepare the way of the Reformation. In some respects it also exhibits the germ of the *Reine Vernunft* of Kant. The book was always a great favorite with Luther, who freely owned himself to be under the deepest obligations to it. "Next to the Bible and St. Augustine," he says, "from no book which I have met have I learned more of what God, Christ, man, and all things are." The sound theology which pervades the work, though clothed in a somewhat mystical garb, conveyed much light to the Reformer's mind. The fundamental thought which the book contains is thus described by Ullman: "If the creature recognise itself in the immutable Good, and as one therewith, and live and act in this knowledge, then it is itself good and perfect. But if, on the contrary, the creature revolt from that Good, it is then evil. All sin consists in apostatizing from the supreme and perfect Good, in making self an object, and in supposing that it is something, and that we derive from it any sort of benefit, such as existence, or life, or knowledge, or ability. This the devil did, and it was by this alone he fell. His presuming that he, too, was something, and that something was his, his 'I' and his 'me' and his 'my' and his 'mine,' were his apostasy and fall. In the self-same way Adam also fell. Eating the apple was not the cause of his fall, but his arrogating to self his 'I' and 'me' and 'mine.' But for this, even if he had eaten seven apples, he would not have fallen. Because of it, however, he must have fallen although he had not tasted the one. So is it with every man, in whom the same thing is repeated a hundred times. But in what way may this apostasy and general fall be repaired? The way is for man to come out of self (isolation as a creature) and enter into God. In order to do this two parties must concur, God and man. Man cannot do it without God, and God could not do it without man; and therefore it behooved God to take upon him human nature and to become man, in order that man might become God. This once took place in the most perfect way in Christ, and as every man should become by grace what Christ was by nature, it ought to be repeated in every man, and in myself among the rest; for were God to be humanized in all other men, and all others to be deified in him, and were this not to take place in me, my fall would not be repaired. In that way Christ restores what was lost by Adam. By Adam came selfishness, and with it disobedience, all evil, and corruption. By Christ, in virtue of his pure and divine life transfusing itself into men, came the annihilation of selfishness, obedience and union with

God, and therein every good thing, peace, heaven, and blessedness." The *Deutsche Theologie*, which thus unfolded Protestant truth so clearly before the Reformation, has since 1621 been inscribed in the Romish Index of prohibited works.

At the Reformation period, Paracelsus (Theophrastus Bombast of Hohenheim, born A.D. 1493, d. 1541) was among the first to show a decided leaning to mysticism, though medicine, not theology, was his peculiar faculty. He was by no means a partisan of Luther, although he was himself a zealous Reformer. His theological mysticism was mixed up with medicine, astronomy, astrology, alchemy, and natural history. From a similar medley Jacob Böhme, at a later date, extracted religious comfort. But the first of the Reformed party who gave to mysticism a definite shape was Valentine Weigel, minister of Ischopping, near Meissen, in Saxony; he died A.D. 1588. Mysticism has often made a close approach to pantheism, and so in his system he said that God had pity on himself in pitying man; for since the believer is by his act of faith raised above himself and abandons the soul to God, so God is conscious of his own being in man. Thus Spinoza declared that God is only self-conscious in the self-consciousness of man. Man is a microcosmal power, and in him the world is exhibited in miniature reflection. During his life Weigel had the worldly wisdom to keep his thoughts to himself, and subscribed the *Formula Concordiæ* as a good Lutheran—really to avoid inconvenience, as stated in a posthumous writing, and not from inner conviction. In his *Postils* he complains earnestly of the sluggish spirit of the existing schools of theology; their bulky bodies of doctrine, their confession, their commonplaces and table-talk, as well as their far-famed Formula of Concord. All such beggarly elements of instruction he would sweep away, and go to the Word of God alone for light. Imputed righteousness was a doctrine, he said, that could only have been devised by Antichrist. Thus he also, though a professed Reformer, was in many points at direct antagonism with Luther and Melancthon.

The most unintelligible of Mystics, however, was Jacob Böhme (q. v.). Light, he declared, had been revealed to him that held him in a state of ecstatic rest; and thoughts were inspired by the revelation that he seems never to have had the power of communicating to others. After a silence of fifteen years he wrote the *Aurora* (A.D. 1612), which was followed by other similar coruscations. His reveries show a strange mixture of the naturalism afterwards developed by Schelling and the wilder theosophy of the ancient Gnostics. Thus he affirmed God and nature to be essentially one; and this dualized principle, without which neither nature as a whole, nor any integral portion of it, can exist, is the Deity. As to be self-engendered is the essence of the Deity, so nature and the external world is the substance of that self-generation. In the fall of Lucifer, where a spirit of light should have been engendered, there issued forth a spirit of fire. It is the principle of life of all creatures, the very heart of their existence. All that is gross and hard, dark and cold, terrible and evil, has its origin in the fall of Lucifer, the Prince of this world. But intimately as his spirit interpenetrates the mass of existence, he is not wholly one with it. The spirit of life is there also, held captive, as it were, under the covenant of death, yet not extinguished. The confines of the rival kingdoms touch each other in man, and keep up a perpetual contest between Love and Rage. In the material world the Creator is born as a creature in the quickened life of the spirit; the stars are nothing else than powers of God; and all three persons of the Trinity are ever present in the universe. The Father is the occult foundation of all; the Son in the heart of the Father is the quickening spirit of life and love, of tenderness and beauty. The Spirit is universally present. From nature and its internal development Böhme professed to have gained his knowledge of philosophy and astrotheology. He was indebted to no human lore; his only book was the book of nature, ever open before his soul. It is true he had learned much from the Theurgists who preceded him, particularly Cornelius Agrippa and Paracelsus, but the grand source of the knowledge which he professed to communicate in his mystical writings was an inward illumination, which he claimed to have received from the Spirit of God, whereby he became minutely acquainted with the essences, properties, and uses of all the objects in nature. Schlegel has been able to trace in these ravings the afflatus of a poetical mind of high order, and he does not scruple to rank Böhme with the master-minds that have taken their theme from the unseen world— Dante, Milton, and Klopstock. Hallam can see nothing in them—nothing better than the incoherence of madness (*Literature of the Middle Ages*, III, iii, 20). Böhme was followed in the same form of mysticism by the Rosicrucians and Freemasons, and by secret societies, which so abounded in the 16th century.

Of a very different stamp was Arndt's mysticism. It means a thoroughly spiritual religion. His principal works are the four books of *True Christianity*, and his devotional collection, the *Paradise of Christian Virtues*. They maintain their high character, and are still used in many households throughout Germany. But they encountered a vehement opposition when they first appeared, more especially from Osiander the younger, who managed to extract from them eight several heresies; the main gravamen being that Arndt slights school learning by his advocacy of practical piety, and of such "popish" Mystics as Thomas à Kempis and Tauler. Moreover, by his doctrine of the illumination and indwelling of the Holy Spirit he trenches upon the Lutheran theory of justification by faith alone and the orthodox doctrine of grace. J. Gerhard's *Meditationes Sacræ* (A.D. 1606), his *Schola Pietatis* and *Postils*, are works of a similar tone of thought to Arndt's, and they met with similar reception at first; as Gerhard said, "If any writer upholds pious practical Christianity, and aims at something higher than mere theological learning, he is straightway branded as a Rosicrucian or Weigelian." J. Val. Andreä, grandson of Jacob Andreä, who took a prominent part in setting up the Lutheran Formula of Concord, was of the same school. In his younger years he accepted the Rosicrucian mystery (A.D. 1602), but more in jest than in earnest. His later writings (A.D. 1617–1619) are conceived in a spirit of mystical piety. His endeavor evidently was to expose and put down the religious and political follies of the age, and uphold what he deemed to be spiritual Christianity. But he wrote in the spirit of Lucian; and it is often difficult to see where irony ends and earnest principle begins. His more liberal acceptation of the *Formula Concordiæ* made him many enemies among the high orthodox Lutherans. The Pietist Spener said of him: "If I could raise any from the dead for the good of the Church, it should be Valentine Andreä." It was owing to Arndt's influence that the mocking, scoffing spirit which seemed natural to Andreä was replaced by something higher and worthier of a Christian man.

But if Protestantism has had its Mystics, Romanism has not been altogether wanting in these religious enthusiasts. In France, in the 16th century, appeared St. Francis de Sales, and in Spain, St. Theresa and St. John of the Cross; all of them making their mystical doctrines subservient to the interests of the Mother Church. "Nowhere," says Mr. Vaughan, "is the duty of implicit self-surrender to the director or confessor more constantly inculcated than in the writings of Theresa and John of the Cross, and nowhere are the inadequacy and mischief of the principle more apparent. John warns the Mystic that his only safeguard against delusion lies in perpetual and unreserved appeal to his director. Theresa tells us that whenever our Lord commanded her in prayer to do anything, and her confessor ordered the opposite, the divine guide enjoined obedience to the human, and would influence the mind of the confessor

afterwards, so that he was moved to counsel what he had before forbidden! Of course; for who knows what might come of it if enthusiasts were to have visions and revelations on their own account? The director must draw after him these fiery and dangerous natures, as the lion-leaders of an Indian pageantry conduct their charge, holding a chain and administering opiates. The question between the orthodox-and the heterodox mysticism of the 14th century was really one of theological doctrine. The same question in the 16th and 17th was simply one of ecclesiastical interests." According to the mystical doctrine of St. Theresa, there are four degrees of prayer: (1) simple mental prayer; (2) the prayer of quiet, called also pure contemplation; (3) the prayer of union, called also perfect contemplation; (4) the prayer of rapture or ecstasy. The raptures and visions of this female saint of Romanism have gained for her a high name. But the mysticism of John of the Cross wore a different aspect. He delighted not in ecstatic prayer like Theresa, but in intense suffering. His earnest prayer was that not a day might pass in which he should not suffer something.

In the history of mysticism the 17th century was chiefly distinguished by the Quietist controversy. The most remarkable exhibition of Quietism is to be found in the writings of Madame Guyon. Thus, when describing her experience, she observes, "The soul passing out of itself by dying to itself necessarily passes into its divine object. This is the law of its transition. When it passes out of self, which is limited, and therefore is not God, and consequently is evil, it necessarily passes into the unlimited and universal, which is God, and therefore is the true good. My own experience seemed to me to be a verification of this. My spirit, disenthralled from selfishness, became united with and lost in God, its Sovereign, who attracted it more and more to himself. And this was so much the case that I could seem to see and know God only, and not myself. . . . It was thus that my soul was lost in God, who communicated to it his qualities, having drawn it out of all that it had of its own. . . . O happy poverty, happy loss, happy nothing, which gives no less than God himself in his own immensity—no more circumscribed to the limited manner of the creation, but always drawing it out of that to plunge it wholly into his Divine Essence. Then the soul knows that all the states of self-pleasing visions, of intellectual illuminations, of ecstacies and raptures, of whatever value they might have been, are now rather obstacles than advancements, and that they are not of service in the state of experience which is far above them, because the state which has props or supports, which is the case with the merely illuminated and ecstatic state, rests in them to some degree, and is pained to lose them. But the soul cannot arrive at the state of which I am now speaking without the loss of all such supports and helps. . . . The soul is then so submissive, and perhaps we may say so passive—that is to say, is so disposed equally to receive from the hand of God either good or evil—as is truly astonishing. It receives both the one and the other without any selfish emotions, letting them flow and be lost as they came." This quotation contains the substance of the doctrine which pervades the mystical writings of Madame Guyon. The whole may be summed up in two words, "disinterested love," which she regarded as the perfection of holiness in the heart of man. A similar, if not wholly identical, doctrine was inculcated at the same period by Molinos in Italy, in a book entitled *The Spiritual Guide*. Quietist opinions were then evidently on the advance in the different countries of Europe, and among their supporters were some of the most illustrious men of the day, of whom it is sufficient to name Fénelon, archbishop of Cambray. But the high character for piety and worth of the leading Quietists made them all the more obnoxious to the Jesuits. Nor was the hostile spirit which was manifested towards the Quietists limited to the Jesuits alone; the celebrated Bossuet, also, was one of the most bitter persecutors of Madame Guyon, and succeeded in procuring the public condemnation of her writings. Fénelon was for a time conjoined with Bossuet in opposing Guyon, but all the while he was conscious that his own opinions did not differ from hers. At length, in 1697, he openly avowed his sympathy with the sentiments of the Mystics in a work which, under the name of the *Maxims of the Saints*, was devoted to an inquiry as to the teachings of the Church on the doctrines of pure love, of mystical union, and of perfection. The publication of this treatise gave rise to a lengthened and angry controversy. Bossuet sought to invoke the vengeance of the government upon his heretical brother, and he had even hoped to call down upon him the fulminations of the pope. In the first object he was successful; in the second he was, for a time at least, disappointed. A war of pamphlets and treatises now raged at Paris, the chief combatants being Bossuet on the one side and Fénelon on the other. The *Maxims* were censured by the Sorbonne, and their author was persecuted by the king of France; but pope Innocent XII declined for a time to pronounce a sentence of condemnation upon Fénelon, of whom he had been accustomed to say that he had erred through an excess of love to God. At length, with the utmost reluctance, and in measured terms, he sent forth the much expected anathema, and Fénelon submitted to the decision of the Roman see. Madame Guyon, after a long life of persecution, thirty-seven years of which were spent in prison, died in 1717. Among the Quietists of the 17th century may be mentioned Madame Bourignon and her accomplished disciple, Peter Poiret; and among those of later times, the fascinating Mystic, Madame de Krüdener.

Vaughan, in his work, *Hours with the Mystics*, institutes a comparison between the Mystics of France and Germany up to this time, and is led thus to comment on the characteristics of these two exponents of mysticism: "Speaking generally, it may be said that France exhibits the mysticism of sentiment, Germany the mysticism of thought. The French love to generalize and to classify. An arrangement which can be expressed by a word, a principle which can be crystallized into a sparkling maxim, they will applaud. But with them conventionalism reigns paramount—society is ever present to the mind of the individual—their sense of the ludicrous is exquisitely keen. The German loves abstractions for their own sake. To secure popularity for a visionary error in France, it must be lucid and elegant as the language—it must be at least an ingenious and intelligible falsehood; but in Germany the most grotesque inversions of thought and of expression will be found no hinderance to its acceptability, and the most hopeless obscurity may be pronounced its highest merit. In this respect German philosophy sometimes resembles Lycophron, who was so convinced that unintelligibility was grandeur as to swear he would hang himself if a man were found capable of understanding his play of *Cassandra*. Almost every later German Mystic has been a secluded student—almost every Mystic of modern France has been a brilliant conversationalist. The genius of mysticism rises in Germany in the clouds of the solitary pipe; in France it is a fashionable Ariel, who hovers in the drawing-room, and hangs to the pendants of the glittering chandelier. If Jacob Böhme had appeared in France, he must have counted disciples by units, where in Germany he reckoned them by hundreds. If Madame Guyon had been born in Germany, rigid Lutheranism might have given her some annoyance; but her earnestness would have redeemed her enthusiasm from ridicule, and she would have lived and died the honored precursor of German pietism."

The modern mysticism of Germany is chiefly remarkable for its excessive *irreligiousness*, and its close alliance with a congeries of metaphysical clouds, misnamed philosophy, which, by essaying to pass beyond the limits of the human faculties, turns day-dreams into logical systems, and resolves all truth and all religion into the discovery that there is no God, or that God is but a name for the universe. The infidelity which in England took the form of natural religion, and in France that of ribaldry and ridicule, assumed in Germany the garb of speculation and of sentimental feeling. To the speculations of Kant, of Fichte, and of Schelling, as well as to the claims of divine revelation, Friedrich Henry Jacobi, in his work on *Divine Things*, opposed that intuitive and immediate knowledge of divine things which he denominated faith, mental feeling, or reason, and which has acquired for his philosophy the name of mysticism. It is a revival of the reveries of Böhme, of the Gnostics, and of the Orientals. Passing through such modifications as it could receive from the learned piety of Schleiermacher, the critical acumen of De Wette, the poetry of Novalis, and the picturesque genius of Carlyle, we now find it exciting to something like vitality the negative theology of Unitarianism in America and in England. By the side of these speculative Mystics we find also in modern times the imaginative Mystics, whose system is less the invention of something new and false than the perversion of what is old and true. To this branch of mysticism belongs the mystical interpretation of the Scriptures, the originator of which, as we have seen, is supposed to have been Philo the Jew, and the character of which pervaded the writings of Hermes, Justin, Clemens of Alexandria, Origen, Gregory of Nyssa, Ambrosius, Jerome, Augustine, Gregory the Great, Bede, Maurus, and Hugo de St. Caro.

In England we see it espoused in the spiritualizing of Solomon's Temple by Bunyan, and Brown's parallels of O.-T. facts with the history of the Jews, etc. Mr. William Law (author of the *Serious Call*, etc.), and the very able opponent of bishop Hoadly, degenerated in the latter part of his life into all the singularities of mysticism; and some suppose that his extravagant notions were one means of driving the celebrated Gibbon into a state of infidelity. "Mr. Law," says Vaughan, "supposed that the material was the region which originally belonged to the fallen angels. At length the light and Spirit of God entered into the chaos, and turned the angels' ruined kingdom into a paradise on earth. God then created man, and placed him there. He was made in the image of the Triune God (whom, like the Hutchinsonians, he compares to 'fire, light, and spirit'), a living mirror of the divine nature, formed to enjoy communion with Father, Son, and Holy Ghost, and to live on earth as the angels do in heaven. He was endowed with immortality, so that the elements of this outward world could not have any power of acting on his body; but by his fall he changed the light, life, and spirit of the world. He died, on the very day of his transgression, to all the influences and operations of the Spirit of God upon him, as we die to the influences of this world when the soul leaves the body; and all the influences and operations of the elements of this life were open to him, as they are in any animal, at his birth into this world; he became an earthly creature, subject to the dominion of this outward world, and stood only in the highest rank of animals. But the goodness of God would not leave man in this condition: redemption from it was immediately granted; and the bruiser of the serpent brought the life, light, and spirit of love once more into the human nature. All men, in consequence of the redemption of Christ, have in them the first spark, or seed, of the divine life, as a treasure hid in the centre of our souls, to bring forth by degrees a new birth of that life which was lost in paradise. No son of Adam can be lost except by turning away from the Saviour within him. The only religion which can save us must be that which can raise the light, life, and Spirit of God in our souls. Nothing can enter the vegetable kingdom till it have vegetable life in it, or be a member of the animal kingdom till it have the animal life. Thus all nature joins with the Gospel in affirming that no man can enter into the kingdom of heaven till the heavenly life is born in him. Nothing can be our righteousness or recovery but the divine nature of Jesus Christ derived to our souls." But the eminent Swedish theologian, Emmanuel Swedenborg, figures more conspicuously than these, if we regard him *merely* as an expositor of the Scriptures. As he, however, ascribes his spiritual interpretations to a special source, he will elsewhere occupy a more distinct and appropriate place, and we now simply advert to him as believing and teaching that God had made him the vehicle of new revelations. We refer our readers to the articles NEW JERUSALEM CHURCH and SWEDENBORG for details of his views and their progress.

We are not altogether strangers to mysticism even in our own day. Only a few years have elapsed since we were asked to believe in the supernatural revelations made to the followers of Edward Irving (q. v.); and the Spiritualists of North America profess to hold converse with the spiritual existences of another world. See SPIRITUALISM. But, passing by these, we find a class of Mystics in the Intuitionists on both sides of the Atlantic, who substitute the subjective revelation of consciousness for the objective revelation of the written Word. As examples of practical mysticism we must here refer also to the history of the Beghards, the Flagellants, Münzers, Anabaptists, and the famous Peasants' War in Germany, and the institution of the Jesuits.

Another fact is worthy of notice in connection with this subject. It is that mysticism has always been most flourishing in times of general religious formalism—a striking illustration of the tendency of any extreme to generate its opposite. The laws of Brahminism brought forth the mystic Buddhism; the Jewish Talmudism gave rise to the mystic Cabala (q. v.); the Spanish theology of the Inquisition found its counterpoise in the mysticism of the Alombrados; Jesuitism in quietism and Jansenism; the old Protestant scholastic orthodoxy in Protestant mysticism.

Enough has now been said to show plainly that the theology of the true Mystics exhibits two distinct phases: a side towards earth, on which the legend on the medal is obscure and without meaning; and an obverse side, bright with the light of heaven; union with the Eternal through sacramental grace is its impress of truth, and flowing from that grace a loving exercise of the great duties of Christian life. It is closely allied with *Quietism.* A very different kind, and yet an essential form of mysticism, is that avowed by Schlegel; one closely similar to the rhapsodical notions of Plotinus, when he says that whereas human consciousness, in which subject and object are insuperably blended together in idea, cannot form to itself a notion of the Absolute, which is unity, still an adequate idea of the Absolute may be gained by the contemplative or intuitive faculty, independently of thought or consciousness; it is a rapid illumination, a sudden rapture, too fleeting for analysis, for it eludes reflection and baffles consciousness. Reflection is, in fact, its death. In this mystical condition of the mind all distinction between subject and object vanishes. There is no longer the Deity on the one hand, the soul on the other. The soul identifies itself with the Deity. It is on this side that mysticism passes into pantheism.

See Danz, *Universalwörterbuch d. Theolog. Literatur,* p. 681; Malcom, *Theological Index,* p. 317 sq.; Winer, *Handbuch,* i, 501 sq.; Herzog, *Real-Encyklop.* x, 152 sq.; Bretschneider, *Systematische Entwickelung,* p. 22; Tholuck, *Susismus seu Theosophia Persarum pantheistica* (Berlin, 1821); Berger, *Disputatio de mysticism* (Harlem, 1819); Höfling, *Mysticismus* (Erlangen, 1832); Theremin, *Ueber d. Wesen d. mystischen Theologie* (*Abendstunden,* Berlin, 1833); Heinroth, *Gesch. u. Kritik. d. Mysticismus aller bekannten Völker u. Zeiten* (Leips. 1830, 8vo); Görres, *Die christl. Mystik* (Regensb. 1836); Helfferich, *Die christl. Mystik* (Hamb. 1842); Lisko, *Die Heilslehre d. Theologie* (Stuttg. 1857); Hamberger, *Stimmen aus dem Heiligthum,* etc. (Stuttg. 1857); Greith,

Die Deutsche Mystik im Prediger-Orden (Freib. 1861, 8vo); Pfeiffer, *Deutsche Mystiker im 14 Jahrhund.* (Leips. 1845–57); Noack, *Die christliche Mystik im Mittelalter, u. in d. neueren Zeit* (Königsb. 1853, 8vo); Ranke, *Hist. of the Reformation;* Lord Herbert, *Memoirs;* Coleridge, *Aids to Reflection;* Parker, *Discourse of Matters pertaining to Religion;* Cockburn, *The Delusions and Errors of Antoina Bourignon,* etc.; Stowell, *On the Work of the Spirit,* p. 258 sq.; Vaughan, *Hours with the Mystics: a Contribution to the History of Religious Opinion* (Lond. 1856, 2 vols.); Bergier, *Dict. de Théologie,* vi, 287; Migne, *Dict. de Mystique chrétienne;* Heckethorn, *Hist. of Secret Societies of all Ages and Countries* (Lond. 1874), pt. iv; De Staël's *Germany,* pt. ii, ch. v; *Meth. Qu. Rev.* Jan. 1853, p. 105, 161; Jan. 1860; April, 1860, p. 277; Jan. 1869, p. 49; *Bibl. Sacra,* Jan. 1851, p. 51; Jan. 1854, p. 546; *Lond. Rev.* Jan. 1857, art. ii; *Edinb. Rev.* lxxiv, 102, 195; *New-Englander,* v, 348; *Retrospective Rev.* i, 288; *Christian Qu.* July, 1873, art. vii; *Blackwood's Mag.* 1854, i, 66 sq. (Myst. in China); *Christian Examiner,* xxxvii, 308; *Brownson's Rev.* Oct. 1863, p. 428; *Brit. and For. Ev. Rev.* Sept. 1854, p. 572; Kitto, *Journ. of Sac. Lit.* 1854, p. 546; *Westminster Rev.* Oct. 1853; Oct. 1870, p. 219; *Christian Remembrancer,* Jan. 1866, p. 86; *Jahrb. deutsch. Theol.* 1867, ii, 362; *Zeitschr. hist. Theol.* Oct. 1850, p. 231; Jan. 1859, p. 49; *Brit. Qu.* Oct. 1874, art. i. A complete account of the host of mystical writers till 1740 is given in Arnold's *Kirchen-Historie* (Schaffhausen, 1742). See also the Church histories of Alzog, Gieseler, Milman, Niedner, Kurtz, Hardwick (*M. A. and Ref.*), Mosheim, Waddington; Hagenbach, *Hist. of Doctr.* (Index in vol. ii); Neander, *Christian Dogmas,* p. 604, 630; Ullman, *Ref. before the Ref.* ii, 44 sq., 185 sq.; Fisher, *Hist. Ref.* p. 65, 67 sq., 245; Stoughton, *Eccl. Hist. of England,* i, 482; ii, 262, 369–385; Hurst's Hagenbach, *Ch. Hist. of the 18th and 19th Centuries* (Index in vol. ii); Morell, *Hist. of Modern Philosophy,* ii, 332 sq., 356 sq.; *Lect. on the Philos. Tendencies of the Age,* lect. iii; Ueberweg, *Hist. of Philos.* i, 358, 400, 433, 435, 436, 467 sq.; ii, 20, 23, 54, 115, 213. 222; Lewes, *Hist. Philos.* (see Index in vol. ii).

Myth, a Greek term ($\mu\tilde{v}\vartheta o\varsigma$), which, however, is not to be found in the Sept. Even in the Apocrypha the word occurs but once ($\mu\tilde{v}\vartheta o\varsigma$ $\check{\alpha}\kappa\alpha\iota\rho o\varsigma$, Eccles. xx, 19, A.V. "an unseasonable tale"), and that in a general sense; while, in one other passage (Bar. iii, 23), $\mu\upsilon\vartheta\acute{o}\lambda o\gamma o\iota$, "authors of fables," has a somewhat doubtful meaning. In the N. T., however, the word occurs five times, and always in a severely disparaging sense, and in every instance is rendered "fables" in our version. Thus Timothy is warned against "*fables* and endless genealogies, which minister questions rather than godly edifying" (1 Tim. i, 4); and against "profane and old wives' fables" ($\beta\varepsilon\beta\acute{\eta}\lambda o\upsilon\varsigma$ $\kappa\alpha\grave{\iota}$ $\gamma\rho\alpha\omega\delta\varepsilon\tilde{\iota}\varsigma$ $\mu\acute{v}\vartheta o\upsilon\varsigma$, iv, 7). These "fables" are opposed to "the truth," and Titus is forbidden to give heed $'\textrm{I}o\upsilon\delta\alpha\ddot{\iota}\kappa o\iota\varsigma$ $\mu\acute{v}\vartheta o\iota\varsigma$. Lastly, in 2 Pet. i, 16 they are characterized as $\sigma\varepsilon\sigma o\phi\iota\sigma\mu\acute{\varepsilon}\nu o\iota$, "cunningly devised," and are contrasted with the sober testimony of eye-witnesses (comp. $\pi\varepsilon\pi\lambda\alpha\sigma\mu\acute{\varepsilon}\nu o\iota$ $\mu\acute{v}\vartheta o\iota$, Diod. Sic. i, 93). Just so in Greek $\mu\tilde{v}\vartheta o\iota$ are opposed to $\iota\sigma\tau o\rho\acute{\iota}\alpha$ (comp. Auson. *Prof. Carm.* 21, 26, "Callentes mython plasmata et historiam"). It is obvious, therefore, that in the N. T. a myth is used in its latest sense to express a story invented as the vehicle for some ethical or theological doctrine, which, in fact, has been called in later times an ethopœia or philospheme. Yet the condemnation is *special* and not general, and cannot point with dissatisfaction to myths, which, like those of Plato, are the splendidly imaginative embodiment of some subjective truth, and which claim no credence for themselves, but are only meant to be regarded as the vehicles of spiritual instruction (see archbishop Trench *On the Parables,* ch. ii, where he distinguishes between "myth," "fable," "parable," "allegory," etc.). That there is nothing in *such* "myths" to deserve reprobation, nay more, that they are a wise form of teaching, is clear from the direct quotation of mythical stories by Jude (ver. 9, 14), and from the use of strictly analogous modes of conveying truth (allegory, fable, parable, etc.) in other parts of the Bible, as well as in the writings of all the wisest of mankind. It must, then, have been the doctrines involved, and not the "mythical" delivery of them, which awoke the indignation of the apostles; and if, as Tertullian thought (Adv. Valent. iii), and as is now generally believed, the "myths" alluded to were the Gnostic mythology of the "Æons," of which the seeds may have been beginning to develop themselves when the pastoral epistles were written, we can easily understand how they would appear to bear the stamp of "philosophy and vain deceit." Theodoret, however, on Tit. i, 14, refers the "Jewish fables" to the Mishna ($\tau \eta \nu$ $\upsilon \pi'$ $\alpha \upsilon \tau \widetilde{\omega} \nu$ $\kappa \alpha \lambda o \upsilon \mu \acute{\epsilon} \nu \eta \nu$ $\delta \epsilon \upsilon \tau \acute{\epsilon} \rho \omega \sigma \iota \nu$, Alford, ad loc.).

No satisfactory definition of the word "myth" has ever been given, partly because of the manifold varieties of myths, and partly because the word has been used in several distinct senses. In Homer it is equivalent to $\lambda \acute{o} \gamma o \varsigma$ (Il. xviii, 253), and Eustathius remarks that in later times it came to mean $\psi \epsilon \upsilon \delta \eta \varsigma$ $\lambda \acute{o} \gamma o \varsigma$ (Il. a, 29), to which definition Suidas adds that it was $\lambda \acute{o} \gamma o \varsigma$ $\psi \epsilon \upsilon \delta \eta \varsigma$, $\epsilon \iota \kappa o \nu \acute{\iota} \zeta \omega \nu$ $\tau \eta \nu$ $\alpha \lambda \eta \vartheta \epsilon \iota \alpha \nu$. Plutarch, less accurately, confounds it with plausible fiction ($\lambda \acute{o} \gamma o \varsigma$ $\psi \epsilon \upsilon \delta \eta \varsigma$ $\acute{\epsilon} o \iota \kappa \grave{\omega} \varsigma$ $\alpha \lambda \eta \vartheta \iota \nu \widetilde{\omega}$), and in the Etymologicum Magnum it is made, in its technical sense, to mean a veiled or enigmatical narration ($\mu \widetilde{\upsilon} \vartheta o \varsigma$ $\sigma \eta \mu \alpha \acute{\iota} \nu \epsilon \iota$ $\delta \acute{\upsilon} o$ . . . $\tau \acute{o} \nu$ $\tau \epsilon$ $\sigma \kappa o \tau \epsilon \iota \nu \grave{o} \nu$ $\lambda \acute{o} \gamma o \nu$ . . . $\kappa \alpha \grave{\iota}$ $\tau \grave{o} \nu$ $\alpha \pi \lambda \widetilde{\omega} \varsigma$ $\lambda \acute{o} \gamma o \nu$). Neither the etymology nor the history of the word help us much. It is derived from $\mu \nu \acute{\epsilon} \omega$, to initiate, or $\mu \acute{\upsilon} \omega$, to shut, and archbishop Trench thinks that it must therefore have originally meant the word shut up in the mind, or muttered with the lips (Synon. of the N. T. [2d ser.] p. 174), though he admits that there is no trace of this in actual use; and as, at first, $\mu \widetilde{\upsilon} \vartheta o \varsigma$ merely means "word," we may even derive it from an onomatopœia of the simplest consonantal utterance (m). It is not until Pindar's time (Ol. i, 47; Nem. vii, 34; vi, 1) that it is used of that which is "mentally conceived, rather than historically true;" and in Attic prose it assumes its normal later sense of any legend or tradition of the prehistoric times. If, however, we analyze the modern use of the word, we shall find that these historical myths, or amplified legends of the remote past, generally mingled with the marvellous, do not properly represent our notion of myths any more than the well-understood philosophemes to which we previously alluded. We must learn, too, to distinguish between the myths and the rationalistic explanations thrust into them by the critical knowledge of a later age. If we would understand the true nature, for instance, of the Greek myths, we must discard from them the timidly rationalistic suggestions of Hecatæus, the severely common-sense views of Palœphatus, and the unsympathizingly sceptical rashness of Euêmerus, no less than the profound moral intentions which have so often been transferred to them by the speculative genius of a Bacon or a Coleridge.

A myth proper, then, is neither a philosopheme nor a legend. It is best described as a spontaneous product of the youthful imagination of mankind—the natural form under which an infant race expresses its conceptions and convictions about supernatural relations and prehistoric events. It is neither fiction, history, nor philosophy; it is a spoken poetry, an uncritical and childlike history, a sincere and self-believing romance. It does not invent, but simply imagines and repeats; it may err, but it never lies. It is a narration, generally marvellous, which no one consciously or scientifically invents, and which every one unintentionally falsifies. "It is," says Mr. Grote, "the natural effusion of the unlettered, imaginative, and believing man." It belongs to an age in which the understanding was credulous and confiding, the imagination full of vigor and vivacity, and the passions earnest and intense. Its very es-

sence consists in the projection of thoughts into the sphere of facts ("der Grund-Trieb des Mythen das Gedachte in ein Geschehenes umzusetzen" [Creuzer, Symbolik, p. 99]). It arises partly from the unconscious and gradual objectizing of the subjective, or confusing mental processes with external realities; and partly from investing the object with the feelings of the subject—that is, from imaginatively attributing to external nature those feelings and qualities which only exist in the percipient soul.

The myth, then, belongs to that period of human progress in which the mind regards "history as all a fairy tale." Before the increase of knowledge, the dawn of science, and the general dissemination of books, men's fancies respecting the past, and the dim conjectures of nascent philosophy, could only be preserved by these traditional semi-poetic tales; to borrow the fine expression of Tacitus, "Fingunt simul creduntque." So far from being startled by the marvellous and the incredible, they expected and looked for it; while discrepancies and contradictions were accepted side by side, because the critical faculty was wholly undeveloped. "The real and the ideal," says Mr. Grote, "were blended together in the primitive conception; . . . the myth passed unquestioned, from the fact of its currency, and from its harmony with existing sentiments and preconceptions" (Hist. of Greece, i, 610). To the intensity of a fresh imagination, and the necessary weakness of the youth of language, we can trace the origin of a vast number of myths. In those early days men looked at all things with the large, open eyes of childish wonderment. The majority of phenomena which they saw and enjoyed were incapable of other than a metaphorical or poetical description; and even if language had been more developed it would have responded less accurately to their thoughts, because they seriously transferred their own feelings and emotions to the world around them, and made themselves the measure of all things. Thus the hunter regarded the moon and stars which "glanced rapidly along the clouded heaven" as a "beaming goddess with her nymphs;" and

"Sunbeams upon distant hills,
Gliding apace with shadows in their train,
Might, with small help from fancy, be transferred
Into fleet Oreads sporting visibly."
Wordsworth, Excursion, bk. iv.

Thus the manifold aspects of nature, imaginatively conceived and metaphorically described, furnished at once a large mythology; and when these elements were combined and arranged for the purpose of illustrating early scientific or theological conceptions, and were corrupted by numberless erroneous etymologies of words, whose true origin was forgotten, we have at once the materials for an extensive and sometimes inscrutable mythology. In the early stage of the myth, confined to the period when everything is personified, it is as difficult to distinguish between what was regarded as fancy and what was believed as fact as it is to this day in the rude and grotesque legends of Polynesians and North American Indians. But in a later time, when myths were preserved in writing and systematized into dogmas, the poetical imaginative faculties had often well-nigh evaporated, and that which had originally been meant as half a metaphor was prosaically hardened into a real and marvellous fact. Thus in many myths, as they were finally preserved, we may see the mere misconceptions of a metaphor, and the guesses of a most imperfect etymology, mingling in two distinct streams with the original simple poetic tale. Any one who considers the evanescent "tradition" of untutored polytheism as it is displayed among modern savages, may watch, even at the present day, the growth and swift diffusion of myths; but we must look into various histories of civilized people (and especially into that of Greece) to see such myths first erroneously systematized into definite narratives, to be deliberately believed—then partially and timidly rationalized—next contemptuously rejected—and finally restored to their true rank as the most interesting relics of a primitive society, and the earnest teachings of a yet unsophisticated religious philosophy.

This subject would require a volume to explain it adequately; and, indeed, it has occupied many important volumes. All that we have here attempted is to remove a groundless and injurious prejudice against the word. Whether or not there be any myths in the Bible, and especially in the earlier books, is a question which must be settled *purely on its own merits*. See MYTHICAL THEORY. It is, however, undesirable that the mere *word* "myth" should be avoided by those who undoubtedly regard some of the Biblical narratives as containing mythical elements. Even men like Bunsen and Ewald bowed to popular prejudice in shunning the *word;* and of the English theologians, who rely so much on their authority, scarcely one (with the exception of Dr. Davidson) has ventured in this particular to desert their guidance. Yet the word "myth" is far more reverent and far less objectionable than "fable," which some would substitute for it; and it is, as Dr. Davidson has pointed out, far more honest than circumlocutions which mean the same thing (*Introd.* i, 146). It will be observed that we are here giving no opinion whatever as to the *fact* of the existence of scriptural myths, but merely pleading that those Biblical critics who understand the true nature of myths, and, rightly or wrongly, believe that here and there in the Hebrew records a mythic element may be traced, should not hesitate to express their conviction by the term which is most suitable and most likely to secure for the subject a clear and fair discussion.

The following are a very few of the more important books on the subject of myths: O. Müller, *Prolegomena zu einer Wissenschaftlichen Mythologie* (Götting. 1825 [transl. by J. Leitch, Lond. 1844]); Grimm, *Deutsche Mythologie;* Buttmann, *Mythologos;* Hermann, *Ueber das Wesen und die Behandlung d. Mythologie;* Löbeck, *Aglaophamus;* Creuzer, *Symbolik und Mythologie der Alten Völker;* Nitzsch, *Helden-Sage der Griechen;* Böttiger, *Kunst-Mythologie d. Griechen;* Kavanagh, *Myths traced to their primary Source through Language* (1856). The subject has of late years received three important contributions—Mr. Grote's *History of Greece*, vol. i; Prof. Max Müller's *Essay on Greek Mythology* (Oxford Essays, 1856); and Cox, *Mythology of the Aryan Nations* (Lond. 1873, 2 vols. 8vo). See MYTHOLOGY.

Mythical Theory, an attempt to destroy the sacred character of Scripture by considering its contents as myths similar in their nature and origin to those of ancient mythology. It is the result of the theological systems of Kant, Hegel, Semler, Eichhorn, Woolston, and has found its fullest development in Strauss's *Life of Jesus*, and his *Old Faith and New*. The only question we can consider here is whether the sayings of the O. and N. T. can or cannot really be considered as myths. In the first place, it is worthy of remark that the word μῦϑος, derived from μύω, *to close the eyes*, has the same root as *mystery* and *mystic*, and points to the shadowy conceptions of the soul, the thoughts which find next an expression in words. Hence it represents not merely the expression, but also the narrative, especially such as finds its origin in the vague ancient times, and consequently fables and sayings undeserving of belief (1 Tim. iv, 7, γραώδεις μύϑους παραιτοῦ; comp. 2 Tim. iv, 4, where it is opposed to the ἀλήϑεια; Tit. i, 14, Ἰουδαϊκοὶ μῦϑοι), and generally every tradition unworthy of being believed (1 Tim. i, 4; μῦϑοι σεσοφισμένοι, 2 Pet. i, 16). The ancients called untrustworthy sayings μυϑολόγημα, and the narration of them μυϑολογία. But by the word *myths* was formerly, and until of late, understood not only the history of the gods, but also many other traditions which rest on but slight or sometimes no historical foundation. Here we have, then, to establish the difference between myths and tradition. The latter is the verbal relation of a fact, at first very cor-

rect, but generally becoming obscured in the course of time by additions and embellishments added to it. In modern times the distinction has become still more marked; as myths are made to be fables resting on an idea only, and developed as if they were truth, though generally connected either with persons, places, or circumstances which have really existed, while by tradition is understood the transmission of real facts or events connected with an idea. Strauss, in his *Life of Jesus*, defines myths as "the historical garb (of the original Christian ideas) used in the aimless poetical tradition (of the early Church) which composes the whole of the Gospel." It is in the nature of myths to be often a sort of symbol of the thoughts from which they sprang. This connection between them is well established in Ullmann, *Historisch oder Mythisch* (Hamb. 1838, p. 56 sq.). Both are realizations of an idea; in the symbol by signs, in the myth by words. "The symbol expresses the immediate and permanent connection between the supernatural and the physical. The myth can take its rise in historical elements which it assimilates, or simply in the thoughts; this establishes the distinction between historical and philosophical myths, between which extremes, of course, there are many intermediates." Both myths and tradition are, then, distinct from history, but form the vague mist out of which history steps forth. This leads to a distinction between the historical period of a people's existence, or that when tradition commences to be certain, and the mythical period. Now to the Bible student and to every Christian arises the question, first clearly proposed by Herder, whether in the original history of mankind, and especially of the chosen people, the same rule holds good that the time of tradition was preceded by a mythical period. This proposition may probably be admitted in a modified form; but the expression *myths* must be rejected, as many erroneous views would otherwise become entangled with it, and because "we are used to hear it especially applied to the fantastic productions of the poets of heathen religions" (Ullmann, p. 58). Yet it cannot be denied that the O. T. contains passages the sense of which is traditional and mythic, and that acute criticism is required to get at real historical events in their true order, not only in the apocryphal books, but even in those recognised as canonical. The necessity of such criticism, which in former times was altogether neglected as useless, has become evident after the attacks of freethinkers and deists, and especially since the rationalists have brought forth their theory of myths and traditions to attack the reality of miracles, "as these are never to find a place in history."

Dr. M'Clintock (in the preface to his translation of Neander's *Life of Christ*, N. Y. 1848, p. xiv sq.) has thus sketched the origin and progress of the mythical process of criticism, as the natural outgrowth of the rationalistic form which infidelity assumed in Germany:

"The declared aim of the rationalists was to interpret the Bible on *rational* principles; that is to say, to find nothing in it beyond the scope of human reason. Not supposing its writers to be impostors, nor denying the record to be a legitimate source, in a certain sense, of religious instruction, they sought to free it from everything *supernatural;* deeming it to be, not a direct divine revelation, but a product of the human mind, aided, indeed, by Divine Providence, but in no extraordinary or miraculous way. The *miracles*, therefore, had to be explained away: and this was done in any mode that the ingenuity or *philosophy* of the expositor might suggest. Sometimes, for instance, they were no miracles at all, but simple natural facts, and all the old interpreters had misunderstood the writers. Sometimes, again, the *writers* of the sacred history misunderstood the facts, deeming them to be miraculous when they were not; e. g. when Christ 'healed the sick,' he merely prescribed for them, as a kind physician, with skill and success; when he 'raised the dead,' he only restored men from a swoon or trance; when he 'subdued the storm,' there was simply a happy 'coincidence,' making a strong impression upon the minds of the disciples; when he fed the 'five thousand,' he only set an example of kindness and benevolence which the rich by-standers eagerly followed by opening their stores to feed the hungry multitude, etc. But even this elastic exegesis, when stretched to its utmost capacity, would not explain every case: some parts of the narratives were stubbornly unyielding, and new methods were demanded. For men who had gone so far, it was easy to go farther—the text itself was not spared: this passage was doubtful, that was corrupt, a third was spurious. In short, 'criticism,' as this desperate kind of interpretation was called, was at last able to make anything, and in a fair way to make *nothing*, out of the sacred records. But still the rationalist agreed with the orthodox supernaturalist in admitting that there was, at bottom, a basis of substantial truth in the records, and asserted that his efforts only tended to free the substantive verity from the envelopments of fable, or perversion with which tradition had invested it. The admission was a fatal one. The absurdities to which the theory led could not long remain undetected. It was soon shown, and shown effectually, that this vaunted criticism was no criticism at all; that the objections which it offered to the Gospel history were as old as Porphyry, or, at least, as the English Deists, and had been refuted again and again; that the errors of interpretation into which the older expositors had fallen might be avoided without touching the truth and inspiration of the evangelists; and, in a word, that there could be no medium between open infidelity and the admission of a supernatural revelation. During the first quarter of the present century the conflict was waged with ardor on both sides, but with increasing energy on the side of truth; and every year weakened the forces of rationalism. Still, the theological mind of Germany was to a considerable extent unsettled: its Tholuck and Hengstenberg stood strong for orthodoxy; its Twesten and Nitzsch applied the clearest logic to systematic theology; its Marheineke and Daub philosophized religiously; its Bretschneider and Hase upheld reason as the judge of revelation; while not a few maintained the old rationalism, though with less and less of conviction, or at least of boldness.

"It was at this point that Strauss conceived the audacious idea of applying the *mythical* theory to the whole structure of the evangelical history. All Germany has been more or less infected with the mytho-mania since the new school of archæologers have gone so deeply into the heathen mythology. 'A mythis omnis priscorum hominum cum historia tum philosophia procedit,' says Heyne; and Bauer asks, logically enough, 'if the early history of every people is mythical, why not the Hebrew?' The mere application of this theory to the sacred records was by no means original with Strauss: he himself points out a number of instances in which Eichhorn, Gabler, Vater, etc., had made use of it. His claim is to have given a completeness to the theory, or rather to its application, which former interpreters had not dreamed of; and, to tell the truth, he has made no halting work of it. That Jesus lived; that he taught in Judæa; that he gathered disciples, and so impressed them with his life and teaching that they believed him to be the Messiah—this is nearly the sum of historical truth contained in the evangelists, according to Strauss. Yet he ascribes no fraudulent *designs* to the writers; his problem is, therefore, to account for the form in which the narratives appear; and this is the place for his theory to work. A Messiah was expected; certain notions were attached to the Messianic character and office; and with these Christ was invested by his followers. 'Such and such a thing must happen to the Messiah; Jesus was the Messiah; therefore such and such a thing must have happened to him.' 'The expectation of a Messiah had flourished in Israel long before the time of Christ; and at the time of his appearance it had ripened into full bloom; not an indefinite longing, either, but an expectation defined by many prominent characteristics. Moses had promised (Deut. xviii, 15) "a prophet like unto himself," a passage applied, in Christ's time, to the Messiah (Acts iii, 22; vii, 37). The Messiah was to spring of David's line, and ascend his throne as a second David (Matt. xxii, 42; Luke i, 32); and therefore he was looked for, in Christ's time, to be born in the little town of Bethlehem (John vi, 42; Matt. ii, 5). In the old legends the most wonderful acts and destinies had been attributed to the prophets: could less be expected of the Messiah? Must not his life be illustrated by the most splendid and significant incidents from the lives of the prophets? Finally, the Messianic æra, as a whole, was expected to be a period of signs and wonders. The eyes of the blind were to be opened; the deaf ears were to be unstopped; the lame were to leap, etc. (Isa. xxxv, etc.). These expressions, part of which, at least, were purely figurative, came to be literally understood (Matt. xi, 5; Luke vii, 21 sq.); and thus, even before Christ's appearance, the image of Messiah was continually filling out with new features. And thus many of the legends respecting Jesus had not to be newly invented; they existed ready-made in the Messianic hopes of the people, derived chiefly from the Old Testament, and only needed to be transferred to Christ and adapted to his character and teachings.'

"These extracts contain the substance of Strauss's theory; his book is little more than an application of it to the individual parts of the history of Christ as given in the evangelists. A few instances of his procedure will suffice. He finds the key to the *miraculous conception* in Matt. i, 22: 'All this was done that it might be fulfilled which was spoken of the Lord by the prophet, saying,'

etc. 'The birth of Jesus, it was said, must correspond to this passage; and what was to be, they concluded, really did occur, and so arose the myth.' The account of the star of the Magians, and of their visit from the East, arose from a similar application of Numb. xxiv, 17; Psa. lxxii, 10; Isa. lx, 1–6, etc. The temptation of Christ was suggested by the trials of Job; its separate features helped out by Exod. xxxiv, 28; Lev. xvi, 8, 10; Deut. ix, 9, etc. The transfiguration finds a starting-point in Exod. xxxiv, 29–35. So we might go through the book.

"The appearance of the work, as we have said, produced a wonderful sensation in Germany; greater, by far, than its merits would seem to have authorized. It was the heaviest blow that unbelief had ever struck against Christianity; and the question was, what should be done? The Prussian government was disposed to utter its ban against the book; and many evangelical theologians deemed this the proper course to pursue in regard to it. But Dr. Neander deprecated such a procedure as calculated to give the work a spurious celebrity, and as wearing, at least, the aspect of a confession that it was unanswerable. He advised that it should be met, not by authority, but by argument, believing that the truth had nothing to fear in such a conflict. His counsel prevailed; and the event has shown that he was right. Replies to Strauss poured forth in a torrent; the Gospel histories were subjected to a closer criticism than ever; and to-day the public mind of Germany is nearer to an orthodox and evangelical view of their contents than it has been for almost a century.

"Besides the general impulse given by Strauss to the study of the four Gospels, he has done theology another good service. His book has given a deadly blow to *rationalism* properly so called. Its paltry criticism and beggarly interpretations of Scripture are nowhere more effectually dissected than in his investigations of the different parts of the history and of the expositions that have been given of it. In a word, he has driven rationalism out of the field to make way for his myths; and Neander, Eberhard, and others have exploded the myths; so that nothing remains but a return to the simple, truthful interpretations which, in the main, are given by the evangelical commentators."

In his *New Life of Jesus* (authorized translation, Lond. 1865, 2 vols. 8vo) Strauss thus defines his modified and later position (p. 213): "I have, mainly in consequence of Baur's hints, allowed more room than before to the hypothesis of conscious and intentional fiction. This may properly be called *myth* as soon as it has gained belief and passed into the legend of a people or a religious sect; for its having done so invariably shows at the same time that it was formed by its author not merely upon notions of his own, but in connection with the consciousness of a majority." He therefore still maintains that "the myth, in its original form, is not the conscious and intentional invention of an individual, but a production of the common consciousness of a people or religious circle, which an individual does indeed first enunciate, but which meets belief for the very reason that such individual is but the organ of this universal conviction" (p. 206); and he proceeds to explain how in this way arose the account of the birth of Jesus in Bethlehem, and the disappearance of his body from the tomb. Yet he adds, "But when we thus point out that an unconscious invention of such accounts was possible far beyond the limits within which they are generally considered admissible, we do not mean to say that conscious fiction had no share at all in the evangelical formation of myths. The narratives of the fourth Gospel especially are for the most part so methodically framed, so carried out into detail, that, if they are not historical, they can apparently only be considered as conscious and intentional inventions" (p. 208). Accordingly he discards the Gospel of John altogether as being purely fictitious. This is the suicidal act of the mythical theorists; for once brought to the alternative of receiving or rejecting the Gospel records as a simple question of *veracity*, their battery is unmasked, and the argument becomes one of bold infidelity. Paley has proved, long ago, that the N.-T. writers had no possible motive or opportunity for either self-deception or imposture.

Certain critics before Strauss had attempted to apply the theory of historical mythus to the Gospel narrative. By *historical mythus* is meant the adornment of actual facts by the imagination. Strauss, however, went further than this, and adopted what he calls the principles of philosophical mythus, i. e. "the expression of an idea in the form of an imaginary biography." But the weak point in Strauss's system, at which it finally broke down, was that he did not assert the whole Gospel to be mythical; he admitted certain statements in the N.-T. histories as facts. Here, then, his system was as great a failure as any other. The very aim of his method was to exclude everything capricious or hypothetical; the result of its application was to leave the field as much open to caprice and hypothesis as before. Nor does his eventual denial of the truthfulness of John's Gospel mend his system; it only introduces a fresh element of discrimination and consequent perplexity. Late researches go much deeper into the idea of the myth and its application, particularly in the work of Schelling, *Ueb. d. Mythen d. ältesten Welt* (in Paulus, *Memorabilien*); Creuzer; F. Baur, of Tübingen, *Symbolik u. Mythologie, oder die Naturreligion d. Alterthums* (Stuttg. 1824–25, 8vo); Ottfried Müller, of Göttingen, *Prolegomena zu einer Wissenschaftlichen Mythologie* (Götting. 1825); A. Batke, *D. bibl. Theol. d. A. Test.* (Berl. 1835). In the O. T. they consider as mythical the history of creation and of the fall of Adam, the consequent punishment, the flood, the origin of the various nations, and the election of the Jewish people, as well as their covenant with Jehovah; the history of the patriarchs, the stay in Egypt of a family which grew into a nation (although, as shown by remaining monuments, this is based on a fact), their egress from Egypt, the giving of the law on Mount Sinai, the forty-years' journey through the wilderness, the account of the manner in which the Israelites came into possession of the Promised Land. Then a great deal in the following books, as also in the later history of the people and of the kings, especially in the form as we find it in the Book of Chronicles, where all is made to promote the priestly interest; the greater part of the history of the prophets, and even passages in the latest history of the people, as the apocryphal books, contain myths concerning the Maccabees. All through, tradition is connected with the myths which form an important element in these narratives, and both are in the whole history of the Israelites connected, in true Oriental style, with the historical element. These views, but often still more sweeping and exaggerated, were at that time advanced cautiously, and used to explain many passages in Scripture with some show of reason; the more as, all line of demarcation being destroyed by the generalization of some assertions, everything came to be measured by the same standard. The absurdities of these views, and their impiety, called into existence an opposite party which rejected the assertion of any myths being contained in the canonical Scriptures; and the views of the latter have gradually prevailed among the more candid and careful even of German critics. Traces, however, of this mythical theory in an obscure or subdued form are seen in Stanley's *Lectures on the Hist. of the Jewish Church;* having evidently come over from Ewald's destructive and arbitrary method of treating Jewish history in his *Israelit. Volk.* A sounder and soberer criticism, however, has found means to restore the narratives of both the O. and the N. T. to their proper rank as genuine history. See RATIONALISM.

Mythology (from μῦϑος, a tale, and λόγος, a word) is, according to Pococke (*India in Greece*, p. 2, note), intended strictly as a term synonymous with "invention," having no historical basis. Yet by usage the word is confined to fictions made in the early periods of a people's existence, for the purpose of presenting their religious belief, and generally their oldest traditions, in an attractive form. The tendency to create myths in this way seems inherent in every people; certainly there is no people so sunk into the brute as to be without them. And, what is more noteworthy, the systems of mythology have by no means ceased to exist even in our own day. They have only taken different shapes, and have been more widely diffused. The name is

changed, while the essence remains. In losing their character of celestial reference they have become more earthly and less splendid and imposing, but their vitality is as great as ever. We might almost say of the gods as some do of the relics of saints of the Romish Church, that the more they are divided the more they multiply. The mystery with which the popular fancy delights to envelop them serves instead of the immortal ambrosia which ministers to their heavenly life. "Nothing," says De Gubernatis, "clings to the earth more closely than a superstition. A scientific truth requires years and sometimes centuries before it can obtain general acceptance. The ancient myth gives us the germ of many existing traditions, and in the same manner the current popular legends often explain the enigma of the old celestial personifications" (*Zoological Mythology*, vol. i, *Introd.*).

Myths may be divided into several classes. The most important is the moral and theological. The latter of these two is of course the more important; for it is in the myth that the oldest theology of all non-Christian nations is embodied. "Mythology," says one, "is not occupied merely or mainly with strange fancies and marvellous fictions, invented for the sake of amusement, but contains the fundamental ideas belonging to the moral and religious nature of man as they have been embodied by the imaginative faculty of the most favored races. It is this dominance of the imagination, so characteristic of the early stages of society, which gives to myth its peculiar dramatic expression, and stamps the popular creed of all nations with the character of a poetry of nature, of man, and of God." Hence arises the great importance of mythological study for the religious student, now so universally recognised.

Mythology, or, more strictly speaking, religious mythology, may be taken in a wider or a narrower sense. In its wider signification it includes all that was believed or might be affirmed concerning the gods of any polytheistic system—not only *theology*, or the doctrine concerning their nature, attributes, and operations, but *their interferences* in the history of the world. From the very nature of the case, the myth-producing faculty exercises itself with exuberance only under the polytheistic form of religion; for there only does a sufficient number of celestial personages exist whose attributes and actions may be clothed in a historical dress. There is nothing, however, to prevent even a monotheistic people from exhibiting certain great ideas of their faith in a narrative form, so as by prosaic minds to be taken for literal historical facts. The first of these divisions answers to the doctrine concerning God found in the Scriptures; the other to the manifestation of God in the events of the world, and especially in Jewish history. Besides strictly theological myths, there are physical myths, that is, fictions representing the most striking appearances and changes of external nature in the form of poetical history; in which view the connection of legends about giants, chimeras, etc., with regions marked by peculiar volcanic phenomena, has often been observed. *It is difficult indeed, in polytheistic religions, to draw any strict line between physical and theological myths;* as the divinity of all the operations of nature is the first postulate of polytheism, and every physical phenomenon becomes the manifestation of a god. Again, though it may appear a contradiction, there are historical myths; that is, marvellous legends about persons who may with probability be supposed to have actually existed. So intermingled, indeed, is fact with fable in early times that there must always be a kind of debatable land between plain theological myth and recognised historical fact. The land is occupied by what are called the heroic myths; that is, legends about heroes, concerning whom it may often be doubtful whether they are merely a sort of inferior and more human-like gods, or only men of more than ordinary powers whom the popular imagination has elevated into demigods. Schelling, in his philosophy of mythology, uses the word in a somewhat broad meaning. He says that "these (divine, or mythological) personalities are at the same time thought of both in certain *natural* and in certain *historical* relations to one another. Kronus is called a son of Uranus; this is a *natural*—when he emasculates and dethrones his father, this is a *historical*, relation. As, however, natural relations in the wider sense are historical, this element is sufficiently indicated when we speak of it as the historical one" (*Lect.* i, p. 7). And he goes on to remark that by their very nature the gods of heathenism as mythological beings have a historical character. They enter into the world of events in that part of the system of heathen religions, or rather of some religions, which speaks of their birth and of their relations among themselves, aside from any manifestations to men or interferences in human affairs. But if we make a distinction between the doctrinal part of polytheism, or of any particular religion, as that of India or Greece, and the historical part from which and from its cultus the doctrinal part, or the religious faith, is ascertained, we shall not be far out of the way. For the *doctrinal* part we refer to the article POLYTHEISM. For the sake of greater clearness, however, we shall, by way of preface, proceed to enumerate some of the principles which ought to be borne in mind when we treat of mythology.

We mention (1) that the divine power or life-giving energy in nature was divided up in heathenism into many separate powers, which were personified, and even became to the heathen mind persons, endowed with separate wills, desires, and intelligence. (2) These divine powers, or gods, cast off their connection with the natural object out of which they grew, so that the connection in the end was no longer obvious to the heathen mind. In this way they entered into various relations to a nation, a tribe, or a class of men; they acquired special moral qualities or attributes of various kinds; and thus all the interests of society in all its subdivisions, all arts and employments, everything in the physical world and among men, was placed under their care. (3) They were conceived of as having human passions and desires; they had distinctions of sex—originally because *active* causes, as the sun, were aptly conceived of as masculine, and *passive*, like the earth, as feminine; they had marriages among themselves, and as they assumed human or other shape at will, they could have connections with human beings also. (4) As objects of nature originally, and as many in number, they all had limited powers, and, while they were immortal, had had a beginning of their existence. The theogony—Hesiod's, for instance—is a part of the cosmogony which in several religions of heathenism was devised—somewhat later than the rise of mythology—to explain the original condition of the world and the way the gods came into existence. As man comes into being by procreation, so in general the existence of the gods is in the same way accounted for. Matter itself is for the most part conceived of as eternal. (5) When the mythological process was in full activity, not only did powers of nature become persons before the imagination and faith of the polytheist, but moral powers or causes also, abstract and general conceptions, feelings, and the like, were turned into personified agents, or even into persons. Thus among the Greeks, Themis, or *justice*, Nemesis, or *retribution*, the Moirai (shares, allotments, *fates*, Latin *Parcœ*), became personified, and even assumed personal existence, together with a multitude of others. And so by the side of the gods, properly so called, a multitude of subordinate beings, who grew out of such personifications, were worshiped among the Greeks and Romans, and formed a portion of a very large class which may be called *secondary divinities*, consisting, among others, of representatives of the life of smaller objects in nature, such as wood, fountain, and other nymphs and spirits; or of dæmons attendant on higher gods, and of heroes, or the spirits of deceased men, as also of demigods, or men with a divine father or moth-

er, who played a part second to no other in classical mythology. (6) The mythological age cannot, on account of our want of historical records, have any exact limits assigned to it. It began in the earliest infancy of nations. We see the mythological spirit in the Vedas, which point back to an age from 1500 to 2000 years anterior to the birth of Christ. We find the Greek mythology fully mature in the age when the Homeric poems were written, and a rude philosophy working up its materials in the Hesiodic poems. Centuries must have elapsed before Homer, during which men looked at nature and the world in this spirit. The poets collected the myths of various parts of Greece, and gave to them a general Grecian stamp, but they did not originally invent them, nor were the gods imported from Egypt, the affirmation of Herodotus to the contrary notwithstanding. The end of this mythologizing spirit is also indefinite. Some few historical events are intermingled with myths, but the connection was later than the myth. To say that they ceased when history began is to say no more, properly speaking, than that for a time mythology and the historical spirit were in conflict, and that, as the result, mythology was looked on as the history of the past.

So far as the actions and interferences of the gods form a part of mythology, it was in no sense a product of *imposture*. No priests or poets, or persons sustaining both characters, invented it. The poet and his hearers had the same faith, and their imaginations were in the same mythological condition: they honestly believed in the general doctrines of the theology, and the general system of divine interference in the affairs of men, of which they introduced the particulars into their poetry. Otherwise they could have met with no responsive chord in the souls of the people; or, if unbelieving themselves, they would not have searched out and reproduced the myths all through the epic age and afterwards. It is folly to suppose that the men of the myth-making times, or of the epic times, played with religion, or looked with critical eyes on the fables of the poets; or, for a long time, were injured in their moral sensibilities by the immoralities and grossness of many portions of the stories which were recited to them by the rhapsodists. This, however, is to be observed: (1) That the epic poets of the Homeric period, and of the cyclical school afterwards, must have felt free to transform and work over and add to the myths which they received or gathered as their stock in trade. This is no more than Christian believers, such as Milton or Klopstock, have done, without the least suspicion that they were practicing a fraud, or irreverently tampering with sacred things. (2) The logographs or mythographs—the collectors of mythology into one corpus, the translators into prose of the epic *sagas—these persons* did allow themselves to make alterations; they may have invented connections between myths, so as to make them fit into their framework and form one whole; they may to some extent have given an improved version of one or another of the fables, under the conscious or unconscious influence of a rationalizing spirit. (3) The lyric poets in making use of the same materials went a little further. Pindar is offended by the immoral acts imputed to the gods, and thus we see that a higher moral standard is beginning to cause a conflict between religious myths and the moral sense. This is more evident afterwards, and was one of the causes of the scepticism of later Greece. We have on record a remarkable story relating to Stesichorus, one of the earliest lyric poets. In the beginning of an ode he had indulged in invectives against Helen, and, as a retribution for his evil speaking, lost his eyesight. He then composed his Helena, in which his version of her story was that she never went to Troy, but her phantom, or *eidōlon*, took her place; his eyesight was thereupon restored. This furnished to Euripides the argument of the drama of Helena. The nucleus of truth here is that the poet deserted the received fable for another which was thought to be new with him (Stesich. *Frag.* in Bergk, 29; Herm. *Praef.* in Eurip. *Hel.;* Bernhardy, *Gesch. Griech. Lit.* ii, 473). (4) The tragic poets indulged in still greater liberties. Æschylus and Sophocles, being religious believers, still respected the myths; while Euripides, an unbeliever, cared little for them except as materials for his verse. (5) In a still later age they were mere materials for works of poetry and art; and that a poet interwove them in his narrative is no proof that he received them as true. It must be observed, also, that in the mouth and recollection of the people myths could not remain *exactly fixed.* They changed from age to age. The spot where the events were first reputed to happen had afterwards many competitors. The actors, especially the minor actors, varied. The poets chose what suited them best, or what first presented itself. Hence it happens that a more antique form of a myth is sometimes picked out of the fragments of some obscure writer, or of some modern author like Pausanias, who went about among the people, or had access to authorities now lost.

The main inquiry is, How did the myths arise, if neither priest nor poet, neither fraud nor conscious invention, was the source of the great mass of them? When we say that they arose by the power of the imagination looking at the world as being full of life, or by the mythologizing process, we say nothing. When we draw analogies from modern myths—as the story of Roland, or the Holy Grail, or the epic of Arthur and his Knights—or trace the marvellous alterations which the life of Alexander the Great underwent in a series of poems and prose narratives, to be found in all the languages of Europe and in some of those of Asia, we still fall short of the explanation (comp. Grote, *Hist. of Greece*, i, end). For in the first place there is in most of the modern myths a germ of fact, as, for instance, in the story of Roland; but the myths relating to the gods had no intrinsical, but only physical, facts for their foundation. When we come to the myths of the heroic times of Greece, there must have been historical events in some shape, perhaps very much distorted, out of which they grew. The machinery in the epic stories founded on these myths—in other words, the interventions of the gods—were conformed to a belief of an age when the material was first chosen for the songs of the rhapsodists; but the difficulty still remains how the religious element of the myths became united with the rest. It is easy enough to see that a story like that of Roland, or a tradition of a siege of Troy, possessing sources of interest for the national mind, should by and by grow in the multitude of its details, be worked over, be altered in the mouth of the people or by the poets—this is what happens on a small scale every day; but it is hard to account for the turning of celestial phenomena into events of history. This does not happen now. The power to do it is lost. If, for instance, the passage of the sun through the signs of the Zodiac—a yearly occurrence—becomes, through some faith of the ancient mind and some power of the imagination, the series of labors of a demigod like Hercules, struggling against monsters on the earth, and doing his work in its particulars once for all, we must say that there is no analogy for this in the present state of the world. The world of physical nature and the world of history are separated now by fixed limits. How in the mythological age did a fact of nature turn into a fact of history? That is the great difficulty which we encounter while speculating on mythology, and it meets us in all the fables concerning the gods of such a nation as Greece, India, or ancient Germany. Mythology must continue a mystery until this is explained.

In attempting a solution of a part of this problem, we must bear in mind the conception of the gods already spoken of, and the sway of the imagination looking out on the life of the world, and conceiving of it as directly originated by superhuman spiritual causes, and not as yet recognising, to the degree that we do, the control of secondary, physical laws. Take a single instance, that of Apollo. We assume here that Apollo was at first a sun-god; this, although no traces of such an identification appear in the poets before Æschylus, and although it has been denied by some writers on mythology (as by Voss, *Mythol. Briefe*, ii, 378 sq.), is now admitted by the later and best scholars, in whose hands the Greek religion has been cleared of many of its difficulties (as, e. g., Creuzer, Welcker, Preller, and others). And it was the sun-god with a personality after the fashion of men, although the sun, *Helios*, still retained a place—a subordinate place—in Greek worship, just as Demeter, the earth-goddess, entered into the events of the world by the side of Gæa, *earth*, whose action was nearly confined to the myths of the cosmogony. The sun was thought to produce pestilence through the excessive heats of summer and autumn. Apollo therefore was conceived of as originating pestilential disease. The sun's rays are naturally thought of as darted forth from the body of the sun itself. Apollo now became an archer, the god of the silver-bow; and when at the beginning of the Iliad *evil disease* was sent through the army before Troy, it was because Apollo was angry at the treatment which his priest, Chryses, met with from Agamemnon. Here we have moral ideas, the god's protection of an injured suppliant, and relations which only a personal existence could assume. The god came down from Olympus—where we have a society of the upper gods under Zeus—he shot his arrow into the army, the mules and dogs first, then the men, were smitten and died. But this sun-god has human feelings and can be propitiated; he can turn away his darts and heal disease. Perhaps here, too, a physical phenomenon may explain the attribute, that as the sun generates pestilence when there is an undue amount of moisture and heat, so his tempered rays bring health. However this may be, the *author* of pestilence became the *arrester* of it; he is called Hekaërgos, the *driver off*, and in the Doric dialect *Apellon*, the averter, which in common Greek became Apollon. As an averter, he is the *curer* of disease—Pæon or Pæan, the *healer*. His connection with music and poetry is more accidental; and his relations to political and social life (which were so important that he became the leading divinity of Greece) must be explained on historical grounds. His name, *Phœbus*, the bright or pure, brings him again into connection with the sun and with purifying rites. He was a source of inspiration as well at Delphi as to others besides the priestess of the oracle—for instance, to the Sibyls. All this, however, does not reach the difficulty. It is quite conceivable that mythological divinities should thus arise, as well as that events which are of common occurrence should be attributed to a special god. But go beyond such events, and you get into deeper water. Take the story of Niobe, for instance, and its explanation by two of the principal mythologers, Welcker (*Gr. Götter.* iii) and Preller (*Gr. Mythol.* ii, 283). Omitting details, Niobe, daughter of Tantalus, the mother of many children, exalted herself against Leto (Latona) because she had given birth to two children only, Apollo and Artemis. Accordingly the angry god avenged his mother; the children of Niobe were shot down, and she wasted away in grief. She was turned into stone, and her stone image was shown on Mount Sipylus, not far from Magnesia, in Asia Minor. This is an Asiatic myth, naturalized in Greece proper, and it signifies the decay of the products of the earth. Niobe is Rhea, the earth-mother, whose multitude of offspring, born in spring, are withered by the god of light in autumn; or, as Welcker explains it, the new or renewed nature (Niobe being from the root denoting *new*), losing her children by the solar heat, mourns for them like Rachel. What renders this fable very remarkable is the stone on Mount Sipylus, which many travellers describe (comp. Hamilton, *Asia Minor*, i, 49, 50) as having the resemblance of an image. Now, whether these or other explanations deserve the preference, we have an annually recurring event turned into a historical and personal event that happened once for all. Here the difficulty comes up again, and is coming up continually. The myth of Cybele and Attis, that of Adonis or Thammuz, that of Osiris, in the same way probably arose out of annually recurring physical phenomena, and yet they stood before the ancient mind as individual events that did not repeat themselves. In these myths dead gods represent the annual decay of life in nature. And so with much more certainty can we interpret the rape of Proserpine in a physical way. She is snatched by the underground king—Hades, or the invisible one—and carried to his abode within the earth to be his wife. Here the myth takes the form of a stealing of a bride, which can be traced in Greece, and even now is found in the practice of many tribes. In consequence of the protests and grief of Demeter, it was arranged that she should be on earth with her mother two thirds of the year, and one third below with her husband, Hades. This threefold division clearly points to the division of the season in the early times of Greece into spring, summer, and winter (literally, *eär, early* time; *theros, hot* time; and *cheima*, either *snow*-time, from a root extant in Sanscrit, or *pouring*-time, rainy time, from Greek χέω). Thus the principle of vegetative life manifests itself in spring and summer only. This myth is the most important one that the Greeks had, as it lay at the foundation of the worship and mysteries at Eleusis. We have explained it in its main features to our satisfaction; but, supposing that we have been successful, the conversion of a recurring physical phenomenon into a historical event which appears in it we find hard to explain. We may say the gods became persons: their attributes, before physical, are now personal attributes; what they do must have a historical quality, must be like human actions; so that if anything physical was attributed to them before, it would be incongruous with their new personal, non-physical nature. But still this turning-point is dark to us, because we are other men than those of the mythological period; we have no longer the mythological faculty in its full exercise—nay, it is all but dead. The anthropomorphic tendency—which men cannot escape from in speaking of the God of the Scriptures whenever they are exalted in their feelings—aided the mythological process, as well as the desire to express an object of worship in human form. But this pertains rather to the article POLYTHEISM, where it will be spoken of more at length.

Not all nations are equally mythological, and some which have historical myths to show are not rich at all in religious myths. The Aryan race had in most of its divisions, as among the Hindûs, the Greeks, the Germans and Northmen, and the Slavonians, a great richness of conception and imagination in this respect; but to none was it given as to the Greeks to stamp the impress of beauty on their mythology, so that their art and poetry, although built on mythology, still charms the Christian world. The Romans were poor in the number of their religious myths, for which the reason may be that they were formal and conscientiously scrupulous in their worship rather than free and gay; or possibly their myths may have been driven into oblivion by early culture derived from Greece. The Shemitic nations and Egypt had also a poor mythology, copious as the pantheon of the last mentioned was. It is said that the myth of Isis, Osiris, and Typhon was their only one. Thus it must either have expelled others from circulation, or none ever existed. Probably there were other myths in remote times. The Persian religion was of Aryan origin, although in centring all interest on the lasting strife between Ormusd and Ahriman it seems to have somewhat chilled the myth-making power. Its pantheon of inferior gods or dæmons was copious enough, but the grand moral idea swallowed up every other. Their myth-making faculty is exercised in their cosmogony and eschatology, but

concerns itself little with special historical relations between man and the divinities. The primitive tribes of this continent were far from wanting in this power, although the forms of their myths are like the imaginings of children. All this shows that mankind are much the same in all races, that resemblances do not necessarily prove one or another race to have been the borrower, and that the religions of nature, man being what he is, have a necessary existence. Again, the myths of a religious character, in which the gods enter into human history, show a craving on the part of man for intercourse with the gods. It was no strange thing that myths should arise where there was no revelation, or where a primitive revelation had been lost; it was equally not strange that a real revelation should take the historical form.

There are certain myths which narrate the origin of the world and the births of the gods. These cosmogonical and theogonical narratives are found alike among the Indians of this continent, among the Greeks, the Syrians, in the Teutonic race, and elsewhere. These of course can be, in great part, nothing else than early human speculations put into a religious mythic shape. They are the rude, childish philosophy of early men, who try to solve the riddles presented to human reflection without knowledge of law and of the world. We believe we may affirm it to be a general truth that no natural religion conceives of a creation out of nothing, and to a great extent the gods had no eternal existence. There was, then, a necessity of a primitive form or stuff out of which the life and thought of the world was evolved. In the Greek speculation on the first origin of things, the rudest shape of matter was the first, and the progress was towards the more perfect, until their thought reached the present condition of things. In Hesiod's *theogony* there is a strange mixture of true personalities and allegorical ideas, but a connection of one with another, a birth or evolution, runs through all except the first. Chaos came to be (ἐγένετο); then the broad-breasted Earth, and Tartarus in the dark recess of spacious Earth, and Eros (most beautiful among the immortal gods). From Chaos Erebus and Night were born (ἐγένοντο); from Night Æther and Day, the progeny of Night and Erebus. Earth first bare starry Uranus to cover her over on every side, with the Hills and the Pontus, without sexual love; then to Uranus she bore many children—the Titans, among whom was Kronus (Saturn), the Cyclops, and the hundred-handed ones. Uranus hid his children, as they were born, in a cavern below the earth, but Kronus mutilated him with the advice of Gæa, and reigned in his stead. From Kronus and Rhea a new class of gods were born, whom the god swallowed, lest any of them should seize his throne, which Uranus and Gæa forewarned him of as being his destiny. When, however, Zeus was born, he was privily conveyed away, and a stone wrapped up in an infant's clothing was swallowed in his stead by Kronus. These children, with the stone, Kronus was made to disgorge, and Zeus, overcoming his father and his Titans, took the throne. In this strange medley, where allegorical beings and such as never received divine honors are put among the gods, we find the Titans playing a great part, who can have had no veneration as gods in the earliest Greek religion. We find also three dynasties: Uranus and Gæa, Kronus and Rhea, and Zeus with Hera. Schelling, following an earlier writer, supposes this to be a tradition of three successive forms of worship, the first and second of which were dualistic. But there is no evidence within the Greek records worth anything going to show that Uranus was ever an object of worship. It is probable that the word itself is connected with Varuna, a highly honored Aryan divinity of the Vedic times. The prevalence, however, of such a worship in Greece, or of a worship of Kronus (i. e. either of *time personified*, or of a divinity corresponding in part with the Roman Saturnus, and having also some Phœnician characteristics drawn from Moloch), prior to that of Zeus, cannot be made out. Nor is there any proof that the Greeks held to a dualism something like that of the Chinese. On the contrary, the Vedic gods, worshipped seven or eight centuries before Hesiod, show that in that early age a polytheism had already been evolved. As was said once before, the whole theogony shows a philosopher with his materials before him, using the cement of his own reflections to unite them together in one structure. We do not mean to say that one man did all this, but that it was not popular tradition. This was necessarily so, for the popular mind knew nothing of a cosmogony. It had no facts to work upon, as it had in the formation of the religions of nature as she appears in the present order of things. We might go on and speak of the cosmogonies of other nations, but the Greek system— the clearest of all—will show, we think, that the part of mythology in which this is treated of is neither popular nor of the very earliest origin.

It is a very interesting inquiry whether any *primeval traditions of mankind*, facts pertaining to the general history of man and of the world, have mingled with the mythologies of heathenism. On the one hand, if there is a tradition of a great fact appearing with marked variations in different countries, and perhaps assuming a local character, the universality is a proof of common origin, notwithstanding the variations; and the presumption is against its being propagated from one part of the world to another, since all things else in mythology seem confined to a particular race or continent. On the other hand, if a myth contains an explanation of some interior conviction of human nature, as the sense of evil, or of a lapse of man from a better state, this may be explained on psychological grounds. To begin with the last kind of myths, the tradition of a former golden age can easily be accounted for on the principle that memory blots out what is evil in the past, and at its time hard to bear, so that the age of our fathers, our youth when we are old, the early history of a nation, are surrounded with a golden halo. As to traditions of a lapse, a departure from the idea of man, they are found in a number of mythologies, but they may all be the product of reflection. Let us take the Prometheus myth for a sample, as it appears in Hesiod. Omitting some of the details, we find that Prometheus —surnamed from his forethought, as his brother Epimetheus was from thinking after he acted—tried to cheat Zeus in respect to the offering of a victim. In revenge, Zeus would not let men have fire. Prometheus, however, who is really a fire-genius or dæmon, stole it out of heaven, carrying it in a hollow stalk, and thus again provoked the wrath of the god. The latter bound Prometheus in chains to a rock, and tormented him by sending an eagle to devour his liver, which grew daily as fast as it was eaten, until Hercules killed the bird and set the victim free. As a punishment to mankind for receiving the fire, a woman was fashioned, endowed with various gifts by the gods, and sent to Epimetheus. She brought with her as a kind of outfit a jar or cask, such as was used in housekeeping. Epimetheus was not wise enough to adopt the advice of his brother to reject the gift. The woman opened the jar, which was full of pains and death-bringing diseases, unknown before, and in consequence of this act they were scattered abroad. Only Hope stayed within the jar's cover. To this we add from the *Prometheus Bound* of Æschylus the striking trait that a condition of the prisoner's deliverance was that some god should suffer in his place (Hesiod, *Theog.* 507–516; *Op.* 43–104; Æschylus, *Prom.* 1027). There is no objection against finding a tradition of a fall in this myth arising from the fact that a state of misery, and not one of sin, is contemplated. That is just the difference between heathenism and revelation, that the former, although conscious of evil, yet finds it hard to come up to the idea of sin. The *resemblances* between this fable and the third chapter of Genesis are plain enough. Prometheus, the fire-bringer,

the introducer of the arts into the world, may stand for the tree of knowledge, and Pandora may stand for Eve. "Our woe" came by a woman in both narratives. But the *differences* are still greater. There is in the fable no temptation of man to evil; he is quite passive, and the craft of his benefactor is the cause of his calamity. Woman does not lead him into sin, but is contrived expressly for his suffering. And, what adds to the awkwardness of the myth in its present form, the race of man was made, and had offered religious homage to the gods, before Pandora spread maladies over the world. It was no progenitor who entailed evil on his posterity, but the god sent evil on a race already spread over the earth. We are disposed, therefore, to regard the story as a Greek invention, rather than as a distorted tradition of the primeval times. When the more recent form of the myth makes it the condition of the liberation of Prometheus that a god shall take his place of suffering, some have found in this particular an adumbration of the Christian doctrine of vicarious suffering; but to admit this would be to admit that heathen myths make as near an approach to the highest truths of the Gospel as is made by the Old Testament itself.

There is, however, another class of myths that have to do with the great fact of the flood, which no local phenomena, happening here and there over the world, can account for, and which could not be originated by the reflecting or observing mind. Traditions of a flood are very numerous, and confined to no one or two races. According to a remark of Bunsen (in his *Christianity and Mankind*, iv, 121), they are not to be met with in the myths of the Turanian or Hamitic races; the tribes of Africa have retained but slender traces of a flood at the best; but in China, Hindostan, Persia, Greece, Babylon, in the *Edda*, and through the tribes of North and South America, they present themselves to us as a part of the mythologies. In many local traditions it is the land of the tribe which is visited with a deluge, but this is no objection against their common origin. In Greece there were fables of three deluges, one of which, Deucalion's, was in Thessaly, that of Ogyges in Bœotia or Attica, and one was localized in the island of Samothrace. Pindar's simple story makes mention of the water overwhelming the earth, of its being forced back by the wisdom of Zeus, and then of Deucalion and Pyrrha coming down from Mount Parnassus to their home at Locrian Opus, where they had a posterity of stones. The destruction of the men of the iron age, the building of an ark by Deucalion at the suggestion of Prometheus, the copious rains bringing on a flood, the death of all men but a few who fled to the highest mountains, the floating of the ark nine days and nights until it struck on Parnassus, are particulars given by mythographers and later poets. The renewal of the human race by Deucalion and Pyrrha throwing stones behind their backs is a play of words between λαός, *people*, and λᾶας, *stone*, as Max Müller and others remark. This myth seems to have been known to Hesiod; and Deucalion is engrafted into the genealogies of the Hellenic race. It is possible that some story imported from foreign parts was its foundation. Across the Atlantic, in a widely different race, we find a tradition which repeats the story of the renewal of men in the time of Deucalion and Pyrrha. The Caribbean tribe of the Tamanakas, on the Orinoco, say that a man and a woman, the only persons saved in a deluge, threw the fruit of the Mauritia-palm over their heads, and thus created a new race (J. G. Müller, *Amer. Urrelig.* p. 229, and Humboldt there cited). We have only room to refer to two other traditions of a flood. One is that of India, which first appears in the *Mahabharata*, as an episode which Bopp has translated (Berlin, 1829). In this myth Manus, a rigidly ascetic prince, was on the bank of the Wirini, when a small fish called for his protection against larger ones, and was put by him into a dish. The fish outgrew the vessel, was then removed into a lake, then, again outgrowing its dwelling, into the Ganges, and from the Ganges into the ocean. As it entered the ocean it told Manus that a great deluge was at hand, that he must build a ship with sails, go into it with the seven wise men, and provide himself with all the seeds known to the Brahmins. The fish promised to appear with a horn, to which Manus should tie his vessel, and so pass over the waters in safety. Many years the fish towed the ship of Manus over the fulness of waters. At length he gave orders to bind the ship to the highest point of Himavan (the Himalayas), which is called, says the poet, "ship-fastening," Naubandhanam, until this day. Then the fish said to Manus, "I am the lord of creatures, even Brahma; higher than me there is nothing." And he bade him renew the race of created things and the worlds, which by means of strict penance he was to accomplish. The deluge of Xisuthrus, which seems half borrowed from the narrative in the Scriptures, is reported by Berosus, who was born under Alexander the Great. Xisuthrus, king of Babylon, was warned by Saturn (Bel) that a flood would come upon the earth in which all men would perish, and was ordered to conceal his books in one of the cities called Heliopolis, and to build a vessel into which he could go with his relations and friends, with birds, beasts, and quadrupeds, together with all necessary food. When the flood was abating he repeated the experiment of Noah, sending out birds, which twice returned, but the third time went their way. He now broke a hole in the vessel, and disappeared, being translated among the gods, with his wife, his son, and the ark-builder. Fragments of that vessel, Berosus is made to say, are still to be seen on a mountain in Armenia. The same story was known to Nicolaus of Damascus, a friend of Herod the Great. Josephus (*Ant.* i, 3, 6), who mentions this, says that all who have recorded the history of barbarian nations have mentioned the deluge and the ark. The story which made the Armenian mountains the landing-place from the ark seems to have circulated in that country before it received Christianity (comp. Wiseman's *Lect.* p. 290, Amer. ed. of 1837). To this Babylonian flood myth can now be added an Assyrian one, discovered by George Smith, the decipherer of cuneiform records, who published two or three years since the life of Assurbanipal, one of the last Assyrian kings, and a contemporary of Manasseh, from the clay tablets recording his reign, and has since found new tablets made for the same king, on which the myth referred to is narrated. It is far more mythological than the Babylonian tradition, and seems to be of later origin, but does not materially differ from the earlier known account, while the name of the ark-builder, which is Sisit, is evidently identical with Xisuthrus. It is worthy of mention that M. Lenormant, in a memoir on this newly-found Assyrian myth, with some plausibility, shows how the story passed from Assyria into India, and was not indigenous in the latter country. We might strengthen our position by the aid of other similar myths, but for this we have no space. What but a tradition of a great fact can have led men all over the world to have a common story of a deluge inwoven in their mythology, the very variations of which—and they are very great—point to a great antiquity of the story, as well as to its independent working up? We close the subject with some remarks of Prof. Welcker's (*Griech. Götterl.* i, 770) on the Greek myths relating to the flood. These, he says, were not inferences from observations of their own. "Only a great event, a covering of the earth with water over wide regions, was sufficient to make a deep impression on human memory, and to produce a story formed with such beautiful simplicity, and spread so widely among the original nations of Asia." See DELUGE.

Nothing remains, according to our plan, but to say a few words on the explanations of the myths of heathendom, especially by the ancients. Great difficulties and uncertainties attend such explanations, because in very many cases the myths are not homogeneous, and because the minds that created them were in a condition

unlike our own. To the Greeks especially this was a subject of deep interest, and a number of solutions were offered; most of which were unsuccessful, because the Greeks of a historic and philosophic age could not comprehend their own remote ancestors. The spirit to attempt such solutions began perhaps in scepticism, and especially in moral revolt from the low conceptions of the mythology. Xenophanes, the founder of the early Eleatic school, more than five hundred years before Christ, says, in an extant fragment of a poem, that "Homer and Hesiod ascribed everything to the gods that was shameful and blamable among men, as to steal, commit adultery, and deceive one another;" and, in another place, that "those who say the gods are born are equally impious with those who say that they die." He also inveighed against the anthropomorphisms of mythology, and rejected a plurality of gods (comp. Nägelsbach, *Posthom. Theol.* p. 428). Such utterances so early could not but meet with responses. The race was not ready to give up its faith in the only divinities known to it; some compromise was therefore necessary; and even the sceptics felt themselves bound to account for the series of events in the mythological times, and for the belief in the gods itself. One of the explanations was the *historical.* Thus Hecatæus of Miletus (about B.C. 520) taught that the myth of Cerberus owed its origin to a poisonous snake lying by the great cavern of Tænarum, in Southern Laconia, which was accounted an opening into the subterranean world. Herodorus of Heraclea turned Atlas into an astrologer and Prometheus into a Scythian king, who was troubled by a river gnawing away, so to speak, the fat of his land by its floods, but was freed from the plague by Hercules changing the course of the stream. The river was called the Aëtus, or eagle river, whence the fable of the eagle consuming the liver of Prometheus (see Lobeck, *Aglaoph.* ii, 987 sq.). So Herodotus mentions a version of the story of *Io,* which made her the daughter of the king of Argos, whereas modern students of mythology regard her as one of the forms of the moon-goddess. This method reminds us of the older rationalists—Paulus, for instance—who nibbled at the supernatural without daring to deny it, and are now deservedly almost forgotten. The gods themselves, however, were not as yet explained away.

A new form of the historical interpretation appeared in the 3d century B.C., which is called, after the name of its founder, Euemerus (Euhemerus, Evemerus), a Sicilian Greek of Messene, who enjoyed the acquaintance of Cassander (ob. 296 B.C.). This man published a book called *Sacred Records,* which claimed to give authentic accounts of Zeus and other gods, drawn from sacred titles and inscriptions found in the most ancient temples, and especially in one of Zeus Triphylius, on an Indian island called Panchæa. His theory was that the gods were deceased men deified: "Great personages in the confusions of uncivilized life, being desirous of obtaining from the common mass of men greater admiration and respect, feigned that they had a certain extraordinary and divine power, on which account they were thought by the multitude to be gods." We have nearly followed the words of Sextus Empiricus (ix, 7, p. 394, ed. Bekker). Lactantius (*Inst.* i, § 2) says that Euemerus stated that Zeus lived on Mount Olympus, and was much resorted to for the settlement of disputes by those who had found out anything new and useful to society. The poet Ennius translated this book into Latin, and, although Cicero speaks of it (*De Nat. Deor.* i, 42, 118) as entirely overthrowing religion, it had great currency as a rational account of the religious system. It was accepted by some of the Christian fathers, and a theory of polytheism somewhat like it was advocated by some of the scholars two centuries ago. Euemerus was without question a forger of records; but the theory found favor (1) because some of the old fables spoke of the birth and reign of Zeus in Crete, and even of his death and burial, and so also of the death of other gods; (2) because the interval between gods and men in Greek polytheism was not very wide, and was almost obliterated by the bestowal of divine honors on such men as Alexander the Great. Heathenism destroyed itself just by destroying all essential differences between the divine and the human. (3) Although the man does not seem to have been an atheist, it was a convenient theory for getting rid of the popular gods, now offensive to philosophy and morality (comp. Hoeck, *Creta*, iii, 326, 337).

The *physical* explanation was forced upon the minds of thinking men by noticing the veneration paid to heavenly bodies, the earth, and the elements, in almost all nations. This was obvious enough in the religions of Phœnicia and Egypt. The great mother, or Cybele, the leading divinity of Asia Minor, was the earth-goddess, according to a generally received interpretation which Lucretius (ii, 601 sq.) gives at large. Etymology was used in the service of this theory. A Roman could hardly fail to perceive the connection between Jupiter or Diespiter (Jovis or Diovis) and *divum*, the clear, broad heaven, or sky; or to notice that the phrases *sub Jove* and *sub Divo* are identical in sense. The poet Ennius, in a line cited by Cicero, says, "Look on this bright space on high which all invoke as Jove." The pantheistic philosophy of the Stoics adopted this explanation of the objects of popular religion. Varro, who was a Stoic, thought that the authors of religion in the old time believed in a world-soul, and that the principal gods were symbolical of the principal portions of the world. Jupiter was *heaven*, and branched out into various manifestations, while the female principal was *earth* under many names. The Stoics supported their philosophy by etymologies as worthless. Saturnus, or *Time*, is so called because it is saturated (satur), so to speak, with years. He swallowed his children, which means that duration consumes the spaces of time, and is filled with times past, without being full.

Another method of explanation may be called the *allegorical*, which was generally a way of conveying moral or philosophical truth, without necessarily asserting in all cases that the old mythology meant just what the philosophers made it to mean. Philo deals with the history of the Old Testament just in the same way. An instance may be found of this and other interpretations in Plutarch's essay on Isis and Osiris. Isis is the principle which receives ideas, Osiris is reason, Typhon unreason, and so on. The same method applied to the mysteries of Eleusis brought into them, as we suppose, the doctrine of the immortality of the soul. A playful specimen of this method is found in Plato's *Gorgias*, where he explains the perforated vessels of the Danaïdes to mean the souls of men whose desires are unbounded; administering supplies to the desires, yet never able to satisfy them. A ridiculous specimen of a physical interpretation is the explanation of the alternate appearance of Castor and Pollux above ground by the two celestial hemispheres, the one under, the other above, the earth (Sextus Empiricus, p. 399, ed. Bekker).

The scientific study of mythology commenced with the ancient nations who produced it, specially with the acute and speculative Greeks. The great mass of the Greek people, indeed—of whom we have a characteristic type in the traveller Pausanias—accepted their oldest legends, in the mass, as divine and human facts; but as early as the time of Euripides, or even before his day, in the case of the Sicilians Epicharmus and Empedocles, we find that philosophers and poets had begun to identify Jove with the upper sky, Apollo with the sun, Juno with the nether atmosphere, and so forth; that is, they interpreted their mythology as a theology and poetry of nature. This, indeed, may be regarded as the prevalent view among the more reflective and philosophical heathens (who were not, like Xenophon, orthodox believers) from the age of Pericles, B.C. 450, to the establishment of Christianity. But there was an altogether opposite view, which arose at a later period

under less genial circumstances, and exercised no small influence both on Greek and Roman writers. This view was first prominently put forth by the Messenian Euemerus in the time of the first Ptolemies, and consisted in the flat prosaic assertion that the gods, equally with the heroes, were originally men, and all the tales about them only human facts sublimed and elevated by the imagination of pious devotees. This view seemed to derive strong support from the known stories about the birth and death of the gods, especially of Jove in Crete; and the growing sceptical tendencies of the scientific school at Alexandria were of course favorable to the promulgation of such views. The work of Euemerus accordingly obtained a wide circulation; and having been translated into Latin, went to nourish that crass form of religious scepticism which was one of the most notable symptoms of the decline of Roman genius at the time of the emperors. Historians, like Diodorus, gladly adopted an interpretation of the popular mythology which promised to swell their stores of trustworthy material; the myths accordingly were coolly emptied of the poetic soul which inspired them, and the early traditions of the heroic ages were set forth as plain history, with a grave sobriety equally opposed to sound criticism, natural piety, and good taste. In modern times, the Greek mythology has again formed the basis of much speculation on the character of myths and the general laws of mythical interpretation. The first tendency of modern Christian scholars, following the track long before taken by the fathers, was to refer all Greek mythology to a corruption of Old-Testament doctrine and history. Of this system of interpreting myths we have examples in Vossius, in the learned and fanciful works of Bryant and Faber, and very recently, though with more pious and poetic feeling, in Gladstone. But the Germans, who have taken the lead here, as in other regions of combined research and speculation, have long ago given up this ground as untenable, and have introduced the rational method of interpreting every system of myths, in the first place, according to the peculiar laws traceable in its own genius and growth. Ground was broken in this department by Heyne, whose views have been tested, corrected, and enlarged by a great number of learned, ingenious, and philosophical writers among his own countrymen, specially by Buttmann, Voss, Creuzer, Müller, Welcker, Gerhard, and Preller. The general tendency of the Germans is to start—as Wordsworth does in his *Excursion*, book iv—from the position of a devout imaginative contemplation of nature, in which the myths originated, and to trace the working out of those ideas, in different places and at different times, with the most critical research and the most vivid reconstruction. If in this work they have given birth to a large mass of ingenious nonsense and brilliant guess-work, there has not been wanting among them abundance of sober judgment and sound sense to counteract such extravagances. It may be noticed, however, as characteristic of their over-speculative intellect, that they have a tendency to bring the sway of theological and physical symbols down into a region of what appears to be plain, historical fact; so that Achilles becomes a water-god, Peleus a mud-god, and the whole of the *Iliad*, according to Forchhammer, a poetical geology of Thessaly and the Troad! Going to the opposite from Euemerus, they have denied the existence even of deified heroes; all the heroes of Greek tradition, according to Uschold, are only degraded gods; and generally in German writers a preference of transcendental to simple and obvious explanations of myths is noticeable. Creuzer, some of whose views had been anticipated by Blackwell, in Scotland, is specially remarkable for the high ground of religious and philosophical conception on which he has placed the interpretation of myths; and he was also the first who directed attention to the Oriental element in Greek mythology—not, indeed, with sufficient discrimination in many cases, but to the great enrichment of mythological material, and the enlargement of philosophical survey. In the most recent times, by uniting the excursive method of Creuzer with the correction supplied by the more critical method of O. Müller and his successors, the science of comparative mythology has been launched into existence; and specially the comparison of the earliest Greek mythology with the sacred legends of the Hindûs has been ably advocated by Max Müller in the *Oxford Essays* (1856). In France, the views of Euemerus were propounded by Banier (1739); and generally the French scholars, such as Raoul Rochette and Petit Radel, show a distinct national tendency to recognise as much of the historical element as possible in mythology. By the British scholars mythology is a field that has been very scantily cultivated. Besides those already named, Bulfinch and Gould have done something in gathering material, but Payne Knight, Mackay, Grote in the first volumes of his history, Keightley, and Freeman are the only names of any note, and their works can in nowise compete in originality, extent of research, in discriminating criticism, or in largeness of view, with the productions of the German school. The best for common purposes is Keightley; the most original, Payne Knight. In this country some service has been rendered to this department of recent study by Profs. Hadley and Whitney, and by the Rev. James Freeman Clarke.

The charm which mythology threw over polytheism, its fascinations for the imaginative faculty, its connection with idolatry and with worship, its appeals to the senses, the vantage-ground which it had in a life-struggle with a severe holy monotheism in more ways than one—these topics will be duly considered in the article on POLYTHEISM, to which we must refer the reader for a list of some of the best books on the heathen religions and mythologies likely to be of special interest to the theological student. See NORSE MYTHOLOGY. (T. D. W.)

N.

Na'ăm (Heb. *id.* נַעַם, in pause נָעַם, *pleasantness;* Sept. Ναάμ v. r. Νοόμ), the last named of the three sons of Caleb the son of Jephunneh (1 Chron. iv, 15). B.C. cir. 1618.

Na'ămah (Heb. *Naämah'*, נַעֲמָה, *pleasant*), the name of two women and also of a place.

1. (Sept. Νοεμά; Josephus, Νοομάς, *Ant.* i, 2, 2.) The daughter of the Cainite Lamech and Zillah, and the sister of Tubal-cain (Gen. iv, 22). B.C. cir. 3549. The family was one of inventors; and as few women are named, the Jewish commentators ascribe suitable inventions to each of them. Naamah is affirmed by them to have invented the spinning of wool and making of cloth. In the Targum of pseudo-Jonathan, Naamah is commemorated as the "mistress of lamenters and singers;" and in the Samaritan Version her name is given as *Zalkipha*. According to others she was distinguished merely by her beauty (see Kalisch, *Genesis*, p. 149). Hence some have unduly pressed the coincidence with Venus the consort of Vulcan, or with certain Syrian mythologies (Bunsen, *Aegyptens Stelle* [Goth. and Hamb. 1845–57], i, 344 sq.).

2. (Sept. Νααμά, Νοομά, v. r. Μαχιάμ, Ναανάν, etc.; Josephus, Νοομάς, *Ant.* viii, 8, 9.) An Ammonitess, the only one of the numerous wives of Solomon that appears to have borne him a son. She was the mother of Rehoboam (q. v.), and probably queen dowager (1 Kings xiv, 21, 31; 2 Chron. xii, 13). B.C. 973. She must consequently have been one of those foreign women whom Solomon took for wives and concubines, and among whom Ammonites are expressly mentioned (1 Kings xi, 1). The Vatican copy of the Septuagint calls her "the daughter of Ana, the son of Nahash;" but this, besides being wanting in the Hebrew, is part of a long passage which is not found either in the Hebrew or in the Alexandrian copy of the Septuagint, and is therefore of no authority.

3. (Sept. Νααμά v. r. Νωμάν), a city in the plain of Judah, mentioned between Beth-dagon and Makkedah (Josh. xv, 41). The associated names indicate a locality much west of Hebron. See JUDAH, TRIBE OF. The requirements correspond tolerably well with that of a modern village marked by Van de Velde on his *Map* as *Naamah*, two miles S.E. of Ascalon (2d. ed. *N'aliah*, three miles); but Capt. Warren (in the *Quar. Statement* of the "Pal. Explor. Fund," April, 1871, p. 91) suggests *Naameh*, six miles N.E. of Yebna (Van de Velde, *Naamy*, six miles N. by E.). See NAAMATHITE.

Na'ăman (Heb. *Naäman'*, נַעֲמָן, *pleasantness*, as in Isa. xvii, 10), the name of two men.

1. (Sept. Νοεμάν; but in 1 Chron. Νοαμά and Νοομά, v. r. Μααμάν.) The second of the sons of Bela the son of Benjamin (Gen. xlvi, 21), apparently exiled by his father (1 Chron. viii, 4, 7), and the head of the family of the NAAMITES (Numb. xxvi, 40); possibly the same elsewhere (1 Chron. vii, 7) called UZZI. B.C. post 1856. See JACOB.

2. (Sept. Ναιμάν, and so the best MSS. of the N. T., but Rec. Text Νεεμάν; Josephus, Ἄμανος, *Ant.* viii, 15, 5.) The commander of the armies of Benhadad II, king of Damascene Syria, in the time of Joram, king of Israel. B.C. cir. 885. Through his valor and abilities Naaman held a high place in the esteem of his king; and although he was afflicted with leprosy, it would seem that this did not, as among the Hebrews, operate as a disqualification for public employment. Nevertheless the condition of a leper could not but have been in his high place both afflicting and painful; and when it was heard that a little Hebrew slave-girl, who waited upon Naaman's wife, had spoken of a prophet in Samaria who could cure her master of his leprosy, Benhadad furnished him with a letter to his traditionary enemy king Joram; but as this letter merely stated that Naaman had been sent for him to cure, the king of Israel rent his clothes, suspecting an intention to fix a quarrel on him. Elisha, hearing of the affair, sent for Naaman, who came to the door of his house, but, as a leper, could not be admitted; nor did Elisha come out to him, but sent him word by a servant to go and dip himself seven times in the Jordan, and that his leprosy would then pass from him. He was, however, by this time so much chafed and disgusted by the apparent neglect and incivility with which he had been treated, that if his attendants had not prevailed upon him to obey the directions of the prophet, he would have returned home still a leper. But he went to the Jordan, and having bent himself seven times beneath its waters, rose from them clear from all leprous stain. He now returned to Elisha, full of gratitude, avowing to him his conviction that the God of Israel, through whom this marvellous deed had been wrought, was great beyond all gods; and declaring that henceforth he would worship him only. He asked permission to take with him two mules' burden of earth. His purpose in this has been disputed, but it was probably to set up in Damascus an altar to Jehovah. He might have heard that an altar of earth was necessary (Exod. xx, 24). The natural explanation is that, with a feeling akin to that which prompted the Pisan invaders to take away the earth of Aceldama for the Campo Santo at Pisa, and in obedience to which the pilgrims to Mecca are said to bring back stones from that sacred territory, the grateful convert to Jehovah wished to take away some of the earth of his country, to form an altar for the burnt-offering and sacrifice which henceforth he intended to dedicate to Jehovah only, and which would be inappropriate if offered on the profane earth of the country of Rimmon or Hadad. We may compare this request with the custom which once prevailed among Christians of carrying away water from the holy river Jordan; and, perhaps more aptly, with a custom still practiced by many Jews of burying a portion of earth from Jerusalem with every one of their number who dies in a foreign land. It would seem, however, that Naaman's faith extended no further than acknowledging the superiority of Jehovah to the gods of other nations so far as his words are naturally understood (2 Kings v, 15). The Talmud regards him as a proselyte of the second class (Gittin, 57). Naaman further requested permission to attend his king in the temple of the idol Rimmon, and bow before the god. Some (e. g. Niemeyer, Charakt. v, 371) have indeed referred these expressions to his past acts of idolatry; but this construction cannot be sustained. Nor is it needed to shield Elisha from the imputation of sanctioning the worship of Rimmon; for his words in the 19th verse are simply the usual Hebrew formula of farewell, and do not imply assent to Naaman's requests. See Stackhouse, Hist. Bible, iv, 869 sq.; Cotta, Vindiciæ verbor. Naaman (Tübingen, 1756). The grateful Syrian would gladly have pressed upon Elisha gifts of high value, but the holy man resolutely refused to take anything. His servant, Gehazi, was less scrupulous, and hastened with a lie in his mouth to ask in his master's name for a portion of that which Elisha had refused. The illustrious Syrian no sooner saw the man running after his chariot than he alighted to meet him, and happy to relieve himself in some degree under the sense of overwhelming obligation, he sent him back with more than he had ventured to ask. This narrative, containing all that is known of Naaman, is given in 2 Kings, ch. v. See ELISHA. Naaman's appearance throughout the occurrence is most characteristic and consistent. He is every inch a soldier, ready at once to resent what he considers as a slight cast either on himself or the natural glories of his country, and blazing out in a moment into sudden "rage," but calmed as speedily by a few good-humored and sensible words from his dependants, and, after the cure has been effected, evincing a thankful and simple heart, whose gratitude knows no bounds and will listen to no refusal. See GEHAZI. How long Naaman lived to continue the worship of Jehovah while assisting officially at that of Rimmon we are not told. When next we hear of Syria, another, Hazael, apparently held the position which Naaman formerly filled. But the reception which Elisha met with on this later occasion in Damascus probably implies that the fame of "the man of God," and of the mighty Jehovah in whose name he wrought, had not been forgotten in the city of Naaman. A Jewish tradition, at least as old as the time of Josephus (Ant. viii, 15, 5), identifies him with the archer whose arrow, whether at random or not, struck Ahab with his mortal wound at Ramoth-Gilead (1 Kings xxii, 34). The expression is remarkable— "because that by him Jehovah had given deliverance to Syria" (ver. 1). It seems, however, to point to services of a more important kind for Syria, though not related in Scripture. But inasmuch as the advantage they won for Syria, and the position they tended to acquire for Naaman, were incidentally to subserve the divine purposes towards Israel, they may perhaps on this account have been ascribed to Jehovah. Naaman himself, and partly by reason of the very greatness he had thus acquired, was to become all unwittingly an instrument of promoting the divine glory—in some sense even more than those who had directly to do with the cause and kingdom of Jehovah. It is singular that the narrative of Naaman's cure is not found in the present text of Josephus. Its absence makes the reference to him as the slayer of Ahab, already mentioned, still more remarkable. It is quoted by our Lord (Luke iv, 27) as an instance of mercy exercised to one who was not of Israel, and it should not escape notice that the reference to this act of healing is recorded by none of the evan-

gelists but Luke the physician. See Kitto, Daily Bible Illust. ad loc.; Keil, Comment. on Kings, ad loc.; Hantzschel, Naaman Syrus (Brem. 1773); Rogers, Naaman (Lond. 1642); Bingham, Naaman the Syrian (Lond. 1865); Bullock, The Syrian Leper (Lond. 1862).

Na'ämathite (Heb. Naämathi', נַעֲמָתִי, a Gentile from some unknown place, Naamah; Sept. ὁ Μιναῖος, but in Job ii, 11, ὁ Μιναίων βασιλεύς; Vulg. Naamathites), the epithet applied to Zophar, one of the three friends of Job (Job ii, 11; xi, 1; xx, 1; xlii, 9). B.C. cir. 2200. Some commentators have thought that he was so named as being a resident of the above NAAMAH (q. v.), in the tribe of Judah (Josh. xv, 41); but this is not at all probable from the locality and age of Job (see Spanheim, Hist. Jobi, xiv, 11). Job's country, Uz, was in Arabia; his other two friends, Eliphaz the Temanite, and Bildad the Shuhite, were Arabians; and hence we may conclude that Naamah was likewise in Arabia (Cellarius, Geogr. ii, 698). See JOB. "If we may judge from modern usage, several places so called probably existed on the Arabian borders of Syria. Thus in the Geographical Dictionary (Marásid el-Ittália) are Noam, a castle in the Yemen, and a place on the Euphrates; Niameh, a place belonging to the Arabs; and Noami, a valley in Tihameh. The name Naamán (of unlikely derivation, however) is very common. Bochart (Phaleg, cap. xxii), as might be expected, seizes the Sept. reading, and in the 'king of the Minæi' sees a confirmation to his theory respecting a Syrian, or northern Arabian settlement of that well-known people of classical antiquity. If the above Naamah could be connected with the Naamathites, these latter might perhaps be identical with the Mehunim or Minæans, traces of whom are found on the south-western outskirts of Judah; one such at Minois, or el-Minyay, a few miles below Gaza. But this point is too hypothetical for acceptance." See ZOPHAR.

Na'ämite (Heb. Naämi', נַעֲמִי; Sept. Νοεμανί), a title of the family descended from NAAMAN (q. v.), the grandson of Benjamin (Numb. xxv, 40). The name is a contraction, of a kind which does not often occur in Hebrew. Accordingly the Samaritan Codex presents it at length—"the Naamanites."

Na'ärah (Heb. Naärah', נַעֲרָה, a girl, as often; Sept. Νοορά v. r. [by interchange] Θωαδά), the second of the two wives of Ashur (q. v.), of the tribe of Judah, by whom he had four sons (1 Chron. iv, 5, 6). B.C. cir. 1618. See also NAARAN; NAARATH.

Na'ärai (Heb. Naäray', נַעֲרָי, youthful; Sept. Νοορά v. r. Νααραί), an Arbite, the son of Ezbai, a military chief in David's army (1 Chron. xi, 37), B.C. cir. 1015; incorrectly called PAARAI in 2 Sam. xxiii, 35 (see Kennicott, Dissert. p. 209 sq.). See DAVID.

Na'äran (Heb. Naäran', נַעֲרָן, boyish; Sept. Νααράν v. r. Νααρνάν and Νοοράν), a town in the territory of Ephraim, on the south-eastern border, between Bethel and Jericho (1 Chron. vii, 28). In Josh. xvi, 7 the name is NAÄRATH (q. v.).

"In 1 Sam. vi, 21 the Peshito-Syriac and Arabic versions have respectively Naarin and Naaran for the Kirjath-jearim of the Hebrew and A. V. If this is anything more than an error, the Naaran to which it refers can hardly be that above spoken of, but must have been situated much nearer to Beth-shemesh and the Philistine lowland."

Na'ärath, or rather NA'ÄRAH (Heb. Naärah', נַעֲרָה, girl, as in NAARAH; with ה local נַעֲרָתָה; Sept. εἰς Νααραθά v. r. αἱ Κῶμαι; Vulg. Naaratha, Auth. Vers. "to Naarath"), a town on the boundary between Benjamin and Ephraim, between Ataroth and Jericho (Josh. xvi, 7); elsewhere called NAARAN (1 Chron. vii, 28); probably the Noörath (Νοοράθ) of Eusebius (Onomast. s. v.), five miles from Jericho, and, according to

Reland (*Palæst.* p. 903, 907), identical with the *Neara* (Νεαρά) of Josephus (*Ant.* xvii, 13, 1); and possibly with the *Noöran* (נוערן) of the rabbins (*Vaijikra Rabo.t*, 23). Schwarz (*Palest.* p. 147, 169) fixes it at "*Neama*," also "five miles from Jericho," meaning perhaps *Nawaimeh*, the name of the lower part of the great Wady Mutyah, or el-Asas, which runs from the foot of the hill of Rümmon into the Jordan valley above Jericho, and in a direction generally parallel to the Wady Suweinit (Robinson, *Bib. Res.* iii, 290). It was probably in the vicinity of one of the strong springs along the edge of the hills north of Jericho, such as Ain-Duk, Ras el-Ain, etc.; perhaps at the "high, conical mountain" called *et-Nejamen* (Robinson, *Later Bibl. Res.* p. 202). See TRIBE.

Naäsenes (from the Heb. נחש, *nachash, a serpent*), serpent-worshippers. See OPHITES.

Na'äshon (Exod. vi, 23). See NAHSHON.

Na'ässon (Ναασσών), the Græcized form (Matt. i, 4; Luke iii, 32) of the Heb. name NAHSHON (q. v.).

Na'äthus (Νάαϑος, Vulg. *Naathus*), one of the family of Addi, who renounced their Gentile wives after the exile, according to 1 Esdr. ix, 31; but there is no name corresponding in the Heb. list, Ezra x, 30.

Naatsuts. See THORN.

Na'bal (Heb. *Nabal'*, נָבָל, *foolish*, as often [comp. 1 Sam. xxv, 25]; Sept. Ναβάλ), one of the characters introduced to us in David's wanderings, apparently to give one detailed glimpse of his whole state of life at that time (1 Sam. xxv). Nabal himself is remarkable as one of the few examples given to us of the private life of a Jewish citizen. His history, doubtless, might be paralleled by that of many a well-to-do Oriental of later times. He was a descendant of Caleb, who dwelt at Maon (probably the modern Mâin, seven miles S.E. of Hebron), when David, already anointed to be king of Israel, was with his adherents on the southern borders of Palestine. B.C. 1060. Some, however, understand that he was simply a resident of that part of the country which bore from its great conqueror the name of Caleb (1 Sam. xxv, 3; xxx, 14; so the Vulgate, A. V., and Ewald). He was himself, according to Josephus (*Ant.* vi, 13, 6), a Ziphite, with his residence at Emmaus, a place of that name not otherwise known, on the southern Carmel, in the pasture lands of Maon. (In the Sept. of xxv, 4 he is called "the Carmelite," and the Sept. reads "Maon" for "Paran" in xxv, 1.) With a usage of the word which reminds us of the like adaptation of similar words in modern times, he, like Barzillai, is styled "very great," evidently from his wealth. His wealth, as might be expected from his abode, consisted chiefly of sheep and goats, which, as in Palestine at the time of the Christian æra (1 Sam. xxv) and at the present day, fed together. The tradition preserved in this case the exact number of each—3000 of the former, 1000 of the latter. It was the custom of the shepherds to drive them into the wild downs on the slopes of Carmel, in Judah, which lay in the lowlands to the south, and corresponded very much to the territory of the Jehâlin Arabs. These Arabs have the same sort of possessions which the sacred narrative ascribes to Nabal; that is, numerous flocks of sheep and goats, but few cows (Robinson, *Res.* ii, 176–180; Wilson, *Lands of the Bible*, ii, 710). It was while the shepherds were on one of these pastoral excursions that they met a band of outlaws, who showed them unexpected kindness, protecting them by day and night, and never themselves committing any depredations (xxv, 7, 15, 16). Such protection is generally so highly valued in the East that a suitable present to the protecting party is understood as a matter of course; and in most instances the proprietor of the flocks is happy to bestow it cheerfully and liberally. Once a year there was a grand banquet on Carmel, when they brought back their sheep from the wilderness for shearing—with eating and drinking "like the feast of a king" (xxv, 2, 4, 36). It was on one of these hilarious occasions—the harvest-seasons of the shepherd—that Nabal came across the path of the man to whom he owes his place in history. Ten youths were seen approaching the hill; in them the shepherds recognised the slaves or attendants of the chief of the freebooters who had defended them in the wilderness. To Nabal they were unknown. They approached him with a triple salutation — enumerated the services of their master, and ended by claiming, with a mixture of courtesy and defiance characteristic of the East, "whatsoever cometh into thy hand for thy servants (the Sept. omits this—and has only the next words), and for *thy son* David." The great sheepmaster was not disposed to recognise this unexpected parental relation. He was a man notorious for his obstinacy (such seems the meaning of the word translated "churlish") and for his general low conduct (xxv, 3, "evil in his doings;" xxv, 17, "a man of Belial"). Josephus and the Sept., taking the word *Caleb* not as a proper name, but as a quality (to which the context certainly lends itself), add "of a disposition like a dog"—cynical—κυνικός. On hearing the demand of the ten petitioners, he sprang up (Sept. ἀνεπήδησε), and broke out into fury, "Who is David? and who is the son of Jesse?"—"What runaway slaves are these to interfere with my own domestic arrangements?" (xxv, 10, 11). The moment that the messengers had gone, the shepherds that stood by perceived the danger which their master and themselves would incur. To Nabal himself they dared not speak (xxv, 17). But the sacred writer, with a tinge of the sentiment which such a contrast always suggests, proceeds to describe that this brutal ruffian was married to a wife as beautiful and as wise as he was the reverse (xxv, 3). See ABIGAIL. To her, as to the good angel of the household, one of the shepherds told the state of affairs. She, with the offerings usual on such occasions (xxv, 18; comp. xxx, 11; 2 Sam. xvi, 1; 1 Chron. xii, 40), loaded the asses of Nabal's large establishment—herself mounted one of them, and, with her attendants running before her, rode down the hill towards David's encampment. David had already made the fatal vow of extermination, couched in the usual terms, of destroying the household of Nabal, so as not even to leave a dog behind (xxv, 22). In this, unquestionably, he erred; for whatever David might, on the score of reciprocity of kindness, have naturally thought himself justified in asking, he yet had no right to exact it as a debt, and still less to resent the refusal of it as an injury. (See Hamberger, *Jusjuram. Davidis*, Jen. 1723.) But acting in the heat of passion, David did not allow his determination to slumber; he ordered four hundred of his men to gird on their armor and go with him to smite Nabal and his house with the edge of the sword. At this moment, as it would seem, Abigail appeared, threw herself on her face before him, and poured forth her petition in language which both in form and expression almost assumes the tone of poetry — "Let thine handmaid, I pray thee, speak in thine audience, and hear the words of thine handmaid." Her main argument rests on the description of her husband's character, which she draws with that mixture of playfulness and seriousness which above all things turns away wrath. His name here came in to his rescue. "As his name is, so is he: Nabal [*fool*] is his name, and folly is with him" (xxv, 25; see also ver. 26). Furthermore, by the wise counsel she contrived to introduce into her address respecting the proper way of meeting opposition and bearing hardship in the Lord's cause, and how much better it was to leave the work of retribution to him than to take it prematurely into one's own hand, she convinced David of sin in resolving to avenge himself on Nabal. Better thoughts now prevailed with him, and he said, "Blessed be the Lord God of Israel, which sent thee this day to meet me; and blessed be thy advice, and blessed be thou which hast kept me this day from coming to shed blood." She returned with the news of David's recantation of his vow. Nabal was then at the height of his orgies. Like the revellers of Palestine in the later times of the monarchy, he had drunk to excess, and his wife dared not communicate to him either his danger or his escape (xxv, 36). At break of day she told him both. The stupid reveller was suddenly roused to a sense of that which impended over him. "His heart died within him, and [he] became as a stone." It was as if a stroke of apoplexy or paralysis had fallen upon him. This seems, however, to have been only a temporary recoil of feeling, from which he again recovered —yet not to any proper sense of his past misconduct or true amendment of life. For, as one still amenable to the just displeasure of Heaven, it is said of him that "about ten days after, the Lord smote Nabal, that he died" (xxv, 37, 38). The shock seems to have been the exciting cause of a malady that carried him off about ten days after. (See Wedel, *Exercit. med. dec.* ix, 10 sq.) The suspicions entertained by theologians of the last century that there was a conspiracy between David and Abigail to make away with Nabal for their own alliance (see Winer, s. v. Nabal), have entirely given place to the better spirit of modern criticism; and it is one of the many proofs of the reverential as well as truthful appreciation of the sacred narrative now inaugurated in Germany, that Ewald enters fully into the feeling of the narrator, and closes his summary of Nabal's death with the reflection that "it was not without justice regarded as a divine judgment." According to the (not very probable) Sept. version of 2 Sam. iii, 33, the recollection of Nabal's death lived afterwards in David's memory to point the contrast of the death of Abner—"Died Abner as Nabal died?" David, not long after, evinced the favorable impression which the good-sense and comeliness of Abigail had made upon him by making her his wife. See Ewald, *Isr. Gesch.* ii, 556; Stackhouse, *Bibl. Hist.* iv, 178 sq.; Niemeyer, *Charakt.* iv, 153 sq.; G. L. Dathe, *De famœ vindicta Dav. ergo Nabalem* (Leips. 1723); Schöttgen, *Moralische Gedanken über D. und N.* (F. ad O. 1714). See DAVID.

Nabari′as (Ναβαρίας, Vulg. *Nabarias*), apparently a corruption (1 Esdr. x, 44) for the ZECHARIAH of Neh. viii, 4.

Nabathæans (Ναβαταῖοι [but Απoταῖοι, Ptol. vi, 7; see below], *Nabatæi*), mentioned in Isa. lx, 7, under the name "Nebaioth," as a pastoral tribe of Arabia, in connection with Kedar (comp. Pliny, v, 12), but with no definite specification of locality. See NEBAIOTH. In the period after the exile, the Maccabæan captains Judas and Jonathan found the Nabathæans after pressing forward beyond the Jordan three days' journey into the Arabian Desert (1 Macc. v, 24; ix, 35), and it seems clear that they were then in the district adjoining Gilead, near the cities of Bozrah and Carnaim. Josephus (*Ant.* i, 2, 4) and Ammianus Marcellinus (xiv, 8) calls the whole region between the Euphrates and the Red Sea *Nabatene* (Ναβατηνή); and the latter makes the Nabathæans the immediate neighbors of Roman Arabia, i. e. of the district containing Bozrah and Philadelphia. Other writers, after the Christian æra, place this people on the Ælanitic gulf of the Red Sea (Strabo, xvi, 777), but extend their territory far into Arabia Petræa, and make Petra, in Wady Musa, their capital city (Strabo, xvi, 779; xvii, 803; Pliny, v, 12; vi, 32; Diod. Sic. ii, 48; iii, 43; xix, 94). The Nabathæans were considered a rich people (Dionys. *Perieg.* 955); most of them lived a nomadic life, but many prosecuted a regular and important carrying trade through this region (Diod. Sic. xix, 94; Apul. *Flor.* i, 6). They were governed by kings. Pompey, when in Syria, sent an army against them and subdued them (Joseph. *Ant.* xiv, 3, 3; 6, 4). They submitted formally to the Romans in the time of Trajan (Dio. Cass. lxviii, 14; Ammian.

Marcel. xiv, 8). The chief cities of the Nabathæans may have stood in the vicinity of Bozrah (q. v.), in Edom; and the accounts which Greek and Roman writers give respecting the Nabathæans do not perhaps refer exclusively to this particular tribe, but the name with them may include other Arabian tribes, as the Edomites; yet it is probable that a branch of the nomadic Nabathæans at an early period wandered eastward as far as the Euphrates, in the neighborhood of which lie the Nabathæan morasses (*Nabat*, "*paludes Nabathæorum;*" Golius, cited by Forster, *Geog. of Arabia*, i, 214, note; comp. Strabo, xvi, 767). Ptolemy (vi, 7, 21) mentions Nabathæans in Arabia Felix (comp. Steph. Byz. s. v. p. 578), unless, with recent editions, we read in this place Ἀποταῖοι, which, however, some suppose to be simply another form of the name (but comp. Reland, *Palæst.* p. 90 sq.; Cless, in Pauly's *Realencykl.* 377 sq.). In Genesis (xxv, 13; xxviii, 9; xxxvi, 3; comp. 1 Chron. i, 29) the Nabathæans are mentioned in genealogical connection with Nebaioth (q. v.), the first-born son of Ishmael and brother of Kedar; and a son of Ishmael named *Nabat* appears in Arabian tradition (Abulfed. *Annal.* i, 22), but not as the ancestor of this tribe, who are said to be descended from another Nabat, a son of Mash, and a descendant of Shem. On these traditions the supposition has been based that the Nabathæans were not Arabians, but Aramæans; and Beer believed that remnants of their Aramæan language were concealed in the inscriptions at Sinai (Robinson, *Bibl. Research.* i, 544; comp. Quatremère, *Mémoires sur les Nabatéens*, Par. 1835; Ritter, *Erdk.* xii, 111 sq.), but the unbroken Biblical genealogy cannot be set aside on behalf of the fragmentary and uncertain traditions of Arabia (Winer, ii, 129). The name of the Nabathæans occurs on the cuneiform inscriptions (q. v.). See Smith, *Dict. of Gr. and Rom. Geog.* s. v. Nabatæi; the duke of Luynes, in the *Revue Numismatique* (new series, Par. 1858, vol. iii); the count de Vogué, in the *Mélanges d'Archéologie Orientale* (Par. 1868); Vincent, *Commerce of the Ancients in the Indian Ocean* (Lond. 1807), ii, 275 sq.; Nöldeke, in the *Zeitschr. der deutsch. morgenl. Gesellschaft*, xxv, 113 sq. See PETRA.

Nab′athites (Ναβατταῖοι, Ναυαταῖοι v. r. Ναβατέοι; Vulg. *Nabathæi*), another form (1 Macc. v, 25; ix, 35) for the NABATHÆANS (q. v.).

Nable is the ecclesiastical term for a stringed instrument with a triangular, sonorous box. It only differed from the psaltery in form and having shorter strings (Walcott, *Sacred Archœol.* s. v.).

Na′both (Heb. *Naboth′*, נָבוֹת, *fruits*, according to Gesenius, but *pre-eminence* according to Fürst; Sept. Ναβούθ, v. r. Ναβουθαί, Ναβοθαί; Josephus, Νάβουθος, *Ant.* viii, 13, 7), an Israelite of the town of Jezreel in the time of Ahab, king of Israel. B.C. cir. 897. "He was the owner of a small portion of ground (2 Kings ix, 25, 26) that lay on the eastern slope of the hill of Jezreel. He had also a vineyard, of which the situation is not quite certain. According to the Hebrew text (1 Kings xxi, 1) it was in Jezreel, but the Sept. renders the whole clause differently, omitting the words 'which was in Jezreel,' and reading instead of 'the palace,' 'the *threshing-floor* of Ahab, king of Samaria.' This points to the view, certainly most consistent with the subsequent narrative, that Naboth's vineyard was on the hill of Samaria, close to the 'threshing-floor' (the word translated in A. V. 'void place') which undoubtedly existed there, hard by the gate of the city (1 Kings xxiv). The royal palace of Ahab was close upon the city wall at Jezreel. According to both texts, it immediately adjoined the vineyard (1 Kings xxi, 1, 2, Heb.; 1 Kings xxi, 2, Sept.; 2 Kings ix, 30, 36), and it thus became an object of desire to the king, who offered an equivalent in money, or another vineyard, in exchange for this. Naboth, in the independent spirit of a Jewish landholder (comp. 2 Sam. xxiv; 1 Kings xvi), refused. Perhaps the turn of his expression implies that his objection was mingled with a religious scruple at forwarding the acquisitions of a half-heathen king: 'Jehovah forbid it to me that I should give the inheritance of my fathers unto thee.' Ahab was cowed by this reply; but the proud spirit of his wife, Jezebel, was roused. She and her husband were apparently in the city of Samaria (1 Kings xxi, 18). She took the matter into her own hands, and sent a warrant in Ahab's name, sealed with Ahab's seal, to the elders and nobles of Jezreel, suggesting the mode of destroying the man who had insulted the royal power. A solemn fast was proclaimed, as on the announcement of some great calamity. Naboth was 'set on high' in the public place of Samaria (the Heb. word which is rendered, here only, 'on high,' is more accurately 'at the head of,' or 'in the chiefest place among' [1 Sam. ix, 22]. The passage is obscured by our ignorance of the nature of the ceremonial in which Naboth was made to take part; but, in default of this knowledge, we may accept the explanation of Josephus, that an assembly [ἐκκλησία] was convened, at the head of which Naboth, in virtue of his position, was placed, in order that the charge of blasphemy and the subsequent catastrophe might be more telling); two men of worthless character accused him of having 'cursed God and the king.' He and his children (2 Kings ix, 26), who else might have succeeded to his father's inheritance, were dragged out of the city and despatched the same night. The place of execution there, as at Hebron (2 Sam. iii), was by the large tank, or reservoir, which still remains on the slope of the hill of Samaria, immediately outside the walls. The usual punishment for blasphemy was enforced (Lev. xxiv, 16; Numb. xv, 30). Naboth and his sons were stoned; their mangled remains were devoured by the dogs (and swine, Sept.) that prowled under the walls; and the blood from their wounds ran down into the waters of the tank below, which was the common bathing-place of the prostitutes of the city (comp. 1 Kings xxi, 19; xxii, 38, Sept.). Josephus (Ant. viii, 15, 6) makes the execution to have been at Jezreel, where he also places the washing of Ahab's chariot." This narrative is remarkable as the only mention in the Scriptures of a woman as able to write, and some have inferred, but needlessly, that the letters mentioned in 1 Kings xxi, 8 must have been written by an amanuensis. The state of female education in the East has probably always, as now, been such that not one woman in ten thousand could write at all. Coquerel (in the Biographie Sacrée) thinks that the reason why the children of Naboth perished with him —being perhaps put to death by the creatures of Jezebel—was that otherwise the crime would have been useless, as the children would still have been entitled to the father's heritage. But we know not that Naboth had any sons; and if he had sons, and they had been taken off, the estate might still have had an heir. It is not unlikely that a custom like that of escheat in modern times obtained in Israel, giving to the crown the property of persons put to death for treason or blasphemy. On Naboth's death, accordingly, Ahab obtained possession of his inheritance. The perpetration of this crime brought upon Ahab and Jezebel the severest maledictions, which shortly after were carried into effect. The only tribunal to which he remained accountable pronounced his doom through a prophet. "This was the final step in Ahab's course of wickedness, and as he was in the act of taking possession, Elijah met him and announced the awful doom which awaited him and his queen and children. A kind of repentance on the part of the king led to another announcement of a certain modification of the retribution, which was not to come during Ahab's lifetime. But in that very plot of ground, and apparently quite close to the city, his son, king Jehoram, was met by Jehu, who mortally wounded him with an arrow. The king sank dead in his chariot, and Jehu bade his attendant captain take up the body and cast it into the portion of the field of

Naboth. As he was doing so he was reminded by Jehu that they both had been riding behind Ahab at the time when the Lord laid this burden upon him, 'Surely I have seen yesterday (אֶמֶשׁ, yesternight) the blood of Naboth and the blood of his sons. saith the Lord; and I will requite thee in this plat, saith the Lord' (2 Kings ix, 21-26). This passage seems to imply two circumstances which are not mentioned in the earlier history: that Naboth's sons were put to death as well as himself, and that Ahab took possession the very day after the judicial murder." The English version renders the words thus: "In the place where dogs licked the blood of Naboth, shall dogs lick thy blood, even thine" (1 Kings xxi, 19). But the fulfilment is recorded as taking place in the pool of Samaria (xxii, 38), "And they washed out the chariot in the pool of Samaria, and the dogs licked up his blood." Kimchi explains this by saying that the water of this pool ran to Jezreel; but Schwarz (Palest. p. 165) identifies Jezreel with Serain, sixteen miles from Sebaste, where the pool stood, and on a higher level. Accordingly, he insists that the rendering "on the spot" is wrong, and that בַּמָּקוֹם should be rendered "in place of," i. e. "in punishment for" (comp. Hosea ii, 1). See Kitto, Daily Bible Illustr. ad loc. See AHAB; ELIJAH; JEZEBEL; JEZREEL.

Nabuchodono'sor (Ναβουχοδονόσορ), the Græcised form in the Apocrypha (1 Esdr. i, 40, 41, 45, 46; Tob. xiv, 15; Jud. i, 1, 5, 7, 11, 12; ii, 1, 4, 19; iii, 2, 8; iv, 1; vi, 2, 4; xi, 7, 23; xii, 13; xiii, 18) of the name of the Babylonian king NEBUCHADNEZZAR (q. v.).

Nacchianti (Latin Naclantus), GIACOMO, an Italian prelate noted as a theologian, was born at Florence near the opening of the 16th century. He joined the Dominicans, and taught theology for some time at Rome. In 1544 he was created bishop of Chiozzia, in the territory of Venice. In this capacity he attended the Council of Trent, and there distinguished himself by his scholarship and his liberality. He went so far as to condemn the position of those Romanists who desired equal recognition for the Church writings as for inspired. He declared that "the placing of Scripture and tradition on the same level was impious" (comp. Sarpi, i, 293; Mendham, Memoirs of the Council of Trent [Lond. 1834], p. 59, 60). He died at Florence, April 24, 1569. We quote of his works, Scripturæ sacræ medulla (Venice, 1561, 4to):—Enarrationes in Epistolam Pauli ad Ephesios, in maximum pontificatum, etc. (Venice, 1570, 2 vols. 8vo):—Digressiones et Tractationes (Venice, 1657, 2 vols. fol.). See Hoefer, Nouv. Biog. Générale, xxxvii, 108; Wessenberg, Kirchen-Versammlungen, iii, 211; Ranke, Hist. of the Papacy, i, 151; Hardwick, Hist. of the Reformation, p. 282.

Naccus is the name of the richly embroidered red horse-blankets which ornament the horses of the papal incumbent, especially at the coronation ceremonies of the pope.

Nachash. See SERPENT.

Nachmanides (or **Nachmani** = Ben-Nachman), MOSES (also called by the Jews Ramban, רמב"ן, from the initial letters ר' משה בן נחמן, R. Moses ben-Nachman; the Pious Teacher [הרב המאמין], the Great Master [הרב הגדול], and by Christian writers Moses Gerundensis), a Jewish writer of considerable note in the literary history of the Iberian peninsula, was born at Gerona, in Catalonia, about 1194. So extraordinary was his proficiency in the Biblical and Talmudical writings, that he wrote an elaborate Treatise on the Rights of Primogeniture and Vows (הלכות בכורות ונדרים) when he was scarcely fifteen years of age (1210), for which he obtained the title of "the Father of Knowledge," and composed his commentaries (חדושים) on the greater part of the Talmud (1217-

1223) before he was thirty. His Talmudical learning was no doubt mainly acquired after study of the writings of Moses Maimonides, which Nachmanides got hold of while yet a youth, and under the erudite instruction of the noted rabbi Jehudah the Pious, of Paris, whose pupil he was. About the year 1262, while practicing as a physician in his native place, he delivered, by request, a discourse in Saragossa before James I, king of Aragon, and the magnates of the Church and State, in defence of Judaism. This remarkable address (דרשה), which has for its text Psa. xix, 9, "The law of the Lord is perfect," etc., and is an important contribution to Biblical exegesis, the Christology of the O. T., and the understanding of Judaism, was first published in 1582, with the title תורת יהוה תמימה, wherewith it commences; then at Prague, 1595; and with corrections and notes by the learned and industrious Adolph Jellinek (Leipsic, 1853). In the year 1263 king James I of Aragon issued a decree that, in order to put a stop to the daily disputes which took place between the Jews and the Dominican friars who had studied Arabic and Hebrew, a public disputation should be held at Barcelona. The Jews on their part nominated as their advocate Moses Nachmanides, while the Christians were represented by Fra Pablo Christiani, a converted Jew. This disputation, which took place before the king and the court, lasted four days (July 20–24). As usual in similar cases, each party claimed the victory. Nachmanides circulated this disputation among his brethren, as Pablo Christiani and his friends gave an incorrect report of it; and the pope, Clement IV, was so incensed at it that he wrote to James I of Aragon, urging on his majesty to banish Nachmanides from his dominions. Thereupon the septuagenarian had to leave (1266) his native place, his two sons, his college with numerous disciples, and his friends. He went to the Holy Land, which he reached Aug. 12, 1267. The disputation referred to was first published, with omissions and interpolations, and an exceedingly bad Latin translation, by Wagenseil, in his *Tela ignea Satanæ* (Altorf, 1681). It was then published in the collection of polemical writings entitled מלחמת חובה, where it is the first of the series, and is called וכוח הרמ"בן עם פראי פולו, *The Discussion of Ramban with Fra Paolo* (Constantinople, 1710); and recently again by the erudite Steinschneider, *Nachmanidis Disputatio publica pro fide Judaica a. 1263, e cod. MSS. recognita* (Berl. 1860), to which are added learned notes by the editor, and Nachmanides's exposition of Isa. liii. In Palestine Nachmanides completed and revised his stupendous *Commentary on the Pentateuch*, an archæological and mystical work which he had begun nearly twenty years before (1249–1268). "Physician by profession, thoroughly conversant not only with Hebrew, Chaldee, Syriac, and Arabic, but also with Greek, Latin, Spanish, etc., master of the whole cycle of Talmudic, Midrashic, and exegetical literature, and intimately acquainted with the manners, customs, and geography of the East, he frequently quotes medical works (ספר הרפואות, and ספרי נסיונות), clears up medical difficulties (comp. comment. on Gen. xxx, 14; xlv, 26; xlvi, 15; Lev. iii, 9; xi, 11; xii, 4; xiii, 3, 42; Numb. xxi, 9), explains difficult terms by comparing the Hebrew with other languages (comment. on Gen. xlix, 12, 20; Exod. xxx, 23, 34; xxxii, 1; Lev. xi, 11; xiii, 29; xix, 20; Deut. xiii, 2, 4; xxxiii, 30), criticises Christian versions (Gen. xli, 45; Numb. xi, 17), explains the customs and geography of the East (Gen. xi, 28 xxxiv, 12; xxxviii, 18, 24), gently and reverentially attacks the rationalistic views of Maimonides about miracles and revelation, and controverts and exposes, in unsparing language, Aben-Ezra's scepticism, concealed in unbelieving, mystical doctrines. See ABEN-EZRA. Being a thorough believer in the Cabala, Nachmanides, though explaining the obvious sense of the Bible, yet maintains that

each separate letter is imbued with a spiritual and recondite potency, and forms a link in the grand chain of revelation, and that those who are initiated in the secrets of the Cabala can, by the combination of these letters, penetrate, more than ordinary readers, into the mysteries of Holy Writ. When it is remarked that no less than fifteen Jewish literati, of different periods, have written super-commentaries on this remarkable production, the importance of this commentary, and the influence it exercised on Biblical exegesis and the Jewish literature, will easily be comprehended" (Ginsburg, in Kitto). This commentary, which is alternately denominated חדושי תורה, פרוש, or באור על התורה, פרוש נחמני and סתרי תורה, was first published before 1480; then in Lisbon, 1489; Naples, 1490; Pesaro, 1514; Salonoikai, 1521; with the comments of Rashi, Aben-Ezra, etc. (Constantinople, 1522); with the Hebrew text of the Pentateuch, and the Five Megilloth, the Chaldee Paraphrase, the Comment of Rashi, and the super-commentary of Aboab on Nachmanides (Venice, 1548); and, besides many other editions, lately in the excellent Pentateuch and Five Megilloth, containing the Hebrew text, the Chaldee Paraphrases, the Commentaries of Rashi, Aben-Ezra, Rashbam, Seforno, etc. (Vienna, 1859, 5 vols.). Nachmanides also wrote a commentary on Job (פרוש על איוב), which was first published in Bomberg's Rabbinical Bible (Venice, 1517), and was incorporated in Frankfurter's Great Rabbinical Bible (Amsterd. 1724–27). See FRANKFURTER. But that Nachmanides was not the author of this commentary has been proved by Dr. Frankel, in his *Monatsschrift*, 1868, p. 449 sq. The cabalistic commentary on the Song of Songs, which is ascribed to him, belongs to his teacher Asariel. Besides the works already mentioned, Nachmanides wrote a number of cabalistical, dogmatical, ethical, and religio-polemical works, as שַׁעַר הַגְּמוּל, on reward and punishment (Naples, 1490; latest edition, Warsaw, 1873):—סוֹד הַחִבּוּר or אִגֶּרֶת הַקֹּדֶשׁ, on the sanctity of marriage (Rome, 1546, and often since):—ס' הָאֱמוּנָה וְהַבִּטָּחוֹן, also שַׁעַר אֱמוּנָה, a large cabalistic work on prayers, the natural law, the decalogue, the attributes of God, etc. (Venice, 1601; latest ed. Warsaw, 1873):—פֵּרוּשׁ סֵפֶר יְצִרָה, a commentary on the book Jezirah (q. v.), printed together with the book Jezirah (Mantua, 1562, and often):—ס' הַגְּאֻוּלָה, on the redemption from captivity, in sections, of which a part of the second section was published by Asar de Rossi in his *Meor Enajim* (Mantua, 1574, and often). He also wrote some poems, of which one is especially beautiful, and is generally used in the synagogical service for the first day of the new year—the מָרֹאשׁ מִקַּרְמֵי עוֹלָמִים. In the division of the synagogues, caused by the writings of Maimonides (q. v.), he took the part of the latter, probably more on account of the esteem he felt for this great man than for any sympathy with his opinions. Maimonides intended to give Judaism a character of unity, but he produced the contrary. His aim was to harmonize philosophy and religion, but the result was a division in the synagogue, which gave birth to a philosophism called Cabala, and to this newly-born Cabala Nachmanides became converted, though he was at first decidedly adverse to this system. But one day the Cabalist who was most zealous to convert him was caught in a house of ill-fame, and condemned to death. He requested Nachmanides to visit him on the Sabbath, the day fixed for his execution. Nachmanides reproved him for his sins, but the Cabalist declared his innocence, and that he would appear at his house on this very day after the execution, and partake with him the Sabbath meal. According to the story, he did as he promised, as by means of the cabalistic mysteries he effected his escape, and an ass was executed in his stead, and he himself was suddenly transported into Nachmanides's house! From that time

Nachmanides became a disciple of the Cabala, and was initiated into its mysteries, the tenets of which pervade his numerous writings. Thus in the introduction to his *Commentary on the Pentateuch* he remarks, "We possess a faithful tradition that the whole Pentateuch consists of names of the Holy One (blessed be he!); for the words may be divided into sacred names in another sense, so that it is to be taken as an allegory. Thus the words בראשית ברא אלהים, in Gen. i, 1, may be divided into three other words, e. g. בראש יתברא אלהים. In like manner is the whole Pentateuch, which consists of nothing but transpositions and numerals of divine names." Nachmanides died at Acre (Ptolemais) about 1270, leaving a number of disciples. See Ginsburg, in Kitto, *Cyclop.* s. v.; Steinschneider, *Catalogus Libr. Hebr. in Biblioth. Bodleiana*, col. 1947–65; Fürst, *Biblioth. Judaica*, iii, 2–8; Perles, in Frankel's *Monatsschrift für Gesch. u. Wissenschaft d. Judenth.* viii, 81 sq., 113 sq.; Grätz, *Gesch. d. Juden*, vii, 41–50, 54 sq., 78–80, 132–144, 417 sq.; De Rossi, *Dizionario storico degli autori Ebrei*, p. 236 sq. (Germ. transl. by Hamberger); id. *Biblioth. Judaica Antichristiana* (Padua, 1800), p. 74 sq.; Lindo, *Hist. of the Jews in Spain and Portugal* (Lond. 1848), p. 68 sq.; Finn, *Sephardim*, p. 199 sq.; Basnage, *Hist. of the Jews* (Taylor's transl.), p. 655, 656 sq., 660; Da Costa, *Israel and the Gentiles* (New York, 1855), p. 299 sq.; Ginsburg, *The Kabbalah*, etc. (Lond. 1865), p. 108 sq.; Dessauer, *Gesch. d. Israeliten*, p. 307 sq.; Braunschweiger, *Gesch. d. Juden in den Roman. Staaten* (Würzburg, 1865), p. 165, 181; Jost, *Gesch. d. Judenth. u. s. Sekten*, iii, 13, 37, 73; Etheridge, *Introd. to Hebr. Literature*, p. 251 sq., 358, 408; Sachs, *Religiöse Poesie d. Juden in Spanien*, p. 135 sq., 321 sq.; Delitzsch, *Zur Gesch. d. Jüdischen Poesie*, p. 39, 65, 85; Ginsburg, *Levita's Massoreth Ha-Massoreth*, p. 124; id. *Jacob Ibn-Adonijah's Introd. to the Rabbinic Bible*, p. 10, 39, 40; Zunz, *Literaturgesch. d. Synagogalen Poesie*, p. 478; Cassel, *Leitfaden für Gesch. u. Literatur*, p. 67 sq.; Schmucker, *Hist. of the Modern Jews*, 149 sq.; Steinschneider, *Jewish Literature*, p. 89. (B. P.)

Na′chon (Heb. *Nakon'*, נָכוֹן, *prepared;* Sept. Ναχών, v. r. Ναχώρ and even 'Ωδάδ), a name given only as identifying a *threshing-floor* near which Uzzah was slain, for laying his hand upon the ark (2 Sam. vi, 6). It is doubted whether this be a proper name, denoting the owner of the floor, or merely an epithet applied to it, i. e. *the prepared floor* (so the Targum of Jonathan; comp. Buxtorf, *Lex. Rabb.* col. 2647). This floor could not have been far from Jerusalem, and must have nearly adjoined the house of Obed-edom, in which the ark was deposited. In the parallel text (1 Chron. xiii, 9) the place is called the *floor of Chidon*, which some suppose to be another name of the owner (Talm. Bab. *Sotah*, iii, fol. 35). See CHIDON. Another method of identifying the two names is to regard Nachon as derived from נכה, *to smite*, because Jehovah smote Uzzah there; and Chidon as containing a figurative allusion to the divine javelin which smote him. In any case PEREZ-UZZAH (q. v.) afterwards became the local designation of the spot.

Na′chor, a more accurate form of the name NAHOR (q. v.), meaning: (*a*) Abraham's grandfather (Luke iii, 34), (*b*) his brother (Josh. xxiv, 2).

Nachshon BEN-ZADOK, a Jewish writer of the early period in the development of post-Christian Judaism, was gaon at the academy of Sura or Sora, A.D. 890–898. He is the author of a great number of questions and answers (שְׁאֵלוֹת וּתְשׁוּבוֹת), and wrote explanations of difficult passages in the Talmud, which explanations are reprinted in the *Responsa Gaonim* (Berl. 1848), ed. Cassel. To Nachshon is also attributed the perpetual calendar (*Iggul di R. Nachshon*), founded upon a period of nineteen years, which was

proved to be not quite correct by the learned Spaniards of the 10th and 11th centuries, but was, nevertheless, made the foundation of calendar tables (לוּחוֹת, from לוּח, a table), by some later writers, as Jacob ben-Asher, at Toledo, and has retained a place in some works nearly to the present time. This same Nachshon is probably also the author of the chronicle entitled סדר תנאים ואמוראים, a treatise upon the Tanaim and Amoraim, critically edited by Luzzatto in *Kerem chemed*, (1839), iv, 184 sq. See Grätz, *Gesch. d. Juden*, v, 280; Fürst, *Bibl. Judaica*, iii, 9; Steinschneider, *Catalogus Libr. Hebr. in Biblioth. Bodleiana*, p. 2020; Scaliger, *De Emendatione Temporum*, ii, 132 sq.; Luzzatto, *Calendario Ebraïco per venti secoli*; Schwarz, *Der Jüd. Kalender* (Breslau, 1872), p. 78. (B. P.)

Nachtigall (Latin *Luscinius*), OTTOMAR, a Roman Catholic polemic, was born at Strasburg about 1487. After having studied belles-lettres and jurisprudence at the universities of Paris, Louvain, Padua, and Vienna, he visited a large part of Europe, particularly Hungary and Italy, and even some parts of Asia. During this time he was in holy orders. On his return to Germany he preached in different places, among others at Augsburg, where he joined the famous Geiler of Kaisersberg. In 1514 he returned to his native town, where for several years he gave lessons in Greek, a language in which he excelled, in the convent of St. Ulric at Augsburg. In 1528 he was removed from his chair, on account of his sermons against the doctrines of Luther. The following year he established himself at Freiburg, in Brisgau, where he continued to preach against the Reformed doctrines. He died about 1535. Nachtigall was renowned among his contemporaries for his extensive and varied learning, and was very satirical, Erasmus and Hutten being the special subjects of his satire. The following are his works, *Carmen heroicum Græcum quo J. Geileri Kaisersbergii obitum decantat* (Strasburg, 1510, 4to):—*Institutiones musicæ* (Strasburg, 1515 and 1536, 4to; Augsburg, 1542, 4to):—*Progymnasmata Græcæ litteraturæ* (Strasburg, 1517 and 1523, 4to):—*Grunnius sophista, sive Pelagus humanæ miseriæ, quo docetur utrius natura ad virtutem et felicitatem propius accedat, hominis an bruti animantis* (Strasburg, 1522, 8vo; see Schelhorn, *Amœnitates litterariæ*, vol. x):—*Evangelica Historia, e Græco versa* (Augsburg, 1523, 4to). Nachtigall himself finished a German translation of this version of the Gospels, which in some respects may be compared to a concordance, under the title *Joci et sales* (Augsburg, 1524, 8vo; Frankfort, 1602, 8vo). Nachtigall has also made a German translation of the Psalms of David (Augsburg, 1524, 4to), and published editions of classical writers. See Hoefer, *Nouv. Biog. Générale*, s. v.; Schelhorn, *Amœnitates litterariæ*, vi, 455; Nicéron, *Mémoires*, vol. xxxii; Rotermund's *Supplement* to Jöcher's *Allgem. Gelehrten-Lexikon*, s. v. (J. H. W.)

Na′dab (Heb. *Nadab'*, נָדָב, *liberal* [see Simonis *Onom. V. T.* p. 409]; Sept. Ναδάβ), the name of four men.

1. (Josephus, Νάβαδος, *Ant.* iii, 8, 1 and 7.) The eldest (Exod. vi, 23; Numb. iii, 2) of the four sons of Aaron by Elisheba, who were anointed, with their father, to be priests of Jehovah (Exod. xxviii, 1). B.C. 1657. He, his father and brother, and seventy old men of Israel, were led out from the midst of the assembled people (Exod. xxiv, 1), and were commanded to stay and worship God "afar off," below the lofty summit of Sinai, where Moses alone was to come near to the Lord. Subsequently he, with his brother Abihu, offered incense with strange or common fire to the Lord, instead of that which had been miraculously kindled and was perpetually kept burning upon the altar of burnt offerings; and they were immediately consumed by a fire from the presence of God (Lev. x, 1, 2; Numb. iii, 4; xxvi, 61). They left no children (1 Chron. xxiv, 2). From the injunction given (Lev. x, 9, 10) immediately after their death, it has been inferred (Rosenmüller, ad loc.) that the brothers were in a state of intoxication when they committed the offence. The spiritual meaning of the injunction is drawn out at great length by Origen, *Hom.* vii, in *Levit.* On this occasion, as if to mark more decidedly the divine displeasure with the offenders, Aaron and his surviving son were forbidden to go through the ordinary outward ceremonial of mourning for the dead. See J. D. Frobösen, *Gedanken v. d. Sünde Nadabs u. Obihu,* in the *Brem. u. Verd. Bibl.* i, 4, p. 159 sq.; J. Medhurst, in the *Bibl. Hagan.* iv, 70–76; Bp. Hall, *Contemplations,* ad loc.; Saurin, *Discour. Historiques,* ii, 354; *Dissert.* p. 531; A. Littleton, *Sermons,* p. 303; J. Dickson, *Discourses,* p. 183; C. Simeon, *Works,* i, 613; R. P. Buddicom, *Christian Exodus,* ii, 1. See ABIHU.

2. (Josephus, Νάδαβος, *Ant.* viii, 11, 4.) Son and successor of Jeroboam on the throne of Israel (1 Kings xiv, 20). B.C. 951. He followed the deep-laid but criminal and dangerous policy of his father (xv, 26). In the latter part of his reign, "Gibbethon, in the territory of Dan (Josh. xix, 44), a Levitical town (xxi, 23), was occupied by the Philistines, perhaps having been deserted by its lawful possessors in the general self-exile of the Levites from the polluted territory of Jeroboam. Nadab and all Israel went up and laid siege to this frontier town. A conspiracy broke out in the midst of the army, and the king was slain by Baasha, a man of Issachar. Abijah's prophecy (1 Kings xiv, 10) was literally fulfilled by the murderer, who proceeded to destroy the whole house of Jeroboam. So perished the first Israelitish dynasty. We are not told what events led to the siege of Gibbethon, or how it ended, or any other incident in Nadab's short reign. It does not appear what ground Ewald and Newman have for describing the war with the Philistines as unsuccessful. It is remarkable that when a similar destruction fell upon the family of the murderer Baasha twenty-four years afterwards, the Israelitish army was again engaged in a siege of Gibbethon (1 Kings xvi, 15)." See GIBBETHON. In 1 Kings xv, 25 Nadab is assigned a reign of two years, but a comparison of the connected events and dates show that it lasted little, if any, over one year; so that the reckoning must have been made out by the usual proleptic method, which computed the years as beginning at the normal point of the Jewish calendar, i. e. the 1st of Nisan preceding. See CHRONOLOGY.

3. The first named of the two sons of Shammai, in the tribe of Judah, and the father of two sons (1 Chron. ii, 28, 30). B.C. post 1618.

4. The fifth named of the eight sons of Jehiel, "the father [founder] of Gibeon ;" a Benjamite of Gibeon (1 Chron. viii, 30; ix, 36). B.C. perhaps cir. 1013.

Nadab'atha (Ναδαβάϑ v. r. Γαβαδάν; Syriac, *Nobot; Vulg. Madaba*), "a place from which the bride was conducted by the children of Jambri (q. v.) when Jonathan and Simon attacked them (1 Macc. ix, 37). Josephus (*Ant.* xiii, 1, 4) gives the name as *Gabath* (Γαβαϑά). Jerome's conjecture (in the Vulgate) can hardly be admitted, because *Medeba* was the city of the Jambrites (see ver. 36) to which the bride was brought, not that from which she came. That Nadabatha was on the east of Jordan is most probable ; for though, even to the time of the Gospel narrative, by 'Chanaanites'—to which the bride in this case belonged—is signified Phœnicians, yet we have the authority (such as it is) of the Book of Judith (v. 3) for attaching that name especially to the people of Moab and Ammon ; and it is not probable that when the whole country was in such disorder a wedding *cortége* would travel for so great a distance as from Phœnicia to Medeba. On the east of Jordan the only two names that occur as possible are *Nebo*— by Eusebius and Jerome written *Nabo* and *Nabau*— and *Nabathæa.* Compare the lists of places round

es-Salt, in Robinson, 1st ed. iii, 167–70." See GABATHA.

Nadal, BERNARD H., D.D., a distinguished minister of the Methodist Episcopal Church, was born in Talbot County, Md., March 27, 1812. He was converted in 1832; and after the necessary preparatory studies, which he pursued in private, he was admitted as a preacher in the old Baltimore Conference in 1835. His subsequent fields of labor as a pastor were Luray Circuit, Va.; St. Mary's Circuit, Md.; Bladensburg, Md.; City Station, Baltimore ; Lewisburgh, Va.; Lexington, Va.; Columbia Street, Baltimore ; Carlisle, Pa.; High Street, Baltimore ; City Station, Baltimore ; Foundry Church, Washington ; Sands Street, Brooklyn ; First Church, New Haven ; Wesley Chapel, Washington ; Trinity Church, Philadelphia. During his entire pastoral life he was a close student, and made up for the absence of an early college training by extraordinary application afterwards. In 1848, while stationed at Carlisle, Pa., he graduated at Dickinson College, having pursued his studies in the college in connection with his pastoral work. During a part of his pastorate in Carlisle he taught a class in the college. In 1849 he was appointed agent of Baltimore Female College ; but as it was thought inexpedient at that time to prosecute the agency, he consented to supply for that year the pulpit of an Independent Church in Baltimore. From 1854 to 1857 he was professor in Indiana Asbury University. In the latter year he returned to the Baltimore Conference, and became presiding elder of Roanoke District in Western Virginia. This was a time when the great waves of agitation on the subject of slavery were rolling fiercely over the Border States. Dr. Nadal entered vigorously into the contest, and boldly and successfully defended the position of his Church and Conference on the subject. By his sermons and addresses he exerted a marked influence in favor of the national government during the war of the rebellion. He enjoyed the friendship of president Lincoln, and poured forth in an able discourse his sorrow at his death. In 1867 he accepted the professorship of historical theology in the Drew Theological Seminary at Madison, and after the decease of Dr. M'Clintock (q. v.) he was also acting president of the institution ; but he was removed by death shortly afterwards, June 20, 1870. Dr. Nadal was an able and forcible preacher, and maintained to the last a high rank in the pulpit. Many of his discourses on special occasions were printed and widely read, and exhibited a high order of pulpit eloquence. He was also well known as a vigorous and polished writer, and contributed very largely to the periodical literature of his time. He was one of the editorial staff of *The Methodist,* whose editor, Dr. Crooks, said of him that "in writing he was almost without a peer in the American Methodist Church.' Dr. Nadal's thorough scholarship, fine social qualities, and his ability to communicate instruction, made him an efficient and popular instructor, and his professional career in both the institutions which he served was marked by enthusiasm, energy, and success. A volume of his *Sermons* (entitled *New Life Dawning,* etc.) was published under the editorship of Prof. Buttz, with a *Memoir* prefixed (N. Y. 1873, 12mo).

Nadasdy, THOMAS, a Hungarian Protestant divine of some note, flourished during the Reformation movement of the 16th century. But little is known of his personal history. He was distinguished by unusual attainments, power, wealth, zeal, and generosity in supporting the cause of the Gospel. He died in 1553. " Nadasdy had been a strong pillar in the Church in a day when every man was with one hand building the walls of Zion and with the other holding a weapon." See Craig, *Hist. of the Prot. Church in Hungary* (Bost. 1864), p. 92, 93.

Nænia (i. e. a *dirge* or lamentation, equivalent to the Greek ϑρῆνος) is the term used to describe the Roman funeral songs, uttered either by the relatives of the deceased or by hired persons. At Rome Nænia was personified and worshipped as a goddess, and even had a chapel, which, however, as in the case of all other gods in connection with the dead, was outside the walls of the city, near the porta Viminalis. As Næniæ are compared with lullabies, and as they seem to have been sung with a soft voice, as if a person was to be lulled to sleep, the object of this worship was probably to procure rest and peace for the departed in the lower world. See Augustine, De Civ. Dei, vi, 9; Arnobius, Adv. Gent. iv, 7; vii, 32; Horace, Carm. iii, 28, 16; Festus, p. 161, 163, ed. Müller.

Naga (a Sanscrit word signifying *snake*) designates in Hindû mythology a monster, regarded as a demigod, and having a human face with the tail of a serpent and the expanded neck of a cobra de capello. The worship of the snake-gods is termed Naga Panchami. These gods, of whom, among the Hindûs, Vasûki is the lord and Manûsa the queen, reside in regions immediately under the earth, supposed to be the seat of exhaustless treasures, the blaze of which supplies the absence of the solar radiance. The race of these beings is said to have sprung from Kasyapa (q. v.), in order to people the regions below the earth (Patala). The principal Nagas, of which there are about a dozen, are propitiated with offerings of milk and ghee. The fifth lunar day of Sravana is held sacred to the Nagas. On that day ablutions are performed in the pool sacred to Vasûki, the lord of the Nagas. By observing this ceremony the Nagas are pleased, and the votaries are believed to rest free from the dread of serpents. See Moor, *Hindû Pantheon*, s. v.; Coleman, *Hindû Mythol.* p. 254.

Nagara, ISRAEL BEN-MOSES, a Jewish writer, was a native of Spain, but flourished at Damascus near the closing part of the 16th century. He was a celebrated poet, and was wont to attend the mosques to collect their musical tunes, to which he adapted Hebrew or Chaldee verses. His works were, זְמִירוֹת יִשְׂרָאֵל, a collection of religious poems in three parts (Isafet, 1587; Venice, 1606):—מְשָׂחֶקֶת בַּתֵּבֵל, a metrical homily on contempt for the world (Venice, 1580, 1599):—מֵימֵי־ יִשְׂרָאֵל, *The Waters of Israel*, a *mélange*, poetical, epistolary, and oratorical, arranged under six heads, designated by the waters mentioned in the Bible: 1. מֵי הַשִּׁלֹחַ, *Waters of Siloah*; 2. מֵי מְנוּחוֹת, *Waters of Quietude*; 3. מֵי מְרִיבָה, *Waters of Strife*; 4. מֵי מָצוֹר, *Waters of Besieging*; 5. מֵי זָהָב, *Gold Waters*; 6. מֵי מָרִים, *Bitter Waters* (Venice, 1605). See Fürst, *Biblioth. Judaica*, iii, 12; De Rossi, *Dizionario* (Germ. transl.), p. 240; Lindo, *Hist. of the Jews in Spain*, p. 360; Etheridge, *Introd. to Hebr. Lit.* p. 462; Margoliouth, *Modern Judaism Investigated*, p. 245; Jost, *Gesch. d. Judenth. u. s. Sekten*, iii, 275; Grätz, *Gesch. d. Juden*, ix, 421, 422; Delitzsch, *Zur Gesch. d. Jüd. Poesie*, p. 56; Zunz, *Zur Gesch. u. Literatur*, p. 229; *Literaturgesch. d. synagogalen Poesie* (Berl. 1865), p. 419. (B. P.)

Nagarjuna or **Nagasena**, one of the most celebrated Buddhistic teachers or patriarchs—the thirteenth—according to some, lived about 400 years, according to others, about 500 years after the death of the Buddha Sakyamuni (i. e. 143 or 43 B.C.). He was the founder of the Mâdhyamika school, and his principal disciples were Aryadeva and Buddhapâlita. According to the tradition of the Buddhas, he was born in the south of India, in a Brahminical family. Even as a child he studied all the four Vedas; later he travelled through various countries, and became proficient in astronomy, geography, and magical arts. By means of the last he had several amorous adventures, which ended in the death of three companions of his, but in his own repentance, and, with the assistance of a Buddhist mendicant, in his conversion to Buddhism. Many miracles are, of course, attributed to his career as propagator of this doctrine, especially in the south of India,

and his life is said to have lasted 300 years. See E. Burnouf. *Introd. à l'Hist. du Buddhisme Indien* (Par. 1844); Spence Hardy, *Manual of Buddhism* (Lond. 1853).

Nagasena. See NAGARJUNA.

Nagdilah, SAMUEL BEN-JOSEPH, HA-LEVI, surnamed *Han-nagid* (the prince or chief), a Jewish writer, was born at Cordova in 993. He was a pupil of Chajug (q. v.), and a contemporary of Ibn-Ganach (q. v.). When in 1015 rabbi Chanoch, under whose instruction he acquired extensive Talmudical learning, died, R. Samuel succeeded to the chief rabbinate of Spain, with the title of prince (Nagid). Owing, however, to the intestine wars between the rival Moorish chiefs for supremacy, many inhabitants quitted Cordova, among whom was also Samuel ha-Levi, who went to Malaga, where he kept a druggist's shop. His profound knowledge of Arabian literature and his beautiful writing brought him to the notice of Alkas ben-Alarif, prime minister of Habus ibn-Moskan of Granada, who made him his secretary, and on his death-bed recommended his sovereign to be guided by him. In 1020 he was himself made prime minister, and in 1027 secured the crown to Badis, the eldest son of the deceased king, although the grandees had sought to place Balkin, the younger son, on the throne of his father. Nagdilah zealously cultivated poetry and science, in which he himself excelled, and to the encouragement of which he devoted a large portion of his wealth. He collected and purchased many copies of the Talmud, Mishna, and other books, which, to disseminate learning, he distributed gratuitously, and he was the indefatigable patron both of Spanish and foreign authors. Besides a treatise which he wrote against Ibn-Ganach in defence of his teacher Chajug, entitled הַשָּׂגַת הַחַשָּׂגָה, he is best known as the author of a good treatise on the methodology of the Talmud, of which a condensed German translation is given by Pinner in his introduction to the treatise *Berakoth*; he also wrote the *Son of Proverbs*, בֶּן־מִשְׁלֵי (or parables), consisting of poems which are represented as profound and magnificent, and of which some pieces are given by Dukes in his *Rabbinische Blumenlese*. He is also said to have written a commentary on the Pentateuch (פ׳ עַל הַתּוֹרָה), of which that on the Book of Numbers alone is preserved in MSS. (Bodleian Libr. No. 152); and according to Ibn-Ezra (*Yesod Mora*, init.; *Moznaim*, pref.) he wrote also a grammatical work consisting of twenty-two books, entitled סֵפֶר הָעֹשֶׁר, which Aben-Ezra praises above all similar efforts that had preceded it, but which is also lost. Nagdilah died in 1055. See Fürst, *Bibl. Jud.* iii, 14 sq.; De Rossi, *Dizionario storico degli Autori Ebrei* (Germ. transl.), p. 240 sq.; Grätz, *Gesch. d. Juden*, vi, 18 sq.; Jost, *Gesch. d. Judenth. u. s. Sekten*, ii, 406; Dessauer, *Gesch. d. Israeliten* (Breslau, 1870), p. 289; Braunschweiger, *Gesch. d. Juden in d. Roman. Staaten*, p. 34 sq.: Lindo, *Hist. of the Jews in Spain*, p. 49 sq.; Finn, *Sephardim*, p. 174; Da Costa, *Israel and the Gentiles*, p. 252; Etheridge, *Introd. to Hebr. Literature*, p. 105, 247; Margoliouth, *Modern Judaism Investigated* (Lond. 1843), p. 243; Steinschneider, *Jewish Literature*, p. 136; Dukes, *Rabbinische Blumenlese* (Leips. 1844), p. 55, 58, 219, and his *R. Sam. ha-Nagid u. s. Werke*, in נַחַל קְדוּמִים (Hanover, 1853), ii, 1–40; Delitzsch, *Zur Gesch. d. Jüd. Poesie*, p. 144, 149; Munk, *Samuel ha-Nagid*, in his notice on Abu'l-Walid Merwan, etc. (Par. 1851), p. 90–109; Grätz, *Blumenlese Neuhebr. Dichtungen* (Bresl. 1862), p. 33; Kämpf, *Nichtandalusische Poesie Andalusischer Dichter* (Prague, 1858), p. 157 sq.; Sachs, *Religiöse Poesie der Juden in Spanien* (Berl. 1843), p. 216; Fürst, *Hebrew and Chaldee Lexicon*, introd. p. xxviii; Kalisch, *Hebrew Grammar* (Lond. 1863), ii, 24 sq.; Kimchi, *Liber Radicum* (ed. Biesenthal et Lebrecht [Berol. 1847]), p. xlvi sq.; Cassel, *Leitfaden für Jüd. Gesch. u. Literatur* (Berl. 1872), p. 59 sq. (B. P.)

Nag'gè [rather *Nangæ*] (Ναγγαί v. r. Ναγαί; comp. Sept. Ναγαί for *Nogah*, נֹגַהּ, 1 Chron. iii, 7), one of the ancestors of Christ in the maternal line, the son of Maath (rather of Semei), and father of Esli (Luke iii, 25); corresponding to NEARIAH (q. v.), the son of Shemaiah, and father of Elioenai in the Davidic lineage (1 Chron. iii, 22, 23). B.C. 350.

Nagot, FRANÇOIS - CHARLES, a French ascetic writer, was born at Tours, April 19, 1734. Admitted into the congregation of the priests of Saint-Sulpice, he was sent as professor of theology to the Seminary of Nantes. He was made superior of the house of the Robertins at Paris in 1769, afterwards of the small seminary of Saint-Sulpice, then director of the large seminary. The revolution decided him, in 1791, to come to this country and settle at Baltimore, where Pius VI had just created an episcopal see, comprising at that time all the territory of the United States. At the Monumental City he succeeded in establishing a seminary, and a college which still enjoys all the privileges of a university. He retained the management of these houses till the year 1810, when he was obliged by infirmities to resign. He died at Baltimore, April 9, 1816. His principal writings are, *Relation de la conversion de quelques Protestants* (1791, 1794, 12mo) :—*La Doctrine de l'Écriture sur les miracles* (Paris, 1808, 3 vols. 12mo; a translation of an English work by George Hay) :— *Vie de M. Olier, curé de Saint-Sulpice* (1813, 8vo) :—in manuscript different translations of works of English piety. See Hoefer, *Nouv. Biog. Générale,* s. v.

Nagpur or **Nagpore,** an extensive inland province of British India, belonging in its civil administration to the Bengal, and in its military to the Madras presidency, extends immediately north-east of the Nizam's dominions, in lat. 17° 15′–23° 5′ N., long. 78° 3′–83° 10′, and has an area of 76,432 square miles, with a population of 4,650,000. The north part of the province is mountainous in character. The climate is not healthy, and is especially insalubrious in the extensive tracts of low, marshy land which abound in the province. The Gonds, supposed to be the aborigines, are the most remarkable class of the inhabitants. They rear fowls, swine, and buffaloes; but their country, forming the south-eastern tracts—about one third of the whole—is covered with a dense jungle, swarming with tigers. In the more favored districts, where the inhabitants are more industrious, rice, maize, flax, and other seeds and vegetables are extensively cultivated. The rajahs of Nagpur, sometimes called the rajahs of Berar, ruled over a state formed out of a part of the great Mahratta kingdom. The dynasty, however, died out in 1853, and the territory came into possession of the British. The province has five divisions. Its capital, Nagpur, has a population of 115,000. Inclusive of its extensive suburbs, it is seven miles in circumference. It contains no important edifices. The great body of the inhabitants live in thatched mud tents, interspersed with trees, which prevent the circulation of air and secrete moisture, thus rendering the town unnecessarily unhealthy. Missions are sustained here by the Church of England and other Protestant bodies, but little progress has as yet been made in converting the natives.

Nag's-Head Consecration designates the questionable way in which Roman Catholics assert that the apostolical succession was preserved in the Church of England. They aver that on the passing of the first Act of Uniformity in the first year of queen Elizabeth's reign, fourteen bishops vacating their sees, and all the other sees excepting that of Llandaff being vacant, there was a difficulty in maintaining the hitherto unbroken succession of bishops from apostolical times; and that, as Kitchin of Llandaff refused to officiate at Parker's consecration, the Protestant divines procured the help of Scory, a deprived bishop of the reign of Edward VI, and all having met at the Nag's-Head tavern,

in Cheapside, they knelt before Scory, who laid a Bible on their heads or shoulders, saying, " Take thou authority to preach the Word of God sincerely ;" and they rose up bishops of the New Church of England! The story, which was first told by a Jesuit, Sacro Bosco, or Holywood, forty-five years after the event, intelligent Romanists themselves deny. Thus it is discredited by the Roman Catholic historian Lingard, and is carefully refuted by Strype in his life of Parker. The facts of the case are best stated in archbishop Bramhall's account of the Nag's-Head fable (*Works,* p. 436), and is the shortest and fullest refutation of the story : " They say that archbishop Parker and the rest of the Protestant bishops in the beginning of queen Elizabeth's reign, or at least sundry of them, were consecrated at the Nag's Head, in Cheapside, together, by bishop Scory alone, or by him and bishop Barlow, without sermon, without sacrament, without solemnity, in the year 1559 (but they know not what day, nor before what public notaries), by a new, fantastic form. All this they maintain on the supposed voluntary report of Mr. Neale (a single malicious spy), in private to his own party, long after the business pretended to be done. We say that archbishop Parker was consecrated alone at Lambeth, in the church, by four bishops, authorized thereunto by commission under the great seal of England, with sermon, with sacrament, with due solemnities, on the 17th day of December, A.D. 1559, before four of the most eminent public notaries in England, and particularly the same public notary was principal actuary both at cardinal Pole's consecration and archbishop Parker's." We may add that the election took place in the chapter-house at Canterbury, and the confirmation at St. Mary-le-Bone's church in Cheapside. Scory, then elected to the see of Bedford; Barlow, formerly bishop of Wells, then elected to Chichester; Coverdale, formerly of Exeter, and never reappointed to any see ; and Hodgkin, suffragan of Hereford, were the episcopal officers who officiated at the consecration. The Nag's-Head story probably arose from the company having possibly gone from Bow church, after the confirmation, to take a dinner together at the tavern hard by, according to the prevailing custom. The due succession of bishops in the English Church it would seem the Nag's-Head's fable has never proved to have broken. Prof. Döllinger, at the recent Congress of the Old Catholics at Bonn (August, 1875), held that there can be no controversy regarding the legitimacy of Anglican ordinations, which was questioned last year by Orientals. He said there was no doubt of their succession. When, under queen Elizabeth, the present Episcopal Church was founded, those who disagreed were dismissed, and discussion turned on the legitimacy of archbishop Parker's nomination. Of this there was no doubt. It was proved by his journal, the Register, and by contemporary history. To doubt it would be like the doubting of the man who sought to show that Napoleon I was a myth. The succession of the Romish Church could be disputed. Things had occurred which would become formidable weapons if anybody cared to use them. But there was no room for doubt as to succession in the Anglican Church. See Courayer, *Validity of the Ordinations of the English* (Oxford, 1844, new ed.) ; Baily, *Ordinum Anglicanorum defensio* (Lond. 1870); Soames, *Hist. of the Reformation,* iv, 691 sq.; Wordsworth, *Eccles. Biog.* iii, 383, n.; Hardwick, *Ch. Hist. of the Reformation,* p. 226 ; Burnet, *Hist. of the Reformation,* ii, 624; Baxter, *Ch. Hist.* p. 481; *Engl. Rev.* vi, 198; *Ch. Rev.* 1868 (July), p. 301; *Meth. Quar. Rev.* 1874 (Jan.), p. 159. See also PARKER (*archbishop*).

Na'halal (Heb. *Nahalal'*, נַהֲלָל, *pasture* ; Sept. Νααλώλ v. r. Ναβάαλ, and even Σελλά; Vulg. *Naälol;* Auth. Vers. once " Nahallal," Josh. xix, 15), a city, in the tribe of Zebulun, on the border of Issachar (Josh. xix, 15), but inhabited by Canaanites tributary to Israel (Judg. i, 30, where the name is " Nahalol"), given with its "suburbs" to the Merarite Levites (Josh. xxi, 35). It is mentioned between Kithlish and Shimron. Eusebius erroneously locates it E. of the Jordan (*Onomast.* s. v. Νειλά). "The Jerusalem Talmud (*Megillah*, chap. i; *Maaser Sheni*, chap. v), as quoted by Schwarz (*Palest.* p. 172) and Reland (*Palæst.* p. 717), asserts that Nahalal (or *Mahalal*, as it is in some copies) was in post-Biblical times called *Mahlul;* and this Schwarz identifies with the modern *Malul*, a village in the plain of Esdraelon under the mountains which enclose the plain on the north, four miles west of Nazareth, and two from Japhia; an identification concurred in by Van de Velde (*Memoir*, s. v.). One Hebrew MS. (30 Kennicott) lends countenance to it by reading מהלל, i. e. *Mahalal*, in Josh. xxi, 35. If the town was in the great plain, we can understand why the Israelites were unable to drive out the Canaanites from it, since their chariots must have been extremely formidable as long as they remained on level or smooth ground." This site, however, has been appropriated by Porter to that of the ancient MARALAH (q. v.).

Naha'liël (Heb. *Nachaliël'*, נַחֲלִיאֵל, *possession* [or *valley*] *of God;* Sept. Νααλιήλ v. r. Μαναήλ), the fifty-fourth encampment of the Israelites in the wilderness, between Mattanah and Bamoth (Numb. xxi, 19); apparently in the northern part of the plain Ard Ramadan, south-east of Jebel Humeh, perhaps on the northern branch of Wady Wâleh (Burckhardt, ii, 635). See EXODE. It lay "beyond," that is, north of the Arnon (ver. 13), and between Mattanah and Bamoth, the next after Bamoth being Pisgah. It does not occur in the catalogue of Numb. xxxiii, nor anywhere besides the passage quoted above. By Eusebius and Jerome (*Onomast.* s. v. Naaliel) it is mentioned as close to the Arnon. Mr. Grove, in Smith's *Dict.*, suggests that "its name seems to imply that it was a stream or wady, and it is not impossibly preserved in that of the *Wady Encheyle*, which runs into the Mojeb, the ancient Arnon, a short distance to the east of the place at which the road between Rabba and Aroer crosses the ravine of the latter river. The name *Encheyle*, when written in Hebrew letters (אנחילה), is little more than נחליאל transposed." See, however, MATTANAH.

Nahal'lal (Josh. xix, 15). See NAHALAL.

Na'halol (Heb. *Nahalol'*, נַחֲלֹל, *pasture;* Sept. Νααλώλ v. r. Εναμμάν and Δομανά; Vulg. *Naälol*), a slightly different orthography (Judg. i, 30) for the name NAHALAL (q. v.).

Na'ham (Heb. *Nach'am*, נַחַם, *consolation;* Sept. Ναχέμ v. r. Ναχαΐμ, Ναχέϑ), a brother of Hodiah, the second or Jewish wife of Mered; and "father" of Keilah and Eshtemoa (1 Chron. iv, 19). B.C. post 1612. He seems to have been the same called ISHBAH (q. v.) in ver. 17. See MERED.

Naham'ani (Heb. *Nachamany'*, נַחֲמָנִי, *repenting* or *compassionate;* Sept. Ναεμανι), one of the Jews who returned with Zerubbabel from the captivity (Neh. vii, 7). B.C. 536. His name is omitted in the parallel list of Ezra ii, 2.

Na'harai [others *Nahar'aï* or *Nahara'ï*] (1 Chron. xi, 39). See NAHARI.

Naharaïm. See ARAM-NAHARAIM.

Na'hari (Heb. *Nacharay'*, נַחֲרַי, *snorer;* Sept. Ναραί v. r. Ναχώρ; Vulg. *Naarai;* A. V. [in later ed.] "Nahar" [the more correct form] in 1 Chron. xi, 39; Sept. Ναχαραί; Vulg. *Naharai* in 2 Sam. xxiii, 37), a Berothite, one of David's chieftains, and armor-bearer of Joab, son of Zeruiah (1 Chron. xi, 39; 2 Sam. xxiii, 37). B.C. cir. 1013.

Na'hash (Heb. *Nachash'*, נָחָשׁ, *serpent*, as often; Sept. Ναάς; Joseph. Ναάσης; Vulg. *Naäs*), the name

of two persons. For the city of Nahash (Auth. Vers. Chron. iv, 12, marg.), see IR-NAHASH.

1. A king of the Ammonites, near the beginning of Saul's reign. B.C. 1092. A message came from the people of Jabesh-gilead soliciting immediate help against the fierce hostility of this Ammonitish chief. He had apparently acquired a name for his military achievements before directing an assault against the city of Jabesh (see 1 Sam. xii, 12); for though it was a well-fortified place, and the largest town in the transjordanic territory of Manasseh, the inhabitants seem to have thought it a hopeless matter to contend against so formidable an adversary. They were ready to submit to his supremacy if he would enter into covenant with them on somewhat reasonable terms; but as he, in the pride and insolence of power, declared he would insist on plucking out all their right eyes, and casting it as a reproach on Israel, the inhabitants were obliged to appeal to their fellow-countrymen. The mutilating barbarity proposed to the inhabitants of Jabesh-gilead by Nahash is a practice that was formerly very common in the East. Mr. Hanway, in his *Journey in Persia*, gives several instances of it. See EYE. Accordingly the inhabitants of Jabesh-gilead obtained a truce of seven days, and despatched messengers to Gibeah to inform Saul of their extremity (1 Sam. xi, 1–4). Saul felt the greatness of the emergency, and took prompt measures to relieve the place and discomfit the army of Nahash. See JABESH-GILEAD. In this he was perfectly successful; and neither Nahash nor his people ventured any more to attack Israel during the reign of Saul. See SAUL. If we might rely on the testimony of Josephus (*Ant.* vi, 5, 3), Nahash himself fell in the rout that ensued. But of this the sacred narrative is entirely silent; and the probability is (for we have no reason to suppose Nahash to have been an official designation or a common name among the Ammonites) that the Nahash whom Saul discomfited was the same who afterwards showed kindness to David. How this kindness was exhibited, or at what particular time, we are not told; but we can have little doubt that it occurred some time during the fierce persecutions which David endured at the hands of Saul, when the king of Ammon, like the king of Gath, might deem it a stroke of policy, in respect to Saul, to befriend the man whom he was pursuing as an enemy. Jewish traditions affirm that it consisted in his having afforded protection to one of David's brothers, who escaped alone when his family were massacred by the treacherous king of Moab, to whose care they had been intrusted by David (1 Sam. xxii, 3, 4), and who found an asylum with Nahash. (See the *Midrash* of R. Tanchum, as quoted by S. Jarchi on 2 Sam. x, 2.) See DAVID. David was not unmindful of the kindness he had received from Nahash; and wishing to cultivate peaceful relations with his son and successor Hanun, he sent messengers to condole with him on receiving intelligence of the death of Nahash (2 Sam. x, 2). By the folly of Hanun this well-meant embassy turned into the occasion of a bloody war, which placed David for a time in some peril, but from which he at last emerged completely triumphant. See HANUN.

Mention is made in the history of David's flight from the presence of Absalom of a "Shobi, the son of Nahash of Rabbah of the children of Ammon," coming along with others to David at Mahanaim, with food and refreshments (2 Sam. xvii, 27–29). It is possible that this was a son of Nahash, the former king, though it cannot be regarded as at all certain. That an Ammonite, however, should at such a time have so readily proffered his liberality to David is a striking proof that even after the terrible Ammonitish war there still were bosoms among the children of Ammon which stood well affected to the person and the cause of David. See SHOBI.

2. A person mentioned once only (2 Sam. xvii, 25) in stating the parentage of Amasa, the commander-in-chief of Absalom's army. Amasa is there said to have been the son (perhaps illegitimate) of a certain Ithra, by Abigail, "daughter of Nahash, and sister (Alex. Sept. *brother*) to Zeruiah." B.C. ante 1023. By the genealogy of 1 Chron. ii, 16 it appears that Zeruiah and Abigail were sisters of David and the other children of Jesse. The question then arises, How could Abigail have been at the same time daughter of Nahash and sister to the children of Jesse? To this four answers may be given:

1. The universal tradition of the rabbins is that Nahash and Jesse were identical (see the citations from the Talmud in Meyer, *Seder Olam*, 569; also Jerome, *Quæst. Hebr.* ad loc.). "Nahash," says Solomon Jarchi (in his commentary on 2 Sam. xvii, 25), "was Jesse the father of David, because he died without sin, by the counsel of the serpent" (*nachash*); i. e. by the infirmity of his fallen human nature only.

2. The explanation first put forth by Prof. Stanley (*Hist. of the Jewish Church*, ii, 50), that Nahash was the king of the Ammonites, and that the same woman had first been his wife or concubine—in which capacity she had given birth to Abigail and Zeruiah—and afterwards wife to Jesse, and the mother of his children. In this manner Abigail and Zeruiah would be sisters to David, without being at the same time daughters of Jesse. This has in its favor the guarded statement of 1 Chron. ii, 16 that the two women were not themselves Jesse's children, but sisters of his children; and the improbability (otherwise extreme) of so close a connection between an Israelite and an Ammonitish king is alleviated by Jesse's known descent from a Moabitess, and by the connection which has been shown above to have existed between David and Nahash of Ammon.

3. A third possible explanation is that Nahash was the name, not of Jesse, nor of a former husband of his wife, but of his wife herself. There is nothing in the name to prevent its being borne equally by either sex, and other instances may be quoted of women who are given in the genealogies as the daughters, not of their fathers, but of their mothers: e. g. Mehetabel, daughter of Matred, daughter of Mezahab. Still it seems very improbable that Jesse's wife would be suddenly intruded into the narrative, as she is if this hypothesis be adopted.

4. The most natural supposition under all the circumstances is that Abigail and Zeruiah were sisters of David merely on the mother's side; and that the mother, before she became the wife of Jesse, had been married to some person (apparently an Israelite, but otherwise unknown) named Nahash, to whom she had borne Abigail and Zeruiah. This seems to be countenanced by the peculiar manner in which they are mentioned in the genealogy of Chronicles — not as Jesse's daughters, but as David's sisters — as if their relationship to him were what alone entitled them to a place in it.

Na'hath (Heb. *Nach'ath*, נַחַת, *rest*, as often), the name of three men.

1. (Sept. Ναχόθ, Gen. xxxvi, 13; Ναχώθ, ib. 17; Ναχέθ, 1 Chron. i, 37.) The first named of the four sons of Reuel, the son of Esau, and a prince (A. V. "duke") among the Edomites (Gen. xxxvi, 13, 17). B.C. cir. 1890.

2. (Sept. Καινάθ v. r. Κνάθ, Νάαθ.) A Kohathite Levite, son of Zophai or Zuph, and ancestor of Samuel the prophet (1 Chron. vi, 26). B.C. cir. 1280. He is the same with TOAH (1 Chron. vi, 34) and TOHU (1 Sam. i, 1).

3. (Sept. Ναέθ.) A Levite, appointed by Hezekiah one of the overseers of sacred offerings in the Temple under Cononiah and Shimei (2 Chron. xxxi, 13). B.C. cir. 725.

Nahavendi, BENJAMIN BEN-MOSES (בנימין בן משה נהונדי), a celebrated Jewish commentator of the Karaite sect, flourished about A.D. 800, and derived his name from his native place, Nahavend, in ancient Media. He not only immortalized his name by effecting a reformation and consolidation in the opinions of his sect, and by being next in importance to Anan, the founder of this sect, but he greatly distinguished himself as an expositor of the Hebrew Scriptures. He wrote (in Hebrew), *A Commentary on the Pentateuch*, in which he illustrates the Mosaic enactments by copious descriptions of the manners and customs of the East (comp. Pinsker, *Likute Kadmonioth*, p. 72, Appendix):— *A Commentary on Isaiah*, in which he denies the supposed Messianic prophecies (comp. Jephet on Isaiah liii):—*A Commentary on the Book of Daniel*, in which *days* (xii, 12) are made to mean *years* (comp. Pinsker, *ibid.* p. 32, Appendix; Jephet, at end of Daniel):—*A Commentary on the Five Megilloth*—the Canticles, Ruth, Esther, Lamentations, and Ecclesiastes—interpreting the first and last of these allegorically. Pinsker (*ibid.* p. 109-111, Appendix) gives a specimen of this commentary, the MS. of which exists in the Paris library:—*A Book of Commands* (ספר מצוה), in which he propounds the Karaitic mode of explanation of Scripture, in opposition to the Rabbinic expositions:— *The Book of Legal Enactments* (ס' הַדִּינִין), also called מַשְׂאֵת בִּנְיָמִין, *The Tribute of Benjamin*, which treats exclusively of the penal and civil laws of the Mosaic code, printed at Eupatoria, 1834. Besides these exegetical and practical works, Nahavendi seems also to have composed a dogmatic work, which contains speculations about God and creation and the soul. The soul, in his view, has no separate existence, but is only part of the body, and can expect no life and no retribution apart from its bodily connection. God comes into no immediate relation with the world. His creation and providence are all through mediators, second causes, spiritual forces (δυνάμεις), words (λόγοι), angels of various kinds and degrees. Nahavendi denied that God spoke directly to Moses, or that any word had come to patriarchs or prophets from one too exalted for all human intercourse, and would allow no anthropomorphic conceptions of the divine nature. In several minor points of practice he departed from the teaching of Anan, particularly as to the observance of the Sabbath, the killing of the paschal lamb, and the validity of the marriage bond. A lawful marriage, according to Nahavendi, requires more than purchase, contract, and cohabitation; it must have the preliminaries of betrothal, taking home, bridal presents, religious covenant, and the presence of witnesses, to be lawful. That the services which he rendered for the cause of his co-religionists were highly appreciated by them may be seen from the fact that in consequence of his scriptural teaching they discarded the name Ananites, and henceforth called themselves *Karaites* (קראים), i. e. *Scripturalists*, or *Bene-Mikra* (בני מקרא), *Baale-Mikra* (בעלי מקרא), followers of the Bible, in contradistinction to the *Baale ha - Kabala* (בעלי הקבלה), followers of tradition. See Pinsker, *Likute Kadmonioth*, p. 44 sq.; Fürst, *Bibl. Judaica*, iii, 15; id. *Das Goldene Zeitalter der Karäischen Literatur, Benj. Nahâwendi*, in *Sabbath-Blatt*, 1846, p. 86; id. *Gesch. d. Karäerthums*, i, 71 sq., 157 sq.; Ginsburg, in Kitto's *Cyclop.* s. v.; id. *The Karaites, their History and Literature*; Grätz, *Gesch. d. Juden*, v, 203 sq., 451 sq., 468 sq.; Jost, *Gesch. d. Judenth. u. s. Sekten*, ii, 344. See KARAITES. (B. P.)

Nah'bi (Heb. *Nachbi'*, נַחְבִּי, *hidden*; Sept. Ναβί v. r. Ναβά; Vulg. *Nahabi*), the son of Vophsi, of the tribe of Naphtali; one of the twelve spies sent by Moses to explore the land of Canaan (Numb. xiii, 14). B.C. 1657.

Na'hor (Heb. *Nachor'*, נָחוֹר, *snorting*; Sept. and N. T. Ναχώρ; Josephus Ναχώρης; Vulg. *Nachor*: A. V. "Nachor," Josh. xxiv, 2; Luke iii, 34), the name of two men.

1. Son of Serug, father of Terah, and grandfather of Abraham (Gen. xi, 22–25; Luke iii, 34). He died at the age of 148 years. B.C. 2174.

2. Grandson of the preceding, being a son of Terah, and brother of Abraham and Haran (Gen. xi, 26; Josh. xxiv, 2). The order of the name of Terah is not im-

No certain traces of the name of Nahor have been recognised in Mesopotamia. Ewald (*Geschichte*, i, 359) proposes *Haditha*, a town on the Euphrates just above Hit, and bearing the additional name of *el-Naura*; also another place, likewise called *el-Na'ura*, mentioned by some Arabian geographers as lying farther north; and

GENEALOGY OF ABRAHAM'S FAMILY.

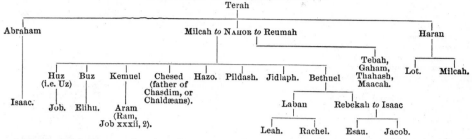

probably inverted in the narrative; in which case Nahor, instead of being younger than Abraham, was really older. B.C. ante 2163. He married Milcah, the daughter of his brother Haran; and when Abraham and Lot migrated to Canaan, Nahor remained behind in the land of his birth, on the eastern side of the Euphrates—the boundary between the Old and the New World of that early age—and gathered his family around him at the sepulchre of his father (Gen. xi, 27–32; comp. 2 Sam. xix, 37). Coupling this with the statement of Judith v, 8 and the universal tradition of the East, that Terah's departure from Ur was a relinquishment of false worship, an additional force is given to the mention of " the god of Nahor" (Gen. xxxi, 53) as distinct from the God of Abraham's descendants. Two generations later Nahor's family were certainly living at Haran (Gen. xxviii, 10; xxix, 4). Like Jacob, and also like Ishmael, Nahor was the father of twelve sons; and further, as in the case of Jacob, eight of them were the children of his wife, and four of a concubine, Reumah (Gen. xxii, 21–24). Special care is taken in speaking of the legitimate branch to specify its descent from Milcah—"the son of Milcah, which she bare unto Nahor." It was to this pure and unsullied race that Abraham and Rebekah in turn had recourse for wives for their sons. But with Jacob's flight from Haran the intercourse ceased. The heap of stones which he and "Laban the Syrian" erected on Mount Gilead (Gen. xxxi, 46) may be said to have formed at once the tomb of their past connection and the barrier against its continuance. Even at that time a wide variation had taken place not only in their language (ver. 47), but, as it would seem, in the Object of their worship. The "God of Nahor" appears as a distinct divinity from the "God of Abraham and the Fear of Isaac" (ver. 53). Doubtless this was one of the "other gods" which before the call of Abraham were worshipped by the family of Terah, whose images were in Rachel's possession during the conference on Gilead, and which had to be discarded before Jacob could go into the presence of the "God of Bethel" (Gen. xxxv, 2; comp. xxxi, 13). Henceforward the line of distinction between the two families is most sharply drawn (as in the allusion of Josh. xxiv, 2), and the descendants of Nahor confine their communications to their own immediate kindred, or to the members of other non-Israelitish tribes, as in the case of Job the man of Uz, and his friends, Elihu the Buzite of the kindred of Ram, Eliphaz the Temanite, and Bildad the Shuhite. Many centuries later David appears to have come into collision —sometimes friendly, sometimes the reverse—with one or two of the more remote Nahorite tribes. Tibhath, probably identical with Tebah and Maacah, are mentioned in the relation of his wars on the eastern frontier of Israel (1 Chron. xviii, 8; xix, 6); and the mother of Absalom either belonged to or was connected with the latter of the above nations.

Nachrein, which, however, seems to lie out of Mesopotamia to the east. Others have mentioned *Naarda*, or *Nehardea*, a town or district in the neighborhood of the above, celebrated as the site of a college of the Jews (Smith, *Dict. of Geogr.* s. v. Naarda).

Nah'shon (Heb. *Nachshon'*, נַחְשׁוֹן, *sorcerer;* Sept. and N. T. Ναασσών, but Ναασσῶν, Numb. i, 7; A. V. " Naashon," Exod. vi, 23; "Naason," Matt. i, 4; Luke iii, 32), the son of Aminadab, and prince of the children of Judah (as he is styled in the genealogy of Judah, 1 Chron. ii, 10) at the time of the first numbering in the wilderness (Exod. vi, 23; Numb. i, 7, etc.). B.C. 1657. His sister, Elisheba, was wife to Aaron, and his son, Salmon, was husband to Rahab after the taking of Jericho. From Elisheba being described as "sister of Naashon," we may infer that he was a person of considerable note and dignity, which his appointment as one of the twelve princes who assisted Moses and Aaron in taking the census, and who were all "renowned of the congregation, . . . heads of thousands in Israel," shows him to have been. No less conspicuous for high rank and position does he appear in Numb. ii, 3; vii, 12; x, 14, where, in the encampment, in the offerings of the princes, and in the order of march, the first place is assigned to him as captain of the host of Judah. Indeed, on these three last-named occasions he appears as the first man in the state next to Moses and Aaron, whereas at the census he comes after the chiefs of the tribes of Reuben and Simeon. Nahshon died in the wilderness, according to Numb. xxvi, 64, 65, but no further particulars of his life are given. In the N. T. he occurs twice, viz. in Matt. i, 4, and Luke iii, 32, in the genealogy of Christ, where his lineage in the preceding and following descents is evidently copied from Ruth iv, 18–20; 1 Chron. ii, 10–12.

Na'hum (Heb. *Nachum'*, נַחוּם, *consolation;* a name likewise found as נחם in the Phœnician inscriptions, [Gesenius, *Monum. Phœn.* p. 134, 137]; and in the form Νάουμος in a Greek inscription given by Böckh, *Corp. Inscr.* iv, 3; Sept. Ναούμ; comp. Luke iii, 25), the seventh of the minor prophets, according to the arrangement of both the Hebrew and Greek. (In this and the following article we give a copious exposition of all the topics of interest relating to the whole subject). Of the author himself we have no more knowledge than is afforded us by the scanty title of his book, "the book of the vision of Nahum the Elkoshite," which gives no indication whatever of his date, and leaves his origin obscure. The site of Elkosk, his native place, is disputed, some placing it in Galilee, with Jerome, who was shown the ruins by his guide (*Præm. in Nah.*); so Cyril (ad loc.). Capernaum, literally "village of Nahum," is supposed to have derived its name from the prophet. Schwarz

(*Descr. of Pal.* p. 188) mentions a *Kefar Tanchum,* or *Nachum,* close on Chinnereth, and two and a half English miles north of Tiberias. "They point out there the graves of Nahum the prophet, of rabbis Tanchum and Tanchuma, who all repose there, and through these the ancient position of the village is easily known." Others (after Assemani, *Bibl. Orient.* i, 525; iii, 352) locate Nahum's birthplace in Assyria, where the tomb of the prophet is still visited as a sacred spot by Jews from all parts. Benjamin of Tudela (p. 53 Heb. text, ed. Asher) thus briefly alludes to it: "And in the city of Asshur (Mosul) is the synagogue of Obadiah, and the synagogue of Jonah the son of Amittai, and the synagogue of Nahum the Elkoshite." See ELKOSH. Mr. Layard, who visited the place, says (*Nineveh,* i, 197), "It is held in great reverence by Mohammedans and Christians, but especially by Jews, who keep the building—a modern one—in repair. The tomb is a simple plaster box, covered with green cloth, and standing at the upper end of a large chamber. There are no inscriptions nor fragments of any antiquity about the place; and I am not aware in what the tradition originated, nor how long it has attached to the village of Alkosh." Gesenius regards both the above locations of Elkosh as very doubtful (*Thesaurus,* s. v.). Those who maintain the latter site assume that the prophet's parents were carried into captivity by Tiglath-pileser, and planted, with other exile colonists, in the province of Assyria, the modern Kurdistan, and that the prophet was born at the village of Alkush, on the east bank of the Tigris, a few miles north of Mosul. (So Eichhorn, *Einl.* iv, 390; Ritter, *Erdk.* ix, 742; and others.) Ewald is of opinion that the prophecy was written there at a time when Nineveh was threatened from without. Against this it may be urged that it does not appear that the exiles were carried into the province of Assyria proper, but into the newly-conquered districts, such as Mesopotamia, Babylonia, or Media. The arguments in favor of an Assyrian locality for the prophet are supported by the occurrence of what are presumed to be Assyrian words: הַצָּב, ii, 8; מִנְזָרַיִךְ, טַפְסְרַיִךְ, iii, 17; and the strange form מִלְאָכֵכֶה in ii, 14, which is supposed to indicate a foreign influence. In addition to this is the internal evidence supplied by the vivid description of Nineveh, of whose splendors it is contended Nahum must have been an eye-witness; but Hitzig justly observes that these descriptions display merely a lively imagination, and such knowledge of a renowned city as might be possessed by any one in Anterior Asia. The Assyrian warriors were no strangers in Palestine, and that there was sufficient intercourse between the two countries is rendered probable by the history of the prophet Jonah. There is nothing in the prophecy of Nahum to indicate that it was written in the immediate neighborhood of Nineveh, and in full view of the scenes which are depicted, nor is the language that of an exile in an enemy's country. No allusion is made to the captivity; while, on the other hand, the imagery is such as would be natural to an inhabitant of Palestine (i, 4), to whom the rich pastures of Bashan, the vineyards of Carmel, and the blossoms of Lebanon were emblems of all that was luxuriant and fertile. The language employed in i, 15 and ii, 2 is appropriate to one who wrote for his countrymen in their native land. In fact, the sole origin of the theory that Nahum flourished in Assyria is the name of the village Alkush, which contains his supposed tomb, and from its similarity to Elkosh was apparently selected by mediæval tradition as a shrine for pilgrims, with as little probability to recommend it as exists in the case of Obadiah and Jephthah, whose burial-places are still shown in the same neighborhood. This supposition is more reasonable than another which has been adopted in order to account for the existence of Nahum's tomb at a place the name of which so closely resembles that of his native town. Alkush, it is suggested, was founded by the Israelitish

exiles, and so named by them in memory of Elkosh in their own country. Tradition, as usual, has usurped the province of history. According to pseudo-Epiphanius (*De Vitis Proph.* in *Opp.* ii, 247), Nahum was of the tribe of Simeon, "from Elcesei, beyond the Jordan, at Begabar (Βηγαβάρ; *Chron. Pasch.* 150 B. Βηταβαρή),") or Bethabara, where he died in peace and was buried. In the Roman Martyrology the 1st of December is consecrated to his memory. For the period in which he lived, see the discussion below as to the date of his writing.

NAHUM, BOOK OF. The same uncertainty and dispute have prevailed on many points affecting the prophecy as have been detailed above respecting the prophet.

1. *Place of Writing.*—This largely depends upon the location of his birthplace. Dr. Davidson, in his *Introduction to the Old Testament,* confesses that the testimonies in favor of the Galilæan authorship are older and better; but still prefers to think that Nahum was an Assyrian by residence, "because the analogy of prophecy and internal phenomena favor this opinion." But Prof. Stähelin justly remarks that the absence of all reference in the prophecy to the Hebrew exiles in Assyria, among whom the prophet is supposed, on this hypothesis, to have been born and brought up, is an "internal phenomenon" which is quite decisive against the supposition; and with regard to the alleged "analogy of prophecy" being opposed to the idea that a prophet living so far from Nineveh as Galilee could utter predictions of so much circumstantiality against it, it is hard to see how such a statement can be reconciled with such circumstantial prophecies as those directed against Babylon by Isaiah and other certainly Palestinian prophets.

2. *Date of the Prophecy.*—This is even more uncertain than its place of writing. In the *Seder Olam Rabba* (p. 55, ed. Meyer) Nahum is made contemporary with Joel and Habakkuk in the reign of Manasseh. Syncellus (*Chron.* p. 201 d) places him with Hosea, Amos, and Jonah in the reign of Joash king of Israel, more than a century earlier; while according to Eutychius (*Ann.* p. 252) he was contemporary with Haggai, Zechariah, and Malachi, and prophesied in the fifth year after the destruction of Jerusalem. Josephus (*Ant.* ix, 11, 3) mentions him as living in the latter part of the reign of Jotham. "About this time was a certain prophet, Nahum by name; who, prophesying concerning the downfall of Assyrians and of Nineveh, said thus," etc.; to which he adds, "and all that was foretold concerning Nineveh came to pass after one hundred and fifteen years." From this Carpzov concluded that Nahum prophesied in the beginning of the reign of Ahaz, about B.C. 742. Modern writers are divided in their suffrages. Bertholdt thinks it probable that the prophet escaped into Judah when the ten tribes were carried captive, and wrote in the reign of Hezekiah. Keil (*Lehrb. d. Einl. in d. A. T.*) places him in the latter half of Hezekiah's reign, after the invasion of Sennacherib. Vitringa (*Typ. Doctr. proph.* p. 37) was of the like opinion, and the same view is taken by De Wette (*Einl.* p. 328), who suggests that the rebellion of the Medes against the Assyrians (B.C. 710), and the election of their own king in the person of Deïoces, may have been present to the prophet's mind. But the history of Deïoces and his very existence are now generally believed to be mythical. This period also is adopted by Knobel (*Prophet.* ii. 207, etc.) as the date of the prophecy. He was guided to his conclusion by the same supposed facts, and the destruction of No Ammon, or Thebes, of Upper Egypt, which he believed was effected by the Assyrian monarch Sargon (B.C. 717-715), and is referred to by Nahum (iii, 8) as a recent event. In this case the prophet would be a younger contemporary of Isaiah (comp. Isa. xx, 1). Ewald, again, conceives that the siege of Nineveh by the Median king Phraortes (B.C. 630-625) may have suggested Nahum's

prophecy of its destruction. The existence of Phraortes at the period to which he is assigned is now believed to be an anachronism. See MEDES. Junius and Tremellius select the last years of Josiah as the period at which Nahum prophesied; but at this time not Nineveh, but Babylon, was the object of alarm to the Hebrews. The arguments by which Strauss (*Nahumi de Nino Vaticinium*, prol. c. 1, 3) endeavors to prove that the prophecy belongs to the time at which Manasseh was in captivity at Babylon, that is, between the years 680 and 667 B.C., are not convincing. Assuming that the position which Nahum occupies in the canon between Micah and Habakkuk supplies, as the limits of his prophetical career, the reigns of Hezekiah and Josiah, he endeavors to show from certain apparent resemblances to the writings of the older prophets—Joel, Jonah, and Isaiah—that Nahum must have been familiar with their writings, and consequently later in point of time than any of them. But a careful examination of the passages by which this argument is maintained will show that the phrases and turns of expression upon which the resemblance is supposed to rest are in no way remarkable or characteristic, and might have been freely used by any one familiar with Oriental metaphor and imagery without incurring the charge of plagiarism. Two exceptions are Nah. ii, 10, where a striking expression is used which only occurs besides in Joel ii, 6, and Nah. i, 15 (Heb. ii, 1), the first clause of which is nearly word for word the same as that of Isa. lii, 7. But these passages, by themselves, would equally prove that Nahum was anterior both to Joel and Isaiah, and that his diction was copied by them. Other references which are supposed to indicate imitations of older writers, or, at least, familiarity with their writings, are Nah. i, 3 compared with Jon. iv, 2; Nah. i, 13 with Isa. x, 27; Nah. iii, 10 with Isa. xiii, 16; Nah. ii, 2 [1] with Isa. xxiv, 1; Nah. iii, 5 with Isa. xlvii, 2, 3; and Nah. iii, 7 with Isa. li, 19. For the purpose of showing that Nahum preceded Jeremiah, Strauss quotes other passages in which the later prophet is believed to have had in his mind expressions of his predecessor with which he was familiar. The most striking of these are Jer. x, 19 compared with Nah. iii, 19; Jer. xiii, 26 with Nah. iii, 5; Jer. i, 37, li, 30 with Nah. iii, 13. Words which are assumed by the same commentator to be peculiar to the times of Isaiah are appealed to by him as evidences of the date of the prophecy. But the only examples which he quotes prove nothing : $\check{\text{s}}$etep, *shéteph* (Nah. i, 8, A. V. " flood"), occurs in Job, the Psalms, and in Proverbs, but not once in Isaiah; and מְצוּרָה, *métsûrâh* (Nah. ii, 1 [2], A. V. " munition"), is found only once in Isaiah, though it occurs frequently in the Chronicles, and is not a word likely to be uncommon or peculiar, so that nothing can be inferred from it. Besides, all this would be as appropriate to the times of Hezekiah as to those of Manasseh. That the prophecy was written before the final downfall of Nineveh, and its capture by the Medes and Chaldæans (cir. B.C. 625), will be admitted. The allusions to the Assyrian power imply that this was still unbroken (i, 12; ii, 13, 14; iii, 15–17). The glory of the kingdom was at its brightest in the reign of Esarhaddon (B.C. 680–660), who for thirteen years made Babylon the seat of the empire; and this fact would incline us to fix the date of Nahum rather in the reign of his father Sennacherib, for Nineveh alone is contemplated in the destruction threatened to the Assyrian power, and no hint is given that its importance in the kingdom was diminished, as it necessarily would be, by the establishment of another capital. That Palestine was suffering from the effects of Assyrian invasion at the time of Nahum's writing seems probable from the allusions in i, 11, 12, 13; ii, 2; and the vivid description of the Assyrian armament in ii, 3, 4. At such a time the prophecy would be appropriate; and if i, 14 refers to the death of Sennacherib in the house of Nisroch, it must have been written before that event. The capt-

ure of No Ammon, or Thebes, has not been identified with anything like certainty. It is referred to as of recent occurrence, and it has been conjectured with probability that it was sacked by Sargon in the invasion of Egypt alluded to in Isa. xx, 1. These circumstances seem to determine the fourteenth year of Hezekiah (B.C. 712) as the period before which the prophecy of Nahum could not have been written. The condition of Assyria in the reign of Sennacherib would correspond with the state of things implied in the prophecy; and it is on all accounts most probable that Nahum flourished in the latter half of the reign of Hezekiah, and wrote his prophecy soon after the date above mentioned, either in Jerusalem or its neighborhood, where the echo still lingered of " the rattling of the wheels, and of the prancing horses, and of the jumping chariots" of the Assyrian host, and "the flame of the sword and lightning of the spear" still flashed in the memory of the beleaguered citizens. The arguments in favor of this date, adduced by Eichhorn (in his *Einleit.*), supporting the same conclusion reached by Vitringa (*Typus Doctr. Proph.* p. 37), have not been overthrown by Davidson in his late *Introd. to the O. T.*; and it may therefore be regarded as measurably acquiesced in by the majority of modern critics.

As to the above attempt to fix the date of Nahum's prophecy by comparing parts of it with similar passages in the writings of Isaiah (viz., Nah. iii, 5 with Isa. xlvii, 2, 3; Nah. iii, 7, 10 with Isa. li, 19 sq.; Nah. ii, 1 with Isa. lii, 1, 7; Nah. ii, 3 with Isa. lii, 8), the resemblance between these passages, it is alleged, is so close that the one writer must have had the other before him when composing his own oracles; and as it is assumed that Nahum was the copier, and as Isaiah's writing must be placed in the latter part of the reign of Hezekiah, it is concluded that Nahum must have written towards the close of that reign or early in the following. But allowing the similarity of the passages, everything else in this argument is mere assumption, any part of which may be reversed with equal probability; and accordingly we find that while Keil and Otto Strauss hold Nahum for the borrower, Delitzsch and Nägelsbach attribute this to Isaiah. The supposed allusion to Sennacherib's invasion in i, 14 has been thought to find support from the words אָשִׂים קִבְרֶךָ, which, joined as the accents direct with what precedes, may be rendered, " I will make it [the house of thy gods] thy grave," and may be viewed as referring to the slaughter of Sennacherib in the temple of his deity (Isa. xxxvii, 38). But to this much weight cannot be attached; for, on the one hand, the rendering in the A. V. is quite as likely to be the correct one as that suggested, and, on the other, it by no means follows that when a man's grave is said to be made in any place it means that in that place he is to be murdered.

The results of the above discussion may be briefly summed up thus : that Nahum was a native of Galilee; that upon the invasion and deportation of the ten tribes he escaped into the territory of Judah, and probably took up his residence in Jerusalem, where he witnessed the siege of the city by Sennacherib, and the destruction of the Assyrian host, in the reign of Hezekiah; and that probably soon after that memorable event, which proved "the beginning of the end" of the Assyrian power, and taking occasion from it, the Spirit of prophecy chose him to be the instrument of predicting the final and complete overthrow of Nineveh and her empire—an empire which had been built up by violence and cruel oppression, and which was justly doomed to perish by the extremities of fire and sword. Nahum was a contemporary of Isaiah and Micah.

3. *Contents.*—As the title " the burden of Nineveh" imports, the prophecy of Nahum is directed against that proud city, and falls into three parts. The *first* (i) contains the introduction (1–10) and the theme of the prophet's oracle (11–14). The *second* (ii) sets forth

the calamity which should come upon the Assyrian empire. The *third* (iii) recapitulates the reasons for the judgments that should be thus inflicted, and announces the certainty of their coming. The whole forms one continuous composition. There is no ground for the opinion which some (Huet, Kalinsky, Bertholdt) have maintained that the three parts of the book were produced at different times.

To descend to details, the prophecy commences with a declaration of the character of Jehovah, "a God jealous and avenging," as exhibited in his dealings with his enemies, and the swift and terrible vengeance with which he pursues them (i, 2–6), while to those that trust in him he is "good, a stronghold in the day of trouble" (i, 7), in contrast with the overwhelming flood which shall sweep away his foes (i, 8). The language of the prophet now becomes more special, and points to the destruction which awaited the hosts of Assyria who had just gone up out of Judah (i, 9–11). In the verses that follow the intention of Jehovah is still more fully declared, and addressed first to Judah (i, 12, 13), and then to the monarch of Assyria (i, 14). And now the vision grows more distinct. The messenger of glad tidings, the news of Nineveh's downfall, treads the mountains that were round about Jerusalem (i, 15), and proclaims to Judah the accomplishment of her vows. But round the doomed city gather the destroying armies; "the breaker in pieces" has gone up, and Jehovah musters his hosts to the battle to avenge his people (ii, 1, 2). The prophet's mind in vision sees the burnished bronze shields of the scarlet-clad warriors of the besieging army, the flashing steel scythes of their war-chariots as they are drawn up in battle array, and the quivering cypress-shafts of their spears (ii, 3). The Assyrians hasten to the defence: their chariots rush madly through the streets, and run to and fro like the lightning in the broad ways, which glare with their bright armor like torches. But a panic has seized their mighty ones; their ranks are broken as they march, and they hurry to the wall only to see the covered battering-rams of the besiegers ready for the attack (ii, 4, 5). The crisis hastens on with terrible rapidity. The river-gates are broken in, and the royal palace is in the hands of the victors (ii, 6). And then comes the end; the city is taken and carried captive, and her maidens "moan as with the voice of doves," beating their breasts with sorrow (ii, 7). The flight becomes general, and the leaders in vain endeavor to stem the torrent of fugitives (ii, 8). The wealth of the city and its accumulated treasures become the spoil of the captors, and the conquered suffer all the horrors that follow the assault and storm (ii, 9, 10). Over the charred and blackened ruins the prophet, as the mouthpiece of Jehovah, exclaims in triumph, "Where is the lair of the lions, the feeding place of the young lions, where walked lion, lioness, lion's whelp, and none made [them] afraid?" (ii, 11, 12). In reverse of this the downfall of Nineveh was certain, for "behold! I am against thee, saith Jehovah of Hosts" (ii, 13). The vision ends, and the prophet, recalled from the scenes of the future to the realities of the present, collects himself, as it were, for one final outburst of withering denunciation against the Assyrian city, not now threatened by her Median and Chaldæan conquerors, but in the full tide of prosperity, the oppressor and corrupter of nations. Mingled with this woe there is no touch of sadness or compassion for her fate; she will fall unpitied and unlamented, and with terrible calmness the prophet pronounces her final doom: "All that hear the bruit of thee shall clap the hands over thee; for upon whom has not thy wickedness passed continually?" (iii, 19).

4. The *genuineness* of this prophecy has never been called in question. The words in the inscription, מַשָּׂא נִינְוֵה, have been subjected to suspicion by some on the ground that, as the proper commencement of the writing follows, they are probably a later addition;

but, as Hävernick remarks, there is nothing unfit in the arrangement which makes the announcement of the subject precede the announcement of the author, and therefore nothing improbable in the supposition that both parts of the inscription came from the same pen—that of the author.

5. *Style.*—As a poet, Nahum occupies a high place in the first rank of Hebrew literature. In proof of this it is only necessary to refer to the opening verses of his prophecy (i, 2–6), and to the magnificent description of the siege and destruction of Nineveh in chap. ii. His style is clear and uninvolved, though pregnant and forcible; his diction sonorous and rhythmical, the words re-echoing to the sense (comp. ii, 4; iii, 3). According to Eichhorn, the most striking characteristic of his style is the power of representing several phases of an idea in the briefest sentences, as in his description of God, the conquest of Nineveh, and the destruction of No Ammon. "The variety in his manner of presenting ideas discovers much poetic talent in the prophet. The reader of taste and sensibility will be affected by the entire structure of the poem, by the agreeable manner in which the ideas are brought forward, by the flexibility of the expressions, the roundness of his turns, the exquisite outline of his figures, by the strength and delicacy, and the expression of sympathy and greatness, which diffuse themselves over the whole subject."

Some words and forms of words are almost peculiar to Nahum; as, for example, סְעָרָה for שְׂעָרָה, in i, 3, occurs only besides in Job ix, 17; קֻנֹּא for קַנָּא, in i, 2, is found only in Josh. xxiv, 19; תְּבוּנָה, ii, 9 [10], is only found in Job xxiii, 3, and not in the same sense; הֵדַ, in iii, 2, is only found in Judg. v, 22; פְּלָדוֹת and רָעַל, ii, 3 [4], נָהַג, ii, 7 [8], בּוּקָה and מְבוּקָה, ii, 10 [11], מִנְזָרִים, iii, 17, and כְּתָה, iii, 19, do not occur elsewhere. The unusual form of the pronominal suffix in מַלְאָכֵכֵה, ii, 13 [14], נַפְשׁוּ for נַפְצוּ, iii, 18, are peculiar to Nahum; מֵצָר, iii, 5, is also found in 1 Kings vii, 36; זוֹבֵר, iii, 17, occurs besides only in Amos vii, 1; and the foreign word טַפְסַר, iii, 17, in the slightly different form טִפְסָר, is found only in Jer. ii, 27.

6. *Confirmation by History.*—We should expect a prophecy so entirely occupied with the overthrow of Nineveh to admit of frequent and useful illustration from the recent literature of the Assyrian monuments. And our expectation is not disappointed. One of Nahum's latest commentators, Dr. Otto Strauss, has made large use of this newly-opened source in his work, published in 1853, *Nahumi de Nino Vaticinium explicavit, ex Assyriis Monumentis illustravit*, etc. His prolegomena, especially in the chapters "De rebus Assyriorum" and "De indole Vaticinii," are full of new and valuable matter; and in his commentary he frequently quotes and applies to the elucidation of the text the writings of Botta, Layard, Rawlinson, and Bonomi, and thus fully vindicates the truth of a remark made by the last-named author that in the sculptures of Khorsabad and Nimrûd "we possess an authentic contemporary commentary upon the prophecies." See also Vance Smith, *Prophecies relating to Nineveh* (Lond. 1857); Breiteneicher, *Nineve und Nahum* (Munich, 1861). The predictions of the prophet have been remarkably fulfilled. The city of Nineveh was destroyed about 607 or 606 B.C., or about a century after the prophecy of Nahum was uttered. The recent researches of Dr. Layard in the ruins of Nineveh throw a striking light upon the prophecy of Nahum, denouncing, nearly 2500 years ago, the fall of Nineveh. We can but glance at a few of these, and compare them with the words of the prophet. The "recently uncovered pavement at the gateway, marked with the ruts of the chariot wheels," tallies exactly with Nah. iii, 2, where the prophetic vision presents the man of God, rapt into future times, "the noise of the whip, and the noise of the rattling of the wheels,

and of the prancing horses, and of the bounding war-chariots." The "ivory ornaments, the metal bowls, vases, and saucers, most beautifully embossed and en-graved, denoting by the style of sculpture a very ad-vanced stage of civilization," tally with the prophet's description of the "store and glory of the pleasant fur-niture" (Nah. ii, 9). The "buried city and its orna-mental remnants, fragile with rust," and their destina-tion in their mutilated condition to the museums of modern nations, recall Nahum iii, 6 and i, 14: "I will cast my filth upon thee;" "I will make thy grave; I will set thee as a gazing-stock." See NINEVEH.

7. *Commentaries.*—The following are the special ex-egetical helps on this prophecy alone: Theophylact, *Commentaria* (in *Opp.* vol. iv); Julian of Toledo, *Com-mentarius* (in the *Bibl. Max. Patr.* vol. xii); Biblian-der, *Exegesis* (Tigur. 1534, 8vo); Luther, *Enarratio* (in *Opp.* iv, 475; also in German, ed. Agricola, 1555); De la Huerga, *Commentarius* (Lugd. 1558, 1561, 8vo); Chy-træus, *Explicatio* (Viteberg. 1565, 8vo; also in *Opp.* ii, 341); Selnecker, *Auslegung* [includ. Jon. and Hab.] (Leips. 1567, 4to); Pintus, *Commentarius* [includ. Dan. and Lam.] (Corimb. 1582; Colon. 1582, 8vo; Ven. 1583, 4to; Autun, 1595, 8vo; also in *Opp.*); Drusius, *Lectiones* [includ. Hab. etc.] (Lugd. 1595, 8vo); Gesner, *Expositio* (Vitemb. 1604, 8vo); Crocius, *Commentarius* (Brem. 1620, 1627, 12mo); Tarnovius, *Commentarius* (Rost. 1623, 4to); De Quiros, *Commentarii* [includ. Mal.] (His-pali, 1623, fol.; Lugd. 1623, 4to); Ursinus, *Hypomne-mata* [includ. Obad.] (Francf. 1652, 8vo); Hafenreffer, *Commentarius* [includ. Hab.] (Stuttg. 1663, 4to); Abar-banel, *Commentarius*, ed. Sprecher (Helmst. 1703, 4to); Aben-Ezra, *Comment.* (Heb. and Lat., ed. Lund, Upsal. 1705, 4to; Lat. only, ed. Stenhagen, Upsal. 1705, 8vo); Van Hoeke, *Explicatio* [includ. five other minor proph.] (Ludg. Bat. 1709, 4to; also in Germ., Frkf. and Lpz. 1710, 4to); Wüld, *Meditationes* (Francf. 1712, 4to); Kalinsky, *Observationes* (Vratislav, 1748, 4to); Lessing, *Observa-tiones* [includ. Jon.] (Chemnitz, 1780, 8vo); Conz, *Erklärung* (in Stäudlin's *Beiträge*, Stuttg. 1786, p. 72 sq.); Agrell, *Observationes* (Upsal. 1788, 4to); Wahl, *Uebersetz.* (in his *Magazin* [Halle, 1790], iii, 62 sq.); Grimm, *Erklärung* (Düsseld. 1790, 8vo; Greve, *Inter-pretatio* [includ. Hab.] (Amst. 1793, 4to); Svanborg, *Notæ* (Upsal. 1806, 4to); Frähn, *Curæ* (Rost. 1807, 4to); Neumann, *Anmerk.* (Bresl. 1808, 8vo); Middeldorpf, *Uebersetz.*, with *Anmerk.* by Gurlitt (Hamb. 1808, 8vo); Kreenan, *Expositio* (Hardev. 1808, 4to); Björn, *Vatic. Nah.* [includ. Lam.] (Hafn. 1814, 8vo); Justi, *Erläut.* (Lpz. 1820, 8vo); Schröder, *Harfenklänge* [includ. Joel and Hab.] (Hildesh. 1827, 8vo); Rosenmüller, *Scholia* (Lips. 1827, 8vo); Philippson, *Uebers.* [includ. Hos. etc.] (Halle, 1828, 8vo); Hölemann, *Illustratio* (Lips. 1842, 8vo); Edwards, *Notes* (in the *Biblioth. Sacra*, 1848, p. 551 sq.); Strauss, *Nineve*, etc. (in Lat., Lps. 1853; in Germ. ib. 1858, 8vo); Breiteneicher, *Nineve und Nah.* (Munich, 1861, 8vo); Reinke, *Aelt. Version.* (Munich, 1867, 8vo). See PROPHETS, MINOR.

Nahum OF GIMSO (the present Jimzu, near Lydda), a rabbi noted for his great exegetical knowledge, was a disciple of Jochanan ben-Zachai (q. v.), and one of the most prominent Tanaite teachers. He had a school of his own, and is reported as the hero of many wonderful adventures, and even the name of his native place was *hagadically* interpreted as having been his usual excla-mation: "This also intends to benefit" (*garn-su l'-toba*). He was severely tried, and, with rabbinical resignation, he viewed his trials as so many consequences of his own hardness and unkindness. Many stories regarding his personal history are afloat. Thus the following ex-travagant story is told of him: On one occasion he carried to the house of his father-in-law some valu-able presents. A poor person asked him for assistance while he was engaged unloading the beasts which had carried the rich burden. Nahum bade him wait; but before he was at leisure to attend to him, the person who asked his help had sunk down from want and

exhaustion. In grief for an unkindness which had caused the poor man's death, he invoked blindness upon his eyes, and paralysis upon his hands and feet. These imprecations were soon verified, and Nahum gladly suf-fered in order to expiate, as he thought, his sin. Ac-cordingly, when his pupils, at the sight of his sufferings, exclaimed, "Alas! that we see thee in such suffering," he replied, "Nay, rather, alas! if ye did not see me so suffering." In theology, Nahum was distinguished as an original thinker, and followed Hillel's (q. v.) method of Biblical interpretation. The latter had laid down a number of rules, the so-called מדות ז (seven rules), according to which the meaning of the text was to be ascertained. To these exegetical principles Nahum added another canon, important in the development of Rabbinism, called "*the rule of extension and restriction*" (*Ribbuj u-mi'ut*), according to which certain articles and prepositions in the text were now stated to serve not only a grammatical purpose, but also to indicate that the obvious meaning of the text required either to be enlarged or else restricted. This rule, which, as will be readily conceived, opened a wide door to fanciful inter-pretation, was generally adopted, but found also oppo-nents, especially in Nechuajah ben Ha-Kanah (q. v.). See Grätz, *Gesch. d. Juden* (Leipsic, 1866), iv, 21 sq.; Jost, *Gesch. d. Juden. u. s. Sekten*, ii, 26–89; Edersheim, *His-tory of the Jews* (Edinburgh, 1857), p. 157 sq.; Frankel, *Hodegetica in Mishnam* (Leipsic, 1859), p. 99. (B. P.)

Naiads (from Gr. νάειν, *to swim*) is the name of the nymphs who figure in Greek and Roman mythology. They presided over fresh waters, and were supposed to inspire those who drank of them with oracular powers and the gift of poetry. They could also restore sick persons to health. They are represented in works of art as beautiful maidens, half draped, with long hair.

Na'idus (Ναΐδος, Vulg. *Raanas*), one of the priests, the "sons" of Pahath-Moab, who had taken foreign wives after the captivity (1 Esdr. ix, 31); evidently the BENAIAH (q. v.) of the Heb. text (Ezra x, 30).

Naigon, JACQUES ANDRÉ, a modern French infidel of note, was born at Paris or at Dijon in 1738. He was intended to be an artist, either painter or sculptor, and was afforded all the opportunities to secure him distinc-tion in his profession. But brought in contact with the eminent philosophers of his time, especially with Diderot and Holbach, Naigon was inspired with a love for study, and he soon began to write for the pub-lic, at first under a nom-de-plume, and later under his own signature, and ably defended his friends from the severe and just attacks of the theological and critical world. He was himself inclined to accept a more sub-stantial philosophy than Diderot and Holbach taught, but by his defence of these wild thinkers he was led away, until he taught and thought as they did. Thus in his *Théologie Portative* (Lond. and Amsterd. 1768, 12mo) he defines the soul as an unknown substance, which in a certain way controls our body, but which we can never definitely know. Spirituality he defines as an occult quality, invented by Plato, perfected by Des Cartes, and changed into an article of faith by the theologians. Immortality is not much better treated: "It is essential for the Church that our soul be immor-tal; as without it we could not very well find employment for the ministers in churches—it would force the clergy to bankruptcy." In the same manner he treats the doc-trine of Free Will, and all other theological dogmas. Engaged as editor on the philosophical portion of the *Encyclopédie Méthodique* (*Dictionnaire des philosophes anciens et modernes* [Par. 1791–94, 3 vols. 8vo]), he there incorporated his views, and laid down doctrines clearly evincing a philosophy of fatalism, materialism, and even atheism. He entered the political life, but was not as notably successful. He died Feb. 28, 1810. His works are largely collections of ancient philoso-phers. He also edited the writings of his friends Diderot and Holbach; and assisted in an edition of Rousseau's and Montaigne's works. See Damiron, *Mémoires pour servir à l'histoire de la Philosophie au dix-huitième siècle*, vol. ii, pt. viii; *Dictionnaire des Sciences philosophiques*, vol. iv, s. v.   (J. H. W.)

Nail [for fastening] is the rendering of two Heb. words in the A. V.

1. יָתֵד, *yathêd* (from *piercing*), which usually denotes a (wooden) peg, pin, or nail (of any material), as driven into a wall (Ezek. xv, 3; Isa. xxii, 25); and more especially a tent-pin driven into the earth by a mallet to fasten the tent (Exod. xxvii, 19; xxxv, 18; xxxviii, 31; Isa. xxxiii, 20; liv, 2). It was one of these pins which Jael used in fastening to the ground the temples of Sisera (Judg. iv, 21, 22). Hence to drive a pin or to fasten a nail presents among the Hebrews an image of a fixed dwelling, a firm and stable abode (Isa. xxii, 23). This image is still frequent among the Arabs (see Marac. p. 597; Beidav. *Apud Salium*, p. 518). See TENT. In the passages in Exodus these tabernacle-pins are said to have been of copper (see Lightfoot, *Spicil.* in Exod. § 42; Joseph. *Ant.* v, 5, 4); in Judges the material is not mentioned; we should most naturally think of some metal, yet the Sept. uses πάσσαλον, which suggests that it was a wooden pin. A pin or nail is also, by a further application of the metaphor, applied to a prince, on whom the care and welfare of the state depends (Zech. x, 4), where the term פִּנָּה, *corner-stone*, is applied to the same person denoted by the word "nail." So also Ezra ix, 8. All these allusions refer to large nails, or pins, or cramps, used in applications requiring great strength. See Thomson, *Land and Book*, iii, 149.

2. מַסְמֵר, *masmer'* (a *point*, only in the plur.; also מַסְמְרוֹת, Jer. x, 4; מַסְמְרִים, 1 Chron. xxii, 3; מַסְמְרִים, Isa. xli, 7), is applied to ordinary and ornamental nails. There is in Eccles. xii, 11 a very significant proverbial application, "The words of the wise are as nails fastened," etc.; that is, "they sink deep into the heart of man." In this passage the figure is generally understood to refer to nails driven into a wall, but which Ginsburg understands of the tent-pins above mentioned, whose use for holding fast is contrasted with the use of goads for driving cattle forward, the entire verse in his opinion having reference to pastoral life. The golden nails of the Temple are denoted by this word. We are told that David prepared iron for the nails to be used in the Temple; and as the holy of holies was plated with gold, the nails also for fastening the plates were probably of gold. Their weight is said to have been fifty shekels, equal to twenty-five ounces, a weight obviously so much too small, unless mere gilding be supposed, for the total weight required, that the Sept. and Vulg. render it as expressing that of each nail, which is equally excessive. To remedy this difficulty, Thenius suggests reading five hundred for fifty shekels (1 Chron. xxii, 3; 2 Chron. iii, 9; Bertheau, *On Chronicles*, in *Kurzgef. Handb.*).

' Nail," Vulg. *palus*, is the rendering of πάσσαλος in Ecclus. xxvii, 2. In the N. T. we have ἧλος and προσηλόω in speaking of the nails of the Cross (John xx, 25; Col. ii, 14). See CROSS.

Nail [of the finger], צִפֹּרֶן, *tsippo'ren*, so called from *scraping*), occurs in Deut. xxi, 12, in connection with the verb עָשָׂה, *'asâh*, "to make" (Sept. περιονυχίζω, Vulg. *circumcido*, A. V. "pare," but in marg. "dress," "suffer to grow"), which Gesenius explains "make neat." Much controversy has arisen on the meaning of this passage; one set of interpreters, including Josephus and Philo, regarding the action as indicative of mourning, while others refer it to the deposition of mourning. Some, who would thus belong to the latter class, refer it to the practice of staining the nails with henna. The word *asah*, "make," is used both of "dressing," i. e. mak-

ing clean the feet, and also of "trimming," i. e. combing and making neat the beard, in the case of Mephibosheth (2 Sam. xix, 24). It seems, therefore, on the whole to mean "make suitable" to the particular purpose intended, whatever that may be; unless, as Gesenius thinks, the passage refers to the completion of the female captive's month of seclusion, that purpose is evidently one of mourning—a month's mourning interposed for the purpose of preventing on the one hand too hasty an approach on the part of the captor, and on the other too sudden a shock to natural feeling in the captive. Following this line of interpretation, the command will stand thus: The captive is to lay aside the "raiment of her captivity," viz. her ordinary dress in which she had been taken captive, and she is to remain in mourning retirement for a month with hair shortened and nails made suitable to the same purpose, thus presenting an appearance of woe to which the nails untrimmed and shortened hair would seem each in their way most suitable (see Job i, 20). If, on the other hand, we suppose that the shaving the head, etc., indicate the time of retirement completed, we must suppose also a sort of Nazaritic initiation into her new condition, a supposition for which there is elsewhere no warrant in the law, besides the fact that the "making," whether paring the nails or letting them grow, is nowhere mentioned as a Nazaritic ceremony, and also that the shaving the head at the end of the month would seem an altogether unsuitable introduction to the condition of a bride. We conclude, therefore, that the captive's head was shaved at the commencement of the month, and that during that period her nails were to be allowed to grow in token of natural sorrow and consequent personal neglect. See Joseph. *Ant.* iv, 8–23; Philo, περὶ φιλανθρ. ch. 14, vol. ii, p. 394 (ed. Mangey); Clem. Alex. *Strom.* ii, ch. 18; iii, ch. 11; vol. ii, p. 475, 543 (ed. Potter); Calmet, Patrick. *Crit. Sacr.* on Deut. xxi, 12; Schleusner, *Lex. V. T.* περιονυχίζω; Selden, *De Jur. Nat.* v, xiii, p. 644; Harmer, *Obs.* iv, 104; Wilkinson, *Anc. Eg.* ii, 345; Lane, *M. E.* i, 64; Gesenius, *Thes. Hebr.* p. 1075; Michaelis, *Laws of Moses*, art. 88, vol. i, p. 464 (ed. Smith); Numb. vi, 2, 18. See PARE.

In Jer. xvii, 1 the same Heb. word occurs in the sense of the "*point*" of a stylus or metallic pen, which was often tipped with adamant or diamond (Pliny, *Hist. Nat.* xxxvii, 4, 15). See PEN.

In Dan. iv, 33; vii, 19, the cognate Chald. טְפַר, *tephar'*, occurs of the *claws* of a bird or beast.

Nail, NICHOLAS, a French martyr to the Protestant cause, was born at Mans in the first quarter of the 16th century. He was of humble origin, and earned his daily bread on the shoemaker's bench. He was working in Lausanne, Switzerland, when the Reformed doctrines began to gain the attention of the people, and Nail became himself interested, and finally embraced the new views. Determined that his countrymen should share the great blessing he had come to enjoy, he quitted Lausanne for Paris with a pack of books and tracts. In the French capital he was discovered circulating these heretical productions, and was seized by the police Feb. 14, 1553; and though he openly confessed to have freely circulated these books, because they contained the truth he espoused, he yet refused to make known his friends and assistants even after he had been put to the torture. Refusing also to point out the people who had bought his books or had become his disciples, he was finally tried, sentenced to death, and led to the Place Maubert, from which a crowd of witnesses had passed to heaven in the smoke and flames of the funeral pile. In order to prevent Nail from speaking to any one on the way, a new torture was devised. A large wooden gag was put into his mouth, by which his jaws were burst asunder, and the blood streamed down his neck. Yet, though his mouth was stopped, by gesticulations and motions, and by lifting his eyes heavenward, he still made known his firm trust in the presence of his Saviour.

As he passed before a hospital on which an image of the Virgin was placed, an effort was made to compel him to show reverence to it by crossing himself and bowing his head, but he turned from it with indignation. This threw the rabble into a wild rage. Having arrived at the place of execution, Nail was bound with a rope to a roller over the funeral pile, divested of his apparel, and daubed all over with fat and powder. Next the entire mass was set on fire with bundles of straw, so that his whole body began to burn. Then he was drawn up and down on the roller over the wood-fire, which was burning under him. But he remained true to all his pledges, and was enabled to endure patiently this torture. He was heard to call continually on the name of the Lord after he began to burn, the string which tied the gag in his mouth having been burned, and his lacerated mouth being again set free. With prayers and praises his spirit passed from his suffering body into the presence of the Lord. See Hurst, *Martyrs to the Tract Cause*, p. 117, 118.

Naillac, PHILIBERT DE, the grand-master of the Order of the Knights of St. John of Jerusalem, was born about 1340 of a noble family. But little is known of his personal history. He became master of this order in 1376, and engaged in the Crusades, and was greatly distinguished by his valor and skill in warfare. He was prominently engaged in the battle of Nicopolis, and served the Christian interests by his treaties with the Saracens. Thus he concluded a treaty with the sultan of Egypt, which gave the Christians permission to enclose the Holy Sepulchre at Jerusalem with a wall; to maintain six knights of the Order of St. John within the city, free from all tribute, who should be permitted to carry on the hospitable duties of their profession in favor of all pilgrims led thither by devotion; that Christian slaves might be redeemed, either by purchase or by exchange with a Saracen; and that convents might be maintained in Jerusalem and in the other principal cities of the Holy Land. In 1415 internal dissension threatened the very existence of the Order of St. John. Naillac's wise counsels prevented all disgraceful proceedings; and when he died, in 1421, "he left the fraternity, at whose head he had been placed for so many years, at union with itself, at peace with its neighbors, and in a most flourishing state of prosperity." See Boissat, *Hist. des Chevaliers de St. Jean de Jerusalem*; Porter, *Knights of Malta*, i, 291 sq., 313. (J. H. W.)

Nails IN THE CRUCIFIX. In the 13th century three are portrayed, one foot of the Crucified overlying the other without the hypopodion. James de Voragine first mentions the change, which Ayala, bishop of Galicia, attributes to the Albigensian heretics. Benedict XIV pronounced the nail preserved in St. Cross, Rome, to be authentic. See CRUCIFIX. On Irish crosses the Saviour's feet are represented tied with a cord, and his arms drooping (Walcott, *Sacred Archæol.* s. v.). See CROSS.

Nain (Gr. Ναΐν; according to Simon, from Heb. נָאִין, *nain'*, *green pastures*; so written in the Eastern versions of the N. T., but Schwarz, *Palest.* p. 169, writes נעים, as if from נָעִין, *gracefulness*), a town (πόλις) of Palestine, mentioned only in the N. T. as the place where Jesus raised the widow's son to life (Luke vii, 11–17). Josephus speaks of a Nain, but it was different from this, being situated in the south (*War*, iv, 9, 4). The site of Nain is described by Jerome as being two miles south of Tabor, near Endor (*Onomast.* s. v. Naim; Eusebius has twelve miles, but the error is probably that of a copyist writing ιβ instead of β. Neither this number, however, nor that of Jerome, is accurate). Phocas places it north of Tabor (see Reland, *Palæst.* p. 904). As its name has always been preserved, it was recognised by the Crusaders, and has often been noticed by travellers up to the present day. It has now dwindled to a mean village called *Nein* (according to De

Saulcy [*Dead Sea*, i, 75], *Nayin*, pronounced by the Arabs exactly as Ναΐν), which contains remains of very ancient buildings, with a fountain (Tristram, *Land of Israel*, p. 130). It stands on a bleak, rocky slope, on the northern declivity of Jebel ed-Duhy (the "hill Moreh" of Scripture, and the "Little Hermon" of modern travellers), directly facing Tabor, from which it is four miles distant, and two and a half miles south-west of Endor. It is a small, poor hamlet, of some twenty houses, or rather huts. Round the houses, however, are pretty extensive ruins; and there are some traces of what appears to be an ancient wall. The most interesting antiquities are tombs, hewn in the rock, a short distance east of the village. It was in this direction our Lord approached, and probably to one or other of those very tombs they were bearing the corpse when he met and arrested the mournful procession (see Thomson, *Land and Book*, ii, 158). The situation of Nain is extremely beautiful. At the foot of the slope on which it stands is the great plain of Esdraelon, bounded on the north by the graceful wooded hills of Galilee, over which the snow-capped summits of Hermon and Lebanon appear. See Robinson, *Bib. Res.* ii, 361; Van de Velde, *Syria and Palestine*, ii, 382; Stanley, *Sinai and Palestine*, p. 357; Porter, *Hand-book to Syria*, p. 358.

Nai'oth (Heb., margin, *nayoth'*, נָיוֹת, *dwellings*; text, *Nevayoth'*, נְוָיֹת; Sept. Ναυάθ, v. r. Ναυϊώθ and Αὐάθ; Vulg. *Najoth*), or, more fully, "Naioth in Ramah," a place in which Samuel and David took refuge together, after the latter had made his escape from the jealous fury of Saul (1 Sam. xix, 18, 19, 22, 23; xx, 1). "Naioth" occurs both in Heb. and A. V. in 1 Sam. xix, 18 only. The Sept. supplies ἐν 'Ραμά in that verse. The Vulg. adheres to the Hebrew. It is evident from ver. 18 that Naioth was not actually in Ramah, Samuel's habitual residence, though from the affix it must have been near it (Ewald, iii, 66). In its corrected form (*Keri*) the name becomes a mere appellation, and from an early date has been interpreted to mean the huts or dwellings of a school or college of prophets over which Samuel presided, as Elisha did over those at Gilgal and Jericho. This appears first in the Targum-Jonathan, where for Naioth we find throughout בֵּית אוּלְפָּנָא, "the house of instruction," the term which appears in later times to have been regularly applied to the schools of the rabbis (Buxtorf, *Lex. Talm.* col. 106); and there ver. 20 is rendered, "And they saw the company of scribes singing praises, and Samuel teaching, standing over them," thus introducing the idea of Samuel as a teacher. Jerome, in his notice of this name in the *Onomasticon* (s. v. Namoth), refers to his observations thereon in the "libri Hebraicarum quæstionum." As, however, we at present possess these books, they contain no reference to Naioth. Josephus calls it "a certain place named *Galbaath*" (Γαλβαάθ), and distinguishes it from Ramah (*Ant.* vi, 11, 5). R. Isaiah and other Jewish commentators state that Ramah was the name of a hill, and Naioth of the place upon it. See RAMAH.

Naironi, ANTONIO-FAUSTO, a Maronite savant, was born about 1635 at Ban, on Mount Lebanon, and was a nephew of Abraham Ecchellensis. Naironi was educated at Parma; and after a voyage to Syria to procure works relative to his Protestant brethren, he became professor of the Syriac language in the College de Sapience in 1666, and occupied this chair until 1694. He died at Rome Nov. 3, 1707. We have of his works, *Officia sanctorum juxta ritum ecclesiæ Maronitarum* (Rome, 1656, 1666, fol.):—*De saluberrima potione cahue seu cafe nuncupata discursus* (Rome, 1671, 12mo; translated into Italian by Fred. Vegilin [Rome, 1671] and by Paul Bosca [Milan, 1673], and into French):—*Dissertatio de origine, nomine ac religione Maronitarum* (Rome, 1679, 8vo; a work eclipsed by the learned researches of Assemani):—*Evoplia fidei catholicæ Romanæ histori-*

co-dogmaticæ (Rome, 1694, 8vo), in which is found a large number of curious facts in the civil and religious history of the East. See Hoefer, *Nouv. Biog. Gén.* s. v.

Naitore, CHARLES, a French painter and engraver, whose works were mostly on sacred subjects, was born at Nismes in 1700. He studied under François le Moine, and was employed to finish several works left incomplete at the death of that master. Little is recorded of the circumstances of his life. His chief merit seemed to have consisted in the correctness of his design; his coloring is criticised as feeble and cold. The principal works of Naitore adorn the apartments of the first story of the Chateau Versailles, the Hôtel de Soubise, and the chapel of Les Enfans Trouvés, at Paris. In 1755 he was appointed director of the French Academy at Rome, which honorable office he filled until 1775. He died, according to Dumesnil, in 1777. There are a few etchings by Naitore executed from his own designs in a free and spirited manner. Among his works on sacred subjects are *The Crucifixion, with Mary Magdalene at the foot of the Cross, The Adoration of the Magi,* and the *Martyrdom of St. Fered.*

Nakdan, SAMSON or SIMSON, a Jewish writer noted for his mastery of the Hebrew tongue, and hence surnamed "the Grammarian," flourished about 1240. He was familiar with the best works of his Spanish coreligionists, such as those of Chajug (q. v.), Jona ibn-Ganach (q. v.), Parchon (q. v.), Aben-Ezra (q. v.), and other grammarians, and is the author of a grammatical work entitled חבּוּר הקוֹנים, or שׁמשׁוֹני 'ס, which discusses the vowel-points and accents. Elias Levita refers to this work of Samson Nakdan in his *Massoreth ha-Massoreth,* but it has not as yet appeared in print. Excerpts of it, however, have been published in Abicht's *Accentus Hebr. ex antiquissimo usu lectorio vel musico explicati,* etc.; acced. *Porta accentuum Lat. conversa et notis illustr.* (Leips. 1713); Delitzsch, in *Jesurun,* p. 16, 86, 92, 192, 249, 252; comp. Fürst, *Bibl. Jud.* iii, 16; De Rossi, *Dizionario* (Germ. transl.), p. 242; Wolf, *Bibliotheca Hebræa,* i, 1152; iii, 1160; iv, 1003; Geiger, *Schimschon ein Lexicograph in Deutschland,* in the *Wissenschaftl. Zeitschrift für Jüdische Theologie,* v, 413–30; Ginsburg, in Levita's *Massoreth ha-Massoreth* (Lond. 1867), p. 257; Kalisch, *Hebr. Grammar* (Lond. 1863), ii, 29; Zunz, *Zur Geschichte u. Literatur,* p. 113, 114. (B. P.)

Naked. The Hebrew word עָרוֹם, *arom',* rendered "naked" in our Bibles, means absolute nakedness in such passages as Job i, 21; Eccles. v, 15; Mic. i, 8; Amos ii, 16; but in other places it means one who is ragged or poorly clad (John xxi, 7; Isa. lviii, 7), in the same sense as γυμνός in James ii, 15, which does not indeed differ from a familiar application of the word "naked" among ourselves. A more peculiar and Oriental sense of the word is that in which it is applied to one who has laid aside his loose outer garment, and goes about in his tunic. When, therefore, Saul is described as having lain down "naked" (1 Sam. xix, 24), we are to understand that he had laid aside his flowing outer robe; and it was thus that Isaiah went "naked" and barefoot (Isa. xx, 2; comp. John xxi, 7). Our use of the word "undress," to denote simply a dress less than that which we consider full and complete, corresponds to this signification of the word. See DRESS. This word is also used metaphorically to signify *put to shame, stripped of resources, void of succor, disarmed.* Thus in Jer. xlix, 10, "I have made Esau bare," etc., signifies the destruction of the Edomites, God having exposed them defenceless to their invaders. The "nakedness of a land" (Gen. xlii, 9) signifies the weak and ruined parts of it where the country lies most open and exposed to danger. "Naked" is also put for discovered, known, manifest. So in Job xxvi, 6, "Hell is naked before him;" the unseen state of the dead is open to the eyes of God. St. Paul says in the same sense, "Neither is there any

creature that is not manifest in his sight; but all things are naked and open unto the eyes of him with whom we have to do" (Heb. iv, 13). Nakedness also signifies sin or folly. Thus in Gen. iii, 7 it is indicative of sin in general; in Exod. xxxii, 25; 2 Chron. xxviii, 19; Ezek. xvi, 36, it is put for idolatry; and elsewhere in the Scriptures for all kinds of vice, but idolatry in particular.

Nakir is the name of one of the angels or dæmons who attend the dead at burial, according to the belief of the Indian Mussulmans. The *Nakir* and *Monkir,* as these angels are called, attend the body soon after it is interred, set it upright in the grave, and question the soul, which it is believed they have power to recall to the corpse for the sake of examination. The question from the angels is, Who is thy Lord, and who is thy prophet, and what is thy religion? They who can answer in the orthodox formula, "There is no god but God, and Mohammed is his prophet," are dismissed with honor, and their rest is visited with sweet airs from paradise. The unbelievers are beaten with iron maces, and gnawed by dragons, till they fill the cemeteries with howlings, which are audible alike to angels and jins, but mercifully withheld from men, whose nerves might be less equal to the sound, or their hearts more moved to compassion. See Trevor, *India, its Natives and Missions,* p. 149, 227.

Nala is in Hindû mythology the name of a monkey chief, who, according to some authorities, built for Rama (q. v.) the bridge from continental India to the island of Ceylon.

Naldi, ANTONIO, an Italian theologian, was born at Faenza towards the close of the 16th century. He was of a noble family, and had embraced religious life among the Théatins, and was distinguished for his learning and piety. He died at Rome in 1645. We have of his works, *Questiones practicæ in foro interiori usu frequente* (Bologne, 1610, 1624, 1646, 4to) :—*Resolutiones practicæ casuum conscientiæ, in quibus præcipue de justitia contractus livelli vulgo nuncupati, et de cambiis agitur* (Brescia, 1621, 4to) :—*Adnotationes ad varia juris pontificii loca* (Rome, 1632, fol.; Lyons, 1671, fol.; and in the *Corpus juris canonici,* Lyons, 1661, 2 vols. 4to) :—*Summa theologiæ moralis* (Brescia, 1623; Bologne, 1625). See Hoefer, *Nouv. Biog. Générale.* s. v.; Mittarelli, *De Litteratura Faventina,* p. 124.

Naldini, BATTISTA, an Italian painter who devoted himself to religious subjects, was born at Florence in 1537. He first studied under Jacopo Carrucci, called Il Pontormo, and afterwards under Angiolo Bronzino. According to Baglioni, he visited Rome during the pontificate of Gregory XIII, and painted several altar-pieces for the churches, among which is a picture of the *Baptism of Christ* in La Trinità de' Monti, and the *Martyrdom of St. John the Baptist* in the church of that saint. On returning to Florence he was chosen by Vasari coadjutor in his works in the Palazzo Vecchio, and retained by him about fourteen years. Vasari makes honorable mention of Naldini even when a young man, commending him as skilful, vigorous, expeditious, and indefatigable. Naldini painted many pictures at Florence, especially the *Deposition from the Cross* and the *Purification* at S. Maria Novella, praised by Borghini for their judicious composition, correct design, elegant attitudes, beautiful coloring, and excellent perspective. His pictures are criticised by Lanzi as having the knee-joints too large, the eyes too widely opened, and generally marked with a certain fierceness; the coloring often characterized by changeable hues. In teaching his scholars, he followed the prevailing method of employing them to design after the chalk drawings of Michael Angelo, and giving them his own finished paintings to copy. He was living in 1590. See Spooner, *Biog. Hist. of the Fine Arts,* ii, 606.

Nalson, John, a clergyman of the English Church, was born about the year 1638. He became rector of Doddington, and afterwards prebend of Ely. He died in 1686. His chief writings were several historico-political works defending the action of Royalists in their treatment of king Charles I; the principal publication is *An Impartial Collection of the Great Affairs of State from the Beginning of the Scotch Rebellion in* 1639 *to the Murder of King Charles I.* This work is valuable because of its fairness and truthfulness, and is much used as a reference.

Nalson, Valentine, an Anglican divine, was born in 1641. But little is known of his personal history. He was prebend of York near the opening of the 18th century, and died in 1724. He published shortly before his death *Twenty Sermons* (Lond. 1724, 8vo).

Nalton, JAMES, an English divine, flourished about the middle of the 17th century. He was expelled from the English Church and compelled to flee to Holland in 1622, on pretence of being implicated in what was called Love's Plot, but really because of his non-conformity. He published occasional sermons—1646, 1661, 1664—and is recommended by Baxter for his piety as well as learning. He died in the year 1662. Twenty of his sermons were published after his death (in 1677) by Matthew Poole (q. v.), who commended them highly. See *Gen. Biog. Dict.* s. v.; Allibone, *Dict. of Brit. and Amer. Authors,* s. v.

Namaqualand, an African country lying south of the Orange River, and now absorbed in Cape Colony, is divided into the greater and the lesser. The former comprises all the region north of Cape Colony, extending from the Orange River, lat. 29° 30′, to Walfish Bay, lat. 23°, and stretching inland from the west coast to the Kalihari Desert, comprehending an area of about 100,000 square miles. The Little Namaqualand is the territory south of the Orange River, and, though very rich in mineral resources, is a barren-looking country, and with only a few bays, notwithstanding it has a coastline of over one hundred miles. The native tribes perhaps number about 50,000 souls. They are mainly confined to the region called Great Namaqualand, north of the Gariep or Orange River, and the country a few miles south of it, as far as the Kamiesbergen. They are a pastoral people of rather predatory habits, and live under the rule of their chiefs, whose powers, however, are of a very limited nature. Differing from the Bosjesmen Hottentots, the Namaquas are a tall, well-made, active people, although presenting the usual peculiarities of the race, such as the light olive complexion, the oblique eye, and short tufted hair. Both men and women have remarkably small and neat hands and feet. The lower limbs of the women, however, are very thick and ungainly, especially as they advance in years, when they assume a dropsical appearance. The Namaquas are less influenced by the surrounding civilization of Europeans and missionaries than the more energetic and civilized Bastard races, who, in point of civilization and appearance, are very little inferior to the ordinary Dutch Boer of Cape Colony. "The Namaquas," says Chapman, "are in many respects a strange people, and one hardly knows what to make of their character and feelings. The missionaries told me as a fact that when once a party were going out on a cattle-lifting expedition, they very innocently asked them to pray for their success" (i, 428). The Namaquas speak a dialect of the Hottentot language, which, however, differs considerably from that used by other tribes of that people. Mission stations of the Rhenish and Wesleyan societies have been for many years established among them, and in a few localities, near Cape Colony, with considerable success; and the New Testament and some elementary works have been translated into the Namaqua dialect. Many of the southern Namaquas possess wagons and oxen, and are employed in the transport of copper ore from the mines of Little Namaqualand to the shipping port at Hondeklip Bay. A few of the peculiar customs of the Hottentot tribes, described by Kolben nearly 200 years ago, may still be traced among the more remote tribes of the Namaquas; but the constant contact with the Cape Colonists, and the efforts of the missionaries, have partially civilized this race, so that an ordinary Hottentot is quite as respectable a savage, or perhaps more so than his Betjouana or Amakosa brethren. Information on Namaqualand may be found in the travels of Moffat, Campbell, Chapman, and Le Vaillant. See AFRICA; HOTTENTOTS; NATAL.

Namaquas. See NAMAQUALAND.

Name (Heb. *shem,* שֵׁם; Gr. ὄνομα). On the names of persons in Oriental countries, and especially in ancient Israel, the following particulars may be noticed. (See Hauptmann, *De Hebræor. ὀνοματοθεσίᾳ* [Gera, 1757]; Schwarz, *De nomin. V. T. propriis* [Gött. 1743].)

(1.) A name among the Hebrews was given to the male child at the time of its circumcision, but it is probable that previous to the introduction of that rite the name was given immediately after its birth. All Oriental proper names have a special significance, which is more or less obvious, and generally may be ascertained. This meaning is often alluded to or explained in the Old Testament (Gen. xxvii, 36; 1 Sam. xxv, 25; Ruth i, 20). But some have attempted to show that the ex-

Namaqua Kraal.

planations given in the Pentateuch of the names of the patriarchs, etc., are not historically correct, on the ground that they are mutually inconsistent, or that they violate the analogies of the language; and refer them to a desire on the part of the writer to interweave the name significantly with the narrative (see Ewald, *Isr. Gesch.* i, 429). Those of modern nations, e. g. the English and Germans, have also their meaning, but it is more difficult to discover, as these languages do not preserve the roots in so pure a form as Oriental tongues. In early times they were conferred (by the mother, as Gen. iv, 1, 25; xix, 37 sq.; xxix, 32 sq.; xxx, 18, 20 sq.; xxxv, 18; 1 Sam. i, 20; iv, 21; comp. Isa. vii, 14; *Odys.* xviii, 6; Eurip. *Phœniss.* 57; yet also by the father, Gen. xvi, 15; xvii, 19; xxi, 3; Exod. ii, 22; Hosea i, 4 sq.; see Tournefort, *Voyage*, ii, 434) sometimes in reference to remarkable circumstances preceding or attending the child's birth, to peculiarities of its bodily constitution, to a wish connected with its future, or as an expression of endearment; sometimes borrowed from religion, and in this case applied both as a pious remembrancer and an omen of good. Sometimes the name had a prophetic meaning (Isa. vii, 14; viii, 3; Hosea i, 4, 6, 9; Matt. i, 21; Luke i, 13, 60, 63). In these classes belong many compounded in Hebrew with אֵל, יְהוּ, יוֹ (comp. Hengstenberg, *Pent.* i, 267 sq.), just as the Assyrian, Aramæan, and Phœnician names with Nebo (Nebu), Bel, Baal; the German Gottlieb, Gotthold, Ehregott, Christlieb, etc.; and the Tyrian names, Ἀσταρτος, Δελαιάσταρτος, in Josephus, *Apion*, i, 18 (on which see Hamaker, *Miscell. Phœnic.* p. 213; Fromann, *De cultu deorum ex ὀνοματοθεσίᾳ illustra.* [Altdorf, 1745]). For examples of the first class, see Gen. xxv, 25 sq.; xxix, 32 sq.; xxx, 6 sq.; xxxv, 18; xli, 51; 1 Sam. ii, 20; iv, 21; comp. Rosenmüller, *Morgenl*, i, 139, 173; Seetzen, in Zach's *Correspondenz*, xix, 214; Gesen. *Com. in Jes.* i, 303; Bohlen, *Genes.* p. 292. Such names take various forms among the Shemitic nations, following in each language the name it applies to God; e. g. Hannibal (חַנִּיבַעַל) and John (יוֹחָנָן); Abibal (אֲבִיבַעַל) and Abijah (אֲבִיָּה); Ezrubaal (עֶזְרוּבַעַל) and Azriel (עַזְרִיאֵל). See Ludolf. *Histor. Æth.* iv, 3. See BAALIM. The terms of endearment are appropriated especially to girls, and are often taken from the names of valued animals and plants (רָחֵל, Rachel, *a sheep;* תָּמָר, Tamar, *palm-tree;* צִבְיָה, Zibia, *roe;* צִפֹּרָה, Zipporah, *sparrow;* קְצִיעָה, Keziah, *cassia*). Comp. Hartmann, *Pentat.* 276 sq. On the transfer of names from animals to children, see Bochart, *Hieroz.* i, 2, 43; Simonis *Onomast.* p. 16, 390 sq. At a later period, when a sufficient number of words had become proper names by usage, a suitable choice was made among them, or the child took the father's name (Tobit i, 9; Luke i, 59; Josephus, *Ant.* xiv, 1, 3; *War*, v, 13, 2; Euseb. *H. E.* i, 13, 5), or yet oftener the grandfather's (1 Sam. xxii, 9; xxiii, 6; xxx, 7; 2 Sam. viii, 17. See Elsner, *Observ.* i, 176 sq.; Simonis *Onomast. V. T.* p. 17; comp. Eustath. *Ad Iliad.* 581, 4). This was the case also with the Phœnicians (see Gesen. *Monum. Phœn.* p. 100), and is still with the Egyptians (*Descript. de l'Égypte*, xxiii, 59 sq.), Frieslanders, and Danes. Sometimes that of a highly-esteemed kinsman was taken (comp. Luke i, 61; Lightfoot, *Hor. Hebr.* ad loc.; Rosenmüller, *Morgenl.* v, 158). In the Roman period we meet with many persons who were named by prefixing *Bar*, בַּר, *son*, after the Aramæan custom, to the names of their fathers; as in the N. T. *Bartholomew, Bartimeus, Barjesus, Barabbas.* Many of these were originally only surnames, as in Matt. xvi, 17, but by custom the personal name was entirely dropped (as in Arab., e. g. Ibn-Sina). But some Orientals, at the birth of a son, put off their own names, and thenceforth bear that of the child, with the prefix Abu, *father*, e. g. Abu-Nausel; comp. Arvieux, *Nachr.* ii, 292. According to Ge-

senius (*Isa.* i, 278), a person in earlier times was sometimes accosted or described as the son of this or that man, in order to disparage him, either because the father was obscure, or because the personal merit of the son would thus be questioned. But, besides, there are many Hebrew proper names which cannot be classed among appellatives; the roots of which, however, have been preserved. These have received proper attention in modern Lexicons. (See Gesenius, *Geschichte Hebr. Sprache.* On the formation of Hebrew proper names, see Ewald, *Ausführl. Lehrb. de Hebr. Spr.* p. 491 sq.). It must further be observed that (*a*) among the later Jews many old names were commonly shortened or otherwise modified in form; e. g. Lazarus for Eleazar. This shortening of names in the N. T. has been examined by Winer (*Gram. N. T.* p. 113 sq.: comp. besides J. C. Mylius, *Diss. de varietat. V. T.* p. 12; Simonis *Onomast. V. T.* p. 12). Aramæan names, also, had crept in among those of true Hebrew origin—as *Martha, Tabitha, Cephas.* (*b*) After the age of the Seleucidæ, Greek names came into circulation; as *Lysimachus*, 2 Macc. iv, 29; *Antipater*, 1 Macc. xii, 16; *Berenice, Herod* (among these must be reckoned *Andrew*, see Joseph. *Ant.* xii, 2, 2; although Olshausen [*Bibl. Comment.* i, 321] would refer it to the Hebrew נָדַר, *to dedicate*); especially those Hebrew names which had been translated in the Greek versions; as *Dositheus*, Δωσίθεος, 2 Macc. xii, 19; or *Theodotos*, Θεόδοτος, 2 Macc. xiv, 19; 3 Macc. i, 4; comp. the Hebrew גְּבַדִיאֵל, רוֹזְבָר, זְבַדְיָה; Nicodemus or Nicolaus, Νικόδημος, Νικόλαος, comp. בִּלְעָם; Menelaus, Μενέλαος, comp. אוֹנִיָּה, Josephus, *Ant.* xii, 5, 1. Instead of these, a Greek name of somewhat similar form and meaning was sometimes used; as Ἄλκιμος (comp. אֶלְקִים), Ἰάσων, etc. Ἰησοῦς, Jesus, is also a Hebrew name, approaching a Greek form. See JESUS. (On Ὀνίας, Σίμων, *Hyrcanus*, see Simonis *Onomast. N. T.* p. 152.) The custom thus introduced was confirmed by increasing intercourse with the Greeks, and even some Latin names crept into Judæa. The names *Philip, Ptolemy, Alexander*, etc., were not rare (comp. especially Joseph. *Ant.* xiv, 10, 22). Jews took Latin names on various occasions; some, for instance, on emancipation from Roman slavery. Among Egyptian Jews, Greek names were in use still earlier (comp. Philo, ii, 528). (*c*) Here we find in part the reason why, in later times, some of the Jews bore two names at once; e. g. *Johannes Marcus, Jesus Justus* (Col. iv, 11). Other occasions were these: *Bar* was prefixed to the name of the father for a surname, as *Joseph Barsabas;* or it was acquired on some special occasion, as *Simon Cephas* or *Peter, Joses Barnabas*, Ἰωνάθαν Ἀπφοῦς (1 Macc. ii, 5), *Simon Canaanites* (comp. also Josephus, *War*, v, 11, 5), or given to distinguish persons of the same name in one family or neighborhood; a distinction usually made in the Talmud by adding the name of the father, or of a trade or profession; elsewhere by that of one's residence or birthplace, as *Mary Magdalene, Judas Iscariot.* A complete catalogue of all the proper names used by Jews is given by Hiller, *Onomast. Sacrum* (Tübing. 1706); J. Simon, *Onomast. V. T.* (Hal. 1741), in connection with his *Onomast. N. T. et libr. V. T. apocrapha* (ibid. 1762); comp. B. Michaelis, *Observatt. philol. de nomin. prop. Hebr.* (Hal. 1729), and his *Diss. nomina quædam propr. V. et N. T. ex virilib. in mulietria*, etc., *versa suo restituens sexui* (Hal. 1754); Potts, *Sylloge*, vii, 26 sq. There is a useful catalogue of Phœnician and Carthaginian proper names in Gesenius, *Monumenta Phœn.* p. 395 sq.

(2.) The name was naturally given for the most part by the parents, but sometimes a number of their kinsmen and friends would agree in bestowing one; as in Ruth iv, 17; Luke i, 59. Not seldom in the course of life this was changed for a new name which was full of significance among those who gave it; or was at first added to the original name, and gradually took its place. The latter happened with Cephas (Peter) and Barnabas. But princes often changed their names on their accession to the throne, as the popes do now (2 Kings xxiii, 34; xxiv, 17); comp. Joseph. *Ant.* xvi, 9, 4; Justin, x, 3; Ctes. *Pers.* 56; Ludolf, *Histor. Æthiop.*; Paulsen, *Regier. d. Morgenl.* p. 78. This was done even in the case of private persons on entering upon public duties of importance. See Numb. xiii, 16; comp. John i, 42; Acts iv, 36. This is still customary with monks on taking the vows of cloister life. To this head must be referred also the incident in 2 Sam. xii, 25, where the prophet Nathan, on assuming the charge of Solomon's education, gave him the name Jedediah. So in reference to important epochs in life (Gen. xxxii, 28; comp. xvii, 5, 15; Judg. vi, 32). The appellation Boanerges, which Jesus gave to James and John (Matt. iii, 17), seems not to have been a permanent name, but simply the expression of an opinion as to their talents and disposition. In Gen. xli, 45; Dan. i, 7; v, 12, the change of name takes place, not so much in reference to the change of circumstances or occupation as because Joseph and Daniel were in lands where their former Hebrew names were not understood or not readily pronounced. On the change of Saul's name to Paul, see PAUL. Comp. Harmar, *Observ.* iii, 368; J. H. Stuss, *De mutatione nomin. sacra et profana* (Goth. 1735), iii, 4; Hackett, *Illust. Script.* p. 83; Thomson, *Land and Book*, i, 179; Nöldeke, *Hebr. u. Arab. Eigennamen*, in the *Zeitschr. f. deutsch. morgenl. Gesellschaft*, 1861, p. 806. See PROPER NAMES.

Name OF GOD. By this term we are to understand: 1, God himself (Psa. xx, 1); 2, his titles peculiar to himself (Exod. iii, 13, 14); 3, his word (Psa. v, 11: Acts ix, 15); 4, his works (Psa. viii, 1); 5, his worship (Exod. xx, 24); 6, his perfections and excellences (Exod. xxxiv, 6; John xvii, 26). The properties or qualities of this name are these: 1, a glorious name (Psa. lxxii, 17); 2, transcendent and incomparable (Rev. xix, 16); 3, powerful (Phil. ii, 10); 4, holy and reverend (Psa. cxi, 9); 5, awful to the wicked; 6, perpetual (Isa. lv, 13). See Hannam, *Anal. Comp.* p. 20.

Namer. See LEOPARD.

Names, CHRISTIAN. The modern practice of giving names at baptism is most probably in accordance with primitive usage, and might have been adopted from the custom of the Jews naming their children when they circumcised them. No mention of the practice is made by the writers of the New Testament, or by the Church fathers, Justin Martyr, Tertullian, Origen, Cyprian, or by any other of the early ecclesiastical writers. In fact, we find that many of these writers, and others, such as Constantine, Ambrose, Augustine, and Gregory, retained their original names after they had received adult baptism. There are, however, numerous instances of persons receiving new names at their baptism; and it appears that it was customary to register the names of all candidates, when they were received as catechumens, in the registers of the Church, and those of their sponsors also. The Church, grounding its practice on James ii, 7, compared with 1 Peter iv, 15, required that the name of the person to be baptized should have some reference to the Christian religion, as some Christian virtue; and in accordance with such a purpose seems to have been the practice of the early Christians of Rome, whose names, as recorded on the marble slabs of the Catacombs, appear beautifully and designedly expressive of Christian sentiment or character (see Withrow, *Catacombs of Rome*, p. 454, 457). St. Chrysostom advised the Christians of his day that the names ought to refer to some holy persons; and the Council of Trent, in its various provisions for baptism, advised that the name given to the baptized should be taken from some saint (Barnum's *Romanism*, p. 450). The Council of Nice forbade the use of names of heathen gods (comp. Bates's *Christ. Antiquities*); and the Church

of England, in the 16th century, forbade all names of heathen origin (Soames, *Elizabethan Religious History*, p. 39). "Of old," says Hart (*Eccl. Records*), "the bishop used to pronounce the person's name at the time of confirmation; and if it was desirable that the name given at baptism should be altered, it might be done by the bishop pronouncing a new name when he administered the rite. This custom was continued in our reformed liturgy till the last revision in the time of king Charles II."

Names OF CHRISTIANS, *in early ages*, are manifold, besides those found in the N. T. Thus the Church fathers used various appellations in describing Christians: *Catholics*, for while the Church remained one and undivided, it was properly called Catholic; *Ecclesiastics*, men of the Church; *Dogmatics*, men of the doctrine; *Gnostics*, men of knowledge. The names of reproach and derision heaped upon Christians were almost endless. The following are of importance in illustrating the condition of the primitive Church: *Jews*, for at first they were regarded merely as a Jewish sect; *Nazarenes*, always used in a bad sense; *Galilæans*, a name used by Julian the Apostate, who died with these words on his lips, "*Vicisti, O Galilæe;" Greeks*, for by the ancient Romans this was a term expressive of suspicion and contempt; *Magicians, Sibyllists*, from their being charged with corrupting the Sibylline books; *Sarmentitii*, from the *fagots* with which fires were kindled around martyrs at the stake; *Semaxii*, from the *stake* to which they were bound; *Parabolani*, from their being exposed to wild beasts; Βιαθάνατοι, *self-murderers*, because of their fearlessness of death; Ἄθεοι, *atheists*; Νεώτεροι, *new lights*; Σταυρολάτραι, *worshippers of the cross*; *Plautinæ prosapiæ homines, pistores*, men of the race of Plautus, bakers (Plautus is said to have hired himself to a baker to grind in his mill); *Asinarii*, worshippers of an ass; *Abjecti, Creduli, Fatui, Hebetes, Idiotæ, Imperiti, Lucifugæ, Simplices, Stulti, Stupidi*, etc.

Nanæ'a (Ναναία). The last act of Antiochus Epiphanes was his attempt to plunder the temple of Nanæa at Elymais, which had been enriched by the gifts and trophies of Alexander the Great (1 Macc. vi, 1–4; 2 Macc. i, 13–16). The Persian goddess Nanæa, called also *Aanœtis* (Ἀναῖτις, Strabo, xv, p. 733), is apparently the Moon goddess, of whom the Greek *Artemis* was the nearest representative in Polybius (quoted by Josephus, *Ant.* xii, 9). Beyer calls her the "Elymæan Venus" (*ad Joh. Seldeni*, etc. *addit.* p. 345), and some have identified Nanæa with *Meni* (q. v.), and both with the planet *Venus*, the star of luck, called by the Syrians *Nani*, and in Zend *Nahid*, or *Anahid*. See DIANA. Elphinstone in 1811 found coins of the Sassanians with the inscription NANAIA, and on the reverse a figure with nimbus and lotus-flower (Movers, *Phön.* i, 626). It is probable that Nanæa is identical with the deity named by Strabo (xi, p. 532) as the *numen patrium* of the Persians, who was also honored by the Medes, Armenians, and in many districts of Asia Minor. Other forms of the name are Ἀναία, given by Strabo, Αἴνη by Polybius, Ἀνεῖτις by Plutarch, and Ταναῖς by Clemens Alexandrinus, with which last the variations of some MSS. of Strabo correspond. In consequence of a confusion between the Greek and Eastern mythologies, Nanæa has been identified with Artemis and Aphrodite, the probability being that she corresponds with the Tauric or Ephesian Artemis, who was invested with the attributes of Aphrodite, and represented the productive power of nature. In this case some weight may be allowed to the conjecture that "the desire of women" mentioned in Dan. xi, 37 is the same as the goddess Nanæa. "This female deity," Stuart remarks, "under different names, was worshipped in Africa, Syria, Phœnicia, Cyprus, Greece, Rome, Babylonia, Persia, and other countries. The Mylitta (= Heb. מוֹלֶדֶת, *generatrix*) of the East was the Venus of the West, the Neith of Egypt, the Astarte of the Syrians, the Anais or Anaitis of the Armenians, all uniting in the worship of the power which represented maternal productiveness. . . . Antiochus, it seems, paid little or no regard to this idol" (*Commentary on Dan.* ad loc.). In 2 Macc. ix, 1, 2, there appears to be a different account of the same sacrilegious attempt of Antiochus; but the scene of the event is there placed at Persepolis, "the city of the Persians," where there might well have been a temple to the national deity. But Grimm considers it far more probable that it was an Elymæan temple which excited the cupidity of the king. See Gesenius, *Jesaia*, iii, 337, and Grimm's *Commentar* in the *Kurzgef. Handb.* ad loc.

Nance, JOHN, an Anglican clergyman, flourished in the early part of this century. He was educated at Oxford, and became fellow of Worcester College. He then took holy orders, and was made rector of Old Romney. Later he became master of the grammar-school at Ashford, Kent. He died after 1816. He published *Sermons on various subjects* (1807, 8vo):—*A Letter from a Country Clergyman to his Parishioners, on the Arguments and Practices of some of the Modern Dissenters* (1809, 8vo):—*An Address to the Members of the Church of England* (1811, 8vo). See *Dict. of Living Authors*, s. v.

Nandi is in Hindû mythology the name of a white bull, regarded as the vehicle of Siva (q. v.).

Nanian Manuscript (CODEX NANIANUS, designated as U of the Gospels, now in the Library of St. Mark, Venice, where it is numbered I, viii), so called from a former possessor, is an uncial codex of the 9th or 10th century, containing the four Gospels, carefully and luxuriously written in two columns of twenty-two lines each on a 4to page, with ornaments in gold and colors. It has the Eusebian canons in the margin. It accords with the Alexandrine recension. Münter first sent some extracts from it to Birch, who used them for his edition. Tischendorf collated the MS. in 1843, and Tregelles in 1846, and they compared their work for mutual correction at Leipsic. See Scrivener, *Introd.* p. 117; Tregelles, in Horne's *Introd.* iv, 202. See MANUSCRIPTS, BIBLICAL.

Specimen of the *Codex Nanianus* (containing Mark vi, 18: Βάν-τοσ αυτου | εισ τὸ πλοῖο | παρεκάλει àν | τον ὁ δαιμο | νισθεισ ἱνα).

Nanini, GIOVANNI - MARIA, an Italian composer, was born about 1540 at Vallerano. He studied harmony in the school of Goudimel with Palestrina. From 1571 to 1575 he performed the duties of chapel-master in the church of Sainte Mary, and in 1577 he entered the college of singers in the pontifical chapel. He was director of a school in composition, which was the first of its kind established at Rome by an Italian. According to M. Fétis, this master is to be regarded as one of the most learned men of the Roman school, and his productions deserve to be placed immediately after those of Palestrina. Several of his motets are still sung, among others at Christmas matins a *Hodie nobis cælorum rex*, which is truly beautiful. He died at Rome March

11, 1607. He published, *Motetti* (Venice, 1578, 4to, 2 books):—*Madrigali a cinque voci* (ibid. 1579–1586, 4 vols. 4to, 4 books):—*Canzonette a tre voci* (ibid. 1587, 4to). Many fragments of his scattered through several collections are still known; and in manuscript there are fugues, litanies, masses, psalms, and a treatise on counterpoint. His younger brother, Giovanni-Bernardino, was also chapel-master at Rome. He was among the first to abandon the old style for new music with organ accompaniment. To him we also owe, *Madrigali* (Venice and Rome, 1598–1612, 3 parts, 4to):—*Motecta* (Rome, 1608–1618, 4 parts, 4to):—*Salmi* (ibid. 1620, 4to). See Hoefer, *Nouv. Biog. Générale*, s. v.

Nanni DI BACCIO BIGIO, a Florentine sculptor and architect, lived in the first part of the 16th century. He studied sculpture under Raffaelle de Montelupe, and produced the statue of pope Clement VII in the Minerva at Rome, and a good copy of Michael Angelo's *Piety*, which he executed, it is said, under his direction for the church of the Madonna dell' Anima. After having studied architecture under Lorenzetto, he was employed upon St. Peter's Church by Antonio de San-Gallo. It is known that Michael Angelo, succeeding San-Gallo, commenced by destroying all that his predecessor had done, discharging all those who had worked under his orders. Hence the hatred that Nanni bore to the prince of the Florentine school. De Quincey says, "Nanni has left no work of his own to assure him a distinguished place among the architects of his time, and perhaps he would have ill deserved one in the history of architecture if his rival, whom he twice overreached by intrigue, had not given him a kind of celebrity." Michael Angelo having been commissioned to restore the bridge Santa-Maria over the Tiber, Nanni took the work from him, and accomplished it so that at the first inundation the bridge was carried away. Afterwards he succeeded in joining Michael Angelo in the work upon St. Peter's. Michael Angelo protested with his usual vivacity, and proved the ignorance of Nanni, who, says Vasari, was dismissed under disgrace. Several considerable edifices of Rome have been built after his designs, particularly the palaces Ricci and Salirati. See Hoefer, *Nouv. Biog. Générale*, s. v.

Nanni, GIROLAMO, a Roman painter of religious subjects, called "*Il Poco e Buono*," flourished about 1643. His talents were ordinary, and he deserves little notice, except for his studious disposition and slowness of execution. He was employed by Sixtus V in several considerable works, and whenever requested by the director to hasten operations, he always answered "poco e buono" (little and good), which expression gained him his surname. There are a number of his pictures at Rome, among which are the *Annunciation* in the church of the Madonna dell' Anima, and two subjects from the life of St. Bonaventura in St. Bartolomeo dell' Isola.

Nanok or **Nannuk**, the founder of the sect of the Seikhs, which has now grown into a powerful nation, was originally a Hindû of the Khetore caste, and was born, in 1469, at Talawandy (now called Rhaypore), a small village of Lahore, Hindostan. He is said to have travelled through most of the countries in India, and even into Persia and Arabia, preaching his doctrines in peace, and preserving an unaffected meekness and simplicity of manners. He died at Rawu, a village to the north of Lahore, in 1539. The unity, omniscience, and omnipotence of God were some of the principal tenets taught by Nanok. Not less than 100,000 persons in different countries adopted the tenets of Nanok before his decease, and considered him as their guru, or religious guide. See SEIKHS.

Nantes, Council of. Two important ecclesiastical assemblages were held in the city of Nantes, France, besides those of the Huguenots (q. v.). The first Church council was held about the year 1127, under the count

Conon; Hildebert, archbishop of Tours, presiding. It was ruled that children by an incestuous marriage should have no share in the succession of their parents; and that the children of priests should not receive holy orders except they should first have taken monastic vows. Anathema was pronounced against those who plundered shipwrecked property (*Conc.* tom. x, p. 918). A second Church council was held there in 1264; Vincent, archbishop of Tours, presiding. Nine canons were published. The most important (2) forbids the number of monks in any priory or abbey to be diminished (5) forbids to set more than two dishes before the bishop in visitation, and orders that if more have been prepared they shall be given to the poor; (6) forbids pluralities; (7) forbids, under pain of excommunication, to demand toll of the clergy (*Conc.* tom. xi, p. 826).

Nantes, Edict of, is the name of a famous decree published by Henry IV of France, April 13, 1598, guaranteeing to his Protestant subjects the liberty of serving God according to the dictates of their conscience, and security for the enjoyment of their civil rights and privileges. The decree had been made necessary by many causes, the most important of which was Henry's own defection from the Protestant faith, and probable consequent alliance with the Romanists against those he once loved. See HUGUENOTS. There can be no doubt that Henry IV simply left the Protestant fold to secure the protection of Rome and its allies for his throne and realm. His own political actions after apostasy reveal such a cause. (See, however, for a defense of this king's apostasy, Jervis, *Hist. of the Church of France*, i, 199 sq.) Once a Romanist, he determined for the sake of pleasing the papal host to do all in his power to weaken the Huguenots, and thus indirectly largely assisted their persecution. Yet though Henry had quitted the Protestants in order to strengthen himself, he had still to learn that a great source of trouble and perplexity would come to him from those he had considered too weak to be worth his friendship or attention even. When suddenly forced to declare war against Spain, Henry found himself deprived of the support and aid of some of his most valuable citizens. They were Protestants, and after 1594, when the truce for hostilities had expired, and no guarantee as to their future had been granted them, they had declared themselves "a state within the state." They would only hold their own strongholds, and refused to take up arms in defence of a realm that failed to afford them the protection to which their citizenship entitled them. Even Romanists saw the folly of the king's course, and propositions were finally made to renew the edict of 1577, or, what is the same, the Edict of Nantes (1591), which had never yet taken effect because of the opposition of Parliament. The Reformed demanded more. In 1597 a meeting was called at Loudun to effect a reconciliation. It failed to bring about the much-desired result. Another meeting was called at Vendôme, but it also failed; for the Protestants feared the direct influence of the court, which was in the immediate vicinity, and the meeting was adjourned to Saumur. By the close of 1597, however, the different parties came to an understanding. France had been successful. Spain was in favor of peace, and in the hour of prosperity Henry was inclined to grant favors. The result was an agreement for the edict; and on the same day on which the peace with Spain was settled by the signature of the king, the edict obtained the king's approval and hand and seal (May 2, 1598). It was in reality a new confirmation of former treaties between the French government and the Huguenots, by which all verdicts against them were erased from the rolls of the courts, and their unlimited liberty of conscience was recognised. The preamble to this most important document, the Magna Charta of Protestant liberty in France, specifies, curiously enough, as the royal motive for issuing it, the necessity of completely and securely re-establishing the Catholic religion in those localities where

it had been abolished during the late troubles; viz. Béarn, La Rochelle, Nismes, Montauban, etc. "Now that it had pleased God to grant repose to the kingdom from the destruction of civil war, the king felt it his duty to make provisions for the public worship and service of God among all classes of his subjects; and if it was impossible at present that all could be brought to agree in one and the same external form of worship, at all events there might be uniformity of spirit and purpose; and such regulations might be adopted as should obviate all danger of public disturbance or collision. Accordingly he had determined to enact and promulgate a law on this subject—universal, distinct, positive, and absolute —a perpetual and irrevocable edict; and he prayed God that his subjects might be led to accept it, as the surest guarantee of their union and tranquillity, and of the re-establishment of the French empire in its ancient power and splendor." Then follow the enacting clauses, comprised in ninety-two articles. Those who professed the "so-called Reformed religion" were to enjoy henceforth full and complete liberty of conscience, and the free exercise of their public worship throughout the realm of France, though not without certain restrictions. All seigneurs possessing the right of "haute justice" might assemble for worship with their families, their tenants, and others they chose to invite; landowners of a lower grade were not to hold meetings consisting of more than thirty persons. Huguenots were to be freely admitted to all colleges, schools, and hospitals; they might found, endow, and maintain educational and charitable institutions; and their religious books might be published in all places where their worship was authorized. They were to be eligible to all public employments on equal terms with Catholics, and on accepting office were not to be bound to take any oaths, or to attend any ceremonies repulsive to their conscience. A new court, called the "Chambre de l'Édit," was instituted in the Parliament of Paris, composed of a president and sixteen councillors, of whom one, or two at the most, were to be Protestants. Other similar courts were established in Guienne, Languedoc, and Dauphiné. These were to take cognizance of all cases arising between Protestants and Catholics. Besides the privilege granted to the holders of fiefs, the Reformed worship was legalized in one town or village in every bailage throughout France. In certain specified places, however, it was altogether prohibited: at the court or residence of the sovereign for the time being; at Paris, and within a radius of five leagues round the capital; and in all military camps, with the exception of the personal quarters of a Protestant general. It was also excluded from Rheims, Dijon, Soissons, Beauvais, Sens, Nantes, Joinville, and other towns, in virtue of separate arrangements made by Henry with the local nobles. The Huguenots were enjoined to show outward respect to the Catholic religion, to observe its holydays, and to pay tithes to the clergy. They were to desist from all political negotiations and cabals, both within and beyond the realm; their provincial assemblies were to be forthwith dissolved; and the king engaged to license the holding of a representative synod once in three years, with the privilege of addressing the crown on the condition of the Reformed body, and petitioning for redress of grievances. There were, in addition, fifty secret articles which did not appear on the face of the edict. By one of these the king confirmed the Huguenots in possession (for eight years) of all the cautionary towns which had been granted to them by the treaty of 1577. Several of these were places of considerable strength and importance; including La Rochelle, Montauban, Nismes, Montpellier, Grenoble, Lectoure, Niort, etc. The expense of maintaining the Huguenot garrisons was to be defrayed by a royal grant of 80,000 crowns per annum. From this period the Reformers or Huguenots (who then counted 760 churches) had a legal existence in France, but gradually their political strength was crushed by the mighty despotism of Richelieu—

who, however, never dreamed of interfering with their liberty of worship. Neither did his successors, Mazarin and Colbert. The edict had indeed been confirmed by Louis XIII in 1610, and by Louis XIV in 1652; but under the influence of a "penitence" as corrupt and sensual as the sins which occasioned it, this same Louis XIV, after a series of detestable dragonnades (q. v.), signed a decree for the revocation of the edict, October 18, 1685, at the instigation, it is generally believed, of the Jesuits and their willing handmaid, Madame de Maintenon, the mistress of the king. Although its provisions had, in fact, long been repealed by various ordinances forbidding the profession of the Reformed faith under severe penalties, the act of revocation was the death-knell of the Huguenots. It authorized the destruction of all Protestant churches, and prohibited all public and private worship; it banished all Protestant pastors from France; demanded the closing of all Protestant schools, and parents were forbidden to instruct their children in the Reformed faith, but enjoined to bring them up in the Roman Catholic religion. If any persons were detected in the act of attempting to escape from France, men were condemned to the galleys for life, and women were imprisoned for life. Such were some of the inhuman provisions of the edict of Revocation. The result of this despotic act was that, rather than conform to the established religion, 400,000 Protestants—among them the most industrious, the most intelligent, and the most religious of the nation—quitted France, and took refuge in Great Britain, Holland, Germany, Switzerland, and America. The loss to France was immense; the gain to other countries, no less. Composed largely of merchants, manufacturers, and skilled artisans, they carried with them their knowledge, taste, and aptitude for business. From them England, in particular, learned the art of manufacturing silk, crystal glasses, and the more delicate kinds of jewelry. Many besides these, whom the vigilance of their enemies guarded so closely as to prevent their flight, were exposed to the brutal rage of the soldiery, and assaulted by every barbarous form of persecution that might tend to subdue their courage, and thus engage them to a feigned and external profession of popery. See Michelet, *Louis XIV et la Révocation de l'Édit de Nantes*, p. 284 sq.; Benoit, *Hist. de l'Édit de Nantes* (1693), iii, 127 sq.; Ranke, *Französ. Gesch.* vol. ii; Morney, *Mémoires et Correspondence* (Par. 1824), vol. v; Wessenberg, *Gesch. d. Kirchenversammlungen*, iv, 277, 280, 281; Seebohm, *Protest. Revol.* p. 267; *Edinb. Rev.* lxxx, 68 sq.; Smiles, *Hist. of the Huguenots*, and his *Huguenots after the Revocation*, p. 1-19, 24, 44, 45, 78; Weiss, *Hist. des Refugiés*, p. 1 sq.; Bray, *Revolt in the Cevennes*, p. 4-7, 13, 19, 49 sq., 214, 313; Smedley, *Hist. of the Ref. Church in France*, iii, 42, 44 sq., 92, 231; De Felice, *Hist. of Prot. in France*, bk. i, pt. xviii, xx; bk. iv, ch. xvii; and other works referred to under HUGUENOTS.

Nanteuil, CÉLESTIN, a French artist noted for his contributions to sacred art, was born at Rome in 1813. He studied under Langlois and Ingres, and exhibited his first work, a *Holy Family*, in 1833, followed by *A Beggar* (1834), and *Christ Healing the Sick* (1837); but he was mainly employed as a lithographer, and in the course of about thirty years executed more than 2000 vignettes for literary and musical publications. Among his more recent paintings are, *The Temptation* (1851):— *The Vine* (1853):—*Souvenirs of the Past* and *The Kiss of Judas* (1858), the latter after Van Dyck, of which he also produced an admirable engraving. He died at Paris in 1873.

Na'ömi (Heb. *Noömi'*, נָעֳמִי, *my delight*; Sept. Νοομμείν, v. r. Νωεμίν, Νοεμμείν, Νοεμμεί, Νοομμεί, Νωεμείν, Νωεμμείν; Vulg. *Noemi*), a woman of Bethlehem in the days of the early judges; wife of Elimelech, mother of Mahlon and Chilion, and mother-in-law of Ruth (Ruth i, 2, etc.; ii, 1, etc.; iii, 1; iv, 3, etc.). B.C. cir. 1363. The significance of her name contributes to

the point of the paronomasia in i, 20, 21, though the passage contains also a play on the mere sound of the name, "Call me not Naomi (pleasant), call me Mara (bitter): ... why then call ye me Naomi, seeing the Lord hath testified (*anâh*, עָנָה) against me?" See RUTH.

Naös (ναός, the Greek technical name for *a temple*) is used to designate the body of the church. See NAVE. The earlier Christians were averse to using this word with reference to their worship, on account of the use of it by the heathen. It was their boast that they had neither temples nor altars. But this is to be understood only relatively, by way of distinction between Jewish and heathen rites. When the danger of sympathizing either with Judaism or heathen idolatry had ceased, and a suspicion of such union could not be supposed to exist, Christians felt less hesitation in calling their churches temples, especially as this was the name rendered familiar to them by the Old-Testament Scriptures. The words ναός and *templum* are of frequent occurrence in the writings of Lactantius, Ambrose, Eusebius, and Chrysostom, and the phraseology was common in the 4th century. See Neale, *Hist. East. Ch. Introd.* (see Index in vol. ii); Coleman, *Christian Antiquities* (see Index); Walcott, *Sacred Archæology*, s. v.

Na'phish (Heb. *Naphish'*, נָפִישׁ, *refresher;* Sept. Ναφές; Vulg. *Naphis*), the eleventh named of the twelve sons of Ishmael, patriarch and prince among the Ishmaelites (Gen. xxv, 15; Chron. i, 31). B.C. post 1077. In 1 Chron. v, 19 (Sept. Ναφισαῖοι, A.V. "Nephesh") the name of the ancestor is given to the tribe descended from him, who are classed among the Hagarites (q. v.), defeated by the transjordanic tribes on their settlement in Canaan. "Naphish, in the three passages in which the name occurs, is grouped with Jetur. Jetur was unquestionably identical with the Greek Ituræa and modern Jedûr; a small province situated at the eastern base of Hermon, and bordering on Damascus and Bashan. Jetur and Naphish were allies, and apparently dwelt together. The Israelites took from them 50,000 camels, 250,000 sheep, and 2000 asses. They were manifestly a pastoral people, like the great modern tribes of the Anizeh, some of which have flocks and herds equally numerous. Then, having conquered the people and captured their cattle, we are told that 'the children of the half-tribe of Manasseh *dwelt in the land: they increased from Bashan unto Baal-Hermon, and Senir, and unto Mount Hermon.'* From this it may be concluded that the people of Naphish had a settled home situated between the range of Hermon and Bashan—that is, along the eastern declivities of the mountains." "They have not been identified with any Arabian tribe; but identifications with Ishmaelitish tribes are often difficult. The difficulty in question arises from intermarriages with Keturahites and Joktanites, from the influence of Mohammedan history, and from our ignorance respecting many of the tribes, and the towns and districts, of Arabia. If the Hagarenes went southwards, into the province of Hejr, after their defeat, Naphish may have gone with them, and traces of his name should in this case be looked for in that obscure province of Arabia." They doubtless became afterwards amalgamated with the Ishmaelitish clans, and so lost to late history. See ARABIA.

Naph'isi (Ναφισί v. r. Ναφεισεί; Vulg. *Nasissin*), one of the Temple servants whose "sons" returned from the exile (1 Esdr. v, 31); evidently the NEPHISHESIM (q. v.) or NEPHUSIM of the Heb. texts (Neh. vii, 52; Ezra ii, 50).

Naph'tali (Heb. *Naphtali'*, נַפְתָּלִי, *my wrestling*, see Gen. xxx, 8; Sept. Νεφθαλί, but fourteen times Νεφθαλει, as Gen. xxx, 8; eight times Νεφθαλείμ, as Gen. xxxv, 25; once Νεφδαλίμ, as 1 Kings iv, 15; N. T. and Josephus, Νεφθαλείμ; Vulg. O. T. *Nephthali*; but sometimes *Nephtali*, as Gen. xxx, 8; N. T. *Nephthalim*;

Auth. Ver. N. T. "Nephthalim"), the sixth son of Jacob, and his second by Bilhah, Rachel's handmaid, born B.C. 1915, in Padan-Aram. (In the following account of this patriarch and the tribe descended from him we bring together a general view of the whole subject.) At his birth, the origin of the name is thus explained (Gen. xxx, 8) : "And Rachel said, With *wrestlings* of God have *I wrestled*" (נַפְתּוּלֵי אֱלֹהִים נִפְתַּלְתִּי, i. e. according to the Hebrew idiom, "immense wrestlings;" ἀμηχάνητος οἷον, "as if irresistible," is the explanation of the name given by Josephus, *Ant.* i, 19, 8) "with my sister; and I have prevailed; and she called his name *Naphtali*." Both the Septuagint and Latin versions mistake the meaning and spoil the force of this passage (Gen. xxx, 8). Onkelos and the Syriac version represent Rachel as having entreated God by prayer, and this seems to be the correct idea (see Kalisch, ad loc.). By his birth Naphtali was thus allied to Dan (Gen. xxxv, 25); and he also belonged to the same portion of the family as Ephraim and Benjamin, the sons of Rachel; but, as we shall see, these connections appear to have been only imperfectly maintained by the tribe descended from him. At the migration to Egypt four sons are attributed to Naphtali (Gen. xlvi, 24; Exod. i, 4; 1 Chron. vii, 13). Of the individual patriarch not a single trait is given in the Bible, as up to the time of Jacob's blessing the twelve patriarchs his name is only mentioned in two public lists (Gen. xxxv, 25; xlvi, 24); but in the Jewish traditions he is celebrated for his powers as a swift runner, and he is named as one of the five who were chosen by Joseph to represent the family before Pharaoh (*Targ. Pseudojon.* on Gen. l, 13 and xlvii, 2). In the *Testament of the Twelve Patriarchs* Naphtali dies in his one hundred and thirty-second year, in the seventh month, on the fourth day of the month. That work explains his name as given "because Rachel had dealt deceitfully" (ἐν πανουργίᾳ ἐποίησε). It also gives the genealogy of his mother: "Balla (Bilhah), the daughter of Routhaios, the brother of Deborah, Rebekah's nurse, was born the same day with Rachel. Routhaios was a Chaldæan of the kindred of Abraham, who, being taken captive, was bought as a slave by Laban. Laban gave him his maid Aina or Eva to wife, by whom he had Zelipha (Zilpah)—so called from the place in which he had been captive— and Balla" (Fabricius, *Cod. Pseudepigr. V. T.* p. 659, etc.).

NAPHTALI, TRIBE OF. The blessing pronounced by Jacob upon Naphtali was very short; but the language is obscure, and its interpretation has occasioned considerable controversy. In the English version it reads thus, "Naphtali is a hind let loose; he giveth goodly words" (Gen. xlix, 21). The Septuagint translates the first clause, Νεφθαλεὶ στέλεχος ἀνειμένον, "Naphtali is a wide-spread tree." The translators must either have had before them or they must have invented a different pointing of the Hebrew text (אֵילָה instead of אַיָּלָה. The former, equivalent to אֵיל or אלון, signifies "a strong tree," *arbor robusta;* but especially an "oak" or "terebinth." Gesenius, *Thesaurus,* p. 47). The second clause is made to correspond, ἐπιδιδοὺς ἐν τῷ γεννήματι κάλλος, "putting forth in its fruit beauty," or "giving forth goodly boughs." Here the pointing must have been different from the Masoretic. Instead of אֹמֶר, "words," they read אֶמֶר, "shoots" or "leaves." This view has been substantially adopted by Bochart and many modern commentators. Bochart examines the text minutely, and translates, "Nephthali est ut arbor surculosa, edens ramos pulchritudinis," id est, "egregios et speciosos" (*Opera*, ii, 895 sq.; comp. Stanley, *S. and P.* p. 355). The translation of this difficult passage given by Ewald (*Geschichte*, ii, 380),

"Naphtali is a towering Terebinth;
He hath a goodly crest,"

gives it an allusion at once to the situation of the tribe at the very apex of the country, to the heroes who towered at the head of the tribe, and to the lofty mountains on whose summits their castles, then as now, were perched. The only reasons for the change are that it gives a better sense, and it seems to accord more with Moses's blessing in Deut. xxxiii, 23. The great fruitfulness of the tribe would thus be indicated, and the nature of the country they were to occupy. This translation, however, is opposed to the Masoretic text, and to the interpretations of the best Jewish writers (Bochart, l. c.). The present reading, too, when thoughtfully considered, is as appropriate as the other. This, like the other blessings of the patriarch, was intended to shadow forth under poetic imagery the future character and history of the tribe. "Naphtali is a hind let loose," or "a graceful hind"—timid and distrustful of its own powers, swift of foot to elude its enemies; but when brought to bay fierce and strong to defend its life. These were the qualities shown by Naphtali. They left several of their cities in the hands of the Canaanites (Judg. i, 33); they had not confidence to fight alone, but when assailed they made a noble defence (Judg. v, 18), and united with others in pursuit of a flying foe (vi, 35). Their want of self-confidence was chiefly shown in the case of Barak; and then, too, they displayed in the end heroic devotion and unwearied alacrity. "He (that is, Naphtali; the masc. חַפְתָּן proves this) giveth goodly words." The tribe was to be famous for the beauty of its language. It probably possessed poets and writers whose names have not come down to us. We have one noble ode ascribed in part at least to a Naphtalite (Judg. v, 1. See Kalisch, *On Gen.* xlix, 21).

During the sojourn in Egypt Naphtali increased with wonderful rapidity. Four sons went down with their father and Jacob; and at the exodus the adult males numbered 53,400 (Numb. i, 43). It thus held exactly the middle position in the nation, having five above it in numbers, and six below. But when the borders of the Promised Land were reached its numbers were reduced to 45,400, with four only below it in the scale, one of the four being Ephraim (Numb. xxvi, 48–50; comp. 37). The leader of the tribe at Sinai was Ahira ben-Enan (Numb. ii, 29); and at Shiloh, Pedahel ben-Ammihud (xxxiv, 28). Among the spies its representative was Nahbi ben-Vophsi (xiii, 14).

During the march through the wilderness Naphtali occupied a position on the north of the sacred tent with Dan, and also with another tribe, which, though not originally so intimately connected, became afterwards his immediate neighbor—Asher (Numb. ii, 25–31). The three formed the "camp of Dan," and their common standard, according to the Jewish traditions, was a serpent or basilisk, with the motto, "Return, O Jehovah, unto the many thousands of Israel" (*Targ. Pseudojon.* on Numb. ii, 25).

Jacob's blessing had special reference to the character and achievements of the tribe; that of Moses to the nature of their territory—"*O Naphtali, satisfied with favor, and full with the blessing of the Lord: possess thou the west and the south*" (Deut. xxx, 23). A more literal and more accurate rendering of the Hebrew would be, "Naphtali, replete with favors, and full of the blessings of Jehovah; possess thou the west and Darom." The word רָם, *Yam*, which in the A. V. is translated "west," evidently means "the sea;" that is, the Sea of Galilee, which lay in part within the territory of Naphtali. The Hebrew term דָּרוֹם, *Darom* ("a circuit," from the root דור = Arab. *dâr*, "to go round;" see Gesenius, *Thesaurus*, s. v.), is most probably a proper name equivalent to *Galil* ("a circuit"), or Galilee, the name given in Josh. xx, 7, xxi, 32, and elsewhere, to a district amid the mountains of Naphtali [see GALILEE], of which Darom may have been the older appellation. "The sea and Darom" would thus signify the region by the Lake of Galilee and the mountains to the north of it. Both the Sept. and Vulgate render םי "the sea" (see also the Chaldee rabbi Salomon, Bochart, Ainsworth, Montanus, and others). The possessions allotted to Naphtali are described in Josh. xix, 32–39. The lot of this tribe was not drawn till the last but one. The two portions then remaining unappropriated were the noble but remote district which lay between the strip of coast-land already allotted to Asher and the upper part of the Jordan, and the little canton or corner, more central, but in every other respect far inferior, which projected from the territory of Judah into the country of the Philistines, and formed the "marches" between those two never-tiring combatants. Naphtali chose the former of these, leaving the latter to the Danites, a large number of whom shortly followed their relatives to their home in the more remote but undisturbed north, and thus testified to the wisdom of Naphtali's selection. The territory thus appropriated was enclosed on three sides by those of other tribes. It lay at the north-eastern angle of Palestine. On the east the tribe was bounded by the Jordan and the lakes of Merom and Galilee; on the south by Zebulun; on the west by Asher; and on the north apparently by the river Leontes. Hammath was one of its cities, and it has been satisfactorily identified with the ruins around the warm springs a mile south of Tiberias. Consequently, to Naphtali belonged the whole western shore of the Sea of Galilee. See TRIBE. Naphtali possessed a greater variety of soil, scenery, and climate than any of the other tribes. Its northern portions are the highlands of Palestine. The sublime ravine of the Leontes separates its mountains from the chain of Lebanon, of which, however, they may be regarded as a prolongation. The scenery is here rich and beautiful. The summit of the range is broad, presenting an expanse

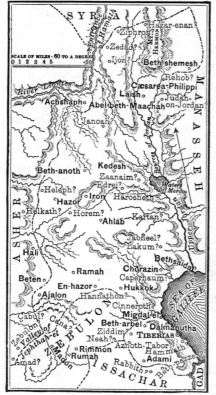

Map of the Tribe of Naphtali.

of undulating table-land, ornamented with broad belts and irregular clumps of evergreen oak, and having here and there little upland plains, covered with verdure, and bordered with thickets of arbutus and hawthorn. In the centre of this park-like region lie the ruins of the sanctuary of the tribe, the northern city of refuge, Kedesh-Naphtali. The ridge rises gradually towards the south, and culminates at Safed, which has an elevation of nearly three thousand feet. Two other peaks, a few miles westward, are one thousand feet higher, and are the loftiest points in Western Palestine (see Van de Velde, Memoir, p. 177). On the western brow of the ridge the tribes of Asher and Naphtali joined, the former having allotted to it the western slopes and narrow plain of Phœnicia (Josh. xix, 24–30). On the east the mountains of Naphtali break abruptly down in gray cliffs and wooded slopes into the rich valley of the Jordan. On the north brow of these slopes stands the massive castle of Hunîn, probably the ancient Beth-Rehob; and twelve miles south of it, commanding the waters of Merom, are the ruins of Kasyûn, which may perhaps mark the site of the capital of the northern Canaanites—Hazor. The Jordan valley, though soft, and in places marshy, is extremely fertile. Here the people of Sidon established at an early period an agricultural colony to supply their city with grain and fruits. The region, or "circuit," around Kedesh was anciently called Galil, a name subsequently extended to the whole of Northern Palestine; and as a large number of foreigners settled among the mountains—descendants of the Canaanites, and others from Phœnicia and Syria —it was called "Galilee of the Gentiles." See GALILEE. According to Josephus (Ant. v, 1, 22), the eastern side of the tribe reached as far as Damascus; but of this—though not impossible in the early times of the nation and before the rise of the Syrian monarchy— there is no indication in the Bible. The question was recently discussed in the Journal of Sacred and Classical Philology by Thrupp and Tregelles (Nos. for 1855, 1856), who both favor the idea of a much wider extension in that direction than has usually been supposed; but their arguments have not sufficed to convince Ewald, who reviews them in his eighth Jahrbuch, and who very justly thinks that the statement of Josephus ought not to be pressed. The southern section of Naphtali was the garden of Palestine. The little plains along the shore of the Sea of Galilee, and the vales that run up into the mountains, are of unrivalled fertility. Josephus describes the plain on the shore of the lake, then called Gennesaret, as an earthly paradise, where the choicest fruits grew luxuriantly, and where eternal spring reigned. His words are not much exaggerated; for now, though more a wilderness than a paradise, its surpassing richness is apparent. The shore is lined with a wide border of oleander; behind this is a tangled thicket of the lote tree; and here and there are clumps of dwarf palms. The plain beyond, except the few spots cultivated, is covered with gigantic thistles (Josephus, War, iii, 10, 8; Robinson, Bib. Res. ii, 402). Thus Naphtali had a communication with the Sea of Galilee, the rich district of the Ard el-Huleh and the Merj Ayûn, and all the splendidly watered country about Banias and Hasbeya, the springs of Jordan. But the capabilities of these plains and of the access to the lake, which at a later period raised Galilee and Gennesareth to so high a pitch of crowded and busy prosperity, were not destined to be developed while they were in the keeping of the tribe of Naphtali. It was the mountainous country ("Mount Naphtali," Josh. xx, 7), which formed the chief part of their inheritance, that impressed or brought out the qualities for which Naphtali was remarkable at the one remarkable period of its history. This district, the modern Belad-Besharah, or "land of good tidings," comprises some of the most beautiful scenery and some of the most fertile soil in Palestine (Porter, p. 363), forests surpassing those of the renowned Carmel itself (Van de Velde, i, 293); as rich in noble and ever-varying prospects as any country in the world (ii, 407). As it is thus described by one of the few travellers who have crossed its mountains and descended into its ravines, so it was at the time of the Christian æra — "the soil," says Josephus (*War.* iii, 3, 2), "universally rich and productive; full of plantations of trees of all sorts; so fertile as to invite the most slothful to cultivate it."

The following is a list of all the localities in the tribe, with their probable identification:

Abel-beth-Maachah.	Town.	*Abil el-Karub.*
Abel-maim.	do.	{See ABEL-BETH-MAA-CHAH.
Adamah, or Adami.	do.	*Damieh?*
Ahlab.	do.	*El-Jish.*
Ajalon.	do.	*Jalun.*
Arbel.	do.	See BETH-ARBEL.
Aznoth-Tabor.	do.	[*Kurn-Hattin*]?
Baal-gad, or Baal-hermon.	do.	{See CÆSAREA-PHILIP-PI.
Beth-anath.	do.	*Ainata.*
Beth-arbel.	do.	*Irbid.*
Beth-shemesh.	do.	*Mejdel esh-Shems.*
Cæsarea-Philippi.	do.	*Banias.*
Capernaum.	do.	*Tell-Hum?*
Chinnereth, or Cinnereth, or Cinneroth.	{Town. Region. Lake.	[*Abu-Shusheh*]? See GENNESARETH.
Chorazin.	Town.	*Bir-Kerazeh?*
Dalmanutha.	do.	*Ain el-Barideh?*
Dan, or Dan-jaan.	do.	See LAISH.
Edrei.	do.	*Tell-Khuraibeh?*
En-hazor.	do.	[*Tell-Hazur.*]
Gennesareth.	Plain.	{N.W. shore of Lake Tiberias.
Gennesareth.	Lake.	*Bahr-Tubariyeh.*
Hammath, or Hammon, or Hammothdor.	Town.	*Hammam?*
Haroseth.	do.	*Tuleil Girsh?*
Hazar-enan.	do.	[*Hasbeya*]?
Hazor.	do.	*Hazur.*
Heleph.	do.	*Beitlif?*
Hermon.	Mount.	*Jebel es-Sheikh.*
Horem.	Town.	*Hurah?*
Hukkoth.	do.	*Yakuk.*
Ijon.	do.	*Tell-Dibbin?*
Iron.	do.	*Khurbet-Yarun.*
Jahneel.	do.	[*El-Janneh*]?
Janoah.	do.	*Kulat Hunin?*
Kartan.	do.	[*El-Katanah*]?
Kedesh, or Kishion.	do.	*Kades.*
Laish, or Leshem.	do.	*Tell-Kadi?*
Lakum.	do.	{[Ruins E. of Tell-Akbara]?
Magdala, or Migdal-el.	do.	*El-Mejdel.*
Nekeb.	do.	See ADAMI.
Rakkath.	do.	See HAMMATH.
Ramah.	do.	*Rameh.*
Rehob.	do.	*Deir Ruheib?*
Shepham.	do.	{See CÆSAREA-PHILIP-PI.
Tiberias.	do.	*Tubariyeh.*
Zaanaim, or Zaanium.	do.	[*Ain Mellahah*]?
Zedad.	do.	[*Jedeida*]?
Ziddim, or Zer.	do.	*Hattin?*
Ziphron.	do.	[*Kaukaba*]?

Three of the towns of Naphtali were allotted to the Gershonite Levites: Kadesh (already called Kedesh-in-Galilee), Hammoth-dor, and Kartan. Of these, the first was a city of refuge (Josh. xx, 7; xxi, 32). It should be noticed that in the list of fortified towns at Josh. xix, 35-38 only sixteen cities are enumerated (or but thirteen if we join as one the names not connected by the conjunction), whereas the sum calls for nineteen. The difference is probably to be made up by including such of those mentioned in the preceding verses as lay within the territory of the tribe and had walls. The enumeration, like the rest in this and the adjoining chapters, is not exhaustive (see Keil, ad loc.).

Naphtali, on account of its position, was in a great measure isolated from the Israelitish kingdoms. Yet it had its share in those incursions and molestations by the surrounding heathen which were the common lot of all the tribes (Judah perhaps alone excepted) during the first centuries after the conquest. One of these, apparently the severest struggle of all, fell with special violence on the north of the country, and the leader by whom the invasion was repelled—Barak

of Kedesh-Naphtali—was the one great hero whom Naphtali is recorded to have produced. How gigantic were the efforts by which these heroic mountaineers saved their darling highlands from the swarms of Canaanites who followed Jabin and Sisera, and how grand the position which they achieved in the eyes of the whole nation, may be gathered from the narrative of the war in Judg. iv, and still more from the expressions of the triumphal song in which Deborah, the prophetess of Ephraim, immortalized the victors and branded their reluctant countrymen with everlasting infamy. Gilead and Reuben lingered beyond the Jordan among their flocks; Dan and Asher preferred the luxurious calm of their hot lowlands to the free air and fierce strife of the mountains; Issachar, with characteristic sluggishness seems to have moved slowly if he moved at all; but Zebulun and Naphtali, on the summits of their native highlands, devoted themselves to death, even to an extravagant pitch of heroism and self-devotion (Judg. v, 18):

"Zebulun are a people that threw away their lives even unto death—
And Naphtali, on the high places of the field."

Naphtali was one of Solomon's commissariat districts, under the charge of his son-in-law Ahimaaz; who with his wife Basmath resided in his presidency, and doubtless enlivened that remote and rural locality by a miniature of the court of his august father-in-law held at Safed or Kedesh, or wherever his residence may have been (1 Kings iv, 15). Here he doubtless watched the progress of the unpromising new district presented to Solomon by Hiram—the twenty cities of Cabul, which seem to have been within the territory of Naphtali, perhaps the nucleus of the Galilee of later date. The ruler of the tribe (נְגִיד)—a different dignity altogether from that of Ahimaaz—was, in the reign of David, Jerimoth ben-Azriel (1 Chron. xxvii, 19). In later times the Naphtalites appear to have resigned themselves to the intercourse with the heathen which was the bane of the northern tribes in general, and of which there are already indications in Judg. i, 33; comp. Isa. ix, 1. The location by Jeroboam within their territory of the great sanctuary for the northern part of his kingdom must have given an impulse to their nationality, and for a time have revived the connection with their brethren nearer the centre. Nominally subject to Samaria, it was separated from it by the plain of Esdraelon, over which so often swept the devastating hordes of the "Children of the East," and the powerful armies of Syria. The usual route of the Syrian expeditions was along the east base of Hermon, and across the Jordan at Jacob's bridge. The Naphtalites in their mountain fastnesses thus generally escaped their devastations. But whenever the enemy marched through the valley of Cœle-Syria, then Naphtali bore the first brunt of the onset. In the reigns of Baasha, king of Israel, and Asa, king of Judah, this tribe was the first to suffer from the invasion of Benhadad, king of Syria, who "sent the captains of the hosts which he had against the cities of Israel, and smote all Cinneroth, with all the land of Naphtali" (1 Kings xv, 20), especially "all its store cities" (2 Chron. xvi, 4). At length, in the reign of Pekah, king of Israel (cir. B.C. 730), Tiglath-pileser overran the whole of the north of Israel, swept off the population, and bore them away to Assyria (2 Kings xv, 29). It is perhaps worth while adding that Tobit belonged to Naphtali, for he tells us that "in the time of Enemessar (or Shalmaneser), king of the Assyrians, he was led captive out of Thisbe, which is at the right hand of that city which is called Kedesh of Naphtali, in Galilee, above Aser;" that he came with his brethren to Nineveh, and that the Most High gave him grace and favor before Enemessar, who made him purveyor to the palace (Tobit i, 5; vii, 3).

But though the history of the tribe of Naphtali ends here, and the name is not mentioned again except in the well-known citation of Matthew (iv, 15), and the mystical references of Ezekiel (xlviii, 3, 4, 34) and of the writer of the Apocalypse (Rev. vii, 6), yet under the title of Galilee—apparently an ancient name, though not brought prominently forward until the Christian æra—the district which they had formerly occupied was destined to become in every way far more important than it had ever before been. After the captivity the Israelites again settled largely in Naphtali, and its southern section became the most densely populated district in Palestine. It became the principal scene also of our Lord's public labors. After his brethren at Nazareth rejected and sought to kill him, he "came down" (Luke iv, 31) from the uplands and dwelt in "Capernaum, which is upon the sea-coast, in the borders of Zabulon and Nephthalim" (Matt. iv, 13). The new capital of Galilee had recently been built by Antipas, and called after the emperor, Tiberias. Other towns — Magdala, Capernaum, Chorazin, and Bethsaida — dotted the shore, which teemed with life and industry. Vast multitudes followed Jesus wherever he went (Mark ii, 1–12; Matt. xiii, 1–23, etc.). The greater number of his beautiful parables were spoken here; and it was the scene of most of his miracles (Porter, Hand-book, p. 430, 431). Then the words of Isaiah were fulfilled as they are quoted and applied by Matthew (iv, 15, 16): "The land of Zabulon, and the land of Nephthalim, the region of the sea [that is, of the Sea of Galilee; the same district called "the sea" in Deut. xxxiii, 23], Peræa [the proper name of the country beyond Jordan], Galilee of the Gentiles [called "Darom" in Deut. xxxiii, 23] — the people which sat in darkness saw great light; and to them which sat in the region and shadow of death light is sprung up." The details of this tribe's history, as well as the account of its sufferings and heroic resistance during the campaign of Titus aud Vespasian prior to the destruction of Jerusalem, are given elsewhere. See PALESTINE.

Naphtali is now almost a desert. A mournful silence reigns along the shores of the Sea of Galilee. There are still a few populous villages among the mountains; but Safet and Tiberias are the only places of any importance within the boundaries of the tribe, and they are fast falling to ruin.

NAPH'TALI, MOUNT (הַר נַפְתָּלִי, Sept. ὄρος Νεφθαλεί, Vulg. Mons Nephtali), the mountainous district which formed the main part of the inheritance of Naphtali (Josh. xx, 7), answering to "Mount Ephraim" in the centre and "Mount Judah" in the south of Palestine. See NAPHTALI.

Naphthar (νέφθαρ, Vulg. Nephthar), the name given by Nehemiah, according to the account in the Apocrypha, to the substance (not the place, as the Vulg.) which after the return from Babylon was discovered in the dry pit where at the destruction of the Temple the sacred fire of the altar had been hidden (2 Macc. i, 36; comp. 19). The legend is a curious one; and it is plain, from the description of the substance— "thick water," which, being poured over the sacrifice and the wood, was kindled by the great heat of the sun, and then burned with an exceedingly bright and clear flame (ver. 32)—that it was either the same as or closely allied to the naphtha of modern commerce (petroleum). The narrative is not at all extravagant in its terms, and is very probably grounded on some actual occurrence. The only difficulty it presents is the explanation given of the name: "Naphthar, which is, being interpreted, cleansing" (καθαρισμός), and which has hitherto puzzled all the interpreters. It is perhaps due to some mistake in copying. A list of conjectures will be found in Grimm (Kurzgef. Handb. ad loc.), and another in Reland's Diss. de vet. Ling. Pers. lxviii. The writer adds, "But many men call it Nephi." The identity of the names with naphtha is obvious. The place from which this combustible water was taken was enclosed by the "king of Persia" (Artaxerxes Longimanus), and

converted into a sanctuary (such seems to be the force of ἱερὸν ποιεῖν, ver. 34). In modern times it has been identified with the large well called by the Arabs Bir-eyûb, situated beneath Jerusalem, at the confluence of the valleys of Kidron and Hinnom. This well, the Arab name of which may mean the well of Joab or of Job, and which is usually identified with En-rogel, is also known to the Frank Christians as the "Well of Nehemiah." According to Dr. Robinson (Bib. Res. i. 332, note), the first trace of this name is in Quaresmius (Elucidatio, etc., ii, 270–4), who wrote in the early part of the 17th century (1616–25). He calls it "the well of Nehemiah and of fire," in words which seem to imply that such was at that time its recognised name: "Celebris ille et nominatus puteus, Nehemiæ et ignis appellatus." The valley which runs from it to the Dead Sea is called Wady en-Nar, "Valley of the Fire;" but no stress can be laid on this, as the name may have originated the tradition. A description of the Bir-eyûb is given by Williams (Holy City, ii, 489–95), Barclay (City, etc., p. 513–16), and by the careful Tobler (Umgebungen, etc., p. 50). At present it would be an equally unsuitable spot either to store fire or to seek for naphtha. One thing is plain, that it cannot have been En-rogel (which was a living spring of water from the days of Joshua downwards) and a naphtha well also. See BITUMEN.

Naph'tuhim (Heb. Naphtuhim', נַפְתֻּחִים, prob. of Egyptian origin, but of uncertain meaning [see below]; Sept. Νεφθαλείμ, Gen. x, 13; Νεφθαλίμ, 1 Chron. i, 11, v. r. Νεφθωσείμ, Νεφθονείμ; Vulg. Nephtheim and Nephthuim), a Hamitic tribe of Mizraim's descendants (Gen. x, 13; 1 Chron. x, 11). The plural form of the name seems to indicate a tribe sprung from Naphteh. Jonathan (Chald. Chron.) interprets it פְּנַטְסְכְנָאֵי, Pentaschœni, i. e. inhabitants of Pentaschœnum, a city in Lower Egypt, twenty Roman miles from Pelusium. Saadias renders it Curamanii. Bochart (Phal. iv, 29) compares Nephthys, the name of an Egyptian goddess, sister and wife of Typhon; which, according to Plutarch (De Iside, c. 38), means τῆς γῆς τὰ ἔσχατα καὶ παρόρια, the ends of the earth or land, i. e. the sea-shore; and so the Coptic interprets Naphtuhim. Michaelis (Spicileg. i, 268 sq.) understands the name to belong to the desert between Egypt and Asia, near the Sirbonian lake, which the Egyptians call the exhalations of Typhon. See also Jablonsky, Opusc. i, 161; Schulthess, Paradies, p. 152. But Miss F. Corbaux ("Rephaim," in the Journ. of Sac. Lit. 1851, p. 151) identifies this tribe with the original Memphites, whose capital, "the dwelling of Ptah," Na-Ptah, is contracted in Hebrew into Naph (נף). "If we may judge from their position in the list of the Mizraites, according to the Masoretic text (in the Sept. in Gen. x they follow the Ludim and precede the Anamim, Ἐνεμετιείμ), immediately after the Lehabim, who doubtless dwelt to the west of Egypt, and before the Pathrusim, who inhabited that country, the Naphtuhim were probably settled at first, or at the time when Gen. x was written, either in Egypt or immediately to the west of it. In Coptic the city Marea and the neighboring territory, which probably corresponded to the older Mareotic nome, is called piphaiat or piphaiad, a name composed of the word phaiat or phaiad, of unknown meaning, with the plural definite article pi prefixed. In hieroglyphics mention is made of a nation or confederacy of tribes conquered by the Egyptians called 'the Nine Bows,' a name which Champollion read Naphit, or, as we should write it, NA-PETU, 'the bows,' though he called them 'the Nine Bows' (or 'nine peoples,' Brugsch, Geogr. Inschr. ii, 20). It seems, however, more reasonable to suppose that we should read (ix) PETU, 'the Nine Bows,' literally. It is also doubtful whether the Coptic name of Marea contains the word 'bow,' which is only found in the forms pite (S. masc.) and phit (M. fem. 'a rainbow'); but it is possible that the second part of the former may have been originally the same as the latter. It is noteworthy that there should be two geographical names connected with the bow in hieroglyphics, the one of a country, MERU-PET, 'the island of the bow,' probably MEROË, and the other of a nation or confederacy, 'the Nine Bows, and that in the list of the Hamites there should be two similar names, Phut and Naphtuhim, besides Cush, probably of like sense. No important historical notice of the Nine Bows has been found in the Egyptian inscriptions: they are only spoken of in a general manner when the kings are said, in laudatory inscriptions, to have subdued great nations, such as the Negroes, or extensive countries, such as Kish, or Cush. Perhaps, therefore, this name is that of a confederacy or of a widely spread nation, of which the members or tribes are spoken of separately in records of a more particular character, treating of special conquests of the Pharaohs or enumerating their tributaries." "It appears more probable, however, to identify the Naphtuhim with the city of *Naphata* or *Napata*, the capital of an ancient Ethiopian kingdom, and one of the most splendid cities in Africa (Strabo, xvii, p. 820; Pliny, *Hist. Nat.* vi, 35; Ptolemy, iv, 7). Strabo states that Napata was the royal seat of queen Candace, a fact which may connect one of the most ancient tribes of the Old Testament with an incident in apostolic history (Acts viii, 27). The city and its territory lay upon the southern frontier of Mizraim, at the great bend of the Nile in Soudan, and having the desert of Bahiuda on the south. The ruins of the city on the banks of the river are extensive and splendid, consisting of pyramids, temples, sphinxes, and sculptures. The modern name is *Meroë* or *Merawe*; though some geographers do not adopt this view (Ritter, *Erdkunde*, i, 591). The connection of this city with Egypt is shown by the character of its ruins. There is a temple of Osiris and another of Ammon; and there is a necropolis on whose gateway Osiris is figured receiving gifts as the god of the lower world. Two lions of red granite of beautiful workmanship were found here, and brought to England by lord Prudhoe, afterwards duke of Northumberland. They are at present in the British Museum (Hoskins, *Travels*, p. 161, 288; Layard, *Nin. and Bab.* p. 157; Kalisch, *On Genesis*, p. 265; Smith, *Dict. of Gr. and Rom. Geog.* ii, 396)."

Napier, *Lord* JOHN, of Merchiston, Scotland, celebrated specially as a mathematician, but noted also as a religious writer, was born in 1550. He studied at the University of St. Andrews, Edinburgh, after which he travelled through France, Italy, and Germany. Upon his return home he applied himself especially to mathematics, in which he secured a great and lasting reputation by his discovery of logarithms. He, however, also devoted some time to the study of theology. His work on the Revelation indicates the most acute investigation. It is a most curious and learned work on the Apocalypse, and is entitled *A plaine Discovery of the whole Revelation of St. John, set down in two Treatises; whereunto are annexed certain Oracles of Sibylla* (5th ed., corrected and amended, Edinb. 1645, 4to). In the dedication he gives some advice to king James on religious matters, and on the propriety of reformation in his own "house, family, and court." It was translated into French, Dutch, and German. Napier was in a certain sense an adventist. He looked for an early consummation of the millennium. The date he believed to be about 1688. Napier died April 3, 1617. See *Life, Writings, and Inventions of John Napier*, by the Earl of Buchan and Walter Minto (1787); Mark Napier, *Memoirs of J. Napier* (1834); Chambers, *Biog. Dict. of Scotsmen*, s. v.; Darling, *Cyclop. Bibliog.* ii, 2152; Allibone, *Dict. of Brit. and Amer. Authors*, s. v.; *Westminster Rev.* July, 1835.

Napkin, the rendering in the A. V. of σουδάριον, Vulg. *sudarium* in Luke xix, 20; John ii, 44; xx, 7; which, however, is rendered "handkerchief" in Acts xix, 12, where it is associated with aprons, σιμικίνθια: they are classed together, inasmuch as they refer to objects of a very similar character. Both words are of Latin origin: σουδάριον = *sudarium*, from *sudo*, "to sweat" (the Lutheran translation preserves the reference to its etymology in its rendering, *schweisstuch*); σιμικίνθιον = *semicinctium*, i. e. "a half girdle." Neither is much used by classical writers; the *sudarium* is referred to as used for wiping the face ("candido frontem sudario tergeret," Quintil. vi, 3) or hands ("sudario manus tergens, quod in collo habebat," Petron. *in fragm. Trugur.* cap. 67); and also as worn over the face for the purpose of concealment (Sueton. *in Neron.* cap. 48): the word was introduced by the Romans into Palestine, where it was adopted by the Jews, in the form סידרא, as = מִשְׁפָּחַת in Ruth iii, 15. The *sudarium* is noticed in the N. T. as a wrapper to fold up money (Luke xix, 20)—as a cloth bound about the head of a corpse (John xi, 44; xx, 7), being probably brought from the crown of the head under the chin—and, lastly, as an article of dress that could easily be removed (Acts xix, 12), probably a handkerchief worn on the head like the *keffieh* of the Bedouin. The *semicinctium* is noticed by Martial, xiv, *epigr.* 153, and by Petron. *in Satyr.* cap. 94. The distinction between the *cinctus* and the *semicinctium* consisted in its width (Isidor. *Orig.* xix, 33): with regard to the character of the σιμικίνθιον, the only inference from the passage in which it occurs (Acts xix, 12) is that it was easily removed from the person, and probably was worn next to the skin. According to Suidas, the distinction between the *sudarium* and the *semicinctium* was very small, for he explains the latter by the former, σιμικίνθιον · φακιόλιον ἢ σουδάριον, the φακιόλιον being a species of head-dress: Hesychius likewise explains σιμικίνθιον by φακιόλιον. According to the scholiast (*in Cod. Steph.*), as quoted by Schleusner (*Lex.* s. v. σουδάριον), the distinction between the two terms is that the *sudarium* was worn on the head, and the *semicinctium* used as a handkerchief. The difference was probably not in the shape, but in the use of the article; we may conceive them to have been bands of linen of greater or less size, which might be adapted to many purposes, like the article now called *lungi* among the Arabs, which is applied sometimes as a girdle, at other times as a turban (Wellsted, *Travels*, i, 321). See APRON; HANDKERCHIEF.

Napkins are used in some Christian churches, e. g. in those of the Romish communion, in the ministration of the Lord's Supper, and the custom is claimed to be of patristic or even apostolic origin. There is certainly evidence that linen and silk cloths were used as far back as the 6th century to cover the eucharistic elements previous to consecration and administration. Oftentimes their "altar napkins," as they were usually called, were richly adorned, and very costly. There is notice of such practice in the pontificate of Vitalienus, in the 7th century. The emperor Constantius, when visiting at Rome the church of St. Peter, presented a piece of gold-embroidered altar napkin: "Super altare pallium auro textile" (*In Vitaliam*, 135, 15). In the 8th century pope Zacharias presented to the same altar a napkin of the same make, enriched furthermore by precious jewels, and ornamented with a representation of Christ's nativity: "Fecit vestem super altare beati Petri ex auro textam, habentem nativitatem Domini Dei et Salvatoris Jesu Christi, ornavitque eam gemmis pretiosis" (Anast. *In Zach.* 219, 5). The expressions "in altari," "super altare," to designate such altar-cloths, make it plain that they were not used like altar-cloths in our day, but were napkins used as we see linen used in the communion service in the churches of to-day. Priers thinks that these cloths served the double purpose of altar-cloths and napkins, covering both altar and the elements consecrated thereon. See Martigny, *Dict. des Antiquités Chrétiennes*, p. 427 sq.

Naples, an Italian province, deserves treatment

here as it was formerly an independent kingdom which, together with Sicily, constituted the territory known as the Two Sicilies, and, occupying the south end of the Italian peninsula, consisted of the continental territory of Naples and the insular dependency of Sicily. Extending over an area of 429 square miles, it contained, in 1881, a population of 1,021,858 souls. The article ITALY has already pointed out the part which this province has played in the history of the booted land, yet it may not be inappropriate to add here a few supplementary notes, to afford our readers a better résumé of the historical data of Naples.

In ancient times this territory was divided into numerous petty states independent of each other, and its inhabitants were of various races. Many of the ancient Italian states arose from Greek colonies which had been founded previous to the 7th century B.C. The ancient historical importance of Naples is attested by the splendor of its cities and the warlike renown of its population. On its conquest by the Romans, the great Neapolitan cities severally adopted the municipal, federative, or colonist form of government, and gradually assimilated their laws and customs to those of their conquerors. After the downfall of the Western Empire Naples was seized by Odoacer, but soon afterwards (A.D. 490) it was subjected by the Goths, and in the following century by the Lombards, who established in it various independent duchies, as Benevento, Spoleto, Salerno, Capua, etc. Most of these were overthrown by invading bands of Arabs, Saracens, and Byzantines. While the last were yet in power, Sergius (A.D. 875), then duke of Naples, is accounted to have been in secret and friendly intercourse with the Saracens, and after direct interference on the part of the pope, a churchman secured for a time control of the country. He, however, fell into the same unhallowed policy as Sergius, and gave the papacy much trouble. Finally, the whole country was subdued by the Normans in the 11th century. They subsequently erected Naples and Sicily into a kingdom, and established a new political, ecclesiastical, and military system. To the Norman dynasty succeeded that of the Hohenstaufen, whose rule was marked by an immense intellectual and social advancement of the people; but the vindictive enmity with which the papal see regarded this dynasty, provoked by the independent policy pursued here by Frederick II (see Lea, *Studies in Ch. Hist.* p. 399, 192), led to the invasion of Naples by Charles of Anjou, who, notwithstanding the heroic resistance of king Manfred, at the battle of Benevento (1266) annihilated the power of the Hohenstaufen. The ascendency of Charles of Anjou was further effectually secured by the treacherous defeat and decapitation (1268) of Konradin, the last male heir to the throne. By the *Sicilian Vespers* (q. v.) the island of Sicily was, however, wrested in 1282 from his grasp, and became an appanage of the Spanish crown. The predominance of the Neapolitan Guelph, or papal party, during the glorious reign of Robert I; the depraved licentiousness of his heiress and granddaughter, Joanna; the fearful ravages committed by predatory bands of German mercenaries and by the plague; the futile attempts of the Anjou sovereigns to recover Sicily; and the envenomed feuds of rival claimants to the throne, are the leading features of the history of Naples during the rule of this dynasty, which expired with the profligate Joanna II in 1435, and was followed by that of Aragon, which had ruled Sicily from the time of the Sicilian Vespers. During the tenure of the Aragon race, various unsuccessful attempts were made by the house of Anjou to recover their lost sovereignty; and the country, especially near the coast, was repeatedly ravaged by the Turks (1480). In fact, after the death of Alfonso, the first ruler of the Aragon dynasty, the country groaned under a load of misery. Wars, defensive and offensive, were incessant; the country was impoverished; and a conspiracy of the nobles to remedy the condition of affairs was productive of the most lam-

entable results, both to the conspirators themselves and to the other influential Neapolitan families. In 1495 Charles VIII of France invaded Naples, and though he was compelled to withdraw in the same year, his successor, Louis XII, with the treacherous assistance of Ferdinand (the Catholic) of Spain, succeeded in conquering the country in 1501. Two years afterwards the Spaniards under Gonzalvo di Cordova drove out the French, and the country from this time became a province of Spain. Sicily had previously (1479) been annexed to the same kingdom. During the two centuries of Spanish rule in Naples, the parliaments which had existed from the time of the Normans fell into desuetude, the exercise of supreme authority devolved on viceroys; and to their ignorance, rapacity, and oppressive administration may safely be ascribed the unexampled misery and abasement of this period. But not only in secular affairs did the Spanish rule prove baneful to this Italian territory. Protestantism had early gained a footing here, and the Spaniards therefore worked zealously to introduce the Inquisition. The repugnance of the people caused it to be delayed for some time; but in the early part of 1564 the institution was finally and firmly established there, and its victims soon increased (see Giannone, *Histoire Civile de Naples*, bk. xxxii, ch. v, § 11). The severe persecutions which now threatened all who were not loyal to Rome caused many to quit their native country, and thus the misery of this unfortunate land was only intensified (see Baird, *Protestantism in Italy*, p. 87, 88; Ranke, *Hist. of the Papacy*, i, 161 sq.). In 1647 the Neapolitans rebelled and renounced their Spanish allegiance, but the Spaniards succeeded in quelling the rebellion. At the opening of last century Naples fell to Austria, and Sicily was secured by Savoy. In 1720, however, both Sicilies were reunited under the Austrian rule, and in 1735 were given to Don Carlos, third son of Philip V of Spain, who ascended the throne as Charles I, and founded the Bourbon dynasty. His reign was marked by equity and moderation; great reforms were effected in the administration of public affairs, science and literature were encouraged, and splendid works of public utility were erected throughout the kingdom. It was during his reign that Pompeii and Herculaneum were discovered. His successor, Ferdinand IV, followed in the course of legislative reform; but on the proclamation of the French Republic (1789) his states were invaded by a French army, and the kingdom of Naples was erected into the Parthenopean Republic (1799). Ferdinand retired with his court to Sicily, and for a brief period enjoyed the restoration of his sovereign rights in Naples; but a second invasion by Napoleon (1806) ended in the proclamation of his brother, Joseph Bonaparte, as king of Naples; and on this latter assuming the Spanish crown, in 1808, that of Naples was awarded to Joachim Murat, brother-in-law of Napoleon. After the defeat and execution of Murat in 1815, the Bourbon monarch, Ferdinand IV, was restored. The liberal insurrectionary movements in Naples in 1821 and 1830 were the forerunners of the Revolution of 1848; and in each case the party of progress was combated by the respective kings with ruthless severity and perfidious concessions, to be cancelled and avenged with sanguinary fury when the disarmed and credulous patriots were at the mercy of the sovereigns. In 1859 the efforts of Garibaldi brought about the Italian war, which finally resulted in freeing all Italian territory from foreign rule, and thus Naples was incorporated as part of the newly-established Italian kingdom. See ITALY. The city of Naples is noted as the place in which the liquefaction of the blood of St. Januarius (q. v.) takes place.

Napoleon, GIACOPPO, a Roman prelate of great note, was the descendant of the distinguished Roman house of the Orsini, and flourished after the opening of the 14th century. He was the head and representative of the Italian cardinals at the time of the decease of pope Clement V in 1314, whom he had greatly disliked and bitterly opposed in all his measures, and exerted himself in the elevation of James of Cahors as pope John XXII. Cardinal Napoleon was a great favorite with the Romans, and therefore enjoyed much influence at the papal court. He was the cardinal of St. Peter's, and known generally only as such. Upon the decease of pope Gregory XI in 1376, the papal conclave had great difficulty in choosing a successor. The cardinal of St. Peter's aspired to the pontificate, and the Romans anxiously looked for his elevation; but the conclave considered him too old, and the archbishop of Bari was elevated as pope Urban VI. During the insurrection consequent upon the election of pope Innocent VII, the cardinal was killed in 1404. See Milman, *Hist. Lat. Christianity*, vii, 16, 477, 478.

Napoli (or *Nauplia* or *Nabulus*), a city of Palestine, supposed to be the ancient SHECHEM (now *Nablus*), and situated about thirty miles north of Jerusalem, is noted in ecclesiastical history as the seat of a Church council held there in 1120, which was convoked by the patriarch Guermondus and king Baldwin, and was attended by ten prelates and several distinguished secular princes. The canons published by this council are lost. Its object was reform in the Church. See Labbé, *Concil.* x, 884.

Napoli, CESARE DI, a Sicilian painter, flourished at Messina about 1583. According to Hackert, he studied in the academy of Polidoro da Caravaggio at Messina, and was one of his most distinguished disciples. He was a perfect imitator of his master's style, and executed some excellent works for the churches.

Narada. See NAREDA.

Naraka, the hell of the Hindûs, according to Manu (q. v.), is divided into twenty-one cells or apartments, each of them 10,000 yojanas in length, breadth, and height. The walls are said to be nine yojanas in thickness, and of so dazzling a brightness that they burst the eyes of those who look at them, even from the distance of 100 yojanas. Each hell is so enclosed that there is no possibility of escape from it. Manu, the celebrated Hindû Moses, gives a general description, dwelling with considerable detail on the tortures which await the impious in the other world. "They will be mangled (in these hells) by ravens and owls; they will swallow cakes boiling hot, walk over burning sands," etc. The Purânas, of course, also furnish an account of Naraka, and they are indeed far more systematic. The Vishnu-Purâna, for instance, not only names twenty-eight such hells, but distinctly assigns each of them to a particular class of sinners. Thus a man who bears false witness, or utters a falsehood, is condemned to the hell *Raurava* (i. e. fearful); one who causes abortion, plunders a town, kills a cow, or strangles a man, goes to the hell *Rodha* (i. e. obstruction); the murderer of a Brahmin, stealer of gold, or drinker of wine, goes to the hell *Súkara* (i. e. swine); and so on. Besides these twenty-eight hells, however, which the Purâna names, we are told of " hundreds and thousands of others in which sinners pay the penalty of their crimes." See HINDUISM.

Narasingha (a Sanscrit word from *nara*, "a man," and *singha*, "a lion," i. e. the *man-lion*) is the name, in Hindû mythology, of the fourth avatar of Vishnû. It is related that Hiranyakasipu, by his penances and sacrifices in honor of Brahma, had obtained as a boon from that deity that he should possess universal monarchy, and be wholly exempt from death or injury from every god, man, or creature in existence. Having now nothing to fear, his arrogance and impiety became insufferable. He had, however, a son of a wholly different character, and remarkable for his piety and virtue. The son, reproving his father's wickedness, once said to him that the Deity was present everywhere. "Is he in that pillar?" said the angry tyrant. "Yes," replied the son. Thereupon Hiranyakasipu, in contempt, struck the pillar with his sword, when the stony mass fell asun-

der, and a being, half man and half lion, issuing from its centre, tore to pieces the impious wretch who had thus insulted and defied the divine Power. See Moor, *Hindû Pantheon*, p. 17, 120; Coleman, *Hindû Mythology*, p. 18 sq.

Narayana is a Sanscrit word of somewhat uncertain etymology, commonly supposed to signify *moving upon the waters*, and applied in the Hindû mythology to the universal divine Spirit, which existed before all worlds (comp. Gen. i, 2). In this sense Narayana may be regarded as another name for Brahm (q. v.), but it is also frequently used as one of the many appellations of Vishnû. See Moor, *Hindû Pantheon*, p. 102.

Narayani is the consort (or *sakti*) of Narayana, considered as Vishnû, and hence a name of Lakshmi (q. v.).

Narbonne, COUNCILS OF (*Concilium Narbonense*), were held from the 5th to the opening of the 17th century. Several of these have an important bearing on the ecclesiastical history of France, and have made the name of this old city famous. Narbonne is situated in Southern France, fifty-five miles from Montpellier, and was called by the Romans *Narbo Martius*. Being only eight miles from the sea, the place was an important commercial centre. It was the second settlement founded in South Gallia by the Romans, and was considered by them an important acquisition, both for its strength and as the key to the road into Spain. Under Tiberius it flourished greatly; the arts and sciences being cultivated with success, and its schools rivalling for a long time those of Rome. There is reason to believe that Narbonne was known to the Greeks 500 B.C. About A.D. 309 it became the capital of Gallia Narbonensis, and contained among other buildings a capitol, theatre, forum, aqueducts, triumphal arches, etc. It was taken in 719 by the Saracens, who planted there a Moslem colony, and destroyed the churches. In 859 it came into the hands of the Northmen. During the 11th and 12th centuries it was a flourishing manufacturing city, but subsequently it fell into comparative decay, and is now entirely destitute of any monument of its former splendor. The first council was held there in 589, Migetius, archbishop of Toledo, presiding, and eight Gallican bishops attending. Its only important action was the confirmation of the acts of the Council of Toledo (589). The second and third council, held there in 791 and 1054 respectively, are of no special import. The fourth, however, was of great consequence, inasmuch as enactments were made against the spread of the Reformation, then beginning to extend on the Continent. This council was held in 1227, Peter, archbishop of Narbonne, presiding; twenty canons were published. The second, third, and fourth relate to excommunicated persons and to the Jews: the latter, in canon 3, are directed to carry upon the bosom the figure of a wheel to distinguish them, and are forbidden to work on Sundays and festivals. Canon 4 orders them to pay yearly at Easter a certain sum for each family, as an offering to the parish church. Canons 13, 14, 15, and 16 are directed against heretics, and charge the bishops to station in every parish spies to make inquiry into heresies and notorious crimes, and to give in their report to them. Count Raymond, the count de Foix, the viscount Besiers, the people of Toulouse, and all heretics and their abettors, were publicly excommunicated, and their persons and property given up to the attacks of the first aggressor (Labbé, *Conc.* xi, 304). The fifth council was held in 1235, and there the archbishops of Narbonne, Arles, and Aix, assisted by several other prelates, by the pope's command, drew up a grand rule concerning the penances, etc., which the preaching friars (lately appointed inquisitors in those parts) should impose upon heretics, i. e. upon those whom they had exempted from prison on account of prompt surrender within the specified time of grace, and voluntary information against themselves and others. They were directed to come to church every Sunday, bearing the cross, and to present themselves to the curate between the singing of the epistle and the gospel, holding in their hands the rod with which to receive chastisement; to do the same at all processions; to be present every Sunday at mass, vespers, and sermons; to carry arms at their own expense in defence of the faith and of the Church against the Saracens, etc. Those heretics who had not so surrendered themselves, or who in any other way had rendered themselves unworthy of indulgence, but who nevertheless submitted to the Church, were ordered to be imprisoned for life; but as their number was so great that it was impossible to build prisons sufficient to contain them, the preaching friars were permitted to defer their imprisonment until they had received the pope's instructions. As for those who refused obedience, who would neither enter the prison nor remain there, they were abandoned to the secular arm without further hearing, as were also the relapsed. The rest of these twenty-nine canons are conceived in the same cruel spirit—a spirit very contrary to that of the Church and of the early councils, and equally wanting in wisdom, mildness, and charity (Fleury, *Hist. Ecclésiastique; Labbé, Conc. xi, 487*). A sixth council, held April 15, 1374, Peter, archbishop of Narbonne, presiding, promulgated twenty-eight canons, aimed at the suppression of provincial councils and the preaching of laymen or excommunicated priests, encouraging heresy hunting, forbidding burial to the excommunicated, and granting an indulgence to those who pray for the pope (Labbé, *Conc.* [App.] xi, 2493). A seventh council, held in 1551, Alex. Zerbinet, vicar-general of the cardinal-archbishop of Narbonne, presiding, promulgated sixty-six canons, of which the first contains a confession of faith, made necessary by the spread of liberalism and the Reformation, and the second to the ninth relate to the qualifications of candidates for orders; the tenth forbids ordination of the diseased, maimed, or stutterers; the thirteenth to the twenty-fourth relate to the life, habits, etc., of the clergy, and betray a great decline of Christianity in the priesthood, as there were canons passed against their frequenting of taverns, gambling, etc.; the fifty-second directs medical men to exhort their patients to confess to their priests (Labbé, *Conc.* xv, 5). An eighth council, held in 1607, archbishop Louis de Vervins of Narbonne presiding, and seven other bishops attending, published forty-nine canons of faith and discipline, similar to those enacted in most of the synods held after the Council of Trent. The most important is the second canon, which forbids any person to possess or read the Scriptures in the French version without the bishop's consent in writing. The thirty-ninth canon forbids dancing, and eating and buying and selling in churches; also forbids dogs in churches; orders cleanliness, etc. (Labbé, *Conc.* xv, 1573). See also Wessenberg, *Gesch. der Kirchenversammlungen*, ii, 59; Hefele, *Concilien Geschichte* (see Index in vol. v); Landon, *Manual of Councils*, s. v.

Narbonni, MOSES (also called *Mestre Vidal*), a Jewish writer of note, was born about 1300. His father, Joshua of Narbonne, was a resident of Perpignan, and being deeply interested in the Jewish, i. e. Maimonidistic philosophy, instructed his son in that branch of science. Vidal cultivated also metaphysics, and admired likewise Averroes or Avicebron (q. v.), whose works he especially commented upon. His knowledge he enlarged by travelling from 1345 to 1362. He was obliged to leave his place when the populace massacred the Jews at the time that the "black death" was ravaging all Europe, and he not only lost all his property, but also, what was more painful to him, all his books. This, however, did not prevent him from finishing his great work at Soria—a commentary on Maimonides's *More Nebuchim*, באור לספר מורה נבוכים (lately edited by Goldenthal [Vienna, 1852]), which he commenced at Toledo in 1355, and which has been rendered into Latin by R. Solomon bar-Maimon, and pub-

lished by Is. Euchel (Berlin, 1791; Wien, 1818: Sulzbach, 1828, etc.). Vidal also translated into Hebrew from the Arabic of Algazali: 1, on the Unity of God:—2, on Divine Providence:—3, on the Utility of Logic. He died in 1362. See Fürst, *Bibl. Judaica*, iii, 17; Grätz, *Gesch. d. Juden*, vii, 352, 353 (Leipsic, 1873); Etheridge, *Introd. to Hebr. Literat.* p. 261; De Rossi, *Dizionario* (Germ. transl.), p. 242 sq.; Lindo, *Hist. of the Jews in Spain*, p. 159; Finn, *Sephardim*, p. 394; Jost, *Gesch. d. Judenth. u. s. Sekten*, iii, 84; Munk, *Mélanges*, p. 592 sq.; and *Philosophie des Juifs* (Germ. transl. by B. Beer), p. 33 sq., 113 sq.; Zunz, *Additamenta zum Leipziger Katalog d. Hebr. cod.* p. 325 sq. (B. P.)

Narcis′sus (Gr. Νάρκισσος, a well-known flower, comp. νάρκη), a Roman, among whose kinsmen (so Auth. Vers. in marg. renders τοὺς ἐκ τοῦ Ναρκίσσου, text has "household") or friends were Christians, whom Paul salutes (Rom. xvi, 11). A.D. 55. Neander (*Pflanz.* i, 384) supposes him to be the same with Narcissus, freedman and private secretary of the emperor Claudius (Pliny *H. N.* xxxiii, 47; Sueton. *Claud.* 38), who exercised unbounded influence over that emperor, but was put to death on the accession of Nero, A.D. 54 (Tacitus, *Annal.* xiii, 1, 57, 65; Dio Cass. lx, 34). But this is inconsistent with the probable date of the Epistle. "Dio Cassius (lxiv, 3) mentions another Narcissus, who probably was living in Rome at that time; he attained to some notoriety as an associate of Nero, and was put to an ignominious death with Helius, Patrobius, Locusta, and others, on the accession of Galba, A.D. 68. His name, however (see Reimar's note, ad loc.), was at that time too common in Rome to give any probability to the guess that he was the Narcissus mentioned by St. Paul. A late and improbable tradition (Pseudo-Hippolytus) makes Narcissus one of the seventy disciples, and bishop of Athens."

Narcissus, ST., bishop of Jerusalem, was born about the year 98. One of the most worthy priests belonging to the clergy of Jerusalem, he was over eighty years old when he was elected to succeed Dolichianus, twenty-ninth bishop from the apostles. Notwithstanding his advanced age, he governed his Church with the zeal and vigor of youth. He presided in 197 at the Council of Cæsarea, in Palestine, where it was decided that the Passover should be celebrated on Sunday. Three evil-disposed Christians accused him of an atrocious crime, and sustained their false slanders by oaths. Although the Church placed no faith in their affirmations, Narcissus profited by this circumstance to follow a long-cherished desire to live in the desert. He left Jerusalem about 199, and no one could discover the place of his retreat. Divine justice, the story goes, soon overtook his persecutors: the first died with his family by the burning of his house; leprosy attacked the second, and the third became blind. Feeling himself called of God to resume the care of his Church, Narcissus left his solitude in 207; and on arriving at Jerusalem he found his see occupied by another bishop, named Gordius, who had been elected during his absence. Both governed this diocese, it is said, until the death of Gordius again left Narcissus sole possessor of the see. Extreme age having at last rendered him unfit for episcopal duties, he took as coadjutor Alexander, bishop of Flaviade, who about 212, with the approval of the clergy and of the people, consented to take charge of the Church at Jerusalem. This is the first example of a bishop being transferred from one see to another, and given as coadjutor to a living bishop, although it is true Alexander was rather the successor of Narcissus, who had simply the honor of the episcopate. He is universally spoken of as a man of austere piety, verging on asceticism. A great number of miracles are attributed to St. Narcissus. He died in the year 216, Oct. 29, which day is kept in his memory by the Roman Catholics. See Butler, *Lives of the Saints*, iv, 309–311; Jerome, *De viris Illustribus*, c. 73; Eusebius, *Hist.*

Eccles. vi, x; Pressensé, *Hist. of the Martyrs and Apologists*, p. 263, 264; Burton, *Eccles. Hist.* p. 449, 464, 479, 480. (J. H. W.)

Nard. See SPIKENARD.

Nardi, ANGELO, an Italian painter of religious subjects, who, according to Palomino, passed the greater part of his life in Spain, flourished about 1645. He studied under Paolo Veronese, and imitated the style of that master in all his works. It is probable that Nardi attained a good degree of excellence, as Philip IV appointed him painter to the court. There are a number of his pictures in the churches at Madrid, among which the most esteemed are the *Annunciation*, of the Society of S. Justo; the *Nativity* and *Conception* in the church of the Franciscans; the *Guardian Angel*, and *St. Michæl the Archangel*, in the church of the Barefooted Carmelites. Nardi died at Madrid in 1660. See Spooner, *Biog. Hist. of the Fine Arts*, ii, 608.

Nardin, JEAN FRÉDÉRIC, an eminent French Protestant divine, was born at Montbéliard in 1687. He went to Germany after having acquired a thorough classical knowledge, and studied theology at the University of Tübingen. He then became successively pastor at Hericourt in 1714 and at Blamont in 1718. He died in 1728. In the unity of a discourse his sermons are models of composition; the arrangement is natural, the language pleasing, the thoughts original and instructive. A collection of his sermons was published under the title *Le prédicateur évangélique, ou Sermons* (4th ed. Paris, 1821, 4 vols. 8vo). See *Cyclop. Bibliograph.* ii, 2153; Hoefer, *Nouv. Biog. Générale*, s. v.

Nareda (or **Narada**) is the name of a Hindû divinity, a son of Brahma and Suraswati. He was regarded as the messenger of the gods and the inventor of the *vina*, or Hindû lute. He is described not only as a wise legislator, but also as an astronomer, a musician, and a distinguished warrior. His name is frequently met with in Hindû mythology See Coleman, *Hindû Mythology*, p. 7.

Nareg (or **Naregatsi**), GREGORY, an Armenian ascetic writer, was born in 951. He was placed while young in the convent of Nareg, of which one of his relatives was the abbot, and remained there until his death, which occurred Feb. 27, 1003. Gregory is now well known by the name of the place where he flourished and distinguished himself. He enjoyed the reputation of a saint among his countrymen. He left a *Collection of pieces on mystical theology*, which is often too obscure through sublimity of style (the best editions are those of Constantinople, 1774, 12mo, and Venice, 1789, 12mo):—*Homilies:—Hymns:—*and a *Commentary on the Canticles.* See Hoefer, *Nouv. Biog. Générale*, s. v.

Nares, Edmund, D.D., an English divine of note, was born of noble and distinguished parentage at London in 1762, and was educated at Westminster School, where he continued till the year 1779, and then removed to Christ Church, Oxford, under the tuition of Dr. Randolph, afterwards bishop of London. After taking his bachelor's degree, he was elected a fellow of Merton College in 1788, but did not take his master's degree till the year following. In 1792 he entered into holy orders, and was soon afterwards presented to the cure of St. Peter's in the East by the college of which he was a member, and there he officiated for some years with great and deserved popularity. He vacated his fellowship in 1797, on his marriage, and soon after was presented with the rectory of Biddenden. In 1814 he was given the professorship of modern history at Oxford, on which occasion he took his degree of D.D. He flourished in this position until after 1816. He died at Biddenden, Kent, Aug. 20, 1841. His publications are, *An Attempt to show how far the Philosophical Notion of a Plurality of Worlds is consistent with the Language of Scripture* (1802, 8vo):—*Sermons composed for Country Congregations* (1803, 8vo):—*A View of the Evidences of Christianity at the Close of the pretended Age of Reason* (in eight sermons preached as Bampton Lectures, 1805, 8vo):—*A Sermon preached at the Primary Visitation of the Archbishop of Canterbury at Ashford* (1806, 4to):—*A Letter to the Rev. F. Stone, M.A., in Reply to his Visitation Sermon* (preached at Danbury, in Essex, 1807, 8vo):—*The Duty and Expediency of Translating the Scriptures into the Current Languages of the East* (a sermon preached before the University of Oxford, 1807, 4to):—*A Jubilee Sermon* (preached Oct. 25, 1809, 8vo):—*Remarks on the Version of the New Testament lately published by the Unitarians* (1810, 8vo):—*Thinks I to Myself* (1811, 12mo; 9th ed. 1813):—*A Sermon* (preached at Oxford before the University on Commencement Sunday, and published at the request of the vice-chancellor, 1814, 8vo):—*Discourses on the Three Creeds,* etc., *with a copious and distinct Appendix to each Set of Sermons* (ibid. 1819, 8vo):—*Life of William Cecil, Earl of Burghley* (ibid. 1828–31, 3 vols. 4to). See Darling, *Cyclop. Bibliogr.* ii, 2155; Allibone, *Dict. of Brit. and Amer. Authors*, s. v.; *Dict. Living Authors*, s. v.

Nares, James, D.M., an eminent English composer of sacred music, was born at Stanwell, Middlesex, in 1715. He was educated as a chorister at King's Chapel, London. In 1734 he was appointed organist at York Cathedral, and in 1756 organist and composer to king George II, and in the following year master of the choristers in the royal chapel, which position he held until 1780. He died in 1783. He composed several anthems and services for the royal chapel, and published *Twenty Anthems in Score,* which is still in constant use in the cathedrals of Great Britain. See Chappell, *Hist. of Music* (Lond. 1874 sq., 4 vols. 8vo).

Nares, Robert, archdeacon of Stafford, a distinguished English divine, son of the preceding, was born in 1753, and was educated at Westminster School and at Christ Church, Oxford, where he was made M.A. in 1778. He entered into holy orders at once, and became successively rector of Sharnford, Leicestershire, preacher of Lincoln's Inn, and assistant librarian at the British Museum. Appointed archdeacon of Stafford in 1799, he became also prebendary of Lincoln, rector of St. Mary's, Reading, canon of Lichfield, and rector of All-Hallows, London Wall. Dr. Nares was editor of the first series of the *British Critic,* a High-Church literary review. He died in 1829. Among his works we notice, *Discourses preached before the Hon. Society of Lincoln's Inn* (Lond. 1794, 8vo):—*A connected and chronological View of the Prophecies relating to the Christian Church* (in twelve sermons, preached 1800 to 1804 at the Lecture founded by the Right Rev. W. Warburton, bishop of Gloucester [Lond. 1805, 8vo]):—*Essays and other occasional Compositions* (Lond. 1810, 2 vols. 8vo):—*On the Influence of Sectaries, and the Stability of the Church* (Lond. 1813, 8vo):—*The Veracity of the Evangelists demonstrated* (1815):—*Sermons on Faith and other Subjects* (Lond. 1825, 8vo). See Darling, *Cyclop. Bibliogr.* ii, 2156; Allibone, *Dict. of Brit. and Amer. Authors*, s. v.

Narni, GIROLAMO DE, a celebrated Capuchin preacher, one of the most noted of Italian pulpit orators, flourished at Rome in the early part of the 17th century. Very little is accessible to us of his personal history; but we know that he was one of the principal promoters of the scheme to support and enlarge the *Propaganda* (q. v.), and that as a man and preacher he was highly esteemed among Romanists. "He commanded," says Ranke, "general reverence by a life which procured for him the reputation of a saint, and in the pulpit he displayed a fulness of thought, solidity of expression, and majesty of delivery which captivated everybody. Bellarmine, on one occasion, as he came from hearing Narni preach, said he thought that one of St. Augustine's three wishes had been granted to him, that, namely, of hearing St. Paul preach" (*Hist. of the Papacy in the 16th and 17th Centuries*, ii, 69, 244).

Narnszewicz, ADAM STANISLAUS, an eminent Polish prelate, noted especially as a historical writer, and surnamed the Tacitus of his country, was born in Lithuania in 1733. He entered the Order of Jesuits in 1748; travelled through Germany, France, and Italy; was appointed professor at Nassau, and became bishop of Smolensk in 1773, and of Luck in 1790. He died at Janowiecz, in Galicia, in 1796. His most important work is a *History of Poland* (Warsaw, 1780 sq., 8 vols.).

Narthex (Gr. νάρϑηξ, signifying a plant with a long stalk, but applied by the Greeks to any oblong figure) is the technical term used in ecclesiastical architecture to designate that part of the early Christian churches which formed an outer division, and may be properly termed an "ante-temple," it being within the church, yet separate from the rest by a railing or screen, and being the part to which catechumens and penitents were admitted. See CHURCH. The term *narthex* is supposed to have been given to it on account of its oblong shape, in this respect resembling a rod or staff (ferula). It was the long and narrow part extending along the front of the church. Here were usually three entrances: one on the west side, another on the south, and another on the north. The chief entrance or great door was at the west, opposite the altar: it was called, after the corresponding gate in the Jewish Temple, the *beautiful* or *royal gate*. The gates and doors consisted of two folding leaves. The doors leading from this part into the nave were appropriated to the various classes of the members, and named accordingly, "the priests' door," "the men's door," etc. In the vestibule, or πρόναος, in the stricter sense, the catechumens and *audientes* had their station. Here also heretics and unbelievers stood. In the πρόπυλα, or portico, funerals were performed; in large churches meetings for ecclesiastical purposes were held there, and in later times the water-font was also placed there, instead of being, as formerly, outside the walls of the church—in the *exedræ*, or buildings adjoining the church. In this fountain persons entering were accustomed to wash their hands and face. See FONT. See Farrar, *Eccles. Dict.* s. v.; Martigny, *Dict. des Antiquités*, s. v.; Coleman, *Christian Antiquities*, p. 723–25; Bingham, *Christian Antiquities*, ii, 286–290; Siegel, *Christl. Alterthümer*, ii, 876; Riddle, *Christian Antiquities;* Walcott, *Sacred Archæol.* s. v.; Neale, *History of the Eastern Church* (Introd.).

Nary, CORNELIUS, an Irish Roman Catholic divine noted for his scholarly attainments, was born in the county of Kildare in 1660, and was educated at Kilkenny, where he graduated in 1684 and took holy orders; he then went to Paris to continue his studies at the Irish College in the French capital, and remained there six or seven years, attaining the principalship of the institution. In 1695 he was honored with the doctorate in philosophy by the University of Cambrai, and was made preceptor of count Antrim. A little later he was appointed to one of the large churches in Dublin, and he died in that city March 3, 1738. Nary wielded an able pen, and wrote much in defence of his faith (1705, 1728, 1730, 3 vols.). His other and more important works are, *The New Testament translated, with Marginal Notes* (Lond. 1705; Dublin, 1718, 8vo):—*The Holy Bible, with Notes* (Dublin, 1719):—*A New History of the World* (Dublin, 1720, fol.). For an estimate of Nary's Scripture versions, see Lewis, *Hist. of Engl. Transl.* p. 356–363 (8vo ed.).

Nasafi, Al, an Arabian theologian and poet, was born at Naksheb or Nasaf in 1069. He was of the Hanefite sect, and has written more than a hundred works, as many in prose as in verse, upon all branches of Mussulman tradition and law. He died at Samarcand in 1143. His principal works are *al-Mandhuma*, a work in verse upon all disputed points among the different Mussulman sects. It exists in manuscript in the Royal Library at Paris, No. 1385, and in the Bodleian

Library at Oxford, No. 1243. The *Mandhuma* has been commented upon, in 1275, by Mahmud ben-Daud, surnamed Alluluï al-Bokhari Alfulhanji. This commentary is likewise found in manuscript in the Royal Library at Paris, No. 1387. Another is in the library at Leyden, in manuscript, No. 359. Nasafi afterwards wrote *Akaïd*, a brief treatise on Moslem doctrine (manuscript, No. 407, in the Royal Library, Paris). There is a commentary of the *Akaïd* by Saadeddin Masud ben-Omar al-Taftazani, which has in its turn been commented upon by Turkish mullahs. We have, lastly, from Nasafi a moral poem in stanzas of five distichs, treating of the vanity of this life. The verses of each stanza turn upon the same rhyme, and this runs successively through all the letters of the alphabet. This poem is found in manuscript in the Royal Library at Paris, No. 1418.

Nasafi, Aühadeddin (or **Ahuadeddin**), AL, an Arabian doctor, who flourished at Shiraz towards the close of the 13th century. The particulars of his life are not known. He wrote a curious poem, in seventy-six verses, upon the principal dogmas of the Sunnites, or orthodox Mussulmans, under the title *Kelamât nesmaha al-Shineh*. This poem was published, with a Latin translation, by J. Uri, under the title *Carmen Arabicum, vel verba doctoris al Nasafi de religionis sunniticæ principiis numero vincta* (Oxford, 1770, 4to).

Nasafi, Hafededdin Abul-Baracat Abdallah, AL, an Arabian doctor, died at Bagdad in 1315. He composed a commentary on the *Mandhuma*, under the title *al-Masfi* or *al-Mosaffi* (in manuscript in the Royal Library at Paris, No. 1386):—*Kenez al-hahaïk*, a treatise on Mohammedan jurisprudence, in manuscript (ibid. No. 473):—*Omdat al-akaïd*, a treatise on metaphysics, in manuscript (ibid. No. 412). See Hoefer, *Nouv. Biog. Générale*, s. v.

Nasalli, IGNACE, an Italian cardinal, was born at Parma Oct. 7, 1750. Early entering the ecclesiastical career, he began his novitiate in the Society of Jesus; when Clement XIV was obliged to suppress this order, Pius VII made him successively prelate of his house, referendary of the two signatures, civil lieutenant of the tribunal of the cardinal-vicar, and one of the members of the ecclesiastical immunity. In 1815 he was sent to Spain to conciliate the people, and to confer with Ferdinand VII upon different communications that this prince had sent to the pope; but on arriving at Barcelona he found that he could not continue his route to Madrid without an express permission from the court. This was one consequence of the notices made in the name of Ferdinand VII on the publication of the pope's bulls in Spain. Nasalli returned to Parma, where he was chargé d'affaires from the court of Rome. In November, 1818, he became apostolic nuncio to the Helvetian Confederation, and Dec. 27, 1819, was declared archbishop of Tyre in partibus. Nominated in July, 1823, minister plenipotentiary to the court of the Netherlands, two months after he was sent to that of Prussia to conclude an agreement between these two governments; he succeeded in this mission to Brussels as well as Berlin. As a reward for his services, Leo XII created him cardinal of the title of Sainte-Agnes without the walls, in the consistory of June 25, 1827. Nasalli, who in 1814 had powerfully contributed to the restoration of the Jesuits, in whose favor he had formerly published several articles, continued in his new position to feel the greatest interest in this order. He died at Rome Dec. 2, 1831. See Hoefer, *Nouv. Biog. Générale*, s. v.; Nicolini, *History of the Jesuits;* Steinmetz, *History of the Jesuitical Order* (see Index in vol. ii). (J. H. W.)

Nas'bas (Νασβάς, Vulg. *Nabath*), the nephew of Tobit who came with Achiacharus to the wedding of Tobias (Tob. xi, 18). Grotius considers him the same with Achiacharus the son of Anael, but according to the Vulgate they were brothers. The margin of the A. V. gives "Junius" as the equivalent of Nasbas.

Nascio, the name of a Roman divinity, who presided over the birth of children, and was accordingly a goddess assisting Lucina in her functions, and analogous to the Greek Eileithya. She had a sanctuary in the neighborhood of Ardea.

Naselli, FRANCESCO, a distinguished Italian painter who devoted himself largely to sacred subjects, was of noble birth, and flourished at Ferrara about the opening of the 17th century. Lanzi says he practiced drawing from the naked model with assiduity, and studied and copied the works of Caracci and Guercino. By such practice he formed an excellent style of his own on a large scale, soft with vigorous coloring and rapid execution, inclining in those of his fleshes to a sunburned hue. He made many excellent copies of the works of those masters which are in the churches of his native place and in private cabinets. Among these is his *Communion of St. Jerome*, from Agostino Caracci. He was exceedingly industrious and persevering, although in easy circumstances and of noble rank. He painted at the Scala in competition with one of the Caracci, Bonone, and Scarsellino; and, according to Lanzi, was deemed not unworthy of those eminent artists. Among his principal works are the *Nativity*, in the cathedral; the *Assumption*, in S. Francesco; and several representations of the *Last Supper*, in private institutions. He died at Ferrara in 1630.

Nash, Frederick K., a Presbyterian minister, was born at Hillsborough, N. C., Feb. 14, 1813. He was a child of the covenant, and many of his relatives were ministers of the Gospel. With such associations and counsellors, he soon identified himself with God's people. During his college course at the University of North Carolina he became converted, and on returning he united himself with the Hillsborough Church. Though young, he was soon after elected a ruling elder. He studied law in his father's office; was admitted to the bar, but while practicing he was led to consider the claims of the ministry. Convinced that it was his duty thus to serve God, he placed himself under the care of Orange Presbytery, N. C., April 24, 1835, and immediately commenced his studies in the Union Theological Seminary at Prince Edward, Va. In 1837 he was licensed, and in 1838 was ordained pastor of Unity Church. This relation was dissolved in 1842. In 1843 he was without any regular charge. During 1844-45 he labored as stated supply for Rutherford and Little Britain churches, in the bounds of Concord Presbytery. In 1846 he began preaching in Centre Church, and there he labored until he died, Dec. 31, 1861. Mr. Nash was an active member of the presbytery and synod. He was chairman of the committee to prepare the resolutions adopted by his presbytery when they seceded from the General Assembly of the Presbyterian Church. He was also appointed as a commissioner to the Southern Assembly. As a preacher, he was clear, practical, and pungent, with the special ability of saying the right word at the right time. See Wilson, *Presb. Hist. Almanac*, 1863, p. 193.

Nash, Michael, a Wesleyan preacher noted as a writer on dogmatic theology, flourished near the close of last century. But little is known of his personal history. Of his works, however, several remain of value to this day. He wrote an able defence of the Christian truths against the attacks of modern infidelity in his *Paine's Age of Reason measured by the Standard of Truth* (1794, 8vo). See *Dict. of Living Authors* (Lond. 1816, 8vo), s. v.

Nash, Treadway Russel, an English divine noted for his antiquarian labors, was born near the opening of last century. He was educated at Worcester College, Oxford, where he took his degree of D.D. in 1758. He was a man of fortune, and died at his seat in Worcestershire in 1811. Dr. Nash published collec-

tions for a history of Worcestershire (2 vols. fol.):—a splendid edition of *Hudibras* (3 vols. 4to):—and some papers in the *Archæologia*. See Allibone, *Dict. of Brit. and Amer. Auth.* s. v.

Nasi, Abraham, BEN-CHIJA, surnamed the *Astronomer*, a Jewish savant of note (in Marseilles), was born in 1065, and died in 1136. He held the office of *Zachib es-Shorta*, præfectus prætorianibus, and was much esteemed for his proficiency in astronomy. His writings are highly valued. He wrote—1, a description of the form of the earth, the arrangement of the firmament, and revolutions of the planets (צוּרַת הָאָרֶץ 'ס:—(וְתַבְנִית כַּדּוּרֵי הָרָקִיעַ וְסֵדֶר מַחֲלַךְ כּוֹכְבֵיהֶם 2, a highly moral work, entitled *Meditations of a Penitent Soul, on reaching the Gates of Repentance* (הֶגָיוֹן 'ס הַנֶּפֶשׁ, edit., with an essay by S. L. Rapaport, by E. Freimann (Leips. 1860), in four parts: (a) on man's origin and wondrous nature; (b) on the duties of life; (c) on the return to God by penitence; (d) on dying well, and on the close of this life:—3, a work on arithmetic and the intercalation:—4, another on the planets, the two spheres, and the Greek, Roman, and Mohammedan calendars:—5, a work on geometry, with an explanation of spherical triangles, and the conversion of angles and circles (*Mishnath ha-Middoth*, the first geometrical work edited in Hebrew by Steinschneider [Berl. 1864]):—6, a treatise on music, and on *Megillath ha-Megaleh*, the volume of the Revealer, on the redemption of Israel, the resurrection of the dead, and the advent of Messiah, the date of which he ventured to predict by an astronomical computation (comp. his חֶשְׁבּוֹן הָעִבּוּר 'ס on the mathematical and technical chronology of the Hebrew, Nazarites, Mohammedans, etc. Printed for the first time and edited, in Hebrew, by H. Filipowski [Lond. 1851]), and which should have taken place, according to him, in the year 5118 of the world = A.D. 1358. See Grätz, *Hist. of the Jews*, vi, 110; Braunschweiger, *Gesch. d. Juden in den Roman. Staaten*, p. 59 sq.; Fürst, *Bibl. Judaica*, i, 6; De Rossi, *Dizionario*, s. v. (Germ. transl.), p. 81; Lindo, *Hist. of the Jews in Spain*, p. 53; Finn, *Sephardim*, p. 189. (B. P.)

Nasi, Jehudah. See HAKKODESH.

Nasiah (בֶּן־הַנְּשִׂיאָה), MOSES BEN-ISAAK, a Jewish writer who flourished some time during the Middle Ages in England. When and where he was born it is difficult to say. All that is known of him is that he wrote a grammar entitled לְשׁוֹן לִמּוּדִים, the preface of which has been published by L. Dukes in *L. B. d. Orients*, 1844, c. 518, 519. Later he wrote a dictionary under the title סֵפֶר הַשֹּׁהַם, in 180 sections, with an elaborate introduction, entitled יְסוֹד שְׂעָרִים, which, based on the labors of Ibn-Chajug (q. v.), Ibn-Ganach (q. v.), and especially Parchon, endeavors to surpass them in completeness and logical arrangement.—Fürst, *Bibl. Jud.* iii, 18; Kalisch, *Hebrew Grammar* (Lond. 1863), ii, 28; L. Dukes, *Ausführliche Notiz über Moses ibn-Nasia, wie auch Auszüge aus seinen Werken*, reprinted in the *Jewish Chronicle*, 1849, No. 37, 38, 41-43, 46, 48. (B. P.)

Nasini, GIUSEPPE NICCOLO, an Italian painter who devoted himself largely to religious art, was born at Siena, according to Della Valle, in 1664. He first studied under his father Francesco, an artist of little note, but afterwards entered the school of Ciro Ferri, and became one of his ablest disciples. He was deficient in correctness of design and dignity of character, but possessed a fertile imagination, and a resolute and commanding execution, which peculiarly qualified him for grand fresco works. At the recommendation of Ciro Ferri, he was employed by the grand-duke of Tuscany to paint in the Palazzo Pitti, from the designs of P. da Cortona, the *Four Ages of Man*, in emblematical subjects, which he finished to the satisfaction of his employer. There are many of his subjects at Siena, Foligno, and Florence, among which his masterpiece is supposed to be the *St. Leonardo*, in Madonna del Pianto, at Foligno. At Rome he was commissioned to paint the ceiling of the Capella Bracciana, the church de SS. Apostolis, and the large Prophets of the Lateran Cathedral, competing with Luti and the first artists then at Rome. Bartsch mentions a print by Nasini, representing the *Virgin and the Infants Jesus and John* in a landscape, with cherubs flying in the air; designed in the style of Ciro Ferri, and engraved with great delicacy, in the manner of P. S. Bartoli. Nasini died in 1736.

Nasir, ISAAC, a famous Jewish philosopher devoted to Cabalism, who flourished about 1100, is the author of a cabalistic work entitled מַסֶּכֶת אֲצִילוּת, the *Treatise on the Emanations*, in which he introduces the prophet Elijah as speaking and teaching under the four names of Eliah ben-Joseph, Jaresiah ben-Joseph, Zechariah ben-Joseph, and Jeroham ben-Joseph, and propounding the system of the Cabala (q. v.). This remarkable treatise was first published by R. Abraham, (Vilna, 1802); it was then reprinted, with all its faults, in Lemberg, 1850; and in 1853 by Dr. Jellinek, in his *Auswahl Kabbalistischer Mystik* (part i, גִּנְזֵי חָכְמָה הַקְּבָּלָה). See Ginsburg, *The Kabbalah*, p. 109, where an analysis of this treatise is given; Fürst, *Bibl. Jud.* iii, p. 18. (B. P.)

Na'sith (Νασίθ v. r. Νασί; Vulg. *Nasit*), one of the Temple servants whose posterity returned from Babylon (1 Esdr. v, 32); evidently the NEZIAH (q. v.) of the Heb. text (Ezra, ii, 54).

Nasmith, David, a Scottish philanthropist, born of respectable parentage at Glasgow March 21, 1799, was distinguished for his zeal in promoting religious and benevolent associations. He founded in 1826 the Glasgow City Mission, and having subsequently visited England, Ireland, France, and the United States of America, he established missions in their principal cities. The London City Mission, which began its operations in 1835 with four missionaries, numbered in 1856 upwards of three hundred. Nasmith also founded the London Female Mission, the Adult School Society, and other similar institutions. He died in 1839. See *English Cyclopædia*, s. v.; Thomas, *Dict. of Biog. and Mythol.* p. 1657.

Nasmith, James, an English divine, was born at Norwich in 1740, and was educated at Benet College, Cambridge. He took the degree of D.D. in 1797; and his last preferment was the rectory of Leverington, in the Isle of Ely, where he died in 1808. Dr. Nasmith published *A Catalogue of Benet College Library:*—an edition of the *Itineraries of Simon and William of Worcester* (8vo):—a new edition of Tanner's *Notitia Monastica*, etc. See Allibone, *Dict. of Brit. and Amer. Authors*, s. v.

Na'sor, THE PLAIN OF (τὸ πεδίον Νασώρ; Vulg. *campus Asor*), the scene of an action between Jonathan the Maccabee and the forces of Demetrius (1 Macc. xi, 67; comp. 63). It was near Cades (Kadesh-Naphtali) on the one side, and the water of Gennesar (Lake of Gennesareth) on the other, and therefore may be safely identified with the HAZOR which became so renowned in the history of the conquest for the victories of Joshua and Barak. In fact the name is the same, except that through the error of a transcriber the N from the preceding Greek word has become attached to it. Josephus (*Ant.* xiii, 5, 7) gives it correctly, Ἀσώρ.

Nassarians, or NOSAIRI, a Mohammedan sect of the Shiite party, formed in the two hundred and seventieth year of the Hegira, received its name from Nasar, in the environs of Kûfa, the birthplace of its founder. These religionists occupy a strip of Mount Lebanon, and are tributary to the Turks. They have about eight

hundred villages, and the chief town is Sasita, eight leagues from Tripoli. Here their sheik resides. Their manners are rude, and corrupted by remnants of heathenish customs, which remind us of the Lingam worship. Although polygamy is not allowed, yet on certain festival days they permit the promiscuous intercourse of the sexes. They are divided, after the manner of the Hindûs, into numerous castes, which oppress one another. They profess to be worshippers of Ali, believe in the transmigration of souls, but not in a heaven or hell. They are friendly to Christians, and observe some of their festivals and ceremonies, but without understanding their meaning. A spiritual head, *sheik khalil*, directs their religious concerns, and travels among them as a prophet. The opinion, formerly current, that this sect were Syrian Sabians, or disciples of St. John, has been completely exploded by Niebuhr, and by the accounts of Rousseau, the French consul at Aleppo. See D'Herbelot, *Bibliothèque Orientale*, s. v. See CHRISTIANS OF ST. JOHN.

Nassau, until the recent re-establishment of the German Empire an independent duchy of Germany, but now constituting the southwestern part of the Prussian province of Hesse-Nassau, is situated between 49° 50' and 50° 50' N. lat., and 7° 30' and 8° 45' E long. It is bounded on the west and south by the Main and the Rhine, the Prussian-Rhenish provinces, and the former grand-duchy of Hesse; on the east by the extinct Hesse and Frankfort territories; and on the north by the province of Westphalia. It covers an area of 1808 square miles, with a population of 468,311 in 1866. The country possesses very great physical advantages. In its southern districts, nearly the whole of its area is occupied by the Taunus Mountains, whose highest point, the Great Feldberg, attains an elevation of about 2750 feet. This range includes within its boundaries the fertile valleys known as the Rheingau. The northern part of the duchy includes the barren highlands of the Westerwald, whose most considerable peak, the Salzburger Head, is nearly 2000 feet high. Besides the Rhine and the Main, which are the boundary rivers, Nassau is traversed from east to west by the Lahn, which becomes navigable at Weilburg, and is augmented by the confluence of numerous other streams, as the Weil, Ems, Aar, Dill, Elbe. The productiveness of the soil is proved by the excellent quality of the numerous vegetable products, which include corn, hemp, flax, tobacco, vegetables, and fruits, especially grapes, which yield some of the best of Rhenish wines. In the more mountainous districts, iron, lead, copper, and some silver are obtained, also much good building-stone, marble, and coal; the chief mineral wealth is, however, derived from the numerous springs, which, directly and indirectly, bring the province a clear annual gain of nearly 100,000 dollars. The most noted of these springs, of which there are more than one hundred, are Wiesbaden, Weilbach, Langen-Schwalbach, Schlangenbad, Ems, Fachingen, Selters, Soden, and Geilnau.

In tracing the history of Nassau to its earliest origin, we find that the districts now known by that name were anciently occupied by the Allemanni, and on the subjugation of the latter people by the Franks became incorporated first with the Frankish, and next with the German Empire. Among the various chiefs who raised themselves to independent power in this portion of the Frankish territories, one of the most influential was Otto of Laurenburg, brother of king Conrad I, who became the founder of two distinct lines of princes. The heads of these lines were Walram and Otto, the sons of count Henry I, who, in 1255, divided the land between them. Walram II, the elder, was the progenitor of the house of Laurenburg, which, towards the close of the 12th century, assumed its present name of Nassau from the name of its chief stronghold; while Otto, the younger, by his marriage with the heiress of Gelders, founded the line of Nassau-Gelders, whose last male representative died in 1423, but which still survives through a female branch in the family now occupying the throne of the Netherlands. This junior branch of the house of Nassau, by inheritance from a collateral representative, acquired possession, in 1544, of the principality of Orange; and since that period the representatives of the Otto line have been known as princes of Orange (q. v.). The Walram line, which in 1292 gave an emperor to Germany in the person of Adolf of Nassau, was subdivided by the descendants of that prince into several branches, until, by the successive extinction of the other lines, the Nassau-Weilburg family, which last reigned over the duchy, was left, in 1816, the sole heir and representative of the Walram dynasty in Germany. Nassau was declared a duchy in 1806, and in 1817 duke William granted a new constitution; but during the first sittings of the assembly dissensions arose between the ducal government and the people's representatives, which resulted in an estrangement of ruler and ruled, and were not quieted until 1834. In 1836 Nassau joined the German Zollverein, and its material prosperity thereafter rapidly developed. In 1839 the last duke of Nassau came to the throne in the person of Adolphus William. He experienced the revolutionary days of 1848, but remained in possession of his territory until 1866, when Prussia deposed him because of his alliance with Austria. He is now a pensioner of the Prussian government.

Christianity was introduced among the people of Nassau at a very early date, probably during the period of Rome's world rule, after its emperors had become Christians. The presbyter Lubertius, who flourished in the 4th century, preached in these domains; but no stronghold was made here for Christianity until the days of Boniface in the 8th century, about 739. In the 10th and 11th centuries many churches were built and Christianity was fortified by schools. The people, however, were but poorly educated, and at the dawn of the Reformation this country was far behind other German territories. About 1530 Nassau declared for the new faith, and in 1534 joined the Smalcald league. At first decided Lutherans, the Nassau Protestants gradually turned over to the views of the Reformed Church, and in 1582 the theologians of Nassau, protesting against the monster Ubiquity in the Form of Concord, were induced to adopt the Heidelberg Catechism, and in consequence of its relation to the house of Orange, Nassau was brought to accept the ecclesiastical system which prevailed in the Netherlands. (See Staubing, *Kirchen-u. Ref.-Gesch. Oranien-Nass. Lande* [Hadam, 1804]; Hase, *Ch. Hist.* p. 413.) In 1817 the Protestants of Nassau constituted an *Evangelical United Church,* and a theological seminary is supported at Herborn, where all who look towards the ministry are obliged to spend one year after finishing a university curriculum. Nearly half the population of Nassau belong to the Roman Catholic Church, which is under the ecclesiastical jurisdiction of the bishop of Limburg, who is assisted by a board of commissioners, located at Eltville, on the Rhine. There are also about 8000 persons who belong to the Jewish and other persuasions. Ample provisions are made in the territory for popular education, in furtherance of which there are upwards of 700 elementary schools, with about 1000 teachers, 10 normal schools, a gymnasium, various training, polytechnic, military, and other educational institutions. See Vogel, *Beschreib. d. Herzogth. Nassau* (Wiesb. 1843–44); Schliephake, *Gesch. v. Nassau* (ib. 1864–70, 3 vols. 8vo).

Natal, a British colony, and noted seat of an Anglican bishopric, is situated on the south-east coast of Africa, about 800 miles east-north-east of the Cape of Good Hope, between the 29th and 31st parallels of south latitude. Its north-eastern boundary is the Tugela, or Buffalo River, which divides it from Zululand, and its southwestern boundary is the Umzimculu, separating it from Kaffraria proper. A lofty and rugged range of mountains, called the Quathlamba, or Drakenberg, divides it from the Free State and Basutuland, and it contains a well-defined area of about 16,145 square miles, according to the British parliamentary accounts of 1872, with a population of 250,352, of whom 17,821 are whites, and 5227 Indian coolies, the remainder being natives of the soil, called Zulus, or Zulu-Kaffirs (see KAFFIRS), remnants of the different tribes which originally occupied the territory, but by persecution and warfare were dispersed, and only came together again since the British occupation of Natal.

History.—The region now forming the colony of Natal derives its name (*Natalis Jesu*) from its being discovered by the Portuguese on Christmas-day, 1497. It was visited and favorably reported upon towards the close of the 17th century, and later by Dampier, Woods Rogers, and several Dutch navigators. Subsequently a Dutch expedition purchased the territory from some native chiefs. Its colonization was not fairly projected, however, until about 1822, when it was visited by several white traders from the Cape, who found the country in possession of the Zulu chief Chaka, who ruled in a most sanguinary manner over all the tribes, from the Umzimculu to the St. Lucia River. He was killed and succeeded by his brother Dingaan in 1838; but the latter having treacherously murdered a party of emigrant Dutch Boers, who had paid him a friendly visit by invitation to buy land, he was attacked and finally destroyed by the Boers, who at that time had emigrated from Cape Colony in large numbers, and who made his brother Panda paramount chief in his stead, and then settled themselves down in the country as his lords and masters. The British government, however, now interfered; and after a severe struggle on the part of the Boers, the country was formally proclaimed a British colony on May 12, 1843, since which time it has progressed very satisfactorily, and bids fair to become one of the most valuable dependencies of the British crown on the African continent. Natal is governed by a lieutenant-governor, nominally subordinate to, although really independent of, the governor of the Cape, and has recently received a constitution somewhat similar to that of Cape Colony. Municipal institutions have been granted to the principal towns.

Climate, etc.—The coast region, extending about twenty-five miles inland, is highly fertile, and has a climate almost tropical, though perfectly healthy. Sugar, cof-

Natal from the Sea.

fee, indigo, arrow-root, ginger, tobacco, and cotton thrive amazingly, and the pine-apple ripens in the open air with very little cultivation. The midland terrace is more fit for the cereals and usual European crops, while on the higher plateau, along the foot of the mountains, are immense tracts of the finest pasturage for cattle and sheep. Coal, copper, iron, and other minerals are found in several places; and there is no doubt when the great mountain-range is properly explored that it will be found very rich in mineral wealth. Since the discovery of diamonds near the Vaal River, large and valuable gems of this class have been exported through Natal. The climate is very salubrious; the thermometer ranges between 90° and 38°, but the heat, even in summer, is seldom oppressive. The mean temperature at Pietermaritzburg, the capital, is 3.5° above that of Cape Town. The winter begins in April and ends in September; the average number of rainy days being thirteen. In the summer season the thunder-storms are very frequent and severe. The annual rainfall on the coast is about thirty-two inches. Inland, it varies a good deal in different districts, and is greatest in summer. The south-east is the prevailing wind here in the summer months, as in Cape Colony. Occasionally the sirocco from the north-west is felt, which generally terminates in a thunder-storm.

The natives of Natal, belonging to the same ethnological family as the Kaffirs, are split up into numerous petty tribes, each tribe having a chief of its own, who, however, is amenable to British authority. Constant jealousies and animosities exist among these tribes, and nothing but fear of the British government prevents them from destroying each other. The greater part of the natives in this colony dwell on locations assigned them by government, and over each location is placed a white magistrate, to keep order, to collect the annual tax, which is seven shillings per hut, settle their numerous disputes, etc. When cases presented by the natives are not satisfactorily settled by the magistrates, they have the privilege of appealing to the lieutenant-governor of the colony. These Zulus of Natal are a pastoral people, and disinclined to agricultural pursuits, yet under the influence of the British they have extensively engaged in them, and are fast developing the

A Zulu Group.

resources of the country. They are trusted by the Europeans, and even favored, except by the Boers.

Evangelization.—Much has been done for the civilization of the natives of Natal. As early as 1835 missionaries of the American Board for Foreign Missions commenced to preach Christ to them, but the severe persecutions which all Europeans suffered until the British made Natal a colonial possession prevented all successful propagation of the Christian faith for a long time. After the colonial establishment of Natal the Wesleyans went out in force, and greatly promoted the work inaugurated by the American Missionary Society agents, who continued their labors with renewed vigor, and to this day remain in that field. In 1845 the Norwegian Missionary Society sent her missionaries to this territory, and in 1847 Berlin missionaries augmented the already strong force of Christian workers. Another German missionary society, that of Hermannsburg, in Hanover, sent helpers in 1854, and soon found several stations wherein to preach Christ. Still more recently missions in Natal were founded by the Anglican establishment, through the agency of the now world-renowned rationalist, bishop Colenso, in 1853. His efforts secured much interest for Natal, and caused it to be made a diocese, and he himself became its superintendent in 1855. His departure from the orthodox faith caused his removal; but he still continues his interest in colonial missionary labors, however inconsistent his efforts for the propagation of the Christian faith may seem with his avowed theory of Scripture interpretation. Very recently the Missionary Society of the Reformed Church of Holland has established several stations, and it is also meeting with much success in spreading Christianity among the Zulus. The American mission, which is served chiefly by Presbyterian and Congregational ministers, in 1870 maintained nineteen stations and out-stations, with twelve churches, and about five hundred native members. The Roman Catholics also labor in Natal in force, and maintain a bishopric. Aside from conversions which have been effected, the natives are not only benefited, at least indirectly, in their morals, but their mental cultivation has been greatly improved. Schools are numerous and well patronized. In 1870 there were seventy-nine schools sustained by the British colonial government, with an average attendance of 1797 pupils, besides a large number of excellent schools maintained by the missionaries in different parts of the country, prominent among which are the American mission schools in the coast range, and those of the Church of England, of the Wesleyans, and of the Free-Church of Scotland. The colonial schools are under the control of a superintendent of education, and Natal, it is said by those who are competent eye-witnesses, boasts a superior school system. See Mann, *The Colony of Natal* (Lond. 1860); Muire, *The British Col. of Natal* (1869); Grout, *Zululand, or Life among the Zulu-Kaffirs of Natal and Zululand* (Phila. 1865, 12mo), especially valuable on mission work up to 1860; Chapman, *Travels in the Interior of South Africa* (Lond. 1868, 2 vols. 8vo), vol. i, ch. i sq.; Grundemann, *Missions-Atlas*, pt. i, § 15; Newcomb, *Cyclop. of Missions*, s. v.; *The Quarterly Review* (London), vol. lviii, art. i.

Natal days, a name applied in early ecclesiastical language, especially in martyrologies and funerary inscriptions, not only to the natural, but also to the spiritual birth. See NATALITIA. The term was also used in many ways, thus: (1) *Natales episcopatus*, the days of a bishop's ordination, observed as an annual festival. (2) *Natalis Christi*, day of our Lord's birth (Christmas). See CHRISTMAS. (3) *Natales martyrum*, anniversaries of the martyrs; their sufferings and death being called their nativity. (*Commemorations of martyrs* may be traced back to an early date. The feasts of the Innocents and of the Maccabees were celebrated before the time of Chrysostom. See MARTYRS, FESTIVALS OF THE.) (4) *Natales urbium*, the two annual days kept in memory of the foundation of the two great cities,

Rome and Constantinople. (5) *Natales genuini*, in memory of the emperor's birthday, and (6) *Natales imperii*, in memory of his inauguration. Ordinary birthdays were forbidden to be celebrated in Lent. (7) *Natalis calicis*, the Thursday of Easter. (8) The day of baptism was also called *Nativitas spiritualis*. See Eadie, *Eccles. Cyclop.* s. v.; Bingham, *Antiquities of the Christian Church*, ii, 158, 1124, 1170; Aschbach, *Kirchen-Lex.* iv, 296; Riddle, *Christian Antiquities* (see Index); Siegel, *Christl. Alterthümer* (see Index in vol. iv); Martigny, *Dictionnaire des Antiquités*, s. v. Natale.

Natale (Latin *Natalis*), IERONIMO, a Spanish Jesuit, was born at Majorca in 1507. An intimate friend of Ignatius Loyola, he entered the Society of Jesus in October, 1545. After having executed several commissions at the Council of Trent, in Africa, and in Sicily, he established at Messina a college, in which he taught theology and Hebrew from 1552. He was afterwards charged by the founder of his order to promulgate in Sicily, Portugal, and Spain the constitutions of the society. Nov. 1, 1554, he was made vicar-general to Ignatius Loyola. Pope Julius III designated Natale in the following year to accompany cardinal Morone, legate of the holy chair, to the Diet of Augsburg. June 19, 1558, after having declined the chief command of the society, which was given to Lainez, he was nominated assistant for Germany and France, and undertook in the interest of the order several missions to Spain under Philip II. In March, 1566, he energetically sustained before the Diet of Augsburg the rights of the Church and of the holy chair, and on his return to Rome solicited, as vicar-general of Francis Borgia, the confirmation of the Order of Ignatius from Gregory XIII. At last he spent several years in Flanders, where he consecrated his time to the work by which he is principally known, and which is much sought after by amateurs for the engravings with which it is ornamented. He died at Rome April 3, 1580. His principal work is, *Adnotationes et meditationes in Evangelia quæ in sacrosancto missæ sacrificio toto anno leguntur, cum eorumdem Evangeliorum concordantia historiæ integritati sufficienti. Accessit et index historiam ipsam Evangelicam in ordinem temporis vitæ Christi distribuens* (Antw. 1594, fol., engraved title, 595 pages). This work, of which the price is still very high, is ornamented with 153 plates engraved upon copper by Jerome brothers, Wierix, and Collaert, from designs by Martin de Vos and Bernardin Passeri. These engravings, copied and engraved upon steel, have served to illustrate a *Vie de Jésus Christ*, by abbot Brispot (Paris, 1853, 2 vols. fol.), at the head of which is found a notice of Natalis and an explanation of the engravings:— *Scholiæ in Constitutiones et Declarationes sancti Patris nostri Ignatii et admonitiones pro superioribus* (preserved in MS. form in the library of the Jesuits at Rome). See Hoefer, *Nouv. Biog. Générale*, s. v.

Natali, Carlo, called *Il Guardolino*, an Italian painter and architect who devoted himself largely to sacred subjects, was born at Cremona about 1590. He studied successively under Andrea Mainardi and Guido Reni; and subsequently resided during a number of years at Rome and Genoa, observing all that was most valuable, and exerting his own talents in the art. Among his best paintings is his *St. Francesca Romana*, in the church of S. Gismondo at Cremona, which Lanzi ranks above mediocrity. Natali did not execute many works in painting, being principally devoted to architecture. His edifices are principally at Genoa and Cremona; but none of them are mentioned. He was living in 1683.

Natali, Francesco, a painter who devoted himself mostly to sacred art, was the brother of Giuseppe, whose style he adopted, and whom he nearly approached, and even surpassed in dignity. He executed many works on a large scale for the churches in Lombardy and Tuscany. He was also much employed at the courts of the dukes of Massa, Modena, and Parma, in which latter city he died in 1723.

Natali, Gio. Battista, an Italian painter and architect, the son of Carlo Natali, devoted himself to secular and religious subjects. He was born at Cremona about 1630, and was instructed in both arts by his father, and afterwards went to Rome for improvement, where he pursued his studies under P. da Cortona. On returning to Cremona he was employed for the churches, and established a school of painting upon the principles of Cortona, although without many followers. There is a large painting by him in the Predicatori displaying some skill, representing the *Holy Patriarch burning heretical books*, which Lanzi says is not unworthy of a follower of Cortona. As an architect, none of his works are mentioned. He died about 1700.

Natali, Giuseppe, an eminent painter of sacred and secular art, was born at Casal Maggiore, in the Cremonese territory, in 1652. According to Zaist, possessing a natural genius for the art, he went to Rome, notwithstanding the opposition of his father; and from thence to Bologna, where he assiduously studied the works of Dentone, Colonna, and Mitelli, the most famous perspective and architectural painters of the age. He flourished precisely at the period which the architectural painters consider the happiest for their art. Lanzi says, "He formed a style at once praiseworthy for the grandeur and beauty of the architecture, and the elegance of the ornamental parts judiciously introduced. He gratifies the eye by presenting those views which are the most charming, and gives it repose by distributing them at just distances. In his grotesques he retains much of the antique, shunning all useless exhibitions of modern foliages, and varying the painting from time to time with small landscapes. The softness and harmony of his tints elicited great commendation." Natalis found abundant employment, and decorated many churches and public edifices. He also executed a great many oil paintings, which were in the highest repute. He died in 1722.

Natalia, a term used in the early Church for the days on which martyrdom was suffered by some of her number, as if they were birthdays; and just as the heathens used to have festivities on memorable days, so these early Christians used to celebrate annually such birthdays of martyrs into the kingdom of God. The graves of the departed were visited, and after a time festivities were allowed. See Hase, *Ch. History*, p. 68. See also NATALITIA.

Natalis THE THEODOTIAN. See THEODOTIUS.

Natalis (NOEL), **Alexander**, a distinguished Roman Catholic theologian, was born at Rouen Jan. 19, 1639. He studied at first in the Dominican school of his native city, and joined that order in May, 1655. His talents having attracted the attention of his superiors, he was sent to Paris, where he first studied, then taught, theology, and received the degree of D.D. in 1675. Colbert appointed him to write a history of the Church, and in consequence he published in 1677 the first volume of his *Selecta historiæ ecclesiasticæ capita et in loca ejusdem insignia dissertationes historicæ, criticæ, dogmaticæ*, the twenty-fourth and last volume of which appeared in 1686. It extends down to the close of the Council of Trent. It is written in the spirit of Gallicanism, learnedly, but in a dry, scholastic style. This was followed by the *Historia ecclesiastica Veteris Novique Testamenti* (Paris, 1699; Lucca, 1754; Bingen-on-the-Rhine, 1785-90), one of the most important works of the Gallican school, but the character of which is more dogmatic and polemic than historical. The free, Gallican spirit of this work caused it to be condemned by pope

Innocent XI, who by a bull of July 13, 1684, forbade the reading of Natalis's works under penalty of excommunication. Natalis, however, did not retract, but defended his work, and it was finally withdrawn from the Index by pope Benedict XIII. In 1706 Natalis became provincial of his order. His sight began to fail him in 1712, and, becoming entirely blind, he was obliged to discontinue his labors. He died in the convent of the Jacobins at Paris, Aug. 21, 1724. His principal works, besides the above, are, *Theologia dogmatica et moralis* (Paris, 1693, 1703, 1743, 1768):—*Præcepta et regulæ ad prædicatores verbi divini informandos:—Expositio literalis et moralis* (S. S. Evangeliorum), etc. (editio novissima, Paris, 1769, 2 vols. 4to), etc. See Herzog, *Real-Encyklopädie*, x, 222 sq.; Mosheim, *Eccles. Hist.* vol. ii; Hase, *Ch. Hist.* p. 8; Schaff, *Hist. Christian Ch.* i, 28; Hagenbach, *Hist. Doctr.* ii, 199, 206; *Ch. Remembrancer*, 1862, p. 35; *Bibliotheca Sacra*, vii, 59. (J. H. W.)

Natalis, Cæcilius, is the name of the person who maintains the cause of paganism in the dialogue of Minucius Felix entitled *Octavia*. See MINUCIUS. Various conjectures have been made as to who this Natalis was, but there are no sufficient data for deciding the question.

Natalis, Michael, a Flemish engraver and student of sacred art, was born at Liege about 1589. After acquiring the elements of design under Joachim Sandrart, he visited Antwerp, and studied engraving under Charles Mallery. From thence he went to Rome, and adopted the style of Cornelius Bloemært, which he followed with some success. He engraved a number of plates after the great Italian masters; also a part of the plates in the Giustiniani Gallery, in concert with Regnier Persyn, Theodore Matham, and others. On returning to Flanders he was invited to Paris, where he resided some time. His plates are executed with the graver in a free, open style, but are deficient in taste. His drawing is frequently incorrect, and the effect is usually cold and heavy, but his strokes are clear and regular, and he handled the burin with great facility. His portraits are his best productions. A list of his principal plates is given in Spooner's *Biog. Hist. of the Fine Arts*, ii, 609.

Natalitia, i. e. *natal days* of the saints. Tertullian and other ancient writers use the words *natalitia* and *natales* in speaking of martyrs, not meaning their natural birth, but their nativity to a glorious crown in the kingdom of heaven. See above, NATAL DAYS. In this sense, Tertullian says St. Paul was born again by a new nativity at Rome, because he suffered martyrdom there. He explains it on the ground that the death of a martyr is not properly a death, but an endless life; for the sake of which all things are to be endured, and death itself to be despised. See Tertullian, *De Cor. Mil.* cap. 3; *Oblationes pro defunctis, pro natalitiis, annua die facimus; Conc. Laod.* can. 51, Μαρτύρων γενέθλια; Ambrose, *Hom.* 70; Bingham, *Antiquities of the Christian Church*, ii, 1161; Walcott, *Sacred Archæology*, s. v.

Natansohn, JOSEPH SAUL, a rabbi of note, was born in the year 1808. He received a strictly religious education in conformity with the traditions of his family, and even as a youth showed great mental ability and rare diligence. When hardly nineteen years of age he composed, together with his brother-in-law, the deceased Marcus Wolf Ellinger, a learned work entitled מִפְרָשֵׂי הַיָּם, novellas on the Talmudical treatise *Baba Kama* (Lemberg, 1828), which at the time received the highest acknowledgment from rabbinical scholars. He finally entered the rabbinate, not for enjoyment, but rather to devote himself zealously to rabbinic studies. Indeed he spent his whole life in the study of rabbinic lore, the fruit of which were several learned works, as מָגֵן גִּבּוֹרִים מְאִירַת עֵינַיִם (Wilna, 1839):—, comments upon the Orach Chajim (the Jewish ritual), in two

parts (Lemberg, 1832–37):—הַגָּהוֹת חֹשׁ "ס, critical notes on the Talmud, to be found in the edition of the Talmud (Slobuta, 1824–30; Vienna, 1832–46):—מְעַשֵּׁה אלפס, comments upon Alfasi's *Sefer ha-Halachoth*, published with Alfasi's work and commentaries (Presburg, 1836). When in the year 1840 religious disputes began in the Jewish community of Lemberg, he sided with the conservatives, but when the strife became more intense and reckless, he withdrew from all participation in the matter, and devoted his time to study. From all parts of the world the most difficult questions were sent to him. Being considered the highest authority in ritual questions, his opinion was sought for from afar off. In the year 1858 Natansohn was appointed to the rabbiship of Lemberg, which position he held until his death, March 3, 1875. See Fürst, *Bibl. Jud.* iii, 28 sq.; *Jewish Messenger*, New York, 1875. (B. P.)

Nataph. See STACTE.

Natatorium (a *swimming-place*), a term used by some writers when describing the baptistery.—Farrar, *Eccles. Dict.;* Bingham, *Antiquities of the Christian Church*, ii, 310.

Na'than (Heb. *Nathan'*, נָתָן, *given*, i. e. by God; Sept. Ναθάν, but in the later books Νάθαν, and so Josephus, *Ant.* vii, 3, 3; but Ναθάνα of the prophet, *Ant.* vii, 4, 4, etc.), the name of five or six men.

1. The eleventh in descent from Judah, being the son of Attai and father of Zabad (1 Chron. ii, 36). B.C. post 1612.

2. An eminent Hebrew prophet in the reigns of David and Solomon. If the expression "first and last," in 2 Chron. ix, 29, is to be taken literally, he must have lived late into the life of Solomon, in which case he must have been considerably younger than David. At any rate he seems to have been the younger of the two prophets who accompanied him, and may be considered as the latest direct representative of the schools of Samuel. A Jewish tradition mentioned by Jerome (*Qu. Heb.* on 1 Sam. xvii, 12) identifies him with the eighth son of Jesse (2 Sam. v, 14); but of this there is no probability. He first appears in the consultation with David about the building of the Temple. B.C. cir. 1043. He begins by advising it, and then, after a vision, withdraws his advice, on the ground that the time had not yet come (2 Sam. vii, 2, 3, 17). See Ewald, *Isr. Gesch.* ii, 592. He next comes forward as the reprover of David for the sin with Bathsheba; and his famous apologue on the rich man and the ewe lamb, which is the only direct example of his prophetic power, shows it to have been of a very high order (2 Sam. xii, 1–12). B.C. 1035. There is an indistinct trace of his appearing also at the time of the plague which fell on Jerusalem in accordance with the warning of Gad. "An angel," says Eupolemus (Euseb. *Præp. Ev.* ix, 30), "pointed him to the place where the Temple was to be, but forbade him to build it, as being stained with blood, and having fought many wars. His name was Dianathan." This was probably occasioned by some confusion of the Greek version, διὰ Νάθαν, with the parallel passage of 1 Chron. xxii, 8, where the blood-stained life of David is given as a reason against the building, but where Nathan is not named. B.C. cir. 1017. On the birth of Solomon he was either specially charged with giving him his name, Jedidah, or else with his education, according as the words of 2 Sam. xii, 25, "He sent [or "sent him"] by [or "into"] the hand of Nathan," are understood. B.C. cir. 1034. At any rate, in the last years of David, it is Nathan who, by taking the side of Solomon, turned the scale in his favor. He advised Bathsheba; he himself ventured to enter the royal presence with a remonstrance against the king's apathy; and at David's request he assisted in the inauguration of Solomon (1 Kings i, 8, 10, 11, 22, 23, 24, 32, 34, 38, 45). B.C. cir. 1015. His son Zabud occupied the post of "king's friend," perhaps succeeding Nathan (2 Sam.

xv, 37; 1 Chron. xxvii, 33); and Azariah, another of his sons, occupied a high place in the king's court (1 Kings iv, 5). He assisted David by his counsels when he reorganized the public worship (2 Chron. xxix, 25). B.C. 1014. This is the last time that we hear directly of his intervention in the history. His influence may be traced in the perpetuation of his manner of prophecy in the writings ascribed to Solomon (comp. Eccl. ix, 14–16 with 2 Sam. xii, 1–4). He left two works behind him—a life of David (1 Chron. xxix, 29), and a life of Solomon (2 Chron. ix, 29). The last of these may have been incomplete, as we cannot be sure that he outlived Solomon. The consideration in which he was held at the time is indicated by the solemn announcement of his approach—"Behold Nathan the prophet" (1 Kings i, 23). The peculiar affix of "the prophet," as distinguished from "the seer," given to Samuel and Gad (1 Chron. xxix, 29), shows his identification with the later view of the prophetic office indicated in 1 Sam. ix, 9. His grave is shown at *Halhul* near Hebron (see Robinson, *Bib. Res.* i, 216, note).

3. A native of Zobah, in Syria; the father of Igul, one of David's mighty men (2 Sam. xxiii, 36; 1 Chron. xi, 38). B.C. cir. 1040.

4. A son of David (2 Sam. v, 14; 1 Chron. xiv, 4), from whom the evangelist Luke has reckoned the genealogy of Mary the mother of Jesus (Luke iii, 31). B.C. cir. 1032. See GENEALOGY. In 1 Chron. iii, 5 Nathan is said to have been "the son of David by Bathshua," i. e. Bathsheba, but the rendering has been questioned. To him must probably be referred the words of Zech. xii, 12 (see Henderson, *Min. Proph.* ad loc.), though some have interpreted it as the house of the prophet Nathan standing for the family of the prophets. See DAVID.

5. One of the head men who returned from Babylon with Ezra on his second expedition, and whom he despatched from his encampment at the River Ahava to the colony of Jews at Casiphia, to obtain thence some Levites and Nethinim for the Temple service (Ezra viii, 16). B.C. 459. "That Nathan and those mentioned with him were laymen appears evident from the concluding words of the preceding verse, and therefore it is not impossible that he may be the same with the son of Bani, who was obliged to relinquish his foreign wife (Ezra x, 39); though on the other hand these marriages seem rather to have been contracted by those who had been longer in Jerusalem than he, who had so lately arrived from Babylon, could be." B.C. 458.

Nathan ben-Jechiel, also called *Aruk* (ערוך), or *Baal ha-Aruk* (בעל הערוך), from the fact that he is the author of the celebrated lexicon denominated *Aruk*, a distinguished Jewish lexicographer, was born in Rome about 1030, where, like his ancestors before him and his descendants after him, he was held in the highest veneration for his extraordinary learning, and it was said of him, "peritum omnis generis scientiarum fuisse." Though busily engaged in faithfully discharging the responsible duties devolving upon him as rabbi of the Jewish community in the Eternal City, and in attending to the Hebrew academy of which he was the president, R. Nathan devoted all his spare time for the greater part of his life to the writing of that important lexicon which has obtained such a world-wide celebrity. From the words of the epilogue which R. Nathan himself appended to it (*this lexicon was completed on Tuesday, the nineteenth day of the month on which the Temple was destroyed by the despised one* [i. e. Ab=end of July], 4861 *after the creation* [=A.D. 1101], 1033 *after the destruction of the burned Temple*, 1413 *of the Seleucian æra*), it will be seen that he finished this lexicon A.D. 1101. According to Mr. Etheridge, the work was finished in the year 4865, answering to A.D. 1105; it may be that he read בשנת דתתסה ליצירה instead of דתתסא. Five years after the completion of the work Jechiel died, A.D. 1106. The lexicon is de-

nominated *Aruk* (ערוך), from ערך, *to arrange, to set in order*), i. e. *arrangement* of the words in alphabetical order, and extends over the Mishna, both the Gemaras, the Midrashim, and all the Chaldee paraphrases of the O. T. "The importance of this work, both to the understanding of the ancient expositions of the Bible and the criticism of the text of the Chaldee paraphrases, can hardly be overrated, inasmuch as R. Nathan, in explaining the words, embodied the interpretations of the ancient sages preserved by tradition, and adopted the ancient and correct readings. So comprehensive is this lexicon, and so highly was it appreciated, that it not only superseded and buried in oblivion a lexicon also called *Aruk*, compiled by Zemach ben-Paltoi, who was gaon in Pumbaditha, A.D. 871–890, but simply left for his future supplementors to compile and rearrange the rich materials which R. Nathan amassed. In this, however, they did not always succeed" (Ginsburg). Notwithstanding the subsequent labors of Buxtorf, Landau, and others, in the field of Hebræo-Aramaic lexicography, the *Aruk* of Nathan Jechiel still holds its pre-eminence. Its definitions are remarkable for their substantial import and verbal precision, and it is even quoted by David Kimchi (q. v.) in his famous ספר השרשים, s. v. דרדר, נץ, פקע, שכר. It was published at Pisauri, 1515, and often afterwards. An edition was published at Amsterdam in 1655, with the additions of B.-Musafia (q. v.), which edition was republished by M. I. Landau with his own notes, in 5 vols., under the title מערבי לשוֹן, or *Rabbinisch - Aramäisch - Deutsches Wörterbuch zur Kenntniss des Talmuds, der Targumim u. Midraschim*, etc. (Prague, 1819–24). A convenient edition of the *Aruk*, with the supplements of Mussafia, De Lonsano, and Berlin, has been published by H. Sperling (Lemberg, 1857); still later annotations to the *Aruk*, with emendations and critical notes, appeared by R. Lindermann, under the title ספר שריד בערכין (Berl. 1864; see Frankel, *Monatsschrift*, 1865, p. 393 sq.); and a still later edition was published by Lonsano and Berlin (Lemberg, 1865), and the latest edition is that of Lemberg (1874, 2 vols.). To the honor of R. Nathan be it said—though it does not redound to the glory of modern scholarship—that his *Aruk* is still the only clew to the ancient Jewish writings which are so important to Biblical literature and exegesis. See the masterly biography of R. Nathan by Rapaport in the Hebrew annual entitled *Bikure ha-Itim* (Vienna, 1829), x, 1–79; xi (ibid. 1830), 81–90; Geiger, in *Zeitschrift der Deutschen Morgenländischen Gesellschaft*. xii, 142 sq., 357 sq.; xiv, 318 sq.; Steinschneider, *Catalogus Libr. Hebr. in Biblioth. Bodleiana*, No. 2040–2043; id. *Bibliograph. Handbuch*, p. 99 sq.; Kitto, *Cyclop.* s. v.; Fürst, *Biblioth. Judaica*, iii, 20 sq.; De Rossi, *Dizionario storico degli autori Ebrei*, p. 140 sq. (German transl.); Etheridge, *Introd. to Jewish Literature*, p. 284 sq.; Grätz, *Gesch. d. Juden*, vi, 76; Braunschweiger, *Gesch. d. Juden in den Roman. Staaten*, p. 56; Basnage, *History of the Jews*, p. 625 (Taylor's transl.); Dernburg, in Geiger's *Zeitschrift für Jüd. Theologie*, iv, 123 sq.; Bleek, *Einleitung in das Alte Testam.* p. 100; Kimchi, *Liber radicum* (ed. Lebrecht u. Biesenthal), p. xxxix; Buxtorf, *Lexicon Talmudicum*, etc., p. ix, ed. B. Fischer (Leips. 1869); (N. Y.) *Jewish Messenger*, Jan. 8, 1874. (B. P.)

Nathan ha-Babli, one of the most distinguished Mishnaic doctors, was a native of Mêshan, in Babylonia. In consequence of his high birth, as his father was the prince of the captivity in Babylon, and his marvellous knowledge. of the law, both divine and human, which he acquired as a student in the country of his adoption, he was created vicar (אבברת רין) of the patriarch Simon II ben-Gamaliel II, A.D. 140–163. In the Talmud he is often quoted as a profound scholar of the law (*Horajoth*, 13 b; *Baba Kama*, 23 a; *Baba Mezia*, 117 b), and he materially contributed to the compilation of the Mishna, as he himself compiled a Mishna, which is referred to as *Mishnath de Rabbi Nathan* (משנת דרבי נתן), and which Jehudah the Holy (q. v.) made use of in the redaction of the present Mishna. Besides this *corpus juris*, he is also the author of, 1, the *Aboth of R. Nathan* (אבות דרבי נתן), being a compilation of the apothegms and moral sayings of the Jewish fathers (אבות), interspersed with traditional explanations of divers texts of Scripture, consisting of forty-one chapters. Both the historian and moral philosopher will find this work an important contribution to the literary and philosophical history of antiquity. It is printed in the different editions of the Talmud after the tractate *Yebamoth*, and has also been published separately with various commentaries (Venice, 1622; Amsterdam, 1778), and with two excellent commentaries (Wilna, 1833), translated into Latin, with notes, by Francis Taylor (Lond. 1654), under the title of *R. Nathanis Tractatus de Patribus, Latine cum notis*, but in its present form contains later interpolations:—2, of the *Forty-nine Rules* (ארבעים ותשע מדות), a work of mathematical import, and which Geiger thinks was written by a later author of the same name. See Fürst, *Bibl. Jud.* iii, 19 sq.; *Kultur- u. Literaturgesch. der Juden in Asien* (Leips. 1849), p. 16 sq.; Zunz, *Die Gottesdienstlichen Vorträge der Juden* (Berl. 1832), p. 108 sq.; Steinschneider, *Catalogus Libr. Hebr. in Biblioth. Bodleiana*, col. 2032 sq.; Geiger, *Wissenschaftliche Zeitschrift* (Leips. 1847), vi, 19 sq.; Grätz, *Gesch. d. Juden*, iv, 187, 201, 203, 204; Jost, *Gesch. d. Judenth. u. s. Sekten*, ii, 110 sq., 123; Etheridge, *Introd. to Hebr. Lit.* p. 77; Dukes, *Rabbin. Blumenlese* (Leips. 1844), p. 39; Delitzsch, *Zur Gesch. d. Jüd. Poesie*, p. 33; Frankel, *Hodegetica in Mischnam* (Leips. 1859), p. 187–191; Ginsburg, *The Essenes, their History and Doctrines* (Lond. 1864), p. 22; art. *Sadducees*, in the 3d ed. of Kitto's *Cyclop. of Bibl. Lit.* iii, 731 sq., note, reprinted in part in Smith's *Dict. of the Bible* (Amer. ed.), iv, 2778, note. (B. P.)

Nathan, Isaac, BEN-KALONYMOS, a Jewish writer of great celebrity, flourished near the opening of the 15th century. The exact date of either the birth or death of this author of the first Hebrew concordance, who traces his lineage to the royal family of David, has not as yet been ascertained. All that we know with certainty is that he lived at Avignon, Montpellier, or Arles in the time of Benedict XIII, and that his writings were called forth by the conduct of this antipope towards the Jews, which was as follows. This pope, Peter de Luna by name, who was declared a schismatic, heretic, and perjurer, and who was deposed by the Council of Pisa (1409), but was still recognised on the Pyrenean peninsula, thought that he would secure the general recognition of his claims to St. Peter's chair if he could bring about the conversion of the Spanish Jews. He therefore issued a summons (1412), with the sanction of his patron, Ferdinand the Just, king of Aragon, to all the learned rabbins to hold a public controversy at Tortosa, and appointed the learned Jewish physician, Joshua Lorqui—or Geronimo de Santa Fé, as he was called after his conversion—to prove to them from the Talmud and other Jewish writings that the Messiah, whose advent the Jews were daily expecting, had already come in the person of Jesus Christ. To escape the threatening dangers, sixty of the most celebrated Jewish literati of Aragon answered the summons. They were headed by don Bidal ben-Benevenisti, Ibn-Labi of Saragossa, Joseph Albo, the famous author of the *Ikarim*, Sechariah ha-Levi Saladin, Astruc Levi, Bonastruc Desmaëthe, Ibn-Joseph, Ibn-Jachja, etc., and this most famous *controversy of Tortosa* lasted twenty-one months (from February, 1413, to November, 1414). Benedict XIII presided at the meetings, and in the first session, which was held Feb. 7, 1413, he thus addressed the Jews: "Ye learned Hebrews, know that I have not

come here to discuss which religion is true, yours or ours. I am certain mine is the truest. Your law was formerly the only true law, but it is now abrogated. You are convoked here solely by Geronimo, who has engaged to prove to you that the Messiah has come by the evidence of your Talmud, which was composed long since by rabbins far superior to yourselves in wisdom; therefore be careful of your arguments." Two treatises were prepared for this controversy by Joshua Lorqui, or Geronimo de Santa Fé, the antipope's champion, entitled *Tractatus contra perfidiam Judæorum et contra Talmud*, printed in the *Bibliotheca Maxima Patrum*, tom. xxvi, and separately in *Hebræomastix* (Frankf. a. M., 1602). It was in reply to these tracts that R. Nathan wrote the work entitled תוכחת מתעה, *Correction of the Misguided*, which has not as yet been published. To the same cause is to be ascribed his Hebrew concordance, entitled אור זרוע, מאיר נתיב, or רחובות, which was designed to enable his brethren to rebut the attacks on Judaism, by helping them to find easily the passages of the O. T. quoted in support of the Messiahship of Jesus of Nazareth, and by aiding them to see what legitimate construction can be put on these passages in accordance with the context in which they occur. This concordance, to which R. Nathan devoted eight years of his life (1437–1445), and in which he adopted the plan of the Latin concordance of Arlotti, general of the order of Minorites (cir. 1290), first appeared with an elaborate introduction (פתיחת הקונקורדאנסיס) in Venice, 1523, then again, with the introduction castrated by the Inquisition (ibid. 1564, and Basle, 1581). The great value of this work can be best ascertained from what Jacob ben-Chajim, who carried through the press the Rabbinic Bible (1524–25) in Bomberg's printing-establishment, where the concordance appeared only a few months previously, says of it in his celebrated introduction (transl. by Ginsburg, Lond. 1867): "But for a certain book, called *Concordance*, the author of which is the learned R. Isaac Nathan, who lived some forty years ago, published in our printing-office at Venice, I could not have corrected the verses. This is a precious work; it embraces all the points of the Holy Bible, and explains all the sacred Scriptures by stating all nouns and verbs, with their analogous forms, and giving at the heading of every noun and verb an explanation, saying the meaning of the word is so and so, and branches out in such and such a manner, and comments upon each one separately. It also marks the division of each chapter, and the number of chapters in every prophetical book, and tells in which chapter and verse every word occurs. The advantage to be derived from this book is indescribable; without it there is no way of examining the references of the Massorah, since one who studies the Massorah must look into the verse which the Massorah quotes, and which, without a concordance, would take a very long time to find, as you might not know in which prophet the passage referred to occurs, and if you knew the prophet, you still might not know the chapter and verse. Besides, all the world is not so learned in the Scriptures. Whosoever has this concordance does not require any more the lexicon of Kimchi, for it contains all the roots, whereunto is added an index of all the verses in the Bible; none of them is wanted. In conclusion, without it I could not have done the work which I have done." Nathan's concordance was also translated into Latin by Reuchlin (Basle, 1556), and was inserted by the Minorite Maria di Calasio, in his four-volume concordance (Rome, 1622). It is the basis both of Buxtorf's and Fürst's concordances. See Steinschneider, *Catalogus Librorum Hebr. in Bibliotheca Bodleiana*, col. 1141–1143; id. *Bibliographisches Handbuch*, p. 100; Fürst, *Bibliotheca Judaica*, iii, 22; Grätz, *Gesch. der Juden* (Leips. 1875), viii, 150, 151; Kitto, *Cyclop. s. v.*; Wolf, *Bibl. Hebr.* ii, 681; Le Long, *Bibl. Sacra* (ed. Boernes), ii, 398; De

Rossi, *Dizionario storico degli autori Ebrei*, p. 125 (German transl.); id. *Bibliotheca Judaica Antichristiana*, p. 76 sq.; Etheridge, *Introd. to Hebr. Literature*, p. 289; Lindo, *Hist. of the Jews of Spain and Portugal*, p. 209 sq.; Milman, *Hist. of the Jews* (new ed. New York, 1870), iii, 299 sq. (B. P.)

Nathan'aël (Ναθαναήλ, but Ναθανάηλος in 1 Esdr. ix, 22; for the Heb. נְתַנְאֵל, *given of God*, i. q. Θεόδορος; comp. *Nathan*), the name of three men in the Apocrypha and one in the N. T. See also NETHANEËL.

1. A brother of Samaras the Levite, in the time of Josias (1 Esdr. i, 8); evidently the NETHANEEL (q. v.) of the Heb. text (2 Chron. xxv, 9).

2. One of the "sons of Phaisus" who renounced their Gentile wives after the captivity (1 Esdr. ix, 32); evidently the NETHANEEL (s. v.) of the Heb. text (Esdr. x, 22).

3. Son of Samael and father of Eliab among the ancestry of Judith (Jud. viii, 1), and therefore a Simeonite (ix, 2). See JUDITH.

4. One of the earliest disciples of our Lord, concerning whom, under that name at least, we learn from Scripture little more than his birthplace, Cana of Galilee (John xxi, 2), and his simple, truthful character (John i, 47). We have no particulars of his life. Indeed the name does not occur in the first three Gospels. We learn, however, from the evangelist John that Jesus on the third or fourth day after his return from the scene of his temptation to that of his baptism, having been proclaimed by the Baptist as the Lamb of God, was minded to go into Galilee. He first then called Philip to follow him, but Philip could not set forth on his journey without communicating to Nathanael the wonderful intelligence which he had received from his master the Baptist, namely, that the Messiah so long foretold by Moses and the prophets had at last appeared. Nathanael, who seems to have heard the announcement at first with some distrust, as doubting whether anything good could come out of so small and inconsiderable a place as Nazareth—a place nowhere mentioned in the Old Testament—yet readily accepted Philip's invitation to go and satisfy himself by his own personal observation (John i, 46). What follows is a testimony to the humility, simplicity, and sincerity of his own character from One who could read his heart, such as is recorded of hardly any other person in the Bible. Nathanael, on his approach to Jesus, is saluted by him as "an Israelite indeed, in whom there is no guile"—a true child of Abraham, and not simply according to the flesh. So little, however, did he expect any such distinctive praise, that he could not refrain from asking how it was that he had become known to Jesus. The answer, "before that Philip called thee, when thou wast under the fig-tree, I saw thee," appears to have satisfied him that the speaker was more than man—that he must have read his secret thoughts, and heard his unuttered prayer at a time when he was studiously screening himself from public observation, as was the custom with pious Jews (Tholuck, *Comment. on John*, ad loc.). The conclusion was inevitable. Nathanael at once confessed, "Rabbi, thou art the Son of God; thou art the King of Israel" (John i, 49). B.C. 25. The name of Nathanael occurs but once again in the Gospel narrative, and then simply as one of the small company of disciples to whom Jesus showed himself at the Sea of Tiberias after his resurrection. B.C. 29. On that occasion we may fairly suppose that he joined his brethren in their night's venture on the lake —that, having been a sharer of their fruitless toil, he was a witness with them of the miraculous draught of fishes the next morning—and that he afterwards partook of the meal, to which, without daring to ask, the disciples felt assured in their hearts that he who had called them was the Lord (John xxi, 12). Once therefore at the beginning of our Saviour's ministry, and once

after his resurrection, does the name of Nathanael occur in the sacred record.

This scanty notice of one who was intimately associated with the very chiefest apostles, and was himself the object of our Lord's most emphatic commendation, has not unnaturally provoked the inquiry whether he may not be identified with another of the well-known disciples of Jesus. It is indeed very commonly believed that Nathanael and *Bartholomew* are the same person. The evidence for that belief is as follows: John, who twice mentions Nathanael, never introduces the name of Bartholomew at all. Matt. x, 3; Mark iii, 18; and Luke vi, 14, all speak of Bartholomew, but never of Nathanael. It may be, however, that Nathanael was the proper name, and Bartholomew (son of Tholmai) the surname of the same disciple, just as Simon was called Bar-Jona, and Joses, Barnabas. It was Philip who first brought Nathanael to Jesus, just as Andrew had brought his brother Simon, and Bartholomew is named by each of the first three evangelists immediately after Philip; while by Luke he is coupled with Philip precisely in the same way as Simon with his brother Andrew, and James with his brother John. It should be observed, too, that as all the other disciples mentioned in the first chapter of John became apostles of Christ, it is difficult to suppose that one who had been so singularly commended by Jesus, and who in his turn had so promptly and so fully confessed him to be the Son of God, should be excluded from the number. Again, that Nathanael was one of the original twelve, is inferred with much probability from his not being proposed as one of the candidates to fill the place of Judas. Still we must be careful to distinguish conjecture, however well founded, from proof. To the argument based upon the fact that in John's enumeration of the disciples to whom our Lord showed himself at the Sea of Tiberias Nathanael stands before the sons of Zebedee, it is replied that this was to be expected, as the writer was himself a son of Zebedee; and, further, that Nathanael is placed after Thomas in this list, while Bartholomew comes before Thomas in Matthew, Mark, and Luke. But as in the Acts Luke reverses the order of the two names, putting Thomas first and Bartholomew second, we cannot attach much weight to this argument. St. Augustine not only denies the claim of Nathanael to be one of the Twelve, but assigns as a reason for his opinion that whereas Nathanael was most likely a learned man in the law of Moses, it was, as Paul tells us (1 Cor. i, 26), the wisdom of Christ to make choice of rude and unlettered men to confound the wise (*in Johan. Ev.* ch. i, § 17). St. Gregory adopts the same view (*on John* i, 33, ch. 16, B). In a dissertation on John i, 46, to be found in *Thes. Theo. philolog.* ii, 370, the author, J. Kindler, maintains (*Nath. vere Israelites* [Viteb. 1680]) that Bartholomew and Nathanael are different persons.

There is a tradition that Nathanael was the bridegroom at the marriage of Cana (Calmet), and Epiphanius (*Adv. Hær.* i, § 223) implies his belief that of the two disciples whom Jesus overtook on the road to Emmaus Nathanael was one. The following additional monographs are extant: Lange, *Nath. confessio* (Lips. 1755); Pignatelli, *De Apostolatu Nath. Barth.* (Par. 1560); Robert, *Nathanaël Barth.* (Duaci, 1519); Hartmann, *Examen Jo.* i, 47 (Aboæ, 1753). See BARTHOLOMEW.

Nathani'as (Ναθανίας), one of the "sons of Maoni" who renounced their Gentile wives taken after the return from Babylon (1 Esdr. ix, 34); evidently the NATHAN (q. v.) of the Heb. text (Ezra x, 39).

Nathaniel, called in Arabic *Abul-Barkat Hïbat Allah bar-Malka*, was one of the medical coryphæi of the Mohammedan dominions in the 12th century, and was also distinguished as a philosopher and Hebraist, on which account he was designated *Wachidal-Zeman*, i. e. "the only one of his time." He tried his skill on the

Book of Ecclesiastes (*Koheleth*), but his commentary, which is written in Arabic, has never been published; the MS. is in the Bodleian Library at Oxford. Isaac ibn-Ezra, son of the great commentator, celebrated Abul-Barkat's commentary on Koheleth in a poem (see Dukes, *Kokbe Jizchak*, 1848, p. 21 sq.), in which he declares that this Solomonic book will henceforth (A.D. 1143) go by the name of him who has so successfully unlocked its meaning. Comp. Grätz, *Gesch. d. Juden*, vi, 280 sq.; *Zeitschrift der Morgenländischen Gesellschaft*, 1859, p. 711 sq.; Ginsburg, *Historical and Critical Commentary on the Book of Ecclesiastes*, p. 58; Pocock, *Notæ Miscellaneæ ad Portam Mosis* (London, 1740), i, 196, where a specimen of this commentary is given. (B. P.)

Na'than-Mel'ech (Hebrew, *Nethan'-Me'lek*, נְתַן־מֶלֶךְ, i. e. *Nathan of* the *king*; Sept. Nαϑὰν βασιλεύς), a eunuch (A. V. "chamberlain") in the court of Josiah, by whose chamber at the entrance to the Temple were the horses which the kings of Judah had dedicated to the sun (2 Kings xxiii, 11). B.C. 628.

Nathus, FABIAN, a German divine, flourished in Bohemia during the anti-Reformation period of the 16th century. But little is known of his personal history. He was preaching at Prague, holding at the same time the professorship of Oriental languages at the university of the Bohemian capital, when the victories of Ferdinand II subjected Bohemia to Romish rule and to Jesuitic interferences. Up to 1615 the Bohemians had been favored with Protestant preaching in the German tongue, out of respect for the elector of Saxony and at his intercession; but the Jesuits, determined that all Protestant ideas should be crushed, caused the *States* to pass an edict forbidding even preaching in German, and consequently brought about also the dismissal of those who had preached in the German; and on Oct. 29, 1622, the last four Lutheran clergymen who had remained in the country were obliged to leave. Among these was Nathus. He went to Brunswick, Germany, and there died about 1640. Nathus was an able defender and propagator of the Reformed doctrines, and deserves to be ranked among those who suffered martyrdom for conscience' sake. Although he did not die at the stake, he yet suffered expulsion from the field of his labor and separation from the flock which deeply loved him. See Pescheck, *The Reformation and Anti-Reformation in Bohemia* (Lond. 1846, 2 vols. 8vo), ii, 32–33, 414. (J. H. W.)

Nation. This word in the Auth. Ver. generally represents the Heb. גּוֹי, i. e. *the nation as a body politic;* in plur. גּוֹיִם, esp. of foreign nations, the GENTILES (q. v.); usually in the Sept. ἴϑνος, ἴϑνη, Vulg. *gens, gentes.* Sometimes it represents the Heb. עַם, which means esp. *the* PEOPLE (q. v.), Sept. λαός; in poetry, לְאָמִים, לְאֹם; and in Chald. אֻמָּה. It means sometimes all the inhabitants of a particular country (Deut. iv, 34), the country or kingdom itself (Exod. xxxiv, 10; Rev. vii, 9); sometimes countrymen, natives of the same stock (Acts xxvi, 4); sometimes the father, head, or original of a people (Gen. xxv, 23). In the prophets the term "nations" is often used as a general name for the heathen or Gentiles (Isa. ix, 2; comp. Matt. iv, 15). See ETHNOLOGY.

National Church. See CHURCH AND STATE.

National Covenant. See COVENANT.

National Deities. See MYTHOLOGY; POLYTHEISM.

National Synods. Provincial and national synods have, by immemorial practice of the Roman Catholic Church, the right of condemning heresies and errors, and of correcting abuses of all kinds in particular churches. Paul of Samosata, Photinus, Sabellius, Arius, Eustathius, Apollinaris, the Donatists, Pelagians, etc.,

were all condemned in particular councils in the first instance. The particular councils of Arles, Orange, Carthage, Toledo, Gangra, etc., pronounced judgments in controversies of faith; not to speak of more recent decisions of the same kind. The objection of Bossuet, who found fault with the principle of the English Reformation, viz., that every national Church was a complete body in itself, and might examine and reform errors and corruptions in doctrine and worship, falls therefore to the ground, in view of the practice of his own Church. See Bossuet, *Variations;* Fleury, *Hist.* l. 157, s. 37; Palmer, *On the Church*, i, 417; Walcott, *Sacred Archæol.* s. v.; Aschbach, *Kirchen-Lexikon*, s. v. National Synoden. See SYNODS. (J. N. P.)

Native TREE is probably the meaning of the Heb. word אֶזְרָח, *ezrâch* (Sept. κέδρος τοῦ Λιβάνου, Vulg. *cedrus Libani*), in Psa. xxxvii, 35. It is difficult to see upon what grounds the translators of the A. V. have understood it to signify a "bay-tree:" such a rendering is entirely unsupported by any kind of evidence. Most of the Jewish doctors understand by the term *ezrâch* "a tree which grows in its own soil"—one that has never been transplanted; which is the interpretation given in the margin of the A. V. Some versions, as the Vulg. and the Arabic, follow the Sept., which reads "cedar of Lebanon," mistaking the Hebrew word for one of somewhat similar form. Celsius (*Hierob.* i, 194) agrees with the author of the sixth Greek edition, which gives αὐτόχϑων (*indigena*, "one born in the land") as the meaning of the Hebrew word: with this view rabbi Solomon and Hammond (*Comment. on Ps.* xxviii) coincide. Dr. Royle (Kitto's *Cycl. Bib. Lit.* art. "Ezrach") suggests the Arabic *Ashruk*, which he says is described in Arabic works on materia medica as a tree having leaves like the *ghar* or "bay-tree." This opinion must be rejected as unsupported by any authority. Perhaps no specified tree is intended by the word *ezrâch*, which occurs in several passages of the Hebrew Bible, and signifies "a native," in contradistinction to "a stranger" or "a foreigner." Comp. Lev. xvi, 29: "Ye shall afflict your souls . . . whether it be one of your own country (הָאֶזְרָח, *hâ-ezrâch*) or a stranger that sojourneth among you." The epithet "green," as Celsius has observed, is by no means the only meaning of the Hebrew word; for the same word occurs in Dan. iv, 4, where Nebuchadnezzar uses it of himself—"I was *flourishing* in my palace." In all other passages where the word *ezrâch* occurs it is evidently spoken of *a man* (Cels. *Hierob.* i, 196). In support of this view we may observe that the word translated "in great power" more literally signifies "to be formidable," or "to cause terror," and that the word which the A. V. translates "spreading himself," more properly means to "make bare." The passage then might be thus paraphrased: "I have seen the wicked a terror to others, and behaving with barefaced audacity, just as some proud native of the land." In the Levitical law the oppression of the stranger was strongly forbidden, perhaps therefore some reference to such acts of oppression is made in these words of the Psalmist. See BAY-TREE.

Nativité, JEANNE LE ROYER, DE LA, a French female fanatic, was born at La Chapelle Janson, near Fougères (Brittany), Jan. 24, 1732. Received as lay sister in the convent of the Urbanists de Fougères, where she had been admitted as a domestic at the age of eighteen, this girl, without education, believed she had divine visions and revelations. Her successive confessors, to whom she related them, sought to calm her troubled imagination; but one of them, less enlightened or more credulous, confirmed the sister in her pious reveries. The abbot Genet wrote at her dictation what she pretended to have seen or heard; and on the death of this ecclesiastic, which occurred in 1817, the manuscripts that he possessed were sold to a bookseller, who published them under the title of *Vie et Révélations de la sœur de la*

Nativité (1817, 3 vols. 12mo). In it are found numerous and extraordinary revelations, in which she predicts many things concerning the Church and the end of the world; also a *Recueil d'autorités* in support of these revelations. The abbot Tresvaux placed the name of Jeanne Le Royer in his *Galerie des saints et autres personnes pieuses de la Bretagne*, making a continuation to the work of don Lobineau on this subject. A new edition of the work of the sister de la Nativité was made in 1819 (4 vols. 8vo and 12mo). The 4th volume, supplementary, was dictated by the sister to some nuns who enjoyed her confidence; like the others, it contains details which might be severely criticised. The author of *L'Ami de la religion et du roi* gave an analysis and an extract from this work, warning his readers "that not all the revelations of the sister are to be believed as implicitly true," a precaution which seems superfluous. She died at Fougères Aug. 15, 1798. See Hoefer, *Nouv. Biog. Générale*, s. v.

Nativity OF CHRIST. The birth of our Saviour was exactly as predicted by the prophecies of the Old Testament (Isa. vii, 14; Jer. xxxi, 22). He was born of a virgin, of the house of David, and of the tribe of Judah (Matt. i; Luke i, 27). His coming into the world was after the manner of other men, though his generation and conception were extraordinary. The place of his birth was Bethlehem (Mic. v, 2; Matt. ii, 4,6), whither his parents were wonderfully conducted by Providence (Luke ii, 1, 7). The time of his birth was foretold by the prophets to be before the sceptre or civil government departed from Judah (Gen. xlix, 10; Mal. iii, 1; Hag. ii, 6, 7, 9; Dan. ix, 34). The exact year of his birth is not agreed on by chronologers, but it was about the four thousandth year of the world; nor can the precise season of the year, the month, and day in which he was born be ascertained. See CHRONOLOGY. The Egyptians placed it in January; Wagenseil in February; Bochart in March; some, mentioned by Clement of Alexandria, in April; others in May; Epiphanius speaks of some who placed it in June, and of others who supposed it to have been in July; Wagenseil, who was not sure of February, fixed it probably in August; Lightfoot on the 15th of September; Scaliger, Casaubon, and Calvisius in October; others in November; and the Latin Church in December. It does not, however, appear probable that the vulgar account is right; the circumstance of the shepherds watching their flocks by night agrees not with the winter season. Dr. Gill thinks it was more likely in autumn, in the month of September, at the feast of Tabernacles, to which there seems some reference in John i, 14. The Scripture, however, assures us that it was in the "fulness of time" (Gal. iv, 4); and, indeed, the wisdom of God is evidently displayed as to the time when, as well as the end for which Christ came. It was in a time when the world stood in need of such a Saviour, and was best prepared for receiving him. The date of the Nativity is discussed in most treatises on chronology. See also Jarvis, *Introd. to Hist. of the Church*; Strong's *Harmony and Exposition*, Append. ii; *Stud. und Kritiken*, 1846, iv, 1007; *New-Englander*, 1847, p. 215 sq.; Anon. *The Month of the Nativity* (Lond. 1848, 24mo); and the monographs cited by Volbeding, *Index Programmatum*, p. 10, 12, 13; Hase, *Leben Jesu*, p. 45, 46, 50. See JESUS CHRIST.

NATIVITY OF CHRIST *commemoratea*. The early Christian Church, it is now established beyond question, observed as a holy day the supposed day on which the Saviour of the world beheld this mortal sphere. See, however, the article CHRISTMAS. We may here add simply that Bingham insists upon it that in the early Church the day of Christ's nativity was kept with the same veneration and religious solemnity as the Lord's day; for they had always sermons on this day, of which there are many instances in the writings of Chrysostom, Nazianzen, Basil, Ambrose, Augustine, Leo, and others. Neither did they let this day ever pass

without a solemn communion; for Chrysostom, in this very place, invites his people to the holy table, telling them "that if they came with faith, they might see Christ lying in the manger, for the holy table supplied the place of the manger; the body of the Lord was laid upon the holy table, not as before, wrapped in swaddling clothes, but invested on every side with the Holy Spirit" (Chrysostom, *Hom*. 31, *de Philogonio*, i, 399). And that the solemnity might be more universally observed, liberty was granted on this day to servants to rest from their ordinary labors, as on the Sabbath and the Lord's day. This is particularly mentioned by the author of the Apostolical Constitutions (*Constit*. lib. 8, cap. 33): "Let servants rest from their labor on the day of Christ's nativity, because on this day an unexpected blessing was given unto men, in that the Word of God, Jesus Christ, was born of the Virgin Mary for the salvation of the world." All fasting was as strictly prohibited on this festival as on the Lord's day; and no one, without suspicion of some impious heresy, could go against this rule, as appears from what pope Leo says of the Priscillianists, that they dishonored the day of Christ's nativity and the Lord's day by fasting, which they pretended they did only for the exercise of devotion in an ascetic life; but in reality, it was to affront the days of his nativity and resurrection, because with Cerdon, and Marcion, and the Manichees, they neither believed the truth of the Saviour's incarnation nor his resurrection. Therefore, in opposition to these and such like heresies, the Church was always very jealous of any one who pretended to make a fast of the nativity of Christ. Finally, to show all possible honor to this day, the Church obliged all persons to frequent religious assemblies in the city churches, and not go to any of the lesser churches in the country, except some necessity of sickness or infirmity compelled them so to do (*Conc. Aurelian*. i, can. 27). The laws of the state prohibited all public games and shows on this day as on the Lord's day.

Some students of ecclesiastical antiquity hold the observance of Christ's nativity to be derived from the Encænia, or feast of dedication of churches; others suppose, as is stated in the article CHRISTMAS, that it was designed to supersede the *Saturnalia*. It is, however, most natural to conclude that, in an age when the clergy were disposed to multiply festivals, the analogy of other events in the Saviour's history may have suggested the propriety of marking his nativity with a distinct celebration. It was at first observed on the 6th of January; but towards the end of the fourth century we have two distinct festivals, namely, that of the nativity of Christ, on December 25th, and that of the baptism, probably the circumcision, of Jesus, on January 6th.

The festival of the nativity is in the Roman Catholic Church not only distinguished by the advent, but by the observance of three saints' days immediately after it. Wheatly gives this singular reason for the collocation of these days: "None are thought fitter attendants on Christ's nativity than those blessed martyrs who have not scrupled to lay down their lives for him, from whose birth they received life eternal." He says, "Accordingly, we may observe three kinds of martyrdom: the first, both in will and deed, which is the highest; the second, in will, but not in deed; the third, in deed, but not in will. So the Church commemorates these martyrs in the same order: St. Stephen first, who suffered death both in will and in deed; St. John the Evangelist, who suffered martyrdom in will, but not in deed (being miraculously delivered out of the caldron of burning oil, into which he was put in Rome); the holy Innocents last, who suffered in deed and not in will—for though they were not sensible on what account they suffered, yet it is certain they suffered for the cause of Christ, since it was on account of his birth that their lives were taken away" (*Commentary on the Book of Common Prayer*, sec. iv, p. 200). Other fanciful reasons have been assigned. It is uncertain at what time these festivals began to be observed in connection with that of the nativity. Some Roman Catholic divines in the Middle Ages represented the nativity on the stage. See MYSTERIES. Thus St. Francis, about three years before his death, with papal permission, celebrated Christ's nativity. "A manger was prepared by his direction, and the whole scene of the miraculous birth represented. The mass was interpolated before the prayers. St. Francis preached on the Nativity. The angelic choirs were heard; a wondering disciple declared that he saw a beautiful child reposing in the manger (Milman, *Lat. Christianity*, v, 265). The nativity of Christ has been the frequent subject of students of sacred art. The engraver and the painter have in all ages since the birth of the Saviour been busy in the treatment of this historic event on stone and on canvas. We insert here illustrations of several engravings on stone and glass which are regarded as superior specimens of sacred art by Christian archæologists. See

Antique Representations of the Nativity.

Manne, *Diss. on the Birth of Christ*; Lardner, *Credibility*, i, 1; ii, 796, 963; Gill, *Body of Divinity, on Incarnation*; Bishop Law, *Theory of Religion*; Newton, *Review of Ecclesiastical History*; Dr. Robertson, *Sermon on the Situation of the World at Christ's Appearance*; Buckminster, *Sermons*; Edwards, *Redemption*, p. 313, 316; Robinson, *Claude*, i, 276, 317; John Edwards, *Survey of all the Dispensations and Methods of Religion*, vol. i, ch. xiii; Bingham, *Antiquities of the Christian Church*, ii, 114 sq.; *Engl. Rev.* vi, 82 sq. See ADVENT.

Nativity, Gospel of. See GOSPELS, SPURIOUS.

Natronai (II) BEN-HILAI, a very learned rabbi of his time, whose opinion was regarded as an authority, flourished as gaon of the famous college in Sura after the middle of the 9th century (859–869). His correspondence was a very large one; and even the Jewish congregations of Lucena, in Spain, asked him questions on matters of religion, which he answered in Arabic, contrary to his predecessors, who only understood the Hebrew and Chaldee. In answer to the question whether it is lawful to put the points to the synagogal scrolls of the Pentateuch, he distinctly declared that points are not Sinaitic (i. e. sacred), having been invented by the sages, and put down as signs for the reader; and moreover, since it is prohibited to us to make any additions from our own cogitations, lest we transgress the command, "Ye shall not add," etc. (Deut. iv, 2), we must not put the points to the scrolls of the Law. See Grätz, *Gesch. d. Juden*, v, 248; Fürst, *Bibl. Judaica*, iii, 24;

Ginsburg, in Leorta's *Massoreth ha-Massoreth*, p. 44 sq.; Fürst, *Gesch. d. Karäerthums*, i, 114, 179. (B. P.)

Natta, JACOPE, a Christian convert from Judaism, of whose history little or nothing is known, excepting that he flourished in the 17th century, and is the author of a treatise written in Italian, *Ragionamento della venuta del Messia contro la dureza ed ostinazione Ebraica*, i. e. a dissertation on the advent of the Messiah against the hardness and pertinacity of the Jews (Venice, 1629; Milan, 1644). From his treatise we may assume that he was an Italian Jew by birth. See Wolf, *Bibl. Hebr.* iii, 518; Jöcher, *Allgemeines Gelehrten-Lexikon*, s. v.; Fürst, *Bibl. Jud.* ii, 25; Kalkar, *Israel u. d. Kirche*, p. 83.

Natural is the rendering in the A. V. of the N. T. for two Greek words of somewhat kindred signification: 1, as opposed to *artificial*, φυσικός, applied only to the *animal* nature of men (Rom. i, 26, 27; Jude x) or beasts (2 Pet. ii, 12); 2, as opposed to *spiritual*, ψυχικός, applied to *inanimate* objects (1 Cor. xv, 44, 46), and to men in their *unconverted* state (1 Cor. ii, 14), or as *depraved* (James iii, 15; Jude xix). See CARNAL.

Natural Ability. See INABILITY.

Natural History OF THE BIBLE. This will be found discussed under the subdivisions BOTANY, ZOOLOGY, etc. We add here a few general treatises on the subject: Scheuzer, *Hist. Nat. Biblicæ* (August. 1731–5, 4 vols. fol.); Harris, *Nat. Hist. of Bible* (new ed. Lond. 1833, 12mo); Carpenter, *Scripture Nat. Hist.* (Lond. 1828, 8vo); Simson, *Hieroglyphica animalium*, etc. (Edinb. 1622–4, 4 pts. 4to); Franzius, *Animalium Hist. Sacra* (Amst. 1643); Bochart, *Hierozoicon* (L. Bat. 1714, 2 vols. fol.); Vallesius, *Sacra philosophia* (Lugd. 1588, 8vo); Ursinus, *Arboretum Biblicum* (Norimb. 1699, 2 vols. 8vo); Hiller, *Hierophyticon* (Traj. 1725, 4to); Celsius, *Hierobotanicon* (Amst. 1748, 2 vols. 8vo); Rosenmüller, *Bibl. Botany and Mineralogy* (transl. from German) (Edinb. 1840, 12mo); Schwarz, *Nat. Hist. of Palest.* (in Heb. תּוֹצְרת הָאָרֶץ, Jerusalem, 1845, 8vo); Fletcher, *Scripture Nat. Hist.* (Lond. n. d. 2 vols. 16mo); Morris, *Bible Nat. Hist.* (Lond. 1852, 16mo); Young, *Scripture Nat. Hist.* (new ed. Lond. 1851, 12mo); Duns, *Bible Nat. Science* (Lond. 1863–5, 2 vols. 8vo); Tristram, *Nat. Hist. of Bible* (Lond. 1868, 12mo); "Nat. Hist. of Bible," in *Lond. Quarterly*, July, 1863; "Biblical Botany," in *Brit. and For. Evang. Rev.* Jan. 1864.

Natural Laws. See NATURE, LAWS OF.

Natural Religion. See RELIGION.

Natural Theology is that department of study which treats of the existence and attributes of God as revealed to us in the *natural* world. Since no book can be accepted by us as coming from any being until we have proof of the existence of such a being, natural theology is *to us* the foundation of all revealed religion. Even if we infer the existence of the being and his character from the character of the book itself, the process is the same in kind as inferring his existence and character from any other work, so that the proof which we have from the Bible of the existence of God cannot be higher *in kind* than that which we have from nature.

1. *Method of Proof.*—Natural theology sets out with the assumption that every event must have a cause, and that there may be such relations between causes and effects—such combinations of matter and force in producing specific results, that the existence of a Designer may be inferred, and his attributes and character may thus be revealed. Until these positions are granted, no step can be taken in this science. If they are not to be accepted, then a science of natural theology is impossible. The truth of these assumptions is found in the intuitive beliefs of the human mind.

Natural theology now claims as its field of investigation not only the whole natural world, but also the physical, intellectual, and moral nature of man.

2. *Claims as a Science.*—It being now conceded by all that the present order of things had a beginning—in

this sense, at least, that there was a time when not a single species of plants or animals now upon the earth had an existence, in fact that there was a time when there was no living thing upon the earth—it is a fair question to ask, How came all these animals and plants here, with all their complex relations for the continuance of the species? How came man here? The hypothesis that living species have always existed as they now are being abandoned, two other hypotheses only seem possible: (1) That animals and plants have been produced as the resultants of forces eternally inherent in matter; (2) That they have been produced by the design and organizing power of a personal being. Both of these hypotheses have their supporters, though those who accept the latter by no means agree as to the method in which creative power has been manifested in the production of species. It is certain that the large majority of students of nature have seen, in its different departments, such combinations to produce specific results, such likeness to the works of man—contrivances differing from his only in their grandeur and perfection —that they have believed in a being who has originated, by some method, all the living things upon the earth. The existence of man is taken as proof of the existence of a being like him in the elements of personality, though infinitely above him in wisdom and power. It is claimed that belief in the existence of a personal God is reached by the same process of thought by which every science has been built up, and by which all the conclusions in common life are reached; that the necessary principles of belief, careful investigation, and sound induction all aid in proving the existence of a personal Creator from the works of nature. It is claimed that no scientific process has been more legitimate, and no inference in actual life more in accordance with the common-sense wisdom of the world, than the investigations and the results reached in natural theology. This claims, therefore, a place among the sciences, relying upon the nature of the processes by which its conclusions are reached. Its claim has been, and still is, admitted by a large majority of the ablest students of nature and of man.

That natural theology, as it has now been defined, has any just claim to scientific rank is utterly denied by a class of philosophers, positivists, who seek to limit all investigation to observed phenomena, ignoring or denying both efficient and final causes; and also by those who, without denying the abstract doctrine of final causes, affirm that we have no evidence of final cause in the works of nature. They regard the adaptation which we see in nature simply as the result of materials and forces mutually limited in producing the existing forms. The conclusions of such writers are well expressed in the words of Büchner: "Our reflecting reason is the sole cause of this apparent design, which is nothing but the necessary consequence of the combination of natural materials and forces" (*Force and Matter*, p. 90).

3. *Arguments.*—(1.) The history of the race proves that there has been at all times and in all places, except among the most degraded tribes, some notion of God, or gods, or some supernatural agents to be feared and worshipped. It is claimed by Sir John Lubbock and others that the most degraded tribes are without any notion of a Supreme Being; and it is asserted that deaf mutes are in the same condition till they are instructed. Granting all the facts stated, the conclusions may be fairly questioned. It does not follow that there is no idea of God present in the mind because it has not forced its way up into language, or because it cannot be detected in our imperfect intercourse with degraded savages and uneducated mutes. So constantly has the notion of a God appeared in all ages, that it has been claimed by some that the idea of God is *innate*. This doctrine, at the present time, is accepted only in this modified form, if at all, that the capabilities of the human mind are such that in its perfect development the idea of God is surely reached in the study of nature and man.

An *à priori* proof of the existence of God has been accepted by some, from the supposed power of the human mind to form a conception of a perfect being. The inference is made from such a power of the mind that a being must exist to correspond to the conceptions of it. This argument in some of its forms has been accepted and enforced by Des Cartes, Leibnitz, Dr. Samuel Clarke, and other eminent philosophers. As it involves subtile metaphysical distinctions, it is certainly not fitted to impress the popular mind; and it has failed to satisfy such acute metaphysicians as Reid and Stewart, who surely could not be charged with undue scepticism.

(2.) The *teleological* argument may fairly be made to include the study of nature and the study of man as a physical, intellectual, and moral being. It is simple in form, readily apprehended, and has been enforced among thinking men in all ages. Socrates and Cicero are well known among the ancients for their arguments on this subject. The Bible appeals to nature for illustrations of the power and goodness of God. His existence is taken for granted in the first verse of Genesis, on the ground that there is in nature proof of the existence of such a being. In the New Testament we have the testimony of Paul to the fulness and value of this proof (Rom. i, 19-20), and among the fathers there have been able writers on this subject. Since the time of Paley, whose name is best known of all those who have entered this field, writers in large numbers have appeared, who have written treatises professedly on this subject, or have treated it indirectly in connection with scientific discussions. Some of the ablest arguments have been made in this way; and of late years great additions have been made, directly and indirectly, to such writings (see *Literature* below).

It has been objected to the argument from design that, at best, it only proves the existence of a worker, or world-builder; that it is only in man that we have proof of the existence of a personal Creator. It may be added that the creator of man is not necessarily the self-existent God. But the existence of man's creator proves that there must be a self-existent, personal God.

After we reach the proof that our Creator is a personal being, loving justice and truth, we must wait for him to declare whether he is the Almighty or not— whether he shall swear by himself or one greater. Thus we join natural theology to revelation. Natural theology declares a Creator of man, of the heavens and the earth. He declares himself to be the *Almighty*, which we know from the laws of our belief must exist. We seek for a cause of what we see, and cannot stop till we find one adequate and necessarily eternal.

4. *Counter Tendencies of the Present Day.*—As already intimated, the *positive philosophy*, of which Comte is the father, would render the science of natural theology impossible. This science assumes the existence of efficient causes, and rests for its proof upon final causes. Both efficient and final causes positive philosophy forbids us to name as having any relation to science. If they exist, they are to be to us as though they were not.

The doctrine of *evolution*, which, in some of its forms, is now accepted by many scientific men, is supposed by some to weaken or destroy the proof for the existence of a Creator. This result is claimed by some who hold the doctrine, and denied by others of the same school. For one who accepts the doctrine of causality, belief in the existence and wisdom of a designer will not be affected at all by the time required or the secondary agencies employed in producing results. The only question that could arise would be in reference to power. When a certain effect is reached, as the production of a tree or animal, with all their complex relations, such an effect demands belief in a cause adequate to produce such a result; and if there is evidence of wisdom and skill in it, the evidence is there irrespective of the time or secondary agencies concerned in its production. The belief that a being of low rank can be raised to a higher rank by any process of development or natural selection, without the same agency in kind as would be required to produce the being of high rank directly, can arise only by ignoring the plainest principles of causality. Whatever may be the final conclusions of science in regard to the origin of species, they cannot affect the argument for design in the creation of species, nor materially change the teachings of natural theology. If any difficulty arises, it will be found in harmonizing the teachings of science with the Bible account of creation as to the mode in which the creative power was manifested.

5. *Literature.*—Xenoph. *Memorabilia;* Plato, *Laws,* x; Cicero, *De Natura Deorum;* Des Cartes, *Princip. Philos.;* Leibnitz, *Theodice;* Augustine, *Confess.;* Derham, *Phys. Theology;* Nieuwentyt, *Relig. Philos.;* Dr. Samuel Clarke, *Boyle Lect. and Sermons,* vol. ii; Paley, *Natural Theology;* the *Bridgewater Treatises;* Chalmers, *Nat. Theology;* Tulloch, *Theism;* McCosh and Dickie, *Typical Forms,* etc.; Hitchcock, *Rel. of Geol.;* Cooke, *Rel. of Chem.;* Agassiz, *Contrib. to Nat. Hist. U. S.* vol. i; Chadbourne, *Nat. Theol.* (N. Y. 1867, 8vo); Jackson, *Philos. of Nat. Theol.* (Lond. 1874); Cocker, *Theistic Conception,* etc. (N. Y. 1875); Godwin, *Christ and Humanity* (N. Y. 1875); Gillett, *Nat. Theol.* (N. Y. 1874, 12mo); Wiseman, *Con. between Science and Revealed Relig.;* Bushnell, *Nat. and Supernatural;* President Hopkins, in the *Am. Quar. Obs.* vol. i; Child, *Benedicite;* Molloy, *Geol. and Rev.;* Foster (J.), *On Nat. Religion and Social Virtue;* Grose (John), *Rational Ethics;* Jevon, *System. Morality on the Grounds of Nat. Rel.;* Priestley, *Institutes of Nat. Rel.;* Wilkins, *Principles of Nat. Rel.;* Thompson, *Christian Theism;* Zöckler, *Theol. naturalis;* Amer. *Presb. Rev.* July, 1866, art. i; *Amer. Ch. Qu. Rev.* April, 1869, art. ii; *Mercersburg Rev.* 1860; *North Am. Rev.* Jan. 1865; Oct. 1865; July, 1867; *New-Englander,* Jan. 1868; Oct. 1874; Jan. 1875; *Bibliotheca Sacra,* April, 1868; Oct. 1868; *Westminster Rev.* Jan. 1854; Jan. 1867; *Presb. Qu. and Princet. Rev.* April, 1875, art. viii; *Meth. Qu. Rev.* July, 1865, p. 519 sq. See THEOLOGY. (P. A. C.)

Naturalism is the name given to those systems of the philosophy of *nature* which explain the phenomena by a blind force acting necessarily. This doctrine is to be found in Lucretius, and was held by Leucippus and Epicurus. The *Système de la Nature* of D'Holbach, the *Traité de la Nature* of Robinet, and the *Philosophie de la Nature* of Delisle de Sales, also contain it. In theology the term *naturalism* is applied to all those forms of belief or speculation which deny the doctrine of a personal God as the author and governor of the universe; being thus opposed to *Theism* (q. v.). See Literature appended to article NATURAL THEOLOGY.

Naturalists. This name, which has now become nearly obsolete in a theological or philosophical sense, has been used to designate two sections of the anti-christian school which rejects belief in supernatural causes or operations. (1) The name has been mostly used by German writers for those who identify God with nature, but who are more generally known as Pantheists. (2) By English writers it is generally taken as signifying those who consider natural religion to be sufficient for man's guidance and happiness without any supernatural revelation. But these latter may be subdivided also into two classes, the *first* of which has received the name of "Philosophical Naturalists," who accept revelation as containing truth, but as being at the best only a reduplication of natural religion, and so unnecessary. The name is rarely found in works written later than the 18th century, when it was used by Kant in Germany and by Boyle in England; and the school formerly known as Naturalists are now called Pantheists and Rationalists.

Nature. I. *New.- Test. Usage of the Word.*—In

James i, 23; iii, 6, the Greek is γένεσις, -εως; elsewhere, as Rom. i, 26, φύσις. It is variously used for, 1, the laws of the natural or moral world (Rom. i, 26; ii, 14; xi, 21, 24). 2. Birth, origin, or natural descent: "Jews by nature" (Gal. ii, 15; Rom. ii, 27); "Which by nature are no gods" (Gal. iv, 8). 3. *Genus, kind:* "For every kind (marg. '*nature*') of beasts," etc., "is tamed, and hath been tamed of mankind" (marg. "*nature of man*" [James iii, 4]). 4. The native mode of thinking, feeling, acting, as unenlightened and unsanctified by the Holy Spirit: "The natural man receiveth not the things of the Spirit of God" (1 Cor. ii, 14; comp. Eph. ii, 3). 5. *Nature* also denotes a customary sense of propriety: "Doth not nature itself teach you that, if a man have long hair, it is a shame unto him?" (1 Cor. xi, 14). It was the national custom among both the Hebrews and Greeks for men to wear the hair short.

II. *Philosophical Import of the Word.*—"The term *nature* is used sometimes in a wider, sometimes in a narrower extension. When employed in its most extensive meaning, it embraces the two worlds of mind and matter. When employed in its more restricted signification, it is a synonyme for the latter only, and is then used in contradistinction to the former. In the Greek philosophy, the word φύσις was general in its meaning; and the great branch of philosophy, styled '*physical* or *physiological*,' included under it not only the sciences of matter, but also those of mind. With us, the term *nature* is more vaguely extensive than the terms *physics, physical, physiology, physiological,* or even than the adjective *natural;* whereas, in the philosophy of Germany, *natur* and its correlatives, whether of Greek or Latin derivation, are in general expressive of the world of matter in contrast to the world of intelligence" (Sir W. Hamilton, Reid's *Works,* p. 216, note).

"The word *nature* has been used in two senses, viz., actively and passively; energetic (=*forma formans*), and material (=*forma formata*). In the first it signifies the inward principle of whatever is requisite for the reality of a thing as *existent;* while the *essence,* or essential property, signifies the inner principle of all that appertains to the *possibility* of a thing. Hence, in accurate language, we say the essence of a mathematical circle or geometrical figure, not the *nature,* because in the conception of forms, purely geometrical, there is no expression or implication of their real existence. In the second or material sense of the word *nature,* we mean by it the sum total of all things, as far as they are objects of our senses, and consequently of possible experience—the aggregate of phenomena, whether existing for our outer senses or for our inner sense. The doctrine concerning *nature* would therefore (the word *physiology* being both ambiguous in itself, and already otherwise appropriated) be more properly entitled phenomenology, distinguished into its two grand divisions, somatology and psychology" (Coleridge, *Friend,* p. 410).

Nature, Divine. See article GOD, in vol. iii, p. 908 sq.

Nature, Human. See BODY; IMAGE OF GOD; SOUL; SPIRIT.

Nature, Laws of. In the question raised under this title the following points must be considered: (1) the substance itself of nature; (2) the forces working in and through it; and (3) their production always of identical results under identical circumstances. This immutable connection is intuitively considered as an inherent necessity, the result of experience as assumed by reason. On the other hand all the known laws of nature are sometimes considered as a whole, termed then *natural law,* by virtue of which all nature forcibly working, and by the combination of all its inherent forces, gives rise to all effects. In this sense, however, natural law can only be fully appreciated by contrast. This is afforded in two ways by theology, in which it gives rise to theories that have attained at times undue preponderance. We find it first in the domain of apologetics and dogmatics, where natural law requires the creative power of the living God to explain not only the creation, but also the preservation of the universe. We find it next in the province of morals, where the distinction between the causality of the natural forces and those of the human will, between the necessities of nature and the freedom of man, and, in short, between natural law and moral law, is to be established. In both instances the laws of nature are opposed to the effects of freedom; but in dogmatics it is the freedom of the Creator as the absolute master of his creation, while in ethics it is the freedom of man as the *membrum præcipuum* of the earthly creation.

I. *In Dogmatics*, the first point which arises is to ascertain whether the laws of nature, inherent in the creature and in the world, admit of or exclude the co-operation of God; and in the latter case whether, according to the pantheistic idea, nature itself is God; or whether, according to the deistical theory, God, after creating the universe, left it to the exclusive guidance of natural laws. The answer to these questions settles also that of the admissibility of miracles. It is well known that Schleiermacher, and still more emphatically Strauss, have denied the existence of miracles from the standpoint of natural laws. Schleiermacher (*Der Christl. Glaube*, § 46) says that religious consciousness, as a simple feeling of dependence, "is identical with the knowledge that all which afflicts or influences us is caused by and results from natural causes;" and (§ 47) "that the interests of piety can never give rise to the necessity of so arranging a fact that it should be placed in such immediate dependence from God as to deny its taking its source in the general laws of nature." Every absolute miracle disturbs the whole order of nature, both negatively as regards the past, as the miracle contradicts all previous observations, and thus appears to suppress the usual working of nature; and positively with reference to the future, "in which everything is changed at once from what it would have been had not the miracle occurred, so that every miracle not only disturbs forever the whole connection of the original organization, but every new miracle also annuls the preceding, in so far as they have come to be counted among the working agencies." See MIRACLES. It will be sufficient for our present purpose to refer to R. Rothe's answer to the views of Schleiermacher (in the *Studien u. Kritiken*, 1858, i, 27–40): "If the course of the universe is an arithmetical sum, the factors of which, including also the free motives, are in themselves invariable quantities; or if the divine government of the world is something like the clock-work of a music-box, in which the melodies to be played were from all eternity pinned in the cylinder, then, certainly, there can be no room in the universe for miracles. These have for their basis a positive independence with respect to God, although not interfering with absolute dependence upon him; there is a real distinction and separation between the divine causality and that of the creature, and also in the operation of freedom in the world. ... I respect the laws of nature, and rejoice at every advance we make in their knowledge. God himself has subjected to them the forces of nature; but he has not subjected to them his liberty or his almighty will. He has retained undisturbed his absolute liberty, and his sovereignty in the universe he has created. Miracles prove that the laws of nature, while they are the greatest power in the world, are yet subject to the government of him who created them, the ever-living God." Thus the laws of nature are the work of the eternal Law-giver and loving Governor.

II. *In Ethics* we have to consider the connection between inanimate and unreasoning creation and personalities, or, in other words, the relation between natural and moral law. The distinction is generally drawn by the definition that natural law implies a *state* of being, moral law a *volition*. The first belongs to the domain of necessity, the latter to the province of free-will.

VI.—28

Schleiermacher has, indeed, sought to lessen and even to destroy this distinction of the *phænomena* and *noumena* of Kant and Fichte, i. e. of a theoretical and a practical reason of an object and a subject; and for that purpose has resorted to Schelling's philosophy of identity. This system consists in upholding the unity of nature and spirit, and points to the "will" ever arising from dead nature. Thus in his interesting treatise, *Ueber d. Unterschied zwischen Natur- und Sittengesetz* (in his *Sämmtliche Werke*, III, ii, 397–417), he seeks to equalize them. According to the common view (p. 400), the natural law must contain a general expression of what *really* occurs in and through nature, and the moral law of what should occur in and through reason in her domain. Yet here we find again the obligation of the moral law based upon the existence of the mind, and of the respect for the law to which its observance relates. On the other hand (p. 409, 413) the natural law is also connected with an obligation, implying that all does not fully and perfectly proceed according to the law. Thus monstrosities and diseases stand in the same relation to the laws of nature, in whose domain they occur, as immorality and disobedience do to the moral law. Among the elementary forces and processes of nature we find vegetation and animalization; but abortion and disease, in nature, are not the effects of a new principle; they are only a deficiency of those of vegetation and animalization. So also "in the domain of spiritual life we find deviations corresponding to its nature, which we find in that of vegetation and animalization. We even find others, having their origin not in intelligence itself, but in the fact that the mind in its state of earthly existence must become a centre, and as such must in an oscillating life appear inefficient sometimes in view of the subordinate functions." Thus by the side of reason and its laws there exists also a deficiency, and the deviations, in which the mind-force appears inadequate to the work, are in fact nothing but what we call evil and immorality. The two laws are therefore essentially similar. The difference of obligation is simply this: "It is only through the intervention of the mind-force that the individuality becomes free, and a mental life alone is a complete life. Hence it is merely on this point that the obligation is directed to the will." This theory of Schleiermacher agrees perfectly with his general view of ethics as a science, with which he opposed in his time the exaggeration of the feeling of duty, considering ethics especially as the chief good. But quite as evident, in the given theory, is the disadvantageous connection under which this definition of the natural and moral law is placed by Schleiermacher. It lies in the rejection of liberty, and therefore of the positive and essential prevalence of evil. The "intellectual" process is looked upon as similar to the vegetative and animalizing; the mind appears only as perceptive; evil takes its source only in quantitative oscillations, and in the relative weakness of the moral principles. The spiritual life is placed in the light of a natural process, and thus we find again in Schleiermacher's ethics the same naturalism as in dogmatics. Such is the pantheistic side of Schleiermacher's system, the conclusions of which have led many into an atheistical materialism that goes so far as to consider thought itself but "a secretion of the brain." It must be the aim therefore of theology to overcome this pantheistic leaven, and to establish the limits of the power of the laws of nature, so as to prevent natural necessity being supposed to annul God's creative power and human liberty. It must show that the Spirit of the Lord is liberty, and not nature, and that God is all in all. See Herzog, *Real-Encym.* x, 224 sq. See LAW.

Nau, MICHEL, a French missionary, was born at Paris in 1631, of distinguished, noble parentage. He joined the Jesuits in 1656, and his superiors, after having intrusted to him the direction of the studies of the two princes De Longueville, appointed him to the missions in the East. He travelled over Mesopotamia,

Syria, Persia, and Armenia, where his zeal, and the conversions that he wrought, more than once excited the Mussulmans against him. Exhausted in strength, he returned to France in 1682, and died at Paris March 8, 1683. We have of his works, *Voyage nouveau de la Terre Sainte, enrichi de plusieurs remarques servant à l'intelligence de la Sainte Écriture* (Paris, 1679 and 1702, 12mo; a book at the same time curious, edifying, and useful):—*Ecclesiæ Romanæ Græcæque vera effigies et consensus, ex variis tum recentibus, tum antiquis monumentis. Accessit religio Christiana contra Alcoranum defensa* (Paris, 1680, 4to):—*L'État présent de la religion Mahométane* (Paris, 1681, 1685, 1687, 2 vols. 12mo), an extended translation of the preceding Latin book. See Hoefer, *Nouv. Biog. Générale*, s. v.

Naudæus, PHILIP, a French Protestant theologian, was born at Metz in 1654. In 1687 he was obliged to flee to Berlin in consequence of religious persecutions. He became a member of the Academy of Berlin, and died in 1729. As a theologian he was chiefly distinguished for his ultra-Calvinistic views. He steadfastly upheld the doctrine of strictly supralapsarian predestination, and of purely imputative justification, and opposed all the concessions which the most distinguished theologians of the early part of the 18th century were disposed to make. We therefore find him involved in numberless controversies, not only with Bayle and the mystic Poiret, but also, on account of his defence of the old system, with Le Blanc, La Placette, Osterwald, and even with the theological faculty of Frankfort. In his principal work on this subject, *La souveraine perfection de Dieu dans les divins attributs et la parfaite integrité de l'Écriture prise au sens des anciens reformés*, he says, "God is so absolutely perfect that he acts only for his own self and his own glory; so that he alone knows what agrees with his perfection and his glory, and we can form no judgment whatever of it." From this he proceeds to show that supralapsarianism is alone logical, and all other views inconsistent and unavailing, whether Arminian, Lutheran, or less strictly Calvinistic. He maintained, however, that the infralapsarian doctrine did but apparently contradict supralapsarianism. His efforts to counteract the tendencies of the times were unavailing, and his works did not exert much influence. See Hering, *Beiträge z. Geschichte d. evang.-reform. Kirche in den Preuss.-Brandenb. Ländern*, ii, 170; Chauffepié, *Dictionnaire*, s. v.; Schweizer, *Gesch. d. Centraldogmen in d. reform. Kirche*, ii, 765–820; Gass, *Dogmengesch*. iii, 295.

Naudé, GABRIEL, a French bibliographer, noted for his defence of Kempis as the author of *De Imitatione Christi*, was born at Paris in 1600. He displayed at an early age a great aptitude for philological and critical studies. He studied medicine at Paris, but took his doctor's degree in that science at Padua. On his return to Paris in 1628 he published his work, *Apologie pour les grandes Personnages faussement accusés de Magie* (1629). In 1631 he accompanied the papal nuncio, cardinal De' Bagni, on his return to Rome, and he was appointed his librarian. While he was at Rome the controversy concerning the authorship of the book *De Imitatione Christi* began. See KEMPIS, THOMAS À. The Benedictines claimed the authorship for one of their order, John Gersen, abbot of Vercelli; while the regular canons of St. Geneviève claimed it for Thomas à Kempis. Naudé, being in Italy, was requested to examine several manuscripts of the work in question. His report was unfavorable to the claims of the Benedictines, who were much incensed against him, and accused him of bad faith. The affair then came before the courts in the shape of a charge of defamation; the suit lasted for years, and was at last compromised. In 1640 cardinal De' Bagni died, and Naudé, after remaining some time with cardinal Barberini, the nephew of the reigning pope, Urban VIII, was recalled to Paris in 1642, and appointed librarian to cardinal Mazarin. In this capacity he travelled through

several parts of Europe to collect books and manuscripts to enrich his patron's library, which was afterwards sold according to a sentence of the Parliament of Paris, during the civil war of the Fronde, to the great sorrow of Naudé, who attempted to prevent what he considered an act of barbarism (comp. his *Avis à Nosseigneurs du Parlement sur la Vente de la Bibliothèque du Cardinal Mazarin*, 1652). On receiving an invitation from queen Christina of Sweden to be her librarian, Naudé went to Stockholm in 1652, where he was very well received. The climate of Sweden not agreeing with his health, he set out to return to Paris, but on his way home died suddenly in 1653. Naudé was a decided opponent of the Huguenots, and urged severe measures for their extinction. He claimed that France suffered by permitting Protestantism to spread in its borders. Protestant writers are wont to claim, and that of course justly, that the stagnation of trade in France was consequent upon the removal of the Huguenots; but Naudé claims that "had all the heretics in France been cut off, the country would afterwards have enjoyed perfect tranquillity." Yet to his credit it must be said that, however self-opinionated and paradoxical, Naudé was a man of irreproachable character, and a truly learned man. Many are the eulogies and epitaphs which have been written in his honor. See Jacob, *Gabrielis Naudæi Tumulus* (1659); Sainte-Beuve, *Portraits littéraires* (1855).

Naudi is the name of a bull which the Hindûs regard as sacred because he is the *vahan* of Nahardeva, or Siva (q. v.), just as the Egyptians regarded Apis as the soul of Osiris (q. v.). The Egyptians believed that when Apis ate out of the hands of those who went to consult him the answer was favorable. "The Hindûs," says Bartolomeo, "place rice and other articles before their doors as the animal passes along in their processions, and if he stop to taste them, consider it as a fortunate event. This, at least, he is very prone to do, to the serious injury of the Hindû shopkeepers, as he wanders, not in his most sacred capacity, through the streets of Calcutta and other towns." Naudi is held in great reverence among the Hindûs, and is one of the most sacred emblems of Siva. Naudi is by some described as the emblem of justice. See Coleman, *Mythology of the Hindûs*, p. 64.

Naudi, ANGELO, an Italian painter of religious subjects, flourished in the 16th century. He was a pupil and imitator of Paul Veronese. Naudi went to Spain, where, according to Palomino, he passed the greater part of his life, and executed many works for the churches at Madrid, which are highly commended by the author above mentioned. He was appointed court-painter by king Philip, in whose service he continued a long time. See Spooner, *Biog. Hist. of the Fine Arts*, ii, 610.

Naueshwer, a name among the Hindûs for a subordinate incarnation of their god *Vishnu* (q. v.), described as having taken place at Alemdy, near Poonah, about, as some state, 700, or, according to others, 200 years ago. Naueshwer is stated to have been a religious ascetic, and to have been buried alive at Alemdy, where his tomb is seen under a splendid temple, and where he yet appears (for, although buried, he is not dead) to pious, if at the same time wealthy visitors. See Coleman, *Mythology of the Hindûs*, p. 390.

Na'üm (Gr. Ναούμ, for the Heb. *Nahum*, q. v.), the son of Esli and father of Amos, in the maternal ancestry of Christ (Luke iii, 25); apparently the same with JO-HANAN (q. v.), the son of Elioenai (1 Chron. iii, 24). See GENEALOGY OF CHRIST.

Naumann, JOHANN GOTTLIEB, a noted German composer of music, both sacred and profane, was born of very humble parentage near Dresden, Saxony, in 1741. Though Naumann had to struggle against poverty and hardships, his industry never relaxed. He pursued his studies until he made himself one of the first musicians of his age. In 1765 he was appointed composer to the elector of Saxony. He died of apoplexy in the year 1801. His compositions, which were very numerous, include works of every kind—operas, oratorios, songs, cantatas, odes, compositions for the pianoforte, symphonies, etc. For the last years of his life he devoted himself altogether to the composition of sacred music, and left many valuable works in the library of the chapel of Dresden.

Naumburg Convention was a meeting of German evangelical rulers and states, held at Naumburg-on-the-Saale from January 20 to February 8, 1561, with a view to harmonizing the evangelical parties in Germany by subscribing anew the Augsburg Confession of 1530. The Protestant German Church was sadly divided on dogmatic grounds; the Council of Trent was to meet again, and the desire of the princes who met at Augsburg was to give by their subscription of the Augsburg Confession, not only a uniform Confession to the Church, which might bring about the long-desired peace between the dissenting parties, but also to present to the council a harmonious body and union within the Protestant Church. Since the beginning of the Reformation, the German as well as the Swiss Protestant Church had been not only in a constant fight with the Romish Church, but also with each other, which since Luther's death had not diminished, but rather increased. The new edition of the Augsburg Confession, which Melancthon published in 1540, made him the mark of those zealots who adhered to the dead letter of Luther, and who attacked and charged him with apostasy, while his adherents the "Philippists," as they were called, were charged in connection with their master with "crypto-Calvinism." Besides the Calvinistic and crypto-Calvinistic controversies, the *Interimistic* (q. v.), *Adiaphoristic* (q. v.), *Majoristic* (q. v.), *Osiandrian, Staniarian, Synergistic,* and *Flacian* controversies disturbed the peace of the Protestant Church. All attempts of the Protestants to have peace among themselves and with the Church of Rome were in vain; but this object was never lost sight of whenever a good opportunity offered itself. Thus in 1557, Feb. 11, a colloquy was held at Worms for this purpose, but Flacius frustrated it. Another effort was made in the following year, when the Roman king Ferdinand was to be proclaimed emperor at Frankfort-on-the-Main; some of the Protestant princes charged Melancthon to prepare a declaration on the controverted points, in which declaration the princes acknowledged a full harmony with the Augsburg Confession, asserted it to be their own confession, and incorporated it into the Frankfort Recess, March 18, 1558; agreeing at the same time to have a friendly understanding on such points of the controversy as might need yet a fuller explanation, but that for the present "nothing should be taught, preached, or propagated which was not in harmony with their confession as laid down in the Recess." But this attempt was also in vain, since some, especially the Flacians, would not accept the Frankfort Recess. The same must be said of the attempt made by the duke John Frederick of Saxony to convene the states and theologians of Lower Saxony at Magdeburg, May 16, 1558. When in the next year, at the Diet of Augsburg, the emperor Ferdinand promised to try to convene a council in order to do away with all religious controversies, which seemed the more likely now that pope Paul IV was succeeded by Pius IV, the evangelical rulers said more clearly that something ought to be done to bring union and peace into the Church. The Church of Rome was wont to reproach the Protestants that they did not know which Augsburg Confession to accept, the one originally made by Luther, and known as the *Confessio Invariata,* or the one doctored by Melancthon, and known as the *Confessio Variata.* To take away this reproach, it was necessary in the first place to agree which form of the Augsburg Confession should be the basis of their creed, and in the sec-

ond place to effect a union of the whole Protestant body, in order to appear before the council as a phalanx strong in union and unanimous and harmonious in faith. To bring about this result, especially through the exertions of the duke Christopher of Würtemberg, the Naumburg Ecclesiastical Convention was convened. In the first place, the duke Christopher came to an understanding with the elector Frederick III, and his son-in-law, duke John Frederick, that all should subscribe anew the Augsburg Confession of 1530, accept the Apology and the Smalcald articles, remain steadfast in their confession, tolerate no sects in their lands, and forbid their theologians to renew their attacks. They also agreed to invite the other rulers and states to appear at a convention to be held, where every effort for a union should be made on the basis of these stipulations. After the landgrave Philip of Hesse and the duke John Frederick had approved of this plan, the elector August of Saxony issued a proclamation, Dec. 6, 1560, summoning all evangelical rulers and states to meet at Naumburg Jan. 20, 1561, for the purpose of subscribing anew the Augsburg Confession, by means of which at the future council a unanimous and firm confession could be presented. There were present or represented by delegates all the Protestant rulers of Germany, with the exception of the dukes Henry and William of Luneburg, who, like king Frederick of Denmark, declared in a letter that they would accept all the resolutions of the assembly. The tenth session, January 29, brought about the result that the confession of 1530, as compared with the different editions of 1540 and 1542, should be the common confession of all, and that in the preface to the new edition the essential harmony of the Apology and the *Variata* of 1540 should be emphasized. This new edition, which was to be presented to the emperor, was signed by the elector Frederick of the Palatinate, the elector August, the landgrave Wolfgang of Zweibrücken, duke Christopher of Würtemberg, margrave Charles of Baden, landgrave Philip of Hesse, count William of Hohenstein in behalf of the elector of Brandenburg, count Otto von Seelen in behalf of the palatine George, George Albinus in behalf of the margrave John of Brandenburg, Wolf von Koderitz in behalf of the margrave George Frederick of Brandenburg, count Ludwig von Eberstein in behalf of the duke Barnim of Pomerania, Christian Kissaw in behalf of the duke's brother, Joh. Trockenbroot in behalf of the princes of Anhalt, and Sebastian Glaser in behalf of the count of Henneberg. Some of the delegates and princes, however, especially duke Ulrich of Mecklenburg and John Frederick of Saxony, induced by Flacian theologians, refused to subscribe the preface, because it was not severe enough in anathematizing the Lutheran errors and sects. The latter even left Naumburg at the fifteenth session, February 3, thus frustrating the union among the Protestants, which was almost achieved, and causing the discord to appear more conspicuous. On the same day the imperial and papal delegates made their appearance, and presented the breve of pope Pius IV, which invited the Protestants to the council; they were especially loud in their praises of the forthcoming council, as the best means of settling all the pending questions. The rulers and states promised to take the matter into consideration; the result of it was that they not only returned the breve in which they were addressed as "beloved sons," against which address they protested, since they wished neither the pope to be their father nor them to be his sons; but they also refused to attend the council, as in no way would it meet their demands. Finally, they also addressed a letter to the kings of France and Navarre in behalf and favor of the persecuted Huguenots in France, accompanying the same with a copy of the newly-subscribed Augsburg Confession; they also sent a copy to England, Scotland, and Sweden. After having delivered to the imperial delegates a letter for the emperor, the convention was closed on Feb. 8, 1561. See Calinich, *Der Naumburger Fürstentag* (Gotha, 1870);

Gieseler, *Church History*, iv, 220, notes; Hase, *History of the Christian Church*, p. 404; Wessenberg, *Gesch. der Kirchenversammlungen des 16ten u. 17ten Jahr.* iii, 358, 359; Planck, *Geschichte der Protest. Theologie*, iii, 111, 124, 183; Wendecker, *Neue Beiträge zur Geschichte d. Reformation*, vol. ii; Dr. Beck, *Johann Fredrich der Mittlere*, etc. (Weimar, 1858), i, 356 sq.; Gelbke, *Der Naumburgische Fürstentag*, etc. (Leipsic, 1793); Salig, *Vollständige Historie der Augsburg. Confession*, vol. iii; Heppe, *Geschichte des Deutschen Protestantismus in den Jahren* 1550–1581.

Nauplia, or *Napoli di Romania*, a seaport town of Greece, and capital of an eparchy of its own name, situated fifty-eight miles south-west of Athens, with a population of 8543 in 1870, was the seat of the Greek government after the independent establishment of the modern kingdom in 1829, and is noted in ecclesiastical history as the place of a national synod held there July 15 to 27, 1833, for the purpose of regenerating the Greek Church. The synod was convened by the then ministers of public worship and of education, instead of the patriarch, who resided at Constantinople, and was subject to Turkish influence. There were many causes for the convocation of the Nauplia Synod, not the least of which was the proper placing of all episcopal officers, many of them having been consecrated during the war of freedom, and being therefore without patriarchal ordination. At the time of the calling of the Nauplia Synod there were in the Church of Greece twenty-two *canonical*, or regularly consecrated prelates, and twelve uncanonical episcopates, i. e. such as had not patriarchal ordination; and besides these some twenty ex-bishops, deprived of their sees by the troubles of the times. The council was therefore called to settle the following two propositions, and they were approved by the twenty-six prelates who attended the synod:

(1.) The Eastern Orthodox and Apostolic Church of Greece, which spiritually owns as head of the Christian faith Jesus Christ our Lord, is dependent on no external authority, while she preserves unshaken dogmatic unity with all the Eastern orthodox churches. With respect to the administration of the Church which pertains to the crown, she acknowledges the king of Greece as her supreme head, as is in nothing contrary to the holy canons.

(2.) A permanent synod shall be established, consisting entirely of archbishops and bishops, appointed by the king, to be the highest ecclesiastical authority, after the model of the Russian Church.

The divisions of the dioceses of the kingdom followed next. Their number was definitely fixed at ten; and it was ordered that each province should constitute a diocese, which should bear the name of the province, and that the city which was the principal seat of the bishopric should be the capital of the province. Since, however, by degrees fifty-three Greek bishops came forward who all needed some provision, forty provisional sees were erected for such of them as were still able to superintend a diocese; the remainder were provided for in some other manner. The names of the definitive sees were as follows, the provisional bishoprics we have not thought worth while to insert:

Corinth and Argolis	See of	Corinth.
Achaia and Elis	" "	Patræ.
Messenia	" "	Cyparissia.
Arcadia	" "	Mantinea.
Laconia	" "	Sparta.
Acarnania and Ætolia	" "	Missolonghi.
Phocis and Locris	" "	Amphissa.
Attica and Bœotia	" "	Athens.
Eubœa	" "	Chalcis.
The Cyclades	" "	Hermopolis.

It was further arranged that in case of any vacancy of the provisional sees it should not be filled up, but the see should be united to the permanent diocese of the province, whose bishop had his seat in its capital; but this arrangement has not altogether been carried out. The synod is composed of a president, four members, who must be bishops, a secretary, a royal commissioner, and supernumerary members. See Neale, *Introd. Hist. of the Holy East. Ch.* pt. i, vol. i, p. 60–61.

Naur, ELIAS ELKILDSEN, a Danish divine and educator, noted, however, mainly as a hymnologist, flourished in the early part of the last century. He was a professor in the gymnasium at Odensee, in Funen, and died in 1728. He is known by us simply as the author of the Danish hymn translated by Sabine Barney Gould, "When my tongue can no more." See Miller, *Singers and Songs of the Church*.

Nausea, FRIEDRICH, a German theologian and ecclesiastical diplomatist, was born about 1480 at Bleichfeld, or at the village of Weissenfeld, near Würzburg. After having studied the canon law, he became preacher in the cathedral of Mayence in 1526, and a short time after secretary of cardinal Campeggio; in 1534 he was called to Vienna as preacher of the imperial court, and in 1541 was promoted to the bishopric of that city. He assisted at the Conference of Spire, and was sent to the Council of Trent as ambassador of the Roman emperor. Although a declared adversary of the Protestants, he counselled to employ no violence against them, but to have recourse to discussion, in which he excelled. He died at Trent Feb. 6, 1550. He was renowned as one of the first preachers of his time. We have of his works, *Oratio ad Erasmum ut is proximo in Spira statuum conventui intersit* (Vienna, 1524, 4to):—*Ad Carolum I, pro sedando plebeio in Germania tumultu* (Vienna, 1525, 8vo):—*Miscellaneorum libri ii, prior pro horis canonicis, alter pro missa apologeticus* (Mayence, 1527, 4to):—*Homiliarum centuriæ tres* (Cologne, 1530; ibid. 1532):—*Libri mirabilium vii* (Mayence, 1531, and Cologne, 1532, 4to; contains details of several extraordinary events of the time):—*Predigten über alle Evangelien des Jahres* (Mayence, 1535, fol.).—*Sermones quadragesimales* (Cologne, 1535, fol.):—*In Erasmum monodia* (Cologne, 1536, 8vo):—*De puero literis instituendo consilia* (Cologne, 1536):—*Ad Paulum III rerum conciliarum libri v* (Leipsic, 1538, fol.):—*Liber i responsorum ad aliquot Germanicæ nationis adversus sedem apostolicam gravamina* (Cologne, 1538, fol.):—*De Antichristo* (Vienna, 1550, 4to):—*De novissima mortuorum resurrectione* (Vienna, 1551, 4to; Cologne, 1555, 8vo):—*De consummatione hujus sæculi* (Cologne, 1555, 8vo):—*Libri iii methodi de ratione concionandi* (printed several times):—sermons, funeral orations, works of controversy, etc. Nausea had himself given, in 1547, a catalogue of his writings, published and in manuscript, which is found in the series of *Epistolæ miscellaneæ ad Fr. Nauseam*: several of the latter perished at the burning of Vienna in 1525 (see Hummel, *Neue Bibliothek von seltenen Büchern*, 5th part). The *Œuvres complètes* of Nausea have been collected in one volume folio (Cologne, 1616). See Hoefer, *Nouv. Biog. Générale*, s. v.

Nausiphãnes, a Greek philosopher, was attached to the teachings of Democritus, and, according to Sextus Empiricus, was a disciple of Pyrrho. He had a large number of pupils, and was particularly famous as a rhetorician. Epicurus was at one time one of his hearers, and as the latter could not deny this, although he was anxious to be considered a self-taught man, he was obliged to content himself by abusing him, and maintaining that he had learned nothing from him. See Smith, *Dict. of Gr. and Rom. Myth. and Biog.* ii, 1145.

Nautæ (ναῦται, *sailors*) was the name sometimes given in the early Church to the *presbyters* (q. v.), just as by similitude the catechumens were sometimes called ναυτολόγοι, or ναυστολόγοι, with reference to the well-known comparison of the Church with a ship, and to the circumstance that the catechumens took their station in the church at the end of the nave. See Riddle, *Christian Antiquities*, p. 461. See also NAUTOLOGI.

Nautolŏgi (Ναυτολόγοι, *collecting passengers*), a name frequently given to catechists in the early Church. In some authors it was usual to compare the Church to a ship. See NAUTÆ. The bishop was (ὁ πρωρεύς) *the pilot*, the presbyters (οἱ ναῦται) *the mariners*, the deacons (οἱ τοίχαρχοι) *the chief rowers*, the catechists (οἱ

$\nu\alpha\nu\tau\nu\lambda\acute{o}\gamma\omicron\iota$) those who were to admit passengers into the ship, and to contract with them for their fare. This was properly the catechist's duty, to show the catechumens the conditions on which they were to be admitted into the Christian ship.

Nautologoi. See NAUTOLOGI.

Nauvoo. See MORMONS.

Navagero, BERNARDO, an Italian cardinal, was born at Venice in 1507. He was called to the most important positions of trust in the gift of the republic, being successively sent from home as ambassador to Dalmatia, Constantinople, France, Rome, and the court of the emperor. The doge, Pierre Lando, sought his alliance, and caused him to marry Istriana Lando, his granddaughter, who died some years after her marriage with Bernardo. The latter sought consolation in study and religion, and chose the ecclesiastical career. Pope Pius IV, judging that the place of a man so distinguished was in the sacred college, created him cardinal Feb. 26, 1561, and gave him the bishopric of Verona. He was afterwards sent as legate to Trent, where he assisted at the closing of the council. He died at Verona May 27, 1565. We have by this cardinal *Addresses,* and the *Life of Pope Paul IV.* Augustin Valerio has given the life of Bernardo Navagero in his book entitled *De cautione adhibenda in edendis libris* (Padua, 1719, 4to, p. 61–98). See Manin, *Elogio del Cardinale Navagero* (1814); Aubery, *Hist. des Cardinaux.*

Navarre, HENRY OF. See HUGUENOTS.

Navarrette, Alonzo, a Spanish missionary, who was decapitated in Japan, June 1, 1617. He joined the Dominicans of Valladolid, and was sent as missionary to Japan. He departed with several of his colleagues in 1594, and made many proselytes. His success troubled the Japanese priests, who denounced him to the cobo. Navarrette was brought to trial. It was proved that the missionaries were seeking to produce a change in the state; and the first of his order, Navarrette, was condemned to be beheaded. We have of his works, *Epistola ad fratres ordinis in Japonis,* and several other letters to the Dominican missionaries in Japan. See Hoefer, *Nouv. Biog. Générale,* s. v.

Navarrette, Baltazar, a celebrated Spanish theologian of the 17th century, joined the Dominicans of Saragossa. He taught letters and theology in different colleges of his order. He is especially known by his *Controversiæ in D. Thomæ ejusque scholæ defensio* (Valladolid, 1605, 1609, 1634, 3 vols. fol.), a work of celebrity still in Spain, though not as much esteemed for its learning as for its casuistry. Navarrette has left other works of theology, mentioned by Echard. See Hoefer, *Nouv. Biog. Générale,* s. v.; *Gen. Biog. Dict.* xi, 174.

Navarrette, Domingo Fernandez, a noted Spanish missionary, born at Peñafiel, Old Castile, in 1610; joined the Dominican Order, and in 1647 was sent to the Philippine Islands, and became professor of theology at Manilla. Later he went to China, and penetrated beyond the precincts where Europeans were then tolerated. He was made superior of his order, and rendered efficient service for the cause of Christian missions; but during a time of persecution he was driven from the country, and reached home, barely saving his life, in 1673. He

went to Rome, and strongly protested before the authorities against the Jesuitical accommodation theory as tending to delay the Christianizing of China. That his honesty and piety were appreciated is apparent in his appointment to the see of Santo Domingo in 1678. He died in Santo Domingo in Dec., 1689. He wrote *Tratados históricos, políticos, ethicos, y religiosos de la monarquia de China* (Madrid, 1676, fol.); the second volume was suppressed by the Inquisition, and the third never printed. The volume published contains an excellent account of the political and religious condition of the Chinese in his times. See Churchill, *Collection of Voyages and Travels.*

Navarrette, Juan Fernandez, surnamed *El Mudo* (i. e. the mute), a Spanish artist of sacred subjects, was born at Logroño in 1526. Losing both his power of speech and sense of hearing, he studied painting in the monastery of the Hieronymites at Estrella, and afterwards in Italy as a pupil of Titian. He died about 1575. All his works are on sacred subjects, and nearly all of them are preserved in the Escurial.

Navarro, JUAN SIMON, a Spanish painter who devoted himself mostly to sacred art, flourished at Madrid about 1650. He attained considerable distinction. There is a *Holy Family* by him, which is well colored, but inferior. In a convent of the Carmelites at Madrid there are two of his pictures, representing a *Nativity* and an *Epiphany.*

Nave (Greek $\nu\alpha\acute{o}\varsigma$) is the technical term applied to the part of a church ecclesiastically constructed west-

Nave of York Minster.

ward of the choir in which the general congregation assembles; in large buildings it consists of a central division or body, with two or more aisles, and there is sometimes a series of small chapels at the sides beyond the aisles; in smaller buildings it is often without aisles, but has frequently two or more, and sometimes one. In the cathedrals and conventual churches the nave was generally separated from the choir by a screen, which in most instances still remains; on the western side of this, next the nave, one or more altars were occasionally placed; one is recorded, for instance, to have stood thus at Canterbury Cathedral previous to the fire in 1174; the same arrangement appears also to have been formerly common in France, though, with but very few exceptions, the old screens have been removed to make way for light, open partitions. Previous to the Reformation the pulpit was always placed in the nave, as it still is at Ely and Chichester, and always in Roman Catholic churches on the continent; the font also stood there, usually near the west end, sometimes in the middle, and now and then in an aisle, or adjoining one of the pillars. We occasionally find the word *navis* applied instead of *nave;* but there is no relation between the words, since *navis* is from the Greek word ναῦς, *a ship*, and nave from ναός, *a temple*. Other names were sometimes given to it descriptive of its uses, such as *oratorium laici*, ἐκκλησία, *the assembly, quadratum populi*, in allusion to the square form of this part, as distinguished from the semicircular chancel. In some of our old writers the word is written *nef*. The reader will find a full description of the various parts of an ancient church under the word CHURCH. See Farrar, *Eccles. Dict.* s. v.; Riddle, *Christian Antiquities* (see Index); Wolcott, *Sacred Archæol.* s. v.; Parker, *Gloss. of Archit.* s. v.; Neale, *Hist. East. Ch.* (Introd.).

Nave (בַּג, *gab*, anything convex or arched, as the back of an animal, Ezra x, 12; boss of a shield, Job xv; 26), the rim or arch of a wheel. The word occurs in describing the wheels of the ten bases of brass, upon which the levers stood, in the court of Solomon's Temple (1 Kings vii, 33). See LAVER.

Nave (Lat. *Navæus*), **Joseph de**, a Belgian theologian, was born at Viesme, near Liege, in 1651. He was professor of philosophy at Louvain, and in the Seminary of Liege. He was provided with a prebend in the cathedral of St. Paul, but resigned his benefice on account of feeble health. His connections with Opstraët, Arnauld, Du Vaucel, and Quesnel show that he shared their sentiments; and the last having addressed to him a letter some days before his death, he requested it to be placed in his coffin with a New Testament. He died at Liege April 10, 1705. We have of his works, *Memoir containing Reasons for not withdrawing the Seminary of Liege from the Control of the Secular Theologians*. This memoir, written in Latin, offers details as curious as piquant. It was translated into French by P. Quesnel, but it did not have the effect that Nave expected. The Jesuits took possession of the seminary, which gave occasion for another article, *Deux lettres d'un ecclésiastique de Liege* (1699, 4to and 12mo): —*Le fondement de la conduite à la vie et à la piété Chrétienne* (Liege, 1705, 12mo). See Hoefer, *Nouv. Biog. Générale*, s. v.

Nave (Lat. *Navæus*), **Mathias de**, a Belgian theologian, was born at Warnant, in Hesbaye, about 1590. He was received into the University of Douai as doctor of theology, and became in 1620 curate of the collegiate church of St. Peter in that town; some years after prebendary of the church of Seclin; and lastly, July 13, 1633, canon of the cathedral of Tournay, where the censorship of books published in the diocese was intrusted to him. He died at Tournay in 1660. His principal works are, *Annotationes in summæ theologiæ et sacræ Scripturæ præcipuas difficultates, item duo sermones de sanctis Piato et Eleutherio, patronis Tornacensium* (Tournay, 1640, 4to) :—*Prælibatio theologica in festa*

sanctorum (Tournay, 1635, 4to, and Douai, 12mo):— *Encomium sancti Josephi, Virginis Deiparæ sponsi* (Douai, 1627, 12mo; a new edition under this title):— *Sponsus Virginis decoratus corona xxxi gemmarum splendoribus coruscante* (Douai, 1636, 12mo) : — *Catechesis, sive de sacramentorum institutione, etc., conciones xvi* (Douai, 1633, 12mo) :—*Orationes tres signi crucis et orationis efficacia et D. Thomæ Aquinatis laudibus* (Douai, 1630, 4to). He was the editor of a work by Michel de Nave, his uncle, entitled *Chronicon apparitionum et gestorum sancti Michaelis archangeli* (Douai, 1632, 8vo). The latter, born at Warnant, in Hesbaye, in 1539, died at Tournay Nov. 20, 1620, was successively prebendary and official of Arras, archdeacon and vicar-general of Tournay. His work, extracted largely from Colvenerius and Pantaléon, is filled with sentiments and details of erudition; but it is written without discrimination. See Hoefer, *Nouv. Biog. Générale*, s. v.

Na'vè (Ναυή, Ecclus. xli, 1). See NUN.

Navel (שֹׁר, *shor*, or שֹׁרֶר, *shorer'*, or שָׁרִיר, *sharir'*, to *knot* as a cord), the umbilical connection of the fœtus with the mother (Ezek. xvi, 4), hence the abdomen where it is attached (Job xl, 16; figuratively, Prov. iii, 8); finally, the *bodice* or vestment of that part of the person (Cant. vii, 2).

Navez, FRANÇOIS JOSEPH, an eminent Belgian painter, celebrated for his devotion to sacred art, was born at Charleroi Nov. 17, 1787, and studied at Brussels, and at Ghent, where he gained a prize. He early became noted for his artistic qualities; yet he continued his studies, and, not contented with the advantages afforded him at home, went to Paris, where he became a pupil of the celebrated J. L. David, and subsequently studied in Italy under distinguished masters. On his return to the Belgian capital, Navez rose rapidly to distinction. He was made professor in the normal school and director of the Academy of Fine Arts, and was generally acknowledged the most eminent master of the academical school of painting. He died in 1869. Among his works are, *Hagar in the Desert, Meeting of Isaac and Rebecca, Raising of the Son of the Shulamite Woman, Prophet Samuel, Ascension of the Virgin, Marriage of the Virgin, Jesus Sleeping*, and the *Virgin and the Infant Jesus.*

Navigation. The situation of Palestine on the Mediterranean, and the navigable inland sea of Tiberias, accounts for the frequent allusions in Scripture to ships and navigation. In the Old Testament only the Mediterranean commerce is spoken of, especially that of Palestine and the neighboring coasts; for Joppa in Philistia (Jonah i, 3; 2 Chron. ii, 16; comp. 2 Macc. xii, 3) and Tyre in Phœnicia (Isa. xxxiii, 1; Ezek. xxvii; comp. Acts xxi, 7) were in ancient times famous ports for the ships of distant nations (סֹחֵר אַנְשֵׁי, Prov. xxxi, 14), and afterwards the chief marts of Phœnician commerce. The Israelites soon became acquainted with the Phœnicians by coasting voyages (2 Chron. ii, 16), and the tribes of Zebulon (Gen. xlix, 13), Dan, and Asher (Judg. v, 17) seem to have been especially active in trade. After the Edomitish ports Elath and Eziongeber were conquered and annexed to his kingdom, Solomon established a commerce there, which Jehoshaphat afterwards endeavored in vain to revive. In the days of the Maccabees, Joppa was a Jewish seaport (1 Macc. xiv, 5); but Herod the Great opened Cæsarea, a larger and better harbor (Josephus, *War*, iii, 9, 3). Yet even then the Jews had no commerce of their own. The merchant fleets of Babylon are mentioned (Isa. xliii, 14), the ships of Tarshish (Isa. xxiii, 1), and the reed-boats of the Nile (Isa. xviii, 2). Many of the scenes of the Gospels are on the shore of the Sea of Genesareth, where afterwards the Jews had 230 ships, with four men in each (Josephus, *War*, ii, 21, 8). Jesus stood in one of the fishing-boats, and preached to the people on the shore (Matt. xiii, 2; Luke v, 3). He crossed the lake repeatedly (Matt. viii, 23; ix, 1; xiv,

13 sq.; John vi, 17). Some of his first disciples were owners of such boats (Matt. iv, 21; John xxi, 3; Luke v, 3). The vessels of the Egyptians (Diod. Sic. i, 57) and Phœnicians were adorned with brass, purple streamers, etc. The ships of Tyre were the most stately, and the most highly ornamented (Ezek. xxvii; comp. Camenz, De nave Tyria, Viteb. 1714). The deck was of cypress wood; the masts were pine (or cedar) trees ($\sigma\kappa\epsilon\tilde{\upsilon}o\varsigma$, Acts xxvii, 17, according to Kuinöl, ad loc.); the sails were of the Egyptian byssus, colored variously (comp. Ezek. xxvii, 7, and Hävernick, ad loc.). The oars were of oak (ver. 6). Tackling and rudder are not expressly mentioned, though some (as Umbreit) find the latter in הֹבֵל. Others understand it of the mast (see Gesen. Thes. i, 440). But in the New Testament the rudder or helm ($\pi\eta\delta\acute{\alpha}\lambda\iota o\nu$) is mentioned (James iii, 4; Acts xxvii, 40; in which latter passage it must be remarked that the larger ships had two rudders, one at each end; Ælian, V. H. ix, 40; Hygin. Astron. iii, 36; comp. Fab. 14; Heliod. Æth. v, 22; comp. Deyling, Observat. i, 295 sq.). Some had even four, two on each side (see Tacitus, Annal. ii, 6). The 27th and 28th chapters of Acts inform us in several particulars of the equipment of the larger merchant vessels in the Roman period. It was a "ship of burden" in which Paul was taken to Rome. But the ships of burden were built rounder and deeper than the ships of war (Cæsar, Bell. Gall. iv, 22, 25), and sometimes extraordinarily large (Cicero, Fam. xii, 15); therefore used only on the sea and large streams (Pliny, vi, 36), and were driven more by sails than by oars, whereas the ships of war always had from two to five rows (banks) of oars, or even more; hence called biremes, triremes, etc. ($\tau\rho\iota\acute{\eta}\rho\epsilon\iota\varsigma$, 2 Macc. iv, 20). On the pointed projecting front was the prow, carrying the figure-head ($\pi\alpha\rho\acute{\alpha}\sigma\eta\mu o\nu$, Acts xxviii, 11), from which the ship was named (see Tacit. Ann. vi, 34; Ovid, Trist. i, 10, 1 sq.). But the image of the guardian deity stood on the stern (puppis, Virgil, Æn. x, 156 sq.; Silv. Italicus, xiv, 410; Eurip. Iphig. Aul. 240 sq.). Sometimes the figure-head ($\pi\alpha\rho\acute{\alpha}\sigma\eta\mu o\nu$) may have been the statue of the god (comp. Herod. iii, 37 sq.; Ovid, Metam. iii, 617). Each ship had a life-boat ($\sigma\kappa\acute{\alpha}\phi\eta$, Acts xxvii, 16, 30, 32; comp. Cicero, Invent. ii, 51), several anchors (עוּגִּין, Mishna, Baba Bathra, v, 1) fastened with ropes (Arrian, Alex. ii, 4, 8; Acts xxvii, 29, 40; comp. Cæsar, Bell. Civ. i, 25; Josephus, Life, 33), and the sounding-line ($\beta o\lambda\acute{\iota}\varsigma$, comp. Acts xxvii, 28) to measure the depth in places where they wished to cast anchor. Among the sails, one in particular was called $\dot{\alpha}\rho\tau\acute{\epsilon}\mu\omega\nu$ (Acts xxvii, 40; Auth. Vers. "mainsail"), which was spread when a moderate force of wind was desired (comp. Schol. ad Juv. xii, 68), but its exact position cannot be determined. Modern writers understand it to be the "topsail." The girding the ship with strong cables, to prevent her from dashing to pieces on the rocks (Acts xxvii, 17), is often mentioned by ancient writers (Polyb. xxvii, 3, 3; Horace, Od. i, 14, 6 sq.; see Scheffer, Milit. Nav. ii, 5). The various expedients of mariners, when danger threatened the ship, are vividly described in Acts xxvii. First, they lightened the ship (ver. 19), then tried to reach the shore in the boats; then threw the freight into the sea (ver. 38; comp. Jonah i, 5), and the crew and passengers floated to the shore on boards and fragments of the wreck (Acts xxvii, 44). The master of a transport was called $\nu\alpha\acute{\upsilon}\kappa\lambda\eta\rho o\varsigma$ (ver. 11), and was generally a different person from the pilot, $\kappa\upsilon\beta\epsilon\rho\nu\acute{\eta}\tau\eta\varsigma$ (see Cicero, Inv. ii, 51). The former is called רַב הַחֹבֵל (Jonah i, 6), which some would render gubernator, "pilot." The crew are called in Hebrew מַלָּחִים (Ezek. xxvii, 9, 26, 29; Jonah i, 5), from whom the steersmen (חֹבְלִים, Ezek. xxvii, 27, 29) are distinguished. The Sept. renders the former by $\kappa\omega\pi\eta\lambda\acute{\alpha}\tau\alpha\iota$, rowers, the latter by $\kappa\upsilon\beta\epsilon\rho\nu\tilde{\eta}\tau\alpha\iota$, pilots; perhaps correctly. The ancients, by keeping close to the shore, and following all its sin-

uosities, in early times made their voyages very long (comp. 1 Kings x, 22). The same custom is said still to prevail on the Red Sea (Niebuhr, Trav. i, 258; Irwin, Trav. p. 100, 126 sq.). When they ventured out on the high seas, they were guided, having no compasses, by certain well-known stars, as the Pleiades, the Great and the Lesser Bear, Orion, etc. (Odys. v, 272; Polyb. ix, 14–17; Virgil, Æn. iii, 201 sq.; Ovid, Met. iii, 594 sq.; Arrian, Alex. vi, 26, 9). But the Greek and Roman mariners used to call upon the Dioscuri, Castor and Pollux, for deliverance from peril, these being universally considered the tutelary deities of navigation. Through dread of winter storms, ancient navigation was confined to the summer months (Acts xxvii, 9; Philo, Opp. ii, 548). The Romans considered the sea open from March to the time of the equinox (Veget. Mil. v, 9; Propert. i, 8, 9; Cæsar, Gal. iv, 36; v, 23), and ships which were under way at harvest-time sought a safe harbor for winter-quarters (Acts xxvii, 12). See also Schlözer, Vers. einer allge. Gesch. d. Handels u. der Schifffahrt in den Aeltesten Zeiten (Rostock, 1760); Le Roy, La Marine des anciens peuples (Paris, 1777); Berghaus, Gesch. d. Schifffahrtskunde bei d. vorn. Völk. d. Alterth. (Leips. 1792); Benedict, Vers. d. Gesch. d. Schifff. u. d. Hand. bei d. Alten (Leips. 1809); Baumstark, s. v. Navigatio u. navis, in Pauly's Real-Encyklop. v, 428 sq. See SHIP.

Navilieres, PIERRE, a French martyr to the cause of the Reformation doctrines, flourished near the middle of the 16th century. In 1552 Navilieres finished his theological studies at the seminary in Lausanne, under the eminent theologians Beza and Viret. Navilieres returned in this year to France, probably to his native place, Limoges. On the way he was seized and imprisoned for his Reformed opinions, and after due trial for heresy was, with four other students from Lausanne, condemned to death. An appeal to the king delayed the execution of the sentence for one year, and during this time they were kept in prison. Pierre Navilieres had become a Protestant against the protestations and entreaties of his parents, who now used every effort to save his life, and therefore urged him to renounce his principles. His uncle went to Lyons, and implored him with bitter tears to recant. But the young man continued steadfast. In a letter to his father's family he said: "Our Saviour tells us that we must leave father and mother, and wife and children, and follow him. I am confident of eternal life, because I have been cleansed by the blood of Christ from all my sins. Now, my dear friends, whose condition is better, yours or mine? My time will not be long, although I have now been in chains a year and a day. My dark, damp prison is far more pleasant to me than your elaborately ornamented parlors. The jailer's keys sound more sweetly to my ears than all the music of your splendid instruments. I am happy in the shades of death, for I am ready to lay aside this mortality and enter into God's rest. Now I ask you, Do you have such joys as these? Are your large revenues, your grand equipages, and the music of your singers able to give you the peace which I have?" All efforts for his retraction of the unpopular doctrines having proved futile, and the intervention of the Swiss authorities even having failed to stay the judgment of the courts, Navilieres was finally executed, May 16, 1553. Previous to his execution he had published a confession of his faith, which for some time was widely circulated and read among the people of France, and exerted a powerful influence for the Protestant cause. See Hurst, Martyrs of the Tract Cause, p. 136 sq.

Nawawi, MOHIEDDIN ABU-ZAKARIAH YAHIAH, el, an Arabian historian and doctor, was born in 1233 at Nawas, a borough near Damascus, in which city he died in 1277. He belonged to the Sofite sect of the Mohammedans. Nawawi composed a Commentary on the Koran; Critical Rules for History, etc. These writings, however, still remain in manuscript. The principal work of Nawawi is his *Mussulman Biographical Dictionary*, entitled *Kalib tehasib al-amsah* (Book of the Concordance of Names). The first section of it was published, with the Latin translation, under the title *Liber concinnitatis nominum, sive vitæ illustrium virorum*, with notes, by H. F. Wüstenfeld (Göttingen, 1832, 4to). This first section contains, besides the preface, only the life of the prophet Mohammed. M. Wüstenfeld afterwards published, in English, the first six parts, under the title *The Biographical Dictionary of Illustrious Men, chiefly at the beginning of Islamism* (Göttingen, 1841–44, 8vo). See Hoefer, *Nouv. Biog. Gén.* s. v.

Naylor, JAMES, an English religious enthusiast, noted for his fanatical excesses, was born at Ardsley, near Wakefield, in Yorkshire, about the year 1616. James, of humble but honorable parentage, with a limited education, started out in life, and married and settled in Wakefield parish about 1638. In 1641 he became a private soldier in the Parliamentary army, in which he was afterwards made a quartermaster, but quitted it on account of sickness in 1649. After his return home he was converted under the preaching of the Quaker George Fox (1651), and became so enthusiastic a religionist that the next year he believed himself divinely required to quit his relations and go abroad to preach Quakerism. Though poor, he started out unhesitatingly, relying on that divine aid which he believed himself sure to receive. He was a man of excellent natural parts, and acquitted himself so well, both in word and writing, that many joined his society through his ministry. He came to London towards the beginning of 1655, in which city a meeting of Quakers had been established by the ministry of Edward Burrough and Francis Howgill, two eminent Quakers from Westmoreland. Here Naylor preached with so much applause that the distinction which he acquired occasioned his fall; for some inconsiderate women, setting him up in their esteem above Howgill and Burrough, went so far as to disturb them in their preaching. These men, besides giving to the women a deserved reproof, complained of it to Naylor. But he, instead of passing censure, suffered himself to be wrought upon by the reiterated and passionate complaints of the inconsiderate women, especially one Martha Simmons (the chief engine of the mischief), and became estranged from the leading Quakers, who would not suffer him to give ear to the flatteries of such misadvised adherents. In the year 1656 he suffered imprisonment in Exeter; and about this time several deluded persons addressed him by letter in terms of great extravagance. He was called "the everlasting Son of Righteousness," "Prince of Peace," "the only-begotten Son of God," "the fairest of ten thousand;" and during his confinement in Exeter jail some women knelt before him and kissed his feet. About this time George Fox, returning from the West, where he had himself suffered a rigorous imprisonment, called on James Naylor in the Exeter prison and reproached him for his defection and excesses. On his release from imprisonment Naylor repaired to Bristol, where his followers formed a procession, and led him into that city in a manner which they intended to resemble the entrance of Christ into Jerusalem. His Quaker friends turned away from him disheartened, and the British authorities, displeased with such exhibitions of religious extravagance, brought him soon to trial, and he was declared guilty of blasphemy by Parliament, and sentenced to a double whipping at different times, branding, boring of the tongue with a hot iron, and imprisonment and hard labor during pleasure. This sentence, though illegal and barbarous, and as wide from the mark of good-sense as Naylor's own excesses, was fully inflicted upon the unhappy man, who, when the delirium of fanaticism was over, humbly acknowledged and lamented the delusion under which he had labored. He wrote while in prison at Bridewell to his friends, regretting his past conduct. After his confinement, which lasted for two years, he again held fellowship with the Quakers, and

enjoyed their confidence and esteem. He died in 1660. The severe measures of Parliament against Naylor have been frequently condemned. It is urged by Nonconformists that the punishment was inflicted in order to prove a terror to all Quakers, who were greatly hated at that time in England. The probability is that Naylor was not in his right mind when he perpetrated those wild, fanatical excesses; at least so judges Southey, who says in *The* (Lond.) *Quarterly Review* (vol. x, p. 107), " He (i. e. Naylor) recovered both from his madness and his sufferings, and his after-life was a reproach to those who, in the hardness of their hearts and the blindness of their understandings, had treated insanity like guilt." Naylor's writings were collected into an octavo volume, and printed in 1716. Of his theological treatises, which bear dates from 1653 to 1656, some were in answer to others by Ellis Bradshaw, Enoch Hewitt, Richard Baxter, Thomas Moore, Jeremy Ives, Thomas Collier, etc. A relation of his *Life, Conversion, Examination, Confession, and Sentence* was published in 1657 (4to). A Memoir of his *Life, Ministry, Trial, and Sufferings* was brought out in 1719 (8vo); and more recently his *Life* has been published by the eminent Quaker apologist, Joseph Gurney Bevan. See *Biog. Brit.* s. v.; Sewel, *Hist. of the Quakers;* Watts, *Biblioth. Brit.* s. v.; *Gen. Biog. Dict.* s. v.; Neal, *Hist. of the Puritans*, vol. iii (Supplem.); Burton, *Parliam. Diary*, i, 46–173; Baxter, *Ch. Hist. of England*, p. 611; and Whittier, in the *Democratic Review*, March, 1846.

Nazaræans is the name of a Jewish sect mentioned by Epiphanius (*Hær.* xviii). The name is probably derived from *netsir*, a *branch* (Epiphanius also writes it *Nasaræans* and *Nassaraians*), and, if we are right in identifying this sect with the Genistæ (q. v.), signifies a branch of the true stock. The sect aimed at a patriarchal religion in place of a Mosaic Judaism. They canonized the patriarchs, and did not exclude Moses and Joshua from that society. They allowed that a law was given to Moses, but asserted that this law was lost, and that the Pentateuch is corrupt or supposititious. They practiced circumcision, kept the Sabbath and the Jewish festivals, rejected the sacrifice of animals, and ate no flesh. It follows from this that they rejected the history of Genesis as well as the laws of Moses; but whether they professed to found their doctrine on tradition or on a new revelation is not told. They were found in Galaaditis, Basanitis, and other parts beyond Jordan. See NAZARENES.

Nazaréne, an epithet given to our Lord. There are two Greek words for this designation—Ναζαρηνός (only Mark i, 24; xiv, 67; xvi, 6; Luke iv, 34); and (elsewhere) Ναζωραῖος—both derived from Ναζαρέθ, Nazareth of Galilee, the place of the Saviour's childhood and education. These two Greek words occur in the New Testament nineteen times; twice only are they rendered Nazarene (Matt. ii, 23; Acts xxiv, 5); everywhere else by the words "of Nazareth," as Matt. xxi, 11. This appellative is found in the New Testament applied to Jesus by the dæmons in the synagogue at Capernaum (Mark i, 24; Luke iv, 34); by the people, who so describe him to Bartimæus (Mark x, 47; Luke xviii, 37); by the soldiers who arrested Jesus (John xviii, 5, 7); by the servants at his trial (Matt. xxvi, 71; Mark xiv, 67); by Pilate in the inscription on the cross (John xix, 19); by the disciples on the way to Emmaus (Luke xxiv, 19); by Peter (Acts ii, 22; iii, 6; iv, 10); by Stephen, as reported by the false witness (Acts vi, 14); by the ascended Jesus (Acts xxii, 8); and by Paul (Acts xxvi, 9). At first it was applied to Jesus naturally and properly, as defining his residence. In process of time, however, other influences came into operation. Galilee was held in disesteem for several reasons: its dialect was provincial, rough, and strange (Buxtorf, *Lex. Talmud;* Mark xiv, 70); its population was impure, containing not only provincial Jews, but also heathen, as Egyptians, Arabians, Phœnicians (Strabo, *Geog.* xvi, 523); its people were seditious (Josephus, as cited in Schleusner, s. v. Γαλιλαῖος); whence also the point of the accusation made against Paul, as "ringleader of the sect of Nazarenes" (Acts xxiv, 5). Nazareth was a despised part even of Galilee, being a small, obscure place. Accordingly its inhabitants were held in little consideration everywhere. Hence the name Nazarene (Kuinöl, in Matt. ii, 23) became a term of reproach (Wetstein, in Matt. ii, 23, 26, 71), and as such, as well as a mere epithet of description, it is used in the New Testament. "The name still exists in Arabic as the ordinary designation of Christians, and the recent revolt in India was connected with a pretended ancient prophecy that the *Nazarenes*, after holding power for one hundred years, would be expelled." See NAZARETH.

In Matt. ii, 23, it is said of Jesus, "And he came and dwelt in a city called Nazareth; that it might be fulfilled which was spoken by the prophets, He shall be called *a Nazarene.*" This citation has received the following explanations (Spanheim, *Dubia Evangelica*, ii, 538–648; Wolf, *Curæ Philologicæ*, i, 46–48; Hengstenberg, *Christology of the O. T.* ii, 106–112): 1. It is generally thought that the evangelist does not limit himself to a quotation from any single prophet, but alludes to the several passages of the prophets where the Messiah is spoken of as "despised of men," as Psa. xxii; Isa. liii. (See Paulus, Rosenmüller, Kuinöl, Van der Palm, Gersdorf, Olshausen, Ebrard, Davidson, Lange, and others, ad loc.) 2. But many (as Bauer, Gieseler, in the *Stud. u. Krit.* 1831, p. 588 sq.; De Wette, Bretschneider, 3d ed.) find here an allusion to the passages where the Messiah is called נֵצֶר, *nêtser*, a branch or sprout (Isa. xi, 1; see Hengstenberg, *Christol.* ii, 1 sq.). "This explanation, which Jerome mentions as that given by learned (Christian) Jews in his day, has been adopted by Surenhusius, Fritzsche, Krabbe (*Leben Jesu*), Drechsler (on Isa. xi, 1), Schirlitz (*N.-T. Wörterb.*), Robinson (*N.-T. Lex.*), and Meyer. It is confirmed by the following considerations· (1) *Nêtser*, as Hengstenberg, after De Dieu and others, has shown, was the proper Hebrew name of Nazareth. (2) The reference to the etymological signification of the word is entirely in keeping with Matt. ii, 21–23. (3) The Messiah is expressly called a *Nêtser* in Isa. xi, 1. (4) The same thought, and under the same image, although expressed by a different word, is found in Jer. xxiii, 5; xxxiii, 15; Zech. iii, 8; vi, 12, which accounts for the statement of Matthew that this prediction was uttered 'by the *prophets*' in the plural." It seems, however, rather refined for so general a quotation; nor does it after all point especially to any particular passage of the Old Testament as being cited. Moreover, the ζ in Ναζωραῖος cannot correspond to צ, but to ז (see Olshausen, ad loc.; so Bengel, who derives the word from נֵזֶר, *a crown*). 3. Others have supposed a direct quotation from some lost prophecy (Chrysostom, Theophylact, Clericus, etc., ad loc.), or from some apocryphal book (Ewald), or that it is a traditional prophecy (Calovius; Alexander, *Connection and Harmony of the Old and New Testaments*), all which suppositions are refuted by the fact that the phrase "by the prophets," in the New Testament, refers exclusively to the *canonical* books of the Old Testament. Nor is there any evidence elsewhere of such a source. 4. Many would make Ναζωραῖος = נָזִיר, *Nazarite*, i. e. one especially *consecrated* or *devoted* to God (Judg. xiii, 5); but this does not at all accord with our Saviour's character (see Matt. xi, 19, etc.), nor with the Sept. mode of spelling the word, which is generally Ναζιραῖος, and never Ναζωραῖος. (See Schleusner's *Lex. to LXX*, ad verb.) See NAZARITE. 5. "Recently a suggestion, which Witsius borrowed from Socinus, has been revived by Zuschlag and Riggenbach, that the true word is נֹצֵר or נֹצְרִי, *my Saviour*, with reference to Jesus as the Saviour of the

world, but without much success (Zuschlag, in the *Zeitschrift für die Lutherische Theologie*, 1854, p. 417–446; Riggenbach in the *Stud. u. Krit.* 1855, p. 588, 612)." See JESUS.

Nazarenes is the name of a Jewish Christian sect whose members continued to observe all the obligations and ceremonies of the law of Moses after the mother Church of Jerusalem had abandoned it. The sect was the Pella branch of the Jerusalem Church, which did not join in the change made on the appointment of Marcus, the first Jerusalem bishop of the uncircumcision. See JUDAIZING CHRISTIANS. The Nazarenes are not named by the earlier historians and fathers of the Church; Irenæus, Hippolytus, Tertullian, Origen, Clement, and Eusebius are silent regarding them; and the accounts and notices which we have of them are furnished by Epiphanius, Augustine, Theodóret, Philaster, Jerome, and Isidore; but from these it is clearly apparent, as we shall presently show, that the Nazarenes and Ebionites were identical, and that the former, as has been supposed by some Unitarian scholars, was really composed only of such primitive Christian converts from Judaism who retained their Jewish prejudices despite their conversion; and that their faith respecting Jesus Christ, which is unjustly claimed to have been Socinian —i. e. that Jesus was a mere man—is not to be taken as an illustration and evidence of the faith of the early Church. For the sake of clearing up this question we append a full examination of the early writers of the Church who have furnished us any clew regarding the Nazarenes and their relation to the early orthodox Church. See NAZARÆANS.

I. Of the Church fathers who wrote regarding the Nazarenes, the earliest, Epiphanius, states that the Nazarenes flourished principally in Berœa, in Cœle-Syria, in Decapolis at Pella, and in Basanitis, and that from thence, after the retreat from Jerusalem, the sect had its beginning. Epiphanius adds that he could not ascertain the date of the sect as compared with the Simonians, Corinthians, and others—a statement which points to a sect not formed by one leader whose date could not be ascertained, but to a party gradually separating from the Church. Jerome speaks (*Catal. Scriptt. Eccl.* s. v. *Matthæus*) of the Nazarenes who dwell at Berœa using St. Matthew's Hebrew Gospel, and this implies an early formation of the party. Epiphanius, in his prefatory index, defines the Nazarenes as confessing Jesus to be Christ and the Son of God, but as living in all things according to the law. Augustine (*Hæres.* ix) describes them as confessing Christ to be the Son of God, but observing the law, which Christians are taught to keep, not carnally, but spiritually. From all this it is clear that the Nazarenes were Jewish Christians, forming themselves into a party in Pella and its neighborhood after the retreat from Jerusalem, and passing by degrees into a distinct sect. But there were two classes of Jewish Christians—the one apostolic and orthodox, who did not impose the observance of the law as necessary to salvation, who acknowledged the mission of St. Paul, and recognised the communion of the Gentiles; the other Pharisaic and sectarian, who maintained the universal obligation of the law, and denounced St. Paul as a transgressor. In inquiring to which of these two classes the Nazarenes belonged, it must be noticed, in the first place, that the community at Pella was composed of those converts who joined the Church of Jerusalem in her exile, of those Hellenistic fugitives whose national feelings and love of their city was not so strong as in the native Jews, and of those native Jews who had formed connections in their new residence which overpowered their national feelings. It was a community predisposed to accept in the spirit as well as the letter the decree of the Council of Jerusalem. In the next place the Ebionites and the Nazarenes are contrasted. But it was the Ebionites (q. v.) who held the universal obligation of the law. When, therefore, we read in Jerome (in *Isa.* i. t. 3, p. 4 [ed. 1616]),

"Audiant Ebionæi, qui post passionem abolitam legem putant esse servandam. Audiant Ebionitarum socii, qui Judæis tantum, et de stirpe Isrælitici generis hæc custodienda decernunt," it can hardly be doubted that the "Ebionitarum socii" are the Nazarenes. This sect is thus identified as, in its origin at least, a branch of the orthodox Church of Jerusalem. The Church of Jerusalem had been under the apostles of the circumcision, and at the time of the retreat to Pella had "a literature consisting, on the one hand, of most of the New Testament, except the Gospel of St. John, and on the other of works treating of the much-studied old Halachah and Haggadah law, and others largely dependent on poetic fancy;" "with rites wherein Jewish and Christian practices are still found side by side, circumcision and baptism, hallowing of the Sabbath and of the Lord's day, Passover, perhaps, and Eucharist." These are the surroundings amid which we place the sects of the Nazarenes and its origin (Sinker, Testamenta xii Patriarcharum [Camb. 1869], p. 124). The last-made quotation, the words of which were used with reference to the author of the Testamenta of the twelve patriarchs, leads us to a remarkable book which proceeded from the school, and probably from the very sect under consideration. This book and the writings of the Ebionite school have been much studied of late, and in the hands of German scholars have thrown considerable light on the history of the early Church. In noticing it as an example of the theology of the Nazarenes, it must be remembered that we are entirely ignorant of its author, of the position he held in the Judæo-Christian Church, and of the degree of acceptance his book met with. In short, we are entitled to assume that it is a representative book. But it is known from other authority that the author was of the Nazarene school, and we are thus entitled to gather from his book the broad and distinctive characters of the school. Finer shades of doctrine, and doctrines that are not distinctive, must be referred to the standard formed by the teaching of the apostles as supervening upon the tenets of the Jewish Church. Lardner's summary of the writer's doctrine may be first given. The writer speaks of the nativity of Christ, the meekness and unblamableness of his life, his crucifixion at the instigation of the Jewish priests, the wonderful concomitants of his death, his resurrection, and ascension. He represents the character of the Messiah as God and man, the Most High God among men eating and drinking with them; the Saviour of the world, of the Gentiles and Israel, as eternal High-Priest and King. He likewise speaks of the effusion of the Holy Spirit upon the Messiah, attended with a voice from heaven; his unrighteous treatment by the Jews, and their desolations and the destruction of the Temple on that account; the call of the Gentiles; the illuminating of them generally with new light; the effusion of the Spirit upon believers, but especially and in a more abundant measure upon the Gentiles. Here little notice is taken of Christ's miracles; however, he speaks of the Messiah as a "man who renews the law in the power of the Most High," in which expressions the working of miracles seems to be implied. Here are also passages which seem to contain allusions to the Gospels of St. Matthew, St. Luke, and St. John, the Acts of the Apostles, the Epistle to the Ephesians, the First to the Thessalonians, the First to Timothy, the Epistle to the Hebrews, the First Epistle of St. John, and the Book of Revelation. As far as was consistent with his assumed character, the author declares the canonical authority of the Acts of the Apostles and the Epistles of St. Paul (Credibility, etc. ii, 363). Here the recognition of St. John's Gospel and Epistles, and of St. Paul's Epistles, shows that the Nazarenes, at the later period of this book, were not without the teaching of full catholic Christianity. The question will arise again, with regard to a still later period, "What was Nazarene doctrine respecting the divinity of our Lord?" At the period we have now before us it is just to the Nazarenes, as Jewish Christians,

to assimilate their confession, that Jesus is Christ and the Son of God, with St. Peter's confession, without attributing to them any limited meanings of the term, such as were devised at a later time. The passages may be seen quoted and commented upon in the third chapter of Sinker's work, in which Dorner's remark is quoted, "that the words," from Levi, xviii, "imply that the relation of Christ to the Father is as close as is that of a human son to his father." Christ's birth of a virgin is referred to in Joseph, xix; his pre-existence in Dan, vi; Simeon, vi. On these points we may believe the Nazarenes to have been orthodox. The ethics of the "Testaments" are sufficiently characterized in the remark, "that the view held as to the law of God is the same which we find in St. James's Epistle, the old Mosaic law completed and developed by Christ, and that thus the author recognises the moral bearing of Christianity, not as a contrast, but as a continuation of the old religion" (Sinker's Testam. xii Patriarch. p. 121). The subject of priesthood—the priesthood of our Lord primarily, of the ministers of the Gospel secondarily—requires a more distinct notice. Judah (sec. 21) is made to say, "God gave Levi the priesthood, to me the kingdom, and subjected the kingdom to the priesthood. To me he gave things of earth, to him things of heaven. As heaven surpasses earth, so God's priesthood surpasses an earthly kingdom." The "Testaments" represents Christ as combining in himself the offices of High-Priest and of King, and states consequently that he is to spring from the tribe of Levi as well as from the tribe of Judah (Sim. vii; Dan, v). This identifies, or at least tends to identify, Christ's priesthood with the priesthood of Aaron, contrary to the teaching of the Epistle to the Hebrews. This opinion of the descent of the Virgin Mary from both Judah and Levi might doubtless be held by men of piety and catholicity, who might further repudiate the inference to which it seems naturally to lead; but, on the other hand, it is certain that the opinion, made to rest, as it must, upon much legendary matter, would connect itself with heresy more readily than the historical Davidic genealogy. It would suit the purpose of those who denied that the Word was made flesh to represent the genealogy as a myth, setting forth a transmission of office. It would be more complete if it set forth a transmission of priesthood as well as the royalty of our Lord. The Gnostics were all of them Docetæ (Iren. cxi, 77), and there is nothing unreasonable in the supposition that Docetic teachers in later times laid hold of this opinion, if it were current in the community of the Nazarenes, and endeavored through it to instil their heresy. In that case we should have a reason for the disquisition regarding the priesthood and the royalty, with which Epiphanius introduces his account of the Nazarenes, the relevancy of which is not otherwise very clear. The opinions of the author of the "Testaments" regarding the ministry of the Church are stated clearly in the Testament of Levi. In sect. 3 the universe in the times of the Gospel is described as of seven spheres. Three represent the outer world—the world of unbelievers; the third containing the encampments of the ministers of retribution on the ungodly. The fourth, fifth, and sixth represent the Church, taking the word church in its widest sense; the fourth being the sphere of the saints, the fifth of the ministry, the sixth of ministering angels of intercourse. The fifth is occupied by angels of the face of God. They minister and make atonement before the Lord for all the ignorances (ἀγνοίαις) of the just. They offer to the Lord the reasonable service of a sweet-smelling savor and an unbloody offering. Again, in sect. 8, after the robing of Levi, it is said that Levi's offspring shall be divided into three ranks of office. Two appear to belong to the body of Levites and to the Aaronic priesthood; the third clearly belongs to the Christian ministry. For the third possesses a new name; a King arises from Judah and creates a new priesthood, which is κατὰ τὸν τύπον τῶν ἐθνῶν εἰς πάντα τὰ ἔθνη. The ethnic type is the priesthood of Melchisedek. A passage in Theophilus of Antioch makes this designation easier: "Melchisedek was the first priest of all the priests of the Most High God. From his time priests were found in all the earth" (*To Autol.* ii, cap. 31). This new priesthood shall set in order the table of the Lord, and of it shall be priests, judges, and scribes; i. e. priests in ministering, judges in discipline, scribes in teaching. The only objection which can be made to this description is that the Christian ministry is made to descend from Levi. If the newness of their priesthood were lost sight of, the Christian ministry would be at once identified with the Aaronic priesthood. From this affiliation of the ministers of the Gospel to Levi we are inclined to contend, supposing that the "Testaments" justly represent the belief of the Jewish Christians, that the lower or spurious sacerdotalism which has found place in the Church is of Judaic, not of Gentile, origin. That the Hebrews found a difficulty in appreciating a true import of the history of Melchisedek is clear from the Epistle to the Hebrews. A sense of this difficulty may have led the author of the "Testaments" to refrain from an explicit mention of Melchisedek. Of another author of this school, Aristo of Pella, we have very short fragments (Routh, *Reliquiæ*, p. 93–97). One fragment is important. Aristo speaks of Jesus as the Son of God, the Creator of the world (see Wescott, *On the Canon*, p. 105–107; and Prof. Lightfoot, *St. Paul and the Three*, p. 294, n. 2).

II. It may next be inquired whether the Nazarenes in later times fell into heresy. Augustine accuses them only of Judaizing (*De Hæres.* ix; *Contr. Faust*, xix, 4; *Contr. Crescon. I*, xxxi, 36; *Epist. ad Hieron.* lxxxii; ii, 16; *De Bapt. contr. Donat.* vii, 1). Epiphanius having briefly defined them in the prefatory index as Judaizers, begins in the work itself (*Hæres.* xxix) with stating that they hold the same opinions as the Corinthians, but in his seventh chapter he professes his inability to say whether they did or did not hold Corinthian doctrine regarding Christ. This quite sets aside his previous statement, which may be referred to his well-known proneness to make charges of heresy. In his Commentary on Isaiah Jerome calls the Nazarenes the Hebrews that believe in Christ (in *Isa.* cap. ix, t. 3, p. 33 [ed. 1616]), giving the Nazarene explanation of the prophecy that Christ's doctrine delivered the land of Zebulon and Naphtali from . . . Jewish traditions, that by St. Paul's preaching the Gospel shone among the Gentiles, and at length the whole world saw the clear light of the Gospel (see also *Ad August. Ep.* 89, t. ii, p. 266 [ed. 1616]). Accordingly Lardner writes, "It might easily be shown that the Nazarean Christians did not reject St. John's Gospel, nor hold any principles that oblige them to reject or dislike it" (*Jewish Testimonies*, cap. i, vol. vi, p. 387 [Kippis's ed. 1861]). On the other hand, Theodoret (*De Hær. fab.* ii, 2) accuses the Nazarenes of denying Christ's divinity; but the later authority of Theodoret cannot outweigh the mass of earlier testimony in their favor.

III. Adopting, then, the conclusion that the Nazarenes retained their orthodox creed, it remains to be asked whether they retained their position in the Church, or whether, while free from heretical error, they were yet sectarian. There is no historical information to enable us to answer this question; but there does not appear to be any sufficient reason why the Church of Jerusalem, when it renounced Judaism, should exclude the Church of Pella from communion simply for its retention of national customs; and certainly there was no reason why the Church of Pella should renounce communion with Jerusalem. The general observance for some centuries of the decree of the Council of Jerusalem (Judaizers), enforcing on Gentiles abstinence from things strangled and from blood, implied also (it may fairly be argued) a liberty to the Jews to continue in the observance of their national law; while canons intended to prevent Gentile churches from adopting Jewish customs do not

apply to the Nazarenes. On the other hand, the strong condemnations of the Nazarenes as heretics by Epiphanius and Augustine can be fully explained only on the supposition that the Nazarenes had become the authors of a schism by renouncing communion with the Church. Augustine states in several places that the Nazarenes were called by some *Symmachians* (q. v.). See Gieseler, *Von den Nazaräern u. Ebioniten* (in Stäudlin u. Tzschirner's *Archiv*, vol. iv, st. 2); Schwegler, *Das Nachapostolische Zeitalter*, p. 179 sq.; Schliemann, *Die Clementinen nebst d. verwandten Schriften*, etc. (Hamb. 1844); Haag, *Histoire des dogmes Chrétiens*, i, 109; ii, 22; Tayler, *Hippolytus and the Christian Church*, p. 70; Hagenbach, *History of Doctrines*, i, 55, 56, 170; ii, 328, 344; Schaff, *History of the Christian Church*, i, 212; Mosheim, *Eccles. Hist.* i, 222, 400; Riddle, *Christian Antiquities*, p. 182, 185; Neander, *Ch. Hist.* i, 349 et passim; Pressensé, *Heresy and Christian Doctrine*, p. 78; *Church Rev.* vol. xx; and especially the article in Blunt, *Dict. of Sects, Heresies*, etc., s. v.

Naz'areth (ἡ Ναζαρές or Ναζαρέτ; usually thought to be a Græcized derivative from נֵצֶר, *a sprout*, Aram. נַצְרָאת, see Hengstenberg, *Christol.* ii, 1 sq.; comp. Keim, *Gesch. Jesu* [Zur. 1867], i, 318; but Hitzig, in the *Heidelb. Jahrbüchern*, 1870, p. 50, conjectures somewhat wildly an original form, נָזְרַת, with the signif. "goddess of success"), the place of residence (but not the birthplace) of our Lord. In the following account we bring together whatever is known respecting this interesting locality. See JESUS.

1. *Scripture Mention.*—Nazareth was the town of Joseph and Mary, to which they returned with the infant Jesus (εἰς τὴν πόλιν ἑαυτῶν) after the accomplishment of the events connected with his birth and earliest infancy (Matt. ii, 22). Previous to that event, the place is altogether unknown to history. In Old-Testament Scripture it is never once named, though a town could hardly fail to have existed on so eligible a spot from early times. Josephus, though personally familiar with the whole district in which it lies, is equally silent regarding it. The secluded nature of the spot where it stands, together with its own insignificance, probably combined to shroud it in that obscurity on account of which it would seem to have been divinely chosen for the rearing of God's incarnate Son. As his forerunner, John the Baptist, "was in the desert," unnoticed and unknown, "till the day of his showing unto Israel," so the great Messiah himself, till his public ministry began, was hidden from the world among the Galilæan hills.

The other passages of Scripture which refer expressly to Nazareth, though not numerous, are suggestive and deserve to be recalled here. It was the home of Joseph and Mary (Luke ii, 39). The angel announced to the Virgin there the birth of the Messiah (Luke i, 26–28). The holy family returned thither after the flight into Egypt (Matt. ii, 23). Nazareth is called the native country (ἡ πατρὶς αὐτοῦ) of Jesus: he grew up there from infancy to manhood (Luke iv, 16), and was known through life as "The Nazarene." He taught in the synagogue there (Matt. xiii, 54; Luke iv, 16), and was dragged by his fellow-townsmen to the precipice in order to be cast down thence and be killed (εἰς τὸ κατακρημνίσαι αὐτόν). "Jesus of Nazareth, king of the Jews," was written over his cross (John xix, 19), and after his ascension he revealed himself under that appellation to the persecuting Saul (Acts xxii, 8). The place has given name to his followers in all ages and all lands, a name which will never cease to be one of honor and reproach. See NAZARENE.

The origin of the disrepute in which Nazareth stood (John i, 47) is not certainly known. All the inhabitants of Galilee were looked upon with contempt by the people of Judæa because they spoke a ruder dialect, were less cultivated, and were more exposed by their position to contact with the heathen. But Nazareth labored under a special opprobrium, for it was a Galilæan and not a southern Jew who asked the reproachful question, whether "any good thing" could come from that source. The term "good" (ἀγαθόν), having more commonly an ethical sense, it has been suggested that the inhabitants of Nazareth may have had a bad name among their neighbors for irreligion or some laxity of morals. The supposition receives support from the disposition which they manifested towards the person and ministry of our Lord. They attempted to kill him; they expelled him twice (for Luke iv, 16–29 and Matt. xiii, 54–58 relate probably to different occurrences) from their borders; they were so wilful and unbelieving that he performed not many miracles among them (Matt. xiii, 58); and, finally, they compelled him to turn his back upon them and reside at Capernaum (Matt. iv. 13).

2. *Location.*—Nazareth is a moderate journey of three days from Jerusalem, seven hours, or about twenty miles, from Akka or Ptolemais (Acts xxi, 7), five or six hours, or eighteen miles, from the Sea of Galilee, six miles west from Mount Tabor, two hours from Cana, and two or three from Endor and Nain. It is situated among the hills which constitute the south ridges of Lebanon, just before they sink down into the plain of Esdraelon. The traveller, coming from the south, ascends the mountain range by a steep and rugged path, which, winding onwards and upwards through the hills, brings him suddenly into a small sequestered hollow among their summits; and here, nestling close in at the base of the loftiest of the encircling heights, he beholds—what must ever be to the Christian one of the most profoundly interesting scenes on the face of this earth—the home for thirty years of the Saviour of the world. The surrounding heights vary in altitude; some of them rise to 400 or 500 feet. They have rounded tops, are composed of the glittering limestone which is so common in that country, and, though on the whole sterile and unattractive in appearance, present not an unpleasing aspect, diversified as they are with the foliage of fig-trees and wild shrubs, and with the verdure of occasional fields of grain. Our familiar hollyhock is one of the gay flowers which grow wild there. The enclosed valley is peculiarly rich and well cultivated: it is filled with cornfields, with gardens, hedges of cactus, and clusters of fruit-bearing trees. Being so sheltered by hills, Nazareth enjoys a mild atmosphere and climate. Hence all the fruits of the country—as pomegranates, oranges, figs, olives—ripen early and attain a rare perfection.

In speaking of the precise position of Nazareth, there is some discrepancy among travellers: Stanley says, "The village stands on the steep slope of the *southwestern* side of the valley" (*Sinai and Palestine*, p. 365). Wilson (*Lands of the Bible*, ii, 92) observes that "the village of Násirah, or Nazareth, stands on the *eastern* side of the basin in which it is situated." Thomson (*Land and Book*, ii, 131) seems to place it on the *western* side. Dr. Porter (*Hand-book for Syria and Palestine*, ii, 359) has described Nazareth as lying at the

bottom of "the hill on the *north* side" of the little plain. An inspection of the accompanying plan shows that it lies at the foot and partly up the slope at the *north-western* angle of the valley.

Of the identification of the ancient site there can be no doubt. The name of the present village is *en-Názirah*, the same, therefore, as of old; it is formed on a hill or mountain (Luke iv, 29); it is within the limits of the province of Galilee (Mark i, 9); it is near Cana (whether we assume *Kana* on the east or *Kana* on the north-east as the scene of the first miracle), according to the implication in John ii, 1, 2, 11; a precipice exists in the neighborhood (Luke iv, 29); and, finally, a series of testimonies (Reland, *Palæst.* p. 905) reach back to Eusebius, the father of Church history, which represent the place as having occupied an invariable position.

3. *History.*—Of the condition of Nazareth during the earlier centuries of the Christian æra next to nothing is known. Eusebius, in his *Onomasticon*, alludes to it as a village near Mount Tabor. Epiphanius speaks of it as formerly a town, but in his day only a village. Helena, the mother of Constantine, is related to have built the first church of the Annunciation here. In the time of the Crusaders, the episcopal see of Bethsean was transferred there. The birthplace of Christianity was lost to the Christians by their defeat at Hattin in 1183, and was laid utterly in ruins by sultan Bibars in 1263. Ages passed away before it rose again from this prostration. In 1620 the Franciscans rebuilt the church of the Annunciation, and connected a cloister with it. In 1799 the Turks assaulted the French general Junot at Nazareth; and shortly after 2100 French, under Kleber and Napoleon, defeated a Turkish army of 25,000 at the foot of Mount Tabor. Napoleon himself, after that battle, spent a few hours at Nazareth, and reached there the

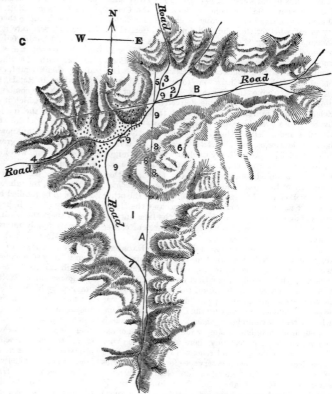

Map of the Valley of Nazareth (by Dr. J. S. Jewell).

A. Valley, about 2 miles long; B. 1 mile long; C. Hills with a *wely*. 1. Wide part of the valley; 2. Fountain of the Virgin; 3. Chapel of Annunciation; 4. Entrance from west; 5. Usual camping-place; 6. Limestone spur; 7. Entrance from south; 8. Artificial caves; 9. Hedges of cactus.

northern limit of his Eastern expedition. The earthquake which destroyed Safed in 1837, injured also Nazareth. No Jews reside there at present, which may be ascribed perhaps as much to the hostility of the Christian sects as to their own hatred of the prophet who was sent "to redeem Israel."

4. *Traditionary Localities.*—Epiphanius, in his book against heresies, written in the latter half of the 4th century, states that, from times prior to those of Josephus, onward to the reign of the elder Constantine, none but Jews were allowed to live in it. Being himself a native of Judæa, and born, as is believed, of Jewish parents, his information on such points as these is not likely to have been incorrect. If so, it effectually overturns all confidence in those many monkish traditions of which the modern Nazareth is full. If several centuries elapsed before Christians resorted to it, or dwelt in it at all, it must needs have been utterly impossible to identify, as those traditions pretend to do, the precise locality of any one of the memorable incidents from which it derives its undying fame.

In the 6th century, although, so far as appears, no trace had been found of either the house of Joseph and Mary or of the scene of the annunciation, those who trade in discoveries of that kind were then already at work. Antoninus Martyr, who in the course of that century went from Tyre to visit Nazareth, found there a synagogue, in which, as he was told, "had stood the very bench on which, along with the children of the place, Jesus in his childhood had sat; but which, to keep it out of the hands of the Christians, the Jews had carried off" (*De urbibus et vicis Palæstinæ*). In the immediately succeeding century, however, almost everything of which tradition boasts at the present day in Nazareth had become an accepted and firmly-established belief of that superstitious age. Writing of the holy places in the 7th century, Adamnanus expressly mentions one great church as having been built over the site of the house in which our Lord was brought up; and another on the spot where the angel Gabriel appeared to the Virgin, to announce to her that divine mystery which has made her blessed among women. Phocas, a writer of the 12th century, alludes to the same traditions, as still studiously cherished; and specially notices the fountain, in a small cave beneath a splendid church, as that at which Mary was wont to drink, and where the angel appeared to her; and also to the house of Joseph as having been changed into a most beautiful place of Christian worship. Tradition, however, is not always sufficiently careful of its own consistency. For it would have us to believe that this house of Joseph, which in the 12th century had been so transmuted, was, in its original form of Joseph's dwelling, carried away bodily from Nazareth by the hands of angels, and set down on the hill above Fiume, at the head of the Adriatic Gulf; and that from thence, after a short stay in the plain below, it was conveyed across the sea to the eastern slope of the Apennines, where, as the *santa casa*, within the magnificent church of our Lady of Loretto, it stands to this day, and continues to be the most frequented and honored of all the holy places in the world! Those who are able to get over all the other difficulties connected with this marvellous story, will not be much embarrassed by the fact that, while the actual house of Joseph, wherever it stood, was no doubt built of the grayish-white limestone of which the whole country around Nazareth is formed, the *santa casa* at Loretto is built of a dark-red stone, to which there is nothing like in all the land of Judæa. Although the miraculous transportation of the holy house took place, according to the tradition regarding it, about the close of the 13th century, there is no trace of the existence of the tradition itself till near the end of the 15th century. That this monstrous fable should have been formally recited and canonized in a bull of the lettered and luxurious sceptic, pope Leo X, serves only to show that there is no delusion too gross for the Papal Church to practice

on human credulity and superstition. There can be little doubt that Nazareth itself had nothing whatever to do with the originating of a story which tended so directly to injure its own renown by robbing it of one of its most precious treasures. The theory of its invention suggested by Stanley is in all probability the true one. "Nazareth was taken by sultan Khalil in 1291, when he stormed the last refuge of the Crusaders in the neighboring city of Acre. From that time not Nazareth only, but the whole of Palestine was closed to the devotions of Europe. The Crusaders were expelled from Asia, and in Europe the spirit of the crusades was extinct. But the natural longing to see the scenes of the events of the sacred history—the superstitious craving to win, for prayer, the favor of consecrated places—did not expire with the crusades. Can we wonder that, under such circumstances, there should have arisen the feeling, the desire, the belief that if Mohammed would not go to the mountain, the mountain must come to Mohammed? The house of Loretto is the petrifaction, so to speak, of the last sigh of the crusades!" (*Sinai and Palestine*, p. 448, 449). The existence of this purely European tradition has proved a source of considerable perplexity to the Franciscan monks of Nazareth; for while the pope's bull and the infallibility of their Church compel them to receive it, they find it somewhat puzzling to harmonize it with what they have to show, and to contend for, within the walls of their own convent. To illustrate this awkward conflict of incompatible claims, Stanley exhibits, at the head of his chapter on the subject, diagrams of the ground-plan of the holy house at Loretto and of the site of the same pretended house at Nazareth—plans which by no possibility can be made to agree.

The extensive edifice which now occupies the place of the church built on the same spot by the Crusaders was begun in the early part of the 17th century, that of the Crusaders having lain in ruins for more than 300 years. The modern structure has been gradually enlarged, and now constitutes, with its numerous conventual buildings, by much the most imposing object that meets the traveller's eye as he comes in sight of Nazareth. It is the Latin convent, and includes within its high-walled enclosure the church already spoken of, the Church of the Annunciation. The church itself is nearly a square of seventy feet, divided, by four massive piers which support the vaulted roof, into nave, choir, and aisles. The piers and walls are covered with canvas hangings, painted, in imitation of tapestry, with Scripture scenes. The sacred grotto, the true holy place, is beneath the floor of the church, and is entered by a broad flight of fifteen steps which lead down into it. Here there is first a vestibule of twenty-five feet by ten, from which a low-arched opening admits the visitor into an inner chamber of the same size—the veritable scene, according to the tradition of the Latin Church, of the ever-memorable Annunciation. Within this *sanctum*, and directly opposite the entrance into it, is a marble altar; and beneath it on the floor a marble slab, with a cross in the centre, professedly marking the place where the Virgin stood when she received the message from on high. On the marble pavement of the grotto is this inscription: *Hic Verbum caro factum est.* From the roof of this grotto the fragment of a granite column hangs, and beneath it the lower part of what the monks allege to be the same column remains inserted in the floor; the middle part of the column, they say, having been broken in pieces by the Saracen infidels in order to bring down the roof. Unfortunately the two parts of the column are of different kinds of stone—the one being of gray granite, the other of Cipolino marble, betraying the clumsiness with which the contrivance has been executed. In another chamber, above and behind the altar, there is an apocryphal picture which claims to represent the "*vera imago Salvatoris nostri, Domini Jesu Christi, ad Regem Abgarum missa.*"

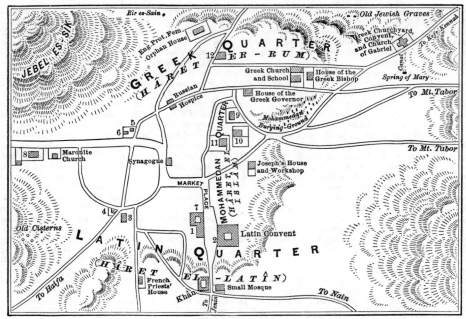

Plan of Nazareth.

1. New quarters of the Latin Convent; 2. Church of the Annunciation; 3. Protestant Church; 4. Protestant Parsonage; 5. Protestant Mission School; 6. Protestant Missionary's House; 7. Convent of French Nuns; 8. The "Mensa Christi;" 9. House of the Mufti; 10. House of the Turkish Governor; 11. Mosque; 12. Mission Hospital.

At some distance from the Latin convent is a modern church, also belonging to the Latins, within which is shown a piece of an old wall—part, as their tradition would have it believed, of Joseph's workshop. In another chapel is the *mensa Christi*, a large table-shaped fragment of solid rock, rising about three feet above the floor, on which, it is told, our Lord ate with his disciples both before and after his resurrection. Finally there is the synagogue from which Jesus was dragged by the multitude to the brow of the hill on which the city stood, with the design of casting him down.

Such are the "chief sights" in Nazareth which the Latin Church has to show, and in which it glories. The Greek Church, also, has something to exhibit, for she too has her Church of the Annunciation. It is located over a fountain, said to be that mentioned in one of the apocryphal gospels as adjoining the scene of that event. It is at a short distance from the present public fountain, and is sometimes distinctively called the Chapel of the Angel Gabriel.

Two localities possess, though in different ways, a certain interest which no one will fail to recognise. One of these is the "Fountain of the Virgin," situated at the north-eastern extremity of the town, where, according to one tradition, the mother of Jesus received the angel's salutation (Luke i, 28). Though we may attach no importance to this latter belief, we must, on other accounts, regard the spring with a feeling akin to that of religious veneration. It derives its name from the fact that Mary, during her life at Nazareth, no doubt accompanied often by "the child Jesus," must have been accustomed to repair to this fountain for water, as is the practice of the women of that village at the present day. Certainly, as Dr. Clarke observes (*Travels*, ii, 427), "if there be a spot throughout the Holy Land that was undoubtedly honored by her presence, we may consider this to have been the place; because the situation of a copious spring is not liable to change, and because the custom of repairing thither to draw water has been continued among the female inhabitants of Nazareth from the earliest period of its history." The well-worn path which leads thither from the town has been trodden by the feet of almost count-

less generations. It presents at all hours a busy scene, from the number of those, hurrying to and fro, engaged in the labor of water-carrying. (See the cut, vol. iii, p. 632, of this *Cyclopædia*.)

The other place is that of the attempted Precipitation. We are directed to the true scene of this occurrence, not so much by any tradition as by internal indications in the Gospel history itself. A prevalent opinion of the country has transferred the event to a hill about two miles south-east of the town. But there is no evidence that Nazareth ever occupied a different site from the present one; and that a mob, whose determination was to put to death the object of their rage, should repair to so distant a place for that purpose is entirely incredible. The present village, as already stated, lies along the hill-side, but much nearer the base than the summit. Above the bulk of the town are several rocky ledges over which a person could not be thrown without almost certain destruction. But there is one very remarkable precipice, almost perpendicular and forty or fifty feet high, near the Maronite church, which may well be supposed to be the identical one over which the infuriated townsmen of Jesus attempted to hurl him. The singular precision with which the narrative relates the transaction deserves a remark or two. Casual readers would understand from the account that Nazareth was situated on the summit, and that the people brought Jesus down thence to the brow of the hill as if it were between the town and the valley. If these inferences were correct, the narrative and the locality would then be at variance with each other. Even Reland (*Palæst.* p. 905) says: "Ναζαρέθ—urbs ædificata *super rupem*, unde Christum precipitare conati sunt." But the language of the evangelist, when more closely examined, is found neither to require the inferences in question on the one hand, nor to exclude them on the other. What he asserts is that the incensed crowd "rose up and cast Jesus out of the city, and brought him to the brow of the hill on which the city was built, that they might cast him down headlong." It will be remarked here, in the first place, that it is not said that the people either went up or descended in order to reach the precipice, but simply that they took the Saviour to it, wherever it was; and, in the second place, that it is not said that the city was built "on the brow of the hill," but equally as well that the precipice was "on the brow," without deciding whether the cliff overlooked the town (as is the fact) or was below it. It will be seen, therefore, how very nearly the terms of the history approach a mistake and yet avoid it. As Paley remarks in another case, none but a true account could advance thus to the very brink of contradiction without falling into it. See PRECIPITATION.

5. *Present Condition.*—Modern Nazareth belongs to the better class of Eastern villages. It has a population of 3000 or 4000: a few are Mohammedans, the rest Latin and Greek Christians. There is one mosque, a Franciscan convent of huge dimensions, but displaying no great architectural beauty, a small Maronite church, a Greek church, and perhaps a church or chapel of some of the other confessions. Protestant missions have been attempted, but with no very marked success. Most of the houses are well built of stone, and have a neat and comfortable appearance. As streams in the rainy season are liable to pour down with violence from the hills, every "wise man," instead of building upon the loose soil on the surface, digs deep, and lays his foundation upon the rock ($\dot{\epsilon}\pi\dot{\iota}$ $\tau\dot{\eta}\nu$ $\pi\dot{\epsilon}\tau\rho\alpha\nu$) which is found so generally in that country at a certain depth in the earth. The streets or lanes are narrow and crooked, and after rain are so full of mud and mire as to be almost impassable.

A description of Nazareth would be incomplete without mention of the remarkable view from the tomb of Neby Ismail on one of the hills behind the town. It must suffice to indicate merely the objects within sight. In the north are seen the ridges of Lebanon and, high above all, the white top of Hermon; in the west, Carmel, glimpses of the Mediterranean, the bay and the town of Akka; east and south-east are Gilead, Tabor, Gilboa; and south, the plain of Esdraelon and the mountains of Samaria, with villages on every side, among which are Kana, Nein, Endor, Zerin (Jezreel), and Táannuk (Taanach). It is unquestionably one of the most beautiful and sublime spectacles (for it combines the two features) which earth has to show. Dr. Robinson's elaborate description of the scene (*Bib. Res.* ii, 336, 337) conveys no exaggerated idea of its magnificence or historical interest. It is easy to believe that the Saviour, during the days of his seclusion in the adjacent valley, often came to this very spot, and looked forth thence upon those glorious works of the Creator which so lift the soul upward to him.

Nazareth has long been distinguished for the peculiar beauty of its women. Antoninus Martyr found many there in the 6th century, who pretended to have received this gift from the Virgin Mary; and travellers state that their descendants retain it still.

See, in addition to the above-cited authorities, Lightfoot, *Horæ Heb.* p. 918; Quaresmius, iii, 834; Schulz, *Leitungen,* v, 192; Richter, *Wallf.* p. 57; Schubert, iii, 169; Burckhardt, ii, 583; Scholtz, *Reis.* p. 247; Hackett, *Illustr. of Script.* p. 301; Bonar, *Land of Promise,* p. 397; Sepp, *Das Heil. Land,* ii, 73; Tobler, *Nazareth in Palästina* (Berlin, 1868).

Naz'arite [or, rather, *Nazirite*] (Heb. *Nazir,* נָזִיר, fully נְזִיר אֱלֹהִים, *a Nazarite of God;* Sept. properly Ναζιραῖος, as in Judg. xiii, 7; Lam. iv, 7; but often εὐξάμενος or ἁγιασμένος; Vulg. *Nazaræus;* Talmud, נזירה), the name given to such Israelites, whether male or female, as consecrated themselves to Jehovah by a peculiar vow prescribed in Numb. vi. (In the treatment of this subject we present a general view, referring to other heads for details on collateral points. See Vow.

1. *The Name and its Signification.*—The term נָזִיר comes with the verb נָזַר, signifying *to bind,* and thence *to separate.* Hence we have the cognate נֵזֶר (*nézer*),

denoting a crown or diadem, which binds the head; the hair (Jer. vii, 29), which forms a natural crown; and consecration to God as a *nazir,* which is a separation from certain things that symbolize all that separates or hinders from union with God. The concrete נָזִיר occurs sixteen times in the Old Testament. It denotes, in general, one who is separated from certain things and unto others, and so distinguished from other persons, and consecrated unto God. In two passages (Gen. xlix, 26; Deut. xxxiii, 16) it appears in the phrase נְזִיר אֶחָיו, *one separated from his brethren,* a touching description of Joseph, as he was in the providence of God separated from his brethren by their jealous cruelty for twenty years, and at the same time exalted above them in point of nearness to God and rank among men during the latter period of his life. In two others (Lev. xxv, 5, 11) it denotes that which is separated from common use. It is applied to the vine, while it remained untouched during the sabbatical and the jubilee years. "That which groweth of its own accord of thy harvest thou shalt not reap, neither gather the grapes of thy *nazir*" (ver. 5), that is, of thy vine in the year of its separation from common use. "A jubilee shall that fiftieth year be unto you; ye shall not sow, neither reap that which groweth of itself in it, nor gather its *nazirs*" (ver. 11), that is, the vines of the jubilee year. There are here two deviations from custom: the vine is not pruned, and its spontaneous produce is not gathered for consumption. It is remarkable that Joseph, in the context of Gen. xlix, 26, is figuratively represented as "a fruitful bough, even a fruitful bough by a well, whose branches run over the wall" (ver. 22); in other words, a young shoot from a fruitful tree, spreading forth its richly-laden branches in all the unrestrained luxuriance of nature. The verb נָזַר (*nazár*) is found in ten passages, two of which precede the Book of Numbers. In Lev. xv, 13 we read, "Thus shall ye separate the children of Israel from their uncleanness;" and in Lev. xxii, 2, "Speak unto Aaron and to his sons, that they separate themselves from the holy things of the children of Israel," namely, when they themselves are in their uncleanness, as is explained in the next verse. In these cases the separation is between the holy and the profane; and this usage naturally leads to the special meaning of the term *nazir* in the other twelve places in which it occurs.

According to others the word נֵזֶר, *a diadem,* contains the original idea of נזר, which will then radically signify *to crown,* and the hair is regarded as a crown to the person. The Nazarite in that view is *the crowned one,* because, as we are told in Numb. vi, 7, he has "the crown of God upon his head" (נזר אלהיו על ראשו), evidently referring to his distinguishing badge of the freely growing and profuse mass of hair, which was considered an ornament (2 Sam. xiv, 25, 26), and which he was not allowed to cut off (Numb. vi, 5), because therein his vow chiefly consisted (Judg. xii, 5); and this is confirmed by Numb. vi, 9, where it is said, "If he defiled his head diadem (ראש נזרו), he is to shave his head." Hence also the signification of נזר, *ornamental hair, long hair* (Jer. vii, 29 with Numb. vi, 19); while the vine again, laden with fruit, is called *Nazirite,* or more probably *Nazir,* נָזִיר, i. e. *the crowned* (Lev. xxv, 5, 11); because in its uncut state, when its head is covered with grapes and foliage, it is as much adorned with a diadem as the head of the Nazarite with the abundant hair, just as we call the foliage of a tree its crown. Besides, the vine hills rising in the different parts of Palestine, and resembling heads covered with hair, may have suggested this figure to the Oriental mind, since the summits of mountains are called their *heads* (ראש) in Hebrew (Gen. viii, 5; Exod. xvii, 9, 10; xix, 20; Amos i, 2), and the foliage is not unfrequently compared to the hair or wool (צמרת) of animals (Ezek. xvii, 3, 22;

xxxi, 3, 10, 14; see Saalschütz, *Das Mosaische Recht*, p. 158).

2. *Origin of the Custom.*—The germs of the custom now under consideration reach farther back than the sojourn in the wilderness. The manner in which the topic is introduced in the Book of Numbers (ch. vi) indicates that the *nazir* was not unfamiliar to the minds of the Israelites. The application of the term to the undressed vine of the sabbatical year in a previous book (Levit.) tends to the same conclusion. A custom of this kind might have readily grown up during the long sojourn in Egypt, and have there served as a protest against the prevalent idolatry. Cyril of Alexandria considered that letting the hair grow, the most characteristic feature in the vow, was taken from the Egyptians. This notion has been substantially adopted by Fagius, Spencer, Michaelis, Hengstenberg, and some other critics. Hengstenberg affirms that the Egyptians and the Hebrews were distinguished among ancient nations by cutting their hair as a matter of social propriety; and thus the marked significance of long hair must have been common to them both. The arguments of Bähr, however, to show that the wearing of long hair in Egypt and all other heathen nations had a meaning opposed to the idea of the Nazaritish vow, seem to be conclusive. The head of the Nazarite was perhaps considered as adorned with its growth of hair (Lampe, in *Miscell. Gron.* iv, 107 sq.), which, as a kind of crown, showed his consecration, and the touch of a knife or razor was a profanation of that which belonged to God. In other ancient nations it was usual to promise a god, especially in times of danger, the offering of the hair of the head or of the beard; and sometimes the hair was offered without a vow, especially by new-married women. (Compare Spencer, *Legg. rit.* iii, 6, 1; Doughtæi *Analect.* i, 97.) So among the Egyptians (Diod. Sic. i, 18, 83 sq.), the Syrians (Lucian, *Dea Syr.* c. 60), the Greeks (Homer, *Iliad*, xxiii, 41 sq.; Plut. *Thes.* c. 5; Theodoret, *Quæst. in Lev.* 28; Wachsmuth, *Hellen. Alterthum*, ii, 558), the Rómans (Suet. *Ner.* 11; Martial, ix, 17, 3 sq.), and the Arabians (see *Koran*, ii, 192; Hamas, p. 2 sq.). But the most striking resemblance to the Jewish custom is that found by Morier among the modern Persians. "It frequently happens after the birth of a son, that if the parent be in distress or the child be sick, or that there be any other cause of grief, the mother makes a vow that no razor shall come upon the child's head for a certain period of time, and sometimes for all his life. If the child recovers and the cause of grief be removed, and if the vow be but for a time, so that the mother's vow be fulfilled, then she shaves his head at the end of the time prescribed, makes a small entertainment, collects money and other things from her relations and her friends, which are sent as *nezers* (offerings) to the mosque at Kerbelah, and are there consecrated" (*Second Journey*, p. 109). The abstinence of priests among the ancient Egyptians from certain kinds of food, as a token of peculiar sanctity, is a kindred ordinance (Porphyr. *Abstin.* iv, 7); and some have supposed that the Nazaritish vow had an Egyptian origin, and was simply modified by the Hebrews to accord with their system (Spencer, *Legg. Rit.* iii, 6, 1; Michaelis, *Mos. R.* iii, 27); but the resemblances cited from the Egyptian priesthood are too fragmentary to support the theory. Indeed, the abstinence of the priests was not in the nature of a vow, but was a qualification for their sacred office. And although they were required to practice celibacy, we do not find that wine was forbidden to them. Besides, each feature of the Nazaritish vow is so intimately associated with Hebrew ideas and practices that the search for a foreign origin is wholly unnecessary. The reflections of Ewald (*Isr. Gesch.* ii, 403 sq.) on this subject are too elaborate. Without reason, some, especially Roman Catholic writers, have thought that the first traces of monachism were to be found in this institution. See G. Less, *Super lege Mos. de Nasiræatu, prima eaque antiquissima vitæ*

Monast. improbatione (Gött. 1789). Comp. Michaelis, *Orient. Biblioth.* vi, 235 sq. The only resemblance is in the general purpose, there is none in the nature of the vow. See Dassov, *Vota Monast. et Nasiræor. inter se collata.* (Kil. 1703); comp. Carpzov, *Appar.* 151 sq., 799 sq.; Reland, *Antiq. Sacr.* ii, 10; Bähr, *Symbol.* ii, 430 sq.; G. F. Meinhard, *de Nasiræis* (Jen. 1676); Zorn, *in Miscell. Leips. Nov.* iv, 426 sq. See HAIR.

3. *What constituted a Nazarite.*—The special vow whereby one bound himself to be a *Nazarite* (נֶדֶר נָזִיר) involved the following three things: (*a.*) He is to abstain from wine and strong drink—or as Onkelos, who renders מחמד חדת ועתיק רין ושכר by רין ושכר, and the ancient Jewish canons will have it, from old and new wine—vinegar made of wine or strong drink; liquor of grapes; grapes either moist or dried; and, in fact, from every production of the vine—even from the very stones and skin of the vine. According to the Jewish canons, however, "strong drink made of dates, or such like, is lawful for the Nazarite" (Maimonides, *Hilchoth Neziruth*, v, 1). (*b.*) He must refrain from cutting the hair off his head during the whole period of his Nazariteship. (*c.*) He must avoid every contact with the dead, even if his parents or brothers or sisters were to die during his Nazariteship.

If he was accidentally defiled by death suddenly occurring on his premises, he was obliged to observe the legal purification of seven days (comp. Numb. xix, 14); cut off his hair on the seventh day—which in this case was not burned, but buried (Mishna, *Temura*, vi, 4; and Maimonides, ad loc.); bring on the eighth day two turtle-doves or two young pigeons to the priest—one for a sin-offering and the other for a burnt-offering; hallow his head, offer a lamb of the first year as a trespass-offering, renew his vow, and begin again his Nazariteship, as the days which had passed since the commencement of his vow were lost through this interruption (Numb. vi, 1–12). His desecration by a dead body is alone mentioned, because it might happen without his will; whereas the other two conditions of his vow were in his own power, and, it was presumed, would not be violated. According to the later penalties of the Talmud, men and women who, after taking the Nazaritish vow, cut their hair or plucked it off with their hands, or defiled themselves by wilfully coming in contact with dead bodies, or partook of wine, received forty stripes (*Nazir*, iv, 3; Maimonides, *Hilchoth Nezir*, v, 2, 6, 8, 11). So rigid were the regulations that the Nazarite was not allowed to comb his hair lest some of it might be torn out, but he was permitted to smooth it with his hands (*Nazir*, vi, 3).

As the Mosaic law says nothing about the formality of the Nazaritish vow, and as all other declarations were binding wherever and whenever made (Deut. xxiii, 24), we may accept the ancient Jewish canons that the vow was made in private, and that it was binding even if a man or woman simply said, "Behold, I am a Nazarite!" (הרינ־ נזיר), or repeated, "I also become one," when hearing any one else make this declaration (Mishna, *Nazir*, i, 3; iii, 1; iv, 1). A father could make a vow for his son before he was thirteen years of age, but not a mother for hers (Numb. xxx, 8; *Sota*, iii, 8; *Nazir*, iii, 6). A man had the power to annul his wife's vow (*Nazir*, iv, 1; Maimonides, *Hilchoth Neziruth*, ii, 17), but not his slave's, and in case he did prohibit him to perform it, he was bound to fulfil it as soon as he was set at liberty (*Nazir*, ix, 1).

The vow seems to have been resorted to, like prayer, by pious people, under extraordinary exigencies, such as in cases of sickness (Josephus, *War*, ii, 15), or when starting on a long journey (Mishna, *Nazir*, i, 6), or when wishing for children (*ib.* ii, 7; ix, x).

4. *Accomplishment of the Nazarite's Vow, and the Offerings connected therewith.*—When the time of his Nazariteship was accomplished, the Nazarite had to present himself before the door of the sanctuary with three sac-

rifices, corresponding to the three prohibitions of Nazaritism — (a) A he-lamb of the first year for a burnt-offering; (b) a ewe-lamb also of the first year for a sin-offering; and (c) a ram for a peace-offering. With the latter "he had to bring six tenth-deals and two thirds of a tenth-deal of flour, from which were baked twenty cakes, viz. ten unleavened cakes and ten unleavened wafers. These twenty cakes were anointed with a fourth part of a log of oil, as fixed by a law of Moses from Sinai, and were all brought in one vessel" (Maimonides, Hilchoth Neziruth, viii, 1). Besides these extraordinary cakes and wafers, he had to bring the ordinary meat-offering and drink-offering appointed for all sacrifices (comp. Numb. xxviii). These three sacrifices were designed both as an atonement for the sins which the Nazarite unconsciously committed during his Nazariteship, and as an expression of thanksgiving to Him by whose grace he had happily fulfilled the time of his vow. After the priest had offered these sacrifices—sin-offering first, burnt-offering second, and peace-offering third (Maimonides, Hilchoth Neziruth, viii, 3)—the Nazarite cut off his Nazir head (נזרו ראש)—i. e. the hair which was his Nazaritish pledge—at the door, threw it into the fire under the peace-offering, or, as the ancient Jewish canons have it, under the caldron in which the peace-offering was boiled (Mishna, Nazir, vi, 8). Thereupon "the priest took the boiled shoulder of the ram, one of the ten unleavened cakes from the basket, and one of the unleavened wafers, laid them on the Nazarite's hand, put his hands under those of the owner, and waved it all before the Lord" (Mishna, Nazir, vi, 9). "The fat was then salted and burned upon the altar, while the breast and the fore-leg were eaten by the priests after the fat was burned; the cake, too, which was waved, and the boiled shoulder, were eaten by the priests, but the remaining bread and the meat were eaten by the owners" (Maimonides, Hilchoth Maase ha-Corbanoth, ix, 9–11). Besides these sacrifices which were ordained, the Nazarite also brought a free-will offering proportioned to his circumstances (Numb. vi, 13–21). In the time of the Temple there was a Nazarite chamber in the woman's court in the south-east corner, where the Nazarites boiled their peace-offerings, cut off the hair of their heads, and cast it into the fire under the caldron. They were, however, also allowed to cut off their hair in the country. "But whether the Nazarite cut it in the country or in the sanctuary, he was obliged to have the hair cast under the caldron, and was not allowed to do it before the appointed time for opening the door of the court, as it is written, 'the door of the tent' (Numb. vi, 8); which does not mean that he is to cut off his hair before or at the door, for that would be treating the sanctuary with contempt" (Mishna, Middoth, ii, 5; Nazir, vi, 8; Maimonides, Hilchoth, Neziruth, viii, 3). The assertion, therefore, of Dr. Howson (Life and Epistles of St. Paul, i, 499), and others, that the vow recorded in Acts xviii, 18 cannot be regarded as a regular Nazaritish vow, because it is said that Paul "shaved his head in Cenchreæ," and because it "was not cut off at the door of the temple where the sacrifices were offered, as was required by the law of the Nazarite," is at variance with the practice of the Jews in the days of our Saviour. One could also take upon himself one of the obligations of a Nazarite, and then send his sacrifices through a Nazarite, as may be seen from the following remark: "He who said, 'Lo, I take upon myself the shaving of a Nazarite,' is bound to bring the offerings of shavings for cleanness, and may offer them through any Nazarite he pleases. Or if he says, 'I take upon myself half the offerings of a Nazarite,' or 'I take upon myself half the shaving of a Nazarite,' he has only to bring half the sacrifices, and can send them through any Nazarite he likes, and that Nazarite pays those offerings from his own" (Maimonides. Hilchoth Neziruth, viii, 18). This circumstance, which evidently arose from the fact that the offerings required from a

full Nazarite were beyond the means of the pious poor, and which made it also an act of piety for a rich man to pay the necessary expenses, and thus enable his poorer brethren to complete their vow (Josephus, Ant. xix, 6, 1), explains Acts xxi, 23, 24, 26, where we find that St. Paul could only take upon himself a part of the vow, then proceed with the poor Nazarites to the temple, and offer through them, and thus make them partake of his charges about the sacrifices. The Gemara (quoted by Reland, Ant. Sac.) states that Alexander Jannæus contributed towards supplying nine hundred victims for three hundred Nazarites. See PAUL.

5. Duration of the Nazaritish Vow.—As the Bible says nothing about the duration of the Nazaritish vow, but leaves every one who takes it to fix his own time, the administrators of the Mosaic law were obliged to specify a certain number of days as the lowest period for Nazariteship, since it not unfrequently happened that some took the vow without mentioning any definite time whatever, while others, if they could take it for a few days, would vow too often, and thereby diminish its solemn character. Hence the Jewish canons determined that "if any one says, I will be a Nazarite, without mentioning expressly how long, he cannot be a Nazarite less than thirty days; and even if he says, I take upon myself to be a Nazarite with an exceedingly great Nazariteship, it is not to be more than thirty days, because he expressed no time. If he mentions less than thirty days, e. g. if he says I am a Nazarite for one day or ten days or twenty days, he is nevertheless a Nazarite for thirty days, for there is no Nazariteship for less than thirty days. This is a law transmitted by tradition. But if he mentions a time more than thirty days, e. g. if he says thirty-one days, or forty, or a hundred days, or a hundred years, he must be a Nazarite during the said period, neither less nor more" (Maimonides, Hilchoth Neziruth, iii, 1–3; Mishna, Nazir, i, 3; iii, 1; vi, 3; Joseph. War, ii, 15, 1). The ancient expositors connect the fixing of the indefinite vow at thirty days, with the words, "he shall be holy" (יהיה קדש, Numb. vi, 5), by the exegetical rule called Gematria (סתם נזירות שלשים יום שנאמר קדש יהיה, יהיה שלשים בגמטריא), where יהיה (10+5+10+5=30) amounts to thirty (comp. Siphri, ad loc.). It will be seen from this that there were some who took the Nazaritish vow for life. These are called עולם נזירי (Nazaræi nativi), perpetual Nazarites, in contradistinction from those who took the vow for a limited period (Nazaræi votivi), and are therefore called נזירי ימים, Nazarites for a certain number of days, or נזירי זמן קצוב, Nazarites for a short time. The Bible mentions three Nazarites for life: Samson, Samuel, and John the Baptist. Fathers, and mothers with the consent of their husbands, could devote their prospective children to perpetual Nazaritism (1 Sam. i, 11; Mishna, Nazir, ix, 5), in which case the mother abstained during her pregnancy from wine and strong drink and unclean things (Judg. xiii, 4; Luke i, 15). These life-long Nazarites were afterwards divided into two classes, viz. נזירי עולם, ordinary perpetual Nazarites, and נזירי שמשון, Samson-Nazarites, and the distinction between the two was that the former were allowed to diminish their hair when it became too heavy, if they were willing to bring the three appointed sacrifices, and were obliged to bring a sacrifice in case they became defiled; while the latter were not allowed to diminish their hair, however heavy, but were not required to bring a sacrifice in case they became defiled (Mishna, Nazir, i, 2), because Samson brought no sacrifice after he was defiled by contact with the jaw-bone of a dead ass (Judg. xv, 16). Of course, any one who wished to become a Samson-Nazarite had distinctly to say so (כשמשון הריני) when he took the vow. One instance is related of Helena, queen of Adia-

bene (of whom some particulars are given by Josephus, *Ant.* xx, 2), who, with the zeal of a new convert, took a vow for seven years in order to obtain the divine favor on a military expedition which her son was about to undertake. When her period of consecration had expired she visited Jerusalem, and was there informed by the doctors of the school of Hillel that a vow taken in another country must be repeated whenever the Nazarite might visit the Holy Land. She accordingly continued a Nazarite for a second seven years, and happening to touch a dead body just as the time was about to expire, she was obliged to renew her vow, according to the law in Numb. vi, 9, etc. She thus continued a Nazarite for twenty-one years (*Nazir*, iii, 6).

5. The *meaning* of this interesting ordinance has been largely discussed by Philo Judæus, Maimonides, Abarbanel, and other Jewish writers. The following theories have been maintained by them and by modern writers:

(1.) Some consider it as a symbolical expression of the divine nature working in man, and deny that it involved anything of a strictly ascetic character. Several of the Jewish writers have taken this view more or less completely. Abarbanel imagined that the hair represents the intellectual power, the power belonging to the head, which the wise man was not to suffer to be diminished or to be interfered with by drinking wine or by any other indulgence; and that the Nazarite was not to approach the dead because he was appointed to bear witness to the eternity of the divine nature. Of modern critics, Bähr appears to have most completely trodden in the same track. While he denies that the life of the Nazarite was, in the proper sense, ascetic, he contends that his abstinence from wine, and his not being allowed to approach the dead, figured the separation from other men which characterizes the consecrated servant of the Lord; and that his long hair signified his holiness. The hair, according to his theory, as being the bloom of manhood, is the symbol of growth in the vegetable as well as the animal kingdom, and therefore of the operation of the divine power.

(2.) Others see in Nazaritism the principle of stoicism, and imagine that it was intended to cultivate and bear witness to the sovereignty of the will over the lower tendencies of human nature. The philosophical Jewish doctors, for the most part, seem to have preferred this view. Thus Bechai speaks of the Nazarite as a conqueror who subdued his temptations, and who wore his long hair as a crown, "quod ipse rex sit cupiditatibus imperans præter morem reliquorum hominum, qui cupiditatum sunt servi." He supposed that the hair was worn rough, as a protest against foppery. But others, still taking it as a regal emblem, have imagined that it was kept elaborately dressed, and fancy that they see a proof of the existence of the custom in the seven locks of Samson (Judg. xvi, 13-19).

(3.) Many regard it wholly in the light of a sacrifice of the person to God. Philo has taken this view of the subject. In his work, *On Animals fit for Sacrifice*, he gives an account of the Nazaritish vow, and calls it ἡ εὐχὴ μεγάλη. According to him the Nazarite did not sacrifice merely his possessions, but his person, and the act of sacrifice was to be performed in the completest manner. The outward observances enjoined upon him were to be the genuine expressions of his spiritual devotion. To represent spotless purity within, he was to shun defilement from the dead, at the expense even of the obligation of the closest family ties. As no spiritual state or act can be signified by any single symbol, he was to identify himself with each one of the three victims which he had to offer as often as he broke his vow by accidental pollution, or when the period of his vow came to an end. He was to realize in himself the ideas of the whole burnt-offering, the sin-offering, and the peace-offering. That no mistake might be made in regard to the three sacrifices being shadows of one and the same substance, it was ordained that the vic-

tims should be individuals of one and the same species of animal. The shorn hair was put on the fire of the altar in order that, although the divine law did not permit the offering of human blood, something might be offered up that was actually a portion of his own person. Ewald, following in the same line of thought, has treated the vow of the Nazarite as an act of self-sacrifice; but he looks on the preservation of the hair as signifying that the Nazarite is so set apart for God that no change or diminution should be made in any part of his person, and as serving to himself and the world for a visible token of his peculiar consecration to Jehovah.

(4.) In all such disquisitions there is a basis of truth, combined with an element of error derived from the speculations of the age or of the individual. From a review of all the particulars of this institute, it is to be inferred that it was *a typical representation of a holy life*, forming, in the case of individuals, prominent examples of that fidelity to covenant engagements, for the interests of righteousness, which should have been found in the whole community of Israel. It exhibits to the view a practical symbol of that separation from sin which is coincident with dedication to God. It is a part of that system of teaching by figures which was adapted to a comparatively unsophisticated age. It was not in itself a principle or law for the regulation of conduct, as stoicism or asceticism, but a divinely appointed emblem of a duly regulated life. The symbolical character of the nazirate is manifest from its constitution. It was not incumbent upon any individual or order of men, and therefore possessed no inherent moral obligation. In its ordinary form it lasted only thirty, or, at most, one hundred days. It prohibited not merely intoxicating drink, but every product of the vine, whereas for purely moral purposes the Scripture simply enjoins temperance in all things. It imposed two other restrictions which are not in themselves moral, but only typical or ceremonial, namely, leaving the hair unpolled, and taking no part in the last offices that involved contact with the dead.

A symbol thus regulated by a divine ordinance must have had a profound significance. Accordingly it sets forth, in a striking and beautiful manner, the leading features of a life devoted to God. It originates in a solemn resolve of the free-will, and is in this respect an interesting emblem of a godly life, which is the spontaneous outgoing of a heart renewed by the Spirit of God. It prescribes abstinence from every product of the vine. The intoxicating quality of the juice of the grape, by which reason is clouded and unbalanced, is laid hold of as the fit representative of sin, which darkens the intellect and corrupts the will. And every part of the vine is prohibited, not because it was the forbidden fruit, as some Jewish doctors affirm (Lightfoot on Luke i, 15; Magee, *On the Atonement*, illust. xxxviii), but because this symbolic act conveys the obvious lesson to refrain from sin in every shape and of every degree, since the slightest deviation from rectitude indicates a depraved nature as truly as the most enormous transgression. The growth of the beard is an index of manhood; and the unshorn locks present a striking display of the unrestrained luxuriance of corporeal growth and beauty. They are therefore emblematic of power, liberty, youth, and beauty, and of the unreserved exertion of all our faculties in the service of our Maker and Saviour. The determinate choice of that which is right and good is the principle of a holy life, and the coming forth of that choice into full effect is the beauty of holiness. The flowing locks are equally expressive of childlike simplicity and feminine grace, and therefore of that confiding dependence and yielding devotedness which are characteristic of the new-born child of God. This thought is well brought out by Fairbairn (*Typol.* ii, 419), in harmony with Ainsworth and Baumgarten. But the softness of a faithful heart must be combined with the energy of a valiant spirit, to constitute the perfection of the godly or Christian character. Samson,

Samuel, and John the Baptist were no less distinguished for manly fortitude than for humble deference to the will of God. Defilement by a dead body is the third thing to be avoided. The dead body is the victim of death; the penalty of sin. It has, therefore, been the seat of that moral corruption, contact with which conveys ceremonial defilement.

6. *Relation of Nazaritism to the Levitical Economy.*— As the priestly office presupposed that purity of life of which the Nazarite was an emblem, it is natural that they should present some points of correspondence. Thus the priests were to abstain from wine or strong drink when they went into the tabernacle of the congregation to perform their official functions (Lev. x, 9). But this was obviously a salutary precaution against their being disqualified in mind or body for the proper discharge of their duties. Hence they were not prohibited from other products of the vine; and when not officiating they were under no restriction but the ordinary one of temperance. The high-priest, also, upon whom was "the crown (נֵזֶר) of the anointing oil of his God," was not to touch any dead body, or defile himself for his father or his mother (Lev. xxi, 11, 12). But the ordinary priests were not placed under the same restraint, plainly because a substitute could in this case be found for one who was under a temporary defilement. Maimonides (*More Nebochim*, iii, 48) speaks of the dignity of the Nazarite, in regard to his sanctity, as being equal to that of the high-priest. The abstinence from wine enjoined upon the high-priest on behalf of all the priests when they were about to enter upon their ministrations, is an obvious but perhaps not such an important point in the comparison. There is a passage in the account given by Hegesippus of St. James the Just (Eusebius, *Hist. Eccl.* ii, 23), which, if we may assume it to represent a genuine tradition, is worth a notice, and seems to show that Nazarites were permitted even to enter into the Holy of Holies. He says that St. James was consecrated from his birth neither to eat meat, to drink wine, to cut his hair, nor to indulge in the use of the bath; and that to him alone it was permitted (τούτῳ μόνῳ ἐξῆν) to enter the sanctuary. Perhaps it would not be unreasonable to suppose that the half sacerdotal character of Samuel might have been connected with his prerogative as a Nazarite. Many of the fathers designate him as a priest, although St. Jerome, on the obvious ground of his descent, denies that he had any sacerdotal rank (see Ortlob, *Thes. Nov. Theol.-Philol.* i, 587).

The Nazir did not sequester himself from the engagements or enjoyments of domestic or social life. His vow usually lasted, not for life, but for a number of days determined by himself. He did not therefore form a fraternity, but continued as an individual to participate in the ordinary affairs of every-day life. This vow merely afforded to persons of a certain temperament, in a peculiar state of religious feeling, or in entering on a particular enterprise, a course of typical observance, in which the higher tone of a devout imagination might find a definite and legitimate scope. Such a mode of action, when undertaken with a proper sense of its symbolic import, in accordance with the sanction of the Deity, was well calculated to cultivate pure desires and promote holy tempers in the devotee himself, and at the same time to convey useful and impressive lessons to those who were intelligent and respectful witnesses of his conduct during the time of his separation.

7. *Later Notices.*—The Nazaritish vow was practiced with more or less frequency during all periods of the Old-Testament history. Ewald supposes that Nazarites for life were numerous in very early times, and that they multiplied in periods of great political and religious excitement. We have already found traces of its observance in Judges and 1 Samuel. Amos introduces the Lord expostulating with the people, because, when he had raised up young men for Nazarites, they had given them wine to drink (Amos ii, 11, 12). Jeremiah laments the miserable change that had come over the Nazarites (princes, Gesen., Blayney) in consequence of the desolations of the holy city and land (Lam. iv, 7, 8). This lamentable state of things was the natural result of the national defection. The Nazaritish vow then sprang from an earnest heart as a solemn protest against the formality of the times. It was a cry from some one who had not bowed the knee to the Baal of the age—a welcome ray of hope amid the darkness that overshadowed the Church. It was therefore to be expected in the days of apostasy and peril. Individual piety and personal circumstances might bring it forth in all conditions of the Church militant.

In the time of Judas Maccabæus we find the devout Jews, when they were bringing their gifts to the priests, stirring up the Nazarites of days who had completed the time of their consecration to make the accustomed offerings (1 Macc. iii, 49). From this incident, in connection with what has been related of the liberality of Alexander Jannæus and Herod Agrippa, we may infer that the number of Nazarites must have been very considerable during the two centuries and a half which preceded the destruction of Jerusalem. The instance of St. John the Baptist and that of St. James the Just (if we accept the traditional account) show that the Nazarite for life retained his original character till later times; and the act of St. Paul in joining himself with the four Nazarites at Jerusalem seems to prove that the vow of the Nazarite of days was as little altered in its important features. The case of Helena, queen of Adiabene, has already been cited. Grätz (*Gesch. der Juden*, iii, 80) compares Nazarites and Essenes (q. v.).

8. *Literature.*—In addition to the works repeatedly cited above, especially the Talmudic treatise *Nazir*, and the commentary called *Siphri*, we may mention Michaelis, *Laws of Moses*, ii, 284 sq.; Bähr, *Symbolik des Mos. Cultus*, i, 364; ii, 416, 430; Ewald, *Alterthüm.* p. 96 sq.; *Critici Sacri* ad loc. Num.; Hengstenberg, *Egypt and Moses*, p. 190; Keil, *Bibl. Archäologie*, i, 322; and on Paul's vows the monograph of Reineccius, *De Paulo Nasiræo* (Weissenf. 1720). Others are cited by Volbeding, *Index*, p. 45, 168; and by Danz, *Wörterb.* p. 689.

Nazarites, a Christian sect in Russia and Hungary. Originally they were only known in the neighborhood of Szegedin, but more recently they have spread over the greater part of Hungary. Between the Danube and the Theiss they now number 80,000. The most of their adherents are in the Magyar districts. They profess to derive their confession from the New Testament alone. They hold God to be one in essence, but three in person— Father, Son, and Spirit. Their sacraments are two—Baptism and the Lord's Supper; adults only being baptized, and that by immersion by any male member in good standing, and baptism being essential to salvation. They have no ministers, consider marriage a civil ceremony, recognise no Sabbath—for which they find no injunction in the New Testament, though they worship on that day for convenience' sake—are singularly charitable and moral in their daily lives, refuse to take oaths or to bear arms, and take no part in political affairs. In order to escape from the latter, the parents of the young men, or in case of inability the parishes, hire substitutes for them.

Nazarus, St., a martyr of the first ages of the Church, was put to death at Milan, and is still celebrated in Brittany. Son of a superior Roman and pagan officer, and a Christian mother, whom the Church honors under the name of St. Perpetua, he adopted the maternal faith, renounced the employment of his father, and devoted himself to preaching. He was arrested at Milan with a young boy, named Celsus (vulgarly called Céols), and put to death under some pretext not well known. Their bodies, buried in the environs of Milan, were found about 395 by St. Ambrose, bishop of that city, and carried to the Church of the Apostles, which this prelate had built. "Many relics of St. Nazarus are distributed," say fathers Richard and Giraud, "so that it can scarcely be told which are the true ones." The Church celebrates the fête of St. Nazarus and St. Celsus on the 28th of July. See Hoefer, *Nouv. Biog. Gén.* s. v.

Nazrey, WILLIS, an African bishop of the colored British Methodist Episcopal Church in Canada, was born about 1820. He entered the ministry in 1850, and preached for some time in Canada, gaining friends everywhere by his consistent Christian walk and work. He labored zealously for the promotion of the Gospel cause among his African brethren, and was finally selected by them as their bishop after the separation of the Canadian Church from the Methodist Episcopal Church of the United States. Besides the responsible work of the episcopacy, bishop Nazrey had charge of the *Messenger*, the Canadian paper of the colored Methodists. Bishop Nazrey. died in August, 1875, at Shelburne, N. S.

Nazzari, Bartolomeo, an Italian painter who devoted himself to sacred and secular art, was born, according to Tassi, in the territory of Clusane, in the Bergamese, in 1699. After studying at Venice under Angelo Trevisani, he went to Rome, and finished his course under Benedetto Luti and Francesco Trevisani. He settled at Venice, and became an excellent painter of history and portraits. He visited various capitals of different German and Italian states, and gained a great reputation for his portraits of princes and of their courtiers, also for his heads of youths and old men, drawn from life, very fancifully dressed and decorated. Among his best historical productions is a *Holy Family with St. Anne*, at Pontremoli. He died in 1758. See Spooner, *Biog. Hist. of the Fine Arts*, ii, 610.

Nazzari, Francesco, an Italian ecclesiastical savant, was born about 1634 near Bergamo. He was still young when he was given a philosopher's chair in the College of Sapience at Rome. Following the advice of Michel-Ange Ricci, afterwards cardinal, he undertook in 1668 to establish a literary journal in Italian, for which the *Journal des Savans*, which appeared a short time before in Paris, served him as a model. His associates, Ricci, J. Lucio, Salvator and Francesco Serra, Tommaso de Giuli, J. Pastrizi, and Ciampini, agreed to furnish him with extracts from works in foreign languages. He took upon himself the analysis of the French books, and the revision of all the articles which should be sent to him. He issued this journal, entitled *Giornale de letterati*, until the month of March, 1675, from the office of Tinassi; but forced, in consequence of a difference with the latter, to yield his duties to Ciampini, he formed a new society, and published, under the same title, a continuation, which was printed at the office of Cerrara until the end of 1679. After having been attached as secretary to Jean Lucio, a Dalmatian savant, he accompanied, in 1686, the geometrician Auzout to France, and it is said was very useful to him in the observation of eclipses and celestial revolutions. He died at Rome Oct. 19, 1714. By his will he left his wealth and his library to the Church of the Bergamasques, and founded at Rome a college for the scholars of his province. Besides the journal that he has edited, and which has been reprinted at Bologna, with additions, we owe to Nazzari an Italian version of the *Exposition de la doctrine de l'Église catholique*, by Bossuet (Rome, 1678, 8vo), and an edition of the *Lettere discorsive de Diomede Borghesi* (Rome, 1701, 4to). See Hoefer, *Nouv. Biog. Générale*, s. v.

Ndâ is the name of a religious secret association among the people of Southern Guinea, in West Africa. It is confined to the adult male population, and is thus described by Mr. Wilson, who, from his long residence in the country, acquired an intimate acquaintance with its peculiar customs: "It [i. e. the association] is headed by a spirit of this name, who dwells in the woods, and appears only when summoned by some unusual event—at the death of a person connected with the or-

der, at the birth of twins, or at the inauguration of some one into office. His voice is never heard except at night, and after the people have retired to rest. He enters the village from the wood-side, and is so bundled up in dry plantain leaves that no one would suspect him of belonging to the human species. He is always accompanied by a train of young men, and the party dance to a peculiar and somewhat plaintive air on a flute-like instrument as they parade through the streets. As soon as it is known that he has entered the village, the women and children run away to their rooms to hide themselves. If they should have the misfortune to see Ndâ, or should be discovered peeping at him through the cracks of the houses, they would be thrashed almost to death. Perhaps no woman has ever had the temerity to cast eyes upon this mysterious being. Ndâ frequently stops in front of the dwelling of a man who is known to have rum in his possession, and exacts a bottle, in default of which his property would be injured. The leading men of the village show the utmost deference to his authority, no doubt for the purpose of making a stronger impression upon the minds of the women and children. If a distinguished person dies, Ndâ affects great rage, and comes the following night with a large posse of men to seize the property of the villagers without discrimination. He is sure to lay hands on as many sheep and goats as are necessary to make a grand feast, and no man has any right to complain. Many take the precaution to lock up their sheep and other live stock in their dwelling-houses the night before, and in this way alone can they escape the ravages of this monster of the woods, who is sure to commit depredations somewhat in proportion to the importance and rank of the man who has died. The institution of Ndâ, like that of Mwetyi, is intended to keep the women, children, and slaves in subjection. I once heard a man who belonged to the order acknowledge that there was no such spirit; 'but how,' said he, 'shall we govern our women and our slaves if we do away with the impression that there is such a being.'"

Ndengei, the highest and principal deity worshipped by the Fiji Islanders. Ndengei is to them an impersonation of the abstract idea of eternal existence. He is subject to no emotion or sensation, nor to any appetite except hunger. They believe that this god manifests himself in a variety of forms from age to age, but he is actually worshipped in the form of a huge serpent. According to the Fijians, Ndengei passes a monotonous existence in a gloomy cavern—the hollow of an inland rock near the north-east end of Viti Leon; evincing no interest in any one but his attendant Uto, and giving no signs of life beyond eating, answering his priest, and changing his position from one side to the other. There are points in this description which remind one of the Chronos of Greek mythology. The word Ndengei is supposed by some to be a corruption of the first part of the name Tangasoa, or great Tanga, the chief deity of Polynesia; but whether this idea be well founded or not, great veneration is entertained for Ndengei, as they believe that to this deity the spirit goes immediately after death, either to be purified or to receive sentence. All spirits, however, are not allowed to reach the judgment-seat of Ndengei, for the road is obstructed by an enormous giant wielding a large axe, with which he attacks all who pass him, and those who are wounded dare not present themselves to Ndengei, and are obliged to wander about in the mountains. "At Rewa," says captain Wilkes, of the American exploring expedition, "it is believed that the spirits first repair to the residence of Ndengei, who allots some of them to the devils for food, and sends the rest to Mukalon, a small island off Rewa, where they remain until the appointed day, after which they are all doomed to annihilation. The judgments thus attributed to Ndengei seem to be ascribed rather to his caprice than to any desert of the departed soul." See Williams, *Fiji and the Fijians*, ed. by Rowe (Lond. 1870, 12mo), ch. vii. (J. H. W.)

Ne'äh (Heb. *Neäh'*, נֵעָה [with the definite article], the *shaking* or *settlement* or *descent*; Sept. Αννουά [but Vat. MS. omits]; Vulg. *Noa*), a town in the tribe of Zebulun, on the southern border east of Rimmon (Josh. xix, 13). Eusebius and Jerome (*Onomast.* s. v. Anna) speak only of another place by the same name ten miles south of Neapolis. As Neah is stated to have been not far from Rimmon ("methoar," i. e. "which pertains to" Neah), it lay perhaps at the modern site *Nimrin*, a little west of Kurn Hattin (Robinson, *Later Researches*, p. 341, note). See TRIBE.

Neal, DANIEL, an English dissenting divine and ecclesiastical writer of considerable eminence, was born in London Dec. 14, 1678. His early education was received at Merchant Tailors' School. About 1696 or 1697 he was offered a foundation at St. John's College, Oxford; but feeling that he could not conscientiously meet the religious demands involved in his acceptance, he went to a dissenter's academy, conducted by the celebrated Rev. Thomas Rowe, to whom Dr. Watts addressed his animated ode, called *Free Philosophy*. After three years' study in this school, he went abroad and studied in the Dutch universities of Utrecht and Leyden. Near the close of 1703 Neal returned to England, enjoying at this time the society of the afterwards celebrated Dr. Lardner. Shortly after his return home he was ordained minister of the Independent body, and became assistant to Dr. Singleton, the pastor of a congregation in Aldersgate Street; and at the death of the latter was chosen as successor. He continued in this position until within a year of his death, which occurred April 4, 1743. As a pastor, Mr. Neal met with more than usual success; even as a young man, while yet the assistant of Dr. Singleton, men of all stations came to hear him preach; and so largely did his congregation increase that when he ministered to his people as sole pastor a new church had to be secured. He was known far beyond the pale of his own congregation, and frequently invited to lecture in the interests of Christianity and on Protestant polemics. Mr. Neal had an easy, agreeable manner, both in the style and in the delivery of his sermons, free from affectation. In conversation, he knew how to mix grave and prudent instruction or advice with a becoming cheerfulness, which made his company pleasing and profitable. Yet, notwithstanding these official duties, in the discharge of which he was eminently faithful, he found leisure for valuable literary labors; and the name of Daniel Neal will for some time to come figure prominently in English ecclesiastical history. His chief work is the *History of the Puritans*, which is written with great minuteness and accuracy, though it reflects seriously and often unjustly on the English establishment, and frequently palliates the errors of the Puritans. It was originally published in 4 vols. 8vo, the first of which appeared in 1732, and the second, third, and fourth in 1733, 1736, and 1738 respectively. It has since passed through many editions (Amer. ed. revised, corrected, and enlarged with additional notes by John O. Charles, A.M. [N. Y. 1844], 2 vols. 8vo, and often since). The first volume was reviewed by Dr. Maddox, bishop of St. Asaph, and the remaining volumes by Dr. Zachary Grey. To the former Neal himself replied; and an answer was given to the latter by Dr. Toulmin, in an edition of Neal's *History* published in 1793-7. Various opinions have been expressed on the character and value of Neal's *History*, yet no English critic has ever questioned Neal's honesty. Bishop Warburton considered it grossly unjust to the Anglican establishment, but he never impugned Neal's integrity. Bickersteth, himself of the establishment, calls it "a valuable and instructive history, with a strong bias in favor of his subjects, but an upright mind" (*Christian Student*, p. 514). The truth is, Neal is about as far from the mark, as a historian, as Heylin; and Disraeli has well said that "Heylin, in his *History of the Presbyterians*, blackens

them as so many political devils; and Neal, in his *History of the Puritans*, blanches them into a sweet and almond whiteness" (*Miscell. of Lit.* ed. 1840, p. 298; comp. p. 307, 308). Neal's other publications are a number of separate *Sermons*, 1722, 1723, 1726, 1727, 1735 (nine are in a collection of *Lectures* by several divines, 1735, 2 vols. 8vo):—*A Solemn Prayer against the Plague*, 1721:—three *Tracts* in vindication of his *History of the Puritans*, 1720, 1734, 1739; and the following works: 1. *History of New England*: containing an account of the civil and ecclesiastical affairs of the country to the year 1700; to which is added an Appendix, containing their charter, their ecclesiastical discipline, and their municipal laws (Lond. 1720, 2 vols. 8vo; again, 1747, 2 vols. 8vo; see Dr. Watts's *Letter* to Dr. Cotton Mather, 1720, in *Mass. Hist. Coll.* vol. iv):—2. *Narrative of the Method and Success of Inoculating the Small-Pox in New England, by Mr. Benjamin Colman*, etc. 1722, 8vo. See *Life* by Dr. Toulmin, in Neal's *History of the Puritans*; Wilson's *Hist. of Dissenting Churches*; Bogue and Bennett's *Hist. of Dissenters*, ii, 374; *Funeral Sermon on Neal*, by Jennings; Skeats, *Hist. Free Churches of England*, p. 257, 258, 280, 306; *Prot. Dissent. Mag.* vol. i; Smyth's *Lects. on Mod. Hist.* Lects. xi, xviii; Mosheim's *Eccles. Hist.*; Thomas Moore's *Memoirs* (1853), iv, 159; Lowndes, *Bibl. Man.* 1823; Watts's *Bibl. Brit.* s. v.; Darling, *Cyclop. Bibliog.* ii, 2160; *Lond. Quar. Rev.* x, 90 (by Robert Southey); *North Amer. Rev.* lx, 215 (by E. P. Whipple; see his *Essays and Reviews*, i, 208); *Meth. Quar. Rev.* v, 54 (by D. Belcher); *Princeton Rev.* xvii, 1; *Christ. Rev.* viii, 481; *Christ. Exam.* xxxviii, 126 (by A. Lamson); *Church Rev.* vol. ix; *Amer. Presb. Theol. Rev.* Jan. 1867. (J.H.W.)

Neale, John Mason, a noted English divine, celebrated as a hymnologist and writer of ecclesiastical history, and as a successful educator, was born in London Jan. 24, 1818, and was educated at Cambridge University, Trinity College, class of 1840, where he took the members' prize in 1838, and the Seatonian prize for a sacred poem nine times between 1845-61. Neale entered into holy orders in 1842, and became incumbent of Crawley, in Sussex, which position he held until 1846, when he was appointed warden of the Sackville College, East Grinstead. He died at East Grinstead, Aug. 6, 1866. Of High-Church proclivities, he identified himself with the various movements of the Ritualists, and in 1855 caused a sisterhood to be founded, named St. Margaret. Neale was a voluminous writer, his publications being some seventy in number. His most important work is his *History of the Holy Eastern Church*, vols. i and ii forming a general introduction (London, 1850, 8vo); vols. iii and iv covering the *Patriarchate of Alexandria* (ibid. 1847, 8vo); vol. v treating of the *Patriarchate of Antioch* (ibid. 1874, 8vo). This work is highly esteemed by all students of Oriental Church history. It is a learned and laborious work, and in the parts of which it treats forms a valuable compend. Based as it is on the original sources, it is an invaluable contribution to ecclesiastical history, and it is to be regretted that Mr. Neale did not live to complete it. See *Edinb. Review*, cvii, 322 sq. Other valuable works by Mr. Neale are, *Sequentiæ ex missalibus Germanicis* (1852):—*Mediæval Preachers and Mediæval Preaching* (1857):—*History of the so-called Jansenist Church of Holland* (1858):—*Commentary on the Psalms* (1860):—*Essays on Liturgiology and Church History* (1863):—*The Liturgies* (in Greek) *of St. Mark, St. James, St. Clement, St. Chrysostom, and St. Basil* (1868). Dr. Neale figures as a hymnologist substantially, as in so many other departments of Christian labor, not so much because of his original contributions as for his antiquarian researches, especially his translations of ancient and mediæval hymns. His most valued translation is that of the celebrated poem of Bernard of Clugny, entitled *De Contemptu Mundi*, portions of which are found in many of our best hymn-books in the three hymns, "Brief life is here our portion," "For thee, O dear, dear country," and "Jerusalem the golden." Among his contributions to hymnology, besides those already mentioned, are, *Mediæval Hymns, Sequences, etc.* (1851; also a second edition):—*Hymni Ecclesiæ* (1851):—*Hymns for Children* (sixth edition, 1854):—*Hymns for the Sick:*—*Hymns of the Eastern Church* (1863; new edition, with introduction, 1871):—*Carols for Christmas-Tide* (1853). Several of his hymns have become the common property of English-speaking people. Dr. Schaff has incorporated two of them in his *Christ in Song*, p. 125, 286. (J. H. W.)

Neale, Leonard, D.D., an American Roman Catholic prelate, was born in the state of Maryland in 1746, and was educated at the Roman Catholic college in Baltimore. He entered holy orders after he had enjoyed further superior educational advantages at home and abroad, and rapidly rose to distinction. In 1800 he was consecrated coadjutor to archbishop Carroll of Baltimore, and in 1815 became his successor in the archiepiscopate. Archbishop Neale died at Georgetown, D. C., June 18, 1817. He was highly respected by the Protestants of this country for his Christian zeal and his broad views on religious toleration.

Neale, Samuel, a highly-esteemed Quaker preacher, was born in Dublin, Ireland, in 1729. He began preaching at the age of twenty-two years, and travelled in England, Holland, and Germany, everywhere preaching the Gospel of Christ. In 1753 he returned from this journey, and settled within the compass of Edenberry and Rathangan. He died about 1760. See Janney, *Hist. of Friends*, iii, 282.

Neander, Christoph Friedrich, a German theologian and hymnologist, was born at Ekau in 1724, and was educated at Halle from 1740 to 1743. He entered the ministry, and became pastor at Kubillen, a place in the German province of West Russia; in 1755 at Gränzhof, in the same vicinity; in 1775 at Doblensch; and in 1785 was honored with the superintendency of the whole province. He died in 1802. Neander wrote many Christian songs, of which a collection was published at Riga in 1772, and so extensive was the circulation that several editions were reached. The third edition was brought out in 1779. He also prepared a hymn-book for the province. See E. von der Recke, *Leben des Christoph Friedrich Neander*, herausgegeben von Tiedge (Berlin, 1804, 8vo).

Neander, Daniel Amadeus, a German Protestant prelate of distinction, was born at Lengenfeld, in Saxony, Nov. 17, 1775, and was educated at the University of Leipsic. He entered the ministry, and became pastor at the little village of Flemmingen, near Naumburg; in 1817 was made pastor and superintendent at Merseburg; in 1823 court preacher, and a little later counsellor to the minister of cultus and pastor of St. Peter's at Berlin; in 1829 first general superintendent of the province of Brandenburg, and director of the Consistory; and finally, in 1830, bishop of the Evangelical Church. In 1853, by his own request, he was granted a supernumerary relation, and after 1865, when he was relieved of all ecclesiastical duties, he lived quietly in retirement until his death, Nov. 18, 1869. The bishop enjoyed the confidence and esteem of the Prussian Church, to which he rendered great service in 1829 by settling the controversy which then agitated it, because of the intended introduction of the king's agenda for the communion service into the liturgy. "This difficult controversy was finally settled principally by an arrangement proposed by bishop Neander, according to which a new revision of the liturgy was to be made by the ecclesiastical authorities, with special reference to the most important objections (1829). As this presented to the worshippers a choice of several forms, and paid respect to provincial usages, and as the rights of the Church were preserved and were duly honored by the government, it was accepted without difficulty. Accordingly, since 1830, the agenda has possessed the authority of law, and but *one*

evangelical national Church has been known in Prussia (Hase, *Ch. Hist.* p. 568). Bishop Neander wrote, *Die erste merkwürdige Geistererscheinung des* 19 *Jahrh.* (Dresden, 1804); published some of his *Sermons* (Berl. 1826, 2 vols.); and edited with Bretschneider u. Goldhorn the *Journal für Prediger.* (J. H. W.)

Neander, Joachim, a German Reformed minister, noted as the first and the best of the hymn-writers of the Reformed Church, and also as a participant in the Labadistic movement, was born at Bremen, probably about 1650. He studied theology in the high school of Bremen, where he became acquainted with and adopted the principles of Untereyk. In his early career as a student he was wild and careless, and much given to jesting about religious matters. Thus one day he and two of his comrades went into St. Martin's Church, with the intention of making a jest of the service, but the sermon touched his conscience so deeply that he determined to visit the preacher in private, and from that time he began to lead a more circumspect life. His love of the chase, however, still clung to him; and on one occasion he followed his game on foot so far that night came on and he utterly lost his way among rocky and woody hills, where the climbing was difficult even in daylight. He wandered about for some time, and suddenly discovered that he was in a most dangerous position, and that one step forward would have thrown him over a precipice. A feeling of horror came over him that almost deprived him of the power of motion; and in this extremity he prayed earnestly to God for help, vowing an entire devotion of himself to his service in the future. All at once Neander's courage returned; he felt as if a hand were leading him, and, following the path thus indicated, he at length reached his home in safety. From that day he kept his vow, and a complete change took place in his mode of life. From Bremen Neander went to continue his studies for the ministry at Heidelberg; and upon the completion of his university course visited with classmates at Frankfort-on-the-Main, where he made the acquaintance of the Pietists who flourished there at that time under the leadership of the noted Spener, with whom Neander formed a warm friendship which lasted through life. In 1674 Neander was made rector of the Latin school at Dusseldorf, and he distinguished himself greatly by his success both as a teacher and a preacher. His zeal and his Labadistic tendencies, however, carried him too far, and in 1676 he was dismissed from the school, as well as forbidden to preach until he should make reparation. As he refused to comply with the demand of the school authorities he was obliged to quit the town, and though his pupils loved him so dearly that he could have held his place by encouraging them to insubordinate measures, he counselled submission and left the place. It was summer time, and, feeling himself utterly friendless, he wandered out to a deep and beautiful glen near Mettmann on the Rhine, and there he lived for some months in a cavern which is still known by the name of "Neander's Cave." It was during the period of this retreat that the greater part of his hymns were written. Finally, on Feb. 17, 1677, he signed a confession of his errors, condemning the schism of the Labadists, and all reunion held without the participation of the ministers and elders. He rose at once in popular favor, and shortly after his return to Bremen, in 1679, was made third pastor of St. Martin's—the very church he had once entered in mockery; but he only preached there one year, and died at Easter in 1680. Neander's hymns, 71 in number, appeared for the first time in 1679, under the title, A u. Ω, *Joachim Neanders Glaub- u. Liebesübung, aufgemuntert durch einfältige Bundeslieder u. Dankpsalmen*, etc. Some of them were first introduced in the Darmstadt Hymn-book in 1698, and approved of afterwards in the synods of Julich, Cleve, and Berg in 1731, and of Mark in 1734. Some of them had been set to music composed by Neander himself. Neander's style in his hymns is unequal; occasional harshness contrasts with fine musical lines, but there is a glow, a sweetness, and a depth about his hymns that have made many of them justly and lastingly popular among the German people. See Max Göbel, *Geschichte d. christl. Lebens i. d. rheinisch-westphälischen Kirche*; Kohlmann, *Joachim Neander, s. Herkommen u. s. Geburtsjahr*, in the *Reform. Kirchenzeitung* (1856); Reitz, *Historie d. Wiedergeborenen*; Winterfeld, *Evangelischer Kirchengesang*; Koch, *Gesch. des Kirchen-Liedes*; Winkworth, *Christian Singers of Germany*, p. 284–288; Saunders, *Evenings with the Sacred Poets*, p. 112–115.

Neander, Johann August Wilhelm, universally conceded to be by far the greatest of ecclesiastical historians, and surnamed the father of modern Church history, was born in the university town of Göttingen, Germany, January 15, 1789, a time memorable as introducing the fearful drama of the French Revolution, when the moral atmosphere was infected with deadly poisons, and black and thickening clouds were spread over the political and religious horizon. He was the son of a Jewish merchant, *Mendel* by name, who at one time had been prominent in commercial circles; but, reduced by reverses, was now travelling in little out-of-the-way country towns, selling such goods as could be easily carried about, and would find a ready market among the poorer classes. Mendel was honorably connected by blood-ties with some of the best of German Jewish families, among them the Mendelssohns. He was a pious Jew, and David, as the boy was named at circumcision, was carefully trained religiously and intellectually. At eight years of age he was admitted as student to the Johanneum Gymnasium at Hamburg, whither his parents had removed. At this place the Jewish boy enjoyed the friendship and daily association of Varnhagen von Ense, Chamisso, the poet, Wilhelm Neumann, the composer, etc. Already the abstract, lofty, and pure genius of Neander was beginning to show itself. It is related that a bookseller in the town was struck with the frequent visits to his shop of a bashful, ungainly boy, who used to steal in and seize upon some erudite volume that no one else would touch, and utterly lose himself for hours together in study. This was no other than our David Mendel. Plato and Plutarch were his favorite classics; and many a spare hour out of school not spent in that old book-stall was devoted to the study of these ancient masters of wisdom. The modern writers also engaged his attention; and thoughtfully he perused several works on Christianity, among them that famous work of Schleiermacher entitled *Discourses on Religion*, which appeared in 1799, addressed to the cultivated despisers of religion, and aiming to show the evils arising in society out of indifference to the Christian faith and the practices which it demands. The thoughtful Jewish boy was struck with the reasonable demands made of humanity by a self-sacrificing Saviour; was convinced that he who taught such ethics and demanded of his followers such a life was more than man. Long was the struggle between a faithful adherence to what his parents, especially his pious mother, had taught him; but finally, convinced of his false position, no obstacles could hold him back, and in 1806 he publicly renounced Judaism, and was baptized, adopting, in allusion to the religious change which he had experienced, the name of *Neander* (from the Greek νέος ἀνήρ, i. e. *new man*), and as his Christian or baptismal names those of his Christian teacher, Johann Gurlitt, then principal of the Johanneum, and of his friends August Varnhagen and Wilhelm Neumann. Neander's sisters and brothers, and later his mother also, followed his example. In the year of his admission into the Christian Church he went to Halle as a student of theology, devoting himself with wonderful ardor and success to his task. Neander's favorite professor was he whose work had caused the Jew to embrace Christ as the Messiah, and Schleiermacher in turn greatly interested himself in his convert and student. But much more intimate was Neander's relation to Prof. Knapp,

then the only Pietistic representative at Halle. The sudden defeat of the Prussians at Jena, Oct. 14, 1806, threw Halle open to the French invaders, and three days later the students of that high school were forced to quit it and seek elsewhere educational advantages. Neander went to Göttingen, and there he studied for three years under Planck, then in the zenith of his reputation as a Church historian; he next returned to Hamburg, expecting to enter the ministry, but was prevented in this step by a call as lecturer to the University of Heidelberg. He had been here only a short time when he was appointed extraordinary professor of theology, so great was his success as a lecturer. In 1813 the then newly-established University of Berlin needed a professor of Church history. Neander had created considerable sensation by his monograph on *Julian and his Times*, and the well-informed king of Prussia selected Neander for the vacant chair. Schleiermacher, De Wette, and Marheineke were already engaged, and Neander soon figured as prominently as any of his colleagues. For the remainder of his life he was ardently at work for the advancement of Christianity and in the interests of the university. He especially enjoyed immense celebrity as a lecturer. Even Schleiermacher had a limited circle of auditors compared with the throngs who went to hear Neander. Students flocked to him not only from all parts of Germany, but from the most distant Protestant countries. Many Roman Catholics, even, were among his auditors; and it is said that there is hardly a great preacher in Germany who is not more or less penetrated with his ideas. Perhaps no professor was ever so much loved by his students as Neander. He used to give the poorer ones tickets to his lectures, and to supply them with clothes and money. In 1822–3 Möhler, the distinguished Roman polemic, was one of Neander's hearers; and after paying a tribute to the different celebrated theologians of the university, he alludes in these highly eulogistic terms to the noted Church historian: " Neander embraces everything, even to the most profound. What study of original authorities, what judgment, what deep religiousness, what earnestness, what clearness and precision in the representation; how living, how attractive is the picture of the times which Neander delineates! In how masterly a manner does he know how to describe the men who were the ruling spirits of their times; with what undeviating justice does he apportion praise or blame to each! ... Neander's prelections will be ever memorable to me; they will have decided influence on my Church historical labors. His private life is pervaded by enlightened piety; it is simple as the conduct of a village schoolmaster; his character is lovable and unassuming in the highest degree; he knows in Berlin no street but that which leads him to the university; he knows no persons but his professional colleagues; but Origen, Tertullian, Augustine, Chrysostom, St. Bernard, the letters of Boniface, and so on—he knows these profoundly. His demeanor is, on account of its total want of polish, laughable, but no one laughs at him for it; unbounded is the reverence and love which his students, the respect which his colleagues, the regard which the government, show towards him" (Wörner, *Joh. A. Möhler, ein Lebensbild* [Regensb. 1866], p. 72–74).

Neander labored earnestly in many ways up to a few days of his death, and when the final earthly hour of work had passed he calmly said to the sorrowing friends who gathered about him, "I am weary; I will now go to sleep;" and, as they conducted him to his bed, the place of his last repose, he whispered, with a voice of mellowing affection, "Good-night, good-night." He slumbered for four hours, and then gently and almost imperceptibly "breathed himself into the silent and cold sleep of death." This occurred on July 14, 1850. In his death this good man was honored as in his life. The day of his obsequies was observed as a public holiday in Berlin. A vast procession followed the remains to the grave, stretching the length of full two miles.

The hearse was surrounded by students bearing lighted candles; in front of the body, Neander's Bible and Greek Testament were carried. The carriages of the king and princess of Prussia followed in the procession; and at the grave a solemn choral was sung by a thousand voices, and a discourse was pronounced by his friend, the noted Dr. Krummacher.

In his outward appearance Dr. Neander was a real curiosity, especially in the lecture-room. Dr. Schaff thus described him in his "Sketches of German Divines," as foreign correspondent of the *New York Evangelist*: "Think of a man of middle size, slender frame, homely, though a good-natured and benevolent face, dark and strongly Jewish complexion, deep-seated but sparkling eyes, overshadowed with an unusually strong, bushy pair of eyebrows, black hair flowing in uncombed profusion over the forehead, an old-fashioned coat, a white cravat carelessly tied—as often behind or on one side of the neck as in front—a shabby hat set aslant, jack-boots reaching above the knees; think of him either sitting at home, surrounded by books on the shelves, the table, the few chairs, and all over the floor, or walking Unter den Linden and in the Thiergarten of Berlin, leaning on the arm of his sister Hannchen or a faithful student, his eyes shut or looking half-way up to heaven, talking theology in the midst of the noise and fashion of the city, and presenting altogether a most singular contrast to the teeming life around him, stared at, smiled at, wondered at, yet respectfully greeted by all who knew him; or, finally, standing on the rostrum, playing with a couple of goose-quills which his amanuensis had always to provide, constantly crossing and recrossing his feet, bent forward, frequently sinking his head to discharge a morbid flow of spittle, and then again suddenly throwing it on high, especially when roused to polemic zeal against pantheism and dead formalism, at times fairly threatening to overturn the desk, and yet all the while pouring forth with the greatest earnestness and enthusiasm, without any other help than that of some illegible notes, an uninterrupted flow of learning and thought from the deep and pure fountain of the inner life, and thus, with all the oddity of the outside, at once commanding the veneration and confidence of every hearer: and you have a picture of Neander, the most original phenomenon in the literary world of this 19th century" (reprinted in his *Germany— its Universities, Theology, and Religion*, p. 269, 270).

Neander was never married, and belonged to those exceptions where celibacy is a necessity and duty, and a means of greater usefulness in the kingdom of God. A congenial sister kept house for Neander, and attended to his wants with the most tender care. The childlike intercourse of this original couple had something very touching. He was almost as helpless as a child in matters of dress, and the story runs that he once started off for the lecture-room in his morning-gown and *sans culottes*, but was happily overtaken by the watchful sister; also, that once, in trying a new pair of pantaloons, he kept on the old ones, drew the left half over the right leg, and cut the other off with a pair of scissors as superfluous! *Si non e vero, e ben trovato.* His clothing was of the most simple sort, and hardly fit for a gentleman. His moderation in eating and drinking reminded one of the self-denial of old ascetics, like St. Anthony of Egypt, who ate only once every three days, and then felt ashamed, as an immortal spirit, to be in need of earthly food. Yet Neander was extremely hospitable, and invited his friends often to dinner, and while they were enjoying the provisions of the table he talked to them theology and religion, or branched out occasionally into harmless humor and the more trifling topics of the day, as far as they came to his notice. His heart was open to friendship, and his faithful memory seldom forgot one who once had made an impression upon him, though he were only a transient visitor. Every stranger with proper recommendations was cordially welcome in his study at the fixed hour of conver-

sation (between five and seven in the evening), or at his table, and he showed himself as obliging as could possibly be expected from a man so unpractical and helpless as Neander. Generally he plunged at once into the deepest theological discussions, opening his mind most freely with little prudential regard to men or circumstances. So he shocked many a Puritan and Presbyterian by inviting them to dinner on Sunday, but always won their esteem and love by the ensemble of his theology and character. He spoke English fluently, although not quite correctly. The students he gathered around him one evening every week to a social tea and familiar conversation. There he gave free vent to all that agitated his mind, and rejoiced or troubled his heart, concerning the state of the Church and the movements of theological science.

As a man and a Christian, Dr. Neander was universally esteemed. Indeed his character, religiously considered, is of so noble a Christian type that it calls for special notice. Ardently and profoundly devotional, sympathetic, cheerful, profusely benevolent, and without a shadow of selfishness resting on his soul, he inspired universal reverence, and was himself, by the mild and attractive sanctity of his life, as powerful an argument on behalf of Christianity as his writings. The childlike simplicity of his character was beautiful. Everything like vanity and pretence was as foreign to him as if he dwelt on a different planet. A recent German writer calls him a "Protestant monk or saint, whose world was the cloister of the inner man, out of which he worked and taught for the good of the Church." We do not wonder when it is said that Neander's salutary influence on the religious sentiments and state of Germany are far above that of any other man in this century. He was one of the chief promoters of the changes introduced into the Protestant establishment of Prussia, and of the compromise of the Lutheran and Calvinistic confessions. He is also believed to have contributed more than any other single individual to the overthrow, on the one side, of that anti-historical rationalism, and, on the other, of that dead Lutheran formalism, from both of which the religious life of Germany had so long suffered. His influence was so great as to lead very many of the young men of the fatherland to embrace the vital doctrines of Christianity, for his own theological views were more positive and evangelical than those entertained by any of his colleagues. He shared with the most orthodox of them the opinion that religion is based upon feeling. The Christian "consciousness" was the sum of his theology. "By this term," said he, "is designated the power of the Christian faith in the subjective life of the single individual, in the congregation, and in the Church generally: a power independent and ruling according to its own law—that which, according to the word of our Lord, must first form the leaven of every other historical development of mankind." Neander's motto, "Pectus est, quod theologum facit," unfolds his whole theological system and life career. The Germans call his creed "Pectoralism," in view of the inner basis of his faith. With him, religion amounts to nothing without Christ. Nor must Christ be the mere subject of study; the soul and its manifold affections must embrace him. The barrenness of Judaism is done away in him, and the emptiness of rationalistic criticism is successfully met by the fulness found in Christianity. Sin is not merely hurtful and prejudicial, but it induces guilt and danger. It can be pardoned only through the death and mediation of Christ. The illustrations of devout service to be found in the history of the Church should serve as examples for succeeding times. Neander therefore spent much of the careful labor of his life in portraying prominent characters; for it was his opinion that individuals sometimes combine the features of their times, the virtues or the vices prevalent; and that if these individualities be clearly defined the Church is furnished with valuable lessons for centuries. The work which he published when but twenty-two years of age, *Julian the Apostate* (Leips. 1812; transl. by G. V. Cox, N. Y. 1850, 12mo), was the beginning of a series of similar monographs designed to show the importance of the individual in history, and to point out great crises in the religious life of man. He subsequently produced *St. Bernard* (Berl. 1813):— *Gnosticism* (1818):—*St. Chrysostom* (1821, 2 vols.):— *Denkwürdigkeiten aus der Gesch. des Christenthums und des geistlichen Lebens* (1822, 3 vols.; 3d ed. 1845–46); in an English dress, entitled *The History of the Christian Religion and Church during the first Three Centuries*, transl. by Henry John Rose (2d ed. Lond. 1842, 2 vols. 8vo):—*Tertullian* (1826):—*Geschichte der Pflanzung und Leitung der Kirche durch die Apostel* (Hamb. 1832–33, 2 vols.; 4th ed. 1847; *History of the Planting and Training of the Christian Church by the Apostles*, transl. from the German by J. E. Ryland [Lond. 1851, 2 vols. sm. 8vo]):—*Das Leben Jesu Christi in seinem geschichtlichen Zusammenhange*, written as a reply to Strauss's work (Hamb. 1837; 5th ed. 1853; *The Life of Jesus Christ in its historical Connection and historical Development*, transl. from the 4th German ed. by John M'Clintock, D.D., LL.D., and Charles E. Blumenthal [N. Y. 1848, 8vo]):— *Wissenschaftliche Abhandlungen*, published by Jacobi (Berl. 1851):—*Geschichte der Christlichen Dogmen*, also published by Jacobi (1856); in English entitled *Lectures on the History of Christian Dogmas* (Lond. 1857, 2 vols. 12mo). To these may be added a few practical commentaries and essays. By far the most important of these works is his *Life of Christ*, which has a polemic aim against Strauss. This is, however, only a small part of its merits; and but for the notes an ordinary reader would not detect any such specific tendency. It unfolds the life of the Saviour from the record with great clearness and skill; it invests the outlines thus obtained with the fresh colors of life, without resorting to forced constructions and vain imaginings; and, above all, it seeks, with childlike humility and reverence, to learn and exhibit the mind of the Spirit. The characteristic of spirituality, strongly stamped upon all the works of this great writer, is especially prominent here. None, we think, can read the book without becoming not merely acquainted with the facts of the life of Christ, but more anxious than ever to drink in its spirit. Nor let us forget, in our judgment of what may appear to us even grave errors of opinion in the book, that its author has fought for every step of ground that has been gained of late years by spiritual religion in Germany; and while we lament the "dimness" which this great man confesses with such Christianlike humility, let us acknowledge the grandeur of his idea of the kingdom of God, and the earnestness of his devotion to it. His starting-point and many of his paths are different from ours; it must therefore gladden one's heart, and may perhaps confirm one's faith, to see that Neander reaches, after all, the general results of evangelical theology.

Neander's greatest literary treasure to the world has proved to be, however, his *Allgemeine Geschichte der christlichen Religion und Kirche* (Hamb. 1825–52; 3d ed. 1851–56, 6 vols. 8vo), which treats of the history of the Church from the apostolic age to the Council of Basle in 1430. It is accessible to English readers in the excellent translation of Prof. Joseph Torrey, under the title of *General History of the Christian Religion and Church* (from the second and improved edition [Boston, 1847, 5 vols. 8vo]; and reprinted at Edinburgh and London). Neander sets out in this work with the idea that Christianity is a life-giving spirit, awakened in the mind by the influence of divine truth on the heart; that it recognises no distinction of spiritual authority among men, no priesthood, properly so called, no holy days, and no ordinances in the technical sense of the word; although it naturally assumes forms accommodated to the circumstances of the times, and adapts itself to every stage in human culture. This Christianity is a leaven that takes hold of whatsoever is divine in man, quickening it,

struggling with the contrary elements—with Judaism, with heathenism, with all the worldly and sinful propensities of the soul—gradually modifying or overcoming them, and destined eventually to ferment the whole mind of our race. The history of its workings, developments, and manifestations in these respects is the history of the Christian religion and Church. He exhibits extraordinary talent in bringing out, in a generic way, the hidden life of Christianity, and representing it as a leavenlike power that pervades and sanctifies society from within. He thus restores the religious and practical element to its due prominence in opposition to the coldly intellectual and critical method of rationalistic historians; yet without thereby wronging in the least the claims of science, or running into narrow sectarian extremes, like the pietistic Arnold. Says Dr. Hurst: "The various influences hitherto employed against rationalism had proceeded as far towards its extinction as it was possible for them to go. Philosophy and doctrinal theology had spent their efforts. The history of the Church having always been treated mechanically, it was now necessary that the continued presence and agency of Christ with his people should be carefully portrayed. The progress of the Church needed to be represented as more than growth from natural causes, such as the force of civilization and education. It was necessary to show that a high superintending Wisdom is directing its path, overcoming its difficulties, and leading it through persecution and blood to ultimate triumph. Neander rendered this important service. He directed the vision of the theologian to a new field, and became the father of the best Church historians of the nineteenth century" (*Hist. of Rationalism*, p. 252, 253). Neander no doubt sometimes went too far in his liberality; and by trying to do full justice even to heretics and sectarians, he was in danger sometimes—like Arnold and Milner, although of course in a far less degree—of doing injustice to the champions of orthodoxy and the Church. The cry is therefore, on the part especially of Churchmen, who would claim for the objectivity of the Church a like import with the objectivity of the Gospel, that there is in Neander a want of the proper appreciation of the objective, realistic element in Church history. Now it is true that Neander is more the historian of the invisible kingdom of Christ in the hearts of its individual members than of the visible Church in its great conflict and contact with a wicked world. Yet one need but turn to Neander's pages for a delineation of ecclesiasticism in the Middle Ages—the time when objectiveness was most vigorous in the Church—to be convinced that Neander well understood how to value this quality, when it was the natural form of the growth of the Christian life. The internal and most personal were certainly of more importance to him than anything else. Says Jacobi, Neander's pupil and devoted follower: "When the predominant Christian power was connected with the objective forms of the Church, as in the time of Abelard, he regarded their ascendency as warranted, without justifying the contemporary suppression of the germs of truth, and the reprehensible means which were employed in particular cases. And is it not confirmed by the experience of all ages that there is no fault to which the traditionary Church party is more prone than suspicion of every deviation, and suppression of even such dissent as is legitimate? If in modern times individualism has increased to a bewildering excess, has it not been one principal reason why the rights of individuals to form their own views of the gospel were not acknowledged as they deserved, either in the Middle Ages or in the later decennia of the Reformation—to say nothing of the most flourishing period of Protestant orthodoxy? Would Dr. Kurtz be willing to defend the manner in which Wickliffe, Huss, and John Arndt were treated in the name of orthodoxy; and how, according to his notions, would Luther have been justified in setting himself against the objectivity of the Church, unless, with

Neander and Luther himself, he holds higher still the objectivity of the Gospel? It was not Neander's wish to set aside the objectivity of the Church, or to subordinate it to the individual, but to contract its sphere, in order to give the latter liberty of action, and that the pious members of the Church might testify of the Gospel against the Church. But it is not easy to perceive what is to be gained by the maintenance of the objectivity of the Church, especially in the department of historical study, if not a word is to be said for the other factor of [Christian] life.... We know not why it should be a matter of reproach to Neander that he more or less contrasts what belongs to Christianity generally, with that which merely belongs to the Church. Is there an ecclesiastical communion which dare maintain that its system, taken as a whole, is in every particular a pure expression of the Gospel? Is it, therefore, a fact that these two—the Christian and the ecclesiastical—are everywhere striving at a reconcilement not yet completed, and therefore must be regarded more or less in contrast, relatively, and according to the stage of the Church's development?" (Preface to *Lectures on Dogma* by Neander, i, 9, 10). It must be confessed, too, that Neander's theology in many respects falls short of the proper standard of orthodoxy. He did not admit the binding authority of the symbolical books. His views on inspiration, on the sanctification of the Lord's day, and even on the Trinity, are somewhat loose and latitudinarian. His best disciples in this respect have gone beyond his position and become more churchly. But then it must be considered, 1st, that he rose in an age of universal rationalism, and was one of the earliest pioneers of evangelical faith and theology in Germany; 2d, that this very liberalism and, if we choose to call it, latitudinarianism, served as a bridge for many who could not otherwise have been rescued from the bonds of scepticism; 3d, that these defects did not weaken his general conviction of the divine character of Christianity, nor affect his unfeigned, deep-rooted piety. Many of his pupils and followers may surpass him in orthodoxy, but few can be found in any age in whom doctrine was to the same extent life and power, in whom theoretic conviction had so fully passed over into flesh and blood, in whom the love of Christ and man glowed with so warm and pure a flame, as in the truly great and good Neander. Any defects, if Neander's work can really be said to have defects, cannot blind any one to their real excellences and immortal merits. He is emphatically the evangelical regenerator of this branch of theology, and has made it a running commentary on Christ's previous promise to be with his people to the end of the world, and even with two or three of his humblest disciples where they are assembled in his name. Thus Church history becomes to the intelligent reader a book of devotion as well as useful and interesting information, or to use Neander's own words in the preface to the first volume of his large work, "a living witness for the divine power of Christianity, a school of Christian experience, a voice of edification, instruction, and warning, sounding through all ages for all who will hear." He everywhere follows the footsteps of the Saviour in his march through the various ages of the Church, and kisses them reverently wherever he finds them. He traces them in the writings of an Origen and a Tertullian, a Chrysostom and an Augustine, a Bernard and a Thomas Aquinas, a Luther and a Melancthon, a Calvin and a Fénelon. Christ was to him the divine harmony of all the discords of confessions and sects, or as he liked to repeat after Pascal, "En Jésus Christ toutes les contradictions sont accordées."

Neander, it must be conceded, is not a model as a *writer* of Church history. His style is too monotonous and diffuse, without any picturesque alteration of light and shade, flowing like a quiet stream over an unbroken plain. Yet did he so enrich the department of Church history with material contributions gained by a thorough mastery, independent investigation, and scrupulously conscientious use of the sources, and present a so much more methodical treatment of the subject as to gain for himself the approval of all, and he has come to be universally acknowledged the father of modern Church history, marking by his efforts in this field of sacred learning an epoch as clearly as Flacius (q. v.) did in the 16th, Arnold (q. v.) in the 17th, or Mosheim in the 18th century. "In spite of all faults," says Schaff, "Neander still remains, on the whole, beyond doubt the greatest Church historian thus far of the 19th century. Great, too, especially in this, that he never suffered his renown to obscure at all his sense of the sinfulness and weakness of every human work in this world. With all his comprehensive knowledge, he justly regarded himself as, among many others, merely a forerunner of a new creative epoch of ever-young Christianity; and towards that time he gladly stretched his vision, with the prophetic gaze of faith and hope, from amid the errors and confusion around him. 'We stand,' says he, 'on the line between an old and a new, about to be called into being by the ever-fresh energy of the Gospel. For the fourth time an epoch in the life of our race is in preparation by means of Christianity. We, therefore, can furnish, in every respect, *but pioneer work* for the period of the new creation, when life and science shall be regenerated, and the wonderful works of God proclaimed with new tongues of fire' (*Leben Jesu*, 1st ed. p. ix sq.)" (*Hist. Apostol. Ch.* p. 106). A complete edition of Neander's writings has been brought out in recent years (Gotha, 1862–66, 13 vols. 8vo); and his name will go down to future generations as the philanthropic founder of a home for little wanderers called the "Neander Haus." An American institution of learning, the Rochester Theological Seminary, prides itself on the possession of his library. See Farrell, *Memorial of A. Neander* (1851); Krabbe, *August Neander, ein Beitrag z, dessen Karakteristik* (Hamb. 1852); Kling, *Dr. August Neander, ein Beitrag z. d. Lebensbilde*, in "Stud. u. Krit." of 1851; *Zum Gedächtniss August Neander's* (Berlin, 1850); *Neuer Nekrolog d. Deutschen* (1850, p. 425); Hagenbach, *Neander's Verdienste um d. Kirchengeschichte*, in the "Stud. u. Krit." of 1851; Baur, *d. Epochen d. Kirchlich. Geschichte;* Schaff, *Recollections of Neander*, in "Mercersburg Review," Jan. 1851; and in *Kirchenfreund* (1851), 283 sq.; and *Hist. Apost. Ch.* p. 95–107; Uhlhorn, *d. ältere Kirchengesch. in ihren neueren Darstellungen*, etc.; Saintes, *Rationalism*, p. 265 sq.; *Bib. Sacra*, April, 1851, art. vii; Jan. 1850, p. 77 sq.; Schwarz, *Neueste Deutsche Theologie* (Leips. 1864), ch. i; Kahnis, *Hist. German Protestantism*, p. 272 sq.; Hurst, *Hist. of Rationalism*, p. 249 sq.; Farrar, *Crit. Hist. Free Thought*, p. 251 sq.; *Brit. Qu. Rev.* Nov. 1850; Oct. 1868; *Brit. and For. Ev. Rev.* July, 1868, p. 601 sq.; *New-Englander*, 1865; *Ch. Remembrancer*, 1862, p. 39; *Meth. Qu. Rev.* April, 1848, p. 248; 1847, p. 308; Jan. 1851, p. 143, 181; July, 1852, p. 485; Jan. 1853, p. 102; 1857, p. 203; April, 1865, p. 469; *North Brit. Rev.* Feb. 1851.

Neäp′olis (Νεάπολις, *New City*, a frequent name in Græco-Roman times, like *Newtown* with us; see below), the place in Northern Greece where Paul and his associates first landed in Europe (Acts xvi, 11); where, no doubt, he landed also on his second visit to Macedonia (Acts xx, 1), and whence certainly he embarked on his last journey through that province to Troas and Jerusalem (Acts xx, 6). Philippi being an inland town, Neapolis was evidently the port; and hence it is accounted for that Luke leaves the verb which describes the voyage from Troas to Neapolis (εὐθυδρομήσαμεν) to describe the continuance of the journey from Neapolis to Philippi. The distance from Philippi was ten miles (Strab. vii, 330; Appian, *Bel. Civ.* iv, 106; Ptolemy, iii, 13, 9; Pliny, iv, 11). It was probably the same place with *Datum* (Δάτον), famous for its gold mines (Herod. ix, 75; comp. Böckh's *Pub. Econ. Athens*, p. 8, 228). The town of Neapolis was within the bounds of the province of Thrace (Pliny, *N. H.* iv, 18); but the emperor Vespasian attached it to Macedonia (Suetonius, *Vesp.* 8); and hence, while Pliny locates it in Thrace, Ptolemy (iii, 13) and Strabo (vii, 330) assign it to Macedonia. During the great battle of Philippi the fleet of Brutus and Cassius lay in the bay of Neapolis (Appian, *Bel. Civ.* iv, 106), which Appian states was nine miles distant from their camp at Philippi. Neapolis, therefore, like the present *Kavalla*, which occupies this position, was on a high rocky promontory jutting out into the Ægean. The harbor, a mile and a half wide at the entrance and half a mile broad, lies on the west side. The indifferent roadstead on the east should not be called a harbor. Symbolum, 1670 feet high, with a defile which leads into the plain of Philippi, comes down near to the coast a little to the west of the town. In winter the sun sinks behind Mount Athos in the southwest as early as four o'clock P.M. The land along the eastern shore is low, and otherwise unmarked by any peculiarity. The island of Thasos bears a little to the S.E., twelve or fifteen miles distant. Plane-trees just beyond the walls, not less than four or five hundred years old, cast their shadow over the road which Paul followed on his way to Philippi. The shore of the mainland in this part is low, but the mountains rise to a considerable height behind. To the west of the channel, which separates it from Thasos, the coast recedes and forms a bay, within which, on a promontory with a port at each side, the town was situated (Conybeare and Howson, *Life and Ep. of St. Paul*, i, 308). From the time that Paul visited this place Christianity has, to a greater or less extent, existed in it. In the 6th and 7th centuries it was a bishop's see, but it is now represented by a small seaport (Leake, *Northern Greece*, iii, 180). It has a population of five or six thousand, nine tenths of whom are Mussulmans, and the rest Greeks. For fuller or supplementary information, see Smith, *Dict. of Class. Geog.* ii, 411; comp. PHILIPPI. The following arguments on the identity of the place are of interest to students:

Cousinéry (*Voyage dans la Macédoine*) and Tafel (*De Via Militari Romanorum Egnatia*, etc.) maintain, against the common opinion, that Luke's Neapolis was not at Kavalla, the inhabited town of that name, but at a deserted harbor ten or twelve miles farther west, known as *Eski*, or *Old Kavalla*. Most of those who contend for the other identification assume the point without much discussion, and the subject demands still the attention of the Biblical geographer. It may be well, therefore, to mention with some fulness the reasons which support the claim of Kavalla to be regarded as the ancient Neapolis, in opposition to those which are urged in favor of the other harbor.

First, the Roman and Greek ruins at Kavalla prove that a port existed there in ancient times. Neapolis, wherever it was, formed the point of contact between Northern Greece and Asia Minor at a period of great commercial activity, and would be expected to have left vestiges of its former importance. The antiquities found still at Kavalla fulfil entirely that presumption. One of these is a massive aqueduct, which brings water into the town from a distance of ten or twelve miles north of Kavalla, along the slopes of Symbolum. It is built on two tiers of arches, a hundred feet long and eighty feet high, and is carried over the narrow valley between the promontory and the mainland. The upper part of the work is modern, but the substructions are evidently Roman, as is seen from the composite character of the material, the cement, and the style of the masonry. Just out of the western gate are two marble sarcophagi, used as watering-troughs, with Latin inscriptions, of the age of the emperor Claudius. Columns with chaplets of elegant Ionic workmanship, blocks of marble, fragments of hewn stone, evidently antique, are numerous both in the town and the suburbs. On some of these are inscriptions, mostly in Latin, but one at least in Greek. In digging for the foundation of new houses the walls of ancient ones are often brought to light, and sometimes tablets with sculptured figures, which would be deemed curious at Athens or Corinth. For fuller details, see *Bibliotheca Sacra*, Oct. 1860. On the contrary, no ruins have been found at Eski Kavalla, or Paleopoli, as it is also called, which can be pronounced unmistakably ancient. No remains of walls, no inscriptions, and no indications of any thoroughfare leading thence to Philippi, are reported to exist there. Cousinéry, it is true, speaks of certain ruins at the place which he deems worthy of notice; but, according to the testimony of others, these ruins are altogether inconsiderable, and, which is still more decisive, are modern in their character. Cousinéry himself, in fact, corroborates this, when he says that on the isthmus which binds the peninsula to the mainland, "on trouve les ruines de l'ancienne Néapolis ou celles d'un château reconstruit dans le moyen âge." It appears that a mediæval or Venetian fortress existed there; but, as far as is yet ascertained, nothing else has been discovered which points to an earlier period. Colonel Leake did not visit either this Kavalla or the other, and his assertion that there are "the ruins of a Greek city" there (which he supposes, however, to have been Galepsus, and not Neapolis) appears to rest on Cousinéry's statement. But, as involving this claim of Eski Kavalla in still greater doubt, it may be added that the situation of Galepsus itself is quite uncertain. Dr. Arnold (note on Thucyd. iv, 107) places it near the mouth of the Strymon, and hence much farther west than Leake supposes. According to Cousinéry, Galepsus is to be sought at Kavalla.

Secondly, the advantages of the position render Kavalla the probable site of Neapolis. It is the first convenient harbor south of the Hellespont, on coming from the east. Thasos serves as a natural landmark. Tafel says, indeed, that Kavalla has no port, or one next to none; but that is incorrect. The fact that the place is now the seat of an active commerce proves the contrary. It lies open somewhat to the south and south-west, but is otherwise well sheltered. There is no danger in going into the harbor. Even a rock which lies off the point of the town has twelve fathoms alongside of it. The bottom affords good anchorage; and although the bay may not be so large as that of Eski Kavalla, it is ample for the accommodation of any number of vessels which the course of trade or travel between Asia Minor and Northern Greece would be likely to bring together there at any one time.

Thirdly, the facility of intercourse between this port and Philippi shows that Kavalla and Neapolis must be the same. The distance is ten miles, and hence not greater than Corinth was from Cenchreæ and Ostia from Rome. Both places are in sight at once from the top of Symbolum. The distance between Philippi and Eski Kavalla must be nearly twice as great. Nature itself has opened a passage from the one place to the other. The mountains which guard the plain of Philippi on the coast-side fall apart just behind Kavalla, and render the construction of a road there entirely easy. No such defile exists at any other point in this line of formidable hills. It is impossible to view the configuration of the country from the sea and not feel at once that the only natural place for crossing into the interior is this break-down in the vicinity of Kavalla.

Fourthly, the notices of the ancient writers lead us to adopt the same view. Thus Dio Cassius says (*Hist. Rom.* xlvii, 35) that Neapolis was opposite Thasos (κατ᾽ ἀντιπέρας Θάσου), and that is the situation of Kavalla. It would be much less correct, if correct at all, to say that the other Kavalla was so situated, since no part of the island extends so far to the west. Appian says (*Bell. Civ.* iv, 106) that the camp of the Republicans near the Gangas, the river (ποταμός) at Philippi, was nine Roman miles from their triremes at Neapolis (it was considerably farther to the other place), and that Thasos was twelve Roman miles from their naval station (so we should understand the text); the latter distance appropriate again to Kavalla, but not to the harbor farther west.

Finally, the ancient Itineraries support entirely the identification in question. Both the Antonine and the Jerusalem Itineraries show that the Egnatian Way passed through Philippi. They mention Philippi and Neapolis as next to each other in the order of succession; and since the line of travel which these Itineraries sketch was the one which led from the west to Byzantium, or Constantinople, it is reasonable to suppose that the road, after leaving Philippi, would pursue the most convenient and direct course to the east which the nature of the country allows. If the road, therefore, was constructed on this obvious principle, it would follow the track of the present Turkish road, and the next station, consequently, would be Neapolis, or Kavalla, on the coast, at the termination of the only natural defile across the intervening mountains. The distance, as has been said, is about ten miles. The Jerusalem Itinerary gives the distance between Philippi as ten Roman miles, and the Antonine Itinerary as twelve miles. The difference in the latter case is unimportant, and not greater than in some other instances where the places in the two Itineraries are unquestionably the same. It must be several miles farther than this from Philippi to Old Kavalla, and hence the Neapolis of the Itineraries could not be at that point. The theory of Tafel is that Akontisma, or Herkontroma (the same place, without doubt), which the Itineraries mention next to Neapolis, was at the present Kavalla, and Neapolis at Leuter, or Eski Kavalla. This theory, it is true, arranges the places in the order of the Itineraries; but, as Leake objects, there would be a needless detour of nearly twenty miles, and that through a region much more difficult than the direct way. The more accredited view is that Akontisma was beyond Kavalla, farther east.

The name NEAPOLIS likewise occurs as that of two cities in Palestine.

a. In the form *Nablus*, it has survived as the name

given during the Roman age to the ancient city of *Shechem.* The change appears to have taken place during the reign of Vespasian, as upon the coins of that reign we first find the inscription, "*Flavia Neapolis,*" the former title taken from Flavius Vespasian (Eckhel, *Doctr. Nummor.* iii, 433). Josephus generally calls the city Sichem; but he has Neapolis in *War*, iv, 8, 1; and the words of Epiphanius afford sufficient proof of the identity of Sichem and Neapolis, Ἐν Σικίμοις, τοῦτ' ἔστιν, ἐν τῇ νυνὶ Νεαπόλει (*Adv. Hær.* iii, 1055; see Reland, *Palæst.* p. 1004). For a description and history of this city, see SHECHEM.

b. Neapolis was also the name of an ancient episcopal city of Arabia, whose bishops were present at the councils of Chalcedon and Constantinople. Porter discovered an inscription at the ruined town of *Suleim*, at the western base of Jebel Hauran, near the ancient Kenath, which shows that Suleim is the episcopal *Neapolis* (Porter's *Damascus*, ii, 85; Reland, *Palæst.* p. 217; S. Paulo, *Geogr. Sac.* p. 296).

Neäri'ah (Heb. *Neäryah'*, נְעַרְיָה, *servant of Jehovah*; Sept. Νωαδία, v. r. Νααρία and Νεαρία; Vulg. *Naariah*), the name of two men.

1. The second named of the four sons of Ishi, captains of the 500 Simeonites who in the reign of Hezekiah drove the Amalekites from Mount Seir, and settled there (1 Chron. iv, 41-43). B.C. cir. 715.

2. The fourth named of the six sons of Shemaiah; father of Elioenai, Hezekiah, and Azrikam, a descendant of David (1 Chron. iii, 22, 23). B.C. cir. 350. He is apparently identical with NAGGE (q. v.) in the genealogy (q. v.) of Christ (Luke iii, 25).

Ne'bai (Heb. *Neybay'*, נֵיבָי, *fruitful*; text נוֹבָי, *Nobay'*; Sept. Νωβαί v. r. Βωναί; Vulg. *Nebai*), one of the chief of the people who sealed the covenant with Nehemiah (Neh. x, 19). B.C. cir. 410.

Nebai'oth (Heb. *Nebayoth'*, נְבָיוֹת, Gen. xxviii, 9; xxxvi, 3; 1 Chron. i, 29; elsewhere defectively נְבָיֹת, *heights*; Sept. Ναβαϊώϑ, but in Gen. xxv, 13 v. r. Ναβαιώϑ; in xxviii, 9 v. r. Ναβεώϑ; in Isa. xi, 7 v. r. Ναναταῖοι; Vulg. *Nabajoth*; A. V. "Nebaioth" in 1 Chron. i, 29; Isa. lx, 7; elsewhere "Nebajoth"), the name of a man and of a people after him.

1. The first-born son of Ishmael (Gen. xxv, 13; 1 Chron. i, 29), and the prince or *sheik* (נָשִׂיא, rendered by Jerome φύλαρχος) of one of the twelve Ishmaelitish tribes, which, as well as the territory they occupied, continued to bear his name in after-times (Gen. xxxv, 16; comp. ch. xvii, 20). B.C. cir. 2000. One of Esau's wives, Mahalath, otherwise called Bashemath, is expressly designated as "the sister of Nebaioth" (Gen. xxviii, 9; xxxvi, 3); and by a singular coincidence the land of Esau, or Edom, was ultimately possessed by the posterity of Nebaioth. See below. See NEBAJOTH.

2. A tribe of Ishmaelites, descendants of the above, who, in common with the other Ishmaelites, first settled in the wilderness "before" (i. e. to the east of) the other descendants of Abraham; i. e. in the great desert lying to the east and south-east of Palestine (Gen. xxv, 18; xxi, 21; xvi, 12; and see ARABIA). In Gen. xxv, 16 the English Version speaks of the Ishmaelitish "towns and castles," but the former word in the original signifies "a movable village of tents" (the *horde* of the Tartars), and the latter seems to denote folds for cattle and sheep. Both expressions thus point to a nomadic life, which the tribe of Nebaioth seem to have followed for ages afterwards, inasmuch as in the days of Isaiah the "rams of Nebaioth" are mentioned (Isa. lx, 7) as gifts which the Bedouin, or "Men of the Desert," would consecrate to the service of Jehovah. The territory at first occupied by Nebaioth appears to have been on the south-east of Palestine, in and around the mountains of Edom. There Esau met and became allied with them. As their numbers and their flocks increased, they were

forced to wander more into the south and east so as to secure pasture; and they were brought into connection with their brethren the children of Kedar, with whom Isaiah associates them (lx, 7). It is somewhat remarkable that this celebrated Arab tribe is so seldom mentioned in the Bible. Three times the name occurs in Genesis, once in the genealogies of Chronicles (i, 29), and once in Isaiah; after his age we hear no more of them in Scripture. See BENE-KEDEM.

After the close of the O.-T. canon, both Jewish and heathen writers frequently mention an Arabian tribe called *Nabatæi*, or *Nabathæans* (Ναβαταῖοι), as the most influential and numerous of all the tribes of that country. Josephus says regarding the descendants of Ishmael, "These inhabited all the country from the Euphrates to the Red Sea, and called it *Nabatene*" (Ναβατηνή; *Ant.* i, 13, 4). He regards the Nabatæi as descendants of Nebaioth. Jerome affirms that Nebaioth gave his name to all the region from the Euphrates to the Red Sea (*Comm. in Gen.* xxv, 13). Arabic writers mention the tribe of *Nabat* in Babylonian Irak; but the name is written *Nabath* (D'Herbelot, *Bib. Orient.* s. v. Nabat; Pocock's *Spec. Hist. Arab.* p. 46, 268). The question of their identity depends upon particulars which we here present:

From the works of Arab authors M. Quatremère (*Mémoire sur les Nabatéens,* Paris, 1835, reprinted from the *Nouveau Journ. Asiat.* Jan.–March, 1835) proved the existence of a nation called *Nabat* or *Nabit*, pl. *Anbát* (*Sihâh* and *Kámûs*), reputed to be of ancient origin, of whom scattered remnants existed in Arab times, after the æra of the Flight. The Nabat, in the days of their early prosperity, inhabited the country chiefly between the Euphrates and the Tigris, Bein en-Nahrein and El-Irak (the Mesopotamia and Chaldæa of the classics). That this was their chief seat and that they were Aramæans, or, more accurately, Syro-Chaldæans, seems, in the present state of the inquiry (for it will presently be seen that, by the publication of Oriental texts, our knowledge may be very greatly enlarged), to be a safe conclusion. The Arabs loosely apply the name Nabat to the Syrians, or especially the eastern Syrians, to the Syro-Chaldæans, etc. Thus El-Mesûdi (ap. Quatremère, *l. c.*) says, "The Syrians are the same as the Nabathæans (Nabat). . . . The Nimrods were the kings of the Syrians whom the Arabs call Nabathæus. . . . The Chaldæans are the same as the Syrians, otherwise called Nabat (*Kitâb et-Tenbîh*). The Nabathæans . . . founded the city of Babylon. . . . The inhabitants of Nineveh were part of those whom we call Nabit or Syrians, who form one nation and speak one language; that of the Nabit differs only in a small number of letters; but the foundation of the language is identical" (*Kitâb Mur'j ed-Dhahab*). These and many other fragmentary passages sufficiently prove the existence of a great Aramæan people called Nabat, celebrated among the Arabs for their knowledge of agriculture, and of magic, astronomy, medicine, and science (so called) generally. But we have stronger evidence to this effect. Quatremère introduced to the notice of the learned world the most important relic of that people's literature, a treatise on Nabat agriculture. A study of an imperfect copy of that work, which unfortunately was all he could gain access to, induced him to date it about the time of Nebuchadnezzar, B.C. cir. 600. M. Chwolson, professor of Oriental languages at St. Petersburg, who had shown himself fitted for the inquiry by his treatise on the Sabians and their religion (*Die Sabier und der Sabismus*), has since made that book a subject of special study; and in his *Remains of ancient Babylonian Literature in Arabic Translations* (*Ueber die Ueberreste der Alt-Babylonischen Literatur in Arabischen Uebersetzungen*, St. Petersburg, 1859), he has published the results of his inquiry. Those results, while they establish all that M. Quatremère had advanced respecting the existence of the Nabat, go far beyond him both in the antiquity and the importance which M. Chwolson claims for that people. Ewald, however, in 1857, stated some grave causes for doubting this antiquity, and again in 1859 (both papers appeared in the *Göttingesche Gelehrte Anzeigen*) repeated moderately but decidedly his misgivings. M. Renan followed on the same side (*Journ. de l'Institut*, April-May, 1860); and more recently M. de Gutschmid (*Zeitschrift d. deutsch. morgenländ. Gesellschaft*, xv, 1–100) has attacked the whole theory in a lengthy essay. We recapitulate, as shortly as possible, the bearings of this remarkable inquiry, as far as they relate to the subject of the article.

The remains of the literature of the Nabat consist of four works, one of them a fragment: the "Book of Nabat Agriculture" (already mentioned), the "Book of Poisons," the "Book of Tenkelâsha the Babylonian," and the "Book of the Secrets of the Sun and Moon" (Chwolson, *Ueberreste*, p. 10, 11). They purport to have been translated, in the year 904, by Abû-Bekr Ahmad Ibn-Alî, the Chaldæan of Kissin, or Keisi, better known as Ibn-Wahshûyeh. The "Book of Nabat Agriculture" was, according to the Arab translator, commenced by Daghrith, continued by Yanbushadh, and completed by Kuthami. Chwolson, disregarding the dates assigned to these authors by the translator, thinks that the earliest lived some 2500 years B.C., the second some 300 or 400 years later, and Kuthami, to whom he ascribes the chief authorship (Ibn-Wahshiyeh says he was little more than editor), at the earliest under the sixth king of a Canaanitish dynasty mentioned in the book, which dynasty Chwolson—with Bunsen—makes the same as the fifth (or Arabian) dynasty of Berosus (Chwolson, *Ueberreste*, p. 58, etc.; Bunsen, *Egypt*, iii, 432, etc.; Cory, *Ancient Fragments*, 2d ed. p. 60), or of the 13th century B.C. It will thus be seen that he rejects most of M. Quatremère's reasons for placing the work in the time of Nebuchadnezzar. It is remarkable that that great king is not mentioned, and the author or authors were, it is argued by Chwolson, ignorant not only of the existence of Christianity, but of the kingdom and faith of Israel. While these and other reasons, if granted, strengthen M. Chwolson's case for the antiquity of the work, on the other hand it is urged that even neglecting the difficulties attending an Arab's translating so ancient a writing (and we reject altogether the supposition that it was modernized, as being without a parallel, at least in *Arabic* literature), and conceding that he was of Chaldæan or Nabat race—we encounter formidable intrinsic difficulties. The book contains mention of personages bearing names closely resembling those of Adam, Seth, Enoch, Noah, Shem, Nimrod, and Abraham; and M. Chwolson himself is forced to confess that the particulars related of them are in some respects similar to those recorded of the Biblical patriarchs. If this difficulty proves insurmountable, it shows that the author borrowed from the Bible, or from late Jews, and destroys the claim of an extreme antiquity. Other apparent evidences of the same kind are not wanting. Such is the mention of Ermisa (Hermes), Agathadîmân (Agathodæmon), Tammuz (Adonis), and Yânan (Ionians). It is even a question whether the work should not be dated several centuries after the commencement of our æra. Anachronisms, it is asserted, abound—geographical, linguistic (the use of late words and phrases), historical, and religious (such as the traces of Hellenism, as shown in the mention of Hermes, etc., and influences to be ascribed to Neoplatonism). The whole style is said to be modern, wanting the rugged vigor of antiquity (this, however, is a delicate issue, to be tried only by the ripest scholarship). And while Chwolson dates the oldest part of the "Book of Agriculture" B.C. 2500, and the "Book of Tenkelûsha" in the 1st century A.D. at the latest (p. 136), Rénan asserts that the two are so similar as to preclude the notion of their being separated by any great interval of time (*Journal de l'Institut*).

Although Quatremère recovered the broad outlines of the religion and language of the Nabat, a more extended knowledge of these points hangs mainly on the genuineness or spuriousness of the work of Kuthami. If M. Chwolson's theory be correct, that people present to us one of the most ancient forms of idolatry; and by their writings we can trace the origin and rise of successive phases of pantheism, and the roots of the complicated forms of idolatry, heresy, and philosophical infidelity, which abound in the old seats of the Aramæan race. At present we may conclude that they were Sabians (Sabium, i. e. "apostates"), at least in late times, as Sabæism succeeded the older religions; and their doctrines seem to have approached (how nearly a further knowledge of these obscure subjects will show) those of the Mendæans, Mendaites, or Gnostics. Their language presents similar difficulties; according to M. Chowlson it is the ancient language of Babylonia. A cautious criticism would (till we know more) assign it a place as a comparatively modern dialect of Syro-Chaldee (comp. Quatremère, *Mém.* p. 100-103).

Thus, if M. Chwolson's results are accepted, the "Book of Nabat Agriculture" exhibits to us an ancient civilization, before that of the Greeks, and at least as old as that of the Egyptians, of a great and powerful nation of remote antiquity; making us acquainted with sages hitherto unknown, and with the religions and sciences they either founded or advanced; and throwing a flood of light on what has till now been one of the darkest pages of the world's history. But until the original text of Kuthami's treatise is published we must withhold our acceptance of facts so startling, and regard the antiquity ascribed to it even by Quatremère as extremely doubtful. It is sufficient for the present to know that the most important facts advanced by the latter—the most important when regarded by sober criticism—are supported by the results of the later inquiries of M. Chwolson and others. It remains for us to state the grounds for connecting the Nabat with the Nabathæans.

As the Arabs speak of the Nabat as Syrians, so conversely the Greeks and Romans knew the Nabathæans (Sept. οἱ Ναβαττaῖοι and Ναβαταῖοι; Alex. Ναβατέοι; Vulg. *Nabuthæi*; classical writers, Ἀναταῖοι or Ναταταῖοι, Ptol. vi, 7, § 21; Ναβάται, Suid. s. v.; Lat. *Nabathæi*) as Arabs.

While the inhabitants of the peninsula were comparative strangers to the classical writers, and very little was known of the further-removed peoples of Chaldæa and Mesopotamia, the Nabathæans bordered the well-known Egyptian and Syrian provinces. The nation was famous for its wealth and commerce. Even when, by the decline of its trade (diverted through Egypt), its prosperity waned, Petra is still mentioned as a centre of the trade both of the Sabæans of Southern Arabia [see SHEBA] and the Gerrhæans on the Persian Gulf. It is this extension across the desert that most clearly connects the Nabathæan colony with the birthplace of the nation in Chaldæa. The famous trade of Petra across the well-trodden desert-road to the Persian Gulf is sufficient to account for the presence of this colony; just as traces of Abrahamic peoples [see DEDAN, etc.] are found, demonstrably, on the shores of that sea on the east, and on the borders of Palestine on the west, while along the northern limits of the Arabian peninsula remains of the caravan stations still exist. Nothing is more certain than the existence of this great stream of commerce, from remote times, until the opening of the Egyptian route gradually destroyed it. Josephus (*Ant.* i, 12, 4) speaks of Nabatæa (Ναβαταιά, Strabo; Ναβατηνή, Josephus) as embracing the country from the Euphrates to the Red Sea—i. e. Petræa and all the desert east of it. The Nabat of the Arabs, however, are described as famed for agriculture and science; in these respects offering a contrast to the Nabathæans of Petra, who were found by the expedition sent by Antigonus (B.C. 312) to be dwellers in tents, pastoral, and conducting the trade of the desert; but in the Red Sea again they were piratical, and by seafaring qualities showed a non-Shemitic character.

We agree with M. Quatremère (*Mém.* p. 81), while rejecting some of his reasons, that the civilization of the Nabathæans of Petra, far advanced on that of the surrounding Arabs, is not easily explained except by supposing them to be a different people from those Arabs. A remarkable confirmation of this supposition is found in the character of the buildings of Petra, which are unlike anything constructed by a purely Shemitic race. Architecture is a characteristic of Aryan or mixed races. In Southern Arabia, Nigritians and Shemites (Joktanites) together built huge edifices; so in Babylonia and Assyria, and so too in Egypt, mixed races left this unmistakable mark. See ARABIA. Petra, while it is wanting in the colossal features of those more ancient remains, is yet unmistakably foreign to an unmixed Shemitic race. Further, the subjects of the literature of the Nabat, which are scientific and industrial, are not such as are found in the writings of pure Shemites or Aryans, as Rénan (*Hist. des Langues Sémitiques*, p. 227) has well observed; and he points, as we have above, to a foreign ("Couschite," or partly Nigritian) settlement in Babylonia. It is noteworthy that 'Abd-el-Latif (at the end of the fourth section of his first book, or treatise—see De Lacy's ed.) likens the Copts in Egypt (a mixed race) to the Nabat in El-'Irak.

From most of these and other considerations we think there is no reasonable doubt that the Nabathæans of Arabia Petræa were the same people as the Nabat of Chaldæa; though at what ancient epoch the western settlement was formed remains unknown. That it was not of any importance until after the captivity appears from the notices of the inhabitants of Edom in the canonical books, and their absolute silence respecting the Nabathæans, except (if Nebaioth be identified with them) the passage in Isaiah (lx, 7).

Lastly, did the Nabathæans, or Nabat, derive their name, and were they in part descended, from Nebaioth, son of Ishmael? Josephus says that Nabatæa was inhabited by the twelve sons of Ishmael; and Jerome, "Nebaioth omnis regio ab Euphrate usque ad Mare Rubrum Nabathena usque hodie dicitur, quæ pars Arabiæ est" (*Comment. in Gen.* xxv, 13). Quatremère rejects the identification for an etymological reason—the change of *th* to *t*; but this change is not unusual; in words Arabicized from the Greek the like change of τ generally occurs. Rénan, on the other hand, accepts it, regarding Nebaioth, after his manner, merely as an ancient name unconnected with Biblical history. The Arabs call Nebaioth *Nâbit*, and do not connect him with the Nabat, to whom they give a different descent; but all their Abrahamic genealogies come from late Jews, and are utterly untrustworthy. When we remember the darkness that enshrouds the early history of the "sons of the concubines" after they were sent into the east country, we hesitate to deny a relationship between peoples whose names are strikingly similar, dwelling in the same tract. It is possible that Nebaioth went to the far east, to the country of his grandfather Abraham, intermarried with the Chaldæans, and gave birth to a mixed race, the Nabat. Instances of ancient tribes adopting the name of more modern ones, with which they have become fused, are frequent in the history of the Arabs [see MIDIAN]; but we think it is also admissible to hold that Nebaioth was so named by the sacred historian because he intermarried with the Nabat. It is, however, safest to leave unsettled the identification of Nebaioth and Nabat until another link be added to the chain that at present seems to connect them.

We have not entered into the subject of the language

of the Nabathæans. The little that is known of it tends to strengthen the theory of the Chaldæan origin of that people. The duc de Luynes, in a paper on the coins of the latter in the *Revue Numismatique* (new series, vol. iii, 1858), adduces facts to show that they called themselves Nabat, נבט. It is remarkable that while remnants of the Nabat are mentioned by trustworthy Arab writers as existing in their own day, no Arab record connecting that people with Petra has been found. Caussin believes this to have arisen from the Chaldæan speech of the Nabathæans, and their corruption of Arabic (*Essai sur l'Hist. des Arabes avant l'Islamisme*, i, 38).

It is thus doubtless true that a tribe called Nabat existed at a comparatively early period in Mesopotamia; but may they not have been a branch of the family of Nebaioth? May they not have migrated thither, as sections of the great tribes of Arabia are wont to do now—for instance, the Shummar, whose home is Jebel Shummar, in Central Arabia, where they have villages and settlements; but large sections of the tribe have long been naturalized among the rich pastures of Mesopotamia. In fact, there are few of the great Arabian tribes which do not pay periodical visits to the banks of the Euphrates and Tigris, and which have not branches established there. So it probably was with the tribe of Nebaioth. They visited Mesopotamia, attracted by the water and pasture; then some of them settled there; then from close intercourse with the learned Chaldæans, they may have acquired a taste for their literature, and may have in part adopted their language and their habits of life; and at length, when driven out of Central Asia by the rising power of the Assyrians, Medes, and Persians, they carried these back among their brethren in Arabia. Such, at least, is a probable solution of a difficult question. There can be no doubt that the descendants of Nebaioth settled originally in and around Edom; that in the time of Isaiah they were an influential tribe living in Western Arabia beside the children of Kedar; that the *Nabathæans* occupied the same region in the time of the Maccabees (1 Macc. v, 24 sq., B.C. cir. 161; comp. 1 Macc. ix, 33–37; Josephus, *Ant*. xii, 8, 3); and that Josephus considered these Nabathæans to be the descendants of Ishmael. From these facts it may be fairly inferred that the *Nabathæans* of the classic authors, the tribe *Nebaioth* of the sacred authors, and the *Beni-Nabat* of the Arabs, were identical (Forster, *Geog. of Arabia*, i, 209 sq.; Kalisch, *On Gen.* p. 481; Jerome, *Comment. in Isaiam*, lx, 7).

It would appear that the descendants of Esau, having at first sought an alliance with the Ishmaelites among the mountains of Edom, afterwards succeeded in forcing them to leave their strongholds and migrate to the deserts of Arabia. After a long interval the Ishmaelites returned, and, having expelled the Edomites (or *Idumœans*), took possession of their ancient country. The date of this conquest is unknown; but it was probably about the time of the second captivity, for then the Persians were all-powerful in Central Asia, and would naturally drive back the Arab tribes that had settled there (comp. Diod. Sic. ii, 48); and then also we know that the Idumæans, as if driven from their own mountains, settled in Southern Palestine. But be this as it may, we learn that about B.C. 312 Antigonus, one of the successors of Alexander the Great, sent an army against the Nabathæans of Petra; the city was taken and plundered in the absence of the men, who were at the time attending a great fair in another locality; on the retreat of the army, however, with their booty, they were attacked and cut to pieces by the Nabathæans. Another expedition was sent, but was unsuccessful (Diod. Sic. xix, 104–110). At this period the Nabathæans, like their forefathers, were rich in flocks and herds; they were also, like the Ishmaelites in the time of Jacob, the carriers of spices and merchandise between Arabia and Egypt; and for the protection of their wealth and the furtherance of their commerce they had erected strong cities in the interior of their country, Edom, and on the shores of the Ælanitic Gulf. Idumæa Proper, or Edom, now became the centre of their influence

and power. They gradually advanced in civilization and commercial enterprise, until nearly the whole traffic of Western Asia was in their hands (Diod. Sic. ii, 48–50; iii, 42–43). From their capital, Petra, caravan roads radiated in all directions—eastward to the Persian Gulf and Mesopotamia; northward to Peræa, Damascus, and Palmyra; westward to Palestine and Phœnicia; and southward to the seaports on the Ælanitic Gulf and Red Sea, and to Egypt (see *Tabula Peutingeriana*; *Tab. Theodosiana*; Strabo, xvi, 778–780; Forster, *Geog. of Arabia*, i, 222). When a new route for commerce between the East and the West was opened through Egypt, the Nabathæans became its determined opponents. They built war-galleys and plundered the merchant fleets in the Red Sea; and they also attacked and pillaged such caravans as ventured to convey the spices of Arabia and the merchandise of Persia and Syria by any other way than their own (Diod. Sic. iii, 43; Strabo, xvi, 777; Arrian, *Periplus*).

During the height of their power the country of the Nabathæans embraced the whole of Edom, the eastern shore of the Ælanitic Gulf and the Red Sea to the parallel of the city of Medineh, the desert plain of Arabia to the mountains of Nejd; while on the north-west and north it was bounded by Palestine and Bashan (Strabo, xvi, 767, 777, 779; 1 Macc. v, 25–28; ix, 35; Diod. Sic. ii, 48; Epiphan. *Adv. Hœres.* p. 142). It is true Josephus and Jerome state that the Nabathæans occupied the whole country between Egypt and the Euphrates; but by Nabathæans they seem to have meant all the descendants of Ishmael (comp. Reland, *Palæst.* p. 90; Kalisch, *On Gen.* p. 482). It is not known at what time the Nabathæans gave up the patriarchal form of government and elected a king. The first mention of a king is about B.C. 166, in the reign of Antiochus Epiphanes (2 Macc. v, 8). All their kings appear to have been called either *Aretas* or *Obodas*, and the kingdom was known among classic writers as the "Kingdom of Arabia," sometimes taking the addition *Petræa*, apparently from the capital city Petra. Alexander Jannæus was defeated by Obodas, king of Arabia (Josephus, *Ant*. xiii, 13, 5); and a few years later Antiochus Dionysius of Syria was killed in battle against the Arabians, and *Aretas* their king seized Damascus (xiii, 15, 1, 2; *War*, iv, 7, 8). The kings of Arabia are often mentioned in connection with the conquest and occupation of the province of Syria by the Romans (Josephus, *Ant*. xiv, 5, 1; xv, 6, 2; xvi, 7, 8). A few years before the Christian æra a Roman expedition under the command of Ælius Gallus was sent into Arabia. After various obstacles he at last reached Λευκή Κώμη, or Albus Pagus, the emporium of the Nabathæans, and the port of Petra, which was probably at or near Elath (Strabo, xvi, 4, 22, 24; Dion Cassius, liii, 27; Arrian, *Periplus Maris Eryth.*). The Nabathæan king, Obodas, received him with professions of friendship, and appointed his minister Syllæus to guide the army. By his treachery it was conducted through arid deserts until it was almost destroyed by thirst and disease (Strabo, xvi, 780). The Stoic philosopher Athenodorus spent some time in Petra, and related to Strabo with admiration how the inhabitants lived in entire harmony and union under excellent laws. Pliny also repeatedly speaks of the Nabathæans (*Hist. Nat.* v, 11; vi, 28; xii, 27); and classes along with them the Cedrei, exactly as Kedar and Nebaioth are placed together in Isa. lx, 7. Herod Antipas married a daughter of Aretas, king of the Nabathæans (Matt. xiv, 3, 4); and it appears to have been the same Aretas who captured Damascus, and governed it by an ethnarch at the time of Paul's conversion (Acts ix, 25; 2 Cor. xi, 32). The kingdom of the Nabathæans was overthrown in A.D. 105 by Cornelius Palma, governor of Syria, and was annexed to the Roman empire (Dion Cass. lxviii, 14; Eutrop. viii, 2, 9).

The Nabathæans had, as we have seen, early applied themselves to commerce, especially as carriers of the products of Arabia, India, and the far-distant East, which, as we learn from Strabo, were transported on camels from the above-mentioned Leukè Komè to Petra, and thence to Rhinocoloura (El 'Arish) and elsewhere. But under the Roman dominion the trade of these regions appears to have been widely extended. The passage of merchants and caravans was now made more practicable by military ways. From Elath, or Ailah, one great road had its direction northwards to the rich and central Petra; thence it divided and led on one side to Jerusalem, Gaza, and other ports on the Mediterranean; and on the other side to Damascus. Another road appears to have led directly from Ailah along the Ghor to Jerusalem. Traces of these routes are still visible in many parts. These facts are derived from the specifications of the celebrated *Tabula Theodosiana*, or *Peutingeriana*, compiled in the 4th century. According to this, a line of small fortresses was drawn along the eastern frontier of Arabia Petræa towards the desert, some of which became the sites of towns and cities, whose names are still extant. But as the power of Rome fell into decay, the Arabs of the desert again acquired the ascendency. They plundered the cities, but did not destroy them; and hence those regions are still full of uninhabited yet splendid ruins. Even Petra, the rich and impregnable metropolis, was subjected to the same fate; and now exists, in its almost inaccessible loneliness, only to excite the curiosity of the scholar and the wonder of the traveller by the singularity of its site, its ruins, and its fortunes.

In the course of the 4th century this region came to be included under the general name of "Palestine," and was called *Palæstina Tertia*, or *Salutaris*. It became the diocese of a metropolitan, whose seat was at Petra, and who was afterwards placed under the patriarch of Jerusalem. With the Mohammedan conquest in the 7th century its commercial prosperity disappeared. Lying between the three rival empires of Arabia, Egypt, and Syria, it lost its ancient independence; the course of trade was diverted into new channels; its great routes were abandoned; and at length the entire country was quietly yielded up to the Bedouin of the surrounding wilderness, whose descendants still claim it as their domain. During the 12th century it was partially occupied by the Crusaders, who gave it the name of *Arabia Tertia*, or *Syria Sobal*. From that period it remained unvisited by Europeans, and had almost disappeared from their maps, until it was partially explored, first by Seetzen in 1807, and more fully by Burckhardt in 1812; and now the wonders of the Wady Mûsa are familiarly known to all. See PETRA.

See Reland, *Palæstina Illustr.* p. 90 sq.; Vincent, *Commerce of the Ancients*, ii, 272 sq.; Ritter, *Gesch. d. Petr. Arabiens*, in the "Trans. of the Berlin Acad." 1824; Forster, *Mohammedanism Unveiled*, and *Geography of Arabia*; Robinson, *Sketches of Idumæa*, in "Amer. Bib. Repos." 1833; and *Bibl. Researches*, vol. ii; Cleas, in Pauly's *Real-Encyklopädie*, p. 377 sq.; Quatremère, *Mémoire sur les Nabatéens* (*Extrait du Nouveau Journal Asiatique*), Paris, 1835; Schwarz, *Palest.* p. 215. See NABATHÆANS.

Neba'joth (Gen. xxv, 13; xxviii, 9; xxxvi, 3). See NEBAIOTH.

Nebal'lat (Heb. *Neballat'*, נְבַלָּט; Gesenius, *hidden wickedness*; Fürst, *firm soil*; Dietrich, *projection*; Sept. Ναβαλλάτ [but most copies omit]), a town (probably of Dan) occupied by the tribe of Benjamin (Neh. xi, 34). It is identified by Schwarz (*Palest.* p. 134) with the large village *Beit-Nebâla*, five English miles northeast of Ramleh (Van de Velde, *Memoir*, p. 336).

Ne'bat (Heb. *Nebat'*, נְבָט; Gesenius, *sight*; Fürst, *cultivation*; Sept. Ναβάτ), the father of Jeroboam (q.v.), king of Israel, in connection with whom he is always mentioned as a descendant of Ephraim, living in Zereda, a city of Manasseh (1 Kings xi, 26, etc.; 2. Chron. ix, 29, etc.). B.C. cir. 1000. The Jewish tradition pre-

served in Jerome (*Quæst. Hebr. in lib. Reg.*) identifies him with Shimei of Gera, who was a Benjamite.

Nebbia, Cesare, a reputable Italian painter, whose works were mostly of a religious character, was born at Orvieto about 1536. He studied under Girolamo Muziano, whose style he adopted, and assisted him in the important works he executed for Gregory XIII in the Vatican and the Capella Gregoriana. Assisted by Gio Guerra da Modena, Nebbia superintended the works projected by Sixtus V, intrusting the completion of his designs to the younger painters. They were extensively employed during the five years' reign of that pontiff in the chapel of S. Maria Maggiore, the library of the Vatican, the Scala Santa, and the Lateran and Quirinal palaces. Nebbia was much inferior to Muziano in dignity and grandeur, but possessed a fertile invention and great facility of execution. Lanzi says there are some beautiful pictures by him finely colored, as the *Epiphany*, quite in Muziano's style, in the church of S. Francesco at Viterbo. Among his principal works at Rome, Baglioni mentions the *Coronation of the Virgin* in S. Maria de' Monti, and the *Resurrection* in S. Giacomo degli Spagnuoli. He died at Rome in 1614.

Nebbia, Galeotto, an old Italian painter much devoted to sacred subjects, was a native of Castellaccio, near Alessandria, and flourished at Genoa about 1480. In the church of S. Brigida in that city are two altarpieces by him which are esteemed for their antiquity and originality. The first represents the *Archangels*, and the second *St. Pantaleone and other Martyrs*. Lanzi says they are remarkably well executed for the time: the figures represented on a gold ground, with the draperies extremely rich, with stiff and regular foldings, not borrowed from any other school. The grado, or step, is ornamented with minute histories—somewhat crude, but displaying much diligence and care in finishing.

Nebentrost, GEORGE, a Bohemian Protestant divine, who was obliged to quit his native land during the Anti-Reformation movement at the close of the 16th century, was born at Annaberg in 1577. After having, by due preparation, fitted himself for the ministry, he preached for two years at Dobritzschei and Neschwitz; was then exiled, and resided three years at Pressnitz and Annaberg; and was then again a minister of the Protestant doctrines at Jöhstadt, where he suffered much during the Thirty-years' War. He died in 1657, on the same day on which he had, fifty-eight years before, begun his clerical duties in Bohemia. See Pescheck, *The Ref. and Anti-Ref. in Bohemia*, ii, 405.

Ne'bo (Heb. *Nebo'*, נְבוֹ, prob. of Chaldæan origin, see below, No. 1), the name of a heathen deity, and of three places in or around Palestine. In treating of them we give a general description with references to collateral heads for further details.

1. (Sept. Ναβώ, v. r. Ναβαῦ and [in Isa.] even Δαγών; Vulg. *Nabo*.) The title of a Chaldæan idol or god which occurs both in Isaiah (xlvi, 1) and Jeremiah (xlviii, 1), being the name of a well-known deity of the Babylonians and Assyrians. The original native name was, in Hamitic Babylonian, *Nabiu*; in Shemitic Babylonian and Assyrian, *Nabu*. It is reasonably conjectured to be connected with the Hebrew נבא, "to prophesy" (see Gesenius, *Thes. Heb.* p. 841), whence the common word נביא, "prophet" (Arab. *Neby*). Nebo was the god who presided over learning and letters. He is called "the far-hearing," "he who possesses intelligence," "he who teaches or instructs." Generally, however, he enjoys the high-sounding titles of "Lord of lords," "Holder of the sceptre of power," etc. Hence Layard thinks the name is derived from the Egyptian *Neb*, "Lord" (*Nineveh and Bab.* p. 77). The wedge or arrow-head—the essential element of cuneiform writing —appears to have been his emblem; and hence he bore

✝ ✝ the name of *Tir*, which signifies "a shaft or arrow." His general character corresponds to that of the Egyptian *Thoth*, the Greek *Hermes*, and the Latin *Mercury*. Astronomically he is identified with the planet nearest the sun, called Nebo also by the Mendæans, and Tir by the ancient Persians.

Cuneatic form of the name *Nebo*.

Nebo was of Babylonian rather than of Assyrian origin. In the early Assyrian Pantheon he occupies a

Image of Nebo. (In the British Museum.)

very inferior position, being either omitted from the lists altogether, or occurring as the last of the minor gods. The king supposed to be Pul first brings him prominently forward in Assyria, and then apparently in consequence of some peculiar connection which he himself had with Babylon. A statue of Nebo was set up by this monarch at Calah (Nimrud), which is now in the British Museum. It has a long inscription, written across the body, and consisting chiefly of the god's various epithets. In Babylonia Nebo held a prominent place from an early time. The ancient town of Borsippa was especially under his protection, and the great temple there (the modern Birs-Nimrud) was dedicated to him from a very remote age. See BABEL, TOWER OF. He was the tutelar god of the most important Babylonian kings, in whose names the word *Nabu*, or Nebo, appears as an element: e. g. Nabo-nassar, Nabopolassar, Nebu-chadnezzar, and Nabonadius or Labynetus; and appears to have been honored next to Belmerodach by the later kings. Nebuchadnezzar completely rebuilt his temple at Borsippa, and called after him his famous seaport upon the Persian Gulf, which became known to the Greeks as Teredon or Diridotis—"given to Tir," i. e. to Nebo. The worship of Nebo appears to have continued at Borsippa to the 3d or 4th century after Christ, and the Sabæans of Haran may have preserved it even to a later date. (See Rawlinson's *Herodotus*, i, 637–640; and his *Ancient Monarchies*, i, 140 sq.; and compare Norberg's *Onomasticon*, s. v.; Chwolson, *Sabier; Münter, Babylonien*, p. 15.)

2. (Sept. Ναβαῦ; Vulg. *Nebo*.) A name of the mountain (הַר) from which Moses took his first and last view of the Promised Land (Deut. xxxii, 49; xxxiv, 1). It is so minutely described that it would seem impossible not to recognise it: in the land of Moab; facing Jericho; the head or summit of a mountain called "the Pisgah," which again seems to have formed a portion of the general range of the "mountains of Abarim." Its position is further denoted by the mention of the valley (or perhaps more correctly the ravine) in which Moses was buried, and which was apparently one of the clefts of the mount itself (xxxii, 50)—"the ravine in the land of Moab facing Beth-Peor" (xxxiv, 6). Josephus, speaking of the death of Moses, says of Abarim, "It is a very high mountain opposite Jericho, and one that affords a prospect of the greater part of Canaan" (*Ant.* iv, 8, 48). Eusebius and Jerome say that Nebo is a

mountain "over the Jordan opposite Jericho in Moab, . . . and until this day it is shown in the sixth mile west of Heshbon" (*Onomast.* s. v. Nabau). In another place they locate it between Heshbon and Livias (*ibid.* s. v. Abarim). Gesenius derives the name Nebo from the root נבה, "to project;" and hence נבו would signify *a projection* (*Thesaurus*, p. 841). Others trace the name to the heathen deity *Nebo*, and suppose that there was an ancient high place on the peak where that deity was worshipped (Stanley, p. 294). For fuller information, see Ritter, *Pal. und Syr.* ii, 1176 sq., 1186 sq.; Porter, *Hand-book*, p. 299; Drew, *Scripture Lands*, p. 96; Reland, *Palæst.* p. 342, 496.

Yet, notwithstanding the minuteness of the scriptural descriptions, till lately no one succeeded in pointing out any spot which answers to Nebo. Viewed from the western side of Jordan (the nearest point at which most travellers are able to view them) the mountains of Moab present the appearance of a wall or cliff, the upper line of which is almost straight and horizontal. "There is no peak or point perceptibly higher than the rest; but all is one apparently level line of summit without peaks or gaps" (Robinson, *Bib. Res.* i, 570). "On ne distingue pas un sommet, pas la moindre cime; seulement on aperçoit, çà et là, de legères inflexions, *comme si la main du peintre qui a tracé cette ligne horizontale sur le ciel eût tremblé dans quelques endroits*" (Chateaubriand, *Itinéraire*, part 3). "Possibly," continues Robinson, "on travelling among these mountains, some isolated point or summit might be found answering to the position and character of Nebo." Three such points have been named.

1. Seetzen (March 17, 1806; *Reise*, i, 408) seems to have been the first to suggest the *Jebel Attarûs* (between the Wady Zerka-main and the Arnon, three miles below the former, and ten or twelve south of Heshbon) as the Nebo of Moses. In this he is followed (though probably without any communication) by Burckhardt (July 14, 1812), who mentions it as the highest point in that locality, and therefore probably "Mount Nebo of the Scripture." This is adopted by Irby and Mangles, though with hesitation (*Travels*, June 8, 1818).

2. Another elevation above the general summit level of these highlands is the *Jebel 'Osha*, or *Ausha*', or *Jebel el-Jil'âd*, "the highest point in all the eastern mountains," "overtopping the whole of the Belka, and rising about 3000 feet above the Ghôr" (Burckhardt, July 2, 1812; Robinson, i, 527 note, 570).

But these eminences are alike wanting in one main essential of the Nebo of the Scripture, which is stated to have been "facing Jericho," words which in the widest interpretation must imply that it was "some elevation immediately over the last stage of the Jordan," while 'Osha and Attarûs are equally remote in opposite directions, the one fifteen miles north, the other fifteen miles south of a line drawn eastward from Jericho. Another requisite for the identification is that a view should be obtainable from the summit, corresponding to that prospect over the whole land which Moses is said to have had from Mount Nebo. The view from Jebel Jil'âd has been briefly described by Dr. Porter (*Handbook*, p. 309), though without reference to the possibility of its being Nebo. Of that from Jebel Attarûs no description is extant, for, almost incredible as it seems, none of the travellers above named, although they believed it to be Nebo, appear to have made any attempt to deviate so far from their route as to ascend an eminence which, if their conjectures be correct, must be the most interesting spot in the world.

3. De Saulcey is the first traveller who discovered the name still extant in *Jebel Nebbah*, an eminence on the eastern shore of the Dead Sea, not far from its northern end (*Voyage en Terre Sainte*, i, 289 sq.). The duc de Luynes, however, appears to have been the first to actually visit and accurately locate the summit (*Voyage*, under April 13, 1864). Mr. Tristram next visited it, and

he graphically describes the outlook from its top (*Land of Israel*, p. 536 sq.; comp. also his *Land of Moab*, p. 338 sq.). The place in question lies nearly four miles southwest of Hesban. Prof. Paine, of the American Exploring Party, carefully examined it, and has given a detailed report of his researches and conclusions (in the "Third Statement" of the Am. Pal. Exploration Soc., N. Y. Jan. 1875), in which, while admitting the identity of the modern and ancient names and localities, he enters into a minute argument to prove that Pisgah was a specific title of the particular spot on which Moses stood rather than a general name of the entire range, as usually held. See PISGAH.

3. (Sept. Ναβαὒ; Vulg. *Nebo, Nabo*.) A town on the eastern side of Jordan, situated in the pastoral country (Numb. xxxii, 3), one of those which were taken possession of and rebuilt by the tribe of Reuben (ver. 38). In these lists it is associated with Kirjathaim and Baalmeon or Beon; and in another record (1 Chron. v, 8) with Aroer, as marking one extremity, possibly the west, of a principal part of the tribe. In the remarkable prophecy uttered by Isaiah (xv, 2) and Jeremiah (xlviii, 1, 22) concerning Moab, Nebo is mentioned in the same connection as before, though no longer an Israelitish town, but in the hands of Moab. It does not occur in the catalogue of the towns of Reuben in Joshua (xiii, 15–23); but whether this is an accidental omission, or whether it appears under another name—according to the statement of Numb. xxxii, 38, that the Israelites changed the names of the heathen cities they retained in this district—is uncertain. In the case of Nebo, which was doubtless called after the deity of that name, there would be a double reason for such a change (see Josh. xxiii, 7). There is nothing positive except the name to show that there was a connection between Nebo the town and Mount Nebo. The notices of Eusebius and Jerome (*Onomast.*) are confused, but they rather denote that the two were distinct, and distant from each other. The town (Ναβὦρ, Nabo) they identify with Nobah and Kenath, and locate it eight miles south of Heshbon, where the ruins of el-Habis appear to stand at present; while the mountain (Ναβαὒ, Nabau) is stated to be six miles east (Jer.) or west (Euseb.) from the same spot. But the former statement is certainly an error; and hence we may presume that the town and the mountain were not distinct, especially as we find the associated towns (Medeba and Baal-meon) in the same vicinity. In the list of places south of es-Salt given by Dr. Robinson (*Bib. Res.* iii, App. p. 170) one occurs named *Neba*, which may be identical with Nebo. It perhaps indicates the ruins now extant on the present Jebel *Nebbah*, or Mount Nebo (above).

4. (Sept. Ναβοῦ v. r. Ναβὦ; in Neh. Ναβιαᾶ v. r. Ναβία; Vulg. *Nebo*.) The children of Nebo (*Bene-Nebo*), to the number of fifty-two, are mentioned in the catalogue of the men of Judah and Benjamin who returned from Babylon with Zerubbabel (Ezra ii, 29; Neh. vii, 33; in the latter passage, "the other Nebo," for some not very obvious distinction). Seven of them had foreign wives, whom they were compelled to discard (Ezra x, 43). The name occurs between Bethel and Ai and Lydda, which, if we may trust the arrangement of the list, implies that it was situated in the territory of Benjamin to the north-west of Jerusalem. It is possibly the modern *Beit-Nûbah*, about twelve miles north-west by west of Jerusalem, eight from Lydda, and close to Yalo; apparently the place mentioned by Jerome (*Onomast.* Anab and Anob; and *Epit. Paulæ*, § 8) as Nob the city of the priests (though that identification is hardly admissible), and both in his and later times known as *Bethannaba* or *Bettenuble*. It became cele-

VI.—29

brated in the time of the Crusades as the site of *Castellum Arnaldi*, built by the patriarch of Jerusalem to defend the road to the holy city (Will. Tyr. xiv, 8). It was afterwards visited by Richard of England in A.D. 1192 (Robinson, *Bib. Res.* ii, 254; Porter, *Hand-book*, p. 286).

It is possible that this Nebo was an offshoot of that on the east of Jordan; in which case we have another town added to those already noticed in the territory of Benjamin which retain the names of foreign and heathen settlers.

A town named *Nomba* is mentioned by the Sept. (not in Heb.) among the places in the south of Judah frequented by David (1 Sam. xxx, 30), but its situation forbids any attempt to identify this with Nebo.

Nebrissensis is the surname of the Spanish Erasmus, Antonio de Lebrixa. See LEBRIJA.

Nebuchadnez'zar (Heb. and Chald. *Nebukadnetstsar'*, נְבוּכַדְנֶאצַּר, 2 Kings xxv, 22; 2 Chron. xxxvi, 6; xxxvii, 7, 10, 13; Jer. xxvii, 6, 8, 20; xxviii, 3; xxix, 1, 3; xxxiv, 1; xxxix, 5; Dan. i, 1; also in the shorter forms, נְבֻכַדְנֶאצַּר, 2 Kings xxiv, 1, 10, 11; xxv, 1, 8; 1 Chron. vi, 15; Jer. xxviii, 11, 14; Dan. i, 18; ii, 1; נְבוּכַדְנֶצַּר, the usual form; and נְבֻכַדְנֶצַּר, Dan. iv, 37; v, 18; Sept. Ναβουχοδονόσορ), or (in Jer. and Ezek. only, but in them always except the passages noted above) NEBUCHADREZ'ZAR (q. v.) (which Hitzig [*Jerem.* p. 191] rightly considers the original form), called by Berosus (ap. Josephum), Ναβουχοδονόσορος; by Abydenus (ap. Eusebium, *Præp. Evang.*), Ναβουθρόσορος; and by Strabo, the only writer among the Greeks by whom he is named (xv, 687), Ναυκοοκοδρόσορος, besides Ναβοκολάσαρος, which appears in the Canon of Ptolemy. This name, *Nabuchodonosor*, has passed from the Septuagint into the Latin Vulgate, and into the authorized English version of the books of Judith and Tobit. This monarch was the greatest and most powerful of the Babylonian kings. His name, according to the native orthography, is read as *Nabukuduri-utsur*, and is explained to mean "Nebo (q. v.) is the protector against misfortune," *kuduri* being connected with the Hebrew בִּרְדוֹר, "trouble" or "attack," and *utsur* being a participle from the root נָצַר, "to protect." (According to others, the middle term *kudur* is connected with the Perso-Greek κέδαρις, "a crown;" Oppert refers it to an Arabic *kudur*, "a young man;" while Sir H. Rawlinson thinks it means "a landmark.") The rarer Hebrew form, used by Jeremiah and Ezekiel — *Nebuchadrezzar* — is thus very close indeed to the original. The Persian form, *Nabukudrachara (Beh.*

Na - bi - uv - ku - du - ur - ri - u - su - ur

Nebuchadnezzar's name in cuneiform. (From Ménant, *Grammaire Assyrienne*, p. 321.)

Inscr. col. i, par. 16), is less correct. This (also written *Nabokhodrossor*) is supposed to be the assumed name of one of the rebels subdued by Darius Hystaspis. It is there easily read, being transcribed in another column, and hence is readily recognised elsewhere when found in the pure Babylonian writing, as it often is on bricks and fragments from the ruins near Hillah (Layard, *Nineveh*, ii, 141).

1. Nebuchadnezzar was the son and successor of Nabopolassar, the founder of the Babylonian empire. (See No. 5 below.) He appears to have been of marriageable age at the time of his father's rebellion against Assyria, B.C. 625; for, according to Abydenus (ap. Euseb. *Chron. Can.* i, 9), the alliance between this prince and the Median king was cemented by the betrothal of Amuhia, the daughter of the latter, to Nebuchadnezzar, Nabopolassar's son. Little further is known of him during his father's lifetime. It is suspected, rather than

proved, that he was the leader of a Babylonian contingent which accompanied Cyaxares in his Lydian war [see MEDES], by whose interposition, on the occasion of an eclipse, that war was brought to a close, B.C. 610. (Herodotus terms this leader Labynetus [i, 74]; a word which does not rightly render the Babylonian *Nabu-kuduri-uzur*, but does render another Babylonian name, *Nabu-nahit*. Nabopolassar *may* have had a son of this name; or the Labynetus of Herod. i, 74 may be Nabopolassar himself.) At any rate, a few years later, he was placed at the head of a Babylonian army, and sent by his father, who was now old and infirm, to chastise the insolence of Pharaoh-Necho, king of Egypt. This prince had recently invaded Syria, defeated Josiah, king of Judah, at Megiddo, and reduced the whole tract, from Egypt to Carchemish on the upper Euphrates [see CARCHEMISH], which in the partition of the Assyrian territories on the destruction of Nineveh had been assigned to Babylon (2 Kings xxiii, 29, 30; Beros. ap. Josephus, *c. Ap.* i, 19). Necho had held possession of these countries for about three years, when (B.C. 606) Nebuchadnezzar led an army against him, defeated him at Carchemish in a great battle (Jer. xlvi, 2-12), recovered Cœle-Syria, Phœnicia, and Palestine, took Jerusalem (Dan. i, 1, 2), pressed forward to Egypt, and was engaged in that country or upon its borders when intelligence arrived which recalled him hastily to Babylon. Nabopolassar, after reigning twenty-one years, had died, and the throne was vacant; or, as there is some reason to think, Nebuchadnezzar, since he appeared to be the "king of Babylon" to the Jews, had really been associated with his father (Jer. iv, 1; Dan. i, 1). In some alarm, however, about the succession, he hurried back to the capital, accompanied only by his light troops; and crossing the desert, probably by way of Tadmor or Palmyra, reached Babylon before any disturbance had arisen, and entered peaceably on his kingdom (B.C. 604). The bulk of the army, with the captives—Phœnicians, Syrians, Egyptians, and Jews—returned by the ordinary route, which skirted instead of crossing the desert. It was at this time that Daniel and his companions were brought to Babylon, where they presently grew into favor with Nebuchadnezzar, and became persons of very considerable influence (Dan. i, 3-20). See DANIEL. The sacred vessels taken from Jehovah's house were transferred by Nebuchadnezzar to his temple at Babylon (Isa. xxxix; 2 Chron. xxxvi, 6, 7). See BABYLON; CAPTIVITY.

Within a few years after Nebuchadnezzar's first expedition into Syria and Palestine, disaffection again showed itself in those countries. Jehoiakim—who, although threatened at first with captivity (2 Chron. xxxvi, 6), had been finally maintained on the throne as a Babylonian vassal—after three years of service "turned and rebelled" against his suzerain, probably trusting to be supported by Egypt (2 Kings xxiv, 1). Not long afterwards Phœnicia seems to have broken into revolt; and the Chaldæan monarch, who had previously endeavored to subdue the disaffected by his generals and allies (2 Kings xxiv, 2), once more took the field in person, and marched first of all against Tyre. Having invested that city in the seventh year of his reign (Josephus, *c. Ap.* i, 21), and left a portion of his army there to continue the siege, he proceeded against Jerusalem; which submitted without a struggle (B.C. 598). According to Josephus, who is here our chief authority, Nebuchadnezzar punished Jehoiakim with death (*Ant.* x, 6, 3; comp. Jer. xxii, 18, 19, and xxxvi, 30), but placed his son Jehoiachin upon the throne. Jehoiachin reigned only three months; for, on his showing symptoms of disaffection, Nebuchadnezzar came up against Jerusalem for the third time, deposed the young prince (whom he carried to Babylon, together with a large portion of the population of the city, and the chief of the Temple treasures), and made his uncle, Zedekiah, king in his place. Tyre still held out; and it was not till the thirteenth year from the time of its first invest-

ment that the city of merchants fell (B.C. 585). Before this happened, Jerusalem had been totally destroyed. This consummation was owing to the folly of Zedekiah, who, despite the warnings of Jeremiah, made a treaty with Apries (Hophra), king of Egypt (Ezek. xvii, 15), and on the strength of this alliance renounced his allegiance to the king of Babylon. Nebuchadnezzar commenced the final siege of Jerusalem in the ninth year of Zedekiah—his own sixteenth year (early in B.C. 589)—and took it nearly two years later (latter part of B.C. 588). One effort to carry out the treaty seems to have been made by Apries. An Egyptian army crossed the frontier, and began its march towards Jerusalem; upon which Nebuchadnezzar raised the siege, and set off to meet the new foe. According to Josephus (*Ant.* x, 7, 3) a battle was fought, in which Apries was completely defeated; but the scriptural account seems rather to imply that the Egyptians retired on the advance of Nebuchadnezzar, and recrossed the frontier without risking an engagement (Jer. xxxvii, 5-8). At any rate, the attempt failed, and was not repeated; the "broken reed, Egypt," proved a treacherous support, and after an eighteen months' siege Jerusalem fell. Zedekiah escaped from the city, but was captured near Jericho (Jer. xxxix, 5), and brought to Nebuchadnezzar at Riblah in the territory of Hamath, where his eyes were put out by the king's order, while his sons and his chief nobles were slain. Nebuchadnezzar then returned to Babylon with Zedekiah, whom he imprisoned for the remainder of his life; leaving Nebuzar-adan, the captain of his guard, to complete the destruction of the city and the pacification of Judæa. Gedaliah, a Jew, was appointed governor, but he was shortly murdered, and the rest of the Jews either fled to Egypt or were carried by Nebuzar-adan to Babylon (B.C. 582).

The military successes of Nebuchadnezzar cannot be traced minutely beyond this point. His own annals have not come down to us; and the historical allusions which we find in his extant inscriptions are of the most vague and general character. It may be gathered from the prophetical Scriptures and from Josephus that the conquest of Jerusalem was rapidly followed by the fall of Tyre and the complete submission of Phœnicia (Ezra xxvi-xxviii; Joseph. *c. Ap.* i, 21); after which the Babylonians carried their arms into Egypt, and inflicted severe injuries on that fertile country (Jer. xlvi, 13-26; Ezra xxix, 2-20; xxx, 6; Joseph. *Ant.* x, 9, 7). But we have no account of these campaigns on which we can depend. Josephus adds that Megasthenes, in his fourth book, refers to the same subject, and thereby endeavors to show that Nebuchadnezzar exceeded Hercules, and conquered a great part of Africa and Spain. Strabo adds that "Sesostris, king of Egypt, and Tearcon, king of Ethiopia, extended their expedition as far as Europe, but that Navokodrosor, who is venerated by the Chaldæans more than Hercules by the Greeks, . . . marched through Spain to Greece and Pontus." Our remaining notices of Nebuchadnezzar present him to us as a magnificent prince and beneficent ruler rather than a warrior; and the great fame which has always attached to his name among the Eastern nations depends rather on his buildings and other grand constructions than on any victories or conquests ascribed to him.

2. We are told by Berosus that the first care of Nebuchadnezzar, on obtaining quiet possession of his kingdom after the first Syrian expedition, was to rebuild the temple of Bel (*Bel-Merodach*) at Babylon out of the spoils of the Syrian war (ap. Joseph. *Ant.* x, 11, 1). He next proceeded to strengthen and beautify the city, which he renovated throughout, and surrounded with several lines of fortification, himself adding one entirely new quarter. Having finished the walls and adorned the gates magnificently, he constructed a new palace, adjoining the old residence of his father—a superb edifice which he completed in fifteen days! In the grounds of this palace he formed the celebrated "hanging garden," which was a plaisance, built up with huge stones

to imitate the varied surface of mountains, and planted with trees and shrubs of every kind. Diodorus, probably following Ctesias, describes this marvel as a square, four *plethra* (four hundred feet) each way, and fifty cubits (seventy-five feet) high, approached by sloping paths, and supported on a series of arched galleries increasing in height from the base to the summit. In these galleries were various pleasant chambers; and one of them contained the engines by which water was raised from the river to the surface of the mound. This curious construction, which the Greek writers reckoned among the seven wonders of the world, was said to have been built by Nebuchadnezzar for the gratification of his wife, Amuhia, who, having been brought up among the Median mountains, desired something to remind her of them. Possibly, however, one object was to obtain a pleasure-ground at a height above that to which the mosquitoes are accustomed to rise. This complete renovation of Babylon by Nebuchadnezzar, which Berosus asserts, is confirmed to us in every possible way. The Standard Inscription of the king relates at length the construction of the whole series of works, and appears to have been the authority from which Berosus drew. The ruins confirm this in the most positive way, for nine tenths of the bricks *in situ* are stamped with Nebuchadnezzar's name. Scripture also adds an indirect but important testimony in the exclamation of Nebuchadnezzar recorded by Daniel, "Is not this great Babylon *which I have built?*" (Dan. iv, 30).

But Nebuchadnezzar did not confine his efforts to the ornamentation and improvement of his capital. Throughout the empire, at Borsippa, Sippara, Cutha, Chilmad, Duraba, Teredon, and a multitude of other places, he built or rebuilt cities, repaired temples, constructed quays, reservoirs, canals, and aqueducts, on a scale of grandeur and magnificence surpassing everything of the kind recorded in history, unless it be the constructions of one or two of the greatest Egyptian monarchs. "I have examined," says Sir H. Rawlinson, "the bricks *in situ*, belonging perhaps to a hundred different towns and cities in the neighborhood of Bagdad, and I never found any other legend than that of Nebuchadnezzar, son of Nabopolassar, king of Babylon" (*Com. on the Inscr. of Assyria and Babylonia*, p. 76, 77). "Nebuchadnezzar," says Abydenus, "on succeeding to the throne, fortified Babylon with three lines of walls. He dug the *Nahr Malcha*, or Royal River, which was a branch stream derived from the Euphrates, and also the Acracanus. He likewise made the great reservoir above the city of Sippara, which was thirty parasangs (ninety miles) in circumference, and twenty fathoms (one hundred and twenty feet) deep. Here he placed sluices or flood-gates, which enabled him to irrigate the low country. He also built a quay along the shore of the Red Sea (Persian Gulf), and founded the city of Teredon on the borders of Arabia." It is reasonably concluded from these statements that an extensive system of irrigation was devised by this monarch, to whom the Babylonians were probably indebted for the greater portion of that vast network of canals which covered the whole alluvial tract between the two rivers, and extended on the right bank of the Euphrates to the extreme verge of the stony desert. On that side the principal work was a canal of the largest dimensions, still to be traced, which left the Euphrates at Hit, and skirting the desert ran south-east a distance of above four hundred miles to the Persian Gulf, where it emptied itself into the bay of Grane.

The wealth, greatness, and general prosperity of Nebuchadnezzar are strikingly placed before us in the Book of Daniel. "The God of heaven" gave him, not a kingdom only, but "power, strength, and glory" (Dan. ii, 37). His wealth is evidenced by the image of gold, sixty cubits in height, which he set up in the plain of Dura (Dan. iii, 1). The grandeur and careful organization of his kingdom appear from the long list of his officers, "princes, governors, captains, judges, treasurers,

counsellors, sheriffs, and rulers of provinces," of whom we have repeated mention (ver. 2, 3, 27). We see the existence of a species of hierarchy in the "magicians, astrologers, sorcerers," over whom Daniel was set (ii, 48). The "tree, whose height was great, which grew and was strong, and the height thereof reached unto the heavens, and the sight thereof to the end of all the earth; the leaves whereof were fair, and the fruit much, and in which was food for all; under which the beasts of the field had shadow, and the fowls of heaven dwelt in the branches thereof, and all flesh was fed of it" (iv, 10–12), is the fitting type of a kingdom at once so flourishing and so extensive. It has been thought by some (De Wette, Th. Parker, etc.) that the Book of Daniel represents the satrapial system of government (*Satrapen-Einrichtung*) as established throughout the whole empire; but this conclusion is not justified by a close examination of that document. Nebuchadnezzar, like his Assyrian predecessors (Isa. x, 8), is represented as a "king of kings" (Dan. ii, 37); and the officers enumerated in chap. ii are probably the authorities of Babylonia proper, rather than the governors of remoter regions, who could not be all spared at once from their employments. The instance of Gedaliah (Jer. xl, 5; 2 Kings xxv, 22) is not that of a satrap. He was a Jew; and it may be doubted whether he stood really in any different relation to the Babylonians from Zedekiah or Jehoiachin; although, as he was not of the seed of David, the Jews considered him to be "governor" rather than king.

3. Towards the close of his reign the glory of Nebuchadnezzar suffered a temporary eclipse. As a punishment for his pride and vanity, that strange form of madness was sent upon him which the Greeks called lycanthropy (λυκανθρωπία); wherein the sufferer imagines himself a beast, and, quitting the haunts of men, insists on leading the life of a beast (Dan. iv, 33). Berosus, with the pardonable tenderness of a native, anxious for the good fame of his country's greatest king, suppressed this fact; and it may be doubted whether Herodotus in his Babylonian travels, which fell only about a century after the time, obtained any knowledge of it. Nebuchadnezzar himself, however, in his great inscription appears to allude to it, although in a studied ambiguity of phrase which renders the passage very difficult of translation. After describing the construction of the most important of his great works, he appears to say, "For four years (?) . . . the seat of my kingdom . . . did not rejoice my heart. In all my dominions I did not build a high place of power, the precious treasures of my kingdom I did not lay up. In Babylon, buildings for myself and for the honor of my kingdom I did not lay out. In the worship of Merodach, my lord, the joy of my heart, in Babylon the city of my sovereignty, and the seat of my empire, I did not sing his praises, I did not furnish his altars with victims, nor did I clear out the canals" (Rawlinson's *Herod.* ii, 586). Other negative clauses follow. It is plain that we have here narrated a suspension—apparently for four years—of all those works and occupations on which the king especially prided himself—his temples, palaces, worship, offerings, and works of irrigation; and though the cause of the suspension is not stated, we can scarcely imagine anything that would account for it but some such extraordinary malady as that recorded in Daniel.

It has often been remarked that Herodotus ascribes to a queen, Nitocris, several of the important works, which other writers (Berosus, Abydenus) assign to Nebuchadnezzar. The conjecture naturally arises that Nitocris was Nebuchadnezzar's queen, and that, as she carried on his constructions during his incapacity, they were by some considered to be hers. It is no disproof of this to urge that Nebuchadnezzar's wife was a Median princess, not an Egyptian (as Nitocris must have been from her name), and that she was called, not Nitocris, but Amyitis or Amyhia; for Nebuchadnezzar, who married Amyitis in B.C. 625, and who lived after this marriage more than sixty years, may easily have married again after the decease of his first wife, and his second queen may have been an Egyptian. His later relations with Egypt appear to have been friendly; and it is remarkable that the name Nitocris, which belonged to very primitive Egyptian history, had in fact been resuscitated about this time, and is found on the Egyptian monuments to have been borne by a princess belonging to the family of the Psammetiks.

The nature of Nebuchadnezzar's disease and recovery has been much debated. Origen strangely allegorizes the story (ap. Hieron. *in Dan.*) as a representation of the fall of Lucifer. Bodin (in *Demonol.*) maintains that Nebuchadnezzar underwent an actual metamorphosis of soul and body, a similar instance of which is given by Cluvier (*Append. ad Epitom. Hist.*) on the testimony of an eye-witness. Tertullian (*De Pœnit.*) confines the transformation to the body only, but without loss of reason, of which kind of metamorphosis St. Augustine (*De Civ. Dei*, xviii, 18) reports some instances said to have taken place in Italy, to which he himself attaches little credit; but Gaspard Peucer asserts that the transformation of men into wolves was very common in Livonia. Some Jewish rabbins have asserted that the soul of Nebuchadnezzar, by a real transmigration, changed places with that of an ox (Medina, *De rectâ in Deum fid.*); while others have supposed not a real, but an apparent change, of which there is a case recorded in the life of St. Macarius, the parents of a young woman having been persuaded that their daughter had been transformed into a mare. The most generally received opinion, however, is that Nebuchadnezzar labored under that species of hypochondriacal monomania which leads the patient to fancy himself changed into an animal or other substance, the habits of which he adopts. Jerome probably leaned to this opinion: "Who does not see," he observes, "that *madmen* live like brute beasts" (*in Dan.* iv, 4). To this disease of the imagination physicians have given the name of Lycanthropy, Zoanthropy, or Insania Canina. See DISEASE. In Dan. iv, 15 (iv, 12, according to the Latin) there seems to be an allusion to some species of insanity in the expression, "Even with a band of iron and brass" (*alligetur vinculo ferreo et æreo*, Vulg.); and the loss and return of reason is very clearly intimated in ver. 34, "Mine understanding returned to me, and I blessed the Most High." (See also Virgil, *Eclog.* vi; Drummond Hay, *Western Barbary*, p. 65; B. Reckenberger, *De Nebucadn. ab hominibus expulso*, Jen. 1733; Bertholdt, *Daniel*, i, 290; Heinroth, *Seelenstör.* i, 65; Ader, *De ægrotis in Evang.* p. 31, etc.; Meade, *Med. Sac.*; Müller, *De Nebuchadnezz.* μεταμορφώσει, Lips. 1747.)

The idea of an allegory has been revived in modern times, especially by De Wette (*Einleitung*, p. 257), who considers the accounts in Daniel too improbable, if literally understood, although he admits that they may have been founded on historical traditions. He considers the whole of the narrative in Daniel as referring to Antiochus Epiphanes, who he asserts is also signified by Belshazzar. This hypothesis assumes that the Book of Daniel is spurious, contrary to the New Testament and other ancient testimony (Hengstenberg, *Authent. des Dan.* p. 100 sq.). See DANIEL.

Some have fancied that there was an allusion to the disease of Nebuchadnezzar in the passage of Berosus quoted by Josephus (*c. Apion.* i, 20): "Nabuchodonosor, after he had commenced the aforesaid wall, falling into a sickness, died." Abydenus (ap. Eusebium, *Præpar. Evang.* ix, 41), having cited the passage from Megasthenes already referred to, adds, upon the authority of the same writer, a speech of Nabuchodonosor, wherein, having been struck by some god, he foretold the destruction of Babylon by a "Persian mule," assisted by a Mede, the former boast of Assyria, after which he instantly vanished. A reference has been supposed to exist in these words to Nebuchadnezzar's madness and

consequent disappearance, but there is at most, as De Wette observes, only a traditional connection between them. Jahn (*Hebrew Commonwealth*) conceives the whole to be a tradition made up from his prophetic dreams, his insanity, and from Daniel's explanation of the well-known handwriting in the banqueting-hall of Belshazzar.

After an interval of four, or probably seven years (Dan. iv, 16), Nebuchadnezzar's malady left him. As we are told in Scripture that "his reason returned, and for the glory of his kingdom his honor and brightness returned;" and he "was established in his kingdom, and excellent majesty was added to him" (Dan. iv, 36), so we find in the Standard Inscription that he resumed his great works after a period of suspension, and added fresh "wonders" in his old age to the marvellous constructions of his manhood. He died in the year B.C. 561, at an advanced age (83 or 84), having reigned forty-three years. A son, Evil-Merodach (q. v.), succeeded him.

4. The character of Nebuchadnezzar must be gathered principally from Scripture. There is a conventional formality in the cuneiform inscriptions, which deprives them of almost all value for the illustration of individual mind and temper. Ostentation and vainglory are characteristics of the entire series, each king seeking to magnify above all others his own exploits. We can only observe as peculiar to Nebuchadnezzar a disposition to rest his fame on his great works rather than on his military achievements, and a strong religious spirit, manifesting itself especially in a devotion, which is almost exclusive, to one particular god. Though his own tutelary deity and that of his father was Nebo (Mercury), yet his worship, his ascriptions of praise, his thanksgivings, have in almost every case for their object the god Merodach. Under his protection he placed his son, Evil-Merodach. Merodach is "his lord," "his great lord," "the joy of his heart," "the great lord who has appointed him to the empire of the world, and has confided to his care the far-spread people of the earth," "the great lord who has established him in strength," etc. One of the first of his own titles is, "He who pays homage to Merodach." Even when restoring the temples of other deities, he ascribes the work to the suggestions of Merodach, and places it under his protection. We may hence explain the appearance of a sort of monotheism (Dan. i, 2; iv, 21, 32, 34, 37), mixed with polytheism (ii, 47; iii, 12, 18, 29; iv, 9), in the scriptural notices of him. While admitting a qualified divinity in Nebo, Nana, and other deities of his country, Nebuchadnezzar maintained the real *monarchy* of Bel-Merodach. This deity was to him "the supreme chief of the gods," "the most ancient," "the king of the heavens and the earth." These expressions are all applied to Merodach by Nebuchadnezzar in his inscriptions. It was *his* image, or symbol, undoubtedly, which was "set up" to be worshipped in the "plain of Dura" (iii, 1), and *his* "house" in which the sacred vessels from the Temple were treasured (i, 2). Nebuchadnezzar seems at some times to have identified this, his supreme god, with the God of the Jews (ch. iv); at others, to have regarded the Jewish God as one of the local and inferior deities (ch. iii) over whom Merodach ruled.

The genius and grandeur which characterized Nebuchadnezzar, and which have handed down his name among the few ancient personages known generally throughout the East, are very apparent in Scripture, and indeed in all the accounts of his reign and actions. Without perhaps any strong military turn, he must have possessed a fair amount of such talent to have held his own in the east against the ambitious Medes, and in the west against the Egyptians. Necho and Apries were both princes of good warlike capacity, whom it is some credit to have defeated. The prolonged siege of Tyre is a proof of the determination with which he prosecuted his military enterprises. But his greatness lay especially in the arts of peace. He saw in the natural fertility of Babylonia, and its ample wealth of waters, the foundation of national prosperity, and so of power. Hence his vast canals and elaborate system of irrigation, which made the whole country a garden; and this must have been a main cause of the full treasury, from which alone his palaces and temples can have received their magnificence. The forced labor of captives may have raised the fabrics; but the statues, the enamelled bricks, the fine woodwork, the gold and silver plating, the hangings and curtains, had to be bought; and the enormous expenditure of this monarch, which does not appear to have exhausted the country, and which cannot have been very largely supported by tribute, must have been really supplied in the main from that agricultural wealth which he took so much pains to develop. We may gather from the productiveness of Babylonia under the Persians (Herod. i, 192, 193; iii, 92), after a conquest and two (three?) revolts, some idea of its flourishing condition in the period of independence, for which (according to the consentient testimony of the monuments and the best authors) it was indebted to this king.

The moral character of Nebuchadnezzar is not such as entitles him to our approval. Besides the overweening pride which brought upon him so terrible a chastisement, we note a violence and fury (Dan. ii, 12; iii, 19) common enough among Oriental monarchs of the weaker kind, but from which the greatest of them have usually been free; while at the same time we observe a cold and relentless cruelty which is particularly revolting. The blinding of Zedekiah may perhaps be justified as an ordinary Eastern practice, though it is the earliest case of the kind on record; but the refinement of cruelty by which he was made to witness his sons' execution before his eyes were put out (2 Kings xxv, 7) is worthier of a Dionysius or a Domitian than of a really great king. Again, the detention of Jehoiachin in prison for thirty-six years for an offence committed at the age of eighteen (2 Kings xxiv, 8), is a severity surpassing Oriental harshness. Against these grave faults we have nothing to set, unless it be a feeble trait of magnanimity in the pardon accorded to Shadrach, Meshach, and Abednego when he found that he was without power to punish them (Dan. iii, 26).

It has been thought remarkable that to a man of this character God should make vouchsafed a revelation of the future by means of visions (Dan. ii, 29; iv, 2). But the circumstance, however it may disturb our preconceived notions, is not really at variance with the general laws of God's providence as revealed to us in Scripture. As with his natural, so with his supernatural gifts, they are not confined to the worthy. Even under Christianity, miraculous powers were sometimes possessed by those who made an ill use of them (1 Cor. xiv, 2-33). And God, it is plain, did not leave the old heathen world without some supernatural aid, but made his presence felt from time to time in visions, through prophets, or even by a voice from heaven. It is only necessary to refer to the histories of Pharaoh (Gen. xli, 1-7, 28), Abimelech (xx, 3), Job (Job iv, 13; xxxviii, 1, 1; xl, 6; comp. Dan. iv, 31), and Balaam (Numb. xxii-xxiv), in order to establish the parity of Nebuchadnezzar's visions with other facts recorded in the Bible. He was warned, and the nations over which he ruled were warned through him, God leaving not himself "without witness" even in those dark times. In conclusion, we may notice that a heathen writer (Abydenus), who generally draws his inspirations from Berosus, ascribes to Nebuchadnezzar a miraculous speech just before his death, announcing to the Babylonians the speedy coming of the "Persian mule," who with the help of the Medes would enslave Babylon (Abyd. ap. Euseb. *Præp. Ev.* ix, 41).

5. The Canon of Ptolemy the mathematician, who flourished about the commencement of the Christian æra, consists of a catalogue, arranged in chronological order, of the kings of Babylon, commencing with Nabonassar, who reigned B.C. 747, and ending with Nabon-

ned, B.C. 556. According to this catalogue, Nabopolassar (Ναβουπολάσαρος), who died B.C. 625, was succeeded by Nabocolassar (Ναβοκολάσαρος), B.C. 605. This Nabocolassar is therefore presumed to be the Nebuchadnezzar of Scripture (for the Canon of Ptolemy, see *Table Chronologique des Règnes*, etc., par l'Abbé Halmy, Paris, 1819). Nabopolassar, the father of Nabocolassar, is supposed to have been the first Chaldæan monarch of Babylon, and to have disunited it from the Assyrian empire, of which it had hitherto formed a part (Jahn's *Hebrew Commonwealth*). According to a fragment of Alexander Polyhistor, reported by Syncellus in his *Chronographia*, it was this sovereign who destroyed the city of Nineveh, B.C. 612, which, according to Eusebius (*Chron.* p. 46), he effected in conjunction with Astyages, the eldest son of Cyaxares, king of the Medes (see also Tobit xiv, 15, where the latter is named Assuerus). The following extract, preserved by Josephus, from the lost Chaldæan history of Berosus, priest of the temple of Bel (B.C. 268), will be found to throw considerable light on the Scripture narrative: "When his father Nabuchodonosor heard that the governor whom he had set over Egypt and the places about Cœle-Syria and Phœnicia had revolted from him, while he was not himself able any longer to undergo hardships, he committed to his son Nabuchodonosor, who was still but a youth, some parts of his army, and sent him against the enemy. So when Nabuchodonosor had given him battle, and fought with the rebel, he overcame him, and reduced the country from under his subjection and made it a branch of his own kingdom. But about that time it happened that his father Nabuchodonosor fell ill, and ended his life in the city of Babylon, when he had reigned twenty-one years; and when he learned that his father Nabuchodonosor was dead—having settled the affairs of Egypt and the other countries, and also those that concerned the captive Jews, and the Phœnicians, Syrians, and Egyptians, and having committed the conveyance of them to Babylon to certain of his friends—he hastily crossed the desert, with a few companions, into Babylon. So he took upon him the management of public affairs, and of the kingdom which had been kept for him by one of the chief Chaldæans, and he received the entire dominions of his father, and ordered that when the captives came they should be placed in colonies in the most proper places of Babylonia" (*Ant.* x, 11; see also *Apion.* i, 19; Euseb. *Chron. Armen.* i, 59; Volney, *Recherch. Nouv. sur l'hist. Ancienne*, iii, 151 sq.). It will be observed that both Nebuchadnezzar (styled by some *the Great*) and his father are here equally named Nabuchodonosor, but in the citation of the same narrative from Berosus by Josephus (*c. Apion.* i, 19) the father of Nebuchadnezzar is called Nabolassar (Ναβολάσσαρος), corresponding nearly with the Nabopolassar of Ptolemy; which has induced some to suppose the name Nabuchodonosor in the former citation to be an error of transcription. Some consider the Nabuchodonosor of the Book of Judith to be the same with the Saosduchin of Ptolemy, who was contemporary with Manasseh. Some foundation has thus been afforded for considering Nebuchadnezzar as a general name for Babylonian sovereigns (Prideaux, *Connect.*); this, however, is considered by Whiston as a groundless mistake (Whiston's *Josephus*, note on ch. ix). The similarity of the two names may have led to their being sometimes confounded. The conqueror of Nineveh is also called by the name of Nebuchodonosor in Tobit xiv, 15 (in the Greek, for the Latin ends with ver. 14), and is on this account styled by some *Nebuchadnezzar the First*, a designation first applied to him by rabbi David Ganz, in the age of the world 3285.

According to Ptolemy's Canon, the reign of Nabocolassar is made to commence two years later than that of the Nebuchadnezzar of Scripture. Probably the first capture of Jerusalem (Dan. i, 1) took place during the last years of the reign of Nabopolassar, in the expedition mentioned by Berosus (*ut sup.*), but the Canon of

Ptolemy dates the commencement of his reign from the death of his father, when he became sole king of Babylon (De Wette's *Introd.* § 253, note). See CHRONOLOGY.

Although Herodotus does not name Nebuchadnezzar, he is supposed by some to allude to the expedition of Pharaoh-Necho against Babylon, when he observes that "Necho, after an engagement at Magdolus in Egypt, took Cadytis, a great city of Syria." It is conjectured that he may have confounded Migdol, in Egypt, with Megiddo, and that Cadytis was the same with Jerusalem (El Kadosh, "the holy city") (Jahn's *Hebrew Commonwealth*).

6. One other point in the life of Nebuchadnezzar, connecting it with Scripture, may be glanced at. In the Book of Daniel (ch. iii) there is abruptly introduced an account of a golden image which Nebuchadnezzar set up in the plain of Dura, its inauguration being heralded in solemn pomp to all parts of the kingdom. The image was probably one of his patron-god, Bel-Merodach; and the dedication of such a statue is in perfect keeping with his intense religiousness, which is apparent from his numerous and cordial inscriptions of thanks and homage to the same divinity, after whom also he named his son and successor. The adoration paid to the image was a test of loyalty. To worship the king's god simply at the king's command was such a spectacle of national conformity as an Oriental despot would naturally delight in. Some have supposed that the image represented the king himself, who, in this way, claimed divine honors—an insanity found in Persian, Egyptian, and Seleucid monarchs—in the Grecian Alexander and the Roman Caligula. This is not a likely conjecture. The Jews as a body, it would seem, were not invited to the festival, being aliens and captives. But it is said that the image itself was out of all shape—sixty cubits high, and only six cubits broad—that is, in the proportion of ten to one. Now it is evident from the story that its height was for the sake of its being visible to an immense concourse gathered on a plain, and it is therefore probable that a tall pedestal is included in the measurement; or it may have been an obelisk with a bust on the summit of it (Münter, *Relig. d. Bab.* p. 59; Hengstenberg, *On Daniel*). Diodorus Siculus (lib. ii) informs us that one of the images of massy gold found by Xerxes in the temple of Bel measured forty feet in height, which would have been fairly proportioned to a breadth of six feet, measured at the shoulders. Prideaux supposes that this may have been the identical statue erected by Nebuchadnezzar, which, however, Jahn conceives was more probably only gilt, as a statue of gold could scarcely have been safe from robbers in the plain of Dura; but this conjecture of Jahn seems by no means necessary. Dur—Dura—signifies a plain, and in such a plain, yet vulgarly called Dowair, to the south-east of Babylon, M. Oppert found the pedestal of what must have been a colossal statue. There is no hint that the image was of solid gold, as some objectors imagine. Anything plated with gold was, in popular phrase, called golden (comp. Exod. xxx, 1–3; xxxix, 8, etc.). The description of the process of forging idols in Isa. xl, 19 shows us the plating of the figures. Herodotus mentions a large golden statue of Bel, and then refers to another and much smaller one, which, in contrast, he says, was of "solid gold." The grand demonstration, and the assemblage of "princes, governors, captains, judges, treasurers, counsellors, sheriffs, and all the rulers of the provinces," must have marked some important epoch—the conclusion of some great wars or works, followed by such prosperity and repose as is indicated by the phrase, "I Nebuchadnezzar was at rest in mine house, and flourishing in my palace." It is a strange rationalistic freak on the part of Lengerke, Bleek, and De Wette to regard all this chapter of Daniel as a mere legend, dimly picturing out the cruelties and idolatries of Antiochus Epiphanes.

7. *Literature.*—See Schröder, *Nebuchadn. Chaldæor.*

rex (Marb. 1719); Schröer, *Imper. Babyl.* p. 260 sq.; Lochner, *De Nino Nebuchadnezare* (Stadæ, 1736); Maier, *Statua Nebuchadnezaris* (Jen. 1693); Müller, *De Nebuchadnezaris μεταμορφ.* (Lips. 1747); Offerhaus, *De rebus sub Nebuchadnezare gestis* (Gröning. 1734); Seelen, *De stipendiariis Nebuchadnezaris* (Lubeck, 1737); *Jour. Sac. Lit.* April, 1853, p. 32; Rawlinson, *Evidences*, p. 127, 133; *Ancient Monarchies*, ii, 50 sq. See BABYLONIA.

Nebuchadrez'zar (Heb. *Nebuchadrets'tsar*, נְבוּכַדְרֶאצַּר; Sept. Ναβουχοδονόσορ), a less usual but more correct form (Jer. xxi, 2, 7; xxii, 25; xxiv, 1; xxv, 1, 9; xxix, 21; xxxii, 1, 28; xxxv, 11; xxxvii, 1; xxxix, 1, 11; xliii, 10; xliv, 30; xlvi, 2, 13, 26; xlix, 28, 30; l, 17; li, 34; lii, 4, 12, 28, 29, 30; Ezek. xxvi, 7; xxix, 18, 19; xxx, 10) of the name of king NEBUCHADNEZZAR (q. v.).

Nebushas'ban (Heb. *Nebushazban'*, נְבוּשַׁזְבָּן [written in the text with a small final *n*, for which some copies have, perhaps by error, a *z*], from *Nebo*, and Persian *chésban*, "votary," i. e. *adorer of Nebo*; Sept. omits, but some copies have Ναβουσεζβάν or Ναβουσαρσελχίμ; Vulg. *Nabusezban*), the Rabsaris (q. v.) or chief chamberlain of the Babylonian court, sent by Nebuchadnezzar, in connection with the two other chief dignitaries, Nebuzaradan (the Rab-tabbachim, or chief of the body-guard) and Nergal-sharezer (the Rab-mag, or head of the Magians), to release Jeremiah from prison on the capture of Jerusalem (Jer. xxxix, 13). B.C. 588. "Nebu-shasban's office and title were the same as those of Ashpenaz (Dan. i, 3), whom he probably succeeded. In the list given (ver. 3) of those who took possession of the city in the dead of the night of the 11th Tammuz, Nebushasban is not mentioned by name, but merely by his title Rab-saris. So at the Assyrian invasion in the time of Hezekiah, Tartan, Rab-saris, and Rab-shakeh, as the three highest dignitaries, addressed the Jews from the head of their army (2 Kings xviii, 17). Possibly these three officers in the Assyrian court answered to the three named above in the Babylonian.

Nebuzar'adan (Heb. *Nebuzaradan'*, נְבוּזַרְאֲדָן, for signif. see below; Sept. Ναβουζαρδάν v. r. Ναβουζαρδάν; Josephus, Ναβουζαρδάνης, *Ant.* x, 9, 1 and 2; Vulg. *Nebuzardan*), the Rab-tabbachim, i. e. chief of the slaughterers or executioners (A. V. "captain of the guard"), a high officer in the court of Nebuchadnezzar, apparently (like the Tartan in the Assyrian army) the next to the person of the monarch. He appears not to have been present during the siege of Jerusalem; probably he was occupied in the more important operations at Tyre, but as soon as the city was actually in the hands of the Babylonians he arrived, and from that moment everything was completely directed by him. B.C. 588. It was he who decided, even to the minutest details of fire-pans and bowls (2 Kings xxv, 15), what should be carried off and what burned, which persons should be taken away to Babylon, and which left behind in the country. One act only is referred directly to Nebuchadnezzar—the appointment of the governor or superintendent of the conquered district. All this Nebuzaradan seems to have carried out with wisdom and moderation. His conduct to Jeremiah, to whom his attention had been directed by his master (Jer. xxxix, 11), is marked by even higher qualities than these, and the prophet has preserved (xl, 2–5) a speech of Nebuzaradan to him on liberating him from his chains at Ramah, which contains expressions truly remarkable in a heathen. He seems to have left Judæa for this time when he took down the chief people of Jerusalem to his master at Riblah (2 Kings xxv, 18–20). Six years afterwards he again appeared (Jer. lii, 30). Nebuchadnezzar in his twenty-third year made a descent on the regions east of the Jordan, including the Ammonites and Moabites (Josephus, *Ant.* x, 9, 7), who escaped when

Jerusalem was destroyed. See MOAB. Thence he proceeded to Egypt (Joseph. *ibid.*), and, either on the way thither or on the return, Nebuzaradan again passed through the country and carried off seven hundred and forty-five more captives (Jer. lii, 30).

The name, like Nebu-chadnezzar and Nebu-shasban, contains that of *Nebo* the Babylonian deity. The other portion of the word is less certain. Gesenius (*Thes.* p. 839 *b*) translates by *Mercurii dux dominus*, taking the זַר as = שֵׂר, "prince," and אֲדָן as = אֲדוֹן, "lord." Fürst, on the other hand (*Handwb.* s. v.), treats it as equivalent in meaning to the Hebrew *rab-tabbachim*, which usually follows it, and sometimes occurs by itself (2 Kings xxv, 18; Jer. xl, 2, 5). To obtain this meaning he treats the first member as = Pers. *sar*, Sansc. *ciro*, "chief," as Gesenius; but compares the last member of the name to the Sansc. *dâna*, from *dô*, "to cut off." Gesenius also takes *zaradan* as identical with the first element in the name of Sardan-apalus. But this latter name is now explained by Sir H. Rawlinson as Assur-dan-i-pal (Rawlinson's *Herod.* i, 460).

Neceres is the name which the Turks give to a clan of people inhabiting the mountains about Jebily, in Syria, who are of a very strange and singular character. It is the principle of the Neceres to adhere to no certain religion; chameleon like, they put on the color of religion, whatever it be, which is reflected upon them by the persons with whom they happen to converse. With Christians, they profess themselves Christians; with Turks, they are good Mussulmans; with Jews, they pass for Jews; being such Proteuses in religion that nobody was ever able to discover what shape or standard their consciences are really of. See Broughton, *Biblioth. Hist. Sacra*, ii, s.v. See NASSARIANS.

Necessarians. See NECESSITARIANS.

Necessary Doctrine and Erudition (*for any Christian man*) is the title of a book which the English people received from their sovereign, Henry VIII, in the year 1543, in connection with the legal prohibition of reading the Scriptures. In contradistinction to the *Institution of a Christian Man* (q. v.), which was called the "Bishops' Book," the present formulary was called the "King's Book." The *Necessary Doctrine* was not, like the other, sanctioned by the authority of Convocation, but was composed by a committee originally nominated by the king, their compositions receiving the stamp of his personal approbation. Henry himself had a considerable share in the execution of the work, the chief part of which was corrected by his own hand; and evidence still remains of the diligence with which he had collected and compared the opinions of his bishops and divines on the different points of discussion. The Preface was probably written by himself, and, among other matter, contains a vindication of the late prohibition of the Bible. Cranmer also wrote a portion of it—that concerning faith. But while it was evangelical in doctrine, it was popish in other things, affirming transubstantiation, calling marriage a sacrament, and maintaining the seven sacraments of Romanism. As an authorized formula it retained authority till the king's death. This work has occasioned in the present day much discussion and dispute, arising from the prejudices of its readers. One party has confidently appealed to it as a criterion of the opinions of the Reformers on many doctrinal points, in opposition to the Church from which they had separated; another party has condemned it in the most unqualified terms, as leaning even in doctrine towards popery rather than Protestantism. For a full account of the plan and contents of this work, see Carwithen, *Hist. of the Church of England*, vol. i, ch. vii; see also Palmer, *On the Church*, i, 468 sq., 481 sq.; Eadie, *Eccles. Cyclop.*; Eden, *Theol. Dict.*; Farrar, *Eccles. Dict.*; Burnet, *Ref.* i, 459, 586; iii, 624; *Amer. Theol. Rev.* Feb. 1860, p. 172; *Bib. Sacra*, 1865, p. 350; 1863, p. 891.

Necessitarians, an appellation which may be given to all who maintain that moral agents act from necessity. See the article NECESSITY. Some object not only to the name, but to the dispute on a subject so perplexing as the explanation of the most consistent mode of divine government, and insist that the theme should be left entirely to the future sphere, where even the truth, according to Milton, has never yet dawned. Says the poet:

"Others apart sat on a hill retired,
In thoughts more elevate, and reason'd high
Of providence, foreknowledge, will, and fate,
Fixed fate, free-will, foreknowledge absolute;
And found *no end—in wandering mazes lost!*"

Dr. Watts thinks it probable that the discussion of this subject will constitute one of the sublime employments of the blessed in the heavenly world.

Necessity, DOCTRINE OF. I. *Definition.*—In metaphysics, according to the common statement, "necessity" is that quality of a thing by which it cannot but be, or whereby it cannot be otherwise. When in a proposition which affirms anything to be true there is a fixed invariable connection between the subject and the predicate, then that thing is understood to be necessary. Necessity is opposed to chance, accident, contingency, and to whatever involves the idea of uncertainty and of possible variation. It is usually distinguished in philosophy and theology into physical, metaphysical or logical, and moral.

1. *Physical* necessity has its origin in the established order and laws of the material universe. It is founded in the relation of cause and effect, and implies that where certain causes or forces are present certain effects must uniformly and inevitably follow. "By natural [or physical] necessity, as applied to men," says Edwards, "I mean such necessity as men are under through the force of natural causes. Thus men placed in certain circumstances are the subjects of particular sensations by necessity; they feel pain when their bodies are wounded; they see the objects presented before them in a clear light when their eyes are opened; so by a natural necessity men's bodies move downwards when there is nothing to support them" (*Works*, ii, 13, Carter's ed.).

2. *Metaphysical* or *logical* necessity expresses "the nature of our belief in certain fundamental truths, such as the reality of a material world, the law of causation, and the axioms of mathematics." Logical necessity is characteristic of truths or ideas, as physical necessity is of events or phenomena in the material world. "It is alleged by some philosophers that the truths held by us as most certain are the result of experience. Others contend that such first principles as the axioms of mathematics are not only true, but *necessarily* true; we not only do believe them, but we *must* believe them. Such necessity, it is argued, cannot come from mere experience, and therefore implies an innate or intuitive source. Hence the theory of necessary truth is only another name for the theory of intuitive truth." This necessity, as characteristic of certain truths, may be grounded in the impossibility of conceiving the opposite to be true. Thus Dr. Whewell, in his *Philosophy of the Inductive Sciences* (i, 54, 55), teaches that necessary truths are those in which we not only learn that the proposition *is* true, but see that it *must* be true; in which the negation of the truth is not only false, but impossible. That there are such truths cannot be doubted. We may take, for example, all relations of number. We cannot, by any freak of thought, imagine three and two to make seven. John Stuart Mill, in his *System of Logic*, argues against the theory of necessary truths, especially that the common mathematical axioms are such truths. Dr. Samuel Clarke, in his argument for the existence of God, reasons from a belief in the existence of the Divine Being being necessary in this sense. "So," says Edwards, "the eternal existence of being, generally considered, is necessary in it-

self, because it would be in itself the greatest absurdity to deny the existence of being in general, or to say there was absolute and universal nothing" (*Works*, ii, 11). Besides the meaning of the term necessary in connection with intuitive, or *à priori* truths, the truth of a statement is sometimes said to be necessary by reason of its being implied in another. "Thus if we say that all the apostles were Jews, it follows necessarily that Peter was a Jew." Here is involved the general axiom of syllogistic reasoning that what is true of a whole class is true of each individual, which axiom may be itself an intuitive or necessary truth. But each particular proposition or conclusion from premises is necessary, because it is *implied* in the premises, or because "to withhold assent from it would be to violate the above axiom." This is, more strictly, *logical* necessity. See LOGIC.

3. *Moral necessity* has reference to the volitions and actions of rational agents, and is intended to express the connection between these volitions and actions and certain moral causes, as inclinations, desires, or motives generally. Whether there be any connection which, strictly speaking, may be termed necessary between such motives and the volitions and actions of men, or whether independent of them the will has a self-determining power, is an inquiry which has always largely engaged the attention of both philosophers and theologians. See WILL. The term which stands opposed to necessity in the history and literature of the subject is liberty, or freedom. See LIBERTY.

The consciousness of mankind in general, the Christian consciousness especially, has always asserted the fact of freedom, even in connection often with theories that have been called theories of necessity. The freedom of the will was strongly and almost universally affirmed, with little or no qualification or psychological analysis, as the doctrine of the Church during the ante-Nicene period. "All the Greek fathers, as well as the apologists Justin Martyr, Tatian, and Athenagoras, also the theologians of the Alexandrian school, Clement and Origen, exalt the autonomy, self-determination (αὐτε-ξούσιον) of the human soul with the freshness of youth and a tincture of Hellenistic idealism, but also influenced by a practical Christian interest" (Hagenbach, *Hist. of Doct.* i, 155). With this the Platonic and Aristotelian philosophy was in harmony. Its ethics presupposes freedom. The forms in which the idea of necessity appears in the early history of philosophy, and in the popular sentiment of the first Christian centuries, are those of materialism and fatalism.

II. *Historical Development of the Necessitarian Idea.*—
1. In the early Greek philosophy we find all things—the cosmos—subjected to a materialistic necessity, of which the conceptions of matter and mind peculiar to the materialistic philosophy of the present day are in some measure a reproduction. Heraclitus (about B.C. 500) "assumes as the substantial principle of things ethereal fire," identifies it with the Divine Spirit, the λόγος, or the eternal all - embracing order, which is according to him immanent, as the universal principle of the constant flux of all things. Democritus, with his theory of atoms, according to which "the soul consists of fire, smooth and round atoms, which are also atoms of fire," held that the motion or rest of the atoms is not due to "an all-ruling Mind," but to natural necessity. The Stoics reproduced the doctrine of Heraclitus, affirming matter and force as two ultimate principles, that the working force in the universe is God, "that the rise and decay of the world are controlled by an absolute necessity; this necessity is at once fate (εἱμαρμένη) and the providence (πρόνοια) which governs all things. In the human soul, which is a part of the Deity, or an emanation from the same, is a governing force (τὸ ἡγεμονικόν), to which belong representation, desires, and understanding." As the attention of these philosophers was directed mainly to the universe of nature instead of man, making their philosophy cosmological rather than an-

thropological, they seem not to have attempted any special explanation of the phenomena of volition, or any logically rigorous application of their doctrines of necessity to the working of the human will. In their ethics they speak of men's action as if they were free. Heraclitus "calls upon each individual to follow in his thought and action the universal reason." Democritus says, "Not the act as such, but the will determines moral character." "The Sage alone is free; he is lord also over his own life, and can lawfully bring it to an end according to his own free self-determination." Later, in the more theological Greek philosophy, as that of Philo, "God alone is free; everything finite is involved in necessity." In the less philosophical and more popular thought of the time, human action was sometimes viewed as under the control of a fate which stands in some magical way in intimate connection with the stars, or with other objects in nature. Such views were held by some of the Gnostics.

2. In the more special and systematic treatment of Christian doctrines following the Council of Nice, the theologians undertook to harmonize the doctrines of the freedom of the will and divine predestination and foreknowledge. The heathen philosophy already noticed, in attempting to be theological, had so conceived of the Divine Being in relation to the world as to bring both men and things under a necessity, physical or fatalistic. Christianity, much more decidedly theological, now undertook to give a philosophy of God's relations to human action. In the controversy on the freedom of the will between Augustine and the Pelagians, the point of dispute was the relation of the will in its activity to the grace of God. Freedom was affirmed on both sides, each asserting that its own was the true idea of freedom. The differences consist in the degree and manner of influence upon the soul ascribed to divine grace. The views of Augustine are historically of much importance in the presentation of this subject, as they have formed the basis of the Calvinistic view in modern times. "This general view has been designated a theory of necessity, though its adherents object to the term as ambiguous and misleading. Augustine looked upon grace as the active principle of life, generating as an abiding good that freedom of the will which is entirely lost in the natural man." Pelagius admitted that man stands in need of divine aid; "but he supposed this grace of God to be something external, and added to the efforts put forth by the free-will of man." "He has not the conception of a life unfolding itself; he only recognises the mechanical concatenation of single acts." Augustine "recognises in the grace of God an inspiration of love (*inspiratio dilectionis*), and considers this the source of everything. It was not the view of Augustine that man is like a stone or stick, upon whom grace works externally; he could conceive of grace as working only in the sphere of freedom" (Hagenbach, *Hist. of Doctrines* i, 301, 302). In accordance with the idea and definition of the will and its freedom, which distinguishes the Latin from the Greek anthropology (comp. Shedd, *Hist. of Doct.* i, 61), Augustine's idea of freedom is *self*-determination, as distinguished from *in*determination. In his view the activity of the will proceeds purely from within the man himself, and this is freedom. In all the conditions in which he contemplates man—namely, as unfallen, as fallen, and as renewed—there is self-determination, that is, the "human will moves towards a proposed end by its own self-motion." The will is free in evil, even when by virtue of the moral condition of the man it can will nothing else but evil, because it delights in evil. Hence in the will of Adam, as created, there was an inclination to holiness, but at the same time also, united with it, the possibility of sinning (*possibilitas peccandi*). In the fallen Adam, the activity of the will is inclination to sin, "the unforced, free, self-originating, self-moved energy of the creature." It is freedom in sin, but at the same time a necessity or certainty of sinning. In the renewed, or in those in whom

there is any holy activity, the motion or determination of the will from the very beginning is conditioned upon the grace of God working in the soul in some wonderful hidden way ("interna et occulta, mirabili ac ineffabili potestate") to produce voluntary action in holiness. This is the truest freedom, and its highest development consists in the *non posse peccare*, the *felix necessitas boni*. This grace Augustine designates as irresistible. "By this he meant, not that the human will is converted unwillingly or by compulsion, but that the divine grace is able to overcome the utmost obstinacy of the human spirit" (Shedd, *Hist. of Doct.* i, 73). Augustine's idea and explanation of the activity of the will are from the theological point of view rather than the psychological.

In the scholastic period, as two representatives of its views, we may mention Thomas Aquinas on the one hand, and Duns Scotus on the other. Aquinas held that "the will depends upon the understanding; that which appears good is necessarily sought after; but necessity arising from internal causes, and reposing on knowledge, is freedom." The will is not subject to the necessity of compulsion, but to that necessity which does not destroy freedom—the necessity of striving after ends. Duns Scotus maintained, on the contrary, that "the human will is not determined by the understanding, but has power to choose with no determining ground."

In the German mysticism, which grew up in the 13th and 14th centuries out of scholasticism, the will was treated as subordinate to the knowing faculty, and extreme emphasis was laid on the presence in the divine nature of the element of natural necessity. "True union with God takes place in cognition; knowledge, which is God's action in man, is the foundation of all essence, the ground of love, the determining power of the will."

3. With the decline of scholasticism, and the rise of the spirit of the Reformation, the views of the phenomena of volition are modified by the fact that philosophy becomes more independent of the current theology in its interpretation of the universe of nature and mind. But in their views and methods they largely influence each other. Des Cartes emphasized human freedom; but, as according to his theory the will has no power of itself over the body, his disciples, as Malebranche, introduced the doctrine of Occasionalism—that God by his direct agency moves the body in accordance with our will. Spinoza, developing and transforming the Cartesian dualism into a pantheism, making God the immanent cause of the totality of finite things, holds that God works according to the inner necessity of his nature, in which consists his freedom; that he produces all finite effects only indirectly through finite causes; that there is no such thing as human freedom independent of causality, but that all events, including all acts of volition, are determined by God, though through finite causes, and not immediately. In the seventh definition of his Ethics he defines freedom and necessity as follows: "That thing is called free which exists by the sole necessity of its nature, and the determining cause of whose activity is in itself alone. But that is called necessary, or rather constrained, which owes its existence to another, and whose activity is the result of fixed and determinable causes." Spinoza's idea of free agency differs but little from that of Augustine, as being self-determination; and he "rightly seeks for the proper opposite of freedom, not in necessity taken generally, but in a distinct kind of necessity, namely, constraint, which is to be defined as necessity having its source, not in the nature of the subject of constraint, but in something foreign to that nature (whether in the internal or external world), and overruling the endeavors to which that nature itself gives rise" (Ueberweg, *Hist. of Phil.* ii, 68). Leibnitz, whose philosophy, like that of Des Cartes and Spinoza, was fundamentally theistic, maintained the power of self-determination in the soul; that "freedom, not as an exemption from law, but as the power of de-

VI.—29*

ciding for one's self according to known law, belongs to the essence of the human spirit;" but in place of the natural operation of the spirit upon or through the body, and of the occasionalism of Des Cartes's disciples, Leibnitz substituted the theory of pre-established harmony, "that God, at the beginning, so created soul and body that, while each follows the law of its internal development with perfect independence, each remains at the same time at every instant in perfect agreement." Kant's doctrine of the activity of the will as presented in his *Critique of the Practical Reason*, is given by Ueberweg as follows: "Kant defines the word *maxim* as denoting a subjective principle of willing; the objective principle, on the contrary, which is founded in the reason itself, is termed by him the *practical law;* he includes both together under the conception of the practical *principle*, i. e. a principle which contains a universal determination of the will, involving several practical rules. All the ends to which *desire* may be directed furnish sensuous and egotistic motives for the will, all reducible to the principle of personal happiness or self-love. But a rational being, on the other hand, in so far as he is rational, conceives his practical universal laws as principles, which are fitted to direct the will, not by their matter, but only in view of their form. The will which is determined by the mere form of universal law is independent of the law of sensible phenomena, and therefore free. A free will can only be determined by the mere form of a maxim, or by its fitness to serve as a universal law. Hence his categorical imperative of morals. Self-determination in conformity to the categorical imperative he terms 'autonomy of the will.' The opposite of this is the 'heteronomy of arbitrary choice.' Thus in the moral law, or categorical imperative, he finds a law of causality through freedom. The conception of cause is here employed only with practical intent, the determining motive of the will being found in the intelligible order of things. The freedom which man has as a personal being, not subject to the universal mechanism of nature, is the faculty of being subject to peculiar practical laws, given by his own reason; in other words, every person is subject to the conditions of his own personality." Developments, somewhat diverse from these views of Kant, are found in the philosophy of J. G. Fichte, raising self-determination to a creative activity of the Ego; in that of Schelling, who held "that only in God is man capable of freedom, that the freedom of man was exercised in an intelligible act done before time, that as an empirical being man is subject to necessity resting on his non-temporal self-determination;" in that of Hegel, in his philosophy of spirit, the development of which "is the gradual advance from natural determinateness to freedom, through the *momenta* of subjective, objective, and absolute spirit;" in the philosophy and theology of Schleiermacher, who made prominent the feeling of freedom in connection with the feeling of dependence; in the philosophy of Schopenhauer, in which motives are one of the forms of causality, the action of which is known not only from without, but from within, so that we learn by experience the mystery of the production of effects by causes in its innermost nature; in the philosophy of Herbart (1776–1841), defined by himself as "the elaboration of conceptions," according to which freedom of the will is the assured supremacy of the strongest masses of ideas over single affections or impressions; and in that of Beneke, who reduced all the phenomena of self-consciousness to four fundamental processes, under which certain feelings and judgments arise regarding the comparative worth of processes, which feelings and judgments control the tendencies of the moral agent and determine the will, so that "moral freedom consists in such a decided preponderance, and such a firm establishment of the moral nature in man, that his volition and action are determined by it alone." These views are necessitarian in general, in the sense that the volitions, or choices, and actions, are regarded as determined by, or in accordance with, reasons, motives, principles, desires, feelings, judgments, or, in general, certain prevolitional conditions.

In England as on the Continent the impulse accompanying the Reformation occasioned a freer and more prolific discussion of the freedom of the will among other theological and philosophical topics. In the empirical method of Bacon, and its decided direction of the attention to physical sciences, we have a line of thought, the tendency of which was to reduce the phenomena of volition to some law either *analogous* to the law of cause and effect observed in physical phenomena, or *identical* with it, and a part of it, giving a physical or materialistic necessity. Hobbes plainly declares that the activity of the will is from necessary causes, and he does not distinguish this necessity from ordinary physical causation. See LIBERTY. Locke, in the first edition of his *Essay*, asserts the necessitarianism of Hobbes. "In later editions a power to suspend the determinations of the will is accorded." "That which immediately determines the will from time to time," he says, "to every voluntary act is the uneasiness of desire, fixed on some absent good." In 1715 appeared Anthony Collins's argument for necessity. He states his view thus: "First, though I deny liberty in a certain meaning of the word, yet I contend for liberty as it signifies a power in man to do as he wills or pleases. Secondly, when I affirm necessity, I contend only for moral necessity, meaning thereby that man, who is an intelligent and sensible being, is determined by his reason and his senses; and I deny man to be subject to such necessity as is in clocks, watches, and such other things, which for want of sensation and intelligence are subject to an absolute physical or mechanical necessity." Dr. Samuel Clarke replied to Collins, affirming "that all proper action of the soul is *ipso facto* free action; that the laws which determine the judgment of the understanding next preceding any activity are diverse from those which pertain to the production of the action itself." Hartley followed Collins in his theory of the will, modifying it, however, by his peculiar doctrine of medullary vibrations, and the action of the soul dependent upon them by association. He thus in a measure anticipated the physiological and associational psychology of James Mill, John Stuart Mill, Bain, and Herbert Spencer. The necessitarians found their most effective champion in Priestley, who took up the materialistic theories and deduced from them their logical consequence, which he called a "philosophical" necessity. According to John Stuart Mill, "the law of causality applies in the same strict sense to human actions as to other phenomena." "Correctly conceived," he says, "the doctrine of Philosophical Necessity is simply this: that given the motives which are present to an individual's mind, and given likewise the character and disposition of the individual, the manner in which he will act may be unerringly inferred" (*System of Logic*, ii, 405, 406). He allows at the same time a power in the mind to co-operate in the formation of its own character, and complains of the application of the term necessity to the doctrine of cause and effect in human character as improper. But causation with him means "nothing but invariable, certain, and unconditional sequence," with no "mysterious constraint or compulsion" in the cause over the effect. Alexander Bain considers the will as "a collective term for all the impulses to motion or action. It is absurd to ask whether such a power is free." Dr. Reid (1710–1796), in opposition to the various forms of necessity, denies that every action is performed with some view or from some motive. Dugald Stewart, however, concedes "that for every action there must be a motive;" but maintains that "liberty as opposed to necessity means that the connection between motives and actions is not a necessary connection like that between cause and effect." "The question," he says, "is not concerning the *influence* of motives, but concerning the *nature* of that influence." This is most truly the pivotal point

of the whole controversy. For the opinions of Hamilton and Mansel, see LIBERTY.

4. In this country a fresh theological importance was given to this subject by Jonathan Edwards, who based his theory of voluntary action on the doctrine of moral necessity, taking pains to distinguish it from natural or physical necessity. See LIBERTY. His treatise was directed against the doctrine of the self-determining power of the will as advocated by Arminian writers, endeavoring to prove at the same time that this necessity was not inconsistent with liberty. This moral necessity he defines as "that necessity of connection and consequence which arises from such moral causes as the strength of inclinations or motives, and the connection which there is in many cases between these and such certain volitions and actions" (*Works*, ii, 13). One great purpose in his work was to reply to the objection that the Calvinistic notions of God's moral government are contrary to the common-sense of mankind. Freedom, as involving the self-determining power of the Arminians, he argued, would involve contingency and the absence of certainty. This would exclude foreknowledge. The views of Edwards have been modified, and controverted even, by Calvinistic theologians. The term moral necessity is still used to characterize the theories of those who affirm that the will is determined or determines itself under the influence of motives, as distinguished from the theories of those who affirm a "power to the contrary," or "the power or immunity to put forth in the same circumstances either of several volitions," or such an independence of motives as to make the action of the agent contingent and uncertain, and not certainly or necessarily determined by them. It is applied also to the theories of those who hold to Augustinian and Calvinistic views of the operation of divine grace upon the will. In general they object, and it is acknowledged with justice in some respects, to the term necessity as confusing, and in its associations implying ideas which they disown, since they assert the freedom of the will as the condition of moral obligation and moral divine government. Some, as Dr. Hodge, propose and use the term certainty, as distinguished from necessity on the one hand and contingency on the other. Dr. Hodge teaches that freedom consists in the fact that a man's "volitions are truly and properly his own, determined by nothing out of himself, but proceeding from his own views, feelings, and innermost dispositions, so that they are the real, intelligent, and conscious expression of his character, or of what is in his mind." "We hold," says Dr. M'Cosh, "that the principle of cause and effect reigns in mind as in matter. But there is an important difference between the manner in which this principle operates in body and in spirit. In all proper mental operations the causes and the effects lie both within the mind. Mind is self-acting substance. We hold that the true determining cause of every given volition is not any mere anterior incitement, but the very soul itself by its inherent power of will."

III. *Objections to this Theory.*—The anti-necessitarians notwithstanding allege that the doctrine of necessity, in the light of these various interpretations of Calvinistic theologians, "charges God as the author of sin; that it takes away the freedom of the will; renders man unaccountable to his Maker; makes sin to be no evil, and morality or virtue to be no good; and that it precludes the use of means, and is of the most gloomy tendency. The necessitarians, on the other hand, deny these to be legitimate consequences of their doctrine, which they declare to be the most consistent mode of explaining the divine government; and they observe that the Deity acts no more immorally in decreeing vicious actions than in permitting all those irregularities which he could so easily have prevented. All necessity, say they, does not take away freedom. "The actions of a man may be at one and the same time both free and necessary. Thus it was infallibly certain that Judas would betray Christ, yet he did it voluntarily; Jesus Christ necessarily [?] became man, and died, yet he acted freely. A good man does naturally and necessarily love his children, yet voluntarily. They insist that necessity does not render actions less morally good; for, if necessary virtue be neither moral nor praiseworthy, it will follow that God himself is not a moral being, because he is a necessary one [i. e. necessarily such; rather such by nature]; and the obedience of Christ cannot be good, because it was necessary [?]. Further, say they, necessity does not preclude the use of means; for means are no less appointed than the end. It was ordained that Christ should be delivered up to death; but he could not have been betrayed without a betrayer, nor crucified without crucifiers." That it is not a gloomy doctrine, they allege, because nothing can be more consolatory than to believe that all things are under the direction of an all-wise Being, that his kingdom ruleth over all, and that he doeth all things well. They also urge that to deny necessity is to deny the foreknowledge of God, and to wrest the sceptre from the hand of the Creator, and to place that capricious and undefinable principle, the self-determining power of man, upon the throne of the universe. In these statements there is obviously a confused use of terms in different meanings, so as to mislead the unwary. For instance, *necessity* is confounded with *certainty;* but an action may be certain, though free—that is to say, certain to an omniscient Being, who knows how a free agent will finally resolve; but this certainty is, in fact, a quality of the prescient Being, not that of the action, to which, however, men delusively transfer it. Again: God is called a necessary Being, which, if it mean anything, signifies, as to his moral acts, that he can only act right. But then this is a wrong application of the term necessity, which properly implies such a constraint upon actions, exercised *ab extra,* as renders choice or will impossible. But such necessity cannot exist as to the Supreme Being. Again: the obedience of Christ unto death was necessary—that is to say, unless he had died, guilty man could not have been forgiven; but this could not make the act of the Jews who put him to death a necessary act —that is to say, a forced and constrained one; nor did this necessity affect the act of Christ himself, who acted voluntarily, and might have left man without salvation. That the Jews acted *freely* is evident from their being held liable to punishment, although unconsciously they accomplished the great designs of heaven, which, however, was no excuse for their crime. Finally: as to the allegation that the doctrine of free agency puts man's self-determining power upon the throne of the universe, that view proceeds upon notions unworthy of God, as if he could not accomplish his plans without compelling and controlling all things by a fixed fate; whereas it is both more glorious to him, and certainly more in accordance with the Scriptures, to say that he has a perfect foresight of the manner in which all creatures will act, and that he, by a profound and infinite wisdom, subordinates everything without violence to the evolution and accomplishment of his own glorious purposes.

"The doctrine of necessity is nearly connected with that of predestination, which of late years has assumed a form very different from that which it formerly possessed; for, instead of being considered as a point to be determined almost entirely by the sacred writings, it has, in the hands of a number of able writers, in a great measure resolved itself into a question of natural religion, under the head of the philosophical liberty or necessity of the will; or, whether all human actions are or are not necessarily determined by motives arising from the character which God has impressed on our minds, and the train of circumstances amid which his providence has placed us? The Calvinistic doctrine of predestination is that 'God, for his own glory, hath foreordained whatsoever comes to pass.' The scheme of philosophical necessity, as stated by the most celebrated necessitarian of the age, is, 'that everything is predetermined by the Divine Being; that whatever has been, must have been; and that whatever will be, must be; that all events are preordained by infinite wisdom and unlimited goodness; that the will, in all its determinations, is governed by the state of mind; that the state of mind is in every instance determined by the Deity; and that there is a continued chain of causes and effects, of motives and actions, inseparably connected, and originating from the condition in which we are brought into existence by the Author of our being.' On the other hand, it is justly remarked that 'those who believe the being and perfections of God, and a state of retribution, in which he will reward and punish mankind according to the diversity of their actions, will find it difficult to reconcile the justice of punishment with the necessity of crimes punished. And they that believe all that the Scripture says on the one hand of the eternity of future punishments, and on the other of God's compassion to sinners, and his solemn assurance that he desires not their death, will find the difficulty greatly increased.' It is doubtless an article of the Christian faith that God will reward or punish every man hereafter according to his actions in this life. But we cannot maintain his justice in this particular, if men's actions be necessary either in their own nature or by the divine decrees. Activity and self-determining powers are the foundation of all morality; and to prove that such powers belong to man, it is urged that we ourselves are conscious of possessing them. We blame and condemn ourselves when we do amiss; but guilt, and inward sense of shame, and remorse of conscience are feelings which are inconsistent with the scheme of necessity. It is also agreed that some actions deserve praise, and afford an inward satisfaction; but for this there would be no foundation, if we were invincibly determined in every volition: so that approbation and blame are consequent on free actions only. Nor is the matter at all relieved by bringing in a chain of circumstances as motives necessarily to determine the will. This comes to the same result in sound argument as if there was an immediate *co-action* of omnipotent power compelling one kind of volitions only; which is utterly irreconcilable to all just notions of the nature and operations of will, and to all accountability. Necessity, in the sense of irresistible control, and the doctrine of Scripture, cannot coexist."

IV. *Roman Catholic* theologians recognise also two other kinds of necessity, namely, a necessity of means, and a necessity of precept. Baptism they consider as a necessity of means, or absolute necessity, because it is the only means of salvation instituted by Christ; so that no one can be saved who has not been baptized, whether it be by his own fault or not. Communion is only a necessity of precept. If a man voluntarily refuses to participate in the Lord's Supper, he is deserving of condemnation; but if he was only involuntarily deprived of participating in it, he is not guilty.

See Priestley, *A Free Discussion of the Doctrines of Materialism and Philosophical Necessity* (Lond. 1778, 8vo); Bray, *Philosophy of Necessity;* Clarke, *Boyle Lectures* for 1704; Crombie, *Essay on Philos. Necessity;* Toplady, *On Christian and Philos. Necessity;* Butler, *Analogy,* ch. vi; Copleston, *Inquiry into the Doctrine of N. Graves on Calvinistic Predestination;* Jackson, *Defence of Human Liberty;* Tucker, *Light of Nature;* Watson, *Theol. Institutes,* ii, 350; Hodge, *Christian Theology* (see Index); *Amer. Theol. Rev.* Jan. 1860; Oct. 1861; *Amer. Presb. and Theol. Rev.* Jan. 1865; *North British Rev.* vol. x; and the literature under WILL.

Necham, Neckham, or **Nequam,** ALEXANDER, an English monk, noted as a universal scholar, a proficient in the whole circle of science, including canon law, medicine, and theology, was born at St. Albans in 1157; lived and studied at Paris, and after his return to his native country was made abbot of Cirencester, and died in 1217. He is the author of a great variety of works remaining in MS. But the most important of all his productions, including many theological and philosophical works, is his *De Naturis Rerum*, which is believed to have had quite a large circulation towards the close of the 12th century. It has recently been edited and published by the noted English antiquarian, Thomas Wright, who has written much about Necham in the *Biog. Brit. Lit.* (Anglo-Norman Period), p. 449–50. The *De Naturis Rerum* (Lond. 1863) aims to interest the student of nature in the Author of nature. It is iconoclastic in tendency, and rejects the aid of art in religious ceremonies. See, besides Wright, *Biog. Brit. Lit.*, Piper, *Einleitung in die Monumentale Theologie*, p. 557–59; Cave, *Historia Literaria*, s. v.

Ne'cho (Heb. *Neko'*, נְכוֹ, an Egyptian name; Sept. and Josephus, Νεχαώ; fully פַּרְעֹה נְכוֹ, *Pharaoh-Necho*, 2 Kings xxiii, 29, 33, 34, 35, etc.; once Heb. נְכֹה, *Nekoh'*, Jer. xlvi, 2; Herodotus, Νεκώς; on the twofold appellation of this king on the monuments, see

Hieroglyph of Necho.

Rosellini, *Monum. Stor.* ii, 131 sq., tab. 9), an Egyptian king, son and successor (according to Herodotus, ii, 158) of Psammetichus, and contemporary of the Jewish king Josiah (B.C. 609). The wars and successes of Pharaoh-Necho in Syria are recorded by sacred as well as profane writers, affording a striking instance of agreement between them. On coming to the throne he organized powerful fleets on the Mediterranean and the Red Sea. Having engaged some Phœnician sailors, he sent them on a voyage of discovery along the coasts of Africa. According to Herodotus (iv, 42, 3), they circumnavigated that continent from the Arabian Gulf by the Pillars of Hercules (Gibraltar) to Egypt, and related that in the south they had the sun on their right hand, which that historian could not believe. Most modern writers consider this testimony sufficient, and the voyage attested (see Grote, *Hist. of Greece*, iii, 283 sq.; Beck, *Welt-Gesch.* i, 595 sq.; comp. Pliny, *Hist. Nat.* ii, 67; Arrian, *Rer. Ind.* ad fin.). Necho undertook to check the growth of Babylonian power, and with this view collected a powerful army, and entering Palestine, followed the route along the sea-coast of Judæa, intending to besiege the town of Carchemish on the Euphrates. But Josiah, king of Judah, offended at the passage of the Egyptian army through his territories, resolved to impede, if unable to prevent, their march. Necho sent messengers to induce him to desist, assuring him that he had no hostile intentions against Judæa, "but against the house wherewith I have war; for God commanded me to make haste." This conciliatory message was of no avail. Josiah posted himself in the valley of Megiddo, and prepared to oppose the Egyptians. Megiddo was a city in the tribe of Manasseh, between forty and fifty miles to the north of Jerusalem, and within three hours of the coast. It is apparently confounded by Herodotus with Magdolus in Egypt. In this valley the feeble forces of the Jewish king, having attacked Necho, were routed with great slaughter. Josiah being wounded in the neck with an arrow, ordered his attendants to take him from the field. Escaping from the heavy shower of arrows with which their broken ranks were overwhelmed, they removed him from the chariot in which he had been wounded, and placing him in a "second one that he had," they conveyed him to Jerusalem, where he died (2 Kings xxiii, 29, 30; 2 Chron. xxxv, 20 sq.). See JOSIAH. Necho continued his march to the Euphrates. But three months had scarcely elapsed when, returning from the capture of Carchemish and the defeat of the Chaldæans, he learned that, though Josiah had left an elder son, Jehoahaz had caused himself to be proclaimed king on the death of his father, without soliciting Necho to sanction his taking the crown. Incensed at this, he deposed Jehoahaz

(apparently having summoned him to Riblah), and carried him a prisoner to Jerusalem. On arriving there, Necho made Eliakim, the eldest son, king, changing his name to Jehoiakim; and taking the silver and gold which had been levied upon the Jewish nation, he returned to Egypt with the captive Jehoahaz, who there died (2 Kings xxiii, 31 sq.; 2 Chron. xxxvi, 1-4). Herodotus says that Necho, after having routed the Syrians (the Jews) at Magdolus, took Cadytis, a large city of Syria, in Palestine, which, he adds, is very little less than Sardis (ii, 159; iii, 5). By Cadytis there is scarcely a doubt he meant Jerusalem; the word is only a Greek form of the ancient, as well as the modern, name of that city. In the fourth year after this expedition Necho again marched into Syria, and advanced to the Euphrates. Here Nebuchadnezzar completely routed his army, recovered the town of Carchemish, and, pushing his conquests through Palestine, took from Necho all the territory belonging to the Pharaohs, from the Euphrates to the southern extremity of Syria (2 Kings xxiv, 7, 8; Jer. xlvi, 2; 2 Chron. xxxvi, 9). See NEBUCHADNEZZAR. Necho soon after died, and was succeeded by Psammetichus II (Wilkinson's *Anc. Egyptians*, i, 157 sq.). See EGYPT. According to Manetho (Euseb. *Chron. Armen.* i, 219), Necho was the sixth king in the twenty-sixth dynasty, successor of Psammetichus, and as there had been another of the same name, he was properly Necho the Second. The period of his reign was, according to Manetho, six, according to Herodotus sixteen, years (consult Gesenius, *Jesaia*, i, 596). See Larcher, *Ad Herod.* ii, 158 sq.; iv, 42; Diod. i, 33, and Wess. ad loc.; Strabo, i, 56; Heeren, *African Nat.* ii, 374, 389; Bunsen, *Ægyptens Stelle in der Welt-Geschichte*, iii, 141 sq. See PHARAOH.

Nechites. See NICITAS.

Nechosheth. See BRASS; COPPER.

Nechunjah BEN-HA-KANAH, a famous rabbin at Jamnia, who, like his contemporary Nahum of Gimso (q. v.), had a school and method of his own, was a disciple of Hillel (q. v.), and a contemporary and equal colleague of Jochanan ben-Zachai (q. v.). Nechunjah strictly adhered to his teacher's method of Biblical interpretation, and decidedly opposed Nahum's additional rule of "extension and restriction." He was of a mild and compliant character, and is said to have chiefly occupied himself with mystical theology. So much was this the case, that later tradition ascribed the composition of the oldest cabalistic works to him or to his father, viz., the books *Bahir* (סֵ׳ הַבָּהִיר) and *Peliah* (סֵ׳ הַפְּלִיאָה), which, however, belong to a later time. Like his colleague, Jochanan ben-Zachai, Nechunjah reached a good old age. Himself a living protest against the supposed worldliness of some of his contemporaries, his recorded motto was, "Every one who takes upon himself the yoke of the law is set free from the yoke of the kingdom and the yoke of conformity to the world; but to every one who discards the yoke of the law shall be given the yoke of the kingdom and the yoke of the fashions of this world" (*Aboth*, iii, 5). It is interesting to notice that Nechunjah was one of the few who were wont to ejaculate a short prayer both when entering the college and again when leaving it. He assigned the following reasons for this unusual practice: "When I enter," he said, "I pray that I may not be the occasion of error; and when I leave I bless the Lord for my calling" (*Beracoth*, iv, 2). Later writers (Bartol. iv, 246, etc.) have, without sufficient reason, supposed that he became a convert to Christianity. Certainly both the ground and the objects of his prayers savor more of the pride of the Pharisee than of the spirit of the Christian. See Grätz, *Gesch. d. Juden* (Leipsic, 1866), iv, 22; Jost, *Gesch. d. Juden. u. s. Sekten*, ii, 26; De Rossi, *Dizionario storico* (Germ. transl.), p. 245; Edersheim, *History of the Jews*, p. 158; Etheridge, *Introd. to Hebrew Literature*, p. 65; Frankel, *Hodegetica in Mishnam* (Leipsic, 1859), p. 99. (B. P.)

Neck (usually עֹרֶף, *o'reph*, as Gen. xlix, 8; Lev. v, 8; often צַוָּאר, *tsavvar'*, as Gen. xxvii, 16; and same in Chald., as Dan. v, 7; once the plur. cognate צַוְּרֹנִים, Cant. iv, 9; also גָּרוֹן, *garôn'*, prop. *throat*, Isa. iii, 16; or the plur. cognate, גַּרְגְּרֹת, Prov. iii, 22; once מַפְרֶקֶת, *maphre'keth*, 1 Sam. iv, 18; Gr. τράχηλος), a part of the human frame used by the sacred writers with considerable variety and freedom in figurative expressions, though seldom in such a way as to occasion difficulty to a modern reader. With reference to the graceful ornament which a fine neck gives, especially to the female form, it is said of the spouse in the Canticles, "Thy neck is like the tower of David, builded for an armory" (iv, 4); or, as it is again, "like a tower of ivory" (vii, 4). The neck, however, being that part of the body through which in man, and still more in the lower animals, the life is frequently destroyed, it is sometimes taken as the representative of the animal life; hence "to lay down the neck" (Rom. xvi, 4) is a strong expression for hazarding one's life; to "give one the necks of one's enemies" (2 Sam. xxii, 41) was to surrender their life into his hands; also "to reach even to the neck," or "to the midst of the neck" (Isa. viii, 8; xxx, 28), was to approach the point of overwhelming destruction, which, in Hab. iii, 13, takes the peculiar form of "discovering the foundation to the neck"—the allusion in the last passage being to the foundation of a house, which is like the neck upon which the head rests. But by much the most common reference was to beasts of burden, which bore upon their neck the yoke whereby they did service, and as such were viewed as emblems of men in their relation either to a good or a bad, to a true or a false service. Christ invites all to "take up his yoke" (upon their neck understood), in other words, to yield themselves obediently to his authority (Matt. xi, 29); and a stiff or hardened neck is a familiar expression for an unpliant, rebellious spirit. In the contrary direction, many passages in the prophets convey threatenings of coming judgment by the hands of enemies under the form of laying bands or yokes upon the people's necks (Deut. xxviii, 48; Isa. x, 27; Jer. xxvii, 2). Hence putting the feet on the neck is a usual expres-

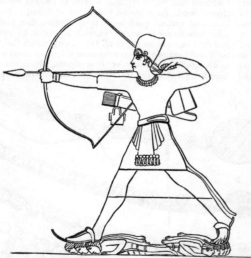

Ancient Egyptian treading the Conquered under Feet.

sion in the East for triumphing over a fallen foe. In the numerous battle-scenes depicted on the monuments of ancient Egypt and Assyria, we see the monarchs frequently represented treading on the necks of their enemies; and a similar practice obtained among the Hebrews. When Joshua had conquered the five kings, he "said unto the captains of the men of war which went

Darius trampling upon a Captive. (From the rock of Behistun [q. v.].)

with him, Come near, put your feet upon the necks of these kings. And they came near, and put their feet upon the necks of them" (Josh. x, 24; comp. 2 Sam. xxii, 41). In India, when people are disputing, should one be a little pressed, and the other begin to triumph, the former will say, "I will tread upon thy neck, and after that beat thee." A low caste man insulting one who is high is sure to hear some one say to the offended individual, "Put your feet on his neck." Nor was this custom peculiar to the East: Quintus Curtius, relating the particulars of a single combat between Dioxippus, an Athenian, and Horratus, a Macedonian, says that, in the end, the former, closing with the latter, struck up his heels, and threw him with great violence on the ground; then, after taking his sword from him, he *set his foot upon his neck*, and was about to dash out his brains, when the king (Alexander) interposed his authority to prevent him. See TRIUMPH.

Necker, JACQUES, an eminent financier and religious statesman, father of the noted French female writer, Madame de Staël, was born of distinguished parentage Sept. 30, 1732. He was sent to Paris in his youth, and was employed in the house of Thellusson, the great banker, who, after a time, took him into partnership. Necker realized a very large fortune, and retired from business at forty years of age. He now began to aspire to official situations, and wrote several works on financial affairs, which made him favorably known. One of these works, a memoir upon the French finances, suggesting the means of making up the deficiency in the revenue, and forwarded to the minister Maurepas, the president of the council of finances, so delighted this French statesman that he obtained for the author, from Louis XVI, after some hesitation, as Necker was an alien and a Protestant, the appointment of director of the treasury in 1776. Necker was appointed director-general of finances in June, 1777, but without a seat in the council; being averse to imposing new taxes, he endeavored to make up the national income by economy and loans. In 1781 he published his *Compte Rendu*, which disclosed for the first time the state of the revenue and expenditure of France, and made him numerous enemies, and he resigned in May, 1781. He withdrew to Switzerland, where he purchased an estate at Copet, on the banks of the Leman Lake, and there he wrote his work *Sur l'Administration des Finances*, 1784. In 1787 Necker returned to Paris, where he wrote against Calonne, who had just been dismissed from his office of comptroller-general of the finances, and he was in consequence banished from the capital, but was soon after recalled. In the following year (August, 1788), on the resignation of Brienne, and at the suggestion of that minister, Louis XVI appointed Necker director-general of finances, as the only man capable of restoring order in the administration. The king had already promised the convocation of the states-general, and Necker urged him to keep his promise. But he failed as a statesman in not arranging beforehand a plan for the sittings of those states, so as to prevent the collision that took place on their first meeting. In fact Necker was a financier, but not a statesman; he was a philosopher and a man of letters, but not a jurist or a legislator, and he was thus considered by a man well qualified to judge of these matters. His second ministry was short. Unable to check or direct the popular storm, and not enjoying the confidence of the court, Necker, unwilling to become the reproach of the agitators, quitted his place and the kingdom. On the 11th of July, 1789, he set off for Switzerland. After the taking of the Bastille, the National Assembly demanded the recall of Necker, and Louis complied. Necker was received in triumph, but his popularity was short-lived. He did not go far enough to please the movement-men. In December of the following year, 1790, he gave in his resignation to the National Assembly, which received it with cool indifference. He spent the remainder of his life in Switzerland, in retirement and study, and wrote several political tracts. He had written, several years before, a work, *De l'Importance des Opinions Religieuses* (translated into English under the title *Of the Importance of Religious Opinions* [London, 1788, 8vo]). This work is eminently able and serviceable to Christianity. In 1800 he published his last and greatest work on the religious view of morality. This work is highly esteemed, and secured a prominent rank for Necker as a moralist. He died April 9, 1804. His works were collected and published by his accomplished daughter in 15 vols. 8vo (1821). See Madame de Staël, *Vie privée de M. Jacques Necker* (1804–1821); Lanjuinais, *Études biograph. sur Antoine Arnauld, P. Nicole, et J. Necker* (1823); Sainte-Beuve, *Causeries du Lundi*, vii, 329 sq.; *Edinb. Rev.* Jan. 1803; *Engl. Cyclop.* s. v.; Darling, *Cycl. Bibliog.* ii, 2166.

Necker, *Madame*, née SUSANNAH CURCHOD, a noted French philanthropist, was born in 1739, in the mountain village of Grassy, situated between the Pays de Vaud and Franche-Comté. Her father, a pastor of the Swiss Church, was a man of considerable talents; her mother was descended from an ancient family of Provence, who had fled to Switzerland on the revocation of the Edict of Nantes. She was the wife of minister Necker, and she greatly distinguished herself during his terms of office in every possible form of benevolence. She erected a hospital in Paris with her own money, was a great reformer of prison abuses, and

surrounded herself with the most distinguished men of the time, among them Buffon, Diderot, D'Alembert, who offered her the homage due to her great learning and her rare goodness of heart. She died in 1795, the year after publishing her *Réflexions sur le Divorce* (Lausanne, 1794, 8vo), an elaborate plea for the indissolubility of marriage. Her complete writings were published by her husband in 5 vols. 8vo (1798–1801). See Gibbon, *Memoirs;* Marmontel, *Mémoires;* Barrère de Vieuzac, *Esprit de Madame Necker* (Paris, 1808, 8vo).

Neckere, LEO DE, D.D., an American Roman Catholic prelate who flourished in the first half of this century, was born about the close of the last century, and after taking holy orders rose rapidly to the most distinguished offices in the gift of the Church. He was consecrated bishop of New Orleans in 1829, and died September 4, 1833.

Necklace is a word that does not occur in the A.V. of the Bible, but represents a piece of personal ornament anciently, as well as still very commonly, worn by both sexes in Oriental countries. It seems to be specially denoted in Heb. by רָבִיד, *rabid'* (so called from *binding* the neck), a *collar* or ornamental "chain" for the neck (Gen. xli, 42; Ezek. xvi, 11). See CHAIN. Necklaces, we learn from the Scriptures, were made sometimes of silver and gold, sometimes of a series of jewels, sometimes of coral (Exod. xxxv, 22; Numb. xxxi, 50). Three necklaces were commonly worn, one reaching lower than the other; from the one that was suspended to the waist there was hung a bottle of perfume, filled with amber and musk, called כָּתֵּי נֶפֶשׁ, *bottey' néphesh,* "houses of the soul" (Isa. iii, 20, margin). See ATTIRE. Among the ancient Egyptians handsome and richly ornamented necklaces were a principal part of the dress, both of men and women; and some idea may be formed of the number of jewels they wore, from those borrowed by the Israelites at the time of the Exodus, and by the paintings of Thebes. They consisted of gold, or of beads of various qualities and shapes, disposed according to fancy, generally with a large drop or figure in the centre. Scarabæi, gold, and carnelian bottles, or the emblems of Goodness and Stability, lotus flowers in enamel, amethysts, pearls, false stones, imitations of fishes, frogs, lions, and various quadrupeds, birds, reptiles, flies, and other insects, shells and leaves, with numerous figures and devices, were strung in all the variety which their taste could suggest; and the museum of Leyden possesses an infinite assortment of those objects, which were once the pride of the ladies of Thebes. Some wore

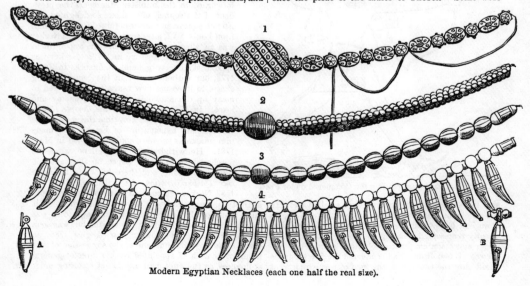

Modern Egyptian Necklaces (each one half the real size).

simple gold chains in imitation of string, to which a stone scarabæus, set in the same precious metal, was appended; but these probably belonged to men, like the *torques* of the Romans. A set of small cups, or covered saucers, of bronze gilt, hanging from a chain of the same materials, were sometimes worn by women, a necklace of which has been found belonging to a Theban lady — offering a striking contrast in their simplicity to the gold leaves inlaid with lapis lazuli, red and green stones, of another she wore, which served, with many more in her possession, to excite the admiration of her friends (Wilkinson, *Anc. Egyptians*, i, 339 sq.). The modern Egyptian ladies are equally fond of wearing necklaces, often of the richest description; the Arabic term for them is *ekd*, and the Egyptians have a great variety; but almost all of them are similar in the following particulars: 1. The beads, etc., of which they are composed are, altogether, not more than ten inches in length; so that they would not entirely encircle the neck if tied quite tight, which is never done: the string extends about six or seven inches beyond each extremity of the series of beads; and when the necklace is tied in the usual manner there is generally a space of three inches or more between these extremities; but the plaits of hair conceal these parts of the string. 2. There is generally, in the centre, one bead or other ornament (and sometimes there are three, or five, or seven) differing in size, form, material, or color from the others. The necklaces mostly worn by ladies are of diamonds or pearls. In the annexed engraving (p. 910), the first necklace is of diamonds set in gold. The second consists of several strings of pearls, with a pierced flattish emerald in the centre. Most of the pearl necklaces are of this description. The third is called *libbeh*. It is composed of hollow gold beads, with a bead of a different kind (sometimes of a precious stone, and sometimes of coral) in the centre. This and the following are seldom worn by any but females of the middle and lower orders. The fourth is called, from its peculiar form, *sha'ir* (which signifies "barley"). It is composed of hollow gold. We give a side view (A) and a back view (B) of one of the appendages of this necklace. There is also a long kind of

Ancient Egyptian Necklaces.

B is composed of small covered cups, of bronze gilt. I *b* is the other end of I *a*. These leaves are of gold, inlaid with lapis lazuli and green and red stones. M *a*, a sort of gold *torques* or chain, of which a stone scarabæus found in gold forms the centre ornament. U, in the possession of the late Mr. Madox. V W X Y Z, gold catches of necklaces, one sliding into the other.

necklace, reaching to the girdle, and composed of diamonds or other precious stones, which is called *kiládeh*. Some women form a long necklace of this kind with Venetian sequins, or Turkish or Egyptian gold coins (Lane, *Modern Egyptians*, ii, 405). The Arab females of Palestine at the present day are especially given to wearing necklaces composed of strings of gold coin, which are their own property, and cannot be taken even for debt (Thomson, *Land and Book*, i, 185). See ORNAMENT.

Neco'dan (Νεκωδάν, Vulg. *Nechodaïcus*), given (1 Esdr. v, 37) as the name of the head of one of the Israelitish families who had lost their pedigree in Babylon; in place of the NEKODA (q. v.) of the Heb. text (Ezra ii, 60).

Necrodeipnon (Gr. νεκρός, *dead*, and δεῖπνον, a *meal*) was the name of a funeral feast among the ancient Greeks. It commonly took place at the house of the nearest relative of the deceased, and was usually attended by all the friends and relatives, it being regarded as a sacred duty to be present on the mournful occasion. See MOURNING.

Necrology (from Gr. νεκρός, *dead*, and λόγος, *discourse*, or enumeration) is the name given in the Roman Catholic Church to a book anciently kept in churches and monasteries, wherein were registered the names of benefactors of such establishments, the time of their death, and the days of their commemoration; as also the deaths of the priors, abbots, religious canons, etc. This record was also called *Calendar* and *Obituary.* The name of Necrology was anciently given sometimes to what is now designated generally as *Martyrology* (q. v.).

When the diptychs fell into desuetude, necrologies, obituaries, books of the dead, books of annals or anniversaries, and books of life took their place as records in cathedrals and collegiate churches and minsters of the names of the deceased. The Benedictines adopted them at the beginning of the 6th century. When an abbot or distinguished monk died, a messenger, carrying a brief or roll, a kind of encyclical letter, rode to the various associated abbeys or churches to apprise them of his decease, and left a schedule containing his own name and that of the dead, and the date of his arrival. The new name was then inserted in the several obituaries. These were read after the martyrology at prime, but in a monastery after the rule. The names were recited on their several anniversaries, and in the case of a benefactor the *De profundis* and a special prayer were sung. The abbot was commemorated by the words, "The deposition of lord abbot N." All others had the simple affix "obiit," i. e. he died. First were read out the names of abbots, then monks, provosts, precentors, and in succession those of sacristans, bishops, priests, sovereigns, and soldiers. Saints were also included; and for convenience a single volume generally comprised the monastic rule, the martyrology, and obituary. The gifts of benefactors were often recited; but sometimes only a general commemoration of all brethren and familiars of the order was made, followed by the words, "Requiescat in pace"—may he rest in peace —uttered by the president, and closed by an "amen" chanted by the whole chapter. Cowell says that at the prayer of the prothesis the Greeks had their names inserted in the catalogue, and deposited a present in money, which formed a considerable portion of a country priest's income. See Walcott, *Sacred Archæology*, p. 396, 397; Martigny, *Dictionnaire des Antiquités Chrétiennes*, p. 432, 433; Martène, *De Antiq. Monach. ritib.* vol. i, pt. i, ch. v.

Necromancer (Heb. דֹּרֵשׁ אֶל־הַמֵּתִים, *one who inquires of the dead*; Sept. ἐπερωτῶν τοὺς νεκρούς). In many ancient nations there were jugglers who professed to be able by incantations to call up the dead from the under world, chiefly to consult them on the mysteries of the present or future. Already in Homer's time this practice had been introduced (see *Odys.* xi, 24 sq.); and the belief in such enchantments, notwithstanding the mockery of the better instructed few (Cicero, *Tusc.* i, 16, 37), kept its ground among the common people in pagan lands down to the latest times (comp. Plin. xxx, 5 sq.; Herodian, iv, 12, 8; Dio Cass. lxxvii, 15; Tertullian, *Apol.* xxiii; *De Anima*, lvii). Particular places were commonly supposed to be, as it were, entrances to Orcus (νεκυομαντεῖα), where, on invocation, the shades would actually appear; for example, at Lake Aornos in Epirus and Lake Avernus in Lower Italy (Cicero, *Tusc.* ut sup.; Heyne, *Excur.* ii sq., ad Virg. *Æn.* vi); and at Heraclea on the Propontis (Herod. v, 92, 7; Diod. Sic. iv, 22; Pausan. ix, 30, 3; Plutarch, *Cim.* vi; Strabo, v, 244). The Eastern Magi were especially famed for necromantic skill (Herodian, *ut sup.*; comp. Strabo, xvi, 762). Necromancy (אֹבוֹת; Talm. דְּרִישׁוּ אֶל הַמֵּתִים; see Othonis *Lex. Rabb.* p.

171) had also found an entrance among the Israelites, especially when idolaters were on the throne (2 Kings xxi, 6; 2 Chron. xxxiii, 6; Isa. viii, 19; xxix, 4, comp. xix, 3, where the Egyptian enchantments are mentioned). In the Law the consultation of these men was forbidden as a heathen superstition (Lev. xix, 31), and they who disobeyed were threatened with death (Lev. xx, 6; Deut. viii, 11). Saul, in his distress, caused the shade of Samuel to be summoned from Sheol by an enchantress (1 Sam. xxviii, 7 sq.; comp. J. C Harenburg in *Iken. Nov. Thesaur.* i, 639 sq.; E. F. Schmersahl, *Nat. Erklär. der Gesch. Sauls mit d. Betrügerin zu Endor* [Gera, 1780]; Hensler, *Erläut. des 1 B. Sam.* p. 88 sq.; *Exeget. Handbuch. A. T.* iv, 251 sq.; Böttcher, *De Inferis*, i, 111 sq.). Dathe believed in the actual appearance of Samuel by a miracle (comp. Döderlein, *Theol. Biblioth.* iii, 331); and the conception the people formed of this apparition, which was not essentially altered by the poets and prophets, afforded a very natural basis for such superstitions. To the spirits thus evoked the enchanter lent a low, soft, almost whispering voice (Isa. viii, 19; comp. xix, 3), as seemed natural for such shades; just as the Greeks and Romans also applied the words τρίζειν (τρύζειν; *Iliad*, xxxiii, 101; *Odys.* xxiv sq.; Lucian, *Menip.* or *Necromant.* xi) and *stridere* (Statius, *Thebais*, vii, 770; Claudian, *In Rufin.* i, 126; Petronius, *Sat.* cxxii, 17; comp. Virgil, *Æn.* iii, 39 sq.) to the returning manes. It is by no means proved that the necromancers produced this muttering and whispering by ventriloquism, although the Septuagint usually renders the Hebrew אוֹב by the Greek ἐγγαστρίμυθος (according to Galen, the ἐγγαστρίμυθοι are so called because, speaking with the mouth closed, they seem to speak from the belly; comp. Josephus, *Ant.* vi, 14, 2). The meaning of the word has been much discussed (see Thenius, *On* 1 *Sam. xxviii*, 3; Knobel, *Prophetism. d. Hebr.* i, 241 sq.; Böttcher, *De Inferis*, i, 101 sq.). Ventriloquism was certainly one of the arts of ancient jugglers (Aristoph. *Vesp.* 1019 sq. See also Leo Allat. *De Engastrimytho*, also in the *Tractat. Bibl.* of the *Critici Sacri*, vi, 331 sq.; Dickinson, *Delph. Phœniciss.* p. 91 sq.; Gesenius, *Comment. on Isa.* i, 605 sq., 853; Van Dale, *De Idolat. p.* 608 sq.; Millii *Dissertat. Sel.* No. 12, also in Ugolini's *Thesaur.* xxiii; Tjeeuk, in the *Commentat. Societ. Scient. Vlissing.* i, 546 sq.; Potter, *Greek Archæol.* i, 758 sq.; Heyne, *Excurs.* i, ad Virg. *Æn.* vi). See DÆMON; SORCERY. In most parts of Greece, necromancy was practiced by priests or consecrated persons in the temples; in Thessaly, it was the profession of a distinct class of persons called Psychagogoi ("Evokers of Spirits"). The practice of it in that country was ultimately connected with many horrid rites, in which human blood, half-burned portions of bodies from funeral piles, the immature fœtus cut out of the womb, etc., were employed; sometimes human beings were slain, that their spirits might be consulted ere they finally passed into the lower world. The establishment of Christianity under Constantine caused necromancy to be placed under the ban of the Church. There are evident traces of necromancy in some of the older Norse and Teutonic poems. The mediæval belief in the evocation of spirits belongs rather to sorcery than to necromancy. See Peucer's *Commentarius de præcipuis divinationum generibus* (Zerbst, 1591); *N. A. Review*, lxxx, 512. See DIVINATION; MAGIC.

A species of necromancy, called *Rochester knockings*, from Rochester, N. Y., where it originated, and *spirit-rappings*, from the *raps* by which departed spirits are said to give their responses, has recently prevailed extensively in the United States, and produced no small amount of fanaticism and infidelity. See *Brit. Quar. Rev.* Oct. 1875, art. vi. See MESMERISM; SPIRITUALISM.

Necropolis (νεκρόπολις, *city of the dead*), a term applied to the cemeteries in the vicinity of ancient cities. It occurs in classical antiquity only as applied to a suburb of Alexandria, lying to the west of that city, having many shops and gardens, and places suitable for the reception of the dead. The corpses were received and embalmed in it. Here Cleopatra, the last of the Ptolemies, applied the asp to her breast, to avoid the ignominy of being led in triumph by Augustus. The site of the necropolis of ancient Alexandria seems to have been where are now the catacombs, consisting of galleries and tombs hollowed out of the soft calcareous stone of which the city is built, and lying at the extremity of the city. See ALEXANDRIA. The term necropolis is now, however, used in a much more extended sense, and applied to all the cemeteries of the ancient world. These consisted either of tombs constructed in the shape of houses and temples, and arranged in streets, like a city of the dead; or else of chambers hollowed in the rock, and ornamented with façades, to imitate houses and temples. Such cemeteries are to be distinguished from the *columbaria*, or subterraneous chambers of the Romans, in which their urns were deposited; or the rows of tombs along the Via Appia; or the cemeteries of the Christians, whose bodies were deposited in the ground. See CATACOMBS. The most remarkable necropolises are at Thebes, in Egypt, situated in a place called Kurneh, on the left bank of the Nile, capable of holding three thousand persons, and which it is calculated must at least have contained five thousand mummies; those of El-Kab, or Eileithyia; of Beni-Hassan, or the Speos Artemidos; and of Madfun, or Abydos; of Siwah, or the Oasis of Ammon. See EGYPT. In Africa, the necropolis of Cyrene is also extensive; and those of Vulci, Corneto, Tarquinii, and Capua are distinguished for their painted tombs [see TOMB], and the numerous vases and other objects of ancient art which have been exhumed from them. Large necropolises have also been found in Lycia, Sicily, and elsewhere. See Strabo, xviii, p. 795-799; Plutarch, *Vit. Anton.*; Letronne, *Journal des Savans* (1828), p. 103; Dennis, *Cities and Cemeteries of Etruria*, i, 412; ii, 276-358. See CEMETERY.

In this connection we may notice that consorting or living with the dead has been observed as a characteristic of diseased melancholy. Individuals have inhabited graveyards, preferring the proximity and association of corpses with which they had no tie to the cheerfulness and comforts of home; and there is recorded one notorious case, in which a gentleman, although on bad terms with his wife while alive, carried her body with him through India, scandalizing the natives, and outraging the feelings of all, by placing the coffin under his bed. This hideous tendency may enter into certain developments of cannibalism, where the feast is celebrated in memory of a departed friend rather than in triumph over a slain foe (Chambers). Among the Arabians the *ghouls* are fairies that are supposed to feed on human flesh. Symptoms of this *necrophilism* may be traced in the Gadarene maniacs of the Gospels (Matt. vii, 28, etc.). See DÆMONIAC.

Necrothaptæ (Gr. νεκρός, dead, and Ѳάπτω, to *bury*) is one of the names by which the ancient Greeks called the undertakers at funerals. Among the Romans they were called *Libitinarii*, from the goddess *Libitina*, who presided over funerals (Livy, xl, c. 19; Plutarch, *Quæst. Roman.*).

Nectar was the drink of the immortal gods, according to the early Greek poets, and was served around to them by the hands of *Hebe* or *Ganymede*. It is confounded by some of the ancient writers with ambrosia, the food of the gods. Thus Sappho and Alcman make nectar the food of the gods, and ambrosia their drink. But nectar is the name given by Homer, Hesiod, Pindar, and the Greek poets generally, and by the Romans, to the beverage of the gods. Homer describes nectar as resembling red wine, and represents its continued use as causing immortality. By the later poets, nectar and ambrosia are represented as of most delicious odor; and

sprinkling with nectar, or anointing with ambrosia, is spoken of as conferring perpetual youth, and these acts are assumed as the symbols of everything most delightful to the taste.

Nectaria is the name of a celebrated deaconess in the early Christian Church. She flourished in the latter half of the 4th century, and was the cause of the deposition of a certain Elpidius by the synod of Rimini, as he had ordained her for an office of which she proved herself unworthy by breaches of confidence and perjury. See Sozomen, *Historia Ecclesiastica*, bk. iv, ch. 24.

Nectarius is the name of two patriarchs of the Eastern Church who figure prominently in ecclesiastical history.

1. The first, who is most widely known, was a native of Tarsus, and with the assistance of the emperor Theodosius became patriarch of Constantinople after the deposition of Gregory (q. v.) Nazianzen, and immediately before Chrysostom. Nectarius's occupancy of the episcopal chair between two such men would have required extraordinary merit to make him conspicuous. But, in truth, though he does not seem to merit the epithet applied to him by Gibbon, "the indolent Nectarius," the fact of his having been appointed at all is the most remarkable feature in his personal history. When Gregory Nazianzen (q. v.) resigned his office (A.D. 381), it was during the meeting of the second œcumenical council at Constantinople. Nectarius, a senator and a man of the highest family, was at this time intending to visit his native place, and previously waited on Diodorus, the bishop of Tarsus, who was in Constantinople as a member of the council. Diodorus, along with the other bishops, was perplexed as to whom they should nominate to the vacant see. Struck by the majestic appearance and white hair of Nectarius, and taking for granted that he was a Christian and had been baptized, Diodorus requested Nectarius to postpone his departure, and recommended him to Flavian, bishop of Antioch, as a fit person to succeed Gregory. Flavian laughed at the strange proposal; but, to oblige his friend, put Nectarius's name last on the list, and together with the other bishops presented it to the emperor. To the astonishment of all, Theodosius selected Nectarius, and persisted in his choice, even when it was ascertained that this candidate for episcopal honor had not yet been baptized, and had never proposed publicly to join the Church. The bishops at last acceded to the wishes of the monarch who had so rigidly opposed the Arians, while the people, attracted probably by his gentle manners and the venerable appearance of the man, presenting as he did every way a strong contrast to Gregory, loudly applauded the choice. Nectarius was baptized, and, before he had time to put off the white robes of a neophyte, he was declared bishop of Constantinople. Most important matters came under the consideration of the council over which, it is probable, he was now called to preside. He showed his discretion by putting himself under the tuition of Cyriacus, bishop of Adana, but we can hardly believe that Nectarius took any active part in the theological questions which were discussed. It is doubtful whether the canons that were enacted under the name of the second œcumenical council were not passed at two different sessions, a second taking place in 382. But this does not matter much, as they all bear the name of this council. The principal business transacted in the council, considered in a theological point of view, related to the conforming and extending of the Nicene Creed, mainly to meet the opinions of the Macedonians. The creed thus enlarged is that used at the mass of the Roman Catholic Church. Other canons regulated discipline, the restriction of the authority of each bishop to his own diocese, and the restoration of penitent heretics. The most important article of all, however, historically considered, was one which was conceded not more on account of the natural propriety of the arrangement than the personal favor which the emperor bore to Nectarius. It was decreed that as Constantinople was *New Rome*, the bishop should be next in dignity to the bishop of Rome, and hold the first place among the Eastern prelates. This, which at first was a mere mark of dignity, became a source of substantial power, embroiled Constantinople with Rome, and was pregnant with all those circumstances that have marked this important schism. Nectarius was the first who held the dignity of *ex officio* head of Eastern bishops as patriarch of Constantinople. These canons were signed July 9, 381. The zeal of Theodosius in the extirpation of Arianism led to the summoning of a council (not œcumenical) at Constantinople in July, 383. There assembled the chiefs of all the sects. By the advice of Sisinnius, afterwards a Novatian bishop, given through Nectarius, the emperor ensnared his opponents into an approval of the writings of the early fathers. He then required of each sect a confession of its faith, which, having read and considered, he condemned them all, and followed up this condemnation by the most stringent laws, for the purpose of entirely rooting them out. As might have been expected, Nectarius was obnoxious to the Arians; and we find that in 388, while the emperor Theodosius was absent in Italy opposing Maximus, a rumor that had falsely spread of the defeat and death of the prince excited their hopes, and they broke out in riot, in the course of which they set fire to the house of Nectarius. The most important act of his office occurred in 390, when Nectarius, alarmed by the public odium which had been excited by the seduction of a woman of quality by a deacon, abolished the practice of confession which had been introduced into the Eastern Church—a penitential priest (*presbyter pœnitentiarus*) having been appointed, whose office it was to receive the confessions of those who had fallen into sin after baptism, and to prescribe for them acts of penitence previously to their being admitted to partake of the privileges of the Church. The officer of the confessional, while seeking to do his duty, provoked such scandal in the Church that it seemed advisable not to continue an office which was likely to do more harm than good (Neander, *Ch. Hist.* ii, 181; Schaff, *Ch. Hist.* iii, 357, 358). According to Balsamon (Hardouin, *Concil.* i, 955), the last council (not œcumenical) at which Nectarius presided was held in Constantinople in 394, regarding a dispute between Agapius and Bagadius in relation to the bishopric of Bostria, this council deciding that the consent of several bishops of a province is necessary to confirm the deposition of one of their number. Nectarius survived his patron, Theodosius, two years, dying Sept. 27, 397. He seems to have borne his honor meekly, and to have acted with great discretion. In the subtle controversies that agitated the Church we learn that he avoided discussion himself, and was guided by the advice of men better skilled in the puzzling dialectics of the time. If the conjecture of Tillemont (*Histoire Ecclésiastique*, ix, 466) be correct, Nectarius was married, and had one son. His brother, Arsatius, succeeded John Chrysostom as patriarch of Constantinople (comp. Fleury, *Histoire Ecclésiastique*, vols. iv and v; Socrates, *Historia Ecclesiastica*, v, 8, 13; Sozomen, *Hist. Eccles.* vii, 8, 9, 14, 16; viii, 8, c. 23). Nectarius is said to have been the author of a *Homilia in Theodorum martyrem*, which was first published among the discourses of Chrysostom (Paris, 1554), and has since been several times reprinted. The decision of the synod concerning Agapius and Bagadius is contained in Freher's *In Jure Græco-Romano*, iv, 247. See Oudin, *Comment.* i, 686; Tillemont, ix, 486; Fabricius, *Bibliotheca Græca* (ed. Harl.), ix, 309; x, 833; xii, 390; Cave, *Hist. Literaria*, i, 277; Smith, *Dict. Greek and Rom. Biog. and Mythol.* s. v.; *Edinb. Rev.* 1867 (July), p. 58.

2. The second Nectarius was patriarch of Jerusalem in the 17th century. Little is known of his history. According to Fabricius, he was born in Crete, educated at Athens under Theophilus Corydales, and while yet a young man entered a convent of Mount Sinai. He succeeded Paisus as patriarch of Jerusalem. A strict partisan of Greek orthodoxy, he opposed both the other parties, and endorsed the Confession of Mogilas in 1662 (*Conf. libr. symb. eccl. Or.* [ed. Kimmel] p. 45). During his patriarchate the Romish emissaries were very active in endeavoring to persuade the Greek Christians of Palestine, suffering under the yoke of the Turks, to unite with the Church of Rome; among them a Franciscan, named Peter, was especially active in distributing five tracts in defence of the papal authority. These tracts Nectarius answered by the publication of another, entitled Κατὰ τῆς ἀρχῆς τοῦ Παππᾶ (Jasii. 1681; Lond. 1702, 8vo), which is a fair refutation of the five principles laid down in the Roman Catholic tracts: 1st, of unity in the primitive Church; 2d, of the harmony of the two principal divisions of the Church in the apostolic time; 3d, of the sole authenticity of the Church of Rome; 4th, of the necessity of the monarchial government of the Church. To the first point Nectarius answers that the union of the Church means the unity between the members of the spiritual Church, which still exists, and this alone constitutes the true Church. To the second, he replies by historical documents showing that, though identical in point of doctrine, the Greek and the Latin churches differed in their form of worship and Church government in the 2d century. To the third, he answers by proving the alteration of the symbols in the Roman Church. Admitting the fourth in principle, he says that the king and head of the Church being Christ, there can be no other head, but naturally an aristocratic organization. He also wrote a work in Greek against the doctrines of Luther and Calvin, which was translated into Latin by Renaudot, who published it, together with Gennadius's *Homilies on the Eucharist*, etc. (Paris, 1709, 4to). Nectarius is said to have also written a history of the Egyptian empire down to sultan Selim. See Fabricius, *Bibl. Græca* (ed. Harl.), ix, 310; Kimmel, l. c. *Præf.* p. 75; *Nic. Comnenus in prænott. mystagog. respons.* vi, sec. 2. (J. N. P.)

Necusia (νεκύσια), a name for the offerings among the ancient Greeks and Romans on the anniversary of the day of the death of a relative. According to some the Necusia were the same with the *Genesia*.

Nedabi'ah (Heb. *Nedabyah'*, נְדַבְיָה, *moved of Jehovah*; Sept. Ναβαδίας v. r. Δενεθεί; Vulg. *Nadabia*), the eighth and last mentioned of the sons of Jeconiah; a descendant of David, and nephew of Zedekiah, king of Judah (1 Chron. iii, 18). B.C. cir. 560.

Nedarim. See TALMUD.

Nedusia is a surname of *Athene*, derived from the river *Nedon*, on the banks of which she was worshipped. See MINERVA.

Needham, John, an English dissenting minister who flourished in the first half of the last century, was for some years pastor of the Baptist Church at Hitcham, Suffolk, and afterwards removed to Bristol (in 1746), where he remained until 1787. He is of interest principally as the author of the pleasant harvest hymn, "To praise the ever-bounteous Lord," found in many of our best collections of hymns.

Needham, John Turberville, an English Roman Catholic divine, noted as a scientist, was born in London in 1713, and educated at the College of Douai, where he entered into orders. He removed to the Continent after having attained celebrity as a scientist, and finally became rector of the Academy of Sciences and Belles-lettres at Brussels, where he died in 1781. Mr. Needham wrote observations inserted in Buffon's *Natural History: Inquiries concerning Nature and Religion:—Idée sommaire, ou vue générale du système physique et métaphysique sur la génération*, etc. See his life, by abbé Mann, in the memoirs of the Royal Academy of Sciences at Brussels; *Lond. Monthly Review*, vol. lxx; Hutton, *Mathematical and Philos. Dict.* s. v.

Needle (Gr. ῥαφίς) occurs in the Bible only in the proverb "to pass through a needle's eye" (τρύφημα) (Matt. xix, 24; Mark x, 25; Luke xviii, 25); for which see CAMEL. Among the ancient Egyptians some needles were of bronze, from three to three and a half inches in length; but as few have been found, we are not able to form any opinion respecting their general size and quality, particularly of those used for fine work, which must have been of a very minute kind (Wilkinson, *Anc. Eg.* ii, 345). See NEEDLEWORK. The use of the needle as

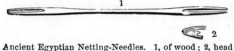

Ancient Egyptian Needles of Bronze. (In the Museum of Alnwick Castle.)

a female accomplishment may be traced up to the earliest times. It was an art in which the ladies of ancient Egypt particularly excelled, as do their descendants at the present day; and the Hebrew females also no doubt acquired great perfection in it during their residence in that country, as we read of the embroidery of the sacerdotal robes and curtains of the tabernacle (Exod. xxviii, 39; xxvi, 36); and also of "a prey of divers colors of needlework, of divers colors of needlework on both sides" (Judg. v, 30). That the ladies of Assyria and Babylonia also excelled in various kinds of needlework Layard has shown from the recently exhumed monuments of Nineveh (see *Nineveh*, etc., ii, 315 sq.). In the British Museum may be seen some needles for sewing, made of bronze, taken from the Egyptian remains; there are likewise some spindles and netting-needles made of wood, nine inches to nine inches and a half in length; and also some skeins of thread, a portion of which is dyed of a reddish color. See EMBROIDERY.

Ancient Egyptian Netting-Needles. 1, of wood; 2, head of another of bronze.

Needlework occurs in the Auth. Ver. twice (Judg. v, 30; Psa. xlv, 14) as a translation of the Heb. רִקְמָה, *rikmah'*, properly *variegated work* (elsewhere "broidered work"); and also of the cognate רֹקֵם, *rokem'* (Exod. xxvi, 36; xxvii, 16; xxviii, 39; xxxvi, 37; xxxviii, 18), properly an *embroiderer* (as elsewhere rendered). In Exodus the embroiderer is contrasted with the "cunning workman," *chosheb'* (חֹשֵׁב): and the consideration of one of these terms involves that of the other. Various explanations have been offered as to the distinction between them, but most of these overlook the distinction marked in the Bible itself, viz., that the *rokem* wove simply a variegated texture, without gold thread or figures, and that the *chosheb* interwove gold thread or figures into the variegated texture. We conceive that the use of the gold thread was for delineating figures, as is implied in the description of the corslet of Amasis (Herod. iii, 47), and that the notices of gold thread in some instances and of figures in others were but different methods of describing the same thing. It follows, then, that the application of the term "embroiderer" to *rokem* is false; if it belong to either it is

Ancient Egyptian Embroidered Dresses. (From Champollion, *Monuments de l'Égypte.*)

to *chosheb*, or the "cunning workman," who added the figures. But if "*embroidery*" be strictly confined to the work of the *needle*, we doubt whether it can be applied to either, for the simple addition of gold thread, or of a figure, does not involve the use of the needle. The patterns may have been worked into the stuff by the loom, as appears to have been the case in Egypt (Wilkinson, iii, 128; comp. Her. l. c.), where the Hebrews learned the art, and as is stated by Josephus (ἄνθη ἐνύφανται, *Ant.* iii, 7, 2). The distinction, as given by the Talmudists, and which has been adopted by Gesenius (*Thesaur.* p. 1311) and Bähr (*Symbolik*, i, 266), is this, that *rikmah*, or "needlework," was where a pattern was attached to the stuff by being sewn to it on *one* side, and the work of the *chosheb* when the pattern was worked into the stuff by the loom, and so appeared on *both* sides. This view appears to be entirely inconsistent with the statements of the Bible, and with the sense of the word *rikmah* elsewhere. The absence of the figure or the gold thread in the one, and its presence in the other, constitutes the essence of the distinction. In support of this view we call attention to the passages in which the expressions are contrasted. *Rikmah* consisted of the following materials, "blue, purple, scarlet, and fine twined linen" (Exod. xxvi, 36; xxvii, 16; xxxvi, 37; xxxviii, 18; xxxix, 28). The work of the *chosheb* was either "fine twined linen, blue, purple, and scarlet, *with cherubims*" (Exod. xxvi, 1, 31; xxxvi, 8, 35), or "*gold*, blue, purple, scarlet, and fine twined linen" (xxviii, 6, 8, 15; xxxix, 2, 5, 8). Again, looking at the general sense of the words, we shall find that *chosheb* in-

Embroidered Dress of Sardanapalus III. (From the Assyrian Sculptures in the British Museum.)

volves the idea of invention, or *designing* patterns; *rikmah*, the idea of *texture* as well as *variegated color*. The former is applied to other arts which demanded the exercise of inventive genius, as in the construction of engines of war (2 Chron. xxvi, 15); the latter is applied to other substances, the texture of which is remarkable, as the human body (Psa. cxxxix, 15). Further than this, *rikmah* involves the idea of a regular disposition of colors, which demanded no inventive genius. Beyond the instances already adduced, it is applied to tessellated pavement (1 Chron. xxix, 2), to the eagle's plumage (Ezek. xvii, 3), and, in the Targums, to the leopard's spotted skin (Jer. xiii, 23). In the same sense it is applied to the colored sails of the Egyptian vessels (Ezek. xxvii, 16), which were either checkered or worked according to a regularly recurring pattern (Wilkinson, iii, 211). Gesenius considers this passage as conclusive for his view of the distinction, but it is hardly conceivable that the patterns were on one side of the sail only, nor does there appear any ground to infer a departure from the usual custom of working the colors by the loom. The ancient versions do not contribute much to the elucidation of the point. The Sept. varies between ποικιλτής and ῥαφιδευτής, as representing *rokem*, and ποικιλτής and ὑφαντής for *chosheb*, combining the two terms in each case for the work itself—ἡ ποικιλία τοῦ ῥαφιδευτοῦ for the first, ἔργον ὑφαντὸν ποικιλτόν for the second. The distinction, as far as it is observed, consisted in the one being *needle-work* and the other *loom-work*. The Vulgate gives generally *plumarius* for the first, and *polymitarius* for the second; but in Exod. xxvi, 1, 31 *plumarius* is used for the second. The first of these terms (*plumarius*) is well chosen to express *rokem*, but *polymitarius*, i. e. a weaver who works together threads of divers colors, is as applicable to one as to the other. The rendering in Ezek. xxvii, 16, *scutulata*, i. e. "checkered," correctly describes one of the productions of the *rokem*. We have lastly to notice the incorrect rendering of the word שָׁבַץ in the A. V.— "broider," "embroider" (Exod. xxviii, 4, 39). It means stuff worked in a *tessellated* manner, i. e. with square cavities such as stones might be set in (comp. ver. 20). The art of embroidery by the loom was extensively practiced among the nations of antiquity. In addition to the Egyptians, the Babylonians were celebrated for it, but embroidery in the proper sense of the term, i. e. with the needle, was a Phrygian invention of later date (Pliny, viii, 48). There are three words for "*weaver*" employed in the descriptions of textures used in the tabernacle and the garments of the priest: 1. אָרֵג, *orég*, the simpler *weaver*, who wrought in one color, even though that color were blue (Judg. xvi, 13; Isa. lix, 5; Exod. xxviii, 32; xxxix, 22, 27); 2. רֹקֵם, *rokém*, the *color-weaver*, who wrought in textures of at least three colors, as he wove cloth made of blue, purple, and scarlet threads, and twined linen (Exod. xxvi, 36; xxvii, 16; xxviii, 39; xxxix, 29); 3. חֹשֵׁב, *choshéb*, the *embroiderer*, who wrought in the same colors and materials as the color-weaver or *rokem*, but always with an additional thread, producing figures (Exod. xxvi, 1, 31; xxviii, 6, 8, 15; xxix, 3) (Paine, *Temple of Solomon*, p. 12). See *Art of Needlework from the Earliest Ages*, by the countess of Wilton (Lond. 1840). See EMBROIDER; WEAVE.

Neef (or **Neefs**), **James**, a Flemish engraver who devoted himself mostly to sacred and secular art, was born at Antwerp, according to Nagler, about 1610. There are various dates assigned for his birth, but Nagler is probably correct, as there are prints by Neef extant dated 1632 and 1633. His last print recorded is dated 1645. He engraved a number of plates after Rubens, Vandyck, and other celebrated Flemish painters. His drawing is correct, but stiff and mannered, and his heads often have an extravagant expression; but his prints are much esteemed. They are executed entirely with the graver, which he handled with great facility. Among his works are, *The Fall of the Angels:—The Meeting of Abraham and Melchisedec:—The Crucifixion, with the Virgin and St. John:—St. Augustine:—The Martyrdom of St. Thomas:—The Judgment of Paris:— The Triumph of Galatea* (all these are after Rubens): —*Christ and his Six Penitents:—Job and his Wife:— The Martyrdom of St. Lievin:—Christ's offering to Magdalen* (all these after Gerard Segers):—*Christ brought before Pilate*, after J. Jordaens:—*St. Roch interceding for the Persons attacked by the Plague*, after Erasmus Quellinus.

Neef, Jean, a Belgian ascetic writer, was born at Mechlin in 1576. He belonged to the Order of the Hermits of St. Augustine, in which he filled the office of prior. In 1625 he was appointed provincial for Flanders and Cologne. He died at Mechlin, June 28, 1656. His works are, *Vita sanctæ Monicæ* (Antwerp, 1628):— *Horologium monasticæ perfectionis* (Louvain, 1630):— *De tertiariis ordinis Sancti Augustini* (Antwerp, 1632): —*Eremus Augustiniana floribus honoris et sanctitatis vernans* (Louvain, 1638, 4to), in which is found the life of St. Augustine, and a great number of notices of the remarkable personages of his order:—*Le Nouveau Testament*, in Flemish. See André, *Bibl. Belgica*, ii, 700.

**Neefs, PETER, called *the Old,* an eminent Flemish

painter who mostly confined himself to the cultivation of ecclesiastical art, was born at Antwerp in 1570. He was a disciple of the elder Henry Steenwyck, whose manner he closely imitated. He painted views of churches and convents, especially interiors, preferring those in the Gothic style of architecture. He possessed a profound knowledge of perspective, and represented his subjects, with all their rich ornaments and every architectural member, with strict truth, and yet without betraying the appearance of anxious labor. Every object is marked with minute precision, and finished with an exquisite touch and a light pencil. His bright, clear pictures, in which he avoided the darkish-brown coloring sometimes observable in the works of his master Steenwyck, are the most esteemed. Being an indifferent designer of figures, he often got F. Francks, Van Thulden, Velvet Breughel, or Teniers to paint the figures; those of the two last greatly enhance the value of the pictures of Neefs. He died in 1651. His son, Peter Martin (called *the Young*), painted in the same style, and chose the same subjects as his father, but was by no means equal to him.

Neely, PHILIP P., a minister of the Methodist Episcopal Church, South, was born in Rutherford County, Tenn., Sept. 9, 1819. He was converted in 1836, and in 1837 joined the Tennessee Conference, and was appointed junior preacher on Jackson Circuit, West Tennessee. On the division of the conference he became a member of the Memphis Conference, and was stationed at Holly Springs, Miss., in 1841. During the two years following he was stationed in Huntsville, Ala.; in 1844 was appointed president of the Columbia Female College; in 1846 travelled as agent of the Transylvania University. In 1848 he was transferred to the Alabama Conference, and labored in its boundaries until his death at Mobile, Ala., Nov. 9, 1868. See *Min. Ann. Conf. M. E. Church, South*, p. 233.

Neëmi'as (Νεεμίας v. r. Νεμουσί), the Græcised form (Ecclus. xlix, 13; 2 Macc. i, 18, 20, 21, 23, 31, 36; ii, 13) of the name of NEHEMIAH (q. v.).

Neercassel, JAN VAN, an eminent Dutch prelate, was born at Gorkum in 1623, and after a thorough education entered into holy orders. He joined the congregation of the Oratory, taught theology at Mechlin and at Cologne, then was nominated archdeacon of Utrecht, and finally, in 1661, was elevated to the bishopric of that city under the title of Bishop of Castoria. In 1663 he became the only bishop of the five hundred thousand Catholics scattered throughout Holland, and governed his vast diocese with such great solicitude that he succeeded in re-establishing ecclesiastical discipline. Neercassel enjoyed the greatest consideration even among Protestants. He was in correspondence with eminent scholars and divines, among these Bossuet, who highly esteemed Neercassel's writings. He died at Zwolle in 1686. Bishop Neercassel was in sympathy with the French Jansenists, and several of them, among others Dr. Arnauld himself, found in his episcopate a refuge. Neercassel himself remained in peace with Rome; but the successor he had pointed out was not chosen on account of the interference of the Jesuits, who feared that M. van Heussen might prove a schismatic, and finally Coddes, one of the three whom the Society of Jesus proposed to the papal see, was elevated. We have of Neercassel's works, *De Sanctorum et præcipue B. Mariæ cultu* (Utrecht, 1675, 8vo), translated into French by abbé Le Roy (Paris, 1679, 8vo):—*Tractatus de lectione Scripturarum, in quo Protestantium eas legendi praxis refellitur, Catholicorum vero stabilitur* (Emmerich, 1677, 8vo), translated into French (Cologne, 1680, 8vo):—*Amor pœnitens, seu de recto usu Clavium* (Emmerich, 1683, 12mo); in a new edition, given the following year, the author suppressed the propositions which had displeased at Rome; the *Amor pœnitens* was translated into French (Utrecht, 1741, 3 vols. 12mo). See

Du Pin, *Les Auteurs Ecclésiastiques* 17me *Cent.*; Hoefer, *Nouv. Biog. Générale*, s. v.; Tregelles, *The Jansenists* (Lond. 1861, 12mo), p. 54, 55. (J. H. W.)

Neesing (an obsolete word for *sneezing*) is found only in Job xli, 10, as a rendering of עֲטִישָׁה, *atishah'* (which occurs only there), from an otherwise unused root signifying *to sneeze* (q. v.).

Nefasti, DIES, i. e. *unlawful days,* a term among the ancient Romans for those days on which neither courts of justice nor the assemblies of people could be held; afterwards they were dedicated chiefly to the worship of the gods. Numa Pompilius is said to have been the originator of the *dies nefasti.*

Neff, FELIX, a philanthropic Swiss Protestant divine, was born in 1798 at a small village near Geneva. While yet a youth he enlisted as a soldier in the Genevese service, where his excellent conduct and superior qualifications soon procured him advancement. But he became obnoxious to his brother-officers by the unbending principles and the high-toned purity of his life, the result of the careful teachings of his widowed and pious mother. He was advised to leave the army for the pulpit, and finally resolving to follow this advice, he resigned his commission in 1819. He now offered himself for the work of a catechist or parish missionary, and labored for two years in that capacity in several of the Swiss cantons, and afterwards for six months at Grenoble. But when he desired to be ordained, he found that religious scruples prevented his connecting himself with the Established Church of Geneva, while from his being a foreigner he could not hope to receive ordination through the Protestant Church of France. He was therefore advised to repair to England, where he was ordained, May 19, 1823, in Mr. Clayton's chapel in the Poultry; and a few days afterwards left London to return to the scene of his former labors at Mens. However gratifying his reception among that attached people, his benevolent mind fixed on another place, in a wild and sequestered portion of the High Alps, as more urgently in need of his services. The consistory of the Protestant churches permitting, he entered on his pastoral charge in 1824. Thus this devoted minister, who might have enjoyed comfort and leisure in the beautiful and fertile vales of Languedoc, chose to settle in a poor and wildly extending Alpine district, comprising not less than seventeen isolated villages within a circuit of eighty miles. There was one part of his parish, the Val Fressinière, where the inhabitants were so low socially, as well as uncivilized in the most common arts of life, as to be scarcely removed in many respects above the condition of barbarism. Neff perceived that his first step must be to supply the want of education, and, unable to pay a teacher, he joined the duties of a schoolmaster to those he already bore. Having at length succeeded in interesting the people in his efforts, he induced them to build a school-house, he directing the workmen, and acting at once as architect and mason. But such excessive labor exhausted his constitution, and he died April 12, 1829, leaving a name entitled to be ranked among the best benefactors of his fellow-creatures. See Gilly, *Memoirs of Neff, and of his Labors among the French Protestants of Dauphiné, a Remnant of the Primitive Christians of Gaul* (Lond. 1832, 8vo); Bost, *Life of Felix Neff* (Lond. 1855); Jamieson, *Cyclop. of Relig. Biog.* p. 349; Darling, *Cyclop. Bibliog.* ii, 2166; *The London Quarterly Review,* April, 1833. (J. N. P.)

Negaïm. See TALMUD.

Negation is in philosophical parlance the absence of that which does not naturally belong to the thing we are speaking of, or which has no right, obligation, or necessity to be present with; as when we say a stone is inanimate or blind or deaf, i. e. has no life, sight, or hearing (Watts, *Logic,* pt. i, ch. ii, § 6). According to the scholastic theologian, Thomas Aquinas (*Summa theolog.* pt. i, qu. 48, art. v), "simple *negation* denies to a thing

some certain realities which do not belong to the nature of the same. *Privation,* on the contrary, is deficiency in some reality which belongs to the nature of the being." See PRIVATION. In simple apprehension there is no affirmation or denial; so that, strictly speaking, there are no negative ideas, notions, or conceptions. In truth, some that are so called represent the most positive nullities; as infinity, immortality, etc. But in some ideas, as in that of blindness, deafness, insensibility, there is, as it were, a taking away of something from the object of which these ideas are entertained. This is, however, privation (στέρησις) rather than negation (ἀπόφασις), and in general it may be said that *negation* implies some anterior conception of the objects of which the negation is made. Absolute negation is impossible. We have no idea of nothing—it is but a word. "*Nihilum,* or *nothing,*" says Clarke, "is that of which everything can truly be denied, and nothing can be truly affirmed. So that the idea of *nothing* (if I may so speak) is absolutely the negation of all ideas. The idea, therefore, either of a finite or infinite *nothing* is a contradiction in terms" (*Answer to Seventh Letter*). *Nothing,* taken *positively,* is what does not but may exist, as a river of milk; taken *negatively,* it is that which does not and cannot exist, as a square circle, a mountain without a valley. Nothing positively is *ens potentiale.* Nothing negatively is *non ens.* See Krauth's Fleming, *Vocabulary of Philos.* p. 345, 346.

Negeb. See SOUTH COUNTRY.

Neges (or more commonly CANUSIS) is the name of an order of Japanese monks or secular priests who officiate in the *mias* or temples. They are either maintained by the endowment money of the mia to which they may happen to belong, or by a pension from the Dairi; but their principal support is derived from the voluntary contributions of the devotees. The Canusis wear, as a badge of their office, either a white or yellow robe over their ordinary dress. Their cap, which is made in the shape of a boat, is tied under the chin with silken strings. Upon this cap are tassels with fringes to them, which are longer or shorter according to the rank of the person who wears them. Their beards are close shaven, but their hair is very long; the superiors, however, wear it curled up under a piece of black gauze. At each ear is a long piece of silk, which comes forward over the lower part of the face. The order of the Canusis depends, with respect to spiritual concerns, on the decision of the Dairi, and with regard to temporal matters they are subject, like all other ecclesiastics, to the authority of the judge of the temple, who is appointed by the secular monarch. The superiors of the Canusis are remarkable for their pride and contempt of the common people. They are to be seen scattered throughout all the provinces and cities of the empire. The leading monks reside at Miaco; but, though invested with great authority and influence over the people, they are always subject to the imperial authority, which punishes ecclesiastical delinquents with death. The Canusis, in their discourse to the people, dwell chiefly on points of morality. They preach from a rostrum or pulpit, and alongside of them is placed the tutelar idol of the sect or order to which they belong, and to this the devotees present their free-will offerings. On each side of the pulpit there is a lighted lamp suspended from the canopy, and a little below it is a desk or pen for the younger priests, where some of them sit and others stand. The preacher wears a hat upon his head shaped like an umbrella, and holds a fan in his hand. Before commencing his sermon he appears to meditate for a little, then rings a small bell by way of enjoining silence upon his audience; and after quiet is obtained he opens a book which lies upon a cushion before him, containing the moral precepts and fundamental principles of the religion of his sect. Having chosen his text, he delivers his discourse, which is usually clear and vigorous in its language, and strictly methodical in its arrangement. The peroration very often consists of a high-flown eulogium upon the order to which the preacher belongs. The audience are called upon, by the ringing of a little bell, to kneel down and say their prayers, sometimes before and sometimes after the sermon. On certain days set apart for the dead, the Japanese priests, as well as monks, sing the Namanda to the sound of little bells for the repose of their deceased friends. See Macfarlane, *Japan* (Lond. 1852, 8vo), bk. iv.

Neg'inah, properly NEGINATH (נְגִינַת, *neginath'*), occurs in the title of Psa. lxi, "to the chief musician upon Neginah." If the present reading be correct, the form of the word may be compared with that of Mahalath (Psa. liii). But the Sept. (ἐν ὕμνοις) and Vulg. (*in hymnis*) evidently read "Neginoth" in the plural, which occurs in the titles of five Psalms, and is perhaps the true reading. Whether the word be singular or plural, it is the general term by which all stringed instruments are described (Smith). In the singular it has the derived sense of the *music of stringed instruments* (1 Sam. xvi, 16; Isa. xxxviii, 20); and of *songs to be accompanied with stringed instruments* (Psa. lxxvii, 7), especially a *song of derision* (Job xxx, 9). See NEGINOTH.

Neg'inoth (נְגִינוֹת, *neginoth'*, *songs* with instrumental accompaniment, see NEGINAH; Sept. ὕμνοι; Vulg. *hymni*) is found in the titles of Psa. iv, vi, liv, lv, lxvii, lxxvi, and the margin of Hab. iii, 19 (text "stringed instruments"), and there seems but little doubt that it is the general term denoting all stringed instruments whatsoever, whether played with the hand, like the harp and guitar, or with a plectrum. It thus includes all those instruments which in the A. V. are denoted by the special terms "harp," "psaltery" or "viol," "sackbut," as well as by the general descriptions "stringed instruments" (Psa. cl, 4), "instruments of music" (1 Sam. xviii, 6), or, as the margin gives it, "three-stringed instruments," and the "instrument of ten strings" (Psa. xxxiii, 2; xcii, 3; cxliv, 9). "The chief musician on *Neginoth*" was therefore the conductor of that portion of the Temple choir who played upon the stringed instruments, and who are mentioned in Psa. lxviii, 25 (נֹגְנִים, *nogenim*). The root (נָגַן = κρούειν) from which the word is derived occurs in 1 Sam. xvi, 16, 17, 18, 23; xviii, 10; xix, 9; Isa. xxxviii, 20, and a comparison of these passages confirms what has been said with regard to its meaning. The author of the *Shilte Haggibborim*, quoted by Kircher (*Musurgia*, i, 4, p. 48), describes the Neginoth as instruments of wood, long and round, pierced with several apertures, and having three strings of gut stretched across them, which were played with a bow of horsehair. It is extremely doubtful, however, whether the Hebrews were acquainted with anything so closely resembling the modern violin. See MUSICAL INSTRUMENTS; PSALMS.

Nego. See ABED-NEGO.

Negombo, Negosi, and **Nepindi** are the names by which the African negroes of Congo, Angola, etc., designate three of their priests.

1. The *Negombo* is looked upon both as a priest and a prophet. He not only professes to foretell future events, but he ascribes to himself likewise an innate virtue of healing all manner of diseases. He is always sufficiently provided with a vast variety of medicaments, the virtues whereof are so deeply impressed on the minds of the negroes that the failure of Negombo's prescriptions is always imputed to the patient.

2. The *Negosi* must take to himself eleven wives, and, as is usual among African tribes, he also acts the part of a magician. When any native meditates revenge upon an enemy, he applies to the Negosi, who cuts off some locks of his hair, and, binding them together, throws them into the fire, uttering all the while various imprecations on the enemy, and all his possessions and kin.

3. The *Nepindi* styles himself master of the elements, and pretends to control thunder, lightning, and storms. To manifest his power, he raises large heaps of earth contiguous to his habitation. After he has finished the usual sacrifices and magical operations, a little animal, they say, creeps out from the foot of one of these, which raises itself by slow degrees, and at last takes its flight towards the heavens. Then thick clouds darken the skies, and thunder, lightning, and rain immediately ensues. See Cavazzi, *Ittor. descrizione de Congo*, etc.

Negores, a religious sect in Japan, which derives its origin from Cambodoxi, a disciple of Xeaca. The sect consists of three classes. The first, who are less numerous than the others, devote themselves to the worship of the gods and the performance of religious ceremonies; the second employ themselves in military affairs, and the third in the preparation of weapons of war. The Negores, as a body, are so numerous and influential that the emperor finds it necessary to secure their favor. They are scrupulously careful about the lives of inferior animals, but their quarrels with each other often end in bloodshed. See Gardner, *Faiths of the World*, ii, 524; Broughton, *Bibliotheca Histor. Sacra*, ii, s. v.

Negosi. See NEGOMBO.

Negri (or **Negro**), **Francesco**, an Italian Reformer noted for his philological attainments, was born of a noble and ancient family in Bassano, in the Venetian territory, in 1500. Gifted with an active and penetrating mind, he became an excellent student. He entered the Order of Benedictines. The principles of the Reformation preached in Germany and Switzerland penetrating Italy at this time, Negri came forward as one of the first to adopt the new doctrines, and promptly abandoning his order, he went to Germany, joined Zwingli, and accompanied the great Swiss Reformer to the conferences of Marburg in 1529, and assisted at the Diet of Augsburg in 1530. Negri defended with eloquence the famous Protestant profession of faith known under the name of the Confession of Augsburg. He afterwards returned to Italy; but that country offering no security to the preachers of the Reformed doctrines, he went back to Germany. He stopped some time at Strasburg, then at Geneva, and finally settled at Chiavenna, a small village of the Grisons, where he married, and became the teacher of a school. His small salary scarcely sufficed to support his family. It appears that he attempted to better his position by going again to Geneva; but he was not more fortunate than before, and he returned to Chiavenna, where he died some time posterior to 1559. In his last years Negri departed from the theological platform of his old teachers, Luther and Zwingli, and embraced Socinianism. We have of his works, *Turcicarum rerum commentarius* (Paris, 1538, 8vo), translated by Paul Giovo:—*Rudimenta grammaticæ, ex auctoribus collecta* (Milan, 1541), reprinted under the title of *Canones grammaticales* (Peschiaro, 1555, 8vo):—*Ovidii Metamorphosis in epitomen Phalencis versibus redacta* (Zurich, 1542; Basle, 1544):—*Tragædia de libero arbitrio* (Geneva, 1546, 4to, and 1550, with additions). This singular dramatic allegory upon one of the most disputed questions between the Catholics and the Reformers is rare and recherché; the denouement of the piece is the triumph of Justifying Grace over king Free-Will, who is beheaded, and over the pope, who is recognised as Antichrist. The drama was translated into French under the title *La tragédie du roi Franc-Arbitre* (Villefranche [Geneva], 1559, 8vo). We also have of Negri's works, *De Fanini Faventini ac Dominici Bassanensis morte, qui nuper ob Christum in Italia Romani pontificis jussu impie occisi sunt, brevis historia* (Chiavenna, 1550, 8vo), one of his rarest and most curious books:—*Historia Francisci Spieræ civitatulani qui quod susceptam semel Evangelicæ veritatis professionem abnegasset, in horrendum incidit desperationem* (Tübingen, 1555, 8vo). See Roberti, *Notizie storico-critiche della* *vita e delle opere di Franc. Negri, apostata Bassanese del secolo xvi* (Bassano, 1839, 4to); *Dizionario istorico* (ed. De Bassano); Brunet, *Manuel du Libraire* (Index); Hoefer, *Nouv. Biog. Gén.* xxvii, 618, 619. (J. H. W.)

Negri, Girolamo, an Italian humanist, was born at Venice in 1494. After having been vicar of the bishops of Belluno and Vicenza, he became secretary of cardinal Cornaro, and later of cardinal Contarini. Negri obtained afterwards a canonicate at Padua. He died at Padua in 1577. According to the judgment of Sadolet, he wrote Latin with purity and great elegance. We have of his works, *Epistolæ et Orationes* (Padua, 1579, 4to, and Rome, 1767). At the head of this last edition is found a biography of Negri, written by abbé Costanzi. See Foscarini, *Storia della letteratura Veneziana.*

Negri, Salomon (Arabic, *Soleyman Alsadi*), a Greek philosopher, was born at Damascus in the latter part of the 17th century. Instructed by the Jesuit missionaries in the Greek and Latin languages, he came to Paris, and continued his studies at the Sorbonne. He afterwards went to London, and in 1701 to Halle, where he remained four years, giving lessons in Arabic, among others to the celebrated Michaelis. The climate of Germany being injurious to his health, he went to Italy, and afterwards established himself at Constantinople, where he was ordained priest of the Greek Church. The war brought him again to Italy. He sought, but without success, to found at Venice, and later at Rome, a school where he would have taught Arabic, Syriac, and Turkish. He then returned to Halle, where he again passed sixteen months; and finally settled in London, and there obtained employment as interpreter of the Oriental languages. He died there in 1729. Negri has given Arabic translations of the *Psalms* and the *New Testament,* published under the auspices of the British and Foreign Bible Society. The *Psalms* appeared in 1725 (8vo); the *New Testament* in 1727 (4to). These two versions have been severely criticised by Reiske (see Baumgarten, *Nachrichten von merkwürdigen Büchern,* iii, 283). We have likewise a Latin translation of the *Vie de Gabriel Bachtishusia* (in the *Opera* of Freind). Lastly, he has published in the *Freiwilliges Hebeopfer* a *Conversation* which he had in Constantinople with a Turkish mollah. See *Memoria Negriana* (Halle, 1764, 4to); Rotermund, *Supplement* to Jöcher, *Gelehrten-Lexikon,* s. v.; Hoefer, *Nouv. Biog. Générale,* xxxvii, 616.

Negri, Virginia - Angélica - Paula - Antonia, an Italian nun, was born in 1508 at Milan. She early left the world to enter the new monastery of the Angelicas of St. Paul, to the foundation of which she had contributed, and became teacher of the novices. Full of zeal for the propagation of her faith, she travelled over Vicenza, Udine, Padua, Verona, Brescia, preaching everywhere repentance and purity of life. The sick and the poor also became the object of her care, and several hospitals owe their foundation to her. Among the number of conversions that she made, we mention that of Alphonse, marquis of Guaste, governor of the Milanese, whom she comforted by religious counsels on his death-bed. Many of her converts entered the congregation of the Clercs of St. Paul. Calumny did not spare her; and her enemies, seeking to prove her a visionary, found the means to immure her in the convent of the Clarissas. John of Salazar, an Italian prelate, then archbishop of Luciano, was named to examine her conduct, and recognised the falsity of the accusations. A woman of superior mind, she wrote well. She was well versed in Latin. She died at Milan April 4, 1555. We have of her works, *Lettere spirituali della devota e religiosa Angelica Paula Antonia de Negri* (Venice, 1547, 4to; Milan, 1563, 8vo). Another edition, published at Rome (1576, 12mo), is preceded by the life of Virginia Negri by J. B. Fontana de Conti. The spiritual letters, to the number of seventy-two, are

divided into three parts, and for unction and piety offer some resemblance to those of Saint Catharine of Sienna. There is also attributed to Negri, *Esercizio particolare d'una serva del Signore* (Brescia, 1577, 12mo). See *Biblioth. mediol. scriptorum,* ii, 993; Arisi, *Cremona litterata;* Augustinus, *Ab Ecclesia, Teatro delle done letterate,* p. 271.

Negrillos or **Negritos** (Spanish, diminutive of *Negroes*) is the name given by the Spaniards to certain Negro-like tribes inhabiting the interior of some of the Philippine Islands, and differing essentially both in features and manners from the Malay inhabitants of the Eastern archipelago. Among the planters and villagers of the plains they bear the name of *Itas* or *Ajetas* (pronounced *Abetus*). They are also called by the Spaniards *Negritos del Monte,* from their inhabiting the mountainous districts for the most part; and one of the islands where they are most numerous bears the name of *Isla de los Negros.* These Negritos are also known by the names *Aeta, Aigta, Ite, Inapta,* and *Igolote* or *Igorote.* They bear a very strong resemblance to the Negroes of Guinea, but are much smaller in size, averaging in height not more than four feet eight inches, whence their appellation. They are described as a short, small, but well-made and active people, the lower part of the face projecting like that of the African Negroes, the hair either woolly or frizzled, and the complexion exceedingly dark, but not quite so black as that of the Negroes. The Spaniards describe them as small, more slightly built, less black, and less ugly than the Negroes —*Menos Negros y menos feos.* All writers concur in speaking of them as sunk in the lowest depths of savagedom, wandering in the woods and mountains, without any fixed dwellings, and with only a strip of bark to cover their nakedness; sleeping in the branches of the trees, or among the ashes of the fires at which they had cooked their food. Their only weapons are the bow and arrow; and they live upon roots, wild fruits, and any sort of animals that they can surprise in their haunts or conquer in the chase. By the Malays they

Negritos of Luzon.

are despised and hated; and the buffalo-hunters in the woods, when they meet with them, do not scruple to shoot them down like wild beasts or game. "It has not come to my knowledge," says Mallat, "that a family of these Negroes ever took up their abode in a village. If the Mohammedan inhabitants make slaves of them, they will rather submit to be beaten to death than undergo any bodily fatigue; and it is impossible, either by force or persuasion, to bring them to labor.... Prompted by an irresistible instinct to return to the place of their birth, they prefer a savage life to all the charms of civilization. It has occurred that individuals, who have taken Negritos during their infancy, and made sacrifices to give them an education, have found themselves suddenly abandoned by them" (ii, 95). The same writer, an ecclesiastic, speaks of them as gentle and inoffensive in their manners, whenever he himself came in contact with them; and although informed that some of them were cannibals, he was not inclined to believe the report. Dr. Carl Scherzer, the historian of the circumnavigation of the *Novara*, when at Manilla, had an opportunity of seeing a Negrita girl whom he thus describes: "This was a girl of about twelve or fourteen years of age, of dwarf-like figure, with woolly hair, broad nostrils, but without the dark skin and wide everted lips which characterize the Negro type. This pleasing-looking, symmetrically-formed girl had been brought up in the house of a Spaniard, apparently with the pious object of rescuing her soul from heathenism. The poor little Negrilla hardly understood her own mother-tongue, besides a very little Tagal, so that we had considerable difficulty in understanding each other." According to Spanish statements, the Negritos are found only in five of the Philippine Islands, viz. Luzon, Mindoro, Panay, Negros, and Mindanao, and are estimated at about 25,000 souls. A few exist, however, in the interior of some of the other islands in the Eastern archipelago; and they are scattered also, though in small numbers, through certain islands of Polynesia. They are altogether an island people, and are hence treated of by Prichard under the designation of Pelagian Negroes. By Dr. Pickering they are regarded as a distinct race, resembling the Papuan, but differing from it in the diminutive stature, the general absence of a beard, the projecting of the lower part of the face or the inclined profile, and the exaggerated Negro features. The hair, also, is more woolly than that of the Papuans, though far from equalling that of the Negroes in knotty closeness. By Latham the Negritos are classified under the subdivision of "Oceanic Mongolidæ, C," which subdivision is further modified by him into the designation of "Amphinesians" and "Kelænonesians." Müller, in his *Allgemeine Ethnographie* (Vienna, 1873), classifies them among the Papuans of the pure type, but Wallace considers them a totally distinct race, and, connecting them with the inhabitants of the Andaman Islands, in the Bay of Bengal, is of opinion that they are probably of Asiatic rather than of Polynesian origin; and Peschel, in his *Volkerkunde* (2d ed. Leipsic, 1875), prefers to call them Asiatic Papuans, in distinction from Australian Papuans. The Negritos out of the Philippine Islands are found for the most part in the islands embraced under the latter designation, as New Guinea, New Ireland, Solomon's Isles, Louisiade, New Caledonia, and Tasmania or Van Diemen's Land. Except in the last-mentioned island, however, the Negritos, strictly speaking—that is, the blackish people with woolly hair —do not preponderate over the other native tribes less strongly marked with Negro features; while in Tasmania itself the race has almost entirely disappeared, amounting at present to not more than two or three dozen souls. Dr. Pickering is of opinion that "the Negrito race once occupied more space than it does at this time, and that it has in many instances preceded the dissemination of other races." We conclude with a description of a Negrito native of Erromango (the island where the missionary Williams was murdered), supplied

to Dr. Pickering by Horatio Hales, his associate in the United States exploring expedition. "He was about five feet high," says Mr. Hales, "slender and long limbed; he had close woolly hair, and retreating arched forehead, short and scanty eyebrows, and small snub nose, thick lips (especially the upper), a retreating chin, and that projection of the jaws and lower part of the face which is one of the distinctive characteristics of the Negro race. ... Placed in a crowd of African blacks, there was nothing about him by which he could have been distinguished from the rest."

The Negritos have no religion, and adore no star. It appears, however, that they have transmitted to the Sanguianes (a brown race inhabiting the neighborhood), or have learned from the latter, the practice of worshipping for a day a rock or the trunk of a tree in which they find a resemblance to some animal or other. Then they leave it, and think no more about idols until they meet with some other fantastical form, which becomes a new object of an equally frivolous worship. Living in a state altogether primitive, these savages possess no instruments of music; and their language, which resembles the chirruping of birds, contains only a few words incredibly difficult of acquisition by the stranger who tries to learn them. They are faithful in marriage, and have only one wife. When a young man has made his choice, his friends or parents ask the consent of the girl. It is never refused. The day is chosen, and in the morning, before sunrise, the girl is sent into the forest, where she hides herself, or not, according to her inclination towards her suitor. An hour afterwards the young man is sent to seek her; and if he has the good luck to find her, and bring her back to her friends before sunset, the marriage is consummated, and she is his wife forever. But if, on the contrary, he returns without her, he must give up all further claim. Old age is very much respected among the Negritos, and it is always one of the eldest who governs their assemblies. All the savages of this race live in great families of sixty or eighty, and stray in the forests without any fixed residence. They hold the dead in great veneration. For several years they resort to their graves for the purpose of depositing a little tobacco and betel upon them. The bow and arrows of the deceased are suspended over his grave on the day of interment, and, according to their belief, he emerges every night from the grave to go hunting. They do not always wait for the death of the afflicted before burying them. Immediately after the body has been deposited in the grave it becomes necessary, according to their usages, that the death should be avenged. The hunters of the tribe go out with their lances and arrows to kill the first living creature they meet with, whether a man, a stag, a wild hog, or a buffalo. When on a journey in search of a victim, they take the precaution of breaking off the young shoots of the shrubs they pass by, leaving the ends hanging in the direction of their route, in order to warn neighbors and travellers to avoid the path they are taking in search of a man or a beast to be offered up; for if one of their own people fall into their hands, even he is sacrificed as the expiatory victim. See Mallat, *Les Philippines*, etc. (Paris, 1846, 2 vols. 8vo), ii, 94 sq.; De la Gironière, *Vingt Années aux Philippines* (Paris, 1853), p. 294 sq.; Earl, *Native Races of the Indian Archipelago* (Lond. 1853), ch. vii, viii; Semper, *Die Philippinen u. ihre Bewohner* (Würzburg, 1869).

Negro (from Latin *niger*, "black") is the name generally applied to the African natives. This is, however, an incorrect use of the word, for Negro races inhabit only portions of the African continent, principally between lat. 10° N. and 20° S. The Negro has no connection, at least not intimately, with the races inhabiting Northern Africa, such as the Egyptians, Berbers, Assyrians, Nubians, etc. The southern extremities of Africa, too, are comparatively free from Negroes; they are inhabited by the Hottentots (q. v.). The Kaffres (q. v.) are sometimes classed with the Negroes.

In some of the border countries a strict classification of their inhabitants is difficult, as they have considerably intermixed. The Negro, too, is not at all confined to the African continent, but is found in various parts of Asia and its islands, and throughout America and the West Indies, whither he was originally carried for bondage servitude. See SLAVERY. In Blumenbach's fivefold division of mankind the Negroes occupy the first place under the variety *Ethiopian*, which likewise embraces the Kaffres, Hottentots, Australians, Alforians, and Oceanic Negroes. In Latham's threefold division they are placed among the *Atlantidæ*, and form the primary subdivision of *Negro Atlantidæ* in that author's classification; while in Pickering's elevenfold division they occupy the last place in his enumeration of the races of mankind. Physically the Negro is distinguished by a soft and silky skin, dull cherry-red in the infant, and growing black very soon; it differs from that of the whites principally in the greater amount of pigment cells in the *Rete Malpighii* (the epidermis being uncolored), and in the greater number of cutaneous glands. His hair is generally called woolly, though improperly, for it differs but little from that of the other races except in color, and in its curled and twisted form, and is rather harsh and wiry. His lips are thick, the lower part of his face prognathic, or projecting like a muzzle. His skull, which is very thick and solid, is long and narrow, with a depressed forehead, prominent occiput and jaws, a facial angle of $70°$ to $65°$. According to Camper's lateral admeasurement, the head of the Negro shows an angle of $70°$, while that of the European shows one of $80°$, on which difference of $10°$, as he considered, depends the superior beauty of the latter. There is not much dependence, however, to be placed on such a mode of admeasurement; and the same may be said of Blumenbach's vertical method. According to this, a considerable difference would appear to exist between the skull of the Negro and that of the European. "But," says Dr. Prichard, "I have carefully examined the situation of the foramen magnum in many Negro skulls; in all of them its position may be accurately described as being exactly behind the transverse line bisecting the antero-posterior diameter of the basis cranii. This is precisely the place which Owen has pointed out as the general position of the occipital hole in the human skull. In those Negro skulls which have the alveolar process very protuberant, the anterior half of the line above described is lengthened in a slight degree by this circumstance. If allowance is made for it, no difference is perceptible. The difference is in all instances extremely slight; and it is equally perceptible in heads belonging to other races of men, if we examine crania which have prominent upper jaws. If a line is let fall from the summit of the head at right angles with the plane of the basis, the occipital foramen will be found to be situated immediately behind it; and this is precisely the case in Negro and in European heads." There is, in fact, neither in this respect—the conformation of the Negro skull—nor in any other, solid ground for the opinion hazarded by some writers, and supported either through ignorance or from interested motives by many persons—that the Negro forms a connecting link between the higher order of apes and mankind. The skin, hair, skull, lips, maxillary profile, and general facial appearance of the Negro, are not, however, the only features that distinguish him in a great degree from the European, and seem to stamp him as a distinct variety of the human race. "In the Negro," says Prichard, "the bones of the leg are bent outwards. Soemmering and Lawrence have observed that the tibiæ and fibulæ in the Negro are more convex in front than in Europeans; the calves are very high, so as to encroach upon the upper part of the legs; the feet and hands, but particularly the former, are flat; and the os calcis, instead of being arched, is continued nearly in a straight line with the other bones of the foot, which is remarkably broad." As to the supposed excessive length of

the forearm in the Negro, a circumstance also dwelt upon as showing an approach to the anthropoid apes, facts are altogether against the statement; there being no greater difference than is observable in individuals of any other variety of mankind. His height is seldom six feet, and rarely below five and a half; and as a rule the Negro figures are fine, especially their torso. Seen from behind, the spine usually appears depressed, owing to the greater curvature of the ribs; the nates are more flattened than in other races, and join the thighs almost at a right angle instead of a curve. Besides these characteristics may be mentioned the projecting upper edge of the orbit; broad, retreating chin, and great development of lower part of the face; small eyes, in which but little of the yellowish-white ball is seen; small, thick ears, standing off from the head, with a small lobe and a general stunted look; black iris; very wide zygomatic arches, giving large space for the muscles of the lower jaw; large and transverse opening of the nasal cavity. The pelvis is long and narrow, its average circumference being from twenty-six to twenty-eight inches, instead of thirty to thirty-six as in the whites; this shape in the female, according to Vrolik and Weber, corresponds to the characteristic shape of the Negro head; those writers considering it as a type of degradation, as it approaches that of the *quadrumana* in the more vertical direction of the iliac bones and their less width, in the smaller breadth of sacrum, and in the consequent less extent of the hips.

In the skin of the Negro there is much oily matter, and he perspires profusely, which serves to keep him in health. The Negro flourishes under the fiercest heats and unhealthy dampness of the tropics, notwithstanding the virulent epidemics and endemics of the country where the white man soon dies; he has less nervous sensibility than the whites, and is not subject to nervous affections; is comparatively insensible to pain, bearing surgical operations well; the effects of opium and other narcotics appear rather in the digestive, circulatory, and respiratory functions than in the cerebral and nervous system; he is little subject to yellow fever, and more to yaws and other cutaneous affections; he is generally very torpid under disease. The senses of the Negroes are acute; the voice in the males is hoarse and not powerful, and in the females high and shrill. They are fond of music, and have many ingeniously contrived musical instruments, generally of a noisy character; they have a keen sense of the ridiculous, and are of a cheerful disposition; though cruel to their enemies and prisoners, and setting little value on human life, they are naturally kind-hearted, hospitable to strangers, and communicative of their joys and sorrows; the females are remarkably affectionate as mothers and children, and as attendants on the sick, even to foreigners. They are less dirty in their persons and dwellings than most other barbarous races. They are ready to receive instruction, and to profit by it up to a certain point; quick to perceive the beauty of goodness, they generally appreciate the services of the missionaries in their behalf, and were not their teachings counteracted by the intoxicating drink brought by traders, they would probably in time, in outward observances if not in reality, merit the name of semi-Christian communities. The custom of polygamy prevails among all the Negro tribes, and where these are constituted into nations or kingdoms, as in Dahomey, the sovereign has often as many as two or three thousand wives, whom he occasionally disposes of as presents to his chief officers and favorites. In those parts of Africa where the slave-trade has flourished the Negro is lowest in the stage of civilized life. In other parts he shows a capacity for practicing the arts of life. Negroes are ingenious in the construction of their dwellings and in the manufacture of their weapons; they have some knowledge of the working of iron and other metals; they manufacture arms, dress and prepare the skins of animals, weave cloth, and fabricate numerous useful household utensils. Neither are they altogether deficient in a knowledge of agriculture. These marks of civilization are, for the most part, apparent in the districts either wholly or partially converted to Mohammedanism. Mungo Park, in his account of Sego, the capital of Bambarra, describes it as a city of 30,000 inhabitants, with houses of two stories high, having flat roofs, mosques in every quarter, and ferries conveying men and horses over the Niger. "The view of this extensive city," he says, "the numerous canoes upon the river, the crowded population, and the cultivated state of the surrounding country, formed altogether a prospect of civilization and magnificence which I little expected to find in the bosom of Africa."

The languages of the various nations and tribes of Negroes are very numerous. Vocabularies of nearly 200 languages have been brought from Africa by the Rev. Dr. Koelle. "A slight examination of these vocabularies," says Mr. Edwin Norris, "seems to show that there are among the Negro idioms a dozen or more classes of languages, differing from each other at least as much as the more remote Indo-Germanic languages do." To these Negro idioms Dr. Krapf has given the name of *Nigro-Hamitic Languages.* These may perhaps have affinities with some of the other African tongues, but not with any of the great well-defined families of languages. For further information upon this subject, as well as upon the classification of the different Negro races, we must content ourselves with referring to Dr. Prichard's *Natural History of Man,* and especially to a learned note by Mr. Edwin Norris in vol. i of that work (p. 323). It has been said that no Negro nation ever possessed a literature, or had the ingenuity to invent an alphabet, and until recently this was probably true; but Christian missionaries have discovered a tribe in Western Africa, named *Vei,* which possess a well-constructed written language, with books, the invention of one of their number still living, who presents a case as remarkable as that of the invention of the Cherokee alphabet. Among the Negro race there is a great variety, greater, perhaps, than among any other family, yet while the several tribes have these clearly distinctive peculiarities, they yet bear a strong general resemblance to each other, not only in their physical appearance, but in their intellectual capacities, moral instincts, customs, and manners.

The religion of the Negroes is but a debased *fetich* worship [see FETICHISM], except where Mohammedanism has made them acquainted with an ethical religion. Those who have not accepted the teachings of the Koran (q. v.) make fetiches of serpents, elephants' teeth, tigers' claws, and other parts of animals, at the dictation of their *fetich man,* or priest. They also manufacture idols of wood and stone, which they worship; and yet, under all this, they have some idea of a Supreme Being. They believe in good and evil spirits, and are perpetually practicing incantations to ward off the baneful influence of their spiritual enemies. In Eastern Africa, Speke (*Discovery of the Source of the Nile,* p. 243) mentions that on one occasion, "as there was a partial eclipse of the moon, all the Wanguana [a Negro race] marched up and down from Rumanika's to Nuanagi's huts, singing and beating our tin cooking-pots to frighten off the spirit of the sun from consuming entirely the chief object of their reverence, the moon." Lander (*Niger Expedition,* ii, 180, 183) mentions that at Boussa, in Central Africa, an eclipse was attributed to an attack made by the sun on the moon. During the whole time the eclipse lasted the natives made as much noise as possible, "in the hope of being able to frighten away the sun to his proper sphere, and leave the moon to enlighten the world as at other times." They make prayers and offerings to their idols, and have sacred songs and festivals, dances, ceremonies, and places; and they have priests and holy men, who are also magicians and doctors. They believe generally in an after-life (see Lubbock, p. 139, 140), without, however, any distinctive idea of retribution, and some tribes hold the

transmigration of the human soul into a gorilla, or other beast, bird, reptile, or fish; they are very superstitious, and have great fear of ghosts and apparitions. Their religion, in fact, is one altogether of fear; and as this leads to cruelty, we find them for the most part indifferent to the sacrifice of human life. They sacrifice animals, and in some parts they even offer up human victims to propitiate their deities. They are cruel to their enemies and prisoners, and often shed blood for the mere savage delight they experience in seeing it flow from their victims. We need only allude to the inhuman *customs,* as they are called, of Dahomey, and the *Yam* and *Adai customs* of the Ashantees, as described by Bowdich, in support of this statement. The Negroes are easily influenced by the teachings of ethical religions, and the converts made for Mohammedanism are believed to be very numerous [see MOHAMMEDANISM]; Christian missionaries have met with success also. The Romanists were early workers among them, but in recent years the Protestants have been most successful in propagating Christianity among them. For further details regarding the civil, social, and religious condition of the Negroes, and of missions among them, see the articles AFRICA; KAFFRES; LIBERIA; MANDINGOES; PO, FERNANDO; YOMBA. Of the condition and prospects of the Negroes in the various countries into which they have been imported during the prevalence of the slave-trade we have not room to speak here, but refer to the article SLAVERY. They are found in all the West India Islands, to the number of about 3,000,000; in the United States, Brazil, Peru, and other parts of South America; also in the Cape de Verde Islands, Arabia, Morocco, etc. In the British West India Islands they were emancipated from slavery in 1834, and in those belonging to France in 1848. Indeed, slavery now exists nowhere in the West Indies, with the exception of Cuba and Porto Rico. In the United States the Negroes amount to about 6,700,000; they are now liberated, and enjoy civil rights, and some occupy prominent positions in ecclesiastical and political life, and in all the other walks of life many are rising to influence and power.

The Negroes figure in history from very ancient date. They were not much known by the Hebrews and the Homeric Greeks, to judge from the writings at our command, but the Egyptians became acquainted with Negroes, about B.C. 2300, through the conquests of their rulers, and we find Negroes represented on Egyptian monuments as early as B.C. 1000. For nearly thirty-five centuries the type has remained unchanged in Egypt. The Greeks first knew them in the 7th century B.C., their Ethiopians being merely any people darker than the Hellenic, like the Arabs, Egyptians, Libyans, or Carthaginians, none of whom are Negroes. The typical Negroes of the Guinea coast are generally rude and nearly naked savages, of a deep black color and ugly features; in the interior many of the tribes, like the Fan, and others visited since 1855 by Paul du Chaillu and Winwood Reade, are fierce cannibals, but fine-looking, warlike, ingenious, and skilful in the working of iron. Those on the Slave Coast are more degraded, selling their neighbors to slave-dealers. In the vast region explored by Livingstone, Barth, Du Chaillu, Burton, Speke, Baker, Schweinfurth, and other recent travellers, there are many tribes more or less savage, for an account of which the reader is referred to the respective special notices in this work, and chiefly to the narratives of these explorers.

The father of English ethnology, Dr. Prichard, thought that the original pair must have been Negroes, and that mankind descended from them. His words are: "It must be concluded that the process of nature in the human species is the transmutation of the characters of the Negro into those of the European, or the evolution of white varieties in black races of men. We have seen that there are causes existing which are capable of producing such an alteration, but we have no facts which induce us to suppose that the reverse of this change could in any circumstances be effected. This leads us to the inference that the primitive stock of men were Negroes, which has every appearance of truth" (*Researches*, p. 233). It is not a little remarkable that although Blumenbach and Prichard were both advocates for the unity of man, they materially differed in their argumentation. Blumenbach saw in his five varieties of man nothing but degeneracy from some ideal perfect type. Prichard, on the contrary, could imagine no arguments, or knew of any facts, to support such a conclusion. Prichard, however, was not alone in this supposition, for Pallas, Lacipède, Hunter, Dornik, and Link were also inclined to the same view. See Hunt, in *Memoirs of the Anthropol. Society of London*, vol. i, art. i; see also in these memoirs, same vol., art. ii; Prichard, *Researches into the Phys. Hist. of Mankind*, i, 199–211 (3d ed.); Latham, *Varieties of Man*, p. 469 sq.; Nott, *Types of Mankind*, p. 260; Quatrefages, *Unité de l'Espèce Humaine* (Paris, 1861); Lubbock, *Origin of Civilization*, ch. iv–vi; *Trans. of the Ethnological Society of London*, vol. i, new series, p. 317 sq.; Casalis, *Les Bassoutos ou Vingt-trois années de séjour et d'observations au sud d'Afrique* (Paris, 1859), especially p. 257–268; Burton, *Lake Regions of Central Africa*, (1861), vol. i; Görz, *Reiseskizzen aus Nordost-Afrika* (1855), i, 162 sq., 175 sq.; Reade, *Savage Africa*, ch. xxxvi; Pruner Bey, *Memoir on the Negro; Wanderings in West Africa*, vol. i and ii; the Rev. Henry J. Cox, D.D., in *Methodist Quarterly Review*, Jan. 1875, art. iv; and in the same Review, April, 1874, art. iv; *Blackwood's Magazine*, May, 1866, art. iii. See also the recent publications on Africa by the celebrated travellers Barth, Livingstone, Speke, Chapman, and Schweinfurth.

Negrone or **Nigrone**, PIETRO, called *Il Giovane Zingaro* ("the young Gypsy"), a painter of the Neapolitan school who devoted himself mostly to sacred art, was born at Calabria about 1505. Dominic says he first studied under Gio. Antonio d'Amato, afterwards under Marco Calabrese; and he commends him as an accomplished and diligent artist. In S. Agnello, at Naples, there is a picture of *The Virgin and the Infant in the Clouds, with Saints and a Glory of Angels*; also in S. Maria Donna Romata are two pictures by him, representing the *Adoration of the Magi* and the *Scourging of Christ*, painted in 1541. He died, according to Lanzi, about 1565.

Negroponte, FRA FRANCESCO, or ANTONIO, a monk of the Capuchin order, who flourished at Venice in the early part of the 15th century; he devoted himself to the cultivation of sacred art, and was a noted painter, whose works. according to Kugler, resemble those of Jacobello del Fiore.

Nehalennia, a pagan goddess, the origin of whose name it is difficult to trace, was worshipped in ancient Gaul and Germany. An image of this female deity was first discovered in 1646 in Zealand, among some ruins which had long been covered by the sea. Several images have since been discovered in France, Germany, and Italy. Youth seems to have been one of her attributes. She is sometimes represented sitting and sometimes standing. Montfaucon, in his *Antiquities*, gives seven pictures of this goddess. She is represented carrying a basket of fruit, with a dog at her side. The resemblance of her name with the Greek νέα σελήνη (new moon) may trace a connection to the goddess Diana; others think her an ocean deity. See Bescherelle, *La Mythologie Illustrée*, p. 78; Grimm, *Deutsche Mythologie*, s. v.; Mallet, *Northern Antiquities*.

Nehel'amite (Heb. *Nechelami'*, נֶחֱלָמִי, with the art.; Sept. Αἰλαμίτης v. r. Ἐλαμίτης, Νεελαμίτης, Αἰλαμί), an appellation of a man named Shemaiah, a false prophet, who went with the captives to Babylon (Jer. xxix, 24, 31, 32). The name is no doubt formed from

that either of Shemaiah's native place or the progenitor of his family; which of the two is uncertain. See SHEMAIAH. No place called *Nehelam* is mentioned in the Bible, or known to have existed in Palestine, nor does it occur in any of the genealogical lists of families. It resembles the name which the Sept. has attached to Ahijah the prophet, namely, the Enlamite—ὁ Ενλαμεί; but by what authority they substitute that name for "the Shilonite" of the Hebrew text is doubtful. The word "Nehelamite" also probably contains a play on the "dreams" (*chalam*) and "dreamers," whom Jeremiah is never wearied of denouncing (see ch. xxiii, xxvii, xxix). Fürst, however, thinks (*Heb. Lex.* s. v.) that there is an allusion to the failure of an inheritance (נחל), as threatened. The Targum gives the name as *Chelam*, חֵלָם. A place of this name [see HELAM] lay somewhere between the Jordan and the Euphrates.

Nehemi'ah (Heb. *Nechemyah'*, נְחֶמְיָה, *comforted by Jehovah*; Sept. Νεεμίας v. r. Νεεμία; Josephus, Νεεμίας, *Ant.* xi, 5, 6), the name of three men.

1. The second named of the "children of the province," who had been carried away by Nebuchadnezzar, and lived to return with Zerubbabel to Judæa (Ezra ii, 2; Neh. vii, 7). B.C. 536. He was not the same as No. 3 (see Carpzov, *Introd.* i, 341 sq.).

2. Son of Azbuk, of the tribe of Judah; ruler in half the town of Bethzur, in the mountains of Judah, who took a leading part in rebuilding the wall of Jerusalem (Neh. iii, 16). B.C. 445.

3. The son of Hachaliah (Neh. i, 1) and brother of Hanani (Neh. vii, 7). He was apparently of the tribe of Judah, since his fathers were buried at Jerusalem, and Hanani his kinsman seems to have been of that tribe (Neh. i, 2; ii, 3; vii, 2). Some think he was of priestly descent, because his name appears at the head of a list of priests in Neh. x, 1–8; but it is obvious, from Neh. ix, 38, that he stands there as a prince, and not as a priest—that he heads the list because he was head of the nation. The Vulgate, in 2 Macc. i, 21, calls him "*sacerdos* Nehemias" (comp. Rambach, *Præf. in Neh.* p. 112; Carpzov, *Introd.* i, 338); but this is a false version of the Greek, which has ἐκέλευσε τοὺς ἱερεῖς Νεεμίας, and not ὁ ἱερεύς, which the Latin would require. The Syriac agrees with the Greek. The expression in ver. 18, that Nehemiah offered sacrifice," implies no more than that he provided the sacrifices. Others, with some probability, infer, from his station at the Persian court and the high commission he received, that he was, like Zerubbabel, of the tribe of Judah and of the house of David (Carpzov, *Introductio*, etc., i, 339). Malalas of Antioch (*Chronogr.* vi, 160) singularly combines the two views, and calls him "Nehemiah the priest, of the seed of David."

While Nehemiah was cupbearer in the royal palace at Shushan, in the twentieth year of Artaxerxes Longimanus (q. v.), or B.C. 447, learning the mournful and desolate condition of the returned colony in Judæa (Neh. i, 2 sq.; comp. Kleinert, in the *Dörpt. Beiträg.* i, 243 sq.), he obtained permission of the king to make a journey to Jerusalem, and there to act as lieutenant or governor (Heb. פֶּחָה, Neh. v, 14. On the title of honor given to Nehemiah [Neh. viii, 9; x, 1], Tirshatha', תִּרְשָׁתָא, see Gesen. *Thesaur.* s. v.; Benfey, *Monatsnam.* s. 196, identifies it with the Zend *thvôrestâ*, "commander." But in Neh. vii, 65, 70, this title denotes not Nehemiah, but Zerubbabel, as is evident from Ezra ii, 63–70). Being furnished with this high commission, which included letters to the satraps and subordinates, and enjoying the protection of a military escort (ii, 9), Nehemiah reached Jerusalem in the year B.C. 446, and remained there till B.C. 434, being actively engaged for twelve years in promoting the public good (v, 14). "It is impossible to overestimate the importance to the future political and ecclesiastical prosperity of the

Jewish nation of this great achievement of their patriotic governor. How low the community of the Palestine Jews had fallen is apparent from the fact that from the 6th year of Darius to the 7th of Artaxerxes there is no history of them whatever; and that even after Ezra's commission, and the ample grants made by Artaxerxes in his 7th year, and the considerable re-enforcements, both in wealth and numbers, which Ezra's government brought to them, they were in a state of abject 'affliction and reproach' in the 20th of Artaxerxes: their country pillaged, their citizens kidnapped and made slaves of by their heathen neighbors, robbery and murder rife in their very capital, Jerusalem almost deserted, and the Temple again falling into decay. The one step which could resuscitate the nation, preserve the Mosaic institutions, and lay the foundation of future independence, was the restoration of the city walls. Jerusalem being once again secure from the attacks of the marauding heathen, civil government would become possible, the spirit of the people and their attachment to the ancient capital of the monarchy would revive, the priests and Levites would be encouraged to come into residence, the tithes and first-fruits and other stores would be safe, and Judah, if not actually independent, would preserve the essentials of national and religious life. To this great object, therefore, Nehemiah directed his whole energies without an hour's unnecessary delay. By word and example he induced the whole population, with the single exception of the Tekoite nobles, to commence building with the utmost vigor, even the lukewarm high-priest Eliashib performing his part. In a wonderfully short time the walls seemed to emerge from the heaps of burned rubbish, and to encircle the city as in the days of old. The gateways also were rebuilt, and ready for the doors to be hung upon them. But it soon became apparent how wisely Nehemiah had acted in hastening on the work. On his very first arrival, as governor, Sanballat and Tobiah had given unequivocal proof of their mortification at his appointment, and before the work was commenced had scornfully asked whether he intended to rebel against the king of Persia. But when the restoration was seen to be rapidly progressing, their indignation knew no bounds. They not only poured out a torrent of abuse and contempt upon all engaged in the work, but actually made a great conspiracy to fall upon the builders with an armed force and put a stop to the undertaking. The project was defeated by the vigilance and prudence of Nehemiah, who armed all the people after their families, and showed such a strong front that their enemies dared not attack them. This armed attitude was continued from that day forward. Various stratagems were then resorted to to get Nehemiah away from Jerusalem, and if possible to take his life." But in the face of these difficulties he rebuilt, or repaired, the city wall, not without serious opposition from parties of Samaritans, finishing the work in fifty-two days (Neh. vi, 15); reformed abuses, redressed grievances (ch. v), introduced law and order (ch. vii), and revived the worship of God (ch. viii sq.). A strange fable is told of his discovering again the holy fire (2 Macc. i, 18 sq.). The account in 2 Macc. ii, 13 of the compilation by Nehemiah of the Old-Testament writings is disbelieved by Eichhorn (Apokr. p. 255 sq.), and is rightly estimated by Hengstenberg (Auth. d. Dan. p. 241 sq.). See ESDRAS, BOOKS OF. It should be added that the son of Sirach, in celebrating Nehemiah's good deeds, mentions only that he "raised up for us the walls that were fallen, and set up the gates and bars, and raised up our ruins again" (Ecclus. xlix, 13). In his important public proceedings, which appear all to have happened in the first year of his government, Nehemiah enjoyed the assistance of Ezra (q. v.), who is named on several occasions as taking a prominent part in conducting affairs (Neh. viii, 1, 9, 13; xii, 36). Ezra had gone up to Jerusalem thirteen years before, and lived to be Nehemiah's fellow-laborer. These contemporaries are equally emi-

nent among the benefactors of the Jewish people—alike patriotic and zealous, though not uniform in character, or the same in operation. In the character of Ezra we find no indication of the self-complacency which forms a marked feature in that of Nehemiah. The former, in accordance with his priestly calling, labored chiefly in promoting the interests of religion, but the latter had most to do with the general affairs of government; the one was in charge of the Temple, the other of the state. Nehemiah refused to receive his lawful allowance as governor from the people, in consideration of their poverty, during the whole twelve years that he was in office, but kept at his own charge a table for 150 Jews, at which any who returned from captivity were welcome. Nehemiah returned to Persia B.C. 434, but soon heard of new abuses creeping in among the Jews, and he determined to visit Judæa again. The time of this second journey is indefinitely stated as "after some days" (xiii, 6, 7), which many have understood as meaning a single year; but this is not long enough to account for such abuses as would require Nehemiah's presence. Prideaux (Connection, i, 520 sq.; comp. Jahn, Archäol. II, i, 272 sq.; Einleitung, ii, 288 sq.) has shown sufficient reason for referring it to the second half of the reign of Darius Nothus, say B.C. 410. (But Hävernick, Einleitung ins A. T. ii, 324, holds a medium view, dating this visit B.C. cir. 424. See further, Michaelis on Nehemiah xiii; Clericus, ad idem; Petavius, Doctrina Temp. xii, 25; Cellarius, Dissertat. p. 130; Jour. of Sac. Lit. Jan. 1862, p. 446.) See SEVENTY WEEKS. After his return to the government of Judæa, Nehemiah enforced the separation of all the mixed multitude from Israel (Neh. xiii, 1–3), and accordingly expelled Tobiah the Ammonite from the chamber which the high-priest, Eliashib, had prepared for him in the Temple (xiii, 4–9). Better arrangements were also made for the support of the Temple service (xiii, 10–14), and for the rigid observance of the Sabbath (xiii, 15–22). One of the last acts of his government was an effort to put an end to mixed marriages, which led him to "chase" away a son of Joiada, the high-priest, because he was son-in-law to Sanballat the Horonite (xiii, 23–29). It is not unlikely that Nehemiah remained at his post till about the year B.C. 405, towards the close of the reign of Darius Nothus, who is mentioned in xii, 22. See DARIUS. At this time Nehemiah would be between sixty and seventy years old, if we suppose him (as most do) to have been only between twenty and thirty when he first went to Jerusalem. That he lived to be an old man is thus quite probable from the sacred history; and this is expressly declared by Josephus, who (Ant. xi, 5, 6) states that he died at an advanced age. Of the place and year of his death nothing is known. "On reviewing the character of Nehemiah, we seem unable to find a single fault (unless it be a slightly Ciceronian egotism) to counterbalance his many and great virtues. For pure and disinterested patriotism he stands unrivalled. The man whom the account of the misery and ruin of his native country, and the perils with which his countrymen were beset prompted to leave his splendid residence, and a post of wealth, power, and influence, in the first court in the world, that he might share and alleviate the sorrows of his native land, must have been pre-eminently a patriot. Every act of his during his government bespeaks one who had no selfishness in his nature. All he did was noble, generous, high-minded, courageous, and to the highest degree upright. But to stern integrity he united great humility and kindness, and a princely hospitality. As a statesman he combined forethought, prudence, and sagacity in counsel, with vigor, promptitude, and decision in action. In dealing with the enemies of his country he was wary, penetrating, and bold. In directing the internal economy of the state, he took a comprehensive view of the real welfare of the people, and adopted the measures best calculated to promote it. In dealing both with friend and foe, he was utterly free from favor or fear, conspicuous for the simplicity with which he aimed only at doing what was right, without respect of persons. But in nothing was he more remarkable than for his piety, and the singleness of eye with which he walked before God. He seems to have undertaken everything in dependence upon God, with prayer for his blessing and guidance, and to have sought his reward only from God." See Randall, *Nehemiah the Tirshatha* (Lond. 1874).

NEHEMIAH, BOOK OF, the latest of all the historical books of Scripture, both as to the time of its composition and the scope of its narrative in general, and as to the supplementary matter of ch. xii in particular, which reaches down to the time of Alexander the Great.

1. *Authorship.*—This book, which bears the title דִּבְרֵי נְחֶמְיָה, *Nehemiah's Words*, was anciently connected with Ezra, as if it formed part of the same work (Eichhorn, *Einleitung*, ii, 627). This connection is indicated by its first word, וַיְהִי, "*And* it came to pass." It arose, doubtless, from the fact that Nehemiah is a sort of continuation of Ezra (q. v.). Some ancient writers called this book the second Book of Ezra, and regarded that learned scribe as the author of it (Carpzov, *Introductio*, etc., p. 336). There can, however, be no reasonable doubt that it proceeded from Nehemiah, for its style and spirit, except in one portion, are wholly unlike Ezra's. Here we find no Chaldee documents, as in Ezra, though we might expect some from ch. ii, 7, 8, 9, and ch. vi, 5; and here also the writer discovers a species of egotism never manifested by Ezra (Neh. v, 14-19; Eichhorn, *Einleitung ins A. Test.* ii, 619).

While the book as a whole is considered to have come from Nehemiah, it consists in part of compilation. He doubtless wrote the greater part himself, but some portions he evidently took from other works. It is allowed by all that he is, in the strictest sense, the author of the narrative from ch. i to ch. vii, 5 (Hävernick, *Einleitung*, ii, 304). The account in ch. vii, 6-73 is avowedly compiled, for he says in ver. 5, "I found a register," etc. This register we find also in Ezra ii, 1-70, hence it might be thought that our author borrowed this part from Ezra; but it is more likely that they both copied from public documents, such as "the Book of the Chronicles" (דִּבְרֵי הַיָּמִים), mentioned in Neh. xii, 23. Had Nehemiah taken his list from Ezra, we might expect agreement, if not identity, in the contents; but the two records vary much in details, and are only reconciled with difficulty. "The second part (ch. viii, ix, x) is said to be marked by a strong *Levitical* or *priestly* bias, different from the tone of the rest of the book, whose interests all tend in the direction of *civil* society; also by different words and phrases, and by the use of the third person, instead of the first, when speaking of Nehemiah. Hence critics differ in their opinions, some ascribing these chapters to Ezra, some making them the composition of an unknown author in a later age. The third portion (ch. ix, xii, xiii) is again pronounced to be the work of Nehemiah, though with certain additions, which (in the estimation of these critics) are seen to be excrescences, or which betray a different authorship, chiefly on account of chronological facts which are irreconcilable with the supposition that Nehemiah wrote them.

"The most of the supposed difficulties vanish, or rather give place to a conviction of the unity of the book, as soon as we take the proper position for looking at the events narrated, as they would appear to Nehemiah, the narrator of his own feelings and transactions. Such a person does not write exactly in the order of time; nor do events seem in the same proportion to each other in his eyes and in the eyes of many of his readers. This is notorious to every reader of memoirs and biographies, particularly autobiographies. If at times there be something peculiar in the arrangements of this book of Nehemiah, as we have indicated that there is also in

Ezra, this ought to be admitted as a consequence of the writer's own state of mind or circumstances. Certainly those who have written later than the date of these books of Ezra and Nehemiah, and have endeavored to arrange their details in a different order to suit their own purposes, have effected little as to the point of consecutiveness. This is seen in the case of the tolerably respectable compiler of the third Book of Esdras, which is preserved in the Apocrypha.

"On the other hand, the book appears from the course of the life of Nehemiah (see below) to be a continuous record, written in a lively, distinct, and energetic manner, such as is admitted by every one to be very suitable to the circumstances in which it is said to have been composed. This is a fact which strikes us in reading all the accounts—the building of the ruins, the earlier and the later reforms, and the sacred services at the feast of tabernacles. Of course such different subjects are not described in the self-same words or style; and this diversity illustrates the working of Nehemiah's mind as that of a man deeply interested in the affairs in which he took an active part. It is only a perverted ingenuity which would make these differences an evidence that ch. viii, ix, x have come from a different author. Those who wish to go into the particulars of a verbal criticism may find the materials in Keil's *Introduction to the Old Testament*. He shows how the difference in the use of the names of God is suitable to the different circumstances in which they are used; how the language of the Levites in prayer is naturally more akin to the language of the law of Moses and of the Psalms than to that of plain history; how the expression, 'the nobles and the rulers,' which is frequent elsewhere, is wanting in this section; while instead of it we once meet with the Mosaic term, 'chief of the fathers,' or rather, 'heads of the fathers' houses' (ch. viii, 13); though he might have mentioned that still a different expression is found in this disputed section, and in a passage which is confessedly genuine (ch. x, 29, and iii, 5); and that Ezra is not named among those who signed the covenant, because he acted the part of 'mediator' in the transaction, as Moses had done before. This pre-eminent position assigned to Ezra necessarily threw even Nehemiah somewhat into the background, and led him to speak of himself in the *third* person instead of in the *first*, as in the rest of his book. Indeed this was the more natural and more distinct, because the first person plural, 'we,' 'our,' is used throughout the account of the sealing (ch. ix, x), which sufficiently marks the writer as an eye-witness and party in the transaction, yet one who wished not to appear singled out from his countrymen, except where this was unavoidable on account of his official capacity. When he does so mention himself it is with the addition, 'the Tirshatha,' a peculiar word, of uncertain origin and meaning, though unmistakably an attributive title of the governor. Perhaps he may have used this title rather than another, in these descriptions of ecclesiastical affairs, because of the title being given to Zerubbabel, the governor whom God had so greatly honored in the restoration of the church, while it occurs nowhere else.'

The mention of Jaddua as a high-priest (ch. xii, 11, 22) has occasioned much perplexity. This Jaddua appears to have been in office in B.C. 332, when Alexander the Great came to Jerusalem (Joseph. *Ant.* xi, 8); how then could he be named by Nehemiah? Some (e. g. Vitringa, Rambach) suppose the 10th and 11th verses to be a later addition, which seems to be the only reasonable solution; others (Hävernick, Keil) endeavor to show that Nehemiah wrote it, supposing that he lived to be an old man, so as possibly to see the year B.C. 370; and that Jaddua had at that time entered on his office, so that he filled it for about forty years, i. e. till B.C. 332 (see especially Hävernick's *Einleitung*, ii, 320-324). But this Davidson rightly thinks improbable (see Horne's *Introd.* ii, 694). Some finally resort to the belief that Jaddua is only mentioned here as having been born, but not as yet an incumbent of high-priesthood. It is difficult in that case to see why he is named at all, as the writer could not have foreseen that he would ever fill the office. See JADDUA. A similar addition by a still later hand, probably some member of the so-called "Great Sanhedrim," perhaps Simon the Just, its president, has evidently been made in the list of the Davidic line (1 Chron. iii, 23–24), which comes down to the 3d century B.C. See GENE-ALOGY OF OUR LORD. This leads to a presumption of an occasional interpolation of these few genealogical items, which (as in the case of the notice of the death of Moses in Deut. xxxiv, 5–12) do not affect the general authorship of the book. See EZRA, BOOK OF.

2. As to the *date* of the book, it is not likely that it came from Nehemiah's hand till near the close of his life. Certainly it could not have been all written before the expulsion of the priest recorded in ch. xiii, 23–29, which took place about the year B.C. 413.

3. The *canonical character* of Nehemiah's work is established by very ancient testimony. It should be noticed, however, that this book is not expressly named by Melito of Sardis (A.D. 170) in his account of the sacred writings; but this creates no difficulty, since he does mention Ezra, of which Nehemiah was then considered but a part (Eichhorn, *Einleitung*, ii, 627). Thus the Book of Nehemiah has always had an undisputed place in the Canon, being included by the Hebrews under the general head of the Book of Ezra, and as Jerome tells us in the *Prolog. Gal.* by the Greeks and Latins under the name of the second Book of Ezra. See ESDRAS, FIRST BOOK OF. "There is no quotation from it in the N.T., and it has been comparatively neglected by both the Greek and Latin fathers, perhaps on account of its simple character, and the absence of anything supernatural, prophetical, or mystical in its contents. St. Jerome (*ad Paulinam*) does indeed suggest that the account of the building of the walls, and the return of the people, the description of the priests, Levites, Israelites, and proselytes, and the division of the labor among the different families, have a hidden meaning; and also hints that Nehemiah's name, which he interprets *consolator a Domino*, points to a mystical sense. But the book does not easily lend itself to such applications, which are so manifestly forced and strained that even Augustine says of the whole Book of Ezra that it is simply historical rather than prophetical (*De Civit. Dei*, xviii, 36). Those however who wish to see St. Jerome's hint elaborately carried out may refer to the Ven. Bede's *Allegorica Expositio in Librum Nehemiæ, qui et Ezræ Secundus*, as well as to the preface to his exposition of Ezra; and, in another sense, to Bp. Pilkington's Exposition upon Nehemiah, and John Fox's Preface (*Park. Soc.*). It may be added that Bede describes both Ezra and Nehemiah as *prophets*, which is the head under which Josephus includes them in his description of the sacred books (*C. Ap.* i, 8)."

4. The *contents* of the book have been specified above in the biography of the author. The work can scarcely be called a history of Nehemiah and his times; it is rather a collection of notices of some important transactions that happened during the first year of his government, with a few scraps from his later history. The contents appear to be arranged in chronological order, with the exception perhaps of ch. xii, 27–43, where the account of the dedication of the wall seems to be out of its proper place: we might expect it rather after ch. vii, 1–4, where the completion of the wall is mentioned.

"The whole narrative gives us a graphic and interesting account of the state of Jerusalem and the returned captives in the writer's times, and, incidentally, of the nature of the Persian government and the condition of its remote provinces. The documents appended to it also give some further information as to the times of Zerubbabel on the one hand, and as to the continuation of the genealogical registers and the succession of the

high-priesthood to the close of the Persian empire on the other. The view given of the rise of two factions among the Jews—the one the strict religious party, adhering with uncompromising faithfulness to the Mosaic institutions, headed by Nehemiah; the other, the gentilizing party, ever imitating heathen customs, and making heathen connections, headed, or at least encouraged by the high-priest Eliashib and his family—sets before us the germ of much that we meet with in a more developed state in later Jewish history from the commencement of the Macedonian dynasty till the final destruction of Jerusalem. Again, in this history as well as in the Book of Ezra, we see the bitter enmity between the Jews and Samaritans acquiring strength and definitive form on both religious and political grounds. It would seem from iv, 1, 2, 8 (A. V.), and vi, 2, 6, etc., that the depression of Jerusalem was a fixed part of the policy of Sanballat, and that he had the design of raising Samaria as the head of Palestine, upon the ruin of Jerusalem, a design which seems to have been entertained by the Samaritans in later times. The book also throws much light upon the domestic institutions of the Jews. We learn incidentally the prevalence of usury, and of slavery as its consequence, the frequent and burdensome oppressions of the governors (v, 15), the judicial use of corporal punishment (xiii, 25), the continuance of false prophets as an engine of policy, as in the days of the kings of Judah (vi, 7, 12, 14), the restitution of the Mosaic provision for the maintenance of the priests and Levites and the due performance of the Temple service (xiii, 10–3), the much freer promulgation of the Holy Scriptures by the public reading of them (viii, 1; ix, 3; xiii, 1), and the more general acquaintance with them arising from their collection into one volume, and the multiplication of copies of them by the care of Ezra the scribe and Nehemiah himself (2 Macc. ii, 13), as well as from the stimulus given to the art of reading among the Jewish people during their residence in Babylon [see HILKIAH]; the mixed form of political government still surviving the ruin of their independence (v, 7, 13; x), the reviving trade with Tyre (xiii, 16), the agricultural pursuits and wealth of the Jews (v, 11; xiii, 15), the tendency to take heathen wives, indicating, possibly, a disproportion in the number of Jewish males and females among the returned captives (x, 30; xiii, 3, 23), the danger the Jewish language was in of being corrupted (xiii, 24), with other details which only the narrative of an eye-witness would have preserved to us. Some of these details give us incidentally information of great historical importance.

"(*a.*) The account of the building and dedication of the wall (iii, xii) contains the most valuable materials for settling the topography of Jerusalem to be found in Scripture. See JERUSALEM.

"(*b.*) The list of returned captives who came under different leaders from the time of Zerubbabel to that of Nehemiah (amounting in all to only 42,360 adult males, and 7337 servants), which is given in ch. vii, conveys a faithful picture of the political weakness of the Jewish nation as compared with the times when Judah alone numbered 470,000 fighting men (1 Chron. xxi, 5). It justifies the description of the Palestine Jews as 'the remnant that are left of the captivity' (Neh. i, 3), and as 'these feeble Jews' (iv, 2), and explains the great difficulty felt by Nehemiah in peopling Jerusalem itself with a sufficient number of inhabitants to preserve it from assault (vii, 3, 4; xi, 1, 2). It is an important aid, too, in understanding the subsequent history, and in appreciating the patriotism and valor by which they attained their independence under the Maccabees.

"(*c.*) The lists of leaders, priests, Levites, and of those who signed the covenant, reveal incidentally much of the national spirit as well as of the social habits of the captives, derived from older times. Thus the fact that *twelve* leaders are named in Neh. vii, 7 indicates the feeling of the captives that they represented the *twelve* tribes, a feeling further evidenced in the expression 'the men of the people of Israel.' The enumeration of twenty-one and twenty-two, or, if Zidkijah stands for the head of the house of Zadok, twenty-three chief priests in x, 1–8, xii, 1–7, of whom nine bear the names of those who were heads of courses in David's time (1 Chron. xxiv) [see Jehoiarib], shows how, even in their wasted and reduced numbers, they struggled to preserve these ancient institutions, and also supplies the reason of the mention of these particular twenty-two or twenty-three names.

"(d.) Other miscellaneous information contained in this book embraces the hereditary crafts practiced by certain priestly families, e. g. the apothecaries, or makers of the sacred ointments and incense (iii, 8), and the goldsmiths, whose business it probably was to repair the sacred vessels (iii, 8), and who may have been the ancestors, so to speak, of the money-changers in the Temple (John ii, 14, 15); the situation of the garden of the kings of Judah by which Zedekiah escaped (2 Kings xxv, 4), as seen in iii, 15; and statistics, reminding one of Domesday-Book, concerning not only the cities and families of the returned captives, but the number of their horses, mules, camels, and asses (ch. vii): to which more might be added."

5. In respect to *language and style*, this book is very similar to the Chronicles of Ezra. Nehemiah has, it is true, quite his own manner, and, as De Wette has observed, certain phrases and modes of expression peculiar to himself. He has also some few words and forms not found elsewhere in Scripture; but the general Hebrew style is exactly that of the books purporting to be of the same age. Some words, as מְצִלְתַּיִם, "cymbals," occur in Chron., Ezra, and Neh., but nowhere else. הִתְנַדֵּב occurs frequently in the same three books, but only twice (in Judg. v) besides. אִגֶּרֶת or אִגַּרְתָּא, "a letter," is common only to Neh., Esth., Ezra, and Chron. בִּירָה, and its Chaldee equivalent, בִּירְא, whether spoken of the palace at Susa or of the Temple at Jerusalem, are common only to Neh., Ezra, Esth., Dan., and Chron.: יָגֵל to Neh. and Dan., and Psa. xlv. The phrase אֱלֹהֵי הַשָּׁמַיִם, and its Chaldee equivalent, "the God of Heavens," are common to Ezra, Neh., and Dan. מְפֹרָשׁ, "distinctly," is common to Ezra and Neh. Such words as פַּרְדֵּס, מְדִינָה, סָגָן, and such Aramaisms as the use of חָבַל, i, 7, רְמַלֶּךְ, v, 7, מִדָּה, v, 4, etc., are also evidences of the age when Nehemiah wrote. As examples of peculiar words or meanings, used in this book alone, the following may be mentioned: שָׁבַר בְּ, "to inspect," ii, 13, 15; מֵאָה, in the sense of "interest," v, 11; אוּף (in Hiph.), "to shut," vii, 3; מוֹעַל, "a lifting up," viii, 6; הֻדֹרוֹת, "praises," or "choirs," xii, 8; תַּהֲלוּכָה, "a procession," xii, 32; מִקְרָא, in the sense of "reading," viii, 8; אֹצָרָה, for אֲצָרִירָה, xiii, 8, where both form and sense are alike unusual. The Aramæan form, יְהוֹדָה, Hiph. of יָדָה, for יוֹדֶה, is very rare, only five other analogous examples occurring in the Heb. Scriptures, though it is very common in Biblical Chaldee. The phrase אִישׁ שָׁלְחוֹ הַמַּיִם, iv, 17 (which is omitted by the Sept.), is incapable of explanation. One would have expected, instead of בְּיָדוֹ, הַמַּיִם, as in 2 Chron. xxiii, 10. הַתִּרְשָׁתָא, "the Tirshatha," which only occurs in Ezra ii, 63; Neh. vii, 65, 70; viii, 9; x, 1, is of uncertain etymology and meaning. It is a term applied almost exclusively to Nehemiah, and seems to be more likely to mean "cupbearer" than "governor," though the latter interpretation is adopted by Gesenius (*Thes.* s. v.).

The text of Nehemiah is generally pure and free from corruption, except in the proper names, in which there is considerable fluctuation in the orthography, both as compared with other parts of the same book and with the same names in other parts of Scripture; and

also in numerals. Of the latter we have seen several examples in the parallel passages of Ezra ii and Neh. vii; and the same lists give variations in names of men. So does xii, 1–7, compared with xii, 12, and with x, 1–8. A comparison of Neh. xi, 3, etc., with 1 Chron. ix, 2, etc., exhibits the following fluctuations: Neh. xi, 4, *Athaiah* of the children of Perez = 1 Chron. ix, 4, *Uthai* of the children of Perez; v, 5, *Maaseiah* the son of Shiloni = v, 5, of the Shilonites, *Asaiah*; v, 9, *Judah* the son of Senuah (Heb. Ha-senuah) = v, 7, *Hodaviah* the son of Hasenuah; v, 10, Jedaiah the son of Joiarib, Jachin = v, 10, Jedaiah, Jehoiarib, Jachin; v, 13, *Amasai* son of Azareel = v, 12, *Maasai* son of Jahzerah; v, 17, Micah the son of *Zabdi* = v, 15, Micah the son of *Zichri* (comp. Neh. xii, 35). To these many others might be added.

6. *Commentaries.*—The special exegetical helps on the Book of Nehemiah are not numerous: Bede, *In Nehemiæ allegorica expositio* (in *Opp.* iv; and *Works*, by Giles, i, 1); Brenz, *Comment. in Nehemiæ* (in *Opp.* ii); Wolphius, *In Nehemiæ librum commentaria* (Tigur. 1570, fol.); Strigel, *Argumentum et Scholia* (Lips. 1571, 1572, 8vo); Pilkington, *Expositio* on certain chapters (Lond. 1585, 4to; also in *Works*, p. 275); Pempel, *Explanatio* [includ. Ezra and Dan.] (in *Works*, Lond. 1585); Rambach, *Adnotationes* (in his work on the O. T. iii, 107); Sanctius, *Commentarii* [includ. Ruth, etc.] (Lugd. 1628, fol.); Ferus, *Erklärung* (Mayence, 1619, 8vo); Crommius, *In hist. Nehemiæ*, etc. [includ. other books] (Lovan. 1632, 4to); Lombard, *Commentarius* [includ. Ezra] (Par. 1643, fol.); Trapp, *Commentary* [includ. Ezra, etc.] (Lond. 1656, fol.); Jackson, *Explanation* [includ. Ezra and Esth.] (Lond. 1657, 4to); De Oliva, *Commentarii* [includ. other books] (Lugd. 1664, 1679, 2 vols. fol.); Bertheau, *Commentary* [includ. Ezra and Esth.] (in the *Exeg. Handb.* Leips. 1862, 8vo); Barde, *Étude critique et exégétique* (Tübing. 1861, 8vo); also, Lange's and Keil and Delitzsch's *Bible-works.* See Commentary.

Nehemi′as (Νεεμίας v. r. Ναιμίας), the Græcized form (retained in the A.V. of the Apocrypha) of the name Nehemiah (q. v.), namely, (a) The contemporary of Zerubbabel and Jeshua (1 Esdr. v. 8); (b) The governor, son of Hachaliah (1 Esdr. v, 40).

Ne′hiloth (Heb. *Nechiloth′*, נְחִילוֹת, with the art.; the plur. of נְחִילָה, which, however, is not found), occurs only in the title of Psa. v, where the A. V. renders "upon Nehiloth" (אֶל־הַנְּחִילוֹת). The Sept., Aquila, Symmachus, and Theodotion translate ὑπὲρ τῆς κληρονομούσης, and the Vulgate, "*pro ea quæ hæreditatem consequitur*," by which Augustine understands the Church. The origin of their error was a mistaken etymology, by which Nehiloth is derived from נָחַל, *nachál*, "to inherit." Hengstenberg maintains that the title with this derivation has a mystical or spiritual meaning, "for the inheritance," or "upon the lots," i. e. of the righteous and the wicked. Other etymologies have been proposed which are equally unsound. In Chaldee נְחִיל, *nechil*, signifies "a swarm of bees," and hence Jarchi attributes to Nehiloth the notion of multitude, the psalm being sung by the whole people of Israel. R. Hai, quoted by Kimchi, adopting the same origin for the word, explains it as an instrument, the sound of which was like the hum of bees, a wind instrument, according to Sonntag (*De tit. Psa.* p. 430), which had a rough tone. Michaelis (*Suppl. ad Lex. Heb.* p. 1629) suggests, with not unreasonable timidity, that the root is to be found in the Arab. *nachala*, "to winnow," and hence to separate and select the better part, indicating that the psalm, in the title of which Nehiloth occurs, was "an ode to be chanted by the purified and better portion of the people." It is most likely, as Gesenius and others explain, that it is derived (instead of נְחִלֹּת) from the root חָלַל, *chalál*, "to bore, perforate," whence חָלִיל, *chalil*, a flute or pipe (1 Sam. x, 5; 1

Kings i, 40), so that Nehiloth is the general term for perforated wind-instruments of all kinds, as Neginoth denotes all manner of stringed instruments. The title of Psa. v is therefore addressed to the conductor of the Temple choir who played upon flutes and the like, and these are directly alluded to in Psa. lxxxvii, 7, where (חֹלְלִים, *cholelim*) "the players upon instruments" who are associated with the singers are properly "pipers" or "flute-players." See FLUTE. Others, like Aben-Ezra among rabbinical commentators, and Hitzig among living scholars, understand it to be the name of an air to which the psalm was sung, "after, or according to, the inheritance." Fürst suggests that *Nehiloth* was a musical choir, having their chief seat at a town which bore a cognate name, perhaps Hilen (1 Chron. vi, 58; comp. his explanation of *Neginoth*). The use of the preposition אֶל in this connection does not justify the rendering "upon," but requires us to understand that the psalm under consideration was to be chanted *in imitation* or in the style of (*à la*) the air or musical instrument in question. See PSALMS.

Ne'hum (Heb. *Nechum'*, נְחוּם, if genuine, i. q. *Nahum*, i. e. *consoled*, but prob. by erroneous transcription for רְחוּם, i. e. *Rechum*; Sept. Ἰναούμ, but most MSS. have Ναούμ; Vulg. *Nahum*), one of the Israelites who returned from Babylon with Zerubbabel (Neh. vii, 7); called REHUM (q. v.) in the parallel list (Ezra ii, 2).

Nehush'ta (Heb. *Nechushta'*, נְחֻשְׁתָּא, *copper*; Sept. Νεεσθά v. r. Ναισθά; Vulg. *Nohesta*), the daughter of Elnathan of Jerusalem, wife of Jehoiakim, and mother of Jehoiachin, kings of Judah (2 Kings xxiv, 8). B.C. cir. 616.

Nehush'tan (Heb. *Nechushtan'*, נְחֻשְׁתָּן, *of copper*, with the art.; Sept. Νεεσθάν, v. r. Νεσθάν and even Νεσθαλεί; Vulg. *Nohestan*), a contemptuous name given to the copper ("brazen") serpent which Moses had made during the plague in the wilderness (Numb. xxi, 8 sq.), and which the Israelites worshipped (2 Kings xviii, 4). See BRAZEN SERPENT. "One of the first acts of Hezekiah, upon coming to the throne of Judah, was to destroy all traces of the idolatrous rites which had gained such a fast hold upon the people during the reign of his father Ahaz. Among other objects of superstitious reverence and worship was this singular metallic effigy, which was preserved throughout the wanderings of the Israelites, probably as a memorial of their deliverance, and according to a late tradition was placed in the Temple. The lapse of nearly a thousand years had invested this ancient relic with a mysterious sanctity which easily degenerated into idolatrous reverence, and at the time of Hezekiah's accession it had evidently been long an object of worship, 'for unto those days the children of Israel did burn incense to it,' or as the Hebrew more fully implies, 'had been in the habit of burning incense to it' (הָיוּ מְקַטְּרִים, *had been incense-burners*). The expression points to a settled practice. It is evident that our translators by their rendering, 'And he called it Nehushtan,' understood with many commentators that the subject of the sentence is Hezekiah, and that when he destroyed the brazen serpent he gave it the name Nehushtan, 'a brazen thing,' in token of his utter contempt, and to impress upon the people the idea of its worthlessness. This rendering has the support of the Sept. and Vulgate, Junius and Tremellius, Münster, Clericus, and others; but it is better to understand the Hebrew as referring to the name by which the serpent was generally known, the subject of the verb being indefinite—and one called it '*Nehushtan.*' Such a construction is common, and instances of it may be found in Gen. xxv, 26; xxxviii, 29, 30, where our translators correctly render 'his name was called,' and in Gen. xlviii, 1, 2. This was the view taken in the Targ. Jon. and in the Peshito-Syriac, 'And they called it Nehushtan,' which Buxtorf approves (*Hist.*

Serp. Æn. cap. vi). It has the support of Luther, Pfeiffer (*Dub. Vex.* cent. 3, loc. 5), J. D. Michaelis (*Bibel für Ungel.*), and Bunsen (*Bibelwerk*), as well as of Ewald (*Gesch.* iii, 622), Keil, Thenius, and most modern commentators." See HEZEKIAH. "The fact of the preservation of the brazen serpent till the time of Hezekiah is, as Bunsen remarks, a sufficient guarantee not only for the historical truth of the narrative in Numbers, but also for the religious significancy of the symbol; for had it been, as some have supposed, an image of Satan, it would not have been suffered by David or Solomon to remain (*Bibelwerk*, v, 217). The fact also that it is referred to by our Lord as in some sense resembling him (John iii, 14, 15), not only vouches for the same things, but further imposes on us the duty of seeking in it a deeper significancy than that which the mere narrative of Moses would lead us to attach to it. We may, therefore, dismiss at once all the attempts of rationalists to resolve the facts of the Mosaic narrative into mere ordinary occurrences; such as that of Bauer, who finds in the cure of the Israelites by looking at the brazen serpent only an instance of the curative power of the imagination (*Hebr. Gesch.* ii, 320), or that of Paulus, who thinks that the brazen serpent being at some distance from the camp, and the sight of it moving the Israelite who had been bitten to walk to it, the motion thereby produced served to work off the effects of the poison, and so tended to a cure (*Comment.* iv, 1, 198 sq.); or that of Hofmann, who ingeniously suggests that the brazen serpent was the title of a rural hospital, where medicine and doctors were to be found by those who had faith to go for them. It is sad to see a man like Bunsen falling back on the old exploded rationalistic explanation of this occurrence. 'The fixing of the gaze on the image brought the mind to a state of repose, and so made the bodily cure possible' (*Bibelwerk*, v, 217), as if this were all! We may pass over also the notion of Marsham, according to whom the serpent of brass was an implement of magic or incantation borrowed from the Egyptians, who he says 'imprimis μαγείᾳ τινὶ ἐπιχωρίῳ ob serpentum incantationem celebrantur' (*Canon Chron.* p. 148); for this is so purely gratuitous, and so opposed to the narrative of Moses, as well as the religious principles and feelings which he sought to inculcate (comp. Lev. xix, 26), that it must be at once rejected (see Deyling, *Obs. Sac.* ii, 210 sq.). The traditionary belief of the ancient Jews is that the brazen serpent was the symbol of salvation, and that healing came to the sufferer who looked to it as the result of his faith in God, who had appointed this method of cure." See Schachan, *De serpentis ænei significatione* (Lubec. 1713); Nölting, *De serp. æn. Servatoris typo* (Jen. 1759); Huth, *Serpens exaltatus non contritionis sed conterendi imago* (Erlang. 1758). See SERPENT.

Nei'ël [many *Ne'iel*] (Heb. *Neïel'*, נְעִיאֵל, *dwelling-place of God*; Sept. Ναιήλ v. r. Ἀνιήλ, Ἰναηλ; Vulg. *Nehiel*), a town in the territory of Asher, near the southern or south-eastern border (Josh. xix, 27). Eusebius and Jerome (who call it the "village *Bætoanœa*," Βαιτοαναιά) place it in the mountain (Carmel), sixteen miles east (N.?) of Cæsarea Palæstina, where medicinal springs were found (*Onomast.* s. v. Aniel, Ἀνιή λ, the reading of the Alexand. MS. of the Sept. in the above passage); a position which exactly agrees with that of the modern village *Bistan*, adjoining the spring Ain-Haud, a short distance east of Athlit (Van de Velde, *Map*). The description of the boundary is quite indistinct at this point [see TRIBE]; and if we regard merely the associated names Jiphthah-el (the present Jefat) and Cabul (now Kabul), we might locate Neiel at the modern *Miar* (supposing a mere interchange of liquids in the name), a village conspicuously situated half-way between them (Robinson, *New Res.* iii, 87, 103); although Beth-emek (q. v.) is mentioned immediately before Neiel, and lies much farther interior (at Amkah). Keil (*Comment. on*

Josh. ad loc.) thinks that the statement of the text assigns both these latter places a position south of the border and within Zebulon; while Knobel (*Commentar*, ad loc. Josh.) is inclined to identify Neiel with the NEAH of Josh. xix, 13, which, however, lay too far east. For other views, see Rosenmüller, *Scholia*, ad loc.

Neigh (צָהַל, *tsahal'*, prop. *to be clear* or bright; hence to emit a sharp sound, as of a *shout*, so often; spoken of the neighing of a horse [Jer. viii, 16; xiii, 27; l, 5, 8] and the bellowing of a bull [Jer. l, 11]; but in both cases as indicative of lustful desire).

Neighbor (usually רֵעַ, *réä,* elsewhere "friend;" ὁ πλησίος, one's *nearest* dweller). This word in its general sense signifies a person near, and one connected with us by the bonds of humanity, and whom charity requires that we should consider as a friend and relation (Deut. v, 20). At the time of our Saviour the Pharisees had restrained the meaning of the word neighbor to those of their own nation or to their own friends, holding that to hate their enemy was not forbidden by the law (Matt. v, 43). But our Saviour informed them that the whole world were neighbors; that they ought not to do to another what they would not have done to themselves; and that this charity extended even to enemies. The beautiful parable of the Good Samaritan is set forth to illustrate this principle (Luke x, 29–37). See CHARITY.

Neil, JOHN, a Presbyterian minister, was born in 1804 in Antrim Co., Ireland. His parents, emigrating to the United States, settled upon a farm in Washington Co., Pa. He was early taught the great truths of the Bible, and the way of salvation according to the faith and practice of the Associate Reformed Presbyterian Church. He was educated at Washington College, Washington, Pa.; studied theology at the Associate Reformed Seminary at Alleghany City, Pa.; was licensed in 1836, and in 1838 was ordained pastor of the three congregations of Mount Jackson, Centre, and Mahoning, Pa. In 1849, after laboring earnestly and faithfully for eleven years, he was released from Mahoning congregation; in 1857, on account of failing health, he also resigned Centre congregation, continuing thereafter his labors with the Mount Jackson congregation until 1860, when he became unable to preach and retired from the ministry. He died in 1861. Mr. Neil was a close student of the Scriptures. As a preacher he was more instructive than attractive. He always endeavored to make thorough pulpit preparation, and often wrote his sermons a second time before delivery. See Wilson, *Presb. Hist. Almanac,* 1863, p. 361.

Neile, John, D.D., an English divine, flourished in the reign of king James II as dean of Ripon. He was born about the beginning of the 17th century, and was noted among his contemporaries. See Stoughton, *Eccles. Hist. of Eng.* ii, 197.

Neile, Richard, D.D., an English prelate of considerable note, flourished in the reign of king James I, i. e. some time about the opening of the 17th century. He was born near the close of the 16th century, and after due educational training became a school-teacher, but afterwards took holy orders, and rapidly rose to positions of influence. He was finally elevated to the episcopate, and successively held the sees of Rochester, Lichfield and Coventry, Lincoln, Durham, and Winchester, and was then made archbishop of York, promotions which are said to have been secured by Neile by most base and unchristian conduct. He was subservient to the interests of king James at the expense of his own manhood, and is generally spoken of as the ecclesiastical courtier of king James's reign. Says Perry (*Eccles. Hist.* i, 205), "If we were to write down against this prelate all that is deliberately said of him by his metropolitan, archbishop Abbot (Collett's *State Trials,* vol. ii), his character (i. e. Neile's) would be by no means a flattering one." Abbot was bid to beware of

VI.—30

him, for that "he was ever and in all things naught. That he did all the worst offices that ever he could, and was still stirring the coals to procure to himself a reputation." "I know not," said another, "what the bishop of Lichfield does among you, but he hath made a shift to be taken for a knave generally with us." Though the friend and ally of Laud, he was yet far his inferior, and Neile is universally spoken of as "neither conspicuous for learning nor for diligence in his office. He did not preach once in twelve years, ... but knew how to please both James and Charles. He was one of a class of men of whom the Church of England can never be proud." Archbishop Neile died in 1640. See Perry, *Hist. of the Ch. of Eng.* i, 191 sq.

Neill, Hugh, an American divine of the colonial period, came to this country about the opening of the last century, and labored in Pennsylvania and New Jersey. In the mother country he was a Nonconformist, and labored for years as Presbyterian minister both in England and in New Jersey, where he greatly distinguished himself. He was ordained to holy orders in the Anglican establishment in 1749 by the bishop of London, and was at once appointed to missionary work. During the following fifteen years—the extent of his work in this country—his sympathies were especially directed to the negro race, whose love and confidence he gained. He died about 1770. See Anderson, *Hist. of the Ch. of Eng. in the Colonies and foreign Dependencies of the British Empire,* iii, 379–81, 457; Hawkins, *Eccles. Hist.* p. 126 sq.

Neill, William, D.D., an eminent Presbyterian divine, was born near McKeesport, Alleghany Co., Pa., in 1778. His parents were killed by Indians while he was yet a child, so that he was raised by friends. He was engaged in a store at Canonsburg, Pa., when the question of duty being brought to his mind and heart he soon decided upon the ministry. He pursued his preparatory studies in the Old Academy, which afterwards became Jefferson College, Pa.; graduated at Princeton College in 1803, and acted as tutor there, during which time he studied theology. In 1805 he was licensed by the New Brunswick Presbytery; in 1806 was ordained pastor of a Church at Cooperstown, N. J.; in 1809, of the First Church, Albany, N. Y.; in 1816, of the Sixth Church, Philadelphia, where he continued to labor until 1824, when he was called to the presidency of Dickinson College, at Carlisle, Pa., then under the control of the Presbyterians. There Dr. Neill labored for five years, when long-continued difficulties, which could not be controlled, prompted him to resign, and by the action of the trustees the college passed into the hands of the Methodists. On leaving Carlisle, in 1829, he became secretary and general agent for the Board of Education, which office he held for two years. In speaking of his duties at that time, he says, "I was their factotum, had the office in my dwelling, kept the records, wrote the letters, travelled, preached, collected funds, and prepared the reports, without even a boy to go on errands; but, harder than all, I had to contend with the American Education Society, and the prejudices of the people against all denominational boards. ... However, we made some progress; a few hundred dollars were collected, a few beneficiaries were registered, and the people began to come slowly under the shadow of their own standard." Finding the work too hard and incompatible with his duty to his family, he resigned, and in 1831 retired to Germantown, and there betook himself again to the duties of the pulpit. He preached until 1842, when he removed to Philadelphia, and remained without charge until his death, Aug. 8, 1860. Dr. Neill was deemed one of the most useful ministers of his day. His preaching was clear and replete with Gospel truth, persuasive and tender. His active mind often found expression in the religious press. He published, *Lectures on Biblical History* (1846, 1855):—*Practical Exposition of the Epistles to the*

Ephesians (1850):—*The Divine Origin and Authority of the Christian Religion* (1854):—*A Discourse reviewing a Ministry of Fifty Years* (1857). He also for some years edited the *Presbyterian Magazine*, and contributed papers to several of the religious periodicals. After his death there was published a volume of his *Sermons* with his *Autobiography*, and a *Commemorative Discourse* by the Rev. Dr. J. H. Jones. See Wilson, *Presb. Hist. Almanac*, 1861, p. 102; Allibone's *Dict. of Authors*, s. v.; *American Presbyterian Reunion Memorial Volume*, 1837–1871, p. 128–133. (J. L. S.)

Neilson, JOHN, a Scotch martyr to religious liberty, was a nobleman of considerable influence in Galloway. He had enjoyed superior educational advantages, was by nature quite talented, and enjoyed an unblemished character. But he was a Covenanter, and consequently subjected to severe persecutions on the part of the Anglican clergy. When the people of Galloway rose in self-defence, he joined them; and, notwithstanding the cruel treatment which he and his family had received from Turner, Mr. Neilson argued strenuously and successfully against the proposal of some to put the oppressor to death. As the prelates could not conceive that the persecuted Presbyterians would have dared to rise in self-defence unless there had been a widely extended conspiracy, they determined to extort a confession of the nature and extent of this plot from such of the prisoners as were certain to be acquainted with it if it existed. For this reason they resolved to put Neilson to the torture of the *boot*. In vain did they crush his leg in this fearful engine of torture; shrieking nature attested his agony, but his soul was clear of the guilt wherewith he was charged, and he would not blacken it by making a false acknowledgment of a crime of which he was innocent. When the persecutors found that they could extort nothing from him but groans and anguish, they condemned him to suffer, along with his guiltless friends, the shorter pangs of death. See Hetherington, *Hist. of the Church of Scotland*, p. 230; Wodrow, ii, 53.

Neisser Brothers. See MORAVIANS.

Neith is the name of the female divinity of *wisdom* among the ancient Egyptians. Her name, which means "I came from myself," leads to the supposition that she was an impersonation of nature. She was chiefly worshipped in the Delta, where a city was built bearing her name. Her temple, the largest in Egypt, was at Sais, the kings of which called themselves her sons. It was open to the sky, and bore an inscription, "I am all that was, and is, and is to be; no mortal has lifted up my veil, and the fruit which I brought forth is the sun." Ranking next to Ptah, the most exalted of Egyptian divinities, she is to the female deities what Ptah (q. v.) is to the male; and indeed so closely are the functions of the two commingled or confounded in some representations of them that Neith may be briefly defined as the female counterpart of the great *demiurgus*. Ptah is the primary *paternal* element in nature, Neith the primary *conceptive* element. He is the father of the sun, she is the mother of the same luminary, and one of her titles is consequently "the great con-engenderer of the sun" (Bunsen, i, 386; Kenrick, i, 390). Ptah is the primordial fire, while Neith is the primordial space or chaos, self-producing, coeternal with him, and co-equal; or, in other words, the "feminine ether" everywhere diffused as the material basis of all forms of created existence. Neith is called

Figure of Neith. (From the Egyptian Monuments.)

also *Muth*, the universal mother and queen of heaven. Neith wears the red crown of Lower Egypt, indicating the proper seat of her worship; but her monuments are found in the upper region also. By reversing her hieroglyphic signs NT (i. e. by reading them in the European instead of the Asiatic manner), may have been formed *Athene*, the patron goddess of Athens, which city was supposed to have been founded from Sais. The owl, her favorite bird, is also found upon the coinage of the Delta; but the virgin mother of Egypt seems to have had little else in common with the Minerva who sprang full armed from the brain of Jupiter. See MINERVA. A statue of Neith is preserved in the Egyptian Room of the British Museum. Neith is generally represented in green, a sign that she was connected with the under world, and invisible to mortals; a festival of "Burning Lamps" was held in her honor. See Bunsen, *Egypt's Place in History*, vol. i; Kenrick, *Anc. Egypt under the Pharaohs*, vol. i; Rougé, in *Revue Archéologique* (huitième année), p. 40 sq.; Hardwick, *Christ and other Masters*, ii, 248 sq.; Baur, *Symbolik und Mythologie*, vol. ii, pt. i, p. 43; Trevor, *Ancient Egypt*, p. 134, 187, 152.

Neithe is the name of a Celtic divinity who was superstitiously reverenced even in Christian Scotland. The primitive signification of the name is *to wash* or *purify* with water, and the name was probably given to this divinity because she is the presiding spirit of the water element. She was the goddess of fountains, which to this day are regarded with particular veneration over every part of the Highlands. "The sick, who resort to them for health," says Brand (*Popular Antiquities of Great Britain*, ii, 376), "address their vows to the presiding powers and offer presents to conciliate their favor. The presents generally consist of a small piece of money or a few fragrant flowers." See the article HOLY WELL.

Nekam, a Mohammedan martyr to the Christian cause, flourished near the middle of the 11th century. He was of an influential family, but, convinced of the errors of Mohammedanism, he embraced Christianity and became a Jacobite. His parents and friends forsook him, and he consequently retired to the church of St. Michael at Moctara, where, after a short stay, he was urged by the monks to retreat with them to the convent of S. Macarius. He refused to join them, on the ground of his obligation to publicly confessing Christ, especially among his former associates, in order that they too might become Christ's servants on earth. He went to Cairo, and there boldly presenting himself in the public streets, was imprisoned and condemned to death, because of his apostasy. All efforts to reclaim him, or to feign madness in order that his life might be saved, he refused as improper means, and he was consequently beheaded. The corpse was given up to his friends and buried near the church of Moctara, but the patriarch Abd-el-Messiah removed it within the building, and erected an altar in honor of the noble martyr. See Neale's *Hist. Holy East. Ch.* (*Patriarchate of Alexandria*, ii, 215, 716).

Ne'keb (Heb. *id.*, but only with the art., הַנֶּקֶב; Sept. καὶ Ναβώκ, v. r. Ναβόκ, Νακέβ; Vulg. *quæ est Neceb*), given in our version as one of the towns on the boundary of Naphtali (Josh. xix, 33 only), apparently between Adami and Jabneel. A great number of commentators, from Jonathan the Targumist and Jerome (*Vulgate* as above) to Keil (*Josua*, ad loc.), have taken this name as being connected with the preceding—Adami-han-Nekeb (i. e. *Adami* [*of*] *the Cavern*) (so Junius and Tremellius, "Adamæi fossa"); and indeed this is the force of the accentuation of the present Hebrew text. But on the other hand the Sept. gives the two as distinct, and in the Talmud the post-biblical names of each are given, that of han-Nekeb being *Tsiadathah* (צִיירדתא, *Gemara Hieros.* Cod. Megilla, in Reland, *Palæst.* p. 545, 717, 817; also Schwarz, *Palestine*

p. 181). Of this more modern name Schwarz suggests that a trace is to be found in "*Hazedhi*, three English miles N. from al-Chatti." Hackett suggests *Neckev*, near Ramah, on the road to Akka (*Illust. of Script.* p. 240). Both these suggestions, however, are superfluous. See ADAMI.

Neko'da (Heb. *Nekoda'*, נְקוֹדָא, *distinguished*; Sept. Νεκωδά, v. r. Νεχωδά and Νεκωδάν), the head of a family of the "Temple servants" who returned with Zerubbabel from Babylon (Ezra ii, 48; Neh. vii, 50). B.C. 535. A man of the same name is mentioned in Ezra ii, 60; Neh. vii, 62, as the progenitor of certain persons who on the return from Babylon had lost their pedigree, from which it would seem that they claimed to be Israelites; but as the Nethinim are mentioned immediately before, and neither of the associated names occurs again, we may presume that they were finally determined to be descendants of the above-named non-Israelite (see Keil, ad loc.). See NETHINIM.

Nekoth. See SPICES.

Nélis, CORNEILLE FRANÇOIS DE, a learned Belgian prelate, was born in Mechlin June 5, 1736. He was educated at the University of Louvain, and took the degree of licentiate May 6, 1760. Almost immediately he became principal of the College of Mechlin, and, in addition, the management of the library of the Academy was intrusted to him. He made himself advantageously known to the literary world by several *Dissertations* upon various points of history and philosophy. He was nominated canon of Tournay in 1765, and in 1767 vicar-general of that city; he also held for a time the vicariate-general over the province of Tournaisis. Upon the exclusion of the Society of Jesus from the country in 1773, he was designated as a member of the royal commission for the studies instituted at Brussels. The archduke Maximilian, afterwards elector of Cologne, having appreciated his merit in a visit that Nélis made to the Belgian provinces, signalized him to the emperor Joseph II, who nominated Nélis to the bishopric of Antwerp, Oct. 25, 1784. Although he owed his elevation to the house of Austria, his conscience was greatly alarmed by the religious innovations that the emperor Joseph II wished to introduce; and as early as May 22, 1786, he addressed remonstrances to the government concerning the order of publishing from the pulpit the proclamations of the police and others, and several days after representations upon the suppression of societies, processions, and upon impediments that invalidate marriage. The same year he opposed the imperial edict which instituted a new form of concourse for conferring benefices; later he wrote against the suppression of episcopal seminaries. The death of Joseph II wrought some changes, and on July 19, 1793, Nélis, who had shown himself one of the most ardent enemies of France, wrote to the emperor Francis II to justify and excuse his conduct during the Brabançonne revolution. The 21st of April following he went to Brussels, where the states were convened, and was cordially welcomed by the emperor. But the revolution advanced rapidly, and at the approach of the French army Nélis, who had everything to fear, fled in haste from Antwerp, June 28, 1794. He sought first an asylum at Breda, but could not long remain in that town, and made his way to Rotterdam, and in 1795 went over into Germany. After having sojourned several months at Göttingen and at Osnabrück, then in Switzerland at Zurich, near Lavater, of whom he was an intimate friend, he passed to Bavaria, and shortly after to Italy, where he dwelt successively at Florence, Parma, Bologna, Rome, and Naples. He found at last a welcome hospitality in a convent of Camaldules near Florence, where he died, August 21, 1798. We have among the works of this prelate, *Éloge funèbre de l'empereur François I* (Louvain, 1765, 4to, in Latin; Brussels, 1766, 4to, in Latin and French):—*Éloge funèbre de Marie-Thérèse* (Brussels, 1780, 4to and 8vo). This eulogy, written in French, is considered much superior

to the one composed by the abbé de Boismont:—*Belgicarum rerum Prodromus, sive de historia Belgica ejusque scriptoribus præcipuis commentatio* (Parma, 1795, 8vo). M. de Reiffenberg paid it the greatest eulogy in his edition of the *Chronique rimée de Philippe Mouskes:—L'Aveugle de la Montagne, ou entretiens philosophiques* (1789, 1793, 2 vols. 8vo; enlarged edition, Parma, 1795, 8vo; Rome, 1797, 4to). In the collections of the Academy of Brussels, 1777, and following year, are found the following, by Nélis: *Mémoire sur l'ancien Brabant; sur la vigogne et l'amélioration de nos laines; sur la pierre Brunehaut dans le Tournaisis; sur la constitution municipale et sur les privilèges accordés aux villes des Pays-Bas; sur les écoles et sur les études d'humanités.* We also have from Nélis numerous *Mandements* and *Lettres pastorales,* either in Flemish or in French. Among the manuscripts that he has left, two especially are of interest, *Questionum Camaldulensium libri quatuor,* and *Europæ fata, mores, disciplinæ, ab ineunte sæculo XV usque ad finem sæculi XVIII.* These two works were on the point of being published when death removed their author, who bequeathed them to the convent of the Camaldules, where he had found an asylum. See *Synopsis actorum ecclesiæ Antwerpiensis,* etc., by De Ram; *Mémoires de l'Académie des Sciences de Bruxelles,* passim; *Documents particuliers.*—Hoefer, *Nouv. Biog. Générale,* s. v.

Neller, GEORG CHRISTOPH, *Count,* a German canonist, was born at Aub (bishopric of Würzburg) in 1710. He entered holy orders in 1748, was nominated professor of the canon law at Trèves, where he received a canonicate; he next became counsellor of the elector of Trèves, and was then elevated to the dignity of count palatine. He died at Trèves in 1783. We have of his works, *Principia juris publici ecclesiastici Catholicorum ad statum Germaniæ accommodata* (Frankfort, 1746 and 1768, 8vo):—*De Concordatis Germaniæ* (Trèves, 1748):—*De Jurisprudentia Trevirorum sub Romanis* (ibid, 1752):—*De Jurisprudentia Trevirorum Belgica* (ibid, 1752):—*Jurisprudentia Trevirorum ante-Romana, sub Romanis, sub Francis et sub Germanis,* in the *Prodromus historiæ Trevirensis* of Montheim:—*Kurzer Unterricht von den alt-römischen, fränkischen, trierischen und rheinländischen Pfennigen und Hellern* (ibid. 1763):—*Dissertatio in Dagoberti diploma Horrense* (ibid. 1770):—many juridical dissertations, united in one collection, published at Trèves in 1776 (4to). See Meusel, *Lexikon,* s. v.; Weidlich, *Nachrichten,* vol. ii and iv.

Nelli, Nello, an Italian painter of Pisa who flourished in the 13th century, is remembered as the author of a *Madonna* painted on panel in the old church of Tripalle at Pisa, signed *Nerus Nellus de Pisa me pinxit,* 1299. See Spooner, *Biog. Hist. of the Fine Arts,* ii, 616.

Nelli, Suora Platella, an Italian paintress of a noble family, who devoted herself to religious as well as to secular art, was born at Florence in 1523. She became a nun in the Dominican Convent of St. Catherine at Florence, and without other assistance than a collection of designs by Fra. Bartolomeo di S. Marco, she attained considerable excellence in painting. Her productions are generally in the style of that artist, although she also imitated other masters. Among them are a picture of the *Crucifixion,* with a number of small figures finished; a *Descent from the Cross,* said to be after a design by Andrea del Sarto in the church of her order at Florence; and an *Adoration of the Magi,* of her own composition, possessing great merit. She died in 1588.

Nello, BERNARDO DI GIO FALCONI, an old painter of Pisa, whose works were mostly of a religious character, flourished about 1390. He was a distinguished artist in his time, and Lanzi says he still merits consideration. He painted many pictures in the Cathedral at Pisa. He is supposed to be the same as *Nello di Vanni,* who with other Pisan artists painted in the Campo Santo in the

14th century. See Spooner, *Biog. Hist. of the Fine Arts*, ii, 614.

Nelson, David, M.D., an American Presbyterian minister and educator, was born near Jonesborough, in East Tennessee, Sept. 24, 1793. He was educated at Washington College, and after graduating in Philadelphia returned to Kentucky at the age of nineteen, intending to practice medicine; but the war of 1812 having commenced, he joined a Kentucky regiment as surgeon, and proceeded to Canada. He afterwards accompanied the army of generals Jackson and Coffee to Alabama and Florida, and after the establishment of peace settled finally at Jonesborough, where he resumed his medical practice with great success. While away at war he had become estranged from his early religious convictions, and in part at least espoused infidel theories. He now became more seriously convinced of his dependence on God, and, reawakened and converted, he determined to forsake a lucrative professional career for the purpose of entering the ministry, and was licensed to preach in April, 1825. He preached for some three years in Tennessee, where he was at the same time connected with the *Calvinistic Magazine*, published at Rogersville. In 1828 he became pastor of the church of Danville, Ky., succeeding his brother Samuel. In 1830 he removed to Missouri, and was chiefly instrumental in establishing Marion College, of which he became the first president. In 1836 Dr. Nelson, who was a warm emancipationist, owing to a disturbance growing out of the slavery question, removed to Illinois, and at Oakland, near Quincy, established an institute for the education of young men, especially for such as were preparing to become missionaries. Here he exhausted his pecuniary means, and died Oct. 17, 1844. His most remarkable work is his *Cause and Cure of Infidelity* (1836 and often). The manuscript of *Wealth and Honor*, which he intended for publication, was lost after it passed from his hands. He also wrote many occasional articles on missions, baptism, etc., which appeared in the *New York Observer* and other papers of the day. See Sprague, *Annals of the American Pulpit*, iv, 677; *Hist. of Presbyterianism in Kentucky*, p. 330. (J. H. W.)

Nelson, John (1), an eminent Methodist lay preacher, was one of the ablest of the assistants of the Wesleys in their evangelical movement in the last century. He is generally acknowledged the chief founder of Methodism in Yorkshire, a portion of England in which it has had signal success down to our day. Nelson was born near the close of the 17th century. He was the descendant of humble but honorable parentage, and was early apprenticed to a stone-mason, a trade at which he became proficient, and at which he worked nearly all his life, even in the midst of his evangelizing labors. He was converted under the preaching of John Wesley in 1711, at Moorfields. Nelson's home was in Bristol. He had led an upright life from his youth, and had at the time of his conversion an humble but a happy home, a good wife, good wages, good health, and a stout English heart. He had long been distressed by the sense of moral wants which his life failed to meet until the light came under the preaching of Wesley. The sad and trying days of Nelson are thus narrated by his biographer: "Something he believed there must be in true religion to meet the wants of the soul, otherwise man is more unfortunate than the brute that perishes. Absorbed in such meditations, this untutored mechanic wandered in the fields after the work of the day, discussing to himself questions which had employed and ennobled the thoughts of Plato in the groves of the Cephissus, and agitated by the anxieties that had stirred the souls of Wesley and his associates at Oxford. His conduct was a mystery to his less thoughtful fellow-workmen. He refused to share in their gross indulgences; they cursed him because he would not drink as they did. He bore their insults with a calm philosophy; but having as 'brave a heart as ever English-

man was blessed with' (Southey), he would not allow them to infringe on his rights; and when they took away his tools, determined that if he would not drink with them he should not work while they were carousing, he fought with several of them until they were content to let him alone in his inexplicable gravity and courage. He also went from church to church, for he was still a faithful churchman, but met no answers to his profound questions. He visited the chapels of all classes of Dissenters, but the quiet of the Quaker worship could not quiet the voice that spoke through his conscience, and the splendor of the Roman ritual soon became but irksome pomp to him. He tried, he tells us, all but the Jews, and hoping for nothing from them, resolved to adhere steadily to the Church, regulating his life with strictness, spending his leisure in reading and prayer, and leaving his final fate unsolved. Whitefield's eloquence at Moorfields, however, attracted him thither, but it did not meet his wants. He loved the great orator, he tells us, and was willing to fight for him against the mob, but his mind only sank deeper into perplexity. He became morbidly despondent; he slept little, and often awoke from his horrible dreams dripping with sweat and shivering with terror. Wesley came to Moorfields; Nelson gazed upon him with inexpressible interest as he ascended the platform, stroked back his hair, and cast his eye directly upon him. 'My heart,' he says, 'beat like the pendulum of a clock, and when he spoke I thought his whole discourse was aimed at me.' 'This man,' he said to himself, 'can tell the secrets of my heart; he has shown me the remedy for my wretchedness, even the blood of Christ.' He now became more than ever devoted to religious duties, and soon found the peace of mind he had so long been seeking. He records with dramatic interest the discussions and efforts of his acquaintances to prevent him from going too far in religion. They seem to have been mostly an honest, simple class like himself; they thought he would become unfit for business, and that poverty and distress would fall upon his family. They wished he had never heard Wesley, who, they predicted, would 'be the ruin of him.' He told them that he had reason to bless God that Wesley was ever born, for by hearing him he had become sensible that his business in this world was to get well out of it. The family with whom he lodged were disposed to expel him from the house, for they were afraid some mischief would come on either themselves or him from 'so much praying and fuss as he made about religion.' He procured money and went to pay them what he owed them, and take his leave; but they would not let him escape; 'What if John is right, and we wrong?' was a natural question which they asked among themselves. 'If God has done for you anything more than for us, show us how we may find the same mercy,' asked one of them. He was soon leading them to hear Wesley at Moorfields. One of them was made partaker of the same grace, and he expressed the hope of meeting both in heaven. With much simplicity, but true English determination, he adhered to his religious principles at any risk. His employer required work to be done during the Sabbath on the exchequer building, declaring that the king's business required haste, and that it was usual in such cases to work on Sunday for his majesty. Nelson replied that he would not work on the Sabbath for any man in England, except to quench fire, or something that required the same immediate help. His employer threatened him with the loss of his business. He replied that he would rather starve than offend God. 'What hast thou done that thou makest such an ado about religion?' asked his employer; 'I always took thee for an honest man, and could trust thee with five hundred pounds.' 'So you might,' replied the sturdy Methodist, 'and not have lost one penny by me.' 'But I have a worse opinion of thee now than ever,' resumed the employer. 'Master,' replied Nelson, 'I have the odds of you there, for I have a much worse opinion of myself than you can have.' The honest man was not dismissed, nor again asked to work on Sunday, nor were any of his fellow-workmen." Immediately after his conversion he wrote to his wife, who was in the country, and to all his kindred, explaining his new method of life, and exhorting them to adopt it. Soon after he went to visit them at Bristol, and was met with considerable opposition. But he was only the more encouraged to holy living, and faithfully studied the sacred writings to fortify himself in his new opinions. Ere long his friends were converted, and he held meetings in his house, reading, exhorting, and praying with such of his neighbors as would come to bear. The number soon increased so considerably that he was obliged to stand in his door in order to reach all who were within the house and in the yard. In a very short time the character of the community began to change; ale-houses were deserted, and six or seven converts made weekly. But not only the people had changed, Nelson himself had become another man; his sermons from being quite private had become public; indeed, he had become a preacher, and one of such power that Wesley, when hearing of the success attending Nelson's modest labors, set out at once to visit and direct him. Nelson was made one of Wesley's helpers, and the band of rustic followers one of his united societies. Thus Methodism started in Yorkshire, and thus opened the career of one of the ablest lay-preachers in modern times. Nelson's labors were so successful that Wesley invited him to leave his home and assist in spreading Methodism in other parts of England, and soon he became almost as abundant in labors and sufferings as the Wesleys, and his influence over the working classes equal to that of John Wesley himself. Not even Whitefield possessed more power over the common people. Indeed, "without Nelson and similar lay-preachers, Methodism could not have been sustained as it was. The souls which the leaders of the movement saved, were by these more carefully matured" (Skeats, p. 372, 373). Nelson's good-sense, cool courage, sound piety, and apt speech secured him success wherever he went. He spread Methodism not only in Yorkshire, but in Cornwall, Lincolnshire, Lancashire, and other counties. He was a man of such genuine spirit and popular tact that his worst opposers usually became his best friends. Like Wesley and Whitefield, he was persecuted and annoyed by the established clergy and their tools. His house at Bristol was pulled down; at Nottingham squibs were thrown in his face; at Grimsby the rector headed a mob to the beat of the town drum, and, after supplying them with beer, called upon them to "fight for the Church." Fighting for the Church meant the demolition of the house in which Nelson was living, and its windows were forthwith pulled down and the furniture destroyed (Nelson's Journal, p. 92). But the preaching of the Yorkshire mason soon stopped all such proceedings. The drummer of Grimsby, who had been hired by the rector to beat down Nelson's preaching on the day after the riot, was one of the witnesses of its power. After beating for three quarters of an hour he stood and listened, and soon the tears of penitence were seen rolling down his cheeks. Such was Nelson's power over his audience. The clergy, determined to stay his influence, finally caused him to be impressed into the army, on his return to Bristol, as a vagrant, without visible means of living. Though he protested and tried to prove this charge unjust, he was yet taken and made a soldier. But even in his bonds Nelson did not cease to preach; and when he was forcibly compelled to wear the uniform, he boldly declared that he despised war, and that no one could ever compel him to enter any other service than that of the Prince of Peace, to whom he had dedicated himself. He remained a preacher even amid the din of arms, admonished his comrades against cursing and other sins, distributed tracts among them, and appointed prayer-meetings. All this involved him in new sufferings and persecutions, and he finally sank in the midst of this ill-

treatment; and when, in order to save his life, it became necessary to dismiss him in 1744, he again resumed evangelizing labors, but died before the close of that year. See Stevens, Hist. of Methodism, i, 136, 176, 193, 205, 227, 249; ii, 153; Southey, Life of Wesley, chap. xiv; Skeats, Hist. of the Free Churches of Eng. p. 373; Hurst's Hagenbach, Ch. Hist. of the 18th and 19th Centuries, i, 453 sq.; Porter, Compendium of Methodism, p. 43 sq. See also his own Journal.

Nelson, John (2), D.D., an American Congregational minister, was born in Worcester, Mass., in 1785, and graduated at Williams College. In 1813 he was ordained pastor of the Congregational Church in Leicester, where his whole ministerial life, extending over a period of fifty-eight years, was passed. He died Dec. 6, 1871. From 1844 he had a colleague, and for eighteen years previous to his death was an invalid. See Appleton's Annual Cyclopædia, 1871, p. 591.

Nelson, Joseph. LL.D., an American educator, was born about 1794, and was educated at Rutgers College, New Brunswick, N. J., class of 1815. He was made professor of languages in 1826, but resigned this position in 1829. He was a distinguished classical scholar and teacher. During his professorship in Rutgers College he was blind, yet so thoroughly versed in his authors and so capable as an instructor that he was enabled to perform the duties of his chair with great acceptance. His other senses were remarkably acute. It is said that he could accurately tell the size of a room by the sound of the stamp of his foot upon the floor. He retired from active duty at the close of his professorship, and died in the city of New York in 1830. (W. J. R. T.)

Nelson, Matthew, a minister of the Methodist Protestant Church, was born in Prince Edward County, Va., April 7, 1781. In 1795 his father, colonel Ambrose Nelson, a descendant of the "old Scotch Tom," removed to Danville, Ky. Together with his brother Thomas, who was born in 1779, Matthew was converted in 1801-1802, and together these brothers were baptized while upon their knees in the Kentucky River. They exhibited such interest in the promotion of holy living that they were shortly after licensed to exhort by the Methodist Episcopal Church which they had joined, and in a very brief period were made preachers and admitted into the Kentucky Conference by bishop McKendree. Thomas preached for several years in Ohio, Mississippi, Louisiana, Kentucky, and Tennessee, when his health failed, and he was placed on the superannuated list. He then went South, and the time and place of his death are not known. Matthew preached until 1815, when he located. When the question of lay-representation first agitated the Methodist Episcopal Church, he took sides for the reform, and was elected delegate for Kentucky to the Baltimore Convention. He was a member of that body when it formed the constitution of the Methodist Protestant Church, and thereafter his membership was in that branch of Methodism. He made, however, no distinction in his treatment of Methodists, and his house was the home of Methodist preachers generally. In 1837 he removed to Rutherford Co., Tenn., and there continued to be the same zealous promoter of Methodism. He died in 1856. His children joined the Methodist Episcopal Church without any opposition on his part. See McFerrin, Methodism in Tennessee, ii, 134-137.

Nelson, Robert, a pious and learned English divine, noted as the author of various works in practical divinity which have long been held in very high estimation, was born at London June 22, 1656. He studied at St. Paul's School, London, and at Trinity College, Cambridge, and was while a young man elected a Fellow of the Royal Society. He was intimate with Halley, with whom he travelled in France and Italy. While at Rome he met with and married in 1682 Lady Theophila Lucy, widow of a baronet, and daughter of the earl of Berkeley. This lady, under the influence of the celebrated French Romanist, Bossuet—an intimate friend of Nelson—some time after their marriage became a Roman Catholic, to his great grief. Nelson's mind had been much occupied with the consideration of both the practical and controversial points in divinity, and his chief friends were eminent divines in the English Church, particularly Bull, Hickes, Lloyd, and Tillotson—the last was one of his most valued associates. Nelson not only employed his own powers of persuasion, both verbal and literary, but called in the aid of his friend, archbishop Tillotson; both were, however, unsuccessful, the lady continuing in the Romish communion till her death. His first work, *Transubstantiation contrary to Scripture, or the Protestant's Answer to the Seeker's Request* (1688), appears to be the substance of his considerations on this subject. He was strongly attached to king James II. He was the zealous promoter of all works of charity, having the ability as well as the disposition to give what true benevolence prompted. In helping to build churches, found schools, disseminate useful books, and enforce the laws against crime, he worked most effectually. At the Revolution he scrupled to take the oaths to king William, and remained a nonjuror till the year 1709, when on the death of Dr. Lloyd, the last survivor of the deprived nonjuring bishops, except Dr. Keen, he by Dr. Keen's advice returned to the Church of England as then established. He died Jan. 16, 1715, at Kensington, and was buried in the cemetery of St. George the Martyr by the Foundling Hospital. Robert Nelson wrote *A Companion for the Festivals and Fasts of the Church of England*, etc. (16th ed. Lond. 1736, 8vo). It is still one of the best works of the kind; several abridgments of it have appeared. Bickersteth praises it, but deplores the "great want of evangelical principles and unction" (*Christian Student*, p. 429), probably because Nelson espouses Bull's views on justification:—*The Practice of true Devotion in Relation to the End as well as the Means of Religion*, etc. (7th ed. Lond. 1726, 12mo):—*The great Duty of frequenting the Christian Sacrifice, and the Nature of the Preparation required* (5th ed. Lond. 1714, 12mo):—*An Address to Persons of Quality and Estate* (Lond. 1715, 8vo):—*The whole Duty of a Christian, by way of Question and Answer* (9th ed. Lond. 1727, 12mo):—*Instructions for them that come to be Confirmed* (Lond. 1823, 12mo). He published also a *Life of Bishop Bull*, together with the latter's works (Lond. 1714, 3 vols. 8vo; see Debary, *History of the Ch. of England*, 1685-1717, p. 346 sq.), and the works of *Kettlewell* (Lond. 1719, 2 vols. fol.). See Secretan, *Life of Nelson;* Perry, *Hist. of the Church of Scotland*, iii, 69; Palin, *Hist. of the Church of England*, 1688-1717, p. 37 sq.; *Engl. Cyclop.* s. v.; Darling, *Cyclop. Bibliog.* ii, 2166.

Nelson, Stephen Smith, an American Baptist minister, was born in Middleborough, Mass., Oct. 5, 1772, graduated at Brown University in 1794, and was licensed to preach in 1796. After supplying the Church at Hartford for two years, he was ordained pastor there in 1798, occasionally preaching in the neighborhood, particularly at Middletown. While in Hartford he took an active part in preparing "the Baptist Petition," an address to the Legislature on the subject of the grievances of "Dissenters" from the "Standing Order," which finally severed, in Connecticut at least, the union between Church and State in 1818. He was also appointed to prepare and forward a congratulatory address to Mr. Jefferson on his election as president of the United States. In 1801 he resigned his charge in Hartford, and became principal of a large academy at Sing Sing (then Mount Pleasant), but in consequence of the war with Great Britain he removed in 1815 to Attleborough, Mass., where his labors were very successful, and he afterwards had for a while charge successively of the churches in Plymouth, Mass., and Canton, Conn. In 1825 he removed to Amherst, Mass., where he continued

preaching occasionally until his death, Dec. 8, 1853. See Sprague, *Annals of the Amer. Pulpit*, vi, 366.

Nelson, Lady Theophila. See NELSON, ROBERT.

Nelson, Thomas. See NELSON, MATTHEW.

Nemæan Games, one of the four great festivals of ancient Greece, deriving its name from *Nemëa*, where it was celebrated, as Pindar tells us, in honor of Zeus. The games consisted of horse-racing, chariot-racing, running, wrestling, boxing, throwing the spear, shooting with the bow, and other warlike exercises. The victors were crowned with a chaplet of olive, and afterwards of green parsley. The Nemæan games were regularly celebrated twice in the course of every Olympiad. They appear to have been discontinued soon after the reign of the Roman emperor Hadrian. See GAMES.

Nemalah. See ANT.

Nemar. See LEOPARD.

Nemeius was a frequent surname of *Zeus*, and under it he was worshipped at Nemea, where games were celebrated in his honor. See NEMÆAN GAMES.

Nemesiăci was the name which was given to the officers of the goddess Nemesis, who presided over good fortune, and was the dispenser of faith. See NEMESIS.

Nemĕsis (Νέμεσις, *vengeance*), a female Greek divinity, is most commonly described, according to Hesiod, as a daughter of Night, though some call her a daughter of Erebus (Hygin. *Fab.* præf.) or of Oceanus (Tzetz. *Ad. Lyc.* 88; Pausan. i, 33, 3; vii, 5, 1). Nemesis was a personification of the moral reverence for law, of the natural fear of committing a culpable action, and nence of conscience, and for this reason she was mentioned together with Αἰδώς, or Shame. In course of time, when an enlarged experience convinced men that a divine will found room for its activity amid the little occurrences of human life, she came to be considered as the personification of the righteous anger of the gods, and as the power who constantly preserves or restores the moral equilibrium of earthly affairs—preventing mortals from reaching that excessive prosperity which would lead them to forget the reverence due to the immortal gods, or visiting them with wholesome calamities in the midst of their happiness. Hence originated the latest and loftiest conception of Nemesis as the being to whom was intrusted the execution of the decrees of a strict retributive providence—the awful and mysterious avenger of wrong, punishing and humbling evil-doers in particular. Nemesis was thus regarded as allied to Até and the Eumenides. She is represented as the regulator of human affairs, disbursing at pleasure happiness or unhappiness, the goods and ills of life. She was also looked upon as an avenging deity, and as inflexibly severe to the proud and insolent (Pausanius, i, 33, 2). There was a celebrated temple sacred to her at Rhamnus, in Attica, about sixty stadia distant from Marathon; hence Nemesis was sometimes called also *Rhamnusia* or *Rhamnusis*. In this temple there was a statue of the goddess, made from a block of Parian marble, which the Persians had brought thither to erect a trophy of their expected victory at Marathon. Pausanias says that this statue was the work of Phidias (Pausan. i, 33, 2, 3), but Pliny ascribes it to Agoracritus, and adds that it was preferred by M. Varro to all other statues which existed (*Hist. Nat.* xxxvi, 4, 3). A fragment, supposed by some to be the head of this statue, was found in the temple of Rhamnus, and was presented to the British Museum in 1820 (*Elgin and Phigaleian Marbles*, i, 120; ii, 123). She was represented in the older times as a young virgin, resembling Venus; in later times as clothed with the tunic and peplus, sometimes with swords in her hands and a wheel at her foot, a griffin also having his right paw upon the wheel; sometimes in a chariot drawn by griffins. Nemesis is a frequent figure on coins and gems. The practice of representing the statues of Nemesis with wings was first introduced after the time of Alexander the Great by the inhabitants of Smyrna, who worshipped several goddesses under this name (Pausan. vii, 5, 1; ix, 35, 2). According to a myth preserved by Pausanias, Nemesis was the mother of Helena by Zeus; and Leda, the reputed mother of Helena, was only her nurse (Pausan. i, 33, 7); but this myth seems to have been invented in later times to represent the divine vengeance which was inflicted on the Greeks and Trojans through the instrumentality of Helena. There was also a statue of Nemesis in the Capitol at Rome, though we learn that this goddess had no name in Latin (Pliny, *Hist. Nat.* xxviii, 5). See Smith, *Dict. of Greek and Roman Biog. and Myth.* s. v.; Vollmer, *Mythologisches Wörterbuch*, s. v.; Westcott, *Hand-book of Archæology*, p. 194, 195.

Nemesius, an ancient Christian philosopher of the Greek Church, noted as the author of a work entitled Περὶ φύσεως ἀνϑρώπου, was, according to the title of the work, bishop of Emisa or Emesa, in Phœnicia, and he is also mentioned as such by Anastasius Nicenus (*Quæst. in S. Script.* ap. *Biblioth. Patrum*, vi, 157 [ed. Paris, 1575]). The time in which he lived cannot be determined with much exactness, as the only ancient writers by whom he is quoted or mentioned are probably Anastasius and Moses bar-Cepha (*De Parad.* i, 20, p. 55 [ed. Antw. 1569]). He has sometimes been confounded with the heathen præfect of Cappadocia, Nemesius, praised by Gregory Nazianzen, who corresponded with him. It would seem, however, from the fact that his work mentions no author posterior to the 4th century, but often Apollinaris and Eunomius, that he lived some time in the 5th century; Ritter opines about the middle of that century, as the expressions he uses concerning the union of the Logos and the human nature (p. 60, ed. Antw.) resemble the views sanctioned by the Council of Chalcedon. But there is no express reference to Nestorius and Eutychius, nor to the standing term of the two natures. At the same time there are evident references to the christology of Theodore of Mopsuestia, so that we may place the work at about the close of the first decade of the 5th century. The work was formerly attributed to Gregory of Nyssa, an error arising probably by a confounding of this treatise with that entitled Περὶ κατασκευῆς ἰνϑρώπου. This mistake occurred the more readily from the great similarity of the views of the two writers. Yet in Nemesius the philosophical argument appears only occasionally in close connection with the Christian dogma, which, however, he always considers as decisive. He defended the theory of the freedom of the will against the doctrine of fatalism, and also held fast to some of the ancient philosophical views concerning the nature of the soul, pre-existence, and, in a certain sense, metempsychosis, while the Church rejected the doctrine of Origen. (Comp. here, however, bishop Fell, *Annotationes*, p. 20 [ed. Oxon. 1671].) After Christian theology had experienced the influence of philosophy (and especially of the eclectic Platonism of the 2d century), and thus received a scientific character, philosophy became absorbed in it without ceasing to exist, and thus we find Origen, Athanasius, and Augustine renowned both as philosophers and as theologians. But as dogmatics only attained the form of a traditional system in the 4th century, under the influx of Greek theology, there arose, besides theology, a sort of neutral ground, given up to special philosophical questions. Plato and Aristotle came again into honor. Nemesius, at least as regards method, sought to imitate the latter, but had not his power. His investigations are chiefly of a psychological nature. For him, as for Plato, the soul is an immaterial substance, involved in incessant and self-produced motion. The soul existed before it entered the body. It is eternal, like all suprasensible things. It is not true that new souls are constantly coming into existence, whether by generation or by direct creation. The opinion is also false that the world is destined to be destroyed when the number of souls shall have been completed; God will not destroy

what has been well put together. Nemesius rejects, nevertheless, the doctrine of a world-soul, and of the migration of the human soul through the bodies of animals. In considering the separate faculties of the soul, and also in his doctrine of the freedom of the will, Nemesius largely follows Aristotle. Every species of animal, he says, possesses definite instincts, by which alone its actions are determined; but the actions of man are infinitely varied. Placed midway between the sensible and the suprasensible worlds, man's business is to decide by means of his reason in which direction he will turn —this is his freedom. The work was extensively used by J. Philoponus, John of Damascus, Elias Cretensis, etc. The first Greek edition was published by Nicasius Ellebodius (Antw. 1565, 8vo), with a Latin translation; the next by bishop Fell (Oxon. 1671, 8vo), and the last and best by C. F. Matthæus (Halle, 1802, 8vo). It is also published in Migne's *Patrologie Grecque*. It was translated into English by George Wither (Lond. 1636, 12mo), into German by Österhammer (Salzburg, 1819, 8vo), into French by J. B. Thibault (Paris, 1844, 8vo), and into Italian by Domin. Pizzimenti (8vo). See Ritter, *Gesch. d. christl. Phil.* ii, 461 sq.; Fabricius, *Bibl. Græca*, vii, 549 sq.; Bayle, *Dict. Histor. et Crit.* s. v.; Brucker, *Hist. Crit. Philosoph.*; Ueberweg, *Hist. of Philos.* i, 347, 349; Alzog, *Patrologie*, § 57; Haller, *Bibl. Anat.*; Smith, *Dict. of Greek and Roman Biog. and Mythol.* vol. ii, s. v.; Haag, *Hist. des Dogmes Chrétiens*, i, 245; ii, 70.

Nemez, FREDERIC, a noted Waldensian prelate, flourished in the first half of the 15th century in Bohemia. He was consecrated priest in the convent of the Bohemian capital, Sept. 4, 1433, by bishop Nicholas Philibert, a legate of the Council of Basle. In 1434 Nemez, together with another priest, also a Waldensian, and consecrated at the same time with himself, was sent to Basle, where the council was at open variance with the pope; and in full convention of the clergy they were consecrated bishops by prelates of the Church of Rome. It was done at the instance of the Calixtines [see HUSSITES], whom the council was anxious to propitiate and please. Thus the Waldensians in Bohemia secured the episcopal succession. Nemez died near the middle of the 15th century. See Butler, *Ch. Hist.* ii, 349.

Nemĭnè Contradicente, or *Nem. Con.*, is a term used in ecclesiastical councils to indicate that there is no opposition to a given measure proposed.

Nemĭnè Dissentiente, or *Nem. Diss.*, "No one dissenting." This term also is very often found in journals of conventions, and other documents containing business proceedings.

Nemu'el [according to analogy *Nem'uĕl*] (Heb. *Nemuël'*, נְמוּאֵל, *spread of God*, or perhaps for *Jemuel*; Sept. Ναμουήλ; Vulg. *Namuel*), the name of two Hebrews.

1. The first named of the five sons of Simeon (1 Chron. iv, 24), and progenitor of the Nemuelites (Numb. xxvi, 12). He is elsewhere (Gen. xlvi, 10) called JEMUEL (q. v.).

2. First-named son of Eliab, of the tribe of Reuben, and brother of Dathan and Abiram (Numb. xxvi, 9). B.C. cir. 1619.

Nemu'elites (Heb. *Nemuëli'*, נְמוּאֵלִי, Gentile appellative from נְמוּאֵל, *Nemuel*; Sept. Ναμουηλι; Vulg. *Namuelitæ*), a family in the tribe of Simeon, descended from his first-born (Numb. xxvi, 12). See NEMUEL.

Nennius, of Bangor, in Wales, a noted British monastic, flourished in the first part of the 9th century (comp. *Historia Britonum*). Vossius (*De Historicis Latinis*) says that he lived in the early part of the 7th century, but he assigns no authority for this assertion. In the history Nennius states himself to have been a Briton, and not a Saxon, and a disciple of the holy bishop Elbodus, or Elvodug. He wrote a history of

Britain, *Historia Britonum*, or, as it is sometimes styled, *Eulogium Britanniæ*, which, he says at the beginning, he compiled from all he could find—"from the Roman annals and the chronicles of the fathers, as well as from the writings of the Scots and the Angli, and from the traditions of our ancestors." The history begins with a fabulous genealogy of Brutus, grandson of Æneas, who reigned in Britain. The author afterwards relates the arrival of the Picts in North Britain, and of the Scots in Ireland; and, after a brief and confused narrative of the Roman conquest and empire in Britain, he comes to the Saxon invasion and gradual subjugation of the country. The manuscript of Nennius was mutilated and interpolated by a transcriber, who signs himself "Samuel," and "a disciple of Beularius Presbyter," and who acknowledges that he left out what he thought useless in Nennius's work, and added what he gathered from other writers concerning the towns and wonders of Britain: see end of ch. lxiv of Nennii Banchoriensis *Eulogium Britanniæ*, edited by C. Bertram, and published together with *Gildas* and *Richard, the Monk of Westminster* (Copenhagen, 1757, 8vo). Such is the common account of Nennius; but it is, to say the least, doubtful whether such a person ever existed, and whether the history ascribed to him was not the fabrication of a much later age. Though the work existed earlier, the name of Nennius is not mentioned in connection with it earlier than the 13th century. It is in any case of little value, but even that little is of course greatly reduced if it be the production of an age much later than it professes to be. The question will be found fully discussed in Mr. Wright's *Biographia Britannica Literaria* (Anglo-Saxon period), p. 137–142; the Introduction to Mr. Stevenson's valuable variorum edition of the *Historia Britonum;* Schoell, *Diss. de Eccles. Britonum Scotorumque Historiæ Fontibus*, p. 29–37. A translation of Nennius, by the Rev. W. Gunn, was published in London (1819, 8vo), and reprinted in the *Six Old English Chronicles*, published as a volume in Bohn's "Antiquarian Library" (1848). (J. N. P.)

Neo-Arians. See ARIANS; SOCINIANS; UNITARIANS.

Neo-Cæsarēa, Council of (*Concilium Neocesarense*), was held at Neo-Cæsarea, in Pontus, about the year 314, shortly after the Council of Ancyra. It was composed, for the most part, of the same bishops who assisted at the latter, and Vitalis of Antioch is believed to have presided. Fifteen canons of discipline were published. The most important acts are: 1, enjoining the degradation of priests who marry after ordination— a very important measure, and of interest to the inquiring student into the history of celibacy (see Lea, *Hist. of Sacerdotal Celibacy*, p. 48, 49); 2, depriving of communion, through life, women who, having married two brothers, refuse to dissolve the marriage; 6, permitting to baptize women with child whenever they will; 7, forbidding priests to be present at the second marriage of any person; 8, forbidding to confer holy orders upon a layman whose wife has committed adultery: orders that if she has committed adultery after his ordination he shall put her away, and declares that if he shall continue to live with her he cannot retain the ministry committed to him; 11, forbidding to admit any one, however well qualified, to the priesthood under thirty years of age, because the Lord Jesus Christ at that age began his ministry; 13, directing that, where both are present, the city priests shall celebrate the holy eucharist in preference to those from the country; 14, declaring that the Chorepiscopi are after the pattern of the Seventy, and permitting them to offer; 15, ordering that there shall be seven deacons in every city, as is approved by the book of Acts. See Labbé, *Conc.* i, 1480; Landon, *Manual of Councils*, p. 420, 421; Neander, *Ch. Hist.* ii, 147, 156, 318.

Neocŏri (*νεωκόροι, temple-sweepers*) is the title which the officers bore who were attached to the pagan temples in ancient Greece. Their office was originally to sweep the temple, and perform other menial services connected with it. In course of time these duties were intrusted to slaves, and the *Neocori* came to occupy a higher position, superintending the temples, guarding the treasures, and regulating the sacred rites. In some towns there was a regular college of *Neocori*, and the office, having considerable honor attached to it, was sought by persons even of high rank. In the time of the emperors nations and cities eagerly sought the title of *Neocori*, and counted it a special privilege to have the charge of a temple. Thus in the Acts of the Apostles we learn that the city of Ephesus was *Neocora* to the great goddess Diana. See Gardner, *Faiths of the World*, p. 525; Broughton, *Biblioth. Historica Sacra*, s. v. See DIANA.

Neology (from νέος, *new*, and λόγος, *doctrine*), a term synonymous with καινοδοξία, καινοτομία, is expressive of a tendency to novelty, not from a feeling of its superiority, but simply on account of its newness. The word is not classically used, yet νεολογία would not be contrary to the analogy of language, and would be equivalent to the *nomina mutare* (as Cicero, *De Fin.* iii, 5, says of Zeno: "Non tam rerum inventor fuit, quam novorum verborum"). Neology, then, is an unnecessary innovation in language, thought, or usage, and dangerous in so far as it disturbs continuity and is the result of fancy. In theology the term is used especially to designate the rationalistic theories opposed to revealed religion which have obtained such success among certain German and English theologians. These resort to the novel expedient of reducing the standard of the doctrine and facts of Scripture to the level of unassisted human reason. See RATIONALISM. (J. H. W.)

Neo-Manichæans was the name of a Christian sect which, like the Priscillianists and Paulicians, denied the resurrection of the flesh; and, like the Quakers and Swedenborgians of our own day, thought that after death the soul became the inhabitant of a spiritual body. In other respects the Neo-Manichæans held the views of the Manichæans (q. v.).

Neomenia or Noumenia (Gr. *new moon*), a festival of the ancient Greeks at the beginning of every lunar month, which was (as the name imports) observed upon the day of new moon in honor of all the gods, but especially of Apollo, who was called Νεομηνιος, because the sun is the first author of all light, and whatever distinction of times and seasons may be taken from other planets, yet they are all owing to him as the original and fountain of those borrowed rays by which they shine. This festival was observed with games and public entertainments made by the richer class, to whose tables the poor flocked in great numbers. The Athenians at these times offered solemn prayers and sacrifices for the prosperity of their country during the ensuing month in Erectheus's temple, in the Acropolis, which was kept by a dragon, to which they gave a cake made of honey. The Jews had their Neomenia, or feast of the new moon, on which peculiar sacrifices were appointed. They made on this day a sort of family entertainment and rejoicing. Thus David tells Jonathan, "Behold, to-morrow is the new moon, and I should not fail to sit with the king at meat," etc; and Saul, we find, took it amiss that he did not attend. The most celebrated Neomenia of all others was that at the beginning of the civil year, or first day of the month Tisri. No servile labor was performed on that day; and they offered particular burnt sacrifices, and sounded the trumpets of the Temple. The modern Jews keep the Neomenia only as a feast of devotion, which any one may observe or not, as he pleases. In the prayers of the synagogue they read from Psa. cxiii to cxviii. They bring forth the roll of the law, and read therein to four persons. They call to remembrance the sacrifice that used to be offered on this day in the Temple. See NEW MOON.

Neonomians (from the Greek νέος, *new*, and νόμος, *law*) is the appellation of those Christians who regard Christianity as a *new law*, mitigated in its requisitions for the sake of Christ. Neonomianism has many modifications, and has been held by Arminians as well as Calvinists—persons very greatly differing from each other in the consequences to which they carry it, and in the principles from which they deduce it. One opinion is that the new covenant of grace which, through the medium of Christ's death, the Father made with men consists, according to this system, not in our being justified by faith, as it apprehends the righteousness of Christ, but in this, that God, abrogating the exaction of perfect legal obedience, reputes or accepts of faith itself, and the imperfect obedience of faith instead of the perfect obedience of the law, and graciously accounts them worthy of the reward of eternal life. Towards the close of the 17th century a controversy was agitated among the English Dissenters, in which the one side (who were partial to the writings of Dr. Crisp) were charged with antinomianism, and the other (who favored those of Mr. Baxter) were accused of neonomianism. Dr. Daniel Williams was a principal writer on what was called the neonomian side. He teaches as follows:

"1. God has eternally elected a certain definite number of men whom he will infallibly save by Christ in the way prescribed by the Gospel. 2. These very elect are not personally justified until they receive Christ and yield themselves up to him, but they remain condemned while unconverted to Christ. 3. By the ministry of the Gospel there is a serious offer of pardon and glory, upon the terms of the Gospel, to all that hear it; and God thereby requires them to comply with the said terms. 4. Ministers ought to use these and other Gospel benefits as motives, assuring men that if they believe they shall be justified; if they turn to God, they shall live; if they repent, their sins shall be blotted out; and while they *neglect* these duties they cannot have a personal interest in these respective benefits. 5. It is by the power of the Spirit of Christ freely exerted, and not by the power of free will, that the Gospel becomes effectual for the conversion of any soul to the obedience of faith. 6. When a man believes, yet is not that very faith, and much less any other work, the matter of that righteousness for which a sinner is justified, i. e. entitled to pardon, acceptance, and eternal glory, as righteous before God; and it is the imputed righteousness of Christ alone for which the Gospel gives the believer a right to these and all saving blessings, who in this respect is justified by Christ's righteousness alone. By both this and the fifth head it appears that all boasting is excluded, and we are saved by free grace. 7. *Faith* alone receives the Lord Jesus and his righteousness, and the subject of this faith is a *convinced, penitent soul*; hence we are justified by faith alone, and the *impenitent* are not forgiven. 8. God has freely promised that all whom he predestinated to salvation shall not only savingly believe, but that he by his power shall preserve them from a *total* or a *final apostasy.* 9. Yet the believer, while he lives in this world, is to pass the time of his sojourning here with fear, because his warfare is not accomplished, and it is true that if he draw back God will have no pleasure in him. These, with the like cautions, God blesseth as means to the saints' perseverance, and these by ministers should be so urged. 10. The law of innocence, or moral law, is still so in force that every precept thereof constitutes duty, even to the believer; every breach thereof is a sin deserving of death: this law binds death by its curse on every unbeliever, and the righteousness for or by which we are justified before God is a righteousness (at least) adequate to that law, which is Christ's alone righteousness; and this so imputed to the believer that God deals judiciously with him according thereto. 11. Yet such is the grace of the Gospel that it promiseth in and by Christ a freedom from the curse, forgiveness of sin, and eternal life to every sincere believer; which promise God will certainly perform, notwithstanding the threatening of the law."

Dr. Williams maintains the conditionality of the covenant of grace; but admits with Dr. Owen, who also uses the term *condition*, that "Christ undertook that those who were to be taken into this covenant should receive grace enabling them to comply with the terms of it, fulfil its conditions, and yield the obedience which God required therein." On this subject Dr. Williams further says: "The question is not whether the first (viz., regenerating) grace, by which we are enabled to perform the condition, be absolutely given. This I affirm, though that be dispensed ordinarily in a due use

of means, and in a way discountenancing idleness, and fit encouragement given to the use of means." The following objection, among others, was made by several ministers in 1692 against Dr. Williams's *Gospel Truth Stated*, etc.: "To supply the room of the moral law, vacated by him, he turns the Gospel into a new law, in the keeping of which we shall be justified for the sake of Christ's righteousness, making qualifications and acts of ours a disposing subordinate righteousness whereby we become capable of being justified by Christ's righteousness." To this, among other things, he answers:

"The difference is not (1) whether the Gospel be a new law in the Socinian, popish, or Arminian sense. This I deny. Nor (2) is faith or any other grace or act of ours any atonement for sin, satisfaction to justice, meriting qualification, or any part of that righteousness for which we are justified at God our Creator's bar. This I deny in places innumerable. Nor (3) whether the Gospel be a law more new than is implied in the first promise to fallen Adam, proposed to Cain, and obeyed by Abel to the differencing of him from his unbelieving brother. This I deny. (4) Nor whether the Gospel be a law that allows sin when it accepts such graces as true, though short of perfection, to be the conditions of our personal interest in the benefits purchased by Christ. This I deny. (5) Nor whether the Gospel be a law the promises whereof entitle the performers of its conditions to the benefits, as of debt. This I deny. The difference is—1. Is the Gospel a law in this sense, namely, God in Christ thereby commandeth sinners to repent of sin and receive Christ by a true operative faith, promising that thereupon they shall be united to him, justified by his righteousness, pardoned, and adopted; and that, persevering in faith and true holiness, they shall be finally saved; also threatening that if any shall die impenitent, unbelieving, ungodly, rejecters of his grace, they shall perish without relief, and endure sorer punishments than if these offers had not been made to them? 2. Hath the Gospel a sanction, that is, doth Christ therein enforce his commands of faith, repentance, and perseverance by the foresaid promises and threatenings, as motives to our obedience? Both these I affirm, and they deny: saying, the Gospel in the largest sense is an absolute promise without precepts and conditions, and a Gospel threat is a bull. 3. Do the Gospel promises of benefits to certain graces, and its threats that those benefits shall be withheld and the contrary evils inflicted for the neglect of such graces, render these graces the condition of our personal title to those benefits? This they deny, and I affirm," etc.

It does not appear to have been a question in this controversy whether God in his Word commands sinners to repent and believe in Christ, nor whether he promises life to believers and threatens death to unbelievers; but whether it be the Gospel under the form of a new law that thus commands or threatens, or the moral law on its behalf, and whether its promises to believing render such believing a condition of the things promised. In another controversy, however, which arose afterwards among the same people, in the Assembly of 1720, it became a question whether God did by his Word, call it law or Gospel, command unregenerate sinners to repent and believe in Christ, or do anything else which is spiritually good. Of those who took the affirmative side of this question one party maintained it on the ground of the Gospel being a new law, consisting of commands, promises, and threatenings, the terms or conditions of which were repentance, faith, and sincere obedience. But those who first engaged in the controversy, though they allowed the encouragement to repent and believe to arise merely from the grace of the Gospel, yet considered the formal obligation to do so as arising merely from the moral law, which, requiring supreme love to God, requires acquiescence in any revelation which he shall at any time make known. The Hopkinsians of America are believed in their teachings to espouse the same views. Not only do they fearlessly set forth the extent, spirituality, and unflinching demands of the law; they think it necessary also to urge upon sinners the *legal dispensation*, if we may so speak, of the Gospel. See Watson, *Dict. of Theology*, s. v.; Hagenbach, *Hist. of Doctrines*, ii, 431; Chauncey *Neonomianism Unmasked*; Buchanan, *Doctrine of Justification*; Hetherington, *Hist. of the Church of Scotland*, p. 341 (on the anti-Neonomian side). See MODERATES.

Neophyte (from νέος, *new*, and φυτόν, a *plant*), i. e. *newly planted*, was a word used in the Eleusinian and other mysteries to designate a person recently initiated. In the early Church it was the name given to converts to Christianity who had just received baptism. After that solemn ceremony they wore white garments for eight days, from Easter eve until the Sunday after Easter, which was hence called *Dominica in albis*, i. e. the Sunday in white. (These garments were usually made of white linen, but sometimes of more costly materials.) They were also subject to a strict discipline or probation for a much longer period. At first they were considered unfit for the priestly office, on the grounds of 1 Tim. iii, 6, where the word is rendered "novice," and explained by Gregory the Great to have been used in allusion to "their being newly planted in the faith" (*Epp.* 6, v; *Ep.* 51). Neophytes differed from catechumens (q. v.), inasmuch as the persons were supposed to have not only embraced the doctrines of the Church, but also to have received baptism. Paul, in the passage referred to, directs Timothy not to promote a neophyte to the episcopate; and this prohibition was generally maintained. The duration of this exclusion was left for a time to the discretion of bishops, but several of the ancient synods legislated regarding it. The third council of Arles (524) and the third of Orange (538) fix a year as the least limit of probation. Ecclesiastical history offers, however, a few instances in which this rule was departed from, as in the appointment of Ambrosius as bishop; but these exceptions were not frequent. In the modern Roman Catholic Church the same discipline is observed, and extends to persons converted not alone from heathenism, but from any sect of Christians separated from the communion of Rome. The time, however, is left to be determined by circumstances. The Roman Catholic missionaries still give the name of neophytes to the Jews, Mussulmans, or pagans who are converted to Christianity, and the Church grants them numerous privileges in order to induce others to follow their example (see Ferrari, *Biblioth. canonica*, s. v. Neophytus, No. 3). Gregory XIII established at Rome a special college for young neophytes, where they are instructed to become afterwards missionaries in their native countries; it is called the College of the Propaganda, and is one of the most richly endowed and privileged seminaries of the Roman Church. The name neophyte is also applied in Roman usage to *newly-ordained priests*, and sometimes, though more rarely, to the *novices* of a religious order. See Bergier, *Dict. de Théologie*, s. v.; Martigny, *Dict. des Antiquités*, p. 433–435; Siegel, *Christliche Alterthümer*, iii, 17 sq.; Riddle, *Christian Antiquities*, p. 313, 522; Walcott, *Sacred Archæology*, s. v.

Neophȳtus. A short but curious tract, published by Cotelerius in his *Ecclesiæ Græcæ Monumenta*, ii, 457–462, bears this title: Νεοφύτου πρεσβυτέρου μοναχοῦ καὶ ἐγκλειστοῦ περὶ τῶν κατὰ χῶραν Κύπρον σκαιῶν, *Neophyti Presbyteri Monachi et Inclusi, de Calamitatibus Cypri*. It gives a brief account of the usurpation of the island by Isaac Comnenus, its conquest, and the imprisonment of Isaac by Richard Cœur de Lion, king of England, and the sale of the island to the Latins (as the writer represents the transaction) by Richard. The writer was contemporary with these transactions, and therefore lived about the close of the 12th century. He was a resident and probably a native of Cyprus. There are several MSS. in the different European libraries bearing the name of Neophytus. Of these a MS. formerly in the Colbertine Library at Paris contained thirty *Orationes*, evidently by this Neophytus; a *Catena in Canticum*, and some others on theological subjects, are of more dubious authorship, but they may be by the same author; a *Demonstratio de Plautis*, and one or two chemical treatises, are by another Neophytus, surnamed Prodromenus; and *Definitiones et Divisiones Summariæ totius Aristotelis Philosophiæ*, and *Epitome in Porphyrii quinque voces et in Aristotelis Organon*, are apparently by a third writer of the same name. See Cotelerius, *l. c.*, and notes in col. 678, 679; Du Cange, *Glossarium Med. et Inf. Græcitatis; Index Auctorum*, p. 29; Fabricius, *Bibliotheca Græca*, v, 738; viii, 661, 662; xi, 339, etc.; Cave, *Hist. Litt.* ad ann. 1190, ii, 251 (ed. Oxford, 1740, 1742); Smith, *Dict. Greek and Rom. Biog. and Mythol.* s. v.

Neo-Platonism, an eclectic philosophy nearly coeval in origin with Christianity, but developed in an anti-Christian and pantheistic direction. The term, taken in the wider sense, may be defined as that form or method of philosophizing which, recognising or claiming Plato as leader, incorporated with his views other, especially Oriental, conceptions, and sought by means of such composite or eclectic philosophical results to harmonize or, at the least, to reconcile the teachings of the various ancient schools of philosophy; in the narrow, and perhaps the more common acceptation, it is applied to the doctrinal system of the philosophical school founded at Alexandria, in Egypt, by Ammonius Saccas, in the first half of the 3d century after Christ, and continued by his pupils and successors not only in the city of its origin, but also in other places. Plotinus, one of the earliest and most eminent of its disciples and masters, taught at Rome, and the term *Romano-Alexandrian* is sometimes applied to it.

Many of the early Christian writers advocated the employment of the philosophical methods to elucidate and establish the doctrines of the Gospel, and were, consequently, to a greater or less extent imbued with the spirit and favored the professed objects of the Neo-Platonists, i. e. the conciliation of philosophy and religion; but the pagan school, especially during its later history, was characterized by an intense hostility to Christianity, as well as by theosophical views and theurgic practices. The influence of this form of philosophy did not disappear entirely with the suppression of its schools by Theodosius in the 6th century, but traces of it may be seen even in the scholasticism of the Middle Ages (notably in the writings of Erigena, who flourished in the 9th century); and after the revival of literature, in what are styled the modern times, the impress of this type of Platonism appears with more or less distinctness in the philosophical systems of Pletho, Ficinus, Paracelsus, and others of the 15th and 16th centuries, as well as, subsequently, in those of Gale and Cudworth, and in the speculations of Schelling and his school in regard to the identity of subject and object. In fact, the spirit of Neo-Platonism has impregnated subsequent religious as well as philosophical thought in such a way and to such an extent as to make a careful examination of its history and doctrines an object worthy of the serious attention of those minds who are anxious to distinguish the truth which saves from the error which misleads and destroys.

I. *History.*—The rise and development of this philosophy may, for our present purpose, be sufficiently exhibited by, *first*, an outline of the causes tending to produce it, followed, *secondly*, by a brief sketch of the lives and opinions of only the most prominent characters who either, as precursors, prepared the way for its introduction and establishment, or, as founders and disciples of the school, expounded and defended its doctrines. To this we shall add a summary of its general principles (mainly abridged from Schwegler) and some observations on its relations to Christianity; and, lastly, such a list of works on the subject as will enable any one so desiring to inform himself more fully.

1. *Subjective Causes.*—Aside from the very great influence manifestly exerted by Oriental ideas in shaping the character and tendencies of the philosophy of the period in which Neo-Platonism had its birth, there were internal causes at work, growing out of the unsatisfactory results of the preceding pagan philosophics, and the want felt, especially by earnest and thoughtful spirits, of something different—something which gave better promise of satisfying the longings of the human

race for a solution of the problem of its origin and destiny. Instead of giving clearer light and purer life to men groping after the knowledge of God and themselves, the development of the old philosophies had ended in scepticism and moral debasement. This result was disappointing and disheartening. Scepticism promised contentment of spirit, but, instead, produced only the opposite, viz. the necessity for an unceasing opposition to all positive assertions; and in place of the rest sought for, it gave only an unappeasable disquiet, which, in turn, begat a yearning for a condition absolutely satisfying and removed from all sceptical objections. This longing for something absolutely certain found historical expression in Neo-Platonism.

Zeller (as given in Ueberweg, p. 222) says: "The feeling of alienation from God and the yearning after a higher revelation are universal characteristics of the last centuries of the ancient world. This yearning was, in the first place, but an expression of the consciousness of the decline of the classical nations and of their culture, the presentiment of the approach of a new æra; and it called into life not only Christianity, but also, before it, pagan and Jewish Alexandrianism, and other related developments."

2. *Objective Causes.*—The conquests of Alexander the Great, extending from the Mediterranean to the Indus, brought the Occidental and Oriental peoples and civilizations into nearer relations with each other, and thereby opened up new fields for philosophical research to the active and inquiring Hellenic race on one side, while, on the other side, the disciples of Zoroaster and the gymnosophists of India were, in like manner, made acquainted with the opinions and speculations of the Greek philosophers. The Hebrew, whose home lay between these extremes, contributed also his share to the common stock, and enlarged thereby the common fund of relatively new ideas. The succession of the Romans to the empire of the civilized world still further increased this fund, and enlarged the sphere of philosophical activities. The results of this mutual action and reaction of the East and the West upon each other were made more permanent by Alexander's policy of planting colonies and founding cities among the nations brought under his sway. The city in Lower Egypt founded by and named after him, and, with masterly foresight, located on the pathway of the commercial intercourse of nations for that and succeeding ages, became naturally also the great central point of philosophical intercourse and reciprocal culture. At this focus of the intellectual activity as well as emporium of the trade and commerce of the times the natives of various lands met together, and discussed and compared philosophies and faiths. Here was the soil where once flourished the ancient wisdom and learning of Egypt, the origin of whose civilization was referred by a proud priesthood far back into the shadows of unhistorical æras. Here were found advocates of the Greek polytheism, with its poetic conceptions of divinities peopling mountain and dale, forest and stream, land and sea, and with a cultus adjusted to the mercurial temperament of that race. Here also were Roman representatives of the statelier and graver character of a nation notable for its deep religious sentiment. Here, too, the Jewish scribe, proud of the antiquity of his people and of their divinely-given law, upheld the doctrine of the unity of God taught in his sacred books, and pointed to their purer teachings and sublimer truths. The Persian discoursed of his master Zoroaster, of the two principles, the good and the evil one, struggling for the mastery of the world, and of the magical knowledge possessed by the priests and philosophers of his land. The Brahmin, wandering from the far Ganges, brought with him his ascetic mysticism and pride of caste, the doctrine of a quiescent supreme divinity, in whose repose purified souls found happiness, and of a trinity of active forces or emanations therefrom—the Creator, the preserver, the destroyer. Here too, in the appointed time,

appeared the heralds of a new and diviner philosophy, whose roots, planted in the soil of man's primeval home, and kept alive by Jehovah's care through all the mutations of history, were destined in the fulness of the times to grow up into that Apocalyptic tree of life whose "leaves were for the healing of the nations." In this, the cosmopolitan city of the world of that epoch, the philosophical conceptions of monism, of dualism, of monotheism, of polytheism, of magism, of mysticism, and of asceticism, found a common point of contact and a common field of combat. Out of their conflicts was evolved that type of eclectic philosophy which, under the name of Neo-Platonism, supplanted in the pagan world the classical philosophies, and, in its later periods, assuming an intensely hostile attitude to Christianity, became the representative and type of all heathen philosophy and religions, contesting with the new faith the dominion over the mind and conscience of man. With this end in view, it became a syncretism in object as well as form, and sought to array under its banners all the influences and forces of paganism to enable it to resist and turn back the aggressive movements of its despised but dreaded rival. But these supreme efforts of an effete philosophy and faith could not long withstand the onward sweep of the purer and soul-satisfying philosophy of the Gospel, and soon triumphant Christianity was relieved from this burden of conflict with the opposing powers of this world by the extinction of this last of the pagan schools. The triumph of Christianity was the triumph of the idea of monotheism, of the doctrine of the divine unity, over both dualism and polytheism and their allied conceptions and influences. Monotheism, as a world-religious idea, belonged to the Jews, to whom it was given by revelation; its triumph with Christianity was therefore the triumph "of the religious idea of the Jewish people, stripped of its national limitations, and softened and spiritualized" (Ueberweg).

It may not be inappropriate even here to call attention to the fact that this revealed conception of God was lodged with a people whose home was near the centre of the olden world—the pivot, so to speak, about which the movements of ancient social and religious life revolved.

3. *Biographical History.*—(1.) The earliest in point of time, as well as one of the most important, of those philosophers whom we shall mention as among the precursors of Neo-Platonism was Philo (commonly surnamed Judæus, to distinguish him from Greek writers of the same name), born about twenty or twenty-five years before Christ, at Alexandria, in Egypt. He belonged to an illustrious and, according to some authorities, to a priestly family of the Jewish race. Josephus (*Ant.* xviii, 8) speaks of him as "a man eminent on all accounts, brother to Alexander the Alabarch, and one not unskilful in philosophy." He was of the sect of the Pharisees, and, by reason of his learning and good repute, was placed by his co-religionists, when he was already advanced in life, at the head of an embassy sent A.D. 39–40 to Rome, to repel before Caligula the accusations of the Greeks of Alexandria against the loyalty of the Jews of that city, and to plead in behalf of his race for the uninterrupted exercise of their religion, and against the desecration of their holy places by setting up statues of the emperor therein. His embassy was fruitless so far as its immediate object was concerned, for the prejudiced and enraged Caligula refused to see them; but that emperor's death in the following year put a stop to the persecution he had ordered.

Philo's works are mainly commentaries, with separate titles, on the chief subjects of the Pentateuch. He employed the allegorizing method of interpreting the Scriptures which was in use by the cultivated Jews of his native city, and sought thereby to harmonize the philosophy of religion with that of Plato, Aristotle, and others. His theology, consequently, was a "blending of Platonism and Judaism." He taught that God should be worshipped as a personal being, yet conceived of as the most general of existences: $\tau\grave{o}$ $\gamma\epsilon\nu\iota\kappa\acute{\omega}\tau\alpha\tau\acute{o}\nu$ $\grave{\epsilon}\sigma\tau\iota\nu$ $\grave{o}$ $\vartheta\epsilon\acute{o}\varsigma$ (Legis Alleg. vol. ii). He is $\tau\grave{o}$ $\check{o}\nu$, the existing; is above all human knowledge and virtue, and even "above the idea of the Good" ($\kappa\rho\epsilon\acute{\iota}\tau\tau\omega\nu$ $\tau\epsilon$ $\mathring{\eta}$ $\mathring{\alpha}\rho\epsilon\tau\mathring{\eta}$ $\kappa\alpha\grave{\iota}$ $\kappa\rho\epsilon\acute{\iota}\tau\tau\omega\nu$ $\mathring{\eta}$ $\grave{\epsilon}\pi\iota\sigma\tau\acute{\eta}\mu\eta$, $\kappa\alpha\grave{\iota}$ $\kappa\rho\epsilon\acute{\iota}\tau\tau\omega\nu$ $\mathring{\eta}$ $\alpha\mathring{\upsilon}\tau\grave{o}$ $\tau\mathring{\alpha}\gamma\alpha\vartheta\grave{o}\nu$ $\kappa\alpha\grave{\iota}$ $\alpha\mathring{\upsilon}\tau\grave{o}$ $\tau\grave{o}$ $\kappa\alpha\lambda\acute{o}\nu$, De Mundi Opificio, i, 2); the absolute is reached not by demonstration ($\lambda\acute{o}\gamma\omega\nu$ $\mathring{\alpha}\pi o\delta\epsilon\acute{\iota}\xi\epsilon\iota$), but by clear insight ($\grave{\epsilon}\nu\alpha\rho\gamma\epsilon\acute{\iota}\alpha$). Divinity and matter are the two first principles, existing from eternity: the Divinity is "being, real, infinite, immutable, incomprehensible to human understanding" ($\check{o}\nu$); matter is "non-existing ($\mu\mathring{\eta}$ $\check{o}\nu$), having received from the Divinity a form and life." In creation, Deity, unwilling to come into contact with impure matter, employed as his instruments "incorporeal potencies or ideas," the highest of which, the creative one ($\pi o\iota\eta\tau\iota\kappa\acute{\eta}$), is in Scripture named God ($\vartheta\epsilon\acute{o}\varsigma$); the second, the ruling one ($\beta\alpha\sigma\iota\lambda\iota\kappa\acute{\eta}$), is called Lord ($\kappa\acute{\upsilon}\rho\iota o\varsigma$): these potencies are conceived of as independent personal beings who have appeared to men. "The highest of all the divine forces is the Logos," in which the world of ideas finds its place. The Logos is the image of God, and the type after which the world is formed, and the manifestation of the Deity, making and ruling the world, and serving as the Mediator between God and man. The conception of an incarnate Logos was, however, impossible to Philo, who regarded matter as impure. This conception forms one of the fundamental doctrines which separate Christianity from the Alexandrian theosophy. Philo refers the doctrine of ideas to Moses ($M\omega\ddot{\upsilon}\sigma\acute{\epsilon}\omega\varsigma$ $\grave{\epsilon}\sigma\tau\grave{\iota}$ $\tau\grave{o}$ $\delta\acute{o}\gamma\mu\alpha$ $\tau o\tilde{\upsilon}\tau o$, $o\mathring{\upsilon}\kappa$ $\grave{\epsilon}\mu\acute{o}\nu$), and has given to it a character, arising from his own religious conceptions, which has so transformed the Platonic theory as to interfere "with the correct historical comprehension of Platonism even down to our own times" (Ueberweg). Sharpe (Hist. of Egypt, ii, 111) thinks that the writings of Philo "explain how Platonism became united to Judaism, and again show us the point of agreement between the New Platonists and the Platonic Christians."

(2.) Of the Greeks who may be classed among the forerunners in the movement tending to harmonize the doctrines of Plato with the speculations of Oriental philosophy we can notice only (i) Thrasyllus of Mendes (died A.D. 36), who arranged all the works of Plato admitted by him to be genuine into nine tetralogies, and combined with Platonism certain mystical Neo-Pythagorean speculations founded on numbers and the Chaldæan astrology; and (ii) Plutarch of Chæronea (born about A.D. 40, and died about A.D. 120), the author of the well-known biographies. He was a pupil of Ammonius of Alexandria (not Saccas), and taught at Athens during the reigns of Nero and Vespasian. Plutarch's doctrines deviate less from pure Platonism than those taught by the Neo-Platonists proper of the school of Alexandria, yet he is regarded by some as standing "next to Philo both in age and character as a representative of Oriental tendencies in Greek philosophy." So far as the Grecian systems are concerned, while holding mainly to Plato and controverting the views of the Stoics and Epicureans, he evinced little regard for the dialectics of Platonism, and was a strong believer in the Stoic doctrine of a Providence. In regard to Oriental doctrines, while profoundly reverent of the ancient cultus of his country, and opposed to the introduction of foreign superstitions and Jewish and Syrian rites, he, from the Greek point of view, sought to reconcile the philosophy of religion with the true interpretation of the worship of Isis and Osiris. He distinguished (as did Philo) between an absolute God whose essence is unknown to us and a creating power or energy which formed the world. Isis corresponds to the latter, and connects the creation with Osiris, the supreme and invisible one. The world is the offspring of two distinct principles, one inherently good, and the other inherently evil (the dualism of Zoroaster), whose battle-ground is the soul of man. Besides one supreme God, Plutarch

recognised the divinities of the popular faiths as well as the existence of dæmons, some good, some evil, as necessary mediators between the divine and human.

(3.) L. Apuleius (born about A.D. 130), a teacher of the Platonic and Aristotelian philosophies at Medaura, in Numidia, was a Latin representative of the then prevailing tendency to the assimilation of Oriental and Occidental philosophy. Holding that it was derogatory to the proper conception of God to have him burdened with the superintendence of things, he assigns to him, as the ministers who direct "mundane events," hosts of dæmons, whose abode is in the air, and who are the objects of the religious ceremonies both of the Greeks and the barbarians, and also of the practice of magic. He speaks of a trinity of divine faculties, immutable, eternal, viz. God himself, the divine Reason, and the World-Soul.

(4.) Numenius of Apamea, in Syria, who flourished in the latter half of the second century after Christ, showed in his writings (of which fragments only have come down to us) even a stronger tendency towards Oriental ideas, and referred the origin of Greek philosophy to Jewish, Egyptian, Magian, and Brahminical sources. Suidas (s. v.) quotes him as styling Plato the Attic Moses ($\tau\grave{\iota}$ $\gamma\acute{\alpha}\rho$ $\grave{\epsilon}\sigma\tau\iota$ $\Pi\lambda\acute{\alpha}\tau\omega\nu$ $\mathring{\eta}$ $M\omega\sigma\mathring{\eta}\varsigma$ $A\tau\tau\iota\kappa\acute{\iota}\zeta\omega\nu$;). So highly was he esteemed by the Neo-Platonists of the following periods that some authors regard him as the real founder of the Alexandrian school, an honor denied him by the Alexandrians themselves because of his Syrian origin and non-residence in their midst. He further developed the conception of a trinity in the divine Being, who was incorporeal, by distinguishing therein, 1st, a perfectly intelligent, immutable, eternal, supreme God; 2d, a world-maker, or demiurgos; and, 3d, the world. These he terms father, son, and grandson ($\pi\acute{\alpha}\pi\pi o\varsigma$, $\check{\epsilon}\kappa\gamma o\nu o\varsigma$, $\mathring{\alpha}\pi\acute{o}\gamma o\nu o\varsigma$), and ascribes the doctrine to both Plato and his master, Socrates. Numenius also held that the soul is immortal and immaterial, and that its descent into the body from its former incorporeal state implies previous moral delinquency—a conception indicating an acquaintance with Jewish and Christian doctrines on the fall of man. Cronius, described by Porphyry as a friend of Numenius, and who shared his opinions, was, according to Suidas (s. v. $\Omega\rho\iota$-$\gamma\acute{\epsilon}\nu\eta\varsigma$), the author of writings studied by the Christian Origen.

(5.) Some of the writings popularly attributed to the mythical Hermes Trismegistus treat of religious and philosophical subjects in the style and from the standpoint of Neo-Platonism, and are classed among the productions of the Egyptian Platonists. The reputed author was the Egyptian Thot or Theut, identified with the Greek Hermes, who, as the fabled author of all the discoveries and productions of the human mind, the source of all knowledge and thought, the embodied Logos, was dignified with the title of $T\rho\grave{\iota}\varsigma$ $M\acute{\epsilon}\gamma\iota\sigma\tau o\varsigma$, thrice greatest (may there not be in this name a reference to the Neo-Platonic trinity?). Some of these writings "belonged to the school of Philo, and were known to Plutarch; others are of a much later date, and not unaffected by the influence of Christianity." The Poimander, one of the largest and most important of these works still extant, seems to have been composed in imitation of the Pastor of Hermas. It gives views of nature, the world, God, and the human soul quite in the spirit of Neo-Platonism, but with such occasional admixture of Oriental, Jewish, and Christian ideas as to show the syncretism peculiar to the philosophy of the time.

(6.) Ammonius, called Saccas from his vocation of corn-porter (lived from about A.D. 175 to 250), is usually regarded as the founder of the Alexandrio-Roman school of Neo-Platonism. He was born of Christian parents, and by them trained in the principles of their faith, but probably apostatized when his mind became absorbed in the study of heathen philosophy. Though of humble origin, and destitute of the advantages of early culture, his enthusiastic love of knowledge and his great natural abilities enabled him to overcome the disadvantages surrounding him, and to found a school of philosophy, and to attract to it pupils whose subsequent fame as philosophers made the name of their master illustrious. Of these the most prominent were Plotinus, the two Origens, the philologist Longinus, and Herennius. Ammonius left no written record of his opinions, and we are indebted to his disciples, especially Plotinus, for what knowledge we possess of his doctrines. His aim in general was to show the agreement, if not substantial identity, of the systems of Plato and Aristotle.

(7.) Plotinus was the first to develop and systematize in written form the Neo-Platonic doctrines. He was born at Lycopolis, a city of Upper Egypt, A.D. 205, and was so delicate and sickly as to prevent his early training; consequently he was twenty-eight years of age before he had so far completed his preparatory education as to be able to turn his attention to philosophy. After he had tried several teachers without satisfaction, a companion took him to hear Ammonius lecture, and so pleased was Plotinus that he exclaimed, "This is the man of whom I was in search !" He attended upon the teaching of Ammonius for eleven years, when, desirous of visiting the Brahmins and the Magi to learn their philosophy, he joined the ill-fated expedition of the emperor Gordian against the Persians. After the death of that emperor Plotinus with difficulty escaped to Antioch, and thence repaired to Rome, where at the age of forty years he established himself as a teacher of philosophy, and remained in Italy until his death, A.D. 270. According to the statement of Porphyry (*Vita Plotini*, ch. ii), he had agreed with his fellow-disciples, Herennius and Origen, not to divulge the doctrines of their master, Ammonius; but Herennius having broken this promise, and being followed by Origen, Plotinus felt himself no longer bound to silence in this respect, and made public these doctrines, at first in oral lectures, which afterwards, by the solicitations of friends, he was induced to publish in written form for the use of a few select hearers. At various times he added to the number of his written compositions, until, at his death, the whole, as edited and published by his pupil, Porphyry, amounted to fifty-four books. In this number, fifty-four, Porphyry was delighted to have the multiple of the perfect mystic numbers, six and nine; and the whole were arranged in six enneads or groups of nine treatises each. The following summary of their contents is from Donaldson (in his continuation of Müller), viz.: "The *first* comprised the moral positions; the *second*, the physical discussions; the *third*, the theory of the world; the *fourth* treated of the soul; the *fifth*, of the intellect and ideas; the *sixth*, of entity, unity, and the good. Again, the first three *enneads*, the fourth and fifth, and the last, formed three separate bodies ($\sigma\acute{\omega}\mu\alpha\tau\alpha$)." Plotinus enjoyed in an extraordinary degree the esteem, or rather reverence, of his followers, upon whom his ascetic virtues, his mysticism and enthusiasm, made the impression of a divine inspiration and participation in divinity. These feelings were doubtless intensified by the display of energy and tireless activity of a spirit encased in so frail a body as his. For this body he felt a true ascetic's contempt, as was shown by his answer to Amelius's importunate request that he would sit for his likeness. Said he, "Is it not sufficient to carry about the image which nature has placed around us, and must one leave behind a more lasting image of this image, as though it were something worth looking at?" (Donaldson). His asceticism and contempt for the body show the influence of Oriental ideas on his mind.

A fundamental principle of the philosophy of Plotinus is the identity of the subject and the object, of the cogniser and thing cognised. The office of philosophy should be to gain "a knowledge of the One . . . the essence and first principle of all things," not by a process of thought or reasoning, but by an immediate intuition.

This One is variously styled by him the Being, the One, the Good ($\tau\grave{o}$ $\ddot{o}\nu$, $\tau\grave{o}$ $\ddot{\epsilon}\nu$, $\tau\grave{o}$ $\dot{\alpha}\gamma\alpha\vartheta\acute{o}\nu$). The three elements of being are *Unity*, or the One, described as original, pure light, pervading space; *Intelligence*, the $\nu o\tilde{\nu}\varsigma$, emanating from the One, and contemplating it in order to comprehend it; the *World-Soul*, an emanation from the Nous. These constitute the Trinity of Plotinus. The One is exalted above the Nous, as that stands above the soul, which is immaterial and immortal. Plotinus teaches that the One "is elevated above the sphere of the Ideas," which are emanations from the One, constituting in their unity the Nous, in which they are immanent and "substantially existent and essential parts." The Soul, being the image ($\epsilon\ddot{\iota}\delta\omega\lambda o\nu$) and product of the Nous, "turns in a double direction towards the Nous, its producer, and towards the material, which is its own product." The souls of men, in consequence of their descent into bodies, have forgotten their divine origin, have become estranged from the Good, or One. Hence the true duty of man is to seek to return to God by means of virtue, philosophy, and especially by the ecstasy, or immediate intuition of the Deity and union with him. Porphyry states that Plotinus attained to this unification with God four times in the six years he spent with him. This Plotinian view reminds us of the Hindû philosophy. The most eminent of the disciples of Plotinus were Amelius and Porphyry.

(8.) Amelius (whose true name was Gentilianus) flourished in the latter half of the 3d century after Christ, and, according to Suidas (s. v.), was a native of Apamea, in Syria, but according to Porphyry (whose opinion is the more probable one), of Ameria or Amelia, in Umbria. Led by the study of the works of Numenius, whom he greatly admired, to embrace the principles of the Alexandrian Neo-Platonic school, he became a regular attendant on the lectures of Plotinus at Rome, and was the means of converting Porphyry to the doctrines of Plotinus, and afterwards, in conjunction with him, of inducing Plotinus to publish his writings. His principal work aimed to show the differences between Numenius and Plotinus, and that the latter could not justly be charged with plagiarism of the former's doctrines. If he did not himself eventually become a Christian, he appears to have highly approved of St. John's definition of the Logos, and is supposed to be the Platonist referred to by St. Augustine as having declared that the beginning of the Gospel by St. John ought to be written in letters of gold, and put in the most conspicuous place in every church. After the death of his master, Plotinus, he retired to Apamea, in Syria, and died there. According to Ueberweg, "he distinguished in the Nous three hypostases, which he styled three demiurges, or three kings: $\tau\grave{o}\nu$ $\ddot{o}\nu\tau\alpha$, $\tau\grave{o}\nu$ $\ddot{\epsilon}\chi o\nu\tau\alpha$, $\tau\grave{o}\nu$ $\dot{o}\rho\tilde{\omega}\nu\tau\alpha$. Of these, the second participated in the real being of the first, and the third in the being of the second, enjoying at the same time the vision of the first (Procl. in *Plat. Tim.* 93 d.). Amelius maintained the theory (opposed by Plotinus) of the unity of all souls in the World-Soul (Jamblichus, *Ap. Stob. Ecl.* p. 886, 888, 898)."

(9.) Porphyry, the greatest disciple of Plotinus, and the famous opponent of Christianity, was born, according to some accounts, at Batanæa (the Bashan of Scripture), in Syria, according to others, at Tyre, A.D. 233, and died about A.D. 304, probably at Rome. His proper name was Malchus (same as the Shemitic word Melek, *a king*), which his friend Amelius changed to the corresponding Greek form, Basileus, for which latter term his master, Longinus, substituted the adjective Porphyrius ($\Pi o\rho\varphi\acute{\nu}\rho\iota o\varsigma$), "clad in purple." He was first a pupil of Origen at Cæsarea, then of Longinus at Athens, and finally, at the age of thirty, he joined the school of Plotinus at Rome. He wrote a book in opposition to the doctrines of his teacher, to which Amelius replied, and, having convinced Porphyry of his errors, secured a formal recantation of them. Porphyry henceforth was an ardent supporter of Plotinus's views, and gained so fully his confidence and esteem that he was selected by him to execute the delicate and responsible task of arranging and publishing his writings. He also wrote a biography of Plotinus, which is the source of most of our knowledge of the life of that philosopher. His claims to consideration as a philosopher rest less on any originality of thought and research than on his ability and earnestness as an expounder and defender of Plotinian doctrines, on a perspicacity of style rare in that age, and also on the extent of his learning. His doctrine was in its character more practical and religious than that of Plotinus. The end of philosophizing, according to him, is the salvation of the soul. His Syrian origin and Oriental training, as well as his temperament, made him more inclined than Plotinus to the tenets of the Neo-Pythagoreans and to the advocacy of thaumaturgy, whether he sincerely believed in it or not. His views on these matters, however, appear to have been modified in his later years. While probably he had little faith in the old Greek polytheism, he bitterly opposed Christianity, and wrote a work in fifteen books against its doctrines, and especially against the divinity of Christ. This work, which excited vigorous opposition, and called forth numerous replies from Christian writers, was destroyed publicly by the order of the emperor Theodosius, A.D. 435. We are consequently indebted for our knowledge of its nature and merits to the notices and arguments of its opponents. From these we learn that in the *first* book Porphyry set forth what he deemed to be contradictions in the Scriptures, which he claimed were therefore not infallible; in the *third* he treated of the interpretation of Scripture, repudiating Origen's allegorical fancies; in the *fourth* he opposed the narrative of Sanchoniathon to the Mosaic history; and in the *twelfth* and *thirteenth* he maintained that the prophecies of Daniel were written after the events predicted, thus seeking to nullify their force as proofs of the inspiration of the Jewish Scriptures. It is much to be regretted by the Christian world that this work, written by one of the most learned and earnest opposers of Christianity in the age of the Council of Nice, has not been preserved. It would doubtless throw much light on the social and religious condition of the times, and give us a clearer insight into the causes then at work to promote the triumph of Christianity over paganism. Socrates (*Hist. Eccles.* iii, 23) asserts that Porphyry was an apostate from the Christian faith, and wrote this work in revenge for indignities from Christians, but his statement is not generally accepted as correct.

(10.) Jamblichus (died about A.D. 330), a native of Chalcis, in Cœle-Syria, was a pupil of Porphyry, and the head of the Syrian school of Neo-Platonism, in which a fantastical theurgy was favored. He made use of philosophy merely to confirm polytheistic worship, and strove to justify superstition on speculative grounds. His system was elastic enough to include all the classical and Oriental divinities except the Christian, together with those of Plotinus, and many others created by his own fancy. Miracles were attributed to him by some of his disciples, who even spoke of him as "the divine," or "most divine." However, he was in fact far inferior to his master, Porphyry, and cannot be commended either for originality of thought or grace of style. The exaggerated estimate of him by the emperor Julian, viz. that he was inferior to Plato only in the age in which he lived, can be accounted for only on the ground of that emperor's partiality for those who advocated the principles of paganism. The theodicy of Jamblichus rests, as did that of Plotinus and Porphyry, upon the principle of the multiplicity of the hypostases in the unity of the divine nature (Simon), but he assumed an absolutely first *One*, above the One of Plotinus, and wholly without attributes—an ineffable first essence (ἡ πάντη ἄρρητος ἀρχή). Next to this stands the Plotinian One. From this latter is produced the *intelligible world*, consisting of three elements; and from

this in turn emanates the *intellectual world*, consisting also of three members, the Nous, Power, and the Demiurge (subdivided into seven, a favorite Pythagorean number). This triadic arrangement extends also to the sphere of pyschology. He carried to "a great length the mysticism and extravagances of his age," and determined and arranged, according to a fantastical numerical scheme, the number and order of the polytheistic gods, angels, dæmons, and heroes recognised by him. The sensible world occupies the last place. He maintained the doctrine of a union with God (ὁραστικὴ ἔνωσις), not through the ecstasy, as did the earlier Neo-Platonists, but by means of theurgic rites and ceremonies. Of his writings only a few are extant. The most important are [1] Περὶ Πυθαγόρου αἱρέσεως, *On the Sect of Pythagoras*; and [2] Περὶ μυστηρίων, *On the Mysteries*, where, in the character of an Egyptian priest named Abammon, he replies to Porphyry's letter to Anebo, and "endeavors to refute various doubts respecting the truth and purity of the Egyptian religion and worship, and to prove the divine origin of the Egyptian and Chaldæan theology, as well as that men, through theurgic rites, may commune with the Deity" (Smith, s. v.). Jamblichus had many followers, some of whom, however, rejected the belief in magic and theurgy. One of his immediate disciples, Theodorus of Asine, drew up a still more complicated triadic system, and thus assisted in the transition to the doctrines of Proclus.

(11.) The next important character whom we have space in this sketch to mention is the emperor Julian, commonly styled "the Apostate," because, having renounced the Christian faith, in which he had been trained, he became one of its most virulent and dangerous foes, and an earnest and influential friend and patron of Neo-Platonism and the old heathen cultus. Julian (born A.D. 331; died of a wound received in battle with the Persians, A.D. 363) was a nephew of Constantine the Great, and succeeded Constantius, A.D. 361. It appears that he had secretly apostatized from Christianity some years before ascending the throne; and after that event he publicly avowed himself a convert to paganism, and put forth his best efforts to re-establish its doctrines and worship throughout the empire over which he reigned. Aware, however, of the strong foothold which Christianity had obtained, and of the failure in the past of direct and open persecution to break its power over the minds of men or to stop its progress, he judged it prudent at first to adopt other methods, and to clothe his purpose in the garb of humanity and freedom of conscience. He accordingly proclaimed entire toleration for all parties, while he gave the whole influence of his position and patronage to the adherents of his own faith, conferring his favors equally on the old supporters of paganism and whatever proselytes he could attract to it. Without adopting fully either the unfavorable accounts of his conduct and motives given by Christian writers, or the fulsome laudations of him by heathen authors, it may justly be said that "his talents, his principles, and his deeds were alike extraordinary." Boasting of a philosophy which affected to look with complacent contempt upon Christians as ignorant worshippers of "a dead Jew," he was himself, in fact, so superstitious as to attach supreme importance to the mystic rites and juggleries of polytheistic worship. Scorning all evidence of the miracles of Christ, he lent a ready ear to the absurdest theurgic follies. How little of sincerity there was in his pretensions to impartial fairness towards all the subjects and faiths of his empire was shown by his treatment of the Christians, not stopping in the end even short of open persecution. How little reliance for success over the doctrines of the Galilæans, as he contemptuously styled the Christians, he really placed upon the inherent superiority of his vaunted philosophy may be seen from the admissions of a modern writer, deemed to be a not unfriendly critic of his character and aims. Gibbon says:

"A prince, who had studied human nature, and who possessed the treasures of the Roman empire, could adapt his arguments, his promises, and his rewards to every order of Christians, and the merit of a seasonable conversion was allowed to supply the defects of a candidate, or even to expiate the guilt of a criminal. As the army is the most forcible engine of absolute power, Julian applied himself with peculiar diligence to corrupt the religion of his troops. . . . The holy name of Christ was erased from the Labarum; and the symbols of war, of majesty, and of pagan superstition were so dexterously blended that the faithful subject incurred the guilt of idolatry when he respectfully saluted the person or image of his sovereign. The soldiers passed successively in review; and each of them, before he received from the hand of Julian a liberal donation, proportioned to his rank and services, was required to cast a few grains of incense into the flame which burned upon the altar. . . . By the frequent repetition of these arts, and at the expense of sums which would have purchased the service of half the nations of Scythia, Julian gradually acquired for his troops the imaginary protection of the gods, and for himself the firm and effectual support of the Roman legions" (*Hist. of Decline*, etc., ii, 430, 431 [Harper's ed. N. Y. 1852]).

Julian's work against the Christians (Κατὰ Χριστιανῶν) shared the fate of the similar one by Porphyry, and we are indebted to the reply of Cyril for such extracts from it as are extant. The plans and purposes of Julian against the Christian faith were overruled by him who is Master alike of philosophers and kings, and later tradition reports of him that, gathering into his hand the blood flowing from his wound, he cast it into the air, with the words, Νενίκηκας Γαλιλαῖε, "Thou hast conquered, O Galilæan."

Julian's successor, Jovian, proclaimed emperor on the field, responded to the acclamations of the troops by declaring himself a Christian, and that he "could not hope for divine protection, or the success of their arms, were he to take the command of men trained up in the principles of the late emperor Julian." The soldiers replied, "You shall command Christians. The oldest of us were trained by Constantine, the next by Constantius, and the reign of Julian has been too short to bind any men among us to his persuasions." Jovian soon issued an edict which "placed the Christian religion on a legal basis," and put an end to the persecution of its followers. Thus imperial power, princely learning, philosophy falsely so called, and lavish prodigality of treasure had been employed in vain to overthrow the temples of God erected in the hearts of men.

(12.) "In practical life Neo-Platonic philosophy was unable to vie with Christianity; its mission was simply the preservation of the olden learning, science, and art." When, therefore, the political direction given to it during the reign of Julian had failed to renovate "the ancient cultus and the ancient faith," its representatives applied themselves anew to scientific pursuits, especially to the study and exegesis of Plato and Aristotle. The "philosophy became again a mere matter of the school," whose seat was transferred to Athens, where Plutarch, the son of Nestorius (born about A.D. 350, and died 433), taught. This Plutarch was styled by the later Neo-Platonists "the Great," to distinguish him from the historian and Platonist who lived in the reign of Trajan. He appears to have been a Syncretist, and to have maintained, after Jamblichus, the efficacy of theurgic rites for uniting man with God. According to Proclus, he "distinguished between the One, the Nous, the Soul, the forms immanent in material things and matter." Syrianus, his pupil and a teacher of Proclus, wrote a commentary on the metaphysics of Aristotle, whose philosophy he considered as a stepping-stone to that of Plato.

(13.) Proclus (A.D. 411–485), surnamed Διάδοχος, "the Successor," was by far the most celebrated of the later Neo-Platonists, "the Scholastic among the Greek philosophers." He was born at Byzantium, spent his youth at Xanthus, studied at Alexandria, and subsequently at Athens under Plutarch and his daughter, Asclepigenia, and Syrianus. During his travels he was initiated into the mysteries and arcana of theurgy, and was wont to say that it had been revealed to him in a dream that he was the last link of the Hermaic chain (σειρὰ Ἑρμαϊκή), i. e. of the men consecrated by Hermes to preserve by perpetual tradition the esoteric doctrines of the mysteries. His biographer, Marinus, tells of his wonderful precocity, his quick comprehension, and extraordinary memory; of his ascetic virtues, his scrupulous observance of the mystic rites, his fastings, vigils, his profound knowledge of the Orphic and Chaldæan mysteries; and says that in several instances the gods appeared to him. In philosophy his aim was to combine, according to the principles of dialectics, the mass of transmitted philosophy, enlarged by additions of his own, into a rigidly scientific form. His theology rests on the same general principles as that of Plotinus, with the same hypostases in the same order, but differing in the particular that each hypostasis is divided into a new trinity. There is but one real principle of things, unity, from which all things emanate by triads—all reality being subject to this triadic development. That which is produced is at once like and unlike its cause; so far as it is like it is immanent in the cause, and so far as it is unlike, it is separated from it. The development is a *descending* one, from the higher to the lower. All things tend to return to their source, unity. Out of this first essence issue a plurality of unities, all "exalted above being, life, reason, and our power of knowledge, that operate in the world, and are the agents of Providence, the gods." After the unities follow "the triad of the *intelligible, intelligible-intellectual*, and *intellectual* essences," of which the second participates in the first, and the third in the second. The Intelligible or Being (οὐσία) includes three triads. The *intelligible-intellectual* sphere contains female divinities, and is subdivided into inferior triads. The *intellectual essences* "are arranged according to the number seven," by a sevenfold division of which Proclus makes up seven hebdomads of intellectual essences. Souls emanate from the intellectual, are by nature eternal, are divine, of dæmons and of men. The human soul possesses freedom of will, and is therefore responsible. Matter is neither good nor evil, but is the source of natural necessity.

(14.) Among the adherents and teachers of Neo-Platonism in the early part of the 5th century was the celebrated female philosopher Hypatia, whose life, genius, learning, beauty, accomplishments, and untimely fate have been made, by a writer of distinction recently deceased, the groundwork of an interesting and vivid picture of the social condition, the philosophical conflicts, and the religious animosities of that age (*Hypatia, or Old Foes with a New Face*, by Charles Kingsley, Lond. 1872, cr. 8vo). She was the daughter of Theon, and by him was taught philosophy and mathematics. Her learning and eloquence were such as to entitle her to the honor of presiding over the Neo-Platonic school at Alexandria, where she lectured to large audiences. Having incurred the enmity of some ignorant bigots among the Christian populace of that city, she was one day seized in the street, dragged from her carriage into one of the churches, and most cruelly murdered by a mob of fanatics headed by one Peter, a reader of one of the churches. Her tragic death made her a martyr among the pagans, while the spirit and conduct of her murderers merit the execration of Christians, whose principles were thereby grossly violated.

(15.) Boethius, the author of the *Consolation*, a work which was the most influential medium for the transmission of Greek philosophy to the West during the early part of the Middle Ages, was one of the last Neo-Platonists of antiquity. Other less conspicuous names follow in the history of the school, whose doctrines continued to be taught publicly until, in the year A.D. 529, the emperor Justinian by an edict forbade the teaching of philosophy at Athens, and confiscated the property of the Platonic school. In consequence of this edict, Damascius, Simplicius, and other teachers of the heathen philosophy, fled to the protection of Chosroes, king of Persia; but, disappointed in their hopes of gaining new life and honors for their philosophy, they were glad to avail themselves of the terms of peace between the Persians and the Romans to return to their country again in A.D. 533. Thus ended as an organized system of doctrines this type of Hellenic philosophy, which a recent author regards "as a progressive evolution out of the combined action of Platonism, Judaism, and mysticism before the Christian æra, completed by the additional forces of Christianity and Aristotelianism in the 1st and 2d centuries of the Christian æra, and thus the result of seven centuries of growth and conflict in human thought" (*American Cyclopædia*).

II. *Résumé of General Principles.* — 1. Viewed from the stand-point of doctrine regarding the number of first principles, Neo-Platonism was a monism, as it traced all things back ultimately to the Absolute One, but its conceptions of the Deity as manifested were not monotheistic in the Jewish and Christian sense, but pantheistic. It rejected the Biblical idea of an *objective revelation* of man's relations to God, and of the means by which man could attain to a saving knowledge of him, and claimed to unite man with the Deity by a *subjective intuition*, called the ecstasy, wherein the subject, man's soul, and the object, the Absolute, or God, are so intimately united as to lose their separate identity. This unification with God is attainable by asceticism and profound contemplation, and, according to some later Neo-Platonists, by theurgic and magic rites. This conception of a mystic blending, so to speak, of the human with the divine gave to Neo-Platonism its peculiar character, in contrast with the purely Grecian systems of philosophy.

2. Closely connected with this theory of the ecstasy stands the doctrine of the three cosmical principles, the Neo-Platonic trinity. To the two hitherto admitted ones, viz. the reason and the soul, they added a third one, as the ultimate uniter of all distinctions, the primal One. This One is inexpressible and inconceivable. All things are derived from it not by division, which would diminish it, but by a radiation or flowing forth, as rays of light from the sun. This conception of the first as producer, in relation to the second, gives a basis for their doctrine of emanations.

3. The Neo-Platonic doctrine of emanations represents the world as outflowing from God in such a manner that each remoter emanation is possessed of a lower degree of perfection than its principle. Fire gives forth heat, snow causes coldness, odorous substances exhale odors, and every organism, so soon as it has reached its full development, begets something like itself. So the perfect and eternal One, in the overflow of his perfections, allows to proceed from himself (but without himself being weakened or diminished thereby) that which is also ever-enduring and, next to himself, the best, viz. the Reason or World - Intelligence, his own immediate reflection and image. The Reason is, next to the primal One, the most perfect, and contains in itself the world of ideas.

As the Reason emanates from the primal One, so the World-Soul flows forth from the Reason as its image, and in turn gives rise to sensible matter, the last and lowest of the emanations. In this way is the World-Soul the plastic artist of the visible universe, which closes the series of emanations. The aim of the emanation theory is attained in a continuous process from God to the sensible world. Individual souls, like the World-Soul, partake of the life of the Reason and of the Sensible, just as a sun-ray touches alike the sun and the earth. From the world of reason, their original and proper home, they have descended, each in its allotted time, not voluntarily, but following an inherent

necessity, into the corporeal world, yet without entirely forsaking the world of ideas. The soul's true vocation, then, is to seek to regain its proper home, to free itself from participation in the corporeal, in order that it may ascend again into the world of ideas, and attain the ultimate aim of all its desires and efforts, immediate union with God through the ecstatic vision of the primal One, into whom it sinks unconscious and loses itself.

III. *Concluding Observations.* — Neo - Platonism and Christianity, though opposing forces in the religious movements of their age, mutually influenced the doctrinal developments of each other. This fact is apparent not only from an examination of individual writers, but much more from a comparison of the parallel history of each. The works of Justin Martyr, Clement of Alexandria, Origen, Augustine, and other Christian writers of the early ages of the Church, abound in evidences of the influence of the philosophic spirit. On the other hand, a glance at the historical development of Neo-Platonism reveals a corresponding action of Christian ideas on it. Their opposition to each other arose naturally from the relative positions occupied by each. Neo-Platonism was a merely human religio-philosophical eclecticism, seeking to found a universal religion under the form of a philosophy which readily accepted the religious conceptions of all nations, and claimed to select the wheat from the chaff of all previous systems. Christianity, as a system of revealed truth, was of necessity exclusive. It could accept no modification of its dogmas, could agree to no alliance with differing creeds. Neo-Platonism was the creed of philosophers lifted, in their conceit, above the vulgar crowd, and despising the illiterate. Christianity was open to all grades and conditions of men. In her fold the learned and the unlearned were alike welcomed as redeemed by the blood of her divine Master. The one made a fruitless effort to revive the life and vigor of the heathen past; the other labored, and not in vain, for the future, wherein Christ "shall see of the travail of his soul, and shall be satisfied." The one seemed to hold itself aloof from contact with the suffering, and made no effort to elevate the lowly; the other sought alike the rich and the poor, relieved the suffering, comforted the sorrowing, and encouraged the weary by the hope of rest from their labors. From the fires of persecution the one came forth purified as gold tried in the furnace, the other vanished as the stubble. Neo-Platonism, though claiming to be eclectic, did nothing to unite men by means of its philosophy. Christianity, with its "mighty and all-embracing message," and its exhibition of love and self-sacrifice, welded together the hearts of men better than the force of power or the cold abstractions of the intellect, proving that the foolishness of the Gospel is wiser than the wisdom (philosophy) of men, and that the weak things of God are stronger than men.

IV. *Literature.*—The original sources of information embrace the works of Philo-Judæus, Plutarch, Apuleius, Plotinus, Porphyry, Jamblichus, Julian, Eunapius (Βίοι φιλοσόφων καὶ σοφιστῶν), Sallustius (Περὶ Θεῶν καὶ κόσμου), Proclus, Suidas, the early Christian apologists and fathers, and the Church historians—Eusebius, Socrates, Sozomen, Theodoret, and Evagrius. To these may be added among modern or secondary sources, several of which have been freely used in the preparation of this article, and often without special acknowledgment: Ritter, *Hist. of Ancient Philosophy* (Morrison's transl., Lond. 1846, 4 vols. 8vo), see Index in vol. iv; Müller, *Hist. of the Literature of Ancient Greece* (continued by Donaldson, Lond. 1858, 3 vols. 8vo), see Index in vol. iii; Ueberweg, *Hist. of Philosophy from Thales to the Present Time* (N. Y. 1872, 2 vols. 8vo), see Index in vol. ii; Tennemann, *Manual of the Hist. of Philosophy* (Bohn's ed., Lond. 1852, 8vo), see Index; Lewes, *Hist. of Philosophy*, vol. ii; Butler, *Hist. of Ancient Philosophy*, vol. ii; Hardwick, *Christ and other Masters* (3d ed. Lond. 1874, post 8vo), see Index; Schwegler, *Gesch.*

der Philosophie im Umriss (3d ed. Stuttgard, 1857, 8vo; also Prof. Seelye's transl., N. Y. 1860, 12mo), p. 97–101; Fichte, *De philosophiæ novæ Platonicæ origine* (Berl. 1818); Vogt, *Neu-Platonismus und Christenthum*, pt. i; *Neu-platonische Lehre* (nach Plotin) (1836); Kirchner, *Die Philosophie des Plotin* (Halle, 1832); Ullmann, *Einfluss des Christenthums auf Porphyrius* (in *Stud. u. Krit.* 1854); Simon, *Hist. de l'École d'Alexandrie* (Paris, 1845, 2 vols. 8vo); Kingsley, *Alexandria and her Schools* (1854); Barthélemy St. Hilaire, *De l'École d'Alexandrie* (Paris, 1845); Vacherot, *Hist. critique de l'École d'Alexandrie* (Paris, 1846–50, 3 vols. 8vo); Ennemoser, *Hist. of Magic* (Bohn's ed., Lond. 1854, 2 vols. cr. 8vo), i, 443–457; Ruffner, *The Fathers of the Desert* (N. Y. 1850, 2 vols. 12mo), i, 180–188; Mosheim, *Institutes of Eccles. Hist.* (Murdock's transl., New Haven, 1832, 3 vols. 8vo), see Index to vol. i, s. v. Plato; Neander, *Lectures on the Hist. of Christian Dogmas* (Lond. 1858, 2 vols. 16mo), see Index; id. *Church Hist.* (Bohn's ed., 10 vols. post 8vo), see Index; id. *Julian the Apostate and his Generation* (transl. by Cox, Lond. 12mo); Townsend, *Eccles. and Civil Hist.* etc. (Lond. 1847, 2 vols. 8vo), i, 412–419; Milman, *Hist. of Christianity from the Birth of Christ to the Abolition of Paganism in the Roman Empire* (Engl. and Amer. editions), see Index; Schaff, *Hist. of the Apostolic Church* (N. Y. 1874, 8vo), p. 154, 155; and *Hist. of the Christian Church* (N. Y. 1870, 2 vols. 8vo), see Index. Consult also Smith, *Dict. of Gr. and Rom. Biog. and Mythol.; Hoefer, Nouv. Biog. Générale;* the encyclopædias under the appropriate names and titles; and the articles in the following periodicals: the *London Quarterly*, July, 1857, p. 308 sq.; *Revue des deux Mondes*, May 15, 1866, p. 498 sq.; *Biblical Repository*, 1834. See also ALEXANDRIAN SCHOOL. (J. W. M.)

Neo-Platonists. See NEO-PLATONISM.

Neo-Pythagoreans. See PYTHAGOREANS.

Neo-Sabellians. See SABELLIANS.

Neo-Samosatians. See SAMOSATIANS.

Neostadiensium Admonitio CHRISTIANA DE LIBRO CONCORDIÆ, *quem vocant, a quibusdam theologis nomine quorumdam ordinum Augustanæ confessionis edito* (Neostad. in Palatinatu, 1581). Under this title the Reformed theologians assembled by Johann Casimir at Neustadt published a work against the Lutheran Formula of Concord. Most of these theologians were driven out of Heidelberg by elector Ludwig, who sided with the Lutheran party, but were well received by the zealous Calvinist John Casimir. He appointed a number of them to the gymnasium at Neustadt, which remained a Reformed seminary as long as Heidelberg continued Lutheran, i. e. from 1576 to 1583. This *Admonitio*, composed by Ursinus, and therefore also contained in the Ursini *Opera* (ii, 486 sq. [Heidelb. 1612]), is the most important of the Lutheran protests against the Formula of Concord, and closely connected with the *Historia der Augsburger Confession* (published at Neustadt in 1580). It consists of a lengthy introduction on the evils of party feeling, the unavoidableness of doctrinal differences, etc., and of twelve chapters, treating, 1, on the person of Christ and restoration of the true doctrine; 2, same concerning the Eucharist; 3, reply to the false accusations against our Church on account of certain dogmas; 4, on the authority of the Confession of Augsburg; 5, on the true meaning of that confession; 6, of the authority of Luther; 7, of the unjust judgment passed on our doctrine in the Book of Concord; 8, of the false assertions contained in that work; 9, of the contradictions contained in it; 10, of the conduct of the theologians concerning the Formula of Concord, and of the duty of the Christian state in ecclesiastical controversies; 11, of the evils attending the carrying out of the Formula of Concord; 12, exposition of the true and correct manner of establishing unity in the Christian Church. It is a remarkable work. Thus on page 115 we read:

"The importance of the Confession of Augsburg is sometimes greatly exaggerated, as when it is held that any one who departs even from the letter of it is a heretic. Besides, we do not dissent from its real meaning. The canonical books alone are divine, and form the sole rule of doctrine. All other works on doctrine may indeed possess ecclesiastical authority, but not divine, and can only be received in so far as they agree with the Scriptures. Among them are œcumenical works which no one has a right of his private authority to alter, while there are others peculiar to some churches which are less to be observed, as one can be a member of the Universal Church without endorsing them, and because other churches have the same right of drawing up particular confessions according to their requirements. They do not abolish the decisions of the Universal Church; nor do they decide on what is truth or what error, but only on what does or does not agree with the doctrines of their Church. They therefore cannot be looked upon as symbols, as is attempted to be done concerning the Confession of Augsburg and the Formula of Concord, which would then be obligatory for all Christians. It is neither possible nor advisable to impose on all churches the same formula; it is therefore better to allow every Church liberty to draw up its own confession according to its requirements and to the necessities of controversy, provided they all hold fast to the fundamental truths of Christianity. This is the case with several confessions of the present time, which are all necessary, and the Confession of Augsburg has no privilege over any other, however good it may be in itself. Neither of it nor of any other can it be said that whosoever rejects it is a heretic. It was framed in the early days of the Reformation, when light was only beginning to struggle against papal obscuration, and many points were yet imperfectly defined. It were both wrong and absurd to forbid learned teachers, and even the framers of the confession themselves, from making the doctrines profit by their increased experience, or even establishing them in a clearer and better manner. Besides, this confession is only the work of a few, and framed under the pressure of circumstances amid a disturbed Diet; consequently under fear of danger, and the necessity of dealing most gently with papal abuses. It is therefore neither as full nor as explicit as many would desire, and requires subsequent improvements."

This extract suffices to show that the *Admonitio Neost.* is yet worthy of a careful perusal. The chapter on the authority of Luther is especially remarkable for its true evangelical character, but it is least read by those whom it may benefit most. The party of the Formula of Concord attacked the *Admonitio*, and it was defended by the opponents of the formula, particularly by Ursinus himself (*Opp.* vol. ii). See Herzog, *Real-Encyklopädie*, x, 263 sq.; Krauth, *The Conservative Reformation and its Theology*, p. 288 sq.

Neot, ST., a learned English monastic of the Anglo-Saxon period, noted as the preceptor as well as kinsman and friend of king Alfred, was born towards the middle of the first half of the 9th century. He is believed to have been first bred for a soldier's life, but while yet a youth to have grown tired of the world, and retired to the abbey of Glastonbury, about 850, for a solitary and devoted life. He studied assiduously, and it is said that even there he became eminent for his literary attainments, and that the fame of his learning drew to Glastonbury a great number of scholars eager to profit by his instruction. The Anglo-Saxon *Life of Neot* seems to indicate that at this period of his life he made several visits to Rome. After a residence of some years at Glastonbury, Neot was seized with an eager desire to live in greater solitude, and he quitted his abbey, accompanied by a single attendant named Barius, to seek a place suitable to his purpose. At length he settled among the woods of Cornwall, in a beautifully retired spot, near a village previously known by the name of Ham-Stoke, but afterwards called from him Neot-Stoke, and in more modern times distinguished by the simple appellation of St. Neot's. He there built himself a hermitage, and remained in it with his single companion during seven years, at the end of which period he began again to conceive the idea of returning to the world. His biographers tell us that he went to Rome to consult with the pope, by whose advice he returned to his once solitary dwelling, and founded there a small monastic house, into which he gathered some monks, and was himself constituted their first abbot. According to his biographers, he at this time received frequent visits from his kinsman king Alfred, who held him in the highest respect, and he urged his royal relative to turn his mind from the vanities of the world. It is pretended that it was by his advice that Alfred re-endowed the English school at Rome and sent offerings to the pope, and that his influence with the pope procured for Alfred many apostolic favors. Some writers of very suspicious authority have gone still further, and asserted that not only did St. Neot originate the idea of the foundation of the University of Oxford, which they affirm was first laid by Alfred, but that he and Grimbald were the first two professors there. If we can put any faith in the stories told by the biographers, Neot must have died in or a little before the year 877; but all our information relating to him is extremely uncertain. His festival was kept on the 31st of July. He was buried at St. Neot's in Cornwall, where his bones remained in peace until 974, when they were carried away by stealth to the newly-founded monastery of St. Neot's in Huntingdonshire, and were there deposited in a handsome chapel. The old bibliographers (Bale, Pits, etc.) attribute to Neot several writings, as *Annals of the Earlier Part of Alfred's Reign:—Sermons and Exhortations:—A Letter to Pope Martin on the Subject of the English at Rome:* —and a book of *Exhortations to King Alfred.* We may observe that there is less authority for making him the author of these writings than for making him professor at Oxford. St. Neot is described as "humble to all, affable in conversation, wise in transacting business, venerable in aspect, severe in countenance, moderate even in his walk, upright, calm, temperate, and charitable." Two towns in England bear his name. His attributes are the pilgrim's staff and wallet. He is commemorated by the Church of Rome October 28th. There are several lives extant of St. Neot, but they are all filled more or less with legendary matter. The one on which the others were probably based was composed towards the beginning of the 11th century. The most ancient of the lives now extant is a sketch in Anglo-Saxon, which has been printed in the Rev. G. C. Gorham's *History and Antiquities of Eynesbury and St. Neot's* (Lond. 1820–1824, 2 vols. 8vo). This is the most valuable of any remains regarding St. Neot. See also Wright, *Biographia Britannica Literaria* (Anglo-Saxon period), p. 381–383; Clement, *Hand-book of Legendary and Mythological Art*, p. 233. (J. H. W.)

Nepa(u)l, an independent kingdom of India, comprising a portion of the southern slope of the Himalayas, bounded on the N. by Thibet, on the S. and W. by British India, and on the E. by Sikkim, a protected state, is situated in long. 80° 15′–88° 15′ E. It is 500 miles in length by about 100 miles in average breadth, covers an area of 50,000 square miles, and has a population estimated at 2,000,000. The kingdom is separated from the plains of India by the long, narrow strip of land, resembling an English down, but unhealthy, called the Terai, which extends along the whole southern border. North of this, and running parallel with it, is the great forest of Nepaul, from eight to ten miles broad. North of this strip is a tract of hilly country, and above that are two tracts of greater elevation, the first of which may be called mountainous, while the second might appropriately be called Alpine, if it did not comprise among its mountains peaks which, like Mount Everest and Dhawalagiri, attain almost twice the elevation of Mont Blanc. The principal rivers are the Kurnalli, the Rapti, the Gunduk with its great tributaries, and the Sun Kosi. The climate, most unhealthy in the Terai, is healthy and pleasant in the hilly and mountainous districts, suggesting that of Southern Europe. In the *Valley of Nepaul*—the district surrounding the capital—the heat of Bengal, which is felt in the hollows, may be exchanged for the cold of Russia by ascending the slopes of the hills which enclose it. The soil is extremely rich and fruitful. Barley, millet, rice, maize, wheat, cotton, tobacco, sugar-cane, pine-apple, and various tropical fruits are cultivated. Gold has not been

found, but iron and copper mines are worked. The capital of the country is Khatmandu. The inhabitants consist of a variety of races, but the dominant people are the Ghurkas, a tribe of Mongol origin, Hindûs in religion, who conquered the country about the close of the 18th century. Their chief occupation is war. Many Hindûs from Chiton settled in Nepaul at the time of the Mohammedan invasion, and some of them have preserved their blood pure to the present time, while others have intermarried with Chinese and Tartars. The Hindûs are found chiefly in the west; the east is populated by aboriginal tribes, among which are the Newars, Magars, Gurungs, Jariyas, Dhenwars, Bûtcas, Mhanjas, and Bhanras. The most important of these are the Newars, who constitute the agriculturists and artisans of the country. They are ingenious and peaceable, though excessively dirty; of middle size and great strength, with round flat faces, small eyes, broad noses, and open countenances. They are Buddhists, but have a priesthood of their own, and reject the Thibetan model of Buddhism as it prevails among the other aboriginals of Nepaul. They as well as others of the aborigines practice polyandry to some extent. Thirteen dialects are spoken in Nepaul, but only two of the dialects possess any literature, and they are the dialects of the two most prominent tribes—the Newars and Ghurkas.

Of the history of Nepaul little is known until the invasion of the Ghurkas (1768); it seems never to have been subject to the Mogul or any other great Asiatic conquerors. A war in which it became involved with Thibet in 1790 led to hostilities with the emperor of China, who, regarding himself as the protector of the lamas, in 1792 sent an army of 70,000 men against the Nepaulese, and checked the extension of their territory to the northward. A treaty of commerce was concluded with the British in 1792, and from 1802 to 1804 Katmandu was the residence of a representative of the British government. Repeated encroachments of the rajah upon the East India Company's territories led the British to declare war in 1814, and they consequently invaded the country on the western frontier, where their troops met repeated losses, and their commander, Gen. Gillespie, was slain. In the following year, however, the campaign under Sir David Ochterlony was attended with very different results. The victory of Malome, the capitulation of the famous Nepaulese commander Amîr Singh, and finally the rapid advance of the victor towards Katmandu, obliged the Nepaulese monarch to make peace, and a treaty in March, 1816. Throughout

Natives of Nepaul.

the mutiny of 1857 the Nepaulese cultivated the friendship of the British, and the prime minister, Jung Bahadûr, defeated the last remnant of the rebels in December, 1859. The policy of the government towards foreigners, however, is exceedingly exclusive. Much valuable information concerning the country is contained in the work on *Nepaul and Thibet*, by B. H. Hodgson, formerly British minister at Katmandu (1874). See also Oliphant, *A Journey to Katmandu* (1852); Col. Kirkpatrick, *Account of the Kingdom of Nepaul* (Lond. 1811); *Edinburgh Review*, July, 1840, art. i; *Blackwood's Magazine*, 1852, pt. ii, p. 86; 1860, pt. i, p. 509; and the article Gorkhas in the *American Cyclopædia*.

Nepenthè (from Gr. *νή, not*, and *πένθος, grief*), is the name of a magic potion mentioned both by Greek and Roman poets, which was supposed to make persons forget their sorrows and misfortunes. It was the juice or infusion of a plant now unknown. Homer says it grew in Egypt, and that Helen learned its use from the Egyptians. According to Theodorus Siculus the Theban women also knew the secret of making it.

Nephalia (Gr. *νηφάλιος, sober*) were festivals and sacrifices of the ancient Greeks, but more especially of the Athenians, and received their name from the circumstance that no wine was offered, but only milk, mead, and other mild liquors. The vine, the fig-tree, and the mulberry were prohibited from being used in the Nephalia because they were looked upon as symbols of drunkenness. See Broughton, *Bibliotheca Historica Sacra*, ii, 162.

Ne'pheg (Heb. *id.* נֶפֶג, *sprout;* Sept. Ναφέκ, Exod. vi, 21; Ναφήγ, 2 Sam. v, 15; Ναφέγ, 1 Chron. iii, 7; Ναφάγ v. r. Ναφάθ, 1 Chron. xiv, 6), the name of two Hebrews.

1. The second-named son of Izhar, a Kohathite of the tribe of Levi (Exod. vi, 21). B.C. cir. 1760.

2. The ninth-named son of David, born at Jerusalem (2 Sam. v, 15; 1 Chron. iii, 7; xiv, 6). B.C. cir. 1020.

Nephes Ogli (i. e. *Son of the Holy Spirit*) is a title given in the East to certain persons who are supposed to be born after an extraordinary manner, e. g. of a mother that is a virgin. We are told that there are Turkish young women who live in certain retired places where they never see a man. They go but seldom to the mosques, and when they come thither they stay there from nine till twelve at night, and accompany their prayers with so many distortions of the body and cries that their strength is quite exhausted, and they often fall to the ground in a swoon. If from that time they find themselves with child they pretend it is by the favor of the Holy Spirit; and for this reason the children they bring forth are called *Nephes Ogli*. The Nephes Ogli thus pretended to be miraculously born are looked upon as persons who have the gift of working miracles, and it is claimed that their hair or pieces of their garments cure all sorts of diseases. See Broughton, *Bibliotheca Historica Sacra*, ii, 162; Hottinger, *Hist. Orient.* p. 295.

Népheth, a word occurring only in the phrase שְׁלֹשֶׁת הַנָּפֶת, *three of the height*, i. e. *the triple height* (Josh. xvii, 11). The name seems to refer to the three places just mentioned—Endor, Taanach, and Megiddo—which were elevated above the plain; comp. *Tricollis; Tremont* (Gesenius, s. v.). But the Targum renders *tres regiones*, "three countries," which is followed by the Auth. Version. The Latin (after the Sept. τὸ τρίτον Νοφέθ) has *tertia pars urbis Nopheth*, "the third part of the city Nopheth," and is followed by Luther. Schwarz (*Palest.* p. 149), with less probability, gives "the three Nepheth, meaning three places of the same name in the neighborhood of Dor," and finds a village *Naphatha* two miles and a half south-east of Dor (comp. Josh. xii, 23). See Keil, ad loc.

Nephew is used in the old English sense of *grand-*

son as a rendering of נֶכֶד (*néked*, Job xviii, 19; Isa. xiv, 22; *progeny*, especially a "son's son," as rendered in Gen. xxi, 23), and ἔκγονον, a *descendant* (1 Tim. v, 4). See KINDRED.

Ne'phi (Νεφθαεί v. r. Νεφθάς; Vulg. *Nephi*), the name given by many (παρὰ τοῖς πολλοῖς) to the substance otherwise called (2 Macc. i, 36) NAPHTHAR (q. v.).

Nephilîm (נְפִילִים) occurs only in the plural form, and in the two passages (Gen. vi, 4; Numb. xiii, 33) where it is rendered in the English version "giants." This meaning is given by all the old versions (Sept. γίγαντες; Aquila, ἐπιπίπτοντες; Symm. βιαῖοι; Vulg. *gigantes;* Onk. גִּבָּרַיָּא; Luther, *tyrannen*), and is demanded by the latter passage. "The word is derived either from פָּלָה or פָּלָא (= 'marvelous'), or, as is generally believed, from נָפַל, either in the sense to throw down, or to *fall* (= fallen angels [Jarchi]; comp. Isa. xiv, 12; Luke x, 18), or meaning ἥρωες, *irruentes* (Gesen.), or *collapsi* (by euphemism, Böttcher, *De Inferis*, p. 92); but certainly not 'because men fell from terror of them' (as R. Kimchi). That the word means *giant* is clear from Numb. xiii, 32, 33, and is confirmed by נְפִלָא, the Chaldee name for 'the aery giant' Orion (Job ix, 9; xxxviii, 31; Isa. xiii, 10; Targ.), unless this name arise from the *obliquity* of the constellation (*Gen. of Earth*, p. 35). We now come to the remarkable conjectures about the origin of these *Nephilim* in Gen. vi, 1–4. (An immense amount has been written on this passage. See Kurz, *Die Ehen der Söhne Gottes*, etc. [Berlin, 1857]; Ewald, *Jahrb.* 1854, p. 126; Govett's *Isaiah Unfulfilled;* Faber's *Many Mansions* [*J. of Sac. Lit.* Oct. 1858], etc.) We are told that 'there *were* Nephilim in the earth,' and that afterwards (Sept. καὶ μετ' ἐκεῖνο) the 'sons of God' mingling with the beautiful 'daughters of men' produced a race of violent and insolent *Gibborim* (גִּבֹּרִים). This latter word is also rendered by the Sept. γίγαντες, but its meaning is more general. It is clear, however, that *no statement* is made that the Nephilim themselves sprang from this unhallowed union. Who, then, were they? Taking the usual derivation (נָפַל), and explaining it to mean 'fallen spirits,' the Nephilim seem to be identical with the 'sons of God;' but the verse before us militates against this notion as much as against that which makes the Nephilim the same as the Gibborim, viz. the *offspring* of wicked marriages. This latter supposition can only be accepted if we admit either (1) that there were two kinds of Nephilim—those who existed before the unequal intercourse, and those produced by it (Heidegger, *Hist. Patr.* xi), or (2) by following the Vulgate rendering, *postquam enim ingressi sunt*, etc. But the common rendering seems to be correct, nor is there much probability in Aben-Ezra's explanation that אַחֲרֵי־כֵן ('after that') means אַחַר הַמַּבּוּל (i. e. 'after the deluge'), and is an allusion to the Anakims." We may remark, however, that the Hebrew word *Nephilim* may rather be taken in an active sense=*those who fall* upon others, i. e. the violent tyrants of those days (Aquila, ἐπιπίπτοντες); and this agrees with the evident lawlessness of the times. See ANTEDILUVIANS.

Ne'phis (Νιφίς, v. r. Νηφίς, Φινίς; Vulg. *Liptis*), given (1 Esdr. v, 21) as one of the heads of the families that returned from Babylon, in place of NEBO (q. v.) in the Heb. list (Ezra ii, 28), perhaps by some confusion with the MAGBISH following.

Ne'phish (1 Chron. v, 19). See NAPHISH.

Nephish'esim (Neh. vii, 52). See NEPHUSIM.

Neph'tali (Tob. i, 2, 4, 5). See NAPHTALI.

Neph'thalim (Tob. vii, 3; Matt. iv, 13, 15; Rev. vii, 6). See NAPHTALI.

Nephthys, the sister and wife of Typhon, the evil god of the ancient Egyptians. To Osiris she bore

Anubis, who is represented with the head of a dog. Nephthys belongs to the third order of deities, as classified by Sir J. G. Wilkinson in his *Materia Hieroglyphica*. In Egyptian theogony she personified the unfruitful earth, and was therefore the symbol of sterility. Nephthys also represented the ocean, and hence it is possible that the god of the classic nations, Neptune, was derived from the Egyptians.

Nephto'äh [some *Neph'toäh*] (Heb. *Nephto'äch*, נִפְתּוֹחַ, *opened*; Sept. Ναφθώ v. r. Μαφθώ; Vulg. *Nephthoa*), the name of a spring (עַיִן, A. V. "fountain," "well"), and apparently a streamlet (מַיִם, A. V. "water," "waters") issuing from it (or perhaps a watering-place for cattle), on the border between Judah and Benjamin. Its position is described with considerable minuteness. From the valley of Hinnom the northern boundary of Judah was drawn to the top of the hill on the west, that is, in the direction of the Convent of the Cross; and the border was drawn from the top of the hill *unto the fountain of the water of Nephtoah*, and thence to Kirjath-jearim (Josh. xv, 8, 9). A similar description of the southern boundary of Benjamin is given in Josh. xviii, 14–16; and the name is not again mentioned in Scripture. Its site appears to have been unknown to Jerome and Eusebius; they do not mention it in their *Onomasticon*. From the above passages it might be inferred that the waters of Nephtoah lay somewhere in or near a direct line between Jerusalem and Kirjath-jearim. Nephtoah was formerly identified with various springs, especially *Ain Karim*, or Fountain of the Virgin of mediæval times (Doubdan, *Voyage*, p. 187; see also the citations of Tobler, *Topographie*, p. 351; and Sandys, iii, 184), and even the so-called *Well of Joab* in the Kedron valley (*Mislin*, ii, 155); but these, especially the last, are unsuitable in their situation as respects Jerusalem and Kirjath-jearim, and have the additional drawback that the features of the country there are not such as to permit a boundary-line to be traced along it. Schwarz (*Palest.* p. 268 sq.) finds a large spring near the castle of Al-Burak, the water of which was once carried by an aqueduct to Jerusalem, in which openings were made in order that passers-by might draw water; and that it was thence called *Mè Nephto'ach*, מֵי נִפְתּוֹחַ, *the opened water*. But this is fanciful. Recent geographers have pretty generally agreed to identify Nephtoah with *Ain Lifta*, a fountain near the village of that name, two and a half miles north-west of Jerusalem (Barclay, *City of the Great King*, p. 544; Tobler, *Dritte Wanderung*, p. 202; comp. *Topographie*, p. 343 sq.; Stewart, *Tent and Khan*, p. 349). The spring—of which a view is given by Dr. Barclay—is very abundant, and the water escapes in a considerable stream into the valley below. This, however, cannot be reconciled with the statement in 1 Sam. x, 2, that Rachel's sepulchre lay near the border of Benjamin, and it is nearly three miles south of the valley of Hinnom. Consequently, from the top of the hill on the west of Hinnom the border must have turned southward [see TRIBE], and we must look for the waters of Nephtoah on the south or south-west of Jerusalem. About a mile and a half from Jerusalem, on the road to Rachel's tomb, and close to the convent of Mar-Elyas, is an old well, which some have identified with Nephtoah (*Narrative of Mission to Jews*, June 13). It is, however, a mere well. A much more probable site is *Ain Yalo*, in Wady el-Werd, three miles south-west of the city. It is a small fountain, whose waters flow into a large pool, and are drawn off to irrigate some gardens. Its water is esteemed at Jerusalem, whither it is conveyed in skins on the backs of donkeys (Porter, *Hand-book*, p. 232; Robinson, *Bib. Res.* iii, 265). In front of the fountain are some ruins. There is another larger and much more beautiful fountain a mile farther down the valley, called *Ain Haniyeh*, said by tradition to be the fountain in which Philip baptized the eunuch (Barclay, p. 548). It is ornamented with a niched façade and Corinthian pilasters. See Porter, *Handbook for Palestine.*

Nephu'sim (Heb. *Nephusim'*, נְפוּסִים, so the marg.; but the text has *Nephisim'*, נְפִיסִים, expansions; Sept. Νεφουσίμ v. r. Ναφεισών; Vulg. *Naphusim*), the head of a family of "Temple servants" who returned from Babylon with Zerubbabel (Ezra ii, 50). B.C. cir. 535. The parallel text (Neh. vii, 52) has (less correctly, it would seem) NEPHISHESIM (Heb. *Nephishesim*, נְפִישְׁסִים, marg.; but text has *Nephushesim'*, נְפוּשְׁסִים; Sept. Νεφωσάς, v. r. Νεφωσασεί, Νεφωσαείμ, Νεφωσασείμ; Vulg. *Naphussim*). See NETHINIM.

Nepindi. See NEGOMBO.

Nepomuk, JOHN. See JOHN OF NEPOMUK.

Nepos, an Egyptian bishop, who flourished in the first half of the 3d century, was a believer in Chiliasm and in the literal interpretation of Scripture, and consequently an opponent of Origen's system. He wrote a work, Ἔλεγχος ἀλληγοριστῶν, now lost, which was at the time considered by his party in Egypt as an incontrovertible argument in favor of Christ's earthly kingdom. This, like all similar works, was undoubtedly based on the Apocalypse, but we possess no particulars as to the manner in which he represented the millennium. Gennadius says that he separated the resurrection of the just from that of the unjust, which is to occur only at the end of the millennium, accompanied by all the circumstances described in Rev. xx, probably because he everywhere understood it in a literal sense. Bishop Dionysius of Alexandria complained that many neglected the Scriptures for this work of Nepos, in which they believed they discovered great secrets. He found himself even obliged, after the death of Nepos, to convene at Arsinoë an assembly of presbyters and teachers for the purpose of examining into the doctrines of the work. The meeting lasted three days, and ended in all renouncing the Chiliast doctrine. Still Dionysius, in view of the reputation of Nepos and of his work, thought it necessary to refute the doctrines therein contained, and he wrote for that purpose his Περὶ ἐπαγγελιῶν, which, from its being a general refutation of Chiliasm, was by Jerome considered as directed against Irenæus, and by Theodoret as against Cerinthus. The fragments of this work contained in Eusebius are the sources of our knowledge concerning Nepos and his party. It reproved the doctrine of Nepos in a very gentle manner, and in nowise justifies the representation that Nepos was formally condemned, as has been asserted in later times (*Libell. synod.* in Mansi, *Coll. conc.* i, 1017). According to Fulgentius (in *Pint. Arian.* c. 2), who also considers Nepos a heretic, his party still counted adherents in the 6th century. See Eusebius, *Hist. Eccles.* vii, 24 sq.; Gennadius, *De Dogm. Eccles.* c. 55; Tillemont, *Mém.* iv, 261 sq. (ed. Venet.); Walsch, *Ketzerhistor.* vol. ii; Schupart, *De chiliasmo Nepotis* (Giessen, 1724); Walsch, *Einleitung in die Religionstreitigkeiten der luth. Kirche*, ii, 559; Neander, *Church Hist.* i, 652; Guericke, *Ancient Church Hist.* p. 196. (J. N. P.)

Nepotism is a word invented in ecclesiastical language to express a peculiar characteristic of many high ecclesiastics in Roman Catholic countries, and more particularly of popes, a propensity, namely, to aggrandize their family by exorbitant grants and favors conferred on members of it; literally on nephews (Latin *nepotes*). Many of the highest and wealthiest families of the Roman nobility owe their elevation entirely to this species of patronage. Nepotism was first practiced, and that to a very considerable degree, by pope Nicholas III (q. v.), towards the close of the 13th century; reproachfully he was called the patriarch of papal nepotism. In the 15th century it found most prominent practice under Sixtus IV (q. v.), and he may be said to have carried nepotism to its highest pitch, and to have given rise to much scandal in the Romish Church. Alexander VI

(q. v.) is only second to the preceding pope (see Butler, *Eccles. Hist.* ii, 129, 132; Fisher, *Hist. of the Ref.* p. 45). Alexander V had no relations on whom to lavish his friendship, but he found an opportunity to practice nepotism towards the order to which he belonged prior to his elevation to the papacy. As early as the 16th century strong efforts were made to stay this evil practice. Pope Pius IV and his successors labored for this end. But nepotism was not successfully circumscribed until the 17th century by popes Innocent XI and XII, the latter of whom subjected, by a bull under date of July 28, 1692, all cardinals to an oath against the practice of nepotism. See Leti, *Il Nepotismo di Roma* (Amst. 1667; in Latin, entitled *Nepot. Rom.* [Stuttg. 1669]); Ranke, *Hist. of the Papacy;* Ffoulkes, *Divisions of Christendom,* i, 561; Milman, *Hist. of Latin Christianity,* vi, 141, 530; vii, 272, 302; viii, 171; Cartwright, *On Papal Conclaves,* p. 180–183; Wessenberg, *Gesch. der Kirchenversammlungen* (see Index in vol. iv).

Neptunalia is the name of a festival anciently celebrated at Rome in honor of Neptune (q. v.) on the 23d of July. Little information is accessible as to the manner in which this festival was kept, but it would appear that huts were wont to be erected with the branches and foliage of trees, where people probably feasted and amused themselves in various ways.

Neptune, an ancient Roman god of the waters. It is doubtful whether he was originally a marine deity, for the old Italians were the very opposite of a maritime people, yet his name is commonly connected with *nato,* to swim; hence at an earlier period he may have borne another designation, afterwards forgotten. When the Romans became a maritime power, and had grown acquainted with Grecian mythology, they, in accordance with their usual practice, identified him with the Greek god whom he most resembled. This was *Poseidōn,* also *Poteidan* (connected with πότος, *a drink;* πόντος, *the sea;* and ποταμός, *a river*). Poseidon appears in his most primitive mythological form as the god of water in general, or the fluid element. He was the son of Cronos (Saturn) and Rhea, and a brother of Jupiter. On the partition of the universe among the sons of Cronos, he obtained the sea as his portion, in the depths of which he had his palace near Ægæ, in Eubœa. Here also he

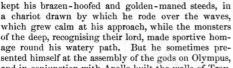

Figure of Neptune.

kept his brazen-hoofed and golden-maned steeds, in a chariot drawn by which he rode over the waves, which grew calm at his approach, while the monsters of the deep, recognising their lord, made sportive homage round his watery path. But he sometimes presented himself at the assembly of the gods on Olympus, and in conjunction with Apollo built the walls of Troy. In the Trojan war he sided with the Greeks; nevertheless he subsequently showed himself inimical to the great sea-wanderer Ulysses, who had blinded his son Polyphemus. He was also believed to have created the horse, and taught men its use. The symbol of his power was a trident, with which he raised and stilled storms, broke rocks, etc. According to Herodotus, the name and worship of Poseidon came to the Greeks from Libya. He was worshipped in all parts of Greece and Southern Italy, especially in the seaport towns. The Isthmian games were held in his honor. Black and white bulls, boars, and rams were offered in sacrifice to him. Neptune was commonly represented with a trident, and with horses or dolphins, often along with Amphitrite, in a chariot drawn by dolphins, and surrounded by tritons and other sea-monsters. As befitted the fluctuating element over which he ruled, he is sometimes figured asleep or reposing, and sometimes in a state of violent agitation. See Vollmer, *Mythologisches Wörterbuch,* s. v.; Westcott, *Hand-book of Archæol.* p. 166, 167.

Nepveu, FRANÇOIS, a French ascetic author, was born April 28, 1639, at St. Malo. Admitted in 1654 into the Society of Jesus, he was professor of the humanities, rhetoric, and philosophy, and afterwards occupied different positions; at the time of his death, which occurred in February, 1708, he was rector of the college of Rennes. All his works treat of practical religion or morality; they have frequently been reprinted even in our day, and translated into several languages. The principal are, *De l'Amour de Jésus-Christ* (Nantes, 1684, 12mo; 5th ed. Paris, 1756, 12mo):—*Exercices intérieurs pour honorer les mystères de Jésus-Christ* (Paris, 1791, 2 vols. 12mo; Lyons, 1836, 12mo):—*Retraite selon l'esprit et la méthode de St. Ignace* (Paris, 1687, 12mo):—*Manière de se préparer à la mort* (Paris, 1693, 1697, 12mo): —*Pensées et réflexions Chrétiennes pour tous les jours de l'année* (Paris, 1695, 4 vols. 12mo, and 1850, 8vo); transl. twice into Latin (Ingolstadt, 1727, and Heidelberg, 1774, 4 vols. 8vo); into Flemish (1837, 1839, 4 vols. 4to); twice into German (1752 and 1829); and twice into Italian (1715 and 1842):—*L'Esprit du Christianisme, ou la conformité du Chrétien avec Jésus-Christ* (Paris, 1700, 12mo):—*Conduite Chrétienne* (Paris, 1704, 12mo): —*Retraite spirituelle* (Paris, 1708, 12mo). Nepveu is also the author of the philosophical theses maintained in 1679 by Louis de la Tour d'Auvergne, prince de Turenne, and remarkable not only for their extent and solidity, but still more because they are ornamented with symbols, inscriptions, and vignettes, due to the good taste of J. Charles de la Rue. See Moréri, *Grand Dictionn. Histor.* s. v.; Hoefer, *Nouv. Biog. Générale,* s. v.

Nequiti is the name of a secret association among the natives of Congo, who celebrate their mysteries in dark and sequestered places, where none but the initiated are allowed to enter.

Ner (Heb. *id.* נֵר, *light;* Sept. Νήρ), a Benjamite, according to 1 Chron. viii, 33, father of Kish and Abner, and grandfather of king Saul. B.C. cir. 1140. Abner was, therefore, uncle to Saul, as is expressly stated in 1 Sam. xiv, 50. But some confusion has arisen from the statement in 1 Chron. ix, 36, that Kish and Ner were both sons of Jehiel, whence it has been concluded that they were brothers, and consequently that Abner and Saul were first cousins. The explanation of this, however, is that there was an elder Kish, uncle of Saul's father, or, rather, Ner's grandfather. See SAUL. "The name Ner, combined with that of his son Abner, may be compared with Nadab in ver. 36, and Abinadab, ver. 39; with Jesse, 1 Chron. ii, 13, and Abishai, ver. 16; and with Juda, Luke iii, 26, and Abiud, Matt. i, 13." Gesenius, misled by 1 Sam. ix, 1, gives the following genealogy (*Thesaur.* p. 9):

Abiel
|
Kish   Ner
| |
Saul.   Abner;

but the following seems better to reconcile the passages on the subject:

Abiel
|
Ner
|
Abner.   Kish
|
Saul.

See ABIEL; KISH; SAUL.

Nerd. See SPIKENARD.

Nereids ($\nu\eta\rho\epsilon\hat{\imath}\delta\epsilon\varsigma$) was the name of the Greek seanymphs. They were fifty in number, and were daughters of *Nereus*, the old man of the sea. They were generally represented as very beautiful maidens, and sometimes as half woman and half fish. The Nereids were regarded as favorable to sailors. They were worshipped in several parts of Greece, but more especially in seaport towns.

Figure of a Nereid.

Nereus (Gr. $N\eta\rho\epsilon\acute{v}\varsigma$), a marine divinity in classic mythology, was represented as a wise and prophetic old man, and was believed to dwell at the bottom of the sea with his beautiful daughters the *Nereids*. He was regarded as ruling principally over the Ægean Sea, and was believed occasionally to appear to men in different shapes, predicting what should befall them in the future. The poets feigned that he could assume various forms like Proteus, and would only reveal the future when, having exhausted his powers of transformation, he was reduced to his original shape. Nereus yielded his place to Poseidon, and gave him his daughter Amphitrite. His attribute was the trident. He frequently appears in ancient works of art.

Ne'reus ($N\eta\rho\epsilon\acute{v}\varsigma$), a Christian at Rome to whom, with his sister, the apostle Paul sent his salutation (Rom. xvi, 15). A.D. 55. "The name may be of Hebrew origin, נֵר or נֵרֵר; or it may be, as Grotius suggests, from the Sabine *Nerio*, a word, according to Aulus Gellius, signifying 'virtus et fortitudo' (*N. A.* xiii, 22), and with which *Nero* and *Nerienes*, the wife of Mars, stand allied." "Origen conjectures that he belonged to the household of Philologus and Julia. Estius suggests that he may be identified with a Nereus who is said to have been baptized at Rome by St. Peter. A legendary account of him is given in Bolland, *Acta Sanctorum*, May 12; from which, in the opinion of Tillemont (*H. E.* ii, 139), may be gathered the fact that he was beheaded at Terracina, probably in the reign of Nerva. His ashes are said to be deposited in the ancient church of SS. Nereo ed Archilleo at Rome. There is a reference to his legendary history in bishop Jeremy Taylor's sermon, *The Marriage-ring*, pt. i."

Nereus, ST., a martyr of the early Christian Church, was a eunuch and servant of St. Domitilla (q. v.). Refusing to abjure his faith, he was, with his mistress, banished by Domitian into a little isle on the coast of Terracina, called Pontia. Afterwards, amid the persecutions under Trajan, Nereus suffered martyrdom with his mistress. The ancient Church kept a festival in memory of these faithful ones, and St. Gregory the Great thus alludes to the great solemnity: "These saints, before whose tomb we are assembled, despised the world and trampled it under their feet, when peace, plenty, riches, and health gave it charms." St. Nereus is commemorated in the Church of Rome May 12. See Butler, *Lives of the Saints*, ii, 311, 312.

Ner'gal (Heb. *Nergal'*, נֵרְגַּל [in pause נֵרְגָּל]; Sept. Ἐργέλ v. r. Νηργέλ; Vulg. *Nergel*), one of the chief Assyrian and Babylonian deities (2 Kings xvii,

30), seems to have corresponded closely to the classical *Mars*. He was of Babylonian origin, and various derivations of the name have been suggested. Fürst traces it to נרג, *to break in pieces*, with ל added; Gesenius identifies it with the Sabian *Nerig*, the *l* being appended as the mark of a diminutive, which was a sign of endearment; Von Bohlen compares the Sanscrit *Nrigal*, *man-destroyer*, spoken of a fierce warrior, and corresponding to *Merodach*; and Rawlinson says the name "is evidently compounded of the two Hamitic roots— *air*, a man, and *gula*, great; so that he is *the great man*, or *the great hero*" (*Ancient Monarchies*, i, 171; ii, 256). "His monumental titles are — 'the storm-ruler, 'the king of battle,' 'the champion of the gods,' 'the male principle' (or 'the strong begetter'), 'the tutelar god of Babylonia,' and 'the god of the chase.' Of this last he is the god pre-eminently; another deity, *Nin*, disputing with him the presidency over war and battles. It is conjectured that he may represent the deified Nimrod— 'the mighty hunter before the Lord'—from whom the kings both of Babylon and Nineveh were likely to claim descent. See NIMROD. The city peculiarly dedicated to his worship is found in the inscriptions to be Cutha or Tiggaba, which is in Arabian tradition the special city of Nimrod. The only express mention of Nergal contained in sacred Scripture is in the above passage, where 'the men of Cutha,' placed in the cities of Samaria by a king of Assyria (Esar-haddon?), are said to have 'made Nergal their god' when transplanted to their new country—a fact in close accordance with the frequent notices in the inscriptions, which mark him as the tutelar god of that city. Nergal's name occurs as the initial element in *Nergal*-shar-ezar (Jer. xxxix, 3 and 13); and is also found, under a contracted form, in the name of a comparatively late king—the Abenn*erigus* of Josephus (*Ant.* xx, 2, 1). Nergal appears to have been worshipped under the symbol of the 'Man-Lion.' The Shemitic name for the god of Cutha was *Aria*, a word which signifies 'lion' both in Hebrew and Syriac. *Nir*, the first element of the god's name, is capable of the same signification. Perhaps the habits of the lion as a hunter of beasts were known, and he was thus regarded as the most fitting symbol of the god who presided over the chase. It is in connection with their hunting excursions that the Assyrian kings make most frequent mention of this deity. As early as B.C. 1150, Tiglath-pileser I speaks of him as furnishing the arrows with which he slaughtered the wild animals. *Assur-dani-pal* (Sardanapalus), the son and successor of Esar-haddon, never fails to invoke his aid, and ascribes all his hunting achievements to his influence. Pul sacrificed to him in Cutha, and Sennacherib built him a temple in the city of Tarbisa, near Nineveh; but in general he was not much worshipped either by the earlier or the later kings (see the *Essay* of Sir H. Rawlinson in Rawlinson's *Herodotus*, i, 631-634)." The rabbinical commentators believe that this idol was in the form of a cock, since the somewhat similar word, תַּרְנְגוֹל, *tarnegol*, in the Talmud, means a cock (Selden, *Dii Syr.* ii, 8, p. 317 sq.; Schwarz, *Palest.* p. 80). In curious coincidence with this tradition Layard gives two figures of a cock on Babylonian remains, showing its ancient worship by that people (*Nineveh and Babylon*, p. 158). Norberg, Gesenius, and other inquirers into the astrolatry of the Assyrians and Chaldæans, conclude that Nergal is the same as the Sabian name for the planet Mars. Both among the Sabians and Arabians it means *ill-luck*, *misfortune;* and it was by no means peculiar to the mythology of the West to make it the symbol of bloodshed and war. The Sabian Mars was typified as a man holding in one hand a drawn sword, and in the other a human head just cut off; his garments were also red, no doubt from the hue which the body of the planet presents to the

Engraved Gem from Babylon.

Cylinder in the British Museum.

eye. Among the southern Arabs his temple was painted red; and they offered to him garments stained with blood, and a warrior (probably a prisoner), who was cast into a pool. It is related of the caliph Hakim that in the last night of his life, as he saw the planet Mars rise, he murmured, " Dost thou ascend, thou accursed shedder of blood? then is my hour come;" and at that moment the assassins sprang upon him from their hiding-place (Mohammed Abu-Taleb, ap. Norberg, *Onomast.* p. 105; *Bar-Hebræus*, p. 220). See Gesenius, *Thesaur.* p. 913, and *Comment. zu Jesa*, ii, 344; Nork, *Bibl. Mythol.* i, 60 sq.; Lanci, *Paral. alla illust. del. Sac. Script.* i, 284; Wichmanshausen, *Diss. de Nergal. Cuth. Idolo* (Viteb. 1707).

Ner'gal-share'zer (Hebrew *Nergal'-Sharets'er*, נֵרְגַל־שַׂרְאֶצֶר; Sept. Νηργελσασασάρ, Vat. MS. Νεριγλισσάρ v. r. Μαργανασάρ, Μαργαννασάρ, Νηργελσαρασάρ; Ναγαργᾶς v. r. Νηργέλ, all in Jer. xxxix, 3; also Νηργέλ καὶ Σαρασάρ, ver. 13; Vulg. *Neregel et Sereser*), the name apparently of two persons among the "princes of the king of Babylon," who accompanied Nebuchadnezzar on his last expedition against Jerusalem, B.C. 588. The first part of the name is the god *Nergal* (q. v.), and Sharezer is supposed from the Zend to mean *prince of fire* (Gesen.).

1. The first of these is mentioned only in Jer. xxxix, 3, without any other designation or notice.

2. "The other has the honorable distinction of Rab-mag (רַב־מָג), and it is to him alone that any particular interest attaches (Jer. xxxix, 3). In sacred Scripture he appears among the persons who, by command of Nebuchadnezzar, released Jeremiah from prison (Jer. xxxix, 13); profane history gives us reason to believe that he was a personage of great importance, who not long afterwards mounted the Babylonian throne. This identification depends in part upon the exact resemblance of name which is found on Babylonian bricks in the form of *Nergal-shar-uzur;* but mainly it rests upon the title *Rubu-emga,* or Rab-mag, which this king bears in his inscriptions, and on the improbability of there having been, towards the close of the Babylonian period —when the monumental monarch must have lived— two persons of exactly the same name holding this office. See RAB-MAG. Assuming on these grounds the identity of the scriptural ' Nergal-Sharezer, Rab-mag,' with the monumental ' *Nergal-shar-uzur, Rab-emga,*' we may learn something of the prince in question from profane authors. There cannot be a doubt that he was the monarch called *Neriglissar* or *Neriglissoor* by Berosus (Josephus, *c. Ap.* i, 30), who murdered Evil-Merodach, the son of Nebuchadnezzar, and succeeded him upon the throne. This prince was married to a daughter of Nebuchadnezzar, and was thus the brother-in-law of his predecessor, whom he put to death. His reign lasted between three and four years. He appears to have died a natural death, and certainly left his crown to a young son, Laborosoarchod, who was murdered after a reign of nine months. In the Canon of Ptolemy he appears, under the designation of *Nerigassolassar,*

as reigning four years between Illoarudamus (Evil-Merodach) and Nabonadius, his son's reign not obtaining any mention because it fell short of a year. A palace built by Neriglissar has been discovered at Babylon. It is the only building of any extent on the right bank of the Euphrates. See BABYLON. The bricks bear the name of Nergal-shar-uzur, the title of Rab-mag, and also a statement — which is somewhat surprising — that Nergal-shar-uzur was the son of a certain ' Belzikkar-iskun, *king of Babylon.*' The only explanation which has been offered of this statement is a conjecture (Rawlinson's *Herodotus*, i, 518) that Bel-zikkar-iskun may possibly have been the ' chief Chaldæan' who (according to Berosus) kept the royal authority for Nebuchadnezzar during the interval between his father's death and his own arrival at Babylon. See NEBUCHADNEZZAR. Neriglissar could scarcely have given his father the title of king without some ground; and this is at any rate a possible ground, and one compatible with the non-appearance of the name in any extant list of the later Babylonian monarchs. Neriglissar's office of RAB-MAG will be further considered under that word. It is evident that he was a personage of importance before he mounted the throne. Some (as Larcher) have sought to identify him with Darius the Mede; but this view is quite untenable. There is abundant reason to believe from his name and his office that he was a native Babylonian—a grandee of high rank under Nebuchadnezzar, who regarded him as a fitting match for one of his daughters. He did not, like Darius Medus, gain Babylon by conquest, but acquired his dominion by an internal revolution. His reign lasted from B.C. 559 to B.C. 556."

Ne'ri (Νηρί), the son of Melchi and father of Salathiel, according to Luke's genealogy of Jesus (iii, 27, 28); probably identical with the NERIAH (q. v.) of the O. T. (Jer. li, 59). See GENEALOGY OF OUR LORD.

Neri, FILIPPO DE', ST., the founder of the Congregation of the Oratory, was born of a noble family at Florence, July 22, 1515. His character, even in boyhood, foreshadowed the career of piety and benevolence to which he was destined, and he was commonly known among his youthful companions by the name of " good Philip." On the death of his parents he was adopted by a very wealthy uncle, with whom he lived for some time at San Germano, near Monte Cassino, and by whom he was recognised as his destined heir. But he relinquished all these prospects for a life of piety and charity; and, after having considerably advanced in his studies at his native place, he decided to set out for Rome, where he hoped to have greater opportunities for charitable labors. He went to the Italian capital in 1533, and there arduously devoted himself to philosophical and theological studies in the Augustine schools. But he by no means confined himself to his intellectual improvement. He won the esteem and reverence of all by his extraordinary devotion to the Church and to the poor and needy and forsaken. He abounded in charitable labors, instructing children who had no teachers, caring for the sick, reclaiming vicious persons, and engaging in all manner of enterprises requiring a benevolent disposition and a pious soul. (The particulars of his life, some of which are very curious, have been fully narrated by his biographers Bacci and Gallonio.) In the pursuit of these objects he displayed a sincerity and a single-heartedness which naturally enough exposed him to the sneers and the slanders of the worldly, the prudish, and the sticklers for outward decorum. But he cared little for the opinion of such people, and went on unmindful of all opposition or want of interest. Neither money nor labor did he spare to accomplish his purposes. Thus he founded an asylum for poor and sick strangers, and other houseless or helpless persons, in which they were sheltered until they were able to return to their home. Realizing his need of closer alliance with the Church, he decided finally to take holy orders, and on May 23,

1551, was ordained priest in the church of the Lateran. The year previous to his admission into the priesthood he had exerted himself for the conversion of several associates of his, and he succeeded with Salviati, a brother of the cardinal of that name, and Tarugio, who afterwards became a cardinal, and Baronius, so celebrated in ecclesiastical history as a writer, and some others. No sooner had their zeal been enlisted in the interests of the Church than he banded them together in a confraternity for the care of poor pilgrims visiting Rome, and other houseless persons, as well as of the sick generally, which still subsists, and which has numbered among its associates many of the most distinguished members of the Roman Catholic Church. This confraternity is noteworthy, moreover, as having been the germ of the far more celebrated Congregation of the Oratory (q. v.), which was founded by St. Philip in concert with these friends. Besides the general objects above indicated, and the spiritual duties designed for the personal sanctification of the members, the main object of this association was the moral instruction and religious training of the young and uneducated, who were assembled in chapels or oratorios, for prayer and for religious and moral instruction. The personal character of Neri, the unselfish devotedness of his life, his unaffected piety, his genuine love of the poor, his kindly and cheerful disposition, and, perhaps, as much as any of the rest, a certain quaint humor, and a tinge of what may almost be called drollery which pervaded many of his sayings and doings, contributed to popularize his institute. Besides being a man of education and general information, he could readily enter into the spirit of the respective pursuits of all whom he sought out for his assistance, and thus so greatly endeared himself to every one who was brought in contact with him. Many and peculiar were the means he used to further his purpose. Thus, e. g., indirectly Neri became the founder of the *Oratorios* (q. v.). As a further means of withdrawing youth from dangerous amusements, sacred musical entertainments (thence called by the name of *oratorio*) were held in the oratory, at first consisting solely of hymns, but afterwards partaking of the nature of sacred operas or dramas, some of which were written by distinguished writers, such as Zeno and Metastasio, except that they did not admit the scenic or dramatic accompaniments of these more secular compositions; the parts were sung, like those of an opera, with this difference, that the singers were stationed in a gallery of the chapel. The chapel being called in Italian "Oratorio," i. e. a place of prayer, came to be applied to the performance, and the congregation or order constituted by Neri hence took the name of *Fathers of the Oratory*. Besides the musical entertainments, religious and literary lectures also formed part of his plan, and it was in the lectures originally prepared for the Oratory that, at the instance of Neri, the gigantic *Church History* of Baronius had its origin. But though Neri's great characteristics were simply charity and a cheerful piety, the people, who greatly revered him, believed him to be a more than commonly endowed saint, and he was by them said to have the power of working miracles and curing possession. He no doubt wrought miracles in freeing people from the possession of evil spirits, for, as he himself said, the idea of being possessed of evil spirits was not to be too readily received, and its best remedy is cheerfulness, as it often arises only from melancholy. These precepts he carried into practice to such an extent that, having been accused of allowing and even encouraging worldly pleasures, such as dancing, etc., among his disciples, he was suspended from his functions as confessor and preacher; he was even complained of to the pope as trying to found a new sect. The accusation, however, did not prevail, and he was soon after restored. In 1570 the nocturnal meetings of his society, held simply for devotional and charitable purposes as above spoken of, were made the ground of new accusations, yet he became but the more confirmed in his peculiar views. Some have ac-

cused him of triviality, but it is more likely that he meant his practices as a check to the sanctimonious, pharisaical gravity and decorousness which prevailed in Rome after 1560. Though pressed on several occasions to accept the office of cardinal, he steadily declined. Theiner relates that when Henry IV, of France, joined the Roman Catholic Church in 1593, the pope refused to revoke the excommunication pronounced against the prince; a total separation of the French from the Roman Church seemed unavoidable, but Baronius having occasion to confess the pope, Neri forbade his granting him the absolution unless he promised to grant it in turn to the king. This plan succeeded, and Henry IV rewarded the order by munificent donations. The Brotherhood of the Oratory was regularly organized by the pope in 1575; according to its regulation the members are all equal, and have to perform in turn all the menial duties necessary in the community. (They show yet an inscription said to have been traced by the hand of the great Church historian: "Caes. Baronius, cocus perpetuus.") All the affairs of the communities were to be decided by the majority of votes. Neri, more prudent than other founders of ascetic organizations, did not suffer the members of the Oratory to bind themselves by perpetual vows as do the monks, preferring that the spirit of charity and sacrifice should alone unite them, and for this end each member had to pay a monthly fee for the expense of the house, as the lodgings alone were free. The institution was approved by Gregory XIII in 1575, and it soon spread over Italy, France, and other countries. The congregation "De l'Oratoire" has produced many distinguished men, Baronius and Massillon among others. Study, preaching, and the education of youth are the chief occupations of its members. Being bound by no vows, any member of the Oratory can at any time withdraw with all his property. The present Oratory, Sta. Maria at Vallicella (Rome), was the residence of Neri after 1583. It has a good library, and the oratorios continue to be performed, especially from All-saints' Day (Nov. 3d) to Palm Sunday. Neri resigned the office of superior of the community in favor of Baronius, and died a few years afterwards, May 25, 1595. He was canonized in 1662 by Gregory XV. Some of his letters, and his *Ricordi*, or advice to youth, have been published, as well as two sonnets out of many which he composed. The regulations he left for the guidance of his order were published in 1612. Neri was an amiable, virtuous, and religious man, and his example had a great influence on the clergy of Rome. See Gallonio, *Vita beate Phil. Nerii* (Rome, 1600); *Vita Phil. Nerii* (Munich, 1610); *Vide y Hechos de S. Filipe Neri* (1613); Bacci, *Vita di S. Filippo Neri* (1622); Vasquez, *S. Filipe Neri Epitome de sua Vita* (1651); Manni, *Raggionamenti sulla vita di F. Neri* (1786); *Vie de St. Philippe de Neri* (1847); Faber, *Spirit and Genius of St. Phil. Neri* (1850); Ranke, *Hist. of the Papacy*, i, 323–367 sq.; Hase, *Ch. Hist.* p. 462. See also ORATORY, CONGREGATION OF THE.

Neri′ah (Heb. *Neriyah′*, נֵרִיָּה, *Jehovah is my lamp*, or *lamp of Jehovah*, also [Jer. xxxvi, 14, 32; xliii, 6] in the prolonged form *Neriya′hu*, נֵרִיָּהוּ; Sept. Νηρίας [v. r. Νηρί in Jer. xliii, 3]; Vulg. *Nerias*, but *Neri* in Jer. xxii, 12), the son of Maaseiah, and father of Seraiah (Jer. li, 59) and Baruch (Jer. xxxii, 12, 16; xxxvi, 4, 8, 14, 32; xliii, 3, 6; xlv, 1). He appears to be the same with NERI (q. v.) in our Lord's maternal ancestry (Luke iii, 27, 28; see Strong's *Harmony and Expos. of the Gospels*, p. 17). B.C. cir. 620.

Neri′as (Νηρίας), the Græcized form (Bar. i, 1) of the name of NERIAH (q. v.), the father of Seraiah and Baruch (Jer. xlv, 1; li, 59).

Another Nerias or Neriah is mentioned by Josephus (*Ant.* x, 9, 6), and also by the Jewish record *Seder Olam*, as a high-priest, son of Uriah and father of Odeas or

Hosaiah; but the reference is probably to AZARIAH, 15 (2 Chron. xxxi, 10). See HIGH-PRIEST.

Nero, a Roman emperor, celebrated in the history of the world as a tyrant and a debauchee, figures in ecclesiastical annals chiefly because of the intolerant and persecuting spirit which he manifested towards the followers of Jesus in the Eternal City. His full name was *Nero Claudius Cæsar Drusus Germanicus* (originally *Lucius Domitius Ahenobarbus*). He was the son of Domitius Ahenobarbus and of Agrippina, daughter of Germanicus, and was born in 37 at Antium. After the marriage of his mother, in third nuptials, with her uncle, the emperor Claudius, Nero was adopted by that prince, and Nero's name changed as above given. His education was carefully looked after. He was placed under the tuition of the philosopher Seneca (q. v.), and appears to have improved his opportunities. He is said to have persevered in his studies, and to have made great progress especially in the Greek language, of which he exhibited a specimen in his sixteenth year by pleading in that tongue the rights or privileges of the Rhodians and of the inhabitants of Ilium; but he possessed little oratorical skill (Suetonius, *Nero,* c. 7; Tacitus, *Annales,* xii, 58). Nero was so much trusted by Claudius that he finally married him to his daughter Octavia. When he was about seventeen years of age Nero's abandoned mother poisoned her husband, Claudius, and by means of her criminal favors succeeded in raising her son to the throne (A.D. 54), over whom she expected to exercise the most absolute control. Nero himself shortly after disposed of the rightful heir, Britannicus, by poison, and thus became sole and undisputed ruler. For the first few years his public conduct, under the control of Burrhus and Seneca, was unexceptionable; in private, however, he disgraced himself by the most odious vices, and his mother endeavored to retain her influence by shamefully complying with his inclinations. But after a time, even with all her efforts, she perceived her hold to slacken, and noticed how he disregarded her advice and refused her requests. Gradually the two became estranged from each other. Nero was accused of criminal love for Ætia, a woman of low birth, and of improper relations with Poppæa, the wife of Otho, who succeeded Nero on the throne. This maddened his mother, and she frequently abused him with the most contemptuous language; reminded him that he owed his elevation to her, and threatened that she would inform the soldiers of the manner in which Claudius had met his death. Nero was thus kept in constant dread of revolt and assassination, and finally, in A.D. 59, he caused this detestable woman to be murdered. Now, fearing no rival in power, he gave full scope to the darkest traits of his character. The low servility into which the Roman senate had sunk at this time may be estimated from the fact that it actually issued an address congratulating the hateful matricide on the death of Agrippina. Nero himself, on the other hand, confessed that he was ever haunted by the ghost of his murdered mother. The affairs of the empire were at this time far from tranquil. In A.D. 61 an insurrection broke out in Britain under queen Boadicea, which was, however, suppressed by Suetonius Paulinus. The following year saw an unsuccessful war against the Parthians in Armenia. At home matters were not much better. The emperor was lampooned in verse; the senate and priesthood, alike venal, were also satirized by audacious malcontents; his most valued friend Burrhus died; and Seneca, disgusted with the licentiousness of the court, had quitted the capital. And the worst was yet to come. In June, A.D. 64, a terrible conflagration broke out in Rome, and for six days and seven nights the fire raged with the greatest fury; even after it was supposed extinguished it broke forth again and continued for two days longer. A vast territory experienced the results of this conflagration. Out of the fourteen districts into which the city was divided, three were totally destroyed, and in seven of the others

it left only a few half-ruined houses. Not only the temples and public buildings, as well as private houses, but also monuments of all kinds, masterpieces of art, and libraries were destroyed, and a great number of lives lost. Although the emperor remained at Antium during the early part of the conflagration, and only returned to Rome when the fire approached his palace, the people generally accused him of having purposely set fire to the city, and preventing its being put out, in order to build up a finer one on its ruins. In compliance with his orders the sufferers were relieved, and such as built again were aided by the state; but this did not allay the general suspicion, as he was said to have ascended the tower of Mæcenas during the fire, and there recited verses on the downfall of Troy. All the processions and sacrifices which he commanded for the purpose of appeasing the gods, as well as the vast sums he squandered among the people, did not allay the suspicion. Indeed Dion and Suetonius expressly accuse him, but these writers, it is well known, were always inclined to favorably receive any scandal. Tacitus (*Ann.* xv, 38) thinks the matter doubtful, or at least all his efforts to determine Nero's part in the case failed to convince of guilt. So doubtful was Nero's character that the belief of his guilt was general at the time, and ever since the world has been inclined to judge him the perpetrator of the crime. Church historians thus treat him. Even the liberal-minded Rénan, who in his *L'Antéchrist* (Paris, 1873) has furnished the latest, fullest, most spirited, and probably most accurate delineation of Nero and his time, believes this emperor to have caused the conflagration, in order to rebuild the city in greater splendor and more artistic form, and thus give renown to his reign. Says Rénan: "Rome, above all things, preoccupied his [i. e. Nero's] thoughts. His project was to rebuild it from top to bottom, and to name it afresh—Neropolis. For a century past it had been one of the wonders of the world. In size it rivalled the ancient capitals of Asia, and its edifices were fine, strong, and solid. But its streets appeared mean to the taste of the day: for that taste tended more and more to vulgar and decorative construction, it aspired to broad effects such as rejoice the heart of gaping sightseers, and it condescended to a thousand tricks unknown to the ancient Greeks. At the head of the whole movement was Nero. The new Rome which he imagined was something like the Paris of our own day—one of those artificial cities, built to order, in planning which the great point aimed at is to catch the admiration of visitors from the country and of foreigners" (p. 136–143). To remove all suspicion from himself, Nero spread the report that the Romans should regard the Christians as the authors of the fire—that mysterious sect who, like the Jews in the Middle Ages, were generally hit upon as the cause of all otherwise inexplicable calamities; and, as if Nero himself believed them guilty of this crime, he now inaugurated a series of persecutions which have made his name a byword for cruelty and inhumanity. See NERONIAN PERSECUTIONS. But while busy persecuting the Christians, Nero found time to carry forward his scheme for the embellishment of Rome. He rebuilt in great magnificence the burned districts, and reared for himself on the Palatine Hill a splendid palace, called, from the immense profusion of its golden ornaments, the *Aurea Domus,* or Golden House; and in order to provide for this expenditure, and for the gratification of the Roman populace by spectacles and distributions of corn, Italy and the provinces were unsparingly plundered. In A.D. 65 a powerful conspiracy was formed for the purpose of placing Piso upon the throne, but it was discovered by Nero, and the principal conspirators were put to death. Among others who suffered on this occasion were Lucan and Seneca; but the guilt of the latter is doubtful. In the same year Poppæa died, in consequence of a kick which she received from her husband while she was in an advanced state of pregnancy. On the death of Poppæa Nero wished to marry Antonia,

Palace of the Cæsars at Rome.

daughter of the emperor Claudius, and his sister by adoption, but she refused, and was in consequence put to death. He however married Statilia Messalina, having first caused her husband Vestinus to be killed. Nero also executed or banished many persons highly distinguished for integrity and virtue. His vanity led him to seek distinction as a poet, a philosopher, an actor, a musician, and a charioteer, and he received sycophantic applauses, not only in Italy, but in Greece, to which, upon invitation of the Greek cities, he made a visit in 67. But in 68 the Gallic and Spanish legions, and after them the Prætorian Guards, rose against him to make Galba emperor, and Nero was obliged to flee from the city and conceal himself in the house of a freedman, Phaon, about four miles distant. The senate, which had hitherto been most subservient, declared him an enemy of his country, and the tyrant ended his life by suicide, June 11, 68, just as the Roman soldiers were approaching his hiding-place (Dion. Cas. lxi–lxiii; Tacit. Ann. xiii–xv; Sueton. Nero). Nero was a lover of arts and letters. The Apollo Belvedere is supposed by Thiersch (Epochen der bildenden Kunst unter den Griechen, p. 312) and some other writers to have been made for this emperor. He also possessed much taste as a poet and histrionic performer. But he was, notwithstanding these accomplishments, a licentious voluptuary, and scrupled not to commit any crime that would tend to gratify his lust or strengthen his power. Yet, as Rénan has well observed, "one cannot absolutely say that the wretch was without a heart, nor deficient in a certain sentiment of the good and the beautiful. So far from being incapable of friendship, he often showed himself a good comrade; and it was precisely this that rendered him cruel. He was determined to be loved and admired for his own sake; and was irritated against those who did not manifest towards him these feelings" (p. 126–132). The words of Suetonius, "Elatus inflatusque tantis velut successibus, negavit quenquam Principum scisse quid sibi liceret" (Nero, § 37), we think, sum up in most admirable conciseness the character and work of this strange ruler. It was during Nero's reign that the war commenced between the Jews and Romans which terminated subsequently in the destruction

Coin of Nero, with façade of the Macellum Augusti. (From the British Museum.)

of Jerusalem by Titus, and the overthrow of the Jewish polity. According to the personnel given by Rénan (L'Antéchrist, p. 173), "Nero had a bad face, lowering looks, blue eyes, chestnut hair dressed in rows of curls, a terrible lip, and the air (wicked and stupid at the same time) as of a great silly doll, supremely self-satisfied, puffed up with vanity." Although repeatedly alluded to, he is not expressly named in the text of the New Testament (see Acts xxv, 11, etc.; Phil. i, 12, 13; iv, 22); but in the subscription (probably spurious) to the Second Epistle to Timothy he is called Cæsar Nero (Καῖσαρ Νέρων). Many authors refer to Nero the prophecy by John (Rev. xiii, 11–18) of the beast with two horns, and interpret the 18th verse as referring to the Hebrew name of Nero, נֶרוֹן קֶסַר, which amounts numerically to 666, the number there given; since, written more nearly in Roman style, נְרוֹ קֶסַר, it amounts to 616, which Irenæus testifies was the number found in many manuscripts in his day (see Stuart, Apoc. ii, 457 sq.; Benary, Zeitschrift für Speculative Theologie, 1836, vol. i, pt. ii; Bibliotheca Sacra, 1843, p. 332 sq.; 1844, p. 84 sq.). See REVELATION, BOOK OF. Nero was the emperor before whom Paul was brought on his first imprisonment at Rome, A.D. 56–58; and in the persecution of the Christians by Nero in the year A.D. 64 the apostles Peter and Paul are supposed to have suffered martyrdom. All the authorities furnishing facts in Nero's life are collected by Tillemont (Hist. des Empereurs, vol. i). See the monographs cited by Volbeding, Index Programmatum, p. 95, 97; and compare also Rénan's L'Antéchrist, and the original authorities quoted there; Merivale, Hist. of the Romans under the Empire; Diderot, Essai sur les Règnes de Claude et de Néron; and the Church historians quoted in the article on NERONIAN PERSECUTIONS. (J. H. W.)

Nerol, TOBIJJA, ha-Kohen, was born at Metz in 1652. After the death of his father, who had held the office of rabbi, in 1659, Nerol went to Worms, thence to Padua, where he studied medicine. He then moved to Constantinople, where he was introduced as physician to the sultan Achmet III. At the beginning of the 18th century Nerol went to Venice, thence to Palestine, and died at Jerusalem in 1729. He is the author of an encyclopædical work entitled ס', מַעֲשֵׂה טוֹבִיָּה, divided into three parts: the first part, which is called עוֹלָם קָטָן, treats of metaphysics, physical sciences, astronomy, and natural philosophy; the second part, which is called עוֹלָם חָדָשׁ, treats of geography, physiology, pathology, therapeutics, anatomy, and surgery; the third part, which is called עוֹלָם הָעֶשִׁיָּה, treats of the different diseases. This valuable work was first published at Venice in 1707, and often since. See Fürst, Bibl. Jud. iii, 2829; Carmoly, Histoire des Médecins Juifs, i, 247–251; L. B. d. Orients (1850), c. 579; Leipziger Acta Eruditorum (1721), p. 533; Unschuldige Nachrichten zum Jahre (1722), p. 531. (B. P.)

Neroni, BARTOLOMEO, called Maestro Riccio, a distinguished Italian painter, who devoted himself especially to sacred art, flourished about 1573. He studied under Giovanni Antonio Razzi, whom he assisted in his works, and whose daughter he married. Lanzi says that Neroni, after the death of the four great pillars of the Sienese school, sustained its reputation and probably educated one of its restorers. His pictures unite the style of Razzi with a certain resemblance to the manner of Vasari in the distribution of his tints. He had excellent abilities in perspective, especially in representing scenery; Andreani has engraved a specimen. He was also greatly skilled in architecture, and had a pension from the magistrates of Lucca for his assistance in the public works. In Siena, at the Osservanti, is a Crucifixion by him, with a great number of figures; and in the church of the Derelitte a Descent from the Cross entirely in the style of Razzi.

See Spooner, *Biographical History of the Fine Arts*, ii, 614.

Neronian Persecutions were really the first severe trials which the Christians of Rome had to endure. They occurred in A.D. 64, and were instigated by Nero (q. v.) himself. Although we possess no positive information as to the manner in which the first Christian community was established at Rome, it appears certain that it was not originally instituted by the apostles. It is more probable that the frequent intercourse of the Roman Jews with Palestine and Jerusalem led at an early time to the introduction of the new doctrines, the believers still remaining connected with the synagogues. They became gradually more numerous; and the frequent controversies which here, as in other cities, arose among the Jews, partly on their own tenets, partly concerning the person and the coming of Christ, led at last to open disturbances, and gave occasion to the emperor Claudius to publish in 41 a strict edict banishing *all* the Jews, including those who acknowledged Christ. The edict, however, did not receive a very severe execution, only the leaders, such as Aquila, whom we find mentioned in the N. T., being banished. As to the others, there was probably some alleviation made in the decree; but while allowed to remain at Rome, they were not permitted to assemble in the synagogues until a new edict, promulgated about the end of the same year, again restored them this privilege also, and guaranteed the Jews religious liberty throughout the empire. This temporary closing of the synagogues, however, led the Christians to organize places of worship for themselves, and to form an independent community. Their number now increased so rapidly that St. Paul, who had been informed of their position by Aquila at Corinth, expressed in his Epistle to the Romans the desire to visit them, which he fulfilled three years later, when he was led as a prisoner from Cæsarea to Rome, remaining there a while, and laboring for the new religion with such success that Tacitus speaks of the Christians of Rome as "an *immense* multitude." The rapid increase of the Christians made them of course unpopular at Rome. Suetonius, in his *Nero* (chap. xvi), speaks of them as a "*dangerous* sect." They were mistrusted because they abstained from participation in the sacrifices and other heathen ceremonies, and were hated because they were believed secretly at work against the peace of Roman citizens. They were accused of misanthropy, and were suspected of all manner of crimes. But no open intent to persecute them manifested itself until Nero ordered ceremonies after the great fire, and the Christians failed to participate. They were now accused as the authors of the conflagration; first, probably, by friends of the court, in order to turn public animosity from Nero, who was by many believed to have favored the burning of Rome. See NERO. The emperor himself took up the public rumor, and acted upon it as a verity. "He inflicted," says Tacitus, "the most exquisite tortures on those men, who, under the vulgar appellation of Christians, were already branded with *deserved* infamy," and a vast multitude, or as Tacitus has it, "ingens multitudo," were put to death in the most shocking manner. Indeed, it appears from the detailed accounts of Tacitus that Nero's proceedings were quite different from mere capital executions according to the Roman law; for the Christian martyrs were not simply put to death, but their execution was made to gratify the bloodthirstiness of the tyrant, and to serve as an amusement to the people. Says Rénan:

"Though persuaded that the conflagration was the crime of Nero, many serious Romans saw in this *coup* a means of delivering the city from an intolerable pest. Tacitus, notwithstanding some qualms of pity, was of this opinion; and as to Suetonius, he reckons among the meritorious acts of Nero the punishment which he had inflicted on the partisans of a new and mischievous superstition. Yet these punishments were something absolutely frightful. Never before had such refinements of cruelty been witnessed. Almost all the Christians who were arrested were of the humble class; and the usual punishment of such unfortunates, when treason or sacrilege was laid to their charge, was to be thrown to wild beasts, or to be burned alive in the amphitheatre, with an addition of cruel scourgings. One of the most hideous characteristics of Roman manners was that they converted punishments into a fete, and public executions into a public entertainment. Persia, in moments of fanaticism and terror, had used frightful forms of torture; and on more than one occasion had tasted a sombre kind of pleasure in inflicting them. But never before the establishment of Roman dominion had these horrors been made a public diversion, a subject for peals of laughter and applause. The amphitheatres had become the regular places of execution, and the tribunals of justice furnished materials for the sport. The roads that converged to Rome were crowded with the criminals of the whole world, to provide victims for the circus and amusement for the populace. . . . But, this time, to the barbarity of the executioner was added a touch of derision. The victims were reserved for a fete, to which (no doubt) an expiatory character was attached. Roman annals had known few days so extraordinary. The *ludus matutinus*, usually devoted to combats of animals, saw to-day an unheard-of procession. The condemned persons, sewn up in skins of wild beasts, were thrust out into the arena to be torn by dogs; others were crucified; others again were clothed in tunics dipped in oil, pitch, or rosin, and then found themselves attached to stakes, and reserved to illuminate the nocturnal festivities. When dusk came on, these living torches were set on fire. Nero offered for the spectacle his magnificent gardens beyond the Tiber, on the site of the modern Borgo and in the precincts of the Church of St. Peter" (p. 163–165).

But physical suffering was not enough to satisfy the infernal malice of the heathen world against these pure and patient servants of the Crucified One. Moral tortures, mental anguish, brutal and Satanic invasions of all that a Christian holds most sacred and most inviolable, must be undergone by them ere the baptism of blood was complete, ere the infant Church could be (like her Master) "made perfect through sufferings." The pen almost refuses to write, the brain almost refuses to conceive, the atrocities which followed. The heart and conscience of the reader can do no more, even now at the distance of 1800 years, than cry to heaven, with the souls of the slain under the Apocalyptic altar, "How long, O Lord, holy and true, dost thou not judge and avenge this blood on them that dwell on the earth?" (Rev. vi, 10).

"Women, and even virgins, were mixed up with these horrible sports; and nameless indignities were inflicted on them, as part of the festivities. It had become an established usage under Nero to force condemned persons to play in the amphitheatre mythological scenes which involved at least the death of the actor. These hideous operas, to which the application of ingenious mechanism lent an astonishing effect, were the novelties of the day. Greece would indeed have recoiled with surprise had such attempts been suggested to her, to supplement æsthetics by ferocity, to make torture minister to art! The unhappy wretch was introduced into the arena richly dressed as a god or a hero destined to death. He then represented by his sufferings some tragic scene of pagan myth, consecrated by the works of poets and sculptors. Sometimes it was Hercules, frantic and burning on Mount Œta, and madly tearing from his flesh the tunic of blazing pitch. Sometimes it was Orpheus torn in pieces by a bear, Dædalus thrown from heaven and devoured by beasts, Pasiphaë undergoing the attacks of the bull, or Attys put to death. . . . Nero, no doubt, was present at these spectacles. As he was nearsighted, he used to wear a concave emerald in his eye to serve as an eye-glass for watching the combats of gladiators. He loved to make a parade of his knowledge as a connoisseur in sculpture. . . . Worthy of a connoisseur like him must have been the plastic forms and the colors presented by a human frame palpitating under the teeth of beasts; by a poor timid maiden with chaste gestures veiling her nudity, and then tossed by a bull and torn in pieces on the pebbles of the arena! Yes, he was there, in the front rank, on the *podium*, supported by vestals and curule magistrates" (p. 157–173).

So great were the sufferings of the tormented that even the pagan historian is forced to confess that "pity arose for the guilty, though they deserved the severest punishment, since they were put to death, *not for the public good, but to gratify the cruelty of one man*" (*Annales*, xv, 44). But even the cruelty of Nero is not generally adjudged sufficient ground for all these executions, and it is believed by some that the powerful Poppæa Sabina, proved by Josephus (*Ant.* xx, 8) to have been a convert to Judaism, mainly instigated the severity of this persecution. It is thought by some that the apostle

Paul lost his life on this occasion. Wieseler (*Chronol. Synopse der vier Evangelien* [1843], p. 531) places the execution of Paul in the beginning of the year 64, and the crucifixion of Peter in the Neronian persecution, therefore some months later. Tradition places the death of both apostles in the Neronian persecution, and some witnesses, as Jerome and Gelasius, put both martyrdoms on the same day; but others, as Arator, Cedrenus, Augustine, separate them by an interval of one year or less. That Paul suffered first, before the outbreak of the persecution properly so called, seems to be indicated by the easier mode and the locality of his death; for in the persecution itself his Roman citizenship would hardly have been respected; and the scene of that persecution was not the Ostian Way, but the Vatican across the Tiber, where Nero's gardens and the circus lay (comp. Tacitus, *Ann.* xiv, 14; and Bunsen, *Beschreibung der Stadt Rom.* ii, 1, p. 13 sq.). At the same time, this persecution, notwithstanding the statement of Orosius, does not seem to have extended through all the provinces, but rather to have been restricted to Rome and the surrounding country.

Shortly after the death of Nero, July 11, 68, the belief commenced to gain adherents among the people that he was not dead. They expected him to return from the East as a great conqueror, and this induced several adventurers to assume his name and create insurrections. As for the Christians, the remembrance of that terrible persecution, their manner of interpreting the Book of Revelations, and still more the Sibylline Oracles, led them for several centuries to believe that Nero was still living, and even that he would appear at the latter day as the Antichrist or with him. Says Schaff: "The report arose first among the heathen that Nero was not really dead, and would come forth again from his concealment; according to Tacitus (*Hist.* ii, 8), 'Sub idem tempus Achaja atque Asia falso exterritæ, velut Nero adventaret, vario super exitu ejus rumore, eoque pluribus vivere eum fingentibus credentibusque.' Among the Christians this rumor took the form that Nero would return as Antichrist, or (according to Lactantius) as the forerunner of Antichrist. That such an expectation arose, at least afterwards, in the Church, though merely as the private opinion of individuals, is plain from Augustine, *De civitate Dei*, lib. xx, cap. 19, where he says that by the 'mystery of iniquity' (2 Thess. ii, 7) some understood Nero, and then proceeds: 'Unde nonnulli ipsum (Neronem) resurrecturum et *futurum Antichristum* suspicantur. Alii vero nec eum occisum putant, sed subtractum potius, ut putaretur occisus; et vivum occultari in vigore ipsius ætatis, in qua fuit, quum crederetur exstinctus, donec suo tempore reveletur et restituatur in regnum. Sed multum mihi mira est hæc opinantium tanta præsumptio.' Lactantius mentions a similar opinion (*De mort. persec.* c. 2) with a reference to a passage in the Sibylline Oracles (lib. iv, p. 525, ed. Ser. Gallæus), which, however, refers not at all to Antichrist, but probably to the appearance of the pseudo-Nero in the time of Titus (comp. Tacitus, *Hist.* i, 2) as to a past fact, as Thiersch has shown (*Kritik der N.-Test. Schriften*, 1845, p. 410 sq.) against Bleek. Altogether erroneous is the view of Ewald, Lücke, and others, who charge this superstition respecting Nero as the future Antichrist upon the author of the Apocalypse; taking the beast, which 'was, and is not, and yet is' (xvii, 8, 11), to be Nero. This betrays an exceedingly low, unworthy view of this holy book" (*Hist. Apostol. Ch.* p. 347). Yet very recently this "low and unworthy view" of the Apocalypse has found general favor in England, and in France also. Not only has the rationalistic Rénan espoused it, but several of the British conservative reviews, in notices of *L'Antéchrist*, commend Mr. Rénan's researches as to the authorship and object of the Apocalypse. The *name* of the Antichrist is believed by Rénan to be found in chap. xiii, 18, which (number of the beast) amounts to precisely 666, and signifies, if to each Hebrew letter is given its numerical

value, Νέρων Καῖσαρ, or נרון קסר, well known in that form by sight to all the provincials on their coin and standards and inscriptions (comp. *Edinburgh Review*, Oct. 1874, art. viii; and see under NERO, above). See Pauly, *Real-Encyklopädie d. Klass. Alterthumswissenschaft*, pt. v, p. 576–591; Kortholt, *De persecutionibus ecclesiæ primitivæ sub imperatoribus ethnicis* (Kilon. 1689); Walch, *De Romanorum in tolerandis diversis religionibus disciplina publica* (in the *Nov. Commentt. Soc. Reg.* [Gött. 1733, vol. iii]); Lehmann, *Studien z. Gesch. d. apost. Zeitalters* (Greifw. 1856, 4to); Masson, *Histoire critique de la République des lettres*, viii, 74, 117; ix, 172, 186; Toinard, *Ad Lactant. de Mortibus Persequutorum*, p. 398 (ed. Du Fresnoy); Tillemont, *Hist. des Empereurs*, i, 564; Baratier, *De successione Romanor. Pontificum*, cap. v, p. 60; Mosheim, *Commentaries*, i, 97, 120; Schaff, *Hist. of the Apostolic Church*, p. 395; id. *Hist. of the Christian Church*, i, 162, 305; Mosheim, *Eccles. Hist.* (1st cent. in vol. i); Neander, *Ch. Hist.* i, 94; Leckey, *Hist. Europ. Morals*, i, 274, 326, 456; Burton, *Eccles. Hist.* p. 190, 195, 200, 203, 231, 237, 242, 322; Gieseler, *Eccles. Hist.* i, 56 sq.; Riddle, *Hist. of the Papacy*, i, 5 sq.; *Meth. Quar. Rev.* Jan. 1875, p. 127–131; *Christian Quarterly*, April, 1874, p. 275–277; *Journal of Sacred Literature*, vol. xxvi.

Nerses is the name of three great dignitaries who have become much distinguished in the history of the Armenian Church.

1. NERSES I, THE GREAT, was a great-grandson of Gregory Photistes, the apostle of the Armenians, and was born at Vagharchabad about 310. In the year 364 he was elected bishop, and in 366, at the Council of Walarsckapat, the clergy of the country appointed him as their catholicos, or patriarch. At that time it was also decided that in future the patriarchs of Armenia should no more be consecrated by the archbishop of Cæsarea, but that their own bishops should appoint and consecrate them. In his position as patriarch Nerses exhibited his great talents, especially with regard to Church discipline, his care for the poor, and other matters pertaining to his office. Twice Nerses went to Constantinople in behalf of the Armenian king Arsaces, who had revolted against the emperors Valentinian and Valens. He succeeded in appeasing the former, while the latter banished him. Theodosius the Great, Valens's successor, recalled Nerses from his banishment, and retained him a short time at Constantinople, in order to be present at the second œcumenical council in the year 381. He then returned to Armenia, where he died in 384, being poisoned by the young king, Para. His son was Sahak the Great (q. v.). See Lequien, *Oriens Christianus*, i, 1375.

2. NERSES KLAJETSI, i. e. *Klajeman* (called also *Nerses IV*, catholicos of Armenia, and *Shnorhali*, i. e. "the Pleasant," because of his oratorical talents), was born between 1098 and 1100. He was the son of an Armenian prince, who destined him for the clerical order. In connection with his brother Gregory he was at first educated by the catholicos Gregory Wkajaser, i. e. μαρτυροφίλος, and afterwards by Stephanus, the abbot of the "red monastery" (Karmir Wankh), who, when Nerses was ready to enter into holy orders, consecrated him as deacon, and shortly afterwards as priest. By the unanimous desire of the clergy, Nerses accepted in 1166 the high dignity of bishop, in which position he remained until his death in 1173. When, in 1165, he accidentally met with the son-in-law of the emperor Manuel Comnenus (q. v.), he took the opportunity to address a letter to the emperor, in which he showed that there was no real dogmatical difference between the Armenian and Greek churches, and that the Armenian Church, when speaking of *one* nature of Christ, takes the word in the sense of person; the same also can be said of the liturgical and ritual differences in both churches. This letter gave rise to a correspondence between the two churches, which aimed at the union of both. The emperor sent the philosopher Theorianus, who held a disputation with the Armenian abbot, John Uthman, the result of which was a mutual acknowledgment of their agreement in dogmatical as well as liturgical and ritual points. This disputation was first published by John Leunclavius (Basle, 1578), in Greek and Latin, and republished more fully by Angelo May in his *Scriptorum veterum nova collectio* (Romæ, 1822), vol. vi. Nerses, however, died before he received the consent of all the Armenian bishops to those points which the emperor, in a letter dated December, 1172, had made the basis of the union, viz., 1, to excommunicate all those who accept *one* nature in Christ—Eutyches, Dioscurus, Severus, Timothy the hunch-backed, and the like; 2, they should acknowledge two natures in Christ, as well as two wills and two energies ($\dot{\epsilon}\nu\dot{\epsilon}\rho\gamma\epsilon\iota\alpha\iota$), but *one* person; 3, they should omit the words *qui crucificus es* in the Tersanctus; 4, to celebrate the Greek festivals—the annunciation of Mary, March 25; the birth of Jesus, Dec. 25; his circumcision on the 1st and his baptism on the 6th of January; his presentation in the Temple, Feb. 2; and all the festivals of the Lord, the Blessed Virgin, of John the Baptist, the holy apostles, etc.; 5, the myron should be prepared with olive-oil; 6, to use at the communion leavened bread, and wine mixed with water; 7, to allow the laity as well as the clergy, with the exception of the penitents, during divine service and communion to remain in the church; 8, to acknowledge the fourth, fifth, sixth, and seventh œcumenical councils; and, 9, that the catholicos should only be appointed by the Greek emperor. Nerses was a fruitful writer and a learned theologian. Of great importance for the history of the Church and doctrines are his epistles, which he wrote as bishop and catholicos with reference to theological disputes and ecclesiastical questions, and which were published at Constantinople (1825) and Venice (1858), where also (in 1833) a Latin translation by Capelletti was published. Nerses excelled, too, as a poet, and he is said to have introduced rhyme into Armenian poetry. The Armenians regard him as their Homer. His greatest poem is *Jesus the Son*, a poetical epitome of the Old and New Testaments in 3825 verses; and the *Word of Faith*, an epitome of the four Gospels in 1502 verses. His spiritual songs are found in the hymn-books of the Armenian Church. In 1824 an edition of his poems and works was published at Venice. See Monike, in Ilgen's *Zeitschrift für hist. Theologie*, i, 87 sq.; Lequien, *Oriens Christianus*, i, 1399; Galanus, *Conciliatio*, vol. i, ch. xix.

3. NERSES LAMBRONENSIS (originally *Sembat*), a relative of Nerses IV, and son of the duke of Lambron, was born in 1133. He was very talented, and when sixteen years old he was appointed abbot of the monastery of Skyrra, near Constantinople. When he heard of this appointment he concluded to retire into the desert. He was prevented from doing this by his mother, who took him to Hromkla, that he might be consecrated by his uncle Nerses, which the latter did, giving him at the same time his name, Nerses. Shortly afterwards he retired into the monastery on the Black Mountain, where the learned Stephanos became his teacher. Nerses's oratorical talents were soon discovered by the monks, and he was obliged to preach in the church at Lambron, which he did with such satisfaction that, although only eighteen years of age, he was offered the abbacy of the monastery of Skyrra and the bishopric of Lambron. All these honors, however, he declined, and in order to give himself entirely to his studies he went with his teacher into the desert. In the year 1176 Nerses was appointed archbishop of Tarsus and Lambron, and also abbot of the monastery of Skyrra. In the year 1179 he was delegated by the catholicos Gregory to open the synod which was to convene at Hromkla for the purpose of bringing about the union between the Armenian and Greek churches, by an acceptance of the Confession of the Council of Chalcedon (q. v.) and the doctrine of two natures. This union which was about to be consummated was, however, frustrated by the

death of the emperor in 1180. In the midst of the ensuing revolts, wars, and troubles of the time, the whole matter was entirely forgotten. The hatred of the Greeks against the Armenians was again renewed, especially when the latter connected themselves with the Latin crusaders. In order to justify himself as well as his people against the Greeks, who represented them to the Latins as Eutychians (q. v.), the catholicos Gregory, in 1184, sent a delegation to pope Lucius III, who in return answered the letter by sending the insignia of the patriarchate, together with a Roman liturgy and epistle, which Nerses translated; the latter also consented to some changes which the Roman clergy had proposed, especially that the main ecclesiastical festivals should be celebrated with the other churches at one and the same time, which caused great dissatisfaction among the Oriental-Armenian clergy. Nerses died in 1192, and was buried in the monastery of Skyrra, whose abbot he was, and is commemorated in his Church on July 17. He wrote, *Explanation of the Ecclesiastical Orders and Liturgy of the Mass* (Venice. 1847):—*Address at the Opening of the Council at Hromkla* (ibid. 1784; in a Latin transl., ibid. 1812, 1838, and in a German by Neumann, Leips. 1834):—*Commentaries on different Books of the Bible*:—*Biographies of the Fathers, especially the Anchorites, Addresses, and Homilies* (Venice, 1838):—*Explanation of the Nicene Symbol* (Constant. 1736):—*A Panegyric on Nerses Klajensis* (St. Petersburg, 1782; Madras, 1810; Constant. 1826); besides translations from the Latin, Syriac, and Greek. See Lequien, *Oriens Christianus*, i, 1345. See also Herzog, *Real-Encyklopädie*, xix, 85 sq.; xx, 210 sq.; *Theologisches Universal-Lexikon*, s. v.; *Biography of the Saints*, vol. v; Neumann, *Versuch einer Geschichte der armenischen Literatur* (Leips. 1836), p. 148; Tchamtchenang, *Hist. of Armenia* (Venice, 1783–4, 3 vols.), iii, 58 sq.; Gieseler, *Church History* (Smith's transl.), ii, 617; Kurtz, *Lehrbuch d. Kirchengeschichte* (Mitau, 1874), p. 190, 214; Jöcher, *Allgemeines Gelehrten-Lexikon*, s. v. Nierses; Cave, *Historia literaria scriptorum ecclesiasticorum*, p. 591, 596; Malan, *Life and Times of St. Gregory the Illuminator*, with Introd. on the *Hist. of the Armenian Church*, p. 35 sq.

Nerva, MARCUS COCCEIUS, the thirteenth Roman emperor, noted for his kindness to the early Christians, was born at Narnia, in Umbria, in A.D. 27, according to Eutropius (viii, 1), or in A.D. 32, according to Dion (lxviii, 4). His family originally came from Crete; but several of his ancestors rose to the highest dignities in the Roman state. His grandfather, Cocceius Nerva, who was consul in A.D. 22, was a great favorite of the emperor Tiberius, and was one of the most celebrated jurists of his age. We learn from Tacitus that he put an end to his own life (*Ann.* vi, 28). Marcus Cocceius Nerva is first mentioned as a favorite of Nero, who bestowed upon him triumphal honors in A.D. 66, when he was prætor elect. The poetry of Nerva, which is noticed with praise by Pliny and Martial, appears to have recommended him to the favor of Nero. Nerva was employed in offices of trust and honor during the reigns of Vespasian and Titus, but he incurred the suspicion of Domitian, and was banished by him to Tarentum. On the assassination of Domitian, Sept. 18, A.D. 96, Nerva succeeded to the sovereign power, chiefly through the influence of Petronius Secundus, commander of the Prætorian cohorts, and of Parthenius, the chamberlain of the palace. The mild and equable administration of Nerva is acknowledged and praised by all ancient writers, and formed a striking contrast to the sanguinary rule of his predecessor. He discouraged all informers, recalled the exiles from banishment, relieved the people from some oppressive taxes, and granted toleration to the Christians. Many instances of his clemency and liberality are recorded by his contemporary, the younger Pliny. Nerva allowed no senator to be put to death during his reign, and practiced the greatest economy in order to relieve the wants of the poorer citizens. But his impartial administration of justice met with little favor from the Prætorian cohorts, who had been allowed by Domitian to indulge in excesses of every kind. Enraged at the loss of their benefactor and favorite, they compelled Nerva to deliver into their hands Parthenius and their own commander Petronius, both of whom they put to death. The excesses of his guards convinced Nerva that the government of the Roman empire required greater energy both of body and mind than he possessed, and he accordingly adopted Trajan, who possessed both vigor and ability to direct public affairs, as his successor, and associated him with himself in the government. By this action Nerva evinced clearly that he possessed good sense and a noble character. He died Jan. 27, A.D. 98, after a reign of sixteen months and nine days (Dion, lxviii, 4). Though he had set at liberty those who had been condemned under the intolerant reign of Domitian because they had apostatized from the pagan faith and adopted the new religion, Nerva yet failed to secure to his Christian subjects any lasting benefits, since their religion was not recognised by any public act as a *religio licita*, and hence the severe persecutions under Trajan may easily be explained. Christianity having been diffused peacefully under Nerva, had spread considerably; no sooner was Trajan on the throne than the fury of its enemies, which had been held in check, broke forth with increased violence. See the article TRAJAN. See Schaff, *Ch. Hist.* i, 163; Hase, *Ch. Hist.* p. 38; Neander, *Ch. Hist.* i, 96; Gibbon, *Decline and Fall of the Roman Empire* (Harper's ed., Index in vol. vi); Burton, *Eccles. Hist.* p. 279, 284, 298, 299; Hagenbach, *Kirchengesch. d. ersten drei Jahrhunderte*, ch. vii; Tillemont, *Hist. des Empereurs*, vol. ii; Smith, *Dict. of Greek and Roman Biogr. and Mythol.* vol. ii, s. v. (J. H. W.)

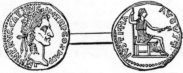

Coin of the Emperor Nerva.

Nervet, JEAN, a French prelate, was born in 1442 at Evreux. He early joined the Order of St. Augustine. Louis XI, having found talent in Nervet, attached him to his person in the capacity of almoner (1474), and selected him afterwards for confessor. His virtues and his rare prudence attracted towards him many people of consideration at the court, where he remained until the accession of Charles VIII. Nervet became successively prior of Sainte-Catherine-la-Couture of Paris, counsellor of state, abbé of Juilly, and bishop of Megara *in partibus*. He was educated at the University of Paris, and cultivated letters; he was one of the protectors of the Hellenist Chéradame. Nervet died November 2, 1525, and was buried in the cloister of Juilly. See Desfontaines, *Jugement sur les écrits nouveaux*, viii, 168; Archon, *Hist. ecclés. de la chapelle des Rois de France*, ii, 416; Dom Toussaint du Plessis, *Catalogue des abbés de Juilly; Gallia Christiana*, iv, 787, and viii, 1677.

Nescient Philosophy. See PHILOSOPHY.

Nesher. See EAGLE.

Nesmond, François de. See NESMOND, HENRI DE.

Nesmond, Henri de, a French prelate and academician, was born at Bordeaux about 1645. He descended from a family originally from Ireland, and was the son of a president in the Parliament of Bordeaux. Henri was afforded superior educational advantages, and early entered upon an ecclesiastical career. The success of his preaching caused him to be made successively abbé of Chézy (May 26, 1682) and bishop of

Montauban (Sept. 3, 1687). The differences which existed between the court of France and the holy chair delayed the papal bulls of his appointment until Oct. 13, 1692. Intrusted with the government of a diocese in which were a large number of Protestants, he succeeded by his instructions, and still more by the mildness of his zeal and his exemplary manners, in bringing many of them into the Church. He was received as counsellor in the Parliament of Toulouse April 26, 1695, was transferred to the archbishopric of Alby Aug. 15, 1703, and became abbé of the Mas-Garnier in 1715, and archbishop of Toulouse Nov. 5, 1719. In this capacity he was called upon to address Louis XIV and Louis XV in the name of the province of Languedoc. The former of these princes loved to hear him, and called him the finest speaker of his kingdom. M. de Nesmond succeeded Fléchier in the French Academy June 30, 1710. Nesmond died at Toulouse, May 27, 1727. All his wealth he left to the poor and to the hospitals. His *Discourses and Sermons*, etc., were collected and published (Paris, 1734, 12mo). One of his cousins, FRANçOIS DE NESMOND, who made him his heir, was born at Paris, Sept. 21, 1629; became bishop of Bayeux Aug. 9, 1661; and died June 16, 1715, dean of the bishops of France, in his diocese, where his memory is held in great veneration through the benefits which he has conferred. See D'Alembert, *Hist. des membres de l'Acad. Franç.* iv, 347; *Gallia Christiana* vol. xiii.

Nessa is the name of an intercalary month introduced by the ancient Arabians to bring the lunar, every third year, into conformity with the solar year. The use of this month was forbidden by Mohammed in the Koran.

Nesse, CHRISTOPHER, an English divine, was born December 26, 1621, at North Cowes (Yorkshire), and was educated at St. John's College, University of Cambridge. He took holy orders, and obtained a benefice at Cottingham, in the vicinity of Hull, as well as the lectureship in the parish of Leeds. Rejected by the established Church for non-conformity in 1662, he went to London, and took charge of a dissenting congregation in Salisbury Court, Fleet Street, with which he remained connected for thirty years. He died at London, December 26, 1705. Nesse is the author of a large number of theological and other works; but he has made himself known principally by the work entitled *History and Mystery of the Old and New Testaments, logically discussed and theologically improved* (Lond. 1690–96, 4 vols. fol.); to this work Matthew Henry is thought to owe much of his most valuable material for his *Exposition*. Other works of Nesse's of value are, *The Christian's Walk and Work on Earth:—The Christian's Crown and Glory:—Church History, from Adam: —Antidote against Popery:—A Divine Legacy:—A Discovery of the Person and Period of Antichrist* (Lond. 1679, 8vo):—*The Reigns of Times* (1681, 4to):—*Life of Pope Innocent XI*. John Dunton tells us that this book was written for him, and that the whole impression was sold in a fortnight. See Wilson, *Hist. of Dissenting Churches;* Granger, *Biog. Hist. of England*, v, 78 sq.; Allibone, *Dict. of Brit. and Amer. Authors*, ii, 1408, 1409; Hook, *Eccles. Biography*, vii, 400. (J. H. W.)

Nessus, the god of a river in Thrace which bore the same name.

Nest (קֵן. *ken*, from קָנַן, *to build*; κατασκήνωσις, lit. a *tent-dwelling*). The law in Deut. xxii, 6, 7 directs that if one falls in with a bird's-nest with eggs or young, he shall allow the dam to escape, and not take her as well as the nest. The reason Maimonides (*Moreh Nebuchim*) gives for this is, "The eggs on which the dam is sitting, or the young ones which have need of her, are not, in general, permitted to be eaten; and when the dam is allowed to escape she is not distressed by seeing her young ones carried off. It thus frequently happens that all are untouched, because that which might be taken may not be lawfully eaten." He adds, "If the law, then, be thus careful to prevent birds and beasts (for he had been alluding to the instances of this humanity of the law) from suffering pain and grief, how much more mankind!" See LAW OF MOSES.

The ingenuity with which a bird's-nest is constructed, its perfect adaptation to its intended purpose, its compactness, its hollow form, its warmth, the different materials of which it is composed, its lining, the industry and perseverance with which it is collected and put together, the art with which it is concealed—all these and other points render it impossible to look on the more elaborate specimens of birds'-nests without strong admiration. It is true there are very numerous gradations in the perfection of what we may call *art* in these structures—from the shallow cavity scratched in the ground by the partridge, to the purse of the oriole, exquisitely woven of horse-hair, and suspended from a twig, or the tiny cup of the humming-bird compactly felted of silk-cotton, and ornamented with lichens; but this endless variety is only the more admirable, because we see that each form is perfect in its kind, and answers its own purpose better than any other could have done. Various as are the materials selected by birds for the formation of their nests, they are generally chosen for one prominent quality, namely, the warmth of the young (Job xxix, 18).

The eagle is remarkable for the jealousy with which its domestic economy is removed far from human intrusion. Jehovah alludes to this in his contest with his servant Job (xxxix, 27, 28): "Doth the eagle mount up at thy command, and make her nest on high? She dwelleth and abideth on the rock, upon the crag of the rock, and the strong place: from thence she seeketh the prey, and her eyes behold afar off." The loftiness of the eagle's nest was proverbial, it was "among the stars" (Obad. 4); and "to make his nest as high as the eagle" was a phrase by which the prophets reproved the pride and ambition of man (Jer. xlix, 16 ; Hab. ii, 9). ₋ee EAGLE.

Another bird remarkable for the inaccessible localities in which it incubates is the rock-dove. See DOVE. Clefts in lofty precipices, deep holes in beetling cliffs, and shelves in dark caverns, are chosen by this bird. The narrow passes between towering rocks that cleave the elevated region on both sides of the Dead Sea are perforated with clefts and caves, which are numerously tenanted by blue rock-doves. The prophet Jeremiah takes occasion from this derisively to exhort Moab, in the prospect of his desolation by the Chaldæan king, to imitate the rock-dove: "O ye that dwell in Moab, leave the cities, and dwell in the rock, and be like the dove that maketh her nest in the sides of the hole's mouth" (Jer. xlviii, 28). It was doubtless the resemblance in habit between the rock-dwelling inhabitants of Idumæa and the rock-dove, both of whom were probably full in view from the summit of Pisgah, that suggested the metaphor which Balaam used of the Kenite, "Strong is thy dwelling-place, and thou puttest thy nest in a rock" (Numb. xxiv, 21). See KENITE.

The *gallinaceæ* usually lay their eggs in great numbers, often in a nest carelessly made on the ground, and with very little precaution against accidents or interferences from others of the same species. Hence they frequently fail in incubation, or even desert their nest. This seems to be the point of the allusion of the prophet Jeremiah: "As the partridge sitteth on eggs, and hatcheth them not; so he that getteth riches, and not by right, shall leave them in the midst of his days, and at his end shall be a fool" (Jer. xvii, 11). Such a nest we may suppose to have been in the mind of the prophet Isaiah, in the self-gratulatory soliloquy which he puts into the mouth of the conquering king of Assyria: "And my hand hath found as a nest the riches of the people; and as one gathereth eggs that are left, have I gathered all the earth: and there was none that moved

the wing, or opened the mouth, or peeped [piped]" (Isa. x, 14). A nest *on the ground*, containing *many eggs*, from which the chicks emerge *active* and *fledged*, and in which they can utter their feeble *piping*, is the figure here, and suits some gallinaceous species.

Most birds, however, resort to trees for the fabrication of their nests; and in Palestine the thick foliage of the cedars would afford peculiar advantages of shelter and concealment. The dominion exercised over the surrounding nations by the great empire of Assyria is symbolized by Ezekiel under the figure of a lofty and far-spreading cedar in Lebanon, in whose boughs all the fowls of the heaven made their nests (Ezek. xxxi, 3–6), and a like comparison indicated to Nebuchadnezzar his royal power (Dan. iv, 21). Jeremiah apostrophizes the inhabitants of Lebanon, as "making their nests in the cedars" (xxii, 23); and in the beautiful picture of nature in Psa. civ, the cedars of Lebanon which God hath planted are brought before us as the place "where the birds make their nests;" while "as for the stork, the fir-trees are her house" (ver. 17); perhaps the flat summits of old trees, a more exposed situation than in the cedar forest. See STORK.

The propensity of the swallow to affix its nest to human edifices, and of the sparrow to bring up its young in the haunts of men, is elegantly glanced at by the Psalmist, when he contrasts their familiarity with his own exile from the sanctuary (Psa. lxxxiv, 2, 3). See BIRD.

Nesterfield, ECCLESIASTICAL COUNCIL OF (*Concilium Nesterfeldense*), was held about the year 703, under Bertwald, archbishop of Canterbury, in which Wilfred of York was a second time deposed; he appealed to Rome, and his case was considered in a council held there in that year. See Inett, *Orig. Anglicanæ*, i, 133. See also WILFRED OF YORK.

Nestor, or LETOPIS NESTEROVA, the Russian Venerable Bede, the most revered name in the whole compass of his country's literature, was born in 1056. At the age of seventeen he entered the convent of Peczerich, at Kiew, where he remained until his death, about 1116. But little is known of his personal history. In the Palericon of his convent there is this beautiful testimony to his life: "Nestor labored industriously on his annals, thought of eternity, served and pleased his Creator, and died at a good old age peacefully." His *Chronicle of Russia,* which is his life-work, comes down to 1115; it has been continued by Sylvester, a monk of Kiew, afterwards bishop of Perejaslaw, and others, to 1206. There are several manuscript copies of it, and they differ somewhat from each other, so that they have become the subject of many interesting investigations both to Russian and foreign historians. They were published by Radziwill or Königsberg at St. Petersburg (1767, 4to), from a manuscript found at Königsberg, and considered by the critics as the most trustworthy extant. The first critical edition, however, was published in Germany, with a German translation by Schlözer (Gött. 1802–1809, 5 vols. 8vo), carrying the work up to the year 980; a German translation of the whole work was brought out at Leipsic in 1774, but it is faulty. The latest and best edition, entitled *Chronicon Nestoris textus, versio Latina et glossarium* (ed. Miklosisch), was brought out at Vienna (1860 sq.). This *Chronicle* is highly prized by the Russians as the oldest annals of their history. Nestor wrote also a *Patericum Peczericum,* which is a sort of biography of some of the abbots and saints of the convent of Kiew, and very valuable as the oldest document treating of Russian ecclesiastical history. Though interspersed with many absurdities and superstitions, it was first published in 1661, and has been reproduced since in divers forms. Nestor was a very learned man in his time. He understood perfectly the Greek language, and read the Byzantine historians, from whom he translated many passages, and inserted them in his *Chron-*

icle. His information he obtained from contemporaneous traditions (probably also from still more ancient Lätopisses), and he derived great advantage from the recollections of his brother in the cloister, the monk Jan, who died in 1106, at the age of ninety-one years, and who was born consequently in 1015, i. e. one year previous to the death of grand-prince Waldimir. Much, however, of Nestor's work consists of what he was enabled to record as a contemporary and an eye-witness. Truth shines evidently in all his writings. His style is equal, and resembles the Biblical books. The persons whom he mentions are made to speak in the language of the historical books of the Old Testament. He frequently interweaves sentences taken from Holy Writ, and subjoins pious moral reflections. His illustrious editor, Schlözer, says of him: "Without this brother of the cloister, what should we ever have known about the entire history of the Upper North down to the 11th century? But this *Chronicle* is still more important in relation to the people for which it was written; who, by following the example of its author, acquired a taste for reading and writing, and never lost those arts again through all the melancholy times and centuries of actual barbarism that followed." See Karamsin, *Gesch. des russichen Reiches*, vol. viii; Strahl, *Gesch. des russichen Staates*, i, 458 sq.; id. *Beiträge z. russ. Kirchengeschichte* (Halle, 1827), i, 90 sq.; *Göttinger gel. Anzeigen*, 1807, p. 263 sq.; Schlözer, *Proben russicher Annalen*, p. 27 sq.; and the biography in his edition of Nestor, i, 9 sq.; Piper, *Einleitung in die Monumentale Theologie*, § 95; Stanley, *Lect. Hist. East. Church*, p. 388; Otto, *Hist. of Russian Literature*, p. 300 sq.   (J. H. W.)

Nestorian Monastics are a class of devotees among the Nestorians (q. v.), claiming to be of the Order of St. Anthony, though they do not strictly adhere to the rules of that or any other order, and are but insignificant in number. They probably were quite powerful as a monastic body at one time, for there are a large number of monasteries now extant in the Nestorian country which these devotees named and supported. Most of these monasteries are now deserted, especially those upon the River Tigris; the rest have but few inmates except that of Ormûz, which is the most considerable, and in that there are only about fifty monks. This monastery is the residence of the patriarchs, and takes its name from Hormisdas, one of the Nestorian saints.

Nestorian Monk.

There are some other monasteries in Persia, the most considerable of which is that near Tauris. They have about twenty double convents, that is, both for monks and nuns, who have separate habitations, though but one common church. While the monks are employed in bodily labor the nuns prepare their victuals. The religious Nestorians eat no fish, drink no wine. Their Lents are six in number; viz., the grand Lent of the universal Church; that of the Apostles, which begins fifteen days before the festival of St. Peter; that of the Assumption of Our Lady; that of the Exaltation of the Holy Cross, each of fifteen days; that of Elias, or the Ninevites, which lasts eight days; and that of Christ's Nativity, which continues twenty-five days. The Nestorian monks are habited in a black gown tied with a leathern girdle. They wear, instead of a capuche, a blue turban. The nuns are habited after the same manner, excepting that they tie a kind of black veil about their heads and under their chins. They must be forty years old before they take the monastic habit. If a monk desires to quit his convent to marry, he asks leave of the pasha, and the bishop is obliged to consent to it for fear the monk might turn Mohammedan. See Brunel, *Histoire des Clergés Seculier et Regulier*, ii, 44-47.

Nestorians, a sect of early Christians, so called after Nestorius (q. v.), are generally regarded as the Protestants in Eastern Christianity, they having always opposed the regard for Mary as more than woman, and having in many other respects preserved the orthodox doctrines and authorized usages of the early Church of Christ. As a sect they claim to be of earlier origin than the age of Nestorius, and date their conversion back to the preaching of the apostle Thomas, hence some of them are called *Thomas Christians* (see below). There is besides a tradition prevalent among the Nestorians which makes them of Jewish descent, and claims for their ancestry Ur of the Chaldees, and Abraham, the patriarch; hence they sometimes call themselves *Chaldœans* (see below). But though these claims may have no foundation, it is yet to be conceded that the Nestorians are probably the oldest, as they certainly are the purest, of the Oriental churches, although, as we shall presently see, they are guilty of more or less Christological heresy, and hold some absurd superstitions, and maintain, as a sect, a service which is little more than mere formalism.

I. *Doctrinal Position.*—In the article NESTORIUS is set forth the controversy which agitated the Eastern Church in the 4th and 5th centuries regarding the person and nature of Christ, arising out of the use of ambiguous terms—$\dot{\nu}\pi\acute{o}\sigma\tau\alpha\sigma\iota\varsigma$ and $\pi\rho\acute{o}\sigma\omega\pi o\nu$ [see HYPOSTASIS]—and how peace was finally restored between the Syrian and Egyptian churches by the confession drawn up by Theodoret. It remains now to point out how the opposition organized in order to sustain Nestorius in his course, after deposition from the patriarchate, finally developed such strength as to prove a formidable antagonism to the Cyrillites, making necessary further action on the part of the emperor, who finally caused the expulsion of all Nestorians from the Roman empire, and by this action only gave development to Nestorianism in the East, by an independent and new sect, as is generally believed in the West, or by auxiliarizing an already existing sect of like tendency, as the Nestorians of to-day generally claim.

It will be seen in the article on Nestorius that, notwithstanding his deposition, his devoted and persistent adherents favored the doctrines Nestorius had taught. Including the diocesan synods and the schismatical assemblies, there were not less than nineteen or twenty meetings during the first twenty years of the controversy. Mercator gives them in order: he makes out that there were four at Rome, at Alexandria, and Constantinople; two at Ephesus; two at least held by the Orientals; and others at Antioch, Berœa, and elsewhere. Most of these we treat under their respective titles. The second at Constantinople, held Oct. 25, 431, was for the election of Maximin in succession to Nestorius; and the third, which was rather a consultation of bishops with the emperor, was for considering the best means of re-establishing the peace of the Church. The Council of Chalcedon (A.D. 451) was assembled to condemn the opposite heresy, that of Eutyches. It not only did so, but incidentally confirmed the decision of the Council of Ephesus, and expressly adapted the term $\vartheta\varepsilon o\tau\delta\kappa o\varsigma$. Two years later a council at Constantinople, among other things, condemned a letter of Ibas of Edessa that had renounced the term $\vartheta\varepsilon o\tau\delta\kappa o\varsigma$. Gelasius, bishop of Rome (A.D. 492-496), also synodically condemned the Nestorians. But whatever their favor or condemnation at papal Rome, so troublesome did these faithful Nestorians become to the government that the emperor saw himself obliged to second the efforts of the special Church council which he had called, to settle this great Christological question advisedly and finally by the expulsion from his dominions of all who failed to accept the Ephesian decision. It was thus that Nestorianism was transplanted to Assyria, and especially to Persia, where it has ever since maintained its ground, finding immediately upon its appearance there protection from the government—such favors being prompted, probably, by political opposition to Constantinople.

This colonization of Nestorianism, however, was not begun by the emperor's illiberal policy. It had taken rise much earlier. Presbyter Ibas (q. v.), for the simple purpose of giving the Persian Christians an intelligent account of the controversy, had written a letter to Mares, bishop of Hardoshir, in Persia, shortly after the union of patriarch John of Antioch and of Cyril, in which he clearly established the merits of the controversy, condemning what was amiss in Cyril, and commending only what he believed worthy of support in Nestorius, but yet evincing greater sympathy for the latter. So much moderation did Ibas exhibit in his letter, and so earnestly did he plead for peace in the Church, that the missive was not without influence. He had besides furnished Syriac translations of the works of Diodorus of Tarsus and of Theodore of Mopsuestia; and thus having an opportunity to examine for themselves into the merits of the controversy, the Assyrian and Persian Christians were numerously won over to Nestorius. Further strength was given to Nestorianism, especially in Persia, by the expulsion of the teachers from Edessa, where Nestorius's views had found willing and enthusiastic exponents. Among those whom the Persians gained over for their own Church by this intolerant policy of bishop Rabulas of Edessa we notice particularly Barsumas, who, as bishop or metropolitan of Nisibis (A.D. 435-489), contributed in no small degree to the propagation of Nestorian views in Persia and the reduction of the Cyrillites. Supported by Nerses (q. v.) the leper, also driven out of Edessa, Barsumas founded a new theological school at Nisibis. He also used his influence with the king of Persia to have him confirm the Persian Christians in their aversion to the Cyrillian Council of Ephesus, and in their adhesion to the Antiochian and Nestorian theology; and he even so far controlled king Feroze that this monarch expelled those Christians who had espoused the Cyrillian views, and set Nestorians in their place, putting them in possession of the principal seat of ecclesiastical authority in Persia, the see of Seleucia, which from that time to our own day has always been filled by the patriarch of the Nestorians. Indeed, such was the zeal and success of Barsumas that the Nestorians who still remain in Chaldæa, Persia, Assyria, and the adjacent countries, consider him really their parent and founder. He certainly contributed much, not only to the upbuilding of Nestorianism in Persia, but to its spread into Egypt, Syria, Arabia, India, Tartary, and China, whence went his theological students from the school at Nisibis. "The Nestorians," says Mosheim (Eccles. Hist. i, 93), "after they had obtained a fixed residence in Persia, and had located the

VI.—31

head of their sect at Seleucia, were as successful as they were industrious in disseminating their doctrines in the countries lying without the Roman empire. It appears from unquestionable documents, still existing, that there were numerous societies in all parts of Persia, in India, in Armenia, in Arabia, in Syria, and in other countries, under the jurisdiction of the patriarch of Seleucia during this (the 6th) century." Of the 7th century he says (ibid. i, 499), "The Christian religion was in this century diffused beyond its former bounds, both in the Eastern and Western countries. In the East, the Nestorians, with incredible industry and perseverance, labored to propagate it from Persia, Syria, and India among the barbarous and savage nations inhabiting the deserts and the remotest shores of Asia. In particular, the vast empire of China was enlightened by their zeal and industry with the light of Christianity." In A.D. 498 a Church council convened at Seleucia, and by this body the Nestorian doctrine was made the faith of the Persian Church. The dogmas then adopted amount to what follows: 1. That in the Saviour of the world there were two hypostases, or persons, of which the one was divine, or the Eternal Word, and the other human, or the man Christ Jesus; 2. That these two hypostases had only one outward appearance; 3. That the union between the Son of God and the Son of Man was formed in the moment of the Virgin's conception, and is never to be dissolved; 4. That this union was not of nature or person, but of will and affection; 5. That Christ was to be carefully distinguished from God, who dwelt in him as in a temple; 6. That Mary was to be called the mother of Christ ($X\rho\iota\sigma\tau o\tau\delta\kappa o\varsigma$), and not the mother of God ($\Theta\varepsilon o\tau\delta\kappa o\varsigma$). How far Nestorius himself maintained these views will never clearly appear, as his own expositions of Christology are only extant in fragments, and they even are full of contradictions; but certainly the doctrine as here laid down by the Council of Seleucia involves a denial of the unity of Christ's character. "The Nestorian Christ," says Dr. Shedd, in his History of Christian Doctrine, "is two persons—one divine, and one human. The important distinction between a 'nature' and a 'person' is not observed, and the consequence is that there are two separate and diverse selves in Jesus Christ. Instead of a blending of the two natures into only one self, the Nestorian scheme places two selves side by side, and allows only a moral and sympathetic union between them. The result is that the acts of each nature derive no character from the qualities of the other. There is no divine humiliation, because the humanity is confessedly the seat of humiliation, and the humanity is by itself, unblended in the unity of a common self-consciousness. And there is no exaltation of the humanity, because the divinity is confessedly the source of the exaltation, and this also is insulated and isolated for the same reason. There is God, and there is man; but there is no God-man."

II. Ecclesiastical History.—When the Sassanidæ, by restoring the Zoroastrian mode of worship, had overthrown the empire of the Parthians, the previous good understanding came to an end, as they required theirs to be not only the predominant, but the only religion of the empire. Yet the later rulers of this dynasty appear to have cared more for politics than for religion, and the Christians, i. e. the Nestorians, were left in peace, except in times of war against the Greek emperors. Pherozes (or Feroze or Firuz), as we have seen above, had been well disposed by Barsumas in favor of the Nestorians, but he had bitterly opposed the Roman Catholics, and persecuted them. Cavades, or Cobad, his successor (448-531), after he came back from the land of the Huns, whither he had fled out of prison, commenced against the Greek empire a war which lasted four years, and which led to a persecution of the Christians. (He had commanded the community of women. This led to an insurrection of the nobility, and Cavades was thrown into prison, whence his sister managed to help him escape and flee the country. His brother, Jamapes, who was appointed in his place, recalled the obnoxious law; and as it had probably had also a demoralizing effect on the Christians, Badæus, then patriarch of the Nestorians, with the assent of this new and more liberal ruler, held a synod to remedy the evil.) According to Barhebræus (*Bibl. Or.* ii, 409), Cavades reascended the throne with the aid of the Greeks, and sought to force the Nestorians to unite again with the Romish Church. This, however, does not appear trustworthy. About the end of Cavades's reign a schism took place among the Nestorians, which is said to have lasted twelve years, and during this time two patriarchs, Nerses and Elisæus, were elected by the opposing parties, each of which in turn appointed bishops from among his followers. After Nerses had died in prison and Elisæus had been deposed by a synod, the bishops elected Paulus, who however filled the office but a few months, and was succeeded by Mar Aba I, or "the Great" (536–552), a Magian converted to Christianity. He translated the liturgy of the Nestorians from the Greek into Syriac; and this version continues in use at the present day among the Nestorians. Mar Aba I showed also great activity in restoring order and discipline in the Church, visiting the different dioceses, sending pastoral addresses to distant churches, and holding in 544 a synod in which it was declared that neither patriarchs nor bishops should thenceforth be allowed to marry—a regulation which has ever since been observed in the Nestorian Church. He also confirmed the former canons, and ordered that, while adhering strictly to the Nicene Creed, the system of Theodore of Mopsuestia should form the basis of the Scripture exegesis. On account of the previously mentioned schism, when there were often two bishops appointed to the same see, Mar Aba I deposed the unworthy dignitaries; and in cases where two equally deserving filled the office, he retained the oldest, and the other had to return to his former condition until the office became vacant again. Patriarch Ezechiel (577–580), as soon as he entered into office, held a synod (Feb., 577), whose principal result was the promulgation of an edict against the Messalians. As the Monophysites had made great progress in Persia under Cavades, and especially under Chosroes I (531–579) [see KHOSRU], Jacob Baradæus appointed as œcumenical metropolitan, in the place of the imprisoned patriarch, a metropolitan of the East, Achudemes, whom Barhebræus considers as the first maphrian (q. v.) of the East. Chosroes, according to popular tradition, became a Christian in the latter part of his life, and recommended his successors to avoid war with Greece. As for himself, he seems to have been often at war with that country, and to have on those occasions persecuted the Christians. His son, Hormuzd IV, as also Chosroes II, proved more friendly to the Nestorians, especially the latter, who compelled all Christians in the empire to join them. He afterwards, however, persecuted them on account of their having elected Gregorius as patriarch against his will; and after Gregorius's death, in 608, he forbade their appointing another. The office remained vacant for twenty years, until Shiruje (Siroës), the son of Chosroes II, ascended the throne. He proved favorable to the Christians of all denominations. His successors also left them in peace, being too weak and too much occupied in preserving their position and life to do otherwise.

Under the caliphs the Nestorians were seldom persecuted; on the contrary, they claim that they received several charters, the authenticity of some of which, however, is doubted. The first, they say, was obtained by patriarch Jesujab of Gadala (628–647), who saw the last Persian kings. He went himself to Mohammed, and asked him for it. It was printed by Gabriel Sionita (Paris, 1630). Indeed, Mohammed is supposed to owe his imperfect knowledge of Christianity to a Nestorian monk, Sergius; and it is therefore but natural to suppose that from him the sect received many privileges, so that it obtained great consideration among the

Arabians, and exerted an influence upon their culture, and thus upon the development of philosophy and science in general. The words of the world's savant, Alexander von Humboldt, in the second volume of his *Kosmos* (Stuttg. and Tübing. 1847, p. 247 sq.), on the connection of Nestorianism with the culture and physical science of the Arabians, are worthy of note here: "It was one of the wondrous arrangements in the system of things that the Christian sect of the Nestorians, which has exerted a very important influence on the geographical extension of knowledge, was of service even to the Arabians before the latter found their way to learned and disputatious Alexandria; that Christian Nestorianism, in fact, under the protection of the arms of Islam, was able to penetrate far into Eastern Asia. The Arabians, in other words, gained their first acquaintance with Grecian literature through the Syrians, a kindred Shemitic race; while the Syrians themselves, scarcely a century and a half before, had first received the knowledge of Grecian literature through the anathematized Nestorians. Physicians who had been educated in the institutions of the Greeks, and at the celebrated medical school founded by the Nestorian Christians at Edessa, in Mesopotamia, were, as early as the times of Mohammed, befriended by him and by Abu-Bekr, in Mecca." Jesujab also obtained another charter from Omar, together with complete exemption from taxes for himself, his brothers, servants, and followers, which it is said lasted until the beginning of the 14th century. Ali gave Maremes, a follower of Jesujab, then bishop of Nisibis, on account of his having supplied his army with food, a recommendation for all his followers to spare the Christians. Similar securities were given to their patriarchs by Muktedir-billah, Kader-billah, and their successors, and Jesujab of Adiabene (650–660) was able to write to Simeon, metropolitan of Persia, that the Arabs were not only not opposed to Christianity, but held it in high respect, showing great regard to the priests and people, and even supporting the churches and convents. As the Nestorians were distinguished for their learning and activity, many of them held high official positions. They were especially renowned, as we have already learned from Humboldt, as physicians and as secretaries to the caliphs, and so highly and favorably were these regarded that no election of patriarchs or other important ecclesiastical event took place without their being consulted. In this manner the Nestorians acquired great preponderance over the other Christian sects, and the caliphs Kajim-beamr-illah and Muktedir-billah declared officially that the patriarch Sabarjesu (surnamed Zanbur) and Ebedjesu should have authority not only over the Nestorians, but also over the Roman Catholics, or Melchites (q. v.), and the Jacobites (q. v.). With the exception of a short persecution under Harûn-al-Raschid, we find but two during that entire period: the first, chiefly directed against the Nestorians, by Mutewekkil, was occasioned by his physician, Bochtjesu, having displeased him; the second, by Hakim-beamr-illah, was directed with great vigor against all Christians, and even against the Jews, but it of course did not extend beyond his own dominions of Syria, Palestine, and Egypt. The power of the physicians and secretaries also proved injurious at length, as they went so far as to arbitrarily appoint and depose patriarchs, making the caliphs confirm their action. (Christianity, it may be stated here, had been introduced into Arabia at a very early period. Both the Nestorians and the Jacobites sought this field to propagate their own doctrines, and the former proved successful in that undertaking. Under the caliphs they spread not only in Arabia, but through Syria and Palestine, and under Mar Aba II [patriarch 742–752] a bishop had to be appointed for the Nestorians distributed throughout Egypt. This bishop was subject to the see of Damascus; in later times they had also a metropolitan of Egypt. The bishops of the different parts of Arabia were at first subject to the metropolitans of Persia, to whose diocese belonged also the East Indies, the western shores of which, at least, were still Christian in the early part of the 7th century.)

After Bagdad had been built and become the abode of the caliphs, the patriarchs selected it also as their residence in A.D. 762. They were elected there, but ordained at Seleucia. Ananjesu II was the first patriarch elected at Bagdad. The patriarch was called *yazelich*, i. e. catholicos, and in the 13th century the yazelich had no less than twenty-five metropolitans under his supervision. Says an ecclesiastical historian: "The Nestorians had now become widely extended. They occupied, almost to the exclusion of other Christian sects, the region which forms the modern kingdom of Persia, in all parts of which they had churches. They were numerous in Armenia, Mesopotamia, and Arabia. They had churches in Syria and in the island of Cyprus. They had churches among the mountains of Malabar in India. They had numerous churches in the vast regions of Tartary, from the Caspian Sea to Mount Imaus, and beyond, through the greater part of what is now known as Chinese Tartary, and even in China itself. The names of twenty-five metropolitan sees are on record, which of course embraced a far greater number of bishoprics, and still more numerous societies or churches." Mar Aba II resided at Wasit, and after the building of Sermeura by Mutasim, in the year 220 of the Hegira, some of the patriarchs chose it as their residence. When Hulagu Khan took Bagdad, in 1258, patriarch Machicha caused the Christians of all sects to assemble in a church, and saved them by stratagem from the hands of the Mongols. Hulagu and most of his followers were not badly disposed towards the Christians, and particularly towards the Nestorians, partly because of a common enmity against the Mohammedans, and partly because their religion, Buddhism, had borrowed so much of its form from Nestorianism, and also because a large number of their wives were at least nominal Christians, and some of their leaders too. This was especially the case in the land of the Keraït, or Krite-Tartars, where, according to divers accounts, Nestorianism had been flourishing since the 11th century, and whose rulers seem to have embraced it. Their title, Ung(h), or Bang Khan, could readily be derived from a perversion of the name John, and thus have given rise to the tradition of the presbyter or priest John [see JOHN, PRESTER] being a mighty king, which afterwards, when its fictitious character was recognised, was transferred to the (until then unknown) Christian king of Ethiopia (see Gould, *Myths of the Mid. Ages*, p. 30 sq.; Mosheim, *Historia Tartarorum Eccles.* [Helmst. 1741]; Neander, *Kirchengesch.* v, 84 sq.). Zenghis Khan himself took to wife a daughter of his vanquished enemy Bang Khan, Toghrul, and his son Jaghatai, according to Marco Polo, became a Christian. The family of the Bang Khan of Tenduch remained also allied to the imperial family down to the days of Marco Polo; and the chief of the Minorites, John of Monte Corvino, succeeded in inducing a prince of that country, successor of the Bang Khan, whom he calls George, together with a large number of his followers, to become reconciled with the Romish Church in 1292. This union, however, was of but short duration, as his son in 1299, with all his adherents, returned to Nestorianism. The same John of Monte Corvino (q. v.) built the first Christian church at Peking, with the assent of Kublaï Khan, and baptized six thousand people, for which he was by the pope appointed *Archiepiscopus Cambaliensis*. Assemani gives the names of a number of Christian princes or rulers of the family of Zenghis Khan. Arghun Khan, who reigned after the return of the family to Mohammedanism, promised to become a Christian after taking Jerusalem. Kaigatu, son of Abaga, was a Christian, according to Haytho. Cassan was at first in favor of the Mohammedans, who had aided him in ascending the throne, and his general, Neuruz, persecuted the Christians, but he changed after-

wards, and greatly favored them. Chodabende, second son of Arghun, called by the Tartars Oldshaïtu, was led by his mother to become a Christian, like her, and was baptized under the name of Nicholas, but after her death he returned to Islamism, and took the name of Mohammed Ghaiath-ed-din; his son, Abu Saïd, surnamed Behadur Khan, was probably of the same religion, as were also his followers, under whom the empire was divided between several dynasties. It remained thus divided until Timur reunited it. After him the Turcomans ruled over Mesopotamia, Chaldæa, Media, and Persia. His successors founded the Mongol empire in India and the Turkish empire in Western Asia.

The long and uninterrupted peace enjoyed by the Christians under the rule of the Arabs and Mongols had led to a great expansion of Nestorianism in Eastern Asia. Hulagu had (according to Haytho) given to Christians the command of camps and of whole states, and appointed a palace in Bagdad for the residence of patriarch Machicha. Abaga Khan confirmed this gift, but Machicha was obliged to leave the town on account of a disturbance he had himself occasioned (by causing a Christian renegade to be thrown into the Tigris), and retired to Arbela. The return of Achmed Khan, Chodabende, and their successors to Islamism put an end to the favor of the Christians, but we find no evidence of their being really oppressed until the reign of Timur, who persecuted both Christians and Mohammedans. Communications with the distant East were now broken up, and the churches there gradually died out. Islamism, on the contrary, gained ground daily, and destroyed the Christian communities in Tartary and India. The same was subsequently done in Persia by the fanatical Shiites. and in other parts of Asia by the Mohammedan dynasties. To these causes must be added that the popes, especially since the appearance of the Mongols, who showed themselves favorable to the Christians, maintained an active correspondence with their princes, and sent missionaries who opposed the Nestorians, till, with the single exception of a few communities scattered through India, and now known as *Thomas Christians*, they were almost entirely confined to the wild mountains and the valleys of Kurdistan and to Armenia. Here, under the Turkish dominion, they remain to this day, with a separate patriarch, who from 1559 till the 17th century resided at Mosul, but has since dwelt in an almost inaccessible valley on the borders of Turkey and Persia. They are very ignorant and poor, and have been much reduced by war, persecution, disease, and want.

III. *Nestorians of the Church of Rome.*—A portion of the Nestorians, especially those in cities, united from time to time, under the name of *Chaldæans*, with the Roman Church, subject to a patriarch of their own. He resided first at Bagdad, and afterwards at Mosul; but a division arising among them, in 1551 the patriarchate became divided, at least for a time, and a new patriarch was consecrated by pope Innocent IX, whose successors fixed their residence in the city of Ormuz, in the mountainous parts of Persia. where they still continue, distinguished by the name of *Simeonites*.

It is difficult to determine the early relation of the Christians of Persia to the see of Rome, yet without a brief review of their early history it is not well possible to understand the progress of Romanism in the Nestorian country, and we therefore insert here as much as is essential for the purpose of affording the reader a complete history of Nestorianism. It is very likely that Christianity was introduced into Persia as early as the days of the apostles, but the whole history of the empire at that time is so uncertain that it is impossible to arrive at any definite statements as to its progress. Under the Arsacides, who were thoroughly indifferent in religious matters, it is likely that the Church was permitted to spread unmolested, and Barhebræus and others only mention one persecution of short duration. Trajan, however, persecuted the Christians as far as his power extended throughout the provinces during his wars. The bishop of the chief town of Seleucia-Ctesiphon gradually became the head of the Christian Church in Persia and the more remote Eastern countries. Yet when Papa, bishop of Seleucia, sent Simeon and Shadost as his representatives to the Council of Nice (A.D. 325), we still find a John, bishop of Persia, sent also to the same assembly as representative of the churches of Persia and the East Indies. And although Jaballaha, archbishop of Seleucia, in the synod of A.D. 420, invested the bishops of Persia with the office of metropolitans, it is only Jesujab of Adiabne (654-660), his pupil and successor Georgius (660-680), or, finally, Timotheus (778-820), who brought them into absolute subjection to the see of Seleucia. But as the frequent wars with the Romans rendered the journey difficult and sometimes impossible, it was at last neglected, and Shachlupha, who died in 182 (according to Amru in 244; see Assemani, *Bibl. Or.* iv, 42), was the first who was ordained at Seleucia. They thus acquired a certain degree of independence. Papa, the successor of Shachlupha, received the title of archbishop; subsequent ones took that of patriarch, and claimed the same rank as those of the Western Church. This, Assemani states (*Bibl. Or.* iii, 427; iv, 80), was first done by Babæus (498-503) at a synod held in 499. He calls him the first Nestorian bishop of Seleucia, and asserts that his three predecessors—Dadjesu, Babæus, and Acacius—remained true to the Roman Catholic doctrine, and to their obedience to the see of Antioch. Yet Dadjesu already held a synod (430-465), in which it was declared that no complaints or accusations could ever be brought against the bishop of Seleucia, to whom all owed unquestioning obedience. In the Arabic *Synodicon* and *Nemocanon* it is further stated that it is not allowable to complain of him to the Western patriarchs, nor to appeal to them from his decisions: this is by Assemani considered as a later Nestorian interpolation. But Babæus and Acacius must have been weak prelates, for it appears from the canons of the times that the morals of the clergy became very lax under their rule; and Acacius, who formerly belonged to the school of Edessa, and therefore held the Nestorian doctrines, being sent to Constantinople as Persian ambassador, joined there in anathematizing Nestorius, but after his return never acted against the Nestorians. He complained also, according to Barhebræus (see Assemani, *Bibl. Or.* iii, 383, note), that Xenajas, monophysite bishop of Mabug (Hierapolis), known by the Greek name of Philoxenus, as the translators of the N. T. into Syriac called him, denominated him and his adherents "Nestorians," while he had no knowledge whatever of Nestorius nor of his heresy (!). This seems, then, to be the origin of the name. They called themselves "Chaldæans," a name which now is used only for the Nestorians reconciled with the Romish Church; they claim that the appellation of Nestorians is wrong, as Nestorius never was their patriarch, and they do not even understand his language, and that, moreover, he is posterior to them. Although these early patriarchs did not venture to break openly with the see of Rome, Babæus—originally a layman, and, as such, married— who filled the see of Seleucia after a two-years' vacancy, was the first to act towards it in a fearless manner. He held a synod in which it was declared, 1, that all that had passed between Barsumas and Acacius (who had excommunicated each other) should be forgotten, and their correspondence destroyed; 2, that the patriarch, bishops, priests, and monks should be allowed to marry one wife (not several, as had previously been sometimes the case; see Assemani, *De catholicis seu patriarchis Chaldæorum et Nestorianorum Commentarius* [Rome, 1775, 4to], p. 18); 3, that the patriarch of Seleucia was entitled to absolute obedience; 4, that the bishops should meet their metropolitan every two years instead of yearly, and the patriarch every four instead of every two years, to consider Church matters, and that in the month of October, the patriarch having the privi-

lege of calling the meeting earlier. Barhebræus says, in reference to the second canon, that Babæus commanded his successors to marry under penalty of interdict, and ordered also the bishops and presbyters to marry again after their wife's death, which is evidently an erroneous statement (see *Bibl. Or.* p. 429). His successors were of the same opinions: all the episcopal sees were filled by Nestorian bishops, and they all sought to increase their party. Besides them there labored also for the same object a number of writers, and particularly the monks of numerous convents which they established in Assyria, and among whom we must notice as the most ancient and most renowned those of Nisibis. They produced not only learned theologians and efficient priests, but also distinguished physicians and philosophers; they translated the Greek classics, namely, Aristotle, Hippocrates, and Galen; they were in that age of darkness the only depositaries of learning, and the teachers of the surrounding barbarians. They had schools in many parts of the country. Besides the school at Nisibis, there was founded at about the same time, by Æacius, also from Edessa, a school at Seleucia. It was revived in 530, and was in existence as late as 605. A school was also established at Dorkina in A.D. 585. At Bagdad were two schools in 832, and two others were in its neighborhood. Schools existed besides at Terhana, Mahuza, Maraga, and Adiabene, in Assyria, and at Maraga, in Aderbijan. There were also schools in Elam, Persia, Korassan, and Arabia. The school at Nisibis had a three-years' course of study. The studies, to a great extent, were theological; but to the study of the Bible there was added in the schools generally the study of grammar, rhetoric, poetry, dialectics, arithmetic, geometry, music, astronomy, medicine, etc. (comp. Anderson, *Oriental Churches*, i, 168).

The first among the Nestorians who embraced Roman Catholicism was the metropolitan Sahaduna, who was sent by Siroës, king of Persia, as ambassador to the court of Byzantium, together with the newly-elected patriarch, Jesujab of Gadala, in 628. Shortly afterwards king Heraclius took a journey to Assyria, and invited many Nestorians and Monophysites to join the Romish Church. Sahaduna, declared free by patriarch Maremes, was excommunicated by his successor Jesujab of Adiabene for having three times openly professed Nestorianism, and as often recanted again. Their second reunion with the Romish Church was merely fictitious. Pope Innocent IV had sent some bishops with an address to Rabban Ara, vicar of the East (not "patriarch," as Raynaldus has it), who was a Nestorian. Ara answered with true Oriental devotion in 1247, and recommended to the pope the archbishop of Jerusalem and his brethren in Syria, adding to it a confession of faith drawn up by the archbishop of Nisibis, and signed by two other archbishops and three bishops, in which Mary was designated as χριστοτόκος. This is also the nature of the works of the Jacobite patriarch Ignatius, and of the maphrian John. Pope Nicholas IV, in 1288, sent an address, together with a confession of faith, to patriarch Jaballaha (1281-1317), to which his successor, Benedict XI, obtained an answer in 1304, in which the Church of Rome is called the mother and teacher of all others, and the pope the head pastor of Christianity. From these expressions, and from the accompanying apparently orthodox confession of faith, Assemani concludes that Jaballaha connected himself with the Romish Church. However true this inference may have been of Jaballaha's individual opinions, they certainly exercised no influence over his followers. At the beginning of the 14th century pope John XXII made a vigorous effort for the total suppression of the Nestorians. He sent letters to the patriarch of Jerusalem on the subject (A.D. 1326). By this time both Nestorians and Jacobites (who held the Eutychian heresy that there was but one nature in Christ) had exclusive establishments. In the pope's letter it is stated that both these sects "habentes illic distinctas ecclesias, in quibus errores et hæreses hujusmodi, non sine magnis suarum et muttorum aliorum animarum periculis publice dogmatisan." The patriarch is accordingly urged to exterminate them. On the other hand, during the pontificate of Eugenius IV, in 1445, a number of Nestorians residing in the island of Cyprus, together with their metropolitan, Timothy of Tarsus, were induced by the missionary archbishop Andreas to join the Romish Church. A more enduring reunion took place in the 16th century; the Nestorians were already greatly reduced in numbers, and, with the exception of the Christians of St. Thomas in India, were all restricted again within the limits of the mountains of Kûrdistan. The patriarchate had become hereditary, the nephew succeeding the uncle in that office. At the death of patriarch Simeon in 1551, his nephew, Bar Mama, with the aid of the only remaining metropolitan, Ananjesu, assumed the office. The three remaining bishops of Arbela, Salmas, and Aderbijan (which in themselves were sufficient to elect a patriarch), assembled a number of priests, monks, etc., at Mosul, and elected John Sulaca, monk or abbot of the convent of Hormuzd, as patriarch. In order to give their patriarch an advantage over Simeon Denha Bar Mama, they sent him to Rome to be ordained. On his return he was made prisoner in Amid (Diarbekir), at the instigation of his rival, according to Assemani, and killed in prison. Another was at once appointed in his place, and matters continued thus for about one hundred years. Simeon Denha, however, sustained by those Nestorians who had remained true to their Church, did not surrender his office, but retained it until his death in 1559, when his adherents appointed another, who, as well as his successors after him, took the name of Elias. Among them was one who, at the request of pope Paul V, sent, in 1607 and 1609, orthodox confessions of faith to Rome, and in a synod held a short time before his death at Amid (in 1617) submitted to the pope's requisitions. The union which resulted was, however, disturbed again by his successors. At last, in 1684, pope Innocent XI appointed a patriarch, who resided in Amid (Diarbekir), as his successors afterwards did, and took the name of Joseph, which they have retained. Since then there is a patriarch of the Chaldæans (Nestorians who have united with the Church of Rome) who is named Joseph, and resides at El-Kushmur, Mosul (in the convent of St. Hormisdas); while there is another for the Nestorians, called Simeon, who claims also to be the "patriarch of the Chaldæans." He resides in the mountains of Kûrdistan, near Julamerk. The present Chaldæan community in the East—composed of converts from the Nestorians to the papacy—may be set down as not exceeding 20,000 souls, scattered from Diarbekir to the frontiers of Persia, and from the borders of Tyari to Bagdad—a district which once contained a vast Nestorian population. Many of these "Chaldæans" sigh for a reform in their Church. The Chaldæan portion of Nestorians, i. e. the Romanized Nestorians, are governed by a patriarch and six bishops, but these have lately been pensioned by the Propaganda, the patriarch receiving a yearly salary of 20,000 piastres, or £200, and the bishops sums varying from 2000 to 8000 piastres each. Through the influence of the French embassy in 1845, Mar Zeya obtained a firman from Constantinople acknowledging him as patriarch of the Chaldæans. This was the first recognition by the Ottoman Porte of the new community. But the patriarch soon discovered that his functions were virtually exercised by the Propaganda. He grew weary of the interference of the Latin missionaries, and resisted their demands. Various charges were brought against him in consequence, and he was summoned to Rome to answer for himself. He chose rather to resign his office, and was succeeded in 1846 by Mar Yûsef. In effect, the Chaldæans have no longer an independent existence. They are a section of the Romish Church, their connection with which, while on the one hand it has introduced among them schools and education after the European manner, has on the other infected them with deeper superstitions; and the only benefit which they have derived from a change of name and communion is the promise of political protection from France, with occasional presents of ecclesiastical vestments, pictures of saints, and rosaries—"Gifts," says Mr. Badger, "which they know not how to use, and show no disposition to learn." It is worthy of note that, notwithstanding the number of the Church rituals, and the extent of country over which they are scattered, there is a striking uniformity in all the copies now in use both among the Nestorians and "Chaldæans," except where these latter have omitted parts of the original text, or altered it to suit their present conformity with Rome. The only way of accounting for this coincidence is afforded by the operation of that canon which made it obligatory upon all the metropolitans and bishops to appear in person or by proxy to testify of their faith and obedience before the catholicos—that is, the patriarch. Yet it appears that there is no standard confession of faith—nothing entitled to be considered a symbol of the doctrines held by this community. See CHALDÆANS; NESTORIAN MONASTICS.

IV. The *Christians of St. Thomas*, in East India, are a branch of the Nestorians. They are named after the apostle Thomas, who is supposed to have preached the Gospel in that country. It is probable also that during the persecution in Persia a number of Christians emigrated to India. A bishop and priest, it is said, went in 345 from Jerusalem to Malabar. Cosmas Indicopleustes (in the 6th century, about 530) speaks of a Church in Malabar. At Calliana there was a bishop ordained in Persia, and in the island of Ceylon a Church with a presbyter, deacon, etc., also ordained in Persia, but these served simply for the Persian merchants in the island, the inhabitants not being Christians. About 570 Bud, the presbyter, visited the churches of India as periodeutes (an office still existing among the Nestorians; see Assem. *Bibl. Or.* iii, 219), but Jesujab of Adiabene (patriarch, 850-860) complained in his letters to Simeon, the metropolitan of Persia, that through his fault and that of his predecessors the churches of India were in a very bad state (it was patriarch Timotheus who first gave them a metropolitan [see below]), and that Christianity had almost died out in Korassan. He commanded the readers no longer to obey their bishop, who was deposed by a synod of Seleucia, and to elect a new one to be sent to him for ordination. It is probable that Christianity spread thence into China, and a stone monument discovered there (whose authenticity there does not seem to be any reasonable ground to doubt) testifies to the success of the Nestorian Church from the time of its introduction under Jesujab of Gadala in 636-781. Salibazacha (patriarch, 714-726) appointed the first metropolitan of China. About the same time there were also metropolitans appointed to Herat and Samarcand. Nestorianism spread subsequently also into Tartary.

But to return to the Nestorians of St. Thomas. They first attained to a metropolitanate in the 8th century. The first incumbent of the office was patriarch Timotheus (A.D. 778-820), and since then their bishops also have been immediately appointed by the patriarchs. They secured from the different governments great privileges, which date chiefly from the beginning of the 9th century. This and their great increase in numbers led them to establish a state and to elect a king, after the death of which their little kingdom fell into subjection to the emperor of Cochin-China. In consequence of the quarrels of the Indian princes with each other—quarrels of which the Mohammedans knew how to take advantage—they were gradually much oppressed, and in 1502 they were induced to offer the crown to the renowned Vasco de Gama, who had landed on their shores. Their connection with the patriarch of the Nestorians appears to have soon come to an end. About 1120-1130 their spiritual chief is said to have gone to Constantinople for the purpose of being made bishop, and thence to Rome. In after-times the Indian churches were reduced to a very small number, only one deacon remaining, who held all ecclesiastical offices. On this account Georgius and Josephus were sent in 1490 to the Nestorian patriarch Simeon to ask him to give them a bishop. They were both ordained priests, and the two monks, Thomas and John, sent back with them as bishops. John remained in India, settling at Cranganor, but Thomas soon went back again. Patriarch Elias († 1502) instituted three monks, Jaballaha as the metropolitan, Jacob and Denha as bishops, and sent them with Thomas to India. They found Mar John still alive, and stated that they discovered 30,000 Christian families, distributed in twenty provinces; later Portuguese authorities restrict the number to 16,000 families. These gradually declined, being oppressed in many ways, and were thus led to place themselves under the protection of Portugal, offering to recognise king Emmanuel as their only ruler. This led to their ruin, for they were then treated worse than ever by the native princes, and afterwards oppressed by the Portuguese. Papal emissaries—namely, Jesuits—were sent to them, who sought to subject them to the pope by violence and cunning. The archbishop of Goa, Alexius Menez (q. v.), obliged them to recognise the decisions of the synod held in 1599 at Diamper, so that but few communities, and those lost in the mountains, remained true to the faith of their forefathers (comp. Marsden, *Hist. of Christian Churches and Sects,* p. 99).

Two centuries had elapsed without any particular information concerning the Nestorian Christians in the interior of India. It was doubted by many if they were still in existence, when they were visited by Dr. Claudius Buchanan in 1807. He found in the neighborhood of Travancore the Syrian metropolitan and his clergy. They were much depressed, but they still numbered fifty-five churches. They made use of the liturgy of Antioch, in the Syrian language. They had many old and valuable copies of the Scriptures. One of these, a Syrian manuscript of high antiquity, they presented to Dr. Buchanan, by whom it was placed in the university library at Cambridge. He describes the doctrines of the Syrian Christians as few in number, but pure, and agreeing in essential points with those of the Church of England. There were then, he computed, 200,000 Syrian Christians in the south of India, besides the Indians who speak the Malabar language, and are subject to the Church of Rome. Dr. Buchanan thus describes the appearance of Mar Dionysius the metro-

politan: "He was dressed in a vestment of dark-red silk, a large golden cross hung from his neck, and his venerable beard reached below his girdle. On public occasions he wears the episcopal mitre, and a muslin robe is thrown over his under garment; and in his hand he bears the crosier, or pastoral staff. He is a man of highly respectable character in his Church; eminent for his piety, and for the attention he devotes to his sacred functions." Later visitors speak in less glowing terms of this interesting people. Their general ignorance seems to have been much greater than Dr. Buchanan was led to suppose, and they observe superstitions with which he does not appear to have been made acquainted. But in 1853, almost simultaneously with the restoration of the patriarchate of the Chaldæans, those subject to the Romish Church threw off the yoke out of hatred towards the Jesuits. The barefooted Barnabites have, in recent times, been trying with more zeal than success to bring them again into the Romish communion. The Christians of St. Thomas are still considered to number about 70,000, forming an independent state under the protectorate of Great Britain, and governed by their priests and elders. They honor the memory of Theodore and Nestorius in their Syriac liturgy, and adhere to the Nestorian patriarchs. See CHRISTIANS OF ST. THOMAS.

Besides these Nestorians, there are yet some 200,000 Jacobites around the coasts of Malabar and Travancore. These appear to have gone there only since the 16th century, perhaps on account of the above-mentioned reaction against Romanism. The Jacobite patriarch sent Gregory of Jerusalem as metropolitan to India; the office of maphrian was afterwards held successively by Andreas, Basilius, John, and Thomas, who in 1709 and 1720 wrote to the Jacobite patriarch Ignatius. In his last letter, among other information, he states that in 1709 Gabriel of Nineveh, who was sent to him as metropolitan by patriarch Elias, and whom he received because he recognised two natures and two persons in Christ, had since been discovered by him to be a heretic (Nestorian). Anterior conversions to Jacobitism as well as the existence of anterior Jacobite communities in India appear doubtful. To this must be added that there are said to be four Jacobite bishops in India, one of whom resides in Cochin-China. See JACOBITES.

V. We now return to the *Nestorians of Persia* and the neighboring countries. Like the Christians of St. Thomas, these too had perished from the knowledge of European Christendom, and their existence had been almost forgotten when the missionary enterprise of the

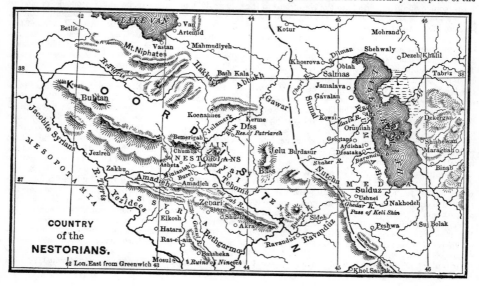

COUNTRY of the NESTORIANS.

American Protestant churches again brought them into notice. Attention was particularly called to them in 1830 by Messrs. Smith and Dwight, missionaries of the American Board of Commissioners for Foreign Missions, who, while on an exploring missionary tour, visited the Nestorians. They embodied their observations in a publication entitled *Researches.* From this source and other works of Badger (below quoted), and Dr. Anderson's *Oriental Missions,* we derive the following statements: Dividing the Turkish from the Persian empire is a wild range of mountains, now called Kûrdistan, which includes within its boundaries portions of the ancient Assyria, Media, and Armenia. In the most inaccessible parts of this district the Nestorians dwell, about 100,000 strong. They are still governed by "meliks," or kings, chosen from their own people by the popular voice irregularly expressed. The office of these chiefs is usually hereditary in the same family. The Turkish government, however, is making vigorous efforts, through the agency of the neighboring Kûrds, to reduce these independent Nestorians to a state of vassalage. Dwelling in these mountainous recesses, their independence is dearly purchased; they find it difficult to obtain a bare subsistence, and many of them are miserably poor: numbers travel abroad and beg as a profession. Their fare is coarse and their manners rude. During the summer many of them descend to the plains of Orûmiah, at the foot of the Kûrdistan range, and here a considerable body of Nestorian Christians, estimated at about 40,000, have fixed their residence. They have a tradition that their ancestors came down from the mountains to live on the plain five or six hundred years ago. It is probable that they were entirely swept away from this province during the devastations of Timurlane, but there are monuments of their residence here at an earlier period. The oldest mosque in the city of Orûmiah was once a Christian church. The Nestorians of the plain partake in their manners of the urbanity of the Persians, and they themselves denominate their fellow-Christians, the mountaineers, wild men. Though suffering oppression and extortion from the Mohammedans, their circumstances are tolerable for a people in bondage. The country is fertile, and the industrious among them are surrounded with plenty. Their character is bold, generous, kind, and artless. Oppression has not broken their spirit; they are still brave and restless, and, so far as a subject people can be, independent. The Nestorians of the mountains, with all their rudeness and even ferocity, possess the same traits of kindness and generosity. The hungry man will divide his last morsel of bread with a stranger, or even with a foe. The Nestorians of the plain, as a matter of calculation, lay in liberal stores for their poor countrymen of Kûrdistan, when, pinched with want, they come down in the winter to seek subsistence. In their language, as in Arabic, the missionaries found no word for *home;* and there is no need of it, for the thing itself is wanting. The house consists of one large room, and is generally occupied by several generations. In that one room all the work of the family is performed. There they eat, and there they sleep. The beds consist of three articles—a thick comfortable filled with wool or cotton beneath, a pillow, and one

heavy quilt for covering. On rising they "take up their beds" and pile them on a wooden frame, and spread them down again at night. The room is lighted by an opening in the roof, which also serves for a chimney; though, of course, in a very imperfect manner, as the inside of every dwelling that has stood for any length of time bears witness. The upper part of the walls and the under surface of the roof—we can hardly call it ceiling—fairly glitter, as if they had been painted black and varnished, and all articles of clothing, books, and household utensils are saturated with the smell of creosote. The floor, like the walls, is of earth, covered in part with coarse straw mats and pieces of carpeting; and the flat roof, of the same material, rests on a layer of sticks, supported by large beams; the mass above, however, often sifts through, and sometimes during a heavy rain assumes the form of a shower of mud. Bad as all this may seem, the houses are still worse in the mountain districts, such as Gawar. There they are half under ground, made of cobble stones laid up against

Nestorian House in the Jyari.

the slanting sides of the excavation, and covered by a conical roof with a hole in the centre. They contain, besides the family, all the implements of husbandry, the cattle, and the flocks. These last occupy "the sides of the house" (1 Sam. xxiv, 3), and stand facing the "decana," or raised place in the centre, which is devoted to the family. As wood is scarce in the mountains, and the climate severe, the animal heat of the cattle is a substitute for fuel, except as sun-baked cakes of manure are used once a day for cooking, as is the practice also on the plain. In such houses the buffaloes sometimes break loose and fight furiously, and instances are not rare when they knock down the posts on which the roof rests, and thus bury all in one common ruin. The influence of such family arrangements, even in the most favored villages of the plain, on manners and morality need not be told. It is equally evident that in such circumstances personal tidiness is impossible, though few in our favored land have any idea of the extent of such untidiness. The total number of the Nestorian Christians, exclusive of the Jacobites or monophysite Syrians, and the Chaldæans or converts to the Romish faith, was computed by the American missionaries, in

Nestorian Woman and Child.

1840, at 140,000; 100,000 in the mountains, and 30,000 or 40,000 in the plain. Later travellers would make the figure a little larger, and it is now generally stated as 150,000.

The patriarch of the Nestorian Church (who is always chosen from the same family, and invariably takes the name of Shamun or Simon) resides at Diz, a village in one of the most inaccessible parts of the Kûrdish mountains. In early times, as we have seen, the patriarch resided at Seleucia; after A.D.752 at Bagdad; later he established himself at Elkush. Since the quarrel of the rival candidates and the defection of the Chaldæans to Rome, about the close of the 16th century, the patriarch has taken refuge in the mountains. He professes only to wield spiritual power, but among the mountaineers his word is law, both in matters spiritual and temporal. Among the Nestorians of Orûmiah his power is more limited; he seldom ventures to come among them; and being thus be-

Nestorian Bishop.

yond the reach of the full exercise of his authority, the people have become lax in their regard for his spiritual prerogatives; still they look up to him with respect and veneration. The patriarch does not receive the imposition of hands at his consecration, since it cannot be performed by his inferiors; but all orders of the clergy, from the deacon to the metropolitan, are ordained by him with the imposition of hands. Under the Nestorian patriarch are eighteen bishops, four of whom reside in the province of Orûmiah. A diocese varies in size from a single village to twenty or thirty. The bishops ordain the inferior clergy, make annual visitations, and superintend the diocese. Besides deacons and priests, there are archdeacons, subdeacons, and readers. The office of metran, or metropolitan, is distinct from that of the patriarch, although, it is true, they are often united in the same person. The canons of the Nestorian Church require celibacy, but only of the episcopal orders. They

also demand from these higher ecclesiastical orders abstinence from animal food, even from their infancy. The mother of the candidate for the episcopate or patriarchate must observe the same abstinence while she nurses the infant. The Nestorian bishops do not defend these practices from Scripture, but only as matters of propriety (this restriction, however, is not always observed, and was violated only recently by bishop Mar Yohann in 1859). Neither celibacy nor abstinence from animal food are required of the inferior clergy, nor do monasteries or convents exist among the Nestorians proper. The clergy are usually poor. They cultivate the ground, or teach a few scholars, or gain a small pittance by marriage fees and small contributions. It can be no matter of surprise that some of them can scarcely read. When visited by the American missionaries in 1833, a majority of them could merely chant their devotions in the ancient Syriac, and even some of the bishops were in the same predicament. The Syriac Bible has since been distributed freely among them, and the state of general knowledge is improved. The patriarch receives an annual contribution, collected for him by the bishops; it seldom exceeds three hundred dollars. The Romish agents leave no measures untried, of force or fraud, to seduce the Nestorian Church and even its patriarchs. A few years ago a Jesuit offered to the Nestorian patriarch ten thousand dollars, it is said, on condition that he would acknowledge the papal supremacy. He made answer in the words that Simon Peter once addressed to Simon Magus, "Thy money perish with thee." A more adroit overture was made afterwards, though with as little success, in the offer to canonize Nestorius.

Religion, in the proper sense, is in a low condition. The vice of lying is almost universal among clergy and laity; intemperance is very prevalent. The Sunday is to a great extent regarded only as a holiday, and profaneness and some other vices are very common. Still a venerable remnant exists of a primitive Church, founded, as they invariably maintain, not by Nestorius, but in apostolic times by Thomas the Apostle (q. v.). It is beset with dangers on every side. The artifices of the Jesuits are unceasing and sometimes successful. Recently a patriarch was brought over by violence to the Church of Rome. On the other hand, the Mohammedans attempt to proselyte. Nestorian girls are occasionally kidnapped or decoyed away, and become the wives of the followers of the false prophet. Some hardened culprits apostatize for the sake of escaping punishment, but these are all the triumphs of which the Mohammedans can boast.

The sword of the Moslem has not spared the Nestorians. They are grievously oppressed and ground down with taxes and impositions. The Nestorians are marked out alike by religion and nationality as victims of oppression. However great their wrongs, they can hope for little redress, for a distant court shares in the plunder taken from them, and believes its own officials rather than the despised rayahs whom they oppress. Even when foreign intervention procures some edict in their favor, these same officials, in distant Orûmiah, are at no loss to evade its demands. The Nestorian is not allowed a place in the bazaar; he cannot engage in commerce. And in the mechanic arts he cannot aspire higher than the position of a mason or carpenter, which, of course, is not to be compared to the standing of the same trades among us. When our missionaries went to Orûmiah a decent garment on a Nestorian was safe only as it had an outer covering of rags to hide it. The lofty spirit of the mountaineers in 1843 ventured to rebel, and an indiscriminate massacre was the penalty. "What can we do?" said they to the European visitors who inquired the cause of their rebellion; "if we descend into the plains, build villages, plant vineyards, and till the barren soil, we are so overwhelmed with taxations and impositions of every kind that our labor, though blessed of God, is of no profit to ourselves. If we take refuge in the mountains, even here we are liable every year to be hunted like partridges. Such is our lot; but God is merciful." Mr. Badger, who visited the Kûrds, on behalf of the Society for Promoting Christian Knowledge, relates that as he passed through Marden, a village on one of the summits of the mountain range, in 1843, he saw in the market-place several human heads rolling in the dust which had been brought in as trophies by the soldiers of Mohammed Pasha. "The next day," he says, "I saw a large number of horses, asses, mules, and even cows, laden with booty taken from the same people, the Kûrds of a neighboring district. Among these there were loads of human heads, and a number of prisoners, some of whom were to be impaled on the morrow. The collector of taxes in the district had embezzled a sum of money, and the Kûrds were ordered to make good the deficiency. As they were unable or unwilling to comply, a troop of Albanians was sent against them, who plundered the refractory villages, massacred about a hundred and fifty persons, and committed other excesses too horrible to relate. Such is Ottoman rule."

The creed and practice of the Nestorians are more simple and more scriptural than those of the Greek or any other Oriental Church. They entertain the deepest abhorrence of image worship, auricular confession, and purgatory. Their doctrinal tenets lie under suspicion; yet the American missionaries do not hesitate to vouch for their correctness. Mr. Perkins was sent out by the American Board of Foreign Missions, and lived among them six years, laboring with considerable success. "On the momentous subject of the divinity of Christ," he says, "in relation to which the charge of heresy is so violently thrown upon them by the papal and other Oriental sects, their belief is orthodox and scriptural." Mr. Badger also judges favorably of their orthodoxy. He thinks that, although in error with respect to the language in which they express their belief with regard to the second person in the Trinity, the Nestorians hold, nevertheless, in effect the true Catholic doctrine as it is revealed in Holy Scripture, and as it was set forth by the Council of Ephesus.

Several writers have lately made English translations of the Nestorian rituals. These are so overlaid with Oriental figure and sentiment that to ascertain their exact meaning on the points at issue is, however, by no means an easy task. We make a single extract from a service for the Holy Nativity: "Blessed art thou, O Virgin, daughter of David. Since in thee all the promises made to the righteous have been fulfilled, and in the race of prophecy has found rest; for after a wonderful manner thou didst conceive as a virgin without marriage, and in a wonderful way thou didst bring forth the Messiah, the Son of God; as it is written, the Holy Spirit formed him in thee, and the Word dwelt in him by union, without conversion or confusion, the natures continuing to subsist unchanged, and the persons also, by their essential attributes, the divinity and humanity subsisting in one parsopa of filiation. For the Lord is one, the power is one, the denomination ruling over all is one, and he is the ruler and disposer of all by the mysterious power of his divinity, whom we ought ever to thank and worship, saying, Blessed is the righteous One who clothed himself with Adam's [humanity], and made him Lord in heaven and earth" (Badger, ii, 34). But though the ritual does not clearly develop the Christological dogmas, it is certain that the Nestorian Church is the only body outside of Protestantism (excepting the Moravians and Waldensians) which acknowledges, as do the churches which appeared at the Reformation, or came out of these, the *supreme* authority of the Holy Scriptures, and holds no doctrine or practice essential to salvation which may not be proved from Holy Writ. Indeed, the reverence in which the Nestorians hold the inspired volume has made them the fortunate possessors of some of the most ancient and valuable MSS. in existence. Their ancient language was the Syriac, of which the modern vernacu-

lar is a dialect, corrupted by contractions and inversions and a great number of Persian and Turkish words. Among their books are some very ancient copies of the Scriptures in Syriac. Several of these are at least six hundred years old. They also possess a copy of the N. T. which purports to be fifteen hundred years old. These copies are regarded by them with much veneration, and are used with great care; they are wrapped in several covers, and when taken into the hands are as reverently kissed as the Jews do their MSS. of the O. T. used for synagogal service. It must not be supposed, however, that they are the possessors of very large numbers of MSS. Dr. Grant found in the library of the patriarch not more than sixty volumes, all in manuscript, and a part of these were duplicates. Indeed, they have no works of value, except on devotional subjects. Once an educated people, the Nestorians are now perfectly illiterate. Very little attempt has been made to reduce the vernacular language to writing, and the printing-press was unknown to them until the advent of the American missionaries. The only books they possess are the Church rituals; to be able to read these, and to write fairly, is considered a high education, and is all that is desired, even from candidates for holy orders. Except the priests, few or none can read; and even of these but few can do more than merely repeat their devotions in an unknown tongue, while neither they nor their hearers know anything of the meaning. The N. T. is read in the old Syriac; but this differs considerably from the dialect in common use, and it is read withal in such a manner as to be almost unintelligible. The laity are regular in attendance at church, where they hear a liturgy of great beauty, partly chanted and partly mumbled. Certain prayers are familiar to all ranks, and persons devoutly disposed are often seen retiring to a corner of the church to pray in secret. There is no sermon to arouse reflection or to sustain faith, by impressing the conscience and the understanding; no lecture to expound the difficulties of Scripture. Thus the main body of the Nestorians are only nominal Christians, and such they must probably remain until more favored nations come to their relief. True, their religious principles are more simple and scriptural than those of other Oriental churches, and they are not guilty of so many corrupt practices as the Papal and Greek churches. But the life and power of Christianity are departed in a large measure, and scarcely a symptom of spiritual vitality was apparent when the American missionaries first met them. The existence of such a people for seventeen hundred years, among hostile nations and circumstances so disastrous, is a matter of astonishment; and their own preservation, too, of so much of the pure doctrine of the Gospel as they still retain is remarkable. Their liturgical books recognise seven sacraments, but confession is infrequent, if not altogether disused. Marriage is dissoluble by the sentence of the patriarch; communion is administered in both kinds; and although the language of the liturgy plainly implies the belief of transubstantiation, yet it is said not to be popularly held among them. The fasts are strict, and of very long duration, amounting to very nearly one half the entire year. They pray for the dead, but are said to reject the notion of purgatory. Monasteries and convents do not exist among this branch of the Nestorians. "They have no relics such as are common in the Church of Rome," says Mr. Badger (*Nestorians and their Ritual*, ii, 136), yet "they believe the remains of the martyrs and saints to be endowed with supernatural virtues;" and they invoke the Virgin and the saints, asking for their prayers to Christ. They have no pictures or images in their churches, and are much opposed to the use of them. The only symbol among them is a plain Greek cross, which they venerate highly. The sign of the cross is used in baptism and in prayer; a cross is engraved over the low entrances of their churches, and kissed by those who enter, and the priests carry with them a small silver cross, which is often kissed by the people. They are very scrupulous respecting their religious ceremonies and fasts. Many Nestorians would rather die than violate their periodical fasts, yet are they very far from Protestant in their ideas respecting their daily life; even their most intelligent ecclesiastics seem to have hardly any idea of the meaning of regeneration. Indeed, the Nestorians, take them as a whole class, are ignorant and superstitious; lying, profanity, and intemperance are common vices.

VI. *Missions among the Nestorians.* — Probably no Christian mission in modern times has been so satisfactorily conducted, or so decidedly happy in its influences and results, as that among the Nestorians, in all its branches. British and American missionaries have labored among the Nestorians since the year 1833. The missionaries sent forth by the American Board of Commissioners for Foreign Missions were the first of Protestant missionaries to occupy the field, and it is generally conceded that their labors have met thus far with a success beyond the most sanguine expectations, proving clearly that these efforts for the evangelization of the Nestorians are owned and blessed by the great Head of the Church. The first missionary of the American Board of Commissioners for Foreign Missions was Mr. Justin Perkins, who was taken from Amherst College, where he was teaching at the time of this appointment. In the instructions given to him the main object of the mission was defined to be to bring about a change which would "enable the Nestorian Church, through the grace of God, to exert a commanding influence in the spiritual regeneration of Asia." Considering the past history of Nestorianism, its present state, and the character of the people attached to it, it was hoped that, brought again to a fuller knowledge of the truth, and to feel the regenerating and sanctifying power of truth attended by the influences of the Spirit, the members of that belief would again become, not only themselves true disciples of Christ and heirs of life, but efficient laborers in the great work of building up Christ's kingdom throughout the world. Mrs. Perkins joined in the work, and together they studied the language and customs of the people whom they were to serve until, in 1835, Dr. Grant, a physician, of Utica, N. Y., joined them. Dr. Grant's professional character served to secure the favor of the Persian governor, and the Nestorian bishops and priests at once gave them their cordial co-operation in the prosecution of their missionary labors, regarding them not as rivals, but as coadjutors with them in a necessary work of instruction and improvement among the people. The first thing which these excellent men attempted, after having obtained a mastery of the language, ancient and modern, was to commence the establishment of schools. One, for boys, was opened in 1836; it began in a cellar, with seven pupils. A school for girls was opened in 1838. It commenced with four scholars, taught by Mrs. Dr. Grant. As the result of her exertions, it is said that "hers was the privilege of creating such a public sentiment in favor of the education of woman that her successors have found the gates wide open before them, and often wondered at the extent and permanence of the influence she acquired." In 1843 the first female boarding-school was started by advice of Miss Fidelia Fiske, who, after graduation at Mount Holyoake, joined this mission in 1843. In this school, which was established at Orûmiah, nearly two hundred women have been educated, of whom about one half were hopefully pious. Many of the young women after leaving the seminary have married young men who had been educated in the male seminary. For some years there have been some seventy schools, with about twelve to thirteen hundred pupils of both sexes in annual attendance. It is estimated that about six thousand persons have learned to read, most if not all of whom possess and read the sacred Scriptures. A high school at Orûmiah (which is the principal seat of the American mission), opened and

presided over by the late excellent professor Stoddard for several years, has been blessed in an extraordinary manner. Of the many young men who may be considered as graduates, more than two hundred and thirteen left the seminary hopefully pious. Of the many others who did not complete a full course of studies not a few left it giving good evidence of piety; and better than all, many of the young men who left the seminary are now faithful preachers of the Gospel, efficient teachers in the village schools, or otherwise useful Christians.

In 1840 the first printing-press was set up in Orûmiah by the ingenious and efficient missionary printer, Mr. Breath, who died in 1861. The Nestorians, who formerly had no printed copies of the sacred Scriptures, or any part of them, now have the Bible in both the ancient and vernacular languages, printed in parallel columns. Through the exertions of the missionaries they now have also quite a literature, embracing many volumes of religious books and tracts, together with spelling-books, geographies, arithmetics, etc. A monthly periodical, called *The Rays of Light*, is published, and read with much delight by the people; and there are now publishing two smaller periodicals, entitled *Night of Toil* and *Signet Ring*. In all, eleven thousand volumes have been printed at the mission press. Native printers and bookbinders have been so well trained that since the death of Mr. Breath they have progressed without American help in this direction. The missionaries have, from the first, labored much in the good work of imparting the Gospel by oral instruction in Orûmiah, and in the villages far and wide. Until 1868 all plans for the forming of separate churches were opposed; the missionaries therefore formed no churches, wisely preferring to promote the regeneration of the national churches—a good work and noble in purpose; but finding by experience that the old Church, as such, could not be reformed, or, as Dr. Anderson has it, "that the dead Church could not be galvanized into spiritual life" (ii, 312), it was at last determined that all who sought the higher life, and found it not in the national Church, should form reunions on the apostolic basis. There are now of such societies seventeen, with seventy-three congregations, and seven hundred and sixty-seven members. The attempt at separation from the national Church has resulted in the formation of a High-Church party, supported by Anglican High-Churchmen. The Church of England has, however, refused to send missionaries into this field, and the only injury done by this movement to the American mission work is the delay which it has caused in bringing the independent societies into self-supporting condition. There are no doubt many others who are truly pious, though they receive the sacraments in the national churches. Indeed, the missionaries preach much in the national churches, and enjoy the confidence of the patriarch and of many priests. It can certainly be asserted that the Gospel is now preached among the Nestorian people not by the missionaries only. When the mission was commenced the ecclesiastics were not preachers, and their public religious services were not preaching services. But bishops and priests have been pupils in the schools, and bishops and priests have felt the force of truth—have become new creatures in Christ Jesus, and are now, in some cases, zealous and impressive preachers. And some young men who have been educated at the seminary, and have become apparently devoted Christians, have been ordained by the bishops of their Church, and are thus fully introduced into the work of the ministry. The patriarch has at times opposed, and some of the bishops, in 1867, prohibited the pious helpers of the mission from preaching in their dioceses; but, to a great extent, the whole field is and has been open to them, and among them are some who make extensive tours, not only on the plain, but in the mountain districts, as zealous and able evangelists. Take it all in all, the influence of the mission upon the condition and morals of the people has been most salutary. They have readily imbibed the spirit of Christian civilization, and faithfully observed all the precepts of the Gospel. The influence of spiritual religion upon the pupils and their friends is manifest in all their daily walks in life, and their example is making a deep impression on those who have not yet been made objects of religious instruction. The schools that have been organized in the villages now help to support themselves; the mission having made it a rule to furnish no teacher, except in new villages, where a part of the support was not assumed by the people. In the year 1861 upwards of five hundred dollars were contributed for the support of missions, and since then the sum has considerably increased. The missionary zeal is growing constantly, and the Nestorians are anxious to become the bearers of the truth to other Asiatic peoples. At the annual convention of helpers and representatives of the Nestorian churches held in Oct., 1867, a demand was made for special mission fields; and in 1870 the mission resolved that they considered it a duty urged upon them to embrace at once within their efforts the Armenians and the Mussulman sects of Central Persia; and they expressed the hope that the Board would

heartily endorse their action, and help them to carry it out without delay. The Board approving such a step, the Nestorians have since labored among the Armenians in Russia, and the same people at Tabriz, Hamadan (the ancient Ecbatana), Teheran, Ispahan, in Persia, and the numerous villages in the intervening regions—descendants, to a great extent, of Armenians carried captive, in 1605, from the regions of Ararat by shah Abbas the Great.

Since the autumn of 1870 the Nestorian mission has passed from the control of the American Board of Commissioners for Foreign Missions to the care of the Presbyterian Board of Foreign Missions, and it is expected that the work so gloriously begun will be prosecuted by that body with equal zeal and success. This mission, being on the western borders of Persia and the eastern borders of Turkey, in the very heart of the Mohammedan world, and on the dividing line of its two great sects, the *Sûnies* and *Shiites*, certainly occupies a position of transcendant importance. We insert below a table from Dr. Anderson's work on *Oriental Missions* (ii, 498–9), showing the laborers employed, etc.

VII. *Probable Origin of the Nestorian People.*—We have seen above that the Nestorians claim to have

MISSION TO THE NESTORIANS.

Ordained Missionaries.	Wives of Missionaries.	Time of Entering.	Time of Leaving.
* Justin Perkins, D.D.		November, 1835.	May 28, 1869.
	Mrs. Charlotte Perkins	November, 1835.	———, 1857.
* Albert L. Holladay		June 7, 1837.	Spring, 1846.
	Mrs. Anne Y. Holladay	June 7, 1837.	Spring, 1846.
* William R. Stocking		June 7, 1837.	June, 1853.
	Mrs. Jerusha R. Stocking	June 7, 1837.	June, 1853.
* Willard Jones		November 17, 1839.	———, 1844.
	Mrs. Miriam Jones	November 17, 1839.	Winter, 1844.
* A. H. Wright, M.D.		July 25, 1840.	* January 4, 1865.
	Mrs. Catharine A. Wright	June 14, 1843.	August, 1859.
* Abel K. Hinsdale		June, 1841.	* December 26, 1842.
	* Mrs. Sarah C. Hinsdale	June, 1841.	October 21, 1844.
* Colby C. Mitchell		June, 1841.	* June 27, 1841.
	* Mrs. Eliza A. Mitchell	June, 1841.	* July 12, 1841.
* James Lyman Merrick		December, 1842.	Summer, 1845.
	* Mrs. Emma Merrick	December, 1842.	Summer, 1845.
Thomas Laurie, D.D.		November 11, 1842.	November 10, 1844.
	* Mrs. Martha F. Laurie	November 11, 1842.	* December 16, 1843.
* David T. Stoddard		June 14, 1843.	* January 26, 1857.
	* Mrs. Harriet Stoddard	June 14, 1843.	* August 2, 1848.
	Mrs. Sophia D. Stoddard	June 26, 1851.	July, 1858.
* Joseph G. Cochran		September 27, 1847.	* November 2, 1871.
	Mrs. Deborah W. Cochran	September 27, 1848.	
George W. Coan		October 13, 1849.	
	Mrs. Sarah P. Coan	October 13, 1849.	
* Samuel A. Rhea		June 26, 1851.	* September 2, 1865.
	* Mrs. Martha Ann Rhea	July 1, 1852.	* September 16, 1857.
	Mrs. Sarah Jane Rhea	October 25, 1860.	May, 1869.
* Edwin H. Crane		October 20, 1852.	* August 27, 1854.
	* Mrs. Ann E. Crane [afterwards Mrs. P. O. Powers]	October 20, 1852.	November, 1857.
* Thomas L. Ambrose		November 27, 1858.	August, 1861.
John H. Shedd		November 11, 1859.	———, 1870.
	Mrs. Sarah Jane Shedd	November 11, 1859.	
* Amherst L. Thompson		July 2, 1860.	* August 25, 1860.
	Mrs. Esther E. Thompson	July 2, 1860.	Summer, 1861.
Benjamin Labaree		October 25, 1860.	
	Mrs. Elizabeth E. Labaree	October 25, 1860.	
Henry N. Cobb		October 25, 1860.	Autumn, 1862.
	Mrs. Matilda E. Cobb	October 25, 1860.	Autumn, 1862.
Missionary Physicians.			
* Asahel Grant, M.D.		October 15, 1835.	* April 24, 1844.
	* Mrs. Judith S. Grant	October 15, 1835.	* January 14, 1839.
* F. N. H. Young, M.D.		October 25, 1860.	Summer, 1863.
T. L. Van Norden, M.D.		October 6, 1866.	
	Mrs. Mary M. Van Norden	October 6, 1866.	
Assistant Missionaries.			
* Edwin Breath		November 7, 1840.	* November 18, 1861.
	Mrs. Sarah Ann Breath	October 13, 1849.	Summer, 1862.
	* Miss Fidelia Fiske	June 14, 1843.	July 15, 1858.
	Miss Catharine A. Myers [afterwards Mrs. Wright]	June 14, 1843.	August, 1859.
	Miss Mary Susan Rice	November 20, 1847.	
	* Miss Martha Ann Harris [afterwards Mrs. Rhea]	July 1, 1852.	* September 16, 1857.
	Miss Aura Jeannette Beach	July 2, 1860.	September, 1862.
	* Miss Harriet N. Crawford	July 2, 1860.	May, 1865.
	Miss Nancy Jane Dean	October 19, 1868.	

The asterisk (*) placed before a name denotes that the person is deceased. When placed before a *date*, in the right hand column, it denotes that the person died *at the time there indicated*, and in the field.

been early instructed in Christian truths. Dr. Grant, a learned American missionary, has recently put forth an argument to show that the Nestorians are the descendants of the lost tribes of Israel. He cites as proof of his theory their Jewish physiognomy, the frequency of those proper names which occur in the Old Testament, the peculiarities of their customs, and other points of resemblance. His proofs are not regarded as satisfactory by his co-missionaries, nor by Mr. Badger, who contests his facts. It is a question, however, of detail and research, and we can only here make mention that such a theory of their origin is espoused, and refer to Dr. Grant's and Mr. Badger's writings. One service of the Nestorian Church certainly partakes much more of a Jewish than a Christian character: this is a commemoration for the dead celebrated in all the mountain villages once a year, on some Saturday in the month of October. For some days previous to the festival each family prepares its offerings. These consist of lambs and bread, which are carried into the church-yard. After the people have partaken of the holy eucharist, the priest goes out, cuts several locks of wool off the fleeces, and throws them into a censer. While a deacon swings this to and fro in the presence of the guests the priest recites an anthem, in which the oblation is offered to the Lord, and prayers are made both for the living and the dead. The service concluded, the lambs and the bread are divided among the company. Many come from distant villages to join in the commemoration. Those who can afford it kill a lamb and distribute bread and other provisions among the poor, after the death of their relations, hoping that the offerings will, in some way, profit the souls of the departed. Dr. Grant mentions another sacrifice which is offered occasionally as a thank-offering for blessings received. A lamb is slain before the door of the church, when a little of the blood is put on the door and lintel; the right shoulder and breast belong to the officiating priest, and the skin is also given to the priest as was required in the law of burnt offerings (Lev. vii); but these strange customs may have been derived from the Mohammedans, who often sacrifice a lamb with the same intention at the doors of their shrines throughout Turkey, and sprinkle the building with the blood, after which the animal is distributed among the people of the village. As might be expected in a people so ignorant, the Nestorians are superstitious. They observe many fasts. Their ritual contains offices for the purification of those who have touched the corpse of an unbeliever, and a service for the purification of unclean cisterns and fountains, some parts of which are extremely beautiful. The Nestorians place a high value on charms and talismans, and the clergy are generally the authors of these profane and absurd effusions which they transcribe and sell to the people.

VIII. *Literature.*—The works extant on the history of Nestorianism are very numerous. In Malcom's *Theological Index* is a long list of such works; the most important are, Doucin, *Histoire du Nestorianisme* (1689); Franzius (Northolti), *Dissertationes;* Le Quien, *Oriens Christianus;* Schröder, *Liberati Historia controversiæ Nestorianæ.* In the foregoing account, besides the usual materials, the *Breviarium* of Liberatus, who was archdeacon of Carthage, written cir. A.D. 564, and the works of Marius Mercator, already referred to under Nestorius (q. v.), have been largely relied upon. On the Nestorian side appear the sermons of Eutherius; and Assemani, *De Syris Nestorianis,* in his *Bibliotheca Orientalis* (Rom. 1719–1728 sq.), tom. iii, pt. ii (quoted by Dr. Hey, bk. iv, art. ii, § 9), gives a catalogue of 198 writers, with more in an appendix, who are called Syrian Nestorian writers: "but the New Testament is one book so reckoned, and Clemens Romanus one author." See also Ebedjesu (Nestorian metropolitan of Nisibis, † 1318), *Liber Margaritæ de veritate fidei* (a defence of the Nestorians), in Mai's *Script. vet. nova. collect.* pt. x, ii, 317; Gibbon, *Decline and Fall of the Roman Empire,* ch.

xlvii, near the end; Hohlenberg, *De originibus et fatis ecclesiæ Christianæ in India orientali* (Havniæ, 1822, 8vo); Hagenbach, *Hist. Doctrines,* i, 20, 241, 275; ii, 35, 117, 344, 363; Hardwick, *Hist. Mid. Ages* (see Index); Lea, *Hist. Sacerdotal Celibacy,* p. 97 sq.; Haag, *Hist. des Dogmes Chrétiens,* i, 190–192; ii, 119, 139, 166, 289, 320; Bruns, *Neues Repertorium f. d. theol. Literatur u. kirchliche Statistik;* Ritter, *Erdkunde;* Justin Perkins, *A Residence of Eight Years in Persia* (Andover, 1843, 8vo); Ainsworth, *Travels and Researches in Mesopotamia,* etc.; Layard, *Nineveh and its Remains;* Perkins, *Eight Years spent among the Nestorian Christians* (New York, 1843); Buchanan, *Christian Researches in the East;* Smith and Dwight, *Researches in Armenia, with a Visit to the Nestorian and Chaldæan Christians of Orûmiah and Salmas* (Bost. 1833, 2 vols. 8vo); *Woman and her Saviour in Persia* (Bost. 1863); Etheridge, *Rituals of the Syrian Churches;* Grant, *The Nestorians* (1841); Badger, *The Nestorians and their Rituals* (Lond. 1852, 2 vols.); Wiltsch, *Kirchliche Geographie u. Statistik,* i, 214 sq.; Wiggers, *Kirchliche Statistik,* vol. i, pt. ii, § 73 sq.; Newcomb, *Cyclop. of Missions,* p. 553 sq.; Anderson, *Hist. of the Missions of the A. B. C. F. M. in the Oriental Churches,* vols. i and ii; Grundemann, *Missions-Atlas,* pt. ii, No. 3; *The Wesleyan Methodist Magazine,* July and August, 1852; *North British Review,* vol. xi; xxxviii, 247; *Ch. Remembrancer,* 1862, p. 65; *Princeton Rev.* 1842, p. 59; Kitto, *Jour. Sac. Lit.* Jan. 1853, p. 513; *Meth. Quar. Rev.* July, 1854, p. 462; 1843, p. 479; 1841, p. 483.

Nestorius, a celebrated theologian of the 5th century, noted as the founder of the Nestorians (q. v.)—an important and early sect of Christians—was born, according to the ecclesiastical historian Socrates, who has written his life, at Germanicia, a city in Northern Syria, near the opening of the 5th century. He received his theological education, it is supposed, under the Monophysite Theodore of Mopsuestia. Nestorius was ordained to the priesthood at Antioch, where he was made a presbyter, and where he was "esteemed and celebrated," says Neander, "on account of the rigid austerity of his life and the impressive fervor of his preaching." The popularity of his pulpit gifts attracted to him large and attentive audiences, and he became a great favorite with the people generally. The Church—which was then greatly divided on the doctrine of the motherhood of Mary, some holding her to be the mother of God, others regarding her simply in the modern evangelical light—looked upon Nestorius as the man eminently fit by his sound, practical judgment and his vast theological learning for a clearing process in this mystifying dogma; and so general was the opinion that Nestorius could unite all Christian believers of the East that the people hailed with great satisfaction and joy his elevation (A.D. 428) to the patriarchate of Constantinople, which had been sought for by more prominent ecclesiastics, whom the emperor had passed by because of their rivalry. In Constantinople Nestorius was looked to as a second Chrysostom, and a restorer of the honor of his great predecessor against the detraction of his Alexandrian rival. But no sooner was Nestorius promoted to this elevated and responsible position than he began to display an intemperate zeal, which partook more of the bigotry of the monk than the general tolerant spirit which was becoming his character and position as a minister of Christ. His very first efforts when once seated in the patriarchal chair were directed towards the extirpation of heretics, including Arians and Novatians, Quartodecimani and Macedonians, who at that time abounded in the capital of the East and its subordinate dioceses. Indeed Nestorius's course had been foreshadowed in his inaugural discourse, in which, addressing the emperor Theodosius II, or the Younger, he gave utterance to these violent expressions: "Give me a country purged of all these heretics, and in exchange for it I will give you heaven. Help me to subdue the heretics, and I will help you to conquer the Persians." Nor did his fury against the heretics find vent only in words; he proceeded to deeds of persecution which, by exciting tumults among the people, led to the effusion of blood. The Pelagians alone, with whose doctrine of free-will (but not of original sin) he sympathized, he treated indulgently, receiving to himself Julian of Eclanum, Cœlestius, and other banished leaders of that party, interceding for them in 429 with the emperor and with the pope Celestine, though, on account of the very unfavorable reports concerning Pelagianism which were spread by the layman Marius Mercator, then living in Constantinople, his intercessions were of no avail (comp. Schaff, *Ch. Hist.* iii, 716). While thus busily engaged in the persecution of others, Nestorius raised up even among the orthodox party in the Church a numerous host of enemies, who were not long in accusing him also of heresy. Having been trained in the strict Antiochian doctrine as to the clear distinction between the divine and human natures of Christ, he and his friend Anastasius, whom he had brought with him from Antioch, could not fail to disapprove of some expressions then current in the Church, which evidently proceeded upon confused notions in respect to the two natures of Christ. One expression in particular, the title Θεοτόκος, or Mother of God, applied to the Virgin Mary, more especially taken in connection with the excessive veneration of the Virgin which had begun to prevail, called forth the strongest reprobation on the part of Nestorius. Along with his friend Anastasius he took occasion in his public discourses to state, in the most emphatic manner, his objections to the certainly very bold and equivocal expression *mother of God*, which had already been sometimes applied to the Virgin Mary by Origen, Alexander of Alexandria, Athanasius, Basil, and others, and which, after the Arian controversy, and with the growth of the worship of Mary, had passed into the devotional language of the people (comp. Schaff, *Ch. Hist.* iii, 716, also 582, 583). The sense, or monstrous nonsense, of this term of course was not that the creature bore the Creator, or that the eternal Deity took its beginning from Mary, which would be the most absurd and the most wicked of all heresies, and a shocking blasphemy; but the expression was intended only to denote the indissoluble union of the divine and human natures in Christ, and the veritable incarnation of the Logos, who took the human nature from the body of Mary, came forth God-Man from her womb, and as God-Man suffered on the cross. For Christ was born as a *person*, and suffered as a *person;* and the personality in Christ resided in his divinity, not in his humanity. So, in fact, the reasonable soul of man, which is the centre of the human personality, participates in the suffering and the death-struggle of the body, though the soul itself does not and cannot die. The Antiochian theology, however, could not conceive a human nature without a human personality, and this it strictly separated from the divine Logos. Therefore Theodore of Mopsuestia had already disputed the term *theotokos* with all earnestness. "Mary," he says, "bore Jesus, not the Logos, for the Logos was, and continues to be, omnipresent, though he dwelt in Jesus in a special manner from the beginning. Therefore Mary is strictly the mother of *Christ*, not the mother of *God*. Only in a figure, *per anaphoram*, can she be called also the mother of God, because God was in a peculiar sense in Christ. Properly speaking, she gave birth to a man in whom the union with the Logos had begun, but was still so incomplete that he could not yet (till after his baptism) be called the Son of God." He even declared it "insane" to say that God was born of the Virgin; "not God, but the temple in which God dwelt, was born of Mary." In a similar strain Nestorius and his friend Anastasius argued from the pulpit against the *theotokon*. Nestorius proposed the middle expression, mother of *Christ* (Χριστοτόκος), because Christ was at the same time God and man. He delivered several discourses on

this disputed point. "You ask," he says in his first sermon, "whether Mary may be called *mother of God*. Has God, then, a mother? If so, heathenism itself is excusable in assigning mothers to its gods; but then Paul is a liar, for he said of the deity of Christ that it was without father, without mother, and without descent (Heb. vii, 3: ἀπάτωρ, ἀμήτωρ, ἄνευ γενεαλογίας). No, my dear sir, Mary did not bear God; . . . the creature bore not the uncreated Creator, but the man who is the instrument of the Godhead; the Holy Ghost conceived not the Logos, but formed for him, out of the virgin, a temple which he might inhabit (John ii, 21). The incarnate God did not die, but quickened him in whom he was made flesh. . . . This garment, which he used, I honor on account of the God which was covered therein and inseparable therefrom; . . . *I separate the natures, but I unite the worship.* Consider what this must mean. He who was formed in the womb of Mary was not himself God, but God assumed him [*assumsit*, i. e. clothed himself with humanity], and on account of him who assumed, he who was assumed is also called *God.*" A controversy now ensued in which the enemies of Nestorius, not comprehending the danger which he saw to be involved in the use of the word *theotokos*, charged him most unjustly with holding the Photinian and Samosatenian views, which asserted that Jesus was born of Mary as a mere man; or, in other words, they accused him of denying the divinity of Christ. The question was very keenly agitated, both among the clergy and laity, whether Mary was entitled to be called the mother of God. In this dispute Nestorius took an active part, adhering firmly to the doctrine of the school of Antioch. Dupin (*Bibliothèque*, i, 442, ed. 1722) thus summarizes his views as expounded by himself: 1. He expressly rejected the error of those who said that Christ was a mere man, as Ebion, Paul of Samosata, Photinus. 2. He maintained that the Word was united to the humanity in Christ Jesus, and that this union was most intimate and strict. 3. He maintained that these two natures made one Christ, one Son, one Person. 4. And that this Person may have either divine or human properties attributed to him. But his words contradicted this formal enunciation of his doctrine. His illustrations proved that he did not allow the hypostatic union, but admitted a moral union only. A contemporary writer (Marius Mercator, *Opera* [Paris, 1673, ed. Garnier]), who lived in the first half of the fifth century, says that Nestorius was sound in most of the Catholic truths on this question taken seriatim. He was sound "de persona divina assumente," also "de natura humana assumpta," and also "de tempore, quo primum extitit unio;" all these positions being demonstrated by extracts from extant sermons and other writings of Nestorius. But he was unsound "de genere unionis." He certainly allowed only a moral union, "Deus et homo unum tantum moraliter." Hence the incarnation according to him was "ἐνοίκησις, ἀνάληψις, ἐνέργεια, ἐνανθρώπησις." There were two natures in Christ, and the properties in each should be very carefully distinguished—" duæ in Christo reipsa hypostases; secernenda singulorum idiomata." Nor would he allow human attributes to be predicated of the divine nature of Christ: "Nec quæ unius tribuenda alteri, nisi καθ᾽ ὁμονυμίαν, vel σχετικῶς." Rogers (*Parker Soc.* p. 55) quotes an opposite passage in this connection: Φησὶ γὰρ ἐνωθῆναι τὸν Θεὸν λόγον τῷ ἐκ Μαρίας ἀνθρώπῳ, ὥσπερ εἴ τις φίλος φίλῳ ἕνωσιν διὰ σχέσεως ποιοῖτο (Nicephorus, xviii, 48). He denied therefore that God the Son had endured human suffering or gone through human experiences, and he necessarily rejected, according to the above view, the term Θεοτόκος, and proposed Χριστοτόκος as an alternative. There is abundant proof from his works of his denial of the hypostatic union. He compared the union of the two natures in Christ to marriage; he spoke of Christ's humanity being the habit, the temple of his divinity. He said that Thomas had touched him that was risen again, and honored him that raised him up. He believed "hominem Deificatum, et non verbum carnem factum," that Christ became God by merit and not by nature. At some meetings at Ephesus, preliminary to the council, Nestorius said he would not admit that a child could be God. Acacius, bishop of Melitana, at the council said that he had heard a bishop of the party of Nestorius say "that he that suffered for us was a distinct person from the Word" (Dupin, i, 640). Nestorius proposed an alteration of phraseology in order to overcome this difficulty. He suggested that there would be no difficulty if we said the divine Jesus Christ knew men's thoughts, the human Jesus Christ was hungry, and the like (see Dr. Hey's Lect. iv. He speaks of the cruelty of the persecution of Nestorius, and does "not scruple to say that the Council of Ephesus erred in treating Nestorius with too great severity"). Practically it became clear that his doctrine amounted to teaching that there were two persons in Christ, and it was so felt at the time. See HYPOSTATICAL UNION. Thus the word theotokos became the watchword of the orthodox party in the Nestorian controversy, as the term homoousios had been in the Arian; opposition to the word θεοτόκος meant denial of the mystery of the incarnation, or of the true union of the divine and human natures in Christ. Unquestionably the Antiochian Christology, which was represented by Nestorius, did not make the Logos truly become man. It asserted indeed, rightly, the duality of the natures, and the continued distinction between them; it denied, with equal correctness, that God, as such, could either be born, or suffer and die; but it pressed the distinction of the two natures to double personality. It substituted for the idea of the incarnation the idea of an assumption (πρόσληψις) of human nature, or rather of an entire man, into fellowship with the Logos, and an indwelling of Godhead in Christ (ἐνοίκησις in distinction from ἐνσάρκωσις). Instead of God-Man (θεάνθρωπος), we have here the idea of a mere God-bearing man (ἕνωσις καθ' ὑπόστασιν); and the person of Jesus of Nazareth is only the instrument, or the temple, in which the divine Logos dwells. The two natures form, not a personal unity (θεοφόρος, also θεοδόχος, from δέχεσθαι, God-assuming), but only a moral unity, an intimate friendship or conjunction (συνάφεια). They hold an outward, mechanical relation to each other, in which each retains its peculiar attributes (ἰδιώματα), forbidding any sort of communicatio idiomatum. This union is, in the first place, a gracious condescension on the part of God (ἕνωσις κατὰ χάριν, or κατ' εὐδοκίαν), whereby the Logos makes the man an object of the divine pleasure, and in the second place an elevation of the man to higher dignity and to sonship with God (ἕνωσις κατ' ἀξίαν, καθ' υἱοθεσίαν). By virtue of the condescension there arises, in the third place, a practical fellowship of operation (ἕνωσις κατ' ἐνέργειαν), in which the humanity becomes the instrument and temple of the Deity and the ἕνωσις σχετική culminates. Theodore of Mopsuestia, the able founder of the Antiochian Christology, set forth the elevation of the man to sonship with God (starting from Luke ii, 53) under the aspect of a gradual moral process, and made it dependent on the progressive virtue and meritoriousness of Jesus, which were completed in the resurrection, and earned for him the unchangeableness of the divine life as a reward for his voluntary victory for virtue. The Antiochian and Nestorian theory amounts therefore, at bottom, to a duality of persons in Christ, though without clearly avowing it. It cannot conceive the reality of the two natures without a personal independence for each. With the theanthropic unity of the person of Christ it denies also the theanthropic unity of his work, especially of his sufferings and death; and in the same measure it enfeebles the reality of redemption. From this point of view Mary, of course, could be nothing more than mother of the man Jesus, and the predicate theotokos, strictly understood, must appear absurd or blasphemous. Nestorius would admit no more than

that God passed through (transiit) the womb of Mary. Cyril charges upon Nestorius (Epist. ad Cœlest.) that he does not say the Son of God died and rose again, but always only the man Jesus died and rose. Nestorius himself says, in his second homily (in Mar. Merc. p. 763 sq.): "It may be said that the Son of God, in the wider sense, died, but not that God died. Moreover the Scriptures, in speaking of the birth, passion, and death, never say God, but Christ, or Jesus, or the Lord—all of them names which suit both natures. A born, dead, and buried God cannot be worshipped." "Pilate," he says in another sermon, "did not crucify the Godhead, but the clothing of the Godhead, and Joseph of Arimathæa did not shroud and bury the Logos" (in Mar. Merc. p. 789 sq.).

Nestorius by this controversy had opened a question which went beyond the usual theological arena. The sentiment of venerating Mary had spread so greatly among the people that it touched the most vehement passions, and he was, therefore, not only resisted by theologians of the opposite camp, viz., the Alexandrians, but by the people, and was rejected in public by some of his own clergy even. He accordingly, enraged at the contempt shown to his authority as patriarch, hesitated not to issue orders that the most refractory should be seized, and forthwith beaten and imprisoned. One of these, Proclus by name, who had at a former period applied in vain for the patriarchate of Constantinople, rendered himself peculiarly conspicuous by the bitter hostility which he evinced to the opinions of Nestorius. This man having, on one occasion, been called to preach in the presence of his patriarch, took occasion, in the course of his sermon, to extol the Virgin Mary as the mother of God, and charged all who refused to acknowledge her as such with being believers in a deified man. Proclus, in the course of his discourse, praised Mary as "the spotless treasure-house of virginity; the spiritual paradise of the second Adam; the workshop in which the two natures were annealed together; the bridal chamber in which the Word wedded the flesh; the living bush of nature, which was unharmed by the fire of the divine birth; the light cloud which bore him who sat between the cherubim; the stainless fleece, bathed in the dews of heaven, with which the Shepherd clothed his sheep; the handmaid and the mother, the Virgin and Heaven." The sermon was received with loud applause, and Nestorius found it necessary to defend his own doctrine against the misrepresentations of the preacher. Nestorius's middle term of Χριστοτόκος, which he had adopted to prevent a schism in the Church, failed longer to satisfy any except his most devoted associates; and a considerable party, composed both of clergy, monks, and Church members, refused outright to recognise Nestorius as their ecclesiastical superior. They even renounced all Church fellowship with him. The patriarch accordingly convened a synod at Constantinople in A.D. 429, which deposed some of the most violent of the clergy as favorers of Manichæan doctrines by denying the reality of Christ's humanity. In a short time, however, the Nestorian controversy, which had raged so violently in the Church and patriarchate of Constantinople, extended far beyond these narrow limits, and soon another eminent opponent appeared to harass Nestorius. This one was Cyril, bishop of Alexandria, who had previously exhibited a violent persecuting spirit against pagans, Jews, and heretics. He took the field, moved by interests both personal and doctrinal, and used every means to overthrow his rival in Constantinople, as his like-minded uncle and predecessor, Theophilus, had overthrown the noble Chrysostom in the Origenistic strife. The theological controversy was at the same time a contest of the two patriarchates. In personal character Cyril stands far below Nestorius, but he excelled him in knowledge of the world, shrewdness, theological learning, and acuteness, and had the show of greater veneration for Christ and for Mary on his side; and in his opposition to the abstract separation of the divine and human he was in the right, though he himself pressed to the verge of the opposite error of mixing or confusing the two natures in Christ. (Comp. in particular his assertion of an ἕνωσις φυσική in the third of his Anathematismi against Nestorius; Hefele [Conciliengesch. ii, 155], however, understands by this not a ἕνωσις εἰς μίαν φύσιν, but only a real union in one being, one existence.) Cyril, as if to blind the eyes of his antagonists, opened the controversy by mild and apparently suave measures. He simply wrote to Nestorius remonstrating against the views of the Constantinopolitan patriarch. Cyril published two letters addressed to Egyptian monks, in which he assailed the opinions of Nestorius, without, however, alluding to or once mentioning his name. The appearance of these writings excited no light sensation in the East, and gave great offence to Nestorius, against whom they were so plainly levelled. Cyril followed this up by a solemn protest, and finally launched out by vehement and bitter denunciations of Nestorius and his doctrine, declaring the latter at variance with the very essence of Christianity. An epistolary altercation now took place between the two patriarchs, which continued for some time, with considerable bitterness on both sides. To bring about Nestorius's removal from the patriarchate, Cyril addressed the emperor, the empress Eudocia, and the emperor's sister Pulcheria, who took a lively interest in Church affairs; and when these efforts failed to bring about the much desired result, he finally determined to rouse the pope against Nestorius, and therefore caused the sermons of that patriarch to be translated and sent to Rome, and at the same time urged his holiness to take summary measures for the vindication of pure doctrine. Celestine, moved by orthodox instinct, and flattered by the appeal to his authority, summoned a synod to meet at Rome, and with their sanction decided that the clergy excommunicated by Nestorius should be restored to the fellowship of the Church; and, further, that if within ten days after receiving the sentence pronounced at Rome, Nestorius should not give a written recantation of his errors, he should be forthwith deposed from his office as patriarch and excommunicated, "ab universalis ecclesiæ catholicæ communione dejectus." Cyril having thus found at last the opportunity of humbling his rival, took it upon himself to execute the sentence of the Roman synod. Summoning a synod of Egyptian bishops at Alexandria, Cyril despatched a letter, A.D. 430, in the name of the synod to Nestorius, in which, conformably to the sentence pronounced at Rome, he called upon him to recant, and concluded with twelve anathemas against his presumed errors, thus formally setting forward the Egyptian creed in opposition to the Antiochian system, as expressed by Theodore of Mopsuestia. The controversy now completely altered its aspect, being converted from a personal into a doctrinal dispute. By orders of John, patriarch of Antioch, a refutation of the Egyptian anathemas was published by Theodoret, bishop of Cyros, a town on the Euphrates; and this refutation, which was written with great severity, called forth an equally violent reply from the pen of Cyril. Nestorius, on his part, treated the deputies sent from Celestine and Cyril with the utmost contempt, and answered the anathemas of Cyril by sending twelve counter anathemas, in which he accused his opponents of the heresy of Apollinaris (q. v.).

The controversy had now become so general and critical that it was thought to be absolutely necessary to summon a general council, and therefore the emperor, Theodosius II, in connection with his Western colleague, Valentinian III, issued a proclamation to all the metropolitans of his empire to meet in œcumenical council at Ephesus about Pentecost of the following year. Cyril and Nestorius arrived at Ephesus at the appointed time, the former authorized temporarily to represent the pope, Celestine, and accompanied by a great number of Egyptian bishops, who came to act as his

devoted tools. The bishop of the city in which the council was assembled was the friend of Cyril, and such was the extent of influence arrayed against Nestorius that he found it necessary to solicit from the imperial commissioner a guard to protect his person and the house in which he resided. A number of the Syrian bishops were prevented from reaching Ephesus in time for the opening of the council, and having waited sixteen days beyond the time appointed by the emperor, Cyril insisted on commencing proceedings, and accordingly on June 22, 431, he opened the synod with 200 bishops. The bishop of Hippo, St. Augustine, was to have presided at the Council of Ephesus, but he died in the latter part of the year 430. Nestorius refused to attend till all the bishops had assembled, and having been formally invited three several times to appear and answer the various charges, oral and written, laid against him, his refusals to obey the summons of the synod were construed as an admission on his own part of his guilt, and it therefore proceeded to his condemnation. The bishops unanimously cried, "Whosoever does not anathematize Nestorius, let himself be anathema; the true faith anathematizes him; the holy council anathematizes him. Whosoever holds fellowship with Nestorius, let him be anathema. We all anathematize the letter and the doctrines of Nestorius. We all anathematize Nestorius and his followers, and his ungodly faith, and his ungodly doctrine. We all anathematize Nestorius," etc. (Mansi, iv, 1170 sq.; Hefele, ii, 169). Then a multitude of Christological expressions of the earlier fathers and several passages from the writings of Nestorius were read, and at the close of the first session, which lasted till late in the night, the synod, in which, says Schaff, "an uncharitable, violent, and passionate spirit ruled the transactions," after many tears, as its members declared, constrained by the laws of the Church, and by the letter of the Roman bishop, Celestine, pronounced sentence in the following terms: "The Lord Jesus Christ, by Nestorius blasphemed, has ordained by this most holy synod that the Nestorius above named be excluded from the episcopal dignity, and from sacerdotal fellowship" (Mansi, iv, 1211; Hefele, ii, 172). This sentence was no sooner passed than, by orders of Cyril, it was publicly proclaimed by heralds through the whole city. It was also formally announced to the emperor. Meanwhile John, bishop of Antioch, with about thirty Syrian bishops, arrived at Ephesus a few days after the council headed by Cyril had met and deposed Nestorius, and, on learning what had been done, they declared the proceedings of that council null and void, proceeded to form a new council, or conciliabulum—yielding nothing to the heated violence of the other—in the dwelling of the celebrated Theodoret (q. v.), under the protection of the imperial counsellor and a body-guard, and declared itself to be the only regular one. The conciliabulum, in turn, now deposed Cyril and Memnon, bishop of Ephesus, and excommunicated the other members who had taken part in the proceedings of the Cyrillian councils until they should manifest penitence and condemn the anathemas of Cyril (Mansi, iv, 1259 sq.; Hefele, ii, 178 sq.). The sentence against the two bishops was made known throughout the city, and formally communicated to the emperor. In the midst of this conflict of councils the deputies of the Roman bishop appeared at Ephesus, and, according to their instructions, gave their formal sanction to all the proceedings of Cyril and his council. The emperor, however, on hearing the report of his commissioner, lost no time in despatching a letter to Ephesus by the hands of an imperial officer, conveying his royal pleasure that the disputed question should be carefully considered, not by any party in the assembly, but by the whole council in common, and until this was done no one of the bishops could be permitted to return to his diocese or to visit the court. Cyril and his party, seeing the evident leaning of the emperor in favor of Nestorius, resorted to various expedients for the purpose of enlisting the influence of the court for themselves, and at length they succeeded in prevailing upon the feeble and vacillating emperor, through the intervention of Theophilus's sister, to confirm the deposition of Nestorius, although he had agreed to withdraw his objection to the word "theotokos," mother of God. Thus, finally forsaken by the court, which had so long protected him against his numerous and powerful enemies, Nestorius saw himself deserted by many of the bishops of his party; and though John of Antioch and a number of the Eastern bishops stood firm for a time, John and Cyril were ultimately brought to an agreement, and both retained their sees. The compromise which was effected between the two prelates and the emperor was brought about mainly by the following steps. John of Antioch sent the aged bishop Paul of Emesa a messenger to Alexandria with a creed which he had already, in a shorter form, laid before the emperor, and which broke the doctrinal antagonism by asserting the duality of the natures against Cyril, and the predicate *mother of God* against Nestorius (Mansi, v, 305; Hefele, ii, 246; Gieseler, I, ii, 150). "We confess," says this symbol, which was composed by Theodoret, "that our Lord Jesus Christ, the only-begotten Son of God, is perfect God and perfect man, of a reasonable soul and body subsisting ($\vartheta εὸν τέλειον καὶ ἄνϑρωπον τέλειον ἐκ ψυχῆς λογικῆς$ [against Apollinaris] $καὶ σώματος$); as to his Godhead begotten of the Father before all time, but as to his manhood born of the Virgin Mary in the end of the days for us and for our salvation; of the same essence with the Father as to his Godhead, and of the same substance with us as to his manhood ($ὁμοούσιον τῷ πατρὶ κατὰ τὴν ϑεότητα, καὶ ὁμοούσιον ἡμῖν κατὰ τὴν ἀνϑρωπότητα$. Here *homoousios*, at least in the second clause, evidently does not imply numerical unity, but only generic unity); for two natures are united with one another ($δύο γὰρ φύσεων ἕνωσις γέγονε$, in opposition to the $μία φύσις$ of Cyril). Therefore we confess *one* Christ, *one* Lord, and *one* Son. By reason of this *union*, which yet is *without confusion* ($κατὰ ταύτην τὴν τῆς ἀσυγχύτου$ [against Cyril] $ἐνώσεως ἔννοιαν$), we also confess that the holy Virgin is *mother of God*, because God the Logos was made flesh and man, and united with himself the temple [humanity] even from the conception; which temple he took from the Virgin. But concerning the words of the Gospel and Epistles respecting Christ, we know that theologians apply some which refer to the *one person* to the two natures in common, but separate others as referring to the two natures, and assign the expressions which become God to the Godhead of Christ, but the expressions of humiliation to his manhood" ($καὶ τὰς μὲν ϑεοπρεπεῖς κατὰ τὴν ϑεότητα τοῦ Χριστοῦ, τὰς δὲ ταπεινὰς κατὰ τὴν ἀνϑρωπότητα αὐτοῦ παραδιδόντας$). This compromise of principle with which John of Antioch was thus made chargeable roused a large party in his own diocese, and many of the Syrian bishops withdrew from all fellowship with him. A schism followed in various parts of the Eastern Church. Nestorius, on the other hand, at his own request, was assigned to his former cloister at Antioch, and on Oct. 25, 431, Maximian was nominated as his successor in Constantinople. Upon the death of this patriarch in A.D. 433, however, a large party at Constantinople demanded the restoration of Nestorius, threatening that if their wish was refused they would set fire to the patriarchal church; but so strong was the influence exercised by the opponents of the deposed patriarch that the vacant dignity was conferred upon his early adversary, Proclus. Cyril, seeing the strength of Nestorius's friends, determined now that his opponent should be forever removed beyond the possibility of exercising any longer any influence in the Church; and the Antiochians, having saved the doctrine of two natures, were gradually won over by persuasives in various forms to consent to the sacrifice of the person of Nestorius for the sake of the unity of the Church. Finally, in A.D. 435,

an imperial edict appeared which condemned Nestorius to perpetual banishment in the Greater Oasis of Upper Egypt. "The unhappy Nestorius," says a Church historian, "was now dragged from the stillness of his former cloister of Euporpius, before the gates of Antioch, in which he had enjoyed four years of repose, from one place of exile to another—first to Arabia, then to Egypt—and was compelled to drink the bitter cup of persecution which he himself, in the days of his power, had forced upon the heretics." To his credit, be it said, he bore his sufferings with resignation and independence. In his exile Nestorius busied himself by the writing of several theological works. Thus he wrote a history of his life and of his theological controversy, in which he sought to vindicate himself against the reproaches of both friends and foes, significantly entitled a *Tragedy*. (Fragments in Evagrius, *Hist. Eccles.* i, 7, and in the *Synodicon adversus Tragœdiam Irenæi*, c. 6. That the book bore the name of *Tragedy* is stated by Ebedjesu, a Nestorian metropolitan. The imperial commissioner, Irenæus, afterwards bishop of Tyre, a friend of Nestorius, composed a book concerning him and the ecclesiastical history of his time, likewise under the title of *Tragedy*, fragments of which, in a Latin translation, are preserved in the so-called *Synodicon*, in Mansi, v, 431 sq.) Various accounts are given of the circumstances which led to his death, but in one thing all are agreed, that his last years were embittered by many acts of harsh and cruel persecution. The precise time or place of his death has not been ascertained, but he is believed to have died previous to A.D. 450, when the Eutychian controversy began to attract notice. The account given by Evagrius, that Nestorius's death was caused by a disease in which his tongue was eaten by worms, rests, according to Evagrius himself, on a single and unnamed authority. The more probably authentic narratives ascribe his death to the effects of a fall. He was still living A.D. 439, when Socrates wrote his history (*Hist. Eccles.* vii, 34). The Monophysite Jacobites are accustomed from year to year to cast stones upon his supposed grave in Upper Egypt, and have spread the tradition that it has never been moistened by the rain of heaven, which yet falls upon the evil and the good. The emperor, who had formerly favored him, but was now turned entirely against him, caused all his writings to be burned, and his followers to be named after Simon Magus, and stigmatized as Simonians. But though this be his memory in the East, in the West the sad fate and upright character of Nestorius, after having been long abhorred, has in modern times, since Luther, found much sympathy; while Cyril, by his violent conduct, has incurred much censure. Walch (*Ketzerhist.* v, 817 sq.) has collected the earlier opinions. Gieseler and Neander take the part of Nestorius against Cyril, and think that he was unjustly condemned. So also Milman, who would rather meet the justice of the divine Redeemer loaded with the errors of Nestorius than with the barbarities of Cyril, but does not enter into the theological merits of the controversy (*Hist. of Latin Christianity*, i, 210). Petavius, Baur, Hefele, and Ebrard, on the contrary, vindicate Cyril against Nestorius, not as to his personal conduct, which was anything but Christian, but in regard to the particular matter in question, viz., the defence of the unity of Christ against the division of his personality. Dorner (ii, 81 sq.) justly distributes the right and wrong, truth and error, on both sides, and considers Nestorius and Cyril representatives of two equally one-sided conceptions, which complement each other. Cyril's strength lay on the religious and speculative side of Christology, that of Nestorius on the ethical and practical. Kahnis (*Dogmatik*, ii, 86) gives a similar judgment. Perhaps it is nearest the truth to concede that Nestorius was possessed of an honest and pious zeal, but was wanting in that prudence and moderation by which zeal should have been controlled.

Literature.—On the sources are to be consulted—(1.)

In favor of Nestorius: Nestorius, Ὁμιλίαι, *Sermones; Anathematismi.* Extracts from the Greek original in the *Acts* of the Council of Ephesus; in a Latin translation in Marius Mercator, a North African layman who just then resided in Constantinople (*Opera*, ed. Garnerius [Paris, 1673], pt. ii; and better ed. Baluzius, Paris, 1684); also in Gallandi, *Bibl. vet. P. P.* (viii, 615–735), and in Migne's *Patrol.* (tom. xlviii). Nestorius's own account (Evagrius, *Hist. Eccles.* i, 7) was used by his friend Irenæus (bishop of Tyre till 448) in his *Tragœdia s. comm. de rebus in synodo Ephesina ac in Oriente toto gestis*, which, however, is lost; the documents attached to it were revised in the 6th century in the *Synodicon adversus Tragœdiam Irenœi* (in Mansi, v, 731 sq.). In favor of Nestorius, or at least of his doctrine, Theodoret († 457) in his works against Cyril, and in three dialogues entitled Ἐρανιστής (Beggar). Comp. also the fragments of Theodore of Mopsuestia († 429).

(2.) *Against Nestorius:* It has been shown that the great opponent of Nestorius was Cyril of Alexandria. He published Ἀναθεματισμοί, five books κατὰ Νεστορίου, and several Epistles against Nestorius and Theodoret, in vol. vi of Aubert's ed. of his *Opera* (Paris, 1638 [in Migne's ed.], tom. ix). These aim to prove that the Virgin Mary was θεοτόκος, and not χριστοτόκος. But there are besides a great number of writers against Nestorius and his heresy whose works are extant. Among these are, Socrates, *Hist. Eccles.* vii, c. 29–35 (written after 431, but still before the death of Nestorius; comp. c. 34); Evagrius, *Hist. Eccles.* i, 2–7; Liberatus (deacon of Carthage about 553), *Breviarium causæ Nestorianorum et Eutychianorum* (ed. Garnier, Paris, 1675; and printed in Gallandi, *Bibl. vet. Patrum*, xii, 121–161); Leontius of Byzantium (monachus), *De sectis;* and *Contra Nestorium et Eutychen* (in Gallandi, *Bibl.* xii, 625 sq., and 658–700). Besides these should be mentioned Philastrius, Epiphanius, Theodoret, Faustus, Maxentius, Marius Mercator, and many others. A complete collection of all the acts of the Nestorian controversy, see in Mansi, iv, 567 sq.; and v, vii, ix.

Of later literature, see Petavius, *Theolog. dogmatum,* tom. iv (*de incarnatione*), lib. i, c. 7 sq.; Garnier, *De hæresi et libris Nestorii,* in his edition of the *Opera Marii Mercator.* (Paris, 1673; newly edited by Migne, Paris, 1846); Gibbon, *Decline and Fall of the Roman Empire,* ch. xlvii; Jablonski, *De Nestorianismo* (Berol. 1724); Gengler (R. C.), *Ueber die Verdammung des Nestorius* (in *Tübinger Quartalschrift,* 1835, No. 2); Schmid, *Vera Nestorii de unione naturarum in Christo sententia* (Jena, 1794, 4to); Salig, *De Eutychianismo ante Eutychen* (Wolfenb. 1723, 4to); Schröckh, *Kirchen-Geschichte,* xviii, 176–312; Walch, *Ketzerhist.* v, 289–936; Schaff, *Ch. Hist.* iii, 714–733; Neander, Torrey's transl. ii, 446–524; iv, 44 sq.; and his *Hist. of Dogma.* p. 329, 331–333, 336, 393; Gieseler, *Kirchen-Geschichte,* i, div. ii, p. 131 sq. (4th ed.); Baur, *Gesch. der Dreieinigkeitslehre,* i, 693–777; Dorner, *Person of Christ,* ii, 60–98; Hefele (R. C.), *Conciliengesch.* ii, 134 sq.; Milman, *History of Latin Christianity,* i, 195–252; Neale, *History of the Holy Eastern Church (Patriarchate of Alexandria),* i, 233–277; Wright, *Early Christianity in Arabia,* § ix; Stanley, in his *History of the Eastern Church,* has seen fit to ignore the Nestorian and the other Christological controversies —the most important in the history of the Greek Church; Liddon, *Bampton Lectures on the Divinity of Christ,* p. 121, 257, 463; comp. also W. Möller, art. Nestorius, in Herzog's *Real-Encykl.* x, 288–296. See also the literature appended to the article NESTORIANS.

Net. There are in Scripture several words denoting different kinds of nets, and this, with the frequency of images derived from them, shows that nets were much in use among the Hebrews for fishing, hunting, and fowling. Indeed, for the two latter purposes nets were used to an extent of which now, since the invention of fire-arms, a notion can scarcely be formed. The various terms applied by the Hebrews to nets had reference either to the construction of the article or to its use and objects. To the first of these we may assign the following terms: (1.) מִכְמָר, *mikmár,* or מַכְמֹר, *makmor,* which occurs only in Psa. cxli, 10; Isa. li, 20, where it denotes a hunter's net, is derived from כָּמַר, *kamár,* to *plait or interweave;* but a longer word, from the same source, מִכְמֹרֶת, *mikmóreth* (A. V. "drag"), denotes the net of fishermen (Isa. xix, 8; Hab. i, 15, 16). (2.) שֶׂבָךְ, *sebák,* or (in its fem. form) שְׂבָכָה, *sebakáh,* which is derived from שָׂבַךְ, *sabák,* to *twine,* and designates an actual hunting-net in Job xviii, 6 (A. V. "snare"); but elsewhere is applied to network or latticework, especially around the capitals of columns ("network, wreathen-work," etc., 1 Kings vii, 18, 20, 41, 42; 2 Kings xxv, 17; 2 Chron. iv, 12, 13; Jer. lii, 22, 23), and also before a window or balcony ("lattice," 2 Kings i, 2). To the second head we may assign the following: (3.) חֵרֶם, *chérem,* which denotes a net for either fishing or fowling. It is derived from חָרַם, *charám,* signifying *to shut up;* and the idea is. therefore, founded on its shutting in the prey. It occurs (in this sense) in Hab. i, 16, 17; Ezek. xxvi, 5, 14; xlvii, 10; Zech. xiv, 11, etc. In Eccles. vii, 26 it is applied by an apt metaphor to female entanglements. (4.) מָצוֹד, *matsód,* or מָצוּד, *matsúd* (with the corresponding feminine forms, מְצוֹדָה, *metsodáh,* and מְצוּדָה, *metsudáh*), from the root צוּד, *tsúd, to lie in wait,* occurs in the sense of a *net* for fishes (Eccles. ix, 12) or animals (Job xix, 6; Psa. xlvi, 11; "snare," Ezek. xii, 13; xvii, 20; "to be hunted," Ezek. xiii, 21); metaphorically of the *prey* caught (Prov. xii, 10), or of female blandishments ("snare," Eccles. vii, 26). (5.) רֶשֶׁת, *résheth,* the most common term, from יָרַשׁ, *yarásh, to get possession of,* is applied to a corded *meshwork* of any description, whether for catching birds (Prov. i, 17) or other animals (Job xviii, 8; Psa. ix, 15; x, 9; xxv, 15; xxxi, 4; xxxv, 7, 8; lvii, 6; cxl, 5; Prov. xxix. 5; Lam. i, 13; Ezek. xii, 13; xix, 8; xxxii, 3; Hos. v, 1; vii, 12), or as a screen for sifting ashes from the fire (Exod. xxvii, 4, 5; xxxviii, 4). What distinction other than these vague intimations there may have been between the various nets described by the Hebrew terms we are unable to decide. In the New Testament no other net than that for fishing is mentioned. (6.) The most general word which describes it (δίκτυον, from δικεῖν, *to throw,* occurring in Matt. iv, 20, 21; Mark i, 18, 19; Luke v, 2, 4, 5, 6; John xxi, 6, 8, 11) is usually confined to fishing-nets by classical writers, although sometimes applied to the nets of hunters. (7.) Another word to describe a net, ἀμφίβληστρον (from ἀμφιβάλλω, *to cast around*), occurs in Matt. iv, 18; Mark i, 16, which, like *chérem* above, is founded on the idea of enfolding or shutting in the prey. (8.) A special kind was the σαγήνη (from σάττω, *to load*), whence our word *seine,* a large hauling or draw-net; it is the term used in the parable of the draw-net (Matt. xiii, 47).

The metaphorical references to the net are very nu-

Piece of an Ancient Egyptian Fishing-net, with leads, etc., attached. (From the Berlin Museum.)

merous: it was selected as an appropriate image of the subtle devices of the enemies of God on the one hand (e. g. Psa. ix, 15; xxv, 15; xxxi, 4), and of the unavertable vengeance of God on the other (Lam. i, 13; Ezek. xii, 13; Hos. vii, 12). See SNARE.

1. *Fishing-nets.*—We have no direct information concerning the fish-nets of the Hebrews, but suppose that they were not materially different from those of the ancient Egyptians, concerning which we now possess very good information, and which are more than once mentioned in Scripture (Isa. xix, 8). The Egyptians constructed their nets of flax-string: the netting-needle was made of wood, and in shape closely resembled our

own (Wilkinson, *Anc. Egypt*. ii, 95). See NEEDLE. The usual fishing-net among this people was of a long form, like the common drag-net, with wooden floats on the upper and leads on the lower side. The leads were occasionally of an elongated shape, hanging from the outer cord or border of the net; but they were most usually flat, and, being folded round the cord, the opposite sides were beaten together; and this method continues to be adopted by the modern Egyptians. The net was sometimes let down from a boat, but those who pulled it usually stood on the shore, and landed the fish on a shelving bank. This mode, however, was more adapted to river than to lake fishing; and hence in all the detailed examples of fishing in the New Testament the net is cast from and drawn into boats, excepting in one case where, the draught being too great to take into the boat, the fishers dragged the net after their boats to the shore (John xxi, 6, 8). Sometimes in shallow water a smaller net was used

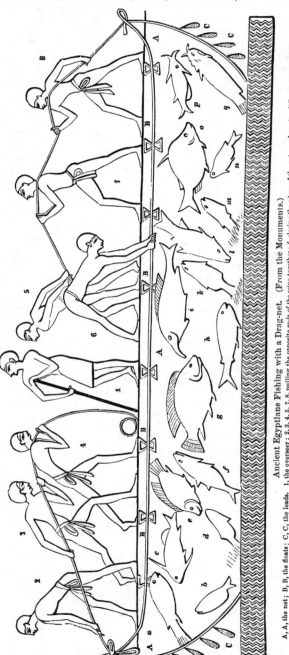

Ancient Egyptians Fishing with a Drag-net. (From the Monuments.)

A, A, the net; B, B, the floats; C, C, the leads. 1, the overseer; 2, 3, 4, 5, 7, 8, pulling the opposite ends of the seine together; 6, closing the edges of the net. *a, b, c,* etc., different kinds of fishes.

Ancient Egyptian Fowling Scene. (From the Monuments.)

Figs. 1, 2, 3, pull the rope that the net may collapse; 4 makes a sign with his hand to keep silence and pull; at *p* the rope is fixed· at *f, g, e,* are geese and baskets of their eggs; *h* are pelicans; *i* and *n*, papyrus plants.

furnished with a pole on either side, to which it was attached; and the fisherman, holding one of the poles in each hand, thrust it below the surface of the water, and awaited the moment when a shoal of fish passed over it.

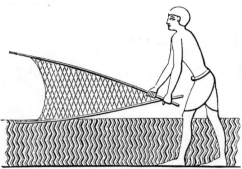

A sort of Landing-net used by the Ancient Egyptians. (From the Monuments.)

This, or a smaller landing-net, likewise secured the large fish, which had been wounded with the spear or entangled with the hook. In the large cut given on p. 978 the fishermen in the boat, excepting the master, are almost naked, as are also those who have occasion to wade in the water in hauling the net to the shore. Such seems also to have been the practice among the Hebrew fishermen; for Peter, when he left the boat to hasten on shore to his risen Lord, "girt his fisher's coat unto him, for he was naked" (John xxi, 7); although, in this case, the word "naked" (q. v.) must be understood with some latitude. For modern fishing-nets in Palestine, see Thomson, *Land and Book*, ii, 79 sq. See FISHING.

2. *Fowling-nets.*—These were also in common use among the Hebrews, and the references to them in the Bible receive striking illustration from the representations on the Egyptian monuments. The ancient Egyptians either caught the birds in large clap-nets or in traps; and they sometimes shot them with arrows, or felled them with a throw-stick, as they flew in the thickets. The trap was generally made of network, strained over a frame. It consisted of two semicircular sides or flaps, of equal size, one or both moving on the common bar, or axis, upon which they rested. When the trap was set, the two flaps were kept open by means of strings, probably of catgut, which, the moment the bait that stood in the centre of the bar was touched, slipped aside, and allowed the two flaps to collapse, and thus secured the bird. Another kind, which was square, appears to have closed in the same manner; but its construction was different, the framework running across the centre, and not, as in others, round the edges of the trap. So skilful were they in making traps that they were strong enough to hold the hyæna; and in the one which caught the robber in the treasury of Rhampsinitus the power of the spring or the mechanism of the catch was so perfect that his brother was unable to open it or release him. Similar in ingenuity, though not in strength, were the nets made by the convicts banished to Rhinocolura by Actisanes, which, though made of split straws, were yet capable of catching many of the numerous quails that frequented that desert region at a particular period of the year. The clap-net was of different forms, though on the same general principle as the traps. The larger ones consisted, like the smaller ones above, of two sides or frames, over which the network was strained (see next page); at one end was a short rope, which they fastened to a bush or a cluster of reeds, and at the other was one of considerable length, which, as soon as the birds were seen feeding in the area within the net, was pulled by the fowlers, causing the two sides to collapse. As soon as they had selected a convenient spot for laying down the net, in a field or on the surface of a pond, the known resort of numerous wild fowl, they spread open the two sides or flaps, and secured them in such a manner that they remained flat upon the ground until pulled by the rope. A man, crouched behind some reeds growing at a convenient distance from the spot, from which he could observe the birds as they came down, watched the net, and, enjoining silence by placing his hand over his mouth, beckoned to those holding the rope to keep themselves in readiness till he saw them assembled in sufficient numbers, when a wave of his hand gave the signal for closing the net (Wilkinson, *Ancient Egyptians*, ii, 181 sq.).

"Birds formed an article of food among the Hebrews (Lev. xvii, 13), and much skill was exercised in catching them. The following were the most approved methods: (1.) The trap (פַּח), which consisted of two parts—a net, strained over a frame, and a stick to support it, but so placed that it should give way at the slightest touch; the stick or springe was termed מוֹקֵשׁ (Amos iii, 5, 'gin;' Psa. lxix, 22, 'trap'); this was the most usual method (Job xviii, 9; Eccles. ix, 12; Prov. vii, 23). (2.) The snare (צַמִּים, from צָמַם, *to braid;* Job xviii, 9, A. V. 'robber'), consisting of a cord (חֶבֶל, Job xviii, 10; comp. Psa. xviii, 5; cxvi, 3; cxl, 5) so set as to catch the bird by the leg. (3.) The net, as above. (4.) The decoy, to which reference is made in Jer. v, 26, 27—a cage of peculiar construction (כְּלוּב)—was filled with birds, which acted as decoys; the door of the cage was kept open by a piece of stick acting as a springe (מֵשְׁחִית), and closed suddenly with a *clap* (whence perhaps the term *kelûb*) on the entrance of a bird. The partridge appears to have been used as a decoy (Ecclus. xi. 30)." See FOWLING.

3. *Hunting-nets.*—These, as has already been seen, were

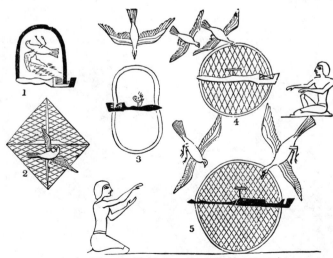

Ancient Egyptian Bird-traps. (From the Monuments.)

Fig. 1. Trap closed, and the bird caught in it; the network of it has been effaced, as also in Fig. 3. The other traps are open.

of universal use among the Hebrews. "The objects for which hunting is practiced indicate the various conditions of society and the progress of civilization. Hunting, as a matter of necessity, whether for the extermination of dangerous beasts or for procuring sustenance, betokens a rude and semi-civilized state; as an amusement, it betokens an advanced state. In the former, personal prowess and physical strength are the qualities which elevate a man above his fellows and fit him for dominion, and hence one of the greatest heroes of antiquity is described as a 'mighty hunter before the Lord' (Gen. x, 9), while Ishmael, the progenitor of a wild race, was famed as an archer (Gen. xxi, 20), and Esau, holding a similar position, was 'a cunning hunter, a man of the field' (Gen. xxv, 27). The latter state may be exemplified, not indeed from Scripture itself, but from contemporary records. Among the accomplishments of Herod, his skill in the chase is particularly noticed; he kept a regular stud and a huntsman (Josephus, *Ant.* xvi, 10, 3), followed up the sport in a wild country (*Ant.* xv, 7, 7) which abounded with stags, wild asses, and bears, and is said to have killed as many as forty head in a day (*War*, i, 21, 113). The wealthy in Egypt and Assyria followed the sports of the field with great zest; they had their preserves for the express purpose of keeping and hunting game (Wilkinson's *Anc. Egyptians*, i, 215; Xen. *Cyrop.* i, 4, 5, 14), and drew from hunting scenes subjects for decorating the walls of their buildings, and even the robes they wore on state occasions. The Hebrews, as a pastoral and agricultural people, were not given to the sports of the field; the density of the population, the earnestness of their character, and the tendency of their ritual regulations, particularly those affecting food, all combined to discourage the practice of hunting; and perhaps the examples of Ishmael and Esau were recorded with the same object. There was no lack of game in Palestine; on their entrance into the land the wild beasts were so numerous as to be dangerous (Exod. xxiii, 29); the utter destruction of them was guarded against by the provisions of the Mosaic law (Exod. xxiii, 11; Lev. xxv, 7). Some of the fiercer animals survived to a late period, as lions (Judg. xiv, v; 1 Sam. xvii, 34;

2 Sam. xxiii, 20; 1 Kings xiii, 24; xx, 36) and bears (1 Sam. xvii, 34; 2 Kings ii, 24); jackals (Judg. xv. 4) and foxes (Cant. ii, 15) were also numerous; hart, roebuck, and fallow deer (Deut. xii, 15; 1 Kings iv, 23) formed a regular source of sustenance, and were possibly

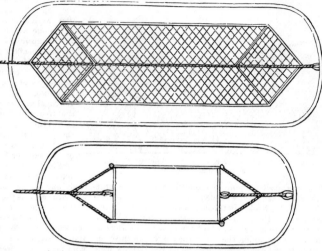

Ancient Egyptian Clap-nets. (From the Monuments.)

preserved in enclosures. The manner of catching these animals was either by digging a pitfall (שַׁחַת), which was the usual manner with the larger animals, as the lion (2 Sam. xxiii, 20; Ezek. xix, 4, 8); or, secondly, by a trap (פַּח), which was set under ground (Job xviii, 10), in the run of the animal (Prov. xxii, 5), and caught it by the leg (Job xviii, 9); or, lastly, by the use of the net, of which there were various kinds, as for the gazelle (?) (Isa. li, 20, A.V. 'wild bull'), and other animals of that class. The game selected was generally such as was adapted for food (Prov. xii, 27), and care was taken to pour out the blood of these as well as of tame animals (Lev. xvii, 13)." All this is admirably and fully illustrated on the Egyptian monuments. Among the ancient Egyptians, in hunting, a space of considerable size was sometimes enclosed with nets, into which the animals were driven. The spots thus enclosed were usually in the vicinity of the water brooks to which they were in the habit of repairing in the morning and evening; and having awaited the time when they went to drink, the hunters disposed their nets, occupied proper positions for observing them unseen, and gradually

Deer-shooting within a Netted Enclosure. (From the Kuyunjik Gallery, British Museum.)

closed in upon them. The usages of the Egyptians, and, so far as can be ascertained, of other Oriental nations, in this respect, correspond with the intimations of Julius Pollux (*Onomast.* v, 4), who states that two kinds of nets were employed in this mode of hunting. One, a long net, called by the Greeks δίκτυον, was furnished with several ropes, and was supported on forked poles, varying in length to correspond with the inequalities of the ground over which it extended. The others were smaller nets, called ἐνόδια, for stopping gaps. These practices are obviously alluded to in such passages as Job xix, 6; Psa. cxl, 5; Isa. li, 20. The method in which the net was applied is familiar to us from the descriptions in Virgil (*Æn.* iv, 121, 151 sq.; x, 707 sq.); it was placed across a ravine or narrow valley, frequented by the animals for the sake of water, and the game was driven in by the hunters, and then despatched either with bow and arrow or spears (comp. Wilkinson, i, 214). The Assyrian monuments likewise confirm this method of taking game. See HUNTING.

Netchaëf, INNOCENT, a Russian prelate and writer, was born in 1722, and was educated for the Church; and, after filling various offices of distinction, was made archbishop of Pskof and of Riga. He died at St. Petersburg, Jan. 24, 1799. Netchaëf is known as the author of several *Sermons,* published by the holy synod in 1775, to be read in the pulpit; and by the following works: *Of the Manner of Confessing Children* (Moscow, 1769 and 1795, 8vo):—*Counsels of a Bishop to a Priest* (St. Petersburg, 1790 and 1795):—*Preparations for Death* (St. Petersburg, 1793). The celebrated poet Derjavin has composed the epitaph of Netchaëf's tomb, which may be seen in a cell of St. Alexandre-Nevski. See *Dictionnaire historique des écrivains ecclésiastiques de l'Église Gréco-russe,* s. v.

Nethan'eël (Heb. *Nethanel',* נְתַנְאֵל, *given of God;* Sept. Ναθαναήλ), the name of ten Hebrews. See also NATHANIEL.

1. A son of Zuar and phylarch of Issachar at the time of the exode (Numb. i, 8; ii, 5; vii, 18, 28; x, 15). B.C. 1657.

2. The fourth son of Jesse, and brother of king David (1 Chron. xi, 14). B.C. cir. 1070.

3. A priest who blew a trumpet before the ark when David brought it from Kirjath-Jearim to Jerusalem (1 Chron. xv, 24). B.C. 1043.

4. A Levite, father of the scribe Shemaiah (1 Chron. xxiv, 6). B.C. ante 1014.

5. A porter of the Temple, fifth-named son of Obed-edom of the family of Korhites in the tribe of Levi (1 Chron. xxvi, 4). B.C. cir. 1014.

6. One of five "princes" who were commanded by Jehoshaphat, on his accession, to teach the law from the book, in connection with priests and Levites, through the cities of Judah (2 Chron. xvii, 7). B.C. 912.

7. A chief Levite, brother of Conaniah and Shemaiah, who gave offerings when Josiah renewed the observance of the passover in Jerusalem (2 Chron. xxxv, 9). B.C. 628.

8. Fourth named of six sons of Pashur, of the "sons of the priests," who were found by Ezra to have taken idolatrous wives (Ezra x, 22). B.C. 458.

9. A priest, "son" of Jedaiah, "chief of the fathers," in the days of the high-priest Joiakim (Neh. xii, 21). B.C. cir. 446.

10. A priest's son, and brother of Zechariah, who bore a trumpet at the dedication of the walls of Jerusalem (Neh. xii, 36). B.C. 446. Possibly he was identical with 9.

Nethani'ah (Heb. *Nethanyah',* נְתַנְיָה, also in the prolonged form *Nethanya'hu,* נְתַנְיָהוּ, 1 Chron. xxv, 12; 2 Chron. xvii, 8; Jer. xxxvi, 14; xl, 8; xli, 9, *given of Jehovah;* Sept. Ναθανίας, v. r. in 2 Kings xxv, 23 Μαθθανίας), the name of four Hebrews.

1. Third named of four sons of Asaph, who were ap-

pointed by order of David to minister in the Temple. He was chief of the fifth division of sacred musicians (1 Chron. xxv, 2, 12). B.C. cir. 1015.

2. A Levite, one of those sent with "princes" and priests, on the accession of Jehoshaphat, to teach the law through the cities of Judah (2 Chron. xvii, 8). B.C. cir. 912.

3. Son of Shelamiah and father of Jehudi (q. v.) (Jer. xxxvi, 14). B.C. cir. 638.

4. Son of Elishama (q. v.) of the royal family of Judah, and father of Ishmael (q. v.) who murdered Gedaliah (2 Kings xxv, 23, 25; Jer. xl, 8, 14, 15; xli, 1, 2, 6, 7, 9, 10, 11, 12, 15, 16, 18). B.C. cir. 620.

Nether. See NITRE.

Netherlands. See BELGIUM AND HOLLAND.

Netherlands Missionary Society. See the article MISSIONS in this volume, especially p. 358.

Neth'inim (Heb. *Nethinim,* נְתִינִים) is the name given in the post-exilian books of the Hebrew Scriptures to the hereditary Temple servants who were assigned to the Levites to do the subordinate and menial work.

1. *Name and its Signification.*—The name נתינים, which is the plural of נתין, passive adjective from נתן, *to give,* "to set apart, to denote," properly denotes *given,* "the devoted," i. e. to do the menial work of the sanctuary for the Levites, and, like other terms of office, has become the appellative of that class of men who were thus allotted as hereditary Temple servants to assist the Levites. Hence they are called ἱερόδουλοι by Josephus (*Ant.* xi, 5, 6), while the Vulg. (*Nathinaei*), the Chaldee (נתיניך), Luther (*Nethinim*), the Zurich Bible, Coverdale, Matthew's Bible, the Geneva Version, the Bishops' Bible, and the A. V. uniformly retain the original in all the seventeen passages in which it occurs, except that the A. V., following the example of the preceding English versions, incorrectly adds the plural termination *s* ("*Nethinims*") to the Hebrew ים, which is already plural, as it does in "cherubims." The Sept., however, is inconsistent both in its spelling and rendering of it. Thus, in nine places out of the seventeen it has οἱ Ναθινίμ, Alex. Ναθινείμ (Ezra ii, 70; vii, 7, 24; viii, 20 [twice]; Neh. iii, 26; vii, 46, 73; x, 28); in three οἱ Ναθιναῖοι (Ezra ii, 43 [Vat. Ναθινίμ]; Neh. xi, 3, 21); in two οἱ Ναθανείμ [Vat. Ναθανίμ] (Ezra ii, 58; Neh. vii, 60); in one Ἀθανείμ (Ezra viii, 17); in another it takes ברית הנתינים for one word, and substitutes for it Βηθαναθινίμ (Neh. iii, 31); and in another place again it translates נתינים by οἱ δεδομένοι (1 Chron. ix, 2). Theodoret's explanation of נתינים, δόσις Ἰαώ, τουτέστι, τοῦ ὄντος Θεοῦ (*Quæst. in. i. Paralip.*), which is also that of Bochart, "*dedititios* appellavit, quod se sponte dededissent" (*Phaleg,* lib. ii, cap. i; *Opp.* i, 67, ed. Lugduni, 1692), is both contrary to the grammatical meaning of the word, which, as "*Pail*" *participle,* can only be *those given,* and not *who voluntarily gave themselves,* and at variance with facts.

2. *Origin and Duties of the Nethinim.*—It is the unanimous voice both of Jewish tradition (comp. *Jebamoth,* 78 b; *Midrash Jalkut* on Josh. ix, 27) and the best Jewish commentators (comp. Rashi and Aben-Ezra on Ezra ii, 43; Kimchi on Josh. ix, 20) that the Gibeonites whom Joshua consigned forever to be the hewers of wood and the drawers of water, i. e. the perpetual menial servants (לברית אלהי) of the sanctuary (Josh. ix, 21-27), are the original caste denominated *Nethinim* in the post-exilian period; and there is no valid reason for rejecting this ancient tradition. As these Gibeonites or sanctuary slaves were greatly diminished by the bloody persecutions of Saul, and in the massacre at Nob (2 Sam. xxii, 1-19), and moreover, as the reorganization and extension of the sanctuary service effected by the royal Psalmist both rendered the work of the Levites

very laborious and demanded an increase of the existing staff of menial servants, "David and the princes [after him] gave (נתן) the *Nethinim* (or *these given ones*, הנתונים) for the service of the Levites" (Ezra viii, 20). From the ancient practice of consigning aliens and captives of war to do both the menial work of the people at large and of the priests and Levites (Numb. xxxi, 25-47; Deut. xxix, 10), which also obtained among the Syrians, Phœnicians, the Greeks, and other nations of antiquity, and which still obtains among the Arabs, who devote slaves to the service of the Kaaba at Mecca and to the sepulchre of the Prophet at Medina (Burckhardt, *Travels in Arabia*, i, 288, etc.; ii, 166, etc., 174, 181), there can be little doubt that the thinned ranks were recruited by David and the other princes from the captives taken in battle. Indeed, their foreign names given in the catalogue of those who returned from Babylon (Ezra ii, 43-58) fully confirm this view. As this newly-increased and reorganized staff, founded upon the remnant of the aboriginal Gibeonites, was now formally and *exclusively given* by David to the Levites (Ezra viii, 20), just as the Levites themselves, by the command of God, were given to the priests (Numb. viii, 19; xviii, 2-6), their primitive name was no more applicable to them, because the new accession, constituting the majority, were no Gibeonites, and because they were no more the servants of the sanctuary at large, but were *a gift* to the Levites. It was for this reason that they were henceforth called *Nethinim* (נתונים), *the given ones*, i. e. to the Levites, the very expression used with regard to the Levites when they in their turn were given to the priests. See Levite. Being thus given to them, the Nethinim had to relieve the Levites of every menial and laborious work connected with the sanctuary. They had to draw and carry the water, hew and fetch the wood, and attend to everything which the Levites ordered them to do; and because they were so entirely at the disposal of the Levites, therefore the Bible prescribes no special duties for the Nethinim.

3. *Number of the Nethinim, their Locality, Revenues, and Social Position.*—We must not forget that the Levites were *given* to Aaron and his sons, i. e. to the priests as an order, and were accordingly the first Nethinim (נתונם, Numb. iii, 9; viii, 19). At first they were the only attendants, and their work must have been laborious enough. The first conquests, however, brought them their share of the captive slaves of the Midianites, and 320 were *given* to them as having charge of the Tabernacle (Numb. xxxi, 47), while 32 only were assigned specially to the priests. This disposition to devolve the more laborious offices of their ritual upon slaves of another race showed itself again in the treatment of the Gibeonites. They, too, were *given* (A. V. "made") to be "hewers of wood and drawers of water" for the house of God (Josh. ix, 27), and the addition of so large a number (the population of five cities) must have relieved the Levites from much that had before been burdensome. We know little or nothing as to their treatment. It was a matter of necessity that they should be circumcised (Exod. xii, 48) and conform to the religion of their conquerors, and this might at first seem hard enough. On the other hand, it must be remembered that they presented themselves as recognising the supremacy of Jehovah (Josh. ix, 9), and that for many generations the remembrance of the solemn covenant entered into with them made men look with horror on the shedding of Gibeonitish blood (2 Sam. xxi, 9), and protected them from much outrage. No addition to the number thus employed appears to have been made during the period of the Judges, and they continued to be known by their old name as the Gibeonites. The want of a further supply was, however, felt when the reorganization of worship commenced under David. Either the massacre at Nob had involved the Gibeonites as well as the priests (1 Sam. xxii, 19), or else they had

fallen victims to some other outburst of Saul's fury, and though there were survivors (2 Sam. xxi, 2), the number was likely to be quite inadequate for the greater stateliness of the new worship at Jerusalem. It is to this period accordingly that the origin of the class bearing this name may be traced. The Nethinim were those "whom David and the princes appointed (Heb. *gave*) for the service of the Levites" (Ezra viii, 20). Though their number is nowhere given up to the time of the Babylonian captivity, yet the fact that the aboriginal *Hieroduli*, i. e. the Gibeonites, consisted of the population of five cities when the service of the sanctuary was not so imposing makes it pretty certain that the Nethinim with whom David and the other princes replenished the thinned ranks at the time when the Temple worship required a large staff of menial servants must have counted their thousands. As a matter of convenience, they most probably lived within the precincts and in the immediate neighborhood of the Temple, and must have been supported by the contributions of the people. We have more decided information about them in the post-exilian records. Only 612 Nethinim returned from Babylon—392 with Zerubbabel (Ezra ii, 58; Neh. vii, 60), and 220 with Ezra (Ezra viii, 20)—under the leadership of Ziha and Gispa (Neh. xi, 21), who, as their foreign names indicate, were of their own body. But even this small number had to be coaxed in order to get them to return from exile, as is evident from Ezra viii, 17, where they are addressed as *brethren* of Iddo, a chief of the Levites. It is evident from the whole context (Ezra viii, 15-19), which speaks of securing Iddo's interests to procure Levites as well as Nethinim, that he was not *a Nathin*, but a *distinguished Levite* who had great influence both among his own Levitical brethren and the Nethinim who were under his control. Some of them lived in Ophel, which they helped to rebuild (Neh. iii, 26; xi, 26), because of its proximity to the Temple; while others, as in the pre-exilian period, dwelt with the Levites in their own cities (Ezra ii, 70). They were under the control of a chief of their own body (Ezra ii, 43; Neh. vii, 46). Belonging to the Temple, they, like the other sacred ministers, were exempted from taxation by the Persian satraps (Ezra vii, 24), and were maintained from the Temple treasury and (מעשר שני) the second tithes (*Jebamoth*, 86 b; *Jerusalem Maaser Sheni*, v, 15; *Jerusalem Sota*, ix, 11; comp. Herzfeld, *Geschichte des Volkes Israel*, i, 138-140). Though they conformed to the Jewish religion (Exod. xii, 48; Deut. xxix, 11; Josh. ix, 9; Neh. x, 28), they occupied a very low position, and were even ranged below the *Mamzer* (ממזר), or illegal offspring, as may be seen from the following order of precedence given in the Mishna: "A priest is before a Levi, a Levi before an Israelite, an Israelite before a *Mamzer*, a *Mamzer* before a *Nathin*, a *Nathin* before a proselyte, and a proselyte before a manumitted slave" (*Horajoth*, iii, 8). The Nethinim were restricted to intermarriage among themselves, and if a Jew or Jewess married one of them, though all the valid ceremonies were performed, the issue shared in all the degrading disqualifications of the Nethinim (Mishna, *Kiddushin*, iii, 12; iv, 1; *Jebamoth*, ii, 4); and they were even excluded from the privileges of being exempt from military service, allotted to newly-married people and to those who were faint-hearted (Deut. xx, 7, 8, with Mishna, *Sota*, viii, 3-6). If a woman was suspected of being deflowered by any one, or if she had an illegitimate child, it was ascribed to a Nathin, and the offspring took the degraded position of the Nathin, notwithstanding the assertion of the mother that the father of the child was a priest, unless she could adduce proof to support her assertion (Mishna, *Kethuboth*, i, 8, 9). If a court of justice (בית דין) gave a decision, and one of the members of the court was found to be a Nathin, the judgment was invalid, inasmuch as he was not regarded as a legal number of the congregation (עדה) specified in Lev. iv, 13; Numb. xxxv, 24 (Mishna, *Horajoth*, iii, 1). Eventually they seem to have been merged in the mass of the Jewish population, as no allusion to them occurs in the Apocrypha or New Testament. Their number, at all events, was then insufficient for the service of the Temple; whence, as Josephus tells us (*War*, ii, 17, 6), a festival, called Ξυλοφορία (Xylophoria), was established, in which the people, to supply the deficiency, were obliged to bring a certain quantity of wood to the Temple for the use of the altar of burnt-offering. See Schröder, *De Nethinæis* (Marb. 1719); Will, *De Nethinæis Levitarum famulis* (Altdorf, 1745); Lampe, in *Miscell. Groning.* i, 463 sq., 539 sq.; Pfeffinger, in *Ugolin. Thesaur.* vol. xiii. See GIBEONITE; TEMPLE.

Neton. Macrobius, in his *Saturnalia*, mentions that the Accitani, an Iberian tribe, worshipped under the name of *Neton* a statue of Mars adorned with rays of light.

Neto'phah (Heb. *Netophah'*, נְטֹפָה, *distillation*; Sept. Νετωφά in Ezra, v. r. Νεφωτά; but Ἀνετωφά in Neh., v. r. Ἀτωφά; Vulg. *Netopha*), a town in Palestine, fifty-six of whose people returned from captivity with Zerubbabel (Ezra ii, 22; Neh. vii, 26). Two of David's guard, Maharai and Heleb or Hildai, leaders also of two of the monthly courses (1 Chron. xxvii, 13, 15), were Netophathites, and it was the native place of at least one of the captains who remained under arms near Jerusalem after its destruction by Nebuchadnezzar: for the "villages of the Netophathites" were the residence of the Levites (1 Chron. ix, 16), a fact which shows that they did not confine themselves to the places named in the catalogues of Josh. xxi and 1 Chron. vi. From another notice we learn that the particular Levites who inhabited these villages were singers (Neh. xii, 28). That Netophah belonged to Judah appears from the fact that the two heroes above mentioned belonged, the one to the Zarhites—that is, the great family of Zerah, one of the chief houses of the tribe—and the other to Othniel, the son-in-law of Caleb. To judge from Neh. vii, 26, it was in the neighborhood of, or closely connected with, Bethlehem, which is also implied by 1 Chron. ii, 54, though the precise force of the latter statement cannot now be made out. From the number of Netophathites who returned from captivity, the place was probably only a small village, which indeed may account for its having escaped mention in the lists of Joshua. The Netophathites seem to have been a warlike race, if we may judge from the fact that one of the great military leaders of the Jews during the rule of the viceroy Gedaliah was Seraiah from that place (2 Kings xxv, 23; Jer. xl, 8). A remarkable tradition, of which there is no trace in the Bible, but which, nevertheless, is not improbably authentic, is preserved by the Jewish authors, to the effect that the Netophathites slew the guards which had been placed by Jeroboam on the roads leading to Jerusalem to stop the passage of the first-fruits from the country villages to the Temple (Targum on 1 Chron. ii, 34; on Ruth iv, 20, and Eccles. iii, 11). Jeroboam's obstruction, which is said to have remained in force till the reign of Hoshea (see the notes of Beck to Targum on 1 Chron. ii, 54), was commemorated by a fast on the 23d Sivan, which is still retained in the Jewish calendar (see the calendar given by Basnage, *Hist. des Juifs*, vol. vi, ch. xxix). Netophah is not mentioned by Eusebius and Jerome, and although in the Mishna reference is made to the "oil of Netophah" (*Peah*, vii, 1, 12), and to the "valley of Beth-Netophah," in which artichokes flourished, whose growth determined the date of some ceremonial observance (*Shebiith*, ix, 7), nothing is said as to the situation of the place. The latter may well be the present village of *Beit Nettif*, which stands on the edge of the great valley of the Wady es-Sumt (Robinson, *Bib. Res.* ii, 16, 17; Porter, *Hand-book*, p. 248), but can hardly be the Netophah of the Bible, since it is not near Beth-

lehem, but in quite another direction. It may, however, be the place mentioned (as above) by the rabbins (see Reland, *Palæst.* p. 650, 909). The only name in the neighborhood of Bethlehem suggestive of Netophah is that which appears in Van de Velde's map (1858) as *Antûbeh*, and in Tobler (*Dritte Wand.* p. 80) as *Um-Tûba*, attached to a half-ruined village about two miles north-east of Bethlehem and a wady which falls therefrom into the Wady en-Nar, or Kidron. See NETOPHATHI.

Neto'phathi (Neh. xii, 28) or **Neto'phathite** (so A. V. in the sing., except 1 Chron. ii, 54; ix, 16, "Netophathites," Heb. everywhere *Netophathi'*, the form corresponding to "Netophathite" and "Netophathites," always with the art. הַנְּטֹפָתִי, a Gentile from *Netophah*; Chron. [plene] הַנְּטוֹפָתִי; Sept. Νετωφαθί, as 1 Chron. ii, 54, etc., but Νετωφατίτης, 2 Sam. xxiii, 28; Νετωφαθίτης, 2 Kings xxv, 23; Νετωφατί, 1 Chron. xxvii, 15; Νετουφάτ, 1 Chron. xxvii, 13; Νετωφαθί, Jer. xl, 8; with v. r. Νωτεφατί; once mistakenly rendered ἀπὸ ἐπαυλέων, Neh. xii, 28), an inhabitant of Netophah (q. v.). The Netophathites are called sons of Salma (1 Chron. ii, 54), probably the founder of the village (2 Sam. xxiii, 28, 29; Jer. xl, 8).

Netovtshins, a sect of Russian dissenters who are described by Dr. Pinkerton in his account of the Greek Church in Russia as very ignorant and much divided in opinion. They go under the general name of *Spasova Soglasia*, or the Union for Salvation. Their leading tenet is that Antichrist has come and begun his ruin of the Church, and has put an end to everything good, and that a gradual extinction of all holiness is now going on. The Netovtshins appear to be an offshoot of the *Pomorane* (q. v.). See Platov's *Present View of the Russian Church.*

Netpe or **Nutpe,** an Egyptian female deity, is spoken of as daughter to the Sun, wife of Seb, and mother of Typhon, the god of evil among the ancient Egyptians. According to a myth, she was represented as seated on the tree of life, and sprinkling healthful water upon the souls of men. In one form she personifies the abyss of heaven, represented as a female figure, stretched across the aerial vault, with her arms and legs enclosing the earth. She was thought to be the *Rhea* of the Greeks. See Trevor, *Ancient Egypt*, p. 147, 149.

Nets. See HAWK.

Netter, THOMAS OF WALDEN (generally known as *Thomas Waldensis*), an eminent English Roman Catholic Church historian of the early part of the 15th century, was born at Walden, Essex. He joined the Carmelites, and rose in course of time to prominence in his order in England. He was placed first in London, and afterwards at Oxford, where he became a professor, first of philosophy and then of divinity. He zealously contested the opinions of Wickliffe both in the schools and in the pulpit; was elected provincial of his order; and by command of King Henry IV attended the Council of Pisa in 1409. By Henry V he was appointed privy counsellor and confessor, and sent to the Council of Constance, where he distinguished himself by his speeches against the Wickliffites and Hussites. He likewise possessed the favor of Henry VI, and went to France with the intention of being present at his coronation at Paris, but he died on his journey at Rouen in 1430. He wrote a number of works; the Bodleian Library at Oxford possesses numerous MSS. of his, for instance, a list of all the heresies, under the title of *Catalogus Zizaniorum.* But his only published work is his *Doctrinale antiquitatum fidei Ecclesiæ Catholicæ* (Paris, 1521, 1523, 1532; 2d ed. Salamanca, 1556; 3d ed. Venice, 1571, with notes by a Carmelite monk named Rubeo; 4th ed. Venice, 1757, with notes by Blanciotti). The work is divided into six books: i, of God and Christ; ii, of the body of Christ, the Church, and its members; iii, of monachism; iv, of the begging monks and monastic property; v, of the sacraments; vi, of other parts of divine worship. The book is simply a criticism of the Lollards and of Wickliffe's whole system. It is still held in great esteem by Roman Catholics. Among his other writings we notice commentaries on Genesis, Exodus, Leviticus, the Acts of the Apostles, the Epistle of Paul to the Romans, and the first Epistle of Peter, and a multitude of dissertations, disputations, sermons, letters, etc., which are enumerated in Freheri *Theatrum Vir. Erud. Clar. Moreri*. See Lechler, *Wiclif u. d. Lollarden* (1874, 1875): Niedner's *Zeitschrift f. histor. Theologie*, 1853, p. 559–572; Hook, *Eccles. Biog.* vii, 401; Hardwick, *Ch. Hist. Mid. Ages*, p. 393, n. 6; p. 394, n. 3. (J. N. P.)

Nettle is the rendering in the Auth. Ver. of two Hebrew words. See also THORN.

1. *Chârûl'*, חָרוּל (so called from its *pricking* or *burning*; Sept. φρύγανα ἄγρια; Vulg. *sentes, urtica*, and *spina*), occurs in three places in Scripture. Thus in Prov. xxiv, 30, 31, "I went by the field of the slothful, etc., and, lo, it was all grown over with thorns, and nettles (*charullim*, חֲרֻלִּים) had covered the face thereof." So in Job xxx, 7 it is stated that he was insulted by the children of those whom he would formerly have disdained to employ, and who were so abject and destitute that "among the bushes they brayed; under the *nettles* they were gathered together;" and in Zeph. ii, 9, "Surely Moab shall be as Sodom, and the children of Ammon as Gomorrah, even the breeding of *nettles*, and salt-pits, and a perpetual desolation." Considerable difficulty has been experienced in determining the plant which is alluded to in the above passages, which, as Celsius says, "has been sparingly mentioned, and not minutely described by the sacred writers." The majority of translators and commentators have thought that some thorny or prickly plant is intended by the *charul*, on account of the other plants which are mentioned along with it. Hence brambles, the wild plum, thistles, etc., have been severally selected; but nettles have had the greatest number of supporters. Celsius, however, prefers the *Zizyphus Paliurus*, or the plant called *Christ's thorn*, as best suited to the contexts. The *cactus*, or prickly pear, would be a very suitable representative, in many respects, as it is largely used in Palestine for a hedge or fence, and grows to the height of eight or ten feet. But there is this great objection to many of the plants proposed, that they are of too slow growth to suit the passage in Proverbs, which implies a rapid and general intrusion of the plant in question. All these determinations, however, amount to nothing more than conjectures, because, as Rosenmüller says, the cognate languages have not this word, and also because "the Greek translators of Alexandria in the first and last of the three places in which the Hebrew word occurs entirely deviate from our present Hebrew text; but in Job they translate *charul* by *wild shrubs*." It does not appear that a thorny plant is necessarily meant by the term. All that is implied is that neglected fields will become covered with *weeds*, and that these will be of a kind such as idlers may take shelter under. This passage, indeed, seems to preclude any thorny plant or nettle, as no one would voluntarily resort to such a situation; and Bar-Bahlul, as quoted by Celsius (ii, 168), considers *pease*, or rather vetches, to be intended. Moreover, it is worthy of remark that there is an Arabic word not unlike *charul* which is applied to plants apparently suitable to all the above passages. The word *khardul* applies to different species of *mustard*, and also to plants which are employed for the same purposes as mustard. Some of the wild kinds of mustard spring up in corn-fields, and become very troublesome. One of these, indeed, *sinapis arvensis*, is abundant in corn-fields, where it is a pernicious weed, and also in waste ground when newly disturbed. Khardul is that indigenous in Asia. Some of the species are

found in Syria and Palestine; and Russell mentions the above (*sinapis arvensis*), or charlock, as common in the neighborhood of Aleppo. It is also widely diffused in Europe (see Decandolle, *Syst. Natural.* ii, 615). See MUSTARD.

2. *Kimmôsh'*, קִמּוֹשׁ, *kimôsh'*, קִימוֹשׁ, and *kimmâshôn*, קִמָּשׂוֹן, occur, the first in Isa. xxxiv, 13, the second in Hos. ix, 6, and the third in Prov. xxiv, 31, where it is mentioned along with *charul*, which we believe to indicate *charlock*. The field of the slothful is there described as being grown over with thorns (*charullim*), "and nettles (*kimshon*) had covered the face thereof." In Isaiah it is said, "And thorns (*choach*) shall come up in the palaces, *nettles* (*kimosh*) and brambles in the fortresses thereof." Hos. ix, 6, "The pleasant places for their silver, *nettles* (*kimosh*) shall possess them; thorns (*choach*) shall be in their tabernacles." Though different interpretations have been given of this word (Sept. ἀκάνθινα ξύλα, ἄκανθα, ὄλεθρος; Vulg. *urtica*), as thorns, thistles, wild camomile, etc., the greatest number of authors have united in adopting *nettles*, chiefly in consequence of the authority of Jewish writers. Thus, Rosenmüller says, rabbi Tanchum, on Hos. ix, 6, explains *kimosh* by the common nettle, in Pococke's *Comment. on Hosea*. So rabbi Ben-Melech, as quoted and translated by Celsius (*Hierobot.* ii, 207), speaks of it as a kind of nettle, commonly called *urtica*. Nettles spring up rapidly in deserted as in inhabited places, in fields, ditches, and road-sides, especially where there is some moisture in the soil or climate. They are found in tropical situations as well as in temperate climes, but the springing up of nettles in deserted places is rather a European than an Oriental idea. See THORN.

Nettleton, ASHAEL, D.D., a Congregational minister of note, was born April 21, 1783, at North Killingworth, Conn. He graduated at Yale College in 1809; entered the ministry May 28, 1811; and from 1812 to 1822 travelled as an evangelist through Connecticut and parts of Massachusetts and New York. He had originally intended to become a missionary; but his preaching was attended with such great success, hundreds being converted by his labors, that he concluded to stay at home and continue in this work. In 1822 his health failed, and he almost ceased preaching for two years, but afterwards resumed the work, spending his winters in the South, and visiting England, Scotland, and Ireland in 1831. On his return, in 1832, he was appointed professor of pastoral theology in the then newly-organized theological seminary at East Windsor; but he did not accept this office, and simply took up his residence in the place and lectured occasionally to the students. He died May 16, 1844. Dr. Nettleton was a decided opponent to the New Haven theology, and in sermons and addresses took frequent opportunity to combat it. His only publication was a compilation, *The Village Hymns* (1824). After the doctor's death there was published *Remains of the late Rev. A. Nettleton, D.D., consisting of Sermons, Outlines and Plans of Sermons, Brief Observations on Texts of Scripture, and Miscellaneous Remarks* (edited by Bennet Tyler, D.D. [Hartford, 1845, 12mo]), of which the *Christian Review* (Oct. 1846, p. 171) spoke in terms of high commendation. The "Remains" was remodelled in some parts, and brought out by Bonar in 1854. See, besides this and the review referred to, Sprague, *Annals of the Amer. Pulpit*, ii, 542; Drake, *Dictionary of American Biography*, s. v. (J. H. W.)

Neubrigensis, WILLIAM (called also *Petit* or *Parvus*), canon of the Augustine convent of Newbury, was born at Bridlington in 1136. He gave early promises of great talent, and was on that account educated in the convent. At the request of the superiors of a neighboring convent he wrote a commentary on Solomon's Song, and afterwards a *Historia Rerum Anglicarum*, which he dedicated to Ernald, abbot of Rivaulx.

This history, divided into five parts, embraces the period from William I to 1197. The first book, in which he mainly follows Henry of Huntingdon, extends to the time of Stephen, and is merely an introduction to the most important part of the work, which treats of the history of his own times, and is the best chronicle of that period. He evinces, for his age, remarkable critical acumen, a great spirit of observation, and fine discrimination. Although not completely free from the prejudices of the Middle Ages, the author is worthy of the name of historian. The work was first published at Antwerp in 1567, then at Heidelberg in 1587, Paris in 1610–1632, and at Oxford (by Hearne) in 1719. The best edition is one corrected from two MSS. of the 13th century by H. C. Hamilton, for the English Historical Society (1856). Neubrigensis is believed to have died about 1208. See Herzog, *Real-Encyklopädie*, x, 298; Cave, *Hist. Lit.* ii, 253.

Neuenar (Lat. *Neuenarius* or *Nevenarius*), HERMANN, *Count*, a learned German prelate, was born in 1491 in the town of Julich. He entered into holy orders; became provost of the College Church of Aix-la-Chapelle, afterwards of the Cathedral of Cologne; and lastly, in 1524, chancellor of the high school in that city. He possessed great knowledge, and defended Reuchlin against the attacks of the Dominicans of Cologne. In agreement with Hutten and Camerarius upon literary questions, he separated himself from them on the subject of religious reform, and voted against the innovators at the Diet of Augsburg. He died at Augsburg in 1530. We have of his works, *Oratio in comitiis Francofurtensibus pro Carolo Romanorum rege recens electo* (Frankfort, 1519, and Hanover, 1611, fol.): —*Oratio gratulatoria ad Carolum V* (1519), reprinted, as well as the preceding piece, in the third volume of the *Scriptores* of Freher:—*Epistola ad Carolum V* (Schelestadt, 1519, 4to), written to engage that prince to favor classical studies:—*Brevis enarratio de origine et sedibus Francorum* (Cologne, 1521, 4to; Anvers, 1585); in this work, reprinted with others in vol. i of the *Scriptores* of Duchesne, the author is among the first to combat the erroneous opinion regarding the Trojan origin of the Franks:—*De Morbo seu febri sudatoria, vulgo sudore Brittanico vocato* (Cologne, 1529, 4to): —*Carmina* (Leipsic, 1529):—*Annotationes aliquot herbarum*, in vol. iii of the *Herbarium Brunsfeldii* (Basle, 1540):—*De Gallia Belgica commentariolus* (Anvers, 1584, 4to). Neuenar also gave the first edition of the *Vie de Charlemagne* and of the *Annales* of Eginhard (Cologne, 1521, 4to), and of the *Art vétérinaire* of R. Végèce (Basle, 1528, 4to); he also translated into Latin several Greek epigrams in the collection of Soter, published at Cologne in 1528; his translation of the *Psalms* and other fragments from the Bible are found in the *Psalmi* published (Hagenau, 1532, 8vo) by one of his nephews, who has placed at the beginning of it a *Vie de Neuenar*, reproduced in the *Noctes academicæ* of J. Fr. Christ; his *Poem on the Death of the Saviour* is inserted in the *Hymni sacri* of G. Fabricius; finally, several letters of Neuenar are found in the correspondence of Reuchlin. See Burckhardt, *Analecta*, and *De fatis linguæ Latinæ*, p. 337; Hartzheim, *Bibl. Coloniensis*; Buschius, *Vallum humanitatis*; Paquot, *Mémoires*, vol. xvi.

Neufchâtel. See SWITZERLAND.

Neufchâtel, Berthold de, a Swiss prelate, was born in the latter part of the 11th century, of noble origin. After filling several important ecclesiastical offices, he was elected bishop of Basle in 1122. He followed the custom of the prelates of noble birth, and went to join the aulic cortège of the Roman king, and neglected the affairs of his diocese. We find him at Strasburg in 1123; in 1124 he was a member of the assembly of Mayence, where he favored the pretensions of Philip of Swabia, aspiring to the empire after the death of Henry V. But the majority of votes was in favor of Lothaire, and

Lothaire, proclaimed emperor, commenced by treating Berthold as an enemy. Berthold had some difficulty with the monks of Saint-Blaise. The emperor wished to hear the cause, and declared himself in favor of the monks. Berthold was restored to the good graces of the emperor in the year 1130; but a few years later, in 1134, he was obliged to abdicate, and died not long after. The motive of this abdication is not well known. It is believed, however, to have been enjoined upon him by Innocent II. See *Basilea Sacra*, p. 191; *Monuments de l'Histoire de l'ancien évêché de Bâle*, published by M. Trouillat, passim.

Neufchâtel, Charles de, a French prelate, who lived in the latter part of the 15th century, was the son of Jean de Neufchâtel (q. v.). Charles was chief singer in the Cathedral of Besançon when Quentin Ménart governed that church. When the latter died, the age of Charles did not permit the canons to confer upon him the vacant title by vote of election; they could simply make him a candidate, and this they did. Charles had for competitor the celebrated cardinal of Arras, Jean Jouffroy. Yet the credit of his family prevailed over the power of the cardinal; after having been made a candidate by the canons of Besançon, he was nominated by the pope. The city of Besançon had itself wished this nomination, the facile and benevolent character of Charles giving it hope that his administration would be peaceful. He met their expectations, and even wished, in the year 1471, to efface the last trace of the discords which had troubled the government of his predecessor; he consented then to the destruction of the Château de Brigilles, newly rebuilt, and the citizens pledged themselves, through gratitude to him, to pay 600 florins in gold. In the mean time, the civil tumults being appeased, the city and church of Besançon were desolated by foreign war. After the death of Charles the Bold, the French, united to the Lorraines, invaded the Franche-Comté, and made great ravages. Charles de Neufchâtel at first resisted the enemy's forces; but Louis XI was a very skilful prince, who knew how to intimidate and corrupt. The duke Maximilian, learning that Charles de Neufchâtel had taken sides with France, declared he had forfeited his office, and even obliged him to leave his archiepiscopal palace. Charles then retired, and enjoyed the society and protection of king Louis, who, as the story goes, assigned him a pension of 4000 livres. Charles de Neufchâtel was at the court of France in the year 1480, when Louis, bishop of Bayeux, died. The king immediately nominated Neufchâtel administrator of that church (March 6). He could not indeed institute as bishop a confirmed archbishop; he could simply, by a sort of incardination, place him over the government of a vacant bishopric. Thus the canons of Besançon, deprived of their living archbishop, had not the right to give him a successor. Charles received for some time the revenues from his archbishopric, which, joined to his pension and his salary as administrator, made him one of the richest prelates of the kingdom. Neufchâtel died towards the close of the 15th century. His body was transported to Bayeux, his heart to Besançon. See *Gallia Christ. vetus*, vol. i; Dunod, *Histoire de l'Église de Besançon*, vol. i; L'Abbé Richard, *Hist. des Dioc. de Besançon et de S. Claude.*

Neufchâtel, Henri de, another Swiss prelate, flourished in the first part of the 13th century. His father, Ulric III, was count of Neufchâtel. At first provost of the church of Basle, and coadjutor to bishop Berthold of Ferrete, he established himself upon the episcopal seat in 1262. He was a man proud of his origin and of his alliances, and would yield to no one, not even the sovereign princes. From the first he engaged in an armed warfare with Rudolph of Hapsburg, his relative. They quarrelled about the castles of Brisach and of Neuenburg. The two armies had for chiefs the count and the bishop, and took as many strong places, and desolated as many boroughs and farms in the name of the one as of the other. In 1268, Henry of Neufchâtel carried by assault Hertenberg, Blotzheim, and Rheinfelden, although the latter place was accounted impregnable; Rudolph in turn besieged Toggenburg: there interposed in the affray the peasants, ill-treated by count Rudolph, who rushed suddenly upon the castles of Auggen, Gervesch, and Froschbach, and demolished them. Desolation reigned everywhere in the year 1269, when the two adversaries concluded to close the strife by a treaty. But they finally failed to agree, and reopened the war. In 1272, Rudolph, making each day new progress, ruined the Château de Tieffenstein, and carried conflagration even to the suburbs of Basle, and finally besieged the episcopal city. Henry, though for a long time he had valiantly opposed, now found himself unable to prolong the struggle, and signed a truce Sept. 22, 1273. His death occurred the following year, Sept. 13, 1274. One does not find in the life of Henry de Neufchâtel any acts properly belonging to a bishop. Absolutely destitute of all ecclesiastical science, ignorant of or despising his episcopal duties, he acted the part of a valiant warrior and a skilful captain, and this part alone he was by education and general training fitted to play in life. See *Annales Colmarienses*, apud Urstisium, passim; Herrgott, *Genealog. Habsb.* vol. ii, passim; *Basilea Sacra*, p. 237; *Monum. de l'Hist. de l'ancien évêché de Bâle*, collected by M. Trouillat, vol. ii, passim.

Neufchâtel, Jean de, a French prelate of note, was born in Neufchâtel, Switzerland, about 1335. Belonging to one of the most important houses of the county of Bourgogne, and son of Thibaut, baron de Neufchâtel, and of Jeanne de Châlons, he became at fifteen canon of Autun, then prior of St. Peter of Abbeville and of Notre-Dame of Bar-le-Duc. Ordained priest in Besançon, he appeared as a candidate for archbishop of that city, but failed to secure support, and was content to be consecrated in 1371 bishop of Nevers, whence he passed in October, 1372, to the see of Toul. The emperor Charles IV gave him, in 1377, letters-patent which invested him with temporal power and recognised him as a prince of the empire. Robert de Genève, his relative, having become pope under the name of Clement VII, made him, in 1378, one of his chamberlains, and on October 23, 1383, created him cardinal. Jean in the following year resigned his bishopric, the administration of which he resumed May 29, 1385. He became, in December, 1392, bishop of Ostia and of Velletri, and two years after concurred in the election of Pierre de Lune, otherwise known as Benedict XIII, whom he crowned at Avignon in October, 1394. Jean was long obedient to him; but, afflicted by the schism which rent the Church, he used all means to bring it to an end, and ceased not to solicit Benedict XIII to resign; yet Neufchâtel died without having been able to triumph over the obstinacy of Pierre de Lune. On the day of his death, which occurred in Avignon, October 4, 1398, a fire consumed his palace, and his ashes, collected by his friends, were deposited in the Carthusian Monastery of Villeneuve-les-Avignon. See *Gallia Christiana*, vol. xii and xiii; Aubery, *Histoire des cardinaux.*

Neugard, TRUDPERT, a German Roman Catholic theologian, was born at Villingen, in Baden-Baden, January 23, 1742; studied with the Benedictines, who have a monastery at that place, and joined that order in 1759. In 1765 he was ordained to the priesthood, and in 1767 was made teacher of the Oriental languages and hermeneutics at the theological school in Freiburg. Four years later he was recalled to his monastery, and was given the care of the younger brethren of his order. In 1807, after the secularization of this convent, Neugard went to Austria and lived in monastic retirement. He died about 1815. He left in MS. some historical and ascetical writings. He compiled a history of several

monasteries, and assisted on a number of large works: e. g. the *Germania Sacra*, etc. See Waitzenegger, *Gelehrten- u. Schriftsteller-Lexikon*, iii, 340-343.

Neuilly, Fulk of. See FULCO.

Neukomm, *Chevalier* SIGISMUND, a celebrated German composer, noted for his devotion to sacred music, was born at Salzburg in 1778. He was related to the Haydn family, and, evincing musical talents at a very early age, he was placed under the Haydn brothers for instruction. From Michael Haydn, the elder brother — author of *The Creation* — Neukomm acquired that predilection for sacred music which distinguished him throughout his career. At the age of twenty he went to Vienna to study under Joseph Haydn, who received his young relative most kindly and made him his pupil; and the friendship thus begun lasted without interruption during the whole of the great master's life. Neukomm's close and unbroken intercourse with Joseph Haydn, and admiration of his genius, had a sensible effect on the formation of his own style, which is marked not only with Haydn's regularity, symmetry, and clearness, but with many of Haydn's characteristic traits of musical phraseology. After having gained a high reputation in Germany, Russia, France, Italy, and South America, Neukomm went to England in 1829, and his reception by the public was such as to induce him to pass much time in that country. His residence in England was an active period of his life. It was while there that his greatest works were composed, among them the oratorios of *Mount Sinai* and *David*. *Mount Sinai*, originally set to German words, was afterwards adapted by him to an English version of the text, and performed for the first time at the Derby Musical Festival of 1831. *David*, the poem of which was originally written in English, was composed expressly for the Birmingham Musical Festival, and performed in 1834. During the same period he gave the English public many vocal pieces, both sacred and secular, which obtained general popularity. Among these, his sacred cantatas, *Miriam, The Prophecy of Babylon*, and *Absalom*, are remarkable for their grandeur, expression, and complete adaptation of the music to English poetry, for Neukomm was a perfect master of the English language. *The Sea* was for a long time the most popular song of the day; and though it has given place to newer favorites, it is still frequently heard, and always with pleasure. Neukomm's latest work is *Twenty Psalms selected from the authorized English Version*, for the use of singing-schools, choral societies, churches, and chapels of every persuasion. It was written for the Association for the Revival of Sacred Music in Scotland, and published by that body at Edinburgh in 1853. It possesses great value. The most beautiful of the Psalms are selected, and the music, in a plain and simple style, has the grand and solemn beauty which characterizes Neukomm's sacred works. Neukomm died at Paris, April 3, 1858. His residence for a few years previous had been alternately at London, Paris, and Bonn. There is scarcely a branch of his art which he has left untouched. A collection of voluntaries for the organ—an instrument on which Neukomm was one of the greatest performers in Europe—is among the most important works produced by him in England. His instrumental compositions, symphonies, quartets, sonatas, etc., are very numerous and of much merit; but it is on his great sacred works that his permanent fame will rest. In the course of his long life Neukomm received many of the honors due to the highest distinction in his art. He was invested with several orders of knighthood in France, Portugal, and Prussia; was a member of the Royal Academy of Arts in Prussia, and of most of the principal musical institutions and societies in Europe and the United States. The doctorate of music was conferred on him by the University of Dublin, and he was one of the jury of the great London Exhibition in 1851. For several years before his death he was afflicted with an ophthalmic complaint, at one time almost amounting to deprivation of sight, but he partially recovered from it. See Fétis, *Biographie Universelle des Musiciens*, s. v.; *English Cyclop.* s. v.; *Esquisse biographique de Sigismond Neukomm par lui même*, in *La Maîtrise* (Paris, 1859).

Neuman, Johann Georg, a German theologian, was born in 1661 at Hertz, near Merseburg. He was educated at the University of Wittenberg, and became in 1690 professor of poesy and librarian in his alma mater, and in 1692 obtained a theologian's chair; he was called later to the dignity of provost of the court chapel. His death occurred in 1709. Neuman was one of the principal adversaries of Spener. He wrote more than a hundred and twenty dissertations upon theological, historical, and literary subjects, most of which are collected in his *Primitiæ dissertationum* (Wittenberg, 1700, 1707, and 1716, 8vo), and in his *Programmata academica* (ibid. 1707 and 1722, 4to). He also published the biographies of several theologians; among them Hunnius, Hutter, Runge, etc. See Schönbach, *Vita Neumanni* (1716, 8vo); Raufft, *Leben der chur-sächsischen Theologen*, vol. ii; Faber, *Nachrichten von der Schloss-Kirche zu Wittenberg*; Gass, *Dogmengesch.* iii, 57; Erdmann, *Biographien der Pröbste zu Wittenberg*.

Neuman, John Nepomaceæ, D.D., a Roman Catholic prelate, was born in Bohemia, March 28, 1811, and came to this country upon the completion of his university course at the high school in Prague. He took holy orders at New York in 1836, and subsequently entered the Order of the Most Holy Redeemer. After filling several appointments as priest, he was consecrated bishop of Philadelphia March 28, 1852, and he held that episcopal see until his decease, Jan. 5, 1860. Bishop Neuman was generally esteemed and much beloved by his people. He was a man of more than ordinary ability.

Neumann, Carl Friedrich, a distinguished German Orientalist, ethnographer, and historian, was born, of Jewish parents, Dec. 22, 1798, at Reichmannsdorf, near Bamberg. Without any means, but by hard study and diligence, he was enabled in the year 1817 to go to Heidelberg to attend the lectures there. In 1818 he joined the Christian Church, taking instead of his former name, *Bamberger*, that of *Neumann*, under which he became known to the literary world. Upon the completion of his studies at Heidelberg and Munich, he was appointed in 1821 as professor at the Gymnasium of Speier, but on account of his liberal views he had to give up his position in 1825. He next went to Venice, where he studied the Armenian language with the Mechitarists in the monastery of St. Lazarus; he then continued his Oriental studies at Paris and London; and in 1830 went to India and China, with a view to becoming thoroughly acquainted with the Chinese language and literature. He there collected a library of about 12,000 volumes, chiefly on Chinese literature; and after his return he was appointed, in 1833, professor at Munich, where he lectured on the Chinese and Armenian languages and literature, on ethnography, universal and German history, until the year 1852, when he was discharged on account of his liberal religious and political views. He settled at Berlin in 1863, and there he remained until his death, which occurred March 17, 1870. He was a close student of political and philosophical phases in history, and was greatly devoted to republican institutions. The American government he admired, and warmly met every American who had occasion to see him. He freely mingled in foreign society at Berlin, and was much sought after by all literature-loving strangers in the German capital. He wrote, *Mémoirs sur la vie et les ouvrages de David, philosophe Arménien* (Paris, 1829):—*Catechism of the Shamans* (from the Chinese, 1831):—*Pilgerfahrten buddhistischer Priester aus China nach Indien* (Leipsic, 1833):—*Lehrsaal des*

Mittelreichs (Munich, 1836):—*Versuch einer Geschichte der armenischen Literatur* (Leipsic, 1836):—*Translations from the Chinese and Armenian, with Notes and Illustrations* (London, 1839):—*Geschichte des englischen Reiches in Asien* (Leipsic, 1857, 2 vols.):—*Geschichte der Vereinigten Staaten von Amerika* (Berlin, 1863–1866, 3 vols.), besides a number of essays, which were published in the *Zeitschrift* of the German Oriental Society (i, 91–128, 217–237; iv, 33–43, 225–243; vii, 141–155; xviii, 294). A translation of his *Hoei Schein, or the Discovery of America by Buddhist Monks in the 5th Century*, was published at London in 1874. See Kalkar, *Israel u. die Kirche* (Hamburg, 1869), p. 128; *Literarischer Handweiser*, 1870, p. 487 sq.; Kurz, *Gesch. d. deutschen Literatur*, iv, 867, 925; *For. Quar. Rev.* xxi, 126, 255. (J. H. W.)

Neumann, Caspar, a German theologian, noted as a Hebraist, was born at Breslau, in Silesia, Sept. 14, 1648. After graduating at the Gymnasium of St. Magdalen, he went in 1667 to Jena to study theology. Three years later he published his dissertation on the Roman Catholic Church (*Dissertatio de Ecclesia Catholica*), and the university conferred on him the title of "magister." He soon commenced lecturing on Church history, and his lectures were attended by a great many students. At the recommendation of the divines of Jena, duke Ernest the Fious, of Gotha, appointed him as the fellow-traveller of his son, prince Christian, with whom Neumann went through Germany, Switzerland, Southern France, Savoy, and Upper Italy. In 1678 he was appointed by the successor of the duke court-preacher in Altenburg. A year later the authorities of his native place appointed him to the diaconate of St. Mary Magdalen, and in 1689 as pastor of the same church and assessor of the consistory. In 1697 he became superintendent of the evangelical churches and schools, pastor of St. Elizabeth, and first professor of theology at the gymnasia. He died Jan. 27, 1715. Besides devotional works, he wrote תּוֹלְדוֹת 'ס, *Genesis linguæ sanctæ Vet. Test.* (Norimb. 1696):—*Exodus linguæ sanctæ e captivitate Babylon. tentatus in Lexico etymologico Hebræo-biblico* (ibid. 1697–1700):—מִפְתַּח בְּרִחעֶבֶּר, *Janua ad significationem hieroglyphicam litterarum Ebraicarum*, etc. pt. iii (Breslau, 1712):—*De punctis vocalibus* (ibid. 1715). Possessed of great learning, he was likewise a very pious and saintly man, full of love for humanity. He is also the author of thirty-nine hymns, which are yet to be found in many hymn-books. The best known is his *Herr, auf Erden muss ich leiden* (English translation in Choral-book for England, No. 66, "Lord, on earth I dwell sad-hearted"). See Tacken, *Life of M. Casp. Neumann* (Breslau and Leipsic, 1741); Koch, *Gesch. d. deutschen Kirchenliedes*, v, 456 sq.; Jöcher, *Gelehrten-Lexikon*, iii, 881; supplement by Rottermund, v, 563; Knapp, *Evangelischer Liederschatz*, p. 1339, s. v.; Fürst, *Biblioth. Judaica*, iii, 30; Steinschneider, *Bibliogr. Handbuch*, p. 101; Bleek, *Einleitung. in das A. Test.* p. 132; Keil, *Introduction to the Old Testament*, ii, 175. (B. P.)

Neumann, Joachim, a noted German educator and Hebraist, was born at Brody, in Austrian Poland, in the year 1778 or 1779, of Jewish parentage. Up to his thirteenth year he received his education in the house of his father, which he then left for Posen, where he was enabled to satisfy his thirst for knowledge. Towards the end of the last century he obtained an appointment as teacher in a celebrated Jewish school at Dessau, where he remained until the year 1807. During his residence there he took part with three other learned Jews in publishing a German translation of the twelve minor prophets, which was accompanied by a Hebrew commentary. At that time a great change had taken place among the Jews living in different parts of Prussia with regard to their social position. About the year 1790 the king of Prussia granted the Jews who had obtained permission to live in Breslau an exemption from the taxes which had formerly been imposed on them when obtaining such permission, on the condition that they should establish a school for the poor children of their community. This led to the founding of William School in 1791, and in 1807 Neumann was invited to become the head master and inspector of that school. For about nineteen years he had charge of that institution, i. e. from 1807 to 1826. During his connection with this school Neumann had been on terms of the most intimate friendship with professors Steffens and Scheibel, who were the means of bringing him to the knowledge of the truth as it is in Christ. Satisfied of the necessity of accepting Christ as the Messiah, he was baptized on April 16, 1826, together with his wife and three sons, in the parish church of St. Elizabeth, by professor Scheibel, having as one of the sponsors professor Braniss, of the University of Breslau, his brother-in-law. Neumann was now engaged as a teacher of Hebrew in the university, in which, besides professor Braniss, professor Fischer, professor of chemistry—another brother-in-law of his—were distinguishing themselves. Neumann died suddenly, March 3, 1865. His second son is now professor of medicine in the University of Breslau. Neumann wrote, besides his *Commentary on Amos, Nahum, Haggai, Zechariah, and Malachi,* which was published at Dessau in 1805, under the title, קְצָת תְּרֵי עֲשַׂר עִם הָא וּבֵאוּר, a Hebrew Chrestomathy in 2 vols. (Breslau, 1821). See Fürst, *Bibl. Jud.* iii, 30; Steinschneider, *Bibliographisches Handbuch* (Leipsic, 1859), p. 101; *Jewish Intelligencer,* 1865. (B. P.)

Neumark, Georg, a German musician and author of a great number of sacred songs, commonly heard in the evangelical churches of Germany, was born in Thuringia about the year 1621. His parents, who were poor, soon after went to reside at Mullhouse, in France, which accounts for his having often been considered a native of that city. In 1643 he went to study law at the University of Königsberg, where Simon Dach, the centre of the Königsberg school of poetry, was professor of poetry and poet-laureate. Dach was also a great musician. Under his influence the young law student became, like the professor, a musician and a poet. When a student Neumark frequently suffered for want of food. In 1651 he went to live at Hamburg. There his poverty was so great that he was obliged to pawn his violdi-gamba, a six-stringed instrument then in use, upon which he played very skilfully. In the midst of his sufferings he refused every unworthy method of seeking a livelihood, and preserved his simplicity of life and his trust in God. An attendant of the Swedish ambassador being greatly moved by a hymn which Neumark had sung, accompanying it upon his viol, which the Jew pawnbroker had permitted him to use, sought him out, learned his story, and afterwards repeated it to his master. The result was the young poet was appointed secretary of the ambassador. His first act on receiving the joyful news of his appointment was to redeem his viol. Then, as expressive of the way in which his faith had been justified by the issue, he composed his most famous hymn, *Wer nur den lieben Gott lässt walten,* translated into our tongue in the *Lyra Germanica* of Susanna Winkworth as "Leave God to order all thy ways." In 1651 he settled at Weimar, where he was appointed by duke William IV librarian of the royal archives. He lived a life of cheerful confidence in God, often giving expression to his pious sentiments in Christian hymns, and died at Weimar, July 8, 1681. Besides his numerous poetical productions, which were often published, Neumark wrote also some historical essays in Latin, such as *Horti historici, manuale et libellus precatorius:—Comœdiæ de Caliste et Lysandro,* etc., a history of the successful society to which he belonged:—*Hochsprossender poetischer Palmbaum* (Nuremberg, 1670). The American Tract Society has published an English version of his hymns. See Miller's *Singers and Songs of*

the Church; Koch, *Gesch. des Kirchenliedes,* vol. i, ii, and iv; Herzog, *Real-Encyklop.* x, 300.

Neumark, Jehuda Löb (BEN-DAVID), OF HANAU, a Jewish writer of note, flourished near the opening of the 18th century. He died April 9, 1723. Jablonski (q. v.) mentions Neumark in the preface to his *Biblia Hebraica cum notis Hebraicis* (Berlin, 1699) as the author of a Hebrew Grammar, entitled שֹׁרֶשׁ יְהוּדָה (Frankfort-on-the-Main, 1693), which was long used and valued. In the preface to this grammar Neumark gives a history of the best Hebrew grammarians, and criticises very sharply the neglect of Hebrew philology. See Fürst, *Bibl. Judaica,* iii, 31; De Rossi, *Dizionario storico degli autori Ebrei,* p. 245 (Germ. transl.); Kalisch, *Hebr. Grammar,* ii, 35; Steinschneider, *Bibliographisches Handbuch,* p. 101; *Catalogus Libr. Hebr. in Bibl. Bodleiana,* p. 1364; Zunz, *Monatstage des Kalenderjahres,* p. 18 (Berlin, 1872; Engl. transl. by the Rev. B. Pick in *Jewish Messenger,* New York, 1874). (B. P.)

Neumeister, ERDMANN, a German Protestant divine and author of numerous hymns, was born at Uechtritz, near Weissenfels, May 12, 1671. He studied first at the school of Pforta, and afterwards at the University of Leipsic. In 1697 he became pastor at Bibra, in Thuringia, and filled successively the same office at Eckartsberga, Weissenfels, Sorau, and Hamburg, where he died, while pastor of the church of St. Jacob, Aug. 18, 1756. He was an opponent both of pietism and of chiliasm, and held fast to the old orthodoxy. Neumeister is best known by his hymns, of which he wrote about 700; some of them are truly excellent, and still in use. Among these we notice, "Gott macht ein grosses Abendmahl," etc.; "Jesus nimmt die Sünder an," etc. (Engl. transl. in Mill's *Horæ Germanicæ,* p. 73, "This man sinners doth receive"); "Wie Gott will!" also "Will ich sagen" (Engl. transl. in *Hymns from the Land of Luther,* p. 155, as "Thou wilt, my God, I ever say"); and "Lass irdische Geschäfte stehn," etc. He wrote also a *Specimen dissertationis historico-criticæ de poetis Germanicis.* His poetical works are, *Fünffache Kirchenandachten* (1716 and 1717):—*Fortgesetzte fünffache Kirchenandachten* (1726):—*Evangelischer Nachklang* (1718-1729):—*Zugang zum Gnadenstuhl.* See Herzog, *Real-Encyklopädie,* x, 301; Koch, *Gesch. des deutschen Kirchenliedes,* v, 371 sq.; Döring, *Die Deutschen Kanzelredner,* s. v.; Knapp, *Evangelischer Liederschatz,* p. 1339 sq. (J. H. W.)

Neuser, ADAM, a German Socinian theologian, was born in Swabia in the 16th century. Educated in Lutheranism by his parents, who belonged to that communion, he entered the Reformed Church, after having finished his studies, probably because he sought greater liberty of thought than he could find in the Lutheran Church. He then established himself in the Palatinate, and soon gained the good-will of the elector, who appointed him pastor of St. Peter's Church of Heidelberg, and who even formed the project of giving him a professor's chair in the university of that city. But this prince wishing in 1569 to introduce into his states the ecclesiastical discipline of the Church of Geneva, Neuser strongly resisted the innovation, perhaps not so much because it departed from the civil power as because this discipline, by an excessive rigor, would have caused an intolerable weight of ecclesiastical despotism over the Reformed Church of the Palatinate. This bold opposition deprived him of the good graces of the elector, and he was dismissed from the pastorate. Neuser now openly espoused Socinianism, to which he had long inclined, and he exerted himself to spread its principles among his friends. Sylvanus, pastor at Ludemburg, joined him in this design, which was communicated to Georg Blandrata, physician of the vaïvode of Transylvania, and to some other ministers who professed the Socinian opinions. It is related that Neuser and Sylvanus sought to assure themselves of the protection of the sultan Selim, but that they were betrayed by the ambassador of the vaïvode of Transylvania, whom they had charged with this negotiation, and that he delivered their letters to the elector palatine. Whatever may be the true history of it, they were certainly arrested, and conducted to Amberg. Sylvanus was decapitated in 1572; Neuser succeeded in escaping from his prison, and, after having wandered over the country for some time, arrived in Constantinople, where he became a Mussulman, and died in the Mohammedan faith, Oct. 11, 1576. As might be expected, the memory of this restless and adventurous man has not been spared. He has been accused, though without apparent ground, of all vices, among others of drunkenness. It is just to add that those who have painted him in black colors recognise, however, by a singular contradiction, that there never was anything to reprimand in his conduct except his departure from orthodoxy, and this, of course, must be regretted. We are assured that he obtained a great ascendency over the people of the Palatinate, and that he owed this extraordinary consideration as well to his religious zeal as to his eloquence. It is a pity that a man of his ability should have suffered himself to be led away from his moorings to land finally in Mohammedanism. The biographical *Lexikon* of Jöcher assures us that he has left no printed work; the *Biographie Universelle*, on the contrary, pretends that his writings are numerous, and that they have been collected by the Socinians. The *Bibliothèque des Anti-Trinitaires*, which calls him *Neusner*, quotes but one—*Scopus Septimi Capitis ad Romanos* (Ingolstadt, 1583, 8vo). His letter to Selim, if it be authentic, is found in the collection of Mieg—*Monumenta pietatis et litteraturæ* (Frankfort, 1702, 4to), pt. i, p. 318; vol. iii of the *Mélanges tirés de la Bibliothèque de Wolfenbüttel* has another letter of Neuser, containing the apology for his conduct, dated at Constantinople the Wednesday before Easter of the year 1574. See Jöcher, *Gelehrten-Lexikon*, s. v.; Hoefer, *Nouv. Biog. Générale*, s. v.; Gass, *Dogmengesch.* ii, 21. (J. H. W.)

Neuss, HEINRICH GEORG, D.D., a German Lutheran theologian, was born, March 11, 1654, at Elbingeroda, in the duchy of Brunswick. He received his early education at Osterwick, Quedlinburg, and Halberstädt. Being very poor, he accepted the private tutorship in the house of Dr. Reccius, in Wernigerode, a position which he held for three years, until, in 1677, he was enabled to go to Erfurt, where he studied theology. In 1683 he was appointed conrector at Blankenburg, and in the next year rector. In 1690 he became adjunct to the Rev. Chr. Schmidt in Wolfenbüttel, and then deacon at the church of St. Henrici. Here he became intimately connected with two other pious ministers, who commenced to hold private meetings for devotional purposes. Soon, however, these meetings were openly spoken against, especially under the lead of Fr. Ulr. Calixt, of Helmstädt, who wrote against chiliasm, and the result was that in 1692 an edict was issued which forbade such pietism as heresy. These three men then left Wolfenbüttel. Neuss was called to Hedwigsburg, and three years later, in 1695, the duke Rudolph Augustus appointed him superintendent in Remmlingen; and in 1696 count Ernest von Stolberg called him to Wernigerode as pastor primarius at St. Sylvester and George, and superintendent and councillor of the consistory. Neuss died there Sept. 30, 1716. Besides some theological works, he also published a collection of 134 hymns, entitled *Hebopfer* (heave-offering). The best known of his hymns is his "Ein reines Herz, Herr schaff in mir" (Engl. transl. by E. Cox, in *Hymns from the German*, p. 176, "A new and contrite heart create"). Comp. Koch, *Gesch. d. deutsch. Kirchenliedes*, iv, 425 sq.; v, 573 sq.; Jöcher, *Gelehrten-Lexikon*, iii, 888; supplement by Rottermund, v, 589 sq.; Wezel, *Hymnopoeographia* (Herrnstadt, 1721), ii, 240 sq.; Winterfeld, *Der evang. Kirchengesang* (Leips. 1845), ii, 522–533. (B. P.)

Neustadt, Bible of, is the title of a revision of Luther's version of the Scriptures made at Neustadt in 1588 by the Reformed Church to express more clearly the Calvinistic notions of that body. The master spirit in this revision was David Pareus. In 1595 the *Biblia Herbornensia* was brought out by the Reformed body, and it met with less opposition. See, however, the articles PAREUS (DAVID) and SIEGWART.

Neuville, Charles Frey de, a French pulpit orator, brother of the following, was born in the diocese of Coutances, Dec. 23, 1693. He was educated in the college of the Jesuits at Rennes, who, recognising his ability, initiated him into their order in 1710. He taught belles-lettres and philosophy for eighteen years, when he made his début in the pulpit, where he had great success (1736). After the dissolution of his society, his presence, quite inoffensive, was tolerated in France, and, under the protection of the king and queen, he lived unmolested but retired. His death occurred July 13, 1774, in St. Germain-en-Laye. We have of his works, *Oraison funèbre de M. le Cardinal de Fleury*, etc. (Paris, 1743, 4to, and often):—*Oraison de très-haut, très-puissant seigneur Charles-Auguste Foucquet de Belle-Isle, duc de Gisors, pair et maréchal de France*, etc. (Paris, 1761, 4to):—*Sermons* (Paris, 1777, 8 vols. 12mo; Lyons, 1778, 8 vols. 12mo). These sermons have been translated into German by J.-B. Dily (Vienna, 1777–80, 8 vols. 8vo) and by Priest. Joh. Buchmann (Augsburg, 1841, 12mo); into Spanish by Juan-Antonio Pellicer, Juan Ceron, and Pontela (Madrid, 1784); into Italian (Venice, 1774, 1786, 1793). Neuville had collected three volumes of *Observations hist. et crit.*, but the fear of wrong interpretations and of compromising his editors determined him, some days before his death, to throw his manuscript into the fire. Biographers have often confounded this ecclesiastical orator with his brother, and with Anne Joseph de la Neuville. See Caballero, *Bibliothecæ scriptorum Societatis Jesu* (Rome, 1814–16, 4to); Aloïs et Alphonse de Backer, *Bibl. des écrivains de la Compagnie de Jésus*, 1st series, p. 519, 520.

Neuville, Pierre-Claude Frey de, a French theologian, was born at Grandville, Sept. 5, 1692. His family were originally from the canton of Basle, and went for some unknown cause to dwell in Brittany. Neuville entered, Sept. 12, 1710, the Society of Jesus, where he occupied honorable and responsible positions. Twice he was provincial. He was a good preacher. When his order was threatened with dissolution (1763), he did not await persecution, but retired to Rennes, where he died in August, 1775. We have of his works, *Sermons* (Rouen, 1778, 2 vols. 12mo):—*Observations sur l'institut de la Société de Jésus* (Avignon, 1761, 1762, 1771, 12mo):—*Lettre d'un ami de la vérité à ceux qui ne haïssent pas la lumière, ou réflexions critiques sur les reproches faits à la Société de Jésus relativement à la doctrine* (12mo). See Raymond Diosada Caballero, *Bibliothecæ scriptorum Societatis Jesu* (1814–16, 4to); Feller, *Supplement de la France littéraire; Nouvel appel à la raison des écrits et libelles publiés par la passion contre les Jésuites de France* (Brussels, 1761, 12mo); Aloïs et Alp. de Backer, *Bibliothèque des écrivains de la Compagnie de Jésus;* Barbier, *Dict. des Anonymes*, No. 9643; *Catalogus personarum et officiorum provinciæ Franciæ Societatis Jesu*, ann. 1759, p. 3.

Neuville (DE PLESSIS-BARDOUL), **Roland de**, a noted French prelate, was born in 1530. He was abbé of St. James of Montfort when, in 1562, he was nominated bishop of St. Pol-de-Léon by the protection of the duke d'Étampes, in the place of Roland de Chauvigné. Though he may have assisted at the Council of Tours (1583), and may have subscribed to the edicts of toleration published in 1588, Neuville showed himself none the less a violent persecutor of the Protestants; he himself boasted of not having left a single heretic in his diocese. He died in Rennes, Feb. 5,

1613, after fifty years' episcopate. The library of Lyons possesses, No. 441, a very beautiful *Missale ecclesiæ Gallicæ*, folio, written in magnificent Gothic characters and illuminated with excellent vignettes, which appears to have been the property of Roland de Neuville.

Nevay, JOHN, a noted Scotch Presbyterian minister, who flourished in the days of the English Revolution as pastor of Newmills, in the parish of London, was identified with the struggle for the independence of the Kirk, and in 1647 gained unenviable notoriety by the severe measures which he counselled general Leslie to adopt against the British soldiery. But, though severe with his opponents in religion, Mr. Nevay cannot be said to have lacked in religious devotion and Christian zeal. He is commended by his contemporaries of the Kirk for soundness in the faith, shining piety in conversation, and great diligence in attending all the parts of his ministerial functions, particularly church judicatories; one who was always very zealous in contending against steps of defection contrary to the work of reformation carried on in that period. See *Scots Worthies*, p. 287.

Neve, Francois de, a Flemish painter of sacred art, was born at Antwerp, according to Balkema, in 1625. He studied for some time the works of Rubens and Vandyck, and afterwards visited Rome for improvement, where he resided several years. On returning to Flanders he painted a number of good historical works which gained him considerable reputation; but he afterwards painted heroic landscapes with subjects from history or fable, in which he evinced great fertility of invention and refinement of taste. Bartsch mentions fourteen etchings by this artist, executed in a slight but very masterly style, embellished with figures correctly drawn and ingeniously grouped. Neve died in 1681. See Spooner, *Biog. Hist. of the Fine Arts*, ii, 615.

Neve, Timothy (1), D.D., an English divine, was born at Wotton, in Shropshire, in 1694, and was educated at St. John's College, Cambridge University. After graduation he taught for a while at Spalding, then took holy orders, and was made minor canon of Peterborough; while there he was a joint-founder of "The Gentleman's Society," of which he was for a long time secretary. He was afterwards successively prebendary of Lincoln, archdeacon of Huntingdon, and rector of Alwalton, in Huntingdonshire, where he died in 1759. Dr. Neve was chaplain to the bishop of Lincoln, Dr. Thomas, and is spoken of by his contemporaries as a worthy man and a close student. He published one sermon, entitled *Preaching with Authority* (Oxf. 1747, 8vo), and several astronomical papers which have been republished in this country in the *Philadelphia Transactions;* also an essay on the *Invention of Printing.*

Neve, Timothy (2), D.D., an eminent English divine, son of the preceding, was born at Spalding in 1724. He studied at Corpus Christi College, Oxford, of which he was elected fellow in 1747. He became successively chaplain of Merton College, rector of Geddington (in 1762) and of Middleton Stoney; was elected Margaret professor of divinity at Oxford, and installed prebendary of Worcester in 1783. He died in 1798. He was an able theologian and scholar. He published a sermon preached before the earl of Westmoreland, chancellor of the University of Oxford, on July 8, 1759, and entitled *The Comparative Blessings of Christianity:—Eight Sermons preached, in 1781, at the Lecture founded by the Rev. John Bampton* (Oxf. 1781, 8vo):—*Seventeen Sermons on various Subjects* (ibid. 1798, 8vo):—*Animadversions on Phillips's Life of Cardinal Pole* (ibid. 1766, 8vo). See Darling, *Cycl. Bibliographica*, ii, 2169; *Gen. Biog. Dict.* s. v.; Hook, *Eccles. Biog.* vii, s. v.

Nevil(le), THOMAS, D.D., an English theologian of the Elizabethan period, noted for his strict adherence to the Calvinistic doctrines in a sharp and decisive form,

was born at Canterbury, educated at the University of Cambridge, and became a fellow of Pembroke Hall, Cambridge, in 1570. Ten years after we find him proctor of the university, and in 1582 presented to the mastership of Magdalen College. In 1590 he was promoted by the queen to the deanery of Peterborough. In 1593 he was appointed to the mastership of Trinity College, and in March, 1594, resigned the rectory of Doddington, on being presented to that of Teversham, near Cambridge. In 1595 he was concerned in the controversy which originated at Cambridge from the public declaration of William Barret, fellow of Caius College, against the doctrine of predestination and falling from grace. On these points, the general persuasion being then favorable to the system of Calvin, Barret was called before some of the heads of the Church, and compelled to retract his Arminian opinions. The dispute, however, which was referred by both parties to archbishop Whitgift, occasioned the well-known conference of the divines at Lambeth (1595), where they agreed on certain propositions, in conformity with Calvin's principles, commonly called the *Lambeth Articles* (q. v.). Dr. Neville and his brethren soon after had to complain of Dr. Baro(n), lady Margaret professor of divinity, for maintaining some doctrines respecting universal salvation diametrically opposite to those of the Lambeth Articles, in consequence of which he was removed from his station in the university. (For a full account of this, see the life of Peter Baro(n); Collier, *Eccles. Hist.* ii, 647; and Strype, *Annals*, iv, 322.) In 1597 Neville was promoted to the deanery of Canterbury. He was in this position on the accession of king James to the throne of England, and was by archbishop Whitgift, in his own name and of all the bishops and clergy, sent into Scotland to give his majesty assurance of their unfeigned duty and loyalty, and to know what commands he had for them to observe concerning ecclesiastical causes; recommending also the Church of England to his favor and protection. The Puritans had always hoped much for the Presbyterian cause from this king, and the Anglican clergy were therefore doubly anxious as to the result of this mission, which was evidently intended to win him over to the support of the Anglican establishment. It proved that Dr. Neville was the right man for this mission. He impressed the king favorably, and was given the assurance that he (i. e. James) would uphold the government of the late queen as she had left it. This answer was quite in conformity with king James's recent action in Scotland (see the article JAMES I in vol. iv). He was inclined to Romanism, but fearing to offend by such an extreme departure, he halted in the Anglican camp, and from henceforth favored Episcopalianism. Neville himself was the frequent recipient of king James's favor. Thus the king, when on a visit to Cambridge in 1615, accepted the hospitality of Dr. Neville, then at Trinity College. Dr. Neville died in 1615, shortly after king James had visited him. By his munificence to Trinity College Dr. Neville has secured to himself the gratitude and admiration of posterity. He expended more than £3000 in rebuilding that fine quadrangle which to this day retains the name of Neville's Court. He was also a contributor to the library of the college, and a benefactor to Eastbridge Hospital in his native city. See Hook, *Eccles. Biog.* vii, 402–404; Stoughton, *Eccles. Hist.* i, 19; Soames, *Elizabethan Religious History*, p. 454, 471–473, 517; Froude, *Hist. of Eng.* (see Index in vol. xii). (J. H. W.)

Nevin, THOMAS, an Irish Presbyterian divine, flourished after the opening of the 18th century as pastor of a church in Downpatrick. This church belonged at that time to the synod of Ulster, which was then greatly agitated by the question whether any Presbyterian ministers could refuse to sign a confession on the ground that by such an act they gave up the right of private judgment. Mr. Nevin belonged to the party who at the synod of 1721 refused to subscribe to the Westminster Confession, and were therefore named

Non-Subscribers. They were open to much suspicion; and after the synod of 1723, when the controversy regarding the propriety of intercommunion among the subscribers and non-subscribers had become general, Mr. Nevin, having carelessly expressed himself on the Trinitarian doctrine, was forthwith accused of heresy, and brought to trial in the synod of 1724; and though "satisfactory proofs were laid before the synod of Mr. Nevin's orthodoxy in this cardinal point of the Saviour's Deity, . . . the synod, disregarding these testimonies, and fully aware of Mr. Nevin's determination not to clear himself, under existing circumstances, by any declaration or subscription, resolved not to inquire further into the truth or relevancy of this accusation, but simply to require of him an immediate declaration of his belief in the Supreme Deity of Christ. With this demand, as was to be expected, he refused to comply, as the principle so frequently avowed by the non-subscribers that to clear himself by any such method was directly sinful; but he added that his refusal did not proceed from any disbelief of the doctrine of the Supreme Deity of Christ. Nothing, therefore, could be held to be proved against him, beyond the fact of his being a non-subscriber, like the rest of his party. Yet it was moved that, as Mr. Nevin had refused to make the declaration required of him, the synod should hold no further ministerial communion with him, nor proceed any further in his trial. This motion was carried." By the peculiar nature of the sentence passed on him, Mr. Nevin, though deprived of ministerial communion with the synod, was yet suffered to enjoy his ministerial character, and he therefore remained pastor of Downpatrick. He died about 1730. See Killen's Reid, *History of the Presbyterian Church in Ireland,* iii, 206 sq., 219 sq.

Nevins, WILLIAM, D.D., a noted Presbyterian minister, was born in Norwich, Conn., Oct. 13, 1797. After a mercantile education, he entered Yale College in 1812, and graduated in 1816. He then became a member of the Princeton Theological Seminary, and was licensed to preach at Lisbon, Conn., in September, 1819. On Oct. 19, 1820, he was ordained and installed pastor of the First Presbyterian Church in Baltimore. His health having become impaired, he went for some time to St. Croix to try the effects of a milder climate. Not deriving any benefit from it, however, he returned to Baltimore, and there died, Sept. 14, 1835. Dr. Nevins published two sermons in the *National Preacher,* and five tracts through the American Tract Society. Shortly after his death there was published a selection of his manuscripts, entitled *Select Remains,* with a memoir by Rev. William S. Plumer, D.D. His contributions to the *N.Y. Observer* were published about the same time in two small volumes, entitled *Thoughts on Popery* and *Practical Thoughts.* A volume of *Sermons,* selected by himself, was printed in 1837. All of his publications were most acceptable at the time of their appearance, and have continued to exert an influence for good to this time. As a pastor and preacher Dr. Nevins was deservedly popular. See, besides the memoir already referred to, Sprague, *Annals,* iv, 629.

Nevis, a small but beautiful and fertile island of the West Indies, belonging to Great Britain, forms one of the group of the Lesser Antilles, and lies immediately south-east of St. Christopher, from which it is separated by a strait called the Narrows, two miles wide. It is circular in form, rises in a central peak to the height of about 2500 feet, and has an area of 45 square miles. Population (1871), 11,735, of whom only a small proportion, not more than one fifth, is white. Charlestown, a seaport, with a tolerable roadstead, situated on the south-west shore of the island, is the seat of government, consisting of a government council and general assembly. The principal products are sugar, molasses, and rum. Nevis was colonized by English emigrants from St. Christopher in 1628, was taken by the French in 1706, and restored by the peace of Utrecht; it was taken again by the French in 1782, but restored by the peace of 1783. The Romanists have many adherents in Nevis. The Wesleyans, who were the first Protestant missionaries to preach in the West Indies, established a station at Gingerland, and are laboring there with some appearance of ultimate success. At Charlestown the United Presbyterian Mission is pushing the work of evangelization, especially among the blacks.

Additional Note on the Mormons.—Since our article on this subject was written, the collision between the Mormon authorities and the United States government —which is still the supreme and sole general civil administration in the territory, Congress having steadily refused to admit Utah as a State in the Union without such stipulations on the subject of polygamy, and especially safeguards to loyalty, as the Mormons are unwilling to accept—has resulted in the federal court taking possession of the Mormon premises in Salt Lake City, practically confiscating, or at least occupying and controlling, them, on the ground of treason; and it is said that the Mormons are secretly preparing for another migration, this time to Mexico, where they have purchased a large tract of land, so as to be beyond our jurisdiction. The temple is nearly completed, although likewise in the hands of the general government; but it is not to be used by the Mormons as a place of worship, for which indeed its interior construction is not adapted, but for purposes of ecclesiastical ceremony and general office work. The denunciatory tone of Mormons is now greatly moderated; and although the old style of declamation on the subject of civil power is still maintained, its tone is greatly softened, and all talk of open or forcible rebellion is abandoned. Criminal suits have been instituted, and are still pending before the U. S. courts, also against many leading Mormons for bigamy, adultery, and other unchaste practices, and in consequence polygamy is generally abandoned, at least in public, by the sect as a whole. The general aspect of the situation points to a speedy disruption of the Mormon community in Utah, especially as the influx of non-Mormon immigrants is gradually but surely overpowering them.